FICTION CORE COLLECTION

SEVENTEENTH EDITION

CORE COLLECTION SERIES

FORMERLY
STANDARD CATALOG SERIES

CHRISTI SHOWMAN FARRAR, GENERAL EDITOR

CHILDREN'S CORE COLLECTION
MIDDLE AND JUNIOR HIGH CORE COLLECTION
SENIOR HIGH CORE COLLECTION
PUBLIC LIBRARY CORE COLLECTION: NONFICTION
PUBLIC LIBRARY CORE COLLECTION: FICTION

FICTION
CORE COLLECTION

SEVENTEENTH EDITION

EDITED BY

EVE-MARIE MILLER

LIZA OLDHAM

AND

CHRISTI SHOWMAN FARRAR

H. W. Wilson
A Division of EBSCO Information Services
Ipswich, Massachusetts
2014
GREY HOUSE PUBLISHING

ISBN 978-0-8242-1234-6

Abridged Dewey Decimal Classification and Relative Index, Edition 15 is © 2004-2012 OCLC Online Computer Library Center, Inc. Used with Permission. DDC, Dewey, Dewey Decimal Classification, and WebDewey are registered trademarks of OCLC.

Fiction Core Collection, 2014, published by Grey House Publishing, Inc., Amenia, NY, under exclusive license from EBSCO Information Services, Inc.

A catalog record for this title is available from the Library of Congress.

PRINTED IN THE UNITED STATES OF AMERICA

CONTENTS

PREFACE

FICTION CORE COLLECTION is a selective list of classic and contemporary works of adult fiction either written or translated into English. The Core Collections are also available in electronic format via EBSCO*host*, updated weekly.

What's new in this Edition?

A new feature is the identification of titles that are considered "most highly recommended." These titles constitute a short list of the essential books in a given category or on a given subject. For supplemental titles, please consult the online database. A star (★) at the start of an entry indicates that a book is a "most highly recommended" title.

This edition includes more than 9,000 book titles. Of these 9,000 titles, over 2,500 titles are new since the 16th edition. New editions and new translations are added as they are published. In preparing this edition the editors and advisors have made an extensive review of genre fiction: mystery, romance, western, and science fiction, in particular, in an attempt to fill in genre gaps. As with other types of fiction, both literary quality and popularity are taken into consideration in preparing these lists.

This is the first edition of the FICTION CORE COLLECTION published under EBSCO Information Services. As such, users may notice some formatting and indexing changes that reflect differences in book processing procedures and the merging of two bodies of metadata. These changes include, but are not limited to, the repeated listing of author names within Part 1 and the inclusion of a Names Index preceding the Title and Subject Index. As with any transition, there have been adjustments and challenges, but EBSCO is committed to the FICTION CORE COLLECTION, and to all of the titles in the Core Collections line. EBSCO invites feedback from Core Collections customers at corecollections@ebsco.com

Scope and Coverage

The items in the FICTION CORE COLLECTION are considered appropriate for libraries serving adult readers and have been selected with guidance from review sources and the advice of librarian advisors with expertise in fiction. Titles selected for inclusion include popular works deemed to have lasting value to readers as well as new literary and genre titles that have been recognized as significant achievements in their respected areas of literature.

Books listed are both hardcover and paperback editions published in the United States, or published in Canada or the United Kingdom and distributed in the United States. Out-of-print titles have been retained in the belief that good fiction is not obsolete simply because it happens to go out of print.

FICTION CORE COLLECTION is a guide to works of fiction only. Users who seek literary criticism, literary history, biographies of authors, and books on the writing of fiction are referred to FICTION CORE COLLECTION's companion publication, PUBLIC LIBRARY CORE COLLECTION: NONFICTION.

Organization

The Core Collection is organized into two parts: the List of Fictional Works and the Indexes.

Part 1. List of Fictional Works. Books are listed alphabetically under main entry, usually the author. Each entry also includes information about publisher, date of publication, paging, price, ISBN, and Library of Congress control number; a descriptive abstract; and excerpts from reviews when possible.

Part 2. Indexes. The index to books in the List of Fictional Works is divided into two parts: a Name Index and a Title and Subject Index. Access is also provided by genre, form, and literary technique within the Title and Subject Index. This access is one of the Collection's most important features and is especially valued by readers' advisors.

ACKNOWLEDGMENTS

H. W. Wilson and EBSCO Information Services express special gratitude to the following librarians who both advised the company in editorial matters and assisted in the selection and weeding of titles for this Core Collection.

Advisory Board

Beth Anderson
Reference Librarian
Ann Arbor District Library
Ann Arbor, MI

Jennifer Baker
Fiction and Readers' Advisory
  Librarian
The Seattle Public Library
Seattle, WA

Angela Carstensen
Director of Library and
  Media Services
Convent of the Sacred Heart
New York, NY

Leigh Anne Focareta
Senior Librarian
Carnegie Library of Pittsburgh
Pittsburgh, PA

Megan McArdle
Library Services Manager
Berkeley Public Library
Berkeley, CA

Don Wentworth
Senior Staff Librarian
Reference Service Department
Carnegie Library of Pittsburgh
Pittsburgh, PA

The following EBSCO librarians were instrumental in the creation of this collection:

Jennifer Sawtelle
Kendal Spires
Gabriela Toth
Emily Tragert
Brittany Wylde

DIRECTIONS FOR USE OF THE
CORE COLLECTION

USES OF THE COLLECTION

FICTION CORE COLLECTION is designed to serve a number of purposes:

As an aid in purchasing. The Core Collection is designed to assist in the selection and ordering of titles. Annotations are provided for each title along with information concerning the publisher, ISBN, price, and availability.

As an aid in user service. Every title in this Core Collection is a recommended work and can be given with confidence to a user who expresses a need based on topic, genre, etc. Reader's advisory and user service are further aided by information about sequels, series, and companion volumes; by the descriptive and critical annotations; and by the subject headings in the Title and Subject Index.

As an aid in collection maintenance. Information about titles available on a subject facilitates decisions to rebind, replace, or discard items. If a book has been deleted from the Core Collection in this edition because it is no longer in print, that deletion is not intended as a sign that the book is no longer valuable or that it should necessarily be weeded from the collection.

ORGANIZATION

The Core Collection consists of two parts: the List of Fictional Works and the Indexes.

Part 1. List of Fictional Works

Part 1 lists works of fiction in alphabetical order by the last name of the author or by title, if the title is the main entry. References are made from variant forms of authors' names, from names of joint authors, and from names of editors or compilers of short story collections.

Each listing consists of a full bibliographical description. Prices, which are always subject to change, have been obtained from the publisher, when available, and are as current as possible. Entries include notes regarding sequels and publication history, and, whenever possible, an evaluation from a quoted source. The following is an example of a typical entry and a description of its components:

DeLillo, Don

★The **angel** Esmeralda. Scribner 2011 213p $24

ISBN 978-1-4516-5584-1

LC 2011-33996

This book offers a collection of short stories. Various stories include the following themes: "the dread embodied in a child's random abduction ('The Runner'), the sense of doom experienced by a jailed financial crook as he listens to a litany of crisis and chaos on TV ('Hammer and Sickle') and . . . a sexual encounter on a remote tropical island ('Creation'). . . . [T]he title story . . . [is a] tale of two nuns set in . . . the South Bronx during the 1970s, at its worst." (America)

"DeLillo's first collection of short fiction, compiling stories written between 1979 and 2011, serves as a liberating reminder that terror existed long before there was a war on it." (N Y Times Book Rev)

The name of the author, Don DeLillo, is given in conformity with *Anglo-American Cataloguing Rules,* 2nd edition, 2002 revision. The star at the start of the title indicates this is a "most highly recommended" title. The title of the book is *The angel Esmeralda.* The book was published by Scribner in 2011.

The book has 213 pages. If it were part of a series, then the series name would follow the page count. It sells for $24. (Prices given were current when the Collection went to press.)

The ISBN (International Standard Book Number) is included to facilitate ordering. The Library of Congress control number is provided when available.

Following are two notes supplying additional information about the book. The first is a description of the book. The second is a critical note from the *New York Times Book Review.* Such annotations are useful in evaluating books for selection and in determining which of several books on the same subject is best suited for the individual reader. Notes are also made to describe special features, sequels and companion volumes, editions available, and publication history.

Part 2. Indexes

The Title and Subject Index is a single alphabetical list of all the books entered in the Core Collection. Each book is entered under title, which is followed by the name of the author under which the entry for the book will be found in Part 1. Books are also listed under their main subjects or themes, as well as under headings for genre, form, or literary technique, if appropriate. Subject headings and subject cross references are printed in capital letters.

"See" references are made from forms of names or subjects that are not used as headings. "See also" references are made to related or more specific headings.

The following are examples of Index entries for the book cited above:

Title   The **angel** Esmerelda. DeLillo, D.

Subject   **SHORT STORIES**
                 DeLillo, D. The angel Esmerelda

The Name Index is a list of names and pseudonyms used by authors included in Part 1. This list is included as a separate index for ease of reference, readers' advisory, and display creation.

FICTION CORE COLLECTION

SEVENTEENTH EDITION

FICTION CORE COLLECTION

Seventeenth Edition

A

Abani, Christopher
GraceLand. Farrar, Straus, and Giroux 2004
321p $24
ISBN 0-374-16589-0
LC 2003-12705
"This book works brilliantly in two ways. As a convincing and unpatronizing record of life in a poor Nigerian slum, and as a frighteningly honest insight into a world skewed by casual violence, it's wonderful." N Y Times Book Rev

Abbott, Lee K.
All things, all at once; new and selected stories.
Norton 2006 365p $26.95
ISBN 0-393-06137-X; 978-0-393-06137-6
LC 2005-27348
"With his distinctive literary voice, Abbott claims the short story as his own territory and populates it with 40-ish men with bellies going soft who are products of their pasts—which may include duty in Vietnam—trying to make their best of the present. In these sometimes loosely linked stories, which fall into the author's categories of boy-girl, buddy-buddy, father-son, and futuristic or wacky, Abbot virtually grabs the reader by the neck with his opening sentences and doesn't let go. His territory is the Southwest, often small-town Deming, New Mexico, the hometown to which his protagonists tend to return as adults." Booklist

Abbott, Megan E., 1971-
Bury me deep. Simon & Schuster Paperbacks
2009 240p il pa $15
ISBN 978-1-4165-9909-8; 978-1-4165-9909-6
LC 2008-30676
Working "from a true crime, the infamous Brighton Trunk Murders of 1934, Edgar-winner Abbott brings the era to life, inhabiting the 'bright-eyed and twitchy-tailed' party girls in all their enthusiasm and desperation. Her nearly stream-of-consciousness narration is direct and powerful, straight from Marion's addled and passionate brain. . . . But for all the classic-noir simplicity, such as the use of repetition rather than elaboration for emphasis, her prose carries an urgency that brings hardboiled crime fiction kicking and screaming into the modern age." Kirkus

Abbott, Megan E., 1971-
Dare me; a novel. Megan Abbott. Reagan Arthur Books 2012 290 p. $24.99
ISBN 0316097772; 9780316097772
LC 2011051323

This novel tells the story of cheerleaders and best friends Addy Hanlon and Beth Cassidy. Addy has always followed Beth's leadership, but the young and cool new coach "Colette French draws Addy and the other cheerleaders into her life," leaving Beth unsettled and jealous. A suicide "focuses a police investigation on Coach and her squad." When "Addy tries to uncover the truth behind the death," she "learns that the boundary between loyalty and love can be dangerous terrain." (Amazon.com)
"Abbott has a keen sense for the beauty, danger, and vulnerability of teenage girls; her spare, elegant prose cuts straight to the heart of the high school pecking order and brings the girls' world to life." LJ

Abbott, Megan E., 1971-
The end of everything; a novel. Little, Brown
2011 246p $23.99
ISBN 978-0-316-09779-6; 0-316-09779-9
LC 2010-31574
"Lizzie Hood and Evie Verver are two 13-year-old girls who have been best friends for years. A few weeks before their eighth-grade graduation, Evie disappears after school. As the last person to see Evie, Lizzie suddenly becomes the star witness, attention she both covets and dreads. When Lizzie remembers seeing a maroon car cruising in front of their school, the police focus on Harold Shaw, an insurance agent whose car matches her description. Yet Shaw is nowhere to be found, and neither is Evie. As the investigation reaches a fever pitch and Lizzie pursues her own leads, she wonders how well she really knew her friend. Evie's boisterous, joke-cracking father lends emotional support. Abbott . . . expertly captures the nuances of lost innocence and childhood friendships, without ever losing an undercurrent of menace." Publ Wkly

Abbott, Megan E., 1971-
The song is you; [by] Megan Abbott. Simon & Schuster 2007 242p $23
ISBN 978-0-7432-9171-2; 0-7432-9171-9
LC 2006-51229
The author uses a "real-life crime—the disappearance of actress Jean Spangler from Los Angeles in 1949—as her hook to spin a downbeat tale about a journalist-turned-studio-flack, Gil 'Hop' Hopkins. Hop was with Spangler, a stunner but a second-rate acting talent, the last night she was seen, and harbors guilt over leaving her in the company of a famous acting and singing duo, Marv Sutton and Gene Merrel, who have a reputation for rough play. Hop's efforts at amateur sleuthing unearth a blackmail ring and a possible mob connection to Spangler's disappearance. Abbott deserves credit for resurrecting this virtually forgotten case

and concocting a plausible fictional solution to a true crime." Publ Wkly

Abe, Kobo

The **woman** in the dunes; translated from the Japanese by E. Dale Saunders; with drawings by Machi Abé. Knopf 1964 239p il

Original Japanese edition, 1962

The protagonist of this novel "is Niki Jumpei, an amateur entomologist who, on a weekend trip from the city, discovers a bizarre village in the dunes where residents live in deep sand pits. Imprisoned with a widow in one of the pits, he must shovel the omnipresent sand that threatens to bury the community. The novel relates Niki's attempts to escape the pit, his relationship with the woman, and his gradual acceptance of a new identity." Merriam-Webster's Ency of Lit

Abercrombie, Joe

Before they are hanged. Pyr Books 2008 543p pa $15.98

ISBN 978-159102-641-9; 1-59102-641-5

LC 2007-51694

Sequel to: The blade itself

"As savage Northmen invade Angland, the northernmost province of the unwieldy Union, honorable, hardworking Union soldier Colonel West watches his notions of civilized warfare erode in one horrible battle after another. In Dagoska, a southern city threatened by Gurkish soldiers and left undefended as Union troops head to Angland, dreadfully maimed Inquisitor Glokta employs tortures and deceptions to ferret out conspiracies against the king. Ignoring these worldly concerns, disreputable magus Bayaz of Calcis drives a squabbling little band through a wasteland in search of a relic that can open a gate to the realm of demons. Abercrombie leavens the bloody action with moments of dark humor, developing a story suffused with a rich understanding of human darkness and light." Publ Wkly

Followed by: Last argument of kings

Abercrombie, Joe

The **blade** itself. Pyr 2007 531p pa $15

ISBN 978-1-59102-594-8; 1-59102-594-X

LC 2007-28499

This is a "fantasy novel full of enough ironic and slightly self-deprecating humor and Scorcese-esque violence to make the average hipper than thou non-fantasy reader want to learn more about the genre . . . , yet filled with enough touchstones to make your average Tolkien weaned fantasy reader quite happy indeed." Blade & Thruster

Followed by: Before they are hanged

Abercrombie, Joe

The **heroes**; 1st ed. Orbit 2011 xi, 541p.p ill.

ISBN 9780316044981; 0316193569; 9780316193566

This fantasy novel tells the story of a "three-day battle . . . set in the same world as [author Joe] Abercrombie's First Law Trilogy. . . . Union commander Lord Marshal Kroy coordinates the fight with the aid of a motley group of incompetent, self-important officers. . . . Col. Bremer dan Gorst is officially a royal observer who nurses a burning desire to kill or be killed. Leading a much smaller army against the Union is Black Dow, whose grip on the throne of the Northmen is tenuous and based on fear and brutality. Calder, a slippery and cunning egotist, advocates peace while plotting to take Black Dow's place." (Publishers Weekly)

Abercrombie, Joe

Last argument of kings. Pyr Books 2008 639p pa $15.98

ISBN 978-1-59102-690-7; 1-59102-690-3

LC 2008-482104

Concluding title in the author's First Law sword & sorcery trilogy that began with The blade itself and Before they are hanged

"Abercrombie is a fresh new talent, presenting a dark view of life with wit and zest, and readers will mourn the end of this vivid story arc." Publ Wkly

Abercrombie, Joe

Red country; Orbit 2012 464 p.

ISBN 0316187216; 9780316187213

In this novel by Joe Abercrombie "Shy South . . . [will] have to sharpen up some bad old ways to get her family back. . . . She sets off in pursuit with only a pair of oxen and her cowardly old step father Lamb for company. But it turns out Lamb's buried a bloody past of his own. . . . Their journey will take them across the barren plains to a frontier town gripped by gold fever, through feud, duel and massacre, high into the unmapped mountains to a reckoning with the Ghosts." (Publisher's note)

Ablow, Keith R.

Compulsion; {by} Keith Ablow. St. Martin's Press 2002 321p

ISBN 0-312-26641-3

LC 2001-58861

"Clevenger does not spout jargon, and if you can get past the unnerving glibness, he comes across with fascinating clinical insights into murderers and other psychos." N Y Times Book Rev

Abraham, Daniel

An **autumn** war. Tor 2008 366p $25.95

ISBN 978-0-7653-1342-3; 0-7653-1342-1

LC 2008-16974

Third volume in the author's Long Price Quartet; earlier titles: A shadow in summer; A betrayal in winter

In this fantasy, "powerful elementals called andat are enslaved by poets to work for the city-states of the Khaiem. The ongoing struggles of familiar, aging characters-poet Maati, his ex-lover Liat, the mercenary Sinja, and Otah, now the reluctant ruler of his Khaiem city-occupy much of the story, but a new voice drives the plot. Gen. Balasar Gice, of the rival Galt Empire, is convinced that the andat are a threat to mankind and wants to eliminate them for good. As Gice's plan comes to fruition, everyone must confront changes in their world that go beyond anything they'd ever imagined. New readers will find Abraham's deft storytelling style accessible, but returning fans will most appreciate the growth of the world and the characters." Publ Wkly

Abraham, Daniel

A **shadow** in summer. Tor 2006 331p $24.95

ISBN 0-765-31340-5

LC 2005-16832

This is a "fine example of high fantasy that, in its presentation of the poet-andat relationship, offers a new and striking take on the age-old question of the power of magic and the responsibilities of the magician. But what is most stisfying about the book is the degree to which it bends the conventions of the genre in interesting ways." Sci Fic Wkly

Abraham, Pearl

The **romance** reader. Riverhead Bks. 1995 296p

ISBN 1-573-22015-9

LC 95-964

"Abraham's intense, sensitive prose and her ability to create vivid scenes and memorable characters augment this authentic, often disturbing, look at Hasidic home life and beliefs." Publ Wkly

Abrahams, Peter

Dog on it; a Chet and Bernie mystery. [by] Spencer Quinn. Atria Books 2008 305p $25

ISBN 978-1-4165-8583-1; 1-4165-8583-4

"Chet the Jet is a dog who failed K-9 school (cats in the open country played a role in his demise), but now he is a dedicated PI and works with Bernie, owner of the Little Detective Agency. The story is told entirely from Chet's point of view, which will delight dog-loving mystery readers, but the book is also an excellent PI tale, dogs aside, as Chet and Bernie investigate the disappearance of a teenage girl whose developer dad may be up to no good. . . . Excellent and fully fleshed primary and secondary characters, a consistently doggy view of the world, and a sprightly pace make this a not-to-be-missed debut." Booklist

Abrahams, Peter

Hard rain. Dutton 1988 374p

ISBN 0-525-24581-2

LC 87-18947

"Jessie is an appealingly ordinary heroine, a resilient working mother. And each of the characters she encounters on her descent into a violent world of personal and political deception is vividly drawn. 'Hard Rain,' which takes its title from a Bob Dylan song, is infused with a knowing, affectionate feeling for the pop culture of the 1960's." N Y Times Book Rev

Abrahams, Peter

Nerve damage. William Morrow 2007 304p $24.95

ISBN 978-0-06-113797-6; 0-06-113797-9

LC 2006-47092

"Sculptor Roy Valois has never recovered from the tragic death of his beloved wife, Delia, in a helicopter accident while on a humanitarian mission to Honduras. Delia worked for the Hobbes Institute, 'a think tank specializing in third-world economic problems.' Roy's internal scars have kept him at a distance from others, even as the effects of asbestos exposure in his youth begin to ravage his body. When a chance remark leads Roy to search out the text of his already written obituary for the New York Times, he finds a minor error concerning the Hobbes Institute. That niggling loose thread obsesses the artist, but his efforts to set the record straight reveal that much of what he knew about his wife was a lie." Publ Wkly

"The care with which Abrahams brings his characters to life sets him apart from most thriller writers working today." New Yorker

Abrams, David

Fobbit. Black Cat 2012 372 p. $15

ISBN 0802120326; 9780802120328

This book is a "satire of the Iraq War. . . . The Fobbits of the title are U.S. Army support personnel, stationed at Baghdad's enclave of desk jobs: Forward Operating Base Triumph. . . . The soul of the book is Staff Sgt. Chance Gooding Jr., a public relations NCO who spends his days crafting excruciating press releases and fending off a growing sense of moral bankruptcy." (Publishers Weekly)

Abu-Jaber, Diana

Birds of paradise; a novel. W. W. Norton & Co. 2011 362p $25.95

ISBN 978-0-393-06461-2; 0-393-06461-1

LC 2011-14575

"After 13-year-old Felice Muir runs away from her Miami home. . . , her mother, Avis, retreats to her kitchen, where she creates elaborate pastries as part therapy, part offering to her absent daughter. Felice's father, Brian, buries himself in his lawyering and fantasizes about the young Cuban woman in the office next door, and her brother, Stanley, throws himself into the organic market he's opened in lieu of going to college. They all vacillate between willing themselves to forget Felice and constant wondering—why she left, where she is, if she's alive—until the approach of her eighteenth birthday and a storm named Katrina upsets their fragile holding patterns. Abu-Jaber . . . employs her descriptive talents in bringing Miami to steamy, pulsing life, but it is Birds of Paradise's neither predictable nor merely haphazard momentum and its rich cast of characters that make us feel we're in deliciously capable hands." Elle

Abu-Jaber, Diana

Crescent. Norton 2003 349p hardcover o.p. pa $13.95

ISBN 0-393-05747-X; 0-393-32554-7 pa

LC 2002-152907

"Sirine's now-deceased missionary parents were Iraqi and American; she's been raised since she was nine by her beloved Iraqi uncle. Her world is his house, the cafe where she is chef, and the air of Los Angeles. She's nearly 40, and inside her pale skin and green eyes she feels the rhythms of her uncle's Arabic stories and the scent of Eastern spices. Hanif ('Han'), a professor of Arabic literature at the local university comes to the cafe for the tastes of home, and he and Sirine fall into an affair of wild, sweet tenderness. . . . Abu-Jaber's language is miraculous, whether describing the texture of Han's skin or Sirine's way with an onion. It is not possible to stop reading." Booklist

Abu-Jaber, Diana

Origin; a novel. W.W. Norton & Co. 2007 384p $24.95

ISBN 978-0-393-06455-1; 0-393-06455-7

LC 2007-4963

"For all its internal chill, the drama that unfolds around fingerprint expert Lena Dawson is a struggle toward spring and the light. Haunting and compelling, Origin combines the traditions of the crime novel with an examination of Lena's unusual upbringing. It's a little film noir, a bit independent-woman-detective thriller, and winningly fresh in its approach." PopMatters

Achebe, Chinua

★ Things fall apart. Astor-Honor 1959 215p $15.95

ISBN 0-8392-1113-9

First published 1958 in the United Kingdom; first United States edition published by McDowell, Obolensky

"The novel chronicles the life of Okonkwo, the leader of an Igbo (Ibo) community, from the events leading up to his banishment from the community for accidentally killing a clansman, through the seven years of his exile, to his return. The novel addresses the problem of the intrusion in the 1890s of white missionaries and colonial government into tribal Igbo society. It describes the simultaneous disintegration of its protagonist Okonkwo and of his village. The novel was praised for its intelligent and realistic treatment of tribal beliefs and of psychological disintegration coincident with social unraveling." Merriam-Webster's Ency of Lit

Aciman, Andre A.

Call me by your name; [by] André Aciman. Farrar, Straus and Giroux 2007 248p $23

ISBN 0-374-29921-8

LC 2006-11720

"When Oliver, a handsome young American philosopher, arrives in a seaside town in Italy to work on a book about Heraclitus, as the guest of an Italian professor, the son of the house, Elio—seventeen, studious, moody, and ravenous—falls for him. Elio's edgy rapture as he forms himself in relation to another plays out against the background of a scorching Mediterranean summer, and Aciman introduces a small universe of characters who are themselves altered by the charged air that surrounds the lovers: Elio's mother, who calls Oliver il cauboi (the cowboy); his generous, hazy father; and the households cantankerous cook, who every morning carefully cracks open the American's soft-boiled eggs." New Yorker

Aciman, André

Eight white nights; [by] Andre Aciman. Farrar, Straus and Giroux 2010 360p $26

ISBN 978-0-374-22842-2; 0-374-22842-6

LC 2009-25415

This "novel unfolds over eight snowy nights in Manhattan. The unnamed narrator arrives at a swank party, where he meets a beautiful young woman named Clara. The two strike up a flirtatious exchange that carries them through an affair, and which makes up a large chunk of the narrative. Clara's speech is peppered with puns and neologisms that are meant to lend an air of sophistication but which make her sound like a disturbed adolescent. 'For your nymphormation, namphibalence strikes women too,' she says, after tonguing her friend Beryl in front of some men. Happily, Aciman's gifts as a poet of desire outshine the high jinks." New Yorker

Aciman, André

Harvard Square; a novel. André Aciman. 1st ed. W.W. Norton & Co Inc. 2013 304 p. (hardcover) $25.95

ISBN 039308860X; 9780393088601

LC 2012050738

This book's narrator, "a young Jewish man originally from Egypt, is a graduate student at Harvard in the mid 1970s. After failing exams he questions his goal of a career in academia. When he's not studying, he frequents Cambridge bars and restaurants that cater to a Middle Eastern clientele, and there he meets Kalaj, a man of Tunisian descent with a magnetic personality. With much in common, the two bond and spend the fall carousing in Cambridge and reminiscing about their pasts." (Library Journal)

Ackroyd, Peter

The fall of Troy. Nan A. Talese 2007 212p $23

ISBN 978-0-385-52290-8

LC 2007-7208

First published 2006 in the United Kingdom

Ackroyd's "evocation of the landscape, the weather and the conditions of the Hissarlik dig are brilliant, and his minor characters are deftly brought to life. Above all, he manages to suggest, in a book which is less slight than it may appear, that men who meddle with the gods do so at their peril." Sunday Telegraph

Ackroyd, Peter

The trial of Elizabeth Cree; a novel of the Limehouse murders. Talese 1995 261p

ISBN 0-385-47707-4

LC 94-37348

First published 1994 in the United Kingdom with title: Dan Leno and the Limehouse Golem

"Well-known but incidental Victorian 'characters'—Karl Marx and the novelist George Gissing—converge in this mystery/anti-suspense fiction about a former music-hall actress, Elizabeth Cree, and her husband, an apparent serial killer. Chapters of Mr. Cree's diary alternate with transcripts of Mrs. Cree's trial for his murder and sections of third-person narrative." New Yorker

Adams, Alice

After the war; a novel. Knopf 2000 305p $25

ISBN 0-375-40683-2

LC 99-47104

Adams' final novel, set in 1940s North Carolina, "picks up where her previous book, 'A Southern Exposure,' left off. Cynthia Baird, a transplanted Yankee, is floating from one affair to another while her husband, Harry, is off fighting in Europe; her housekeeper, Odessa, the moral center of this particular universe, keeps turning out her ham biscuits; the local girls, including Melanctha Byrd, who is heading North to Radcliffe . . . are growing sly and eager to leave town. There are so many subplots—about race relations, sex, politics, and adolescence—that it's as if Adams wanted both to capture an era entirely and to make things, this once, come out right. The result is lovely, tender, and a little hokey, like that moment just before the birthday candles are blown out." New Yorker

Adams, Alice

A **southern** exposure; a novel. Knopf 1996 305p

ISBN 0-679-44452-1

LC 95-16109

"Though this plot teeters on the edge of soap opera, it never slips into the slush, thanks in part to the sobering imminence of war, which casts an air of gravity over all these amorous proceedings. Ms. Adams's breezy, wistful lyricism perfectly captures this lovely place and golden time, just before things got so damn serious forever." NY Times Book Rev

Adams, Alice

★ The **stories** of Alice Adams. Knopf 2002 622p $30

ISBN 0-375-41285-9

LC 2002-70940

"Taken together, these stories betray the changing mores of the past half-century; taken in sequence, they trace the changes in the American short story over the past 40 years, some of those changes wrought by Adams herself." Publ Wkly

Adams, Douglas

The **hitchhiker's** guide to the galaxy; 25th anniversary illustrated collector's ed.; Harmony Books 2004 271p il $35

ISBN 1-4000-5293-9

LC 2004-558987

First published 1980

"Based on a BBC radio series, . . . this is the episodic story of Arthur Dent, a contemporary Englishman who discovers first that his unpretentious house is about to be demolished to make way for a bypass, and second that a good friend is actually an alien galactic hitchhiker who announces that Earth itself will soon be demolished to make way for an intergalactic speedway. A suitably bewildered Dent soon finds himself hitching . . . rides throughout space, aided by a . . . reference book, The Hitchhiker's Guide to the Galaxy, a compendium of 'facts,' philosophies, and wild advice." Libr J

Adams, Douglas

Life, the universe, and everything. Harmony Bks. 1982 227p hardcover o.p. pa $12.95

ISBN 0-517-54874-7; 0-345-41890-6 pa

LC 82-15470

Third volume in The hitchhiker's series

"Arthur Dent and his motley crew do tie up most of the loose ends and manage to prevent the destruction of the universe, but the first two novels . . . 'must' be read to understand the situation, and even then it's confusing." Libr J

Followed by So long, and thanks for all the fish

Adams, Douglas

Mostly harmless. Harmony Bks. 1992 277p hardcover o.p. pa $12.95

ISBN 0-517-57740-2; 0-345-37933-0 pa

LC 92-25457

"A Grebulon reconnaissance ship with faulty programming, a news reporter suffering from a bad case of missed opportunities, a fugitive from the new 'improved' offices of the Hitchhiker's Guide to the Galaxy, and a hitchhiker lost in a parallel universe come together in grand style in the fifth installment of Adams's best-selling 'trilogy.'" Libr J

Adams, Douglas

The **restaurant** at the end of the universe. Harmony Bks. 1981 250p hardcover o.p. pa $12.95

ISBN 0-517-54535-7; 0-345-41892-1 pa

LC 81-6563

Second volume in The hitchhiker's series

First published 1980 in the United Kingdom

"Poor uprooted Arthur Dent finds himself swept along in the wake of Zaphod Beeblebrox, former President of the Galaxy, as Zaphod searches for the man who rules the Universe. They and their companions tumble from one scrape into another, with the erratic aid of Zaphod's dead great-grandfather and Marvin, their perpetually depressed robot. Adams's lively sense of the ridiculous has concocted many hilarious episodes, though the inspired lunacy of the first book has become rather uneven here. Still, this is one of the best pieces of sf humor available." Libr J

Followed by Life, the universe, and everything

Adams, Douglas

So long, and thanks for all the fish. Harmony Bks. 1985 204p hardcover o.p. pa $7.99

ISBN 0-517-55439-9; 0-345-39183-4 pa

LC 84-19350

Fourth volume in The hitchhiker's series

Arthur Dent "returns to a supposedly destroyed Earth to build a hyperspace bypass. The night of his return, Arthur falls in love with a sedated girl (her brother says she's 'barking mad'), only to lose her, then accidentally find her twice more. She is Fenchurch, the girl who in . . . 'Guide' . . . discovered the secret of Earth's potential happiness moments before it was demolished. Her 'madness' stems from the time when Earth should have been destroyed, and wasn't, but when all the dolphins disappeared. . . . The humor is still off-the-wall, but less forced and more gentle than the other books. . . . The series seems to be winding down, but it is still an addictive commodity to its fans." SLJ

Followed by Mostly harmless

Adams, Henry

★ **Democracy**; an American novel. introduction by Arthur Schlesinger, Jr. Modern Library 2003 xx, 209p pa $12.95

ISBN 0-375-76058-X

LC 2002-19645

First published anonymously 1880

"A social and political satire based on the corruption of the second Grant administration, the book includes characters modeled on President Hayes and James G. Blaine. A charming and intelligent young widow, Madeleine Lee, moves to Washington 'to touch with her own hands the massive machinery of society.' She finally rejects an offer of marriage from a senator who has compromised his moral integrity for political advantage." Reader's Ency. 3d edition

Adams, Lorraine

Harbor. Knopf 2004 291p $23.95

ISBN 1-4000-4233-X

LC 2004-40916

This novel "tells the story of Aziz Arkoun, a twenty-four-year-old Arab Muslim from Algeria who enters America illegally by hiding for fifty-two days in the hold of a tanker and swimming into Boston Harbor. Aziz falls in with a group of young Algerians in East Boston, including Rafik, a childhood friend who is now a petty criminal. Hopes for prosperity and safety are dashed: Aziz takes low-paying jobs, is beset by chaotic living arrangements, and, after stumbling across some suspicious secret dealings of Rafik's, gets caught up in the F.B.I. investigation of an international terrorist cell. Though the premise of the novel may seem too topical for its own good, Adams displays a gift for detail and character that takes us fully inside the complex systems of survival, kinship, and religious ideology which form Aziz's world." New Yorker

Adams, Lorraine

The **room** and the chair; a novel. Alfred A. Knopf 2010 315p $25.95

ISBN 978-0-307-27241-6; 0-307-27241-9

LC 2009-24009

"Adams' book is so topical it could be ripped from tomorrow's headlines. It's an inside scoop that reads — given its large cast of characters, its numerous locales and its labyrinthine plot twists — like a much bigger book than its tidy 315 pages. Yet the reader never feels cheated, so good a reporter is Adams, so supple a writer." San Antonio Express-News

Adams, Poppy

The **sister**; a novel. Alfred A. Knopf 2008 273p $23.95

ISBN 978-0-307-26816-7; 0-307-26816-0

LC 2008-1882

Published in the United Kingdom with title: The behaviour of moths

"Ginny and her younger sister Vivien lead an idyllic childhood in West Dorset, England, until Vivien nearly dies in an accident . . . when Ginny is 11 and Vivien is eight. Later, after the pair is expelled from school, a 15-year-old Vivien moves to London, and Ginny stays behind, covering up her mother Maud's alcoholism while trying to assist her father, Clive, with his research on moths and butterflies. After Maud's death and Clive's subsequent dementia, Ginny lives alone in the massive house, a brilliant but increasingly reclusive scientist whose insular world is cracked open when Vivien announces her desire to return and live out her days with Ginny. Long-buried secrets float to the surface as Ginny narrates with scientific precision her life's slow disintegration. Though the lepidopterological jargon and asides can slow things down, Adams expertly captures Ginny's voice and the dynamics of a deeply troubled family as the book barrels toward its chilling conclusion." Publ Wkly

Adams, Richard

Watership Down. Scribner Classics 1974 429p $27.50

ISBN 0-684-83605-4

First published 1972 in the United Kingdom; first United States edition 1974 by Macmillian

"Faced with the annihilation of its warren, a small group of male rabbits sets out across the English downs in search of a new home. Internal struggles for power surface in this intricately woven, realistically told adult adventure when the protagonists must coordinate tactics in order to defeat an enemy rabbit fortress. It is clear that the author has done research on rabbit behavior, for this tale is truly authentic." Shapiro. Fic for Youth. 3d edition

Adams, Sheila Kay

My old true love; a novel. Algonquin Books of Chapel Hill 2004 289p $23.95

ISBN 1-565-12407-3

LC 2003-70809

"Paying keen attention to the nuances of relationships between individuals as well as between people and their geographical and temporal contexts, Sheila Kay Adams writes a uniquely private and complex Civil War novel. Adams elegantly interweaves folk songs and nature into her narrative in ways that never stray from her purpose, which is to tell a family's story." Hist Fic Rev

Adamson, Gil

The **outlander**; a novel. Ecco 2008 389p $25.95

ISBN 978-0-06-149125-2; 0-06-149125-X

LC 2007-41062

First published in 2007 in Canada

"Of course, the Girl Being Chased is one of the most enduring figures of chivalric and chauvinistic literature, a staple of television dramas and horror films. . . . But Gil is short for Gillian, and her strange and complicated heroine has nothing in common with Hollywood's wornout damsels in distress. . . there are pages here you can't read slowly enough to catch every word." Washington Post Book World

Adichie, Chimamanda Ngozi, 1977-

★ **Americanah**; a novel. Chimamanda Ngozi Adichie. 1st ed. Alfred A. Knopf 2013 496 p. (hardcover) $26.95

ISBN 0307271080; 9780307271082

LC 2012043875

In this book, "Ifemelu, beautiful and naturally aristocratic, has the good fortune to escape Nigeria during a time of military dictatorship. . . . Ifemelu's high school sweetheart, Obinze . . . he has been denied a visa to enter post-9/11 America . . . , and now he is living illegally in London, delivering refrigerators and looking for a way to find his beloved. . . . The years pass, and Ifemelu is involved in the usual entanglements." Can they reunite? (Kirkus Reviews)

Adichie, Chimamanda Ngozi, 1977-

Half of a yellow sun. Alfred A. Knopf 2006 435p $24.95

ISBN 978-1-4000-4416-0; 1-4000-4416-2

LC 2005-57784

The author has a "gift for capturing the rhythms of African middle-class life: not just its political awareness but the aspirations and cultural imperatives that lend it its varied character.... For its portrayal of Nigeria's political and cultural past, [this book] is a welcome addition to the corpus of African letters." Times Lit Suppl

Adichie, Chimamanda Ngozi, 1977-
The **thing** around your neck. Alfred A. Knopf 2009 240p $24.95
 ISBN 978-0-307-27107-5; 0-307-27107-2
          LC 2008-41271
"The stories are set both in the United States and in Nigeria, where things continue to fall apart.... Adichie, a brilliant writer whose characters stay with you for a long time, deserves to be more widely known." Libr J

Adiga, Aravind
✓ ★ **Last** man in tower; a novel. Alfred A. Knopf 2011 381p $26.96
 ISBN 978-0-307-59409-9; 0-307-59409-2
          LC 2011-03406
"In the rapidly expanding city of Mumbai, where new buildings sprout like weeds, the construction business isn't just a front for illegal activity, it's a raison d'être. When a less-than-ethical developer tries to lure, and later coerce, a community of longstanding tenants out of their apartment complex, it is only the widowed schoolteacher of 3A who continues to rebuff him.... [Adiga] maps out, in luminous prose, India's ambivalence toward its accelerated growth, while creating an engaging protagonist in the stubborn resident: a man whose ambition and independence have been tempered with an understanding of the important, if almost imperceptible, difference between development and progress." Entertainment Wkly

Adiga, Aravind
✓ The **white** tiger; a novel. Free Press 2008 336p $24
 ISBN 978-1-416-56259-7; 1-416-56259-1
          LC 2007-45527
"In this darkly comic début novel set in India, Balram, a chauffeur, murders his employer, justifying his crime as the act of a 'social entrepreneur.' In a series of letters to the Premier of China, in anticipation of the leader's upcoming visit to Balram's homeland, the chauffeur recounts his transformation from an honest, hardworking boy growing up in 'the Darkness'—those areas of rural India where education and electricity are equally scarce, and where villagers banter about local elections 'like eunuchs discussing the Kama Sutra'—to a determined killer. He places the blame for his rage squarely on the avarice of the Indian élite, among whom bribes are commonplace, and who perpetuate a system in which many are sacrificed to the whims of a few. Adiga's message isn't subtle or novel, but Balram's appealingly sardonic voice and acute observations of the social order are both winning and unsettling." New Yorker

Adler, Elizabeth
✓ **All** or nothing. Delacorte Press 1999 327p
 ISBN 0-385-33380-3
          LC 99-31965

This suspense novel features retired New Orleans homicide detective, now Hollywood Hills private investigator Al Giraud and his partner, law professor and ex-DA Marla Cwitowitz. The wife of electronics executive Steve Mallard hires the duo when her husband becomes the prime suspect in the disappearance of realtor Laurie Martin

Adler, Elizabeth
Fortune is a woman. Delacorte Press 1992 433p
✓ ISBN 0-385-30529-X
          LC 91-24977
"Francie Harrison is the poor little rich girl with a misogynistic father in turn-of-the-century San Francisco. She escapes the doll's world he plans for her and finds love, only to have it disintegrate in the earthquake of 1906. Amidst the destruction, she meets Lai Tsin, an illegal Chinese immigrant, and the strong Yorkshirewoman Annie Aysgarth, who, together, help her build a world for herself. All three profit from the alliance and emerge on top of the business world, rich in friendship as well as treasure.... Writing and characterization are tight, depictions of Nob Hill and Oriental influence ring true, and pacing is superb." Booklist

Adler, Elizabeth
Now or never. Delacorte Press 1997 346p
 ISBN 0-385-31592-9
          LC 96-24146
"Predictably, romantic sparks fly, but there's something mysterious about the beautiful Mallory. Eventually Harry pries his lover's deepest secrets out of her and finds she may hold the clue to the murderer's identity. Nerve-jangling suspense, steamy sex, glamorous characters, and graphic descriptions of the victims' last moments will grab readers' attention." Booklist

Adler, Hans Gunther
Panorama; a novel. [by] H.G. Adler; translated from the German by Peter Filkins. Random House 2010 xxii, 450p $26
 ISBN 978-1-4000-6851-7; 1-4000-6851-7
          LC 2010-15079
Original German edition, 1968
"Adler chronicles various moments in the life of protagonist Josef: unhappy childhood in Prague, brutish boarding school, teenage adventures in the bucolic Czech forest, political and bureaucratic frustrations as a young academic, and, finally, hardship and bleakness in a concentration camp. It is written in a captivating stream-of-consciousness style that wanders yet comes to circle certain salient observations, and readers may note stylistic and philosophical continuities between this and the work of W. G. Sebald, who claimed Adler as a major influence. But, in part, the beauty of this work is that it can't be easily categorized: it's not quite a bildungsroman; it's delightfully if erratically satirical; it's hauntingly bleak yet possesses echoes of the transcendent." Booklist

Adler-Olsen, Jussi
The **absent** one; by Jussi Adler-Olsen; translated by K.E. Semmel. Dutton 2012 406 p. (hardcover) $26.95
 ISBN 9780525952893
          LC 2012021473

This novel, by Jussi Adler-Olsen, is the second book in the "Department Q" series. It follows "detective Carl Mørck, a deeply flawed, brilliant detective newly assigned to . . . Copenhagen's coldest cases. . . . A brother and sister were brutally murdered two decades earlier. . . . But once Mørck reopens the files, it becomes clear that all is not what it seems. Looking into the supposedly solved case leads him to Kimmie, a woman living on the streets, stealing to survive." (Publisher's note)

Adler-Olsen, Jussi

A **Conspiracy** of Faith; Jussi Adler-Olsen. Penguin Group USA 2013 512 p. (hardcover) $26.95

ISBN 0525954007; 9780525954002

This novel, by Jussi Adler-Olsen, is part of the "Department Q" series. "Detective Carl Mørck holds . . . [an] old and decayed message, written in blood. It is a cry for help from two young brothers, tied and bound in a boathouse by the sea. Could it be real? . . . Carl's investigation will force him to cross paths with a woman stuck in a desperate marriage. . . . But enough is enough. She will find out the truth, no matter the cost to her husband--or to herself." (Publisher's note)

Adler-Olsen, Jussi

The **keeper** of lost causes; Jussi Adler-Olsen; translated by Lisa Hartford. Dutton 2011 396 p. (hardcover) $25.95

ISBN 0525952489; 9780525952480

LC 2011014873

This novel, by Jussi Adler-Olsen, first entry in the "Department Q" series, "features the deeply flawed chief detective Carl Mørck, who used to be . . . one of Copenhagen's best. . . . [Now] Carl's been selected to run Department Q, a new special investigations division that turns out to be a department of one. With a stack of Copenhagen's coldest cases to keep him company, . . . Carl may have the last laugh, and redeem himself in the process." (Publisher's note)

Adrian, Chris

The **children's** hospital. McSweeney's Books 2006 615p $24

ISBN 1-932416-60-9

"Adrian's vast floating world of a novel is a marvel. The Children's Hospital is intelligent, seductive and beautifully realized." Hartford Courant

Adrian, Chris

The **great** night. Farrar, Straus and Giroux 2011 292p $26

ISBN 978-0-374-16641-0; 0-374-16641-2

LC 2010-47603

A "retelling of Shakespeare;'s 'A Midsummer Night's Dream.' On Midsummer Eve 2008, three people, each on the run from a failed relationship, become trapped in San Francisco's Buena Vista Park, the secret home of Titania, Oberon, and their court. On this night, something awful is happening in the faerie kingdom: in a fit of sadness over the end of her marriage, which broke up in the wake of the death of her adopted son, Titania has set loose an ancient menace, and the chaos that ensues will threaten the lives of immortals and mortals alike." Publisher's note

"Inventive and scarily beautiful, this could wipe out casual readers, but it is an extraordinary novel." Libr J

Agee, James

★ A **death** in the family. McDowell, Obolensky 1957 339p

"Six-year-old Rufus Follet, his younger sister Catherine, his mother, and various relatives all react differently to the unexpected announcement that Rufus's father has been fatally injured in an automobile accident. The poignancy of sorrow, the strength of personal beliefs, and the comforting love and support of a family are all elements of this compassionate novel." Shapiro. Fic for Youth. 3d edition

Agee, James

Let us now praise famous men; A death in the family, and shorter fiction. Library of America 2005 818p il $35

ISBN 1-931082-81-2

LC 2005-45098

Let us now praise famous men (1941) is a journalistic collaboration with photographer Walker Evans that depicts the lives of Alabama sharecroppers. A death in the family is entered separately. The morning watch (1951) is an autobiographical novella where a twelve-year-old school boy in Tennessee wrestles with religious issues. Several short stories are also included.

Agnon, Shmuel Yosef

★ **Only** yesterday; [by] S.Y. Agnon; translated by Barbara Harshav. Princeton Univ. Press 2000 652p

ISBN 0-691-00972-4

LC 00-21147

"Though Agnon would go on to write much of compelling interest during his remaining 25 years, this would be his masterpiece—a novel that deserves comparison with Kafka's The Trial, Mann's The Magic Mountain and Hermann Broch's The Sleepwalkers as a deployment of the resources of fiction for plumbing those abysses of cultural and personal crisis that haunted so many imaginations in the modernist period." Los Angeles Times Book Rev

Ahmad, A. X.

The **Caretaker**. St. Martin's Press 2013 304 p. (hardcover) $24.99

ISBN 1250016843; 9781250016843

LC 2013006966

This novel "introduces Ranjit Singh, a former captain in the Indian army currently trying to make ends meet as a landscaper on Martha's Vineyard." Singh gets the caretaker position at the home of Sen. Clayton Neals. "Singh's family moves into the Neals's home, but they must flee when a break-in occurs. As they leave, Singh's daughter, Shanti, grabs a doll that contains a hidden microfilm chip that proves to be the key to the family's survival." (Library Journal)

Ahmad, Jamil

The **wandering** falcon. Penguin Books 2011 243p $25.95

ISBN 978-0-241-114515-9; 0-241-14515-5

LC 20110323153

A novel "set in the forbidding remote tribal areas of Pakistan and Afghanistan. . . . [The author] has written [a] . . . portrait of a world of custom and compassion, of love and cruelty, of hardship and survival, a place fragile, unknown, and unforgiving." (Publisher's note)

"A gripping book, as important for illuminating the current state of this region as it is timeless in its beautiful imagery and rhythmic prose." Publ Wkly

Aiken, Joan

The **monkey's** wedding, and other stories. Small Beer Press 2011 203p $24

ISBN 978-1-931520-74-4; 1-931520-74-7

LC 2011-04625

"Brisk, matter-of-fact accounts of annoying mermaids, hospitable devils, unionizing mice and robot prototypes that make flipping light switches an act of menace. And the women range from self-willed wives to beautiful stunt motorcyclists to knitting spinsters. Sometimes they conform to the stereotypes of the times they were created in, but Aiken is full of surprises: Her plots and characters continually wander off the beaten track, leaving far behind what fantasist Lord Dunsany called 'the fields we know.'" Seattle Times

Aira, Cesar

An **afternoon** in the life of a landscape painter. New Directions 2006 87p $12.95

ISBN 978-0-8112-1630-2; 0-8112-1630-6

LC 2005-35053

Original Spanish edition, 2000

"This novella-cum-artistic meditation is about Johann Moritz Rugendas, a 19th century German artist and colleague of explorer Alexander von Humboldt. Rugendas visited Chile, Argentina and Mexico in the hope of recording the flora and fauna through an art conceived as 'physiognomic totality.' During a trip to the Pampas, he is electrified by a convergence of nature and spirituality. The impact of his experience handicaps him physically and psychologically. And his quest to see the Indians of the region ultimately crowns his descent to hell. More than fiction, it is an imaginative chronicle based on Rugendas' correspondence and other historical sources from the era. To which Aira adds the novelistic touch: el beso de la fantasía—the kiss of fantasy. That his protagonist is a European attempting to scientifically codify what he sees—Rugendas is a child of positivism—allows for an unforgettable opportunity to see Latin America from the eyes of a foreigner. Better yet, the foreigner, Rugendas, is re-imagined a la Russian doll by a native, Aira, thus inviting the reader to be simultaneously outsiders and insider." San Francisco Chronicle

Aira, Cesar

Ghosts; translated by Chris Andrews. New Directions 2008 139p pa $12.95

ISBN 978-0-8112-1742-2 pa; 0-8112-1742-6 pa

LC 2008-47193

Original Spanish edition, 1990

A "novel about a migrant Chilean family living in an apartment house under construction in Buenos Aires. New Year's Eve finds the hard-drinking Chilean night watchman, Raúl Vinas, hosting a party with his wife, Elisa, their four small children and Elisa's pensive 15-year-old daughter, Patri. Moreover, ghosts reside in the house: naked, dust-covered floating men, mostly unseen except by Elisa and Patri. The novel engineers a clever layering of metaphorical details about the building, but gradually focuses on Elisa's preparations for the party and her conversations with her daughter about finding a 'real man' to marry. Prodded perhaps by her isolation within the family, Patri accepts the ghosts' invitation to a midnight feast, at her life's peril." Publ Wkly

Aira, Cesar

The **literary** conference; translated by Katherine Silver. New Directions 2010 90p pa $9.95

ISBN 978-0-8112-1878-8 pa; 0-8112-1878-3 pa

LC 2009-45914

Original Spanish edition, 2006

"At a literary conference, César, the protagonist—author and translator by day, mad scientist by night—hatches a plan to rule the world by creating an army cloned from the Mexican author Carlos Fuentes. But César accidentally clones a cell that's not from Fuentes but from Fuentes's silk tie, thus loosing lumbering, thousand-foot-long electric-blue silkworms upon the city of Mérida. Aira writes, 'It seems like the insertion of a different plot line, from an old B-rated science fiction movie.' It sure does. But Aira's writerly self-reference, while hardly subtle, is disarming, and the result is amusing, self-conscious camp." New Yorker

Aira, Cesar

The **seamstress** and the wind; translated by Rosalie Knecht. New Directions 2011 132p pa $12.95

ISBN 978-0-8112-1912-9; 0-8112-1912-7

LC 2011-06006

Original Spanish edition, 1994

The novel "is simultaneously minimalist and epic. Aira's voice is clear, his characters are palpable, and his ideas—elucidations on literary theory, existential ruminations, and thought experiments—are evocative and infectious. The story, which concerns a seamstress and her husband who travel the Patagonia desert in pursuit of their accidentally kidnapped son, careens with each chapter at dizzying speed. Seamstress might be thought confusing and possibly incomplete, because the story's inciting incident—the kidnapped child—goes completely unresolved, even forgotten by the seamstress and her husband. But that is the point: It's part of Aira's style; he is mysterious without obfuscating." Zyzzyva

Akhtar, Ayad, 1970-

√**American** dervish; by Ayad Akhtar. Little, Brown and Co. 2012 357p

ISBN 9780297865445 Weidenfeld and Nicolson; 0316183318 Little, Brown and Co.; 9780316183314 Little, Brown and Co.

LC 2011019737

This book tells the story of "Hayat Shah [who] is a young American in love for the first time. His normal life of school, baseball, and video games had previously been distinguished only by his Pakistani heritage and by the frequent chill between his parents, who fight over things he is too young to understand. Then Mina arrives, and everything changes. . . . Her deep spirituality brings the family's Muslim faith to life in a way that resonates with Hayat as nothing has before." (Publisher's note)

Akst, Daniel

The **Webster** chronicle; a novel. Putnam 2001 311p $24.95

 ISBN 0-399-14812-4

          LC 2001-25679

 Protagonist Terry Mathers "struggles with the declining financial stability of the small-town newspaper he co-owns and edits, his failing marriage, and his long-suffering relationship with his successful television journalist father. While he fights his own demons, he must objectively cover crucial matters in the village of Webster—including the threatened takeover of a local department store by a big chain and allegations of sexual abuse and Satanism at the local preschool." Libr J

 "Akst vividly illustrates the rocky road from ethical journalism to tabloid sensationalism." Booklist

Akunin, Boris

✓**Murder** on the Leviathan; a novel. translated by Andrew Bromfield. Random House 2004 223p il $21.95

 ISBN 1-400-06051-6

          LC 2003-70379

 Original Russian edition, 2000

 "Snappishly witty in Andrew Bromfield's crisp translation, Akunin's dry observations on the moral poverty of the upper classes are drolly set off by his lush descriptions of the material luxuries by which they measure the value of life itself." N Y Times Book Rev

Alam, Saher

✓ The **groom** to have been. Spiegel & Grau 2008 399p pa $14

 ISBN 978-0-385-52460-5; 0-385-52460-9

          LC 2007049047

 "Inspired by Edith Wharton's The Age of Innocence, the narrative transports readers back and forth between Canada and New York as Nasr, a successful young professional, indulges his mother by allowing the family to look for a wife for him, despite his second-generation immigrant's ambivalence about the practice. Readers who enjoyed Vikram Seth's A Suitable Boy, set in India, will find familiar themes in this classic story of love found too late. But there's a considerable twist. We know from the novel's start who Nasr's bride-to-be is but not how the events of 9/11 and its aftermath affect their plans or how a series of misunderstandings with Jameela, the rebellious, contradictory family friend, will change everything for Nasr." Libr J

Alarcón, Daniel, 1977-

 American odysseys; writings by new Americans. The Vilcek Foundation. 1st Dalkey ed. Dalkey Archive Press 2013 600 p. (paperback) $16

 ISBN 1564788067; 9781564788061

          LC 2012049513

 This "anthology is composed of selections from 22 writers recognized by the 2011 Vilcek Prize for Creative Promise, an award given annually to a young American immigrant (Dinaw Mengestu won in 2011). The anthology, with a foreword by Charles Simic, is composed of poetry, short stories, and excerpts of novels. . . . Across the works, identity and memory emerge as common themes of the immigrant experience." (Publishers Weekly)

Alarcon, Daniel

✓ **Lost** City Radio; a novel. HarperCollins 2007 257p $24.95

 ISBN 0-06-059479-9

          LC 2006-046498

 This "is a fable for an entire continent, and is no less pertinent in other parts of the world where different languages are spoken in different climates but where the same ruinous dance is played out." Washington Post Book World

Albert, Elisa

✓ The **book** of Dahlia; a novel. Free Press 2008 276p $23

 ISBN 978-0-7432-9129-3; 0-7432-9129-8

          LC 2007-33839

 "Dahlia Finger, the heroine of this début novel, is a sarcastic, self-absorbed Jewish American Princess, twenty-nine years old and living in a desirable bungalow in Venice, California, bought for her by her lawyer father. She's also, thanks to Albert's control of tone and timing, one of the most likable characters in recent fiction, as self-aware about her bad habits (smoking pot, wallowing in hopelessness, refusing to engage with her broken family) as she is incapable of changing them, even when diagnosed with a 'level four' tumor in the left temporal lobe of her brain. Basing her chapters on a self-help book that Dahlia buys ('It's Up to You: The Cancer To-Do List'), Albert writes with the black humor of Lorrie Moore and a pathos that is uniquely her own, all the more blistering for being slyly invoked." New Yorker

Albert, Susan Wittig

✓The **Darling** Dahlias and the cucumber tree; Susan Wittig Albert. Berkley Prime Crime 2010 xii, 290p (hc) $24.95

 ISBN 9780425234457

          LC 2010010033

 This book "begins in May 1930 in the small town of Darling, Alabama. . . . The Dahlias comprise the 12 members of a gardening club dedicated to beautifying their town while struggling to survive the Depression." (Booklist) They "are still excited about their clubhouse, an old estate . . . whose garden includes a possibly haunted cucumber tree, which might shelter a buried treasure. Also distracting the members -- especially widow and probate clerk Verna Tidwell; legal secretary and freelance journalist Elizabeth 'Lizzy' Lacy, and Mayor Jed Taylor's wife, Ophelia Snow -- are a prison break and the disappearance of drugstore clerk Eva Louise 'Bunny' Scott, the town tart. After Bunny turns up dead in a wrecked stolen van, the ladies investigate." (Publishers Weekly)

Albert, Susan Wittig

✓ **Rosemary** remembered; a China Bayles mystery. Berkley Prime Crime 1995 296p

 ISBN 0-425-14937-4

          LC 95-15062

 In this mystery China Bayles "discovers a dead woman—who resembles herself—in a pick-up truck. China interrupts her herb-shop business to investigate the woman's past and uncovers a small host of likely suspects. The best of small-town Texas." Libr J

Alcott, Louisa May

✓ ★ **Little** women; Little men; Jo's boys; [Elaine Showalter, editor] Library of America, Distributed to the trade in the U.S. by Penguin Putnam 2005 1092p il (The library of America) $40

    ISBN 1-931082-73-1

                    LC 2004-48828

"Little Women (1868-69), set in New England during the Civil War, introduces the charming, unforgettable March sisters Meg, Jo, Amy, and Beth as they begin to make their way into the world. Little Men (1871) follows the intellectual tomboy Jo, now married, into adulthood, as she finds herself the caretaker of a houseful of rambunctious children at Plumfield school. Jo's Boys (1886) returns to Plumfield a decade later. Now grown, Jo's children recount adventures of their own." Publisher's note

Aldiss, Brian Wilson

✓ ★ **Helliconia** spring; [by] Brian W. Aldiss. Atheneum Pubs. 1982 361p

    ISBN 0-689-11196-9

                    LC 81-66036

"Aldiss has not only written a science fiction novel about another world, he has created another universe complete with it's own language and flavor, peopled with colorful characters (both human and otherwise) who engage sympathy and interest." Best Sellers

Followed by Helliconia summer

Aldiss, Brian Wilson

✓ ★ **Helliconia** summer; [by] Brian W. Aldiss. Atheneum Pubs. 1983 398p

    ISBN 0-689-11388-9

                    LC 83-45062

"In this second novel in Aldiss's trilogy, the planet Helliconia . . . is presented as an epic miniature of humanity's loftiest aspirations and basest shortcomings. The action takes place on two levels, represented by the geometrical symbol of the planet's supreme god Akhanaba. Some events proceed along the inner rim, driven by incessant racial wars between the cohabitant Helliconian humans and the 'ahuman' Phagors. Along the outermost rim are the concerns of the king of Borlien . . . and the nefarious intrigues of court hangers-on ranging from chancellors to child prostitutes." Publ Wkly

Followed by Helliconia winter

Aldiss, Brian Wilson

✓ ★ **Helliconia** winter. Atheneum Pubs. 1985 281p

    ISBN 0-689-11541-5

                    LC 84-45607

In this concluding volume of the "trilogy, the planet Helliconia begins its descent into a winter that will last for centuries. Nonhuman phagors, better suited to the changing climate, begin to reclaim their ancient lands, and the plague they bring panics the Oligarchy into ever more repressive measures to stave off a new dark age. As young Luterin Shokerandit learns, however, such civilized willfulness only

subverts the grand, interdependent cycles of the natural world." Publ Wkly

"This conclusion to the Helliconia trilogy ranks as a landmark of fictional world-building." Libr J

Alenyikov, Michael

✓ **Ivan** and Misha; stories. Michael Alenyikov. TriQuarterly Books 2010 199 p.

    ISBN 0810127180; 9780810127180

                    LC 2010024016

This collection of short stories, the 2011 winner of the Northern California Book Award for Fiction, "revolves around a pair of fraternal twins, Ivan and Misha, brought to America as children, along with their father, Louie. Ivan inherited his father's dark good looks and his mother's bipolar disease . . . Misha has his mother's blond coloring and the burden of responsibility for his brother. Both brothers become involved in gay relationships, which strain their own bonds. . . . [The author captures] the world the father and brothers have made for themselves in contemporary New York City, . . . the jitteriness of Ivan's manic episodes, the tensions of urban gay life, and the coping with family acceptance and AIDS." (Libr J)

Alexander, Hannah

   Last resort; Hannah Alexander. Steeple Hill Books 2005 311 p. (pbk.) $6.99; (pbk.) o.p.

    ISBN 9780373785971; 0373785402

                    LC 2005282645

In this romance novel by Hannah Alexander, a Christy Award-Winning author, "Clarissa Cooper, twelve, vanishes near her home -- abducted, evidence suggests, by someone close to her. . . . Noelle Cooper races back to her hometown to help in the search. In the effort to save her young cousin, she steps into a web of secrets that has haunted her family for generations. . . . Nathan Trask will do anything to protect Noelle from danger. Noelle's childhood friend, he might be much more . . . if she dares turn to him." (Publisher's note)

Alexander, Tamera, 1961-

   Rekindled; Tamera Alexander. Bethany House 2006 334p $14.99

    ISBN 0764201085 (pbk.); 9780764201080

                    LC 2005028052

In this book, "[t]en years ago Kathryn Jennings made a vow. For better or worse. And that promise still holds true, even though her marriage has not turned out as she expected. When her husband fails to return home one stormy winter night, she struggles to keep their ranch, but her efforts are blocked at every turn. After a . . . glimpse into her husband's past, Kathryn uncovers a hidden truth. What she wouldn't give to turn back time and be able to love her husband for the man that he was, not for the man she always wanted him to be." (Publisher's note)

Followed by: Revealed (2006)

Alexander, Victoria

   Secrets of a proper lady; Victoria Alexander. Avon Books 2007 375p. $7.99

    ISBN 0060882646; 9780060882648

                    LC 2009510987

In this book, "Lady Cordelia Bannister simply cannot marry a man she has not chosen herself, no matter what her father decrees. So, pretending to be her own companion, she decides to seek out information about her intended by meeting with his secretary—a man who soon beguiles her. But Lady Cordelia doesn't know the truth—the man [she] can't resist is really her intended, Daniel Sinclair. Daniel has nearly won the wager he made with three of London's most eligible bachelors. While two of his compatriots have surrendered to the shackles of marriage, he's remained free to woo any woman he chooses. Yet duty forces him to consider Lady Cordelia, so, determined to find a way to escape honor intact, he continues the masquerade he started." (Publisher's note)

Alexie, Sherman, 1966-
✓ ★ **Blasphemy**; new and selected stories. by Sherman Alexie. Grover Pr 2012 viii, 465 p.p (hardcover) $27.00; (ebook) $24.99

ISBN 0802120393; 9780802120397; 9781921942969

Author Sherman Alexie presents a short story collection. "A son envisions his dead father's 'impossibly small corpse' peering out of his morning omelet in the page-long 'Breakfast.' In 'Gentrification,' a white narrator's do-gooder intentions go predictably awry in his all-black neighborhood. 'Night People' finds a sex-starved insomniac and a connection-hungry manicurist at a 24-hour New York City salon finding common ground in their loneliness and lack of sleep." (Publishers Weekly)

Alexie, Sherman, 1966-
✓ **Flight**; a novel. Black Cat 2007 181p pa $13

ISBN 978-0-8021-7037-8; 0-8021-7037-4

LC 2006-52656

"Many of [the] allegorical, action-packed vignettes tread familiar thematic territory—the continuing fight for survival, the anger of racial divides, the absence of fathers—of Mr. Alexie's earlier works. . . . But with 'Flight,' he takes these themes a step further: he skillfully explores both sides of the proverbial war. Zits witnesses brutal violence through the eyes of whites and Indians, fathers and sons, and he begins to understand what it means to be the hero, the villain and the victim." N Y Times (Late N Y Ed)

Alexie, Sherman
✓ **Indian** killer. Atlantic Monthly Press 1996 420p

ISBN 0-871-13652-X

LC 96-27996

"Sherman Alexie is too good a writer, too devoted to the complexities of a story, to settle for a diatribe. His vigorous prose, his haunted , surprising characters and his meditative exploration of the sources of human identity transform into a resonant tragedy what might have been a melodrama in less assured hands." N Y Times Book Rev

Alexie, Sherman
✓ **Reservation** blues. Atlantic Monthly Press 1995 306p

ISBN 0-871-13594-9

LC 94-46132

"Hilarious but poignant, filled with enchantments yet dead-on accurate with regard to modern Indian life, this tour de force will leave readers wondering if Alexie himself hasn't made a deal with the Gentleman in order to do everything so well." Publ Wkly

Alfieri, Annamaria
✓ **City** of silver; a mystery. Annamaria Alfieri. Minotaur Books 2009 xiv, 317 p.p $24.99

ISBN 031238386X; 9780312383862

LC 2009010489

In this book, "it's 1650, and the Peruvian city of Potosí is under investigation from the King of Spain for producing counterfeit silver coins. Meanwhile, the Grand Inquisitor of New Spain is also investigating . . . the actions of abbess Mother Maria Santa Hilda, who has allowed an apparent suicide, a young woman who died inside the abbey, to be buried in sacred ground. But Mother Maria does not think this was a suicide, and in her attempt to prove her case find out more than even she suspected." (Publisher's note)

Algren, Nelson
✓ ★ The **man** with the golden arm; a novel. Doubleday 1949 343p

"Set in the slums of Chicago, the novel, which won a National Book Award in 1950, tells the story of Frankie Machine (Francis Majcinek) who is said to have a 'golden arm' because of his sure touch with pool cues, dice, his drumsticks, his heroin needle, and his deck of cards. Unable to free himself from his slum environment, Frankie is finally driven to suicide." Reader's Ency. 4th edition

Algren, Nelson
✓ A **walk** on the wild side. Farrar, Straus & Cudahy 1956 346p

A novel about the residents of a slum street in New Orleans during the early years of the Depression

"Algren's vivid writing gives this degenerate cast the power to shock or appall, and if a glimmer of compassion leaks through occasionally it is slapped down before it gets out of hand." Libr J

Ali, Monica
✓ ★ **Brick** lane; a novel. Scribner 2003 369p $25

ISBN 0-7432-4330-7

LC 2003-42795

"Nazeen, a young Bangladeshi woman, moves to London's Bangla Town (around the street of the title) in the mid-nineteen eighties after an arranged marriage with an older man. Seen through Nazeen's eyes, England is at first utterly baffling, but over the seventeen years of the narrative (which takes us into the post-September 11th era), she gradually finds her way, bringing up two daughters and eventually starting an all-female tailoring business. . . . In Ali's subtle narration, Nazeen's mixture of traditionalism, and adaptability, of acceptence and restlessness, emerges as a quiet strength." New Yorker

Ali, Monica
✓ **In** the kitchen; a novel. Scribner 2009 436p $25.99

ISBN 978-1-4165-7168-1; 1-4165-7168-X

LC 2009-01551

"Gabriel plans to serve "Classic French, a modern twist, cooked with precision" in his restaurant. Translated into literary terms, it's a fair description of what Ali herself dishes up in this rich, classically structured novel that tackles big social issues." San Francisco Chron

Ali, Monica

✓ **Untold** story; a novel. Scribner 2011 259p $25

ISBN 978-1-4516-3548-5; 1-4516-3548-6

"After a series of moves from one American town to another, Lydia finally settles in a generic hamlet called Kensington, where she becomes friends with three middle-aged women: a bubbly blonde named Amber; a stressed out, brunette mom named Suzie; and a red-haired, New-Agey realtor named Tevis. These three pals are kinder, gentler versions of John Updike's witches of Eastwick — or maybe older, hipper versions of the gals in Rona Jaffe's 'Best of Everything.' . . . Like Curtis Sittenfeld, who tried to channel Laura Bush in 'American Wife,' Ms. Ali does an engaging job of creating sympathy for her heroine." N Y Times (Late N Y Ed)

Allen, Sarah Addison

The **girl** who chased the moon; a novel. Bantam Books 2010 269p $25; pa $15

ISBN 978-0-553-80721-9; 0-553-80721-8; 978-0-553-38559-5 pa; 0-553-38559-3 pa

LC 2009-42254

Emily Benedict came to Mullaby, North Carolina, hoping to solve at least some of the riddles surrounding her mother's life. But the moment Emily enters the house where her mother grew up and meets the grandfather she never knew—a reclusive, real-life gentle giant—she realizes that mysteries aren't solved in Mullaby, they're a way of life.

"That it is never too late to change the future and that high school sins can be forgiven—these are wonderful messages, but Allen's warm characters and quirky setting are what will completely open readers' hearts to this story. Nothing in it disappoints." Libr J

Allen, Sarah Addison

The **peach** keeper; a novel. Bantam Books 2011 273p $25

ISBN 978-0-553-80722-6

LC 2010-47828

This is a "mystery that seems to solve its own riddle long before the final chapter, a character study interrupted by crisis and a flirtation with magic realism that soon gives way to conventional storytelling. That singularity stands as the novel's selling point, along with Allen's immensely readable prose." Denver Post

Allen, Sarah Addison

✓ The **sugar** queen. Bantam Books 2008 276p $22

ISBN 978-0-553-80549-9; 0-553-80549-5

LC 2007-48178

"Allen's characters are darling, and even the bad guys are charming and charismatic in this novel written as a modern-day fairy tale. In Allen's town of Bald Slope, magic lets books choose their owners and passion fry eggs in their carton. Best of all, it lets friends discover one another in the most mysterious ways." St. Petersburg Times

Allen, Shawn

The **13**; Fall. Robbie Cheuvront and Erik Reed; with Shawn Allen. Barbour Publishing 2012 313 p. (pbk.) $12.99

ISBN 1616267690; 9781616267698

LC 2012462256

In this book by Robbie Cheuvront and Erik Reed, "CIA agent Jonathan Keene is investigating the disappearance of border agents when a man named the Prophet warns of the United States's imminent downfall. Fourteen days later, the West Coast is hit and destroyed. Keene is paired with FBI agent Megan Taylor to stop the terrorists, but before they can act, the country is reduced to the original 13 colonies." (Library Journal)

Allende, Isabel, 1942-

✓ **Daughter** of fortune; a novel. translated from the Spanish by Margaret Sayers Peden. HarperCollins Pubs. 1999 399p hardcover o.p. pa $16.95

ISBN 0-06-019491-X; 0-06-156533-4 pa

LC 99-26021

Original Spanish edition, 1999

"This novel has pretensions, but they are overridden by Allende's riproaring girl's adventure story. . . . Throughout it all, Allende projects a woman's point of view with confidence, control and an expansive definition of romance as a fact of life." Time

Allende, Isabel

✓ ★ **Eva** Luna; translated by Margaret Sayers Peden. Knopf 1988 271p hardcover o.p. pa $14

ISBN 0-394-57273-4; 0-553-38382-5 pa

LC 88-45272

Original Spanish edition, 1987

This "wonderful novel, crammed with the strange and fantastical, the sensuous and the erotic, also speaks powerfully in the cause of freedom." Publ Wkly

Allende, Isabel

✓ ★ The **house** of the spirits; translated from the Spanish by Magda Bogin. Knopf 1985 368p $29.95; pa $16

ISBN 0-394-53907-9; 0-553-38380-9 pa

LC 84-48516

Original Spanish edition, 1982

"The style is superbly controlled (and/or the translation is marvelously sensitive), balancing detail rich in associations with a deadpan humor that completely demystifies things that would be otherwise inexplicable. In other words, sentimentality never intrudes on the emotions you develop for these hopelessly well-meaning people and their equally errant children." Best Sellers

Allende, Isabel

✓ **Island** beneath the sea; a novel. translated from the Spanish by Margaret Sayers Peden. Harper 2010 457p $26.99; pa $14.99

ISBN 978-0-06-198824-0; 0-06-198824-3; 978-0-06-198825-7 pa; 0-06-198825-1 pa

LC 2009-46251

Original Spanish edition, 2009

"In a many-faceted plot, Allende animates irresistible characters authentic in their emotional turmoil and pragmatic adaptability. She also captures the racial, sexual, and entrepreneurial dynamics of each society in sensuous detail while masterfully dramatizing the psychic wounds of slavery. Sexually explicit, Allende is grace incarnate in her evocations of the spiritual energy that still sustains the beleaguered people of Haiti and New Orleans." Booklist

Allende, Isabel, 1942-

✓ ★ **Maya's** Notebook. HarperCollins 2013 400 p. (hardcover) $27.99

ISBN 0062105620; 9780062105622

In this book, set in 2009, "Berkley-born and -bred Maya arrives in Chiloé, an isolated island community in southern Chile, to escape the drug dealers and law enforcement officials on her trail. Her eponymous notebook combines a record of Maya's not-so-gradual immersion into the Chiloé community with her memories of an idyllic childhood and horrifically wayward adolescence." (Kirkus Reviews)

Allende, Isabel

✓ **Portrait** in sepia; translated from the Spanish by Margaret Sayers Peden. HarperCollins Pubs. 2001 304p

ISBN 0-06-621161-1

LC 00-54127

Sequel to Daughter of fortune

Original Spanish edition, 2000

"Through Aurora, Allende exercises her supreme storytelling abilities, of which strong, passionate characters are paramount." Publ Wkly

Allingham, Margery

Crime and Mr. Campion. Doubleday 1959 575p

An omnibus volume containing the complete texts of three mystery novels all starring the British detective Albert Campion. Death of a ghost (1934) is based on art forgery, Flowers for the judge (1936) is about the murder of a publisher and Dancers in mourning (1937) concerns a group of theatrical characters

Allingham, Margery

Three cases for Mr. Campion. Doubleday 1961 604p

"The Gyrth chalice mystery" unravels Mr. Campion's solution to the secret in the locked room of Gyrth Tower; "The fashion in shrouds" involves the theft of dress designs, sixty cages of canaries, and blackmail, as Albert Campion investigates a three-year-old murder; "Traitor's purse" finds Albert Campion, an amnesia victim haunted by an urgency to do something of immense consequence before time runs out

Allison, Dorothy

✓ ★ **Bastard** out of Carolina. Dutton 1992 309p hardcover o.p. pa $16

ISBN 0-525-93425-1; 0-452-28705-7 pa

LC 91-34607

"Set in the rural South, this tale centers around the Boatwright family, a proud and closeknit clan known for their drinking, fighting, and womanizing. Nicknamed Bone by her Uncle Earle, Ruth Anne is the bastard child of Anney Boatwright, who has fought tirelessly to legitimize her child. When she marries Glen, a man from a good family, it appears that her prayers have been answered. However, Anney suffers a miscarriage and Glen begins drifting. He develops a contentious relationship with Bone and then begins taking sexual liberties with her. . . . Unaware of her husband's abusive behavior, Anney stands by her man. Eventually, a violent encounter wrests Bone away from her stepfather." Libr J

Alpert, Mark

Extinction; a thriller. St Martins Pr 2013 384 p. $25.99

ISBN 1250021340; 9781250021342

LC 2012042089

In this thriller, a Chinese "computer program known as Supreme Harmony achieves consciousness." Then, a Chinese government official visits retired army colonel Jim Pierce, seeking "information on the whereabouts of Pierce's estranged daughter, Layla, an accomplished hacker who has been 'investigating the recent arrests of several Chinese dissidents involved in the pro-democracy movement.' Layla's cyber intrusions pose a risk to both the regime and Supreme Harmony." (Publishers Weekly)

Altschul, Andrew Foster

Deus ex machina; a novel. Counterpoint 2011 205p pa $14.95

ISBN 978-1-58243-601-2; 1-58243-601-0

LC 2010-31494

"The novel is a behind the scenes story of an extreme Survivor-like reality show called The Deserted, in which contestants are plane-crashed into remote areas and left to fend for themselves—though in reality, of course, with highly strategic surveillance and manipulation by a nearby television crew. Rather than chapters, the novel is broken up into the weeks of a television season, which sounds more gimmicky than it comes off. Altschul gives the book the kind of seesaw suspense of so much reality television, then undercuts it with some deadly poetic satire." PopMatters

Altschul, Andrew Foster

✓ **Lady** Lazarus. Harcourt 2008 561p $25

ISBN 978-0-15-101484-2; 0-15-101484-1

LC 2007-28550

"The center of this novel, Calliope Bird Morath, is a young poet. The daughter of a Kurt Cobain-like rock god and a minimally talented but outrageously self-promoting rock goddess, Calliope is destined for stardom. Then, when she is 4, her father kills himself in front of her. . . . Calliope is struck silent for years. When she begins to speak, it's in poetry." Sacramento News & Rev

Alvarez, Julia

✓ ★ **How** the Garcia girls lost their accents. Algonquin Bks. 1991 290p hardcover o.p. pa $13.95

ISBN 0-945575-57-2; 1-56512-975-X pa

LC 90-48575

"This is an account of parallel odysseys, as each of the four daughters adapts in her own way, and a large part of Alvarez's accomplishment is the complexity with which these vivid characters are rendered." Publ Wkly

Alvarez, Julia

Yo! Algonquin Bks. 1997 309p $18.95

ISBN 1-56512-157-0

LC 96-24611

Sequel to How the Garcia girls lost their accents

"Yolanda Garcia's mother and sisters are furious at her for having plagiarized their lives in her all-too-celebrated novel. The balance of this novel is a rebuttal of sorts, narrated by her defenders. For everyone else who has come into contact with Yo and her storytelling prowess—from her repressed professor to her downtrodden landlady—life has changed for the better. These high-spirited accounts indulge the pleasing fantasy that we are the heroes not only of our own lives but of everyone else's as well." New Yorker

Amado, Jorge

★ **Dona** Flor and her two husbands; a moral and amorous tale. translated from the Portuguese by Harriet de Onís. Knopf 1969 553p

Original Portuguese edition published 1966 in Brazil

"Dona Flor has such a harridan of a mother (Dona Rozilda) that you would like her to have her cake and eat it, too, and she very nearly does. Dona Flor's first husband, Vadinho, is a scamp, a prevaricator, and a 'shameless lover.' On Carnival Sunday, at the height of the gaiety, filled with rum, he drops dead. Dona Flor is desolate but cuts a handsome figure as a widow. She lives through the wake (a gem of a scene) and her mourning quite well, with memories and her cooking school to sustain her. Then suitors appear. None appeal but Dr. Teodoro Madureira, pharmacist and bassoonist, a pillar of propriety. Dona Rozilda is ecstatic, but the well-rounded Dona Flor has her troubles, for alas, Dr. Teodoro is no lover. Dreams haunt her and strange things begin to happen. Thanks to a Yoruba charm, Vadinho returns to ravish our bewildered heroine, and then the fun begins. Bahia in Brazil is the setting for this delectable rum cake of a novel." Publ Wkly

Amado, Jorge

Gabriela, clove and cinnamon; translated from the Portuguese by James L. Taylor and William L. Grossman. Knopf 1962 425p

Original Portuguese edition published 1958 in Brazil

"Ilhéus, a Brazilian town near Bahia, is fortunate in the wealth it is realizing from its cacao crop. Money flows freely and is spent in cabarets, in bordellos, and on gambling during the period 1925-1926. . . . The removal of a sand bar blocking the harbor is the basis of this fascinating portrait of politics in a provincial Brazilian town. Amado also tells the love story of Nacib, the Arab owner of the most popular café in town, and Gabriela, a child of nature. Amoral rather than immoral, with skin the color of cinnamon and smelling of cloves, Gabriela gives her love readily and freely. Her skillful cooking makes her more valuable to Nacib as a mistress than as a wife. The atmosphere of this entertaining novel is lusty, sensual, and humorous." Shapiro. Fic for Youth. 3d edition

Amend, Allison

A **nearly** perfect copy; a novel. Allison Amend. Nan A. Talese/Doubleday 2013 304 p. (alk. paper) $25.95

ISBN 0385536690; 9780385536691

LC 2012020699

In this novel, by Allison Amend, "Elm Howells has a loving family and a distinguished career at an elite Manhattan auction house. But after a tragic loss . . . , she pursues a reckless course of action that jeopardizes her personal and professional success. Meanwhile, talented artist Gabriel Connois wearies of remaining at the margins of the capricious Parisian art scene, and, desperate for recognition, he embarks on a scheme that threatens his burgeoning reputation." (Publisher's note)

American fantastic tales: terror and the uncanny from Poe to the pulps; Peter Straub, editor. Library of America 2009 746p $35

ISBN 978-1-59853-047-6

LC 2009-927073

"A valuable collection of excellent, often deeply disturbing stories." Kirkus

American fantastic tales: terror and the uncanny from the 1940s to now; Peter Straub, editor. Library of America 2009 713p $35

ISBN 978-1-59853-048-3

LC 2009-927074

This volume's "contents reflect confused and perturbed reactions to radical changes in people's daily lives and the larger world around them during periods of instability beginning around the time of World War II and extending into the dizzying technological changes of the past quarter-century. . . . A terrific, must-have collection." Kirkus

Amidon, Stephen

Security. Farrar, Straus and Giroux 2009 276p $25

ISBN 978-0-374-25711-8; 0-374-25711-6

LC 2008-13850

"Stoneleigh is the 'nuclear-free, dolphin-safe' New England town where Edward Inman outfits the homes of skittish yuppies with motion sensors, panic rooms and CCTV. Doyle Cutler is one of his clients—a wealthy man with a seedy mien, an aversion to shaking hands and a recessive chin (always a bad sign.) These men, respectively, are hero and villain of [the novel] . . . . The book is part campus tale, part mystery, part police procedural. The proportions are well mixed. Stoneleigh's customary tranquility is stirred when Mary Steckl, a local college student, accuses Doyle Cutler of sexually assaulting her. Cutler rebounds with an accusation that Mary's father, a drunk with a criminal record, is the real perp. The town is divided. . . . For all its plot twists, Security is a book stitched of sensible prose. There are no flourishes, no embroidery." N Y Observer

Amirrezvani, Anita

★ **Equal** of the sun; a novel. Anita Amirrezvani. 1st Scribner hardcover ed. Scribner 2012 431 p. (hardcover) $26

ISBN 1451660464; 9781451660463

LC 2011277836

Author Anita Amirrezvani tells the story of "Javaher, a eunuch . . . [and] the loyal servant of Princess Pari, a wise if occasionally headstrong daughter of the shah. . . . He is determined to learn who among the nation's elite is responsible for his father's murder. . . . [The] shah dies and is replaced with his son Isma'il, who begins a reign . . . that threatens to break down the fragile truces with neighboring lands. . . . [Pari] begins a scheme to end his reign, with Javaher serving as assistant, sounding board and spy . . . [which] allows him to navigate the highest and lowest castes of Iranian society." (Kirkus Reviews)

Includes bibliographical references

Amis, Kingsley

★ **Lucky** Jim; a novel. Doubleday 1954 256p

First published 1953 in the United Kingdom

"The title is ironic, since the story is about the comic misfortunes of Jim Dixon, a young lower-middle-class instructor at an English university. The book satirizes the academic 'racket' and cultural pretensions." Reader's Ency. 4th edition

Amis, Kingsley

The **Russian** girl. Viking 1994 296p

ISBN 0-670-85329-1

First published 1992 in the United Kingdom

"What makes 'The Russian Girl' such a jolly good read is precisely {its} scathing level of insight, to say nothing of Amis's dazzling virtuosity with the old bons mots. They litter the floor. He also manages to be very, very funny, even when he's being very, very serious." NY Times Book Rev

Amis, Martin, 1949-

House of meetings. Alfred A. Knopf 2007 256p $23

ISBN 1-400-04455-3

LC 2006-47397

First published 2006 in the United Kingdom

"In previous novels Amis has been something of a metafictioneer, but the outstanding virtue of House of Meetings is its traditional psychological realism. Its themes of the camps, the misery, the overwhelming sense of sin, and the presentation of Russia as an emblem of human fate all recall Dostoyevsky, and, like Dostoyevsky, Amis fails to offer any answer to the question of human evil that the book raises." New Yorker

Amis, Martin, 1949-

★ **Lionel** Asbo; state of England. by Martin Amis. 1st American ed. Alfred A. Knopf 2012 255 p. (paperback) $15.00; (hardcover) $25.95

ISBN 9780307948083; 0307958086; 9780307958082

LC 2012006340

This novel is "two stories, a satirical take on the rise and fall of Lionel Abso, small-time criminal, and the coming-of-age story of Desmond 'Des' Pepperdine." Lionel has been a thug since age three, in and out of prison his whole life. "Des is Lionel's nephew. He is gifted" and "book-smart. . . . When Lionel's not in jail the two live in a . . . housing estate in . . . Diston." Then "Lionel wins the lottery, becomes a multimillionaire and starts living the celebrity life." (Library Journal)

Amis, Martin

★ **London** fields. Harmony Bks. 1989 470p

ISBN 0-517-57718-6

LC 89-49558

"Amis's technical virtuosity is extraordinary. . . . {This is} the most intellectually interesting fiction of the year, and a work beyond the reach of any British contemporary. Amis's figures, like those of Dickens, are caricatures that have their own gigantic reality." London Rev Books

Amis, Martin

★ The **pregnant** widow; inside history. Alfred A. Knopf 2010 370p $26.95

ISBN 978-1-4000-4452-8; 1-4000-4452-9

LC 2009-41689

"When Amis shows us the sexual revolution in action and reaction, when he tells us how people dressed and what it meant, when he depicts the effects of women's sexual aggression on men's egos, how women talked about men and vice versa when he is pretending to be a well-behaved comic-naturalist novelist, the book works. But when he philosophises he can sound just like tedious-clever journalism. . . . And the narrative is slowed and blurred by Amis' unwillingness ever to say anything in a simple or straightforward way." Age

Amis, Martin

Time's arrow; or, The nature of the offense. Harmony Bks. 1991 168p

ISBN 0-517-58515-4

LC 91-4144

This novel "shoots us into the past as it reveals the true identity of a man called Tod Friendly. As Tod lies in a hospital bed, his consciousness distances itself from the present and assesses his life in reverse, like a film run backwards. Every action is reversed and every conversation inverted. This voice, this estranged soul, watches Tod create food and beverages at meals, get paid for bringing items into stores, and grow younger. As his American identity is stripped away, his hideous past as a German doctor and executioner at a Nazi extermination camp is revealed." Booklist

Ampuero, Roberto

The **Neruda** case; Roberto Ampuero; translated by Carolina De Robertis. Riverhead Books 2012 340 p.

ISBN 159448743X; 9781594487439

LC 2012001890

This book by Roberto Ampuero presents a "fictional interpretation of Nobel laureate Pablo Neruda's final days in 1973 . . . Neruda, who's ill with cancer as Chile teeters toward upheaval because of his friend President Allende's reform platform, seeks out unemployed Cuban Cayetano Brulé in Valparaíso and hires him to investigate the whereabouts of a former acquaintance, Dr. Ángel Bracamonte. Never mind that Brulé is no detective. The aging poet-cum-political activist persuades the young Brûlé . . . travel to Mexico City, the last place Neruda saw Bracamonte. The mission seems cut and dried, except Neruda has not only withheld critical information, he has sworn Brûlé to secrecy. Nobody must know the identity of who Brûlé is looking for or why he is looking for him." (Publishers Weekly)

Includes bibliographical references and index.

Amsterdam, Steven

Things we didn't see coming; [by] Steven Amsterdam. Pantheon Books 2010 199p $24

ISBN 0307378500; 9780307378507

LC 2009-17843

This debut collection of linked short stories "follows a single man over three decades as he tries to survive in an increasingly savage apocalyptic world that is at once utterly fantastic and disturbingly familiar. Here, coming-of-age is complicated not only by family troubles and mercurial love affairs, but treacherous weather, unstable governments, pandemic, and technology run amuck." (Publisher's note)

Amsterdam's "unsettling debut story collection . . . envisions a not-too-distant future plagued by pollution, disease, corruption, turbulent climate conditions and a society whose members readily sacrifice morality for survival. Despite their bleakness, each of the nine entries is wildly original and engaging, yet not for the faint of heart or those seeking an optimistic escape from the everyday. . . . Amsterdam's writing is consistently bold and daring, dense yet somehow accessible." Edge

Anatoli, A.

Babi Yar; a document in the form of a novel. {by} A. Anatoli (Kuznetsov). Translated by David Floyd. Farrar, Straus & Giroux 1970 477p

ISBN 0-374-10761-0

Original Russian edition published 1966 in censored form under author's former name A. Kuznetsov; English translation by Jacob Guralsky of this version published 1967 by Dial Press

A documentary novel about the period from 1941 to 1943 in which the Germans systematically murdered some 2,000,000 people, including 50,000 Jews, at the ravine on the outskirts of Kiev known as Babi Yar. The author, who was twelve years old at the time, based his work on interviews, newspaper clippings, diaries and other documents

Anaya, Rudolfo A.

The **man** who could fly and other stories. University of Oklahoma Press 2006 197p (Chicana & Chicano visions of the Américas) $19.95

ISBN 0-8061-3738-X

LC 2005-51426

"The stories showcase 30 years of Anaya's Chicano literary voice, simultaneously innocent and omniscient and always rooted in the landscape, especially the windswept llanos of New Mexico. . . . The characters' passionate force radiates from Anaya's simple prose as they confront ethical dilemmas in varied regional settings." Libr J

Andersen Nexo, Martin

Pelle the conqueror: v1 Childhood; translated from the Danish by Steven T. Murray; edited and with

an afterword by Tiina Nunnally. Fjord Press 1989 244p

LC 89-7837

"Andersen Nexo, who was born in the slums of Copenhagen, ultimately developed Pelle into a proletarian epic hero. In this first, largely autobiographical volume, however, there's scant evidence of his strict social realism. Rather, Andersen Nexo's robust sense of life, his convincing evocation of childhood, his moral vision—and, above all, his brave young hero—make this novel generous and grand." N Y Times Book Rev

Andersen Nexo, Martin

Pelle the conqueror: v2 Apprenticeship; translated from the Danish by Steven T. Murray & Tiina Nunnally; with an afterword by Niels Ingwersen. Fjord Press 1991 224p

In this volume "Pelle begins the journey the European proletariat undertook when the modern capitalistic society was formed; he goes from rural misery and poverty to the same or worse in an urban setting. As a shoemaker's apprentice in the nearest town, he retains some ties with the past but grows into adolescence in a milieu of different values and new people, establishing solidarity with the poorest. . . . With his faults and virtues, endurance and optimism, Pelle is one of literature's most charming heroes." Libr J

Andersen, Laura

The **Boleyn** King; a novel. Laura Andersen. Ballantine Books Trade Paperbacks 2013 368 p. (pbk.) $15

ISBN 0345534093; 9780345534095

LC 2013004505

This novel by Laura Andersen is "the first book in an enthralling trilogy that [imagines]: What if Anne Boleyn had actually given Henry VIII a son who grew up to be king? Henry IX, known as William, is a king bound by the restraints of the regency yet anxious to prove himself. [He] trusts only three people: his older sister Elizabeth; his best friend . . . Dominic; and Minuette, a young orphan. When he and Dominic both fall in love with Minuette, romantic obsession looms over a new generation of Tudors." (Publisher's note)

Anderson, Alison

Darwin's wink; a novel of nature and love. Thomas Dunne Books/St. Martin's Press 2004 288p $23.95

ISBN 0-312-33199-1

LC 2004-17763

"Christian, a disenchanted, 30-something Swiss man haunted by his experiences as a Red Cross worker in Bosnia, comes to Egret Island, . . . off the coast of Mauritius, to work for Fran, a middle-aged, outwardly brusque American naturalist seeking to restore the island to its original, untouched state and the endangered mourner-bird to its previous strength. Like Christian, who left behind a pregnant lover, Fran has also loved and lost; she tries to confine herself to a cerebral approach to work and life, blunting her sexual frissons and painful flashbacks through Darwinian logic. . . . Readers will find the plot distantly secondary to the novel's rich emotional palette, as Anderson captures the expansive beauty of Mauritius and the nuances of human character with languid, sensual and occasionally violet prose." Publ Wkly

Anderson, Catherine
√ **Star** bright; Catherine Anderson. Signet 2009 418 p. geneal. table $7.99
    ISBN 0451225716; 9780451225719
LC 2009510890

In this book, written by "New York Times" best-selling author Catherine Anderson, "[f]aking her own death to escape her murderous husband, Rainie Hall takes refuge in the rural community of Crystal Falls, where she finds work as a bookkeeper on a horse ranch run by dangerously good-looking Parker Harrigan. . . . Rainie fears she can never escape retribution from the man who has sworn to kill her—and that her mere presence could jeopardize everything the Harrigan family holds dear." (Publisher's note)

Anderson, Poul
√ **Genesis**. TOR Bks. 2000 253p
    ISBN 0-312-86707-7
LC 99-58829

"Christian Brannock agrees to have his personality uploaded into a computer so that his mind can explore the stars long after the death of his body. When his billion-year journey brings him back to an Earth that has undergone many cosmic changes, Brannock encounters another uploaded personality who restores to him the wonder of being 'human.' The lyrical approach of this sf master to the meaning of human existence gives his latest effort a surreal, allegorical feel." Libr J

Anderson, Poul
√ **War** of the Gods. TOR Bks. 1997 304p
    ISBN 0-312-86315-2
LC 97-19383

"Anderson writes with a spare style, often relying on the alliterative, rhythmic prose of Scandinavian folklore, giving this epic tale an original spirit and tone. Readers bored with Tolkien-clone fantasies will be enthralled by the intricately detailed world and characters Anderson brings to life here." Publ Wkly

Anderson, Sherwood, 1876-1941
√ ★ **Winesburg**, Ohio. Modern Lib. 1995 231p
    ISBN 0-679-60146-5
LC 94-23229

A reissue of the title first published 1919 by B.W. Huebsch

"A series of twenty-three vignettes, Winesburg, Ohio is a character study of a small town. It highlights individual residents and scrutinizes who they are and why this reality often conflicts with their dreams. The short stories are linked through George Willard, a young newspaper reporter who is disenchanted with the narrow-mindedness of small towns." Shapiro. Fic for Youth. 3d edition

Anderson-Dargatz, Gail
√ A **recipe** for bees. Harmony Bks. 2000 305p
    ISBN 0-609-60451-1
LC 99-25269

First published 1999 in the United Kingdom

"Augusta is a headstrong heroine with prismatic perspectives; her long, never-dull life as told by the gifted Anderson-Dargatz is both charming and impressive in its quiet, cumulative power." Publ Wkly

Anderton, Jo
Debris. Angry Robot 2011 432p (Veiled worlds trilogy)
    ISBN 085766154X pa; 9780857661548 pa

This book tells the story of a woman who "is among the highest in her far-future society -- a skilled pioneer, able to use a mixture of ritual and innate talent to manipulate the particles that hold all matter together. But an accident brings her life crashing down around her ears." (Publisher's note) "Stripped of her powers, bound inside a bizarre powersuit, . . . Tanyana must adjust to a new life collecting 'debris,' the stuff left behind by pions. But as she tries to find who has done all of this to her, she also starts to realize that debris is more important than anyone could guess." (angryrobotbooks.com)

Andrews, Mary Kay
√ **Every** crooked nanny. HarperCollins Pubs. 1992 286p
    ISBN 0-06-017923-6
LC 91-58359

This novel introduces "J. Callahan Garrity, a former cop and failed gumshoe who now runs a cleaning service in Atlanta, Ga. While cleaning the home of snooty society lady Lilah Rose Beemish, Callahan is hired to trace Kristee, the family's Mormon nanny, who has absconded with furs, jewels and, Callahan learns, incriminating business secrets gleaned from Lilah's husband Bo during their affair." Publ Wkly

"This quick-paced thriller provides an intriguing introduction to a delightfully down-to-earth sleuth." Booklist

Andrews, Mary Kay
Irish eyes; a Callahan Garrity mystery. HarperCollins Pubs. 2000 296p $24
    ISBN 0-06-019421-9
LC 99-55680

"Former Atlanta cop Garrity returns to crime solving when her ex-partner, Bucky Deavers, is shot on the way home from a party he finagled her into attending at the Shamrock Society. With the help of the eccentric staff of her housecleaning business, Garrity vows to get to the bottom of the shooting. This is an entertaining, suspenseful romp." Booklist

Andrews, Mary Kay
√ **Ladies'** night; Mary Kay Andrews. St. Martin's Press 2013 458 p. (hardcover) $26.99
    ISBN 1250019672; 9781250019677
LC 2013009101

In this novel by Mary Kay Andrews "Grace Stanton's life as a rising media star and beloved lifestyle blogger takes a surprising turn when she catches her husband cheating. Moving in with her widowed mother . . . is less than ideal. So is attending court-mandated weekly "divorce recovery" therapy sessions with three other women and one man for whom betrayal seems to be the only commonality. The . . .

bonds that develop lead the members of the group to try and find closure." (Publisher's note)

Andrews, Mary Kay

✓ **Summer** rental; Mary Kay Andrews. 1st ed.; St. Martin's Press 2011 viii, 402p

ISBN 9780312642693; 0312642695

LC 2011004404

This book tells the story of "three lifelong friends who grew up together in Savannah--unemployed banker Ellis, model Julia, teacher Dorie--and reunite in Nags Head, N.C., for a month-long holiday at a rundown rental elegantly named the Ebbtide. But when the 30-somethings BFFs, each of whom is struggling with life-changing crises, take in Maryn, a stranger and runaway-wife, the beachy holiday takes on a dangerous edge. To the rescue comes handsome landlord Ty, who's renting out his ramshackle family home in hopes of staving off foreclosure." (Publishers Weekly)

Angell, Roger

Nothing but you; love stories from The New Yorker. edited by Roger Angell. Random House 1997 471p

ISBN 0-679-45701-1

LC 96-43079

Ansa, Tina McElroy

✓ The **hand** I fan with. Doubleday 1996 462p

ISBN 0-385-47601-9

LC 96-6256

Sequel to Baby in the family (1989)

"Ansa writes believably of the spirit world; on the other hand, her inventories of Lena's many material possessions can be overlong and jarring. Yet a strong sense of place and an engagingly eccentric cast of characters keep the narrative moving—and ultimately bring Lena's two worlds together." N Y Times Book Rev

Ansay, A. Manette

✓ **River** angel. Morrow 1998 243p

ISBN 0-688-15243-0

LC 97-31006

"With 'River Angel,' A. Manette Ansay has moved beyond her prior mastery of the family scene to a lucid, eloquent representation of the commingled and conflicting lives of a town." N Y Times Book Rev

Anshaw, Carol

✓ **Carry** the one; Carol Anshaw. Simon & Schuster 2012 253 p.

ISBN 9781451636888; 9781451636895; 9781451656930

LC 2011013428

This book "begins in the hours following Carmen's wedding reception, when a car filled with stoned, drunk, and sleepy guests accidentally hits and kills a girl on a dark country road. For the next twenty-five years, those involved, including Carmen and her brother and sister, craft their lives in response to this single tragic moment. As one character says, 'When you add us up, you always have to carry the one.' Through friendships and love affairs; marriage and divorce; parenthood, holidays, and the modest calamities and triumphs of ordinary days, 'Carry the One' shows how one life affects another and how those who thrive and those who self-destruct are closer to each other than we'd expect." (Publisher's note)

Anthony, Evelyn

The **Janus** imperative. Coward, McCann & Geoghegan 1980 275p

ISBN 0-698-11016-1

LC 79-20768

"Political journalist Max Steiner is interviewing a German politician in Paris when the man is assassinated. His dying word is 'Janus.' As a Hitler Youth 25 years earlier, Steiner had heard another dying man utter the same word in Hitler's Berlin bunker in 1945. He persuades his boss to let him do an in-depth story on the assassination and hurries to Germany to dig into Bunker archives for connections between the two Januses. But as he starts interviewing survivors, a terrorist group is proceeding to murder the same survivors. German intelligence and the CIA become involved, and Steiner's quest ends in a convent in Munich, where some unholy violence takes place." Publ Wkly

This novel has "strong, believable characters, clear prose and good description." West Coast Rev Books

Anthony, Piers

✓ **Split** infinity. Ballantine Bks. 1980 372p il (Apprentice Adept)

ISBN 0-345-28645-6

LC 79-20282

In this first volume of the author's Apprentice Adept series "Stile, the principal character . . . takes his turns between two parallel worlds. His home world of Proton is a strictly regulated mechanized society where wealthy Citizens own serfs who work and compete for them in the Games. These Games are a central feature of the novel and range from tiddlywinks to marathon racing. The fantasy land of Phaze is an organic world into which he escapes to avoid a mysterious killer. There he meets a unicorn, . . . who changes into a woman, and a man who changes into a werewolf, among others. Here he discovers that he can cast magic spells and sets out to find his alter ego." Voice Youth Advocates

Followed by: Blue Adept (1981); Juxtaposition (1982); Out of phaze (1987); Robot Adept (1988); Unicorn point (1989); Phaze doubt (1990)

Anthony, Piers

✓ **Virtual** mode. 1991 304p (Mode)

ISBN 0-399-13661-4

LC 90-42919

"Anthony's 'realism' manages to avoid sleaze, and the lighter parts of the narrative, while indeed light, are seldom frivolous. In addition, Anthony's pacing and world building are up to standard." Booklist

Followed by: Fractal mode (1992); Chaos mode (1993); DoOon mode (2001)

Anton, Maggie

✓ **Rav** Hisda's daughter, book I, apprentice; a novel of love, the Talmud, and sorcery. Maggie Anton. Plume 2012 xxvi, 452 p. (paperback) $16.00

ISBN 0452298091; 9780452298095

LC 2012014785

In this novel by Maggie Anton "Hisdadukh, blessed to be beautiful and learned, is the youngest child of Talmudic sage Rav Hisda. . . . Rome, fast becoming Christian, battles Zoroastrian Persia for dominance while Rav Hisda and his colleagues struggle to establish new Jewish traditions after the destruction of Jerusalem's Holy Temple. Against this backdrop Hisdaduh embarks on the tortuous path to become an enchantress in the very land where the word 'magic' originated." (Publisher's note)

Antunes, Antonio Lobo

✓ The **inquisitors'** manual; translated by Richard Zenith. Grove Press 2003 435p $25

ISBN 0-8021-1732-5

LC 2002-33858

Original Portuguese edition, 1997

"Lobo Antunes, one of the most skillfull psychological portraitists writing anywhere, renders the turpitude of an entire society through an impasto of intensely individual voices." New Yorker

Appelfeld, Aharon

✓ ★ **Badenheim** 1939; [by] Aharon Appelfeld; translated by Dalya Bilu. Godine 1980 148p

ISBN 0-879-23342-7

LC 80-66192

Originally published in Hebrew

"Year after year the regular summer guests, most of them comfortably wealthy middle-class Jews, come to the little resort town Badenheim near Vienna to be entertained, to eat strawberry tarts, to find love. Even in 1939, with the Nazis firmly ensconced in Vienna, no one is allowed to worry, and the few who do are declared mad. In the end, Badenheim is closed off; all its people—guests, musicians, pastry chefs, even the dogs and goldfish of the town—are packed into cattle cars. Still the people delude themselves into thinking that they are going 'home,' back to their origins in Poland, and anyone who doubts this is argued down. The novel ends with the closing of the cattle cars' sliding doors." Libr J

"The most shocking thing about this novel is not its satirical humor, but its charm. Appelfeld manages to treat his appalling theme with grace." N Y Rev Books

Appelfeld, Aharon

✓ **Blooms** of darkness; translated from the Hebrew by Jeffrey M. Green. Schocken Books 2010 279p $25.95

ISBN 978-0-8052-4280-5; 0-8052-4280-5

LC 2009-33532

Original Hebrew edition, 2006

Appelfeld "narrates Blooms of Darkness in a taut, terse present-tense voice that refuses the consolations of retrospect. His decision to use the present tense is particularly shrewd since it eliminates—for the reader, as for Hugo—any possibility of a future. . . Like Anne Frank's diary—a work to which it will draw justified comparison—Blooms

of Darkness, beautifully translated from the Hebrew by Jeffrey M. Green, records a brutal process of education." N Y Times Book Rev

Appelfeld, Aharon

✓ **Until** the dawn's light. Schocken Books 2011 231p $26

ISBN 978-0-8052-4179-2; 0-8052-4179-5

LC 2011-07286

Original Hebrew edition, 1995

This book "depicts the world of early 20th-century Austrian Jews, many of whom have abandoned their ancestral traditions and converted to Christianity. . . . After the Jewish Blanca marries her gentile, ominously named high school classmate Adolf following a whirlwind (but remarkably unromantic) courtship, her life becomes unbearable. Blanca feels herself 'enslaved,' trapped in a marriage to an abusive, bombastically anti-Semitic man. Though she feels hopeless after her mother's death and her father's tragic disappearance, the birth of her son renews Blanca's strength and drives her to an act that will send her and Otto fleeing." Publ Wkly

"A beautiful and affecting novel, Tolstoyan in its compassion for humanity." Kirkus

Apple, Max

The **Jew** of Home Depot and other stories. Johns Hopkins University Press 2007 170p $19.95

ISBN 978-0-8018-8738-3; 0-8018-8738-0

LC 2007-18864

"Comic movies don't often get Oscar nods. In fiction, too, tragedy wears the capital L for Literature, whereas comedy—good luck, happy endings, pleasure itself—is deemed to be the fluffy stuff of chick lit and beach books. With The Jew of Home Depot, his first collection of stories in two decades, Max Apple challenges the canard that misery reveals more about our identity than joy does. . . . The 13 delightful, utterly cynicism-free stories collected here are mostly tales of courtship, and as the title not so shyly suggests, they often star Jews." Washington Post Book World

Archer, Jeffrey, 1940-

✓ **And** thereby hangs a tale. St. Martin's Press 2010 301p $25.99

ISBN 978-0-312-53953-5; 0-312-53953-3

LC 2010-21666

"Archer assembles 15 more of the clever stories for which he is known. They are split between tales of trickery, as with 'Stuck on You,' where an eager young man is played by a diamond thief, and decidedly sentimental stories, such as 'Members Only,' about a man who wants nothing more than to join a private country club. . . . His trademark twists—sometimes a surprise to the reader, sometimes not—and genial tone will endear these mostly cozy stories to his many fans." Publ Wkly

Archer, Jeffrey

✓ **As** the crow flies. HarperCollins 1991 617p

ISBN 0-06-017914-7

LC 90-56105

This novel has the "usual Archer signature: fast-moving plot, romance, high finance, and good natured mockery of

Britain. It uses the conventions of the classic revenge tale, featuring a feud that continues through two generations and the stock characters of the genre: the resourceful hero, the clever childhood sweetheart, the bastard son, the nefarious mother. . . . Archer knows what fast-reading light fiction is all about and dishes it up with panache." Quill Quire

Archer, Jeffrey, 1940-
✓**Best** kept secret; Jeffrey Archer. 1st ed. St. Martin's Press 2013 384 p. (hardcover) $27.99
  ISBN 125000098X; 9781250000989

LC 2013000638

  This historical family saga, by Jeffrey Archer, is book three of "The Clifton Chronicles." It is set in "1945, London. The vote in the House of Lords as to who should inherit the Barrington family fortune has ended in a tie. The Lord Chancellor's deciding vote will cast a long shadow on the lives of Harry Clifton and Giles Barrington. . . . In 1957, Sebastian wins a scholarship to Cambridge, and a new generation of the Clifton family marches onto the page." (Publisher's note)

Archer, Jeffrey
✓A **matter** of honor. Linden Press 1986 399p
  ISBN 0-671-62434-2

LC 86-7405

  "Adam Scott is left a most unorthodox bequest in his father's will that takes him on a terrifying chase across Europe pursuing a priceless icon and being pursued by Soviet, American, and British intelligence forces. Archer cagily impels his well-crafted characters straight into action, then ever so slowly fills in all the dimensions of the struggle in which they are engaged. . . . Scott's steely determination to uphold his family's honor holds the reader's interest, and his skill at eluding the enemy culminates in a master stratagem that gives the story its final twist. A fast-paced and exciting, though corpse-riddled, thriller." Booklist

Archer, Jeffrey
  Only time will tell. St. Martin's Press 2011 386p $27.99
  ISBN 978-0-312-53955-9; 0-312-53955-X

LC 2011-25823

  "This first title from the Clifton Chronicles introduces readers to Harry Clifton, a boy growing up in Bristol whose father mysteriously died a full year before his birth, supposedly killed in WWI. Though Harry dreams of becoming a stevedore like his Uncle Stan, crazy Old Jack Tar shows Harry the truths of the stevedore life and becomes his surrogate father. After hearing an angelic treble voice, Harry decides to join the choir and learns to read. The choir in turn gains him a scholarship to boys' boarding school St. Bede's a gateway to the life his mother wants for him, far from the harbor and shipping industry. He meets scholarly Deakins and wealthy Giles Barrington, who become his best friends, and the three strive to gain acceptance to Bristol Grammar School. Though Giles' father has a particular aversion to Harry, the boys' friendship proves stronger than any paternal dictates." Publ Wkly

Archer, Jeffrey, 1940-
✓The **sins** of the father; Jeffrey Archer. 1st U.S. ed. St. Martin's Press 2012 339 p. (hardcover) $27.99; (paperback) $9.99
  ISBN 1250000971; 9781250000972; 9781429949033; 9781250010407

LC 2011046558

  Author Jeffrey Archer continues his "Clifton Chronicles" book series. "First, Harry is sent to trial and prison. Then Emma Barrington, whose relationship to Harry is murky, departs England for the U.S., leaving behind a child Harry doesn't know has been born. . . . Harry gets out of prison . . . by volunteering for a military special operations group. . . . Emma learns Sefton Jelks, Wall Street attorney, was paid by a wealthy client to finagle Harry into prison. . . . Finally, the cast gathers in post-war England, where a paternity case is settled once and for all." (Kirkus Reviews)

Armstrong, Kelley
✓**Bitten**. Viking 2001 342p
  ISBN 978-0-670-89471-0

LC 00-68590

  This is the first title in the author's Women of the Otherworld series. "Elena Michaels is a self-described 'mutt,' a werewolf who left her secretive pack in upstate New York for a life among humans. In the year since she relocated to Toronto, she's embarked on a career as a journalist and begun a pleasingly mundane relationship with a decent man. All this is jeopardized when she agrees to help her old packmates hunt some troublesome mutts who are converting common criminals to werewolves and leaving a trail of conspicuous carnage. . . . Filled with romance and supernatural intrigue, this book will surely remind readers of Anne Rice's sophisticated refurbishings of the vampire story." Publ Wkly

  Followed by: Stolen (2002); Dime store magic (2004); Industrial magic (2004); Haunted (2005); Broken (2006); No humans involved (2007); Personal demon (2008); Living with the dead (2008); Frostbitten (2009); Waking the witch (2010); Spell bound (2011)

Arnaldur Indridason
✓The **draining** lake; translated from the Icelandic by Bernard Scudder. Thomas Dunne Books 2008 312p $24.95
  ISBN 978-0-312-35873-0; 0-312-35873-3

LC 2008-21257

  Original Icelandic edition, 2004
  "Indridason keeps readers guessing as to the identities of the snitch and the skeleton until the very last pages of this moody investigation into the fatal follies of youth, politics and memory. By novel's end, fittingly, the lake waters begin to rise again, obscuring all." Washington Post Book World

Arnott, Jake
✓The **house** of rumour; Jake Arnott. Houghton Mifflin Harcourt 2013 448 p. (hardcover) $26
  ISBN 0544077792; 9780544077799

LC 2012042359

  This novel, by Jake Arnott, "explores WWII spy intrigue (featuring Ian Fleming), occultism (Aleister Crowley), the West Coast science-fiction set (Heinlein, L. Ron Hubbard, and Philip K. Dick all appear), and the new wave music scene of the '80s. The decades-spanning, labyrinthine plot . . . [is] told through multiple narrators, what at first appears to be a constellation of random events begins to cohere as the work of a shadow organization--or is it just coincidence?" (Publisher's note)

Arnow, Harriette Louisa Simpson

√ The **dollmaker**; [by] Harriette Simpson Arnow. Macmillan 1954 549p

"It is hard to believe that anyone who opens its pages will soon forget {Gertie} and her sufferings as traced in Harriette Arnow's long, heavily packed masterwork." NY Times Book Rev

Arsenault, Emily

√ The **broken** teaglass; a novel. Delacorte Press 2009 370p $25; pa $15

ISBN 978-0-553-80733-2; 0-553-80733-1; 978-0-553-38653-0 pa

LC 2008-39167

"College graduate Billy Webb takes a job at the Samuelson Company, a venerable dictionary publisher in out-of-the-way Claxton, Massachusetts. While he learns the ropes of research reading, defining, and answering the phone, wondering whether his hushed workplace is really the 'real world,' he finds an unusual citation (for the word editrix) from The Broken Teaglass, by Dolores Beekmim. Though it's not the only such excerpt in the files, no such novel has even been published. Stranger still, the story seems to be set at Samuelson. Working with his arch, cryptic colleague Mona Minot, Billy tries to find the rest of the citations, which seem to make reference to murder. . . . [This] novel has a delightful premise, crisply drawn characters, and a subtle sense of humor. Word nerds, too, will enjoy the peeks at the procedure of making a dictionary." Booklist

Arsenault, Emily

In search of the Rose notes. William Morrow 2011 369p pa $14.99

ISBN 978-0-06-201232-6

Drawn back to her old neighborhood and to her former best friend Charlotte when the bones of their babysitter Rose are found, Nora must revisit the events surrounding Rose's disappearance and her own troubled adolescence.

"Instead of dwelling on fear and pain, Arsenault guides the reader through grief, compassion, and understanding in this emotionally complex and deeply satisfying read." Publ Wkly

Arvin, Reed

√ **Blood** of angels; a novel. Reed Arvin. HarperCollins Publishers 2005 viii, 354p (pbk.) $7.99

ISBN 9780060596354; 0060596341; 9780060596347

LC 2004060931

This book tells the story of "Thomas Dennehy, assistant DA of Davidson County, Tenn., [who will] be certified as the first lawyer in the country to have sent the wrong man to the death chamber. As if that isn't enough, he must also prosecute a charismatic member of the local Sudanese community, Moses Bol, accused of killing a prostitute, in a trial that threatens to engulf Nashville in a full-scale race riot. Dennehy is tough, in court and out, and has plenty of . . .

personal problems—primarily an ex-wife for whom he has conflicting feelings and an 11-year-old daughter he adores. . . . While trying to sort through his problems, Dennehy falls for an unlikely lady, Fiona Towns, a local minister and Moses Bol's alibi." (Publishers Weekly)

Asaro, Catherine

√ **Primary** inversion. Tor 1995 317p

ISBN 0-312-85764-0

LC 94-47207

"In a distant future where three empires battle for control of the galaxy, Sauscony Valdoria, the heir apparent of the Skolian Empire, finds herself inexplicably attracted to Jaibriol Qox, the son of the Emperor of Tarnth and the symbol of everything Sauscony has been taught to despise. Asaro's sf debut features strong male and female protagonists and a well-realized far-future world. Blending hard science with a familiar tale of star-crossed lovers." Libr J

Asch, Sholem

The **Apostle**; translated by Maurice Samuel. Putnam 1943 804p

In "'The Apostle,' Sholem Asch has written a book which should stand beside 'The Nazarene.' Its erudition, its essential reverence for the two faiths concerned, its scholarly and dramatic portrayal of the Jew who spread the gospel to the gentiles will call forth the respect of every civilized and intelligent reader." N Y Her Trib Books

Asch, Sholem

The **Nazarene**; translated by Maurice Samuel. Putnam 1939 698p

A novel based on the life of Christ told from three different points of view. First there is the narrative as a modern Polish Jewish scholar hears it from lips of one who claims to be the reincarnation of the Roman military governor of Jerusalem. Then there is the 'fifth gospel' written by Judas Iscariot, and finally there is the story as the young Jew remembers it when he realizes that he himself is the reincarnation of a disciple of the Pharisee, Rabbi Nicodemon.

"Judged purely as a novel, The Nazarene is a superb achievement. Even on the factual side, a work such as Papini's Life is thin beside it. This is because Mr. Asch has taken an infinite amount of trouble to build up an historical background against which the figure of Jesus may move authentically, with that sense of reality which we should expect of fiction as of life." Atlantic

Asimov, Isaac

√ The **complete** stories. Doubleday 1990 2v v1 pa $19.95

ISBN 0-385-41627-X

LC 90-3136

This set contains all of Asimov's science fiction stories including the "collections 'Earth Is Room Enough' and 'Nine Tomorrows' from the 1950s as well as . . . 'Nightfall and Other Stories.'" SLJ

Asimov, Isaac
✓ ★ **Forward** the Foundation. Doubleday 1993
415p (Foundation)
ISBN 0-385-24793-1

LC 92-46655
This volume and Prelude to Foundation predate the other Foundation novels in terms of internal chronology
Although "Asimov leans rather heavily on dialogue to carry the story, we are privileged to learn something more of Seldon, whom Asimov regards as his alter ego—intellectually vigorous, witty, vulnerable, and deeply concerned about the fate of his fallible species." Christ Sci Monit

Asimov, Isaac
✓ ★ **Foundation**. Gnome Press 1951 255p
(Foundation)
"A story of a Galactic Empire of the future, and its successor in the government of the Milky Way." Publ Wkly
Followed by Foundation and empire

Asimov, Isaac
✓★ **Foundation** and earth. Doubleday 1986
356p (Foundation)
ISBN 0-385-23312-4

LC 86-2130
In the fifth novel of the Foundation series "Golan Trevize rejects the vaunted Selden Plan of Foundation and Empire in favor of a bold experiment in galactic unity. To ferret out the reason for his instinctive decision, Trevize embarks on a journey through uncharted space in search of a legendary planet known as Earth. Asimov's latest entry in his epic series features his usual cast of intelligent, likeable characters and just enough action to give substance to this novel of lucid speculations." Libr J

Asimov, Isaac
✓ ★ **Foundation** and empire. Gnome Press 1952
247p (Foundation)
In this second volume of the Foundation series "two groups struggle for control of the world's destiny in a future time when mankind has settled in the Milky Way. Then a mutant appears bringing with him a new threat for everyone." Chicago Public Libr
Followed by Second Foundation

Asimov, Isaac
✓ ★ **Foundation's** edge. Doubleday 1982 366p
(Foundation)
ISBN 0-385-17725-9
The fourth novel in the Foundation series "shows us the Seldon Plan at midpoint and still surprisingly on target in spite of the passage of time and unforeseen events. The focus has narrowed to power struggles between the Foundations, both wishing to be the controlling element in the planned Second Galactic Empire, quite unlike Seldon's idealistic vision. And new players have been introduced into the game." Libr J
Followed by Foundation and earth

Asimov, Isaac
✓ The **gods** themselves. Doubleday 1972 288p

"Imagination is the fount of Isaac Asimov's mastery. The suspense he generates . . . is low-key and subtle, and he has a gifted knack for making wild and indescribable superbeings (for he never quite describes them) seem lifelike, though scarcely human." Best Sellers

Asimov, Isaac
✓ ★ **I,** robot; Bantam hardcover ed.; Bantam
Books 2004 224p (Robot series) $24; pa $7.99
ISBN 0-553-80370-0; 0-553-29438-5 pa

LC 2003-69139
First published 1950 by Gnome Press
"These loosely connected stories cover the career of Dr. Susan Calvin and United States Robots, the industry that she heads, from the time of the public's early distrust of these robots to its later dependency on them. This collection is an important introduction to a theme often found in science fiction: the encroachment of technology on our lives." Shapiro. Fic for Youth. 3d edition

Asimov, Isaac
✓ ★ **Prelude** to Foundation. Doubleday 1988
403p (Foundation)
ISBN 0-385-23313-2

LC 87-33086
This novel and Forward the Foundation are set chronologically prior to other volumes in the Foundation series
This "is vintage Asimov, a novel that places ideas ahead of all its other elements but doesn't stint on characterization or entertaining plot lines. It also contains a fair number of mysteries, and . . . all of this is handled in a simple, direct style that never gets between the reader and the story." West Coast Rev Books

Asimov, Isaac
✓ The **rest** of the robots. Doubleday 1964 556p
Contains two science-fiction mystery novels featuring Elijah Baley: The caves of steel and The naked sun, first published 1954 and 1957 respectively. Short stories included are: Robot AL-76 goes astray; Victory unintentional; First Law; Let's get together; Satisfaction guaranteed; Risk; Lenny; Galley slave.

Asimov, Isaac
✓ ★ **Second** Foundation. Gnome Press 1953
210p (Foundation)
Third book of the Foundation series about the efforts of a group of scientists who are trying to subdue the chaos and conflict of the galactic world. The story centers on fourteen-year-old Arkady Darrell's search for this secret group
Followed by Foundation's edge

Aslam, Nadeem
✓ ★ The **Blind** Man's Garden; Nadeem Aslam.
Alfred A. Knopf 2013 384 p. (First Edition) $26.95
ISBN 0307961710; 9780307961716

LC 2012041083
This book by Nadeem Aslam is a "novel set in Pakistan and Afghanistan in the months following 9/11: a story of war, of one family's losses. Jeo and Mikal are foster brothers from a small town in Pakistan. Jeo is a . . . medical student. Mikal has been a vagabond . . . in love with a woman he

can't have. When Jeo decides to sneak across the border into Afghanistan . . . to help care for wounded civilians . . . Mikal determines to go with him." (Publisher's note)

Includes bibliographical references

Aslam, Nadeem

√ **Maps** for lost lovers; Nadeem Aslam. 1st American ed. Knopf 2005 xii, 379 p o.p.; (pbk.) $14.95

ISBN 1400042429; 9781400076970

LC 2004059428

Kiriyama Prize: Fiction (2005)

In this book, author Nadeem "Aslam . . . explores the interwoven lives of Pakistani immigrants in an English town they have rechristened Dasht-e-Tanhaii, 'the Wilderness of Solitude' or 'the Desert of Loneliness.' The disappearance of Jugnu and Chanda, lovers who broke Islamic law to live in sin, throws the small community into upheaval. The police arrest Chanda's brothers, whom they believe murdered the couple to avenge their family's shame. . . . Aslam depicts an insular ex-pat Pakistani community fighting to preserve its cultural heritage and losing the battle to its Western-born children. . . . At the heart of the turmoil is sexual freedom, and Aslam illustrates the many ways women's lives are restricted and romantic love is denied in the name of religion." (Publishers Weekly)

Aslam, Nadeem

√ The **wasted** vigil. Alfred A. Knopf 2008 319p $25

ISBN 978-0-307-26842-6; 0-307-26842-X

LC 2008-17772

"The prose in The Wasted Vigil is usually so generous with startling perceptions that the reader rarely feels overwhelmed by the social and historical facts that Aslam, writing about a country largely unknown to his readers, has to constantly smuggle into his narrative. . . . Aslam's determination to gaze resolutely at the darkest side of our many cold and hot wars is what gives The Wasted Vigil its depth and power." N Y Rev Books

Atherton, Nancy

√ **Aunt** Dimity digs in. Viking 1998 275p

ISBN 0-670-87061-7

LC 97-34633

"Living in the cottage left to Lori by her mother's close friend, Dimity Westwood, Lori is thankful for the arrival of the local and unmarried Francesca Sciaparelli to aid with the double joys of motherhood. In this corpseless tale, the mystery concerns a document stolen from the vicarage. . . . Asked to resolve the dilemma, Lori, a rare book expert, is aided by Aunt Dimity who communicates with her ghostly handwriting in a special blue journal." Publ Wkly

Atkins, Ace

The **broken** places; Ace Atkins. G.P. Putnam's Sons 2013 368 p. (hardcover) $26.95

ISBN 0399161783; 9780399161780

LC 2013009334

This novel, by Ace Atkins, is an entry in the "Quinn Colson" series. "A year after becoming sheriff, Quinn Colson is faced with the release of an infamous murderer from prison. Jamey Dixon comes back to Jericho preaching redemption,

and some believe him; but for the victim's family, the only thought is revenge. . . . Colson and his deputy, Lillie, . . . [didn't] count on one more unwelcome visitor: a tornado that causes havoc just as events come to a head." (Publisher's note)

Atkins, Ace

√ **Devil's** garden. G.P. Putnam's Sons 2009 354p $24.95

ISBN 978-0-399-15536-9; 0-399-15536-8

LC 2008-46361

"The 1921 rape/manslaughter trial of silent film star Roscoe 'Fatty' Arbuckle provides the gritty backdrop for Atkins's outstanding crime novel, in which Dashiell Hammett, then a Pinkerton operative living in San Francisco, plays a significant role. A wild party Arbuckle throws at San Francisco's posh St. Francis Hotel results in tragedy after an actress, Virginia Rappe, is mysteriously injured and later dies. . . . With enviable ease, Atkins . . . brings to life Hammett, Arbuckle, William Randolph Hearst and other real figures of the period. Those familiar with the historical case will be impressed by how well the book meshes fact and fiction. Genre fans who enjoy the grim realism of James Ellroy's post-WWII Los Angeles will find a lot to like in Atkins's Prohibition-era San Francisco." Publ Wkly

Atkins, Ace

√ The **ranger**. G.P. Putnam's Sons 2011 334p $25.95

ISBN 978-0-399-15748-6; 0-399-15748-4

LC 2011-02785

"Fresh from his tour of duty in Afghanistan, Quinn returns to his hometown of Jericho, Miss., for the funeral of his uncle, Sheriff Hampton Beckett. The sheriff's death was ruled a suicide but Deputy Lillie Virgil believes he was murdered and appeals to Quinn to help find his murderer. But as he tries to find the truth behind his uncle's death, Quinn plunges into a morass of violence and corruption that has overpowered his rural hometown and the environs of remote Tibbehah County. An 'invisible confederacy of crooks' includes a compound of meth dealers, shady land deals and a general disregard for the law. While Quinn acts as the archetypical character who has come to clean up the town, 'The Ranger' avoids stereotypes and clichés. Quinn isn't molded as a superhero but a man struggling with his role and duties as a soldier and what he owes his family and hometown." South Florida Sun-Sentinel

Atkins, Ace

√ **White** shadow. Putnam 2006 370p $24.95

ISBN 0-399-15355-1

LC 2005-56683

This novel "slowly unfurls itself, strolling along with the readers, as it evokes the heat and humidity of a setting where the languorousness stands in sharp contrast to the life and death stakes at hand. Murder, corruption, and organized crime are all present, but the heat seems to suck the speed out of them, so even death is dispatched in slow motion. Ultimately, the atmosphere of this novel is the star. Atkins nails all the period details and describes the city perfectly." PopMatters

Atkins, Ace

✓**Wicked** city. G. P. Putnam's Sons 2008 336p $24.95

ISBN 978-0-399-15457-7

LC 2007-32774

"It's 1954, and the attorney-general-elect of Alabama has been assassinated near a downtown street. Among the gathering crowd stands a young teen still wearing 3-D glasses from the John Wayne movie he's just seen. So begins Ace Atkins' novel, Wicked City, a vivid depiction of the real-life Phenix City, a den of gambling, prostitution and corruption that rivaled any Hollywood creation. Atkins provides a 3-D view through two narrators, an omniscient teller and Lamar Murphy, an ex-boxer enlisted to help solve Albert Patterson's murder. . . . A character warns that the sweetness of Phenix City moonshine masks the embalming fluid that provides its kick. Atkins has likewise crafted a smart tale of a decadent place; Southern sweetness laced with poison." Paste

Atkinson, Kate

✓ ★ **Case** histories; a novel. Little, Brown 2004 312p $23.95

ISBN 0-316-74040-3 Little, Brown; 0-385-60799-7 Doubleday

LC 2004-2379

This novel is set in Cambridge, England. "Olivia Land, youngest and most beloved of the Land girls, goes missing in the night and is never seen again. Thirty years later, two of her surviving sisters unearth a shocking clue to Olivia's disappearance. . . . Theo delights in his daughter Laura's wit, effortless beauty, and selfless love. But her first day as an associate in his law firm is also the day when Theo's world turns upside down. . . . Michelle looks around one day and finds herself trapped. . . . A very needy baby and a very demanding husband make her every waking moment a reminder that . . . she'd made a grave mistake and would spend the rest of her life paying for it—until a fit of rage creates a grisly, bloody escape. As Private Detective Jackson Brodie investigates all three cases, startling connections and discoveries emerge. Inextricably caught up in his clients' grief, joy, and desire, Jackson finds their unshakable need for resolution very much like his own." (Publisher's note)

"The novel is packed with women whose appetites are large, and Atkinson's prose is correspondingly loose and louche: no single point of view predominates, and everyone's thoughts effortlessly rollick along." N Y Times Book Rev

Atkinson, Kate

✓ ★ **Life** After Life; Kate Atkinson. Little Brown & Co 2013 544 p. $27.99

ISBN 0316176486; 9780316176484

This book is the story of Ursula Todd, who has an apparently infinite number of lives. "As she grows, she also dies, repeatedly, in a variety of ways, while the young century marches on towards its second cataclysmic world war. Does Ursula's apparently infinite number of lives give her the power to save the world from its inevitable destiny? And if she can—will she?" (Publisher's note)

Atkinson, Kate

Not the end of the world; stories. Little, Brown 2002 244p il $23.95

ISBN 0-316-61430-0

LC 2003-40117

"While not as intense or unified as Atkinson's full-length work, this is a sharp and wholly original collection." Publ Wkly

Atkinson, Kate

✓**Started** early, took my dog; a novel. Little, Brown and Company 2011 371p $24.99

ISBN 978-0-316-06673-0; 0-316-06673-7

LC 2010-32217

First published 2010 in the United Kingdom

"A delight: an intricate construction that assembles itself before the reader's eyes, populated by idiosyncratic, multidimensional characters and written with shrewd, mordant grace. . . . Atkinson's Jackson Brodie books are like high-wire acts in which she is forever defying gravity (in the form of crime fiction's improbable conventions) by making the work fresh, unpredictable and alive." Salon.com

Atkinson, Kate

✓ ★ **When** will there be good news? Little, Brown & Co. 2008 388p $24.99

ISBN 978-0-316-15485-7; 0-316-15485-7

LC 2008-14738

"As always, Atkinson inhabits her characters with fluency, clarity and a good eye and ear for quirks and habits of mind." Times Lit Suppl

This is the author's third mystery featuring former police officer and private detective Jackson Brodie. "Set mostly around Edinburgh, Scotland, the tale begins with a six-year-old girl escaping an attacker who kills her mother, eight-year-old sister, and baby brother. Atkinson then weaves a plot that connects Brodie to the girl, now an adult, through coincidence and more tragedy, this time a train wreck. Detective Chief Inspector Louise Morse, who has a thing for Brodie, returns to his life, and a new character appears: Reggie, an orphaned 16-year-old girl with a criminal for a brother and a desire to study for her A-levels even though she has dropped out of school." Libr J

Atlee, Alison

★ The **typewriter** girl; Alison Atlee. 1st Gallery Books trade pbk ed Gallery Books 2013 367 p. (paperback) $15

ISBN 1451673256; 1451673272; 9781451673258; 9781451673272

LC 2012007883

In this book, Betsey Dobson travels to the Idensea seaside resort and is hired by manager John Jones. "John, who has spent four years supervising construction of the resort's pleasure railway and indoor amusement park, clashes with Sir Alton Dunning, who wants to maintain his hotel's elegant exclusivity. In addition to completing the park, John's plans also include finding a rich wife. Yet Betsy intrigues him, even after he learns how she was seduced and abandoned" while working as a housemaid. (Library Journal)

Attenberg, Jami

The **melting** season. Riverhead Books 2010
289p $25.95

    ISBN 978-1-59448-896-2; 1-59448-896-7

                           LC 2009-33715

"While Attenberg's story of self-empowerment could easily wear thin, she skillfully keeps it from getting too maudlin and melodramatic. She has a talent for creating strong, interesting characters and situations that keep the story humming along." Chicago Sun-Times

Attenberg, Jami

✓ ★ The **Middlesteins**; Jami Attenberg. Grand Central Pub. 2012 288 p. $24.99

    ISBN 1455507210; 9781455507214

                           LC 2011025990

In "[Jami] Attenberg's multigenerational novel about a Midwestern Jewish family, shifting points of view tell the story of the breakup and aftermath of Edie and Richard Middlestein's nearly 40-year marriage as Edie slowly eats herself to death. . . . When complications surrounding Edie's diabetes precipitate Richard's filing for divorce, the already tightly wound [daughter-in-law] Rachelle becomes obsessed with the family's physical and moral health." (Publishers Weekly)

Atwood, Margaret, 1939-

✓ **Alias** Grace. Talese 1996 468p il

    ISBN 0-385-47571-3

                           LC 96-21689

This "novel is based on the case of Grace Marks, who in 1843 was sentenced to life imprisonment for her role in the murders of her employer and his mistress. In this fictional rendition, three men try to spring the beautiful alleged murderess from prison, by way of religion, pre-Freudian analysis, and chicanery." New Yorker

"Always a powerful writer, Atwood outdoes herself with compelling prose, expert control of the material, and fine attention to historical detail." Libr J

Atwood, Margaret, 1939-

✓ The **blind** assassin. Talese 2000 521p $26

    ISBN 0-385-47572-1

                           LC 99-462109

"Within the novel, stories produce anguish and arousal, charges and vindications, guilt and vengeance. For readers of the novel, all this may foster something like delight, although the fictional universe is hardly a pleasant one." Women's Rev Books

Atwood, Margaret, 1939-

✓ ★ **Cat's** eye. Doubleday 1989 446p

    ISBN 0-385-26007-5

                           LC 88-24345

First published 1988 in Canada

Elaine Risley, the narrator of this novel, "is a Canadian painter of some renown who, at 50, has returned to her childhood city of Toronto for a retrospective of her work. The dull, provincial city of her youth has become world class in the intervening years . . . but in the week she is there her interest in the city's new galleries and restaurants and shops and, in many ways, in the retrospective itself, is only glanc-

ing. Her focus, and the novel's, is all on the past." N Y Times Book Rev

"Atwood's achievement is the decoding of childhood's secrets, and the creation of a flawed and haunting work of art." Time

Atwood, Margaret, 1939-

✓ ★ The **Handmaid's** tale; with an introduction by Valerie Martin. Everyman's Library 2006 xxxiii, 350p

    ISBN 0307264602

                           LC 2006042618

First published 1986 by Houghton Mifflin

This is a new edition of Atwood's 1986 novel with an introduction by Valerie Martin. The book is "set in the near future, in a fundamentalist Christian totalitarian state called the Republic of Gilead. . . . Because of environmental pollution, the number of fertile women is low and those who can still bear children are effectively prisoners of the government. When the Christian fundamentalists took power they removed fertile women from their husbands and children and sent them to live with government leaders—or 'Commanders'—and their infertile wives—so that they could conceive and bear children who would then be raised by the Commanders and their wives as their own. The novel is narrated by one of these fertile women, called Handmaids." (N Y Rev Books)

"A gripping suspense tale, The Handmaid's Tale is an allegory of what results from a politics based on misogyny, racism, and anti-Semitism." Ms

Atwood, Margaret, 1939-

✓ **Life** before man. Simon & Schuster 1980 317p

    ISBN 0-671-25115-5

                           LC 79-20281

This "is a powerful, introspective view of contemporary marriage and the changing roles of the sexes. . . . {This novel} returns to the survival and identity theme of Atwood's early thematic guide to Canadian literature, but at a level that transcends the national. With men and mores rooted in the prehistoric past, Atwood forces us to confront a harrowing present that anticipates an ecologically and culturally doomed future." Choice

Atwood, Margaret, 1939-

✓ The **year** of the flood; a novel. Nan A. Talese/ Doubleday 2009 448p $26.95

    ISBN 978-0-385-52877-1; 0-385-52877-9

                           LC 2009-05901

"Structurally, the book can be overwhelming. The story begins with the end and is told from the disparate points of view of Ren, a young sex-club trapeze dancer; Toby, who becomes one of God's Gardeners; and Adam One, the leader of the Gardeners. Narratives jump back and forth in time to show how and why the destruction came about. Keeping the story line straight can be challenging because of the multiple narrators, but it's easy enough to tell the good guys from the bad guys. The good guys are green. (Not literally, although in a book like this, that is a possibility.) Atwood gives each main character an imaginative life history." Dallas Morning News

Atxaga, Bernardo

✓**Seven** houses in France; Bernardo Atxaga; translated from the Spanish by Margaret Jull Costa. Farrar Straus & Giroux 2012 250 p. (paperback: alk. paper) $15.00; (hardcover) $29.40

ISBN 1555976239; 1846554470; 9781555976231; 9781846554476

LC 2011507407

This historical novel "is set in the Belgian Congo in the early part of the last century, [where] the arrival of a devout and taciturn young officer into a contingent of colorful colonial soldiers on a remote jungle outpost on the River Congo sets off a . . . chain of events." The marksman, Chrysostome Liège, is abused by his commander, Captain Biran, who is "engage[d] in a risky contraband scheme with his covetous subordinate, the psychotic Lieutenant Van Thiegel." (Publishers Weekly)

Aubert, Rosemary

✓The **ferryman** will be there; an Ellis Portal mystery. Bridge Works 2001 258p $22.95

ISBN 1-882593-44-8

LC 00-52900

"Portal's indomitable integrity and checkered past make his ministrations to the troubled girls utterly believable and moving. This is quickly becoming a very special series." Booklist

Auchincloss, Louis

✓The **book** class. Houghton Mifflin 1984 212p

ISBN 0-395-36138-9

LC 84-522

"In 1908 a group of Park Avenue debutantes begins to meet once a month to discuss books, past and present. 'The Book Class' endures for 64 years, creating a lasting and telling impression on the son of one of its members, the novel's narrator, Christopher Gates. These pampered and seemingly fragile women, whose lives are filled with great passion, disappointment, and tragedy, exude an aura of power and mystery which fascinates Gates and which he probes throughout his life." Libr J

"Auchincloss may work on a small canvas, but no one excels his finely etched portraits of sophisticates of good breeding and inherited wealth." Publ Wkly

Auchincloss, Louis

✓Her infinite variety. Houghton Mifflin 2000 224p $25

ISBN 0-618-02191-4

LC 99-47302

This novel "relates how a Depression-era Vassar graduate named Clara Longcope—the shrewd and beautiful daughter of a Yale professor—charms and manipulates her way to the pinnacle of New York society." N Y Times Book Rev

"An astute and witty novel about a woman who disdains the old values of money and class in favor of a feminine meritocracy in the world of business." Publ Wkly

Auel, Jean M.

✓★ The **Clan** of the Cave Bear; a novel. Crown 1980 468p (Earth's children)

ISBN 0-517-18918-6

LC 80-14581

"It's subject matter, its vast research . . . make this fictional excursion into prehistory a thing of wonder. But it's an enjoyable story, too, though leisurely and not notable for the quality of its prose. . . . The depiction of how the cave-dwelling Neanderthals lived—how they performed their totemistic rituals, gathered medicinal plants, slew mammoths and other animals—is solid, convincing and sometimes exciting." Publ Wkly

Followed by The Valley of Horses

Auel, Jean M.

✓The **land** of painted caves. Broadway Books 2011 757p (Earth's children) $30

ISBN 978-0-517-58051-6; 0-517-58051-9

LC 2010-21873

The sixth and final book in the author's Earth's Children series which began with The Clan of the Cave Bear (1980)

"Ayla is the mate of Jondalar, the mother of Jonayla, their infant daughter, and an acolyte of the First of the Zelandonii, the spiritual leaders of the caves of her husband's people. But all is not well with Ayla. She is separated from her husband and daughter while training for her new position, which takes a terrible physical toll on her health, and her innovative ideas and unusual history create conflict among the people. . . . Though one must occasionally suspend disbelief that one young woman, no matter how intelligent, can really be responsible for introducing concepts such as animal husbandry, sign language, and the role of men in sexuality and conception, the book is compelling." Libr J

Auslander, Shalom

✓Hope; a tragedy. Shalom Auslander. Riverhead Books 2011 292 p.

ISBN 9781594488382

LC 2011046843

The novel tells the story of "a young Jewish business writer and his family, who buy a house in rural New York. They find that their purchase has included a whole lot more than they bargained for. The protagonist, Solomon Kugel, discovers there's a secret tenant in the attic - none other than Holocaust writer-victim Anne Frank. The iconic Anne Frank, now very old, miraculously survived the Nazi death camps and took up residence in this bucolic enclave, camping in Kugel's attic and writing a book about her life. Kugel targets . . . all sorts of social worries, such as anti-Semitism; and oddities from gluten allergies to the tanning fad to the real estate business." (NPR)

Austen, Jane

✓★ **Emma**; with an introduction by Marilyn Butler. Knopf 1991 xlvii, 498p $19

ISBN 0-679-40581-X

LC 91-52988

First published 1815

"Emma is a pretty girl of sterling character and more will than she can properly manage. She thinks she knows what is best for everybody, and is a prey to many deceptions. She is imposed upon, and imposes upon herself; it is a long while before she sees things as they are, and recognizes where her own happiness lies. Her hero is one of Jane's sober, clear-eyed, and perfect men. The Fairfax and Churchill subplot furnishes a comedy of dissimulation contrasting didactically with Emma's honesty. A formidable snob and vulgarian, Mrs. Elton, and a good-natured bore, Miss Bates, who would be insufferable outside these pages, are among the more laughable characters." Baker. Guide to the Best Fic

Austen, Jane

★ **Mansfield** Park; with an introduction by Peter Conrad. Alfred A. Knopf 1992 xxxvii, 488p $21

ISBN 0-679-41269-7

LC 91-58689

First published 1814

"Her most considerable piece of work, not in mere dimensions, but in the mastery of a difficult problem. . . . In truth, nowhere is the difference between true comedy and satire better exemplified." Baker. Guide to the Best Fic

Austen, Jane

Northanger Abbey. Vintage Classics 2007 241p pa $6.95

ISBN 978-0-307-38683-0; 0-307-38683-X

LC 2007-281091

First published 1818

"Though not published until 1818, this was written 1798-9 and entitled 'Susan', revised in 1803 and sold for publication; it may perhaps have been rewritten or touched up later, before it appeared posthumously. Begun as a parody of sentimentalism and the romantics, it developed into the genre which was to be peculiarly Jane Austen's—the portrayal in sober and faithful tints of the quiet middle-class life she knew; the satire restrained, the comedy all-pervasive." Baker. Guide to the Best Fic

Austen, Jane

Persuasion. Alfred A. Knopf 1992 xxxvii, 260p $18

ISBN 0-679-40986-6

LC 91-53181

First published 1818

"The heroine, Anne Elliott, and her lover, Captain Wentworth, had been engaged eight years before the story opens but Anne had broken the engagement in deference to family and friends. Upon his return he finds her 'wretchedly altered,' but after numerous obstacles have been overcome, the lovers are happily united." Gerwig. Handb for Readers and Writers

Austen, Jane

★ **Pride** and prejudice; introduction by Anna Quindlen. Modern Library 1995 281p $14.95

ISBN 0-679-60168-6

LC 95-6310

First published 1813

"The characters are drawn with humor, delicacy, and the intimate knowledge of men and women that Miss Austen always shows." Keller. Reader's Dig of Books

Austen, Jane

★ **Sense** and sensibility; with an introduction by Peter Conrad. Knopf 1992 xxxix, 367p $16

ISBN 0-679-40987-4

LC 91-53182

First published 1811

"A study of character and manners in a very delicate, precise, miniature style; the characters just everyday people, drawn as they are without exaggeration; the minute differences of human nature delicately penciled; the satire directed against mere commonplace foolishness, conceit, and vulgarity, rather than vice or eccentricity. In truth, the social failings and personal foibles are self-revealed rather than satirized and make spontaneous comedy." Baker. Guide to the Best Fic

Auster, Paul

The **Brooklyn** follies. Holt 2006 306p $24

ISBN 0-8050-7714-6

LC 2005-40201

This "is a departure for Auster. Instead of tight plotting and theoretical figure work, there is domestic realism. The result is a novel far more passionately American than Auster's previous ones." Times Lit Suppl

Auster, Paul

In the country of last things. Viking 1987 188p

ISBN 0-670-81445-8

LC 86-40257

"Imagine an American city in the near future, populated almost wholly by street dwellers, squatters in ruined buildings, scavengers for subsistence. Suicide clubs offer interesting ways to die, for a fee, but the rich have fled with their jewels, and those who are left survive on what little cash trade-in centers will give them for the day's pickings. This . . . dreamlike fable about a peculiarly recognizable society, now in the throes of entropy, focuses on the plight of a young woman, Anna Blume." Publ Wkly

This novel "is distinguished by an uncanny grasp of the day-to-day realities of homelessness. This is a scary but highly relevant book." Libr J

Auster, Paul

★ **Invisible**. Henry Holt and Co. 2009 308p $25

ISBN 978-0-8050-9080-2; 0-8050-9080-0

LC 2009-02237

This novel "novel opens in New York City in the spring of 1967, when twenty-year-old Adam Walker, an aspiring poet and student at Columbia University, meets the enigmatic Frenchman Rudolf Born and his silent and seductive girfriend, Margot. Before long, Walker finds himself caught in a perverse triangle that leads to a sudden, shocking act of violence that will alter the course of his life. Three different narrators tell the story of Invisible, a novel that travels in time from 1967 to 2007 and moves from Morningside Heights, to the Left Bank of Paris, to a remote island in the Caribbean." Publisher's note

Auster, Paul

Oracle night. Holt 2003 243p $23

ISBN 0-8050-7320-5

"A novelist writing about a novelist writing about an editor reading a novel: these Russian dolls might come across as merely cute, were it not for the fact that the lucid Mr Auster is a natural storyteller, with a seemingly inexhaustible trove of yarns at his disposal. All of the stories within stories are compelling in their own right." Economist

Auster, Paul

✓ **Sunset** Park. Henry Holt and Co. 2010 309p $25

ISBN 978-0-8050-9286-8; 0-8050-9286-2

LC 2009-45726

"The novel is graphically sexual and, more surprisingly, insistently phallic. This is a little bewildering until, as the novel progresses, one comes to accept that, for Auster's characters, the body – in its fragility and strength – is one of the only certainties in a time of increasing darkness. In a way, Sunset Park is Auster's most Whitmanesque novel and it's very entertaining." Globe and Mail

Austin, Lynn

✓ **All** she ever wanted; Lynn Austin. Bethany House 2005 400p (pbk.) $14.99

ISBN 0764228897; 9780764228896

LC 2005018574

In this book, "Kathleen Seymour's carefully constructed world starts to collapse when her teenage daughter, Joelle, is caught shoplifting and a row with her boss leaves Kathleen unemployed. After a few sessions with a therapist, Kathleen tries reconnecting with her daughter by taking her to a party hosted by the estranged family members Kathleen left years ago. Through multiple points of view and . . . [several] flashbacks to previous generations, [author Lynn N.] Austin . . . illustrates how shame and bad choices can affect families for years." (Publishers Weekly)

Ausubel, Ramona

No one is here except all of us; Ramona Ausubel. Riverhead Books 2012 336p.

ISBN 9781594487941

LC 2011046846

'This novel takes place "[i]n 1939, [when] the families in a remote Jewish village in Romania feel the war close in on them. Their tribe has moved and escaped for thousands of years-across oceans, deserts, and mountains-but now, it seems, there is nowhere else to go. . . . At the suggestion of an eleven-year-old girl and a mysterious stranger who has washed up on the riverbank, the villagers decide to reinvent the world: deny any relationship with the known and start over from scratch. . . . Time and history are forgotten. Jobs, husbands, a child, are reassigned. And for years, there is boundless hope. But the real world continues to unfold alongside the imagined one, eventually overtaking it, and soon our narrator-the girl, grown into a young mother-must flee her village, move from one world to the next, to find her husband and save her children, and propel them toward a real and hopeful future." (Publisher's note)

Avallone, Silvia

Swimming to Elba; Silvia Avallone; translated by Antony Shugaar. Viking 2012 308 p. (hardcover) $25.95; (paperback) $16.00; (audiobook) $59.95

ISBN 0670023582; 9780670023585; 9780143123651; 9781455154623

LC 2011043895

This book by Silvia Avallone "is set in the industrial town of Piombino, [Italy]. . . . At the novel's heart are two families linked together by their 13-year-old daughters, Anna and Francesca, who have been best friends since early childhood. . . . The girls only have eyes for each other until Anna's head is turned by all the attention the two receive from men. . . . The girls' bond is torn apart, setting them both on potentially risky paths." (Booklist)

Avery, Ellis

The **last** nude; Ellis Avery. Riverhead Books 2012 310 p. $25.95

ISBN 1594488134; 9781594488139

LC 2011027708

This book relies on historical events that occurred "[i]n 1927 . . . [when] Polish artist Tamara de Lempicka encountered 17-year-old Rafaela while in Paris's Bois de Boulogne and took her home, using her as a model for six significant paintings (including Beautiful Rafaela) and briefly becoming her lover. . . . Inspired by these bare facts, [author Ellis] Avery . . . has crafted a . . . work that imagines the relationship between artist and model." (Library Journal)

Includes bibliographical references.

B

Babel', I.

✓ ★ The **complete** works of Isaac Babel; edited by Nathalie Babel; translated with notes by Peter Constantine; introduction by Cynthia Ozick. Norton 2001 1072p il maps $39.95

ISBN 0-393-04846-2

LC 2001-44036

In addition to the stories this volume contains sketches, journalistic pieces, a diary, plays, and screenplays

"Few writers possess Babel's level of genius and temerity, and this first complete collection should acquaint more readers with his unjustly neglected work." Publ Wkly

Includes bibliographical references

Babson, Marian

Canapes for the kitties. St. Martin's Press 1997 220p

ISBN 0-312-16929-9

LC 97-16232

"When Lorinda Lucas, a well-known mystery writer in Brimful Coffers, kills off her popular fictional heroines, neighboring writers rebel. Old and new resentments (that even involve local cats Had-I, But-Known, and Roscoe) lead to murder." Libr J

Babson's "lighthearted good humor and skewed view of the world enliven every page of this charming morsel of a mystery." Publ Wkly

Baca, Jimmy Santiago

The **importance** of a piece of paper. Grove Press 2004 225p $22

ISBN 0-8021-1765-1

LC 2003-57089

"The rural Southwest landscape of Baca's short stories is inhabited by outsiders: drug addicts and convicts, absentee mothers and runaways. Baca's first collection of fiction . . . paints a picture of Chicano life that is at once cruel and sweetly redemptive." Publ Wkly

Bachelder, Chris

Abbott awaits; a novel. Louisiana State University Press 2011 180p (Yellow shoe fiction) pa $18.95

ISBN 978-0-8071-3722-2; 0-8071-3722-7

LC 2010-24227

"Absent underlying intrigue, this novel relies on its particularly well-developed protagonist and his profound observations. And with no need to race to the next plot point, the book can spend lavish time unpacking tiny events. . . . [The novel] will work best for readers who enjoy the same things as Abbott himself, the puzzling together of little moments, the search for ways to learn their meaning." Paste

Bacigalupi, Paolo

The **windup** girl. Night Shade Books 2009 361p $24.95; pa $14.95

ISBN 978-1-59780-157-7; 978-1-59780-158-4 pa

In this novel Bacigalupi follows the interconnected stories of several people caught "in the genome industry's web: We have a covert 'calorie man' called Anderson who tries to sniff out uncontaminated genomes for a Monsanto-esque multinational called AgriGen; a 'yellow card' Chinese refugee named Hock Seng who is trying to climb to the top of the energy-generator black market in Thailand; Environment Ministry shock troops Jaidee and Kanya, whose job is to protect Thailand from contaminated genomes, foreign imports, and dirty energy; and the mysterious whore Emiko, a genetically-engineered 'windup' person abandoned by her former owner in Thailand, where GMO people are illegal. We follow these characters through every eschelon of Thai society, from backroom meetings between government officials to backroom performances at the strip club where Emiko is fetishistically degraded every night. . . . One of the strengths of The Windup Girl, other than its intriguing characters, is Bacigalupi's world building. You can practically taste this future Thailand he's built." io9

Bacon, Charlotte

Split estate. Farrar, Straus and Giroux 2008 290p $25

ISBN 978-0-374-28183-0; 0-374-28183-1

LC 2007-42856

"The story opens shortly after Laura King—wife, mother of two teenagers and longtime depressive—jumps to her death from an Upper East Side apartment. Shocked and devastated, Arthur, her doting lawyer husband, decides to move his family back to his childhood home in the small town of Callendar, Wyoming—a place where he never quite fit in, being more comfortable with a book than astride a horse. Bacon adeptly captures the less obvious and less pretty aspects of the King family's grief, particularly Arthur's complete loss of confidence—as if his wife's decision to end her life has exposed him as inadequate. Lucy, Arthur's salty, independent mother, might be grateful for the company that Arthur and the kids provide, but she also struggles to overcome her frustration with her only child's nebbishy ways—as well as her own sense of culpability. . . . There are no easy resolutions here, just haunting meditations on character that are as compelling as they are austere." Time Out N Y

Baggott, Julianna

Pure; Julianna Baggott. Grand Central Publishing 2012 431p.

ISBN 9781455503063; 9781455503032; 9781611733563; 9781455503056

LC 2011010209

Alex Award (2013)

This book is set "sometime in the unspecified future, [where] a series of detonations as all but destroyed the world. A handpicked few were given refuge in the Dome, a high-tech bubble designed to withstand environmental disaster. Those left outside were not so fortunate. The intensity of the explosions not only devastated the landscape but changed forever those who survived it, fusing people with animals, with objects, with the earth." It follows Pressia, a "survivor . . . In a few days' time, on her 16th birthday, Pressia will be claimed by the OSR . . a paramilitary force that terrorizes the ravaged city. She will be 'untaught to read' and either trained as a killer or, if her deformations are too debilitating, used for target practice. . . . Meanwhile, life in the Dome has its own privations. The younger inhabitants, known as Pures because of their unblemished bodies, are being subjected to a series of 'codings,' devised to enhance their physical capabilities and suppress potentially rebellious behavior." (N Y Times)

Bahr, Howard

The **Judas** Field; a novel of the Civil War. H. Holt 2006 292p $25

ISBN 978-0-8050-6739-2

LC 2005-055011

The author "recreates this seminal moment in American history with prose that is vivid, unflinching and often incantatory. The book's pace and detail are wrenching, and it is starkly devoid of romanticism. Within the battlefield scenes, Bahr's accomplishment is magnificent: a fully realized depiction of controlled mass butchery on a field of blood, body parts and utterly obliterated human beings. The reader puts down the book with a sense of shock to find he is not actually inside a level of hell." Washington Post Book World

Bail, Murray

★ **Eucalyptus**; a novel. Farrar, Straus & Giroux 1998 255p

ISBN 0-374-14857-0

LC 98-5880

"In this contemporary Australian fairy tale, a widower named Holland acquires a sprawling property in New South Wales and plants it with hundreds of varieties of eucalyptus . . . , when it is time for his daughter, Ellen, to wed, he offers her hand to the suitor who can name each specimen on his estate. In the meantime, Ellen encounters a handsome stranger under a coolabah who courts her with stories that prove to be less random than they appear. The novel's categorizations and mysteries become a playful inquiry into the nature of storytelling, with an unpredictable conclusion." New Yorker

Bainbridge, Beryl

The **birthday** boys. Carroll & Graf Pubs. 1994 189p

ISBN 0-7867-0071-8

LC 94-1264

First published 1991 in the United Kingdom

"The story of Capt. Robert Scott's second expedition is narrated by Scott himself and the four men who perished along with him in the frigid weather and miserable conditions of Antarctica. Beginning with their June 1910 departure from Cardiff on the 'Terra Nova,' and ending with the terrible journey by sled back to the ship in March 1912, the five men consecutively recount their journey through an emotional as well as physical landscape." Libr J

Bainbridge, Beryl

Every man for himself; Beryl Bainbridge. Carroll & Graf Publishers 1996 224 p.

ISBN 0786703490

LC 96032518

This novel "takes place on the ill-fated Titanic. The story is narrated by Morgan, a young American, and follows the events between boarding and rescue by the Carpathia." (Libr J)

"Bainbridge hits a tremendous pace as her story reaches its climax. In a remarkably concise book, shot through with laconic wit, she establishes complex characters who engage first the reader's curiosity, then affection. The elegiac theme extends far beyond the historical event." New Statesman (1913)

Bainbridge, Beryl

The **girl** in the polka-dot dress. Europa Editions 2011 162p pa $15

ISBN 978-1-60945-056-4; 1-60945-056-6

"The pleasures of the episodic novel emerge from Bainbridge's unerring sense of the never-ending queerness of both people and the world. As with a David Lynch film, the audience is taken on an awfully strange adventure; puzzling over what it's really all about (or wondering if it's truly about anything at all) is part of the allure." Globe and Mail

Baker, Dorothy

★ **Young** man with a horn. Houghton Mifflin 1938 243p

"Rick Martin is not interested in school but is intrigued by music. Learning how to play the jazz trumpet from black musicians, Rick becomes a genius in the art of 'swing' and quickly rises to fame in the Phil Morrison orchestra. The inability to cope with success, as well as a bad marriage and gin, lead to his fatal end." Shapiro. Fic for Youth. 3d edition

Baker, Jo

The **undertow**; Jo Baker. Alfred A. Knopf 2012 335 p.

ISBN 0307957098; 9780307957092

LC 2012002079

This historical novel by Jo Baker traces "a family, constructed over decades, through relationships, wars and secrets . . . Starting in London in 1914, it introduces young sweethearts William and Amelia Hastings. . . . Amelia, pregnant with Billy, will always stay faithful to William's memory . . . and when shipmate George Sully . . . threatens, Amelia and Billy see him off together. Billy has a talent for cycling, but his prospects . . . are clouded by issues of money and class, and then World War II intervenes. Billy survives to marry Ruby . . . The couple's first child is Will, partly disabled by Perthes disease. . . . Clever Will achieves academic success at Oxford, but marries unhappily. It's with his artistic daughter Billie that the book reaches its . . . conclusion." (Kirkus)

Baker, Kage

★ The **bird** of the river. Tor 2010 268p $25.99

ISBN 978-0-7653-2296-8; 0-7653-2296-X

LC 2010-30146

"A vivid setting . . . with minimal fantasy elements, agreeably complemented by solid plotting, mysteries, surprises and characters that grow in the telling. A sparkling farewell from a writer whose illustrious career proved all too brief." Kirkus

Baker, Kage

The **graveyard** game. Harcourt 2000 298p

ISBN 0-15-100449-8

LC 00-27790

"When the cyborg known as Mendoza disappears out of grief for her murdered lover, fellow operatives Joseph and Lewis begin a search through time for her and discover some unpleasant secrets about their employer–Dr. Zeus Incorporated, otherwise known as The Company. . . . [This installment] spans centuries and includes stops in late 20th-century Hollywood and early 21st-century London, among other times and places." Libr J

Baker, Kage

The **house** of the stag. Tor 2008 350p $25.95

ISBN 978-0-7653-1745-2; 0-7653-1745-1

LC 2008-30212

"Baker's fantasy is completely different from her science fiction, but it's just as good. Gently humorous and ironic, Gard is a character readers will pull for as he moves from foundling to outcast to slave to ruler. Baker's worldbuilding is consistently topnotch, and the various supporting characters are just as well drawn as her antihero." Romantic Times

Baker, Kage

★ **In** the garden of Iden; a novel of the company. Harcourt Brace & Co. 1998 329p

ISBN 0-15-100299-1

LC 97-23284

"The initial assignment for 18-year-old Mendoza, transformed into an immortal cyborg by the 24th-century Company, is to retrieve from Renaissance England an endangered plant that cures cancer. Posing as a Spanish lady accompanying her doctor father, she falls in love with the mortal Nicholas Harpole, secretary to the owner of Iden Hall and its exotic gardens. Amidst the raging Catholic/Protestant powerplays revolving around the English throne and the fervent religious bloodlust of common folk, Mendoza is torn between her task and her love. Baker's story comments powerfully on religious hypocrisy and xenophobia." Libr J

Baker, Kage

The **life** of the world to come. TOR Books 2004 334p $25.95

ISBN 0-7653-1132-1

LC 2004-49574

"Cyborg biologist Mendoza has been exiled to the extremely distant past to live her immortal span farming maize and lettuce for wealthy tourists of the twenty-fourth century. She occasionally reminisces about the man she loved in, first, the sixteenth, and then, the nineteenth century. Then, one day, he crash-lands in her cornfield. It isn't precisely he, of course, but someone from the same Company project named Alec Checkerfield. . . Most of the story is his, from childhood spent on a sailing ship to his youth and education in London to growing wealth and power. As he discovers ever more about his parentage and the power of Dr. Zeus, Inc., to manipulate people and the world, he determines to bring the Company down. Mendoza provides him the key tidbit that, after 2355, Dr. Zeus' knowledge is blank. That time will be Alec's window of opportunity. Alec is quite a character, especially for the sedate twenty-fourth century, and in Baker's skillful hands, his story is well told and engrossing." Booklist

Baker, Kage

Mendoza in Hollywood; a novel of the company. Harcourt 2000 334p

ISBN 0-15-100448-X

LC 99-14949

"Assigned, along with other time-traveling members of the Company, to Cahuenga Pass, CA, in 1862, Mendoza discovers firsthand the dangers and pleasures of living in the American West during the Civil War. Haunted by dreams of a long-lost lover and pursued by his ghost, Mendoza struggles to come to terms with her personal past while fulfilling her duties to the future–with mixed results. Baker's latest tale of the wisecracking cyborg mercenaries from the 24th century combines historical detail and fast-paced action with a good dose of ironic wit and a dollop of bittersweet romance." Libr J

Baker, Kage

Mother Aegypt and other stories. Night Shade Books 2004 249p $27

ISBN 1-892389-75-4

"Told with splendid clarity, the 13 tales in this collection . . . are deceptively simple and seem, at first, to be comfortably folkloric. Each then takes a distinctive turn, often an O. Henry twist, and becomes indelibly the author's own." Publ Wkly

Baker, Kage

Not less than gods. Tor 2010 319p $25.99

ISBN 978-0-7653-1891-6; 0-763-1891-1

LC 2009-40728

"The first in a new set of novels, set in the same world as the author's Company series. . . . Here the author lays out the back story of Edward Alton Bell-Fairfax, a genetically engineered Company operative who first appeared in

Mendoza in Hollywood (2000). The brilliant Edward is born into privilege in 1824 England. In his 20s, he meets the mysterious Dr. Nennys, who says that Edward was created to be part of a secret organization, possessed of amazing technology—and that Edward has important work to do. The novel's adventurous Victorian setting, full of anachronistic technology from automatons to night-vision goggles, is reminiscent of steampunk—and fans of that popular subgenre may find much to enjoy." Kirkus

Baker, Kage

Sky coyote; a novel of the company. Harcourt Brace & Co. 1999 310p

ISBN 0-15-100354-8

LC 98-16833

"Fresh from a cushy R&R after a supervisory stint in the Inquisition, time-hopping cyborg Facilitator Joseph jaunts to 16th-century Alta California. There, cybernetically outfitted with fur and paws, he apotheosizes to the cannily entrepreneurial Chumash Indian tribe so he can collect them and their entire biosystem for Company studies in the remote future." Publ Wkly

The author "blends accurate historical research and arch comedy to produce an entertaining tale of time travel and mythic adventure." Libr J

Baker, Kage

√ The **sons** of heaven. Tor 2007 430p $25.95

ISBN 978-0-7653-1746-9; 0-7653-1746-X

LC 2007-9541

This is the concluding volume of the "saga of The Company and its immortal, time-traveling minions. As this volume opens, it is very nearly July 9, 2355, the end of recorded time, after which there is only silence regarding the fate of humankind. Various factions of cyborgs, mortals and other mysterious entities have differing opinions about what should occur after that date, and some of their plans involve armed insurrection and genocide. From the first volume, 'In the Garden of Iden,' Botanist Mendoza has always been at the center of the narrative, and for a certain subset of Baker's readers, Mendoza's star-crossed love affairs with three eerily similar men across literally countless centuries inspire the most devotion to the series. Others may find Mendoza something of an annoying pill and prefer the adventures of the supporting cast, especially Preservationist Lewis and Facilitator Joseph, two secret agents never sure of who their true enemies might be. No matter. 'The Sons of Heaven' gives equal time to both Mendoza and her subordinates, and Baker resolves the apocalyptic conflict with flair and enviable skill." San Francisco Chronicle

Baker, Kevin

√ **Strivers** Row. HarperCollins 2006 550p $26.95

ISBN 0-06-019583-5

LC 2005-52679

In this "novel—the final volume of a New York trilogy called 'City of Fire' [previous titles: Dreamland and Paradise Alley]—Kevin Baker plunges into the world of Harlem in the early 1940's to imagine the lives of two African-American men. . . . One of his main characters was known in the 'real' world of 1943 as Malcolm Little, a rootless 18-year-old who would later become famous as Malcolm X. The other is the invention of Baker: a young, bourgeois, light-skinned Harlem clergyman named Jonah Dove. Malcolm is poor. Jonah is comfortably middle-class. In different ways, each is tormented by the world. . . . In the end, Baker has written a brave, honorable work, taking us into a vanished world that should be better known. More important, he imagines his human subjects with a sense of pity and compassion and embrace, thus making them visible in ways that are fresh and new." N Y Times Book Rev

Baker, Lori

★ The **Glass** Ocean; Lori Baker. Penguin Group USA 2013 352 p. $25.95

    ISBN 1594205361; 9781594205361

LC 2013007696

This novel "is narrated by red-haired, six-foot-plus Carlotta Dell'oro, who relates the story of her parents' lives. On an 1841 expedition aboard the Narcissus, during which he's expected to sketch sea creatures, Leonardo Dell'oro falls for remote, lovely Clotilde Girard, whose father funded the voyage. Leonardo brings Clotilde to remote Whitby, England, when her father goes missing, but they aren't the perfect couple." (Library Journal)

Baker, Nicholson, 1957-

The **anthologist**. Simon & Schuster 2009 243p $25

    ISBN 978-1-4165-7244-2; 1-4165-7244-9

LC 2009-01205

"The narrator, Paul Chowder, is a poet who is struggling to write the introduction to an anthology of rhyming poems he's collected. He's also trying to win back Roz, the woman who has just left him. These dilemmas make for some enlightening, absorbing reflections on poetry, the creative process, and life itself. While Chowder admits that he despises teaching, the narrative offers a wonderful explanation of what poetry is and the relationship between form and meaning. In the process, Chowder comes to understand himself better and pulls out of a slump. The novel's subtle sense of humor comes through as Chowder deals with injured fingers, a misbehaving dog, and the perils of reading his poetry in public." Libr J

Baker, Nicholson, 1957-

House of holes; a book of raunch. Simon & Schuster 2011 262p $25

    ISBN 978-1-4391-8951-1; 1-4391-8951-X

LC 2010-47433

This novel is comprised of "a series of fantasies that a very imaginative 14-year-old boy might have: They all involve metamorphoses that enable more sexual possibilities than are human. Genitals can be swapped, people can shrink to miniature size (you can guess where they go). These transformations occur, to a long list of characters, in a parallel universe, an uninhibited plane of existence (perhaps something like the unconscious) that resembles nothing more than a high-end holiday resort. It has a sprawling landscape of beaches, hotel rooms and parodic attractions (Upskirt Street, the masturboats, pussyboarding). Magical objects – the Belt of Jingly Bells, the Cable of Induhash, drops from King Bohuslav's beard – can heal and arouse. You get to this House of Holes through actual holes in the real world – the end of a straw, the back of a clothes dryer. The land of enchantment is run by a matter-of-fact headmistress, the plump, fif-

tyish Lila, who assigns and withholds its pleasures. . . . You might think this is too adolescent to be arousing, but you'd be surprised by the effect prolonged exposure to all this mad splashing might have. It's a bit repetitive, for sure, and the characters are hard to tell apart, which doesn't really matter, as there is no unifying plot. They are interchangeable bodies, reflecting the theme of mutability in their own stories." Globe and Mail

Baker, Tiffany

The **little** giant of Aberdeen County; a novel. Grand Central Pub. 2009 341p $24.99

    ISBN 978-0-446-19420-4; 0-446-19420-4

LC 2008-774

"In an upstate New York backwater, Truly, massive from birth, has a bleak existence with her depressed father and her china-doll-like sister, Serena Jane. Truly grows at an astonishing rate—her girth the result of a pituitary gland problem—and after her father dies when Truly is 12, Truly is sloughed off to the Dyersons, a hapless farming family. Her outsize kindness surfaces as she befriends the Dyersons' outcast daughter, Amelia, and later leaves her beloved Dyerson farm to take care of Serena Jane's husband and son after Serena Jane leaves them. Haunting the margins of Truly's story is that of Tabitha Dyerson, a rumored witch whose secrets afford a breathtaking role reversal for Truly." Publ Wkly

"Baker enters Alice Hoffman territory in this parable about beauty and ugliness, meanness and mercy and magic, and does it with considerable dark humor." Hartford Courant

Bakker, Gerbrand

The **twin**; translated from the Dutch by David Colmer. Archipelago Books 2009 343p $25

    ISBN 978-0-9800330-2-1; 0-9800330-2-0

LC 2008-45725

Original Dutch edition, 2006; this translation first published 2008 in the United Kingdom

"Helmer Van Wonderen ditches university to return home to the family farm in north Holland when his twin brother, Henk, is killed in a car accident. Nearly forty years later, Helmer, now 57, ponders the path his life has taken while waiting for his invalid father to die. The catalyst arrives in the form of Riet, Henk's teenage sweetheart, who now has an adolescent son. Helmer has inherited the life of his dead twin, and Bakker's great skill is to characterise the mixture of grief, guilt, rage and regret that shadows Helmer, without resorting to caricature or clunky exposition." TNT Magazine

Bakopoulos, Natalie

The **green** shore; a novel. Natalie Bakopoulos. 1st Simon & Schuster hc. ed. Simon & Schuster 2012 353 p. (paperback) $15.00; (hardcover) $25.00

    ISBN 9781451633948; 1451633920; 9781451633924

LC 2011032325

This novel by Natalie Bakopoulos presents "a family drama and revolutionary romance set during the Greek military junta of 1967-1974. . . . 21-year-old Sophie is dancing at her leftist boyfriend Nick's Athens apartment when soldiers barge in and arrest suspected student dissidents. Refusing to break contact with Nick and his fellow activists or abandon the liberal political convictions inherited from her family,

Sophie sinks dangerously deeper into antijunta resistance." (Publishers Weekly)

Baldacci, David

√ **Absolute** power. Warner Bks. 1996 469p

ISBN 0-446-51996-0

LC 95-22956

"The action begins when a grizzled professional cat burglar gets trapped inside the bedroom closet of one of the world's richest men, only to witness, through a one-way mirror, two Secret Service agents kill the billionaire's trampy young wife as she tries to fight off the drunken sexual advances of the nation's chief executive. Running for his life, but not before he picks up a bloodstained letter opener that puts the president at the scene of the crime, the burglar becomes the target of a clandestine manhunt orchestrated by leading members of the executive branch. Meanwhile, Jack Graham, once a public defender and now a high-powered corporate attorney, gets drawn into the case." Publ Wkly

Baldacci, David

√ **Deliver** us from evil. Grand Central Pub. 2010 406p $27.99

ISBN 978-0-446-56408-3; 0-446-56408-7

LC 2010-01140

Sequel to: The whole truth (2008)

"We become intensely involved in the story, wishing we could step inside the book and clue its two protagonists into what's going on. The only problem—for fans of Shaw, anyway—is that, in Reggie, Baldacci has created such an interesting and engaging character that he might have made Shaw redundant." Booklist

Baldacci, David

√ **Divine** justice. Grand Central Pub. 2008 387p $27.99

ISBN 978-0-446-19550-8; 0-446-19550-2

LC 2008-33072

In this installment in the author's Camel Club series, "Oliver Stone (aka John Carr, ex-CIA assassin) is wanted dead by his enemies and alive by his friends. Stone is on the run after assassinating the two men responsible for the death of his family and his friend Milton. Now Stone's former superior, Gen. Macklin Hayes, enlists tracker Joe Knox to locate Stone so Hayes can silence Stone forever. During Stone's flight from the law, a random act of kindness by Stone forces him on an unwanted detour to Divine, VA. There, Stone's continued good deeds might end up costing him his life as he quickly gets tangled in the hidden web of deceit to which the town owes its prosperity. . . . Fans will welcome this latest tale about the charismatic Stone and his exceedingly loyal friends with its fast-paced action and intriguing plot twists." Libr J

Baldacci, David

√ **One** summer. Grand Central Publisher 2011 337p $25.99

ISBN 978-0-446-58314-5; 0-446-58314-6

LC 2010-41020

"Baldacci's muscle-bound style doesn't do subtle: He is best at choreographing fight scenes, rescues and dire brushes with severe weather, all of which, thankfully, are here in abundance." Kirkus

Baldacci, David

√ The **simple** truth. Warner Bks. 1998 470p

ISBN 0-446-52332-1

LC 98-22548

"The crime being covered up is stale beer compared to the Supreme Court setting, but as with a scenic drive, the destination of a Baldacci cliff-hanger is less important than the route taken." Booklist

Baldacci, David

√ **Total** control. Warner Bks. 1997 520p

ISBN 0-446-52095-0

LC 96-32869

"Sidney Archer is devastated when she hears that the plane carrying her husband to Los Angeles has crashed. But her nightmare begins when she learns he'd traded identities and flown to Seattle instead. Evidence suggests that Jason Archer was selling corporate secrets to a high-tech rival. Soon Sidney herself is caught in a web of intrigue as wealthy men vie for more power and money." Libr J

Baldwin, James

√ ★ **Another** country. Dial Press (NY) 1962 436p

This novel is set in "New York City and focuses mainly on Harlem society. The death—perhaps suicide—of the main character, Rufus Scott, is representative of the treatment individuals receive in an environment which is essentially hostile and which erects barriers to their desire for love." Camb Guide to Lit in Engl

Baldwin, James

√ **Early** novels and stories. Library of Am. 1998 970p $35

ISBN 1-88301-151-5

LC 97-23028

Contents: Go tell it on the mountain; Giovanni's room; Another country; Going to meet the man

Baldwin, James

√ ★ **Giovanni's** room; a novel. Dial Press (NY) 1956 248p

"We meet the narrator, known to us only as David, in the south of France, but most of the story is laid in Paris. It develops as the story of a young American involved both with a woman and with another man, the man being the Giovanni of the title. When a choice has to be made, David chooses the woman, Hella." N Y Times Book Rev

"Mr. Baldwin has taken a very special theme and treated it with great artistry and restraint." Saturday Rev

Baldwin, James

√ ★ **Go** tell it on the mountain. Knopf 1953 303p $15.95; pa $6.99

ISBN 0-679-60154-6; 0-440-33007-6 pa

This novel is an "autobiographical story of a Harlem child's relationship with his father against the background of his being saved in the pentecostal church." Benet's Reader's Ency of Am Lit

Baldwin, James

Going to meet the man. Dial Press (NY) 1965 249p

Contents: The rockpile; The outing; The man child; Previous condition; Sonny's blues; This morning, this evening, so soon; Come out the wilderness; Going to meet the man

Baldwin, James

If Beale Street could talk. Dial Press (NY) 1974 197p hardcover o.p. pa $12.95

ISBN 0-803-74169-3; 0-307-27593-0 pa

"Tish, aged 19, and Fonny, 22 years old, are in love and pledged to marry, a decision hastened by Tish's unexpected pregnancy. Fonny is falsely accused of raping a Puerto Rican woman and is sent to prison. The families of the desperate couple search frantically for evidence that will prove his innocence in order to reunite the lovers and provide a safe haven for the expected child. There is some explicit sex but it is not treated in a sensational manner, nor is the use of street language gratuitous." Shapiro. Fic for Youth. 3d edition

Baldwin, James

Tell me how long the train's been gone; a novel. Dial Press (NY) 1968 484p

Leo Proudhammer, a successful black "actor has a serious heart attack on stage. Barbara King, his leading lady . . . and in a strange way his inamorata, stays by his side. In a series of flashbacks . . . Leo relives his past from his Harlem boyhood on. Although he learned early to hate 'the man,' Leo's own betrayal as a man and as a human being is not limited to the white man's corruption. It encompasses his painful relationship with his brother, who lures him into homosexuality. Paralleling this story is the tale of Leo's career. The third thread is his bisexual private life in which the two main figures are white Barbara, his true but unattainable love, and black Christopher, worshipful and available." Publ Wkly

Baldwin, Joshua

The **Wilshire** sun. Turtle Point Press 2011 104p pa $10.50

ISBN 978-1-933527-46-8

LC 2010-935786

"Written in the first person and partially in an epistolary style, with a clearly unreliable narrator, the novella bears hallmarks of Nathanael West and seems to knowingly invite comparison. Surreal and paranoid, Jacob's story encapsulates the legend of Los Angeles as told by an outsider. Jacob, a young writer from Brooklyn, lives with his mother and aunt and aspires to move to Los Angeles with a work acquaintance to write screenplays. After a false start lands him back in New York, he finally makes it to L.A. for good. However, life in the city doesn't provide the fecund creative experience he'd anticipated, and his tenuous mental state declines rapidly. The ensuing narrative becomes ever more dreamlike, and the fictional letters he writes to and from imaginary people . . . grow more nonsensical, treating readers to a tantalizing glimpse beyond the edge of sanity." Publ Wkly

Baldwin, Rosecrans

You lost me there. Riverhead Books 2010 296p $25.95

ISBN 978-1-59448-763-7; 1-59448-763-4

LC 2009-48671

Dr. Victor Aaron, "a widower in his late 50s, is the sort of genius (he's a leading Alzheimer's researcher) who's a dolt when it comes to understanding emotions, either in himself or others. his subspecialty is misunderstanding women, a masculine weakness the author probes with delicacy as Victor mourns the loss of his wife, Sara. By way of diary-like notes she left behind, Sara is, you see, equally the narrator of this scientifically erudite fiction. And a good storyteller she is, too, since in life she was a successful playwright and screenwriter. The story teeters as it concludes, but Baldwin keeps his balance with sharply drawn secondary characters." Entertainment Wkly

Ball, Jesse

The **curfew**; a novel. Vintage Books 2011 194p pa $15

ISBN 978-0-307-73985-8; 0-307-73985-6

LC 2011-01509

"The novel mixes humour and pathos in equal measure, and resembles the absurdities found in the fiction of Kafka and the plays of Samuel Beckett – giving the novel a bit of darkly comic richness. It's a strange, unsettling read, one that lingers with you." PopMatters

Ball, John Dudley

In the heat of the night; by John Ball. Harper & Row 1965 184p

"Virgil Tibbs is found with a full wallet in the waiting room of a railroad station in Wells, a small town in the Carolinas. Because he is black he becomes the prime suspect for the murder of the town's musical director. The local police chief learns that Tibbs is a homicide expert from the Pasadena police department and enlists his assistance. Tibbs solves the crime, despite the bigotry to which he is exposed." Shapiro. Fic for Youth. 2d edition

Ballantyne, Lisa

The **guilty** one; Lisa Ballantyne. William Morrow 2013 480 p. $14.99

ISBN 0062195514; 9780062195517

LC 2012013279

This novel, by Lisa Ballantyne, "is a psychological thriller about the darkness in each of us. . . . Solicitor Daniel Hunter is called to defend 11-year-old Sebastian who has been charged with the murder of a young boy on a London playground. While examining Sebastian's life in order to save it, Daniel can't help but be transported to his own difficult youth spent in foster care--a time when the one he trusted the most was the one who betrayed him." (Publisher's note)

Ballard, J. G., 1930-2009

★ The **complete** stories of J.G. Ballard. W.W. Norton & Company 2009 1199p $35; pa $24.95

ISBN 978-0-393-07262-4; 0-393-07262-2; 978-0-393-33929-1 pa; 0-393-33929-7 pa

LC 2009-18456

"An astonishing record of a vibrant and vital mind at work. This volume includes 92 stories, most of which are set in some kind of nightmarish future world or alternate 'visionary present,' to use Ballard's phrase from his introduction to the book. The variety of stories here is impressive, even dizzying." Libr J

Includes bibliographical references and index

Ballard, J. G., 1930-2009

★ The **day** of creation. Farrar, Straus & Giroux 1988 254p

ISBN 0-374-13527-4

LC 87-37525

First published 1987 in the United Kingdom

The narrator of this novel, Dr. Mallory, "is a physician with the World Health Organization, working in a mythical central African country, who launches what appears to be a vain search for water to forestall the desertification of the region. He accidentally releases the flow—and in fact thinks he is the creator—of a new river. . . . {He later} embarks on a dangerous journey to find its source and destroy it." Books Can

Ballard, J. G., 1930-2009

Empire of the Sun; a novel. Simon & Schuster 1984 279p hardcover o.p. pa $13

ISBN 0-671-53051-8; 0-7432-6523-8 pa

LC 84-10630

"This novel is much more than the gritty story of a child's miraculous survival in the grimly familiar setting of World War II's concentration camps. There is no nostalgia for a good war here, no sentimentality for the human spirit at extremes. Mr. Ballard is more ambitious than romance usually allows. He aims to render a vision of the apocalypse, and succeeds so well that it can hurt to dwell upon his images." N Y Times Book Rev

Followed by The kindness of women (1991)

Ballard, J. G., 1930-2009

Kingdom come; J.G. Ballard. Liveright 2012 304 p. $24.95

ISBN 0393081788; 9780393081787; 9780871404039

LC 2011041724

In this book, set in a fascist suburban future, mental patient Duncan Christie is held for the murder of a man shot and killed at the mall. "This seems to be a cut-and-dried case, even to Richard Pearson, narrator and son of the victim, but a few anomalies crop up." Plus, "Pearson has other problems, for he has recently lost his job . . . . Pearson watches with some amazement the rise of quasi-fascist elements in this quasi-suburban setting that's starting to create its own reality." (Kirkus)

Ballard, J. G., 1930-2009

Millennium people. W.W. Norton & Company 2011 288p $26.95

ISBN 978-0-393-08177-0; 0-393-08177-X

LC 2010-52504

First published 2003 in the United Kingdom

"Ballard is a natural surrealist; his is a world where the unthinkable is commonplace and rationality chucked in the towel long ago. . . . Ballard's phrasing is as sure as ever. He writes wonderfully well about London. His characterization is as vivid as it is strange. An extremely unsettling novel. Reading it is like having all the planks that underpin your life removed one by one and being forced to confront the brutality and emptiness that lies below." Scotsman

Ballestrini, Nanni

Sandokan; a novel. translated by Antony Shugaar. Melville House 2009 158p (Contemporary art of the novella) pa $13

ISBN 9781933633800; 1933633808

LC 2009-29731

Original Italian edition, 2004

A "first-person narrative in which the despondent resident of a small southern Italian town tells how his community was engulfed and made utterly unlivable by an ultra-violent clan of Camorra (that region's version of the Mafia). He talks in an uninterrupted, frequently unpunctuated flow of despondent, bloody, ripped-from-the-headlines reportage, spilling his guts, though he seems to know that no matter what he says or who he says it to, the regime of inescapable corruption will continue. His voice spikes with rage and deepens with sorrow as he relates in a pounding rush the slow, then sudden, death of a region where violence was always in the blood and was seemingly just waiting for some force to unleash it." PopMatters

Balogh, Mary

More than a mistress. Delacorte Press 2000 343p

ISBN 0-385-33531-8

LC 99-462117

"When Jane Ingleby tries to stop a duel, Jocelyn Dudley, Duke of Tresham, is wounded. So it's surprising that she ends up employed as his nurse—and ultimately his mistress as well. But as their relationship blossoms, Jocelyn commits the unpardonable sin of falling in love. In this refreshingly unconventional romance, which boasts an outspoken, memorable heroine, the author again pushes the edges of the genre." Libr J

Balogh, Mary

The **secret** mistress. Delacorte Press 2011 309p $24

ISBN 978-0-385-34331-2; 0-385-34331-0

LC 2010-52864

Balogh "pairs a staid young nobleman with a vivacious debutante in this topnotch tale. When the headstrong Lady Angeline Dudley, sister of the wealthy duke of Tresham, is accosted by the rakish Lord Windrow, she immediately falls for the ordinary-looking gentleman who intervenes. Her rescuer, Edward Ailsbury, is the earl of Heyward, whose family-unaware of his affection for his bluestocking confidante, Eunice Goddard-plans to match him with the very eligible Angeline. An unusually accurate portrayal of Regency society, laden with colorful period detail, makes a sparkling backdrop, and the supporting characters are delightful." Publ Wkly

Balogh, Mary

Seducing an angel. Delacorte Press 2009 325p $23

ISBN 978-0-385-34105-9

LC 2009-01662

"Cassandra Belmont, the widowed Lady Paget, is in London on a desperate mission. Rumored to have killed her husband and banished penniless from his estate by the heir, Cassie has no option but to find a protector for herself and her small household—and wealthy, young, angelically handsome Stephen Huxtable, Earl of Merton, seems the perfect choice. Marriage is definitely not her goal, nor is it his, until an impulsive public kiss changes everything. The gradually developing relationship between these fully realized, three-dimensional characters is complex, believable, and exquisitely rendered." Libr J

Balogh, Mary

Simply love. Delacorte Press 2006 311p $22

ISBN 978-0-385-33883-7; 0-385-33883-X

LC 2005-58262

This novel brings "together lovely Anne Jewell, a teacher at Miss Martin's School for Girls in Bath, and Sydnam Butler, the horribly disfigured steward for the Wales estate of the Duke of Bewcastle. Anne and her son have been invited on holiday with the Bedwyn clan. Neither Anne nor Sydnam is comfortable in company, he because of the injuries he sustained in the Peninsular Wars and she because as a rape victim she is the unwed mother of a nine-year-old. The two connect, and Anne soon discovers that she is pregnant. They marry, but that is only the beginning of their story. Both have had so much pain in their lives, neither one feels worthy of love. Balogh has once again crafted a sensuous tale of two very real people finding love and making each other's lives whole and beautiful." Booklist

Balogh, Mary

Simply magic. Delacorte Press 2007 326p $22

ISBN 978-0-385-33823-3; 0-385-33823-6

LC 2006-48480

"Susanna Osbourne is enjoying a perfectly lovely holiday in the countryside until she meets the wealthy nobleman Peter Edgeworth. Despite Susanna's best efforts to let Peter know she has no interest whatsoever in him, the viscount, who is visiting a friend at a neighboring estate, insists on flirting with her. Peter's persistent charm gradually melts Susanna's icy reserve, and the two end up sharing one wonderfully romantic afternoon together. But then Susanna disappears, forcing Peter to solve the mystery of her past if he is to have any chance at all of a life with her. . . . Balogh continues her superb Simply romance series featuring four teachers from Miss Martin's School for Girls with another exquisitely crafted Regency historical that brilliantly blends deliciously clever writing, subtly nuanced characters, and simmering sensuality into a simply sublime romance." Booklist

Balogh, Mary

Simply perfect. Delacorte Press 2008 343p $22

ISBN 978-0-385-33824-0

LC 2007-24314

A title in the authors's Regency series centering on Miss Martin's School for Girls. "Falling in love with the heir to a dukedom is the last thing practical, compassionate headmis-

tress Claudia Martin has in mind when she agrees to take her charity students to spend part of the summer at a country estate. But fate has a way of shaking things up, and as Claudia and Joseph, the Marquess of Attingsborough, are thrown together, a wary friendship and respect expand into a love that for all its passion seems doomed from the start. Class lines are clearly drawn in this emotionally rich romance that pits a pair of beautifully delineated, appropriately conflicted protagonists against the snobbish rigidity of the social structure of the times." Libr J

Balogh, Mary

Slightly dangerous. Delacorte Press 2004 344p

ISBN 0-385-33811-2

LC 2003-70091

This is the "culmination of Balogh's wonderfully entertaining Bedwyn series, in which each sibling in the aristocratic family finds the love of his or her life. Wulfric, the eldest brother, is known for his icy reserve, and, in fact, the formidable duke effectively stopped marriage-minded pursuits and was content with his mistress until she died. Invited to a house party, he unhappily finds himself in the company of Christine Derrick, the klutzy, impoverished widow of a viscount's brother. Two more unsuitable lovers have never been imagined, but Balogh, famous for her believable characters and finely crafted Regency-era settings, forges a relationship that leaps off the page and into the hearts of her readers. The sixth title in a series would seem an unlikely point to begin, but Balogh includes the other five Bedwyn siblings and their loves in such a way as to delight readers familiar with them, and entice readers new to the series to read the previous installments." Booklist

Balzac, Honore de

The **country** doctor; Translated by Ellen Marriage; introd. by Marcel Girard. Dutton 1961 xxv, 290p

Original French edition, 1833. Part of the series: Scenes of provincial life

The device with which this character study is held together concerns the visit of Pierre Joseph Genastas, an ex-soldier, who is searching for the saintly doctor Benassis. "A minute description of country life in the hilly region about Grenoble; the agricultural doings, the wretchedness of the peasantry, and M. Benassis' persevering attempts to ameliorate their condition, furnish a good example of Balzac's indefatigable realism. In this practical philanthropist, the reformed sinner who becomes a public benefactor, an ideal figure is created, a great soul, unselfish, full of love for man, unconquerably patient." Baker. Guide to the Best Fic

Balzac, Honore de

Cousin Bette; translated from the French by James Waring. Knopf 1991 xliii, 484p

ISBN 0-679-40671-9

LC 91-52964

Original French edition, 1846. Part of the series: Scenes of Parisian life

"This powerful story is a vivid picture of the tastes and vices of Parisian life in the middle of last century. Lisbeth Fischer, commonly called Cousin Bette, is an eccentric poor relation, a worker in gold and silver lace. The keynote of her character is jealousy, the special object of it her beautiful and nobel-minded cousin Adeline, wife of Baron Hector Hulot. The chief interest of the story lies in the development of her character, of that of the unscrupulous beauty Madame Marneffe, and the base and empty voluptuary Hulot. . . . Gloomy and despairing . . . {it is} yet terribly powerful." Keller. Reader's Dig of Books

Balzac, Honore de

✓ ★ **Pere** Goriot (Old Goriot) a new translation: responses, contemporaries and other novelists, twentieth-century criticism. translated by Burton Raffel; edited by Peter Brooks. W.W. Norton & Co. 1998 370p map pa $11.25

ISBN 0-393-97166-X

LC 97-19938

Original French edition, 1835. Part of the series: Scenes of Parisian life

"Goriot, a retired manufacturer of vermicelli, is a good man and a weak father. He has given away his money in order to ensure the marriage of his two daughters, Anastasie and Delphine. Because of his love for them, he has to accept all kinds of humiliations from his sons-in-law, one a 'gentilhomme,' M. de Restaud, and the other a financier, M. de Nucingen. Both young women are ungrateful. They gradually abandon him. He dies without seeing them at his bedside, cared for only by young Rastignac, a law student who lives at the same boarding house, the pension Vauquer." Haydn. Thesaurus of Book Dig

Bambara, Toni Cade

Gorilla, my love. Random House 1972 177p

ISBN 0-394-48201-8

Contents: My man Bovanne; Gorilla, my love; Raymond's run; The hammer man; Mississippi Ham Rider; Happy birthday; Playin with Punjab; Talkin bout Sonny; The lesson; The survivor; Sweet town; Blues ain't no mockin bird; Basement; Maggie of the green bottles; The Johnson girls

Bambara, Toni Cade

The **salt** eaters. Random House 1980 295p

ISBN 0-394-50712-6

LC 79-4806

"Velma Henry has tried suicide and survived and now sits on a stool in the Southwest Community Infirmary in Clayborne (a Southern city) listening to faith healer Minnie Ransom ask a hard question about what she wants. Fitfully she asks herself some questions, too, and in the process remembers what happened, fingers the past, absents herself from her own healing to recollect other times, other places, other folks, as she mentally travels abroad in Clayborne in search of answers." Publ Wkly

This novel "with its beautiful, difficult prose, is a work at once intensely personal and political that will assure Bambara's place in black American fiction." Libr J

Bank, Melissa

✓ The **girls'** guide to hunting and fishing. Viking 1999 288p $23.95

ISBN 0-670-88300-X

LC 98-48590

"Often funny, poignant, and well sprinkled with razor-sharp wit, Jane's search for love (usually in all the wrong places) is going to be familiar to many." Booklist

Bank, Melissa

✓ The **wonder** spot; Melissa Bank. Viking 2005 324p (pbk.) $14.00; o.p.

ISBN 9780143037217; 0670034118 (acid-free paper)

LC 2004061189

This book follows "Sophie Applebaum, a sarcastic, self-deprecating middle child from a suburban Jewish family who moves from a fish-out-of-water adolescence to a how-did-I-get-here adulthood. . . . Sophie's (mis)adventures in life and love include an attempt to use lyrics from Bob Dylan's 'It Ain't Me, Babe' to argue against the necessity of attending Hebrew school and a penchant for imagining her future life with men she barely knows." Also described in the story are "a grandmother's slip into senility, Sophie's mother's dip into infidelity, a brother's turn toward Orthodox Judaism. Through it all, Sophie never quite escapes the sense of being a 'solid trying to do a liquid's job'" (Publishers Weekly)

Banks, Iain, 1954-2013

✓ The **hydrogen** sonata; Iain M. Banks. Orbit 2012 517 p. (hardcover) $25.99

ISBN 0316212377; 9780316212366; 9780316212373; 9780316212380; 9781619695481

LC 2012944666

This novel, by Iain M. Banks, is a science fiction story set in space. "[T]he Gzilt . . . [have] made the collective decision to . . . Sublime, elevating themselves to a new and . . . complex existence. Amid preparations though, the Regimental High Command is destroyed. . . . Vyr Cossont appears to have been involved. . . . Aided only by an . . . android and a suspicious Culture avatar, Cossont must complete her last mission given to her by the High Command." (Publisher's note)

Banks, Iain, 1954-2013

✓ **Matter;** a Culture novel. [by] Iain M. Banks. Orbit 2008 593p $25.99

ISBN 9780316005364; 0316005363

LC 2007-941828

This novel in the author's series about "the Culture, an interstellar posthuman civilization of incredible wealth and technological sophistication, centers on three siblings: Ferbin and Oramen, the misfit heirs of conquering King Hausk of the Sarl, who rules a backward and patriarchal realm deep beneath the surface of the artificial 'Shellworld' Sursamen, and their exiled sister, Djan, now a powerful agent of the Culture's Special Circumstances division. When King Hausk is murdered, Ferbin narrowly avoids the conspirators and sets out across the galaxy to ask Djan's help with revenge against the killer, now serving as Oramen's regent. Soon they learn of the horrific forces a hidden enemy is about to unleash on Sursamen, and must race to save the home that has rejected them both. Beautifully written and filled with memorable characters and startling technology" Publ Wkly

Banks, Iain, 1954-2013

Stonemouth; a novel. by Iain Banks. Pegasus Crime 2012 357 p. $25.95

ISBN 1605983829; 9781605983820

LC 2012462689

In this book, "Stewart Gilmour . . . has returned . . . to Stonemouth, the Scottish town of his upbringing. . . . [H]e had to flee Stonemouth after falling foul of a local crime family. . . . Donald Murston, the current head of the family, has given him grudging permission . . . to attend the funeral of Donald's father Joe. . . . [W]e find that the funeral is merely a pretext for him to determine what happened to the first and only love of his life, Donald's daughter Ellie." (TLS)

Banks, Iain

Surface detail; [by] Iain M. Banks. Orbit 2010 627p pa $14.99

ISBN 978-0-316-12340-2; 0-316-12340-4

LC 2010-932993

"This is another novel concerning the Culture, Banks's 9000-year-old humanoid civilisation in which hedonism rules, anyone can be immortal and downloading your brain onto a computer is routine. The Culture is unhappy that the elephant-aliens use the brain-downloading technology to send their citizens to online heaven or hell after their death. Torture and sadism being a familiar theme of Banks, he dwells on the virtual hell, of course, sparing us none of the gory details. There are other Banksian leitmotifs, such as the archvillain wielding absolute power in his own, relatively backward civilisation, whose comeuppance at the hands of the Culture you long for. The best character is an avatar representing an arrogant and foulmouthed warship, which takes sadistic glee in fulfilling the role it was designed for killing other ships and their crew. Its charged relationship with a vulnerable humanoid in its care forms a welcome counterpoint to the cut and thrust of the incessant space battles. . . . Combining deep philosophical questions with the fast-paced multiple sub-plots that are standard in Banks's novels these days, there's something here for everyone." New Scientist

Banks, Oliver T.

The **Caravaggio** obsession; a novel. by Oliver Banks. Little, Brown 1984 230p

ISBN 0-316-08022-5

LC 83-17497

"When a friend in the art auction business is killed in New York, Amos {Hatcher} tracks art and murder to Rome. There he is thwarted by the police and threatened by quasi-radical thugs. Amos soon realizes that his friend's murderer, the ringleader of the robberies, is obsessed with that earlier dark genius, the painter Caravaggio. Banks crams his story with history and lore in ways that are essential to the plot and fascinating to even the most culture-resistant reader. The spirit of Caravaggio and the desperate, beautiful city of Rome haunt this superlative thriller." Wilson Libr Bull

Banks, Ray

No more heroes. Houghton Mifflin Harcourt 2010 261p $26

ISBN 978-0-15-101459-0

LC 2009-26621

First published 2008 in the United Kingdom

"Though the heavy vernacular and nonstop violence aren't for everyone, Cal's third rough-and-tumble first-person caper . . . should keep most readers rapidly turning pages till the solid plot builds to a payoff in late innings." Kirkus

Banks, Russell

✓ ★ **Affliction.** Harper & Row 1989 355p

ISBN 0-06-016142-6

LC 89-45075

"Wade Whitehouse is a small-town policeman in his early forties made crazy-desperate by a life of chronic failure and intractably self-destructive behavior. Like his father, he's moody, abusive, and a mean drunk. Wade's got a good heart, and he'd like to change his ways, but his desire to reform is thwarted by his baser male instincts. Things just keep getting worse until he finally can't take it anymore, whereupon he snaps and literally runs amok in a mad and murderous rage of Oedipal annihilation before vanishing, ghostlike, into the snow-covered New Hampshire countryside. Wade's tragic saga is related by his younger brother, Rolfe, a bookish history teacher who suppresses his own self-destructive tendencies by submerging himself in scholarly pursuits." Booklist

This novel is "psychological portraiture of a high order, and like all profound portraits it finds in its subject astonishing contradictions." N Y Times Book Rev

Banks, Russell, 1940-

✓**Cloudsplitter**; a novel. HarperCollins Pubs. 1998 758p

ISBN 0-06-016860-9

LC 97-22163

In 1859, five insurrectionists escaped Harpers Ferry, "including Brown's son Owen. In 'Cloudsplitter' Owen decides to tell his tale. He has fled . . . to a California mountaintop, there to remain in seclusion until the end of the century, when one Miss Mayo requests an audience for a biography of John Brown she's researching. Owen responds with this book, a very long suicide note addressed to her but, as he explains, also to his father, his brothers, and others among the already dead. It is Owen's brief for Purgatory, where he expects to meet all those who devoted their lives to John Brown." New Yorker

"To rise above period costume and stately diction, a historical novel must have a saving tincture of anachronism, a point of forced contact with the unfinished business of the present. Cloudsplitter, is brought alive by Owen's ambivalent, recognizably modern consciousness." Nation

Banks, Russell, 1940-

✓**Lost** memory of skin. Ecco 2011 416p $25.99

ISBN 978-0-06-185763-8; 0-06-185763-7

LC 2011276214

This novel by Russell Banks follows "'The Kid,' a young sex offender . . . After a police raid, the Kid meets 'the Professor,' a pompous, rotund man claiming to be researching homelessness. He wants to study--and cure--the Kid in order to prove his theories about society. But just as the study commences, the Professor, claiming that his life is in danger because of past work as a government spy, turns the tables, paying the Kid to interview him instead." (Publishers Weekly)

"Set in a fictional part of Florida in a time of paranoia (possibly the near future), Lost Memory of Skin is the story of a twentyish sex offender (known simply as the Kid) on parole and the affable but troubled sociology instructor (called the Professor) on a misguided mission to help him become better adjusted. The Kid is a wastrel addicted to Internet porn, with only his pet iguana for company, until an unfortunate series of events—beginning with an Internet chat with an underage girl and ending To Catch a Predator–style—lands him in prison. Upon his release, he is forced to live with other sex offenders under a causeway because of a law that keeps them 2,500 feet from anywhere children are playing. The Professor, a behemoth in a suit, begins interviewing the Kid for academic research purposes; as he learns more about the Kid's crime, he begins to reveal his own troubled history, which only undermines his efforts to help. Banks inhabits unsympathetic voices well, and it is a pleasure to see his gift turned to big, semisurreal characters. The grand, rambling examination of guilt and blame takes place against a ravishingly bleak backdrop, lyrically described, while each revelation of character is like a quiet explosion." Time Out N Y

Banks, Russell
✓ ★ The **sweet** hereafter. HarperCollins Pubs. 1991 257p

ISBN 0-06-016703-3

LC 90-56404

In this novel the story "is told by four people: Dolores Driscoll, a school-bus driver in a small town; Billy Ansel, father of two of the children on the bus; Mitchell Stephens, a lawyer; and Nichole Burnell, a student. In the accident on which the story is centered, Ansel loses his children and Nichole is paralyzed. Dolores survives the accident—the plunge of the bus through the guardrail and into the water-filled quarry—and then tries to survive survival. Mitchell Stephens becomes the attorney for the group of parents who mount a lawsuit." Christ Sci Monit

"Banks handles his dark theme with judicious restraint, empathy and compassion." Publ Wkly

Bannister, Jo
✓ **No** birds sing. St. Martin's Press 1996 297p $21.95

ISBN 0-312-14382-6

LC 96-7296

This procedural "about the Castlemere, England, police department boasts a wonderful cast of multidimensional characters: Detective Superintendent Frank Shapiro, Detective Inspector Liz Graham, and the department's wild Irishman, Detective Sergeant Cal Donovan. In this . . . installment in the series, Castlemere is hit by a smash-and-grab gang, train hijackers, and a rapist. Watching Bannister weave these disparate elements together to produce another gripping tale is half the fun." Booklist

Bannon, James
12; James Bannon. Banco Picante Press 2011 260 p. $9.99

ISBN 9780983912439; 0983912432

This science-fiction and psychological thriller revolves around a terminally ill bio-software scientist's attempt to upload his mind into the consciousness of an unborn baby to once again be with the woman he loves. Neuroscientist

Edward Frame's plan results in the creation of Adam, a child born with the mind and awareness of a grown man. The plot follows Adam as he grows into a young man and faces the unintended consequences Edward's actions. "[James] Bannon's debut novel is a science-fiction thriller . . . but . . . ultimately a . . . romance and . . . [an] exploration into the frailty and preciousness of human existence." (Kirkus)

Banville, John, 1945-
Ancient light; John Banville. Alfred A. Knopf 2012 287 p. $25.95

ISBN 0307957055; 9780307957054

LC 2012019891

This novel by John Banville is "about an actor in the twilight of his life and his career. . . . Is there any difference between memory and invention? . . . [This] is the question that haunts Alexander Cleave . . . as he plumbs the memories of his first--and perhaps only--love . . . and of his daughter, lost to a kind of madness of mind and heart that Cleave can only fail to understand." (Publisher's note)

Banville, John, 1945-
✓ ★ The **book** of evidence. HarperCollins Pubs. 1990 219p

ISBN 0-684-19180-6

LC 89-10985

First published 1989 in the United Kingdom

"This novel, the inventive testimony of a murderer more interested in making an impression than escaping conviction, is . . . hauntingly beautiful and original. . . . Mr. Banville shows his uncanny ability to make everything he describes seem new and rare, yet instantly recognisable." Economist

Banville, John
★ **Christine** Falls; a novel. [by] Benjamin Black. H. Holt 2006 340p $25

ISBN 978-0-8050-8152-7; 0-8050-8152-6

LC 2006-43581

"As the story moves from Ireland to Boston, the push and pull of the novel's dual existence as 'literary thriller' becomes almost as absorbing as the plot; the tension between the two halves of that troublesome equation regularly rippling the book's surface. . . . At its best, the prose here is every bit as acute as one would expect from John Banville, even Banville in disguise—the baroque flourishes are held in check . . . , but the stern elegance remains, and its marriage to a thriller's momentum can have startling results." Times Lit Suppl

Followed by: The silver swan (2008)

Banville, John
A **death** in summer; a novel. [by] Benjamin Black. Henry Holt and Co. 2011 308p $25

ISBN 978-0-8050-9092-5; 0-8050-9092-4

LC 2010-43024

"The setup in Benjamin Black's latest Quirke mystery is a classic one: Newspaper tycoon Richard Jewell is dead from what appears to be a self-inflicted gunshot wound; Quirke believes the apparent suicide is really a murder. The ensuing investigation leads Quirke to Jewell's business rival and to members of each of their staffs, who were plucked out of the same orphanage — one that Quirke had spent time in as a child. . . . A word of caution to those new to the series: Each book builds on the last in terms of character development. Though readers will get the gist of Quirke's problem with alcohol and his complicated relationship with his daughter, those back stories provide more context and thus a more comprehensive picture." Seattle Times

Banville, John

Elegy for April; [by] Benjamin Black. Henry Holt and Co. 2010 293p $25

ISBN 978-0-8050-9091-8; 0-8050-9091-6

LC 2009-48156

"Black has found firmer footing with each novel. . . . In Elegy for April, he's nailed down the recipe, the style and pace that allows him to craft a story of suspense while filling it with sharp-eyed, bigger picture observations." Time Out Chicago

Banville, John, 1945-

The infinities. Alfred A. Knopf 2010 273p $25.95

ISBN 978-0-307-27279-9; 0-307-27279-6

LC 2009-48331

First published 2009 in the United Kingdom

"Sure, 'The Infinities' will have you looking up 'invigilate' in the dictionary (I'll save you the time: 'to keep watch') and Googling 'Amphitryon' (a Greek myth dramatized by the 19th century German writer Heinrich von Kleist). But none of this legwork feels like a chore, because 'The Infinities' is constructed as a tantalizing puzzle you're eager to piece together. And Hermes is a delightfully cheeky and amiable narrator, constantly mocking randy old Zeus and guiding us through the multiple worlds of the novel. Moreover, Banville is a glorious stylist whose prose holds sustaining pleasures, both large and small." Newsday

Banville, John

The sea. Knopf 2005 195p $23

ISBN 0-307-26311-8

LC 2005-50418

"What's strangest about 'The Sea' is that the novel somehow becomes simpler and clearer as it gets more self-conscious: a consequence, I suppose, of its author dropping the pretense of being one kind of writer and giving in to his authentic and much more complicated creative nature. This misshapen but affecting novel turns out to be about something even more familiar than the loss of innocence: it's about grief, the misery and confusion the narrator feels on losing his wife." N Y Times Book Rev

Banville, John

The silver swan; a novel. [by] Benjamin Black. Henry Holt and Co. 2008 290p $25

ISBN 978-0-8050-8153-4; 0-8050-8153-4

LC 2007-31567

"Black has created a wonderful protagonist in Quirke. Tortured and guilt-ridden, six months sober and aching to drink, and just a bit more curious and perceptive than he would choose to be, Quirke is a natural detective. Even when he wants to cover up the truth, he can't. No one will thank him, he knows from the start. But that's just another burden he must carry." Boston Globe

Bao Ninh

The sorrow of war; a novel of North Vietnam. translated from the Vietnamese by Phan Thanh Hao; edited by Frank Palmos. Scribner 1995 233p

ISBN 0-679-43961-7

LC 94-22390

Original Vietnamese edition, 1991

"The word classic is bandied about with ridiculous laxity, but in this case it is hard not to fall back on it. Nothing else really fits the elemental simplicity of theme and treatment: love, war, death, disillusionment, betrayal." New Statesman (1913)

Barbash, Tom

The last good chance; a novel. Picador USA 2002 440p $24

ISBN 0-312-28796-8

LC 2002-25847

"Steven Turner is a young journalist exiled at a paper in Lakeland, a decaying port town in rural upstate New York. His best friend, Jack Lambeau, is the Lakeland town planner. An ambitious Ivy League graduate, Lambeau had had difficulty advancing his experimental urban planning ideas in New York City. When Lakeland's mayor, William Hickey, promised him carte blanche for his New Urbanist—style visions, Lambeau agreed to return to his hometown. With evangelical fervor, he tries to revive Lakeland through a glittering lakefront development project. What he doesn't know, and what the mayor does, is that there are tubs of toxic materials illegally dumped under the lakefront. . . .This is a taut, intricate vision of ambition, corruption and love in the postindustrial era." Publ Wkly

Barber, Ros, 1964-

The Marlowe papers; a novel. Ros Barber. St. Martin's Press 2013 464 p. (hardback) $24.99

ISBN 1250017173; 9781250017178

LC 2012037986

In this novel by Ros Barber "Christopher Marlowe reveals . . . that his 'death' was an elaborate ruse to avoid a conviction of heresy; . . . that he continued to write plays and poetry, hiding behind the name of a colorless man from Stratford--one William Shakespeare. This novel . . . in verse gives voice to . . . a cobbler's son who counted nobles among his friends, a spy in the Queen's service, a fickle lover and a declared religious skeptic." (Publisher's note)

Barbery, Muriel

The elegance of the hedgehog; translated from the French by Alison Anderson. Europa Editions 325p pa $15

ISBN 978-1-933372-60-0; 1-933372-60-5

Original French edition, 2006

In this novel, "the unschooled middle-aged concierge of an upper-class Paris apartment building acts like a stereotypical concierge, leaving the television on all day and sharing her quarters with an old, fat cat, but she secretly consumes vast quantities of literature. A few floors above her, the brilliant and prematurely disillusioned twelve-year-old daughter of a 'holier-than-thou-left-wing-intellectual' family is planning arson and suicide, unless she can find something worth living for beyond the 'vacuousness of bourgeois existence.'

a dowdy woman, head of Todd's fan club, whose courage and good sense mark her as the novel's hero." Publ Wkly

Barker, Clive

★ **Imajica**. HarperCollins Pubs. 1991 824p

ISBN 0-06-017922-8

LC 90-56405

"Barker's prodigious imagination delivers magicians, doppelgängers, Boschean creatures of staggeringly various descriptions and a pantheon of gods and goddesses seduced by power and redeemed by love in a story of violence, occasional unconventional eroticism and mesmerizing invention." Publ Wkly

Barker, Clive

★ **Weaveworld**. Poseidon Press 1987 584p

ISBN 0-671-61268-9

LC 87-18602

Barker "creates a fantastic romance of magic and promise that is at once popular fiction and utopian conjuring. . . . There is great wit in the struggle that ensues, and keen attention to the facts of poverty and exile." NY Times Book Rev

Barker, Nicola

Darkmans. Harper Perennial 2008 838p pa $16.95

ISBN 978-0-06-157521-1; 0-06-157521-6

LC 2007-40012

First published 2007 in the United Kingdom

"Darkmans is set in Ashford, the Kent town now best known as the home of the Channel Tunnel's International Passenger Station. But in becoming a 'geographical hub', the town in Barker's imagination is robbed of its history, sterilised in the present, and abandoned to an uncertain future. . . . [The central character, Daniel] Beede, is a diligent local worthy turned Puritan avenger by, and against, the brash homogenisation of his hometown. The novel introduces the reader to a remarkable cast of characters: one circle encompasses Beede's drug-dealing son Kane, his ex-girlfriend Kelly Broad (of the infamous Broad clan) and Gaffar, a Kurdish refugee mildly besotted with Kelly and 'employed' by Kane, who has a morbid fear of salads. Another circle links Beede's chiropodist Elen and her husband, the paranoid, narcoleptic Isidore, and their eerie child-prodigy son Fleet. . . . [The plot] is twisted and braided with an intricacy so delicate you barely notice the links until the whole web engulfs you." Scotland on Sunday

Barker, Pat

Double vision. Farrar, Straus & Giroux 2003 258p $23

ISBN 0-374-20905-7

LC 2003-54736

Barker "writes superbly, with economy and a lovely talent for darting images. The subject matter is dark, and much is left unsaid, but the reader is drawn on, from page to page." Economist

Barker, Pat

★ The **eye** in the door. Dutton 1994 280p

ISBN 0-525-93808-7

LC 93-43833

Unbeknown to each other, the two autodidacts share an allergy to grammatical errors (the concierge considers a misplaced comma an 'underhanded attack') and a love of tea and moments of ineffable beauty. Barbery's sly wit, which bestows lightness on the most ponderous cogitations, keeps her tale aloft." New Yorker

Barclay, Linwood

★ **Trust** your eyes; a thriller. Linwood Barclay. New American Library 2012 498 p. (hardcover) $25.95; (paperback) $9.99

ISBN 0451237900; 9780451237903; 9780451414175

LC 2011053176

This book by Linwood Barclay follows "Thomas Kilbride . . . a map-obsessed schizophrenic. . . . With a computer program . . . he travels the world while never so much as stepping out the door. . . . Then he sees something . . . in a street view of downtown New York City . . . that looks like a woman being murdered. . . . Thomas's brother, Ray . . . humors him with a half-hearted investigation. But Ray soon realizes he and his brother have stumbled onto a deadly conspiracy." (Publisher's note)

Barfoot, Joan

Critical injuries. Counterpoint 2002 336p $25

ISBN 1-58243-208-2

LC 2002-23845

"At 49 Isla revels in her second marriage and loves her advertising career, a happy life forever changed when she walks in on a robbery and the startled gunman, 17-year-old Roddy, shoots. . . . As Isla lies frozen in a hospital bed and Roddy emotionally freezes everyone out as he lies hopeless in jail, their thoughts are remarkably similar as they revisit the people and events that shaped their lives and worry about each other." Booklist

Barker, Clive

The **books** of blood. Putnam 1988 462p

ISBN 0-399-13343-7

LC 88-2404

Omnibus edition of volumes 1-3 of Books of blood originally published 1984 in the United Kingdom; 1986 in paperback in the United States. Volumes 4 and 5 of Books of blood published with title: The inhuman condition and In the flesh

Barker, Clive

Coldheart Canyon. HarperCollins Pubs. 2001 676p

ISBN 0-06-018297-0

LC 2001-279145

Years ago, many film stars and "their colleagues were drawn by the beautiful, rapacious film star Katya Lupi to her magnificent home in Los Angeles's Coldheart Canyon. What kept them at the house, even after death, is the incredible room in its lowest story. Assembled from thousands of painted tiles, that room—brought to California in the 1920s from an ancient monastery in Romania—is literally alive with evil. . . . The room's powers bestow timeless youth on some, including Katya, but give rise to monstrous entities as well. In the present day, into this horrific place enter several modern sorts, most notably A-list film hero Todd Pickett and

First published 1993 in the United Kingdom

This work "succeeds as both historical fiction and as sequel. Its research and speculation combine to produce a kind of educated imagination that is persuasive and illuminating about this particular place and time. . . . The novel's greatest success, however, has to do with the insight it provides into its central doctor-patient relationships." N Y Times Book Rev

Followed by The ghost road

Barker, Pat

★ The **ghost** road. Dutton 1996 278p

ISBN 0-525-94191-6

LC 95-46863

First published 1995 in the United Kingdom

"The Ghost Road is a startlingly good novel in its own right. With the other two volumes of the trilogy, it forms one of the richest and most rewarding works of fiction of recent times. Intricately plotted, beautifully written, skillfully assembled, tender, horrifying and funny, it lives on in the imagination, like the war it so imaginatively and so intelligently explores." Times Lit Suppl

Barker, Pat

★ **Regeneration**. Dutton 1992 251p

ISBN 0-525-93427-8

LC 91-41264

First published 1991 in the United Kingdom

"'Regeneration' is an antiwar war novel, in a tradition that is by now an established one, though it tells a part of the whole story of war that is not often told—how war may batter and break men's minds—and so makes the madness of war more than a metaphor, and more awful." N Y Times Book Rev

Followed by The eye in the door

Barlow, Toby

Babayaga; by Toby Barlow. 1st ed. Farrar Straus & Giroux 2013 383 p. ill. (hardcover) $27.00

ISBN 0374107874; 9780374107871

LC 2013008712

In this book, the "reader is introduced to Zoya, a babayaga, or witch, living in Paris some years after WWII, as she gets rid of a lover who has noticed her failure to visibly age. The messy results lead her to drag in Elga, her mentor; Elga in turn gets heat from a detective and turns him into a flea. Zoya then meets, charms, and falls for a CIA agent named Will who has problems of his own." (Publishers Weekly)

Barnard, Robert

Death of a literary widow. Scribner 1980 192p

ISBN 0-684-16648-8

LC 80-13128

First published 1979 in the United Kingdom with title: Posthumous papers

"Two elderly women, Viola and Hilda, live in the same house, avoiding each other like the plague. Both have been married to the same man, the late writer Walter Mackin, who is the object of a sudden, intense renewal of interest—articles are written about him, his books are reissued. The great concern of the two wives is who will profit from Mackin's posthumous reputation. One of the old ladies dies in a fire, leaving everyone wondering whether she went out in an accidental blaze or as the result of someone's murderous rage." Booklist

Barnard, Robert

A **fall** from grace. Scribner 2007 261p $24

ISBN 978-0-7432-7220-9; 0-7432-7220-X

LC 2006-51427

Leeds cop Charlie Peace is a "newly made inspector, relocating with his wife to the village of Slepton Edge, a move somewhat darkened by the parallel move of Peace's detested father-in-law to a house nearby. . . . Peace and his wife, Felicity, learn that her father had to leave his former village hurriedly, after he struck a young woman. And now the old man is hitting on a teenage girl. Before the Peaces have a chance to figure out how to protect her, the old man is found dead at the bottom of a quarry. Suspects abound, including a clutch of murderous children and Felicity herself. Peace moves into full detective mode with a murder on his doorstep and his wife a prime suspect. This very satisfying riff on the traditional village mystery finds Barnard at the top of his game." Booklist

Barnard, Robert

A **murder** in Mayfair. Scribner 2000 270p

ISBN 0-684-86445-2

LC 99-46962

"When Colin Pinnock becomes a junior minister in the new Labor government, he is full of promise and resolve, until a curt message on a grubby postcard—'Who do you think you are?'—challenges all his assumptions about himself. . . . Barnard is meticulous about building up the suspense as Colin is hounded by the faceless fury bent on ending, or at least ruining, his blameless life. But there's more nasty fun in reading the story as the revenge of the ousted Tories on the cheeky whippersnappers who think they can keep their integrity, not to mention their sanity, once they start playing politics for real." N Y Times Book Rev

Barnard, Robert

Out of the blackout. Scribner 1985

ISBN 0-684-18282-3

LC 85-1694

"An unusual piece of detection in that the central character is searching for himself—who was he before he was taken, with other children, to foster homes in the country during the London blitz? Though the tale is not wholeheartedly crime fiction, a murder is discovered and its ramifications elucidated by the self-searching hero." Barzun. Cat of Crime. Rev and enl edition

Barnes, Djuna

★ **Nightwood**. Modern Lib. 2000 xxxii, 169p

ISBN 0-679-64024-X

LC 99-56308

First published 1936 in the United Kingdom; first United States edition 1937 by Harcourt, Brace

"An account of the tangled sexual and psychological relationships between various expatriates in Paris and Berlin. Narrated in part through an alcoholic haze of stream of consciousness, it owes its reputation as an avant-garde work partially to its frank treatment of lesbianism." Benet's Reader's Ency of Am Lit

Barnes, John

The **armies** of memory. Tor 2006 429p $25.95
ISBN 0-7653-0330-2

LC 2005-18807

"Set in the same far-future universe as A Million Open Doors and A Sky So Big and Black, Barnes's novel concludes the adventures of one of the genre's most distinctive 'special agents,' the cultured, talented, and deadly Giraut Leones. At the same time, the author depicts a future in which the coexistence of divergent human cultures remains a major force in the development of human society. A superb blending of adventure and scientific speculation." Libr J

Barnes, John

The **sky** so big and black. TOR Bks. 2002 315p $24.95
ISBN 0-7653-0303-5

LC 2002-22307

"As always, Barnes's character are beautifully natural. His sense of how the conditions of a place can create a culture and individual sensibilities is outstanding, and here he even allows his slang to evolve." Publ Wkly

Barnes, Jonathan

The **somnambulist**. William Morrow & Co. 2008 353p $23.95
ISBN 978-0-06-137538-5; 0-06-137538-1

First published 2007 in the United Kingdom

"There is much that is strange, magical and darkly hilarious in this book, at least if one savors the sardonic and the bizarre. At various points it recalls Dickens, Alice in Wonderland and Frankenstein, but it remains an original and monumentally inventive piece of work." Washington Post Book World

Barnes, Julian, 1946-

★ A **history** of the world in 101/2 chapters. Knopf 1989 307p
ISBN 0-394-58061-3

LC 89-45266

This book "shapes up not only as Barnes's funniest novel but also his most richly cargoed and imaginatively designed. . . . As satirist and story-teller he has few equals at present." New Statesman Soc

Barnes, Julian

Pulse. Alfred A. Knopf 2011 227p il $25
ISBN 978-0-307-59526-3; 0-307-59526-9

LC 2011-02736

In this collection "Barnes' main focus is on love and intimacy — how it starts, and what accounts for its endurance or failure to thrive. Many of his characters suffer the loss of one of their five senses, or of a close relationship. . . . Interspersed through the first half of Pulse is a quartet of witty, clever dinner party conversations, 'At Phil & Joanna's,' presented with little exposition. The tight-knit group of aging boomers who gather every few months manage to preserve their high spirits even as they banter about serious subjects, including American politics, global warming, health care, 'the marmalade theory of Britishness,' and gender distinctions in talking about love and sex. These snappy running dialogues evoke Barnes' conversational novels . . . . They also demonstrate, along with the other stories in this graceful collection, that Barnes has his finger firmly planted on the pulse of topics that continue to matter to us." NPR

Barnes, Julian, 1946-

★ The **sense** of an ending. Alfred A. Knopf 2011 163p.
ISBN 0-307-95712-8; 978-0-307-95712-2

LC 2011025433

Man Booker Prize (2011)

The novel, a recipient of the Man Booker Prize, takes place in "the North London suburbia. . . . The narrator, Tony Webster, now well into middle age, looks back to his school days when he was one of a group of clever, articulate, and opinionated youths. A few years later one of them, Adrian Finn, commits suicide, and the novel follows Tony's attempts to understand this tragic event. Eventually he discovers that the reasons for it are not at all what he (and the readers) had assumed." (Commonweal)

"Tony Webster, a contented man settling comfortably into middle age, fondly carries his youth with him until a long-ago first love and an old childhood friend begin to haunt his present, forcing him to question the core of his character. Barnes' latest—a meditation on memory and aging—occasionally feels more like a series of wise, underline-worthy insights than a novel. But the many truths he highlights make it worthy of a careful read." Entertainment Wkly

Barnes, Linda

Cold case. Delacorte Press 1997 385p
ISBN 0-385-30614-8

LC 96-38216

"Carlotta isn't as smooth an operator as some of her colleagues . . . but her gung-ho technique works for her and it's easy to get caught up in her enthusiasm." N Y Times Book Rev

Barnes, Linda

The **Perfect** Ghost; Linda Barnes. St Martins Pr 2013 304 p. (hardcover) $24.99
ISBN 1250023637; 9781250023636

LC 2013002519

This novel from Anthony Award-winner Linda Barnes focuses on "Em Moore, an agoraphobe who ghostwrites celebrity biographies under the joint pseudonym T.E. Blakemore, [who] worries whether she can complete her current project—an 'autobiography' of famed actor-director Garrett Malcolm—without her writing partner, Teddy Blake, after his death in a car crash." (Publishers Weekly)

Barnes, Linda

The **snake** tattoo. St. Martin's Press 1989 290p
ISBN 0-312-02643-9

LC 88-30525

Private eye Carlotta Carlyle "is faced with two equally difficult cases: finding a missing teenage girl, who seems to have traded posh suburbia for the moral sewer of Boston's Combat Zone, and helping Beantown cop and longtime friend Mooney, who stands accused of assaulting a supposedly unarmed man in a bar fight." Booklist

"Bright, witty, and a touch sarcastic." Libr J

Barone, Sam

Dawn of empire. William Morrow 2006 483p map $25.95

ISBN 978-0-06-089244-9; 0-06-089244-7

LC 2005-58374

"In the fertile land of Mesopotamia circa 3000 B.C.E., the first cities arose, threatening the existence of nomads who depended on raiding small, defenseless farmsteads and villages for food and slaves. When news reaches the people of one of these cities that the barbaric Alur Meriki have targeted them for their next raid, Eskkar, a nomadic warrior exiled from his clan, assumes the role of war leader and devises a plan to save Orak and its people. . . . Readers will find it hard to put down this dramatic tale of conflict between cultures, bloody warfare, and early diplomacy and statehood as seen through the eyes of a man born to conquer and rule." Libr J

Barone, Sam

Empire rising. William Morrow 2007 465p $25.95

ISBN 978-0-06-089246-3

LC 2007-40485

In this sequel to Dawn of empire, "Lord Eskkar, a former barbarian who earlier saved the city of Akkad from almost-certain defeat, and Lady Trella, an erstwhile slave and his wife, now rule the 'biggest city on the Tigris.' Hoping to crush the bandits marauding in the countryside and extend Akkadian rule, Eskkar dispatches one band of soldiers south from Akkad and leads another north. In Eskkar's absence, Korthac, a newly arrived Egyptian warrior posing as a trader, schemes to infiltrate the city with his followers and seize power. . . . The frenetic action might be predictable, but it's never boring. The setting is convincingly rendered, and the characters—heroes and villains—are sharply drawn. Fans of ancient historical fiction will enjoy this instructive journey to the dawn of civilization." Publ Wkly

Barr, Nevada

Burn; an Anna Pigeon novel. Minotaur Books 2010 378p $25.99

ISBN 978-0-312-61456-0; 0-312-61456-X

LC 2010-21411

In this installment Anna Pigeon is in "New Orleans, staying with a friend, when, believe it or not, somebody tries to put a hex on her. Anna soon suspects that her friend's tenant, an abundantly off-putting fellow named Jordan, might have something to do with it—but why? This is not the first time the author has taken Anna out of her usual rustic settings . . . , but regular readers need not worry: Barr isn't merely rehashing big-city themes she's tackled before. There's a reason why this story needs to be set in the Big Easy, and Barr develops the narrative carefully, never letting the eerie black-magic elements overshadow her solid and suspenseful plotting." Booklist

Barr, Nevada

High country. Putnam 2004 323p $24.95

ISBN 0-399-15144-3

LC 2003-47243

This mystery finds Ranger Anna Pigeon "undercover as a waitress at the famous Ahwahnee Hotel in Yosemite National Park. Four seasonal workers have been missing for two weeks, and not even a professional rescue team can scrounge up a clue. Are they AWOL, or is it foul play? Anna waits tables, plays mom to a couple of twentysomething roommates, takes flak from the dining room manager, and deals with bullies before striking out on her own to figure out what has happened. The gossip among hotel staff and visitors is that there's a gold mine in the Sierra Mountains. Barr's even pace and deft characterizations will please series fans while winning her new readers." Libr J

Barr, Nevada

The **rope**; by Nevada Barr. Minotaur Books 2011 357 p.

ISBN 1410444864; 9781410444868 978-0-312-61457-7

LC 2011035837

This book tells the story of fictional character Anna Pigeon, who, "[i]n 1995 and 35 years old, fresh off the bus from New York City, . . . takes a . . . job as a seasonal employee of the Glen Canyon National Recreational Area. On her day off, Anna goes hiking into the park never to return. . . Anna . . . wakes up, trapped at the bottom of a dry natural well, naked, without supplies and no clear memory of how she found herself in this situation. . . . [I]t soon becomes clear that someone has trapped her there, in an inescapable prison, and no one knows that she is even missing. . . . Anna Pigeon must muster the courage, determination and will to live that she didn't even know she still possessed to survive, outwit and triumph." (Publisher's note)

Barr, Nevada

Winter study. Putnam 2008 370p $24.95

ISBN 978-0-399-15458-4; 0-399-15458-2

"The blizzards, the dangerous ice and the manhunts through the frozen woods are described with crisp, hard-edged beauty. And the wolves, those maligned 'ogres of childhood,' are magnificent." N Y Times Book Rev

Barrett, A. Igoni

Love is power, or something like that; A. Igoni Barrett. Farrar Straus & Giroux 2013 176 p. (paperback) $15

ISBN 1555976409; 9781555976408

LC 2012956123

This collection of short stories, by A. Igoni Barrett, centers on Nigeria. "In these wide-ranging stories, A. Igoni Barrett roams the streets with people from all stations of life. A man with acute halitosis navigates the chaos of the Lagos bus system. A minor policeman, full of the authority and corruption of his uniform, beats his wife. A family's fortunes fall from love and wealth to infidelity and poverty as poor choices unfurl over three generations." (Publisher's note)

Barrett, Andrea

Archangel; Fiction. by Andrea Barrett. 1st ed. W W Norton & Co Inc 2013 238 p. (hardcover) $24.95

ISBN 0393240002; 9780393240009

LC 2013016958

This is a collection of science-focused stories from National Book Award winner Andrea Barrett. "In 'The Ether of Space,' set in 1920, astronomer Phoebe Wells struggles with the implications of Einstein's theories; in 'The Island,' set in 1873, young biologist Henrietta Atkins, initially worshipful of a creationist professor, succumbs to Darwinism. (Publishers Weekly)

Barrett, Andrea

Ship fever and other stories. Norton 1996 254p $21

ISBN 0-393-03853-X

LC 95-14562

Barrett "tells her stories through alternating voices, diaries, letters—whatever seems to hint at the most promising results. Seen against a larger fictional landscape overpopulated with the sensational and affectless, her work stands out for its sheer intelligence, its painstaking attempt to discern and describe the world's configuration." N Y Times Book Rev

Barrett, William E.

★ The lilies of the field; drawings by Burt Silverman. Doubleday 1962 92p

"Homer Smith is an amiable Southern black man. Driving through the Southwest after getting out of the Army, he stops to help four German refugee nuns build a church. After teaching them English and survival skills, he disappears, leaving behind the legend of his faithful help." Shapiro. Fic for Youth. 3d edition

Barry, Brunonia

The lace reader. William Morrow 2008 390p $24.95

ISBN 978-0-06-162476-6; 0-06-162476-4

Self-published 2006

"Set in Salem, Mass., the story is that of a 32-year-old woman who fled when she was 17 to California but returns when her 85-year-old great-aunt, Eva, is reported missing. Like Eva, Towner Whitney is a 'reader,' though she suppresses the talent. Eva could see a picture in a piece of Ipswich lace that would foretell what was to come. . . . Towner ran off after an extended stay in a high-end looney bin, where she ended up following the suicide of her twin sister, Lyndley. It was that, more than anything, that caused her to reject the family heritage of reading minds as well as lace, though such gifts certainly hold a respected place in Salem. Or did until her Uncle Cal, a wife batterer who sexually abused Lyndley, form a fundamentalist cult to torment and harass the modern-day wiccans? That includes Great-Aunt Eva, a wise and knowing woman, who is found dead and may have been murdered. Cal is a suspect, and it seems he also may have killed a young woman carrying his child. This time it's not so easy for Towner to run, but in staying she confronts pervasive menace." N Y Daily News

Barry, Brunonia

The map of true places. William Morrow & Co. 2010 406p $25.99

ISBN 978-0-06-162478-0

"Although marred by unnecessary 'come-to-realize' moments, this woman-in-jeopardy thriller retooled with gothic elements — shifting identities, secrets and portents, a deserted cottage and a missing suicide note — manages to transcend its component cliches." Kirkus

Barry, Kevin

City of Bohane; Kevin Barry. Cape 2011 277 pp.

ISBN 9780224090575; 0224090577

LC 2011431407

The book explores the "imagined, decivilized Irish city" of Bohane, which "has taken 40 years to fall into utter decay. The setting is a rich stew of ethnicities, loyalties, gangster cred, vices and technologically barren conflicts. . . . Pulling the strings on this criminality is Logan Hartnett, a gaunt, pale rake called 'The Albino.' Hartnett is beleaguered by harpy wife Immaculata and protected by a trio of young warriors: ambitious Wolfie Stanners, irrepressible F##ker Burke and razor-cool Jenni Ching, who works all sides with equal aplomb. A 'welt of vengeance' threatens to jump off, after a Cusack of the Rises gets 'Reefed' in Smoketown. . . . Stirring the pot is the fact that Hartnett's mortal enemy, 'The Gant Broderick,' has sashayed back into town." (Kirkus)

Barry, Max

Company. Doubleday 2006 338p $22.95

ISBN 0-385-51439-5

LC 2005-48498

"As bitter as break-room coffee, the novel eviscerates demeaning modern management techniques that treat workers as 'headcounts.' Though Barry's primary target is corporate dehumanization, he's at his funniest lampooning the suits that tread the stage, consumed by the sound and fury of office politics that signify nothing." Publ Wkly

Barry, Max

Lexicon; a novel. Max Barry. The Penguin Press 2013 400 p. (hardcover) $26.95

ISBN 1594205388; 9781101604908; 9781594205385

LC 2012046980

In this novel, there is "a secret society of 'poets' who collect and wield special words to control others. Emily Ruff, a teenager living on the street, has been recruited by the organization but leaves in seeming disgrace. Years later, Wil Parke is caught in a firefight between the factions—over him. He is the only survivor of a horrifying event unleashed by an ultimate word of power. But there is a deeper connection between Wil and Emily and the organization that comes between them." (Library Journal)

Barry, Sebastian, 1955-

On Canaan's side. Viking 2011 256p $25.95

ISBN 978-0-670-022922; 0-670-02292-6

LC 2011-13207

"A masterful novel filled with the bittersweet ruminations of an 89-year-old woman as she reflects on her rich life while contemplating death. . . . A novel to be savored." Kirkus

Barth, John

★ Giles goat-boy; or, The revised new syllabus. Doubleday 1966 xxxi, 710p

"The novel's protagonist, Billy Bockfuss (also called George Giles, the goat-boy), was raised with herds of goats on a university farm after being found as a baby in the bowels of the giant West Campus Automatic Computer (WESCAC). The WESCAC plans to create a being called GILES (Grand-Tutorial Ideal, Laboratory Eugenical Specimen) that would possess superhuman abilities. Billy's foster father, who tends the herd, suspects Billy of being GILES but tries to groom him to be humanity's savior and to stop WESCAC's domination over humans." Merriam-Webster's Ency of Lit

Barth, John

The **sot**-weed factor. Doubleday 1967 806p

Picaresque novel "originally published in 1960 and revised in 1967. A parody of the historical novel, it is based on and takes its title from a satirical poem published in 1708 by Ebenezer Cooke, who is the protagonist of Barth's work. The novel's black humor is derived from its purposeful misuse of conventional litarary devices." Merriam-Webster's Ency of Lit

Barthelme, Donald

★ **Sixty** stories. Putnam 1981 457p

ISBN 0-399-12659-7

LC 81-8646

Barthelme, Frederick

Waveland; a novel. Doubleday 2009 240p $24.95

ISBN 978-0-385-52729-3; 0-385-52729-2

LC 2008-13511

"In this powerfully atmospheric story of loneliness and risk, Barthelme slyly conceals emotional and philosophical intensity beneath the peculiarity of circumstance, the dazzle of hilarious repartee, and the luster of gorgeous prose." Booklist

Bartlett, Don

It's fine by me; Per Petterson, Don Bartlett. Graywolf Press 2012 208 p. (alk. paper) $22.00

ISBN 1555976263; 9781555976262

LC 2012936227

This book, by Per Petterson, follows the character "Arvid Jansen in his youth. . . . Arvid befriends a boy named Audun. On Audun's first day of school he refuses to talk or take off his sunglasses. . . . Audun lives with his mother in a working-class district of Oslo. He delivers newspapers and talks for hours about Jack London and Ernest Hemingway with Arvid. But he's not sure that school is the right path for him and feels that life holds other possibilities." (Publisher's note)

Barton, Emily

Brookland. Farrar, Straus & Giroux 2006 478p $25

ISBN 0-374-11690-3

LC 2005-16269

"So much modern fiction thinks small, feels small. Emily Barton will never be accused of either. The large and complex storytelling in 'Brookland' is divided between a traditional third-person narrative and the much older Prudence's letters to her daughter. Both feature a large and complex cast." N Y Times Book Rev

Bass, Rick

★ **Nashville** chrome. Houghton Mifflin Harcourt 2010 253p $24

ISBN 978-0-54731-726-7; 0-54731-726-3

LC 2010-05732

"Bass gives us Maxine, Bonnie and Jim Ed Brown, three of the five children of Floyd and Birdie Brown; their childhood in the backwoods of post-Depression south-central Arkansas; and their rise to fame as singers and songwriters, members of the fledgling Grand Ole Opry and contemporaries of Elvis Presley. The trio's biggest hit was 'The Three Bells,' and they broke up in 1965. Maxine, who had the strongest pull to fame, went on to release a solo album and write her autobiography. . . . Bass does what he does — sluicing their lives, traveling up Maxine's bloodstream to create a parallel story, a work of fiction full of real names, dates and facts. And when he is done with the Browns, those facts sit, like so many fish bones, on history's clean plate." Los Angeles Times

Bates, Erin

Her Amish man; [a forbidden Eden: a novel] Erin Bates. Gallery Books 2012 293 p. (trade paper) $15

ISBN 1451662092; 1451662106; 9781451662092; 9781451662108

LC 2011051760

This book by Erin Bates is an Amish romance novel. "Because Leah McKenzie's mother was 'shunned' for marrying an outsider, Leah has never known her Amish relatives. Then she is framed for a murder she didn't commit, and she needs somewhere to hide until she can clear her name" so "she heads for her grandmother's home in Illinois." She is soon entranced by the simplicity of the Amish lifestyle and the charms of Amish man John Miller. (Publisher's note)

Bates, H. E.

★ **Fair** stood the wind for France. Little, Brown 1944 270p

A British bomber, returning from a mission over Italy, crashed in occupied France. The members of the crew managed to escape via the underground route, all but the pilot who was too ill. He was cared for by a family of French peasants, whose innate goodness made such an impression on him that when he finally left France he took with him the daughter of the family, as his wife

"An almost unbearable suspense, the romance of the two young people and a true portrait of the little people of France, defenseless but possessed of an enduring power, all these go to make an unforgettable story, beautifully told." Bookmark

Bates, Judy Fong

Midnight at the Dragon Café; Judy Fong Bates. McClelland & Stewart 2004 317 p. Library binding $22.95

ISBN 9781417697786; 0771010982

LC 2004381288

This book, "[s]et in the 1960s, [tells] . . . the story of a young girl, the daughter of a small Ontario town's solitary Chinese family, whose life is changed over the course of one summer when she learns the burden of secrets. Through Su-Jen's eyes, the hard life behind the scenes at the Dragon Café unfolds. . . . Su-Jen's . . . mother, a beautiful but embittered woman, settles uneasily into their new life. Su-Jen feels the weight of her mother's unhappiness as Su-Jen's life takes her outside the restaurant and far from the customs of the traditional past. When Su-Jen's half-brother arrives, smouldering under the responsibilities he must bear as the dutiful Chinese son, he forms an alliance with Su-Jen's mother, one that will have devastating consequences." (Publisher's note)

Battle, Lois

Southern women. St. Martin's Press 1984 404p
ISBN 0-312-74747-0

LC 83-22999

"The author's characters are the type that readers of light fiction enjoy: they possess ordinary urges and desires overlaid with tinges of nobility, tragedy, and/or glamour. The plot unravels quickly but logically, with no artificial twists and turns." Booklist

Bauer, Belinda

Blacklands. Simon & Schuster 2010 221p $23
ISBN 978-1-4391-4944-7; 1-4391-4944-5

LC 2009-08548

"Twelve-year-old Steven's hardscrabble life in tiny Shipcolt, England, on the edge of Exmoor has a predictable monotony: he spends most of his free time with his best friend, Lewis, dodging the local bullies and trying to garner the favor of his mother, Lettie, and his Nan (grandmother), who seem to disapprove of his every move. The two women exist in a state of emotional limbo, still mourning the death of his Uncle Billy, who was abducted and murdered as an 11 year old by a serial killer serving time in a nearby prison. Steven enters into a bold plan—to find his uncle's killer and thus win the affection of his mother and grandmother. But once he begins a secret correspondence with the killer, Steven starts down a treacherous path that could endanger his own life." Libr J

"Bauer displays remarkable talent in pacing, plotting and, most important of all, getting beneath the skin of even her most repellent characters." Kirkus

Bauer, Belinda

Darkside; a novel. Simon & Schuster Paperbacks 2011 287p $15
ISBN 978-1-4516-1275-2; 1-4516-1275-3

LC 2010-28109

"Given the shallow pool of prospective victims and suspects, it takes real skill to write a plausible whodunit about an undetected serial killer running amok in an English village. . . . Arriving in the bleak midwinter to investigate the murder of an elderly woman as she lay paralyzed in her bed, the citybred Detective Chief Inspector John Marvel is so appalled to find himself in the boondocks, obliged to waste his talents 'on the low and the stupid,' that out of sheer spite, he repeatedly subjects the local constable, Jonas Holly, to public humiliation. Jonas, a sweet, conscientious policeman who sacrificed his career ambitions to care for his dying wife, knows he doesn't deserve this ridicule. But the taunting notes the killer leaves behind as he continues his rampage touches some core of guilt Jonas can't bring himself to face. Set against a landscape that would tax anyone's sanity, Bauer's grim tale deploys a morbid wit that's positively wicked." N Y Times Book Rev

Bauer, Carlene

★ Frances and Bernard; Carlene Bauer. Houghton Mifflin Harcourt 2013 195 p. (hardcover) $23
ISBN 0547858248; 9780547858241

LC 2012014028

In this book, set in the late 1950s, "over the course of one long lunch at a writer's workshop, Frances and Bernard begin a journey of love and loss. They banter about writing and the workshop's limitations, and, while falling in love, they struggle with the meaning of religion and the nature of friendship. In the end, their relationship is tested to the limits when Bernard suffers a manic episode." (Library Journal)

Bauermeister, Erica

Joy for beginners. Putnam 2011 272p $24.95
ISBN 978-0-399-15712-7; 0-399-15712-3

LC 2010-26587

This novel "centers around seven women. Kate is a cancer survivor, and the friends that supported her through it all come together to celebrate her recovery. In honor of that, Kate makes a bargain with them. She's going to do something she has always been terrified of: white-water rafting. In return, they each have to do something they've always said they wouldn't. But they don't get to choose. Kate does. The novel tells the story of each of the characters separately. The reader gets to know these women intimately; their pasts, their lives, their hopes, their dreams. Most importantly, their secret fears. The challenges Kate sets for all of them speak to their innermost—and unrealized—longings and sets them on the paths to true happiness and fulfillment." Fort Worth Examiner

Bausch, Richard

Peace; a novel. Knopf 2008 171p $19.95
ISBN 978-0-307-26833-4; 0-307-26833-0

LC 2007-37096

"A story cleanly told — void of trickery or plot shifting, without the faux drama of point-of-view shifts or uninvited monologue on the state of the cultural landscape — well, that's a thing to behold. . . . Bausch, among the most prolific and accomplished story writers of the last two decades, provides a gift to those who like to swallow their stories whole, in one sitting, without digression or narrative handstands." Esquire

Bausch, Richard

Something is out there; stories. Alfred A. Knopf 2010 268p $25.95
ISBN 978-0-307-26627-9; 0-307-26627-3

LC 2009-27437

"In this fine new collection, Bausch presents us with young people and old people; married, single and divorced people; straight and gay people; professional and blue-collar people; and people who are simply layabouts. They make bad choices, occasionally even deadly choices, because they can't help themselves—and because the universe is full of peril and temptation. . . . Again and again, [Bausch] excavates the darkest corners of his characters' lives without giving in to despair." N Y Times Book Rev

Bausch, Richard

★ The **stories** of Richard Bausch. HarperCollins 2003 651p $29.95

 ISBN 0-06-019649-1

LC 2003-42318

"Failure and its exactions this is Bausch's big subject. These 42 stories test the play of hope and disappointment in the lives of spouses and lovers, of parents and children and siblings. And while Bausch does in several instances write with insight and authority from a woman's perspective, it is the sons, fathers and husbands in their daily trials that he registers most memorably. Indeed, so alive are these characters, with their credible flaws, their complaints and loud excitements, that closing the book feels like pushing the door shut on some clamorous party." N Y Times Book Rev

Bausch, Richard

✓ **Thanksgiving** night; a novel. HarperCollins Publishers 2006 403p $24.95

 ISBN 978-0-06-009443-0; 0-06-009443-5

LC 2006-41222

"For all its alternately antic and sly humor, Bausch's novel is also filled with sudden displays of emotion. . . . Old-fashioned novelists tend to be generous, and 'Thanksgiving Night' comes with broad swaths of detail, abundant quirks and lots of human suffering, as well as low-key lyricism." N Y Times Book Rev

Baxter, Charles

✓ The **feast** of love. Pantheon Bks. 2000 308p

 ISBN 0-375-41019-8

LC 99-53088

"An insomniac Mid-western novelist named Charlie Baxter becomes the unwitting audience of a neighbor's midnight confession, and is drawn into a tale of love in its manifold guises—confused, ecstatic, unrequited. We hear the story of Kathryn, who left her husband for the female shortstop of a local softball team; of Diana, a capricious lawyer who doesn't want anyone to want her too much; and of Chloé, a pierced teenager with a strong sense of justice and a doomed passion for a former drug addict. Baxter's novel is a modern Symposium, unexpectedly hilarious in its attempt to get at the evasive truths of love; unlike Plato's treatise, though, its strength lies in its recognition that such truths aren't universal." New Yorker

Baxter, Charles

✓ **Gryphon**; new and selected stories. Pantheon Books 2011 400p $27.95

 ISBN 978-0-307-37921-4; 0-307-37921-3

LC 2010-13785

"The strength of Charles Baxter's 'Gryphon' stories collection is characters who struggle with shame in an age when the burden of knowledge is compounded by the inability to act properly. Most of the stories are set in snowy Midwestern cities whose economic and social misfortunes weigh on his characters like an alp. . . . Baxter's writing is spare but, like a flash of cat eyes in the night, well-crafted images and wit flit onto the pages to keep the narrative moving." Providence J

Baxter, Charles

✓ **Saul** and Patsy. Pantheon Bks. 2003 317p $24

 ISBN 0-375-41029-5

LC 2003-42027

"Baxter's prose is succulent, his characters magnetic, his humor incisive, his decipherment of the human psyche felicitous, and his command of the storyteller's magic absolute." Booklist

Baxter, Charles

✓ The **soul** thief. Pantheon Books 2008 210p $20

 ISBN 978-0-375-42252-2; 0-375-42252-8

LC 2007-18119

"Baxter's evocation of the mindset of Vietnam-era students and the 'hysterical intellectualism' of their parties is gloriously done, especially in its attention to era-specific details." N Y Times Book Rev

Baxter, Stephen

✓ **Evolution**; a novel. Del Rey/Ballantine Bks. 2003 578p $25.95

 ISBN 0-345-45782-X

LC 2002-31422

"As a group scientists gathers in the South Pacific for a conference to save the human race from extinction, their actions represent the culmination of millions of years of struggle by their primate ancestors to survive in an ever-changing world. . . . {Baxter} uses a modern-day story as a frame within which he relates a series of vignettes tracing the history of the evolution of intelligent life on Earth, from its mammalian beginnings in the Cretaceous era to the present. Spanning more than 165 million years and encompassing the entire planet, Baxter's ambitious saga provides both an exercise in painless paleontology and superb storytelling." Libr J

Baxter, Stephen

 Manifold; space. Stephen Baxter. Ballantine Pub. Group 2001 452p (pbk.) $7.99; o.p.

 ISBN 9780345430786; 9780345430779

LC 00050804

This book takes place in "2020. Fueled by an insatiable curiosity, Reid Malenfant ventures to the far edge of the solar system, where he discovers a strange artifact left behind by an alien civilization: A gateway that functions as a kind of quantum transporter, allowing virtually instantaneous travel over the vast distances of interstellar space. . . . [H]e will soon be faced with an impossible choice that will push him beyond terror, beyond sanity, beyond humanity itself. Meanwhile on Earth the Japanese scientist Nemoto fears her worst nightmares are coming true. Startling discoveries reveal that the Moon, Venus, even Mars once thrived with life . . . that was snuffed out not just once but many times, in cycles of birth and destruction." (Publisher's note)

Baxter, Stephen

✓ **Sunstorm**; Arthur C. Clarke, Stephen Baxter. Ballantine Books 2005 324p (Time odyssey) o.p.; (pbk.) $7.99

 ISBN 034545250X; 9780345452511

LC 2004062354

In this science fiction novel, "[h]ostile aliens intend to blow up the Sun and wipe humanity out. . . . In 2037, a giant solar flare disrupts electrical and electronic processes on Earth. Having predicted the flare, genius physicist Eugene Mangles . . . extrapolates . . . that on April 20, 2042, another huge solar eruption will fry the Earth down to the bedrock. . . . [T]he . . . characters—British Astronomer Royal Siobhan McGorran chief among them— . . . come up with the idea of a space shield. . . . Meanwhile, Lieutenant Bisesa Dutt of the British Army, having lived five years in another reality, . . . contacts Siobhan with her suspicions about the mysterious Firstborn, alien intelligences who want to expunge the human race." (Kirkus)

Bayard, Louis

The **black** tower. William Morrow 2008 352p $24.95

ISBN 978-0-06-117350-9; 0-06-117350-9

LC 2008-5059

The author sets his "historical adventure in the streets of Paris as the blood lust of the revolution subsides. It is 1818 when Vidocq, a former convict and the (real-life) founder of the newly created plainclothes investigative force known as the Sûreté, tracks down obscure medical student Hector Carpentier, whose name was found in the pocket of a dead man. As they work through the clues together, they move from the slums of Paris out to the royal gardens of Saint-Cloud. The duo soon realizes that the murders they are investigating may be connected to the whereabouts of Marie Antoinette's lost son, said to have died in the Black Tower." Libr J

Bayard, Louis

The **school** of night; a novel. Henry Holt and Company 2011 338p $25

ISBN 978-0-8050-9069-7; 0-8050-9069-X

LC 2010-24961

A "fabricated account of a secret society of brilliant Elizabethan thinkers who challenge conventional 16th-century wisdom by exercising 'the freedom to speak their minds.' Henry Cavendish, the 21st-century scholar who narrates the story, tumbles to this academic crew when an unscrupulous collector (who would 'lay down his life for a Shakespeare quarto') hires him to search the archives of a fellow bibliophile who committed suicide. Leaving Henry to puzzle out the clues in the library, Bayard shifts the story to Tudor England, where members of the elite circle that meets at Sir Walter Ralegh's Dorset estate are immersed in their esoteric arts. From either perspective, the story is fascinating. And yes, there's a good reason that Shakespeare is not welcome in this company." N Y Times Book Rev

Beach, Edward Latimer

Run silent, run deep; {by} Edward L. Beach. Holt & Co. 1955 364p

"If ever a book has the ring of reality, this is it. From the moment the reader steps aboard a training boat in New London, Conn., to the time when the submarine Walrus dives deeply to avoid the depth charges of the enemy's destroyers, there is awe and respect for the author who created them." N Y Times Book Rev

Beachy, Stephen

Boneyard. Verse Chorus Press 2011 303p il pa $15.95

ISBN 978-1-891241-33-8

LC 2011-15261

"A 'collaborative' novel, the skeleton of which was supposedly assembled by Amish teen Jake Yoder, whose work Beachy claims to have discovered and then saved from the young man's attempts to burn the stories he had come to deem sinful. Convinced the stories were destined for literary greatness — as a rare example of Amish literature, at the very least — USF professor Beachy hung meat on the text where necessary. Verse Chorus Press then agreed to publish the novel, though Beachy's editor, Judith Owsley Brown, expresses her doubt regarding the existence of Yoder in boneyard's preface, extending that skepticism to Beachy's sanity (and that of his therapist) in a series of footnotes that bubble and whisper from the book's margins, occasionally (and quite purposely) distracting from the narrative proper. Boneyard is a grotesque funhouse of kinky sex (often with gas masks on), egregious footnoting, child abuse, delusions of rock 'n' roll grandeur, and he-said-she-said narrative finger-pointing." East Bay Express

Beagle, Peter S.

★ The **last** unicorn. Viking 1968 218p hardcover o.p. pa $14.95

ISBN 0-670-41908-7; 0-451-45052-3 pa

"Beagle is a true magician with words, a master of prose and a deft practitioner in verse. He has been compared, not unreasonably, with Lewis Carroll and J. R. R. Tolkien, but he stands squarely and triumphantly on his own feet." Saturday Rev

Beale, Elaine

Another life altogether; a novel. Spiegel and Grau 2010 402p $26

ISBN 978-0-385-53004-0; 0-385-53004-8

LC 2009-03779

"The novel plays out two major stories Jesse's family collapse and her own coming to terms with her sexuality. Horrified by both her attraction to an older girl and her private admiration for an openly gay classmate tormented by their peers, Jesse tries desperately to find her footing. Beale does a wonderful job describing all of her characters with richness and economy, but as she moves Jesse through this agonizing transformation, Beale is particularly powerful." Boston Globe

Beamer, Amelia

★ The **loving** dead. Night Shade 2010 241p il pa $14.95

ISBN 978-1-59780-194-2; 1-59780-194-1

"Trader Joe's employee Kate encounters her first zombie when she helps her belly-dance instructor fend off the amorous advances of a stranger. Soon the instructor succumbs to zombieism herself — but not before she and Kate make love, excited by pheromones the zombie plague releases at onset. This sexually transmitted disease, which also turns its victims' tongues 'the color of well-done burger' and gives them an appetite for living human flesh, soon reduces California's Bay Area to a shambles. Kate and her housemate Michael take refuge on Alcatraz Island with the help of iPhone apps and Googled research on authentic Haitian zombies. Fast-paced yet thought-provoking fun." Seattle Times

Bear, Elizabeth

All the windwracked stars. Tor 2008 368p (The edda of burdens) $24.95

ISBN 978-0-7653-1882-4; 0-7653-1882-2

LC 2008-34076

A "postapocalyptic melodrama based loosely upon Norse mythology. On the Last Day, the historian Muire fled the battle, leaving her sibling Valkyries to die. More than 2,300 years later, only a single city, Eiledon, has survived as the dying world slowly turns into ice. Ashamed of her cowardice, Muire now vows to keep the last humans safe, but as she slowly pieces together the horrific truth behind the magic that has kept Eiledon standing, she must decide whether it's worth the price." Publ Wkly

The author's "ability to create breathtaking variations on ancient themes and make them new and brilliant is, perhaps, unparalleled in the genre." Libr J

Bear, Elizabeth

Blood and iron. ROC 2006 432p pa $7.99

ISBN 978-0-451-46092-9; 0-451-46092-8

LC 2005-33954

"Ancient grudges and ruthless schemes are simply business as usual to the Faerie court in Bear's complex and involving contemporary fantasy. Seeker, formerly Elaine Andraste, is a changeling bound to the Mebd, the queen of the Daoine Sidhe, to find other changelings and bring them to the Faerie court. There, like legendary Tam Lin, and Seeker's own son, Ian, they entertain the queen until she tires of them. Now the queen needs Seeker to find—and win the heart of—the new Merlin, latest incarnation of a being who, in the hands of the Task—or Promethean—advances. Long-forgotten rivalries and unsuspected blood ties arise to tug at Seeker's loyalties, even as the queen promises to free Ian when she succeeds." Publ Wkly

Bear, Elizabeth

Chill. Spectra/Ballantine Books 2010 310p pa $7.99

ISBN 978-0-553-59108-8

Sequel to: Dust (2008)

"Bear enhances the usual generation ship themes—social amnesia, decaying infrastructure, and mission-threatening grand calamities—with enough new flourishes, including a biotechnology-based class system and cruel experiments based on misapprehensions of Darwin, to keep readers happily engaged." Publ Wkly

Bear, Elizabeth

Ink and steel; a novel of the Promethean Age. Roc 2008 427p pa $14

ISBN 978-0-451-46209-1

LC 2008-746

"Bear reveals the secret war between fae and the Elizabethan court in this dramatic prequel to Blood and Iron and Whiskey and Water. Framed with the intrigues of queens and courtiers, the story focuses on the mutual respect and growing love of Kit Marley (aka Christopher Marlowe) and Will Shakespeare. As Morgan le Fey rescues Kit from assassins, various factions recruit Will to bolster their political machinations with the magic of poetry. Kit pulls Will into Faerie and both are forced to face their own deepest desires and fears, which cannot be resolved until they deal with a power even higher than mortal Queen Elizabeth or fae Queen Mab. Copious quotes and intelligent speculation about their lives and works mark this sensitive and sensual look at the two supreme playwrights of the English Renaissance." Publ Wkly

Bear, Elizabeth

Range of ghosts; Elizabeth Bear. Tor 2012 334p.

ISBN 9780765327543

LC 2011025171

In this fantasy book, "Temur, grandson of the Great Khan, is walking away from a battlefield where he was left for dead. All around lie the fallen armies of his cousin and his brother, who made war to rule the Khaganate. Temur is now the legitimate heir by blood to his grandfather's throne. . . . Once-Princess Samarkar is climbing the thousand steps of the Citadel of the Wizards of Tsarepheth. She was heir to the Rasan Empire until her father got a son on a new wife. . . . These two will come together to stand against the hidden cult that has so carefully brought all the empires of the Celadon Highway to strife and civil war through guile and deceit and sorcerous power." (Publisher's note)

Bear, Elizabeth

Shattered pillars; Elizabeth Bear. Tor Books 2013 336 p. (Eternal sky) (hardcover) $26.99

ISBN 0765327554; 9780765327550; 9781429947770

LC 2012038826

This is Elizabeth Bear's second installment in her Mongolia-inspired fantasy epic series. "The necromancer priest al-Sepehr is bringing war to the world, placing his allies and minions throughout the nations to see them crumble. But beyond his control are Edene, who has stolen the green ring that makes her ruler of the ancient and treacherous realm of Erem; bold imperial scion Temur;" and his companions Samarkar, Hrahima, and Hsiung. (Publishers Weekly)

Bear, Greg

★ Anvil of stars. Warner Bks. 1992 434p

ISBN 0-446-51601-5

LC 91-50411

Sequel to The forge of God

"Bear is superlatively competent in the English language and a master of both technical wizardry and powerful scenes. Throughout the book, he addresses the question of an ethical basis for genocide, leaving the matter sufficiently open to make one wonder whether the story is yet completed." Booklist

Bear, Greg

The collected stories of Greg Bear. TOR Bks. 2002 653p hardcover o.p. pa $17.95

ISBN 0-7653-0160-1; 0-7653-0161-X pa

LC 2002-20466

In addition to Blood music (1985), a novelette where a genetic engineer injects himself with experimental intelligent microorganisms with disasterous results, this "volume subsumes Bear's earlier collections, The wind from a burning woman (1983) and Tangents (1989), while also including more recent work." Anatomy of Wonder 5

Bear, Greg

✓ ★ The **forge** of God. TOR Bks. 1987 474p

ISBN 0-312-93021-6

LC 87-50482

"Three geologists discover an alien artifact in Death Valley and set off a chain of events leading to the discovery that Earth is about to be invaded by two alien races. One race sends out planet-wrecking machines; . . . the other is trying to enlist the survivors of humanity in tracking down and destroying the planet wreckers. The battle over Earth is seen through the eyes of a large cast of well-drawn characters, crowned by a climax of enormous power." Booklist

Followed by Anvil of stars

Beard, Jo Ann

In Zanesville. Little, Brown and Co. 2011 289 p. $23.99

ISBN 978-0-316-08447-5; 0-316-08447-6

LC 2010041808

Alex Award (2012)

The events of the novel take place in the 1970s. In Zanesville is "titled after the Illinois township where the story is set. . . . [The book opens] inside the house of the six children whom the narrator and her best friend, Felicia, babysit all summer." (Bookforum)

This novel is "set in an Illinois factory town in the 1970s. The coming-of-age material is familiar: the panic that accompanies the first sight of a tampon; the drowsy-making thrill of a boy's hand creeping up your back; the impotent worry over a broken parent. And yet somehow Beard makes the daily rituals and discoveries of her nameless 14-year-old narrator and her best friend Felicia ('Flea') epic and profound. These thoughtful, funny, awestruck, slightly peculiar girls are so endearing, so painfully true, that they almost make a reader wish she were back in high school so she could be friends with them." Entertainment Wkly

Beard, Richard

✓ **Lazarus** is dead. Harvill Secker 2011 265 p. $16

ISBN 1609450809; 184655506X; 9781609450809; 9781846555060

In "this alternative theological novel," Richard Beard suggests that "Jesus and Lazarus grew up as best friends and then drifted apart." Here, Lazarus comes down "with a strange and mysterious illness . . . . Beard invests this illness with a mythic quality by having Lazarus contract all of the seven major diseases of ancient Israel." He refuses to summon Jesus to save him, "so Lazarus does in fact die, and Jesus does resurrect him, but the Romans . . . immediately begin to persecute Lazarus." (Kirkus)

Beaton, Kate

✓ **Hark!** A vagrant. Drawn and Quarterly 2011 168p il

ISBN 1770460608; 9781770460607

LC 2011505458

The book offers a collection of comic strips by author Kate Beaton, "a series of short gag cartoons, primarily about history and literature, with a particularly Canadian bent. . . . Comics about long-suffering heroines like Jane Eyre, Laura Secord, and 'Every Lady Scientist in History Who Ever Did Anything Until Now' highlight the absurdities of gender disparity. . . . A number of these comics are driven simply by absurdity itself: a kingdom whose royal mascot is a fat pony; a sexy Batman; and teens who solve crimes in a real-life fashion: by hiding behind the school, smoking weed, and lying about it later." (Quill & Quire)

Includes index.

Beaton, M. C.

✓ ★ **Death** of a hussy. St. Martin's Press 1990 164p

ISBN 0-312-05071-2

LC 90-36883

"Maggie is a devil, all right, but splendid fun as a character. And the mischief she makes in Lochdubh is resolved by Hamish in an easygoing Highland fashion that is no less canny for being so droll." N Y Times Book Rev

Beaton, M. C.

✓ **Death** of a macho man. Mysterious Press 1996 216p

ISBN 0-89296-531-2

LC 96-7268

"Scottish constable Hamish MacBeth, finding his reputation on the line, agrees to a public fight with a tattooed stranger who claims to be a professional wrestler. When someone prevents the match by murdering the stranger, suspicion falls on Hamish, who then investigates." Libr J

"Befuddled, earnest and utterly endearing, Hamish makes his triumphs sweetly satisfying." Publ Wkly

Beaton, M. C.

Death of a Valentine. Grand Central Pub. 2010 246p $23.99

ISBN 978-0-4465-4738-3; 0446547387

LC 2009-06083

"The Highlands' most famous bachelor has a narrow escape in Beaton's amusing update on the irresistible Hamish and his coterie of friends and ex-loves." Kirkus

Beaton, M. C.

✓ **Love,** lies, and liquor; an Agatha Raisin mystery. St. Martin's Minotaur 2006 231p $22.95

ISBN 0-312-34910-6

LC 2006-43407

Agatha Raisin's "ex-husband, James, from whom she has never fully recovered, has given Agatha reason to believe he may want to reconcile. He invites her to join him at the beloved scene of his childhood summer vacations, Snoth-on-Sea. The resort is rundown, the food miserable, and the guests obnoxious. Agatha's shouting match in the dining room with a boorish, insulting woman comes back to haunt her when the woman is found strangled to death, Agatha's scarf around her pudgy neck. Agatha must investigate to clear herself. More murder follows. Another highly satisfying Beaton cozy, this one is long on the kind of social comedy that uses character, plot, and atmosphere to produce the laughter." Booklist

Beattie, Ann
★ **Chilly** scenes of winter. Doubleday 1976 280p
ISBN 0-385-11658-6

"Beattie has an instinct for the grotesque that verges on the edge of real wit and pain. She is obviously a first-rate craftswoman with an eye for idiosyncratic detail." Saturday Rev

Beattie, Ann
Follies; new stories. Scribner 2005 305p $25
ISBN 0-743-26961-6
LC 2004-65087

"The tales in this volume showcase a newly flexible voice that accommodates both the author's patented gift for social observation and her more recent interest in her characters' inner lives, a voice that allows her to move fluently back and forth in time, back and forth from memory to rumination." N Y Times (Late N Y Ed)

Beattie, Ann
My life, starring Dara Falcon. Knopf 1997 307p
ISBN 0-679-45502-7
LC 96-36679

"Dara is a fascinating character, and though she finally gets on the reader's nerves, Beattie has crafted a fine study of obsessive relationships with her usual aplomb." Libr J

Beattie, Ann
The **New** Yorker stories. Scribner 2010 514p $30
ISBN 978-1-4391-6874-5; 1-4391-6874-1
LC 2010-32933

The book presents a compilation of short stories by author Ann Beattie which she has published in the "New Yorker" magazine since the 1970s. "In 'The Burning House,' . . . [a] man destroys the delicate ecosystem that exists among himself, his exwife, their young daughter and his lover (his gay lover—this is all the way back in 1979) by taking a job in San Francisco. . . . By the early 1980s—the pieces later included, for the most part, in her fourth collection, 'Where You'll Find Me'—Beattie's work has changed again. Now the stories are almost all quite brief, six pages or less. . . . 'The New Yorker Stories''s final pieces, which represent Beattie's work since the early '90s, reflect . . . a mellowing. . . . The characters have aging parents, or are ones." (Nation)

"Beattie made her mark as an audaciously understated yet resoundingly on-the-mark writer in the 1970s in the New Yorker, and it is testimony both to her unceasing artistic growth and the magazine's unshakable commitment to exceptional short stories that the final works in this grand retrospective collection are as provocative as the first. Forty-eight Beattie stories appeared in the New Yorker between 1974 and 2006, and until now nearly half remained uncollected. This scintillating volume showcases Beattie's stunning insights into the eternal isolation of individuals and each decade's signature longings and conflicts." Booklist

Beattie, Ann
★ **Picturing** Will. Random House 1989 230p
ISBN 0-394-56987-3
LC 89-42781

Beattie "has almost as many narrative voices as characters in this book, yet the result is never confusing. . . . 'Picturing Will' would be admirable for its technique alone; what makes it Beattie's best novel is her new and fearless way with emotional complexity." Newsweek

Beattie, Ann
Walks with men. Scribner 2010 102p $17; pa $10
ISBN 978-1-4391-7576-7; 1-4391-7576-4; 978-1-4391-6869-1 pa; 1-4391-6869-5 pa
LC 2009-52240

"With its taut telling of a frequently inexplicable and ill-advised romance, and its abrupt, mysterious conclusion, [this work] shares qualities with some of Beattie's iconic short stories. . . . Yet this novella is a deceptively complex work, one that touches on the intricate strangenesses of friendship and marriage, and of life in that indulgent period. . . . Beattie has a brilliant ear for the elliptical way people speak, especially when they are failing to read each other." San Francisco Chron

Beatty, Paul
Slumberland; a novel. Bloomsbury 2008 256p
ISBN 978-1-59691-240-3; 1-59691-240-5
LC 2007-45049

"The protagonist of the novel, DJ Darky, is a Los Angeles DJ who comes to Berlin to be a jukebox sommelier. He is in search of a virtuoso saxophonist, Charles Stone nicknamed the Shuwa who is in many ways his doppelgänger. DJ Darky has created a sonic masterpiece, layering nearly every sound he can find into a flawless testament, a musical ars poetica. Now, despite offers from the gangsta rap community, he wants the Shuwa to play some avant-garde mystical voodoo music over the beat. DJ Darky arrives in Germany, having already declared the end of blackness, to find himself once more the subject of racism amid constant reminders of his obsolete ethnicity. His real quest, we soon learn, is for meaning and a place in the increasingly chaotic post-Cold War world. 'Slumberland' is laugh-out-loud funny in many places, and its wit and satire can be burning, regardless of where they are pointed: blackness or whiteness." Los Angeles Times Book Rev

Beauvoir, Simone de
★ The **mandarins**; a novel. World Pub. 1956 610p
Original French edition, 1954

This "semiautobiographical novel addressed the attempts of post-World War II leftist intellectuals to abandon their elite, 'mandarin' status and to engage in political activism. The characters of psychologist Anne Dubreuilh and her husband Robert were roughly based on de Beauvoir and her lifelong associate Jean-Paul Sartre; de Beauvoir's account of Anne's affair with the American Lewis Brogan was a thinly veiled account of her own relationship with novelist Nelson Algren." Merriam-Webster's Ency of Lit

Beckett, Samuel

✓ ★ **Molloy**, Malone dies, The unnamable; with an introduction by Gabriel Josipovici. Knopf 1997 xliii, 476p $22

ISBN 0-375-40070-2

LC 98-119494

A reissue of the title first published 1959 by Grove Press; Original French editions of Molloy and Malone dies published 1951; The unnamable, 1953. These translations published separately 1955, 1956 and 1958, respectively

The trilogy "is concerned with the search for identity, for the true self which can rest from self-caricature; and as a parallel it is concerned with the true silence which is the end of speech. Molloy, Malone and their final unnamable incarnation are paradigms of humanity in general and of the artist in particular. . . . The trilogy seen as a whole composes one of the most remarkable, most original and most haunting prose-works of the century." Times Lit Suppl

Beckett, Samuel

✓ ★ **Murphy**. Grove Press 1957 282p

First published 1938 in the United Kingdom

"The story concerns an Irishman in London who yearns to do nothing more than sit in his rocking chair and daydream. Murphy attempts to avoid all action; he escapes from a girl he is about to marry, takes up with a kind prostitute, and finds a job as a nurse in a mental institution, where he plays nonconfrontational chess. His disengagement from the world is shattered when his fiancée, with a detective and two new lovers in tow, discovers him. He is killed when someone accidentally turns on the gas in his apartment." Merriam-Webster's Ency of Lit

Begley, Louis

✓ **About** Schmidt; Louis Begley. 1st ed. Alfred Knopf; Distributed by Random House 1996 273p $23

ISBN 0679450335; 9780679450337

LC 96008244

This book tells the story of Schmidt, a "retired lawyer whose lucrative practice was notable for its meticulousness but is now all but anarchistic, . . . [who] misses his late wife and is uneasy alone in their stately Long Island mansion. His sense of isolation is compounded by his estrangement from his only child, Charlotte, whom he uncharitably thinks of as a 'smug, overworked yuppie,' and by his displeasure over her impending marriage to a lawyer he claims not to like because he's a dull-witted workaholic, when, in fact, it's his Jewishness Schmidt can't abide." (Booklist)

Belanger, Andy

✓ **Kill** Shakespeare; the blast of war/ Volume 2. created and written by Conor McCreery and Anthony Del Col; art by Andy Belanger; colors by Ian Herring l; lettering by Chris Mowry, Neil Uyetake, and Shawn Lee; original series edits by Tom Waltz. IDW 2011 148 p.

ISBN 1613770251; 9781613770252

This book, the second volume of the comic book series, presents a "sweeping fantasy of magic, war, betrayal, and love [which] is set in a world where Shakespeare's characters dwell and Shakespeare himself is an absent god struggling with a heavy conscience. The second volume builds to the climactic finale of Hamlet's quest to find the creatorgod Shakespeare and return peace to a land torn apart by an evil army led by Richard III and Lady Macbeth. Joined by love interest Juliet, the warrior Othello, the wise fool Falstaff, and the spy Iago, Hamlet has built an army of rebels, the prodigals, who hold off their enemies while he searches for their creator. But even victory comes at a cost as friends and foes die in a great final battle." (Publishers Wkly)

Belcher, R. S.

The **six**-gun tarot; R. S. Belcher. Tor Books 2013 364 p. (hardcover) $25.99

ISBN 0765329328; 9780765329325; 9781429946988

LC 2012026479

In this debut novel from R.S. Belcher, when "young Jim Negrey and his long-suffering horse find sanctuary in the cattle town of Galgotha, NV, Jim notices that the sheriff bears the marks of a noose round his neck; his deputy calls the coyotes his kin, and a nameless evil inhabits the nearby silver mine." (Library Journal)

Belfer, Lauren

A **fierce** radiance; a novel. Harper 2010 400p $25.99

ISBN 978-0-06-125251-8; 0-06-125251-4

LC 2009-40116

"Belfer fuses fiction and history cleverly and seamlessly. . . . A Fierce Radiance resonates precisely because the characters Belfer creates, and the ones she borrows from history, feel real — as organic and natural as the molds from which these miracle drugs come." USA Today

Bell, Albert A.

✓ The **blood** of Caesar; a second case from the notebooks of Pliny the younger. Ingalls Pub. Group 2008 pa $15.95

ISBN 978-1-932158-82-3; 1-932158-82-0

LC 2007-51907

"When the body of a mason is found in the library of current Princeps (first citizen) Domitian, Pliny the Younger is asked by his mother to find the killer. At the same time, Domitian orders Pliny and his friend Tacitus to find out if there is a real heir to the throne. . . . Readers will delight in the duo's tracing of Caesar's blood line; walking with Pliny through his daily routine is entertaining, too. Outstandingly researched and laden with suspense." Libr J

Bell, Alden

✓ The **reapers** are the angels; a novel. Alden Bell. Henry Holt and Company 2010 225 p. pa $15

ISBN 9780805092431; 0805092439

LC 2009048158

Alex Award (2011)

This book follows "15-year-old Temple," who was "[b]orn into a crumbling society plagued by zombies. . . . When she is assaulted at a safe house, she murders her human attacker, Abraham Todd, and runs from his vengeful brother,

Moses. Temple soon acquires a traveling partner, a slow mute by the name of Maury, and begrudgingly takes responsibility for his care, remembering a young boy she swore to protect but couldn't save. Fleeing Moses, the 'meatskins,' and her own battered conscience, Temple still finds moments of simple joy in the brutal world." (Publishers Weekly)

Bell, Christine

The **Perez** family. Norton 1990 256p

ISBN 0-393-02798-8

LC 89-25569

"Christine Bell is much more than a lighthearted comic novelist. She's one of those writers like Flannery O'Connor or Isak Dinesen: she doesn't so much write stories as spin tales. . . . What may have seemed cartoonish in the middle of the book, you now realize, was mythic, archetypal. What you have been reading turns out to be a profound little parable about the redemptive power of love." N Y Times Book Rev

Bell, Madison Smartt

All souls' rising. Pantheon Bks. 1995 530p

ISBN 0-679-43989-7

LC 95-12339

"Set during the struggle for Haiti's independence in the late 1700s, this intensely imagined epic novel of racial hatred and bloody upheaval illuminates the enmities among the astonishingly complex ethnic populations of the Caribbean island. Bell evokes a society caught in the crucible of violence with superb characterizations, ranging from the arrogant grand blanc plantation owners to the black slaves—including Toussaint L'Ouverture, the leader of the black revolt." Publ Wkly

Bell, Madison Smartt

The **color** of night. Vintage Books 2011 208p $15

ISBN 978-0-307-74188-2; 0-307-74188-5

LC 2010-19104

"As Bell maps Mae's trajectory of mayhem and death in this brilliantly ferocious novel of abuse and survival, this sinister fable of blood lust and madness, he grapples with timeless equations of predator and prey, the sublime and the demonic, the dark ecstasy of destruction and the hell wrought by catastrophic delusion." Kansas City Star

Bell, Madison Smartt

Ten Indians. Pantheon Bks. 1996 264p

ISBN 0-679-44246-4

LC 96-14357

The novel, "told partly from Devlin's viewpoint and partly, in convincing street language, from that of the drug dealers and their women, is spare and cinematic. Devlin, far out on a lonely voyage, saves his honor. Saves his daughter too. But it is the neighborhood that wins. Good ending, good novel." Time

Belle, Jennifer

The **seven** year bitch. Riverhead Books 2010 320p $25.95

ISBN 978-1-59448-755-2; 1-59448-755-7

LC 2010-00147

"The heroines of Jennifer Belle's wry comic novels often feel like a cockeyed cross between Cosmo girl and Woody Allen muse, and her latest, native Manhattanite Isolde Brilliant, is no different. That Isolde's also a laid-off hedge fund manager with a troubled marriage, an infant, and a 40th birthday looming makes The Seven Year Bitch sound heavy; it's not. She flirts with infidelity and navigates satiric set-pieces (fertility-challenged nannies, bad playdate mommies) like a Baby Björn-toting Alice in a kook-infested urban Wonderland. It doesn't add up to much, but it's a fun ride." Entertainment Wkly

Bellow, Saul, 1915-2005

★ The **adventures** of Augie March; with an introduction by Martin Amis. Knopf 1995 xxxvii, 616p

ISBN 0-679-44460-2

A reissue of the title first published 1953 by Viking

"It is a picaresque story of a poor Jewish youth from Chicago, his progress, sometimes highly comic, through the world of the 20th century, and his attempts to make sense of it." Merriam-Webster's Ency of Lit

Bellow, Saul

The **Bellarosa** connection. Penguin Bks. 1989 102p

ISBN 0-14-012686-4

LC 89-32936

"The end of 'The Bellarosa Connection' is abrupt, matter-of-fact, almost offbeat. It is a conclusion, perhaps, in which nothing is concluded, . . . but it is appropriate to the overall pitch and voice of this cannily resourceful entertainment." N Y Times Book Rev

Bellow, Saul

Dangling man. Vanguard Press 1944 191p

This story purports to be the journal of a young man living in Chicago, who gives up his job, expecting to be inducted into the army. Owing to technicalities Joseph is left dangling for almost a year. His journal explains his psychological reactions to idleness, how he passes his time, his growing unrest, and finally the relief when the call comes

"The book is an excellent document on the experience of the non-combatant in time of war. It is well written and never dull—in spite of the dismalness of the Chicago background and the undramatic character of the subject. It is also one of the most honest pieces of testimony on the psychology of a whole generation who have grown up during the depression and the war." New Yorker

Bellow, Saul

★ **Henderson** the rain king; a novel. Viking 1959 341p

This novel, "designed on a grand and mythic scale, records American millionaire Gene Henderson's quest for revelation and spiritual power in Africa, where he becomes rainmaker and heir to a kingdom." Oxford Companion to Engl Lit

Bellow, Saul, 1915-2005

Herzog. Viking 1964 341p

"Beleaguered by the intensity of his introspection, Herzog worries over his life: an intellectual stumped in the middle of his second book—tellingly, an inquiry into Romanticism—a husband brooding over his second failed marriage, and above all a man trying to think his way into clarity, all the while wryly aware that he is the creator of his own paralysis. The epitome of this condition is the spate of letters that Herzog writes—to the living and the dead, to the famous and to his own circle of friends and enemies—but never sends. The letters document Herzog's detailed, vivid, and anxious apprehensions of contemporary American life in Chicago, in New York, and in the more pastoral setting of his retreat in the Berkshires. They also serve as a wonderfully colloquial venue for his irreverent, chatty, but also profound reflections on the fate of the individual in modern society." Benet's Reader's Ency of Am Lit

Bellow, Saul

★ **Humboldt's** gift. Viking 1975 487p
ISBN 0-670-38655-3

"The story of Charlie Citrine, a successful writer and academic plagued by women, lawsuits, and mafiosi, whose present career is interwoven with memories of the early success, failing powers, and squalid death of his friend Von Humboldt Fleischer, whose poetic destiny he fears he may inherit, together with his manuscripts." Oxford Companion to Engl Lit

Bellow, Saul

Mr. Sammler's planet. Viking 1970 313p
ISBN 0-670-33319-0

"Artur Sammler, in his seventies and an escapee from the horrors of Nazi atrocities and the memory of having had to dig himself out of his own grave, theorizes about the possibility of finding a similar escape from the assaults of life in New York City, its muggings, crime, dirt, noise. Living with his bizarre daughter, Shula, also saved from death in Europe but somewhat deranged, perhaps the result of traumas suffered, is not possible, and living with his niece Margotte also has its drawbacks. The most important person to Sammler is his nephew Elya, by whose generosity Sammler and Shula are able to exist. But Elya's escape from the horrors of his own life—his son Wallace's irresponsible behavior and his daughter Angela's sexually promiscuous behavior—is by way of death. For our desire to find relief from the outrages of life in this decade, Bellow has made a metaphor of man's desire to go to the moon." Shapiro. Fic for Youth. 3d edition

Bellow, Saul

Novels, 1944-1953. Library of America 2003 1029p $35
ISBN 1-931082-38-3

LC 2003-40144

Dangling man and The adventures of Augie March are entered separately. The victim (1947) tells the story of Asa Leventhal, who once held a position on a New York trade journal, and had won a certain security, but a few sultry weeks while his wife was away almost wrecked him. The remembrance of his insane mother, and the constant harrying of a Gentile friend, who insisted that Asa had ruined his career, brings him to the verge of insanity.

Bellow, Saul

Novels, 1956-1964. Library of America 2007 794p $35
ISBN 978-1-59853-002-5; 1-59853-002-X

LC 2006-46687

Contents: Seize the day; Henderson the rain king; Herzog, each entered separately

Bellow, Saul

Novels, 1970-1982. Library of America 2010 1064p $40
ISBN 978-1-59853-079-7; 1-59853-0798

LC 2010-924272

"In Mr. Sammler's Planet, the anarchic forces of late-1960s America are set loose on Artur Sammler. . . . A Holocaust survivor living out his latter days in Manhattan, Sammler endures the city's everyday barbarism, as shocking as it is casual, and must contend with absurd complications when a manuscript goes missing. . . . Humboldt's Gift depicts the deep and troubled friendship between the tormented poet Von Humboldt Fleisher and the renowned writer Charlie Citrine. . . . In The dean's December, Albert Corde experiences totalitarianism firsthand when he travels to Bucharest to visit his dying mother-in-law. As a college dean in Chicago he has attracted controversy through his journalism and his role in a racially charged murder trial. Alternating between Romanian and American settings, the novel is . . . [an] indictment of official hypocrisy and corruption on both sides of the Iron Curtain." Publisher's note

Bellow, Saul

Seize the day; with three short stories and a one-act play. Viking 1956 211p

"Seize the Day gives contemporary literature a story which will be explained, expounded, and argued, but about which a final reckoning can be made only after it ripples out in the imagination of the generations of readers to come. I suspect that it is one of the central stories of our day." Nation

Belzer, Richard

I am not a cop! Richard Belzer with Michael Black. Simon & Schuster 2008 260p $24
ISBN 978-1-4165-7066-0; 1-4165-7066-7

LC 2008-9534

A murder mystery that features an actor named Richard Belzer who plays John Munch, a TV detective. "When an old friend of Belzer's, New York City assistant medical examiner Rudy Markovich, disappears under suspicious circumstances, Belzer decides to investigate. After the actor finds a clue referring to four recent deaths, he and Kalisha Carter, the attractive woman his producer assigns to keep an eye on him, dig into those cases." Publ Wkly

"Deft comic timing, the gruff persona, and a lively, if predictable, story will satisfy fans." Libr J

Benaron, Naomi

★ **Running** the rift; Naomi Benaron. Algonquin Books of Chapel Hill 2012 365p.
ISBN 9781616200428; 1616200421

LC 2011026349

Bellwether Prize for Fiction (2010)

This book, the winner of the 2010 Bellwether Prize, tells the story of "Jean Patrick Nkuba, a gifted Rwandan boy. . . . Born a Tutsi, he is thrust into a world where it's impossible to stay apolitical—where the man who used to sell you gifts for your family now spews hatred . . . where your Hutu coach is secretly training the very soldiers who will hunt down your family. Yet in an environment increasingly restrictive for the Tutsi, he holds fast to his dream of becoming Rwanda's first Olympic medal contender in track, a feat he believes might deliver him and his people from this violence. When the killing begins, Jean Patrick is forced to flee, leaving behind the woman, the family, and the country he loves. Finding them again is the race of his life." (Publisher's note)

Includes bibliographical references

Benchley, Peter

Jaws. Random House 2005 311p $15.95
ISBN 1-4000-6456-2

LC 2005-46451

First published 1974

This is a "story about what happens when a great white shark terrorizes a small Long Island town. . . . A woman swimmer is devoured by the shark, and Police Chief Martin Brody insists on closing the beaches. But he's overruled by the town fathers who remind him that the community is dependent on summer visitors for economic survival. Two deaths later, the news can no longer be suppressed and Brody, an oceanographer and a fisherman go after the monster in an exciting chase." Publ Wkly

Bender, Aimee

The **particular** sadness of lemon cake; a novel Aimee Bender. 1st ed. Doubleday 2010 292 p. $25.95
ISBN 0385501129; 9780385501125

LC 2009032541

Alex Award (2011)

This book follows "young, needy Rose Edelstein, who can literally taste the emotions of whoever prepares her food, giving her unwanted insight into other people's secret emotional lives--including her mother's, whose lemon cake betrays a deep dissatisfaction." (Publishers Weekly)

"When her mother begins an affair, Rose can taste that, too. Her brilliant older brother, Joseph, seems to have some type of autism spectrum disorder, though it is never named. Rose grows up and manages what she now considers her food skill, discerning not only the city of production but also the personality and temperament of the growers and pickers. She also draws closer to her father, finally understanding his prepossessions." (Library Journal)

"Nine-year-old Rose Edelstein bids adieu to normality after taking a bite of her mother's lemon cake. Immediately, she is overwhelmed by the emptiness of her mother's life. All food has this effect on her. She can taste emotions, particularly those that are hidden or repressed. . . . While the time period is never specified—the book appears to open in the 1970s—the setting is forever-sunny Los Angeles. Until the emergence of her super sense, Rose had been the unexceptional child of a supposedly unexceptional nuclear family. As we follow her into maturity, however, she discovers she has more in common with her father and her brother Joseph than previously thought. Each of them possesses a special ability as well." Miami Herald

Benet, Stephen Vincent, 1898-1943

The **Devil** and Daniel Webster; illustrated by Harold Denison. Farrar & Rinehart 1937 61 p. ill.
ISBN 9780848807894; 9780895987020

"Jabez Stone, a New Hampshire farmer, receives a decade of material wealth in return for selling his soul to the Devil—Mr. Scratch. When the Devil comes to claim Stone's soul, the farmer has the statesman and orator Daniel Webster argue his case at midnight before a jury of historic American villains." Merriam-Webster's Ency of Lit

Benford, Gregory

Foundation's fear. HarperPrism 1997 425p (Second Foundation trilogy)
ISBN 0-06-105243-4

LC 96-45296

"Mr. Benford picks up the story as Seldon is about to become First Minister to Emperor Cleon I, who rules the 25 million inhabited planets of the galaxy from the imperial capital of Trantor. I have no idea whether anyone unfamiliar with the original Foundation series—which spells out what happened to Seldon and his predictions—will be able to make sense of 'Foundation's Fear.' But for the legions of readers who have long been tantalized by Asimov's cryptic references to psychohistory, Mr. Benford provides some fascinating insights into its development." N Y Times Book Rev

Followed by Foundation and chaos, by Greg Bear

Benford, Gregory

★ **Timescape**. Simon & Schuster 1980 412p
ISBN 0-671-25327-1

"As the world lurches toward disaster, scientists in 1998 try to transmit a warning message to 1962 by means of tachyons. Their story is told in parallel with that of the scientists trying to decode the transmission, and the two plots converge on the possibility of paradox. Unusual for the realism of its depiction of scientists at work; admirably serious in handling the implications of its theme." Anatomy of Wonder 4

Benioff, David

City of thieves; a novel. Viking 2008 258p $24.95
ISBN 978-0-670-01870-3; 0-670-01870-8

LC 2007-42784

In this novel, a writer depicts his grandfather's experiences during the siege of Leningrad. "Having elected to stay in Leningrad during the siege, 17-year-old Lev Beniov is caught looting a German paratrooper's corpse. The penalty for this infraction (and many others) is execution. But when Colonel Grechko confronts Lev and Kolya, a Russian army deserter also facing execution, he spares them on the condition that they acquire a dozen eggs for the colonel's daughter's wedding cake. Their mission exposes them to the most ghoulish acts of the starved populace and takes them behind enemy lines to the Russian countryside. There, Lev and Kolya take on an even more daring objective: to kill the commander of the local occupying German forces." Publ Wkly

Benjamin, Melanie

✓ **Alice** I have been. Delacorte Press 2010 351p il $25

    ISBN 978-0-385-34413-5; 0-385-34413-9

                      LC 2009-35353

A "fictionalized autobiography of Alice Liddell Hargreaves, the real-life inspiration for one of the most beloved characters in children's literature. . . . When we first meet 7-year-old Alice Liddell circa 1859, in the novel's first and best section, she is just a charmingly ordinary little girl: the sprightly, strong-willed fourth child of an Oxford dean who befriends a stuttering math tutor named Charles Dodgson (the Carroll pen name came later). Through their unlikely companionship, Alice finds relief from the often stultifying confines of Victorian girlhood, quickly becoming a favorite subject for both his amateur photography and the tall tales he concocts to entertain her and her sisters. . . . By the time *Alice I Have Been* leaps forward to Alice's early 20s and her star-crossed affair with a sickly young prince, however, the consequences of a lurid, long-ago incident between the author and his young muse have cast an enduring pall over both their lives." Entertainment Wkly

Benjamin, Melanie

✓ The **autobiography** of Mrs. Tom Thumb; a novel. Delacorte Press 2011 424p $25

    ISBN 978-0-385-34415-9

                      LC 2010-52863

"Vinnie's first-person narration grabs you from the opening pages, providing hints of the absorbing and entertaining story to come. The novel is also a delightful cavalcade of late 19th-century Americana, as you travel with Vinnie up and down the Mississippi, head westward via the expanding railroad, and hobnob with New York's rich and famous." Libr J

    Includes bibliographical references

Benjamin, Melanie

    ★ The **aviator's** wife; a novel. Melanie Benjamin. 1st ed. Delacorte Press 2013 416 p. (hardcover) $26.00; (ebook) $26

    ISBN 0345528670; 9780345528674; 9780345534699

                      LC 2012017014

This biographical novel, by Melanie Benjamin, follows Anne Morrow, wife of aviator Charles Lindbergh. "Anne Morrow, the shy daughter of [a] U.S. ambassador, . . . meets Colonel Charles Lindbergh, fresh off his celebrated 1927 solo flight across the Atlantic. . . . The two marry in a headline-making wedding. Hounded by adoring crowds and . . . an insatiable press, Charles shields himself and his new bride from prying eyes, leaving Anne to feel her life falling back into the shadows." (Publisher's note)

Benn, James R.

✓ **Billy** Boyle; a World War II mystery. Soho Press 2006 284p $23

    ISBN 1-569474-33-8

                      LC 2006-42300

"Benn provides historically accurate background and appealing characters, spices the narrative with romance and emotion, and ruminates about the consequences of actions, all in a suitably straightforward prose style. A solid addition to mystery collections." Libr J

Benn, James R.

✓ The **first** wave; a Billy Boyle World War II mystery. Soho Press 2007 294p $24

    ISBN 978-1-56947-471-6; 1-56947-471-0

                      LC 2007-5314

"Take a young Irish cop. Turn him into a lieutenant on Eisenhower's personal staff—one charged with being 'Ike's investigator.' Set him ashore on the coast of French North Africa along with the first wave of invading American troops. And watch the mayhem, mystery, and murder that are bound to follow. Corrupt Vichy French officers steal a shipment of American penicillin, killing a supply sergeant in the process. Benn . . . delivers a cross-genre tale that is at once spy story, soldier story, and hard-Boyled detective. Bullets, babes, and bombs give Billy Boyle a bad time before he solves the case, but you'll have a good time reading about it." Libr J

Benn, James R.

    A **mortal** terror; a Billy Boyle World War II mystery. Soho Crime 2011 345p $25

    ISBN 978-1-56947-994-0

                      LC 2011-18081

"War has taken its toll on First Lt. Billy Boyle, and he's not alone in his misery. It's January 1944, and he's trying to figure out why he has been dispatched to Naples in his sixth outing. . . . Billy, a police detective back home, works for his Uncle Ike (yes, that Ike) as a military private investigator. Simply put, the general trusts Billy because he's family. In this captivating episode, a serial killer from the inside (dubbed the Red Heart Killer because he leaves playing cards on his victims) is targeting Allied officers, moving systematically up the ranks, and it's getting pretty tense in the officers' quarters. Billy is under the gun to find the madman before he runs out of cards. . . . Benn does a superb job of simultaneously capturing the personal anguish of war and creating a splendid adventure novel." Libr J

Bennett, Alan, 1934-

✓ **Smut**; stories. Alan Bennett. 1st U.S. ed. Picador 2012 152 p. (paperback) $14.00; (downloadable audio) $29.95

    ISBN 1250003164; 9781250003164; 9780792785217 unabridged

                      LC 2011035090

Author Alan Bennett's "book consists of two stories, 'The Greening of Mrs. Donaldson' and 'The Shielding of Mrs. Forbes.' In the first, widowed, cash-strapped 55-year-old Mrs. Donaldson rents out a bedroom in her home to a young couple . . . [and takes] a job at the hospital. . . . In Bennett's next tale, Betty is smitten with [her gay] fiancé Graham Forbes. . . . But Graham, who'd married for money, in time startles himself by actually liking Betty. . . . Eventually, Graham's secret comes out--as do others, [and] the Betty/Graham union continues." (Kirkus Reviews)

Bennett, Robert Jackson

✓ **American** elsewhere; Robert Jackson Bennett. Orbit 2012 688 p. $13.99

    ISBN 0316200204; 9780316200202

                      LC 2012016166

In this book by Robert Jackson Bennett, "Mona Bright, a former cop with a tragic past, inherits her long-dead mother's house in Wink, N. Mex., a picture-perfect hamlet built as a support community for a government lab conducting experiments in quantum physics. As Mona pieces together a history that bears no resemblance to the childhood she remembers, Bennett's . . . narrative unveils a chronicle of dysfunction masked by Wink's mechanical obsession with normalcy." (Publishers Weekly)

Bennett, Robert Jackson
The **company** man; Robert Jackson Bennett. 1st ed.; Orbit 2010 466p.
ISBN 9780316054706 pa; 0316054704
LC 2010011247
This book, "an alternate history novel," is set in a reality where "by 1919 . . . 50 years of mind-boggling technological innovations flowing from quiet Lawrence Kulahee have changed the face of the world. After a chance meeting with Kulahee, ruthless entrepreneur William McNaughton realizes the economic potential of the unassuming genius. In short order, the skies are full of airships, the roads with automobiles, and the U.S. becomes the most powerful nation on Earth. . . . Disparities in wealth have produced a society that seems headed towards social collapse. Unrest has spurred the formation of a labor-union movement, many of whose members and organizers are dropping like flies, killed in inexplicable circumstances. . . . Enter quasi-policeman Hayes to sort things out. He's a highly troubled man but also seems to have psychic gifts rivaling in scale the intellectual gifts of Kulahee." (Booklist)

Bennett, Robert Jackson
The **troupe**; Robert Jackson Bennett. Orbit 2012 505 p.
ISBN 9780316187527
LC 2011018068
The author "melds an energetic reimagining of medieval myth with [a] . . . backdrop of impresarios, puppeteers, and amazing feats of strength in this tale of turn-of-the-century vaudevillians. The performances of Hieronomo "Harry" Silenus's quartet leave audiences dazzled yet unable to remember what they have seen. Teen piano prodigy George Carole, believing that Harry is his father, joins the quartet and learns their actual mission: to sing the song of creation that keeps the world alive and safe. As darkness closes in, the exhausted and increasingly fractious performers gamble everything for one more bit of the song." (Publishers Wkly)

Bennett, Vanora
The **queen's** lover. William Morrow 2010 578p $25.99
ISBN 978-0-06-168986-4; 0-06-168986-6
The "tale of young Catherine de Valois, the fifteenth-century French princess sacrificed on the altar of national honor and political expediency. Hastily married off to King Henry V of England as a battle prize, she must learn to navigate the intricacies and intrigues of the English royal court after Henry's untimely death. Luckily, she has Owain Tudor, the Welsh-born controller of her household, to assist her in doing so. Especially unique and compelling is the story of Elizabeth's friendship with feminist poet Christine de Pizan.

Historical fiction with enough heft to satisfy discriminating fans." Booklist

Benson, E. F.
★ **Make** way for Lucia. Harper & Row 1986 1119p
ISBN 0-06-015678-3
LC 86-45639
A reissue of the omnibus edition of six novels and one short story published 1977 by Crowell
These novels were originally published in the United States by George H. Doran Company and Doubleday, Doran & Company

Berg, Elizabeth, 1948-
Home safe; a novel. Random House 2009 260p $25
ISBN 978-1-4000-6511-0; 1-4000-6511-9
LC 2008-49247
"Helen Ames is a popular and prolific writer living in Oak Park, Illinois. . . . But Helen has lost her ability to write. Her inner world is as stunned and hushed as her cherished home in the wake of her husband's sudden death. Dan took care of everything, leaving Helen free to dwell in her imaginary worlds. Now she is bereft and confused. Tessa, her beautiful, patient, funny daughter, a beauty editor at a woman's magazine, is trying to help, as is Helen's outspoken best friend, Midge. And at least Helen is financially secure. Or not. Where has her money gone? Did Dan have a secret life? Or was he planning a glorious surprise? Berg is a tender and enchanting storyteller who wisely celebrates the simple, sustaining elements of life, from comfort food to birdsong to a good laugh." Booklist

Berg, Elizabeth
The **last** time I saw you; a novel. Random House 2010 244p $25
ISBN 978-1-4000-6864-7; 1-4000-6864-9
LC 2009-40008
"As the novel opens one of the graduates of the small-town high school, a woman named Dorothy Shauman, prepares herself for . . . [her 40th high school reunion]. Divorced and nearly sixty Dorothy plays with the fantasy of seducing Pete Decker, her high school class's heart-throb. We soon get to meet Pete, among other former class mates, and discover that he's got literal heart problems, as well as a dead marriage, and though his looks have held up nothing much else about him has. Candy Sullivan, the class vamp, is suffering also, with a shattering medical diagnosis. Meanwhile some of the other graduates, the nerds of the original class, seem to have made reasonably good lives for themselves. As the narrative moves us toward the main event, we feel sympathy for these people, as much as we would for ourselves, which points up the success of Berg's gentle, but never bowdlerized, renderings of the hopes and desires of this rather large cast of everyday characters." Chicago Trib

Berg, Elizabeth
Once upon a time, there was you; a novel. Random House 2011 280p $26
ISBN 978-1-4000-6865-4; 1-4000-6865-7
LC 2010-49690

"In St. Paul, Minn. John — a phlegmatic architect — is just beginning to date again. One day he gets a call from his ex-wife, Irene, in San Francisco, worried that their 18-year-old daughter Sadie has not come back from a weekend away with friends and does not answer her cell phone. Sadie, feeling smothered by her high-strung, controlling mother, had actually been on her way to a tryst with her new boyfriend but, frustrated by his tardiness, had accepted a ride from a stranger who turns out to be the archetypal villain of a horror story. As often happens in a Berg novel, the plot seems momentarily derailed into stereotype at this point. But, once again, Berg manages to restrain the melodrama through a lucky coincidence. . . . Berg's psychological wisdom about love, family, and aging always make her well-paced novels a good read." Providence J

Berg, Elizabeth, 1948-

★ **Tapestry** of fortunes; a novel. Elizabeth Berg. Random House 2013 240 p. (hardback) $26

ISBN 0812993144; 9780679644699; 9780812993141

LC 2012033033

In this novel, by Elizabeth Berg, "four women venture into their pasts in order to shape their futures. . . . Cecilia Ross . . . moves into a[n] . . old house in Saint Paul, . . . with . . . three housemates: Lise, the home's owner . . . ; Joni, a top-notch sous chef . . . ; and Renie, the . . . most mercurial of the group, who is trying to rectify a teenage mistake. These women embark on a journey together in an attempt to connect with parts of themselves long denied." (Publisher's note)

Berg, Elizabeth

√ **We** are all welcome here; a novel. Random 2006 187p hardcover o.p. pa $15

ISBN 1-4000-6161-X; 0-8129-7100-0 pa

LC 2005-48956

"It is the summer of 1964. In Tupelo, Mississippi, the town of Elvis's birth, tensions are mounting over civil-rights demonstrations occurring ever more frequently—and violently—across the state. But in Paige Dunn's small, ramshackle house, there are more immediate concerns. Challenged by the effects of the polio she contracted during her last month of pregnancy, Paige is nonetheless determined to live as normal a life as possible and to raise her daughter, Diana, in the way she sees fit—with the support of her tough-talking black caregiver, Peacie." Publisher's note

"Full of humor, devoid of self-pity, with lively characters that rise above their circumstances, this is the story of an adolescent accepting adult responsibilities, encountering the temptations of boys and booze, and experiencing the tensions between race and class in the 1960s." SLJ

Berg, Elizabeth

√ ★ **What** we keep; a novel. Random House 1998 272p

ISBN 0-375-50099-5

LC 97-42070

As the novel "opens, Ginny is flying to California to join her sister in a meeting with their mother, whom neither daughter has seen for 35 years. Ginny uses her travel time to reflect upon her memories of the summer when her mother withdrew from the family and became an outsider in her daughters' lives. Berg's precise, evocative descriptions create vivid images of Ginny's physical world, while Berg's understanding and perception are an eloquent testimony to Ginny's emotional turmoil." Libr J

Berger, Thomas

Arthur Rex. Delacorte Press/Seymour Lawrence 1978 499p

ISBN 0-440-00362-8

LC 78-7241

This is a "splendid, satiric retelling of the legend of Camelot. . . . The curious truth is that Mr. Berger's revisions are most authentic, most profound, when the admixture of parody is strongest. At those times—a good three-fourths of the book—he is never merely a parodist after all, but also a compelling yarnspinner in his own right." N Y Times Book Rev

Berger, Thomas

√ ★ **Being** invisible; a novel. Little, Brown 1987 262p

ISBN 0-316-09158-8

LC 86-20897

"There is much in 'Being Invisible' to celebrate—the pleasures of invention, humor, surprise, of Mr. Berger's enraged, unforgiving view. That so much of his vision seems neither freakish nor admonitory but rather, oddly tonic, says something about the era in which we live. . . . It is a sign of the times that we feel such affection for Thomas Berger's dogged, cranky courage, and for the denizens of his unwelcoming and chaotic corner of the fictional world." N Y Times Book Rev

Berger, Thomas

√ **Little** Big Man. Dial Press (NY) 1979 xxii, 440p

"The author purports to write the story of Jack Crabb, adopted Cheyenne, gunfighter, buffalo hunter, and survivor of Custer's last stand, whom he has located at the Marville Center for Senior Citizens. In the few months before his death at the self-professed age of 111, Crabb recounts his version of life in the Old West." Shapiro. Fic for Youth. 3d edition

Followed by The return of Little Big Man (1999)

Berger, Thomas

√ ★ **Neighbors**. Delacorte Press/Seymour Lawrence 1980 275p

ISBN 0-440-06556-9

LC 79-20307

Berger "quickly conditions the reader to expect the unexpected but manages to be consistently surprising nevertheless, introducing new twists and outrages that not even the most warped spectator could have foreseen. The novel adopts a formal, almost fussy style to convey lunacy, as if Berger were describing low deeds to a maiden aunt. . . . {The book} is not at all interested in being socially redeeming, and those who read books to gain warm feelings or philosophic nuggets will come away from this one empty-handed and probably angry. . . .What Berger has produced is a tour de force." Time

Bergman, Megan Mayhew

Birds of a lesser paradise; stories. Megan Mayhew Bergman. Scribner 2012 224 p.

ISBN 9781451643350; 9781451643367; 9781451643374

LC 2011019400

This book features a "collection of [short] stories, most of them revolving around motherhood, animals and conflicting loyalties. . . . [In] "Housewifely Arts," a single mom drives her 7-year-old son nine hours south to a roadside zoo near Myrtle Beach in hopes of hearing one last time her mother's voice . . . or rather the perfect mimicry of that voice by the 36-year-old African gray parrot. . . . In "The Cow That Milked Herself," a young mother-to-be gets an ultrasound in the office of her husband, a loving but distracted and harried veterinarian. . . . In "Every Vein a Tooth," a woman who shelters refugee animals . . . watches helplessly as her boyfriend . . . drifts away. . . . The woman's response is . . . to carry on as she always has, no matter the human consequences." (Kirkus)

Berlinski, Mischa

Fieldwork. Farrar, Straus and Giroux 2007 320p $24

ISBN 978037429916-3; 0-374-29916-1

LC 2006-16214

The narrative "focuses on Martiya van der Leun, who has committed suicide in a Thai women's prison, where she was serving a 50-year sentence for murdering an American missionary. A young farang (white and foreign) journalist named Mischa Berlinski learns that Martiya was an American anthropologist who for years lived with a tribe called the Dyalos to study its mysterious culture. Mischa finds Martiya's story—and exactly why she committed the crime—so oddly compelling that he dedicates his life to understanding Martiya's fate." Libr J

"With its offbeat style, Berlinski's consummate fieldwork—fictional though it may be—produces an intricate whodunit, both disturbing and entertaining." Washington Post Book World

Berman, Sabina

Me, who dove into the heart of the world; a novel. Sabina Berman; translated by Lisa Dillman. 1st U.S. ed. Henry Holt and Co. 2012 242 p. (hardcover) $24.00

ISBN 0805093257; 9780805093254

LC 2011045668

This novel by Sabina Berman is "narrated by. . . Karen Nieto, an autistic savant whose idiosyncrasies prove her greatest gifts. . . . Karen . . . finds freedom not only in the love and patient instruction of her aunt but eventually at the bottom of the ocean swimming among the creatures of the sea. . . . [H]er gifts with animals are finally put to good use at the family's fishery. Her plan is brilliant: Consolation Tuna will be the first humane tuna fishery on the planet." (Publisher's note)

Berne, Suzanne

A **perfect** arrangement; a novel. Algonquin Bks. 2001 301p $23.95

ISBN 1-56512-261-5

LC 00-69451

The author provides a "probing, intelligent exploration of a contemporary family with a strong sense of entitlement, whose future turns out to be anything but certain." N Y Times Book Rev

Bernhard, Thomas

Frost; translated from the German by Michael Hofmann. Alfred A. Knopf 2006 341p $25.95

ISBN 1-4000-4066-3

LC 2006-40886

Original German edition, 1963

"A student's increasingly erratic dispatches over 27 days comprise this obsessive first novel by Bernhard. . . . An unnamed medical student is sent from Vienna by his supervisor, an eminent surgeon named Strauch, to undertake 'precise observation' of the surgeon's brother, a famous painter who has suddenly left the city for the 'dismal' village of Weng. After 'systematically inveigling' himself into the company of the painter under the pretense of being a vacationing law student, the student slowly feels his own mood and mental attitudes being subsumed by the painter's paranoid outbursts and disjointed monologues. Weng itself, located in a grim valley still bearing the grisly traces of WWII, is a hotbed of murky scandal. . . . Bernhard's glorious talent for bleak existential monologues is second only to Beckett's, and seems to have sprung up fully mature in his mesmerizing debut." Publ Wkly

Bernhard, Thomas

★ The **loser**; translated from the German by Jack Dawson; afterword by Mark M. Anderson. Knopf 1991 189p

ISBN 0-394-57239-4

LC 90-45942

Original German edition, 1983

"Dawson's translation is superb. . . . The Loser is undoubtedly one of the most fascinating works of contemporary Austrian literature, and given its extraordinary meditations on art, the artist, and the reception of the creative process, it is a work that should find international readership." American Book Rev

Bernhard, Thomas

★ **Woodcutters**; translated from the German by David McLintock. Knopf 1987 181p

ISBN 0-394-55152-4

LC 87-45123

Original German edition, 1984

"Mr. Bernhard's portrait of a society in dissolution has a Scandinavian darkness reminiscent of Ibsen and Strindberg, but it is filtered through a minimalist prose of obsessive repetition and ever so slight modulations." N Y Times Book Rev

Bernhardt, William

Dark justice. Ballantine Pub. Group 1999 389p
ISBN 0-345-40738-5

LC 98-28182

On a book-signing tour in Washington State attorney Ben Kincaid "inadvertently gets involved in a group called Green Rage, a conservationist organization wrestling with the local logging industry in a life-or-death struggle. One of the members of the group has been charged with a horrible murder—and who is the alleged perp? None other than {a} man Ben defended six years ago. To defend him again, Ben has to go up against prosecutor Granville 'Granny' Adams, who, despite her moniker, is attractive and tough as nails. She is bound and determined to win this case. In the meantime, subplots swirl and crash around Ben's feet, but these only serve to enrich the entertainment value of this wonderfully riveting read." Booklist

Bernheimer, Kate

Horse, flower, bird; stories. Coffee House Press 2010 185p il pa $14.95
ISBN 978-1-56689-247-6; 1-56689-247-3

LC 2010-16257

"This is a collection of eight imaginative if not downright unusual tales that will delight readers but also evoke sadness and loneliness. . . . . Bernheimer's passion for fairy tales is evident in every story she spins, which should come as no surprise—she is founder and editor of Fairy Tale Review. . . . [Her] work provides a refreshing contrast to most available fiction. It is no stretch to compare her to Aimee Bender or Kelly Link." Libr J

Berry, Jedediah

✓ The **manual** of detection. Penguin Press 2009 278p $25.95
ISBN 978-1-59420-211-7

LC 2008-44753

This is Berry's debut novel. "In an unnamed city always slick with rain, Charles Unwin toils as a clerk at a huge, imperious detective agency. All he knows about solving mysteries comes from the reports he's filed for the illustrious detective Travis Sivart. When Sivart goes missing and his supervisor turns up murdered, Unwin is suddenly promoted to detective, a rank for which he lacks both the skills and the stomach. His only guidance comes from his new assistant, who would be perfect if she weren't so sleepy, and from the pithy yet profound Manual of Detection. . . . Unwin mounts his search for Sivart, but is soon framed for murder, pursued by goons and gunmen, and confounded by the infamous femme fatale Cleo Greenwood." (Publisher's note)

"Charles Unwin, a meek detective-agency clerk, is set on the trail of a legendary adversary after the disappearance of a colleague. He's handed the rulebook of the title, but it gets him only so far; the vast bureaucratic agency and the nightmarish villain remain mysterious, and the nameless nocturnal city in which the story takes place presents its own series of surrealistic bewilderments. When the central conflict eventually clarifies, it's somewhat disappointing that it is a 9/11 allegory. More valuable is Berry's ability to create the feeling of inhabiting a strange and haunting dream, with its own persuasive logic and somnambulant pacing." New Yorker

Berry, Steve

The **Charlemagne** pursuit; a novel. Ballantine Books 2008 509p il $26
ISBN 978-0-345-48579-3; 0-345-48579-3

LC 2008-28357

"Using his connections in the federal government, Cotton [Malone] asks to see a classified file that details the mission that resulted in his father's death. He knew his father died on a submarine but none of the shocking details about where or why he died. But Cotton is not the only person who wants this file, and they kill to get it. Nazi missions to the Antarctic, ancient societies, and a valuable artifact from Charlemagne's tomb all play key roles as Malone uncovers the truth. So much is going on that there is enough material for two good books, let alone one great one." Libr J

Berry, Steve

✓ The **third** secret; a novel. Steve Berry. Ballantine Books 2005 400 p. map (hc.: alk. paper) $24.95
ISBN 0345476131; 034547614X

LC 2005045759

This book's background takes place in "Fatima, Portugal, 1917: The Virgin Mary appears to three peasant children, sharing with them three secrets, two of which are soon revealed to the world. The third secret is sealed away in the Vatican, read only by popes, and not disclosed until the year 2000. . . . Vatican City, present day: Papal secretary Father Colin Michener is concerned for the Pope. . . . When Pope Clement sends Michener to the Romanian highlands, then to a Bosnian holy site, in search of a priest, . . . [he] finds himself embroiled in murder, . . . deceit, and his forbidden passion for a beloved woman. . . . [I]n Germany, . . . he learns that the third secret of Fatima may dictate the very fate of the Church–a fate now lying in Michener's own hands." (Publisher's note)

Berry, Wendell

✓ **Jayber** Crow; a novel. Counterpoint 2000 363p
ISBN 1-58243-029-2

LC 00-35889

"Orphaned at 4 by the flu epidemic of 1918, and again at 10, when age claims the elderly relatives who took him in, Jonah 'Jayber' Crow finds a valued place as a humble barber in a Kentucky river township. He finds love, too, though he never speaks of it." Booklist

Berry, Wendell

★ **That** distant land; the collected stories of Wendell Berry. Shoemaker & Hoard 2004 440p $26
ISBN 1-593-76027-2

LC 2003-25213

"Set in a small Kentucky farming village, this collection of Berry's Port William stories illuminates the evolution of rural American life over the course of the 20th century. In 23 stories, Berry chronicles Port William from the 1880s to the 1980s, evoking the connectedness of the small town's denizens to each other and to the land." Publ Wkly

The **Best** American mystery stories of the century; Tony Hillerman, editor; Otto Penzler, series editor; with an introduction by Tony Hillerman.

Houghton Mifflin 2000 813p hardcover o.p. pa $17.95

ISBN 0-618-01267-2; 0-618-01271-0 pa

"This anthology is a cornerstone volume for any mystery library." Publ Wkly

Best American mystery stories [date] Otto Penzler, series editor. Houghton Mifflin

Annual. First published 1997. Editors vary

An annual volume of mystery stories culled from a variety of magazines, collections, and anthologies. Loren D. Estleman, Lawrence Block, Michael Connelly, Joyce Carol Oates, Bill Pronzini, Hannah Tinti, James Lee Burke, and Holly Goddard Jones are among the authors represented

★ The **best** American noir of the century; edited by James Ellroy & Otto Penzler; with an introduction by James Ellroy. Houghton Mifflin Harcourt 2010 731p $30

ISBN 978-0-547-33077-8

LC 2010-17204

This anthology "features noir of the literary kind. For those of you for whom the shot glass is always half empty and the forecast is always grim, you can't do much better this sterling collection of 39 tales from the darkness at the edge of town, full of characters doomed to bad choices and worse luck. You can gripe about the editors' definition of noir or some of their omissions, but they've done a great job here, offering lesser known tales by such expected perpetrators as Cornell Woolrich, Jim Thompson, James M. Cain, Mickey Spillane, Evan Hunter and Patricia Highsmith as well as a few outliers, such as Dorothy B. Hughes, David 'Rambo' Morrell and Lorenzo 'Sleepers' Carcaterra and a few authors even the most devoted noir devotee may not be familiar with. Tod Robbins, anyone?" Mystery Scene

The **Best** American short stories; selected from U.S. and Canadian magazines. Houghton Mifflin

This annual series began in 1915 under the editorship of Edward J. O'Brien with title: Best short stories. Editors vary

An annual anthology of stories by American and Canadian writers culled from a variety of magazines. Authors represented include: Raymond Carver, Alice Munro, Tobias Wolff, John Updike, Rick Bass, and Jamaica Kincaid

The **Best** American short stories 2012; edited by Tom Perrotta and Heidi Pitlor. Mariner Books 2012 356 p. $14.95

ISBN 0547242107; 9780547242101

This short story anthology, edited by Tom Perrotta and Heidi Pitlor, is the 2012 edition of "The Best American series" of short fiction and nonfiction. "Each volume's series editor selects notable works from hundreds of magazines, journals, and websites." Authors included within this edition include Nathan Englander, Mary Gaitskill, Roxane Gay, Jennifer Haigh, Steven Millhauser, Alice Munro, Lawrence Osborne, Eric Puchner, George Saunders, Kate Walbert, and others." (Publisher's note)

The **Best** from Fantasy & Science Fiction; 1st-20th, 22nd-24th series. Doubleday 1952 23v

24th series published by Scribner. No volume bearing 21st series designation published; Special 25th anniversary volume published instead

Collection culled from a journal, founded in 1949, that "continues to publish an unusual number of first stories and award winners, to discover new, literary writers, to maintain a circulation of about half to two-thirds that of the most popular magazines, and to remain the most consistently reliable magazine in the field." New Ency of Sci Fic

The **Best** from fantasy & science fiction: the fiftieth anniversary anthology; edited by Edward L. Ferman and Gordon Van Gelder. Doherty Assocs. 1999 381p $24.95

ISBN 0-312-86973-8

LC 99-40560

"This anthology includes 22 stories published . . . between 1993 and 1998. . . . Their authors include such luminaries as Ursula Le Guin, Gene Wolfe, and Ray Bradbury, and the distinguished if less conspicuous likes of Paul Di Filippo, Terry Bisson, and Esther Friesner." Booklist

Best of the Best American short stories, 1915-1950; edited by Martha Foley. Houghton Mifflin 1952 369p

How the Devil came down Division Street, by N. Algren; I'm a fool, by S. Anderson; The blue sash, by W. Beck; Nothing ever breaks except the heart, by K. Boyle; Horse thief, by E. Caldwell; Sex education, by D. Canfield; The enormous radio, by J. Cheever; The wind and the snow of winter, by W. V. Clark; Boys will be boys, by I. S. Cobb; Christ in concrete, by P. Di Donato; Hand upon the waters, by W. Faulkner; My old man, by E. Hemingway; The peach stone, by P. Horgan; Haircut, by R. Lardner; Man on a road, by A. Maltz; Prince of darkness, by J. F. Powers; Resurrection of a life, by W. Saroyan; Search through the streets of the city, by I. Shaw; The interior castle, by J. Stafford; How beautiful with shoes, by W. D. Steele; The women on the wall, by W. Stegner; Dawn of remembered spring, by J. Stuart; A wife of Nashville, by P. Taylor; The catbird seat, by J. Thurber; A curtain of green, by E. Welty

Betts, Doris

★ **Souls** raised from the dead; a novel. Knopf 1994 339p

ISBN 0-679-42621-3

LC 93-30900

"Mary's life and death are superbly and unsentimentally accomplished. . . . Yet none of this should sound grim, only appropriately sad, because Ms. Betts seems to be possessed of high spirits and a generous wisdom. And that is what buoys up her characters and makes a lot of the proceedings very funny even as her people struggle with their anger and bewilderment." N Y Times Book Rev

Beukes, Lauren

Zoo city; Lauren Beukes. Angry Robot 2011 317 p. (pbk.) $15

ISBN 9780857662163

LC 2010475248

Arthur C. Clarke Award (2011)

This book, the winner of the 2011 Arthur C. Clarke Award, offers a "parallel world . . . [where] those who cause someone's death are both blessed and cursed with companion animals who mark them as killers while giving them special powers. In a run-down slum in Johannesburg, journalist and former addict Zinzi December uses the power provided by her Sloth to find lost objects, supplementing her meager income by running 419 scams. When a rich client is murdered, Zinzi is drawn into an investigation that involves teen pop stars, sleazy record producers, and ethics-challenged newspapermen." (Publishers Weekly)

Beverley, Jo

✓ **Winter** Fire; Jo Beverley. New American Library 2003 311p (pbk.) $7.99

ISBN 0451210654

LC 2004572913

In this book, "Genova Smith convinces her employers, the elderly Trayce ladies, to let her bring an abandoned baby with them to a Christmas party at Rothgar Abbey, even as she does her best to get the Marquess of Ashart, the man she mistakenly believes to be the father, to accept responsibility for his actions. Ash has no intention of claiming the child, but he agrees to accompany his great aunts to the holiday fete. . . . When she is caught with Ash in a seemingly compromising situation, Genova agrees to a pretend betrothal but has no intention of giving in to her desires for the wickedly handsome Ash." (Booklist)

Bezmozgis, David

✓ The **free** world. Farrar, Straus & Giroux 2011 356p

ISBN 0-374-28140-8; 978-0-374-28140-3

LC 2010-33122

In this novel, after "refusing the Kremlin's order to relocate to Israel, the Jewish Krasnansky family of 1978 Russia makes their way across Italy at the sides of thousands of other immigrants." (Publisher's note)

The novel "opens on the platform of Vienna's Western Terminal, where 'the representatives of Soviet Jewry — from Tallinn to Tashkent — roiled, snarled, and elbowed to deposit their belongings onto the waiting train.' Among them are two brothers, Alec and Karl Krasnansky, their wives, children and elderly parents, all jostling west from Riga, Latvia toward Rome. The novel takes place in 1978 during the five-month interlude the family spends in Italy awaiting word on where they will go: America, Canada, Australia or Israel. The gifted Bezmozgis is interested in what must be left behind, what is and is not in the suitcases. His characters must navigate the pull of places and relationships, language and ideologies. One must weigh whether to keep or end a pregnancy. Out of the stream of the everyday, Bezmozgis brings his considerable talent for observation and humor." Cleveland Plain Dealer

Bezos, MacKenzie

Traps; by MacKenzie Bezos. Alfred A. Knopf 2013 224 p. (hardcover) $24.95; (ebook) $74.85

ISBN 0307959732; 9780307950291; 9780307959737; 9780307959744

LC 2012029032

In this novel, by MacKenzie Bezos, "the paths of four very different women intersect, briefly but significantly, in ways that will change each of them forever. . . . Dana is a . . . security guard trained in special ops . . . but is terrified of committing to the man she loves. Lynn is a fiercely independent older woman living alone in Nevada. . . . Jessica is a reclusive movie star. . . . Vivian is a seventeen-year-old prostitute who will do anything to protect her twin babies." (Publisher's note)

Bhattacharya, Rahul

✓ The **sly** company of people who care; Rahul Bhattacharya. 1st American ed. Farrar, Straus and Giroux 2011 278p.

ISBN 0374265852; 9780374265854; 978-0-374-26585-4; 0-374-26585-2

LC 2010047596

"The narrator of this novel journeys into Guyana's interior to seek answers about the country's past." (N Y Times Book Rev)

Bierce, Ambrose

★ The **complete** short stories of Ambrose Bierce; compiled with commentary by Ernest Jerome Hopkins. Doubleday 1970 496p

ISBN 9780803260719

LC 79103758

The **Big** book of adventure stories; edited and with a introduction by Otto Penzler; foreword by Douglas Preston. Vintage Crime/Black Lizard 2011 874p pa $25

ISBN 978-0-307-47450-6; 0-307-47450-X

LC 2011-02226

"Otto Penzler has ranged far and wide to make this anthology. (What fun he must have had!) It is divided into 11 sections: Sword & Sorcery; Megalomania Rules; Man vs. Nature; Island Paradise; Sand and Sun; Something Feels Funny; Go West, Young Man; Future Shock; I Spy; Yellow Peril; In Darkest Africa. Much of it is, as Mr. Penzler happily warns readers, politically most incorrect. Almost all the authors are more than comfortable with the idea of Anglo-Saxon superiority, and lesser breeds are treated with disdain and contempt—even when there is reason to fear their vile schemes and vindictive nature. . . . The range of stories Mr. Penzler has collected is wide, the range of talent too." Wall Street J

Bilenchi, Romano

★ The **chill**; translated from the Italian by Ann Goldstein. Europa 2009 99p pa $15

ISBN 978-1-933372-90-7

Original Italian edition, 1982

"Following an unnamed teenager's initiation into adulthood in Tuscany in the Fascist years, [this novelette consists of] a series of episodes of alienation, narrated in a frank, flat voice. In a sickeningly swift eighty pages, the protagonist becomes aware of the petty and vicious nature of his fellow-townspeople, of his increasing estrangement from friends and family, and of his first grotesque (if fascinating) stirrings of sexuality. Manipulated and dominated by the adults around him, he concludes that 'it wasn't possible to live among other people if all of a sudden they could attack one another with such ferocity.' Most coming-of-age novels illuminate the tumultuous inner world of adolescence; Bilenchi's reveals the brutality of the adulthood that surrounds it." New Yorker

Bill, Frank

Crimes in southern Indiana; stories. Farrar, Straus and Giroux 2011 272p
   ISBN 978-0-374-53288-8
                                  LC 20110756
"When the first character you meet is named Pitchfork, and when the first thing Pitchfork does is press the barrel of a .45 to his nephew's forehead and a sawed-off shotgun to his son's forehead, and when this opening comes off as tame compared to all that follows, you know you're not in the nostalgic Indiana of new-mown hay and moonlight on the Wabash. You're in Frank Bill's Indiana, Southern Indiana, which in Bill's ever violent and never dull stories becomes a blend of Midwest Gothic and country pulp." Seattle Times

Billingsley, ReShonda Tate

Let the church say amen; ReShonda Tate Billingsley. Pocket Books 2004 ix, 277p (pbk.) $6.99
   ISBN 0743477146; 9780743477147
                               LC 2004050397
This book tells the story of "Reverend Simon Jackson [who] has always felt destined to lead, and he's done a good job of it -- having transformed his small Houston church into one of the most respected and renowned in the region. But while the good Reverend's been busy tending his flock, his family's gone astray. His nineteen-year-old daughter, Rachel, gives new meaning to 'baby mama drama.' David, the oldest at twenty-seven, has been spiraling into a life of crime ever since his promising football career came to an end. Blessedly, Jonathan, Simon's beloved middle child, is in control of his life and is poised to take his side as associate pastor -- or so everybody thinks." (Publisher's note)

Bilyeau, Nancy

The **chalice**; a novel. Nancy Bilyeau. 1st Touchstone hardcover ed. Simon & Schuster 2013 496 p. (hardcover) $26.99; (paperback) $16.00
   ISBN 1476708657; 9781476708652; 9781476708669
                               LC 2012031205
   Sequel to: The crown
In this historical novel by Nancy Bilyeah, "England's bloody power struggle between crown and cross threatens to tear the country apart. Novice Joanna Stafford has tasted the wrath of the royal court . . . and escaped death at the hands of those desperate to possess the power of an ancient relic. . . .Despite the possibilities of arrest and imprisonment, she becomes caught up in a shadowy international plot targeting Henry VIII himself." (Publisher's note)

Binchy, Maeve

 ✓ ★ **Circle** of friends. Delacorte Press 1991 565p
   ISBN 0-385-30149-9
                                LC 90-3944
   First published 1990 in the United Kingdom
"There is nothing fancy about 'Circle of Friends.' There is no torrid sex, no profound philosophy. There are no stun-

ning metaphors. There is just a wonderfully absorbing story about people worth caring about. And that is a rare pleasure." N Y Times Book Rev

Binchy, Maeve

 ✓ The **glass** lake. Delacorte Press 1995 584p
   ISBN 0-385-31354-3
                                LC 94-36104
   First published 1994 in the United Kingdom
   This novel "focuses on the inhabitants of a small town in Ireland. Helen, wife and mother of the McMahon household, is presumed to have drowned in a nearby lake. Actually, she shook off her dull, staid life and fled to London with her lover. Successful at business, she yearns for some communication with her now teenaged daughter, Kit. She begins a casual correspondence with Kit under the guise of being an old friend of her mother." Libr J

Binchy, Maeve

 ✓ ★ **Silver** wedding. Delacorte Press 1989 306p
   ISBN 0-385-29826-9
                                LC 89-1276
"An elegant literary construction, a comedy of manners as well as a soap opera. Each chapter has its own story, yet each story connects with all the others to produce a satisfying whole. Add to this a sly, understated tone and you have a book that's an effortless pleasure to read." NY Times Book Rev

Binchy, Maeve, 1940-2012

 ✓ A **week** in winter; by Maeve Binchy. 1st U.S. ed. Alfred A. Knopf 2013 336 p. (hardcover) $26.95
   ISBN 0307273571; 9780307273574
                                LC 2012039948
In this book, Stone House is a rundown house in western Ireland. "When Chicky Starr decides to buy the property and turn it into a hotel, the town thinks she's gone crazy. The project brings unexpected peace and understanding to Chicky and her staff," but the "first out-of-towners arrive with disappointment, disgrace, and doubt." Yet "all experience a catharsis on the cliffs and trails and in the gardens that can be found in the surrounding countryside." (Library Journal)

Binchy, Maeve

 ✓ **Whitethorn** Woods. A.A. Knopf 2007 339p $25.95
   ISBN 978-0-307-26578-4; 0-307-26578-1
                                LC 2006-48803
   First published 2006 in the United Kingdom
"Story by story, voice by voice, Binchy builds the fictional community of Rossmore so that, by the end of the novel, we know Rossmore's inhabitants better than our own neighbours . . . . Few contemporary novelists match Binchy's gift for giving us the world through her characters' eyes." Toronto Globe and Mail

Binet, Laurent, 1972-

✓ ★ **HHhH**; Laurent Binet; translated from the French by Sam Taylor. Farrar, Straus and Giroux 2012 327 p.

ISBN 0374169918; 9780374169916

LC 2011046063

In this book, which "tak[es] its title from the German for 'Himmler's brain is called Heydrich,' [author Laurent] Binet . . . tells two stories: primarily that of the daring mission to assassinate Reinhard Heydrich, the prominent Nazi Protector of Bohemia and Moravia known as . . . 'The Man with the Iron Heart.' . . . It is also, however, the metafictional tale of Binet's struggles with shaping the story." (Publishers Weekly)

Bingham, Harry

✓ ★ **Talking** to the dead; a novel. Harry Bingham. Delacorte Press 2012 337 p. $26

ISBN 0345533739; 9780345533739; 9780345533746

LC 2011041365

In this novel, by Harry Bingham, "a young woman undone by drugs and prostitution, her six-year-old daughter dead alongside her. But then detectives find . . . the platinum credit card of a very wealthy . . . steel tycoon. What is a heroin-addicted hooker doing with the credit card of a well-known . . . man who died months ago? This is the question that the most junior member of the investigative team, Detective Constable Fiona Griffiths, is assigned to answer." (Publisher's note)

Bingham, Sallie

✓ **Mending**; new and selected stories. Sarabande Books 2011 260p $23; pa $16.95

ISBN 9781936747009; 1936747006; 9781936747016 pa; 1936747014 pa

LC 2011-06208

"Spanning 50 years, this omnibus of Bingham's tight, sparkling short fiction includes stories from her earliest collection, The Touching Hand (1967), to her latest, Red Car (2008). . . . [Her work] remains sharp and deliciously unsettling, ripe for discovery by a new generation of readers." Publ Wkly

Birch, Carol

✓ ★ **Jamrach's** menagerie. Doubleday 2011 295p il $25.95

ISBN 978-0-385-53440-6; 0-385-53440-X

LC 2010-38082

"Jaffy's experience could well move the reader as profoundly as it changed the narrator." Kirkus

Bird, Sarah

✓ The **gap** year; a novel. Alfred A. Knopf 2011 301p $25.95

ISBN 978-0-307-59279-8

LC 2010-51495

"The title alludes to the break in a mother-daughter relationship during the daughter's senior year of high school. Single mom Camilla feels her daughter, Aubrey, beginning to pull away from her, especially after Aubrey embarks on a romance with classmate Tyler. Add in the sudden reappearance of Aubrey's father, who years ago left the family to join a cultlike religion (it might sound familiar to fans of certain Hollywood types), and gaps in this family open and close at blinding speed. The narrative alternates between Camilla's current perspective over the course of a few days and Aubrey's retelling of the previous year. This technique makes for a compelling read and builds to a satisfying and surprisingly tender conclusion." Libr J

Bird, Sarah

✓ The **Yokota** Officers Club; a novel. Knopf 2001 367p

ISBN 0-375-41214-X

LC 2001-89763

The author "nails the voice of Bernie in a delicate balance of confused, shy child vs. the bright emerging woman she has become. Bird's masterly use of the tricky technique of children revealing adult subtleties is breathtaking." Libr J

Bishop, Anne

✓ **Written** in red; a novel of the Others. Anne Bishop. Roc 2013 448 p. (hardcover) $26.95

ISBN 0451464966; 9780451464965

LC 2012036432

In this novel, Meg Corbyn is a Cassandra sangue, a blood prophet who sees the future when her skin is cut. Along with others like her, she has lived under the tight reins of her Controllers, with no actual experiences of the real world. Knowing that eventually blood prophets lose their usefulness and, usually, their lives, Meg seeks refuge at the Lakeside Courtyard, a part of the city owned and operated by the Others—shapeshifters and other supernatural creatures." (Library Journal)

Bisson, Terry

✓ **Numbers** don't lie; Terry Bisson. Tachyon Publications 2005 176p

ISBN 1892391325; 9781892391322

This collection of science fiction short stories is centered around "Wilson Wu. . . . No piker, Wu manages to walk, in 'one long step for mankind,' from an auto repair garage in a nondescript part of Brooklyn directly to the moon in 'The Hole in the Hole.' He even brings back half of a dune buggy left behind by astronauts and casually explains the situation as 'a periodic incongruent neotopological metaeuclidean adjacency.' In the second tale, 'The Edge of the Universe,' Wu saves the expanding universe from shrinking. Finally, he patches 'a hole in the fabric of space-time' in 'Get Me to the Church on Time.'" (Publishers Weekly)

Black mask; a magazine.

The **Black** Lizard big book of Black Mask stories; edited and with a foreword by Otto Penzler; introduction by Keith Alan Deutsch. Vintage Crime/Black Lizard 2010 1116p pa $25

ISBN 978-0-307-45543-7

LC 2010-24508

"Launched by H.L. Mencken and George Jean Nathan in the 1920s, Black Mask would springboard the careers of a handful of writers, raising the level of penny dreadful pulp mysteries to that of literature, while also publishing plenty of quickly hacked-out swill. This gathers the cream produced by legends like Dashiell Hammett (the godfather of hardboiled detective fiction), Erle Stanley Gardner, Raymond Chandler, Carroll John Daly, Cornell Woolrich, and other aces. There are more than 50 stories in all, including 'The Maltese Falcon' (the original serialized version, which differs from the published novel, is reproduced here for the first time since its initial 1929 publication), Chandler's 'Try the Girl' (which, ultimately, became Farewell, My Lovely), and Horace McCoy's 'Dirty Work.' Each author receives a brief bio and the stories sport original artwork—it's a complete education on vintage crime mysteries between two covers. . . . A hefty hunk of hardboiled heaven and a noir lover's dream." Libr J

Black, Benjamin

Vengeance; a novel. Benjamin Black. Henry Holt and Co. 2012 320 p. $26

ISBN 0805094393; 9780805094398

LC 2012001842

This detective novel is the fifth in a series "featuring Inspector Hackett . . . and Dr. Quirke, the laconic pathologist. . . . Two families, one Catholic, one Protestant, have been in business together for generations, and the lowlier Clancys have finally come to resent the haughty Delahayes. When the two patriarchs die mysteriously at sea, Hackett and Quirke consider the surviving family members." (Booklist)

"A seductively moody and shrewdly damning tale of privilege, arrogance, vengeance, and a touch of madness." Booklist

Black, Cara

Murder below Montparnasse; Cara Black. Soho Press 2013 319 p. (hardcover) $25.95

ISBN 1616952156; 9781616952150

LC 2012032374

This novel, by Cara Black, is an episode in the "Aimée Leduc Investigation" mystery series. "A long-lost Modigliani portrait, a grieving brother's blood vendetta, a Soviet secret that's been buried for 80 years--Parisian private investigator Aimée Leduc's current case is her most exciting one yet. . . . Aimée has to find the painting, stop her attackers, and figure out what her long-missing mother . . . has to do with all this." (Publisher's note)

Black, Cara

Murder in Belleville; Cara Black. Soho 2000 341 p. map (hardcover) $23

ISBN 1569472114; 9781569472118

LC 00041012

In this book by Cara Black, "sassy detective Aimee Leduc . . . receive[s] a puzzling, urgent call from her friend Anais. . . . Aimee witnesses a car bombing. . . . By questioning locals, she discovers that the dead woman, Sophie, had an alias, Eugenie Grandet, and lived what looked like a dual life. . . . As Aimee searches deeper for clues, she attracts the kind of attention of ruthless people who would rather she didn't snoop." (Publishers Weekly)

Black, Cara

Murder in Clichy; Cara Black. Soho Press 2005 284 p. map (hardcover) $24

ISBN 1569473838; 9781569473832

LC 2004048242

This book is part of author Clara Black's Aimée Leduc series. "Aimée Leduc, a private investigator based in Paris, has been introduced to the Cao Dai temple by her partner, René. . . . A Vietnamese nun asks her for a favor--to hand over a check and bring a package back to the temple. But this act of kindness ends in a stranger's death and leaves her with a bullet wound in the arm, a check for 50,000 francs and a trove of ancient jade artifacts whose provenance is a mystery." (Publisher's note)

Black, Cara, 1951-

Murder in Passy. Soho Press 2011 273p $25

ISBN 978-1-56947-882-0; 1-56947-882-1

LC 2010-34816

This Aimée Leduc investigation "finds the Paris PI's world turned upside down with the arrest of her godfather and longtime mentor, Commissaire Morbier, for murder. Worse yet, the victim—Morbier's inamorata, Xavierre d'Eslay—was with Aimée minutes before her death by strangulation. To clear Morbier, Aimée must dig deep as his fellow officers close rank and refuse to cooperate. Helping Aimée are her detective agency partner, René; her cousin, Sebastian; and her former policeman lover, Melac, who may or may not have an agenda of his own during the investigation. Though Xavierre lived a life of privilege in the posh suburb of Passy, Aimée discovers her past is shrouded in secrecy, linked to Basque separatists and terrorist acts." Publ Wkly

"Leduc is always a reliable and charming guide to the city's lesser-known corners." Seattle Times

Black, Cara

Murder in the Bastille; Cara Black. Soho Press 2003 276 p. (hardcover) $24

ISBN 1569473242; 9781569473245

LC 2002042625

In this book by Cara Black, part of the Aimée Leduc series, "after a mysterious attack leaves her blinded. . . Aimee and her partner, computer expert Ren Friant, face dual dilemmas. . . . The diminutive Ren must become the eyes of the team while Aimee makes do as best she can with her other senses. Meanwhile, with her attacker still on the loose and the police off on a wrong scent chasing a serial killer, Aimee remains a vulnerable target." (Publishers Weekly)

Black, Cara

Murder in the Marais; Cara Black. Soho Press 1999 354 p. (hardcover) $22

ISBN 1569471592; 9781569471593

LC 98052070

In this book by Cara Black, part of the Aimée Leduc series, "[p]rivate investigator Aimée Leduc . . . discovers the body of an elderly Jewish woman whose forehead has been inscribed with a swastika. With the arrival of a German trade delegation, meanwhile, the existence of a powerful covert group comprising former SS officers becomes clear. Aimée's subsequent investigation exposes the connection between a war-time romance gone wrong and the modern-day murder." (Library Journal)

Black, Cara

Murder in the rue de Paradis; Cara Black. Soho Crime 2008 305 p. map (hardcover) $24.00

ISBN 9781569474747; 1569474745

LC 2007009194

This novel, by Cara Black, is an episode in the "Aimée Leduc Investigation" mystery series. "As Aimée is about to find happiness at last, Yves, her fiancé of a single night, is killed. . . . Finding out who cut her lover's throat involves Aimée in Kurdish and Turkish politics as she tries to track down his contacts above and beneath the streets of Paris." (Publisher's note)

Black, Cara

Murder in the Sentier; Cara Black. Soho Press 2002 322 p. (hardcover) $24.00

ISBN 1569472785; 9781569472781

LC 2002017566

This book is the third in author Cara Black's Aimée Leduc series. It follows "the daughter of an American, Sydney Leduc, who disappeared when Aimee was eight years old, and a Parisian cop, Jean-Claude Leduc, . . . from whom she inherited a detective agency. . . . Aimée has always wanted to know the truth about her missing mother, so when she gets a phone call from a woman . . . claiming to have known her mother in prison she agrees to meet the mysterious caller." (Publishers Weekly)

In this mystery, sleuth Aimee Leduc scours Paris' Second Arrondissement "in pursuit of a tip to the whereabouts of her American mother, a political fugitive since the early 1970's for her anarchist activities with a group very much like the Baader-Meinhof gang. The plot that has Aimee pounding the cobblestones of this quaint quarter is a circular affair that entails much chasing after aging urban guerrillas who tend to be incoherent, hostile or dead when found. . . . But if it lacks design, the story provides a street map to this idiosyncratic area." N Y Times Book Rev

Black, Elizabeth

The **drowning** house; a novel. Elizabeth Black. Nan A. Talese/Doubleday 2013 288 p. (alk. paper) $25.95

ISBN 0385535864; 9780385535861

LC 2011046222

In this novel by Elizabeth Black "photographer Clare Porterfield's once-happy marriage is coming apart, unraveling under the strain of a family tragedy. When she receives an invitation to direct an exhibition in her hometown of Galveston, Texas, she jumps at the chance to escape her grief and reconnect with the island she hasn't seen for ten years. There Clare will . . . search for answers about her troubled past and her family's complicated relationship with the wealthy and influential Carraday family." (Publisher's note)

Black, Lisa

Blunt Impact; Lisa Black. Severn House Pub Ltd 2013 224 p. (hardcover) $28.95

ISBN 072788252X; 9780727882523

This novel, by Lisa Black, is an entry in the author's "Theresa Maclean" mystery series. "Forensic scientist Theresa MacLean is puzzled by the questionable death of a female construction worker at a Cleveland building site. A witness to the death--a young girl nicknamed Ghost--may be able to help. . . . Soon Theresa finds herself in a race against time to protect Ghost from an unknown killer before he is able to find the little girl and silence her for good." (Publisher's note)

Black, Lisa

Evidence of murder; Lisa Black. 1st ed. William Morrow 2009 345 p. (hardcover) $24.99

ISBN 0061544485; 9780061544484

LC 2008025028

This is the second book by Lisa Black to feature forensic investigator Theresa MacLean. Here, "Jillian Perry has been found dead in the woods, leaving behind a husband of three weeks and a young daughter. The police can't determine how she died—her body shows no visible marks, and the autopsy reveals nothing suspicious—and the leading theory is that she purposely wandered into the forest and succumbed to the freezing weather. But" Theresa suspects something else. (Publisher's note)

Includes bibliographical references (p. 345)

Black, Lisa

Takeover. William Morrow 2008 341p $24.95

ISBN 978-0-06-154445-3; 0-06-154445-0

LC 2007-45606

As this thriller "opens, thirty-eight year old forensic scientist Theresa MacLean is working a murder scene along with her cousin, homicide detective Frank Patrick, and his partner, Theresa's fiancé, Paul Cleary. The deceased is a middle-aged man whose head had been bashed in. His name is Mark Ludlow, and he had worked as an examiner for the Federal Reserve Bank of Cleveland. Coincidentally, two armed men later enter that same bank in an apparent robbery attempt. Since the Federal Reserve is no ordinary savings and loan, the perpetrators fail to get their hands on any ready cash. Knowing that they cannot escape without being gunned down by snipers, the two criminals, Lucas Parrish and Bobby Moyers, take hostages while they consider their options. Much to Theresa's horror, her future husband, Paul, is among the people being held captive. . . . Black skillfully creates a claustrophobic and tension-laden atmosphere." Mostly Fiction

Black, Lisa

Trail of blood; Lisa Black. 1st ed. William Morrow 2010 393 p. map (hardcover) $24.99

ISBN 0061989339; 9780061989339

LC 2010002953

In this suspense novel, by Lisa Black, "seventy-five years ago, a madman nicknamed the Torso Killer terrorized Cleveland. . . . And he was never caught. Today, forensic scientist Theresa MacLean is called to an abandoned building where a desiccated, decapitated body has been found in a room that's been sealed off for years. Although there's no immediate proof, everyone assumes the same thing: that the newly discovered corpse was a Torso Killer victim." (Publisher's note)

Includes bibliographical references

Blackmoore, Stephen

✓ **City** of the lost; Stephen Blackmoore. Daw Books 2012 217 p. (pbk.) $15

ISBN 0756407028; 9780756407025

LC 2011277148

"A head-shakingly perfect blend of zombie schlock, deadpan wit, startling profanity, desperate improvisation and inventive brilliance." Kirkus

Blackmore, R. D.

✓ **Lorna** Doone; a romance of Exmoor. edited with an introduction and notes by Sally Shuttleworth. Oxford University Press 2009 xxix, 680p (Oxford world's classics) pa $13.95

ISBN 978-0-19-953759-4; 0-19-953759-3

First published 1869

A romantic love-story of Exmoor and the North Devon Coast of England, telling of the outlaw Doones, the maid brought up in the midst of them, and plain John Ridd's herculean power and his service to James II during Monmouth's Rebellion

"The scenic descriptions of the lovely region befits the tale, and many local worthies have their lineaments preserved here. Though 'Lorna Doone' made little stir at the time of its appearance, it has had innumerable imitations since, and it initiated a return to . . . romanticism in historical fiction." Baker. Guide to the Best Fic

Blackstock, Terri

✓ **Shadow** in serenity; Terri Blackstock. Zondervan 2011 352p.

ISBN 9780310332312; 9780310332329

This book tells the story of Carny Sullivan, who "grew up in the zany world of a traveling carnival. Quaint and peaceful Serenity, Texas, has given her a home, a life, and a child. Logan Brisco is the smoothest, slickest, handsomest man Serenity, Texas has ever seen. But Carny Sullivan knows a con artist when she sees one . . . [F]rom his Italian shoes to his movie-actor smile, Logan has the rest of the town snowed. Carny is determined to reveal Brisco's selfish intentions before his promise to the townspeople for a cut in a giant amusement park sucks Serenity dry. Yet, as much as she hates his winning ways, there is a man behind that suave smile, a man who may win her heart against her will." (Publisher's note)

Blackwell, Elise

✓ **Grub**. Toby Press 2007 353p $24.95

ISBN 978-1-59264-199-4; 1-59264-199-7

In this contemporary retelling of George Gissing's 'New Grub Street' set in New York City, Blackwell "focuses on a smoothie out for money and fame but intrigued by the daughter of a bitter, fading man-of-letters: Jackson Miller, Margot and her father Andrew Yarborough. Equally important are a novelist struggling to sell a second novel, produce a third and not lose his ambitious wife, and the wife, who turns to her own pragmatic pen: Eddie and Amanda Renfros." PopMatters

"A mordantly witty, thoroughly stimulating absolutely wonderful, satire of the New York literary world and of the price of being a literary success in America." Islamorada Free Press

Blackwood, Caroline

Never breathe a word; the collected stories of Caroline Blackwood. Counterpoint 2010 366p $26

ISBN 978-1-58243-569-5; 1-58243-569-3

LC 2009-38105

"It is clear that we read for pleasure; what is less obvious are the varieties of pleasures we experience. Pleasing isn't always pleasant. Take Caroline Blackwood's stories they are rare in their brutal exposure and are deeply troubling to read. Yet 'Never Breathe a Word' is nothing less than a marvelous slide into an emotional abyss. In Blackwood's stories, women — almost always women — have quietly slipped outside their conventional roles. . . . They inhabit danger zones of keen intelligence, amused manipulation and something else — self-indulgence, or maybe self-importance. They are sometimes funny, unwittingly revealing and rarely nice. At the core, they're out of sync with underlying societal assumptions, women who are unselfconsciously and dominantly at the center of their worlds." Los Angeles Times Book Rev

Blake, Robin

✓ **A dark** anatomy; Robin Blake. Macmillan 2011 359 p. map $11.04

ISBN 023074835X; 9780230748354

LC 2011431238

In this mystery novel, "[t]he Lancashire estate of Garlick Hall is the scene of a gruesome murder and Titus Cragg, lawyer and coroner, is called upon to investigate and arrange a coroner's jury. When Dolores Brockletower, the wife of the squire, is found with her throat cut in the woods near her home, Titus calls upon his friend doctor Luke Fidelis to help investigate. . . . [W]hen the corpse is stolen . . . it is obvious someone is willing to go to great lengths to prevent an investigation." (Kirkus)

Blake, Sarah

The **postmistress**. Amy Einhorn Books 2010 326p $25.95

ISBN 978-0-399-15619-9; 0-399-15619-9

LC 2009-24532

"Frankie Bard is an American radio gal reporting from the Blitz in London, desperate for her dawdling countrymen back home to understand the need to enter World War II. Frankie's tough and fun. She can quip and quaff as quick as any of her male colleagues. She's one of three terrifically moving women — each of whom responds in her own way to the horrors of the war — in Sarah Blake's novel. Frankie's reports of an escalating conflict, and the terrifying waves of Jews flung from their homes, hold a young bride named Emma Fitch spellbound in tiny Franklin, Mass. Emma longs for a letter from her doctor husband, who has left her behind so that he can care for London's wounded and fallen. Yet it isn't Emma who first learns of the doctor's fate — it is Iris James, the town's postmistress, who delivers, daily, the letters that change people's lives. Iris, an ungainly 40-year-old with unflattering red lipstick and a crush on the town mechanic, ultimately proves to be the heart of Blake's novel." Entertainment Wkly

Bland, Eleanor Taylor

See no evil; a Marti MacAlister mystery. St. Martin's Press 1998 274p

ISBN 0-312-16910-8

LC 97-39642

"Detective Marti MacAlister, of the Lincoln Prairie police department, wonders how she and her partner will find the murderer of a young woman who 'fell' to her death on the rocky shores of Lake Michigan. A homeless black man has not seen his best friend in days and wonders what has happened. And a crafty stalker wonders how best to massacre Marti, her kids, and her housemates." Libr J

"Bland tightens the suspense with realistic details and subplot twists before wrapping the narrative up in a satisfying solution." Publ Wkly

Blatty, William Peter

Dimiter. Forge 2010 302p $24.99

ISBN 978-0-7653-2512-9; 0-7653-2512-8

LC 2010-13285

"In 1973 Albania, a nameless prisoner is arrested by authorities and put through horrific torture, but he refuses to reveal his name or purpose. A year later in Jerusalem, a doctor contemplates a series of seemingly mystical occurrences at his hospital, while his police-detective friend still mourns the deaths of his wife and son. All three are brought together by a mystery involving murder, international intrigue, and Christian belief. Blatty's greatest strength has also always been his most mockable weakness: his complete, unabashed sincerity. Dimiter is so unhampered by the agonies of irony and self-awareness that it's occasionally impossible to read with a straight face. . . . And yet that same unwinking intensity gives the story its power." A.V. Club

Blatty, William Peter

★ The **exorcist**. Harper & Row 1971 340p

ISBN 0-06-010365-5

"Blatty has done his homework. He discourses, a bit bookishly, on the history of possession and the relation of autosuggestion to masked guilt. . . . Blatty maintains headlong thrust, slowly increasing Regan's agony until the reader winces; no more, a part of us says, but of course we want more because Blatty handles the horror so well." Newsweek

Bledsoe, Alex

The **hum** and the shiver. Tor Books 2011 349p $15.99

ISBN 978-0-7653-2744-4

LC 2011021573

"Bledsoe turns standard urban fantasy tropes on their head by reimagining modern elves as a tiny, isolated ethnic group unsure of their own origins, like the Lemkos of Poland or the Melungeons of the southern Appalachians. The plot is a bit thin, but the slowly unfolding mystery of the Tufa is a fascinating and absorbing masterpiece of world-building." Publ Wkly

Bledsoe, Alex

Wisp of a thing; Alex Bledsoe. 1st ed. Tor 2013 352 p. (hardcover) $25.99

ISBN 0765334135; 9780765334138

LC 2013003720

In this novel, by Alex Bledsoe, named in "'Kirkus Reviews'" Best Fiction Books of 2011, "touched by a very public tragedy, musician Rob Quillen comes to Cloud County, Tennessee, in search of a song that might ease his aching heart. All he knows of the mysterious and reclusive Tufa is what he has read on the internet: they are an enigmatic clan of swarthy, black-haired mountain people whose historical roots are lost in myth and controversy." (Publisher's note)

Blew, Mary Clearman

Jackalope dreams. University of Nebraska Press 2008 390p (Flyover fiction) $24.95

ISBN 978-0-8032-1588-7; 0-8032-1588-6

LC 2007-23271

"Blew's prose is as hardscrabble and finely whittled as her Montana subjects. . . . [She has woven] disparate elements—the death of the old West, the crazed militiamen, women both weak and strong, all-seeing children, the creeping destruction of drugs—into a tautly beautiful book." PopMatters

Block, Brett Ellen

The **language** of sand; a novel. [by] Ellen Block. Bantam Books Trade Paperbacks 2010 276p pa $15

ISBN 978-0-440-24575-9; 0-440-24575-3

LC 2009-52876

"After the tragic death of her husband and son, Abigail Harker leaves her career as a lexicographer in Boston to become the caretaker of an old lighthouse on an island off the coast of North Carolina. Arriving on Chapel Isle in the off-season, Abigail imagines she will find peace and solitude while coming to know the island her late husband loved as a child. However, things are not quite as she imagines. The quaint lighthouse turns out to be a dilapidated wreck with a sordid past; the ambience proves to be both prickly and mysterious; and her memories of the life she left behind follow Abigail everywhere." Booklist

"Block writes gracefully about heartache and the mending of an injured soul, and the smalltown backdrop is pleasant without being kitschy." Publ Wkly

Block, Francesca Lia

The **elementals**; Francesca Lia Block. St. Martin's Press 2012 272 p. (hardcover) $24.99

ISBN 1250005493; 9781250005496; 9781250018427

LC 2012028277

This novel, by Francesca Lia Block, follows "Ariel Silverman, facing the challenges of her first years away at college in Berkeley, California. . . . Ariel is haunted by the disappearance of her best friend, Jeni, who vanished without a trace. . . . Ariel wonders if she will be fully alive, until she meets three mysterious . . . young people living . . . in the Berkeley hills. Through them Ariel will unravel the mystery of her best friend's disappearance and face a chilling choice." (Publisher's note)

Block, Lawrence

All the flowers are dying. Morrow 2005 288p $24.95

ISBN 0-06-019831-1

LC 2004-53643

"Although Scudder's hunt for the killer turns into a companionable tour of colorful neighborhoods, his thoughts on the city run deep and reflect real feelings about its humanity." N Y Times Book Rev

Block, Lawrence

★ The **burglar** in the library; a Bernie Rhodenbarr mystery. Dutton 1997 342p

ISBN 0-525-94301-3

LC 96-37537

"Panting after a copy of 'The Big Sleep' inscribed by Raymond Chandler for Dashiell Hammett ('the ultimate association copy in American crime fiction'), Bernie drags Carolyn to an inn, 'a genuine English country house' in the Berkshires, so he can relieve the unsuspecting owners of this treasure. But before he can pull the heist, the inn is snowbound, the phone lines are cut, the bridge is down and Bernie's ex-girlfriend shows up with her new husband. What next? A body in the library? Yes, and, even better, the drollest sendup of a murder-in-a-teacup mystery that you will ever hope to beg, borrow—or steal." N Y Times Book Rev

Block, Lawrence

A **drop** of the hard stuff; a Matthew Scudder novel. Mulholland Books/Little, Brown and Co. 2011 319p $25.99

ISBN 978-0-316-12733-2

LC 2010-41792

"More than any of the previous entries, the mystery in A Drop of the Hard Stuff is interwoven with the 12-Step program that's such an intimate part of Scudder's life. Told in flashback, the story begins when Scudder bumps into a childhood neighbor at an AA meeting. Matt and Jack Avery were casual friends for a brief period during their youths, but as adults they drifted to opposite sides of the law – Scudder joining the police while Avery opted for a life of crime. Apart from a brief glimpse a rookie cop Scudder got of Avery in a police lineup years back, the two haven't seen each other in decades. . . . While Matt still harbors reservations about the A.A. program, Jack's on the 9th step, which requires him to make amends to the people he's harmed. It's during this process that Jack is brutally murdered. Since the cops won't spend much time searching for the murderer of a 'known criminal,' Jack's sponsor asks Matt to investigate. . . . Another solid entry in one of mystery's most reliable series." Spinetingler

Block, Lawrence

✓ **Eight** million ways to die. Arbor House 1982 319p

ISBN 0-87795-405-4

LC 81-71698

This "novel is both a rousing private-eye story and an extended meditation on the whimsical ways of death—through freak accident, premeditated murder, and self-destruction. Private eye Matthew Scudder solves murders while he battles his own alcoholism. . . . In {this} tale, a 23-year old prostitute, Kim Dakkinen, wants out of 'the life' and asks Scudder to speak to her pimp, Chance. Scudder does, and a few days later Kim is found stabbed to death. Chance does the unexpected by hiring Scudder to find Kim's murderer, and while Scudder investigates, another one of Chance's

prostitutes commits suicide; then another slashing occurs. A magnificently plotted, sensitive portrayal of two kinds of death—the kind that comes as an intruder and the kind that comes as an invited guest." Booklist

Block, Lawrence

Getting off; a novel of sex and violence. by Lawrence Block writing as Jill Emerson. Hard Case Crime 2011 335p $25.99

ISBN 978-0-8576-8287-1; 0-8576-8287-3

This novel's "nymphomaniacal, blonde protagonist is also a sociopathic serial killer who drifts from town to town murdering her many men, motivated by lingering rage and abandonment issues left over from father/daughter incest that spilled over into patricide. Deceptively innocent, Kit Tolliver isn't just a sex maniac (and remorseless knife-wielding maniac), she's a pathological liar who changes her name and life story with unnerving ease to lull her victims. Reflecting her rootless existence, Getting Off unfolds chapter by chapter like a series of linked short stories, in each of which she meets and disposes of a new man. She's icy and clinical about murder, but constantly overheated about sex. Aimless, she picks up some semblance of a life goal (and the novel picks up the threads of its loosely woven plot) when she realizes that of all the men she's had, five have survived—which is unforgivably sloppy of her, and ought to be corrected. With the same skill he's shown in his more mainstream work, Block slowly ratchets up the intensity and violence, using each successive murder either to give a deeper glimpse into Kit's twisted psyche, or push her one step further toward her psychotic but somehow distortedly logical goal." AV Club

Block, Lawrence

★ **Hit** me; a Keller novel. Lawrence Block. Mulholland Books 2013 352 p. $26.99

ISBN 0316127353; 9780316127356; 9780316224147

LC 2012019988

This book by Lawrence block opens with "philatelist and killer for hire John Keller . . . living in New Orleans under a new name with his wife, Julia, and their baby daughter. Despite having a legitimate job in real estate, Keller can't resist resuming his old life. . . . In inventive ways, Keller deals with a cheating wife in Dallas, a 'felonious monk' in New York City, a cruise ship in Florida with a protected witness aboard, and a wandering husband in Denver." (Publishers Weekly)

Block, Lawrence

✓ **Killing** Castro. Hard Case Crime 2009 204p pa $6.99

ISBN 978-0-8439-6113-3; 0-8439-6113-9

First published 1961 by Monarch under the pseudonym Lee Duncan with title: Fidel Castro assassinated

An "absorbing yarn about five men vying for a $100,000 prize put on Fidel Castro's head by a mysterious guy named Hiraldo. Bounty hunter Ray Garrison only works on his own; hardened murderer Michael Turner is paired with 19-year-old Jim Hines, avenging his brother's execution; and Earl Fenton, longing to do some good before he dies of cancer, teams up with jack-of-all-trades Matt Garth, who just wants the money. As they make their way to the Cuban coast, sympathetic locals support the five would-be killers in their titular goal despite their penchant for rape and mayhem. Passages discussing Castro's life and times add depth to this intense, taut thriller, just as good now as it was in 1961." Publ Wkly

Block, Lawrence

✓ The **sins** of the fathers; a Matthew Scudder novel. introduction by Stephen King. Dark Harvest 1992 179p

ISBN 0-913165-66-2

First published 1976 in paperback

This novel introduced the then-hard-drinking ex-cop Matt Scudder. "The father of murdered Wendy Hanniford comes to Scudder to try to find out more about his errant daughter—not to find her killer, who was apparently her living partner, a brittle young man who was found in the street raving and covered with her blood and who killed himself shortly after he was arrested. In his dour, methodical, oddly empathetic way, Scudder finds out a great deal, altering several lives in the process. . . . This is a fine opportunity to get in on the start of what has become one of the most rewarding PI series currently in progress." Publ Wkly

Block, Lawrence

✓ A **ticket** to the boneyard; a Matthew Scudder novel. Morrow 1990 302p

ISBN 0-688-09070-2

LC 90-5710

The author "has a fine nose for the pungencies of New York's after-dark street life, and he gives his hero wonderful opportunities to swap syllables with the city's most articulate riffraff. This is primo stuff, and Scudder doesn't get any sharper than when he's interviewing transvestite hookers, desk clerks in fleabag hotels and bouncers in gay leather bars." N Y Times Book Rev

Block, Lawrence

✓ ★ **When** the sacred ginmill closes. Arbor House 1986 239p

ISBN 0-87795-774-6

LC 85-18682

"The writing is realistic in the best sense of the word. There are no artificial heroics, forced lines of dialogue or false moves. Mr. Block knows his New York and the way people speak." N Y Times Book Rev

Bock, Charles

✓ **Beautiful** children; a novel. Random House 2008 417p $25

ISBN 978-1-4000-6650-6; 1-4000-6650-6

LC 2007-4166

"In the no-man's land of Bock's Vegas there remain only the survival strategies of the hopelessly inept young. I cannot think of another novelist who has dared to attack this most pressing and complex issue so ferociously." Washington Post Book World

Bock, Dennis

✓ The **ash** garden; a novel. Knopf 2001 281p $23

ISBN 0-375-41302-2

LC 2001-29872

"Bock's writing is both dense and immensely readable, as engaging when it focuses on life's minutiae as when it explores life's catastrophes. The Ash Garden is difficult to forget and it rewards repeated readings in a way that few novels can." Quill Quire

Bognanni, Peter

✓ The **house** of tomorrow; Peter Bognanni. Amy Einhorn Books/G.P. Putnam's Sons 2010 354p o.p.; (pbk.) $15

ISBN 0399156097; 9780425238882

LC 2009023542

Alex Award (2011)

This book follows teenager Sebastian Prendergast, who "lives in Iowa's first geodesic dome with his grandmother, a devout follower of futurist philosopher Buckminster R. Fuller. But when Nana has a stroke, Sebastian is thrown together with Janice and teenage Jared Whitcomb, who were touring the home when Nana was stricken. Soon, Sebastian and Jared form an unlikely bond via the great teenage tradition of punk rock, starting their own band despite the objections of everyone around them and Sebastian's lack of musical ability . . . And while Jared succeeds to some degree in socializing Sebastian—teaching him about music, smoking, and curse words—Sebastian ends up getting more than he bargained for when the two get caught up in Whitcomb family drama." (Publishers Weekly)

"Sebastian's first stumble out of the woods into the sweet and vicious real world may not break any new ground, but it's worthwhile, distracting and delightful. Bognanni . . . captures that breath we take before we jump out into our life" Minneapolis Star Tribune

Bohjalian, Christopher A.

The **night** strangers; a novel. [by] Chris Bohjalian. Crown 2011 378p $25

ISBN 978-0-307-39499-6; 0-307-39499-9

LC 2010-45401

"Chip Linton is at the controls of a jet that flies into a flock of birds and goes down in Lake Champlain. Although Linton does everything correctly, an errant wave tips the plane over. Thirty-nine of the 48 people aboard die, and the captain's life, obviously, is changed forever. His lawyer wife, Emily, and their 10-year-old twins decide they need to start over. So they leave Pennsylvania for the small town of Bethel, N.H. But things do not get better. The ghost of several drowned passengers haunts him, particularly Ashley, a young girl, and her dad. They are stuck in purgatory and alone. Linton believes he's responsible, and that Ashley deserves company, and he's prepared to kill his own daughters to provide it. He's crazy, of course or is he? The denouement is not only unexpected but is also perfect and true to the story. Bohjalian is a terrific writer and parsimonious in the way he issues information, slowly building an increasing sense of dread and excitement." Minneapolis Star Tribune

Bohjalian, Christopher A.

✓ The **sandcastle** girls; a novel. Chris Bohjalian. Doubleday 2012 299 p. $25.95

ISBN 0385534795; 9780385534796

LC 2011050285

In this book, "Elizabeth Endicott, a recent Mount Holyoke graduate, accompanies her Bostonian banker father on his philanthropic mission to Aleppo, Syria, to aid Armenian refugees fleeing atrocities committed by the Ottoman government. Her friendship with Armenian engineer Armen . . . flourishes . . . in letters. Years later, Laura Petrosian, seeking out a photograph of a woman rumored to be her Armenian grandmother, uncovers these letters." (Library Journal)

"Bohjalian powerfully narrates an intricately nuanced romance with a complicated historical event at the forefront." LJ

Bohjalian, Christopher A.
Secrets of Eden; a novel. [by] Chris Bohjalian. Shaye Areheart Books 2010 370p $25
ISBN 978-0-307-39497-2
LC 2009-23946
"Alice Hayward, the town of Haverill knows, is a battered wife, struggling to find meaning in her life with her brutal husband. The same day that she is baptized by the town's minister, Stephen Drew, she is murdered by her husband, who then turned a gun on himself. These facts emerge in the book's first dozen pages, and the rest of the novel rotates around the events of that night. Four narrative voices, with varying degrees of directness, tell their versions of the story: the Reverend Drew, who has a not entirely spiritual connection with Alice; state's attorney Catherine Benincasa, concerned that the full story may not yet have been told; self-help author Heather Laurent, a specialist in angels who's haunted by her own parents' murder/suicide; and the Haywards' daughter Katie, a newly orphaned highschooler sorting out the messiness left behind." Seattle Times

Bohjalian, Christopher A.
Skeletons at the feast; a novel. by Chris Bohjalian. Shaye Areheart Books 2008 372p map $25
ISBN 978-0-307-39495-8; 0-307-39495-6
LC 2007-40800
"Inspired by the World War II diary of an East Prussian woman, Skeletons describes the horrific final months of the war as a motley crew of characters struggle to make their way across the Polish countryside to reach British and American lines. With Russian troops on their flanks and remnants of the Third Reich dotted dauntingly here and there, their journey is a daring and terrifying exodus. Key to the group are Uri Singer, a German Jew who dove to freedom from a train headed to Auschwitz and thereafter assumes the identity of various dead German soldiers; Anna Emmerich, a daughter of Prussian aristocrats who is fleeing with her family; and Callum Finnella, a Scottish prisoner of war who hides in the Emmerich family wagon and has become Anna's lover." Rocky Mountain News

Bohman, Therese
Drowned; by Therese Bohman; translated by Marlaine Delargy. Other Press 2011 217 p. (trade pbk.: acid-free paper) $14.95
ISBN 1590515242; 9781590515242; 9781590515259
LC 2011049352
In this book, "[a]cademic burnout Marina leaves art history behind and travels to rural Skåne to stay with her older sister, Stella, and Stella's much older boyfriend,

well-known writer Gabriel." Marina and Gabriel begin an affair. When Stella drowns, Marina begins to question whether Gabriel might be responsible for her sister's death. (Publishers Weekly)

Boianjiu, Shani
The people of forever are not afraid; a novel. Shani Boianjiu. 1st ed. Hogarth 2012 338 p. (hardcover) $24.00; (ebook) $72.00
ISBN 0307955958; 9780307955951; 9780307955968
LC 2012008962
This novel, by Shani Boianjiu, follows three Israeli women soldiers. "Yael, Avishag, and Lea grow up together in a tiny, dusty Israeli village. . . . When they are conscripted into the army, their lives change in unpredictable ways, influencing the women they become and the friendship that they struggle to sustain. . . . They drill, constantly, for a moment that may never come. They live inside that single, intense second just before danger erupts." (Publisher's note)

Bolaño, Roberto, 1953-2003
2666; translated from the Spanish by Natasha Wimmer. Farrar, Straus and Giroux 2008 898p $30
ISBN 978-0-374-10014-8; 0-374-10014-4
LC 2008-18295
Original Spanish edition, 2004
"More vast and more lurid than his previous novels that have been translated into English, '2666' is not Roberto Bolaño's masterpiece but almost a compendium, in individual scenes, of the qualities that made him a great writer. His themes are violence, dislocation, and the sexiness of literature, and here these strands are recombined endlessly, in Europe, Detroit, and Mexico, through multiple narrators and prose styles. The action converges on the Sonoran desert, where Bolaño anatomizes, in brutal and eerie detail, the true-life murders of hundreds of women, most of which remain unsolved. By the end, after close to nine hundred pages, the reader will be impressed by the range and power on display but might wish that the novel cohered, rather than merely concluding." New Yorker

Bolano, Roberto
Amulet; translated from the Spanish by Chris Andrews. New Directions 2006 184p $19.95
ISBN 978-0-8112-1664-7; 0-8112-1664-0
LC 2006-23507
Original Spanish edition, 1999
This is a "curiously joyful novel that delights in its storytelling even as it struggles with the question of how art might be sustained under conditions resolutely opposed to it." Harper's

Bolano, Roberto
★ By night in Chile; translated from the Spanish by Chris Andrews. New Directions 2004 130p pa $13.95
ISBN 0-81121-547-4 pa
Original Spanish edition, 2000
"Postwar Chilean politics and literature infuse this densely learned, richly evocative novel. In Chris Andrews's lucid translation, Bolano's febrile narrative tack and occasional surreal touches bring to mind the classics of Latin

American magic realism; his cerebral protagonist and non-fiction borrowings are reminiscent of Thomas Bernhard and W. G. Sebald." N Y Times Book Rev

Bolano, Roberto

√ **Distant** star; translated from the Spanish by Chris Andrews. New Directions 2004 149p pa $14.95

ISBN 0-8112-1586-5

LC 2004-19033

Original Spanish edition, 1996

"'The melancholy folklore of exile' pervades this novel, which describes the divergent paths of three young Chilean poets around the time of Pinochet's coup. At university, the unnamed narrator and his friend are fascinated by a mysterious new member of their poetry workshop. Alberto Ruiz-Tagle is 'serious, well mannered, a clear thinker,' but his poems seem false, as if his true work were yet to be revealed. It becomes apparent that this is literally the case when Allende's government falls: as an Air Force officer for the new regime, he becomes famous for writing nationalist slogans in the sky. (The left-wing narrator, now in jail, reads them from his prison yard.) Bolano's spare prose lends his narrator's account a chilly precision—as if the detachment of his former classmate had become his country's, and his own." New Yorker

Bolano, Roberto

√ **Last** evenings on Earth; translated from the Spanish by Chris Andrews. New Directions 2006 219p $23.95

ISBN 978-0-8112-1634-0; 0-8112-1634-9

LC 2006-3819

"These 14 bleakly luminous stories are all told in the first person by men (usually young) who yearn for something just out of their grasp (fame, talent, love) and who harbor few hopes of attaining what they desire. . . . The stories are similar, in theme and voice (though not in locale), and they are perfectly calibrated: Bolaño limns the capacity of a voice to carry despair without shading into bitterness." Publ Wkly

Bolano, Roberto

√ **Monsieur** Pain; translated by Chris Andrews. New Directions 2010 134p $22.95

ISBN 978-0-8112-1714-9; 0-8112-1714-0

LC 2009-37431

Original Spanish edition, 1999

"Paris, 1938: Two shadowy Spaniards seem to be stalking Monsieur Pain, a middle-aged mesmerist hopelessly in love with a young widow, who appears with a desperate plea: She needs his help to heal Monsieur Vallejo, a Peruvian dying of inexplicable hiccups. Monsieur Pain tries to visit the ailing man in the clinic, which turns out to be a Kafkaesque maze of circular halls and hostile nurses. Meanwhile, the mysterious Spaniards issue Pain a cash bribe and a demand: Under no circumstances must he use his occult abilities to heal the Peruvian. The Peruvian in question is none other than the poet César Vallejo, widely considered one of the most innovative surrealists of the 20th century. Bolaño draws on actual facts the real Vallejo was hospitalized in Paris in 1938, and his wife called in practitioners of occult sciences when doctors failed to cure him to weave his brilliant, noir-steeped fictional world. As Pain wanders

the rainy streets of Paris, convinced of a plot to assassinate Vallejo, haunted by his own complicity and helpless rebellion, we enter a hallucinatory dreamscape flooded with resonant symbols." San Francisco Chron

Bolano, Roberto

★ **Nazi** literature in the Americas; translated from the Spanish by Chris Andrews. New Directions 2008 227p $23.95

ISBN 978-0-8112-1705-7; 0-8112-1705-1

LC 2007-37800

Original Spanish edition, 1996

This novel, "a wicked, invented encyclopedia of imaginary fascist writers and literary tastemakers, is Bolaño playing with sharp, twisting knives. As if he were Borges's wisecracking, sardonic son, Bolaño has meticulously created a tightly woven network of far-right litterateurs and purveyors of belles lettres for whom Hitler was beauty, truth and great lost hope. Cross-referenced, complete with bibliography and a biographical list of secondary figures, Nazi Literature is composed of a series of sketches, the compressed life stories of writers in North and South America who never existed, but all too easily could have. Goose-stepping caricatures a la 'The Producers' they are not; instead, they are frighteningly subtle, poignant and plausible." N Y Times Book Rev

Includes bibliographical references

Bolano, Roberto

√ ★ The **savage** detectives; translated from the Spanish by Natasha Wimmer. Farrar, Straus & Giroux 2007 577p il $27

ISBN 978-0-374-19148-1; 0-374-19148-4

LC 2006-22176

Original Spanish edition, 1998

"'Though the fragmented narrative can be frustrating at times, the late-20th-century panorama emerging from the cacophony is simultaneously frightening and spectacular. At every turn, Bolaño examines the individual lives history discards. The result is a large, sprawling and—most of all—sublime novel." Paste

Bolaño, Roberto, 1953-2003

√ The **skating** rink; translated by Chris Andrews. New Directions 2009 182p $21.95

ISBN 978-0-8112-1713-2; 0-8112-1713-2

LC 2009-10724

Original Spanish edition, 1993

"Set in the fictional Spanish seaside town of 'Z' and told from the points-of-view of an alternating trio of narrators—Remo Morán, former poet-turned-businessman; Enric Rosquelles, corrupt civil servant; and Gaspar Heredia, illegal immigrant, campground nightwatchman and our authorial stand-in—the novel revolves around Nuria Martí, an aspiring Olympic skater whose beauty will compel Morán and Rosquelles in ways neither had previously imagined. To help Martí in her training, Rosquelles embezzles city funds to transform a dilapidated mansion on the outskirts of the city into a fully operational regulation-sized skating rink. Meanwhile, Martí begins a casual romance with Morán, the more physically attractive (and apparently well-endowed) of the two rivals. And here, the initial pieces are set. Add in Heredia's fixation with two of the campground's residents,

Carmen, a former opera singer, and Caridad, a mysterious, taciturn girl, and it seems inevitable that these actions will culminate in disaster. . . . The novel traverses territories of escalating and unstable passion, but not without occasional comedy." Faster Times

Bolaño, Roberto, 1953-2003

✓ ★ The **Third** Reich; a novel. translated from the Spanish by Natasha Wimmer. 1st American ed. Farrar, Straus and Giroux 2011 277p. $25

ISBN 9780374275624; 9781250013934

LC 2011025798

Original Spanish edition, 2010

This book tells the story of "Udo Berger and his girl-friend Ingeborg, Germans in their 20s, [who] arrive on Spain's Costa Brava for their vacation. . . . War games are Udo's passion, and he's the German champion . . . [and] he's brought with him a World War II game, the eponymous Third Reich. . . . [T]he core of the novel [is] the game and . . . [Udo's] obsession with a mysterious, badly scarred guy known as El Quemado (the Burn Victim). . . . No one is sure of his background; South America? There's even a sugges-tion he's the re-incarnation of an Incan warrior. At first Udo idealizes him as a Noble Savage, but he's plenty smart, a po-etry lover. Udo teaches him the game; El Quemado catches on fast. Power shifts from the cocksure Udo to his humble opponent as the German crumbles, on the board and off." (Kirkus)

"Not long after his death, [Bolaño's] heirs discovered an unpublished manuscript, The Third Reich, written more than 20 years ago, and now translated into English by Na-tasha Wimmer. While it might not feature the narrative fire-works of his award-winning The Savage Detectives (1998) or the epic sprawl of 2666, it's no less brilliant. . . . The novel chronicles a month in the life of Udo Berger, a young German on vacation in northeast Spain with his girlfriend, Ingeborg. Udo is a prodigy, a widely respected master of 'war games' — a type of strategy-based board game popu-lar among hobbyists in the 1970s and 1980s. He plans to use his time off to research an article he's writing about The Third Reich, a challenging World War II simulation . . . . His plans are derailed, though, once he and Ingeborg meet Charly, a charming, impulsive fellow German tourist, and El Quemado ('The Burned One'), a mysterious beach dweller who shows an unexpected interest in the game. After Charly disappears while windsurfing, it doesn't take long for Udo to realize that no amount of skill or strategy can keep his life from falling apart." NPR

Boll, Heinrich

✓The **clown**; translated from the German by Leila Vennewitz. McGraw-Hill 1965 247p

Original German edition, 1963

This novel revolves around the loss of meaning in the life of Hans Schnier, a twenty-seven-year-old clown and mime who returns home to Bonn after a disastrous perfor-mance tour. Flashbacks reconstruct Schnier's life in Hitler's Germany and his bitter experiences of the postwar period

"What Schnier (and the author) seem to be asking is: How can an honest man profess Christianity when Christian culture in the West failed to stop the rise of Nazism . . . and when the Church thrives in a society that worships nothing

but the values of the marketplace? Hard questions but em-bodied in a bitter and brilliant book." NY Times Book Rev

Boll, Heinrich

✓The **silent** angel; translated by Breon Mitchell. St. Martin's Press 1994 182p

ISBN 0-312-11064-2

LC 94-2052

Written in 1950; first German edition, 1992

"While the bleakness Böll portrays might have made German publishers wary in 1950, the artistry of his portrayal makes 'The Silent Angel' a rich novel, one still pertinent to our own hunger for the bread of meaning amid the rubble of history. Heinrich Böll's gift to us is the skill with which he captures its first pangs." NY Times Book Rev

Bolton, S. J.

✓**Now** you see me. Minotaur Books 2011 395p il $25.99

ISBN 978-0-312-60052-5; 0-312-60052-6

LC 2011-08751

"On the anniversary of the original Ripper's first killing, Det. Constable Lacey Flint is horrified to find a dying wom-an, 'her abdomen . . . a mass of scarlet,' leaning against the detective's car in a London car park. The guilt-ridden Flint wonders whether different actions on her part might have saved the victim's life or caught the killer. The connection with the 1888 autumn of terror becomes clear after a journal-ist receives a letter obviously derived from some of the cor-respondence Scotland Yard received back then, ostensibly from the Ripper himself. By coincidence, Flint is something of a Ripper expert, and her knowledge proves useful in what develops into a multiple murder investigation. Avoiding gra-tuitous violence, Bolton . . . skillfully plays with the reader's expectations." Publ Wkly

Bond, Larry

✓**Exit** plan; Larry Bond. Forge 2012 412 p.

ISBN 0765331462; 9780765331465; 9781429957052

LC 2011277667

This "military action novel" depicts a "tale of SEAL ad-ventures and global politics. . . . [T]wo high-level members of the Iranian military conclude that their nuclear engineers won't be able to build an atomic weapon anytime soon. They come up with a desperate plan: pretend to be readying a nuclear test to trick the Israelis and Americans into imple-menting a first strike. This action will secure the backing of the rest of the Arab world in a regional war against Israel. Proof of this plan rests with two disaffected Iranians, Shirin Naseri, who works in a nuclear lab, and her husband, Yousef, an officer in the country's air defenses. After the couple offer proof to the CIA, a SEAL team sets out to bring them out of Iran." (Publishers Weekly)

Bond, Michael

Monsieur Pamplemousse. Beaufort Bks. 1985 191p

ISBN 0-8253-0267-6

LC 84-24444

First published 1983 in the United Kingdom

Pamplemousse is a "gastronomic detective, an under-cover critic for a prestigious Gallic dining guide. With his faithful bloodhound, Pommes Frites, Pamplemousse—a former inspector with the Sureté—investigates the cuisine of his favorite hotel-restaurant, La Langoustine. There, misfortune strikes: the specialty of the house is served to him with a man's head inside. . . . Mystery takes a back seat to fine food and hilarious characters in this ribald, side-splitting farce." Publ Wkly

Borchardt, Alice

The **silver** wolf. Ballantine Bks. 1998 451p
ISBN 0-345-42360-7

LC 98-4802

"As Charlemagne consolidates his empire through a combination of wars and strategic marriages, a young girl who possesses the power to transform herself into a silver wolf becomes a reluctant pawn in a game of politics and survival. Against the decadent and barbaric backdrop of Rome in the Dark Ages, the author . . . spins a love-story tinged with the supernatural. Borchardt's sensual prose and period detail provide a lush setting for her tale of a woman struggling to reconcile her human and wolf natures." Libr J

Borges, Jorge Luis

★ **Collected** fictions; translated by Andrew Hurley. Viking 1998 565p
ISBN 0-670-84970-7

LC 98-21217

This is a collection of all the stories written by Borges over a 50-year period

"A Borges invention . . . always takes the reader on a roller-coaster ride into some previously unsuspected dimension. This collection of the great magician's work is a new translation and includes one piece never before put into English." Atl Mon

Borland, Hal

When the legends die. Lippincott 1963 288p hardcover o.p. pa $6.50
ISBN 0-553-25738-2

"Thomas Black Bull, a Ute Indian, is being reared in the traditional Native American way when his parents are forced to flee from the world of the white man. After the death of his parents Tom is returned to the white world, where he suffers the disintegration of his native heritage and traditions as he experiences school, sheep herding, and rodeo life. Following a serious accident at a rodeo he returns to the mountains and is drawn back into his past." Shapiro. Fic for Youth 3rd edition

Bornikova, Phillipa

Box office poison; by Phillipa Bornikova. Tor Books 2013 316 p. (hardcover) $24.99
ISBN 0765326833; 9780765326836

LC 2013015151

In this novel by Phillipa Bornikova "elves start getting all the roles in Hollywood. [When] human actors sue . . . the Screen Actors Guild . . . forces the two sides into arbitration. Linnet Ellery, a human lawyer working for a vampire law firm, [serves] as arbitrator. Linnet discovers that there are . . . forces . . . determined to shatter the . . . peace between elves, vampires, werewolves, and humans. Someone has been co-

ercing . . . elven actors into committing . . . acts of violence against humans." (Publisher's note)

Bornikova, Phillipa

This case is gonna kill me; Phillipa Bornikova. Tor 2012 318 p. (paperback) $14.99
ISBN 0765326825; 9780765326829; 9780765333896; 9781429977913

LC 2012011473

In this novel, by Phillipa Bornikova, "[l]aw, finance, the military, and politics are under the sway of long-lived vampires, werewolves, and the elven Alfar. . . . Linnet Ellery is . . . beginning her career in a powerful New York 'white fang' law firm. . . . But strange things keep happening to her. . . . However, there's apparently more to Linnet Ellery than a little old-money human privilege. More than even she knows." (Publisher's note)

Bosse, Malcolm J.

The **warlord**. Simon & Schuster 1983 717p
ISBN 0-671-44332-1

"This book is a must for the student of China as well as those interested in human nature. It is a complicated story and cannot be skimmed or read between loads at the laundromat. This story is for those who enjoy 'hunkering down' in the sun and traveling to exotic places, where they must deal with contradictions, love and hate, peace and violence, confusions, and Marxist loyalty, and ultimately betrayal." Best Sellers

Followed by Fire in heaven

Boswell, Robert

Century's son. Knopf 2002 307p $24
ISBN 0-375-41237-9

LC 2001-38101

"Morgan, whose first name has fallen away 'from disuse,' was once a fearless labor organizer for his fellow sanitation workers; it was his uncompromising idealism that led Zhenya, his college-professor wife, to fall in love with him. But, ten years later, Morgan has abandoned his activism; he spends his days collecting garbage and contemplating his decline, which began when his son hanged himself, at the age of twelve. As if the Morgan marriage didn't have enough to deal with, Zhenya's father, the famous Russian writer Peter Ivanovich Kamenev, is coming to visit. . . . A moving portrait of a family both torn apart and united by grief." New Yorker

Boswell, Robert

The **heyday** of the insensitive bastards; stories. Graywolf Press 2009 258p $24
ISBN 978-1-55597-524-1; 1-55597-524-0

LC 2008-941562

"Some of the stories are very short sketches or vignettes of brief encounters of a sexual or violent nature, while the longer stories are more novelistic and include large casts of characters and complex narratives. Boswell, whose style and subject matter is somewhat reminiscent of Tobias Wolff and Robert Stone, is a virtuoso of descriptive prose, and handles the psychological and emotional imagery with skill." Libr J

Boucher, Christopher

How to keep your Volkswagen alive. Melville House 2011 239p pa $15

ISBN 978-1-935554-63-9; 1-935554-63-8

This book "is set in a zany, modern-day western Massachusetts, where time is literally money, inanimate objects walk and talk, words take on new meaning, and, like the narrator's ever-shifting metaphors, the landscape alters its form at will. Based on a veritable hippie bible, a 1969 Volkswagen maintenance manual, Boucher's loosely structured, surreal interpretation portrays a man struggling to raise his sickly, illegitimate son, a 1971 VW Beetle (he often vomits oil) who was born shortly after the narrator's father was abducted and killed by a Heart Attack Tree. When the narrator sets out to investigate his father's death, his attempts to save time to heal his ailing son result in one long how-to on fatherhood. . . . With wicked, postmodern playfulness and a heart of tenderness, Boucher introduces a supercharged novel that reaffirms the vast and rousing possibilities of fiction." Booklist

Includes bibliographical references

Boulle, Pierre

✓★ The **bridge** over the River Kwai; translated by Xan Fielding. Vanguard Press 1954 224p

Original French edition, 1952

"In 1942 the Japanese military under the command of Col. Saito orders its British prisoners of war to construct a bridge over the 400-foot-wide River Kwai in the Siamese jungle. Complications arise when prisoner Col. Nicholson insists that officers not be treated like regular lower-class soldiers. Medical officer Clipton is much more humane, and this difference brings the two fellow prisoners into frequent conflict. When the bridge is finally completed, a British demolition team prepares to destroy it." Shapiro. Fic for Youth. 3d edition

Boulle, Pierre

✓★ **Planet** of the apes; translated by Xan Feilding. Ballantine 2001 268p pa $6.99

ISBN 0-345-44798-0

First published 1963 by Vanguard Press; published in the United Kingdom with title: Monkey planet

"In this Swiftian fable Boulle gives full play to his not inconsiderable gift for irony and satire." Libr J

Bourne, Joanna

★ The **black** hawk; Joanna Bourne. Berkley Sensation 2011 336p.

ISBN 9780425244531 pa; 9781410447456

LC 2012659025

This espionage thriller tells the story of two spies. "Adrian Hawker spied on France for England while Justine DeCabrillac gathered intelligence for the Police Sècrete. They were teens when they met in Paris in 1794, and as they grew up, their paths crossed often in a changing world. Sometimes they were on the same side, and sometimes they were opposed, but it was inevitable that they fall bittersweetly in love, knowing that any minute duty could take precedence over passion. Their tempestuous love affair unfolds in flashbacks, alternating with scenes from 1818 London, where somebody tries to kill Justine and frame Hawker, now head

of the British Intelligence Service with as many enemies in England as in France." (Publishers Weekly)

Bourne, Joanna

The **forbidden** rose. Berkley Sensation 2010 392p (Berkley Sensation historical romance) pa $7.99

ISBN 978-0-425-23561-4; 0-425-23561-0

A glittering French aristocrat is on the run, disguised as a British governess. England's top spy has a score to settle with her family. But as they're drawn inexorably into the intrigue and madness of Revolutionary Paris, they gamble on a love to which neither of them will admit.

The author "delivers another addictively readable installment in her loosely connected Spymaster novels, a flawless romance in which an espionage-steeped plot is deftly balanced with a lusciously sensual love story." Booklist

Bourne, Joanna

My lord and spymaster. Berkley Sensation 2008 324p pa $7.99

ISBN 978-0-425-22246-1; 0-425-22246-2

"Jess Whitby, daughter of suspected spy Josiah Whitby, is doing everything in her power to exonerate her imprisoned father. In order to free him, she must prove that someone other than her father is the Cinq, a notorious mole. But Jess has met her match in Capt. Sebastian Kennett, wealthy bastard son of an English nobleman, equally as clever at keeping tabs on Jess as she is at tracking him. Sebastian is responsible for Josiah's arrest; Jess believes that Sebastian may be the Cinq; their mutual attraction proves a lovely foil for their suspicious minds. Glimpses of the leads' sordid pasts add depth, and Bourne's consummate way with a story line and an explosive denouement do the rest." Publ Wkly

Bourne, Joanna

The **spymaster's** lady. Berkley Publishing Group 2008 373p pa $7.99

ISBN 978-0-425-21960-7

"Annique Villiers, the elusive spy known as the Fox Cub, has outwitted, outmaneuvered and outfoxed every man she's ever met, until British spymaster Robert Grey steps into a French prison. Grey's mission is to capture the Cub and uncover exactly what she knows and who she works for. As enemies, they hate one another; as fellow prisoners they must band together to escape. Their truce is filled with suspicion, but there's also a spark of something more a forbidden passion that threatens their missions." Romantic Times

Bova, Ben

✓**Jupiter**. TOR Bks. 2001 368p

ISBN 0-312-87217-8

LC 00-48021

"Assigned by the New Morality, Earth's conservative ruling coalition, to act as its agent at a research station in orbit around the planet Jupiter, astrophysicist Grant Archer finds himself torn between his faith in God and his loyalty to science. . . . {This is a} first-rate adventure that combines hard science with human drama to create a challenging and compelling tale of courage and conviction." Libr J

Bova, Ben

✓ **Leviathans** of Jupiter. Tor 2011 477p $24.99

ISBN 978-0-7653-1788-9; 0-7653-1788-5

LC 2010-36115

"To prove that the massive symbionts, named Leviathans, that inhabit Jupiter's atmosphere possess intelligence, physicist Grant Archer readies a deep-pressure manned probe for immersion in the giant planet's deadly cloud cover. Equally anxious to thwart his attempt, millionaire Katherine Westfall seeks to outmaneuver Archer in her bid for the top spot in the International Astronautical Authority (IAA) by any means possible—including murder. Bova's novels revolving around the planets . . . contain common themes—rebellion against political and religious interference in space colonization, human courage, and the desire to reach the stars; his latest addition provides all that as well as fully realized characters and a fast-action plot." Libr J

Bova, Ben

✓ ★ **Mars**. Bantam Bks. 1992 502p

ISBN 0-553-07892-5

LC 91-29466

"A Native American geologist finds himself the center of political controversy as he becomes one of the first humans to set foot on the red planet. Bova's imaginary chronicle of the first human mission to Mars offers a field day for science buffs as his characters experience the challenges of exploring Earth's nearest neighbor." Libr J

Followed by Return to Mars

Bova, Ben

✓ **Mars** life. Tor 2008 432p hardcover o.p. pa $7.99

ISBN 978-0-7653-1787-2; 0-7653-1787-7; 978-0-7653-5724-3 pa; 0-7653-5724-0 pa

LC 2008-20388

Sequel to: Return to Mars (1999)

"Bova deftly captures the excitement of scientific discovery and planetary exploration. This compelling story, balancing action and plausible political intrigue, will easily be enjoyed by both fans and newcomers." Publ Wkly

Bova, Ben

✓ **Return** to Mars. Avon Bks. 1999 403p

ISBN 0-380-97640-4

LC 99-21635

Sequel to Mars

"Where Bova shines is in making science not only comprehensible but entertaining." N Y Times Book Rev

Followed by: Mars life (2008)

Bova, Ben

✓ **Saturn**. TOR Bks. 2003 412p $24.95

ISBN 0-312-87218-6

LC 2003-40216

"Bova is definitely the man to do justice to the astronomical marvels of the Saturnian system with its enormous potential as a second home for humanity, especially in the complex environments of its moons. Loud, prolonged applause, then, for the strengths of this book." Booklist

Bowen, Elizabeth

✓ The **heat** of the day. Knopf 1949 372p

Essentially this novel presents character studies of Stella Rodney, and the two men who loved her. The background is London after Dunkirk, a London of blitzes and buzz bombs; and peaceful Ireland. The two men are Robert Kelway, Stella's lover, and the mysterious Harrison, who betrays Kelway's secret in order to gain Stella for himself

"Miss Bowen's novel expertly flicks the rawness of several unsolved queries concerning loyalty and love and ponders the degree to which human beings are strangers to each other. More densely written than her earlier work, this study of behavior is a soberly shocking, compassionate baring of the confused and vulnerable human heart." N Y Her Trib Books

Bowen, Peter

Badlands. St. Martin's Minotaur 2003 250p $23.95

ISBN 0-312-26252-3

LC 2002-37196

Montana sheriff Gabriel Du Pré's "suspicions are aroused when the Host of Yahweh immediately destroys the ranch buildings, sells the livestock and erects a makeshift metal chapel for secret rites. Soon, reportsof mass murders and suicides bring in cautious FBI agents ever mindful of the Waco debacle. Du Pré's blunt speech and sometimes opaque thought patterns can be hard to follow, but his pursuits of wrongdoers over cliffs, canyons and arid river beds are truly riveting." Publ Wkly

Bowles, Paul

Collected stories & later writings. Library of America 2002 1062p $40

ISBN 1-931082-20-0

LC 2002-19452

Fifty-two of the short stories in this volume have appeared in the five books: The delicate prey (1950); A hundred camels in the courtyard (1962); The time of friendship (1967); Things gone and things still here (1977); and Midnight mass (1981). Six selected later stories are also included. Up above the world (1966) is a novella where an American couple visiting Central America have a frightening experience with an apparently wealthy local couple. Their heads are green and their hands are blue (1963) is a collection of travel essays.

Includes bibliographical references

Bowles, Paul

★ The **sheltering** sky. New Directions 1949 318p

"Port and Kit Moresby, an American couple of independent means, have been traveling aimlessly for 12 years. By the time they reach Morocco they have become disaffected and alienated. They take up with a series of unreliable, rootless wanderers. On a trip to the interior Port contracts typhoid fever—out of apathy he has neglected to be vaccinated—and dies. Kit has an affair with an Arab and joins his household, but their relationship soon falls apart. Kit is found and returned to Oran. She is teetering on the brink of insanity and finds an opportunity to disappear into the crowded bazaar." Merriam-Webster's Ency of Lit

Bowles, Paul

The **sheltering** sky; Let it come down; The spider's house. Library of America 2002 938p $35
ISBN 1-931082-19-7
LC 2002-19453

The sheltering sky is entered separately. "In Let It Come Down (1952), Bowles plots the doomed trajectory of Nelson Dyar, a New York bank teller who comes to Tangier in search of a different life and ends up giving in to his darkest impulses. . . . The Spider's House (1955) . . . is set against the end of French rule in Morocco. Its characters—ranging from a Moroccan boy gifted with spiritual healing power to an American writer who regrets the passing of traditional ways—are caught up in the clash between colonial and nationalist factions, and are forced to confront cultural gulfs widened by political violence." Publisher's note

Bowles, Paul

The **stories** of Paul Bowles; introduction by Robert Stone. Ecco Press 2001 657p $39.95
ISBN 0-06-621273-1
LC 2001-51231

"Earthy, violent and comfortable with corruption, these deeply affecting stories are distinguished by their lyrical rhythms and meticulous regard for language." Publ Wkly

Box, C. J.

✓**Back** of beyond. Minotaur Books 2011 372p $25.99
ISBN 978-0-312-36574-5
LC 2011-10134

"A disgraced cop with a history of alcoholism, Cody Hoyt is also a bulldog investigator. When his AA sponsor turns up dead, Cody determines that the killer is one of 14 dudes on a weeklong expedition in Yellowstone National Park; Cody's son is also on the trip. While struggling to figure out who and why, and where they are in the wilderness, Cody also searches for redemption on behalf of his friend." Libr J

Box, C. J.

✓**Blood** trail. G.P. Putnam's Sons 2008 301p $24.95
ISBN 978-0-399-15488-1; 0-3991-5488-4
LC 2007-44776

"When a hunter is butchered in Wyoming, game warden Joe Pickett and his boss, Randy Pope, set off to investigate. Soon, it becomes clear that someone is systematically killing hunters. Caught between the people who hunt and those who are opposed to hunting, not to mention facing one of the most dangerous cases of his career, Pickett must find a way to bring the killer to justice before more deaths occur. . . . [Box's] sense of place and talent for character development are on a par with those of James Lee Burke." Libr J

Box, C. J.

✓**Force** of nature; C.J. Box. G. P. Putnam's Sons 2012 385 p. (Joe Pickett novel)
ISBN 039915826X; 9780399158261
LC 2011047681

In this book, "set just weeks after fugitive Nate Romanowski's double loss of his lover and a trusted ally, . . .

Nate realizes that his former Air Force mentor is hunting him down and systematically eliminating all his known associates. A bloody confrontation along the Twelve Sleep River injures Nate and sets the tone for a series of violent attacks stretching from Colorado into Wyoming and Idaho. Getting ever closer to Nate's best friends, game warden Joe Pickett and his wife Marybeth, the killer taunts his intended victims. Nate, up against a skilled falconer, expects only the worst outcome, but still he perseveres. And Joe, always honorable, plans to save Nate's life, no matter what it takes." (Libr J)

Box, C. J.

✓★ **Free** fire; by C.J. Box. G.P. Putnam's Sons 2007 352p map o.p.; (pbk.) $7.99; o.p.
ISBN 9780399154270; 9780425221242; 0399154272
LC 2007000539

In this book, "Joe Pickett, having recently been fired from his job as a Wyoming game warden, is working on his father-in-law's ranch when he receives a call from the governor's office . . . [regarding] Clay McCann, a lawyer who slaughtered four campers in cold blood in a far-off corner of Yellowstone National Park. After the murders, McCann immediately turned himself in at the nearest park ranger station. . . . [But] the crimes were committed in a thin sliver of land with zero residents and overlapping jurisdiction, the so-called free-fire zone. McCann had taken advantage of a loophole in the law: neither the state of Wyoming nor the federal government can try him for his crime, so he walks out of prison a free man. Governor Rulon . . . wants his own investigation into the murders. The governor will reinstate Joe as a game warden if he'll go to Yellowstone to investigate." (Publisher's note)

Box, C. J.

✓The **highway**; C. J. Box. Minotaur Books 2013 400 p. (hardcover) $25.99
ISBN 0312583206; 9780312583200
LC 2013009869

In this novel by C.J. Box "two sisters set out across . . . Montana [and] the girls . . . simply vanish. Former police investigator Cody Hoyt, . . . convinced by his son and his former rookie partner, Cassie Dewell, . . . begins the drive . . . to the girls' last known location. This . . . landscape is the hunting ground for a killer whose viciousness is outmatched only by his intelligence. Can Cody Hoyt battle his own demons and find this killer before another victim vanishes on the highway?" (Publisher's note)

Box, C. J.

✓**Nowhere** to run. G.P. Putnam's Sons 2010 356p $25.95
ISBN 978-0-399-15645-8; 0-399-15645-3
LC 2009-46027

"Joe Pickett, exiled to the 'warden's graveyard' in a remote district of southern Wyoming, has one week left before regaining his old job in Twelve Sleep County, where his family still lives. On a final horseback patrol, however, a routine citation for unlicensed fishing turns into a deadly confrontation with twin brothers Caleb and Camish Grim, whose anger at the government is downright murderous. The first hundred pages are as good as anything Box has written, highlighting both the dangerous beauty of the West and the risks of a job where a lone civil servant interacts with a well-armed populace. As events escalate and a complex conspiracy comes to light, momentum is maintained by the dogged determination of Pickett, who could have walked away, and probably should have, but didn't." Booklist

Box, C. J.

Open season; C.J. Box. G.P. Putnam 2001 293p. (pbk.) $7.99; (acid-free paper) o.p.

ISBN 9780425185469; 0399147489

LC 00050992

Anthony Awards: Best First Novel (2002), Macavity Awards: Best First Mystery Novel (2002)

This book "introduc[es] Wyoming game warden Joe Pickett . . . [who] is struggling to fill the shoes of his mentor, legendary Vern Dunnegan, as warden of Twelve Sleep County, and trying to support his wife and growing family on the meager salary he makes. The hours are long, the work hard but satisfying, and Joe's honesty and integrity would pay off if he could avoid 'bonehead moves' like . . . allowing a poacher to grab Joe's firearm from him. When that . . . poacher turns up dead and bloodied in Joe's woodpile with only a cooler containing unidentified animal scat, his life, livelihood and family will never be the same. . . . [The plot includes] local political and bureaucratic intrigue, a high-stakes pipeline scheme and an endangered species that Joe's eldest daughter 'discovers.'" (Publishers Weekly)

Box, C. J.

Out of range; C.J. Box. G.P. Putnam's Sons 2005 308p. (acid-free paper) o.p.; (pbk.) $7.99

ISBN 0399152911; 9780425209455

LC 2004060141

In this "fifth Joe Picket novel, . . . the Wyoming game warden is temporarily transferred from his backwater base, Saddlestring, to Jackson, a sophisticated tourist mecca, to replace warden Will Jensen, who apparently shot himself to death. Joe has his doubts about Will's 'suicide,' but little time to investigate given other distractions: a vast and remote territory to patrol, questionable practices by a hunting outfitter, pressure to approve an exclusive housing development on a wildlife trail and protests by animal rights activists. At home, Joe's contentious wife, Marybeth, deals with mysterious threats and daughter Sheridan's teenage angst. To complicate matters further, Joe's reputation as a hard-headed law enforcer, unwilling to play politics, precedes him." (Publishers Weekly)

Box, C. J.

Savage run. Putnam 2002 272p

ISBN 0-399-14887-6

LC 2001-57872

"Two creepy, cold-hearted guys carry out orders from an unseen other as they murder a famous environmental activist, a noted environmental writer, and the country's most powerful @green' congressman. Called in after the first murder (by explosion), which also killed several animals in his part of the Wyoming wilderness, game warden Joe Pickett begins to suspect a broader conspiracy. With a few clues from his part-time librarian wife, Pickett moves the investigation forward." Libr J

Boyagoda, Randy

Beggar's feast; Randy Boyagoda. Pintail 2012 321 p. $16

ISBN 0670066583; 9780670066582

LC 2010671074

In this book, "[Randy] Boyagoda follows the life of Sam Kandy, born in 1899 in a small village in Ceylon (present-day Sri Lanka) and determined to rise above his lot. Singularly focused on his desire to achieve greatness and return to his village as a man to be respected and feared, Sam exhibits few redeeming qualities as he leaves a swath of broken lives in his path. Ironically, his ultimate success is brought about by a chance encounter and the will of a woman 30 years his junior." (Library Journal)

Boyd, William

Ordinary thunderstorms; a novel. Harper 2010 403p $26.99

ISBN 978-0-06-187674-5; 0-06-187674-7

First published 2009 in the United Kingdom

"The wonderfully ambiguous ending shows justice served through savvy exploitation of Internet social networks, a shareholder meeting and the sensation-hungry modern media. . . . Fine entertainment, and even finer as a thoughtful exploration of the intersections of different people in a modern metropolis." Kirkus

Boyd, William

Waiting for sunrise; a novel. William Boyd. Harper 2012 353 p.

ISBN 9780061876769

LC 2011036857

This book follows, "former espionage agent . . . Lysander Rief . . . [who,] having gone to consult a Freudian psychoanalyst . . . encounters Hettie Bull, a highly strung expat Englishwoman. . . . [T]hey begin an affair. But she accuses him of raping her and he's arrested, only to be rescued by British diplomatic officials, kicking off a web of intrigue that enmeshes Rief in ever more mysterious circumstances." (Publishers Weekly)

Boyden, Joseph

Three-day road; a novel. Joseph Boyden. Viking 2005 354 p. o.p.; (pbk.) $15

ISBN 0670034312; 9780143037071

LC 2004066149

CBA Libris Awards (Canadian Booksellers Association): Fiction Book of the Year (2006), Roger Writers' Trust Fiction Prize (2005)

This book follows "Cree Indians Xavier Bird and Elijah Whiskyjack [who] join the Canadian Army in 1915 . . . expect[ing] to go to France, become warriors and kill Germans. What they don't expect is that the war will drive one of them mad and make the other a morphine-addicted cripple. . . . Elijah is outgoing and boastful, while Xavier is quiet and reserved, but both are deadly efficient soldiers. A parallel story line tells of Niska, Xavier's aunt, a Cree Indian prophet and healer, as she tells of the sad decline of Cree culture and waits for her nephew to come home. . . . [O]ne of the men's addiction to drugs and killing causes him to take extreme risks; when he finally commits murder to hide the ugly truth, his friend sees only one solution to save his own soul." (Publishers Weekly)

Boyer, Rick

The **Daisy** Ducks; a Doc Adams suspense novel. Houghton Mifflin 1986 276p

ISBN 0-395-35289-4

LC 86-3016

"If you like action-suspense novels, Doc Adams could become addictive. Boyer's smooth style creates a character with charisma and a story that moves like a freight train at full throttle—powerfully swift." Best Sellers

Boykin, Kim

The **wisdom** of hair; Kim Boykin. Berkley Books 2013 304 p. (paperback) $15

ISBN 0425261050; 9780425261057

LC 2012035919

This novel focuses on "Zora Adams, daughter of an alcoholic Judy Garland impersonator. When Zora reaches her 19th birthday, she leaves her codependent mother. Under the watchful eye of her favorite former English teacher, Zora enrolls in the Davenport School of Beauty, where she finds a kindred spirit in the beautiful stylist Sarah Jane. When she meets hard-drinking professor Winston Sawyer, she becomes infatuated. Can Zora save him?" (Library Journal)

Boyle, Elizabeth

Along Came a Duke; Rhymes with Love. Elizabeth Boyle. Avon 2012 384 p.

ISBN 0062089064; 9780062089069

In this historical romance novel, author Elizabeth Boyle launches the Rhymes with Love Regency series with this . . . Cinderella story. The duke of Preston is the worst sort of rake, ruining young men with reckless wagers and seducing innocent misses during parties. Tabitha Timmons is an orphan who lives with her aunt and uncle and works her fingers to the bone as a scullery maid. A sensible girl who speaks her mind, she immediately pegs Preston as a ne'er-do-well. It takes a late-night dinner and an impromptu dancing lesson for her to sense hints of Prince Charming. Tabitha may be naive about many things, but she is resourceful and practical when it comes to saving herself from greedy relatives interested in her inheritance." (Publishers Weekly)

Boyle, Elizabeth

Mad about the duke. Thorndike Press 2011 384p

ISBN 9780061783500

LC 2010042211

Romantic Times Reviewers' Choice Award: Best Historical (2010)

In this book, "James Lambert St. Maur Thurston Tremont, agree[s] to work for Elinor Sterling, the second dowager Lady Standon. After mistaking James for the Duke of Hollindrake's man of business, Elinor proceeds to hire him as her new matchmaker. While Elinor already has come up with her own list of potential husbands—all dukes and nothing but dukes—she wants James to vet the candidates," and James is mad his name is not on the list. (Booklist)

Boyle, T. Coraghessan, 1948-

Road to Wellville; a novel. Viking 1993 476p il

ISBN 0-670-83766-0

LC 92-50731

The author "evokes the world of the senses with remarkable skill. As always, his prose is a marvel, enjoyable from beginning to end, alive with astute observations, sharp intelligence and subtle musicality. Possibly as an effect of his highly developed style, Mr. Boyle's vision has been one of the most distinctive and original of his generation." N Y Times Book Rev

Boyle, T. Coraghessan, 1948-

San Miguel; T. Coraghessan Boyle. Viking 2012 367 p. (hardcover) $27.95

ISBN 0670026247; 9780670026241; 9780670026296

LC 2012004731

This historical novel by T. C. Boyle "portrays two families living and working on barren San Miguel Island off the coast of California. In 1888 Marantha Waters leaves her comfortable life on mainland California and moves out to San Miguel with her adopted daughter and husband. . . . Years later, in 1930, Elise Lester, newly wed at 38, moves to San Miguel with her husband, Herbie, a World War I veteran." (Library Journal)

Boyle, T. Coraghessan

★ The **tortilla** curtain. Viking 1995 355p

ISBN 0-670-85604-5

LC 95-1970

"What Boyle does, and does well, is lay on the line our national cult of hypocrisy. Comically and painfully he details the snug wastefulness of the haves and the vile misery of the have-nots. . . . Americans of every stripe will find themselves rooting for Cándido and América, right up to the riproaring deus ex machina ending that screams out that we are all in this together." Nation

Boyle, T. Coraghessan

When the killing's done. Viking 2011 369p $26.95

ISBN 978-0-670-02232-8; 0-670-02232-2

LC 2010-46488

"The novel never reduces its narrative to polemics—there are no heroes here—while underscoring the difficult decisions that those who consider themselves on the side of the angels must face. Narrative propulsion is laced with delicious irony in this winning novel." Kirkus

Boyle, T. Coraghessan

Wild child; stories. Viking 2010 304p $25.95

ISBN 978-0-670-02142-0; 0-670-02142-3

LC 2009-26518

In this "collection of short stories, Boyle captures characters facing a range of critical turning points. Some of these moments are quiet: An unexpected emotional connection is made in a rundown recording studio ('Three Quarters of the Way to Hell'); a college graduate wonders whether she should accept a menial dog-sitting job ('Admiral'). Others are more obviously dramatic: A woman encounters an escaped tiger in her suburban garden ('Question 62'); a Venezuelan baseball player discovers his mother has been kidnapped ('The Unlucky Mother of Aquiles Maldonado'). In Boyle's world, they all have the potential to become peak experiences. While the scenarios may be surreal, the characters experiencing them are decidedly down-to-earth." Boston Globe

Boyle, T. Coraghessan
✓The **women**; a novel. Viking 2009 451p $27.95
    ISBN 978-0-670-02041-6; 0-670-02041-9
                    LC 2008-42462

"Boyle's latest novel takes on the architect Frank Lloyd Wright by examining his notoriously tumultuous relationships with four women, each unique in her own histrionic way. Narrated in reverse chronological order by a fictional Japanese apprentice, the book is extremely readable and deftly builds a portrait of the artist as pure egoist. Unfortunately, the novel avoids any sustained consideration of Wright's relationship to his art—a passion arguably more important in forming his genius than any of the women in his life were. Still, it proves an effective showcase for Boyle's own strengths as a craftsman. His prose is full of vivid descriptions and turns of phrase that pop with a preternatural precision." New Yorker

Boyle, T. Coraghessan
✓ **World's** end; a novel. Viking 1987 456p
    ISBN 0-670-81489-X
                    LC 87-40023

"The themes Mr. Boyle develops as his story shuttles between epochs make us grasp in new terms their connection with the American social and political experiment. His mastery of history is the secret of the accomplishment here. Mr. Boyle has lost none of the qualities that marked him a wit writer before, but now he has challenged his own disengagement; passion, need and belief breathe with striking force and freedom through this smashing good novel." N Y Times Book Rev

Boyne, John
The **absolutist**; John Boyne. Other Press 2011 309 p. (trade paperback) $16.95; (ebook) $14.99; (audiobook) $40.95
    ISBN 1590515528; 9781590515525; 9781590515532; 9781452629360
                    LC 2012000433

This book by John Boyne "documents the lives of two inseparable men navigating the trenches of WWI and the ramifications of a taboo involvement. . . .Tristan Sadler [is] a soldier en route to visit his dead comrade Will Bancroft's older sister Marian in Norwich, England. . . . The story oscillates between Sadler's trip in 1919 to return Will's letters to Marian, and recollections of wartime, including a forbidden and fleeting homosexual affair with Bancroft." (Publishers Weekly)

Boyne, John
✓ **Crippen**; a novel of murder. Thomas Dunne Books 2006 337p $24.95
    ISBN 978-0-312-34358-3; 0-312-34358-2
                    LC 2005-56011
    First published 2004 in the United Kingdom

"Boyne starts with the basic facts. . . but he has altered the story to suit his dramatic needs and authorial whims. The result of his reinvention is a dark comedy that is supremely readable, always suspenseful, sometimes laugh-out-loud funny and, finally, a monumental piece of misogyny. In Boyne's sardonic telling, Cora Crippen was a monster who richly deserved to die, and her long-suffering husband was a man more sinned against than sinning." Washington Post Book World

Boyne, John
The **house** of special purpose; by John Boyne. Other Press 2012 480 p. (paperback) $16.95
    ISBN 1590515986; 9781590515983; 9781590515990
                    LC 2012030175

In this historical novel, by John Boyne, "eighty-year-old Georgy Jachmenev is haunted by his past--a past of death, suffering, and scandal. . . . Living in England with his beloved wife, Zoya, Georgy prepares to make one final journey back to the Russia he once knew and loved. . . . As Georgy remembers days gone by, we are transported to St. Petersburg, to the Winter Palace of the czar, in the early twentieth century--a time of change, threat, and bloody revolution." (Publisher's note)

Bracewell, Patricia
Shadow on the crown; Patricia Bracewell. Viking 2013 xi, 416 p.p map (hardcover) $27.95
    ISBN 0670026395; 9780670026395
                    LC 2012028932

This book by Patricia Bracewell "begins with Emma of Normandy crossing the 'Narrow Sea' in 1002 C.E. to marry the much older King Aethelred. Emma is ill-prepared for the trials that come with her new position. . . .The king, regretting the hasty decision of 'taking a Norman slut to wife,' quickly tires of his demanding new bride; jealous rivals vie for Emma's crown; and the threat of a Viking invasion constantly looms." (Publishers Weekly)

Bradbury, Malcolm
✓ **To** the Hermitage. Overlook Press 2001 498p $27.95
    ISBN 1-58567-131-2
                    LC 00-50147

"The book is overextended, but it is also lively, thought provoking and, in its portrait of contemporary Russia, vividly chilling. For patient readers of a scholarly inclination and with a liking for the stranger corners of history, this will be a treat." Publ Wkly
    Includes bibliographical references

Bradbury, Ray, 1920-2012
★ **Bradbury** stories; 100 of his most celebrated tales. Morrow 2003 893p hardcover o.p. pa $17.95
    ISBN 0-06-054242-X; 0-06-054488-0 pa
                    LC 2003-42189

"This massive retrospective of self-selected Bradbury stories offers a compendium of his eccentrics, misfits, losers, and small-town dreamers, who typically inhabit an uncanny setting or confront a strange, unsettling situation." Libr J

Bradbury, Ray

✓ ★ **Dandelion** wine; a novel. Avon Books 1999 267p $15.95

ISBN 0-380-97726-5

LC 98-93914

First published 1957 by Doubleday

A novel about one summer in the life of a twelve-year-old boy, Douglas Spaulding: the summer of 1928. The place is Green Town, Illinois, and Doug and his brother Tom wander in and out among their elders, living and dreaming, sometimes aware of things, again just having a wonderful time. Doug's big discovery that summer was that he was alive.

"The writing is beautiful and the characters are wonderful living people. A rare reading experience—highly recommended to all libraries." Libr J

Followed by Farewell summer (2006)

Bradbury, Ray, 1920-2012

✓ ★ **Fahrenheit** 451. Simon & Schuster 2003 190p $23

ISBN 0-7432-4722-1

LC 2003-66160

First published 1953 in paperback by Ballantine Bks.

Dystopian novel about a bookburner official in a future fascist state.

Bradbury, Ray

✓ The **illustrated** man. Doubleday 1951 251p

In this work "the stories are given a linking framework; they are all seen as magical tattoos becoming living stories, springing from the body of the protagonist." Sci Fic Ency

Bradbury, Ray

✓ ★ The **Martian** chronicles. Avon Books 1997 268p $15.95

ISBN 0-380-97383-9

LC 96-95071

First published 1950 by Doubleday

This book's "closely interwoven short stories, linked by recurrent images and themes, tell of the repeated attempts by humans to colonize Mars, of the way they bring their old prejudices with them, and of the repeated, ambiguous meetings with the shape-changing Martians." Sci Fic Ency

Bradbury, Ray

✓ ★ **Something** wicked this way comes. Avon Bks. 1999 293p $15.95; pa $7.99

ISBN 0-380-97727-3; 0-380-72940-7 pa

A reissue of the title first published 1962 by Simon and Schuster

"We read here of the loss of innocence, the recognition of evil, the bond between generations, and the purely fantastic. These forces enter Green Town, Illinois, on the wheels of Cooger and Dark's Pandemonium Shadow Show. Will Halloway and Jim Nightshade, two 13-year-olds, explore the sinister carnival for excitement, which becomes desperation as the forces of the dark threaten to engulf them. Bradbury's gentle humanism and lyric style serve this fantasy well." Shapiro. Fic for Youth. 3d edition

Bradford, Barbara Taylor

The **Ravenscar** dynasty. St. Martin's Press 2007 484p $25.95

ISBN 978-0-312-35460-2; 0-312-35460-6

LC 2006-50979

This is the "first installment of a projected trilogy centering on internecine power struggles within the early 20th century incarnation of the centuries-old Deravenel clan and their London-based family business. A suspicious hotel fire causes the death of patriarch Richard Deravenel along with that of one of his sons, his brother-in-law and his young nephew, forcing tall, handsome, bright, seductive, 17-year old Edward Deravenel out of Oxford into the world of commerce. He and cousin Neville Watkins (a successful businessman in his own right) plot to avenge their fathers' and brothers' deaths and seize the company, currently under the stewardship of a delusional absentee executive whose ambitious (and French) wife is behind the skullduggery. Edward's longtime friend, Will Hasling, also joins the fray, and Neville has his own motivations." Publ Wkly

Bradford, Barbara Taylor

★ A **woman** of substance. Doubleday 1979 755p

ISBN 0-385-12050-8

LC 77-9231

"It's a life worth the telling, and Ms. Bradford has told it well, sparing no detail. She writes competently, if not extraordinarily, against an accurate and well drawn historical background." West Coast Rev Books

Followed by Hold the dream

Bradley, Alan

I am half-sick of shadows; Alan Bradley. Delacorte Press 2011 297 p.

ISBN 9780385344012 (hardback); 9780345532152 (ebook); 0385344015

LC 2011022373

This book tells the story of "the precocious Flavia de Luce -- an eleven-year-old-sleuth with a passion for chemistry and a penchant for crime solving. . . . [W]hen a film crew arrives at Buckshaw, the de Luces' decaying English estate, to shoot a movie starring the famed Phyllis Wyvern . . . nobody is prepared for the evening's shocking conclusion: a body found, past midnight, strangled to death with a length of film." (Publisher's note)

"Despite the murder and subsequent investigation, 'Shadows' is more about the de Luce family than anything else. . . . [T]he real plot revolves around Flavia's simultaneous desire to understand more about he de Luces and nervousness about what she might learn." (arts.nationalpost.com)

Bradley, Alan

A **red** herring without mustard; a Flavia de Luce novel. Delacorte Press 2011 399p $23

ISBN 978-0-385-34232-2

LC 2010-49325

"Think preteen Nancy Drew, only savvier and a lot richer, and you have Flavia de Luce, an 11-year-old sleuth of the English gentry who's morbidly interested in both corpses and poison (she's got a chemistry lab in the attic). When a body turns up on the lawn of the family estate — skewered by an heirloom sterling lobster fork — she gets to work. Don't be fooled by Flavia's age or the 1950s setting: A Red Herring isn't a dainty tea-and-crumpets sort of mystery. It's shot through with real grit." Entertainment Wkly

Bradley, Alan

Speaking from among the bones; a Flavia de Luce novel. Alan Bradley. Delacorte Press 2012 400 p. (ebook) $24

ISBN 0385344031; 9780345538680; 9780385344036

LC 2012028396

In this mystery novel by Alan Bradley, part of the Flavia de Luce series, "Eleven-year-old amateur detective and ardent chemist Flavia de Luce . . . finds . . . the body of Mr. Collicutt, the church organist, . . . [in a] patron's saint's tomb. . . . Who held a vendetta against Mr. Collicutt, and why would they hide him in such a sacred resting place? The irrepressible Flavia decides to find out." (Publisher's note)

Bradley, Alan

★ The **sweetness** at the bottom of the pie; Alan Bradley. Delacorte Press 2009 373p (pbk.) $15

ISBN 9780385343497; 9780385342308

LC 2008041787

Agatha Awards: Best First Novel (2009), Arthur Ellis Awards: Best First Novel (2010), Dilys Award (2010), Macavity Awards: Best First Mystery Novel (2010)

This book follows "11-year-old sleuth Flavia de Luce. . . . In an early 1950s English village, Flavia is preoccupied with retaliating against her lofty older sisters when a rude, redheaded stranger arrives to confront her eccentric father, a philatelic devotee. Equally adept at quoting 18th-century works, listening at keyholes and picking locks, Flavia learns that her father, Colonel de Luce, may be involved in the suicide of his long-ago schoolmaster and the theft of a priceless stamp. The sudden expiration of the stranger in a cucumber bed, wacky village characters with ties to the schoolmaster, and a sharp inspector with doubts about the colonel and his enterprising young detective daughter mean complications for Flavia." (Publishers Weekly)

"Mystery fans, Anglophiles, and science buffs will delight in this book and may come away with a slightly altered view of what is possible for a headstrong girl to achieve." SLJ

Bradley, Alan

The **weed** that strings the hangman's bag; a Flavia de Luce mystery. Alan Bradley. Delacorte Press 2010 364p map $24

ISBN 9780385342315

LC 2009043002

This is the second mystery novel featuring girl detective Flavia de Luce, introduced in The Sweetness at the Bottom of the Pie (2009). When master puppeteer Robert Porson's "van breaks down in the village of Bishop's Lacey, Flavia . . . helps Rupert and his charming assistant, Nialla, put together a performance in the local church. . . . But even as the newcomers . . . set the stage for Jack and the Beanstalk, there are signs that something just isn't right: Nialla's strange bruises and solitary cries in the churchyard, Rupert's unexplained disappearances and a violent argument with his BBC

producer, the disturbing atmosphere at Culverhouse Farm, and the peculiar goings-on in nearby Gibbet Wood—where young Robin Ingleby was found hanging. . . . While the local police do their best to keep up with Flavia in solving Rupert's murder, his killer may pull Flavia in way over her head." (Publisher's note)

Bradley, Jane

You believers. Unbridled Books 2011 406p $25.95

ISBN 978-1-60953-046-4

LC 2010-47173

"When Katy Connor goes missing, her boyfriend and her mother spend the first week in a perpetual state of limbo, too scared to think the worst but, as the days go by, too numb to hope for her return. It's only Shelby Waters, the woman who heads an all-volunteer search-and-rescue team, who seems to know just what they need to hear and what they should be doing to locate their missing loved one. Shelby is motivated by her own private grief over her older sister, who was murdered years ago, her body scattered in the woods. In a riveting narrative, Bradley offers both unending compassion and a chilling assessment of the kind of harm that people are able and willing to inflict on one another. In heartrending detail, she lays out the ruined lives and broken hearts inevitably left in the wake of those ubiquitous missing posters tacked up in store windows. Harrowing reading from a gifted writer." Booklist

Bradley, Marion Zimmer

The **mists** of Avalon. Ballantine Pub. Group 2000 876p $30; pa $16.95

ISBN 0-345-44118-4; 0-345-35049-9 pa

LC 00-712415

A reissue of the title first published 1982 by Knopf

This retelling of the Arthurian legend is dominated by the character of Morgan le Fay (here called Morgaine), the powerful sorceress who symbolizes the historical clash between Christianity and the early pagan religions of the British Isles." Publ Wkly

Other novels in the Avalon series written with Diana L. Paxson are: The forest house (1993); Lady of Avalon (1997); Priestess of Avalon (2000). Following Bradley's death Paxson continued the series with: Ancestors of Avalon (2004); Ravens of Avalon (2007); Sword of Avalon (2009)

Braff, Joshua

Peep show; a novel. Algonquin Books of Chapel Hill 2010 266p il pa $13.95

ISBN 978-1-56512-508-7

"The novel is narrated by David Arbus, a 17-year-old amateur photographer living in 1970s New York. David's parents are divorced, and he struggles to find a place for himself somewhere between their radically different worlds: His mother, Mickey, is a baal teshuva, a kind of ultra-religious Jewish born-again, whereas his father, Marty, runs the Imperial, a burlesque theater in Times Square. Despite its title and narrative framing, which focuses on David as he grows up and takes lots of pictures along the way, 'Peep Show' really revolves around David's 15-year-old sister, Debra, who follows her mother into Orthodoxy as David goes to work for and live with Marty." San Francisco Chron

Braffet, Kelly

Save yourself; a novel. Kelly Braffet. Crown Publishers 2013 352 p. (alk. paper) $25

ISBN 0385347340; 9780385347341

LC 2012048148

In this book, set in Ratchetsburg, Pa., "Patrick Cusimano blames his brother, Mike, for the fact that, their father, John, was sent to prison for the hit-and-run death of a child while in an alcoholic haze. Mike believes that if Patrick hadn't called the police, their father would never have been arrested, despite the damaged, bloody car. The residents of Ratchetsburg also fault the brothers for waiting 19 hours before calling the police." (Publishers Weekly)

Bragg, Melvyn

The **soldier's** return. Arcade Pub. 2002 384p $25.95

ISBN 1-55970-639-2

LC 2002-21558

First published 1999 in the United Kingdom

"Bragg weaves a powerful, deeply moving story of a family and a society torn apart by war. His straightforward prose and the measured pace of his writing allow readers to savor every nuance of life in a small town in postwar England, and the depth and reality of his characters and his ability to bring the horrors of war alive are nothing short of brilliant." Booklist

Bragg, Melvyn

A **son** of war; a novel. Arcade Pub. 2003 426p $25.95

ISBN 1-559-70686-4

LC 2002-44058

This sequel to A soldier's return "finds Sam and Ellen Richardson and their son, Joe, still in the dreary slums of Wigton, waiting for their chance for a new council house in a developing outskirt. Times are tough, and they are barely scraping by." Libr J

"A hauntingly evocative slice of postwar life." Booklist

Bragi Olafsson

★ The **ambassador**; translated from the Icelandic by Lytton Smith. Open Letter 2010 298p pa $15.95

ISBN 978-1-934824-13-9; 1-934824-13-5

LC 2010-28002

Original Icelandic edition, 2006

"Ólafsson's dark, delightful tale of an alcoholic Icelandic poet representing his country at a poetry festival in Lithuania brims with mordant commentary and beguiling narrative cul-de-sacs. The book begins with one of many nods to Gogol as Sturla Jón Jónsson buys an expensive overcoat that he will promptly lose at the festival. Then the situation worsens: Sturla gets mixed up with a Salomé-inspired striptease gone wrong, is accused of plagiarizing in his latest book, gets harassed by a garlic-breath prostitute, and resorts, in a moment of desperation, to thievery." Publ Wkly

Bragi Olafsson

★ The **pets**; a novel. translated from the Icelandic by Janice Balfour. Open Letter 2008 157p $14.95

ISBN 978-1-934824-01-6; 1-934824-01-1

LC 2008-926608

Original Icelandic edition, 2001

"A horribly amusing tale about a man who is stuck under a bed, a semiliterate translation of R Kelly's Trapped in the Closet writ small. It's a witty and comical trifle." Brick Wkly

Brand, Max

Beyond the outposts. Five Star 1997 254p

ISBN 0-7862-0745-0

LC 97-9308

Earlier version of this story was serialized in 1925 in Western Story magazine

This western adventure follows the "journeys of young Lew Dorset as he searches for his father, an escaped convict. His skill with firearms gets him a job as a hunter with a trader's freight train heading onto the prairies to barter with the Indians. There he meets young Chuck Morris, and together they take on a Cheyenne attack party. Finding shelter in a Sioux village, they absorb the native culture. . . . Lew goes on to play a decisive role in a battle between the Sioux and Pawnee, but returns to find that Chuck has deserted his wife and son. His attempts to reconcile them culminate in great danger and, ultimately, a threat to his life." Publisher's note

Brand, Max

Chinook; a north-western story. Five Star 1998 271p

ISBN 0-7862-1155-5

LC 98-22718

"Joe Harney heads to Alaska during the great gold rush of 1898 and finds himself impressed by a great wolf dog owned by Andrew Steen, a crusty, bad-tempered loner. When Harney saves Steen's life, Steen grudgingly agrees that they can travel overland together. On that harsh journey, they meet Kate Winslow and learn that she's headed for Circle City to meet up with a man who wants her dead. This is a tale of the tough and often ruthless folks who risked their lives to get to the frozen north and, with any luck, to find their fortune." Publisher's note

Brand, Max

★ The **collected** stories of Max Brand; edited, with story prefaces, by Robert and Jane Easton; introduction by William Bloodworth. centennial ed; University of Neb. Press 1994 xx, 342p $40

ISBN 0-8032-1244-5

LC 93-43938

Brand, Max

Fugitives' fire. Putnam 1991 184p

ISBN 0-399-13587-1

LC 90-8478

This novel originally appeared 1928 in Western story magazine as two novelettes: Prairie pawn and Fugitive's fire

This novel features fugitive plainsman Paul Torridon. "A prisoner of the mighty Cheyenne Nation, young Torridon lives in pampered misery. The Cheyenne, who call him

'White Thunder,' are convinced of his supernatural talents and expect him to deliver good luck in battle and rain in drought. He is richly rewarded for his 'mystical favors,' but he dreads the day his good luck and horse sense will fail, revealing him as only too mortal—and losing him his scalp in the bargain." Publisher's note

Brand, Max

The **gentle** desperado. Dodd, Mead 1985 195p
ISBN 0-396-08715-9

LC 85-10321

This novel is comprised of three stories originally published in Western Story Magazine under the pseudonym, George Owen Baxter

"Robert Fernald was a deadly fighter, but he didn't really believe it, not even when he outgunned his opponents. To his enemies, he looked like a kid, too mild-mannered to be a threat. But then he went after Tom Gill and his men who were preying on the Larkin ranch, forcing handsome young Beatrice Larkin into bankruptcy. Everyone said it would take an army to stop the rustlers from driving the stolen cattle through the mountain passes—until Fernald faced tough Tom Gill himself in a showdown." Publisher's note

Brand, Max

In the hills of Monterey; a western story. Five Star 1998 239p
ISBN 0-7862-0988-7

LC 97-38421

"The wealthiest landowner in the province of Spanish-controlled Alta California has sent away to Spain for a suitable bridegroom for his beautiful daughter, Ortiza Tarabal. Francisco Valdez arrives with his slave, an Englishman known as El Rojo, a courageous man who has made some enemies among the ruling class, but has the devotion of the Indians. El Rojo also has the very dangerous love of Ortiza Tarabal, despite her betrothal to Francisco Valdez and the wrath of her father." Publisher's note

Brand, Max

Max Brand's best western stories; edited with a biographical introduction by William F. Nolan. Dodd, Mead 1981 3v

LC 81-3204

Brand, Max

★ The **Stingaree**. Dodd, Mead 1968 216p
"Jimmy Green is a wild, half-Indian, half-civilized, thirteen-year-old who is undisputed king of the small village of Fort Anxious. One day, a tramp wanders into the village, and ultimately into the life of Jimmy, changing it from the complacent existence of a boy into the desperate flight of a fugitive. The stranger, also known as the Stingaree, has come from Alabama to revenge the death of his partner by the leading citizen of Fort Anxious. Although he succeeds in forcing the man to confess, he is thwarted by the police in his attempt to kill Stanley Parker. The Stingaree, along with Jimmy Green, an Indian companion, and a wild dog is forced to flee into the wilderness, beginning one of the best chase episodes." Libr J

Brand, Max

Stolen gold: a western trio. Five Star 1999 255p
ISBN 0-7862-1333-7

LC 98-52067

"The three short novels collected here were all published in pulp magazines during the 1920s. . . . In the title piece, former convict Reata is duped into abandoning his hard-won domestic bliss to search for treasure. The second tale finds a drifter accused of murder. His only hope for justice is the daughter of the sheriff who captured him. The third tale features a good samaritan drawn into a web of duplicity when he tries to help a newlywed whose husband is suddenly seized by a local lawman." Booklist

Brand, Max

The **survival** of Juan Oro. Five Star 1999 259p
ISBN 0-7862-1325-6

LC 98-42372

This tale "was born as a magazine serial in 1925. Now published in book form with the author's original material restored, the story tells of Juan Oro, who, raised by Yaquis and captured by the forces of Don José Fontana, is apprenticed to outlaw Matias Bordi after promising to murder Bordi once he has learned the ways of a killer. But Juan's feelings for Bordi are such that he cannot keep his promise. . . . Mainstream western fare from a master of the genre." Booklist

Brandon, John

✓**Arkansas**. McSweeney's Books 2008 230p $22
ISBN 978-1-932416-90-9

"The novel jumps from perspective to perspective—even dabbling in the second person to tell Frog's story—and at times it can be difficult to keep track of a narrative that is constantly slipping in time to provide back story on different characters. Brandon's writing is so sparse it sometimes feels blasé, but the tension between his hardboiled prose and his characters' appealing naïveté makes the novel work." Portland Mercury

Braun, Lilian Jackson

✓ The **cat** who ate Danish modern. Dutton 1967 192p

The "adventure of Koko, The Siamese, and his Watson, Jim Qwilleran. The 'Daily Fluxion' assigns Jim to mastermind a new Sunday supplement called, of all things, 'Gracious Abodes.' But the shocking consequences of the first few issues makes Jim realize that he is back in his own field, crime reporting, and that only Koko can help with the answers." Libr J

"The mystery is mild, the satire on interior decorating fads and fancies amusing, and the Siamese cat who helps play detective delightful." Publ Wkly

Braun, Lilian Jackson

✓The **cat** who brought down the house. Putnam 2003 228p
ISBN 0-399-14942-2

LC 2002-68138

"Thelma Thackery, in her 80s, comes back to Pickax after a long Hollywood career in food. She's turning the old opera house into a revival movie theater, sparks a few other local delights, but can't seem to get her ne'er-do-well nephew to do well at all. Qwill plugs away at old lies and a death in Thelma's family. We learn stuff through his newspaper column and his journal entries, and through the responses of his Siamese cat, KoKo. All the murders are offstage: the fun part is in food, clothing, and the quotidian joys of small-town life." Booklist

Braun, Lilian Jackson

✓The **cat** who sang for the birds. Putnam 1998 244p

ISBN 0-399-14333-5

LC 97-19094

In this mystery featuring Jim Qwilleran and his sleuthing Siamese cats, "the crime—involving fraud, bribery, and arson—centers on the murders of a 93-year-old woman and a young butterfly painter. Equally important to the story and to reader enjoyment are an adult spelling bee (developed and promoted as a baseball game complete with competing teams and pinch spellers), the painting of librarian Polly Duncan's portrait, and Qwill's brief experience with lepidopterology." Booklist

Braun, Lilian Jackson

✓The **cat** who smelled a rat. Putnam 2001 229p

ISBN 0-399-14665-2

LC 00-34198

"Jim 'Qwill' Qwilleran is still enjoying life in the small town of Pickax in Moose County. . . . Having moved into his winter residence, a condominium near his lady-love, head librarian Polly, the wealthy Qwill and his Siamese cats, Koko and Yum Yum, are awaiting the 'Big One'—the first blizzard of the season. A drought has caused a series of fires in the abandoned mine shafts around Pickax—or is it arson? When a member of the citizens' firewatch patrol is killed, a sinister plot unfolds." Booklist

Braun, Lilian Jackson

✓ ★ The **cat** who went underground. Putnam 1989 223p

ISBN 0-399-13431-X

LC 88-32185

"Qwill's saving grace is that he is properly humble before the superior intelligence of his pets, while the author is shrewd enough to balance the cats' amazing antics with many amusing character studies of the Mooseville natives." N Y Times Book Rev

Brave new worlds; edited by John Joseph Adams. Night Shade Books 2011 481p pa $15.99

ISBN 978-1-59780-221-5

"Familiar classics by such luminaries as Shirley Jackson, Ursula K. Le Guin, and J.G. Ballard rub shoulders with new standouts in this dark anthology of 33 dystopian futures and alternate worlds. In Joseph Paul Haines's 'Ten with a Flag,' a government uses confusion to manipulate the governed. Sarah Langan's 'Independence Day' shows a tyrannical future U.S. through a teenager's eyes. Matt Williamson's 'Sacrament' offers the torturer's perspective on his 'art.' Adam-Troy Castro's 'Of a Sweet Slow Dance in the Wake of Temporary Dogs' asks how much of our souls we would surrender for nine days of guaranteed happiness plus one of horror. Grinding inevitability runs through Vylar Kaftan's

interactive 'Civilization.' Most of the stories are bleak, many are hopeless, and all serve as powerful warnings of what we may let ourselves become." Publ Wkly

Braybrooke, June

Every eye; [by] Isobel English; with an introduction by Neville Braybrooke. David R. Godine 2006 151p $23.95

ISBN 1-57423-199-5; 978-1-57423-199-1

LC 2006-2858

First published 1956 in the United Kingdom

"Hatty, the narrator of this exquisite 1956 novel, is a piano teacher who was born with a lazy eye. Though her vision has been repaired, a lingering feeling of isolation makes it seem that 'this outward sign was only the visible proof of inward impediment.' Hatty's voice on the page vividly conveys her sense of 'discordancy' with others, as the action shifts between recollections of adolescence and young-adulthood in grim, gray England and her considerably cheerier present, travelling through a Technicolor Spain with a new, much younger husband. The true marvel of the novel lies in the taut interweaving of these narratives: past informing present and present recasting past. Enlightenment is kept satisfyingly in abeyance until a rapturous conclusion on a mountaintop in Ibiza." New Yorker

Brennan, Marie

✓A **natural** history of dragons; a memoir by Lady Trent. Marie Brennan. Tor 2013 336 p. (hardcover) $16.99

ISBN 0765331969; 9780765331960

LC 2012038819

In this book, "Isabella, Lady Trent, is a naturalist and adventurer in a country that . . . resembles 19th-century England, yet fantastical creatures roam. . . . Isabella has been obsessed with studying dragons since childhood, but a formal scientific career is off limits to a woman. Instead she . . . join[s] [her husband's] "expedition to see the wild dragons of Vystrana. Along the way, Isabella solves a mystery and proves her worth as a naturalist." (Publishers Weekly)

Brennan, Marie

✓With fate conspire. Tor 2011 526p $27.99

ISBN 978-0-7653-2537-2; 0-7653-2537-3

LC 2011-18987

"The fourth and, for now, final book in Brennan's Onyx Court series. . . . It focuses on a new set of characters, and a new threat to the existence of the Onyx Hall, the faerie realm which lies beneath London's heart. . . . The year is 1884. The Onyx Hall is crumbling, threatened with dissolution in the face of the construction of the inner Circle of the London Underground — an iron ring around London. The Hall cannot survive, and without its protection, the fae will be forced to flee. Only the Queen's will holds the fabric of the Hall together, but Lune has not been seen in public in years. While her Prince of the Stone, a bricklayer's son, strives to maintain some measure of order, unscrupulous powers in the lawless Goblin Market scheme for ways to build their own kingdoms out of the coming ruin, and other fae seek means of finding safety in a city that will not welcome them openly." Publisher's note

"An absorbing finale to a series that has grown richer with every installment." Kirkus

Brennan, Thomas

Doktor Glass; Thomas Brennan. Ace Books 2013 314 p. (pbk.) $15

ISBN 0425258173; 9780425258170

LC 2012030179

This steampunk mystery is set at the end of the 19th century. Soon, "the Transatlantic Span, which links Liverpool and New York City via a mammoth suspension bridge, will open for business. Inspector Matthew Langton is distracted from the excitement, though, by the recent death of his wife and a tricky murder case involving a plot to assassinate the Queen." (Booklist)

Brennert, Alan

Palisades Park; Alan Brennert. St Martins Pr 2013 432 p. (hardcover) $25.99

ISBN 0312643721; 9780312643720

LC 2013000634

This novel focuses on Palisades Park in New Jersey. "Opening in 1922, when young Eddie Stopka visits the park, and closing in 1974, with Eddie's daughter witness to its demolition, the novel traces the ups and downs of this classic park during its heyday—and of the Stopkas' similarly variable fortunes." (Publishers Weekly)

Breslin, Jimmy

★ The **gang** that couldn't shoot straight. Viking 1969 249p

ISBN 0-670-33396-4

"By no means a great work, this is still a strong indictment of American society—police, politicians, criminals, and the 'silent'—that deserves to offend more than Sicilians." Choice

Breslin, Jimmy

Table money. Ticknor & Fields 1986 435p

ISBN 0-899-19312-9

LC 85-28880

This "saga concerning the Morrisons of Queens, New York—from their late-nineteenth-century arrival in the U.S. to the present day—is painfully stereotypical in its depiction of the men (a long line of hard-drinking, male chauvinistic, and irresponsible tunnel workers) and their beleaguered, long-suffering women. Generation after generation repeats the same mistakes—dying too soon from alcoholism, giving birth too early in life—and even when Owen Morrison, the latter-day lad whose story takes up most of the book, wins the Congressional medal of honor in Vietnam, he finds that his hero's badge is virtually worthless on the gray borough streets and in the perilous tunnel that epitomizes his clan's plight." Booklist

Brett, Simon

Mrs. Pargeter's package. Scribner 1991 224p

ISBN 0-684-19286-1

LC 90-27463

First published 1990 in the United Kingdom

"Avoiding the treacly simpering typical of so many British cozy mysteries, Brett keeps us chuckling with a steady stream of dryly noted cultural tidbits, while still supplying a wide-ranging plot that hangs together elegantly." Booklist

Brett, Simon

★ **Murder** unprompted; a Charles Paris novel. Scribner 1982 160p

ISBN 0-684-17659-9

LC 82-5578

"Here Paris is less drunk than usual, which enables us to believe that he can think as shrewdly as he does. And the situation is delightful: he gets at last a chance to act in a play that may move to a big West End theater if all goes well in the tryouts. The interplay among the cast is splendid, funny, and also touching. Murder in full view, on the first night, might bring good publicity, but other troubles develop—the whole mess handled in masterly fashion." Barzun. Cat of Crime. Rev and enl edition

Brett, Simon

The **torso** in the town; a Fethering mystery. Berkley Prime Crime 2002 340p

ISBN 0-425-18502-8

LC 2002-18482

"A dinner party in a richly restored country house in a Sussex village that is 'riddled with class consciousness' is interrupted by a scream. A body, arms and legs neatly removed, has been discovered in the cellar. There to witness the discovery is an outsider, a middle-aged woman from the seaside village of Fethering. The woman, Jude brings news of the grisly find back to her pal Carole Seddon another middle-aged woman from Fethering, in hopes that a little mystery will pull her out of a depression brought on by a lapsed love affair. . . . The ladies from Fethering once again proceed totally outside the bumbling police investigation in a somehow utterly credible way, gaining access and insight where the police can't." Booklist

Brewer, Sonny

The **poet** of Tolstoy Park; a novel. Sonny Brewer. Ballantine Books 2005 xi, 254p map $21.95; (pbk.) $15

ISBN 034547631X; 9780345476326

LC 2005297258

This work of historical fiction "chronicles the real-life journey of Henry Stuart, who, in 1925 at the age of 67, is diagnosed with consumption and told he only has a year to live. Henry decides to leave his home in Idaho. . . . [He] chooses a small plot of land in Fairhope, Alabama, as his final residence, and he corresponds with a man named Peter Stedman in order to get the supplies to build a house. On the train to Alabama, Henry gives his shoes away to a porter and determines to live out the rest of his days in solitude. But life might have other plans for him: on the final leg of his journey he meets a friendly schoolteacher named Kate, and Peter also seeks to develop a rapport with Henry. Henry tries to shut them all out until one life-altering night gives him a new perspective." (Booklist)

Brill, Amy

The **movement** of stars; Amy Brill. Riverhead Books 2013 400 p. (hardcover) $27.95

ISBN 1594487448; 9781101602058; 9781594487446

LC 2012027241

In this book, introverted Quaker "Hannah Gardner Price spends her days working at the local Nantucket Atheneum and her nights scanning the stars in search of a comet that she hopes will earn her a prestigious King of Denmark Prize. . . . Hannah soon finds herself at a crossroad when her father announces he's remarrying and moving to Philadelphia, meaning Hannah must either marry . . . or abandon her night-sky vigils." She embarks on a controversial interracial relationship. (Bust Magazine)

Brin, David

✓★ **Brightness** reef. Bantam Bks. 1995 514p

ISBN 0-553-89015-8

LC 95-17601

"Brin's rich world-building easily equals that displayed in classic series such as Herbert's Dune and Asimov's Foundation. Brin's resumption of Uplift is most welcome." Booklist

Followed by Infinity's shore

Brin, David

★ **Earth**. Bantam Bks. 1990 601p

✓ ISBN 0-553-05778-2

LC 90-4

"In the mid-21st century, as the world is attempting to reconcile humanity's furious technological progress with its depletion of the planet's vanishing resources, the discovery of a pair of singularities (miniature black holes) deep in the Earth's core abruptly transforms an ongoing struggle for preservation into a desperate battle to prevent the Earth's imminent destruction. Combining the fast pacing of a techno-thriller with a unique array of characters, the author . . . delivers a thoughtful, persuasive message of hope and warning that embraces today's issues and tomorrow's possibilities." Libr J

Brin, David

✓ **Existence**; David Brin. Tor 2012 556 p. (hardcover) $27.99

ISBN 9780765303615; 9781429946964

LC 2012017272

This science fiction book tells the story of "Gerald Livingston [who] is an orbital garbage collector. For a hundred years, people have been abandoning things in space, and someone has to clean it up. But there's something spinning a little bit higher than he expects, something that isn't on the decades' old orbital maps. An hour after he grabs it and brings it in, rumors fill Earth's infomesh about an 'alien artifact.' Thrown into the maelstrom of worldwide shared experience, the Artifact is a game-changer. A message in a bottle; an alien capsule that wants to communicate. The world reacts as humans always do: with fear and hope and selfishness and love and violence. And insatiable curiosity." (Publisher's note)

Includes bibliographical references

Brin, David

★ **Heaven's** reach. Bantam Bks. 1998 447p

ISBN 0-553-10174-9

LC 98-4914

"Brin's intellectual fertility is as prodigious as ever; indeed, readers coming to his work for the first time may feel a bit daunted. Brin doesn't fill all parts of his vast canvas with equal skill but manages enough of it at the top of his form to please all Uplift followers and many others as well." Booklist

Brin, David

✓ **Infinity's** shore. Ban tam Bks. 1996 524p

ISBN 0-553-10173-0

LC 96-32346

Second volume in the Uplift trilogy. "On the planet Jijo, the painfully developed cooperation among six sapient races (humans included) is rapidly crumbling under the impact of contact from space. The visitors include the dolphin crew of the ship Streaker and the Rothen, the race who may have 'uplifted' to intelligence most of the races of Jijo, except the humans, who because of their unique status are in greater peril than ever. The ensuing tale is well paced, immensely complex {and} highly literate." Publ Wkly

Followed by Heaven's reach

Brink, Andre P. (Andre Philippus), 1935-

★ The **other** side of silence; [by] André Brink. Harcourt 2003 311p

ISBN 0-15-100770-5

LC 2002-32748

First published 2002 in the United Kingdom

This novel "takes as its point of departure a German program at the turn of the twentieth century whereby women were shipped out to Germany's colonies in South-West Africa (now Namibia) to be wives—or, failing that, sexual fodder—for the colonizers. Brink's protagonist, Hannah X., an abused orphan from Bremen, is eager for the imagined romance of the desert, but life in the colonies turns out to be even worse than what she has known before. . . .Brink's powerful and brutal story is an effective response to those who suspected that the end of apartheid would leave him without a subject, and a shrewd meditation on the dehumanizing power of hatred." New Yorker

Brink, Andre P. (Andre Philippus), 1935-

★ **Philida**; a novel. by Andre Brink. Vintage Books 2012 310 p. (paperback) $15

ISBN 0345805038; 9780345805034

LC 2012031043

This book, "set on South Africa's Cape ('Caab') in the 1830s as slavery is being abolished, and four characters and one outsider narrate the action. Philida is the most sympathetic, seeking justice when a promise of freedom from her 'baas' with whom she bore four children is reneged on, and she is put to auction." (Library Journal)

"With alternating present-tense viewpoints, the aching personal drama is set against the history of lechery, power, and violent abuse... [a] stirring novel." Booklist

Bristow, Gwen

Jubilee Trail. Crowell 1950 564p

The Jubilee Trail was the traders' name for the great Spanish Trail, which in the 1840's led from Santa Fé to Los Angeles. This long novel describes the trek of a gently bred New York girl and her trader husband, along that trail. When she was left a widow and penniless, Garnet and the variety girl she had befriended managed to make their living. The story closes about the time of the California gold discovery

Brkic, Courtney Angela

The **First** Rule of Swimming; by Courtney Angela Brkic. Little, Brown and Co. 2013 384 p. $26
ISBN 0316217387; 9780316217385

In this novel by Courtney Angela Brkic "Magdalena does not panic when she learns that her younger sister has disappeared. A free-spirit, Jadranka has always been prone to mysterious absences. But when weeks pass with no word, Magdalena leaves the isolated Croatian island where their family has always lived and sets off to New York to find her sister. Her search begins to unspool the dark history of their family, reaching back three generations to a country torn by war." (Publisher's note)

Brockmann, Suzanne

Born to darkness; Ballantine Books 2012 416p.
ISBN 9780345521279; 9780345521293
LC 2012003863

This book is set "in the not-too-distant future, [in which] Boston is a war zone. A new drug, Destiny, keeps people in perfect physical shape while driving them insane. It's manufactured from the hormones of preteen girls procured by the nefarious Organization. Trying to combat the tide are empath Michelle 'Mac' Mackenzie of the Obermeyer Institute, which teaches 'Greater-Thans' to harness their supernatural powers for good, and blacklisted former Navy SEAL Shane Laughlin. The Greater-Thans race to save the girls before the Organization discards them." (Publishers Weekly)

Brockmeier, Kevin

The **brief** history of the dead; Kevin Brockmeier. Pantheon Books 2006 252p $22.95
ISBN 0375423699
LC 2005-48882

"The City is inhabited by the recently departed, who reside there only as long as they remain in the memories of the living. Among the current residents of this afterlife are Luka Sims, who prints the only newspaper in the City, with news from the other side; Coleman Kinzler, a vagrant who speaks the cautionary words of God; and Marion and Phillip Byrd, who find themselves falling in love again after decades of marriage. On Earth, Laura Byrd is trapped by extreme weather in an Antarctic research station." (Publisher's note)

"Although it never quite lives up to its promising premise, the novel's Borges-like spirit will appeal to select readers." Booklist

Brockmeier, Kevin

The **Illumination**. Pantheon Books 2011 257p $24.95
ISBN 0375425314; 9780375425318
LC 2010-20732

In the aftermath of a fatal car accident, a private journal of love notes written by a husband to his wife passes into the keeping of a hospital patient, and from there through the hands of five other suffering people.

"For a novel so relentlessly fixed on elucidating human suffering in all its permutations, 'The Illumination' is surprisingly uplifting. This is a testament to Brockmeier's considerable stylistic gifts — the man writes exquisite sentences — and to the palpable compassion with which he frames each of his characters." Cleveland Plain Dealer

Brockmeier, Kevin

The **view** from the seventh layer. Pantheon Books 2008 267p $21.95
ISBN 978-0-375-42530-1; 0-375-42530-6
LC 2007-23404

"This work compiles 13 wondrous tales—four fables, eight stories, and one choose-your-own-adventure. . . . [Brockmeier's] stories have a bit less of the troubling, possibly ironic distancing that can be a pitfall in the fiction of peers like David Foster Wallace. Instead, we're invited to empathize with the characters via his clean lines and attentive crafting. The comparisons to Italo Calvino are certainly valid (Calvino's novel The Baron in the Trees is even referenced), and yet Brockmeier's tales feel distinctly contemporary." Libr J

Brockway, Connie

The **golden** season; Connie Brockway. Onyx 2010 388p. (pbk.) $7.99
ISBN 9780451412836; 0451412834
LC 2010479420

This book follows "Lydia Eastlake, . . . the toast of the town . . . [who] never thought her considerable fortune would ever run out. Now she is left with one option if she doesn't want to learn how to economize: find a wealthy man to marry before word of her financial reversal gets out. After meeting kind and sexy Captain Ned Lockton, Lydia thinks she may have found her perfect match, but what she doesn't know is that Ned, whose own family is rapidly draining the ancestral coffers, is hunting for a spouse too, and only heiresses need apply." (Booklist)

Brockway, Connie

★ The **Lady** Most Willing; A Novel in Three Parts. Julia Quinn, Eloisa James, Connie Brockway. Avon 2012 384 p. $7.99
ISBN 0062107380; 9780062107381

This historical romance is "set in 1819 Scotland. Laird Taran Ferguson goes to great drunken lengths to kidnap four young women—and John Shevington, duke of Bretton, by accident—in hope of finding brides for his nephews, Byron (an English earl) and Robin (improbably, a French count). No one takes Taran seriously or feels at all endangered or coerced, but while they're all stuck in his castle waiting out a storm, romance blossoms of its own accord." (Publishers Weekly)

"Clever, engaging, funny, and guaranteed to keep the pages turning, this well-written Regency "novel in three parts" by popular authors Quinn, Eloisa James, and Connie Brockway is a pure delight..." LJ

Bronsky, Alina

The **Hottest** Dishes of the Tartar Cuisine; translated from German by Tim Mohr. Europa Editions 2011 304p.

ISBN 9781609450069 pa

This book tells the story of "Rosa Achmetowna . . . [who] lives in a cramped Soviet apartment with her husband, teenage daughter Sulfia, and a nosy, disagreeable roommate. . . . [W]hen the 'rather stupid' Sulfia winds up pregnant, Rosa immediately tries a variety of crude home remedies for aborting Sulfia's baby—but nine months later, Aminat is born." (Publishers Weekly)

"When Aminat, now a wild and willful teenager, catches the eye of a sleazy German cookbook writer researching Tartar cuisine, Rosa is quick to broker a deal that will guarantee all three women a passage out of the Soviet Union. But as soon as they are settled in the West, the . . . dysfunctional ties that bind mother, daughter and grandmother begin to fray." (Publisher's note)

Bronte, Anne

The **tenant** of Wildfell Hall. Modern Lib. 1997 510p

ISBN 0-679-60279-8

LC 97-14200

First published 1848

"This epistolary novel presents a portrait of debauchery that is remarkable in light of the author's sheltered life. It is the story of young Helen Graham's disastrous marriage to the dashing drunkard Arthur Huntingdon—said to be modeled on the author's wayward brother Branwell—and her flight from him to the seclusion of Wildfell Hall. Pursued by Gilbert Markham, who is in love with her, Graham refuses him and, by way of explanation, gives him her journal. There he reads of her wretched married life. Eventually, after Huntingdon's death, they marry." Merriam-Webster's Ency of Lit

Bronte, Charlotte

★ **Emma**; by Charlotte Brontë and Another Lady J.M. Dent 1980 201p

Fragments of a story left unfinished at Brontë's death form the opening two chapters of this novel completed by Constance Savery

"In the full-blown literary manner and circuitous storytelling characteristic of Charlotte Brontë, . . . an intriguing melodrama unrolls in this tale of wrongs finally righted. Most wronged is adolescent Martina, deprived of her natural mother by the machinations of her stepbrothers, led on by their sister, the cruel, enigmatic beauty Emma. The events that lead to familial reconciliation include Martina's sentence to ladies' boarding school, abduction to a French convent and graveyard visitations before some fancy detective work by an old friend unravels the ingenious but dastardly plot. The author of this Gothic romp is obviously steeped in the period and felicitous style of the brilliant English novelist, providing entertainment on the same grand scale." Publ Wkly

Bronte, Charlotte

★ **Jane** Eyre; [by] Charlotte Brontë with an introduction by Lucy Hughes-Hallet. Knopf 1991 xxxviii, 284p $20

ISBN 0-679-40582-8

LC 91-52968

First published 1847

"In both heroine and hero the author introduced types new to English fiction. Jane Eyre is a shy, intense little orphan, never for a moment, neither in her unhappy school days nor her subsequent career as a governess, displaying those qualities of superficial beauty and charm that had marked the conventional heroine. Jane's lover, Edward Rochester, to whose ward she is governess, is a strange, violent man, bereft of conventional courtesy, a law unto himself. Rochester's moodiness derives from the fact that he is married to an insane wife, whose existence, long kept secret, is revealed on the very day of his projected marriage to Jane. Years afterward the lovers are reunited." Reader's Ency. 4th edition

Bronte, Emily

★ **Wuthering** Heights; with an introduction by Katherine Frank. Knopf 1991 xxxiii, 385p $22

ISBN 0-679-40543-7

LC 91-52969

First published 1847

Forced by a storm to spend the night at the home of the somber and unsociable Heathcliff, Mr. Lockwood has an encounter with the spirit of Catherine Linton. He gradually learns that Catherine's father, Mr. Earnshaw, had taken in Heathcliff as a young orphan. Heathcliff and Catherine began to fall in love, but after Mr. Earnshaw's death Catherine's brother treated Heathcliff in a degrading manner and Catherine married rich Edgar Linton. Heathcliff gradually worked his revenge against those who injured him.

Includes bibliographical references

Brook, Meljean

The **Iron** Duke. Berkley Sensation 2010 378p il pa $15

ISBN 978-0-425-23667-3; 0-425-23667-6

LC 2010-28988

"Airships, zombies, nanotechnology, outlandish secondary characters, and a complicated heroine . . . make for a complex, gripping read." Publ Wkly

Brooker, Barbara Rose

The **Viagra** diaries; Barbara Rose Brooker. Gallery Books 2012 288 p. (paperback) $16

ISBN 145168861X; 9781451688610; 9781451688627

LC 2012014410

In this book, divorced retiree Anny Applebaum "supplements [her] inadequate social security with money she earns writing a newspaper column for seniors. Her editor, a young woman who likes and admires her, has to inform her that their boss plans to cut the column unless she can come up with topics that attract more readers." Anny starts documenting her online dating experiences, which makes the column a national success. (Kirkus)

Brookmyre, Christopher

When the Devil Drives; a Liberty Lane mystery. by Christopher Brookmyre. Pgw 2013 288 p. (hardcover) $24

ISBN 080212089X; 9780802120892

In this book, "young women are being scooped off the streets of 1839 London under the cover of darkness, and folks think the devil himself is driving the coach. When the bodies of two victims are later positioned near prominent London monuments, the fear factor rises. Even Liberty Lane, a female private investigator, is shaken by this development. She has been probing the disappearance of a young man's fiancée—who has been murdered—and her client is AWOL." (Library Journal)

Brookmyre, Christopher

Where the bodies are buried; Christopher Brookmyre. Atlantic Monthly Press 2012 293 p. $25

ISBN 0802120253; 9780802120250

Originally published: London: Little, Brown, 2011.

In this book, Christopher "Brookmyre . . . introduces Det. Insp. Catherine McLeod and PI Jasmine Sharp in . . . [this] Glasgow crime series. . . . [P]erceptive Catherine looks into the murder of a drug dealer, ... while inexperienced Jasmine searches for her PI uncle/boss, who went missing while working a case involving a family that disappeared decades before. Jasmine's only lead is Glen Fallan, a professional assassin who's rumored to have been dead for 20 years." (Publishers Weekly)

"Red herrings and plot convolutions abound, but it's Brookmyre's sense of the city and its no-nuance criminals that makes this one a winner." Booklist

Brookner, Anita

★ Brief lives. Random House 1991 260p

ISBN 0-394-58548-8

LC 90-38904

First published 1990 in the United Kingdom

"This short, subtle, beautifully organised and orchestrated novel positively gains from the deliberate restraint and detachment of the writing." London Rev Books

Brookner, Anita

Family and friends. Pantheon Bks. 1985 187p

ISBN 0-394-54616-4

LC 85-6373

"Anita Brookner's prose is impeccably elegant and she is unsentimental with it. . . . There is a closeness of atmosphere, almost claustrophobic, in Family and Friends, as if we were alternating between a discreetly perfumed lady's boudoir and the smoking room of a superior gentleman's club. There is no mistaking the originality as well as the skill and consistency with which the novel so beautifully conforms to its genre and its intentions." N Y Rev Books

Brookner, Anita

★ Hotel du Lac. Pantheon Bks. 1985 184p

ISBN 0-394-54215-0

LC 84-20641

First published 1984 in the United Kingdom

The tone of this novel is "oddly detached, very small-scale, faintly humorous. . . . It is by means of this very remoteness that Edith manages to hold our interest throughout this achingly uneventful holiday, with its empty chasms of time, its murmuring respectability, its dining room scattered sparsely with people who mean nothing to her. . . . There are some uncomfortable patches. . . . But generally, the writing is graceful and attractive." N Y Times Book Rev

Brookner, Anita

Undue influence; a novel. Random House 2000 231p $24

ISBN 0-375-50334-X

LC 99-36282

"The novel contains a fine brace of supporting characters whose behavior implicitly reflects on Claire's fall into limbo, and Brookner's narrative skill works like a scalpel exposing the complexity of each of their lives." Publ Wkly

Brooks, Albert, 1947-

2030; the real story of what happens to America. St. Martin's Press 2011 375p $25.99

ISBN 978-0-312-58372-9; 0-312-58372-9

LC 2010-54560

A novel set in the year 2030. "Cancer has been cured, global warming is an acknowledged reality, people have robot companions, and the president is a Jew—and oy vey does he have his hands full with an earthquake-leveled Los Angeles and a growing movement by the young to exterminate the elderly. And when the Chinese offer to rebuild L.A. in exchange for a half-ownership stake in Southern California, President Bernstein is faced with a decision that will alter the future of America. Brooks's sweeping narrative encompasses a diverse cast of characters, including an 80-year-old Angelino left homeless by the earthquake, a trust fund brat with a grudge against the elderly, and a teenage girl saddled with debt after her father's death, all of whom get brought together just in time for a climactic hostage crisis. Brooks's mordant vision encompasses the future of politics, medicine, entertainment, and daily living, resulting in a novel as entertaining as it is thought provoking, like something from the imagination of a borscht belt H.G. Wells." Publ Wkly

Brooks, Bill

Frontier justice; a John Henry Cole story. Bill Brooks. Five Star 2012 322 p. (hardcover) $25.95

ISBN 1432826077; 9781432826079

LC 2012016329

This is Bill Brooks' second John Henry Cole story. Here, Cole "hits the trail of revenge after his partner, Ike Kelly, is found dead, apparently the victim of a gigantic, vengeful black man named Leviticus Book. Cole is joined on the trail by bounty hunter Will Harper in an arduous pursuit through bad winter weather and worse luck, taunted all the while by Book, who, with his big Sharps rifle, makes both Cole and Harper seem like fools." (Booklist)

Brooks, Bill

Winter kill; a John Henry Cole story. by Bill Brooks. Five Star, A part of Gale, Cengage Learning 2013 262 p. (A John Henry Cole story) (hardcover) $25.95

ISBN 1432826344; 9781432826345

LC 2013005469

In this Western novel, by Bill Brooks, "John Henry Cole was three miles out of town on his small ranch waiting out the storm that was quickly killing his cattle and horses and starting to feel a little crazy himself. . . . [Then] Teddy Green a Texas Ranger arrives in Cheyenne and seeks Cole's help in locating Ella Mims, a woman who once lived in Cheyenne and with whom Cole had once been intimate. Green wants to question her concerning her involvement in a murder in Denver City." (Publisher's note)

Brooks, Geraldine
Caleb's crossing. Viking 2011 306p $26.95
ISBN 978-0-670-02104-8; 0-670-02104-0
LC 2010-51207

In this book, the narrator, "Bethia Mayfield, grow[s] up in the tiny settlement of Great Harbor amid a small band of pioneers and Puritans. . . . As often as she can, she slips away to . . . observe . . . [the] native Wampanoag inhabitants. At twelve, she encounters Caleb, the young son of a chieftain, and the two forge a tentative secret. . . . Bethia's minister father tries to convert the Wampanoag, awakening the wrath of the tribe's shaman, against whose magic he must test his own beliefs. One of his projects becomes the education of Caleb, and a year later, Caleb is in Cambridge, studying Latin and Greek among the colonial elite. There, Bethia finds herself reluctantly indentured as a housekeeper and can closely observe Caleb's crossing of cultures." (Publisher's note)

A historical novel "inspired by Caleb Cheeshahteaumauck, the first Native American to graduate from Harvard. Brooks brings the 1660s to life with evocative period detail, intriguing characters, and a compelling story narrated by Bethia Mayfield, the outspoken daughter of a Calvinist preacher. While exploring the island now known as Martha's Vineyard, Bethia meets Caleb, a Wampanoag native to the island, and they become close, clandestine friends. After Caleb loses most of his family to smallpox, he begins to study under the tutelage of Bethia's father. Since Bethia isn't allowed to pursue education herself, she eavesdrops on Caleb's and her own brother's lessons. Caleb is a gifted scholar who eventually travels, along with Bethia's brother, to Cambridge to continue his education. Bethia tags along and her descriptions of 17th-century Cambridge and Harvard are as entertaining as they are enlightening." Publ Wkly

Brooks, Geraldine
People of the book. Viking 2008 372p
ISBN 9780670018215
LC 2007-18082

"In 1996, Hanna Heath, an Australian rare-book expert, is offered the job of a lifetime: analysis and conservation of the famed Sarajevo Haggadah, which has been rescued from Serb shelling during the Bosnian war. Priceless and beautiful, the book is one of the earliest Jewish volumes ever to be illuminated with images. . . . In Bosnia during World War II, a Muslim risks his life to protect it from the Nazis. In the hedonistic salons of fin-de-siècle Vienna, the book becomes a pawn in the struggle against the city's rising anti-Semitism. In Venice during the time of the inquisition, a Catholic priest saves it from burning. In Barcelona in 1492, the scribe who wrote the text sees his family destroyed by the agonies of enforced exile. And in Seville in 1480, the reason for the Haggadah's extraordinary illuminations is finally disclosed.

Hanna's investigation unexpectedly plunges her into the intrigues of fine art forgers and ultranationalist fanatics." (Publisher's note)

"When an Australian rare-book conservator named Hanna Heath finds a butterfly wing, a salt crystal, a white hair, and bloodstains in the recently rediscovered Sarajevo Haggadah, a late-medieval illuminated codex of uncertain provenance, she sets out to solve the mystery of the book's origins. To her disappointment, analysis of the specimens reveals little. . . . Brooks, beginning where science leaves off, uses Hanna's finds as entry points to richly imagined historical landscapes peopled by the Haggadah's creators, protectors, and would-be destroyers—a female Muslim slave in Convivencia Spain, a Jewish doctor in fin-de-siècle Vienna, an alcoholic priest in seventeenth-century Venice. Their narratives alternate with Hanna's own, and the final, multilayered effect is complex and moving." New Yorker

Brooks, Geraldine
Year of wonders; a novel of the plague. Viking 2001 308p
ISBN 0-670-91021-X
LC 00-52757

"In 1665, the intense young pastor of a plague-stricken Derbyshire village persuades his parish to quarantine itself from the outside world. This selfless decision leads to the deaths of two-thirds of the inhabitants but saves the surrounding towns, as it did in the case of the historical village that inspired the tale. The novel glitters with careful research into such arcana as seventeenth-century lead-mining, sheep-farming, and of course, medicine, but its true strength is a deep imaginative engagement with how people are changed by catastrophe. . . . A rare few—including the narrator, a young widow who is a servant of the pastor—discover new strengths and abilities." New Yorker

Brooks, Max
★ **World** War Z; an oral history of the zombie war. Crown 2006 342p $24.95
ISBN 0-307-34660-9
LC 2006-9517

"Brooks tells the story of the world's desperate battle against the zombie threat with a series of first-person accounts 'as told to the author' by various characters around the world. A Chinese doctor encounters one of the earliest zombie cases at a time when the Chinese government is ruthlessly suppressing any information about the outbreak that will soon spread across the globe. The tale then follows the outbreak via testimony of smugglers, intelligence officials, military personnel and many others who struggle to defeat the zombie menace. Despite its implausible premise and choppy delivery, the novel is surprisingly hard to put down." Publ Wkly

Brooks, Terry
The **druid** of Shannara. Ballantine Bks. 1991 423p (Heritage of Shannara)
ISBN 0-345-36298-5
LC 90-42424

In the second novel in the Heritage of Shannara tetralogy "Walker Boh, the 'Dark Uncle,' embarks on a perilous journey to recover the black Elfstone and restore the lost druid keep of Paranor." Libr J

"Broadening the landscape of his magic world, Brooks has produced a deep and thoughtful fantasy." Publ Wkly

Followed by The elfqueen of Shannara

Brooks, Terry

First king of Shannara. Ballantine Bks. 1996 489p

ISBN 0-345-39652-9

LC 95-52321

"To defend his followers and escape subjugation from the evil Warlock Lord, Druid Bremen must possess the magical Black Elfstone. This . . . answers fans' questions about the early history of the Shannara family." Libr J

Brooks, Terry

The **measure** of the magic; legends of Shannara. Del Rey/Ballantine Books 2011 383p $27

ISBN 978-0-345-48420-8; 0-345-48420-7

LC 2011-14440

Sequel to: The bearer of the Black Staff (2010)

Sider Ament, the "wielder of the power of the Black Staff, is dead. With his dying breath, he has given possession of the Black Staff over to Panterra Qu, a young Tracker. Panterra, though, doesn't know how to unlock the power of the Staff. Time is not on his side, however. The Elf king of Arborlon has been assassinated, and Trolls are massing for an invasion. Elsewhere, Panterra's companion, Prue Liss, is desperately trying to find her way back to safety. Trolls hunt her, but if that were all, it would be bad enough. Coming in their wake is a darker and more sinister foe: The Ragpicker, a Demon bent on locating magic. In particular he seeks the Black Staff, and whomever happens to possess it will fall under his assault. The main storyline Brooks weaves with Panterra is extraordinarily fun. The tension is ramped up as Panterra struggles to understand the Staff and how to control it. Throw in the mystery and the conspiracy surrounding the death of the King of the Elves, and you have more than enough excitement and intrigue." Bookreporter

Brooks, Terry

The **sword** of Shannara; illustrated by the Brothers Hildebrandt. Random House 1977 726p il

ISBN 0-394-41333-4

LC 77-151532

"Reminiscent of Tolkien's fantasies though lacking the originality of his vision and the beauty of his language, this is still an engrossing saga of hardship and adventure with well-maintained action that will keep readers captive right up to a nicely-wrought finish." SLJ

Followed by The Elfstones of Shannara

Brooks, Terry, 1944-

Wards of Faerie; Terry Brooks. Del Rey 2012 371 p. (Dark legacy of Shannara) (hardcover) $28

ISBN 0345523474; 9780345523471

LC 2012020292

This epic fantasy novel, by Terry Brooks, is part of the "Dark Legacy of Shannara" series. "When the world was young, . . . the Elfstones warded the race of Elves and their lands, keeping evil at bay. . . . Thousands of years later, tumultuous times are upon the world. . . . The young Druid Aphenglow Elessedil has stumbled upon the secret account of an Elven girl's heartbreak and the shocking truth about the vanished Elfstones." (Publisher's note)

Brower, Brock

Blue dog, green river. Godine 2005 107p $23.95

ISBN 1-56792-280-5

LC 2004-16528

This novella tells the "tale of a dog's redemption. A former chicken thief, Blue Dog finds herself locked up in the pound with her hindquarters full of buckshot. Enter Paul Nozik, a river guide who decides to reform the canine criminal. A year later, while rafting a string quartet down Utah's Green River, Nozik becomes separated from his pal. Bitten by a rattlesnake and shot at by angry drunks, Blue Dog is knocked into the river toward the rapids. Struggling ashore, she sees a campfire and a naked man playing a flute. Is it Kokopelli, the ancient rock-art deity, come to life? Or is Blue Dog merely hallucinating from the snake venom? In alternating chapters, Brower weaves together the dual threads of Blue Dog's odyssey and Nozik's search. Brower does a good job capturing the life and culture of raftsmen; Blue Dog's thoughts are pure delight, and by the time Blue Dog is reunited with Nozik, the line between reality and the supernatural has become comfortably blurred." Booklist

Brown, Carrie

The **hatbox** baby; a novel. Algonquin Bks. 2000 333p $22.95

ISBN 1-56512-299-2

LC 00-44208

"Confirmed bachelor Dr. Leo Hoffman is a pioneer in neonatal intensive care who finances his research into and medical care of destitute babies by charging admission to his educational programs at fairs and amusement parks. During the summer of 1933, while working at his premature baby exhibit at the Chicago World's Fair, he saves the life of a special 'premie'—and finds love in the process. . . . This is a moving story about complex, interesting characters who love deeply." Libr J

Brown, Carrie

★ **Lamb** in love; a novel. Algonquin Bks. 1999 336p $21.95

ISBN 1-56512-203-8

LC 98-44580

The author "reveals her characters not as others perceive them but as they are able to see one another, and as they come to understand themselves. Norris and Vida are full of depth and longing, passion and poetry, that continually startle and delight." N Y Times Book Rev

Brown, Charles Brockden

Three Gothic novels. Library of America 1998 914p $40

ISBN 978-1-88301-157-4

LC 97-46701

"Wieland; or The Transformation (1798) is a novel of a religious fanatic preyed upon by a sinister ventriloquist. . . . A relentlessly dark exploration of guilt, deception, and compulsion, it creates a sustained mood of irrational terror in the midst of the Pennsylvania countryside. In Arthur Mervyn; or Memoirs of the Year 1793 (1799), Brown draws on his own experiences to create indelible scenes of Philadelphia devastated by a yellow fever epidemic, while telling the story of a young man caught in the snares of a professional swindler. Edgar Huntly; or Memoirs of a Sleepwalker (1799) fuses traditional Gothic themes with motifs drawn from the American Wilderness in a series of eerily unreal adventures that test the limits of the protagonist's self-knowledge." Publisher's note

Brown, Dale

Hammerheads. Fine, D.I. 1990 478p
ISBN 1-556-11170-3

LC 89-46026

"This smooth blend of plot, action and gadgetry supports the debatable argument that drug smuggling can be checked by military methods. But forget ideologies—Hammerheads is a reader's delight from first page to last, a model of the genre." Publ Wkly

Brown, Dale

Storming heaven. Putnam 1994 399p
ISBN 0-399-13931-1

LC 94-12213

"Over the top? Sure. But the author's view about the vulnerability of U.S. airports to aerial attack reads almost plausibly, and Cazaux is a fascinating monster." Booklist

Brown, Dan

The **Da** Vinci code; a novel. Doubleday 2003 454p $24.95
ISBN 0-385-50420-9

LC 2002-40918

"In a two-day span, American symbologist Robert Langdon finds himself accused of murdering the curator of the Louvre, on the run through the streets of Paris and London, and teamed up with French-cryptologist Sophie Neveu to uncover nothing less than the secret location of the Holy Grail. It appears that a conservative Catholic bishop might be on the verge of destroying the Grail, which includes an alternate history of Christ that could bring down the church. . . .The story is full of brain-teasing puzzles and fascinating insights into religious history and art." Booklist

Brown, Dan

The **lost** symbol; a novel. Doubleday 2009 509p $29.95
ISBN 978-0-385-50422-5; 0-385-50422-5

As this novel opens Harvard University symbologist Robert Langdon is "quietly brewing a cup of coffee at home in Cambridge one Sunday morning when he gets a call asking him, in the name of his dear friend and mentor, Peter Solomon, to fly immediately to Washington to fill in for a canceled guest speaker at an illustrious gathering. Many of the attendees at the meeting are expected to be Freemasons and they are gathering in a building rich with Masonic history. So it makes sense that Langdon will be addressing the group on the symbolism found in the architecture of the US capital. Eager to be of service to Solomon, Langdon jumps on a private jet and speeds to Washington only to discover that his mentor, who is a high-level Mason, is in serious trouble, threatened by a deranged loner who hopes to learn the inner secrets of the Masonic world." Christ Sci Mon

Brown, Dee Alexander

★ **Creek** Mary's blood; a novel. [by] Dee Brown. Holt, Rinehart & Winston 1980 401p il
ISBN 0-03-044281-8

LC 79-9060

"Through the words and memories of Dane, grandson of Creek Mary (or Akusa Amayi), we follow the history of the men, children, and grandchildren in the life of that indomitable exemplar of the American Indian. The action—and there is plenty of it—takes place in the period after the Revolutionary War and continues through the nineteenth century. The customs, rituals, courting, fighting, and celebrating are all described in detail. One of the most painful sections of the book depicts the forced removal west of the Mississippi of Indian tribes. . . . The relationships among the various tribes—Creek, Cheyenne, Cherokee, and others—is of great interest. Many famous names are recalled, among them Tecumseh, Andrew Jackson, Teddy Roosevelt, and the great chiefs Crazy Horse and Sitting Bull." Shapiro. Fic for Youth. 3d edition

Brown, E. R.

Almost criminal; by E. R. Brown. Dundurn Press 2013 285 p. ill. (paperback) $17.99
ISBN 1459705831; 9781459705838

LC 2013376771

This novel, written by E.R. Brown, focuses on Randle Kennedy, "British Columbia's most prolific producer of boutique marijuana," who meets Tate MacLane who is "brilliant, miserable, and broke. Randle wants a fresh face to front his transactions. Tate desperately needs a mentor and yearns for respect. Soon Tate finds out that it's harder to get out of the business than to get in." (Publisher's note)

Brown, Eleanor

The **weird** sisters; Eleanor Brown. Amy Einhorn Books/G.P. Putnam's Sons 2011 320p.
ISBN 0399157220; 9780399157226; 978-0-399-15722-6

LC 2010029599

"There is no problem that a library card can't solve. The Andreas family is one of readers. Their father, a . . . Shakespeare professor who speaks almost entirely in verse, has named his three daughters after famous Shakespearean women. When the sisters return to their childhood home, ostensibly to care for their ailing mother, but really to lick their wounds and bury their secrets, they are horrified to find the others there. . . . But the sisters soon discover that everything they've been running from—one another, their small hometown, and themselves—might offer more than they ever expected." (Publisher's note)

Brown, Joe David

Addie Pray; a novel. Simon & Schuster 1971 313p
ISBN 0-671-20962-0

"Brown has a special feeling for the Depression-era South. . . . {Addie's speech} is vulgar, pungent country talk, which adds greatly to the book's easygoing charm. Looking at Long Boy with his floozy, she observes that 'he got that silly, dazed grin like a tom cat being choked to death with cream.' Like that extravagant expression, the book is a long tall, oldtime tale. But as Addie might put it, in the right hands that kind of yarn has a lot of prance left." Time

Brown, Karen

The **longings** of wayward girls; a novel. Karen Brown. Washington Square Press 2013 336 p. $15

ISBN 1476724911; 9781476724911

LC 2012044427

In this novel, "back in the '70s, a quiet middle-class neighborhood is rocked by the disappearance of two young girls who vanish five years apart. Sadie Watkins bears a close resemblance to the first, 9-year-old Laura Loomis, and is grudgingly forced to play with the second, Francie Bingham. Francie, with her awkward appearance, unhappy home life and a desire to be liked, makes an easy target for Sadie and her best friend, Betty." Now an adult, Sadie must confront her past. (Kirkus Reviews)

Brown, Larry

★ **Joe**; a novel. Algonquin Bks. 1991 345p

ISBN 0-945575-61-0

LC 91-12026

A novel about "poor 'white trash' in rural Mississippi. Joe Ranson is a middle-aged redneck with a soul. He fights and spits, drinks beer by the gallon from a cooler embedded in his truck, and endures bad relationships with women. But within the society he inhabits, he is a moral man, more or less following the rituals and established 'codes' of fair play. Unfortunately, he is involved in a classic feud, the roots of which are never revealed, that threatens to destroy him. Also destined to cross paths with Joe is the nomadic Jones family. Gary Jones is a hardworking and painfully naive teenager. His father is pure evil, his mother nearly insane, and his siblings barely human. Joe offers Gary work, fueling hope that these two very different men will learn enough from each other to save themselves." Booklist

Brown, Rita Mae

Dolley; a novel of Dolley Madison in love and war. Bantam Bks. 1994 382p

LC 93-44429

The author re-creates a "critical year in the life of the fourth president's wife, who loved politics and her husband and who had a great gift for friendship. In 1814, Napoleon's war with Britain spilled into its former colonies, and redcoats marching toward under-defended Washington constitute the backdrop of Brown's slice of Dolley Madison's life. Brown vivifies the capital hostess and covert political manipulator's doings by interspersing snippets from an imaginary diary with the main narrative. . . . Brown's Dolley Madison is full-blown and vibrant." Booklist

Brown, Rita Mae

Murder at Monticello; or, Old sins; [by] Rita Mae Brown & Sneaky Pie Brown; illustrations by Wendy Wray. Bantam Bks. 1994 298p il

ISBN 0-553-08140-3

LC 94-16711

"Tiger cat Mrs. Murphy and corgi Tee Tucker . . . help Mary Minor 'Harry' Haristeen, postmistress of Crozet, Virginia, solve a nearly 200-year-old mystery. It begins with a skeleton discovered in a slave cabin during restorations at Monticello—and continues with the present-day murder of Kimball Haynes, head of archaeology there, who has discovered secrets of miscegenation recorded in a doctor's long-hidden journals. . . . An entertaining treat for animal-loving mystery/history fans." Booklist

Brown, Rita Mae

Southern discomfort. Harper & Row 1982 249p

ISBN 0-06-014928-0

LC 81-47683

The author "seems to understand the way in which dark passions and unspeakable desires become magnified among a people segregated by unnatural laws concerning race, class and social position. She portrays well the suffering incurred by trying to defy such a system; she also captures the earthy quality of those who do what they must to get by." Best Sellers

Brown, Rita Mae

Wish you were here; [by] Rita Mae Brown & Sneaky Pie Brown; illustrations by Wendy Wray. Bantam Bks. 1990 242p il

ISBN 0-553-05881-9

LC 90-1071

"Mary Minor ('Harry') Haristeen, divorce in the works, runs the post office in Crozet, Virginia, with a pet cat and dog at her side. After two spectacularly gruesome murders rock the community, Harry attempts to gather helpful clues, while the pets (who converse with each other) do their best to protect her." Libr J

"Ms. Brown writes with wise, disarming wit about her country-bred characters and their not-always-neighborly ways." N Y Times Book Rev

Brown, Rosellen

★ **Before** and after. Farrar, Straus & Giroux 1992 354p

ISBN 0-374-10999-0

LC 92-81571

This novel begins "on the day that Carolyn Reiser, a New Hampshire pediatrician with two teenage kids, gets called to the emergency room. A girl has been bludgeoned to death. The chief suspect is Carolyn's son and he has disappeared." Newsweek

Brown is "tenacious in her examination of each major character. Deftly, artfully, she strips away the delicate shelter of conventional relationships." N Y Times Book Rev

Brown, Rosellen

Half a heart. Farrar, Straus & Giroux 2000 402p

ISBN 0-374-44013-1

LC 00-22926

"Miriam, a rich Houston housewife with three children, has a secret in her past: during a teaching stint at a black college in the Sixties, she had an affair with a black professor and gave birth to a daughter. When the baby's father challenged her for custody of the child, Miriam gave up without a fight and fled to Houston, soon marrying a rich doctor. For years she suffered feelings of guilt and loss yet felt smug that she wasn't as superficial or racist as her friends. As her own mother's health deteriorates, Miriam suddenly tracks down her daughter, Veronica, now 17 and entering Stanford.

Veronica, for her part, intends to milk her new family for money for college." Libr J

"The situation is an intriguing one rendered all the more so by Brown's skillful and sympathetic handling of her two central characters." Time

Brown, Rosellen

Tender mercies. Knopf 1978 259p

ISBN 0-394-42741-6

LC 78-1315

"What impresses one most about Tender Mercies is its dignity and restraint. While we learn a great deal about the physical details of paralysis, catheters and such, Brown makes no case for any horror of the body, nor does Laura's suffering prompt a garish loathing of the universe. . . . The language is spare and clean, with flashes of quiet poetry, perfectly suited to the plain but by no means simple New Englanders it portrays." Saturday Rev

Brown, Sandra

The **alibi**. Warner Bks. 1999 490p

ISBN 0-446-51980-4

LC 99-31444

"When Charleston real estate developer Lute Pettijohn is murdered in the penthouse suite of the posh hotel he recently built, there is no shortage of likely suspects; Pettijohn is one of the most hated men in town. On the same night that the murder occurs, assistant district attorney Hammond Cross attends a county fair, where he meets a mysterious woman who refuses to tell him her name. . . . Later, when a witness places the woman, now identified as respected psychologist Dr. Alex Ladd, at the scene of the crime, she becomes the number one suspect. . . . A web of labyrinthine relationships becomes ever more intricate until the identity of the killer is revealed, a shock that would be implausible in a less carefully constructed tale." Publ Wkly

Brown, Sandra

The **crush**. Warner Bks. 2002 474p

ISBN 0-446-52704-1

LC 2002-25896

"Dr. Rennie Newton thought she was doing the right thing when she voted to acquit contract killer Ricky Lozada while serving on a jury. After all, the prosecution had not proved its case. But when Lozada is released, he begins calling her and leaving her flowers. When a rival doctor at Rennie's hospital is murdered, suspicion falls on Rennie, and the police suspect she has a connection to Lozada. Detective Wick Threadgill, who has deeply personal reasons to hate Lozada, begins to investigate Rennie. . . . This novel delivers a menacing villain and page-turning suspense." Booklist

Brown, Sandra

The **witness**. Warner Bks. 1995 422p

ISBN 0-446-51631-7

LC 94-42733

"This story pivots on the relationship between Kendall Deaton Burnwood, an idealistic public defender, and U.S. Marshal John McGrath, who is returning her to Prosper, S.C., as a material witness when their car crashes into a ravine in Georgia. With her three-month-old in tow, Kendall tries repeatedly to abandon John, who's hobbled by temporary amnesia and a leg injury. Kendall fears the town of Prosper for good reason: it's where she witnessed her husband and father-in-law, ringleaders of a white-supremacist vigilante group, ritualistically execute one of her clients. . . . The push-pull generated by John's memory loss and Kendall's terror sparks a sexual tension that is deftly and vividly consummated, and secrets keep popping out until the last page." Publ Wkly

Brown, Stacia M.

Accidents of providence; Stacia M. Brown. Houghton Mifflin Harcourt 2012 x, 259p.p

ISBN 0547490801; 9780547840116; 9780547490809

LC 2011015933

This work of historical fiction tells the story of a murder case "against Rachel Lockyer, an unmarried glovemaker's apprentice, for breaking the 1624 'Act to Prevent the Destroying and Murdering of Bastard Children.' No one questions that Rachel buried her infant daughter; the case hinges on whether the child was born dead. . . . [Criminal investigator Thomas] Bartwain is increasingly uneasy, especially when he finds a flaw in the law. Meanwhile Rachel remains largely silent . . . because she does not want to expose William Walwyn, who has been her adulterous lover. . . . Walwyn is a well-known leader of the Levelers, a human-rights advocacy group that originally supported [political leader Oliver] Cromwell and is now under attack. . . . Events in the plot are based on historical incidents." (Kirkus)

Browne, Marshall

Eye of the abyss. Thomas Dunne Bks. 2003 290p $23.95

ISBN 0-312-31156-7

LC 2003-47297

"Like the shifting reality of Schmidt's life, the changes in his character are as subtle as they are harrowing, a triumph of Browne's clean, exacting style." N Y Times Book Rev

Browne, Robert

The **paradise** prophecy. Dutton 2011 401p il $25.95

ISBN 978-0-525-95223-7

LC 2011-13477

"When saint-like pop singer Gabriela Zuada is found burned to a crisp in her dressing room after a performance in São Paulo, Brazil, on the last night of her Glory Revealed World Tour, Bernadette Callahan, field agent for the top-secret government spy agency known as Section, investigates. After other horribly burned bodies surface, Milton scholar Sebastian 'Batty' LaLaurie persuades Bernadette that Gabriela's demise is no ordinary murder. Indeed, Beelzebub, Belial, Moloch, and Mammon—a quartet of fallen angels who appropriate human 'skins' as a disguise—are behind the deaths as well as an unholy plot to release Satan to rule over humankind. Only the archangel Michael and his band of puny but courageous humans can defeat the demons. The author . . . offers consistently smart prose and an ending that points to future thrillers set in this fascinating world." Publ Wkly

Browne, S. G.

Lucky bastard; S.G. Browne. Gallery Books 2012 358 p.

ISBN 1451657196; 9781451657197; 9781451657203

LC 2011050997

This "supernaturally themed comedy" novel from "[S.G.] Browne introduces P.I. Nick Monday . . . [who] is . . . one of the few hundred people in America who are able to poach luck, and then sell it on the black market. . . . Nick's trouble begins when a knockout named Tuesday Knight breezes in with an offer of $100,000 to recover her father's stolen luck. Not long after, a Chinese crime boss named Tommy Wong tries to strong-arm Nick into poaching a particularly rare form of luck. Meanwhile, a couple of government agents are on Nick's tail, and who knows what motivates the mysterious Scooter Girl orbiting around the whole scene." (Kirkus)

Browner, Jesse

Everything happens today. Europa Editions 2011 216p pa $15

ISBN 978-1-60945-051-9; 1-60945-051-5

"Sixteen-year-old Wes, the protagonist of this literary experience of teenage angst, attends Manhattan's elite Dalton School but lives downtown in the Village. A modern Holden Caulfield with an iPhone (though he's both smarter and more interesting than Salinger's antihero), Wes tolerates a mentally absent father, cares for a slowly dying mother, and protects his younger sister. The narrative proceeds organically through Wes's turmoil about losing his virginity to the 'wrong' person. As he comes to grips with his fears, the unexpected happens; he is pleasantly surprised by life and rediscovers the authenticity of a real human relationship. . . . has crafted a stupendous, thought-provoking, devilishly delicious novel that reads like Zen koan meets Portrait of the Artist as a Young Man with some modern 'english' that sets the plate spinning." Libr J

Brownrigg, Sylvia

The delivery room. Counterpoint 2008 399p pa $14.95

ISBN 978-1-58243-424-7; 1-58243-424-7

LC 2008-13102

First published 2006 in the United Kingdom

"The Delivery Room is, despite its contemporary themes, an old-fashioned novel, one full of texture and detail, in which character and plot are patiently dissected and illuminated so that a larger picture might become apparent." Times Lit Suppl

Brownrigg, Sylvia

Morality tale; a novel. drawings by Monica Scott. Counterpoint 2008 224p il $24

ISBN 978-1-58243-404-9; 1-58243-404-2

LC 2007-43783

"Contemplating Sylvia Brownrigg's short new novel, the adjective 'quirky' comes to mind. Bold, dry, eccentric, 'Morality Tale' cries out for a descriptive term that can pinpoint its oddness along with its likability. 'Quirky' it will have to be, for this curious, teasing, idiosyncratic and strangely charming book." San Francisco Chron

Bruen, Ken

Cross. St. Martin's Minotaur 2008 288p $23.95

ISBN 978-0-312-34142-8; 0-312-34142-3

LC 2007-42421

First published 2007 in the United Kingdom

"As a result of a shooting meant to kill Galway PI Jack Taylor . . . , Cody, his young apprentice and surrogate son, lies comatose and close to death in the hospital. Meanwhile, Taylor tries to make sense of the brutal murder by crucifixion of a young man and the burning death of the victim's sister." Libr J

"Bruen riffs on different meanings and implications of the word cross throughout, and his insights into pain, loss and Irishness are unforgettable." Publ Wkly

Bruen, Ken

The guards. St. Martin's Minotaur 2003 291p $23.95

ISBN 0-312-30355-6

LC 2002-35855

"Ousted from Ireland's police force, the Garda Siochana (or Guards), Jack Taylor ekes out a living on the unmodernized margins of Galway. . . .When Ann Henderson walks into the pub that serves as Taylor's office, asking him to prove that her daughter Sarah was not a suicide but a murder victim, Taylor finds himself investigating a sex-and-murder tangle—and in love." Booklist

"Bruen's astringent prose and death's-head humor keep this quest for redemption from getting maudlin, just as his 'tapestry of talk' makes somber poetry of the bar-stool laments that serve as dialogue." N Y Times Book Rev

Bruni, Sarah

The Night Gwen Stacy Died; Sarah Bruni. Mariner Books/Houghton Mifflin Harcourt 2013 288 p. $14.95

ISBN 0547898169; 9780547898162

LC 2012040352

In this book, "Iowa doesn't suit Sheila, not from where she is standing at the edge of everything, dreaming in French and planning her future with a taxidermied coyote as a confidant. It is a good thing she has plans for after high school: she is going to get out of this small town she does not understand and where she is not understood and head to Paris. The random element introduced to disrupt Sheila's carefully planned schedule is Peter, the only one who is as much an outsider as she is." (Library Journal)

Brunner, John

★ Stand on Zanzibar. Grove Press 1968 505p

"Extrapolating from current politics, social and sexual mores, the communications revolution, the use of computers, brainwashing, drug use, psychology, philosophy, and sociology, Brunner has fashioned a mammoth work that is an intricate tapestry depicting a possible future. The dozens of characters interspersed in a complex fashion make the novel difficult to read but well worth the effort. Brunner's brand of cynicism and radical social commentary may not appeal to the taste of all readers, but in the time that has elapsed since the publication of the book, we have seen changes that bear startling similarities to several of Brunner's predictions." Shapiro. Fic for Youth. 3d edition

Brunt, Carol Rifka

✓**Tell** the wolves I'm home; a novel. Carol Rifka Brunt. Dial Press 2012 360 p. (hbk.: acid-free paper): $25

 ISBN 0679644199; 081299292X; 9780679644194; 9780812992922

           LC 2011027932

 Alex Award (2013)

 Carol Rifka Brunt's novel "is an exploration of an unlikely friendship that blossoms in the wake of a terrible loss. It's 1987, and 14-year-old June Elbus is reeling from the death of her beloved uncle Finn, a famous painter who has succumbed to AIDS. . . . Finn's death leaves a gaping hole in June's life, and she's shocked when Toby, her uncle's lover and the man her mother holds responsible for his death, makes a bid to fill that emptiness by contacting June secretly." (Booklist)

Bryson, Ellen

✓The **transformation** of Bartholomew Fortuno; a novel. Henry Holt and Co. 2010 331p $26

 ISBN 978-0-8050-9192-2; 0-8050-9192-0

           LC 2009-45214

 "Bartholomew is a wonderful character who doesn't struggle against his self-image but revels in it, challenging audiences with his bravado. . . . A rich tapestry of romance, illusory science, criminal trickery and human intrigue. Let the show begin." Kirkus

Buchan, John

 ★ The **thirty**-nine steps. Doran, G.H. 1915 231p

 "A bored, well-to-do Englishman, Richard Hannay, returns home to England after growing up in South Africa. Drifting between his club and the sights of London, he is drawn into the confidences of a secret agent in the thick of espionage. The agent is murdered in Hannay's apartment and Richard finds himself on the run from Scotland Yard and the cult of the 'Black Stone.'" Shapiro. Fic for Youth. 3d edition

Buchanan, Cathy Marie

 ★ The **painted** girls; Cathy Marie Buchanan. Riverhead Books 2013 368 p. $27.95

 ISBN 1594486247; 9781594486241

           LC 2012038433

 In this novel by Cathy Marie Buchanan, "following their father's sudden death, the van Goethem sisters find their lives upended. . . . Marie throws herself into dance and is soon modeling in the studio of Edgar Degas. . . . There she meets a wealthy male patron of the ballet. . . . Meanwhile Antoinette, derailed by her love for the dangerous Émile Abadie, must choose between honest labor and the more profitable avenues open to a young woman of the Parisian demimonde." (Publisher's note)

 "Buchanan brings the unglamorous reality of the late-19th-century Parisian demimonde into stark relief while imagining the life of Marie Van Goethem, the actual model for the iconic Degas statue Little Dancer Aged Fourteen... the moving yet unsentimental portrait of family love, of two sisters struggling to survive with dignity, makes this a must-read." Kirkus

Buchanan, Edna

 Love kills; a Brit Montero novel. Simon and Schuster 2007 308p $25

 ISBN 978-0-7432-9476-8; 0-7432-9476-9

           LC 2006-39050

 "Miami crime reporter Britt Montero, on the mend emotionally after losing her fiance in a shootout . . . , decides work is the best medicine. Her first case is actually an old one. The body of Nathan York is excavated by construction workers. Years earlier York was the subject of Britt's first big story. He was a militant advocate for men's rights in custody cases and would snatch children from their mothers and deliver them to their estranged fathers. Britt is also trying to track down Marsh Holt, the Honeymoon Killer. A hunky thirtysomething lothario operating with aliases in various states, Holt married a string of women across the country who all suffered fatal 'accidents' while on their honeymoons." Booklist

Buchanan, Edna

 Suitable for framing. Hyperion 1995 243p

 ISBN 0-7868-6047-2

           LC 94-33133

 Miami News crime reporter Britt Montero "confronts a mystery that cuts close to the bone: why she's suddenly losing her journalistic edge. Chance puts her on the spot to see a young woman killed and her toddler injured in the most horrible of a recent string of carjackings. Since then, however, the scoops have been gravitating toward young Trish Tierney, Britt's protégé and the News's newest reporter. Britt doggedly works her contacts in the Miami Police, especially Det. Bill Rakestraw, who is investigating the juvenile ring apparently responsible for the car thefts." Publ Wkly

 "Busy, busy plot but Buchanan's streamlined prose and genuine affection for Miami's weirdness make it a quick and entertaining read." Booklist

Buchanan, Edna

 You only die twice; a Britt Montero mystery. Morrow 2001 292p $24

 ISBN 0-380-97655-2

           LC 00-49543

 "When the body of a beautiful woman is found floating offshore, seaweed in her hair, veteran Miami News police-beat reporter Britt Montero gets the call. . . . Britt senses a good story in the making, and when the body remains unclaimed and foul play is established, she is sure of it. A fingerprint check identifies the well-cared-for mermaid as Kaithlin Jordan of the prominent department store family. One problem: she's been dead for 10 years, and her husband is scheduled to be executed for her murder." Publ Wkly

 "A fascinating amalgam of red herrings, misdirection, and guilt by personality. . . . An intelligent, thoroughly entertaining crime novel." Booklist

Buck, Pearl S.

 ✓ ★ The **good** earth. Washington Square Press 2004 357p (Contemporary classics) pa $14

 ISBN 0-7432-7293-5

 First published 1931 by Day

 This novel set in prerevolutionary China "describes the rise of Wang Lung, a Chinese peasant, from poverty to the position of a rich landowner, helped by his patient wife, O-lan. Their vigor, fortitude, persistence, and enduring love of the soil are emphasized throughout. Generally regarded as Pearl Buck's masterpiece, the book won universal acclaim for its sympathetically authentic picture of Chinese life." Reader's Ency. 4th edition

Buckley, Fiona

The **doublet** affair; a mystery at Queen Elizabeth I's court: featuring Ursula Blanchard. Fiona Buckley. Scribner 1998 294 p. (hbk.) o.p.; (pbk.) $22.99

ISBN 0684838427; 9780743489089

LC 98043016

This book follows "Ursula Blanchard, . . . lady-in-waiting to Queen Elizabeth I, [who] is the only female spy employed by the queen's right-hand man, William Cecil. . . . Ursula is requested by the queen and Cecil to retire temporarily from court and to stay . . . at the home of Leonard and Ann Mason, who are suspected of harboring sympathies for the Catholic Mary, Queen of Scots. Working undercover as a governess, Ursula seeks to gather information on a conspiracy that may involve a London clockmaker and the Masons' tutor. She is helped significantly by her married servants, Fern Dale and Roger Brockley. . . . Ursula finds her life threatened but forges on, unraveling the conspiracy and, ultimately, making a fateful decision regarding her future." (Publishers Weekly)

Buckley, Fiona

The **fugitive** queen; an Ursula Blanchard mystery at Queen Elizabeth I's court. Fiona Buckley. Scribner 2003 277 p. $24

ISBN 074323751X

LC 2003045736

This historical novel "feature[s] Ursula Blanchard, half-sister, confidant and agent of Queen Elizabeth I. In 1568, the queen summons Ursula to court ostensibly because Ursula's ward, Penelope Mason, has been paying too much attention to a married music master. Ursula travels with Penelope to the north of England to find a husband for her ward, but her real mission is to convey a very private verbal message directly to Mary Tudor, formerly Queen of Scots, who's held captive in isolated Bolton Castle. Ursula also seeks to learn what role Mary may have had in the recent mysterious death of her husband, Lord Darnley. Ursula suffers considerable pain, anxiety and concern for her own daughter in the process." (Publishers Weekly)

Buckley, Fiona

Queen of ambition; an Ursula Blanchard mystery at Queen Elizabeth I's court. Fiona Buckley. Scribner 2002 286p. $23

ISBN 0743202643

LC 2001049558

In this novel, "Ursula Blanchard, lady-in-waiting and espionage agent to Queen Elizabeth I, . . . deal[s] with murder and intrigue in [author Fiona] Buckley's fifth . . . Elizabethan mystery. . . . In the early summer of 1564, Ursula is at Withysham, her country manor house, where she and her eight-year-old daughter are waiting for the plague to end in France. . . . Meanwhile, Queen Elizabeth is preparing a Royal Progress to Cambridge University. Ordered to court ear-

lier than expected, Ursula learns that the queen's Secretary of State, Sir William Cecil, is fearful about a student play to be presented to the queen just after she enters the town and greets the public. Ursula and her good friend, Rob Henderson, are sent ahead to investigate." (Publishers Weekly)

Buckley, Fiona

Queen without a crown; Fiona Buckley. Crème de la Crime 2012 240p.

ISBN 9781780290140

This book follows Ursula Blanchard, a "spy and lady-in-waiting" for Queen Elizabeth I of England. "Elizabeth wants Ursula to sniff out possible traitors by visiting targeted sites near the border. The queen knows Ursula is already working on a case for a young royal messenger named Mark, who . . . needs to clear his late father's name. The father was wrongfully accused of a poisoning death some 20 years ago, and only proof of innocence will satisfy the parents of Mark's intended. . . . Ursula gets a break in this cold case from a portrait artist. If Ursula can find the portrait of Mark's father, she might save Mark from a broken heart. Since the painting is probably in a home near the Scottish border, she combines her two missions. Before long, the clever and gutsy Ursula is riding for her life." (Libr J)

Buckley, Fiona

Queen's bounty; Fiona Buckley. Creme de la Crime 2012 240 p.

ISBN 1780290241; 9781780290249

In this novel by Fiona Buckley "Ursula Blanchard . . . is in trouble when she's accused of witchcraft. . . . An outbreak of smallpox, accusations against a servant who had once been convicted as a witch and books on witchcraft found in the home of some friends are evidence enough to persuade a zealous sheriff to investigate. Ursula and her longtime comrade in spying, Roger Brockley . . . attempt to show that Ursula has been set up by a vengeful but unknown enemy." (Kirkus)

Buckley, Fiona

Queen's ransom; a mystery at Queen Elizabeth's court: featuring Ursula Blanchard. Fiona Buckley. Scribner 2000 348p $23.00

ISBN 0684862670

LC 99036455

This novel features "Ursula Blanchard, the heroine of [author Fiona] Buckley's . . . historical mystery series, of which this is the third entry. . . . This time out, the 27-year-old lady-in-waiting is sent on a dangerous mission to France on the brink of civil war. In an effort to mitigate the threats from Spain and France, 28-year-old Queen Elizabeth I wishes to negotiate accords among the warring French Catholics and Protestants, and to secure her support among the latter. Since Ursula had planned to accompany the father of her deceased husband (Luke Blanchard) on a trip to retrieve his young ward from the Loire valley, Elizabeth entrusts her with a letter to be personally delivered to Catherine, Queen of France. . . . On her guard, she sets out for Paris to complete her mission." (Publishers Weekly)

Includes bibliographical references

Buckley, Fiona
A **Rescue** for a Queen; Fiona Buckley. Severn House Pub Ltd 2013 224 p. (hardcover) $28.95
ISBN 1780290403; 9781780290409
This is Fiona Buckley's 11th Tudor mystery. Here, in "1571, Ursula Blanchard, half-sister to the queen, is planning a quiet country life after the death of her devoted husband of six years, Hugh Stannard. But Sir William Cecil, England's secretary of state, wants her" to accompany her surrogate daughter Margaret Emory to the Netherlands for Margaret's marriage to cattle farmer Antonio van Weede so that Ursula can "learn whatever she can about conspiracies against [Queen] Elizabeth." (Publishers Weekly)

Buckley, Fiona
The **siren** queen; an Ursula Blanchard mystery at Queen Elizabeth I's court. Fiona Buckley. Scribner 2004 277p $25
ISBN 0743237528; 9780743237529
LC 2004045284
This book follows "Ursula Blanchard, half sister to Queen Elizabeth I and occasional spy for the realm. . . . While paying a reluctant visit to the seemingly foolish duke of Norfolk to discuss the possibility of an early betrothal for her young daughter, Ursula learns that her host has been conducting an ill-considered correspondence with the incarcerated Mary, queen of Scots. Determined to leave the duke's estate before the impressionable Meg becomes even more besotted with the icy Edmund Dean, she is prevented from returning home by the brutal murders of a courier and a servant. As Ursula attempts to untangle a treasonous web of deceit and double-cross, she places her own life in danger in order to protect the queen and the sister she has pledged to love and serve in secrecy." (Booklist)

Buckley, William F.
Elvis in the morning. Harcourt 2001 328p il $25
ISBN 0-15-100643-1
LC 00-54484
In 1959 Orson Killere, whose mother works for the U.S. Army in Wiesbaden, "decides to 'liberate' two dozen Elvis records from the PX for German teens who can't afford them. His crime is reported in Stars and Stripes, and PFC Presley, stationed nearby, holds a private concert at Orson's home. Orson and Priscilla are soon regular visitors to Presley's off-base quarters. She ultimately moves to Memphis and, years later, becomes Mrs. Presley; Orson is expelled from the University of Michigan as a premature college radical, wanders the country, stumbles into the computer business, and throughout the 1960s and 1970s, plays a small but important role in the King's often troubled life." Booklist

Buckley, William F.
★ **Mongoose**, R.I.P; a Blackford Oakes novel. [by] William F. Buckley, Jr. Random House 1988 322p
ISBN 0-394-55931-2
LC 87-28344
"The best of the Blacky books, this is an entertainment of the Graham Greene order that truly entertains, excites, and edifies. . . . The story builds with considerable suspense up to Blackford's horrendous dilemma on the day of JFK's assassination." Natl Rev

Buehlman, Christopher
Between two fires; Christopher Buehlman. Ace Books 2012 426 p. (hardcover) $25.95
ISBN 1937007863; 9781937007867
LC 2012011957
In this novel by Christopher Buehlman "Thomas, a disgraced knight, has found a young girl alone in a dead Norman village. An orphan of the Black Death, . . . she tells Thomas . . . that the fallen angels under Lucifer are rising in a second war on heaven, and that the world of men has fallen behind the lines of conflict. . . . As hell unleashes its wrath, and as the true nature of the girl is revealed, Thomas will find himself on a macabre battleground of angels and demons, saints, and the risen dead." (Publisher's note)

Buehlman, Christopher
Those across the river. Ace Books 2011 357p $24.95
ISBN 978-0-441-02067-6
LC 2011005232
Moving to rural Georgia, a failed academic plans to write a history of his family's old plantation and the horrors that occurred there but instead discovers a sense of unspoken dread among the townspeople and a long-standing debt of blood.
"Buehlman delivers a creepy, suspenseful, and well-crafted . . . [book] set in post-Depression era South. The action begins early and never lets up. Recommended for horror fans and those willing to be scared enough to want to stay out of the woods!" Libr J

Buffett, Jimmy
A **salty** piece of land. Little, Brown and Co 2004 462p $27.95
ISBN 0-316-90845-2
LC 2004-16508
"Perhaps it is because Buffett has long been a writer of lyrics that his prose style now seems to flow in a fresh, fanciful, finely imagined fashion. . . . What makes the incredible so credible to the reader, what makes the old lighthouse shine again, is the spiritual savvy Buffett has gleaned from the beach of life as he's wandered in the raw poetry of time." N Y Times Book Rev

Bujold, Lois McMaster
The **paladin** of souls. Eos 2003 456p hardcover o.p. pa $7.99
ISBN 0-380-97902-0; 0-380-81861-2 pa
LC 2003-40884
Sequel to The curse of Chalion
"Three years free of the madness that kept her imprisoned in her family's castle, Ista is finally released from her last remaining duties by the death of her mother. She undertakes a pilgrimage, but doesn't get far before she is overtaken by trouble, sorrow, need, and a host of other adversities. Chalion is in trouble again, thanks to the plots, counterplots, machinations, and follies of men and of gods. . . . What really keeps one turning the pages is the fascinating cast of characters—not that the plot is anything to sneeze at." Booklist

Bulgakov, Mikhail Afanas'evich

★ The **master** and Margarita; translated from the Russian by Michael Glenny. Knopf 1992 xxvii, 446p $19

ISBN 0-679-41046-5

LC 91-53220

Written in the 1930s. Original Russian edition published 1966-67 in censored form. This translation, first published 1967 by Harper, is based on the unexpurgated version that was subsequently published 1973 in the Soviet Union

This novel "juxtaposes two planes of action—one set in Moscow in the 1930s and the other in Jerusalem at the time of Christ. The three central characters of the contemporary plot are the Devil, disguised as one Professor Woland; the 'Master,' a repressed novelist; and Margarita, who, though married to a bureaucrat, loves the Master. The Master has burned his manuscript and gone willingly into a psychiatric ward when critics attacked his work—a portrayal of the story of Jesus. Margarita sells her soul to the Devil in order to obtain the Master's release from the psychiatric ward. A parallel plot presents the action of the Master's destroyed novel, the condemnation of Yeshua (Jesus) in Jerusalem." Merriam-Webster's Ency of Lit

Bull, Emma

Territory. Tor 2007 318p hardcover o.p. pa $7.99

ISBN 978-0-312-85735-6; 0-312-85735-7; 978-0-8125-4836-5 pa; 0-8125-4836-1 pa

LC 2007-9534

"In 1881, the Arizona town of Tombstone, rich in minerals for the taking, becomes a magnet for men and women possessing special gifts or hungry for more power than they already have. To this region of natural magic come Wyatt Earp, a master of sorcery; Doc Holliday, whose power belongs to those who can take it; Chow Lung, a Chinese doctor with his own strange abilities; Mildred Benjamin, a writer of Western adventure and a true visionary; and Jesse Fox, a man with a talent for taming horses, among other gifts." Libr J

"Readers will think about the story long after it ends, savoring the writing and imagining what the characters might do next." Publ Wkly

Bull, Emma

War for the Oaks. Orb 2001 332p pa $14.95

ISBN 978-0-765-30034-8; 0-765-30034-6

LC 2001-27117

First published 1987 by Ace

"Guitarist and singer Eddi McCandry has just left a floundering band and is organizing a new one when a phouka, a man who at times is a talking dog, becomes her guardian at the behest of the Faerie Folk. Eddi soon finds herself involved with warring Faerie groups, the Seelie Court and its noble queen versus the Unseelie Court, ruled by the evil Queen of Air and Darkness. The Seelie Court has chosen Eddi because there's 'power in a mortal soul that all of Faerie cannot muster.' Eddi's tart humor helps lend reality. . . . For many readers, the fey qualities of the wispy fantasy may be enough; Eddi even labels her new band Eddi and the Feys. The strength of the novel, however, is in the non-fantasy scenes. These demonstrate a sure knowledge of rock music and the field, and contribute to the climax, a struggle between Eddi and the dark queen at a concert." Publ Wkly

Bunn, T. Davis

Lion of Babylon; Davis Bunn. Bethany House 2011 378p.

ISBN 9780764209932; 0764209930; 9780764209055 pa; 0764209051 pa

LC 2011008207

This book tells the story of "[a]n unlikely American operative [who] has to infiltrate the inner circles of Iraqi politics and culture to save the life of a friend and three companions who have gone mysteriously missing. Marc Royce is surprised to be taken in by an Iraqi family that thinks the disappearances may be connected to the kidnapping of dozens of children." (Publishers Weekly)

"Marc must unravel the truth in a covert operation requiring utmost secrecy -- from both the Americans and the insurgents. But even more secret than the undercover operation is the underground dialogue taking place between sworn enemies. Will the ultimate Reconciler between ancient enemies, current foes, and fanatical religious factions be heard?" (Publisher's note)

Buntline, Ned

The **hero** of a hundred fights; collected stories from the dime novel king, from Buffalo Bill to Wild Bill Hickock. edited and introduced by Clay Reynolds. Union Square Press 2011 438p $24.95

ISBN 978-1-4027-5842-3

LC 2010-34423

"Buntline's knowledge of the Western landscape derived from seeing it through the window of a passenger coach traveling from Council Bluffs, Iowa, to San Francisco in 1869; everything else, Reynolds says, was 'contrivance and coincidence.' Even so, Reynolds makes a solid case that Ned Buntline is a real pioneer and, as much or more than James Fenimore Cooper, is a progenitor of the Western genre. The Hero of a Hundred Fights, especially with Reynolds's excellent introductory essay, is a good showcase for the great rascal and his work." Dallas Morning News

Includes bibliographical references.

Bunyan, John

The **pilgrim's** progress; edited with an introduction and notes by W.R. Owens. Oxford University Press 2003 lvi, 333p il (Oxford world classics) pa $8.95

ISBN 0-19-280361-1

LC 2003-283122

First published 1678

"The 'immortal allegory,' next to the Bible the most widely known book in religious literature. It was written in Bedford jail, where Bunyan was for twelve years a prisoner for his convictions. It describes the troubled journey of Christian and his companions through this life to a triumphal entrance into the Celestial city. Bunyan 'wrote with virgin purity utterly free from mannerisms and affectations; and without knowing himself for a writer of fine English, produced it.'" Pratt Alcove

Includes bibliographical references

Burdett, John

Bangkok 8. Knopf 2003 317p $24

ISBN 1-400-04044-2

LC 2002-40658

"The narrator, a Buddhist cop named Sonchai Jitplecheep, finds himself plunged into a dangerous investigation of the deaths of his partner Pichai Apiradee and U. S. Embassy Sgt. William Bradley. Sonchai is an unusual character on several levels, from the mysteries of his violent past to his conversations with the ghost of Pichai. His ambiguous feelings toward Kimberley Jones, an American FBI agent brought in to work the case, reflect his upbringing as the child of a Thai mother and an unknown American father. . . .The mix of detective work, Bangkok street life, the Thai sex trade and drug smuggling forms a powerful mélange of images and insight." Publ Wkly

Burdett, John

Bangkok haunts. Alfred A. Knopf 2007 305p $24.95

ISBN 978-0-307-26318-6; 0-307-26318-5

LC 2007-61472

In this installment featuring Buddhist Bangkok police detective Sonchai Jitpleecheep, "a murdered prostitute proves to be—even more in death than she was in life—a femme fatale of special magnitude. As in previous episodes, the pleasures derive less from Burdett's baroque plotting (in this case including former Khmer Rouge hired killers, a pornography ring debased even by Bangkok standards, and a death by torture involving elephants) than from the vivid portrait he paints of contemporary Thai life and mores." New Yorker

Burdett, John

Bangkok Tattoo. Knopf 2005 301p $24

ISBN 1-400-04045-0

LC 2005-5593

A mystery featuring Rayal Thai police detective Sonchai Jitpleecheep. "A devout Buddhist, Sonchai makes complex karmic calculations to justify his roles as law-bending cop and part-time papasan at his mother's gogo bar. When the bar's biggest moneymaker is suspected of killing her john, who turns out to be C.I.A., Sonchai initiates a coverup that eventually involves Muslim separatists in southern Thailand and American operatives eager to exploit post-9/11 paranoia for career advancement. The plot showcases Burdett's sly riffs on Third World stereotypes, Buddhism, and the gustatory pleasures of fried grasshoppers. It's a giddy, occasionally over-the-top performance, but mesmerizing: a comic tour of the underbelly of Bangkok in pursuit of both a murderer and the sublime." New Yorker

Burdett, John

The godfather of Kathmandu. Alfred A. Knopf 2010 295p $25.95

ISBN 978-0-307-26319-3

LC 2009-38459

"Though the novel is top-heavy with redundant interview-interrogations, Sonchai's wry narrative voice (think: exotic Philip Marlowe) keeps us hooked. . . . A blissfully nutty caper that brings back fond memories of the late lamented Ross Thomas' crazy-quilt crime fiction." Kirkus

Burdick, Eugene

Fail-safe; by Eugene Burdick & Harvey Wheeler. McGraw-Hill 1962 286p

"With mounting tension this gripping thriller tells of a possible nuclear holocaust. An American attack squadron is accidentally and irretrievably launched to obliterate Moscow. The frantic U.S. president and the Russian premier begin a dramatic hotline race against time to halt the bombers' flight and prevent disaster. The crisis is seen through the eyes of several characters, and their differing perceptions provide an effective story-telling technique." Shapiro. Fic for Youth. 3d edition

Burgess, Anthony

A clockwork orange; the restored edition. Anthony Burgess; edited with an Introduction and notes by Andrew Biswell. W.W. Norton & Co. 2012 246 p. (hardcover) $24.95

ISBN 0393089134; 9780393089134

LC 2012029687

This book is the 50th anniversary edition of Anthony Burgess's novel, which offered a "nightmare vision of the future told in its own fantastically inventive lexicon." Editor "Andrew Biswell, PhD, director of the International Burgess Foundation, has taken a close look at the three varying published editions alongside the original typescript to recreate the novel as Anthony Burgess envisioned it." (Publisher's note)

"Paradox is at the heart of this book, as this newly restored, fiftieth-anniversary edition makes more clear than ever...a fitting publication of a book that remains...shocking and thought provoking." Booklist

Includes bibliographical references

Burgess, Matt

★ Dogfight, a love story; a novel. Doubleday 2010 290p $24.95

ISBN 978-0-385-53298-3; 0-385-53298-9

LC 2009-41885

"With an acute ear for dialogue and the poetry of the street, Burgess . . . gives us the pizzerias and bodegas, playgrounds and schoolyards, barbershops and bowling alleys of his home turf. His is a cliché-free depiction of gritty urban reality, reminiscent of Richard Price. But Burgess's city novel is less Clockers than Portrait of the Artist as an Ambivalent Drug Dealer, less an inner city whodunit than an outer borough how-will-he-do-it." N Y Times Book Rev

Burke, Alafair

Angel's tip. Harper 2008 342p il $23.95

ISBN 0-06-156102-9; 978-0-06-156102-3

LC 2008-3071

Rookie New York City police detective Ellie Hatcher "is out on her morning run when she discovers the corpse of a teenage girl who's been strangled, stabbed, and shorn of her blond hair. The 19-year-old had been visiting the Big Apple with friends and hitting all the clubs while on break from college. Her murder creates a whirlwind of bad publicity for the city, but the NYPD breaks the case very quickly-or have they? Turns out there are weird similarities to some cold cases that Hatcher's deceased partner had been checking out, and she is unconvinced they have the right perp. . .

. . Lots of suspense and plot twists galore keep the pages turning, but the story lines about Hatcher, her boyfriend, her brother, and her partner deserve the credit for making this novel a winner." Libr J

Burke, Alafair

Long gone; a novel of suspense. Harper 2011 357p $24.99

ISBN 978-0-06-199918-5; 0-06-199918-0

At the outset of this novel, "37-year-old Alice Humphrey, the daughter of controversial film director Frank Humphrey, meets charming Drew Campbell at a sparsely attended Manhattan art opening; he asks if she would like to manage the fledgling Highline Gallery. While the job appears too good to be true, Alice, who's been unemployed for eight months, accepts the offer. All goes well until Alice finds Drew dead in the gallery a few weeks later. The police regard Alice as the prime suspect in the murder of 'Drew Campbell,' who was not the man he claimed to be. Evidence against her includes paperwork supposedly showing that she leased the gallery space. Feeling trapped, Alice wonders if she's being set up and if it has anything to do with her famous father. Alice must dig deep into her family's checkered history if she's to prove her innocence. Burke skillfully orchestrates the mounting tension and claustrophobia of Alice's world collapsing in on itself." Publ Wkly

Burke, James Lee, 1936-

★ **Black** cherry blues. Little, Brown 1989 290p

ISBN 0-316-11699-8

LC 89-7977

"A stunning novel that takes detective fiction into new imaginative realms. . . . All the main characters in this darkly beautiful, lyric saga carry heavy emotional baggage, and Robicheaux's sleuthing is a simultaneous exorcism of demons of grief, loss, fear, rage, vengeance." Publ Wkly

Burke, James Lee, 1936-

Feast day of fools; a novel. Simon & Schuster 2011 463p $26.99

ISBN 978-1-4516-4311-4

LC 2011-06468

Interviewing an alcoholic Native American who witnessed a murder along the Texas-Mexico border, Sheriff Hack Holland and his deputy, Sam Tibbs, recognize the work of serial killer Preacher Jack Collins in an investigation that is assisted by the enigmatic Anton Ling.

"The intricately plotted narrative takes numerous unexpected turns, and Burke handles his trademark themes of social justice and corruption with his usual subtlety." Publ Wkly

Burke, James Lee

The **glass** rainbow; a Dave Robicheaux novel. Simon & Schuster 2010 433p $25.99

ISBN 978-1-4391-2829-9; 1-4391-2829-4

LC 2010-07485

"Here, investigating the deaths of seven women, Robicheaux goes down a tortuous path that leads to both Louisiana's lowest criminal swamp scum and members of its gilt-edged aristocracy, with the titular stained-glass window at the center of it all. Burke occasionally stumbles (every

character we meet seems to end up playing an improbably crucial role in the plot), but the venerable author still writes with the same intensity, and moral avidity, that energizes his equally aged hero. And while there are plenty of villains for that hero to face — including, aptly, a Delta oil tycoon — Burke's finely developed understanding of the human race prevents anything from getting too black-and-white." Entertainment Wkly

Burke, James Lee

★ **Heaven's** prisoners. Holt & Co. 1988 292p

ISBN 0-8050-0665-6

LC 87-26878

"There is a pronounced streak of poetry in Mr. Burke's prose. He has the knack of combining action with reflection; he has pity for the human condition, and even his villains can have some sympathetic and redeeming qualities. Mr. Burke writes in an unhurried manner, but the book never loses tension because he is so wrapped up in his characters and their locale." N Y Times Book Rev

Burke, James Lee

Last car to Elysian Fields; a Dave Robicheaux novel. Simon & Schuster 2003 335p $25

ISBN 0-7432-4542-3

LC 2003-54386

"Dave Robicheaux, an Iberia Parish homicide detective with an 'abiding anger' for the corrupters of innocence and the despoilers of beauty, is roped into investigating {legendary R & B guitarist Junior} Crudup's fate by Jimmie Dolan, a priest whose moral crusades cause mobsters to put out a hit on him. Burke's heavies make great showpieces, but Max Coll, a stone killer who repents of his sins and causes all kinds of mayhem trying to do penance, knocks them all off the shelf. In the absence of plagues of locusts, a good hit man can really clean up a dirty town." N Y Times Book Rev

Burke, James Lee, 1936-

Light of the world; a Dave Robicheaux novel. James Lee Burke. Simon & Schuster 2013 560 p. (Hardcover) $27.99

ISBN 1476710767; 9781476710761

LC 2013008797

In this book by James Lee Burke "Louisiana Sherriff's Detective Dave Robicheaux and his longtime friend and partner Clete Purcel are vacationing in Montana's spectacular Big Sky country when a series of suspicious events leads them to believe their lives—and the lives of their families—are in danger. Could convicted sadist and serial killer Asa Surette be loose on the streets of Montana?" (Publisher's note)

Burke, James Lee

Rain gods. Simon & Schuster 2009 434p $25.99

ISBN 978-1-4391-2824-4; 1-4391-2824-3

LC 2009-12166

Hackberry Holland "is the sheriff of a sleepy Texas town near the Mexican border, the last stop for the aging Hack after a tumultuous personal life and an up-and-down career as a politician and lawyer. His downshifted lifestyle is torn asunder when Hack discovers the bodies of nine illegal aliens, buried in a shallow grave behind a church. The trail leads to a troubled Iraq vet, who knows something about the killings, and his country-singer girlfriend, both now on the run from various baddies who want to make sure the kids don't tell anyone what they know. Hack and his deputy, Pam Tibbs, who has a romantic interest in her boss despite his insistence that he is much too old for her, join the chase. . . . Burke fans will notice much that is familiar here—the lyricism, the minor key, the elegiac refrain—but the melody is new and haunting. And, besides, you just have to love a guy with a name like Hackberry." Booklist

Burke, James Lee

A **stained** white radiance. Hyperion 1992 305p
ISBN 1-562-82980-7

LC 91-34213

In this novel "the 'venal and meretricious' bear the unmistakable stench of the modern world: a drug-dealing mobster out to settle scores, a trio of swastika-sporting members of the Aryan Brotherhood, and, lurking on the respectable fringe, an impeccably coiffed former Klansman intent on snagging a senate seat. . . . Dave tackles them all, of course, and in the end establishes a tenuous calm into which he and his family are able to retreat. But the elegiac tone dominates." Booklist

Burke, James Lee

The **tin** roof blowdown; a Dave Robicheaux novel. Simon & Schuster 2007 373p $26
ISBN 978-1-4165-4848-5; 1-4165-4848-3

LC 2007-4847

"In Mr. Burke's universe, some of the saddest storm victims are those who committed terrible sins in a time of crisis and wish they could undo the transgressions. But like George Pelecanos's Washington, Mr. Burke's New Orleans is a place where the destinies of ghetto-bred young black men are all but determined at birth. Mr. Burke sometimes shows an overheated, lyrical bent, and the extremes of Hurricane Katrina make it especially pronounced. . . . Whether invoking William Blake's tiger or Voltaire's Candide, Dave thinks big. He reaches for literary as well as biblical terms to convey the apocalyptic magnitude of New Orleans's collapse." N Y Times (Late N Y Ed)

Burke, Jan

Disturbance. Simon & Schuster 2011 354p $25
ISBN 978-1-4391-5284-3; 1-4391-5284-5

LC 2010-41942

"Despite her reporter's nose for trouble, Irene Kelly's life has almost returned to normal, the Las Piernas News Express wobbles along in defiance of its financial woes, and with the help of her husband, Frank, and a good therapist, she has recovered from the debilitating post traumatic stress disorder that haunted her after her near fatal encounter with notorious serial killer Nick Parrish. Then she receives some unwelcome news: Parrish, once thought permanently paralyzed by the injuries he sustained fleeing recapture, is walking again. And the rumor among the Moths, Parrish's online fan club, is that he is coming after Irene." Publisher's note

Burke, Jan

Remember me, Irene; an Irene Kelly mystery. Simon & Schuster 1996 303p
ISBN 0-684-80343-7

LC 95-52186

In this episode Southern California news reporter Irene Kelly is "married to her longtime lover, cop Frank Harriman. One day at a bus stop, Irene has a disturbing encounter with a homeless wino, only later discovering that the man, Lucas, was once her close friend, a gifted statistician who managed to get even the math-impaired Irene excited about numbers. Lucas has obviously fallen on hard times, so when Irene gets a cryptic message asking her to meet him, she's curious to learn more. But when she goes to the rendezvous, she discovers his dead body—and opens a Pandora's box of troubles. . . . Exciting action, clever dialogue, solid writing, and a smart, likable heroine produce a well-deserved thumbs-up." Booklist

Burke, Shannon

Black flies. Soft Skull Press 2008 185p pa $14.95
ISBN 978-1-59376-191-2; 1-59376-191-0

LC 2007-46762

"It would have been easy for Black Flies to slip into slumming mode, or a voyeuristic inventory of gruesome catastrophes and macho heroism. But Burke's gripping prose, as unadorned as the book's burned-out backdrop, calmly builds toward a larger conundrum: What happens when horrors become commonplace? A gifted stylist, the author makes a thoughtful stab at showing what constant danger can do to an ambulance worker and to a neighborhood's inhabitants." Time Out N Y

Burney, Claudia Mair

Wounded; a love story. Claudia Mair Burney. David C. Cook 2008 362 p. (pbk.) $14.99
ISBN 9781434799388

LC 2008931895

In this book, "[p]oor in health but rich in faith, Gina Merritt—a young, broke, African-American single mother—sits in a pew on Ash Wednesday and has a holy vision. When it fades, her palms are bleeding. Anthony Priest, the junkie sitting beside her, instinctively touches her when she cries out, but Gina flees in shock and pain. A prize-winning journalist before drugs destroyed his career, Anthony is flooded with a sense of well-being and knows he is cured of his addiction. Without understanding why, Anthony follows Gina home to find some answers. Together they search for an answer to this miraculous event and along the way they cross paths with a skeptical evangelical pastor, a gentle Catholic priest, a . . . religious zealot, and a . . . transvestite drug dealer." (Publisher's note)

Burnford, Sheila

Bel Ria. Little, Brown 1978 215p
ISBN 0-316-77139-2

LC 77-21082

First published 1977 in the United Kingdom

"A realistic portrayal of wartime life, and an unsentimental but delightful picture of a remarkable animal, self-reliant, independent, and loving." Libr J

Burnford, Sheila

★ The **incredible** journey; with illustrations by Carl Burger. Little, Brown 1961 145p il

"A half-blind English bull terrier, a sprightly yellow Labrador retriever, and a feisty Siamese cat have resided for eight months with a friend of their owners, who are away on a trip. Then their temporary caretaker leaves them behind in order to take a short vacation. The lonely trio decides to tackle the harsh 250-mile hike across the Canadian wilderness in search of home, despite the human and wild obstacles the group will encounter." Shapiro. Fic for Youth. 3d edition

Burns, Charles

★ **Black** hole; Charles Burns. Pantheon Books 2005 1 v. ill. $29.95

ISBN 9780375714726; 9780375423802; 037542380X

LC 2005046431

Eisner Awards: Best Graphic Album - Reprint (2006); Harvey Awards: Best Graphic Album - Previously Published (2006); Ignatz Awards: Outstanding Anthology or Collection (2006)

This book takes place in "[s]uburban Seattle, [in] the mid-1970s. We learn from the out-set that a strange plague has descended upon the area's teenagers, transmitted by sexual contact. The disease is manifested in any number of ways—from the hideously grotesque to the subtle (and concealable)—but once you've got it, that's it. There's no turning back. As we inhabit the heads of several key characters—some kids who have it, some who don't, some who are about to get it—what unfolds isn't the expected battle to fight the plague, or bring heightened awareness to it , or even to treat it. What we become witness to instead is a fascinating and eerie portrait of the nature of high school alienation itself—the savagery, the cruelty, the relentless anxiety and ennui, the longing for escape. And then the murders start." (Publisher's note)

Burns, Olive Ann

★ **Cold** Sassy tree. Ticknor & Fields 1984 391p $28; pa $13.95

ISBN 0-89919-309-9; 0-618-91971-6 pa

LC 84-8570

"Young Will Tweedy lives in a small Georgia town called Cold Sassy in the early 1900s. He is hard working (when pushed) because he has chores to do at home and work to do at his Grandpa Blakeslee's store. That still leaves him time to plan practical jokes with his pals and to overhear family dramas. The biggest drama begins when Grandpa, only three weeks after the death of his wife whom he had dearly loved, marries Miss Love Simpson—young enough to be his daughter. Miss Love has to face not only the town gossip, but also rejection from Will's Mother and Grandpa's other daughter. The story has humor, excitement, and realistic family confrontations." Shapiro. Fic for Youth. 3d edition

Followed by Leaving Cold Sassy: the unfinished sequel (1992)

Burnside, John

Glister. Nan A. Talese/Doubleday 2008 375p $25.95

ISBN 978-0-385-52764-4; 0-385-52764-0

"What is most beautiful, and most frightening, about the novel itself is its melancholy awareness of how desperate our acts of devotion can be in places like this toxic town, how terrible the things we can learn to love." N Y Times Book Rev

Burroughs, William S.

★ **Naked** lunch; the restored text edited by James Grauerholz and Barry Miles. Grove Press 2003 289p pa $14

ISBN 978-0-8021-4018-0; 0-8021-4018-1

LC 2001-23190

First published 1959 in France; first published 1962 in the United States

"An autobiographical novel that discards . . . conventional narrative prose . . . to present a surrealistic vision of a liberated, hallucinatory counterculture set in opposition to a mass-produced, technological society bent on mass destruction. In this and the books of the next few years, Burroughs relied on such techniques as random cutting and pasting to create an extreme montage effect. Surviving obscenity trials in the U. S., Naked Lunch became an icon of the emancipated sixties." Benet's Reader's Ency Am Lit

Burroway, Janet

Bridge of sand. Houghton Mifflin Harcourt 2009 328p $25

ISBN 978-0-15-101543-6; 0-15-101543-0

LC 2008-22758

"Dana is at a loss after burying her husband, a Pennsylvania senator, a few miles from the United 93 crash on 9/11. Her marriage had almost ended when Graham was diagnosed with cancer, and she nursed him to the end before beginning the task of selling her home. Originally from the South, she heads back to Georgia, aimlessly driving and thinking about her future. She decides to visit her grandmother's house, only to find it has been turned into a strip mall. Once again at loose ends, she looks up old friend Cassius Huston, and they begin an affair, which is problematic because she is white, and he is black. . . . [Burroway] crafts memorable characters while challenging readers' assumptions about race, love, and family." Libr J

Burrowes, Grace

The **heir**; Grace Burrowes. Sourcebooks Casablanca 2010 471 p.

ISBN 1402244347; 9781402244346

In this romance novel, "The earl of Westhaven is determined to avoid his father's marital machinations by remaining in sweltering London while Society departs for the country. Westhaven takes great pleasure in his well-run household until his new housekeeper, Anna Seaton, mistakes his intentions toward a chambermaid and knocks him flat with a fireplace poker. Anna is too educated and polished to have been born to service, but she makes a tender nurse. As their affections grow, Westhaven believes he's found a candidate for marriage who would please him and satisfy his father, but Anna refuses Westhaven's proposal. Her hidden background contains ugly obligations, and she's determined to keep outrunning them even as he tries to change her mind." (Publishers Weekly)

Burrowes, Grace

Lady Louisa's Christmas knight. Sourcebooks Casablanca 2012 374 p. $7.99

ISBN 1402268637; 9781402268632

This is Grace Burrowes' sixth Regency romance novel. "When Lady Louisa Windham, middle daughter of the duke of Moreland, is subjected to the unwelcome advances of an unscrupulous fortunehunter, family friend Sir Joseph Carrington defends her honor and offers marriage. It looks like a happy match for a couple already falling in love, but Louisa's youthful literary folly is ripe for scandal should it come to light, Sir Joseph has far too many secrets . . . , and both are being blackmailed." (Publishers Weekly)

Burrowes, Grace

Lady Maggie's secret scandal; Grace Burrowes. Sourcebooks Casablanca 2012 416p $7.99

ISBN 9781402263774

In this romance novel, "thirty, independent, and firmly on the shelf, Lady Magdalene Windham, the adopted illegitimate daughter of the Duke of Moreland, lives a quiet, sedate life. But Maggie is being plagued by her past, and when her reticule goes missing--and with it some letters she is desperate to have back--she goes to her family's discreet, incredibly observant private investigator, Benjamin Hazlit, the one man who can help her. Although he hides it, Ben quickly realizes that Maggie is not revealing the whole truth; getting her to trust him with her secrets--or her heart--is not going to be easy." (Libr J)

Burrowes, Grace

The **soldier**; Grace Burrowes. Sourcebooks Casablanca 2011 410 p.

ISBN 140224567X; 9781402245671

This historical romance novel is a "Regency-era tale of a duke's illegitimate son and a countryside baker. Rewarded for his military service with a title and a long-neglected estate, Devlin St. Just's attempt to find peace is disrupted by the young bastard daughter of the estate's previous owner. Feeling responsible for her, Devlin invites little Winnie and her aunt, Emmaline Farnum, into his home. Emmie feels swept along but can't resist the opportunity to stay close to her niece. As Emmie and Devlin become confidantes, her friendship, insight, and ample charms help him heal from his emotional war wounds, but Emmie's precarious position in the community and shattering secrets drive her to flee even if it means leaving Winnie--and her heart--behind." (Publishers Weekly)

Buruma, Ian

The **China** lover. Penguin Press 2008 392p $26.95

ISBN 978-1-594-20194-3; 1-594-20194-3

LC 2008-18201

"A teenage singer and actress, Yoshiko Yamaguchi rose to stardom in Japanese-occupied Manchuria in the 1930s, appearing in a series of propaganda films. After the war, she worked in pro-American movies in occupied Japan, before switching to Hollywood and reinventing herself there as a diplomat's wife, a journalist and a prominent Japanese politician. Her career forms the narrative thread of Ian Buruma's evocative novel, which spans roughly 50 years of Japan's tumultuous modern history. Buruma uses Yamaguchi's bizarre story as a metaphor for Japan's own shifting identity, from militaristic dictatorship to America-besotted, postwar ruin, to economically rejuvenated modern nation. . . . Yamaguchi's story is divided into three parts, each narrated by a different man and each paralleling a different phase of Japan's reinvention. This ambitious approach brings her world vividly to life." Scotsman

Busch, Frederick

The **night** inspector; a novel. Harmony Bks. 1999 278p il $23

ISBN 0-609-60235-7

LC 99-11890

The novel "is a marvelously dark-hued story by a master craftsman, and watching mastery at work provides at least a part of the pleasure of reading it." N Y Times Book Rev

Busch, Frederick

Rescue missions; stories. W.W. Norton & Co. 2006 316p $24.95

ISBN 978-0-393-06252-6; 0-393-06252-X

LC 2006-13011

"'Need trumps love,' in the words of one of Busch's indelible characters, and need in all its permutations infuses the final collection of stories from this master of the genre. Whether it's the obligation of a son to his dying father, the unfulfilled duty of a soldier fresh from the war in Iraq, or the demand for revenge of a former lover, the drive for recognition, connection, and affirmation is revealed as an essential life force. In Busch's hands, it thrums with an elegiac cadence, so subtle at times as to be barely perceptible, so strong at others as to take one's breath away." Booklist

Bushnell, Candace

The **Carrie** diaries. Balzer + Bray 2010 272p $18.99

ISBN 978-0-06-172891-4; 0-06-172891-8

LC 2009-53562

Tells the story of Manhattan columnist Carrie Bradshaw's high school years, her relationships with her peers, and how she became a writer.

"It would have been easy to write a coming-of-age story about Carrie Bradshaw that ham-fistedly foreshadows everything fans of the franchise know will come to pass. But Bushnell nails something harder: telling another chapter in the story of a cherished character that stands on its own." Entertainment Wkly

Bushnell, Candace

Lipstick jungle. Hyperion 2005 353p $24.95

ISBN 0-7868-6819-8

LC 2005-46379

"Victory Ford, Wendy Healy, and Nico O'Neilly are three movers and shakers in Manhattan who still find time to lunch at the hottest restaurants. . . . Victory is a world-famous fashion designer whose spring collection failed to impress at New York's all-important fashion week. As the president of Parador Pictures, Wendy is gearing up for the film she hopes will finally snag her the coveted Best Picture Oscar. Nico, editor in chief of Bonfire magazine, is working her way up the corporate ladder. The ladies' love lives are just as interesting as their careers. Victory is being courted by an eccentric billionaire; Wendy's handsome, lazy husband has just demanded a divorce; and married Nico finds herself drawn into a fling with a handsome, younger male model. Readers who want to immerse themselves in the trendy world of New York's high society will find themselves at home in this scintillating novel." Booklist

Butcher, Jim

Changes; a novel of the Dresden files. Roc/New American Library 2010 441p $25.95

ISBN 978-0-451-46317-3; 0-451-46317-X

LC 2010-01202

Chicago wizard/private detective Harry Dresden's "ex-girlfriend Susan informs him that he's got a daughter, who's just been kidnapped by the Red Court of the vampires, as part of their interminably long war against the wizards of the White Council. Curveball or not, Butcher takes this premise and barrels through Harry's recent history, demolishing everything in sight. Old allies are lost, old enemies finally dispatched, and nearly every hovering, delicately-balanced element of Butcher's established status quo is thrown into disarray. It's actually a quite remarkable effect. Again, despite the arbitrariness of the premise, Butcher uses it to fantastic effect." io9

Butcher, Jim

Ghost story; a novel of the Dresden files. Roc 2011 481p $27.95

ISBN 978-0-451-46379-1

LC 2011-20254

"Harry Dresden's back for another adventure against forces far greater than himself—business as usual for Chicago's favorite wizard. Except this time he has a bit of a handicap. He's dead, and he's been sent back to solve the mystery of his murder and make a last stab at saving the people he loves." Booklist

"This stunning, exciting series entry with its heart-stopping action will shock and thrill Butcher fans." Libr J

Butcher, Jim

✓Proven guilty; a novel of the Dresden files. Jim Butcher. ROC 2006 404p o.p.; (paperback) $9.99

ISBN 0451460855 (hardcover); 9780451461032

LC 2005030130

In this novel, "Harry Dresden, Chicago's only consulting wizard, takes on phobophages, creatures that feed on fear who attack a horror film convention, in the . . . eighth installment of [author Jim] Butcher's increasingly complicated Dresden Files series. . . . Harry finds that fighting monsters is only the prelude to maneuvers amid the warring wizards of the White Council and the vampire Red Court. Less and less V.I. Warshawski with witchcraft, Harry aims his deductive powers at political intrigues rather than crime solving. . . . Harry, taking on an apprentice, has to face up to the consequences of his all-too-human failings." (Publishers Weekly)

Butcher, Jim

Side jobs; stories from the Dresden files. Roc 2010 418p $25.95

ISBN 978-0-451-46365-4; 0-451-46365-X

LC 2010-28768

"Eleven tales, 20022010, complete with author's notes and chronology, embellishing the exploits of Chicago's Harry Dresden, licensed PI and professional wizard, ranging from an apprentice piece written two years before the Dresden Files series achieved liftoff to an unpublished novelette set hours after the end of Changes (2010)." Kirkus

Butcher, Jim

Small favor; a novel of the Dresden files. Roc 2008 423p $23.95

ISBN 978-0-451-46189-6; 0-451-46189-4

LC 2007-42136

"There is a lot going on in this book, which is the tenth installment in the bestselling series about that other wizard named Harry. With so many factions, and so many agendas involved, it's easy to get a little lost in the chaos and confusion, but Jim Butcher clearly has it all mapped out, and he's obviously moving around a growing number of pieces on the board as he positions them for the inevitable final conflict at some point down the road. . . . New relationships are forged and old ones tested, some plans are thwarted while others are set into motion, and at the end, there's the distinct sensation of change and growth in Harry Dresden's world." SF Site

Butler, Blake

There is no year; a novel. Harper Perennial 2011 403p il pa $15.99

ISBN 0061997420; 9780061997426

LC 2010-52256

This novel depicts "the psyches of a mother, a father, and their son." (Bookforum)

"Butler's ambitious, kohl-smudged novel is built around a deeply dysfunctional family that moves into a languidly nightmarish home already populated by moldy-toothed imposter-people. They oust the imposters and settle into the house, a decaying structure filled with mystery: a mysterious, all-controlling egg; endless holes, tunnels and secret passages; a room stuffed floor-to-ceiling with hair; and an army of ants that pours out of the wall cracks 'in hordes of slow procession.' Amid the dark-side chaos, the family develops a deep distrust of and disassociation from one another — even while remaining a family. . . . Forget beginnings, middles and ends too: Each page is, it appears, constructed to stand alone as a discrete language study as much as it's meant to play a part in the whole. . . It is also unexpectedly riveting, totally original and frequently funny." Denver Post

Butler, Gwendoline

Death lives next door; the first Inspector Coffin mystery. St. Martin's Press 1992 191p

ISBN 0-312-08175-8

LC 92-1581

First published 1960 in the United Kingdom

"Keeping her detective in the wings, {Butler} begins by focusing her narrative on a gang of shabby, bitter academic types in Oxford, at the center of which dysfunctional clique is the famous and slightly mysterious Marion Manning, watched by a man who in time will claim to be her long lost husband. Everything in Marion's past is weird, and as Coffin is drawn out of London into this narrow little world, it is the investigation of this mysterious past that forms the heart of the book. Butler's regulars shouldn't pass up the chance for this peek at Coffin's past." Booklist

Butler, Octavia E.
  Adulthood rites. 1988 277p (Xenogenesis)
  ISBN 0-446-51422-5

                      LC 87-34620

In the second novel in the Xenogenesis trilogy "the alien Oankali have rescued the dying remnants of humanity after Earth's nuclear war. Now, though, the children of the two races, called constructs, are resented and feared by the original survivors. This is the story of one such construct, Akin, who possesses an adult mind and voice before he is two years old. Stolen by a barren human community, he grows up knowing both races." Publ Wkly

  Followed by Imago

Butler, Octavia E.
  ★ **Dawn**; [by] Octavia Butler. Warner Bks. 1987 264p (Xenogenesis)
  ISBN 0-446-51363-6

                      LC 87-6195

In this first volume in the Xenogenesis trilogy "a band of nuclear holocaust survivors is in the hands of an alien race that offers to save them. The price is high though: the survivors must participate in the evolution of the aliens by bearing children that incorporate some of the aliens' characteristics. Butler is one of the few sf writers who can handle effectively a slow-moving plot that emphasizes characters' emotions. Her command of the language is superior, and her aliens are quite convincing creations." Booklist

  Followed by Adulthood rites

Butler, Octavia E.
  Imago. Warner Bks. 1989 264p (Xenogenesis)
  ISBN 0-446-51472-1

                      LC 88-27975

First published 1985 in the United Kingdom

The concluding volume of the Xenogenesis trilogy "considers a post-holocaust humanity whose only chance for survival is to be absorbed by the alien Oankali. Totally uninterested in domination, this race thrives on a symbiosis that Earthlings find difficult to credit. That distrust hampers the narrator, an ooloi (neuter) named Jodahs, as it tries to find life partners in the same ratio as its five parents: a human couple, an Oankali couple and itself, the essential ooloi who joins all five and melds their genetic legacy. Butler's achievement here is less the abstract reassignment of sexual roles than a warmth and urgency that dramatizes and personalizes these conflicts and transformations." Publ Wkly

Butler, Octavia E.
  ★ **Kindred**; 25th anniverary ed; Beacon Press 2003 287p (Black women writers series) pa $14
  ISBN 0-8070-8369-0

                      LC 2003-62862

First published 1979 by Doubleday

"Dana, a well-educated contemporary African American woman, suddenly finds herself pulled into the past to save the life of a distant ancestor, an early-19th-century southern white boy named Rufus Weylin. Although she returns to the present moments later, she soon finds herself saving Rufus again and again. Although only a short time passes for her between each bout of time travel, years pass for Rufus, who gradually grows into adulthood and becomes a slave owner.

This sometimes painful novel features superb character development." Anatomy of Wonder 5

  Includes bibliographical references

Butler, Robert Olen
  Hell; a novel. Grove Press 2009 232p $24
  ISBN 978-0-8021-1901-8; 0-8021-1901-8

"Butler's lust for the tabloid romp and his stream of the never-ending punch line both irritates and illuminates. The reader's taste will have to be the final arbiters of worth." Publ Wkly

Butler, Samuel
  ★ The **way** of all flesh. Knopf 1992 374p $17
  ISBN 0-679-41718-4

                      LC 92-52916

First published posthumously 1903; first Everyman's library edition 1933

The theme of this semi-autobiographical novel "is the hypocrisy and smug complacency of English middle-class life, and particularly the relationship between parents and children, which is traced through several generations of the Pontifex family. . . . 'The Way of All Flesh' is generally regarded as a very original work: it exercised considerable influence on later English writers. 'It contains records of the things I saw happening rather than imaginary incidents,' said the author. Undoubtedly this novel has a strong vein of autobiography." Haydn. Thesaurus of Book Dig

Buzzelli, Elizabeth Kane
  Dead dogs and Englishmen; Elizabeth Kane Buzzelli. Midnight Ink 2011 346 p.
  ISBN 0738718785; 9780738718781

                      LC 2011005658

This book follows "gruff Deputy Dolly Wakowski," who in this episode of the series "finds herself pregnant, [and] [f]reelancer Emily Kincaid. . . . Their lives keep intersecting over murders . . . that Emily helps Dolly solve while writing them up fro the Northern Statesman. This time they must identify the dead (Mexican?) woman shot in the back of the head in a deserted house. . . . Off the pair go to question migrants, who are skipping town at an alarming rate after dead dogs are left on their doorsteps. Meanwhile, Emily's ex . . . has befriended eccentric Cecil Hawke, and convinced the wealthy Englishman that Emily can edit his manuscript. . . . But when Emily starts reading, the manuscript is . . . about two friends on a killing spree, one of whom has a gnawed-off finger just like Cecil's." (Kirkus)

Byatt, A. S. (Antonia Susan), 1936-
  Angels and insects; two novellas. Turtle Bay Bks. 1993 339p
  ISBN 0-679-40512-7

                      LC 92-56806

First published 1991 in the United Kingdom

"In 'Morpho Eugenia' penniless young entomologist William Adamson has just returned from a 10-year expedition in the Amazon. William is taken in by a titled clergyman with scientific pretensions, and soon marries his benefactor's beautiful daughter. Unable to undertake another Amazon adventure, he studies domestic ant colonies and discovers indecent parallels between the insects and his new family. 'The Conjugial Angel' involves a circle of spiritualists, chief among them Alfred Tennyson's sister Emily, in her youth engaged to Arthur Hallam, the man immortalized in Tennyson's In Memoriam. Emily has been branded faithless for having married years after Hallam's death, . . . but she is uncompromising in her pursuit of Hallam's ghost. . . . Complex and captivating, this fluid volume recasts itself on every page." Publ Wkly

Byatt, A. S. (Antonia Susan), 1936-

The **children's** book; a novel. Alfred A. Knopf 2009 675p $26.95

ISBN 0-307-27209-5; 978-0-307-27209-6

LC 2009-16334

Byatt's novel ranges from the Victorian era through World War I. "When Olive Wellwood's oldest son discovers a runaway named Philip sketching in the basement of the new Victoria and Albert Museum—a talented working-class boy who could be a character out of one of Olive's magical tales—she takes him into the storybook world of her family and friends—a world that conceals more treachery and darkness than Philip has ever imagined and that will soon be eclipsed by far greater forces." (Publisher's note)

"This is a moving book. Its words are beautifully chosen. . . . Everything connects. A S Byatt is Gaudi and Christopher Wren rolled into one." Scotsman

Byatt, A. S.

★ **Possession**; a romance. Modern Lib. 2000 605p

ISBN 0-679-64030-4

LC 99-56297

A reissue of the edition first published 1990 by Random House

"Intelligent, ingenious and humane, {this} bids fair to be looked back upon as one of the most memorable novels of the 1990s." Times Lit Suppl

Byatt, A. S. (Antonia Susan), 1936-

★ **Ragnarok**; A.S. Byatt. Grove Press 2011 177p. ill.

ISBN 1-84767-064-4; 978-1-84767-064-9; 9780802129925; 9780753188842

LC 2011508517

"Recently evacuated to the British countryside and with World War Two raging around her, one young girl is struggling to make sense of her life. Then she is given a book of ancient Norse legends." (Publisher's note)

Includes bibliographical references.

Byers, Michael

Percival's planet; a novel. Henry Holt and Co. 2010 414p $27

ISBN 978-0-8050-9218-9; 0-8050-9218-8

LC 2009-40107

This "novel, set mainly in the 1930s, tells the true story of the search for Pluto and those looking for it as their lives swing slowly and surely into alignment. Michael Byers occasionally gets bogged down in his prodigious research, but his characters remain strong enough to pull you in. They may be attempting to better understand the vast expanse of the universe, but what Byers has created is really just an endearing story of underdogs, both the ragtag crew of astronomers and the tiny celestial body they're hoping to find." Entertainment Wkly

Bynum, Laura

Veracity; a novel. Pocket Books 2010 376p $25

ISBN 978-1-4391-2334-8; 1-4391-2334-9

LC 2009-24707

"While most probably aren't going to label Veracity an instant classic, Bynum does manage to follow the traditional tenets of dystopian literature and still add a few twists and turns that make the book suspenseful, engaging, and thought-provoking. Until the last few chapters, which feel a bit rushed and simplistic, Veracity is a remarkably good read and a read that, at times, seems entirely too plausible for comfort." PopMatters

Bynum, Sarah Shun-Lien

Ms. Hempel chronicles. Harcourt 2008 193p $23

ISBN 978-0-15-101496-5; 0-15-101496-5

LC 2008-08924

"Ms. Hempel's consciousness is a joy to inhabit. Kind, scrupulous, curious, wistful, and odd, she has the vitality of a bright, nervous child, overlaid by the premature worldweariness of someone in their late twenties. . . . This is not a saccharine novel, and heartache, sexual confusion, and resignation rear their heads." Bookforum

Byrd, Max

Grant; a novel. Bantam Bks. 2000 362p $23.95

ISBN 0-553-09633-8

LC 99-56577

"As he covers Grant's potential candidacy and approaching death for the Washington Post, Nicholas Trist, a veteran of the Civil War who lost an arm at the battle of Cold Harbor (in which Grant was the commanding general), interacts with the major political and literary lights of the time. Washington in the 1880s resembles Washington of the 1990s: love affairs, leaks to the newspapers, jockeying for advantages, and even a best-selling anonymous novel purporting to give the inside scoop on Washington politicos. Historical fiction doesn't get any better than this." Booklist

Byrd, Sandra

Roses have thorns; a novel of Elizabeth I. Sandra Byrd. Howard Books 2012 317 p. geneal table (paperback) $14.99

ISBN 1439183163; 9781439183168

LC 2012022886

This book by Sandra Byrd presents "the story of a Swedish noblewoman in Queen Elizabeth I's court." It "draws on Lady Helena von Snakenborg's actual experiences as lady-in-waiting and close companion to the Virgin Queen. Helena . . . was scarcely 17 when chosen to accompany Swedish Princess Cecelia on a visit to the English court in 1564. Immediately upon arrival, Elin catches the eye of Lord Northampton and stays on when Cecelia leaves, becoming a maid of honor to the queen." (Kirkus Reviews)

Byrd, Sandra

✓ The **secret** keeper; a novel of Kateryn Parr. Sandra Byrd. Howard Books 2012 331 p. (pbk.) $14.99
ISBN 1439183147; 9781439183144
LC 2011034743
In this novel, by Sandra Byrd, "Juliana St. John is the daughter of a prosperous knight. Though her family wants her to marry the son of her father's business partner, circumstances set her on a course toward the court of Henry VIII and his last wife, Kateryn Parr. . . . As Juliana learns the secrets of King Henry VIII's court, she faces threats and opposition, learning truths about her own life that will undo everything she holds dear." (Publisher's note)
Includes bibliographical references

Byrd, Sandra

✓ To die for. Howard Books 2011 332 p.
✓ ISBN 9781439183113 pa
LC 2010048161
This book tells "the story of Meg Wyatt, . . . the best friend to Anne Boleyn since their childhoods on neighboring manors in Kent. . . . [A]s Anne's favor rises and falls, so does Meg's. And though she's pledged her loyalty to Anne no matter what the test, Meg just might lose her greatest love—and her own life—because of it. Meg's childhood flirtation with a boy on a neighboring estate turns to true love early on. When he is called to follow the Lord and be a priest she turns her back on both the man and his God. Slowly, though, both woo her back through the heady times of the English reformation. In the midst of it, Meg finds her place in history, her own calling to the Lord that she must follow, too, with consequences of her own." (Publisher's note)
Includes bibliographical references.

Byrne, Trevor

Ghosts and lightning. Doubleday 2009 209p $24.95
ISBN 978-0-385-53127-6; 0-385-53127-3
LC 2009-20031
"Denny Cullen, the antihero of this raucous and sometimes profound début novel, is twenty-six, on the dole, and generally drunk or doped up. Returning home to Dublin after his mother's death, Denny drifts through a series of drug-addled parties, funerals, séances, and other adventures with his alcoholic lesbian sister; a childhood friend who's become a Buddhist junkie; and the friend's hooligan brother. The group forms a witty and often disturbing portrait of the Irish underclass . . . , and the story is inventively narrated in a thick Irish brogue, saturated with profanities and folkloric allusions." New Yorker

Bá, Gabriel

✓ ★ **Daytripper**; Fábio Moon & Gabriel Bá; with coloring by Dave Stewart; lettering by Sean Konot; [introduction by Craig Thompson]. Vertigo 2011 247p chiefly col. ill.
ISBN 9781401229696; 9781451713947
LC 2010941519
This graphic novel, winner of the Eisner Award, tells the story of "Brás de Oliva Domingos, [who] writes obituaries for a Brazilian paper but dreams of writing novels like his famous father and seizing love and life as his friend Jorge

urges. We glimpse nine episode is Brás's life: first kiss, glimpse of true love, son's birth, and more--and at the end of each episode comes 'what if?' What if Brás dies that day? Readers are presented with nine obituaries for Brás at different ages, i.e., nine endings to his story." (Libr J)

C

Cabot, Sally

Benjamin Franklin's Bastard; Sally Cabot. HarperCollins 2013 288 p. (hardcover) $25.99
ISBN 0062241923; 9780062241924
LC 2013015099
This historical fiction novel, by Sally Cabot, follows "the story of Benjamin Franklin and his bastard son, and the women who loved them both. William Franklin, the son of Benjamin and his favorite mistress, Anne, is raised by Deborah, Benjamin's wife. A steadfast loyalist, he and his father cannot reconcile their wildly disparate views, causing a rift in the bond both thought unbreakable." (Publisher's note)
"Cabot shines in her descriptions of colonial life, in her fictionalized rendition of Ben Franklin's charismatic personality and wide-ranging intellect, but especially in interpreting Franklin the man through Anne, a fully-realized, memorable character. It is Anne who brings imagined reality's magic to the narrative. Intriguing historical fiction; a laudable interpretation of colonial life." Kirkus

Cadwalladr, Carole

The **family** tree. Dutton 2005 384p il $23.95
ISBN 0-525-94842-2
LC 2004-52756
"Set in late-20th-century Britain, the novel is narrated by Rebecca Monroe, a pop culture researcher who tells of her marriage to Alistair, a behavioral geneticist; her childhood leading up to her mother's suicide; and her grandmother's doomed biracial romance with Cecil, a Jamaican immigrant. In an effort to better understand herself, the child she can't decide whether or not to have, and the people she still can't believe make up her family, Rebecca considers both sides of the nature/nurture debate, with any romantic notions she might be on the brink of reaching debunked by her husband's passionless scientific postulations. Cadwalladr explicates her tale with a slew of definitions, scientific charts and graphs, detailed family anatomies, examples of deductive fallacies and footnotes expounding on such essential '70s pop culture references as Dallas and The Sale of the Century. Her mastery of time and place, wry humor and sporadic bouts of self-doubt will endear her to readers, while her fascination with the choices people make combined with a morbid curiosity about her own fate add depth and texture to this utterly winning tale of one lovable, dysfunctional family." Publ Wkly

Cain, Chelsea

✓ **Heartsick**. St. Martin's Minotaur 2007 326p $23.95
ISBN 978-0-312-36846-3; 0-312-36846-1
LC 2007-18005

"In addition to spiky characters, Cain has a crisp voice, a wicked sense of humor, and an imagination for all the horrors that can unfold in a locked basement." Entertainment Wkly

Cain, Chelsea

Kill you twice; Chelsea Cain. Minotaur Books 2012 336 p. (hardcover) $25.99

ISBN 9780312619787; 9781250014887

LC 2012013604

In this mystery novel, part of a series following "the 'Beauty Killer,' Gretchen Lowell . . . Portland, Oregon, police detective Archie Sheridan . . . is healing, slowly, from all the wounds, physical and psychological, that Gretchen has inflicted upon him, and Gretchen is safely ensconced in the Oregon State Mental Hospital. . . . Archie gets a call from Gretchen's psychiatrist with a message that the killer Archie is hunting is after Gretchen's child." (Booklist)

Cain, Chelsea

Let me go; Chelsea Cain. Minotaur Books 2013 336 p. (hardcover) $25.99

ISBN 0312619812; 9780312619817

LC 2013009825

This novel by Chelsea Cain focuses on Detective Archie Sheridan and "with escaped serial killer Gretchen Lowell on the loose . . . Archie finds himself crashing a masked ball on a private island owned by Jack Reynolds, a . . . drug kingpin. Archie's nemesis and sometimes lover has something special in mind for [him]. On Halloween Eve, with time running out, and the life of someone close to Archie on the line, Archie knows his only chance is to give Gretchen exactly what she wants." (Publisher's note)

Cain, James M.

The **cocktail** waitress; James M. Cain. Hardcase Crime 2012 272 p. (hardcover) $23.99; (paperback) $14.95; (ebook) $11.99

ISBN 1781160325; 9781781160329; 9781781160343; 9781781160350

In this book by James M. Cain, "following her husband's death in a suspicious car accident, beautiful young widow Joan Medford is forced to take a job serving drinks in a cocktail lounge to make ends meet. . . . At the job she encounters two men who take an interest in her, a handsome young schemer . . . and a wealthy but unwell older man who rewards her for her attentions with a $50,000 tip and an unconventional offer of marriage." (Publisher's note)

Cain, James M.

The **postman** always rings twice, double indemnity, Mildred Pierce and selected stories. Alfred A. Knopf 2003 xxxix, 594p (Everyman's library) $25

ISBN 978-0-375-41438-1; 0-375-41438-X

LC 2003-277292

The postman always rings twice, (1934) is the tale of a drifter who stumbles into a job, into an erotic obsession, and into a murder. Double indemnity (1934) is a story of blind passion, duplicity, and murder. Mildred Pierce (1943) is the tale of a woman with a taste for shiftless men and an unreasoned devotion to her monstrous daughter. Also included here are five stories: Pastorale; The baby in the icebox; Dead man; Brush fire; The girl in the storm

Caldwell, Erskine

★ **God's** little acre. Viking 1933 303p

"A Georgia 'cracker,' Ty Ty Walden, has devoted 15 years to digging for gold on his farm. Always a 'religious man,' he has set aside one acre whose income shall go to the church, but has had to shift 'God's little acre' constantly, so as not to interfere with the digging. Ty Ty's sincere but adaptable morality appears also in the shiftless lives of his children." Oxford Companion to Am Lit. 6th edition

Caldwell, Erskine

★ **Tobacco** road. Scribner 1932 241p

"Jeeter Lester is an impoverished Georgia sharecropper who lives on Tobacco Road with his starving old mother, his sickly wife, Ada, and his two children, sixteen-year-old Dude and Ellie May, who has a harelip. A third child, Pearl, has been married at the age of twelve to Lov Bensey, a railroad worker. When Jeeter's widowed preacher sister, Bessie Rice, induces Dude to marry her by buying him a new automobile, Dude accidentally wrecks the car and kills his grandmother. Pearl runs away from Lov Bensey; Ellie May happily goes to live with him; and Jeeter and Ada, left alone one night, perish when their shack burns down." Reader's Ency. 4th edition

Caldwell, Ian

The **rule** of four; [by] Ian Caldwell & Dustin Thomason. Dial Press 2004 372p $24

ISBN 0-385-33711-6

LC 2003-70124

"A Princeton student has only twenty-four hours to complete his senior thesis—hardly the nail-biting stuff of thrillers, except that the thesis in question purports to solve the mystery of an erotic fifteenth-century allegory littered with ciphers and algorithms. . . . As the student races to meet his deadline, mayhem engulfs the campus: a chase through steam tunnels beneath the grassy quads, an inferno at the school's toniest eating club, and nude frolics in the snow (this last not fiction but a real Princeton tradition). The authors . . . keep up a frantic, somewhat exhausting pace, but the most riveting action sequences take place inside the mind, as the hero wrestles with the manuscript." New Yorker

Caldwell, Taylor

Captains and kings. Doubleday 1972 640p

This novel follows the growth of an Irish immigrant family from complete poverty to a position of wealth and political power. Joseph Armagh is ruled by the desire for money and overcome by ambition for his children. Along the way the family seems to have acquired a curse, so that the second generation of Armaghs reaps only misfortune and destruction

"Through all this saga one cannot help but find some parallels with the Kennedy saga, set back to the period 1850-1915. Portraits of some characters, rather bitterly slanted, are certainly more than coincidental." Publ Wkly

Caldwell, Taylor

Dear and glorious physician. Doubleday 1959 574p

"Gripping and absorbing reading that illuminates a period and highlights the development of a man being prepared for God's purpose. The sweep and greatness of the story dwarf any defects in style." Wis Libr Bull

Caldwell, Taylor

Testimony of two men. Doubleday 1968 605p

"Jonathan Ferrier is the central character. He is dedicated to perfection—to perfect asepsis when few doctors yet acknowledged or even knew the need for it in 1901, and to perfect truth in human relations. Ironically, he himself has been tried for the murder of his wife and justly acquitted. The verdict was not acceptable to his community. Since they are incapable of the perfection he vocally demands, the people around him hate him and are delighted by an apparent opportunity to condemn him." Libr J

"Caldwell combines incisive characterization with an absorbing description of nineteenth-century medical practices." Booklist

Caletti, Deb

He's gone; a novel. Deb Caletti. Bantam Books Trade Paperbacks 2013 352 p. (alk. paper) $15

ISBN 0345534352; 9780345534354; 9780345534361
LC 2012025421

In this mystery novel, "after arguing with her husband at a party the night before, Dani Keller wakes to find him gone. Her first thought is that he is punishing her with his absence . . . . As the days pass, however, Dani starts asking scarier questions: Did Ian leave her for good? Has he run away with another woman? Did he have an accident? Is he lying hurt somewhere . . . or worse? Why can't she remember what happened the night of the argument, after they got home?" (Library Journal)

"Though the opening pages seem to promise a suspense novel--and the close delivers a well-executed plot twist--this is in essence the story of a woman's growing self-knowledge, perfectly executed at an appropriately measured pace." Kirkus

Calisher, Hortense

The **collected** stories of Hortense Calisher. Arbor House 1975 502p

ISBN 0-87795-115-2

Callihan, Kristen

Firelight. Forever 2012 400 p. (pbk) $5.99

ISBN 9781455508594

This book tells the story of "Miranda Ellis, [who] has an unearthly talent for creating fire from thin air. Lord Benjamin Archer has lived for decades under the influence of a dark curse and wears a black mask over his disfigured face. After Miranda's family is ruined, she weds Benjamin for his money and is surprised when passion and romance follow. Shortly after the wedding, Benjamin stands accused of a gruesome series of homicides. As he and Miranda hunt the true killer, Miranda soon sees the innocent, passionate man behind the mask, while wary Benjamin begins to trust in his wife's love even though it endangers them both." (Publishers Weekly)

Calling the wind; twentieth century African-American short stories. edited and with an introduction

by Clarence Major. HarperCollins Pubs. 1993 xxv, 622p hardcover o.p.

ISBN 0-06-018337-3
LC 92-52620

This "could become the anthology of black American short fiction for wide use in the high school and college classroom as well as by the general reading public." Booklist

Calvino, Italo

★ **Baron** in the trees; translated by Archibald Colquhoun. Harcourt 1977 217p pa $12

ISBN 0-15-610680-9
LC 76-039704

Original Italian edition, 1957; this translation first published 1959 by Random House

Calvino's "status as one of Italy's greatest writer's was confirmed by the acclaim which met the fantasy, The baron in the trees (1957), in which a nineteenth-century nobleman opts to pursue life without ever setting foot on the ground. The story examines the meeting-points of reality and imagination." Good Fiction Guide

Calvino, Italo

★ **If** on a winter's night a traveler. Knopf 1993 254p $18

ISBN 0-679-42025-8
LC 92-54302

Original Italian edition, 1979; this is a reissue of the edition published 1981 by Harcourt Brace Jovanovich

The novel "begins with a man discovering that the copy of a novel he has recently purchased is defective, a Polish novel having been bound within its pages. He returns to the bookshop the following day and meets a young woman who is on an identical mission. They both profess a preference for the Polish novel. Interposed between the chapters in which the two strangers attempt to authenticate their texts are 10 excerpts that parody genres of contemporary world fiction, such as the Latin-American novel and the political novel of eastern Europe." Merriam-Webster's Ency of Lit

Calvino, Italo

Invisible cities; translated from the Italian by William Weaver. Harcourt Brace Jovanovich 1974 165p

ISBN 0-15-145290-3

Original Italian edition, 1972

"Italo Calvino is recognized as one of the consummate stylists among writers today, a novelist whose superbly imaginative mind conjures up metaphorical fables of exquisite beauty to transcribe his personal visions of man and the universe." Choice

Calvino, Italo

Mr. Palomar; translated from the Italian by William Weaver. Harcourt Brace Jovanovich 1985 130p

ISBN 0-15-162835-1
LC 85-5490

Original Italian edition, 1983

"There is an almost perfect sense of complementary relationships: Calvino is delicate and strong, his precision is lyric and mathematic; the equation between perceiver and perceived is made infinitely and effortlessly complex but remains exact. The care which Calvino has lavished on the formal arrangement of his book should not, however, lead us to think that it offers only a formal resolution of compositional intricacies, for Mr. Palomor is a work of cunning dialectics that goes beyond the delight in paradoxes for which Calvino is lazily praised." New Statesman (1913)

Calvo, Javier

Wonderful world; a novel. translated by Mara Faye Lethem. Harper 2009 470p $27.99

    ISBN 978-0-06-155768-2; 0-06-155768-4

                             LC 2009-280005

    Original Spanish edition, 2007

"The protagonist, Lucas, is a 33-year-old antiques dealer in Barcelona who finds himself embroiled simultaneously with two gangs of thieves who may have been allies of his late father, even as his horrifically awful mother is suing him for control of the family business. Meanwhile, his best friend is his 12-year-old neighbor, a fatherless girl named Valentina, who regards herself as the greatest living Stephen King expert ('excerpts' from King's newest novel are sprinkled throughout the book). Other cultural references ranging from psychedelic rock and heavy metal to horror movies and superhero comics abound, while the novel's action is overlaid by a patina of Quentin Tarantino–like violence. Surreal, sexy, wildly funny, self-indulgent, and wretchedly excessive, Wonderful World is clearly not for all readers, but it will have its passionate advocates and has all the earmarks of a cult favorite in the making." Booklist

Cameron, Peter

  ★ The city of your final destination. Farrar, Straus & Giroux 2002 312p $24

    ISBN 0-374-28197-1

                             LC 2001-51127

In this "novel, Omar Razaghi, a graduate student in Kansas by way of Iran and Canada, travels to Uruguay to research a biography of Jules Gund, a critically ignored expatriate writer who published only a single novel before his death. In an attempt to obtain permission to proceed with his work, Omar finds himself entangled in, and even falling a bit in love with, the family Jules left behind: his homosexual brother, Adam; Jules's wife, Caroline; and his mistress Arden. . . . The characters discover themselves not through the books they have read (as Omar first believes) or the places they have been (as the title would suggest) but through Cameron's precisely rendered conversations." New Yorker

Cameron, Peter

Coral Glynn; Peter Cameron. Farrar, Straus and Giroux 2012 210 p.

    ISBN 0374299013; 9780374299019

                             LC 2011034926

This book tells the story of "Coral, a nurse, sent to Hart House in 1950 to tend the dying Mrs. Hart." (Libr J) Her son Major Hart "has an aversion to spending the rest of his life alone. He had been badly wounded in the war and has few social contacts beyond his childhood friend Robin, who's in love with the major. . . . Hart somewhat ambivalently returns some of Robin's affection, but . . . he and Coral get engaged. . . . On their wedding night their marriage is immediately thwarted by Inspector Hoke, who's investigating a mysterious murder that occurred in the woods near Hart House. . .

. Uncertain whether Coral has any culpability in the crime, Hart urges her to disappear to London, where she lives for two years. . . . Their on-again/off-again relationship teeters on the brink until Coral finally makes up her mind." (Kirkus)

Campbell, Bebe Moore

Brothers and sisters. Putnam 1994 476p

    ISBN 0-399-13929-X

                             LC 94-14196

"Set in the heart of a Los Angeles still troubled by the aftermath of the April riots, the novel draws a . . . portrait of the internal and external conflicts regarding race experienced by characters of varied backgrounds. The story centers on Esther Jackson, an African American with a promising career in banking who is torn between her need to succeed professionally and her loyalty to other people of color." Libr J

"What makes 'Brothers and Sisters' different from the traditional potboiler is Ms. Campbell's genuine attempt to address the complexities of race in the modern age." N Y Times Book Rev

Campbell, Bebe Moore

Your blues ain't like mine. Putnam 1992 332p

    ISBN 0-399-13746-7

                             LC 91-45518

"Written in poetic prose, filled with masterfully drawn and sympathetic characters that a less able hand might have rendered in stereotypes, this first novel blends the irony of Flannery O'Connor's fiction and the poignance of Harper Lee's." Publ Wkly

Campbell, Bonnie Jo

American salvage; stories. Wayne State University Press 2009 170p pa $18.95

    ISBN 978-0-8143-3412-6; 0-8143-3412-1

                             LC 2008-51203

"Campbell's knockout short stories about postindustrial rural Michigan portray damaged, discarded, and busted-broke people rich in yearning, forgiveness, and love." Booklist

Campbell, Bonnie Jo

★ Once upon a river; Bonnie Jo Campbell. W. W. Norton & Co. 2011 348p. map $25.95

    ISBN 978-0-393-07989-0; 0-393-07989-9; 9780393341775

                             LC 201101499

'This novel, a National Book Award and National Book Critics Circle Award finalist, tells the story of "Margo Crane, a beauty whose unflinching gaze and uncanny ability with a rifle have not made her life any easier. After the violent death of her father, in which she is complicit, Margo takes to the Stark River in her boat, with only a few supplies and a biography of Annie Oakley, in search of her vanished mother. But the river . . . is a dangerous place for a young woman traveling alone, and she must be strong to survive, using her knowledge of the natural world and her ability to look unsparingly into the hearts of those around her. Her river odyssey through rural Michigan becomes a defining journey, one that leads her beyond self-preservation and to the decision of what price she is willing to pay for her choices." (Publisher's note)

"What happens to Margo unfolds as a gripping story, old-fashioned in its fullness of event and character development. And all the while, an assured Campbell narrates in a graceful, gliding, confident voice that steers the action smoothly from one bend in the plot to the next — a demonstration of outstanding skills on the river of American literature." Entertainment Wkly

Campbell, Drusilla

When She Came Home; Drusilla Campbell. 1st ed. GCP 2013 336 p. (paperback) $14.99

ISBN 1455510351; 9781455510351

LC 2012040688

In this novel, by Drusilla Campbell, "Frankie Byrne Tennyson . . . , after bravely serving her country in Iraq . . . [is] finally come home. Home to a husband . . . [with] lingering feelings of abandonment. . . . Home to a daughter whose painful encounters with bullies can only be healed by a mother's love. And home to a father who still can't accept his daughter's decision to serve. . . . But the most difficult part about coming home lies within Frankie herself." (Publisher's note)

Camus, Albert

★ The **fall**; translated from the French by Justin O'Brien. Knopf 1957 147p

Original French edition, 1956

"A former Parisian lawyer explains to a stranger in an Amsterdam bar his current profession of judge-penitent. His bitter honesty prevented him first from winning his own self-esteem through good deeds, then from exhausting his own self-condemnation through debauchery. Knowing that no man is ever innocent, he is still trying to forestall personal judgment by confession, by judging others, and by avoiding any situation demanding action." Reader's Ency. 4th edition

Camus, Albert

✓ The **plague**; translated from the French by Stuart Gilbert. Knopf 1948 278p hardcover o.p. pa $12.95

ISBN 0-394-44061-7; 0-679-72021-9 pa

Original French edition, 1947

"Using an epidemic of bubonic plague in an Algerian city as a symbol for the absurdity of man's condition, Albert Camus has in this novel articulated his firm belief in mankind's heroism in struggling against the ultimate futility of life. The plague makes everyone in the city intensely aware both of mortality and of the fact that cooperation is the only logical consolation anyone will find in the face of certain death. Though each character, from doctor to priest, represents some aspect of mankind's attempts to deal with the absurd, none is a cardboard figure. The reader cares what happens to the men depicted here. One takes pleasure in the moments of deep human connection that leave us with the conviction that men are, on the whole, admirable." Shapiro. Fic for Youth. 3d edition

Camus, Albert

★ The **stranger**; translated from the French by Matthew Ward. Knopf 1988 123p $25

ISBN 0-394-53305-4

LC 83-48885

Original French edition, 1942; published in the United Kingdom with title: The outsider

This novel "reveals the 'Absurd' as the condition of man, who feels himself a stranger in his world. Meursault refuses to 'play the game,' by telling the conventional social white lies demanded of him or by believing in human love or religious faith. The unemotional style of his narrative lays naked his motives—or his absence of motive—for his lack of grief over his mother's death, his affair with Marie, his killing an Arab in the hot Algerian sun. Having rejected by honest self-analysis all interpretations which could explain or justify his existence, he nevertheless discovers, while in prison awaiting execution, a passion for the simple fact of life itself." Reader's Ency. 4th edition

Canin, Ethan

✓ **America** America; a novel. Random House 2008 458p $27

ISBN 978-0-679-45680-3; 0-679-45680-5

LC 2008-2341

"Sifter is, at times, too perfect a lead, and his Saline coming-of-age is an idealized yesteryear, a mythic America encased in amber. But it is so passionately imagined that it is hard to resist Mr. Canin's retreat to simpler times and his vision of those who would forfeit comfort for the possibility of unknown highs (or lows)." N Y Sun

Canin, Ethan

✓ The **palace** thief. Random House 1994 205p

ISBN 0-679-41962-4

LC 93-26888

This "book presents us with four beautifully told long short stories. In each, a man muses over his past and realizes how little control he has had over pivotal moments in his life. . . . Canin proves himself adept at articulating moments of profound embarrassment followed by flashes of self-knowledge that are either invigorating or demoralizing. Moving and memorable." Booklist

Cannell, Dorothy

How to murder your mother-in-law. Bantam Bks. 1994 261p

ISBN 0-553-07493-8

LC 93-31149

"After insisting that husband Ben's parents celebrate their anniversary with them at Merlin's Court, Ellie {Haskell} is dismayed when her in-laws reveal that their religious differences (she's Catholic, he's Jewish) prevented their legal marriage. . . . Then Ellie's father-in-law is caught skinny-dipping with a female friend, prompting mother-in-law Magdalene to leave him. Ellie seeks solace from friends in the village and discovers that everyone is suffering from a surfeit of mothers-in-law. A commiseration session among the afflicted daughters-in-law results in several vividly imagined murder scenarios—which, unfortunately, begin to happen." Booklist

Cannell, Stephen J.

Vertical coffin. St. Martin's Press 2004 335p $24.95

ISBN 0-312-30425-0

LC 2003-58567

A thriller featuring LAPD cop, Shane Scully. "In this latest outing, he finds himself in the middle of a law enforcement territorial war when he begins to investigate the murder of one of his friends from the Los Angeles County Sheriff's Department. It seems as if both the sheriff and the feds arrived at the scene of the crime even though neither of their communications systems were compatible with the LAPD frequency. Shane is teamed with a female sheriff, and together they find themselves without friends in any law enforcement agencies. . . . Cannell is, quite simply, one of the best police procedural writers today." Libr J

Cantrell, Rebecca

The **blood** Gospel; James Rollins and Rebecca Cantrell. William Morrow 2013 496 p. (hardcover) $27.99

ISBN 006199104X; 9780061991042

LC 2012031044

In this novel, by James Rollins and Rebecca Cantrell, "a military forensic expert, . . . a Vatican priest[,] and . . . a brilliant but disillusioned archaeologist" explore a recently discovered tomb. "But a brutal attack at the site sets the three on the run, thrusting them into a race to recover what was once preserved in the tomb's sarcophagus: a book rumored to have been written by Christ's own hand, a tome that is said to hold the secrets to His divinity." (Publisher's note)

Canty, Kevin

★ **Everything**; a novel. Nan A. Talese/Doubleday 2010 282p $25.95

ISBN 978-0-385-53330-0; 0-385-53330-6

LC 2009-48197

This "novel chronicles a year's worth of turmoil in the lives of five appealingly aimless Montanans. Layla, a bright college student, and her heavy-drinking father, RL, fall into parallel adulterous romances—she with Edgar, a promising young painter, he with Betsy, an ex-girlfriend undergoing cancer treatment. Meanwhile, June, a friend of both father and daughter, struggles to put the death of her husband behind her. Canty's urgent, at times impressionistic prose generates moment after moment of intense emotion, falling flat only occasionally, and his characters are self-aware enough to keep the story from sinking into melodrama. As their conflicts play out against the changing seasons of the increasingly encroached-upon Bitterroot Valley wilderness—with its larches, bluebirds, and streams full of rainbow trout—we come to share their bafflement at the passage of time." New Yorker

Capote, Truman

★ **Breakfast** at Tiffany's: a short novel and three stories. Random House 1958 179p

ISBN 0-394-41770-4

"'Breakfast at Tiffany's' tells the story of haunting and neurotic Holiday Golightly, Texan child-bride, girl-about-New York and friend of gangster czar, Sally Tomato, in a remarkable novelette that bears the Capote trademark of neat prose, multiple dimensions and unusual atmosphere." Ont Libr Rev

Capote, Truman

★ The **complete** stories of Truman Capote; By Truman Capote, introduction by Reynolds Price. Random House 2004 300p $24.95

ISBN 0-679-64310-9; 9780812994377

LC 2004-46876

"Ranging from the gothic South to the chic East Coast, from rural children to aging urban sophisticates, all the unforgettable places and people of [Truman] Capote's oeuvre are here, in stories as elegant as they are heartfelt, as haunting as they are compassionate. Reading them reminds us of the miraculous gifts of a beloved American original." (Publisher's note)

"Now, for the first time, all of Capote's short stories are being published together, an event that signifies a renewed appreciation of his overall contribution to literature, for evidence is presented in this one volume that he should be ranked as a major American short story writer." Booklist

Capote, Truman

★ The **grass** harp. Random House 1951 181p

"After the death of his parents, Collin goes to live with his two aunts, Verna and Dolly. The former is wealthy and practical, the latter, whimsical and romantic. Dolly produces a cure for dropsy that she bottles and sells through the mail. Verna is ready to take over the operation and realize a large profit. To avoid this scheme, Collin, Dolly, and Catherine, a servant, go off to live in a treehouse, where they are joined by other eccentric characters. When Dolly dies, Collin is ready for his independence, having learned a valuable lesson about love and nonconformity." Shapiro. Fic for Youth. 3d edition

Caputo, Philip

Acts of faith. Knopf 2005 669p $26.95

ISBN 0-375-41166-6

LC 2004-48982

"Mr. Caputo writes with such authority that he's able to invest events that might seem improbable in another novelist's hands with an uncommon degree of verisimilitude, delineating not only the viewpoints of his Western visitors, but also those of the Sudanese rebels and their Islamic opponents with equally sure-handed drama and psychological ballast" N Y Times (Late N Y Ed)

Caputo, Philip

Crossers. Alfred A. Knopf 2009 447p $26.95

ISBN 978-0-375-41167-0; 0-375-41167-4

LC 2009-19096

"Having lost his wife—and himself—on 9/11, Gil Castle finally leaves his high-power job, sells his home, and heads across country with his dog to stay in a small, primitive shack on the Arizona ranch of relatives he hardly knows. Soon after rescuing a Mexican man who wanted only to get to America but got trapped in a nasty drug deal, Gil is forced to consider the moral issues surrounding the border crossing of both drug runners and desperate illegals. What he doesn't know will soon hurt him: a woman who masterminds a drug cartel across the border is planning to wreak vengeance on his family for a past offense." Libr J

This "is at once a color-filled action tale; a generational saga with a moral; a touching love story; and a bold lesson in history and its inevitabilities." Dallas Morning News

Caputo, Philip

★ **Horn** of Africa. Holt & Co. 1980 487p
ISBN 0-03-042136-5

LC 79-27513

"Three men, two Americans and one Englishman, embark on a mission as mercenaries in Africa, involving gun-running and clandestine warfare. Their capacity for violence is related to events and drives in their own lives. Nordstrand, the most amoral of them, is a character that is indelibly drawn as are the horrible experiences lived through in desert treks. This author has been compared to Joseph Conrad and Graham Greene in his exploration of the deepest recesses of man's soul." Shapiro. Fic for Youth. 3d edition

Carcaterra, Lorenzo

Apaches. Ballantine Bks. 1997 336p
ISBN 0-345-40101-8

This novel opens with the "brutal kidnapping of an innocent 12-year-old girl. But the kidnapper has made a deadly mistake. He has brought Boomer Frontieri back to life, back to the streets. And back into action. A New York City detective forced to retire after being wounded in a drug bust, Boomer thirsts to return to the life he loved—the life of a cop. When an old friend turns to him for help, Boomer has the excuse he needs." Publisher's note

Card, Orson Scott, 1951-

Alvin Journeyman. TOR Bks. 1995 384p (Tales of Alvin Maker)
ISBN 0-312-85053-0

LC 95-22693

Fourth title in the Tales of Alvin Maker series. "Driven from the Wobbish country by a girl's false accusation, {Alvin} returns to his birthplace in Hatrack River and promptly finds himself on trial for stealing the golden plough from Makepiece Smith and also facing lynching for helping fugitive slaves. Meanwhile, Alvin's younger brother, Calvin, is peddling his own Maker's skills with more profit if many fewer scruples, both in America and in Europe. . . . From beginning to end, this novel is full of riches." Booklist

Followed by Heartfire

Card, Orson Scott

Children of the mind. TOR Bks. 1996 349p (Ender's Game) hardcover o.p. pa $15.95; pa $8.99
ISBN 0-312-85395-5; 0-765-30474-0 pa;
9780812522396 pa

LC 95-53262

At the beginning of this fourth series title "Ender Wiggin has placed part of his consciousness and memory in two other bodies, one named after his brother Peter, the other after his sister Valentine. His own body is literally crumbling, and that is not the only problem. A human fleet is on the way to the planet of Lusitania to stop the deadly descolada virus by destroying the planet; meanwhile, the powers that be are also shutting down Ender's friend Jane, the sentient interstellar computer network who makes faster-than-light travel—and,

therewith, discovery of the planet of origin of the descolada virus—possible." Booklist

Followed by Ender's shadow

Card, Orson Scott, 1951-

Earth Afire; by Orson Scott Card and Aaron Johnston. 1st ed. Tor 2013 400 p. (hardcover) $25.99
ISBN 0765329050; 9780765329059

LC 2012043815

This book, written by Orson Scott Card and Aaron Johnston, takes place one hundred years before the novel "Ender's Game." "This is the story of the First Formic War. Victor Delgado beat the alien ship to Earth, but just barely. Not soon enough to convince skeptical governments that there was a threat. They didn't believe that until space stations and ships and colonies went up in sudden flame. And when that happened, only Mazer Rackham and the Mobile Operations Police could move fast enough to meet the threat." (Publisher's note)

Card, Orson Scott

Earthfall. TOR Bks. 1995 350p (Homecoming)
ISBN 0-312-93039-9

LC 94-41993

"This action-packed, plot-rich installment features Card's typical virtues—well-drawn characters and a story driven by complex moral issues." Publ Wkly

Followed by Earthborn

Card, Orson Scott, 1951-

Earth unaware; Orson Scott Card and Aaron Johnston. Tor 2012 368 p. (hardcover) $24.99
ISBN 0765329042; 9780765329042; 9781429946568

LC 2012011661

This science fiction novel, by Orson Scott Card and Aaron Johnston, is a prequel to the "Ender's Game" series. "Humanity was slowly making their way out . . . of the Solar System. . . . The mining ship . . . El Cavador's telescopes pick up a fast-moving object coming in-system. . . . It's massive and moving at a significant fraction of the speed of light. . . . This is humanity's first contact with an alien race. The First Formic War is about to begin." (Publisher's note)

"Card's gift for strong, memorable characters combined with screenwriter Johnston's (Invasive Procedures, with Card) flair for vivid scene-building results in a standout tale of sf adventure that gives "Ender" series fans fascinating backstory to the classic Ender's Game." LJ

Card, Orson Scott

Ender's game. TOR Bks. 1991 xxi, 226p $24.95; pa $6.99
ISBN 0-312-93208-1; 0-8125-5070-6 pa
A reissue of the title first published 1985
ALA YALSA Margaret A. Edwards Award (2008)

"The key, of course, is Ender Wiggin himself. Mr. Card never makes the mistake of patronizing or sentimentalizing his hero. Alternately likable and insufferable, he is a convincing little Napoleon in short pants." N Y Times Book Rev

Card, Orson Scott

Ender's shadow. Doherty Assocs. 1999 379p (Ender's Game) $24.95; pa $7.99

ISBN 0-312-86860-X; 0-812-57571-7 pa

LC 99-35824

ALA YALSA Margaret A. Edwards Award (2008)

In this fifth installment "Card has added a parallel novel that occupies the same time frame as Ender's Game, and chronicles many of the same events. Children are being tested, the best and the brightest being placed into a school where they will be trained for the eminent and final fight to the death between humanity and the insectlike 'Buggers.' Shadow shifts from Ender to Bean as the protagonist and presents the events from Bean's perspective, with his own unique viewpoints. Complex three-dimensional characters, a strong story line, and vivid writing all combine to make this an exceptional work." SLJ

Followed by Shadow of the Hegemon

Card, Orson Scott, 1951-

The **Gate** Thief; Orson Scott Card. 1st ed. St. Martin's Press 2013 380 p. (hardcover) $24.99

ISBN 0765326582; 9780765326584

LC 2012049548

This book by Orson Scott Card follows "Danny North, the 16-year-old incarnation of the messenger/trickster god Thoth-Mercury-Hermes-Loki. . . . He's just coming into his full powers as a gate mage when some of the old gods set out to kill him. He's also so filled with 'innate goodness' that he can fend off all the hot girls who want him and subdue his own adolescent hormones. Naturally, he takes on the task of saving Earth and defeating the forces of evil." (Publishers Weekly)

Card, Orson Scott

Keeper of dreams. TOR 2008 656p $27.95

ISBN 978-0-7653-0497-1; 0-7653-0497-X

LC 2007-46720

"These short science fiction, fantasy and 'literary' stories, along with a handful of Hatrack River tales (related to the Alvin Maker series) and four stories 'written by a Mormon, about Mormon culture, for Mormon readers,' illustrate Card's fascination with complex child protagonists. . . . Card intended several of the included stories, like the powerful 'In the Dragon's House,' to open novels not yet written, but even on their own they provide significant examples of his perennial themes: morality, salvation and redemption." Publ Wkly

Card, Orson Scott

★ **Maps** in a mirror; the short fiction of Orson Scott Card. TOR Bks. 1990 675p $19.95

ISBN 0-312-85047-6

LC 90-38896

This collection features "46 pieces by an exceptional writer. Card's talents are represented by fantasy, science fiction, horror, poetry, and the stories that launched his sagas of Alvin Maker and Ender Wiggins. A substantial amount of autobiographical discussion of each story's origin enhances the volume's high value." Booklist

Card, Orson Scott

Seventh son. Doherty Assocs. 1987 241p (Tales of Alvin Maker) hardcover o.p. pa $6.99

ISBN 0-312-93019-4; 0-812-53305-4 pa

LC 86-51490

"This beguiling book recalls Robert Penn Warren in its robust but reflective blend of folktale, history, parable and personal testimony, pioneer narrative." Publ Wkly

Card, Orson Scott

Speaker for the Dead. TOR Bks. 1986 415p (Ender's Saga) $25.95; pa $7.99

ISBN 0-312-93738-5; 9780812550757 pa

LC 85-51765

In this second title in the series Ender Wiggin becomes "Speaker for the Dead out of remorse over his role in the unnecessary destruction of the Buggers. In his new identity, Wiggin plays a vital role in preventing war when a second nonhuman intelligent race—even more incomprehensible than the Buggers—is discovered. This book lacks the sheer dramatic power of Ender's transformation from child into warlord as portrayed in its predecessor. However, it benefits from increased dramatic unity, a well-developed background and supporting cast on the colony planet Lusitania, and the author's customarily stylish writing." Booklist

Followed by Xenocide

Card, Orson Scott

Xenocide. 1991 394p (Ender's Game) hardcover o.p. pa $15.95; pa $7.99

ISBN 0-312-93208-1; 0-312-86187-7 pa; 9780812509250 pa

LC 90-27108

Third title in the author's distant future series about Ender Wiggin. "As an armed fleet from Starways Congress hurtles through space towards the rebellious planet Lusitania, Ender Wiggin, his sister Valentine, and his family search for a miracle that will preserve the existence of three intelligent and vastly different species. As a storyteller, Card excels in portraying the quiet drama of wars fought not on battlefields but in the hearts and minds of his characters." Libr J

Followed by Children of the mind

Carey, Edward

Alva & Irva; the twins who saved a city. Harcourt 2003 207p il map $24

ISBN 0-15-100782-9

LC 2002-13701

This novel is "mock epical in its consequential-ridiculous tone. . . .and comedically symphonic in the precision and daffy chasteness of its diction. For all its ludicrousness, it is honorably pathetic, too—a genuine human comedy," Booklist

Carey, Jacqueline

Banewreaker; Jacqueline Carey. Tor 2004 431p map (pbk.) $7.99

ISBN 9780765344298; 9780765305213; 0765305216

LC 2004048093

The background for this fantasy novel takes place at a time when "the Seven Shapers dwelled in accord and

Shaped the world to their will. But Satoris, the youngest among them, was deemed too generous in his gifts to the race of Men, and so began the Shapers' War, which Sundered the world. Now six of the Shapers lay to one end of a vast ocean, and Satoris to the other, reviled by even the race of Men. Satoris sits in his Darkhaven, surrounded by his allies. Chief among them is Tanaros Blacksword, immortal Commander General of his army. . . . Now there is a new prophecy that tells of Satoris's destruction and the redemption of the world. To thwart it, Satoris sends Tanaros to capture the Lady of the Ellylon, the beautiful Cerelinde, to prevent her alliance with the last High King of Men." (Publisher's note)

Carey, Jacqueline
Dark currents; agents of Hel. Jacqueline Carey. Roc 2012 368 p. $26.95
ISBN 0451464788; 9780451464781
LC 2012007049
This urban fantasy novel tells the story of "Daisy Johanssen," who lives in a Michigan town that is a tourist destination and "home to a thriving 'eldritch community' of supernatural entities, thanks to the presence of the local underworld controlled by the Norse goddess Hel." Daisy is Hel's assistant as well as a clerk at the human police station. She "is called in to help investigate the drowning of a local college boy when signs of both foul play and magical residue are found on the body." (Publishers Weekly)

Carey, Jacqueline
Kushiel's dart. Tor 2001 701p
ISBN 0-312-87238-0
LC 2001-21945
"Making a marvelous debut, Carey spins a breathtaking epic starring an unflinching yet poignantly vulnerable heroine. The tale blends Christianity and paganism with fascinating results." Booklist
Followed by Kushiel's chosen (2002) and Kushiel's avatar (2003)

Carey, Jacqueline
★ Kushiel's Scion; Jacqueline Carey. Warner Books 2006 xii, 753p map (pbk.) $7.99; o.p.; o.p.
ISBN 9780446610025; 044650002X; 9780446500029
LC 2005023648
This volume of the "Legacy series marks the start of a new trilogy set in Terre d'Ange, the author's reimagined Renaissance world. The story picks up where volume three, 'Kushiel's Avator' (2003), left off, though Imriel nó Montrève de la Courcel, a prince of the blood, now narrates in place of the . . . heroine of the previous books, Phèdre nó Delauney. As a boy, Imriel is abandoned by his treasonous parents and subjected to terrible indignities by pirates. Later rescued and adopted by Phèdre, he grows into a position of authority and learns many skills, including sexual prowess. He has a torrid affair with a married woman, and finally survives a terrible siege at a walled city he courageously defends." (Publishers Weekly)

Carey, Peter, 1943-
★ The **chemistry** of tears; by Peter Carey. Alfred A. Knopf 2012 229 p.
ISBN 0307592715; 9780307592712
LC 2012005880
"The principal narrator of Peter Carey's . . . novel is [museum horologist] Catherine Gehrig." Her "boss . . . gives her a new project to work on, a set of tea chests containing the parts of a nineteenth-century mechanical bird, along with a stack of notebooks written by a man named Henry Brandling. . . . Two parallel quests begin: in 1854, Henry, . . . find[s] someone who will make a bird for his young son . . .; in 2010, Catherine . . . tries to unravel his story and rebuild his bird." (Times Literary Supplement)

Carey, Peter, 1943-
His illegal self. Alfred A. Knopf 2008 272p $24.95
ISBN 978-0-307-26372-8; 0-307-26372-X
LC 2007-42862
"Hippie communal disintegration has been done before, and better by T.C. Boyle in 'Drop City,' but Carey keeps us reading with his vivid lyricism, his finely tuned sense of the ridiculous and his focus on two very specific characters: a boy aching for mother love and a woman who is trying to make sense of having maternal love thrust upon her. In the end, this is a love story, an unconventional but emotionally compelling one." St. Louis Post-Dispatch

Carey, Peter
★ **My** life as a fake. Knopf 2003 266p $24
ISBN 0-375-41498-3
LC 2003-52746
This work "is so confidently brilliant, so economical yet lively in its writing, so tightly fitted and continuously startling in its plot that something, we feel, must be wrong with it. It ends in a bit of a rush, and left several questions dangling in this reader's mind. Unfortunately, to spell out those questions would be to betray too much of an intricate fictional construct where little is as it first seems and fantastic developments unfold like scenes on a fragile paper fan." New Yorker

Carey, Peter
★ **Parrot** and Olivier in America. Knopf 2010 379p $26.95
ISBN 978-0-307-59262-0; 0-307-59262-6
LC 2009-47435
Olivier-Jean-Baptiste de Clarel de Garmont "has been bundled off to America at the behest of his mother, who suffered brutally under the French Terror of 1793 and thinks only of how to save her son from a similar fate. Accompanying him is Parrot, an English orphan with artistic aspirations, trained as a printer, who is yoked to Olivier de Bah-bah Garmont as servant, gadfly and spy. Both men wrestle with demon love: Olivier for his democratic American girl who can never be taken to home to Paris and maman; Parrot for his mistress, a beautiful and lusty painter, all that smeary wine and meat and fat glistening on her lips, and whose talent outstrips his own. In short, it's a buddy novel. But what a novel! . . . . Funny, bawdy, brainy and moving, Parrot & Olivier in America is an utter delight." Globe and Mail

Cargill, C. Robert

Dreams and Shadows. HarperCollins 2013 448 p. $24.99

ISBN 0062190423; 9780062190420

In this book, "[C. Robert] Cargill chronicles the friendship and adventures of Ewan, stolen as a baby by the fairy-goblin crossbreeds called Bendith Y Mamau, and Colby, an eight-year-old who encounters a djinn. . . . The two boys travel from the faerie lands known as the Limestone Kingdom, a realm filled with creatures of myth—Coyote, changelings, the Wild Hunt, and more—to Austin, Tex., where they must learn to navigate the often treacherous path to adulthood." (Publishers Weekly)

Carkeet, David

✓Double negative; David Carkeet. Felony & Mayhem Press 2008 246 p. o.p.; $14.95

ISBN 9781933397085; 9781590203002

LC 2008046001

This book's murder-mystery plot is set at the Wabash Institute, which is "[d]edicated to the study of toddlers and their development of verbal skills . . . [and] home to a nest of sublimely cranky academics. When one of them is bludgeoned to death, Jeremy Cook–the Institute's premier scholar and the book's . . . hero–becomes the prime suspect. To clear his name, Cook resolves to solve the case, even if it means taking time off from his hobby of teaching imaginary words to the Institute's tiny 'subjects.'" (Publisher's note)

Carkeet, David

✓From away. Overlook 2010 288p $25.95

ISBN 978-1-590-20304-0

"Stranded in Montpelier, Vermont, by a late-winter car crash, Denny [Braintree] botches a one-night stand before realizing that people in town think he's Homer Dumpling, who disappeared from Montpelier three years before. Sliding into Homer's life and home, Denny is untroubled by being fired from his job at The Fearless Modeler magazine—and little troubled by being the prime suspect in the death of the woman he failed to bed. There's a crime here that Denny must solve, but Carkeet is much more interested in character—Denny's and Homer's. Denny recalls a less-operatic version of Ignatius O'Reilly from A Confederacy of Dunces, and his gift for saying the wrong thing generates much of the book's humor. The very unwillful Homer is sad, soulful, and affecting. Recommend this one to crime fans looking for something new." Booklist

Carlson, Ron

✓Five skies. Viking 2007 244p $23.95

ISBN 0-670-03850-4; 978-0-670-03850-3

LC 2006-51760

"High in the desert plains of southern Idaho, three men gather for a summer of hard work: an aging rancher, whose wife was killed in a freak accident; a nineteen-year-old fleeing both family and law; and an engineer whose career is built on precision but whose brother died in a poorly planned stunt. Time and talk, so often friends to Carlson's characters, slowly heal the wounds, but the men's commission, a ramp for a Knievel-style canyon jump, makes hazardous any hope for moral uplift and serves, in the end, as the stage for tragedy." New Yorker

Carlson, Ron

The signal. Viking 2009 184p $25.95

ISBN 978-0-670-02100-0; 0-670-02100-8

LC 2008-46690

Carlson "evokes the rugged solace of nature with grace and simplicity, his unadorned prose reminiscent of Cormac McCarthy's. He's as adept at describing the stark beauty of the wild as he is at reflecting the contradictory nature of human interaction. And on the treacherous ground between passion and sentimentality, he never loses his footing." PopMatters

Carlyle, Liz

The Bride Wore Pearls; Liz Carlyle. HarperCollins 2012 422 p. (paperback) $7.99

ISBN 0061965774; 9780061965777

In this Victorian-era romance novel, by Liz Carlyle, "the rules of danger and desire are the only rules that apply for the mysterious men of the St James Society. . . . The third book in her . . . series, [it] . . . is a . . . story of a very proper lady who flees her home in a far corner of the British Empire, entrusting her safety and her heart to a dangerous outlaw in Victorian London." (Publisher's note)

Carlyle, Liz

The bride wore scarlet; Liz Carlyle. Avon 2011 375 p. (paperback) $7.99

ISBN 0061965766; 9780061965760

LC 2012658231

This book is part of Liz Carlyle's Fraternitas paranormal Victorian trilogy. Here, "Anaïs de Rohan has spent much of her life training, hoping to join the male-only Fraternitas. The earl of Bessett reluctantly allows her to accompany him on a mission to Brussels where they must pose as husband and wife in order to rescue a young child who has the ability to see into the future. The pretense leads to real attraction that Bessett and Anaïs find impossible to ignore." (Publishers Weekly)

Carlyle, Liz

One touch of scandal; Liz Carlyle. Thorndike Press 2011 375 p. (paperback) $7.99

ISBN 0061965758; 9780061965753

LC 2012656201

This, the first in Liz Carlyle's supernatural Victorian trilogy, "introduces a governess in desperate straits. Grace Gauthier is about to get engaged to her employer when someone murders him. Dodging suspicious police, Grace goes to a London gentlemen's club in search of a man who knew her father. Instead of finding the family friend, she encounters Lord Ruthveyn, a part-Indian war hero who agrees to help her prove her innocence." (Publishers Weekly)

Carnoy, David

The big exit; David Carnoy. Overlook Press 2012 319 p. $25.95

ISBN 1590205154; 9781590205150

In this crime novel by David Carnoy "Richie Forman is freshly out of prison. By night, he makes a living impersonating Frank Sinatra in San Francisco's lounges and corporate parties. But then his ex-best friend--the man who stole his fiancée while he was in prison--is found hacked to death in his garage, and Richie is the prime suspect." (Publisher's note)

Carr, Caleb

★ The **alienist**. Random House 1994 496p
ISBN 0-679-41779-6

LC 93-32766

"A society-born reporter and an enigmatic abnormal psychologist—the 'alienist' of the title—are recruited in 1896 by New York's reform police commissioner Teddy Roosevelt to track down a serial killer who is slaughtering boy prostitutes. The investigators are opposed at every step by crime bosses and the city's hidden rulers (including J. Pierpont Morgan); they distrust the alienist's novel methods and would rather conceal evidence of the murders than court publicity." (Libr J)

"A society-born police reporter and an enigmatic abnormal psychologist—the 'alienist' of the title—are recruited in 1896 by New York's reform police commissioner Teddy Roosevelt to track down a serial killer who is slaughtering boy prostitutes. The investigators are opposed at every step by crime bosses and city's hidden rulers (including J. Pierpont Morgan); they distrust the alienist's novel methods and would rather conceal evidence of the murders than court publicity." Libr J

Followed by The angel of darkness

Carr, Robyn

The **Wanderer**; A thunder point novel. Robyn Carr. Harlequin Books 2013 377 p. (paperback) $7.99
ISBN 0778314472; 9780778314479

This novel, by Robyn Carr, is set in a small town "on the Oregon coast. . . . Locals love the land's unspoiled beauty. Developers see it as a potential gold mine. When newcomer Hank Cooper learns he's been left an old friend's entire beachfront property, he finds himself with a community's destiny in his hands. Cooper has never been a man to settle in one place, and Thunder Point was supposed to be just another quick stop. But Cooper finds himself getting involved with the town." (Publisher's note)

Carriger, Gail

Blameless. Orbit 2010 374 p.
ISBN 0316074152; 9780316074155

In this novel, after "[q]uitting her husband's house and moving back in with her horrible family, Lady Maccon becomes the scandal of the London season. Queen Victoria dismisses her from the Shadow Council, and . . . Lord Akeldama, unexpectedly leaves town. To top it all off, Alexia is attacked by homicidal mechanical ladybugs, indicating, as only ladybugs can, the fact that all of London's vampires are now very much interested in seeing Alexia quite thoroughly dead. While Lord Maccon elects to get progressively more inebriated and Professor Lyall desperately tries to hold the Woolsey werewolf pack together, Alexia flees England for Italy in search of the mysterious Templars. Only they know enough about the preternatural to explain her increasingly inconvenient condition, but they may be worse than the vampires." (Publisher's note)

Carriger, Gail

Changeless; Gail Carriger. Orbit 2010 388 p.
ISBN 0316074144; 9780316074148

LC 2010515877

In this novel, "Alexia Tarabotti, the Lady Woolsey, awakens in the wee hours of the mid- afternoon to find her husband, who should be decently asleep like any normal werewolf, yelling at the top of his lungs. Then he disappears - leaving her to deal with a regiment of supernatural soldiers encamped on her doorstep, a plethora of exorcised ghosts, and an angry Queen Victoria. But Alexia is armed with her trusty parasol, the latest fashions, and an arsenal of biting civility. Even when her investigations take her to Scotland, the backwater of ugly waistcoats, she is prepared: upending werewolf pack dynamics as only the soulless can. She might even find time to track down her wayward husband, if she feels like it." (Publisher's note)

Carriger, Gail

Heartless. Orbit 2011 385p (The Parasol Protectorate) pa $7.99
ISBN 978-0-316-12719-6

While dealing with a sister who has joined the suffragette movement, Madame Lefoux's latest mechanical invention, and a plague of zombie porcupines, Lady Alexia Maccon must save Queen Victoria from an angry ghost who wants her dead in this fourth novel in the Parasol Protectorate series.

"With action, intrigue, and, above all, proper manners, this excellent series will have broad appeal to readers of steampunk, urban fantasy, and paranormal and historical romance." Libr J

Carriger, Gail

Soulless; the manga. Gail Carriger, Rem; art and adaptation, Rem; lettering, JuYoun Lee. 1st Yen Press ed. Yen Press 2012 224 p. ill. (some col.) (paperback) $12.99
ISBN 031618201X; 9780316182010

LC 2010414717

Alex Award (2010).

This Manga graphic novel adaptation of the book by Gail Carriger tells the story of "Alexia Tarabotti [who] is laboring under a great many social tribulations. First, she has no soul. Second, she's a spinster whose father is both Italian and dead. Third, she was rudely attacked by a vampire, breaking all standards of social etiquette. . . . Alexia accidentally kills the vampire -- and then the appalling Lord Maccon (loud, messy, gorgeous, and werewolf) is sent by Queen Victoria to investigate." (Publisher's note)

Carriger, Gail

Timeless. Orbit 2012 402 p.
ISBN 0316127183; 9780316127189

This novel is the fifth in Gail Carriger's "Parasol Protectorate" series. "Two years after moving into vampire Lord Akeldama's third closet, the soulless Lady Alexia Maccon receives a summons from the world's oldest vampire, who requests an audience with Alexia's soul-stealing, scene-stealing two-year-old daughter, Prudence. Accompanying them to Egypt are Alexia's werewolf husband, Conall; the mysterious inventor Madame Lefoux; and Alexia's best friend, fluttery actress Ivy Tunstell, and her family and colorful theatrical troupe. Back in London, beta werewolf Professor Lyall and new pack member Biffy find love in unexpected places while investigating nefarious goings-on." (Publisher's Weekly)

Carroll, James
  Fault lines. Little, Brown 1980 248p
    ISBN 0-316-13012-5

LC 80-36756

"Mr. Carroll has told his story from all the characters' points of view—which is to say that the narrator's voice jumps from one character's mind to another's even within a single conversation. And by doing so he's made his people too strong and complex to be reduced to mere agents of the action." Books of the Times

Carroll, Jonathan
  The **ghost** in love. Sarah Crichton Books/Farrar, Straus and Giroux 2008 308p $25
    ISBN 978-0-374-16186-6; 0-374-16186-0

LC 2008-7877

"Ben Gould hits his head on the sidewalk in an accident that should have killed him. Somehow he survives, but he's changed in ways that he cannot understand. So starts a magical tale in which Ben talks to his dog, Pilot; the ghost sent to monitor Ben falls in love with his girlfriend; and a mysterious knife-wielding man threatens them all. . . . Love, memory, and balancing the needs of our many selves are themes in this occasionally scary, often luminous work of unconventional fantasy." Libr J

Carroll, Susan
  Midnight bride; Susan Carroll. Ballantine Books 2001 307p. (pbk.) $6.99; o.p.
    ISBN 9780345436368; 0345433971

LC 20010269593

This book offers a "19th-century historical romance. . . . [It tells] the story of Dr. Valentine St. Leger, . . . who possesses a supernatural gift for healing others by absorbing their pain into his own body. . . . Kate Fitzleger . . . has loved Val ever since she came to his English country village when she was adopted by a local. Not one to let family tradition stand in her way, Kate sets out to find a book of sorcery in Prospero's deserted tower. She steals the wizard's tome and, disregarding his warning, casts a spell on her beloved. In the meantime, a sickly midnight visitor appears at Val's home bearing a magic crystal that once belonged to the St. Legers. The talisman has a strange effect on Val, curing his disabled leg and stirring his darker passions." (Publishers Weekly)

Carson, Tom
  Daisy Buchanan's daughter. Paycock Press 2011 628p pa $24.95
    ISBN 978-0-931181-34-4; 0-931181-34-8

"Messy and sprawling Carson's book may often be, it's also a very engaging showcase for the most distinctive voice to be found in any recent American novel. . . . The tone is punchy, profane and endlessly lively, somehow synthesizing Damon Runyon, Thomas Pynchon and the heroine of a screwball comedy." Globe and Mail

Carter, Angela
  ★ **Burning** your boats; the collected short stories. with an introduction by Salman Rushdie. Holt & Co. 1996 462p
    ISBN 0-8050-4462-0

LC 95-26312

"Gathered from 30 years of Carter's writing life, this collection is arranged chronologically to reveal her evolution as a writer as well as her consistent preoccupation with the Gothic. . . . As her friend Salman Rushdie writes in his moving introduction, Carter is not an easy read, but there are many rewards for the persistent." Libr J

Carter, Angela
  ★ **Nights** at the circus. Viking 1985 294p
    ISBN 0-670-80375-8

LC 84-40459

"Carter describes a locale as exotic to the traditional reader as her women are to Walser and, by implication, all men; and she undercuts accepted Western history as she goes." New Republic

Carter, Stephen L.
  The **emperor** of Ocean Park. Knopf 2002 657p $26.95
    ISBN 0-375-41363-4

LC 2001-38227

This "tale of ambition, revenge and the power of familial obligations is set in the privileged environs of an Ivy League law school, Martha's Vineyard, and Washington, D.C. Oliver Garland is the demanding but emotionally distant patriarch of an elite, affluent African American family used to special privileges and close relationships with the powerful in government, business, and the criminal underworld. Oliver's death sparks renewed interest in his political career—as a vitriolic conservative, embittered by a failed bid for the U.S. Supreme Court—and concern in many quarters about 'arrangements' he has made in the event of his demise. Garland's son Talcott, a law professor, is very reluctantly drawn into the intrigue. . . . An elegantly nuanced novel, with finely drawn characters, a challenging plot, and perfect pacing." Booklist

Carter, Stephen L.
  Jericho's fall. Alfred A. Knopf 2009 355p $25.95
    ISBN 978-0-307-27262-1

LC 2009-03814

"I'm not sure how much of 'Jericho's Fall' is possible or even makes sense. Characters occasionally make decisions that seem driven more by plot than by reason. Yet it's all great fun — and I couldn't help but smile as I watched a CIA director being stalked for a change." Boston Globe

Carter, Stephen L.
  New England white. Alfred A. Knopf 2007 555p $24.95
    ISBN 978-0-375-41362-9; 0-375-41362-6

LC 2006-19721

Carter "creates an invigorating and often scathing portrait of the Carlyles' community. He refutes political correctness, preferring to explore the contradictions warring within Julia. . . . [He] is equally intense in his portrayal of the Carlyles' outwardly perfect, inwardly turbulent marriage, a delicate balance of duty and endurance, even love of a sort." PopMatters

Carter, Stephen L.

Palace council. Alfred A. Knopf 2008 513p $26.95

ISBN 978-0-307-26658-3; 0-307-26658-3

LC 2007-52134

"Set primarily in the years between 1954 and 1974—what Carter calls the 'two decades' of the sixties—this political thriller leaves virtually no important person or event unturned. Richard Nixon, Langston Hughes, and dissident groups all play roles as the action shifts from Harlem to Washington and Saigon. After Eddie Wesley stumbles upon the body of a prominent lawyer who died clutching the talisman of a secret society in his fist, he finds himself caught up in the machinations of spies and assassins. Untangling the so-called Palace Council's purpose gains new urgency when Eddie's sister suddenly vanishes. At the same time, Aurelia, the ex-girlfriend for whom he still carries a torch, is on her own path to discovering the enigmatic group's secrets. . . . Carter offers a finely drawn picture of the complicated black social world." New Yorker

Cartwright, Justin

Other people's money; Justin Cartwright. Bloomsbury USA 2011 288p.

ISBN 9781608192731

LC 2011003212

This is a novel by the author of To Heaven by Water (2009). "Tubal and Co. is a small, privately owned bank in England. As the company's longtime leader, Sir Harry Tubal, slips into senility, his son Julian takes over the reins—and not all is well. The company's hedge fund now owns innumerable toxic assets, and Julian fears what will happen when their real value is discovered. Artair Macleod, an actor manager whose ex-wife, Fleur, was all but stolen by Sir Harry, discovers that his company's monthly grant has not been paid by Tubal. Getting no answers from Julian, he goes to the local press, and an eager young reporter begins asking questions. Bit by bit, the reporter discovers that the grant money is in fact a payoff from Fleur, written off by the bank as a charitable donation, and a scandal breaks." (Publisher's note)

Cartwright, Justin

The promise of happiness. Thomas Dunne Books/St. Martin's Press 2006 308p $23.95

ISBN 0-312-34880-0

LC 2005-49381

First published 2004 in the United Kingdom

"Cartwright's novel is wonderfully well written. The savage irony and probing moral questioning nicely balance each other out, and as an exploration of contemporary Englishness—'proud, ironic and ridiculous all at once'—it is unsurpassed." N Y Times Book Rev

Carver, Raymond

★ Collected stories; [William L. Stull & Maureen P. Carroll, editors] Library of America 2009 1019p $40

ISBN 978-1-59853-046-9; 1-59853-046-1

LC 2009-23633

"The Library of America Collected Stories is a fascinating event . . . if you haven't read it you cannot claim, in the fullest sense, to have read Raymond Carver." Tmes Lit Suppl

Carver, Tania

Cage of Bones; Tania Carver. W W Norton & Co Inc 2013 288 p. $25.95

ISBN 160598406X; 9781605984063

This horror novel, by Tania Carver, begins "as a building awaits demolition, a horrifying discovery is made inside the basement: a cage made of human bones--with a terrified, feral child lurking within. Unbeknownst to Detective Inspector Phil Brennan and psychologist Marina Esposito, they have disturbed a killer who has been operating undetected for thirty years. A killer who wants that boy back." (Publisher's note)

Carver, Tania

The creeper; Tania Carver. Pegasus Crime 2012 448 p. (hardcover) $25.95

ISBN 1605983594; 9781605983592

This thriller crime novel, by Tania Carver, follows a stalker-serial killer. "Suzanne Perry is having a vivid nightmare. Someone is in her bedroom, touching her, and she can't move a muscle. She wakes . . . [and] sees a polaroid stuck to the window. . . . Detective Inspector Phil Brennan of the Major Incident Squad has a killer to hunt. A killer who stalks young women, . . . and ultimately tortures and murders them in the most shocking way possible." (Publisher's note)

Carver, Tania

The surrogate; a novel. Pegasus Crime 2011 438p $25.95

ISBN 978-1-60598-256-4

"A serial killer is on the loose in Colchester, England, where pregnant women are being brutally slain, their babies ripped from their wombs. Veteran officer Phil Brennan is desperate to solve the mystery. After the third such murder occurs, this time with the baby almost certainly taken alive, Phil and his team call upon their colleague, psychologist Marina Esposito, to assist in profiling and capturing the killer. Pregnant, Marina is drawn deeper and deeper into the hunt for a monster. . . . This well-written . . . novel grips the reader from the start, with plenty of violence, gore, and psychological suspense." Libr J

Cary, Joyce

★ The horse's mouth; a novel. Harper & Row 1950 311p

The third volume in the trilogy that began with Herself surprised (1948) and To be a pilgrim (1949)

First published 1944 in the United Kingdom

"The book is crammed with characters and picaresque episodes, and its fire and gusto never once flag. It is a comic hymn to life, but it has nobility as well. Depicting low life, it blazes with an image of the highest life of all—that of the creative imagination." Burgess. 99 Novels

Casey, John

✓ ★ **Compass** rose; a novel. Alfred A. Knopf 2010 355p $27.95

ISBN 978-0-375-41025-3; 0-375-41025-2

LC 2010-10520

"Though the plot is a bit overcluttered — Casey has stuffed it with deaths, land grabs, scandals, mother-daughter feuds — the characters shine so brightly that it's easy to forgive a little narrative excess. This isn't a great novel, like Spartina. But it's a very good one." Entertainment Wkly

Casey, John

✓ ★ **Spartina**. Knopf 1989 375p

ISBN 0-394-50098-9

LC 88-45765

It is the author's "fearless romantic insistence on lyric, even mythic symbolism, coupled with the relentless salt-smack clarity of realistic detail, that makes 'Spartina' just possibly the best American novel about going fishing since 'The Old Man and the Sea,' maybe even 'Moby-Dick.'" N Y Times Book Rev

Cash, Wiley

✓ ★ A **land** more kind than home; a novel. Wiley Cash. William Morrow 2012 309 p. (hardcover) $24.99

ISBN 0062088149; 9780062088147; 9780062088239; 9780062088246

LC 2011022819

In this book, set "up beyond Asheville, near where Gunter Mountain falls into Tennessee . . . Jess Hall is the 9-year-old son of Ben and Julie and beloved younger brother of gentle Stump, his mute, autistic sibling. Clem Barefield is county sheriff, a man with a moral code as tough, weathered and flexible as his gun belt. Adelaide Lyle, once a midwife, is now community matriarch of simple faith and solid conscience. Carson Chambliss is pastor of River Road Church of Christ. He has caught Stump spying, peering into the bedroom of his mother Julie, while she happened to be entertaining the amoral pastor. . . .Chambliss convinces Julie to bring Stump to the church to be cured by the laying on of hands. There, Stump suffers a terrible fate." (Kirkus Reviews)

Castellani, Christopher

All this talk of love; a novel. by Christopher Castellani. Algonquin Books of Chapel Hill 2013 320 p. $13.95

ISBN 9781616201708

LC 2012030841

In this book by Christopher Castellani, "it's been fifty years since Antonio Grasso married Maddalena and brought her to America. That was the last time she would see . . . everything she knew and loved in the village of Santa Cecilia, Italy. . . . But . . . ['their] American-born daughter . . . hatches the idea to take the entire family back to Italy. . . . It is an idea that threatens to tear the Grasso family apart." (Publisher's note).

Castellanos Moya, Horacio, 1957-

✓ ★ **Senselessness**; translated from the Spanish by Katherine Silver. New Directions 2008 142p pa $15.95

ISBN 978-0-8112-1707-1; 0-8112-1707-8

LC 2008-2235

Original Spanish edition, 2005

"The book's narrator, a hapless copy editor, arrives in an unnamed Central American country in order to 'manicure' an exhaustive, 1,100-page report on the military's abuses of the indigenous population." Time Out N Y

Castellanos Moya, Horacio, 1957-

✓ ★ **Tyrant** memory; translated from the Spanish by Katherine Silver. New Directions 2011 270p pa $15.95

ISBN 978-0-8112-1917-4; 0-8112-1917-8

LC 2011-02587

"Haydee is surrounded by a host of vibrant and resilient family and friends, whose lives of relative comfort evoke the grande bourgeoisie 'decent people' society that she inhabits. . . It's an extremely appealing world, both exotic and restrained. The literary style is no less interesting, with sharp divisions between the dignified voice of Haydee recording events in her diary and the bawdy Clemente's attempts to leave El Salvador, narrated playwright style. It's truly innovative writing which the accomplished Moya carries off with ease, while simultaneously managing to let the serious, yet politically recalcitrant, Pericles dominate the work, despite his near total absence from any of the events recorded." Metro Eireann

Castillo, Linda

Breaking silence; 1st ed.; Minotaur Books 2011 320p (Kate Burkholder thrillers)

ISBN 9780312374990

LC 2011005103

When the fatal accidents of three Amish farmers are proven to be murders, former Amish woman Kate investigates a possible link between the killings and recent hate crimes, a case that is complicated by a dark secret and her precarious relationship with agent John Tomasetti. (Publisher's note)

"In addition to creating exceptionally well drawn characters and crafting a gripping plot that takes some shocking turns on the way to a heart-pounding conclusion, Castillo probes with keen sensitivity the emotional toll taken by police work." Booklist

Castillo, Linda

Gone missing; a novel. Linda Castillo. Minotaur Books 2012 277 p. (Kate Burkholder thrillers)

ISBN 0312658567; 9780312658564; 9781250010902

LC 2012005483

Author Linda Castillo tells the story of a missing Amish teenager on Rumspringa. "A missing child is a nightmare to all parents, and never more so than in the Amish community, where family ties run deep. When the search for the presumed runaway turns up a dead body, the case quickly becomes a murder investigation. And chief of Police Kate Burkholder knows that in order to solve this case she will have to call upon everything she has to give not only as a

cop, but as a woman whose own Amish roots run deep."
(Publisher's note)

Castillo, Linda
Her last breath; Linda Castillo. Minotaur Books
2013 320 p. (hardcover) $25.99
ISBN 0312658575; 9780312658571
LC 2013006979
In this book by Linda Castillo "an . . . Amish woman .
. .is the central figure in a story that reveals a dark side of
Painters Mill and its . . . Amish world. What . . . seems like
a tragic . . . car accident suddenly takes on a more sinister
cast as evidence emerges that nothing about the crash is accidental. Desperate to find out who killed her best friend's
husband and why, Kate begins to suspect she is . . . on the
trail of a cold blooded killer." (Publisher's note)

Castillo, Linda
Sworn to silence. Minotaur Books 2009 336 p.
(Kate Burkholder thrillers)
ISBN 978-0-312-37497-6; 0-312-37497-6
LC 2008-45671
Kate Burkholder, a former Amish resident of Painters
Mill, is returning as police chief sixteen years after a series
of brutal murders took place there, but when a new victim is
found under her watch, she struggles with a secret that could
hurt both her and her family. (Publisher's note)
"Deeply flawed characters in a distinctive setting make
this a crackling good series opener." Booklist

Castro, Joy
Hell or high water; a novel. Joy Castro. Thomas
Dunne Books 2012 352 p. (hardcover) $25.99
ISBN 1250004578; 9781250004574; 9781250015112
LC 2012009377
In "this suspense novel . . . the central crime is the kidnapping of a college girl from a packed restaurant. The nerve
center for the book is the features section of the New Orleans
Times-Picayune, where heroine Nola Céspedes churns out
entertainment pieces and yearns for an actual news story.
Her editor assigns her to an in-depth feature on the rehabilitation of sex offenders. As Nola (her Cuban single mother
thought the name would give her daughter roots) interviews
victims and offenders, she realizes that her story is evolving
into an investigation of the college girl's disappearance and
probable fate. Most of the book follows Nola on her interviews." (Booklist)

Cather, Willa
★ **Death** comes for the archbishop. Knopf 1992
xxvii, 297p $17; pa $11.95
ISBN 0-679-41319-7; 0-679-72889-9 pa
First published 1927
"Bishop Jean Latour and his vicar Father Joseph Vaillant together create pioneer missions and organize the new
diocese of New Mexico. . . . The two combine to triumph
over the apathy of the Hopi and Navajo Indians, the opposition of corrupt Spanish priests, and adverse climatic and
topographic conditions. They are assisted by Kit Carson and
by such devoted Indians as the guide Jacinto. When Vaillant
goes as a missionary bishop to Colorado, they are finally
separated, but Latour dies soon after his friend, universally

revered and respected, to lie in state in the great Santa Fe cathedral that he himself created." Oxford Companion to Am
Lit. 6th edition

Cather, Willa
Early novels and stories. Library of Am. 1987
1336p $40
ISBN 0-940450-39-9
LC 86-10704
Omnibus edition of four novels: O pioneers! (1913); The
song of the lark (1915); My Antonia (1918); One of ours
(1922) and the story collection—The troll garden (1905)

Cather, Willa
Later novels. Library of Am. 1990 988p
ISBN 0-940450-52-6
LC 89-64130

Cather, Willa
A lost lady. Knopf 1923 173p
"The story of Marian Forrester is told by Niel Herbert,
a Midwestern youth. Married to rugged old empire-builder
Captain Forrester, Marian's graciousness sets her much
above her commonplace neighbors. She becomes the lover
of his friend, Frank Ellinger, however; and after the Captain's death due to a stroke, the lover of Ivy Peters, the man
who acquires her home. Peters marries, and the impoverished Marian returns to the West, a 'lost lady' in the eyes
of her youthful admirer, Niel. He later hears that Marian,
married to a wealthy Englishman, won the respect and admiration of all in her new surroundings." Haydn. Thesaurus
of Book Dig

Cather, Willa
★ **My** Antonia; with an introduction by Lucy
Hughes-Hallett. Knopf 1996 xxxiii, 272p $20
ISBN 0-679-44727-X
LC 96-223945
First published 1918 by Houghton Mifflin
"Told by Jim Burden, a New York lawyer recalling his
boyhood in Nebraska, the story concerns Antonia Shimerda,
who came with her family from Bohemia to settle on the
prairies of Nebraska. The difficulties related to pioneering
and the integration of immigrants into a new culture are
clearly portrayed." Shapiro. Fic for Youth. 3d edition

Cather, Willa
★ **O** pioneers! edited with an introduction and
notes by Marilee Lindemann. Oxford University
Press 2008 xxxi, 179p (Oxford world's classics)
pa $9.95
ISBN 978-0-19-955232-0
LC 2009-291007
First published 1913 by Houghton Mifflin
"The heroic battle for survival of simple pioneer folk in
the Nebraska country of the 1880's. John Bergson, a Swedish farmer, struggles desperately with the soil but dies unsatisfied. His daughter Alexandra resolves to vindicate his faith,
and her strong character carries her weak older brothers and
her mother along to a new zest for life. Years of privation,
are rewarded on the farm. But when Alexandra falls in love
with Carl Linstrum, and her family objects because he is

poor, he leaves to seek a different career. After Alexandra's younger brother Emil is killed by the jealous husband of the French girl Marie Shabata, however, Carl gives up his plans to go to the Klondike, returns to marry Alexandra and take up the life of the farm." Haydn. Thesaurus of Book Dig

Includes bibliographical references

Cather, Willa

✓ **Sapphira** and the slave girl. Knopf 1940 295p

This novel "centers on the family's matriarch, Sapphira Colbert, and her attempt to sell Nancy Till, a mixed-race slave girl. Sapphira's plot is foiled by her husband Henry and their widowed daughter Rachel Blake. A confident, strong-willed invalid, Sapphira has earned the respect of many of her slaves despite her subtle cruelty toward Nancy. Henry is a pious miller whose simple upbringing and passivity contrast with the aristocratic and manipulative nature of his wife. Henry's nephew Martin, a suave but lecherous ex-soldier, tries to seduce Nancy. Rachel, who helps Nancy flee to Canada, remains at odds with Sapphira over the issue of slavery until the death of Rachel's daughter reconciles the pair." Merriam-Webster's Ency of Lit

Cather, Willa

Shadows on the rock. Knopf 1931 280p

"A product of Cather's interest in Catholicism, this work is an episodic narrative of life in Quebec during the last days of Frontenac, centered upon the life of Cécile Auclair, a child recently emigrated from Old France." Benet's Reader's Ency of Am Lit

Cather, Willa

✓ The **song** of the lark. Houghton Mifflin 1915 580p

This novel "tells the story of Thea Kronborg, a Colorado girl, the daughter of a Swedish clergyman, who has a talent for music. She goes to Chicago to study, has an unhappy love affair with Fred Ottenburg, a wealthy young man who cannot obtain a divorce to marry her, and eventually becomes a soprano at the Metropolitan Opera House in New York City, famous for her Wagnerian roles." Reader's Ency. 3d edition

Cather, Willa

✓ **Willa** Cather's collected short fiction, 1892-1912. University of Neb. Press 1970 3v in 1

ISBN 0-8032-0770-0

First published 1965. This edition includes an attributed unsigned story: The elopement of Allen Poole

Caunitz, William J.

Chains of command. Dutton 1999 323p $23.95

ISBN 0-525-94514-8

LC 99-28778

"Christopher Newman deserves a hunk of credit for finishing the last book of his good friend William J. Caunitz, who died before he could complete the job himself. Whoever did what, this is one of the best police procedurals you're likely to read this season. The procedures are impeccable, the dialogue gleefully flouts all rules of grammar and the characters are poster children for their representative neighborhoods." N Y Times Book Rev

Caunitz, William J.

One Police Plaza. Crown 1984 369p

ISBN 0-517-55029-6

LC 83-14323

"This story details the tenacious search of a New York police detective for the murderer responsible for a heinous crime. Lt. Dan Malone is called in on the murder and is caught up in the apparent inconsistencies of the case. Despite threats, direct orders and attempts on his life, Malone refuses to back off. His tenacity pays off, . . . and he is able to solve the murder. The murder, though, includes elements of international terrorism and espionage as well as internal departmental vigilante activities." Best Sellers

The author "expertly depicts the stark reality of the police officer's life and work, and his hard-edged prose drives the story to a stunning conclusion." Booklist

Cave, Nick

The **death** of Bunny Munro. Faber and Faber 2009 278p $25

ISBN 978-0-86547-910-4; 0-86547-910-0

LC 2009-25424

"When we meet long-since-gone-to-seed Bunny Munro, he's shacked up with the latest prostitute, multitasking by phoning to comfort his mentally disturbed wife Libby. A sex-obsessed peddler of beauty products, Bunny numbs himself by limiting his input to the next selfish pleasure. Returning home, he finds Libby has slashed all his clothing and hung herself in a locked bathroom. Instead of comforting their nine-year-old son Bunny Junior, the once-charming lothario fills himself with poisons, packs his bonnet full of inventory and hits the road with his son for a series of misguided lessons about manhood. . . . Profane and profound by turns—not for everyone, but Cave still knows how to command an audience." Kirkus

Celine, Louis-Ferdinand

✓ ★ **Journey** to the end of the night; translated from the French by John H. P. Marks. Little, Brown 1934 509p

Original French edition, 1932

"Ferdinand Bardamu, the cynical, disillusioned hero, wanders aimlessly through war-torn Europe, surrounded by destruction and putrefaction. Man, as Céline portrays him, attempts to flee from the solitude of his existence and the impossibility of helping his fellow humans but succeeds only in embracing evil and death. The novel caused a scandal when it was published because of the coarseness of its language and the unrelieved blackness of its pessimism. Yet the language is a highly original attempt to reproduce the proletarian argot that reflects the horror and intimacy of war, and the pessimism shows Céline's desire to arouse the reader and make him aware of his condition." Reader's Ency. 4th edition

Celona, Marjorie

Y; a novel. by Marjorie Celona. Free Press 2013 350p.

ISBN 9781451674385; 9781451674422

LC 2012009396

This book by Marjorie Celona is "about a wise-beyond-her-years foster child abandoned as a newborn on the doorstep of the local YMCA. . . . Bounced between foster homes,

Shannon endures abuse and neglect until she finally finds stability with Miranda, a kind but no-nonsense single mother. . . .Yet Shannon defines life on her own terms, refusing to settle down, and never stops longing to uncover her roots." (Publisher's note)

A **Century** of great Western stories; edited by John Jakes. Forge 2000 525p hardcover o.p. pa $18.95
ISBN 0-312-86986-X; 0-312-86985-1 pa
LC 99-462096

This anthology of 30 short stories includes pieces by such writers as Owen Wister, Zane Grey, Max Brand, Bill Pronzini, Elmer Kelton and Marcia Muller.

"Romance, murder, action, mystery and suspense are mixed with hefty doses of moral dilemma, guilt and redemption in these carefully plotted tales. . . . Many of the stories are appearing here for the first time since they were published in the pulps of the '30s, '40s and '50s, but their appeal is as fresh as ever." Publ Wkly

Includes bibliographical references

Cervantes Saavedra, Miguel de

★ **Don** Quixote de la Mancha; [by] Miguel de Cervantes; translated, with a critical text based on the first editions of 1605 and 1615, and with variant readings, variorum notes, and an introduction by Samuel Putnam. Modern Library 1998 xl, 1239p $25.95
ISBN 0-679-60286-0
LC 97-47415

Original Spanish edition, published in two parts, 1605 and 1615

"Originally conceived as a comic satire against the chivalric romances then in literary vogue, the novel describes realistically what befalls an elderly knight who, his head bemused by reading romances, sets out on his old horse Rosinante, with his pragmatic squire Sancho Panza, to seek adventure. In the process, he also finds love in the person of the pleasant Dulcinea. Contemporaries evidently did not take the book as seriously as later generations have done, but by the end of the 17th century it was deemed highly significant, especially abroad. It came to be seen as a mock epic in prose, and the 'grave and serious air' of the author's irony was much admired. In the history of the modern novel the role of Don Quixote is recognized as seminal." Merriam-Webster's Ency of Lit

Cervantes Saavedra, Miguel de

Three exemplary novels; translated by Samuel Putnam; illustrated by Luis Quintanilla. Viking 1950 xxi, 232p il

Part of a collection first published 1613 in Spain

Rinconete and Cortadillo is a picaresque novella about thieves in early 17th century Seville. Man of glass is a philosophical tale set in 17th century Italy about a man intent on exposing the lie upon which human existence is based. The colloquy of the dogs describes life in 17th century Spain

Chabon, Michael

★ The **amazing** adventures of Kavalier and Clay; a novel. Random House 2000 639p $26.95
ISBN 0679450041
LC 00-29063

Joe Kavalier, a Czech war refugee, and his American-born cousin Sammy Clay are {this} novel's protagonists. They create a comic-book crusader known as the Escapist. . . . A young artist with Harry Houdini's ability to pick locks while holding his breath, Kavalier has escaped Nazi-occupied Czechoslovakia by hiding in a coffin containing the mythic Golem of Prague." (Time)

"Themes are masterfully explored, leaving the book's sense of humor intact and characters so highly developed they could walk off the page." Newsweek

Chabon, Michael

★ **Telegraph** Avenue; a novel. Michael Chabon; photographs by Malik Johnson. 1st ed. Harper 2012 480 p. (hardcover) $27.99; (trade paperback) $15.99; (ebook) $21.99; (paperback) $27.99
ISBN 0061493341; 9780061493348; 9780061493355; 9780062124609; 9780062201454 (large print)
LC 2012001355

This book by Michael Chabon is "anchored by Brokeland Records, a funky used-vinyl paradise. . . . The proprietors are . . . Archy Stallings and high-strung Nat Jaffe, whose wives, too, work together, in a midwifery partnership. . . . A difficult birth puts Gwen and Aviva's business in jeopardy, just as Archy and Nat face potentially insurmountable competition in the form of a planned megastore." (Booklist)

Chabon, Michael

The **Yiddish** policemen's union; a novel. HarperCollins Publishers 2007 414p $26.95
ISBN 978-0-00-714982-7; 0-00-714982-4
LC 2006-49751

"Though the ultimate secret behind the murder that kick-starts the story involves a religious-political scheme that tips over clumsily into surreal satire, the remainder of the book is so authoritatively and minutely imagined that the reader, absorbed in the plight of [the author's] shambling hero, really doesn't mind. . . . Mr. Chabon has so thoroughly conjured the fictional world of Sitka—its history, culture, geography, its incestuous and byzantine political and sectarian divisions—that the reader comes to take its existence for granted." N Y Times (Late N Y Ed)

Champlin, Tim

Beecher island; a western story. Five Star 2010 218p $25.95
ISBN 978-1-59414-830-9
LC 2009-50455

"Kansas 1868. Matt Talbot is one of a trio of scouts who are meeting with a Cheyenne chief, Bull Bear. After the meeting, some renegade Cheyennes attack the scouts, killing one and leaving another for dead. Talbot manages to escape in one piece, but he soon learns that making his way out of this now-hostile territory unscathed is only the beginning. Surviving the attack will require more than being physically unharmed, as putting his near-death experience behind him is a lot tougher than he'd imagined it would be. The prolific Champlin turns in another deft performance, combining sharply defined characters with a solid story and just the right amount of period detail. An engaging western but also one that delivers plenty of psychological insight." Booklist

Chandler, Raymond

★ The **big** sleep. Knopf 1939 277p

"A tale of degeneracy in southern California, in which two Hollywood heiresses become mixed up in blackmail and murder; and Philip Marlowe is the private detective, who tells the story." Washington, D.C. Public Libr

Chandler, Raymond

The **high** window. Knopf 1942 240p

"This early exploit of Philip Marlowe's is certainly high in the merit list. The Pasadena scene, the characterization, the tough-yet-literate style match the complex plot, involving counterfeiting and blackmail. Just how the photograph of the victim was obtained is glossed over, but all other details are clearly etched." Barzun. Cat of Crime. Rev and enl edition

Chandler, Raymond

The **lady** in the lake. Knopf 1943 216p

"A young wife has been missing for a month and Marlowe is hired by the husband whom she is about to leave for another man. The exposition of situation and character is done with remarkable pace and skill. . . . The scene shifts to Little Fawn Lake, where talk between a local woman, the caretaker of the missing wife's cabin, and Marlowe produces speculation about the absent girl, her lover, and also the missing wife of the caretaker; whereupon comes the dramatic discovery of the corpse in the lake. It is 'not' Marlowe's quarry. From then on this superb tale moves through a maze of puzzles and disclosures to its perfect conclusion. Marlowe makes a greater use of physical clues and ratiocination in this exploit than in any other. It is Chandler's masterpiece and true detection." Barzun. Cat of Crime. Rev and enl edition

Chandler, Raymond

Later novels and other writings. Library of Am. 1995 1076p $35

ISBN 1-883011-08-6

LC 94-43705

The lady in the lake and The long goodbye are entered separately; The little sister is included in The midnight Raymond Chandler. In Playback (1958), "Marlowe is weakening (by his own standards), since he takes on an impossible girl who is running away from a quite imaginary threat and forces her to trust him. There is some silly back-and-forth with $5,000 of traveler's checks, a double fornication without much zest, and at last a transatlantic phone call summoning Marlowe to marry his true love." Barzun. Cat of Crime. Rev and enl ed

Chandler, Raymond

★ The **long** goodbye. Houghton Mifflin 1953 316p

Detective Philip Marlowe provides moral support for Terry Lennox who is running away to Mexico because he thinks he committed a murder

This novel is one of Chandler's "most meticulously plotted and by some stretches his most corrosive. What he gives us here is painful if exciting pleasure." N Y Her Trib Books

Chandler, Raymond

Raymond Chandler; collected stories. with an introduction by John Bayley. Knopf 2002 xxxvii, 1299p $27.50

ISBN 0-375-41500-9

"To read these 25 stories, 22 of which were originally published in the 1930s, consecutively is to watch Chandler's craft develop. . . . Only Chandler fanatics will want to read every word of this encyclopedic volume, but anyone with any interest in the history of hard-boiled fiction should sample its groundbreaking wares." Booklist

Includes bibliographical references

Chandler, Raymond

Stories and early novels. Library of Am. 1995 1199p $35

ISBN 1-883011-07-8

LC 94-45462

The big sleep and The high window are entered separately. Pulp stories includes the following titles: Blackmailers don't shoot; Smart-aleck kill; Finger man; Nevada gas; Spanish blood; Guns at Cyrano's; Pick-up on Noon Street; Goldfish; Red wind; The king in yellow; Pearls are a nuisance; Trouble is my business; I'll be waiting

Farewell, my lovely (1940), a mystery featuring Philip Marlowe, is a "model of complexity kept under control, with a holocaust at the end. Its contents are the now familiar ones of political and personal corruption, double-crossing, and the woman killer." Barzun. Cat of Crime. Rev and enl edition

Chang, Lan Samantha

All is forgotten, nothing is lost. W. W. Norton & Company 2010 208p $23.95

ISBN 978-0-393-06306-6; 0-393-06306-2

LC 2010-17503

"Among the many threads Chang elegantly pursues— the fraught relationships between mentors and students, the value of poetry, the price of ambition—it is her indelible portrait of the loneliness of artistic endeavor that will haunt readers the most in this exquisitely written novel about the poet's lot." Booklist

Chao, Patricia

Mambo peligroso; a novel. Patricia Chao. HarperCollins 2005 x, 300p o.p.; (pbk.) $13.95

ISBN 0060734175; 9780060734183

LC 202004054019

In this book, "[w]hen Catalina Ortiz Midori walks into a shabby New York dance studio for her first mambo class, she has no idea her life is about to change. A Japanese-Cuban immigrant who has lost touch with her Cuban roots, Catalina is mesmerized by the one-eyed teacher, El Tuerto, a titan of the New York mambo scene, and drawn to the dazzling technique of Wendy Cardoza, a Bronx 'mambera' who is one of its reigning queens. Catalina's apprenticeship with them, and her growing obsession with the world of mambo . . . will

. . . draw her into a sinister Miami exile scheme through her disreputable cousin Guillermo." (Publisher's note)

Includes bibliographical references

Chaon, Dan

Await your reply; a novel. Ballantine Books 2009 324p $25

ISBN 978-0-345-47602-9; 0-345-47602-6

LC 2009-21245

"Lucy is a recent high school graduate who leaves a small town in Ohio with her high-school teacher after her parents are killed. Only just above-average in intelligence, she's led to believe she's a stellar thinker by her witty, Maserati-driving, Yale-educated history teacher, George Orson. Miles is searching for his long-gone twin brother, Hayden, a probable schizophrenic. Flashbacks to the twins' childhoods reveal that Miles feels inferior to Hayden, who antagonized him throughout childhood. . . . College student Ryan, who was adopted, leaves a structured life in small-town Iowa to live with his biological father. . . . These stories, at first, present a lot of detail but not a lot of direction, but all the ink spent on backstory and character development prove to be worth it when the characters' lives intersect, and the novel turns from stories about people trying to find themselves to a page-turning mystery." Pittsburgh Post-Gazette

Charlton, Blake

Spellbound. Tor 2011 409p $24.99

ISBN 978-0-7653-1728-5; 0-7653-1728-1

LC 2011-13451

"Ten years after the events of Spellwright (2010), the physician Francesca DeVega discovers that her city of Avel is now secretly controlled by the demon Typhon, in preparation for the Disjunction, a prophesied demonic invasion. She is apparently key to Typhon's plot to recruit Nicodemus Weal, the outlaw spellwright destined to play a (as yet undefined) role in the Disjunction and whose cacography causes him to misspell most magical texts and prevents him from touching other living beings. Tensions rise as the city becomes overrun by various political, religious and magical factions who have their own beliefs about the looming Disjunction. To make matters worse, the Savanna Walker, Typhon's half-draconic creation, roams the streets, causing blindness and aphasia; a second threatened dragon remains hidden. As Francesca (at first reluctantly) joins Nicodemus in his quest to thwart Typhon, find the second dragon and recover the emerald that will cure his cacography, she learns one more devastating truth—about herself. Middle volumes are always tricky, but Charlton succeeds brilliantly here." Kirkus

Charlton, Blake

★ Spellwright. Tor 2010 350p $24.99

ISBN 978-0-7653-1727-8; 0-7653-1727-3

A "a fantastic first novel, set in an intriguing world of magic based on the written word. Charlton uses his own experiences with dyslexia to create a protagonist, Nicodemus, whose learning disability could unmake the world. Reading Spellwright as a bibliophile is a real treat, and the focus on language, reading, writing and understanding as a wizardly trait is something that seems somewhat new, and honestly, something long overdue in the fantasy realm." Io9

Charyn, Jerome

Johnny One-Eye; a tale of the American Revolution. W.W. Norton & Co. 2008 479p $25.95

ISBN 978-0-393-06497-1; 0-393-06497-2

LC 2007-34343

"What 'Johnny One-Eye' lacks in narrative momentum it handily supplies in antics and atmosphere. Here are the founding fathers out on a lark; here is the Revolution waged at the gaming table and in the bedroom. . . . Charyn hasn't woven a taut narrative from a lurching plot. What he has done is to create a rollicking tale in which — true to the dictates of the genre — our hapless rogue makes good. That he should do so in Washington's 'runt of a republic' isn't such a stretch. When you think about it, the American Revolution was something of a picaresque too." International Herald Tribune

Charyn, Jerome

The secret life of Emily Dickinson; a novel. W.W. Norton 2010 348p $24.95

ISBN 978-0-393-06856-6; 0-393-06856-0

LC 2009-38977

"Charyn's novel breezily chronicles the chaotic emotional life of Emily Dickinson. Unfazed by the challenging lack of event in his subject's biography, Charyn recasts her life, from the early years in Mount Holyoke to her death, in 1886, as a drama of desire, peopled by such figures as the handyman at school, an alcoholic scholar who introduces her to rum, and a clergyman whose sermon she attends in Philadelphia. . . . Between assignations with her various paramours, Emily agonizes over her writing, nearly goes blind, and both yearns for her father's affection and longs to escape his possessive oversight." New Yorker

Chase, Loretta Lynda

Miss Wonderful; Loretta Chase. Berkley Sensation 2004 342p $7.99

ISBN 9780425194836; 0425194833

LC 2004574938

This book tells the story of "Alistair Carsington [who] . . . wishes he didn't love women quite so much. To escape his worst impulses, he sets out for a place far from civilization: Derbyshire . . . where he hopes to kill two birds with one stone: avoid all temptation, and repay the friend who saved his life on the fields of Waterloo. But this noble aim drops him straight into opposition with Miss Mirabel Oldridge, a woman every bit as intelligent, obstinate, and devious as he—and maddeningly irresistible. Mirabel Oldridge already has her hands full keeping her brilliant and aggravatingly eccentric father out of trouble. The last thing she needs is a stunningly attractive, oversensitive and overbright aristocrat reminding her she has a heart." (lorettachase.com)

Chase, Loretta

Not quite a lady; Loretta Chase. HarperCollins 2007 372p $6.99

ISBN 0061231231; 9780061231230 pa

LC 2007583781

This romance novel follows "Darius Carsington, fifth son of the earl of Hargate, [who] spends his life in two pursuits: '(1) studying animal behavior, especially breeding and mating behavior, and (2) devoting his leisure hours to emulating this behavior'—with women. But his demanding father finds Darius's interests worthless and gives him a choice: either marry or go to work renovating his father's recently acquired countryside estate. Darius chooses the latter, making him neighbors with Lady Charlotte Hayward, a beautiful woman who's vowed never to marry. . . . Behind her vow, though, Charlotte hides a shameful 10-year-old secret that she's loathe to reveal . . . but nonetheless finds herself falling hard for Darius." (Publishers Weekly)

Chase, Loretta

Scandal wears satin; Loretta Chase. Avon 2012 371 p.

ISBN 0062100319; 9780062100313

In this novel by Loretta Chase a "family scandal has made" dressmaker Sophy Noirot "an enemy of one of society's fashion leaders, . . . leaving her little patience for a big, reckless rakes like the Earl of Longmore. . . . But when Longmore's sister, Noirot's wealthiest, favorite customer, runs away, Sophy can't let him bumble after her on his own. In hot pursuit with the one man who tempts her beyond reason, she finds desire has never slipped on so smoothly." (www.lorettachase.com)

Chase, Loretta

✓Your scandalous ways; Loretta Chase. Avon 2008 374p pa $6.99

ISBN 006123124X; 9780061231247

LC 2008-577455

"A world-weary British spy and master of disguises living in Regency Venice, James Cordier has been dispatched by the government to retrieve highly sensitive letters in courtesan Francesca Bonnard's possession. A few mishaps later, it's clear that Cordier isn't the only one wanting something from the notorious Francesca, who fled England following an affair that left her humiliated, divorced and friendless. Lord Elphick, her ex-husband, is a man with multiple mistresses and great political ambitions. Cordier's mission and Francesca's inability to ever trust a man again lead the two into a marvelously and intricately danced tango of a romance." Publ Wkly

Chase, Loretta Lynda

The last hellion; [by] Loretta Chase. Five Star 1999 393p (Five Star standard print romance series)

ISBN 0-7862-1989-0

LC 99-26433

"When Vere Mallory, the seventh Duke of Ainswood and the last of the infamous 'Mallory Hellions,' ends up in the mud after being properly slugged by an outspoken, crusading journalist of Amazonian proportions, he decides to teach her a lesson—and ends up learning a few things himself. Well-matched, appealing protagonists, a lively, witty writing style, and excellent dialog complement this compelling story that addresses some of the more relevant social issues of the Regency era." Libr J

Chase, Loretta Lynda

Lord of scoundrels. Five Star 1999 352p (Five Star standard print romance series)

ISBN 0-7862-2252-2

LC 99-45472

"A young woman sets out to save her brother from the influence of the wicked Marquess of Dain and falls under the 'Devil's' spell herself in this classic Regency-set historical." Libr J

Chase, Loretta Lynda

Silk is for seduction. Avon 2011 371p (Avon historical romance) pa $7.99

ISBN 978-0-06-163268-6

"With a sharp eye for both upper-class society and the cutthroat world of high-class London mantua makers, Chase mixes snappy dialogue, erotic tension, and the fanciful styles of the era into a sparkling love story as Marcelline's strategy ensnares not only Clevedon's patronage but his heart." Publ Wkly

Chase-Riboud, Barbara

Sally Hemings; a novel. Viking 1979 348p

ISBN 0-670-61605-2

LC 78-12682

A novel about the relationship between Thomas Jefferson and his mistress Sally Hemings, a slave, whom he lived with for thirty-eight years

"If it indeed existed, the relationship must have been much as the author depicts it in this fine first novel: a mixture of love and hate, of tenderness and cruelty, and of freedom and bondage. The book is well researched, well written, insightful, and entertaining." Libr J

Followed by The President's daughter

Chatterjee, Upamanyu

English, August; an Indian story. introduction by Akhil Sharma. New York Review Books 2006 326p (New York Review Books classics) pa $14.95

ISBN 1-59017-179-9

LC 2005-22842

First published 1988 in India

"This satiric novel chronicles the reluctant coming of age of a privileged young man who has just entered the prestigious Indian Administrative Service. Posted to a small town deep in the interior, he finds himself a foreigner in his own country, wary of cholera, defenseless against mosquitoes, and shocked by the sight of a tribal woman: 'They exist, he shrieked silently, outside arty films about tribal exploitation and agrarian reform.' In revolt, he sneaks out of meetings, pretends to be the son of Antarctic explorers, and smokes copious amounts of pot. He's an avatar of the Western slacker: overeducated, bored, plagued with doubts, and incapable of action. Still, Chatterjee's story is uniquely Indian, as he plumbs his hero's fear of being 'just one more urban Indian bewitched by America's hard sell in the Third World.'" New Yorker

Chatwin, Bruce

Utz. Viking 1989 154p

ISBN 0-670-82497-6

LC 88-40310

"The hero of Mr. Chatwin's provocative short novel is a successful survivor. He is part Jewish but has managed to survive Hitler. . . . {Utz is} required to bequeath the collection to the state, and what he does about that insult to his elegant eighteenth-century companions becomes his own peculiar final solution. Mr. Chatwin has created an intriguing proposition—that obedient passivity can amount to successful rebellion." Atlantic

Chaudhuri, Amit

The **immortals**. Alfred A. Knopf 2009 333p $25.95

ISBN 978-0-307-27022-1; 0-307-27022-X

LC 2009-24461

This novel, "set in Bombay during the nineteen-seventies and eighties, traces the relationship between the middle-class Senguptas and their music teacher, Shyamji. Nirmalya Sengupta, a son of privilege, urges purity in art—the ustads, ragas, and shrutis of Indian classical music—while Shyamji succumbs to the exigencies of the marketplace and Hindi film music. . . . Not much happens—Sengupta's father ascends the corporate ladder, his mother takes part in recitals and shyly hopes for a record contract, and Sengupta himself discovers philosophy—but Chaudhuri lovingly evokes a fractious, contradictory city caught between tradition and modernization." New Yorker

Chayefsky, Paddy

Altered states; a novel. Harper & Row 1978 184p

ISBN 0-06-010727-8

LC 77-11542

"What makes this shocking fantasy work is not only Chayefsky's dramatic skill . . . but also the authority of his prodigious research in chemistry, biology, and medicine. . . . The result is a marvelous and exciting work of the imagination." Saturday Rev

Chazin, Suzanne

Flashover. Putnam 2002 332p

ISBN 0-399-14850-7

LC 2001-48772

"Fans of Patricia Cornwell will appreciate the gritty, realistic details Chazin provides concerning the techniques used to investigate suspicious fires. The appealing main character and the fast pace will keep readers turning the pages into the wee hours." Booklist

Cheever, John

★ **Bullet** Park; a novel. Knopf 1969 245p

LC 69-14730

The author "mixes compassion and high comedy brilliantly, holding up to view an America that is fatally schizoid in many of its manifestations. The confrontation that finally comes between Hammer and Nailles is a horrifying dark allegory of our times." Publ Wkly

Cheever, John

Collected stories and other writings. Library of America 2009 1040p $35

ISBN 978-1-59853-034-6

LC 2008-935565

Cheever, John

Complete novels. Library of America 2009 933p $35

ISBN 978-1-59853-035-3

LC 2008-935642

The Wapshot chronicle (1957) depicts a "venerable Massachusetts family in decline. . . . The Wapshot scandal [1964] continues their story by moving beyond the archetypal Yankee village of St. Botolphs and taking its characters abroad and into the planned communities of postwar America, quietly teetering on the brink of nuclear Armageddon. . . . The taut satire Bullet Park (1969), with its scathing indictment of suburbia, shows Cheever taking his novelistic gifts in a new, darker direction. But it scarcely could have prepared readers for the stunning achievement of Falconer [1977], a prison novel unlike anything in Cheever's fiction. . . . At the novel's center is Ezekiel Farragut, a college professor and drug addict serving time for murdering his brother. Within the dehumanizing confinement of the prison, he falls in love with a hustler named Jody. . . . Oh What a Paradise It Seems (1982), the novella with which the volume concludes, is a tale of a May–December relationship that also sounds an elegiac note of protest against the degradation of the environment." Publisher's note

Cheever, John

★ **Falconer**. Knopf 1977 211p

ISBN 0-394-41071-8

"John Cheever uses prison as an emblem for the world in this stunning novel about love, mysticism, and man's relationship with God. . . . The surface events include a prison riot, a massacre of prison cats by an enraged guard who had his steak stolen by one of them, a homosexual love affair, and a couple of breathtaking escapes, one by Farragut's lover, who dons a cassock to escape in a helicopter with a visiting bishop. Woven in and out are threads of Farragut's past life, his relationship to his wife and the other women in his life, the secret behind his hatred for his brother." Choice

Cheever, John

Oh, what a paradise it seems. Knopf 1982 99p

ISBN 0-394-51334-7

LC 81-48109

"Ever more boldly the celebrant of the grand poetry of life, Cheever, once a taut and mordant chronicler of urban and suburban disappointments, now speaks in the cranky, granular, impulsive, confessional style of our native wise men and exhorters since Emerson. The pitch of his final page is positively Transcendental." New Yorker

Cheever, John

★ The **Wapshot** chronicle. Harper & Row 1957 307p

"Based in part on Cheever's adolescence in New England, the novel takes place in a small Massachusetts fishing village and relates the breakdown of both the Wapshot family and the town. Part One focuses on Leander, a gentle ferryboat operator harried by his tyrannical wife and his eccentric sister; he eventually swims out to sea and never returns. Part Two chronicles the disastrous lives of Leander's sons, Coverly and Moses. Told in a comic rather than a tragic vein, the novel uses experimental prose techniques to convey a nostalgic vision of a lost world." Merriam-Webster's Ency of Lit

Followed by The Wapshot scandal

Cheever, John

The **Wapshot** scandal. Harper & Row 1964 309p

This sequel to The Wapshot chronicle "continues the tale of the decline of the fortunes of the Wapshot family and of the mythical New England town of St. Botolphs. The 'scandal' is the discovery that Aunt Honora has never paid her income taxes, and the principal disaster stems from the long-standing oversight. The novel also traces the misfortunes of two Wapshot nephews, Coverly, a public relations man at a missile site, and Moses, an alcoholic. Despite the somberness of the main line of events, the book is not depressing; it is lighted by the high gloss of Mr. Cheever's style, by glints of humor, and especially by the warm glow of human fortitude under stress." Libr J

Chekhov, Anton Pavlovich

Early short stories, 1883-1888; edited by Shelby Foote; translated by Constance Garnett. Modern Lib. 1999 642p

ISBN 0-679-60317-4

LC 98-20049

Following his introduction Foote presents seventy of Chekhov's early stories

Chekhov, Anton Pavlovich

Later short stories, 1888-1903; edited by Shelby Foote; translated by Constance Garnett. Modern Lib. 1999 628p

ISBN 0-679-60316-6

LC 98-20048

This volume contains forty-two short stories

Chekhov, Anton Pavlovich

Longer stories from the last decade; {by} Anton Chekhov; translated by Constance Garnett. Modern Lib. 1993 611p

ISBN 0-679-60063-9

LC 93-14536

Chen, Da

Brothers; a novel. Shaye Areheart Books 2006 421p $25

ISBN 1-4000-9728-2

LC 2005-36267

"Da Chen has achieved something that sounds simple but is, in fact, close to impossible: he brings the Western reader into the guts of the conflict, the agonies and the revelations of events that shook the world's largest population in the 35 years after 1960, when Shento and his brother were born. Make no mistake, this is not contemporary history retold. This is magnificent fiction. It transcends the events it chronicles and does what fiction at its best should do: it changes our internal landscape." Washington Post Book World

Chen, Pauline A.

The **red** chamber; Pauline A. Chen. 1st ed. Alfred A. Knopf 2012 381 p. (ebook) $80.85; (paperback) $16.00; (hardcover) $26.95

ISBN 0307701573; 9780307958419; 9780307946560; 9780307701572

LC 2012005050

This book by Pauline Chen presents a "reimagining of the Chinese classic 'Dream of the Red Chamber,' set . . . [in] eighteenth-century Beijing. . . . When orphaned Daiyu leaves her home in the provinces to take shelter with her cousins in the Capital, she is drawn into a world of opulent splendor, presided over by the ruthless, scheming Xifeng and the prim, repressed Baochai. . . . She finds herself entangled in a web of intrigue and hidden passions." (Publisher's note)

Cheng, Bill

★ **Southern** Cross the Dog; Bill Cheng. HarperCollins 2013 336 p. (hardcover) $25.99

ISBN 0062225006; 9780062225009

This book, by Bill Cheng, follows how "the bonds between three childhood friends are upended by the Great Mississippi Flood of 1927. In its aftermath, one young man must choose between the lure of the future and the claims of the past. Having lost virtually everything in the fearsome storm--home, family, first love--Robert Chatham embarks on an odyssey that takes him through the deep South, from the desperation of a refugee camp . . . into the Mississippi hinterland." (Publisher's note)

Chenoweth, Emily

Hello goodbye; a novel. Random House 2009 273p $25

ISBN 1400065178; 9781400065172

LC 2008-38496

"In the winter of 1990, Helen Hansen—counselor, wife, and mother in the prime of her life—is diagnosed with an inoperable brain tumor. The following August, Helen, her husband Elliott, and their daughter, Abby, a freshman in college, take a trip to northern New Hampshire, where Helen will be able to say goodbye." (Publisher's note)

"Elliott is the headmaster of a shabby private school in Ohio; his wife, Helen, is a juvenile-court counsellor. When a doctor tells Elliott that his wife has a terminal brain tumor, he plans a vacation at a grand New England hotel. . . . Old friends are invited, for what they learn will be their final visit with Helen, but neither she nor her daughter, Abby, is told how sick Helen really is. Chenoweth writes with a restraint that allows minor gestures to become elegantly weighted with meaning." New Yorker

Cherryh, C. J.

The **collected** short fiction of C.J. Cherryh. DAW Bks. 2004 642p $23.95

ISBN 0-7564-0217-4

"Cherryh demonstrates a fine flair for compact storytelling that encompasses science, fantasy, and myth." Libr J

Cherryh, C. J.

Finity's End. Warner Bks. 1997 471p

ISBN 0-446-52072-1

LC 96-37992

In this Merchanter universe novel, "The ship Finity's End, seriously shorthanded after the Union-Alliance War, returns to the Pell station to reclaim Fletcher Neihart, who grew up on the station after his mother was left there during the war. Young Fletcher, however, has a real gift for dealing with Pell's native inhabitants and no interest in being frog-marched aboard Finity's End or adjusting to the role of a new crew member." Booklist

"Despite an abundance of exciting action, this is character-driven drama that represents old-fashioned SF at its very best." Publ Wkly

Cherryh, C. J.

✓★ **Foreigner**; a novel of first contact. DAW Bks. 1994 378p

ISBN 0-88677-590-6

LC 94-179662

"Cherryh plays her strongest suit in this exploration of human/alien contact, producing an incisive study-in-contrast of what it means to be human in a world where trust is non-existent." Libr J

Followed by Invader

Chesnutt, Charles Waddell

★ **Stories**, novels, & essay; Stories, novels, & essays. [by] Charles W. Chesnutt. Library of Am. 2002 939p $35

ISBN 1-931082-06-5

LC 2001-38120

The house behind the cedars (1900) is "concerned with a light-complexioned black woman who is undecided whether to enjoy comfort as a white man's mistress or the sincere love of a black man." Oxford Companion to Am Lit. 6th edition

Includes bibliographical references

Chesterton, G. K.

Father Brown mystery stories; selected and edited with an introduction by Raymond T. Bond. Dodd, Mead 1962 246p

Chesterton, G. K.

✓The **Father** Brown omnibus; with a preface by Auberon Waugh. Dodd, Mead 1983 993p

ISBN 0-396-08159-2

First omnibus edition published 1933; this is a reissue of the 1951 edition analyzed in Short story index, with a new preface by Auberon Waugh

Chesterton, G. K.

✓The **innocence** of Father Brown. Lane 1911 334p

Contents: The blue cross; The secret garden; The queer feet; The flying stars; The invisible man; The honour of Israel Gow; The wrong shape; The sins of Prince Saradine; The hammer of God; The eye of Apollo; The sign of the broken sword; The three tools of death

Cheuse, Alan

✓**Song** of slaves in the desert. Sourcebooks Landmark 2011 500p $25.99

ISBN 978-1-402242-99-1; 1-402242-99-9

LC 2010-48514

"Sent by his father to observe and evaluate his uncle's South Carolina rice plantation as a possible business investment, New York Jew and fledgling entrepreneur Nathaniel Pereira is horrified by his first brush with the brutal realities of slavery. Especially struck by the irony of how a people who themselves lived in bondage for so long could now own slaves, he is torn between his conscience and his duty. His moral dilemma becomes even more complex after he becomes captivated by Liza, a beautiful slave who harbors a shattering secret. A parallel story, passed through the generations from mother to daughter, chronicles the odyssey of one slave family from sixteenth-century Timbuktu to the antebellum South." Booklist

Includes bliographical references and index.

Chevalier, Tracy

✓**Burning** bright. Dutton 2007 311p $24.95

ISBN 978-0-525-94978-7; 0-525-94978-X

LC 2006-26898

A novel set in late 17th-century London. "After a tragic death in the family, the Kellaways are persuaded by a traveling circus owner to move to the bustling city, where they discover that they live next door to the famous William Blake: printer, poet, and political radical. A streetwise girl named Maggie befriends the youngest boy, Jem, and their coming-of-age adventures eventually provide material for Blake's Songs of Innocence and Experience. In addition, the French Revolution has made everyone jittery, and the family is soon caught up in the excitement and uncertainty of political unrest; they also face economic hardship, struggling daily to earn enough to stay together. Chevalier's vivid descriptions and unusual mix of characters make this story an easy pleasure to read." Libr J

Chevalier, Tracy

✓★ **Girl** with a pearl earring. Dutton 2000 240p hardcover o.p. pa $16

ISBN 0-525-94527-X; 0-452-28702-2 pa

LC 99-32493

Chevalier examines the world of artist Johannes Vermeer and the city of Delft in the 17th century through the eyes of Griet, an illiterate 17-year-old. In this novel the fictional character of Griet, a servant in the Vermeer household, acts as the model for the artist's portrait Girl With a Pearl Earring.

The author "has done very well in creating the feel of a society with sharp divisions of status and creed. . . . Griet is a memorable character—reserved, wary, observant, and, although she does not know it, afflicted with a serious and ultimately dangerous crush on her employer. The situation makes a fine story, which is exceptionally well told." Atl Mon

Chevalier, Tracy, 1962-

✓★ The **last** runaway; Tracy Chevalier. Dutton 2013 320 p. $26.95

ISBN 0525952993; 9780525952992

LC 2012034693

This is New York Times bestselling author Tracy Chevalier's seventh novel. Here, "leaving home after suffering a disappointment, English Quaker Honor Bright ends up in 1850 Ohio, where she finds folks—even Quakers—pragmatically unprincipled and becomes involved in the Underground Railroad." (Library Journal)

"Chevalier offers a cast of strong characters wrestling with thorny personalities, the harsh realities of the frontier, and the legal and moral complexities of American slavery." Booklist

Chevalier, Tracy

✓**Remarkable** creatures. Dutton 2010 312p $26.95

ISBN 978-0-525-95145-2; 0-525-95145-8

LC 2009047614

The author provides the "minutiae of everyday life and an evocative, almost visceral response to the visual world. . . . But the vividness of context, of object and image, engage the reader far more than the urgency of character. This book works better as tableau than as living narrative." Cleveland Plain Dealer

Chiang, Ted

✓The **life** cycle of software objects. Subterannean Press 2010 150p $25

ISBN 978-1-59606-317-4; 1-59606-317-3

"Ana Alvarado is a former zookeeper turned software tester. When Blue Gamma offers her a job as animal trainer for their digients—digital entities, spawned by genetic algorithms to provide pets for players in the future virtual reality of Data Earth—she discovers an unexpected affinity for her charges. So does Derek Brooks, an animator who designs digient body parts. The market for digients develops and expands, cools and declines after the pattern of the software industry. Meanwhile Ana, Derek, and their friends become increasingly attached to their cute and talkative charges, who are neither pets nor children but something wholly new. But as Blue Gamma goes bust and Data Earth itself fades into obsolescence, Ana and the remaining digient keepers face a series of increasingly unpleasant dilemmas, their worries sharpened by their charges' growing awareness of the world beyond their pocket universe, and the steady unwinding of their own lives and relationships into middle-aged regrets for lost opportunities." Publ Wkly

Chiaverini, Jennifer

✓ ★ **Mrs.** Lincoln's dressmaker; a novel. Jennifer Chiaverini. Dutton 2013 352 p. (hardcover) $26.95

ISBN 0525953612; 9780525953616

LC 2012036366

In this novel, freed slave Elizabeth "Lizzy" Keckley "gains fame as a dressmaker for Northerners and Southerners alike . . . . She becomes the modiste for Mary Todd Lincoln and is privy to the innermost workings of the Lincoln White House, Mary Todd's reckless spending, President Lincoln's death, and his widow's subsequent penury. When Lizzy writes a memoir about her experiences, she's denigrated by the public." (Publishers Weekly)

Child, Lee

61 hours; a Reacher novel. Delacorte Press 2010 383p $28

ISBN 0-385-34058-3; 978-0-385-34058-8

LC 2009-52804

In this installment Jack Reacher "enters a small South Dakota burg during a snowstorm. First he helps a busload of senior citizens. Then he assists local cops seeking to protect the key witness in an upcoming trial against a crystal-meth ring. Just to keep things lively, Child tosses in a crooked cop conspiring with the bad guys, a riot at a local prison, a ruthless Mexican drug lord, and Susan Turner, a brunette who's working Reacher's old job as head of an Army special-investigations unit (Susan, who digs up a telling morsel in Reacher's history, seems poised to play a significant role in future volumes). Child is a superb craftsman of suspense, juggling several plots and keeping his herrings well-rouged. . . . Best of all, this is a rare series book that reads like a stand-alone. Everything you need to know about Jack Reacher is contained within its pages." Entertainment Wkly

Child, Lee

The **affair**; a Reacher novel. Delacorte Press 2011 405p $28

ISBN 978-0-385-34432-6

"In this 16th novel in the . . . Reacher franchise, Child goes back to small-town Mississippi in 1997. Women have been murdered near a secret Ranger base. The Rangers are suspected, and the official investigation is a mess. Reacher is sent to town disguised as a bum to keep one eye on what might be a flawed army investigation, the other on a series of similar killings in the town, and if he had a third eye, he would use it to cover his back. . . . Exciting and suspenseful, with deceit and cover-ups, violence, and sex, this is another great entry in Child's compelling series." Libr J

Child, Lee

Bad luck and trouble; a Jack Reacher novel. Delacorte Press 2007 377p $26

ISBN 978-0-385-34055-7; 0-385-34055-9

LC 2006-31931

"Throughout the book, Reacher remains fanatically interested in codes, fractions, cube roots and probabilities. The [author] who devises all this must also be acutely aware of formulas, because he is smart enough to avoid them. . . . In the world of Mr. Child's novels, what matters, and dazzles, is what works on the page." N Y Times (Late N Y Ed)

Child, Lee

Echo burning. Putnam 2001 354p

ISBN 0-399-14726-8

LC 00-45910

Jack Reacher is "hitching a ride in Lubbock, Tex., when the Mexican wife of a sadistic landowner picks him up and gets his macho dander up with an ugly tale of physical abuse and mental torture. Although he refuses to play hit man for Carmen Greer, he agrees to hang around the family spread, keep the nasty in-laws at bay and see what happens when her husband gets out of prison for tax evasion. But things go wrong, and soon Reacher is looking for a criminal lawyer." N Y Times Book Rev

"Reacher is a one-man wrecking crew nourished only by the hunt. For anyone who thinks the hard-boiled genre is growing soft around the edges." Booklist

Child, Lee

The **enemy**; a Jack Reacher novel. Delacorte Press 2004 393p $25

ISBN 0-385-33667-5

LC 2003-65282

"Known for his hold-your-breath action scenes, Child proves equally adept at portraying how a criminal investigation uses the smallest of building blocks . . . to construct a compelling circumstantial case." Booklist

Child, Lee

The **hard** way; a Jack Reacher novel. Delacorte Press 2006 371p $25

ISBN 0-385-33669-1

LC 2005-51946

"The imperfections Child adds to his protagonist's character this time out, such as Reacher's not catching onto all of the questionable dealings early on in the novel, give Reacher a much-needed vulnerability. . . . [This is a] breathless, well-paced thriller that will satisfy die-hard fans and newcomers." Denver Post

Child, Lee

Nothing to lose. Delacorte Press 2008 407p $27

ISBN 978-0-385-34056-4; 0-385-34056-7

LC 2007-43735

Jack Reacher "hitchhikes into Colorado, where he finds himself crossing the metaphorical and physical line that divides the small towns of Hope and Despair. Despair lives up to its name; all Reacher wants is a cup of coffee, but what he gets is attacked by four thugs and thrown in jail on a vagrancy charge. After he's kicked out of town, Reacher reacts in his usual manner—he goes back and whips everybody's butt and busts up the town's police force. In the process, he discovers, with the help of a good-looking lady cop from Hope, that a nearby metal processing plant is part of a plan that involves the war in Iraq and an apocalyptic sect bent on ushering in the end-time. With his powerful sense of justice, dogged determination and the physical and mental skills to overcome what to most would be overwhelming odds, Jack Reacher makes an irresistible modern knight-errant." Publ Wkly

Child, Lee

One shot; a Jack Reacher novel. Delacorte Press 2005 376p $25

ISBN 0-385-33668-3

LC 2004-58246

"Mr. Child's idea of heroism has nihilism around the edges but a fierce, fighting spirit at its core. In marked contrast to the brooding figures who otherwise dominate contemporary detective stories, Reacher is not one for self-doubt. His is a two-fisted decency. But Mr. Child also gives him amazing powers of deduction, a serious conscience and the occasional touch of tenderness. It's a wildly improbable mixture, one that can't be beat." N Y Times (Late N Y Ed)

Child, Lee

Persuader; a Jack Reacher novel. Delacorte Press 2003 342p $24.95

ISBN 0-385-33666-7

LC 2002-34965

"What makes the novel really zing, though, is Reacher's narration—aunique mix of the brainy and the brutal, of strategic thinking and explosive action, moral rumination and ruthless force, marking him as one of the most memorable heroes in contemporary thrillerdom." Publ Wkly

Child, Lee

A **wanted** man; a Reacher novel. Lee Child. Random House Inc. 2012 416p.

ISBN 9780385344333; 9780440339366

LC 2012018420

Author Lee Child's book opens with "four people in a car, hoping to make Chicago by morning. An hour behind them, a man lies stabbed to death in an old pumping station . . . Within minutes, the police are notified. Within hours, the FBI descends, laying claim to the victim without ever saying who he was or why he was there. All [protagonist] Reacher wanted was a ride to Virginia. All he did was stick out his thumb. But he soon discovers he has hitched more than a ride. He has tied himself to a massive conspiracy that makes him a threat--to both sides at once." (Amazon)

Child, Lee

Without fail. Putnam 2002 374p

ISBN 0-399-14861-2

LC 2001-48849

This "novel is a stunner, packed with extraordinary detail regarding executive protection and overlaid with a genuine mystery that will baffle even the most astute armchair crime buffs." Booklist

Child, Lee

Worth dying for; a Reacher novel. Delacorte Press 2010 384p $28

ISBN 978-0-385-34431-9; 0-385-34431-7

LC 2010-23100

In this installment, "Reacher happens into a situation tailor-made for his blend of morality and against-the-odds heroics. While passing through an isolated Nebraska town, the ex-military cop persuades the alcoholic local doctor to treat Eleanor Duncan, who's married to the abusive Seth, for a 'nosebleed.' Reacher later breaking Seth's nose prompts members of the Duncan clan, who are involved in an illegal trafficking scheme, to seek revenge. Reacher, who easily disposes of two hit men sent to get him, winds up trying to solve a decades-old case concerning a missing eight-year-old girl. . . . Crisp, efficient prose and well-rounded characterizations (at least of the guys in the white hats) raise this beyond other attempts to translate the pulse-pounding feel of the Die Hard films into prose." Publ Wkly

Childress, Mark

Crazy in Alabama. Putnam 1993 383p

ISBN 0-399-13855-2

LC 92-38334

"It is a measure of Mr. Childress's skill as a novelist—not to mention a triumphant example of style over content—

that he soon had me eating out of his hand. I don't know how he did it but he managed to confront every cliché, every convention of the genre head on and pound it into submission, so that his novel seems not only fresh and original but also positively inspired." NY Times Book Rev

Choi, Susan

A **person** of interest; a novel. Viking 2008 356p $24.95

ISBN 978-0-670-01846-8; 0-670-01846-5

LC 2007-19873

"Lee is a surly Asian-American mathematics professor, who, twice divorced and estranged from his only daughter, has spent his life at a drab state school in the Midwest, a place 'only recently somewhat renowned' for a popular computer-science professor, Rick Hendley, whose office is next door to Lee's. When Hendley is killed by a mail bomb, Lee becomes a 'person of interest' to the F.B.I., and a suspenseful confrontation in the Idaho mountains ensues. But the story's true focus is Lee's fraught sense of his past: a friend whose wife he stole, his failure to achieve youthful ambitions, his 'immigrant's sense of hopeless illegitimacy and impending exposure.'" New Yorker

Chopin, Kate

Complete novels and stories. Library of America 2002 1071p $40

ISBN 1-931082-21-9

LC 2002-19450

At fault (1890) is a melodrama set in Louisiana centered on a love triangle between a young widow, a St. Louis businessman who purchases timber rights to her plantation, and his alcoholic wife. The awakening (1899) depicts a Southern woman's revolt against her husband and her quest for sexual and emotional fulfillment

Christensen, Inger

Azorno; translated from the Danish by Denise Newman. New Directions 2009 104p pa $13.95

ISBN 978-0-8112-1657-9

LC 2009-16786

Original Swedish edition, 1967

"The book's central drama is also its opening one. It is the question of which woman meets Azorno on page eight, page eight being that of the mysterious novel within the novel ostensibly. The eponymous Azorno is cited as the protagonist of Sampel's book, yet Sampel is also called Azorno, both by himself and by the women who may or may not surround him in reality. . . . The novel's kaleidoscope of females—Xenia, Louise, Randi, Katarina, Bathsheba—all write novels or letters, but beyond existing on the page to the reader at hand (which is to say Christensen's) they are themselves written by one another in turn, defined as characters within each others' dramas. . . . It is to the novel's credit that it asks more questions than it ever answers. Just whose daydream this is we never know for sure, but at Christensen and Newman's combined best it feels like our own." Harvard Crimson

Christensen, Kate

The **Astral**; a novel. Doubleday 2011 311p $25.95

ISBN 978-0-385-53091-0; 0-385-53091-9

LC 2010049794

"The Astral is a huge, rose-colored apartment building in the rapidly gentrifying Brooklyn neighborhood of Greenpoint. For decades, it has been the . . . home of the poet Harry Qucik and his wife, Luz, who raised two children in their . . . top-floor apartment." (Publisher's note)

"A masterpiece of comedy and angst. Think Gulley Jimson of Joyce Cary's The Horses Mouth transported from 1930s London to present-day Brooklyn." Kirkus

Christensen, Kate

✓The **great** man; a novel. Doubleday 2007 305p $23.95

ISBN 978-0-385-51845-1; 0-385-51845-5

LC 2007-5927

"At the center of this snippy comedy of manners is a New York-based painter and philanderer, Oscar Feldman, whose oeuvre consists of boldly rendered female nudes. That Oscar has been dead for a few years barely matters to the constellation of elderly women in his orbit: his long-suffering wife, Abigail, who rarely leaves her Upper West Side apartment; Teddy, his soignée bohemian mistress, moldering in Greenpoint; his sister Maxine, an abstract painter who is equally preoccupied with female flesh, and considered by some a greater talent. When two feckless biographers descend, looking for the inside scoop, Oscars big secret, hanging in plain view, becomes a vehicle for both rapprochement and revelation." New Yorker

Christensen, Kate

Trouble; a novel. Doubleday 2009 320p $26

ISBN 978-0-385-52730-9; 0-385-52730-6

LC 2008-31416

"Josie Dorvillier, a Manhattan therapist, is trapped in a loveless marriage to an academic. When her best friend from college, a rock star whose best days are behind her, draws ridicule on a celebrity blog for her affair with a much younger television actor, the two friends decide to escape to Mexico City for an uncharacteristically debauched vacation of mescal, marijuana, and men. The subject matter teeters on the edge of tabloid, and the sex scenes with Latin lovers are sometimes just cheesy, but Christensen . . . generally eschews sentimentality, spinning a stylish, even occasionally suspenseful story of middle-aged sexual awakening and female friendship." New Yorker

Christie, Agatha

✓★ The **A.B.C.** murders; a Hercule Poirot mystery. Black Dog & Leventhal Publishers 2006 252p $12

ISBN 1-57912-624-3; 978-1-57912-624-7

LC 2006-45734

First published 1936 by Dodd, Mead & Company

This novel is "about a serial killer who announces his apparently unmotivated killings in advance to Poirot; the only clue is a railway guide left at the scene of each crime. In the opinion of many critics, this is one of Dame Agatha's greatest detective novels." Ency of Mystery & Detection

Christie, Agatha

✓ ★ **And** then there were none. St. Martin's Griffin 2004 264p pa $12.95

ISBN 0-312-33087-1

LC 2004-41165

First published 1939 in the United Kingdom with title: Ten little niggers; first United States edition, 1940, by Dodd, Mead. Variant title: Ten little Indians

"A tour de force on the following trapeze: invitations go out to a group of people, all of whom have been responsible for the death of someone by negligence of intent. The island on which the party is gathered is owned by the would-be avenger of all those deaths. The events and the tension produced by the gradual polishing off of the undetected culprits are beautifully done. One improbability, well hidden, makes the whole thing plausible." Barzun. Cat of Crime. Rev and enl edition

Christie, Agatha

The **body** in the library. Dodd, Mead 1942 245p

"The body that turns up in the married colonel's library is that of a dancing hostess from a neighboring seaside hotel. The setting is St. Mary Mead, whence Miss Marple has drawn her knowledge of human evil and duplicity and applies it to the case at hand, predicting a second murder and averting a third." Barzun. Cat of Crime. Rev and enl edition

Christie, Agatha

✓ ★ **Curtain**. Dodd, Mead 1975 238p

ISBN 0-396-07191-0

"In this her last book, which contrives Poirot's death proprio motu, the old grand master shows that her powers of invention and execution remained strong and fresh till the end. Her villain acts villainous in an entirely new way and from an original yet convincing motive. As for Poirot's performance, it is charged with a new purposefulness, ending in a fine display of moral conscience. The story may have one or two moments of weak writing and even an unparsable sentence, but it is an astonishing piece of work nevertheless." Barzun. Cat of Crime. Rev and enl edition

Christie, Agatha

Endless night. Dodd, Mead 1968

First published 1967 in the United Kingdom

"A sharp break with all her previous work: none of her usual detectives. No résumé would be fair since the impact of the book depends upon a skillfully worked-out volte-face involving two characters. The creator of Roger Ackroyd has done it again, in a different way, but without any pretense at detection." Barzun. Cat of Crime. Rev and enl edition

Christie, Agatha

The **Hollow**. Putnam 1992 296p

ISBN 0-399-13727-0

LC 91-31855

First published 1946; copyright renewed 1974

"A triumph of Christie's art, not so much of characterization—for the detective story does not really permit true character study—but of motive-building. That is where A.C. is unrivaled. She knows how to make plausible the divergence between action and motive that maintains uncertainty until the physical clues, the times, and other objective facts mesh with motive to disclose the culprit. The great art is to multiply the ambiguities of feeling, action, and gesture without falling into obvious patterns about greed, revenge, and the like. Here the familiar figure of the able, virile, brilliant man whom women go for is admirably sketched and provided with three possible women murderers and their possibly jealous men. In addition, an elderly femme folle very well done—and Poirot." Barzun. Cat of Crime. Rev and enl edition

Christie, Agatha

✓ **Mrs.** McGinty's dead. Dodd, Mead 1952 243p

First published 1951 in the United Kingdom with title: Blood will tell

"A Poirot story with Mrs. Oliver thrown in for humor, otherwise, an ingenious plot involving the discovery of one of the offspring of some scandals of 20 years earlier, so as to account for the murder of a charwoman who presumably found an incriminating photograph. Complex and well handled, as well as amusing." Barzun. Cat of Crime. Rev and enl edition

Christie, Agatha

✓ The **murder** at the vicarage; a detective story. Dodd, Mead 1930 319p

Colonel Protheroe, the heartily disliked squire of St Mary Mead, is the victim. The fact that his wife is desperately in love with another man seems to have supplied motive for murder on the part of two people at least. But shrewd Miss Marple points out several other possibilities

"The plot of this tale is intricate. . . . But it is well constructed and holds the reader's attention on the problem of who wanted Col. Protheroe out of the way. The byplay between the vicar and his flirtatious wife is also an amusing innovation." Barzun. Cat of Crime. Rev and enl edition

Christie, Agatha

✓ ★ **Murder** in the Calais coach. Dodd, Mead 1934 302p

A man is murdered on a train going from Istanbul to Calais. The famous detective Hercule Poirot happens to be on board and unravels the mystery

"This is the tour de force in which Agatha makes conspiracy believable and enlivens it by a really satisfying description of the Taurus Express (part of the Orient system)." Barzun. Cat of Crime. Rev and enl edition

Christie, Agatha

✓ A **murder** is announced. Dodd, Mead 1950 248p

"A well-told story—her 50th—of blackmail and murder in an English village. Miss Marple does the detecting, and the author plays very fair with the reader in the laying down of a trail leading to the unmasking of a most satisfactory least likely person." Barzun. Cat of Crime. Rev and enl edition

Christie, Agatha

The **murder** of Roger Ackroyd. Dodd, Mead 1926 306p

"Roger Ackroyd, a retired business man, is found dead in his study shortly after the suicide of the woman he was to have married. Suspicion and the police point to Ackroyd's adopted son as the murderer, but the outcome of the story is a complete surprise. As in others of Miss Christie's tales, the mystery is solved by . . . M. Poirot." Booklist

Christie, Agatha
★ The **pale** horse. Dodd, Mead 1962 242p
First published 1961 in the United Kingdom

"This story relies on Mrs. Oliver without Poirot: detection is carried out by an oldish-young scholar called Mark Easterbrook, and what he investigates is superbly organized murder compounded with black magic. A classic treatment of the paralytic suspect-cum-wheelchair is thrown in for good measure." Barzun. Cat of Crime. Rev and enl edition

Christie, Agatha
Three blind mice and other stories. Dodd, Mead 1950 250p

A collection of eight stories and one novelette most of the puzzles solved either by Miss Marple or Hercule Poirot. The title story is a novelette, first published 1948, which was also published with the title: The mousetrap, and appeared as a play with that title. It involves a murder at a boarding-house where several people have taken shelter during a snowstorm. After a policeman arrives on skis, another murder takes place

Christie, Agatha
Towards zero. Blakiston 1944 256 p.

"Agatha has always liked the combination of the big house on the cliff, the large party composed of relatives and in-laws at odds with one another, plus a couple of mysterious and possibly good-for-nothing male visitors. All these give sufficient reason for fastening the murder(s) upon almost any one of the group. The present brew is one of her best servings, enhanced by almost too many cleverly arranged clues, some of them laid by the murderer to bring off a double bluff. Poirot functions only to the extent of being wished for by Insp. Battle, who is solid and acceptable." Barzun. Cat of Crime. Rev and enl edition

Chung, Catherine
✓ **Forgotten** country; Catherine Chung. Riverhead Books 2012 304 p.
ISBN 9781594488085
LC 2011047577

In this book, "[o]n the night Janie waits for her sister, Hannah, to be born, her grandmother tells her a story: Since the Japanese occupation of Korea, their family has lost a daughter in every generation, so Janie is charged with keeping Hannah safe. . . . Years later, when Hannah inexplicably cuts all ties and disappears, Janie embarks on a mission to find her sister and finally uncover the truth beneath her family's silence." (Publisher's note)

Church, James
✓ **Bamboo** and blood; James Church. Thomas Dunne Books / St. Martin's Minotaur 2008 294p $13.99
ISBN 9780312372910; 0312372914
LC 2008030116

This book takes place "[i]n the winter of 1997, [when,] trying to stay alive during a famine that has devastated much of North Korea, Inspector O is ordered to play host to an Israeli agent who appears in Pyongyang. When the wife of a North Korean diplomat in Pakistan dies under suspicious circumstances, O is told to investigate, with a curious proviso: Don't look too closely at the details, and stay away from the question of missiles. O knows he can't avoid finding out what he is supposed to ignore on a trail that leads him from the dark, chilly rooms of Pyongyang to an abandoned secret facility deep in the countryside, guarded by a lonely general; and from the streets of New York to a bench beneath a horse chestnut tree on the shores of Lake Geneva, where the Inspector discovers he is up to his ears in missiles---and worse." (Publisher's note)

Church, James
A **drop** of Chinese blood; James Church. Thomas Dunne Books 2012 304 p. map (hardcover) $24.99
ISBN 0312550634; 9780312550639; 9781250017925
LC 2012033780

In this novel by James Church "Major Bing . . . [is] the long-suffering chief of the Chinese Ministry of State Security operations on the border with North Korea. . . . As suddenly as she shows up. . . a woman Headquarters wants closely watched . . . mysteriously disappears across the river into North Korea, leaving in her wake both consternation and a highly sensitive assignment for Bing to bring back from the North a long missing Chinese security official." (Publisher's note)

Church, James
✓ The **man** with the Baltic stare; James Church. Minotaur Books 2010 279 p. $24.99
ISBN 0312372922; 9780312372927
LC 2009047482

This book by James Church, part of the Inspector O series, is set "five years after . . . Inspector O was allowed to leave the Ministry of People's Security. . . . A summons to Pyongyang drags him back into the fray. . . . He must go to Macau to solve the murder of a high-priced prostitute, whose corpse was chopped up into pieces. The local authorities suspect the killer to be the young man being groomed to become the new leader of North Korea." (Publishers Weekly)

Chute, Carolyn
✓ The **Beans** of Egypt, Maine. Ticknor & Fields 1985 215p
ISBN 0-899-19314-5
LC 84-8840

The author "vividly evokes the substitutions rural poverty must make for everything from drinking glasses to romance, yet her imaginary Egypt can also echo with Old Testament allusions. The writing is uneven: sometimes striking and provocative, but mainly hovering uncomfortably between (perfectly caught) rural Maine speech patterns and a more literary spareness." Libr J

Other titles about the inhabitants of Egypt, Maine are: Letourneau's Used Auto Parts (1988) and Merry men (1994)

Chute, Carolyn

The **school** on Heart's Content Road. Atlantic Monthly Press 2008 384p $24

ISBN 978-0-87113-987-0; 0-87113-987-1

This novel, set in rural Egypt, Maine, focuses on "a 15-year-old boy, Mickey Gammon, who has been ground down by poverty and the public schools. He earns money working odd jobs for the Border Mountain Militia, patriots with an equal love of Bible and country, and commanded by Vietnam veteran Rex York. Through Rex, Mickey meets, and ultimately joins, a utopian community called The Settlement — home-schoolers, radical agrarians and anti-corporate types living where even Google Maps can't find them. They're led by the polygamous Gordon St. Onge with such a religious fervor that his followers refer to him as 'the prophet.' Gordon collects lost children just as he does wives; he also has taken in a 6-year-old named Jane, whose mother has been arrested on trumped-up drug charges. In a plotline with shades of Waco and the YFZ Ranch, authorities pressure Jane to act as a spy inside the Settlement. Characters and plotlines burst forth and multiply . . . . But get past the political screeds and Chute's disdain for the media and capitalism, and this is a profoundly human novel. Her language is both down-home and inventive, idiosyncratic and real." USA Today

Ciotta, Beth

Her Sky Cowboy; Beth Ciotta. Signet Eclipse 2012 342 p. $7.99

ISBN 0451238478; 9780451238474

This steampunk romance novel is set in "an alternate Victorian England. Spunky airship mechanic Amelia Darcy is smitten with an obsession for flight and a longtime yen for Tucker Gentry, the Sky Cowboy, an American . . . antihero." After her father's death, she competes for a scientific prize, encounters Tucker, and the "two pursue an airborne quest for Leonardo da Vinci's fabled ornithopter while fending off sky pirates employed by dastardly and lascivious Lord Bingham." (Publishers Weekly)

Ciotta, Beth

His Clockwork Canary; The Glorious Victorious Darcys. by Beth Ciotta. Penguin Group USA 2013 352 p. (paperback) $7.99

ISBN 0451239997; 9780451239990

This is the second book in Beth Ciotta's Glorious Victorious Darcys series. Here, "amateur engineer Simon Darcy is hellbent on restoring the Darcy family's fame and fortune before his older twin, Jules, can do so. Simon intends to find the original clockwork propulsion system brought by the Mod Peace Rebels from the love-not-war-making 1960s." (Publishers Weekly)

Cisneros, Sandra

★ The **house** on Mango Street. Knopf 1994 134p $24

ISBN 0-679-43335-X

LC 93-43564

Originally published 1984 by Arte Publico Press

This is "a composite of evocative snapshots that manages to passionately recreate the milieu of the poor quarters of Chicago." Commonweal

Clancy, Tom

Against all enemies; [by] Tom Clancy; with Peter Telep. G.P. Putnam's Sons 2011 756p $28.95

ISBN 978-0-399-15730-1

LC 2011-12458

"Max Moore is a former Navy SEAL who is working with the Special Activities Division (SAD) of the CIA. He's a new warrior for a dangerous time, possessed with a skill set that combines lethal fighting abilities with a canny intelligence and an almost inhuman amphibian capability that made him a legend among his SEAL instructors. Clancy and Telep insert Moore into a battle with two fronts, resulting in a long but always engrossing tale that will keep you up and happily bleary-eyed for at least a couple of nights. The basis for Against All Enemies is a story that has circulated for several years, strongly confirmed by some and vigorously denied by others. There are variations, but the main thrust of it concerns an unholy agreement between one of the Mexican drug cartels and the Taliban, involving drugs and access to the United States at its southern border, with one dirty hand washing the other." Bookreporter

Clancy, Tom

Clear and present danger. Putnam 1989 656p

ISBN 0-399-13440-9

LC 89-10287

"A president decides that drug smuggling has become a 'clear and present danger' to national security. The response is a complex and covert military campaign against the 'Colombian Cartel.' Clancy presents the technology of special operations and the details of light infantry warfare with his usual facility. Superior even to his descriptions of tools and techniques, however, is Clancy's analysis of the legal and moral problems of operating in a twilight zone, where the rules are ambiguous and an open society makes secrecy impossible." Publ Wkly

Clancy, Tom

★ The **hunt** for Red October. Naval Inst. Press 1984 387p $27.95

ISBN 0-87021-285-0

LC 84-16569

"Based on a true incident—the attempted defection of a Soviet destroyer in 1975—the plot concerns the defection of the 'Red October', a Soviet submarine carrying 26 Seahawk missiles able to destroy 200 cities. Russia's fleet is ordered to find and destroy the sub; the U.S. Navy wants to find it and get it to an American port. An 18-day, 4,000-mile hunt across the Atlantic ensues." Booklist

Clancy, Tom

Patriot games. Putnam 1987 540p $27.95

ISBN 0-399-13241-4

LC 87-6910

"On a visit with his wife and daughter in London, Ryan stumbles onto an attempt by a new Irish revolutionary group to kidnap the Prince and Princess of Wales and their eldest son. Using his Marine Corps training, Ryan saves the royals (which leads to several visits between the Ryans and the residents of Buckingham Palace), but Ryan becomes the target of the surviving terrorists." Publ Wkly

Clark, Carol Higgins

✓ **Decked**; a Regan Reilly mystery. Warner Bks. 1992 230p

ISBN 0-446-51549-3

LC 91-50639

This mystery, finds "private detective Regan Reilly returning to Oxford for her tenth reunion. Discovery of a dead classmate's body on the estate of a former professor and his eccentric aunt, however, dampens any festivity. Regan accompanies the aunt on a week-long cruise to New York after someone poisons the original companion, but stays in touch with police. Danger lurks on the boat, of course, and Regan figures things out just in time." Libr J

Clark, Clare

Beautiful lies; Clare Clark. 1st U.S. ed. Houghton Mifflin Harcourt 2012 500 p. (hardcover) $26.00; (ebook) $26.00

ISBN 0151014671; 9780151014675; 9780547840598

LC 2012023346

Author Clare Clark's book provides a "portrait of the Victorian era, encompassing socialist politics, spiritualism, economic crisis, tabloid journalism, Buffalo Bill's Wild West, and family secrets. Maribel Campbell Lowe is the wife of an earnest MP, whose passion for the socialist cause puts his political career at risk . . . When a devious newspaper editor comes close to revealing her past, and destroying her reputation and her husband's career, bright, resourceful Maribel must take a stand." (Publishers Weekly)

Clark, Clare

Savage lands. Houghton Mifflin Harcourt 2010 406p map $25

ISBN 978-0-15-101473-6; 0-15-1014-73-6

LC 2009-18048

This is a "good old-fashioned (that is, slow and deliberate) 19th-century novel, with all the weight of material detail and all the unexpected turns of plot and shifts of time and place that we expect from such productions. The physical world of Louisiana, its bursting ripeness and rot, becomes a metaphor for the characters' inner lives, and this is undoubtedly where the novel's strength lies." N Y Times Book Rev

Clark, Marcia

★ **Guilt** by association. Little, Brown & Company 2011 368 p.

ISBN 9780316129510; 0316129518

LC 2010031573

In this book, "[s]omeone has been watching D.A. Rachel Knight--someone who's Rachel's equal in brains, but with more malicious intentions. It began when a near-impossible case fell into Rachel's lap, the suspectless homicide of a homeless man. In the face of courthouse backbiting and a gauzy web of clues, Rachel is determined to deliver justice. She's got back-up: tough-as-nails Detective Bailey Keller. As Rachel and Bailey stir things up, they're shocked to uncover a connection with the vicious murder of an LAPD cop a year earlier. Something tells Rachel someone knows the truth, someone who'd kill to keep it secret." (Publisher's note)

Clark, Marcia

✓ **Guilt** by degrees; a novel by. Marcia Clark. Little, Brown and Co. 2011 441 p.

ISBN 9780316129534

LC 2011034636

In this book, "[Marcia] Clark brings back Los Angeles DA Rachel Knight in this sequel to . . . "Guilt by Association." This new book opens with a gruesome murder of a cop followed by the street killing of a homeless man. Knight is soon following a treacherous path to find the killer, dodging department politics along the way. We learn more about Knight's disturbing childhood and her love life, as her gal pals--a fellow district attorney and a badass cop--share their work and their lives, bringing additional depth to the tale. But it is the antagonist, a psychopath with a brutal backstory and nerves of steel, who dominates the show." (Libr J)

Clark, Martin

The legal limit. Knopf 2008 356p $24.95

ISBN 978-0-307-26835-8; 0-307-26835-7

LC 2007-042861

This is a "model for how to write a literary thriller with a wry sense of humor. . . . Compelling characters, surprising twists, rich details, all told in a knowing voice that will affect the way you view destiny, God, the human condition and the heady concept of justice." Oregonian

Clark, Mary Higgins

The Anastasia syndrome and other stories. Simon & Schuster 1989 318p

ISBN 0-671-67367-X

LC 89-38841

In the title novella a "noted woman historian sets to work on a study of the British Civil War, juggling her research schedule with a love affair with a rising politician. But her writing is interrupted by strange mental sequences that seem to transport her back to Cromwell's time and involve her in plots against the monarchy. Moreover, these troubling events out of the past are mirrored in the present as a series of terrorist bombings seems to follow the historian's path around England." Booklist

Clark, Mary Higgins

Before I say goodbye. Simon & Schuster 2000 332p

ISBN 0-684-83598-3

LC 00-266596

"Nell MacDermott, a Manhattan political columnist with her eye on her grandfather's Congressional seat, has been hearing voices since she was 10 years old. But she doesn't tap into her gifts until her husband, Adam, dies in a boating accident and a sympathetic aunt takes her to a medium. Suddenly Nell is seeing black auras and having insights into her husband's shady character and dodgy business deals. There are limits to her powers, however, and she fails to spot the villain who is setting her up to die." N Y Times Book Rev

"The elements of Clark's plot masterfully converge to reveal the killer. A fast-paced, fun ride that leaves the reader guessing until the end." Booklist

Clark, Mary Higgins

The **cradle** will fall. Simon & Schuster 1980 314p

ISBN 0-671-25268-2

LC 80-121

"The story centers on what assistant prosecutor Katie De Maio may have seen when she was recovering in the hospital from a car accident. Katie believes, but isn't sure, that she saw a doctor load the body of a young woman into the trunk of a car. Katie has seen clearly, but she doesn't know it. The doctor, a fertility expert who murders his unsuccessful experimental subjects, has seen Katie and determines to get rid of her." Booklist

Clark, Mary Higgins

A **cry** in the night. Simon & Schuster 1982 317p

ISBN 0-671-43128-5

LC 82-10289

In this neo-Gothic thriller "the clues are so subtle, so delicately woven into the fabric of the heroine's life, that even the reader begins to believe, with the heroine, that she herself is either criminal or insane." West Coast Rev Books

Clark, Mary Higgins

Daddy's little girl. Simon & Schuster 2002 291p

ISBN 0-7432-0604-5

LC 2002-21112

This novel's "heroine is Atlanta investigative journalist Ellie Cavanaugh, who was seven when her sister, Andrea, 15, was beaten to death by 20-year-old Rob Westerfield, scion of the wealthiest family in a small Westchester town. Now Westerfield is up for parole, so Ellie, now 30, returns home to speak out against him. When Westerfield is released, Ellie begins to write a book aimed at re-proving his guilt. . . . With its textured plot, well-sketched secondary characters, strong pacing and appealing heroine, this is Clark at her most winning." Publ Wkly

Clark, Mary Higgins

★ **Loves** music, loves to dance. Simon & Schuster 1991 319p

ISBN 0-671-67364-5

LC 91-10757

"This Cinderella story turned sour reaffirms that Mary Higgins Clark deserves her reputation for creating splendid suspenseful fiction. Though the novel's characters are simple in more ways than one . . . the plot—surprisingly upbeat and thoroughly engaging—more than makes up for this flaw." N Y Times Book Rev

Clark, Mary Higgins

Nighttime is my time. Simon & Schuster 2004 370p $25.95

ISBN 0-7432-0607-X

LC 2004-273751

This book features "three females in peril, all targets of a serial killer who fancies himself a night-hunting predator. . . . The Owl kills his first victim, then it's off to attend his 20th high school reunion at Stonecroft Academy in Cornwall-on-Hudson, where he intends to do in the last several women who humiliated him when he was a geeky high school student. . . . The game here is figuring out which

of the men who come to the reunion, all former nerds, is the Owl." Publ Wkly

Clark, Mary Higgins

No place like home. Simon & Schuster 2005 368p hardcover o.p. pa $7.99

ISBN 0-7432-6489-4; 1-4165-7955-9 pa

LC 2005-42535

"At One Old Mill Lane, in Mendham, N.J., 10-year-old Liza Barton wakes to find her stepfather, Ted Cartwright, attacking her mother, Audrey. Liza grabs a gun in defense, but in the ensuing melee Audrey is killed and Ted is wounded. Dubbed 'Little Lizzie Borden,' Liza is taken away and almost convicted of murdering her mother and attempting to kill the lying, scheming Ted. Twenty-four years later, Liza, now known as Celia Foster Nolan, has just been presented with a surprise birthday present from her new husband, Alex: the house at One Old Mill Lane." Publ Wkly

Clark, Mary Higgins

On the street where you live. Simon & Schuster 2001 317p $26

ISBN 0-7432-0602-9

LC 2001-272623

"In the 1890s, three young women in the upscale seaside village of Spring Lake died at the hands of an unidentified killer. In the present day, two young women have disappeared from town—and their killer, whose first-person ruminations vein the third-person narrative, is preparing to strike again. His final target will be Emily Graham, an ambitious young attorney just moved to Spring Lake from upstate New York, where she'd been victimized by a stalker. . . . Clark's prose ambles as usual, but it takes readers where they want to go—deep into an old-fashioned tale of a damsel in delicious distress." Publ Wkly

Clark, Mary Higgins

Remember me. Simon & Schuster 1994 306p

ISBN 0-671-86708-3

LC 94-8762

"Just what is the mysterious presence that seems to haunt Menley Nichols and baby Hannah in their spectacular rented Cape Cod mansion? Menley is still trying to recover from the horror of her two-year-old son Bobby's death on the railroad crossing. Lawyer husband Adam is too busy dashing to and from New York, and defending a local hunk suspected of doing away with his wealthy bride, to be much help. And so the presence moves in on Menley, Rebecca style, with eerie middle-of-the-night sound effects and rocking cradles. As always with Clark, there are several plots going on at once, which are miraculously blended and resolved in the finale." Publ Wkly

Clark, Mary Higgins

The **second** time around. Simon & Schuster 2003 302p $26

ISBN 0-7432-0606-1

LC 2003-271798

"Financial columnist Marcia 'Carley' DeCarlo finds herself squarely in the middle of a bizarre story about the mysterious disappearance of Nick Spencer, founder of the medical research firm Gen-stone, which had been on the brink of developing a cancer vaccine. When it's discovered that Spencer apparently stole thousands of investment dollars and either lied about or sabotaged the progress of the vaccine's development, Carley can't believe it. . . . Under the guise of doing an in-depth story on Nick Spencer, Carley conducts her own investigation, discovering dark forces behind Gen-stone's demise. The prolific and ever-popular Clark isn't the subtlest crime writer, but she knows how to spin an intriguing tale, and this time she's created a convincing heroine in Carley." Booklist

Clark, Mary Higgins

The **shadow** of your smile; a novel. Simon & Schuster 2010 319p $25.99

ISBN 978-1-4391-7226-1; 1-4391-7226-9

LC 2009-43894

"When a deceased nun, Sister Catherine, becomes a candidate for sainthood . . . , Monica Farrell, a 31-year-old Manhattan pediatrician, becomes the target of those who don't want her to inherit what's left of a fortune created by her unknown grandfather, Alex Gannon, with whom Catherine had a secret love child before she took up holy orders. That child, given up for adoption, became Monica's father. Monica must now testify whether two boys became cancer-free due to prayers to Sister Catherine so she can qualify for beatification. . . . Clark skillfully mixes spiritual questions with down and dirty deeds as she reveals Gannon Foundation funds have been steadily siphoned off by greedy heirs and associates who will stop at nothing, even murder, to keep their criminal misbehavior under wraps." Publ Wkly

Clark, Mary Higgins

Stillwatch. Simon & Schuster 1984 302p

ISBN 0-671-46952-5

LC 84-14058

"Pat Traymore arrives in the nation's capital to produce a TV documentary on Sen. Abigail Jennings, rumored to be the President's choice to succeed the ailing, retired Vice-President. Disregarding dire warnings, Pat moves back into the house where, when she was a baby, her father had killed her mother and himself and tried to kill her too. The young woman begins to suspect something not quite admirable in Jenning's background as her research gets under way." Publ Wkly

Clark, Mary Higgins

A **stranger** is watching. Simon & Schuster 1978 314p

ISBN 0-671-23071-9

"When Steve Peterson's son and girl friend disappear, there is no apparent connection between this event and the murder of Steve's wife several years earlier. The latter crime had supposedly been solved, and, indeed, the convicted murderer is about to be executed. However, the kidnapping, the murder, and the execution are linked, as it turns out, and the common denominator is an expert mechanic and full-time psychopath named Arty." Best Sellers

Clark, Mary Higgins

★ **Two** little girls in blue. Simon & Schuster 2006 322p $25.95

ISBN 0-7432-6490-8

LC 2006-42254

"Before leaving for a black-tie affair in New York City, Margaret and Steve Frawley celebrate the third birthday of their twin girls, Kathy and Kelly, with a party at their new home in Ridgefield, Conn. Later that night, when Margaret can't reach the babysitter, she contacts the Ridgefield police. The frantic couple return home to find the children missing and a ransom note demanding $8 million. Though the Frawleys meet all the conditions, only Kelly turns up in a car along with a dead driver and a suicide note saying that Kathy has died. But Kelly's telepathic messages from her sister keep telling her differently, and Margaret won't give up hope. Even the most skeptical law enforcement officers and the FBI, who pursue suspects from New York to Cape Cod, begin to believe Kelly is on to something. Clues from ordinary people lead to a riveting conclusion. Rivaling Clark's debut–Where Are the Children?–this suspense thriller is certain to send terror into the heart of any parent." Publ Wkly

Clark, Mary Higgins

Weep no more, my lady; a novel. Simon and Schuster 1987 315p

ISBN 0-671-55664-9

LC 87-4760

"Although this novel is not quite as tightly plotted as other of Clark's best-sellers, . . . the author's legions of fans will find much to enjoy here—characters aplenty, multiple motives, and enough surprises to keep the action chugging along." Booklist

Clark, Mary Higgins

Where are the children? Simon & Schuster 1975 223p

ISBN 0-671-21942-1

This tale is "set against a background of Cape Cod in the dead of winter. Nancy Eldredge's past hides a terrible secret. She was once tried and almost convicted of the murder of her two young children from a first marriage. . . . She is now happily married again with another little boy and girl. When these children vanish from their front yard in a snowstorm, Nancy's past is raked up and the local police are certain she has killed again." Publ Wkly

Clark, Nancy

The **Hills** at home. Pantheon Bks. 2003 481p $25

ISBN 0-375-42203-X

LC 2002-72314

"The plot is mild and ambling, and the darker emotions are kept strictly offstage, but plot and angst are not the point. The point is the revelation of a particular kind of life, and at that the book succeeds brilliantly." N Y Times Book Rev

Clark, Wahida

Thug lovin' Wahida Clark. Grand Central Pub. 2009 342 p.
ISBN 0446178098; 9780446178099
LC 2008051427

This book is the fourth novel in Wahida Clark's 'Thug' series, in which "Tasha and Trae Macklin have reformed somewhat but are still in urban grit mode. . . . [T]he couple's moved to L.A. although Trae briefly returns to the East Coast for some revenge killing after his cousin Shaheem's murdered. Three years later, Tasha has three children and . . . Trace opens up a flashy nightspot, Club New York. To do this, he makes a connection with Charles Li, a Chinese mobster, and his dangerous daughter, Charli. Then Sabeerah, a devious young witness to Trae's New Jersey crime, moves to L.A. and tries to blackmail Trae. In another plot line net. Rick Bryant, the couple's neighbor, gets involved with Kyra, Tasha's old friend, whose hubby, Marvin, is using drugs." (Publishers Weekly)

Clark, Walter Van Tilburg

★ The **Ox**-bow incident. Random House 1940 309p

"Rustlers are systematically stealing cattle near Bridger's Gulch, Nevada, in the late 1880s. After a cattleman is killed, an illegal posse is formed to apprehend the criminals. In a remote valley they surprise three men, hold a makeshift trial, and hang the three. Soon afterward it is discovered that the wrong men have been punished. This is a western with psychological insight." Shapiro. Fic for Youth. 3d edition

Clarke, Arthur C.

★ **2001**: a space odyssey. New Am. Lib. 1968 221p hardcover o.p. pa $7.99
ISBN 0-451-45799-4 pa

Astronauts of the spaceship Discovery, aided by their computer, HAL, blast off in search of proof that extraterrestrial beings had a part in the development of intelligent life forms on Earth millions of years ago.

"By standing the universe on its head, the author makes us see the ordinary universe in a different light. . . . [This novel becomes] a complex allegory about the history of the world." New Yorker

Clarke, Arthur C.

2010: odyssey two. Ballantine Bks. 1982 291p
ISBN 0-345-30305-9
LC 82-6850

"The Soviet Union and the United States send a joint mission, which includes Dr. Heywood Floyd, to find out what happened to David Bowman, HAL, and the 'Discovery'. . . . Clarke has written a sequel to the movie, not the book, but it doesn't matter. This is another gripping adventure for which there is bound to be much demand." Libr J

Clarke, Arthur C.

2061: odyssey three. Ballantine Bks. 1987 279p
ISBN 0-345-35173-8
LC 87-47811

"Clarke transforms his grasp of science into informed speculation while unleashing, with the understated skill of a master storyteller, several stunning narrative twists." Booklist

Clarke, Arthur C.

3001: the final odyssey. Ballantine Bks. 1997 263p
ISBN 0-345-31522-7
LC 96-49490

"3001 can stand alone from its predecessors in Clarke's Space Odyssey saga and is an intelligent romp, distinguished by Clarke's usual and inimitable wit and an unusual (perhaps unwelcome) strain of grumpiness about religion." Booklist

Clarke, Arthur C.

★ **Childhood's** end. Ballantine Bks. 1953 214p hardcover o.p. pa $13.95
ISBN 0-345-44405-1 pa

This novel is "paradigmatic of Clarke's more speculative, transcendental novels. Structured as a succession of apocalytic revelations, it depicts the sudden metamorphosis of humanity, under the protective midwifery of the alien Overlords, into the next evolutionary stage, a group mind that ultimately merges with the cosmic Overmind, destroying the Earth in the process. . . . The alien other that transcends humanity yet paradoxically represents humanity's destiny is a recurring theme in the author's speculative novels." New Ency of Sci Fic

Clarke, Arthur C.

★ The **collected** stories of Arthur C. Clarke. TOR Bks. 2001 966p hardcover o.p. pa $19.95
ISBN 0-312-87821-4; 0-312-87860-5 pa
First published 2000 in the United Kingdom

"Although most of these stories date from between 1946 and 1970, seven earlier tales, rescued from what would now be called fanzines, extend coverage back to 1937, and a few snippets stretch it toward the present. At least two dozen stories bear titles that are household words among sf readers. . . . The stories demonstrate Clarke's dazzling and unique combination of command of the language, scientific and other kinds of erudition, and inimitable wit." Booklist

Clarke, Arthur C.

★ The **Garden** of Rama; by Arthur C. Clarke and Gentry Lee. Bantam Bks. 1991 441p (Rama)
ISBN 0-553-07261-7
LC 91-2888

This is the third title in the Rama saga. "Trapped aboard the massive Raman spacecraft as it leaves Earth's solar system, three cosmonauts begin a 13-year voyage toward an unknown destination. Combining the best of space adventure (as the spacefarers encounter other life forms within the multi-habitat vessel) with human drama (as children are born and raised in an unearthly environment), this third novel in the Rama cycle asks as many questions as it answers." Libr J

Followed by Rama revealed

Clarke, Arthur C.

The **hammer** of God. Bantam Bks. 1993 226p
ISBN 0-553-09557-9
LC 93-22096

Expanded version of a short story that appeared 1992 in Time magazine

This is "vintage Arthur C. Clarke. While he takes pains to persuade readers that the threat of destruction from outer space is real, he is optimistic about humanity's ability to meet any challenge if its keeps its collective head." N Y Times Book Rev

Clarke, Arthur C.

Rama II; by Arthur C. Clarke and Gentry Lee. Bantam Bks. 1989 420p (Rama)

ISBN 0-553-05714-6

LC 89-15152

In this second installment in the Rama saga "another Rama appears in our galaxy with the same shape, the same unearthly vistas, and even more creatures running wild over its spacescapes. A childlike genius, a beautiful medical officer, and a deeply religious military man form the nucleus of the good guys, anxious to explore, befriend the creatures, and discover the true purpose of the spacecraft." Booklist

Followed by The Garden of Rama

Clarke, Arthur C.

Rama revealed; {by} Arthur C. Clarke and Gentry Lee. Bantam Bks. 1994 466p (Rama)

ISBN 0-553-09536-6

LC 93-31459

"Fans of skillfully crafted hard sf . . . will find plenty of Clarke and Lee's fascinating scientific speculations vividly given form in the marvels of Raman technology." Booklist

Clarke, Arthur C.

★ Rendezvous with Rama. Harcourt Brace Jovanovich 1973 303p (Rama)

ISBN 0-15-176835-8

This work contains "flights of prose where the language fairly purrs. And here too one finds the questioning and probing of man and his place in the cosmos that marks good fiction and good science fiction." Libr J

Followed by Rama II

Clarke, Brock

An arsonist's guide to writers' homes in New England; a novel. Algonquin Books Of Chapel Hill 2007 303p $23.95

ISBN 978-1-56512-551-3; 1-56512-551-7

LC 2006-100732

"This straight-faced, postmodern comedy scorches all things literary, from those moldy author museums to the excruciating question-and-answer sessions that follow public readings. There are no survivors here: women's book clubs, literary critics, Harry Potter fans, bookstores, English professors, memoir writers, librarians, Jane Smiley, even the author himself—they're all singed under Clarke's crisp wit." Washington Post Book World

Clarke, Brock

Exley; a novel. Algonquin Books of Chapel Hill 2010 303p $24.95

ISBN 978-1-56512-608-4

LC 2010-15518

"Frederick Exley's classic 1968 account of his epic alcoholism, A Fan's Notes, bears the oxymoronic subtitle 'A Fictional Memoir.' It is the space between those words, between real and fabricated memory, that Clarke examines in his flawed but forceful new novel, Exley. Miller is a precocious 9-year-old who lives in a cloud of self-delusion, especially when it comes to his dad, an acolyte of A Fan's Notes who may or may not be in a coma at the VA hospital. The boy goes on a search for the inconveniently dead Exley, a mission that is ultimately less about finding the truth than avoiding it. With humor as black as Exley's liver, Clarke picks apart the fictions we tell one another — and those we tell ourselves." Entertainment Wkly

Clarke, Lucy

Swimming at night; a novel. Lucy Clarke. Touchstone 2013 384 p. (hardcover) $24.99

ISBN 1451683391; 9781451683394; 9781451683417; 9781451683424

LC 2012946644

In this book, "British sisters Katie and Mia couldn't be more different. Older sibling Katie is the responsible one, ... Mia, on the other hand, is the wild child," unemployed and abusing drugs. When Mia is found dead in Bali during her impromptu world travels, "Katie can't believe the authorities, who've declared it a suicide. But all Katie has to go on is Mia's travel journal . . . . Determined to find answers, she leaves her fiancé behind and retraces Mia's journey." (Booklist)

Clarke, Richard A., 1951-

The scorpion's gate; Richard A. Clarke. G. P. Putnam's Sons 2005 305p map $24.95

ISBN 0399152946

LC 2005048875

In this book, set "in the near future, . . . [a] radical new government has taken over Saudi Arabia and renamed it Islamyah; an oil crisis looms; and Iran, Iraq, and China prepare to invade Islamyah while a power-mad U.S. secretary of defense plots his own invasion and the reestablishment of the corrupt Saudi monarchy. Only a few intelligence operatives from the United States and England are aware of what's happening and work desperately to forestall an unnecessary war." The author is best known as a "former [U.S.] national coordinator for security and counterterrorism." (Library Journal)

Clarke, Susanna

★ Jonathan Strange & Mr. Norrell; illustrations by Portia Rosenberg. Bloomsbury 2004 782p il $27.95

ISBN 1-582-34416-7

LC 2004-2402

"This fantasy novel is set in early-nineteenth-century England, where two men, Gilbert Norrell and his pupil Jonathan Strange, revive the once-thriving practice of the dark arts. After aiding the British against Napoleon, the magicians fall out over interpretations of wizardly philosophy. Meanwhile, a malevolent fairy accidentally set loose by Norrell enchants, among others, Strange's wife. Clarke's ability to construct a fully imagined world-much of it explained in long, witty footnotes-is impressive." New Yorker

Claudel, Philippe

The **investigation**; a novel. Philippe Claudel; translated from the French by John Cullen. Random House 2012 221 p.

ISBN 0385535341; 9780385535342

LC 2011034662

In this satire-mystery by Philippe Claudel, translated by John Cullen, "[t]he Investigator . . . has been assigned to conduct an Investigation of a series of suicides (twenty-two in the past eighteen months) that have taken place at the Enterprise, a huge, sprawling complex located in an unnamed Town. . . . Time and time again, regulations hamstring him, street layouts befuddle him, and all the while he senses someone watching him, recording his every movement." (Publisher's note)

Clavell, James

Gai-Jin; a novel of Japan. Delacorte Press 1993 1038p

ISBN 0-385-31016-1

LC 92-42129

The sixth volume in the author's Asian saga depicts the political and social intrigue that resulted when Japan slowly opened its doors to foreigners or gai-jin. This novel "opens in 1862 with a fictionalized version of the assassination of a British citizen, Charles Richardson, by samurai traveling with the rebellious lord of Satsuma on the great national highway known as the Tokaido. It ends with the British bombardment of Kagoshima in 1863, a seminal event on the road to the Meiji Restoration, which brought feudal Japan into the modern era." N Y Times Book Rev

Clavell "melds plot-driven storytelling and colorful characterization in vibrant collaboration with an exotic, dynamic setting." Publ Wkly

Clavell, James

King Rat; a novel. Little, Brown 1962 406p

Third novel in the author's Asian saga

This novel "is strong in narrative detail, penetrating in observation of human nature under stress, and thought-provoking in its analysis of right and wrong." Cincinnati Public Libr

Clavell, James

Noble house; a novel of contemporary Hong Kong. Delacorte Press 1981 1206p

ISBN 0-440-06456-2

LC 80-26889

Fourth novel in the author's Asian saga

"Ian Dunross, head of Struan's, an old and respected China trade firm in Hong Kong, makes his appearance in the middle of a typhoon, and from there to the very end of this . . . saga the action never lets up. This action takes place during one week of 1963, with two plots going, and dozens of participants. . . . Along the way we are treated to the sights, sounds, smells, and history of Hong Kong. There is international finance and banking, the workings of multinational companies, smuggling of narcotics and gold, insight into how the Chinese regard sex, and their marvelously pragmatic view of how the world works." Libr J

Clavell, James

★ **Shogun**; a novel of Japan. Atheneum Pubs. 1975 808 p.

ISBN 0-689-10565-7

First novel in the author's Asian saga

"Clavell creates a world: people, customs, settings, needs and desires all become so enveloping that you forget who and where you are. 'Sh'ogun' is history infused with fantasy. It strives for epic dimension and occasionally it approaches that elevated state. It's irresistible, maybe unforgettable." N Y Times Book Rev

Clavell, James

Tai-Pan. Delacorte Press 1983 590p

ISBN 0-440-08724-4

LC 82-18339

Second novel in the author's Asian saga

A reissue of the title first published 1966 by Atheneum

"The backgrounds—Hong Kong, the sailing ships, the trading preserve in Canton—surge with life, and the plot is neatly dovetailed with history. Superb storytelling; an utterly absorbing book." Publ Wkly

Clavell, James

Whirlwind. Morrow 1986 1147p

ISBN 0-688-06663-1

LC 86-11293

Fifth novel in the author's Asian saga

"Clavell has done a fine job . . . . of delineating the geography and politics of a country in turmoil. He seems less successful with the characters, however, as many of his Iranians are thinly disguised stereotypes. Still, the novel is rife with corporate and multinational intrigue, political drama, and romance." Booklist

Clay, Heather

Losing Charlotte. Alfred A. Knopf 2010 261p $24.95

ISBN 978-0-375-41538-8; 0-375-41538-6

LC 2009-23439

"Highly recommended for those who enjoy themes about family and sibling relationships and fans of women's fiction à la Elizabeth Berg, Anne Lamott, Alice Hoffman, and Jodi Picoult." Libr J

Cleage, Pearl

Babylon sisters; a novel. Ballantine Books/One World 2005 292p $23.95

ISBN 0-345-45609-2

LC 2004-51909

"For more than 17 years, Catherine Sanderson has not revealed the identity of her daughter's father and has kept the child's existence hidden from him. However, the universe, teenage curiosity, and two new work assignments conspire to put Catherine's past and present on a collision course. The plot is spun around a tale of women's empowerment, modern-day slavery, betrayal, and the survival of African American community institutions." Libr J

The author's "intelligent, lively narrative hits numerous notes–domestic drama, romance, thriller–right in tune." Publ Wkly

Cleage, Pearl

I wish I had a red dress. Morrow 2001 323p $24

ISBN 0-380-97733-8

LC 00-54620

"With humor and sparkling dialog, Cleage balances the dark, abusive relationships of Joyce's clients with the delightfully healthy love between Joyce and Nate and the strength of women's friendships." Libr J

Cleage, Pearl

What looks like crazy on an ordinary day-- a novel. Avon Bks. 1997 244p

ISBN 0-380-97584-X

LC 97-17708

"Despite the early bad news, Cleage's funny, irreverent, and hopeful novel is stunningly real and evocative of the conditions behind the high unemployment, aimlessness, and drug culture that permeate the urban landscape and have invaded smaller towns as well." Booklist

Cleave, Chris

★ Gold; a novel. Chris Cleave. Simon & Schuster 2012 336 p.

ISBN 1451672721; 9781451672725; 9781451672732; 9781451672749

LC 2011043699

This "novel [is] about the world of professional cycling. Zoe Castle and Kate Meadows met at age 19 trying out for the British Cycling Team and have been friends and rivals for 13 years now. Kate might have more natural ability, but Zoe is the more driven of the two. Kate is married to a fellow racer, Jack Argall, and they have an eight-year-old daughter, Sophie, who suffers from leukemia. Zoe is pursued by her own demons and has a tabloid reputation for sleeping around, which doesn't sit well with her agent. Things begin to heat up when the International Olympic Committee changes its rules so that only one cyclist, either Zoe or Kate, will be eligible to compete in the 2012 London Games." (Publishers Weekly)

Cleave, Chris

Little Bee. Simon & Schuster 2009 271p $24

ISBN 978-1-4165-8963-1; 1-4165-8963-5

LC 2008-30689

First published 2008 in the United Kingdom with title: The other hand

"The novel begins in the middle of the story when Little Bee is illegally released from a prison outside of London after two years of incarceration for attempting to sneak into the country. . . . Without any papers, legal documentation or identification, Little Bee is forced to visit the only person she knows in England—Sarah Summers. . . .Sarah Summers and her husband, Andrew O'Rourke, met Little Bee on a beach in Nigeria. Having grown apart in their marriage, Andrew and Sarah traveled to Nigeria to get away from city life. Inadvertently, the couple stumbles across Little Bee and her sister while taking a romantic walk on the beach, only to be surrounded by a group of mercenaries intent on killing the girls. . . . In a gruesome twist, the soldiers agree to let the girls live if Andrew will cut off his middle finger. As Andrew is unable to comply with their terms, Sarah picks up a machete and slices off her own finger—effectively dooming their marriage. The soldiers initially take both girls away, but in the end spare Little Bee. When she appears at Sarah and Andrew's household outside of London, a series of tragic, beautiful and emotionally turbulent events unfold which will change all of their lives forever." PopMatters

Cleave, Paul

Cemetery Lake; a thriller. by Paul Cleave. 1st Atria paperback ed. Atria Books 2013 416 p. (paperback) $16

ISBN 1451677839; 9781451677836

LC 2012047800

This is Paul Cleave's third Christchurch mystery, introducing PI Theodore Tate. "Two years earlier, the grown daughter of bank manager Henry Martins asked Tate, then a policeman, to investigate what she believed to have been her father's murder. Tate found nothing, but now the second husband of Martins's widow has died, possibly of poisoning. Martins's body is exhumed . . . and three bodies surface in a lake adjacent to the cemetery, one belonging to a missing 19-year-old girl." (Publishers Weekly)

Cleaver, Steven

Saving Erasmus; a novel. Steven Cleaver. Paraclete Press 2007 182p $21.95

ISBN 9781557254986; 1557254982

LC 2006037285

In this novel, chosen by "Library Journal" as a 2007 Best Christian Fiction title, "[w]hen fresh seminary graduate, Andrew Benoit, is sent to the tiny parish of Erasmus, he soon encounters the Angel of Death who threatens to destroy the town. . . . Along the way, Andrew follows many paths of inquiry, discovering the history of the American cinema, encounters with medieval saints, fear of the apocalypse, the Angel of Death, and conversations with a curious group of mystics who meet at the Instant Coffee Cup. This modern-day Jonah tries desperately to save a small town only to discover that he himself is the one who needs saving." (Publisher's note)

Clement, Hal

Heavy planet; the classic Mesklin stories. Orb 2002 414p il pa $20.99

ISBN 978-0-765-30368-4; 0-765-30368-X

LC 2002-32481

This volume includes the novel Mission of gravity (1954) and its sequel, Star light (1971), as well as the short stories Under and Lecture Demonstration. Also included is Whirligig world, the essay Clement published in Astounding in 1953 that describes the process he used to create the high-gravity planet Mesklin

Mission of gravity is a "first-rate story of First Contact between explorers from Earth and a most unhuman sentient native species, to the benefit of both, rejecting the cliché that one still sees in movie and TV SF that alienness equals evil. . . . A major work." Anatomy of Wonder 4

Clement, Hal

Noise. TOR Bks. 2003 252p $23.95

ISBN 0-7653-0857-6

LC 2003-55987

"Linguist Mike Hoani arrives on the water planet Kainui to study the evolution of the language of its original Polynesian colonists. His travels on a planet with no fixed land except for floating artificial cities plunge him into a maritime adventure that tests his knowledge of both language and human nature." Libr J

Clements, Rory

✓ **Revenger**; Rory Clements. Bantam Books 2011 429p.

ISBN 9780385342841; 0385342845

LC 2010053015

Dagger Awards: CWA Ellis Peters Historical Award (2010)

This book tells the story of "John Shakespeare, the playwright's older brother, [who] has left the intelligence world behind to teach at a small school, but he's drawn back into the treacherous world of spying by two powerful and competing rivals -- the earl of Essex and Queen Elizabeth's new spymaster, Sir Robert Cecil. Essex asks Shakespeare to find the truth behind the mysterious disappearance of the colonists of Roanoke, Va. One of them has reportedly been seen walking the streets of London, and Essex wants the intelligencer to confirm or dispel those rumors. Meanwhile, Cecil, who fears that Essex's scheming threatens the monarch, seeks to have Shakespeare work as a double agent." (Publishers Weekly)

Cleverly, Barbara

✓ The **last** kashmiri rose; Barbara Cleverly. Carroll & Graf Publishers 2002 287P $14.00

ISBN 9781616950026; 0786710594

LC 2002073834

In this book, set "[i]n a land of saffron sunsets and blazing summer heat, an Englishwoman has been found dead, her wrists slit, her body floating in a bathtub of blood and water. But is it suicide or murder? The case falls to Scotland Yard inspector Joe Sandilands, who survived the horror of the Western Front and has endured six sultry months in English-ruled Calcutta. Sandilands is ordered to investigate, and soon discovers that there have been other mysterious deaths, hearkening sinister ties to the present case. Now, as the sovereignty of Britain is in decline and an insurgent India is on the rise, Sandilands must navigate the treacherous corridors of political decorum." (Publisher's note)

Cleverly, Barbara

Strange images of death. Soho Constable 2010 314p $25

ISBN 978-1-56947-632-1; 1-56947-632-2

LC 2009-49928

"This latest chapter in the life and times (1926) of Scotland Yard Detective Joe Sandilands has our intrepid hero on the way to a holiday on the French Riviera, including some idealized assignations with gorgeous Frenchwomen. That's the plan after he deposits his niece, Dorcas, with her father at an art colony in a French castle known as Chateau du Diable. Of course, Dorcas and Joe arrive just in time for dinner and a mystery. It seems there's a vandal in the house. The local count wonders if Joe will consult. Then there's a 600-year-old dead woman to investigate. This is the best Sandilands book so far. And if you haven't already discovered the series, it's a perfect spot to begin." Globe and Mail

Clinch, Jon

✓ **Finn**; a novel. Random House 2007 287p $23.95

ISBN 978-1-4000-6591-2; 1-4000-6591-7

LC 2006-45802

"Shocking and charming. Clinch creates a folk-art masterpiece that will delight, beguile and entertain as it does justice to its predecessor. . . . In Finn, Clinch expands the bloodlines and scope of the original story and casts new light on the troubled legacy of our country's infamous past." N Y Post

Clinch, Jon

Kings of the earth; a novel. Random House 2010 393p $26

ISBN 978-1-4000-6901-9; 1-4000-6901-7

LC 2009-34377

"As children, brothers Vernon, Audie, and Creed Proctor slept in the same bed in the family's dilapidated farmhouse in upstate New York. Decades later, now semiliterate grown men, they still sleep in the same bed. They're indifferent to any twentieth-century societal considerations—e.g., hygiene—except the tending of their dairy cows. But Vernon, who believes he has cancer, dies in bed, and state troopers arrest Creed for murder. Area residents, who know the Proctors largely as reclusive oddities or even pariahs, reject the idea that Creed is capable of murder and donate money for his legal defense. . . . Spanning nearly 60 years, the story is narrated in multiple voices: the brothers; their neighbor, who tries to protect them from things they don't understand; a state trooper; and others. It's an odd but intriguing story, made both odder and more intriguing by the fact that it is based on real people and real events." Booklist

Cline, Ernest

✓ **Ready** player one; [by] Ernest Cline. Crown Publishers 2011 374p. $24

ISBN 978-0-307-88743-6; 0-307-88743-X; 9780307887450; 9780307887443; 9780307887436

LC 2011015247

Alex Award (2012)

The events in this novel take place in 2044. Many of the students of 1980s trivia are interested in that particular time period "because a billionaire inventor, James Halliday, died and left behind a mischievous legacy. Whoever first cracks Halliday's series of '80s-related riddles, clues and puzzles that are included in a film called 'Anorak's Invitation' will inherit his fortune." (N Y Times (Late N Y Ed))

"Cultural items from VH1's I Love the 80's series and early G4 programming like Icons or Portal cover a basic swath of the material, but Monty Python, John Hughes, Dungeons & Dragons, WarGames, Blade Runner, Pac-Man, Rush, and infinitely more highly regarded geek cultural touchstones appear both as delightful inclusions and ingenious plot devices. Ready Player One lends itself easily to mash-up comparisons, since in its more complicated passages, it amounts to long strings of cultural references pumped through well-worn story arcs. The adventure comedy of Mike Judge's Idiocracy meets South Park's Imaginationland with a dash of Willy Wonka, except all of the cynicism has been replaced by sheer geeky love." A.V. Club

Cline, Rachel

What to keep; a novel. Rachel Cline. 1st ed; Random House 2004 290p $23.95

ISBN 1-400-06183-0

LC 2003-54810

"Divided into three sections, the story follows the life of Denny Roman, a daughter of brilliant but socially dysfunctional parents, and her relationship with Maureen, the family's de facto life secretary, who teaches Denny how to accept the good parts of herself and her parents and not obsess over the bad." Libr J

Close, Jennifer

Girls in white dresses. Alfred A. Knopf 2011 293p $24.95

ISBN 978-0-307-59685-7; 0-307-59685-0

LC 2011-03397

"As long as there are young people moving to New York to fulfill their vague postcollegiate dreams, there will be books about them. Close's Girls in White Dresses is breezier than most, a lightly sardonic chronicle of a group of recent Boston College grads whose ambitions seem to hinge largely on finding a decent guy and a doorman building without a rodent problem. If the stakes seem low, they are. . . . Still, there's a thread of melancholy running through Dresses that hints at something deeper and truer: not just the adventure of being young, but the unmooring of it, too." Entertainment Wkly

Clute, John

★ **Appleseed**. TOR Bks. 2002 337p $25.95

ISBN 0-765-30378-7

"Nathaniel 'Stinky' Freer captains his ship, the Tile Dance, through space with the aid of a conjoined AI. . . . On a seemingly routine mercantile contract to the planet Trencher, he's nearly killed by the rampaging, cannibalistic, self-devouring alien, Opsophagos. On returning to his ship, Stinky discovers that he's somehow acquired two new AIs and that he has a stowaway: a topiary parthogenete, Mamselle Cunning Earth Link, who holds the key to the location of the planet where there are plaque-eating lenses. Opsophagos remains in hot pursuit as Stinky meets the mythic Johnny Appleseed, rediscovers his lady love and has a sexual encounter that just might save the universe." Publ Wkly

Coady, Lynn

The **antagonist**; Lynn Coady. Alfred A Knopf 2013 304 p. $25.95

ISBN 0307961354; 0887842968; 9780307961358; 9780887842962

In this book, 40-year-old "Gordon 'Rank' Rankin discovers that a close friend from university days has used him as a primary character in a novel. Infuriated with Adam's portrayal of him as a teenager, Rank begins to blister Adam with angry e-mails to set the record straight and, ultimately, to come to terms with Rank's own deeply conflicted feelings about himself and his life." (Booklist)

Coben, Harlan, 1962-

Caught. Dutton 2010 388p $27.95

ISBN 978-0-525-95158-2; 0-525-95158-X

LC 2010-02056

"As usual with Coben, there are dark secrets from the past, plenty of quips and pithy insults, and some colorful specimens along the trail. Despite the touchy subject matter, 'Caught' earns a PG-13 rating. We're not talking soaring prose here, but Coben is an engaging companion." Portland Oregonian

Coben, Harlan

Darkest fear. Delacorte Press 2000 285p

ISBN 0-385-33433-8

LC 99-89788

"The Bolitar thrillers are always leavened with humor, no matter how grim the content, and this one is no exception. Even so, the darkness of the plot and the seriousness of the theme—the reponsibilities of parenthood—give this installment added impact." Booklist

Coben, Harlan

Gone for good. Delacorte Press 2002 340p

ISBN 0-385-33558-X

LC 2001-55292

"Through Klein, the psychological suspense turns on the question of guilt, surely but also on the transcendence of familial love and forgiveness. Watching Klein decide among dangerous alternatives, as the clockwork plot keeps picking up speed, is breathtaking." Booklist

Coben, Harlan

Hold tight. Dutton 2008 416p $26.95

ISBN 978-0-525-95060-8; 0-525-95060-5

LC 2007-51582

"The story is about Tia and Mike Baye, whose son, Adam, has been somewhat isolated since his best friend killed himself. The parents, not knowing where he is going and what he is doing, consider putting some sophisticated spyware on their son's computer. Even though troubled by their invasion of his privacy they do so, anyway, using their worries about his welfare as an excuse. Once they find out where Adam is going and what he is doing, Mike all but abandons his medical practice to search for him and interact with some very dangerous people. Coben's style is laid back initially, but it builds into a strong, smart, suspenseful novel including at least five different storylines. " Deseret News

Coben, Harlan, 1962-

The **innocent**; by Harlan Coben. Dutton 2005 388p $26.95

ISBN 0525948740

LC 2005001627

This book tells the story of Matt Hunter, who "accidentally killed another boy in a fight he was trying to break up. Now, five years after his release from prison, . . . he answers a call from [his wife] Olivia and sees a video of her wearing a blonde wig, walking around a strange hotel room with a strange man. . . . [T]he unknown man keeps tugging on Matt's leash by phoning him with further taunts." Other "plot lines [include] a young woman's search for information about her birth mother, . . . a Vegas stripper murdered ten years ago, and the much more recent death of Sister Mary Rose, a nun with breast implants. . . . As Matt starts to notice details about a mysterious car that's been following him and the weather outside Olivia's hotel room, though, the pieces of the puzzle start to fall together." (Kirkus)

"A paralegal, devoted husband and soon-to-be father, Matt Hunter has a not-so-secret past: when he was 20, in an attempt to break up a fistfight, he killed a man and served four years in prison for it. He's been out five years, living in his New Jersey hometown, and life is pretty good. But when his beloved wife, Olivia, goes away on a business trip, he receives 15 seconds of digital video on his camera phone showing her in a hotel room with another man. Meanwhile, Loren Muse, Essex County homicide investigator, is working on an unusual case: an autopsy of a nun reveals breast implants, which hint at a previous, not so holy life. After the FBI is called in, evidence links Matt to the nun killing. . . . All the characters have extensive, interesting histories, which makes their actions believable under the extreme circumstances that engulf them." Publ Wkly

Coben, Harlan
Just one look. Dutton 2004 370p $25.95
ISBN 0-525-94791-4
LC 2004-2329
"While flipping through a set of newly developed photographs, Grace Lawson comes across an old picture of four people, one of whom resembles her husband, Jack. When she shows him the photo, he denies being the person or knowing anyone involved. Later that night, with the photo in his possession, Jack flees the house and promptly vanishes. When Grace uncovers proof that one of the strangers in the picture is now dead, her picture-perfect life starts to unravel. With each thriller, Coben just gets better and better." Libr J

Coben, Harlan
No second chance. Dutton 2003 338p $24.95
ISBN 0-525-94729-9
LC 2002-192530
"The novel, spanning 18 months and jumping between the father and the kidnappers, sets off depth charges of meets, double-crosses, near-misses, and vengful acts. Coben holds it together with his hero's determination and smarts." Booklist

Coben, Harlan
One false move. Delacorte Press 1998 322p
ISBN 0-385-32369-7
LC 97-51206
"After four paperback appearances, sports agent/sleuth Myron Bolitar makes his hardcover debut in a stylish mystery distinguished by memorably quirky characters and smart, tough narration." Publ Wkly

Coben, Harlan, 1962-
Stay close; Harlan Coben. Dutton 2012 400p.
ISBN 9780525952275
LC 2012001871
In this book, "three people are haunted by the disappearance of Stewart Green 17 years earlier in Atlantic City: photographer Ray Levine; housewife Megan Pierce; and Detective Broome, who investigated the disappearance and befriended Green's wife and kids. The disappearance of Carlton Flynn on February 18, the same date Green went missing, helps reignite the smoldering case, pointing the way to other victims and a strange pattern. Flynn's case also results in a pair of preppie, very scary sadists calling themselves Ken and Barbie entering the scene." (Publishers Weekly)

Coben, Harlan
The **woods**. Dutton 2007 404p $26.95
ISBN 978-0-525-95012-7; 0-525-95012-5
LC 2007-8329
The author "has created another surprising and emotional story that will remain with the reader long after the last page is finished. One of Coben's best." Libr J

Cockey, Tim
Hearse case scenario. Hyperion 2002 338p
ISBN 0-7868-6711-6
LC 2001-24188
In this mystery "Hitchcock Sewell, Baltimore's wisecracking mortician/sleuth, sets out to exonerate his hapless childhood friend, Lucy, accused of murdering her low-life boyfriend, Shrimp Martin. Sure, Lucy shot him, but she wasn't the one who killed him." Publ Wkly

Cockey, Tim
Murder in the hearse degree. Hyperion 2003 324p $22.95
ISBN 0-7868-6712-4
LC 2002-27458
Wisecracking undertaker Hitchcock Sewell "finds out that his former squeeze, Libby Gellman, is back in town with her two children but sans husband and nanny. The nanny, surprisingly pregnant, is more than geographically distant: she's fallen from a very high bridge and drowned. Or was she pushed? The police support a knee-jerk suicide theory. The nanny's loyal mother doesn't. So Hitch sets off to see exactly what happened. . . . Brimming with humor—much of it dark—this book is perfect for the reader who has finished all the books by Janet Evanovich or Sue Grafton and doesn't know what to read next." Libr J

Cocteau, Jean
The **impostor**; translated from the French by Dorothy Williams. Noonday Press 1957 132p
Original French edition, 1923; first English translation published 1925 by Appleton with title: Thomas the imposter
The setting of Cocteau's short novel "is the First World War; his imposter, a French youth, too young for the services, who in a borrowed uniform and under a borrowed name succeeds in obtaining a post in a curious nursing unit run by a Polish princess and her daughter. He plays the part he has adopted so well that in the end he succeeds in convincing even himself of his authenticity, and having finally been adopted as their mascot by a unit of Marines dies in the end a gallant death." Times Lit Suppl

Coe, Jonathan
The **closed** circle. Knopf 2005 367p $25
ISBN 0-375-41415-0
LC 2004-57789
"While Coe's political sensibility is readily apparent, this novel, with its incredibly well developed characters and its immensely engaging narrative, is no polemical tract. It's a compelling, dramatic and often funny depiction of the way we live now—both savage and heartfelt at the same time." Publ Wkly

Coe, Jonathan

✓ The **rain** before it falls. Alfred A. Knopf 2008 240p $23.95

    ISBN 978-0-307-26803-7; 0-307-26803-9

                            LC 2007-43487

    First published 2007 in the United Kingdom

"Following the death of her Aunt Rosamond, niece Gill is named executrix of her estate and inherits a series of cassettes that Rosamond recorded on the eve of her demise. The cassettes detail Rosamond's tumultuous connection with her cousin Beatrix, as well as Beatrix's daughter Thea and granddaughter Imogen. Rosamond intended the tapes for Imogen, but Gill can't locate her. Gradually, the tapes reveal the unhappiness of these relationships and the tragedies of these women's lives. In the recordings, Rosamond often displays an irritating passivity, while the manipulative, volatile Beatrix is revealed as a bitch—not that this genteel novel makes use of such a term. . . . If Rosamond's temperament makes for a somewhat mannered novel, it's nevertheless an absorbing one." Village Voice

Coe, Jonathan

    ★ The **Rotters'** Club. Knopf 2002 419p

    ISBN 0-375-41383-9

                          LC 2001-42523

    First published 2001 in the United Kingdom

"The Rotter's Club, for all its occassional overegging and its self-conscious deployment of issues, is a superior entertainment. The pages seem to turn themselves, and Coe's oblique humor allows the romantic and satirical to combine without undercutting each other." New Statesman (1913)

Coe, Jonathan

✓ The **terrible** privacy of Maxwell Sim. Alfred A. Knopf 2011 314p $26.95

    ISBN 9780307594815

                          LC 2010-35997

    First published 2010 in the United Kingdom

The author "broadly satirizes the disconnectedness of modern life with the story of Maxwell Sim, who has 70 Facebook friends but no one he can turn to when his wife and daughter leave him. After a trip to Australia to reconnect with his estranged father leads nowhere, Trevor, one of Max's few real friends, offers him an unusual gig: drive a Prius to the northernmost tip of the British Isles as part of a promotion for a startup eco-toothbrush company. Max takes a meandering route that allows him to visit his ex-wife, check in on his father's long-empty apartment, and pay a visit to the parents of his childhood friends. He also develops a romantic fixation on the voice coming from his GPS, which he names Emma. . . . Coe has a lot of fun skewering the way technology and social media have become buttresses of society." Publ Wkly

Coel, Margaret

    Blood memory. Berkley Prime Crime 2008 305p $24.95

    ISBN 978-0-425-22345-1; 0-425-22345-0

                          LC 2008-22197

"The story sails along like an eagle riding the wind, and Coel provides plenty of plausible misdirection before revealing the surprising hand behind the plot to take her life.

. . . Coel does a nice job of making Denver and the nearby environs into a charming 'character'—not the easiest task." Daily Camera (Boulder, Co.)

Coel, Margaret

    The **dream** stalker. Berkley Prime Crime 1997 244p

    ISBN 0-425-15967-1

                          LC 96-54797

"Arapaho lawyer Vicky Holden opposes the plan to construct a nuclear waste facility on the Wind River Reservation, but she receives death threats and the enmity of her people for her pains. Good friend John O'Malley, Jesuit priest at the local mission, believes that a murdered Indian he found has some connection to Vicky's troubles, so he investigates—against police advice. Financial problems at the mission, the personal crises of the new assistant, and O'Malley's own temptations of the flesh lend realistic touches to the author's usual commendable plotting and characterization." Libr J

Coel, Margaret

    The **ghost** walker. Berkley Prime Crime 1996 243p

    ISBN 0-425-15468-8

                          LC 95-26164

"Coel's Catholic Irish Jesuit priest and his Arapaho friends and neighbors, each with individual worldviews and sensibilities, make for interesting contrasts in this excellent mystery that focuses on the strange place Native Americans occupy in their own land." Booklist

Coetzee, J. M.

✓ ★ **Age** of iron. Random House 1990 198p

    ISBN 0-394-58859-2

                          LC 90-8310

"The word 'shame' throbs through the text like a recurrent pain. The principal character thinks she is dying of it. . . . One can, of course, read her death as a metaphor for the doom of liberalism in South Africa. . . . But Age of Iron is about dying as much as it is about apartheid, and that raises it above the level of a political novel or a roman à thèse, and gives resonance to the political message." N Y Rev Books

Coetzee, J. M.

✓ **Diary** of a bad year. Viking 2007 231p $24.95

    ISBN 978-0-670-01875-8; 0-670-01875-9

                          LC 2007-27378

The "essays create a compelling, even lovable, portrait of a chilly and curmudgeonly aging writer. . . . Anya, in the last 90 pages, transcends her gestural, schematic treatment, and becomes a complex, compassionate individual." Boston Globe

Coetzee, J. M.

✓ ★ **Disgrace**. Viking 1999 220p

    ISBN 0-670-88731-5

"A novel that not only works its spell but makes it impossible for us to lay it aside once we've finished reading it. . . . Coetzee's sentences are coiled springs, and the energy they release would take other writers pages to summon." New Yorker

Coetzee, J. M.

Elizabeth Costello. Viking 2003 230p $21.95

ISBN 0-670-03130-5

LC 2003-60849

"There is no justice in the ability of youth to shame age, and yet it's a fundamental fact of the embodied life. Coetzee's unflinching exploration of this desolate and strangely beautiful terrain represents the cruelest and best use to which literature can be put." N Y Times Book Rev

Coetzee, J. M.

Foe. Viking 1987 157p

ISBN 0-670-81398-2

LC 86-40267

First published 1986 in the United Kingdom

"In adding to Defoe's repertory company, Coetzee has introduced urgencies that are neither fresh nor illumined, only brilliantly disguised. Flashing back and forward, scattering allusions, adopting a series of poses and styles, the author is less reminiscent of a prior novelist than of contemporary street mimes who build hints until the audience shouts in recognition." Time

Coetzee, J. M.

★ Life & times of Michael K. Viking 1984 184p

ISBN 0-670-42789-6

LC 83-47860

First published 1983 in the United Kingdom

"Born with a harelip and brought up in an uncaring orphanage, Michael K. struggles through a desperate life in South Africa. When his sick mother persuades him to bring her back to her homeland, he must endure not only the terrible journey, pulling her in a cart he has made, but also risk the dangers of military checkpoints since he does not have the necessary permits. His undying attachment is to the land, but he is not allowed to remain the gardener he wishes to be. The details of Michael's suffering in camps, hospitals, and labor gangs are harrowing and underscore a courage that never forsakes him." Shapiro. Fic for Youth. 3d edition

Coetzee, J. M.

Slow man. Viking 2005 265p $24.95

ISBN 0-670-03459-2

LC 2005-54693

"What saves Slow Man from being a sterile, self-referential literary exercise is the vividness of the characters who animate it. Coetzee writes in a degree-zero style, purposely flat and unemphatic-he must be a translator's dream-yet in this book he has found a new access of warmth and humor, and displays a vivifying fondness for his characters. It is his triumph in Slow Man to bring a world into being with a minimum of literary effects." New Republic

Coetzee, J. M.

★ Summertime. Viking 2009 256p $25.95

ISBN 978-0-670-02138-3; 0-670-02138-5

LC 2009-37527

"In the early seventies, a young unpublished writer returns to his native South Africa after a disgrace abroad. His name is John Coetzee, and he both is and isn't the Nobel-winning author of this unorthodox book. Where the real

Coetzee had a wife and children at the time, his doppelgänger shares a crumbling house with his widowed father and engages in fitful affairs with married women, one of whom judges him 'autistic' in bed. These 'facts' emerge from interviews conducted by a biographer nearly four decades later, after Coetzee's (imagined) death. At stake is what it means to commit oneself: to a person, a place, a moral imperative. . . . Not since 'Disgrace' has he written with such urgency and feeling." New Yorker

Cohen, Joshua

Four new messages; Joshua Cohen. Farrar Straus & Giroux 2012 193 p. (alk. paper) $14.00

ISBN 1555976182; 9781555976187

LC 2012936219

This collection of short stories, by Joshua Cohen, "capture[s] the pathos and absurdity of life in the age of the internet." Story characters include "a hapless drug dealer in Princeton . . . , a frustrated pharmaceutical copywriter . . . , a father visiting NYU with his daughter [who] remembers a former writing teacher, . . . [and] an aspiring journalist. . . . Highbrow and low-down, these four . . . stories explain what happens when the virtual begins to colonize the real." (Publisher's note)

Cohen, Joshua

Witz; the story of the last Jew on earth. Dalkey Archive Press 2010 817p pa $18.95

ISBN 978-1-56478-588-6; 1-56478-588-2

LC 2009-46093

"In this ambitious novel, Benjamin Israelien—born full grown, bearded, and wearing glasses—is the last living Jew, a national celebrity and Messiah-like great hope for an America terrified of losing God's grace. In more than eight hundred pages of dense, often self-amused prose, he tours in a big revival show, visits Holocaust sites ('Whateverwitz' in 'Polandland'), and even makes a brief sojourn in space with a tentacled alien named Doktor Froid. 'Witz,' as Cohen explains, means 'joke,' and the novel overflows with puns, allusions, and Borscht Belt zingers, in an incantatory modernist style. But the story, which, for all its intellectual energy, values cleverness above clarity, is a bleak one, in which the flesh is cursed, life is absurd, and the end is near." New Yorker

Cohen, Leah Hager

The grief of others. Riverhead Books 2011 371p $26.95

ISBN 978-1-59448-805-4; 1-59448-805-3

LC 2011-09414

"Occasionally, the action of Cohen's novel seems forced when it moves outside the family circle, particularly when John goes to his job managing the theatrical scene shop at a community college. Sometimes, too, in shifting the perspective from one character to another, Cohen lets her own voice intrude, breaking the spell she's cast. But those are quibbles about a novel that's otherwise graceful, satisfying, and closely observed." Boston Globe

Cohen, Leah Hager

Heart, you bully, you punk. Viking 2003 $23.95
$23.95

ISBN 0-670-03167-4

LC 2002-69191

"Cohen offers a bittersweet love story involving a 31-year-old math teacher at a Brooklyn private school, her star pupil, and the student's father. Ann James, the star student, breaks both heels when she slips (or jumps?) from the top of the bleachers. Her injuries render her immobile for a time; to help her keep up in math, Ann's teacher, Esker, volunteers to tutor her at home. After meeting Ann's father, Wally, Esker begins, despite herself, to fall in love with him. . . . Cohen demonstrates that there can be beauty even in sadness." Booklist

Cohen, Leah Hager

House lights. W. W. Norton 2007 302p $24.95

ISBN 978-0-393-06451-3; 0-393-06451-4

LC 2007-06910

The novel is "artfully constructed. By virtue of their length, novels forgive undisciplined descriptive flights, but Cohen writes with the scrupulousness of someone fashioning a short story, in which even the smallest details must bear their weight of significance." N Y Times Book Rev

Cohen, Robert

Inspired sleep; a novel. Scribner 2001 399p $25

ISBN 0-684-85079-6

LC 00-57337

"Smartly observed and stylishly written, Cohen's new novel is crammed with incidental pleasures. Yet underneath its clever examination of our current love affair with pharmaceuticals lie unsettling questions about the myths we choose to live by: it's not the interpretation of dreams but the meaning of our waking hours that is up for grabs here." New Yorker

Coldsmith, Don

The long journey home. Forge 2001 400p $24.95

ISBN 0-312-87617-3

LC 00-48459

Coldsmith portrays a "Native American athlete who bears an intentional resemblance to the great Jim Thorpe. . . . This well-researched piece of historical fiction interweaves a compelling life story with many of the pivotal events of the early twentieth century." Booklist

Coldsmith, Don

Tallgrass; a novel of the Great Plains. Bantam Bks. 1997 454p

ISBN 0-553-10632-5

LC 96-19672

Coldsmith's saga concerns "the opening of the Santa Fe Trail. Starting with the coming of the Spanish conquistadors in 1541, his work spans 300 years to a time when the fur trade has died, Eastern Native Americans have been relocated onto lands west of the Mississippi, and conflict is building between the Plains Indians and Eastern interlopers, both Indian and white. Coldsmith focuses on a tribe of Pawnee and

the devastation that contact with whites brings. This powerful novel demonstrates the diversity of the Native American culture while treating the tribes and their history with dignity and understanding." Libr J

Cole, Teju

Open city; a novel. Random House 2011 259p $25

ISBN 978-1-4000-6809-8; 1-4000-6809-6

LC 2010-08927

"Cole's writing is assured, his ideas are well developed, and his imagery is delicious. . . . His readers will be those who understand that all stories are interconnected, that literature is not mere entertainment, and that art is nothing if not an extended conversation spanning eras, nations and languages. The novel's importance lies in its honesty." N Y Times Book Rev

Colegate, Isabel

★ The shooting party. Viking 1981 195p

ISBN 0-670-64064-6

LC 80-54194

First published 1980 in the United Kingdom

"The time is October 1913, the place an estate in Oxfordshire where Sir Randolph Nettleby and his wife are hosting the biggest shoot of the season. Brought together are the privileged in pursuit of pleasure. For these guests shooting is a special ritual with the shooters, gamekeepers, beaters, and servants all playing specific roles, and the sport is marvelously and meticulously described. Woven through the story are the portrayals of the gentry, the allusions to romantic and adulterous affairs, the relationship between the classes, and the feeling of the vast changes soon to overtake the Edwardian period. The rising tension that accompanies the final hours of the shooting on this day explodes into unexpected tragedy." Shapiro. Fic for Youth. 3d edition

Colegate, Isabel

Winter journey. Counterpoint 2001 199p

ISBN 1-58243-122-1

LC 00-64449

First published 1995 in the United Kingdom

"Colegate employs a varied cast of background characters who, in addition to their fully dimensional portrayals, provide insight into Britain's still potent class system. In Colegate's assured hands, the natural landscape is rendered as clearly as her characters' interior landscapes, and she accomplishes this in a slim text remarkable for its lucidity, humor and precise observation." Publ Wkly

Coleman, Ashley

Murder mamas; Ashley & JaQuavis. Urban Books 2011 236 p.

ISBN 1601625006; 9781601625007

LC 2011276990

Street Lit Book Medal Award: Author(s) of the Year (2012)

In this book, "Aries is a beautiful woman with an ugly secret—she's part of the Murder Mamas, a crew of murderers for hire. . . . Her husband and son in Barbados have no idea of her true identity and the things she's done, and she's happy to keep it that way. Unfortunately, Case has other plans for Aries. He's got a score to settle with Macy, a former partner who stole the woman he loved. Case might have let things go, except for one thing: Macy left behind the thug lifestyle to become the mayor of Los Angeles, and his new 'clean up the streets' campaign is seriously cutting into Case's business. . . . Aries still has an unpaid debt with Case, and he hunts her down to tell her he's willing to cancel the debt—only if she completes the hit on Macy." (Publisher's note)

Coleman, Ashley

Murderville; first of a trilogy. Ashley Coleman, JaQuavis Coleman. Cash Money Content 2011 272 p.

ISBN 9781936399000; 9781936399024

LC 2011922348

Street Lit Book Medal Award: Author(s) of the Year (2012)

This book, the first of a trilogy, focuses on "[t]wo children from Sierra Leone, Liberty and A'shai, [who] are brought together by chance only to be forced apart by the most inevitable and tragic fate. . . . Liberty is dying of a fatal heart condition. . . . A'shai blames himself for not protecting Liberty, but all Liberty asks is for A'shai to tell her a story, to help her remember what brought them to this point. . . . As Liberty lies dying, A'shai walks her though their past, reliving their ill-fated journeys through the streets. Their story will take them from an arranged marriage, through Mexico's drug cartel, child brothels, hustling in Detroit, to escaping the high-powered heads of L.A.'s underworld." (Publisher's note)

Coleman, JaQuavis

The **dopeman's** wife; JaQuavis Coleman. Urban Books 2009 vi, 230 p.p

ISBN 1601621590; 9781601621597

LC 2009504291

This book tells the story of a young woman named Nautica's journey through a world of drugs, crimes, and dangerous men. After her relationship with "Zion, a gangster who moves 20 bricks of coke to lock down Flint, MI, turns horrifyingly abusive. . . . Nautica relieves him of $80,000 and motors to Baltimore. But on the way she must deal with hookers, pimps, psychos, and, finally, . . . gangster Tical, the drug boss of B-more. . . . [Then,] hoods from Flint show up. Tical might be able to save her, but chances of a happy ending are slim. The backstory sets streetwise Nautica on a journey powered by cocaine and ecstasy to phenomenal wealth dripping with bling." (Libr J)

Coleridge, N. D.

The **adventuress**; a novel. N.D. Coleridge. St. Martin's Press 2013 368 p. (hardcover) $25.99

ISBN 1250028256; 9781250028259

LC 2013010084

This novel by N.D. Coleridge "follows the rise . . . of Cathy Fox. From her humble beginnings as a matron's assistant at a top girls' boarding school, Cath embarks on a journey that will take her from a Portsmouth backstreet to the boardrooms of the global empires. With a cast of footballers, media moguls, lords and dukes, Coleridge charts the rise of a

woman who will not be denied, right to the very pinnacle of society—a Royal Wedding." (Publisher's note)

Coleridge, Nicholas

Godchildren. Thomas Dunne Books 2008 551p $25.95

ISBN 978-0-312-38258-2; 0-312-38258-8

LC 2008-19639

First published 2002 in the United Kingdom

"This wickedly enjoyable novel about a venal British billionaire and his godchildren shows a moribund class society being rapidly dismantled by global wealth. The property and shipping tycoon Marcus Brand's six godchildren include a Scottish aristocrat whose snobbery outstrips his dwindling inheritance, a debonair London gigolo, and a socialist Birmingham boy who pulls himself up by his bootstraps to become a capitalist with a heart of gold. While the story of who triumphs is predictable, Coleridge dissects the social mores of Cap Ferrat and Lyford Cay with skill, noting sartorial codes with the precision of Tom Wolfe." New Yorker

Colette

★ The **collected** stories of Colette; edited, and with an introduction, by Robert Phelps; translated by Matthew Ward, et al. Farrar, Straus & Giroux 1983 605p

ISBN 0-374-12629-1

LC 83-16449

"Includes two novellas that rank as classics, not only in Colette's canon, but in all of 20th century French literature. The Tender Shoot is the story of a singularly nasty middle-aged roué's pursuit of a 15-year-old peasant girl. Upon this squalid tale, Colette lavished her most lyrical language and poetic fancies, heightening the sense of evil. . . . As Colette remarked of her writing, her 'great landscape was always the human face.' No work demonstrates this better than The Kepi, the portrait of a doomed 46-year-old French lieutenant." Time

Colette

★ The **complete** Claudine; Claudine at school, Claudine in Paris, Claudine married, Claudine and Annie. translated by Antonia White. Farrar, Straus & Giroux 1976 632p

Omnibus edition of four semi-autobiographical novels written by Colette in 1900-1903. The first three appeared under the pen name of her husband and the fourth novel was published under both their names. These translations have copyright dates 1956, 1958, 1960 and 1962 respectively. Variant title for English translation of third volume: Indulgent husband; of final volume: Innocent wife

In the first novel we meet Claudine as a precocious school girl peeping and spying on both her contemporaries and her boarding school teachers. The second novel depicts a girl approaching womanhood discovering the exciting world of Paris and meeting a varied assortment of escorts. Claudine married is not so much the story of the heroine's marriage as the story of Claudine's love affair with Rézi, another married woman. The final volume has Claudine as one of its principal characters, but it is largely the story of an innocent young wife, who during the absence of her domineering husband begins to see more of her sister-in-law and her sophisticated friends and her eyes open to the true ways of life and love

Colette

Six novels. Modern Lib. 697p

Colfer, Eoin, 1965-

√ Plugged; a novel. Overlook Press 2011 254p $24.95

ISBN 978-1-59020-463-4

LC 2011025335

"Outrageous characters, . . . uproariously funny plot twists, and brutal, nonstop action make this a sure-fire winner." Publ Wkly

Colfer, Eoin, 1965-

Screwed; Eoin Colfer. Penguin Group USA 2013 304 p. $25.95

ISBN 1468301705; 9781468301700

LC 2013022339

This book by Eoin Colfer "adds and entirely new chapter to the adventures and misadventures of Daniel McEvoy, the down-on-his-luck Irish bouncer at a seedy New Jersey bar who, with the help of a motley crew of unlikely characters, solved a bizarre string of murders--including the one of the girl he loved. But people around him continue to die mysteriously, and Daniel is called into action once again." (Publisher's note)

Coll, Susan

Acceptance; a novel. Farrar, Straus and Giroux 2007 286p $23

ISBN 978-0-374-23719-6; 0-374-23719-0

LC 2006-15896

This "sendup of the college admissions process is set in a tony suburb of Washington, D.C. A group of overachieving students . . . fight for what seems an ever-narrowing pool of Ivy League spots (the only ones that matter), state-university scholarships (for the rare student who is financially challenged), and liberal-arts places ('safeties'). The view from the other side of the desk is provided by a character in the admissions department of a newly popular college in upstate New York, which is trawling for kids whose parents can pay for new campus facilities. Coll is alert to the comedy— and the pathos—of a system that leads highschool seniors to solicit recommendation letters from their pediatricians." New Yorker

Collins, Brandilyn

Crimson eve; Brandilyn Collins. Zondervan 2007 342p (Kanner Lake series) (pbk.) $14.99

ISBN 0310252253; 9780310252252

LC 2007012727

This book is "the 3rd book in [author] Brandilyn Collins' Kanner Lake series. . . . [The story follows] Carla Radling [who] is targeted by a hit man and is unsure . . . why someone wants her dead. She . . . stumbles into safety, but on the run, she can never be sure who to trust. The story unfolds through present day action and the diary entries from Carla's 16 year old diary." (rbclibrary.wordpress.com)

Collins, Ciarán

★ The **gamal**; Ciarán Collins. Bloomsbury USA 2013 480 p. (alk. paper) $17

ISBN 1608198758; 9781608198757

LC 2012046539

In this novel by Ciarán Collins "Charlie has a story to tell, about his best friends Sinead and James and the bad things that happened. Charlie has promised Dr Quinn he'll write 1,000 words a day, but it's hard to know which words to write. And which secrets to tell. This is the story of the dark heart of an Irish village, of how daring to be different can be dangerous, and how there is nothing a person will not do for love." (Publisher's note)

Collins, James

Beginner's Greek; a novel. Little, Brown, and Co. 2008 441p

ISBN 9780316021555; 0-316-02155-5

LC 2007-11690

"Whenever Peter [Russell] boards a plane, which is often, due to his Wall Street job, he wonders whether this will be the flight on which he meets the woman of his dreams. Then, on a trip from New York to Los Angeles, it actually happens: A woman sits next to him who is not only beautiful, but on page 500 of one of Peter's favorite books. They talk (or rather, Holly talks and a smitten Peter tries his best to answer intelligibly). They learn about each other's favorite books, their families, their jobs. It looks as if this might be love at first sight. . . . Five hours later, they land in L.A. and promise to meet for dinner. But when Peter gets to his hotel, her phone number has vanished from his shirt pocket. Years later, when he and Holly meet again, she's on the arm of a womanizing but charming author who also happens to be Peter's closest friend. The two eventually marry, and, resigned, Peter marries the dull but sweet Charlotte." BookPage

Collins "has a rare ability to satirize without becoming nasty, and periodically gives romantic clichés a good tweak." Christ Sci Monit

Collins, Max Allan

Black hats; a novel of Wyatt Earp and Al Capone. [by] Patrick Culhane. William Morrow 2007 304p $24.95

ISBN 978-0-06-089253-1; 0-06-089253-6

LC 2006-48611

This novel "has the young and reckless son of the late "Doc" Holliday being protected and guided by a 70-year-old Wyatt Earp in a New York City gangland war over a large supply of hard liquor. Did Johnny Holliday Jr. give gangster Al Capone the three knife scars on his cheek responsible for the "Scarface" nickname? That's just part of the story. Collins has outdone himself in this tale of bad guys, bullets, and booze set at the start of the Prohibition era." Libr J

Collins, Max Allan

√ Bye bye, baby. Forge 2011 336p $24.99

ISBN 978-0-7653-2179-4; 0-7653-2179-3

Set in 1962, this Nate Heller novel finds the Chicago PI "looking into the death of Hollywood icon Marilyn Monroe. The book's first half covers the movie star's last two months, as she tries to deal with attacks on many fronts—by the movie studio that fired her; by her abusive ex-husband, Joe

DiMaggio; and by the Kennedys. By the time a drug overdose claims her, there's no shortage of people who wanted her dead. Heller, Monroe's sometime lover, who refuses to buy the official line that she committed suicide, steps on powerful toes with his usual tenacity and stubbornness to reach the truth. Collins convincingly portrays the real-life players in the drama, who include Jimmy Hoffa and Frank Sinatra." Publ Wkly

Collins, Max Allan

Quarry's ex. Hard Case Crime 2011 223p pa $9.95

ISBN 978-0-85768-286-4; 0-85768-286-5

"With Quarry's Ex, Collins takes us back to the mid-career of his brutal hero, a Vietnam vet and former hitman now hiring himself out to rich targets to kill their would-be killers. In Ex, his client proves to be a low-budget action film director who also turns out to be married to Quarry's betraying ex-wife Joni. Taking a cover job as unit publicity manager for Hard Wheels 2, a piece of video store fodder being filmed in Las Vegas, our hero seeks out Nick Varnos, a contractor who specializes in kills that look like accidents. Quarry's task becomes twofold: figure out how Varnos intents to off director Arthur Stockwell and identify the person responsible for putting out the hit on the director in the first place. . . . Collins tells his cynical little tale with plenty of tough wit; he especially has fun with his narrator's take on the dying days of drive-in moviemaking." Seattle Post-Intelligencer

Collins, Max Allan

Target Lancer; Max Allan Collins. Forge 2012 320 p. (hardcover) $25.99

ISBN 0765321807; 9780765321800; 9781429947060

LC 2012019943

This historical suspense novel, by Max Allan Collins, portrays the conspiracy to assassinate U.S. President John F. Kennedy. "Long before November 22, 1963, Nathan Heller, . . . knows that a conspiracy is in the works. . . . After being interrogated by gangsters and contacted by U.S. Attorney General Robert Kennedy, Heller realizes that he may be the one person who can prevent a devastating political assassination." (Publisher's note)

Collins, Michael

Death of a writer; a novel. Bloomsbury Pub. 2006 307p $24.95

ISBN 978-1-59691-229-8; 1-59691-229-4

LC 2006-1950

This novel is as "caustic as it is brilliant, a concoction of academic satire, German philosophy and literary criticism mixed up as a haunting murder mystery that will leave you disoriented—and deeply amused." Washington Post Book World

Collins, Michael

Lost souls; Michael Collins. 1st American ed; Viking 2004 260p $23.95

ISBN 0-670-03328-6

LC 2003-64535

"Collins's style, which alternates between the clipped prose of a cop novel and some surreally introspective pas-sages, gives the book the prose feel of a David Lynch film." Publ Wkly

Collins, Wilkie

★ The **moonstone**. Knopf 1992 473p $19
ISBN 0-679-41722-2

LC 92-52918

First published 1868

This novel "concerns the disappearance of the Moonstone, an enormous diamond that once adorned a Hindu idol and came into the possession of an English officer. The heroine, Miss Verinder, believes her lover, Franklin Blake, to be the thief; other suspects are Blake's rival and three mysterious Brahmins. The mystery is solved by Sergeant Cuff, possibly the first detective in English fiction." Reader's Ency. 4th edition

Collins, Wilkie

★ The **woman** in white. Knopf 1991 xxxvii, 569p $20
ISBN 0-679-40563-1

LC 91-52971

First published 1860; first Everyman's library edition 1910

"Practically the first English novel to deal with the detection of crime. The plot is based on the resemblance between the heroine and a mysterious woman in white, and involves an infamous attempt to obtain the heroine's money." Lenrow. Reader's Guide to Prose Fic

Colucci, A. J.

The **colony**; A.J. Colucci. Thomas Dunne Books 2012 294 p. (hardcover) $24.99

ISBN 1250001293; 9781250001290; 9781250017314

LC 2012035593

In this book by A. J. Colucci, "two years after a geneticist releases a huge queen ant in Manhattan's Riverside Park, New York City comes under attack from a vicious new species of ant. . . . As the death toll rises, the ambitious mayor calls on Paul O'Keefe, a leading ant expert, for solutions. When Paul is stymied, the federal government snatches his ex-wife, entomologist Kendra Hart, from her research project in New Mexico." (Publishers Weekly)

Colwin, Laurie

A **big** storm knocked it over; a novel. HarperCollins Pubs. 1993 259p

ISBN 0-06-017019-0

LC 92-56219

"The novel makes the idea of happy endings for decent people seem entirely plausible, almost inevitable—no small feat for a writer these days and no small pleasure for a reader." N Y Times Book Rev

Colwin, Laurie

Family happiness; a novel. Knopf 1982 271p
ISBN 0-394-52511-6

LC 82-23

"What is so striking about this wrenching novel is not the plot itself . . . but, rather, the absolutely convincing way that Colwin portrays Polly's slow awakening to selfhood." Booklist

Colwin, Laurie

Goodbye without leaving. Poseidon Press 1990 253p

ISBN 0-671-70706-X

LC 90-6797

This novel follows the "progress of Geraldine Cole-shares' life, from mediocre graduate student to rock 'n' roll backup singer to wife and mother. She seems happily married to Johnny Miller, a lawyer but a music fanatic at heart. She worries (but not too much) about what she is doing with her life, and what it all means." Libr J

"The tone here is disarmingly light, the humor intimate, and the plot inventive. A cheerfully irreverent look at an identity crisis and its unexpected resolution." Booklist

Colwin, Laurie

Happy all the time; a novel. Knopf 1978 213p

ISBN 0-394-50190-X

LC 78-2425

Set in New York City, this love story involves four quite normal people, "two men, two women. The men are cousins and close friends, the women are very different from each other, but full of spunk and individuality. Guido and Holly come together first, Vincent and Misty meet later. The men, long-time associates, are terribly nervous about their women liking each other. The women, in turn, eye each other warily. What we, as readers are treated to, however, is one of the most engaging and funniest dual courtships in a long time. The dialogue is sparkling and crisp, the encounter situations perfectly believable and perfectly ridiculous, as these four people, who really are 'happy all the time,' go through the 'angst' of realizing it." Publ Wkly

Company, Flavia

The **Island** of Last Truth; Flavia Company. Europa Editions 2012 124 p. (paperback) $15

ISBN 1609450817; 9781609450816

This novel, by Flavia Company, is "a story of many mysteries, principal among them, the true identity of the enigmatic Dr. Matthew Prendel. Legend has is that Prendel, . . . had been shipwrecked years before the story opens in contemporary New York. . . . He survived thanks to an incredible stroke of luck, while his entire crew perished. . . . Or perhaps . . . something darker was at play. . . . The only thing sure is that Matthew Prendel disappeared for five whole years." (Publisher's note)

Compton, Jodi

Thieves get rich, saints get shot; a novel. Crown Trade 2011 291p $23

ISBN 978-0-307-58808-1

LC 2010-45403

Sequel to: Hailey's war (2010)

"Hailey Cain, tough girl/West Point dropout, resurfaces in Los Angeles as second-in-command enforcer to Serena 'Warchild' Delgadillo, the leader of a Latina female gang. Rejected by the Army because of a brain tumor she knows will kill her, and rejected as well by her adored cousin CJ, who can't manage the unconventional lifestyle that allows Hailey to cope with her shortened life, Hailey plunges into a maelstrom of hijacking, deadly gang rivalry, and identity theft. . . . Readers fascinated by Hailey's conflict between

her aching heart and her canny head will hope she continues raising Cain." Publ Wkly

Conde, Maryse

✓ **I,** Tituba, black witch of Salem; translated by Richard Philcox; foreword by Angela Y. Davis; afterword by Ann Armstrong Scarboro. University Press of Va. 1992 227p

ISBN 0-8139-1398-5

LC 92-8134

Original French edition, 1986

"Part historical novel, part literary fable, part exploration of the clash of irreconcilable cultures, {this} is most of all an affirmation of a courageous and resourceful woman's capacity for survival." N Y Times Book Rev

Conklin, Tara

The **house** girl; a novel. Tara Conklin. 1st ed. William Morrow Paperbacks 2013 384 p. (hardcover) $20.99; (paperback) $14.99; (ebook) $20.99

ISBN 0062207393; 9780062207395; 9780062207517; 9780062207524

LC 2012027370

This book follows "Lina Sparrow . . . a first-year associate at a prestigious New York law firm; in 1852, Josephine Bell is the titular 'house girl,' a slave on a Virginia farm. Assigned to work on a class-action suit involving slavery reparations, Lina searches out a suitable plaintiff for the case. . . . Lina's father, an artist, suggests that Lina research the story of Josephine, speculated to be the real artist behind paintings attributed to . . . her white master." (Publishers Weekly)

Conley, Robert J.

✓ **Mountain** windsong; a novel of the Trail of Tears. University of Okla. Press 1992 218p

ISBN 0-8061-2452-0

LC 92-54150

"Its historical accuracy and its political correctness aside, the novel is a timeless love story about young people buffeted by a changing world over which they have no control." Booklist

Conlon, Edward

✓ ★ **Red** on red; Edward Conlon. 1st ed.; Spiegel & Grau 2011 442p

ISBN 9780385519175; 9780385519182

LC 2010017534

This book "tells the . . . story of two NYPD detectives, Meehan and Esposito: one damaged and introspective, the other ambitious and unscrupulous. Meehan is compelled by haunting and elusive stories that defy easy resolution, while Esposito is drawn to cases of rough and ordinary combat. A fierce and unlikely friendship develops between them and plays out against a tangle of mysteries: a lonely immigrant who hangs herself in Inwood Hill Park, a serial rapist preying on upper Manhattan, a troubled Catholic schoolgirl who appears in the wrong place with uncanny regularity, and a savage gang war that erupts over a case of mistaken identity." (Publisher's note)

Conn, Brian

The **fixed** stars; thirty-seven emblems for the perilous season. FC2 2010 311p pa $19.95

ISBN 978-1-57366-153-9; 1-57366-153-8

LC 2009-38689

"An intricate, innovative, and beautifully realized book about a far-future society contending with mysterious plagues and its own violent customs, The Fixed Stars is speculative fiction at once challenging and deeply rewarding, alive with a kind of mythic strangeness." Rain Taxi

Connell, Evan S.

✓ **Deus** lo volt! chronicle of the Crusades. Counterpoint 2000 462p

ISBN 1-58243-065-9

LC 99-54831

What enlivens Connell's historial fiction "is first, his boyish fascination with how much has been buried alongside the victims: lost books and alphabets, artworks, cities, enigmatic treasures of all kinds. Second, there is the glittering anger of his style." Yale Rev

Connell, Evan S.

Lost in Uttar Pradesh; new and selected stories. Counterpoint 2008 359p $27

ISBN 978-1-59376-175-2; 1-59376-175-9

LC 2007-43829

"The stories in 'Lost in Uttar Pradesh' — seven of which are published here for the first time — vary in setting and length, but it is not hard to identify the common thread running through them: Connell's characters, whether recurring or simply enjoying a walk-on, find themselves suddenly shellacked by the realization that the world is not as it appears — moral, ordered, progressing toward some comprehensible end but is, in fact, the opposite. . . . If these narratives sometimes feel less like fully realized stories and more like fragments of an ongoing conversation Connell is having with the world, so be it — what he's working to do here is express both rage and its futility, and it's fascinating to watch this theme morph and play out in various scenarios." Star Tribune (Minneapolis, Minn.)

Connell, Evan S.

✓ ★ **Mr.** Bridge; [by] Evan S. Connell, Jr. Knopf 1969 369p

"Mr. Connell's art is one of restraint and perfect mimicry. His chapters are admirably short, his style is brevity itself. . . . Rarely has a satirist damned his subject with such good humor." N Y Times Book Rev

Connell, Evan S.

✓ ★ **Mrs.** Bridge; [by] Evan S. Connell, Jr. Viking 1959 254p

"India Bridge is a country club matron in Kansas City. Her husband, a successful lawyer, is seldom home so Mrs. Bridge copes—not too well—with her children, who are very different from one another. Ruth, the eldest, keeps aloft; Douglas, the youngest, is mostly off on his own projects and not interested in the fine rules of behavior that Mrs. Bridge finds essential. She seems able to communicate most easily with Carolyn, the middle child. We follow the family as the children grow. Mrs. Bridge, eager to be a proper upper-middle-class wife and mother, finds no happiness despite her affluence and good intentions." Shapiro. Fic for Youth. 3d edition

Connelly, Joe

Crumbtown. Knopf 2003 259p $23

ISBN 0-375-41364-2

LC 2002-72930

"Set in a phantasmagoric dreamscape that is part New York City slum and part absurd parallel universe, Crumbtown is a place in which little is as it appears. The story centers on Don Reedy, in prison for a Robin Hood-style bank robbery, who is freed from jail to act as a consultant on a TV show based on his life. Once out, he quickly falls for Rita, a Russian émigré bartender, and teams up with half twins Tim and Tom, his former partners-in-crime, who sold him out to the police 15 years earlier. With them, he plots a new robbery set to take place during the filming of the bank robbery scene of the TV show. The result is a wildly inventive and darkly satiric take on a world constantly shifting and media image." Libr J

Connelly, Karen

The **lizard** cage. Nan A. Talese 2007 430p $26

ISBN 978-0-385-51818-5; 0-385-51818-8

LC 2006-44565

First published 2005 in Canada

"A thrilling, vital excoriation of the military junta that has ruled Burma for decades. . . . Karen Connelly's language and imagery evoke the short stories and poems that trickle out of Burma, by turns fearful and violent, beautiful and rancid." Wall Street J

Connelly, Michael, 1956-

The **black** ice. Little, Brown 1993 322p

ISBN 0-316-15382-6

LC 92-33500

Harry Bosch is a "smart, determined LAPD homicide detective who's driven by an inner sense of justice. This time out he arrives early on the scene of a fellow officer's suicide; then he's told it's not his case: back off. Fat chance. Harry senses the officer may have gone over to the bad guys and was killed when he tried to tiptoe back to the right side of the tracks. At every turn, Harry is confronted by dirty cops struggling to save their collective butts by lying and misdirecting the investigation. . . . A powerful novel." Booklist

Connelly, Michael

Blood work. Little, Brown 1998 393p

ISBN 0-316-15399-0

LC 97-28240

"Terry McCaleb was an FBI profiler specializing in serial killers until his heart gave out. After waiting two years for a heart transplant, he's just happy to be alive—until Graciela, a beautiful woman with a disturbing story, draws him back into the game. Graciela's sister Glory was killed in a convenience story robbery, and she's come to seek McCaleb's help in solving the crime. . . . High suspense, masterful plotting, and smart prose make this a superior thriller." Libr J

Connelly, Michael

The **brass** verdict; a novel. Little, Brown and Company 2008 422p $26.99

ISBN 978-0-316-16629-4; 0-316-16629-4

LC 2008-19374

"If this were no more than a standard legal thriller, it would still be hard to put down. But for all the glee we might take in watching Mickey in action—psychoanalyzing the jury pool, shredding the credibility of a prosecution witness or faking civility to a powerful judge—The Brass Verdict is not just a conventional legal thriller but also a complicated morality play." N Y Times Book Rev

Connelly, Michael, 1956-

City of bones; a novel. Little, Brown 2002 393p

ISBN 0-316-15405-9

LC 2001-38399

This is the latest installment in Mr. Connelly's crime series featuring LAPD detective Harry Bosch. The story revolves around "the long-undiscovered murder of a 12-year-old boy, whose skeletal remains are found high up in the Hollywood hills. Harry had a sad childhood himself, so he is especially drawn to a case that involves long-term abuse, as indicated by many signs of trauma to the boy's bones. . . . So Harry begins analyzing the crime scene, which is perilous and remote. He finds a 1975 quarter that helps pinpoint the year of the murder, and he talks to those who live nearby. Usual suspects abound." (N Y Times (Late N Y Ed))

This mystery opens with "the discovery of a human bone in the densely wooded hills around Laurel Canyon. Once the recovered skeleton is identified as that of a 12-year-old boy who had been repeatedly abused before his death, some 20 years earlier, Harry Bosch, the Los Angeles homicide detective . . . can go on the hunt for the killer. But before he does, Connelly works those initial scenes into a taut mini-drama in which even minor characters, like the elderly doctor whose dog dug up the first bone, play standout roles that burn with conviction." N Y Times Book Rev

Connelly, Michael

★ The **closers**; a novel. Little, Brown 2005 403p $26.95

ISBN 0-316-73494-2

LC 2005-00076

"In Los Angeles in 1988, a sixteen-year-old girl disappeared from her home and was later found dead of a gunshot wound to the chest. The death appeared at first to be a suicide but some of the evidence contradicted that scenario, and detectives came to believe this was in fact a murder. Despite a by-the-book investigation, no one was ever charged. Now Detective Harry Bosch is back with the LAPD with the sole mission of closing unsolved cases, and this girl's death is the first he's given." Publisher's note

"Like James Ellroy and John Fante, both of whose work is referred to here, Mr. Connelly continues to make his doomy, secretive Los Angeles a living, breathing character in his stories." N Y Times (Late N Y Ed)

Connelly, Michael

A **darkness** more than night; a novel. Little, Brown 2001 418p

ISBN 0-316-15407-5

LC 00-31025

This mystery pits L.A.P.D. detective Harry Bosch and former FBI profiler Terry McCaleb against each other. "When approached by an old L.A.P.D. pal, McCaleb jumps at the chance to help on a baffling murder case, the ritualistic details of which suggest a serial killer. It doesn't take McCaleb long to focus in on a prime suspect: Bosch. . . . Readers familiar with Bosch's bend-but-don't-break morality won't be stumped for long, but Connelly's . . . novel is otherwise flawless, cleverly conceived, superbly plotted and morally complex." Publ Wkly

Connelly, Michael

Echo Park; a novel. Little, Brown and Co. 2006 405p $26.99

ISBN 978-0-316-73495-0; 0-316-73495-0

LC 2006-9809

"What puts Connelly in the top rank of modern procedural writers and, perhaps, into the ranks of the better modern L.A. writers of any genre is his willingness to accept that there aren't always easy answers in Bosch's life, or sometimes any answers at all. . . . That sense of uncertainty and dread, combined with Bosch's going from middle age to the precipice of old age, informs every page of this novel." Washington Post Book World

Connelly, Michael, 1956-

The **fifth** witness; a novel. Little, Brown and Company 2011 421p $27.99

ISBN 978-0-316-06935-9; 0-316-06935-3

LC 2011-00576

"Mickey Haller has fallen on tough times. He expands his business into foreclosure defense, only to see one of his clients accused of killing the banker she blames for trying to take away her home. Mickey puts his team into high gear to exonerate Lisa Trammel, even though the evidence and his own suspicions tell him his client is guilty. Soon after he learns that the victim had black market dealings of his own, Haller is assaulted, too—and he's certain he's on the right trail." Publisher's note

"The story line is compelling, intense, and terrifying while providing an in-depth look at the mortgage crisis that is surprisingly interesting." Libr J

Connelly, Michael

★ The **Lincoln** lawyer; a novel. Little, Brown 2005 404p $26.95

ISBN 0-316-73493-4

LC 2005-12863

"The book is haunted by Mickey's worst nightmare: the thought of having to defend an innocent man. He starts out without the foggiest idea of what to do with someone like that. But by the end of the story an Honest Abe conscience has begun to kick in. That's when Mickey becomes a Connelly character through and through." N Y Times (Late N Y Ed)

Connelly, Michael

Lost light; a novel. Little, Brown 2003 360p $25.95

    ISBN 0-316-15460-1

LC 2002-36848

"The cop who failed to collar the person who strangled Angela Benton on her 24th birthday can't do much about it now; having taken a bullet in the spine, he's paralyzed from the neck down. But the man can talk, and he talks Harry Bosch into taking the cold case. . . . Despite some shockingly sunny developments in his personal life, Bosch wears his depression like armour, making him the perfect hero for our paranoid age." N Y Times Book Rev

Connelly, Michael

The narrows; a novel. Little, Brown 2004 404p $25.95

    ISBN 0-316-15530-6

LC 2003-25681

"Expertly juggling the narrative between Bosch's brooding, hardboiled voice and a broader third-person perspective that takes in the points of view of Walling and the Poet, Connelly builds tension exponentially through superb use of dramatic irony." Booklist

Connelly, Michael

Nine dragons; a novel. Little, Brown and Co. 2009 377p $27.99

    ISBN 978-0-316-16631-7; 0-316-16631-6

LC 2009-28913

In this adventure LAPD detective Harry Bosch "suspects that the shooting death of an L.A. liquor store owner is linked to a dangerous triad with tentacles that reach across the sea to China. Warned to stop pursuing leads on the case, Harry naturally ignores the threats and continues the investigation until he is presented with a video revealing the kidnapping of his 13-year-old daughter Maddy in Hong Kong. . . . Connelly's crime thriller plots are often nothing more or less than boilerplate melodramas with a unique twist in the third act, but credit must be given for creating one of the most enduring, endearing, and tenacious heroes in a genre often overcrowded with hardboiled creations." PopMatters

Connelly, Michael

The overlook; a novel. Little, Brown and Co. 2007 225p $21.99

    ISBN 978-0-316-01895-1; 0-316-01895-3

LC 2007-1954

This novel, which was originally serialized in the New York Times magazine, reunites Harry Bosch "with his former flame, FBI agent Rachel Walling. Bosch must break in a new partner, rookie Iggy Ferras, when they're called to look into the execution of physicist Stanley Kent on a Mulholland Drive overlook. When a special FBI unit, headed by Walling, arrives and tries to usurp his case, claiming it's a matter of national security, Bosch refuses to back down. Walling's focus on the potential theft of radioactive material from the hospital where Kent was lending his expertise to cancer treatment and her unwillingness to share information only make Bosch more determined to solve the case. . . . The scramble to investigate threats to national security, justified

or otherwise, is a timely subject and one on which Connelly puts a brilliant new spin." Publ Wkly

Connelly, Michael

The scarecrow; a novel. Little, Brown and Co. 2009 419p $27.99

    ISBN 978-0-316-16630-0

LC 2009-00855

This novel "begins with Jack McEvoy — the crime reporter who was the hero of Connelly's 1996 The Poet— being given two weeks' notice at the Los Angeles Times. He's expected to spend his last days training his replacement: a young reporter whose real advantage, for the bosses, is that her salary is much lower than Jack's. . . . Jack decides that the ultimate 'fuck you' to the paper will be a final story so good that the suits will look like fools to fire him. He decides on the case of a teen gangbanger charged with a stripper's rape and murder. It doesn't take long for Jack to suss out that the police have the wrong man, and to link the murder with another that makes it clear both are the work of a serial killer. The Scarecrow is swift and engrossing, and it marks a development that has needed to happen in Connelly's novels for a while." Boston Phoenix

Connelly, Michael

Void moon; a novel. Little, Brown 2000 391p $32

    ISBN 0-316-15406-7

LC 99-37054

"Cassie Black, a crack burglar whose specialty is stealing from high rollers who break the bank in Las Vegas, ignores the astrological warning of a bad moon and inadvertently rips off a courier for the Chicago mob. 'Sometimes you can steal too much,' Cassie tells her panicked accomplice when they finish counting the mob's $2.5 million down payment for the Cleopatra Casino. 'We just did.' Connelly makes shrewd work of the manhunt, cranking up the suspense to keep Cassie a whisker ahead of her pursuer, a techno-savvy psycho named Jack Karch, who is so adept at ruining a perfectly good hand that they call him the Jack of Spades." N Y Times Book Rev

Connolly, John, 1968-

Bad men; a thriller. Atria Books 2004 392p $25

    ISBN 0-7434-8784-2

LC 2003-69639

"The small island of Sanctuary, off the coast of Maine, was once the scene of a bloody massacre. Now, three centuries later, evil has again come to the island, a modern-day evil with strange, eerie connections to the events of the late 1600s. Do two police officers have even a remote chance of stopping the carnage? This is one of those novels that refuses to be pigeonholed. It's a thriller; it's a mystery; it's a tale of the supernatural (sort of). At its center is Joe Dupree, the (literal) gentle giant of a cop, a man whose kindness and compassion would appear to make him a bad choice to defend the citizens of Sanctuary from the marauding evil that approaches." Booklist

Connolly, John
    The **book** of lost things. Atria Books 2006 339p
$23

    ISBN 978-0-7432-9885-8; 0-7432-9885-3
                                            LC 2006-049340

    A "novel about a 12-year-old English boy, David, who
is thrust into a realm where eternal stories and fairy tales
assume an often gruesome reality. Books are the magic that
speak to David, whose mother has died at the start of WWII
after a long debilitating illness. His father remarries, and
soon his stepmother is pregnant with yet another interloper
who will threaten David's place in his father's life. When
a portal to another world opens in time-honored fashion,
David enters a land of beasts and monsters where he must
undertake a quest if he is to earn his way back out. Connolly
echoes many great fairy tales and legends (Little Red Riding
Hood, Roland, Hansel and Gretel), but cleverly twists them
to his own purposes." Libr J

Connolly, John
    The **burning** soul; a thriller. Atria Books 2011
406p $26

    ISBN 978-1-4391-6527-0
                                            LC 2011-21367

    Private investigator Charlie Parker "is hired to help Ran-
dall Haight, who is being blackmailed for a past crime in
which he and a friend as teenagers were convicted of killing
a 14-year-old girl. On his release as an adult, Haight was
given a new name and set himself up as a tax accountant in
the small Maine town of Pastor's Bay. But with the disappearance of a local 14-year-old girl, Haight wants to protect
his new life and asks Parker to find the blackmailers. To further complicate matters, there are others in Pastor's Bay who
are not who they seem to be, and Parker finds himself deeply
embroiled in the town's secrets." Libr J

    "An intelligent, plausible thriller, both harrowing and
memorable." Kirkus

Connolly, John, 1968-
    The **infernals**; John Connolly. 1st Atria Books
hardcover ed. Atria Books 2011 311p.

    ISBN 9781451643084 (hc); 9781451643107 (ebook);
9781451643091 (tp)
                                            LC 2011021366

    This book tells the story of "an ordinary English boy, his
loyal dog, and their encounters with demons and dark lords. .
. . Samuel, who is now 13. . . has a bit of an undeserved reputation as a troublemaker, when in reality he and [his dog]
Boswell managed to save the world from an invasion from
Hell." (Kirkus) "[A]n angry demon is seeking revenge for
Samuel's part in foiling the invasion . . . and when Samuel
and . . . Boswell are pulled through a portal into the dark
realm . . . it gets its chance. But . . . the Infernals have not
reckoned on the bravery and cleverness of a boy and his dog,
or the loyalty of Samuel's friend, the hapless demon Nurd,
or the presence of two clueless policemen and the unlucky,
if cheerfully optimistic, driver of an ice-cream van. Most of
all, no one has planned on the intervention of an unexpected
band of little men." (Publisher's note)

Connolly, John
    The **unquiet**; a novel. Atria Books 2007 418p
$25.95

    ISBN 978-0-7432-9893-3; 0-7432-9893-4
                                            LC 2006-101541

    "Daniel Clay, a psychiatrist alleged to have worked with
a child-abuse ring, is missing and presumed dead. His grown
daughter, Rebecca, is being stalked by an ex-con whose own
daughter is missing. Rebecca hires Portland, Maine, investigator Charlie Parker to protect her and dissuade her stalker, a
former contract killer named Merrick who is intent on either
finding his daughter or avenging her death. The case leads
to a very dark chapter in Maine's rural history and to the
still-operational remnants of a syndicate of highly organized
child abusers. Connolly weaves elements of the supernatural into a disturbing, very dark tale. . . . The disquieting
subject, coupled with Connolly's dark, lyrical prose, will
leave unshakable images lurking on the edge of the reader's
consciousness." Booklist

Connolly, Tina
    Ironskin; Tina Connolly. Tor 2012 304 p.
(hardcover) $24.99

    ISBN 0765330598; 9780765330598; 9781429993043
                                            LC 2012019874

    This fantasy novel by Tina Connolly is "set in a gothic,
alternate version of the Victorian era, in the aftermath of a
war with powerful, forest-dwelling beings called the fey. . . .
Jane Eliot, a young teacher and former governess dedicates
herself to teaching the peculiar, stubborn [Dorie] but wonders whether Dorie's disquieting powers can be curtailed.
Jane soon comes to realize that the war with the fey may not,
in fact, be over after all." (Kirkus Reviews)

Conrad, Joseph
    The **complete** short fiction of Joseph Conrad;
edited with an introduction by Samuel Hynes. Ecco
Press 1991 2v

    ISBN 0-88001-307-9 v1; 0-88001-308-7 v2
                                            LC 91-27115

Conrad, Joseph
    Great short works of Joseph Conrad. Harper &
Row 1966 378p

Conrad, Joseph
    ★ **Heart** of darkness; with an introduction by
Verlyn Klinkenborg. Knopf 1993 110p $15

    ISBN 0-679-42801-1
                                            LC 93-1855

    Originally published 1902 in the United Kingdom in the
collection Youth, and two other stories

    "Marlow tells his friends of an experience in the (then)
Belgian Congo, where he once ran a river steamer for a
trading company. Fascinated by reports about the powerful
white trader Kurtz, Marlow went into the jungle in search
of him, expecting to find in his character a clue to the evil
around him. He found Kurtz living a depraved and abominable life, based on his exploitation of the natives. Without
the pressures of society, and with the opportunity to wield
absolute power, Kurtz succumbs to atavism." Reader's
Ency. 4th edition

Conrad, Joseph

★ **Lord** Jim; a tale. Knopf 1992 xxxiii, 437p $19

    ISBN 0-679-40544-5

                        LC 91-53223

First published 1899; first Everyman's library edition 1935

"The title character is a man haunted by guilt over an act of cowardice. He becomes an agent at an isolated East Indian trading post. There his feelings of inadequacy and responsibility are played out to their logical and inevitable end." Merriam-Webster's Ency of Lit

Conrad, Joseph

The **Nigger** of the Narcissus; edited, with an introduction and notes, by Cedric Watts. Penguin Books 1989 151p map pa $12.95

    ISBN 0-14-018094-X

First published 1897 with title: Children of the sea

"All life on board the Narcissus revolves around James Wait, a dying black sailor. Other members of the crew include the strong Captain Allistoun; Craik, an Irish religious fanatic; and Donkin, an arrogant, lazy Cockney. The superstitious sailors cater to Wait, even steal food for him, and rescue him when the ship capsizes during a fierce storm. However, he is also the cause of dissension aboard ship, leading to a near mutiny. The novel is notable not only for its vivid picture of life at sea but also as a study of evolving relationships among men amid the most extreme circumstances." Merriam-Webster's Ency of Lit

Conrad, Joseph

★ **Nostromo**; a tale of the seaboard. Knopf 1992 532p $20

    ISBN 0-679-40990-4

                        LC 91-53185

First published 1904; first Everyman's library edition 1957

"Set in the South American republic of 'Costaguana,' it is an exciting, complicated story about capitalist exploitation and revolution on the national scene and about personal morality and corruption in individuals. Charles Gould's silver mine helps to maintain the country's stability and its reactionary government. Gould's idealistic preoccupation with the mine warps his character and makes him neglect his gentle wife, Dona Emilia. When the revolution comes, Gould puts a consignment of silver in the charge of Nostromo, the magnificent, 'incorruptible' capataz de cargadores ('foreman of the dock workers'). A chance happening makes Nostromo decide to bury the silver and pretend that it was lost at sea. He is eventually killed on the island where his riches are buried, when he is mistaken by his fiancée's father for a prowler. . . . Conrad's characterization is strong, his narration is complex and oblique. The story starts halfway through the events of the revolution and proceeds by way of flashbacks and glimpses into the future." Reader's Ency. 4th edition

Conrad, Joseph

The **portable** Conrad; edited, and with an introduction and notes, by Morton Dauwen Zabel. Viking 1947 760p

Short stories included are: Prince Roman; Warrior's soul; Amy Foster; Outpost of progress; Il Conde; The lagoon; The secret sharer. The novelettes are: Youth; Heart of darkness

Conrad, Joseph

Victory; an island tale. with an introduction by Tony Tanner. Knopf 1998 lxi, 385p $20

    ISBN 0-375-40047-8

                        LC 98-27677

First published 1915

The novel's "central character, Axel Heyst, a Swedish aristocrat, lives on an island in the Malay Archipelego. Influenced by the sceptical philosophy of his father, and trying to avoid forming any attachments, his way of life is challenged when he rescues Lena, who has been touring the islands as part of a Ladies' Orchestra, from the sexual harassment of the hotelkeeper, Schomberg. The novel explores their relationship and the difficulties precipitated by the arrival of the devilish 'Mr Jones' and his two companions." Oxford Companion to 20th-century Lit in Engl

Includes bibliographical references

Conroy, Pat

Beach music. Talese 1995 628p $32.50

    ISBN 0-385-41304-1

                        LC 95-13563

This "is an absolute attic of a book. It's overstuffed. Seemingly every memory, character, place, and event from not only Conroy's life, but from the lives of most of the people he's ever met are in it. And as in a proper attic, you wander through 'Beach Music' dazed and fascinated by the odd, clashing richness of the several lifestyles it contains." Christ Sci Monit

Conroy, Pat

The **lords** of discipline. Bantam Books 2002 561p pa $15

    ISBN 0-553-38156-3

A reissue of the title first published 1980 by Houghton Mifflin

The novel "is engrossing and well written. Pat Conroy . . . writes dialogue that reeks of witty Hollywood repartee, but his descriptions and characterizations are both sensitive and entertaining. He carefully draws Will as the young man who disdains military formalities and defends plebes." Saturday Rev

Conroy, Pat

★ The **prince** of tides. Houghton Mifflin 1986 567p $35

    ISBN 0-395-35300-9

                        LC 86-10689

"Savannah Wingo, a successful feminist poet who has suffered from hallucinations and suicidal tendencies since childhood, has never been able to reconcile her life in New York with her early South Carolina tidewater heritage. Her suicide attempt brings her twin brother, Tom, to New York, where he spends the next few months, at the request of Savannah's psychiatrist . . . helping to reconstruct and analyze her early life." Libr J

Conroy, Pat

South of Broad; a novel. Doubleday 2009 514p $29.95

ISBN 978-0-385-41305-3; 0-385-41305-X

LC 2008-45681

"In the great Southern tradition of storytelling, the city of Charleston, S.C., is the principal 'character' in Pat Conroy's new novel. . . . Like the Southern Gothic masters, William Faulkner and Flannery O'Connor, Conroy understands that a compelling sense of place will lend grace to his narrative, inhabiting the minds of his readers like the mournful strains of an old folk song." Boston Globe

Constantine, K. C.

Blood mud. Mysterious Press 1999 375p

ISBN 0-89296-647-5

LC 98-34909

"Constantine knows that Faulkner was right: the only subject truly worth writing about is the human heart in conflict with itself. The evocation of Mario's fears and inner conflicts, told through agonizingly wonderful dialogue between husband and wife, raises this latest Balzic novel to the level of the best contemporary literature." Booklist

Constantine, K. C.

Brushback. Mysterious Press 1998 278p $29

ISBN 0-89296-646-7

LC 97-10130

"This is another near-perfect game from Constantine. His working-class dialogue is always exacting and evocative, and his detective is a great guy with a good heart and a mouth that just never quits." Publ Wkly

Constantine, K. C.

Family values. Mysterious Press 1997 216p

ISBN 0-89296-545-2

LC 96-23330

Retired Rocksburg, Pa. police chief Mario Balzic is "working on special assignment for the state's Deputy Attorney General, who is bedeviled by a 17-year-old murder case that won't roll over and die. The plot isn't much: Balzic goes around interviewing people involved in the trial of Lester Walczinsky, who is doing serious prison time for killing a couple of no-good drug dealers, and digging up evidence of past perjury and police corruption. Plot doesn't really count for much in Mr. Constantine's books. Character does." N Y Times Book Rev

Constantine, K. C.

Grievance. Mysterious Press 2000 279p

ISBN 0-89296-648-3

LC 99-41380

This mystery, set in Rocksburg, Pa., begins with "the murder of J. D. Lyon, C.E.O. of the local steel outfit that pulled up stakes and relocated to Brazil, tossing this company town into an economic sinkhole. Ruggiero (Rugs) Carlucci, the young police sergeant who recently took over the peacekeeping chores . . . does his best to conduct a fair investigation. But he is driven to distraction by his mother's deteriorating mental state, and his work ethic is compromised by his compassion for the families whose lives were so casually destroyed by the murdered man. . . . The

anguished voices of the broken people in this beat-up town would make a saint weep." N Y Times Book Rev

Constantine, K. C.

Saving room for dessert. Mysterious Press 2002 294p

ISBN 0-89296-763-3

LC 2002-20096

This mystery "focuses on three Rocksburg cops who patrol the Flats, an area of the city known for domestic disputes that often become deadly. Officer William Rayford prays for a thunderstorm that will keep the feuding Bucyks and Hornyaks, not to mention the certifiable Scavellis, indoors. His prayers aren't answered, however, and Rayford and fellow cops Reseta and Canozza all find themselves drawn into a lunatic situation that ends tragically." Booklist

"Constantine is as eloquent as ever in speaking out on the inevitability of violence when people can't find the language to express themselves." N Y Times Book Rev

Cook, Claire

Best staged plans; Claire Cook. 1st ed.; Voice-Hyperion 2011 viii, 238p

ISBN 9781401341176; 9781401341855

LC 2010041839

This book tells the story of Sandra, "a professional home stage based out of the Boston area. Knowledgeable about home design and full of ideas, she somehow can't manage to get her own house ready for the market, thanks to her lacking-off husband and son. When she gets an offer to stage a boutique hotel in Atlanta, she leaps at the chance to run away and get some distance and perspective." (Libr J)

Cook, Elizabeth

Achilles. Picador 2002 115p

ISBN 0-312-28884-0

LC 2001-52398

First published 2001 in the United Kingdom

"This forceful re-creation of the life of Achilles sacrifices nothing to modernity: gods mate violently with mortals, ghosts feast on sheep's blood, and Achilles rages and slays, unburdened by psychology. At the same time, this brief, intense novel is unmistakably modern in intent, turning a war epic into a meditation on the limits of human perfectibility." New Yorker

Cook, Robin

★ Coma; a novel. Little, Brown 1977 306p

ISBN 0-316-15510-1

LC 76-52951

"A female medical student uses her charms and femininity to obtain forbidden charts and computer read-outs on certain patients who have gone into coma on the operating table and never come out of it, remaining like vegetables due to extensive brain damage. Susan feels there is something wrong and sets out to find what it is. As a second-year med student, she knows practically nothing of medical terms or practices, so spends all of her class time in the library trying to learn the terminology before she can try to solve a mystery that has puzzled the finest surgeons in the hospital. She does manage to uncover a ring of doctors who are selling various organs for transplant from the coma victims as soon as they can declare them dead, and is almost a victim herself for her pains." West Coast Rev Books

Cook, Robin

Crisis. G.P. Putnam's Sons 2006 468p $25.95
ISBN 0-399-15357-8

LC 2006-46231

"Dr. Craig Bowman is irritated when problem-patient Patience Stanhope calls him on what he assumes is yet another false alarm. But Craig makes a house call and discovers Patience near death. He rushes her to the hospital but not in time to save her, and the result is a malpractice suit that could cost Craig his livelihood. Alexis, the wife Craig recently reunited with, calls her brother, New York City medical examiner Jack Stapleton . . . , and asks him to come to Boston for advice. Jack, who is less than a week away from his wedding to fellow ME Laurie Montgomery, agrees, despite the fact that he's never liked Craig. But when he travels to Boston and starts to attend Craig's trial, Jack worries that the case is being railroaded by the plaintiff's sleazy lawyer. When Jack performs the autopsy, the results are shocking." Booklist

Cook, Robin

Godplayer. Putnam 1983 368p
ISBN 0-399-12764-X

LC 83-4507

"Someone is playing God on the surgery floor of Boston Memorial Hospital, causing unexplained patient deaths. Pathologist Robert Sieber, with the help of Dr. Cassandra Kingsley, is investigating these 'SSD's,' sudden surgical deaths. Meanwhile Cassi's husband, a top surgeon, is becoming estranged from her, and seems headed for a breakdown. When Cassi herself must be admitted for an eye operation, she isn't aware that she is the Godplayer's next target." Libr J

Cook, Robin

Marker; Robin Cook. Putnam 2005 533p $25.95
ISBN 0-399-15293-8

LC 2005-45812

This book "revisits medical examiners Jack Stapleton and Laurie Montgomery, whose romantic relationship has hit a major bump. Approaching her forty-third birthday, Laurie wants a family and has grown impatient with Jack's reluctance to commit. She walks out on Jack, but she can't avoid him at work. She soon finds herself absorbed in a puzzling case: 28-year-old Sean McGillan has landed on her table, and she can't determine what killed him. Sean had just undergone routine knee surgery, but she can't find any reason why he went into cardiac arrest in his hospital bed. When another young, seemingly healthy patient dies, she suspects foul play." Booklist

"True love runs a rocky course, and the plot thickens before the denouement crackles to an electric edge-of-the-seat finale." Publ Wkly

Cook, Robin

Seizure. Putnam 2003 464p $24.95
ISBN 0-399-14876-0

LC 2003-43225

This "medical thriller centers around two men—Daniel Lowell, a brilliant researcher and Ashely Butler, a power-ful southern senator. Daniel and his girlfriend, Stephanie D'Agostino, are the cofounders of CURE, a medical research company, the existence of which relies heavily on biotechnology legislation that Butler is trying to block. . . . Cook is at his best when focusing on fascinating cutting-edge biotechnology procedures." Booklist

Cook, Robin

Vector. Putnam 1999 404p
ISBN 0-399-14471-4

LC 98-49058

In this "novel, the People's Aryan Army (PAA) is planning a major terrorist attack against a big government building in New York, hoping that will spark nationwide revolution. PAA founder Curt recruits immigrant Russian technician Yuri to prepare bioweapons for the attack. Yuri sets up a basement lab to produce anthrax, and a package 'bomb' becomes the vector for the anthrax when Yuri tries it out on a Greek rug dealer. Desiring proof of the merchant's death, Yuri meets Jack Stapleton from the medical examiner's office, and Jack's sidekick, Laurie, gets involved. . . . Vector is Cook at his best, providing both thrills and an urgent message." Booklist

Cook, Thomas H.

Breakheart Hill. Bantam Bks. 1995 264p
ISBN 0-553-09651-6

LC 94-26639

"Cook has crafted a novel of stunning power, with a climax that is so unexpected the reader may think he has cheated. But there is no cheating here, only excellent storytelling." Booklist

Cook, Thomas H.

The **Chatham** School affair. Bantam Bks. 1996 292p
ISBN 0-553-09652-4

LC 96-4021

"Cook is a marvelous stylist, gracing his prose with splendid observations about people and the lush, potentially lethal landscape surrounding them. Events accelerate with increasing force, but few readers will be prepared for the surprise that awaits at novel's end." Publ Wkly

Cook, Thomas H.

The **cloud** of unknowing. Harcourt 2007 320p $24
ISBN 978-0-15-101260-2; 0-15-101260-1

LC 2006-13951

"Although Cook is maddeningly coy about who actually killed whom, he writes eloquently about the fears that lead people to equate intelligence with madness, suppressing the imagination and taking refuge in mediocrity." N Y Times Book Rev

Cook, Thomas H.

The **fate** of Katherine Carr. Houghton Mifflin Harcourt 2009 276p $25
ISBN 978-0-15-101401-9; 0-15-101401-9

LC 2008-49203

"George Gates has been completely broken by the kidnapping and murder of his eight-year-old son seven years ago. Gates is a former travel writer, much given to writing about places where people disappeared. Now he salves his psyche by writing totally innocuous small features for the local paper. A chance meeting at a bar with the detective who organized the search parties when Gates' son went missing leads Gates into a new interest, a cold case that has obsessed the detective for two decades. Retired missing-persons detective Arlo McBride shows Gates the poems and journal that the 31-year-old missing woman left behind, and both men are pulled into reopening the case." Booklist

"Adept at merging past and present plot lines, Cook eloquently examines the often cathartic act of storytelling." Publ Wkly

Cook, Thomas H.
  Instruments of night. Bantam Bks. 1998 293p
  ISBN 0-553-10554-X
  LC 97-52760

"Although it's easy to miss the very real clues that Cook drops so artfully into the story, there's no ignoring his savage imagery, or escaping the airless chambers of his disturbing imagination." N Y Times Book Rev

Cook, Thomas H.
  The **interrogation**. Bantam Bks. 2002 286p $23.95
  ISBN 0-533-80095-7
  LC 2002-280882

"It's 1952. Three cops take turns grilling one suspect in interrogation Room Number Three. They have 12 hours to solve the murder of a little girl, found strangled to death in a park, before the suspect must be released. . . . The ticking clock, in addition to the economy of scene, makes this an incredibly intense read, culminating in a true shocker of an ending." Booklist

Cook, Thomas H.
  ✓ The **last** talk with Lola Faye. Houghton Mifflin Harcourt 2010 275p $25
  ISBN 978-0-15-101407-1; 0-15-101407-8
  LC 2009-27927

"For the reader who can handle the frenetic jumping between present and past (a narrative strategy that is inherently un-suspenseful), and endure a few annoying red herrings, 'The Last Talk With Lola Faye' will emerge as an eloquent articulation that 'the truths we won't face are the ones that never stop pumping their slow poison into our blood.' It's a story about coming to terms, a thriller whose engine is regret, and for Page, as well as for the reader, it was a talk worth having." Minneapolis Star Tribune

Cook, Thomas H.
  ✓ **Master** of the delta. Harcourt 2008 367p $24
  ISBN 978-0-15-101254-1; 0-15-101254-7
  LC 2007-26506

"Cook writes in a multiplicity of voices and time frames, and with a profusion of literary references that in another context might seem showy. But from the perspective of a learned narrator who has lived long enough to rue the day he tried to play God, the convolutions of both plot and thought—so tortured and twisted and ultimately so futile—are entirely in character." N Y Times Book Rev

Cook, Thomas H.
  Places in the dark. Bantam Bks. 2000 245p
  ISBN 0-553-10563-9
  LC 99-89644

A village on the coast of Maine "is torn apart by the arrival of a young woman, Dora March, who seems to bring death in her path. Dora awakens the interest and passions of two brothers. Central to the brothers' fascination with Dora is their half-knowledge of the childhood trauma that has maimed her spirit. One brother is murdered; Dora flees; the older brother embarks on a quest to find her and rid himself of obsession." Booklist

This novel "is swept along by Cook's artistry, his insights into broken people, his austere imagery of the barren landscapes that attract them." N Y Times Book Rev

Cook, Thomas H.
  ✓ The **quest** for Anna Klein. Houghton Mifflin Harcourt 2011 346p $27
  ISBN 978-0-547-36464-3; 0-547-36464-4
  LC 2010-42696

"Cook's work is elegant, philosophical, and literary. This book is to be treasured, and is bound to earn him new readers." Cleveland Plain Dealer

Cook, Thomas H.
  ✓ ★ **Sandrine's** Case. Pgw 2013 352 p. $24
  ISBN 0802126081; 9780802126085

In this novel, "Sam Madison and his wife, Sandrine, both professors at Georgia's Coburn College (he of literature, she of history) and parents of a grown daughter, appear to have a solid marriage. But below the surface there are problems, which culminate in Sandrine's death from a cocktail of Demerol and vodka. While the coroner rules the death a suicide, the police suspect foul play and soon zero in on Sam as his wife's killer." (Publishers Weekly)

Cooke, Carolyn
  ✓ **Daughters** of the revolution; a novel. Alfred A. Knopf 2011 173p $24.95
  ISBN 978-0-307-59473-0; 0-307-59473-4
  LC 2011-02743

In this novel "the '60s are encroaching upon the prestigious Goode School, where headmaster Goddard Byrd — 'God' for short — stands staunchly opposed to coeducation until Carole Faust, a gifted African-American girl, is admitted via clerical error. The shock waves from this period permeate the decades that follow in unexpected ways, throughout the school and beyond. Cooke's slim but muscular novel asks a lot of the reader, switching perspectives and taking narrative detours. But her exquisitely hewn sentences and fiercely original characters brilliantly capture a moment of social change without ever resorting to simplistic, black-and-white depictions of feminism." Entertainment Wkly

Cooley, Martha
  ✓ The **archivist**; a novel. Little, Brown 1998 328p
  ISBN 0-316-15872-0
  LC 97-38385

The novel "treats serious questions in a humane and passionate manner, and leaves one thinking about these questions long after one has read the last page. Cooley is an accomplished stylist—there's scarcely a graceless or unintelligent sentence in the book—and a subtle chronicler of the inner life." N Y Times Book Rev

Coonts, Stephen

✓ **America**; a Jake Grafton novel. St. Martin's Press 2001 390p

ISBN 0-312-25341-9

LC 2001-34899

"America—the U.S. Navy's most advanced submarine—is pirated on her shakedown cruise by a mysterious crew of terrorists, just two months after the newly launched first satellite in an orbital antimissile system mysteriously disappeared. The missing sub then dispatches its Tomahawk missiles with magnetic pulse warheads to Washington and New York, devastating the government and Wall Street. Jake Grafton thinks these dire deeds are connected, and with various allies, he sets out to prove it and retrieve sub and satellite." Booklist

Coonts, Stephen

Final flight. Doubleday 1988 387p

ISBN 0-385-24555-6

LC 88-12001

Capt. Jake Grafton's "night-flying's over, thanks to failing eyesight. But the fate of the Middle East is hanging in the balance when his F-14 tears off into Mediterranean airspace. Coonts has cast the hero of his first novel, The Flight of the Intruder, as a wing commander aboard an aircraft carrier. He has also thrust him into the bulls-eye of an Arab plot to steal the ship's nuclear weapons. . . . The backdrop is Naples, and the well-detailed lives of Navy pilots. Final Flight has a long fuse, but its detonation is well worth the wait." Publ Wkly

Coonts, Stephen

★ **Flight** of the Intruder. Naval Inst. Press 1986 329p $26.95

ISBN 0-87021-200-1

LC 86-16440

"In the autumn of 1972, despite rumors of peace, United States Navy pilots flew A-6 Intruder attack planes in bombing raids over North Vietnam. Some of these pilots were angered by the relative insignificance of their targets—road intersections, sampan repair yards—which mocked the loss of life incurred carrying out the missions. So when the pilot Jake Grafton's best friend, a bombardier, is killed by a rifle bullet fired randomly from the ground, he decides 'to bomb something worth the trip' and plans a solo, unauthorized raid on Communist Party headquarters in downtown Hanoi." N Y Times Book Rev

Cooper, Isabel

No proper lady; Isabel Cooper. Sourcebooks Casablanca 2011 368p.

ISBN 9781402259524 pa; 9781402259531

This book, named a Best Book of the Year by "Publishers Weekly and "Library Journal," tells the story of "a woman from a dystopian future . . . where humanity is losing the war against demonic forces unleashed by a 200-year-old evil wizard, Alex Reynell. To destroy Reynell, Joan goes back to England in 1888, where magician Simon Grenville becomes

her guide to a completely different way of life. When she practices proper Victorian flirtation on Simon, their heady attraction flairs." (Publishers Weekly)

Cooper, J. California

The **future** has a past; stories. Doubleday 2000 265p $23.95

ISBN 0-385-49680-X

LC 00-34602

Stories about "African-American women struggling to make something of their smalltown lives. . . . Navigating poverty, unwanted pregnancy, single motherhood and inexperience, all Cooper's heroines triumph, to lesser and greater degrees, finding 'real love' despite being surrounded by 'no good men'." Publ Wkly

Cooper, J. California

The **wake** of the wind. Doubleday 1998 373p

ISBN 0-385-48704-5

LC 98-21594

"Two good friends in Africa, Kola and Suwaibu, are taken from Africa and brought to America as slaves. The story of their great-great-great grandchildren, Mordecai (Mor) and Lifee, reunites these friends' families through marriage. Mor and Lifee's life together is chronicled through their marriage, freedom from slavery, the birth of their children and grandchildren, and their deaths." Booklist

Cooper, J. California

Wild stars seeking midnight suns. Doubleday 2006 209p

ISBN 0-385-51133-7

LC 2005-56004

"Cooper's talent for capturing the lives of ordinary people penetrates this collection of short stories. These are simple stories about personal struggles in settings from small towns to urban centers. An awkward young woman, pushed into a loveless marriage by her mother, eventually finds her own way professionally and emotionally. Two successful urban professionals cross paths in a nightclub, and neither is satisfied when the evening ends as so many have–in disappointment. A 14-year-old in love with her best friend's much older brother observes the sexual tensions he stirs in others. Many of the stories are told from the perspective of a narrator, close but far away enough for sharp discernment. Cooper fans will enjoy this collection, and those who are new to her work will appreciate her character development and artful storytelling." Booklist

Cooper, James Fenimore

✓ The **Deerslayer**; or, The first war-path, a tale. with an introduction by Donald E. Pease. Penguin Books 1987 xxvii, 548p il (Penguin classics) pa $12

ISBN 0-14-039061-8

LC 88-104322

This is the first title of the author's Leatherstocking saga featuring Natty Bumppo

First published 1841 in two volumes by Lea & Blanchard

Set in New York State this "is a record of Natty Bumppo's early days as a young hunter brought up among the Delaware Indians, engaged in warfare against the Hurons.

He helps defend the family of Tom Hutter, a settler, from attack. Judith, who is really not Tom's daughter, but a girl of noble birth, loves Natty Bumppo and begs him not to return to the Iroquois, who have released him on parole from capture. Bumppo does return, but is rescued by the intervention of Judith, who thereafter disappears, and the Delaware Chief Chingachgook, who remains a lifelong friend." Haydn. Thesaurus of Book Dig

Followed by The last of the Mohicans

Cooper, James Fenimore

✓ The **last** of the Mohicans; introduction by Leslie A. Fiedler. Modern Library 2001 xxxii, 350p (The Modern Library classics) pa $9.95

ISBN 0-375-75764-3

LC 00-68105

First published 1826

This Leatherstocking tale "presents Chingachgook and his son Uncas as the last of the Iroquois aristocracy. Natty Bumppo, the scout Hawkeye, is in the prime of his career in the campaign of Fort William Henry on Lake George under attack by the French and Indians. The commander's daughters, Cora and Alice Munro, with the latter's fiancé Major Duncan Heyward, are captured by a traitorous Indian but rescued and conveyed to the fort by Hawkeye. Later Munro surrenders to Montcalm, and the girls are seized again by Indians. Uncas and Cora are killed, and the others return to civilization." Haydn. Thesaurus of Book Dig

Cooper, James Fenimore

★ The **Leatherstocking** tales. Library of Am. 1985 2v ea $40

ISBN 0-940450-20-8 v1; 0-940450-21-6 v2

LC 84-25060

These novels "are linked together by the career of Natty Bumppo, or Hawkeye, Cooper's inimitable backwoodsman, a romantic embodiment of the virtues of both races, and of Chingachgook, his Indian counterpart, equally idealized. . . . There is little historical background; but the vivid descriptions of wood, lake, and prairie, and of the daily life of Indian and huntsman, gives the finest imaginable picture extant of natural scenes and human conditions that have long passed away." Baker. Guide to the Best Fic

Cooper, James Fenimore

✓ The **Pathfinder**; or, The inland sea. edited with an introduction and notes by William P. Kelly. Oxford University Press 1992 xxxv, 484p pa $11.95

ISBN 0-19-283989-6

First published 1840

The third in the Leatherstocking tales "finds Natty Bumppo at the age of forty. A small outpost on Lake Ontario is under attack. Mabel Dunham helps in the defense, and with the aid of Pathfinder, Chingachgook, and Jasper Western, a young sailor, the Iroquois are routed. Lieutenant Muir . . . arrests Jasper as a traitor, but when Muir is revealed as the guilty one, he is killed by Arrowhead, a Tuscarora Indian. Jasper wins the love of Mabel." Haydn. Thesaurus of Book Dig

Includes bibliographical references

Followed by The pioneers

Cooper, James Fenimore

✓ The **pilot**; a tale of the sea. edited with an historical introduction and explanatory notes by Kay Seymour House. State University of New York Press 1986 xlvii, 479p il $59.50

ISBN 0-8739-5415-7

LC 84-8765

First published 1823

John "Paul Jones's adventures suggested the plot; which is, in brief, an attempt during the Revolutionary War to abduct some prominent Englishmen for exchange against American prisoners." Keller. Reader's Dig of Books

Includes bibliographical references

Cooper, James Fenimore

✓ The **pioneers**; edited with an introduction and notes by James D. Wallace. Oxford University Press 1999 465p map pa $10.95

ISBN 0-19-283667-6

First published 1822

In this fourth of the Leatherstocking tales Natty "first appears as an older man. The story takes place in the village of Templeton, founded by Judge Temple. The central conflict is between the laws of nature, upheld by Natty, and the laws of civilization. Symbolic of this opposition are two incidents, the first being the settler's hypocritical effort to punish Natty fo killing a deer out of season for food, despite their own slaughter of pigeons purely for sport. The second is over the true ownership of the Judge's lands , which is resolved by the marriage of Elizabeth Temple and Edward Effingham, heir of the true owner. Natty, like Huck Finn, heads for the Far West to escape confining civilization." Reader's Ency. 4th edition

Followed by The prairie

Cooper, James Fenimore

✓ The **prairie**; with an introduction by Blake Nevius. Penguin 1987 xxvi, 386p pa $13

ISBN 0-14-039026-X

LC 87-2891

Sequel to The pioneers

First published 1827

This final installment in the Leatherstocking tales centers on the death of Natty Bumppo. "Cooper contrasts the noble, disinterested Natty with the squatter Ishmael Bush and his family. Lawless and self-seeking, the squatters portend ill for the future of democracy. Cooper's prairie descriptions . . . are derived from the Journals of Lewis and Clark." Reader's Ency. 4th edition

Cooper, James Fenimore

✓ **Sea** tales: The pilot, The red rover. Library of America, Distributed to the trade in the U.S. and Canada by Viking Press 1991 902p $35

ISBN 0-940450-70-4

LC 90-52923

The pilot is entered separately. In The red rover (1827 in United Kingdom and France, 1828 in the United States), "Lt. Henry Ark, an officer in the British Navy about the middle of the 18th century, . . . takes the name Wilder and enlists as a common sailor on board the Dolphin in the hope of tracking down a mysterious pirate, the Red Rover." Reader's Ency. 2nd edition

Coover, Robert
Briar Rose. Grove Press 1996 86p
ISBN 0-8021-1591-8
LC 96-4917
"Coover doesn't just spit in the eye of happily-ever-after; he gouges it out. But what makes Briar Rose more than a cynical tale for adult children is the startling complexity of its vision." Nation

Coover, Robert
Ghost town; a novel. Holt & Co. 1998 147p
ISBN 0-8050-5884-2
LC 98-5713
"Genre isn't the only target of Coover's perversity: the goings on are often hilariously obscene, and perhaps truer to the old West than what we want to imagine. 'Ghost Town' is both warped and scintillating, a cross between 'No Exit' and 'The Canterbury Tales'." New Yorker

Coover, Robert
★ **Noir**. Overlook 2010 192p $24.95
ISBN 978-1-59020-294-4; 1-59020-294-5
LC 2009-40215
"With its flashbacks and glittering allusions, Noir is an exuberant, edgy laugh in the dark. . . . If you're looking for a Sam Spade, Mr. Noir is not your sleuth. He's an empty trench coat, which makes the ending so delicious. If you're a Coover groover, you'll love how the writer gooses this classic subgenre. Noir is an obsidian gem." Dallas Morning News

Coover, Robert
Pinocchio in Venice. Linden Press/Simon & Schuster 1991 330p
ISBN 0-671-64471-8
LC 90-45706
"The ribaldry and the 'fun' are a lot more strenuous and obsessive than self-denial ever was. But then, that is Coover's specialism–the joke on the joker, that the world without soul, far from being easy, is absurdly hard." Times Lit Suppl

Coplin, Amanda
✓★ The **orchardist**; a novel. Amanda Coplin. Harper, an imprint of HarperCollinsPublishers 2012 426 p. $26.99
ISBN 006218850X; 9780062188502
LC 2012005466
This book is set "in the Pacific Northwest during the early years of the 20th century, [where] middle-aged Talmadge tends his orchards, . . . Two barely pubescent sisters, Jane and Delia, both pregnant by an opium-addicted, violent brothel owner from whom they have escaped, touch Talmadge's otherwise stoic heart, and he shelters and protects them until the arrival of the girls' pursuers precipitates tragic consequences." (Publishers Weekly)

Corey, James S. A.
✓ **Abaddon's** Gate; by James S. A. Corey. 1st ed. Orbit 2013 576 p. (paperback) $17
ISBN 0316129070; 9780316129077
LC 2012041860
This novel, written by James S.A. Corey, is the third in the Expanse series. An "alien artifact . . . has appeared in Uranus' orbit, where it has built a massive gate that leads to a starless dark. Jim Holden and the crew of the Rocinante are part of a vast flotilla of scientific and military ships going out to examine the artifact. The emissaries of the human race try to find whether the gate is an opportunity or a threat. But behind the scenes, a complex plot is unfolding, with the destruction of Holden at its core." (Publisher's note)

Corey, James S. A.
✓ **Caliban's** war; by James S. A. Corey. Orbit 2012 624 p. $15.99
ISBN 9780316129060
LC 2011031646
This book by James S. A. Corey "returns to the politically charged future solar system setting of 'Leviathan Wakes.' . . . Eighteen months have passed since the now defunct corporation Protogen tried--with horrifying results--to harness an alien molecule with the power to rearrange living and inanimate matter. . . . The shaky détente among Mars, Earth, and the Outer Planets Alliance shatters after aliens attack Earth and Mars forces on Ganymede, making it look like Earth was the aggressor." (Publishers Weekly)

Corey, James S. A.
✓★ **Leviathan** Wakes; James S.A. Corey. 1st ed. Orbit 2011 582p.
ISBN 9780316129084 pa; 0316129089
LC 2010046442
This book tells the story of "Jim Holden, [who] is XO of an ice-hauler swinging between the rings of Saturn and the mining stations of the Belt. . . . His ship's captain . . . orders Holden and a shuttle crew to investigate what proves to be a derelict. Holden realizes it's some sort of trap, but an immensely powerful, stealthed warship destroys the ice-hauler, leaving Holden and the shuttle crew the sole survivors. This unthinkable act swiftly brings Earth . . . Mars . . . and the . . . Belt to the brink of war. Meanwhile, . . . cynical, hard-drinking detective Miller . . . receives orders to track down . . . a girl. . . . [T]he trail leads towards Holden, the derelict, and what might prove to be a horrifying biological experiment." (Kirkus)

Cornwell, Bernard, 1944-
✓ **1356**; Bernard Cornwell. HarperCollins 2013 432 p. $28.99
ISBN 0061969672; 9780061969676
This book is the fourth book in Bernard Cornwell's Grail Quest series. English archer Sir Thomas of Hookton's lord orders him to find the mystical sword of Saint Peter before the French do, so he 'begins, with his men, a perilous journey of raiding and plundering across southern France. . . . Thomas and his men reach the decisive Battle of Poitiers, a vicious melee that killed thousands, unseated a king, and forced a devastating and short peace on a land ravaged by warfare." (Publishers Weekly)

Cornwell, Bernard, 1944-

The **archer's** tale. HarperCollins Pubs. 2001 374p

ISBN 0-06-621084-4

LC 2001-24333

First published 2000 in the United Kingdom with title Harlequin

"Authentically detailed and appropriately gruesome, the medieval battle scenes fairly crackle with tension; however, what sets Cornwell's work apart from most run-of-the-mill military adventures are his meticulously developed story lines and his razor-sharp characterizations." Booklist

Cornwell, Bernard

✓ **Burning** land; a novel. HarperCollins 2010 336p $25.99

ISBN 978-0-06-088874-9; 0-06-088874-1

"Uhtred the Warlord is the irreverent and conflicted hero of Cornwell's Saxon Tales saga about Alfred the Great. In [this volume] . . . , both he and England are in peril. The Saxons and the Danes are at war, and this puts Uhtred in a precarious position. Worse, he is an unrepentant pagan in a world that is becoming aggressively Christian. After tragedy strikes, he is exiled and determines once again to become a Viking, retrieve the mighty fortress that is his heritage, and get away from not-so-merry England. However, fate pulls him back to help protect the kingdom of Mercia from the Danes. . . . Cornwell makes his subject material come alive." Libr J

Cornwell, Bernard, 1944-

Death of kings. HarperCollins 2011 xii, 320 p.p $27.99

ISBN 9780061969652

LC 2012371564

This book follows Uhtred, an "irreverent but deadly ninth-century Saxon-born, Viking raised warrior" who has sworn loyalty to English leader Alfred the Great. Alfred is dying and "wishes to cement the line of succession, thus guaranteeing his son, Edward, the throne." (Libr J)

Cornwell, Bernard

Enemy of God; a novel of Arthur. St. Martin's Press 1997 396p (Warlord chronicles)

ISBN 0-312-15523-9

LC 96-51740

In the second volume of the Warlord Chronicles trilogy, "having secured the throne of Dumnonia for the infant King Mordred, Arthur seeks to bring peace to the kingdom by uniting the various rival Celtic factions into the 'Brotherhood of Britain.' Derfel, one of Arthur's warriors and the book's narrator, sardonically notes that 'the Round Table, of course, was never a proper name, but rather a nickname.' But Arthur's good intentions are gradually undone: by Merlin's quest for the Thirteen Treasures of Britain; by Lancelot's and Guinevere's ambitions; by Mordred, now an unpleasant young man incapable of wise rule; and by the growing conflict between the old Druid religion and the new Christianity." Libr J

"This complex and superbly wrought narrative easily eclipses the more sanitized and tepid versions of Arthur's exploits." Booklist

Followed by Excalibur

Cornwell, Bernard

✓ **Excalibur**; a novel of Arthur. St. Martin's Press 1998 340p (Warlord chronicles)

ISBN 0-312-18575-8

LC 98-10247

"The action is gripping and skillfully paced, cadenced by passages in which the characters reveal themselves in conversation and thought, convincingly evoking the spirit of the time. Ways of ancient ritual, battle and daily life are laid out in surprising detail." Publ Wkly

Cornwell, Bernard

Gallows thief. HarperCollins Pubs. 2002 297p

ISBN 0-06-008273-9

LC 2001-58334

First published 2001 in the United Kingdom

"After successfully defending his country at Waterloo, Captain Rider Sandman returns to England to face bankruptcy and disgrace. . . . Looking for any type of honest work that will enable him to live and to pay off some of his father's creditors, he accepts an assignment to investigate the circumstances of the brutal rape and murder of the countess of Avebury. Though a hapless young portrait painter has already been convicted of the crime, Sandman begins to suspect well-connected members of the aristocracy have framed him." Booklist

Cornwell, Bernard, 1944-

The **last** kingdom; a novel. Bernard Cornwell. HarperCollins Publishers 2005 333p map o.p.; o.p.; (pbk.) $14.99

ISBN 0060530510 (acid-free paper); 9780060530518; 9780060887186

LC 2004054236

This book is "set in medieval England prior to the unification of the four Anglo-Saxon kingdoms. . . . Northumbria is invaded by the fearless Danes, and Uhtred, the rightful heir to the earldom of Bebbanburg, is captured by the enemy. Raised as a Viking warrior by Ragnar the Terrible, his beloved surrogate father, Uhtred is still torn by an innate desire to reclaim his birthright. Fighting as a Dane but realizing that his ultimate destiny lies along another path, he seizes the opportunity to serve Alfred, king of Wessex, after Ragnar is horribly betrayed and murdered by Kjartan, a fellow Dane. . . . Uhtred awaits his chance to settle the blood feud with Kjartan and to seize Bebbanburg from his treacherous uncle." (Booklist)

Cornwell, Bernard, 1944-

✓ **Lords** of the North; Bernard Cornwell. HarperCollins Publishers 2007 xvii, 317p map $25.95

ISBN 9780060888626 (acid-free paper); 0060888628 (acid-free paper)

LC 2006043627

Sequel to: The pale horseman.

This book, "set in A.D. 878, . . . chronicles the adventures of 21-year-old Saxon warrior Uhtred of Bebbanburg. . . . Uhtred, who despite his Danish upbringing supported King Alfred of Wessex in the fight against the Danes in The Pale Horseman, helps free Guthred, an enslaved Dane, who proclaims himself king of Northumbria. . . . [Uhtred] . . . attempts to destroy such enemies as Kjartan the Cruel, Sven the One-Eyed and Ælfric (Uhtred's thief of an uncle) and woos his beloved Gisela, Guthred's Valkyrie-like sister. Uhtred must overcome many challenges, notably King Guthred's shocking betrayal that leads to Uhtred's spending two years as a shipboard slave." (Publishers Weekly)

Cornwell, Bernard, 1944-
The **pale** horseman; Bernard Cornwell. Harper-Collins 2006 xv, 349p map $22.99; (pbk.) $13.95
ISBN 0060787120; 9780061144837
LC 2005046290
Sequel to: The last kingdom.
This book, "set in ninth-century England . . . continues the story of Uhtred, a young Northumbrian nobleman and warrior who is torn between his Saxon patriotism and his admiration for England's Danish invaders. . . . On one hand, he admires the bloodthirstiness of the Danes and dislikes the sickly, priestlike King Alfred of Wessex, whose hold is tenuous at best. On the other, Uhtred is Saxon, and he and Alfred are the only forces protecting their culture."

Cornwell, Bernard
★ **Rebel**. HarperCollins Pubs. 1993 308p (Starbuck chronicles)
ISBN 0-06-017713-6
LC 92-53344
This first volume of the Starbuck chronicles "follows the adventures of Nathaniel Starbuck, the rebellious and discredited son of a famous Boston abolitionist preacher. Nate flees the North after helping a femme fatale steal money she claimed was hers, winding up in Richmond as Fort Sumter falls and the Civil War begins. Unable to return home, distrusted by Southerners because of his parentage, Nate is taken under the wing of the mercurial and megalomaniacal Washington Faulconer, obsessed with building an independent army, answerable only to him, to fight for the Confederacy. Spanning the period from Sumter's capitulation in April 1861 to the First Battle of Bull Run in July, the book is well paced and filled with the historical details genre fans demand." Publ Wkly
Followed by Copperhead

Cornwell, Bernard
Sharpe's battle; Richard Sharpe and the Battle of Fuentes de Onoro, May 1811. HarperCollins Pubs. 1995 304p il
ISBN 0-06-017677-6
LC 95-10347
This adventure finds Sharpe "fighting the French and the hierarchy of Wellington's army. The encounter takes place in 1811, shortly after the destruction of Almeida (recounted in Sharpe's Gold. It is still Almeida that is under contention, for the French have mounted a massive campaign to supply the scant forces that still hold the fort. On another front, Sharpe is waging a private battle (which nearly gets him court-martialed) against the ferocious French Wolf Brigade. Vintage Cornwell." Booklist

Cornwell, Bernard
Sharpe's devil; Richard Sharpe and the Emperor, 1820-1821. HarperCollins Pubs. 1992 280p
ISBN 0-06-017977-5
LC 91-58360
Sequel to Sharpe's Waterloo
This is a "rousing read, full of invincible characters, deafening broadsides, roaring cannons, and smoking pistols as Cornwell writes of old-fashioned battles, blazing with glory." Booklist

Cornwell, Bernard
Sharpe's fortress; Richard Sharpe and the Siege of Gawilghur, December 1803. HarperCollins Pubs. 2000 294p
ISBN 0-06-019424-3
LC 00-59703
This installment in the Richard Sharpe saga finds "Sharpe, a junior officer in Her Majesty's army, stationed in India in 1803. Struggling to earn the respect of both his superiors and his troops, he . . . runs up against the unscrupulous Sergeant Obadiah Hakeswill. Uncovering an act of treason by Hakeswill, Sharpe must confront his sworn enemy in order to protect himself and recover a cache of stolen jewels. Set against the backdrop of the Maharatta War and the siege of the fortress of Gawilghur, this fast-paced historical adventure features plenty of electrifying military action." Booklist

Cornwell, Bernard
Sharpe's fury; Richard Sharpe and the Battle of Barrosa, March 1811. HarperCollins 2006 337p $24.95
ISBN 0-06-053048-0
In this adventure "Capt. Richard Sharpe, upstart rifleman, performs a sensitive mission for Henry Wellesley, the duke of Wellington's younger brother and special envoy to Spain in Cadiz. . . . A secret cabal of Spaniards who favor a rapprochement with France threatens the alliance between England and Spain in the fight against Bonaparte. The conspirators, who include a murderous priest, Fr. Salvador Montseny, have stolen some unfortunate love letters Wellesley wrote to his prostitute amour, Caterina Blazquez, and plan to use them to embarrass the British. It's up to Sharpe to recover the letters and save the alliance." Publ Wkly
"As in the other Sharpe novels, there is a lot of action here, played out in sturdy prose." Libr J

Cornwell, Bernard
Sharpe's havoc; Richard Sharpe and the campaign in northern Portugal, spring 1809. HarperCollins Pubs. 2003 306p $25.95
ISBN 0-06-053046-4
LC 2002-191284
"It is 1809, and Napoleon has plans to annex the Iberian Peninsula; British troops are sent to help the Portugese in their battle against the French. Sharpe and his small regiment of riflemen are separated from the main body of British troops, and once again find themselves in the thick of the action, which centers in and around the city of Oporto. Complicating matters is Kate Savage, the daughter of a British wine mechant in Oporto, whom Sharpe must find and escort to to safety. Meanwhile, a French spy marries Kate solely

to get his hands on her fortune. The action shifts between battle scenes and the spy, whom Sharpe unmasks. Although the outcome is never in doubt, this nevertheless makes for a rousing story." Libr J

Cornwell, Bernard

Sharpe's prey: Richard Sharpe and the Expedition to Copenhagen, 1807. HarperCollins Pubs. 2002 262p

ISBN 0-06-000252-2

LC 2001-46501

"Richard Sharpe, though stuck in the lowly role of regimental quartermaster, finds himself in the thick of the 1807 British campaign to destroy the Danish navy anchored in Copenhagen before the French can seize the ships and pose another invasion threat. As ever, the story starts fast, here with the murder of an English army officer in London by Captain John Lavisser—a traitor working for the French and as vile a villain as any Sharpe has faced—and scarcely lets up until Sharpe's final confrontation with Lavisser during the British bombardment of Copenhagen." Publ Wkly

Cornwell, Bernard

✓ Sharpe's Trafalgar; Richard Sharpe and the Battle of Trafalgar, October 21, 1805. HarperCollins Pubs. 2001 293p

ISBN 0-06-019425-1

LC 00-53871

First published 2000 in the United Kingdom

"Sharpe finds himself on a homeward-bound ship to England after duty in India. He has some problems adjusting to sea life but learns quickly. When his ship is attacked by the French, Sharpe finds out that the French ship contains a treaty that could cause a new outbreak of hostilities between India and the British. The result is the 1805 Battle of Trafalgar. . . . Cornwell satisfyingly delivers action, adventure, and a great gallery of villains and heroes, plus the usual beautiful lady." Libr J

Cornwell, Bernard

Sharpe's Waterloo; Richard Sharpe and the Waterloo campaign, 15 June to 18 June 1815. Viking 1990 378p

LC 89-40661

Sequel to Sharpe's revenge

"At Waterloo, Lieutenant-Colonel Sharpe serves as military adviser to the Dutch prince of Orange—a hapless military strategist who sends legions to their deaths before Sharpe takes matters into his own hands. . . . Along the way, Sharpe settles an old score with Lord John Rossendale, who previously cuckolded him and helped deprive him of his hard-earned fortune. Cornwell graphically depicts the grime and horror of the battlefield, including cavalry charges, cannon bombardments, and infantry attacks. A sublime work of historical fiction." Booklist

Followed by Sharpe's devil

Cornwell, Bernard

Stonehenge, 2000 B.C. a novel. HarperCollins Pubs. 2000 433p

ISBN 0-06-019700-5

LC 00-24288

A "novel that imagines the history behind Stonehenge. At the story's center are three brothers: Lengar, a warrior who takes the leadership of his tribe through patricide; Camaban, a crippled outcast who transforms himself into a sorcerer and seizes power from Lengar; and Saban, a craftsman who longs for the peaceful days of his father's reign. . . . Cornwell's depictions of the herculean efforts needed to move, shape and raise the stones of Stonehenge sound plausible, and his portrayal of the vitality and brutality of a society slowly creeping toward civilization is deft." N Y Times Book Rev

Cornwell, Bernard, 1944-

Sword song; the battle for London. Bernard Cornwell. Harper 2008 xv, 314p map (hbk.) $25.95

ISBN 9780060888640; 0060888644; 9780007219735; 0007219733; 9780060888664; 0060888660; 9780061370946; 0061370940

LC 2008299876

This book takes place in "[t]he year . . . [of] 885, . . . [when] England is at peace, divided between the Danish kingdom to the north and the Saxon kingdom of Wessex in the south. Uhtred, the dispossessed son of a Northumbrian lord . . . has finally settled down. He has land, a wife, and two children, and a duty given to him by King Alfred to hold the frontier on the Thames. But then trouble stirs: a dead man has risen, and new Vikings have arrived to occupy the decayed Roman city of London. Their dream is to conquer Wessex, and to do it they need Uhtred's help. Alfred has other ideas. He wants Uhtred to expel the Viking raiders from London. Uhtred must weigh his oath to the king against the dangerous turning tide of shifting allegiances and deadly power struggles." (Publisher's note)

Cornwell, Bernard

Vagabond. HarperCollins Pubs. 2002 405p $25.95

ISBN 0-06-621080-1

LC 2002-68884

"Cornwell is meticulous about historical facts and period detail, and his descriptions of butchery with arrow, mace and battleaxe are nothing if not convincing. As expected, the book culminates with battlefieldslaughter on an epic scale." Publ Wkly

Cornwell, Bernard

★ The winter king; a novel of Arthur. St. Martin's Press 1996 431p (Warlord chronicles)

ISBN 0-312-14447-4

LC 96-1421

First published 1995 in the United Kingdom

"Cornwell's Arthur is fierce, dedicated and complex, a man with many problems, most of his own making. His impulsive decisions sometimes have tragic ramifications, as when he lustfully takes Guinevere instead of the intented Ceinwyn, alienating his friends and allies and inspiring a bloody battle. The secondary characters are equally unexpected, and are ribboned with the magic and superstition of the times." Publ Wkly

Followed by Enemy of God

Cortazar, Julio

★ **Hopscotch**; translated from the Spanish by Gregory Rabassa. Pantheon Bks. 1966 564p

Original Spanish edition published 1963 in Argentina

"Considered to be Cortázar's masterwork, it is an open-ended novel; after reading the first 56 chapters, the reader is asked to reread the chapters in a different order. . . . The novel's antihero is Horacio Oliveira, an Argentine existentialist who lives among cultured expatriates in Paris while searching for his telepathic mistress. Returning to Buenos Aires, Oliveira meets Traveler and Talita, who are the doubles of his mistress and himself. None of the characters understands or cares more than superficially about the others, and impulse motivates their choices and actions. Narrative progress in the story is insignificant and its end is inconclusive." Merriam-Webster's Ency of Lit

Cosse, Laurence

A **novel** bookstore; translated from the French by Alison Anderson. Europa Editions 2010 416p pa $15

ISBN 978-1-933372-82-2; 1-933372-82-6

Original French edition, 2009

"The book begins with descriptions of the committee members' menacings, provoking a reader's quick interest and sympathy. Then follows the booksellers' lengthy interview with a sympathetic police inspector, in which the history of their individual lives and mutual enterprise is told. After that, the rest of the plot unfolds. Several mysteries are plumbed, if not necessarily solved, in this most engaging and winning novel." San Francisco Chron

Costello, Mark

Big if. Norton 2002 315p $24.95

ISBN 0-393-05116-1

LC 2002-512

"The novel ends not with a bang but a shiver—in a masterfully orchestrated scene that is vividly cinematic. But true to his materials and vision—and to life—Costello slyly defuses the emotional catharsis in a manner that would be anathema to the feel-good demands of a major Hollywood production." N Y Times Book Rev

Cotter, Bill

Fever chart. McSweeney's Books 2009 305p $22

ISBN 978-1-934781-41-8

LC 2010-292916

Narrator Jerome Coe "describes himself as a 'needy, yellow, luckless, less-than-reliable mutilatee who comes with fallible shutoff valves.' Nevertheless, one is charmed by Jerome from the moment he appears, newly discharged from the Boll Compound for a Variety of Disturbances and patiently tolerating his landlord's lecture on the rudeness of messy suicides. He might be unbalanced . . . , but he is positively Chaplinesque in his plucky forbearance. As a surrealistic series of misadventures, hospitalizations, and unshakable infatuations (alas, women are his weakness) takes him from Massachusetts to New Orleans, it is Jerome versus the world—and we are firmly on his side. . . . Cotter gives only the briefest of nods to plot, but Fever Chart is not about the destination so much as the reckless, driving-with-your-

knees journey, and Jerome Coe is an antihero for the ages." Texas Monthly

Cotterill, Colin

Anarchy and old dogs; Colin Cotterill. Soho Press 2007 viii, 272 p.p

ISBN 978-1-56947-463-1

LC 2006049651

"Digging deep, Dr. Siri finds political roots in a seemingly random killing. . . . Using a twisty mystery as a MacGuffin, [Cotterill] takes droll aim at the absurdities of recent history, all the more fascinating for their plausibility." Kirkus

Cotterill, Colin

The **coroner's** lunch; Colin Cotterill. Soho Press 2004 257 p. $24

ISBN 1569473765; 9781569473764

LC 2004048191

"Confronted by the poisoning of an important official's wife and the sudden appearance of three bodies that may create an international incident between Laos and Vietnam, 72-year-old state coroner Dr. Siri Paiboun keeps his cool in Cotterill's engaging whodunit, set in Laos a year after the 1975 Communist takeover." Pub Wkly

Cotterill, Colin

Curse of the pogo stick; Colin Cotterill. Soho 2008 xii, 240 p.p (hbk. $24

ISBN 1569474850; 9781569474853

LC 2007044006

This novel, by Colin Cotterill, is an entry in the "Dr. Siri Paiboun" series. "A booby-trapped corpse, intended for Dr. Siri, the national coroner of Laos, has been delivered to the morgue. In his absence, only Nurse Dtui's intervention saves the lives of the morgue attendants. . . . Dr. Siri is kidnapped by seven female Hmong villagers . . . so that he will . . . exorcise the headman's daughter whose soul is possessed by a demon, and lift the curse of the pogo stick." (Publisher's note)

Cotterill, Colin

Disco for the departed; Colin Cotterill. Soho Press 2006 viii, 247 p.p $23

ISBN 1569474281; 9781569474280

LC 2005055462

This novel, by Colin Cotterill, is an entry in the "Dr. Siri Paiboun" series. "Dr. Siri Paiboun, reluctant national coroner of the People's Democratic Republic of Laos, is summoned to . . . Huaphan Province. . . . An arm is found protruding from the concrete walk that had been laid from the President's former cave hideout to his new house beneath the cliffs. Dr. Siri is ordered to supervise the disinterment of the body . . . , identify the corpse, and discover how he died." (Publisher's note)

Cotterill, Colin

★ **Killed** at the whim of a hat. Minotaur Books 2011 374p map $24.99

ISBN 978-0-312-56453-7; 0-312-56453-8

LC 2011-08722

"Cotterill combines plenty of humor with fascinating and unusual characters, a solid mystery, and the relatively unfamiliar setting of southern Thailand to launch what may be the best new international mystery series since the No. 1 Ladies' Detective Agency." Booklist

Cotterill, Colin

√ **Love** songs from a shallow grave. Soho 2010 326p $25

ISBN 978-1-56947-627-7; 1-56947-627-6

LC 2010-08171

Laotian "Dr. Siri Paiboun, the nation's official (and only) coroner, is determined to see the humor in his diminished life, finding it bubbling up unexpectedly when he goes to the movies to see a piece of Chinese propaganda called 'The Train From the Xiang Wu Irrigation Plant' or when he reflects on the giant billboards urging everyone to breed pigs. . . . To further engage his quick mind, Siri is sometimes given a puzzle to solve, like the murders of three young women, each killed by a thrust through the heart from an épée, a weapon that 99.9 percent of the Laotian population has never heard of. It's also standard procedure in this series for Cotterill to step back from the case at hand and dispatch Siri on a field trip to some other Communist garden spot in Southeast Asia. This time, he's sent on a diplomatic mission to Cambodia that yields rich evidence of crimes committed by the Khmer Rouge in Phnom Penh. And no, it's not the least bit funny." N Y Times Book Rev

Cotterill, Colin

The **merry** misogynist; Colin Cotterill. Soho Press 2009 viii, 274 p.p $24

ISBN 1569475563; 9781569475560

LC 2009010677

This mystery novel, by Colin Cotterill, is an entry in the author's "Dr. Siri Paiboun Investigation" series. "In . . . 1978 Laos, . . . the corpse of . . . [a woman] turns up in Dr. Siri's morgue. . . . The victim was tied to a tree and strangled. . . . Siri discovers that . . . this has happened many times before. He sets out to investigate this unprecedented phenomenon--a serial killer in peaceful Buddhist Laos." (Publisher's note)

Cotterill, Colin

Slash and burn; Colin Cotterill. Soho Crime 2011 290p.

ISBN 9781616951788; 9781616951160

LC 2011030330

This novel tells the story of "Dr. Siri, . . . Laos's national coroner, . . . [who is] dragged into one last job for the Lao government: supervising an excavation for the remains of U.S. fighter pilot who went down in the remote northern Lao jungle ten years earlier. The presence of American soldiers in Laos is a hot-button issue for both the Americans and the Lao involved, and the search party includes high-level politicians and scientists. But one member of the party is found dead, setting off a chain of accidents Dr. Siri suspects aren't completely accidental. Everyone is trapped in a cabin in the jungle, and the bodies are starting to pile up." (Publisher's note)

Cotterill, Colin

Thirty-three teeth; Colin Cotterill. Soho Press 2005 238 p. $24

ISBN 1569473889; 9781569473887

LC 2004058933

Dilys Award (2006)

This novel, by Colin Cotterill, is an entry in the "Dr. Siri Paiboun" series. "The national coroner of Laos, Dr. Siri Paiboun, . . . with . . . his helpers, the mentally retarded Mr. Geung and Nurse Dtui . . . elucidates the causes of mysterious deaths. But he also communes with the deposed king, whose special channel to the occult has left him, and attends a conference of shamans called by the Communist government to give the spirits an ultimatum: obey party orders or get out." (Publisher's note)

Cotterill, Colin

The **woman** who wouldn't die; by Colin Cotterill. Soho Press 2013 307 p. (hardcover) $25.95

ISBN 1616952067; 9781616952068

LC 2012038332

This novel, by Colin Cotterill, is the ninth book in his "Dr. Siri mysteries" series. "In a small Lao village, . . . a woman was . . . killed. . . . Then, three days later, she was back . . . , clairvoyant, and can speak to the dead. . . . That's why the . . . dead brother of a Lao general has enlisted her to . . . uncover his remains. . . . Coroner Dr. Siri Paiboun and his wife . . . are sent along to supervise the excavation. . . . Except Siri . . . doesn't trust the woman." (Publisher's note)

Coulter, Catherine

√ The **maze**. Putnam 1997 373p

ISBN 0-399-14264-9

LC 97-12343

"San Franciscan Lacey Sherlock was just a teenager, dreaming of studying piano at Berkeley, when her older sister's life was brutally ended by the serial murderer that the media dubbed the String Killer. Now, seven years and one brief mental breakdown later, her career plans have changed. Having completed FBI training and learned to be addressed by her surname, she's assigned to agent Dillon Savich's Criminal Apprehension Unit, which, utilizing Dillon's specialized computer program for profiling, is responsible for pursuing serial killers. This places the obsessed Sherlock exactly where she wants to be when the String Killer strikes again, this time in Boston. It also puts her in position to become romantically involved with her attractive superior." Publ Wkly

Coulter, Catherine

Split second. G. P. Putnam's Sons 2011 419p $26.95

ISBN 978-0-399-15743-1

LC 2011-08016

In this "15th FBI thriller featuring husband-wife agents Dillon Savich and Lacey Sherlock (after Whiplash), Dillon arrives one night at a Georgetown convenience store in Washington, D.C., just in time to thwart an armed robbery. While the robbery, which left one gunman wounded and a female accomplice dead, is never far from his thoughts, Dillon soon has an important case to pursue with Lacey—investigating a serial killer who may be related to the notorious

Ted Bundy and has a chameleonlike ability to change appearances. . . . A tight plot full of unexpected twists will keep readers turning the pages." Publ Wkly

Coulter, Catherine

The **target**. Putnam 1998 372p
ISBN 0-399-14395-5
LC 98-10563

"Coulter's plot doesn't always add up, and she can overdo her penchant for quirky characters . . . but her central figures—wary, quietly resilient Molly, musically gifted Emma and tough, decent Ramsey—make this an absorbing read." Publ Wkly

Coupland, Douglas

Eleanor Rigby; a novel. Bloomsbury 2005 249p $22.95
ISBN 1-582-34523-6
LC 2004-46437

"Liz Dunn is fat, lonely and has no friends. . . . The only exciting incident ever to brighten Liz's life was a class trip to Rome when she was 16, during which she attended a party where she drank so much she can't remember what happened. Nine months after she returned home, she gave birth to a son, an event hidden from her family because of her natural rotundness. Liz gave the child up for adoption and then launched into a life of perpetual loneliness (hence the title's nod to the lonely lady of Beatles fame). All this changes when her now 20-year-old son, Jeremy, shows up. He's a great kid, but his story is tragic-he bounced around foster homes until he could take care of himself, he has multiple sclerosis and his body is rapidly deteriorating. Coupland . . . avoids the pitfalls of weepy melodrama with sarcastic humor, inspired treatment of the weirdness of everyday life and dark mystical interludes." Publ Wkly

Couto, Mia

Sleepwalking land; translated by David Brookshaw. Serpent's Tail 2006 213p pa $14.95
ISBN 1-85242-897-X
Original Portuguese edition, 1992

"Many great novels have shown a world torn to shreds by the brutality of war. To do so, their authors ground their texts in the details of destruction and decay. But Couto's novel stands apart: it shows the world that war creates, a dreamscape of uncertainty where characters and readers alike marvel not at the abnormal becoming normal but at the way we come to accept the impossible as reality." N Y Times Book Rev

Coward, Noel

The **collected** stories of Noel Coward. Dutton 1983 630p
ISBN 0-525-24207-4
LC 83-5704

Cox, Michael

The **glass** of time; the secret life of Miss Esperanza Gorst. narrated by herself. W. W. Norton 2008 586p $24.95
ISBN 978-0-393-06773-6; 0-393-06773-4
LC 2008-23909

An "entirely wonderful mock Victorian novel. . . . It's a melodrama, of course, chock-full of revenge, romance, duplicity, concealed identities and murder most frequent—but melodrama on a grand scale." Washington Post Book World

Cox, Michael

The **meaning** of night; a confession. W. W. Norton 2006 703p $25.95
ISBN 978-0-393-06203-8; 0-393-06203-1
LC 2006-18941

"Cox has delivered almost everything Victorian readers might have expected (mystery, wit, romance, an evil double) and some (explanatory footnotes) they might not. Throughout [the book], he winks slyly at the era's literary conventions while twisting story lines back on one another. The result is a narrative as beguiling as it is intelligent, full of great country houses, epic loves, fierce anger and vicious habits of every sort." N Y Times Book Rev
Includes bibliographical references

Cozarinsky, Edgardo

The **bride** from Odessa; translated from the Spanish by Nick Caistor. Farrar, Straus and Giroux 2004 161p $22
ISBN 0-374-11673-6
Original Spanish edition, 2001

"Any exploration of the past is necessarily incomplete and Cozarinsky has found the perfect form in these fragmentary stories. . . . His prose, as translated by Nick Caistor, is elegant, cool and precise. Occasionally the amassing of clauses might suggest the original Spanish, . . . but this is a book about moving between cultures, between continents and between generations; to be aware of the movement between languages is not necessarily a bad thing." Times Lit Suppl

Cozzens, James Gould

By love possessed. Harcourt Brace & Co. 1957 570p

This novel concerns "49 hours in the life of Arthur Winner, . . . New England lawyer. The stability of Arthur's private and professional worlds is suddenly shaken both by repercussions of unhapppy and indiscreet episodes from his supposedly well-ordered past and by present events involving himself and those close to him." Booklist

Crace, Jim, 1946-

All that follows; a novel. Nan A. Talese/Doubleday 2010 223p $25.95
ISBN 9780385520768; 0-385-52076-X
LC 2009-31130

"During the Bush Administration, Lenny Lessing was a promising British jazz saxophonist whose actions could never quite keep up with his leftist rhetoric. By 2024, he is in full retreat, living off royalties, nursing a bad shoulder, and surfing news channels. But when an old colleague tries to disrupt an international summit and ends up taking a family hostage instead, Len finds himself sucked into events that he would have much preferred to watch on television. Crace's decision to give this Walter Mitty an entire novel to hiccup and stumble through is a risk. . . But the book is not without its unexpected accents—a sinuous evocation of the saxophone, futuristic touches such as dementia-preventing cigarettes, and a tender portrait of Len's faltering marriage—and eventually the antihero's frantic improvisations begin to sound like music." New Yorker

Crace, Jim

Being dead. Farrar, Straus & Giroux 2000 193p
ISBN 0-374-11013-1

LC 99-45082

First published 1999 in the United Kingdom

This novel's two central characters, Joseph and Celice, are biologists. "The story is told in two directions. As it opens, Joseph and Celice are recently dead, victims of a senseless murder. Subsequent chapters alternate between a counterclockwise retracing of the route they took to meet their bloody fate, and . . . descriptions of their physical decomposition." N Y Rev Books

"The style is agile, precise, and vigorous. Words hit their target directly and unerringly. Images are colorful, evocative, forceful." Commonweal

Crace, Jim

The **devil's** larder. Farrar, Straus & Giroux 2001 165p $20
ISBN 0-374-13859-1

LC 2001-23625

Crace has "written a set of teasing tales about how we are never so ignorantly alive as when we are eating ourselves to death. The 64 brief fictions that make up 'The Devil's Larder' are parables and parodies of knowingness. . . . Reading a collection of 64 apparently unconnected brief fictions, numbered and untitled and held together only by the odd title of the book, may not necessarily appear to be a tempting prospect. The form of the book is experimental in that it toys with the reader's willingness (or unwillingness) not to make too much sense of what is going on." N Y Times Book Rev

Crace, Jim

★ The **gift** of stones. Scribner 1989 169p
ISBN 0-684-19070-2

LC 88-31587

First published 1988 in the United Kingdom

"As the fabulist tale unwinds, Crace looks into the role of the artist in society—here, a storyteller—considering both the impact and limits of imagination in guiding us toward new horizons. A marvelous literary effort." Libr J

Crace, Jim, 1946-

★ **Harvest**; Jim Crace. 1st American ed. Nan A. Talese/Doubleday 2013 224 p. (hardcover) $24.95
ISBN 0385520778; 9780385520775

LC 2012026208

Man Booker Prize Shortlist (2013)

This book is set in a premodern English village. "One morning, Master Kent's stable is found burning, and strangers who have peaceably signaled their presence by sending up the customary smoke plume are blamed; their heads are shaved, and the two men are put in stocks. The only one to show them sympathy is odd Mr. Quill, hired to map the village lands." (Library Journal)

Crace, Jim

The **pesthouse**; a novel. Nan A. Talese 2007 255p $24.95
ISBN 978-0-385-52075-1; 0-385-52075-1

LC 2006-26555

"After a forgotten eco-reaction in the distant past, the U.S. government, economy and society have collapsed. The illiterate inhabitants ride horses, fight with bows and swords and scratch a meager living from farming and fishing. But with crop yields and fish runs mysteriously dwindling, most are trekking to the Atlantic coast to take ships to the promised land of Europe, gawking along the way at the ruins of freeways and machinery yards, which seem the wasteful excesses of giants. Heading east, naïve farm boy Franklin teams up with Margaret, a recovering victim of the mysterious 'flux' whose shaven head (mark of the unclean) causes passersby to shun her. Their love blossoms amid misadventures in an anarchic landscape." Publ Wkly

"The story is a gripping, harrowing adventure tale and Crace's language is extraordinary: he has immersed himself in his own kind of variant American idiom . . . which is simple, often beautiful, as tough and workable as leather." New Statesman

Crace, Jim

★ **Quarantine**. Farrar, Straus & Giroux 1998 242p
ISBN 0-374-23962-2

LC 97-61489

First published 1997 in the United Kingdom

"Five people come to the desert of Judea, for a quarantine, a fast of forty days. For four of them, the standard daytime fast will be enough. . . . They are Shim, part-Jew, part-Greek, sophisticate, religious dilettante, sceptic; Aphas, an old man with a new growth, looking for a simple miracle; Marti, the childless wife of a barren marriage, about to be cast off by her philoprogenitive husband; a nameless, perhaps Tourettic nomad, whose hopes remain unintelligible. And Jesus, a callow young man from Galilee with Messianic ambitions. He intends a total fast." Times Lit Suppl

Crace's "prose is startlingly specific about ancient life and Judea's harsh, terrible beauty. Unlike many authors of biblical fiction, he blends his research smoothly into his narrative and adds a leavening pinch of humor." Time

Crafts, Hannah

The **bondswomans** narrative; edited by Henry Louis Gates Jr. Warner Bks. 2002 lxxiv, 338p il $24.95
ISBN 0-446-53008-5

LC 2001-98325

"Published from a manuscript bought at auction by Henry Louis Gates Jr., {this} is quite probably the first novel written by a black woman, as well as the only novel written by a female fugitive slave. It is also one of the few purely firsthand accounts of the slave experience available." N Y Times Book Rev

Includes bibliographical references

Craig, Amanda

Love in idleness; a novel. Talese 2003 340p $23.95

ISBN 0-385-50776-3

LC 2002-43570

"The novel reprises Shakespeare's mercurial farce about Athenian lovers and fairy royalty wandering around a forest at night, falling in and out of besottedness at the instigation of the mischievous Puck." N Y Times Book Rev

Craig, Philip R.

A **shoot** on Martha's Vineyard; a Martha's Vineyard mystery. Scribner 1998 285p map $22

ISBN 0-684-83454-5

LC 97-51141

When "J.W. Jackson's long-time nemesis arrives in town and is murdered, J.W. can avoid suspicion only by finding the murderer. A handsome Hollywood movie scout, meanwhile, takes a shine to Jackson's new wife. A lively and entertaining addition to the series." Libr J

Craig, Philip R.

Third strike; a Brady Coyne/J.W. Jackson mystery. [by] Philip R. Craig and William G. Tapply. Scribner 2007 323p $24

ISBN 978-1-4165-3256-9; 1-4165-3256-0

LC 2007-9103

"Tapply's Boston lawyer, Brady Coyne, responds to an anguished call for help from an old client living on Martha's Vineyard, where the late Philip Craig's ex-cop, J.W. Jackson, is being urged by his wife to investigate the death of a striking ferry boat worker. . . . The two friends pursue their cases separately and together as tensions caused by the ferry strike mount and a murder raises the stakes. This marks the highly enjoyable and poignant end to a short, sweet series." Publ Wkly

Craig, Philip R.

Vineyard enigma; a Martha's Vineyard mystery. Scribner 2002 242p $24

ISBN 0-7432-0523-5

LC 2001-57809

"The arrival on Martha's Vineyard of a strange man in search of two African soapstone eagles creates turmoil for series star J. W. Jackson. Murder, art-world intrigue, and jealousy of his wife's attraction to the man all complicate J. W.'s life." Libr J

Craig, Philip R.

A **vineyard** killing; a Martha's Vineyard mystery. Scribner 2003 229p $24

ISBN 0-7432-0524-3

LC 2002-42878

This installment "begins with a bang: an unknown assailant shoots someone outside the delicatessen where series private investigator J. W. Jackson is eating with his wife. Jackson is soon embroiled in a murder case involving grabby real estate developers and recalcitrant islanders. Off-season atmosphere and the usual high-caliber sleuthing." Libr J

Crais, Robert

Chasing darkness; an Elvis Cole novel. Simon & Schuster 2008 273p $25.95

ISBN 978-0-7432-8164-5; 0-7432-8164-0

LC 2008-10709

"While clearing houses in the path of a forest fire in Laurel Canyon, police officers find the body of Lionel Byrd, an apparent suicide. Three years earlier, Cole, working for Byrd's attorney, uncovered evidence that cleared Byrd of a murder charge. Now new evidence suggests that he was guilty of that murder and six others, two of them committed after Cole helped exonerate him. Torn by guilt, Cole plunges into his own investigation, which leads in startling directions." Publ Wkly

Crais, Robert

Demolition angel; a novel. Doubleday 2000 386p

ISBN 0-385-49584-6

LC 00-29054

"The book features one of the most complex heroines to grace a thriller since Clarice Starling locked eyes with Hannibal Lecter, a deliciously spooky villain in the person of a mad bomber known as Mr. Red, and an aggressively involving plot." Publ Wkly

Crais, Robert

First rule. G.P. Putnam's Sons 2010 308p $26.95

ISBN 978-0-399-15613-7; 0-399-15613-5

LC 2009-36928

"Righteous vengeance, a reckless pace, a stratospheric body count and just enough surprises to keep you turning the pages. The pleasures may be primitive, but they're genuine." Kirkus

Crais, Robert

The **forgotten** man; a novel. Doubleday 2005 352p $24.95

ISBN 0-385-50428-4

LC 2004-61857

"When an apparently homeless man is found shot in an alley, the first officer on the scene tells private investigator Elvis Cole that the dying man claimed to be Cole's father. Cole has never known the identity of his father. His mother was mentally unstable and would often go missing for extended periods. Cole was conceived during such a disappearance, and the only clue his mother gave him was the cryptic comment that his father was a 'human cannonball' in a circus. Long obsessed with finding his father, Cole backtracks through the years to learn the dead man's true identity. As he searches, Cole is unaware that he is the target of an associate of the dead man. . . . A deeply moving, heartfelt mystery." Booklist

Crais, Robert

Indigo slam; an Elvis Cole novel. Hyperion 1997 288p

ISBN 0-7868-6261-0

LC 97-966

In this mystery L.A. shamus Elvis Cole is "approached by three resourceful young children who would like their missing father located. That dad, Clark Hewitt, is soon revealed as a mystery man, a master printer and a possible junkie who fled the witness protection program he entered after informing on a counterfeiting operation run by Russian and Ukrainian mobsters. While Clark's kids clearly revere him, Elvis is suspicious. The feds want Clark back in their care and the Russians want revenge for his squealing." Publ Wkly

Crais, Robert

L.A. requiem. Doubleday 1999 382p
✓ ISBN 0-385-49583-8

LC 98-52921

In this episode L.A. PI Elvis Cole, "drops his adolescent swagger in the heroic act of helping his friend and partner, Joe Pike, to stop the vengeful killer who is framing Pike for his own crimes. The writing doesn't fool around, either, and what starts as a routine search for a rich man's pampered daughter becomes a tense face-off with a killer and a serious examination of the limits of friendship." N Y Times Book Rev

Crais, Robert

The **last** detective; a novel. Doubleday 2003 302p $24.95

ISBN 0-385-50426-8

LC 2002-41507

This Elvis Cole thriller finds the "Los Angeles P. I. racing the clock to rescue his girlfriend's 10-year-old son, Ben, from a team of kidnappers who claim to be paying Cole back for atrocities they say he committed in Vietnam." N Y Times Book Rev

"Fast action, though guys, vivid Los Angeles details, and snappy dialog are Craig's trademarks, and this tale has them all." Libr J

Crais, Robert

✓ **Taken**; Robert Crais. G. P. Putnam's Sons 2012 341p.

ISBN 9780399158278; 0399158278

LC 2012372608

In this book, "the police tell a wealthy industrialist that her missing son has faked his own kidnapping". When "she hires Elvis Cole and Joe Pike" to investigate, "Cole soon determines that it was no fake. The boy and his secret girlfriend have been taken, and are now lost in the gray and changing world of the professional border kidnappers who prey not only on innocent victims but also on one another-buying, selling, and stealing victims like commodities. Fortunately, the kidnappers don't yet know who the boy is, but when Cole goes undercover to try to buy the two hostages back, he himself is taken and disappears. Now it is up to Pike to retrace Cole's steps". (Publisher's note)

Crais, Robert

The **two** minute rule. Simon & Schuster 2006 325p $24.95

ISBN 0-7432-8161-6

LC 2005-57476

"Career criminal Max Holman, a.k.a. the 'Hero Bandit,' has just finished serving ten years in prison for bank robbery and at middle age finally understands that he has to change

his ways. On the day of his release, Holman's estranged police officer son is killed along with three other cops—a tragedy that shatters any hope of reconciliation. When the LAPD quickly closes the case by blaming a junkie who killed himself after the crime, Holman is unconvinced. He persuades the now retired FBI agent who originally arrested him to help him, and the story takes off at breakneck speed. In this superb tale with a likable ex-con protagonist, Crais creates a totally believable world in which good and evil are turned upside down." Libr J

Crais, Robert

The **watchman**. Simon and Schuster 2007 292p $25.95

ISBN 978-0-7432-8163-8; 0-7432-8163-2

LC 2006-38775

"Larkin Barkley, a troubled L.A. woman from a wealthy family, finds herself under the protection of federal agents after emerging uninjured from a serious car accident. Something she saw warrants her death. The bad guys came close to success, probably with an assist from someone charged with her safety. Joe Pike, a former marine, LAPD officer, and mercenary, is hired to protect her on the word of his former police partner. Pike and the girl go underground after another attempt on her life leaves three would-be assassins dead. Pike then enlists his partner, private investigator Elvis Cole, to do the digging while he does the shooting. Cole targets a drug cartel's money-laundering network as the source of the death squads and identifies Barkley's father as the possible link. . . . Fans of the Elvis Cole series have long wished for an installment focusing on sidekick Pike, and their wish is more than granted with this stunningly emotional thriller." Booklist

Cramer, W. Dale

✓ ★ **Bad** ground; W. Dale Cramer. Bethany House 2004 382p $12.99

ISBN 076422784X (pbk.); 9780764227844

LC 2004002023

In this book, "[t]he day before his mother's funeral, newly orphaned 17-year-old Jeremy Prine is given a letter in which she tells him, 'When the time is right I want you to go find your Uncle Aiden. . . . You have something I couldn't give him, and he has something I couldn't give you.' He hitchhikes to where Aiden, aka Snake, works a hard-rock tunnel south of Atlanta, and Jeremy manages to wangle a job. [Author W. Dale] Cramer invites the reader into the life of the rock tunnel workers—hard-bitten, simple men with simple desires—as Jeremy wrestles with change, loss and becoming a man." (Publishers Weekly)

Cramer, W. Dale

Levi's will; a novel. W. Dale Cramer. Bethany House 2005 394p (pbk.) $14.99; o.p.

ISBN 9780764207129; 0764229958

LC 2005004602

Christy Award: Contemporary Stand Alone (2006)

This book begins "[i]n 1943, [when] 19-year-old Will Mullet flees his pacifist Amish community of Apple Creek, Ohio, leaving behind a pregnant girl and a rigid, God-fearing home to find a new life. He enlists in the military, marries a southern belle and tries to erase every trace of his past. But he can't completely disengage from his roots, and nor, he belatedly discovers, does he want to. Levi, Will's father, is slow to accept the prodigal son. Decades pass, and . . . Will's life and relationship with his own children unfolds. . . . [Author W. Dale] Cramer shifts eras and narrative styles from chapter to chapter, sometimes following Will's life in the 1940s as a young single man, sometimes chronicling other decades leading up to and including the 1980s." (Publishers Weekly)

Crane, Elizabeth
You must be this happy to enter; stories. Punk Planet Books 2008 183p pa $14.95
ISBN 978-1-933354-43-9
LC 2007-926133
"Zombies, time travelers, reality TV contestants and even a few normalish folks populate the pages of Elizabeth Crane's quirky, charming new collection. . . . Crane writes like she's running out of air: fast and a little babbly, but she's endlessly entertaining." PopMatters

Crane, Stephen, 1871-1900
The **complete** novels of Stephen Crane; edited with an introduction by Thomas A. Gullason. Doubleday 1967 xvi, 821 p.p
ISBN 9780385041829
LC 67010369

Crane, Stephen, 1871-1900
The **complete** short stories & sketches of Stephen Crane; edited with an introduction by Thomas A. Gullason. Doubleday 1963 790p

Crane, Stephen, 1871-1900
★ **Maggie**: a girl of the streets (a story of New York) an authoritative text, backgrounds and sources, the author and the novel, reviews and criticism, edited by Thomas A. Gullason. Norton 1979 258p
ISBN 0-393-01222-0
LC 78-24596
First published privately in 1893 under the pseudonym Johnston Smith
"Maggie Johnson is the daughter of a brutal father and a drunken mother. She goes to work in a collar factory, falls in love with Pete, a bartender who is a friend of her brother Jimmie, and is seduced by him. Her mother disowns her, she becomes a prostitute; and in despair she finally kills herself. Her final degeneration becomes almost an allegory." Reader's Ency. 4th edition

Crane, Stephen, 1871-1900
The **portable** Stephen Crane; edited, with an introduction and notes, by Joseph Katz. Viking 1969 xxvi, 550p
ISBN 0-670-01068-5

Crane, Stephen, 1871-1900
Prose and poetry. Library of Am. 1984 1379p $40; pa $15.95
ISBN 0-940450-17-8; 1-883011-39-6 pa
LC 83-19908
Maggie: a girl of the streets and The red badge of courage are entered separately. George's mother (1896) focuses on a woman who sacrifices everything for her own son, whom she mistakenly believes to be destined for greatness. The third violet (1896-97) deals with an artist and his bohemian life. In The monster (1898) "Henry Johnson, a black servant in the home of Dr. Trescott, rescues the physician's son from a fire. He is terribly disfigured and loses his sanity, so that no home can be found for him in the town. Horrified by the 'monster,' the townspeople ostracize the doctor and his family because they harbor the man." Oxford Companion to Am Lit. 6th edition

Crane, Stephen, 1871-1900
★ The **red** badge of courage; an episode of the American Civil War. introduced by Wendell Minor. Complete and unabridged ed.; Puffin 2009 215p (Puffin classics) pa $4.99
ISBN 978-0-14-132752-5
First published 1895 by D. Appleton and Co.
"A young Union soldier, Henry Fleming, tells of his feelings when he is under fire for the first time during the battle of Chancellorsville. He is overcome by fear and runs from the field. Later he returns to lead a charge that reestablishes his own reputation as well as that of his company. One of the great novels of the Civil War." Cincinnati Public Libr

Crane, Stephen, 1871-1900
The **red** badge of courage and other stories; with biographical illustrations and pictures of the settings of the stories together with an introduction and captions by Max J. Herzberg. Dodd, Mead 1957 409p il

Crews, Harry
★ A **feast** of snakes. Atheneum 1976 177p
ISBN 0-689-107293
LC 76-8206
The novel is set in the backwoods hamlet of Mystic, Georgia, where the annual festival "begins with the crowning of the high-school Rattlesnake Queen , continues with a pit-bull championship fight, and ends with a Rattlesnake Roundup. The festival this year is a total nightmare: a black girl with a razor emasculates Sheriff Buddy Matlow, Big Joe Mackey kicks his losing dog to death, and Joe Lon Mackey–aged twenty-two, practically illiterate, miserably married, with two screaming babies, his years of glory as an all-around athlete . . . behind him–goes out of control with a twelve-gauge shotgun." New Yorker

Crichton, Michael
★ The **Andromeda** strain. Avon Books 2003 331p pa $7.99
ISBN 0-06-054181-4
First published 1969 by Knopf
"In these days of interplanetary exploration, this tale of the world's first space-age biological emergency may seem uncomfortably believable. When a contaminated space capsule drops to earth in a small Nevada town and all the town's residents suddenly die, four American scientists gather at an underground laboratory of Project Wildfire to search frantically for an antidote to the threat of a worldwide epidemic." Shapiro. Fic for Youth. 3d edition

Crichton, Michael

★ **Jurassic** Park; a novel. Knopf 1990 399p $28.95; pa $7.99

ISBN 0-394-58816-9; 0-345-37077-5 pa

LC 90-52960

This novel "tells of a modern-day scientist bringing to life a horde of prehistoric animals." N Y Times Book Rev

"Crichton is a master at blending technology with fiction. . . . Suspense, excitement, and good adventure pervade this book." SLJ

Followed by The lost world (1995)

Crichton, Michael

Pirate latitudes; a novel. Harper 2009 312p map $27.99

ISBN 978-0-06-192937-3; 0-06-192937-9

LC 2009-49965

The Caribbean, 1665. Pirate captain Charles Hunter, with backing from a powerful ally, assembles a crew of ruffians to take the Spanish galleon, "El Trinidad," guarded by the bloodthirsty Cazalla, a favorite commander of the Spanish king himself.

"Capt. Charles Hunter is the protagonist, a swashbuckling rake from the Massachusetts Bay Colony (with a degree from a new college called Harvard) who is bumming around Jamaica looking for trouble when he hears about a boatload of Spanish booty waiting to be stolen. This being a Crichton novel, Hunter promptly assembles a crackerjack team of 'privateers' — an eagle-eyed helmsman named Enders, the master assassin Sanson, an explosives expert nicknamed simply 'The Jew' — and sails off to raid King Philip's coffers. Along the way he rescues a comely kidnapped Englishwoman from island cannibals, crosses swords with a sadistic villain called Cazalla, and outflanks Spanish gunships with bold tactical maneuvers that would leave Jack Sparrow gasping." Entertainment Wkly

Crichton, Michael

Prey; novel. HarperCollins Pubs. 2002 376p $26.95

ISBN 0-06-621412-2

LC 2002-32338

"Despite its absurd moments, 'Prey' is irresistibly suspenseful. You're entertained on one level and you learn something on another, even if the two levels do ultimately diverge." N Y Times Book Rev

Crichton, Michael

Sphere; a novel. Knopf 1987 385p

ISBN 0-394-56110-4

LC 86-46321

The author "sends a team of civilian experts to the floor of the Pacific to investigate an enormous spaceship that appears to have rested there for some 300 years. In it, they discover a huge sphere, made of a mysterious metal, which they cannot force open despite its having a door. Then, when one of the group inspects the ship on his own, it opens, he enters, and the real fun begins. . . . Crichton's prose, pedestrian but not clumsy, lets the story spin itself out, and few readers who grab its thread will let go until the web is broken in a 'Wizard of Oz'-style ending." Booklist

Crichton, Michael

Timeline. Knopf 1999 449p

ISBN 0-679-44481-5

LC 99-461985

In this novel, a billionaire planning a theme park uses time travel to send historians working on an excavation in the Dordogne back to the France of 1357, where they become involved in a war

"Crichton is a master of an odd hybrid: entertaining novels that educate. 'Timeline' is a page turner and a very lucid look at life in the late Middle Ages. He teaches you how to think like a knight during a joust by putting you in the saddle." Newsweek

Crime novels: American noir of the 1930s and 40s; [edited by Robert Polito] Library of Am. 1997 990p il $35

ISBN 1-88301-146-9

LC 97-2485

The postman always rings twice and The big clock are entered in main catalog. They shoot horses, don't they? (1935) explores the turbulent world of a Hollywood dance marathon. Thieves like us (1937) follows a fugitive band of Oklahoma bank robbers. Nightmare alley (1946) presents a psychological portrait of a doomed carnival hustler. I married a dead man (published 1948 under pseudonym William Irish) is a title of switched identities set in suburbia

Crime novels: American noir of the 1950s; [edited by Robert Polito] Library of Am. 1997 892p $35

ISBN 1-883011-49-3

LC 97-2487

The killer inside me (1952) portrays a small town Texas deputy sheriff who is a psychopathic killer. The talented Mr. Ripley (1955) is about an opportunistic social parasite. Pickup (1955) explores the seedy world of an alcoholic African American painter. Down there (1956; variant title: Shoot the piano player) is a psychological portrait of a barroom pianist. The real cool killers (1959) features Harlem police officers Coffin Ed Johnson and Grave Digger Jones

Cristofano, David

The **girl** she used to be. Grand Central Pub. 2009 241p $22.99

ISBN 978-0-446-58222-3; 0-446-58222-0

LC 2008-03280

"The novel is told from Melody's point of view, and Cristofano is largely able to pull off the female perspective. . . Snappy dialogue and scenes with unpredictable outcomes keep the novel going at a steady pace." PopMatters

Criswell, Millie

What to do about Annie? Millie Criswell. Ivy Books 2001 316p

ISBN 0804119511

LC 2001116593

In this book, "[h]aving grown up in Baltimore's Little Italy with a Jewish father and an Italian mother, Annie Goldman feels caught between two worlds and is determined to flaunt her individuality. She . . . drives Father 'what-a-hunk' Joe Russo crazy with her curve-hugging clothes. Annie once dreamed that she would have a future with Joe, but her hopes were dashed when he left her to join the priesthood. Now, 15 years later, Joe has decided to hang up his rosary beads and give love another try. . . . While the two attempt to rekindle their romance, Annie becomes a part owner of her father's outdated clothing store. . . . Joe has his own problems to contend with as well—namely, his domineering mother and her matchmaking machinations." (Publishers Weekly)

Crombie, Deborah

And justice there is none. Bantam Bks. 2002 318p

ISBN 0-553-10973-1

LC 2002-21459

"For all the picturesque charms of its setting, . . . this is another hard-nosed piece of social criticism from Deborah Crombie, an American author with serious designs on the British cozy mystery." N Y Times Book Rev

Crombie, Deborah

Kissed a sad goodbye. Bantam Bks. 1999 322p $23.95

ISBN 0-553-10943-X

LC 98-50186

"The murder of a beautiful businesswoman in London's Isle of Dogs neighborhood calls both local police and Scotland Yard into play. The Yard's Duncan Kincaid and Gemma James . . . create a psychological profile of the victim and thoroughly investigate the thriving family tea concern." Libr J

Crombie, Deborah

Water like a stone. William Morrow 2007 407p $24.95

ISBN 978-0-06-052527-9; 0-06-052527-4

LC 2006-46841

"As in books by Elizabeth George and P. D. James, the intriguing personal relationships and family dynamics drive this well-crafted, impressive mystery-drama." Booklist

Crompton, Richard

Hour of the Red God; Richard Crompton. Sarah Crichton Books/Farrar, Straus and Giroux 2013 304 p. (Detective Mollel mysteries) (hardcover: alk. paper) $26

ISBN 0374171998; 9780374171995

LC 2012034612

In this mystery novel, Nairobi police detective Mollel, a single parent who lost his wife to the 1998 al-Qaeda bombing of the U.S. embassy, looks into the murder of a fellow Maasai tribe member, a woman whose genitals were freshly mutilated. Mollel's less-than-honest boss, who quickly labels the victim a prostitute, directs him to wrap things up quickly. But the dogged Mollel follows the evidence wherever it leads, even if it means stepping on the toes of the rich and powerful." (Publishers Weekly)

"[Crompton's] debut novel combines a sinuous plot, a wonderfully complex and tragic protagonist, and a remarkable portrait of a city that is simultaneously exotic yet familiar." Booklist

Cronin, A. J.

★ The **citadel**. Little, Brown 1937 401p

"In 1921 Andrew Manson, newly graduated at the top of his medical-school class, accepts his first position as assistant to a dying physician in an impoverished Welsh mining town. Hard-working and conscientious at first, Andrew is promoted to a more socially desirable post in London, where he abandons his principles. A faulty operating-room procedure magnifies his increasing incompetence and jolts him back to a career of integrity." Shapiro. Fic for Youth. 3d edition

Cronin, A. J.

★ The **keys** of the kingdom. Little, Brown 1941 344p

ISBN 0-316-16189-6

"A child of Scottish fisher folk, Father Francis Chisholm, even as a young lad, yearned to enter the Catholic priesthood. After graduation from the seminary and a few years of parish work at home, he was sent to China as a missionary. With the years of toil he acquired saintliness and tolerance. Pestilence and famine, bandits and flood, and unappreciative superiors only served to strengthen his character and fortitude. Excellent character delineation." Libr J

Cronin, Justin

The **passage**; a novel. Ballantine Books 2010 766p $27

ISBN 978-0-345-50496-8

LC 2010-07455

This first novel in a proposed trilogy, "set in the near American future (Texas is now overseen by Gov. Jenna Bush), expertly draws together the parallel story lines of an unusually watchful, stoic little girl named Amy and a covert Army experiment to turn the human body into a bioweapon, using death-row inmates as test subjects. Cronin painstakingly weaves the threads of a narrative so involving and immediate that when he jumps ahead almost a century, it's hard at first to release those characters and invest in the dozens of new ones that emerge in the Stand–meets–The Road journey that follows. The Passage owes a substantial debt to both King's 1978 epic and Cormac McCarthy's 2007 Pulitzer winner, and he is not immune to some of the hoarier tropes of Armageddon fiction (mystical children, cryptic-wisdom-spouting old folks, impossibly arduous vision quests). But his bogeymen, the vampiric, blood-hungry beasts known as 'virals,' are magnificently unnerving, and his power to compel readers to the next page seldom flags." Entertainment Wkly

Crosby, Ellen

The **Viognier** vendetta; a wine country mystery. Scribner 2010 254p

ISBN 978-1-4391-6386-3

LC 2010-07846

Lucie Montgomery "hasn't heard from her old college friend Rebecca Natale for more than a dozen years. Now Rebecca's in Washington, D.C., for a black-tie gala honoring her boss, the wealthy tycoon Sir Thomas Asher. But shortly after lunch with Lucie, Rebecca disappears while on her way to pick up a priceless antique wine cooler that dates back to the War of 1812. Rebecca's clothes are later found at near a Potomac boat house. To find out what happened to her friend, Lucie joins forces with an investment analyst who has a grudge against Sir Thomas. . . . [The novel] feels as light and crisp as the wine Lucie produces on her Montgomery Estate Vineyard." South Florida Sun-Sentinel

Cross, Amanda

The **collected** stories of Amanda Cross. Ballantine Bks. 1997 184p

ISBN 0-345-40817-9

LC 96-42006

"Kate Fansler, a university professor normally involved with things academic, also dabbles in solving mysteries. In these short stories, she deals with cases ranging from missing persons to murder. Cross presents a complex jumble of seemingly enigmatic clues that Kate proceeds to study and resolve into a simple answer based on logic and deduction. The author camouflages the clues, facts, and answers by placing them in total view during the entire story." SLJ

Cross, Amanda

Honest doubt. Ballantine Bks. 2000 259p $22

ISBN 0-345-44011-0

LC 00-41445

In this mystery Kate Fansler serves "as a consultant to private eye Estelle 'Woody' Woodhaven, who is investigating the murder of misogynistic Tennyson scholar Charles Hancock. Woody, a down-to-earth, overweight sleuth, is a likable foil to the elegant, erudite Kate. . . . Devotees of the series may be disappointed at Kate's relatively minor role, but they will be amply compensated by the delightful Woody." Libr J

Cross, Amanda

An **imperfect** spy. Ballantine Bks. 1995 228p

ISBN 0-345-38917-4

LC 94-25357

Academic sleuth Kate Fansler "and husband Reed have each agreed to teach a course at New York's third-rate, racist, and chauvinistic Schuyler Law School, where they investigate the accidental death of the school's only woman professor and try to assist an imprisoned faculty wife who murdered her abusive husband. Highly sophisticated tone, carefully constructed prose, and nicely contrived plot make this a winner." Libr J

Cross, Amanda

The **puzzled** heart. Ballantine Bks. 1998 257p

ISBN 0-345-41883-2

LC 97-22686

This "Kate Fansler mystery starts with the kidnapping, just outside his Manhattan office, of attorney Reed Amhearst, the husband of English professor and amateur sleuth Kate. Told that her husband will be released after she publicly renounces feminism, Kate is frustrated by her unfamiliar powerlessness. She turns to Harriet Furst . . . now part-owner of a detective agency. The innocuous-looking but feisty Harriet and her businesslike partner, Toni, almost effortlessly rescue Reed. The remainder of this entertaining intellectual puzzle concerns the discovery of who kidnapped him and why." Publ Wkly

Cross, Janine

Touched by venom; Janine Cross. ROC 2005 353p o.p.

ISBN 0451460480

LC 2005014310

This book, "set in Malacar, a land with a repressive patriarchal society that both worships and enslaves dragons, . . . introduces headstrong nine-year-old Zarq Darquel, who lives a harsh but not completely unpleasant life as a member of the pottery clan on a dragon estate. When destitution forces her father to sell Waisi, Zarq's beautiful older sister, into sexual slavery, her mother, Kavarria, who belongs to the disdained Djimbi race, tries to save Waisi at all costs, but more tragedy follows. Zarq, her life governed by her mother's madness and obsession, eventually winds up as a sexually mutilated nun caring for retired bull dragons." (Publishers Weekly)

Followed by: Shadowed by Wings (2006)

Cross, Neil

Luther; the calling. Simon & Schuster 2012 326 p.

ISBN 1451673094; 9781451673098

LC 2012462320

This novel by Neil Cross is "the first in a series . . . featuring DCI John Luther . . . [and] takes us into Luther's past and into his mind. It is the story of the case that tore his personal and professional relationships apart and propelled him over the precipice. Beyond fury, beyond vengeance. All the way to murder." (Publisher's note)

Crouch, Katie

Girls in trucks. Little, Brown 2008 241p $21.99

ISBN 978-0-316-00211-0; 0-316-00211-9

LC 2007-30639

"Occasionally allowing us glimpses of the inner lives of her fellow debutantes, Sarah Walters has a fresh and winning voice, and Crouch easily maintains the reader's interest in her funny, painful journey all the way to the last page despite the lack of a conventionally laid-out plot. Girls in Trucks is not exactly experimental fiction—it's told in the linked-short-story format used in books like The Girls' Guide to Hunting and Fishing—but it's not your grandmother's Southern saga either." BookPage

Crouch, Katie

Men and dogs; a novel. Little, Brown and Co. 2010 279p $23.99

ISBN 978-0-316-00213-4; 0-316-00213-5

LC 2009-38523

"Crouch is too smart a writer to craft a damaged-woman-goes-home-again-and-finds-healing-and-redemption story. She knows that real life all too often disappoints, and that happiness is found in how we manage our expectations. Hannah is hardly perfect at the end, but at least she's learned a few things about being a responsible adult. Thanks to the author's sardonic sensibility, there's nothing sappy about those lessons." San Francisco Chron

Crowley, John

Four freedoms. William Morrow 2009 389p $25.99

ISBN 978-0-06-123150-6; 0-06-123150-9

LC 2008-46338

"Although nominally about life at an American aircraft factory during World War II, Crowley's complex and subtle novel is much grander. He explores the minds and hearts of people compelled by history to radically change their lives. Unaccountably optimistic Prosper Olander, orphaned as a child and crippled by a failed surgery, discovers that even he can find important work at a distant aircraft company in rural Oklahoma. Connie Wrobleski, frightened of nearly everything except her infant son, also travels to Oklahoma to reunite with her domineering husband, only to see him desert his family by enlisting. Prosper, Connie, and half a dozen other characters are developed in intricate detail and used as lenses on the massive relocation, dislocation, and societal change caused by the war." Booklist

Crowley, John

Little, big. HarperPerennial 2006 538p (Harper Perennial modern classics) pa $16.99

ISBN 978-0-06-112005-3; 0-06-112005-7

First published 1981 by Bantam

"One of the authentic masterpieces of modern imaginative literature. Painstakingly composed and elegantly structured, it is the sort of book that defies categorization yet lodges permanently in the memories of readers fortunate enough to encounter it." Barnes and Noble

Crowley, John

★ **Lord** Byron's novel; the evening land. William Morrow 2005 465p $25.95

ISBN 0-06-055658-7

LC 2004-63575

"Crowley's real achievement in Lord Byron's Novel is not a convincing imitation of Byron—not even Byron, who was pudgy and pale and walked with a limp, could always pull that off. More persuasive by far is the suffocating world of encryption and code, coincidence and conspiracy, paranoia and parapsychology that Crowley summons from his 19th-century documents and 21st-century decoders." N Y Times Book Rev

Crowley, John

★ The **translator**. Morrow 2002 295p

ISBN 0-380-97862-8

LC 2001-40324

"The fears 'The Translator' conjures seem eerily familiar, like a bad dream we've had before. At the same time, the novel gives us a world so suffused with beauty that its inhabitants manage to speak in fragments of poetry without sounding pompous or absurd." N Y Times Book Rev

Crumey, Andrew

Mr. Mee. Picador 2001 344p

ISBN 0-312-26803-3

"Musing on Rousseau, the French encyclopedists and the vagaries of chance and identity, Crumey . . . has written another novel of ideas in the grand tradition of Calvino, Borges and Kundera." Publ Wkly

Crumley, James

Bordersnakes. Mysterious Press 1996 320p

ISBN 0-89296-573-8

LC 96-34405

"The plot, such as it is, takes the pair from one violent encounter to the next, each with its separate cast of sublimely weird characters. . . . Mr. Crumley saves his fiercest prose for El Paso, where the villains of the piece have their day; but the sheer originality of his style tears up every pit stop on this hellishly funny adventure." NY Times Book Rev

Crumley, James

The **final** country. Mysterious Press 2001 310p

ISBN 0-89296-666-1

LC 2001-30640

"Plot twists and details seem loose and easy, yet every thread is sewn tight as a hardball. This is a brilliant achievement, with Crumley returned to his full powers, seeming to say with each assured sentence, Yeah, I'm an old dog, but I still wag the baddest bone." Publ Wkly

Crumley, James

★ The **last** good kiss; a novel. Random House 1978 259p

ISBN 0-394-41946-4

LC 77-90286

"C. W. Sughrue is hired to trace the missing and drunken writer Abraham Trahearne by the man's divorced first wife, Catherine. Catherine Trahearne is sexy, elegant, and ice-cold. She lives with Trahearne's ancient mother, Edna, across the creek from the house where Trahearne lives with Melinda, his second wife. The plot is episodic and keeps one bleary eye loosely focused on Trahearne's dysfunctional extended family." Murphy. Ency of Murder and Mystery

Crumley, James

★ The **wrong** case; a novel. Random House 1975 272p

ISBN 0-394-49198-3

LC 74-29598

Milton "Milo" Milodragovitch is a private detective in Meriwether, Montana. This case involves the suicide of a homosexual heroin pusher

This is "an exceptionally good example of the genre. Properly deferring to hallowed conventions, Crumley writes about damaged people seen through a haze of jaded romanticism, but he asserts his own tone of voice . . . . Crumley is a vivid writer. He makes Milo much more vulnerable, more involved in this sordid case than Hammett or Chandler would have done." Newsweek

Crummey, Michael

Galore; a novel. Other Press 2011 338p pa $15.95

ISBN 978-1-59051-434-4; 1-59051-434-3

LC 2010-40763

First published 2009 in Canada

Crummey "has created an unforgettable place of the imagination. Paradise Deep belongs on the same literary map as Faulkner's Yoknapatawpha and Garcia Marquez's Macondo." Boston Globe

Cruse, Howard

The **complete** Wendel; by Howard Cruse. Universe Pub. 2011 288 p. ill.

ISBN 0789322161; 9780789322166

LC 2010934608

This book is a compilation of Howard Cruse's comic strip "Wendel," which was published in the newspaper "The Advocate" in the 1980s. "Cruse's feature was an episodic chronicle of life as experienced by young Wendel Trupstock, his lover Ollie and their friends, who collectively represented a particular slice of the American LGBT demographic during a particularly stressful period in recent history, when the afterglow of gay liberation collided with the AIDS epidemic and the ascendancy of Moral Majority-fueled homophobia. Simultaneously a mirror of the days' new events and a comedic portrayal of everyday queer life, drawing Wendel required . . . what the cartoonist calls an "elasticity of tone," balancing lightheartedness with pain, erotic mischief with mundane follies." (Kirkus)

Crusie, Jennifer

Anyone but you; Jennifer Crusie. Harlequin 1996 283p o.p.; o.p.

ISBN 9780373440047; 9780373771387

LC 2007582920

This book tells the story of "Nina Askew, [for whom] turning forty means freedom." She buys a puppy named Fred who "manage[s] to put Nina face-to-face with Alex Moore, her gorgeous, younger downstairs neighbor. Alex looks great on paper—a sexy, seemingly sane, surprisingly single E.R. doctor who shares Fred's abiding love for Oreos—but a ten-year difference in age, despite his devastating smile, is too wide a gap for Nina to handle. Ignoring her insistent best friend, some interfering do-gooders and the ubiquitous Fred—not to mention her suddenly raging hormones—Nina thinks anyone but Alex would be a better bet for a relationship." (jennycrusie.com)

Crusie, Jennifer

Bet me. St. Martin's Press 2004 337p $22.95

ISBN 0-312-30346-7

LC 2003-58182

"Minerva Dobbs thought David Fisk might be the one she's been waiting for, until he dumps her three weeks before her sister Diana's wedding. Min soon realizes just how lucky she is to be rid of David when she overhears him at her favorite bar betting a handsome stranger, Calvin Morrisey, that Cal couldn't bed Min in a month. At first Min debates the idea of giving them both a piece of her mind, but then she remembers she still needs a date for the wedding. Why not use the all-too charming Cal just like he was going to use her, and then dump him? Of course, Min never expected that Cal might turn out to be the 'one.' . . . Finding exactly the right balance between cynicism and optimism, Crusie deftly blends snappy dialogue; quirky, irrepressible secondary characters; and two beautifully matched protagonists struggling against their romantic fate." Booklist

Crusie, Jennifer

Faking it. St. Martin's Press 2002 340p $24.95

ISBN 0-312-28468-3

"Matilda Goodnight has put her days of forging art behind her, but when her niece accidentally sells one of the six paintings she did as the fictitious daughter of a reclusive painter, she fears her secret past will be discovered. Tilda determines to steal the painting from Clea Lewis, the conniving social climber who brought it. But when she sneaks into the house Clea shares with wealthy Mason Phipps, she runs right into Davy Dempsey, who is there to steal back the money Clea took from him. Sparks fly instantly between the two. . . . {This} is an entertaining, fast-paced romp with a pleasing love story at its heart." Booklist

Cullin, Mitch

★ A **slight** trick of the mind; a novel. Nan A. Talese 2005 272p $23.95

ISBN 0-385-51328-3

LC 2004-46038

"Cullin is an unusually sophisticated theorist of human nature, and this book is first and foremost an analysis of Holmes—both as a fictional character and as an embodiment of the human drive to make fictions. . . . As the conclusion of this beautiful novel makes plain, lives aren't like cases or, for that matter, like narratives. They are never solved or resolved: they just one day come to an end." N Y Times Book Rev

Cullin, Mitch

Undersurface; a novel. art by Peter I. Chang. Permanent Press 2002 166p il $24

ISBN 1-57962-077-9

LC 2001-36621

An "account of a Tucson teacher's descent into the lurid, furtive world of illicit gay sex, which lands him in the wrong place at the wrong time when a murder is committed. John Connor is the ordinary, sensitive narrator whose descent begins when he finds himself frequenting adult video stores after his sex life with his wife sours. . . . As a crime narrative based on a true story, the book is a chilling if somewhat dated tale of a misstep morphing into free fall; as a literary character study, Connor's attempt to come to terms with his situation is both haunting and compelling." Publ Wkly

Cumming, Charles, 1971-

√ ★ The **Trinity** Six. St. Martin's Press 2011 356p

ISBN 0-312-67529-1; 978-0-312-67529-5

LC 2010-40197

This novel imagines a sixth man, Sam Gaddis, among the Cambridge spies "Kim Philby, John Cairncross, Guy Burgess, Donald Maclean and Anthony Blunt." (N Y Times Book Rev)

"Over a wine-soaked dinner with his friend Charlotte, Sam Gaddis, university professor and author of several widely unread books on Soviet history, learns a tantalizing piece of information: that the Cambridge Five, a real-life KGB cell that operated in 1930s England, was actually six spies strong, and Charlotte has access to someone who claims to be privy to the sixth spy's memoirs. Gaddis, who is in desperate need of quick cash, happily accepts his friend's offer to collaborate on a book, but when she dies of a heart attack that night, it is up to Gaddis to find her contact—an elderly man named Thomas Neame—and complete the book on his own. Gaddis doesn't realize that Charlotte was actually murdered by an agent of the FSB (the post-Soviet successor to the KBG) because of her interest in the truth about the Cambridge Five. . . . Taut, atmospheric and immersive—an instant classic." Kirkus

Cummins, Ann

Yellowcake. Houghton Mifflin Co. 2007 303p $24

ISBN 978-0-618-26926-6; 0-618-26926-6

LC 2006-23453

"By fusing suspenseful love entanglements with family angst, Native American concerns, grief over the poisoning of the land, penetrating compassion, and ironic humor, Cummins brilliantly conflates the insidious damage wrought by radiation sickness with the maladies of the soul caused by prejudice, poverty, nature's abuse, and love's betrayal." Booklist

Cumyn, Alan

Losing it. St. Martin's Press 2003 365p $24.95

ISBN 0-312-30691-1

LC 2002-31882

"The nuanced persuasive characterization propels the story forward and provides depth and texture. . . . A bonus is that Cumyn spices up this essentially sad story with some horrifyingly funny scenes." Booklist

Cunningham, Elaine

Shadows in the starlight. Tor 2006 286p $23.95

ISBN 0-7653-0971-8

LC 2005-44639

"Fired from the vice squad when a failed bust becomes a bloodbath, Gwen Gelman opens her own P.I. business focused on domestic problems and runaways. Called to investigate a missing-persons case involving the wife and son of someone she dislikes immensely, Gelman begins questioning her own cloudy past and slowly awakens to her changeling heritage. The second installment in a series that began with Shadows in the Darkness [2004] features a wise-cracking, gun-toting heroine and a fast-paced story of an elven legacy rediscovered." Libr J

Cunningham, Michael

By nightfall. Farrar, Straus and Giroux 2010 238p $25

ISBN 978-0-374-29908-8; 0-374-29908-0

LC 2010-12614

"Cunningham is a cool observer of the New York art scene, and he has fun with the contrasts between the makers of art, toiling away in obscurity, and the buyers cocooned in expensive suburbs. His descriptions of the objects themselves are also worth the price of the book. . . . [This] is a good book, even a challenging one. But for a story about the power of passion to upend lives, it lacks juiciness and messiness. Cunningham's prose is so exact and so careful that it actually takes away from the story, putting an arid, intellectual distance between Peter and the reader. The result: Instead of a novel overflowing with flesh and sweat, rage and craziness, Cunningham has given us a well-considered treatise." Cleveland Plain Dealer

Cunningham, Michael

Flesh and blood. Farrar, Straus & Giroux 1995 465p

ISBN 0-374-18113-6

LC 94-24628

"Fairly brief episodes, often occuring years apart, recount key moments in the establishment, disintegration, and reconfiguration of the family. Thoroughly realized action, vivid character delineation, and the splendid control of language guarantee both the unity and powerful impact of this successful novel." Libr J

Cunningham, Michael

★ The hours. Farrar, Straus & Giroux 1998 229p $23

ISBN 0-374-17289-7

LC 98-34188

"After a brief prologue, the stories alternate in an intricate sequence, rather like a rhyme scheme. . . . The whole book does sound a little fussy in description, an exercise in echoes, but it doesn't read that way." N Y Times Book Rev

Cunningham, Michael

★ Specimen days. Farrar, Straus and Giroux 2005 308p $25

ISBN 0-374-29962-5

LC 2005-40518

"As much as Cunningham's novel is haunted by the ghost of Whitman's prophecies, it is profoundly informed by the events of September 11, 2001. . . . Cunningham's brilliantly imagined dystopian future represents the final betrayal of Walt Whitman's joyously democratic America." New Leader

Currie, Ron

Everything matters! [by] Ron Currie, Jr. Viking 2009 305p $25.95

ISBN 978-0-670-02092-8; 0-670-02092-3

LC 2008-46686

"Junior Thibodeau of Waterville, ME—the fourth-smartest person in human history—is born with the certain knowledge that an asteroid will destroy Earth in 36 years. In that case, what is the point of living? In this radical reimagining of Frank Capra's It's a Wonderful Life, Junior tells his own story, while in alternating chapters his wildly dysfunctional family and friends provide commentary." Libr J

Currie, Ron

Flimsy little plastic miracles; a true story. Ron Currie, Jr. Viking 2013 352 p. $26.95

ISBN 0670025348; 9780670025343

LC 2012028931

In this book by Ron Currie Jr., his "protagonist, a blend of fact and fiction from his own life, is so distraught by his father's death, a book lost to fire, and an unreciprocated love that he hides out on a Caribbean island to write a new book about the mess. Then he fakes his own death, which brings him fame, fortune, and big trouble." (Library Journal)

Cusk, Rachel

Arlington Park. Farrar, Straus and Giroux 2007 256p $23

ISBN 978-0-374-10080-3; 0-374-10080-2

LC 2006-7952

First published 2006 in the United Kingdom

"The microscopic detail of daily life offered here could be excruciating for some readers, but for anyone who enjoys an original and imaginative writing style and wry observations of the way people live, it's well worth the read." Rocky Mountain News

Cusk, Rachel

✓ ★ The **Bradshaw** variations. Farrar, Straus and Giroux 2010 234p $25

ISBN 978-0-374-10081-0

LC 2009-31888

First published 2009 in the United Kingdom

"By dropping a man into what Philip Larkin once called 'the hollows of afternoons', and chaining the father to the sink instead, Cusk flips the notion of the unfulfilled, bored mother on its head, and delivers a thought-provoking, rich and powerful study of family life." Scotland on Sunday

Cusk, Rachel

In the fold; a novel. Little, Brown and Co. 2005 262p $23.95

ISBN 0-571-22813-5

LC 2005-02589

This novel is the "cleverest portrait of narcissism since Charles Allen Gilbert's 1892 painting 'All Is Vanity.' Like that image, an optical illusion that can be seen either as a young woman at her mirror or as a human skull, 'In the Fold' is at once a shimmering vision of privilege and a wise meditation on disillusionment." N Y Times Book Rev

Cussler, Clive

✓ **Atlantis** found. Putnam 1999 534p $26.95

ISBN 0-399-14588-5

LC 99-39883

"This is a fascinating story with exotic locations, high-tech wizardry, heart-pounding suspense, the threat of a cataclysmic disaster, resourceful heroes, and an action-packed conclusion—all backed by meticulous research to make this a truly grand adventure." Libr J

Cussler, Clive

Black wind; [by] Clive Cussler and Dirk Cussler. Putnam 2004 530p il $27.95

ISBN 0-399-15259-8

LC 2004-53536

"The story begins toward the end of World War II, and the Japanese have sent two submarines to the West Coast of the U.S. They are carrying a lethal new strain of biological virus, but neither vessel makes it to the designated target. Then, in 2007, a number of sea-lion deaths are reported along the western Alaska Peninsula, and birds and people in the area become sick and die, although no known environmental catastrophe or human-induced culprit is suspected. Called to the scene is Dirk Pitt, the head of the National Underwater Marine Agency, and his two sons, one a marine biologist, the other a marine engineer. Their task is to locate and recover the two subs from the ocean floor. There are the usual harrowing encounters, close calls, daring exploits, and—in the end—annihilation of the bad guys. Another win for NUMA." Booklist

Cussler, Clive

The **chase**. G.P. Putnam's Sons 2007 404p il $26.95

ISBN 978-0-399-15438-6; 0-399-15438-8

LC 2007-17291

"In 1906, the American West is still expanding. With the cities still distant from one another, a ruthless criminal nicknamed 'The Butcher Bandit' takes advantage, robbing banks, killing all witnesses, and seemingly disappearing into thin air. Recruited to end the crime spree is Isaac Bell, one of the best outlaw hunters in the country. His adversary proves to be exceptionally cunning, and Bell will have a tough time not only proving the identity of the killer but also staying alive long enough to catch him. Cussler clearly had a lot of fun writing this. The details of early 20th-century America and the novel's thrill-a-minute pace will add another best seller to his résumé." Libr J

Cussler, Clive

Fire ice; a novel from the NUMA(r) files. {by} Clive Cussler, with Paul Kemprecos. Putnam 2002 434p

ISBN 0-399-14872-8

LC 2002-19050

Previous titles in the Kurt Austin series: Serpent (1999) and Blue Gold (2000), published in paperback

In this thriller Kurt Austin and "the men from NUMA (Native Underwater & Marine Agency) team up with former KGB spies to face down a Russian mobster with czarist aspirations and a zealot's hatred for the 'corruption and materialism' of the Western lifestyle. . . . Cussler is in top form here, working in a role for Old Ironsides and Czar Nicholas II's crown while throwing in enough derringdo and eco-lore to leave his fans breathless." Publ Wkly

Cussler, Clive

Flood tide; a novel. Simon & Schuster 1997 511p

ISBN 0-684-80298-8

LC 97-26660

In this thriller, Dirk Pitt and "his sidekick, Al Giordino, are out to catch a Chinese shipping magnate who smuggles illegal Chinese immigrants into countries around the world to be worked as indentured slaves. On a lake near Seattle, Pitt stumbles across Qin Shang's heavily guarded compound. Pitt is the special projects director for the National Underwater & Marine Agency. . . . Searching the lake with a robotic observation device, Pitt finds heaps of mass-executed Chinese bodies. He then rescues a dozen still-living captives, including beautiful Immigration and Naturalization Service agent Julia Lee." Publ Wkly

Cussler, Clive

Inca gold; a novel. Simon & Schuster 1994 537p

ISBN 0-671-68156-7

LC 94-6577

"A chance rescue of two divers trapped in a Peruvian sinkhole leads series hero Dirk Pitt . . . into a search for lost treasure that involves grave robbers, art thieves and ancient curses. Cussler's latest adventure novel features terrorists who aren't really terrorists and a respected archeologist who is not what he seems: it all boils down to a race between Pitt and some unscrupulous crooks for a cache of Inca gold hidden away from the Spanish and lost since the 16th century. . . . It's pure escapist adventure, with a wry touch of humor and a certain self-referential glee." Publ Wkly

Cussler, Clive

The **kingdom**; [by] Clive Cussler with Grant Blackwood. G. P. Putnam's Sons 2011 392p $27.95
ISBN 978-0-399-15742-4; 0-399-15742-5

LC 2011-09207

In this "adventure featuring treasure hunters extraordinaire Sam and Remi Fargo . . . , the couple get on the trail of a sacred object, the Theurang, 'said to have been a life-sized statue of a manlike creature or . . . the skeleton of the creature itself.' Or maybe it's a chest holding the creature's bones. Reclusive wealthy entrepreneur Charles King (aka 'King Charlie') is also searching for this artifact. King's girlfriend, Zhilan Hsu, and their grown children, Russell and Marjorie, will stop at nothing to fulfill King's deadly demands. . . . Fresh prose, a smart and amusing husband-and-wife team, interesting history and science, and a wildly imaginative plot all add up to a good time for Cussler's many fans as well as series newcomers." Publ Wkly

Cussler, Clive

Lost city; a novel from the NUMA files. [by] Clive Cussler with Paul Kemprecos. Putnam 2004 420p $26.95
ISBN 0-399-15177-X

LC 2004-50556

"Kidnappings, hair's breadth escapes, fierce battles, strange science, beautiful women and plenty of action add up to vintage Cussler." Publ Wkly

Cussler, Clive

Plague ship; a novel of the Oregon files. [by] Clive Cussler; with Jack Du Brul. G.P. Putnam's Sons 2008 515p $26.95
ISBN 978-0-399-15497-3

LC 2008-5426

"Capt. Juan Cabrillo, who heads the Corporation, a covert military company for hire, and the multifaceted crew of the Oregon, a high-tech ship disguised to look like a tramp steamer, take on a group known as the Responsivists. The Responsivists publicly espouse a program of global population control, but are secretly planning a devastating attack on the human race utilizing a virulent virus found aboard an ancient ship that may be Noah's Ark. The authors are up to their usual high standards when in fighting mode." Publ Wkly

Cussler, Clive

The **race**; [by] Clive Cussler and Justin Scott. G. P. Putnam's Sons 2011 404p il $27.95
ISBN 978-0-399-15781-3

LC 2011-19712

Sequel to The spy (2010)

"Evocative period detail, brave men and women and their fabulous flying machines, and nonstop action add up to plenty of fun." Publ Wkly

Cussler, Clive

Sahara; a novel. Simon & Schuster 1992 541p
ISBN 0-671-68155-9

LC 92-5100

"Pepper the plot with human-rights abuse, cannibalism, state-of-the-art weaponry, espionage, and the evil General Zateb Kazim—and you've got more than enough action to keep the Cussler's thrill-craving fans satiated." Booklist

Cussler, Clive

Shock wave; a novel. Simon & Schuster 1996 537p
ISBN 0-684-80297-X

LC 95-30057

"Readers will love this ripsnorting, old-fashioned sea adventure based on only slightly futuristic science. Cussler writes with tremendous confidence, creating bold characters to love or hate. They all act in situations of gripping intensity and palpable reality." Libr J

Cussler, Clive

The **spy**; [by] Clive Cussler and Justin Scott. G.P. Putnam's Sons 2010 436 p. ill. (hardcover) $27.95
ISBN 0399156437; 9780399156434

LC 2010009053

This novel, by Clive Cussler and Justin Scott, is an "Isaac Bell Adventure." "It is 1908, . . . a brilliant American battleship gun designer dies in a sensational apparent suicide. . . . The man's grief-stricken daughter turns to the legendary Van Dorn Detective Agency to clear her father's name. . . . And when more suspicious deaths follow, it becomes clear that . . . an elusive spy . . . is orchestrating the destruction of America's brightest technological minds." (Publisher's note)

Cussler, Clive

The **striker**; an Isaac Bell adventure. Clive Cussler and Justin Scott. G.P. Putnam's Sons 2013 384 p. (hardcover) $27.95
ISBN 0399161775; 9780399161773

LC 2012047881

This novel, by Clive Cussler and Justin Scott, is book 6 in the "Isaac Bell Adventure" series. "It is 1902, and . . . Isaac Bell, only two years out of his apprenticeship at the Van Dorn Detective Agency, has an urgent message for his boss. Hired to hunt for radical unionist saboteurs in the coal mines, he is witness to a terrible accident that makes him think that something else is going on, that provocateurs are at work and bigger stakes are in play." (Publisher's note)

Cussler, Clive

The **thief**; an Isaac Bell adventure. by Clive Cussler and Justin Scott. G.P. Putnam's Sons 2012 408 p. ill. (Isaac Bell novels) (hardcover) $27.95
ISBN 0399158618; 9780399158612

LC 2011052236

This adventure story, by Clive Cussler and Justin Scott, is the fifth "Isaac Bell" novel by the author. "On the ocean liner Mauretania, two European scientists with a dramatic new invention are barely rescued from abduction by the . . . intrepid . . . investigator Isaac Bell. . . . A ruthless espionage agent has spotted a priceless opportunity to give the Germans an edge. It is up to Isaac Bell to figure out who he is, what he is up to, and stop him." (Publisher's note)

Cussler, Clive
Valhalla rising. Putnam 2001 531p
ISBN 0-399-14787-X
LC 2001-19516

"Historical asides of submarine lore, Jules Verne minutiae and references to Viking runes in America add touches of real-life oddity to the mix, and nothing will prepare even longtime Cussler fans for the major surprise he drops at the end." Publ Wkly

Cussler, Clive
White death; a novel from the NUMA files. {by} Clive Cussler with Paul Kemprecos. Putnam 2003 419p $26.95
ISBN 0-399-15041-2
LC 2003-46501

This thriller "chronicles the exploits of Kurt Austin, leader and hero of NUMA's Special Assignment Team. The plot involves Austin and his partner Zavala, who are investigating a feud between a radical environmentalist group and a Danish cruiser. Austin and Zavala must come to the rescue of men trapped on the ship. They find that a giant multinational corporation is seeking to kill anyone who attempts to stop its efforts to control the seas." Booklist

Cutter, Kimberly
The **maid**. Houghton Mifflin Harcourt 2011 287p
ISBN 9780547427522; 978-0-547-42752-2
LC 2011-09146

This book tells "the story of Joan of Arc. . . . After an unremarkable childhood as the youngest of five children in rural France, we see the . . . moment in her adolescence when she first hears heavenly voices. Three saints impart to Joan the sacred mission of both raising an army against England and crowning the dauphin king of France in Reims. [Author Kimberly] Cutter builds a . . . case for how a 15th-century peasant girl from Domrémy could embolden an army to reclaim their land from the English in the name of God. She . . . describes Jehanne's transformation from an innocent, curious child into a confident, driven young woman who conquers souls, brings thousands to her support, and convinces a wary would-be king that she can make him realize his destiny." (Publishers Weekly)

"Was Joan of Arc a messenger from God, a lunatic, or just a petulant kid? She's a little of each in this beautifully written novel, which follows Jehanne from her girlhood to the Hundred Years' War — during which, as a teenager, she insisted that God had commanded her to lead the French army — to her death at 19, burned at the stake in the Rouen marketplace. Cutter presents Jehanne as part mystic, but also part mascot used by France to rally support from the peasants. In The Maid's best scenes, she couldn't be more human." Entertainment Wkly

Czepiel, Kathy Leonard
A **violet** season; A novel. Kathy Leonard Czepiel. 1st Simon & Schuster pbk. ed. Simon & Schuster Paperbacks 2012 254, [10] p.p (trade paperback) $15.00
ISBN 1451655061; 9781451655063; 9781451655087
LC 2011031733

This book "traces a struggling rural family at the turn of the 20th century." Frank Fletcher, in order to pay his debts and regain his share in the Fletcher family's profitable violet farm, brings his daughter Alice to work as housekeeper at a brothel in New York City, though he "tells his wife that Alice is working in a factory. . . . By the time Ida finally learns where Alice is, she has been raped and fallen into a serious depression." (Publishers Weekly)

Czerneda, Julie E.
A **Turn** of Light; Julie E. Czerneda. Penguin Group USA 2013 896 p. $20
ISBN 0756407079; 9780756407070

In this fantasy novel, Julie E. Czerneda introduces the world of Marrowdell "and a beautiful but restless heroine who holds the key to Marrowdell's security. Although she longs to travel beyond the well-trod byways of her village, Jenn Nalynn, the miller's daughter, is moored to Marrowdell by the curse of her birth. Turn-born, she unwittingly provides the balance between Marrodell and the darkly feral Verge." These two worlds "can only coexist if Jenn . . . remains firmly rooted in place." (Booklist)

D

D'Amato, Barbara
Hard evidence; a Cat Marsala mystery. Scribner 1999 255p
ISBN 0-684-83354-9
LC 98-31785

Cat Marsala "tosses her dog a bone bought from an expensive food store, but the bone turns out to be human. What a way to end a pleasant dinner and begin sleuthing." Libr J

"A vivid supporting cast, sprightly yet controlled wit and some fine cooking advice . . . combine to make for another delightful mystery from the ever-reliable author." Publ Wkly

D'Amato, Barbara
Hard road; a Cat Marsala mystery. {by} Barbara D'Amato; and an essay by Brian D'Amato, {The wooden gargoyles: evil in Oz} Scribner 2001 286p $24
ISBN 0-7432-0095-0
LC 2001-31393

"Fans of L. Frank Baum's Oz books and all the history, controversy, and minutiae surrounding them will rejoice in D'Amato's merry weaving of all things Oz into this innovative mystery. Oz references are no mere gloss, however, but provide a satirical, sometimes spooky commentary on the action." Booklist

Includes bibliographical references

D'Amato, Barbara

White male infant. Forge 2002 333p
ISBN 0-7653-0024-9

LC 2002-25029

In this thriller about a baby-selling cartel D'Amato mixes "together a couple who are fighting against their suspicions that their greatly loved adopted son is not who they thought he was; a CNN reporter and her cameraman who see, firsthand, the deplorable conditions in European and Russian orphanages; and an FBI investigation into a highly profitable and corrupt international adoption agency. The separate strands of this complex but riveting story start coming together when the couple find evidence suggesting their son was not orphaned but kidnapped at the same time the CNN reporter discovers her cameraman brutally slain in their Russian hotel. Another D'Amato stunner." Booklist

D'Ambrosio, Charles

The **dead** fish museum. Knopf 2006 236p $22
ISBN 1-4000-4286-0

LC 2005-44672

"A gemlike set of eight stories in which wayward, self-deceiving characters set out to make order of their customary chaos–and realize they are more likely to find unhappy company than catharsis." Publ Wkly

D'Erasmo, Stacey

The **sky** below. Houghton Mifflin 2009 320p $24
ISBN 978-0-618-43925-6; 0-618-43925-0

LC 2008-25673

This "novel tells the story of a misanthropic obituary writer for a dying New York newspaper, who views his life through a series of memory boxes modelled on the assemblage art of Joseph Cornell. 'I assiduously collected interesting junk, filling my pockets with pebbles and wire and old nails: the stuff of transformation,' he says. He narrates the drudgery of the daily grind and scrutinizes his dysfunctional, fatherless childhood, during which he rebelled against his mother by dealing drugs and engaging in sex with men for money. Now nearing forty and spiritually broken, he is given a diagnosis of cancer and travels to a commune in Mexico, where he reluctantly receives the help of a clairvoyant eight-year-old girl. Although the book strays into portentous magic realism, its lyrical prose and telling detail create a powerful atmosphere." New Yorker

D'Souza, Tony

The **Konkans**. Harcourt 2008 320p $25
ISBN 978-0-15-101519-1; 0-15-101519-8

LC 2007-15303

This is "more than an ethnographic study—D'Souza stays character-focused throughout the novel, gently mixing irony and fatalism with a warm affection for humans and the stupid things they do." Washington City Paper

D'Souza, Tony

Mule; a novel of moving weight. Mariner Books 2011 292p pa $14.95
ISBN 978-0-547-57671-8; 0-547-576714

LC 2011-16050

"After the recession and an unexpected baby, James, an out-of-work journalist, agrees to transport a stash of prime-grade weed from California to Florida as a temporary money fix. But when he gets a taste of the fast cash, he becomes addicted to the thrill of the operation, continuing long after money ceases to be a necessity. In Mule, an acutely detailed page-turner, D'Souza depicts the moral free fall of a decent — albeit weak-willed — man so believably, readers may start buying James' brand of hazy moral justification." Entertainment Wkly

D'Souza, Tony

Whiteman. Harcourt 2006 279p $22
ISBN 0-15-101145-1

LC 2005-25459

"One significant virtue of D'Souza's storytelling rests in his ability to present Jack's experiences of African life with a vividness that reveals the continent's allure without sentimentalizing its exoticism. . . . Much of the drama that unfolds in the 12 loosely chronological parts of 'Whiteman' (each a story that could stand on its own) rests in the gentle progression that ferries Jack away from a form of blindness to a new kind of sight." N Y Times Book Rev

Dabbagh, Selma

Out of It. St Martins Pr 2013 $15.00
ISBN 1608198766; 9781608198764; 9789992178744; 9992178744

This novel by Selma Dabbagh "follows the lives of Rashid and Iman as they try to forge paths for themselves in the midst of occupation, religious fundamentalism and the divisions between Palestinian factions. It tells of family secrets, unlikely love stories and unburied tragedies . . . of the modern Arab world." (Author's note)

Dahl, Arne

Bad Blood; by Arne Dahl; translated by Rachel Willson-Broyles. Pantheon Books 2013 341 p. (hardcover) $25.95
ISBN 0375425365; 9780375425363

LC 2012046772

In this novel by Arne Dahl "the Intercrime team is assigned the task of tracking down an American serial killer on the loose in Sweden. Detectives Paul Hjelm and Kerstin Holm of Intercrime's A-Unit take over the investigation. They learn that the method of torture used . . . a highly specialized means of extracting information secretly developed during the Vietnam War. Hjelm and Holm fly to New York, hoping to discover both the killer's identity and the source of his interest in Sweden." (Publisher's note)

Dahl, Arne

Misterioso; translated from the Swedish by Tiina Nunally. Pantheon Books 2011 339p $25.95
ISBN 978-0-375-42535-6

LC 2010-32837

Original Swedish edition, 1999

"It's 1997, and a serial killer is methodically killing Sweden's wealthiest businessmen while listening to a tape of Thelonious Monk's haunting classic Misterioso. The National Police, still traumatized by the unsolved assassination of Prime Minister Olaf Palme a decade before, decide to create a special unit to hunt down the killer. Paul Hjelm, a detective in Stockholm's southern suburbs, is selected as one of the unit's six seemingly mismatched members. . . . [The author] sets a full plate for himself in the first of a series about Hjelm and his colleagues. He describes a once comfortable country fragmented by racial malaise; East European Mafias; a financial collapse brought on by greedy, reckless bankers and government deregulation; postindustrial capitalism; and a gnawing fear that Sweden has lost its way." Booklist

Dahl, Roald

Collected stories; edited and introduced by Jeremy Treglown. Everyman's Library/Alfred A. Knopf 2006 xxxvii, 850p $30

ISBN 978-0-307-26490-9; 0-307-26490-4

First published 1991 in the United Kingdom with title: The collected stories of Raold Dahl. The introduction is new to this volume

"With the inventive power of a Thomas Edison and the imagination of a Lewis Carroll . . . Roald Dahl is a wizard of comedy and the grotesque, an artist with a marvelously topsy-turvy sense of the ridiculous in life." Cleveland Plain Dealer

Dai Sijie

✓ **Once** on a moonless night; translated from the French by Adriana Hunter. Alfred A. Knopf 2008 277p $24.95

ISBN 978-0-307-27158-7

LC 2008-41089

Original French edition, 2007

"This strange and beautiful novel ponders the nature of language, the history of China, filial and romantic love, and intellectual passion. . . . Though it plays with ideas, the novel is most impressive as a stream of striking images and vignettes." N Y Times Book Rev

Daley, Robert

Nowhere to run. Warner Bks. 1996 460p

ISBN 0-446-52063-2

LC 96-3146

"Daley's leads are likable and believable, his French local color is first-rate and his complicated plot turns, buoyed by tension and splashed with violence, work beautifully. The ending isn't happy, but it rings true." Publ Wkly

Daley, Robert

Wall of brass; a novel. Little, Brown 1994 409p

ISBN 0-316-17206-5

LC 94-14185

"When New York City Police Commissioner Harry Chapman is shot while jogging on Manhattan's Upper West Side, his former patrol-car partner, Bert Farber, now chief of detectives, is assigned to find the killer. Farber is also one of three top contenders to replace Chapman as commissioner, and his two chief rivals are doing their best to roadblock him in his search for the killer. Complicating the situation . . . {is} Farber's torrid romance with Chapman's wife, Mary Alice." Publ Wkly

"A tightly plotted, involving tale of law and disorder." Booklist

Dallas, Sandra

The **diary** of Mattie Spenser. St. Martin's Press 1997 229p

ISBN 0-312-15515-8

LC 96-53926

"Beginning in 1865, a week after her wedding in Fort Madison, Iowa, Mattie Spenser confides to her diary as she and her new husband travel by Conestoga wagon to the Colorado Territories. The building of a sod house; the births and deaths of children; the melting of narrow attitudes toward 'loose' women, Indians, and Negroes; and the growth of Mattie as a person are all visible in these pages, full of what seems like genuine details of prairie life." Booklist

Dallas, Sandra

The **Persian** Pickle Club. St. Martin's Press 1995 196p

ISBN 0-312-13586-6

LC 95-31032

This is a "simple but endearing story that depicts small-town eccentricities with affection and adds dazzle with some latebreaking surprises. Dallas hits all the right notes, combining an authentic look at the social fabric of Depression-era life with a homespun suspense story." Publ Wkly

Dallas, Sandra

✓ **Tallgrass**. St. Martin's Press 2007 305p $23.95

ISBN 978-0-312-36019-1; 0-312-36019-3

LC 2006-51271

"Rennie Stroud looks back to 1942, when she was 13, to tell a powerful coming-of-age story. That year, the U.S. government opened a Japanese internment camp outside Ellis, CO, less than a mile from where Rennie and her family farmed sugar beets. Rennie observes the prejudice of some of the townspeople as well as her parents' strong moral code and their entanglement in the emotions of the time. Her father, Loyal, not only shows open support for the Japanese, whom he views as Americans, but offers to hire them to work on the farm. When a young girl is murdered, suspicion naturally turns to the camp, and the town is divided by fear. Dallas's strong, provocative novel is a moving examination of prejudice and fear that addresses issues of community discord, abuse, and rape." Libr J

Dalton, John

The **inverted** forest; a novel. Scribner 2011 323p

ISBN 1-4165-9602-X; 978-1-4165-9602-8

LC 2011-05574

"A story set at a summer camp can go a number of different ways. The Inverted Forest — a gripping, tender, and at times disturbing tale — takes the road less traveled. It's the summer of 1996, and a small group of inexperienced counselors find themselves unprepared to care for more than 100 severely developmentally disabled adult campers from a state facility. A shocking act of violence will affect the young staff for years to come, and Dalton nimbly delves into his characters' perspectives, uncovering past secrets and future dreams (and eventual disappointments). While some of what's described is anything but pleasant, reading it certainly is." Entertainment Wkly

Dams, Jeanne M.

Death in lacquer red; a Hilda Johansson mystery. Walker & Co. 1999 255p

ISBN 0-8027-3329-8

LC 98-45223

"With its fine churches and stately homes, its new industries and bustling downtown, South Bend, Ind., in 1900 looks like paradise to Hilda Johansson, a young Swedish maid who keeps house for the prominent Studebaker family. . . . When Hilda finds the battered body of a missionary lady, the sister of the grand political personage who lives next door, . . . {she} takes it upon herself to solve the crime before people look for a scapegoat among the city's immigrant population." N Y Times Book Rev

Daniel, Susanna

✓ **Stiltsville**; a novel. HarperCollins 2010 310p $24.99

ISBN 978-0-06-196307-0

This is a "love story but not one that should be mistaken for a romance. This lyrically written work, which follows the ebb and flow of a long marriage, is just intimate enough to draw the reader close. It isn't until well into the novel that you realize just how much you've come to care about author Susana Daniel's narrator and her story." Denver Post

Danielewski, Mark Z.

✓ **Only** revolutions. Random House 2006 384p $26

ISBN 0-375-42176-9; 0-385-61138-2

LC 2006-40996

This novel "consists of the dual free-verse narratives of 16-year-old Hailey and Sam, which are meant to be read in tandem; eight pages of Hailey's story are to be read first, then the volume needs to be flipped upside down and read in reverse for Sam's story, until the two narratives meet in the middle. With a Jack Kerouac-like reverence for the open road and a Dr. Seuss-like feel for wordplay, Danielewski tells an epic love story as the two teens travel across time, from the Civil War to the year 2063, in vehicles ranging from a Model T to a Mustang. Though outside forces threaten to undermine them, the two remain forever 16 and madly in love. . . . This creative paean to the velocity of young lovers and the vibrancy of American culture is sure to wow the experimental-fiction camp." Booklist

Dann, Jack

Jubilee. TOR Bks. 2003 441p $27.95

ISBN 0-7653-0676-X

LC 2002-73275

"The 17 stories in this collection illustrate the varied talents of one of the genre's most flexible and enduring writers." Libr J

Danticat, Edwidge

✓ The **dew** breaker. Knopf 2004 244p $22

ISBN 1-400-04114-7

"Beautifully written fiction about the real-life horror that is Haiti. Seamlessly blending the personal and political, it deals with what happens to a country and its people when mothers and fathers disappear for their political transgressions." USA Today

Danticat, Edwidge

✓ The **farming** of bones; a novel. Soho Press 1998 312p $23

ISBN 1-56947-126-6

LC 98-3655

"The book is based on a historical incident in 1937, when Dominican dictator Trujillo ordered the massacre of 15,000 to 20,000 Haitian emigrants living in his country. The Farming of Bones recounts the story through the eyes of Amabelle Désir, a young Haitian woman who is working in the Dominican Republic as the servant to a patrician family." Time

"It's a testament to Danticat's skill that Amabelle's musical, sorrowing voice never falters, even during her stark descriptions of the bloodbath." New Yorker

Danticat, Edwidge

✓ **Krik?** Krak! Soho Press 1995 224p

ISBN 1-56947-025-1

LC 94-41999

The author "touches upon life both in Haiti and in New York's Haitian community, though we spend most of our time in Port-au-Prince and the country town of Ville Rose. The best of these stories humanize, particularize, give poignancy to the lives of people we may have come to think of as faceless emblems of misery, poverty and brutality." N Y Times Book Rev

Danvers, Dennis

The **fourth** world. Avon Eos 2000 336p $23

ISBN 0-380-97761-3

LC 99-52345

"When virtual reporter Santee St. John joins forces with the woman he loves in order to fight for a people's revolution in 21st-century Mexico, he uncovers a conspiracy that introduces a new element into the perennial battle between the First and Third Worlds. The author . . . crafts a mind-bending tale of paranoia, adventure, and unexpected love set in a near-future filled with web addicts deceived by powerful manipulators of the truth." Libr J

Dare, Tessa

✓ **Any** Duchess Will Do; Tessa Bare. HarperCollins Publishers 2013 384 p. (paperback) $5.99

ISBN 0062240129; 9780062240125

This is Tessa Dare's fourth Spindle Cove romance novel. Here, "Griffin York, the marriage-shy eighth Duke of Halford, is dragged to the town by his mother, who orders him to pick a bride. He brashly selects Pauline Simms, a proud tavern serving girl. Griff's mother declares she can turn Pauline into duchess material; Griff retorts that if she fails, he'll be off the hook. He offers Pauline £1,000 to go to London and fail the training," but things become complicated when attraction arises. (Publishers Weekly)

Dare, Tessa

A **lady** by midnight. Avon 2012 374 p. (paperback) $7.99

ISBN 0062049895; 9780062049896

This novel is part of Tessa Dare's Spindle Cove historical romance series. Here, "a young woman [Kate Taylor] searching for her family finds love unexpectedly with a handsome colonel—but the secrets of her heritage threaten to disrupt their romance . . . and their upcoming nuptials." (Publisher's note)

Dare, Tessa

A **night** to surrender. Avon 2011 400 p.

ISBN 9780062049834

In this book, "[Tessa] Dare . . . pairs up an educated spinster and a wounded hero in this . . . the first in the "Spindle Cove series." Lt. Col. Victor "Bram" Bramwell is traveling with fellow soldiers when a flock of sheep stalls them. They set explosives to scatter the sheep, but Susanna Finch, a woman living nearby, gets too close. Fortunately, Bram knocks her out of harm's way just in time. The instant attraction between Susanna and Bram is complicated by Bram's having just inherited a title, a crumbling castle, and the right to summon a militia. The last will be nearly impossible in the peaceful woman-dominated community of Spindle Cove, where few are thrilled by the military newcomers." (Publishers Wkly)

Dare, Tessa

A **week** to be wicked. Avon 2012 375 p.

ISBN 0062049879; 9780062049872

The plot of this romance novel "unites an unlikely pair as a wastrel viscount comes to the aid of a serious scientist. Minerva Highwood asks Colin Sandhurst, Lord Payne, to accompany her on a journey from spinster haven Spindle Cove to Edinburgh, where she plans on winning a prize for her presentation to the geological society. The journey will appear as an aborted elopement, but Minerva is willing to risk social stigma to achieve fame. She promises Colin her cash winnings, as the confirmed bachelor can't access his trust fund until he marries. Minerva and Colin's mishap-filled trip results in passion that neither expected." (Publishers Weekly)

The **dark**; new ghost stories. edited by Ellen Datlow. TOR Bks. 2003 378p $25.95

ISBN 0-7653-0444-9

LC 2003-54336

"Datlow has cast her net beyond the horror genre's usual names and pulled in contributors whose stories are the equal of their best work, as well as mystery, fantasy and SF writers whose tales seem to be the ghost story they've always wanted to tell." Publ Wkly

Dark matter; a century of speculative fiction from the African diaspora. edited by Sheree R. Thomas. Warner Bks. 2000 427p

ISBN 0-446-52583-9

LC 00-22288

"Ranging in variety from the lilting cadence of Nalo Hopkinson ('Greedy Choke Puppy') to the understated bleakness of Derek Bell ('The space traders'), this collection of 28 tales by African American sf and fantasy authors showcases a wealth of talent that spans over 100 years." Libr J

Dark, Alice Elliott

Think of England; a novel. Simon & Schuster 2002 271p $24

ISBN 0-684-86522-X

LC 2002-17554

"Everything in this spare, eccentrically paced book is a pleasure to read, from the exposition of nine-year-old Jane MacLeod's home life in Pennsylvania to a family reunion, thirty-six years later. . . . It's almost impossible to write about the kind of subtle, inward sorrows and tensions that animate this story, and the author manages the challenge handsomely." New Yorker

Darnton, John

Black and white and dead all over. A. A. Knopf 2008 351p $24.95

ISBN 978-0-307-26752-8; 0-307-26752-0

LC 2007-50902

"The assistant managing editor of the New York Globe, a broadsheet newspaper based in midtown Manhattan, is murdered in his office. Suspects include disgruntled beat reporters, ambitious editors, and conniving board members, and the only person who really seems to know what's going on is Bashir, the Afghan coffee-cart guy. Darnton, a forty-year veteran of the Times, precisely plots an old-fashioned murder mystery while also considering the changing nature of modern journalism. . . . Darnton's villain is ultimately undone by a penchant for cliché. Being a psychopathic killer is one thing, but at the Globe hackneyed writing is the real crime." New Yorker

Darnton, John

The **experiment**. Dutton 1999 421p

ISBN 0-525-94517-2

LC 99-28860

"One way to achieve longer life might be to clone people who could provide body parts when yours wear out; clandestine research might reveal better but equally diabolical ways to extend life for those willing to pay large sums. When reporter Jude Harley discovers his apparent twin, a man raised in a mysterious island colony, he joins forces with a beautiful expert on twins, and the three uncover a genetic engineering plot of monstrous proportions, extending into the government and backward into their own childhoods as part of a secret project deep in an Arizona cavern." Libr J

"The central anxieties of 'The Experiment' strongly reflect the velocity of our technologies and the godlike desires of our nature." N Y Times Book Rev

Darnton, John

Mind catcher. Dutton 2002 387p $25.95

ISBN 0-525-94662-4

LC 2002-25540

"This is a dazzling, fast-paced novel that taps into issues about mind-body duality, cyberspace, artificial intelligence, and stem cell research. Well-drawn characters, tense emotions, and philosophical debates provide additional depth to this exciting scientific thriller." Booklist

Darnton, John
Neanderthal. Random House 1996 368p
ISBN 0-679-44978-7

LC 96-11045

"Mat Morrison and Susan Arnot, archaeologists and ex-lovers, are summoned to investigate an odd find: an apparently new Neanderthal skull. They rush to Tadjikistan and foray into some of the least hospitable terrain in Asia. Not too unexpectedly, they find their quarry only to discover a long-lost mentor who is guarding unsettling moral, political, and archaeological secrets that threaten their lives and those of the reclusive Neanderthals. . . . When government agents intrude and threaten the scientific find, the two scientists must survive, rescue their old friend, deceive American and Russian intelligence gatherers, and balance a study of an astounding archaeological find with the interests of the tribes." Libr J

Dau, Stephen
The **book** of Jonas; Stephen Dau. Blue Rider Press 2012 256p
ISBN 9780399158452

LC 2011047494

This book tells the story of "Younis, a perceptive . . . boy in a nameless Central Asian land, [who] is caught up in the war on terror. His village has been destroyed, his family killed, and now he must remake himself as Jonas Iskander, refugee. A charity sends Jonas to live with the Martins, an evangelical family in Pennsylvania. There he attends high school, an outcast . . he is also bullied, until he finally responds to an ugly attack by beating the bully senseless. The school mandates counseling . . . the young refugee's fractured recollections lead the counselor to connect Jonas's story with that of Rose Henderson, whose son, Christopher, went missing while in combat in Jonas' home country. To Rose, trapped in a limbo of loss, Jonas reluctantly tells his story—of the attack on his village and of his mountain cave sanctuary where he was found by the soldier." (Kirkus)

Davenport, Kiana
House of many gods; a novel. Ballantine Books 2006 330p $24.95
ISBN 0-345-48150-X

LC 2005-48174

"Left by her beautiful, tortured mother to be raised by her extended family, little Ana must survive by her wits in a small village on the west coast of Oahu. All the while, she keeps a tight hold on her anger at this abandonment, using it as fuel to fight her way to a good education and to medical school. . . . Davenport mines the depths of emotion and does not shy away from themes of madness and cruelty. Here she follows both Ana and her mother as they encounter love, illness, and redemption, all woven with the mysticism of island lore." Libr J

Davenport, Kiana
The **Spy** Lover; Kiana Davenport. Brilliance Audio 2012 303 p. (paperback) $14.95
ISBN 1612183417; 9781612183411

In this novel, by Kiana Davenport, "a Chinese immigrant serving in the Union Army, a nurse doubling as a spy for the North, and a one-armed Confederate cavalryman find their lives inextricably entwined. Fleeing . . . China, Johnny Tom arrives in America with dreams of becoming a citizen. . . . [On the] Union side, he is promised American citizenship. . . . But first Johnny must survive the butchery of battles and the cruelties inflicted on non-white soldiers." (Publisher's note)

Davidar, David
The **house** of blue mangoes. HarperCollins Pubs. 2002 421p
ISBN 0-06-621254-5

A multigenerational family saga set on the "Dorai estate in a tiny village in southern India. Tamil Christians, the Dorais are fortunate to have the contemplative patriarch Solomon at the helm in 1899, a time of violent unrest. Solomon has high hopes for his good-looking and athletic son, Aaron, but the heir apparent gets drawn into a radical terrorist group, so it's shy and studious Daniel, who makes a fortune in cosmetics, who takes his father's place. An avid student of the history and cultures of India, Davidar tracks the fortunes of the Dorai clan over the course of five turbulent decades as the independence movement coalesces, British rule ends, and India is drawn into two world wars." Booklist

Davidson, Andrew
The **gargoyle**. Doubleday 2008 468p $25.95
ISBN 978-0-385-52494-0; 0-385-52494-3

"Likely to ignite the passion of anyone who loves a mix of romance and the macabre. . . . Nothing [the narrator]—or you—can assume about this spectacularly imaginative journey will help navigate its twists and turns. Before it's all over, like Dante before him, our narrator must visit Hades, and like every chapter of The Gargoyle, that's a hell of a story, too." Washington Post Book World

Davidson, Diane Mott
Killer pancake. Bantam Bks. 1995 301p
ISBN 0-553-09588-9

LC 95-10852

The author "includes recipes as she brings events to a proper boil in this latest lively and satisfying outing for Goldy, who not only solves the mystery but also finds, much to her delight, that coffee can save your life." Publ Wkly

Davidson, Diane Mott
The **last** suppers. Bantam Bks. 1994 283p il
ISBN 0-553-09587-0

LC 94-18886

"Caterer Goldy Bear's wedding would have been perfect except for two minor problems—the priest is killed shortly before the wedding and her fiancé, homicide detective Tom Schultz, is kidnapped from the scene of the crime. Frustrated with waiting for updates from the police, Goldy attempts to find out who ruined her wedding." Booklist

"An appealing mixture of food and crime." Libr J

Davidson, Diane Mott
Prime cut. Bantam Bks. 1998 305p
ISBN 0-553-10001-7

LC 98-33736

In this mystery "Aspen Meadows, Colo., caterer Goldy Schulz is ousted from her kitchen. Bilked, like many other residents, by local contractor Gerald Eliot, her workplace in a shambles, she agrees to help her old teacher, Chef André, as he caters a Christmas catalogue fashion shoot. On the way home from the acrimonious set, she stops by to visit her friend Cameron Burr, whose house has also been ravaged by Eliot. Searching for a coffee pot, she discovers Eliot's dead body." Publ Wkly

Davies, J. D.

Gentleman captain; J.D. Davies. 1st U.S. ed.; Houghton Mifflin Harcourt 2010 336 p. $25
ISBN 0547382618; 9780547382616

LC 2010005737

In this novel by, J. D. Davies, "Captain Matthew Quinton is determined to complete his second mission without loss of life or honor. Rebellion is stirring in the Scottish Isles, and King Charles II needs loyal officers to sail north and face the threat. But aboard His Majesty's Ship the Jupiter, the young 'gentleman captain' leads a resentful crew and has but few on whom he can rely. . . . [He has] a growing conviction that betrayal lies closer to home than he had thought." (Publisher's note)

Includes bibliographical references

Davies, J. D.

The **mountain** of gold; J.D. Davies. Houghton Mifflin Harcourt 2012 359 p. (hardback) $25
ISBN 0547580991; 9780547580999

LC 2011028559

Sequel to: Gentleman Captain

This book "begins when a captured Barbary pirate speaks of . . . a mountain of gold. Rather than hang this enemy of England, King Charles II hands him back over to the man who apprehended him, Capt. Matthew Quinton. Quinton and the pirate devise an expedition to Africa and the treasure, which the king desires for his campaign against the Dutch. . . . Once out to sea, the captain's mission takes on new complications that test his crew and England's reputation as a maritime power." (Library Journal)

"A naval adventure that goes well beyond the usual outlines of the genre to paint a lively portrait of England in the 1600s." Kirkus

Davies, Peter Ho

The **Welsh** girl; a novel. Houghton Mifflin 2007 338p $24
ISBN 978-0-618-00700-4; 0-618-00700-8

LC 2006-15358

This novel is "set during World War II in northern Wales, where German POWs are held in a low-security prison. The intertwining stories involve a farm girl named Esther, who becomes pregnant after being raped by an English soldier; German POW Karsten, who is ashamed of surrendering in battle; and Jewish interrogator Rotheram, who is trying to refute captured Hitler deputy Rudolf Hess's claims of amnesia. From behind the prison fence, Karsten becomes friendly with Esther. He later escapes and hides at Esther's farm. Karsten and Esther share their fears, humiliation, and shame, which eventually leads to an affectionate sexual episode before Karsten gives himself up and returns to prison. . . . The characters are heartfelt and real and events vividly and memorably described." Libr J

Davies, Robertson

The **cunning** man; a novel. Viking 1995 469p
ISBN 0-670-85911-7

LC 94-31874

Robertson "entertains with an old-fashioned fictional mixture that he seems to have invented anew: keen social observations delivered with wit, intelligence and free-floating philosophical curiosity." Time

Davies, Robertson

Fifth business. Viking 1970 308p

The first volume in the Deptford trilogy, followed by The manticore and World of wonders

This novel "achieves a richness and depth that are exceptional in a modern novel and rare at any time. On its simplest and most obvious level it is a remarkably colorful tale of ambition, love and weird vengeance. At its deepest, it is a work of theological fiction that approaches Graham Greene at the top of his form." Book World

Davies, Robertson

The **lyre** of Orpheus. Viking 1989 472p
ISBN 0-670-82416-X

LC 88-40311

Concluding volume of the Cornish trilogy

"This fable about the nature of artistic creation has two major plot lines. One thread concerns the production of an unfinished opera said to have been written by E.T.A. Hoffmann. The other concerns the discovery that the famous art collector Francis Cornish actually passed off one of his own paintings as a 16th-century masterpiece." Merriam-Webster's Ency of Lit

Davies, Robertson

The **manticore**. Viking 1972 310p
ISBN 0-670-45313-7

The second volume in the Deptford trilogy

This book "reflects in its style the buoyancy of the quick mind of its hero as well as his pomposity, his over confidence, and egotism. No doubt about it: Robertson Davies is a manipulator of words and he entrances the reader with a flowing flurry of dialogue and narrative. His book is well written, insightful, and a delightful psychological excursion." Best Sellers

Davies, Robertson

Murther & walking spirits; a novel. Viking 1991 357p
ISBN 0-670-84189-7

LC 91-29844

"The films convey more than sight and sound, making our hero eerily privy to his relatives' thoughts and feelings. Davies has great fun with this device, giving full rein to his sense of drama, love of gritty, historical detail, and delight in satire." Booklist

Davies, Robertson

★ The **rebel** angels. Viking 1982 326p
ISBN 0-670-59063-0

LC 81-51907

First volume in the Cornish trilogy, followed by What's bred in the bone and The lyre of Orpheus

First published 1981 in Canada

"The names of Rabelais and Paracelsus are not gratuitously invoked by the plot. There is a Rabelaisian quality . . . in Mr. Davies's own writing; while the hermetic and heterodox ideas associated with the name of Paracelsus are exploited in a fashion that is at once playful and serious." New Repub

Davies, Robertson

What's bred in the bone. Viking 1985 436p
ISBN 0-670-80916-0

LC 85-40550

Second volume in the Cornish trilogy

"This novel nourishes the brain while it beguiles the senses. Even those who dislike its message must keep it in mind while they scramble for a rebuttal." Time

Davies, Robertson

★ **World** of wonders. Viking 1976 358p
ISBN 0-670-78812-0

Final volume in the Deptford trilogy

"If there is a single dominating theme, it is that we can never escape the consequences of our actions, and to ignore them is to be destroyed. . . . Among contemporary novelists, only Graham Greene has trod this ground and gleaned it so successfully. He and Davies stand alone, each in his own quarter of the field." New Repub

Davies, Valentine

Miracle on 34th Street. Harcourt Brace & Co. 1947 120p
ISBN 0-15-160239-5

"Old Mr. Kringle believed he was Santa Claus, and he looked the part, but the home for the aged decided the delusion made him ineligible as a permanent resident so he went to stay with a friend who was a keeper of Central Park zoo. Quite by accident he became the official Santa Claus in Macy's department store where he inaugurated a new and profitable policy of good will between stores, but an irritated personnel manager tried to have him committed to a mental hospital. The case went to court and the judge was in a dilemma—what would happen to his political career if he declared Santa Claus a myth?" Booklist

"Nice blend of fantasy, fun and humor with the universal and wholesome appeal of the Christmas spirit." Libr J

Davis, Amanda

Wonder when you'll miss me. William Morrow 2003 259p $24.95; pa $12.95
ISBN 0-688-16781-0; 0-06-053426-5 pa

LC 2002-24118

"Davis's writing is at its finest when the protagonist is struggling through the constant trials with her distant mother, her ineffectual teachers, and her one true friend's suicide. . . . The author succeeds in making this character unique, with flaws that teens will relate to. Readers will root for Faith, and the heartwarming conclusion will leave them satisfied." SLJ

Includes bibliographical references

Davis, Claire

Winter range. Picador 2000 262p $23
ISBN 0-312-26140-3

LC 00-34701

"Winters are hard on the eastern edge of Montana, and a couple of bad ones in a row can force a rancher to sell his herd. But Chas Stubblefield refuses to unload his cattle, or even to slaughter them; he is letting them starve to death out on the range as a reproach to the merchants, the banks, and God, who he believes has turned against him. Local wisdom dictates that property is property: if Stubblefield wants to lose his reputation along with his farm, that's his business. But Ike Parsons, the sheriff, is an outsider, and he decides to intervene—a decision that has dire consequences for both his marriage and his community. This fine first novel—part thriller, part love story—explores the gradations between pity and mercy." New Yorker

Davis, Kathryn

The **thin** place. Little Brown 2006 277p $23.95
ISBN 0-316-73504-3

LC 2005-07981

"In the opening pages of this . . . book, three small-town girls discover a man's corpse at the edge of a lake, and one of them, Mees Kipp, mysteriously brings him back to life. Davis writes hallucinatory, literate prose, and adopts a cosmic perspective: she is concerned with nothing less than describing the town's every waking moment. The experiences of Mees's dog, trotting through a clearing that smells of porcupine, stand alongside those of a minister's wife reading her morning paper and 'confronting whatever form the devil had chosen to assume overnight.' In any other book, a magical resurrection would be a central event; for Davis, it's just another moment in a particular place." New Yorker

Davis, Kathryn

★ **Versailles**. Houghton Mifflin 2002 206p $21
ISBN 0-618-22136-0

LC 2002-510048

This "idiosyncratic novel begins when Marie Antoinette, née Maria Antonia Josephina Johanna, Archduchess of Austria, aged fourteen, is riding in a blue-satin-lined carriage on her way to be married to the Dauphin of France. It ends with her death. Except for the brief, witty playlets studded throughout the narrative (in which various minor actors try to figure out what's going on), the Queen tells her own story, and the voice Davis has given her is by turns sage, mercurial, and ravishing. It is also edged with doom, each word bordered in black by the reader's own premonitions." New Yorker

Davis, Lindsey

The **accusers**. Mysterious Press 2004 368p il map $25
ISBN 0-89296-811-7

LC 2003-65008

In this installment Marcus Didius Falco matches his "wits against two sleek lawyers intimately involved with the evident suicide of a Roman senator accused of corruption. Did he or didn't he? Of course, Falco uncovers the truth, though just barely; the ending is a surprise and surprisingly affecting. Meanwhile, the brothers of Falco's beloved Helen continue learning how hard the life of an informer can be and grow up just a little. Topnotch work in a topnotch series." Libr J

Davis, Lindsey

Last act in Palmyra. Mysterious Press 1996 476p

ISBN 0-89296-625-4

LC 95-1612

First published 1994 in the United Kingdom

Court investigator Marcus Didius Falco "was denied a promised promotion into the upper class by the emperor Vespasian after his last escapade, a promotion required for him to marry his lover, the patrician Helena Justina. To get out of town with Helena, he takes on a job for one of the emperor's less trustworthy underlings, heading for Syria to do a little snooping. . . . While sightseeing, Falco and Helena discover, in a cistern, the body of a playwright who had been with an acting troupe out of Rome." Publ Wkly

"A delightful adventure that's charming, witty, intriguing, and clever." Booklist

Davis, Lindsey

★ Master and God; Lindsey Davis. 1st US ed. St. Martin's Press 2012 452 p. (hardcover) $25.99; (hardcover) $25.99; (downloadable audio) $69.95; (paperback) $16.99

ISBN 0312606648; 146680243X; 9780312606640; 9781466802438; 9780792787815; 9781250021557

LC 2012024195

This book is a "novel about the reign of Emperor Domitian (51-96 C.E.). . . . The novel's action revolves around Gaius Vinius, a soldier promoted to the emperor's Praetorian Guard, and Flavia Lucilla, the daughter of a freed slave who takes up her mother's profession as a hairdresser to high-ranking members of society. The two characters navigate wars, fires, business, real estate, scandals, and multiple marriages as Domitian's once-successful reign deteriorates." (Kirkus Reviews)

Davis, Lindsey

Poseidon's gold; a Marcus Didius Falco mystery. Crown 1994 336p

ISBN 0-517-59241-X

LC 94-13060

First published 1993 in the United Kingdom

In this mystery Marcus Didius Falco "is challenged to locate both the art treasure hidden by his deceased brother as well as to clear his own name from a murder charge. His father, an auctioneer of (sometimes fine) art, and Helena, his fiancee, are able assistants. The first-person narrative immediately draws readers into the story. Falco's dry wit surfaces with puns and satirical asides, and the conversations are especially realistic—often with half sentences. Details of Roman art, architecture, military, etc. appear throughout." SLJ

Davis, Lindsey

Three hands in the fountain. Mysterious Press 1999 351p $30

ISBN 0-89296-691-2

LC 98-45058

First published 1997 in the United Kingdom

In this "mystery featuring Marcus Didius Falco, the Roman gumshoe teams with old friend Petronius Longus to discover who is assaulting and murdering young women during festival time and then tossing their chopped-up remains into the city's reservoirs." Libr J

"Davis weaves an intricate, irreverent plot filled with wittily imagined characters." Publ Wkly

Davis, Lindsey

Venus in copper; a Marcus Didius Falco novel. Crown 1992 277p

ISBN 0-517-58477-8

LC 91-37297

First published 1991 in the United Kingdom

A "mystery set in the Rome of Vespasian. Falco, the ancient equivalent of a private detective, ferrets out information for two nouveau-riche women about a 'professional bride' who wants to marry their husbands' business partner. When someone murders the partner, the fiancée hires Falco to find the murderer." Libr J

This novel "demonstrates Davis' solid historical knowledge as well as his quick wit." Booklist

Davis, Lydia

★ The collected stories of Lydia Davis. Farrar, Straus and Giroux 2010 733p $30

ISBN 978-0-374-27060-5; 0-374-27060-0

LC 2009-25451

This volume presents a "body of work probably unique in American writing, in its combination of lucidity, aphoristic brevity, formal originality, sly comedy, metaphysical bleakness, philosophical pressure, and human wisdom. I suspect that The Collected Stories of Lydia Davis will in time be seen as one of the great, strange American literary contributions, distinct and crookedly personal, like the work of Flannery O'Connor, or Donald Barthelme, or J. F. Powers." New Yorker

Davis-Goff, Annabel

This cold country. Harcourt 2002 348p $31

ISBN 0-15-100847-7

LC 2001-3817

A "tale about a young English woman adjusting to new social, political and class demands when she moves to Ireland during World War II. A volunteer in England's Land Army, Daisy Creed works on a farm in Wales. Given the rare wartime occasion to meet an eligible bachelor, she quickly marries Patrick Nugent, a distant Anglo-Irish cousin of her employer. In a matter of days, Patrick is called on duty and Daisy joins Patrick's family in Ireland. Gothic touches abound; the Nugents are eccentrics, their home full of mysteries and reminders of better days." Publ Wkly

"A satisfying story told without sentimentality or melodrama but with a fine eye for detail." Booklist

Dawson, Peter

Rider on the buckskin; a western story. Five Star 2011 198p $25.95

ISBN 978-1-59414-943-6; 1-59414-943-7

LC 2011-04258

Dawson "has a firm grasp of character and action, and the story, in which Rivers winds up in the middle of a range war, falling in love with a beautiful woman and going head-to-head with the men who put him behind bars, is exactly the sort of thing genre fans will eat up. An exciting western." Booklist

Day, Cathy

The **circus** in winter; Cathy Day. 1st ed; Harcourt 2004 274p il $23
ISBN 0-15-101048-X

LC 2003-25033

In this "collection of interrelated short stories, [Day] succeeds in appropriating much of the garish pungency of the world of freaks, geeks and sideshow Houdinis without succumbing to its ready banalities. Although once or twice she treads close to cliche must the revelations of two-bit fortunetellers in fiction always turn out to be true? most of the time she steers clear of tired expectations. This is one circus act that doesn't rely on dependable gimmicks to keep the audience amused." N Y Times Book Rev

De Bernieres, Louis

Birds without wings; Louis de Bernieres. 1st American ed; Knopf 2004 553p $25.95
ISBN 1-400-04341-7

LC 2004-14529

"This epic about the tragedy of borders is likely to cross all borders, moving readers everywhere as it describes the harrowing cost of remaking faraway places in the image of our dreams." Christ Sci Monit

De Bernieres, Louis

★ **Corelli's** mandolin. Pantheon Bks. 1994 437p
ISBN 0-679-43644-8

LC 94-4783

The novel "has at times the rangy, expansive feeling of legend or saga, at other times the cozy intensities of chamber drama. The piece of Greek history it represents is composed of sufferings large and small, of national catastrophes and household agonies." N Y Times Book Rev

De Bernieres, Louis

A **partisan's** daughter. Alfred A. Knopf 2008 193p $23.95
ISBN 978-0-307-26887-7; 0-307-26887-X

LC 2008-17773

This novel's main "characters are Chris and Roza. He's a 40-year-old English pharmaceuticals salesman, locked in a loveless suburban marriage; she's an undocumented Yugoslav girl, scraping out an existence amid the economic hardship of pre-Thatcher 1970s London. They meet when, on an impulse—and for the first time in his life—Chris approaches a girl he believes to be a streetwalker. Roza protests she is not a 'working girl,' but she accepts a ride from him because she judges him, rightly, to be safe and kind. Before they part, she admits that she was once a prostitute, and charged 500 pounds for her services. Obsessed with the idea of sleeping with her, Chris begins to squirrel away money, but in the meantime he regularly visits Roza as friend rather than client, enjoying her company and listening to her stories. . . . Roza shocks Chris with the revelation that she once seduced her father, who was a comrade of Tito, and details her rape

at the hands of a British thug. But Chris, like readers of the novel, is never quite sure when Roza is telling the truth or when she is weaving a tale to make herself more fascinating—to this humdrum man who so obviously adores her, and to herself." BookPage

De Feo, Ronald

Calling Mr. King; a novel. Other Press 2011 291p $14.95
ISBN 978-1-59051-475-7; 1-59051-475-0

LC 2010-54082

"Whether pretending to be a British aristocrat in New York or unsentimentally confronting his dismal childhood, De Feo's hit man is extremely likable, and the novel emerges as a study of the delights and dangers of reinvention." New Yorker

De Giovanni, Maurizio, 1958-

★ The **Crocodile**; Maurizio de Giovanni; translated from the Italian by Antony Sgugaar. Penguin Group USA 2013 336 p. $17
ISBN 1609451198; 9781609451196

In this detective novel, disgraced Sicilian Insp. Giuseppe Lojacono is exiled to Naples and "spends his working days playing computer poker. He gets a chance to exercise his dormant gray cells when a gunman kills a 16-year-old boy, and the detective, one of the first on the scene, notices that the killer left behind some used tissues." He's ignored until "his theory that this death isn't related to organized crime attracts the interest of the investigating prosecutor." (Publishers Weekly)

De Gramont, Nina

Gossip of the starlings; a novel. Algonquin Books of Chapel Hill 2008 276p $22.95
ISBN 978-1-56512-565-0; 1-56512-565-7

LC 2008-5883

"Catherine Morrow and Skye Butterfield both end up at Esther Percy School for Girls after landing in trouble at their previous schools for the well-to-do. Catherine's dad pulled her from the exclusive Waverly after she was caught in bed with her lower-crust boyfriend, John Paul. Skye was expelled from her previous school after a couple of offenses. . . . Both of Skye's transgressions, however, are of the noble variety, which provides convenient campaign spin for her father, the famed and charming U.S. Sen. Douglas Butterfield. Skye chooses Catherine as her closest (and only) friend at Esther Percy, and the two take to toking like it's going out of style (the novel is set in 1984, so in fairness, maybe it was). After a failed excursion to the Butterfields' summer estate, during which Catherine unsuccessfully tries to meld Skye with her old friends, frissons of tension crackle between the two, leading to the sort of high-drama tragedy that only the privileged get to partake in. De Gramont writes with uncommon grace about the hypnotizing effect of fame on Catherine." Time Out Chicago

De Hartog, Jan

★ The **peaceable** kingdom; an American saga. Atheneum Pubs. 1972 677p

This first volume in the author's trilogy about Quaker life "is set in England in 1652-53 and Pennsylvania in 1754-55.

. . . In the first section, Margaret Fell, who falls in love with the Quaker preacher George Fox, must exorcise the passion of sexual desire in order to achieve grace. In her encounters she begins the work of reform in prisons, schools and mental institutions; in her progress she loses her property and possessions and is forced into prison. . . . In the second part of the novel, which takes place in colonial Pennsylvania, (there occur) Indian uprisings, massacres of Indians by whites, several murders of black slaves and ritual retribution by the blacks for the murders." N Y Times Book Rev

Followed by The lamb's war

De Kretser, Michelle

The **Hamilton** case. Little, Brown and Co 2004 307p $24.95

ISBN 0-316-73548-5

LC 2003-60759

Having come of age on the island nation of Ceylon, Sam Obeysekere is a lawyer whose life is guided by the British culture that dominates his homeland. . . . .Sam's undoing arrives in the form of the Hamilton case, a scandalous murder that shakes the upper echelons of island society. Guided by grandiose visions of Sherlock Holmes, he becomes convinced he can solve the mysterious case-and that his good standing with the English will insulate him from the unrest the case has exposed." Publisher's note

De Kretser, Michelle

The **lost** dog; a novel. Little, Brown and Co. 2008 326p il $24.99

ISBN 978-0-316-00183-0; 0-316-00183-X

LC 2007-43331

First published 2007 in Australia

"While staying in a remote cabin trying to finish his book on Henry James, divorced college professor Tom Loxley loses his dog and sets out to find him in the Australian outback. Accompanying him is Nellie Zhang, a highly regarded contemporary artist with a scandal in her past—and a woman with whom Tom would like to be more than just friends. Tom's search for the dog is mirrored by multiple needs: to understand his past as an immigrant from India, to grasp both Nellie's art and her personal history (information about which is doled out in fragments), to be sensitive to his mother's growing disabilities, and to anchor himself in the present." Libr J

This is "an uncompromisingly literary (and literate) book: ferociously intelligent, highbrow, allusive and unflinching." Time

De la Cruz, Melissa

Witches of East End. Hyperion 2011 273p

ISBN 1-4013-2390-1; 978-1-4013-2390-5

LC 2010-52857

This first title in the author's series about witchcraft is "the tale of the Beauchamp women — Joanna and her daughters Freya and Ingrid, who had their powers stripped back in the 17th century. But as they say, magic will out, and the women begin to dabble again just as a bunch of mysterious happenings start plaguing their small Long Island town. De la Cruz balances the supernatural high-jinksery with unpredictable twists and a conclusion that nicely sets up book 2." Entertainment Wkly

De la Mare, Walter

Collected tales; chosen, and with an introduction, by Edward Wagenknecht. Knopf 1950 xxi, 467p

De la Pava, Sergio

A **naked** singularity; a novel. Sergio de la Pava. The University of Chicago Press 2012 678 p. (paperback: alkaline paper) $18

ISBN 0226141799; 9780226141794

LC 2011032343

The author, Sergio de la Pava, "tells the story of Casi, a child of Colombian immigrants who lives in Brooklyn and works in Manhattan as a public defender--one who, tellingly has never lost a trial. . . . [Readers see Casi's] sense of justice and even his sense of self begin to crack--and how his world then slowly devolves. . . . [Pava] takes readers through crime and courts, immigrant families and urban blight, savagery and media satire, scatology and boxing, and even a breathless heist worthy of any crime novel." (Publisher's note)

De la Roche, Mazo

Jalna. Little, Brown 1927 347p

Jalna is the family home of the Whiteoaks. Gathered under its roof are representatives of each generation from the time the grandparents drifted to Canada, via England from India and there built their homestead on a lavish scale. Renny, 37, is the present head of the household which includes Gran—a formidable old lady of 99—two uncles, an aunt, an elderly sister, and four half-brothers. An affectionate, warring group of strong personalities from the old lady down to Wakefield, the youngest, aged nine. Two of the boys marry and bring their wives home

De Lint, Charles

Memory and dream. TOR Bks. 1994 400p

ISBN 0-312-85572-9

LC 94-21752

The author's "multi-voiced, time-shifting narrative . . . . beautifully evokes a sense of creative community, making it almost possible to believe that the rarified aesthetic atmosphere might well be capable of conjuring up a spirit or two." Publ Wkly

De Lint, Charles

Someplace to be flying. TOR Bks. 1998 380p

ISBN 0-312-85849-3

LC 97-37443

"A cab driver and a freelance photographer come together in the town of Newford to explore the existence of the mythical 'animal people' and discover the hidden world that lurks outside their normal perceptions. . . . DeLint's elegant prose and effective storytelling continue to transform the mundane into the magical at every turn." Libr J

De Lint, Charles

Trader. TOR Bks. 1997 352p

ISBN 0-312-85847-7

LC 96-30646

"De Lint is a master at world building, at creating the apt image, and at making grippingly suspenseful a story in which the fate of the characters may have no cosmic significance but is vitally important to them and their closest friends." Booklist

De Lint, Charles

Widdershins. Tor Books 2006 560p $27.95
ISBN 0-765312-85-9

LC 2005-34475

"On her way home from a gig in the small Canadian town of Sweetwater, Celtic fiddler Lizzie Mahone disrupts the feasting of a band of faerie thugs and becomes a target for their hostility, also winning the respect of a pair of Native American spirits. These new complications bring her into the orbit of Jilly Coppercorn, a brilliant painter and a favorite of the many faerie folk who dwell unseen in the nearby town of Newford, and Jilly's friend, master fiddler Geordie Riddell. As familiarly as though he were chronicling the lives of old friends, de Lint . . . spins yet another magical story of the intersections between reality and the faerie and spirit world in this latest addition to the Newford opus." Libr J

De los Santos, Marisa

Belong to me. William Morrow 2008 390p $24.95
ISBN 978-0-06-124027-0; 0-06-124027-3

LC 2007-43197

This sequel to Love walked in follows Cornelia Brown and "her oncologist husband, Teo Sandoval, to suburban Philadelphia. Piper Truitt lives across the street with her husband and two young children. She considers herself the arbiter of style and local propriety. Add to the mix waitress Lake and her son, Dev, who is enrolled in a private academy far superior to his previous California public school. From the outset, Cornelia and Piper are traveling down different paths, while Cornelia and Lake seem to hit it off. . . . But there is more beneath the surface of these women and their motivations than the lovely locale can mask." Libr J

"Smart, funny writing about the risks we take for love." Redbook

De los Santos, Marisa

Love walked in; a novel. Dutton 2006 307p $23.95
ISBN 0-525-94917-8

LC 2005-3281

"Cornelia is a sprightly little thing who's stuck in a rut managing a coffee shop and watching her beloved film classics in her spare time. Then, right out of the movies, 'love walked in,' looking just like a modern-day incarnation of Cary Grant. Martin seems to be perfect for Cornelia, until she meets his ten-year-old daughter, Clare, whom he had failed to mention. When Cornelia learns that Clare's mother, Martin's ex-wife, has disappeared, she steps right into the situation. Narrated by Cornelia and Claire in alternating chapters, this is the story of how two lives intersect and a great relationship blooms from an unexpected seed." Libr J

De Robertis, Carolina

★ **Perla**; by Carolina De Robertis. Alfred A. Knopf 2012 256p.
ISBN 9780307947840; 9780307599599

LC 2011041833

This book tells the story of "Perla, the narrator, . . . [who] is a young university student . . . [with] a dark secret: Her father was a naval officer who during the late 1970s and early '80s helped round up the 'disappeared,' dissidents who were arrested and executed by the military regime, often dropped into the Atlantic Ocean from airplanes. . . . But that legacy becomes unavoidable to her when a man appears in Perla's home, soaked and dank-smelling and constantly thirsty. He's a ghost of one of the disappeared, but also quite real: The water that he can't shake off soaks the apartment. His surreal presence unlocks a host of memories for Perla, and the novel alternates between her perspective, as she recalls her difficult relationship with her father, and the stranger's perspective, as he recalls the horrific rapes and other abuses he suffered while in military custody." (Kirkus)

de Rosnay, Tatiana

Sarah's key; Tatiana de Rosnay. St. Martin's Press 2007 294p $25.95
ISBN 9780312370831; 0312370830

LC 2007010080

This novel begins in "Paris, July 1942 . . . [when] Sarah, a ten-year-old girl, is taken with her parents by the French police as they go door to door arresting Jewish families in the middle of the night. Desperate to protect her younger brother, Sarah locks him in a bedroom cupboard—their secret hiding place—and promises to come back for him as soon as they are released. Sixty Years Later: Sarah's story intertwines with that of Julia Jarmond, an American journalist investigating the roundup. In her research, Julia stumbles onto a trail of secrets that link her to Sarah, and to questions about her own future." (Publisher's note)

De Sa, Anthony

Barnacle love. Algonquin Books of Chapel Hill 2010 226p pa $14.95
ISBN 978-1-56512-926-9; 1-56512-926-1

LC 2010-20929

First published 2008 in Canada

"These beautifully connected stories follow Manuel from Sao Miguel, one of the tiny islands in the Portuguese Azores, to Toronto where he goes to seek a better life for himself. In Canada, he struggles to keep his dreams alive, but success eludes him, and his failure to fulfill his own promise drives him to drink and almost to despair. His son, Antonio, smart and sensitive, wants to admire and respect his father, but sees too clearly his father's many limitations. The family romance — how the father left home with nothing, went to sea, and was miraculously saved from drowning — governs the lives of mother, daughter, and son. But the son wants none of it; he wants to fit in, wants to eat Swanson TV dinners, have a mother who drives him to summer camp and a father who wears a shirt and tie to work. The father's point of view controls the early stories, giving way to the son's in the new world." Boston Globe

Dean, Anna

Bellfield Hall, or, The observations of Miss Dido Kent; Anna Dean. 1st U.S. ed.; Minotaur Books 2010 300 p.
ISBN 0312562942; 9780312562946

LC 2009041130

The book tells the tale of [s]pinster aunt Miss Dido Kent [who] is summoned to Bellfield Hall, the Montague country estate, by her niece Catherine, who wants her to discover why Richard Montague, her fiancé, ran off after declaring he was a ruined man. Before Dido can solve this puzzle, an unknown woman is found murdered in the Hall's shrubbery, and Richard's strange departure makes him a prime suspect. Can Dido discover the truth hidden behind a wealth of secrets, or will this house party have a decidedly unhappy ending? (Libr J)

Bellfield Hall

Observations of Miss Dido Kent

Dean, Anna

A **gentleman** of fortune, or, The suspicions of Miss Dido Kent; Anna Dean. Minotaur Books 2011 335 p.

ISBN 0312596960; 9780312596965

LC 2010042003

Sequel to: Bellfield Hall

In this detective novel, a "murder among the English gentility . . . challenges the inquisitive prowess of Miss Dido Kent. . . . Dido is residing in the fashionable town of Richmond with her cousin, Mrs. Flora Beaumont, when the ladies learn that the charming, eligible bachelor Mr. Lansdale has finally come into his fortune on the death of his invalid aunt. This happy occasion is disrupted by the vicious gossip of Mrs. Midgely, a neighbor who insinuates that Mrs. Lansdale was murdered. . . . When Mrs. Midgely prevails upon the local apothecary to bring the case to the magistrates, Dido gives in to her natural curiosity. By paying visits, eavesdropping in shops and attending to the subtleties of parlor games, Dido aspires to defend Mr. Lansdale's innocence." (Kirkus)

Dean, Anna

A **woman** of consequence; the investigations of Miss Dido Kent. Anna Dean. Minotaur Books / A Thomas Dunne Book 2012 383 p. (Dido Kent mystery)

ISBN 0312626843; 9780312626846; 9781429942560

LC 2012003258

This book, "[s]et in 1806," is "[Anna] Dean's . . . third mystery featuring Miss Dido Kent. . . . Dido writes to her sister, Eliza, of Penelope Lambe's falling and hitting her head at ruined Madderstone Abbey, where the "sweet-tempered, good-natured girl" had gone in the hope of getting a glimpse of the abbey ghost known as the Grey Nun. Penelope's claim to have seen the Grey Nun shortly before losing consciousness leads Dido to investigate Madderstone for herself. The discovery in a drained pool on the abbey grounds of a human skeleton raises the stakes. Dean . . . integrates a wealth of historical detail, especially regarding the rights of women and the inheritance laws in effect in the early 19th century." (Publishers Wkly)

Dean, Debra

The **madonnas** of Leningrad; a novel. William Morrow 2006 231p hardcover o.p. pa $13.99

ISBN 0-06-082530-8; 0-06-082531-6 pa

LC 2005-50233

"Like her adoring museum audiences 60 years earlier, readers will absorb Marina's glorious, lush accounts of clas-sical beauties as she traces them in her mind. Dean eloquently depicts the ravages of Alzheimer's disease and convincingly describes the inner world of the afflicted." Libr J

Dean, Louise

Becoming strangers. Harcourt 2006 307p $24

ISBN 0-15-101174-5

LC 2005-2400

First published 2004 in the United Kingdom

"At a Caribbean resort, elderly Britishers Dorothy and George Davis are thrown together with a younger and more urbane Belgian couple, Annemieke and Jan De Groot. Although this is the Davises' first trip abroad (courtesy of their pushy daughter), it may well be the unhappily married De Groots' last, for Jan is slowly dying of cancer. Although he hopes the holiday will help them become better friends, Annemieke spends most of her time in pursuit of extramarital sexual adventure. George and Dorothy, meanwhile, are coming to terms with the fact that Dorothy is in an increasingly advanced stage of Alzheimer's." Booklist

"Dean peels back the skin of these marriages with an unflinching lack of sentimentality and an immense talent for close observation and evocative, often poetic detail." Atlantic

Dean, Louise

The **old** romantic. Riverhead Books 2011 338p $25.95

ISBN 978-1-59448-779-8

LC 2010-36868

In this novel, "a British family drama set along splintered class lines at a decaying seaside resort, Dean explores the relationships between Nick, a Cambridge-educated divorce attorney; his unctuous brother, Dave; and their father, Ken, a working-class lug who's developed a death obsession in his old age, choosing the lining for his coffin and even having an affair with the embalmer at the local funeral home. There's not much in the way of plot in The Old Romantic, but Dean's razor-sharp observations, coupled with her very real affection for her characters, make the pages fly." Entertainment Wkly

Dean, Louise

This human season. Harcourt, Inc. 2007 374p $23

ISBN 978-0-15-101253-4; 0-15-101253-9

LC 2006-16217

First published 2005 in the United Kingdom

"Christmas is coming in bleak and lawless 1979 Belfast, but there is little cheer for the families of IRA political prisoners or for their prison guards. Alternating chapters follow the stories of Sean Moran, a young man in prison for his part in a car bombing gone awry, and John Dunn, a former British soldier and recent guard recruit." Libr J

"Dean mercilessly heightens the suspense while managing at the same time to confer complexity and even grace on her characters and on their forbidding city." Boston Globe

Dean, Margaret Lazarus

The **time** it takes to fall. Simon & Schuster 2007 305p $24

ISBN 978-0-7432-9722-6; 0-7432-9722-9

LC 2006-52213

"This first novel looks at the tragedy of the Challenger space shuttle from the unique perspective of a teenage girl named Dolores, whose father works for NASA. Dolores is obsessed with becoming an astronaut and keeps a scrapbook of stories associated with the space program that includes a journal of her attendance at the successful launches. After Dolores befriends a schoolmate named Eric, she comes to suspect that his father, the director of launch safety, is having an affair with her mother. Dolores is forced to consider the wobbly direction her young life is beginning to take when her mother leaves the family and when her father is involved in the investigation of the space program's cover-ups after the Challenger disaster. . . . A gripping judgment of American culture with a harrowing depiction in the epilog of the last few minutes in the lives of the Challenger's seven astronauts." Libr J

Dean, Michael

★ **I,** Hogarth. Penguin Group USA 2013 272 p. $26.95

ISBN 1468303422; 9781468303421

This book is a fictional biography of artist William Hogarth. "Born in 1697 . . . , Hogarth was apprenticed to an engraver, only to maneuver his way into tutelage from and assistantship to the court painter Sir James Thornhill. Hogarth's family fractures when father Richard lands in debtors' prison." In a moneylender's mansion, "Hogarth glimpses Kate, a strumpet, the vision unleashing the artist's lifelong appreciation for fleshly sensuality." (Kirkus Reviews)

Dean, S. F. X.

It can't be my grave. Walker & Co. 1984 222p

ISBN 0-8027-5596-8

LC 84-13192

First published 1983 in the United Kingdom

Professor Neil Kelly "is in London for the British publication of his surprise bestseller on the life of John Donne. There an old Oxford chum, now a famous thespian, and his actress wife tell Kelly of the possibility of running their own theater company devoted to lost plays by women writers and funded by tycoon Gordon Fairly. Sir Gordon, a man of power and charm, believes a 16th century female ancestor to have been the author of a newly found play attributed to Shakespeare or Marlowe, and wants to confirm her authorship. He offers Kelly a huge sum to play devil's advocate and prove his theories wrong, but before research can get under way, the rich man is murdered. . . . This mystery is worth reading for the sheer pleasure of its language." Publ Wkly

Deane, Seamus

★ **Reading** in the dark. Knopf 1997 245p

ISBN 0-394-57440-0

LC 96-49635

First published 1996 in the United Kingdom

"A Catholic boy growing up hard by the border between Donegal and Derry is fascinated by the local ghost stories and neighborhood lore, and this fascination leads him to secrets at the heart of a family feud. His search for the truth runs through a labyrinth of Irish detours and delights: elaborate catechisms, mad poets, mute idiots, drunken hyperbole, deathbed revelations, and a clever reprisal involving an unwitting bishop." New Yorker

Deaver, Jeff

The **bodies** left behind; [by] Jeffery Deaver. Simon & Schuster 2008 350p $26.95

ISBN 978-1-4165-9561-8; 1-4165-9561-9

LC 2008-30682

"Deaver plays gotcha with readers so many times you begin to anticipate his tricks, but the biggest twist of all, you'll never see coming. Very engrossing story." Fort Worth Star-Telegram

Deaver, Jeff

The **broken** window; a Lincoln Rhyme novel. [by] Jeffery Deaver. Simon & Schuster 2008 417p $26.95

ISBN 978-1-4165-4997-0; 1-4165-4997-8

LC 2007-48867

"Quadriplegic forensics whiz Lincoln Rhyme and his Glock-toting girlfriend, Amelia Sachs, track a serial killer who uses an all-knowing computer database to frame fall guys. . . . Rhyme still intrigues in his eighth outing, while Deaver's scarily believable depiction of identity theft in a total-surveillance society stokes our paranoia." Entertainment Wkly

Deaver, Jeff

The **Coffin** Dancer; [by] Jeffery Deaver. Simon & Schuster 1998 358p

ISBN 0-684-85285-3

LC 98-13537

Quadriplegic forensic specialist Lincoln Rhyme "is called in to track down a contract killer, known as the Coffin Dancer, who has been hired to eliminate three witnesses in the upcoming federal trial of Philip Hansen. The trial is set to begin just 48 hours from the novel's (literally) explosive beginning. Rhyme and his beautiful assistant, detective Amelia Sachs, have just that much time to ID the Dancer and keep him from murdering the remaining witnesses. . . . The pace, energized by Deaver's precise attention, never flags." Publ Wkly

Deaver, Jeff

Garden of beasts; a novel of Berlin 1936. {by} Jeffery Deaver. Simon & Schuster 2004 404p $24.95

ISBN 0-7432-2201-6

LC 2004-45206

"Top Nazis, including Hitler, Himmler and Göring, make colorful cameos, but it's the smart, shaded-gray characterizations of the principals that anchor the exciting plot." Publ Wkly

Deaver, Jeff

Roadside crosses; [by] Jeffery Deaver. Simon & Schuster 2009 399p $26.95

ISBN 978-1-4165-4999-4

LC 2009-02294

"The web sites mentioned throughout the book are actual live links and add to the fun. Though a couple of subplots get glossed over, the main story resonates. Dance is another exciting series character, and though this series has a ways to go before it achieves the devotion accorded Deaver's Rhyme/Sachs series, it has unlimited potential." Libr J

Deaver, Jeff

The **vanished** man; a Lincoln Rhyme novel.
[by] Jeffery Deaver. Simon & Schuster 2003 399p
$25.95

ISBN 0-7432-2200-8

LC 2002-42826

"Among the crimes rendered with Deaver's customary
grace and wit are sadistic variations on Houdini's Water
Torture Cell, P. T. Selbit's neat trick of sawing a woman in
half and one of Howard Thurston's animal acts, in which he
brought a dead bird back to life." N Y Times Book Rev

Deaver, Jeffery

Carte blanche: 007; the new James Bond novel.
[by] Jeffery Deaver. Simon & Schuster 2011 414p
$26.99

ISBN 978-1-4516-2069-6; 1-451-62069-1

LC 2011-04183

"James Bond returns, rebooted, in this new novel set
in the modern day, where he works for the ODG, a secret
agency of the British government whose task is the 'protect
the realm'. When a text message is intercepted mentioning
an attack and potentially thousands of deaths, 007 is called
in and given carte blanche (the modern equivalent of his old
licence to kill) to save the day. The novel is presented as an
interesting blend of author Jeffrey Deaver, and Bond-creator
Ian Fleming's writing styles." Hungry Reader

Deb, Siddhartha

The **point** of return. Ecco Press 2003 304p
$24.95

ISBN 0-06-050151-0

LC 2002-35300

"To allow Dr. Dam to evolve through most of the book
in a self-generated fog of benevolence and to shatter it in
the last pages is a brillant stroke.... Storytelling of the kind
Deb lavishes, for most of his book, on Dr. Dam is rare and
precious and uplifting." N Y Times Book Rev

Deborde, Rob

Portlandtown; a tale of the Oregon Wyldes. Rob
DeBorde. St. Martin's Griffin 2012 384 p.

ISBN 1250006643; 9781250006646

LC 2012037424

This novel by Rob DeBorde is "a supernatural western.
... When [Joseph Wylde's] father-in-law's grave-digging
awakens more than just ghosts, Joseph invites him into their
home.... Unfortunately, the old man's past soon follows,
unleashing a terrible storm on a city already knee deep in
floodwaters. As the dead mysteriously begin to rise, the Wyldes must find the truth before an unspeakable evil can spread
across the West and beyond." (Publisher's note)

Dee, Ed

The **con** man's daughter. Mysterious Press 2003
279p $23.95

ISBN 0-89296-794-3

LC 2003-50976

"Dee proves a sure hand when depicting the rough life
of cops and criminals—and especially when creating Eddie
Dunne, an amalgam of good and bad." Libr J

Dee, Jonathan

The **privileges**; a novel. Random House 2010
258p $25

ISBN 1-4000-6867-3; 978-1-4000-6867-8

LC 2009-12900

"Smart, socially gifted, and chronically impatient, Adam
and Cynthia Morey ... marry young and have two children
before Cynthia reaches the age of twenty-five. Adam is a rising star in the world of private equity and becomes his boss's
protégé. With a beautiful home in ... Manhattan, gorgeous
children, and plenty of money, they are, by any reasonable
standard, successful. But the Moreys' standards are not the
same as other people's. The future in which they have always believed for themselves and their children—a life of
almost boundless privilege— ... is not arriving fast enough
to suit them." (Publisher's note)

The "tale of a family scaling the heights of finance in
New York City, a family born, nursed and prep-schooled on
the fiscally rich milk of the hedge fund. The novel begins
with the wedding of Cynthia and Adam—two glossy, self-
absorbed 22-year-olds. ... [They] go on to live the life of
insider-trading zillionaires, obtaining the Manhattan penthouse, the villa in Anguilla, the halfhearted charitable trust.
But where a lesser novelist might rely on sarcasm and satire,
Dee opts for old-fashioned complexity. The wedding scene,
a 32-page masterpiece, begins with a panoramic perspective
that dips into the brains of all involved, from the wedding
planner to her stoned son to Cynthia's jealous mother. His
characters are stories in and of themselves, particularly Cynthia, a sexy savant who calls people skanks and pays off her
estranged father's girlfriend to leave his deathbed. Yet Dee
approaches her—and all his characters—with understanding." Time Out N Y

Dee, Jonathan

A **thousand** pardons; a novel. Jonathan Dee.
Random House 2012 224 p. (ebook) $26; (hard-
cover) $26

ISBN 0812993217; 9780679645009; 9780812993219

LC 2012018513

In this novel, by Jonathan Dee, "once a privileged and
loving couple, the Armsteads have now reached a breaking
point. ... Thrust back into the working world, Helen finds
a job in public relations and relocates ... to an apartment
in Manhattan. There, Helen discovers ... she can convince
arrogant men to admit their mistakes, spinning crises into
second chances. Yet redemption is more easily granted in her
professional life than in her personal one." (Publisher's note)

Defoe, Daniel

A **journal** of the plague year; edited with an
introduction and notes by Cynthia Wall. Penguin
Books 2003 xxxviii, 289p (Penguin classics)

ISBN 0-14-043785-1

LC 2003-276684

First published 1722

An account "of the epidemic of bubonic plague in England during the summer and fall of 1665." Reader's Ency.
4th edition

Defoe, Daniel

★ **Moll** Flanders; with an introduction by John Mullan. Knopf 1991 xxxiii, 338p $19

ISBN 0-679-40548-8

LC 91-52994

First published 1722. Variant title: The fortunes and misfortunes of the famous Moll Flanders

"This purports to be the autobiography of the daughter of a woman who had been transported to Virginia for theft soon after her child's birth. The child, abandoned in England, is brought up in the house of the compassionate mayor of Colchester. The story relates her seduction, her subsequent marriages and liaisons, and her visit to Virginia, where she finds her mother and discovers that she has unwittingly married her own brother. After leaving him and returning to England, she is presently reduced to destitution. She becomes an extremely successful pickpocket and thief, but is presently detected and transported to Virginia in company with one of her former husbands, a highwayman. With the funds that each has amassed they set up as planters, and Moll moreover finds that she has inherited a plantation from her mother. She and her husband spend their declining years in a atmosphere of prosperity and ostensible penitence." Oxford Companion to Engl Lit. 6th edition

Defoe, Daniel

★ **Robinson** Crusoe; edited with an introduction by Thomas Keymer and notes by Thomas Keymer and James Kelly. Oxford University Press 2007 368p (Oxford world's classics) pa $7.95

ISBN 0-19-283342-1; 978-0-19-283342-6

LC 2006-26022

First published 1719

"A minutely circumstantial account of the hero's shipwreck and escape to an uninhabited island, and the methodical industry whereby he makes himself a comfortable home. The story is founded on the actual experiences of Alexander Selkirk, who spent four years on the island of Juan Fernandez in the early 18th century." Lenrow. Reader's Guide to Prose Fic

Deford, Frank

The **entitled**; a novel. Sourcebooks 2007 318p $24.95

ISBN 978-1-4022-0896-6; 1-4022-0896-0

LC 2007-10914

"Howie Traveler is the manager of the Cleveland Indians, and Jay Alcazar is his star player. Never quite good enough as a player, Traveler spent two decades in the minors as a coach and manager, building his resume oh so slowly. Alcazar, on the other hand, is the son of a wealthy Cuban immigrant. Even if he hadn't become a baseball star, he would have enjoyed myriad opportunities. The pair share a mundane player-manager relationship until one night Traveler inadvertently spies Alcazar in a physical dispute with a woman trying to escape the star's hotel room. When the woman comes forward with a rape charge, Traveler must balance his career against doing the right thing. In a parallel plot, Alcazar tries to unravel the mystery surrounding his real parents and his birth in Castro's Cuba." Booklist

"More than a terrific baseball book. It's a terrific book, period." Sports Illustrated

Deighton, Len

★ **Berlin** game. Knopf 1984 345p

ISBN 0-394-53407-7

LC 83-48104

The first volume of an espionage trilogy; other volumes are Mexico set and London match

This novel "is a decent entertainment that rattles swiftly along to its payoff. Two things especially recommend it—a devious contrivance of plot that has probably never been used before in an espionage novel; and the city of Berlin, mecca to spies and spy novelists. The second is the greater asset. Although the book is elaborately plotted, its best moments derive from the setting and from the force of this particular setting upon behavior and psychology." N Y Times Book Rev

Deighton, Len

City of gold. HarperCollins Pubs. 1992 375p

ISBN 0-06-017937-6

LC 92-52565

"Story lines concern not just the war but also black-market activities and the efforts of Jewish operatives to arm themselves for the anticipated battle for a homeland. Directing his varied characters and juggling his many subplots, Deighton demonstrates enviable legerdemain." Publ Wkly

Deighton, Len

★ **Funeral** in Berlin; a novel. Putnam 1965 312p

First published 1964 in the United Kingdom

A spy story in which a British agent is involved in smuggling a Russian scientist out of East Berlin with the connivance of a Russian security officer and a German contact man whose loyalties and motives are questionable

The author "writes well of the circles within circles at international crossroads where enemies can be closer than friends, and where horror and humor follow the agent." Libr J

Deighton, Len

★ The **Ipcress** file. Simon & Schuster 1963 287p

First published 1962 in the United Kingdom

"A British secret-service agent is assigned to help recover a kidnapped biochemist. The international intrigue, involving brainwashing, spies, and counter-spies of uncertain loyalties, takes the agent from London to the Far East, to an atomic test site in the Pacific, and behind the Iron Curtain." Shapiro. Fic for Youth. 3d edition

Deighton, Len

London match. Knopf 1985 407p

ISBN 0-394-54937-6

LC 85-40454

"The strength of (this novel) is not in its plot but its characterization. . . . Mr. Deighton portrays each character of his large cast fully and sympathetically. However, the best character is the city of Berlin. It is a living presence, and in some of the descriptions one can almost hear the stones breathing." N Y Times Book Rev

Deighton, Len

Mexico set. Knopf 1985 373p

ISBN 0-394-53525-1

LC 84-48500

The second volume of the spy trilogy that began with Berlin game

"Deighton displays prodigious talent here; while portraying sharply defined, sympathetic, and down-to-earth characters, he slowly but inexorably revs up the plot for a thoroughly exciting and satisfying conclusion." Libr J

Dekker, Ted

Forbidden; Ted Dekker and Tosca Lee. Center Street 2011 384 pp.

ISBN 9781599953540

LC 2011004779

This book tells the story of a world in which "science has found a way to genetically control emotions, and has stripped humans of all emotions but the one necessary for self-preservation -- fear. . . . Early in the story, artist Rom Sebastian is accosted by a stranger in an alley who claims to have known Rom's father, and entrusts him with a parcel . . . which includes a vial of blood and a cryptic message that suggests drinking it 'grants the power to live,' and makes the fateful decision to drink. . . . The blood he has imbibed contains the power to awaken a full spectrum of human emotion . . . [and] the results take him to the highest echelons of power, where he begins to question everything he thought he knew." (urbanchristiannews.com)

Dekker, Ted

Immanuel's veins; Ted Dekker. Thomas Nelson 2010 367p. (hardcover: alk. paper) 25.99

ISBN 9781595540096; 1595540091

LC 2010016894

This book is an "18th century novel set in the Carpathian Mountains. When two warriors are charged by Catherine the Great of Russia to guard two young women at risk of harm, Toma, the narrator and protagonist, must choose between his duty and honor and the passion he feels for one of the two, the beautiful Lucine. When she falls into the hands of a group of descendants of Nephilim—offspring of the angels who bred with humans, as mentioned in Genesis—Toma must rescue her by means of blood and a love he's never known but must come to understand first himself: the blood of Immanuel's veins." (Publishers Weekly)

Dekker, Ted

Mortal; Ted Dekker and Tosca Lee. Faithwords 2012 432 p. (downloadable audio) $59.99; (paperback) $7.99; (hardcover) $24.99; (hardcover) $24.99

ISBN 9781619690943; 9781599953571; 1599953587; 9781599953588

This book, the second in the "Books of Mortals" series, is set "five hundred years into the post-apocalyptic future . . . [where most people] have been emptied of all emotion but fear. . . . Hope rests in Jonathan's ability to reawaken humanity. The megalomaniac Saric, who commands a race of lowly, foul-smelling Dark Bloods, will have something to say about that. So will Saric's sister Feyn, newly revived from a suspended state." (Kirkus Reviews)

Delaney, Edward J.

★ Broken Irish. Turtle Point Press 2011 379p pa $18.50

ISBN 978-1-933527-50-5; 1-933527-50-1

LC 2010-938747

"After alcoholic copywriter Jimmy Gilbride loses his job, a rich entrepreneur offers him a lucrative ghostwriting opportunity; crestfallen widow Colleen mourns her military husband and struggles to raise her secretive 13-year-old son, Christopher, while offering clandestine help to Jeanmarie, a reckless teenage runaway with a sketchy boyfriend. Meanwhile, Father John is retiring from the priesthood with an overwhelming sense of uselessness and a guilty conscience. Christopher starts spending time with Jeanmarie, which doesn't sit well with her boyfriend. As the boy braces for violence and Colleen appeals to the church, blackouts, memory lapses, and liver problems get in the way of Jimmy's new job." Publ Wkly

Delaney, Frank

Ireland; a novel. Frank Delaney. HarperCollinsPublishers 2005 559p (pbk.) $14.99; o.p.

ISBN 9780061244438; 0060563486

LC 2004054202

In this book, "BBC reporter [Frank] Delaney . . . [offers a] fictionalized history of his native country, . . . [Ireland]. In 1951, when Ronan O'Mara is nine, he meets the aging itinerant Storyteller, who emerges out a 'silver veil' of Irish mist, hoping to trade a yarn for a hot meal. Welcomed inside, the Storyteller lights his pipe and begins, telling of the architect of Newgrange, who built 'a marvelous, immortal structure . . . before Stonehenge in England, before the pyramids of Egypt,' and the dentally challenged King Conor of Ulster, who tried, and failed, to outsmart his wife. The stories utterly captivate the young Ronan, . . . with their warriors and kings, drinkers and devils. . . . When Ronan's mother banishes the Storyteller for telling a blasphemous tale, Ronan vows to find him. He also becomes fascinated by Irish myth and legend, and, as the years pass, he discovers his own gift for storytelling." (Publishers Weekly)

Delaney, Frank

The matchmaker of Kenmare; Frank Delaney. 1st ed.; Random House 2011 x, 397 p.p

ISBN 9781400067848; 0679604332; 1400067847; 9780679604334

LC 2010035301

Sequel to: Venetia Kelly's traveling show.

In this book, "[a]s World War II rages on, Ben remains haunted by the mysterious disappearance of his wife, the actress Venetia Kelly. Searching for purpose by collecting stories for the Irish Folklore Commission, he travels to a remote seaside cottage to profile the . . . Matchmaker of Kenmare. Ben is immediately captivated by the forthright Miss Begley, who is remarkably self-assured in her instincts but provincial in her experience. . . . But when Charles Miller, a striking American military intelligence officer, arrives on the scene, Miss Begley develops an intense infatuation and looks to make a match for herself. Miller needs a favor, but it will be dangerous. Under the cover of their neutrality as Irish citizens, Miss Begley and Ben travel to London and

LIST OF FICTIONAL WORKS

effectively operate as spies. As they are drawn more deeply and painfully into the conflict, both discover the perils of neutrality--in both love and war." (Publisher's note)

Delaney, Frank

Venetia Kelly's traveling show; a novel. Random House 2010 427p $26

ISBN 978-1-4000-6783-1; 1-4000-6783-9

LC 2009-028383

"Benedict MacCarthy narrates, looking back to 1932 when he was 18. In that tumultuous year, with the young Republic of Ireland poised for a crucial election, Ben's father abandons his family and his prosperous farm to join Venetia Kelly's Traveling Show. Ben's mother sends him to bring his father home, and so begins the innocent Ben's odyssey and education. His father is mesmerized by the beautiful actress Venetia Kelly.... Soon Ben finds himself in her thrall, rivaling his father for Venetia's attentions. The show mixes tumbling, singing, and broad humor, with Venetia's dramatic recitations of poetry and scenes from Shakespeare rounding out the bill. The finale is Venetia's ventriloquist act with Blarney, an irrepressible dummy who specializes in cutting observations about Irish politics. The complicated plot has many well-drawn characters." Boston Globe

Delany, Samuel R.

★ Stars in my pocket like grains of sand. Bantam Bks. 1984 384p

ISBN 0-553-05053-2

LC 84-45180

This far future novel is the "dual story of Rat Korga, a slave and the last survivor of his devastated world, and Marq Dyeth, an industrial diplomat who introduces Korga to a future galaxy consisting of 6,000 human- and alien-inhabited planets." Booklist

"Reading this novel is like learning another language, only to realize how much it teaches you about your own, and how relative it makes your cultural assumptions." Publ Wkly

Delbanco, Nicholas

Sherbrookes. Dalkey Archive Press 2011 671p pa $19.95

ISBN 978-1-56478-587-9

LC 2011-16861

Originally published by William Morrow and Co. as: Possession (1977), Sherbrookes (1978), and Stillness (1980)

The saga "of a New England clan whose conflicts and celebrations unfold in the shadows of the family manse on its Vermont estate.... This book is not simply the three original novels ... bound together. It isn't a complete revision of the original story, either. Instead, what Delbanco has done is trim the narrative excesses of his younger self and rediscover thematic echoes that occur when three books fit together snugly into one." L A Times Book Rev

Delbanco, Nicholas

What remains. Warner Bks. 2000 200p

ISBN 0-446-52416-6

LC 00-39895

"The mood is elegiac, meditative, yet delicate: a Chopin nocturne, perhaps, played out in words. The horror, the melodrama, is always held back. The memory and effects of the Holocaust are ever present but never dwelled on." N Y Times Book Rev

Delderfield, R. F.

★ To serve them all my days. Simon & Schuster 1972 638p

ISBN 0-671-21371-7

Concerns "the boys and masters of a West Country English public school in the years between World War I and II. ... The central character is David Powlett-Jones, a shell-shocked youngster fresh from the Western Front, when we first meet him; a compassionate headmaster, whose personal life has known its full share of drama, sorrow and love, when we part company with him. In between, Mr. Delderfield has some eminently sane and sensible points to make about what education for life is really like. Academic rivalries, some bitter and vengeful; the loneliness of a small boy whose parents have no real feeling for him, and of a small girl whose mother and twin have died tragically; the development of an intense love affair between a mature man and woman are all elements in the storytelling." Publ Wkly

DeLillo, Don

★ The angel Esmeralda. Scribner 2011 213p $24

ISBN 978-1-4516-5584-1

LC 2011-33996

This book offers a collection of short stories. Various stories include the following themes: "the dread embodied in a child's random abduction ('The Runner'), the sense of doom experienced by a jailed financial crook as he listens to a litany of crisis and chaos on TV ('Hammer and Sickle') and ... a sexual encounter on a remote tropical island ('Creation').... [T]he title story ... [is a] tale of two nuns set in ... the South Bronx during the 1970s, at its worst." (America)

"DeLillo's first collection of short fiction, compiling stories written between 1979 and 2011, serves as a liberating reminder that terror existed long before there was a war on it." N Y Times Book Rev

DeLillo, Don

The body artist; a novel. Scribner 2001 124p

ISBN 0-7432-0395-X

LC 00-58842

"A young widow discovers that a dishevelled, vaguely autistic man has somehow taken up residence in her spare room—and that her dead husband's spirit may or may not be inhabiting her new boarder. This is a fertile premise— the novel plays with questions of identity, presence, ritual, memory, and sanity, and uses those questions to investigate the larger mystery of death—but the book's brevity forces DeLillo to treat his themes sketchily, and at times with an uncharacteristic sentimentality." New Yorker

DeLillo, Don

Cosmopolis; a novel. Scribner 2003 209p $25

ISBN 0-7432-4424-9

LC 2002-30540

"DeLillo, master novelist and seer, tells the surreal, electrifying story of this dehumanized moneyman in English scrubbed so clean and assembled so exquisitely it seems like a new language." Booklist

DeLillo, Don

Falling man; a novel. Scribner 2007 246p $26
ISBN 978-1-416-54602-3; 1-416-54602-2

LC 2006-52306

"Scenes are laid out like cards face up in some mysterious game of solitaire, except that each card, each sequence, seems to carry some larger import. It's not clear even at the novel's end what its finishing up might mean. On one narrative level, the game is already over — the characters are living in an unknown afterworld. But on another level — DeLillo inserts several time-jumps into the pre-Sept. 11 past — we see his terrorist preparing himself. . . . Though the setup feels stylized, it is also riveting." Los Angeles Times Book Rev

DeLillo, Don

★ **Libra**. Viking 1988 456p
ISBN 0-670-82317-1

LC 87-40649

DeLillo's "novel is his own personal vision—though anchored well enough in historical actuality—of what really was behind Lee Harvey Oswald's gun blasts from the book depository that day in Dallas. DeLillo follows Oswald through the marines and during his defection to the Soviet Union, as well as positing a scenario for how he came to be the vehicle for delivering the anti-Castro blow that resulted in Kennedy's death." Booklist

This novel "provokes the reader with its clever use of history, its dramatic pacing and its immaculate and detailed construction." Publ Wkly

DeLillo, Don

The **names**. Knopf 1982 339p
ISBN 0-394-52814-X

LC 82-48012

"Self-absorbed, rootless James Axton is a 'risk analyst' for insuring multinational corporations against political hazards. His ambiguous world—defined by an estranged family and the Iranian revolution—is bizarrely highlighted by the advent of an elusive ritual murder cult, 'The Names.' His compulsion to track down the meaning of the cult (it matches the initials of victims and place names) leads him as far off as India, and deep into 'memory, solitude, obsession, death.'" Libr J

"Nearly every page testifies to DeLillo's exceptional gifts as a writer." New Republic

DeLillo, Don

Point Omega; a novel. Scribner 2010 117p $24
ISBN 1-4391-6996-9; 978-1-4391-6995-7

LC 2009-42232

"Jim Finley, a young filmmaker, attempts to convince Richard Elster, a former secret war advisor, to tell his story on film, an endeavor complicated by the arrival of Richard's daughter from New York and a devastating event that throws everything into question." (Publisher's note)

"An academic, hired by the Defense Department to 'conceptualize' the Iraq War. A struggling postmodern filmmaker who visits the academic in his desert retreat to enlist him as the subject of a documentary. Hitchcock's 'Psycho' slowed down to run at two frames a second, or some 24 hours in all, in an installation at New York's Museum of Modern Art. All three figure in Don DeLillo's spectral, difficult, and some-times brilliant novel, 'Point Omega.' They are linked, but that is to overstate the clarity; it would be truer to say that they haunt each other." Boston Globe

DeLillo, Don

★ **Ratner's** star. Knopf 1976 437p
ISBN 0-394-40083-6

LC 75-36808

This is a "grim, surreal novel, it's protagonist a 14-year-old mathematical genius and Nobel laureate, Billy Twillig, whose mission is to decode the message of a star and to invent a mathematical language to answer it." Oxford Companion to Am Lit. 6th edition

DeLillo, Don

Underworld. Scribner 1997 827p
ISBN 0-684-84269-6

LC 97-13825

"The dialogue is a rockingly comic attack on our mental excreta: the distortions and sound bites of the television age. DeLillo was absent from his fiction before, an unbodied intelligence, but here is an undertow of personal pain he has never touched. This is his most demanding novel and yet his most transparent, giving the reader the privileged intimacy that comes from seeing a writer whole." N Y Times Book Rev

DeLillo, Don

★ **White** noise. Viking 1985 326p
ISBN 0-670-80373-1

LC 84-40375

This "is a stunning performance from one of our finest and most intelligent novelists. DeLillo's reach is broad and deep, combining acute observation of the textures of American life and analytic rigor." New Repub

Delinsky, Barbara

Flirting with Pete; a novel. Scribner 2003 355p $26
ISBN 0-7432-4642-X

LC 2003-42721

"Seamlessly and compassionately weaving Jenny's unsettling past with Casey's uncertain future. Delinsky delivers a scintillating study of each woman's search for answers and absolution." Booklist

Delinsky, Barbara

Lake news. Simon & Schuster 1999 380p
ISBN 0-684-86432-0

The author "plots this satisfying, gentle romance with the sure hand of an expert, scattering shady pasts and dark secrets among some of her characters, while giving others destructive family patterns and difficult family dynamics to contend with." Publ Wkly

Delinsky, Barbara

The **summer** I dared; a novel. Barbara Delinsky. Simon & Schuster 2004 355p $24.95
ISBN 0-7432-4643-8

LC 2004-45339

The "tale of three people quite literally thrown together following a boating accident off the Maine coast that spares them while taking the lives of nine others. At 40 Julia is an obedient wife, dutiful daughter, and devoted mother, and has planned a visit to her aunt Zoe to reflect on her obligation to herself versus her ties to her family. Rescued by fellow passenger Noah Prine, Julia feels connected to him by virtue of their shared tragedy while also being drawn to Kim Colella, the other survivor, whose whereabouts at the time of the crash provide a shadowy subplot. As a gentle romance blossoms between Julia and Noah, each evaluates who they were before the accident and who they hope to become in its aftermath. Once again, Delinsky excels at combining a compelling mystery with an insightful portrayal of captivating people facing challenges both ordinary and dramatic." Booklist

Delinsky, Barbara

Sweet salt air; Barbara Delinsky. 1st ed. St. Martin's Press 2013 416 p. (hardcover) $25.99
    ISBN 1250007038; 9781250007032
                                LC 2013004041
In this novel, by Barbara Delinsky, "Charlotte and Nicole were once the best of friends. . . . But many years, and many secrets, have kept the women apart. . . . When Nicole is commissioned to write a book about island food, she invites her old friend Charlotte back to Quinnipeague, for a final summer, to help. . . . But what both women don't know is that they are each holding something back that may change their lives forever." (Publisher's note)

Delius, Friedrich Christian, 1943-

Portrait of the mother as a young woman; Friedrich Christian Delius; translated from the German by Jamie Bulloch. Farrar, Straus and Giroux 2012 119p.
    ISBN 0374533296; 9780374533298; 9780956284006
                                LC 2011046065
This book follows "the heavily pregnant young narrator" as she "takes a long walk though the streets of Rome. . . . But while that is all that actually happens, her thoughts wander freely, touching often on her absent husband, Gert, a soldier stationed in North Africa. . . . The specific horrors of the war figure little in her thoughts, other than a vague recognition that the Führer who 'places himself above God' should not be obeyed blindly." (Kirkus Reviews)

Dellamonica, A. M.

Indigo Springs; A.M. Dellamonica. 1st ed.; Tor 2009 320p
    ISBN 9780765319470
                                LC 2009031595
In this book, protagonist "Astrid's wastrel father knew the secret of the indigo-blue waters that run beneath the town of Indigo Springs. When Astrid and her friend Sahara learn to use the magic waters for themselves, they begin an experiment in wild magic that escalates into an ecological crisis and drives an irreparable wedge between them." (Library Journal)

Delson, Rudolph

Maynard and Jennica. Houghton Mifflin 2007 300p $24
    ISBN 978-0-618-83448-8; 0-618-83448-6
                                LC 2007-8520

This is a "giddy boy-meets-girl (twice) fable that evolves into an astute portrait of a relationship. The lovers are an odd couple—she a workaholic Princeton grad from California, he an indie filmmaker and New York native who loathes everything outside his home town. Their story is told documentary style, with thirty-five characters taking turns narrating. Each character has an appealing voice, and the chatty arrangement highlights Delson's comic timing. Best is his portrait of New York, which emerges as both fantastical and hilariously recognizable, a unique place defined by its possibilities and worthy of the dreams it inspires." New Yorker

DeMarinis, Rick

Borrowed hearts; new and selected stories. Seven Stories Press 1999 322p $24
    ISBN 1-88836-398-3
                                LC 98-55233
Contents: Under the wheat; Billy Ducks among the pharaohs; Life between meals; The smile of a turtle; Weeds; The handgun; Disneyland; Romance: a prose villanelle; Your story; Pagans; Your burden is lifted, love returns; Medicine man; Safe forever; Paraiso: an elegy; An airman's goodbye; Aliens; Horizontal snow; Wilderness; The Voice of America; Insulation; Borrowed hearts; A romantic interlude; Experience; Fault lines; Feet; Hormone X; Novias; On the lam; Sieze the day; The boys we were, the men we became; The singular we
    "Dark humor, cosmic danger, and unglamorous romance snake through DeMarinis' compelling short stories." Booklist

DeMarinis, Rick

Sky full of sand. Dennis McMillan 2003 250p $30
    ISBN 0-939767-47-3
In this novel, set in El Paso, Uriah Walkinghorse is "suspended somewhere between a 'normal' existence and a descent into the bizarre and desperate world that surrounds him. Strained but strong ties still bind him to his odd assortment of adopted siblings—black and white and Korean—who include a school principal, an addict, a delivery driver and a corporate lawyer. At 42, he has lost his wife, abandoned his quest for a master's and manages derelict apartments of derelicts in exchange for rent. His one accomplishment was a bodybuilding title, Mr. West Side, and he still maintains a diet and exercise program. DeMarinis's exceptionally sharp wit slashes through the prose as Uri undertakes an odyssey through a world of kinky sex, drugs, high finance and the most vicious, most wasted dregs of humanity on either side of the border." Publ Wkly

Demetz, Hanna

The house on Prague Street; translated from the German by the author. St. Martin's Press 1980 186p
    ISBN 0-312-39322-9
                                LC 79-27312
Original German edition, 1970
This autobiographical novel tells the story of Helene Richter whose "adolescence in wartime Czechoslovakia coincides with the Holocaust, which intrudes more and more insistently into her life until its . . . violence destroys her romantic dreams. The house on Prague Street symbolizes her loss of innocence. At first the serene family homestead,

it eventually shelters survivors of Auschwitz whose only familial ties are their shared memories of horror." SLJ

DeMille, Nelson

The **charm** school. Warner Bks. 1988 533p

ISBN 0-446-51305-9

LC 87-34637

"On an unorthodox vacation trip to Russia, Gregory Fisher, a young American tourist, stumbles onto a secret. . . . In a place called Mrs. Ivanova's Charm School, young Russians are being taught to imitate American citizens. And their instructors, none of whom have volunteered for the job, are Americans. . . . The Charm School offers much in the way of action and adventure, but the novel is more than an 'Us vs. Them' shoot 'em up. It is also a fascinating psychological study, one that forces the reader to ponder the true roles of good and evil, in connection with the individual mind as well as with international relations." West Coast Rev Books

DeMille, Nelson

The **gate** house. Grand Central Pub. 2008 677p $27.99

ISBN 978-0-446-53342-3; 0-446-53342-4

LC 2008-26065

A "sequel to The Gold Coast (1990), in which Susan Sutter, then the wife of tax attorney John Sutter, had a torrid affair with Frank Bellarosa, a powerful Mafia boss and the Sutters' neighbor on Long Island's tony Gold Coast, with fatal results for Bellarosa. After divorcing Susan, John sailed the world for three years, then built himself a new life in London. Now John has returned to the small gatehouse that was once part of his ex-wife's family estate, only to find Bellarosa's thuggish son, Anthony, living next door. In another coincidence, Susan has just reacquired the six-bedroom guest cottage where she and John lived as a married couple on her family's former property. Susan and John soon begin to explore an improbable reconciliation, even as they suspect she may be in Anthony's gun sights. The plot more than takes its time getting to its violent and predictable resolution, but DeMille devotees should have plenty of fun along the way." Publ Wkly

DeMille, Nelson

The **general's** daughter. Warner Bks. 1992 454p

ISBN 0-446-51306-7

LC 91-51174

"Paul Brenner, a warrant officer in the army's criminal investigation unit, reluctantly teams with an old flame, Cynthia Sunhill, to investigate the murder of Captain Ann Campbell. Ann's body has been staked down with tent pegs on a rifle range; she's naked but she hasn't been brutalized. She's the daughter of a famous general, just back from the Gulf War, and she's also the Army's poster girl, a graduate with honors from West Point. And yet her chosen specialty, psychological operations, has raised some eyebrows, and Brenner and Sunhill soon discover other dark secrets about her." Booklist

"Characterization in general is fuzzy, though DeMille captures the often unquestioning regimen of life on a military base." Publ Wkly

DeMille, Nelson

The **Gold** Coast. Warner Bks. 1990 500p

ISBN 0-446-51504-3

LC 89-40465

"What makes 'The Gold Coast' glitter is Nelson DeMille's sharp evocation of the vulpine Bellarosa and of Sutter, a wonderfully sardonic, self-mocking man betrayed by a midlife crisis. In his way, Mr. DeMille . . . is as keen a social satirist as Edith Wharton." NY Times Book Rev

DeMille, Nelson

The **lion's** game; a novel. Warner Bks. 2000 677p $36

ISBN 0-446-52065-9

"DeMille artfully constructs a compulsively readable thriller around a troubling story line, slowly developing his villain from a faceless entity into a nation's all-too-human nemesis." Publ Wkly

DeMille, Nelson

Plum Island. Warner Bks. 1997 511p

ISBN 0-446-51506-X

LC 97-7221

"Key to the novel's sway is its boisterous plot, as DeMille expertly melds medical mystery, police procedural and nautical adventure, adding assorted love interests and capping matters with a ferocious storm at sea." Publ Wkly

DeMille, Nelson

Wild fire; a novel. Warner Books 2006 519p $26.99

ISBN 978-0-446-57967-4; 0-446-57967-X

LC 2006-20982

This thriller features "John Corey, the ex-NYPD detective who now works on a government anti-terrorism task force. . . . Bain Madox, a brilliant and probably insane villain, has hatched a fiendishly clever plot to force the U.S. to launch an all-out nuclear attack against the entire Islamic world. It's up to Corey, with the help of his FBI agent wife, to stop Madox before he can detonate nuclear weapons on American soil. Set in 2002, barely a year after 9/11, the novel presents a what-if scenario that's so plausible we have to remind ourselves that DeMille is making the whole thing up. Or is he? As usual, DeMille appears to have done a ton of research; what sets his thrillers apart from those of some of his competitors is the way he seamlessly incorporates real technology and real government organizations into his stories." Booklist

DeMille, Nelson

Word of honor. Warner Bks. 1985 518p

ISBN 0-446-51280-X

LC 85-40005

"The flashbacks to Hue, the pre-trial investigation (involving an attractive female major), the court-martial proceedings, the emotions of the principal characters and the soul-sickness wrought by war (which is the story's effective subtext)—all are depicted with marvelous vividness." Publ Wkly

DeNiro, Alan

Total oblivion, more or less; a novel. Spectra
Ballantine Books 2009 306p pa $15

ISBN 978-0-553-59254-2; 0-553-59254-8

LC 2009-36101

"Macy's adventure is engaging and absorbing, but it
doesn't make much sense. For those conditioned to the logic
of classic science fiction, 'Total Oblivion's' rule-breaking
can be frustrating. But readers who are willing to let go will
be swept away." Los Angeles Times Book Rev

Dennis, Patrick

Auntie Mame; an irreverent escapade. Vanguard
Press 1955 280p

"A fond and somewhat baffled nephew reminisces about
the aunt who guided his young footsteps in her unorthodox,
inimitable fashion. Auntie Mame lived wholeheartedly in
phases; whether she was being show girl, shopgirl, Southern
belle, tweedy authoress, college widow, or society matron,
she played each part to the hilt. Life with Auntie Mame was
infinitely entertaining and unpredictable." Booklist

Followed by Around the world with Auntie Mame (1958)

DePoy, Phillip

The **drifter's** wheel. St. Martin's Minotaur 2008
276p $24.95

ISBN 978-0-312-36203-4; 0-312-36203-X

LC 2008-13401

"The arrival of a young man at Fever Devilin's house in
Blue Mountain, GA, upsets the folklorist's quiet life. The
stranger ends up dead, but Fever is convinced that the deceased man is not the one who visited him. Investigating
this puzzle leads Fever to unraveling the secrets held by a
reclusive but influential family in the area and the possibility that the stranger is really a time traveler come back to
murder again. . . . DePoy's latest concocts a delicious brew
of Southern culture laced with a dollop of the supernatural,
topped by unexpected denouements leaving readers wanting
more." Libr J

Dermansky, Marcy

Twins; Marcy Dermansky. William Morrow
2005 295 p. (pbk.) $14.99; (acid-free paper) $21.95

ISBN 9780060759797; 9780060759780

LC 2004063574

This book follows "two teenagers [as they] struggle with
identity and self determination. To the casual observer, twins
Chloe and Sue are exactly the same. . . . Of course, Chloe
understands that they're very different people, but Sue wants
nothing more than to be one with Chloe, whom she's convinced is prettier, smarter and nicer. The chapters alternate
between the voices of Sue and Chloe, moving . . . through
their high school years with their attendant dramas and tragedies." (Publishers Weekly)

Dermont, Amber

The **starboard** sea; a novel. Amber Dermont.
1st ed. St. Martin's Press 2012 310 p. (hardcover)
$24.99

ISBN 0312642806; 9780312642808; 9781429950978

LC 2011041100

This coming-of-age story is set in 1987. "Reeling from
the suicide of Cal, his sailing partner and first love, Jason
Prosper is sent to Bellingham, a . . . boarding school that
caters to entitled delinquents. There, he befriends Aidan
. . . who helps him come to terms with Cal's death. However, Jason also takes up with a fraternity of pranksters. .
. . After Aidan dies mysteriously during a hurricane, Jason must face the truth about his new friends and school."
(Publishers Weekly)

Desai, Anita

★ **Clear** light of day. Houghton Mifflin 2000
182p pa $13

ISBN 0-618-07451-1

LC 00-61326

First published 1980 by Harper & Row

This work "does what only the best novels can do: it totally submerges us. It takes us so deeply into another world
that we almost fear we won't be able to climb out again." N
Y Times Book Rev

Desai, Anita

Fire on the mountain. Harper & Row 1977 145p

ISBN 0-06-011066-X

LC 77-3788

"In this novel set in the hill country of India, Nanda
Kaul's great-granddaughter is sent to spend the summer
with her, thus breaking the solitude of the old and withdrawn
woman, shattering the privacy she prizes most. But Raka,
too, is clearly an outsider, a child living in and through her
imagination, and one with a talent for disappearing. As Nanda Kaul finds herself attempting to draw out and communicate with the strange and unfathomable Raka, she discovers
in the girl more of herself than she would have believed possible. Meanwhile, Nanda Kaul's lone friend, Ila Das, appears
and hovers always on the brink of hysteria until that hysteria
leads to a shocking rape and murder that is the book's climax." Publ Wkly

"This is a delicate wisp of a story that nevertheless possesses great tensile strength." Booklist

Desai, Kiran

The **inheritance** of loss. Atlantic Monthly 2006
324p $24

ISBN 0-87113-929-4

LC 2005-52416

"In a crumbling, isolated house at the foot of Mount
Kanchenjunga lives an embittered old judge who wants to
retire in peace when his orphaned granddaughter Sai arrives
on his doorstep. The judge's chatty cook watches over her,
but his thoughts are mostly with his son, Biju, hopscotching
from one New York restaurant job to another, trying to stay a
step ahead of the INS, forced to consider his country's place
in the world. When a Nepalese insurgency in the mountains
threatens Sai's new-sprung romance with her handsome Nepali tutor and causes their lives to descend into chaos, they,
too, are forced to confront their colliding interests." (Publisher's note)

This "novel is set in the nineteen-eighties in the northeast corner of India, where the borders of several Himalayan states—Bhutan and Sikkim, Nepal and Tibet—meet. At
the head of the novel's teeming cast is Jemubhai Patel, a
Cambridge-educated judge who has retired from serving a

country he finds 'too messy for justice.' He lives in an isolated house with his cook, his orphaned seventeen-year-old granddaughter, and a red setter, whose company Jemubhai prefers to that of human beings. The tranquillity of his existence is contrasted with the life of the cook's son, working in grimy Manhattan restaurants, and with his granddaughter's affair with a Nepali tutor involved in an insurgency that irrevocably alters Jemubhai's life. Briskly paced and sumptuously written, the novel ponders questions of nationhood, modernity, and class, in ways both moving and revelatory." New Yorker

DeSilva, Bruce
Cliff Walk; a Liam Mulligan novel. Bruce DeSilva. Forge 2012 318 p.
ISBN 076533237X; 9780765332370
LC 2012001817

Sequel to: Rogue Island
This mystery novel features journalist Liam Mulligan and is set "in Providence, Rhode Island. . . . A last-minute assignment to cover a soiree at a Newport mansion finds Mulligan catching a breather on the famed Cliff Walk fronting the mansions and facing the sea. He's just in time to see a man in a tuxedo fall to his death on the rocks below. . . . [Mulligan's] examination into the Cliff Walk murder leads into the porn empire, which has tentacles in so many power brokers' pockets, and into a series of child murders." (Booklist)

DeSilva, Bruce
Rogue island; Bruce DeSilva. Thorndike Press 2010 304 p.
ISBN 0765327260; 9780765327260
LC 2011389934
Macavity Awards: Best First Mystery Novel (2011); Edgar Allan Poe Awards: Best First Novel by an American Author (2011)
This crime mystery novel by Bruce DeSilva follows the journalist Liam Mulligan. "His beat is Providence, Rhode Island, and he knows every street and alley. He knows the priests and prostitutes, the cops and street thugs. He knows the mobsters and politicians--who are pretty much one and the same. Someone is systematically burning down the neighborhood Mulligan grew up in, people he knows and loves are perishing in the flames, and the public is on the verge of panic. With the police looking for answers in all the wrong places, and with the whole city of Providence on his back, Mulligan must find the hand that strikes the match." (Publisher's note)

Desrochers, Suzanne, 1976-
Bride of New France; Suzanne Desrochers. Penguin Canada 2011 294 p. $24.95
ISBN 0393073378; 9780143173380 pa
LC 2012017364
In this book, set "in 1669, Laure is sent across the Atlantic to New France with [her friend] Madeleine as filles du roi. . . . From the moment she arrives in Ville-Marie (Montreal) she is expected to marry and produce children with a brutish French soldier who himself can barely survive the harsh conditions of his forest cabin. But through her clandestine relationship with Deskaheh, an allied Iroquois,

Laure finds a sense of the possibilities in this New World." (Publisher's note)

Deutermann, Peter T., 1941-
The cat dancers; P.T. Deutermann. St. Martin's Press 2005 341p (hbk.) $24.95; (pbk.) $6.99
ISBN 0312333773; 9780312933425
LC 2005046583
In this book, "[w]hen two petty criminals who've brutally murdered three innocent people are turned loose on a technicality, they and others begin to die in horrible ways. A police lieutenant in rural North Carolina, . . . Cam Richter begins to suspect a vigilante group is responsible for the growing body count. Some of his own cops and a group of 'cat dancers' -- outdoors types who like to sneak up on mountain lions and photograph them face on, close up, and teed off -- may count among the members. Of course, Richter himself is also a suspect." (Library Journal)

Deutermann, Peter T.
Darkside. St. Martin's Press 2002 406p maps $24.95
ISBN 0-312-28120-X
LC 2002-68393
An "account of some creepy goings-on at the U.S. Naval Academy in Annapolis. As the book opens, the school is buzzing with the news that a plebe has plummeted from a sixth-story window and died. Amid questions of suicide, a new twist emerges; the plebe was wearing a pair of panties belonging to Midshipman First Class Julie Markham, a perky senior at the academy and an acquaintance of the dead plebe, who then gets drawn into the investigation. Her father, a retired former fighter pilot and academy history professor, hires crack defense lawyer Liz DeWinter, fearing that Markham will somehow be scapegoated by the Navy Criminal Investigation Service." Publ Wkly

Deutermann, P. T., 1941-
★ The ghosts of Bungo Suido; a novel. by P. T. Deutermann. 1st ed. St. Martin's Press 2013 343 p. (hardcover) $25.99
ISBN 1250018021; 9781250018021
LC 2013009264
In this novel by P.T. Deutermann, set during World War II, "America's naval forces face what seems an insurmountable threat from Japan: immense Yamato-class battleships, which dwarf every other ship at sea. Built in secrecy, these ships seem invincible, and lay waste to any challengers. Lieutenant Commander Gar Hammond . . . is now captain of a new submarine. Hammond may be the navy's only hope to locate and stop the Japanese super-ship before it launches." (Publisher's note)

Deutermann, Peter T., 1941-
Pacific glory; P.T. Deutermann. St. Martin's Press 2011 vii, 389p.p
ISBN 9780312599447; 0312599447
LC 2010041944
This book tells "the story of Annapolis friends Marsh Vincent, who barely survives the Savo [Island] debacle [during World War II,] and Mick McCarty, whose dive bombing at Midway sinks a Japanese aircraft carrier that helped dev-

astate Pearl Harbor, and Glory Hawthorne, a woman both love who has become a navy nurse. Having seen the savagery of naval war, Marsh fears he may not have the courage to face it again. Mick, an Annapolis football hero, has problems with alcohol and authority. He fears that he may be grounded. Ultimately, both are off Samar when a small group of tiny escort carriers and destroyers finds itself facing an overwhelming force of cruisers—and the Yamato, the largest battleship ever built." (Booklist)

DeVido, Brian

Every time I talk to Liston. Bloomsbury 2004 276p $22.95

ISBN 1-58234-458-2

The "writing shows quiet purpose in every move, carrying its insider knowledge with easy confidence. DeVido, at his best when showing how men tell stories about themselves with their bodies, pulls off the tricky feat of using boxing action to express character." N Y Times Book Rev

Devoto, Pat Cunningham

The **summer** we got saved; Pat Cunningham Devoto. Warner Books 2005 411p msp hardcover o.p. o.p.; (pbk.) $21.99

ISBN 0446576964; 9780446697156

LC 2004010408

This book, "takes place in Alabama and Tennessee during the early 1960s. Tab is a junior high school girl, . . . her childhood friend, Maudie, is a black polio victim who wears a leg brace and recently survived a fire at the Tuskegee Polio Institute. Tab's father, Charles, is a hardworking farmer descended from one of the founders of the Ku Klux Klan. . . . When Tab and her older sister embark on a secret trip to the Highlander Folk School with their socially conscious aunt, they become unwilling participants in an interracial camp, living with Civil Rights activists. At the same time, Maudie is recruited to help prepare resistant African Americans for voter registration by teaching life skills and reading, and Charles is . . . supporting the candidate running against segregationist George Wallace. The stories converge when the main characters experience the tragic consequences of their involvement with integration." (School Library Journal)

Dew, Robb Forman

The **evidence** against her; a novel. Little, Brown 2001 327p

ISBN 0-316-89019-7

LC 2001-29101

This novel is "set in the small town of Washburn, Ohio. The story begins with three children born on the same September day in 1888, and it ends with those same three, grown and with children of their own, in the summer of 1927. Lily Scofield, her cousin Warren Scofield and Robert Butler, son of the Methodist pastor, grow up as an inseparable group. . . . Even after Lily marries Robert in June 1913, she assumes that Warren will still somehow always be close by. . . . {But he meets} Agnes Claytor, who was a 14-year-old guest at Lily's wedding." N Y Times Book Rev

"A marvel of lyrical understatement, the narrative flows like a river—smooth, with surprising depths, some turbulence and the inexorability of time's passing." Publ Wkly

Dew, Robb Forman

The **truth** of the matter; a novel. Little, Brown 2005 327p $24.95

ISBN 0-316-89004-9

LC 2005-03841

Second title in a trilogy about the Scofield family of Washburn, Ohio; begun with: The evidence against her.

"Agnes Scofield has raised her children as a widow, having lost husband Warren in a car accident in 1930. This loss permeates the way in which Agnes recalls her life–she does not feel, she represses–and affects the relationships she has with her children. During World War II, her children leave home, and Agnes adjusts to single life only to have to readjust when they return to their small Ohio town with spouses and children in tow. The family ultimately finds the homecoming unsettling, as if they are just meeting one another for the first time. Dew's plain writing highlights the characters' inner lives and the wartime environment, yet it carries the reader along effortlessly." Libr J

DeWeese, Dan

You don't love this man; a novel. Harper Perennial 2011 336 p. pa $14.99

ISBN 978-0-06-199232-2; 0-06-199232-1

LC 2010-24949

"Paul is having a stressful day. At 49, he is the manager of a bank branch in an unnamed Pacific Northwest city (which happens to look a lot like Portland). On the morning of his daughter Miranda's wedding day, he gets a call that the branch has been robbed. At the same time, he and his ex-wife realize that they don't know where Miranda is or whether she'll show up for the ceremony. . . . The book follows Paul as he moves through the day of his daughter's wedding, juggling matters at the bank and matters of the heart. Shy and socially awkward, particularly as a young man, Paul's story is told in equal parts through flashback and in present tense." Portland Oregonian

"Life, both mundane and off-kilter, is revealed in this fine novel about a man who may not be as lost as he thinks." Kirkus

Dewitt, Helen

Lightning rods. New Directions 2011 273p $24.95

ISBN 978-0-8112-1943-3; 0-8112-1943-7

This is an "exercise in novel as extrapolation. Ms. Dewitt's method is to introduce a device into the world as we know it and systematically explore how the world reacts to that device. Joe's original moment of epiphany is almost superfluous; the real fun results once the idea exists and must be dealt with. Ms. Dewitt creates the problems, identifies the problems, and then figures out how to solve them. It's an appealingly practical way to think about writing fiction, and one that ignores any distinction between realism and fantasy." N Y Observer

DeWitt, Patrick

Ablutions; notes for a novel. Houghton Mifflin Harcourt 2009 164p $23

ISBN 978-0-15-101498-9; 0-15-101498-1

LC 2008-37772

The "story of an alcoholic, pill-popping, 32-year-old Hollywood bartender in the midst of a slow and steady downward spiral. Told deftly in the second person—a potentially annoying conceit—deWitt's portrayal of the drinking life is staunchly unromantic. (Consider him the anti-Bukowski.) The author, an ex-barman himself, poses the book as 'notes on a novel,' arranged in short, anecdotal snippets that read like the outline for a future, more elaborate project. This risk could have resulted in an underrealized mess, but the result is an accessible, side-splitting story that never buckles under its apparently haphazard structure. The cast of characters—which include a former child star and various tawdry, L.I.I.T.-slurping women—adds background to the main narrative of a man whose life and ambition are drowning in an ocean of Jamesons. . . . Despite its messy topic, the book becomes a welcome rarity: an experimental novel that's also a page-turner." Time Out N Y

DeWitt, Patrick

★ The **Sisters** brothers. Ecco Press 2011 328p il $24.99

ISBN 978-0-06-204126-5; 0-0-6204126-6

LC 2011282605

Governor General's Literary Awards: English-Language Fiction (2011)

Rogers Writers' Trust Fiction Prize (2011)

A novel about the "life and times of two gunslingers, Eli and Charlie Sisters. Contracted by their boss, the mysterious Commodore, the brothers are ordered to hightail it out of 1851 Oregon City and head to California's gold-rush camps. There, they'll meet a dandy named Henry Morris (a man who 'is not above biting') who will lead them to their intended target: prospector Hermann Kermit Warm. The brothers don't really know why the Commodore wants Warm dead, or even whether he's innocent (it wouldn't surprise them if he was), but taking lives is their job, and they set out on the trail with two ramshackle horses. It seems like a plot straight out of a spaghetti western, but from the start, deWitt has more than a few tricks in his saddlebag. Narrated in delicious deadpan by Eli, the kinder of the two brothers, ('Our blood is the same, we just use it differently,' Eli explains) the two men embark on a series of picaresque misadventures. . . . When the brothers finally get to California and find their victim, all expectations are gleefully reversed. The brothers discover that nothing is really what it seems to be, that a career change could be in the works, and the plot peels away like onion skin, revealing startling secrets that lead to a transformative ending as unexpectedly moving as it is satisfying." Boston Globe

DeWoskin, Rachel

Big girl small; Rachel DeWoskin. Farrar, Straus and Giroux 2011 294p. $25

ISBN 978-0-374-11257-8; 9781250002532; 9780374112578; 9781611731132

LC 201033106

Alex Award (2012)

This book tells the story of "a gifted high-school junior whose struggle to fit in is compounded by her height (3' 9"). Judy . . . has just transferred from public high school to Ann Arbor's elite Darcy Arts Academy. . . . She . . . develops an immediate crush on Jeff, who moved to town only a year ago and seems nicer than the other kids in his crowd. . . . They end up drinking with two of his friends. Judy wakes up at his house the next morning naked, with no memory of what happened. Soon enough she learns that a tape is circulating at the school showing her having sex with all three boys. Because of her height, she is considered 'handicapped,' and everyone considers her a tragic victim, making her humiliation worse." (Kirkus)

"Bright and sardonic Judy Lohden, a 16-year-old dwarf freshly enrolled in Ann Arbor's Darcy Arts Academy, falls victim to 'the worst Steven King Carrie prank in the history of dating' at the hands of popular boy Jeff Legassic, who becomes an object of desire as soon as he and Judy meet cute the first week of school. The book opens with Judy hiding out in a seedy motel; throughout the novel, she slowly unveils her secret and reveals her two visions of herself—that of a pretty teenage girl with an hourglass figure who happens to be three feet nine inches tall, and that of a sideshow attraction. It's a rare author who is willing to subject her protagonist to the extreme ranges of degradation and redemption to which DeWoskin subjects Judy; thankfully, she manages it beautifully." Publ Wkly

Dexter, Colin

★ The **daughters** of Cain. Crown 1995 295p

ISBN 0-517-70067-0

First published 1994 in the United Kingdom

In this Inspector Morse case "the crime is the murder of a retired Oxford don, and the stratagem is to make the homicide seem easy to solve. . . . Mr. Dexter is a superb technician who torments the reader with logistical details that contradict every previously established point in his puzzle. Red herrings are a specialty. But the canny author also strews the path with literary quotations to think on, polysyllabic words to look up and characters whose lives are so complicated they turn into richly distracting mini-dramas." N Y Times Book Rev

Dexter, Colin

Death is now my neighbor; an Inspector Morse novel. Crown 1996 347p

ISBN 0-517-70786-1

LC 96-31781

This mystery "involves two senior Oxford dons and their ambitious wives in the death of a young woman with no obvious connections to any of them. Despite a medical scare that leaves him feeling 'unmanned' and has him behaving with uncharacteristic charity, Morse is brilliant at finding the links, filling in the blanks and coming up with the answers to this complicated case—if not to the ultimate questions that trouble his soul." N Y Times Book Rev

Dexter, Colin

The **jewel** that was ours. Crown 1992 275p il

ISBN 0-517-58847-1

LC 91-45245

First published 1991 in the United Kingdom

This mystery finds British Inspector Morse "stymied by the theft of a rare artifact bound for the Ashmolean Museum and by the sudden deaths of both the American woman who owned it and the curator for whom it was intended. Challenged to keep track of several sneaky academics and frisky elderly tourists, the detective noses over British Rail timetables, handwritten notes and a smelly assortment of red herrings." N Y Times Book Rev

"The watertight solution is as tricky as it is dazzling." Booklist

Dexter, Colin
Morse's greatest mystery and other stories. Crown 1995 242p
   ISBN 0-517-79992-8
First published 1993 in the United Kingdom
   Contents: As good as gold; Morse's greatest mystery; Evans tries an O-level; Dead as a dodo; At the Lulu-Bar Motel; Neighborhood watch; A case of mis-identity; The inside story; Monty's revolver; The carpet-bagger; Last call

Dexter, Colin
The **remorseful** day. Crown 2000 363p
   ISBN 0-609-60622-0
                                                            LC 99-59840
First published 1999 in the United Kingdom
   "A two-year-old murder has baffled the police in Burford, a rural English village. Inspector Morse, who excels at this sort of puzzle, refuses to touch it, despite anonymous phone calls offering new evidence. Then his sidekick, Sergeant Lewis, discovers that the inspector knew the murdered woman." Libr J

Dexter, Colin
The **secret** of annexe 3. St. Martin's Press 1987 218p
   ISBN 0-312-01089-3
                                                            LC 87-17590
First published 1986 in the United Kingdom
   "Inspector Morse and Sergeant Lewis investigate a murder committed on New Year's Eve at a hotel in Oxford. Three couples are housed in the hotel annex, and one man, winner of the prize in the fancy-dress contest, is found dead in his room. The first problem facing Morse and Lewis is locating the other five guests, including the victim's wife, all of whom have fled, having registered under fake names and addresses. . . . Engrossed in the story that Dexter tells in his witty and stylish fashion, readers will savor the mystery of the masquerade and the detecting partners' ultimate triumph." Publ Wkly

Dexter, Colin
The **way** through the woods. Crown 1993 296p
   ISBN 0-517-59444-7
                                                            LC 92-40762
First published 1992 in the United Kingdom
   "To say that the investigation is tricky is only to hint at the technical density of the plot, which, once all the tantalizing enigmas have been packed up, hinges on the most basic human frailties. Dazzling." N Y Times Book Rev

Dexter, Colin
The **wench** is dead. St. Martin's Press 1990 200p il
   ISBN 0-312-04444-5
                                                            LC 89-77807
First published 1989 in the United Kingdom

"Mr. Dexter has fashioned a taxing brainteaser for Morse, whose superior wits and famously foul temper tug the reader into the detective's hospital bed to share his single-minded pursuit of the truth." N Y Times Book Rev

Dexter, Pete
   ★ **Deadwood**. Random House 1986 365p
   ISBN 0-394-53669-X
                                                            LC 85-19635
   "Deadwood (is) a vibrant, squalid late-nineteenth-century boomtown nestled in the forbidding Black Hills of the untamed Dakota Territory. When the legendary Wild Bill Hickok guides a wagon train full of prostitutes into the virtually lawless town, he becomes the target of Al Swearingen, a vengeful and cowardly pimp who hires an addlepated sot to kill him. Wild Bill's disquieted final days are spent in the company of a score of rough characters (including a riotously off-color Calamity Jane), each of whom is later bitterly haunted by the freakish circumstances of his murder." Booklist
   This novel "is unpredictable, hyperbolic and, page after page, uproarious; a joshing book written in high spirits and a raw appreciation for the past." N Y Times Book Rev

Dexter, Pete
The **paperboy**. Random House 1995 307p
   ISBN 0-679-42175-0
                                                            LC 94-21523
   "Set in the fetid swamps of northern Florida, the novel concerns the legal case of Hillary Van Wetter, who has been condemned to death for the murder of the county sheriff. Nineteen-year-old Jack James, son of the local newspaper publisher and delivery boy for the daily edition, narrates the story, which begins with Charlotte Bless, an interloping southern floozy just past her prime who takes an obsessive interest in Van Wetter's case. Jack's elder brother, Ward, a reporter in Miami, also detects a story in Van Wetter's predicament and returns to his native Moat County to investigate. He brings along the handsome, ambitious writer Yardley Acheman, whose stylistic flash is matched by his willingness to cut ethical corners. The group's inquiry drives this novel's action, taking them through the swamp, to death row, and on to Daytona Beach." Booklist
   "Dexter's writing is rock-solid, he offers acute observations about the nature of reporting and his grip on the Southern male psyche is unquestionable." Publ Wkly

Dexter, Pete
   ★ **Paris** Trout. Random House 1988 306p
   ISBN 0-394-56370-0
                                                            LC 87-43314
   "Paris Trout, the small-town Georgia store owner . . . sleeps with a sheet of lead under his mattress. He's afraid someone is going to hide under his bed and shoot him in the middle of the night—and for no good reason, as Trout sees it. He was only taking care of business, trying to collect on Henry Ray Boxer's debt. That little black girl, Rosie Sayers, who got shot and killed in the scuffle, shouldn't have got in his way, or the woman with Rosie, who still walks around with Trout's bullet in her chest. . . . Mr. Dexter has created a character whose racism is a blunt, unregenerate fact, as primitive and willful as an earthquake or a rainstorm—and just as sealed off from argument, examination or questions

of mercy. What the town's polite society takes care to disguise in Sunday-go-to-meeting euphemisms, Paris sets in defiant, ugly relief; he makes it easy for them to believe they are innocent of racism." N Y Times Book Rev

Dexter, Pete
Spooner. Grand Central Pub. 2009 469p $26.99

ISBN 978-0-446-54072-8; 0-446-54072-2

LC 2009-06087

"The title character is one Warren Spooner, a kid dogged by the fact that his mother's favorite child, Spooner's twin brother, died at birth. Spooner's dad dies soon afterward. Into the family's life arrives Ottosson, [a] disgraced young naval officer turned schoolteacher. He is a man of great virtues: smart, tough, capable and wreathed in infinite patience. He will need the latter quality in spades to deal with his troubled stepson.... Despite the autobiographical elements in 'Spooner,' the book lacks a narrative arc that permits a complete picture of the protagonist's life. This is not cited as a fault. It is a function of how this picaresque novel serves as a work of memory, real or imagined." Denver Post

Dexter, Pete
Train; a novel. Doubleday 2003 280p $26

ISBN 0-385-50591-4

LC 2003-51946

Lionel "Train" Walk is a "young black caddy at an exclusive L.A. country club in 1953. Train is a self-taught golfer, too, and his natural ability catches the eye of an enigmatic cop, Miller Packard (or 'Mile-Away-Man,' as Train dubs him). As the stories of Train, Packard, and Norah Still, the survivor of a yacht hijacking (and eventually, Packard's wife), interject and ultimately implode, Dexter painstakingly reminds us that noir is all about disappointment, too." Booklist

Dezenhall, Eric
Money wanders. Thomas Dunne Bks. 2002 338p $24.95

ISBN 0-312-28275-3

LC 2001-54335

A "comic caper about a Jewish pollster put to work for an aging South Jersey/Philly Mafia don. Middle-aged Jonah Eastman, a D.C. spin doctor for hire whose business is in the doldrums, is summoned back to his Jersy home by his ailing grandfather Mickey, an old-school Jewish capo for the local Cosa Nostra kingpin, Mario Vanni. Mickey's cryptic deathbed missive to his nervous grandson directs Jonah to take on the don as a client." Publ Wkly

Dial, Connie
Fallen angels; Connie Dial. The Permanent Press 2012 296 p. hardcover o.p. $29

ISBN 1579622747; 9781579622749

LC 2011051392

This crime novel features Capt. Josie Corsino, who is investigating the death of starlet Hillary Dennis. Since the main suspect "Cory is L.A. city councilman Eli Goldman's son, Deputy Chief Eric Bright tells Corsino to go easy on Cory. Other pressures arise: Corsino's son, David, is tied to Cory; Corsino's husband, Jake, is unhappy; and too many

incompetent or corrupt cops hamper her investigation." (Publishers Weekly)

Diamant, Anita
Last days of Dogtown; a novel. Scribner 2005 263p il $25

ISBN 0-7432-2573-2

LC 2005-45191

This novel "weaves together seemingly disparate stories of a dying Massachusetts town. . . . In the early 1800s, Dogtown is a village on Cape Ann populated by spinsters, free slaves, and prostitutes, all of whom are reviled by the surrounding communities. Beginning with the death of a town patriarch and ending when the last resident expires, Dogtown's final days are filled with all the secrets a town can keep. Several characters stand out, including Tammy Younger, the town pariah, and Judy Rhines, whose affair with a free African is kept secret to heartbreaking effect. Diamant has a gift for storytelling and breathes life into this dying town and its eccentric inhabitants." Libr J

Diamant, Anita
★ The red tent. St. Martin's Press 1997 321p $24.95; pa $16.95

ISBN 0-312-16978-7; 0-312-35376-6 pa

LC 97-16825

"Diamant's fiction debut links the passions of the early Israelites to the ongoing traditions of modern Jews, while the red tent of her title (where women retreat for menstruation, childbirth and illness) becomes a resonant symbol of womanly strength, love and wisdom. Despite a few unprofitable digressions, Diamant succeeds admirably in depicting the lives of women in the age that engendered our civilization and our most enduring values." Publ Wkly

Diamond, De'nesha
A gangster and a gentleman; Kiki Swinson, De'nesha Diamond. Dafina 2012 320 p. $15

ISBN 0758251823; 9780758251824

This book contains two novellas, one by Kiki Swinson and one by De'nesha Diamond. In Swinson's "I Need a Gangsta," "Melody Goldman isn't about to let her rich, cheating, ungrateful husband walk out and leave her with nothing" so she hires ex-con Scott Harris to help her." In Diamond's "Gentlemen Prefer Bullets," "publicist Blake Scott" has kept "far, far away from her gangsta kingpin father. But now the only person who can protect her is his enforcer, Eli Hardwick." (Publisher's note)

Diamond, De'nesha
Hustlin' divas; De'nesha Diamond. Dafina Books 2010 343 p.

ISBN 0758247559; 9780758247551

Sequel to: Street Divas. New York: Dafina Books, 2011.

In this novel, "Memphis is the crime capital of America, and no one knows that better than the women born and raised in its mean streets. It's put sisters Ta'Shara and LeShelle on opposite sides of the street game, where blood means nothing and loyalty doesn't last long. It's also got Yolanda, an ambitious drug mule, and Melanie, a police detective, caught up with the same man -- the notorious hustler Python. These four women think they've got the game figured out, but the one man they have in common will have them living double lives and wondering who will come out on top." (Publisher's note)

Diaz, Junot

The **brief** wondrous life of Oscar Wao; Junot Díaz. Riverhead Books 2007 339 p.

ISBN 1-59448-958-0; 978-1-59448-958-7

LC 2007017251

This book tells the story of "a lonely outsider . . . Oscar grows up in a Dominican neighborhood in Paterson,, NJ, as an overweight, homely lover of sf and fantasy. . Reading such books and trying to emulate them in his own writing provide Oscar's only pleasure. What he really wants is love, but his romantic overtures are constantly rejected." Also presented are "glances at the history of the Dominican Republic, focusing on the Rafael Trujillo dictatorship and its effect on Oscar's family. Díaz . . . shifts between Oscar and his sister, mother, and grandfather to give this intimate character study an epic scale, showing that an individual life is the product of family history." (Libr J)

In this novel "Díaz presents a slice of the vast history of Santo Domingo and the intricate past and present of a doomed family. . . . Oscar de León [is] Díaz's sci-fi obsessed, overweight, romantic hero who hopes to someday be the 'Dominican Stephen King.' Oscar is the ultimate outcast both at home and at school. This 'ghetto nerd' lacks the philandering, macho finesse expected of a Dominican male. His bookish manner and unappealing looks relegate his high school experience to the level of 'a medieval spectacle,' an experience 'like being put in the stocks and forced to endure the pelting and outrages of a mob of deranged half-wits.' But this is more than a tale of mere adolescent anguish. Oscar and his family appear to be the hapless victims of a so-called Dominican curse, or the 'fukú,' that has followed them for generations from the shores of their homeland to New Jersey. Díaz weaves the stories of Lola, his troubled but supportive sister, and Belicia, his hardened mother, along with various other family members, to portray a colorful and complex portrait of mad love, old-world superstition, and the continual strivings of a diaspora." Christ Sci Monit

Diaz, Junot

Drown. Riverhead Bks. 1996 208p

ISBN 0-573-22041-8

LC 96-18362

"The 10 tales in this intense debut collection plunge us into the emotional lives of people redefining their American identity. Narrated by adolescent Dominican males living in the struggling communities of the Dominican Republic, New York and New Jersey, these stories chronicle their outwardly cool but inwardly anguished attempts to recreate themselves in the midst of eroding family structures and their own burgeoning sexuality." Publ Wkly

Dibdin, Michael

And then you die; an Aurelio Zen mystery. Pantheon Bks. 2002 183p

ISBN 0-375-42188-2

LC 2002-283086

"You have to read between the lines—in scenes about a broken marriage, an empty home, a discredited occupa-

tion—to understand why Zen is really running for his life." N Y Times Book Rev

Dibdin, Michael

Blood rain; an Aurelio Zen mystery. Pantheon Bks. 2000 273p

ISBN 0-375-40915-7

LC 99-46938

First published 1999 in the United Kingdom

Didbin "uses the somber tones, circuitous locutions and dense plot structure appropriate to a region where every gesture—from a chess game to a political assassination—sends a subtle and dangerous message." N Y Times Book Rev

Dibdin, Michael

A **long** finish; an Aurelio Zen mystery. Pantheon Bks. 1998 261p

ISBN 0-375-40429-5

LC 98-15764

When a leading Piedmontese "vintner is murdered and his son is charged with the gruesome deed, Zen is dispatched from Rome by a notable personage fearful that 'one of the great vintages of the century' will be compromised. . . . The all-embracing sense of place in Dibdin's mysteries extends here to the earthy sights and smells of dark woods (where the truffles grow) and lush vineyards (where the grapes ripen) and ancient farmhouses (where murder is done). Only when Zen learns to look past the beauty of these pastoral scenes can he identify the evil that lives in this village." N Y Times Book Rev

Dibdin, Michael

Medusa; an Aurelio Zen mystery. Michael Dibdin. Pantheon Books 2003 259p $22

ISBN 0-375-42269-2

LC 2003-60893

"A long-dead body found in a mountain tunnel piques the interest of veteran Italian police officer Aurelio Zen (Blood Rain), who is especially intrigued by the inordinate attention paid to the case by the Defense Ministry and his own superior in the Interior Ministry. The corpse turns out to be that of Lt. Leonardo Ferraro, reportedly killed in a plane crash 30 years earlier. Its discovery brings to light a secret right-wing military group that prepared to overthrow the government in the 1970s. . . . Dibdin does a superb job of creating a complex background of Italian politics and society." Libr J

Dibdin, Michael

Ratking; Michael Dibdin. Bantam Books 1989 266p. (pbk.) $13.95; o.p.

ISBN 9780679768548; 055305337X

LC 88-47832

In this book, the winner of the 1988 Gold Dagger award, "Italian Police Commissioner Aurelio Zen is dispatched to investigate the kidnapping of Ruggiero Miletti, a powerful Perugian industrialist. But nobody much wants Zen to succeed: not the local authorities, who view him as an interloper, and certainly not Miletti's children, who seem content to let the head of the family languish in the hands of his abductors -- if he's still alive. Was Miletti truly the victim of professionals? Or might his kidnapper be someone closer to home: his preening son Daniele, with his million-lire wardrobe and his profitable drug business? His daughter, Cinzia, whose vapid beauty conceals a devastating secret?" (Publisher's note)

Followed by: Vendetta (1998)

The **Dick** Francis treasury of great racing stories; edited and introduced by Dick Francis and John Welcome. Norton 1990 221p

ISBN 0-393-02879-8

LC 89-72151

Contents: The dream, by R. Findlay; Silver Blaze, by A. C. Doyle; A glass of port with the proctor, by J. Welcome; Carrot for a chestnut, by D. Francis; The look of eagles, by J. T. Foote; Prime rogues, by M. Keane; The coop, by E. Wallace; The splendid outcast, by B. Markham; I'm a fool, by S. Anderson; Had a horse, by J. Galsworthy; The major, by C. Davy; What's it get you?, by J. P. Marquand; Harmony, by W. Fain; The bagman's pony, by E. de Somerville

First published 1989 in the United Kingdom with title: Great racing stories

Dick, Philip K.

★ The **collected** stories of Philip K. Dick. Underwood/Miller 1987 5v

ISBN 0-88733-053-3

Dick, Philip K.

★ **Do** androids dream of electric sheep? Ballantine Books 1996 244p pa $13.95

ISBN 0-345-40447-5

LC 96-96117

First published 1968

"In a future where technological sophistication has made the ersatz virtually indistinguishable from the real, the hero is a bounty hunter who must track down and eliminate androids passing for human. . . . A key novel in Dick's canon." Anatomy of Wonder 5

Dick, Philip K.

✓ **Five** novels of the 1960s & 70s; Martian timeslip; Dr. Bloodmoney; Now wait for last year; Flow my tears, the policeman said; A scanner darkly. Library of America 2008 1128p $40

ISBN 978-1-59853-025-4

"Martian Time-Slip (1964) unfolds on a parched and thinly colonized Red Planet where the unscrupulous seek to profit from a troubled child's time-fracturing visions. Dr. Bloodmoney, or How We Got Along After the Bomb (1965) chronicles the interwoven stories of a multiracial community of survivors, including the scientist who may have been responsible for World War III. . . . Now Wait for Last Year (1966) explores the effects of JJ-180, a hallucinogen that alters not only perception, but reality. In Flow My Tears, the Policeman Said (1974), a television star seeks to unravel a mystery that has left him stripped of his identity. A Scanner Darkly (1977), the basis for the 2006 film, envisions a drug-addled world in which a narcotics officer's tenuous hold on sanity is strained by his new surveillance assignment: himself." Publisher's note

Dick, Philip K.

✓ ★ **Four** novels of the 1960s; The man in the high castle; The three stigmata of Palmer Eldritch; Do androids dream of electric sheep?; Ubik. Library of America 2007 830p $35

ISBN 978-1-59853-009-4; 1-598-53009-7

LC 2006-48776

"These novels grapple with spirituality, rather than science. In The Man in the High Castle [1962], set in a United States that has been defeated by the Axis powers in World War II, the characters use the ancient Chinese text I Ching to determine their actions. In The Three Stigmata [1965], hallucinogenic drugs provide virtual reality experiences that lead to discussions of the existence and nature of God. Do Androids Dream [1968] features a religion, Mercerism, in which adherents experience real suffering through a machine that registers their empathy for a sacrificial victim. Ubik [1969] utilizes the Tibetan Book of the Dead to examine the existence and consciousness of an afterlife. I don't want this to sound as if Dick is some dry-as-bones, proselytizing prophet. These novels are also funny, thrilling and stimulating. There are shootouts with renegade androids and undercover spies. There are parodies of consumer culture. There are debates about historicity and drug use. Each novel offers a reading experience that is cathartic while reading, yet offers fruit for continued thought afterward." Philadelphia Inquirer

Dick, Philip K.

✓ ★ The **man** in the high castle. Vintage Books 1992 259p pa $12

ISBN 0-679-74067-8

LC 91-50895

First published 1962 by Putnam

"An alternate history in which Germany and Japan won World War II and partitioned the U.S., except for the Rocky Mountain States, which were left in a kind of political limbo. Faction-ridden Nazism oppressively rules the eastern U.S. In the west, the Japanese overlords are reconciling Oriental and American cultural values. . . . This is Dick's most important early book." Anatomy of Wonder 5

Dick, Philip K.

The **minority** report. Pantheon Bks. 2002 103p $12.95

ISBN 0-375-42187-4

LC 2002-72313

Originally published posthumously as a short story

"Police Commissioner John Anderton finds himself at the mercy of his own crime-prevention system when the prescient precogs he's hired to stop crime before it starts peg him as a soon-to-be murderer." Publ Wkly

Dick, Philip K.

VALIS and later novels; edited by Jonathan Lethem. Library of America 2009 849p $35

ISBN 9781598530445

"The collection opens with A Maze of Death (1970). . . . Mysteriously summoned to the planet Delmak-O, a motley group of colonists attempts to survive together in a hostile new world. . . . . . [VALIS (1981) is a] self-portrait of a man confronting a 'Vast Active Living Intelligence System,' torn between conflicting interpretations of what might be gnostic illumination or mental collapse. In The Divine Invasion (1981), the life of a solitary off-world colonist is hijacked by a local alien, who turns out to be the Yahweh of Judeo-Christian tradition. Returning to Earth with his pregnant wife in tow, Dick's hapless Herb Asher finds himself thrust into the middle of an apocalyptic war between Good and Evil. . . . The Transmigration of Timothy Archer (1982), Dick's last novel, is by turns a theological mystery story, a roman à clef, and a starkly disillusioned portrait of contemporary California life. Based loosely on the career of Bishop James Pike, Dick's close friend and a kindred spirit, the novel's title character gives up his comfortable place in the church hierarchy in a tragic quest for enlightenment." Publisher's note

Dickens, Charles

Barnaby Rudge; a tale of the riots of 'eighty. with 76 illustrations by George Cattermole and Hablot K. Browne ('Phiz') and an introduction by Kathleen Tillotson. Oxford Univ. Press 1961 634p il
    ISBN 0-19-254513-2
    First published 1841
    The plot is one of Dickens' weakest. The novel's chief interest lies in its depiction of the riots, shown to have been caused by a government heedless of the needs of its poor." Reader's Ency. 4th edition

Dickens, Charles

★ Bleak House; with the original illustrations by Phiz; introduced by Barbara Hardy. Knopf 1991 xlix, 891p il $23
    ISBN 0-679-40568-2

    LC 91-52974
    First published 1853
    "In this novel, Dickens attacks the delays and archaic absurdities of the courts, which he knew about firsthand." Reader's Ency. 4th edition

Dickens, Charles

A Charles Dickens Christmas; A Christmas carol; The Chimes; The cricket on the hearth. with illustrations by Warren Chappell. Oxford Univ. Press 1976 308p il
    Omnibus edition of the titles first published 1843, 1845 and 1846 respectively, the first and third of which are entered separately. The chimes is a fable about the fears and aspirations of the London poor. A porter and runner of errands, under the influence of the goblins of the church bells and/or a dish of tripe, has a nightmare or vision of awful misfortunes befalling his daughter, but conditions are ameliorated after he awakens

Dickens, Charles

★ A Christmas carol; with illustrations by Arthur Rackham. Knopf 1994 155p il $13.95
    ISBN 0-679-43639-1

    LC 95-163031
    Written in 1843
    "This Christmas story of nineteenth century England has delighted young and old for generations. In it, a miser, Scrooge, through a series of dreams, finds the true Christmas spirit. . . . The story ends with the much-quoted cry of

Tiny Tim, the crippled son of Bob Cratchit, whom Scrooge now aids: 'God bless us, everyone!'" Haydn. Thesaurus of Book Dig

Dickens, Charles

The complete ghost stories of Charles Dickens; edited by Peter Haining. Watts 1983 341p il
    ISBN 0-531-09885-0

    LC 82-13481
    First published 1982 in the United Kingdom
    Contents: Captain Murderer and the Devil's bargain; The lawyer and the ghost; The queer chair; The ghosts of the mail; A madman's manuscript; The story of the goblins who stole a sexton; Baron Koëldwethout's apparition; A Christmas carol; The haunted man and the ghost's bargain; To be read at dusk; The ghost chamber; The haunted house; Mr Testator's visitation; The trial for murder; The signalman; Four ghost stories; The portrait-painter's story; Well-authenticated rappings

Dickens, Charles

The cricket on the hearth; a tale of home. with illustrations by C. E. Brock. Dutton 171p il
    First published in 1846; this is a reissue of an edition first published 1905
    "In this short Christmas fairy tale of a happy English home, the cricket chirps when all is well, and is silent when sorrow enters. Mr. and Mrs. Perrybingle (John and Dot) give refuge to an old stranger, Edward Plummer. John sees the stranger, as a young man, without his disguise, put his arm around Dot. The cricket takes the form of a fairy and counsels him. John does not judge his young wife and is ready to forgive her. However, Edward bursts in with his bride, May Fielding, and explains everything." Haydn. Thesaurus of Book Dig

Dickens, Charles

★ David Copperfield; with the original illustrations by "Phiz"; introduced by Michael Slater. Knopf 1991 xlii, 891p il $25
    ISBN 0-679-40571-2

    LC 91-52995
    First published 1850
    This novel "incorporates material from the autobiography Dickens had recently begun but soon abandoned and is written in the first person, a new technique for him. Although Copperfield differs from his creator in many ways, Dickens uses many early personal experiences that had meant much to him—his own period of work in a factory while his father was jailed, his schooling and reading, his passion for Maria Beadnell (a woman much like Dora Spenlow), and (more cursorily) his emergence from parliamentary reporting into successful novel writing." Merriam-Webster's Ency of Lit

Dickens, Charles

Dombey and Son; with forty illustrations by 'Phiz'; introduced by Lucy Hughes-Hallett. Knopf 1994 xlvii, 889p il $23
    ISBN 0-679-43591-3

    LC 94-4778
    First published 1848

"The proud, unfeeling Mr. Dombey has but one ambition: to have a son so that his firm might be called Dombey and Son. When his son Paul is born, he promises to fulfill this ambition, which overrides even grief at the death of Mrs. Dombey. Young Paul, a delicate, sensitive boy, is quite unequal to the great things expected of him; he is sent to Mr. Blimber's school and gives way under the strain of the discipline. . . . Mr. Dombey is embittered by Paul's death. Florence, his daughter, lives on with him, trying desperately to win his love, but she has succeeded only in incurring his hatred because she lives while her brother died. Dombey marries again, but his second wife, Edith Granger, runs off with Mr. Carker, his business manager. Florence marries the kind young Walter Gay. Dombey's firm fails, and alone and miserable, he finds himself longing for the sweet and kind daughter whom he treated so coldly. The two are reconciled, and Dombey tries to expiate his past through his grandchildren." Reader's Ency. 4th edition

Dickens, Charles
★ **Great** expectations; illustrated by F.W. Pailthrope with an introduction by Michael Slater. Knopf 1992 xxxiv, 469p il $21

ISBN 0-679-40579-8

LC 91-53219

First published 1861

"The first-person narrative relates the coming-of-age of Pip (Philip Pirrip). Reared in the marshes of Kent by his disagreeable sister and her sweet-natured husband, the blacksmith Joe Gargery, the young Pip one day helps a convict to escape. Later he is sent to live with Miss Havisham, a woman driven half-mad years earlier by her lover's departure on their wedding day. . . . When an anonymous benefactor makes it possible for Pip to go to London for an education, he credits Miss Havisham. . . . Pips benefactor turns out to have been Abel Magwitch, the convict he once aided, who dies awaiting trial after Pip is unable to help him a second time. Joe rescues Pip from despair and nurses him back to health." Merriam-Webster's Ency of Lit

Dickens, Charles
✓ **Hard** times. Knopf 1992 299p $19

ISBN 0-679-41323-5

LC 91-58704

First published 1854. Variant title: Hard times for these times

The proprietor of an experimental private school in an English manufacturing town, "Thomas Gradgrind, a fanatic of the demonstrable fact, has raised his children Tom and Louisa in an atmosphere of grimmest practicality. Louisa marries the banker Josiah Bounderby partly to protect her brother who is in Bounderby's employ, and partly because her education has resulted in an emotional atrophy that makes her indifferent to her fate. Tom, shallow and unscrupulous, robs Bounderby's bank and contrives to frame Stephen Blackpool, an honest and long-suffering mill hand. Meanwhile, Louisa's dormant emotions began to awaken, stimulated by disgust for the vulgar Bounderby and the attentions of the charming, amoral James Harthouse. When she runs away to her father and when Tom's guilt is discovered, Gradgrind realizes how his principles have blighted his children's lives. . . . The novel is Dickens's harshest indictment of practices and philosophical justifications of mid-19th-century industrialism in England." Reader's Ency. 4th edition

Dickens, Charles
✓ **Little** Dorrit. Knopf 1992 xxxvii, 836p il $22

ISBN 0-679-41725-7

LC 92-52919

First published 1857

"Satirizes the Civil Service under the style of the Circumlocution Office. Also pictures prison life. Little Dorrit's father being Father of the Marshalsea. The melodramatic element appears in the history of the House of Clennam: with the usual complement of originals: Mr. F.'s Aunt, the Meagles, Pancks, Mr. Nanby, Mr. Casby, Flora Finching, Miss Wade, Tallycoram." Baker. Guide to the Best Fic

Dickens, Charles
✓ **Martin** Chuzzlewit; with forty illustrations by "Phiz"; introduced by William Boyd. Knopf 1994 xlvii, 851p il $20

ISBN 0-679-43884-X

LC 95-136833

"The story's protagonist, Martin Chuzzlewit, is an apprentice architect who is fired by Seth Pecksniff and is also disinherited by his own eccentric, wealthy grandfather. Martin and a servant, Mark Tapley, travel to the United States, where they are swindled by land speculators and have other unpleasant but sometimes comic experiences. Thoroughly disillusioned with the New World, the pair returns to England, where a chastened Martin is reconciled with his grandfather, who gives his approval to Martin's forthcoming marriage to his true love, Mary Graham." Merriam-Webster's Ency of Lit

Dickens, Charles
The **mystery** of Edwin Drood; with 12 illustrations by Luke Fildes and 2 by Charles Collins, and an introduction by S. C. Roberts. Oxford Univ. Press 1956 278p il

ISBN 0-19-254516-7

First published 1870

"This novel Dickens left unfinished at his death. The striking opening scene shows John Jasper, precentor of Cloisterham cathedral, in an opium den. He is the uncle of Edwin Drood, and persecutes with his evil passion Rosa Bud, to whom Drood is betrothed by an arrangement made by the late respective fathers of the two orphans. Actually Edwin is cool to Rosa, and it is another orphan, Neville Landless, who is attracted to her. The sinister Jasper foments a quarrel between Edwin and Neville, not knowing that the engagement had already been broken off. The same night Edwin disappears, and there is circumstantial evidence pointing to Neville as his murderer. The latter is arrested, but as no body has been found, is released. There turns up in the neighborhood a white-haired stranger who calls himself Datchery and acts like a detective on the trail of Jasper. Here the story breaks off with no indication as to how it would have ended." Haydn. Thesaurus of Book Dig

Dickens, Charles

✓ ★ **Nicholas** Nickleby; with an introduction by John Carey. Knopf 1993 lvii, 843p il $24

ISBN 0-679-42307-9

LC 93-1856

First published 1839

After Nicholas Nickleby's father dies bankrupt, Nicholas, his sister and their mother go to London to seek aid from Nicholas' uncle, a moneylender. At the scheming miser's insistence, Nicholas "first serves as usher to Mr. Wackford Squeers, schoolmaster at Dotheboys Hall; the brutality of Squeers and his wife, especially toward a poor, half-witted boy named Smike, causes Nicholas to leave in disgust. Smike runs away from school to follow Nicholas, remaining his follower until he dies. Next Nicholas joins the theatrical company of Mr. Crummles, and finally he secures a good post in a counting house owned by the benevolent Cheeryble brothers, Ned and Charles, self-made merchants ready to help those struggling against ill fortune." Reader's Ency. 4th edition

Dickens, Charles

✓ The **old** curiosity shop; with seventy-five illustrations by Cattermole and `Phiz'; introduced by Peter Washington. Knopf 1995 569p il $24

ISBN 0-679-44373-8

LC 95-75208

First published 1841; first Everyman's library edition 1907

This is the "story of Little Nell Trent and the evil dwarf Quilp. When Little Nell's grandfather gambles away his curiosity shop to his creditor Quilp, the girl and the old man flee London. Nell's friend Kit Nubbles and a mysterious Single Gentleman (who turns out to be the wealthy brother of Nell's grandfather) attempt to find them but are thwarted by Quilp, who drowns while fleeing the law. Little Nell dies before Kit and the Single Gentleman arrive, and her brokenhearted grandfather dies days later." Merriam-Webster's Ency of Lit

Dickens, Charles

Oliver Twist; with twenty-four illustrations by George Cruikshank; introduced by Michael Slater. Knopf 1992 xlvi, 427p il $20

ISBN 0-679-41724-9

LC 92-52899

First published 1837-1838

"A boy from an English workhouse falls into the hands of rogues who train him to be a pickpocket. The story of his struggles to escape from an environment of crime is one of hardship, danger and the severe obstacles overcome." Natl Counc of Teachers of Engl

Dickens, Charles

✓ **Our** mutual friend; with an introduction by Andrew Sanders. Knopf 1994 xliii, 832p $22

ISBN 0-679-42028-2

LC 93-81033

First published 1865

"John Harmon, 'our mutual friend,' will inherit a fortune if he marries Bella Wilfer. He assumes the names of Julius Handford and later John Rokesmith, and his supposed death helps him conceal his identity. John's father's foreman, Nicodemus Boffin, and his wife, Henrietta, help him with the ruse. He enters the employ of Boffin, who has adopted Bella. Bella has had her head turned by wealth, but reforms when her eyes are opened to its evils; she marries Harmon. Other characters are: Jesse Hexam; his son Charley, and daughter, Lizzie; Bradley Headstone, schoolmaster, who is jealous of Eugene Wrayburn's love for Lizzie Hexam; Fanny Cleaver (Jenny Wren), a doll's dressmaker; one-legged Silas Wegg, the villain in the main plot, as Headstone is in the secondary one. Here again Dickens protests against the poor laws through the character Betty Hidger, who fears the workhouse." Haydn. Thesaurus of Book Dig

Dickens, Charles

The **posthumous** papers of the Pickwick Club; with forty-three illustrations by Seymour and "Phiz" and an introduction by Bernard Darwin. Oxford Univ. Press 1959 xxiii, 801p il

ISBN 0-19-254501-9

First published 1837

"Episodes of the doings and foibles of the Pickwick Club. . . . The book is made up of letters and manuscripts about the club's actions. Among the incidents are: the army parade; trip to Manor Farm; the saving of Rachel Wardle from the villain, Alfred Jingle; trip to Eatonsville; Mrs. Leo Hunter's party of authors, including Count Smorltork and Charles FitzMarshall; ice skating. Pickwick's landlady, Mrs. Bardell, faints in his arms and compromises the unsophisticated gentleman. She sues him for breach of promise and an amusing court trial follows. Pickwick refuses to pay damages and is put in Fleet prison. Sam Weller, his faithful servant, accompanies him. Mrs. Bardell is also incarcerated for not paying the costs of the trial. When Pickwick is released he retires to a house outside London, with Weller, and the latter's new bride, Mary, as housekeeper. He dissolves the club and spends his time arranging its memoranda." Haydn. Thesaurus of Book Dig

Dickens, Charles

✓ ★ A **tale** of two cities; with an introduction by Simon Schama and sixteen illustrations by Phiz. Knopf 1993 xxviii, 413p il $20

ISBN 0-679-42073-8

LC 92-73542

First published 1859

"Although Dickens borrowed from Thomas Carlyle's history, The French Revolution, for his sprawling tale of London and revolutionary Paris, the novel offers more drama than accuracy. The scenes of large-scale mob violence are especially vivid, if superficial in historical understanding. The complex plot involves Sydney Carton's sacrifice of his own life on behalf of his friends Charles Darnay and Lucie Manette. While political events drive the story, Dickens takes a decidedly antipolitical tone, lambasting both aristocratic tyranny and revolutionary excess." Merriam-Webster's Ency of Lit

Dickey, James

✓ ★ **Deliverance**. Houghton Mifflin 1970 278p

ISBN 9780385313872

LC 82462524

"The plot revolves around a canoe trip undertaken by four city men as a break in routine and to see a wilderness river before it is dammed. Early in the journey two of the men are attacked by brutal mountaineers and another member of the quartet is killed. Dickey probes the diverse personalities of each man, showing clearly that leadership devolves on the one most able to solve a problem rationally rather than the one most given to theorizing about how to cope with the issue of basic survival." Booklist

Dickey, James

To the white sea. Houghton Mifflin 1993 275p
ISBN 0-395-47565-1

LC 93-1247

WWII Air Force gunner Muldrow is shot down over Tokyo shortly before the "fire raid on that city. His position should be hopeless, but the man comes from a remote region of Alaska, where he grew up hunting, trapping, and studying game. His object is to find similarly cold country, and as he lurks and dodges his way north to Hokkaido, he uses every trick of camouflage and predation that he has learned from hare and wolverine." Atlantic

This novel "allows no easy assumption about nature or violence or war. What makes it so haunting, though, what keeps you reading, is the beauty of the prose." Newsweek

Dickinson, Charles

A shortcut in time. Forge 2003 288p $24.95
ISBN 0-7653-0579-8

LC 2002-34688

"Josh Winkler's settled life changes when he chooses a shortcut to town and ends up 15 minutes in the past. On the same path, he meets Constance, another bewildered time traveler from the year 1908. No one believes them, especialy Josh's doctor wife, who orders neurological tests. To validate their experiences, Josh researches Constance's disappearance in the local library's newspaper archives and discovers that Constance's boyfriend, a suspect in her disappearance, was hanged by an angry mob; Constance needs to find her way back to 1908 to prevent his death." Libr J

"Dickinson conjures a notably mundane environment, then makes it extraorinary" Booklist

Dickinson, Peter

Some deaths before dying. Mysterious Press 1999 251p $27
ISBN 0-89296-696-3

LC 98-37535

Dickinson's "radiant portrait of Rachel does honor to 'her long and steadfast campaign to keep hold of her mind,' just as he dignifies the other aged or inarticulate characters in his story by lending them the clarity of voice to express the thoughts they feared they'd lost forever." N Y Times Book Rev

Dickinson, Peter

★ The yellow room conspiracy. Mysterious Press 1994 261p
ISBN 0-89296-556-8

LC 94-1980

"The yellow room was one of about 50 in Blatchards, an old mansion near Bury St. Edmonds. Owned by Lord Verek-

er, Blatchards was dominated by his five striking daughters whose politics and personal lives in the 1930s and '40s are at the heart of Dickinson's . . . tale. Flashbacks told in alternating chapters by Lucy Vereker, the third daughter, and her lover Paul Ackerley, now near the end of their lives, describe events that culminated in the 1956 fire that destroyed the house, an event that each one thought the other may have, in different ways, engineered. The fire covered up evidence about the death—accident, suicide or murder?—of Gerry Grantworth, the eldest daughter's husband." Publ Wkly

"Like the labyrinthine route one must take to the Yellow Room, the resolution of the mystery is lengthy and winding and delightfully disorienting." N Y Times Book Rev

Dicks, Matthew

Memoirs of an imaginary friend; Matthew Dicks. 1st ed. St. Martin's Press 2012 314 p. (hardcover) $24.99
ISBN 125000621X; 9781250006219; 9781250024008

LC 2012028234

In this novel by Matthew Dicks "imaginary friend Budo . . . thinks constantly of the day when eight-year-old Max Delaney will stop believing in him. When that happens, Budo will disappear. . . . Some people say that [Max] has Asperger's Syndrome, but most just say he's 'on the spectrum.' . . . [When] Mrs. Patterson, the woman who works with Max in the Learning Center . . . kidnaps Max, it is up to Budo and a team of imaginary friends to save him." (Publisher's note)

Dicks, Matthew

Unexpectedly, Milo; a novel. Broadway Books 2010 344p pa $14.99
ISBN 9780307592309 pa; 0307592308 pa

LC 2010-11082

When obsessive-compulsive geriatric nurse Milo Shade "isn't able to make it to a bowling alley where he can bowl a strike or to a karaoke bar to sing '99 Luftballons' in German, he'll dip into his emergency stash of grape jelly jars and get some fast relief by popping their pressure caps. But keeping his increasingly irrational needs a secret from his wife has put such a strain on their marriage that Milo is currently living on his own. The chance discovery of a video camera and a set of confessional tapes made by a woman who has long held herself responsible for the disappearance and probable death of a childhood friend inspires Milo to put his O.C.D. to better use by tracking down the lost friend. The methodical ways he has adopted in pursuit of his weird impulses make Milo a good detective." N Y Times Book Rev

Didion, Joan

A book of common prayer. Simon & Schuster 1977 272p
ISBN 0-671-22491-3

LC 76-50067

Didion's "exposition of situations and details adroitly conceals their significance—until much later their meaning flares before our eyes. This is a remarkably good novel." Newsweek

Didion, Joan

The **last** thing he wanted. Knopf 1996 227p
ISBN 0-679-43331-7

LC 96-17084

"There's an animating tension in Didion's fiction between her achingly sure control as storyteller and stylist and the numbing vagueness of the people she depicts. . . . Didion's novels are thus simultaneously lucid and surreal." New Yorker

Didion, Joan

★ **Play** it as it lays; a novel. Farrar, Straus & Giroux 1970 214p

"Using a phrenetic millieu of drugs, pills, sexual aberrancy, Didion elliptically etches the self-destructive life of Maria Wyeth. Didion with authorial legerdemain skillfully controls the suspense as Maria dangerously exists: she cannot relate and adjust. Her father has told her life was a crap game and to play it as it lays, not the hard way. But Maria plays it the hardest way, trying to anesthetize herself against pain (almost everyone, anything) and pleasure (Kate, her neurally damaged child), and trying to lose herself in the dead-end life around her." Choice

Diehl, William

Primal fear. Villard Bks. 1993 418p
ISBN 0-679-40211-X

LC 92-5728

"Taking the best elements of horror fiction, the psychological thriller, and the legal novel, best-selling author Diehl concocts an especially exciting chiller. . . . The ending may not hold up under a psychiatrist's professional scrutiny, but the general reader will find it an immensely successful finis!." Booklist

Diehl, William

Reign in hell. Ballantine Bks. 1997 437p
ISBN 0-345-41144-7

LC 97-18214

"Illinois state attorney general Vail is called upon by President Lawrence Pennington to seek a trial case against one of the largest militia outfits in the country. The leader of this outfit, Gen. Joshua Engstrom, just happens to be an old adversary of the president, putting Vail in the middle of a dangerous situation. Vail must also relive the past when unwillingly faced with his nemesis from years ago, serial killer Aaron Stampler, who has now become blind Brother Transgression. The meshing of these storylines is intricate yet easily followed as the tension mounts." Libr J

Diehl, William

Show of evil. Ballantine Bks. 1995 483p
ISBN 0-345-37535-1

LC 94-24112

"Defense attorney-turned-district attorney Martin Vail comes to regret having saved a murderer, Aaron Stampler, from the death penalty; Stampler wasn't suffering from multiple personality disorder but was merely a vicious killer who has many more scores to settle. When Stampler proves smart enough to convince an egotistical psychiatrist that he is now sane and can return to society, Vail has to out-think him to save not only his own life but the lives of everyone who contributed to the killer's ten years in a mental institution. The action is gripping, and the characters are well drawn." Libr J

Dierbeck, Lisa

One pill makes you smaller. Farrar, Straus & Giroux 2003 312p $24
ISBN 0-374-22649-0

LC 2002-44675

"This unsettling and disorienting—but also deliciously pop—account of deplorable actions and shattered innocence is a tour de force, a meshing of the myths of the counterculture with the fantastic universe of Lewis Carroll. It's a genuinely original, compulsively readable first novel, sure to stir up controversy." Publ Wkly

Dietrich, William

The **Barbed** Crown; An Ethan Gage Adventure. William Dietrich. HarperCollins 2013 368 p. (hardcover) $26.99
ISBN 0062194070; 9780062194077

In this novel, by William Dietrich, "the sixth tale of rogue and adventurer Ethan Gage . . ., our hero returns to Paris and London. . . . Gage plots revenge on Napoleon Bonaparte for the kidnap of his son. . . . While Ethan spies on the French court, his wife, Astiza, works to sabotage Napoleon's coronation using the Crown of Thorns, a legendary relic said to have come from the Crucifixion itself." (Publisher's note)

Diffenbaugh, Vanessa

The **language** of flowers; Vanessa Diffenbaugh. Ballantine Books 2011 322 p. $25
ISBN 978-0-345-52554-3; 0-345-52554-X; 9780345525567

LC 201051026

The book tells the story of orphan "Victoria [who] was placed with a woman named Elizabeth, on a picturesque Napa vineyard. . . . Unable to trust her turn of luck, the furious little girl tried to sabotage her new situation. . . . But Elizabeth refused to be baited, offering consequences but not ultimatums, making it clear that no matter what, Victoria was there to stay. . . . But something went terribly wrong. We meet the girl as she walks away from her last group home, only to unfurl her sleeping bag at a park on Potrero Hill, scrounge leftovers off cafe tables and begin a job search, with no diploma or work experience. . . . In chapters taking us back to the past, we learn that although Victoria failed at school, Elizabeth recognized that she was bright and curious, and taught her everything about the grapes and the flowers on her vineyard. . . . As an adult, Victoria . . . serendipitously find[s] work at an upscale flower shop." (SFGate)

"After more than 32 homes, 18-year-old Victoria Jones, abandoned as a baby, has given up on the idea of love or family. Scarred, suspicious and defiant, she has nothing: no friends, no money, just an attitude, an instinct for flowers and an education in their meaning from Elizabeth, the one kind foster parent who persevered with her. Now graduating out of state care, Victoria must make her own way and starts out by sleeping rough in a local San Francisco park. But a florist gives her casual work and then, at a flower market, she meets Grant, Elizabeth's nephew, another awkward soul who speaks the language of flowers. Diffenbaugh narrates

Victoria and Grant's present-day involvement, over which the cloud of the past hangs heavy, in parallel with the history of Elizabeth's foster care, which we know ended badly. . . . An unusual, overextended romance, fairy tale in parts but with a sprinkling of grit." Kirkus

Dillard, Annie

The **Maytrees**; a novel. HarperCollinsPublishers 2007 216p $24.95

ISBN 978-0-06-123953-3; 0-06-123953-4

LC 2006-52599

"The good news is that in The Maytrees, despite the big words and the name-dropping . . . there is also good old straight narrative and prose that is often, yes, breathtakingly illuminative." N Y Times Book Rev

Dinesen, Isak

★ **Seven** Gothic tales; with an introduction by Dorothy Canfield. Modern Lib. 1994 422p

ISBN 0-679-60086-8

LC 91-50030

First published 1934 by H. Smith and analyzed in Short story index

"Distinguished by a romantic style and an aura of mystery, these tales of nineteenth-century aristocratic life in northern Europe remain favorites of a wide audience. A major plot device in some stories is the revealing of illegitimacy (sometimes of legitimacy), while a strong element of the supernatural is to be found in others." Shapiro. Fic for Youth. 3d edition

Dinesen, Isak

Winter's tales. Random House 1942 313p

Contents: The sailor-boy's tale; The young man with the carnation; The pearls; The invincible slaveowners; The heroine; The dreaming child; Alkmene; The fish; Peter and Rosa; Sorrow-acre; A consolatory tale

Disch, Thomas M.

The **wall** of America. Tachyon Publications 2008 245p pa $14.95

ISBN 978-1-892391-82-7; 1-892391-82-1

"Decrying but not despairing, this collection of 19 later short pieces by author and poet Disch (1940-2008) lovingly tears into the realities and fantasies of American life. . . . Though sometimes light and slight, these tales show Disch at his masterful, acerbic best." Publ Wkly

Disch, Thomas M.

Word of God: or, Holy writ rewritten. Tachyon 2008 180p $14.95

ISBN 978-1-892391-77-3; 1-892391-77-5

"The book is a memoir and a novel at the same time; spoof and jeremiad; reportage and alternate-world fantasy; the confessional chrestomathy of a lonely man and the card sharpery of a devilish fine grinning God guy, all at the same time. It is a parable of the making of the work of art; it is the work of art." Sci Fi Wkly

Dische, Irene

The **Empress** of Weehawken. Farrar, Straus and Giroux 2007 307p $24

ISBN 978-0-374-29912-5; 0-374-29912-9

LC 2006--101574

"Incredibly witty, beautifully written. . . 'The Empress of Weehawken' is a potent stew of class, sex and religion, as well as cultural and generational clashes, and Dische crafts a glorious misanthrope in her fictionalized version of her grandmother." Newark Star-Ledger

Disher, Garry

★ **Wyatt.** Soho Crime 2011 313p $25

ISBN 978-1-56947-962-9

LC 2011-13484

"With an uncanny ability to hide in plain sight, master thief Wyatt Wareen . . . slips calmly and silently through the streets of Melbourne, Australia. No one—including law enforcement—ever notices or remembers his presence. This calculated anonymity, along with Wyatt's preference for taking low-risk jobs and working alone, has fostered his underworld success. But when he changes his usual MO to join an old contact and his ex-wife on a lucrative jewel heist, the job takes an ugly turn that puts them all at risk. . . . Disher's depiction of Melbourne's underworld is a revelation—undeniably lurid and harsh yet humming with a vibrancy that lends a soulful note to the story. . . . [The author] excels at capturing the complexity and tension of life on the run, and his characters exude a visceral energy as they compete to survive." Libr J

Divakaruni, Chitra Banerjee, 1956-

★ **Oleander** girl; a novel. by Chitra Banerjee Divakaruni. Free Press 2013 304 p. (hardcover) $24

ISBN 1451695659; 9781451695656

LC 2012025671

In this novel, by Chitra Banerjee Divakaruni, "the wild and headstrong Korobi Roy has enjoyed a privileged childhood with her adoring grandparents. . . . However, a sudden heart attack kills Korobi's grandfather, revealing serious financial problems and a devastating secret about Korobi's past. Shattered by this discovery and by her grandparents' betrayal, Korobi decides to undertake a courageous search across post-9/11 America to find her true identity." (Publisher's note)

"Divakaruni... introduces a cast of characters who defy their stereotypes... [and] has crafted a beautiful, complex story in which caste, class, religion, and race are significant factors informing people's world views." LJ

Dixon, Keith

The **art** of losing. St. Martin's Press 2007 243p $24.95

ISBN 978-0-312-35868-6; 0-312-35868-7

LC 2006-50972

"New York City filmmaker Mike Jacobs is so tired of being broke that it seems like a good idea when his friend and producer, Sebby Laslo, suggests they strike it rich by fixing a horse race. Sebby enlists two jockeys to do the heavy lifting, but Mike will have to place the bets with a string of shady bookmakers because Sebby has run out of credit.

First, he needs to establish his credentials by losing a few bets—that's the easy part. The hard part comes when the horses who are supposed to win the fixed race collide and fall en route to the big payoff. One jockey is left paralyzed, the other is overcome by a need to confess, and Mike is left holding the bag for thousands in debts that he has no way of repaying. Just to survive, he'll need to do things he wouldn't have thought himself capable of doing, but he does them all the same. It is a descent into darkness that can only end in calamity, but the reader, swept up in the narrative momentum, can no more look away than Mike can avoid damnation, if not death. Dixon has written a cautionary tale that is not easy to enjoy but even harder to forget." Booklist

Dixon, Stephen
✓ **Frog**. British Am. Pub. 1991 769p
ISBN 0-945167-43-1; 0-945167-41-5 pa
LC 91-12639
"'Frog' is a narrative that leaps forward and lands sideways and flops over backward, croaking in dissonant pitches from chapter to chapter and contradicting itself whenever it pleases. . . . [The book], though billed as a novel, looks very much like a crazy quilt of short stories. Does that matter? Surprisingly, not very much. For no reader can fail to grasp that these often mutually exclusive scenarios for the family of a writer called Howard Tetch convey the jumpy landscape of that writer's mind." N Y Times Book Rev

Dixon, Stephen
I; a novel. McSweeney's Books 2002 338p $18
ISBN 0-9719047-07-0
"Reading this novel made up of interlinked stories can feel like being trapped in a small room with someone who insists on telling you every damn thing that crosses his mind. I., the hero, is an older writer stuck in a life that seems increasingly hard to endure: his wife is chronically ill, his two daughters find him difficult at best, and he is often gripped by an unfocussed and uncontrollable anger. But from this grim material emerges a moving and oddly funny book, as I. takes refuge in reveries of the past, recounting stories of Thanksgiving Day parades, meals in Paris, family quarrels, and the courtship of his wife. He also imagines myriad scenarios that might have happened but didn't; these unlived possibilities underscore the contingency of even our deepest relationships, and the ways in which we can be haunted by the alternatives." New Yorker
Followed by: End of I (2006)

Dixon, Stephen
✓ ★ **Interstate**; a novel. Holt & Co. 1995 374p
ISBN 0-8050-2654-1
LC 94-40174
In this novel, "eight narratives are alternative replays of a . . . moment that transpires in the book's opening pages: an act of random violence in which a man [Nathan Frey]and his two daughters are shot at by punks in a passing van, and one of the girls is killed." Libr J

Dixon, Stephen
Old friends; a novel. Melville House Pub 2004 220p $22.95
ISBN 0-9749609-2-6
LC 2004-16101

"Dixon follows the lives of two writers from the time they meet as young men until late middle age. Neither Irv nor Leonard has achieved any great fame, and though there's a good deal of writerly chatter, it's really background music to the story of the daily struggles of two aging men and their families. Their lives are tragic, but not dramatically so—Leonard slowly fades into Lyme disease-induced dementia while Irv is busy caring for his crippled wife. What makes this book so good is Dixon's ability to invent characters just average enough that readers can identify with the banality of their pain." Publ Wkly

Dobyns, Stephen, 1941-
✓ The **burn** palace; Stephen Dobyns. Blue Rider Press 2013 480 p. $26.95
ISBN 0399160876; 9780399160875
LC 2012028038
In this novel by Stephen Dobyns "a baby is stolen from a local hospital and a huge striped snake put in the bassinet in its place. . . . Meanwhile, packs of murderous coyotes make increasingly daring attacks on the townspeople. Most disturbing of all, locals begin coming forward with stories of strange rituals in the woods. . . . It takes the help of young Hercel McGarity Jr., a 10-year-old who may possess . . . magical powers, to give the people of Brewster a chance to defend themselves." (Publisher's note)

Dobyns, Stephen, 1941-
Saratoga strongbox; a Charlie Bradshaw mystery. Viking 1998 198p $21.95
ISBN 0-670-87692-5
LC 98-2886
This Bradshaw racetrack adventure "begins when his sometime partner, Vic Plotz, agrees to pick up a mysterious suitcase in Montreal for a wealthy Saratoga entrepreneur. Ex-cop Charlie is soon investigating an assortment of strange characters, looking for a murderer." Libr J
"Dobyns keeps a grip on his farcical plot and gives his rambunctious characters plenty of room to win, place and show off." N Y Times Book Rev

Doctorow, Cory
✓ **Down** and out in the Magic Kindgom. TOR Bks. 2003 208p $22.95
ISBN 0-7653-0436-8
LC 2002-73277
"Jules, a relative youngster at more than a century old, is a contented citizen of the Bitchun Society that has filled Earth and near-space since shortage and death were overcome. . . . What Jules wants to do is move to Disney World, join the ad-hoc crew that runs the park and fine-tune the Haunted Mansion ride to make it even more wonderful. When his prudently stored consciousness abruptly awakens in a cloned body, he learns that he was murdered; evidently he's in the way of somebody else's dreams. . . . Doctorow has served up a nicely understated dish: meringue laced with caffeine." Publ Wkly

Doctorow, Cory
Overclocked; stories of the future present. Thunder's Mouth Press 2007 285p pa $15.95
ISBN 978-1-56025-981-7; 1-56025-981-7

"As these stories illustrate, [Doctorow] has a knack for identifying those seminal trends of our current landscape that will in all likelihood determine the shape of our future(s). Add in a recursive affection for past landmarks of SF . . . , and a gentle empathy for the underdogs in such scenarios, and you get a winning narrative and ideational combination." Sci Fi Wkly

Doctorow, Cory

Rapture of the nerds; Cory Doctorow and Charles Stross. Tor 2012 349 p.

ISBN 0765329107; 9780765329103; 9781429944915
LC 2012019450

This novel, by Cory Doctorow and Charles Stross, takes places "at the dusk of the twenty-first century. . . . [T]here's Tech Jury Service: random humans . . . charged with assessing dozens of new inventions and ruling on whether to let them loose. Young Huw, a technophobic, misanthropic Welshman, has been selected, . . . a task he does his best to perform despite an itchy technovirus, the apathy of the proletariat, and a couple of truly awful moments on bathroom floors." (Publisher's note)

Doctorow, E. L.

All the time in the world; new and selected stories. Random House 2011 277p $26

ISBN 978-1-4000-6963-7
LC 2010-42500

"In the preface to his new book, [Doctorow] reiterates a position he has advocated many times: 'You write to find out what you're writing.' . . . . The surprises in this book come at you as slaps on the back of the head. Even while the plots make the surprises seem inevitable the moment you see them, you have to imagine Doctorow's own shock and relief that the story has come so far from its premise. You can only imagine it, though, because the writer and his agenda are nowhere to be found. At the emotional heights of this book, you communicate less with Doctorow than with the presiding god of the world of the story. Doctorow is only the medium. The effect is egoless, frank, spontaneous and altogether wonderful." San Francisco Chron

Doctorow, E. L.

★ **Billy** Bathgate; a novel. Random House 1989 323p

ISBN 0-394-52529-9
LC 88-42820

This is the "story of Billy's education, conducted on an extravagant scale. Doctorow brings a nice sense of moral ambiguity and creates characters who develop or deteriorate at an appropriate pace. His fecund run-on sentences are a pleasure to read. It all adds up to that rarity: a formal literary work that's also hugely entertaining." Newsweek

Doctorow, E. L.

★ The **book** of Daniel; a novel. Random House 1971 303p

ISBN 0-394-46271-8

"The trial of Julius and Ethel Rosenberg in 1950-51 for espionage was a cause célèbre during the fifties. The justice of administering the death penalty to that pair is still argued, particularly by the sons of the Rosenbergs. In this novel,

which is based on that case, Daniel Isaacson tells of the effect of that execution on his childhood, marriage, and career. The whole period of pre-World War II radicalism, the tyranny of the McCarthy era, the peace march on the Pentagon in 1967, the nature of left-wing politics in the United States are the elements that make this a provocative sociopolitical novel." Shapiro. Fic for Youth. 3d edition

Doctorow, E. L.

City of God; a novel. Random House 2000 272p

ISBN 0-679-44783-0
LC 99-53215

"In fall 1999, a brass cross disappears from St. Timothy's Episcopal Church in Manhattan and reappears at an Upper West Side synagogue, forcing clergy deep into a religious mystery." Libr J

Doctorow, E. L.

Homer & Langley; a novel. Random House 2009 208p $26

ISBN 978-1-4000-6494-6; 1-4000-6494-5
LC 2009-06959

"Toward the end of E.L. Doctorow's novel 'Homer & Langley,' narrator Homer Collyer, the real-life Manhattanite notorious for his and his brother Langley's reclusive lifestyle and hoarding of sundry objects, frets about their legacy: 'For what could be more terrible than being turned into a mythic joke? How could we cope, once dead and gone, with no one available to reclaim our history?' In attempting to recover the Collyer brothers' history from those who would reduce their existence to eccentricities, Doctorow probes the inner workings of the brothers' minds and extends their lives well beyond 1947, when the real Collyers died." San Antonio Express-News

"Cunningly panoramic. . . . Doctorow has packed this tale with episodes of existential wonder that capture the brothers in all their fascinating wackiness." Elle

Doctorow, E. L.

Loon Lake. Random House 1980 258p

ISBN 0-394-50691-X
LC 79-5526

"Doctorow has written a myth about the inheritance of America. Many techniques enhance the epic feeling. The novel is set in 1936, yet ranges across the first half of the century, even as it shifts viewpoints from the young man's memories to the poet's verses." Books of the Times

Doctorow, E. L.

The **march**. Random House 2005 363p $25.95

ISBN 0-375-50671-3
LC 2005-46452

"The march in question is that of General William Tecumseh Sherman and his Union soldiers as they slash and burn their way through Georgia and the Carolinas, and the 'march to freedom' as liberated slaves fall in step with the liberating army. But it is also, given the poetic depth of Doctorow's vision, the great march of time and of humanity in all its cruelty and glory. As Doctorow dramatizes the fury, conviction, and chaos of the Civil War, he portrays historical figures, as he is wont to do, most electrifyingly Sherman himself. But he focuses most on brilliantly imagined characters who embody the epic conflicts of that cataclysmic era, including Pearl, the smart and courageous daughter of a slave and slave owner; an excessively clinical military surgeon; the valiant daughter of a Southern judge; a freed slave who becomes a war photographer; and Arly, a scheming Rebel soldier who provides shrewdly comic relief. Doctorow writes with blazing clarity about the 'brutal romance' of war and its gruesome realities, with lyrical splendor about nature, and with wry wisdom and nimble satire about human folly." Booklist

Doctorow, E. L.

★ **Ragtime**. Modern Library 1997 320p $18.95
ISBN 0-679-60297-6

LC 97-42251

This is a reissue of the title first published in 1975 by Random House

"The lives of an upper-middle-class family in New Rochelle; a black ragtime musician who loses his love, his child, and his life because of bigotry; and a poor immigrant Jewish family are interwoven in this early-twentieth-century story. There are cameo appearances by wellknown figures of that period: Houdini, anarchist Emma Goldman, actress Evelyn Nesbit, Henry Ford, and J.P. Morgan, whose magnificent library plays an important part in the story. The book mingles fact and fiction in portraying the era of ragtime." Shapiro. Fic for Youth. 3d edition

Doctorow, E. L.

Sweet land stories. Random House 2004 147p $22.95
ISBN 1-400-06204-7

LC 2003-58780

"As one might expect of Doctorow, the title is ironic. In settings that range across the U.S., most of the alienated characters in the five stories here find life anything but sweet as they struggle to surmount the stigmas of poverty, lack of education and their instincts to gamble against the odds. . . . In this knowing treatment of the cynical abuse of power, Doctorow uses the spare, laconic style endemic to thrillers and builds suspense with sure strokes. Boring like a laser into the failures of the American dream, he captures the resilience of those who won't accept defeat." Publ Wkly

Doctorow, E. L.

The **waterworks**. Random House 1994 253p
ISBN 0-394-58754-5

LC 93-44735

"Martin Pemberton, renegade son of rich, unscrupulous Augustus Pemberton and favorite freelance of the persevering editor of the New York Telegram, . . . narrates this tale. First, Martin claims to have seen his dead father on a horse-drawn omnibus, and then he disappears. The worried editor contacts Inspector Edmund Donne—the only honest cop in 1870s New York, where the Tweed Ring holds sway—and eventually they discover that the ailing Augustus is part of an experiment by the brilliant Dr. Sartorius to prolong the lives of several old men rich enough to foot the bill." Libr J

Doctorow, E. L.

Welcome to Hard Times. Simon & Schuster 1960 180p

"A novel about a small town in the barren West at the close of the last century. . . . The tale revolves around a badman who destroys the town of Hard Times in one day, causally and cruelly; a mayor who is too weak to kill the badman but who is hopeful enough to rebuild the town; and a woman of easy virtue who waits, in terror and hatred, for the return of the bad-man." Springfield Repub

Docx, Edward

The **calligrapher**. Houghton Mifflin 2003 360p $24
ISBN 0-618-34397-0

LC 2003-51149

The novel's "protagonist, Jasper Jackson, is a Londoner whose current job is to transcribe the Songs and Sonnets of John Donne for a wealthy client. Like Donne, Jasper is also a relentless womanizer, a charming cad who lives for love affairs. When the woman of his dreams appears in his own garden, Jasper succumbs to real love for the first time and slowly begins to realize what it feels like to be the pursuer rather than the pursued." Publ Wkly

Docx, Edward

Pravda. Houghton Mifflin Co. 2007 395p pa $13.95
ISBN 978-0-618-53440-1; 0-618-53440-7

LC 2007-8523

Published in Great Britain with title: Self help

The author's "ability to evoke the atmosphere of a city is almost Dickensian. . . . Docx can place you within each heart-stopping moment, speed up and slow down time from one sentence to the next. . . . A gripping read that will engage, delight, and engross." Guardian (London)

Doenges, Judy

What she left me: stories and a novella. Middlebury College Press 1999 173p $22.95
ISBN 0-87451-937-3

LC 99-30945

"Marginal may be the best overall descriptor for these characters, who, whether working class or elite, and despite outward appearances, roil with inner turmoil. Certainly, the sad poignancy and the dark humor of their lives touch us deeply." Booklist

Doerr, Anthony

Memory wall; stories. Scribner 2010 243p $24
ISBN 1-4391-8280-9; 978-1-4391-8280-2

LC 2009-52245

This is a collection of six stories by the author of The Shell Collector (2002), About Grace (2004), and Four Seasons in Rome (2007).

"The characters in these six stories struggle to recall loved ones who are gone, or choose to bury their memories, or are displaced from their homes, left with nothing but memories. Such is Doerr's skill and sensitivity that he seems to be his characters' caretaker rather than their creator. It's as if he possesses a photographic memory of all of their lives, but as a discriminating photographer he knows exactly which pictures to include in the exhibition, and which to leave out, the whole more powerful through their absence." San Francisco Chron

Doerr, Harriet
Consider this, senora. Harcourt Brace & Co. 1993 241p

ISBN 0-15-193103-8

LC 93-21471

This "novel focuses on expatriate Americans in Mexico searching for love, connection and meaning. Three women buy land on the hillside hard by a poverty-stricken village whose inhabitants view them with gentle bewilderment." Publ Wkly

"Doerr instills each of her memorable characters with great dignity and resilience, and bestows upon her entranced readers a deep sense of peace and wonder." Booklist

Doerr, Harriet
★ **Stones** for Ibarra. Viking 1984 214p

ISBN 0-670-19203-1

LC 83-47861

"When Sara and Richard Everton pack up their belongings and mortgage themselves to leave California for a small village in Mexico, their friends think they are crazy. Many of the Mexican natives in the village of Ibarra also consider the two gringos incredible. While Sara restores the house that had belonged to Richard's grandparents, Richard restores a copper mine that had been his family's, and thereby gives employment to many of the villagers. We learn that Richard has leukemia and has been given just a few years to live, but it is the lives of the villagers that are more full of tragedy, religious commitment, and reliance on talismans and prayers. There is a strength among these people and an acceptance of all that life brings which make them memorable. Learning from them, perhaps, Sara finally accepts the inevitability of her husband's death." Shapiro. Fic for Youth. 3d edition

Doerr, Harriet
The **tiger** in the grass; stories and other inventions. Viking 1995 210p

ISBN 0-670-86471-4

LC 95-32391

"In this elegant collection of stories and 'inventions,' never before published in book form, Doerr opens the window on her own past: childhood in California, marriage, . . . child-rearing experiences and the bold decision to return to school after the death of her husband. These are revelatory tales full of tenderness, humor, and gratitude, but the jewels of the collection are Doerr's stories about life in Mexico, the place dearest to her heart." Booklist

Doetsch, Richard
Half-past dawn. Atria Books 2011 356 p.

ISBN 9781439183977; 143918397X; 1439183996; 9781439183991

LC 2011034027

In this story, "Jack Keeler, a district attorney for the city of New York, . . . wakes up one morning to an empty house. He has a stitched-up bullet wound on his chest and a bizarre tattoo covering his arm. Jack has no memory of what happened." After seeing a newspaper article describing a car crash in which he and his wife supposedly died, "Jack begins a desperate mission to restore his life and find answers to what has happened." (Miami Herald) Other elements of the story include "an Asian people out of legend, an assassin who will stop at nothing to avenge his death sentence, and a diary whose contents tell the future." (Publisher's note)

Doherty, P. C.
The **Anubis** slayings; a story of intrigue and murder set in ancient Egypt. St. Martin's Minotaur 2001 308p

ISBN 0-312-27658-3

First published 2000 in the United Kingdom

An historical mystery set in ancient Egypt "where principal judge Amertoke must solve a series of gruesome murders. It is 1497 B.C.E. and the Pharaoh Queen Hatusu (Hatshepsut) is in the process of consolidating power and taking over as ruler after her husband's death. She has just defeated the Mitanni, and formal peace negotiations are in progress. Someone wearing a jackal mask that resembles the god Anubis is poisoning people." Booklist

Doherty, P. C.
The **gates** of hell; a mystery of Alexander the Great. {by} Paul Doherty. Carroll & Graf Pubs. 2003 292p il $24

ISBN 0-7867-1157-4

This mystery revolves "around the military exploits of Alexander the Great and the behind-the-scenes adventures of Telamon, his boyhood friend and personal physician. When Alexander's determination to invade and conquer Halicarnassus, a city inextricably linked to his infamous father, is threatened by an unsettling series of murders within his own inner circle, Telamon must use his considerable powers of detection in order to uncover a treasonous plot linked to the legendary Pythian manuscript. Booklist

Doherty, P. C.
The **godless** man; a mystery of Alexander the Great. {by} Paul Doherty. Carroll & Graf Pubs. 2002 303p $25

ISBN 0-7867-0995-2

LC 2002-67397

"After his mighty victory at the Granicus in 334 B.C., Alexander the Great sweeps deeper into Persia in this multilayered and entertaining mystery, but when his army captures the city of Ephesus, the march of conquest seems doomed to halt in the face of intrigue and multiple murders." Publ Wkly

Doherty, P. C.
The **house** of death; a mystery of Alexander the Great. {by} Paul C. Doherty. Carroll & Graf Pubs. 2001 276p

ISBN 0-7867-0853-0

LC 2001-28828

"Anxious to dominate the Persian empire in 334 B.C.E., Alexander the Great awaits a sign from the gods. He instead finds intrigue, secret agendas, spies, and murder. The appearance of boyhood friend Telamon gives him a trusted ear—he hopes." Libr J

"Fans of ancient historical mysteries will find themselves in superbly practiced hands." Publ Wkly

Doherty, P. C.

The **Mysterium**; a Hugh Corbett medieval mystery. P.C. Doherty. Minotaur Books 2012 312 p.
ISBN 0312678193; 9780312678197; 9781429942409
LC 2012003259

In this murder mystery novel set in 1304 London, England, "[k]eeper of the Secret Seal Sir Hugh Corbett, problem solver for King Edward I, is tasked with solving several murders whose roots may lie deep in the past. Walter Evesham, Chief Justice in the Court of the King's Bench, has been accused of bribery and corruption. His attempts to atone for his sins at the Abbey of Syon are cut short when he's murdered in his locked cell." (Kirkus)

Doig, Ivan

★ The **bartender's** tale; Ivan Doig. Riverhead Books 2012 400 p. $27.95
ISBN 1594487359; 9781594487354
LC 2012017498

In this book, "[a]fter living half his life in Phoenix, Ariz., with his aunt, 12-year-old Russell 'Rusty' Harry comes back to the tiny town of Gros Ventre to live with his father, Tom, the owner of a popular saloon. . . . Rusty entertains himself in the cavernous back room, which Tom operates like a pawnshop." Soon, "12-year-old Zoe Constantine shows up and soon becomes Rusty's partner in crime in the backroom, listening to the bar through a concealed air vent." (Publishers Weekly)

Doig, Ivan

Bucking the sun; a novel. Simon & Schuster 1996 412p
ISBN 0-684-81171-5
LC 96-3814

The author "begins this saga with adultery and death, then moves backward to examine the causes. Just as the building of the mammoth Fort Peck Dam transforms the Montana countryside, it radically alters the lives of its Depression-era inhabitants. In particular, members of the Duff clan abandon subsistence farming and move to the construction boomtowns. There a father, three brothers, and their wives confront the task of building the largest earthen dam in the world, brave the dangers of such labor, and battle among themselves. . . . This richly detailed narrative offers comedy, passion, and adventure." Libr J

Doig, Ivan

★ **Dancing** at the Rascal Fair. Atheneum Pubs. 1987 405p
ISBN 0-689-11764-7
LC 87-18672

Chronologically the first in the author's Montana trilogy
"If the thorny individualism of Rob and Angus results in lives that are never easy, they are rich in incident and growth, beautifully described in Doig's strong, savory prose. America's frontier history comes vividly to life in this absorbing saga filled with memorable characters." Publ Wkly

Doig, Ivan

The **eleventh** man. Harcourt 2008 406p $26
ISBN 978-0-15-101243-5; 0-15-101243-1
LC 2008-10046

In this novel, "11 starters of a close-knit Montana college championship football team enlist as the U.S. hits the thick of WWII and are capriciously flung around the globe in various branches of the service. Ben Reinking, initially slated for pilot training, is jerked from his plane and more or less forced to become a war correspondent for the semi-secret Threshold Press War Project, a propaganda arm of the combined armed forces. His orders: to travel the world, visiting and writing profiles on each of his heroic teammates. The fetching Women's Airforce Service Pilot who flies him around, Cass Standish, is married to a soldier fighting in the South Pacific, which leads to anguish for them both . . . . Meanwhile, Ben's former teammates are being killed one by one, often, it seems, being deliberately put into harm's way. Doig adroitly keeps Ben on track, offering an old-fashioned greatest generation story, well told." Publ Wkly

Doig, Ivan

English Creek. Atheneum Pubs. 1984 339p
ISBN 0-689-11478-8
LC 84-45051

This volume in the Montana trilogy chronologically follows Dancing at the Rascal Fair
This "is a sensitive coming-of-age story as well as a portrait of a society still looking to its frontier past, but about to be engulfed by the future. The result is both highly personal and deeply engaging." Best Sellers

Doig, Ivan

Mountain time; a novel. Scribner 1999 316p
ISBN 0-684-83295-X
LC 99-14324

This novel focuses on "sisters Lexa and Mariah McCaskell. Lexa's marriage to a forest ranger and her days as cook in Alaska are behind her; now sturdy, capable Lexa runs a catering service in Seattle. She lives with rugged environmental journalist Mitch Rozier, another escapee from rough life in northern Montana. At 50, Mitch is facing a double crisis: the newspaper where his column appears is about to fold, and his foxy, rapacious father, Lyle, a notorious land despoiler, is dying of leukemia and has summoned him back to Twin Sulphur Springs. Lexa goes back to Montana, too, bringing her sexy sister, Mariah, just returned to the States after a year-long photographing expedition around the world. Lyle's illness and death unleash complex memories and future shocks." Publ Wkly
"A worthy addition to Doig's impressive saga of the twentieth-century West." Booklist

Doig, Ivan

Prairie nocturne; a novel. Scribner 2003 371p $26
ISBN 0-7432-0135-3
LC 2003-50385

"By multiplying, deepening and texturing the genealogy of the Two Medicine country in the course of six novels, Doig has staked his claim as one of Montana's essential literary witnesses. . . . And no other writer since A.B. Guthrie has been more determined to evoke the supersized grandeur of Big Sky country, especially in a time when it was emptier and more suited to mythologizing than it is today." Washington Post Book World

Doig, Ivan

Ride with me, Mariah Montana. Atheneum Pubs. 1990 324p

ISBN 0-689-12019-2

LC 90-35834

Concluding volume of the author's Montana trilogy

"To explore the meaning of Montana's century of statehood, 65-year-old Jick McCaskill, his photographer daughter Mariah, and her newspaper columnist ex-husband Riley Wright tour the Treasure State in Jick's Winnebago. While Riley writes on-the-scene dispatches and Mariah takes photos of the places they visit, Jick, the narrator, recounts the state's—and his family's—good and bad times. A lengthy picaresque with innumerable well-crafted vignettes, this leisurely novel could easily serve as a tour guide of Montana's historic places. As the miles go by, Riley and Mariah again fall in and out of love, and Jick, a widower, unexpectedly finds a new mate." Libr J

Doig, Ivan

The **whistling** season. Harcourt 2006 345p hardcover o.p. pa $14.95

ISBN 978-0-15-101237-4; 0-15-101237-7; 978-0-15-603164-6 pa; 0-15-603164-7 pa

LC 2005-25457

"Set in the early 1900s, this novel is a nostalgic, bittersweet story about a widower, his three sons, and the year these boys spend in a one-room country schoolhouse. The novel begins with the father, Oliver, hiring a widowed housekeeper named Rose from Minneapolis (her advertisement reads 'Can't Cook but Doesn't Bite'). She arrives with her unconventional brother, Morrie, in tow. Morrie is something of a scholar, and he soon finds himself pressed into service as a replacement teacher. During the course of the novel, these intriguing and unpredictable characters come together in surprising and uplifting ways. This is an affectionate, heartwarming tale that also celebrates a vanished way of life and laments its passing." Libr J

Doig, Ivan

Work song. Riverhead Books 2010 275p $25.95

ISBN 1594487626; 9781594487620; 978-1-59448-762-0; 1-59448-762-6

LC 2009-42647

This novel featuring Morrie Morgan, the hero of The Whistling Season (2006), depicts post-World War I Butte, Montana, in thrall to the Anaconda mining company.

This "sequel to The Whistling Season (2006) begins ten years later in 1919, when Morrie Morgan gets off the train in Butte, MT, "the richest hill on earth," run by Anaconda Copper. He settles into a boardinghouse run by the widow Grace and is befriended by her other boarders, Griff and Hoop, two retired miners who tell Morrie what's going on in town. Scholarly Morrie finds his niche at the public library, the domain of a crusty retired rancher named Sandison, who comes with the territory because the entire library is his own magnificent book collection. Before long, Morrie discovers he's being shadowed by Anaconda's thugs for being a strike agitator." Libr J

Doiron, Paul

Bad Little Falls; a novel. Paul Doiron. 1st ed. Minotaur Books 2012 310 p. ill. (hardcover) $24.99; (paperback) $14.99

ISBN 0312558481; 9780312558482; 9781250010919; 9781250031471

LC 2012007787

This is the "third novel from Edgar-finalist [Paul] Dorion featuring game warden Mike Bowditch." Bowditch has been transferred to Washington County, Maine "after he became an embarrassment to the powers-that-be by shooting a murderer in self-defense." His strict rule-following earns him enemies. One night during a blizzard, veterinarian Doc Larrabee "needs his help with a person suffering from a severe case of frostbite." Further, Bowditch must find the victim's lost partner. (Publishers Weekly)

Doiron, Paul

The **poacher's** son. Minotaur Books 2010 336p $24.99

ISBN 978-0-312-55846-8; 0-312-55846-5

LC 2009-41136

"Along with nostalgic laments about the old-growth woods and modest settlements that have already fallen to civilization, Doiron provides wonderful scenes of present-day bear-tracking and man-hunting through the kind of terrain that attracts hikers, hunters and the odd 'paranoid militia freak' like the one causing so much trouble in this story." N Y Times Book Rev

Dolan, Harry

Bad things happen. Amy Einhorn Books/G. P. Putman's Sons 2009 338p $24.95

ISBN 978-0-399-15563-5

LC 2008-54628

"Although the plot is fairly outlandish, the narrative comes with startling developments and nicely tricky reversals. There's also something appealingly offbeat about the wry, dry tone of its academic humor, which has much to do with the self-important authors who figure in the hectic plot." N Y Times Book Rev

Dolan, Harry

Very bad men. Amy Einhorn Books 2011 412p $25.95

ISBN 978-0-399-15749-3; 0-399-15749-2

LC 2011-06877

Sequel to: Bad things happen (2009)

"Anthony Lark's mission is simple: to kill three of the men involved in a fatally botched bank robbery 17 years ago. He's already dispatched two of his targets—an impressive feat, considering that one of them, Terry Dawtrey, is serving 30 years in Kinross Prison—when he identifies them both and announces his third, nurse practitioner Sutton Bell, in an anonymous letter to Loogan . . . , who promptly shares it with his ladylove, police detective Elizabeth Waishkey. The timely intervention of aspiring tabloid reporter Lucy Navarro saves Bell from Lark's initial attempt and gives Dolan a chance to fill in some back story. . . . Dolan mixes his pitches with an ace's judgment, steadily complicating Lark's quest while keeping the psychology of his characters considerably more plausible than in Loogan's equally baroque debut. The rare crime novel with something for everyone who reads crime fiction." Kirkus

Domingue, Ronlyn

The **mercy** of thin air; a novel. Ronlyn Domingue. Atria Books 2005 310 p.

ISBN 0743278801; 0743278828; 9780743278805

LC 2005045287

This book has "[t]wo strands: first the story of Razi Nolan, growing up in New Orleans in the 1920s, . . . set on breaking the comfortable family mould by making a career as a doctor. Then she falls in love with Andrew O'Connell and her plans become complicated. . . . [O]ne summer morning, she accidentally drowns. By choice, and from where she narrates, she stays between this world and the unknown; every memory of her life remains perfectly intact. More than seventy years later, Razi finds Andrew's once-treasured bookcase at a garage sale. She watches a young couple take it home, Amy and Scott, burdened with secrets of their own. As their . . . relationship unravels, Razi remembers her past with Andrew and how . . . he coped after her death." (Publisher's note)

Dominguez, Carlos Maria

The **house** of paper; illustrations by Peter Sís; translated from the Spanish by Nick Caistor. Harcourt 2005 103p il $18

ISBN 0-15-101147-8

LC 2005-02401

Original Spanish edition, 2004

The author has "written a wonderfully amusing account of how books can dominate the life of the inveterate collector. It is itself a small book, beautifully translated by Nick Caistor and charmingly illustrated by Peter Sis, and you may buy it without worrying about finding room for it on your shelves. I have already found such a place–between a copy of a novel by Italo Calvino and a collection of the stories of Dino Buzzati. It should be happy there, with its Italian cousins, a jewel of whimsy supported on each side by authors from roughly the same tradition." N Y Times Book Rev

Donaldson, Stephen R.

The **Illearth** war. Holt, Rinehart & Winston 1977 407p il (Chronicles of Thomas Covenant, the Unbeliever)

ISBN 0-03-022776-3

LC 77-8621

In this second volume, Lord Foul the Despiser continues his attack against the Land with the Illearth Stone. Covenant and the daughter of the High Lord, Elena, undertake a mission into a mountain region, where they hope they will find the ancient gnostic power that will combat the Stone

Donaldson, Stephen R.

Lord Foul's bane. Holt, Rinehart & Winston 1977 369p il (Chronicles of Thomas Covenant, the Unbeliever)

LC 77-73868

Thomas Covenant, a man burdened with a stigma that has isolated him, is suddenly sent to a mysterious magic world known as the Land. The Land has an immortal enemy—Lord Foul the Despiser—who wishes to destroy it. In

Thomas, who does not believe in the Land's life-restoring powers, Lord Foul thinks he has found the perfect tool for his purpose

Donaldson, Stephen R.

The **One** Tree. Ballantine Bks. 1982 475p (Chronicles of Thomas Covenant, the Unbeliever)

ISBN 0-345-29898-5

LC 81-17596

This is the central volume of the second trilogy about the Land

"Covenant finds that his role as savior of the Land must be shared with another from our world, Dr. Linden Avery. . . . To stop Lord Foul's terrible concatenation of plagues, the Sunbane, they sail with giants on a granite ship in search of the One Tree. Covenant hopes to fashion from it a new Staff of the Law to restore the natural order Foul has overturned." Publ Wkly

Donaldson, Stephen R.

The **power** that preserves. Holt, Rinehart & Winston 1977 379p il (Chronicles of Thomas Covenant, the Unbeliever)

ISBN 0-03-022781-X

LC 77-10814

In this final volume of the first trilogy Covenant makes his way to the stronghold of Lord Foul the Despiser. He is accompanied by his friend Saltheart Foamfollower, a Giant. But it is Covenant who must meet Foul in final combat, to ensure survival for the Land and to achieve salvation for himself

"Below the stirring adventure tale is a poignant and profoundly religious chronicle of a quest for self-esteem and peace." Booklist

Donaldson, Stephen R.

The **runes** of the earth. G.P. Putnam's Sons 2004 xx, 532p (Last chronicles of Thomas Covenant) $26.95

ISBN 0-399-15232-6

LC 2004-50526

"It is 10 years since Thomas Covenant's death, and Linden Avery runs the small mental hospital in which Covenant's widow, Joan, is confined. Roger Covenant, newly turned 21, visits Avery and tries to get his mother released. Failing at that, he kidnaps Joan as well as Avery's adopted son, then commits several murders and flees to the Land, the other world of Covenant sagas. Roger is clearly doing Lord Foul's bidding, and Avery has no choice but to follow him. She discovers that in the Land three and a half millennia have passed. The Haruchai are now called the Masters and distrust Earthpower, and an old man, Anele, who is full of Earthpower, is key to finding the lost and essential Staff of Law. . . . Expect readers to swarm." Booklist

Donaldson, Stephen R.

White gold wielder. Ballantine Bks. 1983 485p il (Chronicles of Thomas Covenant, the Unbeliever)

ISBN 0-345-30307-5

LC 82-20640

This is the concluding volume of the second trilogy about the Land

"At the end of 'The One Tree,' Covenant failed to create a new Staff of Law to deliver the Land from the Sunbane, so he, Linden Avery, and their companions set out across the northern wastes to Revelstone, where Covenant extinguishes the Banefire. The paradox of white gold and venom has set him against his friends, however; when he faces Lord Foul at Mount Thunder, they believe that he will betray the Land, until that enigmatic created being, Vain, achieves his destiny." Libr J

Donaldson, Stephen R.

The **wounded** Land. Ballantine Bks. 1980 497p il (Chronicles of Thomas Covenant, the Unbeliever)
ISBN 0-345-28647-2

LC 79-20644

This is the first volume of the second trilogy about the Land

"In the first of the second trilogy of his adventures, leper Thomas Covenant returns to the mysterious Land after nearly 4000 years have passed there (ten years in earth time). Dr. Linden Avery unexpectedly joins him and goes through the same denial and disbelief he had suffered before. Now the Land is suffering from unending plagues called the Sunbane, inflicted by the evil Lord Foul whom Covenant had defeated but not destroyed on his last visit. Although it is not necessary to have read the previous three to appreciate the breadth and scope of this grim fantasy, for those who have 'The Wounded Land' is absolutely compelling." SLJ

Donoghue, Emma

★ **Room**; a novel. Emma Donoghue. Little, Brown and Co. 2010 321p
ISBN 0316098337; 9780316098335

LC 2010006983

Alex Award (2011), CBA Libris Awards (Canadian Booksellers Association): Fiction Book of the Year (2011), Rogers Writers' Trust Fiction Prize (2010), Indies' Choice Book Awards: Adult Fiction (2011)

"The narrator of Emma Donoghue's 'Room' is a 5-year-old boy. . . . He and his mother have been trapped in the 11-by-11-foot room of the title since the day he was born." (N Y Times (Late N Y Ed))

"Though the story's chilling circumstances reflect the horrors endured by tabloid-famous abductees, Donoghue avoids all sensationalism. Instead, she gracefully distills what it means to be a mother — and what it's like for a child whose entire world measures just 11 x 11." Entertainment Wkly

Donoghue, Emma

The **sealed** letter. Harcourt 2008 396p $26
ISBN 978-0-15-101549-8; 0-15-101549-X

LC 2008-14677

Donoghue "has sifted through court records, newspapers, correspondence, and even Faithfull's later novels. She makes 150-year-old events immediate. . . . What could have been mere Victorian melodrama resonates here with emotional truth." Quill Quire

Donoghue, Emma

Slammerkin. Harcourt 2001 336p $30
ISBN 0-15-100672-5

LC 00-49867

First published 2000 in the United Kingdom

"In her storytelling, the author shrewdly alternates the point of view, a technique that, rather than feeling gratuitous and shticky as it so often does these days, works to put Mary in a delicious pickle, since the satisfaction of her deepest desires, and the revelation of her secret career, could crush those for whom she—and we—come to feel real affection." N Y Times Book Rev

Donoghue, Emma

Touchy subjects; stories. Harcourt 2006 280p $24
ISBN 978-0-15-101386-9; 0-15-101386-1

LC 2005-26170

Donoghue "exhibits adeptness in the short story form in this collection of 19 tales that, without a hint of pretension but with wisdom extending far beyond the placidness of her prose style, isolates aspects of a character or a moment of revelation for a character. . . . Her stories find secure footing where poignancy and humor intersect, and their geniality will prove an asset to librarians encouraging readers exclusively devoted to the novel to–come on–try some short stories." Booklist

Donohue, John J.

Sensei. Thomas Dunne Bks. 2003 258p $23.95
ISBN 0-312-28812-3

LC 2002-32507

"Someone who calls himself Ronin—masterless Samurai—is apparently killing off martial-arts masters across the U.S., and Connor Burke, a university professor and martial-arts student, is brought into the investigation by his brother, a New York detective assigned to the case. Connor recruits his own sensei, Yamshita, and this unusual pair uncover the facts with a combination of mental skill and good, old-fashioned (amateur) detective work." Booklist

Donohue, Keith

Angels of destruction; a novel. Shaye Areheart Books 2009 347p $24
ISBN 978-0-307-45025-8; 0-307-45025-2

LC 2008-21277

"One night in the middle of winter, widow Margaret Quinn hears a tiny rap on her door. To her surprise, she finds a 9-year-old girl shivering in the cold. She shuffles the child into her home and, soon enough, into her heart. Margaret has grown reclusive with the years. A decade earlier, in 1975, her daughter, Erica, ran off with a high school sweetheart to join a West Coast revolutionary group called Angels of Destruction. Not long after, her husband, Paul, died. . . . When the beguiling 9-year-old says she has no family and no home, Margaret's mind races. She names the girl Norah and decides to pass her off as a granddaughter. Norah is her conniving equal, and their bond deepens at breakneck speed. Enrolled in elementary school, Norah befriends a boy named Sean, whose father abandoned him and his mother. Naturally withdrawn, given the circumstances of his life, Sean warms to Norah, who quickly reveals — first to him and later to classmates and adults — ethereal displays of magic." Pittsburgh Post-Gazette

Donohue, Keith
Centuries of June; a novel. Crown 2011 342p $24
ISBN 978-0-307-45028-9; 0-307-45028-7
LC 2010-23574

This is "an episodic novel that's part ghost story, part psychological mystery and part vaudeville show. Think Scheherazade by way of 'Tristram Shandy' by way of 'The Sixth Sense.' . . . For all of its complexity and ambition, 'Centuries of June' captivates mostly in the small things, the little bits of textual and theatrical sleight-of-hand that Donohue pulls off without much apparent effort." Washington Post Book World

Donohue, Keith
The stolen child; a novel. Nan A. Talese 2006 319p hardcover o.p. pa $15
ISBN 0-385-51616-9; 1-4000-9653-7 pa
LC 2005-53828

"On the surface, Donohue may seem to have written a clever debut novel about fairies. But the real triumph of the book is that, while our backs were turned, he has performed a switch and delivered a luminous and thrilling novel about our humanity." Washington Post Book World

Donovan, Anne
Buddha Da. Carroll & Graf Publishers 2004 330p pa $14
ISBN 0-7867-1336-4 pa
LC 2004-45770

"The transcribed brogue and gag-rich premise initially lend Buddha Da a slapstick feel. But as Jimmy's engagement with Buddhism deepens, the novel matures into an astute exploration of Donovan's enormously appealing characters." N Y Times Book Rev

Donovan, Gerard
Young Irelanders; stories. Overlook Press 2008 223p $24.95
ISBN 978-1-59020-030-8

Donovan "writes convincingly about loss and survival in an Ireland where big gaps remain between what his characters want and what they have." Publ Wkly

Doolittle, Sean
Lake country; a novel. Sean Doolittle. Bantam Books Trade Paperbacks 2012 322 p. (paperback) $15.00
ISBN 9780345532145; 9780345533920
LC 2011040262

This novel by Sean Doolittle tells the story of "an ex-marine named Darryl Potter. . . . Five years ago, successful architect Wade Benson killed a young woman when he fell asleep at the wheel. . . . Potter sets out to even the score by kidnapping Benson's twenty-year-old daughter. It's a bad, bad plan, and only Mike Barlowe, Potter's former combat buddy, knows how to stop it. . . . Barlowe races to head off his troubled friend before innocent people get hurt." (Publisher's note)

Dorris, Michael
Cloud chamber; a novel. Scribner 1997 316p
ISBN 0-684-81567-2
LC 96-42544

"Though not unflawed—a few voices sound confusingly similar and a few characters are more types than people— this is a compellingly readable and emotionally satisfying novel, full of secrets and surprises." Booklist

Dorris, Michael
The crown of Columbus; a novel. {by} Michael Dorris, Louise Erdrich. HarperCollins Pubs. 1991 382p
ISBN 0-06-016079-9
LC 90-55964

"Told in the very different voices of college professor lovers Vivian Twostar, Native American single mother, and Roger Williams, poet of an old New England family, the collaborative effort flows smoothly. Although estranged during Vivian's pregnancy, both are working on academic projects concerning the 500th anniversary of the discovery of North America by Columbus. The collision of their two lives is funny, vivid, and life-affirming." Libr J

Dorris, Michael
★ A yellow raft in blue water. Holt & Co. 1987 343p hardcover o.p. pa $14
ISBN 0-8050-0045-3; 0-312-42185-0 pa
LC 86-26947

"The bitter rifts and inevitable bonds between generations are highlighted as a teenaged daughter, mother, and grand matriarch of an American Indian family tell their life stories. Humorous and poignant, with unique characters." SLJ

Dorst, Doug
Alive in Necropolis. Riverhead Books 2008 437p $25.95
ISBN 978-1-594-48987-7; 1-594-48987-4
LC 2008-05817

"Like Dashiell Hammett, Dorst conveys a hard-bitten love of the physical San Francisco, the fog-swallowed town, the sun after rain, the mineshaft drops in temperature. Scenes are rooted in surroundings and the weather. The fiction seems to possess, and be possessed by, its beloved Bay. . . . The ghosts are a prime pleasure here. The prose picks up a quickness in their presence. They are figures out of newsreels, colorful, iconic." N Y Times Book Rev

Dorst, Doug
The surf guru; stories. Riverhead Books 2010 288p $25.95
ISBN 978-1-59448-761-3; 1-59448-761-8
LC 2010-08995

"All of Dorst's stories brim with gumption. They're fun-loving, testosterone-rich yarns. And while his book is an amalgam of voices, moods, styles and forms . . . the stories speak to an important literary pursuit: that of pushing limits, of embracing challenge, no matter the gharials at your toes." N Y Times Book Rev

Dos Passos, John

1919. Harcourt Brace & Co. 1932 473p

In this second volume of the trilogy, the author continues his chronicle of life in America through the war years, giving glimpses of the lives and characters of five young Americans—a low caste sailor, the daughter of a Chicago minister, a young girl from Texas, a radical Jew, a young poet

"'1919' is literally what so many books are erroneously called, 'a slice of life.' With infinite skill that slicing is done by the author, and the raw surface which meets the reader's eye is the actual living, breathing record of a period in its most intense manifestation." Chicago Daily Trib

Followed by The big money (1936)

Dos Passos, John

The **42nd** parallel. Harper 1930 426p

First volume of the author's U.S.A. trilogy

The characters "include Fainy McCreary ('Mac'), who eventually joins the Mexican Revolution; the ruthless J. Ward Moorehouse; Eleanor Stoddard, with whom he has an affair; and Charley Anderson, who later becomes a war hero and airplane manufacturer. These various interlocking strands are designed to show the U.S. on the eve of the First World War, rather than the development of particular individuals." Reader's Ency. 3d edition

Followed by 1919

Dos Passos, John

Manhattan transfer. Harper 1925 404p

"Dos Passos creates a portrait of New York City in the first quarter of this century by telling the stories of many people. They include the daughter of an accountant, who loses hope for any future happiness when her first love commits suicide; a milkman who rises in status to become a union boss; and an immigrant sailor who starts as a bartender and becomes a wealthy bootlegger during Prohibition. There are happy and unhappy endings to these stories, but always the city plays an important role." Shapiro. Fic for Youth. 3d edition

Dos Passos, John

★ **Novels,** 1920-1925. Library of America 2003 873p (The library of America) $35

ISBN 1-931082-39-1

LC 2003-47529

One man's initiation, 1917 (1920) focuses on a young American's experiences in France during a time of war. Three soldiers (1921) describes the lives of three men with three different backgrounds—an Indiana farmboy, an Italian-American store clerk, and a musician hoping to become a composer—and how they cope with life both on and off the battlefield. Manhattan transfer is entered separately.

Dos Passos, John

★ **U.S.A.** Library of Am. 1996 1288p $40

ISBN 1-883011-14-0

LC 95-49282

An omnibus volume containing the trilogy titles: The 42nd parallel, first published 1930; 1919, first published 1932 and The big money, first published 1936

"U.S.A. tries to capture, through a diversity of fictional techniques, the variety and multiplicity of American life in the first decades of the 20th cent.; it presents various interlocking and parallel narratives, against a panoramic collage of real-life events, snatches of newsreel and popular song, advertisements, etc., with a commentary by the author as 'The Camera Eye.'" Oxford Companion to Engl Lit

Doss, James D.

The **night** visitor; a shaman mystery. Avon Twilight 1999 392p

ISBN 0-380-97721-4

LC 99-25049

Ute lawman Charlie Moon and Shaman Daisy Perika are featured in this "blend of modern murder and ancient beliefs, set on the Southern Ute Reservation in Colorado. Charlie investigates a murder associated with a paleontological dig, while Daisy senses a much older injustice. An excellent addition to the series." Libr J

Doss, James D.

The **old** gray wolf; James D. Doss. Minotaur Books 2012 344 p. (hardcover) $25.99

ISBN 0312613717; 9780312613716; 9781250018090

LC 2012035880

In this novel by James D. Doss, part of the Charlie Moon Mysteries series, "former police officer . . . and current rancher Charlie Moon and Chief of Police Scott Parris didn't mean for things to get out of hand, but the purse-snatching LeRoy Hooten left them with little choice when he made a run for it. When Hooten dies due to his injuries . . . the dead man's mother--a widow to a brutal mobster--wastes no time making a call to an old associate to settle the score." (Publisher's note)

Doss, James D.

The **shaman's** bones. Avon Bks. 1997 276p

ISBN 0-380-97424-X

LC 96-52148

"Even though Ute police officer Charlie Moon's elderly aunt, a well-known visionary and shaman, warns him of impending violence on the Colorado reservation, he is ill prepared for what happens. Events begin with an Indian's bad check but escalate to child abandonment, a vicious attack on a female police trainee, murder, and the theft of another shaman's sacred objects. Doss uses setting and atmosphere to heighten the mystical aspects of his subject and astute characterization to enforce its credibility." Libr J

Dostoyevsky, Fyodor

The **best** short stories of Dostoevsky; translated with an introduction by David Magarshack. Modern Lib. 1992 xxvii, 348p

ISBN 0-679-60020-5

LC 92-50214

First Modern Library edition 1955

Contents: White nights; The honest thief; The Christmas tree and a wedding; The peasant Marey; Notes from the underground; A gentle creature; The dream of a ridiculous man

Dostoyevsky, Fyodor

★ The **brothers** Karamazov; translated by Constance Garnett. Modern Library 1996 xxi, 880p $21

ISBN 0-679-60181-3

Written 1880

"The main plot involves Fyodor Pavlovich 'Karamazov' and his four sons: Dmitry, Ivan, Alyosha, and the bastard Smerdyakov. Fyodor Pavlovich, a depraved buffoon, is Dmitry's rival for the affections of the local siren, Grushenka, despite her checkered past and blemished reputation. Fyodor Pavlovich is a model of animation and irrationalism, who enjoys his depravity and is only encouraged by the shock and disapproval of others. After violent quarrels over Grushenka and over Dmitry's disputed inheritance, Fyodor Pavlovich is murdered. Dmitry is arrested and brought to trial for the crime. This basic line of action is complicated throughout the novel by a host of other factors masterfully linked to the main plot. . . . The literal, religious, social, and ethical levels of the novel are buttressed by the psychological probings for which Dostoyevsky is well known." Reader's Ency. 4th edition

Dostoyevsky, Fyodor

★ **Crime** and punishment; translated from the Russian by Constance Garnett; with an introduction by Ernest J. Simmons. Modern Library 1994 xxiv, 629p $19.95

ISBN 0-679-60100-7

Written 1866

"The novel is a psychological analysis of the poor student Raskolnikov, whose theory that humanitarian ends justify evil means leads him to murder a St. Petersburg pawnbroker. The act produces nightmarish guilt in Raskolnikov. The narrative's feverish, compelling tone follows the twists and turns of Raskolnikov's emotions and elaborates his struggle with his conscience and his mounting sense of horror as he wanders the city's hot, crowded streets. In prison, Raskolnikov comes to the realization that happiness cannot be achieved by a reasoned plan of existence but must be earned by suffering." Merriam-Webster's Ency of Lit

Dostoyevsky, Fyodor

The **gambler**; translated by Constance Garnett; edited, with an introduction and notes, by Gary Saul Morson. Modern Library 2003 xlvii, 188p (Modern Library classics) pa $13

ISBN 978-0-8129-6693-0; 0-8129-6693-7

LC 2002-32566

Written 1866

"The gambling mania of the tale's hero, Aleksey Ivanovich, is a reflection of the author's own weakness. The heroine of the story, Polina, is based on Polina Suslova, Dostoevski's lover in 1862-63." Reader's Ency. 4th edition

Dostoyevsky, Fyodor

★ The **idiot**; translated from the Russian by Richard Pevear and Larissa Volokhonsky; with an introduction by Richard Pevear. Everyman's Library 2002 xxxiii, 633p $23

ISBN 0-375-41392-8

LC 2001-33561

Written 1868

"Dostoevsky puts into a world of foolishness, vice, pretence, and sordid ambitions, a being who in childhood had suffered from mental disease, and who with an intellect of more than ordinary power retains the simplicity and clear insight of a child. . . . The deeply absorbing drama in which he is a protagonist turns on the salvation of a woman, Nastasya Filipovna who had been corrupted in young girlhood." Baker. Guide to the Best Fic

Dostoyevsky, Fyodor

Notes from underground; translated from the Russian by Richard Pevear and Larissa Volkhonsky [sic]; with an introduction by Richard Pevear. Knopf 2004 xxxi, 126p $18

ISBN 1-4000-4191-0

LC 2003-59216

Written 1864. Variant titles: Letters from the underworld and Memoirs from underground

"The work, which includes extremely misanthropic passages, contains the seeds of nearly all of the moral, religious, political, and social concerns that appear in Dostoyevsky's great novels. Written as a reaction against Nikolay Chernyshevsky's ideological novel What Is to Be Done? (1863), which offered a planned utopia based on 'natural' laws of self-interest, Notes from the Underground attacks the scientism and rationalism at the heart of Chernyshevsky's novel. The views and actions of Dostoyevsky's underground man demostrate that in asserting free will humans often act against self-interest." Merriam-Webster's Ency of Lit

Dostoyevsky, Fyodor

The **possessed**; a novel in three parts. from the Russian by Constance Garnett. Macmillan Pub. Co. 1913 637p

Original Russian edition, 1892. Variant titles: Demons; The devils

"Loosely based on sensational press reports of a Moscow student's murder by fellow revolutionists, The possessed depicts the destructive chaos caused by outside agitators who move into a moribund provincial town. The enigmatic Stavrogin dominates the novel. His magnetic personality influences his tutor, the liberal intellectual poseur Stepan Verkhovensky, and the teacher's revolutionary son Pyotr, as well as other radicals. Stavrogin is portrayed as a man of strength without direction, capable of goodness and nobility. When Stavrogin loses his faith in God, however, he is seized by brutal desires he does not fully understand. In the end, Stavrogin hangs himself in what he believes is an act of generosity, and Stepan Verkhovensky is received into the church on his deathbed." Merriam-Webster's Ency of Lit

Doughty, Louise

Whatever you love; a novel. Louise Doughty. Harper Perennial 2012 369 p.

ISBN 0062094661; 9780062094667

LC 2011028521

This book, a finalist for the Orange Prize and the Costa Novel Award, looks at "the loss of life, love, and rationality. Laura Needham is a single mother raising two children." Her 9-year-old daughter dies in a hit-and-run accident on page one. "As Laura grapples with her daughter's death, her already complicated relationship with her ex-husband grows more so." Laura slowly loses her mind and "moves to the brink of a breakdown that might end in violence." (Publishers Weekly)

Douglas, Carole Nelson

Cat in a midnight choir; a Midnight Louie mystery. Forge 2002 350p

ISBN 0-312-85797-7

LC 2001-58281

In this adventure Vegas cat sleuth "Louie's human roommate, Temple Barr, and her boyfriend, Max, are interested in a group of mysterious magicians called the Synth. Matters are complicated when a stripper is murdered, and police lieutenant C. R. Molina, a recurring character, identifies Max, also a magician, as a prime suspect. Alternating chapters—third-person human narration playing off against first-person Louie—move the action along briskly." Booklist

Douglas, Carole Nelson

Cat in a neon nightmare; a Midnight Louie mystery. Forge 2003 365p $24.95

ISBN 0-7653-0680-8

LC 2002-45491

In this episode sleuth and supercat Midnight Louie "and his human associates, Temple Barr and Max Kinsella, tangle with the Synth, a gang of outlaw magicians up to no good. Tracking down the elusive renegades takes Louie to a private magic club called Nightmare—imagine the bar in Star Wars but not quite as friendly." Booklist

Dovey, Ceridwen

Blood kin. Viking 2008 183p $23.95

ISBN 978-0-670-01856-7; 0-670-01856-2

LC 2007-019876

In this "novel, the deposed president of an unnamed country is imprisoned in his residence with, among others, his chef, his barber, and his portraitist. These three servants, awaiting their fate, reveal, in alternating chapters, their ties to the president and their reasons for serving his corrupt regime. Dovey connects her main characters to the president first through their work—their tasks of feeding, grooming, and painting give them an uneasy intimacy with the president—and then through various women in their lives. The narratives of these women, halfway through the book, expose the full extent of the president's depravity. In lively, straightforward prose, Dovey gets to the heart of the complicit nature of the master-servant relationship." New Yorker

Dowlatabadi, Mahmoud

The colonel; Mahmoud Dowlatabadi; translated by Tom Patterdale. Melville House 2012 v, 247 p.p (paperback) $17.95

ISBN 1612191320; 9781612191324

LC 2012934610

This Iranian novel, by Mahmoud Dowlatabadi, "begins on a . . . rainy night, when there's a knock on the Colonel's door. Two policemen have come to summon him to collect the tortured body of his youngest daughter. . . . As we watch him struggle with the death of his innocent child, we find him wracked with guilt and anger over the condition of his country, particularly as represented by his own children." (Publisher's note)

Down, David

Masaryk Station; David Downing. Soho Crime 2013 330 p. (hardcover) $26.95

ISBN 1616952237; 9781616952235

LC 2012042044

This book by David Downing, "the sixth novel in the John Russell series . . . opens in 1948 with postwar Berlin and Eastern Europe in disarray. . . . John Russell's situation is just as complex: The Brits and the Americans think he's their double agent, working against the Soviets. . . . Posing as a journalist, he carries out missions in Trieste, Belgrade, and Prague. . . . Meanwhile, Russell's wife, Effi, an actress, faces her own challenges." (Library Journal)

Downie, Ruth

Caveat emptor; a novel of the Roman Empire. Bloomsbury USA 2011 338p $25

ISBN 978-1-59691-608-1; 1-59691-608-7

LC 2010-34525

"Serial physician (medicus) and de facto detective Gaius Petreius Ruso is assigned to investigate the suspicious disappearance of both tax collector Julius Asper and money owed to the coffers of Emperor Hadrian. Ruso traces a path between the Roman command center in Londinium and the northern metropolis (Verulamium) whence Asper and his brother (also 'missing') have presumably fled. When it appears both fugitives were murdered, Asper's pregnant common-law wife begins hurling accusations. Ruso's former servant and present wife Tilla does what she usually does, helping out, investigating on her own and attracting the threatening attentions of assorted suspects. . . . As always, Downie displays a virtuoso's command of pertinent period detail." Kirkus

Downie, Ruth

Medicus; a novel of the Roman Empire. Bloomsbury Pub. 2006 386p $23.95

ISBN 978-1-59691-231-1; 1-59691-231-6

LC 2006-13179

"The plot is suspenseful and fluidly told, but the evolving bond between master and servant is at the heart of this excellent first work, as Downie carefully details the pained conscience of the former and the latter's sorrow that both her family and her country have been ravaged." Libr J

Downie, Ruth

Semper Fidelis; A Novel of the Roman Empire. Ruth Downie. St. Martin's Press 2013 352 p. (hardcover) $26.00

ISBN 1608197093; 9781608197095

This historical novel, by Ruth Downie, is part of the "Novels of the Roman Empire" series. "As mysterious injuries, and even deaths, begin to appear in the medical ledgers, it's clear that all is not well amongst the native recruits to Britannia's imperial army. . . . Bound by his sense of duty and ill-advised curiosity, Ruso begins to ask questions nobody wants to hear. Meanwhile his barbarian wife, Tilla, is finding out some of the answers." (Publisher's note)

Downie, Ruth

Terra incognita; a novel of the Roman Empire. Bloomsbury 2008 384p $23.95

ISBN 978-1-59691-232-8; 1-59691-232-4

LC 2007-44474

"Having just solved the mysterious deaths of several prostitutes . . . , Ruso accepts a posting to the northern border of Roman Britain in the hopes of getting a much-deserved rest and a return to actual medical practice. Instead, he finds himself at the center of an investigation into the death of a Roman soldier. The murder victim's missing head, an over-zealous military aide who doesn't hesitate to use torture to force confessions from the local natives, a drug-addled fellow medic who has confessed to the murder, a stag-headed rabble-rouser, and Ruso's housekeeper all play a part in the drama. Saving this novel from a certain gritty grimness often found in mysteries is Downie's wry and witty humor." Libr J

Downing, David

Potsdam station. Soho Press 2011 340p $25

ISBN 978-1-56947-917-9

LC 2010-39801

This episode finds "well-traveled Anglo-American journalist [John Ressell] in Moscow in the spring of 1945, angling for a way to get back into Berlin, where his German girlfriend is still trapped, before the Reich falls and the Red Army starts exacting its revenge on the surviving populace — starting with the women. Russell gets his pass; but it's not free. He must guide an expedition to Berlin on a secret hunt for documents from the German atomic research program. Downing provides no platform for debate in this unsentimental novel, leaving his hero to ponder the ethics of his pragmatic choices while surveying the ground-level horrors to be seen in Berlin. The assaults on the ear are no less shocking, from the screams of women in the night to the appalling silence at the end of it all." N Y Times Book Rev

Downing, David C.

Looking for the king; an Inklings novel. Ignatius Press 2010 285p $19.95

ISBN 978-1-58617-514-6; 1-58617-514-9

LC 2010-922767

"A story in which the hero and heroine discuss their mid-twentieth century quest for the relics of kings Arthur and Alfred with C. S. Lewis, J. R. R. Tolkien, Charles Williams and other Inklings, and so come away with a deeper understanding not only of history and myth, but of religion and life. The action revolves around two Americans, Tom McCord, a doctoral candidate looking for evidence to prove King Arthur was a real historic figure, and Laura Hartman, a recent college graduate visiting England to figure out a series of strange, repetitive dreams. The dreams revolve around King Alfred (he of Chesterton's Ballad of the White Horse) and the Lance of Longinus which pierced the side of Christ. Inevitably, the two team up (both archeologically and romantically) in a quest to unravel Laura's dreams and Tom's motives in attempting to build his academic reputation. . . . The main characters are well-drawn and engaging, and the Inklings themselves are as quirky in print as they must have been in life." CatholicCulture.org

Doyle, Arthur Conan, Sir, 1859-1930

The **adventures** and the memoirs of Sherlock Holmes; by Arthur Conan Doyle; illustrated by Scott McKowen. Sterling Pub. Co. 2004 vi, 569 p.p ill. (hardcover) $9.95

ISBN 140271453X; 9781402714535

LC 2004016067

This book is a collection of Sir Arthur Conan Doyle's mystery stories featuring detective "Sherlock Holmes, with his unequalled powers of deduction." This edition has illustrations created by Scott McKowen "in scratchboard, an engraving medium which evokes the look of popular art from the period of these stories." (Publisher's note)

Doyle, Arthur Conan, Sir, 1859-1930

The **best** science fiction of Arthur Conan Doyle; edited by Charles G. Waugh and Martin H. Greenberg; with an introduction by George E. Slusser. Southern Ill. Univ. Press 1981 190p (Alternatives)

LC 81-8884

"The 14 pieces inevitably include a couple of Sherlock Holmes stories. They also include 2 of the not-so-readily-available Professor Challenger tales . . . and 10 other stories spread over more than 40 years of the author's career." Booklist

Doyle, Arthur Conan

★ The **complete** Sherlock Holmes; with a preface by Christopher Morley. Doubleday 1960 1122p $27.95

ISBN 0-385-00689-6

First published 1930

This book contains the following four Sherlock Holmes novels: A study in scarlet (1887); The sign of the four (1890); The hound of the Baskervilles (1902); The valley of fear (1915). It also contains fifty-eight Sherlock Holmes stories which were originally published in the following separate volumes: Adventures of Sherlock Holmes (1892); Memoirs of Sherlock Holmes (1894); The return of Sherlock Holmes (1905); His last bow (1917); The case book of Sherlock Holmes (1927).

Doyle, Arthur Conan

The **hound** of the Baskervilles; introduction by Laurie R. King; notes by James Danly. Modern Library 2002 xx, 181p pa $7.95

ISBN 0-8129-6606-6

LC 2002-29505

First published 1902

"By a miracle of judgment, the supernatural is handled with great effect and no letdown. The plot and subplots are thoroughly worked out and the false clues put in and removed with a master hand. The criminal is superb, Dr. Mortimer memorable, and the secondary figures each contribute to the total effect of brilliancy and grandeur combined. One wishes one could be reading it for the first time." Barzun. Cat of Crime. Rev and enl edition

Doyle, Arthur Conan

The **lost** world; being an account of the recent amazing adventures of Professor George E. Challenger, Lord John Roxton, Professor Summerlee, and Mr. E.D. Malone of the Daily gazette. edited with an introduction and notes by Ian Duncan. Oxford University Press 2008 xxxi, 199p pa $10.95

ISBN 978-0-19-953879-9; 0-19-953879-4

LC 2009-290488

"Two professors and two other Englishmen come across a region in the Amazon valley where the Jurassic period still persists, with its flora and fauna, pterodactyls, dinosaurs, iguanodons, and other beasts that we know only in fossil form, still flourishing. The scientific squabbles of Challenger and the other professor provide incidental comedy." Baker. Guide to best Fic

Doyle, Arthur Conan

The **narrative** of John Smith; edited and with an introduction by Jon Lellenberg, Daniel Stashower and Rachel Foss. British Library 2011 138p il $15

ISBN 978-0-7123-5841-5; 0-7123-5841-2

This unfinished novel "provides insights into Conan Doyle's perennial interest in topics such as medicine and religion, and shows flashes of his humour. However, as its editors acknowledge, this is a work in progress; a compendium of ideas, lacking narrative drive." Telegraph (UK)

Doyle, Arthur Conan

The **sign** of four; with an introduction by Graham Greene. Doubleday 1977 134p

First published 1890 in the United Kingdom. Variant title: The sign of the four

Mary Morstan, the future wife of Dr. Watson, engages Holmes to trace her vanished father. Four years after his disappearance, Miss Morstan began receiving an annual gift of a large and lustrous pearl. Now her unknown benefactor has summoned her to a rendezvous outside the Lyceum Theater. As Holmes unravels the mystery, the Agra pearls are seen to be the center of a grim tale of murder and duplicity, which begins in India and ends in a chase through London's dockland

Doyle, Arthur Conan

A **study** in scarlet; with an introduction by Hugh Greene. Doubleday 1977 145p

First published 1887

"A sensational story in two parts: the first deals with adventures in Utah and the wrong committed by two brutal Mormons on a girl and her lover; the second is the history of a mysterious double murder committed in London and, by the agency of Sherlock Holmes, shown to be the work of the wronged lover, who thus, after many years, attains his revenge." Baker. Guide to the Best Fic

Doyle, Arthur Conan

The **valley** of fear; a Sherlock Holmes novel. illustrated by Arthur I. Keller. Doran, G.H. 1915 320p il

First published 1914

"With the exception of 'The Hound of the Baskervilles,' our favorite among the long tales of Sherlock Holmes. Chapter 1 has in its ten pages some of the best wit and humor to be found anywhere, plus the solution of a cipher, and a stunning punch ending. Nor is there any serious letdown as Holmes, Watson, and Inspector MacDonald investigate the murder of John Douglas at Birlstone Manor in Sussex. The shadow of Moriarty appears early and comes into sharper focus at the end of the story after the long—and gripping—interlude dealing with Douglas' life among the 'scowrers' of the Pennsylvania coalfields." Barzun. Cat of Crime. Rev and enl edition

Doyle, Arthur Conan

The **White** Company; by A. Conan Doyle; pictures by N. C. Wyeth. Morrow 1988 366p il $24.99

ISBN 0-688-07817-6

LC 87-62625

First published 1891; this is a reissue of the edition published 1922 by Cosmopolitan Book Corporation

"The Hampshire hero joins an English Free Company, and, in the course of much wandering through France and the Pyrenees, meets with stirring adventures and performs many a deed of valour. The historical situation is that arising out of the Black Prince's decision to espouse the cause of Pedro the Cruel of Castile. Edward III, the Black Prince, Chandos, Sir William Felton, Bertrand du Guesclin, Don Pedro and others appear." Nield. Guide to the Best Hist Novels & Tales

Doyle, Larry

Go, mutants! a novel. Ecco 354p $23.99

ISBN 0-06-168655-7; 978-0-06-168655-9

"J!m (not a typo) is the son of an alien who tried to take over the world. Now he goes to Manhattan High School with his best friends Johnny (a half-man, half-radioactive-ape hybrid) and Larry (a blob with heart). A girl named Marie loves him in spite of his open, giant-brained cranium, though he doesn't realize it. Trouble is, life isn't giving him much breathing room lately. He's changing inside, with impossible-to-predict consequences, and in spite of current trends toward extraterrestrial integration, the norms are just itching for a chance to turn on their unconventional neighbors. Plus there's the school dance to prepare for, and Russ, the sheriff's son, who's just itching for a fight. Doyle packs his story with hundreds of genre references, throwing out names, monsters, and hat-tips to pop-culture icons big and small. Mutants keeps a light tone, and while not every one-liner lands, the ratio is heavily slanted toward the positive." AV Club

Doyle, Roddy

Bullfighting and other stories. Viking 2011 214p $25.95

ISBN 978-0-670-02287-8; 0-670-02287-X

LC 2010-53424

"A kind of composite central character emerges in the course of these 13 stories (many of which have appeared in the New Yorker). He is a middle-aged Dubliner who can't "really imagine life before the children" or marriage. Though he might take an occasional holiday from responsibility (such as the boys' week in Spain detailed in the title story), he is typically conscientious to a comical fault." Minneapolis Star Tribune

Doyle, Roddy

The **dead** republic. Viking 2010 329p $26.95

ISBN 978-0-670-02177-2; 0-670-02177-6

LC 2009-44778

The novel "reads almost like a hallucinatory dream of the making and unmaking of the idea of modern Ireland. While it is not quite the successor to the trilogy's first two novels that fans might have envisioned, it remains a fine if imperfect farewell to one of the more memorable protagonists in recent literature." Denver Post

Doyle, Roddy

The **deportees** and other stories. Viking 2008 242p

ISBN 978-0-670-01845-1

LC 2007-17659

"Sure, Doyle's characters' voices are to the line pitch-perfect, taut and precise. But in the best of these stories it isn't the dialogue. It's the pacing. It's the velocity. As the author explains in an introduction to the book, the stories in The Deportees were serialized in a Dublin newspaper, eight-hundred words per segment, and each story is broken down into sections that can leave them a tad choppy, creating a kind of Doppler Effect. But Doyle's stories are always compressed the way the best short story writers compress." Esquire

Doyle, Roddy

★ **Paddy** Clarke, ha ha ha. Viking 1993 282p

Doyle's "triumph in this novel is to replenish our sense of how children think and speak and explain the adult world to themselves." London Rev Books

Doyle, Roddy

Paula Spencer. Viking 2007 281p $24.95

ISBN 978-0-670-03816-9; 0-670-03816-4

LC 2006-41370

In this novel "novel, Doyle revisits the life of Paula Spencer, the heroine of his 1996 book, 'The Woman Who Walked Into Doors.' A decade on, Paula has been off the bottle for four months and five days, her abusive husband has been shot while robbing a bank, and her four children are—almost—grown: a daughter with a job in sales buys Paula one appliance after another in an effort to make her mom's life work; a son, recovering from heroin addiction, shows up after an absence of nine years, competent and silent; her younger daughter is drinking herself senseless at twenty-two; and her younger son, worried and self-contained, is still in high school. Doyle's depiction of a seething home life is penetrating, and Paula, as she patches a self together from remnants, emerges as an inspiring heroine without a hint of smarminess." New Yorker

Doyle, Roddy

A **star** called Henry. Viking 1999 343p

ISBN 0-670-88757-9

LC 99-25310

"The story is told in the voice of Henry Smart, born into harsh poverty in 1901 in Dublin. By age five, Henry was on his own, living in the streets of the city with his younger brother Victor in tow. . . . Fearless, more man than boy at 14, Henry was among the Irish rebels at the 1916 Easter Rising,

pitching his own personal rage into the onset of Ireland's long and bloody battle for independence. Haunted by memories of a mother ravaged by poverty and repeated childbirths and by the fate of young Victor and his other siblings, Henry throws himself into the fight for the Republic." Booklist

"In Doyle's hands, the grand patriotic narrative is tempered with a sharp sense of humanity and human frailty." Times Lit Suppl

Doyle, Roddy

★ The **woman** who walked into doors. Viking 1996 226p

LC 95-41850

Doyle "is a very, very good writer. 'The Woman Who Walked Into Doors' honors not the female experience in the abstract, but the experience of this one woman, Paula Spencer; it examines it with tenderness, but with fearless clear-sightedness. And it's funny in places too. Paula Spencer is neither a victim nor a flawless Madonna; she inhabits the complexity of her mind and history; she acts to buy a better future for her children." N Y Times Book Rev

Doyon, Stephanie

The **greatest** man in Cedar Hole; Stephanie Doyon. Simon & Schuster 2005 375p o.p.; $24.99

ISBN 0743271335; 9780743271349

LC 2004062600

This book is set "in the small, inbred town of Cedar Hole, [where] mediocrity is the watchword. . . . Bright and good-hearted, [Robert J. Cutler] becomes one of Cedar Hole's prime boosters. . . . Although he is generally regarded as the town's leading citizen, not everyone thinks so highly of him. His wife . . . resents the time he spends on civic activities, and his childhood rival, Francis 'Spud' Pinkham . . . still smarts at the memory of being bested at the Lawn Rodeo contest. When Robert is killed in a traffic accident, Spud begins to think he will inherit Robert's mantle, especially after a spring discovered on his property turns him into a wealthy man." (Booklist)

Dozois, Gardner R.

When the great days come; [by] Gardner Dozois. Prime 2011 358p $24.95

ISBN 978-1-60701-278-8

"This emotionally moving collection of Dozois's recent writing and a selection of his best earlier pieces-including his two Nebula winners, 'The Peacemaker' and 'Morning Child' is a valuable reminder that the renowned Asimov's editor and anthologist also continues, if sporadically, to write significant fiction. . . . Dozois demonstrates his range with classic fantasy, alternate history, and golden age–style horror as well as hard SF." Publ Wkly

Drabble, Margaret, 1939-

A **day** in the life of a smiling woman; complete short stories. Houghton Mifflin Harcourt 2011 xxii, 227p $24

ISBN 978-0-547-55040-4; 0-547-55040-5

LC 2010049798

"The discursive spaciousness of Margaret Drabble's voice and vision lends itself to the long form, as her 17 splendid novels demonstrate. This may help to explain why her 'complete short stories' make up so slender a volume. Drabble, it seems, just didn't have enough time to write short stories (with apologies to Mark Twain). Of those collected here, 14 in all, the earliest dates from the 1950s, the most recent from the 1990s. Some are reed slim, but many glimmer with the irony, lyricism, moral vision and (despite their page counts) amplitude we associate with Drabble's novels. They reflect back to us the last half of the 20th century, albeit in Drabble's often 19th-century voice." N Y Times Book Rev

Drabble, Margaret, 1939-

The **radiant** way. Knopf 1987 407p

ISBN 0-394-56143-0

LC 87-45126

Drabble "charts every hill and dale in the increasingly brighter landscape of middle-class women's roles (a progression that takes place, ironically, as Britain's economic power erodes). Drabble is a master of delicate phrasing set amid a big, robust narrative." Booklist

Followed by A natural curiosity (1989) and The gates of ivory (1992)

Drabble, Margaret

The **sea** lady; a late romance. Harcourt, Inc. 2007 345p $24

ISBN 978-0-15-101263-3; 0-15-101263-6

LC 2006-23778

First published 2006 in the United Kingdom

The author "has a keen sense of the past and the ways in which intellectual fashions evolve. She is pitiless—and very funny—about the flimsiness of Ailsa's various posturings. Where Humphrey craves knowledge, Ailsa craves exposure. Their love affair mirrors the age they are living through. . . . Drabble writes beautifully about the passing of time and the sad, incomplete experience of human love." New Statesman

Drabble, Margaret

The **witch** of Exmoor. Harcourt Brace & Co. 1997 281p

ISBN 0-15-100363-7

LC 97-10952

First published 1996 in the United Kingdom

"Can politics ever amount to more than the conspiracies we hatch against our parents and the spells we cast on our children? The humbling surprise of Drabble's novel is not that it refuses to resolve this question but that we gradually lose our lofty perspective and begin to have an emotional stake in the answer." New Yorker

Dragoman, Gyorgy

The **white** king; translated from the Hungarian by Paul Olchváry. Houghton Mifflin 2007 263p $24

ISBN 978-0-618-94517-7; 0-618-94517-2

LC 2007-36124

"Political and geographical ambiguities are what allow the novel to hover between bildungsroman and historic documentation. The novel swirls between polarities and it is the dichotomous tension that brings joy, freedom and adventure to the story. Dragomán's prose is exuberant and sputters with youthful truthfulness." PopMatters

Drake, David

Grimmer than hell. Baen Bks. 2003 373p $24

ISBN 0-7434-3590-7

LC 2002-34194

"Fourteen short stories and an introduction make up the latest, highly recommended collection from a leading light of military sf. . . . The intoduction puts everything in perspective with a minimum of apologetics, compressing Drake's psychological history since the Vietnam War into a short essay valuable to new and old fans alike." Booklist

Drake, Nick

Egypt; Nick Drake. HarperCollins 2011 x, 335p.p maps

ISBN 9780060765941; 9780060765958

LC 2011276351

In this historical fiction book, "[t]he future of Egypt lies in the hands of chief detective Rahotep in this final installment of Nick Drake's . . . ancient Egyptian trilogy. King Tutankhamun has died without an heir, and his young widow, Queen Ankhesenamun, last of her dynasty, struggles to maintain power and order. To defeat her enemies, she has but one hope: to forge an alliance with the Hittites, a powerful, militant new empire that threatens Egypt's supremacy. The loyal Rahotep, chief detective of the Thebes Medjay—the ancient capital's elite police force—and his friend, the royal envoy Nakht, are sent on a clandestine mission to the Hittite homeland, to persuade the king to agree to a marriage between one of his sons and Ankhesenamun—a union that would bring peace to the region and consolidate the queen's power." (Publisher's note)

Includes bibliographical references

Drake, Nick

Tutankhamun; the book of shadows. Harper 2010 374p map $24.99

ISBN 978-0-06-076592-7; 0-06-076592-5

LC 2009-29458

Sequel to: Nefertiti

First published 2009 in the United Kingdom

In this second title in the author's ancient Egyption trilogy, Rahotep, the stalwart chief detective of the Thebes division, is summoned to the palace to investigate a threat to the newly crowned Tutankhamun. As he begins to piece together the clues, he realizes that a series of mysterious gifts have much in common with a string of sadistic murders plaguing the city.

"Drake seamlessly introduces a serial killer plot line into his vivid evocation of the past. Admirers of such great historical novelists as Robert Graves and Mary Renault will hope that he continues working in the field after concluding this series." Publ Wkly

Includes bibliographical references

Drayson, Nicholas

Guide to the birds of East Africa. Houghton Mifflin 2008 201p $22

ISBN 978-0-547-15258-5; 0-547-15258-2

LC 2008-17183

"With captivating character sketches and glimpses into Kenyan life and politics, Drayson meets the inevitable comparisons to Alexander McCall Smith without breaking a sweat." Publ Wkly

Dreiser, Theodore

★ An **American** tragedy. Boni & Liveright 1925 2v

"Clyde Griffiths, product of a poor and pious home, is driven by ambition to acquire money and social status. He is loved by Roberta, a factory coworker, but is dazzled by Sondra, who would be a passport to the country-club set. When Roberta, pregnant and no longer desirable, becomes an obstacle to Clyde's fulfilling his dream, he plans her death, for which he is caught and convicted." Shapiro. Fic for Youth. 3d edition

Dreiser, Theodore

★ **Jennie** Gerhardt; a novel. Harper 1911 430p

"The fortunes of two families, German and Irish immigrants. Jennie, child of an unsuccessful German, falls a prey to the pleasure-loving son of the enterprising Irishman. Whether of deep-laid purpose or not, the book illustrates the rottenness of a complex social fabric resting on materialism." Baker. Guide to the Best Fic

Dreiser, Theodore

★ **Sister** Carrie; historical editors, John C. Berkey, Alice M. Winters; textual editor, James L.W. West III; general editor Neda M. Westlake; introduction by Alfred Kazin. Penguin Books 1994 499p pa $12.95

ISBN 0-14-018828-2

First published 1900

"A powerful account of a young working girl's rise to the 'tinsel and shine' of worldly success, and of the slow decline of her lover and protector Hurstwood." Oxford Companion to Engl Lit

Dreiser, Theodore

Sister Carrie; Jennie Gerhardt; Twelve men. Library of America 1987 1168p il $40

ISBN 0-940450-41-0

Sister Carrie and Jennie Gerhardt are entered separately. Twelve men (1919) presents brief biographical sketches of twelve men that have influenced the author's life

Dreyer, Eileen

Barely a lady. Forever 2010 418p pa $6.99

ISBN 978-0-446-54208-1

"Five years ago Olivia's husband, Jack, nearly destroyed her life, and now he is about to do it again. Accepting scurrilous rumors as fact, Jack divorced Olivia early in their marriage, leaving her destitute. She has finally rebuilt her life, and now all her hard work is threatened when Jack's old valet suddenly turns up and insists that Olivia accompany him to Waterloo, where Olivia discovers that Jack is badly wounded and attired in a French officer's uniform. Helping her ex could very well destroy Olivia, but she knows Jack is no traitor. . . . [The novel is] addictively readable thanks to exquisitely nuanced characters, a brilliantly realized historical setting, and a captivating plot encompassing both the triumph and tragedy of war." Booklist

Drummond, Laurie Lynn

Anything you say can and will be used against you; stories. HarperCollinsPublishers 2004 250p $23.95

ISBN 0-06-056162-9

LC 2003-51133

"Combining Southern grace and urban brutality, ex-cop Drummond debuts with 10 short stories grouped into five blistering fictional portraits of Baton Rouge policewomen. Each lady is tough even without her bulletproof vest, and all are plagued by death and corruption as they undertake the bracing, dehumanizing enforcement of justice." Publ Wkly

Druon, Maurice

The **Iron** King; a novel. Translated from the French by Humphrey Hare. HarperCollins 2013 368 p. (paperback) $14.99

ISBN 0007491263; 9780007491261

LC 56010197

This book is the first in "a seven-part historical series that chronicles the beginnings of the Hundred Years' War and the fall of the Capetian kings" from author Maurice Druon. At the heart of this entry "is the French monarch, Philip the Fair (1268-1314), grandson of Saint Louis, who rules with an iron fist; it's his persecution of the Knights Templar, including burning its Grand Master at the stake, that sets the stage for his downfall." (Library Journal)

Drury, Allen

★ **Advise** and consent; drawings by Arthur Shilstone. Doubleday 1959 616p il

"Robert A. Leffingwell, a liberal intellectual, is nominated by the President of the United States to be Secretary of State. The lives of four politicians are affected by the fight for his approval in the Senate. A suicide, a surprise witness at the hearings, a vote of censure, and some chicanery highlight the Washington political scene depicted in this novel." Shapiro. Fic for Youth. 3d edition

Drury, Tom

The **driftless** area. Atlantic Monthly Press 2006 215p $22

ISBN 0-87113-943-X

LC 2006-40787

"Deadpan wit, cosmic melancholy, characters both ethereal and down and dirty, predicaments a Beckett character would accept as inevitable, and a porous divide between the living and the dead add up to a delectably unnerving outlaw fairy tale." Booklist

Du Maurier, Daphne

Daphne du Maurier's classics of the macabre; illustrated by Michael Foreman. Doubleday 1987 284p il $18.95

ISBN 0-385-24302-2

LC 87-9108

"Six of du Maurier's best stories admirably illustrated by a watercolorist, Michael Foreman, well able to catch their atmosphere. . . . Careful readers will notice that most of the creepy situations in these stories develop from marital stress and that sexual undertones sound everywhere. All readers ought to savor du Maurier's peerless narrative gift." Booklist

Du Maurier, Daphne

Frenchman's Creek. Doubleday, Doran 1942 310p

"The lovely Lady St. Columb fled by coach from the boredom of London society, and an unloved husband to their wild and unused Cornish coast estate. There she discovered an aristocratic French pirate who secreted his ship and crew in the hidden creek and as a game preyed gaily upon the dull Cornish gentry. {The book describes} the love between the two and the thrilling adventure they shared." Booklist

Du Maurier, Daphne

Jamaica Inn. Doubleday, Doran 1936 332p

"A stirring tale of an old inn on the desolate moors of Cornwall, where Mary Yellan, left alone in the world at her mother's death, took refuge with her aunt. Her uncle, the landlord, directed smugglers who wrecked ships on the nearby coast, and the inn was a place of horror and mystery. Mary's hope of rescuing her aunt, and escaping, was soon complicated by her unwilling interest in the landlord's brother, who stole horses but drew the line at murder." Booklist

Du Maurier, Daphne

★ **Rebecca.** Doubleday 1938 457p $29.95

ISBN 0-385-04380-5

"Rebecca, lovely and charming wife of English aristocrat Maxim de Winter, dies unexpectedly, and the mystery surrounding her death haunts all who remain at the Manderley country estate. Eight months after the sailing accident in which Rebecca lost her life Maxim remarries. Through his new wife's writing, the reader learns the truth about Rebecca's death and character." Shapiro. Fic for Youth. 3d edition

Dubus, Andre, 1959-

Dirty Love; by Andre Dubus III. 1st ed. W W Norton & Co Inc 2013 320 p. (hardcover) $25.95

ISBN 0393064654; 9780393064650

LC 2013017214

This book contains four loosely connected short works. In 'Listen Carefully as Our Options Have Changed,' Mark Welch is a middle-aged project manager who suspects that his wife is having an affair. . . . One shorter work deals with Maria, an overweight bank teller, and the surprising things she discovers about herself after she falls in love for the first time; another follows Robert Doucette, a bartender-cum-poet who cheats on his pregnant wife." (Publishers Weekly)

Dubus, Andre, 1959-

The **garden** of last days; a novel. [by] Andre Dubus III. W.W. Norton 2008 537p $24.95

ISBN 0393041654; 9780393041651; 978-0-393-04165-1; 0-393-04165-4

LC 2008-1294

This is a novel by the author of House of Sand and Fog (1999) and Bluesman (2001). "One early September night in Florida, a stripper brings her daughter to work. . . . April works at the Puma Club for Men. And tonight she has an unusual client, a foreigner both remote and too personal, and free with his money. . . . His name is Bassam. Meanwhile, another man, AJ, has been thrown out of the club for holding hands with his favorite stripper, and he's drunk and angry." (Publisher's note)

The "narrative mostly unfolds at a Florida strip club, and the evening is spent with a terrorist who drives a leased Neon, a stripper who brings her toddler to work, a patron who gets bounced for innocently touching a dancer, and a landlord who, had she not taken ill, might have saved everyone. . . . When the critics weigh in, there will be plenty of chatter about how Dubus so deeply inhabits even the most disturbing characters. And rightly so. But the book's most profound achievement is a far more difficult one: the omnipresence of hope in a hopeless place. [The novel] is riveting and disturbing, as beautiful as it is bleak, and if there are cowards among the cast of broken characters, I couldn't find them." Esquire

Ducker, Bruce

Dizzying heights; the Aspen novel. Fulcrum Pub. 2008 362p il $25.95; pa $16.95

ISBN 978-1-55591-685-5; 978-155591-658-9 pa

LC 2007-51817

The satire "works well, staying lighthearted, with just enough plot twists to keep things interesting, and characters unraveling from stereotypes to more sympathetic individuals over the course of the book. But it's Ducker's use of language that separates his spin on the well-worn form and makes the book his own. Not only does Ducker display a keen sense of intelligence in breaking down the various structures of business, investment, and law and makes them both real and understandable for the reader, but he displays a far more poetic sense of his setting than most comedic writers. The Colorado Ducker describes is in the details, from understandings of local history to the precise and intricate descriptions of the flora and fauna." PopMatters

Ducornet, Rikki

Gazelle. Knopf 2003 189p $21

ISBN 0-375-41124-0

LC 2002-34000

"Lushly detailed yet swiftly paced, this mythic coming-of-age novel archly traces the plexus of sensuality, intelligence, and imagination that defines the human soul." Booklist

Ducornet, Rikki

Netsuke; a novel. Coffee House Press 2011 127p pa $14.95

ISBN 978-1-56689-253-7; 1-56689-253-8

LC 2010-38004

"Our society is numb to explicit depictions of sexual acts. The perversity, decadence, even the depravity that Ducornet renders here feel explosively fresh because their sources are thought and emotion, not the body, and finally there's pathos too, which means the book cannot be dismissed as porn. What interests Ducornet is the magnetic collision of eros and thanatos in their most chthonic, archetypal forms." Boston Globe

Due, Tananarive

Blood colony; a novel. Atria Books 2008 422p $25

ISBN 978-0-7432-8735-7; 0-7432-8735-5

LC 2008-12403

Due "expertly mixes genres and intertwines sociopolitical issues into the framework of a story about a group of ancient African immortals who are battling to end the AIDS/HIV epidemic. Like the late, great Octavia Butler, Due fearlessly tackles contemporary issues." Baltimore Sun

Due, Tananarive

The **good** house. Atria 2003 482p $25
ISBN 0-7434-4900-2

"Due handles the potentially unwieldy elements of her novel with confidence, cross-cutting smoothly from past to present, introducing revelatory facts that alter the interpretation of earlier scenes and interjecting powerfully orchestrated moments of supernatural horror that sustain the tale's momentum." Publ Wkly

Due, Tananarive

My soul to keep. HarperCollins Pubs. 1997 346p
LC 97-4992

"Smart psychological renderings, particularly of familial bonds, and a memorable set of African American protagonists highlight Due's . . . horror novel. Centering around the potent theme of immortality, this briskly told tale adds fresh blood—literally and figuratively—to a genre currently on life support." Publ Wkly

Duenas, Maria

The **time** in between; Maria Duenas; translated by Daniel Hahn. 1st Atria Books hardcover ed. Atria Books 2011 615 p.
ISBN 9781451616880; 1451616880
LC 2011019250

This book "opens during the mid-1930s as Spain is on the brink of civil war and young Sira Quiroga is preparing a simple wedding in Madrid, where she lives. Sira's plans are thrown off track when she meets Ramiro Arribas, the cunning older manager of a typewriter shop who convinces her to embark on an exotic life in Morocco. The future that he envisions for her differs from what he imagines for himself, however, and he abandons Sira after pilfering her inheritance and leaving her saddled with debt. Newly adrift, Sira travels to northern Morocco, where she is reluctantly taken in by Candelaria, a disreputable woman known for housing dispossessed souls. In Candelaria's care, Sira returns to her roots as a dressmaker's apprentice. Realizing her talent with a needle and thread, Candeleria takes advantage, quietly financing Sira's efforts and taking half the profits." (Publishers Weekly)

Includes bibliographical references.

Duffy, Stella

Theodora; actress, empress, whore. Stella Duffy. Penguin Books 2011 352 p. $15
ISBN 0143119877; 9780143119876
LC 2011007869

This book by Stella Duffy presents the fictional "retelling of the true story of a woman (500-548) who rose from lowly beginnings to become Empress of the Byzantine Empire. . . . Theodora was trained as a dancer, singer, and actress who performed on the stage and in the bedrooms of anyone who could afford her, from the time she was a child. . . . When Theodora finds herself cast off in a few short years,

she must make her way back to her beloved Constantinople." (Library Journal)

Includes bibliographical references

Dufosse, Christophe

School's out; translated by Shaun Whiteside. Penguin Books 2007 326p pa $14
ISBN 978-0-14-303811-5

Original French edition, 2002; this translation first published 2006 in the United Kingdom

"At a middle school in Clerval, the teacher of class 9F jumps to his death, in an apparent suicide. Pierre Hoffman, a thirty-two-year-old melancholic literature instructor, is told to take his place and immediately senses something 'unsettling' about the students. Gossip reveals that the entire staff is spooked by 9F, but Hoffman, disregarding warnings, is drawn into a series of creepy events. . . . At its heart, the novel is a subtle and disconcerting meditation on the relationship between teachers and students (Dufossé is a former teacher), and, despite digressive subplots, the central mystery—what's wrong with the students?—enthralls." New Yorker

Dufresne, John

Deep in the shade of paradise. Norton 2002 364p $25.95
ISBN 0-393-02020-7
LC 2001-44487

"The people in this small town are surprisingly endearing, despite their quirks. Numerous asides sprinkled throughout the novel make for a clever and memorable narrative style." Booklist

Dufresne, John

Requiem, Mass. a novel. W. W. Norton & Co. 2008 316p $24.95
ISBN 978-0-393-05790-4; 0-393-05790-9
LC 2008-1343

"The book unfolds like a series of nesting dolls: John meanders around his coastal Florida home, writing his novel, visiting with friends and going on appointments for teaching jobs, while Johnny lives with his mother's worsening condition, his father's absences, his mother's hospitalization and a momentous trip South. Then there are stories within the memoir within the story, including the one a woman tells about her friend, Ginger Rae, who talks of writing a neighbor's suicide note, then claims it's part of a story she herself is writing. John is a very amusing unreliable narrator, and Dufresne's witty, sardonic take on life's fictions leaps off the page." Publ Wkly

Dugoni, Robert

Murder one; a novel. Simon & Schuster 2011 374p $24.99
ISBN 978-1-4516-0669-0; 1-4516-0669-9
LC 2011-05010

In this legal thriller Seattle attorney David Sloane "attends his first public event since his wife's murder a year earlier, a benefit to promote legal aid services, where he literally runs into attorney Barclay Reid, an adversary from a previous case. Reid is also in mourning-for her college age daughter, Carly, who died of a heroin overdose. Reid mounts a charm offensive to persuade Sloane to represent her in a wrongful death suit against the Russian gangster, Filyp Vasiliev, who was behind the heroin sale that killed Carly and who has just beaten federal criminal charges after a judge tossed out crucial evidence at a pretrial hearing. The shooting death of Vasiliev in his Seattle home derails the developing romance between Sloane and Reid as well as the civil case. While many will anticipate the ending twist, Dugoni conveys the legalese in digestible form." Publ Wkly

Duisberg, Kristin Waterfield

The **good** patient; a novel. St. Martin's Press 2003 328p $23.95

ISBN 0-312-30039-5

LC 2002-36877

"From the facile duplicity of Darien's counseling sessions to the innocence of her interior dialogues, Duisberg's first-person narrative is electrifying in its unfeigned candor, harrowing in its unnerving vulnerability." Booklist

Dumas, Alexandre

★ **Camille**; the lady of the camellias. by Alexandre Dumas fils; translated by Edmund Gosse; with a new introduction by Toril Moi. Signet Classic 2004 255p il pa $6.95

ISBN 978-0-451-52920-6; 0-451-52920-0

Original French edition, 1848; first United States edition published 1857 by E.J. Hincken with title: The camelia-lady. Variant title: Lady with the camellias

Camille "is a beautiful courtesan who has become part of the fashionable world of Paris. Scorning the wealthy Count de Varville, who has offered to relieve her debts should she once more become his mistress, she escapes to the country with her penniless lover Armand Duval. Here Camille makes her great sacrifice. Giving Armand, whom she truly loves, the impression that she has tired of their life together, but actually at the request of his family, she returns to Paris and her life of frivolity. The tale concludes with the ultimate tragic reunion of Armand and the dying Camille." Reader's Ency. 4th edition

Dumas, Alexandre

★ The **Count** of Monte Cristo. Modern Library 1996 1462p $25.95

ISBN 0-679-60199-6

LC 96-3397

Original French edition, 1844

"Edmond Dantes, a young sailor unjustly accused of helping the exiled Napoleon in 1815, has been arrested and imprisoned in the Chateau d'If, near Marseille. After fifteen years, he finally escapes by taking the place of his dead companion, the Abbe Faria; enclosed in a sack, he is thrown into the sea. He cuts the sack with his knife, swims to safety, is taken to Italy on a fisherman's boat. From Genoa, he goes to the caverns of Monte Cristo and digs up the fabulous treasures of which the dying Faria had told. He then uses the money to punish his enemies and reward his friends." Haydn. Thesaurus of Book Dig

Dumas, Alexandre

The **last** cavalier; being the adventures of Count Sainte-Hermine in the age of Napoleon. translated by Lauren Yoder. Pegasus Books 2007 751p $32

ISBN 978-1-93364-831-6; 1-93364-831-7

Original French edition, 2005

Originally serialized in a newspaper, this unfinished novel, "nominally concerns a young velvet-suited nobleman 'whose pallor bespoke a strange destiny': to redeem his family's Royalist past, he must serve as a common sailor on a corsair. But Dumas seems only intermittently interested in his hero, lingering instead on Napoleon, still an emperor-in-waiting, bemoaning his marriage to spendthrift Josephine ('I shall keep divorce legal in France, if only so I can leave that woman'). Amid stagecoach heists, assassination attempts, and the occasional tiger hunt, sudden details gleam: a condemned aristocrat requests the services of a barber en route to the scaffold; a lovelorn girl conspires to commit suicide by snakebite." New Yorker

Dumas, Alexandre

★ The **man** in the iron mask; translated by Joachim Neugroschel; introduction by Francine du Plessix Gray. Penguin Books 2003 xxv, 470p (Penguin classics) pa $16

ISBN 978-0-14-043924-3; 0-14-043924-2

LC 2002-193017

Original French edition published 1850 as part of Le Vicomte de Bragelonne

The identity of the man in the iron mask—is an unsolved mystery. Dumas' "iron mask episode is found toward the end . . . of the third volume of 'Vicomte De Bragelonne'. . . . The present volume remains essentially the story of the . . . closing years of those four men who had performed such prodigies—attacking armies, assaulting castles, terrifying death itself—Athos, Porthos, Aramis, and their captain, D'Artagnan." Preface for the reader

Dumas, Alexandre

Short stories. Black, W.J. 1927 10v in 1

Dumas, Alexandre

★ The **three** musketeers; translated with an introduction by Richard Pevear. Viking 2006 704p $35

ISBN 0-670-03779-6

LC 2005-58468

Original French edition, 1844

"Richard Pevear's brisk, agile new translation succeeds, I think, because it does justice to the pure nuttiness of Dumas's writing: the nonindustrial, nonformulaic, downright peculiar qualities that make a work of popular fiction memorable." N Y Times Book Rev

Dumas, Alexandre

Twenty years after; edited with an introduction and notes by David Coward. Oxford University Press 1998 xxv, 845p il pa $15.95

ISBN 0-19-283843-1

LC 99-188043

Sequel to The three musketeers

Original French edition, 1845; first United States edition published 1846 by Taylor, Wilde and Company

"Anne of Austria's regency, the insurrection of the Fronde, and the execution of Charles I of England mark out the period (1648-9)." Baker. Guide to the Best Fic

Followed by The Vicomte de Bragelonne (1848-1850)

Dunant, Sarah

The **birth** of Venus; a novel. Random House 2004 394p $21.95

ISBN 1-400-06073-7

LC 2003-46932

In this novel, "the fictional narrator is Alessandra Cecchi, 14, the daughter of a wealthy cloth merchant in the Florence of Michelangelo and Botticelli. Alessandra yearns to live with a brush in her hand. For that matter, she would be happy just to get out of the house. But it's the 1490s, so her best hope is an agreeable arranged marriage." (Time)

"Part feverish thriller, part historical romance, the story of the outspoken heroine's sentimental education—a comprehensive curriculum including every conceivable transgression—sometimes comes off as a heady blend of Browning's My Last Duchess and Anaïs Nin. But Dunant's skill lies in combining these elements with a finely textured and pertinent depiction of a cultured citizenry in the grip of rampant fundamentalism." New Yorker

Dunant, Sarah

★ **Blood** and beauty; the Borgias: a novel. Sarah Dunant. 1st U.S. ed. Random House Inc. 2013 506 p. map (hardcover) $27

ISBN 1400069297; 9781400069293

LC 2012042215

In this work of "biofiction" by Sarah Dunant presents an "account of Rodrigo Borgia's ascent to the papacy as Alexander VI in 1492 and his subsequent tireless efforts to build a power base through the strategic use of his four children. Cesare is the sly, shrewd son . . . who moves ruthlessly from cardinal to soldier as politics and advancement dictate. Beloved daughter Lucrezia makes one strategic marriage after another while nursing a powerful attachment to Cesare." (Kirkus Reviews)

"...An impressively confident, capable sweep through the corrupt politics and serpentine relationships of a legendary family." Kirkus

Dunant, Sarah

In the company of the courtesan; a novel. Random House 2006 371p $23.95

ISBN 1-4000-6381-7

LC 2005-51649

This historical novel "follows the fortunes of a beautiful, flame-haired courtesan, Fiammetta Bianchini, who, after escaping from the 1527 pillage of Rome, sets up shop in Venice. The novel, narrated by Fiammetta's servant, a dwarf, chronicles the pair's horrific scrapes and their dizzying triumphs, which include Fiammetta's becoming Titian's model for his 'Venus of Urbino.' Along the way, Dunant presents a lively and detailed acccount of the glimmering palaces and murky alleys of Renaissance Venice, and examines the way the city's clerics and prostitutes alike are bound by its peculiar dynamic of opulence and restraint." New Yorker

Duncan, Dave

When the saints; Dave Duncan. Tor 2011 332 p. (Brothers Magnus)

ISBN 0765323486; 9780765323484

LC 2011021617

This book is "set in Jorgary, a fictional country in late 15th-century Central Europe. Certain individuals possess a form of magic called Speaking, which involves invoking saints . . . to work miracles. The Magnus clan has loyally served the kings of Jorgary for centuries. However, Cardinal Zdenek, the real ruler of Jorgary . . . knows that Duke Wartislaw of Pomerania has invaded Jorgary with an army of Wends. . . . The four surviving Magnus brothers, Wulf, Otto, Anton and Vlad, have . . . been dispatched to Gallant to organize the defenses. Young Wulf is a Speaker, powerful but untrained and ignorant of magic's rules, wracked with doubts as to whether his talents truly emanate from saints or demons. Zdenek arranges for another Speaker, from a mysterious organization known as the Saints, to assist with Wulf's education." (Kirkus)

Duncan, Glen

Death of an ordinary man; Glen Duncan. Grove Press 2005 304p pa $13

ISBN 0-8021-7004-8

LC 2004-56727

"As this novel opens, Nathan finds himself falling into darkness and emerges to float above his own funeral. . . . Along with the reader, Nathan pieces together his life and death mosaiclike as he hovers around his family after the funeral, able to sense their feelings and falling into the memories thus invoked. We see his passion for his edgy, intense wife, who ultimately betrayed him with his best friend; we register his concern for his floundering son and budding, tough-as-nails older daughter. We learn that a younger daughter has died and are eventually rubbed raw by the details of her horrific death. Duncan layers on brilliant prose—sometimes a little heavily, as the narrative seems to slow halfway through. In the end, however, he has produced an arresting story, and he writes convincingly and affectingly of the consequences of a child's death, which is pretty rare indeed." Libr J

Duncan, Glen

The **last** werewolf. Knopf 2011 293p

ISBN 0-307-59508-0; 978-0-307-59508-9

LC 2011-11667

"Jake is a werewolf, and after the unfortunate and violent death of his one contemporary, he is now the last of his species. Although he is physically healthy, Jake is deeply distraught and lonely. Jake's depression has carried him to the point where he is actually contemplating suicide—even if it means terminating a legend thousands of years old. It would seem to be easy enough for him to end everything. But for very different reasons there are two dangerous groups pursuing him who will stop at nothing to keep him alive." (Publisher's note)

A "yarn about a Kant-quoting lycanthrope on the run from monster hunters bent on rendering his species extinct. Jake Marlowe, whose name recalls the hero of Joseph Conrad's Heart of Darkness and the author of Doctor Faustus, was infected nearly 200 years ago and has grown weary of the chase and his monthly feedings. Unlike Jeff Lindsay's

Dexter Morgan, the serial killer who targets only fellow killers, Jake is generally less discriminating in his selection of victims. But even he gives in to charitable impulses, of a sort: 'Two nights ago I'd eaten a forty-three-year-old hedge fund specialist. I've been in a phase of taking the ones no one wants.' Jake is not only quite the raconteur, he's also a major horndog — the book's many sex scenes are just as graphic as the kills. 'The werewolf gets dyslexia and a permanent erection,' Duncan notes, while the vampires whose presence makes Jake physically ill are immortal and sexless. Take that, True Blood fans! Duncan creates a world that is completely imagined, if occasionally implausible." Entertainment Wkly

Duncan, Glen

Talulla rising; by Glen Duncan. Alfred A. Knopf 2012 351 p. (hardcover: alk. paper) $25.95; (paperback) $15.00; (ebook) $25.95

ISBN 0307595099; 9780307595096; 9780307742186; 9780307958433

LC 2012005881

Sequel to: The Last Werewolf.

This book by Glen Duncan "finds newly turned werewolf Talulla Demetriou hiding out in a remote hunting lodge . . . mourning her dead werewolf lover, Jake Marlowe, by whom she's pregnant. After Talulla delivers boy-girl befurred twins, vampires kidnap her newborn son as a sacrifice to bring back their mythic progenitor. With baby daughter Zoë in tow, Talulla sets out after the vampires in a quest to regain her son that will bring her in contact with more of her kind." (Publishers Weekly)

Duncker, Patricia

The **strange** case of the composer and his judge; a novel. Bloomsbury USA 2010 262p $15

ISBN 978-1-608-19203-8; 1-608-19203-2 pa

LC 2009-49557

"Duncker has written a tightly plotted thriller that, at times, sags and slows with the density of historical and scientific research. But the book as a whole is an accomplishment — a quick, instantly involving, page-turning mystery, written in fluid, lyrical prose, and populated with characters that are flawed and human and complete." Boston Globe

Dunlap, Phil

Ambush Creek. Avalon Books 2010 202p $23.95

ISBN 978-0-8034-7780-3; 0-8034-7780-5

LC 2010-06234

"When U.S. Marshal Piedmont Kelly is asked by Cochise Sheriff John Henry Stevens to look into the suspicious activity of three unsavory bounty hunters, he rides into what looks like a battle's aftermath, with bullet holes riddling a ranch house, but no sign of those engaged in the gunplay. Kelly finds nothing to indicate that the mysterious rancher living there fit the description of the bounty hunters' quarry, either. Kelly sets out to locate the missing man. Enlisting the tracking skills of his old friend Spotted Dog—the Chiricahua Apache whose life he once saved—they follow four horses from the rancher's house all the way to Desert Belle, a dusty town that holds grim memories for Kelly. They ride straight into a deadly game where $50,000, several lives,

and the survival of the Gilded Lily mine are at stake." Publisher's note

"With a raft of well-drawn, even indelible, characters, the novel also offers a compellingly involved, quite plausible, and tightly woven plot." Booklist

Dunmore, Helen

The **betrayal**. Black Cat 2011 331p pa 14.95

ISBN 978-0-8021-7088-0; 0-8021-7088-9

First published 2010 in the United Kingdom

"In her sequel to The Siege (2002), Dunmore returns to Leningrad in 1952, compressing the anxiety and terror of the postwar Stalinist years into the intimate details of one family's crisis. A sense of doom takes over from the first page when pediatrician Andrei is approached by a nervously sweating colleague who twists his arm to consult on a case they both know will bring trouble. Volkov, the head of State Security, has brought in his 10-year-old son Gorya with a badly swollen leg. X-rays show a cancerous tumor; Gorya's leg must be amputated. Andrei, whose specialty is arthritis, has no expertise in oncology, but Volkov demands he take charge of the case because Gorya likes him. Anti-Semitic Volkov even agrees to Andrei's recommendation of a Jewish surgeon. Although the amputation is successful and Gorya appears on the road to recovery, the surgeon immediately transfers out of Leningrad and recommends Andrei do the same to lower his visibility. Instead, he and his wife Anna, who fell in love during the Nazi's siege on the city, take a fatalistic approach, barely altering their routine. . . . Historical fiction of the highest order." Kirkus

Dunn, Katherine

✓ ★ **Geek** love. Knopf 1989 347p

ISBN 0-394-56902-4

LC 88-45776

"The story begins as the five Binewski children, Arty, Elly, Iphy, Olympia and Baby Chick, gather around Papa Al to hear a revered family tale of their parents' courtship. Mama Crystal Lil interrupts and editorializes as she knits. . . . Papa's story is about how Mama became the geek in his traveling carnival, and all five children are carnival freaks." (Christ Century)

"The narrator is a bald female albino hunchback dwarf, raised in her family's carnival show, Binewski's Fabulon. (By using drugs and other methods, her parents succeeded in producing children with physical 'attributes' perfect for performance in a freak show.) This picaresque tale follows the life of the narrator during her family's carnival existence, through times both strange and awful." Booklist

Dunn, Mark

✓ **Ella** Minnow Pea; a progressively lipogrammatic epistolary fable. by Mark Dunn. MacAdam/Cage Pubs. 2001 205p (alk. paper) $22.00

ISBN 9780967370163; 0967370167

LC 2001042585

This novel "takes place in the present day on the fictional island of Nollop off the coast of South Carolina, where over a century earlier, the great Nevin Nollop invented a 35-letter panagram (a phrase, sentence or verse containing every letter in the alphabet). . . . Nollop was deified for his achievement. . . . Life seems almost utopian in its simplicity until letters of the alphabet start falling from the inscription on the statue erected in Nollop's honor, and the island's governing council decrees that as each letter falls, it must be extirpated from both spoken and written language. Forced to choose from a gradually shrinking pool of words, the novel's protagonists—a family of islanders—seek ways to communicate without employing the forbidden letters." (Publishers Weekly)

Dunn, Sarah

The **big** love. Little, Brown 2004 228p $21.95

ISBN 0-316-73815-8

"Alison Hopkins is devastated when her live-in boyfriend, Tom, walks out of their dinner party and back into the arms of his ex-girlfriend, Kate. Tom is only 33-year-old Alison's second lover, and she wonders if she wouldn't be better off if she had slept with more men. So when Henry, her handsome new boss at the free daily Philadelphia paper for which she writes a relationship column, seems interested in her, Alison seizes the opportunity. . . . Musing on everything from her evangelical Christian upbringing to men behaving badly . . . Alison's engaging voice carries this thoughtful, introspective, smart novel along and raises it far above the average novel about a young woman looking for love in the big city." Booklist

Dunne, Dominick

An **inconvenient** woman. Crown 1990 458p

LC 90-1602

"This is a smart novel because Dominick Dunne understands the distance between Los Angeles society and the spicy bazaars of Hollywood. And what makes Mr. Dunne not only first-rate, but also different from other writers who write about the very rich in late 20th-century America, is his knowledge that there's more to it than getting the labels and the street names right." N Y Times Book Rev

Dunne, Dominick

People like us; a novel. Crown 1988 403p

LC 88-353

"Engaging us in his characters' concerns and then pulling multiple story strands into a tight knot, Dominick Dunne demonstrates with wit and accuracy the delicate, merciless distinction between 'people like that' and 'people like us'." N Y Times Book Rev

Dunne, Dominick

A **season** in purgatory. Crown 1993 377p

LC 92-42352

"The unforgettable Bradley family, their skeletons . . . and peccadillos offer an allure similar to a sidelong glance at tabloid headlines, though here told with wit and skill. Their machinations prove both fascinating and appalling—and always hypnotically readable." Publ Wkly

Dunne, Dominick

Too much money; a novel. Crown Publishers 2009 275p $26

ISBN 978-0-609-60387-1; 0-609-60387-6

LC 2009-39443

Sequel to: People like us

"The novel opens with an Easter luncheon in a vast Park Avenue apartment that ironically marks the decline of its owner, a well-bred old guard woman named Lil Altemus. Gus Bailey, Dunne's alter ego, is in attendance. He's a journalist who works for a high-society magazine and is about to write a novel about widowed Perla Zacharias, one of the wealthiest women in the world, who, because of dubious origins, has been held down from New York society's highest ranks. Zacharias is not happy with the news about the novel and takes appropriate measures to block it. . . . Dunne shows a little more affection for his subjects than Capote, but not that much. Too little sympathy and you have acid satire. Too much and you have a sentimental portrait. Dunne does it just about right. After you finish his portrayal of the very rich, you may somehow be satisfied with the knowledge of just how poorly they live." San Francisco Chron

Dunne, Dominick

★ The **two** Mrs. Grenvilles; a novel. Crown 1985 374p

LC 85-445

"Basil Plant, a semisuccessful novelist tenuously clinging to the fringes of high society, narrates this haunting tale of two women destroyed by the virulence of their own twisted emotions. Alice Grenville, a respected woman of means, is initially appalled when her only son chooses to marry considerably beneath their fashionable set; still, rather than risk Junior's disaffection, Alice grudgingly accepts second-rate actress Ann Arden into her upper-crust family. The pathetic fates of the two Mrs. Grenvilles are sealed when Ann, in a jealous rage, murders her disenchanted husband. In order to avoid the sensationalism of a highly publicized scandal, Alice helps cover up the crime, forever binding herself to the woman she despises most. An affecting and disturbing tragedy replete with vivid portraits of spiritually crippled souls desperately struggling to inject some substance into their empty lives." Booklist

Dunne, John Gregory

Nothing lost. Knopf 2004 335p $24.95

ISBN 1-4000-4143-0

The author "adeptly skewers the pretensions of the politicians, pundits, and celebrities who descend upon the trial, ready to use it to further their own agendas. This is a violent, sexually charged, and, at times, acidly funny tale of power and paranoia in contemporary America." Libr J

Dunne, John Gregory

★ **True** confessions. Dutton 1977 341p

This novel is "about brotherhood, the loss of innocence, and the frailty of the human condition. Corruption-ridden LA in the late 1940s provides the backdrop for this tale of two brothers, a cop and a priest, who are unable to detach themselves from their Irish Catholic milieu. The bizarre murder of a prostitute provides the focal point but not the main subject matter of this work, which is concerned with policeman Tom's investigation and his discovery of seemingly universal weakness among the multitude of characters." Libr J

Dunnett, Dorothy

Caprice and Rondo. Knopf 1998 xxix, 539p (House of Niccolò)

ISBN 0-679-45477-2

LC 97-49458

First published 1997 in the United Kingdom

This seventh book in the House of Niccolo series "opens in 1474 as self-exiled Nicholas, holed up in Danzig with rowdy Polish cronies, licks his wounds from the family feud that destroyed his Scottish bank and alienated him further from his estranged wife (the obdurate, sharp-witted Gelis van Borselen). To protect Europe from the Turks, and to rebuild his financial empire, the globe-trotting Nicholas . . . mixes it up with Crimean Tartars, negotiates with the Shah of Persia and parries with Moscow traders before confronting Gelis in Ghent, where family skeletons tumble out of the closet. As usual, Dunnett brings her early modern financiers and aristocrats glitteringly to life." Publ Wkly

Dunnett, Dorothy

Checkmate. Putnam 1975 581p il

"A thoroughly romantic action yarn which isn't an insult to the intelligence. Intricately plotted, atmospheric, and peopled with characters of magnetic complexity, this series combines literary quality with can't-put-down entertainment." Libr J

Dunnett, Dorothy

Gemini. Knopf 2000 xxxii, 672p il (House of Niccolò) $27.50

ISBN 0-679-45478-0

LC 00-25027

"It's remarkably easy for the neophyte to enter Dunnett's adventurous world, for the author does an outstanding job of keeping each personality distinct and each of the innumerable subplots coherent. . . . Dunnett's work sits triumphantly at the top of a crowded field: it is a sensational, emotionally resonant epic." Publ Wkly

Dunnett, Dorothy

★ Niccolo rising. Knopf 1986 470p (House of Niccolò)

ISBN 0-394-53107-8

LC 86-45306

In the first volume of the House of Niccolò series we meet Claus, later known as Niccolò, "an apprentice at the Bruges branch of the Charetty company, run by the widowed owner. Claus is an enigma, seemingly a buffoon getting into scrapes with Felix, the Charetty heir, but also capable of initiating a courier service in connection with the Charetty commercial and mercenary ventures. In an era of economic and political intrigue, Claus makes the most of all opportunities—romantic and business." Libr J

This novel "displays all the author's strengths: strong characterization, subtle wit (with a dash of slapstick), lively action, and labyrinthine plot." Wilson Libr Bull

Followed by The spring of the ram

Dunnett, Dorothy

Pawn in frankincense. Putnam 1969 486p

Previous titles in this series of interlocking novels about Scottish adventurer Francis Crawford are: The game

of kings (1961); Queen's play (1964) and The disorderly knights (1966)

This installment of Crawford's adventures finds him in "the eastern Mediterranean region searching for his bastard son, who is being held hostage. Plots and counterplots, blood and gore lead to an excruciating climax in the form of a chess contest (a game this is not), in which Crawford and his old adversary Graham Mallett play with living pieces, themselves included. Penalty for capture is death, and Crawford's son, whom he can't recognize, is involved." Libr J

Followed by The ringed castle (1971)

Dunnett, Dorothy

Race of scorpions. Knopf 1990 534p (House of Niccolò)

ISBN 0-394-57107-X

LC 89-45292

"Through precisely rendered scenes, whether depicting a battle on the high seas, the operations of a dye works, a cleverly plotted ambush (using insects) or the gruesome tactics employed to destroy a proud city under siege, Dunnett furnishes fascinating images while spinning her admirable narrative web." Publ Wkly

Followed by Scales of gold

Dunnett, Dorothy

Scales of gold. Knopf 1992 519p (House of Niccolò)

ISBN 0-394-58627-1

LC 91-55554

First published 1991 in the United Kingdom

"Set within a rich tapestry of fifteenth-century Europe and Africa that is woven by a master of historical fiction, Nicholas' travels are constantly endangered by the greedy and vengeful figures he has tangled with in the past as well as by the natural hazards of the period." Booklist

Followed by The unicorn hunt

Dunnett, Dorothy

The spring of the ram. Knopf 1988 469p (House of Niccolò)

ISBN 0-394-56437-5

LC 87-37847

"Dunnett tells this story of love and money against a well-researched background of historical and cultural detail, taking her readers from Europe to Byzantium." Booklist

Followed by Race of scorpions

Dunnett, Dorothy

To lie with lions. Knopf 1996 xxiv, 626p (House of Niccolò)

ISBN 0-394-58629-8

LC 95-50422

First published 1995 in the United Kingdom

This sixth book in the House of Niccolo series focuses on 15th century adventurer Nicholas de Fleury's "marriage to quick-witted, self-sufficient Gelis van Borselen. It's a war of wills, egos and attrition that erupts in 1471 as de Fleury (aka Nicholas vander Poele) snatches his infant son, Jordan, from Gelis's arms and kidnaps the boy, a pawn in a bitter power struggle that will take the lives of friends and rivals. . . . With her usual dramatic flair, Dunnett mixes historical and fictive characters in a tale that sweeps from Venice to Antwerp, Edinburgh, Iceland, France and Cyprus." Publ Wkly

Followed by Caprice and Rondo

Dunnett, Dorothy

The **unicorn** hunt. Knopf 1994 656p (House of Niccolò)

ISBN 0-394-58628-X

LC 93-35692

First published 1993 in the United Kingdom

"Dunnett's writing style is somewhat complex but rich in information. The reader can feel immersed in the environment she creates; the characters (there are many) have well-developed, unique identities." Libr J

Followed by To lie with lions

Dunning, John

★ **Booked** to die; a mystery introducing Cliff Janeway. Scribner 1992 321p $24

ISBN 0-684-19383-3

LC 91-26889

Homicide detective and rare book collector Cliff "Janeway turns in his badge, opens a shop called Twice Told Books on Denver's Book Row and for a time becomes preoccupied with the enchanting lore of his trade. But Janeway discovers that not all book folk are gentlefolk. Two inoffensive book scouts are murdered after making a rare find, and the young clerk in Twice Told Books is dispatched with equal brutality. Thinking like a cop again, Janeway starts suspecting all his new friends on Book Row, including the woman with whom he has fallen in love. . . . This is a soundly plotted, evenly executed whodunit in the classic mode." N Y Times Book Rev

Dunning, John

The **bookman's** wake; a mystery with Cliff Janeway. Scribner 1995 351p

ISBN 0-684-80003-9

LC 94-34328

The author "can't resist writing lengthy, luxurious passages about the craftsmanship of the great print men. Strictly speaking, these eloquent lectures on the art of the printer and the beauty of the book get in the way of the action; but that shouldn't bother anyone who loves books—and their covers." N Y Times Book Rev

Dunning, John

The **sign** of the book; a Cliff Janeway novel. John Dunning. Scribner 2005 353p $25

ISBN 0-7432-5505-4

LC 2004-51190

"Rare books dealer Cliff Janeway agrees to help a friend of a friend, who's accused of murdering her husband. Coincidentally, the victim had an amazing book collection." Libr J

"It's great fun thumbing the pages with Janeway, who knows his business and takes a keen, almost sensual pleasure in a virgin edition." N Y Times Book Rev

Dunning, John

Two o'clock, eastern wartime; a novel. Scribner 2001 478p $26

ISBN 0-7432-0195-7

LC 00-32218

"Dunning masterfully re-creates that brief moment when radio seemed to offer a means of changing the nature of artistic expression. Superb entertainment and fascinating media history." Booklist

Duong Thu Huong

The **zenith**; Duong Thu Huong; translated by Stephen B. Young and Hoa Pham Young. Viking 2012 509 p.

ISBN 0670023752; 9780670023752

LC 2011046011

This novel, by Duong Thu Huong, "offers an . . . imagined account of the final months in the life of President Ho Chi Minh at an isolated mountaintop compound where he is imprisoned both physically and emotionally, weaving his story in with those of his wife's brother-in-law, an elder in a small village town, and a close friend and political ally, to explore how we reconcile the struggles of the human heart with the external world." (Publisher's note)

DuPree, Kia

Silenced; a novel. Kia DuPree. Grand Central Pub. 2011 336 p. $13.99

ISBN 9780446547741 pa

LC 2011000858

In this book, "30-year-old Nicola "Cola" Hampton struggles to keep her family together. Told from the perspectives of both Cola and her young daughter, Teyona ("Tinka"), the novel opens with Cola losing her job and moving Tinka and her older sons--14-year-old Marquan and 12-year-old Taevon--into Sursum Corda, a notorious D.C. housing project. Cola desperately wants to prevent her children from making the same mistakes that she and their fathers have made: Marquan's father is serving a life sentence for murder; Taevon's is a womanizer; and Tinka's has simply disappeared. Despite Cola's best efforts, Marquan steals a car, is associated with a double homicide, and a few years later is charged with capital murder; Taevon deals drugs; and Tinka's boyfriend robs liquor stores and gas stations." (Publishers Wkly)

Duran, Meredith

At your pleasure. Pocket Star Books 2012 387 p. (paperback) $7.99

ISBN 1451606958; 9781451606959

In this Regency romance novel, Adrian Ferrers, the Earl of Rivenham "will let nothing—not the deepening shadow of war, nor the growing darkness within him—interfere with his ambition to restore his family to its former glory. But when tasked by the king to uncover a traitor, he discovers instead a conspiracy—and a woman whose courage awakens terrible temptations." (Publisher's note)

Duran, Meredith

A **lady's** lessons in scandal; Meredith Duran. Pocket Star Books 2011 400p.

ISBN 9781451606935 pa

This book tells the story of "Nell Whitby, [who] has grown up in the slums of London's Bethnel Green. . . . When her mother is on her death bed she tells Nell that she is the daughter of the Earl of Rushden. Nell writes a letter to the earl asking for help for her dying mother, but she never hears from him. . . . After her mother's death, Nell goes to Rushden's home planning to exact her revenge upon him. . . . Being held at gunpoint aside, [Simon St. Maur] views this as his lucky day . . . marrying one of the heiresses of the late Earl of Rushden is a coup even he could never imagine. Simon strikes a bargain with Nell: he will teach her to be a proper lady and she will agree to marry him." (theromance-dish.com)

Durham, David Anthony

Acacia; book one: The war with the Mein. Doubleday 2007 576p $26.95

ISBN 978-0-385-50606-9; 0-385-50606-6

LC 2006-29726

"Leodan Akaran wants only to be a devoted father and political reformer, but his Acacian empire is based on forced labor, drugged pacification, and a dark deal that trades children into slavery. His chance for reform ends abruptly when the Meins, a fierce people subjugated by the Acacians, revolt through assassination, warfare, and biological terror. The four Akaran children scatter to their respective hiding places—and destinies—around the empire. . . . A series opener that combines the moral ambiguity and brutality of George R.R. Martin's Song of Ice and Fire with Guy Gavriel Kay's emotional sweep and Ursula K. Le Guin's ethnic diversity." Libr J

Durham, David Anthony

★ **Gabriel's** story. Doubleday 2001 291p hardcover o.p. pa $13.95

ISBN 0-385-49814-4; 0-385-72033-5 pa

LC 00-25291

In this "novel, set in the eighteen-seventies, Gabriel, a fifteen-year-old black boy from Baltimore, resents his new life on the Kansas plains when his widowed mother marries a homesteader. But then he falls in with a charismatic cowpunch and horse thief, and as they travel west to New Mexico a series of violent episodes brings Gabriel to swift maturity. The moral gravity of Durham's narrative is offset by his attentiveness to the primacy of nature in the Western landscape." New Yorker

Durham, David Anthony

A **walk** through darkness. Doubleday 2002 292p

ISBN 0-385-49925-6

LC 2001-47673

Durham "tells the parallel tales of two men in antebellum America: William, a young fugitive slave, and Morrison, a white man hired to track him. William escapes from Maryland and makes his way toward Philadelphia in search of his pregnant wife, Dover. Morrison, an older Scottish immigrant, has lived a hard, violent life he's not proud of, whose dark secrets—such as his responsibility for the death of his brother—slowly emerge as the story unwinds." Publ Wkly

Durham, Marilyn

The **man** who loved Cat Dancing. Harcourt Brace Jovanovich 1972 246p

"The man who loved Cat Dancing is John Wesley {Jay} Grobart, an ex-army officer who married Cat, a Shoshone squaw, when she was only 14. . . . When we meet Grobart, he is about to rob a train: recently released from prison after serving a 10-year term for the killing of three Indians believed to have raped and killed his wife, he wants money to regain his son. . . . At the same time, we meet Catherine Crocker who is on her way to catch the same train to expedite flight from her husband. Instead of catching the train she is kidnapped by the robbers. . . . The story . . . takes place in the Wyoming Territory of the 1880s." New Repub

Durrell, Lawrence

The **Alexandria** quartet: Justine; Balthazar; Mountolive {and} Clea. Dutton 1962 884p

Omnibus edition of four titles entered separately

Durrell, Lawrence

★ **Balthazar**; a novel. Dutton 1958 250p

The second volume of the Alexandria quartet

"Once again {Durrell} writes of Justine, Melissa, Clea, Nessim, Pursewarden, Scobie, Pombal—but from a fresh point of view. The new insights are provided by the psychiatrist, Balthazar, who convinces the narrator that the first volume of the story was almost wholly inaccurate. . . . So this second volume is a correction and an expansion of the first." N Y Times Book Rev

Followed by Mountolive

Durrell, Lawrence

★ **Clea**; a novel. Dutton 1960 287p

Final volume of the Alexandria quartet

"'The Alexandria Quartet' is one of the major achievements of fiction in our time, distinguished not only by its power of language, by its evocation of a place, by its creation of character, by the drama of many of its incidents, but also by its boldly original design. 'Clea' perfects the work, as a spire crowns a cathedral, but the spire is not to be judged in isolation." Saturday Rev

Durrell, Lawrence

★ **Justine**. Dutton 1957 253p

First volume of the Alexandria quartet

"Set in Alexandria the story concerns the amorous adventures of a penniless young man, a prostitute who lives with him, the rich and beautiful Justine with whom he has an affair, and Justine's husband." Publ Wkly

Followed by Balthazar

Durrell, Lawrence

★ **Mountolive**; a novel. Dutton 1959 318p

Third volume of the Alexandria quartet

First published 1958 in the United Kingdom

The perspective is "that of David Mountolive, the British ambassador: and what appeared to be 'the intrigues of desire' are shown to be intrigues motivated by politics. We learn that the beautiful Jewess, Justine, and her Coptic (Christian) husband, Nessim, are passionately united by a common cause: he believes that the formation of a Jewish state will save other minorities in the Arab world from Muslim domination and he is the leader of a group which is smuggling arms to the Jews in Palestine. The discovery of this conspiracy by Nessim's loyal English friends, Purse-warden and the ambassador, and their reactions to it form the plot line of Mountolive." Atlantic

Followed by Clea

Durrow, Heidi W.

★ The **girl** who fell from the sky; a novel. Algonquin Books of Chapel Hill 2010 264p $22.95

ISBN 978-1-56512-680-0; 1-56512-680-7

LC 2009-27572

"Set in the 1980s and focusing luminously on one unusually sympathetic girl overcoming apocalyptic tragedy and navigating her way through nascent sexuality and racial tensions, Durrow's novel transcends topicality." Christ Sci Monit

Dyachenko, Marina

The **scar**; Sergey Dyachenko and Marina Dyachenko. Tor 2012 336p.

ISBN 9780765329936

LC 2011025177

This book "is the story of a man driven by his own feverish demons to find redemption and the woman who just might save him. . . . Egert is a brash, confident member of the elite guards and an egotistical philanderer. But after he kills an innocent student in a duel, a mysterious man known as 'The Wanderer' challenges Egert and slashes his face with his sword, leaving Egert with a scar that comes to symbolize his cowardice. Unable to end his suffering by his own hand, Egert embarks on an odyssey to undo the curse and the horrible damage he has caused, which can only be repaired by a painful journey down a long and harrowing path." (Publisher's note)

Dybek, Stuart

✓ I sailed with Magellan. Farrar, Straus and Giroux 2003 307p $24

ISBN 0-374-17407-5

LC 2003-49052

The "episodes that intersect and surround young Perry Katzek's upbringing in the Polish-Mexican ghetto of Chicago's South Side are simultaneously daring and compassionate, intimate in detail and mythic in scale. Dybek has the rare ability to dart back and forth in time and slide around recklessly in space while carrying the reader effortlessly with him." Washington Post Book World

Dyer, Geoff

Jeff in Venice, death in Varanasi. Pantheon Books 2009 296p $24

ISBN 978-0-307-37737-1; 0-307-37737-7

LC 2008-23759

This novel is "zany and deceptively light, even as Atman explores the meaning of life and enlightenment. Does it matter whether the unnamed hero of the second part is Jeff or Geoff? Or whether the stories in Venice and Varanasi are the same story? You can read this novel as if you're munching a burger or savoring a ribeye." St. Louis Post-Dispatch

Díaz, Junot, 1968-

★ **This** is how you lose her; Junot Díaz. Riverhead Books 2012 213 p. $26.95

ISBN 1594487367; 9781594487361

LC 2012024051

This short story collection, by Pulitzer Prize-winning author Junot Díaz, "turns . . . to the haunting, impossible power of love--obsessive love, illicit love, fading love, maternal love. . . . At the heart of these stories is the irrepressible, irresistible Yunior, a young hardhead whose longing for love is equaled only by his recklessness--and by the extraordinary women he loves and loses." (Publisher's note)

E

Eagle, Kathleen

Ride a painted pony; Kathleen Eagle. MIRA Books 2006 314p.

ISBN 0778323595; 9780778323594

LC 2007282428

In this book, "Nick Red Shield, who is Sioux, swerves off a rain-slicked Missouri road and comes across an injured white woman in the bushes. Thinking he was the cause, Nick offers 'Joey' shelter at a local motel. The woman's real name is Lauren Davis; her taken name of Joey is the name of her son, who has been kidnapped by his father, Richard Vargas. Richard's friend Jack Reed was supposed to kill Lauren, but couldn't bring himself to finish the job. Lauren and Nick quickly fall for each other; back at Nick's South Dakota ranch, she begins to work his new paint horse, True Colors (Lauren's a former jockey). But Lauren can't let . . . the man she's falling in love with distract her from her primary goal-reuniting with her son." (Publishers Weekly)

Earle, Steve

✓ **I'll** never get out of this world alive. Houghton Mifflin Harcourt 2011 243p $26

ISBN 978-0-618-82096-2; 0-618-82096-5

LC 2010-49825

"Doc has lost his license to practice medicine but still tends to the whores, victims and/or perpetrators of street crime, and occasional unwanted pregnancy in San Antonio's South Presa corridor. Doc is haunted by the ghost of Hank Williams (he might have had a hand in Hank's journey to the grave), and most of the proceeds from his illicit medical practice go to support his own heroin habit. Then a Mexican girl seeking to terminate a pregnancy is brought to his room. Because Graciela bleeds profusely after the procedure, Doc moves her into his room. Soon she insinuates herself into his life and his medical practice, and Doc is feeling the call of the needle much less frequently. While Graciela herself is slow to heal, the patients she touches seem to mend as if by miracle, eventually bringing Doc and the other residents at the boardinghouse unwanted attention from both the church and the law." Libr J

"With its Charles Portis vibe and the author's immense cred as a musician and actor, this should have no problem finding the wide audience it deserves." Publ Wkly

Earley, Tony

The **blue** star; a novel. Little, Brown 2008 286p $23.99

ISBN 978-0-316-19907-0; 0-316-19907-9

LC 2007-9921

Sequel to: Jim the boy

"It's late summer 1941, and Jim Glass, now a high school senior, has an earnest, unshakable passion for classmate Chrissie Steppe. But as straightforward as his feelings are, the circumstances of his nascent romance are complex: Chrissie's family is indebted to their landlord, whose sailor son Bucky claimed Chrissie as his girl before shipping out to serve on the USS California at Pearl Harbor. Throughout Jim's fraught final year at school, he relies on the advice of his uncles, but after Pearl Harbor is bombed, they can't protect him from the war's toll. Questions of patriotism, sexuality and poverty weave their way into a narrative that's deceptive in its simplicity: the growing pains that Jim and his friends experience pack a startling emotional punch." Publ Wkly

Earley, Tony

Jim the boy; a novel. Little, Brown 2000 227p $23.95

ISBN 0-316-19964-8

LC 99-42901

This novel is set in "the Depression-era town of Aliceville, N.C. . . . The story opens on Jim's 10th birthday and ends a year later. In that time, Jim sees the ocean for the first time, plays ball in front of a stopped passenger train that might or might not have Ty Cobb on board, visits his dying grandfather and watches a traveling salesman court his widowed mother." Newsweek

"The genius of a novel like this is Earley's trust in the purity of his style and the plainness of his story. Perhaps all things done very well look simple." Christ Sci Monit

Eastland, Sam

Archive 17; a novel of suspense. Sam Eastland. Bantam Books 2012 262 p.

ISBN 9780345525734; 9780345525758

LC 2011011626

This novel is a "thriller set in the Soviet Union under Stalin (after 2011's Shadow Pass) [in which] . . . much of the book's action [takes place in] Siberia. Countless lives hang on the caprice of Joseph Stalin, including that of Inspector Pekkala, a former czarist guard who served time as a political prisoner before becoming Stalin's (mostly) trusted investigator. In 1939, the dictator sends Pekkala to his old labor camp, Borodok, to look into the murder of Isaac Ryabov, a former cavalry captain and one of the last surviving colleagues of Colonel Kolchak, a close ally of the Russian imperial family. Pekkala must go undercover to catch whoever slit Ryabov's throat and stay in the good graces of Stalin, who fears that Ryabov's demise may pose a threat: to his rule." (Publishers Weekly)

Eastland, Sam

Eye of the Red Tsar; a novel of suspense. Bantam Books 2010 278p $25

ISBN 978-0-553-80781-3; 0-553-80781-1

LC 2009-52898

"The tale is a bit too reliant on flashbacks, but hair-raising action sequences and spellbinding settings make up for that minor flaw." Kirkus

Includes bibliographical references

Eastland, Sam

Shadow pass; a novel of suspense. Sam Eastland. Bantam Books 2011 289 p.

ISBN 055380782X; 9780553807820; 9780553908091

LC 2010027234

In this book, "[d]eep in the Russian countryside, a thirty-ton killing machine known officially as T-34 is being developed in total secrecy. Its inventor is a rogue genius whose macabre death is considered an accident only by the innocent. Suspecting assassins everywhere, Stalin brings in his best—if least obedient—detective to solve a murder that's tantamount to treason. Answerable to no one, Inspector Pekkala has the dictator's permission to go anywhere and interrogate anyone. But the closer Pekkala gets to answers, the more questions he uncovers—first and foremost, why is the state's most dreaded female operative, Commissar Major Lysenkova, investigating the case when she's only assigned to internal affairs?" (Publisher's note)

Ebel, Kathy

Claudia Silver to the rescue; a novel. Kathy Ebel. Houghton Mifflin Harcourt 2013 256 p. (hardcover) $25

ISBN 0547985576; 9780547985572

LC 2012039062

In this novel, by Kathy Ebel, "estranged from her . . . family and fired for an impropriety at work, Claudia Silver is officially in over her head. When her younger sister lands on her doorstep urgently in need of help, twenty-something Claudia desperately wants to offer the rescue that she herself has longed for. But Claudia missteps dramatically, straight into a disastrous love affair that disrupts three very different New York households." (Publisher's note)

Ebershoff, David

The **19th** wife; a novel. Random House 2008 514p $26

ISBN 978-1-4000-6397-0; 1-4000-6397-3

LC 2008-00074

This "novel tells two parallel stories of polygamy. The first recounts Brigham Young's expulsion of one of his wives, Ann Eliza, from the Mormon Church; the second is a modern-day murder mystery set in a polygamous compound in Utah. Unfolding through an impressive variety of narrative forms—Wikipedia entries, academic research papers, newspaper opinion pieces—the stories include fascinating historical details. . . . Ebershoff demonstrates abundant virtuosity, as he convincingly inhabits the voices of both a nineteenth-century Mormon wife and a contemporary gay youth excommunicated from the church, while also managing to say something about the mysterious power of faith." New Yorker

Eberstadt, Fernanda

Rat. Alfred A. Knopf 2010 293p $25.95

ISBN 978-0-307-27183-9; 0-307-27183-8

LC 2009-24849

"A deceptively simple construct written in uncomplicated prose, Eberstadt's Huck-Finn-in-the-Pyrenees premise unfurls into a complex commentary on everything from identity and language to domesticity and terrorism." A. V. Club

Eccles, Marjorie

Last nocturne. A Thomas Dunne Book/Minotaur Books 2010 409p $25.99

ISBN 978-0-312-57793-3; 0-312-57793-1

LC 2009-49633

First published 2008 in the United Kingdom

"Grace Thurley's decision to break her engagement to an exceedingly dull young man and become the paid companion/secretary to a family friend in London seems to augur a conventionally enjoyable novel of romantic suspense set in the first decade of the last century. But with the death of a young artist and the introduction of a second storyline set in Vienna, the book becomes something quite different and far more complex. Grace's developing romance with Guy Martagon, her employer's son, is for the most part secondary to the story of Isobel Amberly, a widow of independent means who has settled in Vienna after her husband's death. She becomes involved with the Franck brothers, artists whose apartment is in the same building as Isobel's. And they are all linked to the young artist whose death is being investigated in London by the sanguine Chief Inspector Lamb and his sergeant Cogan." Denver Post

Echenoz, Jean

Lightning; translated from the French by Linda Coverdale. New Press 2011 142p $19.95

ISBN 978-1-59558-649-0

This is a "fictional portrait of Nikola Tesla (here depicted as Gregor), a talented immigrant who begins life in the U.S. as an underpaid troubleshooter for Thomas Edison but whose exceptional gifts eventually make him Edison's formidable rival. But readers see much more than the extensively chronicled Edison-Tesla rivalry. Probing deep into Tesla's tangled psyche, Echenoz illuminates unexpected tensions. . . . Coverdale's nuanced translation of Echenoz's highly successful French original permits English-speaking readers to contemplate the human mystery that persists long after the scientific puzzles have been solved." Booklist

Echlin, Kim

The **disappeared**. Black Cat 2009 235p pa $14

ISBN 978-0-8021-7066-8

"There is something of Marguerite Duras in these pages, something of the lust between the young Western girl and the Asian man that drove novels like The Lover and The North China Lover. But while Duras focuses mostly on desire, Echlin focuses on absolute love—physical desire coupled with the need to know everything about the beloved, to follow him even to the grave and beyond. . . . [An] exquisite novel." N Y Times Book Rev

Eco, Umberto, 1932-

Baudolino; translated from the Italian by William Weaver. Harcourt 2002 522p $27

ISBN 0-15-100690-3

LC 2002-2345

Original Italian edition, 2000

"In this whimsical yet deadly earnest tale, Eco puts forth the question that perpetually beguiles him and with which he beguiles the rest of us: If a teller of tales tells us he's telling the truth, how can we know for sure what really happened?." New Yorker

Eco, Umberto

Foucault's pendulum; translated from the Italian by William Weaver. Harcourt Brace Jovanovich 1989 641p $33

ISBN 0-15-132765-3

LC 89-32212

Original Italian edition, 1988

This book "is not meant to be easy. . . . {But} great are the rewards for those who actually manage to read it. For while it is not a novel in the strict sense of the word, it is a truly formidable gathering of information delivered playfully by a master manipulating his own invention—in effect, a long, erudite joke." N Y Times Book Rev

Eco, Umberto

The **island** of the day before; translated from the Italian by William Weaver. Harcourt Brace & Co. 1995 515p

ISBN 0-15-100151-0

LC 95-7594

Original Italian edition, 1994

In this novel, set in 1643, "Roberto della Griva is shipwrecked on a ship. His own ship has been rent apart by a storm, and, tied to a plank, he has drifted to the Daphne, anchored in the bay of a South Pacific island. The deserted Daphne has no boat, and Roberto can't swim, so he is effectively a prisoner. As he explores the Daphne, he recalls his life as a young man at the siege of Casale, his years spent in hot philosophical debate in Paris, and his devotion to an adored but unapproachable woman. But there is an intruder on board, which brings to mind Ferrante, the evil twin Roberto imagines he has. The intruder turns out to be a monk obsessed with issues of time and the meridians." Libr J

Eco, Umberto

The **mysterious** flame of Queen Loana; translated from the Italian by Geoffrey Brock. Harcourt, Inc. 2005 469p il $27

ISBN 0-15-101140-0

LC 2004-29105

Original Italian edition, 2004

"Those who don't enjoy the occasional ramble through 'Bartlett's Quotations' may quickly lose patience with 'Queen Loana,' but bookworms will get an added kick out of puzzling out the dozens of literary allusions." Christ Sci Monit

Eco, Umberto

★ The **name** of the rose; translated from the Italian by William Weaver. Harcourt Brace Jovanovich 1983 502p $35

ISBN 0-15-144647-4

LC 82-21286

Original Italian edition, 1982

This novel "is an antidetective-story detective story; as a semiotic murder mystery it is superbly entertaining; it is also an extraordinary work of novelistic art." Harpers

Eco, Umberto, 1932-

The **Prague** cemetery; translated from the Italian by Richard Dixon. Houghton Mifflin Harcourt 2011 444p il

ISBN 0-547-57753-2; 0547577532; 978-0-547-57753-1; 9780547577531

LC 2011-28593

Original Italian edition, 2010

The book "is a novel about the most notorious and insidious forgery of modern times, 'The Protocols of the Elders of Zion.' Put together in tsarist Russia in the early twentieth century and soon exposed as a clumsy police fraud, 'The Protocols' retain an apparently inextinguishable following among people convinced that a Jewish plot for world domination is still creeping toward fulfillment. . . . Eco . . . has . . . construct[ed] a semifictional narrative of how 'The Protocols' might have evolved . . . [he] suggests that 'The Protocols evolved from the mass of half-baked conspiracy literature that accumulated in nineteenth-century Europe." (New York Review of Books)

"An entertaining and melodramatic farrago of 19th-century European hate-mongering that features a sinister cast of anti-Semites, assassins and Satanists. Mr. Eco's sweaty-palmed conceit is that all of the conspiracies invented to spread and justify the period's race hatred can be traced back to one evil (and of course fictitious) mastermind, the creator of the notorious hoax text 'The Protocols of the Elders of Zion.' That man is the hissably malevolent Simone Simonini, a forger of legal documents who begins his narrative with bilious diatribes against Jesuits, Freemasons, women, the French, Italians, Germans and most of all Jews, whom he blames for the world's ills despite having scarcely met any. The novel is partially Simonini's record of his life and deeds, but his confessions are interrupted by someone who seems to be his alter ego, the Jesuit Abbé Dalla Piccola; and both sets of their chronicles are amended at times by a nameless omniscient third-person voice." Wall Street J

Eden, Cynthia

Deadly lies. Forever 2011 384p pa $7.99
ISBN 978-0-446-55925-6

Sequel to Deadly fear (2010) and Deadly heat (2010)

"Still traumatized by a near-fatal encounter with a serial killer, FBI special agent Samantha Kennedy fights to prove herself by tracking a kidnapper who is targeting the sons of wealthy men. She's also navigating an attraction to business owner Max Ridgeway. When Max's stepbrother disappears, he and Samantha must race against time and the ever-changing whims of a brutal killer while confronting their troubled pasts and their shared passion. Eden's characters are complex and likable, and her plot speeds along breathlessly to a surprising and sizzling conclusion." Publ Wkly

Edgarian, Carol

Three stages of amazement; a novel. Scribner 2011 298p $25
ISBN 978-1-4391-9830-8; 1-4391-9830-6

LC 2010-44448

"Edgarian's characters fully inhabit this all-too-familiar world of marital squabbles, wounded pride and unpaid bills. Her depiction of the frustrations and joys of motherhood is hilariously on target, when it's not tragic. Her characters are caught in the rhythms of trying, failing and trying again—patterns that superbly mimic those of everyday life." BookPage

Edge, Arabella

The **god** of spring. Simon & Schuster 2007 340p $24
ISBN 978-0-7432-9484-3; 0-7432-9484-X

LC 2006-46952

First published 2005 in Australia; published in the United Kingdom with title: The raft

This "brilliant and original . . . novel explores the mechanism of creativity through the story of a single painting. . . . The narrative zips along at such a terrific pace that only at the end is there time for reflection upon the all-consuming nature of real art. Page-turning and substantial, a rare combination." London Daily Mail

Edgerton, Clyde

The **Bible** salesman; a novel. Little, Brown and Co. 2008 241p $23.99
ISBN 978-0-316-11751-7; 0-316-11751-X

LC 2007-45410

"Edgerton is a master of comic timing, and 'The Bible Salesman' is a font of wildly creative comedy. . . . But it's the novel's quiet, introspective moments that are most memorable." Richmond Times-Dispatch

Edgerton, Clyde

The **night** train; a novel. Little, Brown and Company 2011 215p $23.99
ISBN 978-0-316-11759-3; 0-316-11759-5

LC 2010-41546

Edgerton's "affinity for simple sentences and clean chapter breaks give this slim novel an almost fable-like power. [His] knowledge about music is on full display, as is his understanding of the subtleties of race relations as the Civil Rights Movement picked up steam." Kirkus

Edgerton, Clyde

★ **Walking** across Egypt; a novel. Algonquin Bks. 1987 216p $17.95
ISBN 0-912697-51-2

LC 86-20645

"Mattie Rigsbee, at 78, is slowing down. She plans her funeral so as not to be a burden; she supports the local Baptist church and entertains herself with hymns at the parlor piano; she tries not to meddle in her children's lives, though she does wish they'd marry; she longs for grandchildren. Then comes Wesley. Reared in an orphanage until he graduated to the reformatory, Wesley touches her heart, revives a life gone to seed. Just as he needs a grandmother's love and stability, so Mattie needs his challenge, dependence, and love." Libr J

This novel is "warm, innocent, and has a charming central character." Booklist

Followed by Killer diller

Edgeworth, Maria

★ **Castle** Rackrent; edited by George Watson; with an introduction by Kathryn J. Kirkpatrick. Oxford University Press 2000 xliii, 127p (Oxford world's classics) pa $11.95

ISBN 0-19-283563-7

LC 94-48873

First published 1800 in the United Kingdom

"This work may be regarded as the first fully developed historical novel and the first true regional novel in English. Set, according to the title-page, 'Before the year 1782', the characters, the life of the country, and the speech, are unmistakably Irish. It is a brief, high-spirited novel, narrated in his old age by the devoted Thady Quirk, steward to three generations of Rackrents." Oxford Companion to Engl Lit. 6th edition

Edghill, India

Queenmaker; a novel of King David's Queen. St. Martin's Press 2002 376p

ISBN 0-312-28918-9

LC 2001-48603

"When Saul, a simple farmer, is crowned the first king of Israel, his youngest daughter, Michal, thus becomes a princess. She meets and falls in love with a devastatingly handsome charmer, David." Booklist

"With its excellent writing, dynamic characters, and galloping pace, Edghill's work is highly recommended for all historical fiction collections." Libr J

Edmonds, Walter D.

Drums along the Mohawk. Little, Brown 1936 592p

A "regional novel about early settlers in the Mohawk river valley in New York state during the Revolutionary war. The little community is made up of . . . individuals to whom Indian raids, British invasions, and militia gatherings are evidences of a distraught world outside. Their own understanding of the difficulties is rather vague. Gil Martin and his wife, clearing their home in the forest, and their not-very-near neighbors, are the main characters." Booklist

Edugyan, Esi

Half-blood blues; Esi Edugyan. Picador 2012 343p.

ISBN 9781250012708

LC 2011044816

Scotiabank Giller Prize (2011)

This novel, shortlisted for the 2011 Man Booker Prize, tells the story of "Hieronymus Falk, a rising star on the cabaret scene [in 1940s Paris, France], [who] was arrested in a cafe and never heard from again. He was twenty years old. He was a German citizen. And he was black. Fifty years later, Sid, Hiero's bandmate and the only witness that day, is going back to Berlin. Persuaded by his old friend Chip, Sid discovers there's more to the journey than he thought when Chip shares a mysterious letter, bringing to the surface secrets buried since Hiero's fate was settled." (themanbookerprize.com)

Edwards, Kim

The **memory** keeper's daughter; Kim Edwards. Viking 2005 x, 401p (pbk.) $15; $24.95

ISBN 9780670034161; 9780143037149; 0670034169

LC 2005042257

British Book Awards (the Nibbies): Popular Fiction Award (2005)

This book "hinges on the birth of fraternal twins, a healthy boy and a girl with Down syndrome. . . . [W]hen young Norah Henry goes into labor, her husband, orthopedic surgeon Dr. David Henry, must deliver their babies himself, aided only by a nurse. Seeing his daughter's handicap, he instructs the nurse, Caroline Gill, to take her to a home and later tells Norah . . . that their son Paul's twin died at birth. Instead of institutionalizing Phoebe, Caroline absconds with her to Pittsburgh. David's deception becomes the defining moment of the main characters' lives. . . . David's undetected lie warps his marriage; he grapples with guilt; Norah mourns her lost child; and Paul not only deals with his parents' icy relationship but with his own yearnings for his sister as well." (Publishers Weekly)

Edwards, Yvvette

A **Cupboard** full of coats. Oneworld Publications 2011 260 p.

ISBN 9781851687978; 1851687971

In this book, which was long-listed for the Man Booker Prize, "fourteen years after the tragic death of her mother, Jinx cannot reconcile her overwhelming sense of guilt and move on with her life. Her marriage has dissolved, her relationship with her young son is in shambles, and she hasn't learned to love since her mother's violent exit from this world at the hands of her lover. But when an unexpected visitor from the past returns, Jinx is forced to face the twisted tale of her mother's last months and uncover secrets." (Booklist)

Edwardson, Ake

Sail of stone; Åke Edwardson; translated by Rachel Willson-Broyles. Simon & Schuster 2012 402 p.

ISBN 1451608500; 9781451608502

LC 2011028497

This book presents "a pair of fresh cases for Erik Winter and Aneta Djanali, of the Gothenburg Police. Though she hasn't made any complaints herself, her neighbors have repeatedly indicated that Anette Lindsten has been attacked. . . . Imagine her surprise when, on a return visit, she finds Anette's father and brother packing up her things--and then her even greater surprise when she learns that Anette has no brother and that the solicitous men were a pair of thieves. . . . Winter, meanwhile, is chasing his own will-o'-the-wisp at the urging of his old girlfriend Johanna Osvald, who's worried because her fisherman father Axel has vanished during a trip to Scotland. It soon becomes clear that Axel was investigating the disappearance of his own father, John Osvald, from a fishing trawler during the war." (Kirkus)

Effinger, George Alec

   George Alec Effinger live! from planet Earth; featuring contributions by Neal Barrett Jr. ... {et al.} Golden Gryphon Press 2005 360p $25.95

     ISBN 1-930846-32-0

                            LC 2004016935

   "Effinger was one of the acknowledged masters of satirical sf and a prolific short story writer whose prodigious stylistic gifts are showcased in this unusual collection selected by his fellow writers and editors. In tribute to Effinger's genius, 16 veteran authors, from Michael Bishop and Jack Dann to Mike Resnick and Neil Gaiman, introduce each selection with personal reflections on Effinger's character and legacy. . . . Constituting a special treat for Effinger's fans are the O. Niemand stories, here introduced by Gardner Dozois, in which Effinger mimics, without caricature, the styles of such literary legends as Steinbeck, Hemingway, and Twain, while in each tale exploring an sf theme." Booklist

Egan, Greg

   Incandescence. Night Shade Books 2008 250p $24.95

     ISBN 978-1-59780-128-7; 1-59780-128-3

   A hard SF novel about the "efforts of the Arkmakers, who live in a neutron star's accretion disk at the center of the galaxy, to develop orbital physics from first principles and save the artificial world created by their more sophisticated ancestors. Meanwhile, Rakesh, a more or less human member of a distant posthuman society, sets off on an unrelated quest to find the Arkmakers and is soon trying to save them from their current danger." Publ Wkly

   Egan "writes clearly and vividly about the cutting edge of science yet doesn't forget that characters are the windows through which the world is viewed." Libr J

Egan, Greg

   Schild's ladder. Eos 2002 342p $25.95

     ISBN 0-06-105093-8

                            LC 2001-55583

   First published 2001 in the United Kingdom

   "Egan writes rather forbidding novels, always grounded in real science and imbued with serious scientific speculations. This is his most uncompromising book to date." Booklist

   Includes bibliographical references

Egan, Greg

   Zendegi. Night Shade 2010 279p $24.95; pa $14.99

     ISBN 978-1-59780-174-4; 1-59780-174-7; 978-1-59780175-1 pa; 1-59780-175-5 pa

   "Zendegi is two stories told in parallel. The first is the story of Martin Seymour, an Australian journalist sent to Iran to cover another disputed election (this one in 2012), and fifteen years afterward, of the new life that he and his family have built in Iran. The second is Nasim Golestani, an Iranian expatriate who, using a new method of electronically mapping human consciousness, has inadvertently created the framework for the future world's most popular MMORPG, 'Zendegi.' Martin and Nasim discover each other by unfortunate happenstance, and while Zendegi is slowly being destroyed, Nasim and the now-dying Martin try to use the game to preserve a copy of his consciousness, to ensure that Martin's son will always have his father." io9

Egan, Jennifer

   The **keep**. Alfred A. Knopf 2006 239p $23.95

     ISBN 1-4000-4392-1

                            LC 2006-11573

   This novel "makes us think hard about one of the murkiest mysteries of all: the mystery of perception, that uncertain border where reality and imagination meet. . . . In a novel full of unexpected shifts and interruptions, it's amazing how deftly Egan builds a logic for her characters." Los Angeles Times

Egan, Jennifer

   ★ A **visit** from the Goon Squad. Knopf 2010 273p il $25.95

     ISBN 0-307-59283-9; 978-0-307-59283-5

                            LC 2009-46496

   "Interlocking narratives circle the lives of Bennie Salazar, an aging former punk rocker and record executive, and Sasha, the passionate, troubled young woman he employs. Although Bennie and Sasha never discover each other's pasts, the reader does, . . . along with the secret lives of . . . other characters whose paths intersect with theirs, over many years, in locales as varied as New York, San Francisco, Naples, and Africa. We first meet Sasha in her mid-thirties, on her therapist's couch in New York City, confronting her longstanding compulsion to steal. Later, we . . . see her as the child of a violent marriage, then as a runaway living in Naples, then as a college student. . . . We meet Bennie Salazar at the melancholy nadir of his adult life—divorced, struggling to connect with his nine-year-old son . . . —and then revisit him in 1979." (Publisher's note)

   This novel is "centered, nominally, on the aging owner of an independent record label and his comely, kleptomania-prone assistant. But it is in fact a frequently dazzling piece of layer-cake meta-fiction, told via a sprawling constellation of characters and linked vignettes that spill from the late '70s Bay Area punk scene to the African plains, the dissolute slums of Naples, and the flush New York suburbs of the '90s boom. Egan's expert flaying of human foibles has the compulsive allure of poking at a sore tooth: excruciating but exhilarating, too." Entertainment Wkly

Eggers, Dave, 1970-

   ★ A **hologram** for the king; a novel. by Dave Eggers. McSweeney's Books 2012 312 p. $25

     ISBN 193636574X; 9781936365746

     National Book Award Finalist (2012)

   Author David Eggers "takes us around the world to show how one man fights to hold himself and his splintering family together in the face of the global economy's gale-force winds. . . . In a rising Saudi Arabian city, far from weary, recession-scarred America, a struggling businessman pursues a last-ditch attempt to stave off foreclosure, pay his daughter's college tuition, and finally do something great." (Publisher's note)

Eggers, Dave, 1970-
   How we are hungry; stories. by Dave Eggers. Vintage Books 2005 218p (pbk.) $15.00
   ISBN 1400095565; 9781400095568

LC 2005042321

This book offers a collection of short stories. "The collection starts with 'Another,' a story of a middle-aged divorcee galloping through the Egyptian deserts and subjecting himself to the pain of the relentless jolting of the horse's gait until he finally learns to absorb its rhythm. His search for more sights and further experiences is endless, and on he goes, disappointed but insatiable, streaming into the wilderness. . . . 'The Only Meaning of the Oil-Wet Water' is a . . . long short story in which Pilar, a dermatologist, flies to Costa Rica to meet her friend Hand . . . in the knowledge that they'll end up having sex, but uncertain what emotions will bind them beyond lust and friendship." (The Guardian)

Eggers, Dave, 1970-
   What is the what; the autobiography of Valentino Achak Deng: a novel. Dave Eggers. McSweeney's 2006 475 p. map (pbk.) $16; $26
   ISBN 9780307385901; 1932416641; 9781932416640

LC 2007276445

This "novel's subtitle, 'The Autobiography of Valentino Achak Deng,' refers to a real-life Sudanese refugee who informs us in a brief preface that 'over the course of many years, I told my story orally to the author. He then concocted this novel, approximating my voice and using the basic events of my life as the foundation.'" The book presents the fictionalized story of Deng's "odyssey from his village in southern Sudan to temporary shelter in Ethiopia to a vast refugee camp in Kenya and finally to Atlanta." (New York Times)

Eggers "has made the outlines of the tragedy in East Africa—so vague to so many Americans—not only sharp and clear but indelible. An eloquent testimony to the power of storytelling, What Is the What is an extraordinary work of witness, and of art." N Y Times Book Rev

Egolf, Tristan
   Skirt and the fiddle; a novel. Grove Press 2002 199p $23
   ISBN 0-8021-1722-8

LC 2002-16442

"Narrator Charlie Evans, a violin virtuoso and orphan of Asian-Afro-American parentage, ends up in a skid-row boarding house in Philth Town, somewhere near New York City. Among the residents is Tinsel Greetz, an anarchist and troublemaker with whom Charlie reluctantly forms a friendship. . . . This energetic and entertaining work seems more like an expanded short story, but the author's vibrant writing and lunatic vision might be especially appealing to a younger . . . audience." Libr J

Ehrenreich, Ben
   Ether. City Lights Books 2011 183p pa $13.95
   ISBN 978-0-87286-518-1; 0-87286-518-5

LC 2011-29377

"The characters are familiar from hardboiled fiction, but Ehrenreich delights in fleshing out their known contours, playfully exposing the strings on his puppets instead of trying to hide them." Los Angeles Times Book Rev

Ehrenreich, Ben
   The suitors; a novel. Counterpoint Press 2006 295p $23
   ISBN 978-158243-335-6

LC 2005-29772

A "novel loosely based on Homer's Odyssey. . . . The suitors of the title are the parade of prospective lovers who line up on the doorstep of heroine Penny (i.e., Penelope) after her husband, Payne, abandons her. As the novel's Odysseus figure, Payne has built a protective palace around his wife, then promptly assembled an army to fight overseas. In his absence, Penny becomes surrounded by lustful ne'erdowells but pines only for Payne until a mysterious stranger appears to capture her fancy and set the stage for her husband's dramatic return. Ehrenreich's odd mixing of psychological insight and full-blooded characterizations with frivolous plot twists and riotous action may not be to everyone's taste, yet it makes for some delicious occasional black comedy." Booklist

Eisenberg, Deborah
   The collected stories of Deborah Eisenberg. Picador/Farrar, Straus And Giroux 2010 992p $22
   ISBN 978-0-312-42989-8; 0-312-42989-4

LC 2010-02081

This volume gathers all the stories from four previously published collections: Transactions in a foreign currency (1986); Under the 82nd Airborne (1992); All around Atlantis (1997); Twilight of the superheroes (2006)

"Eisenberg's tales, their milieus vividly defined, their dialogue unsettlingly real, are long and leisurely; her characters, hyper-observant but helpless. They often have just enough drive and sense of purpose to thrust themselves into the stream of life, but then they are just carried along, baffled or passive. . . . Wry humor surfaces just often enough to keep desolation at bay. After all, while Eisenberg recognizes that there is no escaping selfishness, weakness, and confusion (both intimate and geopolitical)—let alone illness, age, and misfortune—humanity must keep drifting on somehow." Atlantic

Eisenberg, Deborah
   Twilight of the superheroes. Farrar, Straus & Giroux 2006 225p $23
   ISBN 978-0-374-29941-5; 0-374-29941-2

LC 2005-42659

"Using her playwright's ear for dialogue and a journalistic eye for the askew detail, Ms. Eisenberg gives us—in just a handful of pages—a visceral sense of these characters' daily routines, the worlds they inhabit and the families they rebel against or allow to define them. . . . Instead of forcing her characters' stories into neat, arbitrary, preordained shapes, she allows them to grow asymmetrical narratives—narratives that possess all the surprising twists and dismaying turns of real life." N Y Times (Late N Y Ed)

Ekman, Kerstin

God's mercy; translated by Linda Schenck. University of Nebraska Press 2009 389p (European women writers series) $45; pa $21.95

ISBN 978-0-8032-1074-5; 0-8032-1074-4; 978-0-8032-2458-2 pa; 0-8032-2458-3 pa

LC 2008-51843

Original Swedish edition, 1999

"In 1916 Hillevi Klarins, a 25-year-old midwife from Uppsala, Sweden, applies for a position in northern Röbäck, in the rural Blackwater region. She is entering an unknown world, where tensions between native Lapps, Swedes, and nearby Norwegians run high. Though the area has electricity and plumbing, Röbäck remains a place haunted by little people, folk medicine, and a profound distrust of the medical instruments Hillevi carries. Though much happens in God's Mercy, only a few instances are of the 'novelistic crisis' variety. Rather, the book moves slowly through the lives of these people in Blackwater, Sweden as they acclimate to an increasingly modern world." PopMatters

Elias, Gerald

Danse macabre; Gerald Elias. Minotaur Books 2010 278 p. $24.99

ISBN 0312541899; 9780312541897

LC 2010021994

In author Gerald Elias' book, "blind and cranky Daniel Jacobus, a former concert violinist, reluctantly agrees to investigate the murder of maestro René Allard after . . . musician BTower, who had a tumultuous relationship with Allard, is seen standing over the body literally with blood on his hands. As BTower sits on death row . . . , Jacobus . . . uncovers shady activities on Allard's part. Puzzling transactions involving violins, an attempt on Jacobus's life, and the suicide of an elevator operator indicate that Jacobus may be closing in on uncomfortable truths." (Publishers Weekly)

Elias, Gerald

★ **Death** and transfiguration; a Daniel Jacobus novel. Gerald Elias. Minotaur Books 2012 322 p.

ISBN 9780312678357; 9781250014801

LC 2012005488

This book tells the story of "Vaclav Herza . . . [who] has been music director of Harmonium for forty years. . . . It is the eve of the opening of a dramatic new concert hall designed by Herza himself. It is also the eleventh hour of intense contract negotiations with the musicians that have strained relations within the organization. When the acting concertmaster, Scheherazade O'Brien, is summarily dismissed by the despotic Herza for the permanent concertmaster position, an audition she was poised to win, O'Brien slits her wrists and the orchestra becomes convulsed. Now, blind, cantankerous violin teacher Daniel Jacobus . . . investigates Herza's dark past." (Publisher's note)

Eliot, George

★ **Adam** Bede. Knopf 1992 xxxiii, 612p $20

ISBN 0-679-40991-2

LC 91-53187

First published in 1859

"The title character, a carpenter, is in love with a woman who bears a child by another man. Although Bede tries to help her, he eventually loses her but finds happiness with Dinah Morris, a Methodist preacher. Adam Bede was Eliot's first long novel. Its masterly realism—evident, for example, in the recording of Derbyshire dialect—brought to English fiction the same truthful observation of minute detail that John Ruskin was commending in the Pre-Raphaelites. But what was new in this work of English fiction was the combination of deep human sympathy and rigorous moral judgment." Merriam-Webster's Ency of Lit

Eliot, George

★ **Middlemarch**; a study of provincial life. with an introduction by E.S. Shaffer. Knopf 1991 xxxix, 888p $22

ISBN 0-679-40567-4

LC 91-52976

First published 1872

A novel "with a double plot interest. The heroine, Dorothea Brooke, longs to devote herself to some great cause and, for a time, expects to find it in her marriage to Rev. Mr. Casaubon, an aging scholar. Mr. Casaubon lives only eighteen months after their marriage, a sufficient period to disillusion her completely. He leaves her his estate, with the ill-intentioned proviso that she will forfeit if she marries his young cousin Will Ladislaw, whom she had seen frequently in Rome. Endeavoring to find happiness without Ladislaw, whom she has come to care for deeply, Dorothea throws herself into the struggle for medical reforms advocated by the young Dr. Lydgate. Finally, however, she decides to give up her property and marry Ladislaw. The second plot deals with the efforts and failure of Dr. Lydgate to live up to his early ideals." Reader's Ency. 4th edition

Eliot, George

★ The **mill** on the Floss. Knopf 1992 xxxi, 597p $22

ISBN 0-679-41726-5

LC 92-52920

First published 1860

"Deeply significant tragedy of the inner life, enacted amidst the quaint folk and old-fashioned surroundings of a country town (St. Ogg's is Gainsborough). The conflict of affection and antipathy between a brother and sister, and again in the family relations of their father, is a dominant motive; but the emotional tension rises to a climax in Maggie's unpremeditated yielding to an unworthy lover and betrayal of her finer nature. Brother and sister . . . are purified and reconciled only in death." Baker. Guide to the Best Fic

Eliot, George

Romola; introduction by George Kiely; notes by Kimberly VanEsveld Adams and Emily Sohmer Tai. Modern Library xxii, 621p pa $11.95

ISBN 978-0-375-76121-8; 0-375-76121-7

LC 2002-40788

First published in book form 1863

"Based on a special study of Florentine history in the epoch 1492-1509, the days of Lorenzo de' Medici, and the saintliness and all-conquering energy of Savonarola are finely portrayed. 'Romola' is a sternly tragic novel of temptation, crime and retribution." Baker. Guide to the Best Fic

Eliot, George

★ **Silas** Marner; the weaver of Raveloe. Knopf 1993 xxx, 206p $18

    ISBN 0-679-42030-4

                        LC 92-54293

    First published 1861

"Silas Marner is a handloom weaver, a good man, whose life has been wrecked by a false accusation of theft, which cannot be disproved. For years he lives a lonely life, with the sole companionship of his loom: and he is saved from his own despair by the chance finding of a little child. On this baby girl he lavishes the whole passion of his thwarted nature, and her filial affection makes him a kindly man again. After sixteen years the real thief is dicovered, and Silas's good name is restored. On this slight framework are hung the richest pictures of middle and low class life that George Eliot has painted." Keller. Reader's Dig of Books

Elkin, Stanley

★ The **MacGuffin**. Linden Press 1991 283p

    ISBN 0-671-67324-6

                        LC 90-13233

"Here, MacGuffins of adultery, smuggling, and drug abuse merely provide a context for inspired, Joycean word-play based on cliches, shoptalk, and technical jargon. Language itself is the real topic." Libr J

Elkin, Stanley

Stanley Elkin's The magic kingdom. Dutton 1985 317p

    ISBN 0-525-24304-6

                        LC 84-21109

This is a "book by an extraordinary artist in language. It is also extremely funny and its effect is often that of a strong emetic. That combination leaves the reader wondering which way to turn—not perhaps the worst position for a thoughtful reader to be left in. . . . Elkin is gentle yet tough with his forlorn children, funny yet kind with his distrait adults; as a whole, he has written a sensitive book. . . . His book challenges a resilient and imaginative reader." N Y Rev Books

Elkins, Aaron J.

Dying on the vine; Aaron Elkins. Berkley Prime Crime 2012 294 p. $25.95

    ISBN 0425247880; 9780425247884

                    LC 2012035917

Author Aaron J. Elkins' book "takes the man 'known throughout the world of forensic science as the Skeleton Detective' to Tuscany, where he looks into the apparent murder-suicide of Pietro Cubbiddu, the strong-willed patriarch of the famous Cubbiddu wine-making family, and Pietro's wife, Nola. After examining the remains, Gideon concludes that it's an unusual double homicide instead. The family and its confidantes had motive and opportunity for killing the couple--but why push the bodies off a cliff, then shoot them after they're already dead?" (Publishers Weekly)

Elkins, Aaron J.

Good blood; [by] Aaron Elkins. Berkley Prime Crime 2004 293p $23.95

    ISBN 0-425-19411-6

                    LC 2003-62799

In this mystery, forensic anthropologist Gideon Oliver and his park ranger wife, Julie, "are on holiday in Italy, helping a friend host a tour featuring canoeing and bicycle riding. Since neither activity is Gideon's idea of fun, he lounges around the picturesque town of Stresa and is pulled, consequently, into the investigation of recently uncovered bones, which turn out to be connected to a 40-year-old secret baby swap. In turn, the swap is tied to a recent kidnapping involving the wealthy, influential family to which Gideon's tour guide friend is related. . . . This is vintage Elkins: well-drawn supporting characters, lovely scenery, and a bit of interesting science." Libr J

Elkins, Aaron J.

Little tiny teeth; [by] Aaron Elkins. Berkley Prime Crime 2007 292p $23.95

    ISBN 978-0-425-21530-2; 0-425-21530-X

                    LC 2006-103154

"Elkins totally avoids the sin of sloth represented by some mystery writers who habitually underresearch their topics. Elkins always presents a rich buffet of fascinating scientific facts." Booklist

Elkins, Aaron J.

Skeleton dance; a novel. {by} Aaron Elkins. Morrow 2000 246p $23

    ISBN 0-688-15928-1

                    LC 00-23278

"But for all the breezy humor, the satirical treatment of squabbling scientists respectfully illuminates their fascinating work, and in the end it is the scholarship that dazzles." N Y Times Book Rev

Elkins, Aaron J.

Unnatural selection. Berkley Prime Crime 2006 281p $23.95

    ISBN 0-425-21005-7

                    LC 2006-2173

In this installment, "forensic sleuth Gideon Oliver accompanies his second wife, Julie, to an unusual gathering of conservation experts in the Scilly Isles. . . . Frustrated by his passive role and forced to bite his tongue when opinions are voiced that strike him as lacking intellectual rigor, Oliver leaps at a chance to examine some human remains stored at the local museum. His casual look becomes something more when he determines that one humerus bone is a recent relic, leading to his rousing the sleepy local constabulary to a murder probe. When the victim turns out to have belonged to the conservation group, the circle of suspects centers on the surviving members." Publ Wkly

"Elkins keeps things moving with plenty of local atmosphere, compelling characterization, and a refreshingly low level of violence." Natural Hist

Ellis, Bret Easton

Imperial bedrooms. Alfred A. Knopf 2010 169p $24.95

ISBN 978-0-307-26610-1; 0-307-26610-9

LC 2009-41690

Sequel to: Less than zero (1985)

Clay, a successful screenwriter, has returned from New York to Los Angeles to help cast his new movie, and he's soon drifting through a long-familiar circle that will leave him no choice but to plumb the darkest recesses of his character and come to terms with his proclivity for betrayal.

"As with Chandler's work, the details of the twists and turns are beside the point — particularly since Ellis puckishly reveals at the start which character is going to wind up as a corpse in a Tom Ford suit. But the author uses the thriller framework to infuse nerve-rending unease into this look at Tinseltown mores, a dissection that also comes nicely weighted with both bleak hilarity and firsthand authorial experience." Entertaiment Wkly

Ellis, Bret Easton

Lunar Park. Alfred A. Knopf 2005 308p $24.95

ISBN 0-375-41291-3

LC 2005-40923

"The whole book swirls, surreally, pushing the limits of tolerable confusion while sending up laughably familiar horror story shticks. For a while, it looks as if nothing will be resolved. It works precisely because it is a ghost story, replete with eviscerated livestock, freshly dug graves, and messages written in ash—and because everything, ultimately, is resolved." New Criterion

Ellis, David

In the company of liars; David Ellis. G.P. Putnam's Sons 2005 378p (pbk.) $1.99; o.p.

ISBN 9780425204290; 0399152474

LC 2004057342

This "novel is centered on a woman who is on trial for murder-Allison Pagone, a mother caught between competing forces, each represented by someone who may not care if the pressure kills her in the end. A prosecutor wants Allison convicted and put on death row. An FBI agent believes she can squeeze her into ratting on her family. A daughter and an ex-husband need to save their own skins. And circling them all: a group who would prefer to eliminate her quietly and anonymously, but who also are not what they seem. Our first picture of Allison is in the moments following her death. The story then moves backward in time." (vjbooks.com)

Ellis, David

Life sentence. Putnam 2003 390p $24.95

ISBN 0-399-14979-1

LC 2002-68137

"Jon Soliday and Grant Tully share a dirty secret from their teenage years: after a night of drinking and drugs, Soliday climbed through the bedroom window of a beautiful young woman and then blacked out. Consequently, he doesn't remember anything after that—not even how she ended up dead. Via family connections, Soliday eludes prosecution, and 20 years later he is chief legal counsel to Senator Tully, who is running a fierce campaign for governor. . .

. Elegant prose skillfully impels Soliday through a haze of deadly deceit, where no one is who he appears to be." Libr J

Ellis, Warren

Crooked little vein. William Morrow 2007 280p $21.95

ISBN 978-0-06-072393-4; 0-06-072393-9

"Private Detective Michael McGill's gritty life takes a turn for the bizarre when a drug-addicted White House chief of staff enlists him to recover the Constitution. The real Constitution, of course, not the one in the National Archives. This one was handed to the Founding Fathers by aliens, lost in the 1950s, and since traded among the nation's sexual deviants. McGill hits the road with sexpot Trix to track down its current holder." Libr J

"The home of the free and the land of the brave has rarely looked so creepy in this snappily paced homage to William Burroughs's Naked Lunch." Publ Wkly

Ellison, Ralph, 1914-1994

★ **Invisible** man; preface by Charles Johnson. Modern Lib. 1994 xxxiv, 572p $19.95; pa $12

ISBN 0-679-60139-2; 0-679-73276-4 pa

LC 94-176953

A reissue of the title first published 1952 by Random House

"Acclaimed as a powerful representation of the lives of blacks during the Depression, this novel describes the experiences of one young black man during that period. Dismissed from a Negro college in the South for showing one of the founders how Negroes live there, he is used later as a symbol of repression by a Communist group in New York City. After a Harlem race riot, he is aware that he must contend with both whites and blacks, and that loss of social identity makes him invisible among his fellow beings." Shapiro. Fic for Youth. 3d edition

Ellison, Ralph, 1914-1994

Three days before the shooting-- edited by John F. Callahan and Adam Bradley. Modern Library 2010 1101p $50

ISBN 0375759530; 9780375759536

LC 2010-277049

"At his death in 1994, Ralph Ellison left behind roughly two thousand pages of his second unfinished novel. . . . Five years later, Random House published Juneteenth, drawn from the central narrative of Ellison's unfinished epic. Three Days Before the Shooting . . . gathers together in one volume, for the first time, all the parts of that planned opus, including . . . sequences never before published." (Publisher's note)

"Culled from Ellison's drafts, his notes, and those of his wife, Fanny, this book brings together four decades of work, a portion of which was published posthumously as Juneteenth in 1999. The allegorical, lyrical novel is presented in three books in various stages of completion. It centers on the complex relationship between A. Z. Hickman, a blues musician turned preacher, and Bliss, an orphan of undetermined race, whom Hickman raises as a boy preacher. As a teen, Bliss runs off and develops his skills as a flimflammer, ultimately emerging in the U.S. Senate as Senator Sunraider. Hickman searches in vain for Bliss, but when he

LIST OF FICTIONAL WORKS

learns of a threat to Sunraider, the two are reunited in an orgy of reexamination of their lives and circuitous paths. Book 1 is a first-person narrative by McIntyre, a white reporter who witnesses the shooting of Sunraider on the floor of the Senate and the attempt by Hickman to save a man known as a charismatic race-baiter. Book 2, the basis for Juneteenth, traces the relationship between Hickman and Bliss/Sunraider through a dialogue between them, an inner reflection of their coming together and their falling apart. Book 3 includes several fragments of earlier portions of the novel, deeper character portrayals, and alternative paths of action as Ellison struggled to bring all the pieces together. He is masterful at evoking the language of common black folks, preachers, press and politicians, and charlatans and flimflammers." Booklist

Ellory, R. J.
A **quiet** vendetta. Penguin Group 2012 496 p.
ISBN 9781590205082

This book, set in contemporary New Orleans, opens with "the kidnapping of 19-year-old Catherine Ducane, daughter of Louisiana governor Charles Ducane, and the brutal murder of her driver . . . When the FBI agrees to [kidnapper] Ernesto Perez's request to bring Ray Hartmann of the New York district attorney's office to New Orleans, Perez turns himself in. Perez promises to reveal Catherine's whereabouts, but first he must tell his life story as a Mafia hit man to Hartmann. Perez recounts a journey that includes his involvement in at least 19 murders and the mob's links to such figures as the Kennedys, Richard Nixon, and Marilyn Monroe." (Publishers Weekly)

Ellory, R. J.
A **simple** act of violence; R.J. Ellory. Overlook Press 2011 464p.
ISBN 9781590203187

LC 2011016139

This book presents the story of "a serial murder investigation in Washington DC, told in parallel with a history of the most squalid period in the annals of the CIA -- its shocking activities in Nicaragua, financed by the smuggling of tons of cocaine into America." (guardian.co.uk)

Ellory, Roger Jon
The **Anniversary** Man. Overlook 2010 400p $24.95
ISBN 978-1-59020-327-9; 1-59020-327-5
First published 2009 in the United Kingdom

"Ellory is a patient storyteller, willing to stretch beyond the necessities of his plot and illuminate people who occupy the peripheries of his captivating tale. He also doesn't stint in fleshing out his central players, even if in doing so he swings far from the demands of a police procedural." January

Ellroy, James
American tabloid; a novel. Knopf 1995 571p
ISBN 0-679-40391-4

LC 94-42898

"The dizzying number of covert alliances and compromised loyalties that link the Mob, the C.I.A., Howard Hughes, J. Edgar Hoover, and the Kennedys comes across less like a cancer of epic proportions that like a kind of in-

stitutional dyspepsia. Ellroy's tabloidization of this chapter of American history makes it all the more queasy and real." New Yorker

Ellroy, James
★ The **black** dahlia. Mysterious Press 1987 325p

LC 87-7952

"The author manages a gripping re-creation of LA street life in the 1940s, and his characters are powerfully written and terrifyingly real. The bare-bones plot, the slew of false conclusions, and the hazy evocation of the murder victim give the narrative a dreamlike atmosphere, ideal for a tale of immoral heroes and wasted lives." Booklist

Ellroy, James
Blood's a rover; a novel. Alfred A. Knopf 2009 633p $28.95
ISBN 978-0-679-40393-7; 0-679-40393-0

LC 2009-24460

"The final novel of Ellroy's 'Underworld U.S.A.' trilogy, following 'American Tabloid' and 'The Cold Six Thousand,' is a fittingly crazed and violent account of the years 1968 to 1972. Alternating chapters follow three henchmen with ties to a labyrinth of interconnected schemes—one cooks dope for Howard Hughes while facilitating his Vegas hotel takeover; another subverts black militant groups for J. Edgar Hoover; and the third kills revolutionaries in Cuba. Ellroy employs a huge cast and hyper-pulp prose to create a convincingly horrific universe run by the F.B.I., the Mob, and a host of other sinister organizations." New Yorker

Ellroy, James
The **cold** six thousand. Knopf 2001 672p $25.95
ISBN 0-679-40392-2
Sequel to American tabloid

"Ellroy's prose is easy to absorb sentence by sentence, thanks to his simple subject-verb-object constructions, but monstrous as it acquires cumulative force over hundreds of pages. . . . The novel is an exhausting, masochistic, often revelatory rereading of the allegedly idealistic sixties—an assassination, finally, of the decade rather than of its leaders." New Yorker

Ellroy, James
★ **L.A.** confidential. Mysterious Press 1990 496p $32
ISBN 0-89296-293-3

LC 89-40523

This novel focuses on three L.A. policemen: "Trashcan Jack Vincennes, a narcotics cop who makes a little cash on the side by setting up indiscreet celebrities for exposure in a Hollywood scandal sheet; Bad Bud White, whose favorite crime-stopping technique is to 'shoot everyone involved, then look for somebody a bit more intelligent to sort out the bodies'; and Ed Exley, a well-connected officer who believes in 'stern, absolute justice, whatever the price,' provided it doesn't impede his political ambitions." N Y Times Book Rev

The author "merges raw-edged period detail with sleazy celluloid lore, producing a dark and dazzling descent into the criminal underworld of the 1950s." Booklist

Ellroy, James

L.A. noir. Mysterious Press 1998 644p

LC 98-15470

Contents: In Blood on the moon (1984) Hopkins unearths a serial killer; Because the night (1984) concerns the disappearence of a hero cop and a multiple murder; Suicide hill (1986) explores corruption and betrayal when a kidnapping leads to an orgy of violence

Ellroy, James

White jazz; a novel. Knopf 1992 349p

LC 92-52890

"Ellroy's clipped, telegraphic style, his use of real people and real events, and his creation of a world horrifyingly devoid of any conventional morality make White Jazz a harrowing, remarkable read." Booklist

Elwork, Paul

The girl who would speak for the dead. Amy Einhorn Books/G.P. Putnam's Sons 2011 308p $24.95

ISBN 978-0-399-15717-2; 0-399-15717-4

LC 2010-44996

Expanded version of The tea house (2007)

In 1925, at her family's suburban Philadelphia estate, 13-year-old Emily Stewart discovers she can make a loud rapping noise with her ankle. With her sly twin brother, Michael, Emily entertains gullible schoolmates with "knockings" that spirits purportedly make to answer questions about the afterlife. When adults who have suffered the loss of loved ones start consulting her as a spirit medium, her efforts to give them consolation begin to seem increasingly like cruel deceptions. Based loosely on true events from the early 20th century.

"An intricate yet beautifully told story that is less about ghosts and more about secrets and how destructive they can be." Kirkus

Emerson, Earl W.

Pyro. Ballantine Bks. 2004 307p $24.95

ISBN 0-345-46288-2

"Paul Wollf is a veteran Seattle firefighter whose firefighter father died in an arson blaze when Wollf was four. Fueled by his hatred for the killer, he achieves heroics that protect him from political infighting within the department. Work gets more complicated, however, when a new pattern of fires is detected, each one closer to Wollf's station; evidence points to the arsonist who caused his father's death." Libr J

This is a "fast-paced, smoke-filled, gripping story loaded with plot twists, snappy and graphic dialogue, and firefighting lore." Publ Wkly

Emerson, Earl W.

Vertical burn; by Earl Emerson. Ballantine Bks. 2002 340p

ISBN 0-345-44589-9

LC 2001-35969

"One day, life is dandy for John Finney, . . . a veteran of Seattle's fire department. The next day he loses his friend and partner in a fire he suspects was set, and shortly after that he is being framed for arson and targeted for murder by conspirators who are planning to burn down the city's tallest building. . . . Emerson combines an intimate knowledge of fires and fire fighting with an intricate plot played out by characters you can love or hate." Booklist

Emmons, Cai

His mother's son. Harcourt 2003 366p $25

ISBN 0-15-100734-9

LC 2002-2990

"Dr. Jana Thomas has a secret that no one knows—not even her husband. Fifteen years before, she had a different life and a different name, which she abandoned when her younger brother murdered their parents and went on a killing spree at his school. Now Jana has a young son, and she begins to panic when she sees the warning signs that no one noticed in her brother." Libr J

"Those looking for domestic drama and hidden lives will enjoy Emmons' book and find the anxious and troubled character of Jana interesting." Booklist

Emshwiller, Carol

★ The secret city. Tachyon 2007 209p pa $14.95

ISBN 978-1-892391-44-5; 1-892391-44-9

"First and foremost, Emshwiller is a poet—with a poet's sensibility, precision, and magic. She revels in the sheer taste and sound of words, she infuses them with an extraordinary vitality and sense of life." Newsday

Endo, Shusaku

★ Deep river; translated by Van C. Gessel. New Directions 1995 216p

ISBN 0-8112-1289-0

LC 94-38913

This is a "beautifully wrought, lyrically suggestive story. . . . If Christianity holds up to us the lonely individual challenged by a God who entered history, Buddhism gives us people who are ready to surrender, finally, a measure of their human and spiritual particularity and who, with acceptance, join their fellow creatures as part of the great tide of humanity. Mr. Endo manages to merge both of these streams of faith, bringing them together in a flow that is, indeed, deep. His work is a soulful gift to a world he keeps rendering as unrelievedly parched." N Y Times Book Rev

Endo, Shusaku

The final martyrs; translated by Van C. Gessel. New Directions 1994 199p $21.95

ISBN 0-8112-1272-6

LC 94-746

"This deftly translated collection, comprised of stories written as early as 1959 and as late as 1985, also includes semi-autobiographical tales in which Endo deals with the traumatic impact that his parent's divorce had on his boyhood. He also writes with grace, compassion and gentle humor about old age, love betrayed, Japanese tourists and the marks we leave on the lives of others." Publ Wkly

Endo, Shusaku

★ **Silence**; translated by William Johnston. Taplinger 1979 294p

LC 78-27168

Original Japanese edition, 1966; this translation first published 1969 in Japan

"The story is based on events in early 17th-century Japan, when Japanese Christians and Christian missionaries were brutally persecuted. In the novel, Sebastian Rodrigues, a Portuguese seminarian, journeys to Japan to investigate why his former teacher, a missionary to Japan, has chosen apostasy over martyrdom. Pervading the novel is the belief that Christianity is incomparible with Japanese culture. In the end, seeing the selfishness of martyrdom, Rodrigues also chooses apostasy." Merriam-Webster's Ency of Lit

Eng, Tan Twan

The **gift** of rain. Weinstein Books 2008 435p $23.95

ISBN 978-1-60286-024-7; 1-60286-024-6

First published 2007 in the United Kingdom

"Eng's characters are as deep and troubled as the time in which the story takes place, and he draws on a rich palette to create a sprawling portrait of a lesser explored corner of the war. Hutton's first-person narration is measured, believable and enthralling." Publ Wkly

Engel, Howard

The **Cooperman** variations; a Benny Cooperman mystery. Overlook Press 2002 279p $24.95

ISBN 1-58567-233-5

LC 2002-70410

"Readers new to Benny's world may find themselves a little confused from time to time, but this is only a minor inconvenience. Benny is a wonderful narrator, and once readers have spent a few minutes with him, they will feel like they've known him all their lives." Booklist

Engel, Mary Potter

Strangers and sojourners; stories from the low-country. Counterpoint 2004 222p $23

ISBN 1-582-43264-3

LC 2003-20892

"Subtly interweaving the tale of each character, from a 114-year-old black woman to a cross-dressing outcast, Engel allows each to speak in his or her own distinctive voice, each of which she renders with pinpoint accuracy and astounding versatility. Their eccentricities notwithstanding, these are extraordinary characters, endowed by Engel with a sublime grace and humbling spirituality that is both penetrating and poignant." Booklist

Engelmann, Karen

★ The **Stockholm** Octavo; Karen Engelmann. HarperCollins 2012 432 p. $26.99

ISBN 0061995347; 9780061995347

In this book, "political and social intrigue are merged through the medium of the mystical card layout called the Octavo. . . . In the reign of the alternately enlightened and autocratic King Gustav III, his brother Karl and the society doyenne known as the Uzanne scheme to return control of Sweden to the nobility, opposed secretly by the mysteri-

ous gambling club owner Sofia Sparrow, whose prophetic visions link Gustav with the doomed king and queen of France." (Publishers Weekly)

Enger, Lin

Undiscovered country. Little, Brown and Co. 2008 308p $23.99

ISBN 978-0-316-00694-1; 0-316-00694-7

LC 2007-30138

"A modern-day Hamlet story set in rural northern Minnesota. Teenage Jesse's father, the mayor of Battlepoint, apparently committed suicide with his own hunting rifle. But Jesse suspects his Uncle Clay, who had more than one motive for murder. Is Jesse's suspicion simply his inability to accept his father's senseless act? Or is Clay really guilty— and how complicit is Jesse's mother? If Clay is guilty, what should he do about it? The obvious parallels with Shakespeare's play are even acknowledged by some of the characters, but Enger doesn't let this conceit overwhelm the story. He skillfully draws a portrait of small-town life and all its barely concealed secrets and effectively narrates Jesse's torment." Libr J

Englander, Nathan

The **Ministry** of Special Cases. Alfred A. Knopf 2007 339p $25

ISBN 978-0-375-40493-1; 0-375-40493-7

LC 2006-48731

The author "bravely wrangles the themes of political liberty and personal loss with the swift style and knowing humor of folklore. In the spirit of the simple ambiguity of its title, The Ministry of Special Cases is carefully contradictory, wise and off-kilter, funny and sad." N Y Observer

Englander, Nathan

★ **What** we talk about when we talk about Anne Frank; stories. Nathan Englander. Alfred A. Knopf 2012 224p

ISBN 9780307949608; 9780307958709

LC 2011033756

2013 Sophie Brody Medal Honor Book

This book offers a collection of short stories. "The title story . . . is a . . . portrait of two marriages in which the Holocaust is played out as a devastating parlor game. In the . . . [short story] 'Camp Sundown' vigilante justice is undertaken by a group of geriatric campers in a bucolic summer enclave. 'Free Fruit for Young Widows' is a small, sharp study in evil, . . . told by a father to a son. 'Sister Hills' chronicles the history of Israel's settlements from the eve of the Yom Kippur War through the present, a political fable constructed around the tale of two mothers who strike a terrible bargain to save a child." (Publisher's note)

In this book of "eight stories [about Jewish identity and victimhood], three center on a preoccupation with the Holocaust, one on the related subject of anti-Semitism, and another on the also related subject of the loss of dear ones in the Israeli-Arab conflict. . . . In 'Camp Sundown,' a camp for Jewish elders . . . the aged campers decide for reasons that remain unclear that one of their number was actually a concentration-camp guard, and they gather together and murder him." (New Republic)

Enquist, Per Olov

The **book** about Blanche and Marie; translated from the Swedish by Tiina Nunnally. Overlook Press 2006 218p $24.95

ISBN 1-58567-668-3

LC 2005-58523

Original Swedish edition, 2004

"As Enquist fancifully, lugubriously and rapturously riffs on, extends, and wonders after the notebooks (which really exist), Blanche, Marie (suffering the scandal of her adulterous relationship with Paul Langevin) and the conflicted Charcot get alternating POV chapters, and the modern sensibility that sprang from her body—scientifically scrutinized and dissected, but ever resistant to being known or possessed—emerges beautifully." Publ Wkly

Enright, Anne

★ The **forgotten** waltz. W. W. Norton & Co. 2011 263p $25.95

ISBN 978-0-393-07255-6; 0-393-07255-X

LC 2011-21006

"As Gina accepts that she has been forced into a place where she no longer has the power to walk away, The Forgotten Waltz meditates on the way personal responsibility can twist the most well-meaning, loving relationship into a holding tank for accusations and tears.... Enright allows her main character the thrill of remembered joys, without letting her slip away from blame." A V Club

Enright, Anne

The **gathering**. Black Cat 2007 261p pa $14

ISBN 978-0-8021-7039-2; 0-8021-7039-0

"You will love this book or loathe it. It doesn't take prisoners, it doesn't simper or seek to be liked. Abrasively honest and toweringly moving, it grabs and shakes you, rabbiting on in a manic monologue, comical, tragic, lost and profound." Scotsman

Enright, Anne

Yesterday's weather. Grove Press 2008 308p $24

ISBN 978-0-8021-1874-5; 0-8021-1874-7

"Enright's subjects are family, children, love, domestic horror. The stories are strong and hard bitten. Something in them is always snagging and catching on grief, large or small. She is a confident writer, letting stories unfold at their own speed. Her best pieces have a fluid shape that feels close to the way we actually think, choose, muse." Washington Post Book World

Ephron, Amy

One Sunday morning; a novel. Amy Ephron. William Morrow 2005 213p. (pbk.) $12.95; (acid-free paper) o.p.

ISBN 9780060585532; 0060585528

LC 2004059200

This book opens on "[o]ne Sunday morning [when] four women at a bridge party in the elegant Gramercy Park Hotel see a beautiful young woman whom they all know leaving a nearby hotel with a man who is not her husband. The sight of twenty-year-old Lizzie Carswell with Billy Holmes is shocking and potentially ruinous. And though the ladies do not know the whole story -- and despite their mutual promise to keep what they've seen to themselves -- it is only a matter of time before one of them talks . . . with heartbreaking consequences for them all." (Publisher's note)

Epperson, Tom

Sailor; Tom Epperson. Forge 2012 352 p.

ISBN 0765328925; 9780765328922; 9781429998604

LC 2011047593

This book is a thriller novel by Tom Epperson. "After years of suffering the terror of being married to a criminal, [Gina] took the one thing he ever gave her that she wanted—her son, Luke. . . . With her husband behind bars, her father-in-law will stop at nothing for revenge. . . . With a vast network that stretches across the country, every favor is called in to kill Gina and return Luke to his grandfather. Gina can trust no one. . . . So with a gun and stolen diamonds in her purse, and derelicts, the law, and hit men on her tail, Gina takes Luke and runs. . . . then they meet Gray. He says he's a sailor, but he seems to be hiding a lot. And when the time comes, he's the only thing standing between her and the grave." (Publisher's note)

Epstein, Joseph

Fabulous small Jews; stories. Houghton Mifflin 2003 339p $23

ISBN 0-395-94402-3

LC 2002-27621

"Like his emotionally candid, low-key protagonists, Epstein is intrinsically honest. Gratifying and genuine, this collection examines all sorts of respones to the encroachment of old age on human dignity." Publ Wkly

Epstein, Joseph

★ The **love** song of A. Jerome Minkoff and other stories. Houghton Mifflin Harcourt 2010 260p $24

ISBN 978-0-618-72195-5; 0-618-72195-9

LC 2009-34898

"It's a rare and welcome thing to find a collection of short stories that define a place. . . . Epstein delivers one about a neighborhood on the far north of Chicago called West Rogers Park. It is a polyglot area, but Epstein has chosen to write about the Jews who dominate it. . . . If his voice is wry, it is also sympathetic. Life is hard, and he knows it. He invests his collection with a peerless take on a particular slice of Jewish life today. Each story stands strong as a discrete work, but together they become profound." Boston Globe

Epstein, Leslie

The **eighth** wonder of the world; a novel. Handsel Books/Other Press 2006 461p $25.95

ISBN 978-1-59051-250-0; 1-59051-250-2

LC 2006-895

This novel "imagines a wisecracking American architectural genius, Amos Prince, who, after fleeing America, wows Mussolini with the design for a mile-high skyscraper. . . . The novel soon focuses on Amos's young Jewish-American acolyte, Maximilian Shabilian, who shares Prince's obsessive dream of completing the tower and becomes entangled with the architect's dysfunctional family (and, predictably, his beautiful daughter). As World War II intensifies, Amos descends into livid antiSemitism and anti-Americanism, while

Max launches a tragic attempt to save the Jews of Rome by enlisting them to work on the skyscraper." Publ Wkly

In this work, " the tragic and the inane are slyly spliced together, with inflated delusions punctured by sharp barbs of satire." Washington Post Book World

Epstein, Leslie

San Remo Drive; a novel from memory. Handsel Press 2003 238p il $26

ISBN 1-59051-066-6

LC 2002-35547

"There is something of 'The Winter's Tale' in the way Epstein pulls it all together, something of the miraculous second chance. Losing and finding, he shows us love between fathers and sons as the most powerful and enduring in life. . . . In doing so he has given us, along with F. Scott Fitzgerald's 'Last Tycoon,' Budd Schulberg's 'What Makes Sammy Run?' and his own 'Pandaemonium,' one of the four best Hollywood novels ever written." N Y Times Book Rev

Erdrich, Louise, 1954-

★ The **Beet** Queen; a novel. Holt & Co. 1986 338p

ISBN 0-8050-0058-5

LC 86-4788

Second installment in the author's North Dakota Quartet

This novel "concerns a brother and sister, Karl and Mary Adare, who are abandoned by their mother, who runs away with a barnstorming pilot. Flight is a recurring theme in this . . . tale of loneliness set against a stark North Dakota landscape. Karl spends his life as an itinerant salesman, running from his troubled family and his own sexual ambivalence; Mary, who grows up with her aunt and uncle, uses self-reliance as a way of hiding from the pain of human relationships; and Sita, Mary's cousin, retreats into insanity to avoid facing the realization that her idealized dreams of a glamorous life have evaporated. Only Celestine, Mary's friend and the mother of Karl's child, accepts reality on its own terms as she struggles to protect her daughter from the suffering that has engulfed those around her." Booklist

Erdrich, Louise

Four souls. HarperCollins Publishers 2004 210p $23.95

ISBN 0-06-620975-7

LC 2003-65243

Fleur Pillager takes her mother's name, Four Souls, for strength and walks away from her Ojibwe reservation to the cities of Minneapolis and Saint Paul. She is seeking restitution from and revenge on the lumber baron who has stripped her reservation." Publisher's note

Erdrich, Louise

The **last** report on the miracles at Little No Horse; a novel. HarperCollins Pubs. 2001 361p hardcover o.p. pa $14.95

ISBN 0-06-018727-1; 0-06-157762-6 pa

LC 00-47198

"Even the small incidents in this novel are moments of tremendous power, stripped of sentimentality or pretension. Erdrich has developed a style that can sound as serious as

death or ring with the haunting simplicity of ancient legend." Christ Sci Monit

Erdrich, Louise

★ **Love** medicine; new and expanded version. Holt & Co. 1993 367p

ISBN 0-8050-2798-X

LC 93-15166

Original version published 1984

"The story opens in 1981 when June Kashpaw, an attractive, leggy Chippewa prostitute who has idled away her days on the main streets of oil boomtowns in North Dakota, decides to return to the reservation on which she was raised. Before leaving Williston, N.D., however, June takes on one more client and, afterward, decides to walk back to her home. En route she dies in the freezing Dakota countryside. But her memory and the legacy she passes on to her family prompt various relatives and acquaintances to recall their relationships with her and to reminisce about their own lives." N Y Times Book Rev

Erdrich, Louise

The **Master** Butchers Singing Club. HarperCollins Pubs. 2002 289p $25.95

ISBN 0-06-620977-3

LC 2002-68501

"Erdrich is demonstrably capable of pursuing a potent image or theme throughout a narrative. And although this novel's leitmotif of violent, gruesome death is a bit too obvious, its smaller symbols succeed better, perhaps because they're accompanied by less fanfare." N Y Times Book Rev

Erdrich, Louise

The **painted** drum. HarperCollins 2005 277p $25.95

ISBN 0-06-051510-4

LC 2005-40227

"There is searing pain and loss aplenty in this book, but one of Erdrich's strengths as a writer is the way in which she controls emotion. . . . Readers familiar with her works will recognize characters from the North Dakota native families who populate other of her works. But again, it doesn't really matter. Her themes transcend that terrain." Christ Sci Monit

Erdrich, Louise

The **plague** of doves. HarperCollins 2008 313p $25.95

ISBN 978-0-06-051512-6; 0-06-0515512-0

LC 2007-33626

This novel is about the unsolved murder of a farm family, "but it is also an allegory about blood (and bloody) connections that develop as the descendants of killers and victims continue to live alongside one another near the Ojibwe reservation in North Dakota. As always with Erdrich, the bloodlines are both white and Native American, churned by the passions of characters with wonderful names like Mooshum Milk and Holy Track, whose lives and stories make the question of whodunit seem like an afterthought. Mooshum, one of three Indians falsely accused of the 1911 crime and the only one who survives the lynch mob, tells of finding the murdered farm family and the infant who lived. Evelina, his granddaughter, becomes the central narrator of Mooshum's story amidst the intertwining tales of 'deathless romantic encounters' that follow. Evelina and others detail the dramas of her family, including her own budding romantic encounters with the descendant of the murdered family and a nun whose lineage goes back to the lynch mob." N Y Daily News

Erdrich, Louise

The **red** convertible; selected and new stories, 1978-2008. HarperCollins 2009 496p $27.99

ISBN 978-0-06-153607-6; 0-06-153607-5

"Louise Erdrich is an immensely satisfying storyteller who molds her novels from the clay of her short fiction. . . . This anthology returns 30 of those stories, which eventually became parts of 11 novels, to their original, unentangled forms. The book also includes six other stories, some of which are being published for the first time. Like Faulkner, Erdrich has created a fictional community an Ojibwe reservation in North Dakota from which her work can unfold. Her stories stretch back 100 years or more and venture as far away as New Hampshire, looping elliptically, intersecting through a priest, a place, a hidden parentage. But where her novels develop these relationships, 'The Red Convertible,' in dislodging the stories, creates a new arc between them." Los Angeles Times Book Rev

Erdrich, Louise, 1954-

★ The **round** house; Louise Erdrich. 1st ed. Harper 2012 321 p. (ebook) $21.99; (paperback) $14.99; (hardcover) $27.99

ISBN 9780062065261; 9780062065254; 9780062065247; 0062065246

LC 2012005381

Alex Award (2013)

National Book Award: Fiction (2012)

This book by Louise Erdrich, "[s]et on an Ojibwe reservation in North Dakota . . . focuses on 13-year-old Joseph. After his mother is brutally raped yet refuses to speak about the experience, Joe must not only cope with her slow physical and mental recovery but also confront his own feelings of anger and helplessness. Questions of jurisdiction and treaty law complicate matters. Doubting that justice will be served, Joe enlists his friends to help investigate the crime." (Library Journal)

Erdrich, Louise

★ **Shadow** tag; a novel. Harper 2010 255p $25.99

ISBN 978-0-06-153609-0; 0-06-153609-1

LC 2009-33699

"Irene America, the protagonist of . . . [this] novel, is a woman whose identity has never been entirely her own. For while she is both a mother and a serious academic, she is best known as the subject of her husband Gil's esteemed art—large, assertive and overtly sexual portraits that exemplify his love, but also his constant need to subjugate and own her. This power dynamic has always troubled Irene, but at the novel's start, she discovers that Gil has reached a new level in his quest for possession; he is reading her diary in an attempt to both quell and verify fears that the marriage is deteriorating. Unable to confront Gil directly, but unwilling to let him know everything, Irene reacts by creating another hidden diary in which she records the actual truth. She continues to write in the original diary, however, leaving it where she knows her husband will find it and crafting her words in order to manipulate him. . . . Erdrich is a muscular and fearless writer, and she explores her characters with both compassion and criticism and through lyrical and visceral prose." BookPage

Erdrich, Louise

Tracks; a novel. Holt & Co. 1988 226p

ISBN 0-8050-0895-0

LC 88-9321

"Ms. Erdrich is, as always, the generous kind of storyteller, passing along not only everything her characters know, but the story of the stories as well. Giving life and shape and sense to what's happened, she lets the designs spring clear." N Y Times Book Rev

Erickson, Steve

Zeroville. Europa Editions 2007 329p pa $14.95

ISBN 978-1-933372-39-6; 1-933372-39-7

"Over his entire career Erickson has challenged readers with a fiercely intelligent and surprisingly sensual brand of American surrealism that can, at times, seem impenetrable. For this reason, it surprised me that almost everything in Erickson's new novel Zeroville entertains so readily without seeming watered down or slight. Zeroville is funny, sad and darkly beautiful, built around short chapters that allow the author to capture the essential moment and move effortlessly through time." Washington Post Book World

Eriksson, Kjell

The **princess** of Burundi; translated from the Swedish by Ebba Segerberg. St. Martin's Press 2006 300p hardcover o.p. pa $13.95

ISBN 0-312-32767-6; 0-312-32768-4 pa

LC 2005-50965

Original Swedish edition, 2002

"When the badly mutilated body of John Harald Jonsson—a working-class family man and an expert on the tropical fish known as cichlids—is found in the snow in the provincial Swedish town of Libro, homicide detective Ola Haver and his colleague, Ann Lindell, quickly identify a suspect, an embittered sociopath. The brilliance of Eriksson's richly detailed crime novel, . . . lies in its psychological and even sociological insights. Eriksson not only reveals a deep, sympathetic understanding for his large cast of characters but also evokes a pervasive sense of despair, reminiscent of Henning Mankell's, in the face of the violent, amoral nature of contemporary society and the challenges it places on the police." Publ Wkly

Erpenbeck, Jenny

The **book** of words; translated, with an afterword, by Susan Bernofsky. New Directions 2007 96p pa $14.95

ISBN 9780811217064; 0-8112-1706-X

LC 2007-23569

"Erpenbeck's narrator speaks in the language and consciousness of a little girl, attending school, going on day trips with her wet nurse though she's long past the age of breastfeeding, and living in a beautiful country 'where the sun almost always shines'. Darker hints begin to appear. Playmate Alice casually refers to the gunshots heard outside the schoolyard. The wet nurse's young daughter doesn't return home one day, and other people start to disappear, too. There is a nightmare coming, revealed finally when the narrator's father, a high-ranking government official, takes her on a trip into the countryside and calmly tells her of horror upon horror. Erpenbeck . . . eschews specific geographical detail, letting the eeriness rise to the universal. Susan Bernofsky's remarkably fluid translation does a seamless job of capturing Erpenbeck's swirl of language as the voice of her narrator trips along like uninterrupted thought.. . . . This is writing so intense you don't even notice the brevity." Guardian

Erpenbeck, Jenny

Visitation; translated from the German by Susan Bernofsky. New Directions Pub. 2010 151p
ISBN 0-8112-1835-X; 978-0-8112-1835-1
LC 2010-11144

Original German edition, 2008

This novel's "central character is a place. In a grand house and its grounds, by a lake in Brandenburg, a succession of occupants dislodge each other, borne along by the political calamities of 20th century Europe. The Jewish family who own the property in the 1930s are forced to sell while they wait for visas out of the Third Reich. An architect renovates the house; at the end of the second world war, it's requisitioned by the Russian army; then, under the GDR, the architect has to flee for having done illegal business with the west. The place is reclaimed by returning exiles from Siberia, then resold by estate agents. . . . The one person known to all the owners and occupants–and thus the thread that binds the narrative together–is the gardener. Periodic updates are given of his activities, describing his routines in detail. . . . No word is ever heard from him, and Erpenbeck allows no access to his mind, but we end up feeling great relief whenever he reappears, and deep sadness as this increasingly frail figure does what he can to forestall his Eden's incremental slide into ruin. Indeed, the amount of emotional engagement Erpenbeck manages to win from us, in a mere 150 pages, is just one proof of her mastery." Guardian (UK)

Eschbach, Andreas

The **carpet** makers; Andreas Eschbach; translated by Doryl Jensen; [with a foreword by Orson Scott Card]. Tom Doherty Associates Books 2005 300p $24.95; (pbk.) $15.99
ISBN 0765305933 (alk. paper); 9780765314901
LC 2004058866

This book, "[s]et on a low-tech world where the main industry is the manufacture of carpets of human hair," this book presents a "mosaic of stories of myriad people and cultures trapped in stagnation by one powerful man's petty anger. Intended for the emperor on a distant planet, the carpets are so finely made that each carpet maker can only finish one in his lifetime, working with hairs from the bodies of his wives, who are chosen for the quality and color of their tresses. And so life goes, generation after generation, even after rumors and, finally, ships from the new government arrive with word of the emperor's removal. The new interstellar government learns the emperor secretly maintained thousands of carpet-making planets." (Publishers Weekly)

Eskridge, Kelley

Solitaire. Eos 2002 353p $24.95
ISBN 0-06-008857-5
LC 2002-25381

"Eskridge's evocation of Jackal's time in hightech solitary confinement is a stylistic and psychological tour de force. The horrors she confronts, the defenses she mounts, the things she learns are treated with a painful but bracing clarity." N Y Times Book Rev

Esquivel, Laura

★ **Like** water for chocolate; translated by Carol Christensen and Thomas Christensen. Doubleday 1992 245p $26; pa $13.95
ISBN 0-385-42016-1; 0-385-42017-X pa
LC 91-47188

Original Spanish edition published 1989 in Mexico

Set in turn-of-the-century Mexico, this novel relates the story of Tita, "the youngest of three daughters. Practically raised in the kitchen, she is expected to spend her life waiting on Mama Elena and never to marry. Her habitual torment increases when her beloved Pedro becomes engaged to one of her sisters. Tita and he are thrown into tantalizing proximity and manage to communicate their affection through the dishes she prepares for him and his rapturous appreciation. Eventually, Tita's culinary wizardry unleashes uncontrollable forces, with surprising results." Booklist

"A poignant, funny story of love, life, and food which proves that all three are entwined and interdependent." Libr J

Esquivel, Laura

Swift as desire. Crown 2001 207p $22
ISBN 0-609-60870-3
LC 2001-28351

"Júbilo, a former telegraph operator, is suffering from Parkinson's disease; he has gone mostly blind and mute. His daughter, Lluvia, has the ingenious idea of installing telegraph equipment in Júbilo's bedroom. Now her father can tap out his thoughts in Morse code, which a computer program translates into written words. Flashbacks show us the glories and sorrows of Júbilo's life: his discovery of the power of words, his realization that people hardly ever say what they mean and his choice of telegraphy as a career." N Y Times Book Rev

Essex, Karen

Kleopatra. Warner Bks. 2001 385p
ISBN 0-446-52740-8
LC 00-44930

Essex's "rendering of the ancient world's culture and political machinations make this fast-paced treatment of Kleopatra's adventures particularly engaging. Exhaustive research is evident throughout." Publ Wkly

Essex, Karen

Leonardo's swans; a novel. Doubleday 2006 344p $21.95
ISBN 0-385-51706-8
LC 2005-048468

This historical novel revolves around "15th-century Italian sisters Isabella and Beatrice d'Este. Isabella, the elder, more accomplished sister, is engaged to handsome

Francesco Gonzaga, a minor aristocrat, while Beatrice is intended for the future duke of Milan, Ludovico Sforza, who's powerful, unscrupulous and already in possession of a pregnant mistress. It seems, at first, that Isabella will enjoy domesticity with Francesco, while unhappy Beatrice is useful to her husband only as a vehicle for breeding sons—a situation further complicated by Ludovico's infatuation with the more beautiful Isabella. While Isabella encourages her brother-inlaw's overtures, she's actually desperate to sit for his resident artist, Leonardo da Vinci." Publ Wkly

"Readers of Tracy Chevalier's Girl with a Pearl Earring or Sarah Dunant's The Birth of Venus will welcome this novel, which brings Renaissance Italy vividly to life." Libr J

Essex, Karen

Pharaoh. Warner Bks. 2002 408p

ISBN 0-446-53025-5

LC 2002-16802

Sequel to Kleopatra

This second volume in the series, "which picks up as the 22-year-old queen of Egypt returns from exile in Rome, overflows with war, sex, political intrigue and the fruits of Essex's assiduous research on everything from ancient Egyptian religious ceremonies to traffic laws in Julius Caesar's Rome. . . . The careful balance Essex strikes between Kleopatra's intimate emotional life and her statecraft makes this a satisfyingly nuanced and approachable portrait." Publ Wkly

Esterhazy, Peter

Celestial harmonies; a novel. translated by Judith Sollosy. Ecco 2004 846p $29.95

ISBN 0-06-050104-9

LC 2003-53139

Original Hungarian edition, 2000

This Hungarian family saga is "divided into two books, the first containing fragmented glimpses of five centuries of the aristocratic Esterházy family, the second a somewhat more conventional narrative of the family's fortunes under Communism. Animating the book are a number of father figures—among them Esterházy's actual father—that owe much to the Central European literary tradition of the foolish, magical paterfamilias, and perhaps even more to Donald Barthelme's (dead) version. Ultimately, Esterházy's attempt to explode epic until it resembles the shards and mirrors of his own style doesn't quite live up to its ambition, though it yields many extraordinary moments." New Yorker

Estleman, Loren D.

The **adventures** of Johnny Vermillion. Forge 2006 269p $24.95

ISBN 978-0-765-30914-3

LC 2006-42532

"Johnny Vermillion, operator and featured performer of the Prairie Rose Repertory Company, travels the Wild West putting on plays in towns like Lockjaw, Diablo, and Purgatory. But that's just his cover: in fact, he and his small troop are bank robbers. And when a determined Pinkerton agent tips to what Johnny has been up to, an all-out pursuit results, culminating in a wickedly clever trap. Once again, Estleman proves why he is among the best of our contemporary western novelists . . . . Johnny and his merry band of thieves are thoroughly delightful characters, a bunch of good-natured rogues, colorful without being cartoony." Booklist

Estleman, Loren D.

Alone; a Valentino mystery. Forge 2009 268p $24.99

ISBN 978-0-7653-1576-2; 0-7653-1576-9

LC 2009-34609

In this outing, "UCLA film archivist Valentino gets embroiled in a case involving a love letter supposedly written by Greta Garbo in 1950 that is being used to blackmail the husband of the letter's recipient. Who cares, you might ask? But Garbo is still big news, and soon Valentino is tripping over eager media hounds and trying to stay out of the way of the police investigating the death of the blackmailer. . . . [The author] opens the film industry's back door and allows readers to get a glimpse of the world of film preservation. Full of humor and delightful cinema knowledge, this is sure to please mystery fans who love Hollywood." Libr J

Estleman, Loren D.

American detective; an Amos Walker novel. Forge 2007 254p $24.95

ISBN 978-0-765-31224-2; 0-765-31224-7

"Besides yielding the usual gunplay and fisticuffs, along with choice baseball metaphors . . . the well-oiled plot is supple enough to handle the newfangled criminal enterprises that a big-city shamus has to contend with nowadays. But Estleman also delivers some outstanding stuff on the hazards of the profession, including a bone-chilling stakeout on a lonely lake in the dead of night, that could come only from an old pro." N Y times Book Rev

Estleman, Loren D.

★ **Amos** Walker; the complete story collection. Tyrus Books 2010 637p il $32.95

ISBN 978-1-935562-24-5; 1-935562-24-X

"All the elements that have made Estleman one of the best hard-boiled writers of all time—just a notch below Chandler and Hammett—are present in these 32 short stories. Remarkably, he has kept his Detroit-based Amos Walker series (Motor City Blue) fresh after three decades and 20 novels, and any fan of the genre who has yet to encounter the ex-cop turned PI will get a great introduction through this collection. What's most impressive is Estleman's ability to blend sharp-edged language, cynical characters, betrayals, twists, and a memorable narrative voice within the short story format. He also manages to inject dark humor into his work that keeps the violence, corruption, and double-crosses from becoming too grim. . . . Longtime fans will welcome the author's informative introduction." Publ Wkly

Estleman, Loren D.

Black powder, white smoke. Forge 2002 318p $24.95

ISBN 0-7653-0189-X

LC 2002-69266

Honey Boutrille is a "freed slave who kills a white man to save a working girl in the New Orleans brothel he owns. 'Twice' Emerson is a career criminal on the run after a botched train robbery. Most of the time, Honey travels in Texas, while Twice hides out in the West. We know that they will eventually cross paths, but part of this story's charm is how it will happen." Libr J

Estleman, Loren D.
★ The **book** of Murdock. Forge 2010 271p $24.99
ISBN 978-0-7653-1600-4

"This is one of Estleman's best, a smart, tightly wrapped story about an honest lawman who drinks Old Forester and knows the difference between a Presbyterian and a Unitarian." Publ Wkly

Estleman, Loren D.
Frames; a Valentino mystery. Forge 2008 269p $23.95
ISBN 978-0-7653-1575-5; 0-7653-1575-0

LC 2008-4505

"Estleman first introduced Valentino in a series of short stories for Ellery Queen Mystery Magazine and promises that 'Frames' is the first in a series of novels featuring the 'film detective.' As with every Estleman novel, 'Frames' is written in crisp, vivid prose, the characters well-drawn. And the author's meticulous research of movie history adds another layer of richness." San Francisco Chron

Estleman, Loren D.
★ **Gas** City. Forge 2008 299p $24.95
ISBN 978-0-7653-1956-2; 0-7653-1956-X

LC 2007-34927

"The shades of Frank Norris and Upton Sinclair must have been looking over Loren D. Estleman's shoulder when he wrote Gas City. Set in a Midwestern metropolis that grew up around a refinery, his muscular novel initially takes a long view of the cynical bargain struck between civic leaders and organized crime—and only moves in for the kill when a key figure in this devil's dance decides to reform. Like earlier muckraking writers, Estleman is always looking for the tipping point where our frontier values of independent entrepreneurship and community justice tumble into criminality. And his characters never stop asking whether it's possible to go back and get it right." N Y Times Book Rev

Estleman, Loren D.
The **hours** of the virgin. Mysterious Press 1999 296p $23
ISBN 0-89296-683-1

LC 98-48001

"Estleman doesn't write pretty travelogues; the pavements of his mean streets are always slippery with bodily fluids. But for all the noir trappings of his style, with its moody nightscapes of lonely streets and empty rooms, this is one genre author who follows the procedures without debasing the language or insulting the intelligence." N Y Times Book Rev

Estleman, Loren D.
Infernal angels. Forge 2011 270p $24.99
ISBN 978-0-7653-1955-5; 0-7653-1955-1

LC 2011-13480

A "novel featuring Detroit PI Amos Walker. . . . Reuben Crossgrain, proprietor of Past Presence ('Everything you require for the Modern Regressive Lifestyle'), hires Walker to recover 25 TV converter boxes that allow the owner to watch HDTV on an analog set, although the total value of the loss isn't much more than Walker's standard retainer. The detective hits the pavement to identify the likely recipients of the hot items, and his digging soon attracts the attention of ex-Detroit police detective Mary Ann Thaler, who now works in D.C. on homeland security. As the bodies start to drop, Estleman presents a powerful view of the battered inner city, where federally funded housing ends up derelict. Three decades on, Estleman and Walker show no signs of slowing down." Publ Wkly

Estleman, Loren D.
Jitterbug; a novel of Detroit. Forge 1998 303p
ISBN 0-312-86360-8

LC 98-21185

In World War II Detroit "the heat is on Racket Squad leader Lieutenant Maximilian Zagreb and his three detectives . . . when someone starts killing people for hoarding ration coupons. Using some artful manipulation and some very unsubtle pressure, Zagreb leans on a couple of unlikely sources for help. Frankie 'The Conductor' Orr, a local mob boss, and Dwight Littlejohn, a black riveter in an airplane factory, are unwilling participants in Zagreb's efforts to smoke out the killer dubbed Kilroy by the newspapers." Publ Wkly

"This is historical crime drama at its highest level done by a consummate craftsman." Booklist

Estleman, Loren D.
★ The **master** executioner. Forge 2001 270p $23.95
ISBN 0-312-86970-3

LC 2001-23181

This novel set in the 19th century American West follows "Oscar Stone, a professional hangman, as he dispenses justice to axe murderers and army deserters. . . . Stone's calling causes his lovely young wife to flee in revulsion. But {he} is driven to exploit a gift that marries professionalism with mercy." Economist

"Estleman has created an unforgettable character in Stone. . . . A dark, compelling journey into a previously unexplored facet of the old West." Booklist

Estleman, Loren D.
Poison blonde; an Amos Walker novel. Forge 2003 269p $24.95
ISBN 0-7653-0447-3

LC 2002-35242

"Latin singer Gilia Cristobal, the hottest commodity in show business, hires Detroit private eye Amos Walker to get to the botom of a scam involving the singer's designer gowns, but her real problem is blackmail. It turns out she's not really who she claims to be. . . . Walker is a classic hard-boiled private eye. He breathes air heavy with smoke and cordite, he delivers his dialogue through clenched teeth, and he operates by a murky moral code only he understands." Booklist

Estleman, Loren D.

Port hazard; a Page Murdock novel. Forge 2004 301p $24.95

ISBN 0-7653-0190-3

LC 2003-49425

"Deputy U.S. Marshal Page Murdock usually roams the open trails and cow towns of the West in his dead-or-alive search for outlaws and miscreants. Federal judge Harlan Blackthorne has a different venue for Murdock's next assignment: California's Barbary Coast. A militant wing of the Sons of the Confederacy, located in San Francisco, is assassinating anyone who impedes its efforts to revive interest in secession from the union. . . . Estleman, at home in many genres, here mixes noir and the Old West, as Murdock literally walks off the trail and onto the mean streets. A wildly entertaining read with great period atmosphere and dialogue." Booklist

Estleman, Loren D.

Retro; an Amos Walker novel. Forge 2004 286p $24.95

ISBN 0-7653-0448-1

LC 2003-71103

"Estleman makes his strongest stand for the pure, unvarnished glory of the classic American private eye in Retro, whose tongue-in-cheek title tells you what you need to know about Amos Walker." N Y Times Book Rev

Estleman, Loren D.

A smile on the face of the tiger. Mysterious Press 2000 295p $24.95

ISBN 0-89296-706-4

LC 00-22284

Detroit gumshoe Amos Walker, "a serious drinker-thinker who lives by a tough-guy code that went out of fashion with the Edsel, is sick of hearing that he looks as if he just slouched out of a 1950's paperback novel. But when a publisher hires him to find Eugene Booth, a has-been pulp legend who skipped out on a lucrative contract to reissue his best book, Walker finds himself staring at a streaky mirror image of himself—if he lives so long. . . . Estleman pays handsome homage to Goodis and Woolrich and all the other 'paper tigers' to whom he dedicates this wonderful book." N Y Times Book Rev

Estleman, Loren D.

★ Something borrowed, something black; a Peter Macklin novel. Forge 2002 236p $24.95

ISBN 0-312-87863-X

LC 2001-54752

Peter Macklin "has retired from the hit-man business and married Laurie, a young woman who knows nothing of his former career. They're on their honeymoon in Los Angeles when Macklin is forced back into his old calling by a Midwestern crime lord who's interested in expanding his territory. . . . Back in L.A., Laurie is being held hostage. At first she thinks the lanky cowboy named Abilene is just keeping her company while her husband is away 'on business,' but a fist in the face changes her take on things. . . . The story vibrates with letter-perfect details, and the plot, with changing locations and changing points of view, is deftly handled." Publ Wkly

Estrin, Marc

Insect dreams; the half life of Gregor Samsa. BlueHen Bks. 2002 468p

ISBN 0-399-14836-1

LC 2001-35941

This novel follows Kafka's Gregor Samsa "from post-World War I Vienna through the Manhattan Project in Los Alamos, NM. In numerous behind-the-scenes actions, Gregor befriends historical figures like Charles Ives, President Franklin D. Roosevelt, and Robert Oppenheimer, as well as numerous other highly fascinating fictional characters." Libr J

Includes bibliographical references

Etchart, Martin

The last shepherd; by Martin Etchart. University of Nevada Press 2012 203 p. (pbk.: alk. paper) $22

ISBN 087417886X; 9780874178869; 9780874178876

LC 2012017300

This novel, by Martin Etchart, is part of the "West Word Fiction" series. "Mathieu Etchiberri wants . . . to leave his family's Arizona sheep ranch. . . . Then his father is killed in an accident. . . . He travels to the French Pyrenees from which his father . . . came to settle the questions about his legacy. . . . As Matt resolves the mystery of his family, he also discovers his Basque roots and learns the nature of love of family, responsibility, and . . . the needs of a community." (Publisher's note)

Eugenides, Jeffrey

★ The marriage plot. Farrar, Straus and Giroux 2011 406p $28

ISBN 0-374-20305-9; 978-0-374-20305-4

LC 2011-22099

College English major "Madeleine Hanna is writing her senior thesis on Jane Austen and George Eliot." (Publisher's note)

The novel's "plot, as it were, centers on the lopsided love triangle of three bright young things at Brown University, class of '82: WASPy beauty Madeleine Hanna; charismatic manic-depressive Leonard Bankhead; and Mitchell Grammaticus, who is, Madeleine tells herself, exactly 'the kind of smart, sane, parent-pleasing boy she should fall in love with and marry.' But it's the brilliant, volatile Leonard whom she falls for when the pair meet in a Semiotics 211 seminar. . . . If chronicling the Derrida debates and romantic travails of perpetually self-regarding undergrads, even ones as sharply drawn as the trio here, sounds beneath Eugenides' considerable gifts, well, it can feel that way at times. Plot's story line wobbles and ultimately loses its way. Still, there are serious pleasures here for people who love to read: diamond-sharp observations and dazzling sentences." Entertainment Wkly

Eugenides, Jeffrey

Middlesex. Farrar, Straus & Giroux 2002 529p $26

ISBN 0-374-19969-8

LC 2002-19921

A coming of age story about Cal, a hermaphrodite, born in 1960 Detroit as a baby girl and reborn in 1974 as a teenage boy

"Eugenides pitches a big tent, but one of the delights of 'Middlesex' is how soundly it's constructed, with motifs and characters weaving through the novel's various episodes, pulling it tight." N Y Times Book Rev

Eugenides, Jeffrey

★ The **virgin** suicides. Farrar, Straus & Giroux 1993 249p
    ISBN 0-374-28438-5

LC 92-33466

The author's "engrossing writing style keeps one reading despite a creepy feeling that one shouldn't be enjoying it so much. A black, glittering novel that won't be to everyone's taste but must be tried by readers looking for something different." Libr J

Evanovich, Janet

Eleven on top. St. Martin's Press 2005 310p $26.95
    ISBN 0-312-30626-1

LC 2005-47846

Stephanie Plum "no longer wants to work for her cousin Vinnie, the bail bondsman in the Burg, a section of Trenton, New Jersey. Her first three tries at new gainful employment– the button factory, the local dry cleaner, and the infamous Cluck in a Bucket fast-food joint–engender firebombings, exploding cars, and even the death of a local everyone is way too happy to see go. Meanwhile, several local businessmen have disappeared, and a lowlife Stephanie has known since high school is leaving lurid and scary notes in her apartment. Although brimming with lines that will have readers howling with laughter, this installment also allows flashes of insight into the men in Stephanie's life, Morelli the cop and Ranger the bounty hunter, as well as into Stephanie herself and her (over)extended family." Booklist

Evanovich, Janet

Hard eight. St. Martin's Press 2002 311p $25.95
    ISBN 0-312-26585-9

LC 2002-21290

In this adventure Jersey bounty hunter Stephanie Plum drops "everthing to search for a missing child when Mabel Markowitz's granddaughter, Evelyn, skips town with her little girl, Annie, forfeiting Mabel's house as collateral on a child custody bond. . . . For all its zany elements, the plot turns logically on its own comically warped axis." N Y Times Book Rev

Evanovich, Janet

Hot six. St. Martin's Press 2000 294p
    ISBN 0-312-20540-6

LC 00-25208

"Stephanie Plum, Jersey Girl and bounty hunter extraordinaire, is on the hunt for Ranger, her mysterious and sexy co-worker, who has been implicated in a murder. At the same time, she is tracked by thugs Habib and Mitchell, who threaten bodily harm if she doesn't find Ranger for them." Libr J

Evanovich, Janet

One for the money. Scribner 1994 290p $25
    ISBN 0-684-19639-5

LC 93-50733

"A wonderful sense of humor, an eye for detail, and a self-deprecating narrative endow Stephanie Plum with the easy-to-swallow believability that accounts for her appeal as heroine. . . . A witty, well-written, and gutsy debut." Libr J

Evanovich, Janet

Three to get deadly. Scribner 1997 300p $25
    ISBN 0-684-82265-2

LC 96-42176

"Stephanie Plum stands apart from the female series characters who are so popular in crime fiction. She's funnier, tougher, politically incorrect, and just loves her job to death." Booklist

Evanovich, Janet

To the nines; a Stephanie Plum novel. St. Martin's Press 2003 312p il $25.95
    ISBN 0-312-26586-7

"Bounty hunter Stephanie Plum is at it again. Singh has jumped ship, abandoning his fianceé, stealing her dog, and owing his landlord back rent. Through their sleuthing, Stephanie and Ranger track him down in Vegas. Unfortunately, owing to a previous problem with the law, Ranger isn't allowed to go to Vegas. This leaves Stephanie with Lulu and Connie as her traveling companions." Libr J

Evanovich, Janet

Two for the dough. Scribner 1996 301p
    ISBN 0-684-82592-9

LC 95-23888

In this novel bounty hunter Stephanie Plum tracks "a bond jumper through her blue-collar neighborhood known as the 'burg.' A local funeral home, a slimy undertaker and mutilated corpses figure large in the search for Kenny Mancuso, who, having shot an old high school friend in the knee, posted bail with Stephanie's boss, her cousin, and then disappeared. When the old friend is shot again, fatally, Stephanie reluctantly joins forces with her sexy enemy and love interest, Trenton homicide cop Joe Morelli. . . . Readers will likely stay a few steps ahead of the sleuths, but the sharp repartee and Stephanie's slightly cynical but still fond relationship with her family and the burg hold a treasury of urban-style charms." Publ Wkly

Evans, Danielle

Before you suffocate your own fool self. Riverhead Books 2010 232p $25.95
    ISBN 978-1-59448-769-9; 1-59448-769-3

LC 2010-07179

"This debut collection is contemporary, powerful, and very real. While race is a factor throughout, with biracial characters, mixed-race romantic relationships, and plenty of interaction among people of different ethnicities, it remains subsidiary to themes like family relationships, romantic attachments, coming-of-age, belonging, and searching or yearning for direction in life. . . . A smartly written and enjoyable collection from an up-and-coming author." Libr J

Evans, Justin

✓ The **white** devil. Harper 2011 366p

ISBN 9780061728273; 0061728276; 9780061728280 pa; 0061728284 pa

LC 2010051662

"When Andrew Taylor is sent to the Harrow School, a British institution for privileged adolescents, he is spurned by nearly all of his peers, and becomes immersed in a two-hundred-year-old literary mystery when he finds a friend in the school's poet-in-residence." (Publisher's note)

Evans, Nicholas

The **brave**; a novel. Little, Brown and Company 2010 353p $26.99

ISBN 978-0-316-03378-7

LC 2010-11402

"As a student at the Ashlawn Preparatory School in 1959 England, eight-year-old, cowboy-crazy Tommy Bedford . . . is teased for being a bed wetter and gets the shock of his young life when he learns that his sister, glamorous 'Next Big Thing' actress Diane Reed, is really his mother. Soon afterwards, she and Tommy move to L.A., where Diane falls for TV cowboy Ray Montane, and their tortured relationship leads to a horrifying act of violence that has lifelong repercussions for Tommy. In a parallel, present-day plot, 50-ish Tom, now a writer and documentary filmmaker who specializes in the American West, lives in Montana, is divorced and estranged from his adult son, Danny, who has been accused of committing an atrocity while serving in Iraq, for which he will be tried in a military court. Alternating past and present, Evans expertly juggles his twin narratives until they come shatteringly together as father and son yield to the combined weight of the secrets they hide." Publ Wkly

Evans, Nicholas

The **divide**; Nicholas Evans. Putnam 2005 403 p. (hbk.) o.p.; Library binding $31.95

ISBN 0399152067; 9781585476879

LC 2005048723

In this book, "[t]wo skiers . . . find a body encased in ice: . . . Abbie Cooper, wanted for eco-terrorism and murder. Her parents come to claim her body: Ben from Santa Fe, where he lives with his lover Eve, Sarah from . . . Long Island. Sarah's cruel accusation that Ben is responsible for Abbie's death spins the story back to when they were a happy family . . . or at least had the appearance of one. . . . [T]he façade of marital harmony shatters on Ben's 46th birthday at the Divide, a Montana dude ranch, where he meets Eve. . . . Abbie takes her parents' split badly, and her youthful enthusiasm for saving the planet . . . turns dangerous after she meets Rolf, a cell leader for the Earth Liberation Front. . . . Abbie and Rolf go underground to lead a quasi-criminal existence, despite her parents' televised appeals to turn herself in." (Kirkus)

Evans, Nicholas

✓ ★ The **horse** whisperer. Delacorte Press 1995 404p $24.95

ISBN 0-385-31523-6

LC 95-17742

"Evans can give equally clipped but clear descriptions of a prosthetic device or a Montana vista, and the lead charac-

ters emerge through carefully constructed, seemingly effortless scenes and dialog, not in histrionics." Libr J

Evans, Stephanie Jaye

Safe from harm; Stephanie Jaye Evans. Berkley Prime Crime 2013 336 p. (paperback) $15

ISBN 0425253465; 9780425253465

LC 2012045242

This novel, by Stephanie Jaye Evans, is book two in the "Sugar Land" mystery series. "The ominous text message Bear Wells received from his teenage daughter Jo simply said: 'Come home.' The Texas minister never imagined he'd rush back to find her cradling the dead body of her estranged friend Phoebe. . . . The apparent suicide seems like an open-and-shut case. But . . . the deeper [Jo] digs into Phoebe's life, the more she realizes nobody knew her at all." (Publisher's note)

Evaristo, Bernardine

Blonde roots. Riverhead Books 2009 269p $24.95

ISBN 978-1-59448-863-4; 1-59448-863-0

LC 2008-46308

First published 2008 in the United Kingdom

"The whole story is a riotous, bitter course in the arbitrary nature of our cultural values. Don't be fooled; slavery might have ended 150 years ago, but you've still got time to be enlightened by this bracing novel." Washington Post Book World

Eve, Nomi

The **family** orchard. Knopf 2000 316p $25

ISBN 0-375-41076-7

LC 00-40566

This is "a six-generation family memoir recast as fiction. . . . Set almost entirely in Israel, the book spans 160 years of tumultuous Israeli and family history, from the 1830's, when Palestine was part of the Turkish Empire, through the three major waves, or aliyahs, of Jewish immigration, the British mandate, modern statehood and warfare, up to the present. Historical figures and events flit past in the background of the characters' lives." N Y Times Book Rev

"This fascinating novel not only acknowledges that much of family history is imagined or embellished but glories in it." Booklist

Evenson, Brian

Immobility; Brian Evenson. 1st ed. Tor 2012 253 p. (paperback) $14.99; (hardcover) $24.99

ISBN 9780765330970; 0765330962; 1429992883; 9780765330963; 9781429992886

LC 2012000985

In this post-apocalypic novel, by Brian Evenson, "a man who may or may not be named Josef Horkai wakes from what he is told has been 30 years of cold-sleep storage. . . . Rasmus, the leader of the group, tells Horkai that he is . . . needed to retrieve a mysterious cylinder that has been stolen by a rival group. Horkai's legs are useless and . . . [t]o get Horkai where he needs to go, two . . . individuals of limited intelligence, will carry him." (Kirkus Reviews)

Evenson, Brian

The **open** curtain; a novel. Coffee House Press 2006 223p pa $14.95

ISBN 978-1-56689-188-2; 1-56689-188-4

LC 2006-12060

The author "makes a murder committed in 1902 by a grandson of Mormon prophet Brigham Young one of the central plot strands of his latest novel. Raised in a troubled but strict religious home, teenage misfit Rudd gradually pulls away from his oppressive mother, inventing a new family and new world for himself. When he is found at the scene of a double murder with little memory of the preceding events, he forms a unique bond with 19-year-old Lyndi, the daughter of the victims. The two, barely recovered from the gruesome events, start to lose track of time and to call each other by the names of the perpetrators of the 1902 murder. The Mormon angle is not what is most interesting about this uncompromising novel; instead, it's the convincing portrayal of a disturbed young man pushed to the breaking point by social isolation and religious extremism." Booklist

Everett, Percival L.

American desert; [by] Percival Everett. Hyperion 2004 291p $24.95

ISBN 0-7868-6917-8

LC 2003-056757

"While on his way to commit suicide, Ted Street, an untenured English professor and philandering husband, is beheaded in a car accident. Worse, he wakes up at his own funeral, his head clumsily stitched on his neck and his mouth sewn closed. From there, Ted embarks on a wide-ranging cruise through the American landscape, as he is kidnapped by a cult convinced that he is a devil; picked up by the military to be experimented on as a prototype of the perfect soldier; and sheltered by another cult, which worships him as a messiah." New Yorker

"Thoughtful, darkly comic and full of heart, the novel offers a wonderfully unusual story about retrospection and forgiveness." Publ Wkly

Everett, Percival L.

I am Not Sidney Poitier; a novel. [by] Percival Everett. Graywolf Press 2009 234p pa $16

ISBN 978-1-55597-527-2; 1-55597-527-5

"Everett's latest tells the story of a young man named Not Sidney Poitier who bears an uncanny resemblance to the famed actor and is adept at deploying a hypnotic technique called Fesmerism. When Not Sidney is young, his mother dies, but not before becoming an early investor in Ted Turner's enterprises. The boy then moves to Atlanta, into the home of Ted Turner. Despite his vast wealth and celebrity looks, when Not Sidney ventures out into the world as a young adult, he faces bizarre, stinging and potentially deadly forms of racism. . . . Not only is the novel smart and without a trace of pretentiousness, it shows Everett as a novelist at the height of his narrative and satirical powers." Publ Wkly

Everett, Percival L.

Percival Everett by Virgil Russell; Percival Everett. Graywolf Press 2013 256 p. (alk. paper) $15

ISBN 1555976344; 9781555976347

LC 2012952759

This metaphysical novel, by Percival Everett, is "a story inside a story inside a story. A man visits his aging father in a nursing home, where his father writes the novel he imagines his son would write. Or is it the novel that the son imagines his father would imagine, if he were to imagine the kind of novel the son would write?" (Publisher's note)

Everett, Percival L.

The **water** cure; [by] Percival Everett. Graywolf Press 2007 216p $22

ISBN 978-1-55597-476-3; 1-55597-476-7

LC 2007-924763

"Ishmael Kidder, eccentric enough to bring his own food to restaurants, has made a fortune writing romance novels under an assumed name. He divides his time between California and a remote house, with no telephone, in the hills of Taos, N.M. He is also a kidnapper and torturer. . . . If you think Kidder makes an unlikely hero, please take into consideration that the man he kidnaps, transports across state lines, and ties up in his basement is responsible, or so he believes, for the rape and murder of Kidder's 11-year-old daughter, Lane. The Water Cure takes the form of journal in which Kidder reports his wide-ranging thoughts. The terrible sadness is made all the more acute by an underlying dark humor. The text jumps around from Socratic dialogues with his prisoner to silly jokes to meditations on ancient philosophy and aesthetics to memories of his daughter." PopMatters

Evison, Jonathan

All about Lulu; a novel. Soft Skull Press 2008 340p pa $14.95

ISBN 978-1-59376-196-7; 1-59376-196-1

LC 2007-46761

"William Miller Jr. is a scrawny loner whose mother dies of cancer when he is seven years old, leaving him an awkward vegetarian with an ominously macho father and idiot twin brothers in mid-1970s Santa Monica. William's father, Big Bill, remarries a grief counselor named Willow, and Will spends the following decades in love with Louisa (Lulu, as she prefers to be called), his new stepsister. They are close throughout adolescence, but after a summer at cheerleading camp, Lulu returns home distant and hostile, leaving Will to pine for her in solitary desperation. Will finally appears to be on the path to normalcy in the early 1990s when he lucks into a radio talk-show hosting gig, but the stroke of good fortune is short-lived, as he discovers things about Lulu he'd rather not know. Evison provides readers a viciously funny and deeply felt portrayal of a blended family and one man's thwarted longing." Publ Wkly

Evison, Jonathan

The **revised** fundamentals of caregiving; a novel. by Jonathan Evison. 1st ed. Algonquin Books of Chapel Hill 2012 288 p. (hardcover) $23.95; (audiobook) $52.43; (paperback) $14.95; (ebook) $23.95

ISBN 1616200391; 9781616200398; 9781611749007; 9781616203153; 9781616201852

LC 2012002956

In this novel by Jonathan Evison, "when Ben is assigned to tyrannical nineteen-year-old Trevor, who is in the advanced stages of Duchenne muscular dystrophy, he soon discovers . . . the reality of caring for a fiercely stubborn . . . adolescent. . . . The relationship between Trev and Ben evolves into a close camaraderie, and the traditional boundaries between patient and caregiver begin to blur as they embark on a road trip to visit Trev's ailing father." (Publisher's note)

Evison, Jonathan

★ **West** of here; a novel. Jonathan Evison. Algonquin Books of Chapel Hill 2011 486p maps

ISBN 1565129520; 9781565129528; 978-1-56512-952-8; 1-56512-952-0

LC 201020224

"The book charts the trajectory, over 127 years, of Port Bonita, a fictional outpost on the Olympic Peninsula, west of Seattle." (N Y Times Book Rev)

F

Faber, Michel

The **courage** consort; three novellas. Harcourt 2004 232p $23.00

ISBN 0-15-101061-7

LC 2004-5912

"In 'The Courage Consort,' the soprano of a vocal quintet her husband directs progresses from suicidal anxiety to relative equanimity as the group rehearses a difficult new piece that sudden death prevents them from premiering. In 'The Hundred Ninety-Nine Steps,' a woman resolves her trauma over losing a leg and her lover because of a senseless accident; by means romantic and eerie, a handsome young doctor, his late father's dog, and a manuscript in a bottle are the catalysts of her transformation. In the entrancing 'The Fahrenheit Twins'—perhaps a coming-of-age parable—brother and sister Marko'cain and Tainto'lilith, born and reared in arctic isolation, quest far from home for a signal from the universe telling them what to do with their mother's corpse. Faber's literary artistry in all three pieces is consummate." Booklist

Faber, Michel

The **crimson** petal and the white. Harcourt 2002 838p $26

ISBN 0-15-100692-X

LC 2002-24138

"The large themes that interwine the characters with one another—religion, health, sexuality, death, and, reluctantly, love—are juxtaposed against the most minute and intimate details of Victorian life. . . . This massive work is startling and absorbing." Booklist

Faber, Michel

Vanilla bright like Eminem; stories. Harcourt 2007 246p $23

ISBN 978-0-15-101314-2

LC 2006-103560

First published 2005 in the United Kingdom with title: The Fahrenheit twins

"A cunning, sui generis talent. . . . Mr. Faber's clinical detachment serves well the deprivations and frustrations of postindustrial near-manhood. . . . [His] style provides the fun-house unheimlich of an unedited newswire; comas and infanticide evince the same mannered anxiety as train rides and daydreams." N Y Observer

Fairstein, Linda

Bad blood. Scibner 2007 400p $26

ISBN 978-0-7432-8748-7; 0-7432-8748-7

LC 2006-51168

"While Cooper may engage in a few too many action sequences for legal purists, the crisp writing and Fairstein's enviable capacity to translate her own experience as a prosecutor into an accessible plot puts this series a cut above most entries in this crowded subgenre." Publ Wkly

Fairstein, Linda

The **bone** vault; a novel. Scribner 2003 386p $25

ISBN 0-7432-2354-3

LC 2002-26686

A thriller starring Alexandra Cooper, "a Manhattan assistant district attorney. This time out, she and her sidekick, cop Mike Chapman, are drawn into a particularly mysterious case: a Metropolitan Museum of Art intern is found dead in a sarcophagus, and though she's been dead for months, her body is perfectly preserved. When it is discovered that she died of arsenic poisoning, the plot thickens. This is fun reading." Libr J

Fairstein, Linda

Entombed; [by] Linda A. Fairstein. Scribner 2005 400p $26

ISBN 0-7432-5488-0

LC 2004-52189

"Alexandra Cooper returns in another case featuring two seemingly unrelated crimes that the talented sex-crimes prosecutor is hell-bent on connecting. A serial rapist is terrorizing Manhattan's tony Upper East Side. Dubbed the Silk Stocking rapist, his usual M.O. is to terrorize the victim but not kill her. When one girl winds up dead, Alex and her trusted detective partners, Mercer Wallace and Mike Chapman, believe that perhaps a copycat perpetrator is out there who takes his crimes one step further. At the same time, Alex becomes obsessed with the stories of Edgar Allan Poe, especially after a young person's skeleton is found in an old home Poe once inhabited." Booklist

Fairstein, Linda

Killer heat; a novel. Doubleday 2008 370p $26

ISBN 978-0-385-52397-4; 0-385-52397-1

LC 2007-20286

Assistant DA Alexandra Cooper "alternates between the courtroom and crime scenes amid the sweltering summer heat of Manhattan. As she works to convict a serial rapist accused of over 50 rapes in a 35-year-old cold case, verbal and physical threats from vengeance-seeking drug-gang members heat up the courtroom. Alex is called to a crime scene in an abandoned government building, and soon two other young women vanish. Similarities in the cases suggest the possibility of a serial killer, and Alex and colleagues Mike Chapman and Mercer Wallace brave rising temperatures and isolated locations in hot pursuit of the killer. Partly based on a 2006 crime, the novel delivers taut suspense, action-packed chases, historical glimpses of Manhattan, and a smattering of romance." Libr J

Fairstein, Linda

Night watch; Linda Fairstein. Dutton Adult 2012 402 p. (hardback) $26.95
ISBN 0525952632; 9780525952633
LC 2012009632

In this mystery novel by Linda Fairstein, "[w]hile visiting her boyfriend, Luc, an acclaimed chef, in the charming French town of Mougins, NYC prosecutor Alexandra Cooper trips over . . . a serial murder case that just might be her undoing. The local authorities appear clueless about forensics; the only thing they seem capable of doing is pointing a finger at Luc. . . . At the same time, Alex learns that a prominent West African leader living in France is accused of rape by a housekeeper while he was staying in New York, and her colleagues, investigators Mercer and Chapman, get the case. When the couple returns to New York, Alex dives into the rape case as Luc prepares to reopen one of the city's most famous French restaurants, Lutece." (Booklist)

Falconer, Colin

Feathered serpent; a novel of the Mexican conquest. Crown 2002 374p $22.95
ISBN 0-609-61029-5
LC 2002-24711

"Born an Aztec princess and sold into slavery after her father's death, Malinali was at 15 given to conquistador Herman Cortes. A highly intelligent woman gifted in several languages, she made herself indispensable as an interpreter to the Spaniards. Her desire for revenge against Montezuma II, whom she held responsible for the murder of her father, and her belief that Cortes was actually the god Feathered Serpent, coupled with the Spaniards' overwhelming greed for gold, initiated a disastrous sequence of events that led to the fall of the Aztec empire." Libr J

"This enthralling reconstruction of the birth of modern Mexico is rooted in both genuine history and cultural myth." Booklist

Falconer, Delia

The **lost** thoughts of soldiers. Soft Skull Press 2006 151p $16
ISBN 1-933368-17-9
LC 2006-4052

This is an "imagined portrait of the last days of Frederick Benteen, a real-life survivor of the Battle of Little Bighorn whose reputation in history has changed somewhat over the decades. . . . As the novel opens, Benteen is in retirement in Georgia, living out his days quietly and reflecting on the circle of men he knew under Custer's command, when he receives a letter from an admirer in Chicago, who wants his help in setting the record straight about his service during the fateful battle. As Benteen recalls those days, sliding in and out of the past like a man exploring a house he's not been inside for many years, Falconer gently leads the reader through Benteen's life, giving equal weight to his longstanding marriage to his wife Kate and his days on the prairie with the men of the Seventh Cavalry. Despite the subject matter, Falconer writes with a soft touch, mixing subtly poetic images with the occasional burst of crudity and bawdy hu-

mor one might expect of hard-bitten military men in 1876." Boise Wkly

Faletti, Giorgio

A **pimp's** notes; Giorgio Faletti; translated from the Italian by Antony Shugaar. Farrar, Straus and Giroux 2012 325 p.
ISBN 0374231400; 9780374231408
LC 2011046064

Author Giorgio Faletti tells the story of Bravo, the narrator, who "discovers that he's been framed as part of a complicated scheme that's left some of Italy's prominent movers and shakers dead . . . not long after taking a new prostitute under his wing . . . Bravo is a black-humored, streetwise narrator with an appealingly flinty demeanor even when he's in over his head, and he has an excellent femme fatale in Carla, an initially pliable woman who turns out to be much more manipulative than he expected." (Kirkus)

Fallada, Hans

Every man dies alone; translated by Michael Hofmann, with an afterword by Geoff Wilkes. Melville House Pub. 2009 543p il $27
ISBN 978-1-933633-63-3; 1-933633-63-8
LC 2008-27489

Original German edition, 1947

This is a "readable, suspense-driven novel from an author who a) knew what he was doing when it came to writing commercial fiction, and b) had lived through, and so knew intimately, the period he was writing about. This is an extraordinary combination. I hesitate to use a word like 'serendipity,' but cruelly enough, that's exactly what it was. Thus, the characters — and what characters they are, the good, the bad and the ugly of the Berlin working class during the war — are drawn from life. They are alive." Globe and Mail

Fallon, Siobhan

★ **You** know when the men are gone. G.P. Putnam's Sons 2011 226 p. $23.95
ISBN 978-0-399-15720-2
LC 2010029597

This book offers a collection of short stories about "[t]he crucial role of military wives, . . . where the women are linked by absence and a pervading fear that they'll become war widows. In the title story, a war bride from Serbia finds she can't cope with the loneliness and her outsider status, and chooses her own way out. The wife in 'Inside the Break' realizes that she can't confront her husband's probable infidelity with a female soldier in Iraq; as in other stories, there's a gap between what she can imagine and what she can bear to know. In 'Remission,' a cancer patient waiting on the results of a crucial test is devastated by the behavior of her teenage daughter, and while the trials of adolescence are universal, this story is particularized by the unique tensions between military parents and children." (Publishers Weekly)

"In this book of eight stories, connected by young families stationed at Fort Hood, Texas, Siobhan Fallon sees military life as an alternate universe. It can be many times better and so much worse than its civilian counterparts. . . . Fallon is a superb writer with a delicate perception of this raw material. Her characters may be invented or based on people she herself knew as an army wife. In either case, the stories are powerful." Providence J

Farah, Nuruddin

✓ **Crossbones**. Riverhead Books 2011 389p $27.95

ISBN 1-59448-816-9; 978-1-59448-816-0

LC 2011-18748

Third book of a trilogy started with Links (2004). "Accompanied by his son-in-law Malik, Jeebleh arrives in Mogadishu, Somalia, from New York to visit ailing friend Bile, like him a former political prisoner. Jeebleh had left his homeland for the United States, while Bile stayed on with his companion, Cambara, valiantly hoping to effect change from within. Through their connections, journalist Malik sets up interviews, intending to report on pirating in Somalia's coastal waters. Malik's brother Ahl is also in Somalia, seeking to rescue his son, a naive, malleable teen who's been recruited for jihad by an imam in Minneapolis. As the brothers try to navigate a complex network of alliances, readers gain insight into a once beautiful land devastated by civil war, invasions, and the plundering of its natural resources by foreign nations." Libr J

"Gripping but utterly humane thriller set in one of the least-understood regions on earth." Kirkus

Includes bibliographical references

Farah, Nuruddin

✓ **Knots**. Riverhead Books 2006 422p $25.95

ISBN 978-1-59448-924-2; 1-59448-924-6

LC 2006-23107

"Despite its weaknesses, there is beauty in this story of reclamation and resurrection. When Farah's heroine sheds her veil of conformity, it is as if Somalia itself is emerging from a cocoon of despair." Time Out New York

Farah, Nuruddin

✓ **Links**. Riverhead Books 2004 336p $24.95

ISBN 1-573-22265-8

LC 2003-65969

First published 2003 in South Africa

"Jeebleh, settled in the United States with an American wife and grown children, returns to Mogadishu with two purposes. One is to find the burial place of his mother; the other is to try to rescue the kidnapped niece of Bile, an old friend and onetime comrade in the early fight against the dictator Mohammed Siad Barre." N Y Times Book Rev

This novel is "both alien and familiar, a haunting exploration of the desire to help and the attendant costs of doing so." Christ Sci Monit

Farmer, Philip Jose

The **classic** Philip Jose Farmer, 1952-1964--1964-1973; edited and introduction by Martin H. Greenberg; foreword by Isaac Asimov. Crown 1984 2v

Contents: 1952-1964: Sail on! Sail on; Mother; The God business; The Alley Man; My sister's brother; The king of beasts ; 1964-1973: The shadow of space; Riders of the purple wage {novelette}; Don't wash the carats; The jungle rot kid on the nod; The oogenesis of Bird City; The sliced-crosswise only-on-Tuesday world; Sketches among the ruins of my mind; After King Kong fell

Farmer, Philip Jose

The **dark** design. Berkley Pub. Group 1977 412p (Riverworld)

ISBN 0-399-12031-9

LC 77-5138

The third volume of the Riverworld series

"Some threads in the design are loose or overknotted, but the dash and grand scope of the project and this installment of it are compellingly fascinating." Publ Wkly

Followed by The magic labyrinth

Farmer, Philip Jose

The **fabulous** riverboat; a science fiction novel. Putnam 1971 253p

ISBN 9780345419682; 9780399102738 out of print

LC 98096315

This second novel in the Riverworld series "is set in an 'after-Earthlife' of resurrected people over the age of five from time immemorial. The main character is . . . Sam Langhorne Clemens, alias Mark Twain, who attempts to build a metal riverboat. His goal, not obtained in this novel, is to sail upriver to reach the Misty Tower and discover the secret of its guardians, the Ethicals." Libr J

Followed by The dark design

Farmer, Philip Jose

✓ **Gods** of Riverworld. Putnam 1983 331p (Riverworld)

ISBN 0-399-12843-3

LC 83-9552

The fifth volume of the Riverworld series

"The members of the intrepid band that achieved its quest for the end of the River in the previous books now find themselves in command of the Ethicals' polar control center. When they're not trying to track down an unknown enemy, they're building private worlds and resurrecting a few friends. . . . It's the two varieties of god-playing, culminating in a disastrous tea party in Alice Pleasance Liddell's Wonderland, that give the book its interest." Publ Wkly

Farmer, Philip Jose

The **magic** labyrinth. Berkley Pub. Group 1980 339p (Riverworld)

ISBN 0-399-12381-4

LC 80-144

In this fourth volume in the Riverworld series "Farmer brings his large and bizarre cast of characters (including King John Lackland of England, Samuel Clemens, Sir Richard Burton, Hermann Göring, and Alice Liddell, who inspired 'Alice in Wonderland') to the end of their quest and reveals the secret of the Riverworld. For readers prepared to accept it on its own terms, this book will be rewarding, even exciting. Farmer's imagination does not flag from beginning to end." Booklist

Followed by Gods of Riverworld

Farmer, Philip Jose

✓ **To** your scattered bodies go; a science fiction novel. Putnam 1971 221p (Riverworld)

The first volume of the Riverworld series

"The fabulous Riverworld, site of the resurrection of every human being who has died, is one of the great fictional creations. Sir Richard Burton, Victorian explorer and rogue, finds himself reborn and sets off on an epic journey to learn the truth of its existence." Shapiro. Fic For Youth. 3d edition

Followed by The fabulous riverboat

Farnsworth, Christopher

Blood oath. G. P. Putnam's Sons 2010 390p $24.95

    ISBN 978-0-399-15635-9; 0-399-15635-6

                          LC 2009-36951

"Here we have a tale of contemporary guardianship — the fact that unbeknownst to most, a vampire has been part of the American political system for over a hundred years, serving democracy and defending America against opposition from things not usually noticed by your typical American citizen. To this tale arrives Zach Barrows, up and coming political figure. In circumstances that are a little embarrassing (caught en flagrante with Candace, the President's daughter) the result is a promotion of sorts, to being the political liaison officer to Nathaniel Cade. Cade is the vampire: blood-oathed for over 130 years to the President. Much of the book then is spent assisting Cade in dealing with those supernatural issues that appear from time to time. . . . Generally this book is well-written, has a definite film/TV style (perhaps not too farfetched considering that Farnsworth is also a screenwriter) and if you can live with the impracticalities, a solid, fun read." SFFWorld.com

Farrell, James T.

Studs Lonigan; a trilogy. Library of America 2004 988p (The library of America) $35

    ISBN 1-931082-55-3

                          LC 2003-44207

First published as a trilogy 1935 by Vanguard Press

A trilogy "about life among lower-middle-class Irish Roman Catholics in Chicago during the first third of the 20th century. . . . As a boy, William Lonigan (always referred to as 'Studs') makes a slight effort to rise above his squalid urban environment. However, the combination of his own personality, unwholesome neighborhood friends, a small-minded family, and his schooling and religious training all condemn him to the life of futility and dissipation that are his inheritance." Merriam-Webster's Ency of Lit

Includes bibliographical references

Faulkner, William, 1897-1962

★ **Absalom,** Absalom! corrected text. Random House 1986 313p

    ISBN 0-394-55634-8

                          LC 86-6488

First published 1936

"During the summer of 1910, prior to Quentin Compson's leaving the South for his first year at Harvard, old Rosa Coldfield insists upon a private conference with the youth to divulge her recollections of Thomas Sutpen. Driven by a great plan to become a Southern aristocrat, Sutpen builds a mansion, only to see his life ruined. The title of the book reveals the story's basic tragedy: Sutpen's disappointment in his children. One is a spinster and thus has no offspring to continue the family lineage; the other is a son who has disappeared. Sutpen himself falls victim to a murder for retribution. Faulkner depicts the South before and after the Civil War in this powerfully written novel." Shapiro. Fic for Youth. 3d edition

Faulkner, William

★ **As** I lay dying. Modern Lib. 2000 $16.95

    ISBN 0-375-50452-4

This is a reissue of the title first published 1930 by H. Smith

This book focuses on "the Bundrens, a down-at-the-heels family of dirt farmers in Yoknapatawpha County. Who lays dying is Addie Bundren, the mother. . . . . And when Addie Bundren dies, having just once raised herself to the window to look at her coffin, her presumed desires direct the action of the rest of the book, for she has chosen to be buried among her 'own people' in the town of Jefferson, forty miles away." (New York Review of Books)

"Experimental in both subject and narrative structure, this novel treats the events surrounding the illness, death and burial of Addie Bundren, wife of Anse and mother of Cash, Darl, Jewel, Dewey Dell, and Vardaman. It is divided into 59 short interior monologues, predominantly in the present tense, spoken both by the seven members of the family and by various other characters, including the Reverend Whitfield, Dr. Peabody, and the Bundrens' neighbours, Vernon and Cora Tull." Camb Guide to Lit in Engl

Faulkner, William

Collected stories of William Faulkner. Random House 1950 900p hardcover o.p. pa $19.95

    ISBN 0-679-76403-8 pa

"Forty-two short stories, including all from These Thirteen (1931), all but two from Doctor Martino and other stories (1934) and seventeen published in magazines, 1932-1948. . . . Many of the stories deal with characters and incidents related to those in his novels set in the mythical Yoknapatawpha County, Mississippi." Libr J

Faulkner, William

A fable. Random House 1954 437p

    ISBN 0-394-42400-X

"Set in France a few months before the end of World War I, 'A Fable' is both an allegory of the passion of Christ and a study of a world that has chosen submission to authority and the secular values of power and chauvinism instead of the individuality and the exercise of free will. The novel centers on the fate of a young corporal . . . {who} with the aid of twelve companions, incites a mutiny in the trenches which results in a temporary armistice. Betrayed by a member of his own regiment, the corporal is executed for cowardice along with two other military criminals, becoming a martyr to his principles and his belief in humanity." Benet's Reader's Ency of Am Lit

Faulkner, William

The **Faulkner** reader; selections from the works of William Faulkner. Random House 1954 682p

Faulkner, William

Flags in the dust; edited and with an introduction by Douglas Day. Random House 1973 370p

This is the uncut and complete version of Sartoris. "The introduction describes the bibliographic history of the narrative and makes clear that the present work is as complete a reproduction as possible of the extant composite typescript. Emphasis of 'Flags in the dust' is extended from the Sartoris family featured in the later novel to the full range of Faulkner's Yoknapatawpha social structure, resulting in a complete fictional documentation of the intense Faulknerian world which saturated all his writings." Booklist

Faulkner, William

√ ★ **Go** down, Moses; introduction by Stanley Crouch. Modern Lib. 1995 xxii, 367p

ISBN 0-679-60174-0

LC 95-4715

A reissue of the Random House edition published 1942 with title: Go down Moses, and other stories which was analyzed in Short story index

"The voices of Faulkner's South—black and white, comic and tragic—ring through this sprawling tale of the McCaslin clan. The tone ranges from the farcical to the profound. As the title suggests, the stories are rife with biblical themes. Although the seven stories were originally published separately, Go Down, Moses is best read as a novel of interconnecting generations, races, and dreams." Merriam-Webster's Ency of Lit

Faulkner, William

√ The **hamlet**; 3rd ed; Random House 1964 366p
ISBN 0-394-42759-9

First published 1940

First volume in the trilogy about the "Snopes family who descended upon Yoknapatawpha County, Mississippi in the latter years of the nineteenth century. It "tells how Ab Snopes, ex-bushwhacker, horse trader and sharecropper won immunity in Frenchman's Bend because of his reputation as a barn burner and how his son Flem became a clerk in Will Varner's store. Before long other members of the family descend like swarming locusts on the village. . . . Led by Flem, who has set himself up in the world by marrying Eula Varner when she was pregnant with another man's child, they then move on to Jefferson, the county seat." Magill. Masterpieces of World Lit in Dig Form

Followed by The town

Faulkner, William

Intruder in the dust. Random House 1948 247p
√ ISBN 0-394-43074-3

"When Lucas, an elderly Negro, is accused of murdering a white man, Charles, a 16-year-old white boy, works to save him from being lynched. Charles gets the help he needs in his sleuthing from an old aristocratic lady and a young black boy. The trio visits the church graveyard at night to dig up the corpse of the supposed victim. The book can be read as a mystery and, on a deeper level, as a social commentary on the South." Shapiro. Fic for Youth. 3d edition

Faulkner, William, 1897-1962

√ **Light** in August; the corrected text. Modern Library 2002 512p $21.95

ISBN 0-679-64248-X

LC 2001-57933

First published 1932 by Harrison Smith & Robert Haas, Inc.

This novel by William Faulkner chronicles "Lena Grove's resolute search for the father of her unborn child," presenting a "story of perseverence in the face of mortality". Characters include "Reverend Gail Hightower, plagued by visions of Confederate horsemen, and Joe Christmas, a ragged, itinerant soul obsessed with his mixed-race ancestry." (Publisher's note)

The novel "reiterates the author's concern with a society that classifies men according to race, creed, and origin. Joe Christmas, the central character and victim, appears to be white but is really part black; he has an affair with Joanna Burden, a spinster whom the townsfolk of Jefferson regard with suspicion because of her New England background. Joe eventually kills her and sets fire to her house; he is captured, castrated, and killed by the outraged townspeople, to whom his victim has become a symbol of the innocent white woman attacked and killed by a black man. Other important characters are Lena Grove, who comes to Jefferson far advanced in pregnancy, expecting to find the lover who has deserted her, and Gail Hightower, the minister who ignores his wife and loses his church because of his fanatic devotion to the past." Reader's Ency. 4th edition

Faulkner, William

√ The **mansion**. Random House 1959 436p

"Sometimes the reader grows tired of the tough repetitive monologues and the revelations of Southern decay, but in Faulkner there is a massiveness and even a majesty not easily found elsewhere in the American fiction of this century. . . . Turgid and difficult as he is, Faulkner is worth the trouble." Burgess. 99 Novels

Faulkner, William

√ **Novels**, 1926-1929. Library of Am. 2006 1182p $40

ISBN 1-931082-89-8

LC 2005-49444

Soldiers' pay (1926) explores the disillusionment provoked by World War I. Mosquitoes (1927) is a satire of artistic poseurs. In Flags in the dust (published in truncated form in 1929 as Sartoris) Faulkner began his exploration of Yoknapatapha County, Mississippi. The sound and the fury (1929) tells of the decline of the Compson clan

Faulkner, William

√ **Novels**, 1930-1935. Library of Am. 1985 1034p $35

ISBN 0-940450-26-7

LC 84-23424

Contents: As I lay dying; Sanctuary; Light in August; Pylon

Faulkner, William

√ **Novels**, 1936-1940. Library of Am. 1990 1117p map $37.50

ISBN 0-940450-55-0

LC 89-62931

Absalom, Absalom!, The unvanquished, and The hamlet are entered seperately. If I forget thee, Jerusalem (published 1939 with title The wild palms) depicts, in alternating narratives, the "effects of a Mississippi flood on the lives of a hillbilly convict and a New Orleans doctor and his mistress." Oxford Companion to Am Lit. 6th edition

Faulkner, William
   Novels, 1942-1954. Library of Am. 1994 1115p $35
    ISBN 0-940450-85-2
                                 LC 94-2942
    Contents: Go down, Moses; Intruder in the dust; Requiem for a nun; A fable

Faulkner, William
   Novels, 1957-1962. Library of Am. 1999 1008p $35
    ISBN 1-88301-169-8
                                   LC 99-18348
    Contents: The town; The mansion; The reivers

Faulkner, William
   Pylon. H. Smith and R. Haas, Inc. 1935 315p
   The scene is a Southern city where a Mardi Gras celebration is in progress. The action covers four days in the lives of a strange set of people, all of them connected in some way with the airplane contests which are being held in celebration of the opening of a new airport. The main characters are: Shumann, an airplane pilot; Jiggs, his mechanic; Jackson, a parachute jumper; Laverne, Shumann's wife; and a nameless reporter who adopts the group for the time being

Faulkner, William
   The **reivers**; a reminiscence. Vintage Books 1992 305p pa $12.95
    ISBN 0-679-74192-5
                                  LC 92-50095
    First published 1932 by Harrison Smith & Robert Haas, Inc.
    "Told to his grandson as 'A Reminiscence,' Lucius Priest's monologue recalls his adventures in 1905 as an 11-year-old, when he, the gigantic but childish part-Indian Boon Hogganbeck, and a black family servant, Ned William McCaslin, become reivers (stealthy plunderers) of the automobile of his grandfather, the senior banker of Jefferson, Miss." Oxford Companion to Am Lit. 5th edition

Faulkner, William
   Requiem for a nun. Random House 1951 286p
   "Written in three prose sections, which provide the background, and three acts which present the drama in the courthouse and the jail, the novel centers on Temple Drake, one of the main characters of Sanctuary. In the interval of the eight years separating the events of the two books, Temple has married Gowan Stevens and borne two children; she is being blackmailed by Pete, brother of her lover in Sanctuary, and is planning to run away with him when Nancy Manningoe, her black servant, kills Temple's youngest child. Her attempts to gain a pardon from the governor for Nancy finally bring out Temple's own involvement in and responsibility for the crime." Reader's Ency. 4th edition

Faulkner, William
   ★ **Sanctuary.** J. Cape & H. Smith 1931 380p

"Horace Benbow, an ineffectual intellectual, becomes involved in the violent events centering on Temple Drake, a provocative, irresponsible young coed. Temple is raped by Popeye, who murders a man trying to protect her. Popeye is a figure of evil, but is also a victim of his environment. Carried off to a Memphis brothel by Popeye, Temple later protects him and testifies against Lee Goodwin, who is accused of the murder. Benbow defends Goodwin at the trial and unsuccessfully tries to give shelter to Goodwin's common-law wife. Temple's perjured testimony ends all hope for Goodwin, who is lynched by the townspeople." Reader's Ency. 4th edition

Faulkner, William
   Sartoris. Harcourt Brace & Co. 1929 380p
   A more complete version of this novel was published with title: Flags in the dust
   "A saga of the Sartoris family, the novel deals primarily with young Bayard Sartoris' urge for self-destruction. His beloved twin brother, John, having been killed in World War I, Bayard returns home haunted by the memories of his brother, and becomes involved in a number of accidents. Because of his reckless driving, his grandfather, old Bayard Sartoris, rides with him in an attempt to force him to drive carefully, but young Bayard runs the car off a cliff and his grandfather dies of a heart attack. Unable to face either himself or his family, Bayard goes to Ohio to become a test pilot and is killed. . . . Faulkner picks up the beginnings of the Sartoris family in 'The Unvanquished.'" Benet's Reader's Ency of Am Lit

Faulkner, William
   Snopes; The hamlet, The town, The mansion. introduction by George Garrett. Modern Lib. 1994 1065p $27.95
    ISBN 0-679-60092-2
    An omnibus volume of three novels entered separately

Faulkner, William
   Soldiers' pay. Boni & Liveright 1926 319p
   "Lieutenant Donald Mahon, an American in the British air force during World War I, is discharged from the hospital where he has been treated for a critical head wound, and makes his way home to Georgia. The wound leaves a horrible scar, and causes loss of memory and later blindness. On the train from New York he is aided by Joe Gilligan, an awkward, friendly, footloose ex-soldier, and Margaret Powers, an attractive young widow whose husband was killed in the war. Margaret, strangely attracted to the dying, subhuman Donald, decides to go home with him, as does Gilligan, who is in love with her. Their reception in the Georgia town reveals the character of the fickle people." Oxford Companion to Am Lit. 6th edition

Faulkner, William
   ★ The **sound** and the fury; New, corrected ed.; Random House 1984 326p
    ISBN 0-394-53241-4
                                   LC 84-42626
    First published 1929
    "The story is told in four parts, through the stream of consciousness of three characters (the sons of the Compson

family, Benjy, Quentin, and Jason), and finally in an objective account. The Compson family, formerly genteel Southern patricians, now lead a degenerate, perverted life on their shrunken plantation near Jefferson, Miss. The disintegration of the family, which clings to outworn aristocratic conventions, is counterpointed by the strength of the black servants, who include old Dilsey and her son Luster." Oxford Companion to Am Lit. 6th edition

Faulkner, William
    The **town**. Random House 1957 371p
        ISBN 0-394-42452-2
    This second volume in the Snopes trilogy "relates through three narrators of varying reliability the story of Flem Snopes' rise to prominence in the fictional Yoknapatawpha County. Flem's coldly calculated vengeance on his wife, Eula, and her lover culminates in Eula's suicide and Flem's rise to power in Jefferson, the county seat. Because Flem longs for respect as well as money, he turns against the clan of shiftless Snopes cousins who have followed him to town and forces them to leave Jefferson. In his hunger for social validation, he denies his own origins, and the book ends with a hint that the cousins' revenge will follow." Merriam-Webster's Ency of Lit
    Followed by The mansion

Faulkner, William
    ✓ **Uncollected** stories of William Faulkner; edited by Joseph Blotner. Random House 1979 716p
        ISBN 0-394-40044-5
                LC 78-21803
    Contents: Ambuscade; Retreat; Raid; Skirmish at Sartoris; The unvanquished; Vendée; Fool about a horse; Lizards in Jamshyd's courtyard; The hound; Spotted horses; Lion; The old people; A point of law; Gold is not always; Pantaloon in black; Go down, Moses; Delta autumn; The bear; Race at morning; Hog pawn; Nympholepsy; Frankie and Johnny; The priest; Once aboard the Lugger (I); Once aboard the Lugger (II); Miss Zilphia Gant; Thrift; Idyll in the desert; Two dollar wife; Afternoon of a cow; Mr. Acarius; Sepulture South; Gaslight; Adolescence; Al Jackson; Don Giovanni; Peter; Moonlight; The big shot; Dull tale; A return; A dangerous man; Evangeline; A portrait of Elmer; With caution and dispatch; Snow

Faulkner, William
    The **unvanquished**; drawings by Edward Shenton. Random House 1938 293p il
    This is "a collection of interlocking stories. . . . Set during the Civil War, these stories deal with the Sartoris family, whose modern history Faulkner recounted in Sartoris. Composed of seven stories, which first appeared separately in magazines, the book centers primarily on the adventures of Bayard Sartoris and his black companion, Ringo. Colonel John Sartoris and Miss Rosa, Bayard's grandmother, also figure prominently." Reader's Ency. 3d edition

Faulks, Sebastian
    ✓ ★ **Birdsong**. Random House 1996 402p
        ISBN 978-0679776819
                LC 95-23721
    First published 1993 in the United Kingdom

"In 1910, England's Stephen Wraysford, a junior executive in a textile firm, is sent by his company to northern France. There he falls for Isabelle Azaire, a young and beautiful matron who abandons her abusive husband and sticks by Stephen long enough to conceive a child. Six years later, Stephen is back in France, as a British officer fighting in the trenches. Facing death, embittered by isolation, he steels himself against thoughts of love. But despite rampant disease, harrowing tunnel explosions and desperate attacks on highly fortified German positions, he manages to survive, and to meet with Isabelle again. . . . {The author} proves himself a grand storyteller here." Publ Wkly

Faulks, Sebastian
    Charlotte Gray; a novel. Random House 1999 399p
        ISBN 0-375-50169-X
                LC 98-33658
    First published 1998 in the United Kingdom
    Faulks "has written one of those rare books that is adventurous enough to attract a popular audience while thoughtful enough to sustain the more serious reader." Libr J

Faulks, Sebastian
    Devil may care; [by] Sebastian Faulks, writing as Ian Fleming. Doubleday 2008 278p $24.95
        ISBN 978-0-385-52428-5; 0-385-52428-5
                LC 2007-43052
    "Mr. Faulks-writing-as-Fleming does not fall short of the rest of Fleming's posthumous output. Nor does he tinker with the series's surefire recipe for success. What he delivers is a serviceable madeleine for Bond nostalgists and a decent replica of past Bond escapades." N Y Times (Late N Y Ed)

Faulks, Sebastian
    Engleby; a novel. Doubleday 2007 319p $24.95
        ISBN 978-0-385-52405-6
                LC 2007-16044
    Readers are "plunged without introduction into the journals of Mike Engleby, a fiercely intelligent, acerbic and curiously disturbing young man who's studying natural sciences at Cambridge University in the early 1970's. . . . Engleby drinks and smokes a lot, and skulks, and does drugs—but not in a way that could be described as recreational. He pops little blue pills (also unnamed) but never seems to lose his capacity for lucid, almost clinical analysis of his surroundings. . . . Then there's his creepy infatuation with a pretty fellow student, Jennifer Arkland, who disappears in their final year—missing and presumed dead. Has Engleby killed her? The novel generates an unusual kind of suspense, a nagging puzzlement. Jennifer's fate is a worry, of course, but the persistent question is, What's his problem? . . . . The best way to enjoy Engleby is to concentrate, as the bizarre suspense percolates, on Mr. Faulks' exceptionally precise writing." N Y Observer

Faulks, Sebastian
    ✓ **Human** traces; a novel. Random House 2006 563p $25.95
        ISBN 0-375-50226-2
                LC 2005-46683
    First published 2005 in the United Kingdom

"Faulks understands the difficulties inherent in using fiction to convey these complex arguments. He offsets his characters' earnestness—and his own—through attention to settings and plot details. He sends his protagonists to California and Tanzania to fill in pieces of the puzzle. He allows Rebiere to indulge in titillating sexual obsessions. Generally, the effort to entertain succeeds. And Human Traces can be moving, as its characters grapple with the limitations of knowledge and reason. Despite its shortcomings, the book should serve as a popular vehicle for reassessing the history of psychiatry and confronting the mystery of consciousness." Washington Post Book World

Faulks, Sebastian

On Green Dolphin Street; a novel. Random House 2002 351p

ISBN 0-375-50225-4

LC 2001-41753

"The outline of this archetypal love story may sound familiar, but everything about Faulks' telling of it is fresh. . . . It is a love story above all, but it is also a New York story, the sights, sounds, and smells of the city perfectly evoked to capture one of those moments when the forces of change collide with the proprieties of the past." Booklist

Faulks, Sebastian

A week in December. Doubleday 2010 392p $27.95

ISBN 978-0-385-53291-4; 0-385-53291-1

LC 2009-30109

First published 2009 in the United Kingdom

"The events of the novel span seven days close to Christmas, 2007. It's a time when fears of terrorism are, as now, real and the financial markets are on the brink of disaster. Faulks employs a sizable cast, and a fast bicyclist who rides without a light, to reveal a social DNA that reverberates through the present. The characters are introduced on Sunday, Dec. 16, as Sophie Topping begins final preparations for an important dinner party the following Saturday. Her husband, Lance, has recently been elected to Parliament, and this gathering is meant to show party leadership that Lance moves in powerful circles. The guest list is a combination of financial, social, business, journalism and sports figures, culled from Sophie's broad network. From this assemblage, which Faulks will allow the reader to follow over the coming week, several leading characters emerge. . . . This, at its heart, is fiction about folks, and it's darned compelling." Denver Post

Faust, Christa

Choke hold. Hard Case Crime 2011 250p pa $9.95

ISBN 978-0-8576-8285-7

"The second in a series featuring Angel Dare, a hard-bitten former porn star on the run from Croatian mobsters. When Hold opens, our heroine is working as a waitress down in Yuma, Arizona, after her WitSec cover has been violently blown. A chance encounter with a former industry flame, Thick Vic Ventura, forces her out of hiding after Vic is gunned down at the diner where she's been working. The catalyst for this sudden burst of gunplay turns out to be Vic's son Cody Noon, a dumb-ass would-be fighter beholden to an Arizona businessman with ties to south of the border ex-

treme fighting and drug trafficking. Teaming up with Cody's trainer, a somewhat addled former pugilist named Hank 'The Hammer' Hammond, Angel comes up against Mexican thugs and also winds up drawing the attention of the aforementioned Croatian mobsters. It all comes together in a high body count set of showdowns that ends in Las Vegas." Seattle Post-Intelligencer

Faust, Christa

Money shot. Hard Case Crime 2008 250p pa $6.99

ISBN 978-0-8439-5958-1

"Former porn star Angel Dare (nee Gina Moretti), who stopped acting to establish Daring Angels, a firm that manages women in the business, is lured to perform once more by a hot young male star. Instead, she's beaten, raped, shot, and left for dead in the trunk of a car, and that's just the start—all because of money from the international sex trade. With the help of her company's ex-cop security escort, Lalo Malloy, Angel untangles the plot and players, depending finally on nothing but her own resources for the vengeance she craves. A rip-roaring story with nonstop action and an inside look at X-rated movie making, this is clearly not for all readers or collections; but the title (which originated in the porn industry) and cover art are indicators of its contents." Libr J

Fay, Juliette

Deep down true; Juliette Fay. Penguin Books 2011 xi, 399, 13 p.p

ISBN 014311851X; 9780143118510

LC 2010038552

This book tells the story of recent divorcée Dana Stellgarten. "Her 7-year-old, Grady, is struggling with the absence of his father and becoming moody and morose. She discovers that her 12-year-old, Morgan, is bulimic and succumbing to pressure from her popular friends. Her 16-year-old niece, Alder, literally crashes into their lives and begs Dana to take her in for several months. . . . To top it all off, Dana's well-to-do ex-husband is suddenly struggling with his child-care payments." (Booklist)

Fay, Juliette

The **shortest** way home; Juliette Fay. Penguin Books 2013 386 p. $15

ISBN 014312191X; 9780143121916

LC 2012025149

In this novel, by Juliette Fay, winner of the 2012 Library Journal Award for Best Women's Fiction, "Sean has spent twenty years in . . . disaster areas, . . . but when burnout sets in, Sean is reluctantly drawn home to Belham, Massachusetts. . . . There, he discovers that his . . . [family is] having a little natural disaster of their own. When he reconnects with a woman from his past, Sean has to wonder if the bonds of love and loyalty might just rewrite his destiny." (Publisher's note)

Fay, Kim

★ The **map** of lost memories; a novel. Kim Fay. Ballantine Books 2012 viii, 326 p.p (hardcover: acid-free paper) $26.00

ISBN 9780345531346; 9780345531353; 0345531345
LC 2012004142

This adventure novel, by Kim Fay, follows an "expedition to a remote land, where the search for an elusive treasure becomes a journey into the darkest recesses of the mind and heart. In 1925, . . . Irene Blum, . . . [s]killed at acquiring priceless, often illicitly trafficked artifacts, . . . is given a rare map believed to lead to a set of copper scrolls that chronicle the lost history of Cambodia's ancient Khmer civilization." (Publisher's note)

Faye, Lyndsay

✓ The **gods** of Gotham; Lyndsay Faye. Amy Einhorn Books 2012 414 p. $25.95

ISBN 9780399158377
LC 2011047675

This book is "[s]et in 1845 New York City. . . . Timothy Wilde, a 27-year-old former bartender, adjusts to life as a policeman in New York's newly formed police force. . . . In short order on his lower Manhattan beat, he runs across an infanticide and the body of a 12-year-old Irish boy whose spleen has been removed. The investigation the novice detective launches into the boy's murder brings him deep into the heart of human darkness." (Publishers Weekly)

Federman, Raymond

Shhh; the story of a childhood. Starcherone Books 2010 246p pa $18

ISBN 978-0-9842133-0-6
LC 2009-49334

"Federman keeps the story afloat, buoyant, by the clever manner in which he both lightens and darkens each and every turn of the pages. . . . And Raymond Federman could have written a memoir, or a holocaust novel. Instead, he wrote both. " Pank

Feeling very strange; the Slipstream anthology.
✓ James Patrick Kelly & John Kessel, editors. Tachyon Publications 2006 288p pa $14.95

ISBN 978-1-892391-35-X; 1-892391-35-X

"Is slipstream just science fiction and fantasy that doesn't know that it's science fiction or fantasy? Or is it more than that? Decide for yourself by slipping into short stories that are superb, whatever you choose to call them." SciFi.com

Feldman, Ellen

Next to love; a novel. Spiegel & Grau 2011 291p $25

ISBN 978-0-8129-92717
LC 2010-52486

Follows the stories of three young couples whose lives are irrevocably changed in the years following World War II, a period during which they struggle with difficult losses and witness profound transformations in American culture.

"At turns brave, frustrating, and fragile, Feldman's characters live and love with breathtaking intensity, and her deft juggling of several zigzagging plots makes the pages flow past with the force of a slow but mighty river. Equally impressive is her understanding of the period and of the assumptions not only about race and sex but also about keeping private pain private, which made the Greatest Generation not only flawed but often deeply, quietly miserable." Booklist

Fellowes, Julian, 1949-

Snobs; a novel. by Julian Fellowes. St. Martin's Press 2005 265 p. o.p.; o.p.; (pbk.) $15.99

ISBN 0312336926; 9780312336929; 9781250020369
LC 2004065073

"In . . . [this] novel, Julian Fellowes . . . brings us an insider's look at a contemporary England that is still not as classless as is popularly supposed. Edith Lavery, an English blonde with large eyes and nice manners, is the daughter of a moderately successful accountant and his social-climbing wife. While visiting his parents' stately home as a paying guest, Edith meets Charles, the Earl Broughton, and heir to the Marquess of Uckfield, who runs the family estates in East Sussex and Norfolk. To the gossip columns he is one of the most eligible young aristocrats around. When he proposes, Edith accepts. But is she really in love with Charles? Or with his title, his position, and all that goes with it?" (Publisher's note)

Ferber, Edna

✓ **Cimarron**. Doubleday, Doran 1930 388p

"Yancey Cravat was a big, handsome man who quoted Shakespeare and the Bible and knew the law. He started a newspaper in Wichita, Kansas, in whose pages he protested the government's treatment of the Indians. Against the wishes of her family he married Sabra Venable, daughter of an aristocratic Southern family. Then, lured by the newly opened frontier, he took off with her to help settle Oklahoma, where he was instrumental in establishing law and order. Although he could have been governor of the state, his restlessness took him away for weeks, months, and finally years, leaving Sabra with the responsibility for the newspaper. In the lives of these two strong-willed people, and of their son, Cim, Ferber has captured the drama, conflicts, and rewards of life in pioneer America." Shapiro. Fic for Youth. 3d edition

Ferber, Edna

✓ **So** Big. Doubleday, Page 1924 360p

Selina DeJong would look up from her work and say, 'How big is my man?' Then little Dirk DeJong would answer in the time-worn way, 'So-o-o big!' And he was so nicknamed. Though So Big gives the book its title his mother is the outstanding figure. Until Selina was nineteen she traveled with her gambler-father. At his sudden death she secured a teacher's post in the Dutch settlement of High Prairie, a community of hardworking farmers and their thrifty, slaving wives—narrow-minded people indifferent to natural beauty. Soon Selina married Pervus DeJong, a plodding, goodnatured boy. With her marriage the never-ending drudgery of a farmer's wife began. Through all the years of hardship she never lost her gay indomitable spirit. Unfortunately, she was unable to transmit these qualities to her son

Fergus, Jim

The **wild** girl: the notebooks of Ned Giles, 1932; a novel. Hyperion 2005 355p $23.95

ISBN 1-401-30054-5

LC 2004-54161

"After the death of his parents, 17-year-old Giles leaves behind his job at a Chicago country club to join the Great Apache Expedition, a journey organized by citizens of the U.S and Mexico to recover the kidnapped son of a Mexican rancher. Exploring Mexico's Sierra Madres is an opportunity too rich to resist for Giles, who lucks into a job as one of the expedition's photographers. But when he captures the chilling image of a wild Apache girl in a Mexican jail, the young man cannot, in good conscience, turn his back and walk away. . . . Fans of both Larry McMurtry and Louis L'Amour will relish this deftly rendered tale of survival, self-discovery, and the precarious boundaries between man and beast. " Booklist

Fernández, Macedonio, 1874-1952

The **Museum** of Eterna's novel; the first good novel. translated from the Spanish by Margaret Schwartz; preface by Adam Thirlwell; introduction by the translator. Open Letter 2010 xxiv, 238p

ISBN 1934824062; 9781934824061

LC 2009-48625

Original Spanish edition, 1967

This volume opens with some "fifty prologues—including ones addressed 'To My Authorial Persona,' 'To the Critics,' and 'To Readers Who Will Perish If They Don't Know What the Novel Is About.'. . . These pieces cover a range of topics from how the upcoming novel will be received to how to thwart 'skip-around readers' (by writing a book that defies linearity). The second half of the book is the novel itself, a novel about a group of characters (some borrowed from other texts) who live on an estancia called 'la novella.'" (Publisher's note)

This novel "was initiated in 1925 and worked on until [the author's] death in 1952 and is only now available in English. With its 29 prologues of metaphysical indecision and despair, this book never really begins and thus never has to actually end. Its chapters, framed by letters to the critics and to the 'WINDOW SHOPPING READER,' deliver a cumulative script of adoration and gratitude formed around a woman named Eterna, a character based on the author's great love and benefactor, Consuelo Bosch de Sáenz Valiente. . . . Fernández's theme is love in the face of death, and to get to this, he will combine the metaphysics of Schopenhauer with the fatalist frenzy of Poe." Dallas Morning News

Ferrante, Elena

★ The **lost** daughter; translated from the Italian by Ann Goldstein. Europa 2008 125p pa $14.95

ISBN 978-1-933372-42-6; 1-933372-42-7

Original Italian edition, 2006

"In this brutally frank novel of maternal ambivalence, the narrator, a forty-seven-year-old divorcée summering alone on the Ionian coast, becomes obsessed with a beautiful young mother who seems ill at ease with her husband's rowdy, slightly menacing Neapolitan clan. When this woman's daughter loses her doll, the older woman commits a small crime that she can't explain even to herself. Although much of the drama takes place in her head, Ferrante's gift for psychological horror renders it immediate and visceral." New Yorker

Ferrante, Elena

Troubling love; translated from the Italisn by Ann Goldstein. Europa 2006 139p pa $14.95

ISBN 1-933372-16-8

Original Italian edition, 1995

"Delia, a cartoonist living in Rome, receives three incoherent phone calls from her mother, who is supposed to be on her way from Naples; the next day, her mother's nearly naked body washes up onshore at a seaside resort town. In Naples for the funeral, Delia is confronted with the past she tried to disown as she struggles to make sense of the events leading to her mother's drowning. A shadowy figure named Caserta, the man Delia, as a five-year-old, accused her mother of having an affair with, reëmerges as possibly the last person to see her alive. Ferrante's polished language belies the rawness of her imagery, which conveys perversity, violence, and bodily functions in ripe detail. Delia's discovery of the secret of her childhood is made all the more jarring by the story's disorienting mixture of fantasy and reality." New Yorker

Ferraris, Zoe

✓ **Finding** Nouf. Houghton Mifflin 2008 305p $24

ISBN 978-0-618-87388-3; 0-618-87388-0

LC 2007-38411

"Sixteen-year-old Nouf ash-Shrawi, daughter of a wealthy Saudi Arabian family, mysteriously disappears and is eventually found drowned in the desert. . . . Nouf's brother, Othman, asks his friend Nayir Sharqi, a local desert guide, to find out what happened to his sister. Nayir's investigation leads him into unknown territory—notably, the secret realm of women in a segregated Middle Eastern society. In an unusual partnership that challenges his traditional ideas, Nayir works on the case with Othman's fiancée, a laboratory technician in the medical examiner's office. Ferraris's debut novel gives a fascinating peek into the lives and minds of devout Muslim men and women while serving up an engrossing mystery." Libr J

Ferraris, Zoe

✓ **Kingdom** of strangers; a novel. Zoë Ferraris. Little, Brown and Company 2012 363 p.

ISBN 0316074241; 9780316074247

LC 2011046158

In this novel, a "secret grave is unearthed in the desert revealing the bodies of 19 women and the shocking truth that a serial killer has been operating undetected in Jeddah for more than a decade. However, lead inspector Ibrahim Zahrani is distracted by a mystery closer to home. His mistress has suddenly disappeared, but he cannot report her missing since adultery is punishable by death. . . . [This is] a tale of psychological suspense around . . . the sinister forces trafficking in human lives in Saudi Arabia." (Publisher's note)

Ferrell, Monica

The **answer** is always yes. Dial Press 2008 382p $24

ISBN 978-0-385-33929-2

LC 2008-6627

In this "novel, Matthew Acciaccatura, a bullied nerd from Teaneck, New Jersey, in his freshman year at N.Y.U. and hungry to be cool, is spotted by a Manhattan nightclub owner and given the chance to become a promoter. Ferrell chronicles Matt's ascent in the nineties rave culture and his downfall—brought about by his need, when he is faced with someone who symbolizes his childhood torturers, 'to deal a blow here for all loserkind.' Ferrell's . . . inclusion of a 'Pale Fire'-like commentary by a German sociologist seems unnecessary, given the ease with which her exuberant narration evokes her likable protagonist's world." New Yorker

Ferrigno, Robert

Prayers for the assassin; a novel. Robert Ferrigno. Scribner 2006 397p $24.95

ISBN 0-7432-7289-7

LC 2005-51590

"Ferrigno raises important questions about religious freedom while handling the subject of Islamic faith with great insight and evenhandedness. If the plot sometimes overwhelms character development, he still allows his creations to air their own opinions without moralizing. In sum: a fast-paced thriller with timely appeal." Bookmarks Magazine

Ferris, Joshua

✓ ★ The **unnamed**. Little, Brown and Co. 2010 320p $24.99

ISBN 978-0-316-03401-2; 0-316-03401-0

LC 2009-10264

This novel "explores a marriage put to the test by a strange illness that causes the husband, Tim Farnsworth, to walk endlessly. Tim's malady follows the trajectory of most psychological diseases—there is no hard-and-fast diagnosis, no explanation for his behavior and no quick fix. His long-suffering wife, Jane, must wait for a phone call and go retrieve him from wherever he ends up, finding him exhausted, dehydrated and sometimes frostbitten. Their daughter, Becka, watches from the safe haven of her room, distracting herself with indie music and reruns of Buffy the Vampire Slayer. To complicate matters, Tim is a successful partner at a law firm, and when his disease strikes, he has no choice but to skip out of work and wander until his body gives out. Needless to say, he loses his cases and, subsequently, his job." Time Out N Y

"Audacious, risky and powerfully bleak, with the author's unflinching artistry its saving grace." Kirkus

Fesperman, Dan

The **amateur** spy. Alfred A. Knopf 2008 367p $24.95

ISBN 978-1-4000-4467-2; 1-4000-4467-7

LC 2007-47313

First published 2007 in the United Kingdom

"Freeman Lockhart, the Arabic-speaking titular spy, is burdened by guilt for his unwitting participation in horrific blunders as an aid worker in Africa. As Lockhart attempts to retire with his new wife to a Greek island, mysterious strangers play on that guilt to blackmail him into spying on a Palestinian ex-colleague in Jordan. The plot is complex, the sense of place powerful, and the characterization memorable. A parallel plot features an Arab American woman whose story at last converges with Lockhart's." Libr J

Fesperman, Dan

✓ The **double** game; Dan Fesperman. Alfred A. Knopf 2012 355 p. $26.95

ISBN 0307700135; 9780307700131

LC 2012019889

In this spy novel by Dan Fesperman "spook-turned-novelist Edwin Lemaster revealed to up-and-coming journalist Bill Cage that he'd once considered spying for the enemy. More than two decades later, Cage, now a lonely, disillusioned PR man, receives an anonymous note hinting that he should have dug deeper into Lemaster's pronouncement. As the events of Lemaster's past eerily--and dangerously--begin intersecting with those of Cage's own, a 'long stalemate of secrecy' may finally be coming to an end." (Publisher's note)

Fesperman, Dan

The **warlord's** son; a novel. Knopf 2004 319p $23

ISBN 0-375-41473-8

LC 2004-11841

This novel "offers a brilliant picture of what might be called the journalistic condition specifically, the joys, absurdities and horrors of the foreign correspondent's life and it will teach you more than you ever expected to know about tribesmen for whom violence is a given and betrayal is an art." Washington Post

Festing, I. A.

The **birdkeeper**; I.A. Festing. Book Guild 2010 228 p.

ISBN 1846244943; 9781846244940

LC 2010674521

In this novel, "[w]hen two Siberian cranes return to breed at Naagpur, a bird sanctuary in Rajasthan, their presence stirs bittersweet memories in Satchin Rai. The son of a wealthy businessman, Satchin has turned his back on his family obligations and lineage to work as an ornithologist at Naagpur. . . . When he meets Peter, a charming and handsome Englishman, and agrees to be his guide, he becomes strangely drawn to the confident and charismatic tourist. Their ensuing affair and plans to elope together are at once tantalising and terrifying to Satchin, who is torn between family loyalty and this all-consuming passion that dare not speak its name. . . . When Indira Gandhi is assassinated, the country is plunged into violent unrest, and Satchin is further torn between his country, his father and his secret love." (Publisher's note)

Fforde, Jasper

✓ The **Eyre** affair; a novel. Viking 2002 374p hardcover o.p. pa $14

ISBN 0-670-03064-3; 0-14-200180-5 pa

LC 2001-43775

First published 2001 in the United Kingdom

"It's 1985 in England, at least on the calendar; the Crimean War is in its hundred-and-thirty-first year; time travel is nothing new; Japanese tourists slip in and out of Victorian novels; and the literary branch of the special police, led gamely by the beguiling Thursday Next, are pursuing Acheron Hades, who has stolen the manuscript of 'Martin Chuzzlewit' and set his sights on kidnapping the character Jane Eyre, a theft that could have disastrous consequences for Brontë lovers who like their story straight. This rambunctious caper could be taken as a warning about what might happen if society considered literature really important—like, say, energy futures or accounting." New Yorker

Other titles featuring Thursday Next are:

Thursday Next in Lost in a good book (2003)

Thursday Next in Something rotten (2004)

Thursday Next in The well of lost plots (2004)

Fforde, Jasper

Shades of grey; the road to High Saffron. Viking 2009 390p $25.95

ISBN 978-0-670-01963-2; 0-670-01963-1

LC 2009-30813

"The world is wildly but closely imagined, so the result is as internally coherent as it is unlikely. Distinctive wordplay abounds. All the fooling around is built on a good mystery, and Fforde telegraphs no punches. In short, 'Shades of Grey' is everything that Fforde fans love, and distinctly different from what has come before." Denver Post

Fforde, Jasper

Thursday Next in Lost in a good book; a novel. Viking 2003 399p il hardcover o.p. pa $15

ISBN 0-670-03190-9; 0-14-200403-0 pa

LC 2002-71304

Companion volume to: The Eyre affair

First published 2002 in the United Kingdom with title: Lost in a good book

"Time flies—and leaps and zigzags—while reading this wickedly funny and clever fantasy. Would-be wordsmiths and mystery fans will find the surreal genre-buster irresistible." Publ Wkly

Fforde, Jasper

Thursday Next in Something rotten; a novel. Viking 2004 383p $24.95

ISBN 0-670-03359-6

LC 2004-49497

Published in the United Kingdom with title: Something rotten

Thursday Next, "the literary detective is fed up with the bureaucracy and red tape of BookWorld, where the characters and plots of novels are alive and need constant governing. The Council of Genres refuses to accept her resignation as head of JurisFiction, but she returns to her home in the real world anyway—Swindon, England. Here she hopes to regroup, raise her two-year-old son, Friday, and find some way to uneradicate her husband, Landen Parke-Laine. But this may be Next's most complicated caper yet. Still facing unfinished disciplinary action from earlier outings, she must also sort out personality conflicts in Hamlet; protect Danish literature from a book-burning campaign; rescue the president from the realm of the semidead; and manage the underdog Swindon Mallets croquet team to victory in the SuperHoop." Booklist

Fforde, Jasper

Thursday Next in The well of lost plots; a novel. Viking 2004 375p il $24.95

ISBN 0-670-03289-1

LC 2003-62150

First published 2003 in the United Kingdom with title: The well of lost plots

Thursday Next "has beaten a strategic retreat into BookWorld, where as part of the Character Exchange Program, she hides out in an unpublished, by-the-numbers police procedural. She's pregnant, her husband has been killed before he really existed, and her memories of him are being eaten away by a mindworm. She can't rest for long, however; she's still a trainee agent in the BookWorld police force, JurisFiction, and soon fiction itself is under a greater threat than ever before." Booklist

This "is an interesting, enjoyable mix of detective story, fantasy, and literature." SLJ

Fielding, Helen

Bridget Jones's diary; a novel. Viking 1998 271p $22.95

ISBN 0-670-88072-8

LC 98-18687

First published 1996 in the United Kingdom

"Brimming with a deliciously irreverent sense of humor and a keen sense of women's deepest insecurities, Bridget Jones's Diary is a must-read." Booklist

Fielding, Helen

Bridget Jones: the edge of reason. Viking 2000 338p

ISBN 0-670-89296-3

LC 99-86499

Sequel to Bridget Jones's diary

First published 1999 in the United Kingdom

"How can a reader not love this woman—not in spite of her faults but because of them? Bridget tries so hard. Her days are made up of glorious surges of hope followed by instant defeat or rash interpretations, or both." N Y Times Book Rev

Fielding, Henry

★ The **history** of Tom Jones, a foundling. Knopf 1991 xxxvi, 408, 427p $20

ISBN 0-679-40569-0

LC 91-52996

First published 1749. Variant title: Tom Jones

"Squire Allworthy suspects that the infant whom he adopts and names Tom Jones is the illegitimate child of his servant Jenny Jones. When Tom is a young man, he falls in love with Sophia Western, his beautiful and virtuous neighbor. In the end his true identity is revealed and he wins Sophia's hand, but numerous obstacles have to be overcome, and in the course of the action the various sets of characters pursue each other from one part of the country to another, giving Fielding an opportunity to paint an incomparably vivid picture of England in the mid-18th century." Merriam-Webster's Ency of Lit

Fielding, Henry

Joseph Andrews and Shamela; edited by Douglas Brooks-Davies. Oxford University Press 2008 xliv, 410p (Oxford world's classics) pa $9.95

    ISBN 978-0-19-953698-6; 0-19-953698-8

                            LC 2009-290678

"Henry Fielding wrote both Joseph Andrews (1742) and Shamela (1741) in response to Samuel Richardson's book Pamela (1740), of which Shamela is a splendidly bawdy travesty. Joseph Andrews begins as a parody, too, but soon outgrows its origins, and its deepest roots lie in Cervantes and Marivaux. In both stories, Fielding demonstrates his concern for the corruption of contemporary society, politics, religion, morality, and taste. This revised and expanded edition follows the text of Joseph Andrews established by Martin C. Battestin for the definitive Wesleyan Edition of Fielding's works. The text of Shamela is based on the first edition, and two substantial appendices reprint the preliminary matter from the second edition of Richardson's Pamela and Conyers Middleton's Life of Cicero, which is also closely parodied in Shamela." Publisher's note

Fielding, Joy

Charley's web; a novel. Atria Books 2008 437p $24.95

    ISBN 978-0-7432-9601-4; 0-7432-9601-X

                            LC 2007-32674

When Jill Rohmer, a convicted child killer, invites Charlotte "Charley" Webb, a single mom and columnist for the Palm Beach Post, "to collaborate on the 'true story' of what really happened to the three children she was convicted of murdering, Charley at first thinks it sounds like a great idea. Her sister Anne is, after all, a bestselling romance author, so why couldn't Charley have a nonfiction bestseller? Charley meets with Jill's attractive lawyer, Alex Prescott, who secures a book contract. After committing to the project, Charley begins dating Alex. Then Charley learns Jill had an accomplice, someone on the loose whom Jill calls 'Jack.' Fielding pulls out all the stops as the identity of the ruthless murderer becomes obvious, and Charley must race against time to catch the horrible Jack and save his next target—her son." Publ Wkly

Fielding, Joy

Don't cry now; a novel. Morrow 1995 356p

                            LC 94-42095

"Just when things appear to be all worked out, new evidence points Bonnie in a different direction. With Fielding, nothing is as it appears, and like Bonnie, we can't help brooding on the vulnerability of what we all take for granted." Quill Quire

Fielding, Joy

Heartstopper; a novel. Atria Books 2007 387p $24.95

    ISBN 978-0-7432-9598-7; 0-7432-9598-6

                            LC 2006-50801

In this "suspense novel set in tiny Torrance, Florida, a serial killer's journal entries are interspersed with the stunned reactions of various of the town's citizens when two teenage girls go missing. Sandy Crosbie, a highschool English teacher and the mother of two teenagers, has relocated to remote Torrance from Rochester, New York, at the urging of her handsome doctor husband. But his reasons for the move soon become apparent when he leaves her for Kerri Franklin, a 'Barbie clone and Internet paramour extraordinaire.' Sandy, along with the rest of the town's citizens, is jolted out of her self-absorption when the body of the most popular girl in school is found buried in a shallow grave. Now it's up to exhausted, overweight Sheriff John Weber, unhappily married to the TV-addicted Pauline, to calm residents' fears and find out what happened to the pretty blonde teen. But even as he fends off the town's obnoxious mayor, intent on calling in the FBI, Sandy's daughter goes missing. Fielding crafts a suspenseful plot, with a stunner of a twist, while giving her characters a depth of humanity not frequently found in formula fiction." Booklist

Fielding, Joy

Missing pieces. Doubleday 1997 368p

    ISBN 978-0440222873

                            LC 96-40901

"Practical Kate Sinclair, 47, a family therapist married for 24 years and the mother of two teenaged daughters, is losing control of her orderly, settled life. She fights with her rebellious elder daughter, Sara, who's 17. Her mother is diagnosed with Alzheimer's. Even her body is betraying her, as hot flashes startle her metabolism. Meanwhile, a chance encounter with an old high-school sweetheart inflames her in a totally different way. Worst of all, though, is the infatuation of her sexy half-sister, Jo Lynn, with a man on trial for the murder of 13 women." Publ Wkly

"As outlandish as the relationship between sister Jo Lynn and the serial killer seems, Fielding's talent makes it all quite credible." Booklist

Fielding, Joy

See Jane run. Morrow 1991 364p

    ISBN 0-688-08867-8

                            LC 90-22603

"Fielding handles her material with finesse; suspense is maintained at a high level, and the narrative is enriched by Jane's bracing sense of humor and a cast of sharply drawn, articulate characters." Publ Wkly

Fielding, Joy

Tell me no secrets. Morrow 1993 352p

                            LC 92-43692

"When Jess' ex rescues, or seems to rescue, her from the predictably sadistic stalker/rapist, her comment that 'it's just like in the movies' may seem like self-parody. Jess escapes this formula—and becomes not only real, but touching—when she visits her suburban sister and the brother-in-law she despises, when she talks with a woman juror in a rape trial about why the verdict was not guilty, and when we visit with her in her private fear." Booklist

Fields, Jennie

The age of desire; a novel. Jennie Fields. Pamela Dorman Books/Viking 2012 x, 352 p.p $27.95

    ISBN 067002368X; 9780670023684

                            LC 2011042393

This novel, by Jennie Fields, offers a "glimpse into the life of Edith Wharton and the scandalous love affair that threatened her closest friendship. . . . When . . . Edith falls .

. . in love with a dashing younger journalist, . . . it threatens . . . her abiding friendship with Anna . . . Bahlmann--her . . . nurturing friend. . . . As Edith's marriage crumbles and Anna's disapproval threatens to shatter their lifelong bond, the women must face the fragility at the heart of all friendships." (Publisher's note)

Fields, Tricia

Scratchgravel Road; A Mystery. Tricia Fields. St Martins Pr 2013 320 p. (hardcover) $24.99
ISBN 1250021367; 9781250021366

LC 2013002873

This book is Hillerman Prize winner Tricia Fields's second Josie Gray mystery. When Gray "comes across unconscious store clerk Cassidy Harper in the desert, Josie also spots the decaying corpse of immigrant Juan Santiago lying nearby, his body bearing sores of unknown origin. Cassidy later claims to have stumbled on Juan while on a walk, though his wallet is found in her car." (Publishers Weekly)

Fifty years of the best from Ellery Queen's Mystery Magazine; edited by Eleanor Sullivan. Carroll & Graf Pubs. 1991 642p

LC 90-23928

Finch, Charles (Charles B.)

A **beautiful** blue death; Charles Finch. St. Martin's Minotaur 2007 309 p. $24.95
ISBN 0312359772; 9780312359775

LC 2007011273

Followed by: The September Society (2008)

In this mystery novel by Charles Finch "Charles Lenox, Victorian gentleman and armchair explorer, . . . cannot resist the chance to unravel a mystery . . . when his lifelong friend Lady Jane asks for his help. . . . Prudence Smith, one of Jane's former servants, is dead of an apparent suicide. But Lenox suspects something far more sinister: murder, by a rare and deadly poison. . . . Was it jealousy that killed Prudence Smith? Or was it something else entirely?" (Publisher's note)

Finch, Charles (Charles B.)

The **September** Society. St. Martin's Minotaur 2008 310p $26.95
ISBN 978-0-312-35978-2; 0-312-35978-0

LC 2008-3452

"When Oxford student George Payson goes missing, his mother asks Charles Lennox to find him. All avenues of investigation point to foul play, and then Payson's garroted body is found in the Christ Church Meadow. Wealthy, intelligent, Oxford-educated, and a detective of some repute, Charles seeks to determine what role the little-known student club, the September Society, might have played in Payson's death and what lies behind the threats against Payson's friends and now Lennox's beloved Lady Jane Grey. . . . Finch, a superb hand at plotting, gives nothing away, and even the most astute reader will be guessing to the end." Libr J

Finch, Sheila

The **guild** of xenolinguists; with a foreword by Ian Watson. Golden Gryphon Press 2007 281p $24.95
ISBN 978-1-930846-48-7; 1-930846-48-7

LC 2007-6550

A collection of tales about "the Guild of Xenolinguists (later called lingsters), a formal organization devoted to translating the languages of other worlds. Much as Asimov did with the Three Laws of Robotics, Finch creatively examines the conflicts stemming from adherence to the guild's strict rules. The stories span a wide range, from First Was the Word, a brief tale setting the stage for the development of the guild, to the moving A World Waiting and A Flight of Words, which present their protagonists with morally difficult situations—tortured prisoners, conflicting religious beliefs, abortion—that hold significant contemporary resonance." Publ Wkly

Finder, Joseph

Buried secrets. St. Martin's Press 2011 390p $25.99
ISBN 978-0-312-37914-8

LC 2011-04443

"Finder's compulsively readable sequel to Vanished opens fast and never slows down. When 17-year-old Alexa Marcus, the spoiled daughter of Marshall Marcus, a wildly successful money manager, is kidnapped from a Boston club and buried alive in a coffin equipped with an air hose and a video camera (for Internet streaming, of course!), Marshall asks his old intelligence expert friend, Nick Heller, to find her. The search leads into an expanding world of 'buried secrets,' from Marshall's gold-digging trophy wife, Belinda, and his crumbling investment empire to allegations of government funding for covert operations and the Russian mafia. . . . Self-effacing, wry, and ridiculously competent, Heller makes a reasonably engaging protagonist, but this thriller's real star is the suspenseful, expertly paced plot." Publ Wkly

Finder, Joseph

Company man. St. Martin's Press 2005 520p $24.95
ISBN 0-312-31916-9

This is "as much a novel about the chicanery of the business world as it is a mystery story. Takeovers and outsourcing are not news, but Mr. Finder weaves these prospects menacingly throughout the story, as Nick finds himself increasingly undermined by his colleagues." N Y Times (Late N Y Ed)

Finder, Joseph

Killer instinct. St. Martin's Press 2006 406p $24.95
ISBN 0-312-34747-2

LC 2006-40501

This is a "superb story that dazzles with its heart-pounding suspense, even while posing deeper questions about the ethics of business and what we're willing to do to get ahead." Boston Globe

Finder, Joseph

✓ **Power** play. St. Martin's Press 2007 371p $24.95

ISBN 978-0-312-34748-2; 0-312-34748-0

LC 2007-16178

The author's "strong suit is technical expertise, and he fills this book with seductive bits of inside information. . . . Power Play starts cleverly and later devolves into more conventional suspense tactics. But its premise is enough to send chills through corporate boardrooms, and through civilian readers too." N Y Times (Late N Y Ed)

Finder, Joseph

Vanished. St. Martin's Press 2009 388p $25.99

ISBN 978-0-312-37908-7; 0-312-37908-0

LC 2009-13029

The first title in a "new series featuring Nick Heller, a high-powered international investigator and corporate security consultant. Through a brilliant piece of detection, Heller has just tracked down 12 cargo containers packed with $1 billion in cash when he gets a call from his nephew Gabe in Washington, DC. Heller's brother Roger, the kid's stepfather, has vanished, and the boy's mother, Lauren, is in the hospital, the victim of a late-night attack. Both Roger and Lauren work for Gifford Industries, a multibillion-dollar corporation where Roger mostly handled mergers and acquisitions. . . . Using his Special Forces skills and the latest high-tech wizardry, Heller counters lethal adversaries as he peels back layers of secrets that hide not only high-level corporate crimes but the troubled affairs of his own family." Libr J

Findley, Timothy

✓ The **piano** man's daughter. Crown 1996 461p il

ISBN 978-0002243797

LC 96-171372

First published 1995 in Canada

"Set in turn-of-the-century Canada, the story tells, in a series of evocative flashbacks, the engaging tale of Lily Kilworth, and her son, Charlie. Conceived when her mother, Ede, falls in love with a musician, Lily is born in a field of flowers and grows into an odd, lonely child whose world is exotically tip-tilted. As she matures, she becomes more and more alienated from real life, but this doesn't keep her from having a brief, mysterious affair while she's a student in wartime England. The result is her son, Charlie, who has perfect musical pitch and a high tolerance for his mother's eccentric ways. . . . Brilliantly told, powerfully affecting." Booklist

Finney, Jack

From time to time; a novel. Simon & Schuster 1995 303p il

LC 94-24497

In this sequel to Time and again, "time traveler Simon Morley leaves his voluntary exile in the 19th century to visit the 20th century of his origins and finds himself drawn into a desperate attempt to alter the events of history and prevent the onset of World War I." Libr J

"This mind-stretching escapist adventure is studded with period photos and news clippings that function as an integral part of the story." Publ Wkly

Finney, Jack

✓ ★ **Time** and again. Simon & Schuster 1970 399p

The author "re-creates the world of nineteenth-century New York City and at the same time critically appraises modernity. His hero, Simon Morley, agrees to live in the Dakota apartments and, assisted by hypnosis, to share a series of experiences in the year 1882. Eager to cooperate with the U.S. governmental agencies conducting the test Simon observes the manners and mores of the past and falls in love with Julia, a girl of the period. Simon's enthusiasm palls, however, when he is asked to alter historical events in the interest of the agency's evidently nefarious designs." Booklist

Followed by From time to time

Finney, Patricia

Gloriana's torch. St. Martin's Press 2003 452p $24.95

ISBN 0-312-31285-7

LC 2003-58454

This "tale is set on the eve of the sailing of the Spanish Armada in 1588. David Becket, clerk of the ordnance and sometime spy for Elizabeth I, is ordered by the queen to discover the details of a top-secret Spanish plot dubbed the 'Miracle of Beauty.' In addition, Becket is commanded to rescue his fellow English spy and friend, Simon Ames, who has been condemned by the Spanish Inquisition as a heretic. . . . The various threads of this wide-ranging tale of intrigue do not come together neatly, but Finney's vivid prose and the high level of historical imagination on display make for a satisfying read." Publ Wkly

First thrills; high-octane stories from the hottest thriller authors. edited by Lee Child. Forge 2010 367p $25.99

ISBN 978-0-7653-2648-5

LC 2010-19371

Child "offers a mixed bag in this anthology of 25 original stories by members of ITW (International Thriller Writers), divided between fledgling authors and established names. . . . Steve Berry, ITW's current president, provides an afterword." Publ Wkly

Fishburne, Rodes

Going to see the elephant; a novel. Bantam Dell 2009 293p $22

ISBN 978-0-385-34239-1; 0-385-34239-X

LC 2008-28465

"At times Fishburne has trouble maintaining so many moving parts; the inventor story line can feel extraneous, and the love story takes a while to get going. But what saves the book is its sweetness and innocence, and the depiction of Slater in the big city is a pleasure." Publ Wkly

Fitch, Janet

✓ **Paint** it black; a novel. Little, Brown & Co. 2006 387p $24.99

ISBN 978-0-316-18274-4; 0-316-18274-5

LC 2006-10211

"Fitch has given us a courageous and interesting young woman who handles the bad cards she has been dealt with grace and resolve. No one, not even Cinderella, knows better than Josie Tyrell that life isn't fair—and no one, despite some very long odds, seems more likely to transcend the role of victim and succeed with or without her fairy-tale prince." Washington Post Book World

Fitch, Janet

✓ **White** oleander; a novel. Little, Brown 1999 390p $24.95

ISBN 0-316-28526-9

LC 98-50371

"This sensitive exploration of the mother daughter terrain . . . offers a convincing look at what Adrienne Rich has called 'this womanly splitting of self,' in a poignant, virtuosic, utterly captivating narrative." Publ Wkly

Fitzgerald, Conor

The **namesake**; a Commissario Alec Blume novel. Conor Fitzgerald. Bloomsbury 2012 357 p. map (paperback) $16.00; (hardcover) $25.00

ISBN 9781620400128; 9781608198450

LC 2012004284

"Police commissioner Alec Blume looks into the murder of a Milan insurance agent in Fitzgerald's fine third novel featuring the American expat living in Rome. . . . Fitzgerald provides an insightful glimpse into the machinations of Italian police work and the criminal world, where strong family bonds astound even the most perceptive cop." Pub Wkly

Fitzgerald, F. Scott

★ The **beautiful** and damned. Scribner 449p

✓ ISBN 0-684-15153-7

First published 1922; copyright renewed 1950

"Anthony Patch pursues and wins the beautiful and sought-after Gloria Gilbert. He decides that they can survive on his limited income until he comes into a large fortune he stands to inherit from his grandfather. Through the ensuing years, their lives deteriorate into mindless alcoholic ennui. Anthony's grandfather makes a surprise appearance at one of their wild parties and, in disgust, disinherits him. After his grandfather's death, Anthony institutes a lawsuit that takes years to settle. Although the Patches eventually win, by then Anthony's spirit is broken, he and Gloria have grown apart, and they care about nothing." Merriam-Webster's Ency of Lit

Fitzgerald, F. Scott

✓ The **Fitzgerald** reader; edited by Arthur Mizener. Scribner 1963 xxvii, 509p

This representative selection of Scott Fitzgerald's work "includes the whole of his best novel, 'The Great Gatsby,' and considerable parts of his other two important novels, 'Tender Is the Night, and 'The Last Tycoon.' It also includes two novelettes ('May Day' and 'The Rich Boy'), the four or five best short stories from each period of his career, and his four most famous essays." Foreword

Fitzgerald, F. Scott

✓ ★ The **great** Gatsby; preface by Matthew J. Bruccoli. Scribner Classics 1996 170p

ISBN 0684830426

LC 96016596

First published 1925

"The mysterious Jay Gatsby lives in a luxurious mansion on the Long Island shore. . . . Nick Carraway, the narrator, lives next door to Gatsby, and Nick's cousin Daisy and her crude but wealthy husband Tom Buchanan live directly across the harbor. Gatsby reveals to Nick that he and Daisy had a brief affair before the war and her marriage to Tom. . . . He persuades Nick to bring him and Daisy together again but ultimately he is unable to win her away from Tom. Daisy, driving Gatsby's car, runs over and kills Tom's mistress Myrtle, unaware of her identity. Myrtle's husband traces the car and shoots Gatsby, who has remained silent in order to protect Daisy. Gatsby's friends and business associates have all deserted him, and only Gatsby's father, and one former guest attend the funeral." Reader's Ency. 4th edition

Fitzgerald, F. Scott

✓ ★ The **last** tycoon; an unfinished novel. Scribner 163p

ISBN 0-684-15311-4

First published 1941 with The Great Gatsby, and selected stories; copyright renewed 1969

"The work is an indictment of the Hollywood film industry, where Fitzgerald had had a disappointing career as a screenwriter. Monroe Stahr is a studio executive who has worked obsessively to produce high-quality films without regard to their financial prospects. He takes a personal interest in every aspect of the studio. At age 35 he is almost burned out, and the novel is the story of how he loses control of the studio and his life." Merriam-Webster's Ency of Lit

Fitzgerald, F. Scott

✓ **Novels** and stories, 1920-1922. Library of Am. 2000 1082p $35

ISBN 1-88301-184-1

LC 00-24287

Includes bibliographical references

Contents: This side of paradise (1920); Flappers and philosophers (1920); The beautiful and the damned (1922); Tales of The jazz age (1922) ; Tales of the jazz age includes the following stories: The jelly bean; The camel's back; May day; Porcelain and pink; The diamond as big as the ritz; The curious case of Benjamin Button; Tarquin of cheapside; ¿O russet witch!¿; The lees of happiness; Mr. Icky; Jemina, the mountain girl ; Flappers and philosophers includes the following stories: The offshore pirate; The ice palace; Head and shoulders; The cut-glass bowl; Bernice bobs her hair; Benediction; Dalyrimple goes wrong; The four fists

Fitzgerald, F. Scott

✓ ★ The **short** stories of F. Scott Fitzgerald; edited and with a preface by Matthew J. Bruccoli. Scribner Classics 1998 797p $37.50

ISBN 0-684-84250-5

LC 98-121806

Reissue of the 1989 edition analyzed in Short story index

Fitzgerald, F. Scott

✓ **Six** tales of the jazz age, and other stories. Scribner 1960 192p

Contents: The jelly-bean; The camel's back; The curious case of Benjamin Button; Tarquin of Cheapside; "O'Russet witch!"; The lees of happiness; The adjuster; Hot and cold blood; Gretchen's forty winks

Fitzgerald, F. Scott

The **stories** of F. Scott Fitzgerald; a selection of 28 stories. with an introduction by Malcolm Cowley. Scribner 1951 xxv, 473p

ISBN 0-684-15366-1

"The editor has attempted to make the best selection from all stages of Fitzgerald's career; the stories are arranged in chronological groups." Booklist

Fitzgerald, F. Scott

★ **This** side of paradise. Scribner 282p

ISBN 0-684-15601-6

First published 1920; copyright renewed 1948

"Immature though it seems today, the work when it was published was considered a revelation of the new morality of the young in the early Jazz Age; and it made Fitzgerald famous. The novel's hero, Amory Blaine, is a handsome, spoiled young man who attends Princeton, becomes involved in literary activities, and has several ill-fated romances. A portrait of the Lost Generation, the novel addresses Fitzgerald's later theme of love distorted by social climbing and greed." Merriam-Webster's Ency of Lit

Fitzgerald, Penelope

The **blue** flower. Houghton Mifflin 1997 225p pa $13

ISBN 0-395-85997-2 pa

LC 96-52911

First published 1996 in the United Kingdom

This "is a historical novel based on the life of the poet, aphorist, novelist, Friedrich von Hardenberg, a Saxon nobleman who wrote under the name of Novalis. . . . Novalis had a vision of a unique blue flower as the goal of a quest. . . . In the waking life of Fritz von Hardenberg the part of the flower was played by Sophie von Kühn. She is 12 years old when he meets her and at once designates her his future bride and his incarnation of Wisdom. Reluctant parental permission is obtained for their betrothal, but Sophie (as well as not being noble) is tubercular. . . . Their relationship, and Fritz's dealings with his own family and Sophie's, are the main business of the novel." (London Rev Books)

This novel "ranges far beyond itself. It is an interrogation of life, love, purpose, experience and horizons, which has found its perfect vehicle in a few years from the pitifully short life of a German youth about to become a great poet." N Y Times Book Rev

Fitzgerald, Penelope

The **means** of escape. Houghton Mifflin 2000 117p $18

ISBN 0-618-07994-7

LC 00-38914

Contents: The means of escape; The prescription; Desideratus; Beehernz; The axe; The red-haired girl; Not shown; At Hiruharama

"Strange, whimsical, sometimes gothic or bizarre, these tales demonstrate Fitzgerald's cool and civilized wit and the merciless eye she casts on worldly pretensions." Publ Wkly

Flagg, Fannie, 1944-

★ **Fried** green tomatoes at the Whistle-Stop Cafe. Random House 1987 403p

ISBN 0-394-56152-X

LC 87-12813

This novel is "set in a rural hamlet outside of Birmingham, Alabama. Bulletins from a gossipy town newsletter produced in the 1940s by Dot Weems are interspersed with the recollections of Mrs. Cleo (Vinnie) Throughgoode uttered (40 years later) in a nursing home to a depressed, menopausal visitor, Evelyn Couch (whose life is rejuvenated by these Sunday afternoon chats). Flagg also supplies basic narrative passages illuminating the news shared by Dot and Vinnie. The pace of the novel is as swift as the life of the small town is slow—at least it seems slow until Vinnie drops hints of a murder and of riotous pranks played upon the local minister. The story is carefully plotted, with the moods and people of pre- and post-World War II Alabama splendidly evoked." Booklist

Flagg, Fannie, 1944-

Standing in the rainbow; a novel. Random House 2002 493p

ISBN 0-679-42615-9

LC 2002-21977

"Beneath the sentImentality, there's a real celebration of life here, an affirmation that success and happiness are the results of simple kindness gratituder and courage." Sci Monit

Flanagan, Bill

Evening's empire. Simon & Schuster 2010 648p $26.95

ISBN 978-1-4391-4845-7; 1-4391-4845-7

LC 2009-23871

"Assured, often lyrical and true to the world ofthe star-maker machinery behind the popular song. A lively complement to Nick Hornby's High Fidelity, Mark Hudson's The Music in My Head and Laurence Gonzales's Jambeaux." Kirkus

Flanagan, John

Storm peak; a Jesse Parker mystery. [by] John A. Flanagan. Berkley Prime Crime 2010 391p pa $15

ISBN 978-0-425-23525-6

LC 2009-45782

This mystery "marks the debut appearance of Jesse Parker, a former Denver Police detective and hometown boy who returns to Steamboat and helps solve a puzzling rash of murders. The local sheriff, Lee Torrens, and Jesse share a past; they dated each other when they were teenagers. Although Lee is a seasoned and capable law officer, when the body count rises on the local ski hill, she turns to Jesse. . . . He's been in Steamboat Springs two years, subsisting on work as a member of the ski patrol in the winter and laboring in the summer as either a ranch hand or construction worker. When his good friend presses him to help, he reluctantly becomes her newest deputy. . . . [This is an] easy, enjoyable read and a welcome peek into the machinations of survival in a small town." Denver Post

Flanagan, Richard

Gould's book of fish; a novel in twelve fish. Grove Press 2002 404p il

    ISBN 0-8021-1711-2

LC 2001-55747

The novel "tells the story of William Buelow Gould, a convict sent to a penal colony in Van Diemen's Land in the nineteenth century. Gould recounts his life story as he paints the island's native fish, a task given him by the fatuous prison doctor, convinced that such a taxonomic achievement will launch him into British society. As he completes each painting, Gould's story dips into his past, recalling his grim childhood and ill-fated life of crime." Booklist

"This remarkable novel is a meditation on colonialism—indeed, on history itself—couched in the story of an English guttersnipe." New Yorker

Flanagan, Richard

The **unknown** terrorist. Grove Press 2007 320p $24

    ISBN 978-0-8021-1851-6; 0-8021-1851-8

    First published 2006 in Australia

A "page-turning thriller worthy of John le Carré, with a plot so credible a reader might feel it's nonfiction, except for a few too many coincidences. But even those can't dampen the chilling effect of the story, written in a fresh, exhilarating prose style in which the author makes each sentence a small work of art." Seattle Times

Flanagan, Richard

Wanting. Atlantic Monthly Press 2009 256p $24

    ISBN 978-0-8021-1900-1; 0-8021-1900-X

    First published 2008 in Australia

This novel is a "meditation on the nature and character of the Tasmanian landscape and its bloody history; and it is an exploration of the ways human beings imprison themselves emotionally, and label their prisons reason, science, religion; and it is a musing on illusions and lies, on the awful and wonderful implications of desire." Portland Oregonian

Flanagan, Thomas

★ The **tenants** of time. Dutton 1988 824p

LC 87-13632

This "novel is enormously long and unfalteringly rich in its delineation of the sometimes thorny connection between the public associations and private needs and loyalties of people who live energetically, and even recklessly, through times of political turbulence." Commonweal

Flanagan, Thomas

★ The **year** of the French; a novel. Holt, Rinehart & Winston 1979 516p

LC 78-23539

The author "writes well, taking care to approximate . . . the spoken and written language of the time. The result is, I'm convinced, not only a serious book, free of the irony and satire that informs so many of the more literary historical fictions written today, but a distinguished one as well." Newsweek

Flanery, Patrick

Absolution; Riverhead Books 2012 388 p.

    ISBN 9781594488177

LC 2011049338

In this novel, "Sam Leroux has a publisher's assignment to write the biography of a famous South African author, Clare Wald, imperious, reticent, evasive about her writing and disinclined to discuss her catastrophic personal life. . . . Told from alternating points of view, the novel shifts from . . . present to bloody past, from today's fractured economic and social environment to the historic struggle to end apartheid." (Kirkus Reviews)

Flaubert, Gustave

Madame Bovary; provincial ways. translated with an introduction and notes by Lydia Davis. Viking 2010 342p $27.95

    ISBN 978-0-670-02207-6; 0-670-02207-1

LC 2010-10328

"Poor Emma Bovary. She will never escape the tyranny of her desires, never avoid the anguish into which her romantic conceits deliver her, never claim the oblivion she sought from what is perhaps the most excruciating slow suicide ever written. Her place in the literary canon is assured; she cannot be eclipsed by another tragic heroine. Instead, each day she will be resurrected by countless readers who will agonize over the misery she brings herself and everyone around her and wonder at Flaubert's ability to, godlike, summon life from words on a page. The power of 'Madame Bovary' stems from Flaubert's determination to render each object of his scrutiny exactly as it looks, or sounds or smells or feels or tastes. . . . Given the pressure Flaubert applied to each sentence, there is no greater test of a translator's art than 'Madame Bovary.' Faithful to the style of the original, but not to the point of slavishness, Davis's effort is transparent — the reader never senses her presence. For 'Madame Bovary,' hers is the level of mastery required." N Y Times Book Rev

Includes bibliographical references.

Flaubert, Gustave

★ **Sentimental** education; or, The history of a young man. Magee 2v

    Original French edition, 1869

"The background of this novel is the decline and fall of the Monarchy of Louis Philippe and the Revolution of 1848. . . . The hero, Frederic Moreau, has many of the traits of young Flaubert. Madame Arnous, with whom he falls in love, is very like Madame Schlesinger whom Flaubert had admired at Trouville as early as 1836. The subject of the novel is really the futility of existence." Haydn. Thesaurus of Book Dig

Fleishman, Jeffrey

Promised virgins; a novel of jihad. Arcade Pub. 2009 253p $24.95

    ISBN 978-1-55970-897-5; 1-55970-897-2

LC 2008-31205

This novel "does what a good novel is supposed to do. It creates a real, textured, believable world, and it sweeps the reader along at a fast pace that nevertheless doesn't seem hurried. And it's clear that for the characters, what's real is the here and now, and their own memories, not what's happening in a prosperous, peaceful world away. Fleishman's writing captures what war must be like—a startling mix of the mundane, the extraordinary and the ominous." PopMatters

Fleming, Ian, 1908-1964
★ **Casino** Royale. Macmillan 1954 176p
ISBN 9781567310566; 9781612185439
"Against the background of a French resort the book describes Bond's destruction of the French branch of SMERSH, the Soviet espionage ring. The climax of the story is a tense game of baccarat in which Bond ruins the leader of the ring, Le Chiffre. The girl in the case is a compliant Soviet agent named Vesper Lynd, and there is much closely described violence." Wakeman. World Authors, 1950-1970

Fleming, Ian, 1908-1964
Doctor No. Macmillan 1958 256 p.
ISBN 9780425086797; 9781567310542
LC 58011083
The setting is the Caribbean, where James Bond is trying to trace the disappearance of two agents who had trespassed on the isolated island kingdom of the Eurasian Dr. No. The maniacal doctor, equipped with two pairs of steel pincers for hands, dreams of world conquest and is stockpiling a deadly arsenal for that time. Bond, with female companion in tow, survives a manhunt through the island's mangrove swamps to foil the doctor's plans

Fleming, Ian, 1908-1964
From Russia, with love. Macmillan 1957 253p
ISBN 9781567310535; 9780685112106
LC 57010292
James Bond, the British secret agent here meets the Soviet murder organization SMERSH once more. His execution has been ordered but Bond's counter activities seem successful—until the last page

Fleming, Ian, 1908-1964
★ **Goldfinger**. Macmillan 1959 318p
ISBN 9781612185507; 9781567310511
"James Bond, British Secret Service Agent 007, must retrieve British gold from a Mr. Auric Goldfinger whose ruthless obsession is suggesting in his goal—personal possession of half the supply of mined gold in the world." Publ Wkly

Fleming, Ian, 1908-1964
The **man** with the golden gun. New Am. Lib. 1965 183p
ISBN 9780859974400 out of print; 9781840236903
This adventure "begins with a brainwashed Bond ready to do the bidding of the K.G.B. in headquarters of the Secret Service, and thrashes through to a climax in Jamaica where the adversary is Scaramonga, the most ruthless death-dealing instrument forged in the 20th century." Libr J

Fleming, Ian, 1908-1964
On Her Majesty's Secret Service. New Am. Lib. 1963 299 p.
ISBN 9781567310795; 9781840236743
LC 63018007

James Bond, British secret agent 007, forsakes his bachelorhood for Countess Teresa di Vicenzo, who involves him in another adventure with Ernst Stavro Blofeld, head of an international crime syndicate and architect of an atomic blackmail scheme. The story is set against an Alpine background

Fleming, Ian, 1908-1964
You only live twice. New Am. Lib. 1964 240p
ISBN 9780685116319; 9781567310801
LC 64021144
"Bond, near-prostrate from his bride's death, is given a Japanese assignment to snap him out of his torpor. . . . {The story} involves Bond's making up as a Japanese and venturing into the den of a foreign 'death collector,' a madman who has set up a poisonous garden complete with noxious plants, volcanic geysers, snakes, and, in a lake, piranha fish. Very grisly and chilling. The ending is an epitome of horror." Publ Wkly

Fleming, Irene
The **edge** of ruin. Minotaur Books 2010 230p $24.99
ISBN 978-0-312-57520-5; 0-312-57520-3
LC 2009-47481
"Emily Weiss has a problem. Her husband is in jail for a murder he didn't commit; her life's savings are tied up in a fledgling movie company; Thomas Edison's goons are stalking her; the actors she works with are alcoholics or reprobates or, at the very least, they don't understand English. . . . [The novel] is enormously fun: lively and fast-paced, with an engaging heroine who manages to be spunky but never cloying. The story begins with a strong premise, throws in a series of complications (a dead body among them), and takes the reader on a roller coaster to see where it all end up. Oh, and it's also a cliffhanger, in every sense of the word." PopMatters

Fleming, Thomas J.
Dreams of glory; {by} Thomas Fleming. Forge 2000 301p $24.95
ISBN 0-312-87743-9
LC 00-31810
"Set during the frigid, bone-creaking winter of January 1780, when the Revolutionary War had seemingly quieted down, this . . . tale is based on an actual British plot to kidnap George Washington. . . . At the heart of the novel is the elusive British spy Twenty-Six, whose activities touch all the other characters. Meanwhile, Fleming gives us an almost tactile sense of that cold winter and the desperate living conditions of the American troops in contrast to the near luxury of the British." Libr J

Fleming, Thomas J.
When this cruel war is over; {by} Thomas Fleming. Forge 2001 301p $24.95
ISBN 0-312-87204-6
LC 00-48444
"Appearances by such historical figures as John Wilkes Booth and Mary Surratt and reprints of actual letters between President Lincoln and Colonel Gentry foster suspense." Publ Wkly

Flint, Shamini

A **Bali** conspiracy most foul; Inspector Singh investigates. Minotaur Books 2011 292p $25.99
ISBN 978-0-312-59698-9

LC 2011-08728

Sequel to Inspector Singh investigates: a most peculiar Malaysian murder (2010)

"Inspector Singh, wearing his trademark white sneakers, is dispatched from Singapore to Bali, ostensibly to assist in the investigation of a string of nightclub bombings. But that was just an excuse to get him out of Singapore, since he knows nothing about catching terrorists. Which is why he is more than happy to investigate a possible murder connection after the coroner's office finds a skull with a bullet hole among the victims. Paired with a female Australian officer who is in the doghouse after some unfortunate remarks to the media, Singh tackles the unusually difficult case. . . . Flint not only creates fascinating, unforgettable characters; she also brings to life the unique island setting and lifestyle of Bali." Booklist

Flynn, Gillian

Dark places. Shaye Areheart Books 2009 349p $24
ISBN 978-0-307-34156-3; 0-307-34156-9

LC 2008-40244

"Libby Day, the protagonist of Flynn's disturbing second novel, was, as a seven-year-old, the only survivor of her family's brutal murder by her older brother, an event dubbed by the media the 'Satan Sacrifice of Kinnakee, Kansas.' Twenty-five years later, she has become a hardened, selfish young woman with no friends or family. Since the tragedy, her life has been paid for by donations of well-wishers, but, with that fund now empty, Libby must find a way to make money. Her search leads her to The Kill Club, a secret society of people obsessed with the details of notorious murders. As Libby tries to gather artifacts to sell to The Kill Club (whose members, it turns out, doubt the guilt of her brother), she is forced to reëxamine the events of the night of the murder. Flynn's well-paced story deftly shows the fallibility of memory and the lies a child tells herself to get through a trauma." New Yorker

Flynn, Gillian

★ **Gone** girl; a novel. Gillian Flynn. Crown 2012 419 p.
ISBN 030758836X; 9780307588364; 9780307588388
LC 2011041525

In this book, "[w]hen Nick Dunne's beautiful and clever wife, Amy, goes missing on their fifth wedding anniversary, the media descend. . . . And Nick stumbles badly, for, as it turns out, he has plenty to hide, and under the pressure of police questioning and media scrutiny, he tells one lie after another. Juxtaposed with Nick's first-person narration of events are excerpts from Amy's diary, which completely contradict Nick's story and depict a woman who is afraid of her husband." (Booklist)

Flynn, Gillian

Sharp objects; a novel. Shaye Areheart Books 2006 245p $24
ISBN 0-307-34154-2

LC 2005-35046

The author "offers up a literary thriller that's a doozy. . . and she does it with wit and grit, a sort of Hitchcock visits Stephen King, with plenty of the former's offstage and often only implied violence, and the latter's sense of pacing and facility with dialogue. . . . This is not a comfortable novel of touchy-feely family fun. Rather, it is a tough tale told with remarkable clarity and dexterity." Denver Post

Flynn, Michael

Eifelheim. Tor Book 2006 320p $25.95
ISBN 0-7653-0096-6

LC 2006-5468

"Tom, a young historian, obsesses about Eifelheim, a German village that mysteriously disappeared from all maps in 1349. His lover Sharon, a theoretical physicist, occupies herself with testing the limits of conventional theories of time and space. Their interests merge when they discover the remarkable story of Father Dietrich, Eifelheim's parish priest during the Black Death and a believer in travelers from the stars. With a sure grasp of both speculative science and medieval history, Flynn . . . compellingly weaves past and present together in a dialog of faith and science." Libr J

Flynn, Michael

In the Lion's Mouth; Michael Flynn. Tor 2012 303 p. ill
ISBN 0765322854; 9780765322852

LC 2011025168

This book tells the story of a future universe "wherein two human empires, the Confederation of Central Worlds and the United League of the Periphery, struggle for dominance. . . . Bridget ban, a Hound or agent of the League, seeks news of Donovan buigh, a scarred former Shadow, or operative of the Confederation, her former lover. . . . The great powers of the Confederacy, Those of Name, tortured Donovan to fragment his mind into seven distinct personalities. . . . A civil war . . . smolders in the Lion's Mouth the control arm of the Shadows. . . . Donovan miraculously escaped the horrors inflicted by the Names, and now the rebels . . . [intend] to recruit or at least capture him. Unknown to everybody . . . Donovan's separated personalities have begun to communicate and access their common memories, making him even more formidable than before." (Kirkus)

Flynn, Michael

The **January** dancer. Tor 2008 350p il $24.95
ISBN 978-0-7653-1817-6; 0-7653-1817-2

LC 2008-29772

"The characters zip through so many worlds that it's hard to keep track of them, but Flynn includes enough clever references to the long-abandoned Earth to keep the journey amusing. . . . The balladic framework can be heavy-handed at times, but it adds a mythical quality to what could have been run-of-the-mill space fantasy." Washington Post Book World

Flynn, Michael

On the razor's edge; Michael Flynn. Tor 2013 352 p. (hardback) $25.99

ISBN 0765334801; 9780765334800

LC 2013006328

In this book by Michael Flynn "the secret war among the Shadows of the Name is escalating, and there are hints that it is not so secret as the Shadows had thought. The scarred man, Donovan buigh, half honored guest and half prisoner, is carried deeper into the Confederation, all the way to Holy Terra herself, to help plan the rebel assault on the Secret City. Meanwhile, Bridget ban has organized a posse . . . to go in pursuit of her kidnapped daughter." (Publisher's note)

Flynn, Michael

Up Jim River; 1st ed.; Tor 2010 352 p. ill.

ISBN 9780765322845

LC 2009041210

This book tells the story of "the harper Mearana . . . [whose] mother, Bridget ban, has disappeared on mysterious business. Even the Kennel, her employer and one of the galaxy's two sources of secret agents, didn't know what she was looking for or where she went. Mearana is determined, though, to discover her mother's fate. She manages to convince the scarred man . . . who . . . became six or seven personalities after a botched experiment by Those of Name, to join her out of a sense of nostalgia." (Booklist) "Together, they follow Bridget ban's trail to the raw worlds of the frontier, edging ever closer to the de-civilized and barbarian planets of the Wild. Along the way, they encounter evidence that they too are being followed--by a deadly agent of Those of Name." (Publisher's note)

Flyte, Magnus

City of dark magic; a novel. Magnus Flyte. Penguin Books 2012 464 p. $16

ISBN 0143122681; 9780143122685

LC 2012028676

In this romantic mystery novel, "musicologist Sarah Weston has been summoned to Prague to catalog Beethoven manuscripts at the Lobkowicz Palace." Weird stuff happens as she prepares to go, including the apparent suicide of her mentor Sherbatsky. "As Sarah dutifully sifts through the manuscripts, she discovers clues not only about the 'Immortal Beloved,' but also Sherbatsky's strange behavior leading up to his death," which may have had to do with time-travel drugs.. (Kirkus)

Foden, Giles

Turbulence. Alfred A. Knopf 2010 315p $25.95

ISBN 978-0-307-59277-4

LC 2010-1605

First published 2009 in the United Kingdom

"Well-crafted scientific and philosophical speculation dominates a less consistent plotline, making for thought-provoking if only patchily gripping reading." Kirkus

Foer, Jonathan Safran

Everything is illuminated; a novel. Houghton Mifflin 2002 276p il $24

ISBN 0-618-17387-0

LC 2001-51610

"Foer deftly handles the intricate story-within-a-story plot, and the layers of suspense build as the shtetl hurtles toward the devastation of the 20th century while Alex and Jonathan and Grandfather close in on the object of their search. An impressive, original debut." Publ Wkly

Foer, Jonathan Safran

Extremely loud & incredibly close. Houghton Mifflin 2005 326p il $24.95; pa $13.95

ISBN 0-618-32970-6; 0-618-71165-1 pa

LC 2004-65131

The author's "depiction of Oskar's reaction to phone messages left by his father as he awaited rescue in the burning World Trade Center, his description of Oskar's grandfather's love affair . . . and his experiences during the bombing of Dresden—these passages underscore Mr. Foer's ability to evoke, with enormous compassion and psychological acuity, his characters' emotional experiences, and to show how these private moments intersect with the great public events of history." N Y Times (Late N Y Ed)

Follett, Ken

★ Eye of the needle; a novel. Arbor House 1978 313p

LC 77-90670

"An absolutely terrific thriller, so pulse-pounding, so ingenious in its plotting, and so frighteningly realistic that you simply cannot stop reading, this World War II espionage tale is right up there with the best of them." Publ Wkly

Follett, Ken

Fall of giants; book one of the Century trilogy. Dutton 2010 985p $36

ISBN 0-525-95165-2; 978-0-525-95165-0

LC 2010-09279

This is the first installment of Follet's fictional trilogy spanning the entire twentieth century. It "follows the fates of five interrelated families—American, German, Russian, English and Welsh—as they move through the world-shaking dramas of World War I, the Russian Revolution and the struggle for women's suffrage." (Publisher's note)

"Follett entwines fiction and factual events well. Creating characters of numerous, actual historical figures is a big risk. How do you write about Trotsky without being facile? Follett successfully assails the dilemma from a couple of angles, most importantly by knowing a lot about the period but not making the reader aware of how arduously he is working." Chicago Sun-Times

Follett, Ken

Hornet flight. Dutton 2002 420p $26.95

ISBN 0-525-94689-6

LC 2002-37903

"Tale of amateur spies pursued by Nazi collaborators in occupied Denmark in 1941. Harald Olufsen is an 18-year-old physics student who stumbles into espionage when he accidentally discovers a secret German radar installation on the island where he lives. . . . Follett starts out fast and keeps up the pace, revealing how ordinary people who want to do the right thing are undone by their own enthusiasm and inexperience. He also paints a vivid and convincing picture of life in occupied Denmark, of easy collaboration with the

Nazis and of the insidious, creeping persecution of the Jews. Publ Wkly

Follett, Ken

Jackdaws. Dutton 2001 451p

ISBN 0-525-94628-4

LC 2001-37087

This thriller is about a mission "to take out a German telephone exchange near Reims in the last few hours before D-Day. A full-frontal assault led by British SOE (Special Operations Executives) Felicity 'Flick' Clariet and her husband, a French Resistance leader, has failed, leaving the Allies with only a last-minute desperation plan: a team of six women, posing as a cleaning detail, will infiltrate the exchange and dismantle it. . . . The assembled team includes two lesbians, a German transvestite, and a gypsy. All of this may sound like cliched melodrama, but when Follett starts the clock and slips the narrative gearshift into synchromesh, one's literary misgivings are abandoned in the wake of the plot's forward thrust." Booklist

Follett, Ken

Lie down with lions. Morrow 1986 333p

LC 85-25876

This novel is set in "Afghanistan, where the farmers and nomads are battling their Russian invaders. Jean-Pierre, a doctor fresh from residency, has volunteered two years to tend the wounded and offer general medical aid in the Valley of Five Lions; his real motive, however, is to spy on the rebels for the 'KGB'. Jane, his newly pregnant wife, serves as his nurse and his contact with the women of the villages. When local caravans bringing munitions are repeatedly attacked and the men killed, Ellis Thaler, a 'CIA' expert in explosives, arrives to consolidate the rebel's efforts, that he and Jane had been lovers complicates the situation. Separately they deduce Jean-Pierre's treachery. . . . This is fine adventure filled with passion, violence, and tension." Best Sellers

Follett, Ken

Pillars of the earth; Ken Follett. Morrow 1989 973p ill. (hbk.) $34.99

ISBN 0688046592; 9780688046590

LC 89009405

This book takes place in "the twelfth century; the place—feudal England; and the subject—the building of a glorious cathedral. [Author Ken] Follett has re-created the . . . England of the Middle Ages. . . . The vast forests, the walled towns, the castles, and the monasteries become a familiar landscape. Against this . . . backdrop, filled with the ravages of war and the rhythms of daily life, the . . . storyteller draws the reader . . . into the intertwined lives of his characters—into their dreams, their labors, and their loves: Tom, the master builder; Aliena, the ravishingly beautiful noblewoman; Philip, the prior of Kingsbridge; Jack, the artist in stone; and Ellen, the woman of the forest who casts a terrifying curse." (Publisher's note)

"Follett has skillfully crafted an extraordinary epic buttressed by a succession of suspenseful subplots. A towering triumph of romance, rivalry, and spectacle from a major talent." Booklist

Follett, Ken

Triple; a novel. Arbor House 1979 377p

LC 78-73869

"The Egyptians are making nuclear weapons and the Israelis, in order to do the same, are obliged to steal 100 tons of uranium. A group of old acquaintances at Oxford in 1947 come together again in different roles: the Mossad agent who organizes the theft, the disgruntled Palestinian spying for Egypt, the Russian bureaucrat (actually a KGB colonel), and the American become a Mafia don. The hijacking plot is elaborate beyond description." Libr J

Follett, Ken

Winter of the world; Ken Follett. Dutton 2012 940 p.

ISBN 0525952926; 9780525952923

LC 2012004653

This historical novel, by Ken Follett, is the second book in "The Century Trilogy." "[Picking] up right where the first book left off, . . . its five interrelated families . . . enter a time of enormous . . . turmoil, beginning with the rise of the Third Reich, . . . up to the explosions of the American and Soviet atomic bombs. . . . These characters . . . find their lives inextricably entangled as their experiences illuminate the cataclysms that marked the century." (Publisher's note)

Follett, Ken

World without end. Dutton 2007 1014p $35

ISBN 978-0-525-95007-3; 0-525-95007-9

LC 2007-26639

"Some 200 years after Pillars, the town of Kingsbridge is still dominated by its magnificent cathedral. But times have changed. War and plague have dramatically affected the infrastructure of the Middle Ages, shifting the base of power from the noble and religious to the rising merchant and artisan classes. Populated with an immense cast of truly remarkable characters-the rich and powerful, the weak and downtrodden, clergy, guildsmen and nobility-this novel explores the lives and fortunes of the ancestors of the original inhabitants of Kingsbridge." Libr J

Folsom, Allan R.

The day after tomorrow; a novel. by Allan Folsom. Little, Brown 1994 596p

LC 93-30344

"In this ambitious and impressive first novel, Folsom covers vast amounts of territory at breakneck speed. . . . That Folsom manages to instill some genuine tension amidst all this is testimony to his skill." Libr J

Folsom, Allan R.

Day of confession; a novel. [by] Allan Folsom. Little, Brown 1998 566p $35

ISBN 0-316-28755-5

LC 98-5470

"Four days after Cardinal Rosario Parma is assassinated in Rome, hotshot L.A. entertainment lawyer Harry Addison gets a frantic phone message from his estranged brother, Danny, a Vatican priest. Shortly thereafter, Harry hears that Danny has died in a bus explosion. When he flies to Rome to claim the body, he discovers that Danny is the prime suspect in Parma's murder-and that he's still alive. The novel then follows two parallel plots. Harry tries to find Danny and clear his name; meanwhile, the sinister Cardinal Umberto Palestrina, who thinks he's the reincarnation of Alexander the Great, plots to make China the site of a new Holy Roman Empire." Publ Wkly

Fonseca, Isabel
    Attachment. Knopf 2008 305p $23.95
    ISBN 978-0-307-26691-0; 0-307-26691-5
                   LC 2007-42860
    "If all this sounds soap-operatic—well, it kind of is, but the bubbles have heft as well as loft. Except for her clumsy effort to integrate Sept. 11 into the narrative—and, as a sort of dramatic bonus, the 2003 blackout—Ms. Fonseca's exploration of middle-aged displacement, both mental and physical, is intelligent, nuanced and immensely satisfying." N Y Observer

Forbes, Charlotte
    The **good** works of Ayela Linde; a novel in stories. Arcade Pub. 2006 227p $24
    ISBN 1-55970-807-7
                   LC 2005-29294
    "We meet the beautiful and enigmatic 17-year-old Ayela Linde in 1950, in the Texas border town of Santa Rosalia, where she lives with her dressmaker mother and suffers the stigma of illegitimacy with unconcerned defiance. We see her through the eyes of her friend Druanne as they meet their respective suitors at the local pool and dance hall. In the next 15 chapters, different narrators outline their encounters with Ayela, chronicling everything from her tumultuous young marriage to her death in 1999. . . . Forbes presents a delicate gem of a novel in which she moves deftly from narrator to narrator to produce a rich and moving portrait of Ayela in all phases of her adult life against the colorful backdrop of a town with ever-shifting mores and priorities." Libr J

Ford, Ford Madox
    ★ The **good** soldier; a tale of passion. Knopf 1991 (Everyman's library) $24
    ISBN 0-679-40665-4
                   LC 91-52977
    First published 1915 in the United Kingdom
    This novel "consists of the first-person narration of American John Dowell (an archetypally unreliable narrator), who relates the history of relationships that begin in 1904, when his wife Florence meet Edward and Leonora Ashburnham in a hotel in Nauheim. The two couples form a foursome, and meet regularly. In August 1913 the Ashburnhams take their young ward Nancy Rufford to Nauheim with them, and Florence commits suicide. Later that year the Ashburnhams send Nancy to India (where she goes mad) and Edward also commits suicide. Dowell becomes Nancy's 'male sick nurse'; Leonora remarries. The substance of the novel lies in Dowell's growing understanding of the intrigues that lay behind the orderly Edwardian facade both couples had presented to the world." Oxford Companion to Engl Lit. 6th edition

Ford, Ford Madox
    ★ **Parade's** end. Knopf 1992 906p $22
    ISBN 0-679-41728-1
                   LC 92-52922
    A reissue of the title first published 1950; A one volume edition of the author's tetralogy that includes: Some do not (1924); No more parades (1925); A man could stand up (1926); and The last post (1928)
    This series of novels "describes the adventures in love and war of Christopher Tietjens, an old-fashioned gentleman of the English governing class. Ford draws a brilliant picture of the social changes brought about by the First World War. Before the war, Tietjens is nobly faithful to his impossible wife. But trench warfare seems to him a symbol of the disintegration of his whole society. He has a mental breakdown, goes to live with a woman he loves, and gives up his position, wealth, and historic family ties." Reader's Ency. 4th edition

Ford, Jeffrey
    The **drowned** life. Harper Perennial 2008 290, 16p pa $14.95
    ISBN 978-0-06-143506-5; 0-06-143506-6
                   LC 2008-13181
    "This collection of short stories from the author of The Shadow Year contains some of the most unusual and provocative settings and plots this reviewer has ever encountered, which will make it perfect for book talking to patrons. . . . Sometimes shocking, sometimes mesmerizing, sometimes humorous, this collection will please fans of Raymond Carver and Flannery O'Connor." Libr J

Ford, Jeffrey
    The **empire** of ice cream; with an introduction by Jonathan Carroll. Golden Gryphon Press 2006 319p $24.95
    ISBN 1-930846-39-8
                   LC 2005-24035
    "Giants and unidentifiable alien creatures, fairy tales, the intertwining of wonder and terror, and fantastic views of both the strange and the ordinary all appear in this marvelous collection, with Ford's comments on his inspiration and motivations appended to each story. Ford is nothing if not versatile, as this collection confirms to great effect." Booklist

Ford, Jeffrey
    The **shadow** year. William Morrow 2008 289p $25.95
    ISBN 978-0-06-123152-0; 0-06-123152-5
                   LC 2007-37319
    "A masterly literary adventure that is at once a hypnotically compelling mystery and a stunningly evocative portrait of small-town adolescence." Pittsburgh Press

Ford, Richard, 1944-
    Canada; a novel. Richard Ford. Ecco 2012 420p. $27.99
    ISBN 0061692042; 9780061692048
                   LC 2011279175
    This novel tells the story of "15-year-old Dell Parsons, whose world collapses when his parents are jailed for a bank robbery, his twin sister flees, and he is transported across the

border by a family friend to an obscure town in Canada. . . . Segmented into three parts, the narrative slowly builds into a . . . commentary on life's biggest question: Why are we here?" (Library Journal)

Ford, Richard, 1944-

★ **Independence** Day. Knopf 1995 451p
ISBN 0-679-49265-8

LC 95-3126

One is "constantly struck by the rich, dense mixture of Ford's narrative. No one writes better—and with more inventive brio—about the bland wasteland of US suburbia; that shopping-malled, subdivisioned terrain that has rapidly become the true defining landscape of late 20th-century America." New Statesman (1913)

Ford, Richard

The **lay** of the land. Alfred A. Knopf 2006 496p $26.95
ISBN 978-0-679-45468-7; 0-679-45468-3

LC 2006-25570

This third novel featuring sports journalist Frank Bascombe, who appeared previously in The Sportswriter (1986) and Independence Day (1995), finds the protagonist facing health problems (prostate cancer), the end of the Clinton era, and family issues.

This is as "as vibrant a book as any that Richard Ford has written. It bristles with energy, with a natural assurance on the part of its writer. . . . And what a slice of life at the turn of the century and millennium this novel is. There is so much trenchant criticism of what is wrong with American society: the economic royalism, the greed, the lack of common decency and civility in so many walks of life, and above all perspective. . . . As people today read Theodore Dreiser for his acute portraits of industrialized America in its gilded age and Sinclair Lewis for his insights into his nation's struggles to come to terms with 20th-century changes in its social structures, one day readers will turn to Richard Ford to discover just what the United States was like on the homefront during his particular fin de siecle." Christ Sci Monit

Ford, Richard

A **multitude** of sins; stories. Knopf 2002 286p
ISBN 0-375-41212-3

LC 2001-38402

"Tracing the blueprint of human interaction in this latest collection . . . Ford signals the master text of lust standing behind the multitude of small sins he so tersely and poignantly chronicles. To err is human, and, in Ford's worldview, little is so human as the act of cheating on a wife or husband." Publ Wkly

Ford, Richard

Women with men; three long stories. Knopf 1997 255p
ISBN 978-0679776680

LC 97-5832

In these "three powerful long stories, the author explores precarious and complicated relationships between men and women. Each tale revolves around the fractured emotions aroused by the dissolution of a marriage: feelings of failure and the dizzying sense of spinning unsteadily and off

course through life, like a wheel without an axle. . . . All of Ford's magnetic characters seem permanently jet-lagged, woozy with displacement and disappointment, and their troubles escalate accordingly, with surreal and sickening inevitability." Booklist

Ford, Robert

The **student** conductor. Putnam 2003 289p $24.95
ISBN 0-399-15037-4

LC 2003-46514

"This is finally a novel about power—the power of a great conductor driving a well-trained orchestra, the power of the past to enslave us, the power of the future to free us, and the power of the individual to love and to forgive. There is hardly a wrong note, from the moment Ford lifts his baton to the final refrain." Booklist

Forester, C. S.

Admiral Hornblower in the West Indies. Little, Brown 1958 329p

A collection of Horatio Hornblower's adventures set in the West Indies. "The first belongs chronologically with 'Lieutenant Hornblower.' The rest are set nearly 15 years later when, as rear admiral in command of His Majesty's fleet in the West Indies, he faces a new Bonapartist uprising, suppresses the slave trade, stamps out piracy, and maintains British diplomacy during the South American revolutions." Booklist

"Recounted with taste, with psychological insight, and with a sure sense of story. This is top grade adventure fiction." N Y Her Trib Books

Forester, C. S.

★ The **African** Queen. Little, Brown 1935 275p
ISBN 0-89244-065-1

"At her brother's death Rose Sayer is left alone in an isolated African mission. She is determined to fight against the Germans, who have taken her brother's black converts into custody. She joins forces with a Cockney, Alnutt, and they take a long and dangerous trip down-river in Alnutt's dilapidated launch in order to reach the German boat they intend to blow up. The journey points up the differences between this ill-matched pair, and their bravery as well." Shapiro. Fic for Youth. 3d edition

Forester, C. S.

★ **Beat** to quarters. Little, Brown 1937 324p

A sea story of the British navy in the early nineteenth century. Essentially it is a portrait of a man, captain of an English frigate. Hornblower, son of a country doctor, is a man uncertain of his own powers, of his technical skill and of the admiration of his men, yet when he is sent under sealed orders to the Pacific coast of Central America, he accomplishes his mission brilliantly, and fights two successful battles with the same Spanish warship

"There is plenty of action. But there is also an unusual character study." N Y Times Book Rev

Followed by Ship of the line

Forester, C. S.

✓ **Commodore** Hornblower. Little, Brown 1945 384p

"It is a spirited piece of work, and full of interesting detail where matters naval, military, and diplomatic in that year of decision are concerned." Times Lit Suppl

Followed by Lord Hornblower

Forester, C. S.

✓ **Flying** colours. Little, Brown 1939 294p

Third book in a series which began with Beat to quarters and Ship of the line. Captain Hornblower, his crippled first mate, Bush, and his servant, Brown, escape from their escort on the way to Paris to be tried for piracy. The story is of their recapture of an English vessel and return to England, where they are covered with honors

Followed by Commodore Hornblower

Forester, C. S.

✓ **Hornblower** and the Atropos. Little, Brown 1953 325p

This is a series of episodes in the early life of the Captain; a journey across England from Gloucester to London by canal; his part in the funeral of Nelson; and his battles on the coast of Turkey, where he recovers a huge treasure from a sunken English ship

Forester, C. S.

Hornblower and the Hotspur. Little, Brown 1962 344p

ISBN 0-316-28899-3

"The story opens just before Horatio sails on a cruise in his first command. His rank is Commander; his ship something less than a frigate but something more than a sloop; his task to act as the eyes of the Channel Fleet which is to be in position to blockade Brest upon the imminent declaration of hostilities with France. In the course of action Hornblower is detained at sea for almost two years as, in his own inimitable and logically necessary style, he helps cripple the Napoleonic effort to invade England, the last block to conquest of Europe." Best Sellers

Forester, C. S.

Hornblower during the crisis, and two stories: Hornblower's temptation and The last encounter. Little, Brown 1967 174p

ISBN 0-316-28915-9

"Because Forester died before completing this novel, the reader is left with a summary sketch and his own imagination for final details of the plot. For Forester devotees, this will not detract from the essential verve and dash of Hornblower's last chase." Christ Sci Monit

Forester, C. S.

The **last** nine days of the Bismarck. Little, Brown 1959 138p

"Forester describes the pursuit and epic bombardment at sea in World War II when the German battleship 'Bismarck' broke into the Atlantic and sailed toward Brest with the whole British Home Fleet after her. Scenes on board the 'Bismarck' and the British ships have been given dialog to make the telling more vivid." Publ Wkly

Forester, C. S.

Lieutenant Hornblower. Little, Brown 1952 306p

ISBN 0-316-28907-8

The author "interprets the navy, certainly in its Napoleonic period, with the help of a character that represents the navy at its best and action that is grandly exciting without being melodramatic; helped, too, by a sense of order and a mastery of technique that puts his work on a high plane of artistry." Christ Sci Monit

Forester, C. S.

Lord Hornblower. Little, Brown 1946 322p

ISBN 0-316-28908-6

In this "Hornblower novel Horatio continues his adventures and helps defeat Napoleon by aiding the heir to the Bourbon throne to enter France. Barbara goes to the Congress of Vienna to act as hostess for her brother while Horatio returns to France to visit old friends and renew an old love. When Napoleon escapes from Elba danger threatens Hornblower as he forms a guerrilla band in the south of France. But, saved by the defeat of the French at Waterloo, he returns to the arms of Barbara and new honors as Lord Hornblower." Booklist

Forester, C. S.

Mr. Midshipman Hornblower. Little, Brown 1950 310p

ISBN 0-316-28909-4

Chronologically this is the first book of the Hornblower series. "The book details, in a series of incidents, the genesis of the Hornblower career from the day he first stepped aboard ship as a kings-letter man to the day when he received his commission as Lieutenant in a Spanish prison. Actually the story is told as a series of incidents . . . with only a thin thread of continuity connecting them." Best Sellers

Forester, C. S.

Ship of the line. Little, Brown 1938 298p

In this sequel to Beat to quarters, Captain Hornblower is given command of the ship Sutherland and sent to join the forces blockading the Spanish coast in the war with Napoleon

Followed by Flying colours

Forester, C. S.

✓ **To** the Indies. Little, Brown 1940 298p

"The story of Narciso Rich who is lifted suddenly from his quiet life as a successful lawyer to join the swaggering, gold-hungry hidalgos who went with Columbus on his third voyage. He fights Indians at San Domingo, is kidnapped by renegades, shipwrecked off the coast of Cuba, and finally makes his way back to the settlement in time to return on the ship that carried Columbus in chains." Ont Libr Rev

The **forgotten** affairs of youth; Alexander McCall
✓ Smith. Pantheon Books 2011 261 p.

ISBN 9780307379184

LC 2011023394

This book tells the story of "Isabel Dalhousie, . . . a philosopher . . . [and an] Edinburgh-based heroine[, who] is a professional in the field, the editor of a journal, the Review of Applied Ethics. . . . But by this point in the series, Isabel's issues have been put more or less straight: . . . . She is . . . engaged to . . . Jamie, who is helping raise their toddler son, Charlie. . . . Only Isabel's jealous niece Cat, Jamie's former lover, is still a loose cannon, and when mysterious mushrooms from Cat's delicatessen land Isabel in the emergency room, high drama seems about to be let loose. . . . Before long, Isabel is back on her feet and involved in the main mystery of the book. This time, that means helping a colleague, Jane Cooper, a philosopher who has returned on sabbatical to the land of her birth from Australia. Alone and somewhat isolated, Jane, who was adopted, hopes to track her birth father in the hope of gaining some semblance of belonging, and Isabel has both the contacts and the character to act as an amateur sleuth on her behalf." (Boston.com)

Forna, Aminatta

Ancestor stones. Atlantic Monthly Press 2006 317p $24

    ISBN 0-87113-944-8

                   LC 2006-47708

This is an "optimistic, truthful novel and if we accept Ben Okri's notion of writers as 'the barometer of the vitality of the spirit of the nation', then we should be optimistic about an indisputably talented young novelist and for the future of Africa too." Times Lit Suppl

Forna, Aminatta

  ✓ The **memory** of love; Aminatta Forna. Bloomsbury 2010 445p.

    ISBN 978-1-4088-0813-9 Bloomsbury; 1-4088-0813-7 Bloomsbury; 978-0-8021-1965-0 Atlantic Monthly Press; 0-8021-1965-4 Atlantic Monthly Press

                   LC 2010413660

    Commonwealth Writers' Prize: Best Book (2011)

    Commonwealth Writers' Prize: Regional Award: Africa: Best Book (2011)

This book tells the story of "British psychiatrist Adrian Lockheart, [who] has fled his failing marriage in England in the hopes of doing some good in Sierra Leone. Adrian becomes fascinated by two of his patients, elderly Elias Cole, a former university professor, and Agnes, a woman lost in a fugue state. The dying Cole reveals to Adrian . . . how he fell in love with a radical colleague's wife in the late 1960s, while Adrian must piece together the details of Agnes' life. Adrian finds a friend in a haunted young surgeon, Kai, who is contemplating leaving the country. Kai questions some of Adrian's risky decisions, such as his intention to track Agnes down once she leaves the hospital, but it is Adrian's involvement with a local woman from Kai's past that shocks the young doctor." (Booklist)

Forrest, Katherine V.

Apparition alley; a Kate Delafield mystery. Berkley Prime Crime 1997 248p

    ISBN 978-1883523800

                   LC 96-53688

"Wounded by 'friendly fire' during a burglary arrest gone awry, lesbian LAPD homicide detective Kate Delafield must undergo routine—but intrusive—psychological counseling before returning to duty. Meanwhile, officer Luke Taggart, a pariah among their colleagues, wants Kate to represent him at his disciplinary hearing. Luke believes that he has been set up by vindictive cops and that Kate's 'accident' could

be part of the same conspiracy. Aptly described West Hollywood and L.A. settings, great counseling dialog, and subtle plot machinations underscore the author's talent." Libr J

Forrest, Katherine V.

Liberty Square; a Kate Delafield mystery. Berkley Prime Crime 1996 242p

    ISBN 0-425-15467-X

                   LC 95-46809

This mystery "featuring lesbian LAPD homicide detective Kate Delafield is also a moody meditation on the Vietnam War and the conflicted loyalties it engendered. For ex-marine Delafield begrudgingly attends a reunion with her military buddies from a quarter-century past, an event that not only stirs up troubled memories but also sets the scene for a grisly murder whose motives stem from the time when America's Southeast Asia involvement was bloodiest." Booklist

Forrest, Katherine V.

Sleeping bones. Berkley Prime Crime 1999 260p $21.95

    ISBN 0-425-17029-2

                   LC 98-54294

This Kate Delafield "adventure takes her to the famous La Brea tar pits, where she breaks in new partner Joe on a bizarre case of murder. An excellent novel." Libr J

Forster, E. M.

The **collected** tales of E. M. Forster. Knopf 1947 308p

    Contents: The celestial omnibus: The story of a panic; The other side of the hedge; The celestial omnibus; Other kingdom; The curate's friend; The road from Colonus ; The eternal moment: The machine stops; The point of it: Mr. Andrews; Co-ordination; The story of the siren; The eternal moment

Forster, E. M.

  ★ **Howards** End. Knopf 1991 xxxiii, 359p $19

  ✓ ISBN 0-679-40668-9

                   LC 91-52997

    First published 1910

This novel "deals with an English country house called Howards End and its influence on the lives of the materialistic Wilcoxes, the cultural and idealistic Schlegel sisters, and the poor bank clerk Leonard Bast. The Schlegels try to befriend Bast. Mr. Wilcox, whom Margaret Schlegel later marries, gives him financial advice which ruins him. Helen Schlegel becomes his mistress for a short time and bears his son; thereupon Charles Wilcox thrashes and accidentally kills him. The house passes from intuitive, half-mystical Mrs. Wilcox to her husband's second wife Margaret Schlegel, to Margaret's nephew, Leonard Bast's son. Illustrating Forster's motto 'Only connect,' the house brings together three important elements in English society: money and successful business in the Wilcoxes, culture in the Schlegels, and the lower classes in Leonard Bast." Reader's Ency. 4th edition

Forster, E. M.

  ✓ **Maurice**. Norton 1971 256p

"This posthumous novel with a homosexual theme would have been sensational had it been published when written in 1913. Appearing in the 1970's, it is not sensational, but it is an interesting novel—well written as all of E. M. Forster's works are. . . . It is filled with keen insight and sympathetic character analysis, valuable for an understanding of the author and his works." Choice

Forster, E. M.

★ A **passage** to India; with an introduction by P.N. Furbank. Knopf 1991 xxxix, 293p $18

ISBN 0-679-40549-6

First published 1924

"Politics and mysticism are potent forces in India just after World War I. Ronald Heaslop, magistrate of Chandrapore, has asked his mother, Mrs. Moore, to visit him along with his fiancee, Adela Quested. To add to their knowledge of the real India, Dr. Aziz, a young Moslem doctor, offers to take them to the Marabar Caves outside the city. The visit is a shattering experience. Mrs. Moore is struck by the thought that all her ideas about life are no more than the hollow echo she hears in the cave. Adela, entering another cave alone, emerges in a panic and accuses Dr. Aziz of having attacked her in the gloom of the cave. The trial that results from her accusation divides the groups in the city so acutely that a reconciliation appears impossible." Shapiro. Fic for Youth. 3d edition

Forster, E. M.

★ A **room** with a view. Putnam 1911 364p

First published 1908

The novel "is set mostly in Italy, a country which represents for the author the forces of true passion. The heroine, upper-class Lucy Honeychurch, is visiting Italy with a friend. When she regrets that her hotel room has no view, lower-class Mr. Emerson offers the friends his own room and that of his son. Lucy becomes caught between the world of the Emersons and that of Cecil Vyse, the shallow, conventional young man of her own class to whom she becomes engaged on her return to England. Finally, she overcomes her own prejudice and her family's opposition and marries George Emerson." Reader's Ency. 4th edition

Forster, E. M.

A **room** with a view and Howards End. Modern Lib. 1993 533p

ISBN 0-679-60069-8

LC 93-15340

A combined edition of two titles, both entered separately

Forsyth, Frederick

Avenger. Thomas Dunne Bks. 2003 370p $24.95

ISBN 0-312-31951-7

LC 2003-53163

"World War II, Vietnam, Bosnia, and Cambodia take turns commanding center stage, held together by two protagonists: a middle-age lawyer and an aging business tycoon, who have both suffered devastating losses. The tycoon's loss, that of his grandson on a relief mission in Bosnia, becomes subsumed in the mission of attorney Calvin Dexter, grieving father and former 'Nam tunnel rat, whose mission in life is to bring justice to those who have gotten away with

murder. . . . Forsyth's extraordinary care with detail, his solid voice, and his exquisite pacing make this a totally engrossing thriller." Booklist

Forsyth, Frederick

★ The **day** of the jackal. Viking 1971 380p

"Dissident OAS officers hire a mercenary, known by the code name 'Jackal', to assassinate General Charles deGaulle. The officers hope to cash in on the political chaos that would follow. The methodical, ingenious preparations of 'Jackal' are paralleled by the attempts of the combined French law-enforcement agencies to uncover and stop the plot. The suspense is acute." Shapiro. Fic for Youth. 3d edition

Forsyth, Frederick

★ The **dogs** of war. Viking 1974 408p

A "novel about the carefully planned overthrow of the small African state of Zangaro. Behind the coup is a British multimillionaire, seeking control of the mining rites to the platinum within Zangaro's Crystal Mountain. He hires top mercenary Cat Shannon to do most of the planning and to carry out the attack. The bulk of the novel is devoted to each of the detailed transactions of the 100-day operation, from purchasing and smuggling arms to arranging a multitude of clandestine business deals." Libr J

Forsyth, Frederick

The **fourth** protocol. Viking 1984 389p

LC 83-40646

This novel "succeeds magnificently on at least two . . . levels: as a scrupulously detailed study of spy 'tradecraft' and as a testament to the virtues of a well-constructed plot. We want to know what happens in this book not only because of the inherently dramatic situation, but also because we anticipate the sense of resolution that comes when the puzzle's last piece clicks securely into place." Booklist

Forsyth, Frederick

★ The **Odessa** file. Viking 1972 337p

"Young German reporter Peter Miller comes upon the diary of a survivor of a World War II extermination camp at Riga. Its revelations lead him into the deadly pursuit of commandant Roschmann, known as the Butcher of Riga. Roschmann is engaged in an international scheme to destroy the Jewish state. The plan is promoted by the Odessa, a secret organization that protects the identities and fortunes of former SS members. Miller infiltrates the organization to find and expose Roschmann." Shapiro. Fic for Youth. 3d edition

"Forsyth skillfully blends fact and fiction into a suspenseful and detailed story which is often downright chilling in its credibility." Libr J

Forsyth, Frederick

The **veteran.** St. Martin's Press 2001 367p

ISBN 0-312-28691-0

Whispering wind, set during the Indian wars in 1876, focuses on a frontier scout who survived the massacre at the Little Bighorn

These stories "showcase the author's ability to capture character and generate suspense in remarkably few words." Booklist

Fortier, Anne

✓ **Juliet**; a novel. Ballantine Books 2010 447p $25

ISBN 978-0-345-51610-7; 0-345-51610-9

LC 2010-02093

"American Julie Jacobs travels to Siena in search of her Italian heritage—and possibly an inheritance—only to discover she is descended from 14th-century Giulietta Tomei, whose love for Romeo defied their feuding families and inspired Shakespeare's Romeo and Juliet. Julie's hunt leads her to the families' descendants, still living in Siena, still feuding, and still struggling under the curse of the friar who wished a plague on both their houses. Julie's unraveling of the past is assisted by a Felliniesque contessa and the contessa's handsome nephew, and complicated by mobsters, police, and a mysterious motorcyclist. . . . Fortier navigates around false clues and twists, resulting in a dense, heavily plotted love story that reads like a Da Vinci Code for the smart modern woman." Publ Wkly

Fossum, Karin

Bad intentions; translated from the Norwegian by Charlotte Barslund. Houghton Mifflin Harcourt 2011 213p $24

ISBN 978-0-547-48334-4; 0-547-48334-1

LC 2010-49773

Original Norwegian edition, 2008; this translation first published 2010 in the United Kingdom

This Konrad Sejer mystery "focuses on three young men—the disturbingly intuitive Axel Frimann, the bumbling drug addict Philip Reilly, and the painfully sensitive Jon Moreno. They've been friends forever, but something happens that alters the dynamic among them and causes the unbalanced Moreno to abruptly throw himself out of a small boat into a lake outside Oslo called, appropriately, Dead Water. Sejer and his partner, Jacob Skarre, find no evidence of murder, but something is off, as suggested by Frimann and Reilly altering the details of the suicide. When the body of a 17-year-old Vietnamese immigrant, Kim Van Chau, surfaces in another lake, Sejer discovers that the trio were at the same party as Chau the night he went missing." Publ Wkly

Fossum, Karin

Broken; translated from the Norwegian by Charlotte Barslund. Houghton Mifflin Harcourt 2010 265p $25

ISBN 978-0-15-101366-1; 0-15-101366-7

LC 2010-05730

Original Norwegian edition, 2006; English translation first published 2008 in the United Kingdom

"A woman wakes up in the middle of the night. A strange man is in her bedroom. She lies there in silence, paralyzed with fear. The woman is an author and the man one of her characters, one in a long line that waits in her driveway for the time when she'll tell their stories. He is so desperate that he has resorted to breaking into her house and demanding that she begin. He, the author decides, is named Alvar Eide, forty-two years old, single, works in a gallery. He lives a quiet, orderly life and likes it that way—no demands, no unpleasantness. Until the icy winter morning when a young drug addict, skinny and fragile, walks into the gallery." Publisher's note

Fossum, Karin

The **caller**; Karin Fossum; translated from the Norwegian by K.E. Semmel. 1st ed. Houghton Mifflin Harcourt 2012 244 p. (hardcover) $25.00

ISBN 9780547577524

LC 2012005736

This thriller mystery novel, by Karin Fossum, is part of the Inspector Sejer series. "[A] child is covered in blood. . . and Sejer spends the evening trying to understand why anyone would carry out such a sinister prank. Then, just before midnight, somebody rings his doorbell. . . . From his living room window, the inspector watches a figure disappear into the darkness. Inside [an] envelope Sejer finds a postcard bearing a short message: Hell begins now." (Publisher's note)

Foster, Alan Dean

Dinotopia lost. Turner Pub. (Atlanta) 1996 318p

ISBN 978-0441009213

LC 95-41352

"The plot revolves around a band of pirates whose ship miraculously survives the reefs around Dinotopia and who set out to turn what they find there to profit. Will Denison, the nineteenth-century discoverer of the symbiotic humansaurian society, is dragged into taking a leading part in defeating the pirates, most of whom are converted to the Dinotopian way of life. . . . Although the saurian characters are better limned than the human ones, Foster's addition to Dinotopiana will agreeably reward the fantastic place's many fans." Booklist

Foster, Alan Dean

✓ **Kingdoms** of light. Warner Bks. 2001 372p $24.95

ISBN 0-446-52667-3

LC 00-43501

"Foster's brand of storytelling, lighthearted even at the darkest moments, doesn't leave much room for doubt about how it's all going to turn out. Fans of swift-moving plots and imaginative settings will overlook the thin characters and enjoy this pleasant fantasy tale." Publ Wkly

Foster, Alan Dean

The **mocking** program. Warner Bks. 2002 279p

ISBN 0-446-52774-2

LC 2002-22851

"Like Anthony Burgess' A Clockwork Orange, this novel comes with a glossary to help readers translate the characters' slang (a combination of English and Spanish, mostly). Peppered with clever new technology and offbeat characters, the book successfully crosses genres and will appeal to both mystery and sf fans." Booklist

Foster, Alan Dean

✓ **A triumph** of souls. Warner Bks. 2000 406p $24.95

ISBN 0-446-52218-X

LC 99-41376

Concluding volume in the author's Journeys of the Catechist trilogy; previous titles Carnivores of light and darkness (1998) and Into the thinking kingdoms (1999)

"Set in a magical world with prehistoric overtones, the novel offers more wit and wandering than plot, but the inventive situations are engaging and the characters far more complex than they first appear. The ending is clever and will satisfy those who have made the fantastic trek through Foster's whimsical world." Publ Wkly

Foulds, Adam

The **quickening** maze. Penguin Books 2010 258p pa $15

ISBN 978-0-14-311779-7; 0-14-311779-3

LC 2009-40218

First published 2009 in the United Kingdom

"To be sure, there are inherent drawbacks to historical fiction. To guess at the words and thoughts of long gone people risks inaccuracy at best and disservice at worst. Foulds's Clare is a less sophisticated version of the real poet. But the essence of the man, his sweet, courageous, fine spirit, is real enough in this deeply rewarding fiction." Boston Globe

Fountain, Ben

★ **Billy** Lynn's long halftime walk; Ben Fountain. Ecco 2012 307 p.

ISBN 0060885599; 9780060885595

LC 2011275813

This "novel takes place over a single Thanksgiving Day, when the eight soldiers [of the Iraq War] . . . find themselves at the promotional center of an all-American extravaganza, a nationally televised Dallas Cowboys football game. Providing the novel with its moral compass is protagonist Billy Lynn, a 19-year-old virgin from small-town Texas who has been . . . documented by an embedded Fox News camera." (Kirkus Reviews)

Fowler, Karen Joy

The **Jane** Austen book club. Putnam 2004 288p $23.95

ISBN 0-399-15161-3

LC 2003-47244

This novel is essentially a "character study of six people who meet regularly over several months to discuss six of Austen's works. Jocelyn, in her 50s and never married, is the originator of the club, a control freak who handpicked all the members; Sylvia, her good friend, is in a funk because her husband of 32 years has just left her for another woman; Sylvia's daughter, Allegra, is an attractive 30-year-old lesbian who recently broke up with her lover; Prudie is a twentysomething high school French teacher; the much-married Bernadette, 67, is now single; and Grigg, in his 40s, would love to get married." Libr J

Fowler, Karen Joy

★ **Sarah** Canary. Holt & Co. 1991 290p

ISBN 0-8050-1753-4

LC 91-9746

"This novel is similar in scope to E. L. Doctorow's 'Ragtime,' and yet Ms. Fowler's book is as much a dreamscape as a panorama. Each of her 19 chapters has a contemporaneous and often cryptic epigraph from Emily Dickinson's poetry that, amazingly, seems to dictate the narrative that follows." N Y Times Book Rev

Fowler, Karen Joy

Sister Noon; a novel. Putnam 2001 321p $24.95

ISBN 0-399-14750-0

LC 00-46025

"In Gilded Age-era San Francisco, fortyish spinster Lizzie Hayes is by any measure a good woman. She busies herself with worthy, conservative projects, especially her role as volunteer treasurer and fund-raiser for the Ladies' Relief and Protection Society Home. She does what is expected when it is expected. None in her circle suspects that a risk-taking spirit hides just beneath the surface. But when Lizzie crosses paths with the influential—and notorious—Mrs. Mary Ellen 'Mammy' Pleasant, opportunities for intrigue, passion, and subversion abound, and Lizzie plunges in with enthusiasm. This witty novel is a deft blend of historical fact, urban myth, social satire, and romance." Libr J

Fowler, Karen Joy

We Are All Completely Beside Ourselves; Karen Joy Fowler. GP Putnam And Sons 2013 320 p. (hardcover) $26.95

ISBN 0399162097; 9780399162091

LC 2013000988

This novel, by Karen Joy Fowler, follows "the Cooke family: Mother and Dad, brother Lowell, sister Fern, and our narrator, Rosemary, who begins her story in the middle. . . . 'I spent the first eighteen years of my life . . . raised with a chimpanzee,' she tells us. . . . 'She was my twin, my funhouse mirror, my whirlwind other half, and I loved her as a sister.'" (Publisher's note)

Fowler, Karen Joy

What I didn't see and other stories. Small Beer Press 2010 197p $24

ISBN 978-1-932520-68-3; 1-931520-68-2

LC 2010-25911

An "engrossing and thought-provoking set of short stories that mix history, sci-fi, and fantasy elements with a strong literary voice. Whether examining the machinations of a Northern California cult, in 'Always,' or a vague but obviously horrific violent act in the eerie title story, the PEN/Faulkner finalist displays a gift for thrusting familiar characters into bizarre, off-kilter scenarios. Fowler never strays from the anchor of human emotion that makes her characters so believable, even when chronicling the history of epidemics, ancient archeological digs, single family submersibles, or fallen angels." Publ Wkly

Fowler, Therese Anne

★ **Z**; A Novel of Zelda Fitzgerald. Therese Anne Fowler. 1st ed. St. Martin's Press 2013 375 p. (hardcover) $25.99

ISBN 1250028655; 9781250028655

LC 2013003452

This novel by Therese Anne Fowler follows "Jazz Age legends F. Scott and Zelda Fitzgerald. . . . The famous couple have a whirlwind courtship in Montgomery, Ala., where Scott was briefly stationed at the end of WWI, and Zelda was the talk of the town. Then Fowler unfolds the next 20 years: the couple's New York celebrity after 'This Side of Paradise'; the years in Paris with the other 'Lost Generation' expats; and their return to the U.S. to treat Zelda's schizophrenia." (Publishers Weekly)

Fowles, John

★ The **French** lieutenant's woman. Little, Brown 1969 467p

"The setting is Victorian England. The hero is Charles, respectable, well-to-do, thoughtful, progressive. He is engaged to Ernestina, a rich, attractive, but highly conventional girl, but he falls in love with the beautiful, tragic, mysterious Sarah who is known to Lyme Regis (where the action begins) as 'the French lieutenant's woman' because of some disreputable but romantic episode in her past life. The situation, that of the amorous triangle, is familiar in fiction. What makes this book highly original is that it has three possible endings, all different. . . . We have here a highly readable and informative book, compelling, thrilling, erotic, but we are not permitted to relax as if we were reading Dickens or Thackeray. A very modern mind is manipulating us as well as the characters." Burgess. 99 Novels

Fowles, John

The **magus**; a revised version. with a foreword by the author. Little, Brown 1978 656p
ISBN 0-440-35162-6

LC 77-17343

Originally published 1966; this version first published 1977 in the United Kingdom

"With the narrative skill and literary sleight of hand . . . Fowles again provides hours of engrossing entertainment for an audience susceptible to a massive blend of sensuous realism, suspenseful romanticism, hypertheatrical mystification, psychic intervention, and a gallery of unusual or exotic characters in the vivid setting of the golden, craggy, threatening beauty of an isolated Greek island." Booklist

Frame, Janet, 1924-2004

★ **Between** my father and the king; new and uncollected stories. by Janet Frame. Pgw 2013 256 p. (hardcover) $26.00
ISBN 1619021692; 9781619021693

This book is a collection of stories from award-winning late author Janet Frame. "Thirteen of the 28 stories in this collection were unpublished in her lifetime." Included are "The Gravy Boat," "I Got a Shoes," "A Night at the Opera" and "Gorse is Not People." The last three "concern themselves with the insane and the institutions where they waste away, patronized and abused." (Kirkus Reviews)

Frame, Janet, 1924-2004

Prizes; selected short stories. Counterpoint 2009 294p $26
ISBN 978-1-58243-515-2

Frame "is as famous for her epic personal history as for her career. Her first collection, The Lagoon and Other Stories, published in 1954, was written while Frame stayed in a mental hospital. This new anthology spans her lifetime and includes the best of four published collections—The Lagoon and Other Stories, Snowman Snowman: Fables and Fantasies, The Reservoir: Stories and Sketches, and You Are Now Entering the Human Heart—plus five previously unpublished stories. Often melancholy but containing wonderful

detail, imagery, and emotion, her works cover a wide range of topics like childhood, madness, relationships, identity, and more." Libr J

Frame, Janet

Towards another summer. Counterpoint 2009 216p $24
ISBN 978-1-58243-476-6; 1-58243-476-X

LC 2008-50515

Written in 1963; first published 2007 in New Zealand

"Like every writer worth remembering, Frame exploits—or creates on the page, to be absolutely puristic about it—her peculiar sensibility, her private window into the universal.. . . Frame's sad, slyly comic fish-out-of-water story . . . looks back to Virginia Woolf in its focus on the tortuous internal positionings beneath the surface of apparently casual conversation." N Y Times Book Rev

Frame, Ronald

The **lantern** bearers; a novel. Counterpoint 2001 224p $24
ISBN 1-58243-155-8

LC 2001-28897

First published 1999 in the United Kingdom

"Neil Pritchard, told that he will die of cancer within two years, presses forward with his book on the Scottish composer Euan Bone. He also tells in this book the story of his encounter with Bone shortly before the composer's death. Neil, 14 then and a superb boy soprano, was summering with his aunt in a southern Scottish coastal town when Bone enlisted him to help prepare a vocal score based on a Robert Louis Stevenson essay. All went beautifully, and Neil was falling in love with Bone; then his voice changed, ending the collaboration. . . . In a resentful funk, he told the lie that Bone had molested him, which led, Neil came to think, to Bone's demise." Booklist

Francis, Clare

Wolf winter. Morrow 1988 558p
ISBN 0-688-06376-4

LC 87-24209

First published 1987 in the United Kingdom

"The skill with which the author counterpoints her several plot lines to create a mounting sense of tension is exemplary. . . . 'Wolf Winter' has a sure dramatic sense, minutely realized settings and—most important—the sort of casual style that easily delivers the large amounts of information that are essential to this sort of entertainment." N Y Times Book Rev

Francis, Dick

10 lb. penalty. Putnam 1997 273p $24.95
ISBN 0-399-14302-5

LC 97-28020

"As usual in a Francis novel, the sweetest parts are about family; here, especially the growing love and understanding between father and son. The villains aren't particularly scary, but this smooth, nimbly paced charmer isn't really about bad people anyway, but about how the rest of us cope and live, sometimes in their shadow." Publ Wkly

Francis, Dick

★ **Bolt**. Putnam 1987 318p

LC 86-25167

"As adept on a race-course as he is in an Eaton Square drawing room, Fielding is a match for any menace. . . . In mystery circles, Francis again demonstrates that he is both a win and a nice read." Time

Francis, Dick

Even money; [by] Dick Francis and Felix Francis. G.P. Putnam's Sons 2009 350p $26.95

ISBN 978-0-399-15591-8; 0-399-15591-0

LC 2009-24109

"Ever since he started writing with his son Felix, Dick Francis seems to have found fresh inspiration at the racetrack." N Y Times Book Rev

Francis, Dick

Field of thirteen. Putnam 1998 287p $24.95

ISBN 0-399-14434-X

LC 98-28720

"Many of the stories were written in the 1970s and originally appeared in British and American sporting magazines, but a few have never been published before, thus offering a rare and unexpected treat for Francis' legions of loyal fans." Booklist

Francis, Dick

Longshot. Harper & Row 1990 320p

LC 90-41145

"Francis remains one of the most incandescent talents in the mystery game. His plot positively shimmers, and his sleuth easily hurdles that always difficult jump from credible character to believable amateur detective. Perhaps best of all, Francis extracts a wealth of weird and wonderful shadings from his suspects." Booklist

Francis, Dick

Nerve. Harper & Row 1964 273p

"Rob Finn, a young steeplechase jockey, had been near Art Mathews when Mathews shot himself at the Dunstable races. When asked why the man had killed himself, Finn replied, 'Mr Kellar might know.' Then other jockeys began having trouble and finally Finn was involved." Publisher's note

Francis, Dick

Proof. Harper & Row 1985 334p

LC 84-15940

"Wine merchant Tony Beach is engaged to supply a horse trainer's garden party. During the party a horse van careens into the marquee, bringing disaster. One of the casualties is a restaurant owner suspected of serving cheap liquor under false labels, and Beach, as an expert taster, is enlisted to track the bootleggers. Francis gives the same fascinating and authoritative detail about the liquor trade as he does about the racing world (which figures intermittently in this book as background)." Libr J

Francis, Dick

Shattered. Putnam 2000 289p $25.95

ISBN 0-399-14660-1

LC 00-55937

It was young glassblower Gerard Logan's "misfortune to have been entrusted with the videotape of a valuable medical secret by his best friend, a jockey who dies in a dreadful racing accident at Cheltenham. Not having the slightest clue as to the contents of the tape, which is stolen before he can blink, Logan enlists the aid of some brave and burly friends to trace the tape. . . . Francis' formula is made for excitement, not subtlety, so the eerie serenity of the glass blower's studio provides a nice breather from the choreographed displays of bruising action that keep the author on his toes." N Y Times Book Rev

Francis, Dick

Smokescreen. Harper & Row 1973 213p

First published 1972 in the United Kingdom

"Even given Francis's high standards {this novel is} an elegant construction, in which we see the parts and their potentialities, and are as much excited to discover how he put them together as what happens when he does. . . . A symphony tumultuous with thrills." Times Lit Suppl

Francis, Dick

★ **Whip** hand. Harper & Row 1980 293p

First published 1979 in the United Kingdom

"The book contains moments of breathless suspense, much information about the sport of kings, and perceptive insights into Halley's character that explain some of the reasons for the breakdown of his marriage." Shapiro. Fic for Youth. 3d edition

Franck, Julia

The **blindness** of the heart; translated from the German by Anthea Bell. Grove Press 2010 424p $24.95

ISBN 978-0-8021-1967-4; 0-8021-1967-0

Original German edition, 2007; this translation first published 2009 in the United Kingdom

The novel's "central character, Helene Würsich, is the daughter of a printer who returns maimed and ruined from the battlefields of World War I, leaving Helene and her older sister Martha in the power of their mentally unstable mother Selma, 'the foreign woman'—meaning Jewish, in the disapproving view of the local community. Martha, a nurse, develops a taste for drugs while clever but introverted Helen, unsympathetically treated by Selma, never fulfills her potential. A legacy saves the family's fortunes, the girls move to Berlin to live with a racy aunt and Helene falls in love with a student, only to lose him. As the political mood darkens and Selma is incarcerated for possible hereditary disorders, Helene's future is shaped by another man, Wilhelm, a keen supporter of the new regime who nevertheless agrees to risk 'racial disgrace' and arrange false papers certifying her Aryan descent. But their marriage brings no happiness and a prologue and epilogue expose the emotional damage arising from a long sequence of disasters." Kirkus

Frank, Dorothea Benton

Folly Beach. Harper 2011 358p $25.99

ISBN 978-0-06-196127-4; 0-06-196127-2

"The recently widowed protagonist's journey to rediscovering joy and love will thrill readers, especially with the addition of a suavely integrated story-within-a-story involving a one-woman play about the lovers who wrote Porgy and Bess. There's a certain authenticity to the lives Frank tells that will resonate with many women. Frank's telling of this tale will help readers celebrate love and sexuality after 60." Publ Wkly

Frank, Pat

Alas, Babylon; a novel. Lippincott 1959 253p

"This is an extraordinarily real picture of human beings numbed by catastrophe but still driven by the unconquerable determination of living creatures to keep on being alive. The writing is simple and straightforward and practical." New Yorker

Frankel, Laurie

Goodbye for now; a novel. Laurie Frankel. 1st ed. Doubleday 2012 289 p. (paperback) $15.00; (hardcover) $25.95

ISBN 9780307951274; 0385536186; 9780385536189

LC 2011051266

This novel, by Laurie Frankel, follows "Sam Elling[, who] works for an internet dating company . . . [and] meets the love of his life, . . . Meredith. . . . When Meredith's grandmother . . . dies suddenly, Sam . . . create[s] a computer program that will allow Meredith to have one last conversation with her grandmother . . . from all her correspondence. . . . Meredith loves it, and the couple begins to wonder if this is something that could help more people through their grief." (Publisher's note)

Franklin, Ariana

Mistress of the art of death. Putnam 2007 384p $25.95

ISBN 978-0-399-15414-0; 0-399-154140

LC 2006-24710

"It is 1171 in Cambridge, England, and Henry II is beside himself. Four children have been found murdered and mutilated, and the townsfolk of Cambridge are blaming the Jews, who have taken shelter in the castle. King Henry is less concerned about the murderer than the tax revenue he is losing while the Jewish community languishes in the fortress. He appeals to the king of Sicily to send him a master of the art of death—one who can look at the deceased and determine how he or she died. Adelia, a mistress of this art, arrives with a group of returning pilgrims. Along with a eunuch escort named Mansur and Simon of Naples, a Jew with an affinity for detection, she must piece together the mystery of these hideous crimes before the monster kills again. I. . . This novel will surely please mystery fans as well as lovers of historical fiction." Libr J

Franklin, Ariana

The **serpent's** tale. G. P. Putnam's Sons 2008 371p $25.95

ISBN 978-0-399-15464-5

LC 2007-38585

"When Rosamund Clifford, Henry II's mistress, is poisoned, Dr. Vesuvia Adelia Rachel Ortese Aguilar must draw on her formidable forensic skills to try to uncover the killer. The prime suspect is Henry's estranged wife, Queen Eleanor of Aquitaine, who once plotted to overthrow the king. Adelia reunites with Rowley Picot, now a bishop as well as the father of Adelia's child, and the two set out on a dangerous journey, during which they brave a blizzard and Eleanor's band of ruthless mercenaries." Publ Wkly

"This excellent adventure delivers high drama and lively scholarship from its heroine's feminist perspective." N Y Times Book Rev

Franklin, Miles

The **end** of my career; the sequel to My brilliant career. with a foreword by Verna Coleman. Harper & Row 1981 234p

First published 1946 in Australia with title: My career goes bung

"This book is at times a delicious satire on morals and manners. At other times it is a heart-rending tract for feminism. Always it is entertaining and filled with wisdom and universal truths." Christ Sci Monit

Franklin, Miles

★ **My** brilliant career. Putnam 1980 232p

First published 1901 in Scotland

"The novel's heroine, Sybylla Melvyn, a girl of sixteen, rebels against the stagnant life on her parents' dairy farm at Possum Gully and against the inevitable fate of teaching or marriage that awaits her; both forms of 'slavery' are distasteful to her but she sees marriage as particularly degrading. Rescued temporarily by a period with her affluent grandmother at the congenial station homestead, Caddagat, she faces interwoven problems—her sexual ambivalence which is characterized by strong physical attraction to eligible young squatter, Harold Beecham, and an equally strong physical revulsion." Oxford Companion to Australian Lit

Followed by The end of my career

Franklin, Tom

Crooked letter, crooked letter. William Morrow 2010 274p

ISBN 0-06-059466-7; 978-0-06-059466-4

LC 2010005423

"Franklin writes with quiet economy. There are no great flights of dialogue or rambling description; everything is sharply focused to achieve its purpose. The resulting novel winds through its path as crookedly as the letters of its title, and arrives at a nicely achieved ending. It's an ending that isn't without complication but, given what precedes it, a conclusion that is fitting and right." Denver Post

Franklin, Tom

Hell at the breech; a novel. Morrow 2003 520p $23.95

ISBN 0-688-16741-1

LC 2002-40982

"When a storekeeper campaigning for the state legislature is assassinated, Mitcham Beat is swept by a wave of violence that includes lynchings and shootings, barn burnings, and robberies. A gang of hooded men known as the Hell-at-the-Breech gang is terrorizing the community, and the only man to stop them is an aging sheriff ready to retire with his whiskey bottle. It sounds like the wild, wild West, but Franklin. . . has taken a little-known event in Alabama history, the Mitcham Beat War, and transformed it into a Faulknerian tale of bloody revenge and vigilante justice." Libr J

Franklin, Tom

Smonk; or, Widow town; being the scabrous adventures of E.O. Smonk & of the whore Evavangeline in Clarke County, Alabama, early in the last century. . . William Morrow 2006 254p $23.95

ISBN 978-0-06-084681-7; 0-06-084681-X

LC 2006-43835

"E.O. Smonk is an ugly, unwashed, murdering rapist who has terrorized the small town of Old Texas, Ala., for years. In 1911, the town summons Smonk to stand trial, and a nonstop blood-orgy of brutality and destruction is the result. . . . After Smonk's goons assault the Old Texas courthouse and kill the town's menfolk, reformed former Smonk associate turned lawman Will McKissick pursues Smonk. Meanwhile, a posse of Christian deputies chase teenage whore Evavangeline through the Gulf Coast, but the girl is a skilled killer, too, and the trail of her victims spans the region. . . Fast-paced and unrelentingly violent, Franklin's western isn't for everyone, but readers looking for a strange and savage tale can't go wrong." Publ Wkly

Franzen, Jonathan, 1959-

★ The **corrections**. Farrar, Straus & Giroux 2001 568p $25

ISBN 0-374-12998-3

LC 2001-33478

The novel "has the absorbing treacheries of married life, the comic squalors of cruise-shop travel and the shenanigans of global capitalism. It also has language that builds in powerful, rolling strides. And it has characters, the separately unraveling Lamberts, who get very deeply under your skin." Time

Franzen, Jonathan, 1959-

★ **Freedom**. Farrar, Straus and Giroux 2010 562p $28

ISBN 0374158460; 9780374158460

LC 2010-10273

This multigenerational novel follows the fortunes of the Berglund family of St. Paul.

"Patty and Walter Berglund meet at the University of Minnesota, settle in an initially rundown section of St. Paul, and raise two precocious kids. She's a former student athlete rebelling against her politician mom back East; he's a lawyer–turned–environmental advocate bristling at the legacy of his distant, alcoholic dad. Each has a charged relationship with Walter's ex-roommate, alt-rock musician Richard Katz, but the pair's biggest obstacle to happiness is each other — and themselves. Franzen performs a kind of literary MRI on the marriage, micro-slicing its many nuances. He innately grasps how desires can shift in an instant, and how getting what we want can lead to disappointment or self-doubt. And he remains a keen observer of modern culture. . . . Freedom isn't flawless: Patty's journal reads more like Franzen than his character, and he gets sidetracked by quirky tangents. But

this is a deep dive into a fascinating family that feels very real, and fully grounded in our time." Entertainment Wkly

Fraser, George MacDonald

The **reavers**. Alfred A. Knopf 2008 267p $24

ISBN 978-0-307-26810-5; 0-307-26810-1

LC 2007-50904

First published 2007 in the United Kingdom

"Set on the border between England and Scotland, the plot (if it can be called that) revolves around a Spanish effort, led by the mysterious La Infamosa, to kidnap King James and replace him with an impostor. Attempting to foil her are the ravishing Lady Godiva Dacre and her dimwitted companion, Kylie, along with Gilderoy, part-time highwayman and Scotland's best-known secret agent, and Archie Noble, English 'double-nought' secret agent and ostensible hero of the tale. After a series of hilarious complications, the unlikely foursome finds itself at La Infamosa's cave just as the coup is about to take place. A piece of inspired silliness and a worthy companion to the Flashman tales." Libr J

Frayn, Michael

Headlong; a novel. Metropolitan Bks. 1999 342p

ISBN 0-8050-6285-8

LC 99-20717

Martin Clay "seems to have all he might reasonably wish for: a new career as an art historian, a loving wife, an adorable baby daughter, and a summer cottage in the English countryside, where he is supposed to be completing his book on fifteenth-century Netherlandish art. Instead, he stumbles upon an unsigned Brueghel (at least, he's almost positive it's a Brueghel) stashed in a fireplace of his neighbor's crumbling estate. Overwhelmed by high-minded professional curiosity and base greed, Martin resolves to acquire it by whatever means necessary. What follows is part detective story, part art-history lesson, part cautionary tale, and entirely funny." New Yorker

Frayn, Michael

Spies; a novel. Metropolitan Bks. 2002 261p

ISBN 0-8050-7058-3

LC 2001-39840

"A compelling story about secrecy and betrayal. . . . What is truly remarkable about this novel, though, is the way Frayn perfectly captures the dynamics of childhood friendships." Booklist

Frazier, Charles, 1950-

★ **Cold** Mountain. Atlantic Monthly Press 1997 356p $19.95

ISBN 0-87113-679-1

LC 97-275

"After Inman, a Confederate soldier, is gravely wounded outside Petersburg, he decides to flee the war. With his fearsome LeMat's pistol for protection, he sets out for Cold Mountain, where he was raised and where he left Ada, the woman he loves, on uncertain terms four years earlier. In the meantime, Ada, a preacher's daughter transplanted to the country from Charleston, has begun to learn the hard reality of a farmer's life. This novel's landscape is finely drawn, full of dark beauty and presentiment, and so are its characters.

They give voice to a classical, peculiarly American feeling of nostalgia—the pain of returning home" New Yorker

Frazier, Charles, 1950-

Nightwoods; a novel. Random House 2011 259p $26

ISBN 978-1-4000-6709-1; 1-4000-6709-X

LC 2011-14629

"At the center of Frazier's tale — set in Appalachia in the early 1960s — is Luce, a scarred woman with a dark past who's taken a job as the caretaker of an abandoned old lodge. The solitude suits her. . . . But the outside inevitably intrudes on Luce's isolated retreat, first in the form of her recently murdered sister's mute twin children, then with the unexpected appearance of the murderer, Bud, who's chasing the two terrified young witnesses to his crime. Not surprisingly, things get messy, but Nightwoods is no typical thriller. It hits hard because you come to care so much about the characters, all of them drawn with that precise enchanted prose. By the book's climactic scenes in the shadowy mountain forest that gives Nightwoods its title, the unhurried, poetic suspense is both difficult to bear and impossible to shake." Entertainment Wkly

Frazier, Charles, 1950-

Thirteen moons; a novel. Random House 2006 422p $26.95

ISBN 0-375-50932-1

LC 2007-270081

The author "uses his sense of time and place and his lyrical, pointillist prose to give the reader an aching appreciation of the Indians' plight. . . . [He] recounts Will's melancholy adventures with plenty of narrative brio, giving the reader a succession of suspenseful—and in some cases touching— set pieces." N Y Times (Late N Y Ed)

Freda, Joseph

The patience of rivers; a novel. Norton 2003 351p $24.95

ISBN 0-393-05176-5

LC 2002-13330

"It is 1969, and Nick Lauria is spending his final summer before college hanging out with his best friend, Charlie Miles, while working at his family's campgrounds in Delaware Ford, a small New York town just up the road from the farm where Woodstock is to be held. Nick spends his spare time trying to bed Darlene Van Vooren, the youngest of the three gorgeous Van Vooren sisters. But beneath the surface of Nick's idyllic existence, his family is in trouble." Publ Wkly

"This is an appealing coming-of-age tale set to a classic rock soundtrack." Libr J

Freed, Lynn

The curse of the appropriate man. Harcourt 2004 188p pa $13

ISBN 0-15-602994-4

LC 2004-5914

Freed is "expertly equipped to dissect the defiant longings and treacherous pleasures of the daughters and mothers, lovers and adventurers whom she imagines in her fiction." Washington Post Book World

Freedman, Benedict

Mrs. Mike; the story of Katherine Mary Flannigan. by Benedict and Nancy Freedman; drawings by Ruth D. McCrea. Coward-McCann 1947 312p

"At 16, Boston-reared Katherine Mary O'Fallon is sent north to Alberta, Canada, to find relief for the pleurisy from which she has been suffering. While residing with her Uncle John, she falls in love with Mike, a handsome Canadian Mounted Policeman. Life in the wilderness in the early 1900s is harsh, but the newly married couple finds joy and challenge in their adventures." Shapiro. Fic for Youth. 3d edition

Freeling, Nicolas

A dwarf kingdom. Mysterious Press 1996 213p

ISBN 0-89296-615-7

LC 96-11954

In this mystery Inspector Henri Castang "retires from the Brussels police force. Recoiling from the savage murders of two dear friends, Castang and his wife, Vera, retreat to a villa they have inherited in Biarritz. The living is easy, but Castang is too curmudgeonly to fall into a mental stupor. . . . Sure enough, someone kidnaps his infant granddaughter, and the real estate mogul who has been buzzing around his well-situated property grows increasingly menacing. For Castang, there is no escape, after all, from the 'dwarfish greed' or the gnomish values of his constant nemesis, the ruthless power elite of the abominable bourgeoisie." N Y Times Book Rev

Freeling, Nicolas

One more river. Mysterious Press 1998 214p

ISBN 0-89296-616-5

LC 97-52323

"John Charles, a 70-year-old English expatriate living in the south of France, is jolted out of his complacency (as 'a writer of acknowledged distinction, with an individual prose style') when someone takes a shot at him in the garden of his secluded cottage—which his attackers later burn down. 'Pleased to find himself excited' by the violent turn his placid life has taken, Charles thinks he can escape danger by keeping on the move, in a trek that returns him to scenes (and secrets) of his youth in the Netherlands, Germany and England. . . . Despite the fatalism of the bleak ending, this is a wondrous, strange trip through a very fine mind." N Y Times Book Rev

Freeling, Nicolas

Sand castles. Mysterious Press 1990 209p

ISBN 0-89296-372-7

LC 89-43144

First published 1989 in the United Kingdom

"Like his idiosyncratic hero and heroine—he bashes the Dutch, she the French, for example—Freeling rewards with his oblique, subtly comic style." Publ Wkly

Freely, Maureen

Enlightenment. Overlook Press 2008 398p $24.95

ISBN 978-1-59020-074-2; 1-59020-074-8

First published 2007 in the United Kingdom

"In 1970 Istanbul, Jeannie, the daughter of an American CIA agent, falls in love with Sinan, a student radical who is alienated from America by its persistent support of Turkish corruption. Sinan is imprisoned on trumped-up charges, but years later, the lovers reunite and marry, living peacefully for a while. Then, without warning, on a visit to the States, Sinan is arrested by Homeland Security as a suspected terrorist, leaving Jeannie scrambling to reach her husband and recover their child from foster care. When Jeannie, too, disappears, a reporter unearths truths that alter our perception of all that has transpired." Libr J

Freeman, Brian

The **bone** house. Minotaur Books 2011 342p $24.99

ISBN 978-0-312-56283-0; 0-312-56283-7

LC 2010-41088

"The 'ship-in-a-bottle world' of Door County's landscape, the raw beauty of the Lake Michigan coast, the remoteness of harbor towns like Fish Creek (despite being 'choked with tourists in August') are all captured beautifully, and, more importantly, mirror the emotional lives of the characters." Milwaukee J Sentinel

Freeman, Brian

Stripped. St. Martin's Minotaur 2006 368p $24.95

ISBN 978-0-312-34044-5

LC 2006-045827

"Freeman strengthens his plot with well-shaped characters with complex personalities. . . . His new lieutenant resents Jonathan and has saddled him with Amanda Gillen, a thoughtful cop with quite a few secrets. We hope Freeman will have years to excavate Stride's flawed and complicated personality. But Freeman doesn't just invest in his series hero. Each character gets a full-court press. There's not a character that Freeman doesn't make the reader care about." PopMatters

Freeman, Castle

All that I have; a novel. [by] Castle Freeman Jr. Steerforth Press 2009 164p pa $13.95

ISBN 978-1-58642-151-9; 1-58642-151-4

LC 2008-43223

"Sheriff Lucian Wing, the narrator of Freeman's wonderfully wry fourth novel, is a laconic, old-fashioned lawman who discovers an outpost of nefarious Russians in his sleepy Vermont county. Wing's Fargo-esque delivery is hysterical, but what makes this spare tale a standout is Freeman's keen ear for dialogue and his affection for the quietly complex characters of small-town life." People

Freeman, Castle

★ **Go** with me; [by] Castle Freeman, Jr. Steerforth Press 2008 160p $21.95

ISBN 978-1-58642-139-7; 1-58642-137-9

LC 2007-42572

"This nimble thriller is the literary equivalent of a fierce bantamweight fighter: Short but muscular and lightning quick, it packs a surprising punch . . . . Freeman has a flawless ear for dialogue and a sharp eye for quirky detail." People

Freemantle, Brian

Bomb grade. St. Martin's Press 1997 407p

ISBN 0-312-14565-9

LC 96-48769

First published 1996 in the United Kingdom with title: Charlie's chance

"Mr. Freemantle suggests that what makes Charlie's personal life so precarious is exactly what makes him so successful in his profession, since talk filled with deception and evasion is a basic tool of his trade. Watching this spy at work is like watching a stunted genius play Mozart perfectly, even as the rest of his life threatens to crumble around him." N Y Times Book Rev

Freemantle, Brian

Dead men living. St. Martin's Press 2000 345p

ISBN 0-312-24379-0

LC 99-462044

"Siberia's harsh climate and Moscow's volatile politics are in clear focus as slippery, upper-class Brits and powerful Americans toss monkey wrenches into Charlie's plans." Publ Wkly

Freemantle, Brian

Mind /reader. St. Martin's Press 1998 475p

ISBN 0-312-18654-1

LC 98-4484

"Criminal profiler Claudine Carter has joined Europol, Europe's version of the FBI, after her husband's tragic suicide. Hoping to escape her grief, Claudine throws herself into a horrifying case involving a serial killer who is leaving bloody body parts at public sites across Europe. . . . Freemantle is at the top of his form, with a cunningly devious plot, riveting suspense, strong characters, and enough stunning twists to keep even seasoned readers from guessing the shocking conclusion." Booklist

Freethy, Barbara

Golden lies; Barbara Freethy. Signet 2004 408p (pbk.) $8.99

ISBN 978-0451211262; 045121126X

LC 2004574887

In this book, "[w]hen security expert Riley McAllister helps his grandmother haul a wagonload of old junk to the 'Antiques on the Road' show, he doesn't think she'll get more than five dollars for the lot. But the moment the dragon hits TV screens, collectors are on them like a pack of hungry wolves, especially the owner of the House of Hathaway, San Francisco's most prestigious antiques emporium. Against his better judgment, Riley entrusts the dragon to Paige Hathaway for appraisal, which turns out to be a big mistake when the dragon goes missing. Paige and Riley's search for the object d'art takes them on a fast-paced adventure through the streets of San Francisco, from fashionable Union Square to funky Chinatown, where Paige discovers the existence of her half-sister Alyssa Chen." (Publishers Weekly)

Frei, Max

The **stranger's** magic; Max Frei; translated by Polly Gannon and Astamur Moore. Overlook Press 2012 320 p. $27.95

ISBN 1590204794; 9781590204795

This is the third book in the "Labyrinth of Echo" series. Max Frei has "come into some good luck by having been placed in a position of power in the Unified Kingdom, chasing around the ever-weird city of Echo 'to investigate cases of illegal magic and battle trespassing monsters from other worlds.'" Frei "investigates some . . . capers, including the possibility of a palace coup, an attempted murder and a bungled burglary." (Kirkus)

French, Albert
★ **Billy**. Viking 1993 214p
ISBN 0-670-85013-6

LC 93-14676

"The story, once in motion, gathers momentum like a landslide. . . . 'Billy' is tragedy in the classical mode, mythic in the sense that instead of the surprise, the twists of plot we might discover in a more typical contemporary novel, here we are confirmed in our worst dreads as destiny immutably and shockingly unfolds." NY Times Book Rev

French, Marilyn
Her mother's daughter; a novel. Summit Bks. 1987 686p il

LC 87-7061

The author "continues to imbue what used to be dismissed as 'women's issues' with the significance they deserve. . . . Ms. French continues to write about the inner lives of women with insight and intimacy. What she's given us this time is a page-turner with a heart." N Y Times Book Rev

French, Marilyn
★ The **women's** room. Summit Bks. 1977 471p
LC 77-24918

"Dealing with the interlocking lives of dozens of American women, who know each other at some point of time between the 1950s and the 70s, and concentrating in particular on the evolution of Mira from petted baby girl wife to independent womanhood, it speaks from the heart to women everywhere. . . . {The author's} dialogue, her characterizations, her knowledge of the changing relationships, sexual and otherwise, between men and women in a complex world of shifting values, are all extraordinary. Mira, the suburban housewife and mother, the unexpected divorcee groping her way out of a marriage that she never understood, going back to Harvard at 38 as a graduate student, meeting other women, some tougher, some weaker, coming to terms with herself against all odds, even if it means a bleak and lonely parting from a man she loves, is memorable." Publ Wkly

French, Nicci
Beneath the skin. Mysterious Press 2000 378p $24.95
ISBN 0-89296-726-9

LC 00-101483

French "gives the killer terrifying presence through the perverse 'love' letters he sends to his victims. . . . But, in a stylistic twist that is rare for this genre, the focus of the suspense remains locked on his victims, smart, articulate women who reveal their escalating fears in intimate first-person narratives that are insightful and also sad, because the lessons learned come too late." N Y Times Book Rev

French, Nicci
★ **Blue** Monday; Nicci French. Pamela Dorman Books/Viking 2012 322 p. map
ISBN 0670023361; 9780670023363

LC 2011039747

"The abduction of five-year-old Matthew Farraday provokes national outcry and a desperate police hunt. And when his face is splashed over the newspapers, psychotherapist Frieda Klein is left troubled: one of her patients has been relating dreams in which he has a hunger for a child. A child he can describe in perfect detail, a child the spitting image of Matthew. Detective Chief Inspector Karlsson doesn't take Frieda's concerns seriously until a link emerges with an unsolved abduction twenty years ago and he summons Frieda to interview the victim's sister." (Publisher's note)

"With its smart plot, crisp prose, and a stunning final twist, this is psychological suspense at its best. Absolutely riveting." Booklist

French, Nicci
Land of the living. Warner Bks. 2003 341p $23.95
ISBN 0-446-53151-0

LC 2002-33149

In the "opening scenes, 25-year-old Abbie Devereaux finds herself blindfolded and shackled in some filthy hole, the victim of a kidnapping she can't recall. Through sheer luck Abbie escapes her prison, only to realize that no one in authority believes her story. . . . Although the thwarted killer who is still stalking Abbie is too real for us to share her terror of going mad, we're with her all the way in her gritty quest to forge a new identity and discover what went wrong with the old one." N Y Times Book Rev

French, Nicci
Tuesday's gone; Nicci French. Pamela Dorman Books/Viking 2013 384 p. (hardcover) $27.95
ISBN 0670025674; 9780670025671

LC 2012040052

This novel, by Nicci Gerard and Sean French, writing as Nicci French, follows their character Frieda Klein. "A London social worker makes a routine home visit only to discover her client, Michelle Doyce, serving afternoon tea to a naked, decomposing corpse. . . . Chief Inspector Karlsson again calls upon Frieda for help. She discovers that the body belongs to Robert Poole, con man extraordinaire. But Frieda can't shake the feeling that the past isn't done with her yet." (Publisher's note)

French, Tana
★ **Broken** Harbor; Tana French. Viking 2012 464 p. (alk. paper) $27.95
ISBN 9780670023653

LC 2011042397

This crime novel by Tana French follows "Mick 'Scorcher' Kennedy, the Dublin Garda's top homicide detective. . . . When he and his brand-new partner are assigned a savage triple homicide in a distant housing development, abandoned before completion when the Irish housing bubble burst, Scorcher is shaken; the development is located in a place that gave him the best -- and worst -- moments of his life." (Booklist)

French, Tana

Faithful Place; a novel. Viking 2010 400p $25.95

ISBN 978-0-670-02187-1; 0-670-02187-3

LC 2010-03212

"The first thing that Ms. French does so well in 'Faithful Place' is to inhabit fully a scrappy, shrewd, privately heartbroken middle-aged man. The second is to capture the Mackey family's long-brewing resentments in a way that's utterly realistic on many levels. Sibling rivalries, class conflicts, old grudges, adolescent flirtations and memories of childhood violence are all deftly embedded in this novel, as is the richly idiomatic Dublinese." N Y Times (Late N Y Ed)

French, Tana

In the woods. Viking 2007 429p $24.95

ISBN 978-0-670-03860-2; 0-670-03860-1

LC 2006-33498

French sets a vivid scene for her complex characters, who seem entirely capable of doing the unexpected. Drawn by the grim nature of her plot and the lyrical ferocity of her writing, even smart people who should know better will be able to lose themselves in these dark woods. N Y Times Book Rev

French, Tana

The likeness. Viking 2008 448p $25.95

ISBN 978-0-670-01886-4; 0-670-01886-4

LC 2008-003940

"Cassie Maddox, the partner of the self-destructing detective who narrated 'In the Woods,' is drawn into a ménage à cinq of college students living a seeming charmed existence in an Irish country house. One of the five, a girl who is Cassie's doppelgänger and has been living under an alias Cassie once used as an undercover narcotics agent, turns up murdered in a ruined cottage. Cassie is given the unlikely task of pretending to be a woman who was pretending to be a woman whom Cassie once pretended to be. As you might expect, 'The Likeness' wrestles with matters of identity and intimacy as its heroine comes to prefer this triply false life to her real one. The hypnotic prose and eerie atmosphere conspire to make this ostensible mystery novel much, much more than it appears to be." Salon.com

Fresan, Rodrigo

Kensington Gardens; translated from the Spanish by Natasha Wimmer. Farrar, Straus and Giroux 2006 370p $25

ISBN 0-571-22280-3

LC 2006-11391

Original Spanish edition, 2004; this translation first published 2005 in the United Kingdom

"For all its interest in the Peter Pan story, the novel is principally a homage to the 1960s. . . . Fresan is a consummate fan of pop culture . . . as well as a rank Anglophile, and his breathless rendition of an imaginary guest list at the ultimate Swinging Sixties party is the literary equivalent of an episode of the Rock'n'Roll Years television series." Times Lit Suppl

Freud, Esther

Love falls. Harper Perennial 2007 279p pa $13.95

ISBN 978-0-06-134961-4; 0-06-134961-5

"It's the summer of 1981, a mere week before Diana Spencer and Prince Charles are to be married. Lara, just turned 17, is embarking on a trip from London to Tuscany with her scholarly, travel-phobic father, Lambert, whom she has seen only sporadically since her early childhood. They are off to stay with one of Lambert's oldest friends. The expectation is obvious: this girl will come to know her elusive father; she will break out from her troubled, tentative girlhood and become a confident woman. Will she find a fairytale love as well? . . . [While the author's novel] follows this all-too-familiar arc, her depiction of Lara is so charming and observant, her writing so dynamic, that all the cliches of a youthful summer of self-discovery are transcended." N Y Times Book Rev

Freud, Esther

Lucky break; a novel. Bloomsbury USA 2011 310p pa $16

ISBN 978-1-60819-690-6

LC 2011-00971

"Nell, Dan, Jemma, and Charlie are among the nervous young actors arriving at London's renowned Drama Arts school. Dan and Jemma fall instantly in love and become the golden couple, while shy, awkward Nell struggles for recognition, and Charlie sails through on her fabulous looks. During the next 14 years, their fortunes rise and fall as they suffer the humiliation of auditions, make the right contacts, take work on its merits or for the money, and seek to make personal relationships work. . . . Ambition, luck, and jealousy all play their parts in this affecting portrait of the young and the talented." Booklist

Freudenberger, Nell

The dissident. Ecco 2006 427p $25.95

ISBN 978-0-06-075871-4; 0-06-075871-6

LC 2006-42617

This "novel centers on a Chinese performance artist and former political prisoner, who travels to Los Angeles to accept a teaching fellowship at a prestigious girls' school. His hosts are a well-off family whose matriarch, Cece Travers, is trapped in a loveless marriage with Gordon, a psychiatrist obsessed with tracing his genealogy back to 'the crossing ancestor.' A large cast of secondary characters includes Gordon's sister Joan, an accomplished but discontented novelist who stays skinny 'by worrying,' and his charming but irresponsible brother Phil, who is single-mindedly in love with Cece. Freudenberger demonstrates great talent for capturing the subtleties of cross-cultural and intergenerational relationships, as the dissident's struggles with his past and with his art intersect with Cece's unravelling." New Yorker

Freudenberger, Nell

Lucky girls; stories. HarperCollins Pubs. 2003 225p $22.95

ISBN 0-06-008879-6

LC 2003-44875

Contents: Lucky girls; The orphan; Outside the Eastern gate; The tutor; Letter from the last bastion

"A remarkably poised collection of stories about Americans abroad." N Y Times Book Rev

Freudenberger, Nell

✓ ★ The **newlyweds**; a novel. Nell Freudenberger. Knopf 2012 337 p.

ISBN 0307268845; 9780307268846

LC 2011044116

This book by Nell Freudenberger "examines a marriage arranged via the Internet. . . . Amina wanted to escape from her family's straitened circumstances in Bangladesh; George wanted someone who 'did not play games'. . . . So here she is, in the fall of 2005 in . . . Rochester, N.Y., recently married, working in retail while she studies for a teaching certificate. . . . [S]he's uncertain how to bridge the gulf between [her] two selves. She makes a much-needed friend in George's cousin Kim . . . so when it turns out that she and George have been hiding something important from Amina, it's . . . shattering. However, it does prompt George to agree to bring Amina's parents to America, and she goes to collect them in Bangladesh, where several old family conflicts flare anew." (Kirkus Reviews)

Frey, James

Bright shiny morning. Harper 2008 501p $26.95

ISBN 978-0-06-157313-2; 0-06-157313-2

LC 2008-09273

"When not resurrecting L.A.'s history or making lists of gangs, museums, universities, nationalities, homicides and artists, Frey focuses on four main stories: Old Man Joe, a homeless alcoholic whose attempt to help a meth addict goes terribly wrong; Amberton, a top actor whose obsession with a young man almost shatters his perfectly constructed life; Esperanza, a first-generation Latina who finds herself denying her intelligence and her family's dreams for her future just to survive; and Dylan and Maddie, a young couple fleeing abuse and violence in the Midwest who come looking for a house by the ocean only to find a new brand of horror." Newsday

"The worst bits of Morning are probably worse than anything else you'll read this year, but Frey is such a relentlessly entertaining storyteller that you just won't care." Time

Friedman, Daniel

✓ ★ **Don't** ever get old; Daniel Friedman. Minotaur Books 2012 viii, 294 p.p

ISBN 0312606931; 9780312606930

LC 2012005485

This book "introduces a highly unusual hero, 87-year-old, politically incorrect Buck Schatz, a former member of the Memphis PD. . . . [H]e agrees to a request to visit Jim Wallace, a soldier he served with in WWII who's on his deathbed. Wallace reveals that Heinrich Ziegler, the SS officer who ran the POW camp where both Schatz and Wallace were imprisoned, survived the war. On top of that shocker, Wallace reveals that he facilitated the Nazi's escape in exchange for a gold bar." (Publishers Weekly)

Friedman, Michael

Martian Dawn. Turtle Point Press 2006 149p pa $14.95

ISBN 1-885586-44-2

LC 2005-926844

The author "skewers Hollywood pomposity, environmental idealism, spiritual empowerment—and the surprising banality of a human outpost on Mars—with prose that's a marvel of economy, sardonic without excess sarcasm and rife with deadpan humor. Slight but sly, this is a scrumptious literary trifle." Publ Wkly

Fromm, Pete

As cool as I am. Picador 2003 388p $24

ISBN 0-312-30775-6

LC 2003-49869

This "coming-of-age story follows Lucy Diamond of Great Falls, Mont., for two years, from 14 o 16. They're turbulent years, but more so for Lucy because her parents, themselves married as teenagers, are both self-centered, trying to recapture the youth they feel they missed. Chuck, her father, appears only for a few days every few months; he is a charmer, and Lucy has inherited his humor and smart mouth. Though he claims to be a logger, it becomes clear that there must be other reasons for his long disappearances. Lucy's mother, Lainee, frustrated by her absent husband, has a long string of boyfriends, all of whom, like her husband, eventually disappear. Lucy, meanwhile, drifts into an affair with her best friend, scrawny, funny Kenny, whose divorced mother is an alcoholic." Publ Wkly

"Fromm explores the sexual evolution of a cynical teenage girl who has the spunk and wit to survive two flaky parents and the urges of unbridled adolescence." Booklist

Fuchs, Jake

Conrad in Beverly Hills. Raw Dog Screaming Press 2010 263p $29.95; pa $15.95

ISBN 978-1-933293-98-1; 1-933293-98-5; 978-1-933293-99-8 pa; 1-933293-99-3 pa

LC 2010-928478

"Professor Conrad Keppler, in residence at the University of Wisconsin at Cornflower . . . is increasingly obsessed by his childhood memories of growing up in Beverly Hills. He can clearly see his late father, a semi-famous screenwriter, cajoling a host of second-rate producers Conrad dubbed 'the Irvings.' He also remembers his campaign to rescue his dad from life as an 'ass-kissing screenwriter' and restore him to a respectable career writing serious fiction, a campaign that led to their estrangement. When Conrad discovers an unpublished, unfinished story his father wrote about their relationship, he determines, with the help of a beautiful and savvy colleague, to finish the story and write his way to the reconciliation he never actually experienced. Throughout this unusual novel, Conrad proves to be a quirky if brutally honest narrator, revealing his many sexual obsessions, deep-seated confusion over his Jewish identity, and thinning patience for academic protocol. Fuchs, himself the son of a screenwriter, brings a droll sense of humor and a richly detailed sense of place to this original and memorable family story." Booklist

Fuentes, Carlos

The **campaign**; translated by Alfred Mac Adam. Farrar, Straus & Giroux 1991 246p

LC 91-9723

Original Spanish edition, 1990

"The novel takes on huge themes: revolution versus justice, the illusion of human perfectibility, the value of tradition against the appeal to reason. Though set in the past, it is not trapped in it. Mr Fuentes might equally be writing about modern revolutions." Economist

Fuentes, Carlos

The **crystal** frontier; a novel in nine stories. translated from the Spanish by Alfred Mac Adam. Farrar, Straus & Giroux 1997 266p

ISBN 0-374-13277-1

LC 97-11230

Original Spanish edition published 1995 in Mexico

"Leonardo Barroso is an unscrupulous Mexican oligarch whose fortress of a villa is only a short drive from the 'crystal frontier' of the title, and each one of the nine stories comprising this work explores the life of someone touched by him." Libr J

Fuentes, Carlos

★ The **death** of Artemio Cruz; translated from the Spanish by Alfred MacAdam. Farrar, Straus & Giroux 1991 307p

LC 90-43280

Original Spanish edition published 1962 in Mexico; first English translation by Sam Hileman published 1964

"As the novel opens, Artemio Cruz, former revolutionary turned capitalist, lies on his deathbed. He drifts in and out of consciousness, and when he is conscious his mind wanders between past and present. The story reveals that Cruz became rich through treachery, bribery, corruption, and ruthlessness. As a young man he had been full of revolutionary ideals. Acts committed as a means of self-preservation soon developed into a way of life based on opportunism. A fully realized character, Cruz can also be seen as a symbol of Mexico's quest for wealth at the expense of moral values." Merriam-Webster's Ency of Lit

Fuentes, Carlos

Destiny and desire; a novel. translated by Edith Grossman. Random House 2011 415p $27

ISBN 978-1-4000-6880-7; 1-4000-6880-0

LC 2010-15078

Original Spanish edition, 2008

"A towering work. No character enters its pages lightly, and escape for each carries a price. Fuentes's language is rich, evoking character, place and, perhaps most memorably, the human decisions that propel society. It is a novel of wheels turning within wheels and of convoluted but ultimately meaningful connections." Denver Post

Fuentes, Carlos

The **eagle's** throne; translated by Kristina Cordero. Random House 2006 336p $26.95

ISBN 1-4000-6247-0

LC 2006-40806

Original Spanish edition, 2003

While Fuentes is "concerned, as always, about the destiny of his native country, his story focuses more on down-and-dirty political means than serious political ends, leaving us to draw our own conclusions about what sort of good can possibly come of his characters' byzantine strategies and counterstrategies–their opportunistic alliances, their calculated secret-keeping and secret-leaking, their posturing, their watchful waiting, their sly brutalities. What results is the most wickedly entertaining novel of Fuentes's career." N Y Times Book Rev

Fuentes, Carlos

Happy families; stories. translated by Edith Grossman. Random House 2008 331p $26

ISBN 978-1-4000-6688-9; 1-4000-6688-3

LC 2008-02335

Original Spanish edition, 2006

"Certainly, there aren't many 'happy families' to be found in these pages — more like miniature cyclones of emotion that oscillate between loyalty and betrayal, devotion and rebellion. These 16 stories, like most of the author's fiction, spotlight his home country, though more often than not it's portrayed in less-than-rose-colored hues." San Francisco Chron

Fuentes, Carlos

★ The **old** gringo; translated by Margaret Sayers Peden. Farrar, Straus & Giroux 1985 199p

ISBN 0-374-22578-8

LC 85-16266

Original Spanish edition published in Mexico

"We have in this novel a fastidious American governess stranded in Pancho Villa's revolution, where she attracts the erotic interest of an intellectual fellow countryman and a nature-boy Mexican general. On this inanely trite foundation Mr. Fuentes has erected a narrative of brilliant complexity and sophistication, describing brisk military action and philosophically contrasting national character, or social tradition, or styles of revolt, or regional strengths, weaknesses, and prejudices." Atlantic

Fuentes, Carlos

The **years** with Laura Diaz; translated by Alfred MacAdam. Farrar, Straus & Giroux 2000 516p

ISBN 0-374-29341-4

LC 00-37648

"The novel begins in 1999 when photographer Santiago Lopez-Alfare arrives in Detroit to film a documentary about Mexican muralists in the U.S. There he comes across the image of an unnamed woman immortalized on the mural of the famous Diego Rivera. He soon realizes that 'those almost golden eyes, mestizo, between European and Mexican' belonged to his great-grandmother, Laura Diaz. Thereafter, the novel recounts the life of Diaz, from the settlement of her German grandparents in Mexico in the late 1800s . . . to her experience of the Mexican Revolution and its aftermath." Booklist

Fuentes, Norberto

The **autobiography** of Fidel Castro; translated by Anna Kushner. W.W. Norton & Co. 2009 572p il $27.95

ISBN 978-0-393-06899-3; 0-393-06899-4

LC 2009-31601

An abridged version of a two-volume edition originally published in Spanish, 2004

"Most Cubaphiles will find Fuentes' effort to be a masterful act of ventriloquism, offering a Castro who is prideful, intuitively Machiavellian and relentlessly cynical. . . . Fuentes is the beneficiary of the superb editing and translation of Anna Kushner, whose deftness reminds one of Natasha Wimmer." San Francisco Chron

Includes bibliographical references.

Fugard, Lisa

Skinner's drift; a novel. Scribner 2006 304p $25

ISBN 0-7432-7299-4

LC 2005-44145

"Ten years after leaving South Africa, Eva von Rensburg returns to her homeland because her estranged father is dying. Reluctant to visit him, owing to a dark secret she discovered as a child, Eva spends most of her time drinking in her hotel room, making arrangements for his care, and preparing to sell the family farm. Avoiding the past, however, only serves to bring it to the surface, and Eva remembers with guilt and shame the pain and isolation of growing up in a time of political unrest and class distinction. Set against the vivid landscape and wildlife of the African landscape, this first novel conveys a message of redemption and forgiveness that holds true whether it's concerning a country and its people or a father and his daughter." Libr J

Fuller, David

Sweetsmoke; a novel. Hyperion 2008 310p $24.95

ISBN 978-1-40132-331-8; 1-40132-331-6

LC 2008-01939

"In a bizarre bit of literary artifice, Fuller uses quotation marks for white dialogue but not black. (Aren't all men punctuated equal?) And within this framework, Fuller gives Cassius a mostly plain, vaguely bookish vernacular. . . . Yet if you read Fuller's novel mainly for its fast-paced plot, 'Sweetsmoke' can be captivating." N Y Times Book Rev

Fulmer, David

The **blue** door. Harcourt 2008 325p $25

ISBN 978-0-15-101181-0; 0-15-101181-8

LC 2007-19423

A mystery set in 1962 Philadelphia. "Eddie Cero, a welterweight boxer with too many serious injuries, meets up with Sal Giambroni, who hires him to tail a businessman. Eddie discovers he has a natural bent for this work and is soon taking on a three-year-old cold case involving a rising soul singer. Offering a vivid portrait of Philly's heyday as a music scene (think American Bandstand), Fulmer's latest mystery is an excellent choice for patrons who like George Pelecanos and a good dollop of music in their mysteries." Libr J

Fulmer, David

Jass; David Fulmer. Harcourt 2005 334p map o.p.; (pbk.) $14.00

ISBN 0151010250; 9780156031912

LC 2004011620

In this book, set "[i]n the rowdy red-light district of Storyville, four players of the new music they call 'jass' have turned up dead. When Creole detective Valentin St. Cyr begins to investigate, he discovers that every one of the victims once played in the same band, and the only one left alive has gone into hiding. As he digs deeper, Valentin becomes convinced that a shadowy woman is the key to the mystery. His efforts to find her touch nerves, and soon Tom Anderson, known as the 'King of Storyville,' police lieutenant J. Picot, and even the mayor of New Orleans want him off the case. It's all the proof Valentin needs that there is something even larger and darker at the heart of this sordid business." (Publisher's note)

Fulton, Alice

The **nightingales** of Troy; stories of one family's century. W.W. Norton 2008 254p $23.95

ISBN 978-0-393-04887-2; 0-393-04887-X

LC 2008-13206

"These 10 linked short stories by MacArthur fellow Fulton track the lives of four generations of women from Troy, N.Y., where 'love comes to die.' The first story begins in 1908, and subsequent stories are spaced approximately a decade apart, creating a colorful patchwork of the 20th century. . . . Fulton's strengths are in elaborate detail and delicate construction. And many stories also contain moments of blunt violence and unthinking cruelty, providing the tension at the heart of a book that's rich with feeling for its characters yet willing to expose their faults." Publ Wkly

Furnivall, Kate

The **red** scarf; a novel. Berkley Books 2008 470p pa $15

ISBN 978-0-425-22164-8; 0-425-22164-4

LC 2007-40037

"Sophia Morozova's relationship with fragile Anna Fedorina begins through a small act of kindness at a 1930s Siberian labor camp. As the two inmates struggle daily to survive, they increasingly rely on each other for hope and comfort; when Anna falls ill, Sophia escapes, intending to find Anna's lifelong love, Vasily, and rescue Anna. Beautiful and charismatic, Sophia quickly becomes a force to reckon with in the town of Tivil, where she hopes to find Vasily, and her connections with powerful gypsy Rafik, the handsome factory director Mikhail Pashin and the stern but unreadable Aleksei Fomenko become satisfying sources of danger and desire. Furnivall . . . paints a stark picture of rampant scarcity, grim regimentation and blaring propaganda in pre-WWII Soviet Russia." Publ Wkly

Furst, Alan

Blood of victory; a novel. Random House 2002 237p

ISBN 0-375-50574-1

LC 2002-21312

This thriller "revolves around a plan to disrupt the flow of Romanian oil to the Third Reich. As usual, Furst adheres strictly to the rules of the genre: the protagonist, a Russian expatriate writer, is seduced into service both by the prospect of heroism and by a mysterious Frenchwoman, and embarks on a globetrotting, spy-versus-spy adventure. But his debts to convention work in his favor. Densely atmospheric and genuinely romatic, the novel is most reminiscent of the Hollywood films of the forties, when moral choices were rendered not in black-and-white but in smoky shades of gray." New Yorker

Furst, Alan

Dark voyage; a novel. Random House 2004 256p $24.95

ISBN 1-400-06018-4

LC 2004-46674

The protagonist of this novel is "E. M. DeHaan, the captain of the Dutch tramp freighter Noordenham, a ship without a home since the Nazis invaded Holland. It's 1941 when DeHaan accepts . . . his new assignment: disguised as a Spanish freighter, the Noordendam will be deployed on secret assignments for the British." Booklist

Furst, Alan

The **foreign** correspondent; a novel. Random House 2006 273p $24.95

ISBN 1-4000-6019-2

LC 2006-40417

"In an interview in 2002, Furst said that he had difficulty understanding why none of his bestselling novels had yet been filmed. With no apparent preciousness about what might be lost in a transfer to the screen, he added, 'These really are movies.' In a sense, this is true. He has the ability to invent plots that work all on their own, which is, as Somerset Maugham once pointed out, a very rare gift indeed." Atlantic Monthly

Furst, Alan

✓ Kingdom of shadows; a novel. Random House 2001 272p

ISBN 0-375-50337-4

LC 00-32344

"In Paris in 1938, Nicholas Morath, a Hungarian aristocrat, enjoys the benefits of his wealth and breeding—benefits that include the company of a beautiful young Argentine girlfriend and control of a successful advertising firm. But the rumblings of the Third Reich are drawing nearer, and when Morath's uncle and benefactor, Count Janos Polanyi enlists Nicholas to help fight Fascism back in Hungary the playboy becomes a political operative. . . . The novel's most attractive feature is its matter-of-fact suspense: Furst vigilantly restricts Nicholas's perspective, refusing to allow him anachronistic insight into the history being made around him, and this strategy helps reinvigorate one of the century's frequently told stories." New Yorker

Furst, Alan

✓ ★ Mission to Paris; a novel. Alan Furst. Random House 2012 272 p. map (hbk.) $27.00; (hbk.) $27.00

ISBN 1400069483; 9781400069484

LC 2012450028

This book is set in 1938, when "film star Fredric Stahl is on his way to Paris to make a movie for Paramount France. The Nazis know he's coming--a secret bureau within the Reich Foreign Ministry has for years been waging political warfare against France . . . . For their purposes, Fredric Stahl is a perfect agent of influence, and they attack him. What they don't know is that Stahl . . . has become part of an informal spy service being run out of the American embassy in Paris." (Publisher's note)

Furst, Alan

Red gold. Random House 1999 258p

ISBN 0-679-45186-2

LC 98-24409

Sequel to The world at night (1996)

"It's 1941, and Jules Casson is back in Paris, on the run from the Gestapo and trying to stay alive without attracting attention. Drawn back into the resistance by an intelligence officer he knows from Dunkirk, Casson soon finds himself in the middle of an ill-advised plot to smuggle arms to the Communists. It all goes wrong, of course, as Casson and a Jewish girl he falls in love with struggle to tell the good guys from the bad." Booklist

"Furst proves himself a master at capturing the bleak and mean mood of wartime Paris." N Y Times Book Rev

Furst, Alan

★ Spies of the Balkans; a novel. Random House 2010 268p $26

ISBN 978-1-4000-6603-2; 1-4000-6603-4

LC 2010-07755

Furst "is not in the least imitative—he has own style, and intricate sense of detail—but in his hands the mastery of the traditional spy novel has firmly passed to the other side of the Atlantic, and all I can say is that Eric Ambler and Graham Greene would have read his books with pleasure, and that somebody like Orson Welles (think of him playing Harry Lime in The Third Man) or Otto Preminger could have made a marvelous movie out of Spies of the Balkans. A pity that it probably won't happen—somehow, Furst seems to write in black and white, not Technicolor, just as Greene did—but in the meantime, this is a book, written for adults, to sit down and read in one gulp if you can." Daily Beast

Furst, Alan

The **spies** of Warsaw; a novel. Random House 2008 266p $25

ISBN 978-1-4000-6602-5; 1-4000-6602-6

"Rather than Eric Ambler thrillers or Graham Greene entertainments, the comparisons Mr. Furst's novels most often draw, they might more accurately be seen as extended series of Talk of the Town pieces. There's the same soupçon of irony, the expert deployment of detail and, above all, a thick helping of knowingness—only with military secrets, machine pistols and Gestapo agents instead of celebrity quirks or outer-borough oddities." N Y Observer

The **Future** Is Japanese. Haikasoru 2012 365 p. (paperback) $14.99

ISBN 9781421542232

This anthology of Japanese-themed fiction, edited by Nick Mamatas, Masumi Washington, and Haikasoru, contains "thirteen stories from and about the Land of the Rising Sun [which] run the gamut from fantasy to cyberpunk." Topics include "[a] web browser that threatens to conquer the world, . . . [t]he longest, loneliest railroad on Earth, . . . [a]nd yes, giant robots." (Publisher's note)

Fyfield, Frances

★ **Blind** date. Viking 1998 264p

ISBN 0-670-87889-8

LC 98-21218

First published 1992 in the United Kingdom

"Haunted by her sister's murder and humiliated by her failure, as a police officer on the case, to find the killer, {Elizabeth Kennedy} retreats to her womblike quarters in a London church belfry to recover from a near-fatal mugging that just about destroyed whatever strength and dignity she had left. Here she rages over her miserable condition . . . unaware of how close the killer is to her and to her family, and without a clue of the danger to three of her friends." N Y Times Book Rev

The plotting is "masterly, and Fyfield's critique of society—the real concern of the best crime thrillers—is seriously unsettling." Times Lit Suppl

Fyfield, Frances

Undercurrents. Viking 2001 278p $23.95

ISBN 0-670-89636-5

LC 00-43806

First published 2000 in the United Kingdom

"Dark humor occasionally flashes through the narrative, but Fyfield's latest is primarily a grim, tense story about regret, loneliness and leaving well enough alone. In Warbling, she's created a memorable setting. It's a harsh, foreboding town populated by people—disappointed, judgmental, distrustful—who deserve such a place." Publ Wkly

G

Gabaldon, Diana

A **breath** of snow and ashes. Delacorte Press 2005 979p $28

ISBN 0-385-32416-2

LC 2005-51948

Previous titles in the Oulander series: Outlander (1991); Dragonfly in amber (1992); Voyager (1994); Drums of autumn (1997); The fiery cross (2001)

In this sixth title in the Outlander series, the author "unfolds the continuing story of the Frasers, heartbreakingly heroic highlander Jamie and his time-traveling wife Clare. Set during the three years leading up to the American Revolution, this . . . [novel] maps both violent loss and strong family ties. On the eve of war much is changing on Fraser's Ridge and Jamie and Claire encounter much harm. This vivid and haunting novel, therefore, brings an aching sadness, but it is balanced with sheer joy, revelation, and solace. The large scope of the novel allows Gabaldon to do what she does best, paint in exquisite detail the lives of her characters." Booklist

Followed by: An echo in the bone

Gabaldon, Diana

Dragonfly in amber; Diana Gabaldon. Delacorte Press 1992 743p. $17.00

ISBN 9780385302319; 0385302312

LC 9204904

Sequel to: Outlander (1991)

This book "follows time-traveler Claire Randall and her 18th-century Scottish husband, James Fraser, to the court of Louis XV in 1744, as they seek to forestall the disaster due to overtake the Scottish Highlands at the battle of Culloden Moor the following year. Having learned from Claire about the forthcoming disaster, James, the son of a Highland chief, gains Prince Charles's friendship in order to subtly sabotage Jacobite efforts to raise funds for an invasion of Britain. When James is banished, . . . he and Claire leave France convinced they have accomplished their purpose. They . . . [soon] learn of Prince Charles's landing in Scotland and his signing of James's name to a declaration of the Stewart right to rule, effectively forcing the couple to the Jacobite cause and a fate they are unable to prevent." (Publishers Weekly)

Gabaldon, Diana

Drums of autumn; Diana Gabaldon. Delacorte Press 1996 880p (hbk.) $30.00

ISBN 9780385311403; 0385311400

LC 96014035

This novel follows "Claire Randall, the post-WWII bride of historian Frank Randall, [as she] steps through a skew in the Scottish stone circle Craigh na Dun and lands in Revolutionary America and the arms of Highlander Jamie Fraser. . . . [A] believing Catholic, Claire struggles to live a rich and moral life . . . under these extraordinary circumstances. Claire's adventures in 18th-century Charleston alternate with . . . chapters devoted to her 20th-century daughter, Brianna. Raised as Frank Randall's child, Bree discovers that Jamie Fraser is her real sire. She takes off on a harrowing, confrontational quest through time and space with her suitor, Roger Wakefield, in hot pursuit." (Publishers Weekly)

Gabaldon, Diana

An **echo** in the bone. Delacorte Press 2009 820p $30

ISBN 978-0-385-34245-2; 0-385-34245-4

This seventh Outlander title "covers approximately two years during the heart of the Revolutionary War, beginning in July 1776. Brianna and Roger Mackenzie have traveled back through the stones to 1980 to get the health care for their infant daughter that was unavailable in the 18th century. Jamie Fraser and his beloved time-traveling wife Claire, having survived the fire that burned down their home in the hills of North Carolina, are making plans to sail back to Scotland to retrieve Jamie's printing press so he can fight on the American side with the pen instead of the sword. Meanwhile rich, powerful but tormented homosexual Lord John Grey finds himself in coastal North Carolina catching up with his adoptive son William Ransom, who is anxiously waiting to prove his worth in the British army. . . . There's no lack of action in the novel, and the Revolutionary War setting provides an opportunity for the characters to cross paths with such notable luminaries as Benjamin Franklin, Nathan Hale and Benedict Arnold." Romance Reader

Gabaldon, Diana

The **fiery** cross; Diana Gabaldon. Delacorte Press 2001 ix, 979p $30

ISBN 0385315279 (alk. paper)

LC 2001047063

Romantic Times Reviewers' Choice Award: Historical (2001)

This book follows "time traveler Claire Randall, now firmly ensconced in the past with her daughter, Brianna, and Brianna's husband, Roger, [who] finds herself and her . . . husband, Jamie, at a critical juncture. It is 1771, and the first stirrings of the American Revolution are being felt in the mountains of North Carolina where Jamie, despite being a Catholic, has been given an enormous tract of land by the governor and is ordered to raise a militia. Having learned about the Revolution from his 20th-century wife and daughter, Jamie uneasily complies with the governor's orders and is immensely relieved when the crisis passes and the militia is disbanded." (Publishers Weekly)

Gabaldon, Diana

Outlander; Diana Gabaldon. Delacorte Press 1991 627p. (hc) $30.00

ISBN 9780385302302; 0385302304

LC 90019122

RITA Awards: Romance of the Year (1991)

In this novel, "English nurse Claire Beauchamp Randall and husband Frank take a second honeymoon in the Scottish Highlands in 1945. When Claire walks through a cleft stone in an ancient henge, she's somehow transported to 1743. She encounters Frank's evil ancestor, British captain Jonathan 'Black Jack' Randall, and is adopted by another clan. Claire nurses young soldier James Fraser, a gallant, merry redhead, and the two begin a romance. . . . Scenes of the Highlanders' daily life blend . . . with Scottish wit and humor. Eventually Sassenach (outlander) Claire finds a chance to return to 1945, and must choose between distant memories of Frnak [sic] and her happy, uncomplicated existence with Jamie." (Publishers Weekly)

Gabaldon, Diana

Voyager; Diana Gabaldon. Delacorte Press 1994 viii, 870p $30

ISBN 0385302320

LC 93021907

This book, set "more than 20 years after Claire Randall's] trip to 18th-century Scotland," follows the modern-day heroine, "now a doctor and the mother of a daughter fathered by a man from the distant past" as she "seeks to return in search of her beloved." (Library Journal)

Gaddis, William, 1922-1998

Agape agape; afterword by Joseph Tabbi. Viking 2002 113p

ISBN 0-670-03131-3

LC 2002-20676

"Gaddis has compressed 50 years of research on the social history of the player piano into a novel narrated by a dying elderly man who is as concerned with his own physical collapse as he is with his piano-based literary project. . . . As usual, Gaddis's avant-garde style requires patience and staying power from readers, who must parse long, el-liptical sentences that wander from idea to idea while barely advancing the narrative. But his thoughts and ruminations remain fascinating and challenging." Publ Wkly

Includes bibliographical references

Gaddis, William

A **frolic** of his own; a novel. Poseidon Press 1994 586p

ISBN 0-671-66984-2

LC 93-26098

"The medium is exceptionally dense. The mere effort of sorting out the voices, of tracking them, can be exhausting. . . . In any case, I hope the reader will persevere. 'A Frolic of His Own' is an exceptionally rich, even important novel." N Y Times Book Rev

Gaddis, William, 1922-1998

The **recognitions**; William Gaddis; introduction by William H. Gass. Dalkey Archive Press 2012 956p.

ISBN 9781564786913

LC 2011031304

This book "is a . . . work about art and forgery, and the increasingly thin line between the counterfeit and the fake. [Author William] Gaddis anticipates by almost half a century the crisis of reality that we currently face, where the real and the virtual are combining in alarming ways, and the sources of legitimacy and power are often obscure to us." (Publisher's note)

Gaffney, Patricia

Circle of three; a novel. HarperCollins Pubs. 2000 421p $24

ISBN 0-06-019375-1

LC 00-33521

This tale "follows three generations of women through one tumultuous year. The book centers on recently widowed Carrie, who sees the grieving process as a chance to reinvent herself. But for Ruth, her 15-year-old daughter, it simply precipitates the onset of parent/child separation. Dana, Carrie's 70-year-old mother, isn't grieving; she's too busy trying to direct her daughter's life." Libr J

"Gaffney has each woman narrate in turn, providing added dimension to this poignant story of growing up and growing old." Booklist

Gaffney, Patricia

Flight lessons; a novel. HarperCollins Pubs. 2002 388p

ISBN 0-06-018528-7

LC 2001-51934

"At 36, Anna Catalano is going home to the Eastern Shore of Maryland after finding her boyfriend in bed with her boss and best friend. For some reason she is more upset with her friend than with her boyfriend, maybe because history seems to be repeating itself. Anna walked in on her father and her aunt Rosa in the same position 20 years ago, and even though her mother was dead, Anna could never forgive Rosa, the guiding force in her life, although she did absolve her father. Now Anna is returning to help Rosa run the family restaurant, having flitted from job to job and man to man all this time. . . . The novel is filled with touching insights into family relationships." Booklist

Gaige, Amity

Schroder; Amity Gaige. Twelve 2013 288 p. $21.99

ISBN 1455512133; 9781455512133

LC 2012013882

In this novel by Amity Gaige "young Eric Schroder--a first-generation East German immigrant--adopts the last name Kennedy to more easily fit in, a fateful white lie that will set him on an improbable and ultimately tragic course. 'Shroder' relates the story of Eric's urgent escape years later to Lake Champlain, Vermont, with his six-year-old daughter, Meadow, in an attempt to outrun the authorities amid a heated custody battle with his wife." (Publisher's note)

Gaiman, Neil, 1960-

★ **American** gods; a novel. Morrow 2001 465p $26

ISBN 0-380-97365-0

LC 2001-30407

"A noirish sci-fi road trip novel in which the melting pot of the United States extends not merely to mortals but to a motley assortment of disgruntled gods and deities. Early in 'American Gods' we are introduced to Shadow, a man who has been released from prison only to learn that his wife has died in a car crash. With nothing to return home to, Shadow accepts a job protecting Mr. Wednesday, an omniscient one-eyed grifter. . . . Soon the ex-convict finds himself in an alternate universe, where he is haunted by prophetic nightmares and visited by his dead wife." N Y Times Book Rev

Gaiman, Neil

★ **Anansi** boys. William Morrow 2005 336p il $26.95; pa $7.99

ISBN 978-0-06-051518-8; 0-06-051518-X; 978-0-06-051519-5 pa; 0-06-051519-8 pa

LC 2005-47176

"Fat Charlie's life is about to be spiced up–his estranged father dies in a karaoke bar, and the handsome brother he never knew he had shows up on his doorstep with a gleam in his eye. Next thing he knows, Fat Charlie is being investigated by the police, his fiancée's falling in love with the wrong brother, and he finds out that his father was the god Anansi, Trickster and Spider, and that the beast gods of folklore are plotting their own revenge upon his family bloodline. A fun book with a little of everything–horror, mystery, magic, comedy, song, romance, ghosts, scary birds, ancient grudges, and trademark British wit." Libr J

Gaiman, Neil

Fragile things; short fictions and wonders. William Morrow 2006 xxxi, 360p $26.95

ISBN 978-0-06-051522-5; 0-06-051522-8

LC 2006-48135

"Gaiman follows no overarching theme, but that is what makes these stories charming, at times creepy, and good fun. They read like dreams and meditations, with a stream-of-consciousness quality to their presentation. Gaiman also explains some of the inspiration behind the stories to help put them in perspective." Libr J

Gaiman, Neil

Good omens; the nice and accurate prophecies of Agnes Nutter, witch: a novel. [by] Neil Gaiman and Terry Pratchett. Workman 1990 354p

ISBN 0-89480-853-2

LC 90-50362

"The end of the world is nigh! At least according to the prophecies of Agnes Nutter, a witch whose predictions are usually accurate but seldom heeded. Eleven years before the deadly Last Saturday Night, the ancient rivals of good and evil personified by the angelic Aziraphale (otherwise living as a London book dealer) and the demonic devil and former serpent Crowley clash in substituting the Antichrist during the birth of a baby. But the babies are switched as an unexpected third child enters the picture. The confusion picks up pace as witch hunters Sgt. Shadwell and Newton Pulsifer pursue modern Nutter follower Anathema Device. Along the way, countless puns, humorous footnotes, and satirical illusions enliven the story." SLJ

Gaiman, Neil, 1960-

★ The **Ocean** at the End of the Lane; Neil Gaiman. HarperCollins 2013 192 p. (hardcover) $25.99

ISBN 0062255657; 9780062255655

In this speculative fiction novel, by Neil Gaiman, a 7-year old boy seeks to banish an evil spirit with the help of the odd Hempstock family. "Despite his determination and well-developed sense of right and wrong, he's also a scared little boy drawn into adventures beyond his understanding, forced into terrible mistakes through innocence." (Kirkus Reviews)

Gaiman, Neil

Stardust. Avon Bks. 1999 238p hardcover o.p. pa $13.95; $30.00

ISBN 0-380-97728-1; 0-06-114202-6 pa; 9780062200396

LC 98-8773

"Young Tristran Thorn has grown up in the isolated village of Wall, on the edge of the realm of Faerie. When Tristran and the lovely Victoria see a falling star during the special market fair, Victoria impulsively offers him his heart's desire if he will retrieve the star for her. Tristran crosses the border into Faerie and encounters witches, unicorns, and other strange creatures." Libr J

Gaines, Ernest J.

★ The **autobiography** of Miss Jane Pittman. Dial Press (NY) 1971 245p hardcover o.p. pa $6.99

ISBN 0-553-26357-9 pa

LC 77-144380

"In the epic of Miss Jane Pittman, a 110-year-old ex-slave, the action begins at the time she is a small child watching both Union and Confederate troops come into the plantation on which she lives. It closes with the demonstrations of the sixties and the freedom walk she decides to make. This is a log of trials, heartaches, joys, love—but mostly of endurance." Shapiro. Fic for Youth. 3d edition

Gaines, Ernest J.

★ A **gathering** of old men. Knopf 1983 213p
hardcover o.p. pa $11.95

ISBN 0-394-51468-8; 0-679-73890-8 pa

LC 82-49000

"The story opens with the murder of Beau Boutan, a Ca-
jun farmer, on the Louisiana plantation of Candy Marshall, a
headstrong white owner. She claims to have done the shooting because she wished to protect one of her black workers,
Mathu, who has been like a guardian to her following the
death of her parents. In the plan to stand between Mapes,
the local sheriff, and Mathu, Candy has set into motion an
idea that has brought together a group of old black men with
shotguns (unloaded), all claiming to have done the shooting.
The threat of the South's way of punishing blacks by lynching hangs over the story like a pall. It meets opposition from
Beau's young brother who has been friends with a black
fellow-student and team-mate at his university." Shapiro.
Fic for Youth. 3d edition

Gaines, Ernest J.

★ A **lesson** before dying. Knopf 1997 256p
$26; pa $12.95

ISBN 0-679-45561-2; 0-375-70270-9 pa

LC 92-20335

First published 1993

"The story of two African American men struggling
to attain manhood in a prejudiced society, the tale is set in
Bayonne, La. . . in the late 1940s. It concerns Jefferson, a
mentally slow, barely literate young man, who, though an
innocent bystander to a shootout between a white store
owner and two black robbers is convicted of murder, and
the sophisticated, educated man who comes to his aid. When
Jefferson's own attorney claims that executing him would be
tantamount to killing a hog, his incensed godmother, Miss
Emma, turns to teacher Grant Wiggins, pleading with him to
gain access to the jailed youth and help him to face his death
by electrocution with dignity." Publ Wkly

"YAs who seek thought-provoking reading will enjoy
this glimpse of life in the rural South just before the civil
rights movement." SLJ

Gaitskill, Mary

Don't cry; stories. Pantheon Books 2009 226p
$23.95

ISBN 978-0-375-42419-9; 0-375-42419-9

LC 2008-25231

"There is always a moment in a Mary Gaitskill story
when you wince. And then you shrug. The wince means,
'Wow, that's a pretty creepy aspect of human nature to point
out,' while the shrug is a way of acknowledging, 'But it's
true. Life's really like that, isn't it?' The Gaitskill two-step
— that wince-and-shrug maneuver her work inspires — is
what elevates her above other fiction writers who, though
talented, are content to give us surfaces. Gaitskill never
stops at surfaces. She's too adventurous for that, too reckless. " Newsday

Gaitskill, Mary

Veronica. Pantheon 2005 227p $23
ISBN 0-375-42145-9

LC 2005-43143

The author's "fierce, night-blooming new novel is about
a close friendship between two women. But it should not
be confused with anything cozy. Imagine a buddy story
from the mind of William S. Burroughs, illustrated with
images by Robert Mapplethorpe or David Cronenberg, and
you get some idea of the tenderness to be found here. . . .
Ms. Gaitskill writes so radiantly about violent self-loathing
that the very incongruousness of her language has shocking
power." N Y Times (N Y Late Ed)

Galbraith, Douglas

The **rising** sun. Atlantic Monthly Press 2001
535p

ISBN 0-87113-781-X

LC 00-45336

"Galbraith's greatest achievement is in finding a voice
for his narrator, a tone and a vocabulary that sound plausibly
like those of a 17th century clerk without resorting to the
more onerous clichés and archaisms of historical fiction." N
Y Times Book Rev

Galchen, Rivka

Atmospheric disturbances. Farrar, Straus and
Giroux 2008 240p il $24

ISBN 978-0-374-20011-4; 0-374-20011-4

LC 2007-47327

It is on the "level of psychological realism rather than
postmodern invention, that 'Atmospheric Disturbances' succeeds, and where Ms. Galchen displays her real gifts as a
writer. As we come to learn, in a series of dropped hints, the
real story of Leo and Rema and their marriage, it becomes
clear that the particular form of Leo's delusion is anything
but accidental." N Y Sun

Galgut, Damon

The **impostor**. Black Cat 2009 249p pa $14
ISBN 978-0-8021-7053-8 pa; 0-8021-7053-6 pa
First published 2008 in South Africa

"Set in post-apartheid South Africa, this gripping novel
explores the seamier aspects of reconciliation. Adam, adrift
after losing his job to a young black candidate, moves to an
isolated town to write poetry. Boredom sets in, relieved only
by the appearance of an old school acquaintance, Canning,
who invites Adam to spend weekends on his nearby game
farm. There Adam meets Canning's wife, Baby, who is both
alluring and chillingly aloof, and begins to realize that no
one's motives are as pure as they appear. Galgut gives even
seemingly innocuous details sinister overtones: the clicking
of peacocks on a roof, the shuffling steps of Canning's elderly black servants. Beneath a fairly standard thriller plot
(affairs, corruption) runs a critique of contemporary South
Africa, from the venality of those enriched by a reinvigo-
rated economy to the stale pieties of the white liberal class."
New Yorker

Gallagher, Stephen

The **bedlam** detective; a novel. Stephen Gallagher. Crown Publishers 2012 305 p.

ISBN 9780307406644; 9780307952783

LC 2011018605

In this book, "Sebastian Becker . . . his fast-track career
abruptly derailed, contemplates an uncertain future. . . . [H]

e faces 1912 back in his native England, employed as the special investigator to the Masters of Lunacy. Englishmen of property deemed too loopy to look after anyone's property face Bedlams of one sort or another, their property removed from their care. It's up to Sir James Crichton-Browne, acting for His Majesty's Government, to render judgments informed by evidence his special investigator Sebastian provides. The job . . . is nuanced enough to be interesting. And it gets even more so when Sebastian meets Sir Owain Lancaster, a scientist who's been widely respected until he blames the failure of his lavish Amazonian expedition on a series of attacks by horrific monsters only he can see." (Kirkus)

Gallagher, Stephen

The **kingdom** of bones; a novel. Shaye Areheart Books 2007 366p $24.95

ISBN 978-0-307-38280-1; 0-307-38280-X

LC 2007-13288

"Vividly set in England and America during the booming industrial era of the late 19th and early 20th centuries, this stylish thriller conjures a perfect demon to symbolize the age and its appetites, an entity that inhabits characters eager to barter their souls for fame and fortune." N Y Times Book Rev

Galloway, Gregory

As simple as snow; Gregory Galloway. Putnam 2005 308p $23.95

ISBN 9780399152313; 9780425207802; 0399152318 (alk. paper)

LC 2004044500

Alex Award (2006)

In this book which takes place "[i]n a small town near a river not far from a city, the narrator, an unnamed high school sophomore, encounters new Goth arrival, Anna Cayne. . . . The narrator is unsure why anyone would pursue him, . . . but pursue him Anna does, charming him with intriguing postcards, reading recommendations and long walks by the river. He's soon completely, hopelessly in love. But halfway through the story Anna disappears, leaving the narrator and the reader feeling lost and betrayed. The book becomes a search for Anna, complete with ciphers, codes, sightings and buried maps. Does affable art teacher Mr. Devon have something to do with her disappearance? Who was really driving the night fellow student Bryce Druitt slammed his car into the side of the bridge?" (Publishers Weekly)

Galloway, Janice

Clara. Simon & Schuster 2003 425p $25

ISBN 0-684-84449-4

LC 2002-26800

First published 2002 in the United Kingdom

"The Schumanns' marriage was forged of perfectly dissonant material, and Galloway allows the collisions to speak for themselves." N Y Times Book Rev

Galsworthy, John

End of the chapter. Scribner 1934 897p

Sequel to A modern comedy

In Maid in waiting, Denny Cherrell undertakes the vindication of her brother whose army career has been ru-

ined by an American archeological expedition leader's unjust accusations

Galsworthy, John

★ The **Forsyte** saga; with a preface by Ada Galsworthy. Scribner 1922 xx, 921p

In chancery relates the further fortunes of the Forsyte family. Irene Forsyte's first effort toward emancipation from her husband Soames ended with the accidental death of the architect who loved her. Meeting Irene again, after a separation of fifteen years, awakens in Soames the old desire to possess her, and failing of her consent, files for divorce. This action forces his cousin Jolyon into the role of correspondent. Soames eventually marries Annette Lamotte, who presents him with a daughter, Fleur, instead of a longed-for male heir. Jolyon and Irene marry and have a son, Jon

Followed by A modern comedy

Galsworthy, John

A **modern** comedy. Scribner 1929 798p

Sequel to The Forsyte saga

A reissue of the title first published 1929

The white monkey concerns Fleur and Michael Mont, and Fleur's father Soames. A son is born to the couple, thus strengthening the marriage which had been weakened by Fleur's affair with an artist and her unrequited love for her cousin Jon

"In some respects 'A Modern Comedy' is inferior to 'The Forsyte Saga'; it is much less rich in varied and vivid types of character; it is less successful as the portrait of an age. . . . But in other ways 'A Modern Comedy' has the advantage of its predecessor. It has a more organic unity, a clearer and more symmetrical plan, dominated by one great figure as tragic finally as Père Goriot,—the figure of Soames Forsyte. . . . It is that least showy and attractive of the Forsytes, Soames, the villain, who has proved so strong that, against the will of his somewhat puzzled creator he has become the hero of the cycle." Saturday Rev

Followed by End of the chapter

Gander, Forrest

As a friend. New Directions Pub. 2008 106p pa $13.95

ISBN 978-0-8112-1745-3; 0-8112-1745-0

LC 2008-23125

"The story is a small one, with no ambitions to be the Great American Novel or to chronicle our time. It sets itself the task of seeing up close the lines of one man's very particular life, and how those lines are walked and read, stumbled over and misread, by those nearby." N Y Times Book Rev

Gao Xingjian

Buying a fishing rod for my grandfather; stories. translated from the Chinese by Mabel Lee. Harper-Collins Pubs. 2004 127p $17.95

ISBN 0-06-057555-7

LC 2003-51138

Original Chinese edition, 1989

"Though few in number, the stories in this collection are richly diverse. One is a bittersweet reflection of a newlywed on his honeymoon; another a Pinteresque dialogue in a park; a third a traffic accident recounted in realtime with all its voyeuristic detail and authentic philosophical questioning, and still another, a strong memory-driven, first-person tale that follows the mental trail of a man who passes a fishing equipment shop and begins to remember his grandfather. For variety of content, stylistic experimentation, graceful language, and poignant insight, Xingjian is a writer who does it all beautifully." Booklist

Gao Xingjian

Soul mountain; translated from the Chinese by Mabel Lee. HarperCollins Pubs. 2000 510p

ISBN 0-06-621082-8

LC 2001-269378

In this novel "a character called 'I' learns that he does not have lung cancer, as previously diagnosed, and embarks on a journey through China in search of spiritual tranquility." Time

"It is not easy to say what the novel is about—and yet the marvel is that somehow it is still both engaging and elegant." N Y Times Book Rev

Garcia Marquez, Gabriel

★ The **autumn** of the patriarch; translated from the Spanish by Gregory Rabassa. Harper & Row 1976 269p

Original Spanish edition, 1975

"A highly sophisticated novel about an unnamed dictator (the patriarch), who, at the time of his death, is somewhere between 107 and 232 years of age. The patriarch embodies the archtypal evils of despotism, but even more significant is his extreme, and often pathetic, solitude, which becomes increasingly evident with his advancing age and which emerges as the principal theme. Despite its political and psychological overtones, the autumn of the patriarch can best be described as a lyrical novel, whose plot and character development are subordinate to formal design and symbolic imagery." Ency of World Lit in the 20th century

Garcia Marquez, Gabriel

Chronicle of a death foretold; translated from the Spanish by Gregory Rabassa. Knopf 1983 120p $25

ISBN 0-394-53074-8

LC 82-48884

Original Spanish edition published 1981 in Colombia; this translation first published 1982 in the United Kingdom

This "investigation of an ancient murder takes on the quality of a hallucinatory exploration, a deep groping search into the gathering darkness of human intentions for a truth that continually slithers away." N Y Rev Books

Garcia Marquez, Gabriel

Collected novellas. HarperCollins Pubs. 1990 249p

LC 89-46106

English translations of the three novellas included in this volume were first published 1972, 1968 and 1982 respectively

Garcia Marquez, Gabriel

Collected stories. Harper & Row 1984 311p

LC 84-47826

This volume includes stories from the author's three previous collections: No one writes to the colonel, and other stories; Leaf storm, and other stories, and Innocent Eréndira, and other stories

Garcia Marquez, Gabriel

The **general** and his labyrinth; translated from the Spanish by Edith Grossman. Knopf 1990 285p

ISBN 0-394-58258-6

LC 90-52957

Original Spanish edition, 1989

"Seldom has there been a more fitting match between author and subject. Mr. Garcia Márquez wades into his flamboyant, often improbable and ultimately tragic material with enormous gusto, heaping detail upon sensuous detail, alternating grace with horror." N Y Times Book Rev

Garcia Marquez, Gabriel

In evil hour; translated from the Spanish by Gregory Rabassa. Harper & Row 1979 183p

Original Spanish edition, 1968

"The reader is carried along effortlessly in the current of this gifted storyteller's prose. Both heroes and villains elicit sympathy because their basic human foibles, while true to local circumstances, can be recognized by people of any culture." Libr J

Garcia Marquez, Gabriel

Leaf storm, and other stories; translated from the Spanish by Gregory Rabassa. Harper & Row 1972 146p

The title novella (originally published 1955) covers three generations of boom and decline in the mythical Colombian town Macondo. "The small river town changes with the leaf storm of people—strangers who come there as a result of civil war and the establishment of a banana company. Marquez begins with the end, the death of one mysterious wanderer, a doctor who . . . withdraws from the world. As the narrators, a man, his daughter, her young son, reveal the doctor's story, so too do the tellers' own melancholy lives emerge, symbolic yet specific, representing the everlasting variety of man's inhumanity to man." Publ Wkly

Garcia Marquez, Gabriel

Love in the time of cholera; translated from the Spanish by Edith Grossman; with an introduction by Nicholas Shakespeare. Knopf 1997 xxxiii, 422p $22

ISBN 0-375-40069-9

Original Spanish edition published 1985 in Colombia, this is a reissue of the 1988 edition

"The story, which concerns the themes of love, aging, and death, takes place between the late 1870s and the early 1930s in a South American community troubled by wars and outbreaks of cholera. It is a tale of two lovers, artistic Florentino Ariza and wealthy Fermina Daza, who reunite after a lifetime apart. Their spirit of enduring love contrasts ironically with the surrounding corporeal decay." Merriam-Webster's Ency of Lit

Garcia Marquez, Gabriel

Memories of my melancholy whores; translated from the Spanish by Edith Grossman. Knopf 2005 115p $20

ISBN 1-4000-4460-X

LC 2005-43591

Original Spanish edition, 2004

"Measured by the highest standards, Memories is not a major achievement, but its goal is brave: to speak on behalf of the desire of older men for underage girls, or, in other words, pedophilia. The conceptual strategy that Garcia Marquez uses toward this end is to break down the barrier between erotic passion and the passion of veneration." N Y Rev Books

Garcia Marquez, Gabriel

★ **One** hundred years of solitude; translated from the Spanish by Gregory Rabassa. Harper & Row 1970 422p

ISBN 0-06-011418-5

Original Spanish edition published 1967 in Argentina

This novel "relates the founding of Macondo by Jose Arcadio Buendia, the adventures of six generations of his descendants, and, ultimately, the town's destruction. It also presents a vast synthesis of social, economic, and political evils plaguing much of Latin America. Even more important from a literary point of view is its aesthetic representation of a world in microcosm, that is, a complete history, from Eden to Apocalypse, of a world in which miracles such as people riding on flying carpets and a dead man returning to life tend to erase the thin line between objective and subjective realities." Ency of World Lit in the 20th Century

Garcia Marquez, Gabriel

Strange pilgrims; twelve stories. translated from the Spanish by Edith Grossman. Knopf 1993 188p

ISBN 0-679-42566-7

LC 93-12257

"Exile and loss are the principal subjects of these 12 stories . . . which capture with lyrical precision the emotions of disorientation and fear, coupled with a sense of new possibility, experienced by Latin Americans in Europe." Publ Wkly

Garcia y Robertson, R.

Firebird. Tor Books 2006 320p $24.95

ISBN 978-0-7653-1356-0; 0-7653-1356-1

LC 2006-40363

"In the fictitious European country of Markovy, which borders on the Iron Wood, a young girl named Aria rescues Sir Roye de Roye, a knight bearing the precious egg of the Firebird and fleeing from his pursuers. Falling in love with Sir Roye, Aria joins him on his journey to return the egg to its proper nest. Along the way, the pair encounters a host of mythical creatures, from witches to murderers to beasts of the kind in which people no longer believe." Libr J

"Bawdy and bloody, magical and mythic, this joyous novel is sure to please heroic fantasy fans." Publ Wkly

Garcia, Cristina

The **Aguero** sisters. Knopf 1997 299p

ISBN 0-679-45090-4

LC 96-52204

"The story of the middle-aged Agüero sisters—independent Reina, an electrician living in Havana, and thoroughly urbanized Constancia, a successful cosmetics salesperson living in New York—is also the story of how personal tragedy and the legacy of Castro's revolution impact one family's history and collective memory. The narrative is filtered through many voices, both past and present, including the women's parents, famous naturalists, and Reina's daughter, a sometime prostitute who is sick to death of poverty-stricken Havana." Booklist

Garcia, Cristina

★ **Dreaming** in Cuban; a novel. Knopf 1992 244p

LC 91-20755

"While taking very seriously those ideas that have truly riven so many families in recent years, leaving many obsessed with the politics of Cuba, Ms. Garcia also portrays the costliness of such an obsession and the fading of the light between mothers and daughters, between lovers, as communication fails." N Y Times Book Rev

Garcia, Cristina

A **handbook** to luck. Knopf 2007 259p $24

ISBN 978-0-307-26436-7; 030726436X

LC 2006-48736

"García's characters have a lot to teach us about playing life's odds, and about resilience . . . . With an ear for language and its cadence, García writes with humor, tenderness and an intuitive sense of how ordinary people weather fortune's turns. If you long for a 'handbook' that reveals how ordinary people become extraordinary, you are in luck." N Y Daily News

Garcia, Cristina

The **lady** matador's hotel; a novel. Scribner 2010 209p $24

ISBN 978-1-4391-8174-4; 1-4391-8174-8

LC 2009-49749

"García has created a half-magical world in which blood runs close to the surface and flesh is transitory, opening the door to the big questions of existence: Who am I, and what is my purpose in life? The answers she offers — such as they are — come with a sly wit and strong visual style that explodes with color and life." Miami Herald

Garcia, Cristina

Monkey hunting. Knopf 2003 251p $23

ISBN 0-375-41056-2

LC 2002-35916

"For all the ground Garcia covers, the most beautiful and moving parts of her novel are the chapters on Chen Pan's youthful sufferings. Here, horror and wonder alternate unblinkingly, as if they are random occurrences in a dark once-upon-a-time." N Y Times Book Rev

Garcia-Roza, Luiz Alfredo

Alone in the crowd; an Inspector Espinosa mystery. translated by Benjamin Moser. Henry Holt and Co. 2009 225p $23

ISBN 978-0-8050-7959-3; 0-8050-7959-9

LC 2008-50135

Original Portuguese edition published 2007 in Brazil

"At a bank in Rio de Janeiro, pensioner Dona Laureta withdraws her money from the same teller Hugo Breno every month like clockwork. She leaves the bank, goes to the grocery and pharmacy, and then she travels to the police of the Twelfth Precinct in Copacabana. She asks to speak with the chief, but Espinoza is tied up in a meeting. She decides to leave and come back later, but instead is run over by a bus; bystanders believe she was deliberately pushed. The police interrogate Breno who remains a person of interest. Espinoza has him under surveillance. . . . Espinoza is unaware that Breno has been watching him for decades and even came to the same park when they were children. A memory of a child's death makes the cop wonder if the teller was involved. They meet at a restaurant and Hugo tells his story to Espinoza. A day later Laureta's friend is killed. Espinoza is sure that Breno killed both women, but has no evidence. Both adversaries risk their lives with similar yet differing purposes." Mystery Gazette

Garcia-Roza, Luiz Alfredo

December heat; translated by Benjamin Moser. Holt & Co. 2003 273p $23

ISBN 0-8050-6890-2

LC 2002-38825

Original Portuguese edition published 1998 in Brazil

"This time the plot concerns Espinosa's friend, a retired policeman who appears to be the likely suspect when his hooker girlfriend is murdered. Confusing the issue, though, is a series of subsequent murders whose tenuous links to the first are fading as precious time passes." Booklist

"An exciting procedural, infused with exotic ambience, sympathetic detectives, and a little romance." Libr J

Garcia-Roza, Luiz Alfredo

The **silence** of the rain; a mystery. translated by Benjamin Moser. Holt & Co. 2002 261p

ISBN 0-8050-6889-9

LC 2001-51523

Original Portuguese edition published 1996

In this mystery "Inspector Espinosa of the Rio de Janeiro police department, a jaded intellectual who'd rather visit a used bookstore than a crime scene, must catch the murderer of Richardo Carvalho, a corporate executive found shot to death in a parking garage, his briefcase and wallet missing. . . . The sultry Rio setting, whose exotic neighborhoods add definition to the action, and a most unorthodox detective should appeal to police procedural fans with a taste for the offbeat." Publ Wkly

Gardam, Jane

Faith Fox. Carroll & Graf 2003 416p $25

ISBN 0-786-71221-X

First published 1996 in the United Kingdom

Gardam's "characters, Dickensian in their number, variety, and abounding eccentricities, carry on so convincingly that she seems to be channeling, rather than creating, these people." Atl Mon

Gardam, Jane

The **flight** of the maidens. Carroll & Graf Pubs. 2001 278p $25

ISBN 0-7867-0879-4

LC 00-343383

First published 2000 in the United Kingdom

Gardam "has thrown out the usual too-sensitive-for-you boilerplate of the coming-of-age novel, for which we can be thankful. Luckily, the generational conflict that remains is usually all the better for her wry indirection." N Y Times Book Rev

Gardam, Jane

God on the rocks. Europa Editions 2010 195p $15

ISBN 9781933372761 pa; 1933372761 pa

First published 1978 in the United Kingdom; first American edition published 1979 by Morrow

This novel "dexterously exposes the misapprehensions wrought by class, sex, love, and religion among the members of two families in a seaside town in the north of England during the interwar years. Gardam has been compared to Anita Brookner, but her view, though equally dark, is far less dreary. Few can present tragedy with such humor." Atlantic

Gardam, Jane

Last Friends. Penguin Group USA 2013 304 p. (Old Filth trilogy) $16

ISBN 1609450930; 9781609450939

With this book, author Jane Gardam finishes her Old Filth trilogy. Here, "when Sir Terence and Sir Edward die within months of each other, only a few people at their memorial services can personally recall the details of their venerable yet tumultuous lives they led. But old Dulcie, widow of judge William Willy, and Sir Frederick Fiscal-Smith, perennial houseguest of the upper class, share fleeting recollections of earlier lives through reminisces that are clouded with the haze of old age." (Kirkus Reviews)

Gardam, Jane

The **man** in the wooden hat. Europa Editions 2009 233p pa $15

ISBN 1-933372-89-3; 978-1-933372-89-1

This novel tells the story of the fifty-year marriage of the barrister Edward Feathers, "Old Filth", and his wife Betty.

"In this understated novel, Gardam returns to the successful barrister and judge Sir Edward Feathers, the protagonist of her deliciously acerbic 'Old Filth.' The complementary tale, told largely from the point of view of Feathers's wife, Betty, a fellow 'Raj orphan,' begins as the two make 'a prudent marriage not for love,' in Hong Kong after the Second World War. The story briskly follows their fifty-year union from adulterous beginnings and unhappy childlessness to a companionable old age in England, after the handover of Hong Kong." New Yorker

Gardam, Jane

Old Filth. Europa 2006 289p pa $14.95

ISBN 1-933372-13-3

LC 2005-36039

First published 2004 in the United Kingdom

This "novel examines the life of Sir Edward Feathers, a desiccated barrister known to colleagues and friends as Old Filth (the nickname stands for 'Failed in London Try Hong Kong'). After a lucrative career in Asia, Filth settles into retirement in Dorset. With anatomical precision, Gardam reveals that, contrary to appearances, Sir Edward's life is seething with incident: a 'raj orphan,' whose mother died when he was born and whose father took no notice of him, he was shipped from Malaysia to Wales (cheaper than England) and entrusted to a foster mother who was cruel to him. What happened in the years before he settled into school, and was casually adopted by his best friend's kindly English country family, haunts, corrodes, and quickens Filth's heart; Gardam's prose is so economical that no moment she describes is either gratuitous or wasted." New Yorker

Gardam, Jane

★ The **people** on Privilege Hill and other stories. Europa Editions 2008 196p $15.95

ISBN 978-1-933372-56-3

"The 14 stories in Gardam's marvelously titled new collection, The People on Privilege Hill, focus to a large extent on members of her generation (she was born July 11, 1928, soon to turn 80) or that of her parents. These generally feisty individuals recall sometimes troubling events from their prime while they cope with the affronts of aging in a changing world. Not all the stories are winners, but even the slightest offer the pleasures of Gardam's brisk, sharp sensibility. The title story brings back the splendid character Filth from her last novel. He's approaching 90, a widower who's retired to Dorset and misses the warm tropical rains of the Orient, where he practiced law for many years." Christ Sci Monit

Gardam, Jane

The **queen** of the tambourine. St. Martin's Press 1995 226p

ISBN 0-312-13151-8

LC 95-15833

First published 1991 in the United Kingdom

"With devilish wit, Ms. Gardam ushers Eliza into the ranks of heroines driven mad by splendid suburban isolation. . . . Yet Eliza's story takes on more and more sense as it emerges from her tragicomic vignettes." N Y Times Book Rev

Gardiner, John Rolfe

The **Magellan** House; stories. illustrations by Joan Gardiner. Counterpoint 2004 297p il $24

ISBN 1-582-43233-3

LC 2004-4932

"There is something tantalizingly sinister about Gardiner's short stories: a hint of intrigue and a soupçon of the illicit connect them all. This undercurrent of mystery and paranoia provides a thrilling tension that lurks just below the surface." Booklist

Gardiner, Meg

The **Dirty** Secrets Club. Dutton 2008 355p $24.95

ISBN 978-0-525-95066-0; 0-525-95066-4

LC 2007-46757

"As a forensic psychiatrist, Jo Beckett determines whether murder or suicide has been committed in questionable deaths. The San Francisco Police Department needs her services after a string of suspicious suicides. The cops are concerned that more suicides are imminent, and they're right-bodies start piling up, and the pressure is on Beckett to figure out what's going on and how to stop it." Libr J

"As Beckett gets in touch with her inner Rambo, Ericksen's acid-tinged delivery suddenly works just fine." Publ Wkly

Gardner, Lisa

Alone. Bantam Books 2005 324p $24

ISBN 0-553-80253-4

LC 2004-57577

The protagonist of this thriller is "Massachusetts police sniper Bobby Dodge. He meets his match in Catherine Gagnon, who as a girl was snatched, raped and nearly murdered. Now she's the wife of erratic, rich Jimmy Gagnon and mother of perpetually ill four-year-old Nathan. When Bobby kills Jimmy during a hostage situation at the Gagnons, he does it to save Catherine and Nathan. But was it a righteous shoot, or did Catherine engineer the killing? Judge James Gagnon and his wife, Maryanne, think Bobby murdered their son out of lust for Catherine. As other people start dying, very messily, and the DA and cops come down hard on Bobby, Gardner keeps the tension high and the pace fast." Publ Wkly

Gardner, Lisa

Catch me. Dutton 2012 400 p.

ISBN 9781455870561; 9780525952763

LC 2011043577

This book follows the adventures of "Boston Sgt. Det. D.D. Warren." In this case, "Charlene Rosalind Carter Grant, a 28-year-old police dispatch officer with a horrific childhood, expects to be murdered on January 21. One of her two best friends was strangled at home on January 21 two years earlier; exactly a year later, her other best friend suffered the same fate. On January 17, Grant seeks out Warren at a crime scene and asks the homicide detective to investigate her expected murder. Meanwhile, Warren is looking into the execution-style slayings of two pedophiles. Rookie sex crime detective Ellen O brings her expertise to this second case." (Publishers Weekly)

Gardner, Lisa

Hide; Lisa Gardner. Bantam Books 2007 375p. (hardcover) o.p.; (pbk.) $7.99

ISBN 9780553804324; 9780553588088; 0553804324

LC 2006027933

In this book, "Bobby Dodge, once a sniper for the Massachusetts State Police and now a police detective, gets called to a horrific crime scene in the middle of the night by fellow detective and ex-lover D.D. Warren. An underground chamber has been discovered on the property of a former Boston mental hospital containing six small naked mummified female bodies in clear garbage bags. A silver locket with one of the corpses, which may be decades old, bears the name Annabelle Granger. Later, a woman shows up at the Boston Homicide offices claiming to be Annabelle Granger. Her resemblance to Catherine Gagnon . . . helps stoke a romance between her and Bobby both subtle and sizzling.

The suspense builds as the police uncover links between patients at the hospital and long-ago criminal activities." (Publishers Weekly)

Gardner, Lisa

Live to tell; a detective D.D. Warren novel. Lisa Gardner. Bantam Books 2010 388 p. (acid-free paper) o.p.; (pbk.) $7.99

ISBN 9780553807240; 9780553591910

LC 2010003473

This detective novel follows "D.D. [Warren who investigates] . . . the mass murder of a family. . . . While D.D. labors to crack the case with the help of sidekick Alex Wilson, a . . . professor training as a criminologist by taking a police rotation, single mother Victoria is just trying to make it through another day. Her life revolves around her emotionally disturbed son Evan, whose constant death threats and physical abuse rule her every move even though he's only eight. The third vein in the story is Danielle's tale of survival. When she was still a child, Danielle's family was killed by her father, but her life was spared. Adult Danielle, who wonders why, spends her time giving back by working late hours as a pediatric nurse with disturbed children." (Kirkus)

Gardner, Lisa

Love you more; a novel. Bantam Books 2011 356p $26

ISBN 978-0-553-80725-7; 0-553-80725-0

LC 2010-42093

In this novel featuring Boston PD Sgt. Det. D.D. Warren, "D.D.'s former partner and one-time lover, Det. Bobby Dodge, of the Massachusetts State Police, asks her to look into what appears to be a clear-cut homicide case. The evidence suggests that Tessa Leoni, a state trooper colleague of Bobby's, shot and killed her abusive husband, Brian Darby, who may have kidnapped her six-year-old daughter, Sophie. But Tessa won't talk about her bruises, her husband, or what might have happened to her child. D.D. examines every detail about the family, while Tessa uses her skills to manipulate the investigation. . . . Gardner sprinkles plenty of clues and inventive twists to keep readers off-kilter as the suspense builds to a realistic, jaw-dropping finale." Publ wkly

Gardner, Lisa

The neighbor; Lisa Gardner. Bantam Books 2009 373 p. o.p.; o.p.; $7.99

ISBN 9780553807233; 0553807234; 9780553591903

LC 2009009861

Thriller Awards (International Thriller Writers): Best Novel (2010)

This book follows "Boston police detective D. D. Warren," who is investigating the case of a "schoolteacher [who] vanishes from her home, leaving behind a young daughter and a husband. . . [I]t becomes apparent that her departure was not voluntary and the suspects begin to mount up: the not-so-grieving husband, who seems to be hiding some pretty big secrets; a neighbor who happens to be a registered sex offender; one of the victim's students, a boy who might have some misguided feelings for the victim; even the woman's estrange father . . . the woman herself is deeply troubled and is perhaps not quite the innocent victim she appears to be." (Booklist)

Garey, Juliann

Too bright to hear too loud to see; Juliann Garey. Soho Press 2012 289 p. (hbk.: alk. paper) $25

ISBN 161695129X; 9781616951290; 9781616951306

LC 2012026028

This book is the "story of one man's descent into madness and his painful struggle to recover" from manic depression through electric shock treatments. Formerly a movie studio executive, "the tools of [Greyson Todd's] trade—lying, manipulation, negotiation—were skills that came naturally . . . . Greyson snaps under this constant pressure to pretend, leaves his family, and travels around the world, visiting sex clubs in Thailand and disease-ridden villages in Africa." (Library Journal)

Garigliano, Jeff

Dogface; a novel. MacAdam/Cage 2008 360p pa $14

ISBN 978-1-59692-259-4; 1-59692-259-1

LC 2007-15666

"With its bizarre characters, frank dialogue and violence, it belongs somewhere between Louis Sachar's Holes and a Carl Hiaasen comic thriller. . . . Despite the clichés, the novel never loses its freshness." Dallas Morning News

Garner, Helen

The spare room; a novel. Henry Holt 2009 175p $22

ISBN 978-0-8050-8888-5; 0-8050-8888-1

LC 2008-10107

First published 2008 in Australia

"Humour is not just an occasional relief in The Spare Room, it's actually the lifeblood of the book. The old cliché that 'you've got to laugh' in the face of tragedy is given new meaning by Garner. For all the sickness and suffering and thankless service involved in the story, it's only an acute sense of the absurdity of the situation that keeps the heroine . . . sane. Garner's dealings with terminal illness are truly refreshing. Instead of focusing on the sufferer, Nicola, she delves inwards, exploring the impact on the carer. And she dares to express the unspeakable thoughts we often think when confronted by another's illness." PopMatters

Garwood, Julie

The bride. Atria Books 2002 346p

ISBN 0-7434-5292-5

LC 2002-511767

First published 1989 in paperback by Pocket Books

By edict of the king, the mighty Scottish laird Alec Kincaid must take an English bride. His choice was Jamie, youngest daughter of Baron Jamison. While living in the Highlands, Jamie and Alec learn much about each other and about themselves. All the while, someone is out to put a stop to the love that is growing between them.

Garwood, Julie

The ideal man. Dutton 2011 322p $26.95

ISBN 978-0-525-95225-1; 0-525-95225-X

LC 2011-16646

"Dr. Ellie Sullivan witnesses the escape of two criminals and the shooting of an FBI agent. Ellie performs lifesaving surgery on the agent and in the process meets another

FBI agent, Max Daniels. Sparks immediately fly, but for her sake, Max doesn't want Ellie to be considered a witness. Ellie is about to head home for her sister Ava's wedding, an event full of emotional landmines as Ava essentially stole Ellie's old boyfriend. The bigger concern, however, is the whereabouts of Ellie's dangerous stalker, Evan Patterson. The more Max learns about Patterson, the more concerned he is for Ellie's safety, so he becomes her date to the wedding." RT Book Rev

Gash, Jonathan

Prey dancing; a Dr. Clare Burtonall mystery. Viking 1998 272p

ISBN 0-670-87764-6

LC 98-2830

"The unlikely team of cardiologist Clare Burtonall and her lover, male prostitute Bonn, risk murder when they attempt to carry out an AIDS patient's last request." Libr J

"Brilliantly written, mysterious, menacing, and filled with unforgettable characters." Booklist

Gash, Jonathan

A **rag,** a bone, and a hank of hair; the twenty-first Lovejoy novel. Viking 2000 344p

ISBN 0-670-88598-3

LC 99-52654

First published 1999 in the United Kingdom

"Pursued from East Anglia by the usual creditors and angry husbands, Lovejoy descends on London with a private commission to find out who is flooding the trade with bogus gemstones, a quest that takes him from trendy galleries on Chelsea's King's Road to the jumbled stalls of outdoor markets in Bermondsey, Camden Passage and Portobello Road." N Y Times Book Rev

Gash, Jonathan

The **rich** and the profane; a Lovejoy novel. Viking 1999 344p

ISBN 0-670-88346-8

LC 98-38951

First published 1998 in the United Kingdom

Lovejoy "takes on yet another persona when he impersonates a pop music impresario and produces a splashy variety show on the English Channel island of Guernsey—clever cover for an ingenious art fraud that draws the suckers like flies." N Y Times Book Rev

"With this dervish of comic activity and a romp that ends in a circuslike venue, Gash is in top form." Publ Wkly

Gaskell, Elizabeth Cleghorn

★ **Cranford**; [by] Elizabeth Gaskell. Oxford University Press 1998 xxxii, 194p (Oxford world classics) pa $9.95

ISBN 0-19-283209-3

LC 98-204713

First published 1853

This novel "centres on the formidable Miss Deborah Jenkyns and her gentle sister Miss Matty, daughters of the former rector. Moments of drama are provided by the death of the genial Captain Brown, run over by a train when saving the life of a child; by the panic caused in the village by rumours of burglars; by the surprising marriage of the widowed Lady Glenmire with the vulgar Mr. Hoggins, the village surgeon; by the failure of a bank which ruins Miss Matty, and her rescue by the fortunate return from India of her long-lost brother Peter. But the greatest charm of 'Cranford,' which has kept it unfailingly popular, is its amused but loving portrayal of the old-fashioned customs and 'elegant economy' of a delicately observed group of middle-aged figures in a landscape." Oxford Companion to Engl Lit. 5th edition

Gaspar de Alba, Alicia

Desert blood; the Juárez murders. by Alicia Gaspar de Alba. Arte Publico Press 2005 vi, 346p (pbk.) $16.95; o.p.; o.p.

ISBN 9781558855182; 1558854460 (alk. paper); 9781558854468 (alk. paper)

LC 2004055417

Lambda Literary Awards: Lesbian Mystery (2005)

This novel tells the story of a "visiting professor at an L.A. college, Ivon [Villa, who] is smart, beautiful, and gay. She and her partner, Brigit, decide to adopt a baby from Mexico, and Ivon travels to her native El Paso to see the child. On the plane, she reads an article about the murdered bodies of more than 100 women found in the desert outside Juarez. The crime wave hits home when the mother of the baby she was to adopt becomes one of the victims. Then Ivon's little sister, Irene, goes missing after an evening in Juarez. With the help of her cousin and a nervous priest, Ivon desperately searches for Irene while dealing with their accusatory mother and corrupt border patrol officers." (Booklist)

Gass, William H., 1924-

★ **Middle** C; a novel. by William H. Gass. Alfred A. Knopf 2013 416 p. $28.95

ISBN 0307701638; 9780307701633

LC 2012017087

This novel, by William H. Gass, "begins in Graz, Austria, 1938. Joseph Skizzen's father . . . leaves his country for England. . . . In London . . . , he disappears under mysterious circumstances. The family is relocated to a small town in Ohio, where Joseph Skizzen grows up, becomes a decent amateur piano player, in part to cope with the abandonment of his father, and creates as well a fantasy self--a professor with a fantasy goal: to establish the Inhumanity Museum." (Publisher's note)

Gatewood, Robert

The **sound** of the trees; a novel. Holt & Co. 2002 289p $25

ISBN 0-8050-6802-3

LC 2001-51703

This novel "begins on horse back in Depression-era New Mexico with Trude Mason, a taciturn 18-year-old, and his mother fleeing their impoverished family ranch in predawn desperation to escape the escalating brutality of the young man's father. Enroute to Colorado, Trude's steadfastness of purpose is tested by personal tragedy and sharpened by the treachery of man. His fate becomes entwined with that of a girl whom fortune has placed in the hands of scoundrels. . . . Gatewood has created a richly textured tableau threaded with mysticism and sustained by pitch-perfect dialogue laced with quiet dignity." SLJ

Gaus, P. L.

The **names** of our tears; an Amish-country mystery. P.L. Gaus. Plume 2013 256 p. (paperback) $15.00

ISBN 9780452298194

LC 2012045399

This novel, by P. L. Gaus, is part of the author's "Amish-Country Mystery" series. "Ruth Zook returns home to Holmes County, Ohio, carrying a heavy suitcase and a heavier heart. Coerced into becoming a drug mule, Ruth retaliates by destroying her illicit burden and pays for it with her life. When Fannie Helmuth confesses that she was similarly coerced, Sheriff Bruce Robertson realizes that the drug dealers' operation reaches all the way to Florida's Pinecraft Amish community." (Publisher's note)

Gautreaux, Tim

The **missing**. Alfred A. Knopf 2009 375p $25.95

ISBN 978-0-307-27015-3; 0-307-27015-7

LC 2008-46739

"As the floorwalker in New Orleans' best department store in 1921, Sam Simoneaux knows the policy is to lock the store doors when a lost child is not found in 15 minutes. When he fails to implement that policy, kidnappers make off with three-year-old Lily, the pretty and talented daughter of riverboat performers Elsie and Ted Weller. Fired from his job, Sam—who understands the Wellers' grief, having lost a young son to illness—hires on at the riverboat and taps railroad stationmasters for information to find the kidnappers. His initial error is compounded when he finds Lily and makes a moral judgment he has no right to make. But Sam, the victim of a horrendous crime as an infant, goes to great lengths to right his own wrongs without seeking vengeance for wrongs against himself, even in the face of pure evil. Gautreaux . . . displays fluent prose, accomplished storytelling, and strong characterizations in this paean to the indefatigability of the human spirit. An exceptional novel." Booklist

Gavin, Jim

★ **Middle** men; stories. Jim Gavin. Simon & Schuster 2012 224 p.

ISBN 9781451649314

LC 2011045956

This collection of short stories by Jim Gavin presents a "panoramic vision of California, portraying a group of men, from young dreamers to old vets, as they make valiant forays into middle-class respectability. . . . The men in Gavin's stories all find themselves stuck somewhere in the middle, caught half way between their dreams and the often crushing reality of their lives." (Publisher's note)

Gavin, Rick

Beluga; Rick Gavin. Minotaur Books 2012 304 p. (hardback) $24.99

ISBN 9781250015228; 9781250015990; 1250015227

LC 2012030068

In this novel by Rick Gavin "Nick Reid and his compadre Desmond liberated some money from a nasty meth dealer, and now they need to launder it. The brother of Desmond's ex-wife wants a small sum to set up a scheme involving a trailer full of stolen tires. . . . [and] Shawnica insists that Nick and Desmond help her brother out. In the

next few days, they're set upon by a ninja schoolgirl assassin and a couple of Delta gangsters." (Publisher's note)

Gay, William

I hate to see that evening sun go down; collected stories. Free Press 2002 303p $24

ISBN 0-7432-4088-X

LC 2002-73945

Contents: I hate to see that evening sun go down; A death in the woods; Bonedaddy, Quincy Nell, and the fifteen thousand BTU electric chair; The paperhanger; The man who knew Dylan; Those Deep Elm Brown's Ferry Blues; Crossroads Blues; Closure and roadkill on the life's highway; Sugarbaby; Standing by peaceful waters; Good 'til now; The lightpainter; My hand is just fine where it is

"Gay is richly gifted: a seemingly effortless storyteller, a writer of prose that's fiercely wrought, pungent in detail, yet poetic in the most welcome sense." N Y Times Book Rev

Gay, William

Twilight; a novel. MacAdam/Cage 2006 224p $25

ISBN 978-1-59692-058-3; 1-59692-058-0

LC 2006-19865

The "absence of a soothing depth—of motive, reasons, understanding—is one of the great achievements of the novel. It sets up a central tension for the reader, who deaires to know more, while the writer resolutely adheres to the truth of his universe—that such comforts aren't available and that the quiverings of the individual consciousness aren't substantial enough in the face of life's darkly malevolent forces." Paste

Geagley, Brad

Year of the hyenas; Brad Geagley. Simon & Schuster 2005 291p $23; (pbk.) $20

ISBN 074325080X; 9781439124697

LC 2004058979

This book, set in Thebes, Egypt in 1153 B.C., follows "an embittered, self-loathing, near-alcoholic named Semerket, . . . the Clerk of Investigations and Secrets, . . . a cop charged with nailing the killer of [a] beloved local priestess. . . . Semerket learns soon enough that responsibility has fallen on his shoulders precisely because the powers-that-be expect him to collapse under its weight." (Kirkus) "[H]e ultimately uncovers a conspiracy aimed at overthrowing the current pharaoh, Ramses III." (Library Journal)

Gear, Kathleen O'Neal

People of the masks; [by] Kathleen O'Neal Gear & W. Michael Gear. Forge 1998 416p

ISBN 0-312-85857-4

LC 98-8695

"Great trouble begins for two tribes in what is now northeastern North America when Jumping Badger, a sadistic war leader, raids and destroys Paint Rock village and kidnaps the dwarf child Rumbler, whose power in the spirit world is legendary. Blue Raven, Jumping Badger's cousin, believes that the tribes need to work together to survive attacks from fiercer enemies. But as warriors begin to die, Rumbler is accused of casting evil spells, and Blue Raven can no longer protect him." Libr J

Gear, Kathleen O'Neal

People of the mist; [by] Kathleen O'Neal Gear and W. Michael Gear. Forge 1997 432p maps

ISBN 0-312-85854-X

LC 97-14682

"Simple prose brightened by atmospheric detail sweeps this fluid, suspenseful mix of anthropological research and character-driven mystery to a solid, satisfying resolution." Publ Wkly

Gear, Kathleen O'Neal

People of the owl; a novel of prehistoric North America. {by} Kathleen O'Neal Gear and W. Michael Gear. Forge 2003 560p il maps $25.95

ISBN 0-312-87741-2

LC 2003-40019

"Propelled by the Gears' spry storytelling, this sturdy epic skillfully navigates the ancient swamplands of Louisiana, with their lapping brown waters, hanging vines and brooding skies." Publ Wkly

Gear, W. Michael

Coyote summer. Forge 1997 427p

ISBN 0-312-86330-6

LC 97-5762

Sequel to The morning river (1996)

"Richard Hamilton, the hero of this . . . western, rues the day when his father sent him west. Robbed and sold into indentured servitude on a keelboat, this young student of philosophy is forced to forsake his genteel Bostonian manners and breeding. In the harsh Upper Missouri country of the 1820s, it's kill or be killed. Dick learns that early, when he kills a Pawnee to save the life of an Indian woman, Heals Like the Willow. After a raiding party of Crows steals his company's horses, Dick is almost slaughtered himself when he accompanies brutal hunter Travis on a relentless pursuit of the thieves. Gear skillfully intercuts Dick's story with that of Willow." Publ Wkly

Gear, W. Michael

People of the thunder; [by] W. Michael Gear and Kathleen O'Neal Gear. Forge 2009 383p $25.95

ISBN 978-0-7653-1439-0; 0-7653-1439-8

LC 2008-38017

"Set in the 1300s largely in what is now Alabama and Mississippi, this complex novel tracks three wanderers' quest to create peace in violent times. The Sky Hand people control their territory from Split Sky City (Moundville, Ala.), ruled by scheming chief Flying Hawk and his ruthless nephew, war chief Smoke Shield. While they plot to suppress the enslaved Albaamaha people and to conquer their neighbors, three people pursue a mission to restore peace. Old White is a prophet and 'the most dangerous man alive'; Trader is a man with blood on his hands and a stunning secret; Two Petals is a shaman woman who says and does everything backwards. Together this curious trio must bring down Flying Hawk and Smoke Shield. The story is loaded with early Native American lore, spirituality, economics, government and daily life; however, it is not for the squeamish, as it also contains plenty of blood and gore, hideous torture, rape and chilling cruelty. . . . A terrific tale." Publ Wkly

Gee, Sophie

The **scandal** of the season. Scribner 2007 335p $25

ISBN 978-1-4165-4056-4; 1-4165-4056-3

LC 2006-35556

"Written by Alexander Pope at the request of his friend John Caryll, 'The Rape of the Lock' clinched Pope's fame and assured his success. . . [This novel] provides the poem's backstory, portraying not only the beau and belle of the poem (Lord Robert Petre and Arabella Fermor) but also Pope's own coming to terms with his life: his relationship to longtime friends Teresa and Martha Blount, his attraction to and scorn for the fashionable world, and his uncomfortable social position as a cripple and a Catholic." Libr J

"Gee writes with scholarly confidence, underpinning the racy intrigue of her account with a real understanding of the characters and their world." New Yorker

Genazino, Wilhelm

The **shoe** tester of Frankfurt; a novel. translated from the German by Philip Boehm. New Directions 2006 132p pa $14.95

ISBN 978-0-8112-1583-1; 0-8112-1583-0

LC 2006-9105

Original German edition, 2001

"Filled with the hypersensitive observations of a man who claims that he 'hardly thinks at all anymore—I only look round and about,' the novel shows the transformation of this character from someone who willfully closes his eyes to the world to one who looks around and begins to recognize his connections with the rest of the humanity. The author's tongue-in-cheek humor keeps the novel from imploding under its own weight, while the conclusion offers hope for the future. Slow to start, the novel evolves into a delightful exploration of one man's memories and his halting steps toward a new life." Mostlyfiction.com

Genova, Lisa

Left neglected; a novel. Gallery Books 2011 327p $25

ISBN 978-1-4391-6463-1; 1-4391-6463-0

LC 2010-25568

"Some readers will likely find a few of the plot elements a bit too neat. . . . Despite these contrivances, 'Left Neglected' is a novel worth reading for the way it informs a little-known medical condition, as well as the engaging story of a character who transcends what could have been a tragedy to find a fresh appreciation for life." Boston Globe

Gentle, Mary

The **black** opera; a novel of opera, volcanoes, and the mind of God. Night Shade Books 2012 515 p.

ISBN 1597802190; 9781597802192

This historical fantasy novel by Mary Gentle is set in "Naples, [in] the 19th Century. In the Kingdom of the Two Sicilies, holy music has power. Under the auspices of the Church, the Sung Mass can bring about actual miracles like healing the sick or raising the dead. . . . Now the Prince's Men, a secret society, hope to stage their own black opera to empower the Devil himself - and change Creation for the better! Conrad Scalese is a struggling librettist [who] . . .

finds himself recruited to write and stage a counter opera that will, hopefully, cancel out the apocalyptic threat of the black opera, provided the Prince's Men, and their spies and saboteurs, don't get to him first." (Publisher's note)

George, Elizabeth

Believing the lie; Elizabeth George. Dutton 2012 610p. maps

ISBN 1410445151; 9781410445155; 0525952586; 9780525952589

LC 2011043105

This book tells the story of "Inspector Thomas Lynley, [who] is mystified when he's sent undercover to investigate the death of Ian Cresswell at the request of the man's uncle, the wealthy and influential Bernard Fairclough. The death has been ruled an accidental drowning, and nothing on the surface indicates otherwise. But when Lynley enlists the help of his friends Simon and Deborah St. James, the trio's digging soon reveals that the Fairclough clan is awash in secrets, lies, and motives. . . . As the investigation escalates, the Fairclough family's veneer cracks, with deception and self-delusion threatening to destroy everyone." (Publisher's note)

George, Elizabeth

Careless in red; a novel. Harper 2008 626p $27.95

ISBN 978-0-06-116087-5; 0-06-116087-3

LC 2007-44629

"As with George's other books, the reader is soon plunged into a vast back story of relationships and psychologically complex characters. It's a level of literary sophistication readers have come to expect from George." Seattle Times

George, Elizabeth

This body of death; a novel. Harper 2010 692p $28.99

ISBN 978-0-06-116088-2; 0-06-116088-1

LC 2009-35547

"As always, [George's] story is credible and commanding, and her characters — particularly Lynley and Havers — continue to evolve while remaining the reader's old and dear friends. George's perceptive characterizations find a worthy complement in her descriptive powers, which evoke a strong sense of place. . . . A book for neither the faint of heart nor the short of patience, "This Body of Death" is a rich, unsettling work, one whose darkness is lightened by Lynley's steady emergence from grief." Richmond Times-Dispatch

George, Elizabeth

A **traitor** to memory. Bantam Bks. 2001 422p

ISBN 0-553-80127-9

LC 2001-25488

"Violin virtuoso and former child prodigy Gideon Davies suddenly loses his ability to play. As he works with a psychiatrist to regain his gift, Gideon begins to dredge up memories from his childhood. Suddenly, people involved in an incident from his past, beginning with his mother, are being run over by a big black car. Detective Inspector Thomas Lynley and constables Barbara Havers and Winston Nkata are asked to investigate the hit-and-run murders and, like

Gideon, must reconstruct the past in order to understand what is happening in the present." Libr J

George, Elizabeth

What came before he shot her. HarperCollins 2006 548p $26.95

ISBN 0-06-054562-3

LC 2006-43520

"Twelve-year-old Joel Campbell's father was gunned down by thugs, and his mother is confined to a mental institution. Joel and his siblings live with an unwelcoming aunt in a dangerous part of London. His 15-year-old sister, Vanessa, is trading sexual favors for drugs, and his eight-year-old brother, Toby, spends much of his time in an imaginary world called Sose. To gain protection for his vulnerable little brother, Joel gets involved with the Blade, a vicious neighborhood drug dealer. Joel is the boy who, at the end of George's last novel, With No One as Witness [2005], was arrested in the shooting death of Det. Peter Lynley's wife, Helen. This is an unusual sequel in that, rather than taking up where the last book left off, with the expected cast of characters—Barbara Havers, Winston Nkata, and Peter Lynley—it veers off to tell Joel's story." Libr J

"This is crime writing at its finest, with an almost painfully sharp view of the world and evil." Rocky Mountain News

George, Kathleen

Simple; Kathleen George. New York 2012 322 p.

ISBN 0312569149; 9780312569143; 9781250011299

LC 2012016579

In this novel by Kathleen George "Cassie Price is thrilled when she's hired to work at one of Pittsburgh's most prestigious law firms. Young, pretty, and from a sheltered background, Cassie's new life as an adult now includes meeting rich and powerful people, and she may even be having a mysterious affair. But when her lifeless body is discovered, the police are stumped. Suspicion falls on a neighborhood handyman, but Detective Colleen Greer and her boss, Commander Richard Christie, are not sure." (Publisher's note)

George, Margaret

Elizabeth I; a novel. Viking 2011 671p $30

ISBN 978-0-670-02253-3; 0-670-02253-5

LC 2010-35382

"Set in the final 20 years of Elizabeth's reign, George's novel is the portrait of an aging powerful woman, one who struggles at times with her waning sexual allure even as she refuses to let its loss diminish her power. . . . This historical novel has considerable strengths, from impressive detail and a wonderfully evocative setting to dialogue that feels appropriately 'old' without ever veering into hokeyness. George brings the queen's two major foreign-policy challenges — conflict with Spain and with Ireland — to life in a way that feels both immediate and relevant. But these achievements are at times outweighed both by the inclusion of (seemingly) everything that happened in England during the time period covered, and by the jarring choice to divide the story between two first-person narrators: Elizabeth herself, and her cousin, Lettice Knollys, who was wife to one of Elizabeth's favorite courtiers and mother to another. The two narrators slow the pace down — a problem in such a lengthy tome — and the stories don't intersect enough for a reader to gain traction. . . . Nevertheless, the contrast between the two narrative voices successfully illustrates two very different modes of female power: the Virgin Queen vs. the seductive noblewoman." Boston Globe

Includes bibliographical references

George, Margaret

Helen of Troy. Viking 2006 611p $27.95
ISBN 0-670-03778-8

LC 2005-58473

George's "characters are precisely crafted, and the lovely Helen, clear-eyed and intelligent, is a sympathetic narrator. Despite the novel's length, the pages practically turn themselves. An absorbing retelling of the classic Trojan War myth, and a sobering look at the utter futility of trying to change one's fate." Booklist

George, Margaret

The **memoirs** of Cleopatra; a novel. St. Martin's Press 1997 964p
ISBN 0-312-15430-5

LC 96-51071

George "renders her myriad settings, whether in Athens, Syria, Actium or elsewhere, palpably real. The smell of the Alexandrian harbor, the taste of pomegranates, the visual grandeur of the pyramids and the clash of swords all come alive in her hands. Battles physical and political—Caesar's North African campaign, the Alexandrian War, the ill-fated struggle between Antony and Octavian for control of the world—are evoked with skill and passion, as are more domestic conflicts." Publ Wkly

Gerritsen, Tess

The **apprentice**; a novel. Ballantine Bks. 2002 344p $24.95
ISBN 0-345-44785-9

LC 2002-23185

Boston "detective Jane Rizzoli is called to a crime scene out of her jurisdiction. The victim is a wealthy doctor, found with his throat slashed, sitting on the floor of his living room in his pajamas, with a teacup in his lap. His wife is missing, but her nightgown is found folded neatly on a chair in the bedroom. There are unmistakable similarities to the work of serial killer Warren Hoyt, nicknamed 'the Surgeon,' but he is in prison, which leads Rizzoli to suspect a copcat killer." Libr J

Gerritsen, Tess

Body double. Ballantine Bks. 2004 339p $24.95
ISBN 0-375-43374-0

LC 2004-49807

"Medical examiner Dr. Maura Isles has just returned from a trip to France to encounter a grisly discovery. A woman has been found shot to death in front of her home, and the woman is a dead ringer for Maura. The woman, whose name is Anna Leoni, turns out to be Maura's twin; both were given up for adoption 40 years ago. The mystery deepens when Officer Rick Ballard shows up and tells Maura and Detective Jane Rizzoli that Anna was on the run from an abusive boyfriend and under police protection. But that still doesn't answer the question of what led Anna to Maura's door, and

that question leads Maura to trace her sister's steps to an old house in Maine." Booklist

"An electric series of startling twists, the revelation of ghoulishly practical motives and a nail-biting finale make this Gerritsen's best to date." Publ Wkly

Gerritsen, Tess

The **sinner**. Ballantine Bks. 2003 342p $24.95
ISBN 0-345-45891-5

LC 2003-59151

"When two Boston nuns are found brutally beaten—one fatally and one with a scintilla of life left in her—it's up to homicide detective Jane Rizzoli to find the perpetrator. Medical examiner Dr. Maura Isles, nicknamed the Queen of the Dead, has the unlucky fortune to discover that the murdered nun, a young woman about to make her final vows, hid untold secrets from the rest of the aging convent. . . . Woven within the horror of this gruesome story is the old allegory of good versus evil, but relating it through these two fascinating individuals, Gerritsen avoids cliches." Booklist

Gerritsen, Tess

The **surgeon**. Ballantine Bks. 2001 359p
ISBN 0-345-44783-2

LC 2001-35901

Dr. Catherine Cordell "thought she had shot and killed her rapist and would-be murderer two years earlier in steamy Savannah, where he was a surgery intern at her hospital. Now, in Boston, as another hot summer begins, he appears to have miraculously returned and embarked once again on his grisly mission: he rapes women, then surgically removes their wombs. As two intrepid detectives—Thomas Moore and Jane Rizzoli—investigate, Cordell begins to doubt her own memories (or lack of) and discovers that not even her OR is safe." Publ Wkly

"A fascinating story with a gripping plot and believably human characters." Booklist

Gessen, Keith

All the sad young literary men. Viking 2008 242p il $24.95
ISBN 978-0-670-01855-0; 0-670-01855-4

LC 2007-21009

"Gessen's humor is persistently Seinfeldian, avoiding the excesses of savage comedy or satire, or anything like raging spiritual despair, for All the Sad Young Literary Men is a post-postmodernist work of fiction in which spiritual impotence is the great subtextual theme, even as sexual promiscuity is the norm." N Y Rev Books

Gholson, Christien

A **fish** trapped inside the wind. Parthian Books 2011 268p pa $14.95
ISBN 978-1-906998-90-5

This book tells the story of "a small town in Belgium near the French border, [where] on the morning of Saint Woelfred's festival, dead fish lie on the ground, scattered everywhere, as if blown in by the wind. The quarries that were once active now stand empty and will soon be used as toxic waste dumps. Are the fish a sign from the saint? Or simply a cruel trick played by Contexture, the dance group who once stripped naked at the Vatican? . . . Journeys of self-discovery are experienced through the eyes of a magician, a writer, the town Casanova, a clairvoyant married to a drunk, a priest and a Rimbaud scholar: each seeking answers to their individual tribulations." (Publisher's note)

"Like the most finely cadenced, beautifully fanciful works of surrealism, this novel beckons with its subtle nuances before it leaps into a dazzling mastery that will ensnare even the casual reader. The town of Villon, Belgium, is experiencing an extremely odd phenomenon. Dead fish are strewn everywhere. Flung over yards and stoops and fields, the fish puzzle the residents no end as they speculate on the significance of such a bizarre happening. Other intersecting events include a rally meant to protest a decision to use local quarries as toxic dumps and the festival of St. Woelfred, who fled into the wilderness in the seventh century to live out her days reflecting in prayer." Booklist

Ghosh, Amitav
The **glass** palace; a novel. Random House 2001 474p $25.95
ISBN 0-375-50148-7
LC 00-41477

This narrative "stretches from the British invasion of Burma, in 1885, through the country's independence, to the uneasy military rule of the present day. The novel is presided over by the Indian-born Rajkumar, a poor orphan, who falls for Dolly, a servant of the exiled queen. Ghosh renders the polite imprisonment of the Burmese royal family in India and the lush, dangerous atmosphere of teak camps in the Burmese forest with fine detail—a perfect balance for the broad stroke of romance and serendipity that drive the story forward." New Yorker
Includes bibliographical references

Ghosh, Amitav
The **hungry** tide; Amitav Ghosh. Houghton Mifflin 2005 333p map (pbk.) $14.95
ISBN 0618329978; 9780618711666
LC 2004060942

This book is "set in the Sundarbans, a[n] . . . archipelago . . . that's also a fragile ecosystem. . . . A young marine biologist, born in India but raised in Seattle, is investigating the few remaining freshwater dolphins in this alluring landscape, a vast string of islands and mangrove forests in the Bay of Bengal. She is accompanied by a local fisherman, stubbornly devoted to the old ways of life, who acts as her guide, and by a Delhi-based translator revisiting the region to help an aunt sort through some long-lost family papers. To each, the Sundarbans represent something different, but for all they become ' . . . a meeting not just of many rivers, but a roundabout people can use to pass in many directions—from country to country and even between faiths.'" (New York Times)

Ghosh, Amitav
River of smoke. Farrar, Straus and Giroux 2011 522p $28
ISBN 978-0-374-17423-1
LC 2011-24409

Sequel to Sea of poppies (2008)
"Ghosh's fascination with the multicultural ferment of Canton inspires thrilling descriptions of everything from local cuisine to the geopolitics of the opium wars. And his delight in language, especially the inventiveness of pidgin, further vitalizes his canny and dazzling tale, which, for all its historical exactitude, subtly reflects the hypocrisy and horrors of today's drug trafficking." Booklist

Ghosh, Amitav
Sea of poppies. Farrar, Straus and Giroux 2008 515p map $26
ISBN 978-0-374-17422-4; 0-374-17422-9
LC 2008-30854

"An adventure story set in nineteenth-century Calcutta against the backdrop of the Opium Wars. On the Ibis, a ship engaged in transporting opium across the Bay of Bengal, varied life stories converge. A fallen raja, a half-Chinese convict, a plucky American sailor, a widowed opium farmer, a transgendered religious visionary are all united by the 'smoky paradise' of the opium seed. Ghosh writes with impeccable control, and with a vivid and sometimes surprising imagination." New Yorker

Gibb, Camilla
Sweetness in the belly. Penguin Press 2006 338p $23.95
ISBN 1-59420-084-X
LC 2005-53451

First published 2005 in Canada
"Utterly convincing and authentic . . . a novel that will take you to a place so far from yourself that you may wonder, from time to time, whether you are ever coming back." San Francisco Chronicle

Gibbons, Kaye
Charms for the easy life. Putnam 1992 254p
ISBN 0-399-13791-2
LC 92-40690

"A touching picture of female bonding and solidarity. Related with the simple, tart economy of a folktale, the narrative brims with wisdom and superstition, with Southern manners and insights into human nature." Publ Wkly

Gibbons, Kaye
Divining women. G. P. Putnam's Sons 2004 205p $23.95
ISBN 0-399-15160-5
LC 2003-60661

In this "tale of marital strife and female resilience, Gibbons considers conflicts between blacks and whites and men and women within the context of the First World War and the Spanish influenza epidemic. Martha has sent her intelligent daughter, Mary, to North Carolina to help Martha's half-brother, Troop, and his expectant wife, Maureen, and Mary is amazed to find herself in a household as miserable as it is opulent. Troop is a coldhearted, possibly insane despot; lovely and muddled Maureen is his prisoner; and Zollie and Mamie, their kind African American employees, are treated with appalling indifference. The hate, lies, and machinations at work in this psychotic hothouse rival that of the most gothic of southern melodramas, a tradition Gibbons shrewdly subverts as she divines the true nature of feminine power and points the way toward justice in this gorgeously moody and piquant fairy tale." Booklist

Gibbons, Kaye

★ **Ellen** Foster; a novel. Algonquin Bks. 1987 146p $16.95

ISBN 1-56512-205-4

LC 86-22136

"What might have been grim, melodramatic material in the hands of a less talented author is instead filled with lively humor, . . . compassion and intimacy. This short novel focuses on Ellen's strengths rather than her victimization, presenting a memorable heroine who rescues herself." N Y Times Book Rev

Followed by The life all around me by Ellen Foster (2006)

Gibbons, Kaye

The **life** all around me by Ellen Foster. Harcourt 2006 218p $23

ISBN 0-15-101204-0

LC 2005-14552

Sequel to Ellen Foster (1987)

In this sequel, "Ellen is now 15 and driven to succeed. She and her foster mother, Laura, scrape together enough money to send her to an academic enrichment weekend program at Johns Hopkins University, and she composes an ambitious letter to a professor at Harvard asking him to consider her for admission despite her youth. Yet as she writes poetry to finance her trip to Baltimore, Ellen still clings to her hometown and friends." Libr J

Gibbons, Kaye

On the occasion of my last afternoon. Putnam 1998 273p

ISBN 0-399-14299-1

LC 98-12947

"Gibbons is unsparing in her depiction of the gruesome reality of the carnage, and unflinching in her effort to convey the madness of that time and the havoc it wreaked on people's souls." Booklist

Gibbons, Kaye

Sights unseen. Putnam 1995 209p $19.95

ISBN 0-399-13986-9

LC 95-9781

"Gibbons has her quietly heroic narrator relate one wild and poignant incident after another, holding us rapt with wonder and empathy for Maggie and her loving, self-sacrificing family. This is a novel that deserves unwavering attention from start to finish." Booklist

Gibson, William

★ **Neuromancer**; with a new introduction by the author; with an afterword by Jack Womack. 20th anniversary ed; Ace Books 2004 371p $25

ISBN 0-441-01203-5

LC 2004048718

First published 1984

"In a highly urbanized future dominated by cybernetics and bioengineering, anti-hero Case is rescued from wretchedness and given back the ability to send his persona into the cyberspace of the world's computer networks, where he must carry out a hazardous mission for an enigmatic employer. An adventure story much enlivened by elaborate technical jargon and sleazy, streetwise characters—the pioneering 'cyberpunk' novel and arguably the most influential SF novel of the 1980s." Anatomy of Wonder 5

Gibson, William

★ **Pattern** recognition. Putnam 2003 356p $25.95

ISBN 0-399-14986-4

LC 2002-67955

This novel "tells the story of Cayce Pollard, a 'coolhunter' who gets paid to spot hot new trends for marketers. In her private life, Cayce is obsessed with a series of short films that have appeared anonymously on the Internet. . . . Trouble arises when the two sides of Cayce's life short-circuit: a billionaire marketer gets wind of the films and hires her to find their creator, so he can use them as a marketing tool." (Time)

"Cayce Pollard is a brand consultant whose father disappeared on September 11th. She becomes fascinated by mysterious scraps of film footage—seemingly random scenes, luminously shot—that are disseminated on the Web and have spawned cults of viewers. Gibson wisely avoids addressing the import of 9/11 head on, but he somehow establishes a powerful correlative for it in Cayce's strange quest—through the Tokyo red-light district and the Moscow underworld—to find the anonymous filmmaker. In Gibson's eerie vision of our time, the future has come crashing upon us, fragmentary and undecipherable." New Yorker

Gibson, William

Spook country. G.P. Putnam's Sons 2007 371p $25.95

ISBN 978-0-399-15430-0; 0-399-15430-2

LC 2007-3138

This novel portrays a "post-9/11 America, which, in thrall to ubiquitous media and vague threats of annihilation, has 'developed Stockholm syndrome toward its own government.' The convoluted and politically insistent plot involves a missing shipping container, a former rock star, a Cuban-Chinese crime-facilitating family, and an Ativan addict coerced into domestic espionage. Fanciful touches include the creation of virtual art in public spaces using satellite mapping and Wi-Fi; texting in Volapuk, a Cyrillic-Latin amalgam; encrypting data within songs on an iPod; and the C.I.A.'s recruitment of sea pirates in the war on terrorism. (All but the last are verifiably real.) If Gibson's vision has got bleaker, his eye for the eerie in the everyday still lends events an otherworldly sheen." New Yorker

Gibson, William

Zero history. G.P. Putnam's Sons 2010 404p $26.95

ISBN 0-399-15682-8; 978-0-399-15682-3

LC 2010-16974

Third book in Gibson's Bigend Trilogy, which includes Pattern recognition and Spook country

"In 'Spook Country' (2007), [Hubertus] Bigend employed Hollis Henry, former lead singer of the fictional '90s band the Curfew, to investigate 'locative' technologies. Now, in 'Zero History,' Henry reluctantly accepts a second commission from Bigend, to track down the designer behind the super-fashionable but anti-fashion 'secret brand' Gabriel Hounds." (N Y Times Book Rev)

"Hollis Henry finds herself once again under Bigend's employ. This time she is hired to discover the identity of the designer of a secret brand of clothing called Gabriel Hounds, whom Bigend hopes to enlist in his bid to get into the design, contracting, and manufacture of U.S. military clothing (and its inevitable spinoff into the mainstream consumer market). Military contracting, according to Bigend, is essentially recession proof. Meanwhile, the translator and cryptologist Milgrim . . . , a former Ativan addict (now in recovery on Bigend's dime) with 'zero history' (being off the grid, he has no credit or address history), is asked to assist Hollis in her investigation. What begins as a seemingly innocent apparel-related project takes on more sinister overtones when the two are followed from London to Paris by a competitor with shady dealings in the arms trade and a personal ax to grind with Milgrim." Booklist

Gide, Andre

★ The **counterfeiters** (Les faux-monnayeurs) translated from the French of André Gide by Dorothy Bussy. Knopf 1927 365p

Original French edition, 1925

"The novelist Edouard keeps a journal of events in order to write a novel about the nature of reality. The intrigues of a gang of counterfeiters symbolize the 'counterfeit' personalities with which people disguise themselves to conform hypocritically to convention or to deceive themselves. The adolescent boys Bernard Profitendieu and Olivier Molinier, having left home in order to be free to find and develop their true selves, encounter many varieties of hyprocrisy and self-deception in human relationships and barely escape falling into such poses themselves. Both begin by seeking a close emotional tie with Edouard. Each, however, comes to recognize that Edouard is inadequate as an ideal for emulation, particularly when the novelist cannot recognize the psychological reality of the schoolboy Boris' useless suicide, which is an indirect result of the counterfeiters' machinations." Reader's Ency. 4th edition

Gide, Andre

★ The **immoralist**; translated by Richard Howard. Modern Lib. 1984 171p

ISBN 0-394-60500-4

LC 83-42856

Original French edition, 1902. First United States edition, translated by Dorothy Bussy, published 1930 by Knopf; this translation first published 1970 by Knopf

"Michel takes his bride, Marceline, to North Africa, where he develops tuberculosis and becomes hyperconscious of physical sensations, particularly of his attraction to young Arab boys. Back on his French estate after being cured, he is encouraged by his friend Ménalque to rise above conventional good and evil and give free rein to all his passions. When Marceline falls ill with the tuberculosis she caught while nursing him, he takes her south. He neglects her demands on him more and more, however, in order to keep himself free, since his new doctrine demands that the weak be suppressed if necessary for the preservation of the strong. She dies, and he, guilt-ridden and debilitated by his excesses, tries to justify his conduct to a group of friends." Reader's Ency. 4th edition

Gideon, Melanie

Wife 22; a novel. Melanie Gideon. Ballantine Books 2012 380 p.

ISBN 034552795X; 9780345527950; 9780345527974

LC 2012004405

This novel by Melanie Gideon is about "a woman losing herself . . . and finding herself again . . . in the middle of her life. . . . [A]fter almost twenty years of marriage my husband and I seemed to be running out of things to say to each other. But when the anonymous online study . . . showed up in my inbox, I had no idea how profoundly it would change my life. . . . I was assigned both a pseudonym (Wife 22) and a caseworker (Researcher 101). . . . My anonymous correspondence with Researcher 101 has taken an unexpectedly personal turn." (Publisher's note)

Gien, Pamela

The **syringa** tree; a novel. Random House 2006 262p hardcover o.p. pa $13.95

ISBN 0-375-50755-8; 0-375-75910-7 pa

LC 2006-41054

"As the meaning of apartheid unfolds, Lizzie struggles to understand racial laws that force her nanny to carry work papers and hide from the police. Through her eyes, readers see South African townships and experience the indignities that provoked underground resistance movements. Although the protagonist is occasionally cloying, this is part of the book's charm." Libr J

Giffin, Emily

Heart of the matter. St. Martin's Press 2010 386p $26.99

ISBN 978-0-312-55416-3; 0-312-55416-8

LC 2009-45700

"Giffin's chronicle of fluid, almost casual marital disconnect is a powerful cautionary tale. The slow erosion of marriage leaves Tessa with a litany of unanswered questions. . . . While the ending provides no pat answers, as one would hope, there is the very deliberate turning of a page as, despite transgressions, each of the main characters finds a pathway for looking forward and moving ahead." Boston Globe

Gifford, Barry

The **stars** above Veracruz. Thunder's Mouth Press 2006 262p $24

ISBN 1-56025-807-1

LC 2006-282377

"While the stories take place in cities from Berlin to Havana to San Francisco and involve characters as disparate as a prizefighter, a schoolboy, and a one-legged ex-Legionnaire, each concerns the naked bravery of characters stepping into maturity. Gifford's great talent is capturing defining moments with the casual grace of anecdote. Each of these 16 stunning tales makes the anecdotal monumental." San Francisco Magazine

Gilb, Dagoberto

The **flowers**. Grove Press 2008 250p $24

ISBN 978-0-8021-1859-2; 0-8021-1859-3

"A tightly woven narrative about a boy coming of age in a community bubbling with racial tension. It's beautifully rendered in part because Mr. Gilb nails the voice of 15-year-old narrator Sonny Bravo with pinpoint accuracy." Dallas Morning News

Gilchrist, Ellen

The **age** of miracles; stories. Little, Brown 1995 260p

LC 94-37441

In several of the stories in this collection, the author recounts the adventures of her recurring heroine Rhoda Manning. "Elegant, independent, and successful, Rhoda is approaching 60 with unwavering nerve, delighted with the freedom age brings." Booklist

Gilchrist, Ellen

The **cabal** and other stories. Little, Brown 2000 272p $35

ISBN 0-316-31491-9

LC 99-36893

The cabal "takes place in Jackson, Mississippi, upon Caroline Jones' arrival in town to begin a college teaching job. It just so happens that Caroline's arrival coincides with the mental breakdown of the psychiatrist who tends to the wellbeing of the town's artistic elite, a group called 'the Cabal,' all of whom are subsequently threatened with the public revelation of their deep, dark secrets." Booklist

Gilchrist, Ellen

★ **Ellen** Gilchrist: collected stories. Little, Brown 2000 563p $38

ISBN 0-316-29948-0

"Gilchrist is an important voice in contemporary Southern fiction, and this book belongs in every library." Libr J

Gilchrist, Ellen

Flights of angels; stories. Little, Brown 1998 327p $34

ISBN 0-316-31486-2

LC 98-21420

This collection "features some of Gilchrist's familiar, endearingly eccentric narrators. . . . There are also some new, young and engaging characters and, throughout the book, a convincing evocation of the changing South." Publ Wkly

Gill, Bartholomew

Death in Dublin; a novel of suspense. Morrow 2003 294p $24.95

ISBN 0-06-000849-0

LC 2002-32582

"Gill's final novel pits Police Chief Peter McGarr against a thief and murderer: a night watchman at Dublin's Trinity College has been killed and the irreplaceable Book of Kells stolen. McGarr suspects an infamous and most dangerous band of IRA zealots. Excellent work from a tried-and-true hand." Libr J

Gill, Bartholomew

The **death** of an Irish lover; a Peter McGarr mystery. Avon Bks. 2000 265p $23

ISBN 0-380-97797-4

LC 99-58663

"McGarr of the Dublin Police, who is the chief homicide cop in Ireland, is summoned to the village of Leixleap on the

River Shannon to solve a double murder. Two local fisheries officers, known as the 'eel police' for their efforts to control the lucrative trade of eel poaching, are discovered dead at the local upscale inn. The older man and young woman apparently have been killed by a single bullet. The fact that the room was locked at the time of the murders is the least puzzling aspect of this case." Booklist

"The contradictions Gill manages to unearth in one small, placid patch of Irish ground are simply astonishing." N Y Times Book Rev

Gill, Bartholomew

The **death** of an Irish sea wolf; a Peter McGarr mystery. Morrow 1996 296p

ISBN 978-0688141837

LC 96-15680

This novel is "part swashbuckling adventure . . . and part modern detective story about the disappearance of an old man with a dark past. Peter McGarr, head of the Serious Crimes Unit of the Garda Siochana, applies muscle to break through the sullen reserve of the islanders, an inbred lot who glare coldly at all outsiders. Mr. Gill gives a rough tongue to these crusty salts; but when he puts the town behind him and looks out to sea, there's poetry in his voice." N Y Times Book Rev

Gill, Bartholomew

Death on a cold, wild river; a Peter McGarr mystery. Morrow 1993 251p

LC 93-7729

"Gill writes well, setting the tone for introspective passages with evocations of Ireland's wild coastal landscape on one page, while amusing us with witty pub banter on another. . . . Unpredictable, philosophical, funny, and ever so satisfying." Booklist

Gillham, David R.

City of women; David R. Gillham. Amy Einhorn Books 2012 392 p. (hardcover) $25.95; (paperback) $16.00

ISBN 039915776X; 9780399157769; 9780425252963

LC 2012011002

This book is the story of Sigrid Schröder, "an unassuming stenographer stuck in a loveless marriage and living in Berlin [during World War II] with her sour, difficult mother-in-law. But . . . she has . . . a Jewish lover, and if that were not risky enough, Sigrid becomes entangled with a neighbor who is helping to shelter Jews. As the war progresses, and Sigrid's husband is sent to the Russian front, she's drawn deeper into a world where trust is a hard-won commodity." (Publishers Weekly)

Gilman, Charlotte Perkins

The **Charlotte** Perkins Gilman reader; The yellow wallpaper and other fiction. edited and introduced by Ann J. Lane. Pantheon Bks. 1980 208p

LC 80-7711

The editor "has selected representative pieces by the early-twentieth-century American feminist socialist, including her best known (and best) quasi-autobiographical story, 'The Yellow Wallpaper,' plus excerpts from four novels and three writings about utopias." Booklist

Gilman, Charlotte Perkins

Charlotte Perkins Gilman's Utopian novels; edited and with an introduction by Minna Doskow. Fairleigh Dickinson Univ. Press 1999 389p

ISBN 0-8386-3761-2

LC 98-23510

In Moving the mountain, an explorer, lost in Tibet for thirty years, returns to the United States in 1940 and finds a society totally transformed by women

Includes bibliographical references

Gilman, Charlotte Perkins

Herland; with an introduction by Ann J. Lane. Pantheon Bks. 1979 xxiv, 147p

Written in 1915, Herland was serialized in Gilman's monthly magazine, 'The Forerunner.'

"On the eve of World War I, three American male explorers stumble onto an all-female society somewhere in the distant reaches of the earth. Unable to believe their eyes, they promptly set out to find the men of the society, convinced that, since 'this is a "civilized" country . . . there must be men.' . . . {The novel examines} what is masculine and what is feminine, what is culturally learned and what is biologically determined in our society." Publisher's note

Gilman, Charlotte Perkins

With her in Ourland; sequel to Herland. edited by Mary Jo Deegan and Michael R. Hill; with an introduction by Mary Jo Deegan. Greenwood Press 1997 200p $100.95

ISBN 0-313-27614-5

LC 96-51135

Written in 1916, With her in Ourland was serialized in Gilman's magazine, The Forerunner

"He's a brash American adventurer; she's an independent, albeit sheltered, sociologist from Herland, a 2000-year-old, all-female society. Not surprisingly, when Vandyck (Van) and Ellador marry, most everything becomes a point of negotiation, if not contention: sexual relations, family obligations and attitudes about race, class and the welfare state." Publ Wkly

Gilman, Dorothy

The amazing Mrs. Pollifax. Doubleday 1970 234p

Mrs. Emily Pollifax, widow and grandmother, combats international espionage at the request of the C.I.A. in this spy adventure. The scene is Istanbul where Mrs. Pollifax must help a double agent escape. That she does, outwitting the enemy with her own special brand of logic

Gilman, Dorothy

The elusive Mrs. Pollifax. Doubleday 1971 240p

Mrs. Pollifax "the genteel grandmother-heroine swings into action for the CIA by transporting in her hat some forged passports to the Bulgarian underground which turns out to be a group of five amateurs. In her travels Mrs. Pollifax meets some young Americans, one of whom is ostensibly imprisoned for espionage but actually held for ransom, and Mrs. Pollifax involves the underground and a paid in-

former in a daring rescue plan. Amusing spy adventure with more appeal for readers of light fiction than for espionage buffs." Booklist

Gilman, Dorothy

Kaleidoscope; a Countess Karitska novel. Ballantine Bks. 2002 244p $21

ISBN 0-345-44820-0

LC 2002-277874

"Madame Karitska's trade as a fortune teller attracts a strange array of clients, including an artistic woman whose husband abandons her to join a religious cult and an Italian immigrant with a 'cursed' child. Karitska also helps her good friend, Detective-Lieutenant Pruden, solve the hit-and-run death of a young violinist and the murder of a local philanthropist. Her most troubling case, however, occurs when a subway incident leaves her with an attaché case full of diamonds. This {is a} well-written episodic adventure." Libr J

Gilman, Dorothy

Mrs. Pollifax and the whirling dervish. Doubleday 1990 196p

LC 89-25796

"Mrs. Pollifax's present assignment is to pose as the aunt of a C.I.A. agent while the two, in the guise of tourists, verify the bona fides of the informants, matching faces to photographs. To find the seven, Mrs. Pollifax and her escort are expected to spend a week traversing the desert and mountain areas that lie between Fez and the Algerian border. No sooner do they begin their mission than the first informant is murdered—and Mrs. Pollifax herself is in danger of becoming the killer's next victim." N Y Times Book Rev

"The countryside is depicted in great detail, and so are the native people. Gilman's eye for background matches her marvelous sense of adventure." Booklist

Gilman, Dorothy

Mrs. Pollifax pursued. Fawcett Columbine 1995 198p

LC 94-27625

Mrs. Pollifax "discovers a young woman in her hall closet hiding from some men in a white van. Eager as always, she elicits the girl's story, eludes the villains, and enables the CIA to resolve the situation, which involves kidnapping, shady investments, attempted murder, and the grandson of Ubangiba's last king. Agents actually consult reference books for essential background information, and a few literary allusions build character or relate to earlier Pollifax appearances. This fast-moving tale sports a lively, energetic style." Libr J

Gilman, Dorothy

Mrs. Pollifax, innocent tourist. Fawcett Columbine 1997 203p

LC 96-47715

Mrs. Pollifax is on "a trip to the Middle East with her CIA friend Farrell to retrieve a manuscript written by a murdered dissident. The manuscript, thinly disguised as fiction, provides provocative details of Saddam Hussein's reign of terror. The pickup, arranged through an intermediary, proves much more difficult than Farrell or Mrs. Pollifax anticipated, what with smugglers disguised as businessmen, attacks by knife-wielding sheikhs, car chases, and rides on berserk camels. . . . Fun and entertaining, this one is sure to be a hit with the legion of Mrs. Pollifax fans." Booklist

Gilman, Dorothy

A **palm** for Mrs. Pollifax. Doubleday 1973 226p
ISBN 0-385-09134-6

Emily Pollifax "registers as a guest at a posh resort-clinic in Switzerland where the C.I.A. thinks some stolen plutonium has been hidden. In the course of her investigation Mrs. Pollifax discovers the murdered body of her Interpol contact, meets a charming jewel thief who becomes her ally, befriends a frightened little boy who is the son of a leader in a Middle East nation, and escapes through a latrine chute from a mountain top castle where she and the boy are hiding from the killers who intend to use the plutonium to upset the balance of power in the Middle East." Booklist

Gilman, Dorothy

Thale's Folly. Ballantine Pub. Group 1999 199p
ISBN 0-449-00364-7

LC 98-27657

"At first, it seems Gilman is rounding up the usual literary suspects, but her genial and well-paced writing, vivid landscapes, and quirky characters are greater than the sum of the clichés." Booklist

Gilman, Dorothy

The **unexpected** Mrs. Pollifax. Doubleday 1966 216p

A "tale of espionage with the chase in Mexico and through the mountains of Albania. Emily Pollifax, a widow of 63, was startled by her doctor's suggestion that the cure for her depression was a job. The only career that inspired Emily was spying, and despite her lack of qualifications, off she went to CIA headquarters in Langly, Virginia, to apply. How she became a routine courier, and why unexpected developments brought into play every scrap of skill and knowledge she had acquired in her former secure life, is an exciting discovery for the reader." Libr J

Gilman, Felix

★ The **half**-made world. Tor 2010 479p $25.99
ISBN 978-0-7653-2552-5; 0-7653-2552-7

LC 2010-32564

"Sick of predictable books that fill your subgenre bingo card with the same subgenre elements over and over? . . . . Felix Gilman has blended elements from alternate history, Steampunk, Westerns, and epic fantasy to create something truly original." io9

Gilman, Keith

✓ **Father's** Day. Minotaur Books 2009 259p $24.95
ISBN 978-0-312-38365-7; 0-312-38365-7

LC 2009-08003

"Lou Klein, an ex-Philadelphia cop-turned-PI, returns to his old neighborhood and moves into his deceased mother's house. He has been asked to find the missing daughter of one of his oldest friends. Complications arise when Lou's own daughter comes to stay and bodies begin springing up all over Philadelphia with possible connections to his case.

Narrated in a wise-old-guy tone that is matched by Lou's knack for getting under people's skin, this debut takes us on a roller-coaster ride of surprises." Libr J

Gilman, Laura Ann

✓ **Flesh** and fire; Laura Anne Gilman. Pocket Books 2009 374p (hbk.) o.p.; (pbk.) $9.99
ISBN 9781439101414; 9781439126875;
9781439191545

LC 2009012786

In this fantasy novel, "[o]nce, all power in the Vin Lands was held by the prince-mages, who alone could craft spell-wines, and selfishly used them to increase their own wealth and influence. But their abuse of power caused a demigod to break the Vine, shattering the power of the mages. Now, fourteen centuries later, it is the humble Vinearts who hold the secret of crafting spells from wines, the source of magic, and they are prohibited from holding power. But now . . . [s]trange, terrifying creatures, sudden plagues, and mysterious disappearances threaten the land. Only one Vineart senses the danger, and he has only one weapon to use against it: a young slave. His name is Jerzy, and his origins are unknown. . . . Yet his uncanny sense of the Vinearts' craft offers a hint of greater magics within -- magics that his Master, the Vineart Malech, must cultivate and grow." (Publisher's note)

Followed by: Weight of Stone (2012)

Gilman, Laura Anne

Hard magic. Luna 2010 329p pa $14.95
ISBN 978-0-373-80313-2; 0-373-80313-3

"Spinning off a minor character from the Retrievers books (Staying Dead, etc.), Gilman launches an entertaining new series set in her Cosa Nostradamus world of magic-using Talented humans. Following up on a mysterious job lead, college grad Bonita Torres joins the Private Unaffiliated Paranormal Investigations (PUPI), a freelance CSI-style unit for Talent-related crimes. The puppies refine and practice spells until they get their first big case: an apparent double suicide. As they follow the evidence, trail and interrogate suspects, and defend themselves against attacks, the investigators develop comfortable and engaging team dynamics and create the field of forensic magic. Gilman's deft plotting and first-class characters complement her agile blend of science and spell craft." Publ Wkly

Gilmore, Jennifer

✓ **Golden** country; a novel. Scribner 2006 315p $25
ISBN 978-0-7432-8863-7; 0-7432-8863-7

LC 2005-57586

"An ingeniously plotted family yarn. Gilmore's careful planning results in a satisfying blend of story lines, and her refusal to settle on one simple perspective enlivens the myth of the American Dream." N Y Times Book Rev

Gilmore, Jennifer

The **Mothers**; 1st Scribner hardcover ed. Simon & Schuster 2013 288 p. (hardcover) $26
ISBN 1451697252; 9781451697254

LC 2012533117

This third novel from Jennifer Gilmore is the "cry of a woman who desperately wants a baby. Jesse Weintraub, a

FICTION CORE COLLECTION
Seventeenth Edition

history professor in Manhattan, is postcancer and almost 40. After years of trying to get pregnant, she and husband Ramon Aragon pursue open adoption. The chronicle of their 10-year marriage, forged when Jewish Jesse met Spanish-Italian Ramon in Italy, is a paradoxical tale of marital love surmounting cultural and religious differences and then veering into obsessive desperation." (Publishers Weekly)

Gilmore, Jennifer
Something red; a novel. Scribner 2010 307p $25

ISBN 9781416571704; 1416571701

LC 2009-40482

"When their oldest child, Ben, leaves for college, Dennis and Sharon Goldstein—one-time young idealists who became a bureaucrat and a society caterer, respectively—begin to discover their family's secrets. Not only is Sharon having an affair but daughter Vanessa is anorexic. Indeed, it's soon evident that the family secrets transcend generations. The story is told in chapters from the point of view of each family member, detailing Dennis's travel for the U.S. Department of Agriculture and recollections of when his children were young, Sharon's extramarital affair and her relationship with Vanessa, Ben's college experimentation and activism, and Vanessa's high school relationships and eating disorder." Libr J

Gingrich, Newt
Gettysburg; a novel of the Civil War. {by} Newt Gingrich and William Forstchen; and Albert S. Hanser, contributing editor. St. Martin's Press 2003 463p il $24.95

ISBN 0-312-30935-X

LC 2003-41381

"On July 1, 1863, the Army of Virginia, under the command of Gen. Robert E. Lee, and the Army of the Potomac, under Gen. George G. Meade, clashed in deadly combat near Gettysburg, PA. Of course, Union forces won, but Gingrich and Forstchen imagine a different outcome in which Confederate forces do a surprise march around Union lines to flank and cut off the Union troops from their supply and information routes. In the course of their narrative, the authors depict the gallantry and heroism of Lee, Longstreet, Chamberlain, Hancock, Hunt, and many other officers and enlisted men on both sides of the conflict." Libr J

Gingrich, Newt
Grant comes east; a novel of the Civil War. [by] Newt Gingrich, William R. Forstchen and Albert S. Hanser, contributing editor. 1st ed; Thomas Dunne Books\St. Martin's Press 2004 404p il map $24.95

ISBN 0-312-30937-6

LC 2004-43894

This alternate-history sequel to the author's Gettysburg "centers on the Union government's bringing General Grant eastward from his recent victory in Vicksburg; of course, the immediate ramification of Lee's win at Gettysburg . . . is the threatened safety of Washington, D.C.–and further down the line, the possibility of actual and official recognition of the Confederacy by the European powers. Gingrich and Forstchen's readjustments to history are notably original." Booklist

Ginsberg, Debra
The **grift**; a novel. Shaye Areheart Books 2008 337p $23.95

ISBN 978-0-307-38272-6; 0-307-38272-9

LC 2008-947

"Leaving aside any question of tingling paranormal subtext, The Grift presents a lifelike, multishaded rendering of San Diego's blend of cultures, classes, ancestries and motivations. Ms. Ginsberg folds Marina into the lives and complicated romances of the locals like a stripe of colored sand in a painted-desert souvenir bottle. The Grift is a gift with no strings attached, no dark outcome to dread, a satisfyingly voyeuristic vision of a mysterious stranger's supernaturally charged fortune." N Y Times Book Rev

Giordano, Paolo
The **solitude** of prime numbers. Pamela Dorman Books/Viking 2010 271p $25.95

ISBN 978-0-670-02148-2

LC 2009-41165

Original Italian edition, 2008; This translation first published 2009 in the United Kingdom

"Alice has been crippled in a childhood skiing accident, Mattia is consumed by guilt after playing an unintended but key role in his twin sister's disappearance. Upon meeting in their early teens, they develop a frequently uncomfortable yet enveloping friendship. . . . This is a book about communication: in lacking a facility for self-expression, our stunted protagonists exist almost solely, and safely, in their own minds. Despite its heavy subject matter, it reads easily, due in part to the almost seamless translation. A quietly explosive ending completes the novel in just the fashion it was started, as an intimate psychological portrait of two 'prime numbers'—together alone and alone together." Booklist

Giraldi, William
Busy monsters; a novel. W. W. Norton & Company 2011 282p $24.95

ISBN 978-0-393-07962-3; 0-393-07962-7

LC 2011-07710

The book is a novel in which "Charles Homar is a memoirist of only 'mediocre fame,' . . . who is deeply in love with the vaunted Gillian. When she decides to leave him to pursue her burning passion for hunting a giant squid, he more or less loses his mind. On the dubious advice of his macho best friend, Groot, he lets loose with machine-gun fire on the prow of his beloved's sea vessel and subsequently lands in [jail]. . . . Upon release, he hunts for Sasquatch in the wilds of Canada, looks for UFOs in Seattle, and seeks advice about love from a steroid-fueled bodybuilder in suburban New Jersey. Through it all, Homar treats us to a discursive rant on culture high and low, dissing Goethe and Mel Gibson in equal measure." (Booklist)

"Charles is a familiar breed in modern fiction—an emotionally stunted manchild in his thirties prone to speaking in self-congratulatory platitudes. But Charles's life (and grasp on reality) is upended when his fiancée, Gillian, abruptly dumps him for a giant squid. Not literally—Busy Monsters isn't quite that far out there—but she goes in pursuit of this mammoth cephalopod aboard a ship (appropriately) named The Kraken. Charles determines the only way to win her back is through a grand gesture: capturing Sasquatch, a beast of even greater legendary proportions. Charles's journey

brings him cross-country, where he encounters strange creatures and even stranger people. Giraldi's prose throughout
is enveloping but it's also intimate, reading almost like the
lovesick diary entries of Franz Kafka. But beneath the surreal, there's substance: The encounters with fantastical creatures and lampooning of famous epics (like The Odyssey)
are merely set pieces in his Gen-Y ruminations on relationships and mortality." Time Out N Y

Giroux, E. X.

A **death** for a dancer. St. Martin's Press 1985
198p

LC 85-10896

"Barrister Robert Forsythe and his vigilant secretary,
Miss Sanderson, are pressed by another barrister into examining a case involving a body found inconveniently in a
miniature Chinese Temple on one of England's most sumptuous estates. The victim is con artist Katherine St. Croix,
whose demise throws the family of Sir Amyas Dancer into
giddy paroxysms of speculation that can only be relieved,
claims Dancer, by a private investigator. Enter Forsythe and
Sanderson and exit normalcy as the Dancer family surrounds
them with their bizarrely eccentric demeanor." Booklist

Girzone, Joseph F.

Joshua and the city. Doubleday 1995 242p
ISBN 0-385-47420-2

LC 94-41941

In this inspirational novel set in late 20th century New
York "a mysterious stranger named Joshua appears, bringing with him a vision for healing the city's numerous social
ills. As he walks the city streets, Joshua enters the lives of
a number of people who are trapped in the downward spiral
of their society, offering them love and strong hope for a
brighter future. Joshua reaches out to both rich and poor as
he tries to build God's kingdom on Earth." Libr J

Girzone, Joseph F.

Joshua, the homecoming. Doubleday 1999
259p $19.95
ISBN 0-385-49509-9

LC 99-33129

In this inspirational novel set in 20th century America,
the solitary carpenter Joshua returns to the small town of
Auburn after a 20 year absence. Finding fear and spiritual insecurity among the new generation due to the coming Apocalypse, he calms the people with reminders of God's love

Girzone, Joseph F.

The **shepherd**. Macmillan 1990 246p

LC 90-2351

"Girzone's story is a neat picture of where many American Catholics wish their church would head, but it may
be far too unrealistically drawn to have an impact on real
lives." Booklist

Glapion, Jonathan

Batman; Volume 1 Scott Snyder, Greg Capullo,
Jonathan Glapion. DC Comics 2012 176 p. $24.99
ISBN 1401235417; 9781401235413

LC 2011051796

This New York Times Bestseller comic book anthology,
by Scott Snyder and illustrated by Greg Capullo, "begins a
new era of The Dark Knight as with the relaunch of 'Batman,' as a part of DC Comics-The New 52! After a series
of . . . murders rocks Gotham City, Batman begins to realize
that . . . these crimes go far deeper than appearances suggest.
. . . [Batman] discovers a conspiracy going back to his youth
and beyond to the origins of the city he's sworn to protect."
(Publisher's note)

Glass, Julia

I see you everywhere. Pantheon Books 2008
287p $24.95
ISBN 978-0-375-42275-1; 0-375-42275-7

LC 2008-00212

"Mourning, a dish that never grows cold, is the subtext
of I See You Everywhere, but it is only part of the feast.
Rich, intricate and alive with emotion, the book reconstructs
the complicated bonds between Louisa and Clem, making
neither sister a villain, neither a hero." N Y Times Book Rev

Glass, Julia

★ **Three** Junes. Pantheon Bks. 2002 353p
ISBN 0-375-42144-0

LC 2001-55448

A "narrative of the McLeod family during three vital
summers. . . . Paul McLeod, the reticent Scots widower
introduced in the first section, is the father of Fenno, the
central character of the middle section, who is a reserved,
self-protective gay bookstore owner in Manhattan; both
have dealings with the third section's searching young artist,
Fern Olitsky, whose guilt is the wake of her husband's death
leaves her longing for—and fearful of—beginning anew."
Publ Wkly

"Free of gimmickry, 'Three Junes' brilliantly rescues,
then refurbishes, the traditional plot-driven novel." N Y
Times Book Rev

Glass, Julia

The **whole** world over. Pantheon Books 2006
506p $25.95
ISBN 0-375-42274-9

LC 2005-54043

"Glass is too capable to need recipes and four-legged
friends to make her fiction a pleasure. It's a tribute to this
unassuming but conspicuously talented novelist that even
with far too many of them, The Whole World Over so often
manages to sing." N Y Times Book Rev

Glass, Julia

The **widower's** tale. Pantheon Books 2010
402p $25.95
ISBN 978-0-307-37792-0; 0-307-37792-X

LC 2010-02854

"Percy Darling, 70, is the titular widower, a rigid man
still sorely missing his long-deceased wife. He holds the
center of Glass' [novel], . . . set in a bucolic town outside
of Boston. Orbiting around Percy are two grown daughters:
one a divorced flibbertigibbet and the other a renowned oncologist who is as stern with her family as she is open and
available to her patients. Add to the mix a wayward Harvard grandson, a Guatemalan gardener, a gay preschool

teacher, and a salt-of-the-earth artist who reminds Percy that he is still very much alive. It's a large, endearing cast, bursting with emotional and social issues, and Glass slips effortlessly between their individual and enmeshed dramas." Entertainment Wkly

Glavinic, Thomas

Night work; translated from the German by John Brownjohn. Canongate 2008 375p pa $15

ISBN 978-1-84767-184-4; 1-84767-184-5

Original German edition, 2006

"The premise is incredibly simple. Jonas is a young Viennese man with an undemanding and unfulfilling job as an adviser on interior design, and a girlfriend, Marie, who has gone to visit her sister in Scotland for a few days. On July 4 he wakes up, and is surprised by how quiet the streets are. He can't get Marie on her mobile. The television is only showing static snow, on every channel. As he ventures out, he finds that the world is deserted. Every single living being has vanished. Something apocalyptic has happened, and for some reason Jonas has survived it. . . . Night Work is quite self-consciously philosophical. . . . The solitude makes Jonas prone to musing – about God, identity, love, death and memory. None of this jars or seems superfluous to the narrative." Scotsman

Gleason, Robert

End of days. Forge 2011 490p $24.99

ISBN 978-0-7653-2992-9; 0-7653-2992-1

LC 2011-19776

"Among the principal characters are John Stone, gonzo journalist; Kate Magruder, Stone's ex-girlfriend, whose mother uses her media empire to warn the world about the oncoming nuclear Armageddon and who has built a fortress, the Citadel, where she intends to wait out the war; and Ronald 'Cool Breeze' Robinson, a new prisoner in the notorious Texas prison known as Jack Town. And then there are the more bizarre characters: a massive, singing rat known as Sailor, the story's real hero; semi-sentient nuclear weapons; and scores of madmen, killers, sadists, torturers, and evildoers bent on the earth's destruction. It all adds up to a thrilling take on a frighteningly possible future, one that makes the journey in Cormac McCarthy's The Road look like a stroll through the park." Publ Wkly

Gloss, Molly

The **hearts** of horses. Houghton Mifflin Co. 2007 289p $24

ISBN 978-0-618-79990-9; 0-618-79990-7

LC 2007-8521

Gloss bases her novel on "historical accounts of cowgirls in the American West. With obvious appeal for horse lovers, it has a homespun quality, and varies in action between a gentle canter and energetic gallop." Libr J

Glynn, Alan

Bloodland; Alan Glynn. Faber and Faber 2011 417 p.

ISBN 0571275427; 0571275435; 9780571275427; 9780571275434

LC 2011514786

This book follows "a hungry young journalist named Jimmy Gilroy" who is investigating the case of "Susie Monaghan . . . on the cusp of stardom when her life was cut short by a tragic helicopter crash. . . . Before dying, Susie's path had crossed with an unlikely gallery of powerful men: an ex-Prime minister with a carefully guarded secret; the businessman brother of a U.S. Senator angling for the Oval Office; and a billionaire investor with his eye on an extremely rare commodity. Might there also be a link between Susie's death and a deranged security contractor operating in Congo? Piece by piece, Jimmy uncovers a bizarre nexus of coincidence among these disparate people and events." (Publisher's note)

Goddard, Robert

Beyond recall; a novel. Holt & Co. 1998 310p

ISBN 0-8050-5110-4

LC 97-28895

First published 1997 in the United Kingdom

"There's an elegant arc to Goddard's fluid style, which gracefully orchestrates the story over its broad time span and through the ambiguous testimony of its complex characters." N Y Times Book Rev

Goddard, Robert

Found wanting; a novel. Bantam Books Trade Paperback 2011 357p pa $15

ISBN 978-0-385-34362-6

LC 2010-27207

First published 2008 in the United Kingdom

"Masterful writing and a hot pursuit across Europe elevate this novel. Men in gray flannel suits haven't been this exciting in quite some time." Kirkus

Goddard, Robert

★ **Into** the blue. Poseidon Press 1990 415p

ISBN 0-671-70482-6

LC 90-42481

"During this quest, Harry's courage is tested as well as his judgment of people—all of whom turn out to be totally and depressingly human. An everyman's hero, against all mental and emotional odds, Harry finds Heather and renewed self-respect. A very satisfying novel in every way." Booklist

Goddard, Robert

★ **Long** time coming; a novel. Bantam Books Trade Paperbacks 2010 420p pa $15

ISBN 978-0-385-34361-9; 0-385-34361-2

LC 2009-44547

In this thriller the author "shifts effortlessly between 1976, when 68-year-old Eldritch Swan, thought killed in the Blitz, resurfaces from 36 years in an Irish prison, and 1940, when Eldritch, a cocksure secretary for an unscrupulous Antwerp diamond merchant, Isaac Meridor, prepares to leave for America. The older Eldritch, who appears as weird as his given name implies, assures his nephew, Stephen, he'd been framed in Dublin for unspecified offenses against the state, though he admits to helping steal Meridor's Picasso collection. Eldritch needs Stephen's help to prove the collection rightfully belongs to Meridor's wife, daughter, and granddaughter, Rachel Banner. Bit by tantalizing bit the convoluted tale of Eldritch's unknowing involvement in high wartime crimes and misdemeanors during Britain's finest hour emerges, deftly counterpointed by Stephen's growing attachment to Rachel." Publ Wkly

Goddard, Robert

Never go back. Delta Trade Paperbacks 2007 336p pa $12

ISBN 978-0-385-34063-2; 038534063X

LC 2007-6336

First published 2006 in the United Kingdom

"In 1955, Harry Barnett and a group of fellow Royal Air Force servicemen participated in a teaching experiment in a castle on the outskirts of Aberdeen, Scotland. (Each agreed to be a guinea pig in lieu of punishment for bad behavior.) Now, 50 years later, surviving RAF alumni are invited to a reunion at the same royal locale. Though Barnett, now 70, is reluctant to be away from his wife and young daughter in Vancouver, British Columbia, he decides to go. Tragedy strikes when one of the retired servicemen jumps from the train en route from London (or was he pushed?). In the midst of the reunion, a suspicious automobile accident kills another, and suddenly this get-together doesn't seem like such a good plan. Police soon name Harry and former business partner Barry, whose shady financial dealings once landed him in prison, as prime suspects. Certain the violence is linked to the experiments carried out half a century ago, the two men launch an investigation of their own. Goddard's latest offering marks the return of unlikely hero Harry Barnett, star of Into the Blue (1990) and Out of the Sun (1997). It's a crackling good read, with clipped prose, complex characters, and a smart, sinuous plot." Booklist

Godden, Rumer

The **battle** of the Villa Fiorita. Viking 1963 312p

A "novel about the immediate effects of their parent's divorce on two English children who run off to Italy to persuade their mother to return home. She is enjoying a premarital honeymoon, days filled with sun, golden light, quiet and love, with an English film director. The two children crash into this peaceful pattern and the battle lines are drawn, children against adults." Publ Wkly

Godden's "characters live and linger in the mind, and the very feel of golden Italy counterpoints the sharp battle in which both sides so tragically lose." Libr J

Godden, Rumer

★ **Black** Narcissus. Little, Brown 1939 294p

A "story of a small group of Anglican nuns newly settled in a convent, formerly a general's pleasure palace, on a high ledge facing Himalayan winds and snows. How the strange pagan environment and unusual experiences affect each of the Sisters, and how a year's effort to teach and heal the natives come to naught is related in a portrayal impressive for its beauty, poignancy and insight." Bookmark

Godden, Rumer

★ The **greengage** summer; a novel. Viking 1958 218p

"There is real evil in Miss Godden's novel as well as real good: sex and theft and even murder intrude upon her dewy world as baldly as on the daily papers. But even violence she

handles with consummate delicacy. If she allows a moral to creep in, it is that we lose something valuable in gaining maturity." N Y Her Trib Books

Godden, Rumer

Pippa passes. Morrow 1994 171p

ISBN 0-688-13397-5

LC 94-18336

"In less able hands, these highly romantic goings-on would seem contrived, but Godden's graceful storytelling keeps readers enthralled, with gorgeous Venice and the nitty-gritty of the dance troupe's routine providing a convincing backdrop for her winsome ingenue." Publ Wkly

Godey, John

The **taking** of Pelham one two three. Putnam 1973 316p

LC 72-92306

A suspense novel about a "New York subway train that is hijacked by four desperate men who threaten to murder sixteen passengers unless the mayor pays $1 million ransom. . . . Ryder, the brain behind the caper, is an amoral, asexual fatalist who killed for country in Vietnam and for profit as a mercenary in the Congo and Biafra. Longman, bitter at being sacked from his subway-motorman job, is willing to exploit his intimate knowledge of the transit system. Steever is a . . . hood who follows orders and Welcome is a surly Mafia reject who doesn't." Newsweek

"Brutally realistic and coarse in its details and language, but will be popular with suspense story readers." Booklist

Godwin, Gail

Evensong. Ballantine Bks. 1999 405p

ISBN 0-345-37244-1

LC 98-15861

Sequel to Father Melancholy's daughter

Godwin "has created a character who has enough flaws to satisfy contemporary skeptics but who also struggles convincingly with the old-fashioned task of being a good person. For all its leisurely pace, Evensong turns out, near the end, to have wasted few words." Time

Godwin, Gail

★ The **finishing** school. Viking 1985 322p

ISBN 0-670-31494-3

LC 84-40069

"Fourteen, yearning to grow up, and grieving for the world of Southern gentility she left behind when her widowed mother moved them up north to live with a determinedly middle-class aunt, Justin Stokes 'falls in love' that first summer in rural New York. Ursula DeVane, who shares the neighboring old mansion with her reclusive pianist brother, is 44, a sophisticated bohemian who dazzles . . . Justin with her worldliness and her attentions. A cabin in the woods becomes Justin's 'finishing school' as the . . . tale of Ursula's mysterious past unfolds. . . . {This story is} told from the point of view of a grown-up Justin, nearly 30 years later." Libr J

"'The Finishing School' is a strikingly accurate examination of the affinity between adolescence and middle age." N Y Times Book Rev

Godwin, Gail

★ **Flora**; a novel. Gail Godwin. Bloomsbury 2013 288 p. $26

ISBN 1620401207; 9781620401200

LC 2012036741

In this book, "Helen, a writer, looks back to the fateful summer of 1945, when she was a precocious, motherless 10-year-old trying to make sense of a complicated and unjust world. Young Helen lives on a hill in North Carolina in an old . . . house that was once a sanatorium for folks she calls the Recoverers. Raised by her . . . grandmother, whom she worships, Helen is bereft after Nonie's sudden death" and she must live with her guileless cousin Flora. (Booklist)

Godwin, Gail

The **good** husband. Ballantine Bks. 1994 468p

LC 94-5651

Death "is the metaphorical 'good husband' whom brilliant professor Magda Danvers invokes as she lies dying, a process in which she participates with the same intellectual zest she has brought to her scholarship. While her body wastes away from cancer, she is devotedly tended by her own 'good husband,' Francis Lake, a former seminarian 12 years her junior. They are an unlikely pair: self-effacing Francis is content in his role as house husband and general factotum to flamboyant, iconoclastic Magda. In contrast, the union of Alice and Hugo Henry should constitute marital serenity. Hugo is a 50ish Southern novelist temporarily occupying a chair at Aurelia College; Alice is the empathetic editor who shepherded to publication the work on which his celebrity rests. Yet an icy chill has descended between them after the loss, at birth, of their son. And Hugo's prickly abrasiveness has been exacerbated by writer's block." Publ Wkly

"Godwin's intensely drawn characters are vividly portrayed during the most intimate times of love, marriage, and death." Libr J

Godwin, Gail

A **mother** and two daughters. Viking 1982 564p

ISBN 0-670-49021-0

LC 81-65286

"Suddenly widowed Nell Strickland and her two daughters, reunited in grief, are all on the verge of change as the story begins. Bohemian Cate is twice divorced, almost 40, out of a teaching job and threatened by losses, while younger Lydia, who just left her husband, is winning: a college degree, a new lover, and fame as a TV personality. Ambivalent about accommodation and possibility but 'hospitable . . . to whatever came next,' each has created herself anew by the end. The North Carolina setting is as precisely evoked as {are} the many unusual, amusing characters." Libr J

Godwin, Gail

Queen of the underworld; a novel. Random House 2006 336p $24.95

ISBN 0-345-48318-9

LC 2005-48592

"Emma Gant, Godwin's alter ego, is an eager young reporter just out of college, who lands at a Miami paper in 1959 and makes her way through a landscape populated by scheming journalists, Jewish mobsters, Cuban exiles, a schmalzy ex-beauty queen, and the former madam of an 'elite island whorehouse.'" New Yorker

"A master stylist with a dozen novels to her credit, Godwin has never written more voluptuously, nor had as much fun with a character or setting." Booklist

Godwin, Gail

★ **Unfinished** desires; a novel. Random House 2010 393p $26

ISBN 978-0-345-48320-1; 0-345-48320-0

LC 2008-49320

"Told from multiple points of view, 'Unfinished Desires' puts the author's twin talents storytelling and characterization on dazzling display. Godwin brings each of the girls and women fully alive and tells her well-conceived and well-executed story in a leisurely but suspenseful fashion." Richmond Times-Dispatch

Goethe, Johann Wolfgang von

★ The **sorrows** of young Werther, and Novella; translated by Elizabeth Mayer and Louise Brogan; poems translated by W. H. Auden; foreword by W. H. Auden. Modern Lib. 1993 xx, 201p

ISBN 0-679-60064-7

LC 93-5007

A translation of two of Goethe's works, originally published 1774 and 1828 respectively; this is a reissue of the 1971 edition published by Random House

Novella is an example of a specific literary genre, the idyll. A tame tiger which escapes during a fire pursues a princess and is killed. The animal trainer and his family, lamenting its death, persuade the prince, who has been out hunting a lion, to let them tame that animal rather than kill it. According to W. H. Auden it is "a parable about the relation between wild nature and human craft"

"Werther is a sensitive artist, ill at ease in society and hopelessly in love with Charlotte, who is engaged to someone else. This novel, with the eventual suicide of the hero, caused a sensation throughout Europe." Oxford Companion to Engl Lit

Gogol', Nikolai Vasil'evich

The **collected** tales of Nikolai Gogol; translated and annotated by Richard Pevear and Larissa Volokhonsky. Pantheon Bks. 1998 xxii, 435p

ISBN 0-679-43023-7

LC 97-37228

Gogol', Nikolai Vasil'evich

★ **Dead** souls; [by] Nikolai Gogol; translated and annotated by Richard Pevear and Larissa Volokhonsky. Pantheon Bks. 1996 xxiv, 402p

ISBN 0-679-43022-9

LC 95-24357

Original Russian edition, 1842

"Considered one of the world's finest satires, this picaresque work traces the adventures of the social-climbing Pavel Ivanovich Chichikov, a dismissed civil servant out to seek his fortune. It is admired not only for its enduring comic portraits but also for its sense of moral purpose." Merriam-Webster's Ency of Lit

Gogol', Nikolai Vasil'evich

The **overcoat,** and other tales of good and evil; {by} Nikolai V. Gogol; translated with an introduction by David Magarshack. Norton 1965 271p

This collection was first published 1957 in paperback by Doubleday with title: Tales of good and evil

Gohlke, Cathy

I have seen him in the watchfires; Cathy Gohlke. Moody Publishers 2008 331P (pbk.) $13.99

ISBN 9780802487742; 0802487742

LC 2008013224

Christy Award: Young Adult (2009)

In this book, a "Civil War . . . [novel], Robert Glover is . . . 17 years old. Although he promised his father not to join the Union Army until he became of age, circumstances force Robert to head for the war. He must also cope with his mother's growing mental illness and rely on his own faith to carry him through his trials." (Library Journal) "When he unwittingly gets entangled in a Confederate escape plot, Robert must forge his anger and shame into a new determination to save his family. And, perhaps, he must also realize that the saving might not be entirely up to him. Honor and duty to God and country aren't as clear-cut as he hoped them to be." (Publisher's note)

Gohlke, Cathy

Promise me this; Cathy Gohlke. Tyndale House Publishers 2012 407p (softcover) 13.99

ISBN 9781414353074

LC 2011034977

In this book, "[t]aking a break from work to watch the 'Titanic' set sail on its maiden voyage, Michael Dunnagan meets passenger Owen Allen and decides to stow away in hopes of convincing Owen to let him join his uncle's business in America. But the . . . ship strikes an iceberg, and a dying Owen extracts a promise from Michael that he will care for Owen's relatives in America and his sister Annie, still in England. Annie can't bear the thought that Michael lived when her brother was lost, but the two develop a friendship through the letters they exchange. When World War I breaks out and Annie's letters stop, Michael drops everything to find the woman he has come to love." (Libr J)

Gold, Glen David

Sunnyside. Alfred A. Knopf 2009 559p $26.95

ISBN 978-0-307-27068-9; 0-307-27068-8

LC 2009-03804

This novel "novel tells the story of early Chaplin, the beginning of Hollywood as we know it and a young America getting ready to flex its muscles. Sunnyside starts shortly before America's involvement in World War I, on a day when Chaplin is simultaneously spied in hundreds of places around the country. It is told by a young Chaplin, already a star but not yet a legend; an Adonis-like lighthouse keeper; and an overeducated ne'erdowell. While the latter two do cross paths with Chaplin, their story is the story of a war fought by dregs and managed by idiots. . . . Chaplin does not go to war. Instead he tours with archrival Mary Pickford and friend Douglas Fairbanks, raising money for the cause. We travel with Chaplin, underneath that hat with his thoughts as

he blunders his way past self-doubt and contempt and into greatness." BookPage

Goldberg, Myla

Bee season; a novel. Doubleday 2000 275p hardcover o.p. pa $13.95

ISBN 0-385-49879-9; 0-385-49880-2 pa

LC 99-47933

"Some of the events that unfold . . . seem a little contrived. But Goldberg engenders considerable suspense around both Eliza's string of spelling successes and the fates of the other Naumanns." Time

Goldberg, Myla

Wickett's remedy. Doubleday 2005 326p $24.95

ISBN 0-385-51324-0

LC 2005-48103

"In the margins of each page are voices from the dead commenting on or clarifying plot points. . . . There's a lot going on here, some of which is underdeveloped. Other parts are just plain distracting, particularly the notes from beyond, which are more often hokey than profound. But Goldberg is a skillful, smooth writer who has clearly done her research, and readers who can tune out the noise will be rewarded." Time

Golden, Arthur

★ **Memoirs** of a geisha; a novel. Knopf 1997 434p il $26.95; pa $7.99

ISBN 0-375-40011-7; 1-4000-9689-8 pa

LC 97-74747

"Rarely has a world so closed and foreign been evoked with such natural assurance, from the aesthetics of the Kyoto geisha's 'art'—to the fetishized sexuality of Gion in the thirties and forties, at once delicate and crude, repressed and flagrant." New Yorker

Golding, William

★ **Close** quarters. Farrar, Straus & Giroux 1987 281p

LC 87-5351

This second volume of the trilogy begun with Rites of passage is a "tale of the tragic misadventures befalling an 18th century fighting ship now converted to transporting cargo and passengers on the treacherous voyage from England to Australia. The novel is cast as a journal written by Edmund FitzHenry Talbot, a well-meaning, somewhat uncertain, slightly pompous officer and gentleman enroute to Sydney and a career in His Majesty's service. As a result of a green sailor's blunder, the ship's masts shatter, and it founders. Golding's principal achievement is the vivid, detailed depiction of a disintegrating vessel in the tropical seas, its progressive decay, and the wretchedness and despair of its passengers." Publ Wkly

Followed by Fire down below

Golding, William

★ **Darkness** visible. Farrar, Straus & Giroux 1979 265p

LC 79-19206

"A child hideously maimed in the bombing of London during World War II grows up to inspire the messianic fantasies of the people with whom he comes in contact. In Golding's dark world the horrors of the physically deformed are mirrored in—but are no match for—the spiritual monsters who inhabit the novel's strange vision of contemporary life. A powerful contemplation of the evil at the root of human behavior." Booklist

Golding, William

★ **Fire** down below. Farrar, Straus & Giroux 1989 313p

LC 88-18079

Golding is "translucent and economical. In his writing, allegorical motifs are revealed fleetingly in the everyday and in the ordinary. He is at once a complex and highly readable novelist." Economist

Golding, William

The **inheritors**. Harcourt 1962 233p

First published 1955 in the United Kingdom

A narrative "inhabiting the near-animal consciousness of Lok, a Neanderthal man, and describing in his clumsy terms and with great pathos the casual destruction of his species by Homo sapiens. The reader is shown his ancestors, already armed, arrogant, murderous, and corrupt—not superior to the Neanderthalers, only more clever and more evil." Wakeman. World Authors, 1950-1970

Golding, William

★ **Lord** of the flies; introduction by E. M. Forster; with a biographical and critical note by E. L. Epstein; illustrated by Ben Gibson. 50th anniversary ed; Berkley 2003 315p $23.95; pa $13

ISBN 0-399-52920-9; 0-399-50148-7 pa

LC 2003-54825

First published 1954 in the United Kingdom; first United States edition, 1955, by Coward-McCann

"Stranded on an island, a group of English schoolboys leave innocence behind in a struggle for survival. A political structure modeled after English government is set up and a hierarchy develops, but forces of anarchy and aggression surface. The boys' existence begins to degenerate into a savage one. They are rescued from their microcosmic society to return to an adult, stylized milieu filled with the same psychological tensions and moral voids. Adventure and allegory are brilliantly combined in this novel." Shapiro. Fic for Youth. 3d edition

Golding, William

★ **Rites** of passage. Farrar, Straus & Giroux 1980 278p

LC 80-16809

"In a sense the novel seems highly artificial, not only in its careful, detailed recreation of the period, but also in the elaborate system of correspondences and parallels—some clear, some obscure—which underpins the narration. Yet at the same time it is an extremely lively, enjoyable piece of work. Readers who know only the early Golding will be surprised by its humor." Times Lit Suppl

Followed by Close quarters

Goldman, Francisco

Say her name. Grove Press 2011 350p

ISBN 0802119816; 9780802119810; 0-8021-1981-6; 978-0-8021-1981-0

LC 2011283024

Francisco Goldman has written a novel based on a true story: the life and death of his "young wife, Aura Estrada, who died as a result of a bodysurfing accident in Mexico in 2007." (N Y Times (Late N Y Ed))

The author's "wife, Aura Estrada, died unexpectedly in 2007. She was 30 years old, a fiction writer and academic who loved Jorge Luis Borges and Belle & Sebastian and looked, Goldman writes, 'like a Mexican Björk.' This quietly devastating novel finds him grappling with Aura's life and death: the four years they spent as a couple, her childhood and budding literary career, and his own terrible struggle with her loss, which sits in him like 'a hard hollow rectangle filled with tepid blank air.' His story unfolds gently, like a muted conversation in an empty bar, the tone numb and hushed. Goldman doesn't keep his wife's passing a secret — he reveals it in the very first sentence of Say Her Name. But for most of the book he explores the before and after while dancing around the details of what actually happened. The effect is powerful. As the story builds — inevitably, unbearably — toward Aura's last day, Goldman has so convincingly brought her to life that her death still somehow comes as a shock." Entertainment Wkly

Goldman, William, 1931-

★ **Marathon** man. Delacorte Press 1974 309p

"Babe" Levy, a graduate student, spends his free time running, and dreams of being a great marathon runner. The death of his brother in Babe's apartment starts a chain of mysterious and terrifying events. Pursued by government agents and ex-Nazis, Babe struggles to escape being assassinated. The torture scenes may make this suspenseful story an ordeal for some readers." Shapiro. Fic for Youth. 3d edition

Goldman, William, 1931-

The **princess** bride; S. Morgenstern's classic tale of true love and high adventure. the "good parts" version, abridged by William Goldman. Ballantine Books 2003 xli, 429 p.p ill. o.p.; (hbk.) $25

ISBN 0345418263; 9780151015443

LC 2003272241

This book offers the 30th anniversary edition of William Goldman's book "The Princess Bride." "As a boy, William Goldman claims, he loved to hear his father read the S. Morgenstern classic, 'The Princess Bride.' But as a grown-up he discovered that the boring parts were left out of good old Dad's recitation, and only the 'good parts' reached his ears. . . . [With this book, h]e's reconstructed the 'Good Parts Version.' . . . What's it about? Fencing. Fighting. True Love. Strong Hate. Harsh Revenge. A Few Giants. Lots of Bad Men. Lots of Good Men. Five or Six Beautiful Women. Beasties Monstrous and Gentle. Some Swell Escapes and Captures. Death, Lies, Truth, Miracles, and a Little Sex. In short, it's about everything." (Publisher's note)

Goldsborough, Robert

The **missing** chapter; a Nero Wolfe mystery. Bantam Bks. 1993 229p

LC 93-13714

A publisher hires Nero Wolfe and Archie Goodwin "to investigate the death, labeled a suicide, of Charles Childress, an ill-tempered author who had recently angered several people, including his agent, his editor and the possibly corrupt reviewer who had lambasted the latest Childress novel." Publ Wkly

"The publishing details ring true, and . . . Goldsborough does a masterly job with the Wolfe legacy." Booklist

Goldsmith, Olivia

The **First** Wives Club. Poseidon Press 1992 480p

ISBN 0-671-74693-6

LC 91-30959

As the women "stylishly, systematically and nonviolently foil the schemes of their callous former partners, they conquer their own weaknesses and find appreciative friends and lovers who complement rather than rule them. Goldsmith's glitzy, addictive and credible first novel is certain to raise smiles." Publ Wkly

Goldsmith, Olivia

Pen pals. Dutton 2002 359p

ISBN 0-525-94644-6

LC 2001-47418

Protagonist Jennifer Spencer is "a rising star on Wall Street who is working at a prestigious firm and engaged to a brilliant lawyer. To help protect her trusted mentor-boss from exposure, Jennifer agrees to be the point person in an SEC investigation. After everything goes awry, Jennifer finds herself shackled in Jennings, a women's prison not at all like the country club, white-collar crime camp she envisioned. . . . The path from the despair of prison life to female conquest is glorious and satisfying without being man-hating; the cast of characters perfectly blends women from all walks of life, joined by their common goal." Booklist

Includes bibliographical references

Goldsmith, Olivia

Young wives; a novel. HarperCollins Pubs. 2000 512p $25

ISBN 0-06-017553-2

LC 99-48167

This novel features three protagonists: "sweet, innocent Angie, whose uptight but good-looking Boston lawyer husband is two-timing with her best friend; Jada, an African-American heroine who is at once a bank manager, churchgoer and devoted mother . . . and whose husband is a ne'er-do-well lazybones; and houseproud Michelle Russo, whose dream-boat Italian mate is . . . a high-level drug dealer on the side. All three women are put through purgatory by their husbands, crooked lawyers and a bent legal system until . . . they fight back in all-for-one, one-for-all style." Publ Wkly

Goldstein, Lisa

The **uncertain** places; a novel. Tachyon 2011 237p pa $14.95

ISBN 978-1-61696-014-8; 1-61696-014-0

"A darkly compelling modern fairytale. It's Berkeley in the 1970s and Will Taylor falls for chef and scientist Livvy Feierabend who proves to be just one of a tribe of mysterious women — all related — who made an ancient pact that will prevent Livvy from ever truly becoming Will's, unless he can intervene. The Uncertain Places is charming, magical and oddly believable . . . if you completely suspend belief. Goldstein's strong way with a story makes this entirely possible." January

Goldstein, Rebecca

36 arguments for the existence of God; a work of fiction. [by] Rebecca Newberger Goldstein. Pantheon Books 2010 402p $27.95

ISBN 978-0-307-37818-7; 0-307-37818-7

LC 2009-17022

This "is without a doubt the funniest work of existential philosophy you'll read all year. Thoughtful, witty, and – I cannot stress enough – really entertaining, '36 Arguments' is part campus comedy, part romantic farce, part philosophical treatise." Christ Sci Monit

Gonzales, Laurence

★ **Lucy.** Alfred A Knopf 2010 307p $24.95

ISBN 978-0-307-27260-7; 0-307-27260-5

LC 2010-03898

"Lucy is a genetic experiment: part person, part chimpanzee. She looks and sounds just like any normal 15-year-old girl — in fact, she can recite Shakespeare's sonnets by heart — it's just that she sometimes eats bananas without peeling them and swings from treetop to treetop. . . . Splicing DNA has been a science-fiction plot device as far back as the 19th century, when H.G. Wells was mixing the test tubes. But the results were always horrific crimes against nature. Here, the mutant hybrid couldn't be lovelier or more charming — it's the people who behave like monsters. . . . [The author has] Crichton's gift for page-turning storytelling, but also a vivid, literary-grade prose style, and a knack for getting inside his characters' heads." Entertainment Wkly

Goodis, David

Nightfall; a novel. with a new introduction by Bill Pronzini. Millipede Press 2007 213p $40; pa $14

ISBN 978-1-933618-18-0; 1-933618-18-3; 9781933618173 pa; 1933618175 pa

First published 1947 by Messner

"Jim Vanning, a commercial artist living in Manhattan, is being hunted by a group of bank robbers who believe he ran off with $300,000 of their ill-gotten money. He's also being watched by a detective who's trying to suss out what Vanning did with the satchel of cash. Vanning denies stealing the money, but the money hardly matters—the satchel is just a MacGuffin. Nightfall's real story is about Vanning's despair about how to behave rationally when he knows he's being watched and the detective's self-questioning about whether a man can ever act with integrity without falling under suspicion. It's a relatively big theme for a noir, but Goodis keeps the story earthbound, rooting it in cynical observations designed to keep the mood of paranoia going." Washington City Paper

Goodman, Allegra

★ The **cookbook** collector; a novel. Dial Press 2010 394p $26

ISBN 978-0-385-34085-4; 0-385-34085-0

LC 2009-47594

"As the story opens in 1999, twentysomething sisters Emily and Jessamine Bach are a study in contrasts: One's a driven tech executive in Silicon Valley; the other, an impoverished Berkeley grad student/bookstore employee with a penchant for sprout sandwiches and seductive tree huggers. A revolving constellation of characters — Emily's golden-boy fiancé and instant-millionaire colleagues, Jess' brusque, ponytailed boss, George — are made fully flesh and blood by Goodman; sometimes more so, even, than her protagonists. She especially excels at capturing the precipitous rush of the then-nascent tech boom, with its breakneck innovations and backroom intrigues, while simultaneously recounting Jess' increasing absorption into the ornate and distinctly analog world of high-end bibliophilia. Even as Cookbook strikes a rare bum note with a late, left-field revelation, Goodman delivers a novel of impressive élan and real emotional resonance." Entertainment Wkly

Goodman, Allegra

Intuition; a novel. Dial Press 2006 344p $25; pa $13

ISBN 0-385-33612-8; 0-385-33610-1 pa

LC 2005-51940

"The prestigious Philpott Institute in Cambridge, MA, is a virtually closed community dominated by a charismatic leader, oncologist Sandy Glass. Dr. Glass's enthusiasm galvanizes his ambitious scientists to work round the clock when experimental results yield a possible cancer cure, until one young researcher publicizes her suspicions of fraud." Libr J

Goodman, Allegra

Paradise park; a novel. Dial Press (NY) 2001 360p

ISBN 0-385-33416-8

LC 00-49376

"Like Saul Bellow and Philip Roth before her, Goodman has achieved a breakthrough book by discovering and recording a thoroughly uninhibited narrative voice." Time

Goodman, Carol

Arcadia Falls; a novel. Ballantine Books 2010 355p $25

ISBN 978-0-345-49753-6; 0-345-49753-8

LC 2009-44550

"The tone of 'Arcadia Falls,' suffused as it is with foreboding, is a far cry from gloomy. Goodman's touch is sure-handed, even light, dropping hints and shockers with calibrated ease. She knows just what information the reader needs to turn the pages but has enough trust that the same reader won't rush and gobble up paragraphs to reach the finish line, instead pacing the story for a more languid experience where each sentence, layered on top of another, really counts." Los Angeles Times

Goodman, Carol

The **drowning** tree. Ballantine Books 2004 339p

ISBN 0-345-46211-4

LC 2004-47638

"Juno McKay is a glass artist, caught up with running a business and raising a teenaged daughter. A college reunion, which she reluctantly attends, brings up issues from the past and creates new problems when a close friend dies under mysterious circumstances. . . . Filled with descriptions of beautiful Hudson River scenery and references to mythology and art, this gripping novel will hold the reader's attention until the very last page." Libr J

Goodman, Carol

The **night** villa; a novel. Ballantine Books 2008 413p pa $14

ISBN 978-0-345-47960-0; 0-345-47960-2

LC 2008-8519

"The pleasure of a Carol Goodman novel is in her enviable command of the classical canon–and the deft way she [writes] a book that's light enough for a weekend on the beach but literary enough for a weekend in the Hamptons." Chicago Tribune

Goodman, Carol

The **seduction** of water. Ballantine Bks. 2003 357p

ISBN 0-345-45090-6

LC 2002-34463

This "is the story of Iris Greenfeder, a teacher who would rather be a writer, and the secrets her mother kept and her search for the truth about her mother's death." Libr J

"Mystery, folklore, a thoroughly modern romance, a strong sense of place and a winning combination of erudition and accessibility make this . . . novel a treat." Publ Wkly

Goodman, Jo

A **place** called home. Kensington Pub. Corp. 2011 432p.

ISBN 9780821774182

This book tells the story of a man and a woman who "learn they've been named joint guardians for their late friends' three children. . . . Something about Mitch's forthright intensity has always left ad exec Thea feeling off-balance, while Mitch makes no secret of his disdain when Thea offers him financial assistance if he'll take sole guardianship." (Publisher's note) "Neither is prepared to become a parent -- and certainly not alone . . . as they work to solve their separate dilemmas, Thea and Mitch discover that they need each other, as well." (Libr J)

Goodman, Jo

Season to be sinful; Jo Goodman. Kensington Pub. Corp. 2005 431p $6.50

ISBN 0821777750; 9780821777756

LC 2006567129

In this book, "Wyatt Grantham, Viscount Sheridan, is stunned to find three young boys at his door, demanding he right the wrongs of an incident that occurred earlier that evening when he thwarted a determined thief. When he discovers his wily pickpocket is a woman, now gravely injured, he takes his flame-haired attacker under his wing. . . . He finds himself irresistibly drawn [to] the too clever, cheeky Lily. . . . The five years since she left the care of the French convent have been a nightmare for Lily. Her secrets are dangerous - as is the powerful man determined to find her. The handsome Viscount is clearly a gentleman with secrets of his own, but staying with him could mean the difference between life and death for Lily. With each passing day, her handsome host turns Lily's convalescence into an increasingly sensual escape." (Publisher's note)

Goodwillie, David

American subversive; a novel. Scribner 2010 309p $25

ISBN 978-1-4391-5705-3; 1-4391-5705-7

LC 2009-42233

"Aidan Cole is a fundamentally nice Manhattan 30-something who writes a gossipy media blog by day and barhops with oily Latin American playboys by night. . . . Narrating alternating chapters is Paige Roderick, a fundamentally nice 29-year-old terrorist bomber from North Carolina. Radicalized by her brother's death in Iraq, Paige now orchestrates conflagrations at various targets in New York City, including the Barneys building. Paige questions and laments the violence of her work, even as she dutifully carries it out. The unlikely relationship between these two lost souls is the shaky storyline on which Goodwillie hangs his engrossing, sometimes very funny, wildly overstuffed novel. When an anonymous source e-mails Aidan a photograph of Paige departing the scene of a bombing . . . the previously aimless and hedonistic blogger promptly throws himself into pursuing her. She represents something powerful and pure to jaded Aidan." NPR

Goodwin, Daisy

The **American** heiress; a novel. St. Martin's Press 2011 46880p $25.99

ISBN 978-0-312-65865-6

LC 2010-48539

First published 2010 in the United kingdom with title: My last dutchess

"A shrewd, spirited historical romance with flavors of Edith Wharton, Daphne du Maurier, Jane Austen, Upstairs, Downstairs and a dash of People magazine that charts a bumpy marriage of New World money and Old World tradition." Kirkus

Goolrick, Robert

A **reliable** wife; a novel. Algonquin Books of Chapel Hill 2009 291p $23.95

ISBN 978-1-56512-596-4; 1-56512-596-7

LC 2008-49700

Goolrick is a ticky, mannered writer with an unusual love of clauses that can sometimes give you comma whiplash. This, combined with the graphic problems they are having throughout the novel may be enough to turn some readers off. And that would be a shame, because in the middle of this book a secret is revealed that pushes the plot forward. Freed into clearer storytelling, A Reliable Wife relaxes into an entertaining novel full of all kinds of juicy thingsdeception, betrayal, murder, sex, and even love. PopMatters

Goonan, Kathleen Ann

In war times. Tor 2007 348p $25.95

ISBN 978-0-7653-1355-3; 0-7653-1355-3

LC 2007-5165

This is "the story of Sam Dance, who, while studying mathematics and electronics for the Army just before WW II, is seduced by a mysterious female physicist teaching one of his classes. Dr. Hadntz has plans for a device that might end war forever, by changing humanity's seeming need for conflict. From this premise, Goonan weaves a remarkable tale of quantum physics, human nature and jazz." SF Signal

Goonan, Kathleen Ann

Light music. HarperCollins Pubs. 2002 406p $25.95

ISBN 0-380-97712-5

LC 2001-55602

Sequel to Crescent city rhapsody

In this concluding volume of the Nanotech Quartet "the microscopic machines of the 22nd century have gone beyond creating sentient cities and controlling all communications on Earth—they are themselves evolving. When mysterious lights point to an alien presence and disappearing people arouse stark fear, three human survivors, including Argentine refugee Angelina, set out to solve the mystery and measure the threat to humanity. A lot of picaresque adventures ensue. . . . This classic novel of ideas, with state-of-the-art technology as its subject, remains the work of a powerful imagination with a superior command of language." Publ Wkly

Gordimer, Nadine, 1923-

Beethoven was one-sixteenth black; and other stories. Farrar, Straus and Giroux 2007 177p $21

ISBN 978-0-374-10982-0; 0-374-10982-6

LC 2007-33474

"A story narrated by a tapeworm. A vignette about a parrot unhappy at losing his usual cafe perch. A tale about a cockroach trapped inside a Kafka fan's typewriter . . . South African Nobel laureate Nadine Gordimer has come up with some true curiosities in her new short-story collection. . . . At its best, the book offers compelling psychosexual journeys, probing at marital tensions and the hazardous play of memory in the bereaved (Gordimer's husband, Reinhold Cassirer, to whom the book is dedicated, died in 2001). Some tales also afford glancing, revealing takes on life in post-apartheid South Africa." Seattle Times

Gordimer, Nadine

The **conservationist**. Viking 1975 252p

First published 1974 in the United Kingdom

The author probes "the way of life that exists in South Africa today, and some aspects of the tensions that exist among English and Afrikaaners, Blacks, coloreds, Indian shopkeepers. . . . Mehring is rich, white, bored. His farm is a weekend pleasure place to which he once brought the mistress whose flirtations with left wing causes have now exiled her forever. His teenage son won't even come home for the holidays and wants out of all that South Africa stands for. Mehring is kind enough to his blacks, keeps them in their place, avoids his Boer neighbors with whom he has nothing in common. A loner, living for himself, deliberately isolated from any unpleasantness that might intrude, only gradually does he begin to perceive that there are forces at work in nature, in the closeness between the blacks and the land by which some day his way of life will be forever changed." Publ Wkly

Gordimer, Nadine

Get a life. Farrar, Straus & Giroux 2005 187p $21

ISBN 0-14303-792-7

LC 2005-07199

"Gordimer confronts the reader with questions of conservation, social welfare, and emotional ecosystems. The austere Gordimer's mastery of her craft means she never needs to point at herself, thus highlighting the difference between art and performance." Harper's

Gordimer, Nadine

A **guest** of honor. Viking 1970 504p

The hero of this novel, James "Bray is a 54-year-old former administrator for one of Her Majesty's former African colonies. . . . He was cashiered for showing too much sympathy for the local independence movement. After independence, Bray accepts an invitation to return as an educational consultant to Miss Gordimer's nameless, composite, new African nation. His professional commitment to the excruciating process of Third World nation building is complicated because the country's opposing political factions—one moderate, the other revolutionary—are led by two of his former protégés." Time

Gordimer, Nadine

★ **July's** people. Viking 1981 160p

ISBN 0-670-41048-9

LC 80-24877

"When revolution breaks out against the whites in South Africa, Bamford and Maureen Smales are forced to flee. Their black servant July, loyal to them for fifteen years, takes them away to his people in a bush village. His role changes slowly to one not only of savior but also overseer. The change in their manner of living from the good, clean, well-regulated life of 'the ruling class' to that of the customs of July's people raises havoc within both the white and black families and in the delicate tissue of understanding between the Smales and their servant. There is much to be learned from this powerful story written by an author who lives in South Africa and who writes with authority on a subject that has import for any society where race relations or colonial conditions are fragile and explosive." Shapiro. Fic for Youth. 3d edition

Gordimer, Nadine

Jump and other stories. Farrar, Straus & Giroux 1991 256p

ISBN 0-374-18055-5

LC 91-2687

This "collection of tales features an insider's intensity about people caught in the savage particulars of southern Africa today; at the same time, the surprise of the stories and the slash of their endings make the words resonate with the revelations of an ever-widening universe." Booklist

Gordimer, Nadine

Life times; stories, 1952-2007. Farrar, Straus and Giroux 2010 549p $30

ISBN 978-0-374-27053-7; 0-374-27053-8

LC 2010-23403

Gordimer "has been writing for more than 60 years now, but her concerns have been constant: race, justice, the South African land. In a typical story, the landscape is austere, tough and unforgiving, just the sort of thing to bring out the best in a few hardy people, but calculated to wear down the spirits of most others. . . . Some of the stories clearly date to the early days of resistance to apartheid, politically charged and with passing references to the first stirrings of the African National Congress; others take place in the thick of the battle for justice, amid 'beer-serious conversations about the possibility of the end of the world.' Four of the stories are new, an added pleasure for admirers of Gordimer's work. A welcome collection by a master of English prose—lucid and precisely written, if often bringing news only of disappointment, fear and loss." Kirkus

Gordimer, Nadine

Loot, and other stories. Farrar, Straus & Giroux 2003 240p $23

ISBN 0-374-19090-9

LC 2002-42601

In Karma a deceased insurance executive's spirit makes successive returns to earth in various guises. Mission statement is about a middle-aged Englishwoman who has a sexual relationship with a native while working for an international aid agency in an impoverished African country

"This compelling collection presents a bleak view of human existence in general and of Africa's colonial past in particular. Written with a sharp sense of irony, it should be a part of every fiction collection." Libr J

Gordimer, Nadine

★ **My** son's story. Penguin Books 1991 277p pa $9.95

ISBN 0-14-015975-4

LC 91-17273

First published 1990 by Farrar, Straus & Giroux

"Sonny is a teacher of mixed race. He and his wife are . . . sympathetic to the plight of the 'real blacks,' yet ambitious that they may someday be accepted by the whites. Sonny's political education begins when he's fired for helping black children demonstrate in their township. Jailed for promoting boycotts and participating in illegal gatherings, Sonny meets and falls in love with a blond, blue-eyed woman who works for a human-rights organization. Sonny's adolescent son, Will, tells the story of his father's political and erotic development, the resentments and betrayals that ensue." Newsweek

Gordimer, Nadine

None to accompany me. Farrar, Straus & Giroux 1994 324p

ISBN 0-374-22297-5

LC 94-7553

"A novel that raises more questions than it answers, 'None to Accompany Me' is an unflinching and perceptive exploration of people living on the brink of changes—po-

LIST OF FICTIONAL WORKS

litical and personal—with little but their own sense of self-reliance to guide them." Christ Sci Monitor

Gordimer, Nadine, 1923-

No time like the present; Nadine Gordimer. Farrar, Straus and Giroux 2012 421 p.

ISBN 9780374222642; 0374222649

LC 2012930442

The plot of "Nobel laureate [Nadine] Gordimer's . . . novel, . . . set in contemporary South Africa, revolves around Steve, who's Jewish, and Jabulile (Jabu), who's black. Both were 'comrades' in the fight for racial equality. . . . Married and starting a family in a middle-class suburb, they've 'bought ourselves a house while others including comrades . . . are still under tin and cardboard.' . . . [A]s their children grow up, civil and political unrest keeps pace, forcing them to re-evaluate their position in this new South Africa." (Publishers Weekly)

Gordimer, Nadine

The pickup. Farrar, Straus & Giroux 2001 270p $23

ISBN 0-374-23210-5

LC 2001-23041

"Gordimer writes so tenderly and so searchingly about Julie's gradual transcendence of her western self that she manages to hold sceptism at bay." Women's Review of Books

Includes bibliographical references

Gordon, Emily Fox

It will come to me. Spiegel & Grau 2009 267p $24.95

ISBN 978-0-385-52587-9; 0-385-52587-7

LC 2008-29338

"In this campus satire, Ben and Ruth Blau have settled into what appears to be a comfortable routine at their Southern university campus. Ruth, mourning her inability to follow up on an acclaimed early trilogy of novels, drinks a little too much; Ben, working on a manuscript about altruism, shirks bureaucratic duties in the philosophy department. Their lives are disrupted by two arrivals: a new president determined to shake up the staid faculty habits and a popular memoirist and self-help author who prods Ruth to begin writing again." New Yorker

Gordon, Jaimy

★ Lord of Misrule; a novel. McPherson & Co. 2010 294p $25

ISBN 9780929701837; 0-929701-83-6

LC 2010-35030

Gordon "clearly loves the subculture of grifters and ne'er-do-wells whose lives center on a venue that obviously has never and will never bring them success. Her lowlifes have names like Two-Tie, Medicine Ed, Kidstuff and Deucey, and they're capable of speaking a kind of racetrack patois occasionally reminiscent of Damon Runyon characters. . . . Exceptional writing and idiosyncratic characters make this an engaging read." Kirkus

Gordon, Mary

★ The company of women. Knopf 1981 291p

LC 80-5284

"Given its scope, depth, and the perfection of its lyrical passages (which are the more impressive because of Gordon's natural inclination toward the austere), it is fair to call this a brilliant novel." Saturday Rev

Gordon, Mary

★ Final payments. Random House 1978 297p

LC 77-90259

"Isabel Moore spends 11 years almost totally absorbed in caring for her invalid father, who suffered a paralyzing stroke after discovering his daughter in a compromising situation with one of his students. When she is thirty, her father dies; she is freed from responsibility for his welfare but not yet able to accept responsibility for her own life. Her involvement with two men adds complications as, guilt-ridden and filled with religious skepticism, Isabel searches for answers and begins to heal. Two childhood friends, Eleanor, an independent woman, and Liz, a tough married mother of two children, are instrumental in helping Isabel grow toward self-realization." Shapiro. Fic for Youth. 3d edition

Gordon, Mary

The love of my youth. Pantheon 2011 302p $25.95

ISBN 978-0-307-37742-5; 0-307-37742-3

LC 2011-08966

"Miranda and Adam were each other's first love, but they've had no contact for 30 years. Their heady reunion takes place in Rome, a city of myths and ghosts Adam knows well, allowing him to show Miranda, there for an environmental health conference, the sights and allowing Gordon to make the most of gorgeous settings redolent with ancient secrets and sorrows. The ensuing intense conversations between Miranda and Adam are so psychologically intricate and complexly metaphysical and aesthetic that they seem impossibly theatrical. And yet, as the novel deepens in extended flashbacks, their intoxicating exchanges become exquisitely involving. We learn that their blissful love bloomed when they were 16 in the mid-1960s and slowly withered during their twenties as Adam devoted himself to becoming a great pianist and Miranda searched for a way to help make the world a better place. The more they talk on their Roman rambles, the more the reader burns to know what finally drove them apart." Booklist

Gordon, Neil

The company you keep. Viking 2003 406p $24.95

ISBN 0-670-03218-2

LC 2002-44905

"When limousine-leftist lawyer and single dad Jim Grant is unmasked as Jason Sinai, an ex-Weather Underground militant wanted for a deadly bank robbery, he abandons his daughter and goes on the lam. As he evades a manhunt and seeks out old comrades, the author introduces a sprawling cast of drug dealers, bomb-planting radicals turned leftist academics, Vietnam vets, FBI agents and Republicans who collectively ponder the legacy of the '60s." Publ Wkly

343

Gores, Joe

Cons, scams & grifts. Mysterious Press 2001 324p $24.95

    ISBN 0-89296-594-0

                        LC 2001-30637

"Although this episodic caper looks like a free-for-all, {Gores'} brazen schemes require high levels of intelligence and the underlying design of his ploys is quite breathtaking." N Y Times Book Rev

Gores, Joe

Contract null & void. Mysterious Press 1996 309p

    ISBN 978-0446404471

                        LC 96-12769

"Master of surreal comedic style, Mr. Gores keeps finding outlandish assignments for his repo men. But in the inspired ending, aptly called 'Walpurgisnacht,' the plot lines converge and all the insanity, believe it or not, makes perfect sense." N Y Times Book Rev

Gorky, Maksim

Selected short stories; {by} Maxim Gorky; with an introductory essay by Stefan Zweig. Ungar 1959 348p

Gorman, Edward

Bad moon rising; [by] Ed Gorman. Pegasus Crime 2011 196p $25

    ISBN 978-1-60598-260-1

"In 1968, a hippie commune near Black River Falls, Iowa, both horrifies and entices the townsfolk with its uninhibited lifestyle. Sardonic lawyer and investigator McCain becomes involved after the discovery of the body of Vanessa Mainwaring, the teenage daughter of a well-to-do local, at the commune, and a Vietnam vet who's one of its members flees. Interference by a bigoted sheriff, an opportunistic preacher, and a hysterical father makes matters even worse as Sam tries not just to solve the murder but to help the people around him caught in an intensely stressful situation." Publ Wkly

Gorman, Edward

Breaking up is hard to do; [by] Ed Gorman. Carroll & Graff Pubs. 2004 207p $24

    ISBN 0-7867-1296-1

"In late October 1962, with Armageddon looming in the form of the Cuban missile crisis, life went on in Black River Falls, Iowa-except in the case of a young woman found murdered in gubernatorial candidate Ross Murdoch's under-construction bomb shelter. His political dreams dashed, Murdoch hopes to avoid the electric chair and hires young investigator-attorney Sam McCain to represent him. . . . Intelligent writing and great reading." Booklist

Gorman, Edward

Fools rush in; a Sam McCain mystery. [by] Ed Gorman. Pegasus Books 2007 229p $25

    ISBN 978-1-933548-32-3

"Black River Falls, Iowa, 1963: the violence of the civil-rights era lurks behind the double murder of a Peeping Tom photographer and a handsome black lothario, David Leeds, who was dating the daughter of a white Republican senator. Young Sam McCain, a lawyer and sometime private detective, is on the case. Motives are widespread. The senator was having an affair. Local bikers hated Leeds' success with a white woman to whom they could never aspire. The photographer was a blackmailer, and the white ex-boyfriend of the senator's daughter was a violent bully. . . . Readers unfamiliar with this fine series should hop onboard now and watch as an Iowa Mr. Marple starts to behave like a cornbelt Spenser." Booklist

Gorman, Edward

★ **Save** the last dance for me; [by] Ed Gorman. Carroll & Graf Pubs. 2002 230p $24

    ISBN 0-7867-0968-5

A "dead-on perfect journey to the underside of the late '50s and early '60s, exposing the anti-intellectualism and anti-Semitism that lurked beneath the era's placid surface." Booklist

Gorman, Edward

Sleeping dogs; [by] Ed Gorman. Thomas Dunne Books/St. Martin's Minotaur 2008 238p $23.95

    ISBN 978-0-312-36784-8; 0-312-36784-8

                        LC 2007-51733

"Unleashing a new series, Gorman gives us political speechwriter and sleuth-by-necessity Dev Conrad. He's just signed onto the unexpectedly troubled reelection campaign of a U.S. senator, and must deal with dirty tricks, campaign sabotage, a suicide and his increasing suspicions about the very man he's supposed to be helping stay in Congress." January

Gorman, Edward

Ticket to ride; [by] Ed Gorman. Pegasus Books 2009 225p $25

    ISBN 978-1-605980-70-6

An entry in the Sam McCain series set in Black River Falls, Iowa. "It's 1965, different stances on the Vietnam War have divided the town, and the anti-war Sam McCain seems to have found himself on the unpopular side. Things start to heat up when Lou Bennett, whose son was killed in the war, crashes McCain's anti-war rally and starts a fight with the charismatic young protester Harrison Doran. From there, things only get worse: Bennett is found dead the next day, and Doran is arrested under suspicion of murder. With the whole town convinced of Doran's guilt, McCain begrudgingly agrees to defend Doran as a favor to a friend. Complicating things even further are McCain's crush on Bennett's daughter-inl-aw Wendy, and a skeleton in the family closet revels a web of secrets that Black River Falls would have preferred to keep buried and forgotten. The reasons for Gorman's reputation as a first-rate novelist are on full display." Pulp Serenade

Gosling, Paula

The **dead** of winter. Mysterious Press 1996 328p

    ISBN 978-0446404990

                        LC 95-39099

First published 1995 in the United Kingdom

"This complicated puzzler, pivoting from cozy sewing circles to talk of mafia hit men and cocaine dens, comes to its brilliantly staged conclusion at the annual ice festival where Gosling dramatizes the point that smooth and shiny surfaces can hide a lot of treachery." Publ Wkly

Gosling, Paula

A **few** dying words. Mysterious Press 1994 344p

LC 94-18826

"While bracing for the Blackwater Bay's annual Howl— a traditional Halloween celebration of carnival rides and pranks—Sheriff Matt Gabriel agrees to meet with clearly agitated retired pharmacist, Tom Finnegan. While driving to the sheriff's office, however, Finnegan is run off the road. Matt reaches the older man's side before he dies and hears him whisper 'not an accident.'" Publ Wkly

"Good writing, an inventive plot, and a nice balance of humor and horror make this an appealing mystery." Booklist

Gottlieb, Eli

Now you see him. William Morrow 2008 261p $22.95

ISBN 978-0-06-128464-9; 0-06-128464-5

This is a "haunting and affecting potrait not only of an unthinkable act of violence but also a deeply personal grief and the self-questioning that follows a psychologically scarring event." Vancouver Sun

Goudge, Eileen

Garden of lies. Viking 1989 528p

ISBN 0-670-82458-5

LC 88-40395

"Sylvia seizes the opportunity offered by a hospital fire to switch infants, taking a newborn whose appearance resembles her husband. Her true child, fathered by Sylvia's lover, is left to make her own way in the world. Rachel, raised in luxury as Sylvia's daughter, becomes a doctor. When her career is jeopardized, she is defended by Sylvia'a real daughter, who has overcome poverty to become a lawyer. The two women of course compete for the same man, as Sylvia herself tries to decide whether to marry Nikos, her former lover." Libr J

"The characters intrigue, the situations hold attention, and the sex scenes simmer near the boiling point." Booklist

Followed by Thorns of truth

Goudge, Eileen

One last dance. Viking 1999 384p $24.95

ISBN 0-670-88575-4

LC 98-54891

"Ideal for readers looking for a fairy tale: lovely, talented women, handsome men who love them, and little permanent trauma from a violent death and the awful secrets it unleashes." Libr J

Goudge, Eileen

Stranger in paradise. Viking 2001 321p

ISBN 0-670-89987-9

LC 2001-17747

This first volume of a projected trilogy set in Carson Springs, California focuses on "48-year-old Samantha

'Sam' Kiley and her daughters, Alice and Laura. As the story opens, Alice is about to marry Wes Carpenter, a Ted Turner-esque entertainment mogul nearly 30 years her senior. Then Wes's son, Ian, takes a shine to Sam and the two become romantically involved, alarming Sam's daughters and setting the gossipy town abuzz. Laura, divorced because she couldn't bear children, and given to taking in strays, gets a new lease on life when she provides shelter for 16-year-old female runaway Finch." Publ Wkly

Goudge, Eileen

Such devoted sisters. Viking 1992 562p

LC 91-29103

"In 1954, Dolly Drake mails a letter addressed to Senator Joseph McCarthy that contains damning information about her famous film star sister Eve Dearfield. After leaving small-town America for Hollywood, Dolly has had enough of Eve stealing the spotlight. And she can't tolerate Eve stealing her man, either. Ruining the offending sister's career and her life seems the only thing to do. Years later, of course, she's regretting her actions, but Dolly's far away in Manhattan, with her own chocolate store and a lot of money. And it just so happens that Eve's two children, Annie and Laurel, have run away from home looking for Dolly, their long-lost aunt." Booklist

Goudge, Eileen

Thorns of truth. Viking 1998 398p

ISBN 0-670-87942-8

LC 97-53231

"Forty-six years after Sylvie Rosenthal abandoned Rose as a dark-haired newborn and stole blonde, blue-eyed baby Rachel to take her place, their lives are still intertwined, and Rachel still doesn't know the truth. Now Rose has problems of her own: her husband's death a year ago has left her with a law firm to manage; her stepdaughter is a drunk; and her eldest son, Drew, is planning to marry Rachel's mentally unstable daughter, Iris, against his mother's wishes. Rachel's life is starting to fray at the edges, too. Her job running a women's health clinic has caused a rift in her marriage to Brian, and, even medicated, Iris remains a constant worry." Publ Wkly

Goudge, Eileen

Trail of secrets. Viking 1996 443p

ISBN 0-670-86191-X

LC 95-39411

The author's "characters are sympathetic; her expressions of the fierce emotions of motherhood are immediate; and her crafty decision to reveal likely plot turns to her readers but not to her characters will keep all who love a secret riveted." Publ Wkly

Goudge, Elizabeth

Green Dolphin Street; a novel. Coward-McCann 1944 502p

Published in the United Kingdom with title: Green Dolphin country

This novel is set on one of the English Channel Islands and in frontier New Zealand. "The principal characters are two sisters and the boy who had been their neighbor and companion in Green Dolphin Street on the island. The sisters are Marianne, stern and intellectual, and Marguerite, radiant and beautiful. It is Marguerite whom William loves, but when he writes the letter from New Zealand asking her father for her hand he unaccountably confuses the names and it is Marianne, who comes to be his wife." Wis Libr Bull

Gould, Judith

The **best** is yet to come. Dutton 2002 308p $24.95

ISBN 0-525-94659-4

LC 2002-23541

"After years of hard work, Carolina Mountcastle has finally made her flower shop the first choice of New York's most demanding hostesses. Factor in her storybook marriage to successful businessman Lyon, her 16-year-old son Richie and her great friends, and Carolina would appear to have it all. But when her husband suffers a fatal heart attack while traveling abroad for business and a mysterious woman and her daughter appear at the reading of his will, Carolina's world begins to unravel. . . . Gould's page-turning plot and deliciously evil villains distract artfully from some tone-deaf dialogue. . .and the flower descriptions are a delight." Publ Wkly

Gould, Judith

A **moment** in time. Dutton 2001 323p $24.95

ISBN 0-525-94607-1

LC 2001-25334

Valerie Rochelle has "found happiness, much to her society mother's bewilderment, working as a veterinarian in upstate New York. When Teddy, an old family friend, proposes, her mother is ecstatic, but Valerie is less than thrilled. Nonetheless, she accepts, but her reluctance is exacerbated when she pays a house call to the mysterious Stonelair estate to tend to an ailing horse. She and the estate's new owner, Wyn Conrad, connect on a level that she and Teddy never reach. . . . Gould's steamy tale about the lives of the rich and troubled is perfect for a read on the beach." Booklist

Gowdy, Barbara

Helpless; a novel. Metropolitan Books 2007 307p $24

ISBN 978-0-8050-8288-3

LC 2006-47348

This is the "tale of the stalking and kidnapping of a beautiful young mixed-race Canadian girl. . . . Celia, a single mom holding down two jobs to support her beloved daughter, nine-year-old Rachel . . . , is rushed into every parent's nightmare when the deeply creepy Ron, a small-appliance repairman, uses the cover of a Toronto summertime blackout to 'rescue' Rachel from what he sees as her unsavory poverty. With the help of his girlfriend, Nancy, an uneasy accomplice whose thwarted maternal instincts impel her to try to protect Rachel, Ron imprisons the girl in his basement apartment." Libr J

"There is a clean urgency to Gowdy's tale. We are helpless before her sure and beguiling hand because ultimately—and breathlessly—we are drawn in." Vancouver Sun

Gowdy, Barbara

The **romantic**; a novel. Metropolitan Bks. 2003 305p $24

ISBN 0-8050-7190-3

LC 2002-29904

"Each of the characters, even minor ones, has a unique voice and a vivid, quirky personality. Louise's need to have Abel create the world for her resonates with unfulfilled passion." Publ Wkly

Gracie, Anne

The **Autumn** Bride; Anne Gracie. Berkley Pub Group 2013 320 p. $7.99

ISBN 0425259250; 9780425259252

This historical romance novel, by Anne Gracie, is part of the "Chance Sisters Romance" series. When "Abigail Chantry . . . finds . . . Lady Beatrice Davenham, bedridden and neglected. . . . Abby rousts Lady Beatrice's predatory servants and [she, with her sister and two friends] . . . become her 'nieces.' . . . It's the perfect situation, until Lady Beatrice's dashing and arrogant nephew, Max, Lord Davenham, returns from the Orient." (Publisher's note)

Gracie, Anne

To catch a bride; Anne Gracie. Berkley Sensation 2009 308 p. (pbk.) $7.99; (pbk.) $7.99

ISBN 0425230228; 9780425230220

LC 2010414788

This book follows "a cynical, restless nobleman [who] flees an unwanted betrothal and heads to Egypt to track down the long-lost granddaughter of a family friend, . . . [and] the last thing he expects is to find love in the form of an elusive, cross-dressing Arab street urchin. Yet once he snares the fiercely loyal, independent Ayisha, Rafe Ramsey knows she is exactly what he wants--if only he can convince her." (Libr J)

Grady, James

Six days of the condor. Norton 1974 192p

"When a branch of the CIA is mass murdered, Malcolm, the only survivor, becomes the object of an intense chase involving the Washington police, the CIA, the FBI, the NSC, and a host of other intelligence agencies. Trying to stay one jump ahead of his pursuers, Malcolm struggles to find out who within the agency has sold out his comrades." Libr J

Graeme-Evans, Posie

The **island** house; a novel. by Posie Graeme-Evans. Atria Books 2012 451 p. (paperback) $16

ISBN 0743294432; 9780743294430; 9781451672022

LC 2012010046

This novel, by Posie Graeme-Evans, is about "a young archaeologist who unearths ancient secrets. . . . [In the present,] Freya Dane . . . arrives on the ancient Scottish island of Findnar. . . . [In] AD 800, . . . Signy, a Pictish girl, loses her entire family. Taken in by survivors of the island's Christian community. . . . Signy will call out to Freya across the centuries. Ancient wrongs must be laid to rest in the present and the mystery at the heart of Findnar's violent past exposed." (Publisher's note)

Grafton, Sue

★ **A is for alibi**; a Kinsey Millhone mystery. Holt & Co. 1990 274p $27

ISBN 0-8050-1334-2

A reissue of the title first published 1982 by Holt, Rinehart & Winston

"Kinsey Millhone is a cut above the usual woman private eye who flounces through fiction. Millhone is neither a sex bomb nor a detached cerebrum, but a believable, straightforward character." Booklist

Grafton, Sue

B is for burglar. Holt & Co. 1985 229p $27

ISBN 0-8050-1632-5

LC 84-22378

"Grafton's plot is solid p.i. procedural, but it is her sense of style that will truly delight readers. Her characters, from a punk dope pusher to a brave and resourceful eighty-eight-year-old woman, are completely convincing, and Grafton's ear for natural dialogue is among the best in the business." Wilson Libr Bull

Grafton, Sue

C is for corpse; a Kinsey Millhone mystery. Holt & Co. 1986 243p $27

ISBN 0-8050-2818-8

LC 85-24797

Kinsey Millhone "meets a young man, Buddy Callahan, at the gym where she works out and agrees to take his case. He wants her to investigate an auto accident in which he was badly injured because he claims that it was a murder attempt. When a second attempt results in his death, Kinsey, although she no longer has him as a client, pursues the matter and, in a hair-raising finale that takes place in a morgue, she unmasks the murderer." Shapiro. Fic for Youth. 3d edition

Grafton, Sue

D is for deadbeat; a Kinsey Millhone mystery. Holt & Co. 1987 229p $27

ISBN 0-8050-0248-0

LC 86-25843

"Social awareness and human weakness play a great part in the Millhone books, which always manage to finish with a heart-stopping climax." Libr J

Grafton, Sue

E is for evidence; a Kinsey Millhone mystery. Holt & Co. 1988 227p $27

ISBN 0-8050-0459-9

LC 87-28100

"The plot is just fine and does what a plot ought to in a good detective novel: it keeps us turning pages and serves as a vehicle for the really interesting stuff, an unveiling of the characters' foibles by the worldly-wise but uncorrupt private eye." NY Times Book Rev

Grafton, Sue

F is for fugitive; a Kinsey Millhone mystery. Holt & Co. 1989 261p $27

ISBN 0-8050-0460-2

LC 88-27284

Kinsey Millhone "becomes involved in ugly doings in a California coastal town, where she attempts to prove a man's innocence on a 17-year-old murder rap. Floral Beach appears to be a cozy little place, but it's a hotbed of dirty secrets, most of them involving the long-dead Jean Timberlake, a confused yet apparently sexually quite precocious teenager. Kinsey's investigation opens closet doors, and some tawdry skeletons jump out." Booklist

Grafton, Sue

G is for gumshoe; a Kinsey Millhone mystery. Holt & Co. 1990 261p

LC 89-24652

"Millhone, whose background has made her believe that all families are dysfunctional, has unwittingly taken on another case of domestic violence. Grafton excels in this milieu. Never morally oblique, here she is slyly didactic about (among other things) attitudes toward the mentally ill." Newsweek

Grafton, Sue

H is for homicide. Holt & Co. 1991 256p $27

ISBN 0-8050-1084-X

LC 90-25016

Detective Kinsey Millhone is "hired by California Fidelity to investigate a string of fraudulent automobile insurance claims filed by someone named Bibianna Diaz. To track down the elusive Bibianna, Kinsey adopts an undercover identity as Hannah Moore, a wisecracking, reckless vamp. As Hannah, she befriends Bibianna, a sexy young woman on the run. Both are quickly swept up in an evening of kidnapping and gunplay that ends with the two of them in jail. Through her relationship with Bibianna, Kinsey also stumbles onto a much bigger network of crime." N Y Times Book Rev

Grafton, Sue

I is for innocent. Holt & Co. 1992 286p $27

ISBN 0-8050-1085-8

LC 91-45165

Kinsey Millhone "lands the job of hunting up evidence for a wrongful-death suit against a high-living architect who couldn't be nailed in court for his wife's murder. It's a sobering case, weighted with the survivors' anger and suspicions and darkened by their sordid domestic affairs." N Y Times Book Rev

Grafton, Sue

J is for judgment. Holt & Co. 1993 288p $27

ISBN 0-8050-1935-9

LC 92-35769

"Ms. Grafton writes a smart story and wraps it up with a wry twist; but she takes care to sweeten her tart characterizations with amused understanding and, in the case of Jaffe, even affection." N Y Times Book Rev

Grafton, Sue

K is for killer. Holt & Co. 1994 284p $27

ISBN 0-8050-1936-7

LC 94-1242

"Despite an abrupt ending that has the reader frantically paging back for missed clues, the sturdily engineered plot drags Kinsey into the kind of joints that never seem to close: bars, nightclubs, diners, hospital emergency rooms. All this night crawling serves as an eye-opening experience for Kinsey, who is physically exhausted but mentally energized by her encounters with sad young prostitutes and other fascinating creatures of the night." N Y Times Book Rev

Grafton, Sue
  L is for lawless. Holt & Co. 1995 290p $27
    ISBN 0-8050-1937-5
                                        LC 95-12787
In this adventure "private investigator Kinsey Millhone is just doing a favor for a friend—checking the military status of a recently deceased neighbor—when she's sucked into a chase for the spoils of a 1941 bank heist. It's a lively outing with a couple of heart-pounding scenes, some interesting characters . . . and even a little detection. There are also hints of Kinsey's connecting with long-lost relatives, plus a romantic wedding of octogenarians." Libr J

Grafton, Sue
  M is for malice. Holt & Co. 1996 300p $27
    ISBN 0-8050-3637-7
                                        LC 96-30897
"This is a subtle and swiftly moving novel, pleasantly unpredictable, with an agreeable overlay of smoldering romance, as fellow PI and former lover Robert Dietz reenters Kinsey's life. Grafton's heroine—more introspective, yet still feisty and surefooted—leads this finely tuned and at times electrifying tale to a thoroughly satisfying conclusion." Publ Wkly

Grafton, Sue
  N is for noose. Holt & Co. 1998 289p $25
    ISBN 0-8050-3650-4
                                        LC 97-49320
"Even when people are not nice to Kinsey, Grafton always deals fairly with them in this clean, well-constructed story about small-town insecurities." N Y Times Book Rev

Grafton, Sue
  O is for outlaw. Holt & Co. 1999 318p $26
    ISBN 0-8050-5955-5
                                        LC 99-14967
"Everything that has always worked for this first class series works better here: the sturdy plotting, the animated characters, the breezy style and a heroine with foibles you can laugh at and faults you can forgive." N Y Times Book Rev

Grafton, Sue
  P is for peril. Putnam 2001 352p $26.95
    ISBN 0-399-14719-5
                                        LC 00-46024
"Private investigator Kinsey Milhone is hired by Dr. Fiona Purcell to find her ex-husband, Dowan, a prominent physician who vanished with his passport and $30,000 in cash nine weeks earlier. Wondering what she can do that the Santa Rosa police haven't done already, Kinsey takes the case and quickly discovers that the nursing home Purcell administered is being investigated for Medicare fraud." Libr J

Grafton, Sue
  Q is for quarry. Putnam 2002 385p $26.95
    ISBN 0-399-14915-5
                                        LC 2002-68368
"In the summer of 1969, the decomposed corpse of a young white female was discovered near a quarry off California's Highway 1. Her hands had been bound and her throat slashed. Despite months of investigation, 'Jane Doe' remained unidentified and the case unsolved. Now years later, Con Donlan and Stacey Oliphant, the police officers who had found her body, want Kinsey to help them to identify the girl and find her killer before they retire. At the same time, having learned that the body was found on a ranch owned by her estranged grandmother, Kinsey journeys into the past to retrace her own family history. Once again, an intriguing plot, fully drawn characters, and wry humor prove why Grafton's series is one of the best." Libr J

Grafton, Sue
  R is for ricochet; Sue Grafton. G.P. Putnam's Sons 2004 352p $26.95
    ISBN 0-399-15228-8
                                        LC 2004-44599
"Hired by dying millionaire Nord Lafferty to babysit his recently paroled daughter, Reba, Kinsey [Millhone] finds herself entangled in a complex money-laundering scheme when Reba decides to take revenge on the twotiming lover for whom she had gone to prison. Meanwhile, Kinsey's octogenarian landlord resigns himself to a loveless life after his interfering brothers sabotage a budding relationship with a lively widow. And the twice-divorced Kinsey has to decide whether to risk opening her heart to sexy cop Cheney Phillips. As demonstrated here, Grafton's series remains fresh and exciting, with complex plots and well-developed characters." Libr J

Grafton, Sue
  S is for Silence. Putnam 2005 374p $26.95
    ISBN 0-399-15297-0
                                        LC 2005-48923
"Grafton uses the mystery of Violet's disappearance as a window into Serena Station, a sad little hamlet of boarded-up houses, abandoned oil rigs and rusting railroad tracks. Something vital went out of the place when Violet disappeared, and Kinsey's investigation forces the onetime neighbors of this lusty Jezebel to recall her unbridled sexual energy and reflect on their own joyless lives. By alternating Kinsey's brisk first-person narrative with dramatic flashbacks that catch the spirit of the town during its volatile postwar period, Grafton allows Violet to emerge as a dynamic but dangerous life force—irresistible to men, threatening to women and too reckless for her own good." N Y Times Book Rev

Grafton, Sue
  T is for trespass. G. P. Putnam's Sons 2007 387p
    ISBN 9780399154485; 0-399-15448-5
                                        LC 2007-29368
"Gus Vronsky, Kinsey's elderly next-door neighbor, suffers a fall and needs in-home care. A health-care nurse named Solana Rojas is hired, and Kinsey even does the background check, finding nothing out of order. As Gus's condition deteriorates and Solana limits access to her patient,

Kinsey and her landlord, Henry, suspect that something is a little off with Solana-and 'little off' doesn't fully describe this identity thief and true sociopath. Digging around more carefully, Kinsey unearths horrifying details of Solana's past and must act quickly to save Gus. This is vintage Grafton, set in the 1980s but scarily current, carefully plotted, and fast paced." Libr J

Graham, Jo
Black ships; a novel. Orbit 2008 431p map pa $14.99

ISBN 978-0-316-06800-0; 0-316-06800-4

LC 2007-46166

"Born to a slave taken at the fall of Troy, the child named Gull is chosen by the oracle Pythia to succeed her in service to the Lady of Death because of her prophetic visions. When survivors of a later assault on Troy, called Wilusa by its inhabitants, free their enslaved people, Gull accompanies the captain of the seven black ships, the Trojan Prince Aeneas, as they search for a place to call home. Drawing her inspiration from Virgil's The Aeneid, debut author Graham recreates a vivid picture of the ancient world, a mysterious place in which gods and goddesses speak to their chosen." Libr J

Graham, Winston
Bella Poldark; a novel of Cornwall, 1818-1820. Macmillan 2002 530p $29.95

ISBN 0-333-98923-6

Earlier titles in the Poldark series: Ross Poldark (1945); Demelza (1946); Jeremy Poldark (1950); Warleggan 1953); Black moon (1973); The four swans (1976); The angry tide (1977); The stranger from the sea (1981); The miller's dance (1982); The loving cup (1984); The twisted sword (1990)

This is the twelfth and final novel of the Poldark series. "As the story opens, Valentine Warleggan's paternity still poisons the atmosphere, and his financial and marital trouble form a major narrative strand set firmly against the saga's familiar background of Cornwall. Meanwhile, Bella Poldark's desire for a musical career takes her to stages in London and France, where she is involved with rival suitors. Her widowed older sister, Clowance, must also choose between two men of vastly different backgrounds who propose marriage. A host of other characters and subplots, including a series of murders, keeps the action bubbling." Libr J

Grahame-Smith, Seth
Abraham Lincoln: vampire hunter. Grand Central Pub. 2010 336p

ISBN 0-446-56308-0; 978-0-446-56308-6

LC 2009-42988

"When Abraham Lincoln was nine years old, his mother died from an ailment called the 'milk sickness.' Only later did he learn that his mother's deadly affliction was actually the work of a local vampire. . . . When Abe learned the truth, he vowed revenge and kept one passion hidden throughout his life: the brutal elimination of all vampires. His valiant, bloody fight against the undead was all but lost to history, until Grahame-Smith stumbled upon The Secret Journal of Abraham Lincoln. Using the journal as his guide, Seth reconstructs Lincoln's life story and uncovers the role vampires played in the birth, growth, and near-death of our nation." (Publisher's note)

"An engaging and entertaining read that slips both in and out of historical works and genre fun easily." Io9

Gran, Sara
Claire DeWitt and the city of the dead. Houghton Mifflin Harcourt 2011 273p $24

ISBN 978-0-547-42849-9

LC 2010-21449

The novel is "is difficult to categorize, offering a strangely appealing mix of the mystical and the hardboiled. The book is beautifully written in a tight, quirky style that distinguishes Gran as one of the more original writers working today." Miami Herald

Granger, Bill
The **el** murders. Holt & Co. 1987 246p

LC 86-29399

This mystery features "Chicago homicide detective Terry Flynn and his lover, special investigator Karen Kovac. Flynn's case is the mugging-turned-murder of a gay man on an elevated-train platform. Kovac's case is a brutal rape that also takes place on an El platform. Flynn's key witness—the victim's lover—and Kovac's victim prove to be unacceptable witnesses, but neither Flynn nor Kovac retreats from the investigation." Booklist

"The two cases crisscross in this excellent police procedural filled with tough, streetwise characters and swift, rough action." Libr J

Grant, Cecilia
A **gentleman** undone. Bantam Books 2012 359 p.

ISBN 0553593846; 9780553593846

In this historical romance novel, Will Blackshear accepts the invitation from a friend to join him at Beechams, since it will provide him with the perfect opportunity to lighten the pockets of some wealthy gentlemen. What Will does not expect is to be fleeced himself by Lydia Slaughter, the mistress of another gentleman at the club. Lydia did not plan on being at a man's beck and call forever, which means she needs money. Although Lydia has no trouble winning at cards, she does run into some problems investing her hard-won earnings. All of which lead her to offer Will a mutually beneficial business proposal: in exchange for his help in investing her funds, Lydia will help Will sharpen his cardplaying skills. (Booklist)

Grant, Cecilia
A **lady** awakened; Cecilia Grant. Bantam 2012 368 p. (paperback) $7.99

ISBN 0553593838; 9780553593839

This is Cecilia Grant's debut Regency romance. "Determined to protect her estate and tenants from her nefarious brother-in-law, widow Martha Russell must produce an heir soon enough to claim he was fathered by her deceased husband. Her new neighbor, Theophilius Mirkwood, has been banished to the countryside for his rakish ways—but a rake is just what Martha needs. She proposes to pay him for a month of clandestine interludes with the end result of conception." (Publishers Weekly)

Grant, Helen

The **glass** demon; Helen Grant. Bantam Books Trade Paperbacks 2010 305p. ill. pa $15

ISBN 978-0-385-34420-3; 0-385-34420-1; 9780345527585

LC 2011000738

First published 2010 in the United Kingdom.

This book tells the story of "Lin Fox, [who] finds herself in a falling-down castle deep in the woods of Germany while her father attempts to resuscitate his academic career. For generations, the village has lived with the legend of the Allerheiligen Glass–medieval stained glass windows that are said to have been cursed by a demon, bringing death to those who gaze upon them. . . . On Lin's first day, she meets Michel, a mysterious boy who eventually becomes her only ally. . . .What's unclear is if the escalating threats to her family and mounting village deaths are the result of Michel's mad father, or the Glass Demon himself. Combined with the mystery is the story of Lin's everyday teenage concerns: fitting in at school, pining over a crush, and worrying about family dynamics." (School Libr J)

"With its fascinating information on medieval folklore, unique setting, and increasingly claustrophobic sense of terror, this is an exhilarating page-turner that offers a cerebral blend of horror and mystery." Booklist

Grant, Helen

The **vanishing** of Katharina Linden; a novel. Helen Grant. Delacorte Press 2010 287 p. (hbk.) $24; (pbk.) $15

ISBN 9780385344173; 9780440339618; 9780385344180

LC 201003415

First published 2009 in the United Kingdom

Alex Award (2011)

This book follows "ten-year-old Pia Kolvenbach, [who] becomes known in her German hometown of Bad Münstereifel as 'The Girl Whose Grandmother Exploded.' Pia, whose mother is one of only three British citizens in the area, is already familiar with the peculiarities of this insular town, but the ostracism she now faces leaves her with only two confidantes: StinkStefan, a classmate and fellow outcast, and grouchy, secretive Herr Schiller, a source of town lore. Attention soon shifts from Pia when a local girl, Katharina Linden, becomes neither the first nor the last girl to go missing. Pia and Stefan, inspired . . . by Herr Schiller's gruesome stories, become determined to investigate the disappearances." (Library Journal)

"Set in the small German town of Bad Münstereifel during a cold, dreary winter when little girls seem to be disappearing left and right, this dark story gains immeasurably from Grant's choice of narrator: Pia Kolvenbach, who is socially ostracized (shunned as 'the Potentially Explosive Schoolgirl') after her grandmother dies in a bizarre accident. Feeling even more isolated when her English mother and German father begin quarreling, Pia finds companionship with 'StinkStefan,' 'the most unpopular boy in the class,' and Herr Schiller, a kindly old gent who spins terrifying but oddly comforting horror stories. Although thin on plot, the novel has nice atmosphere and takes a tender view of lonely children trying to make sense of a grown-up world." N Y Times Book Rev

Grant, Linda

We had it so good; a novel. Scribner 2011 325p $25

ISBN 978-1-4516-1740-5

LC 2011-04179

"Linda Grant traces the force of time on a group of friends from their hippie days in the Oxford of the late 1960s all the way to the present, through the conventional and unconventional choices they make, the professionals they become, the children they have, the choices those children make. At the center of the novel is the marriage of Stephen and Andrea Newman. He's an American with a Jewish father and a Cuban mother who arrives in England as a Rhodes scholar, making the crossing by boat with one Bill Clinton. She's British, the smart, sensitive daughter of small-time hotel owners in Cornwall. . . . In due course, they fall into bed, into something like love, into a marriage to keep him out of the American draft and then, unexpectedly, into a real marriage of obligations, children, a shared history, a life in London. Time passes. Arranged around this marriage are Grace, Andrea's dear friend, a raving blond beauty with significant psychic scars; Ivan, an advertising man, formerly a freewheeling daredevil given to spouting Reichian theories of the orgone box; Andrea and Stephen' children and parents; their trysts and crushes; their discarded selves." N Y Times Book Rev

Grant, Michael, 1954-

Officer down. Doubleday 1993 437p

ISBN 0-385-41968-6

LC 92-37205

"First a bomb explodes at New York City's police headquarters, killing an officer, then a policewoman is executed. While it is clear that the police are targets of a highly organized group, the motive behind the attacks is kept secret. FBI agent Chris Liberti, DEA undercover agent Donal Castillo, and deputy inspector Dan Morgan form a special task force to identify the people behind the violence. They know a terrorist group known as Punyo Blanco has been formed by the Colombian drug cartels to force the United States to stop pressuring Colombia into action against the drug lords. . . . The plot is timely, the characters realistic, the motive plausible, and the pace electrifying." Libr J

Grant, Mira

Deadline. Orbit 2011 560p

ISBN 9780316081061

This book is set in "2041, a year after Shaun Mason's sister and co-blogger, Georgia, became infected with the zombie virus. . . . After nearly three decades of rampant zombiism, procedures and protocols have evolved to keep humans safe, constrained, and scared. As Shaun struggles to cope with Georgia's death, a doctor from the Centers for Disease Control sets the After the End Times blogging crew to investigating a conspiracy around people with a reservoir condition--a state in which the virus goes live in just one area of the body--and the high death rate among reputable scientists trying to study them." (Publishers Weekly)

Grant, Mira

Feed. Orbit 2010 599p pa $9.99

ISBN 978-0-316-08105-4; 0-316-08105-1

This fantasy is set in a "postapocalyptic 2039. Twin bloggers Georgia and Shaun Mason and their colleague Buffy are thrilled when Sen. Peter Ryman, the first presidential candidate to come of age since social media saved the world from a virus that reanimates the dead, invites them to cover his campaign. Then an event is attacked by zombies, and Ryman's daughter is killed. As the bloggers wield the newfound power of new media, they tangle with the CDC, a scheming vice presidential candidate, and mysterious conspirators who want more than the Oval Office. Shunning misogynistic horror tropes in favor of genuine drama and pure creepiness, McGuire has crafted a masterpiece of suspense with engaging, appealing characters who conduct a soul-shredding examination of what's true and what's reported." Publ Wkly

Grant, Stephanie

Map of Ireland; a novel. Scribner 2008 197p $22

ISBN 978-1-416-55622-0; 1-416-55622-2

LC 2007-45912

"Ann's descriptions of life in Southie are so compelling that some readers may miss those passages, with their very specific, idiosyncratic details, when she steps out of this world she knows best into the wider world. But Grant emerges on the other side with her firm grip on originality, and ultimately, in spite of the wonderful epigraph by Heraclitus — 'Geography is fate' — Ann represents not so much her community, but herself.... Early on, she muses that 'the problem with the movies was that they made you think you had more experience than you actually did.' That, too, is the gift of a well-worded novel. 'Map of Ireland' is admirably ambitious, bold, and smart." Boston Globe

Grant, Susan

Moonstruck; Susan Grant. HQN 2008 378p (pbk.) $6.99

ISBN 9780373772599; 0373772599

LC 2008577267

This science fiction romance novel tells the story of "Coalition starship admiral Brit Bandar [who] was one tough woman. A mere intergalactic treaty could never get her to trust the Drakken Horde. There was too much bad blood between the Coalition and the Horde and, for intensely personal reasons, Brit wasn't sure that she was through spilling it! But now a peaceful accord had made Finn Rorkken, a notorious Drakken rogue, second in command on her starship, and . . . front and center in her thoughts . . . and her heart." (Publisher's note)

Grant, Susan

The **star** princess; Susan Grant. Love Spell 2003 371 p. o.p.

ISBN 0505525410

LC 2003612437

In this book, "Los Angeles filmmaker Ilana Hamilton . . . takes center stage . . . [along with] her alien counterpart, Vash Prince Ché Vedla. . . . Strong, honorable and . . . strait-laced, Ché will do almost anything to ensure the welfare of his people, even submit to an arranged marriage. While his counselors select his bride-to-be, he [travels] . . . to Earth. The traditionalist Vash people have long believed Earth-dwellers to be 'barbarians,' but that doesn't stop Ché from

seeking out Ilana. . . . Inevitably, their feelings for one another intensify, but someone in the Vedla household is determined to spoil their happily-ever-after." (Publishers Weekly)

Grass, Gunter

The **box**; tales from the darkroom. translated from the German by Krishna Winston. Houghton Mifflin Harcourt 2010 194p $23

ISBN 978-0-547-24503-4; 0-547-24503-3

LC 2010-08479

Original German edition, 2008

"The premise is that for his 80th birthday, Grass has asked his children eight in all, with four different mothers to gather together to record their memories of life with their father. The slender book comprises nine sections. Each consists of the children's uninterrupted (and generally unidentified) voices, bracketed by the author's short preface and concluding reflection. . . . While Grass is the subject of their memories, another figure emerges as equally important: Marie, the author's longtime friend and eventual assistant (and perhaps lover), who constantly takes photographs with her old Agfa box camera as a memory aid for his novels. . . . [This novel] should serve as no one's introduction to Grass; its charm and poignancy hinge on prior knowledge of the author's books." San Francisco Chron

Grass, Gunter

The **call** of the toad; translated by Ralph Manheim. Harcourt Brace Jovanovich 1992 248p il

LC 92-20233

This book is a "skillful balancing act that juggles some very timely questions about the conflict between calls for ethnic self-determination and calls for international unity and cooperation." Christ Sci Monit

Grass, Gunter

Cat and mouse; translated by Ralph Manheim. Harcourt, Brace & World 1963 189p

Original German edition, 1961

A novel about Mahlke, a teenager growing up in a Baltic port city during World War II who is set apart from his fellows by his huge Adam's apple. When a classmate attracts a cat to this 'mouse' he launches Mahlke on his career. Mahlke becomes an excellent swimmer and athlete, and later a hero to his nation. But the symbolic cat watching him is a society of petty men and Mahlke is eventually doomed

Grass, Gunter

Crabwalk; translated from the German by Krishna Winston. Harcourt 2002 234p $25

ISBN 0-15-100764-0

LC 2002-13205

"A writer who refuses to avert his eyes from unpleasant truths, Grassremains an eloquent explorer of his country's troubled 20th-century history." Publ Wkly

Grass, Gunter

The **Danzig** trilogy; translated by Ralph Manheim. Harcourt Brace Jovanovich 1987 1030p

ISBN 0-15-123816-2

LC 87-8725

Contents: The tin drum; Cat and mouse; Dog years

Grass, Gunter

★ **Dog** years; translated by Ralph Manheim. Harcourt, Brace & World 1965 570p

Original German edition, 1963

"A monumental parable on 'mass man,' materialism, and transcendence, written in the richly encrusted, playful, brutal, ironic, subtle, sensitive, surrealist, erudite, unique modern baroque. . . . {This novel tells} of Eduard Amsel, rumored to be half Jew, designer of fantastic scarecrows, endlessly ingenious and talented; of Walter Matern, athlete and compulsive tooth grinder, Amsel's blood brother, his defender, and helper until association with a Nazi S. A. group leads him to beat Amsel unmercifully; of Hitler's favorite dog Prinz of notable lineage and the howling dog days echoing down the centuries through World War II and aftermath. The cast is large; the canvas is chiefly Danzig and villages along the Vistula; and the scarecrow prevails as dominant symbol." Booklist

Grass, Gunter

The **flounder**; translated by Ralph Manheim. Harcourt Brace Jovanovich 1978 547p

LC 78-53891

Original German edition, 1977

"Grass's first-person narrator is the legendary fisherman who caught the magic fish and might have fared well had it not been for the foolishness of his wife Ilsebill. Grass uses the well-known fairy tale as a frame for his chronicler to relate his various lives' experiences (between the late Neolithic and {1970}) . . . to his pregnant wife Ilsebill in the course of nine months. While his story unfolds, the fish is on trial in a feminist courtroom after he has been caught again, this time by three women in West Berlin." Libr J

Grass, Gunter

My century; translated by Michael Henry Heim. Harcourt Brace & Co. 1999 280p $31

ISBN 0-15-100496-X

LC 99-38690

Original German edition, 1999

"The best thing {this book} offers non-Germans, even if inadvertently, is the opportunity to hear, or to overhear, how Germans speak to one another about their history when the rest of us are not supposed to be listening." Natl Rev

Grass, Gunter

★ The **tin** drum; translated from the German by Ralph Manheim; with an introduction by John Reddick. Knopf 1993 xxxvii, 551p

ISBN 0-679-42033-9

LC 92-54295

Original German edition, 1959; this translation first published 1962 in the United Kingdom, 1963 in the United States by Pantheon Books

"Oskar Matzerath, born with an unusually sharp mind, describes the amoral conditions through which he has lived in twentieth-century Germany, both during and after the Hitler regime. This strange narrator stops growing when he is three years old and remains three feet tall until some time late, when he decides to grow a few inches more. After the war he escapes to West Germany, where he works in such capacities as an artist's model, a night-club performer, and

a black marketeer. Depicted as a freak (Oskar becomes a hunchback later in his life), this character symbolizes the deformed society of this century. It is through his tin drum, which he uses to stimulate recollections of his life, that Oskar describes his past while he is an inmate in a mental hospital." Shapiro. Fic for Youth. 3d edition

Grass, Gunter

Too far afield; translated from the German by Krishna Winston. Harcourt 2000 658p $30

ISBN 0-15-100230-4

LC 00-29586

Original German edition published 1995

The narrative's "focus is German reunification, in particular, the fate of the German Democratic Republic after the Wall came down in 1989. At the center of the novel are two characters, locked in a sort of political marriage: Theo Wuttke, a former East German cultural figure and longwinded raconteur, and Ludwig Hoffstaller, a professional spy who served for years as Wuttke's shadow. They are both about to turn 70 in this new Germany and are now both employees of the agency responsible for privatizing state-held companies." Booklist

Grau, Shirley Ann

The **keepers** of the house. Knopf 1964 309p

"This multigenerational novel deals with the twentieth-century heirs of a Southern dynasty, their relations to the past, and their involvement in the racial and political complexities of the present. The narrator is Abigail Mason Tolliver, granddaughter of William Howland, whose second wife had been a Freejack Negro. The townspeople have always assumed that she had been no more than William's mistress, but the truth of the legality of their marriage surfaces when Abigail's husband, John Tolliver, enters the race for governor. In addition to leading to Tolliver's defeat, the story of the marriage also incites a mob to burn down the old Howland house. Abigail saves the house but withdraws the economic support that the Howland family has always supplied the town, and lets it 'shrivel and shrink to its real size.'" Shapiro. Fic for Youth. 3d edition

Graver, Elizabeth

Awake. Holt & Co. 2004 288p $23

ISBN 0-8050-6540-7

LC 2003-55253

"Anna Simon has been living in the dark ever since she gave birth to Max, a child with a rare genetic disease for whom even an hour in sunlight could prove fatal. For years, Anna has homeschooled Max and structured her life around his schedule, despite the fact that her husband, Ian, favors mainstreaming and wants Max to attend school with his older brother. When Anna learns of a camp in upstate New York for children with light-sensitivity disorders, she sees room for a compromise between her own and Ian's approaches. . . . And so the summer that Max is nine, the family heads off to Camp Luna. At first, the place seems like the answer to their problems. But as Anna is drawn into life there and gets to know Hal, the camp's charismatic founder, freedom and safety soon prove to be complicated things." Publisher's note

Graver, Elizabeth

The **end** of the point; a novel. Elizabeth Graver. Harper 2013 352 p. (hardback) $25.99

ISBN 0062184849; 9780062184849

LC 2012025261

This book is a "multigenerational story of a privileged family's vacations on Massachusetts' Buzzards Bay. . . . In 1942, wheelchair-bound insurance executive Mr. Porter" brings his wife, three daughters, mother, and servants to summer "at Ashaunt Point, where an Army base has been temporarily set up nearby." Over the course of the novel, years pass and different characters take turns narrating the story. (Kirkus)

Graves, Robert

Claudius, the god and his wife Messalina. H. Smith & R. Haas 1935 583p

"A vivid picture of profligate Rome during the years in which Claudius conquered Britain and instituted many reforms at home. A story complete in itself, though a continuation of 'I, Claudius.'" Booklist

Graves, Robert

Complete short stories; edited by Lucia Graves. St. Martin's Press 1996 331p

ISBN 0-312-16055-0

LC 96-5343

"Graves is a master storyteller, and the stories collected here are both masterly and charming. Especially noteworthy are the sweetly humorous tales about school days in Edwardian England and the breezy, gently witty stories about everyday life in Majorca, Graves's adopted home." Libr J

Graves, Robert

★ **I,** Claudius; from the autobiography of Tiberius Claudius, born B.C. 10, murdered and deified A.D. 54. H. Smith and R. Haas 1934 494p

"Claudius is lame and a stammerer who seems unlikely to carry on the family tradition of power in ancient Rome. Immersing himself in scholarly pursuits, Claudius observes and lives through the plots hatched by his grandmother, Livia, political conspiracies, murders, and corruption, and he survives a number of emperors. He becomes emperor at last and is a just and well-liked ruler, in contrast to those who preceded him." Shapiro. Fic for Youth. 3d edition

Followed by Claudius, the god and his wife Messalina

Graves, Tracey Garvis

Covet; by Tracey Garvis Graves. Dutton 2013 320 p. (hardcover) $25.95

ISBN 0525954074; 9780525954071

LC 2013016256

In this novel by Tracey Garvis Graves, Chris and Claire Canton's marriage is falling apart. "Chris copes by retreating to a dark place where no one can reach him, not even Claire. Claire has never felt so disconnected from Chris. When [she] is hired to do some graphic design work for the police department, her friendship with Officer Daniel Rush grows. Daniel knows that Claire's marital status means their relationship [is] platonic. But it doesn't take long before Claire and Daniel are . . . close to the line that Claire has sworn she'll never cross." (Publisher's note)

Gray, Alasdair

Old men in love; John Tunnock's posthumous papers. introduced by Lady Sara Sim-Jaeger; edited, decorated by Alasdair Gray. Small Beer Press 2010 311p $24

ISBN 978-1-93152069-0

LC 2010-05876

First published 2007 in the United Kingdom

"Setting themselves against the ideal of seamless self-containment that conventional narratives have always sought, Gray's texts are always emphatically open—to question, to commentary. They are democratically accountable, in other words. Bustling as they are with intertextual references and with the entrances and exits of characters, fictional and real, they feel more like a public than a private space. If the novel was traditionally to be enjoyed at home, to be curled up with in a quiet corner, reading Gray can seem more like visiting a busy municipal library." Times Lit Suppl

Gray, Alasdair

★ **Poor** things; episodes from the early life of Archibald McCandless M.D., Scottish public health officer. edited by Alasdair Gray. Harcourt Brace Jovanovich 1993 317p il

ISBN 0-15-173076-8

LC 92-40018

First published 1992 in the United Kingdom

"Mr. Gray contrasts the political and moral bleakness of contemporary Britain with the civic energy that characterized the best of Victorian values, now lost. He underlines the harm done to Scotland. 'Poor Things' is a political book. It is also witty and delightfully written, if at times two-dimensional. Attention to Victorian Glasgow with its civic fountains, domestic interiors and medical schools gives the book texture. It is the characters, and strangely enough its phantasmagoria, that give it life." N Y Times Book Rev

Gray, Juliana

A **Duke** Never Yields; Juliana Gray. Berkley Pub Group 2013 320 p. $7.99

ISBN 0425251187; 9780425251188

In this historical romance novel, by Juliana Gray, "impatient with the strictures of polite British society, Miss Abigail Harewood has decided to live life on her own terms--and the first thing she requires is a lover. When the commanding Duke of Wallingford arrives on the doorstep of her leased holiday castle, she thinks she's found the perfect candidate: handsome, dashing, and experienced in the art of love." (Publisher's note)

Gray, Juliana

How to Tame Your Duke; by Juliana Gray. Berkley Pub Group 2013 320 p. $7.99

ISBN 0425265668; 9780425265666

This book, by Juliana Gray, is set in England in 1888. "Princess Emilie . . . disguise[s] herself as a tutor in the household of the imposing Duke of Ashland, a former soldier disfigured in battle. Emilie can't resist the opportunity to learn what lies behind his forbidding mask. The duke never imagines that his son's tutor and his mysterious . . . beauty are one and the same. When the true identity of his lover is laid bare, Ashland must . . . safeguard both his lady and his heart." (Publisher's note)

Gray, Juliana

A **lady** never lies; by Juliana Gray. Berkley Sensation 2012 311 p.

ISBN 042525092X; 9780425250921

Author Juliana Gray tells the story of "Lady Alexandra Morley, an alluring widow, [who] is desperate to devise a plan to reverse her fortunes. When fate lands her in the arms of Phineas 'Finn' Burke, an attractive inventor, she despairs of ever getting what she needs...until they kiss . . . Despite the brewing scandal, Finn longs to make Alexandra his wife, but he must first convince the maddening lady that their love is the only thing that matters." (Amazon)

Greatest hits; original stories of assassins, hitmen, and hired guns. edited by Robert J. Randisi. Carroll & Graf 2005 318p $26

ISBN 978-0-7867-1581-7; 0-78671-581-2

LC 2006-297413

Randisi "has gathered 15 memorable tales of contract killers, antiheroes paid to carry out murders for a variety of clients and motives. . . . While the moral code that guides the actions of some of the murderers requires a measure of suspension of disbelief, the taut language and suspenseful plot twists that mark virtually all the stories should draw in even non-hardboiled devotees." Publ Wkly

Greaves, C. Joseph

Hard twisted; a novel. C. Joseph Greaves. St. Martin's Press 2012 304 p.

ISBN 1608198553; 9781608198559

LC 2011051902

Author C. Joseph Greaves' book received the 2010 Best Historical Novel award in the SouthWest Writers Annual Writing Contest. "In May of 1934, outside of Hugo, Oklahoma, a homeless man and his 13 year-old daughter are befriended by a Texas drifter . . . [who] lures father and daughter to Texas . . . [There,] the father, Dillard Garrett, mysteriously disappears, and . . . his daughter Lucile begins a one-year ordeal that culminates in four Utah killings and Palmer's notorious Greenville, Texas 'skeleton murder' trial of 1935." (chuckgreaves.com)

Greaves, Chuck

★ **Hush** money; a mystery. Chuck Greaves. Minotaur Books 2012 326 p.

ISBN 125000523X; 9781250005236; 9781466802483

LC 2012004489

In this book, "[w]hen Sydney Everett's Olympic-caliber jumping horse, Hush Puppy, dies suddenly, her law firm jumps into action, sending out young Pasadena, CA, attorney Jack MacTaggart. Sydney is worth watching because another horse she owned died under suspicious circumstances just a few years earlier. Jack . . . learns that Sydney was guilty of insurance fraud that first time, and someone within the club has been blackmailing her ever since. Jack knows he's hot on the trail when the next death turns out to be that of his mentor at the law firm. Stable manager Tara Flynn clues in Jack to the riding club's dirt and also provides romantic interest and an investigative assistant he can trust.

Meanwhile, Jack's other case, about medical insurance, gives him the break he needs." (Libr J)

Grecian, Alex

The **black** country; Alex Grecian. G.P. Putnam's Sons 2013 400 p. (hardcover) $26.95

ISBN 0399159339; 9780399159336

LC 2013003820

This novel, by Alex Grecian, is part of the "Scotland Yard's Murder Squad" series. "When members of a prominent family disappear from a coal-mining village . . . the local constable sends for help from Scotland Yard. . . . Inspector Walter Day and Sergeant Nevil Hammersmith respond. . . . The villagers have intense, intertwined histories. Everybody bears a secret. Superstitions abound. And the village itself is slowly sinking into the mines beneath it." (Publisher's note)

Greeley, Andrew M.

The **bishop** in the West Wing; a Blackie Ryan story. Forge 2002 255p il

ISBN 0-312-86873-1

LC 2001-58284

"Bishop Blackie Ryan is summoned to Washington, D.C., by the newly elected Democratic president to investigate a possible poltergeist. Shortly after his inauguration, President Jack Patrick McGurn, a South Side Chicago Irishman dubbed Machine Gun McGurn by a national media eager to discredit him, is plagued by a series of inexplicable psychic phenomena. . . . An entertaining romp through the West Wing." Booklist

Greeley, Andrew M.

The **cardinal** virtues. Warner Bks. 1990 449p

LC 89-40463

"When Father Laurence ('Lar') McAuliffe, pastor of an affluent suburban Roman Catholic church, acquires an unconventional new assistant, reactionary elements within the congregation of St. Finian's show their displeasure. As Lar and young Father Jamie struggle to minister to the disparate needs of their flock, archdiocesan conservatives attempt to undermine their unorthodox methods. In addition to successfully challenging the ecclesiastical hierarchy, the dynamic spiritual duo also double as matchmakers, salvage disintegrating marriages, counsel spirited teens, and, most impressively, vanquish a regressive secret society flourishing within the clergy. Greeley appears more comfortable in this reversion to his pastoral roots than in his more sensationalistic fictional forays." Booklist

Greeley, Andrew M.

Irish cream; a Nuala Anne McGrail novel. Andrew M. Greeley. Forge 2005 319p $24.95

ISBN 0-7653-0335-3

LC 2004-56322

Psychic Nuala McGrail and her husband, Dermot Coyne "look into mysteries past and present: the first chronicled in the diaries of Father Richard Lonigan, a 19th-century parish priest in Donegal, Ireland, the second involving poor Damian 'Day' O'Sullivan, whom the couple hire to take care of their two Irish wolfhounds. Amid the troubled political and religious environment in Donegal, where mostly poor Catholic villagers are overseen by Protestant Lord Skeffington,

Father Lonigan investigates two shootings while striving to prevent further violence. In present-day Chicago, Nuala and Dermot face opposition to hiring Day O'Sullivan from the lad's father, since Day is not only a profound disappointment to the O'Sullivan family but also a convicted felon." Publ Wkly

Greeley, Andrew M.

Irish lace; a Nuala Anne McGrail novel. Forge 1996 303p

ISBN 978-0312862343

LC 96-24519

"Moving effortlessly between the (fictional) conspiracies of 1864 and 1995 Chicago, Greeley is at his top page-turning form, throwing in a few stinging words about racism and xenophobia and delivering a rousing defense of the Bill of Rights." Publ Wkly

Greeley, Andrew M.

Irish stew! a Nuala Anne McGrail story. TOR Bks. 2002 303p

ISBN 0-312-87188-0

LC 2001-54805

In this adventure, "set at an international music festival in Milan, the McGrails really have their hands full. Not only are there demands on Nuala professionally (in addition to sleuting, she is an international singing star), they must also solve the mystery surrounding one Seamus Costelloe, whose sinister personage is doomed according to Nuala's ESP. As usual with Greeley's fiction, there is a Chicago connection; in addition to everything else going on, Dermot tries to solve the 100-year-old mystery of who started the Haymarket riot. A light, entertaining read." Booklist

Greeley, Andrew M.

Second spring; a love story. Forge 2003 347p $24.95

ISBN 0-7653-0236-5

LC 2002-32549

"In this installation, Charles 'Chucky' O'Malley and his spirited family face the 1970s. Here we find Chucky approaching 50 and stuck in a vicious midlife and spiritual crisis. While O'Malley can count his blessings—an adoring wife, an amazing sex life, a prestigious career, and a large, happy family—he still feels unfulfilled. In addition, he is no longer able to take comfort in his faith. As a photographer of some importance, O'Malley travels the world snapping historical photos and searching for his own happiness." Booklist

Greeley, Andrew M.

September song. Forge 2001 317p

ISBN 0-312-87225-9

LC 2001-33552

Fourth installment in the author's O'Malley Family saga; previous titles A midwinter's tale (1998); Younger than springtime; Christmas wedding (2000)

This installment "focuses on the spitfire Irish Chuck O'Malley and his gorgeous wife, Rosemarie. Set against the turbulent events of the 1960s following the Kennedy assassination, the novel opens with Chuck handing in his resignation as German ambassador to President Johnson. On a first-name basis with all the major political figures of the time,

Chuck strongly opposes Lyndon's position on the Vietnam War. He returns to Chicago with his wife and five children, only to be notified by Bobby (Kennedy, that is) of the historic civil rights march in Selma, Ala. . . . Sprinkled with . . . silly endearments and some chaste love-making scenes, the novel proceeds along a predictable historic course, weaving a Forrest Gump-like path through the '60s." Publ Wkly

Greeley, Andrew M.

White smoke; a novel about the next papal conclave. Forge 1996 384p

ISBN 978-0312858148

LC 96-1412

Bishop John Blackwood "Blackie" Ryan is "in Rome along with his boss, Sean, Cardinal Cronin of Chicago, as the College of Cardinals meets to choose the next pope. Covering the papal conclave is Dennis (Dinny) Molloy, a Pulitzer Prize-winning reporter for the New York Times, and his lovely ex-wife, Patricia McLaughlin, a correspondent for CNN. There is serious dissension in the ranks about whom should be the next spiritual leader of the world's one billion Roman Catholics. . . . While the clergy battle it out, sparks fly between Dinny and Patty as they rediscover each other. The situation heats up when Dinny unearths a new Vatican investment scandal and Cronin collapses." Libr J

Greeley, Andrew M.

Younger than springtime. Forge 1999 348p

ISBN 0-312-86572-4

LC 99-22198

Sequel to A midwinter's tale (1998)

This novel about the O'Malley family of Chicago "chronicles the romantic and spiritual fortunes of returned soldier Chuck O'Malley, who comes home in 1949, having been stationed for two years in postwar Germany. . . . The central image, bookending the novel, is a snapshot Chuck takes of beautiful Rosemarie Clancy, the troubled alcoholic daughter of Chuck's father's best friend. The photo of Rosemarie, in déshabillé, gets Chuck into trouble at Notre Dame and concatenates his search for spiritual meaning within the strict prohibitions of the Church. Chuck and Rosemarie's lifelong mutual attraction permeates the novel, with Greeley shifting focus in the middle of the book to Chuck's father, John. The elder O'Malley tells of how he met Chuck's mother, and the part Rosemarie's father, Jim Clancy, played in the eventual union. John O'Malley's story is deftly set in the center of Chuck's saga." Publ Wkly

Green cane and juicy flotsam; short stories by Caribbean women. Carmen C. Esteves and Lizabeth Paravisini-Gebert, editors. Rutgers Univ. Press 1991 xxix, 273p

ISBN 0-8135-1737-0

LC 91-4788

"Throughout, {this anthology} the race and class issues unique to Caribbean women are explored but in diverse ways and on a small scale, so that one comes away from the book with a uniquely personal sense of a much larger political phenomenon." Booklist

Green, George Dawes

The **juror**. Warner Bks. 1995 420p

LC 94-18831

"Annie Laird is a single mother, a part-time data entry clerk, an aspiring sculptor, and a juror selected for the murder trial of a mob boss. When a suave, handsome art broker buys some of her work and then invites her to dinner, she thinks her luck may be changing. Her supposed admirer, a Wall Street financier and Taoist nicknamed 'The Teacher,' is actually the brains behind the jailed mobster. The Teacher is incredibly charming; he's also a vicious killer. He promises Annie the continued safety of her son and the assurance of a lucrative artistic career in exchange for help in acquitting the mobster. . . . {This novel} is less a courtroom drama than a gripping psychological cat-and-mouse game." Libr J

Green, George Dawes

Ravens. Grand Central Pub. 2009 325p $24.99

ISBN 978-0-446-53896-1; 0-446-53896-5

LC 2008-48331

"When Shaw and Romeo pull up at a convenience store off I-95 in Georgia, their only thought is to fix a leaky tire and be on their way again to Florida—away from their dull Ohio tech-support jobs. But this happens to be the store from which a $318,000,000-million jackpot ticket has been sold. When a pretty clerk accidentally reveals to Shaw the identity of the winning family, he hatches a ferociously audacious scheme: he and Romeo will squeeze the family for half their prize." Publisher's note

Green, Jane

Another piece of my heart; Jane Green. St. Martin's Press 2012 400p (hardcover) $25.99

ISBN 9780312591823; 9781429962735

LC 2011041347

This book tells the story of "Andi [who] has spent much of her adult life looking for the perfect man, and at thirty-seven, she's finally found him. Ethan--divorced with two daughters, Emily and Sophia--is a devoted father and even better husband. Always hoping one day she would be a mother, Andi embraces the girls like they were her own. But in Emily's eyes, Andi is an obstacle to her father's love, and Emily will do whatever it takes to break her down. When the dynamics between the two escalate, they threaten everything Andi believes about love, family, and motherhood--leaving both women standing at a crossroad in their lives . . . and in their hearts." (Publisher's note)

Green, Jane

The **beach** house. Viking 2008 341p $24.95

ISBN 978-0-670-01885-7; 0-670-01885-6

LC 2008-15516

"Set on Nantucket, the novel follows a 65-year-old widow named Nan, who decides to rent rooms in her rambling oceanfront home after a series of bad investments leaves her close to broke. Soon, a disparate group of strangers — men and women — start moving into the beach house. Green shows us the formation of a new kind of family with Nan as its surrogate mother. The book has a warm, bohemian flavor reminiscent of the 'Tales of the City' novels by Armistead Maupin." Connecticut Post

Green, Norman

The **angel** of Montague Street. HarperCollins Pubs. 2003 293p $24.95

ISBN 0-06-018819-7

LC 2002-32885

Silvano Iurata "should never be in Brooklyn in the first place. It's 1973, the city is broke and mean, and he's ben bumming around since he got out of Vietnam, avoiding his Mafia-employed family and keeping clear of his loco cousin, Domenic, who wants to settle and old family quarrel by killing him with his bare hands. But Iurata is on some private redemptive mission, and he figures that if he can find out what happened to his sweet, mildly retarded brother, last seen in Brooklyn Heights, he might be able to give up the dead and rejoin the living. . . . Green writes about mobster families with a knowledge that is unnerving in its intimacy." N Y Times Book Rev

Green, Norman

Shooting Dr. Jack; a novel. HarperCollins Pubs. 2001 288p $25

ISBN 0-06-018822-7

LC 2001-16841

"The sharply drawn characters and the clever nicknames will invite comparisons to Elmore Leonard, but there's little of Leonard's flash and cockiness here, only a gritty realism, an attention to detail, and a resolute avoidance of clichés." Publ Wkly

Green, Tim

The **letter** of the law. Warner Bks. 2000 341p

ISBN 0-446-52299-6

LC 00-22285

Texan Casey Jordan "helps clear Eric Lipton, a law professor at the University of Texas, of the charge of disemboweling and murdering Marcia Sales. An instant before the jury foreman reads the verdict, Lipton whispers his guilt to Jordan. After the trial, suspicion rests on Donald Sales, the victim's father. Distraught with grief, hating Lipton, and humiliated by Jordan's trial accusation of incest, Sales abducts Jordan to teach her some of the pain his daughter suffered." Libr J

Greenberg, Joanne

★ **I** never promised you a rose garden; a novel. [by] Hannah Green. Holt & Co. 1964 300p

ISBN 0-8050-0872-1

"The hospital world and Deborah's fantasy world are strikingly portrayed, as is the girl's violent struggle between sickness and health, a struggle given added poignancy by youth, wit, and courage." Libr J

Greenberg, Joanne

In this sign. Holt, Rinehart & Winston 1970 275p

"The life of deaf-mutes Abel and Janice Ryder is followed from their marriage to their old age. After they leave the cloistered world of the institution for those with their handicap, they are plunged, unprepared, into the terrifying world of the hearing. They are never fully assimilated into that society. When they have a daughter who can hear, they gain new perspectives, but poverty and personal tragedy—

the death of a son—further separate them from others, even from other deaf people. Greenberg's insights into the lives of the deaf are sensitive and painful." Shapiro. Fic for Youth. 2d edition

Greene, Amy

Bloodroot; a novel. Alfred A. Knopf 2010 291p $24.95

ISBN 978-0-307-26986-7; 0-307-26986-8

LC 2009-19483

"As a first novel, Bloodroot has its awkward moments, and some segments that work less well than others. . . . When Bloodroot works, however, its power is awesome, peeling away layers of the human experience like an onion until it reaches a message of redemption. Greene proves herself a newcomer to watch." Wilmington Star News

Greene, Graham

3: This gun for hire, The confidential agent, The ministry of fear. Viking 1952 3v in 1

A one-volume edition of three suspense stories. The titles were first published 1936, 1939 and 1943, respectively

Greene, Graham

★ **Brighton** rock; an entertainment. Viking 1938 358p

"This novel presents the story of Pinkie Brown, a chilling, utterly evil 17-year-old gang leader who marries the plodding Rose in order to insure her silence about his crimes. Both Pinkie and Rose were reared as Roman Catholics, and that background continues to inform their thoughts, if not their actions. In the end Pinkie dies while attempting to kill Rose; later, a priest tells Rose that her love for Pinkie may have saved her, as the mercy of God may have saved Pinkie." Merriam-Webster's Ency of Lit

Greene, Graham

A **burnt**-out case. Viking 1961 248p

"The story opens as Querry, a European who has lost the ability to connect with emotion or spirituality, arrives at a leprosarium in the Belgian Congo. His spiritual aridity is likened to a medical burnt-out-case—a leper who is in remission but who has been eaten up by his disease. Querry is invigorated by his contact with the leprosarium and its inhabitants, and he begins to come to life. Parkinson, an opportunistic journalist, discovers that Querry is a distinguished architect with a lurid past and begins to write sensationalized newspaper articles about him. When Querry innocently consoles the wife of the manager of a local factory, he is shot dead by her husband." Merriam-Webster's Ency of Lit

Greene, Graham

The **captain** and the enemy. Viking 1988 188p

LC 87-40664

The author "wastes not a word in distilling the fictional preoccupations of a lifetime, omitting descriptive padding and elaborate transitions. But stripped down, the narrative runs fast and true across that bleak and poignant emotional landscape that is uniquely, immortally his." Time

Greene, Graham

Collected stories; including May we borrow your husband? A sense of reality {and} Twenty-one stories. Viking 1973 561p

Greene, Graham

The **comedians**. Viking 1966 309p

This "book concerns a back-slidden Catholic, a native of Monaco and owner of a rundown tourist hotel in Haiti; his affair with the German wife of a Latin American ambassador; and his involvement with a rascally British con man and an American Presidential candidate and his wife, in Haiti to propagate the cult of vegetarianism—most of them in varying degrees comedians on the stage of life, running a bluff, playing a role, substituting sham for sincerity." Libr J

Greene, Graham

★ The **end** of the affair. Viking 1951 240p

"The novel is set in wartime London. The narrator Maurice Bendrix, a bitter, sardonic novelist, has a five-year affair with a married woman, Sarah Miles. When a V-1 bomb explodes in front of Bendrix's apartment and Sarah finds Bendrix pinned beneath the front door, she believes him dead. She promises a God in whom she does not believe that she will give Bendrix up if he is allowed to live. Just then, Bendrix walks into the room and Sarah begins her religious journey; she breaks off with Bendrix, railing against God even as she begins to take religious instruction. Gradually she comes to a profound religious faith." Merriam-Webster's Ency of Lit

Greene, Graham

★ The **heart** of the matter; introduction by James Wood. Deluxe ed; Penguin Books 2004 255p (Penguin classics) pa $15

ISBN 0-14-243799-9

LC 2004-275122

First published 1948

"Set in West Africa, it is a suspense story ingeniously made to hinge on religious faith. . . . The hero is Scobie, an English Roman Catholic who has vowed to make his devout wife happy though he no longer loves her. He borrows money from a local criminal to send her out of harm's way to South Africa; then he falls in love with a young woman from a group of castaways whose ship has been torpedoed. The return of his wife, the development of an adulterous affair, and blackmail drive Scobie deeper into deception and lies. Forced to betray someone, he betrays his god and himself, and finally commits suicide." Reader's Ency. 4th edition

Greene, Graham

The **honorary** consul. Simon & Schuster 1973 315p

This "novel relates the story of the politically motivated kidnapping of a minor British functionary near Argentina's Paraguayan border. The novel's major characters exemplify the kinds of personal sacrifices one must make in order to live in good conscience in a world where there is too much tyranny and injustice. A minor machismo novelist endures privation; a priest joins the radical underground movement; a physician gives up a lucrative Buenos Aires practice." Libr J

Greene, Graham

★ The **human** factor. Knopf 1992 xxviii, 338p $18

ISBN 0-679-40992-0

LC 91-53189

A reissue of the title first published 1978 by Simon & Schuster

"In the British Foreign Service 'the human factor' becomes a liability for employees and a conduit for suspense, intrigue, and tragedy. Maurice Castle, head of a division in which information seems to have been leaked, presents a very positive image that appears to assure his innocence, but Davis, directly responsible to him, is an object of speculation. For a secret agent, the normal relationships of love and family are fraught with danger. As is true of many of Greene's novels, there are questions in this book about the loyalty owed to a government whose activities are suspect." Shapiro. Fic For Youth. 3d edition

Greene, Graham

The **last** word and other stories. Reinhardt Bks. 1990 149p

LC 90-81665

"This modest volume gathers uncollected stories from the entire range of Greene's career. The earliest dates from 1923 (!) and the latest from 1989." Libr J

Greene, Graham

The **ministry** of fear; an entertainment. Viking 1943 239p

"Probably the author's least remembered work, one showing the Buchan influence most clearly. A group of Fifth Column Englishmen attempt to corner and murder a neurotic fellow countryman who possesses a piece of military intelligence they want to pass on to Berlin." Smith. Cloak and Dagger Fic

Greene, Graham

Monsignor Quixote. Simon & Schuster 1982 221p

LC 82-5937

"Father Quixote is a humble parish priest despised by his bishop. Through an accidental encounter with a stranded bishop, he is named Monsignor, much to his bishop's and his discomfort. He sets off on a journey with the communist ex-mayor of his town. The philosophy and thinking of the ex-mayor, Sancho, are diametrically opposed to that of the priest, and there is much provocative discussion between them as they follow paths similar to those taken by the priest's fictional forebear, Don Quixote. Some of their adventures bring the priest to some surprising places, such as an x-rated cinema and a church where religion is being commercialized and demeaned. There is much humor as well as theology to involve the reader in this delightful odyssey." Shapiro. Fic for Youth. 3d edition

Greene, Graham

Orient Express. Doubleday, Doran 1933 310p

First published 1932 in the United Kingdom with title: Stamboul train

This is the story of what happened to a number of people who board the Orient Express at Ostend to make the three-day journey across the continent to Constantinople

Greene, Graham

Our man in Havana; an entertainment. Viking 1958 247p

"Set in Cuba before the communist revolution, the book is a comical spy story about a British vacuum-cleaner salesman's misadventures in the British Secret Intelligence Service. Although many critics found fault with the book's overly farcical style, it was also admired for its skillful rendering of the Cuban locale." Merriam-Webster's Ency of Lit

Greene, Graham

The **power** and the glory; introduction by John Updike. Viking 1990 295p hardcover o.p. pa $14

ISBN 0-670-83536-6; 0-14-243730-1 pa

LC 90-50052

First published 1940 with title: The labyrinthine ways

Set in Mexico, this novel "describes the desperate last wanderings of a whisky priest as outlaw in his own state, who, despite a sense of his own worthlessness (he drinks, and has fathered a bastard daughter), is determined to continue to function as priest until captured. . . . Like many of Greene's works, it combines a conspicuous Christian theme and symbolism with the elements of a thriller." Oxford Companion to Engl Lit

Greene, Graham

★ The **quiet** American. Modern Lib. 1992 247p

ISBN 0-679-60014-0

LC 92-50219

First published 1955 in the United Kingdom; first United States edition published 1956 by Viking

"Mr. Greene has always been a master of suspense, and the particular excellence of 'The Quiet American' lies in the way in which he builds up the situation finally to explode the moral problem which for him lies at the heart of the matter." Times Lit Suppl

Greene, Graham

The **tenth** man. Simon & Schuster 1985 157p

LC 84-29830

"A fatal series of events follows, entwining narrative excitement with broader questions of identity, fate, and morality. As always with Greene, the basic plot is heightened by the novelist's compelling view of the human condition." Libr J

Greene, Graham

Travels with my aunt; a novel. Viking 1969 244p

"The book unmistakably turns its back on the Orphic preoccupations with the hereafter that characterized Greene's Catholic novels, and wholeheartedly embraces a Bacchic emphasis on the here and now." N Y Times Book Rev

Greenfeld, Karl Taro

Triburbia; a novel. Karl Taro Greenfeld. Harper 2012 253 p. map

ISBN 0062132393; 9780062132390

LC 2012462007

"In this . . . novel, [Karl Taro] Greenfeld . . . brings to life the capacious lofts, self-involved chefs, and occasional rent control holdouts of Manhattan's affluent TriBeCa neighborhood. . . . Each chapter . . . is told from the perspective of a different local character. . . . Their lives intersect and overlap because their children attend the same school, they're sleeping with one another's spouses, or, in Sadie's case, because she's the babysitter or, in Cooper's case, because she's queen of the fourth grade." (Publishers Weekly)

Greenleaf, Stephen

Blood type; the new John Marshall Tanner mystery. Morrow 1992 283p

LC 91-40057

Greenleaf delivers "incisive social observations, compassionate characterizations and fine writing. . . . As befits an heir of Ross Macdonald, the author maintains his moral grip on what matters." N Y Times Book Rev

Greenleaf, Stephen

False conception; a John Marshall Tanner novel. Penzler Bks. 1994 273p

ISBN 1-883402-87-5

LC 94-17371

"Stuart and Millicent Colbert can't conceive a child, but they have the resources to hire a surrogate mother. San Francisco private eye, Marsh Tanner is employed to investigate the surrogate, Greta Hammond. The catch: Hammond must never know the identity of the Colberts nor that she's being investigated. . . . Tanner novels are never just mysteries; Greenleaf always weaves in a larger human dilemma, and here he does it more successfully than ever before." Booklist

Greenleaf, Stephen

Flesh wounds. Scribner 1996 318p

ISBN 0-684-81583-4

LC 95-24412

Private eye John Marshall Tanner "gives himself the masochistic pleasure of going to Seattle to do a job for an old flame. Although Tanner is still in love with this woman, he agrees to search for her fiancé's missing daughter, a stunning figure model who has run afoul of an exploitative photographer described as 'a carnivore.'. . . He discovers the city's richer, darker colors when he traces the photographer's previous victims to the sex clubs and prostitutes' turf where they ended up after appearing in a pernicious new line of pornography using advanced digital technology." N Y Times Book Rev

"The Tanner series continues to be among the most emotionally and intellectually challenging in the genre." Booklist

Greenleaf, Stephen

Past tense; a John Marshall Tanner novel. Scribner 1997 282p

ISBN 0-684-83249-6

LC 96-35476

San Francisco investigator Tanner, "rushes to the aid of his best friend, a veteran homicide cop named Charley Sleet, who shoots a man dead in open court and refuses to offer any explanation or defense. Tanner is one of the best listeners in the business, and he gets an earful when he goes around interviewing people who knew either Charley or his victim, a creep whose daughter was suing him for sexual abuse. The characters met on these rounds are prime specimens, and their talk is choice." N Y Times Book Rev

Greenleaf, Stephen

Strawberry Sunday; a John Marshall Tanner novel. Scribner 1999 287p

ISBN 0-684-84954-2

LC 98-40955

"The Tanner books often have been built around a specific social or political issue, and this one is no exception. Greenleaf takes a long, hard look at the miserable conditions in which many farmworkers live and toil, and builds a complex, absorbing plot around the topic." Publ Wkly

Greenwood, Kerry

★ **Medea**; by Kerry Greenwood. Poisoned Pen Press 2013 250 p. $24.95

ISBN 1464201439; 1863304916; 9781464201431

LC 97169609

In this novel by Kerry Greenwood "Medea, Princess of Colchis, is a priestess of Hecate. She is the custodian of the wood in which the Golden Fleece is hung. She alone can tame the giant serpent which guards the grove. And then Jason and his Argonauts come along, and she falls . . . in love. She helps him steal the Golden Fleece ans sails with him to claim his throne. And that's when things go wrong... and she must attempt to reclaim her humanity through . . . murder, grief and heavy seas." (Publisher's note)

Includes bibliographical references

Greenwood, Kerry

Out of the black land; Kerry Greenwood. Poisoned Pen Press 2013 250 p. (hardcover: alk. paper) $24.95

ISBN 1464200386; 9781464200380; 9781464200403

LC 2012953055

In this novel by Kerry Greenwood "Eighteenth Dynasty Egypt is peaceful and prosperous under the dual rule of the Pharaohs Amenhotep III and IV, until the younger Pharaoh begins to dream new and terrifying dreams. . . . Ptah-hotep . . . wants to live a simple life . . . but Amenhotep IV appoints him as Great Royal Scribe. . . . Not content with his own devotion to one god alone, the newly-renamed Akhnaten plans to suppress the worship of all other gods in the Black Land." (Publisher's note)

Greer, Andrew Sean

The **path** of minor planets. Picador 2001 273p $23

ISBN 0-312-27556-0

LC 2001-41818

"In this début novel, Greer pinpoints the 'tiny hidden madnesses in ordinary people' with unerring accuracy, and, in prose littered with sparks, makes palpable the longing for the celestial." New Yorker

Greer, Andrew Sean

The **story** of a marriage. Farrar, Straus & Giroux 2008 195p $22

ISBN 978-0-374-10866-3; 0-374-10866-8

LC 2007-46835

"Greer's short novel feels admirably worked over like a long-simmered sauce. He near-brilliantly juxtaposes the nuances of love, sexual awakening and the sometimes suffocating sacrifices marriage demands against broader cultural observations about political turmoil, the physical and emotional effects of war, sexual repression and racism. His book is a perfect mix of what we seek from literature — captivating storytelling; a complex, finely tuned structure; stunning language; and astute observations about both the mundane intricacies of everyday relationships and society as a whole." Los Angeles Times Book Rev

Greer, Robert O.

★ **First** of state. North Atlantic Books 2010 380p $24.95

ISBN 978-1-55643-915-5; 1-55643-915-6

LC 2010-20235

"CJ Floyd is 22 years old, but he seems much older somehow and certainly more disillusioned than his peers in early-1970s Denver. He finds an emotional anchor and kindred soul in Wiley Ames, a World War II amputee and antique dealer. When Wiley is murdered and his case unsolved, CJ vows to find the killer; in the meantime, he throws himself into his uncle Ike's bail-bond business, if only to push his painful memories into the shadows. Five years later one of Ames' most treasured antiques surfaces at a Denver flea market. It's the thread Floyd needs to unravel the murder. This prequel to Greer's always thoughtful and multilayered Floyd series reveals the pain behind the protagonist's curmudgeonly, emotionally guarded personality and his reluctance to employ violence. CJ Floyd is one of crime fiction's hidden gems, and this is a satisfying entry in a rewarding, underappreciated series." Booklist

Gregory, Daryl

The **devil's** alphabet. Ballantine Books 2009 388p pa $15

ISBN 0-345-50117-9; 978-0-345-50117-2

LC 2009-36180

"The larger question, of what eventually might become of these evolutionary exiles as they move into second and third generations, seems to move us back into Theodore Sturgeon territory, and it's fortunately a territory that Gregory has mastered well. The novel's quiet ending, in a snowbound South Dakota winter, is haunting." Locus

Gregory, Daryl

Pandemonium. Del Rey 2008 288p pa $13

ISBN 978-0-345-50116-5; 0-345-50116-0

LC 2008-300445

"Gregory has produced a debut novel that combines suspense, philosophical conundrums, Jungian psychological theory, aspects of American pop culture, and a touch of neuroscience with skillful and ambitious storytelling." Strange Horizons

Gregory, Daryl

Raising Stony Mayhall. Ballantine Books 2011 422p pa $15

ISBN 978-0-345-52237-5

LC 2011-10016

"Driving home in a winter snowstorm, Wanda Mayhall and her three daughters come upon the corpses of a young woman and her infant, frozen by the side of the road. When the infant opens its eyes, Wanda realizes the child is one of the living dead. In spite of everything they know about the zombie outbreak and the ruthless measures taken to prevent its spread, the Mayhalls keep the child, naming him Stony. In doing so, they cross a line that has repercussions encompassing a new vision of what it means to be alive. . . . Part superhero fiction, part zombie horror story, and part supernatural thriller, this luminous and compelling tale deserves a wide readership beyond genre fans. Highly recommended." Libr J

Gregory, Philippa, 1954-

The **Boleyn** Inheritance. Touchstone 2006 518p $25.95

ISBN 0-7432-7250-1; 978-0-7432-7250-6

An historical novel focusing on the family of Henry VIII. "Among the cast, who alternately narrate: Henry's fourth wife, Bavarian-born Anne of Cleves; his fifth wife, English teenager Katherine Howard; and Lady Rochford (Jane Boleyn), the jealous spouse whose testimony helped send her husband, Thomas, and sister-in-law Anne Boleyn to their execution. Attended by Lady Rochford, 24-year-old Anne of Cleves endures a disastrous first encounter with the twice-her-age king—an occasion where Henry takes notice of Katherine Howard. . . . Rich in intrigue and irony, this is a tale where readers will already know who was divorced, beheaded or survived, but will savor Gregory's sharp staging of how and why." Publ Wkly

Gregory, Philippa, 1954-

The **constant** princess; Philippa Gregory. Simon & Schuster 2005 393p $24.95

ISBN 074327248X; 9780743272483

LC 2005052303

This work of historical fiction follows "Katherine of Aragon, the 16-year-old daughter of King Ferdinand and Queen Isabella of Spain. Katherine knows from a very young age that she is promised to marry Prince Arthur, heir to the English throne, and she never wavers in her conviction that she will one day become queen. That determination is sorely tested, however, upon Arthur's premature death after two years of marriage. Although she loves her husband (a passion that is kept hidden from the court), Katherine agrees to his dying wish that he be declared impotent so that she can marry his younger brother, Henry, and eventually reign as queen." (Library Journal)

Includes bibliographical references.

Gregory, Philippa

Earthly joys. St. Martin's Press 1998 440p

ISBN 0-312-19262-2

LC 98-8771

This story centers on "John Tradescant, gardener to several great lords and finally to the king himself during the darkest days of post-Elizabethan England. Tradescant is a loyal vassal of the old school. . . . The first great lord in Tradescant's life, Sir Robert Cecil, is a man of honor and intelligence, but none of his successors measure up. Under King James I and then his son, Charles I, the court sinks into corruption, decadence and greed, drawing Tradescant ever closer to its evil doings. His loyalty also leads him into a passionate and doomed affair with the most charming, favored and unscrupulous member of the court, the Duke of Buckingham. . . . This tale of forbidden love set against the turmoil of a country in chaos makes for both intelligent and satisfying reading." N Y Times Book Rev

Followed by Virgin earth

Gregory, Philippa, 1954-

The **kingmaker's** daughter; Philippa Gregory. 1st Touchstone hardcover ed Simon & Schuster 2012 417 p. map, geneal. table (hardcover) $26.99; (paperback) $16.00

ISBN 145162607X; 9781451626070; 9781451626087; 9781451626148

LC 2012011787

This work of historical fiction by Philippa Gregory follows "Anne Neville . . . the daughter of the Earl of Warwick, who put Edward of York on the throne after battling the Lancasters. . . . The earl uses his daughters as pawns in the fluid political situation. Anne eventually marries Richard, the youngest of the three York brothers after an ill-fated first marriage." (Library Journal)

Includes bibliographical references

Gregory, Philippa, 1954-

The **lady** of the rivers; the cousins war. Philippa Gregory. Touchstone 2011 448 p. $27.99

ISBN 1416563709; 9781416563709

LC 2011015093

This historical novel by Philippa Gregory tells "the story of Jacquetta, mother of . . . Elizabeth Woodville. Given first to a husband who desires only the magical powers she might possess, Jacquetta marries second for love, much below her station. Still, she manages to keep her family in the good graces of the ineffectual King Henry VI, placing them ultimately on the losing side of the Wars of the Roses." (Library Journal)

Includes bibliographical references

Gregory, Philippa, 1954-

The **other** Boleyn girl; a novel. Scribner Paperback Fiction 2002 664p

ISBN 0-7432-2744-1

LC 2001057646

This is "as much a tale of love and lust as it is a saga about an ambitious family who used their kin as negotiable assets. . . . Absorbing tale of a Renaissance family determined to climb as high as they can, whatever the cost." Kirkus

Gregory, Philippa

The **queen's** fool; a novel. Simon & Schuster 2004 504p pa $16

ISBN 0-7432-4607-1

LC 2003-67378

"It is winter, 1553. Pursued by the Inquisition, Hannah Green, a fourteen-year-old Jewish girl, is forced to flee Spain with her father. But Hannah is no ordinary refugee. Her gift of 'Sight,' the ability to foresee the future, is priceless in the troubled times of the Tudor court. Hannah is adopted by the glamorous Robert Dudley, the charismatic son of King Edward's protector, who brings her to court as a 'holy fool' for Queen Mary and, ultimately, Queen Elizabeth. Hired as a fool but working as a spy; promised in wedlock but in love with her master; endangered by the laws against heresy, treason, and witchcraft, Hannah must choose between the safe life of a commoner and the dangerous intrigues of the royal family that are inextricably bound up in her own yearnings and desires." Publisher's note

Gregory, Philippa, 1954-

The **red** queen; Philippa Gregory. Simon & Schuster 2010 382 p. map tab (Cousins' war) $25.99

ISBN 1416563725; 9781416563723; 9781416563938 (ebk.)

LC 2010514092

This novel, by Philippa Gregory, is book 2 in "The Cousins' War" series. "The opposite of her alluring Yorkist rival, plain Lancastrian heiress Margaret Beaufort grows up knowing women are useful only for bearing sons. . . . While England seethes with discord during the turbulent Wars of the Roses, Margaret's transformation from powerless innocent to political mastermind progresses . . . as rival heirs to England's throne are killed in battle, executed, or deliberately eliminated." (Booklist)

Includes bibliographical references

Gregory, Philippa

Virgin earth. St. Martin's Press 1999 576p

ISBN 0-312-20617-8

LC 99-48489

This sequel to Earthly joys "begins as John Tradescant the Younger, Charles I's gardener, sails to the New World in search of rarities for his gardens. Not only does he find exotic plants, but he also glimpses unimagined freedom. His father's death leads John to a marriage of convenience in England. Unwilling to fight for Charles I, he returns to Virginia, where he joins the Powhatan and finds a wife. But eventually John loses his place in the tribe because of his inability to kill settlers. Determined to maintain a commitment to his English family, he goes home to a country buffeted by civil war." Libr J

Gregory, Philippa, 1954-

The **white** princess; Philippa Gregory. Touchstone 2013 544 p. (hardcover) $27.99; (paperback) $16.00

ISBN 1451626096; 9781451626094; 9781451626100

LC 2013931637

In this book, part of the "Cousins" War series, marriage unites the upstart House of Tudor with its long-time enemies, the declining House of York, to rule over volatile 1485 England. . . . Narrator Elizabeth of York . . . still loves the vanquished Richard III when she dutifully marries his triumphant challenger, Henry VII. The royal pair produces an heir and two spares but mistrust continues to abound, particularly between the two mothers-in-law." Publishers Weekly)

Gregory, Philippa

The **wise** woman. Pocket Bks. 1993 438p

LC 93-21824

First published 1992 in the United Kingdom

A novel of "passion and witchcraft in 16th-century England. Growing up as an ill-used apprentice to Morach, the much-feared wise woman of the moors, Alys finds respite by joining an order of Catholic nuns. When young Lord Hugo and his men burn the abbey to the ground during a drunken rampage, Alys is the only one to escape; she flees back to Morach. . . . Attracted to Hugo despite his murderous past, Alys begins to practice witchcraft in earnest to rid him of Catherine and become his wife." Publ Wkly

Gremillon, Helene

The **confidant**; [a novel: secrets can be keep forever] Hélène Grémillon; translated by Alison Anderson. Penguin Books 2012 245 p. (pbk.) $15

ISBN 0143121561; 9780143121565

LC 2012028555

In this book by Helene Gremillon, "Camille Werner receives a[n] unsigned, handwritten letter among the condolence notes after her mother's death. . . . Camille becomes fascinated with the correspondent's tale of a budding romance between two teenage friends, Annie and Louis, in a small town on the cusp of WWII. . . . When he reveals that Annie has a daughter born around the time of Camille's own birth, Camille becomes obsessed with locating Louis and getting the whole story behind his letters." (Publishers Weekly)

Grenville, Kate

The **idea** of perfection. Viking 2002 401p $24.95

ISBN 0-670-03080-5

LC 2001-58133

First published 2000 in the United Kingdom

"Grenville does her characters the honor of taking their pain seriously and is gracious enough to allow them their hard-earned pleasure. Her ability to move between these elements gives her novel a beautiful balance." N Y Times Book Rev

Grenville, Kate

The **lieutenant**. Atlantic Monthly Presss 2009 307p $24

ISBN 978-0-8021-1916-2; 0-8021-1916-6

First published 2008 in Australia

"Grenville's novel, based on the true story of William Dawes, who was among the soldiers accompanying the first prisoners sent to Australia, concerns Daniel Rooke, a lonely, introverted sort whose skill as an astronomer earns him a privileged position in the first colonial mission sent to New South Wales, in 1787. Living apart from his regiment for the purpose of studying stars, Rooke befriends a young Aboriginal girl and begins to compile a vocabulary and grammar of her language. But as tensions between the two groups escalate he must choose between what he feels is right and what he considers his duty. Grenville's thematic relentless-

ness can be stultifying, but the honest beauty of her story wins out." New Yorker

Grenville, Kate

Sarah Thornhill; Kate Grenville. Grove Press 2011 307 p. (paperback) $15.00; (hardcover) $25.00

ISBN 9780802121219; 0802120245; 9780802120243; 9781921758621

LC 2011459910

Sequel to: The secret river

Australian Book Industry Awards: General Fiction Book of the Year (2012)

In this final book of the Thornhill trilogy, "Sarah Thornhill, the youngest daughter of a wealthy yet provincial British ex-convict, grows up in 19th-century Australia learning not to ask questions about her family's past." She has a love affair with a half-Aboriginal man, but "her chance at happiness is shattered by the racial and class prejudice churning within her family and Australia's burgeoning white society." (Library Journal)

Grenville, Kate

The **secret** river. Canongate 2006 334p $24

ISBN 1-84195-682-4

LC 20060365651

First published 2005 in Australia

"On his first night in New South Wales, in 1806, William Thornhill—Thames boatman, thief, banished convict—gazes despairingly into the forest outside his flimsy hut. A spear-wielding Aborigine appears before him, and his dejection turns to rage. All he has is his family—'those soft parcels of flesh,' sleeping behind him—and 'the dirt under his bare feet, his small grip on this unknown place,' and he is not about to give them up to a naked black stranger. The Aborigine responds with equal vehemence: 'Be off, be off!' The episode shows, in miniature, the project of Grenville's magnificent novel—an unflinching exploration of modern Australia's origins. Like the settlers, we instinctively turn away from the ugly truths behind every cleared riverbank and every posted fence. But Grenville's psychological acuity, and the sheer gorgeousness of her descriptions of the territory being fought over, pulls us ever deeper into a time when one community's opportunity spelled another's doom." New Yorker

Grey, Zane

★ **Riders** of the purple sage; edited with an introduction and notes by Lee Clark Mitchell. Oxford University Press 2008 xxxviii, 265p (Oxford world's classics) pa $9.95

ISBN 978-0-19-955387-7

LC 2008-482024

First published 1912 by Harper

"Well handled melodramatic story of hairbreadth escapes from Mormon vengeance in southwestern Utah in 1871." Booklist

Includes bibliographical references

Grey, Zane

West of the Pecos. Harper 1937 314p

"Romantic western which tells of Colonel Terrill, broken by the Civil War, and his tomboy daughter, their efforts to get a start in the new world of the west, the Colonel's brutal murder and Pecos Smith's ride to rescue the girl, left alone in a land of desperados." Wis Libr Bull

Grey, Zane
Woman of the frontier; a western story. Five Star 1998 320p $19.95
ISBN 0-7862-1156-3
LC 98-22717

"This tale, written in 1934, was rejected by magazines because of its vivid portrayal of the hardships of pioneer life, including the rape of Grey's heroine by a renegade Apache. A heavily edited version called 30,000 on the Hoof was finally published in 1940, a year after the author's death. This version, completely restored by Grey's son, Loren, recounts the trials and tribulations of Arizona rancher Logan Huett, his heroic wife, Lucinda, their three sons, and a girl named Barbara, who is abandoned by wagon-train travelers and raised by the Huetts." Booklist

Griesemer, John
Signal & noise. Picador 2003 593p $26
ISBN 0-312-30082-4
LC 2003-42938

Griesemer "has created some fine set pieces of disaster: the failed launch of the Great Eastern, two spectacular fires, a train crash that wrecks Ludlow's invention of a great Civil War cannon and, best of all, a breathtaking storm at sea. At the other end of the scale, the detail that fleshes out the novel's world is equally convincing." N Y Times Book Rev

Griffin, Kate
Glass God; Kate Griffin. Orbit 2013 464 p. (trade pbk.) $15
ISBN 0316187275; 9780316187275; 9780316235525
LC 2013932405

This novel by Kate Griffin features "Sharon Li: apprentice shaman and community support officer for the magically inclined. It wasn't the career Sharon had in mind, but she's getting used to running Magicals Anonymous. When the Midnight Mayor goes missing, leaving only a suspiciously innocent-looking umbrella behind him, Sharon finds herself promoted. Her first task: find the Midnight Mayor. The only clues she has are a city dryad's cryptic message of doom and several pairs of abandoned shoes." (Publisher's note)

Griffin, Kate
Stray souls; Kate Griffin. Orbit 2012 464 p. (trade pbk.) $14.99
ISBN 0316187267; 9780316187268; 9780316231749
LC 2012944764

In this book by Kate Griffin, "when . . . Sharon Li discovers that she is a shaman, her first act is to start Magicals Anonymous, a support group that draws a mix of some of London's more unusual inhabitants. . . . She soon learns that someone is stealing the souls of London's buildings and leeching life from the city. Somehow, she and her tribe of misfits must find out the identity of their enemy and save London from spiritual destruction." (Library Journal)

Griffin, W. E. B.
The **aviators**. Putnam 1988 409p (Brotherhood of war)
LC 88-12657

"Protaganist Johnny is a born soldier who distinguishes himself as a helicopter pilot in Vietnam and is promoted to aide-de-camp to the commanding officer of Fort Rucker. In his new post, he finds himself directly involved with the development of the Army's first Air Assault Division—a new force crucial to meet the challenge of guerrilla warfare in Vietnam. This is the story of Johnny's year of work and crisis, the making and breaking of rules, the development of friendships, and the awakening of love." Libr J

Griffin, W. E. B.
Blood and honor. Putnam 1996 553p
ISBN 978-0515121940
LC 96-19039

"There's no deep moral digging here as there is in, say, le Carré. But Griffin is a savvy old hand and here, working with an exotic setting and a complex plot, delivers the sort of sturdy entertainment his fans expect." Publ Wkly
Followed by Secret honor

Griffin, W. E. B.
By order of the President; W.E.B. Griffin. Putnam 2004 528p $26.95
ISBN 0-399-15207-5
LC 2004-53417

"Proving himself solidly in control of cutting-edge military material, Griffin bases his new series not on wars past but on today's murky exigencies of terrorism and international political intrigue. . . . In the end, there are a few bodies to account for, but it's the meticulous investigation that leaves readers standing on the tarmac waiting for Charley Castillo and his newly minted band of can-do compatriots to touch down and carry them away again on a new adventure." Publ Wkly

Griffin, W. E. B.
Close combat. Putnam 1993 383p (Corps)
LC 92-34677

Set in 1942 the sixth book in the series "revolves around a war bond tour featuring Marine heroes of the Guadacanal Campaign. Series fans will recognize the central characters, among them Marine general and presidential troubleshooter Fleming Pickering, his fighter pilot son Pick, and movie mogul Homer Dillon, a Marine for the duration. Griffin has Marine Corps lore and trivia down pat, and he uses the bond-tour story line to convey the public-relations aspects of modern war." Publ Wkly
Followed by Behind the lines (1995)

Griffin, W. E. B.
Honor bound. Putnam 1994 474p
LC 93-36850

"Griffin's feel for the details of life in the military 50 years ago and the humanity of his characters on all sides of the covert war make this a superior war story in an interesting milieu." Libr J
Followed by Blood and honor

Griffin, W. E. B.

In danger's path. Putnam 1998 549p (Corps)
ISBN 0-399-14421-8

LC 98-18809

The hero of this novel is "Brigadier General Fleming Pickering, head of the OSS' Pacific operations during World War II. . . . Pickering is a can-do kind of guy, whose assignments include the rescue of some American ex-servicemen and their families who are fleeing the Japanese in the Gobi Desert, and the setting up of a weather station in the desert to aid in air attacks on the Japanese. As in Griffin's other novels, this one is packed with adventure." Booklist

Griffin, W. E. B.

The last heroes. Putnam 1997 342p
ISBN 0-399-14289-4

LC 96-39458

First published 1985 in paperback

First volume of the author's Men at War trilogy about the OSS during World War II

It is June 1941 and "no operation may be more critical than the one being conducted by hotshot pilot Richard Candy and his half-German wild-card friend Eric Fulmar: to secure the rare ore that will power a top-secret weapon coveted on both sides of the Atlantic—the atomic bomb." Publisher's note

Followed by The secret warriors

Griffin, W. E. B.

Line of fire. Putnam 1992 414p (Corps)

LC 91-29971

Book five in the Marine Corps saga "is centered mainly on the World War II battle for Guadalcanal, from August through September of 1942. But not only Guadalcanal: in keeping with the form of preceding volumes, Line of Fire is vast in geographical scope, with action occurring in such diverse and far-flung locations as Australia; the Japanese-held island of Buka in the Solomon Sea; Parris Island, South Carolina; and Washington, D.C. The cast is appropriately large and liberally stocked with brave heroes, beautiful heroines, and assorted tough guys, and their adventures are rendered in the wry, salty narrative voice ex-soldiers like Griffin so often employ when they turn to writing." Booklist

Griffin, W. E. B.

Secret honor. Putnam 2000 497p
ISBN 0-399-14568-0

LC 99-35740

In this third novel in the Honor Bound series "a German general works toward the assassination of Adolf Hitler. In Buenos Aires, the general's son, codenamed Galahad, falls under suspicion by the SS after a Nazi operation suddenly goes bad. In the middle of it all is OSS agent Cletus Frade, who knows the identity of them both and what they will do next if they can survive that long. For not only are SS and Abwehr officers hot on their trails in both countries, but the OSS has branded Frade a rogue agent and is determined to shake the truth from him, at whatever cost." Publisher's note

Griffin, W. E. B.

The secret warriors. Putnam 1998 321p
ISBN 0-399-14381-5

LC 97-37485

First published 1985 in paperback

In this second volume of the Men at War trilogy the OSS drops agents into the Belgian Congo to locate and smuggle out uranium ore while avoiding German agents

Followed by The soldier spies

Griffin, W. E. B.

The soldier spies. Putnam 1999 352p $25.95
ISBN 0-399-14494-3

LC 98-33260

First published 1986 in paperback

"Secret agents Major Richard Caniday (who's really not a major) and Eric Fulmar, members of the fledgling OSS, aim to smuggle out of Germany the scientist whose knowledge of metallurgy holds the key to the Third Reich's development of jet engines. . . . Cameos by such historical figures as William 'Wild Bill' Donovan, Joseph P. Kennedy Jr., David Niven and Peter Ustinov lend color." Publ Wkly

Griffin, W. E. B.

Special ops. Putnam 2001 665p (Brotherhood of war) $25.95
ISBN 0-399-14646-6

LC 00-62779

"In 1964, Cuba's Fidel Castro tried to export communism to Africa under the leadership of the legendary Che Guevera, and Special Ops details the efforts of the U.S. military and the CIA to stop him. With the world's attention focused on Vietnam and Europe, the deadly fighting in some of the world's most remote and primitive places went unnoticed. . . . This is an exciting, intriguing, and fast-paced novel about an often-ignored period in our recent history." Libr J

Griffin, W. E. B.

Under fire. Putnam 2002 576p
ISBN 0-399-14788-8

LC 2001-48245

In this novel "Captain Ken 'Killer' McCoy, a protégé of ex-OSS officer Fleming Pickering, who knows a senator, who knows President Truman, has reported to General MacArthur that North Korea will be invaded. The report disappears, McCoy gets busted to the ranks . . . and the Communists start pouring across the thirty-eighth parallel. Truman, suspicious of MacArthur, gets wind of the report, and appoints Pickering and McCoy to the CIA. Boats, bullets, and carrier-launched avengers and corsairs make up the balance of this expansively told story." Booklist

Griffith, Michael

Trophy. TriQuarterly Books/Northwestern University Press 2011 277 p.
ISBN 9780810152182

LC 2010050767

In this novel, "Vada Prickett is a 29-year-old Hose Associate at a car wash in South Carolina, and Darla, the woman he loves, is about to marry his friend, rival, and life-long neighbor, Wyatt Yancey. . . . Vada, as this . . . novel opens, is being crushed to death by Wyatt's latest animal trophy, a stuffed grizzly bear Vada has been helping him to smuggle--against Darla's wishes--into Wyatt's house. It turns out that the cliché is true--at the moment of death, your life does flash before your eyes. Trophy, the account of a man's final, fleeting instant on earth, joins Vada as he attempts to make that flash last as long as possible. As he lies dying, too soon and too absurdly, Vada tries to unravel the mysteries of his life." (Publisher's note)

Griffiths, Elly

The **crossing** places; Elly Griffiths. 1st U.S. ed. Houghton Mifflin Harcourt 2010 303 p. map (Ruth Galloway mystery.) (hardcover) $25

ISBN 0547229895; 9780547229898

LC 2009007006

This book "introduces archeologist Ruth Galloway. . . .When Det. Chief Insp. Harry Nelson asks for her expertise in identifying human remains . . . he's disappointed when Ruth determines they date to the Iron Age. Harry, who's been haunted . . . by the kidnapping of five-year-old Lucy Downey, hoped the bones could bring closure to the girl's family. Drawn into the investigation, Ruth . . . studies the letters Harry has received over the years, presumably from the kidnapper." (Publishers Weekly)

Griffiths, Elly

A **Dying** Fall; A Ruth Galloway Mystery. 1st U.S. ed. Houghton Mifflin Harcourt 2013 400 p. (hardcover) $26.00

ISBN 0547798164; 9780547798165

LC 2013001330

In this book, part of the Ruth Galloway mystery series, "Ruth, a forensic archeologist and teacher, learns of the death by fire of a college friend and colleague, Dan Golding, the day before receiving a letter from Dan requesting her professional opinion. Dan has excavated the bones of a 'Raven King,' who may be Arthur Pendragon. Single mother Ruth and various others . . . take summer holiday trips to the vicinity of the site of the murder and dig." (Publishers Weekly)

Griffiths, Elly

★ The **house** at sea's end; Elly Griffiths. Houghton Mifflin Harcourt 2012 353 p. (Ruth Galloway mystery) (hbk.) $25

ISBN 0547506147; 9780547506142

LC 2011029652

This book is part of a series following forensic archaeologist Ruth Galloway. After the discovery of "skeletons of six men with their arms bound . . . Home Guard veteran Archie Whitcliffe reveals the existence of a secret the old soldiers have vowed to protect with their lives. But then Archie is killed and a German journalist arrives, asking questions about Operation Lucifer, a plan to stop a German invasion, and a possible British war crime." (Publisher's note)

Solid characterization, believable forensic science, great atmosphere, and a mystery that stretches back decades all make this another winner from the talented Griffiths." Booklist

Griffiths, Emily

The **Janus** stone; Elly Griffiths. 1st U.S. ed. Houghton Mifflin Harcourt 2011 327p. (paperback) $14.95; (hardcover) $26.00

ISBN 9780547577401; 9780547237442; 0547237448

LC 2010005740

This mystery novel tells the story of a murder investigation conducted with the help of "archaeologist Ruth Galloway. . . . [W]hen construction workers demolishing a large old house in Norwich uncover the bones of a child beneath a doorway--minus its skull--Ruth is . . . called upon to investigate. . . . When carbon dating proves that the child's bones . . . relate to a time when the house was privately owned, Ruth is drawn ever more deeply into the case." (Publisher's note)

Grimes, Linda

In a fix; Linda Grimes. 1st ed. Tor 2012 334 p.

ISBN 0765331802; 9780765331809; 9781429947534

LC 2012019453

This novel by Linda Grimes focuses on "Ciel Halligan, . . . [a] kind of human chameleon . . . able to take on her clients' appearances and slip seamlessly into their lives, solving any sticky problems they don't want to deal with themselves. . . . Snagging a marriage proposal for her client while on an all-expenses-paid vacation should be a simple job . . . until Ciel's island resort bungalow is blown to smithereens and her client's about-to-be-fiance is snatched by modern-day Vikings." (Publisher's note)

Grimes, Martha

★ The **Anodyne** Necklace. Little, Brown 1983 250p

LC 83-880

"Sixteen-year-old Katie O'Brien, playing her violin in an underground London station to make some money, is mysteriously attacked. From that incident begins a mystery involving the theft of an emeral necklace, the murder of a young man whose fingers have been chopped off, and still another murder. The characters in this absorbing tale include not only the residents of Littlebourne, Katie's village, but some East End Londoners like the Cripps family, whose squalid home and bizarre behavior will not soon be forgotten by the reader. Satirical humor enlivens the careful and patient unraveling done by the special detective featured in Grimes' mysteries—the attractive Scotland Yard Superintendent Richard Jury." Shapiro. Fic for Youth. 3d edition

Grimes, Martha

Belle ruin. Viking 2005 346p $25.95

ISBN 0-670-03461-4

LC 2005-42289

A mystery featuring "precocious 12-year-old Emma Graham. . . . Basking in the glow of newfound fame after narrowly escaping a murder attempt, Emma has her hands full reporting for the local newspaper, waitressing in her mom's seedy hotel restaurant and performing in her brother's low-budget production of 'Medea: The Musical.' She also creates havoc for the hotel's guests, hobnobs with the local sheriff and trades barbs with her archenemy, Ree-Jane Davidow. Nonetheless, Emma's never ending quest to discover the identity of a mysterious girl only she can see, as well as her passion for solving the 20-year-old mystery surrounding a baby kidnapped from the once famous Belle Rouen hotel are always her top priorities. Grimes' pungent prose and catchy dialog breathe life into her charming young narrator and the novels' idiosyncratic cast of characters." Publ wkly

Grimes, Martha

 Biting the moon; a mystery. Holt & Co. 1999 301p

 ISBN 0-8050-5621-1

 LC 98-42823

Grimes "sends two brave girls on a hair raising road trip from Santa Fe, N.M., to Salmon, Idaho, in pursuit of a child molester and animal abuser. . . . At 14, smart, shy Mary Dark Hope needs to come out of her shell, which she does on this coming-of-age odyssey with the big-eyed wonder of a true explorer. The young amnesiac who calls herself Andi Olivier and feels an affinity with the coyotes she frees from traps is more complicated. Too wise for her years, she's a sober realist with a romantic imagination that makes reality bearable." N Y Times Book Rev

Grimes, Martha

 The **Black** cat; a Richard Jury mystery. Viking 2010 323p $25.95

 ISBN 978-0-670-02160-4; 0-670-02160-1

 LC 2009-30814

"When an unknown woman dressed to kill (in Yves Saint Laurent, Alexander McQueen and Jimmy Choo) is found shot to death on the patio of a modest village pub, Jury is pressed into researching high-end designer rags and the women who can afford to wear them. The investigation takes Grimes's Scotland Yard detective into the orbit of women who really know their labels. Grimes also provides colorful roles for several of Jury's longstanding intimates and enemies, including Harry Johnson, a charming psychopath who lives with an intelligent mutt named Mungo." N Y Times Book Rev

Grimes, Martha

 The **case** has altered. Holt & Co. 1997 370p

 ISBN 0-8050-5620-3

 LC 97-20791

"Psychologically complex and muted in tone, with the characters' elliptical relationships reflecting the setting of England's dreamlike fen country, the novel also boasts Grimes's delicious wit." Publ Wkly

Grimes, Martha

 Cold Flat Junction. Viking 2001 390p

 ISBN 0-670-89491-5

 LC 00-43992

"Emma Graham, the 12-year-old narrator of this . . . coming-of-age mystery, related an earlier installment of this story in 'Hotel Paradise,' named for the once grand jewel of the decaying resort town where she lives. . . . [Emma's] obsession with Mary-Evelyn Devereau, a 12-year-old girl who drowned in Spirit Lake 40 years ago, has not gone unnoticed by her good friend the sheriff, who also suspects this observant child of poking into more recent deaths in the Devereau family." N Y Times Book Rev

Grimes, Martha

 Dakota; a novel. Viking 2008 414p $25.95

 ISBN 978-0-670-01869-7

 LC 2007-41715

This novel, featuring the young woman who calls herself Andi Oliver [introduced in the author's Biting the moon], "begins with Andi, who's still unaware of her real name or her past, adrift in the Dakota badlands. After rescuing an abandoned donkey, Andi makes a temporary home for herself in the small town of Kingdom, where she soon creates a stir by standing up to some local bullies. She really begins to shake things up in the placid community, however, when she takes a job at a pig farm to try to save the cruelly treated animals bred there. . . . While one late plot development stretches credibility, Grimes succeeds in sustaining suspense while graphically portraying the ugliness of animal abuse." Publ Wkly

Grimes, Martha

 The **Deer** Leap. Little, Brown 1985 236p

 LC 85-15916

This "novel is set in a Hampshire village and centralized in the quaint local pub of the title. Scotland Yard's Jury is summoned to Ashdown Dean after local mystery writer Polly Praed discovers a body in a telephone kiosk. The murder ties in with a series of pet poisonings and a controversy over blood sports. More murder follows before the unflappable Jury can sort things out in this satisfyingly cozy, old-fashioned tale that has the elegant/macabre feel of Edward Gorey's drawings." Booklist

Grimes, Martha

 The **Dirty** Duck. Little, Brown 1984 240p

 LC 83-25629

The author is an "elegant writer who has a strong touch of poetry in her. Her prose flows limpidly, distinguished by its accurate dialogue, sophistication and quiet humor. She also has a sympathetic understanding of human foibles." N Y Times Book Rev

Grimes, Martha

 The **five** bells and bladebone. Little, Brown 1987 299p

 LC 87-3148

"Visiting his friend Melrose Plant in Plant's ancestral village, Jury is at the local antique shop when Simon Lean's body is found in a flaptop desk. The dealer has just bought the piece from Lady Summerston, mistress of the lush estate of Watermeadows where Simon had lived with his wife Hannah, the lady's granddaughter. Questioning the women, Jury sees the strong resemblance between the widow and Sadie Diver, who was murdered in London's notorious Limehouse district. . . . The splendid mystery has a tragic core, but the gloom is offset by the author's quiet humor." Publ Wkly

Grimes, Martha

 Foul matter. Viking 2003 372p $25.95

 ISBN 0-670-03259-X

 LC 2003-50153

"The serpentine plot is fun to follow, once Giverney realizes the extent of the mischief he has set in motion. But it's the nasty inside stuff—from the Dickensian names for authors and their publishing houses to the barbaric rituals of a power lunch—that incites rolling in the aisles." N Y Times Book Rev

Grimes, Martha
 Help the poor struggler. Little, Brown 1985 225p
LC 85-109

"An epidemic of child murders brings Jury and Chief Superintendent Macalvie, a local colleague, to reconsider the 20-year-old murder of a woman which had been witnessed by the victim's five-year-old daughter." Libr J

"This fine novel features a plot that startles, characters that convince, and an atmosphere that sparkles." Booklist

Grimes, Martha
 The **Horse** You Came In On. Knopf 1993 331p
LC 92-55069

"Notable for its themes of authorship and authenticity and for the cast of delightfully eccentric characters—who gather each day at a blue-collar bar called The Horse You Came In On—this mystery, with its feathery plot and fey, lighthearted tone, moves in quite a different direction than earlier Jury tales. Not bad, just different." Publ Wkly

Grimes, Martha
 Hotel Paradise. Knopf 1996 347p
ISBN 0-679-44187-5
LC 95-49356

Twelve-year-old "Emma Graham, who works as a salad girl at the decaying resort hotel where her mother cooks, loves her mother's food almost as much as she loves investigating situations that stimulate her active imagination—like the mysterious death 40 years earlier of young Mary-Evelyn Devereau, who lived with three ugly aunts and drowned, silk-clad and sad, in nearby Spirit Lake. Emma pursues the Mary-Evelyn mystery with single-minded determination, and during the course of her investigation, finds answers to questions she didn't even know she wanted to ask." Booklist

"Emma's take on the colorful characters in her small-town world . . . makes this both a provocative study of lonely people and a delightful read." Publ Wkly

Grimes, Martha
 I am the only running footman. Little, Brown 1986 206p
LC 86-15305

"Scotland Yard's wise, kind Superintendent Richard Jury must determine if the case of Ivy Childess, strangled in London, is related to a similar crime in Devon. Ivy had left her sometime lover, David Marr, after a tiff in the Footman, so he heads the list of suspects. Jury's interrogation ends with Marr offering a strong alibi, backed by his prestigious family. Calling on the man's sister and other kin, the superintendent senses private fears behind a gracious facade. Jury is right, but his suspicions produce no evidence of collusion until a shocking truth sends him racing to save the killer's third intended victim. An artist at plotting, Grimes concludes this urbanely humorous, knife-edge thriller with a double twist." Publ Wkly

Grimes, Martha
 Jerusalem Inn. Little, Brown 1984 299p
LC 84-15495

Superintendent Richard Jury "taking a brief holiday a few days before Christmas, meets Helen Minton, a woman seeking answers about her past. Their acquaintanceship has no time to warm to love; Helen dies, of poisoning, it turns out. As Jury assists the local officials in the investigation, he chances upon a tangle of details that leads him to snowbound Spinney Abbey where occur a shot gun murder plus the apparent gradual poisoning of another woman." Best Sellers

Grimes, Martha
 The **Lamorna** wink; a Richard Jury mystery. Viking 1999 368p
ISBN 0-670-88870-2
LC 99-33525

This mystery "centers on Jury regular Melrose Plant/ Lord Ardry, along with an intriguing, brilliant police friend of Jury's, Brian Macalvie, as they investigate the disappearance of one woman, the murder of another, and the horrific, four-year-old unsolved death of two children who lived in the Cornwall house Plant is renting. Ultimately, the events converge, and Jury appears to wrap things up." Libr J

Grimes, Martha
 The **man** with a load of mischief. Little, Brown 1981 263p il
LC 81-8251

"This book takes its intriguing title from the scene of one of several crimes perpetrated by a murderer with a macabre sense of humor and a penchant for depositing corpses in the vicinity or on the premises of English pubs. When a man is found strangled and deposited in a beer vat, likable but cunning Inspector Richard Jury spends his Christmas holidays in the 'picture postcard village' of Long Piddleton, determined to solve the growing number of crimes. Deft characterization and portrayal of English pub life add to the appeal of a cleverly contrived tale." Libr J

Grimes, Martha
 The **Old** Contemptibles. Little, Brown 1991 333p
LC 90-48647

Inspector "Jury is considering marriage to recently met widow Jane Holdsworth at the moment her teenaged son Alex finds her dead, apparently a suicide. Alex runs away, and Jury, required, as a suspect, to remain in London, sends old friend Melrose Plant up to the Lakes to learn what he can about the wealthy Holdsworth family, among whom Jane's death is the fourth suspicious one." Publ Wkly

Grimes, Martha
 The **old** fox deceiv'd. Little, Brown 1982 299p
LC 82-7719

"The central mystery that confronts Inspector Richard Jury of Scotland Yard is not whounit, but to whom was it 'dun.' Was the young woman found mutilated with an ice-pick-like instrument Dillys March, the ward of Colonel Titus Crael who left home 15 years previously and recently returned to reclaim her inheritance? Or was the victim Gemma Temple, Dillys' look-alike, who tried to pass herself off as

Dillys to gain the inheritance? The tiny English fishing village of Rackmoor is divided and tormented by this mystery, which threatens to rock its social structure." Booklist

Grimes, Martha

★ The **Old** Silent. Little, Brown 1989 425p

LC 89-31650

"The calm moments in this moody mystery about parental ties and family schisms and relationships thicker than blood are as fine as anything Ms. Grimes has written." N Y Times Book Rev

Grimes, Martha

The **Old** Wine Shades; a Richard Jury mystery. Viking 2006 352p $25.95

ISBN 0-670-03479-7

LC 2005-58460

In this Richard Jury "mystery, the Scotland Yard detective is on suspension because he decided to save lives rather than wait for a warrant in his previous outing . . . . With time on his hands, Jury is ensnared by the intriguing tale spun by Harry Johnson, a man who, apparently, just happens upon him in a London pub, the Old Wine Shades. Despite himself, Jury is drawn in by Johnson's account of the baffling disappearance of a mother, her autistic son and their dog–and the more baffling reappearance of the pet nine months later. The detective diligently follows every lead to determine the fate of the missing people, even as Johnson's digressions into the paradoxes of quantum physics lead Jury to question the truth of the man's narrative. The scheme Jury ultimately detects is ingeniously clever and sufficiently consistent with the personalities Grimes has created to overcome disbelief." Publ Wkly

Grimes, Martha

Rainbow's end; a Richard Jury novel. Knopf 1995 383p

ISBN 0-679-44188-3

LC 94-48876

In this Richard Jury mystery, three women "die suddenly in public places: an aged textile restorer in Exeter Cathedral, a society matron in the Tate Gallery and an American tourist in the ruins of Old Sarum, near Salisbury. The deaths appear to be natural and unrelated, but the clever Brits come up with a connection: both Englishwomen had recently visited Santa Fe, N.M., where the American had a silver shop. Once in the Southwest, Jury follows his wispy lead to eye-catching locations like a movie set in Santa Fe. . . . Meanwhile, back home, Jury's sidekick, Melrose Plant, pays nostalgic visits to people and places from previous novels, while mourning the passing of the grand old pubs." N Y Times Book Rev

Grimes, Martha

The **Stargazey**; a Richard Jury mystery. Holt & Co. 1998 354p

ISBN 0-8050-5622-X

LC 98-21214

"Jury is on the Fulham Road bus when he spots a beautiful blonde in a fur coat and feels compelled to follow her to the Fulham Palace grounds. Later she is found murdered on the palace grounds. But is it really she? Jury doubts it and follows a winding path to the truth." Libr J

Grimes, Martha

The **train** now departing: two novellas. Viking 2000 185p

ISBN 0-670-89154-1

LC 99-53705

This volume "consists of a pair of atmospheric novellas. While both stories center on middle-aged, single women whose careful, well-ordered lives are gradually altered by meals they share with male acquaintances, these two novellas are quite distinct in their ambience and characterization. In 'The Train Now Departing,' Grimes eerily depicts a bright, analytical woman teetering into madness. 'When the Mousetrap Closes' is the story of Edith Parenger, a woman whose desperate loneliness is pitted against her keen powers of observation in an unflinching exploration of the power of illusion." Libr J

Grimes, Martha

The **winds** of change; a Richard Jury mystery. Viking 2004 407p $25.95

ISBN 0-670-03327-8

LC 2004-52636

This Richard Jury mystery involves "the murder of an anonymous five-year-old girl, shot in the back. . . . When he learns that the child was found near a house frequented by pedophiles, he's convinced there's a link. His suspicions grow stronger when the man supposedly behind the operation turns out to be the father of a child who mysteriously disappeared three years before from a country estate." Booklist

Grimsley, Jim

The **ordinary**. Tor Bks. 2004 368p map $24.95

ISBN 0-7653-0528-3

LC 2003-71148

"Set in the same future world as Kirith Kirin (2000) . . . , Grimsley's latest SF novel intimately explores the conflicts between magic and science, subconscious and conscious action, the past and the future. The planet of the tech-using Hormling of Senal is connected to the land of Irion, home of the magic-believing Erejhen, via the mysterious Twil Gate, a portal of unknown origins in the ocean. Although traders on both sides enjoy brisk commerce through the gate, Hormling leaders look more and more to Irion as a means to provide land and resources for their expanding civilization. Translator Jedda Martele, member of a Senal diplomatic mission to Irion, is caught in the middle when the delegation's true purpose is revealed. . . . Grimsley's finely textured societies have a clockwork intricacy that fascinates even as it dispels surprise." Publ Wkly

Grindle, Lucretia

Villa triste; Lucretia Grindle. Grand Central Pub. 2013 640 p. (trade pbk.) $14.99

ISBN 1455505374; 9781455505371

LC 2012951450

In this book, "[Lucretia] Grindle . . . combines a contemporary mystery with historical fiction in her . . . narrative about Italian partisans in World War II and a modern-day police inspector determined to uncover certain truths." The story follows an Italian young woman, Caterina, during the Nazi occupation of Italy. Caterina keeps a journal of her work as a Resistance nurse, which is later found by police

LIST OF FICTIONAL WORKS

Inspector Alessandro Pallioti, eager to solve some related murders. (Kirkus)

Grippando, James
The **abduction**; a novel. HarperCollins Pubs. 1998 386p
ISBN 0-06-018262-8
LC 97-28153

"It's the year 2000, and U.S. Attorney General Allison Leahy is the country's first female presidential candidate. When opponent Lincoln Howe's granddaughter, Kristen, is kidnapped, Leahy—whose own daughter was abducted eight years earlier—is torn between her political advisors, who tell her to stay far away from the investigation, and her memories of her own tragedy. . . . This is a gripping (and frightening) story about the Machiavellian world of American politics." Booklist

Grippando, James
Born to run; a novel of suspense. HarperCollins 2008 328p $25.99
ISBN 978-0-06-155611-1; 0-06-155611-4
LC 2008-23282

Miami attorney Jack Swyteck comes to the aid of his former governor father as he investigates the suspicious hunting death of the vice president.

"Grippando ratchets up the action to a breakneck pace in the last half of the novel, stopping to liberally sprinkle the proceedings with snarky dialogue, pointed satire, and some touching father-son moments." Booklist

Grippando, James
Found money. HarperCollins Pubs. 1999 336p
ISBN 0-06-018263-6
LC 98-24310

"Just before Frank Duffy dies, he tells his physician son, Ryan, that there is $2 million hidden in the attic, and that Frank got the money through blackmail—albeit off someone who 'deserved it.' The level-headed Ryan considers both claims unbelievable—until he finds the money. . . . Meanwhile, Amy Parkins, while struggling to support her daughter and her grandmother and to put herself through law school, receives $200,000 from an anonymous benefactor, apparently Frank Duffy, whom she'd never met. . . . As Ryan and Amy search for the money's source and meaning, they uncover a conspiracy involving high-ranking government officials, multi-billion-dollar corporations and a hidden crime committed on a hot summer night years ago. The final revelation is a real kicker." Publ Wkly

Grippando, James
Hear no evil. HarperCollins Publishers 2004 310p $23.95
ISBN 0-06-056457-1
LC 2003-57138

This "Jack Swyteck mystery finds the Miami defense lawyer in unfamiliar territory. When a woman asks him to defend her against the charge of murdering her husband, Jack is initially reluctant: the victim is a U.S. naval officer; the crime took place at the naval base at Guantanamo Bay; and Jack has almost no experience with military courtroom procedures. But the woman has a very persuasive reason for

Jack to take the case . . . , and soon Jack finds himself fighting for his client's life in an arena that is brand new to him." Booklist

"This character-driven, intricately plotted thriller will keep readers guessing up to the end." Publ Wkly

Grippando, James
The **informant**. HarperCollins Pubs. 1996 360p
ISBN 978-0062024497
LC 96-16310

"Although his prose is stilted, Mr. Grippando, . . . has a nice flair for the grotesque. More to his credit, he has done his homework on F.B.I. forensics, criminal profiling and the internal protocol for backstabbing." N Y Times Book Rev

Grippando, James
A **king's** ransom. HarperCollins Pubs. 2001 426p
ISBN 0-06-019241-0
LC 2001-16786

Grippando's "research into the kidnapping industry currently thriving in Latin America adds a harrowing dose of realism to a taut, well-constructed page-turner." Publ Wkly

Grippando, James
Lying with strangers. HarperCollins 2007 389p $24.95
ISBN 978-0-06-113838-6; 0-06-113838-X
LC 2006-50956

First published in slightly different form 2006 by Madison Park Press for Doubleday Entertainment's book clubs

"Grippando excels at the ordinary-person-in-extraordinary-circumstances story, and this one uses the premise expertly, building enough suspense to keep readers looking in dark corners and over their shoulders." Booklist

Grippando, James
Money to burn; a novel of suspense. Harper 2010 360p $25.99
ISBN 978-0-06-155630-2; 0-06-155630-0
LC 2009-24828

"Michael Cantella is one of the rock stars of his Wall Street investment firm. Despite his fancy job and his fancy second wife, Michael has never gotten over his first wife, Ivy, who died on their honeymoon four years before. Michael gets another shock when, on the eve of his 35th birthday, his accounts are cleaned out, which also affects the firm for which he works. The wipeout is made to look as if Michael was behind it. The FBI accuses him of money laundering and insider trading, his second marriage is over and Michael is the target of a cruel, seemingly invisible hit man. Grippando keeps the energy level high in "Money To Burn" while also showing the behind-the-scenes machinations of money schemes. A surprise twist is not only believable but also seamlessly woven into the plot." South Florida Sun-Sentinel

Grisham, John, 1955-
The **appeal**. Doubleday 2008 358p $27.95
ISBN 978-0-385-51504-7; 0-385-51504-9
LC 2007-44905

369

"It barely matters that the characters in The Appeal are essentially stick figures. What works for Mr. Grisham is his patient, lawyerly, inexorable way of dramatizing urgent moral issues." N Y Times (Late N Y Ed)

Grisham, John

The **brethren**. Doubleday 2000 366p $30

ISBN 0-385-49746-6

LC 00-23841

This suspense novel revolves around two subplots. In the first three ex-judges, serving time in a federal prison in Florida, concoct a blackmail scheme that targets closeted gay men. The second storyline relates the CIA-backed presidential bid of a corrupt congressman

"Every personage in this novel lies, cheats, steals and/or kills, and while Grisham's fans may miss the stalwart lawyer-heroes and David vs. Goliath slant of his earlier work, all will be captivated by this clever thriller that presents as crisp a cast as he's yet devised, and as grippingly sardonic yet bitingly moral a scenario as he's ever imagined." Publ Wkly

Grisham, John

The **broker**. Doubleday 2005 357p $27.95

ISBN 0-385-51045-4

"If you will be satisfied with a workmanlike spy-cum-politics novel, with some first-rate cloak and dagger intrigue, an uplifting vignette of father-son redemption and a poignant pastiche of unrequited love, then 'The Broker' is the book for you." N Y Times Book Rev

Grisham, John

The **chamber**. Doubleday 1994 486p

ISBN 0-385-42472-8

LC 94-11764

"The chamber in question is the gas chamber at the Mississippi State Penitentiary—and for 69-year-old Sam Crayhall, the road thence has been many years long. Sam was twice tried and twice acquitted for murder after a 1967 Ku Klux Klan scare bombing accidentally killed the twin sons of the intended target; 14 years later he was tried a third time, convicted and sentenced to death row. Now, in 1990, a young Chicago lawyer, employed by the firm that represented Sam but which he has just unceremoniously dumped, wants Sam as a client. Adam Hall, the 26-year-old rookie, is Sam Crayhall's grandson. . . . Though the countdown to an execution is a well-worn plot device, it has seldom been as effective, especially in the novel's last 100 pages." Publ Wkly

Grisham, John

The **client**. Doubleday 1993 422p $29.95; pa $7.99

ISBN 0-385-42471-X; 0-440-21352-5 pa

LC 92-39079

"While sneaking into the woods to smoke forbidden cigarettes, preteen brothers Mark and Ricky find a lawyer committing suicide in his car. Mark tries to save the man but is instead grabbed by him and told the location of the body of a murdered U.S. senator—a murder for which the lawyer's Mafia-connected client is accused. Witnessing the successful suicide sends Ricky into shock and Mark into a web of lies, half-truths, and finally into refusal to tell the confided secret to the police. Mark accidentally but fortuitously hires

a lawyer, Reggie Love, who steers him through a maze of FBI agents, legal proceedings, judges, ambitious lawyers, and hit men. . . . This thriller is unique in its theme and in its suspense mixed with humor. A sure 'all-night' read." SLJ

Grisham, John, 1955-

The **confession**. Doubleday 2010 418p $28.95

ISBN 978-0-385-52804-7; 0-385-52804-3; 0385528043; 9780385528047

LC 20100513753

"Death penalty proponents might not rush to buy this book. It's a no-apologies, flagrantly one-sided story that would only annoy the heck out of them. But Grisham is the master of the legal thriller. Readers who share his views as well as those sitting on the fence will find much to love and lament in the tragic story of Donté Drumm." USA Today

Grisham, John

★ The **firm**. Doubleday 1991 421p hardcover o.p. pa $9.99

ISBN 0-385-41634-2; 0-440-24592-6 pa

LC 90-3945

"The aphorism 'between a rock and a hard place' aptly describes the dilemma of a young attorney pressed by the FBI to reveal crime-related secrets of his firm, while also hounded by his employers to simply take his huge salary and zip his lip. No aphorism, though, can convey the suspense, wit, and polished writing of this laser-sharp candidate for the best recent updating of the David and Goliath story." Libr J

Grisham, John

Ford County; stories. Doubleday 2009 308p $24

ISBN 978-0-385-53245-7; 0-385-53245-8

LC 2009-32845

"In Ford County, John Grisham's first collection of stories, we meet a weird and endearing group of misfits with one thing in common: each has lived in Clanton, the seat of fictional Ford County, Mississippi. . . . Grisham's prose is smooth and controlled as he deftly moves between narrators and storylines, and his skilled storytelling makes even the wackier scenes believable. One of Ford County's greatest assets is its abundant but understated humor." BookPage

Grisham, John

The **last** juror. Doubleday 2004 355p $27.95

ISBN 0-385-51043-8

"The novel will satisfy those with an appetite for legal thrillers and those who believe Grisham possesses more talent than those breathless page-turners sometimes reveal. It ranks among his best-written and most atmospheric novels." USA Today

Grisham, John

The **litigators**. Doubleday 2011 385p $28.95

ISBN 978-0-385-53513-7; 0-385-53513-9

LC 2011-56964

This is "standard Grisham fare. It telegraphs much of the plot but remains an enjoyable and entertaining novel that points out the foibles of the justice system from top to bottom." Bookreporter

Grisham, John

A **painted** house; a novel. Doubleday 2001 388p il $27.95

ISBN 0-385-50120-X

LC 2001-266464

"Grisham is about as good a storyteller as we've got in the United States these days. . . . The plots and subplots twine. The pages turn. The characters take on their own lives." N Y Times Book Rev

Grisham, John

The **partner**. Doubleday 1997 366p $30

ISBN 0-385-47295-1

LC 96-54702

"Money is essentially the principal character in {this novel}. It is a very large sum of it—$90 million, to be exact—that has motivated Gulf Coast lawyer Patrick Lanigan to concoct a scheme to disappear. . . . It is money that drove a crooked defense contractor to try to pry loose a huge sum from Washington, and got Patrick's greedy law firm involved in the first place. And it is varying sums of money that enable Patrick to bribe his way out of a collection of indictments against him a yard long—including one for first-degree murder—when he is eventually found in his Brazilian hide-away and brought back to the U.S. to face the music. . . . To call the plot of The Partner mechanical is at least partly a compliment: it is well-oiled, intricate and works smoothly." Publ Wkly

Grisham, John

★ The **pelican** brief. Doubleday 1992 371p $30

ISBN 0-385-42198-2

LC 91-33235

"Mr. Grisham has written a genuine page-turner. He has an ear for dialogue and is a skillful craftsman. Like a composer, he brings all his themes together at the crucial moment for a gripping, and logical, finale." NY Times Book Rev

Grisham, John

Playing for pizza. Doubleday 2007 262p $21.95

ISBN 978-0-385-52500-8; 0-385-52500-1

LC 2007-27656

"Third-string Cleveland Browns quarterback Rick Dockery becomes the greatest goat ever by throwing three interceptions in the closing minutes of the AFC championship game. Fleeing vengeful fans, he finds refuge in the grungiest corner of professional football, the Italian National Football League as quarterback of the inept but full-of-heart Parma Panthers. What ensues is a winsome football fable, replete with team bonding and character-building as the underdog Panthers challenge the powerhouse Bergamo Lions for a shot at the Italian Superbowl. The book is also the author's love letter to Italy." Publ Wkly

Grisham, John

The **rainmaker**. Doubleday 1995 434p $29.95

ISBN 0-385-42473-6

LC 95-2291

"When the modestly sized law firm that contracted for his future services unexpectedly merges with a tony Ivy League firm, . . . {attorney Rudy Baylor} finds himself without a job and bankrupt. . . . To make a living, Rudy finds himself chasing ambulances for a racketeering shyster, leading to his becoming enthralled with a beautiful young woman hospitalized by her husband's murderous attack. When Rudy agrees to represent the parents of a dying 22-year-old denied insurance coverage for bone-marrow transplant, he finds that he is up against the firm that broke contract with him." Publ Wkly

Grisham, John

The **runaway** jury. Doubleday 1996 401p $30

ISBN 0-385-47294-3

LC 96-13872

"In a Mississippi Gulf Coast town, the widow of a lifelong smoker who died prematurely of lung cancer is suing Big Tobacco. Enter Rankin Fitch, a dark genius of jury fixing, who has won many such trials for the tobacco companies and who foresees no special problems here. Enter also a mysterious juror, Nicholas Easter, whom Fitch's army of jury investigators and manipulators can't quite seem to track—and his equally mysterious girlfriend Marlee. . . . The details of jury selection are fascinating." Publ Wkly

Grisham, John

The **street** lawyer. Doubleday 1998 348p $27.95

ISBN 0-385-49099-2

LC 97-47484

"Michael Brock, a slick antitrust lawyer in a blue-chip Washington legal factory, experiences a profound shock when he and other lawyers are held hostage by a deranged man with a legitimate beef—and a gun. Reordering his values, Michael leaves his high-pressure job and sterile marriage to become an advocate for the homeless. In his zeal for his new mission . . . he also steals a file and tries to sue his old firm on behalf of the people they illegally evicted from a valuable piece of real estate." NY Times Book Rev

Grisham, John

The **summons**. Doubleday 2002 341p $27.95

ISBN 0-385-50382-2

LC 2001-58185

Ray Atlee, a 43-year-old law professor in Virginia is summoned to his family's home in Mississippi by his dying father, a respected judge. Following his father's death Ray discovers over $3 million in cash in the study

This Summons "is a swift, no-nonsense story written in a highly effective, uncluttered fashion. . . . Mr. Grisham seems genuinely interested in the questions of conscience that snare Ray, and he makes them matter." N Y Times Book Rev

Grisham, John

The **testament**. Doubleday 1998 435p $30

ISBN 0-385-49380-0

LC 99-186246

"Nate's search for redemption, which might have become hokey, is quite convincing. The big question—what will Rachel do upon learning she has inherited $11 billion—is nicely resolved." N Y Times Book Rev

Grisham, John

A **time** to kill. Doubleday 1993 487p $30
ISBN 0-385-47081-9

LC 93-32545

A reissue of the title first published 1989 by Wynwood Press

In this novel, set in rural Mississippi, local criminal lawyer Jake Brigance defends a black man on trial for murdering the men who raped his daughter

Grodstein, Lauren

★ A **friend** of the family; a novel. Algonquin Books of Chapel Hill 2009 302p $23.95
ISBN 978-1-56512-916-0; 1-56512-916-4

LC 2009-24476

"The novel is spot-on in its depiction of affection and jealousy among longtime friends; boozy suburban bashes; unrequited love; and adjusting to middle age.... [It] beautifully captures the ever-striving angst of parents who will take any step to ensure their children's lives are easier or better." USA Today

Groff, Lauren

★ **Arcadia**; Lauren Groff. Hyperion 2012 291 p.
ISBN 9781401340872

LC 2011009956

This book offers an "examination of life on a commune [that] follows Bit, . . . born in the late '60s in a spot that will become Arcadia, a utopian community his parents help to form. Despite their idealistic goals, the family's attempts at sustainability bring hunger, cold, illness, and injury. . . . The . . . child whose purposeful lack of speech is sometimes mistaken for slowness finds comfort in Grimms' fairy tales and is lost in the outside world once Arcadia's increasingly entitled spiritual leader falls from grace and the community crumbles. . . . [T]he books second half tracks the ways in which Bit, now an adult, . . . has been shaped by Arcadia; a career in photography was the perfect choice for a man who 'watches life from a good distance.'" (Publishers Weekly)

Groff, Lauren

Delicate edible birds and other stories. Hyperion 2009 306p $23.95
ISBN 978-1-4013-4086-5

LC 2008-44002

An "innovative and beautifully written collection that covers a wide swath of humanity, from east coast resort towns, to the early 20th century flu epidemic, to WWII Europe. . . . Even in the less successful stories, Groff's prose is lovely, and when she nails a story—like the title story about journalists fleeing Nazi-occupied Paris—the results are sublime." Publ Wkly

Groff, Lauren

The **monsters** of Templeton; a novel. Voice/Hyperion 2008 364p il map $24.95
ISBN 978-1-4013-2225-0; 1-4013-2225-5

LC 2007-41360

"Forget the ghouls and cheap scares. What Groff is really digging at here is the enigma of the human spirit and how redemption and resilience shape our lives. The Monsters of Templeton is part mystery and part history, generating much of its appeal through the delightfully cranky, persistent Willie and a host of voices—maybe a few too many—from her tangled family tree." PopMatters

Grondahl, Jens Christian

Lucca; translated from the Danish by Anne Born. Harcourt 2003 332p $26
ISBN 0-15-100594-X

LC 2002-154301

Original Danish edition, 1998

"The title character is an actress who has renounced her career (for love) and then blinded herself in a drunken car crash after being dumped by her husband. Her doctor has become an emotional recluse since, or possibly before, being dumped by his wife. Over the course of many pages we get their back stories." N Y Times Book Rev

The author "proves himself to be master of the poetry of small moments that can lead to shattering discoveries." Libr J

Groot, Tracy

Flame of resistance; Tracy Groot. Tyndale House Publishers, Inc. 2012 403 p. (sc) $13.99
ISBN 1414359470; 9781414359472

LC 2011052924

In this book, "years of Nazi occupation have stolen hope from French prostitute Brigitte Durand. But when downed American pilot Tom Jaeger is picked up by the Resistance, she finds herself in the middle of a plot to infiltrate a Germans-only brothel and smuggle out critical intelligence to Tom." (Christianbook.com)

"This is a superior, page-turning entry." Pub Wkly

Gross, Andrew

Eyes wide open. William Morrow 2011 338p $25.99
ISBN 978-0-06-165596-8; 0-06-165596-1

LC 2010-48025

"Estranged from his brother, Jay Erlich is surprised when he gets a call from Charlie. Unfortunately, the news isn't pleasant. Charlie's son is dead. Jay decides to visit his brother to offer comfort and help. As he learns more about his nephew's death, Jay begins to suspect that it's not as straightforward as it may appear. The police don't seem interested in investigating. Since his nephew was mentally ill, the authorities assume he wasn't taking his medication. Jay cannot stop until he knows the truth, but that will open up secrets hidden for almost two decades. The issues of what family truly means, the struggles of mental illness that affect both the victims and those surrounding them, and the bad decisions of the past that come back with a vengeance are all displayed like an open wound. . . . Gross has written his best book to date." Denver Post

Gross, Andrew

Reckless. William Morrow 2010 404p $25.99
ISBN 978-0-06-165595-1; 0-06-165595-3

LC 2009-44799

"A pulsating thriller that turns on international conspiracies and financial sleight of hand. While thrillers wrapped around the economic crisis and stock-market meltdowns are becoming more common, Gross makes 'Reckless' a fresh and original take on the genre." South Florida Sun-Sentinel

Gross, Claudia

   Scholarium; Claudia Gross. Toby Press 2004 400p $19.95

   ISBN 1-592-64056-7

   "The scene is set with a pervasive cloud of impending evil hovering over the Cologne Scholarium. Master Casall's murderer sends perplexing riddles to the frustrated and suspicious faculty. Casall's widow and select students disappear, the prior stirs potions in a shack, and Master Lombardi hides a guilty secret. In the midst of the debate surrounding the murder, brilliantly timed accusations of witchcraft and sorcery emerge, and rumors fly about pagan sex rites on crumbling altars. . . . Gross weaves a fascinating tapestry depicting the birth of the schism between church and state and showing how the search for truth becomes a life-and-death quest for a group of determined scholars." Booklist

Gross, Gwendolen

   When she was gone; Gwendolen Gross. 1st Gallery Books trade pbk ed Gallery Books 2013 304 p. (paperback) $16

   ISBN 1451684746; 9781451684742; 9781451684766

   LC 2012022605

   This novel, by Gwendolen Gross, asks "what happened to Linsey Hart? When the Cornell-bound teenager disappears into the steamy blue of a late-summer morning, her quiet neighborhood is left to pick apart the threads of their own lives and assumptions. Linsey's neighbors are just ordinary people--but even ordinary people can keep terrible secrets hidden close. . . . As the days of Linsey's absence tick by, dread and hope threaten to tear a community apart." (Publisher's note)

Grossman, Austin

   Soon I will be invincible. Pantheon Books 2007 287p $22.95

   ISBN 978-0-375-42486-1; 0-375-42486-5

   LC 2006-33296

   "A heartbreaking genius of staggering evil, Doctor Impossible avenges lost love, a lonely adolescence, and a plethora of foiled doomsday devices. . . . Every comic-book cliché in this witty, stunning debut is lovingly embraced, then turned inside out." Wired

Grossman, David

   Be my knife; translated by Vered Almog and Maya Gurantz. Farrar, Straus & Giroux 2002 307p

   ISBN 0-374-29977-3

   LC 2001-33645

   Original Hebrew edition, 1998

   "When a thirty-three-year-old man named Yair catches a glimpse of Miriam at a class reunion, he senses a bond with her that goes beyond sexual attraction; because he is a practiced philanderer who is in search of something extraordinary, he implores her to enter a ruthlessly honest correspondence with him, on the understanding that they will never meet. . . . Most of the book is devoted to Yair's letters, and so we don't get to hear Miriam's responses until near the end. But it is Grossman's achievement that we understand

from the start that Yair's vision of Miriam (and thus ours) is almost painfully incomplete." New Yorker

Grossman, David

   ★ **Someone** to run with; translated by Vered Almog and Maya Gurantz. Farrar, Straus and Giroux 2004 343p $24

   ISBN 0-374-26657-3

   LC 2002-29778

   Original Hebrew edition, 2000

   In Jerusalem, teenage Assaf "a shy misfit, embarks upon a quixotic journey with a lost dog to find its mistress. Tamar, a caustic fifteen-year-old who can sing Mozart and Leonard Cohen on demand, runs away from home to find the criminals who have ensnared her older brother. A young street musician, in the grip of a heroin habit as formidable as his talent, stumbles through his routines with death close behind. The resulting picaresque is a cross between 'Run Lola Run' and 'Oliver Twist,' and as the reader waits for these solitary odysseys to intersect, the urgency becomes almost unbearable. Grossman evokes teenage nobility and self-hatred in all its pimply particularity, while slyly suggesting that the arduous quest for connections should never be outgrown." New Yorker

Grossman, David

   ★ **To** the end of the land; translated from the Hebrew by Jessica Cohen. Alfred A. Knopf 2010 575p $26.95

   ISBN 978-0-307-59297-2; 0-307-59297-9

   LC 2010-03915

   Original Hebrew edition, 2008

   Grossman "weaves the essences of private life into the tapestry of history with deliberate and delicate skill; he has created a panorama of breathtaking emotional force, a masterpiece of pacing, of dedicated storytelling, with characters whose lives are etched with extraordinary, vivid detail. While his novel has the vast sweep of pure tragedy, it is also at times playful, and utterly engrossing." N Y Times Book Rev

Grossman, Lev

   The **magician** king; Lev Grossman. Viking 2011 400p. $26.95

   ISBN 978-0-670-02231-1; 0-670-02231-4

   LC 2011019733

   Sequel to: The magicians (2009)

   "After Quentin and his old friend Julia leave Fillory on a magical sailing ship, they end up back in Quentin's home in Chesterton, Massachusetts, and only Julia's dark magic can get them back to the realm they have grown to love." (Publisher's note)

   "Quentin Coldwater, the wizard who traveled to a mythical land to be its king in the first book, has gotten past most of his misery and settled into bored complacency, wondering whether hanging out in a castle and getting drunk is really all there is to rulership. Isn't he meant for great things? Shouldn't he be carrying out some giant quest? In the book's opening chapter, the quest he's already on unravels disappointingly, so he decides to embark to the farthest edge of the land he rules, a speck of an island in the middle of the sea, and he winds up on an even stranger journey. The Magicians was terrific, but loose, with a plot that moved from incident to incident with only the barest connecting material. The Magician King, which is better in almost every way, feels as if it might be even looser in the early going, with plenty of opportunities to worry whether Grossman can pull his narrative together. But once he reaches his devastating climax, neatly knitting together story threads readers won't have even realized were major plot points, the novel reaches a level of poignancy the first could only hope to attain." A V Club

Grossman, Lev

The **magicians**; a novel. Viking 2009 402p $26.95; pa $16

ISBN 978-0-670-02055-3; 0-670-02055-9; 978-0-452-29629-9 pa; 0-452-29629-3 pa

LC 2008-55900

"Quentin Coldwater is a geeky high-school senior in Brooklyn who is convinced that happiness and 'the life he should be living' are elsewhere—for example, in the series of nineteen-thirties British adventure novels that he was obsessed with as a child. When Quentin stumbles on a portal that takes him to a college for magicians in upstate New York, he learns that the world depicted in these novels, known as Fillory, is real, and he is forced to square his youthful ideas with the realities that exist there, too—boredom, regret, shame, and despair. Quentin's journey becomes an unexpectedly moving coming-of-age story in which he learns that magical worlds are much like the real one." New Yorker

Grossman, Paul

Children of wrath; Paul Grossman. St. Martin's Press 2012 324 p. (audiobook) $34.95

ISBN 9781611748451; 9780312601911; 9781429988940

LC 2011041101

This thriller novel is "set in early 1930s Berlin. . . . Berlin headlines scream about people being sickened by tainted sausages. Bags of bones show up in the city's sewer system. Detective Willi Kraus quickly learns the bones are the remains of children--and young boys are disappearing from the city. His superiors take the spectacular murder case away from him because he is Jewish and hand him the case of the bad sausages instead. . . . A father himself, he cannot--will not--ignore the boys and the bones." (Kirkus Reviews)

Gruber, Michael

The **book** of air and shadows. William Morrow 2007 466p $24.95

ISBN 978-0-06-087446-9; 0-06-087446-5

LC 2006-46767

This thriller "centers on a hunt for an unknown autographed Shakespeare play. References to this play turn up in seemingly innocuous letters used as filler in the binding of an old book. Mishkin, an intellectual property attorney, comes into possession of some of these documents through his client, a Shakespearean scholar. Crosetti, who discovered the papers while working at a rare-book store, partners with Mishkin to find the play after the scholar's murder." Libr J

"Few thrillers will surpass [this book] when it comes to energetic writing, compellingly flawed characters, literary scholarship and mathematical conundrums." USA Today

Gruber, Michael

The **forgery** of Venus; a novel. William Morrow 2008 318p $24.95

ISBN 978-0-06-087448-3; 0-06-087448-1

LC 2008-2363

"Gruber writes passionately and knowledgeably about art and its history—and he writes brilliantly about the shadowy lines that blur reality and unreality. Fans of intelligent, literate thrillers will be well rewarded." Publ Wkly

Gruber, Michael

The **good** son; a novel. Henry Holt and Co. 2010 383p $26

ISBN 0-8050-9128-9; 978-0-8050-9128-1

"This novel slides in and out of conventional identities with a facility that would be disturbing if it weren't so damn smooth. Adeptly plotted yet philosophical, worldly yet preoccupied with moral truth, it's a book to provoke comparisons with John le Carré and Graham Greene, while at the same time eluding the ideological constraints that weigh so heavy on those masters." Salon

Gruber, Michael

Night of the jaguar. Morrow 2006 372p $24.95

ISBN 0-06-057768-1

LC 2005-40011

This "supernatural thriller completes the trilogy that began with Tropic of Night and Valley of Bones. All feature Miami cop Jimmy Paz, though the real star of this outing is the supposedly dull-witted Jenny Simpson, a gofer for the Forest Planet Alliance. When someone starts murdering Cuban-American businessmen in grisly fashion, suspicion falls on Moie, an Indian from a remote area of Colombia the victims had plans to develop. . . . Summoned out of retirement, Jimmy takes on the case, though he and his seven-year-old daughter, Amelia, are soon troubled by dreams of a jaguar with evil designs on Amelia. Every time Moie glides onto the page, the book shines, but it's Jenny, helping to shelter Moie, who steals the show . . . . Hotly spiced with hit men and guns, demon gods and piranhas, this one offers more social satire than its predecessors, mostly at the expense of do-gooder environmentalists." Publ Wkly

Gruber, Michael

The **return**; a novel. Michael Gruber. Henry Holt and Co. 2013 384 p. (hardback) $28

ISBN 0805091297; 9780805091298

LC 2012045307

In this novel by Michael Gruber "a shattering piece of news awakens [Richard] Marder's buried desire for vengeance, and with nothing left to lose, he sets off to punish the people whose actions, years earlier, changed his life. Uninvited, [an army buddy from Vietnam Patrick] Skelly shows up and together the two of them raise the stakes far beyond anything Marder could have envisioned. Marder learns that good motives and sense of justice can't always protect the people a man loves." (Publisher's note)

Gruber, Michael

Valley of bones. William Morrow 2005 436p $24.95

ISBN 0-06-057766-5

"When a Sudanese oil baron is thrown to his death from his hotel balcony, Miami detective Jimmy Paz finds a mysterious woman named Emmylou Dideroff vehemently praying at the scene of the crime; she quickly becomes the main suspect. The plot immediately thickens as Emmylou begins to write a lengthy confession about her disturbing childhood, how she reformed from a criminal to a woman of God, and what led her to the Miami hotel room that day. Is she crazy or does God really speak to her? Jimmy and criminal psychologist Lorna Wise investigate and are thrown into a whirlwind journey involving prostitution, white supremacists, the Sudanese civil war, and massive government cover-ups." Libr J

Gruen, Sara

Ape house; a novel. Spiegel & Grau 2010 320p $26

ISBN 0-385-52321-1; 978-0-385-52321-9

LC 2010-08928

When a family of bonobo apes who know American Sign Language are kidnapped from a language laboratory, their mysterious appearance on a reality TV show propels scientist Isabel Duncan, together with reporter John Thigpen, on a personal mission to rescue them.

This novel portrays "group of six bonobo apes housed in the fictional Great Ape Language Lab in Kansas City and the humans who either come to love them or seek to profit from their surprisingly advanced communication skills. Led by Bonzi, the matriarch and undisputed leader, the bonobo group includes Sam, the charismatic oldest male, Jelani, an adolescent showoff, and Makena, 'Jelani's biggest fan,' who is pregnant and due any day. Isabel Duncan is a research scientist overseeing the bonobos and their unique ability to communicate via lexigrams on their computers, supplemented by American Sign Language. . . . Gruen enlivens this charming story of their emotional bonding with multiple villains—including Isabel's fiancé, the head of the Great Ape Language Lab, who she discovers has a history of animal cruelty and a desire to profit from the bonobos under his control. There's also a purveyor of porn who sees the bonobos as the perfect stars for his new reality TV show, enticing viewers with their healthy sex lives 24 hours a day. Ape House turns into a romp, but Gruen never loses the thread of the enviable bond Isabel has nurtured with her ape friends." BookPage

Gruen, Sara

Water for elephants; a novel. Algonquin Books 2006 335p il $23.95

ISBN 1-565-12499-5

LC 2005-52700

"Life is good for Jacob Jankowski. He's about to graduate from veterinary school and about to bed the girl of his dreams. Then his parents are killed in a car crash, leaving him in the middle of the Great Depression with no home, no family, and no career. Almost by accident, Jacob joins the circus. There he falls in love with the beautiful performer Marlena, who is married to the circus' psychotic animal trainer. He also meets the other love of his life, Rosie the elephant. This lushly romantic novel travels back and forth in time between Jacob's present day in a nursing home and his adventures in the surprisingly harsh world of 1930s circuses. The ending of both stories is a little too cheerful to be believed, but just like a circus, the magic of the story and the

writing convince you to suspend your disbelief. The book is partially based on real circus stories and illustrated with historical circus photographs." Booklist

Grumbach, Doris

The book of knowledge; a novel. Norton 1995 248p

ISBN 0-393-03770-3

LC 94-37901

"Grumbach's latest novel is grimly compelling in its portrayal of four lives filled with stifled desires, major depression, incest, self-sacrifice, and thwarted love. . . . Grumbach paints a glowing picture of warmth, security, and safety that is shattered by the Great Depression." Booklist

Grunberg, Arnon

Tirza; by Arnon Grunberg; translated from the Dutch by Sam Garrett. Open Letter 2013 452 p. (paperback) $16.95

ISBN 1934824690; 9781934824696

LC 2012044299

In this book, former book editor Jörgen's life has suffered considerably after the 9/11 terror attacks. The "plot centers on a graduation party for Jörgen's eldest daughter, Tirza, who is planning a trip to Namibia with her boyfriend, who reminds Jörgen of Mohammed Atta, the lead 9/11 hijacker. Jörgen is suffering from the hectoring of his shallow, judgmental wife, and his daughters haven't always shown shrewd judgment. . . . But it's also clear that something is broken within Jörgen himself." (Kirkus)

Grunwald, Lisa

The irresistible Henry House; a novel. Random House 2010 412p $25

ISBN 978-1-4000-6300-0

LC 2009-19720

Henry's "story will no doubt garner comparisons to fellow Zelig-like figures Benjamin Button and Forrest Gump. But Grunwald's writing, while sometimes painted in the brushstrokes of allegory, rarely indulges in that kind of soft-focus sentimentality." Entertainment Wkly

Grushin, Olga

The dream life of Sukhanov. G.P. Putnam's Sons 2005 354p $24.95

ISBN 0-399-15298-9

LC 2005-43175

"On one level, Grushin recounts the comfortable life of fiftysomething art critic and former artist Anatoly Sukhanov, who enjoys all the perks of a pre-Gorbachev existence, until the arrival of a mysterious cousin at his family's capacious Moscow apartment. As his secure life begins to fray and then unravel, Sukhanov, who had the potential of brilliance as a young artist but eventually joined the Soviet establishment, is forced to confront the loss of his beloved wife, his two children, his editorship at the country's leading art magazine, in a word, his identity. Though an absorbing chronicle of life at the end of the Soviet era, this is really much more–a meditation on society, art, truth, and life." Libr J

Grushin, Olga

★ The **line**. G.P. Putnam's Sons 2010 322p $25.95

ISBN 978-0-399-15616-8; 0-399-15616-X

LC 2009-42733

"In the world of The Line, no desire, no matter how trifling, is met without a herculean struggle, and Anna's stymied attempts to present her family with something as simple as a date cake sometimes devolve into farce. But for the most part, Grushin expertly maintains a dreamlike tone to sell the novel's more preposterous (albeit historically grounded) elements, and characters who initially appear one-dimensional become intensely empathetic by the novel's end, as they bristle or cave under a society that grinds down the exceptional to make way for the pedestrian." A. V. Club

Guene, Faiza

Kiffe kiffe tomorrow; [translated from the French by Sarah Adams] Harcourt 2006 179p pa $13

ISBN 0-15-603048-9; 978-0-15-603048-9

LC 2005-30456

Original French edition, 2004

"Doria, 15, a child of Muslim immigrants, describes her daily struggle in Paris' rough housing projects in a contemporary narrative that's touching, furious, and very funny." Booklist

Guest, Judith

★ **Ordinary** people. Viking 1976 263p hardcover o.p. pa $13

ISBN 0-670-52831-5; 0-14-006517-2 pa

"When his older brother drowns in a boating accident, seventeen-year-old Conrad Jarrett feels responsible and makes an unsuccessful attempt at suicide. After eight months in a mental institution, Conrad returns home to parents whose marriage is crumbling, friends who are wary of him, and a psychiatrist who works with him to help put the pieces together. The pain of adolescent anxiety and fragile family relationships are authentically depicted." Shapiro. Fic for Youth. 3d edition

Guinn, Matthew

The **resurrectionist**; a novel. Matthew Guinn. W W Norton & Co Inc 2013 304 p. (hardcover) $25.95

ISBN 0393239314; 9780393239317

LC 2013003760

This novel by Matthew Guinn takes place at "South Carolina Medical College, where ... bones of African American slaves, over a century old, are unearthed. Out of the college's dark past, these bones threaten to ... condemn the present. In the ... nineteenth century, Dr. Frederick Augustus Johnston ... purchased a slave. Nemo ("no man") would become ... responsible for procuring bodies for medical study. Insouciant, tormented, and brilliant, and ... almost supernatural, Nemo [seizes] his self-respect." (Publisher's note)

Gulik, Robert Hans van

The **Chinese** bell murders; three cases solved by Judge Dee. a Chinese detective story suggested by three original Chinese plots; with 15 plates drawn by the author in Chinese style. Harper 1959 262p il

First published 1958 in the United Kingdom

Judge Dee, a legendary magistrate and detective, who is based on a real 7th century Chinese person and was the subject of Chinese detective tales during the 17th and 18th centuries, made his American debut in this murder-rape case. The judge solves three interwoven crimes in the provincial city of Pooyang. A postscript provides information on ancient Chinese detection and court procedure and on the Chinese sources of the story

Gulik, Robert Hans van

The **haunted** monastery; a Chinese detective story. {by} Robert van Gulik; with eight illustrations drawn by the author in Chinese style. Scribner 1969 159p il

First published 1961 in Malaysia; first United States edition published 1963 in paperback

This mystery "finds Judge Dee and his family and retainers stranded because of a broken axle and a howling storm. He has to spend the night solving three murders and a problem of impersonation before he can proceed on his journey the following day." Ency of Mystery & Detection

Gulik, Robert Hans van

The **lacquer** screen; a Chinese detective story. {by} Robert van Gulik; with ten illustrations drawn by the author in Chinese style. Scribner 1970 180p il

First published 1962 in Malaysia; first United States edition published 1963 in paperback

This tale is set in 7th century China. Magistrate detective Judge Dee and his lieutenant join the underworld in a district under the Judge's jurisdiction in order to solve three crimes. They share the life of the gangster-boss and his entourage while the underworld people unwittingly help them in their inquiries. The Judge eventually reveals the ugly secret hidden by the panels of a beautiful lacquer screen

Gulik, Robert Hans van

The **Red** Pavilion; a Chinese detective story. {by} Robert van Gulik; with six illustrations drawn by the author in Chinese style. Scribner 1968 173p il

First published 1961 in Malaysia

Judge Dee, "solves more than one knotty criminal problem, all of them stemming out of the fact that he elects to stay in the infamous Red Pavilion on Paradise Island, not knowing it has been the scene of several mysterious deaths in the past. The Chinese atmosphere is suitably exotic and there is a lovely, mistreated courtesan for the judge to protect." Publ Wkly

Gulik, Robert Hans van

The **willow** pattern; a Chinese detective story. by Robert van Gulik; with fifteen illustrations drawn by the author in Chinese style. Scribner 1965 183p il

"This adventure of the legendary Judge Dee, of Seventh Century China, is a strange, brooding tale of crime, cholera, and corruption. . . . The emperor and his court have fled the plague-ridden city and left the judge and his Colonels, Ma Joong and Chiao Tai, in charge of affairs. They quickly become involved in three murders: 'The Case of the Willow Pattern', 'The Case of the Steep Stairs', and 'The Case of the Murdered Bond-Maid.'" Libr J

Gunesekera, Romesh

The **match**; a novel. New Press 2008 308p $24.95

ISBN 978-1-59558-198-3; 1-59558-198-7

LC 2007-21883

First published 2006 in the United Kingdom

"Many a novelist, drizzling throwaway contemporary references over the text, looks clumsy and laboured in the attempt. Here the forty-year narrative arc is traced across a sequence of precisely judged topical allusions, embracing everything from Skants underwear to Cherie Blair's late baby. Each emerges quite naturally from narrative and dialogue. Time never hangs too heavily on the story, but we are encouraged to value the experience of its passing. Few novelists have so skilfully underlined the beauty of patience as a redeeming virtue." Times Lit Suppl

Gunning, Sally

The **rebellion** of Jane Clarke. William Morrow 2010 273p $24.99

ISBN 978-0-06-178214-5; 0-06-178214-9

LC 2010-20340

A historical novel set in the "heart of Revolutionary War-era Boston, where young Jane Clarke has been sent to care for her great-aunt Gill after refusing to marry the man her loyalist father has chosen for her. Not long after settling into her aunt's house near the British Custom House, Jane is thrust into the milieu of violence and intrigue that eventually leads to a declaration of independence by the American colonists. She befriends the bookseller Henry Knox and meets John Adams, who employs her brother as a clerk. As tensions mount, Jane watches the men around her grow more aggressive in their aversion to British rule, and less concerned with truth. When she is caught up in the Boston Massacre, she must come to terms with the importance of honesty over personal and political passions." Publ Wkly

"Gripping, romantic, historically sound, and completely satisfying." Historical Novels Rev

Guo Xiaolu

A **concise** Chinese-English dictionary for lovers. Nan A. Talese/Doubleday 2007 283p $23.95

ISBN 978-0-385-52029-4; 0-385-52029-8

LC 2007-3118

The novel "cleverly courts our assumptions about the chasm between Chinese and Western cultures, only to upend them. It is an utterly captivating, and disorientating, journey both through language and through love." Independent (London)

Guo Xiaolu

Twenty fragments of a ravenous youth. Nan A. Talese/Douleday 2008 204p il $21.95

ISBN 978-0-385-52592-3

LC 2008-1671

"Guo's début novel, first published eleven years ago in China and now reworked in English, distills the rush to modernization through the experience of Fenfang, a young peasant who leaves her village for Beijing. Part of the post-Cultural Revolution generation, Fenfang is untethered from history and profoundly alone, and Guo imbues her flailing efforts to establish herself with a raw, adolescent pain. Pirated books and DVDs provide an education, as Fenfang takes cues from 'Betty Blue,' 'Chungking Express,' Marguerite Duras, and Tennessee Williams, progressing from work as an extra in state film productions to a screenwriting career. Guo is a filmmaker herself, and, if her recurrent homages occasionally cloy, Fenfang's rage to express herself carries an unmistakable autobiographical intensity." New Yorker

Gurganus, Allan

★ The **oldest** living Confederate widow tells all. Knopf 1989 718p

ISBN 0-394-54537-0

LC 88-45870

"In a way, 'Oldest Living Confederate Widow Tells All' is as much about language and myth-making as it is about love and war. Whether one feels that it succeeds depends on how much leeway one is willing to give to this indomitable 'veteran of the veteran,' as Lucy describes herself." N Y Times Book Rev

Gurganus, Allan

The **practical** heart; four novellas. Knopf 2001 322p $25

ISBN 0-679-43763-0

LC 2001-32665

"In 'The Practical Heart,' the narrator recalls the proclivities of his great-aunt, daughter of a Scottish immigrant to Chicago. . . . 'Preservation News' is a fey portrait of a man who has just lost his battle with AIDS but who spent his last breath in the pursuit of the preservation of historic properties. . . . 'He's One, Too' offers an ironically sympathetic portrayal of a married man arrested for lewd acts with a younger man. And in the longest and most moving piece, 'Saint Monster,' a son remembers how the relationship between his ugly but kind father and his beautiful but faithless mother forced him into prematurely dealing with the rawer aspects of adulthood." Booklist

Gurganus, Allan

White people. Knopf 1991 252p

ISBN 0-394-58841-X

LC 90-52943

The novella A hog loves its life concerns a grandfather and his boyish grandson, the other novella Blessed assurance: a moral tale "is a funny, sad, confessional tale told by a man reflecting on his traumatic youth, when he collected funeral insurance premiums from poor blacks. Gurganus is a champion storyteller with particularly American roots, in the tradition of Mark Twain. This is a collection to be savored and reread." Publ Wkly

Gutcheon, Beth Richardson

Five fortunes; a novel. {by} Beth Gutcheon. Cliff St. Bks. 1998 398p

ISBN 0-06-017679-2

LC 97-48926

This is the "story of friendship and support among a group of five women who first meet on a week-long retreat at a health spa in Arizona. . . . During the following year, these strong, independent, and ambitious women face enormous challenges that bring them even closer: private detective Carter quits smoking and takes on drug dealers in L.A., the still vibrant Rae must face her husband's decline from Alzheimer's disease; Amy and her daughter, Jill, resolve old issues; and the recently widowed Laura declares her candidacy for the U.S. Senate." Booklist

Gutcheon, Beth Richardson

More than you know; a novel. [by] Beth Gutcheon. Morrow 2000 269p

ISBN 0-688-17403-5

LC 99-45936

The novel opens "with an old woman named Hannah reminiscing about her youthful fling in the isolated, picturesque Maine coastal village of Dundee. . . . Hannah's romance is interwoven with a deadly love story, set 100 years earlier, that will in turn mysteriously haunt her. . . . The taut facility with which Gutcheon twines the two stories creates real suspense—both in the exact fates of the couples and the identity of the ghost, who grows viciously vengeful. While Gutcheon cannily evokes the ephemerality of passion, she also evinces, with stark and elemental resonance, the way love and hatred shape lives." N Y Times Book Rev

Gutcheon, Beth Richardson

Saying grace; a novel. {by} Beth Gutcheon. HarperCollins Pubs. 1995 312p

LC 95-8677

"As it follows Rue's trials, 'Saying Grace' provides a realistic portrait of both a good school and its gifted leader. Ms. Gutcheon knows private schools, and she knows her craft—and that's a winning combination." NY Times Book Rev

Guterson, David

East of the mountains. Harcourt Brace & Co. 1999 288p $25

ISBN 0-15-100229-0

LC 98-40512

This is the "story of one Ben Givens, a retired Seattle heart surgeon and widower who is dying of colon cancer. As the novel opens, Ben arises, depressed, after a sleepless night. . . . Ben is so depressed that he has decided to kill himself, and he wants to make it appear accidental; he will die while bird hunting in the dry eastern Washington canyons of his youth. With a surgeon's meticulousness, he sets out early with his dogs in his Scout and a cup of steaming lemon tea in hand." N Y Times Book Rev

"Guterson draws compelling characters and creates a haunting sense of place and of humankind's paradoxical relationship with the natural world." Libr J

Guterson, David

Ed King; a novel. Alfred A. Knopf 2011 301p $26.95

ISBN 978-0-307-27106-8; 0-307-27106-4

LC 2011-10255

"Guterson's narrative voice — by turns savage and sad, amused and outraged — becomes a kind of Greek chorus of one. From the self-reverential blather of Seattle liberals to the gaming industry's nihilistic love of violence to the winner-take-all world of software and search engines, Guterson skewers it all. . . . He interweaves the story with enough mythological references to keep even the most ardent classicist entertained." Seattle Times

Guterson, David

The other. Alfred A. Knopf 2008 255p $24.95

ISBN 978-0-307-26315-5; 0-307-26315-0

LC 2007-41098

"With prose that's as careful and quiet as a mountain lion, The Other asks, and helps answer, two of life's most perplexing questions: How do we live in an imperfect world, and what are our obligations to those we love?" Outside

Guterson, David

Our Lady of the Forest. Knopf 2003 323p $25.95

ISBN 0-375-41211-5

LC 2002-43322

"When Ann Holmes starts having visions of the Virgin Mary, the bedraggled teen runaway becomes the last hope for the inhabitants of a dank, economically depressed logging town and the hordes of miracle-seekers who descend on it. In this panoramic, psychologically dense novel, she also becomes a symbol of the intimate intertwining of the sacred and the profane in American life." Publ Wkly

Guterson, David

★ Snow falling on cedars. Harcourt Brace & Co. 1994 345p $25

ISBN 0-15-100100-6

LC 94-7535

"Japanese American Kabuo Miyomoto is arrested in 1954 for the murder of a fellow fisherman, Carl Heine. Miyomoto's trial, which provides a focal point to the novel, stirs memories of past relationships and events in the minds and hearts of the San Piedro Islanders. Through these memories, Guterson illuminates the grief of loss, the sting of prejudice triggered by World War II, and the imperatives of conscience. With mesmerizing clarity he conveys the voices of Kabuo's wife, Hatsue, and Ishmael Chambers, Hatsue's first love who, having suffered the loss of her love and the ravages of war, ages into a cynical journalist now covering Kabuo's trial." Libr J

Guterson, Mary

Gone to the dogs. St. Martin's Griffin 2009 278p pa $13.99

ISBN 978-0-312-54179-8; 0-312-54179-1

LC 2009-10691

"This irreverent novel inverts the romantic-farce convention of the hero as lovable loser. Here it's the heroine who's the ambitionless slob, a grad-school dropout treading water as a waitress and living in a pigsty of an apartment. When she's eighty-sixed by her jock fiancé for an Amazonian white-water-kayaking enthusiast, she's propelled into action: she kidnaps the new girlfriend's dog. With expert deadpan, Guterson keeps the premise from getting too cute." New Yorker

Guthrie, A. B.

★ The **big** sky; [by] A. B. Guthrie, Jr. Sloane 1947 386p

"After a quarrel and fight with his father, 17-year old Boone Caudill leaves his home in Kentucky headed for St. Louis and the west, where he hopes to hunt buffalo and shoot Indians. The story follows his adventurous course, by foot and horseback, to the Mississippi, then by keel boat to the land of the big sky at the headwaters of the Missouri, where for 13 years he leads the typical life of a mountain man for his period and in that short times sees the Indian degraded, the game killed off and the life he loved destroyed." Wis Libr Bull

Guthrie, A. B.

The **way** West. Sloane 1949 340p

A story of an emigrant trek from Independence, Missouri, to Oregon in the 1840s. Dick Summers, one of the principal characters of the author's earlier novel, 'The Big Sky' reappears in this novel

"Where most writers of Western fiction concentrate on what their characters do, Mr. Guthrie concentrates on how they think and feel. It is this emphasis which gives his book depth and sense of reality." Christ Sci Monit

Guttridge, Peter

The **thing** itself; Peter Guttridge. Severn House 2012 213 p. $28.95

ISBN 0727880810; 9780727880819

This novel, by Peter Guttridge, is book three in the "Brighton Mystery" series. "Thriller writer Victor Tempest is dead and his son, the disgraced ex-Chief Constable Bob Watts, is discovering what really happened in the unsolved Brighton Trunk Murder of 1934. At the same time, DS Sarah Gilchrist has a lead that may establish the truth about the Milldean Massacre. If she can stay alive long enough to follow it." (Publisher's note)

Gwyn, Richard

The **color** of a dog running away. Doubleday 2007 305p $21.95

ISBN 978-0-385-51855-0; 0-385-51855-2

LC 2006-11900

First published 2005 in the United Kingdom

"At thirty-three, Lucas, a Welsh-born expatriate, has drifted into a modest but pleasurable life in Barcelona: occasional translation work, long nights in neighborhood bars, strong coffee in local cafés, and comical exchanges with an Andalusian neighbor who rears rabbits on their common roof. But when Lucas falls in love with a stunning woman he encounters at the Miró Foundation his life becomes the stuff of melodrama. . . . At once an absurdist riddle, a romantic quest, and a love letter to our antihero's chosen home, Gwyn's witty and assured first novel is as much about the

different ways you can tell a story as it is about the story itself." New Yorker

H

Ha Jin

The **bridegroom**; stories. Pantheon Bks. 2000 225p

ISBN 0-375-42067-3

LC 00-28405

"In this dazzling collection of stories, set in provincial China in the fairly recent past, most of the protagonists are emerging from the numbing predictability of totalitarianism, realizing that they must abandon the passivity that has insured their survival in the past." New Yorker

Ha Jin

The **crazed**. Pantheon Bks. 2002 323p

ISBN 0-375-42181-5

LC 2002-22427

"Writing with a searing restraint born of long-brewing grief over the Chinese government's surreal savageness, Ha Jin depicts a warped society in which everyone is driven mad by viciousness and injustice. But Ha Jin's dramatic indictment does not preclude love, or the ancient power of story to memorialize, awaken compassion, and shore up hope." Booklist

Ha Jin

A **free** life. Pantheon Books 2007 660p $26

ISBN 978-0-375-42465-6; 0-375-42465-2

LC 2007-6177

"Jin's main character, Nan Wu, is a graduate student in political science studying at Brandeis. He is married to a pretty, resourceful Chinese woman named Pingping. The Wus have a young son, Taotao, who has just been reunited with his parents after four years living with Nan's parents in China. . . . The Tiananmen riots mark a change in Nan's fortunes. Disillusioned about China's future, he drops out of school, determined to make a life in America any way he can. The events of 'A Free Life' move from Boston to New York, where Wu, frustrated in his literary pursuits, learns to be a chef the old-fashioned way by starting as a busboy; and then to the outskirts of Atlanta where Nan and Pingping become the new owners of a local Chinese restaurant named the Gold Wok. At each location Jin creates a rich community of characters — writers, artists, political dissidents, waiters, shopkeepers, even the Dalai Lama makes an appearance — that give this quiet story of modest triumph a universal dimension." Seattle Times

Ha Jin

In the **pond**; a novel. Zoland Bks. 1998 176p

ISBN 0-944072-92-5

LC 98-33493

"When Shao Bin, in post-Cultural Revolution China, is not among the chosen few for new housing, his wife berates him for not bribing the powers that be. Instead, Bin, a factory worker with a talent for cartooning, takes aim against the bosses' corruption and gets his cartoons published. Not surprisingly, the clownishly wicked bosses maintain an arsenal for zapping such gnats, and it seems that the war can have only the grimmest conclusion. But the author is as resourceful as his hero, and the simplicity of the narrative proves deceptive." New Yorker

Ha Jin
Waiting. Pantheon Bks. 1999 308p $24
ISBN 0-375-40653-0

LC 99-21334

This novel "provides a dual education: a crash course in Chinese society during and since the Cultural Revolution, and more leisurely but nonetheless compelling exploration of the less exotic terrain that is the human heart." N Y Times Book Rev

Ha Jin
War trash. Pantheon Books 2004 352p $25
ISBN 0-375-42276-5

LC 2004-43428

"Written in the modest, uninflected prose of a soldier's letter home, Ha Jin's story, a mixture of authentic historical detail and realistic invention, is a powerful work of the imagination whose psychic territory is not the hunger and humiliation of the prison camp but the haunted past that was the old, lost China and the mysterious future that is in the process of becoming Mao Zedong's chimerical new China." Washington Post

Includes bibliographical references

Haasse, Hella S.
In a dark wood wandering; revised and edited by Anita Miller from an English translation from the Dutch by Lewis C. Kaplan. Academy Chicago 1989 574p
ISBN 0-89733-336-5

LC 89-17814

Original Dutch edition, 1949

"This novel exemplifies historical fiction at its best; the author's meticulous research and polished style bring the medieval world into vibrant focus." Libr J

Habila, Helon
Measuring time; a novel. W. W. Norton & Co. 2007 383p pa $13.95
ISBN 978-0-393-05251-0; 0-393-05251-6

LC 2006-30790

In a "story of contemporary Nigeria, twin brothers want to escape their village of Keti, and war seems the best way to fame and glory. But Mamo has sickle-cell disease, and he must stay home, reading his brother's letters about adventures across the border and, later, about the brutal wars in which he fights. The twins' wealthy politician father rejects the 'weak,' sickly son, but an uncle inspires Mamo to attend university, read widely, and teach; by the time the soldier returns many years later, Mamo has been offered work as palace biographer, but, instead of the expected hagiography, he writes a true history of his people." Booklist

"Habila's beautifully (and deceptively) simple style is matched by a story that is strong, clear and richly evocative." New Statesman (London, England: 1996)

Hacker, Christopher
The Morels; Christopher Hacker. Soho Press 2013 368 p. (hardcover) $25.95
ISBN 1616952431; 9781616952433

LC 2012036639

This novel focuses on "Arthur Morel, who as a child was a talented violinist with a flair for self-sabotage, [and who] has just finished his second novel (also called The Morels), a barely fictionalized account of his relationship with his wife Penelope and their son, Will. His book's last scene, however, depicts Arthur and an eight-year-old Will engaging in a sexual act that shocks the public and quickly scuttles his relationship with his family, who are unmoved by his claims of poetic license." (Publishers Weekly)

Haddam, Jane
Bleeding hearts. Bantam Bks. 1994 311p il

LC 93-14466

This mystery "focuses on Valentine's Day as it's celebrated on Philadelphia's Cavanaugh Street, home to retired FBI agent Demarkian and a host of fellow Armenian immigrants. Everyone in the neighborhood is surprised when homely Hanna Krekorian turns up with a new man in her life, but Demarkian is especially shocked when he finds that Hanna's friend is none other than Paul Hazzard, who was once suspected of violently murdering his wife. Hazzard may have some kind of twisted motive for courting Hanna—but what?" Booklist

"Never quite cozy and never quite tough, this tale combines the best of both styles to stunning effect." Publ Wkly

Haddam, Jane
Cheating at solitaire; a Gregor Demarkian novel. St. Martin's Minotaur 2008 391p $24.95
ISBN 978-0-312-34308-8; 0-312-34308-6

LC 2007-49770

"When the outrageous behavior of a movie crew filming on Margaret's Harbor (a fictionalized Martha's Vineyard) results in the death of a crew member, the island's one-person police department requests the assistance of former FBI agent Gregor Demarkian. Moving slowly through the landscape of her story, Haddam turns the island and its ambiance into a vividly visual experience for readers. Brilliantly introspective, intellectual ruminations and multiple narrators—who fully convey the craziness of the paparazzi and the cutthroat attitudes of those with power—intersperse with Haddam's own unique and frequently unexpected conclusions." Libr J

Haddam, Jane
Flowering Judas; a Gregor Demarkian novel. Minotaur Books 2011 370p $25.99
ISBN 978-0-312-64433-8

LC 2011-09102

"In the 12 years since Chester Morton disappeared, his mother has never stopped trying to find out what happened to him. She's handed out flyers, harassed the police, and paid for a roadside billboard asking passersby who may know something to come forward. The billboard has been there all 12 years, and hardly anybody pays attention to it anymore. Then, after Chester's body is found hanging from the billboard—his very recently dead body, mind you—the authorities ask former FBI agent and part-time investigator Gregor Demarkian to find out what's going on. . . . Gregor is such a well-drawn character that readers, within a few pages of meeting him—and even if they've never picked up another Demarkian novel—will feel like they've known him for years." Booklist

Haddam, Jane

Hardscrabble road. St. Martin's Minotaur 2006 309p $24.95

ISBN 0-312-35373-1

LC 2005-54793

"Those new to Haddam will snap up her earlier work based on this captivating literate mystery, which shows how well a classic fair play whodunit can work in a contemporary setting." Publ Wkly

Haddam, Jane

Somebody else's music. St. Martin's Minotaur 2002 328p $24.95

ISBN 0-312-27186-7

LC 2001-58899

"A famous woman writer with a rock-star lover returns to the hometown where as a nerdy teenager she was traumatized by a nearby, still unsolved murder. The rock star asks FBI Behavioral Sciences Unit chief Gregor Demarkian. . . to solve this case—and more." Libr J

"Haddam movingly explores what that means for our lives—past, present and future—and how that happens and why." Publ Wkly

Haddam, Jane

True believers. St. Martin's Press 2001 328p

ISBN 0-312-20929-0

LC 00-51794

"Haddam's large cast pulses with petty jealousies, vanities and fears as they confront the mysteries of life and religion. This is an engrossingly complex mystery that should win further acclaim for its prolific and talented author." Publ Wkly

Haddon, Mark, 1962-

The **curious** incident of the dog in the night-time; Today Show Book Club ed; Doubleday 2003 226p il $24.95

ISBN 0-385-51210-4

Despite his overwhelming fear of interacting with people, Christopher, a mathematically-gifted, autistic fifteen-year-old boy, decides to investigate the murder of a neighbor's dog and uncovers secret information about his mother

"Unable to feel emotions himself, his story evokes emotions in readers—heartache and frustration for his well-meaning but clueless parents and deep empathy for the wonderfully honest, funny, and lovable protagonist. Readers will never view the behavior of an autistic person again without more compassion and understanding." SLJ

Haddon, Mark, 1962-

The **red** house; a novel. Mark Haddon. Doubleday 2012 264 p.

ISBN 0385535775; 9780385535779

LC 2011029883

In this book, "Richard and Angela, estranged siblings, try to mend their past by spending a week together with their families at a house on the Welsh border. But the ingredients are not promising. Richard arrives with his glossy new wife and stuck-up stepdaughter. Angela brings her loveless marriage and duly troubled children. . . . The proximity and forced intimacy of the holiday exposes the many cracks in their relationships." (Economist)

"Refreshingly, Haddon takes the risk of making the ordinary extraordinary and succeeds; each character is poignantly real and each small trauma a revelation." LJ

Haddon, Mark

A **spot** of bother. Doubleday 2006 354p $24.95

ISBN 978-0-385-52051-5; 0-385-5205-1-4

LC 2006-16578

This novel "pulls off the smart trick of delivering fully human characters whose flaws make them almost impossible to live with, then depicts their love for one another as completely convincing." Cleveland Plain Dealer

Hadley, Tessa

The **London** train. Harper Perennial 2011 324p pa $14.99

ISBN 978-0-06-201183-1; 0-06-201183-9

"Cora has abandoned the bright lights of London for Cardiff, where she's found a job at a local library. Meanwhile, Paul has been enticed away from Wales. Their lives, distinct yet connected, form the basis of this enchanting novel, which considers the significance of coincidence and its potential impact upon ordinary lives." Culture Critic

Hadley, Tessa

Married love and other stories; Tessa Hadley. Jonathan Cape 2012 232 p. $14.99

ISBN 0062135643; 9780062135643; 9780224096423

LC 2012358423

In this collection, Tessa Hadley "considers private fears, bad decisions, tipping points and unexpected assertions of free will, via 12 short fictions. . . . 'The Trojan Prince' introduces a young merchant seaman in the 1920s, flirting with the daughter of a wealthy family but ultimately choosing not to respond to her signals of attraction. In 'A Mouthful of Cut Glass,' . . . two college students take their partners home to meet the family and come face to face with the class divide." (Kirkus)

Hadley, Tessa

The **master** bedroom; a novel. Henry Holt and Co. 2007 339p $26

ISBN 978-0-8050-8076-6; 0-8050-8076-7

LC 2006-48781

"Melancholy and starkly emotive, Hadley's enervating tale evokes the raw drama that lies at the emotional nexus between friends and lovers, husbands and wives, parents and children." Booklist

Hadley, Tessa

Sunstroke and other stories. Picador 2007 177p pa $13

ISBN 978-0-312-42599-9; 0-312-42599-6

LC 2007-13103

"Deft and resonant, [these stories] encapsulate moments of hope and humiliation in a kind of shorthand of different lives lived. Hadley never fails to surprise, but her surprises are understated—not the 'aha' fakery of some gimmicky short fiction but the small shift in expectations or results that's deeply felt but doesn't show, like the twitch of a rudder that sets a boat gliding on a new course." N Y Times Book Rev

Hagberg, David
Abyss. Forge 2011 496p $24.99
ISBN 978-0-7653-2410-8; 0-7653-2410-5
LC 2011-07891

When an NOAA scientist has a breakthrough that could enable a sustainable energy source and prevent dangerous weather systems, former CIA director Kirk McGarvey begins a cat-and-mouse chase with a contract killer seeking to trigger a nuclear disaster.

"This is a timely and frightening novel. Readers will be left thinking, This could really happen." Kirkus

Hage, Rawi
De Niro's game. Steerforth Press 2007 277p $23.95
ISBN 978-1-58195-223-0; 1-58195-223-6
LC 2007-23905

First published 2006 in Canada

"This is a grim, flat book. Hage's flatness gives it the right tone of bruised emotion, disconnectedness, and violence; it's what makes this such an effective debut." Quill & Quire

Hagedorn, Jessica Tarahata
Toxicology; [by] Jessica Hagedorn. Viking 2011 225p $25.95
ISBN 978-0-670-02257-1; 0-670-02257-8
LC 2010-35379

"In this engaging novel, Hagedorn employs a number of stylistic tricks. She drops in footnotes to explain dream sequences, creates a section in the form of a literary journal (modeled on the Paris Review), and pauses the narrative to announce digressions and 'a bit of exposition.' These experimental touches don't justify themselves in every instance, but they sustain the story in a lively way. One of the best reasons to read this novel is its beautifully precise descriptions of New York City." Boston Globe

Hagen, George
The Laments; a novel. Random House 2004 370p $24.95
ISBN 1-400-06221-7
LC 2003-66882

This novel "follows the lives of the Laments, a white South African family in the late 20th century. Howard is an engineer who marries the energetic and artistic Julia. In a twist of events, the Laments adopt Will, just delivered by a mother who has abducted their biological infant and is then tragically killed with the abducted child in an automobile accident. A few years later, Will's twin brothers, Marcus and Julius, are born as the Laments begin their nomadic flights from Rhodesia to the Persian Gulf, England, and, finally, the United States." Libr J

Hager, Jean
The spirit caller. Mysterious Press 1997 257p
ISBN 978-0892966400
LC 96-42033

"Hager offers readers a clever, well-written mystery that also provides an intimate and edifying look at Native Americans' beliefs, traditions, and lifestyle." Booklist

Haggard, H. Rider
★ **King** Solomon's mines; introduction by Alexandra Fuller; illustrations by Walter Paget; notes by James Danly. Modern Library 2002 xxv, 264p il pa $9.95
ISBN 0-8129-6629-5
LC 2002-29519

First published 1885

"Highly coloured romance of adventure in the wilds of Central Africa in quest of King Solomon's Ophir; full of sensational fights, bloodcurdling perils and extraordinary escapes." Baker. Guide to the Best Fic

Haggard, H. Rider
★ **She**; edited with an introduction and notes by Daniel Karlin. Oxford University Press 1998 xxxviii, 332p pa $9.95
ISBN 0-19-283550-5

First published 1885

"'She,' or Ayesha, is an African sorceress whom death apparently cannot touch. The young English hero, Leo Vincey, sets out to avenge the murder of his ancestor, an ancient priest of Isis. The setting of this weird romance is an extinct volcano." Univ Handbk for Readers and Writers

Hagy, Alyson
Boleto; a novel. Alyson Hagy. Graywolf Press 2012 251 p.
ISBN 1555976123; 9781555976125
LC 2012931912

This book "opens with Will [Testerman] buying a beautiful 2-year-old filly for a bargain price. She will be a 'development project' for the patient Will. He talks to her a lot, building trust. He won't ride her yet . . . but they'll be going to California together to meet Don Enrique. . . . It turns out Don Enrique is an Argentine businessman who hosts polo games. His manager is a swine. Five frightened, underfed Argentine teenagers do the barn work. Will's fantasy of learning the polo business, unwisely based on a single conversation with the Don, begins to crumble. Will his innate decency hobble him with this tough, mercenary crowd? And can he protect his beloved filly from these rapacious rich folks?" (Kirkus Reviews)

Haig, Matt
The dead fathers club. Viking 2007 328p $23.95
ISBN 0-670-03833-4
LC 2006-50108

First published 2006 in the United Kingdom

This novel is "clearly inspired by Shakespeare's Hamlet, and part of the fun for the reader is discovering the many droll and unforced parallels. But the real draw is the extraordinary voice that Haig has created for his first-person narrator. Given to panic attacks, Philip is a breathless story-teller who seldom stops for punctuation but whose honesty and innocence, which shine from every sentence, are utterly captivating and heartbreakingly poignant. The result is an absolutely irresistible read." Booklist

Haig, Matt

The **humans**; a novel. Matt Haig. Simon & Schuster 2013 304 p. (hardcover: alk. paper) $25
ISBN 1476727910; 9781476727912; 9781476730592
LC 2013003203

In this novel by Matt Haig "an extraterrestrial visitor arrives on Earth. Taking the form of Professor Andrew Martin . . . the visitor is eager to complete the gruesome task assigned him and [return] to the utopian world of his own planet. Unexpectedly, he forges bonds with Martin's family, and in picking up the pieces of the professor's shattered personal life, he begins to see hope and beauty in the humans' imperfections and begins to question the mission that brought him there." (Publisher's note)

Includes bibliographical references

Haig, Matt

The **Labrador** Pact. Viking 2008 341p $23.95
ISBN 978-0-670-01852-9; 0-670-01852-X
LC 2007-19557

First published 2004 in the United Kingdom with title: The last family in England

The "tale of a noble dog's efforts to save his human family from ruin. Prince, the Lab narrator, begins his story on the day he says will be his last. Animals in this world are always talking to each other—and us, though we can't hear what they say. So they're forced to resort to barks and soulful looks. Labradors are bound by the rules of the titular pact, which requires the breed to make the safety of the human family paramount. For Prince, this means trying to keep his family, the Hunters, safe from the machinations of a seductive couple who clearly have designs on Adam and Kate Hunter, the weary parents of two teenagers." USA Today

Haig, Matt

The **possession** of Mr Cave. Viking 2009 244p $25.95
ISBN 978-0-670-02056-0; 0-670-02056-7

First published 2008 in the United Kingdom

"At times, the theme (which plays on the dual meanings of the word 'possession') can seem heavy-handed, but the near-compulsive emphasis on having, holding, keeping and protecting aptly reflects Cave's troubled state of mind. Haig effectively brings readers into Cave's unstable interior world, asking them to inhabit this closed-off, deeply unreliable space along with their narrator." Bookreporter.com

Haig, Matt

The **Radleys**. Free Press 2010 371p $25
ISBN 978-1-4391-9401-0; 1-4391-9401-7
LC 2010-04459

Struggling with overwork and parenting angst, English village doctor Peter Radley endeavors to hide his family's vampire nature until their daughter's oddly satisfying act of violence reveals the truth, an event that is complicated by the arrival of a practicing vampire family member.

"Dr. Peter Radley, his wife, Helen, and their two teenage children, Rowan and Clara, appear to be an ordinary English family living a quiet suburban life — except that they're a family of nonpracticing vampires (or, in the book's AA-like speak, they're following the rules of The Abstainer's Handbook). Rowan and Clara aren't even aware of what they are — or why they must always wear heavy sunblock — until the night Clara has a run-in with a local thug and nature overcomes nurture. With a body to dispose of, Peter must reach out to his estranged practicing-vampire brother, Will, who holds all manner of dark and dirty family secrets. The Radleys is effortlessly sleek and witty." Entertainment Wkly

Haigh, Jennifer

Baker towers; a novel. William Morrow 2005 334p $24.95
ISBN 0-06-050941-4
LC 2004-49073

This novel is "set in Bakerton, a mining town in post-World World II Pennsylvania. Haigh's focus is the Novak family, particularly the five children being raised by their Italian mother after their Polish father drops dead. All five make attempts to escape Bakerton at one point or another; some are successful, others are not. George, a veteran of WW II, neglects his Bakerton fiancee and marries a cold socialite. Dorothy goes to the nation's capital to work, but a nervous breakdown brings her home. Brilliant, cold Joyce thinks her future lies with the military, but she is sorely disappointed. Sandy is the golden son who escapes to dubious success. And Lucy is the youngest, who finds herself in college despite the nagging feeling that she never wanted to leave home in the first place. Haigh creates a real sense of a community and brings her mining town to life through a large cast of minor characters who pass in and out of the Novaks' lives." Booklist

Haigh, Jennifer

The **condition**; a novel. HarperCollins 2008 390p $25.95
ISBN 978-0-06-075578-2; 0-06-075578-4

"The point of view in 'The Condition' shifts repeatedly, as each character replays the relevant scenes of his or her life. This structure adds dimension, but it slows momentum because time doesn't move forward in a linear fashion. Still, the inner lives of these people are so richly developed that they keep us engaged." Chicago Tribune

Haigh, Jennifer

Faith; a novel. Harper 2011 318p $25.99
ISBN 978-0-06-075580-5; 0-06-075580-6
LC 2010-43160

The tale "goes down with deceptive ease. Haigh's smooth prose belies its hard truths. It is relatively easy to tell a story in black and white. The art lies in writing nuanced shades of gray. 'Faith' is painted with a palette of many tones, its outlines of its character sharp and sharply human." Denver Post

Haigh, Jennifer

Mrs. Kimble. Morrow 2003 394p $24.95
ISBN 0-06-050939-2
LC 2002-70304

The title "refers to three women, each of whom marries an opportunist named Ken Kimble. The first wife, Birdie, is Ken's student at a small Christian college. With her, he has two children. Then he seduces another student and deserts his family, leaving Birdie to bring up the children alone. The second Mrs. Kimble is a successful career woman, reassessing her priorities in the wake of her mastectomy. Ken capitalizes on Joan's neediness and sweeps her off her feet. He also ingratiates himself with her uncle, a real estate tycoon. When Joan and Uncle Floyd die, Ken inherits from both. The third Mrs. Kimble had been the first Mrs. Kimble's babysitter. . . . Original and compelling. Libr J

Hailey, Arthur

Airport. Doubleday 1968 440p

"Here are many minor conflicts—of love, sex, business, and psychological problems—all building up to the tremendously exciting scenes of a shattered transoceanic plane trying to make its way back to the airport, and a runway that can't, but must, be cleared." Publ Wkly

Hailey, Arthur

Detective; a novel. Crown 1997 400p

ISBN 978-0517700259

LC 97-1204

"It's a measure of Hailey's skill as a storyteller that he gives up the killer way before the end but still manages to maintain the suspense." Publ Wkly

Hailey, Arthur

Hotel. Doubleday 1965 376p

This novel reveals the inner workings of a large hotel during a hectic week. "Among the many events, the hotel changes ownership, royalty staying at the hotel are involved in hit-and-run deaths, there is an attempted rape, there is a racial incident, and a thief makes off with sizable loot. This is also the story of Peter McDermott. As an honest and intelligent assistant general manager of the St. Gregory Hotel, he thinks quickly and effectively in handling the many problems that beset this gracious old hotel in New Orleans. Yet his personal record is blemished by a single event which may keep him from rising higher in hotel echelons." Libr J

Hailey, Elizabeth Forsythe

A woman of independent means. Viking 1978 256p

ISBN 0-670-77795-1

LC 77-28414

The author "has succeeded in giving us a portrait of a woman, with all her frailties, strengths, failures and victories combining to prove that living a life is an accomplishment." Christ Sci Monit

Haimoff, Michelle

These days are ours; Michelle Haimoff. Grand Central Pub. 2012 290 p.

ISBN 9781455500291

LC 2011012929

This novel, "which unfolds in Manhattan soon after 9/11, chronicles rich kid Hailey's attempts to make a life and come to an understanding with her parents. . . . As the daughter of publishing heavyweights, Hailey knows she'll never trump their accomplishments. Though she's highly connected, she's determined to find a job on her own--and land golden boy Michael Brenner, whose close family and cozy apartment fill a void. Hailey tries to stay on Michael's radar despite his propensity for bed hopping. Unlike Michael, the Pennsylvania-born Adrian, an interloper in Hailey's social circle, works for his rent, and Hailey isn't sure how she feels about him, even though they share a similar thoughtfulness and sense of humor." (Publishers Weekly)

Haldeman, Joe W.

The accidental time machine; [by] Joe Haldeman. Ace Books 2007 278p $23.95

ISBN 978-0-441-01499-6

LC 2007-6935

"Lowly MIT research assistant Matt Fuller toils away in a physics lab until one day he makes an odd discovery. A sensitive quantum calibrator keeps disappearing and reappearing moments later when he hits the reset button. With a little tinkering, Matt realizes that the device functions as a crude, forward-traveling time machine. With visions of Nobel Prizes dancing in his head, he latches it to a car and leaps into the future. The interesting wrinkle here is that each jump ahead is 12 times longer than the last. Matt's successive futures involve jail time, unwelcome celebrity, and assorted holocausts in the earth's climate. He begins to long for his native era. As usual, Haldeman's ingenuity delivers cutting-edge technological speculation and irresistibly compelling reading." Booklist

Haldeman, Joe W.

The coming; {by} Joe Haldeman. Ace Bks. 2000 216p

ISBN 0-441-00769-4

LC 00-29306

"On 1 October 2054, astronomy professor Rory Bell receives a message, 'We're coming,' from an Earthbound object way out in space that will arrive on New Year's Day. Soon Rory, her composer husband, her chief faculty protege, the university president, a mob shakedown artist, a Gainesville cop, the mayor, the governor of Florida, and, finally, the president and her cabinet are all conniving away in response to the momentous announcement. . . . Haldeman's fast-paced, cannily constructed yarn is ultimately most like that granddaddy of first-contact flicks, The Day the Earth Stood Still. Maybe better." Booklist

Haldeman, Joe W.

Forever free; [by] Joe Haldeman. Ace Bks. 1999 277p

ISBN 0-441-00697-3

LC 99-33231

This novel "reintroduces readers to William Mandella {featured in Forever War} who has been living peacefully on the planet called Middle Finger, a refuge for humans who refuse to become part of the group mind known as Man. But after decades of this peace, Mandella and others are tired of living like zoo animals. They're ready for a challenge, and they'd like to see Earth again. So they steal a starship—and embark upon a voyage that will forever change their understanding of the universe . . . and themselves." Publisher's note

Haldeman, Joe W.

Forever peace; {by} Joe Haldeman. Ace Bks. 1997 326p

ISBN 0-441-00406-7

LC 96-52650

"It is 2043, and the U.S. and its allies are waging a seemingly endless war against a loose federation of Third World countries called Ngumi. Julian Class is a draftee, an infantryman, and part of a 'soldier-boy'—a mechanized, armorplated, highly lethal unit run by a squad of men and women all of whom have been 'jacked' or linked together by surgical implantation. Add to the plot mix a plan to build a mammoth particle accelerator on Jupiter's moon, Io, and the rise of a fundamentalist, secretive religious sect, the Hammer of God, to the very highest military ranks." Booklist

The author "writes with uncommon intelligence and acuity about the terror of war and the horror of the human heritage in the middle of the next century." Publ Wkly

Haldeman, Joe W.

★ The **forever** war; [by] Joe Haldeman. St. Martin's Press 1975 236p

"A naturalistic description of a war that lasts more than a thousand years, although the main characters age only a few years because of the relativistic effects of faster-than-light space travel. The situation of the soldiers fighting in this kind of war is complicated, however, by their alienation from their own societies by the time-dilation effect, and their growing disillusionment with the war." New Ency of Sci Fic

Haldeman, Joe W.

Marsbound; [by] Joe Haldeman. Ace Books 2008 296p $24.95

ISBN 978-0-441-01595-5; 0-441-01595-6

LC 2008-19356

"Recalling Robert A. Heinlein's Red Planet and Podkayne of Mars, Haldeman updates the Martian setting while keeping faith in his characters' ability to respond to unexpected challenges." Publ Wkly

Haldeman, Joe W.

Starbound; [by] Joe Haldeman. Ace Books 2010 292p $24.95

ISBN 978-0-441-01817-8; 0-441-01817-3

LC 2009-40932

"Having survived the Others' attempt to annihilate all life on Earth, humanity and its Martian allies are left with the problem of how to respond to the provocation. A military response is probably doomed, since the Others are vastly more powerful than humanity. Carmen Dula joins a hand-picked crew of Martians and humans on a near-light-speed diplomatic mission to the Others' home system, a mission that will certainly maroon the characters decades in the future and may well end in their sudden deaths at the manipulative appendages of the Others." Romantic Times

"Haldeman's crisp storytelling and juicy plot twists keep us captivated throughout." Booklist

Hale, Benjamin

The **evolution** of Bruno Littlemore. Twelve 2011 578p $25.99

ISBN 978-0-446-57157-9; 0-446-57157-1

LC 2010-12098

Bruno, the novel's "singular protagonist, is a 25-year-old chimp born at a zoo and raised by researchers who taught him to read, write, and speak. The trappings of humanity, unfortunately, have come with unexpected wants and desires, and Bruno ends up falling in love with one of his handlers. Deeply. Making your main character a talking ape — and one who engages in a romantic liaison with a human being, no less — is ambitious, to say the least. But from the first page, it is clear that Bruno is more than mere literary gimmickry; he is fascinating and fully formed. You learn as much by what he withholds as by what he provides, and he withholds a lot . . . . Where the novel should be offensive, it is often tender, and where it should be risible, it is genuinely funny." Entertainment Wkly

Hale, Edward Everett

★ The **man** without a country. R. West 1977 106p il

First published 1863 in Atlantic Monthly; this is a reprint of the 1897 edition published by Roberts Bros.

"This long short-story concerns Philip Nolan, a young officer of the United States Army who is tried for the Aaron Burr conspiracy. During the courtmartial he exclaims, 'Damn the United States! I wish I may never hear of the United States again!' The court thereupon sentences him to live out his life on a naval vessel, and never hear news of the United States. The story recounts the mental torments of the countryless prisoner, who after fifty-seven years finally learns that his nation is thriving, and dies happy." Haydn. Thesaurus of Book Dig

Hale, Shannon

Austenland; a novel. Bloomsbury 2007 197p $19.95

ISBN 978-1-59691-285-4; 1-59691-285-5

LC 2006-34165

The author's "charming first book for adults is chick lit with soul. Though there's a laugh on nearly every page— Hale, like Austen, is adept at subtly skewering the ridiculous—there's also the more serious story of a woman learning the difference between fantasy and reality, and discovering that real life can be better than your dreams." Bookpage

Haley, Alex

Mama Flora's family. Delta 1999 462p pa $23

ISBN 0-440-61409-0

First published 1998 by Scribner

In this multigenerational family saga, the "lives of Mama Flora and her family provide a whirlwind survey of the 20th-century black experience. As a young woman in a small Tennessee town, Flora bears a son and sees his father killed at the hands of white racists. She realizes that education is the only way out of poverty. Soon, her daughter becomes a social worker while her son dabbles in communism and enlists to fight in World War II. As Flora lays dying, she can look back on her family and their accomplishments with pride." Libr J

Hall, Adam

Quiller Balalaika. Carroll & Graf/Otto Penzler 2003 242p $24

ISBN 0-7867-1265-1

First published 1996 in the United Kingdom

"The detritus of the cold war in the former Soviet Union comprises self-serving bureaucracies, opportunistic ex-KGBers, and organized criminals who make their U.S. mafioso counterparts seem like mischievous delinquents. Into the mix drops pseudonymous Brit agent Quiller, with the intent of taking out a British national-Basil Seckes, aka Vasyl Sakkas-who is secretly heading up the burgeoning Russian criminal empire. To bring down Sakkas' empire, Quiller needs the help of one Marius Antonov, currently residing in a Gulag prison. Freeing Antonov entails Quiller making his way into the prison and then escaping with his target, no small feat because the prison is virtually escape proof. . . . The book is a typically atmospheric, exciting Quiller adventure." Booklist

Hall, Adam

★ The **Quiller** memorandum. Simon & Schuster 1965 224p

Published in the United Kingdom with title: The Berlin memorandum

"Quiller is a British 'Shadow executive', employed by 'the Bureau', a government agency assigned to carry out delicate tasks, and it is so secret it does not exist. As we follow Quiller's 'brain-think' sequences we learn that during the Second World War he was an infiltrator who arranged escapes from Nazi concentration camps. Quiller and others like him with specialised skills, do the jobs that M15 and M16 cannot do. Quiller is used only at the authorisation of the Prime Minister. In The Quiller Memorandum he exposes a large, well-organised neo-Nazi conspiracy in Berlin." McCormick and Fletcher. Spy Fic

Hall, Adam

Quiller Salamander. Penzler Bks. 1994 247p

ISBN 1-883402-40-9

LC 94-17372

British secret agent Quiller, "bored in London, takes on a rogue assignment—one the Bureau has not sanctioned but which is the private effort of one of the 'controls,' the enigmatic Flockhart. The mission: discover what Pol Pot is up to in his ongoing efforts to return the Khmer Rouge to power. Arriving in Phnom Penh, Quiller finds himself attracted to his first contact, a female French photographer who harbors an important secret, and suspicious of his field director. Following a narrow escape from a Khmer Rouge encampment, Quiller uncovers plans for yet another Cambodian bloodbath." Publ Wkly

"Mr. Hall, a master of intense prose and tense situations, has again come up with a story that wil not disappoint his admirers." N Y Times Book Rev

Hall, Adam

Quiller solitaire. Morrow 1992 286p

ISBN 0-688-10730-3

LC 91-31060

"When a fellow agent who has called upon him for protection is murdered before his eyes, an enraged and embarrassed Quiller pressures his superiors into giving him the dead man's assignment to investigate the murder of a British cultural attache in Berlin. The murder is apparently tied to former East German national Dieter Klaus, a madman who wants to gain attention for his terrorist splinter group." Publ Wkly

Hall, Albyn Leah

The **rhythm** of the road. Thomas Dunne Books 2007 309p il $24.95

ISBN 978-0-312-35944-7; 0-312-35944-6

LC 2006-48680

The author's "writing is captivating and rhythmic—one can almost hear the hum of wheels on asphalt as the story speeds along. . . . It is not a light read and Jo is often difficult to champion, but mature readers may take away powerful lessons on growing up." Voice Youth Advocates

Hall, Barbara

The **music** teacher; a novel. Algonquin Books of Chapel Hill 2009 292p

ISBN 978-1-56512-463-9

LC 2008-41336

"It feels like an ancient story—the tired, disappointed teacher who has long since given up on her own talent meets the young student who truly has a shot at greatness. . . . Pearl Swain is a violin teacher. Her 14-year-old student, Hallie Bolaris, is brimming with promise, but Pearl's vicarious desires become a problem. She crosses too many boundaries and punishes her student for pushing her away. 'The Music Teacher' is a study of the many ways to crush the creative human spirit. 'Did you get anything from me?' Pearl asks her estranged student. The question echoes long after the novel ends." Los Angeles Times Book Rev

Hall, Brian

I should be extremely happy in your company; a novel of Lewis and Clark. Viking 2003 419p $25.95

ISBN 0-670-03189-5

LC 2002-66376

"Narrated in multiple distinct voices, this retelling of the story of Meriwether Lewis and William Clark's legendary expedition is less a historical blow-by-blow than an engaging character study of the two men. Hall focuses on a few significant episodes in the journey—such as the hunting accident that wounds Lewis and causes him to sink into his famous depression—as seen through the eyes of Lewis, Sacagawea, Clark and Toussaint Charbonneau, Sacagawea's French fur trader husband. The result is a memorable portrait of the expedition leaders." Publ Wkly

Includes bibliographical references

Hall, Emylia

The **book** of summers; Emylia Hall. Mira 2012 348 p. (pbk.) $14.95

ISBN 0778314111; 9780778314110

LC 2012372349

This book by Emylia Hall "follows Beth Lowe, a young Englishwoman, as she recalls languid summers spent in Hungary with her mother, Marika. . . . After a family trip to Hungary . . . her mother suddenly announced her intention to stay. . . . Each year after the split, Beth spent summers with

Marika, until a secret comes to light that impels Beth to turn her back on Hungary and her mother. Years later . . . Marika is dead and has left Beth a scrapbook." (Publishers Weekly)

Hall, James W.
  Blackwater sound; a novel. St. Martin's Minotaur 2002 339p $24.95
    ISBN 0-312-20384-5
                                    LC 2001-48594
  "Hall's quiet studies of loners—the old man in his fog of memory, the marlin in the freedom of the deep—are truly haunting." N Y Times Book Rev

Hall, James W.
  Buzz cut; by James W. Hall. Delacorte Press 1996 374p
                                    LC 95-50425
  In this mystery, "Thorn and Sugar take security detail on a luxury Caribbean cruiseship only to find that a brilliant madman named Butler Jack has hijacked the ship for reasons clear only to himself. Butler creates general havoc on board, altering the ship's course, causing near collisions, and randomly killing crew and passengers in spectacularly bloody fashion. Thorn and Sugar slowly unravel the twisted tale of greed and madness that drives the mind of the hijacker, finally reaching a very surprising truth." Libr J

Hall, James W.
  Off the chart; a novel. St. Martin's Minotaur 2003 337p $24.95
    ISBN 0-312-27178-6
                                    LC 2002-191965
  "Yes, we like to imagine ourselves wearing Thorn's deck shoes, in a full-frontal assault on all those who endanger our world, but Hall, unlike most thriller writers, portrays the collateral damage wreaked when rugged individualists go into overdrive. This remains one of the best series in the genre." Booklist

Hall, James W.
  Red sky at night; by James W. Hall. Delacorte Press 1997 326p
    ISBN 0-385-31638-0
                                    LC 96-45621
  "Ensconced in his Key Largo beach house, Thorn seems to have carved a lasting separate peace with the modern world until a senseless crime drives the other side of his personality to the fore, the side that says, 'There's something broken, and I have to fix it.' What's broken this time, though, is Thorn himself, mysteriously paralyzed from the waist down after attempting to confront an apparent prowler. The story begins with the slaughter of several dolphins—killed for their endorphins, the key ingredient in a miracle, pain-killing drug—and extends to Thorn's distant past and his relationship with his best childhood friend, who has been nursing a grudge against Thorn for decades. . . . Popular fiction at its absolute best." Booklist

Hall, James W.
  Rough draft; a novel. St. Martin's Press 2000 335p
    ISBN 0-312-20383-7
                                    LC 99-55532
  In this suspense novel former Miami cop turned mystery writer Hannah Keller is trying to solve the murder of her parents when she finds a "copy of one of her books containing cryptic marginal notes that appear to be a message from the killer. Meanwhile, the FBI is tracking a psycho hit-man who dispatches his victims by crushing their hearts with his bare hands. The psycho is hunting the money launderer who may have killed Hannah's parents, and unbeknownst to her, she becomes the bait in the Bureau's elaborate sting operation. Hall weaves his contrapuntal plot strains beautifully, letting the reader know more than Hannah knows but never enough to be comfortable." Booklist

Hall, Radclyffe
  The **well** of loneliness; with a commentary by Havelock Ellis. Covici 1928 506p
  This autobiographical novel traces "the life of the wealthy young woman Stephen Gordon from birth to her full realization that she is a 'congenital invert' (as she terms it), a lesbian by nature. . . . It is the first full, rich portrait of a lesbian in literature. At the time the publication was an act of outstanding bravery." British Women Writers

Hall, Sarah, 1974-
  The **Beautiful** indifference; Sarah Hall. Faber & Faber Ltd. 2012 208 p.
    ISBN 0571230180; 9780571230174; 0571230172; 9780571230181
                                    LC 2011535401
  This is novelist Sarah Hall's debut short story collection. Settings range "from the heathered fells and lowlands of Cumbria . . . , to the speed and heat of summer London, to an eerily still lake in the Finnish wilderness. . . . The characters within these territories are real-life survivors, but whether it's a frustrated housewife seeking extreme experience or a young woman contemplating the death of her lover, dark devices and desires rise to the surface." (Publisher's note)

Hall, Sarah, 1974-
  Daughters of the north; a novel. HarperPerennial 2007 209p pa $13.95
    ISBN 978-0-06-143036-7; 0-06-143036-6
  Published in the United Kingdom with title: The Carhullan Army
  In this novel, "a series of ecological and geopolitical disasters in Britain has caused all citizens to be herded into urban centers, where women are fitted with contraceptive coils. Hall's work covers familiar fictive ground in imagining a dystopia in which women's bodies have become the battleground for competing ideologies; what is new here, however, is the unflinching focus on physical control. This can make for squeamish reading, as bodies are continually being 'stretched and scoured' in the most vivid terms, but the result is a powerful argument that, when civil institutions, or the bodies of state, are compromised, so, too, is the integrity of the body. The book sometimes lacks suspense, owing, in

part, to the limitations imposed by its framing device, a transcript of a prisoner's statement." New Yorker

Hall, Steven

The **raw** shark texts. Canongate 2007 428p il $24

ISBN 1-84195-902-2

"The novel's great virtue is its structure. Narrative tricks keep the reader surprised. Information is released in pieces, like time-release drugs in a capsule, their order derived from the progressive revelation of truths rather than the forward march of events. Only at the end do we accelerate towards a more conventional action-packed climax, though even that takes place in a sort of collective unconscious. In many ways, this is cyberfiction, a battle between archetypes in a virtual reality." Times Lit Suppl

Hall, Tarquin

The **case** of the deadly butter chicken; from the files of Vish Puri, India's most private investigator. Tarquin Hall. Simon & Schuster 2012 341 p.

ISBN 9781451613155

LC 2011052702

This book is the third in the Vish Puri detective series. Here, Puri tries to solve the case of the mysterious death of Faheem Khan, "a Pakistani cricket-ace's father. . . . Unfortunately, Faheem's son Kamran, bowler for the Kolkata Colts, has gone back to Rawalpindi to mourn. So Puri, who had never met a Pakistani in person before the Khans, must travel across a most-feared border in pursuit of justice." (Kirkus)

Hallgrimur Helgason

101 Reykjavik; a novel. translated by Brian FitzGibbon. Scribner 2003 339p $23

ISBN 0-7432-2514-7

LC 2002-29434

"This novel uses caustic and irreverent humor to paint a vivid picture of Icelandic youth ideas and culture. . . . While the protagonist is confused, depressed, and futureless, the humor saves the book from being depressing." Libr J

Hallinan, Timothy

★ The **fear** artist; Tim Hallinan. Soho Crime 2012 342 p. (hardback) $25.00

ISBN 1616951125; 9781616951122

LC 2012009728

In this book, a man crashes into Rafferty and "dies in his arms, . . . saying three words: 'Helen Eckersley. Cheyenne.' Seconds later, the police arrive, denying that the man was shot." He is interrogated but can't remember the dead man's words. "Rafferty . . . realizes he's under surveillance. . . . [H]e manages to escape . . . and begins a new life as a fugitive. . . . [I]t becomes apparent that he's been caught on the margins of the war on terror, and that his opponent is a virtuoso artist whose medium is fear." (Publisher's note)

Hallinan, Timothy

A **nail** through the heart. William Morrow 2007 328p $24.95

ISBN 978-0-06-125580-9; 0-06-125580-7

LC 2006-47085

In this thriller set in Bangkok, American Poke Rafferty, "author of a series of adventure guidebooks for young men, wants to adopt a street child named Miaow and marry Rose, a former bar girl. When Miaow runs into a former friend from the street named Superman, Rafferty gets roped into trying to track down several mysterious characters who may or may not have something in common. The unraveling of these connections occupies the main action of the novel. . . . In a refreshing deviation from the norm, Timothy Hallinan's real concern lies not with the crafting of a well-paced thriller (which he's done quite successfully), but with turning the classic hardboiled rugged individualist detective of American noir into a man whose greatest concern is the formation of a family. It's enough to make Raymond Chandler roll over in his grave." PopMatters

Halperin, David J.

Journal of a UFO investigator; a novel. [by] David Halperin. Viking 2011 289p

ISBN 978-0-670-02245-8

LC 2010-34999

"While the science fiction talk may put off some, this heartbreaking coming-of-age story of a boy losing and finding his way in this and other worlds will resonate with many readers." Publ Wkly

Halter, Marek

The **book** of Abraham; translated by Lowell Bair. Holt & Co. 1986 722p

LC 85-17582

Original French edition, 1983

The author "begins his tome in 70 A.D. in Jerusalem, when a scribe named Abraham flees the conquering Roman army. The author follows the dynasty of scribes descended from Abraham through the centuries, until he links them to his own real-life ancestors, a line of printers, one of whom worked with Gutenberg in Strasbourg. The book ends with death of Halter's grandfather, a printer, in the Warsaw ghetto, in 1943. The chronicle moves among dozens of cities in Asia and Europe, deftly encapsulating the historical events and social milieu of time and place, as each generation of this family hands down the so-called Book of Abraham, a record of births and deaths that also symbolizes the continuity of the collective Jewish memory." Publ Wkly

Halter, Marek

Messiah; translated by Lauren Yoder. Toby 2008 487p $24.95

ISBN 978-1-59264-216-8; 1-59264-216-0

Original French edition, 1996

"In 1524, David Reubeni—a real-life prince and military envoy of a lost Jewish kingdom—traveled to Venice aiming to establish a Judeo-Christian alliance that would seize Jerusalem from Ottoman control. In Halter's remarkable imagining of David's travels, throngs of followers flock to David as he makes his way through the center of Christendom, mesmerized by the strange man's vast knowledge and regal charm. . . . But David's lofty goals also attract ruthless enemies and eager fanatics who mistake David for a messiah, all of whom jeopardize his mission. The harrowing adventure is satisfying in its ample twists and turns, but Halter's writing of David Reubeni into the historical fabric of premodern Europe—imagining David taking refreshment with Machiavelli, becoming the subject of a sculpture by Michelangelo and suggesting the creation of the College des Lecteurs Royaux to King Francis I—is the book's major pleasure." Publ Wkly

Halter, Marek

Sarah; a novel. Crown Publishers 2004 294p map $22

ISBN 1-400-05272-6

LC 2003-19648

Original French edition, 2003

"Sarah is the favorite daughter of a lord of Ur, a city-state of Sumeria. Raised in luxury and privilege, she defies her father on the day of her marriage and escapes into the lower city, where she meets Abraham of the nomadic mar.Tu people. Although soldiers take her home, she can't forget the young man who captured her heart and imagination. Owing to an injudicious use of infertility herbs in an effort to stave off marriage, Sarah renders herself sterile and is dedicated to the temple of Ishtar, where she serves as a revered Sacred Handmaid of the Blood for several years until she meets Abraham again. This time, she successfully escapes, and the two dedicate themselves to the one, true, invisible God and create a nation." Libr J

Hambly, Barbara

★ Days of the dead. Bantam Bks. 2003 314p il maps $23.95

ISBN 0-553-10954-5

LC 2002-38571

"An extreme case of culture shock awaits Benjamin January. . .when he leaves cosmopolitan New Orleans, a city that loves life, for bellicose Mexico, a country that lives for its dead. Traveling with his bride, Rose, by overland coach in 1835, this Paris-trained surgeon (and former slave) encounters bloodthirsty bandits, fierce soldiers from Santa Anna's army, rebellious Yankees from uncivilized Texas and a hacienda teeming with feuding relatives on the country estate of the Spanish grandee Don Prospero's only son." N Y Times Book Rev

Hambly, Barbara

Dead water; Barbara Hambly. Bantam Books 2004 297p $25

ISBN 0-553-10964-2

LC 2004-40766

This Benjamin January adventure "finds the amateur sleuth investigating a couple of mysteries. The bank that holds all his money has suddenly and suspiciously collapsed, and someone has apparently put a curse on a former student in the small school operated by January's wife, Rose. Just goes to show: New Orleans, circa 1836, is a wild and dangerous place. . . . Where many writers of historical mysteries get bogged down in exposition, or in cataloging details that most readers are not interested in, Hambly keeps things moving, always focused on her characters and her story, and not on showing off the quantity of research she's done." Booklist

Hambly, Barbara

Die upon a kiss. Bantam Bks. 2001 333p

ISBN 0-553-10924-3

LC 00-69666

In antebellum New Orleans "cultural war is declared between rival American and Creole opera houses when an Italian company attempts to open the season for the upstart Americans with an original and provocative version of 'Othello.' The composer is knifed in the alley, the lead soprano is poisoned, a prominent opera patron is murdered, and—oh, yes, the theater is torched. Benjamin January, a former slave and accomplished musician who plays in the orchestra, is well positioned for this backstage investigation." N Y Times Book Rev

Hambly, Barbara

✓ A free man of color. Bantam Bks. 1997 311p hardcover o.p. pa $5.99

ISBN 0-553-10258-3; 0-553-57526-0 pa

LC 96-44942

"A few suspenseful moments not-withstanding, this isn't an action-packed or suspenseful whodunit. Rather, it's a richly detailed, telling portrait of an intricately structured racial hierarchy." Booklist

Hambly, Barbara

Good man Friday; by Barbara Hambly. Severn House 2013 250 p. (hardcover) $29.95

ISBN 0727882554; 9780727882554

This is the 12th installment in Barbara Hambly's Benjamin January mystery series. Here, "when money becomes tight, January takes on an unusual assignment that requires him to leave New Orleans for Washington. Needless to say, 1838 wasn't the safest of times for a free man of color." (Library Journal)

Hambly, Barbara

Graveyard dust. Bantam Bks. 1999 315p

ISBN 0-553-10259-1

LC 98-43456

"Hambly's plot, which revolves around evils confined to no race or class, is complex and often hard to track, but its emotional authenticity, varied cast and rich historical trappings give the novel power and depth." Publ Wkly

Includes bibliographical references

Hambly, Barbara

Patriot hearts; a novel of the founding mothers. Bantam Dell 2007 430p $25

ISBN 978-0-553-80428-7; 0-553-80428-6

LC 2006-24174

This historical novel "opens with First Lady Dolley Madison waiting anxiously for husband 'Jemmy' and deciding what to save if they must flee the White House during the War of 1812. She is thus reminded of her predecessors Martha Washington and Abigail Adams, as well as Sally Hemings, and each of these women has her turn at personal narratives, which take place at critical points in the nation's early years and in their personal lives. The perspective offered is distinctly feminine and gives readers a sense of peeking backstage at a play they know well." Libr J

Hambly, Barbara

Ran away; Barbara Hambly. Severn House 2011 244p.

ISBN 9780727880826

This novel follows the story of fictional character Ben January, who "fled New Orleans to escape its racism, . . . [and] settled in Paris, where he eked out a living as a musician while studying medicine. He met, fell in love with and married Ayasha, who asked him to help out Shamira, a sick, pregnant concubine in the household of Hüseyin Pasha, a wealthy Turk. . . . When Ayasha was abducted and Shamira's fate necessitated exchanging her infant son for her freedom, Ben came to believe Pasha honorable and trustworthy. That's why five years on, back home in New Orleans after Ayasha's death from cholera, Ben disputes the findings that declare that Pasha . . . tossed two of his concubines, Noura and Karida, from a window in his house. With an assist from his current wife Rose and his friend, ex-opium addict Hannibal, Ben steps in to prove Pasha innocent of murder." (Kirkus)

Hambly, Barbara
★ **Sold** down the river. Bantam Bks. 2000 317p $23.95
ISBN 0-553-10257-5
LC 99-54845

A historical mystery "featuring Benjamin January, a freed slave whose Paris education earns him a living in New Orleans and whose refined sense of justice puts him in peril wherever he goes. . . . Ben bends his back to the pain and humiliation of being a slave again when he goes undercover at a sugar cane plantation 20 miles up the river, were a rebellion may be brewing." N Y Times Book Rev

Hambly, Barbara
Those who hunt the night. Ballantine Bks. 1988 296p
LC 88-47803

"The characters are well drawn (in the case of the vampire Don Simon Ysidro, positively compelling) and plausibly motivated, and the historical setting is both well researched and well depicted." Booklist
Followed by Traveling with the dead

Hambly, Barbara
Traveling with the dead. Ballantine Bks. 1995 343p
ISBN 0-345-38102-5
LC 95-30243

Sequel to Those who hunt the night
"Former British espionage agent James Asher is one of the few mortals aware of the existence of vampires. After he stumbles upon a meeting between an Austrian spy and the long-dead Earl of Ernchester, he embarks upon a dangerous journey across Europe to prevent a catastrophic alliance beteen human governments and the inhumane society of the undead." Libr J

Hambly, Barbara
Wet grave. Bantam Bks. 2002 288p
ISBN 0-553-10935-9
LC 2001-43401

"As with any good historical mystery, we are at least as captivated by the characters, dialogue, and environment as we are with the mystery itself." Booklist

Hamid, Mohsin, 1971-
★ **How** to Get Filthy Rich in Rising Asia; by Mohsin Hamid. Riverhead Hardcover 2013 240 p.
ISBN 9781594487293; 1594487294
LC 2012039847

This book, by Moshin Hamid, presents the "tale of a man's journey from impoverished rural boy to corporate tycoon [and] steals its shape from the business self-help books devoured by ambitious youths all over 'rising Asia.' It follows its nameless hero to the sprawling metropolis where he begins to amass an empire built on that most fluid, and increasingly scarce, of goods: water. Yet his heart remains set on something else, on the pretty girl whose star rises along with his." (Publisher's note)

Hamid, Mohsin, 1971-
The **reluctant** fundamentalist. Harcourt 2007 184p $22
ISBN 0-15-101304-7; 9780151013043
LC 2006-21732

The narrator is "a young Pakistani man named Changez. . . . The novel begins a few years after 9/11. Changez happens upon [an] American in Lahore, invites him to tea and tells him the story of his life in the months just before and after the attacks." (N Y Times Book Rev)

"This is a deeply provocative, excellent addition to the burgeoning sub-genre of September 11 novels. But it would be an understatement to call it merely that. Here is a novel rich in irony and intelligence. Hamid shows us the post-September 11 world from another angle. In doing so he offers up a mirror to the complex business of East-West encounters in these troubled times." Sydney Morning Herald

Hamill, Pete
Forever; a novel. Little, Brown 2002 613p $25.95
ISBN 0-316-34111-8
LC 2002-114241

"In 1740, an Irish Jew named Cormac O'Connor heads to New York in pursuit of the man who killed his father and gets tangled up in a rebellion against the English. Through a series of events involving an African slave with shamanistic powers, he is granted eternal life, provided that he never leaves Manhattan. There follows a tour of the city's history through Cormac's eyes: the political corruption and the poverty, but also the majestic growth of the metropolis through its culture, its buildings, and its people." New Yorker

Hamill, Pete
★ **Snow** in August; a novel. Little, Brown 1997 327p hardcover o.p. pa $14
ISBN 0-316-34094-4; 0-446-67525-3 pa
LC 96-36043

"In Brooklyn in 1947, Michael Devlin, an 11-year-old Irish kid who spends his days reading Captain Marvel and anticipating the arrival of Jackie Robinson, makes the acquaintance of a recently emigrated Orthodox rabbi. In exchange for lessons in English and baseball, Rabbi Hirsch teaches him Yiddish and tells him of Jewish life in old Prague and of the mysteries of the Kabbalah. Anti-Semitism soon rears its head in the form of a gang of young Irish toughs out to rule the neighborhood." Libr J

"Mr. Hamill is not a subtle writer, but his gift for sensual description and his tabloid muscularity . . . fit this page turner of a fable." N Y Times Book Rev

Hamill, Pete

Tabloid city; a novel. Little, Brown and Co. 2011 278p $26.99

ISBN 978-0-316-02075-6; 0-316-02075-3

LC 2010-26166

"Just as the last ever edition of the New York World is getting put to bed, veteran editor Sam Briscoe stops the presses for a sensational murder: socialite Cynthia Harding and her personal secretary are found stabbed to death in Harding's Manhattan town house. The story unfolds in time-stamped, you-are-there bursts that follow a large cast, including several journalists; Cynthia's adopted daughter; a disgraced Madoff-like financier; a media blogger; the murdered secretary's husband, a police officer assigned to a counterterrorism task force, as well as their son, a convert to radical Islam; and best of all by the weary and worldly Briscoe himself. Hamill is at his best in the Briscoe portions, rich in print anecdotes and mournful for a passing age." Publ Wkly

Hamilton, Jane

Disobedience; a novel. Doubleday 2000 272p $24.95

ISBN 0-385-50117-X

LC 00-29504

"Henry Shaw is a high school senior when he intercepts e-mail messages between his mother, Beth, a musician and specialist in ancient music, and violin maker Richard Pollico. As he secretly eavesdrops on the liaison between 'Liza38' and 'Rpol,' Henry's emotions, ranging from horror to fear of abandonment to rage to deep sadness, take on a new dimension when he himself falls in love with a girl he meets in summer camp. Meanwhile, his generally bemused and patient father, Kevin, a high school history teacher, seems unaware of Beth's infidelity, since he spends much of his time coaching Henry's rebellious sister, Elvira, 13, who is obsessed with her desire to join a Civil War reenactment disguised as a boy." Publ Wkly

"Hamilton has written a novel so disturbing that no one will enjoy reading it. But 'Disobedience' is so provocative that you must." Christ Sci Monit

Hamilton, Jane

★ **A map** of the world. Doubleday 1994 389p

ISBN 0-385-47310-9

LC 93-45723

This is "not an easy or light read; indeed, it takes on some of the toughest issues of modern life. But the writer's skill in describing a community and a way of life, as well as her insight into the hearts of her characters, render this story difficult to forget." Christ Sci Monit

Hamilton, Jane

The **short** history of a prince; a novel. Random House 1998 349p

ISBN 0-679-45755-0

LC 97-31627

"Hamilton has an amazing way with the varieties of human pain. Her characters live with ordinary and sometimes extraordinary torment, yet her writing remains bouyant and her sensibility full of light." Newsweek

Hamilton, Jane

When Madeline was young; a novel. Doubleday 2006 273p $22.95

ISBN 0-385-51671-1

LC 2006-40238

"Hamilton has never written more finely nuanced or beguiling prose, imagined more fascinating characters, or posed more provocative moral dilemmas. In each surprising permutation, Hamilton offers fresh perspectives on the puzzles of time, memory, and consciousness, and keenly gauges the many shades of guilt and audacity, grief and sacrifice, tenacity and goodness." Booklist

Hamilton, Masha

The **camel** bookmobile. Harper Collins 2007 308p $24.95

ISBN 978-0-06-117348-6; 0-06-117348-7

LC 2006-41316

"Hamilton's portrayal of nomadic culture is lovingly and colorfully told. It's a painterly glimpse into a world that few Westerners will ever see." USA Today

Hamilton, Peter F.

The **dreaming** void. Del Rey/Ballantine Books 2007 630p $26.95

ISBN 978-0-345-49653-9; 0-345-49653-1

LC 2007-29244

"There is a generous cast of characters and a handful of storylines involved here and it takes the overall story a while to get going. But once it does, it feels like putting on a comfortable jacket; space opera is what Hamilton does and he does it well." SF Signal

Hamilton, Peter F.

★ **Great** north road; Peter F. Hamilton. Del Rey/Ballantine Books 2012 976 p. (hardcover: alk. paper) $30

ISBN 034552666X; 9780345526663; 9780345526687

LC 2012033593

In author Peter F. Hamilton's book, "Sid is a solid investigator" who "must navigate through a Byzantine minefield of competing interests within the police department and the world's political and economic elite . . . all the while hunting down a brutal killer poised to strike again. And on St. Libra, Angela," a "convicted slayer . . . newly released from prison, joins a mission to hunt down the elusive alien, only to learn that the line between hunter and hunted is a thin one." (Publisher's note)

Hamilton, Peter F.

Pandora's star. Del Rey\Ballantine Books 2004 758p $26.95

ISBN 0-345-46162-2

LC 2003-68753

"By the 24th century, the vast human Commonwealth has spread from Earth via artificial wormholes. Various benign or seemingly indifferent alien races have been encountered during exploration of new planets, but an astronomer sparks curiosity by announcing that a pair of stars is enclosed by a mysterious energy barrier. Unfortunately, a space expedition discovers that the shield was created to imprison an insatiably greedy mass mind that sees any other race as a mortal threat. When the barrier somehow is lowered, the alien immediately attacks the largely unprepared Commonwealth, while humans begin wondering if yet another inhuman power has manipulated events that unleashed this threat. The author deftly juggles many characters in multiple plot lines." Publ Wkly

Hamilton, Steve

★ The **lock** artist; Steve Hamilton. Minotaur Books 2010 304 p. $24.99

ISBN 0312380429; 9780312380427

LC 2009034523

Dagger Awards: CWA Ian Fleming Steel Dagger (2011), Edgar Allan Poe Awards: Best Novel (2011), Alex Award (2011)

In this book, "traumatized at the age of eight, Michael, now eighteen, is no ordinary young man. Besides not uttering a single word in ten years, he discovers the one thing he can somehow do better than anyone else. Whether it's a locked door without a key, a padlock with no combination, or even an eight-hundred pound safe, . . . he can open them all. . . . [His] talent . . . will make young Michael a hot commodity with the wrong people and, whether he likes it or not, push him ever close to a life of crime. Until he finally sees his chance to escape, and with one desperate gamble risks everything to come back home to the only person he ever loved, and to unlock the secret that has kept him silent for so long." (Publisher's note)

Hamilton-Paterson, James

★ **Gerontius**. Soho Press 1991 264p

ISBN 0-939149-48-6

LC 91-6441

This is a novel based on an episode in the life of Sir Edward Elgar. "In 1923 Sir Edward Elgar, in his mid-60s and acknowledged as England's finest living composer, takes a cruise to the Amazon port city of Manaos. Rootless and dissatisfied, he repudiates his life's work as insignificant. . . . Elgar wants only to escape from himself, but in Manaos he meets a woman from his past." Libr J

Hammett, Dashiell

★ **Complete** novels. Library of Am. 1999 967p $35

ISBN 1-88301-167-1

LC 98-53911

In Red harvest the nameless operative for the Continental Detective Agency in San Francisco known as the Continental Op fights political corruption in the town of Personville, referred to by its citizens as "Poisonville." In The Dain curse Continental Op solves a jewel burglary, multiple murders, and deals with drug addiction and a family curse

Hammett, Dashiell

Crime stories and other writings. Library of Am. 2001 934p $35

ISBN 1-931082-00-6

LC 00-54594

"The first great author in the hard-boiled detective genre, Hammett remains one of the most entertaining, as demonstrated by this largest single gathering ever of his short fiction. This collection's main distinction is that editor Steven Marcus uses the original story texts from their appearance in Black Mask magazine." Publ Wkly

Includes bibliographical references

Hammett, Dashiell

The **glass** key. Knopf 1931 282p

Appointed special investigator in the district attorney's office to track down the murderer of a Senator's son, Ned Beaumont becomes involved with political bosses, bootlegging gangsters and romance

"One of the two best novels by the man who is generally regarded as the creator and still the acknowledged master of the 'hard-boiled' school of detective fiction. Brutal in its subject matter but excellently written." Howard Haycraft

Hammett, Dashiell

★ The **Maltese** falcon. Knopf 1930 276p

This novel "called the best American detective novel by some critics, opens with Space accepting a case from Brigid O'Shaughnessy, a statuesque redhead masquerading as a Miss Wonderly. Almost immediately, his partner, Miles Archer is killed. Spade hated him and has been having an affair with his wife, but feels duty-bound to find his killer. He becomes involved with an odd assortment of characters, each searching for a statue of a black bird, about a foot high, said to be worth a fortune." Ency of Mystery & Detection

Hammett, Dashiell

Nightmare town; stories. edited by Kirby McCauley, Martin H. Greenberg, and Ed Gorman. Knopf 1999 396p

ISBN 0-375-40111-3

LC 99-37237

These "short stories feature enigmatic plots of devilish intricacy, rife with fisticuffs and pistol shots, and populated by stiffs, laconic coppers, lowlifes and droll, world-weary detectives. Sam Spade shows up several times, as does the Continental Op." Publ Wkly

Hammett, Dashiell

★ The **thin** man. Knopf 1934 259p

"Nick Charles, a San Francisco detective, is the narrator. He and his amusing wife, Nora (on a visit to New York), take time out from drinking and dancing to solve the problem of what happened to an inventor whose disppearance coincided with the murder of his mistress-secretary. There is the right amount of underworld, and in lieu of the usual tough stuff we are treated to an adolescent (son of the disappeared-and-deceased), who battens on the more lurid aspects of toxicology and pathology." Barzun. Cat of Crime. Rev and enl edition

"One of the first works to bring humor, and of a distinctly native brand, to the detective story in this country." Howard Haycraft

Hammond, Diane Coplin

Going to bend; a novel. [by] Diane Hammond. 1st ed; Doubleday 2004 293p $23.95

ISBN 0-385-50943-X

LC 2003-51945

"Feisty Petie Coolbaugh and serene Rose Bundy, both 31, have been best friends for years while living in the small fishing town of Hubbard, OR. Despite the intermittent help of Petie's husband and Rose's boyfriend, they must work to support their families. They begin making soups for Soupe-rior's Caf, run by Los Angeles transplants Nadine and her twin brother, Gordon. This collaboration ignites undiscov-ered talents in both Rose and Petie. Set in the late 1980s, this first novel reverberates with a small cast of memorable, working-class characters." Libr J

Hamner, Earl

★ The **homecoming**; a novel about Spencer's Mountain. [by] Earl Hamner, Jr. Random House 1970 115p

"Fifteen-year-old Clay-Boy of 'Spencer's Mountain' is again the protagonist in this short novel set in Virginia in the early 1930's. The story takes place one snowy Christ-mas Eve while the family of nine is anxiously waiting for the father to come home from his out-of-town job. It tells of Clay-Boy's trip to the woods for a Christmas tree, of his encounter with a fabled albino deer, and of his adventures with neighbors as he searches for his father, who is delayed by the storm. This picture of everyday happenings in a small mountain community and of close family relationships amid the hardships of the Depression years is painted with sim-plicity and charm." Libr J

Hamner, Earl

Spencer's Mountain; [by] Earl Hamner, Jr. Dial Press (NY) 1961 247p

An "account of a boy's growing up in a large and impov-erished family in the Blue Ridge Mountains of Virginia. . . . His chief problems are love and the fact that his father feels that a college education is a waste of money." Publ Wkly

"A novel filled with joie de vivre, frank simplicity, a little sinning, and much human goodness." Libr J

Han, Suyin

The **enchantress**. Bantam Bks. 1985 345p

LC 84-45185

"This is an extremely well-told tale of life and love in the 18th Century. History comes alive, and there is a masterful blending of magic and science at a time when the division between the two were not so great." SLJ

Han, Suyin

Till morning comes; a novel. Bantam Bks. 1982 500p il

LC 81-19150

"Told with sensitivity, this is an engrossing story. Al-though her sympathies lie with the Communist uprising, Han does not spare that regime in depicting the purges." Libr J

Hanauer, Cathi

Gone; a novel. Cathi Hanauer. 1st Atria Books hardcover ed. Atria Books 2012 352 p. (hardcover: alk. paper) $24.99

ISBN 145162641X; 9781451626414; 9781451626421

LC 2012016486

This novel, by Cathi Hanauer, follows "Eve Adams, [who] . . . at forty-two, . . . suddenly finds herself with a growing career of her own . . . as [her husband] Eric's career sinks deeper into the slump it slipped into a few years ago. After a dinner . . . Eric drives the babysitter home and . . . doesn't come back. Eve must now shift the family in pos-sibly irreparable ways. . . ." (Publisher's note)

Hand, Dana

Deep Creek. Houghton Mifflin Harcourt 2010 308p map $25

ISBN 978-0-547237480

LC 2009-15395

"Judge Joe Vincent knows all about political capital; he knows he'll soon have zero if he prosecutes the gang of men who massacred nearly three dozen Chinese gold miners on the banks of the Snake River. After all, those Chinese were heathens, soulless; their alleged killers upstanding citizens. Why make trouble for the town of Lewiston when it's 1887 and Idaho Territory is on the verge of statehood? At times in the historical thriller 'Deep Creek,' it's tough to tell who must overcome the harshest ostracism to crack the case: Lee Loi, a private investigator whose Chinese heri-tage closes doors despite his Yale diploma; Grace Sundown, an alluring half-native mountain guide with a mysterious past; or Vincent, the stubborn, maverick small-town judge no longer willing to heed society's politics and prejudices." Seattle Times

Hand, Elizabeth, 1957-

Available dark; a thriller. Elizabeth Hand. Mi-notaur Books 2012 246 p.

ISBN 9780312585945

LC 2011032833

In this mystery novel, a "moody loner heads to Helsinki and beyond, while murder and general creepiness follow. Photographer Cass Neary likes to live under the radar. . . . When Anton Bredahl, a collector of obscure art, contacts Cass to have her verify the authenticity of some prints, the job takes her all the way to Helsinki, where she meets with . . . photographer Ilkka Kaltunnen. . . . These aren't your stan-dard point-and-shoots; they're morbid and macabre scenes of death, almost like stills from a snuff film. Cass . . . starts to grow suspicious of why Anton might want to spend so much on these pictures. . . . Cass hightails it to Reykjavik to locate her old love Quinn. Somehow, finding him enfolds her further into the creepy world she thought she left behind in Helsinki." (Kirkus)

Hand, Elizabeth, 1957-

★ **Generation** loss; a novel. Small Beer Press 2007 265p $24

ISBN 978-1-931520-21-8; 1-931520-21-6

LC 2006-102024

This is a "crossover novel, difficult to classify, uncom-fortable, spiky. Hand is one of those writers who has challenged the restrictions of genre writing. Here, she both fights with and against the conventions of the thriller genre to get at an evil deeper than its mere perpetrator. . . . So although Generation Loss moves like a thriller, it detonates with greater resound. It's a dark and beautiful novel that should not be read by anyone under the age of 30." Washington Post Book World

Hand, Elizabeth

Mortal love. Morrow 2004 364p $24.95
ISBN 0-06-105170-5

LC 2003-62398

"What lies behind the complex, even violent process that we call artistic inspiration? That is the final mystery evoked in Elizabeth Hand's ambitious and richly imagined novel. By tracing the turbulence and reverberations of that process back to its source, Mortal Love offers its readers the satisfactions of a detective thriller. Here, however, the mystery goes deeper than murder. Nothing, Hand convinces us, is quite as mysterious as art." Washington Post Book World

Handke, Peter

★ **Don** Juan; his own version. translated from the German by Krishna Winston. Farrar, Straus and Giroux 2010 101p $22
ISBN 978-0-374-14231-5; 0-374-14231-9

LC 2009-29526

Original German edition, 2004

"In this quick and airy fantasia, the quintessential womanizer becomes instead a sad and mostly passive man, possessing a certain magnetism but emphatically not a seducer, who feels pursued by time itself. Handke's multilayered structure has a sympathetic narrator relaying Don Juan's account of travel through contemporary Europe, the Middle East, and North Africa. Women everywhere are drawn to him, and in his brief affairs he drops into 'womantime,' a dreamlike state free of the usual self-consciousness and sorrow. The novel's action is obscured behind screens of philosophically tinted analysis touching on the nature of relationships, storytelling, and time. And yet the story itself is suffused with the freshness of the French countryside in which it largely takes place." New Yorker

Handke, Peter

★ The **left**-handed woman; translated by Ralph Manheim. Farrar, Straus & Giroux 1978 87p

LC 78-5568

Original German edition, 1976

"There are echoes of Beckett, Sartre, and Kafka in this chilly little novel. . . . Handke at his best handles that moribund trinity of modern themes—alienation, failure of communication and absurdity—with quirky originality." Newsweek

Handke, Peter

Repetition; translated by Ralph Manheim. Farrar, Straus & Giroux 1988 246p
ISBN 0-374-24934-2

LC 87-33065

Original German edition, 1986

"The author invests this process of self-discovery with such originality and marvelous psychological detail that

Filip's journey becomes at one with the writer's and the reader's as well." Booklist

Handler, Daniel

Adverbs. Ecco 2006 272p $23.95
ISBN 0-06-072441-2

LC 2005-52101

This novel is composed of "intertwining vignettes about love in all of its adverbial misery. Each piece, with an adverb for a title, focuses on young men and women negotiating the minefields of intimate relationships. People disappear, only to reappear in later stories skewering assumptions that were first developed in the earlier tales. . . . The stories feature two recurring images: that of the magpie picking up glittering pieces of material and depositing them in other stories, reflecting reality at different angles, and that of a catastrophic explosion—possibly natural, possibly human-made—that destroys everything and everyone in its wake." Libr J

Hanif, Muhammad

A **case** of exploding mangoes. Alfred A. Knopf 2008 323p $24
ISBN 978-0-307-26807-5; 0-307-26807-1

LC 2008-4150

"There are many reasons to read this excellent novel, and one for which it should be celebrated: Hanif has found in Zia a veritable Homer Simpson of theocratic zealotry . . . . The inevitable comparison here is to Dr. Strangelove, and just as the Kubrick film crystallized the absurdities of nuclear escalation into an archetypal cast of idiots-who-run-the-world, Mangoes provides the necessary update." N Y Observer

Hannah, Barry

★ **Long,** last, happy; new and selected stories. Grove Press 2010 459p $27.50
ISBN 978-0-8021-1968-1; 0-8021-1968-9

"'I want to sleep in her uterus with my foot hanging out.' Many such sentences await the dauntless reader in this posthumous collection by the Southern writer Barry Hannah. . . . Only four of the 31 stories here are new; the rest were culled from an almost half century long career. Fans will greet them like old friends. The uninitiated are in for a revelation. Hannah is often compared to Flannery O'Connor and William Faulkner. Despite their shared regional DNA, Hannah's style is sui generis, a poor thing but his own. An inhospitable drunk in his youth and middle age, he was also beholden to the equally demanding inebriations of language. After repeated humiliation and self-injury he beat the bottle. Lucky for us, he never kicked his other habit. He affixed rhythm to ribaldry, tone to transgression. He inspires us to follow his example and express ourselves as we see fit, political correctness be damned." Miami Herald

Hannah, Kristin

Firefly Lane; Kristin Hannah. 1st ed. St. Martin's Press 2008 479p. (hardcover) $23.95
ISBN 0312364083; 9780312364083

LC 2007040442

This book focuses on the friendship between Kate and Tully and their different life paths. "Tully's ambition to be a journalist brings her all the way to network anchor and beyond, while Kate finds love with a man who first had been smitten with Tully. The women have their problems over the years, stemming from Kate's insecurities and Tully's willingness to sacrifice anything for her career, but in the end their friendship endures when it matters." (Library Journal)

Hannah, Kristin

Fly Away; Kristin Hannah. 1st ed. St Martins Pr 2013 416 p. (hardcover) $27.99

ISBN 0312577214; 9780312577216

LC 2013009097

In this novel, by Kristin Hannah, "Tully Hart has always been larger than life, a woman fueled by big dreams and driven by memories of a painful past. She thinks she can overcome anything until her best friend, Kate Ryan, dies. Tully tries to fulfill her deathbed promise to Kate---to be there for Kate's children--but Tully knows nothing about family or motherhood or taking care of people." (Publisher's note)

Hannah, Kristin

Home again; Kristin Hannah. Fawcett Crest 1996 436 p. (pbk.) $6.99

ISBN 0449226352; 9780449226353

LC 97810570

In this book, "[w]hen movie star Angel DeMarco suffers his first heart attack on location near Seattle, his survival depends on a heart transplant. He's medevac-ed to a local hospital famed for its cardiology unit and placed under the care of Dr. Madelaine Hillyard--the pregnant girlfriend he'd abandoned 17 years earlier. Facing death, he's forced to come to terms with his misspent life and attempt to make things right with Madelaine; his saintly priest brother, Francis; and his rebellious teenaged daughter." (Publishers Weekly)

Hannah, Kristin

Home front; Kristin Hannah. St. Martin's Press 2012 390p.

ISBN 9780312577209

LC 2011033805

This novel tells the story of "Michael and Jolene Zarkades [who] have to face the pressures of everyday life---children, careers, bills, chores---even as their twelve-year marriage is falling apart. Then an unexpected deployment sends Jolene deep into harm's way and leaves defense attorney Michael at home, unaccustomed to being a single parent to their two girls. . . . In her letters home, she paints a rose-colored version of her life on the front lines, shielding her family from the truth. But war will change Jolene in ways that none of them could have foreseen. When tragedy strikes, Michael must face his darkest fear and fight a battle of his own---for everything that matters to his family." (Publisher's note)

Hannah, Kristin

On Mystic lake. Crown 1999 323p $19.95

ISBN 0-609-60249-7

LC 98-26448

Annie Colwater "finds herself abandoned after 20 years by a faithless husband and a college-bound daughter. Having no identity of her own after spending her life nurturing them, she returns to her native Mystic, a logging town in Washington State. There she finds her old high school beau in crisis

after his wife's suicide. His depression prevents him from caring for his small daughter, Izzy, who is also emotionally troubled. Annie is able to find meaning again through nurturing others." Libr J

"Never one to gush, {Hannah} is more than ever disciplined in her writing, and the result is a clean, deep thrust into the reader's heart." Publ Wkly

Hannah, Kristin

★ Winter garden. St. Martin's Press 2010 394p $26.99

ISBN 978-0-312-36412-0; 0-312-36412-1

LC 2009-39230

"This tearjerker weaves a convincing historical novel and contemporary family drama with elements of romance. It is sure to please fans of Danielle Steel, Luanne Rice, and Nicholas Sparks." Libr J

Hannah, Sophie

The cradle in the grave. Penguin Books 2011 456p pa $15

ISBN 978-0-14-311994-4; 0-14-311994-X

LC 2011-14075

First published 2010 in the United Kingdom with title: Room swept white

The novel "concludes in a fashion that manages to be both surprising and, in retrospect, somewhat inevitable, which is further testament to Hannah's storytelling prowess. The author has certainly chosen to work with a lot of ingredients here, and yet the subtlety with which she does so makes for a hearty literary meal-one in which each part feels as if it's essential. If good books are those that entertain while simultaneously provoking thought, then this one certainly qualifies." Hartford Examiner

Hannah, Sophie

Little face. Soho Press 2007 310p $25

ISBN 978-1-56947-468-6; 1-56947-468-0

LC 2007-5185

First published 2006 in the United Kingdom

"Upon her return home from her first solo outing after giving birth, Alice Fancourt makes a horrifying discovery— her infant daughter has been replaced with another child, similar of feature to be sure, but not similar enough to deceive a new mother. Alice's husband, David, for his part, is convinced that Alice is delusional; her mother-inlaw, Vivienne, with whom the young couple lives, remains carefully neutral, but it soon becomes evident that she is pursuing her own agenda, at odds with Alice's. Things muddy up considerably when Alice disappears with the baby, calling into question once again the mysterious death of David's first wife. Two narrative voices move the story forward, Alice's and that of Detective Simon Waterhouse." BookPage

"A terrifying mystery of manipulation, counter-manipulation and, finally, astounding revelation. It's a haunting story told with bewitching skill." Scotsman

Hannah, Sophie

The wrong mother. Penguin Books 2009 415p pa $15

ISBN 978-0-14-311630-1; 0-14-311630-4

LC 2009-27521

First published 2008 in the United Kingdom with title: The point of rescue

"Shockingly (and refreshingly) blunt riffs about the violent emotions of motherhood and the familial yearnings of men, along with chilling and darkly funny revelations about lust and loyalty, make this novel one of the season's most absorbing reads." O magazine

Hannan, Chris

Missy. Farrar, Straus and Giroux 2008 304p map $24

ISBN 978-0-374-19983-8; 0-374-19983-3

LC 2007-37475

This novel "traverses the 19th-century American Southwest, a setting colorfully filled with opium smugglers, mule thieves, natives, and Civil War stragglers. Dropped in the center of the action is Dol McQueen, a brassy teenage prostitute struggling to hang on to a fortune in stolen opium. Hannan writes this character with impeccable style, crafting a vivid portrait whose emotional notes ring true. One cannot help but root for Dol as she withdraws onto the wagon trail, her pursuers ever near. This is a fantastic debut novel." Libr J

Hansen, Brooks

The **monsters** of St. Helena. Farrar, Straus & Giroux 2002 306p $24

ISBN 0-374-27019-8

LC 2002-23433

This novel speculates on Napoleon's "second exile on the remote Atlantic island of St. Helena, where he spent his remaining years dictating his memoirs. Because his island residence is incomplete, the emperor-turned-prisoner stays with the Balcombe family, whose 14-year-old daughter Betsy befriends him. . . . As a contrast, the island's haunted history is revealed through its slaves, who all know the story of St. Helena's first exile, fallen nobleman Fernando Lopez, and his connection to the island." Libr J

Hansen, Erik Fosnes

Tales of protection; translated from the Norwegian by Nadia Christensen. Farrar, Straus & Giroux 2002 500p

ISBN 0-374-27240-9

Original Norwegian edition, 1998

"Hansen favors the Russian doll approach to stories, in which one story is nested inside another. His 'serialism' is romantic in the deepest sense—allegories and narratives contain the deep structure of the world, while math and science are merely the mutable surface. The craft of 19th-century fiction and the complexity of 20th-century thought make this a gloriously rewarding novel." Publ Wkly

Hansen, Joseph

★ A **country** of old men; the last Dave Brandstetter mystery. Viking 1991 177p

LC 90-50550

"While investigating the murder of a drug-dealing musician and the kidnapping of a little boy who witnessed the killing, the gay detective stubbornly ignores the conspicuously poor state of his own health. But even as he drags his creaky bones on an exhausting and dangerous hunt for the killer, his fine, strong mind keeps turning to thoughts of

mortality. . . . A cool stylist who never loses control over his emotional voice, Mr. Hansen trusts his lifelike characters to earn our compassion." NY Times Book Rev

Hansen, Joseph

★ **Early** graves; a Dave Brandstetter mystery. Mysterious Press 1987 184p

LC 87-15178

"Gay detective Dave Brandstetter tracks down a serial killer whose victims have all been young men dying of AIDS. Dave, in his 60s, has just returned to L.A. from a business trip, having been met at the airport by his young ex-lover, TV reporter Cecil, when he discovers the body of real-estate developer Drew Dodge on his porch steps. The man's death becomes linked to a string of stabbing murders, and it also becomes clear that he was killed first and then dropped at Dave's." Publ Wkly

Hansen, Joseph

Gravedigger; a Dave Brandstetter mystery. Holt, Rinehart & Winston 1982 183p

LC 81-6381

Insurance sleuth Dave Brandstetter "investigates the possible murder of a runaway teenage girl, who may have died by her own involvement with drugs, a strange cult, and the wrong kind of people. The missing girl's father, a corrupt lawyer engulfed by scandal, has run away, too, leaving Brandstetter with two cold trails and a lot of questions." Booklist

Hansen, Joseph

The **little** dog laughed; a Dave Brandstetter mystery. Holt & Co. 1986 184p

LC 86-12115

"Called in to investigate the death claims filed on the shooting demise of a globe-striding political journalist, insurance sleuth Brandstetter gets embroiled in international skulduggery. The writer was, of course, no suicide, and his death is linked to that of a young Latino sans green card who is from a Central American republic in turmoil." Booklist

Hansen, Ron

★ The **assassination** of Jesse James by the coward Robert Ford. Knopf 1983 304p

ISBN 0-394-51647-8

LC 83-47851

"Hansen's Jesse is in no way romanticized; his interest derives from the complexity of his psychopathology. The Jesse that emerges here is prematurely decrepit; he'll murder when he doesn't need to, but he reads his Bible and talks about God's peace. Canny, intuitive, he seems to welcome the disciple who will betray him, even gives him the pistol for the job. . . . The novel works not despite our knowledge of what will happen, but because of it a sense of fatality hangs over every scene." Newsweek

Hansen, Ron

★ **Atticus**; a novel. HarperCollins Pubs. 1996 247p

ISBN 0-06-018217-2

LC 95-38450

"This is a didactic novel. It says that simplicity, purity and intelligence are good qualities to have. . . . It names great virtues and then looks at them glancingly, from all directions, finding them in unexpected forms. Mr. Hansen writes vigorously, and like an angel—so much so that 'Atticus' may end up giving didacticism a good name." N Y Times Book Rev

Hansen, Ron

Exiles. Farrar, Straus and Giroux 2008 227p $23
ISBN 978-0-374-15097-6; 0-374-15097-4

LC 2007-46836

An historical novel "about 19th-century poet Gerard Manley Hopkins. . . . [It] zeroes in on one short period of Hopkins' life — circa 1875, when, as a Jesuit seminarian in Wales, he read about the death of five nuns in the sinking of a steamship and wrote what became a famous poem, 'The Wreck of the Deutschland.' Hansen conveys a man conflicted by his callings as both a spiritual vessel and a full-blooded artist." Entertainment Wkly

Hansen, Ron

Hitler's niece; a novel. HarperFlamingo 1999 310p
ISBN 0-06-019419-7

LC 99-12656

"On September 18, 1931 Angelika (Geli) Raubal, the niece of Adolph Hitler, was found dead in her room in her uncle's flat, his pistol lying nearby. . . . Hansen's historically based novel offers one plausible scenario, that Hitler himself murdered her in a fit of anger over her attempts to escape his smothering jealousy. Using a variety of sources, including the memoirs and testimony of several of the principals involved, he attempts to dissect the nature of their relationship and show how such a conclusion is reasonable." Libr J

"Hansen's insightful, brilliantly interpretative, and frightening novel does more to illuminate the welter of evil that fueled Hitler than a dozen biographies." Booklist

Hansen, Ron

Isn't it romantic? an entertainment. HarperCollins Pubs. 2003 198p $17.95
ISBN 0-06-051766-2

LC 2002-69082

"This is a preposterous plot, and at its best, 'Isnt It Romantic?' zips along like a Preston Sturges movie. Hansen slicks down his prose so the sentences are swift, and he punctuates them with a dry wit and some genuinely droll ripostes." N Y Times Book Rev

Hansen, Ron

★ **Mariette** in ecstasy. Burlingame Bks. 1991 179p
ISBN 0-06-018214-8

LC 90-56362

"The novel pulls its taut plot-thread smartly along from start to finish, weaving flash-forward patches of dialogue from the investigation of Mariette's 'case' into the unfolding action of her entry into the life of the convent. The finale is a stunner." N Y Times Book Rev

Hansen, Ron

A **wild** surge of guilty passion; a novel. Scribner 2011 256p $25
ISBN 978-1-4516-1755-9

LC 2011-05571

This "is a gripping, entertaining novel. You can feel Hansen's fascination with this story — and his delight at the wealth of material; the memoirs written by both murderers, the news and court reports, the testimony of lesser characters, the secondary material that flowed for years following the trial and execution of Ruth and Gray. The restraint is evident in his measured tone — this is fiction but the author still relies on the factual material — the times, dates, places." Los Angeles Times

Harbach, Chad

The **art** of fielding; Chad Harbach. Little, Brown and Co. 2011 512 p. $25.99
ISBN 0316126691; 9780316126694

LC 2011-14912

In this novel, college shortstop phenom Henry Skrimshander accidentally beans teammate Owen Dunne with a misplaced throw . . . start[ing] a chain reaction on the campus of Westish College. . . . Owen is solicitously visited in the hospital by school president Guert Affenlight, a widower, who falls in love with the seductive gay student. . . . Affenlight's daughter, Pella, after a failed marriage in San Francisco, returns to become part of a love triangle with Henry and Mike Schwartz, the team captain and Henry's unofficial mentor. And just when Henry's hopes of playing for the St. Louis Cardinals come within reach, he suffers a crisis of confidence, even as his team makes a rousing run at the championship. (Publishers Weekly)

"Henry Skrimshander—the gawky, blank-faced star of Westish College's overachieving baseball squad—is a flawless shortstop, the definition of defensive perfection. He's headed for greatness, or at least a major-league contract; big-time scouts and agents are starting to hover. But then . . . something happens. Henry's brain betrays him. He loses confidence, botching even the most routine throws. He has no idea why, and nothing seems to help. . . . Harbach spins this simple premise into a wide-ranging book about desire and loss, friendship and loneliness. It's about baseball, of course, but also campus life, dishwashing, and Moby-Dick (you'll find yourself reaching for a copy to brush up on the famous "Lee Shore" chapter). Most of Harbach's characters are desperately chasing something. Henry's mentor, Mike Schwartz, covets a national championship and a law career. Westish president Guert Affenlight is infatuated with Henry's brilliant roommate, Owen Dunne. Affenlight's daughter, Pella, longs for a fresh start after a bad marriage. Their struggles get tangled up in and amplified by Henry's collapse and make for a rich, engrossing story." Entertainment Wkly

Harding, Georgina

Painter of silence; Georgina Harding. Bloomsbury 2012 312 p. (hardcover: alk. paper) $26.00
ISBN 1608197700; 9781608197705

LC 2011042284

This book, which was "shortlisted for the Orange Prize for Fiction . . . [is] set in Romania and span[s] several decades up the early 1950s". It follows "Safta . . . a daughter of an aristocratic family . . . [whose] past returns in the form of Augustin, a deaf mute from her childhood . . . [who] is found outside a hospital in a provincial town, where she works as a nurse." (Times Literary Supplement)

Harding, Paul
Tinkers. Bellevue Literary Press 2008 191p $14.95
ISBN 9781934137123 pa; 1-934137-12-X pa
LC 2008-39887

"This compact, adamantine début dips in and out of the consciousness of a New England patriarch named George Washington Crosby as he lies dying on a hospital bed in his living room. . . . The story traces Crosby's life back to his hardscrabble Maine childhood, where his father was a tinker and travelling salesman who suffered from epileptic seizures. Crosby's emotional life is dominated by his father's abandonment of the family on learning that his wife was planning to have him institutionalized, but the most memorable parts of Harding's novel may be his depiction of a nineteenth-century landscape complete with mule-drawn carts and 'frozen wood so brittle that it rang when you split it.' In Harding's skillful evocation, Crosby's life, seen from its final moments, becomes a mosaic of memories." New Yorker

Hardwick, Mollie
★ The Duchess of Duke Street; a novel. Holt, Rinehart & Winston 1977 303p
ISBN 0-03-018291-3
LC 76-29903

First published 1976 in the United Kingdom in two volumes with title The Duchess of Duke Street: Book 1: The way up; Book 2: The golden years

An "adaptation of a BBC television series. . . . The setting is 1900 London. Heroine Louisa Leyton sets out to be the best cook in England and ends up running a residential hotel and a catering service. The cast includes: Edward, Prince of Wales, whose interest in Luisa goes beyond her culinary skills; Augustus Trotter, who becomes Louisa's husband for propriety's sake and assists her as butler; and the Honorable Charles Tyrrel, who befriends Louisa in her post-Edward days. Although the episodic format is still evident in this novelization, it does not impair readability. There is enough adventure and humor here to entertain the reader willing to settle for a light-hearted if slightly unbelievable story." Libr J

Hardwick, Mollie
Malice domestic. St. Martin's Press 1986 218p
LC 86-11376

This is the first novel featuring "Doran Fairweather, a humorously perceptive antiques dealer, and her love, the Reverend Chelmarsh, both of whom live in the isolated village of Abbotsbourne, Kent. A wealthy bachelor takes over the village's long-deserted great house. Events move from cozy to chilling when a series of deaths ensues, including a teen suicide. Graceful writing embellishes this stunning tale of evil." Booklist

Hardwick, Mollie
Parson's pleasure. St. Martin's Press 1987 199p
LC 87-4437

This novel takes Doran Fairweather "to Warwickshire to track down the theft of priceless antiques from a rather eccentric elderly member of the aristocracy, Lady Timberlake. What starts off as a working holiday with her boyfriend, the prudish Rodney Chelmarsh, quickly turns serious when one of the leads Fairweather is investigating, a gypsy antiques dealer, is brutally murdered. Chelmarsh is the first to realize that Fairweather's own life may be in jeopardy. Hardwick has managed to breathe fresh life into this fairly conventional mystery. Everything is vaguely familiar, from the cast of dotty characters to the locale, but this only adds to the book's charm." Publ Wkly

Hardy, Thomas
★ Far from the madding crowd; with an etching by H. Macbeth-Raeburn and a map of Wessex. Knopf 1991 xxxiii, 243p $22
ISBN 0-679-40576-3
LC 91-52978

First published 1874
"Bathsheba Everdene is loved by Gabriel Oak, a young farmer who becomes bailiff of the farm she inherits; by William Boldwood, who owns a neighboring farm; and by Sergeant Troy, a handsome inconsiderate young adventurer. She marries Troy, who mistreats her and squanders her money. When he leaves her and is presumed drowned at sea, Bathsheba becomes engaged to Boldwood. Troy, however, reappears, and is murdered by Boldwood, who goes mad as a result of his action and is sent to a mental institution. Bathsheba then marries Gabriel, the steadiest and most faithful of her three suitors." Reader's Ency. 4th edition

Hardy, Thomas
★ Jude the obscure. Knopf 1992 518p $20
ISBN 0-679-40993-9
LC 92-52925

First published 1895
"Jude Fawley, a poor villager, wants to enter the divinity school at Christminster (Oxford University). Sidetracked by Arabella Donn, an earthy country girl who pretends to be pregnant by him, Jude marries her and is then deserted. He earns a living as a stonemason at Christminster; there he falls in love with his independent-minded cousin, Sue Bridehead. Out of a sense of obligation, Sue marries the schoolmaster Phillotson, who has helped her. Unable to bear living with Phillotson, she returns to live with Jude and eventually bears his children out of wedlock. Their poverty and the weight of society's disapproval begin to take a toll on Sue and Jude. . . . The novel's sexual frankness shocked the public, as did Hardy's criticisms of marriage, the university system, and the church." Merriam-Webster's Ency of Lit

Hardy, Thomas
The Mayor of Casterbridge; with an introduction by Craig Raine. Knopf 1993 362p map $18
ISBN 0-679-42035-5
LC 92-54297

First published 1886. Variant title: The life and death of the Mayor of Casterbridge

"Michael Henchard, a hay-trusser, gets drunk at a fair and sells his wife and child for 5 guineas to a sailor, Newson. When sober again he takes a solemn vow not to touch alcohol for 20 years. By his energy and acumen he becomes rich, respected, and eventually the mayor of Casterbridge. After 18 years his wife returns, supposing Newson dead, and is reunited with her husband. She brings with her her daughter Elizabeth-Jane, and Henchard is led to believe that she is his child, whereas she is in fact Newson's. Through a combination of unhappy circumstances, and the impulsive obstinacy of Henchard, troubles accumulate." Oxford Companion to Engl Lit. 6th edition

Hardy, Thomas
★ The **return** of the native. Knopf 1992 xxxix, 497p map $22
ISBN 0-679-41730-3
LC 92-52901
First published 1878
"The novel is set on Egdon Heath, a barren moor in the fictional Wessex in southwestern England. The native of the title is Clym Yeobright, who has returned to the area to become a schoolmaster after a successful but, in his opinion, a shallow career as a jeweler in Paris. He and his cousin Thomasin exemplify the traditional way of life, while Thomasin's husband, Damon Wildeve, and Clym's wife, Eustacia Vye, long for the excitement of city life. Disappointed that Clym is content to remain on the heath, Eustacia, willful and passionate, rekindles her affair with the reckless Damon. After a series of coincidences Eustacia comes to believe that she is responsible for the death of Clym's mother. Convinced that fate has doomed her to cause others pain, Eustacia flees and is drowned (by accident or intent). Damon drowns trying to save her." Merriam-Webster's Ency of Lit

Hardy, Thomas
★ **Tess** of the D'Urbervilles; with an introduction by Patricia Ingham. Knopf 1991 xlviii, 472p map $22
ISBN 0-679-40586-0
LC 91-52998
First published in complete form 1891
"The tragic history of a woman betrayed. . . . Tess the author contends, is sinned against, but not a sinner; her tragedy is the work of tyrannical circumstances and of the evil deeds of others in the past and the present, and more particularly of two men's baseness, the seducer, and the well-meaning intellectual who married her. . . . The pastoral surroundings, the varying aspects of field, river, sky, serve to deepen the pathos of each stage in the heroine's calamities, or to add beauty and dignity to her tragic personality." Baker. Guide to the Best Fic

Hardy, Thomas
Under the greenwood tree; edited with an introduction and notes by Simon Gatrell. 2009 xxxiii, 218p pa $10.95
ISBN 9780199538515; 0199538514
LC 2009-290549
First published 1872
"The first of the Wessex novels proper, the common groundwork of which is a very vivid delineation of the

people of Dorset and the neighbouring counties, and of the natural life and scenery. . . . An idyll of village life, in which the members of a carrier's family and the village life choir, a gathering of rustic oddities, furnish a sort of comic chorus to the love-affairs of a rustic boy and girl." Baker. Guide to the Best Fic

Hardy, Thomas
Wessex tales. Wordsworth 1995 189p map pa $7.95
ISBN 0-19-283558-0
First published 1888

Harington, Donald
★ **Enduring**. Toby Press 2009 498p $24.95
ISBN 978-1-59264-256-4; 1-59264-256-X
This novel "follows the life of Latha Bourne, a resident of Stay More, a small fictional hamlet in the Arkansas Ozarks. Essentially, the narrative is the 106-year-old Latha's life story. She grew up in poverty and was a vibrant and curious child who always asked questions. As she matures into adolescence, she attends the local school and begins to explore her awaking sexuality. At one point, she becomes pregnant and goes to stay with her sister in Little Rock. After the baby is born, her sister has Latha declared incompetent as a mother and has her committed to a psychiatric hospital, where she remains for several years. Finally she escapes and wanders the roads until she meets a wealthy woman, Mildred Cardwell, who gives her a job as a servant. She stays for seven years and reads voraciously from Mrs. Cardwell's extensive library. Finally, she returns home and settles down. Eventually she is reunited with her daughter and, over time, becomes the respected sage of Stay More. When the novel ends, she has withdrawn from the mere ghost of a town to become a hermit." Historical Novel Society
"Elegiac and complex—a feast of Southerly words that will please Harington's many admirers." Kirkus

Harington, Donald
The **pitcher** shower. Toby Press 2005 202p $22.95
ISBN 1-59264-123-7
LC 2006-540298
This "tale of a late-blooming loner finds Harington circling back around the Ozarks town of Stay More, whose lives and times he's faithfully chronicled for a good many years now. Landon 'Hoppy' Boyd is a young projectionist– or 'pitcher shower,' as he calls himself–and Stay More is both hometown and hub on his circuit of the pre-television era sticks. He calls himself Hoppy because he only shows Hopalong Cassidy features, plus a childhood accident left him with a limp. . . . This ultimate outsider's life changes both for better and worse when he picks up a stowaway and then loses his movies to a roving preacher. But this is a novel about the art of storytelling as much as it is about Hoppy himself." Booklist

Harington, Donald
With. Toby Press 2004 491p $19.95
ISBN 1-59264-050-8
"With is as whimsical as a paper-doll show while being deeply rooted in the earth; it gives the Garden of Eden myth

a happy ending, and should find the wide readership that Harington so richly deserves." Washington Post Book World

Harkaway, Nick, 1972-

Angelmaker; by Nick Harkaway. Alfred A. Knopf 2012 496 p. $26.95

ISBN 9780307743626; 9780307595959

LC 2011028261

This book tells the story of Joe Spork, an antique clock repairman who "has turned his back on his family's mobster history and aims to live a quiet life. That orderly existence is suddenly upended when Joe activates a particularly unusual clockwork mechanism. . . . It's a 1950s doomsday machine. Having triggered it, Joe now faces the wrath of both the British government and a diabolical South Asian dictator who is also [his client] Edie's old arch-nemesis. . . . With Joe's once-quiet world suddenly overrun by mad monks, psychopathic serial killers, scientific geniuses and threats to the future of conscious life in the universe, he realizes that the only way to survive is to muster the courage to fight, help Edie complete a mission she abandoned years ago and pick up his father's old gun." (Publisher's note)

Harkaway, Nick, 1972-

The **gone**-away world. Alfred A. Knopf 2008 497p $24.95

ISBN 978-0-307-26886-0; 0-307-26886-1

LC 2008-8701

This novel "is set in a dystopian future where humanity huddles in the shadow of the Jorgmund Pipe. The ragtag bunch of heroes are sent to put out a fire on the Pipe, a mission both dangerous and imperative, since the Pipe, like a vast futuristic Glade room-freshener, releases the only substance that keeps the psychic stinks and foul odours of this post-apocalyptic world at bay. On the way there, the unnamed narrator reminisces about his upbringing, college days, military service, the Go Away Bombs that created their surreal present, and above all his friend Gonzo, to whom he's always felt closer than a brother. Somehow their story brings in ninjas, first loves, pirate-kings, mime-artists, human monsters and, well, monster monsters. . . . The revelation of Gonzo's relationship to his nameless best friend (and the ways in which Harkaway keeps on teasing around us not knowing his name is one of the novel's joys) is both unexpected and obvious. The Gone-Away World is brakes-off fiction." Scotsman

Harkness, Deborah E.

A **discovery** of witches; a novel. Viking 2011 579p $28.95

ISBN 978-0-670-02241-0; 0-670-02241-1

LC 2010-30425

"A riveting tale full of romance and danger that will have you on the edge of your seat, yet its chief strength lies in the wonderfully rich and ingenious mythology underlying the story. Entwining strands of science and history, Harkness creates a fresh explanation for how such creatures could arise that is so credible, you'll have to keep reminding yourself this is fiction." BookPage

Harkness, Deborah

Shadow of night; Deborah Harkness. Viking 2012 584 p. (hardcover) $28.95; (paperback) $17.00

ISBN 9780670023486; 0670023485; 9780143123620

LC 2012005843

In this sequel, newlywed "vampire/scientist Matthew de Clermont" and "historian/untrained witch Diana Bishop" time-travel "to Elizabethan England so Diana can study witchcraft. . . . There, they hope to retrieve magical manuscript Ashmole 782, last seen in Oxford's 21st-century Bodleian library. Diana gets in touch with her inner firedrake, Matthew with his father, but they can't find a tutor for ages, and they can't rescue the manuscript without a trip to Prague." (Publishers Weekly)

Harlan, Thomas

House of reeds. Tor Bks. 2004 414p map $25.95

ISBN 0-7653-0193-8

LC 2003-57060

"Gretchen Anderssen and her team are shunted from long-overdue leave to the investigation of a rumored First Sun artifact on the obscure planet Jagan. There they land in the middle of a 'flowery war' arranged by the priests to improve the emperor's youngest son, Tezozomoc's, reputation. And Gretchen can't get a permit for the main site on Jagan, because of university politics and the archaeologist already working at it. But then she gets a tip about one city's oldest building, the House of Reeds. She befriends an aging member of the other species present, though also nonnative, on Jagan. He is a former gardener, and with him she enters the House of Reeds. . . . The mystery of the longgone forerunners of the empire Gretchen knows develops grippingly." Booklist

Harlem Renaissance: five novels of the 1920s; Rafia Zafar, editor. Library of America 2011 867p $35

ISBN 978-1-59853-099-5; 1-59853-099-2

This collection "leads off with Jean Toomer's Cane (1923), a unique fusion of fiction, poetry, and drama rooted in Toomer's experiences as a teacher in Georgia. . . . Claude McKay's Home to Harlem (1928), whose freewheeling, impressionistic, bawdy kaleidoscope of Jazz Age nightlife made it a best seller, traces the picaresque adventures of Jake, a World War I veteran, within and beyond Harlem. Nella Larsen's Quicksand (1928), the poignant, nuanced psychological portrait of a woman caught between the two worlds of her mixed Scandinavian and African American heritage; Jessie Redmon Fauset's Plum Bun (1928), the richly detailed account of a young art student's struggles to advance her career in a society full of obstacles both overt and insidiously concealed; and Wallace Thurman's The Blacker the Berry (1929), with its anguished, provocative look at prejudice and exclusion as it tells of a new arrival in Harlem searching for love, each in its distinct way testifies to the enduring power of the Harlem ferment." Publisher's note

Harlem Renaissance: four novels of the 1930s; Rafia Zafar, editor. Library of America 848p $35

ISBN 978-1-59853-101-5; 1-59853-101-8

"Langston Hughes's Not Without Laughter (1931)—the poet's only novel, an elegiac, elegantly realized coming-of-age tale suffused with childhood memories of Missouri and Kansas—follows a young man from his rural origins to the big city. George S. Schuyler's Black No More (1931), a satire founded on the science-fiction premise of a wonder drug permitting blacks to change their race, savagely caricatures public figures white and black alike in its raucous, carnivalesque send-up of American racial attitudes. Considered the first detective story by an African American writer, Rudolph Fisher's The Conjure-Man Dies (1932) is a mystery that comically mixes and reverses stereotypes, placing a Harvard-educated African 'conjureman' at the center of a phantasmagoric charade of deaths and disappearances. Black Thunder (1936), Arna Bontemps's stirring fictional recreation of Gabriel Prosser's 1800 slave revolt, which, though unsuccessful, shook Jefferson's Virginia to its core, marks a turn from aestheticism toward political militance in its exploration of African American history." Publisher's note

Harman, Patricia

The **midwife** of Hope River; a novel. by Patricia Harman. HarperCollins 2012 382 p.
ISBN 0062198890; 9780062198891

LC 2012010944

This historical novel, by Patricia Harman, follows "[m]idwife Patience Murphy. . . . Working in the hardscrabble conditions of Appalachia during the Depression, Patience takes the jobs that no one else wants, helping those most in need--and least likely to pay. She knows a successful midwifery practice must be built on a foundation of openness and trust--but the secrets Patience is keeping are far too intimate and fragile for her to ever let anyone in." (Publisher's note)

Harms, Kelly

The **Good** Luck Girls of Shipwreck Lane; Kelly Harms. St. Martin's Press 2013 304 p. $24.99
ISBN 1250011388; 9781250011381

LC 2013003728

In this novel by Kelly Harms "the HomeSweetHome network has just announced that Janine Brown of Davenport, Iowa, is the big winner of its Free House Sweepstakes, and the prize is a . . . dream home in Maine. The network has no idea, however, that two Janine Browns live in Davenport, and they couldn't be more different. While the logistics surrounding the dual contest winners are resolved, Janey and Nean find that they share so much more than the same name and hometown." (Publisher's note)

Harper, Karen

Fall from pride. Mira Books 2011 342p pa $14.95
ISBN 978-0-7783-1249-9

"Sarah Kauffman is an artist who paints murals on barns in her Amish community. When one of the barns mysteriously burns down, the local papers are quick to print the story. State arson inspector Nate MacKenzie drives down to Columbus to work on the case. He and Sarah make an unusual duo—Nate, the outsider with little knowledge of Amish culture, and Sarah, the Amish woman who often feels like an outsider in her own village. As they discover clues about the

crime, they also come to know more and more about one another. . . . Readers will likely enjoy a trip into the heart of Ohio's famed religious community and may be tempted to find out what lies ahead for this unlikely crime-solving couple." Publ Wkly

Harper, Karen

The **Poyson** garden. Delacorte Press 1999 310p
ISBN 0-385-33283-1

LC 98-36420

"Elizabeth Tudor, daughter of Henry VIII and Anne Boleyn, bides her time as her half-sister, Queen Mary I, burns heretics and sickens in the year 1558. Elizabeth's time may be short, however: a murderer, possibly backed by Mary, is poisoning anyone related to the Boleyn family. . . . Closely guarded at Hatfield by Thomas Pope and his wife, Beatrice, Elizabeth nonetheless determines to uncover the mysterious veiled woman behind the poisonings." Publ Wkly

"Elizabeth's active role may strain credulity a bit, but this one is great fun all the same." Booklist

Harper, Karen

The **queene's** Christmas. Thomas Dunne Books 2003 287p map $24.95
ISBN 0-312-30175-8

LC 2003-46822

"It is the Christmas season of 1564, and Elizabeth wants her subjects to enjoy the holidays while she attempts to outwit her devious Catholic cousin, Mary Queen of Scots, who is plotting to steal the throne of England. Elizabeth has planned an elaborate holiday feast, but the preparations go awry when Master Hodge Thatcher, Dresser of the Queene's Privy Kitchen, is found hanging in his workroom adorned with the peacock feathers meant for decorating the roasted bird. Elizabeth must solve the crime before she becomes another victim. The wonderful historical detail mixed with intrigue and authentic Elizabethan recipes enliven this story." Booklist

Harper, Karen

The **tidal** poole; an Elizabeth I mystery. Delacorte Press 2000 290p
ISBN 0-385-33284-X

LC 99-43315

"During her coronation procession into the city of London, Elizabeth I finds herself in the midst of crime and political intrigue. The murders of a lady of the court and another victim may be part of a plot to overthrow her government. This mystery full of scheming Tudors, Seymours, and Dudleys is a page-turner based on historical sources." Booklist

Harrar, George

The **spinning** man. Putnam 2003 341p $24.95
ISBN 0-399-14983-X

LC 2002-74532

"A graceful and subtle writer, Harrar invites us to identify with the philosopher's struggles to maintain his mental equilibrium, even as the novel dangles the possibility that the mind might not always be in control of the body's behaviors." N Y Times Book Rev

Harries, Ann

Manly pursuits. Bloomsbury Pub. 1999 339p $24.95

    ISBN 1-58234-019-6

"This is a fascinating look at the turn of the last century, the infancy of industrialization, and the decline of imperialism, with hints of the decadence of the sexually repressed Victorian era." Booklist

Harrigan, Stephen

Challenger Park. Knopf 2006 397p $24.95

    ISBN 0-375-41205-0

                    LC 2005-49403

"Harrigan makes his all-too-human characters—caring, needy, shortsighted, world-weary, salty-tongued—sympathetic without hiding the personal abysses into which they are drifting, and that is no small accomplishment." Fort Worth Star-Telegram

Harrigan, Stephen

The gates of the Alamo; a novel. Knopf 2000 581p $25

    ISBN 0-679-44717-2

                    LC 99-33437

This novel is set during the struggle between Texans and Mexicans for the Alamo in 1836. Harrigan concentrates "on fictional characters caught up in a struggle not of their own making—an American naturalist, a female innkeeper and her son, {and} Mexican soldiers." Newsweek

    Includes bibliographical references

Harrington, Laura

Alice Bliss; Laura Harrington. Pamela Dorman Books/Viking 2011 306p. $25.95

    ISBN 978-0-670-02278-6; 0-670-02278-0; 9780143121114

                    LC 201049089

This book tells the story of a teenaged girl, Alice Bliss, who "learns that her father, Matt, is being deployed to Iraq. . . . Alice idolizes her father. . . . When he ships out, Alice is faced with finding a way to fill the emptiness he has left behind." (Publisher's note)

"Playwright and lyricist Harrington transforms her one-act musical Alice Unwrapped into a moving debut about loss and survival. Fifteen-year-old Alice has always been closer to her father (they share a love of working with their hands) than to her mother, but when she needs him the most, he's deployed to Iraq. Alice flexes her independence by claiming his workshop as her own and wearing his shirt. She feels a mix of responsibility and resentment toward her precocious little sister and her disengaged mother, and pursues typical teenage rites of passage while fearing the arrival of bad news. When it comes, Alice inspires her family to preserve her father's traditions and to craft new ones in his honor." Publ Wkly

Harrington, Matthew Joseph

The goliath stone; Larry Niven and Matthew Joseph Harrington. Tor 2013 320 p. (hardcover) $24.99

    ISBN 0765333236; 9780765333230

                    LC 2012049701

In this novel, by Larry Niven and Matthew Joseph Harrington, "Doctor Toby Glyer has effected miracle cures with the use of nanotechnology. But Glyer's controversial nanites are more than just the latest technological advance, they are a new form of life. . . . Twenty-five years ago, . . . [a] mission took nanomachinery out to divert an Earth-crossing asteroid. . . . Now, a much, much larger asteroid is on a collision course with Earth--and the Briareus nanites may be responsible." (Publisher's note)

Harrington, Rebecca

Penelope; [a novel] Rebecca Harrington. Vintage Contemporaries 2012 274 p. (pbk.) $14.95

    ISBN 030795031X; 9780307950314; 9780307950338

                    LC 2012003449

This novel by Rebecca Harrington offers a "bildungsroman chronicling the titular character's freshman year at Harvard, and all the supplementary standard collegiate fare--drunken parties and regrettable hookups, pretentious extracurriculars, friends with and without benefits, an incessant pressure to succeed, and the #1 question: Who am I?" (Publishers Weekly)

Harris, Charlaine

Dead reckoning. Ace Books 2011 325p $27.95

    ISBN 978-0-441-02031-7; 0-441-02031-3

                    LC 2010-54261

"God knows it's not easy being Sookie Stackhouse. The telepathic barmaid at the center of so many supernatural occurrences in the sleepy burg of Bon Temps, La., seems to spend most of her time fending off murderous attackers or the romantic advances of vampires, werewolves, shapeshifters and the like. . . . Her relationship with handsome Viking vampire Eric Northman is still acutely complicated — and old flame Bill Compton and werewolf Alcide Herveaux haven't stopped proclaiming their love for Sookie either. And that just might be part of the problem. Certainly, some things have changed in Bon Temps. Right out of the gate, Ms. Stackhouse loses some of her blond locks when her boss Sam Merlotte's bar is fire-bombed, adding insult to the already critical injury of losing business to Vic's Redneck Roadhouse, the new joint in town. Eric is forcing Pam, the vampire he made, to keep a troubling bit of knowledge from Sookie, even as she learns some personal, painful secrets about her beloved late grandmother Adele and comes into possession of a rare magical object called a 'cluviel dor.' " Los Angeles times Book Rev

Harris, Charlaine

A secret rage. Severn House 2011 198p $27.95

    ISBN 978-0-7278-8026-0

    First published 1984 by Houghton Mifflin

"Former model Nickie returns to her hometown to finish college and moves in with her best friend from boarding school. But coming home means more than going back to school, as she must deal with her estranged parents and confront her long-suppressed feelings for her best friend's older brother. Matters are complicated by the presence of a rapist on campus who attacks both Nickie and her advisor. Convinced that the assailant is someone she knows, Nickie sets out to track him down. Mixing a touch of romance with a suspenseful thriller plot, Harris turns out a top-notch read with wide appeal to genre fans." Booklist

Harris, Deborah Turner

The **temple** and the stone; [by] Katherine Kurtz and Deborah Turner Harris. Warner Bks. 1998 456p

ISBN 0-446-52260-0

LC 98-14344

"Following a vision that foretells the formation of a new Temple of Solomon in Scotland, Brother Arnault de Saint Clair, a member of a secret magical order within the Order of the Knights Templar, becomes involved in the struggle for Scottish independence. The authors . . . vividly re-create one of Scottish history's most compelling periods, as Robert the Bruce and William Wallace share the limelight with fictional, but no less credible, characters." Libr J

Includes bibliographical references

Harris, E. Lynn

And this too shall pass; a novel. Doubleday 1996 347p

ISBN 0-385-48030-X

LC 95-38844

Among the African American characters featured in this novel are "Zurich Robinson, a gay pro-football quarterback; MamaCee, aka Miss Cora, his grandmother; Caliph Taylor, a Chicago cop who is devoted to his daughter; successful attorney Tamela Coleman; sports anchor Mia Miller; and gay sports reporter Sean Elliott. The major plot concerns Zurich's acceptance of his gayness and his developing relationship with Sean. Subplots involve Mia and Tamela, who both struggle with their careers, their relationships with men, and one another. . . . Ultimately both fun and moving, the book has something to impress nearly any reader." Booklist

Harris, E. Lynn

If this world were mine; a novel. Doubleday 1997 318p

ISBN 0-385-48655-3

LC 97-18795

"Members of a monthly journal-writing group, four African American friends from college days who all live in the Chicago area, help each other through the dramas of their respective lives. They're all approaching 40 and looking for answers: Riley Woodson, a self-proclaimed Black Princess immured in a stultifying marriage; Yolanda Williams, a media consultant; gay psychiatrist Leland Thompson; and Dwight Scott, a computer engineer simmering with hatred for white people. . . . A supple raconteur, Harris explores the intimacies of friendship with a sensitive eye." Publ Wkly

Harris, E. Lynn

Not a day goes by; a novel. Doubleday 2000 271p $19.95

ISBN 0-385-49824-1

LC 00-38368

"When John 'Basil' Henderson, ex-football player and sports agent on the rise, falls in love with haughty, ambitious Broadway star Yancey Harrington Braxton, it seems like a perfect match. But on the couple's wedding day, which opens the book, the extravagant nuptials are suddenly canceled. The narrative retraces the couple's rocky courtship. . . . Determined to mary, have children, and keep his homosexual proclivities a secret, Basil doesn't realize that Yancey has a few secrets of her own." Publ Wkly

Harris, Joanne

Chocolat; a novel. Viking 1999 242p

ISBN 0-670-88179-1

LC 98-21771

"When Vianne Rocher and her daughter arrive in the small French town of Lansquenet-sous-Tannes, they open a shop specializing in exquisite, voluptuous chocolates. This is the first breath of giddiness the town has ever felt. So isolated is the place, it still rigorously maintains Lenten abstinences, and the town priest takes umbrage at the effrontery of this arriviste scheduling a festival of chocolate for Easter Sunday. . . . Harris' writing conveys a multitude of images and captures the self-absorption of small town life in France." Booklist

Harris, Joanne

Coastliners; a novel. Morrow 2002 350p

ISBN 0-06-019812-5

LC 2001-59045

Harris "expertly weaves her themes of family, community, and loyalty and shows how these values can be affected by money. Most impressively, she vividly depicts how a bleak, patchy strip of land can be synonymous with home." Booklist

Harris, Joanne

Five quarters of the orange. Morrow 2001 307p $25

ISBN 0-06-019813-3

LC 00-48952

"Harris has constructed a multilayered plot, punctuated with scrumptious descriptons of French delicacies and telling depictions of the war's jolting effects on one fragile family. This intense work brims with sensuality and sensitivity." Publ Wkly

Harris, Joanne

Gentlemen and players. William Morrow 2006 422p $24.95

ISBN 0-06-055914-4

LC 2005-47179

First published 2005 in the United Kingdom

"Constantly surprising and wickedly fun, this revenge tale is told by two narrators in alternating chapters. . . . Beyond the book's considerable entertainment value, Harris has written an unsettling reminder of how much our orderly lives depend on a fragile level of trust. Little grains of dishonesty and malice sprinkled in the gears of an organization are almost impossible to detect but can bring down the whole structure." Washington Post Book World

Harris, Joanne

The **girl** with no shadow; a novel. William Morrow 2008 444p

ISBN 978-0-06-143162-3; 0-06-143162-1

LC 2007-36447

"The race against time gives the story intensity, and the three female characters come alive with Harris's trademark shifting narrations. Although it's a bit darker than Chocolat, readers will drink up this pleasurable tale of love." Libr J

Harris, Joanne

Peaches for Father Francis; a novel. Joanne Harris. Viking 2012 453 p. $26.95

ISBN 0670026360; 9780670026364

LC 2012015089

In this novel, by Joanne Harris, "when Vianne Rocher receives a letter from beyond the grave, she has no choice but to follow the wind that blows her back to Lansquenet, the beautiful French village in which eight years ago she opened a chocolate shop and first learned the meaning of home. Vianne, with her daughters, Anouk and Rosette, finds Lansquenet changed in unexpected ways. . . . Most surprising of all, her old nemesis, Father Francis Reynaud, desperately needs her help." (Publisher's note)

Harris, Mark

Bang the drum slowly; by Henry W. Wiggen; certain of his enthusiasms restrained by Mark Harris. Knopf 1956 243p

A baseball novel which centers on Bruce, a black catcher, who is slowly dying of Hodgkin's disease. The narrator tries to keep the matter a secret, but eventually it comes out. The rest of the book concerns the loyalty of Bruce's teammates to their doomed member

"Narrated by 'Author' in the raucous speech of the ball park, yet with an elegiac dignity." Booklist

Harris, Robert

Archangel; a novel. Random House 1999 373p

ISBN 0-679-42888-7

LC 98-33655

"The sinewy plot never slackens, but what makes the book memorable are the vividly observed backgrounds. . . . No less authentic are the fragmented but undead relics of the old Soviet system." Natl Rev

Harris, Robert

Conspirata. Simon & Schuster 2010 340p map $26

ISBN 978-0-7432-6610-9; 0-7432-6620-2

LC 2009-34374

Second title in the author's Roman trilogy, begun with Imperium

"Beginning in 63 B.C.E. and told by Cicero's slave secretary, Tiro, this complex tale continues to chronicle Cicero's political career as he charms, co-opts, and bribes his way into the exalted position of consul, ruler of Rome. . . . With fabulous oratory and trickery, Cicero uncovers and crushes an insurrection, exposing himself to great danger and possible assassination. Riots, murder, civil unrest, corruption, treachery, and betrayal mark Cicero's political legacy, resulting in a battle between him and Julius Caesar. Throughout, however, Tiro remains loyal and remarkably astute." Publ Wkly

Harris, Robert

★ **Enigma**. Random House 1995 320p

LC 95-11335

"As one expects from a thriller-writer, Harris ensures the tension builds inexorably as the plot unfolds. Unlike some, however, he creates characters that linger in the mind, and he never bores his readers with gratuitous technical detail." New Sci

Harris, Robert

★ **Fatherland**. Random House 1992 338p

LC 91-51026

"'Fatherland' is a bleak book. But what concerns the author is the indestructibility of the human spirit, as exemplified by Xavier March. If Hitler's Germany is hell, at least a few angels are floating around." N Y Times Book Rev

Harris, Robert

The **fear** index; Robert Harris. Alfred A. Knopf 2012 285p.

ISBN 0307957934; 9780307957931

LC 2011043472

In this book, the "story takes place over a . . . twenty-four hour period in the life of Dr. Alexander Hoffmann, computer scientist, mathematical genius, and, of late, hedge fund billionaire. It begins . . . when Hoffmann is awoken by an intruder inside his sixty million dollar villa on the shores of Lake Geneva. A confrontation occurs, Hoffmann is injured, and in his attempt to solve just how someone was able to gain entry into his well-guarded palace, Hoffmann comes face to face with the greatest danger he can imagine: himself. . . . Hoffmann . . . began his career as a computer scientist at CERN (European Organization for Nuclear Research) where his work in artificial intelligence involved modeling sophisticated algorithms that programmed computers to teach themselves. It is this mastery of algorithms, and how they train computers to mimic human behavior, that he has turned to such profitable use at Hoffmann Investment Technologies. And it is this mastery that will come to haunt him." (Amazon.com)

Harris, Robert

The **ghost**. Simon & Schuster 2007 335p $26

ISBN 978-1-4165-5181-2; 1-4165-5181-6

LC 2007-29670

"Adam Lang was Britain's longest serving-and most controversial-prime minister of the last half century, whose career ended . . . after he sided with America in an unpopular war on terror. Now, after stepping down in disgrace, Lang is hiding out in . . . Martha's Vineyard to finish his much sought-after, potentially explosive memoir, for which he accepted one of history's largest cash advances. But the project runs aground when his ghostwriter suddenly and mysteriously disappears and later washes up, dead, on the island's deserted shore." Publ Wkly

Harris, Robert

Imperium; a novel of ancient Rome. Simon & Schuster 2006 305p $26

ISBN 978-0-7432-6603-1; 0-7432-6603-X

LC 2006-44393

"Tackling as his subject the brilliant orator and senator Marcus Cicero, Harris adopts the voice of Tiro, Cicero's faithful manservant and confidential secretary. Based on his real-life counterpart, Tiro, often credited as the inventor of shorthand and the author of a biography of Cicero tragically lost during the Middle Ages, narrates the story of his master's rise from relative obscurity to imperium, attainment of supreme power in the state. Thrusting himself upon the tumultuous Roman political scene at age 27, Cicero, an ambitious provincial lawyer, matches wits and wills with political and military heavyweights Caesar, Pompey, and Crassus. . . . A brilliant fictional biography of one of antiquity's most complex and triumphant characters." Booklist

Harris, Robert

Pompeii; a novel. Random House 2003 278p map hardcover o.p. pa $13.95

ISBN 0-679-42889-5; 0-8129-7461-1 pa

LC 2003-58446

"An upstanding Roman engineer rushes to repair an aqueduct in the shadow of Mount Vesuvius, which, in A.D. 79, is getting ready to blow its top. . . . Lively writing, convincing but economical period details and plenty of intrigue keep the pace quick." Publ Wkly

Harris, Thomas

Black Sunday. Dutton 2000 318p $26.95

ISBN 0-525-94555-5

LC 00-24649

A reissue of the title first published 1975 by Putnam

"All is neck and neck, quite excitingly to the very end. . . . The action is . . . very violent (violent sexy episodes, too) and the plot is packed with business. Not a bit believable, but successful entertainment." Libr J

Harris, Thomas

Hannibal. Delacorte Press 1999 486p $27.95

ISBN 0-385-29929-X

LC 99-29774

"Where Silence haunted and tantalized, Hannibal grosses out and gratifies. Yet there's still a basso ostinato of serious questions, and the answers are darker than in Silence." Nation

Harris, Thomas

Hannibal rising; a novel. Delacorte Press 2006 323p $27.95

ISBN 978-0-385-33941-4; 0-385-33941-0

"There are images of morbid beauty here. . . . Harris' handling of the wartime violence is also impressive, as swift and vicious as the blitzkrieg itself." Los Angeles Times

Harris, Thomas

★ Red Dragon. Dutton 2000 348p $26.95

ISBN 0-525-94556-3

LC 00-22500

A reissue of the title first published 1981 by Putnam

"This is a chilling, tautly written, and well-realized psychological thriller. . . . The suspense is sustained by deft characterizations, fascinating crime-lab details, a twisting plot, and understated prose." Saturday Rev

Harris, Thomas

★ The silence of the lambs. St. Martin's Press 1988 338p $24.95

ISBN 0-312-02282-4

LC 88-18203

"Harris places his clues with precision, and his characterizations . . . are superbly developed and richly complex." Booklist

Followed by Hannibal

Harrison, A. S. A.

The silent wife; a novel. A.S.A. Harrison. Penguin Books 2013 336 p. (paperback) $16

ISBN 0143123238; 9780143123231

LC 2013000993

In this novel, by A. S. A. Harrison, "Jodi and Todd are at a bad place in their marriage. Much is at stake, including the affluent life they lead in their beautiful waterfront condo in Chicago. . . . He is a committed cheater. She lives and breathes denial. He exists in dual worlds. She likes to settle scores. He decides to play for keeps. She has nothing left to lose. Told in alternating voices, . . . [the story] is about a marriage in the throes of dissolution." (Publisher's note)

Harrison, Colin

Afterburn. Farrar, Straus & Giroux 1999 438p $25

ISBN 0-374-10205-8

LC 99-13660

"Powerful businessman Charlie Ravich, a former Vietnam POW, thrives on the hectic world of global commerce. Columbia dropout Christina Welles has been in prison for four years when she is mysteriously released. Her boyfriend, Rick, is desperate to find her, believing that mobster Tony V. arranged her release and wants her killed." Libr J

"Harrison writes extremely well, and sections of 'Afterburn' are as elegant as you'll hope to find in any novel." N Y Times Book Rev

Harrison, Colin

The finder; a novel. Farrar, Straus and Giroux 2008 322p $25

ISBN 978-0-374-29949-1; 0-374-29949-8

LC 2007-36574

"A few pages into the story, a young Chinese woman, Jin Li, witnesses the grisly murder of two Mexican girls. The killers are really after Jin Li, who heads a cleaning company that handles document-shredding and other services for Manhattan firms. That role allows for all manner of discreet snooping – and fuels the illegal stock speculating ring led by her brother back in Shanghai. A forlorn firefighter who survived a nightmarish assignment inside the collapsed World Trade Center towers on 9/11 serves as the novel's hero. He's capable, brooding – and often lost in the maze of subplots. When he's on the stage, though, he grabs the reader's attention, as does Bill Martz, a conniving and captivating billionaire who's been burned by a mysterious plunging stock price engineered by You Know Who. Harrison mostly moves his pieces around the board in expert fashion and, Wolfean tics (exclamation points run amok!) aside, writes with a crisp authority. He's done his homework, too, as the detailed aside on sewage services will attest." Christ Sci Monit

Harrison, Colin

The **Havana** room. Farrar, Straus and Giroux 2004 385p $24

ISBN 0-374-29986-2

LC 2003-9238

"Most thrillers begin with a murder or a kidnapping or some other dread deed. 'The Havana Room' begins with a quote from Schopenhauer. The weighty epigraph signals an engagingly unconventional thriller, full of ruminations on the human condition. . . . Colin Harrison keeps the pages turning at a spanking clip." Economist

Harrison, Harry

The **Stainless** Steel Rat joins the circus. TOR Bks. 1999 269p

ISBN 0-312-86934-7

LC 99-34005

Following The Stainless Steel Rat goes to Hell (1996), the master criminal takes on a new assignment. "After taking a job infiltrating a suspicious circus on a four million credit a day retainer, DiGriz finds himself and his family bound up, literally at times, in a planet-wide swindle. Someone is robbing banks and other sources of wealth using The Rat's good name while he dutifully performs his magic act under the big top. Soon DiGriz is hunted by endless factions of the police, his son Bolivar is jailed, his wife Angelina kidnapped, his formerly benevolent employer is getting more sinister by the hour and worst of all, The Stainless Steel Rat is actually losing money!" Publ Wkly

Harrison, Harry

The **Stainless** Steel Rat sings the blues. Bantam Bks. 1994 229p

LC 93-31809

"Caught in the act of robbing the new mint on the planet Paskonjak, master thief Jim DiGriz, a.k.a. the Stainless Steel Rat, is offered a deal by the Galactic League: discover a stolen artifact thought to be somewhere on the prison planet Liokukae within 30 days and go free—or die. In the same vein as previous adventures featuring Harrison's irrepressible antihero . . . this latest outing boasts fast-paced action, a hint of melodrama, and a sizable dose of satirical tweaks at modern culture." Libr J

Harrison, Harry

Stainless steel visions; illustrated by Bryn Barnard. TOR Bks. 1993 254p il

LC 92-43879

"Thirteen of Harrison's robust, fast-paced tales. One is a new tale of his best-known hero, Slippery Jim DiGriz, the Stainless Steel Rat. Another is 'Roommates,' the basis for the movie Soylent Green. The other 11 range widely over Harrison's 40-year career and many interests (not to mention more than a few prejudices). All reflect Harrison's acknowledged status as heir to the pulp tradition of keeping the story moving forward at all costs." Booklist

Harrison, Jamie

Blue Deer thaw; a mystery. Hyperion 2000 271p $22.95

ISBN 0-7868-6422-2

LC 99-27230

"Clement continues to be one of the most interesting and believable mystery heroes working the American turf, and Harrison demonstrates once again that she's among the most talented writers to grace the genre in recent years." Publ Wkly

Harrison, Jamie

An **unfortunate** prairie occurrence. Hyperion 1998 369p

ISBN 0-7868-6260-2

LC 97-24087

The author allows "us to linger in Blue Deer long enough to learn its history, drink in the scenery and laugh at the kinks and quirks of its idiosyncratic residents. No wonder the world-weary Jules came running back home the first chance he got—the place is heaven." N Y Times Book Rev

Harrison, Jim, 1937-

The **English** major. Grove Press 2008 255p $24

ISBN 978-0-8021-1863-9; 0-8021-1863-1

"The protagonist of this wistfully comic novel is a sixty-year-old English teacher turned farmer, whose wife has left him for another man, and who takes to the road in the quixotic pursuit of renaming all the birds and all the states. Along the way, he picks up a neurotic, sex-hungry former student; despairs of road food; wanders into the desert without enough water; and muses on the ways life can suddenly turn upside down. . . . The premise is well-worn, but Harrison has created a character of such appeal and self-deprecating wisdom that even the more fantastical episodes—a nubile young woman cavorting in the nude for his pleasure—acquire a charmingly philosophical air." New Yorker

Harrison, Jim

★ The **farmer's** daughter. Grove Press 2009 308p $24

ISBN 978-0-8021-1934-6; 0-8021-1934-4

"The natural world, from the mountains of Montana to the cold woods of Michigan's Upper Peninsula, do more than serve as a backdrop. Birds, bears, deer, elk, the mountains, the lakes, even the wind have vivid roles in Harrison's dramas. He offers readers such a sense of place that it all seems like home. And characters so vivid and real that The Farmer's Daughter becomes like a chronicle of actual acquaintances, like reading a book describing dear friends." Miami Herald

Harrison, Jim, 1937-

★ The **great** leader; a faux mystery. Grove Press 2011 329p $24

ISBN 978-0-8021-1970-4; 0-8021-1970-0

"Some of the funniest and profoundest bits in 'The Great Leader' are the detective's alcohol-soaked musings just before he passes out. The novel serves up Sunderson's old-school field notes, which range from serious case observations to stream-of-consciousness ramblings. This is all the better, for it is fun to hear police quote Marx to each other in the field, where the outlaw and his pursuer find they have things in common, and where religion and sex intersect under the canopy of trees in the Upper Peninsula." Cleveland Plain Dealer

Harrison, Jim

Returning to earth. Grove 2007 280p $24.95

ISBN 978-0-8021-1838-7; 0-8021-1838-0

LC 2006-50802

"This could almost be Hemingway, in some of the Michigan stories, but it's even more stripped than Hemingway. . . . [The novel] is both familiar and strange, rooted and rootless, endlessly dark and occasionally hilarious." San Diego Union-Tribune

Harrison, Jim

★ The road home. Atlantic Monthly Press 1998 446p $25

ISBN 0-87113-724-0

LC 98-8391

Sequel to Dalva (1988)

"This saga is as homespun as an old quilt. A woman and her grown son, whom she'd put up for adoption, are reunited. An old man makes his peace as he approaches death. Each family member stitches in a piece of the family history. They are such good company you forget they exist nowhere but in Harrison's imagination." Newsweek

Harrison, Kathryn, 1961-

The binding chair; or, A visit from the Foot Emancipation Society: a novel. Random House 2000 312p

ISBN 0-679-45000-9

LC 99-34559

"Harrison's vision is bold and unsparing, portraying a world in which a woman's survival comes at a terrible cost. . . . The novel continually surprises. Its narrative turns and its tonal shifts—from the rhythms of the epic to those of the erotic, with pauses for comedy along the way—are as deft as they are unexpected." N Y Times Book Rev

Harrison, Kathryn, 1961-

Enchantments; by Kathryn Harrison. 1st ed. Random House 2012 314 p.

ISBN 9781400063475

LC 2010053369

This book tells the story of Masha, the daughter of the Russian mystic Rasputin, who after his death "is sent to live at the imperial palace with Tsar Nikolay and his family. . . . Desperately hoping that Masha has inherited Rasputin's miraculous healing powers, Tsarina Alexandra asks her to tend to [Prince] Aloysha, who suffers from hemophilia, a blood disease that keeps the boy confined to his sickbed. . . . Two months after Masha arrives at the palace, the tsar is forced to abdicate, and Bolsheviks place the royal family under house arrest. . . . To escape the confinement of the palace, they tell stories—some embellished and some entirely imagined—about Nikolay and Alexandra's courtship, Rasputin's many exploits, and the wild and wonderful country on the brink of an irrevocable transformation." (Publisher's note)

Harrison, Kathryn, 1961-

Envy; a novel. Kathryn Harrison. Random House 2005 301p (pbk.) $13.95; (hbk.) o.p.

ISBN 9780812973761; 1400063469

LC 2004061429

This book tells the "story of a New York psychoanalyst, Will Moreland, coping with the death of his eldest child, the stagnation of his marriage, his long estrangement from his own twin brother and the breakup of his parents' decades-long bond. After a chance encounter with an old girlfriend at his 25-year college reunion, a woman whose 24-year-old daughter may or may not be his, Will begins to unravel a few knotty, long-hidden truths about himself and the people closest to him. . . . [The novel also includes] explicit sex scenes." (salon.com)

Harrison, Kathryn, 1961-

The seal wife; a novel. Random House 2002 224p

ISBN 0-375-50629-2

LC 2001-48979

"Painterly in its pearlescent evocation of the Alaskan landscape, steeped in myth and the magic of science, this is a delectably moody, erotic, and provocative cross-cultural love story." Booklist

Harrison, M. John

Nova swing. Bantam Books 2007 252p pa $16

ISBN 978-0-553-38501-4; 0-553-38501-1

LC 2007-8288

First published 2006 in the United Kingdom

"The world Harrison has painted for us isn't pretty, and is often incomprehensible. But look around. It's that way already. Nova Swing is witty, mind-expanding, and entertaining. It's a book not to miss." scifidimensions.com

Harrison, Sue

Brother Wind; a novel. Morrow 1994 494p

LC 94-14271

This volume completes the trilogy about "the harsh and dramatic adventures of Kiin, Samiq and other Aleutian Islanders of 9000 years ago. When her husband is killed by Raven (of the Walrus People tribe), Kiin, an accomplished carver, is forced to abandon both her own tribe of the First Men and one of her twin sons and return with the killer to his village. In revenge, Samiq, chief hunter of the First Men and brother of the murdered man, seeks Raven's death. . . . Informed by Native American legends, myths and traditions and replete with convincing recreations of trading practices, seal hunting and vision fasts, this novel offers an emotionally compelling conclusion to a monumental saga." Publ Wkly

Harrison, Sue

Call down the stars. Morrow 2001 446p

ISBN 0-380-97372-3

LC 2001-30541

The concluding volume of the author's Storyteller trilogy set in prehistoric Alaska. This installment "features two storytellers: Yikaas, a young, handsome, and fiery-tempered member of the River People tribe; and Qumalix, a beautiful, clever, and high-spirited member of the Sea Hunters tribe. These two quick-witted characters spend their evenings sparring verbally and weaving tales of their historic ancestors for their gathered tribespeople. . . . Well-written and meticulously researched, Harrison's powerful yarn details the hardships and simplicity faced by prehistoric people while also emphasizing their humanity." Booklist

Harrison, Sue

Cry of the wind. Avon Bks. 1998 448p

ISBN 0-380-97371-5

LC 98-8837

"Harrison's research is clearly reflected in her meticulous attention to details as disparate as the careful sewing of a parka and the rituals of a caribou hunt. Her characters are based on ancient Native American mythologies and storytelling traditions." Publ Wkly

Harrison, Sue

Mother earth, father sky. Doubleday 1990 313p

LC 89-25656

This is "the story of an Aleutian woman living around 7000 B.C. When her village is destroyed by a hostile tribe, Chagak flees to her grandfather in the Whale Hunter tribe. Along the way, she finds safety with old Shuganan, but her trails do not end there. She endures brutalization and childbirth. . . . Harrison's fine first novel is based on thorough research into the lifestyle and beliefs of ancient Aleutians; exquisite detail imparts great viability to her characters." Booklist

Followed by My sister the moon

Harrison, Sue

My sister the moon. Doubleday 1992 449p

LC 91-29102

The second volume in the author's trilogy "picks up 16 years after 'Mother Earth Father Sky' leaves off. . . . The beautiful Kiin is promised to Amgigh, but has been in love with his brother Samiq for years. Violently abused by her father, marriage is a relief for Kiin. But her jealous younger brother brutally kidnaps and rapes her and tries to sell her as a slave into a marriage far from their homeland. The brutality and physical and sexual abuses are vividly portrayed, as well as the rigid roles of men and women." Baya Book Rev

Followed by Brother Wind

Harrison, Sue

Song of the river. Avon Bks. 1997 484p map

ISBN 0-380-97370-7

LC 97-18455

The first book of the Storyteller saga tells the story "of poisonous revenge for the rape of a young woman, K'os, by men from a neighboring village. Most of it transpires several decades after that calamity, when K'os uses her sexual prowess and manipulative abilities to stir up a war with the offenders' village. . . . Complex and well imagined, the interlocking societies of Harrison's ancient Aleutians make a compelling backdrop for this tale of romance and revenge." Booklist

Followed by Cry of the wind

Harrison, Theo

Dragon bound; Thea Harrison. Berkley Sensation mass-market Berkely Sensation 2011 336p

ISBN 9780425241509

LC 2012656675

"When [her] ex-boyfriend blackmails her into stealing from Dragos Cuelebre, Pia knows it's only a matter of time before the powerful dragon tracks her down. But instead of killing her, Dragos finds himself drawn to [her]. When the two are attacked and captured by goblins, Dragos and Pia realize that an old, powerful enemy of Dragos's wants them dead." (Publishers Weekly)

Harrod-Eagles, Cynthia

Blood lines; an Inspector Bill Slider mystery. Scribner 1996 281p

ISBN 0-684-80047-0

LC 96-8555

Inspector Slider investigates the "death of a prominent music critic who comes to a violent end in the men's room of a BBC recording studio. Each plot twist, including one devious turn that throws suspicion on a former member of Slider's murder squad, hangs on the testimony of the complicated characters, who are among the author's finest stock." N Y Times Book Rev

Harrod-Eagles, Cynthia

Blood Never Dies. Severn House Pub Ltd 2012 256 p. $28.95

ISBN 0727882112; 9780727882110

This book by Cynthia Harrod-Eagles, part of the Bill Slider series, "has the London detective inspector investigating a . . . young man's apparent suicide in a shabby flat. Only, as Slider realizes, the man didn't commit suicide, but had his throat slashed after being drugged. The detective unravels the victim's tangle of aliases to identify him as B.J. Corley, a wealthy and distinguished family's highly accomplished scion." (Publishers Weekly)

Harrod-Eagles, Cynthia

Death to go. Scribner 1994 281p

ISBN 0-684-19650-6

LC 93-10374

First published 1993 in the United Kingdom with title: Necrochip

"Murder provides the foundation for this extraordinary novel, but, it's finally an examination of love, love lost, and ways in which people cope with both." Booklist

Harrod-Eagles, Cynthia

Death watch. Scribner 1993 280p

LC 92-30924

First published 1992 in the United Kingdom

"This is a fine example of the British procedural—a simmering rather than boiling narrative, plenty of quick wit, and a splash of romantic intrigue, all skillfully written and solidly plotted." Booklist

Harrod-Eagles, Cynthia

Game over; a Bill Slider mystery. Severn House 2008 234p $28.95

ISBN 978-0-7278-6615-8

In this "11th Bill Slider mystery . . . the detective inspector investigates the murder of civil servant Ed Stonax, a former high-profile BBC correspondent, found dead with his skull smashed on the floor of his West London flat. . . . The various plot lines neatly intersect at the highest levels of government by the end of this appealing English whodunit." Publ Wkly

Harrod-Eagles, Cynthia

Grave music; an Inspector Bill Slider mystery. Scribner 1995 234p

ISBN 0-684-80046-2

LC 94-39222

First published 1994 in the United Kingdom with title: Dead end

"Though readers may guess the murderer early on in this . . . {novel, Slider's} police cohorts, and his violinist love, Joanna, are among the most appealing cast in recent memory. Their relationships, the music world setting, and the clever dialog . . . recommend this to all collections." Libr J

Harrod-Eagles, Cynthia

Killing time; an Inspector Bill Slider mystery. Scribner 1998 313p

ISBN 0-684-83776-5

LC 97-26290

First published 1996 in the United Kingdom

In this mystery London's Inspector Bill Slider's "attention is divided between solving the murder of a male striptease dancer—a case that extends from seedy Soho cabarets to the posh country homes of cabinet ministers—and sorting out the needs and demands of his estranged wife and new lover. . . . Many readers may guess the killer early on, but that shouldn't interfere with their appreciation for the rumpled, empathetic Slider, whose ability to see the complexity in the people around him is both his strength and his weakness." Booklist

Harrod-Eagles, Cynthia

Orchestrated death; a mystery introducing Inspector Bill Slider. Scribner 1992 266p

ISBN 0-684-19388-4

LC 91-29042

First published 1991 in the United Kingdom

"Detective Inspector Bill Slider {is} taken advantage of at work and pummeled verbally at home by his incompatible spouse. His own dissatisfaction leads Slider to become immersed in solving the murder of a beautiful young violin player. With the help of best friend Sergeant Atherton and the sympathetic ear of new-found true love Joanna, Slider uncovers a far-flung conspiracy." Libr J

A novel "remarkable for its rich, romantic tone, assured technique and perfect literary pitch." N Y Times Book Rev

Harrod-Eagles, Cynthia

Shallow grave; a Bill Slider mystery. Scribner 1999 312p $22

ISBN 0-684-83777-3

LC 99-21351

First published 1998 in the United Kingdom

"It isn't Inspector Bill Slider's passion for architectural oddities that brings him to the Mimpriss Estate, but the body on the terrace of the Old Rectory. . . . The way the neighbors tell it, the victim was 'an unprincipled slut,' the unfaithful wife of a local builder, a 'jealous beast' with means and motive to throttle his spouse. But Slider, whose own convulsive extramartial affairs in this refreshingly grown-up series have made him sensitive to the complexities of modern relationships, believes in looking beneath surfaces." N Y Times Book Rev

Harstad, Donald

Code sixty-one; a novel. Doubleday 2002 370p

ISBN 0-385-50118-8

LC 2001-52736

When Deputy Sheriff Carl Houseman, of Nation County Iowa, answers an attempted entry call he "pays little attention to the woman's charge that a vampire was peering in at her. That changes when two bodies are found in the next 48 hours, one across the river in Wisconsin, the other in Iowa, in a small-town mansion. Both victims have deep neck wounds, forcing Houseman to investigative the unthinkable. Initially, the other cops treat both the usually sensible Houseman and a professional vampire hunter who joins the hunt as nuts, but even they become more and more spooked as local Goths make their tastes known. A terrific read—by turns, funny, eerie, and insightful." Booklist

Harstad, Johan

Buzz Aldrin, what happened to you in all the confusion? John Harstad; translated by Deborah Dawkin. 1st English language ed. Seven Stories Press 2011 471p

ISBN 9781609801359

LC 2010048506

This book "tells the story of Mattias, a thirty-something gardener living in Stavanger, Norway, whose idol is Buzz Aldrin, second man on the moon: the man who was willing to stand in Neil Armstrong's shadow in order to work, diligently and humbly, for the success of the Apollo 11 mission. Following a series of personal and professional disasters, Mattias finds himself lying on a rain-soaked road in the desolate, treeless Faroe Islands, . . . a wad of bills in his pocket and no memory of how he had come to be there . . . when a truck approaches him, driven by a troubled fantastic man with an offer that will shortly change Mattias's life." (Publisher's note)

Hart, Brian

Then came the evening; a novel. Bloomsbury USA 2009 272p $25

ISBN 978-1-60819-014-0; 1-60819-014-5

LC 2009-16969

This novel "begins with a calamitous misunderstanding. Bandy Dorner, hungover and in trouble with two police officers, is told that his cabin burned down the night before. Bandy assumes his wife, Iona, was inside, and in a confused fury he shoots one of the cops, killing him. But Iona, we soon learn, did not die in the fire. She took off with her new man earlier that night—just after she burned down the cabin. The rest is fallout. From the early '70s we fast-forward to 1990. Bandy's son, Tracy, conceived not long before the fire, comes to visit his father in an Idaho prison. The young man has left home and plans to refurbish an old house that belonged to Bandy's parents. Bandy gets out of prison not long after the visit and joins his son in fixing up the home. Iona is there, too. Over the next several months, they live together uncomfortably, broken, a family that never was. Then Came the Evening may seem ostentatiously bleak—full of prison beatings, drunken fights, sex with truckers for drugs; and all this in the rugged American West—but Hart avoids macho sentimentalism." Bookforum

Hart, Carolyn G.

Death in paradise; a Henrie O mystery. {by} Carolyn Hart. Avon Bks. 1998 275p

ISBN 0-380-97414-2

LC 97-29701

Hart is at her "best as she tightens the suspense and keeps the killer's identity out of focus until the cliffhanging finale." Publ Wkly

Hart, Carolyn G.

Death walked in; a death on demand mystery. [by] Carolyn Hart. William Morrow 2008 293p $23.95

ISBN 978-0-06-072405-4; 0-06-072405-6

LC 2007-43589

A fortune in gold coins stolen from a house filled with visiting family members lies at the root of this Max and Annie Darling mystery.

"This tight, Agatha Christie-style puzzler will keep readers guessing to the end." Publ Wkly

Hart, Carolyn G.

Letter from home; {by} Carolyn Hart. Berkley Prime Crime 2003 262p $22.95

ISBN 0-425-19179-6

LC 2003-51953

"Set in a small-town America that lives only in memory, this artfully narrated whodunit observes the residents of an unnamed Oklahoma hamlet over the hot and dusty summer of 1944 as they ration their food, count their war dead and turn on their neighbors." N Y Times Book Rev

Hart, Carolyn G.

Mint julep murder. Bantam Bks. 1995 277p

ISBN 0-553-09463-7

LC 94-34244

"Hart combines genteel ambience, southern charm, a likable heroine, and some wonderfully nasty characters into a pleasantly entertaining mystery." Booklist

Hart, Carolyn G.

Murder walks the plank; a death on demand mystery. [by] Carolyn Hart. HarperCollins Publishers 2004 298p $23.95

ISBN 0-06-000474-6

LC 2003-51095

In this installment "mystery bookstore owner Annie Darling plans a mystery cruise as a benefit for the Island Literacy Council of Broward's Rock, South Carolina. Unfortunately, before the mystery is solved, one of the guests falls overboard. Or was she pushed? Annie believes she was pushed and becomes even more convinced when a suspicious death occurs soon after the cruise. Max and Acting Police Chief Cameron believe the two incidents are either accidents or suicides and are unconnected, leaving Annie, Emma Clyde (Broward's Rock's own mystery author), and mystery reader extraordinaire Henny Brawley no choice but to solve the crimes themselves." Booklist

This novel "can only reinforce Hart's high standing among the cozy mystery cognoscenti." Publ Wkly

Hart, Carolyn G.

Resort to murder; a Henrie O mystery. {by} Carolyn Hart. Morrow 2001 294p $24

ISBN 0-380-97773-7

LC 00-59446

"Recovering from pneumonia, Henrie O isn't sure she feels up to the task of dealing with the emotional maelstrom stewing around the Bermuda wedding of her son-in-law, Lloyd Drake, and beautiful Connor Bailey, a wealthy widow. . . . The hotel where the party has gathered witnessed tragedy the year before, when Roddy Worrell, the manager's husband, plunged to his death from a tower. According to rumor, Roddy had been infatuated with Connor, who spurned his advances. When a ghost is sighted at the tower, word spreads that Roddy has come back to haunt Connor. The subsequent death of a hotel employee who knew more than he should about the apparition puts Henrie O on the murder scent once again." Publ Wkly

Hart, Carolyn G.

Scandal in Fair Haven. Bantam Bks. 1994 275p

LC 93-40346

This Henrie O "adventure takes her to Fair Haven, Tennessee, where a local bookstore owner is accused of murdering his wealthy wife. . . . Hart offers a light and lively read with an appealing 'small-town America' ambience, a compelling plot, a potpourri of fascinating characters, and some revealing insights into what makes us humans tick." Booklist

Hart, Carolyn G.

Skulduggery. Five Star 2000 190p $22.95

ISBN 0-7862-2672-2

LC 00-30845

First published 1984 in the United Kingdom

"On a foggy San Francisco night, Jimmy Lee, a twentysomething Chinese man, comes to physical anthropologist Ellen Christie's Russian Hill apartment with the bones of Peking Man, which vanished in China in the chaos of World War II. Jimmy and Ellen quickly join forces, to protect the bones—and each other—from two, chillingly efficient hitmen. . . . The novel combines effective use of the San Francisco setting with solid characterizations and a 'McGuffin' as intriguing as Hammett's falcon." Booklist

Hart, Carolyn G.

Southern ghost. Bantam Bks. 1992 322p

LC 92-2543

"According to the news story published in the Chastain (South Carolina) Courier at the time, leading citizen Judge Augustus Tarrant suffered a fatal heart attack on May 9, 1970, after learning of the accidental shooting death of his 21-year-old son, Ross. What has prompted young Courtney Kimball to hire Max Darling to investigate this family tragedy 22 years later? . . . Hart's southern-gothic mystery offers a wealth of suspects . . . a generous scattering of literary allusions and peripheral ghost stories, and a chain of intriguing flashbacks that will leave most readers puzzled to the end." Booklist

Hart, Carolyn G.

White elephant dead; {by} Carolyn Hart. Avon Twilight 1999 277p $23

    ISBN 0-380-97530-0

                      LC 99-20833

"After demanding that leading citizens of Broward's Rock donate priceless objects to the annual White Elephant sale, a wicked blackmailer turns up dead. The leading suspect is a top customer at Annie Darling's Death on Demand bookstore, so Annie must get involved." Libr J

This "Death on Demand mystery, delivers charming characters, . . . a tantalizing mystery, and plenty of appealing descriptions of coastal landscapes." Booklist

Hart, Carolyn G.

Yankee Doodle dead; a death on demand mystery. {by} Carolyn Hart. Avon Bks. 1998 273p

    ISBN 0-380-97529-7

                      LC 98-13565

Sleuth Annie Darling, "owner of an island resort mystery bookstore, witnesses the murder of a much-hated man during a Fourth of July fundraiser for the local library." Libr J

Hart, Erin, 1958-

The **book** of Killowen; Erin Hart. Scribner 2013 352 p. (hardcover) $26

    ISBN 1451634846; 9781451634846; 9781451634853; 9781451634860

                      LC 2012028465

In this book, by Erin Hart, "an ancient volume of philosophical heresy provides a motive for murder. . . . After a year away from working in the field, archaeologist Cormac Maguire and pathologist Nora Gavin are back in the bogs, investigating a ninth-century body. . . . They discover that the ancient corpse is not alone--pinned beneath it is the body of Benedict Kavanagh, missing for mere months. . . . Both men were viciously murdered, but centuries apart." (Publisher's note)

Hart, Erin, 1958-

False mermaid. Scribner 2010 318p $26

    ISBN 978-1-4165-6376-1; 1-4165-6376-8

                      LC 2009-37969

Forensic archaeologist Dr. Nora Galvin returns home from Ireland "to Saint Paul, MN, in hopes of healing the wound left by her sister's murder three years ago. Still certain that her sister's husband, who is about to remarry, is the killer, Nora resumes the hunt for evidence with the detective who had worked the case and finds a link to the death of another young woman in the same vicinity. Back in Ireland, Cormac Maguire, Nora's sometime partner, is dealing with his own demons." Libr J

"Pinpoint plotting and sure sense of place make this tale a winner." Kirkus

Hart, Erin

Haunted ground; Erin Hart. Scribner 2003 328 p. maps (hardcover) $24

    ISBN 0743235053; 9780743235051

                   .LC 2002030679

In this crime novel, by Erin Hart, "when farmers cutting turf in a peat bog make a grisly discovery--the perfectly preserved severed head of a young woman with long red hair--Irish archaeologist Cormac Maguire and American pathologist Nora Gavin team up in a case that will open old wounds." (Publisher's note)

Hart, Erin

Lake of sorrows; Erin Hart. Scribner 2004 328 p. maps (hardcover) $24

    ISBN 0743247965; 9780743247962

                      LC 2004052234

In this novel, by Erin Hart, "American forensic pathologist Nora Gavin has been called to an archaeological site in the bleak midlands west of Dublin to assist at an excavation where a well-preserved Iron Age body has been found buried in a peat bog. . . . Nora and archaeologist Cormac Maguire, embroiled in a tumultuous love affair, must team up again professionally, and are soon enmeshed in the web of tangled desires and terrible secrets that surround this untimely death." (Publisher's note)

Hart, John

Down river. Thomas Dunne Books/St. Martin's 2007 325p $24.95

    ISBN 978-0-312-35931-7; 0-312-35931-4

                      LC 2007-21540

"A small North Carolina town is torn apart when a power company wants to buy up all the farmland on the river; some residents cling to their bucolic way of life, while others see only dollar signs. Adam Chase's family has owned the largest parcel in the area for centuries, and his father has no desire to sell. But tempers flare, and soon a young woman is severely beaten, a body is found on the Chase farm, and Adam is the chief suspect. Newly arrived after five years away, Adam is the town pariah. His stepmother had accused him of murdering a family friend, and while the court acquitted him, his family and friends did not. While time has softened some, others seem ready to unleash their stored-up anger. This work is reminiscent of Raymond Chandler's novels, hardboiled and rich with evocative metaphors." Libr J

Hart, John

Iron house. Thomas Dunne Books/St. Martin's Press 2011 421p $25.99

    ISBN 9780312380342

                      LC 2011-06909

This book "focuses on two brothers, Michael and Julian, both raised and abused at the Iron House of the title, an orphanage in the mountains of North Carolina. As a boy, Michael flees the place and ends up on the streets of New York City, where Otto Kaitlin, 'the most powerful crime boss in recent memory,' rescues him and fashions him into an accomplished killing machine and a surrogate son. When Kaitlin dies, his real son, Stevan, fueled by a mixture of jealousy and greed, sets out to destroy everything the now grownup Michael has. Stevan kidnaps Michael's girlfriend, Elena, and threatens emotionally fragile Julian, a creative, tortured genius who is now living at the North Carolina mansion of his adoptive parents. Hart deftly interweaves a complex family history story with Stevan's intense, bloody quest for vengeance." Publ Wkly

Hart, John

The **king** of lies. St. Martin's Minotaur 2006 310p $22.95

ISBN 0-312-34161-X

LC 2005-49774

"More than anything else—more than a terrific whodunit, an unsentimental, clear-eyed story of love and forgiveness, and a gripping family saga—The King of Lies is a masterful piece of writing." Raleigh News & Observer

Hart, John

The **last** child. Minotaur Books 2009 373p $24.95

ISBN 978-0-312-35932-4; 0-312-35932-2

LC 2008-45678

After his twin sister Alyssa disappears, thirteen year-old Johnny Merrimon is determined to find her. When a second girl disappears from his rural North Carolina town, Johnny makes a discovery that sends shock waves through the community.

The author has produced "a novel that is elegant, haunting, and memorable. His characters are given an emotional depth that genre characters seldom have, and the graceful, evocative prose lifts his stories right out of their genre and into the realm of capital-L literature. A must-read for every variety of fiction reader." Booklist

Hart, Josephine

★ **Damage**; a novel. Knopf 1991 195p

ISBN 0-679-40135-0

LC 90-53393

"Erotic obsession is a risky subject for fiction. No matter how besotted the victims of this malady may be, their behavior is likely to strike mere witnesses, i.e., readers, as distasteful, hilarious or both. This first novel . . . sidesteps such unintended responses, thanks to old-fashioned British reserve. . . . The understatement works wonders." Time

Hart, Josephine

The **reconstructionist**. Overlook Press 2001 218p $26.95

ISBN 1-58567-170-3

LC 2001-33963

"Jack Harrington, a well-to-do London psychiatrist, immerses himself in the familial problems of his patients' pasts, while admirably repressing his own childhood trauma. His sister, Kate, a seductive writer of 'fluffy things,' is less able to cope with that trauma, and readers learn early on that Jack's good-natured protectiveness toward his sister belies a far more disturbing sort of sibling bond. . . . Hart has packed this little gem of a novel with sparkling aphoristic insights befitting Jack's profession, and her sketches of fragile, child-like characters masquerading as capable adults are deftly drawn." Publ Wkly

Hart, Josephine

Sin; a novel. Knopf 1992 163p

LC 92-53853

This novel "focuses on the sin of envy, embodied here in the person of narrator Ruth, corrosively jealous of her orphaned cousin Elizabeth, raised and cherished by Ruth's parents as their own daughter. Ruth hates the good, gener-ous, kind Elizabeth and waits for the moment when she will be able to break her rival and take everything." Libr J

"Hart has constructed an arch and streamlined melo-drama inlaid with some undeniably shrewd and provocative observations about human nature." Booklist

Hart, Josephine

The **truth** about love; a novel. Alfred A. Knopf 2009 205p $24

ISBN 978-0-307-27261-4

LC 2009-21375

This "novel explores the grief of the O'Hara family in an unnamed Irish town after the violent death of a teenage son. It is 1962, and the boy, who is also unnamed, is blown up in his own backyard while building a bomb. He was at the age when 'warriors' held a special fascination, his father explains, and the Christian Brothers at school had filled his head with stories of Irish heroes who had fought for inde-pendence against the British. . . . It is the second death in the O'Hara family. Shortly before the book opens, a young daughter has died after a long illness, and the loss of a sec-ond child is too great for Mrs. O'Hara, who collapses into a deep depression. . . . [This] is a serious, at times compelling, look at family and memory, despair and redemption." Wall Street J

Harte, Bret, 1836-1902

★ The **best** short stories of Bret Harte; edit-ed, and with an introduction, by Robert N. Linscott. Modern Lib. 1947 x, 517 p.p

ISBN 9780394602509 out of print

LC 47030278

Harte, Bret, 1836-1902

The **Luck** of Roaring Camp, and other tales; with pictures of the author and his environment and illustrations of the setting of the book together with an introduction by Louis B. Salomon. Dodd, Mead 1961 309p il

Haruf, Kent

★ **Benediction**; Kent Haruf. Alfred A. Knopf 2013 272 p. $25.95

ISBN 0307959880; 9780307959881

LC 2012028744

This book looks at the "last, dying days of old Dad Lewis." He "owns a store in a small Colorado town, and his terminal illness draws out the compassion his adult daugh-ter, whom Dad wants to take over the business upon his im-minent passing, and sparks an arousal in his long-devoted wife to seek some degree of resolution to an unhealed family wound." (Booklist)

Haruf, Kent

★ **Eventide**. Knopf 2004 300p $24.95

ISBN 0-375-41158-5

LC 2003-60480

This novel takes up where the author's Plainsong left off, "in the windy high-plains country in and around the tiny town of Holt, Colorado. Distress is general: out on their ranch, two stolid elderly brothers discover loneliness after the wayward girl they took in leaves for college; various troubles—illness, death, basic inability to cope—afflict the adults in town; and some young children are set adrift from disintegrating homes, with dangerous consequences. Every action in Holt casts a long shadow, and the gist of Haruf's story is what happens when those shadows touch. (The results are equal parts grace and calamity.) It's rare that such slow, deliberate prose is this highly charged, but Haruf's writing draws power from his sense of character—its limitations and its possibilities—and how it propels action." New Yorker

Haruf, Kent

★ **Plainsong**. Knopf 1999 301p $27.50

ISBN 0-375-40618-2

LC 99-15606

"From simple strands of language and cuttings of talk, from the look of the high Colorado plains east of Denver almost to the place where Nebraska and Kansas meet, Haruf has made a novel so foursquare, so delicate and lovely, that it has the power to exalt the reader." N Y Times Book Rev

Another available title about the residents of Holt, Colorado is:

Eventide (2004)

Harvey, John

Cold in hand. Harcourt 2008 376p $26

ISBN 978-0-15-101462-0; 0-15-101462-0

LC 2008-5630

"Resnick is now living with a much younger DI, Lynn Kellog, and their relationship is one of the best aspects of this fine crime novel, subtly described and convincing. . . . Cold in Hand reveals modern England in all its most depressing messiness while engaging the reader with characters whose warmth and humanity give real pleasure. There is no melodrama here; all the actions and motives that are eventually revealed are rooted in reality; and yet at the heart of the novel is an event so shocking in the context that it could rival anything in the most lurid thriller." Times Lit Suppl

Harvey, John

Cold light. Holt & Co. 1994 370p

ISBN 0-8050-2046-2

LC 93-6263

"Nice men, murderers, child batterers, discarded lovers, grieving parents, weary probation officers, cynical cops—they all hurt, they all count and they all speak a kind of poetry in this writer's book." N Y Times Book Rev

Harvey, John

A **darker** shade of blue; stories. Pegasus Crime 2012 366 p.

ISBN 1605982849; 9781605982847

This book is "[a] collection of 18 previously published short stories. . . . In 'Billie's Blues' and 'The Sun, the Moon and the Stars,' Charlie [Resnick] tries to help out Eileen, a stripper turned whore turned witness to murder, with dour results. . . . Resnick makes a cameo appearance in 'Trouble in Mind,' which features [author John] Harvey's leading short-story protagonist, Jack Kiley, who . . . notes that Charlie looks like aging lawman Mario Balzic. Kiley, the former footballer and Met copper now eking out a living as a private eye, faces the usual Harvey suspects . . . with the gals usually in for a bad day. Frank Elder, who stars in three

Harvey novels, loses his wife and begins his retirement in 'Due North,' while Tom Whitemore, a minor character in one of the Elder books, faces his own marriage troubles in 'Sack O' Woe.'" (Kirkus)

Harvey, John

Darkness and light. Harcourt 2006 350p

ISBN 978-0-15-101133-9; 0-15-101133-8

LC 2005-37771

In this procedural, retired policeman Frank Elder "grudgingly agrees to try to find Claire Meecham, the older, widowed sister of a friend of his ex-wife's. While poking through the missing woman's Nottingham bungalow, Elder finds nothing untoward other than evidence that Claire was not quite so uninterested in sex, and possible new relationships, as her younger sister believed. Soon after, Elder is surprised when Claire turns up in her home dead, looking at peace, carefully dressed and laid out in the manner of a woman who met a similar fate years earlier—and whose killer was never caught." Publ Wkly

"A satisfying look at the twists and turns of police work, through a man who can't quite leave his former life behind." Arizona Republic

Harvey, John

Easy meat. Holt & Co. 1996 388p

LC 96-7307

"As Resnick's eyes are opened, Mr. Harvey writes with painful urgency about the kind of sexual and psychological abuse that no child can completely outgrow. If this is one of Mr. Harvey's darkest books, it is also one of his most enlightened." N Y Times Book Rev

Harvey, John

★ **Far** cry. Houghton Mifflin Harcourt 2010 500p $26

ISBN 978-0-547-31594-2; 0-547-31594-5

LC 2009-29048

First published 2009 in the United Kingdom

"The architecture of Harvey's storytelling begs to be admired, with its multiple narratives, shifting time lines and elaborate plot details. But it's his handling of difficult characters and provocative themes that gives the book weight. All the adults in this story love children, some selflessly and others in ways that make your skin crawl, and they all react differently when the children they love are taken away from them. Harvey's touch is so subtle, his style so seductive, that he distracts us from the fact that Ruth isn't the only person whose choices are determined, or tragically derailed, by love for a child — even if it's someone else's child." N Y Times Book Rev

Harvey, John

Flesh and blood. Carroll & Graff Pubs. 2004 370p $25

ISBN 0-7867-1359-3

"If anyone could make you feel sorry for a serial killer, it's John Harvey, who always writes with tender feeling about commonplace people killers among them damaged by criminal violence." N Y Times Book Rev

Harvey, John

Gone to ground. Harcourt 2008 387p $25

ISBN 978-0-15-101363-0; 0-15-101363-2

LC 2006-37390

First published 2007 in the United Kingdom

The author, "best known for his now-complete Charlie Resnick series, follows Cambridge police detectives Will Grayson and Helen Walker as they investigate the disfiguring murder of gay film professor Stephen Bryan. Initially focused on Bryan's love life, they soon sense secrets around a book he was writing on '50s movie queen Stella Leonard. Flashbacks from the star's last film add a noir chill to the tale. Bryan's sister, a journalist, uses her position to look into things on her own, with potentially dangerous results as Leonard's family grows fiercely protective. Harvey keeps the devastating secret at the center of the tale well hidden until the end." Rocky Mountain News

Harvey, John

★ **Last** rites. Holt & Co. 1999 312p

ISBN 0-8050-4150-8

LC 98-33766

First published 1998 in the United Kingdom

This final Charlie Resnick mystery "finds Resnick and colleagues attempting to end a local drug war and track down an escaped killer. As always, Resnick slouches his way to understanding, recognizing eventually that the catalyst for much of the mayhem is a love story, as perverted as it is wrenchingly tender. Meanwhile, strands of stories left incomplete in earlier novels come together, some offering more snapshots of wasted lives, others providing glimmers of hope. Harvey ends his story, yes, but he avoids wrapping it all into too neat a package. The great strength of the Resnick series has always been Harvey's grasp of the mess and muddle of human life and his ability to find poetry in the midst of that mess." Booklist

Harvey, John

★ **Still** waters. Holt & Co. 1997 311p

ISBN 0-8050-4149-4

LC 97-12324

"Charlie Resnick, the laconic British police investigator . . . is faced with the death of an abused woman, a friend of his lover, Hannah. At the same time, he tracks down the circumstances of an idiosyncratic art theft. This standard police procedural formula is given a bit of depth by passages detailing relationships, both business and personal, between the members of the Serious Crime Squad." Libr J

Harvey, John

Wasted years. Holt & Co. 1993 339p

LC 93-247

"By now Harvey's economy of prose is a given, as is his ability to pull together the many composite parts—the interlocking crimes, the boozing, infidelity and Resnick's very human bunch of underlings—that make a Charlie Resnick mystery such satisfying reading." Publ Wkly

Harvey, Michael T.

The **Chicago** way; [by] Michael Harvey. Knopf 2007 303p $23.95

ISBN 978-0-307-26686-6; 0-307-26686-9

LC 2007-7796

"Harvey's tightly plotted evocation of the Chicago underworld is set in the present but brings to mind the voices of Chandler and Hammett." New York

Harvey, Michael T.

The **Fifth** Floor; [by] Michael Harvey. Alfred A. Knopf 2008 277p $23.95

ISBN 978-0-307-26687-3; 0-307-26687-7

LC 2008-1484

This Michael Kelly thriller "has the ex-Chicago cop taking on what he thinks is a simple domestic violence case. But when he tails Johnny Woods, a fixer for the city's powerful mayor, to what turns out to be a grisly murder scene, Kelly realizes he's stumbled onto a scandal that began with the great Chicago Fire of 1871. Digging deeper, Kelly unearths what was once considered an urban legend: two of Chicago's most eminent families conspiring to eradicate Irish immigrants by burning down the city's slums. As more bodies pile up and he becomes romantically involved with a judge with secrets of her own, Kelly vows to expose the conspiracy, even if that means putting himself on the wrong side of the city's most powerful men. Harvey's plot twists in all the right places, and his noir-inspired dialogue crackles without sounding showy. Marlowe and Spade would readily welcome Michael Kelly into their fold." Publ Wkly

Harvey, Michael T.

The **third** rail; [by] Michael Harvey. Alfred A. Knopf 2010 285p $24.95

ISBN 978-0-307-27250-8

LC 2009-46502

"The mystery is lumpy and unsurprising, but Harvey unfolds his tale with no preliminaries, no digressions and barely an extra word—just a book—length jolt of pure adrenaline." Kirkus

Harvey, Michael T.

We all fall down; [by] Michael Harvey. Alfred A. Knopf 2011 297p $24.95

ISBN 978-0-307-27251-5

LC 2011-04681

Chicago cop turned private investigator Michael Kelly is on a hunt for the people who poisoned his city by unleashing a pathogen in a subway tunnel.

"A gripping crime novel with a frightening message about very plausible biological warfare." Booklist

Harwood, John

The **ghost** writer. Harcourt 2004 369p $25

ISBN 0-15-101074-9

LC 2003-24918

"Gerard Freeman grows up on the windswept southern coast of Australia in the late 20th century with a controlling mother strangely silent about the details of her childhood in England. His only solace is steadfast English pen friend, Alice, to whom he confides everything. What was Gerard's mother, Phyllis, hoping to escape when she left England?

The protagonist slowly pieces together his mother's past with the aid of short stories written by his great-grandmother, Viola. These cunning tales, filled with supernatural occurrences and séances, are seamlessly embedded in the main narrative, offering Gerard—and readers—enticing clues into his troubled family's history. After Phyllis's death, her newly liberated son travels to England, hoping to learn more and to pursue elusive Alice. As he searches through the country house his mother inhabited long ago, Gerard finds past and present fusing in horrifying fashion." Publ Wkly

Hasek, Jaroslav

★ The **good** soldier Svejk; and his fortunes in the World War. translated and introduced by Cecil Parrott; illustrated by Josef Lada. Knopf 1993 800p $22

ISBN 0-679-42036-3

LC 92-54304

Original Czech edition published 1920-1923 in 4 volumes; this translation first published 1973 by Heinemann

"The novel reflected the pacifist, antimilitary sentiments of post-World War I Europe. The title character is classified as 'feeble-minded'; nevertheless, with the advent of World War I he is drafted into the service of Austria. Naive, instinctively honest, invariably incompetent, and guileless, Schweik is forever colliding with the clumsy, dehumanized military bureaucracy. Schweik's naiveté serves as a contrast to the self-importance and conniving natures of his superior officers and is the main vehicle for Hăsek's mockery of authority." Merriam-Webster's Ency of Lit

Haskell, John

American purgatorio. Farrar, Straus and Giroux 2005 239p $23

ISBN 0-374-10432-8

LC 2004-20087

"The novel becomes more visual and distinct the farther west Jack travels, and an undertow of regret begins to emerge, intimations of a marriage left unfulfilled. Gradually, Haskell creates a penetrating mood of loss. Turn the last page, and you'll realize that this strange, moving book has done just what a first novel should: it has left an impression." N Y Times Book Rev

Haslett, Adam

Union Atlantic; a novel. Nan A. Talese/Doubleday 2009 304p $26

ISBN 978-0-385-52447-6; 0-385-52447-1

LC 2009-11875

A novel about "Doug Fanning, a handsome, renegade Boston securities trader whose imprudent bets on the Japanese markets threaten to cause systemic bank failure. . . . Unfolding in the fictional town of Finden, Massachusetts, the novel's central narrative pits Doug in an oblique battle of wills with his neighbor Charlotte Graves, a former history teacher and dismayed old-school liberal who resents the size and style of his massive new house. While the two ostensibly wrangle over property rights, the real stakes of their disagreement is not taste but ideology—or perhaps better, pathology. . . . Set during the run-up to the invasion of Iraq, Union Atlantic is like a pressure-compacted version of a Tom Wolfe zeitgeist doorstop, complete with a diffuse cast

of characters (bankers, pot-smoking teenagers, a conflicted corporate whistle-blower, the president of the Federal Reserve Bank of New York) and myriad cultural obsessions: about the corporatization of war, the joyless hedonism of American society and the soullessness of suburban life." Time Out N Y

Hassler, Jon

The **dean's** list. Ballantine Bks. 1997 396p

ISBN 0-345-41637-6

LC 97-10177

"In this sequel to Rookery Blues . . ., Hassler revisits Rookery State College in Minnesota some 30 years later. Leland Edwards, one of the faculty in the first book, is now dean of the college. In spite of growing older and more successful, however, he is still striving to understand his family and friends, tentatively exploring new relationship, and often simply trying to survive the follies of campus life in the 1990s." Libr J

Hassler, Jon

★ **Rookery** blues. Ballantine Bks. 1995 484p

ISBN 0-345-39356-2

LC 95-2953

"Rookery is the name of a northern Minnesota state college where five faculty members get together to play the blues as well as endure them. The group—a beautiful singer, a tormented artist, a woebegone novelist, and two English teachers—includes a love triangle, and political strains arise as the members take different sides in a strike. Set in 1969, it feels like 1959—in large part because of its old-fashioned, four-square, apolitical humanism." New Yorker

Followed by The dean's list

Hassler, Jon

The **Staggerford** flood. Viking 2002 199p $24.95

ISBN 0-670-03125-9

LC 2001-56808

"A natural disaster threatens the unique rural charm of Hassler's Minnesota village in the latest installment in his ongoing series. . . . Agatha McGee is the 80-year-old sixth-grade teacher who is beginning to dread the onset of old age, so much so that a local radio personality suggests that she hold her own memorial party in advance to try to get a lift from the tribute. What invigorates Agatha instead is the threat of a flood, which distracts her from her preoccupation with local gossip and causes her to offer shelter to several troubled residents, including a combative mother and daughter as well as several friends and acquaintances." Publ Wkly

Hassman, Tupelo

Girlchild; Tupelo Hassman. Farrar, Straus and Giroux 2012 275 p.

ISBN 9780374162573

LC 2011041209

Alex Award (2013)

In this novel, a "bright young girl must endure family dysfunction and sexual abuse while coming of age in a Reno trailer park during the late 1980s. Life in the Calle de Las Flores trailer park, as Rory Dawn Hendrix tells it, comes with its own unique rituals and social mores. . . . Her hard-drinking mother Johanna . . . entrusts Rory to a sullen teen-age neighbor, Carol. It turns out that Carol's father . . . has been molesting Carol, and preys upon Rory as well. And when he in turn moves away, taking that secret with him, it is left to Rory to rebuild her shattered self-esteem. Taking inspiration from a battered library copy of The Girl Scout Handbook, Rory does a remarkable job raising herself, while trying to let go of the people (and hurts) that no longer serve her." (Kirkus)

Hatcher, Robin Lee

Catching Katie; Robin Lee Hatcher. Tyndale House Publishers 2003 353p o.p.; o.p.

ISBN 0842360999; 9780842360999

LC 2003013281

This book takes place "[i]n 1916 Idaho, [when] Katie Jones has dedicated her life to the campaign for women's suffrage. Until now she has successfully avoided the ties of marriage, fearing it would obscure her message. Will her growing love for childhood chum Ben Rafferty compromise her calling?" (Publisher's note)

Hatoum, Milton

The brothers; translated from the Portuguese by John Gledson. Farrar, Straus & Giroux 2002 240p $23

ISBN 0-374-14118-5

LC 2002-17054

Original Portuguese edition, 2000

"Set in a Lebanese immigrant community in the Brazil-ian port town of Manaus, this is the story of identical twins, Yaqub and Omar, whose lives take radically different paths: one toward professional success in Brazil's metropolis São Paulo, the other to drunken dissipation in the lowly port of his birth. Set against the backdrop of a city whose very char-acter is undergoing radical change, it is also the story of a family on the verge of conflagration from incestuous pas-sion and riddled with secrets and guilt. . . . Hatoum suggests much while fully revealing little; he's content to unfold his lush narrative—replete with the dances, exotic sights, smells and fragrances of his luscious Brazil—one vivid bolt of cloth at a time." Publ Wkly

Havazelet, Ehud

Bearing the body; a novel. Farrar, Straus and Giroux 2007 296p $24

ISBN 978-0-374-29972-9; 0-374-29972-2

LC 2007-09157

"Havazelet's novel won't make you happier, unless it cheers you to admire a writer who doesn't merely describe but actually reproduces experiences that seem simultane-ously universal and intimate. Reading about Sol and Nathan feels like being adopted into a family you might not want to have, precisely because (as with 'The Sopranos') you recognize the similarities it bears to your own." N Y Times Book Rev

Havill, Steven

Race for the dying; [by] Steven F. Havill. Thom-as Dunne Books 2009 322p $25.99

ISBN 978-0-312-38071-7; 0-312-38071-2

LC 2009-17065

"The conclusion to this pleasant and easy read may be a little too pat, but Havill sets up a number of colorful dra-matic situations that ought to please readers who take their westerns neat." Publ Wkly

Havley, Noah

The good father; by Noah Hawley. Doubleday 2012 320p.

ISBN 9780385535533

LC 2011017657

This book tells the story of "[t]he father of a man who assassinates a presidential candidate [and] tries to make sense of his son's crime. . . . Dr. Paul Allen is a success-ful rheumatologist happily living with his second wife and their twin sons in a chic Connecticut enclave. Contact with Daniel, his aloof son from a previous marriage, is sporadic, and when Daniel drops out of Vassar in his first year to 'see the country,' Dr. Allen shrugs it off as a youthful foible, . . . so the Secret Service agents who appear at his door are a great surprise. Daniel, aka Carter Allen Cash, has shot and killed the Democratic presidential front-runner. . . . Despite the overwhelming evidence against Daniel, Dr. Allen won't believe that his son is guilty . . . and becomes convinced of a conspiracy involving a second man." (Publishers Weekly)

Hawke, Ethan

Ash Wednesday; a novel. Knopf 2002 221p

ISBN 0-375-41326-X

LC 2002-20811

"Hawke's text at times reads raw, but the novel's con-versational tone, dual first-person narration and, above all, direct exploration of the simple truths of life and love make this a worthwhile tale and an honest one." Publ Wkly

Hawkes, John

★ The **blood** oranges. New Directions 1971 271p

"This highly rhapsodic, sensual novel suggests both in title and substance the decline of vitality and enlightenment in the characters' lives as in each new day. Reminiscent of Lawrence in the concern with atmosphere and lushness of description, the book is powerfully evocative of a sometimes comic, sometimes hallucinatory sense of timelessness, ob-session, and escape from reality." Choice

Hawkes, John

★ **Second** skin; preface by Jeffrey Eugenides. New Directions 2005 210p

ISBN 0-8112-1644-6

LC 2005-21516

First published 1964

"As with other contemporaries, such as Pynchon, Barth, and Nabokov, and predecessors such as Faulkner, Lautrem-ont, and Blake, Hawkes has succeeded in creating a stylized, imagined world that doubles for the one in which we live and read his novels." Reader's Ency of Am Lit. 2d edition

Hawthorne, Nathaniel

The **Blithedale** romance; with an introduction by Tony Tanner; and explanatory notes by John Dugdale. Oxford University Press 2009 l, 256p (Oxford world's classics) pa $9.95

ISBN 978-0-19-955486-7; 0-19-955486-2

First published 1852

"Blithedale, a Utopian community, is modeled on Brook Farm, the transcendentalist experiment at West Roxbury, Massachusetts, in which Hawthorne had participated ten years before he wrote the novel. Miles Coverdale, the narrator, is a coldly inquisitive observer; in revealing his knowledge of the other members of the community, he reveals himself." Reader's Ency. 4th edition

Hawthorne, Nathaniel

★ **Collected** novels. Literary Classics of the United States 1983 1272p $39.50

ISBN 0-940450-08-9

LC 82-18031

In Fanshawe (1828), two students at Harley College—one normal and outgoing, the other isolated and scholarly—both fall in love with a third student, Ellen Langdon. When Ellen is kidnapped, the isolated Fanshawe rescues her, only to turn down her marriage proposal afterward. The scarlet letter, The House of the Seven Gables, The Blithedale romance, and The marble faun are entered separately.

Hawthorne, Nathaniel

Complete short stories of Nathaniel Hawthorne. Hanover House 1959 615p

Hawthorne, Nathaniel

Doctor Grimshawe's secret; edited, with an introduction and notes, by Edward H. Davidson. Harvard Univ. Press 1954 305p il

Written 1883

"In a New England town in the early 19th century lives Dr. Grimshawe, an eccentric recluse, and two orphans, Ned and Elsie. The children are involved in a secret related to an estate in England, whence the doctor originally came. This estate has lacked a direct heir since the reign of Charles I, when the incumbent disappeared, leaving a bloody footprint on the threshold. After their guardian's death, the children are separated, but meet again years later, in England. Ned, now Edward Redclyffe, is injured while investigating the estate and is befriended by Colcord, his boyhood tutor. Lord Braithwaite, the estate's present owner, invites Edward to live at the Hall, where he meets Elsie, who warns him of a presentiment of danger. He finds the hiding place of an incredibly old man who 'haunts' the Hall, and recognizes him as the Sir Edward Redclyffe of the times of the bloody footprint. When the old man dies, Colcord produces a locket that proves Edward to be the heir." Oxford Companion to Am Lit. 6th edition

Hawthorne, Nathaniel

The **Hawthorne** treasury; complete novels and selected tales of Nathaniel Hawthorne. edited by Norman Holmes Pearson. Modern Lib. 1999 1409p

ISBN 0-679-60322-0

LC 98-47424

This volume includes the complete text of the following novels: Fanshawe, The scarlet letter, The House of Seven Gables, The Blithedale romance, and The marble faun. Also included are stories from twice-told tales, Mosses from an old manse, and The snow-image and other twice-told tales

Hawthorne, Nathaniel

★ The **House** of the Seven Gables; introduction by Mary Oliver. Modern Library 2001 312p pa $8.75

ISBN 0-375-75687-6

LC 00-64585

First published 1851

"Follows the fortunes of a decayed New England family, consisting of four members—Hephzibah Pyncheon, her brother Clifford, their cousin Judge Pyncheon, and other cousin Phoebe, a country girl. At the time the story opens Hephzibah is living in great poverty at the old homestead, the House of the Seven Gables. With her is [her brother] Clifford, just released from prison, where he had served a term of thirty years for the supposed murder of a rich uncle. Judge Pyncheon, who was influential in obtaining the innocent Clifford's arrest, that he might hide his own wrongdoing, now seeks to confine him in an asylum on the charge of insanity. Hephzibah's pitiful efforts to shield this brother, to support him and herself by keeping a scentshop, to circumvent the machinations of the judge, are described through the greater portion of the novel. The sudden death of the malevolent cousin frees them and makes them possessors of his wealth." Keller. Reader's Dig of Books

Hawthorne, Nathaniel

The **marble** faun; or, The romance of Monte Beni. Ohio State Univ. Press 1968 cxxxiii, 610p $83.95

ISBN 0-8142-0062-1

First published 1860

"The novel's central metaphor is a statue of a faun by Praxiteles that Hawthorne had seen in Florence. In the faun's fusing of animal and human characteristics he finds an allegory of the fall of man from amoral innocence to the knowledge of good and evil. . . . The faun of the novel is Donatello, a passionate young Italian who makes the acquaintance of three American artists, Miriam, Kenyon, and Hilda, who are spending time in Rome. When Donatello kills a man who has been shadowing Miriam, he is wracked by guilt until he is arrested by the police and imprisoned. Both of the women are tainted by guilt." Merriam-Webster's Ency of Lit

Hawthorne, Nathaniel

★ The **scarlet** letter; with an introduction by Alfred Kazin. Knopf 1992 xxvii, 273p $18

ISBN 0-679-41731-1

LC 92-52902

"Set in 17th-century Salem, the novel is built around three scaffold scenes, which occur at the beginning, the middle, and the end. The story opens with the public condemnation of Hester Prynne, and the exhortation that she confess the name of the father of Pearl, her illegitimate child. Hester's husband, an old and scholarly physician, just arrived from England, assumes the name of Roger Chillingworth in order to seek out Hester's lover and revenge himself upon him. He attaches himself as physician to a respected and seemingly holy minister, Arthur Dimmesdale, suspecting that he is the father of the child. The Scarlet Letter traces the

effect of the actual and symbolic sin on all the characters."
Benet's Reader's Ency of Am Lit

Hawthorne, Nathaniel

Tales and sketches, including Twice-told tales, Mosses from an old manse, and The snow-image; A wonder book for girls and boys; Tanglewood tales for girls and boys, being a second Wonder book. Library of Am. 1982 1493p $39.50

ISBN 0-940450-03-8

LC 81-20760

The stories in this collection have appeared in the five books: Twice-told tales (1837); Mosses from an old manse (1846); The snow-image (1852); A wonder book for girls and boys (1851); Tanglewood tales for girls and boys, being a second wonder book (1853)

This volume contains all of Hawthorne's tales and sketches, which are arranged in order of their periodical publication

Hawthorne, Nathaniel

Twice-told tales; introduction by Rosemary Mahoney; notes by Gretchen Short. Modern Library 2001 xxiv, 404p pa $10.95

ISBN 0-375-75788-0

LC 2001-31480

First published 1837

Hay, Elizabeth

Garbo laughs. Counterpoint 2003 294p $25

ISBN 1-582-43291-0

LC 2003-11989

A novel set in Ottawa. "Harriet, the Garbo-like star of the book, is a novelist who has developed the curious habit of writing but not mailing confiding letters to her hero, the then still-living film critic Pauline Kael, and discussing, at length, such burning cinematic questions as who is sexier, Cary Grant or Sean Connery, with her sweetly precocious and equality movie-mad son and daughter. As Harriet indulges her grand obsession with movies, she struggles with her less than passionate feelings for her real-life leading man and forges a warm but risky friendship with a new neighbor, the earthy Dinah." Booklist

"This rich, lovely novel makes us think about the ambivalences and contradictions of relationships and the patience of love." Quill & Quire

Hay, Elizabeth

Late nights on air; a novel. Counterpoint 2008 363p $24

ISBN 978-1-58243-408-7; 1-582-43408-5

LC 2007-43785

First published 2007 in Canada

"The plot of this novel is a faint signal, a series of short moments, sometimes funny, sometimes poignant, often flecked with intimations of tragedy. Hay's writing is so alluring and her lost souls so endearing that you'll lean in to catch the story's delicate developments as these characters shuffle along through quiet desperation and yearning." Washington Post Book World

Hay, Elizabeth

A student of weather. Counterpoint 2001 368p

ISBN 1-58243-123-X

LC 00-64445

This novel "begins circa 1930 on the drought-ravished prairies of Saskatchewan, the home of two motherless sisters. The elder, Lucinda, is fair and diligent, Norma Joyce dark and willful, and both fall for a handsome, rambling botanist from fabled Ottawa, Maurice Dove. . . . As the sisters embark on a tragic rivalry that will determine the course of their lives, their story becomes a fairy tale in which solitude, work, art, and desire acquire mystical significance as Hay adroitly weaves their passions into luminous descriptions of extreme weather and the grand cycle of the seasons." Booklist

Hayder, Mo

Birdman; Mo Hayder. 1st ed. Doubleday 1999 327 p. (hardcover) $23.95

ISBN 038549694X; 9780385496940

LC 99015941

In this mystery novel, as the newest member of the Area Major Investigation Pool, Detective Inspector Jack Caffrey "is called to examine the deaths of five women, each found with a bird in her chest cavity. When other investigators take the case in a wrong direction, Caffery risks his new position to find the truth." (Library Journal)

Hayder, Mo

Gone. Atlantic Monthly Press 2011 415p $24

ISBN 978-0-8021-1964-3; 0-8021-1964-6

A crime novel featuring "Detective Inspector Jack Caffery of Bristol's Major Crime Investigation Unit and Sgt. Flea Marley, who heads up the Underwater Search Unit. This artfully constructed procedural opens with a car-jacking that becomes a kidnapping after the thief drives off with a little girl in the back seat. The narrative takes its first chilling turn when Caffery's team detects a pattern of other 'accidental' kidnappings, indicating that the carjacker was stalking little girls all along. More shocks are in store, but for once the visceral thrills don't come at the expense of character. By giving her villain the intelligence to inflict as much emotional as physical pain, Hayder makes him less of a monster and more of a terror." N Y Times Book Rev

Hayder, Mo

Hanging hill; Mo Hayder. Atlantic Monthly Press 2012 432 p.

ISBN 0802120067; 9780802120069

The story in this book "centers around a pair of estranged sisters--one policewoman--and the gruesome homicide of a teenage beauty, which leads them deeper than they ever anticipated into an underground world of sex and violence. One morning in picture-perfect Bath, England, a teenage girl's body is found on the towpath of a canal: Lorne Woods--beautiful, popular, and apparently the victim of a disturbingly brutal murder. . . . Zoe Benedict . . . is convinced the department head needs to look beyond the usual domestic motives to solve the case. . . . When Zoe's investigation turns up evidence that Lorne's attempts to break into modeling had delivered her into the world of webcam girls and amateur porn, a crippling secret from Zoe's past seems determined to emerge." (Publisher's note)

Hayder, Mo

Poppet; Mo Hayder. Pgw 2013 400 p. (hardcover) $25

ISBN 0802121071; 9780802121073

This horror-thriller novel, by Mo Hayder, is part of the "Jack Caffery" series. "Everything goes according to procedure when a patient, Isaac is released into the community from a high security mental health ward. But when the staff realize that he was connected to a series of unexplained episodes of self-harm amongst the ward's patients, and . . . was released in error, they call on Detective Jack Caffery to investigate, and to track Isaac down before he can kill again." (Publisher's note)

Hayder, Mo

Ritual. Atlantic Monthly Press 2008 410p $24

ISBN 978-0-87113-992-4

At the start of this crime novel featuring Det. Insp. Jack Caffery, "Sgt. Phoebe Flea Marley, a police diver, retrieves a severed hand from Bristol harbor. Without a corpse, the investigation stalls, until fingerprints identify the hand as belonging to Ian Mossy Mallows, a known heroin junkie. While Caffery pursues the drug angle, Flea uncovers a possible connection to muti, a brand of African witchcraft and traditional medicine that incorporates body parts into its rituals. Digging deeper, Caffery and Flea discover that Mallows may still be alive and the men responsible may be using muti as a cover for even darker purposes. . . . Hayder vividly evokes torture and drug abuse, but the violence is never gratuitous. Readers looking for visceral thrills need look no further than this gritty English series." Publ Wkly

Hayder, Mo

Skin; Mo Hayder. Bantam Press 2009 384 p. (ebook) $13.00; (paperback) $13.00; (hardcover) $22.00

ISBN 9780802198013; 9780802145178; 9780802119308 out of print

LC 2009437589

In this novel, by Mo Hayder, "when the decomposed body of a young woman is found near some railway tracks just outside Bristol one hot May morning, all indications are that she committed suicide. . . . But DI Jack Caffery is not so sure. . . . Police diver Flea Marley is working alongside Caffery. . . . And then she makes a discovery that changes everything." (Publisher's note)

Hayder, Mo

The treatment; Mo Hayder. 1st ed. Doubleday 2002 357 p. (hardcover) $23.95

ISBN 0385496958; 9780385496957

LC 2002280302

This is Mo Hayder's second Jack Caffery novel. Here, a "man and his wife lie tied up and imprisoned in their own home. When they are discovered, badly dehydrated and bearing the marks of a brutal beating, they reveal one final horror: Their young son has disappeared. Called in to investigate, Jack Caffery uses all the tricks of the forensic inves-

tigator's trade to piece together the scanty clues at the crime scene." (Publisher's note)

Haydon, Elizabeth

Destiny: child of the sky. TOR Bks. 2001 556p $27.95

ISBN 0-312-86750-6

LC 2001-27473

Sequel to: Prophecy: child of earth

"Though obviously inspired by music theory, Norse and Celtic folklore, and seemingly such authors as Tolkien, C.S. Lewis, Patricia A. McKillip, Anne McCaffrey and Palmer Brown (Cheerful), the author uses a fluid writing style to build a world uniquely and compellingly her own." Publ Wkly

Haydon, Elizabeth

Prophecy; child of earth. TOR Bks. 2000 480p $27.95

ISBN 0-312-86751-4

LC 00-26836

Sequel to Rhapsody (1999)

"The skysinger Rhapsody and her two FirBolg companions seek to carve out a place for themselves in a new world even as their lives move inexorably toward the fulfillment of an ancient prophecy. As momentous events take shape around the three heroes, other forces work hard to undermine their hope and bring the powers of evil closer to victory. . . . Haydon's epic saga of the endless battle between light and darkness resounds with the richness of ancient myths reworked into new forms." Libr J

Haydon, Elizabeth

Requiem for the sun. TOR Bks. 2002 462p $27.95

ISBN 0-312-87884-2

LC 2002-28584

First title in a second Rhapsody fantasy/romance trilogy

"Bears for neologisms may growl over words such as coronated and infrastructure, but even they will raise glasses to toast Haydon's generally high levels of achievement in characterization, world building through well-chosen detail, folkloric and musical expertise, and warmth of spirit." Booklist

Haymon, S. T.

A beautiful death. St. Martin's Press 1994 223p

LC 93-37005

First published 1993 in the United Kingdom

Inspector Ben Jurnet "plunges into his deepest fit of melancholia to date when his fiancée is blown to bits by a car bomb. . . . Racked with guilt for surviving the attack that was surely meant for him, the English copper stumbles through his grief, enduring the sympathy of his friends and the glee of his enemies, until he bolts for Ireland in pursuit of a neighborhood youth with terrorist clan connections in the old country. Ms. Haymon, an elegant and assured stylist whose esthetic juices are always stirred by a good, gloomy setting, finds the perfect lyric complement for Jurnet's dismal mood in the gray, misty drizzle of County Donegal in November." N Y Times Book Rev

Haymon, S. T.

Death of a hero. St. Martin's Press 1996 176p
ISBN 978-0312145828

LC 96-27968

"Posthumously published, Haymond's . . . final work details Detective Inspector Ben Jurnet's last case. Although still mourning the death of his fiancée, he investigates the murder of an idealistic protest leader in the local redlight district. A reliable police procedural." Libr J

Haynes, Dana

Crashers. Minotaur Books 2010 343p $24.99
ISBN 978-0-312-59988-1; 0-312-59988-9

LC 2009-46155

"The premise is simple: a crack team of National Transportation Safety Board experts investigate airplane crashes. Normally they take months to sift through wreckage and evidence, but this time they have mere days: if they can't figure out what and who brought down CascadeAir Flight 818, more planes will fall from the sky. The lead characters, the Crashers, are cut from familiar molds: the hotshot engineer, the voice-recorder specialist, the veteran pathologist, and so on. . . . The plot itself relies on familar assembly-cast TV crime dramas, but it is well paced and generates plenty of tension. A solid debut that, with some fine-tuning, could become an engaging series." Booklist

Haynes, Elizabeth

Dark tide; a novel. Elizabeth Haynes. HarperCollins 2012 400 p. (hardcover) $25.99; (paperback) $14.99
ISBN 0062197339; 9780062197320; 9780062197337

LC 2012024422

This novel, by Elizabeth Haynes, is a "thriller about a woman caught in an underworld of corruption and murder. . . . Genevieve has finally . . . [left] the stress of London behind and start a new life aboard a houseboat in Kent. . . . But the night of her boat-warming party, a body washes up, and to Genevieve's horror, she recognizes the victim. . . . The death can't have anything to do with her. Or so she thinks." (Publisher's note)

Haynes, Elizabeth

Into the darkest corner; a novel. Elizabeth Haynes. Harper 2012 400 p. (hbk.) $25.99
ISBN 0062197258 Harper; 9780062197252 Harper

LC 2012371019

In "[Elizabeth] Haynes' debut, a woman is stalked by the former lover who nearly killed her. Because of a dual time frame that introduces us to twitching, OCD- and PTSD-plagued Catherine Bailey in the fall of 2007 and then pulls back to 2003, we know that the gorgeous, too-good-to-be-true guy she meets in a bar on Halloween is . . . too good to be true. . . . The author . . . traces Cathy's evolution from feisty party girl to paralyzed victim too terrified to do anything but wait for the next blow or knife slash." (Kirkus Reviews)

Hays, Tommy

The **pleasure** was mine. St. Martin's Press 2005 255p $23.95
ISBN 0-312-33932-1

LC 2004-51311

This novel depicts the "transformation of a family in which an older man cares for his wife during her descent into Alzheimer's. The transformation begins when Prate Marshbanks, the remarkable, curmudgeonly protagonist, gets a visitor for the summer: his nine-year-old grandson, Jackson, whose mother died in a car accident several years before. But, despite Jackson's grieving presence, Marshbanks remains preoccupied with his own battle to ensure compassionate care for his wife, whom he has had to place in a nursing home. Hays's elegiac, penetrating description of Prate's marriage frames the landscape of this brilliant novel about love, loss, marriage and family. He offers a grim but hopeful treatment of a difficult subject, and his elegant writing and sharp, tender portraits of the Marshbanks make a potent combination." Publ Wkly

Hayter, Sparkle

Bandit queen boogie. Three Rivers Press 2004 290p pa $13
ISBN 1-4000-4744-7 pa

LC 2003-25853

"Two childhood friends travel across Europe the summer after their college graduation. The trip was meant for Chloe and her boyfriend, but after he dumps her, Blackie agrees to go instead. Unfortunately, brokenhearted Chloe is not much fun to be around—until the two decide to start robbing the sleazy married men who proposition them. Chloe soon perks up, getting addicted to the thrill and the possibility of being caught. Although the story centers on Chloe and Blackie, numerous characters and story lines come together when they steal a statue of the Hindu god Ganesh that contains a valuable treasure belonging to an Indian crime boss. . . . The characters are vividly rendered, and Hayter deftly weaves together the varying story lines and settings." Libr J

Haywood, Gar Anthony

Cemetery Road. Severn House 2010 216p $28.95
ISBN 978-0-7278-6851-0; 0-7278-6851-9
First published 2009 in the United Kingdom

"Errol 'Handy' White is working as a handyman in the Twin Cities when he gets word that his old friend, R. J. Burrows, has been murdered in Los Angeles. Handy knows he must return to L.A. to attend the funeral, but he also knows that when he sets foot in L.A., where he, R. J., and another friend, O'Neal Holden, now a rising politician, came up together, a terrible secret is in danger of coming to light. As young men, the three friends dabbled in crime in South Central L.A. until a revenge heist at a drug dealer's home went tragically awry. Handy has been running ever since, from the crime and from himself, but now realizes that if he is to help R. J.'s daughter find her father's killer, his running days are over. Haywood melds an intricately plotted but highly suspenseful thriller to a moving story of belated coming-of-age, as the introspective, deeply troubled Handy forces himself to confront what has gone wrong with his life." Booklist

Hazzard, Shirley

★ The **great** fire. Farrar, Straus & Giroux 2003 278p $24

ISBN 0-374-16644-7

LC 2003-49189

"The time is 1947-48, and the place is, primarily, East Asia. . . . Our hero, and indeed he fills the requirements to be called one, is Aldred Leith, who is English and part of the occupation forces in Japan; his particular military task is damage survey. He has an interesting past, including, most recently, a two-year walk across civil-war-torn China to write a book. In the present. . .he meets the teenage daughter and younger son of a local Australian commander. And, as Helen is growing headlong into womanhood, this novel of war's aftermath becomes a story of love—or more to the point, of the restoration of the capacity for love once global and personal trauma have been shed." Booklist

Hazzard, Shirley

★ The **transit** of Venus. Viking 1980 337p

LC 79-21754

This "is an exceedingly ambitious novel; a stunning and at times bewildering galaxy of ideas. From a literary and intellectual standpoint it is a challenge. . . . Miss Hazzard's greatest achievement in this novel is the suspense she creates from unfinished relationships. Instead of spinning off in different directions through space, these characters collide once again, drawn together by an ineluctable magnetism." Christ Sci Monit

Healy, J. F.

Invasion of privacy; a John Francis Cuddy mystery. {by} Jeremiah Healy. Pocket Bks. 1996 340p

ISBN 978-0671898748

LC 96-1196

"Acting on behalf of successful bank employee Olga Evorova, Boston P.I. John Cuddy scopes out her secretive potential fiancé, a reclusive man of no apparent family or heritage. Cuddy's investigation stirs up trouble: representatives of the Milwaukee mob appear on the scene and apply pressure." Libr J

"The dialogue crackles, the plot is complex and clever, and Cuddy's relationship with his longtime lover faces a crisis in which machismo won't help." Booklist

Healy, J. F.

Shallow graves; a John Cuddy mystery. {by} Jeremiah Healy. Pocket Bks. 1992 282p

LC 91-44059

"On the verge of a big-time modeling career in New York, Boston model Mau Tim Dani is strangled in her apartment. It looks like a burglary gone bad, but her modeling agency, which carried a 'key employee' insurance policy on her with Empire Insurance, wants to know for sure. Boston private eye John Cuddy used to investigate claims for Empire, which is why he's taken aback when the firm hires him to investigate the death." Booklist

"Healy gives his readers an array of distinctive characters while engaging them in a deftly plotted and satisfying story." Publ Wkly

Healy, J. F.

Spiral; a John Francis Cuddy mystery. {by} Jeremiah Healy. Pocket Bks. 1999 359p

ISBN 0-671-00955-9

LC 99-25769

"Boston private investigator John Cuddy is reeling from the death of his love, Nancy Meagher, in an airline disaster. He can barely cope with the present, and the future seems bleak when his past comes calling. A fellow Vietnam vet enlists Cuddy's investigative skills on behalf of their old commander, Nicolas Helides, whose 13-year-old granddaughter was murdered during a party at the Helides' Florida estate." Booklist

Hearon, Shelby

Footprints. Knopf 1996 191p

ISBN 978-0679446415

LC 95-42853

"Shelby Hearon takes a long, speculative look at the moment in the life of a family when a child departs. She has done a fine job of getting at this inevitable conflict between mother and child, between mother and father. She holds it to the light, turns and examines it with a caustic eye. We are the beneficiaries of a clear-eyed view that catches the humor and poignancy of the evolution of a woman's life." N Y Times Book Rev

Hearon, Shelby

Year of the dog; a novel. University of Texas Press 2007 227p (James A. Michener fiction series) $21

ISBN 978-0-292-71469-4; 0-292-71469-6

LC 2006-22585

"This is not just a cute-sad book about loving and losing a dog but instead a complex and very real story of love and loss, changing perspectives, and making the best of what life gives you. In Hearon's more than capable hands, it is a pleasure." Booklist

Heathcock, Alan

Volt; stories. Graywolf Press 2011 207p pa $15

ISBN 978-1-55597-577-7; 1-55597-577-1

This is a collection of eight linked stories set in an imaginary rural town.

"In these eight stories, four previously published in literary journals, the settings are small towns in the mountains and valleys of the northern plains states. No peaceful rural areas exist in Heathcock's imagination. There's a violent death, whether accidental or planned, in every story. The last six stories constitute a terrific cycle, set in the same town, with the repeating characters of sheriff, mayor, and minister and plots that provide climaxes and resolutions that suit the cycle. . . . Heathcock displays a real talent for describing a character in a telling phrase and shows a deep appreciation of the petty and serious violence of daily life. Recommend Volt to fans of Cormac McCarthy, Larry Brown, and Tom Franklin." Booklist

Hedaya, Yael

Eden; a novel. translated [from the Hebrew] by Jessica Cohen. Metropolitan Books/Henry Holt and Co. 2010 486p $35

ISBN 978-0-8050-9265-3; 0-8050-9265-X

LC 2010-07149

Original Hebrew edition 2005

"Hedaya presents the stark realities of middle age against the background of the harsh Israeli countryside. The book is geographically focused on the city of Eden, a rural Israeli town that is the home of several families whose lives become intertwined throughout the course of the novel. Mark and Alona, a separated couple with two young children, find that living apart brings them closer together even though their musings on relationships are often morose and dark. Mark's teenage daughter, Roni, neglected and lonely, finds an outlet for her emotions and energy through poetry and torrid love affairs with older men. One of those men is Eli, a lawyer whose wife, Dafna, has focused all of her energy into getting pregnant, a task that she has failed to accomplish for seven years." Booklist

Hedges, Peter

The **Heights**. Dutton 2010 295p $25.95

ISBN 978-0-525-95113-1; 0-525-95113-X

LC 2009-20781

"Hedges brings a touch of farce into the many twists before the climax. Warmhearted yet unsentimental, a smooth weave of marital and neighborhood dynamics." Kirkus

Heffernan, William

★ The **dead** detective. Akashic 2010 319p $24.95

ISBN 978-1-936070-61-9; 1-936070-61-8

This novel "introduces Harry Doyle, a soulful homicide cop on the Pinellas County police force who owes his life to the officers who resuscitated him at the age of 10 after his crazy mother tried to send Harry and his younger brother to meet Jesus in heaven. A little overwrought, that bit, though more original than clichés like the stripper who lives with her mother and is working her way through college. But, corny conventions and all, this edgy police drama succeeds in capturing the hysteria that grips Tampa residents when a celebrity criminal — a teacher who seduced a 14-year-old student — is found dead in a cypress swamp with her throat cut and the word 'Evil' carved on her forehead. And you've got to admire a cop who rules out suicide in the case of a guy who died in the middle of watching a Bruce Willis movie on pay-per-view television." N Y Times Book Rev

Heffernan, William

The **Dinosaur** Club; a novel. Morrow 1997 303p

ISBN 0-688-14988-X

LC 96-46637

"At age 49, Jack Fallon discovers that his life is plummeting out of control. In one fell swoop, his wife leaves him and corporate downsizing threatens his livelihood. Always the warrior, Jack organizes other fiftyish management employees to fight their ruthless corporate leaders, and the 'Dinosaur Club' is born. Working against formidable odds, the Dinosaurs engage in hilarious hijinks and serious espionage to foil their chief executives. What Jack does not count on is falling in love with Samantha Moore, legal counsel for the corporation. . . . Heffernan is masterly in examining the scruples of corporate downsizing with a discerning eye and blends levity in his cauldron of good and evil." Libr J

Heffernan, William

Red angel; a novel. Morrow 2000 273p $24

ISBN 0-688-16563-X

LC 99-36638

"New York City special investigative detective Paul Devlin leaves behind an apparent gang war to help Adrianna, his Cuban American lover, with a family problem in Cuba. Only after arriving do they discover the death of Adrianna's aunt—widely known in Cuba as a heroine of the Revolution—and learn that members of a voodoo cult have stolen her body. With the assistance of a local policeman and Devlin's New York partner, Devlin and Adrianna struggle against the machinations of the Cuban secret police and other to uncover the truth. Deeply involving, expertly detailed, and strategically plotted." Libr J

Heggen, Thomas

Mister Roberts; with an introduction by David P. Smith. Naval Inst. Press 1992 xxii, 200p $34.95

ISBN 1-55750-723-6

LC 92-9422

A reissue of the title first published 1946 by Houghton Mifflin

"The leisurely narrative is told in a very few incidents, all centering about an admirable young lieutenant miserably defeated in his desire to get into fighting. A quiet, credible story of the corroding effects of apathy and boredom on men who, in battle, might have been heroes." New Yorker

Hegi, Ursula

Children and fire; a novel. Scribner 2011 272p $25

ISBN 978-1-4516-0829-8; 1-4516-0829-2

LC 2011-08398

"A thoughtful, sidelong approach to the worst moment in Germany's history that invites us to understand how decent people come to collaborate with evil." Kirkus

Hegi, Ursula

Stones from the river. Poseidon Press 1994 507p

ISBN 0-671-78075-1

LC 93-33533

"This moving, elegiac novel commands our compassion and respect for the wisdom and courage to be found in unlikely places, in unlikely times." N Y Times Book Rev

Hegi, Ursula

The **vision** of Emma Blau. Simon & Schuster 2000 432p $25

ISBN 0-684-82997-5

LC 99-56392

"Hegi has created a milieu full of sexual energy—the book is often erotic—and has captured both the tension and love endemic to all tight-knit families. Compelling and absorbing, this old-fashioned saga is rife with passion, tragedy, and redemption." Libr J

Hegi, Ursula

The **worst** thing I've done; a novel. Simon and Schuster 2007 260p $25

ISBN 978-1-4165-4375-6; 1-416-54375-9

LC 2006-101171

"Annie is addicted to talk radio, especially the dueling doctors who dispense psychological advice to the desperate. It makes her feel better about her own depressing circumstances, as she seeks to understand just how the special childhood friendship between herself, charismatic Mason, and steadfast Jake went so tragically wrong. When Annie's parents died on the day she married Mason, the three friends agreed to raise Annie's infant sister. But all their youthful optimism slowly begins to pall when the dynamics of their triangular relationship shift in disturbing directions." Booklist

"One of Hegi's most enchanting skills is her ability to recreate setting, here a Long Island coastal community. . . . A moving exploration of grief." Libr J

Heidish, Marcy

A **woman** called Moses; a novel based on the life of Harriet Tubman. Houghton Mifflin 1976 308p

"This fictional life story, told in the first person, is filled with incandescent raw materials, namely the cruelties of slavery, and the itineraries of escape." N Y Times Book Rev

Hein, Christoph

Settlement; a novel. translated by Philip Boehm. H. Holt 2008 323p $27

ISBN 978-0-8050-7768-1; 0-8050-7768-5

LC 2008-09021

Original German edition, 2004

"The rags-to-riches life story of Bernhard Haber, a refugee living in a small East German town following World War II, is told in five segments, each narrated by someone who knew him: a school chum, his first girlfriend, a fellow rabble-rouser, a former lover, and a merchant colleague. As a child, Haber is tormented by townspeople who consider refugees filthy and lazy, and this cements his obsession with revenge in the form of power and wealth. The chillingly single-minded Haber remains fairly one-dimensional, but the side characters are fleshed with excruciating accuracy and detail." Booklist

Heinemann, Larry

Paco's story. Farrar, Straus & Giroux 1986 209p

LC 86-19527

"Mr. Heinemann's carefully crafted, oblique narrative suggests that the right words are not going to be found in ever-more-graphic, frontal approaches to 'gruesome carnage.' Its horrors may be as forcefully conveyed by a haunting scene in a greasy spoon as by the tearing of human flesh." N Y Times Book Rev

Heinlein, Robert A. (Robert Anson), 1907-1988

★ **Citizen** of the galaxy. Scribner 1957 302p

"Although marketed as a juvenile novel, this work was serialized for adults in Astounding. The Horatio Alger hero is in an interstellar setting, except that his lad starts out closer to the edge than Horatio's bootblacks and newsboys: he is a slave on a far planet of a despotic empire. He escapes into space with a nomadic trading company and eventually gets back to Earth, where he assumes (by inheritance!) the headship of a giant financial corporation. This is a bilungsroman, except that the young hero never really grows up; but Heinlein's knack for creating sociologically plausible cultures is well displayed." Anatomy of Wonder 4

Heinlein, Robert A.

Friday. Holt, Rinehart & Winston 1982 368p il

LC 81-13221

"An artificially created superwoman, courier for a secret organization, has to fend for herself when the decline of the West reaches its climax; she ultimately finds a new raison d'être on the extraterrestrial frontier. Welcomed by Heinlein fans as action-adventure respite from his more introspective works." Anatomy of Wonder 4

Heinlein, Robert A.

Job: a comedy of justice. Ballantine Bks. 1984 376p

LC 84-3091

"Alexander Hergensheimer, a minister from an alternate-world America dominated by Bible Belt fundamentalism, is flipped from one alternate world to another in rapid succession, whereby his faith, his endurance, and his love for his Margrethe are supremely tested. There are occasional patches of discursive philosophical, religious, and ethical ramblings here, which will be familiar territory to most of Heinlein's readers. For the most part, however, this tightly written, provocative, and powerful book, with its large cast of intriguing characters and an irresistibly compelling love story, is eminently readable." Booklist

Heinlein, Robert A.

★ The **moon** is a harsh mistress. Putnam 1966 383p

"Colonists of the Moon declare independence from Earth, and contrive to win the ensuing battle with the aid of a sentient computer. Action-adventure with some exploration of new possibilities in social organization and fierce assertion of the motto 'There Ain't No Such Thing as a Free Lunch.'" Anatomy of Wonder 4

Heinlein, Robert A.

The **puppet** masters. Doubleday 1951 219p

ISBN 0-451-07339-8

"Heinlein's paranoia-laden tale of sluglike creatures, arrived in saucer-shaped craft to enslave humans by the particularly gruesome procedure of growing into each person's nervous system from a position on the upper back of the victim—making his or her profile humpbacked." Anatomy of Wonder. 3d edition

Heinlein, Robert A.

Starship troopers; Ace trade pbk. ed.; Ace Books 2006 279p pa $15

ISBN 0-441-01410-0; 978-0-441-01410-1

LC 2006-40451

First published 1959 by Putnam

"Originally intended as a juvenile, although not published as such, this violent novel of interstellar 'war' won a 1960 Hugo but also gained RAH the reputation of being a militarist, even a 'fascist.'" Sci Fic Ency

Heinlein, Robert A.

★ **Stranger** in a strange land. Putnam 1961 408p hardcover o.p. pa $16.95

ISBN 0-441-78838-6 pa

"The hero is a human born of space travelers from earth and raised by Martians. He is brought to the totalitarian post-World War III world that is in many ways depicted as a satire of the U.S. in the 1960s, marked by repressiveness in sexual morality and religion. The plot, which tells how the heroic stranger creates a Utopian society in which people preserve their individuality but share a brotherhood of community, made Heinlein and his novel cult objects for young people dedicated to a counterculture." Oxford Companion to Am Lit. 5th edition

Heinlein, Robert A. (Robert Anson), 1907-1988

Variable star; Robert A. Heinlein and Spider Robinson. Tor 2006 318p (pbk.) $7.99; (hbk.) $24.95

ISBN 9780765351685; 076531312X

LC 2006006865

This science fiction book, based on "a fifties-era outline" by author Robert A. Heinlein, tells the story of "a young space explorer colonizing a new world. After discovering his fiancee and supposed fellow orphan is really a wealthy mogul's granddaughter, struggling musician Joel Johnston gets cold feet and grabs the next outbound starship. With his formative agricultural training on Ganymede, Joel has skills that come in handy tending goats and crops in preparation for landfall on Brasil Novo. Yet his vow to abandon love in favor of farming meets some surprising--and romantically intriguing--challenges." (Booklist)

Held, Rhiannon

Silver; Rhiannon Held. 1st ed. Tor Books 2012 336 p. (paperback) $14.99; (paperback) $7.99

ISBN 0765330377; 9780765330376; 9781429991094; 9780765368157

LC 2012011645

In this book, "Andrew Dare's job as the enforcer for the Roanoke pack of werewolves requires him to work solo. But when a strange and disturbing scent leads him to rogue werewolf, a female called Silver, he ends up joining forces with her. She suffers from a persistent madness and has lost the ability to shift from her human form as a result of torture. Dare and Silver set out across the country in search of a killer who poses a threat to every werewolf on the continent." (Library Journal)

Hellenga, Robert

The **Italian** lover; a novel. Little, Brown 2007 343p $23.99

ISBN 978-0-316-11763-0; 0-316-11763-3

LC 2007-8716

"Hellenga smoothly merges past and present while injecting Margot's story with fresh talent. . . . This being Italy, there are affairs, fiery outbursts and lots of rich food. This being Hellenga, the story is just as rich." N Y Times Book Rev

Hellenga, Robert

Philosophy made simple; a novel. Little, Brown 2006 277p $23.95

ISBN 0-316-05826-2

LC 2005-10883

"Hellenga possesses an exceptionally magnetic voice, enabling him to draw readers in with charm, then hand them profundity. Alone in his new digs, Rudy feels adrift in a strange and confounding world. A Christian radio station declares the Second Coming. An elephant named Norma Jean paints beautiful, brilliantly hued abstract compositions. . . . Supremely wily and compelling, Hellenga turns a human tale of reason versus feeling into a cosmic playoff between order and chaos." Booklist

Hellenga, Robert

★ **Snakewoman** of Little Egypt; a novel. Bloomsbury 2010 342p $25

ISBN 978-1-60819-262-5; 1-60819-262-8

LC 2010-04164

"Jackson Jones is a professor of anthropology who misses life in the Congo, where he did extensive fieldwork on the Mbuti. He's back in southern Illinois, recovering from illness, and not sure what comes next. . . . Into that opening steps Sunny, the beautiful young niece of a deceased friend. She's just been released from prison for shooting her husband, Earl, pastor of the rattlesnake-handling Church of the Burning Bush With Signs Following. . . . Before long, Jackson and Sunny are lovers. She becomes a college student, and he undertakes what he thinks is an academic study of the church. . . . Catfish wrangling, the history of the timpani, how to dress a deer — I'll admit to skipping a few short sections, including instructions for planting a radio transmitter under a snake's skin. Yet the story never flags. A gun appears on the book's first page, and there's no question it'll get fired. Tying up the strands of a story this complex is tricky, but the ending feels both inevitable and moving." Cleveland Plain Dealer

Heller, Jane

Best enemies. St. Martin's Press 2004 341p $24.95

ISBN 0-312-28849-2

LC 2003-61063

"Amy Sherman and Tara Messer, lifelong best friends, are now all grown up and living in New York City. There has always been some friction in their relationship because Amy feels overshadowed by the extravagantly beautiful and elegant Tara (a lifestyle guru). When Amy catches her fiance, Stuart, in a passionate embrace with Tara two weeks before the wedding, she cuts both of them out of her life. The two eventually marry each other, while Amy focuses on her demanding job as publicity director for a major publisher. Four years later, Amy and Tara are thrown together when Amy is assigned to promote Tara's new book. The two women weave a web of deception, with Tara pretending her life is perfect (even though Stuart is a serial womanizer) while Amy invents a rich, handsome boyfriend, whom she then has to produce." Booklist

Heller, Joseph
  ★ Catch-22; a novel. Simon & Schuster 1999 415p $26
    ISBN 0-684-86513-0
               LC 00-265132
  "A comic, satirical, surreal, and apocalyptic novel . . . which describes the ordeals and exploits of a group of American airmen based on a small Mediterranean island during the Italian campaign of the Second World War, and in particular the reactions of Captain Yossarian, the protagonist." Oxford Companion to Engl Lit. 6th edition
  Followed by Closing time

Heller, Joseph
  Closing time; a novel. Simon & Schuster 1994 464p
    ISBN 0-671-74604-9
               LC 94-20604
  "Heller is richly paranoid about state paranoia, and his winning jokes are more vicious than anything even in Catch-22 itself. Besides which, although Closing Time is too often like an electricity grid in danger of fusing, there are many exchanges that display all the old verve." New Statesman Soc

Heller, Joseph
  Good as Gold. Simon & Schuster 1979 447p
    ISBN 0-671-22923-0
               LC 78-23894
  "Dr. Bruce Gold, forty-eight-year-old professor (Jewish) of literature (English) and author of many seminal articles in small journals (unread), finds himself facing the prospect of becoming a high Washington official. The offer comes from Ralph Newsome (Protestant), a presidential aide. . . . {Gold accepts} and soon meets Andrea Conover, the tall, beautiful, gifted daughter (also Protestant) of a wealthy, retired career diplomat (anti-Semite), clearly the suitable mate for a man with a potential of becoming the country's (very first Jewish) Secretary of State." Publisher's note

Heller, Joseph
  Portrait of an artist, as an old man. Simon & Schuster 2000 233p $23
    ISBN 0-7432-0200-7
               LC 00-711802
  "Eugene Pota, the hero, is an aging novelist whose imaginative powers have been in steady decline since his earlier, more successful works. The book is a record of Pota's attempts to cap off his career with another triumph, and consequently a collection of false starts: here a parody of 'The Metamorphosis,' there a Greek-myth burlesque set among lickerish gods. While these set pieces are almost uniformly unsatisfying (only a fantasia that anatomizes the melancholy of nineteenth-century authors really works), there is something bleakly bracing in Pota's obsession with his own literary desiccation." New Yorker

Heller, Joseph
  ★ Something happened. Knopf 1974 569p
    ISBN 0-394-46568-7
  The protagonist of this novel "Bob Slocum, works for a large, nameless company that sells something. What, we never learn. Slocum has a wife without a name, a disgruntled 15-year-old daughter and adorable 9-year-old son, both also unnamed, and a retarded child, Derek, who has a name and nothing else. Slocum lives in terror at his office, where 'there are six people who are afraid of me, and one small secretary who is afraid of all of us. I have one other person working for me who is not afraid of anyone, not even me, and I would fire him quickly, but I'm afraid of him.' Slocum carries his anxieties home. . . . 'Only one member of the family is not afraid of any of the others, and that one is an idiot.' Between these dry equations Slocum circles and recircles the question of what went wrong with his life." Newsweek

Heller, Peter
  ★ The dog stars; a novel. Peter Heller. 1st ed. Alfred A. Knopf 2012 272 p. (hardcover) $24.95; (ebook) $24.95; (paperback) $15.00
    ISBN 0307959945; 9780307959942; 9780307960931; 9780307950475
               LC 2011050429
  This book by Peter Heller "takes place nine years after a superflu has killed off much of mankind. Hig, an amateur pilot living in Colorado, has retreated to an abandoned airport. . . . Hig's one real comfort . . . is his dog, Jasper. But when that comfort is withdrawn, Hig flies west in search of the radio voice that called out to him three years before. Instead, he ends up being shot down and restrained by a doctor named Cima and her shotgun-toting father, a former Navy SEAL." (Publishers Weekly)

Heller, Zoe
  The believers; a novel. HarperCollins 2009 335p $25.99
    ISBN 978-0-06-143020-6; 0-06-143020-X
               LC 2008-24633
  Heller is an "extraordinarily entertaining writer, and this novel showcases her copious gifts, including a scathing, Waugh-like wit; an unerring ear for the absurdities of contemporary speech; and a native-born Brit's radar for class and status distinctions." N Y Times (Late N Y Ed)

Heller, Zoe
  What was she thinking? notes on a scandal. Holt & Co. 2003 258p $23
    ISBN 0-8050-7333-7
               LC 2002-38809
  "Barbara Covett, a sixtyish history teacher, is the kind of unmarried-woman-with-cat whose female friends sooner or later decide she is 'too intense.' Thus when a beautiful new pottery teacher, Sheba Hart. . .chooses Barbara as a confidante, she is deeply, even rather sinisterly, gratified. Sheba's secret is explosive: married with two kids, she is having an affair with a fifteen-year-old student. . . .Equally adroit at satire and at psychological suspense, Heller charts the course of a predatory friendship and demonstrates the lengths to which some people go for human company." New Yorker

Hellstrom, Borge
  Cell 8; by Anders Roslund and Borge Hellstrom. SilverOak 2012 384p $24.95
    ISBN 9781410445117; 1410445119; 9781402787157
               LC 2011041325

This book tells the story of "dour sociopathic copper Ewert Grens" who investigates the seemingly routine case of "John Schwartz, a crooner on a cruise ship between Stockholm and Finland," arrested for assaulting "a drunken passenger harassing females on the dance floor. . . . But the uncooperative prisoner is in fact a man called John Meyer Frey. And Frey, it seems, died several years ago while awaiting execution on death row in an Ohio prison. Grens becomes obsessed with the case -- as does another man, whose life has been ruined buy the unfulfilled retribution he has thirsted for after many years." (independent.co.uk)

Helprin, Mark
Ellis Island & other stories. Delacorte Press 1981 196p
LC 80-18437

This book "consists of a novella (the title story) and ten short stories whose variation in length, content, style, and theme attest to the remarkable versatility of the writer. . . . Written in the first person, 'Ellis Island' is a four-part story— the recollections of an enterprising Jewish immigrant who finds himself temporarily stranded on that famous stepping stone to the New World. His vulnerability to the arbitrary decisions of immigration functionaries, his efforts to keep from being deported, and his attempts to earn a living are adventures told with a whimsical humor by a raconteur with a zest for life." Best Sellers

Helprin, Mark
★ **In** sunlight and in shadow; Mark Helprin. Houghton Mifflin Harcourt 2012 xiv, 705 p.p
ISBN 0547819234; 9780547819235
LC 2012016242

This novel by Mark Helprin focuses on a "love story . . . in postwar America. Harry Copeland, . . . a former paratrooper, . . . [p]ursues [Catherine Thomas Hale], and in time he wins her over, only to find that Catherine harbors many secrets--and that her family harbors more than a few hidden prejudices and is not at all happy when Harry comes a-courting in the place of Catherine's longtime beau." (Kirkus Reviews)

Helprin, Mark
The **Pacific** and other stories. Penguin Press 2004 366p $25.95
ISBN 1-594-20036-X
LC 2004-50505

This collection is "rich in big, life-shaping notions (love, honor, duty, regret) filtered through the language of longing and nostalgia in such a way that the world takes on a kind of fairy-tale luster." Washington Post

Helprin, Mark
A **soldier** of the great war. Harcourt Brace Jovanovich 1991 792p $32
ISBN 0-15-183600-0
LC 90-45987

"In summer 1964, a distinguished-looking gentleman in his seventies dismounts on principle from a streetcar that was to carry him from Rome to a distant village, instead accompanying on foot a boy denied a fare. As they walk, he tells the boy the story of his life. A young aesthete from a privileged Roman family, Alessandro Giuliani found his charmed existence shattered by the coming of World War I. The war led to an onerous tour of duty, inadvertent desertion, near-execution, forced labor, service high in the Italian Alps that took advantage of his . . . skill at mountain climbing, capture by the enemy, and return home, dispossessed of most of his friends and family. Along the way, he gains, loses, and eventually rediscovers love." Libr J

Helprin, Mark
★ **Winter's** tale. Harcourt Brace Jovanovich 1983 673p $35
ISBN 0-15-197203-6
LC 83-273

The author "describes the impossible with microscopic precision, and he summons the moods and myriad landscapes of the city with breathtaking poetry. . . . Again and again Helprin celebrates selfless love, a devotion to beauty, the desire to explore, and an acceptance of responsibility. . . . Helprin's freewheeling use of fantasy at times eclipses his essential seriousness, diminishing the novel as a whole. Yet there is unquestionable genius in the book's marvelous individual pieces." Saturday Rev

Hemingway, Amanda
The **Greenstone** grail; Amanda Hemingway. Del Rey/Ballentine Books 2005 360p hardcover o.p. $16.95; $12.95
ISBN 0345460782; 9780345460790
LC 2004049396

First published 2004 in the United Kingdom.

This book follows Nathan Ward, who "is just your typical 11-year-old of supernatural parentage, until he stumbles on a hidden altar that gives him visions of a green stone cup filled with blood. Soon he begins dreaming of Eos, a world that needs the grail for a spell to ward off a terrible plague. As the dreams become astral excursions, the grail surfaces in Nathan's world, but then is stolen and sent to Eos, at the wrong time and into the wrong hands. While Nathan goes to the rescue, his mother and the venerable grail guardian, Bartlemy Goodman, fend off the village witch, an antiques trader, police and a malevolent river spirit." (Publishers Weekly)

Hemingway, Ernest
Across the river and into the trees. Scribner Classics 1998 272p $26
ISBN 0-684-84464-8
LC 98-159867

"This is the story of a peace-time army colonel, closely resembling the author, who comes to Venice on leave to go duck shooting, to see the young Italian countess he loves, and to make a significant pilgrimage to the place where he, Richard Cantwell (and Nick Adams, Frederic Henry, and the author himself), was wounded in World War I. . . . The novel is Hemingway's weakest. It points up sharply the importance of that war injury in the author's life and work, but in some of its postures and mannerisms it seems to read like a parody of his better fiction." Herzberg. Reader's Ency of Am Lit

Hemingway, Ernest
★ A **farewell** to arms. Scribner Classics 1997
297p $27.50
ISBN 0-684-83788-9

LC 96-53356
A reissue of the title first published 1929
This novel "deals with a love-affair conducted against
the background of the war in Italy. Its excellence lies in the
delicacy with which it conveys a sense of the impermanence
of the best human feelings; the unobstrusive force of its symbolism of mountain and plain; above all the vast scope of its
vision of war—the retreat from Caporetto is one of the great
war-sequences of literature." Penguin Companion to Am Lit

Hemingway, Ernest
The **garden** of Eden. Scribner 1986 247p
ISBN 0-684-18693-4

LC 86-3701
"Whatever its problems, this version of 'The Garden of
Eden' deserves publication for what it says about writing
and for the short story which Hemingway shows us David
writing." Newsweek

Hemingway, Ernest
The **Hemingway** reader; selected with a fore-
word and twelve brief prefaces by Charles Poore.
Scribner 1953 xx, 652p
Partially analyzed in Short story index

Hemingway, Ernest
In our time; stories. Scribner 156p pa $10
ISBN 0-684-82276-8
First published 1930
Several of these "stories" picture episodes in the life of a
growing boy in the timber country of the Middle West
"Of 'stories' in the commonly accepted sense of the
word there are few. . . . Most of the others are psychological
episodes, incidents, sketches . . . call them what you will.
They are soundly and movingly done." Lit Rev

Hemingway, Ernest
Islands in the stream. Scribner 1970 466p
This posthumous novel is divided into three parts: Bimini, Cuba and At Sea. "'Bimini' is Thomas Hudson in the
1930s entertaining the three sons of his two wrecked marriages; they fish; their love leaves him open to his loneliness,
and then the death of two of them leaves him nothing but
lonely. 'Cuba' is Thomas Hudson clandestinely war effort-
ing in about 1942; his other son (the eldest) has been killed
as a pilot; Thomas Hudson drinks; he meets his first wife
who is all he has ever wanted. 'At Sea' is Thomas Hudson
commanding the pursuit of some German U-boat survivors;
the Germans die, and it may be that the wounded Thomas
Hudson is about to too." N Y Rev Books

Hemingway, Ernest
Men without women. Scribner 1927 232p

Hemingway, Ernest
The Nick Adams stories. Scribner 268p pa $12
ISBN 0-684-16940-1
First published 1972

Arranged chronologically, this collection of 24 tales contains all the semi-autobiographical Nick Adams stories
"The volume presents Nick as a child in the northern
woods, as adolescent, as soldier, veteran, writer, husband
and parent. The last Nick Adams story appeared in 1933,
and what surprises here, in these . . . {stories} of varying
length, quality and intent, is their freshness and immediacy."
Publ Wkly

Hemingway, Ernest
★ The **old** man and the sea; illustrations by C.F.
Tunnicliffe and Raymond Sheppard. Scribner Clas-
sics 1996 93p il $20
ISBN 0-684-83049-3

LC 96-11419
A reissue of the title first published 1952
"The old fisherman Santiago had only one friend in the
village, the boy Manolin. Everyone else thought he was unlucky because he had caught no fish in a long time. At noon
on the 85th day of fishing, he hooked a large fish. He fought
with the huge swordfish for three days and nights before he
could harpoon it, but the battle came to nought when sharks
destroyed the fish before Santiago could get back to the village." Shapiro. Fic for Youth. 3d edition

Hemingway, Ernest
★ The **short** stories. Scribner Classics 1997
457p $30
ISBN 0-684-83786-2

LC 96-53349
Originally published 1938 in collection with the play
The fifth column

Hemingway, Ernest
The **snows** of Kilimanjaro and other stories.
Scribner Classics 1995 143p $25
ISBN 0-684-86221-2

LC 95-4764
A reissue of the title first published 1961

Hemingway, Ernest
★ The **sun** also rises. Scribner Classics 1996
222p $25
ISBN 0-684-83051-5

LC 96-11420
A reissue of the title first published 1926
"Set in the 1920s, the novel deals with a group of aimless
expatriates in France and Spain. They are members of the
cynical and disillusioned post-World War I Lost Generation,
many of whom suffer psychological and physical wounds
as a result of the war. Two of the novel's main characters,
Lady Brett Ashley and Jake Barnes, typify this generation.
Lady Brett drifts through a series of affairs despite her love
for Jake, who has been rendered impotent by a war wound.
Friendship, stoicism, and natural grace under pressure are
offered as the values that matter in an otherwise amoral and
often senseless world." Merriam-Webster's Ency of Lit

Hemingway, Ernest

To have and have not. Scribner Classics 1999 174p $25

ISBN 0-684-85923-8

LC 00-266244

A reissue of the title first published 1937

This novel "deals with the effort of Harry Morgan, a native of Key West, to earn a living for himself and his family. He has operated a boat for rental to fishing parties, but, during the Depression of the 1930s, he is forced to turn to the smuggling of Chinese immigrants and illegal liquor. While assisting a gang of bank robbers to escape, he is shot and mortally wounded. He dies gasping, 'One man alone ain't got . . . no chance.'" Reader's Ency. 4th edition

Hemingway, Ernest

The torrents of spring; a romantic novel in honor of the passing of a great race. Scribner 1926 143p

"A burlesque of 'Sherwood Anderson' and the 'Chicago school' of authors, this comic novel tells of Yogi Johnson and Scripps O'Neil, workers in a pump factory in Petosky, Mich.; of Scripp's amours with two waitresses in Brown's Beanery, and of Yogi's adventures with the Indians." Herzberg. Reader's Ency of Am Lit

Hemingway, Ernest

True at first light; edited with an introduction by Patrick Hemingway. Scribner 1999 319p $26

ISBN 0-684-84921-6

LC 98-55510

"The tension of lion and leopard executions is superbly conveyed, as are the joking and teasing among the men and that peculiar, depersonalized alertness that comes with total concentration on the surrounding environment." Atl Mon

Hemmings, Kaui Hart

The descendants; a novel. Random House 2007 283p $24.95

ISBN 978-1-4000-6633-9; 1-4000-6633-6

LC 2006-51098

The narrator this novel, "the scion of the last Hawaiian landowning clan, has floated through his privileged life: marriage to a model given to 'speedboats, motorcycles, alcoholism'; children getting into trouble (cocaine, bullying) at élite schools; membership at a century-old beach club that rejects those with 'unfavorable pedigrees.' But when a catamaran accident leaves his wife in a coma he must wake from his own 'prolonged unconsciousness,' reacquaint himself with his neglected daughters, and track down his wife's lover. Meanwhile, his cousins are urging him to sell the family's vast landholdings for development—to relinquish, in his eyes, the final vestige of their native Hawaiian ancestry. Hemmings channels the voice of her befuddled middle-aged hero with virtuosity, as he teeters between acerbic and sentimental, scoffing at himself even as he grasps for redemption." New Yorker

Hemon, Aleksandar

The Lazarus project; a novel. with photographs by Velibor Bozovic and from the Chicago Historical Society. Riverhead Books 2008 304p il $24.95

ISBN 978-1-59448-988-4; 1-59448-988-2

LC 2008-6834

This novel "hangs upon two linked narratives — the death of Lazarus Averbuch, a turn-of-the-century Jewish immigrant to Chicago who is killed in a wash of bullets, and a contemporary Bosnian immigrant to Chicago who sets out to write Averbuch's tragic story. Together, the two narratives paint a portrait of a world that is as funny as it is terrible, characterized by violence and commerce, populated almost entirely by haves and have-nots, the quick and the dead. And the dead is the subject here. You can push and bully and probe history, but dead is dead. Nobody can bring back life. Not even one of our most talented writers." Esquire

Hemon, Aleksandar

Love and obstacles; stories. Riverhead Books 2009 209p $25.95

ISBN 978-1-59448-864-1; 1-59448-864-9

LC 2008-50340

"The unnamed narrator who appears in each of these eight stories is clearly another version of Hemon, and readers of his earlier books will recognize his progress from feckless Bosnian teenager to bewildered new immigrant to tentative celebrity writer. . . . Hemon shows us the nobility and the absurdity of immigrant life, the cruelty and the openness of American character. He knows both because he is both; and if this in-betweenness makes Hemon a 'nowhere man,' his excellent work also suggests that in between may be the best place for a writer to live." Slate

Hemon, Aleksandar

Nowhere man; the Pronek fantasies. Doubleday 2002 242p $23.95

ISBN 0-385-49924-8

LC 2002-66208

"Pronek's constantly reconfiguring life makes the novel a wild, twisty read, and Hemon's inimitable voice and the wry urgency of his storytelling should cement his reputation as a talented young writer." Publ Wkly

Hempel, Amy

The collected stories of Amy Hempel; with an introduction by Rick Moody. Scribner 2006 409p $27.50

ISBN 0-7432-8946-3

LC 2005-57608

"You could call Hempel part of a movement in the trajectory of the American short story, and Rick Moody, in his intelligent introduction, places her alongside Alice Munro, Grace Paley, Ann Beattie and others—women writers who rise above what he sees as the 'rage' and posturing of their male counterparts. But in the end such comparisons don't matter. Amy Hempel is herself. You read her stories and wonder, Why are they so wonderful? The answer comes to you at the very end of this volume, in a line toward the close of 'Offertory.' 'Because a human being made this.' That's all you need to know." N Y Times Book Rev

Henderson, Eleanor

Ten thousand saints; Eleanor Henderson. Ecco 2011 388p.

ISBN 0062021028; 9780062021021

LC 2011283405

This book is "a coming-of-age story set in the 1980s that departs from the genre's familiar tropes to find a panoramic view of how the imperfect escape from our parents' mistakes makes (equally imperfect) adults of us. Jude Keffy-Horn and Teddy McNicholas are drug-addled adolescents stuck in suburban Vermont and dreaming of an escape to New York City. But after Teddy dies of an overdose, Jude makes good on their dream and forms a de facto family with Teddy's straight-edge brother, Johnny; Jude's estranged pot-farmer father, Lester; and the troubled Eliza Urbanski, who may be carrying Teddy's child. What results is an odyssey encompassing the age of CBGB, Hare Krishnas, zincs, and the emergence of AIDS." (Publishers Weekly)

"Henderson is a versatile ventriloquist, taking us briskly and believably into the minds and hearts of most of her major characters (though Eliza, while briefly vivid, turns into exactly what the boys treat her as, which is a passive plot device). Though it loses some steam as it hurtles toward a happy ending, 'Ten Thousand Saints' is at its best when depicting the punk scene in New York in the 1980s and its amalgam of homeless junkies, vegan Hinduists, early AIDS victims, and antigentrification activists. It's an auspicious debut, and gives us reason to hope that Eleanor Henderson will mature as satisfyingly as her subjects do." Boston Globe

Henderson, William Haywood

Augusta Locke. Viking 2006 419p $24.95

ISBN 0-670-03491-6

LC 2005-53165

"As we move through Gussie's life, starting at the beginning of the 20th century, the landscape of the American west comes across as a living thing. Meanwhile, the characters who pass through her life are well-drawn, memorable, and not at all simple, whether minor players or major figures." Philadelphia Inquirer

Hendrie, Laura

Remember me; a novel. Holt & Co. 1999 373p $24

ISBN 0-8050-6218-1

LC 99-13302

"Rose Devonic is not much liked in the little town of Quedero, NM, famed for its fine embroidery. . . . Rose's little brother and her uncle, regarded as a crazy dreamer/schemer, were killed along with her mother in an accident. Now Rose survives by embroidering for the tourist trade and living off-season for free in the Ten Tribes Motel, whose gruff but devoted proprietor, Birdie, taught her her stitches. But Birdie's sister Alice, who bought the motel for Birdie with the insurance money she got after her sister died in the same accident that felled Rose's family, wants to sell it. Birdie has a stroke, Alice is clearly developing Alzheimer's and Rose ends up caring for them both." Libr J

"Hendrie's beautifully crafted and gutsy novel is animated by an unusual and vivid cast and charged with sharp and knowing humor." Booklist

Henkin, Joshua

Matrimony. Pantheon Books 2007 291p $23.95

ISBN 978-0-375-42435-9; 0-375-42435-9

LC 2006-103202

The author "writes with a winningly anachronistic absence of showiness. There are no big themes or symbols in Matrimony. The idea of matrimony is not treated as a metaphor, nor is it burdened with the weight of heightened realism. This is just a lifelike, likable book populated by three-dimensional characters who make themselves very much at home on the page. This style becomes humorous, not to mention heretical, with academia as the story's backdrop." N Y Times (Late N Y Ed)

Henkin, Joshua

The world without you; Joshua Henkin. Pantheon Books 2012 321 p.

ISBN 0375424369; 9780375424366

LC 2011046780

In this novel, Joshua "Henkin . . . explores family dynamics. . . . One year after the death of their kidnapped journalist son, Leo, in Iraq, David and Marilyn Frankel, non-practicing Jews, call their entire mishpocha to their summer home . . . to attend his memorial service: Clarissa and her husband . . . are having a difficult time getting pregnant; . . . Noëlle, an Orthodox Jew who arrives from Jerusalem with her husband, Amram, and their four children." (Publishers Weekly)

Henley, Patricia

Hummingbird house; a novel. MacMurray & Beck 1999 326p $22

ISBN 1-87844-887-0

LC 98-31274

"The prismatic trajectory of the tale may be deliberate, for the author's message is double-edged; that trying for a better world is necessary, demanding work, but no one can save herself through saving the world." Publ Wkly

Henley, Patricia

In the river sweet. Pantheon Bks. 2002 291p

ISBN 0-375-42127-0

LC 2002-22018

"The heroine, Ruth Anne Bond, is a woman of 50, living in Indiana; Johnny, her husband of nearly 30 years, is the proprietor of an upscale restaurant. Everything seems picture perfect until devoutly Catholic Ruth Anne learns that their only daughter, Laurel, is a lesbian. While she adjusts to this revelation. . .her own secret past catches up with her: she is contacted by Tin, the illegitimate son she conceived with a blind Vietnamese boy when she was a teenager working in a convent in Saigon. . .(The author) balances long, stream-of-consciousness passages with short, potent sentences to wonderful effect, tilling the familiar ground of sexuality and spirituality with originality and grace." Publ Wkly

Henry, April

Learning to fly. St. Martin's Minotaur 2002 308p $23.95

ISBN 0-312-29052-7

LC 2001-58549

"A gruesome freeway pileup (52 vehicles, 14 deaths) has unexpected benefits for a young woman whose hippie parents named her Free: a new identity plus a bag containing $750,000 in drug money. When a passenger in her car, killed in the carnage, is mistakenly identified as Free, suddenly our pregnant, unemployed heroine has a way out of her problems and the money to finance it. She becomes Lydia, and assembles a new life in what she believes is the safe obscurity of another woman's persona. But then two dangerous men start to track her." Publ Wkly

Henry, O.

The **best** short stories of O. Henry; selected and with an introduction by Bennett A. Cerf, and Van H. Cartmell. Modern Lib. 1994 340p $22.95

ISBN 0-679-60122-8

First Modern Library edition published 1945

O. Henry "is best known for his observations on the diverse lives of everyday New Yorkers, 'the four million' neglected by other writers. He had a fine gift of humor and was adept at the ingenious depiction of ironic circumstances, in plots frequently dependent upon coincidence." Oxford Companion to Am Lit. 6th edition

Henry, O.

★ The **complete** works of O. Henry; foreword by Harry Hansen. Doubleday 1953 1692p $15.95

ISBN 0-385-00961-5

Henry, Patti Callahan

And then I found you; Patti Callahan Henry. 1st ed. St. Martin's Press 2013 272 p. (hardcover) $24.99

ISBN 0312610769; 9780312610760

LC 2013004029

Here, Katie Vaughn panics when she thinks her boring boyfriend might propose. She "casts her memory back to the first day of spring when she was 13. She had experienced her first kiss and first brush with love with classmate Jack Adams. She promised to love him always, but now, at age 35, Katie no longer has Jack in her life. A secret she shared with him so long ago has resurfaced, and this has caused Katie to revisit the past and reevaluate her life." (Library Journal)

Henry, Patti Callahan

Coming up for air. St. Martin's Press 2011 261p $24.99

ISBN 978-0-312-61039-5; 0-312-61039-4

LC 2011019507

"Ellie Calvin is caught in a dying marriage, and she knows this. With her beloved daughter away at college and a growing gap between her and her husband – between her reality and the woman she wants to be – she doesn't quite seem to fit into her own life. But everything changes after her controlling mother, Lillian, passes away. Ellie's world turns upside down when she sees her ex-boyfriend, Hutch, at her mother's funeral and learns that he is in charge of a documentary that involved Lillian before her death. He wants answers to questions that Ellie's not sure she can face, until, in the painful midst of going through her mother's things, she discovers a hidden diary – and a window onto stories buried long ago. As Ellie and Hutch start speaking for the first time in years, Ellie's closed heart slowly begins to open. Fighting

their feelings, they set out together to dig into Lillian's history." Publisher's note

"An affecting Southern tale about second chances and banishing the ghosts of regret. . . . Romantic storytelling at its simple best." Kirkus

Henry, Sue

Cold company; an Alaska mystery. Morrow 2002 294p

ISBN 0-380-97882-2

LC 2001-44860

"One of the hallmarks of Henry's series is the beautiful and rugged Alaskan landscape, and she has never used it more effectively than she does here, as spring sets in motion new discoveries." Publ Wkly

Henry, Sue

Dead north; an Alaska mystery. Morrow 2001 280p

ISBN 0-380-97881-4

LC 00-48077

"While driving a friend's Winnebago to Alaska from Idaho, musher Jess Arnold . . . picks up a hitchhiking teenager trying to escape from the abusive stepfather who just murdered his mother. Friends, police, and the murderer all follow." Libr J

This "story offers a tough mystery, compelling characters, vivid scenery, endearing dogs, and a breakneck pace." Booklist

Henry, Sue

Death takes passage; an Alex Jensen mystery. Avon Bks. 1997 292p

ISBN 0-380-97469-X

LC 97-4002

"Henry refreshingly blends classic mystery devices (a missing passenger, double identities, and locked rooms) with frontier and nautical history and the great beauty of Alaskan glaciers, mountains, night skies, and wildlife. In addition, Henry's enjoyable, well-paced novel displays little gratuitous violence and contains an intriguing mix of real and fictional characters." Booklist

Henry, Sue

Death trap; an Alaska mystery. Morrow 2003 273p $23.95

ISBN 0-380-97883-0

LC 2002-33734

"Sidelined from sled-dog racing this season because of a knee injury, musher Jessie Arnold agrees to help out a friend by working the Iditarod booth at the Alaska State Fair. The fun of the fair ends abruptly for Jessie when a man is found dead in a pond on the grounds, and her beloved lead dog, Tank mysteriously disappears from the booth. . . . Interesting developments in Jessie's personal life will please fans of this long-running series." Booklist

Henry, Sue

Murder on the Iditarod Trail. Atlantic Monthly Press 1991 278p

LC 90-20925

"Henry provides suspense and excitement in this paean to a great sporting event and to the powerful Alaskan landscape." Publ Wkly

Henry, Sue

Murder on the Yukon Quest; an Alaska mystery. Avon Twilight 1999 291p

ISBN 0-380-97764-8

LC 99-21641

"Jessie Arnold has run the world-famous Iditarod dogsled race but is a rookie in the demanding Yukon Quest, which begins in Canada's Yukon Territory and extends over 1,000 dangerous miles to the finish line in Fairbanks. But Jessie has plenty of spirit and a fit, well-trained dog team. All of that hardly prepares her, however, for what happens when one of her fellow racers is kidnapped, and Jessie must deliver the ransom, rescue the victim, and capture the bad guys." Booklist

Hensher, Philip, 1965-

King of the badgers. Faber & Faber 2011 436p $26

ISBN 978-0-865-47863-3; 0-865-47863-5

"A rich and ambitious novel, which manages both to offer a convincing picture of different levels of English society today and to explore the shifting certainties of individual lives. It is certainly easier to read than to summarise, and this is as it should be." Scotsman

Hensher, Philip, 1965-

The **Mulberry** empire; or, The two virtuous journeys of the Amir Dost Mohammed Khan. Knopf 2002 486p

ISBN 0-375-41488-6

"Hensher captures the mood of Western Victorian inquiry—mapping, botanizing, writing it all down—that seemed, in its bustle and energy, in its production of information, to underpin the whole imperial ideal. . . . The novel's plotting is smooth, its observations acute, and the minor and major characters are all beautifully drawn." N Y Times Book Rev

Hensher, Philip

The **northern** clemency. Alfred A. Knopf 2008 597p $26.95

ISBN 978-1-4000-4448-1; 1-4000-4448-0

LC 2008-43794

"The English middle class is scrutinized in this sprawling account of two families on an affluent Sheffield housing estate. The Sellerses, carried north by a job transfer with 'the Electricity,' arrive on Rayfield Avenue in 1974, just as Katherine Glover is stamping to death her youngest child's illicit pet snake in front of the house opposite. Despite this traumatic beginning, the Sellerses and the Glovers gradually develop the ties of proximity—teenagers becoming friends, younger children caught up in playground games, wives sharing confidences and glasses of wine. Hensher's attention is on the foreground, revealing ordinary life through impressive, often funny set pieces and assiduously observed dramatic episodes, which almost compensate for the lack of an organized plot." New Yorker

Hensher, Philip, 1965-

Scenes from early life; Philip Hensher. Faber and Faber 2013 320 p. (hardcover: alk. paper) $27

ISBN 0865477612; 9780865477612

LC 2012022169

Philip Hensher's "novel takes the form of a memoir of Bangladesh in the 1970s, a time when both nation and narrator were on their first feet. . . . The novel has 13 chapters in all and they . . . carr[y] . . . detail[s] about Bengali life in the uncertain years before independence and in the period after, when the horrors of the liberation war were still fresh in everyone's minds." (New Statesman)

Henson, Jim, 1936-1990

Jim Henson's tale of sand; written by Jim Henson and Jerry Juhl; as realized by Ramón K. Pérez; colors by Ian Herring with Ramón K. Pérez; lettering and font design by Deron Bennett based on the handwriting of Jim Henson; edited by Stephen Christy. Archaia Entertainment 2012 152 p.

ISBN 1936393093; 9781936393091

This graphic novel "follows its hapless protagonist as he is cast out into the desert by the cheerful Sheriff Tate. . . . The scruffy hero is a pawn in a game whose rules are concealed from him, pursued across a surrealistic southwest U.S. by an implacable hunter and hindered by the eccentric, bizarre inhabitants of the great desolation. The prize waiting for him at the end of the chase, should he survive to reach the end, is one he will never guess at." (Publishers Weekly)

Herbert, Brian

Dune: House Atreides; [by] Brian Herbert and Kevin J. Anderson. Bantam Bks. 1999 604p

ISBN 0-553-11061-6

LC 99-17726

"Set several decades before the first novel in the Dune series, this describes the origins, feuds and schemes that lay the foundation to the saga. "As Emperor Elrood's son plots a subtle regicide, young Leto Atreides leaves for a year's education on the mechanized world of Ix; a planetologist named Pardot Kynes seeks the secrets of Arrakis; and the eight-year-old slave Duncan Idaho is hunted by his cruel masters in a terrifying game from which he vows escape and vengeance." Publisher's note

"Though the plot here is intricate, even readers new to the saga will be able to follow it easily." Publ Wkly

Herbert, Brian

Dune: House Corrino; [by] Brian Herbert and Kevin J. Anderson. Bantam Bks. 2001 496p

ISBN 0-553-11084-5

LC 2001-25777

"As Emperor Shaddam IV seeks to consolidate his power as Emperor of a Million Worlds through the monopoly of the spice trade, other forces array themselves in opposition to his increasingly tyrannical rule. . . . Though dependent on the previous books, this complex and compelling tale of dynastic intrigue and high drama adds a significant chapter to the classic Dune saga." Libr J

Herbert, Brian

Dune: House Harkonnen; [by] Brian Herbert & Kevin J. Anderson. Bantam Bks. 2000 620p

ISBN 0-553-11072-1

LC 00-39804

In the second prequel "the young Duke Leto Atreides seeks to live up to his late father's expectations, [while] his rivals plot to bring about the downfall of House Atreides. Plots and counterplots involving the debauched Baron Vladimir Harkonnen, his Bene Gesserit enemies, and the treacherous schemers of the enigmatic Bene Tleilax escalate the tension among factions of a fragile galactic empire. Though power seems to reside in the hands of the emperor and his elite armies, the fate of many worlds hinges on the destiny of a single planet—the desert world known as Arrakis, or Dune." Libr J

Herbert, Brian

Dune: The Butlerian jihad; {by} Brian Herbert and Kevin J. Anderson. TOR Bks. 2002 621p $27.95

ISBN 0-7653-0157-1

LC 2002-28581

The authors "continue their prehistory of Frank Herbert's 'Dune' series with a new trilogy opener set in the distant past of Herbert's galactic saga. The authors reveal the origins of the Spacing Guild and the Bene Gesserit, as well as the root of the ancient feud between Houses Atreides and Harkonnen. This compelling saga of men and women struggling for their freedom is required reading for Dune fans." Libr J

Herbert, Brian

Paul of Dune; [by] Brian Herbert and Kevin J. Anderson. Tor 2008 512p $27.95

ISBN 978-0-7653-1294-5; 0-7653-1294-8

LC 2008-30213

"Paul Muad'Dib and his army of Fremen desert warriors have succeeded in their overthrow of the Emperor Shaddam IV, but holding onto a universe of fractious planets proves a challenge even for a man revered by his followers as a god. Set in the years following the late Frank Herbert's classic Dune and its sequel, Dune Messiah, . . . [this book] fills in the missing years of empire building and looks into the formative years of Paul's childhood as well as the histories of those closest to him. . . . A priority purchase for libraries of all sizes." Libr J

Herbert, Frank

Chapterhouse: Dune. Putnam 1985 464p (Dune)

LC 84-17979

The sixth Dune novel "is set on the planet Chapterhouse, where the Bene Gesserits have installed their headquarters. They have fled from the slaughtering Honored Matres (a corrupt version of the Bene Gesserits), with plans to transform Chapterhouse into another desert planet on which the valuable melange spice can be produced. The high point of the book is not the climactic raid on and capture of a group of Honored Matres, but rather a chapter in which a former Honored Matre undergoes the ritual spice agony to become a Bene Gesserit Reverend Mother." SLJ

Herbert, Frank

Children of Dune. Berkley Pub. Corp. 1976 444p (Dune)

This third volume in the saga of Dune "centers on the development of twins Leto and Ghanima and their decision to assume the mantle of political and religious leadership spurned by their father. Herbert expands on many of the questions raised in earlier books, especially prescience and the evolution of mankind." Booklist

Followed by God Emperor of Dune

Herbert, Frank

★ **Dune**. Ace Bks. 1999 517p il $27.95

ISBN 0-441-00590-X

First published 1965 by Chilton

"Herbert combines several classic elements: a Machiavellian world of political intrigue worthy of fourteenth-century Italy, a huge cast of characters, and a detailed picture of a culture. Duke Leto Atreides and his family are coerced into exchanging their rich lands for a barren planet, Dune, which produces a unique drug. Duke's son, Paul, becomes the leader of a group that leads the Fremen of Dune against the enemy. This is a science fiction story with sociological and ecological import." Shapiro. Fic for Youth. 3d edition

Other titles about Dune are:

Chapterhouse: Dune (1985)

Children of Dune (1976)

Dune messiah (1969)

God Emperor of Dune (1981)

Heretics of Dune (1984)

Herbert, Frank

Dune messiah. Putnam 1969 220p (Dune)

In this second volume of the Dune series "the Bene Gesserit, a mystic sisterhood, plot to overthrow the god/emperor Paul Atreides, whom they created by special breeding but whom they cannot now control. Presented here via the narrative and quotes from journals and legends of the people of Dune, the imperial intrigue is engineered by such diverse characters as Bene Gesserit Mother Superior, a Tleilaxu face dancer, a 'ghola' re-creation of Paul's dead friend, and the Princess Consort. Paul's eventual victory because of his future-vision makes fascinating reading." SLJ

Followed by Children of Dune

Herbert, Frank

God Emperor of Dune. Putnam 1981 441p (Dune)

LC 80-25149

In the fourth title of the Dune saga "Leto II, the God Emperor, combines melange, a spice drug, with religion in order to control his people. The scene is the planet now called Arrakis, since only a remnant of the desert, Dune, remains. It is 3,500 years after the events of 'Children of Dune,' which ended while Leto was young. After sacrificing his human body to melange in exchange for an estimated four-thousand year rule, Leto is still alive. Gradually the body of Shi-Hulud the Sandworm God is developing in him, while Leto the Emperor lives in the bosom of God, or so his followers believe. . . . His plan for the survival of humanity is the Golden Path, an enforced tranquility overriding man's desire for chaos, especially war." Best Sellers

Followed by Heretics of Dune

Herbert, Frank

Heretics of Dune. Putnam 1984 480p (Dune)
LC 83-16040

"The fifth installment of the 'Dune Cycle' follows the lives of the two children on different planets: On Gammu, a young Duncan Idaho trains relentlessly for the moment that will awaken the memories of his former lives; on Rakis, the fremen-child Sheeana discovers her ability to command the fearsome sandworms of the desert—and becomes an object of worship." Libr J

Followed by Chapterhouse: Dune

Herbert, James, 1943-2013

Ash; James Herbert. Tor 2012 704 p. (hardcover) $29.99
ISBN 0765328968; 9780765328960; 9781429946933
LC 2012033545

In this book by James Herbert, "absinthe-swilling, deeply conflicted paranormal investigator David Ash tackles Comraich Castle in Scotland, an ancient, isolated pile whose sponsors, the Inner Court, comprise a secret organization of British royals and other superrich, shadowy movers and shakers. . . . It turns out to be a sanctuary for war criminals, mass murderers, child molesters, insane dictators and others whose public presence might prove embarrassing or dangerous." (Kirkus Reviews)

Heriz, Enrique de

Lies; translated from Spanish by John Cullen. Doubleday 2007 415p $26
ISBN 978-0-385-51794-2; 0-385-51794-7

Original Spanish edition, 2004

"After a boating accident in a Guatemalan backwater, Isabel, a Spanish anthropologist researching indigenous funeral rites, finds that one of the victims has been misidentified as her. She is strangely reluctant to return to her grieving children and husband in Barcelona, and her subterfuge turns out to be only the most recent instance of a family penchant for self-invention. De Hériz's chapters cut between Isabel's hallucinatory diary entries and her daughter's account of how she and her two brothers go about the business of mourning. The vivid, deadpan pacing recalls the films of Pedro Almodóvar." New Yorker

Herlihy, James Leo

★ **Midnight** cowboy; [by] James L. Herlihy. Simon & Schuster 1965 253p

"An appalling story, told with great skill and important because Joe Buck is a characteristic product of the way we live and yet he cannot be adequately discussed outside of a novel." Saturday Rev

Hermans, Willem Frederik

Beyond sleep; translated from the Dutch by Ina Rilke. Overlook Press 2007 311p $27.95
ISBN 978-1-58567-538-8; 1-58567-583-0
LC 2006-48743

Original Dutch edition, 1967; this translation first published 2006 in the United Kingdom

"Alfred Issendorf is a PhD candidate aiming to guarantee a cum laude degree by proving his mentor professor's pet theory about meteorite impacts in Norway's Finnmark region. Inadequately prepared, Alfred is disappointed by his professor's Norwegian contacts (this is mordant high-comic material), antipathetic to his companion field researchers except for the maudlin Arne, and maddeningly full of himself though he lacks all self-confidence. Stubborn, to boot, he badly bruises a leg in a fall due to his own inattention, and later he willfully takes off in the wrong direction and gets lost. He meets no tragic end, and when he finds one, he is minimally affected. He is also supremely unlovable, tolerable only because he's young and hence may outgrow his self-absorption. He's unpleasant, and so are the other characters. Finally, they're wryly funny, and in that lies the novel's brilliance." Booklist

Hern, Candice

The **bride** sale; Candice Hern. Avon Books 2002 375p.
ISBN 038080901X
LC 2002580398

This romance novel takes place "[i]n 1818 Gunnisloe, [where] Baron James Harkness . . . hears a nearby auction whose bidding and commentary seem strange to him. He . . . is stunned to see a woman on the block instead of cattle. . . . Gilbert Russell sells his wife Verity to 'Lord Heartless' as the locals call James in order to pay off his debts. Though she starts with doubts about her savior due to the rumors that he killed his wife and child, Verity quickly notices his compassion towards people even those not deserving of it. She begins to fall in love with her benefactor and he feels the same attraction, but the secrets he keeps from everyone including her leaves no hope for a real relationship." (thebestreviews.com)

Hern, Candice

Once a gentleman; Candice Hern. Avon Books 2004 373p. (pbk.) $5.99
ISBN 0060565144
LC 2004573984

In this book, "Nicholas Parrish wakes one morning to pounding at the front door of his London townhouse. Standing before him is the irate father of Prudence Armitage and several of her scowling brothers. They accuse him of compromising Prudence, and to his astonishment the woman in question walks out of his study, looking as if she's just been roused from her bed! Prudence had . . . [fallen] asleep at her desk, and when she walks out of the office and sees her family ready to murder the man she had secretly had a crush on, Prudence is appalled. And when a marriage is forced between them, she is devastated. The damage is done, though, and now she's determined to make things right between herself and her new husband." (Publisher's note)

Hernández, Felisberto, 1902-1964

★ **Lands** of memory; translated by Ester Allen. New Directions 2002 190p $24.95
ISBN 0-8112-1483-4
LC 2001-42589

The Lands of memory is an uncoventional fictional autobiography and Around the time of Clements Colling is a bildungsroman about a one-eyed blind piano teacher and his pupil

"Hernandez revels in images that are simple and repetitive: arms, light and shadow, the houses of the wealthy and their odd contents. The stories acquire a luxurious sheen from the ease with which they navigate memories, taking pleasure in recounting them with no intention other than tracking the mind's twists and turns." Publ Wkly

Herron, Mick

Reconstruction. Soho Press 2008 352p $24.95

ISBN 978-1-56947-504-1; 1-56947-504-0

LC 2007-38618

"When young Jaime Segura slips into the South Oxford Nursery School and waves a gun at the teacher, cleaning lady, parent and two little boys he takes hostage, unpleasant things are bound to happen, and they do — but not until Herron has finished surprising us. First off, Jaime is no mad gunman but a fugitive on the run from British intelligence agents who would rather kill him than question him. But if Jaime's role is a bit ambiguous, so is that of certain of his hostages — not to mention all the men outside, armed to the teeth and about to storm the school. In Herrons book, there's no hiding under the desk." N Y Times Book Rev

Hersey, John

★ A **bell** for Adano. Knopf 1944 269p

"The town bell of Adano is transformed into material for a cannon, and its loss symbolizes a moral loss to the very life of the people. When the town falls into the hands of the Americans and the Fascist forces are in retreat, Major Joppolo, a Brooklyn-born Italian, becomes a favorite of the townspeople because of the concern he has for them. Not only does he help Tina find her missing sweetheart, but he finds a replacement for the bell, retrieving it from a U.S. ship named after an Italian-American hero of World War I. To the town's dismay, Major Joppolo is relieved of his command by an American general whose unreasonable orders he ignores." Shapiro. Fic for Youth. 3d edition

Hersey, John

Key West tales. Knopf 1994 227p

ISBN 0-679-42992-1

LC 93-11094

"In this final collection of stories, Hersey focuses on his theme of ordinary people facing momentous events in their lives: death by AIDS, the death of a friend from AIDS, loss of innocence and virginity, meeting the son one had given up for adoption two decades before, or retirement from military service. As interludes, Hersey presents brief, italicized vignettes of the famous or powerful people who have lived in or visited Key West." Libr J

Hersey, John

A **single** pebble. Knopf 1956 181p

"An American engineer's trip by junk up the Yangtze to locate a dam site, as he relates it years later in retrospect, symbolizes the contrast between the Western idea of progress and tempo of living and the passive resignation of China's ancient culture and traditions. With mounting tension, the story brings into focus the subtle relationship between the young engineer and the owner of the junk, his wife, and

the head tracker, Old Pebble, in a drama heightened by the physical grandeur of the Great River." Booklist

Hersey, John

★ The **wall.** Knopf 1950 632p hardcover o.p. pa $17.95

ISBN 0-394-75696-7 pa

"This novel is presented as a journal kept by a diarist during World War II. It tells of life in the Warsaw Ghetto, depicting Jewish interdependence in a struggle for survival. The writer's observations enrich our understanding of Jewish culture. Although the diarist dies of pneumonia in 1944, his escape from the enclosure within which the Germans confined the Jews is a testament to hope and courage." Shapiro. Fic for Youth. 3d edition

Hershon, Joanna

The **German** bride; a novel. Ballantine Books 2008 304p $25

ISBN 978-0-345-46845-1; 0-345-46845-7

LC 2007-32842

"Eva Frank is a young Jewish girl living in 1860s Berlin who has an illicit affair, and the ensuing consequences are devastating. Driven by guilt over the affair, Eva feels compelled to marry and soon finds herself wedded to Abraham, a man whose dream is to move to the American Southwest. Living and adjusting to married life in America brings with it a multitude of problems, most of which are made worse by Abraham being what we now think of as a compulsive gambler and womanizer." Libr J

"Though sometimes stilted, the novel, with its colorful cast, setting and redemptive conclusion, eventually wins the reader over." Publ Wkly

Hess, Joan

Busy bodies. Dutton 1995 246p

LC 94-46120

In this Claire Malloy mystery, "painter Zeno Gorgias, who has recently moved to the small Arkansas town's historic neighborhood, is staging performance pieces, starring a nearly naked young woman with a rubber snake, on his front lawn. Not only are Claire's hyperbolic teenage daughter and her friend involved, but Claire's policeman lover has his hands full with crowd control. Zeno's estranged wife arrives and threatens to have him institutionalized for incompetence; she is found murdered, her body recovered from charred ashes of Zeno's house after it—and half a million dollars' worth of his paintings—are burned." Publ Wkly

Hess, Joan

A **conventional** corpse; a Claire Malloy mystery. St. Martin's Press 2000 275p

ISBN 0-312-24662-5

LC 00-29686

"Arkansas bookseller/sleuth Claire Malloy organizes a mystery convention at Farber College that goes awry. Five major writers and attendant quirks create problems, as does the appearance/disappearance of a hated mystery editor and the suspicious death of an attendee." Libr J

"Offering a teasingly intricate puzzle along with some zinging satire of current publishing trends, Hess has produced another first-rate mystery." Publ Wkly

Hess, Joan

★ **Death** by the light of the moon. St. Martin's Press 1992 227p

LC 91-37884

"Ms. Hess handles the complicated plot logistics with a deft touch, and although her overblown caricatures lack the affection she lavishes on the characters in her 'Maggody' series, she has a warm spot for teen-agers, whose insufferable ways elicit her funniest and kindest satirical swipes." N Y Times Book Rev

Hess, Joan

A **holly,** jolly murder. Dutton 1997 265p

ISBN 0-525-94240-8

LC 97-12895

"Small-town bookstore owner Claire Malloy lets curiosity get the best of her: she attends a Druid winter solstice festival. When the would-be celebrants discover their wealthy benefactor murdered, the Arch Druid (a feisty old lady) asks Claire's help." Libr J

Hess, Joan

Madness in Maggody. St. Martin's Press 1991 231p

LC 90-49306

"Chief of police Arly Hanks, lately of New York City, takes an offhand attitude toward crime or the lack of it in Maggody, Arkansas, until the tamales hit the fan during the grand opening of a supermarket that none of the other merchants in town wants to see succeed. Now Arly's got one death, and reams of rumors to unravel. Although the situation is loaded with humor and small-town high jinks, the solution to the murder shocks Arly so much she promises herself that in the future she will take her job more seriously." Booklist

Hess, Joan

Maggody and the moonbeams; an Arly Hanks mystery. Simon & Schuster 2001 254p

ISBN 0-7432-0229-5

LC 2001-20208

Police chief Arly Hanks, "to her extreme horror, gets railroaded by Mrs. Jim Bob Buchanon into acting as chaperone for a church youth group at Camp Pearly Gates in nearby Dunkicker. Unbeknownst to all, the camp is also the home of a weird commune, the Daughters of the Moon, which is made up of a group of women (known locally as 'Beamers') who sport shaved heads, magenta lipstick, and white robes. The typical Maggody madness and mayhem begins when one of the campers stumbles over the body of a Beamer whose head has been pulverized." Booklist

Hess, Joan

Mischief in Maggody; an Ozarks murder mystery. St. Martin's Press 1988 202p

LC 88-1867

"Maggody, a little Ozark town where nothing ever happens, has problems. Its first female police chief, Arly Hanks, . . . comes back from vacation to find the community in an uproar . . . local prostitute and moonshiner Robin Buchanon has disappeared, leaving behind five hungry children. . . . Arly manages to foist them onto Mrs. Jim Bob while she goes hunting for the mother, whom she finds with her head

blown off in the middle of a marijuana patch. . . . Another death and the public humiliation of two of the town's most righteous citizens take place before peace comes to Maggody once again. Hess writes an engaging tale, although the raunchy characters impart a certain vulgarity to the text." Publ Wkly

Hess, Joan

Misery loves Maggody; an Arly Hanks mystery. Simon & Schuster 1999 285p $22

ISBN 0-684-84562-8

LC 98-28728

Maggody, Arkansas police chief Arly Hanks "investigates after out-of-town police arrest the mayor of Maggody in connection with the death of a riverboat showgirl." Libr J

Hess, Joan

Mummy dearest; a Claire Malloy mystery. St. Martin's Minotaur 2008 309p $24.95

ISBN 978-0-312-36360-4; 0-312-36360-5

LC 2007-51831

On a honeymoon trip to Luxor, Egypt, with her new husband, Lt. Peter Rosen, teenage daughter Caron, and Caron's best friend Inez, Arkansas bookseller Claire Malloy suddenly finds her honeymoon turned upside down when the two girls are chased through back alleys by unknown pursuers and a blonde college student is kidnapped by two young men on horseback.

"Humor, quirky characters, a rich mother-daughter relationship, and the fresh setting all add to this satisfying addition to Hess' long-running series." Booklist

Hess, Joan

Murder@maggody.com. Simon & Schuster 2000 253p

ISBN 0-684-84563-6

LC 99-46821

"Maggody's eccentric inhabitants and Hess's comic touch infuse this cozy with a refreshing dose of spunk, resulting in another triumph for both small-town America and Hess." Publ Wkly

Hess, Joan

Out on a limb; a Claire Malloy mystery. St. Martin's Minotaur 2002 306p

ISBN 0-312-26680-4

LC 2002-69939

"The author deftly juggles the various plot strands, letting the local news reporter fill in the action in which Claire is uninvolved. The surprising denouement comes off with éclat." Publ Wkly

Hesse, Hermann

Demian. Boni & Liveright 1923 215p

Original German edition, 1919

A novel "featuring young Emil Sinclair. Largely through the crude aggression of a school bully, Sinclair becomes troubled by the realization that life consists of conflicting, opposite forces. His confusion is both cleared and compounded by the appearance of a mysterious older boy named Max Demian. Both Demian and his mother become central influences in Sinclair's life, although their encounters are sporadic. In a letter, Demian tells Sinclair of the devil-god Abraxas, who is the embodiment of a fusion of all good and evil, of destruction and creation. When he is wounded in the war, Sinclair has a vision of Demian, in which his death is implied. From that time on, Sinclair feels himself to be the possessor of the wisdom and understanding he had attributed to Demian. The novel is one of Hesse's most poignant statements of the terrors and torments of adolescence." Reader's Ency. 4th edition

Hesse, Hermann

The **fairy** tales of Hermann Hesse; translated and with an introduction by Jack Zipes; woodcut illustrations by David Frampton. Bantam Bks. 1995 xxxi, 266p il hardcover o.p. pa $14.95

ISBN 0-553-37776-0 pa

LC 94-49166

"Quirky and evocative, Hesse's fairy tales stand alone, but also amplify the ideas and utopian longings of such counterculture avatars as Siddhartha and Steppenwolf." Publ Wkly

Hesse, Hermann

Gertrude; translated by Hilda Rosner. Rev. translation; Boni & Liveright 1969 237p

Original German edition, 1910; this translation first published in the United Kingdom

"The story has three major characters: Herr Kuhn, Herr Muoth, and Fräulein Gertrude Imthor, later Frau Muoth. Narrated by the aging Kuhn, the novel recounts his travails as a youth, his success as a composer, his frustrated love for Gertrude Imthor, and his strange friendship with Heinrich Muoth. . . . As a young man Kuhn had his leg crippled in an accident. The physical disability which prevents him from achieving happiness in life, especially with women, measurably accounts as well for his creativity." Saturday Rev

Hesse, Hermann

The **glass** bead game (Magister Ludi) translated from the German by Richard and Clara Winston; with a foreword by Theodore Ziolkowski. Holt, Rinehart & Winston 1969 558p

Original German edition, 1943; first published 1949 in the United States with title: Magister Ludi

This "novel follows the intellectual and spiritual odyssey of Josef Knecht, who lives in a utopian society in the 23rd century. The culture is dominated by a glass-bead game, practiced in its highest form (in which beads are not even used) by an intellectual elite. The game represents a balanced fusion of the active and contemplative disciplines; it is a combination of music and mathematics (art and science) but includes elements from virtually every cultural endeavor. Knecht becomes master of the game (Lat, Magister Ludi) but has doubts about the virtues of pure intellect. He renounces his order and departs to the outer world, where he eventually dies, the tragic result of a life dedicated entirely to the world of the spirit." Reader's Ency. 4th edition

Hesse, Hermann

Narcissus and Goldmund; translated by Ursule Molinaro. Farrar, Straus & Giroux 1968 315p

Original German edition, 1930; English translation published 1932 with title: Death and the lover; also 1959 in the United Kingdom, with title: Goldmund

"Hesse's prose, ranging from lyricism to allegory, and from unabashed sentimentality to an intellectuality of a high order, is not easily rendered into another language. . . . The present version . . . is close to perfection." Saturday Rev

Hesse, Hermann

★ **Siddhartha**; translated by Hilda Rosner. New Directions 1951 153p $16.95; pa $6.95

ISBN 0-8112-0292-5; 0-8112-0068-X pa

Original German edition, 1923

"The young Indian Siddhartha endures many experiences in his search for the ultimate answer to the question, what is humankind's role on earth? He is also looking for the solution to loneliness and discontent, and he seeks that solution in the way of a wanderer, the company of a courtesan, and the high position of a successful businessman. His final relationship is with a humble but wise ferryman. This is an allegory that examines love, wealth, and freedom while the protagonist struggles toward self-knowledge." Shapiro. Fic for Youth. 3d edition

Hesse, Hermann

★ **Steppenwolf**; translated from the German by Basil Creighton. Holt & Co. 1929 309p hardcover o.p. pa $14

ISBN 0-312-27867-5

Original German edition, 1927

"The hero, Harry Haller . . . is torn between his own frustrated artistic idealism and the inhuman nature of modern reality, which, in his eyes, is characterized entirely by philistinism and technology. It is his inability to be a part of the world and the resulting loneliness and desolation of his existence that cause him to think of himself as a 'Steppenwolf' (wolf of the Steppes). The novel, which is rich in surrealistic imagery throughout, ends in what is called the magic theater, a kind of allegorical sideshow. Here, Haller learns that in order to relate successfully to humanity and reality without sacrificing his ideals, he must overcome his own social and sexual inhibitions." Reader's Ency. 4th edition

Hesse, Hermann

Stories of five decades; edited and with an introduction by Theodore Ziolkowski; translated by Ralph Manheim. With two stories translated by Denver Lindley. Farrar, Straus & Giroux 1973 xx, 328p

Heti, Sheila

How should a person be? a novel from life. Sheila Heti. 1st US ed. Henry Holt and Co. 2012 306 p. (paperback) $16.00; (hardcover) $25.00

ISBN 9781250032447; 0805094725; 9780805094725

LC 2011038498

Author Sheila Heti tells the semi-autobiographical story of character Sheila "after she leaves her husband [and] looks to her friends and the world at large to determine how to be. Acts divided into chapters interspersed with conversations transcribed to read like plays follow Sheila from home to New York to Atlantic City in her search for clarity." (Publishers Weekly)

Hewson, David

The **garden** of evil. Delacorte Press 2008 470p $24

ISBN 978-0-385-33957-5; 0-385-33957-7

LC 2007-45762

Roman detective Nic Costa and "his team are just starting to process a crime scene in an artist's shabby studio, where two corpses lie sprawled before a painting of a rapturous female nude redolent of Caravaggio, when they flush out a hooded gunman. The gunman escapes in the ensuing chase, but not before shooting dead Costa's wife of three months, former FBI agent Emily Deacon. While Costa is taken off the case, his rule-bending boss finds a way for him to help on the sly, assisting the unusual art expert—young Sister Agata Graziano—called in to investigate whether the canvas could really be a Caravaggio and what light it might shed on the murders." Publ Wkly

"A thought-provoking blend of art history and mystery, The Garden of Evil is . . . a treat for readers who like their entertainment literate." Richmond Times-Dispatch

Hewson, David

Lucifer's shadow. Delacorte Press 2004 369p $21.95

ISBN 0-385-33794-9

"In 1733, a wealthy patron of the arts supplies a lovely and talented Jewish woman with a Guarneri violin and the venue for her debut as a concert soloist in a world hostile to both women and Jews. In modern Venice, a young scholar is manipulated into selling a stolen antique violin and pretending authorship of a brilliant concerto recently unearthed in his employer's basement. Both stories follow naive young men who fall in love with gifted and troubled women musicians, then become involved in tracking killers who leave behind only traces of their female victims. The pungent canals of beautiful Venice carry readers on a metaphorical journey, tracing the spread of evil through ghetto, church, concert hall, and even the mansions of the elite." Booklist

Hewson, David

A **season** for the dead. Delacorte Press 2004 386p $21.95

ISBN 0-385-33722-1

LC 2003-62522

"Outsized, eccentric characters, a complex story and an abundance of historical detail make this engrossing book more than just another cookie-cutter, religious-nut serial killer thriller." Publ Wkly

Heyer, Georgette

★ **Black** sheep. Sourcebooks 2008 279p pa $13.95

ISBN 978-1-4022-1078-5; 1-4022-1078-7

LC 2007-50205

First published 1966 in the United Kingdom

"A lovely young spinster is both charmed and infuriated by the wealthy, unconventional black sheep uncle of the fortune hunter on whom her young niece has her heart set. This character-driven novel . . . is considered one of Heyer's best." Libr J

Heyer, Georgette

Frederica. Sourcebooks Casablanca 2008 437p pa $13.95

ISBN 978-1-4022-1476-9

LC 2008-43093

First published 1965 by Dutton

"A 37-year-old bachelor, wealthy, imperious, much the man-about-Regency-London, falls irresistibly for a pretty but not beautiful young woman who, at 24, considers herself put on the shelf and wants only to find a good husband for her younger sister. The girl's two impetuous young brothers and their large friendly dog add hilarious complications." Publ Wkly

Heyer, Georgette

The **grand** Sophy. Putnam 1950 307p

"On the Continent, where she had grown up and knew everyone in military, court, and diplomatic circles, Sophy was famous for her delightfully unexpected behavior, and for her irrepressible habit of managing less energetic people for their own good. When she returned to England, Regency London was also amused and startled by her antics, and her Rivenhall cousins, who offered her hospitality, were subjected to a reorganization of their lives. Sophy had learned the value of surprise attack from the Duke of Wellington, and applied it with shock tactics of her own to untangling the eldest Rivenhall cousins from unsuitable engagements, incidentally winning a husband for herself." Booklist

Heyer, Georgette

Penhallow. Doubleday, Doran 1943 309p

A "story about a family of terrorizing and oversexed males, embroiled with one or two victimized females, half-wits, illegitimate boot boys, and others. Very British, rural, and somewhat artificially 'tense.' . . . Here technique is equal to all improbabilities." Barzun. Cat of Crime. Rev and enl edition

Hiaasen, Carl

Bad monkey; Carl Hiaasen. 1st ed. Alfred A. Knopf 2013 336 p. (hardcover) $26.95

ISBN 0307272591; 9780307272591

LC 2013005863

In this book, disgraced cop Andrew Yancy has a chance to redeem himself. New sheriff Sonny Summers "tells Yancy to take a severed, shark-bitten arm snagged by a fisherman to Miami, where DNA identifies the limb as belonging to Nick Stripling, a retiree in his 40s whose boat was wrecked at sea. Stripling's grown daughter, Caitlin Cox, claims . . . that her hated stepmother murdered her father, and Yancy sees proving the stepmother's guilt as a way to return to the force." (Publishers Weekly)

Hiaasen, Carl

Basket case. Knopf 2002 317p

ISBN 0-375-41107-0

LC 2001-38317

"In laying out the tale of Jack Tagger, a maladjusted, middle-aged Florida obituary writer who stumbles across a hot news story in the supposed scuba-diving death of Jimmy Stoma, former lead singer for a band called Jimmy and the

Slut Puppies, Hiaasen skewers both corporate media operations and the world of pop stardom." N Y Times Book Rev

Hiaasen, Carl
✓ **Lucky** you; a novel. Knopf 1997 353p
ISBN 0-679-45444-6

LC 97-36885

"Sharing $28 million worth of lottery money with the holder of one other winning ticket wouldn't seem to be much of a burden to bear, but it is for Bodean Gazzer and his pal Chub, who crave all the cash to launch their own personal hate group, the White Clarion Aryans. The other winner, a black woman named JoLayne Lucks, plans to use her money to save a patch of Florida swamp, but that's before the Aryans assault her and steal the ticket. With the help of maverick journalist Tom Krome, JoLayne attempts to steal it back." Booklist

"Hiaasen writes witty dialogue that crackles, and his characters are eccentrically colorful." N Y Times Book Rev

Hiaasen, Carl
★ **Native** tongue. Knopf 1991 325p
ISBN 0-394-58796-0

LC 91-52713

"Hiaasen writes to a formula with brilliant success. His books are addictive. . . . One may miss the sour bite of bleaker comedy, found in the best crime stories of a more realistic kind, but for entertainment few can match him." London Rev Books

Hiaasen, Carl
✓ **Nature** girl. Alfred A. Knopf 2006 305p $25.95
ISBN 978-0-307-26299-8; 0-307-26299-5

LC 2006-49360

"As usual, Hiaasen throws his colorful characters into an increasingly frenetic mix, and the fun lies in watching how, or if, they'll manage to extricate themselves. One reason Nature Girl works so well is the fact that much of the action is confined to a single island, allowing the characters to intermingle and weave in and out of view." San Francisco Chronicle

Hiaasen, Carl
Sick puppy; a novel. Knopf 2000 341p
ISBN 0-679-45445-4

LC 99-33435

"While there may be nothing laughable about unchecked environmental exploitation, Hiaasen has refined his knack for using this gloomy but persistent state of affairs as a prime mover for scams of all sorts. In Sick Puppy, he shows himself to be a comic writer at the peak of his powers." Publ Wkly

Hiaasen, Carl
Skin tight. Putnam 1989 319p
ISBN 0-399-13489-1

LC 89-31580

"When Mick Stranahan, a retired investigator, is the attempted victim of murder, he becomes a little curious to find out who wants him dead. He trails the killer to a quack plastic surgeon who was a suspect in a murder case Stranahan investigated four years before. Someone is about to blab that the surgeon had a more than passing interest in the old case

and Stranahan gets back in the harness to investigate." West Coast Rev Books

Hiaasen, Carl
Skinny dip; a novel. Alfred A. Knopf 2004 355p $24.95
ISBN 0-375-41108-9

LC 2004-44106

"Joey Perrone and her husband, Chaz, are taking a cruise to celebrate their wedding anniversary. One night, as the rain pours down, Chaz throws Joey overboard. He then proceeds to convince the authorities that he has no idea what happened to her. Unfortunately for him, Joey is rescued and begins to plot her ultimate revenge against her soon-to-be-patsy of a husband. The squirm-inducing mayhem that follows in this sometimes sidesplitting novel almost makes you feel sorry for Chaz. It has rarely been this much fun to read about the act of revenge. All of the trademark characters and Florida locales are used to maximum effect." Libr J

Hiaasen, Carl
Star Island. Alfred A. Knopf 2010 337p $26.95
ISBN 978-0-307-27258-4; 0-307-27258-3

LC 2010-22584

"Trying to follow the plot, which involves a supporting cast of crooked politicians and predatory developers, is a little like walking a puppy. But the outlandish events soar on the exuberance of Hiaasen's manic style, a canny blend of lunatic farce and savage satire." N Y Times Book Rev

Hiaasen, Carl
Stormy weather; a novel. Knopf 1995 335p
ISBN 0-679-41982-9

LC 95-78487

A Florida hurricane "puts on a collision course a demented cast of tourists, scam artists and eccentrics: New York ad exec Max Lamb, who decides to spice up his Orlando honeymoon by taking his bride and his camcorder into the teeth of the storm; Skink, the swamp-dwelling former Florida governor . . . who kidnaps Max in an effort to teach him to respect the land; Edie March, a seductive drifter who hatches a half-baked personal-injury scam with the help of Snapper, a sadistic ex-con; and Augustine, the altruistic son of a jailed drug smuggler, who juggles skulls to relax." Publ Wkly

"The crimes plotted are minor aspects of a fiction that explores the intersection of the grotesque and the human." Libr J

Hiaasen, Carl
★ **Strip** tease; a novel. Knopf 1993 353p
ISBN 0-679-41981-0

LC 93-12358

In among Hiaasen's "freaks and obsessives, his corrupters and corrupted, his brain-dead and his frenetically active, the author has dropped a real honest-to-God human being, an appealing young woman named Erin Grant. Her presence, her history and goals, make the cartoon nastiness around her less cartoony and more nasty than in previous Hiaasen novels." N Y Times Book Rev

Hickam, Homer H.

The **keeper's** son; a novel. [by] Homer Hickam. 1st ed; Thomas Dunne Books 2003 353p $24.95

ISBN 0-312-30189-8

LC 2003-54964

"This is the first novel of a planned series about rough and tumble Coast Guard Lt. Josh Thurlow and his unusual patrol boat crew during WWII. Josh, 31, is a career officer assigned to Killakeet Island, along North Carolina's treacherous Outer Banks. Both he and his father-the keeper of the Killakeet Lighthouse-are haunted by the loss at sea and presumed death of Josh's two-year-old baby brother 17 years earlier. Shaken from his brooding by the appearance of German U-boats, Josh must try to protect the merchant ships torpedoed every night offshore. . . . Well-crafted characters, gripping naval warfare and colorful island life come together in this dynamic and exciting tale." Publ Wkly

Hicks, Robert

The **widow** of the south; Robert Hicks. Warner Books 2005 426p ill., map o.p.; $43; (pbk.) $14.99

ISBN 0446500127; 0446578827 (lg. print); 9780446697439

LC 2005010568

This book, "based on true events in [the author's] hometown, follows the saga of Carrie McGavock, a lonely Confederate wife who finds purpose transforming her Tennessee plantation into a hospital and cemetery during the Civil War. . . . Before the 1864 battle of Franklin, Confederate Gen. Nathan Bedford Forrest commandeers her house as a field hospital. In alternating points of view, the battle is recounted by different witnesses, including . . . Confederate Sgt. Zachariah Cashwell, who loses a leg. By the end of the battle, 9,000 soldiers have perished, and thousands of Confederates are buried in a field near the McGavock plantation. Zachariah ends up in Carrie's care at the makeshift hospital . . . while Carrie fights to relocate the buried soldiers when her wealthy neighbor threatens to plow up the field after the war." (Publishers Weekly)

Includes bibliographical references

Higashino, Keigo

★ The **devotion** of suspect X; Keigo Higashino; translated by Alexander O. Smith with Elye J. Alexander. 1st U.S. ed.; Minotaur Books 2011 298p

ISBN 9780312375065

LC 2010039022

Naoki Prize (Japan) (2005)

This book tells the story of "Yasuko Hanaoka, . . . a divorced, single mother who thought she had finally escaped her abusive ex-husband Togashi. When he shows up one day . . . the situation quickly escalates into violence and Togashi ends up dead on her apartment floor. . . . Yasuko's next door neighbor, middle-aged high school mathematics teacher Ishigami, offers his help, disposing not only of the body but plotting the cover-up step-by-step. When the body turns up and is identified, Detective Kusanagi . . . brings in Dr. Manabu Yukawa, a physicist and college friend who frequently consults with the police. Yukawa . . . went to college with Ishigami. After meeting up with him again, Yukawa is convinced that Ishigami had something to do with the murder." (Publisher's note)

Higashino, Keigo

Salvation for a saint; Keigo Higashino; translated by Alexander O. Smith; with Elye Alexander. St. Martin's Minotaur 2012 330 p.

ISBN 0312600682; 9780312600686; 9781250015860

LC 2012035862

In this novel by Keigo Higashino, "physics professor Manabu Yukawa -- Detective Galileo -- returns in a new case of impossible murder. . . . Yoshitaka, who was about to leave his marriage and his wife, is poisoned by arsenic-laced coffee and dies. His wife, Ayane, is the logical suspect -- except that she was hundreds of miles away when he was murdered. . . . The brilliant mind of Dr. Yukawa . . . must somehow find a way to . . . capture a very real, very deadly murderer." (Publisher's note)

Higginbotham, Susan

Her highness, the traitor; Susan Higginbotham. Sourcebooks 2012 368 p. (pbk.: alk. paper) $14.99

ISBN 1402265581; 9781402265587

LC 2012003465

This historical novel, by Susan Higginbotham, retells the ascension of the English Queen Jane Grey. "Frances Grey harbored no dream of her children taking the throne. Cousin of the king, she knew the pitfalls of royalty and privilege. . . . Jane Dudley knew her husband was creeping closer to the throne, but someone had to take charge, for the good of the country. She couldn't see the twisted path they all would follow." (Publisher's note)

Higgins, George V., 1939-1999

At end of day; a novel. Harcourt Brace & Co. 2000 383p $30

ISBN 0-15-100358-0

LC 99-46414

"The last novel of the late George V. Higgins shows no hint of failing skill or mellowing temper. The dialogue is as raffishly elegant as ever, the action as disconcerting to the lawfully minded, and the author's underlying attitude what it has regularly been—a plague on all your houses. . . . Questions of law and justice, as discussed by the characters, become almost equally unnerving. Higgins was a brilliantly clever, savagely bitter observer of society." Atl Mon

Higgins, George V.

Bomber's law; a novel. Holt & Co. 1993 296p

ISBN 0-8050-2329-1

LC 93-26006

"A whiz of a stylist with a black belt in dialogue, Higgins lets his characters' conversation carry the story. This is our language as it is spoken, full of false stops and loony poetry." Newsweek

Higgins, George V.

A **change** of gravity. Holt & Co. 1997 456p

ISBN 0-8050-4815-4

LC 97-6892

"The story unfolds in a nonlinear way; it does so almost entirely through superb dialogue that reveals character in a far more complex and interesting way than does an omniscient author. . . . Characters often speak continuously for several pages, but convey such nuances about the mores and social strata of their time that we welcome their loquaciousness." N Y Times Book Rev

Higgins, George V., 1939-1999

The **Digger's** game; George V. Higgins. Penguin Books 1988 169 p.

ISBN 0140102523; 9780140102529

LC 87019761

In this book, "Jerry 'Digger' Doherty is an ex-con and proprietor of a workingman's Boston bar, who supplements his income with the occasional 'odd job,' like stealing live checks and picking up hot goods. His brother's a priest, his wife's a nag, and he's got a deadly appetite for martinis and gambling. But when the Digger loses eighteen grand in borrowed money on a trip to Vegas, he quickly finds himself in the sights of mob loanshark 'the Greek,' who will have to make the Digger pay up one way or another. Luckily—if you call it luck—the Digger has been let in on a little job that can turn his gambling debt into a profit, as long as he can pull it off without getting killed." (Publisher's note)

Higgins, George V.

★ The **friends** of Eddie Coyle. Knopf 1972 183p

ISBN 0-394-47327-2

The action of the story "involves a series of bank robberies. Eddie Coyle is a small-time {Boston} crook who is trying to crash the big time by providing the armament for the robbers. His 'friends' use him, are used by him, and ultimately there is double-crossing all the way along the line." Publ Wkly

"Written entirely in riveting dialogue, this novel is a compelling study of motive." Oxford Companion to Am Lit. 6th edition

Higgins, George V.

The **Mandeville** talent. Holt & Co. 1991 278p

ISBN 0-8050-1412-8

LC 91-9232

"The drama in this book comes simply from watching the protagonists' minds work. Higgins makes us believe that the paper trail of contemporary life actually leads not to obfuscation but to clarity." Booklist

Higgins, Jack

Bad company. Putnam 2003 287p $25.95

ISBN 0-399-14970-8

LC 2003-41365

"As the war is drawing to a close in 1945, Hitler gives his diary to an aide for safekeeping. The diary contains an account of a meeting between representatives of Hitler and President Roosevelt at which they discussed ways to negotiate a peace treaty and then to attack Russia. The aide, Max von Berger, is now (in 2003) a billionaire industrialist and a silent partner with an international crime family. Seeking revenge for a killing, Berger vows to reveal the diary's secret that would destroy the current U.S. president. It's up to an American and a British agent to get the diary before it falls into the hands of the president's enemies." Booklist

Higgins, Jack

Cold Harbour. Simon & Schuster 1990 318p

LC 89-26198

A "tale of deception set in World War II Europe. Cold Harbour, a tiny village on the English Channel in Cornwall, is being used by the Special Operations Executive . . . as a base for running secret agents into and out of occupied France. To safeguard that operation, Englishmen masquerading as Germans patrol the Channel in a captured German vessel and fly planes bearing Luftwaffe insignia. But these deceptions are just the beginning. At a French chateau occupied by the German High Command, the resident family—now reduced to an elderly countess and her young niece, AnneMarie—pretend to be collaborators." N Y Times Book Rev

Higgins, Jack

Confessional. Stein & Day 1985 278p

ISBN 0-8128-3025-3

LC 884-40777

"The hero of this spy-thriller is three people—a KGB agent, an ordained Catholic priest and an IRA terrorist, which means that he goes through a lot of cloak-and-dagger changes as he slips from role to role. In 1958 the Russians set up a mock Irish village in the Ukraine to train future KGB agents so that they could more easily blend into the Irish landscape and go about their nefarious activities of destabilizing English-Irish relations by working through the IRA. Mikhail Kelly was a first-rate candidate because his Irish father had been hung by the British as an IRA activist and he had been raised by his Russian mother in Ireland." Best Sellers

Higgins, Jack

Day of judgment. Holt, Rinehart & Winston 1979 263p

LC 78-15043

"The time of the story is Spring 1963, just prior to President Kennedy's planned visit to Berlin. To discredit his good-will tour, members of the East German Intelligence have kidnapped a {Jesuit} Catholic priest known to be a foe of Communism and a member of an organization that has been smuggling refugees from the East into the West. They imprison him in a castle just fifty miles inside the East German border, to try to break his will and make him reveal certain facts that could prove an embarrassment to the Free World, through brainwashing. But they reckon without dedicated people, including members of the Catholic Church and the members of a non-Catholic monastery in the town where they are holding the priest. The rescuers also have the help of a Jesuit father, a woman doctor and a British Intelligence Officer." West Coast Rev Books

The author "has used an episode in history to write a finely crafted thriller with excellent characterization." Booklist

Higgins, Jack

Day of reckoning. Putnam 2000 295p $25.95

ISBN 0-399-14585-0

LC 99-34847

The journalist wife of Sean Dillon's "old comrade Blake Johnson is killed in Brooklyn on orders of her latest object of investigation, Jack Fox, heir apparent to the powerful Solazzo crime family. The law can't touch Fox, but Blake and Dillon can and will. Aided by Dillon's black-ops boss Brigadier Charles Ferguson, and his crew, plus a father/son team of British gangsters, Blake and Dillon strike again and again at Fox's wallet: shutting down his London gambling den; sinking a boat laden with his gold; destroying a cache of his weapons in Ireland; foiling his plans for a major robbery in London. . . . The action is sleek and intensely absorbing." Publ Wkly

Higgins, Jack

Drink with the Devil. Putnam 1996 311p
ISBN 0-399-14154-5

LC 96-3821

This Sean Dillon adventure "finds the former terrorist involved with a group of Irish Protestant paramilitaries in 1985 as they hijack a truck carrying £100 million in gold bullion. Ten years later, Sean is working for British Intelligence when he is ordered to go after the gold again. Now he is to prevent the bullion from disrupting the peace between the Catholics and Protestants. Dillon, boss Brigadier Ferguson, and partner Hannah Bernstein must also deal with the Mafia. They ask 85-year-old Liam Devlin for help, and the IRA legend of past Higgins books is only too pleased to participate. The excitement never lags as each side double-crosses the others." Libr J

Higgins, Jack

The **eagle** has flown; a novel. Simon & Schuster 1991 335p

LC 91-4368

"Mr. Higgins is an expert storyteller, and he goes about 'The Eagle Has Flown' with typical gusto. Everything is carefully arranged, little pieces fitting into other little pieces to form an action-packed mosaic." NY Times Book Rev

Higgins, Jack

★ The **eagle** has landed. Simon & Schuster 1991 399p

LC 90-44042

A revised edition containing the full text of the title first published 1975 by Holt, Rinehart & Winston

"There are elements of heroism, duplicity, and heavy irony, plus considerable bloodshed, in this action-oriented yarn." Christ Sci Monit

Followed by The eagle has flown

Higgins, Jack

Edge of danger. Putnam 2001 273p $25.95
ISBN 0-399-14701-2

LC 00-40268

"Pitting returning antihero Sean Dillon, once of the IRA, now with British intelligence, against an aristocratic English-Arab family bent on vengeance that threatens world order, the story whips along. From London to the Middle East, from Ireland to the White House, it swirls with intrigue and snaps with violence." Publ Wkly

Higgins, Jack

Eye of the storm. Putnam 1992 320p

LC 91-46736

"Early in 1991, while the Gulf war is in full bloom, operatives of Saddam Hussein hire legendary terrorist Sean

Dillon to take the war to the enemy. A master of disguise and subterfuge, Dillon began his career with the IRA, earning the enmity of Liam Devlin—the unforgettable antihero of The Eagle Has Landed, who makes a featured appearance here—and of Martin Brosnan, an American Special Forces hero and IRA member turned college professor. After Dillon's attempt to assassinate former Prime Minster Margaret Thatcher during a visit to France fails, he decides to go after her successor John Major. . . . Although readers can be sure that Dillon's scheme will be foiled, fun remains in the how and why." Publ Wkly

Followed by Thunder point (1993)

Higgins, Jack

Flight of eagles. Putnam 1998 328p
ISBN 0-399-14376-9

LC 97-37582

The author traces the exploits of twins Max and Harry Kelso "from 1917, when their wealthy American father marries a German baroness, through 1944. . . . Upon her husband's death in 1930, the baroness returns to Germany with Max in tow, leaving Harry in the care of his American grandfather. By the early 1940s Max is Germany's premier flying ace–he eventually downs more than 300 Allied planes–and is famed as the Black Baron. Harry, meanwhile, has enlisted with the RAF and distinguished himself equally in the Battle of Britain and beyond. The narrative cuts briskly from one twin's adventures to the other's as the dashing, daring young men intersect with historical greats including Hitler, Himmler, Goring, FDR and Eisenhower." Publ Wkly

Higgins, Jack

Luciano's luck. Stein & Day 1981 238p

LC 881-40330

"It is 1943 and the Allied invasion of Sicily is imminent. General Eisenhower plans to enlist Sicilian Mafia support for the invasion by sending two emissaries into Sicily to sway Luca, the Sicilian 'capo di tutti capi.' Logically, perhaps, one emissary is the chief U.S. capo, Lucky Luciano (who is in prison); the second is Luca's alienated granddaughter. The commando expedition to effect a meeting between these three in German-occupied Sicily forms the basis for a fast-paced, action-crammed plot, suspenseful to the last page. The fictionalized Luciano is sympathetically portrayed, and although the romanticizing of the Mafia figures jars a little, the historical premises are acceptably plausible." Libr J

Higgins, Jack

Midnight runner. Putnam 2002 289p
ISBN 0-399-14833-7

LC 2001-48124

This suspense novel finds "former IRA enforcer Sean Dillon and his present boss, Gen. Charles Ferguson, . . . responding to various revenge gambits by the beautiful and fabulously wealthy half-bedu, half-English Lady Kate Rashid, countess of Loch Dhu and head of the Rashid Bedu tribe of Hazar, whose three brothers were killed by Dillon and his comrades . . . after, among other acts of infamy, a Rashid assassination attempt on U.S. President Jack Cazalet." Publ Wkly

Higgins, Jack

Night of the fox. Simon & Schuster 1986 316p
LC 86-29662

"Taking the form of a continuous flashback, 'Night of the Fox' begins with the aftermath of a U-boat attack off the coast of German-occupied Jersey, which results in the wounded body of an American soldier being washed ashore. For the Allies, Hugh Kelso is a dangerous liability; if the Germans learn what he knows about the proposed Normandy invasion, disaster would be inevitable. British agents Harry Martinique and Sarah Drayton secretly enter Jersey, posing as an SS officer and his mistress. Another form of deception is also taking place, as a gifted Jewish actor arrives on the island, impersonating Field Marshall Rommel and covering for the real 'Desert Fox,' who is in France on secret talks. The three imposters join forces in a daring and dangerous mission." Booklist

"Higgins combines powerful narrative with documentary detail in an exceptional tale that relies upon the interweaving histories of the various characters." Libr J

Higgins, Jack

The **president's** daughter. Putnam 1997 278p
ISBN 0-399-14239-8
LC 96-48654

"Higgins offers the usual cast of characters—beautiful women and tough guys—and exotic locales, including London, Corfu, Sicily, Ireland, France, and the eastern Mediterranean.... {This} is another 'race against the clock' thriller, and Higgins' fans won't be disappointed." Booklist

Higgins, Jack

Rough justice. G.P. Putnam's Sons 2008 326p $25.95
ISBN 978-0-399-15513-0; 0-399-15513-9
LC 2008-8905

This entry in the Sean Dillon thriller series "finds aging, arthritic ex-gangster Harry Salter retired from active operations, leaving Dillon, once the IRA's most feared enforcer, as the real leader of the loose gang of stalwart lads who covertly battle the foes of Western civilization. A newcomer to the team, Maj. Harry Miller, on the surface a mild-mannered MP who's in reality the British prime minister's secret hit man, hooks up with series regular Blake Johnson in Kosovo, where the Russians, intent on reclaiming old glory, are stirring up trouble. Meanwhile, Islamic fundamentalists are intent on bringing Britain to its knees. The action moves swiftly amid a variety of foreign locales, including Moscow, London and Beirut, to a climax that will leave readers asking themselves, evidence to the contrary, whether the great game is really over." Publ Wkly

Higgins, Jack

Storm warning; a novel. Holt, Rinehart & Winston 1976 311p il

"What does work, exceedingly well, are the action at sea scenes, building up to the climax. . . . Basically what we have are decent people on both sides of the war, some of whom survive, some of whom do not, who come together in a desperate attempt to save the lives of the Germans aboard the ship who have fought so bravely to make it home." Publ Wkly

Higgins, Jack

Touch the devil. Stein & Day 1982 251p
LC 82-40080

"Charles Ferguson of British intelligence persuades Devlin {featured in the Eagle novels} to join forces with Martin Brosnan, former comrade in the fight for Irish independence, to find and stop (by killing if necessary) another onetime rebel, Frank Barry, now in the pay of the Soviets. Barry, a cold assassin and thief of NATO secret weapons, is a match in cunning for Devlin and Brosnan, and he learns about the plot against him from a mole in Ferguson's office. He knows that Devlin and Brosnan's lover, Anne-Marie Audin, get help from the British to spirit Brosnan from a French prison, as grim as Devil's Island, where his revolutionary activities have landed him. Anne-Marie takes the two men to her secluded farm house in southern France, where Barry and his hirelings lurk in ambush." Publ Wkly

Higgins, Jack

The **White** House connection. Putnam 1999 323p $25.95
ISBN 0-399-14489-7
LC 98-42577

"Sean Dillon, a former IRA gunman, now works for the British prime minister; Blake Johnson heads a secret office for the U.S. president. Both have their various talents severely tested while trying to stop a vengeful 66-year-old woman who is assassinating members of the Sons of Erin, including a senator, thereby threatening both governments." Libr J

"When it comes to thrillers, Jack Higgins wrote the book. In fact, he wrote lots of them, and this is one of the best." Booklist

Higgins, Jack

The **wolf** at the door. G.P. Putnam's Sons 2010 306p $26.95
ISBN 978-0-399-15612-0; 0-399-15612-7
LC 2009-29452

In this Sean Dillon thriller, "Russian prime minister Vladimir Putin is behind a plot to kill Dillon and other members of the British prime minister's private intelligence army as payback for their being such a thorn in his side over the years. In London, Gen. Charles Ferguson, who's just left a late-night meeting of Commonwealth ministers, is walking toward his car when it explodes, killing his driver. In New York City, Maj. Harry Miller, who's in the U.S. to attend a U.N. meeting, goes for a stroll in Central Park, where he neatly turns the tables on a hired hit man. Extensive flashbacks explain how the attacks on each of the marked men evolved, with much space devoted to the chief assassin, Daniel Holley. Higgins provides a more cerebral story than usual, but he doesn't stint on action." Publ Wkly

Higgins, Kristan

★ The **Best** Man; Kristan Higgins. Harlequin Books 2013 432 p. $7.99
ISBN 0373777922; 9780373777921

In this contemporary romance novel, by Kristan Higgins, "Faith Holland left her hometown after being jilted at the altar. Now a little older and wiser, she's ready to return to the Blue Heron Winery, her family's vineyard, to confront the ghosts of her past, and maybe enjoy a glass of red. After all, there's some great scenery there. . . . Like Levi Cooper, the local police chief." (Publisher's note)

Higgins, Kristan

My one and only; Kristan Higgins. HQN Books 2011 382p.

ISBN 9781611730708; 9780373775576

This book follows "divorce attorney Harper James . . . [who] is horrified when her stepsister, Willa, announces that she's marrying the brother of Harper's ex-husband, Nick Lowery. Harper and Nick married young, and while their relationship quickly flamed out, the spark between them never really died. Due to a travel snafu after Willa's wedding, Harper and Nick are forced to journey across the country together. Soon, Harper is examining the reasons their marriage failed, her unresolved feelings for Nick, and her abandonment issues." (Publishers Weekly)

Higgins, Kristan

Somebody to love; Kristan Higgins. HQN 2012 425 p. $7.99

ISBN 0373776586; 9780373776580

In this romance novel, by Kristan Higgins, "after her father loses the family fortune in an insider-trading scheme, single mom Parker Welles is faced with some hard decisions. First order of business: go to Gideon's Cove, Maine, to sell the only thing she now owns--a decrepit house in need of some serious flipping. When her father's wingman, James Cahill, asks to go with her, she's not thrilled . . . even if he is fairly gorgeous and knows his way around a toolbox." (Publisher's note)

Higgs, Liz Curtis

Grace in thine eyes; Liz Curtis Higgs.. Waterbrook Press 2006 447p maps $14.99

ISBN 1578562597; 9781578562596

LC 2005033536

This book tells the story of "Davina McKie [who] is a bonny lass of seventeen, as clever as they come and a gifted musician. Unable to speak since childhood, she is doted on by her belligerent younger brothers, Will and Sandy, who vow to protect their silent sister. When the lads are forced to depart the glen, Jamie McKie intends to brighten his daughter's summer by escorting Davina to the Isle of Arran. Her cousins make her welcome at the manse, and the parish delights in hearing their talented fiddler. But when she catches the eye of a handsome young Highlander on Midsummer Eve, sheltered Davina is unprepared for the shocking events that follow." (Publisher's note)

Highsmith, Patricia

The **boy** who followed Ripley. Lippincott & Crowell 1980 291p

LC 79-29678

In this novel "two people meet casually, but their fates become inextricably, and dangerously, joined. Tom Ripley is an American expatriate living on the outskirts of Paris; he meets a 16-year-old American runaway, who turns out to be the son of a recently deceased food products tycoon. The boy is haunted by guilt over his father's death and pursued through Europe by kidnappers. Engrossing and shiver packed." Booklist

Highsmith, Patricia

Patricia Highsmith: selected novels and short stories; edited with an introduction by Joan Schenkar. W. W. Norton & Co. 2011 644p $35

ISBN 978-0-393-08013-1; 0-393-08013-7

LC 2010-34589

"Highsmith's first book, 'Strangers on a Train' (1950), is the disturbing tale of a forced folie à deux between an alcoholic young psychopath and the architect he ensnares in a nightmarish, homicidal scheme. Her second novel, 'The Price of Salt' (1952), done under the pseudonym Claire Morgan, is the semi-lyrical chronicle of a love affair between two women. Each a commercial success, these works are quite different in tone and content, but both are done with a skill and an artistry that utterly convince." Los Angeles Times Book Rev

Highsmith, Patricia

Ripley's game. Knopf 1974 267p

"Highsmith uses a matter-of-fact, almost reportorial, tone to effect her measured, driving pace and to construct her tightly woven web. The second half of this literate and imaginative thriller is especially brilliant—all the way to the dazzling last page." Libr J

Highsmith, Patricia

The **selected** stories of Patricia Highsmith; with a foreword by Graham Greene. Norton 2001 724p $27.95

ISBN 0-393-02031-2

LC 2001-30878

Highsmith, Patricia

★ The **talented** Mr. Ripley; Ripley under ground; Ripley's game. Knopf 1999 877p $26

ISBN 0-375-40792-8

LC 99-38147

In Ripley under ground Tom impersonates a dead artist and is drawn into murder when his deception is about to be discovered

In the talented Mr. Ripley "Tom Ripley is hired by the wealthy Herbert Greenleaf to help him find his son, Dickie. Ripley travels to Europe and catches up to Dickie in Italy, meanwhile corresponding with Greenleaf through the mail. Later, after he has assumed Dickie's identity himself, he keeps up the imposture by writing to Dickie's friends and avoiding personal contact. He continues, however, to be 'Tom Ripley' when the occasion demands. Highsmith takes us into the mind of a repellent character but, through the sheer force of her communication of his personality, compels a sympathetic fascination on the part of the reader." Murphy. Ency of Murder and Mystery

Higley, T. L.

Pompeii; L.T. Higley. B & H Books 2011 xxiii, 338p

ISBN 9781433668579; 1433668572

LC 2011282808

This book tells the story of "Ariella, a young Jewish woman fleeing Jerusalem, and Cato, a Roman merchant famous for his wines. During the fall of Jerusalem, the Roman emperor forces Ariella into slavery; she sneaks away one night, disguises herself as a young man, and joins a gladiator troupe. The gladiators soon journey to Pompeii, where her secret is almost exposed. In Pompeii, she meets Cato, who discovers right away that she's a woman and seeks to watch over her. Through a series of adventures, the two begin secretly to attend meetings led by a Jewish slave named Jeremiah, who expounds the Jewish scriptures and talks about the newly emerging Christian sect." (Publishers Weekly)

Hijuelos, Oscar, 1951-2013
Beautiful Maria of my soul; or, the true story of Maria Garcia y Cifuentes, the lady behind a famous song: a novel. Hyperion 2010 340p $25.99

ISBN 978-1-4013-2334-9; 1-4013-2334-0

LC 2009-35386

"The rare sequel that can be enjoyed independently of the original work or as a complement to it. . . . There's a simmering backdrop of revolution in the middle of the book that provides the story with historical heft. And, in the novel's bold ending, Hijuelos seamlessly welds fact and fiction, with the author himself making an appearance to discuss his books with the characters that inhabit them." Cleveland Plain Dealer

Hijuelos, Oscar, 1951-2013
Empress of the splendid season; a novel. HarperFlamingo 1999 342p

ISBN 0-06-017570-2

LC 98-34798

The author "tells his story without condescension or false sentimentality, in the tone of a neighborhood gossip. The literary device of the cleaning lady also provides a new and unexpected angle of vision on Manhattan's old money. . . . Hijuelos reaffirms his place in the front rank of American novelists and forces the Hispanic immigrant experience closer to the center of our cultural consciousness." Natl Rev

Hijuelos, Oscar
The **fourteen** sisters of Emilio Montez O'Brien; a novel. Farrar, Straus & Giroux 1993 484p

ISBN 0-374-15815-0

LC 92-41935

This novel "tells the story of the family of Nelson O'Brien, an Irish immigrant to the U.S. who travels to Cuba as a photographer during the Spanish-American War. There he falls passionately in love and marries the young and beautiful Mariela Montez. After the couple returns to the farm O'Brien owns in a small Pennsylvania town, he works as the local photographer and operates the community's movie theater, while she keeps busy bearing and rearing their 14 daughters and, finally, one son, Emilio Montez O'Brien." Time

Hijuelos, Oscar
★ The **Mambo** Kings play songs of love; a novel. Farrar, Straus & Giroux 1989 407p

LC 89-1248

"The novel alternates crisp narrative with opulent musings—the language of everyday and the language of longing. When Mr. Hijuelos falters, as from time to time he does, it's through an excess of self-consciousness: he strives too hard for all-encompassing description or grows distant

and dutiful in an effort to get period details just right." N Y Times Book Rev

Hijuelos, Oscar
A **simple** Habana melody: from when the world was good; a novel. HarperCollins Pubs. 2002 342p

ISBN 0-06-017569-9

LC 2002-512611

"While there is a faintly contrived air about Levis's experience of the Holocaust. Hijuelos triumphs in capturing the sights and sounds of Habana at the edge of modernity." Publ Wkly

Hilderbrand, Elin
The **island**; a novel. Little, Brown 2010 407p $25.99

ISBN 978-0-316-04387-8; 0-316-04387-7

LC 2010-06268

"Two generations of women come together off the coast of Nantucket as they spend the summer in the family beach cottage. They're all there for different reasons: Chess is trying to mend her broken heart after her ex-fiancé dies in a tragic accident; her sister, Tate, is eager to escape boredom and figure out what she really wants from life; their mother, Birdie, is still coming to terms with her divorce; and Birdie's sister, India, is trying to help them all—while dealing with her own secret pain." Libr J

This tale "zips along with the kind of well-limned romantic drama that keeps poolside readers out of the water for hours." Entertainment Wkly

Hilderbrand, Elin
Silver girl; a novel. Little, Brown and Co. 2011 408p $26.99

ISBN 978-0-316-09966-0; 0-316-09966-X

LC 2011-02750

"Connie is profoundly lonely following her husband's death and the estrangement from her daughter. Meanwhile, Meredith's husband's investment firm has been revealed as a Ponzi scheme, and the ensuing investigation has, in a very Ruth Madoff–like way, separated her from the life she's known. The women retreat to Connie's Nantucket home, where they repair their relationships and their own broken hearts while a series of threatening events keeps Meredith in hiding. Though Meredith's guilty feelings about missing clues to her husband's dishonesty are overwhelming, the kindness shown by people who support her-including Connie's tentative new flame-encourages her to make good where she can. Much of the novel is told in flashback as Connie and Meredith work through their crises, but Hilderbrand's talents keep those memories as resonant as the present day." Publ Wkly

Hilderbrand, Elin
Summerland; a novel. Elin Hilderbrand. 1st ed. Reagan Arthur Books/Little, Brown and Co. 2012 392 p. (hardcover) $26.99; (paperback) $14.99; (audiobook) $59.99

ISBN 031609983X; 9780316099837; 9780316099899; 9781619690769 unabridged

LC 2012004929

In this book by Elin Hilderbrand, "what begins as a graduation night celebration ends in tragedy after a horrible car crash leaves the driver of the car, Penny Alistair, dead, and her twin brother in a coma. The other passengers, Penny's boyfriend Jake and her friend Demeter, are physically unhurt - but the emotional damage is overwhelming, and questions linger about what happened before Penny took the wheel." (Publisher's note)

Hill, Antonio

The **summer** of dead toys; a novel. Antonio Hill. 1st ed. Crown 2013 368 p. (hardcover) $26
ISBN 0770435874; 9780770435875
LC 2012034335

This novel, by Antonio Hill, is part of the author's "Inspector Salgado" series. "His boss . . . assigns Salgado to a routine accidental death: a college student fell from a balcony in one of Barcelona's ritzier neighborhoods. As Salgado begins to piece together the life and world of the victim, he realizes that his death was not all that simple. . . . Hector begins to follow a trail that will lead him deep into the underbelly of Barcelona's high society." (Publisher's note)

Hill, Joe

20th century ghosts; introduction by Christopher Golden. William Morrow 2007 316p $24.95
ISBN 978-0-06-114797-5; 0-06-114797-4
First published 2005 in the United Kingdom

"Hill's subject matter is steeped in the pop culture and tabloid detritus of the past 50 years: serial killers, abducted children, families living on the fault lines between divorce and poverty, horror movies and supernatural fiction. Yet his real focus is an almost obsessively nuanced exploration of the nature of American manhood. The presiding spirits of 20th Century Ghosts are lost boys and damaged men, running for their lives across a blighted, often surreal modern landscape. . . . Hill captures the heartbreaking longing for connection between men whose intelligence and decency aren't always enough to save them from the dark." Houston Chron

Hill, Joe

Heart-shaped box. William Morrow 2007 376p $24.95
ISBN 978-0-06-114793-7; 0-06-114793-1
LC 2006-46548

The author has created a "wild, mesmerizing, perversely witty tale of horror. In a book much too smart to sound like the work of a neophyte, he builds character invitingly and plants an otherworldly surprise around every corner." N Y Times (Late N Y Ed)

Hill, Joe

★ **Horns**. William Morrow 2010 370p $25.99
ISBN 978-0-06-114795-1; 0-06-114795-8

"The strange thing about Horns is that its opening scenes aren't all that strange. Its author, Joe Hill, is able to make Ig's problem seem like the most natural thing in the world. Mr. Hill writes with such palpable enthusiasm that he has no trouble hooking readers. . . . [He] is able to combine intrigue, editorializing, impassioned romance and even fiery theological debate in one well-told story." N Y Times (Late N Y Ed)

Hill, Lawrence

Someone knows my name; a novel. W.W. Norton & Co. 2007 486p $24.95
ISBN 978-0-393-06578-7; 0-393-06578-2
LC 2007-8035

What makes this novel "extraordinary is Hill's ability to transcend the facts—to make something magical out of them. Despite the unpalatable subject matter, he compels our attention and manages to delight. His Aminata is a heroic figure, a little larger than life, residing within and outside of history. You can never forget this character. She embeds herself in your heart." Toronto Star

Hill, Owen

The **incredible** Double. PM Press 2009 128p pa $13.95
ISBN 978-1-60486-083-2; 1-60486-083-9
LC 2009-901377

Clay Blackburn "is not your typical detective. For one thing, he's a book scout: a guy who haunts used bookstores and estate sales, looking for the one or two items of real value. For another, he's a poet, with a couple of chapbooks to his name. Most tellingly, he's the kind of enlightened anarchist who could only come from Berkeley. . . . And yet, a detective Clay is, after his own odd fashion — working without a license and without a net. In 'The Incredible Double,' he is asked to investigate death threats against a drugstore mogul named Jerry Wally (think Sam Walton with an attitude), only to be drawn quickly down the rabbit hole." Los Angeles Times

Hill, Reginald

Arms and the women; an elliad. Delacorte Press 1999 408p $23.95
ISBN 0-385-33279-3
LC 99-35873

"Andy Dalziel and Peter Pascoe, the ranking Yorkshire police officers in this series, marshal the troops when Pascoe's wife, Ellie and their little girl narrowly escape being abducted in broad daylight from their home. Suspicion naturally falls on any number of criminals with deep grudges against Pascoe; but once these obvious bad guys are eliminated, it begins to look as if Ellie has acquired an enemy of her own, perhaps within the circle of strong-minded political activists in her women's rights group." N Y Times Book Rev

Hill, Reginald

Bones and silence. Delacorte Press 1990 332p
LC 89-48836

"Set in a cathedral city which will host a contemporary enactment of medieval mystery plays, Hill's narrative features the police duo Andrew Dalziel and Peter Pascoe looking into a series of related murders and disappearances tied to a builder who is coincidentally constructing garages for the police station. Meanwhile, the galvanizing director of the mystery plays, Eileen Chung, has cast Dalziel as God and the builder in question as Lucifer." Publ Wkly

"A complex, challenging and diverting novel, from one of the most cogent of detective writers." Times Lit Suppl

Hill, Reginald

Child's play. Macmillan 1987 296p

LC 86-8712

This novel "has two plots. One concerns the will of a dotty, wealthy old woman who leaves her money to a son missing in action since 1944 and presumed dead. Hungry, greedy, angry relatives gather to see what can be done about breaking the will. . . . The other side of the story has to do with a tough cop who lives a secret life as a homosexual. Mr. Hill handles this aspect with grace; there also is a good deal of humor in the way Dalziel goes into action when, on orders from above, he has to track down the homosexual. He takes care of things in his own inimitable manner. Mr. Hill, as always, has a fine time jousting against hypocrisy and the hollow men of the bureaucracy." N Y Times Book Rev

Hill, Reginald

Death comes for the Fat Man. HarperCollins 2007 404p $24.95

ISBN 978-0-06-082082-4; 0-06-082082-9

LC 2006-48655

"Hill delivers his usual bundle of literary treats, from a single fragrant reference to Voltaire to the voluptuous visions of earthly delights Dalziel clings to as he hovers near death. Characters major and minor march boldly through the dense plot, confident of being remembered for their singular personalities and inexhaustible verbal resources, while Pascoe, who catches himself trying to keep his boss alive by assuming his 'blunt and brutish' ways, fears he's losing his own identity." N Y Times Book Rev

Hill, Reginald

Dream of darkness; {by} Patrick Ruell. Countryman Press 1991 204p

LC 90-38677

"The story of Sairey's haunted nights and days alternates with selections from her father's memoirs, which detail his diplomatic career in Uganda during the Amin years. Ruell effectively uses these parallel narratives to slowly unravel the mystery of Sairey's mother's death. A gem of a book with a startling finale." Booklist

Hill, Reginald

Good morning, midnight. HarperCollins 2004 433p $24.95

ISBN 0-06-052807-9

LC 2003-67603

Detectives Andy Dalziel and Peter Pascoe investigate "a locked-room suicide. . . . The case seems as closed as the room in which the local businessman's body was found until Hill and Pascoe discover that this suicide was committed 10 years to the day after the victim's father committed suicide in the same way and that the new suicide has left a very damning cassette tape. A cut-and-dried case morphs into a cold-case scenario in this wickedly clever, classic Brit-mystery puzzle, loaded with Yorkshire atmosphere and mordant wit." Booklist

Hill, Reginald

Killing the lawyers. St. Martin's Press 1997 287p

ISBN 0-312-16877-2

LC 97-16249

Joe Sixsmith is a "black PI in the not especially famous English town of Luton. He solves crimes less by detection than by his own brand of scrupulous honesty, which creates a kind of white light in which the bad guys invariably stand out. After Joe's insurance company undervalues his wrecked and beloved old car, he seeks the counsel of a rude and fancy lawyer. The visit ends in shouting—and becomes a case when the lawyer is murdered. Another lawyer in the dead man's firm is killed, and Joe, after being cleared as a suspect, is hired to investigate by a remaining partner in the firm." Publ Wkly

Hill, Reginald

Pictures of perfection; a Dalziel/Pascoe mystery in five volumes. Delacorte Press 1994 307p

LC 93-47449

"The intrepid trio of Sergeant Wield and detectives Dalziel and Pascoe are called to the tiny hamlet of Enscombe to investigate the mysterious disappearance of a rookie constable. When they arrive, however, they find there are more problems than just a missing copper; skulduggery, thievery, forgery, lust, lechery, libel, and passion all lie in wait for the three unwitting chaps. This is an intelligent, stylish, scintillating, witty mystery that transcends its cozy trappings." Booklist

Hill, Reginald

Recalled to life. Delacorte Press 1992 359p

LC 92-1380

"Though Hill relies too much on coincidence, the complex plot here sustains interest. The novel's chief rewards, however, are those of character: Dalziel is a brilliant, bearish delight and the supporting players, including a brash black woman CIA agent, provide a constant parade of pleasures." Publ Wkly

Hill, Reginald

Singing the sadness; a private eye Joe Sixsmith mystery. Thomas Dunne Bks. 1999 251p

ISBN 0-312-24238-7

LC 99-16864

Black private eye Joe Sixsmith "a member of the local choir, is traveling with his fellow singers to the Llanffugiol Choral Festival when the bus passes a burning cottage; without thinking, Joe rushes into the inferno and rescues a woman from the flames. He is pronouced a hero, but there's a mystery brewing: the cottage was supposed to be empty, so who is the woman Joe rescued?" Booklist

Hill, Reginald

The Stranger House. HarperCollins 2005 480p $24.95

ISBN 0-06-082081-0

LC 2005-40274

"Twentysomething Aussie math whiz Samantha Flood has fiery red hair and a fierce determination to learn the truth about her paternal grandmother, an orphan shipped from her native England to Australia under suspicious circumstances. Sober Spaniard Miguel Madero, who experiences ghostly visions and painful sensations in his feet and hands, has abandoned pursuit of the priesthood to engage in research about English Catholics during the Reformation. The paths of Samantha and Miguel (known to all as 'Mig') cross in the tiny English village of Illthwaite, home to the Stranger House, an inn that has hosted weary travelers for more than 500 years. Samantha and Mig, an unlikely duo, are drawn to one another as each discovers secrets simmering beneath the surface of Illthwaite's deceptively serene facade." Booklist

Hill, Reginald

★ The **wood** beyond. Delacorte Press 1996 358p

LC 95-32319

"Chief Inspector Andy Dalziel and Peter Pascoe investigate the discovery of some old bones near a large pharmaceutical research laboratory in Yorkshire. As the case progresses, Pascoe unearths surprising facts about his own grandfather, a World War I soldier." Libr J

"The theme of personal honor in a dishonorable world gives passion to the characters and urgency to their individual causes and obsessions." N Y Times Book Rev

Hill, Reginald

The **woodcutter**; a novel. Harper 2011 519p $25.99

ISBN 978-0-06-206074-7; 0-06-206074-0

LC 2010-53608

"Near the end, a character refers to the fate of 'the dreadful, drab English.' There's nothing drab about this dark and compelling novel, although some of its characters are dreadful human beings." Kirkus

Hill, Robert

When all is said and done. Graywolf Press 2006 220p $20

ISBN 1-55597-442-2

LC 2005-926374

This is a "portrait of an unusual early 1960s American marriage. Myrmy is a stylish and successful Madison Avenue advertising copywriter, wife, and mother. Her hunky and loving husband, Dan, is a war veteran turned tie salesman. Overriding anti-Semitic obstacles, Myrmy has moved her family out of the city into a suburb, where she remains a dynamo while Dan is plagued by strange maladies. Could his troubles be the result of a little radiation experiment conducted by the military? It's hard to find time for a diagnosis with three young boys to care for. Every aspect of this agile, intoxicating, hilarious, and poignant novel is compelling, but what elevates it is the exuberant language. Hill writes with velocity, rhythm, and wit, conveying a world of subtle emotions and social nuance in brilliantly syncopated inner monologues and staccato dialogue, creating a bravura and resounding performance." Booklist

Hill, Ruth Beebe

Hanta yo. Doubleday 1979 834p

LC 77-74792

"The practice of using the multi-generational family story to reflect changing times and/or historical events is almost a genre unto itself. This is such a novel. . . . The historical accuracy, linguistic acrobatics, and ethnological acuity do not limit the book's appeal. A superb style transcends the few minor flaws, and despite the scholarly impression given by the introduction, chronology notes, and glossaries, this book is first and foremost a well-written story." Libr J

Hill, Susan, 1942-

Mrs. de Winter; a novel. Morrow 1993 349p

LC 93-5347

"What happened to Maxim de Winter and his second wife after Manderley burned? This suspenseful 'completion' of Daphne du Maurier's Rebecca begins with the couple's return to England, following a ten-year, self-imposed exile, for the funeral of Maxim's sister Beatrice. In a voice true to the original story, Hill's Mrs. de Winter chronicles Rebecca's continuing shadow on their life; a mysterious wreath bearing a card with the initial 'R' is discovered near Beatrice's grave, and unwelcome visitors include Jack Favell, who has visions of blackmail, and Mrs. Danvers, who seeks revenge." Libr J

Hill, Susan

The **pure** in heart; a Simon Serrailler crime novel. Overlook Press 2007 370p $24.95

ISBN 978-1-58567-928-7; 1-58567-928-3

First published 2005 in the United Kingdom

"A nine-year-old boy is kidnapped in broad daylight while waiting for his school ride outside his home in the British cathedral town of Lafferton, and the case falls squarely in the lap of Detective Chief Inspector Serrailler. It's a copper's worst nightmare—broken and grieving parents, intense media interest, and extreme pressure from the top police brass to solve the case "yesterday." But there are few leads and no apparent motive, and as the days go by and the child isn't found, hope drains away. Although the case hits Simon and his team exceptionally hard, he has other problems to deal with. . . . This is realistic, gritty, and gut-wrenching crime fiction, but it's also a poignant and thoughtful character study." Booklist

Hill, Susan, 1942-

The **risk** of darkness; a Simon Serrailler mystery. by Susan Hill. Overlook Press 2010 374 p. $15.95

ISBN 9780701176822; 1590202902; 9781590202906

LC 2006491232

In this novel by Susan Hill, part of the Simon Serrailler Mystery series, "the . . . opening chapters introduce the two main plot lines: a spate of child abductions that have been unnerving the residents of the British town of Lafferton is pinned on an emotionally disturbed young woman, and a man unhinged by grief over his wife's death goes on a psychotic rampage in pursuit of women who look like her." (Publishers Weekly)

Hill, Susan, 1942-

Shadows in the street; a Simon Serrailler mystery. Susan Hill. Overlook Press 2010 372 p. $24.95

ISBN 9780701179977; 1590204085; 9781590204085

LC 2010444442

In this novel by Susan Hill, part of the Simon Serrailler series, "Two local prostitutes have been found strangled. When the wife of the St. Michael's Cathedral Dean goes missing and then another respectable woman is taken on her way to work, the townspeople grow angry and afraid. Serrailler is in the greatest danger of his life." (Publisher's note)

Hill, Susan

The **various** haunts of men; a Simon Serrailler crime novel. Overlook Press 2007 437p $24.95

ISBN 978-1-58567-876-1; 1-58567-876-7

LC 2006-51546

"Lafferton, an idyllic village just far enough from the madness of London, is a paragon of tranquility and peace, with a lovely cathedral and a stand of ancient stones on 'the Hill.' But then a woman goes missing from there, and then another, and another. Young policewoman Freya Graffham is assigned to investigate the suspected serial killings. Recently transferred from London, she is young, bright, inquisitive, dedicated, and smitten with Detective Chief Inspector Simon Serrailler. . . . As their relationship and the investigation unfold, the killer is revealed in a series of eerie first-person passages. . . . Readers will be instantly drawn to her likable characters and beautiful landscape and will be carried along by the plot, right up to the shocking final twist." Libr J

Hill, Susan, 1942-

The **vows** of silence; a Simon Serrailler crime novel. Susan Hill. Chatto & Windus 2008 328 p. $24.95

ISBN 1590202457; 9780701179991; 9780701180003; 9781590202456

LC 2008426390

This mystery novel by Susan Hill, part of the Simon Serrailler series, follows "enigmatic and brooding [detective] Simon Serrailler. . . A gunman is terrorizing young women in the cathedral town of Lafferton. What, if anything, links the apparently random murders? Is the marksman with the rifle the same as the killer with the handgun?" (Publisher's note)

Hill, Tobias

The **hidden**; a novel. Harper Perennial 2009 353p pa $14.99

ISBN 978-0-06-176825-5; 0-06-176825-1

"Ben Mercer has fled his failed marriage and his studies at Oxford, and a chance encounter brings him to an excavation near Sparta. An ominous mood seems to hang over the ragtag group, consisting of an ineffective American leader, a quartet of Greek laborers, and a clique of young, beautiful foreigners. As Ben gradually ingratiates himself, he begins to realize that half-heard conversations conceal a sin greater than he can face. Chapters of Spartan history—bellicose, sinister, and doomed—offer engrossing thematic and historical context, though the political motives underpinning the final atrocity feel somewhat unconvincing. What's enthralling is the gradual unwrapping of Ben's character, as his own weaknesses and corruptions emerge." New Yorker

Hill, Tobias

The **love** of stones. Picador 2002 396p

ISBN 0-312-28773-9

LC 2001-50038

"Obsessed with finding a legendary stone set called 'The Three Brethren,' [jewel dealer Katharine] Sterne starts her search in Turkey, where she must first locate a rich, ec-

centric British woman who teases her with a lead about the whereabouts of the gems. As Sterne's quest continues, Hill introduces a parallel historical subplot dealing with the provenance of the stones." Publ Wkly

Hillerman, Tony

The **blessing** way. Harper & Row 1970 201p

ISBN 9780060548131; 9780914001126; 9780061808357; 9781442079977

LC 73096009

"When Bergen McKee, a disillusioned anthropologist, goes to the reservation to continue his research on Navajo witchcraft, he finds himself involved in murder, intrigue, adventure, and, worst of all, what appears to be genuine witchcraft. . . . Investigating the crime is Lt. Joe Leaphorn of the Navajo Law and Order Division." Libr J

Hillerman, Tony

★ **Coyote** waits. Harper & Row 1990 292p

ISBN 9781442079946; 9780061808371; 9780060548094

LC 89046098

Lieutenant Joe Leaphorn of the Navaho Tribal Police is investigating the murder of "his fellow policeman Delbert Nez. Meanwhile, {Jim} Chee, the erstwhile medicine man and Tribal Police officer, is also on the trail of Nez's murderer and believes he has already arrested the culprit in the person of a fellow Navajo, the old shaman Ashie Pinto." N Y Times Book Rev

Hillerman, Tony

★ **Dance** hall of the dead. Harper & Row 1973 166p

ISBN 9780061808388; 9781568496955; 9781442079953; 9780060548056

LC 2012450676

Navajo police lieutenant Joe Leaphorn faces a "mystery and possible murder in the disappearance of a Zuni youth and his Navajo best friend shortly before an important annual Zuni religious ceremony." Booklist

Hillerman, Tony

The **dark** wind. Harper & Row 1982 214p

ISBN 9780060548001; 9780062018021

LC 81047793

"Jim Chee of the Navajo Tribal Police is drawn into the mystique of the Hopi tribal ways, which are very different from his own, as he follows a trail that leads him to a father seeking revenge for his son's death, a corrupt lawman and a fortune in cocaine." Publ Wkly

Hillerman, Tony

The **fallen** man. HarperCollins Pubs. 1996 294p

ISBN 9781442079335; 9780060547967; 9780061967771

LC 96029469

This is Hillerman's thirteenth mystery novel set on a Navajo reservation in the Southwest. "On Halloween a human skeleton is discovered near the peak of the 1700-foot-high Ship Rock, . . . a holy site to the Navajos. Could it be the body of Hal Breedlove, a rancher who went missing 11 years ago? Retired tribal police officer Joe Leaphorn, who had investigated the case, approaches newly promoted Lieutenant Jim Chee with his theory. But before they can close the case, an old Navajo guide who was the last man to see Breedlove alive is seriously wounded by a sniper, raising the possibility that Breedlove's death was murder." (Libr J)

"A skeleton is found on a high ledge of Ship Rock mountain, a place sacred to the Navahos. Tribal Police Lieutenant Chee and the now retired Leaphorn suspect correctly that it belongs to a wealthy rancher missing for 11 years, and Chee tries to discover if it is murder or an accidental death. Meanwhile, Leaphron is hired by a lawyer to look into the investigation for the rancher's Eastern family, who want to own his land legally so they can accept a lucrative bid for the mining rights." SLJ

Hillerman, Tony
The **first** eagle; a novel. HarperCollins Pubs. 1998 278p
ISBN 0-06-017581-8
LC 98-6955

"Surrendering to Hillerman's strong narrative voice and supple storytelling techniques, we come to see that ancient cultures and modern sciences are simply different mythologies for the same reality." N Y Times Book Rev

Hillerman, Tony
The **ghostway**. Harper & Row 1985 213p
ISBN 9780060547783; 9781442079991; 9780061967788
LC 84048165

Originally published 1984 in a limited edition by Dennis McMillan Publications

"The story concerns Navaho tribal detective Jim Chee's pursuit of the men who killed three Navaho of the Turkey clan. Chee solves the murders through his knowledge of the Indian way of life, which is gradually being eroded by white culture. As Navaho rituals help to solve Chee's murders, they also reinforce his doubts about the Indian in him. In an entertaining and fact-filled narrative, Hillerman offers a good look at the plight of contemporary Indians in the West. It is an engrossing and intelligent book for mystery fans and armchair anthropologists alike." Booklist

Hillerman, Tony
Hunting badger. HarperCollins Pubs. 1999 275p hardcover o.p. pa $9.99
ISBN 0-06-019289-5; 0-06-196782-3 pa
LC 99-47906

This "mystery opens with the robbery of the Ute casino. The head of security is killed; a Navajo police officer working off-duty as a rent-a-cop is wounded; and the perpetrators flee into canyon country. Back from vacation, Jim Chee is reluctantly drawn into the hunt for the three men. . . . Retired Lt. Joe Leaphorn gets involved when a rancher gives him the names of the perpetrators." Libr J

This offers "several new insights into the mysteries of Navajo culture and a story with enough twists and surprises to make readers glad they checked in." Publ Wkly

Hillerman, Tony
The **Jim** Chee mysteries. HarperCollins Pubs. 1990 566p $26.95
ISBN 0-06-016478-6

Hillerman, Tony
The **Joe** Leaphorn mysteries; three classic Hillerman mysteries featuring Lt. Joe Leaphorn. Harper & Row 1989 499p
LC 89-45079

Hillerman, Tony
Listening woman. Harper & Row 1978 200p
ISBN 9780060547639; 9780061967764; 9781442079984
LC 77011788

In this novel detective "Joe Leaphorn of the Navajo Tribal Police . . . {is} tracking down the murderer of a harmless old man and searching for a missing helicopter used for the getaway in a Brinks-style robbery pulled off by a militant Indian-rights group called the Buffalo Society. The desecration of some ritual sand paintings and the rumor of a sacred cave lead Leaphorn into a violent confrontation with the fanatical Buffalo Society. The terrorists are plotting to avenge the victims of a long-forgotten atrocity by recreating it—with white children as the pawns—in a vicious kidnapping/mass-murder scheme." N Y Times Book Rev

Hillerman, Tony
People of Darkness. Harper & Row 1980 202p
ISBN 9780061808395; 9780060547585; 9781439513040
LC 80007605

"Navajo Tribal Police Detective Jim Chee, constantly confronted by the split between the ways of the Indian and those of the white man, is led into an investigation that challenges and torments him. A wealthy woman asks Chee to find a stolen box of keepsakes, which contains the key to a mysterious Navajo cult called 'The People of Darkness,' a buried Indian, peyote abuse, and danger. Hillerman has written an absorbing mystery and a fascinating cultural study." Booklist

Hillerman, Tony
Sacred clowns. HarperCollins Pubs. 1993 305p
ISBN 9780061808364; 9780060547516; 9781442079960
LC 91050470

This is the twelfth mystery novel featuring Navajo "tribal policemen Joe Leaphorn and Jim Chee. Unorthodox maverick Chee hates detail . . . and works best solo. . . . {Leaphorn} plays strictly by the book. But with a heavy caseload (including two murder cases, a hit-and-run accident, a possible bribery and corruption scandal within the tribe, and a counterfeit racket involving sacred tribal artifacts) and some tricky personal problems (a love match with a lady lawyer for Chee, a trip to China with a female professor for Leaphorn), the two quickly learn the importance of understanding and teamwork." (Booklist)

"Lt. Joe Leaphorn and Officer Jim Chee of the Navajo police resolve personal issues as they investigate the murders of a tribal dancer and a white schoolteacher." Publ Wkly

FICTION CORE COLLECTION
Seventeenth Edition

Hillerman, Tony

The **shape** shifter. HarperCollins 2006 276p $26.95

ISBN 0-06-056345-1

LC 2005-52602

"Only Hillerman could so masterfully connect such disparate elements as an ancient cursed weaving, two stolen buckets of piñon sap and the Vietnam War. The conclusion is sure to startle longtime fans of this acclaimed mystery series." Publ Wkly

Hillerman, Tony

The **sinister** pig. HarperCollins Pubs. 2003 228p hardcover o.p. pa $7.99

ISBN 0-06-019443-X; 0-06-109878-7 pa

LC 2003-42316

"With his usual up-front approach to issues concerning Native Americans such as endlessly overlapping jurisdictions, Hillerman delivers a masterful tale that both entertains and educates." Publ Wkly

Hillerman, Tony

Skinwalkers. Harper & Row 1987 216p hardcover o.p. pa $7.99

ISBN 0-06-015695-3; 0-06-100017-5 pa

In this mystery "Leaphorn has three unsolved murders to contend with, and then an attempt is made on Chee's life. Much to Leaphorn's dismay bone head figures are the sole clues found, indicating the work of a skinwalker or witch. Hillerman's Leaphorn and Chee novels convey the Navaho culture with all its intricacies set forth in a meaningful way." Libr J

Hillerman, Tony

Talking God. Harper & Row 1989 239p

ISBN 9780061967832; 9780060547318

LC 88045914

This "complex tale hinges on the mysterious murder of a man in shiny old shoes who was apparently killed on his way to an ancient tribal ceremony. Leaphorn and Chee's investigation reveals a conflict over ceremonial masks, which in turn takes them from their familiar New Mexico haunts to Washington, D.C., where they must foil an assassination attempt. As in his previous works, Hillerman combines P. D. James' taut, precise narrative style with a consistently sensitive portrayal of the native American experience. The rural landscapes shimmer with realism, while the plot is crafted with skill and passion, like the masks that figure so strongly in the action." Booklist

Hillerman, Tony

A **thief** of time; a novel. Harper & Row 1988 209p

ISBN 9780060547202; 9780061808401

LC 87046147

"When a noted anthropologist arrives at an ancient Anasazi Indian ruin to dig for clay pots, she is at first angry to discover that the pre-Navajo burial site has already been despoiled, then terrified by what looms out of the darkness. Weeks later, Lieutenant Joe Leaphorn, investigating a report to the Navajo Tribal Police that the anthropologist has been stealing precious artifacts, discovers she has also been re-ported as missing. . . . {Then} Officer Jim Chee, on a routine search for missing excavating equipment, finds more than he expected near a similar dig. Leaphorn joins forces with Chee to . . . {solve a} series of murders that seem to have only one thing in common—the beautiful and very valuable Anasazi pots." (Publisher's note)

In this novel "Lieut. Joe Leaphorn and Officer Jim Chee of the Navajo Tribal Police . . . combine forces . . . in the search for a missing archeologist, Prof. Eleanor Friedman-Bernal. A specialist in Anasazi pots, she's on the verge of a major breakthrough—the identification of a specific artist, dead a thousand years—when, beneath a full desert moon, she seems simply to vanish." N Y Times Book Rev

Hillerman, Tony

★ The **wailing** wind. HarperCollins Pubs. 2002 232p

ISBN 0-06-019444-8

LC 2001-51734

"Hillerman is never better than when he is circling a puzzle from various angles, playing with the perceptions of his detectives as well as the reader's." N Y Times Book Rev

Hilton, Erica

Dirty money Honey; Erica Hilton, Nisa Santiago and introducing Kim K. Melodrama Pub. 2011 223 p.

ISBN 1934157449; 9781934157442

LC 2011927243

In this novel, "[a]t only twenty-five, Honey has a long list of exes in her life—an ex-con father, an ex-husband, and an ex-career as an ATF agent. . . . [S]he's now working as a blackjack dealer in one of the most profitable casinos in alluring Las Vegas. Soon, her life's training is put to good use as Honey develops a master plan to get that dirty money! The city is taken by surprise when an armored truck is highjacked in broad daylight. . . . [T]he Las Vegas police are baffled by this blatant crime, and pressure from the public and casino owners drive them to desperation. Honey and her crew of loyal followers pull off one of the most rewarding and masterful heists in Las Vegas history, but not everyone will get to enjoy the loot. Someone has to take the fall." (Publisher's note)

Hilton, James

★ **Good**-bye Mr. Chips; illustrated by H.M. Brock. Little, Brown 1962 132p il $22

ISBN 0-316-36420-7

First published 1934

"In 1870 Mr. Chipping begins a career teaching the classics at Brookfield Boys' Boarding School in England. After teaching three generations of Brookfield boys, Mr. Chips, as he is fondly called, retires to the boarding house directly across the street from the school. He continues to keep a close watch over the new group of boys and host afternoon teas as a way of sharing his reminiscences. This is a warm testimonial to a caring teacher." Shapiro. Fic for Youth. 3d edition

450

Hilton, James

★ **Lost** horizon; a novel. Morrow 1995 262p hardcover o.p. pa $12.95

    ISBN 0-688-14656-2; 0-06-059452-7 pa

                    LC 96-160022

A reissue of the title first published 1933

"Hugh Conway is a British consul at Baskul when trouble erupts in 1931 and all civilians are evacuated. He and three others board a plane lent by a Maharajah. After they are airborne for several hours, they realize that they are headed in the wrong direction. When the pilot finally lands, the passengers find themselves in Shangri-La, a utopian lamasery whose inhabitants know the secret of attaining long life. Believing that war is going to destroy all civilization, the High Lama summons the newcomers to form the nucleus of a new civilization." Shapiro. Fic for youth. 3d edition

Hilton, James

Random harvest. Little, Brown 1941 326p

"Charles Rainier, wealthy business man and M.P., for nearly twenty years unable to recall that period of his life between his World War injury and 1919 suddenly has his memory restored. The dramatic suspense is great as Rainier faces his two pasts, passionately resolved to find the Paula of his lost years, at whatever cost to his present marriage and position. . . . Part of the story is related in the first person by Rainier's secretary and confidante who is interested in psychology." Libr J

Himes, Chester

The **collected** stories of Chester Himes; foreword by Calvin Hernton. Thunder's Mouth Press 1991 429p

                    LC 90-25682

Himes, Chester

★ **Cotton** comes to Harlem. Vintage Books 1988 159p pa $11.95

    ISBN 0-394-75999-0

                    LC 88-40045

First published 1965 by Putnam

In this mystery featuring "Coffin" Ed Johnson and "Grave Digger" Jones " which, revolves around a cotton bale filled with $87,000, [the author] parodies Marcus Garvey's back to Africa movement. Himes treats the black community with humor and respect, but does not hesitate to show blacks victimizing each other." Murphy. Ency of Murder and mystery

Himes, Chester

Yesterday will make you cry. Norton 1998 363p

    ISBN 0-393-04577-3

                    LC 97-40364

Written in 1937; first published in different form 1953 with title: Cast the first stone

"Is Himes's unexpurgated work anything more than a literary footnote? Some phrases still come off as pulp hardball, but the novel's emotional core continues to smolder. Rage tempered with compassion is the backbone of this story—and what makes it eminently worth reading." N Y Times Book Rev

Hines, T. L.

Waking Lazarus; T.L. Hines. Bethany House 2006 293p o.p.; o.p.

    ISBN 0764202049 (alk. paper); 9780764202049

                    LC 2006007776

This book, which was selected by "Library Journal" as one of the 25 Best Genre Novels of 2006, follows "Jude Allman, [who] has died and come back to life three times, becoming a celebrity against his own wishes. . . . [H]e changes his name and withdraws from the public eye, trying to forget all that came before. But the past, like Jude, won't stay buried. A prowling evil circles his adopted hometown of Red Lodge, Montana. Children are disappearing, and Jude may have the key to solving the crimes--hidden inside the mysteries of his own deaths. His days of hiding are over, and now he must face the questions that have haunted him for years." (Publisher's note)

Hirshberg, Glen

The **Snowman's** children. Carroll & Graf Pubs. 2002 324p $24

    ISBN 0-7867-1082-9

"Troubled 29-year-old Mattie Rhodes returns to Detroit in search of hs childhood friend Theresa, a brilliant, strange, and mysterious girl who, even now, haunts him. For a few magical months in 1977, Mattie, Theresa, and their friend, Spencer, the lone black boy bused to their school as part of Detroits' desegregation mandate, form a special bond, united by their outsider status. At the same time, a serial killer called the Snowman has been preying on children, snatching them in broad daylight. . . . As Mattie and Spencer begin to sense that Theresa is in danger of slipping away from them and descending into mental illness, they concoct a desperate plan to save her and instead condemn their families to the nightmare of media publicity." Booklist

Hoag, Tami

Dark horse. Bantam Bks. 2002 435p

    ISBN 0-553-80192-9

                    LC 2002-74583

"A tangled web of deceit and double-dealing makes for a fascinating look into the wealthy world of horses juxtaposed with the realistic introspection of one very troubled ex-cop." Booklist

Hoag, Tami

Dust to dust. Bantam Bks. 2000 354p

    ISBN 0-553-10634-1

                    LC 00-39786

"Minneapolis detective Sam Kovac and his young female partner, Nikki Liska, find themselves hot on the trail of some bad cops. It all starts when they are called to the scene of a homicide, where they find the nude, hanging body of a young Internal Affairs officer, the son of a department hero. Department brass want to declare the case a suicide and close it quickly. But after nosing around a bit, Kovac and Liska begin to suspect something much more sinister. . . . A classic whodunit with many twists and turns and a surprise ending." Booklist

Hoag, Tami

Guilty as sin. Bantam Bks. 1996 470p

ISBN 0-553-09959-0

LC 95-38214

Sequel to Night sins

This suspense novel opens "with an accused kidnapper and child molester sitting in jail awaiting trial. But is the suspect—a respected and beloved college professor—really the author of a devilishly sick scheme to terrorize the families of idyllic Deer Lake, Minn.? Ellen North is the tough county prosecutor, armed with evidence and anger; Tony Costello is the flashy big-town lawyer intent on winning fame and fortune with a headline case; and Jay Butler Brooks is the reporter, a self-centered firebrand who appears to derive pleasure from the suffering of others. . . . As the criminal's clever plot unravels and North and her team come closer to the truth, the tangled relationships that lie just beneath the surface of Deer Lake are tantalizingly revealed." N Y Times Book Rev

Hoag, Tami

Kill the messenger. Bantam Bks. 2004 419p $26

ISBN 0-553-80195-3

LC 2004-47612

Nineteen-year-old L. A. Bike messenger Jace Damon "picks up a package from a shady lawyer, but when he gets to the delivery address, he finds an empty lot; suddenly, someone attacks him and tries to grab the package. The bike messenger takes off, but the attacker pursues him, nearly runs him over with a car, and takes a couple of shots at him. Injured and frightened, Jace returns to Lowell's office only to find the place swarming with cops and the attorney murdered. The plot thickens as Jace attempts to elude both homicide detective Ken Parker, who wants some answers, and a menacing, shadowy figure, who is trying to get that package." Booklist

"A link to Hollywood provides a burst of fresh energy in the later chapters of this character-driven, solidly constructed thriller." Publ Wkly

Hoag, Tami

Night sins. Bantam Bks. 1995 483p

ISBN 0-553-09961-2

LC 94-23910

The "community of Deer Lake, Minn., takes a turn toward Stephen King territory when the local lady doctor's son is snatched by a fiend who leaves enigmatic notes. Attempting to crack the case, feisty feminist Megan O'Malley—who hopes to become the first female field agent for the male-dominated Minnesota Bureau of Criminal Apprehension—finds herself paired with Mitch Holt, the town's love-scarred sheriff (and recovering alcoholic) who is facing assorted personal demons." Publ Wkly

Hoagland, Edward

Children are diamonds; an African apocalypse. by Edward Hoagland. 1st ed. Arcade Publishing 2013 240 p. (hardcover) $23.95

ISBN 161145834X; 9781611458343

LC 2013013603

This novel, by Edward Hoagland, focuses on Hickey, "an American school teacher who . . . goes to Africa as an aid worker. Working for an agency in Nairobi, one of his jobs is to drive food and medical supplies to Southern Sudan to an aid station run by Ruth, a middle-aged woman, who acts as nurse, doctor, [and] feeder of starving children. When the violence . . . in the region increase . . . and aid workers are being slaughtered or evacuated, Hickey is asked to save Ruth." (Publisher's note)

Hoban, Russell

Angelica's Grotto; a novel. Carroll & Graf Pubs. 2001 271p $25

ISBN 0-7867-0878-6

LC 2001-35121

First published 1999 in the United Kingdom

"Harold's esoteric musings on art, sex, philosophy, sailing, and everything in between will not appeal to everyone, but those willing to follow his meandering thoughts will be rewarded by an intelligently bizarre novel." Booklist

Hoban, Russell

Her name was Lola. Arcade Pub. 2003 207p $24

ISBN 1-559-70726-7

LC 2003-20375

"Hoban apparently wants to see how much outrageous artifice and wilful exposure of literary technique he can get away with while still working his magic on the reader. The answer is plenty. Far from being an arid exercise, the novel has great charm and grace." New Statesman

Hoban, Russell

Linger awhile. David R. Godine 2007 132p pa $15.95

ISBN 0-7475-7984-9

LC 2007-123

First published 2006 in the United Kingdom

"Irving Goodman, an elderly and lecherous widower, believes he has fallen in love with a film star, Justine Trimble, the star of 1950s black-and-white cowboy movies. The only hitch is that Justine has been dead for 47 years. Obsessed with her womanly perfection, Irving calls on a hi-tech friend who manages to isolate Justine's 'particles' and, using a customised 'suspension of disbelief', converts the celluloid star into flesh and blood. To the unsuspecting reader, incredulity may interfere at this early stage. Press on, however, and Hoban's world becomes more thought-provoking than absurd. . . . This is, perhaps fortunately, essentially a comic novel. The characters slave to create their impossible dream only to find that their creation (quite literally) is sucking the lifeblood out of them — Hoban is laughing at himself as much as at the rest of us." London Times

Hoban, Russell

★ Riddley Walker; afterword, notes, and glossary by Russell Hoban. Expanded ed; Indiana Univ. Press 1998 235p il

ISBN 0-253-33448-9

LC 98-14996

A reissue of the title first published 1980 by Summit Bks.

"No review can do more than suggest the range and effect of this extraordinary book. It is 'sui generis,' its inspirations both particular and diverse, its references legion, its craft remarkable—contributing to a whole that is vivid, compelling and certainly unforgettable." Encounter

Hobb, Robin

Assassin's apprentice. Bantam Books 1995 356p map

ISBN 0-553-37445-1

LC 94-28942

"As a royal bastard in the household of King Shrewd, a boy called 'Fitz' spends his early years in the king's stables. When the magic in his blood marks him for destiny, he begins receiving secret instruction, by order of the king, in the art of assassination, a calling that places him in the midst of a nest of intrigue and arcane maneuverings. Firmly grounded in the trappings of high fantasy, Hobb's first novel features a protagonist whose coming of age revolves around the discovery of the meaning of loyalty and trust. [A] gracefully written fantasy." Libr J

Followed by: Royal assassin (1996) and Assassin's quest (1997)

Hobb, Robin

The **mad** ship. Bantam Bks. 1999 647p

ISBN 0-553-10333-4

LC 98-51188

In the second volume of the Liveship trilogy "Althea Vestrit is now a seasoned sailor, and with the aid of her family, her lover Brashen Tell, and the curious woodcarver Amber, she restores the abandoned, blind liveship Paragon, the 'mad ship' of the title. Aboard him (Paragon is male), they set out on a bold quest to find and recover the Vestrit family's liveship Vivacia." Booklist

Followed by Ship of destiny

Hobb, Robin

Ship of destiny. Bantam Bks. 2000 581p map

ISBN 0-553-10323-7

LC 00-37839

This is the final volume of the Liveship trilogy. "Unaware of the war that threatens the trading families of Bingtown, Althea Vestrit searches the sea lanes for her stolen liveship—only to discover the truth behind the origin of the sentient vessels. Hobb combines a unique fantasy vision with themes of devotion and selflessness to produce a powerful conclusion to an innovative saga." Libr J

Hobb, Robin

Ship of magic. Bantam Bks. 1998 685p

ISBN 978-0553575637

LC 97-32216

First book in the author's Liveship traders trilogy

"The untimely death of Old Trader Ephron Vestrit deprives his daughter Althea of her inheritance and places her ambitious brother-in-law Kyle in command of the live ship Viveca and the family fortunes. . . . {This novels is} set in a world of sentient ships, merchant traders, ruthless pirates, dangerous treasures, seagoing dragons, and a mysterious elder race. Hobb excels in depicting complex characters; even her villains command respect, if not sympathy, for their actions." Libr J

Followed by The mad ship

Hobson, Laura Keane Zametkin

Gentleman's agreement; a novel. by Laura Z. Hobson. Simon & Schuster 1947 275p

"Phil Green, a member of the editorial staff of 'Smith's Weekly,' is assigned to write a series of ariticles about anti-Semitism in America. He decides to pose as a Jew for six months, and he has some extraordinary experiences." Benet's Reader's Ency of Am Lit

Hockensmith, Steve

Holmes on the range. St. Martin's Minotaur 2006 294p $22.95

ISBN 978-0-312-34780-2; 0-312-34780-4

LC 2005-50406

This western mystery "features Montana cowboys and brothers Gustav and Otto Amlingmeyer (better known as Old Red and Big Red, respectively). One night in 1892, Old Red becomes smitten with Sherlock Holmes on hearing his brother read 'The Red-Headed League' around the campfire during a cattle drive. Determined to follow in his hero's footsteps, Old Red gets the chance to apply the master's methods after some unsavory characters hire the pair to work at a ranch, whose general manager is soon found dead after a stampede. Another man turns up dead, apparently a suicide, just before the British aristocrats who own the ranch arrive to inspect their property." Publ Wkly

"This is a great reworking of the Holmes conceit, and one suspects Hockensmith will have a steady readership as long as the Amlingmeyers are on the case." Booklist

Hockensmith, Steve

On the wrong track. St. Martin's Minotaur 2007 292p $23.95

ISBN 978-0-312-34781-9; 0-312-34781-2

LC 2007-5176

"Cowboy detectives Big Red and Old Red Amlingmeyer are back. . . . This time, they are railroad cops assigned to protect a train from the Give 'em Hell Boys." Libr J

"As a lively Holmes takeoff, as an inventive melding of mystery and western genres, and as a new source of damn good reading, this series demands attention." Booklist

Hodder, Mark

Expedition to the Mountains of the Moon; by Mark Hodder. Pyr 2012 399p

ISBN 9781616145354

LC 2011037544

This book explores "an alternate steampunk universe" in which "famed explorer and polyglot Sir Richard Burton" travels through time in order to prevent both the assassination of Queen Victoria and a previous attempt to avert the murder which led to the twisting of reality. "Meanwhile . . . in 1863, British PRime Minister Lord Palmerston . . . instructs Burton, ostensibly to seek the source of the Nile, actually to recover a third set of psychoactive diamonds left by a now-extinct non-human race, by which means Palmerston hopes to defeat Germany before the world is engulfed in war. In 1914, Burton arrives in East Africa, where an appalling conflict already rages . . . but this time with few memories and little idea of who he is or what he's supposed to do." (Kirkus)

Hodder, Mark

The **strange** affair of Spring Heeled Jack; by Mark Hodder. Pyr 2010 378 p. (pbk.) $17.00

ISBN 9781616142407

LC 2010020632

Philip K. Dick Award (2010)

In this book, "London in the middle of the 19th century suffers from a plague of dog-faced men, thought by some to be werewolves; in addition, a strange apparition bearing a resemblance to the . . . mythical creature known as Spring-Heeled Jack rampages through the city, savagely attacking young women. Lord Palmerston commissions the famous adventurer Sir Richard Burton as a special agent to investigate these occurrences, and Burton acquires the assistance of the notoriously decadent poet and libertine Algernon Charles Swinburne. Together, the mismatched pair traverses the streets of a city filled with mechanical splendors, genetically engineered animals, and unspeakable squalor. Their investigations lead them to the suspicion that they are living in a nonexistent time." (Library Journal)

Hodgen, Christie

Elegies for the brokenhearted; a novel. W. W. Norton & Co. 2010 271p $23.95

ISBN 039306140X; 9780393061406; 978-0-393-06140-6; 0-393-06140-X

LC 2010-11149

This "novel pulls readers into the life of Mary Murphy, who has, along with her older sister, Malinda, endured her mother's five marriages with a silent stoicism. Mary's uncle Mike is the idol of her youth and a semipermanent male presence, despite being 'the chump, the slouch, the drunk, the bum' of the family, until he takes off for New York City and dies of an overdose. A schoolmate's refusal to give Mary and her family a ride results in her mother meeting her fourth husband, an African American who draws Mary out of her shell and becomes a real father. A college roommate then shows her the impossibility of ever leaving family behind. After she graduates, Mary mounts a search for her runaway sister and ends up living a routine existence in a small town in Maine, her only friends a gay pianist and an older German woman, each paralyzed by their past promise."

"Despite its gritty realities, 'Elegies for the Brokenhearted' ultimately has an almost mythic grandeur, in part because the story is propelled by associative rather than linear logic, in part because the action, played out largely in places that are entirely familiar but hardly ever named, acquires a strange universality, and in part because Hodgen's interest lies in questions of blood and parentage — of the ties that bind us together or drive us apart." N Y Times Book Rev

Hodgins, Eric

Mr. Blandings builds his dream house; illustrated by William Steig. Simon & Schuster 1946 237p il

"Expanded from a 'Fortune' short story, this book is an amusing tale of a New York advertiser who found his apartment much too small and bought 50 acres and a farmhouse in the country. Mr. Blandings' trials and tribulations from the time when the architect, after spending a great deal of time and money, decided that the farmhouse should be torn down instead of remodelled until the new home was finished at a cost of $45,000 more than they expected make hilarious reading." Ont Libr Rev

Hodgkinson, Amanda

22 Britannia Road. Pamela Dorman Books/Viking 2011 323p $25.95

ISBN 0-670-02263-2; 978-0-670-02263-2

LC 2010-45353

Silvana is a survivor of the Polish Holocaust. During the war she and her son Aurek hid out in the forest. "They are rescued from a refugee camp by Janusz, the husband and father from whom they were separated at the beginning of the fighting. Janusz brings them to Ipswich, to the small house and garden that give the novel its title." (N Y Times Book Rev)

This "novel moves between wartime Poland and postwar England as it follows the shifting fortunes of Janusz Nowak and his wife, Silvana. Their young marriage is tested by the German invasion as Janusz enlists and Silvana finds herself left behind in Warsaw with their young son, Aurek. Janusz loses his regiment and ends up in England after spending time on a farm in France, where he has a passionate love affair. Silvana and Aurek escape into the forest and endure years of privation and abuse at the hands of their protectors. Their unexpected postwar family reunion is marred by the guilty secrets they each harbor." Libr J

Hoeg, Peter

Borderliners; translated by Barbara Haveland. Farrar, Straus & Giroux 1994 277p

ISBN 0-374-11554-0

LC 94-18892

Original Danish edition, 1993

"The author avoids simple storytelling, preferring instead to explore the nature of time. 'What is time?' are the book's opening words, and later Mr. Hoeg actually provides brief historical passages on the development of theories of time. In a related device, the novel employs a dreamy, associative narrative, moving back and forth through the years, including flash-forwards to the adult Peter's family life. . . . 'Borderliners' is written from the heart, and its portrait of the embittered survivor Peter is moving." N Y Times Book Rev

Hoeg, Peter

The **history** of Danish dreams; translated by Barbara Haveland. Farrar, Straus & Giroux 1995 356p

ISBN 0-374-17138-6

LC 95-18355

Original Danish edition, 1988

A satiric family saga set in Denmark. "Introduced in the first section are four characters born around the turn of the century: Carl Laurids, whose ambitions lead him beyond his estate, where, in the 16th century, the resident count had banned the keeping of time; Amalie Teader, a girl whose delusion that she has been 'chosen' springs from a wealthy and powerful grandmother, who writes a newspaper that predicts the future; Anna Bak, a pastor's innocent child who is deemed worthy of bearing 'the new Messiah'; and Adonis Jensen, the son of roving thieves, who refuses to learn how to steal because of 'his compassion for mankind.' In Part II, which ends at 1939, these four become couples: Carl and Amalie have a golden child, Carsten, for a son, while Anna and Adonis produce rebellious Maria; in the final section, Carsten and Maria marry and have children of their own." Publ Wkly

"If Dreams is regarded not as a novel, but as a marvelous trunkful of loosely related funny bits, . . . it is a great success." Time

Hoeg, Peter

★ **Smilla's** sense of snow; translated by Tiina Nunnally. Farrar Straus Giroux 1993 453p

ISBN 0-374-26644-1

LC 93-17742

Original Danish edition, 1992; published in the United Kingdom with title: Miss Smilla's feeling for snow

"Selfishness, menace and systematic corruption form the fabric of this mysterious novel. Relationships are all based on suspicion, and love has to be 'like a military operation.'. . . Peter Høeg has a remarkable feeling for sinister surprises." Times Lit Suppl

Hoeg, Peter

Tales of the night; translated by Barbara Haveland. Farrar, Straus & Giroux 1998 278p $23

ISBN 0-374-27254-9

LC 97-26664

Original Danish edition, 1990

These "stories take us to eight separate corners of the world on the night of March 19, 1929. . . . The deep despair and foreboding of well-intentioned Europeans victimized by the very culture that was supposed to educate them is often painfully credible. Potent but problematic, this collection lays bare the difficulties of love, even if it must make do without the dazzling lucidity of Hoeg's more recent works." Publ Wkly

Hoeg, Peter

The **woman** and the ape; translated by Barbara Haveland. Farrar, Straus & Giroux 1997 261p

ISBN 0-374-29203-5

LC 96-27289

This novel is "too fresh in its writing and its perceptions to fall into the sentimentality one might expect. An air of freedom surrounds Madelene's eventual abduction by the ape, and though their sexual involvement may seem over the top to some readers, you can't help but be carried along by Hoeg's convictions." Libr J

Hoff, B. J.

River of mercy; BJ Hoff. Harvest House Publishers 2012 304 p. (pbk.) $13.99

ISBN 0736924205; 9780736924207

LC 2012012455

This novel, by B. J. Hoff, is the "conclusion to her . . . Riverhaven Years trilogy. . . . In this third book, young Gideon Kanagy faces a life-changing challenge--and an unexpected romance with his young Amish friend, Emma Knepp. Gideon's sister, Rachel, and the 'outsider' Jeremiah Gant add to the drama with their own dilemma and its repercussions for the entire community of Riverhaven." (Publisher's note)

Hoffman, Alice

At risk. Putnam 1988 219p

LC 87-33240

"The Farrells are your typical New England upper middle class family. Ivan, the father, is an astronomer, and Polly, the mother, is a free lance photographer. Amanda is a typical 11-year old girl with a passion for gymnastics, and Charles is an 8-year old budding biologist, interested in specimens of frogs and insects and books on dinosaurs. Their comfortable lifestyle is shattered when Amanda is diagnosed as having AIDS. The family goes through stages of disbelief, denial, anger, despair, and finally numbing acceptance as Amanda withers away and is hospitalized at the end presumably with death close at hand." West Coast Rev Books

"Such is Ms. Hoffman's tenderness and perceptiveness that we come to care about her creations despite their imperfections the way we would care about those we love despite theirs." N Y Times Book Rev

Hoffman, Alice

Blackbird house. Doubleday 2004 225p

ISBN 0-385-50761-5

LC 2004-07958

"The relationship of the characters to their surroundings is seen as a kind of magical bond, expressed in language that is both eerie and beautiful. The house of the title is one in which, from story to story, we glimpse various families over the course of two centuries. . . . Hoffman lets Blackbird House stand as an emblem for the transforming power of any long-established home, while reveling in the haunting quality of her own distinctive literary style." N Y Times Book Rev

Hoffman, Alice

Blue diary. Putnam 2001 303p hardcover o.p. pa $14

ISBN 0-399-14802-7; 0-425-18494-3 pa

LC 2001-19517

Ethan Ford is "suddenly arrested on suspicion of the rape and murder of teenager Rachel Morris 15 years earlier in Maryland. Ethan confesses to the crime, but says that he is now 'a different man,' who has redeemed himself through exemplary behavior. What this revelation means to his beautiful wife of 13 years, Jorie [and] his 12-year-old son, Collie . . . allows the novel to investigate the themes of devotion, betrayal, guilt and forgiveness in trenchantly effective ways." Publ Wkly

Hoffman, Alice

The **dovekeepers**; a novel. Scribner 2011 504p $27.99

ISBN 978-1-4516-1747-4; 1-4516-1747-X

LC 2011-18099

"Hoffman put years of research into The Dovekeepers, and at times the story slows from a scholar's desire to dwell on details of custom or ritual. But for those like me who'll follow the novelist anywhere, that pacing becomes its own powerful incantation." Entertainment Wkly

Hoffman, Alice

Here on Earth. Putnam 1997 293p

ISBN 0-399-14313-0

LC 97-5382

The novel "is a surprisingly successful recasting of Wuthering Heights. Like that book, it is charged with passion, but unlike their prototypes, the modern-day lovers indulge their lust to their demise. . . . {Hoffman} not only covers the much-furrowed ground of renewing old romances with startling energy, she evokes the tricky relationship between mother and teenage daughter with bitter-sweet insight." Times Lit Suppl

Hoffman, Alice

The **ice** queen; a novel. Little, Brown 2005 224p $23.95

ISBN 0-316-05859-9

LC 2004-26610

"Ever since she was eight years old, Hoffman's narrator, a devoted reference librarian, has believed that her temper tantrum caused her mother's death. Her guilt turned her solitary, stoic, and somewhat misanthropic, and she envisions herself as an ice queen. Even after she is struck by lightning. As her damaged narrator reluctantly joins a lightning-strike-survivor support group, Hoffman dramatizes the bizarre effects experienced by real-life lightning strike survivors, and orchestrates a highly erotic and risky romance between the ice queen and a fellow survivor known as Lazarus, whose breath ignites paper. As Hoffman's spellbinding and wonderfully insightful tale unfurls, she pays charming tribute to librarians, revels in metaphors of hot and cold, and poetically explores the meaning of trust, the chemistry of healing, and the reach of love." Booklist

Hoffman, Alice

Illumination night. Putnam 1987 224p

LC 86-30472

"A young couple's marriage has survived struggles and poverty in a countercultural transplant to the off-season isolation of Martha's Vineyard only to face a more unlikely and dangerous threat. A teen-age girl, who has moved next door to care for her sick grandmother, develops an erotic fixation on the husband. Hoffman probes the mythic connotations of the situation as she supplies convincing portraits of the man and woman and of the young girl who is determined to come between them. . . . All of this is delineated with both depth and clarity in a novel that encapsulates and transforms the characters' experiences into broader symbols of yearning and passion." Booklist

Hoffman, Alice

Local girls. Putnam 1999 197p $22.95

ISBN 0-399-14507-9

LC 98-50632

A collection of "interlinked stories about a Jewish Long Island family locked in a downward spiral after the parents' divorce. Most of the stories are told from the viewpoint of Gretel Samuelson as she moves from high-school years to young adulthood. . . . Hoffman doesn't sentimentalize her characters' lives: the tragedies they suffer are ordinary, after all. She has a light touch and a poet's knack for making diffuse elements fall into place with seeming effortlessness." Publ Wkly

Hoffman, Alice

Practical magic. Putnam 1995 244p

ISBN 0-399-14055-7

LC 94-47013

This novel is set in Massachusetts. "A family of women notorious for their witchcraft is at the book's center: the Owens sisters and the nieces they're raising, Sally and Gillian. The aunts are famous for dispensing potions to the lovelorn, but the old women are pariahs, too; so when Sally and Gillian grow up, they escape to what they hope will be normality, Sally becomes a perfect homemaker and Gillian a wild thing, but their inheritance can't be dismissed." Newsweek

"The tale of the Owenses' struggle is charmingly told, and a good deal of fun. Dark comedy and a light touch carry the story along to a truly Gothic climax." N Y Times Book Rev

Hoffman, Alice

The **probable** future. Doubleday 2003 322p hardcover o.p. pa $13.95

ISBN 0-385-50760-7; 0-345-45591-6 pa

LC 2003-40960

"Filled with vivid (if sometimes sketchy) characters and cinematic descriptions of New England landscapes, this book will be a hit wherever Hoffman is in demand." Libr J

Hoffman, Alice

The **red** garden. Crown Pubs. 2010 270p $25

ISBN 978-0-307-39387-6; 0-307-39387-9

LC 2010-06246

This "a collection of 14 stories set in Blackwell, Mass., a fictional village deep in the woods of the Berkshires. Beginning with Blackwell's founding in 1786 by a handful of inept, unprepared settlers, these stories span more than 200 years. Each one, complete in itself, offers a time-stamped snapshot of the lives of Blackwell's inhabitants — the temporal equivalent of a holograph. If this book has a plot, it is not the usual kind. Instead, against a background of far-off historical events Hoffman sets the ongoing life of one small town and its episodic interaction with the natural world that surrounds it." Boston Globe

Hoffman, Alice

The **river** king. Putnam 2000 324p

ISBN 0-399-14599-0

LC 00-23870

A novel set in the "small Massachusetts town of Haddan, where the locals resent the snotty denizens of a posh prep school. But not all of Haddan's students are privileged and arrogant. Poor, beautiful, and smart, Carlin is attending Haddan on a swimming scholarship and finds most of her peers callow at best. Gus is also smart, self-possessed, and defiant, and he cannot believe his good luck in befriending a girl as amazing as Carlin. But the boys in his dorm despise and torment him, and no one comprehends the severity of his situation. When his body is pulled from the river, Haddan's legacy of suicide is reexamined, but neither Carlin nor Abe, a maverick policeman, believe that Gus killed himself." Booklist

"It can be hard to find an example of good old-fashioned storytelling these days, but storytelling, refreshingly, is Alice Hoffman's strength." N Y Times Book Rev

Hoffman, Alice

★ **Second** nature. Putnam 1994 254p

LC 93-11595

"In the end, Ms. Hoffman suggests that it is love in all its wondrous forms, from a parent's love for a child to the most consuming sexual passion that truly delineates mankind. Her abiding vision of this ineluctable and uniquely human power informs 'Second Nature' with grace and beauty, making it at once her richest and wisest, as well as her boldest, novel to date." N Y Times Book Rev

Hoffman, Alice

★ **Seventh** heaven. Putnam 1990 256p

LC 89-28737

This is "one of those rare novels so abundant with life it seems to overflow its own pages, these aren't the sort of fictional characters who are all used up by the end of the book; on the contrary, they seem ready to leap straight into another volume." Newsweek

Hoffman, Alice

Skylight confessions. Little, Brown and Co. 2007 262p $24.99

ISBN 978-0-316-05878-0; 0-316-05878-5

LC 2006-01391

This novel, "about the magic of love and the perils of fate, may be the saddest book [Hoffman's] ever written, but it is also one of her very best. . . . [Arlie's] ephemeral self is what fuels the tale—she is a fairy-tale creature, to be sure, and yet she is also obviously a flesh-and-blood woman with deep and compelling desires." Baltimore Sun

Hoffman, Alice

The **story** sisters; a novel. Shaye Areheart Books 2009 325p $25

ISBN 978-0-307-39386-9; 0-307-39386-0

LC 2008-51054

"The Story sisters, Elv, Meg, and Claire, are dark-haired beauties clustered in the attic of their old Long Island house, while their lonely mother broods below. Their all-female household, a sly variation on Little Women, is under a grim fairy-tale spell, and not even sojourns with their fairy-god-mother-like grandmother in Paris can protect them. . . . Meg is practical, while Elv and Claire share a tragic secret, and Elv channels her anguish into elaborate, demon-haunted tales of an imaginary parallel world until she discovers more effective means of self-punishment." Booklist

Hoffman, Alice

The **third** angel; a novel. Shaye Areheart Books 2008 278p $25

ISBN 978-0-307-39385-2; 0-307-39385-2

LC 2007-28071

This is the "tale of three women, all terribly in love with the wrong men. The novel is . . . constructed in three sections, narrated in three different time periods. The women in each section stay on the seventh floor of the haunted Lion Park Hotel in London. The first woman, Maddy Heller, stays at the Lion Park in 1999 for her sister's wedding. Her story is compelling in that she is secretly and tragically in love with her sister's fiance. In 1966, the second woman, Frieda Lewis, falls in love with a guest at the hotel: an American rock star and drug addict who happens to be engaged to someone else. And in 1952, the third woman, Bryn Evans, betrays her fiance at the Lion Park, to disastrous results. At the very end of the novel, Hoffman reveals the tragedy of the Lion Park ghost, the suspenseful event that connects all the women in powerful and mystical ways." Rocky Mountain News

Hoffman, Alice

Turtle Moon. Putnam 1992 255p

ISBN 0-399-13720-3

LC 91-37222

"Julian Cash, policeman, and Lucy Rosen, obit writer, both with hardened shells covering events that shattered their younger selves, are thrown together when they try to solve a murder that endangers Lucy's son and the murdered woman's child. In the ensuing days they gradually draw solace from each other and revisit their pasts in search of the solution to the murder; Lucy to Great Neck, New York where she lived after her parents died when she was 16; Julian to the foster mother who raised him and the gumbo-limbo tree where an imprisoned angel waits, the cousin Julian killed in a car accident 20 years earlier." Libr J

"Hoffman handles romance, suspense, and the healing properties of love and understanding with aplomb and a dash of magic." Booklist

Hoffman, Eva

Appassionata. Other Press 2009 265p $25

ISBN 978-1-59051-319-4

LC 2008-42015

First published 2008 in the United Kingdom with title: Illuminations

"Isabel is an accomplished pianist, and on one of her many tours abroad, she encounters the mysterious Chechen rebel Anzor. At first, she is drawn to him and feels sympathy for his cause, and soon enough she enters into an affair with him. They meet clandestinely in various European cities, but as she comes to learn more about his mysterious undertakings and witnesses at close range the havoc they can create, she comes to question her own values and her fragmented, unsettled way of life." Libr J

Hoffman, Eva

The **secret**; a novel. PublicAffairs 2002 265p $25

ISBN 1-58648-150-9

LC 2002-73433

"The time is 2022, the place is Chicago, and Iris Surrey has an unusually close relationship with her chilly mother, Elizabeth. At 17, Iris is wearying of the odd stares she triggers in others, especially when her look-alike mother is with her. Iris wants to learn the identity of her father, which, alas, is not possible; the reader will figure out before Iris does that she is the product of genetic engineering. When Iris uncovers the truth, she goes on an emotional rampage, intent on tracking down any blood relatives in the hope that they will make her feel more authentic." Libr J

This work "is compelling throughout for Hoffman's prose, for her insights on identity, for her reflections on history." N Y Times Book Rev

Hoffman, Jilliane

Retribution. G.P. Putnam's Sons 2004 420p $24.95

ISBN 0-399-15127-3

LC 2003-46502

"In the late 1980s, law student Chloe Larson was brutally raped and left for dead in her New York apartment. Fast-forward 12 years; Chloe, now known as C.J. Townsend, is one of the top prosecutors in Miami. It is in this capacity that she finds herself face to face with the man who terrorized her." Libr J

"The twists and turns are a suspense lover's dream the climax is chillingly good. An absolutely remarkable first outing." Rendezvous Magazine

Hoffman, Nina Kiriki

Catalyst. Tachyon Publications 2006 171p pa $14.95

ISBN 1-892391-38-4

"Kaslin—and Histly, for that matter—are vibrant creations, their psychology utterly credible for smart adolescents. That the book ends with everything but Kaslin and Histly's relationship up in the air may indicate merely that Hoffman knew when she had achieved perfection." Booklist

Hofmann, Gert

★ **Lichtenberg** and the little flower girl; translated and with an afterword by Michael Hofmann. New Directions 2004 245p $19.95

ISBN 0-8112-1568-7

LC 2003-28140

Original German edition, 1994

"Georg Christoph Lichtenberg, an eighteenth-century Göttingen mathematician, physicist, and astronomer, is remembered for the satiric aphorisms he wrote in his spare time, which have been celebrated by luminaries from Nietzsche to Einstein. He was also a dwarf and a hunchback, attributes crucial to this lively fictionalization of his life by the late German novelist, which charts Lichtenberg's love affair with the progress of civilization and, in parallel, his failure to find a wife. Hofmann gives the scientist a delirious, childish glee at the universe's workings, and a sweetness of character that, true to Lichtenberg's biography, eventually wins him the love of a thirteen-year-old beauty. The author shares with his hero a gift for the epigram, which makes the book seem at first a rather weightless affair. But a mass of loneliness and longing just beneath the comedy keeps it from floating away." New Yorker

Hofmann, Gert

★ **Luck**; translated from the German by Michael Hofmann. New Directions 2002 266p $23.95

ISBN 0-8112-1502-4

LC 2002-3556

Original German edition, 1992

"Stripped, spare prose creates the impression that the boy is merely a detached witness to his parents' separation, but subtle clues belie his neutrality. . . .While Hofmann's desolate emotional landsapes and darkly comic observations are not for those seeking a literary lark, readers will appreciate his deft handling of the minimalist plot and his authentic rendering of a precociously perceptive boy baffled by his elders." Publ Wkly

Hogan, Chuck

Devils in exile; a novel. Scribner 2010 312p $26

ISBN 978-1-4165-5886-6; 1-4165-5886-1

LC 2009-43459

"This is a compelling portrait of a good man who makes bad choices and in the end must battle his way out of a destructive and deadly life." Publ Wkly

Holbert, Bruce

Lonesome animals; Bruce Holbert. Counterpoint 2012 272 p. (paperback) $15.95; (hardcover) $24.00

ISBN 9781619021563; 1582438064; 9781582438061

This book is a "Western set during the 1930s" that "follows an amoral lawman hunting an amoral killer in the rugged, rapidly changing rural counties of Washington State." The protagonist Russell Strawl "has superhuman hearing." (Kirkus Reviews)

Holden, Craig

The **jazz** bird. Simon & Schuster 2002 314p $25

ISBN 0-7432-1296-7

LC 2001-32259

This novel "is based on an actual murder that place in Cincinnati in 1927. In addition to its exploration of the Remus murder case, the book offers a portrait of a now-lost Cincinnati, with its jazz clubs, its great Roebling suspension bridge and its neighborhoods with names like Over the Rhine and Eden Park." N Y Times Book Rev

Holland, Cecelia

The **angel** and the sword. Forge 2000 304p $23.95

ISBN 0-312-86890-1

LC 00-30668

Set in "ninth-century Paris, the novel centers on King Charles the Bald's fight to save the city when the continued demands of the Vikings can no longer be met. To his aid comes the young, intensely spiritual Lord Roderick. Roderick is in fact the Princess Ragny, who fled her native Spain and incestuous father by disguising herself as a man. As Roderick, Ragny struggles with her sin of deception, her personal identity, womanhood, and the privileges and restrictions of manhood. She also manages to become a hero in battle. . . . A wonderful story of faith, love, hope, and justice." Libr J

Holland, Cecelia

The **firedrake**. Atheneum Pubs. 1966 243p

A "picaresque tale set in 11th century Germany, Flanders, Normandy and England. The Irish hero, named Laeghaire, the Gaelic spelling of Lear, is a brave, hard-fighting mercenary in the forces of William of Normandy. He is impetuous, brawling, very proud, with a plain and cutting tongue. Laeghaire kills men in battle with no hesitation, but he is haunted with nightmares about an ugly future. He is a restless adventurer, he is briefly a man in love, he is a violent man of action. This vital central character is placed against a colorful medieval background of castles and wild countryside and in the middle of one fight after another." Publ Wkly

Holland, Cecelia
  Jerusalem. Forge 1996 318p
  ISBN 978-0812553970

LC 95-38814

"The narrative structure may be simple, but Holland's masterful layering of subplots, historical detail and multiple perspectives makes for a great read." Publ Wkly

Holland, Cecelia
  An **ordinary** woman; a dramatized biography of Nancy Kelsey. Forge 1999 223p
  ISBN 0-312-86528-7

LC 98-48929

A "fictionalized biography of Nancy Kelsey, the first American woman to reach California. Traveling by horse and on foot, 17-year-old Nancy leaves Missouri with a baby on her hip in search of California's holy grail. Part of the 1841 Bidwell-Bartleson party, Nancy and her husband, Ben, decide against the meandering Santa Fe Trail in order to take a more—direct and uncharted—course directly across the continent: traversing the Great Plains, the Rockies, the desert and the Sierra Nevadas. . . . The thorough research lends authority to a vivid and engaging narrative that suffers only a little from Holland's evident fervent admiration for her heroine." Publ Wkly
  Includes bibliographical references

Holland, Cecelia
  Pacific Street. Houghton Mifflin 1992 260p

LC 91-27314

"The plot's credibility runs a little thin at times, but Holland captures the lawlessness of early San Francisco with style and imagination and tells a story both engaging and romantic." Libr J

Holland, Cecelia
  Pillar of the Sky; a novel. Knopf 1985 534p

LC 84-48659

"Part Christ figure and part avenger, {Moloquin} is companionable with women, but also amazingly brutal. The tale is full of subtleties and contradictions and depicts a long struggle between the forces of change and those favoring stability. . . . This is more a story of power and customs than of Stonehenge and the early Britons." Libr J

Holland, Cecelia
  Valley of the Kings; a novel of Tutankhamun. Forge 1997 231p
  ISBN 978-0312868628

LC 97-5499

First published 1977 by Dutton under the pseudonym Elizabeth Eliot Carter

The first half of the "novel is narrated by a fictionalized Howard Carter, the Englishman who discovered Tut's tomb in 1922. Holland does an excellent job of rendering Carter's strained relationship with his upper-crust patron, Lord Carnarvon, while surrounded by obtuse British bureaucrats, archeologists more interested in treasure than history and a

culture that Carter loves despite its otherness. . . . The second half of the book flashes back to the ancient Egypt of Tut and concerns three common Egyptians—a mason, a beggar and a maid—who are variously damaged and nurtured by the royals, who have their own problems." Publ Wkly

Holland, Isabelle
  A **death** at St. Anselm's. Doubleday 1984 229p

LC 83-11668

"Holland remains one of the best of modern romantic suspense writers. Her characters (except for her maniacal murderer) are believable, and her settings (in this case, a modern urban church) are uncommon without being wildly exotic." Wilson Libr Bull

Holland, Travis
  The **archivist's** story. Dial Press 2007 239p $23
  ISBN 978-0-385-33995-7; 0-385-33995-X

LC 2006-31932

"There is a quiet authenticity about Holland's writing that draws you in, and soon you will find yourself sitting on the edge of your seat, silently cheering for his characters." Libr J

Hollinghurst, Alan
  The **stranger's** child. Alfred A. Knopf 2011 435p $27.95
  ISBN 978-0-307-27276-8; 0-307-27276-1

LC 2011-10256

A tale about "poet-aristocrat Cecil Valance who in the first section of the novel is an omnisexual wildcard, filled with 'airy aggressions' that alarm and/or seduce just about everyone around him. Forty-four years later Cecil is seen, by a young aspiring gay writer contemplating writing his biography, as 'a very minor poet' of World War I 'who just happened to have written lines here and there that had stuck.' He's on school syllabuses. His life was 'dramatic as well as short.' And the people who remember him, loved him and were apparently 'loved back' are still around to be interviewed. The contrast between living Cecil, as extravagant and carnal a creature as they come, and dead Cecil, who posthumously draws all his surviving circle into 'false piety and dutiful suppression,' couldn't be more striking. . . . Hollinghurst divides the novel into five novella-length sections set in 1913, 1926, 1967, 1980 and 2008. In each of them, he demonstrates his knack for conjuring the moments between events, the seeming down time in which the ramifications of turning points in life sort themselves out. His immersion in each period is fluid and free of false notes, collectively fusing into a single symphonic epic." Seattle Times

Hollingshead, Greg
  Bedlam. Thomas Dunne Books 2006 312p $24.95
  ISBN 978-0-312-35474-9; 0-312-35474-6

LC 2006-44416

First published 2004 in Canada

This novel "begins in 1797 with a jolt: in the bedroom of a real (if minor) historical woman surprised by the unexpected arrival of her naked husband, James Tilly Matthews, an escapee from a London madhouse who is soon back within its walls. After this wrenching, lunatic scene, the novel details, in three different narrative voices, a prolonged struggle both to release him and to discover the possibly political reason for his incarceration. Interspersed are the emotional letters husband and wife write to each other and one touching note from their son. . . . 'Bedlam' has no end of gorgeous writing. Ostentatious language is always a danger when using narrators from the distant past, but Hollingshead's descriptions stand tastefully back from such overexuberance." N Y Times Book Rev

Holman, Sheri

Witches on the road tonight. Atlantic Monthly Press 2011 263p

ISBN 0-8021-1943-3; 978-0-8021-1943-8

"Growing up in Depression-era rural Virginia, Eddie Alley's quiet life is rooted in the rumors of his mother's witchcraft. But when he's visited by a writer and . . . photographer researching American folklore for the WPA, . . . Eddie is inspired to pursue a future beyond the confines of his dead-end town. He leaves for New York and becomes a television horror-movie presenter beloved for his kitschy comedy. Though expert at softening terror for his young fans, Eddie cannot escape the guilty secrets of his own childhood. When he opens his family's door to a homeless teenager working as an intern at the TV station, the boy's presence not only awakens something in Eddie, but also in his twelve-year-old daughter, Wallis, who has begun to feel a strange kinship to her [grandmother]." (Publisher's note)

Holman's "prose, at first glance irksomely voluminous (she never uses one word where four will do) somehow manages to make the most extravagant ideas seem both vivid and likely. She also boasts a fine, Gothic imagination, summoning fragments of visceral detail at will . . . [She] evokes the blur between the real and the supernatural as if it were the most straightforward thing, a knack possessed by few writers, though Alice Hoffman immediately springs to mind." N Y Times Book Rev

Holt, Tom

Blonde bombshell. Orbit 2010 362p pa $13.99

ISBN 978-0-316-08699-8

"Driven mad by the 'lethally insidious. . . toxic aural garbage' that is Terran music, the canine inhabitants of the planet Ostar send Mark Two, a bomb so smart it composes violin sonatas, to blow up Earth. Insatiably curious, Mark Two delays its mission, takes human form, and explores Earth to find out why the Mark One bomb vanished. After encountering software revolutionary Lucy Pavlov, a unicorn, two men who probably aren't werewolves, and drunken corporate stooge George Stetchkin, Mark decides not to complete his mission, precipitating confrontations with a third bomb (named Bob) and the entire Ostar war fleet. . . . [A] wickedly funny, take-no-prisoners mashup of love, Armageddon, activists, and one of the universe's most valuable commodities: octopi." Publ Wkly

Holt, Tom

Doughnut; Tom Holt. Orbit 2013 400 p. (paperback) $13.99

ISBN 0316226106; 9780316226097; 9780316226103

LC 2012951499

In this book by Tom Holt, "physicist Theo Bernstein loses his job when he accidentally blows up Switzerland's Very Very Large Hadron Collider. As his life plummets into chaos, he receives an unexpected inheritance from an old friend, Professor Pieter van Goyen, and careens into a world of impossible possibilities that not only defy the laws of physics but also demand a rewrite. In between, Theo travels to many worlds; meets a cast of friends, relatives, and enemies." (Library Journal)

Holt, Victoria

The black opal. Doubleday 1993 275p

LC 92-33830

In this "romantic mystery, Dr. Marline and his ailing wife adopt young Carmel March after she is found wandering among the azaleas on their estate, Commonwood House. Soon she is on her way to a new life in Australia. When Carmel finally returns as a young woman, she realizes that she was hustled away to shield her from a mysterious murder at Commonwood House, and she is convinced that the wrong man has been convicted for the crime." Libr J

Holt, Victoria

Bride of Pendorric. Doubleday 1963 288p

Favel Farrington is a young bride, married to handsome Roc Pendorric. She is fearful that he has chosen her for her money and that she will become another of the legendary brides of Pendorric Castle to die young and tragically

Holt, Victoria

The Judas kiss. Doubleday 1981 400p

LC 81-43138

"Pippa Ewing discovers that her beloved older sister Francine has been murdered as she lay in bed with her husband Baron Rudolph. As evidence accumulates to show that Francine had not married him after all, Pippa is launched on a quest to solve her sister's murder and vindicate her name, a journey that takes her to the duchy of Bruxenstein; a job as a governess; and another encounter with Nordic, handsome Conrad, who had caused Pippa to 'fall down the slippery slope' one romantic evening. Mysteries pile up as two similar midnight fires take the lives of a pious and cruel grandfather and a young countess. . . . Plenty of romance, an agreeable amount of sex, lots of danger and suspense in Gothic and exotic settings ensure that this will please Holt fans." Publ Wkly

Holt, Victoria

Mistress of Mellyn. Doubleday 1960 334p

In this romantic novel set in late 19th century England, the heroine is an attractive, young English governess. "She takes charge of the motherless child of a handsome, arrogant gentleman who lives in a large creepy mansion in Cornwall. The plot is lively and complicated. Eventually, our bright heroine discovers that her little pupil's mother was murdered and she narrowly escapes being murdered herself." Publ Wkly

Holt, Victoria

My enemy the Queen. Doubleday 1978 348p

LC 77-11366

This novel of the Elizabethan era is narrated by Lettice Knollys, cousin of the queen and wife of the Earl of Essex.

"Aware that Robert Dudley is the favorite of Elizabeth I and of dark rumors about the death of his wife, Lettice becomes one of Dudley's closet strumpets anyhow. When her husband dies, the Countess dares the axe by marrying Robert, but then betrays him by carrying on with a young man who becomes her third husband after Dudley dies. All the events of a momentous age are colored by Lettice's vanity, even the beheading of her own son, the second Essex, who supplants his stepfather in the affections of the queen." Publ Wkly

Holt, Victoria

Secret for a nightingale. Doubleday 1986 371p

LC 86-2206

"In this Victorian romance, Susanna Pleydell loses her husband to drugs and her dearly loved child to her husband's neglect. She develops an obsessive hatred for Damien Adair, the physician she holds responsible for both tragedies. She tries to forget by taking up a nursing career, eventually going to the Crimea. There, working beside Dr. Adair, she finds herself attracted to him despite her hatred. . . . This is one of the better Holt novels, with a well-drawn historical background." Libr J

Holthe, Tess Uriza

When the elephants dance; a novel. Crown 2002 368p il

ISBN 0-609-60952-1

A novel set "in the final days of the battle for the Philippines. During MacArthur's assault on Manila, a group of neighbors seek shelter in the cellar of an abandoned house. Cramped, starving and terrified, they begin to tell each other stories in order 'to stay alive when you have died inside'. . . . Full of weird, fantastic twists and folkloric wisdom, the stories become both a touchstone to and a respite from the horrific events unfolding outside." N Y Times Book Rev

Homes, A. M.

This book will save your life. Viking 2006 372p $24.95

ISBN 0-670-03493-2

LC 2005-54697

"Richard Novak's day-trading fortune has given him the good life in the hills above 21st-century Los Angeles, but a heart-attack scare exposes his isolation, and a rapidly expanding sinkhole in his front yard forces him to move to a Malibu rental. These crises throw Richard into the paths of such diverse characters as a donut shop owner, a runaway housewife, and a reclusive, iconic author. His eventual return to humanity culminates in a confrontational and emotional visit with teenage son Ben. . . . Overall, this is an engaging and timely tale told with a balanced mix of dark humor and sympathy for individuals enduring the foibles of everyday living." Libr J

Hood, Ann

The **knitting** circle. W. W. Norton 2007 346p

ISBN 978-0-393-05901-4; 0-393-05901-4

LC 2006-32223

This novel was "written after Hood's own tragic loss, the death of her young daughter, and it is not hard to imagine the ways in which writing this novel must have been both painful and therapeutic. It is a wondrously simple book about something complicated: the nearly unendurable process of enduring after a great loss. The novel, like knitting, seems to make itself up as it goes along, the threads bound and gathered into a whole. In the end, there is something where there once was nothing." Washington Post Book World

Hood, Ann

The **Obituary** Writer; Ann Hood. 1st ed. W W Norton & Co Inc 2013 320 p. (hardcover) $26.95

ISBN 0393081427; 9780393081428

LC 2012040074

This book is set in 1919, where "Vivien Lowe still hunts for a lover lost in the Great San Francisco Earthquake of 1906 even as she writes obituaries to help herself and others become reconciled to loss. Readers eventually uncover her connection to Claire, a young wife and mother who on the day of JFK's inauguration considers whether she should leave her safe, airless marriage for the man she loves." (Library Journal)

Hood, Ann

An **ornithologist's** guide to life. W.W. Norton 2004 237p $23.95

ISBN 0-393-05900-6

LC 2004-6112

"Hood is a seductive storyteller, given her emotionally reckless and nonconformist characters, sensuous detail, precise dialogue, and keen rendition of the inner monologue that so often contradicts what we say and do. She also engineers just the sort of painful and inexplicable familial and romantic predicaments friends spend hours attempting to decipher." Booklist

Hood, Ann

Places to stay the night. Doubleday 1993 275p

ISBN 0-385-42556-2

LC 92-10526

"Hood, an accomplished scene setter and dialogist, works out the consequences of the characters' confusion of dream with fantasy and their groping return to truth with a wonderful frankness that illuminates the lessons of paradox and our belief in romance. An exceptionally fluent tale about the unending process of growing up." Booklist

Hood, Ann

The **red** thread; a novel. W.W. Norton & Co. 2010 304p $23.95

ISBN 978-0-393-07020-0; 0-393-07020-4

LC 2009-42605

"Maya started The Red Thread Adoption Agency, referring to a Chinese saying that a red thread connects people destined to be together. . . . Interspersed throughout are italicized vignettes about Chinese mothers forced by the quota on children and prejudice against girls to make wrenching decisions. The raw and riveting Chinese stories siphon narrative juice from the more conventional American angst that dominates the novel. Still, the tale ends with a pleasing sense that the red thread is more than a myth, especially in Maya's case." Kirkus

Hooker, Richard

★ **MASH**. Morrow 1968 219p hardcover o.p. pa $13

ISBN 0-688-14955-3 pa

LC 68-29610

"Captains Hawkeye Pierce, Duke Forrest, and 'Trapper' John McIntyre, all M.D.'s, are stationed in Korea with the 4077th MASH (Mobile Army Surgical Hospital). The reader is soon involved in many operations and medical jargon. It is, however, the off-duty activities of these three that engages one's attention and laughter. Full of martinis, or bored, or tired, or all three, the men soon start raising hell. . . . Hilarious, occasionally very serious, full of warm, appealing eccentric characters, one could enjoy a very pleasant evening with this sMASHing novel." Libr J

Hooper, Chloe

A **child's** book of true crime. Scribner 2002 238p $23

ISBN 0-7432-2512-0

"Kate Byrne, a primary-school teacher in Tasmania, is having an affair with the father of one of her students. But even as she obligingly plays the part of the slutty young mistress, she waits, like a child, to be punished; her lover's wife has just written a highly colored account of a local sex crime, and Kate is convinced that the older woman means to harm her. Hooper's first novel is at once suspenseful and self-conscious; crammed with fragments of animal fables, erotic fantasies, deaths remembered and foretold, it becomes a witty and unsettling meditation on innocence and experience." New Yorker

Hooper, Kay

Blood sins. Bantam Books 2009 296p $25

ISBN 978-0-553-80485-0; 0-553-80485-5

LC 2008-34883

In this "paranormal thriller, the second in a trilogy (after Blood Dreams) . . . , Noah Bishop, of the FBI's Special Crimes Unit, and Haven, a civilian investigative organization, take on the fanatical Rev. Adam Deacon Samuel. At age 10, Samuel murdered his abusive prostitute mother by using psychic powers, which a few years later increased after lightning struck him during a tent revival. Noah and his colleagues suspect Samuel, the leader of the Church of the Everlasting Sin, of killing at least eight people via supernatural means and of abusing young girls to enhance his powers. Tessa Gray, a Haven operative posing as a recent widow, reluctantly infiltrates Samuel's compound in the small town of Grace, N.C., near where the body of a fellow Haven operative surfaced in a river. Hooper pulls out all the stops in depicting the unholy preacher's apocalyptic breakdown as Noah's elite team tackles one of their nastiest assignments yet." Publ Wkly

Hooper, Kay

Blood ties; a Bishop/Special Crimes Unit novel. Bantam Books 2010 311p $26

ISBN 978-0-553-80486-7; 0-553-80486-3

LC 2009-37219

The conclusion to Hooper's "paranormal thriller trilogy that began with Blood Dreams and Blood Sins. When a serial killer tortures, dismembers, and dumps eight women in eight weeks in Tennessee and adjacent states, Noah Bishop, head of the FBI's Special Crimes Unit, gets on the case, along with Noah's touch-telepath and seer wife, Miranda, and special agent Hollis Templeton, a profiler-in-training and medium who can selfheal and see auras. Hollis and special investigator Diana Brisco, also a medium and healer, travel to the 'gray time,' a corridor between life and death where a young spirit, Brooke, helps them connect the killings to a past threat. Series fans and newcomers alike will appreciate the appendixes, which include bios of Special Crime Unit agents and definitions of their various paranormal abilities." Publ Wkly

Hooper, Kay

Finding Laura. Bantam Bks. 1997 322p il

LC 97-10116

At the Kilbourne estate auction in Atlanta "striking redhead Laura Sutherland is delighted to acquire a beautiful 200-year-old mirror for her collection. But she's no longer convinced her purchase is a bargain when magnetic Peter Kilbourne turns up dead only hours after attempting to buy back the mirror, and the police immediately consider her a suspect. . . . Hooper keeps the intrigue pleasurably complicated, with gothic touches of suspense and a statisfying resolution." Publ Wkly

Hooper, Kay

Haunting Rachel. Bantam Bks. 1998 346p

ISBN 0-553-09950-7

LC 98-607160

"Rachel Grant's fiancé, Thomas, was lost in the jungles of South America ten years ago, just before their wedding, and she has never found another man to replace him. After her parents die in a plane crash, Rachel begins to catch glimpses of a man who looks very much like Thomas, always right before suspicious accidents threaten her life. As the threats become more deadly and Rachel comes to know the mysterious stranger who resembles her dead lover, messages that seem to come from beyond the grave warn her away." Libr J

"The book keeps you on your toes with plenty of suspects and motives to choose from as well as a ghostly intervention or two." Booklist

Hooper, Kay

Stealing shadows. Bantam Books 2000 356p pa $7.99

ISBN 0-553-57553-8

LC 2003-576744

"The first in a . . . 'thrill-ogy' of suspense novels, this is a serial killer tale charged with deeply felt dread and romance that will steal readers' hearts. Cassie Neill has inherited a psychic gift from her mother that is a mixed blessing at best because it enables her to enter the minds of serial rapists and killers. From her aunt, she inherits a house tucked away in a corner of quiet little Ryan's Bluff, North Carolina, where she takes refuge, hoping to distance herself from the grueling work she's done for the Los Angeles Police Department. But, just as there's no rest for the weary, there's no rest for the wicked either, and visions of a deranged man's plans to kill prompt Cassie to visit Ben Ryan, the small town's prosecuting attorney. Skeptical but interested, Ben finds himself drawn toward the oddly bewitching Cassie, just as she is pulled ever further into the psychotic soul of evil." Booklist

Followed by Hiding in the shadows (2000) and Out of the shadows (2000)

Hooper, Tobe

Midnight movie; a novel. [by] Tobe Hooper, with Alan Goldsher. Three Rivers Press 2011 315p pa $14

ISBN 978-0-307-71701-6; 0-307-71701-1

LC 2010-40358

"Hooper leaps from one viewpoint character to the next, never lingering on one scene long enough for the reader to become bored or for the characters to become developed. Though constrained by the conventions of the genre, Hooper demonstrates an undeniable talent, using established horror tropes with considerable skill and ingenuity." Publ Wkly

Hootman, Ramsey

Courting Greta; by Ramsey Hootman. 1st Gallery Books trade pbk ed Gallery Books 2013 376 p. (paperback) $16

ISBN 1476711291; 9781476711294

LC 2013005837

In this novel written by Ramsey Hootman, Samuel Cooke, a cripple and computer genius, "leaves his lucrative career to teach programming to high schoolers" where he meets Greta Cassamajor, "the sarcastic gym coach with zero sense of humor. Hootman upends traditional romance tropes to weave a charming tale of perseverance, trust, and slightly conditional love." (Publisher's note)

Hoover, Michelle

The **quickening**; a novel. Other Press 2010 216p pa $14.95

ISBN 978-1-59051-346-0; 1-59051-346-0

LC 2010-05199

"In Hoover's début, the quiet struggle between two Midwestern farm women has the stark simplicity of a Biblical parable. After the First World War, stoic, industrious Enidina Current and her husband draw life from the hard earth of their fields, but at home Enidina suffers violent miscarriages. Their only neighbors for miles—Mary Morrow, bred to 'walk in heels and carry cups of tea,' and her tempestuous husband—have two boys. Mary, seeing refinement in the town's anemic preacher, bears him an illegitimate son, whose actions eventually set the two families against one another. If Hoover's symbolism, like the characters' heavy-handed surnames, is at times too overt, the book's lament for a lost way of life . . . has a mournful beauty." New Yorker

Hope, Anthony

The **prisoner** of Zenda; being the history of three months in the life of an English gentleman. Holt & Co. 1894 226p

"Rudolf Rassendyll, an Englishman, makes a three month's visit to the kingdom of Ruritania. He arrives on the eve of the coronation of King Rudolf. The king has an enemy in his brother, Duke Michael, who aspires to the throne himself. During the festivities at Zenda Castle, the Duke drugs King Rudolf so that he is unable to attend his own coronation. Later, Rassendyll, . . . succeeds in impersonating the King and is crowned in his stead. In the meantime, Princess Flavia, the king's betrothed, falls in love with Rassendyll, who in turn loves her. After many dramatic and dangerous escapades, duels, and intrigues King Rudolf is rescued from Zenda Castle where he is held prisoner by Duke Michael. Rassendyll and Princess Flavia renounce each other when the King is restored, and Rassendyll returns to England." Haydn. Thesaurus of Book Dig

Horan, Nancy

Loving Frank. Ballantine Books 2007 362p

ISBN 0345494997; 9780345494993

LC 2007-14810

In this historical novel, the author draws upon research into the life of Frank Lloyd Wright to explore his relationship with Mamah Borthwick Cheney.

"In 1904, Frank Lloyd Wright started work on a house for an Oak Park couple, Edwin and Mamah Cheney, and, before long, he and Mamah had begun a scandalous affair. In her first novel, Horan, viewing the relationship from Mamah's perspective, does well to avoid serving up a bodice-ripper for the smart set. If anything, she cleaves too faithfully to the sources, occasionally giving her story the feel of a dissertation masquerading as a novel. But she succeeds in conveying the emotional center of her protagonist, whom she paints as a proto-feminist, an educated woman fettered by the role of bourgeois matriarch. Horan best evokes Mamah's troubled personality by means of delicately rendered reflections on the power of the natural world, from which her lover drew inspiration." New Yorker

Horlock, Mary

The **book** of lies; a novel. Harper Perennial 2011 347p pa $14.99

ISBN 978-0-06-206509-4

LC 2010-46608

In this book set in the 1980s, "fifteen-year-old Cat, a smart, overweight outsider, has pushed her bullying classmate Nicolette off the cliffs without remorse. 'For the most part, I am glad she's gone.' After her confession, Cat tracks back through the previous months, presenting a chronicle of Nic's chillingly shrewd, mean-girl torture. At home, Cat takes refuge in her father's study, relatively untouched since his recent death. A passionate historian, he collected wartime accounts of the German occupation of Guernsey, and excerpts of those testimonies, interspersed with Cat's passages, bring heartrending family revelations. The narrative shifts may initially disorient readers, but their subtle, skillfully built connections underscore Horlock's themes of the powerful, shadowy reach of history and the slippery nature of truth . . . while Cat's indelible, darkly funny voice offers unsparing insights into the adolescent jungle." Booklist

Horn, Dara

All other nights; a novel. W.W. Norton & Co. 2009 363p $24.95

ISBN 978-0-393-06492-6

LC 2008-53412

The author "both unearths a fascinating, relatively unexplored aspect of American history—the role of Jewish Americans in the Civil War—and delivers a novel rich in human emotion and ambiguity. A triumph." Booklist

Includes bibliographical references

Horn, Dara

The **world** to come; a novel. W.W. Norton & Co. 2006 314p $24.95

ISBN 0-393-05107-2

LC 2005-14586

There is "much to be said for this novel. Dara Horn is skillful with words. She is serious about writing 'Jewish literature,' and she knows her Jewish sources and treats them sensitively. Good at describing people and places, she is also good at dialogue. And she has the ability to construct a complex story from a large number of components and to build an utterly coherent whole out of them. The World to Come is architecturally complicated, but as architecture it 'works' beautifully." Commentary

Hornby, Nick

About a boy. Riverhead Bks. 1998 307p

ISBN 1-57322-087-6

LC 97-46499

The protagonist of this satire set in London is 36-year-old underachieving bachelor Will Lightman. "Targeting single mothers, he joins a single parents' group under false pretenses and is soon drawn into the lives of depressed Fiona and her bright 12-year-old son, Marcus. Suddenly, his life is messy and complicated. . . . {Hornby} has an uncanny ability for homing in on wholly contemporary, often serious topics and serving them up in truly hilarious fashion." Booklist

Hornby, Nick

★ **High** fidelity. Riverhead Bks. 1995 323p

ISBN 1-57322-016-7

LC 95-8469

"Owner of a small London record shop and musical snob of a high degree, [thirty-five-year-old protagonist Rob Fleming] . . . finds his life thrown into turmoil when live-in girlfriend Laura suddenly leaves. He embarks on a journey through the past, tracking down old lovers while finding solace with Marie, an American folk/country singer living in London, even as he yearns for Laura's return." Libr J

"Happily, Hornby does not rely on pop-cultural allusion to limn his characters' inner lives, but uses it instead to create a rich, wry backdrop for them." Time

Hornby, Nick

How to be good. Riverhead Bks. 2001 305p

ISBN 1-57322-193-7

LC 2001-19395

"'I'm not a bad person. I'm a doctor,' says Katie Carr, liberal 1990s North London mother of two. This is her hollow mantra, the only comfort that she can feign while her 20-year marriage to surly David falls to pieces. Just when she is about to be kicked out of the house after confessing to an affair, David returns from a visit with an ecstasy-dropping club kid-turned-faith healer named DJ GoodNews a changed—a good—man." Libr J

Hornby, Nick

Juliet, naked. Riverhead Books 2009 406p $25.95

ISBN 978-1-59448-887-0; 1-59448-887-8

LC 2009-23773

"Duncan is a middle-aged Brit living in the dreary seaside town of Gooleness. He's unhealthily obsessed with Tucker Crowe, a mostly obscure American singer-songwriter who hasn't put out an album since the 1980s. Annie is Duncan's girlfriend of 15 years. . . . Annie tolerates Duncan's musical obsession, but when she disagrees with his fawning review of a new Crowe outtakes album, she realizes her boyfriend is a bit of a wanker. She leaves him. Soon, she serendipitously strikes up an email correspondence with Crowe himself, who's been living out of the public eye on a farm in Pennsylvania. Like Annie, he feels like he's wasted the last 15 years of his life. . . . [Hornby] shows how obsessing over music isn't the road to love and self-actualization. It's the road to heartbreak." N Y Post

Hornby, Nick

A **long** way down. Riverhead Books 2005 333p $24.95

ISBN 1-57322-302-6

LC 2004-58837

"Whatever limited consolations the book's survivors find in each other, Hornby resists melodramatic resolutions or glorious moments of redemption, and he doesn't smuggle away or refute all the reasons his characters took with them to the rooftop where they met, the ones that urged them toward the edge rather than down to the ground the slow way, back into the world." N Y Times Book Rev

Horowitz, Anthony

The **House** of Silk; a Sherlock Holmes novel. Mulholland Books 2011 294p $27.99

ISBN 978-0-316-19699-4; 0-316-196991

LC 2011030839

"A year after Sherlock Holmes's death (from natural causes), Watson takes up his pen one last time to recount a case they shared in 1890 that was 'too monstrous, too shocking' to appear in print. The opening is prosaic enough. London art dealer Edmund Carstairs asks for the detective's help after a shadowy figure in a flat cap, apparently an Irish-American thug bent on revenge, surfaces near Carstairs's Wimbledon home. When a murder follows Holmes getting involved, the trail leads him and the good doctor to a powerful secret society known as the House of Silk." Publ Wkly

Hospital, Janette Turner

Due preparations for the plague. Norton 2003 401p $24.95

ISBN 0-393-05764-X

LC 2002-156598

"Using the form of a politico-literary thriller, Janette Turner Hospital has attempted a meta-physical novel of evil. . . .'Due preparations for the Plague'—the title and the frequent quotes from Camus indicate the author's larger intentions—is a descent through Dantean circles of governmental conspiracy and betrayal." N Y Times Book Rev

Hospital, Janette Turner

North of nowhere, south of loss. Norton 2004 286p $24.95

ISBN 0-393-05991-X

LC 2004-54723

"Hospital's strength lies in capturing her character's interior lives with a poet's grace and precision. . . . The collection is thematically linked: each story explores the geographies and memories that define and bind us even as they change shape over time. How we embroider past events or alter and manipulate memories from actual occurrences are key elements in many of the tales." Booklist

Hospital, Janette Turner
Orpheus lost; a novel. W. W. Norton 2007 358p $24.95

ISBN 978-0-393-06552-7; 0-393-06552-9

LC 2007-24023

"Hospital is relentless in her musical and mythological references, even as the novel shifts halfway through from romance to suspense when Mishka goes missing. While the book could be tagged a literary thriller, Hospital chooses to depict not clinical gore but hallucinatory pain. . . . She is fascinated by religious and political fundamentalism, psychological and physical terror—and who succumbs or resists." PopMatters

Hospital, Janette Turner
★ **Oyster.** Norton 1998 400p

ISBN 0-393-04618-4

LC 97-34071

First published 1996 in the United Kingdom

"With language that slips between the surreal and the all-too-real, the sign of the beast and the meteorological formation of a rain cloud {Hospital} delivers a world that is at once our own and a place from another time, from the old West, the Bible." N Y Times Book Rev

Hosseini, Khaled, 1965-
★ **And** the Mountains Echoed; by Khaled Hosseini. Penguin Group USA 2013 404 p. (hardcover) $28.95

ISBN 159463176X; 9781594631764

LC 2013004004

This novel by Khaled Hosseini is "about how we love, how we take care of one another, and how the choices we make resonate through generations. In this tale revolving around not just parents and children but brothers and sisters, cousins and caretakers, Hosseini explores the many ways in which families nurture, wound, betray, honor, and sacrifice for one another; and how often we are surprised by the actions of those closest to us, at the times that matter most." (Publisher's note)

Hosseini, Khaled, 1965-
★ The **kite** runner. Riverhead Bks. 2003 324p $24.95; pa $14

ISBN 1-57322-245-3; 1-59448-000-1 pa

LC 2003043106

The narrator, "a thirty-eight-year-old writer named Amir, recounts the odyssey of his life from Kabul to San Francisco via Peshwar, Pakistan. The protagonist was born into a wealthy family in Kabul. Raised by his father, . . . Amir lives a relatively happy life until the Soviet tanks roll into Afghanistan. Then he and his father flee to Pakistan and end up in America. In the United States, his father becomes a gas-station manager. . . . Amir meets Soraya, the daughter of

a former Afghan general, and soon [marries]. . . . For fifteen years the young couple tries in vain to have children. Then Amir receives a call from Rahim Khan, a friend and former business partner of his now-deceased father. Amir flies to Peshwar to meet with him. Rahim Khan reveals that Hassan, Amir's childhood friend, the presumed son of the family servant Ali, was in reality Amir's half-brother, his father's illegitimate son with Ali's wife. Hassan and his wife were killed by the Taliban. Rahim Khan wants Amir to go to Kabul and bring Hassan's son to Peshwar." (World Lit Today)

"Khaled Hosseini gives us a vivid and engaging story that reminds us how long his people have been struggling to triumph over the forces of violence." N Y Times Book Rev

Hosseini, Khaled, 1965-
A **thousand** splendid suns. Riverhead Books 2007 372p $25.95

ISBN 978-1-59448-950-1; 1-59448-950-5

LC 2007-8679

"The texture of these characters' journey around the craters of their country is no doubt well known to readers of international news. Rendered as fiction . . . , however, it devastates in a new way." Minneapolis Star Tribune

Houellebecq, Michel, 1958-
The **map** and the territory; Michel Houellebecq; translated from the French by Gavin Bowd. First American edition. Alfred A. Knopf 2012 269p.

ISBN 9782081246331; 9780307946539; 9780307701558

LC 2010540592

Prix Goncourt (France) (2010)

This book, which won the French literary prize the Prix Goncourt, tells "the story of an artist, Jed Martin, and his family and lovers and friends. . . . Global fame and fortune arrive when he turns to painting. . . . Then, while his aging father . . . flirts with oblivion, a police inspector seeks Martin's help in solving an unspeakably gruesome crime. . . . Jed Martin somehow discovers serenity and manages to add another startling chapter to his artistic legacy." (Publisher's note)

Houellebecq, Michel, 1958-
The **possibility** of an island; translated from the French by Gavin Bowd. Alfred A. Knopf 2006 337p $24.95

ISBN 0-307-26349-0

LC 2005-54527

Original French edition, 2005

The power of the novel is "limited by its utter nihilism, and its refusal to countenance the possibility of any enduring good in human life. . . . Houellebecq's novel wants to be both a contemporary satire of empty satisfactions and a dystopic fantasy about their unchecked proliferations, provocative in its moral alarums and blasé about the whole business. It's a book fit for an age done in by wanting too musch for itself." Walrus

Hough, Robert
The **stowaway.** Arcade Pub. 2004 232p $24

ISBN 0-679-31146-7

LC 2004-9347

Based on an actual incident, this novel "relates how two stowaways are discovered on a container ship bound for North America. The stowaways, who speak only Romanian, are set adrift and soon drown. Several crew members agonize over this, with Rodolfo, the bosun, particularly afflicted, since he notified the captain of the stowaways' existence, assuming that they would be integrated into the work of the ship. Later, when two more stowaways are discovered, Rodolfo and the rest of the crew must decide whether to obey orders or to follow their conscience." Libr J

"This is a moving, haunting novel, full of deeply sympathetic portraits of common people being uncommonly brave." Publ Wkly

House, Silas

A **parchment** of leaves; a novel. Algonquin Bks. 2002 278p $23.95

ISBN 1-565-12367-0

LC 2002-66570

"This is a moving love story set against a stunningly beautiful background, and House seems to capture it all— the deep emotion, the love of land, the customs of mountain people—in quietly eloquent prose." Booklist

House, Tom

The **beginning** of calamities; a novel. Bridge Works 2005 288p $24.95

ISBN 1-88259-369-3

LC 2002-152049

This novel is "set in the mid-1970s in a blue-collar Long Island town. Shy, awkward, 11-year-old Danny re-creates the Passion of Christ as a school play to be performed for his fellow parochial school students during Holy Week. Impressed by his initiative, Danny's young teacher, Liz Kaigh, gets caught up in producing and directing the piece, whose troupe of players is eventually composed of the class misfits. The author effectively depicts Danny's constant personal angst and spiritual longings within the context of religious suffering but also manages to add a note of dark humor." Libr J

Houston, James D.

Bird of another heaven; a novel. Alfred A. Knopf 2007 337p $25.95

ISBN 978-1-4000-4202-9; 1-4000-4202-X

LC 2006-48726

"Houston gives us an engaging historical detective story, but his novel succeeds most as a richly delineated portrait of 19th-century Hawaii and California populated with characters of real vigor . . . . He keeps his eye on the essential task: making the filaments that link the past to the present and the fiction to the history visible and strong." San Jose Mercury News

Houston, Pam

Cowboys are my weakness; stories. Norton 1992 171p

LC 91-12920

"Short stories, mostly first-person, told with verve and perfect pitch by women entangled with wild men in a cruel world." N Y Times Book Rev

Houston, Pam

Waltzing the cat. Norton 1998 288p

ISBN 0-393-02749-X

LC 98-10562

This collection "is far from perfect, but Houston's vigorous voice and lively take on what it's like to be a woman both physically bold and hopelessly romantic are to be cherished nonetheless." N Y Times Book Rev

Howard, Linda

Cry no more. Ballantine Books 2003 368p

ISBN 0-345-45341-7

LC 2003-45140

"Milla is a woman with a mission: 10 years after her baby son, Justin, was snatched from her arms, she still hunts for him every day. Her dedicated passion led her to start Finders, an agency set up to help others like her find taken loved ones. Although she has learned some sketchy details about Justin's abductors, they never led anywhere; all she has to go on is a name, Diaz. An anonymous tip about Diaz's location leads to a sighting of the one-eyed man who snatched Justin. When one of Finders' generous grantors offers a tip on finding Diaz, alleged to be a dangerous assassin, Milla takes it upon herself to seek Diaz out, only to learn that he is not tied to the abduction but can help find out who is. . . . At once heart-wrenching and thrilling." Booklist

Howard, Maureen

Big as life; three tales for spring. Viking 2001 225p il $23.95

ISBN 0-670-89978-X

LC 2001-17904

"In 'Children with Matches,' a history professor unexpectedly inherits her family's dilapidated estate, while her lover, a famous economist, fears for his life in war-warped Africa. A young Irish woman's beauty brings her nothing but grief until she finds her calling as an army nurse in World War II, in 'The Magdalene.' And Audubon and his longsuffering wife are the subjects of the title story." Booklist

Howard, Maureen

★ **Natural** history; a novel. Norton 1992 393p il

LC 92-7041

This is a "novel always in the midst of breaking free of itself, its pages filled with brilliant variations on the screenplay, the encyclopedia, the diary, and, of course, the history book." New Repub

Howard, Maureen

The **rags** of time; a novel. Viking 2009 238p il $26.95

ISBN 978-0-670-02132-1; 0-670-02132-6

LC 2009-15167

"Like all of Howard's work, 'The Rags of Time' is extremely ambitious, not only in scale but also in points of reference. . . . As such, Howard invites the reader to try to make sense of it all, to stare at the structure whole, as if at one of Joseph Cornell's boxes full of minutely arranged objects, and give it a name and a theme. But looking at her writing from this perspective misses the most interesting part: her sentences. No one writing in English today produces anything quite like them." N Y Times Book Rev

Howard, Ravi

    Like trees, walking; a novel. Amistad 2007 258p $24.95

    ISBN 978-0-06-052959-8; 0-06-052959-8

                                    LC 2006-48442

    "The first day of spring, 1981, Mobile woke to find a badly beaten black teenager hanging from a tree just a few yards off the city's major thoroughfare. A Klan cross burned not far from the lynching. A quarter century after that horror, which went unsolved for years, Howard explores ways Michael Donald's murder changed the black community left behind. Working in a muted prose style, somber and hushed as the family funeral home where Roy, his teen narrator, watches and dreams, Howard tells the story of a community shocked out of normalcy forever, of lives eclipsed and lost as the ripples of a hate crime spread out across Mobile Bay and into the broader world." Paste

Howatch, Susan

    Absolute truths; a novel. Knopf 1995 559p

                                      LC 94-27510

    Sixth in the Church of England series, this novel "is set during the mid-1960s, the period during which the Church of England . . . was rocked by widespread challenges to tradition. Again representing tradition is narrator Charles Ashworth, The Anglican Bishop of Starbridge. . . . Ashworth's archenemy—and doppelgänger—is Neville Aysgarth, the Dean of the Cathedral who is, according to Ashworth, unorthodoxly open to using the trappings of a capitalistic marketplace to benefit the financially deteriorating church building. To make matters worse, Aysgarth is an alleged dipsomaniac and womanizer, who once made a pass at Ashworth's beloved wife, Lyle. When Lyle dies suddenly, the bereaved widower strays dangerously from the fold." Publ Wkly

Howatch, Susan

    Cashelmara. Simon & Schuster 1974 702p

    Divided into six sections, each narrated by a different character, this novel charts "the lives of three generations of the Anglo-Irish de Salis family between 1859 and 1891. They move between London homes, a Warwickshire estate, New York and Boston—where two Lords de Salis find their wives—but end always at the great white house on their Irish estate, Cashelmara. In the background are the simmering troubles between starving Irish tenants and callous English landlords." Christ Sci Monit

    "With a copiousness of detail studded with adventure, rape, depravity, intrigue, and murder, the story plays out with clarity and brilliance." Best Sellers

Howatch, Susan

    Glamorous powers. Knopf 1988 403p

                                      LC 88-45347

    This "novel, the second in the Church of England series that began with 'Glittering Images,' weaves an intriguing and wholly involving story out of the otherwise sober subject of Christian mysticism in the 20th-century Church of England. Howatch's chief characters are a clerical odd couple, rivals since their Cambridge days: Jonathan Darrow, a 60-year-old Anglo-Catholic monk with 'glamorous' psychic

powers, and his Abbot-General, Francis Ingram, a practical, eloquent, urbane man with sophisticated insight into modern psychology. . . . The wisdom of 'Glamorous Powers' lies in the deft way it aligns psychological and spiritual truths to bring about healing in the broadest sense." N Y Times Book Rev

    Followed by Ultimate prizes

Howatch, Susan

    ★ **Glittering** images. Knopf 1987 399p

    ISBN 0-394-56206-2

                                      LC 87-45130

    This, the first in the Church of England series, "takes place in pre-World War II England, just after Edward VIII abdicated to marry the divorced Wallis Simpson. The event is emblematic, for this novel is about marriage and divorce and proper behavior within a religious context. . . . The narrator is a young intellectual cleric, Charles Ashworth, who is sent by the Archbishop of Canterbury to spy on Alex Jardine, the charismatic, liberal Bishop of Starbridge. Ashworth uncovers evidence in Jardine's household—which includes a depressive wife and her pretty female companion—of sexual scandal and a highly irregular interpretation of Anglican dogma. The revelation of the mystery of Starbridge sends Ashworth into a personal crisis of faith." N Y Times Book Rev

    "An ambitious and lifelike work of uncommon depth." Booklist

    Followed by Glamorous powers

Howatch, Susan

    The **heartbreaker**. Knopf 2004 483p $25

    ISBN 1-4000-4147-3

                                      LC 2003-62493

    "Plot improbabilities and long sections of spiritual musing are redeemed by Howatch's strongly drawn characters: if Carta can come across as brittle and prudish, Gavin's self-absorbed cant is continually entertaining." Publ Wkly

Howatch, Susan

    The **high** flyer; a novel. Knopf 2000 500p

    ISBN 0-375-41057-0

                                      LC 99-58953

    First published 1999 in the United Kingdom

    In this novel "success-driven London lawyer Carter Graham is suddenly confronted with phenomena that test the coping abilities of her liberated, modern mind. The quintessential 'high flyer,' Carter has broken through the glass ceiling and become a partner in the prestigious law firm of Curtis, Towers. Recently married to Kim Betz, a handsome banker almost 15 years her senior, Carter lives in the 'right' apartment complex, drives a Porsche and is thinking of having a baby. However, Kim's hidden past (involvement with Nazis, the occult, group sex and an unsavory psychic healer named Mrs. Mayfield) threatens Carter's carefully orchestrated life plan." Publ Wkly

    "A suspense novel mixed with Gothic overtones and spiritual dimensions, this story works on almost every level." Libr J

Howatch, Susan

    Mystical paths; a novel. Knopf 1992 433p

                                      LC 91-58557

"Although this is all rather formulaic, Howatch has discovered that the Christian story is essentially a romance, and she has exploited this with considerable intelligence." Booklist

Followed by Absolute truths

Howatch, Susan

Penmarric. Simon & Schuster 1971 735p

"Throughout the story, the author keeps the reader aware of the great historical precedent and parallel for her fiction; the love of Henry II and Eleanor of Aquitaine; preceding each chapter are two pertinent quotations about that royal couple and the king's progeny. It is a neat and useful device, adding piquancy and historical flavor to an interesting tale." Best Sellers

Howatch, Susan

Scandalous risks. Knopf 1990 385p

LC 90-53076

"With sculptor's hands fashioning rich, lustrous three-dimensional characters, Howatch brilliantly shows how and why the situation between Venetia and her 'Mr. Dean' arose, flourished, then died away." Booklist

Followed by Mystical paths

Howatch, Susan

Ultimate prizes. Knopf 1989 387p

LC 89-45303

This, third novel in the Church of England series, "is narrated by Neville Aysgarth, an ambitious archdeacon in the fictional English diocese of Starbridge. A brilliant administrator with a firm, practical faith in God and the Church of England, Neville has steadily moved up in life by 'chasing the prizes,' overcoming his humble birth and troubled youth to win for himself a perfect wife, a flock of delightful children and a powerful position, all before age 40. During his climb to success he has kept his mind as tidy as his diocese by relentlessly 'ringing down the curtain'—a mental curtain, that is—on disturbing memories and desires. But alas for Neville, his curtain is shortly to be twitched off its rod, first by an infatuation with a young society girl, then by a death in his family." N Y Times Book Rev

Followed by Scandalous risks

Howatch, Susan

The wheel of fortune. Simon & Schuster 1984 973p

LC 84-5357

This "absorbing novel convincingly demonstrates that a family saga can be more than the mere 'show and tell' of one generation following another. By using six different narrators to recount five generations of a 20th-century Welsh family, the author deftly supplies multiple viewpoints of events." Libr J

Howatch, Susan

The wonder-worker. Knopf 1997 529p

ISBN 0-375-40102-4

LC 97-36886

"The setting is St. Benet's, a London parish church, and while every character displays a level of eccentricity verging on the gothic, Howatch's good-humored tone keeps the whole—just—from collapsing." New Yorker

Howe, Katherine

The physick book of Deliverance Dane; a novel. Hyperion 2009 371p $25.99

ISBN 978-1-4013-4090-2; 1-4013-4090-3

LC 2008-51627

"A Harvard doctoral candidate, Connie learns that 'Physick' is the 17th-century word for an herbal remedy, and that Deliverance Dane was a Massachusetts woman who knew this medicinal craft and kept her recipes—which she called receipts—in an almanac. Connie must discover the hidden location of this old volume of spells (there's no better word for what they are), but she discovers so much more along the way: great personal danger, unanticipated self-knowledge and love, in both its natural and preternatural aspects. The Salem witch trials of 1692 epitomize a moment when a society felt threatened by the notion of women's uncanny power. At strategic points in the novel, Howe recreates, with harrowing vividness, intimate scenes from that historical crisis." BookPage

Howells, William Dean

★ Novels, 1875-1886. Literary Classics of the U.S. 1983 1217p $40

ISBN 0-940450-04-6

LC 82-112

A foregone conclusion (1875) describes the love triangle between American expatriate Florida Vervain, American painter Henry Ferris, and lapsed priest Don Ippolito. In A modern instance (1882), Bartley Hubbard, an unscrupulous and philandering journalist is divorced by his wife and subsequently murdered by one of the individuals scandalized in his newspaper. In Indian summer (1886), Theodore Coville, a middle-aged American vacationing in Florence meets an old acquaintance and one of her young friends, eventually sparking relationships with each of them. The rise of Silas Lapham is entered separately.

Howells, William Dean

Novels, 1886-1888. Library of America 1989 881p $35

ISBN 0-940450-51-8

LC 88-82728

"In The Minister's Charge (1886), Lemuel Barker leaves his impoverished farm and comes to Boston hoping to become a published poet. Proud, innocent, and implacably honest, he is quickly plunged into the humiliating depths of urban homelessness. His plight weighs on the conscience of David Sewell, a minister who could not bear to tell Barker how bad his poetry was. . . . In April Hopes (1887) Alice Pasmer is the only daughter of parents whose dwindling investments have forced their return from Europe to New England. When Alice meets Dan Mavering, the easygoing son of a wealthy wallpaper manufacturer, her mother begins a careful campaign to bring about their marriage. . . . The heroine of Annie Kilburn (1888) returns to her Hatboro', Massachusetts, home after eleven years abroad and finds a once-quiet village rapidly turning into a sprawling factory town with paved streets, electric lights, and a department store. Unmarried at thirty-one, the daughter of a prominent 'old' family, she renews ties with old friends and begins a life devoted to good deeds." Publisher's note

Howells, William Dean

The **rise** of Silas Lapham; with an introduction by Kermit Vanderbilt. Penguin Books 1986 xxxi, 368p pa $12

ISBN 0-14-039030-8

First published 1885

"Silas is a crude, uneducated man who makes his fortune by methods not above criticism, but manly and capable of better things when his conscience is awakened—a compendium of human virtues and vices, drawn with insight, tenderness and humor. The efforts of the prosperous Laphams to get into Boston society, with their mistakes and disillusionments, the sentimental tragicomedy of the two daughters, in love with the same young man; and Lapham's business troubles, are more or less neatly woven in to make the plot." Baker. Guide to the Best Fic

Howrey, Meg

Blind sight; Meg Howrey. Pantheon Books 2011 289p. $24.95

ISBN 978-0-307-37916-0; 0-307-37916-7; 9780307739292

LC 201012935

The book tells the story of a teenaged boy, "Luke Prescott, who has been brought up in a bohemian matriarchy by his divorced New Age mother, a religious grandmother, and two precocious half-sisters. . . . Luke is writing his college applications when his father -- a famous television star whom he never knew -- calls and invites him to Los Angeles for the summer. Luke accepts and is plunged into a world of location shooting, celebrity interviews, glamorous parties, and premieres. As he begins to know the difference between his father's public persona and his private one, Luke finds himself sorting through his own personal mythology." (Publisher's note)

"The novel resonates with authenticity, both with its description of the world of women from which Luke emerges and the world of easy celebrity in which he is tempered. Even many of Howrey's minor characters—Luke's sisters, for example—shine . . . . A wonderfully intriguing examination of what makes, and might break, a family." Kirkus

Hoyt, Elizabeth

Scandalous desires; Elizabeth Hoyt. Grand Central Publishing 2011 384p.

ISBN 9780446558938 pa

LC 2011044264

This book tells the story of Silence Hollingbrook, a young widow who "with her brother Winter runs the Home for Unfortunate Infants and Foundling Children . . . [and] bears the shame of everyone thinking [river pirate Mickey O'Connor] took advantage of her. But she has bigger concerns. Mickey has kidnapped the very young Mary Darling from Silence's home. Mary was left on the orphanage's door step a year ago. . . . [Silence] has suspicions that Mickey is Mary's father. . . . Mickey has many enemies, but the biggest threat comes from the vicar of Whitechapel. . . . Word has reached him that Mickey has a daughter and possibly might have feelings for the innocent Silence. Desperate to

keep them safe, Mickey kidnaps Mary, knowing Silence will storm his home to find her." (USA Today)

Hoyt, Elizabeth

Thief of Shadows; Elizabeth Hoyt. Grand Central Pub. 2012 367 p. (pbk.) $7.99; (pbk.) $7.99

ISBN 1455508322; 9781455508327

This book is the fourth in the Maiden Lane romance series. Here, "[t]he masked Ghost of St. Giles rescues orphaned children from" London's street. "Widowed baroness Isabel Beckinhall rescues the unconscious 'ghost' after finding him injured in the street; before she can ascertain his identity, he awakens and begs her to leave his mask in place. Little does she know he is Winter Makepeace, manager of a local orphanage, whom Isabel finds 'dour.'" (Publishers Weekly)

Hrabal, Bohumil

★ **I** served the King of England; [translated by Paul Wilson] Harcourt Brace Jovanovich 1989 243p

ISBN 0-15-145745-X

LC 88-16482

This novel "is a flood of meandering garrulous narration, with dreamlike, filmlike sequences, hyperbolic, grotesque and farcical analogues of familiar historical fact. No sober account, this, of how it might actually have been, yet still it projects through its debunking prism the shallowness, absurdity and cruelty of how it indeed was." Times Lit Suppl

Hrabal, Bohumil

★ **Too** loud a solitude; translated from the Czech by Michael Henry Heim. Harcourt Brace Jovanovich 1990 98p

ISBN 0-15-190491-X

LC 90-4313

"This is indeed Franz Kafka's Prague. . . . The book is funny, in its desperate, knockabout way. Along with Hant'a's incessant reading goes excessive swilling of beer, and the tone throughout is at once strident and woozy, so that the reader has the impression of being trapped in that basement room as the press grinds and the drunken operator rummages through the tatters of a ruined culture." N Y Rev Books

Hubbard, Susan

The **Society** of S. Simon & Schuster 2007 304p $25

ISBN 978-1-4165-3457-0; 1-4165-3457-1

LC 2006-51265

"Hubbard has created a literary mystery that will appeal to the fans of Diane Setterfield's The Thirteenth Tale or Elizabeth Kostava's The Historian. Well written and full of intriguing characters, the novel moves apace as the reader becomes engaged in the hunt for the truth about Ariella and her family." Libr J

Huddle, David

La Tour dreams of the wolf girl. Houghton Mifflin 2002 196p $24

ISBN 0-618-08173-9

LC 2001-16915

"Shifting between two narratives—one concerning an unhappy wife in present-day Vermont, the other involving the 17th-century French painter Georges de La Tour and a

15-year-old model—the novel's premise sounds like a prescription for historical, escapist entertainment. But anyone looking for easy distraction or predictable romance will be disappointed; Huddle's book offers more complex pleasures. A study of the relation between art and life, the novel has an honesty and psychological depth that are at times painfully real and quietly moving." N Y Times Book Rev

Hudgens, Dallas

Season of Gene; a novel. Scribner 2007 211p $24

ISBN 978-1-4165-4148-6; 1-4165-4148-9

LC 2007-11578

"Gruff, conscientious Joe owns a Washington, D.C., car-detailing service and ticket brokerage, while best friend Gene Dellorso manages a local limo service. Joe's the manager and catcher for the Vicodin-and-beer-fueled Whip Spa Yankees, for which Gene also plays. When Gene, 35, collapses dead at a game, his pre-game confessions of an unsalvageable marriage and a desire to flee for Las Vegas aren't the only secrets he's been hiding: a cavalcade of thugs come crawling out of the woodwork all wanting to claim a 1932 vintage bat used by Babe Ruth that's now worth a cool three million." Publ Wkly

Hudgens has "given readers an engaging, knowing glimpse of an odd, but no doubt real, world of arrested development. And he knows his baseball." Booklist

Hudgins, Andrew

The joker; a memoir. Andrew Hudgins. Simon & Schuster 2013 352 p.

ISBN 9781476712710; 9781476712727

LC 2013009292

In this memoir, by Andrew Hudgins, "Hudgins tells and analyzes the jokes that explore the contradictions in the Baptist religion he was brought up in, the jokes that told him what his parents would not tell him about sex, and the racist jokes that his uncle loved, his father hated, and his mother, caught in the middle, was ambivalent about. This book is both a memoir and a meditation on jokes and how they educated, delighted, and occasionally horrified him as he grew." (Publisher's note)

Includes bibliographical references and index.

Hudson, W. H.

★ Green mansions; a romance of the tropical forest. Putnam 1904 315p

"The hero, Mr. Abel, tells the tragic story of his love for the bird girl, Rima, an ethereal maiden whose jungle upbringing has brought her close to the powers and beauty of nature. Abel has just succeeded in awakening the human emotion of love in the half-wild girl when she is killed by a band of savages." Reader's Ency. 3d edition

Huggins, James Byron

Nightbringer; James Byron Huggins. Whitaker House 2004 302p $19.99

ISBN 088368876X (hardcover: alk. paper); 9780883688762

LC 2004018589

In this book, "a centurion, Gaius Cassius Longinus, reappears with a tourist group visiting a newly reopened abbey in the Alps that holds countless precious relics and artifacts, along with a dark past. Gina, an FBI agent, and her two kids are also in the group, which arrives just as bad weather threatens to cut off the abbey from the outside world. After a day of history lessons and getting to know the friendly monks, an ancient, monstrous enemy attacks, and the humans must unite against it. As more is revealed about the nature of the terror during the fight, people begin questioning their identities and beliefs, but there's never any doubt about which side will prevail." (Publishers Weekly)

Hughes, Anita

Market Street; Anita Hughes. St. Martin's Press 2013 304 p. (paperback) $14.99

ISBN 0312643330; 9780312643331

LC 2013002660

In this book by Anita Hughes, "raised to take the reins [of the department store owned by her family], Cassie [Fenton] instead chose marriage, to Aidan, a UC Berkeley professor. . . . Around the time Aidan has an affair with one of his students, Cassie's mother presents her with a project that promises even more turmoil. . . . The work, and a new friendship with James, the architect for the project, gives Cassie the space to decide whether or not to forgive her husband." (Publishers Weekly)

Hughes, Declan

The city of lost girls. William Morrow 2010 297p $24.99

ISBN 978-0-06-168990-1; 0-06-168990-4

LC 2009-41251

"Larger-than-life Irish movie director Jack Donovan has returned to Dublin to make a film, but he's emotionally rattled by cryptic, threatening messages. He seeks out his onetime friend, Dublin PI Ed Loy, for help. Loy signs on, but the disappearances of three beautiful young women from the set—something that also happened when Donovan made films in LA—tell Loy he's looking for a serial killer, and the killer is almost certainly Donovan or one of his faithful retinue, known to Tinseltown buffs as the Gang of Four. . . . Donovan is 'a carouser extraordinaire,' 'a mad wayward bastard' who sings Puccini arias in pubs and mesmerizes nearly every character in the book. Not even the smart, formidable Loy is immune, and neither is the reader." Booklist

Hughes, Declan

The price of blood; an Irish novel of suspense. William Morrow 2008 312p $24.95

ISBN 978-0-06-082551-5; 0-06-082551-0

LC 2007-40667

This Dublin thriller "featuring P.I. Ed Loy portrays the downside of the booming Irish economy. The real estate bubble has many young Dubliners in over their heads, days away from foreclosure and being forced to move into seedy subdivisions teeming with family gangs. His own dwindling bank balance finds Ed taking more domestic disturbance cases than he'd like, stuck doing surveillance in the same seedy subdivisions. When Father Vincent Tyrrell summons him to help with a very different kind of family matter, the change sounds appealing: he's to track down a missing member of the legendary Tyrrell horse racing dynasty. The case seems surprisingly simple after he finds a phone number linked to the missing Tyrrell in the pocket of a corpse while pursuing another matter. But Ed suddenly discovers himself caught in a web of drugs, race fixing, gambling, incest, and serial murder among the rich and famous." Libr J

"The dialogue is spare and edgy, the pacing crisp; Hughes' sense of local color, and particularly his ability to impart it to his readers, is absolutely spot on." BookPage

Hughes, Langston

Laughing to keep from crying. Holt & Co. 1952 206p

Hughes, Langston

Not without laughter. Knopf 1930 324p

This novel portrays the lives of a poor black family in a small Kansas town

"A sympathetic portrayal, unmarred by bitterness or sentimentality, of a people to whom life, no matter how hard, was not without laughter." Booklist

Hughes, Langston

★ **Short** stories of Langston Hughes; edited by Akiba Sullivan Harper; with an introduction by Arnold Rampersad. Hill & Wang 1996 299p hardcover o.p. pa $16

ISBN 0-8090-1603-6

LC 95-19554

"Dating from 1919 to 1963, these pieces vary in theme, covering life at sea, the trials and tribulations of a young pianist and her elderly white patron, a visiting writer's experience in Cuba, a young girl's winning an art scholarship but losing it when it's learned she is black, and an ambitious black preacher trying to gain fame by being nailed to a cross. If you crave good reading don't pass up this gem." Libr J

Hughes, Langston

★ **Simple** speaks his mind. Simon & Schuster 1950 231p

The central figure, is a Harlem black who expresses his views on many subjects, but always from the point of view of his own race. He dislikes whites, and makes no bones of it. Some of his favorite topics are women, landladies especially, parties, and beer

"Simple is completely frank in his opinions about white people; he dislikes them intensely. The race problem is never absent, but the flow of the book is light-hearted and easy." N Y Times Book Rev

Hughes, Langston

Simple stakes a claim. Rinehart 1957 191p

In this book Simple, of Harlem, speaks his mind on a variety of subjects, ranging from housing conditions, to sex magazines

Hughes, Langston

Simple takes a wife. Simon & Schuster 1953 240p

"Before Mr. Jesse B. Semple, the untutored philosopher of the Harlem rooming-house set, can divorce his wife and espouse the morally impeccable Joyce, he has to run the gauntlet of many problems. He discourses on them in Harlem bars over beers he has cadged from his sympathetic and more literate listener. Under the folklike humor

of 'Simple's' monologs runs a bitter undercurrent of racial consciousness." Booklist

Hughes, Langston

Simple's Uncle Sam. Hill & Wang 1965 180p

Hughes, Mary-Beth

Double happiness; stories. Black Cat 2010 201p $14

ISBN 978-0-8021-7074-3; 0-8021-7074-9

"The stories in this excellent collection meander with the sureness of streams discovering their paths. Hughes keeps her prose close to her characters' thoughts, and doles out the most crucial information on the sly. Many stories deal with women or girls coming to terms with the failings, or deaths, of the men in their lives. . . . If some of Hughes's stories can initially seem scattered or arbitrary, further reading nearly always discloses careful but unobtrusive organization, giving even the saddest revelations—and most revelations here are sad—an air of the miraculous." New Yorker

Hughes, Matthew

Hespira; a tale of Henghis Hapthorn. Night Shade Books 2009 233p $24.95

ISBN 978-1-59780-101-0; 1-59780-101-1

This novel features a "planet-hopping, gourmandizing, insufferably self-important private eye named Henghis Hapthorn. His task is to help a young lady who's lost her memories recollect her life. Though Hapthorn has suffered his own loss — his intuition has decamped to a private estate halfway around the world — his investigative skills remain impressive. And Hughes' account of this far future detective at work is grand, elaborate fun. Still, the most engaging thing about 'Hespira' is the Alice-in-Wonderland complexity of this curiouser and curiouser story." Cleveland Plain Dealer

Hughes, Richard Arthur Warren

★ **A high** wind in Jamaica; [by] Richard Hughes; introduction by Francine Prose. New York Review Books 1999 279p hardcover o.p. pa $12.95

ISBN 0-940322-15-3

LC 99-14565

First published 1929 by Harper with title: The innocent voyage

"A family of children living in Jamaica in the 19th century are sent to England after a hurricane has partly destroyed their home. Amiable pirates capture them by mistake, and the children bring about the pirates' ruin: one girl becomes a murderess. The irrationality and impenetrability of the child's amoral world and the horror of the whole situation are brilliantly conveyed." Reader's Ency. 3d edition

The **Hugo** winners; edited by Isaac Asimov. Doubleday 1962 5v

The stories and novelettes included in these volumes won the Hugo Awards from 1939-1982

Hugo, Victor

★ The **hunchback** of Notre Dame; revised translation and notes by Catherine Liu; introduction by Elizabeth McCracken. Modern Library 2002 xxviii, 483p pa $11.95

ISBN 0-679-64257-9

LC 2002-18917

Original French edition, 1930. Variant title: Notre Dame de Paris

The hidden force of fate is symbolized by the superhuman grandeur and multitudinous imageries of the cathedral. "The first part . . . is a panorama of medieval life—religious, civic, popular, and criminal—drawn with immense learning and an amazing command of spectacular effect. These elements are then set in motion in a fantastic and grandiose drama, of which the personages are romantic sublimations of human virtues and passions—Quasimodo the hunchback, faithful unto death; Esmeralda, incarnation of innocence and steadfastness; Claude Frolla, Faust-like type of the antagonism between religion and appetite. Splendors and absurdities, the sublime and the grotesque are inextricably mingled in this strange romance. The date is fixed at the year 1482." Baker. Guide to the Best Fic

Hugo, Victor

★ **Les** miserables; translated from the French by Charles E. Wilbour; with an introduction by Peter Washington. Knopf 1997 xxxvii, 1432p $27

ISBN 0-375-40317-5

LC 98-156450

Original French edition, 1862

"A panorama of French life in the first half of the [nineteenth] century, aiming to exhibit the fabric of civilization in all its details, and to reveal the cruelty of its pressure on the poor, the outcast, and the criminal. Jean Valjean, a man intrinsically noble, thru the tyranny of society becomes a criminal. His conscience is reawakened by the ministrations of the saintly Bishop Myriel . . . and Valjean, reformed and prosperous, follows in the good bishop's footsteps as an apostle of benevolence, only to be doomed again by the law to slavery and shame. The 'demimondaine' Fantine, another victim of society; her daughter Cosette one of those whom suffering makes sublime; Marius, an ideal of youth and love; Myriel, the incarnation of Christian charity, are the leading characters of this huge morality, which is thronged with representatives of the good in man and the cruelty of society. Magnificent description . . . scenes invested with terror, awe, repulsion, alternate with tedious rhapsodies. Realism mingles with the incredible." Baker. Guide to the Best Fic

Hulme, Kathryn

★ **The nun's** story. Little, Brown 1956 339p

"Convent life, with its rigors and its compensations, has seldom been as fairly depicted as in this biographical account. An unhappy love affair was one of the reasons why 'Gabrielle Van der Mal' {fictitious name} entered a convent in Belgium, but her love of God and desire to serve her fellow men were also important influences. For 17 years she tried diligently to discipline her analytical and independent mind through prayer and hard work as a nurse, first in a hospital for the insane, then in a Congo mission, and finally in a TB sanatorium in occupied Holland. Ultimately, she faced the bitter truth that the religious life, with its inflexible authority, was not for her, and she was released from her vows." Libr J

Hulme, Keri

★ **The bone** people; a novel. Louisiana State Univ. Press 1985 450p

ISBN 0-8071-1284-4

LC 85-12937

First published 1984 in New Zealand

"This novel is unforgettably rich and pungent. . . . Set on the harsh South Island beaches of New Zealand, bound in Maori myth and entwined with Christian symbols, Miss Hulme's provocative novel summons power with words, as in a conjurer's spell." N Y Times Book Rev

Humphreys, Helen

Afterimage; a novel. Metropolitan Bks. 2001 240p $23

ISBN 0-8050-6666-7

LC 00-46907

First published 2000 in Canada

"It's 1865, in England, and both Isabelle Dashell and her husband, Eldon, are making pictures. She's intent on mastering a new medium, photography, and he's seeking renown as a cartographer. When Annie Phelan, a sober beauty orphaned by the Irish famine, answers their ad for a housemaid, she becomes Isabelle's muse and Eldon's confidante, and finds herself pressed into the service of art. Inspired by the work of Julia Margaret Cameron, this urgent, well-made novel charts the boundaries where light becomes shadow, and the known can suddenly appear awful and astonishing." New Yorker

Humphreys, Helen

Coventry. W.W. Norton & Co. 2009 192p $23.95

ISBN 978-0-393-06720-0; 0-393-06720-3

LC 2008-37349

First published 2008 in Canada

"During the Second World War, on the night of the devastating Coventry blitz of November 14, 1940, widow Harriet Marsh finds herself navigating the streets of the town as German bombs explode around her. Alone, and still in mourning for the husband she lost in 1914, Harriet finds comfort amid chaos in the close companionship of a young man half her age, helping him search frantically through the burning streets for his mother. Through her use of actual historical records of the bombing, Humphreys evokes the wartime atmosphere of fear and dislocation with great poignancy, but her novel also emphasizes – especially through Harriet's stoicism and resourcefulness – the resilience of the common individual during times of exceptional challenge. . . Humphreys' poetic language and imagery, though at times seemingly at odds with the narrative, frequently bring to vivid life the brutality and violence of that night in 1940." Quill Quire

Humphreys, Helen

The lost garden. Norton 2002 183p $23.95

ISBN 0-393-05183-8

LC 2002-26308

In this novel, set in the English countryside of 1941, "Gwen Davis, a desperately lonely botanist employed by the Royal Horticultural Society to investigate canker in parsnips, has signed up to direct young women agricultural volunteers on an estate requisitioned for the war effort. Humphreys is a metaphysical novelist; for her, intricate emotional content finds specific analogues in the made world—an astonishing photograph or, as here, an overgrown garden that, once cleared, reveals its consoling secrets." New Yorker

Humphreys, Josephine
★ The **fireman's** fair. Viking 1991 263p
ISBN 0-670-83907-8
LC 90-50575

"Rob Wyatt, unmarried at 32, has quit his job as a lawyer, moved out of a luxury apartment to poor housing, sold his Alfa for a cheap used car, and is looking for a new kind of life. Hurricane Hugo almost devastates the southern town in which he lives and also seems to have swept an uprooting storm through his personal life. His unceasing love for Louise, now married to wealthy Frank Camden, becomes not so firm when Billy Poe, 18 years old and naively innocent (or precociously wise) comes into Rob's life. She is a healer in her innocent wisdom and the novel has an ending especially welcome as a change from many violent and depressing contemporary novels." Shapiro. Fic for Youth. 3d edition

Humphreys, Josephine
Nowhere else on earth. Viking 2000 341p
ISBN 0-670-89176-2
LC 00-36666

"In 1864, Rhoda Strong is a teenager of mixed ancestry in Scuffletown, an Indian settlement on the Lumbee River, in North Carolina. As the town's inhabitants find themselves caught between marauding Union soldiers and Confederates attempting to conscript their children for labor, Rhoda falls in love with a local outlaw who is fighting to protect the community. Humphreys has always been a master of telling a larger story through a deceptively intimate narrative, and Rhoda's tale, with its clear, distinct voice, is no exception." New Yorker

Huneven, Michelle
Blame. Sarah Crichton Books 2009 291p $25
ISBN 978-0-374-11430-5; 0-374-11430-7
LC 2008-54299

"Huneven makes Patsy's story unfold like a thriller, creating a sense of urgency and mystery even about everyday matters. . . . Huneven's prose moves like a hummingbird, in small bursts that are improbably fast and graceful." N Y Times Book Rev

Hunt, Andrew
City of saints; Andrew Hunt. Minotaur Books 2012 336 p. (hardcover) $24.99
ISBN 1250015790; 9781250015792; 9781250015808
LC 2012030078

Author Andrew Hunt's book, recipient of the 2011 Hillerman Prize, is "[s]et in 1930 . . . [and] introduces Salt Lake County deputy Art Oveson, a loving family man and committed Mormon. Haunted by the unsolved murder of his father . . . Oveson is finding his way on the job when he gets involved in a complex and politically sensitive homicide. Helen Pfalzgraf . . . was repeatedly run over by a car . . . Oveson must walk a fine line to hang onto his much needed job and his professional integrity as the murder inquiry threatens to uncover some very dark secrets." (Publishers Weekly)

Hunt, Laird
The **exquisite**; a novel. Coffee House Press 2006 246p pa $14.95
ISBN 978-1-56689-187-5; 1-56689-187-6
LC 2006-11901

A tale "set in post-9/11 New York City. Henry has lost his girlfriend, his cats, and his apartment. A beautiful woman he calls Tulip sends him to Aris Kindt, an eccentric old gent fond of herring and esoteric subjects who may be the mastermind behind a mock murder service—people pay strangers to pretend to kill them. But Henry may actually be a murderer. Perhaps he's a patient in a mental ward. Aris Kindt just so happens to be the name of the thief whose body is the subject of Rembrandt's famous autopsy painting, The Anatomy Lesson. Hunt cites W. G. Sebald as the inspiration for what he calls ghost noir, although Paul Auster seems more apt. . . . The result is an edgy and labyrinthine tale of longing, madness, and death." Booklist

Hunt, Laird
Kind one; a novel. by Laird Hunt. Coffee House Press 2012 p. cm.
ISBN 9781566893114
LC 2011046602

This book follows Ginny, who is "married off at a young age to her mother's second cousin" Linus, who "quickly devolves from promising spouse to abusive master of his wife as well as two of his slaves, Cleome and Zinnia, whom the lonely Ginny befriends. . . . Eventually, Linus's reign of violence impels Ginny to" abuse the slaves as well. "But when Linus suddenly dies, the slave girls turn the tables on their brutal mistress and keep her shackled in a shed next to Linus's decaying body." (Publishers Weekly)

Hunt, Rebecca
Mr. Chartwell; a novel. Dial Press 2010 242p $24
ISBN 978-1-4000-6940-8
LC 2010-15012

"It is July 1964, and in London, young library clerk Esther Hammerhans, widowed for two years, decides to rent her late husband's study to a lodger. But when Mr. Chartwell, the prospective tenant, arrives to inspect the premises, Esther is stunned to discover that he is a dog — an enormous, hideous, and loquacious black Labrador. Known more informally as Black Pat, the animal is in town to serve his client, Sir Winston Churchill. About to retire from Parliament and live out his remaining days in his country estate — Chartwell — the 89-year-old Churchill is coping with the return of his lifelong nemesis, what he calls the 'black dog' of depression. A drooling, stinky, but coy combination of The Joker, Hannibal Lecter, and children's book character Clifford, Black Pat is that dog. And visible only to Churchill and to Esther — still raw and reeling from her husband's suicide — he is all but irresistible. . . . [This debut novel] is as delicious as it is audacious." Boston Globe

Hunt, Samantha
The **invention** of everything else. Houghton Mifflin Co. 2007 257p $24
ISBN 978-0-618-80112-1; 0-618-80112-X
LC 2007-9416

"Set in New York City in 1943, the book focuses on Nikola Tesla, the underappreciated Serbian inventor. . . . Hunt's story unfolds over the last week of Tesla's life: He is 86 years old, destitute, and maybe a little crazy. He is also, of course, a genius. Tesla is an ideal person to bring back to life through fiction; technically, he's famous, but he's also largely unfamiliar. Because his actual story is so incredible (he was pals with Mark Twain, he fell in love with a bird, he tried to invent a 'death ray'), it's tricky to separate the pieces of Hunt's account that are drawn from fact from those that she's invented. Tesla is well balanced by the entirely fictional character of Louisa, a sensible, inquisitive young chambermaid who works at the hotel and befriends the inventor after he catches her snooping through his things. A classic sort of heroine, she treats the fading man like an oracle as she juggles her own daily dramas." Village Voice

Hunter, Evan

★ The **blackboard** jungle. Simon & Schuster 1954 309p

"The author has not used his shocking material merely to appall. With a superb ear for conversation, with competence as a storyteller, and with a tolerant and tough-minded sympathy for his subject, he has built an extremely good novel." N Y Her Trib Books

Hunter, Evan

Candyland; a novel in two parts. [by] Evan Hunter and Ed McBain. Simon & Schuster 2001 301p $25

ISBN 0-7432-1316-5

LC 00-49684

This novel "is written in two parts. The first half, attributed to Hunter, probes the psyche of Benjamin Thorpe, a sexually obsessed Los Angeles architect on the prowl in New York. The second half, attributed to McBain, is a police procedural in which a detective, Emma Boyle, investigates the murder of a prostitute and identifies the architect as a prime suspect. The novel is a gimmick, and it is a surprise that it works at all. That it works so superbly is a tribute to the skills of this great storyteller." N Y Times Book Rev

Hunter, Evan

The **Chisholms**; a novel of the journey West. Harper & Row 1976 208p

This novel about the early nineteenth-century pioneer experience "tracks Hadley Chisholm and family, leaving their unproductive Virginia homeland to find a better life in California; the journey {which is followed up to their departure from Fort Laramie in Wyoming} is arduous, to say the least, for every member of the household." Booklist

"An affectingly spare, closely seen recreation of the pioneer spirit and what the search for new opportunity signified." Publ Wkly

Hunter, Evan

Lizzie. Arbor House 1984 430p

LC 83-15642

"The portrait of Lizzie that emerges is fascinating, ultimately sympathetic: a murderess yes, but the victim of the repression and sexual exploitation of her time." Libr J

Hunter, Evan

The **moment** she was gone; a novel. Simon & Schuster 2002 208p $25

ISBN 0-7432-0269-4

LC 2002-70532

"Carella and Meyer must team up on a murder investigation with Fat Ollie Weeks of the 88th because the lion habitat at the Isola Zoo straddles the boundary between the two precincts and one of the lions dragged part of a victim's body onto the 88th's turf. The body in the lion's den leads the detectives to several things: to a burglary, or at least the burglar; to some strange doings by the Secret Service; to some pretty big local drug dealers; and, finally, to some big-time dealers who don't mind leaving bodies strewn about." Libr J

Hunter, Evan

Privileged conversation. Warner Bks. 1996 326p

LC 95-11148

"Mr. Hunter is smart enough to poke fun at the book's echoes of 'Fatal Attraction.' Even better, he has a good feel for Dr. Chapman's midlife crisis and for the petty annoyances of New York social life." N Y Times Book Rev

Hunter, Madeline

The **conquest** of Lady Cassandra. Jove Books 2013 336 p. (paperback) $7.99

ISBN 0515151114; 9780515151114

In this Regency-era historical romance from RITA Award-winner Madeline Hunter, Cassandra Vernham "desperately needs the money she counted on from auctioning her jewels to keep [her aunt] Sophie safe," but the buyer of a pair of her earrings, Yates Elliston, Viscount Ambury, won't pay her. "Not only does Ambury believe the earrings are hot property, he is almost certain they were stolen from his family." (Booklist)

Hunter, Stephen

The **47th** samurai; a Bob Lee Swagger novel. Simon & Schuster 2007 372p $26

ISBN 978-0-7432-3809-0; 0-7432-3809-5

LC 2007-6627

This Bob Lee Swagger adventure "begins in the closing days of World War II, when Bob Lee's father, Earl (Havana), earns the Medal of Honor on Iwo Jima and takes a Japanese officer's samurai sword as a souvenir. Decades later, Bob returns the sword to the dead officer's son and family. But the sword turns out to be historically and politically important, and the Japanese family is slaughtered to get it. This horror causes Bob Lee to obsess about both avenging the family and retrieving the sword. In effect, he becomes a samurai, and his confrontations with the murderers are extremely bloody. Although heavy on both the explanations of Japanese customs and the sordid world of incredibly savage Japanese criminals, this work is compelling, exciting, and satisfying, a dark adventure that will appeal to thriller fans." Libr J

Hunter, Stephen

Black light. Doubleday 1996 463p

LC 95-43079

"Mr. Hunter, who is a powerful and disturbing writer, tells this unholy story in a heroic style that gives mythic sweep to the generational waves of violence that seem to have had no beginning and threaten to have no end." N Y Times Book Rev

Hunter, Stephen

Dead zero; a Bob Lee Swagger novel. Stephen Hunter. Simon & Schuster 2010 406p. (hardcover) $26.00

ISBN 9781439138656; 9781439149935; 9781439138663; 1439138656; 1439138664

LC 2010046773

Sequel to: I, sniper (2009).

In this book, "[s]everal months after the betrayal of a covert operation in Afghanistan leaves a Marine sniper team dead, the target of that mission, top Taliban commander Ibrahim Zarzi (aka 'the Beheader'), changes sides. . . . Zarzi travels to the U.S., where he meets the president and key congressional leaders and offers the State Department its best chance at achieving a stable, reliable Afghan government. Meanwhile, a Marine radio operator receives a message from Gunnery Sgt. Ray Cruz (aka 'the Cruise Missile'), one of the snipers believed to have been killed. Cruz has returned stateside to continue the mission. The FBI calls in retired Marine sniper ace Bob Lee Swagger to help find Cruz before he blows off the Beheader's head, but someone is following 'Bob the Nailer' to get to Cruz first." (Publishers Weekly)

Hunter, Stephen

★ **Dirty** white boys; a novel. Random House 1994 436p

LC 94-15359

"The blood-soaked packaging of Mr. Hunter's big, mythic theme is thrilling, in the manner of the ancient storytellers, with battles fierce enough for a war and characters crazy enough to fight them to the death. There is no place to run for cover from this author's prose—no glades of pretty writing to cool his vision of a land of lost children, forgotten values and total desolation." NY Times Book Rev

Hunter, Stephen

Havana; an Earl Swagger novel. Simon & Schuster 2003 403p $24.95

ISBN 0-7432-3808-7

LC 2003-54461

"Fifty years ago the mob was enjoying huge profits from its extensive Cuban enterprises. The only cause for concern is a young lawyer named Fidel Castro. Under the auspices of the CIA, an assassination plot is advanced and an unsuspecting Earl Swagger, a Medal of Honor winner and legendary tough guy, is brought in as the shooter. The Communists are also interested in Fidel, and Speshnev, a KGB operator, is brought in to protect their investment. Earl and Speshnev soon discover their efforts are better directed at neutralizing the mob, the corrupt government, and their respective spy agencies." Libr J

"Havana's story line bobs and weaves like a prizefighter, taking the reader in many directions, from barely exciting scenes to intense ones." USA Today

Hunter, Stephen

Hot Springs; a novel. Simon & Schuster 2000 478p $25

ISBN 0-684-86360-X

LC 99-88530

Earl Swagger is "a no-nonsense marine who was awarded the Medal of Honor for heroism on Iwo Jima. After the war, Earl works as a foreman in a sawmill. But when he is offered a job training a group of young lawmen whose mandate is to rid Hot Springs, Ark., of its mob-run gambling houses, he eagerly accepts. . . . As Earl's deputies attempt to clean up Hot Springs, Earl's fearlessness makes his boss think he has a death wish. When he hires an investigator to look into Earl's background, the pious myths that surround Earl's father, a respected Arkansas sheriff, are shattered." N Y Times Book Rev

"Once upon a time, hard-boiled implied more than a style; Hunter shows us what the real thing was all about." Booklist

Hunter, Stephen

I, sniper; a Bob Lee Swagger novel. Simon & Schuster 2009 418p $26

ISBN 978-1-4165-6515-4; 1-4165-6515-9

LC 2009-19792

"Someone is killing the aging antiwar radicals of the 1970s and using incredible sniping skills to do it. With bodies piling up, the FBI calls on the skills and knowledge of Bob Lee Swagger . . . , who quickly determines that an American war hero has been framed and then murdered. The chase is on to find out who's responsible and why. As with all of Hunter's Swagger novels, there is much more than meets the eye, with cover-ups and nasty villains galore. Swagger is a loner, a paladin, and a violent and politically incorrect corrector of injustice, a cousin to Lee Child's Jack Reacher." Libr J

Hunter, Stephen

Night of thunder; a Bob Lee Swagger novel. Simon & Schuster 2008 290p $26

ISBN 978-1-4165-6511-6; 1-4165-6511-6

LC 2008-17856

Sixty-three-year-old marksman Bob Lee Swagger is "back on the Montana farm that provides a haven for him and his family. But then he learns that his elder daughter, 24-year-old journalist Nikki, has been left in a coma after a hit-and-run near Bristol, Tenn. While local police are chalking up the accident to some teen, high on meth or NASCAR, Swagger fears that his daughter may be paying the price for his own violent past 87 kills at last count. And so it's off to the mountains of Tennessee and into the heart of the NASCAR Nation. . . . Perhaps few thriller writers out there can match Hunter's skill when it comes to writing about guns — not just in precise listings of caliber, range and impact, but in prose both lyrical and reverent. . . . Hunter succeeds as well in touching on the tragedies of the methamphetamine craze in rural America and later in capturing the throb and hum of the Bristol Motor Speedway." Washington Post Book World

Hunter, Stephen

Pale horse coming; a novel. Simon & Schuster 2001 491p

ISBN 0-684-86361-8

LC 2001-47386

In this sequel to Hot Springs, "Hunter continues the story of Arkansas state cop Earl Swagger. It's 1951, and Swagger is once again called on to clean up an evil empire. Deep in the swamps of Thebes, Mississippi, a prison for black criminals run by a gang of redneck thugs harbors a sinister conspiracy. After rescuing his friend Sam Vincent from Thebes and narrowly escaping from the prison himself, Earl gathers a team of legendary gunfighters . . . and sets out to liberate Thebes the only way he knows how—violently. . . . The character of Earl Swagger, equal parts gristle and determination, remains compelling, both as archetype and as complex human being." Booklist

Hunter, Stephen

Soft target; Stephen Hunter. Simon & Schuster 2011 256 p.

ISBN 9781439138700; 9781439138717; 9781439149942

LC 2011030150

The book, a novel, tells the story of "Ray Cruz . . . a marine sniper . . . Ray is doing a little shopping on Black Friday with his fiancée at 'America the Mall' in rural Minnesota when a gunman kills Santa Claus, and thousands of shoppers are taken hostage in the middle of the ultimate symbol of American consumerism. Terrorists, right? Well, not exactly. The leader of 'Brigade Mumbai' is just a kid who has 'always liked to wreck things.' It's up to Cruz, a human killing machine who finds himself in the wrong place at the right time (but without a gun), to neutralize the assailants before they begin to empty their automatic weapons—and before the headline hunting bureaucrats from the state police can bungle matters completely." (Booklist)

Hunter, Stephen

Time to hunt; a novel. Doubleday 1998 467p

ISBN 0-385-48043-1

LC 97-46985

"Swagger is a near-mythic character without peer in mystery fiction. He was born to soldier but longs to stop. As we revel in his adventures and triumphs, we also experience his pain." Booklist

Hurston, Zora Neale

The **complete** stories; introduction by Henry Louis Gates, Jr. and Sieglinde Lemke. HarperCollins Pubs. 1995 xxiii, 305p hardcover o.p. pa $14.99

ISBN 0-06-016732-7; 0-06-135018-4 pa

LC 91-50438

This collection of Hurston's short fiction contains nineteen stories originally published between 1921 and 1951, arranged in the order in which they were published, and seven previously unpublished stories.

Includes bibliographical references

Hurston, Zora Neale

★ **Novels** and stories. Library of Am. 1995 1041p $35

ISBN 0-940450-83-6

LC 94-25757

Companion volume to Folklore, memoirs, and other writings

This collection contains Hurston's four novels: Jonah's gourd vine, Their eyes were watching God, Moses, man of the mountain, and Seraph on the Suwanee. Also included are nine short stories

"Libraries without a complete set of Hurston's fiction will find this volume a necessary and easy purchase to fill that unfortunate gap." Booklist

Hurston, Zora Neale

★ **Their** eyes were watching God; with a foreword by Edwidge Danticat. HarperCollins Pubs. 2000 xxii, 231p $22; pa $15.95

ISBN 0-06-019949-0; 0-06-112006-0 pa

LC 00-58186

First published 1937 by Lippincott

This novel "treats social problems from a racial and feminist perspective. Janie Crawford, raised by her grandmother in rural poverty, flees her old and dictatorial husband with Joe Starks, an ambitious man who becomes the mayor of Florida's first town run by African Americans. When Joe dies, Janie falls in love with the younger Teacake and follows him to the truck farming area of the Florida swamps. In the floods following a hurricane, he is bitten by a rabid dog and, crazed, attacks Janie. She shoots him, is charged with murder, and finally exonerated. When she returns to the town she and Joe built, she tells her story to a friend." HarperCollins Reader's Ency of Am Lit

Hurwitz, Gregg

The **crime** writer. Viking 2007 301p $24.95

ISBN 978-0-670-06321-5; 0-670-06321-5

LC 2006-52822

"Successful crime-novelist Drew Danner has gained true tabloid fame-as the murderer of his ex-fiance. Found by the police in the midst of a brain-tumor-induced grand mal seizure, with her blood covering his hands and his fingerprints on the murder weapon, Danner seems to be the only person in L.A. who isn't sure he is a killer. Emergency surgery after his arrest removes the tumor, and a temporary insanity defense frees him, but his comfortable life is shattered. He can't live without knowing if he killed a woman he once loved. His only choice is to become a character in a story he hasn't written. Danner's anguish is compellingly described, and the plot has more twists and turns than Mulholland Drive." Booklist

Hurwitz, Gregg

The **survivor**; Gregg Hurwitz. 1st ed. St. Martin's Press 2012 374 p. (paperback) $9.99; (hardcover) $25.99

ISBN 9781250029430; 0312625510; 9780312625511; 9781250009722

LC 2012013914

Library Journal Best Thrillers: 2012

This novel by Gregg Hurwitz follows "36-year-old Nate Overbay. Diagnosed with Lou Gehrig's disease . . . Nate is about to leap off an 11th-floor ledge of a bank building . . . when he notices a robbery in progress. . . . In revenge, the thwarted theft's mastermind, a notorious Ukrainian mobster, vows to brutally kill Nate and his teenage daughter unless Nate can retrieve the robbery's objective: an envelope stored in one of the bank's safe deposit boxes." (Publishers Weekly)

Hurwitz, Gregg
They're watching. St. Martin's 2010 357p $24.99

ISBN 978-0-312-53490-5; 0-312-53490-6

LC 2009-47039

"This is a very well constructed thriller, full of twists and turns and unexpected revelations. Hurwitz frequently sets us up to expect one thing but delivers something entirely different. He keeps us constantly on our toes, and—this is especially good—he keeps us guessing right until the very last pages about exactly who has targeted Patrick and why. Highly recommended, especially for fans of Dean Koontz, Linwood Barclay, and Harlan Coben." Booklist

Hurwitz, Gregg
You're next. St. Martin's Press 2011 407p $24.99

ISBN 978-0-312-53491-2

LC 2011-06869

The Boss Man has an unexpected motive in destroying Mike Wingate, who's worked his way up from the bottom to become a successful home contractor in Lost Hills, California. To protect his family and himself, Mike, who was raised in a foster home, summons his only friend from those days, the formidable Shep, who has grown up to be a career criminal of considerable skill.

"A thriller that grabs readers by the seat of the pants and gives them a Wow, what next! action thrill ride." Kirkus

Huston, Charlie
Already dead. Ballantine Books 2005 268p map pa $14

ISBN 0-345-47824-X

LC 2004-62323

"Huston's intricate, fast-paced, Chandleresque vampire-crime story has plenty of action, violence, and raw language. An excellent story but not for the squeamish in public libraries." Libr J

Huston, Charlie
Caught stealing. Ballantine Books 2004 240p

ISBN 0-345-46477-X

LC 2004-299530

"Having fled California for New York City after an injury cut short his promising baseball career, Hank Thompson settles into an aimless life as an alcoholic bartender. Still, Hank prides himself on making Manhattan a bit more hospitable by helping his friends, so how can he refuse when a neighbor asks him to cat-sit? One lost kidney later, Hank realizes that an Elmore Leonardesque collection of Russian mobsters, short-fused cons, and renegade cops will snuff out all 10 lives he and the cat share between them if that's what it takes to find the not-so-good neighbor. . . . [This book]

definitely belongs on every Elmore Leonard fan's to-read list. One note of caution: Lovers of mystery-solving felines should place paws over eyes during the hair-raising cat torture scene." Booklist

Huston, Charlie
Every last drop; a novel. Del Rey 2008 252p il pa $14

ISBN 978-0-345-49588-4; 0-345-49588-8

LC 2008-26441

New York vampire PI Joe Pitt "has been exiled to the South Bronx. He's doing his best to keep a low profile and eke out enough of a living to keep him in blood, bullets and smokes. It's not easy. He's there on sufferance — despite the tolerance and interest of local boss Esperanza — and he's down to his last three bullets. Staying out of trouble doesn't come naturally to him either. So when Dexter Predo of the Coalition offers him a chance to go back to Manhattan, Joe takes it. Sure, Predo wants him dead but it's not like he's the only one. Joe is sent to spy on Manhattan's new vampire clan: the Cure. They were set up by Amanda Horde a broken, brilliant, teenage millionaire with a soft spot for Pitt — and are dedicated to finding a cure for Vyrus, the cause and carrier of vampirism. Some vampires consider the Cure to be heretics, others, like the Coalition, consider them a threat to the status quo. Dexter Predo wants to know what they are doing and what they have planned for the future. . . . [Huston] has crafted a riveting and enjoyable story." SF Site

Huston, Charlie
Half the blood of Brooklyn; a novel. Del Rey/Ballantine Books 2008 223p map pa $13.95

ISBN 978-0-345-49587-7

LC 2007-28330

"Huston's third Joe Pitt vampire novel . . . takes his Manhattan-based hardboiled hero on a dangerous trip into the undead communities across the bridge in Brooklyn. The various vampire clans in New York are on the brink of conflict. Leadership has fallen apart, and to make things worse, a 'Van Helsing' is running amok and has recently murdered a longtime supplier of contraband blood. Worst of all, Pitt's AIDS-stricken girlfriend, Evie, is in the hospital failing fast. . . . Huston's formidable writing chops are on full display: his action scenes are unparalleled in crime fiction and his dialogue is so hip and dead-on that Elmore Leonard should be getting nervous." Publ Wkly

Huston, Charlie
The mystic arts of erasing all signs of death. Ballantine Books 2009 319p $25

ISBN 978-0-345-50111-0; 0-345-50111-X

LC 2008-35293

"Oddly, given the willfully grisly subject matter and the rocket-like propulsive quality of Huston's short sentences (a paragraph with more than five lines in it comes to seem almost Proustian), this is a book with something tender and almost mushy at its core. The real subjects here are grief and the quest for friendship and family. . . . The dialogue is terrific . . . and Huston is excellent too on Los Angeles. He doesn't so much evoke the city as allow a sense of it to sink into his prose like blood into a carpet." Los Angeles Times Book Rev

Huston, Charlie

The **shotgun** rule; a novel. Ballantine Books 2007 248p $21.95

ISBN 978-0-345-48135-1; 0-345-48135-6

LC 2007-20511

"In the summer of 1983, four teenage boys (a brainiac, a punk rocker, an army wannabe, and an ex-drug-runner) reclaim their stolen bicycle. They also find a crystal-meth lab and rip-off a half a kilo to sell and perhaps buy their dream car with. The dope-pimp Arroyo brothers—led by obese stoner-hippie, Geezer—kick off a vengeful search. Mayhem, much of it over-the-top and delivered in gruesome detail—rocks the California suburb, and dysfunctional parents deal with their own demons while the boys prove surprisingly clever in a tough spot. From a sharp pitch, staccato dialogue and volatile action, durable characters and an intricate plot emerge, demonstrating Huston can still deliver the expected thriller goods." Paste

Huston, Charlie

Skinner; Charlie Huston. Mulholland Books/ Little, Brown and Company 2013 400 p. (hardback) $26

ISBN 0316133728; 9780316133722

LC 2013001055

This novel by Charlie Huston focuses on Skinner, who "founded his career in 'asset protection' on fear. An . . . effective methodology, until Skinner's CIA handlers began to fear him as much as his enemies did and banished him. Now, [a] . . . cyber-terrorist attack is about to end that long exile. His asset is Jae, a roboticist with a gift for seeing the underlying systems violently shaping a new era of global guerrilla warfare." (Publisher's note)

Huston, Charlie

Sleepless; a novel. Ballantine Books 2010 353p $25

ISBN 978-0-345-50113-4; 0-345-50113-6

LC 2009-36889

In this "thriller set in a postapocalyptic Los Angeles, a devastating illness renders the afflicted unable to sleep. In about a year, those with SLP (as the sleepless illness is known) deteriorate and die. Amid the citys rampant violence and lawlessness, LAPD cop Parker 'Park' Haas tries to persuade himself that a future exists for his newborn daughter. As the outside world becomes increasingly dangerous, Park pursues an undercover investigation that takes him deep into the milieu of an online game called Chasm Tide, into which many people have retreated." Publ Wkly

"A writer as skilled as Huston . . . can make an apocalyptic story terrifyingly plausible. Readers prone to depression should approach with care." Kirkus

Huston, Nancy

Infrared; Nancy Huston. McArthur 2011 264 p. $14.00

ISBN 9780802120274; 1770870296

LC 2011505436

This novel, by Nancy Huston, is a "story about a passionate yet emotionally-wounded woman's sexual explorations. . . . After a troubled childhood and two failed marriages, Rena Greenblatt has achieved success as a photographer. . . . Away from her lover, and stuck in Florence, Italy, with her infuriating stepmother and her aging, unwell father, Rena . . . finds herself traveling into dark and passionate memories that will lead to disturbing revelations." (Publisher's note)

Hustvedt, Siri

The **sorrows** of an American; a novel. Henry Holt and Co. 2008 306p $25

ISBN 978-0-8050-7908-1; 0-8050-7908-4

LC 2007-31046

"The novel opens with narrator Erik Davidsen, a psychiatrist, and his sister Inga, an academic, flying from New York City home to Minnesota, where the pair begins the painful process of sorting through the study of their deceased father, Lars. . . [This] is a novel of secrets and ghosts: Lars' ghosts, which follow him back to Minnesota after his service in World War II; Erik, divorced, lonely, plagued by a patient's suicide; the widowed Inga, who learns her husband, famous writer Max Blaustein, led a secret life during their tumultuous marriage. Even Sonia, Inga's 18-year-old daughter, carries painful burdens, including what she saw from her schoolroom window on September 11, 2001. . . . In a lesser writer's hands, this glut of thematic material could wind a novel into a hopeless knot. Hustvedt's facility is such that instead, we are lead through the inseparable interactions of mind and body as her characters move through the story. The effect is exhilarating rather than jarring, as events urge us forward, each secret offering up a truth that in turn unlocks another door." PopMatters

Hustvedt, Siri

What I loved; a novel. Holt & Co. 2003 370p $25

ISBN 0-8050-7170-9

LC 2002-27358

"The imprint of Henry James turns out to have reference not to the novel's prose style, which is cleanly colloquial, but to a tragic vision in which surface decorum hides subterranean upheaval. 'What I Loved' is a rare thing, a page turner written at full intellectual stretch, serious but witty, large-minded and morally engaged." N Y Times Book Rev

Huxley, Aldous, 1894-1963

★ **Brave** new world; a novel. Doubleday, Doran & Co. 1932 311p

"The ironic title, which Huxley has taken from Shakespeare's The Tempest, describes a world in which science has taken control over morality and humaneness. In this utopia humans emerge from test tubes, families are obsolete, and even pleasure is regulated. When a so-called savage who believes in spirituality is found and is imported to the community, he cannot accommodate himself to this world and ends his life." Shapiro. Fic for Youth. 3d edition

Huxley, Aldous, 1894-1963

Collected short stories. Harper & Row 1957 397p

Huxley, Aldous

★ **Point** counter point. Doubleday, Doran & Co. 1928 432p

The book "presents a satiric picture of London intellectuals and members of English upper-class society during the 1920's. Frequent allusions to literature, painting, music, and contemporary British politics occur throughout the book, and much scientific information is embodied in its background. The story is long and involved, with many characters; it concerns a series of broken marriages and love affairs, and a political assassination. The construction is elaborate, supposedly based on Bach's 'Suite No. 2 in B Minor.' It is also a novel within a novel. Philip Quarles a leading character . . . is himself planning a novel, which echoes or 'counterpoints' the events going on around him." Reader's Ency. 4th edition

Huyler, Frank

The **laws** of invisible things. H. Holt 2004 320p $25

ISBN 0-8050-7330-2

LC 2003-51116

This novel "focuses on Michael Grant, a newly divorced doctor who has just moved to North Carolina and joined the practice of widower Ronald Gass, a much older physician. Grant's lonely personal life is soon in turmoil as it intersects with the black Williams family. Soon after his arrival, Grant treats the granddaughter of Rev. Thomas Williams; the little girl dies, probably due to an oversight by Grant. As a favor to the minister, Grant agrees to see his son Jonas, the girl's father, who has bizarre symptoms that Grant thinks may indicate a previously unknown disease; Gass is skeptical, almost scornful of this idea. Within days, Gass dies of natural causes, Jonas is dead from the disease, and Grant himself is hospitalized with the same symptoms." Libr J

Hyland, M. J.

Carry me down. Canongate 2006 334p $23

ISBN 1-84195-740-2

"At 11, John Egan is nearly six feet tall with a deep voice, and he feels like a freak, especially after he wets himself in class. John believes he is a gifted human lie detector, and he himself is a great liar; his obsession is to be famous and have his gift recognized in the Guinness Book of World Records. But why is Dad lying? The child's naive first-person, present-tense narrative brings achingly close his helplessness in a powerful adult world. He may be a giant, but he has no control. Why suddenly is the family moving? Where to? What is wrong? When they land up in the public-housing projects in Dublin, the scary threat seems to be from a brutal street gang, but the real terror turns out to be in the intimacy of his home. Focused on small things, the quiet plain scenes of daily life lead to the surprising and unforgettable climax." Booklist

Hynes, James

Kings of infinite space. St. Martin's Press 2004 341p $24.95

ISBN 0-312-45645-X

LC 2003-58563

This "is social satire that slides smoothly and surreally into horror, and if it loses a little of its emotional heft in the process, you don't really miss it. The glee with which Hynes choreographs an in-office zombie-vs.-stapler fight scene is compensation enough." Time

Hynes, James

★ The **lecturer's** tale. Picador 2001 388p $25

ISBN 0-312-20332-2

LC 00-47836

"The protagonist is Nelson Humboldt, a once bright star in the English department at Midwest University but now reduced to teaching composition classes. Never one to publish much, Nelson's academic career is on the verge of perishing. That is until he realizes he has accidentally (in the literal sense) acquired a magic power over people that allows him to bend them to his will." Booklist

"The culture wars of the ivory tower may be well-charted waters, but Hynes wades in with Swiftian glee." Am Book Rev

Hynes, James

★ **Next**; a novel. Little, Brown and Co. 2010 308p $23.99

ISBN 978-0-316-05192-7; 0-316-05192-6

LC 2009-08490

"This is a book that begins innocently and is careful not to tip its hand, even though there's something very unusual at work. The title signals nothing. The cover art depicts an empty sky. Blurbs on the back allow four very different writers to skip the hosannas and cut to the chase. They find roundabout ways to say that Next took nerve to write, is much more potent than it may initially appear and has an ending that beggars description." N Y Times (Late N Y Ed)

Høeg, Peter

The **elephant** keepers' children; Peter Høeg; translated from the Danish by Martin Aitken. Other Press 2012 499 p. (hardcover: acid-free paper) $27.95

ISBN 1590514904; 9781590514900; 9781590514917

LC 2012015734

This book by Peter Hoeg "concerns two children, 14-year-old Peter and his older . . . sister, Tilte, who go on the run from the authorities . . . following their parents' mysterious disappearance. The parents work in their hometown church . . . where miracles may have occurred during the father's sermons; lately, they have become involved with shady business dealings as well. . . . The children learn . . . that a theft of priceless religious artifacts may be in the works." (Library Journal)

I

Iagnemma, Karl

The **expeditions**; a novel. Dial Press 2008 322p $24

ISBN 978-0-385-33595-9; 0-385-33595-4

LC 2007-18324

"Emotionally powerful and beautifully wrought. . . . One of this novel's many and considerable strengths is the way in which the author refuses to stack the decks for or against either of his protagonists or their prospective ideas—the man of faith and the man of science. Each has his flaws and each his admirable strengths." Los Angeles Times Book Rev

Iagnemma, Karl

On the nature of human romantic interaction. Dial Press (NY) 2003 212cm il $22.95

ISBN 0-385-33593-8

LC 2003-40953

"The meticulousness of science and mathematics is applied to the mysteries of love in Iagnemma's debut collection, which features eight complex, multilayered stories in which protagonists try to balance the demands of the heart against their need for rational, orderly thinking." Publ Wkly

Ignatius, David

Bloodmoney; David Ignatius. W.W. Norton & Co. 2011 372p.

ISBN 9780393078114; 0393078116; 9780393341799

LC 2011003003

This book tells the story of "Sophie Marx, a CIA officer working for the Hit Parade, a new agency offshoot for covert action. Operating well beyond the reach of headquarters, the Hit Parade's minions roam the globe under deep cover with bags of cash and unorthodox marching orders: Buy peace in the borderlands, warlord by warlord. But the Hit Parade has sprung a leak in Pakistan, and its operatives have begun to disappear. Marx must find the leak and plug it before one of two things happens: Either all of the Hit Parade's people are wiped out or the rest of the world discovers all the illegal things they've been up to." (washingtonpost.com)

Ignatius, David

Body of lies; a novel. W.W. Norton & Co. 2007 349p $24.95

ISBN 978-0-393-06503-9; 0-393-06503-0

LC 2006-102362

"Unlike most of the folks writing fiction about the CIA these days, [Ignatius] understands the gestalt of the place and the internal and external pressure under which the agency's denizens operate." Washington Times

Ignatius, David

A **firing** offense. Random House 1997 333p

LC 96-29518

"Thanks to great writing and an all-too-human protagonist, the preaching is kept to a minimum, but the sermon—about good journalism and bad, truth and lies—is there in bold letters." Publ Wkly

Ignatius, David

The **increment**; a novel. W.W. Norton & Co. 2009 390p $26.95

ISBN 978-0-393-06504-6

LC 2008-53857

The author "immerses readers in a totally believable universe. Jargon, geography and detail all ring true as his meticulously crafted, tightly woven tale moves from Washington to London and Iran. The plot grabs everything in its path like a snowball rolling down a hill." Kirkus

Ignatius, David

The **Sun** King; a novel. Random House 1999 305p

ISBN 0-679-44861-6

LC 99-13490

"A thoroughly involving narrative with a sharp, satiric edge, Ignatius's contemporary take on the tragic confluence of love, power and ambition is a sophisticated look at the media mystique and the movers and shakers in our nation's capitol. His stylish, fluent prose, anchored with fine atmospheric detail, gives the story texture and momentum." Publ Wkly

Iles, Greg

Black cross. Dutton 1995 516p

LC 94-34642

This novel "tells the story of a physician from Georgia and a German Jew who manage to forestall Hitler's use of poison nerve gas during World War II by destroying a secret laboratory hidden in a Nazi death camp. The rash plan for infiltrating the camp and destroying the laboratory has been developed by the Allies and led by Winston Churchill and will require nerves of steel, physical and emotional stamina, unparalleled bravery, and incredible luck. If it works, millions of lives will be saved. But there is a horrible price to pay for the larger victory—hundreds of Jewish prisoners interred in the camp may also die. From the very first page, Iles takes his readers on an emotional roller-coaster ride, juxtaposing tension-filled action scenes, horrifying depictions of savage cruelty, and heart-stopping descriptions of sacrifice and bravery." Booklist

Iles, Greg

The **devil's** punchbowl. Scribner 2009 580p $26.99

ISBN 978-0-7432-9251-1; 0-7432-9251-0

LC 2008-49551

Penn Cage, "a former prosecuting attorney-turned-novelist, is now mayor of Natchez, MS, his hometown. But all is not well, for the promises he made as a candidate seem all but impossible to achieve as a working mayor. When one of his childhood friends is murdered a day after contacting him with information concerning dog fighting, prostitution, drugs, and money laundering presided over by the manager of a Natchez gambling casino, Cage takes on an investigation that makes him the target of organized crime, endangers the lives of his family and closest friends, and draws the wrath of the Justice Department and Homeland Security.... Provides a thrill a minute." Libr J

Iles, Greg

The **footprints** of God. Scribner 2003 459p $25.95

ISBN 0-7432-3469-3

LC 2003-45733

"Readers interested in the exploration of religious themes without the usual New Age blather or window-dressed dogma will snap up this novel of cutting-edge science." Publ Wkly

Iles, Greg

Mortal fear. Dutton 1997 564p

ISBN 978-0525937920

LC 97-194514

"Despite the artifice of the characters operating it, the technology involved in their ingenious computer chase—

which gives new meaning to the term 'network'—is fascinating." N Y Times Book Rev

Iles, Greg

Third degree. Scribner 2007 385p $25.95
ISBN 978-0-7432-9250-4; 0-7432-9250-2

LC 2007-48097

"When Laurel Shields, a 35-year-old mother of two, discovers she's pregnant, she can't be sure her physician husband, Warren, is the father. Meanwhile, Warren is in trouble with the IRS. Laurel believes his obsessive search for a document in their Athens Point, Miss., home is related to a federal Medicaid fraud investigation focusing on his medical partner, Kyle Auster. As the Feds prepare to swoop down on Warren and Kyle's office to collect the evidence of false billings and bribes to patients without any actual illnesses, Warren takes Laurel and their two children hostage. Iles squeezes every drop of suspense out of the prolonged standoff between the doctor and the police." Publ Wkly

Iles, Greg

Turning angel. Scribner 2005 501p $25.95
ISBN 0-7432-3471-5

LC 2005-54469

"All this is lurid in the extreme and, in Iles's hands, entirely gripping, but there is more to Turning Angel than sex and scandal. Iles offers an insider's heartfelt picture of a Southern town that is dying because of lousy schools, a failing economy and racial tensions–and, again, there is no reason to think Natchez is unique. Iles populates this town with characters who are all too real and makes clear that its privileged young people no longer live isolated lives. . . . This is a powerful piece of popular fiction." Washington Post Book World

Indridason, Arnaldur

Outrage; an Inspector Erlendur novel. Arnaldur Indridason; translated from the Icelandic by Anna Yates. Minotaur Books 2012 281 p.
ISBN 0312659113; 9780312659110; 9781250012760

LC 2012035781

In this novel by Arnaldur Indridason "Detective Erlunder decides to take a short leave of absence, putting a female detective, Elínborg, in charge while he is gone. . . . [S] he's quickly thrust into a violent and volatile situation with extremely high stakes. Soon, her investigation uncovers a twisted tale of double lives that may be connected to the unsolved disappearance of a young girl. The clock is ticking to solve the case before a serial rapist strikes again." (Publisher's note)

Inman, Robert

Captain Saturday; a novel. Little, Brown 2002 455p $24.95
ISBN 0-316-41502-2

LC 2001-23529

"Peopled with vivid, endearlingly quixotic characters and filled with dead-on insights into a shallow New South that defines itself by club memberships and designer labels, this richly textured epic is paean to the vagaries of the human heart." Publ Wkly

Innes, Hammond

★ The **wreck** of the Mary Deare. Knopf 1956 296p

"When narrator John Sands first sights the freighter 'Mary Deare' from the deck of his salvage boat, she appears to be a ghostly derelict drifting toward the Channel reefs. Boarding her, however, he encounters her specter-ridden captain, Gideon Patch, and becomes dangerously involved in the suspect seaman's desperate attempt to expose the conspiracy behind her last voyage." Booklist

Inness-Brown, Elizabeth

Burning Marguerite. Knopf 2002 237p $23
ISBN 0-375-41196-8

LC 2001-29860

"When James Jack finds his 94-year-old Tante Marguerite frozen in the snow outside their house on a remote New England island, he sets out to give her the very private funeral she desired. . . . The narrative jumps from James Jack's point of view to Marguerite's, as gradually we learn the tragedy of her young life, which led to a period of exile in New Orleans and finally to her return to the isolated island, where she raised James Jack after the sudden death of his parents. This is a remarkably quiet novel, one that draws its power and beauty as much from silence as from human interaction." Booklist

Irving, John, 1942-

3 by Irving. Random House 1980 718p

LC 79-5536

The first of these novels "involves a madcap scheme to liberate zoo animals, the second chronicles the misadventures of a bungling graduate student, and the third features a ménage-à-quatre in academe. . . . Irving's early fictions are noteworthy not only as forerunners to the remarkable Garp but also on their own merits. Possessing much of the same narrative inventiveness, zany wit, and sheer verve that so distinguish Irving's best-seller, they also maintain a Garp-like balance between the humorous and the macabre." Choice

Irving, John

The **cider** house rules; a novel. Modern Library 1999 571p $24.95
ISBN 978-0-679-60335-1; 0-679-60335-2

LC 99-30034

First published 1985 by Morrow

"The Cider House Rules is filled with people to love and to feel for. . . . The characters in John Irving's novel break all the rules, and yet they remain noble and free-spirited. Victims of tragedy, violence, and injustice, their lives seem more interesting and full of thought-provoking dilemmas than the lives of many real people." Houston Post

Irving, John

The **fourth** hand; a novel. Random House 2001 316p
ISBN 0-375-50627-6

LC 2001-18155

This novel's hero, "Patrick Wallingford, is a television reporter whose left hand is eaten by a lion while he is covering a story about the circus in India. Patrick eventually receives a transplanted hand from a man named Otto Clausen, who accidentally shot himself. . . . Otto's widow, Doris, who has chosen Patrick to be the hand recipient, not only declares that she has visiting rights with her late husband's hand, but also sexually assaults Patrick in order to become pregnant with his child." N Y Times

"Irving's set pieces are on that high level of American gothic comedy he has made uniquely his own." Publ Wkly

Irving, John, 1942-

★ **In** one person; a novel. John Irving. Simon & Schuster 2012 425 p.

ISBN 9781451664126; 9781451664133; 9781451664157

LC 2011039707

The novel tells a story of Billy, a boy growing up in the town of First Sister, Vermont in the 1960s, who comes to realize that he is bisexual. John Irving reintroduces "his signature motifs (New England life, wrestling, praising great writers, forbidden sex) while animating a . . . cast of misfit characters within a complicated plot. . . . Billy navigates fraught relationships with men and women and witnesses the horrors of the AIDS epidemic." (Booklist)

Irving, John

The **Hotel** New Hampshire. Dutton 1981 401p

LC 81-2610

The author "keeps us moving, sacrificing rhetoric to pace, as in the most primitive narrative forms, the fable and the fairy tale. In fiction like this, meaning lies near the surface of the story and in the voice of the storyteller." New Repub

Irving, John

Last night in Twisted River; a novel. Random House 2009 554p $28

ISBN 978-1-4000-6384-0; 1-4000-6384-1

LC 2009-14449

"The story, told over five decades starting in 1954, centers on Dominic Baciagalupo, a logging-camp cook; his son, Daniel, who eventually becomes a writer with the pen name Danny Angel; and Dominic's best friend, Ketchum, a tough and loyal logger. Last Night's sentimental tone is established early — the logging industry is struggling, and Dominic is a single father whose wife died in a tragic accident. The logging camp is idyllic in a rustic way — until an incident featuring an eight-inch skillet, a bear, and a philandering sous-chef drives father and son on the lam. Their flight never ends, really — the vengeful force that sends them running is implacable, and wherever Dominic and Daniel run, they can never truly settle. . . . The real story is that Irving, defying the precepts of critics once again, has created another sprawling, sentimental, emotional tale, the kind that readers crave, however snooty or pedestrian their tastes." Entertainment Wkly

Irving, John

★ A **prayer** for Owen Meany; a novel. Modern Library 2002 xxiv, 641p $24.95

ISBN 0-679-64259-5

LC 2002-26479

First published 1989 by Morrow

This novel is set in New Hampshire in the 1950s and 1960s. Owen Meany is a short boy with a squeaky voice,

who foresees his own death and sees himself as an instrument of God. He hits a baseball that kills the mother of John Wheelwright, the novel's narrator. Because of Owen, John becomes a Christian

"Despite its theological proppings, A Prayer for Owen Meany is a fable of political predestination. As usual, Irving delivers a boisterous cast, a spirited story line and a quality of prose that is frequently underestimated even by his admirers. On the other hand, the novel invites trespass by symbol hunters. . . . To get lost in critical rummage would be to miss the point. Irving's litany of error and folly may strike some as too righteous; but it is effective." Time

Irving, John

A **son** of the circus. Random House 1994 633p

LC 93-44750

Irving "is at the peak of his powers in this new novel. He plunges the reader into one sensual or grotesque scene after another with cheerful vigour and a madcap tenderness for life. . . . The author knows what he is doing from first to last, and handles the dozens of strands of his plot with exuberant ease." Economist

Irving, John

Until I find you; a novel. Random House 2005 824p $27.95

ISBN 1-400-06383-3

"The fatal difference between Irving and his master is that in a Dickens novel the smallest components are thematically and even poetically tied to the central idea, rather than unnecessary and irrelevant. Still, Irving is a skillful, powerful writer, and his novels are nearly always worth the considerable time they demand. His latest, Until I Find You, is in many ways characteristic: generous, sprawling, vivid, and, as with all his work, quintessentially masculine." New Leader

Irving, John

A **widow** for one year; a novel. Random House 1998 537p

ISBN 0-375-50137-1

LC 97-49166

"It is clearly not the outline of the plot that makes the book obstinately memorable. Rather, it is Irving's special gift for farcical incident . . . his piercing sense of the wonderful and terrible vulnerability of children, his poetic evocation of the ravages of time." Publ Wkly

Irving, John

★ The **world** according to Garp. Dutton 1978 437p

LC 77-15564

This "is a long family novel, spanning four generations and two continents, crammed with incidents, characters, feelings and craft. The components of black comedy and melodrama, pathos and tragedy, mesh effortlessly in a tale that can also be read as a commentary on art and the imagination." Time

Irving, Washington

★ The **complete** tales of Washington Irving. Doubleday 1975 xxxvii, 798p

Irwin, Stephen M.

The **broken** ones; a novel. Stephen M. Irwin. 1st American ed. Doubleday 2012 356 p. (hardcover) $26.00; (ebook) $78.00; (paperback) $15.95
ISBN 0385534655; 9780385534659; 9780385534666; 9780307744449

LC 2011039733

In this book by Stephen M. Irwin, "the world is reeling from a natural disaster that occurred a few years earlier. In just one day, Earth's poles shifted to affect climate, agriculture, and governmental infrastructure and setting off a global economic crisis. This event is known as Gray Wednesday, the day when the spectral and living worlds became one. . . . Each person is haunted by a ghost, someone from his or her past." (Library Journal)

Irwin, Stephen M.

The **dead** path; a novel. Doubleday 2010 374p $25.95
ISBN 978-0-385-53343-0; 0-385-53343-8

LC 2009-53661

First published 2009 in Australia

"Irwin writes in a lyrical style that expresses both the poignancy of Nicholas's distressing supernatural experiences and the mood of horror those experiences conjure." Publ Wkly

Isaacs, Susan

After all these years. HarperCollins Pubs. 1993 343p

LC 92-56200

Isaacs "has a field day lampooning upper-class mores . . . but also weaves into this thoroughly diverting caper unexpected moments of genuine tenderness and sly social commentary." Publ Wkly

Isaacs, Susan

Almost paradise. Harper & Row 1984 483p

LC 83-48357

"Nicholas is the scion of a wealthy family, although Jane's bloodline is anything but aristocratic. They marry after Jane convinces Nick that his true talent lies with acting rather than law. In no time Nick is the rage of Broadway and Hollywood. The marriage remains idyllic until Jane develops a fear of crowds so great she is unable to walk to her own mailbox. But she continues to make their Connecticut farmhouse the ideal place for her husband to entertain his many guests. The arrangement works for twenty years, as Nick resists the attempts of countless women to seduce him. Nick finally succumbs to a timid film student and Jane takes up with her shrink." West Coast Rev Books

Isaacs, Susan

As husbands go; a novel. Scribner 2010 342p $25
ISBN 978-1-4165-7301-2; 1-4165-7301-1

LC 2009-52241

"The mystery is barely there, but Isaacs' fans will enjoy another sharp-tongued romp through the New York privileged classes and their foibles." Kirkus

Isaacs, Susan

Close relations. Lippincott 1980 270p

LC 80-7858

"Besides being simultaneously romantic, feminist, and political, the novel is also a satire: of Jewish mothers and success-orientation, late-marrying Irishmen, American political campaigns, WASP mores, and human relations." Best Sellers

Isaacs, Susan

★ **Compromising** positions. Times Bks. 1978 248p

LC 77-13896

"Judith Singer is a nice, average Jewish housewife—on the surface—but beneath that placid exterior lurks a secret longing for high adventure. . . . When a local dentist-Lothario is murdered in his office and a neighbor who was his last patient is a suspect, Judith cannot resist getting into the act. Meddling, gossiping, she turns detective, and when she learns that the elegant late Dr. Fleckstein was not only bedding virtually every woman in town but getting them to pose for exceedingly porno photos, there's no stopping her. Enter detective Nelson Sharpe, much more attractive than Judith's stodgy husband. The two make a wild pair of sleuths as Sharpe tracks down the murderer and an accomplice and exposes smug suburban hypocrisy." Publ Wkly

Isaacs, Susan

Lily White; a novel. HarperCollins Pubs. 1996 459p
ISBN 978-0060176075

LC 96-17399

"Susan Isaac's real subject here isn't murder or legal thrills, of course, but the drama and suspense of middle-class women's lives. In her rendition, it's white-knuckle stuff." N Y Times Book Rev

Isaacs, Susan

Magic hour. HarperCollins Pubs. 1991 412p

LC 90-55570

"Best of all . . . is the subplot, an old-fashioned love story (think 1940s movie) in which Brady falls hard for his leading suspect, the dead producer's first wife. There's no good reason why we should buy into this romance—it rests on a totally improbable premise—but Isaacs sets the hook and reels us in anyway." Booklist

Isaacs, Susan

Red, white and blue; a novel. HarperCollins Pubs. 1998 402p
ISBN 0-06-017608-3

LC 98-34568

"It is no easy task to hold a reader's attention when a novel's outcome is obvious from the very first page. But Susan Isaacs has such a knack for entertaining her reader with the details of American pop culture . . . that it's easy to be distracted from the predictability of her plot." N Y Times Book Rev

Isaacs, Susan

Shining through. Harper & Row 1988 402p

ISBN 0-06-015979-0

LC 87-45630

"Linda Voss is a 31-year-old secretary to the dreamiest looking man on Wall Street, international lawyer John Berringer, with whom she is secretly and hopelessly in love: she is a poor girl from Queens, and he boasts an Ivy League background along with his perfect profile. When circumstances lead to their unlikely marriage, however, sexual fireworks keep them together. As World War II engulfs Europe, the Berringers move to Washington, where both become involved in undercover work for the COI, soon to become the OSS. Heartbreak, plus a feeling of kinship for the victims of Nazism, leads Linda, whose childhood was spent in a German-speaking household, to volunteer for a dangerous mission in Berlin." Publ Wkly

"Whether completely believable or not, Isaacs' tale of bravery and romance makes exciting, entertaining reading." Booklist

Isegawa, Moses

Snakepit. Knopf 2004 259p $24

ISBN 0-375-41454-1

LC 2003-60479

This novel is "set in Uganda in the 1970s. . . . Bat Kaanga is a Ugandan just returned to his homeland after two years in Britain. While he completed a postgraduate degree at Cambridge, he watched from afar as 'flag independence [gave] way to economic independence' in Uganda, his chances to make a fortune there increasing with each 'reform' imposed by Idi Amin. Now, when Bat lands a job as Bureaucrat Two in the Ministry of Power and Communications, he feels himself entering the top echelons of government." Publisher's note

"This is a headlong and blurry novel filled with violence and sex, deceit and revenge-a messy, captivating portrait of a desperate time and place." Publ Wkly

Isherwood, Christopher

★ The **Berlin** stories; The last of Mr. Norris; Goodbye to Berlin. with a preface by the author. New Directions 1954 2v in 1

The two titles included in this combined edition were originally published separately; the first in 1935 in the United Kingdom with title: Mr. Norris changes trains and the latter in 1939 by Random House, which is analyzed in Short story index

Goodbye to Berlin contains six short stories or sketches of life in Berlin in the last years before Hitler came to power. Though written in first person by one calling himself Christopher Isherwood, according to the author's statement, the material is not to be regarded as autobiographical. The sketches are entitled: A Berlin diary (Autumn 1930); Sally Bowles; On Ruegan Island (Summer 1931); The Nowaks; The Landauers; A Berlin diary (Winter 1932-3)

The last of Mr. Norris, set in Berlin during Hitler's rise to power, "is the story of the narrator's innocent friendship with odd, corrupt Mr. Norris. While pretending to be a sincere Communist, Mr. Norris is actually selling information to fascists and foreigners. Mr. Norris's masochistic sexual aberrations add to the impression that he is a symbol of the whole corrupt, disintegrating society." Reader's Ency. 4th edition

Ishiguro, Kazuo

An **artist** of the floating world. Putnam 1986 206p

ISBN 0-399-13119-1

LC 85-25759

"Like figures on a Japanese screen, the painter Masuji Ono and his daughters Setsuko and Noriko are fixed in the formal attitudes that even their private conversations reflect. In the postwar 1940s, the father is a relic of traditional Japan, of teahouses, geishas and patterned gardens not yet destroyed by industry and Westernized thinking. He is unable to communicate with his daughters, unsure of the propriety of his wartime nationalism yet unwilling to exchange it for what seem to him doubtful modern values." Publ Wkly

"The tensions stay tight. And this is what makes Mr. Ishiguro not only a good writer but also a wonderful novelist." N Y Times Book Rev

Ishiguro, Kazuo

Never let me go. Knopf 2005 288p

ISBN 1400043395

LC 2004048966

This is a novel by the author of The Remains of the Day (1989). "Kathy, Ruth and Tommy were pupils at Hailsham—an idyllic establishment situated deep in the English countryside. The children there were tenderly sheltered from the outside world, brought up to believe they were special, and that their personal welfare was crucial. But for what reason were they really there? It is only years later that Kathy, now aged 31, finally allows herself to yield to the pull of memory. What unfolds is the . . . story of how Kathy, Ruth and Tommy slowly come to face the truth about their seemingly happy childhoods—and about their futures." (Publisher's note)

This novel is "set in late 1990s England, in a parallel universe in which humans are cloned and raised expressly to 'donate' their healthy organs and thus eradicate disease from the normal population." Publ Wkly

Ishiguro, Kazuo

★ The **remains** of the day. Knopf 1989 245p

LC 89-80445

"Mr. Stevens is a butler of high quality now employed by the American owner of Darlington Hall. His position as butler was quite different when Lord Darlington was his employer. Then there was a large staff, including Miss Kenton, whose friendly overtures to Stevens were met only by his inability to unbend or find some humor as an outlet offsetting his customary snobbish personality. As Stevens reflects on the past the reader gains insight into Lord Darlington's political connections after World War I with important government officials including Ribbentrop, representive of Germany's movement toward a dictatorship. Questions regarding an employee's unquestioning loyalty toward his employer and awareness of the political situation in the period just before Hitler's rise to power make this a thought-provoking novel." Shapiro. Fic for Youth. 3d edition

Ishiguro, Kazuo

The **unconsoled**. Knopf 1995 544p

ISBN 0-679-40425-2

LC 95-15829

In this novel, "prominent concert pianist Ryder is at odds with his surroundings. Ryder arrives in an unidentified European city at a bit of a loss. Everyone he meets seems to assume that he knows more than he knows, that he is well acquainted with the city and its obscure cultural crisis. A young woman he kindly consents to advise seems to have been an old lover and her son quite possibly his own; he vaguely recalls past conversations. The world he has entered is a surreal, Alice-in-Wonderland place where a door in a cafe can lead back to a hotel miles away. The result is at once dreamy, disorienting, and absolutely compelling; Ishiguro's paragraphs, though Proust-like, are completely lucid and quite addictive to read." Libr J

Ishiguro, Kazuo

When we were orphans. Knopf 2000 335p $25

ISBN 0-375-41054-6

LC 00-26120

"Christopher Banks is an Englishman born in early 20th-century Shanghai whose parents disappear mysteriously when he is nine. He is escorted to England, grows up to be a famed detective, and returns to Shanghai, convinced that his parents are still alive and that he must find them." Libr J

"For all its ellipses and evasions, When We Were Orphans, will linger in the mind as an often fascinating, imaginative work of surpassing intelligence and taste." Times Lit Suppl

Itani, Frances

Deafening. Atlantic Monthly Press 2003 378p $24

ISBN 0-87113-902-2

LC 2003-45108

"Grania O'Neill has been deaf since an early childhod fever. . . . Leaving her intimate Canadian hometown for the Ontario School for the Deaf, she learns sign language and finds Jim, who expresses his love for her by describing beautiful sounds. Unfortunately for their marriage, Jim is off to the trenches of World War I, where the sounds (and sights) are horrifying indeed." Booklist

"This novel is not only a beautifully crafted love story but also an exploration of the possibilities of language and the eloquence of silence." Libr J

Itani, Frances

Remembering the bones. Atlantic Monthly Press 2007 282p $24

ISBN 978-0-87113-977-1; 0-87113-977-4

"On the way to a party for Queen Elizabeth II, Georgie Witley, an Anglophile Canadian born the same day, crashes and is thrown from the driver's seat of her car. Lying on her back, like a beetle, at the bottom of a ravine, Georgie dutifully recites a passage from her grandfather's volume of 'Gray's Anatomy': 'Femur, tibia, fibula. Radius, ulna.' The litany of bones anchors Georgie in her broken body, and also helps her to coax eight decades of memories from their hiding places. She reflects on a life given shape by marriage, motherhood, and world war, milestones that she and the

Queen have in common. In unpretentious, quietly penetrating prose, Itani exposes the richness and depth beneath the surface of one ordinary life." New Yorker

Itani, Frances

Requiem; Frances Itani. Atlantic Monthly Press 2012 317 p. $24

ISBN 0802120229; 9780802120229

This book by Frances Itani "examines the internment of Japanese Canadian citizens during WWII and its impact on one family. In 1997, artist Binosuke Okuma drives from Montreal to the site of the camp on the Fraser River where his family has been interned when Bin was very young, and where his father made a decision that would cut him off from his family--and permit him to fulfill his potential as an artist. But at first memories of Bin's wife, Lena, who died of a stroke, chase him." (Publishers Weekly)

Ivey, Eowyn, 1973-

The **snow** child; Eowyn Ivey. Little, Brown and Co. 2012 389p.

ISBN 9780316175661; 9780316175678

LC 2011024937

This book takes place in Alaska in "1920, and frontier living means building your own log cabin with logs you felled yourself. Mabel, born in Pennsylvania, is facing her second winter up north, and she is wilting in the cold and isolation. . . . Jack, is still tainted by grief. He, exhausted by trying to scratch a living from the wilderness, barely talks and never smiles. One evening, though, their mood lifts, and the couple play in the newly fallen snow. They build a little snowman, complete with scarf and mittens. . . . In the morning, nothing remains but a broken heap of snow and a trail of small footprints leading away. . . . Suffice to say that a pale little girl in that same scarf and mittens eventually emerges from the forest and comes to play a crucial role in Jack and Mabel's life. But they have very different ideas about who or what she is, and what she means to them." (The Guardian)

Iyer, Pico

Abandon; a romance. Knopf 2003 353p $24

ISBN 0-375-41505-X

LC 2002-70059

"Lyer's writing is often poetic, and in presenting the Persian diaspora in Southern California, he has an intriguing way of peeling back familiar landscapes to reveal hidden sights." Booklist

J

Jackson, Charles

★ The **lost** weekend. Rinehart 1944 244p

Psychological study of a drunkard. The actual time covered is five days, but in those five days the story of a man's life is told. Don Biram, a sensitive, charming and well-read man, left alone for a few days by his brother, struggles with his overwhelming desire for alcohol, succumbs to it, and in the resulting prolonged agony, goes over much of his life up to and including the long weekend

"It's written with complete lack of literary pretensions; yet Jackson's sheer ability to lick the problems of flashback, stream of consciousness, mind wandering, twisted recollection and alcoholic delirium is spectacular. . . . Its frankness is sometimes shocking but never aimed to shock. The aim, and it is unerring, is always for accuracy and the complete truth" Book Week

Jackson, Jon A.

No man's dog; a Detective Sergeant Mulheisen mystery. Atlantic Monthly Press 2004 355p $24
ISBN 0-87113-920-0

LC 2003-69500

Detective Sergeant Fang Mulheisen retired from the force "to nurse his mother after she was injured in an apparent terrorist bombing of a suburban Detroit courthouse. That bombing has the curious effect of making partners of former antagonists Service and Mulheisen. Joining forces for different reasons to track down the bombers, these strange bedfellows-two of the most appealing, well-grounded characters in the genre-traipse about in the woods near Traverse City, sparring with a local militia roughneck. Jackson tackles the whole Patriot Act mess from an engaging everyman point of view." Booklist

Jackson, Joshilyn

Between, Georgia. Warner 2006 294p $22.99
ISBN 0-446-52442-5

LC 2005-23748

"Underneath all the pyrotechnics, Joshilyn Jackson is cleverly exploring the nature of family and belonging. . . . Jackson loads her novel with eccentrics straight from Southern Gothic central casting, but her writing brims with enough humor to make it compulsively readable." Christ Sci Monit

Jackson, Joshilyn

A grown up kind of pretty; Joshilyn Jackson. Grand Central Pub. 2012 336p.
ISBN 9780446582353

LC 2011004744

This book is about the "Slocumb women [who] suffer from a . . . curse: every 15 years something bad happens. Ginny gave birth to Liza when she was 15. And Liza had Mosey when she was 15. Now it's Mosey who's 15, and she's nervous. But the curse strikes in a different form, bringing a stroke to Liza that renders her mute and crippled, leaving her husband 'Big' to care for her. Wanting to put a pool in the yard for Liza's water therapy, Ginny has a willow uprooted, unearthing the bones of a baby—Liza's baby. This macabre discovery sends Mosey, Ginny, and Big in search of answers about the baby and Mosey's identity." (Publishers Weekly)

Jackson, Neta

Who do I talk to? Neta Jackson. Thomas Nelson 2009 ix, 406p (pbk.) $15.99
ISBN 1595545247; 9781595545244

LC 2009024971

Christy Award: Contemporary Series, Sequels, and Novellas (2010)

In this book, "Gabby Fairbanks's husband locks her out and disappears with her sons. . . . With her frail mother and a mutt named Dandy, Gabby must take refuge at the women's shelter where she works. . . . There, her new friends-including Lucy the bag lady and sisters from the Yada Yada Prayer

Group-prop her up. But a midnight intruder brings unwanted media attention to the shelter and threatens to undermine Gabby's chances of getting her sons back. Still hoping to put her family together again, Gabby puzzles over what to do with the warm attentions of a sympathetic lawyer who rebuilds her confidence and soothes her wounded spirit." (Publisher's note)

Jackson, Sheneska

Caught up in the rapture. Simon & Schuster 1996 270p
ISBN 0-684-81487-0

LC 95-47337

"This first novel is vivid, realistic, and strong, with perfectly fleshed-out characters. Readers will be bound by each word as they watch Jazmine struggle with life and the pursuit of happiness." Libr J

Jackson, Shirley

Come along with me; part of a novel, sixteen stories, and three lectures. edited by Stanley Edgar Hyman. Viking 1968 243p

Jackson, Shirley

★ The haunting of Hill House. Viking 1959 246p hardcover o.p. pa $14
ISBN 0-14-303998-9 pa

"Dr. John Montague, an anthropologist, is interested in the analysis of supernatural manifestations. He rents Hill House, which is reported to be haunted, and plans to spend the summer there with research assistants. Eleanor Vance, one of the researchers, is at first repelled by the house but soon adjusts. Other people come and signs of psychic activity are rampant, many of them centered on Eleanor. When Dr. Montague insists that she leave to insure her safety, the house does not release her." Shapiro. Fic for Youth. 3d edition

Jackson, Shirley

Just an ordinary day. Bantam Bks. 1997 388p

LC 96-23871

This collection includes unpublished and uncollected stories

Jackson, Shirley

★ The lottery and other stories; introduction by Patrick McGrath. Modern Lib. 2000 292p
ISBN 0-679-64039-8

LC 00-36064

A reissue of The lottery; or, The adventures of James Harris, published 1949 by Farrar, Straus

Jackson, Shirley

Novels and stories; [edited by Joyce Carol Oates] Library of America 2010 827p $35
ISBN 978-1-59853-072-8; 1-59853-072-0

LC 2009-943938

Includes the "short novels The Haunting of Hill House (1959), the tale of an achingly empathetic young woman chosen by a haunted house to be its new tenant, and We Have Always Lived in the Castle (1962), the unrepentant confessions of Miss Merricat Blackwood, a cunning adolescent who has gone to quite unusual lengths to preserve her ideal of family happiness." Publisher's note

Jackson, Shirley

We have always lived in the castle. Viking 1962 214p hardcover o.p. pa $14

ISBN 0-14-303997-0 pa

"Since the time that Constance Blackwood was tried and acquitted of the murder of four members of her family, she has lived with her sister Mary Catherine and her Uncle Julian in the family mansion. Mary Catherine takes care of family chores and Uncle Julian is busy with the writing of a detailed account of the six-year-old murders. Cousin Charles's arrival on the scene disrupts the quiet peace of the family, and Mary Catherine's efforts to get rid of him unloose a chain of events that bring everything down in ruins." Shapiro. Fic for Youth. 3d edition

Jacobson, Dan

All for love; a novel. Metropolitan Books 2006 272p $24

ISBN 978-0-8050-8103-9; 0-8050-8103-8

LC 2006-43363

First published 2005 in the United Kingdom

"What makes this so gripping is its prose, sparkling and pungently suggestive. Jacobson's drama of transgression and repression is a compulsive page-turner." Sunday Times (London)

Jacobson, Howard

The **Finkler** question. Bloomsbury 2010 307p pa $15

ISBN 978-1-608-19611-1; 1-608-19611-9

"The book follows Julian Treslove, a nebbishy British gentile who, after years of service at the BBC and a slew of failed relationships, finds himself middle-aged, unmoored and unmarried. Tellingly, his primary romantic fantasy involves a woman expiring in his arms. Treslove's defining quality is being bizarrely tabula rasa: His work is impersonating disparate celebrities at parties; a lover sums him up, 'There's something missing from you.' But Treslove is content with himself and his life until the day he is violently robbed by a woman. In the aftermath, Treslove in memory whittles the robber's commands from 'Your jewels' to 'You're Jules' to 'You Jew.' He comes to the shocking realization that he's been the victim of anti-Semitism and spends the rest of the book obsessively trying to fill that 'something missing' in him with a Jewish identity much to the bafflement of friends and family." San Francisco Chron

Jacobson, Howard

Kalooki nights. Simon & Schuster 2007 450p $26

ISBN 978-1-4165-4342-8; 1-4165-4342-2

LC 2006-50183

First published 2006 in the United Kingdom

"Jacobson spins a loose yarn around Max's inquiry into his old friend's crime, leaving plenty of opportunities for caustic insights and hilarious detours, as when the teen-aged Max, on his first double date, embarrasses himself in front of Isaiah Berlin." New Yorker

Jacobson, Howard

The **mighty** Walzer; Howard Jacobson. St. Martins Press 2011 400 p.

ISBN 9780099274728; 9781608196852

LC 99490230

This "coming-of-age story . . . follows Oliver Walzer, member of an extended Jewish family in 1950s Manchester, England. Surrounded by aunts and steeped in the culture brought over from eastern Europe, Oliver starts as a shy and observant youth who begins to discover himself and the world through his natural gift as a Ping-Pong player. As the years progress, Oliver and his mates also discover girls, and the novel follows his sexual awakening and maturing, as told from the perspective of a painfully self-conscious, perspicacious, and somewhat cynical teenager. Oliver moves beyond his local roots and attends Cambridge but later in life returns to Manchester for a visit." (Libr J)

Jaffe, Rona

Class reunion; a novel. Delacorte Press 1979 338p

LC 78-25838

"In the Fifties, when rules were rules, college campuses were husband-hunting grounds, and 'going all the way' could ruin a girl's reputation, four Radcliffe students pursue the dream of Mr. Right, Marriage, and Living Happily Ever After. Jaffe builds this book around their 20th reunion, using alternate chapters to flash back through the tales of beautiful Annabel, witty Chris, golden girl Daphne, and insecure Emily. {The author focuses on these women's lives} from college romances to crises which rock them—loveless marriage, divorce, adultery both homosexual and heterosexual, murder, nervous breakdown, birth of a mongoloid child." Libr J

Jaffe, Rona

The **room**-mating season. Dutton 2003 326p $24.95

ISBN 0-525-94713-2

LC 2002-73855

"The year is 1963, and college friends Leigh and Cady are determined to begin their adult lives amid the cosmopolitan social whirl of New York City. An ad for roommates brings two more young women into the circle: Vanessa, a sophisticated airline stewardess, and awkward, needy misfit Susan. . . . Jaffe traces the lives of her characters over the next four decades with wit and poignancy." Booklist

Jaime-Becerra, Michael

This time tomorrow. Thomas Dunne Books/St. Martin's Press 2010 295p $24.99

ISBN 978-0-312-60502-5; 0-312-60502-1

LC 2009-40036

The "novel is set in El Monte, a working-class Mexican American community in Southern California. . . . Packed with details of his characters' barely scraping-by existence, Jaime-Becerra's heartfelt debut brings an entire community vividly to life." Booklist

Jakeman, Jane

In the Kingdom of mists. Berley Prime Crime 2004 355p $23.95

ISBN 0-425-19512-0

LC 2003-62800

"The novel tells a dramatic story about crime and perception, art and reality through the eyes of the famous painter, the policeman and a young diplomat. Multilayered and voiced, this is a fascinating attempt to add an extra dimension to this historical crime novel." Guardian

Jakes, John

American dreams. Dutton 1998 495p

ISBN 0-525-94437-0

LC 97-49163

In the second volume of the "Crown family chronicles, Jakes portrays American during the turbulent period from 1906 to 1917. Once again, the story centers on the family of German-American patriarch and Chicago beer baron Joe Crown, whose headstrong daughter Fritzi defies her father to pursue a dreadfully unsuccessful New York stage career. In desperation, she surrenders to the lure of performing in moving pictures, which takes her to 'empty, rural, and uncivilized' Hollywood, where she falls in love and achieves a measure of fame as a comic actress. Meanwhile, her brother Carl gets tossed out of Princeton, goes to work for eccentric car manufacturer Henry Ford, becomes a race-car driver with Barney Oldfield, 'Speed King of the World', and flies as an ace pilot during WWI. Their cousin Paul is a professional news cameraman driven to record the horrors of war." Publ Wkly

Jakes, John

The best western stories of John Jakes; edited by Bill Pronzini and Martin H. Greenberg. Ohio Univ. Press 1991 275p

LC 90-49427

"This collection combines new material with several of Jakes's better efforts published earlier in the pulp magazines of the 1950s." Libr J

Jakes, John

California gold; a novel. Random House 1989 658p

LC 89-3779

"The novel potently conveys the raw, irrepressible vitality of California, but the historical backdrop (especially the 1906 earthquake) outshines the conventional rags-to-riches plot. Jake's impressive research . . . enriches the story considerably." Publ Wkly

Jakes, John

Charleston; a novel. Dutton 2002 506p

ISBN 0-525-94650-0

LC 2002-21251

This novel "details the shifting fortunes of several generations of a powerful southern dynasty, the Bell family, set against the dramatic and fiery backdrop of the American Revolution and the Civil War. Told in three parts, the story follows the lives, loves, and changing fortunes of the Bells and the Charleston aristocracy to which they belonged. Never one to gloss over details, the author manages to show

the bleak horrors of slavery, war, and greed while also confirming the essential goodness of American ideals. Jakes is in tiptop shape here." Booklist

Jakes, John

Great stories of the American West; stories by John Jakes {et al.}; edited by Martin H. Greenberg. Fine, D.I. 1994 290p il

LC 94-071113

"This excellent collection of 19 short stories is a suitable introduction to western fiction or a marvelous way to rekindle one's enthusiasm for the genre." Booklist

Jakes, John

Heaven and hell. Harcourt Brace Jovanovich 1987 700p

LC 87-17652

"Mr. Jakes sets this fictional action against a meticulously detailed historical backdrop. Although his characters are not as vivid as his storytelling, his portrait of a divided, demoralized nation, inflamed with hatred, still emerges as an enjoyable work of popular historical fiction." N Y Times Book Rev

Jakes, John

Love and war. Harcourt Brace Jovanovich 1984 1019p

LC 84-12895

This sequel to North and South "carries forward the entwined sagas of the Hazards of Pennsylvania, industrialists, and the Mains of South Carolina, plantation owners. . . . The story moves from action on the battlefield to the corridors of Washington to the shipyards of Liverpool. It encompasses deeds heroic and dastardly; passions licit and illicit; spying, assassination plotting and cynical profiteering; and the trying out of new military interventions." Publ Wkly

Followed by Heaven and hell

Jakes, John

★ North and South. Harcourt Brace Jovanovich 1982 740p

LC 81-47898

In this first novel of a trilogy the author "introduces two families: The Main family of South Carolina, and the Hazard family of Pennsylvania. The families are basically different. The Mains from the South grow rice and represent the old ways while the Hazards of the North produce iron and are examples of the Industrial Revolution. Their paths converge however, when Orry Main meets George Hazard as the two are entering West Point in 1842. Their friendship is immediate and strong. Orry's family owns slaves, and George, while loving his friend, cannot understand it. As the years pass each grows more entrenched in his beliefs. . . . George's sister Virgilia, an avowed abolitionist, seeks to pry the friendship apart and nearly succeeds. George and Orry's struggles are representative of that which plague the nation." West Coast Rev Books

Followed by Love and war

Jakes, John

On secret service; a novel. Dutton 2000 448p
ISBN 0-525-94544-X
LC 99-47951

"In 1861, Washington was located on the frontier between the Union and Confederacy; despite being the Union capital, it was a hotbed of Confederate sympathizers, some of whom were actual spies and even involved in the conspiracy to assassinate President Lincoln. . . . Jakes follows, throughout the four-year war period, a handful of individuals with intertwined allegiances as they worked both aboveboard and below for their various causes." Booklist

"Numerous historical figures are represented accurately and plausibly, and lesser-known events like the horrific Draft Riots in New York are vividly portrayed." Libr J

Jakes, John

Savannah; or, A gift for Mr. Lincoln. Dutton 2004 288p il $23.95
ISBN 0-525-94803-1
LC 2004-49417

This "historical novel recounts the taking of Savannah by Gen. William Tecumseh Sherman's Union Army during Christmas 1864. Fundamentally, it is the story of Sara Lester and her precocious 12-year-old daughter, Hattie, who has an aversion to General Sherman until she finds herself in need of his help. The novel includes a rich cast of characters who, as Union forces move north, are ultimately left to their own devices. The narrative offers adventure, romance, humor, and crime along with the trials of an American city living under what is, to its citizens, occupation by a foreign army." Libr J

James, Bill, 1929-

Undercover; Bill James. Severn House Pub Ltd 2012 208 p. $27.95
ISBN 1780290284; 9781780290287

In this novel, by Bill James, "[a]fter a gang shooting involving an undercover police officer, Colin Harpur and his boss Assistant Chief Constable Desmond Iles are called to another Force's ground. . . . Harpur can imagine the pressure the officer would have been under. If a gang decided to kill, a spy would have to go along with it. But with careers of fellow officers . . . at risk, Harpur knows that he and Iles have an exceptionally tough inquiry ahead." (Publisher's note)

James, Eloisa

Kiss me, Annabel; Eloisa James. Avon Books 2005 386p $7.99
ISBN 9780060732103; 0060732105
LC 2006567203

This romance novel tells the story of Miss Annabel Essex, whose "chosen spouse is nothing like the impoverished Scottish Earl of Ardmore, who has nothing but his gorgeous eyes, his brain—and his kisses—to recommend him. So what cruel twist of fate put her in a carriage on her way to Scotland with just that impoverished earl and all the world thinking they're man and wife? Sleeping in the same bed? Not to mention the game of words started by the earl—in which the prize is a kiss. And the forfeit . . . Well. They are almost married, after all!" (Publisher's note)

James, Eloisa

★ The ugly duchess; Eloisa James. HarperCollins 2012 366 p. (paperback) $7.99; (ebook) $7.99
ISBN 0062021737; 9780062021731; 9780062197962
LC 2012451739

In this book by Eloisa James, "James Ryburn . . . is forced by his father . . . to marry his best friend, the sweet but notoriously unattractive Theodora Saxby, so her dowry can cover [his] gambling debts. When Theo . . . realizes all they wanted was her money, she demands that Islay leave her--and leave England. . . . When Islay returns to England, he is a very different man, and Theo must decide whether to let him into her heart." (Publishers Weekly)

James, Eloisa

When beauty tamed the beast; [by] Eloisa James. Avon 2011 374p pa $7.99
ISBN 0062021273; 9780062021274; 978-0-06-202127-4
LC 2011658844

This book tells the story of Linnet Berry Thrynne, who is plagued by rumors that she "is carrying a royal bastard -- and, therefore, is now unmarriageable. So she finds herself accompanying the Duke of Windebank to the wilds of Wales as the perfect bride for his son, a brilliant physician and impotent nobleman with a beastly reputation, in order to ensure the succession. But Linnet is not pregnant, and Piers Yelverton, Earl of Marchant, is not impotent. He is, however, in possession of a rather beastly temper, rude manners, and a determination not to marry or fall in love--a challenge that Linnet is more than willing to accept." (Libr J)

"Her vivacious beauty, a rejection by her current princely flirt, and a series of false assumptions have the entire ton gleefully thinking Linnet Berry Thrynne is carrying a royal bastard—and, therefore, is now unmarriageable. So she finds herself accompanying the Duke of Windebank to the wilds of Wales as the perfect bride for his son, a brilliant physician and impotent nobleman with a beastly reputation, in order to ensure the succession. But Linnet is not pregnant, and Piers Yelverton, Earl of Marchant, is not impotent. He is, however, in possession of a rather beastly temper, rude manners, and a determination not to marry or fall in love—a challenge that Linnet is more than willing to accept. . . . Graced with sly humor, addictive dialog, elegant prose, and a skillfully woven subtext, this smart, deliciously sensual twist on a fairy tale classic is a breathtaking addition to James's series of reimagined fairy tales. Readers will be clambering for more." Libr J

James, Henry

The ambassadors; edited with an introduction by Harry Levin. Penguin Books 1986 517p pa $7
ISBN 0-14-043233-7
LC 87-29773

First published 1903 by Harper

"The central character and first 'ambassador,' Lambert Strether, is sent to Paris by Mrs. Newsome, a wealthy widow whom he plans to marry, in order to persuade her son Chad to come home. Chad is deeply involved with a charming French woman, Madame de Vionnet, and the novel deals chiefly with Strether's gradual conversion to the idea that life may hold more real meaning for Chad in Paris than in Woollett, Massachusetts. Strether comes to this conclusion in spite of his discovery that Chad and Mme de Vionnet are, in fact, more than just good friends. After the arrival of a second ambassador, Chad's sister Sarah, Strether decides to return to Woollett, urging Chad to remain in Paris. The essence of the novel is in Strether's remark, 'Live all you can; it's a mistake not to.'" Reader's Ency. 4th edition

James, Henry

The **American**; edited with an introduction and notes by Adrian Poole. Oxford University Press 1999 xxxiv, 400p pa $10.95

ISBN 0-19-283322-7

LC 98-42570

First published 1877 by J. R. Osgood and Company

"With much humour and delicacy of perception, the author depicts the reaction of different American types to the European environment." Oxford Companion to Engl Lit

James, Henry

★ The **Bostonians**. Knopf 1992 394p

ISBN 0-679-41750-8

LC 92-52889

First published 1886 by Macmillan

This was "one of the first American novels to deal more or less explicitly with lesbianism." Reader's Ency. 4th edition

James, Henry

Complete stories, 1864-1874. Library of Am. 1999 972p $40

ISBN 1-883011-70-1

LC 98-53919

James, Henry

Complete stories, 1874-1884. Library of Am. 1999 941p $35

ISBN 1-883011-63-9

LC 98-19252

Includes bibliographical references

James, Henry

Complete stories, 1884-1891. Library of Am. 1999 904p $35

ISBN 1-883011-64-7

LC 98-19250

Includes bibliographical references

James, Henry

Complete stories, 1892-1898. Library of Am. 1996 948p

ISBN 1-883011-09-4

LC 95-23463

James, Henry

Complete stories, 1898-1910. Library of Am. 1996 946p $35

ISBN 1-883011-10-8

LC 95-23462

James, Henry

The **complete** tales of Henry James; edited with an introduction by Leon Edel. Lippincott 1962 12v

James, Henry

Daisy Miller; introduction by Elizabeth Hardwick; notes by James Danly. Modern Library 2002 xxiv, 80p pa $14.50

ISBN 0-375-75966-2

LC 2001-44626

First published 1878

"The book's title character is a young American woman traveling in Europe with her mother. There she is courted by Frederick Forsyth Winterbourne, an American living abroad. In her innocence, Daisy is compromised by her friendship with an Italian man. Her behavior shocks Winterbourne and the other Americans living in Italy, and they shun her. Only after she dies does Winterbourne recognize that her actions reflected her spontaneous, genuine, and unaffected nature and that his suspicions of her were unwarranted." Merriam-Webster's Ency of Lit

James, Henry

★ The **Europeans**; a sketch. edited with an introduction and notes by Ian Campbell Ross. Oxford University Press 2000 pa $14.50

ISBN 0-19-283500-9

LC 00-703219

First published 1878

"Two expatriates, the Baroness Muenster and her brother Felix Young, come to Boston to visit some relatives they have never seen. The baroness futilely tries to make a wealthy marriage, and Felix seeks to paint portraits of the Bostonians he meets. A contrast is drawn between the sophistication of the pair and the strict New Englanders. Felix marries one of his kinswomen, who is eager to escape from her bleak environment." Benet's Reader's Ency of Am Lit

James, Henry

The **golden** bowl. Knopf 1992 596p $22

ISBN 0-679-41733-8

LC 92-52927

First published 1904 by Scribner

Maggie Verver, daughter of an American millionaire living in London, marries an indigent "Italian prince who has had a love affair with Maggie's closest friend, Charlotte Stant. Charlotte visits the pair and continues her intimacy. Then she marries Maggie's father. Everybody tries to keep secret from the others that he or she knows all that has happened or is happening. The complications are solved when Maggie's father goes back to America with Charlotte. James depicts with all the subtlety of his late style the cultural and moral involvements that follow on international marriage and irregular sex relationships." Benet's Reader's Ency of Am Lit

James, Henry

The **Henry** James reader; selected with a foreword and headnotes by Leon Edel. Scribner 1965 626p

Analyzed in Short story index

James, Henry

✓ ★ The **portrait** of a lady. Knopf 1991 xxv, 626p $20

    ISBN 0-679-40562-3

                           LC 91-52999

   First published 1881 by Houghton

"This is one of the best James's early works, in which he presents various types of American character transplanted into a European environment. The story centres in Isabel Archer, the 'Lady,' an attractive American girl. Around her we have the placid old American banker, Mr. Touchett; his hard repellent wife; his ugly, invalid, witty, charming son Ralph, whom England has thoroughly assimilated; and the outspoken, brilliant, indomitably American journalist Henrietta Stackpole. Isabel refuses the offer of marriage of a typical English peer, the excellent Lord Warburton, and of a bulldog-like New Englander, Casper Goodwood, to fall a victim, under the influence of the slightly sinister Madame Merle (another cosmopolitan American), to a worthless and spiteful dilettante, Gilbert Osmond, who marries her for her fortune and ruins her life; but to whom she remains loyal in spite of her realization of his vileness." Oxford Companion to Engl Lit. 6th edition

James, Henry

✓ **Roderick** Hudson; edited with an introduction by Geoffrey Moore and notes by Patricia Crick. Penguin Books 1986 397p pa $12

    ISBN 0-14-043264-7

   First published serially 1875 in The Atlantic Monthly; in book form 1876 by J. R. Osgood and Company

"The titular hero is a talented young American sculptor who goes to study in Rome at the insistance of a wealthy benefactor and becomes gradually disillusioned about his art and utterly demoralized by his experience. He neglects his New England fiancée; becomes involved in a love affair with Christina Light and finally leaps over a cliff." Univ Handbk for Readers and Writers

James, Henry

✓ **Short** novels of Henry James; with eight full-page illustrations. introduction by E. Hudson Long. Harcourt Brace Jovanovich 1961 530p il

   The first, second and the last titles are entered separately. The pupil is entered in a combined edition with: What Maisie knew, In the cage and The pupil. "In 'The Aspern Papers,' an unnamed American editor rents a room in Venice in the home of Juliana Bordereau, the elderly mistress of Jeffrey Aspern, a deceased Romantic poet, in order to procure from her the poet's papers." Merriam-Webster's Ency of Lit

James, Henry

✓ The **short** stories of Henry James; selected and edited with an introduction by Clifton Fadiman. Dodd, Mead 1945 xx, 644p

James, Henry

✓ The **spoils** of Poynton; edited with an introduction by David Lodge and notes by Patricia Crick. Penguin Books 1987 247p pa $13

    ISBN 0-14-043288-4

   First published 1896 by Houghton

"Owen Gareth, heir to the great house at Poynton, spurns his mother's favorite, Fleda Vetch, to marry Mona Brigstock. Old Mrs. Gareth thereupon removes her art treasures from Poynton. Owen was in fact in love with Fleda, and offers her any object she may desire at Poynton, but suddenly the house is ruined by an accidental fire, which ruins the spoils that have warped so many lives." Haydn. Thesaurus of Book Dig

James, Henry

✓ The **turn** of the screw; edited by Allan Lloyd Smith. J.M. Dent 1993 xxxii, 139p pa $8.95

    ISBN 0-460-87299-0

                        LC 94-125860

   First published 1898

This novella "is told from the viewpoint of the leading character, a governess in love with her employer, who goes to an isolated English estate to take charge of Miles and Flora, two attractive and precocious children. She gradually realizes that her young charges are under the evil influence of two ghosts, Peter Quint, the ex-steward, and Miss Jessel, their former governess. At the climax of the story, she enters into open conflict with the children, as a result of which Flora is alienated and Miles dies of fright." Reader's Ency. 4th edition

James, Henry

✓ **Washington** Square. Modern Lib. 1997 248p

    ISBN 0-679-60276-3

                        LC 97-25219

   First published 1881 by Harper

"The novel concerns Catherine Sloper, the shy and stolid daughter of wealthy, urbane, sardonic Dr. Austin Sloper. When young Morris Townsend, who is courting Catherine for her money, learns that her father will disinherit her if she marries him, he leaves her. Renewing his courtship after Dr. Sloper dies and leaves Catherine a small fortune, Morris is rejected sadly but firmly by Catherine, who lives on at Washington Square and is by then a spinster. Thus Catherine, plain and unintelligent, nevertheless withstands the world's assaults." Benet's Reader's Ency of Am Lit

James, Henry

✓ **What** Maisie knew, In the cage, The pupil. Kelley 1936 xxi, 576p $45

    ISBN 0-678-02811-7

   A combined edition of one novel and two novelettes first published 1897, 1898 and 1891 respectively

   What Maisie knew, concerns a twelve-year-old girl whose parents have divorced and re-married. Living alternately with each parent she learns that her stepmother and stepfather are having an adulterous affair, just as she had learned of her parents earlier infidelities. She decides to go to live with her old governess rather than with either parent. In the cage concerns a young woman who works as a telegram dispatcher in a London grocery store. She experiences vicarious enjoyment by imagining details in the lives of her well-to-do customers and even puts off marriage to her working-class fiancé while she tries to aid in the affairs of an aristocratic lady and her lover. But when she learns the unsavory truth about the couple from an outside source she decides to proceed with her marriage at once. The pupil deals with an American student who becomes a tutor for the sickly son of a shabby American family traveling about in Europe, develops a strong attachment to the boy, and tries to help him leave his despicable family—with tragic results

James, Henry

★ The **wings** of the dove. Modern Lib. 1993 711p

ISBN 0-679-60067-1

LC 93-15338

First published 1902 by Scribner

"The story is set in London and Venice. Kate Croy is a Londoner who encourages her secret fiancé, Merton Densher, to woo and marry Milly Theale, a wealthy young American who is dying of a mysterious malady. This, Kate reasons, although Milly will die soon, she will at least be happily in love, Merton will inherit her fortune, and Kate and Merton can marry and be rich. Shortly after Milly learns of Merton's and Kate's motives, she dies, leaving Merton a legacy that he is too guilt-ridden to accept. Kate is unwilling to forgo the inheritance, and she and Merton part forever, their relationship destroyed by Milly's unwittingly prescient gift." Merriam-Webster's Ency of Lit

James, Julie

A **lot** like love. Berkley Sensation 2011 289p (Berkley Sensation contemporary romance) pa $7.99

ISBN 978-0-425-24016-8; 0-425-24016-9

"Jordan Rhodes seems to have it all: money, fame, beauty, and her own successful business doing what she loves, introducing people to exceptional wines. But her twin brother Kyle is serving hard time after crashing Twitter in an emotional reaction to his girlfriend's very public breakup with him. The FBI offers to commute Kyle's sentence to time served if Jordan cooperates by getting one of their people into a very exclusive charity fundraiser. James' sassy, suspenseful sequel to Something About You (2010) exhibits her trademark sizzle and wit while focusing attention on another FBI undercover agent assigned to ferret out the secrets of Chicago's Mob. James pits Nick McCall's bad-boy appeal against Jordan's warm heart in a classic romance trope and concludes with tantalizing hints about future installments set in the same intriguing venue." Booklist

James, Julie

Something about you. Berkley Sensation 2010 323p (Berkley Sensation contemporary romance) pa $7.99

ISBN 978-0-425-23338-2; 0-425-23338-3

"When a high-priced prostitute is murdered in the neighboring hotel room, sole witness Cameron Lynde's safety is in the very capable but unforgiving hands of FBI special agent Jack Pallas, who thinks she sold him out three years ago on a case involving the Chicago Mob. As an assistant U.S. attorney, she's fully cognizant of the risks, especially since the client caught on videotape engaging in kinky sex is the wellknown, married U.S. senator from Illinois, recently appointed chair of the Senate Committee on Banking, Housing, and Urban Affairs. But as the murderer closes in, Jack and Cameron must put aside their differences to stay alive and solve the case." Booklist

"Delivers an addictively readable combination of sharp humor, sizzlingly sexy romance, and a generous measure of nail-biting suspense." Cicago Tribune

James, Marlon

The **book** of night women. Riverhead Books 2009 417p $26.95

ISBN 1-59448-857-6; 978-1-59448-857-3

LC 2008-46309

This "is the story of Lilith, born into slavery on a Jamaican sugar plantation at the end of the eighteenth century. Even at her birth, the slave women around her recognize a . . . power that they—and she—will come to both revere and fear. The Night Women, as they call themselves, have long been plotting a slave revolt, and as Lilith comes of age and reveals the extent of her power, they see her as the key to their plans." (Publisher's note)

This novel "is both beautifully written and devastating. While the gruesome history of slavery in the Americas is a story we may dare to think we already know, every page of 'The Book of Night Women' reminds us that we don't know nearly enough. . . . While his cast includes sadistic plantation owners and vicious overseers, 'house Negroes' and field slaves, James deftly avoids the clichéd melodrama such characters all too often inspire." N Y Times Book Rev

James, P. D.

The **black** tower. Scribner 1975 271p

"Adam Dalgliesh, convalescing after a severe illness, arrives at Toynton Grange (Dorset coast), the rest home for the young disabled, just too late to find out why his old friend Father Baddeley had sent for him. The monk-robed Wilfred Anstey and his staff are an odd lot, as are the few patients, all in wheelchairs. There's already been a suspicious suicide, and Dalgliesh is not satisfied that the old priest's death was caused by myocarditis alone. Handicapped by poor health, he finally manages to unearth the secret of the grange." Barzun. Cat of Crime. Rev and enl edition

James, P. D.

A **certain** justice. Knopf 1997 364p $25

ISBN 0-375-40109-1

LC 97-36889

"In obedience to the classic crime-writing genre, James finally offers up the guilty party, resolving a complicated plot with impeccable logic. But there the symmetry ends, for the moral and emotional questions she asks do not admit of such neatness." N Y Times Book Rev

James, P. D.

Death comes to Pemberley; [a novel] / P. D. James. 1st United States ed. Alfred A. Knopf 2011 291p

ISBN 0571283578; 9780307959850; 9780571283576

LC 2011941315

This book "draws the characters of Jane Austen's . . . novel 'Pride and Prejudice' into a tale of murder and emotional mayhem. Six years since Elizabeth and Darcy embarked on their life together at Pemberley, Darcy's magnificent estate. . . . Elizabeth has found her footing as the chatelaine of the great house. They have two fine sons . . . [and] there is optimistic talk about the prospects of marriage for

Darcy's sister Georgiana. And preparations are under way for their much-anticipated annual autumn ball. Then, on the eve of the ball . . . a coach careens up the drive carrying Lydia, Elizabeth's disgraced sister, who with her husband, the very dubious Wickham, has been banned from Pemberley. She stumbles out of the carriage, hysterical, shrieking that Wickham has been murdered." (Publisher's note)

James, P. D.

Death in holy orders. Knopf 2001 415p
ISBN 0-375-41255-7

LC 2001-88108

In this mystery "almost everything happens behind the closed doors of St. Anselm's, a small Anglican theological college set on a windy cliff abutting the sea. Commander Adam Dalgliesh, as always both wistful and stern, returns to St. Anselm's, where he spent a few blissful boyhood summers, to investigate the death of a student, but the case quickly expands as bodies begin to fall like so many dominoes. It's a pleasure to read James at the top of her form, as she often is here." New Yorker

James, P. D.

★ **Death** of an expert witness. Scribner 1977 322p

LC 77-21530

"Basically James is a novelist who happens to put her character into mystery stories. She is just as much interested in people and their relationships as she is in the conventions of the genre. And being the perceptive and sensitive writer she is, she constructs books that can be read on several levels." N Y Times Book Rev

James, P. D.

Devices and desires. Knopf 1990 433p
LC 89-45305

First published 1989 in the United Kingdom

"As always with P. D. James, the whodunit element is the lagniappe, so interesting are her characters, so absorbing her depiction of time and place, so rich the texture of the tale she tells." N Y Times Book Rev

James, P. D.

Innocent blood. Scribner 1980 311p

LC 79-28699

"What starts things moving in the tale is a young (adopted) woman's determination to find her real parents. This headstrong wish is gratified, creating social difficulties, deep changes in personal relations, the plotting of a murder, the experience of jail, and miscellaneous sexual activity. The diverse characters are admirably drawn and the author's fingerwork in tying and untying threads is as deft as her touches of sordid life and as nimble as her prose." Barzun. Cat of Crime. Rev and enl edition

James, P. D.

The **lighthouse**. Knopf 2005 335p $25.95
ISBN 0-307-26291-X

LC 2005-51039

This novel "is too rooted in genre conventions to count originality as its strong suit. But it has deviousness to burn, and it also offers other enticements. It's the kind of book that boasts a wryly humorous Scrabble scene, not to mention a Scrabble-lover's vocabulary." N Y Times Book Rev

James, P. D.

Original sin. Knopf 1995 416p

LC 94-26094

First published 1994 in the United Kingdom

A mystery featuring Commander Adam Dalgliesh of Scotland Yard. "Innocent House, a nineteenth-century pile on the Thames that accommodates the Peverell Press, presides over this novel of revenge. After Gerard Etienne, the new chairman of the press, announces his plan to sell the house, he ends up dead, with the head of a toy snake stuffed in his mouth. In this elaborate novel, the author . . . does what she does best: shows that guilt and blame have no single address." New Yorker

James, P. D.

The **private** patient. Alfred A. Knopf 2008 416p $25.95
ISBN 978-0-307-27077-1; 0-307-27077-7

LC 2008-27137

"The book begins by introducing investigative journalist Rhoda Gradwyn, whose face is marked by a disfiguring scar. She chooses prominent plastic surgeon George Chandler-Powell to remove it at his private clinic in Cheverell Manor. . . . It's a place where the comfortably situated can have their cosmetic work done in privacy — and not everyone welcomes the arrival of a professional snoop. The evening after her surgery, Gradwyn is murdered. Dalgliesh and his team are called in to solve the mystery, then have to deal with a second murder. . . . The investigation disrupts lives and disturbs secrets far beyond the little group at the manor. James is in excellent form in 'Patient.' She engages the brain as she entertains with apt descriptions and wry asides, and sets the reader to thinking beyond the obvious." St. Louis Post-Dispatch

James, P. D.

The **skull** beneath the skin. Scribner 1982 328p
LC 82-5981

"Fading actress Clarissa Lisle has been receiving frightening notes and is terrified of failing in her comeback performance, a revival of 'The Duchess of Malfi', held on a small private island off Dorset. Her husband hires detective Cordelia Gray to stop the notes. Once on the island, Cordelia discovers that nearly everyone there has a good reason to hate Clarissa, who is soon found gruesomely battered to death. The isolated group of suspects, hidden clues, and macabre atmosphere of an island castle complete with skulls and underground passageways make a pleasant traditional mystery. But James is never superficial, and her in-depth characterizations and excellent writing reveal complex relationships, motives, and human frailties." Libr J

James, P. D.

A **taste** for death. Knopf 1986 459p
LC 86-45273

Sir Paul Berowne, a minister of the Crown, is found with his throat cut in the vestry of St. Matthew's church in London. A tramp has also been killed. Dalgliesh and his assistant Kate Miskin seek the solution to the mystery in the victims' past. All the family members and witnesses have something to conceal

This "book is about murder and the way murder changes everything. . . . It is also about the human condition in London today, enlarged by a sense of the British past that stretches back like a rich and barely dwindling perspective." N Y Times Book Rev

James, P. D.

★ An **unsuitable** job for a woman. Scribner 1973 216p

First published 1972 in the United Kingdom

"In this book James's usual investigator, Chief Superintendent Dalgliesh, plays only a minor part. It is Cordelia Gray, the young, intelligent, and clear-thinking owner of an unsuccessful detective agency, who solves the case. She is hired by Sir Ronald Callender to investigate the death by suicide of his son, Mark. Miss Gray's meticulous research leads her to suspect that Mark was murdered and makes her a prime target for murder. There are suspenseful moments, close calls, and a very surprising encounter, at last, between Cordelia and Supt. Dalgliesh." Shapiro. Fic for Youth. 3d edition

James, Steven

The **queen**; Steven James. Revell 2011 517p

ISBN 9780800719203; 9780800733032 pa

LC 2011014738

This book tells the story of "FBI Special Agent Patrick Bowers, [who] travels to an isolated Wisconsin town to investigate a double homicide . . . [and] uncovers a high-tech conspiracy with ties to the Cold War and the Middle East. Bowers must use all of his considerable experience to get to the root of the conspiracy and solve the murders." (Libr J) "The gruesome homicide of a mother and her four-year-old daughter point to the missing husband as the main suspect, however Bowers thinks otherwise. It's too pat and doesn't explain the FBI's and Chief of Naval Operations interest in the case. . . . As Bowers gets closer to the truth the danger and conspiracy expands to include a radical eco-terrorist group, an assassin and his old archenemy, serial-killer Richard Basque." (thecypresstimes.com)

Jamison, Leslie

The **gin** closet. Free Press 2010 274p $25

ISBN 978-1-4391-5321-5; 1-4391-5321-3

LC 2009-20264

"Stella, in her 20s, is struggling to make ends meet in New York, working for a demanding writer and sleeping with a married man, when she learns that her mother had a runaway sister named Tilly. She tracks her down and finds an aging alcoholic, living in a trailer in Nevada. Tilly tells Stella that she has a son named Abe, a banker in San Francisco, who has offered her a place to stay, if she cleans up. So Stella helps her aunt to detox and they hit the road, moving into Abe's South of Market loft, where the three form a fragile new family, all hoping to make a better story out of their lives. . . . [This] is no escapist fantasy but a slow and steady heartbreak. It is also exquisitely beautiful. Jamison writes like a poet, her imagery breathtaking, her sentences unfurling unpredictably, to the novel's devastating end." San Francisco Chron

Jance, Judith A.

Birds of prey; a novel of suspense. [by] J.A. Lance. Morrow 2001 390p

ISBN 0-380-97407-X

LC 00-59445

"Retired Seattle cop J. P. Beaumont accompanies his newlywed, eightysomething grandmother and her crusty hubby, Lars Jenssen, on an Alaskan cruise to act as a chaperone of sorts. The jaded protagonist is inadvertently forced to masquerade as an FBI agent when Dr. Harrison Featherman's shrill blonde wife Margaret is tossed overboard, and the crime is captured on ship security cameras." Libr J

Jance, Judith A.

Breach of duty; a J.P. Beaumont mystery. [by] J.A. Jance. Avon Bks. 1999 343p

ISBN 0-380-97406-1

LC 98-42112

In this J.P. Beaumont "mystery, the sensitive Seattle police detective, a recovering alcoholic, juggles several mysteries, including the arson-induced death of an older woman and a series of crimes related to the stolen bones of a Native American shaman. Meanwhile, partner Sue Danielson is hounded by her ex-husband, and all three 'cases' move to violent conclusions almost simultaneously." Libr J

Jance, Judith A.

Dead to rights; a Joanna Brady mystery. {by} J. A. Jance. Avon Bks. 1996 373p

LC 96-24634

"When veterinarian Amos Buckwalter is murdered, all fingers point to Hal Morgan, the angry husband of a woman the drunken vet killed in a car accident the previous year. When she alone thinks he's innocent, Brady, herself a bereaved widow, is unsure if her personal feelings are getting in the way of her professional judgment. More deaths follow as the emotionally fragile Brady attempts to juggle her own family problems . . . with the trials of her job and a potential new love interest." Booklist

"Jance skillfully ties the mystery to the southeastern Arizona landscape, its historic mining towns and their modern problems." Publ Wkly

Jance, Judith A.

Devil's claw; a Joanna Brady mystery. [by] J.A. Jance. Morrow 2000 374p

ISBN 0-380-97501-7

LC 00-25805

Set "in Cochise County, Arizona. This time County Sheriff Joanna Brady is working two cases in the weeks before her wedding to Butch Dixon. The first involves the death of her octogenarian handyman, friend, and neighbor, Clayton Rhodes. . . . The other case involves the murder of a woman freshly released from prison after serving eight years for murdering her husband." Booklist

"The Arizona desert, as usual in Jance's mysteries, plays an unforgettable part in this atmospheric tale." Publ Wkly

Jance, Judith A.

Hand of evil; a novel of suspense. [by] J.A. Jance. Simon & Schuster 2007 368p $25.95

ISBN 978-0-4165-3753-3; 1-4165-3753-8

LC 2007-16986

Ali Reynolds "is a strong-minded woman who has fled L.A. in the wake of double disaster: wrongful dismissal from her TV-journalist job and the bizarre murder of her almost-ex-husband. Now carving out a new life in Sedona, she writes a popular blog, an activity that puts her in touch with a variety of people. In Sedona, meanwhile, Ali's allies include her grown son, Chris, and her pal Dave, a homicide detective and possible love interest. The main story among "Hand of Evil's" busy plots involves the elderly matriarch of a prominent family. An unexpected scholarship from this family once allowed a young Ali to attend college. Ali can hardly refuse, therefore, when the elderly lady summons Ali. The matriarch says she was a victim of incest and wants to demonstrate it by having Ali turn her diary into a memoir." Seattle Times

"Jance crowds the book with subplots, and her characters air a lot of opinions about sexual abuse and health care. But sparks between Ali and Dave and an upbeat ending keep this latest Ali outing on track." Publ Wkly

Jance, Judith A.

Kiss of the bees; [by] J. A. Jance. Avon Bks. 2000 389p

ISBN 0-380-97747-8

LC 99-35465

"In Tucson, twenty years ago, a psychopath named Andrew Carlisle brought blood and terror into the home of Diana Ladd Walker and her family [Hour of the hunter]. When Carlisle died in prison, Diana and her husband, ex-county sheriff Brandon Walker, believed their long nightmare was finally over. They were wrong. Their beloved adopted daughter Lani has vanished—a beautiful Native American teenager destined, according to Tohono O'othham legend, to become a woman of great spiritual power. A serial killer is dead, but his malevolence lives on in another—and now the fiend holds Lani's innocent life in his eager hands." Publisher's note

Jance, Judith A.

Lying in wait; a J.P. Beaumont mystery. by J.A. Jance. Morrow 1994 303p

LC 94-15565

"Beau and Sue probe Else's high school romance, the missing accident victim and the Nazi connection before they come up with the killer in this red hot, fast-paced story." Publ Wkly

Jance, Judith A.

Queen of the night; [by] J. A. Jance. William Morrow 2010 358p $25.99

ISBN 978-0-06-123924-3; 0-06-123924-0

LC 2009-38976

This "suspense novel featuring former homicide detective Brandon Walker and his wife, novelist Diana Ladd . . . , spans some 50 years, from a murder in 1959 in San Diego to a rash of killings in Thousand Oaks, Calif., and Tucson, Ariz., in 2009. Interwoven with these crimes are legends of the Tohono O'odham Indians (aka the Desert People) and the lives of such contemporary Native people as Lani Walker, Brandon and Diana's adopted daughter. Jance's masterful handling of a complex cast of characters makes it easy for the reader to appreciate the intricate web of relationships that bind them across generations." Publ Wkly

Jance, Judith A.

Skeleton canyon; a Joanna Brady mystery. {by} J. A. Jance. Avon Bks. 1997 373p

ISBN 978-0380973958

LC 97-3217

"When high-school valedictorian Bree O'Brien is found dead in the southeastern Arizona mountains, suspicion falls on her boyfriend, Ignacio Ybarra, who refuses to explain his fresh cuts and bruises. But the case isn't that simple, as Coshise County Sheriff Joanna Brady learns. . . . Jance's regional knowledge runs deep, whether she writes about troubled Anglo-Hispanic relations along the border or the surprising power of Arizona thunderstorms." Publ Wkly

Jansma, Kristopher

The **unchangeable** spots of leopards; Kristopher Jansma. Viking 2013 272 p. (hardcover) $26.95

ISBN 067002600X; 9780670026005

LC 2012027179

In this novel, by Kristopher Jansma, "the . . . narrator . . . has wanted to become a writer. From the jazz clubs of Manhattan to the villages of Sri Lanka, . . . [the] narrator will be inspired and haunted by the success of his greatest friend and rival in writing, the eccentric and brilliantly talented Julian McGann, and endlessly enamored with Julian's enchanting friend, Evelyn, the green-eyed girl who got away." (Publisher's note)

Jeffries, Sabrina

'**Twas** the night after Christmas; Sabrina Jeffries. Gallery Books 2012 368 p. (hardcover) $19.99

ISBN 1451642466; 1451642504; 9781451642469; 9781451642506

LC 2012015020

In this book by Sabrina Jeffries, "when a meddling but warmhearted lady's companion tries to force a reconciliation between a dowager countess and her son, no one can guess at the resentment and betrayals that will be unearthed. . . . Meanwhile, Camilla and the earl grow ever closer, and for the first time, Devonmont considers marriage, though Camilla knows a match between them is unacceptable." (Kirkus Reviews)

Jemisin, N. K.

The **hundred** thousand kingdoms. Orbit 2010 427p pa $13.99

ISBN 9780316043915

LC 2009-02075

The first volume of the projected Inheritance Trilogy. "When her mother dies mysteriously, outcast barbarian Yeine Darr answers a summons to the grand city of Sky from her grandfather, King Dekarta Arameri. Proclaimed one of three heirs to the throne of the Hundred Thousand Kingdoms, Yeine must learn the customs of the skyborne capital and its ruling elite before she succumbs to their treachery.

Debut author Jemisin creates a mesmerizingly exotic world where fallen gods serve as slaves to the ruling class and murder and ambition go hand in hand." Libr J

Jemisin, N. K.

The **killing** moon; N.K. Jemisin. Orbit 2012 440 p.

ISBN 0316187283; 9780316187282

LC 2011028110

This fantasy novel by N. K. Jemisin takes place in "the ancient city-state of Gujaareh, [where] peace is the only law. Upon its rooftops and amongst the shadows of its cobbled streets wait the Gatherers - the keepers of this peace. Priests of the dream-goddess, their duty is to harvest the magic of the sleeping mind and use it to heal, soothe . . . and kill those judged corrupt. But when a conspiracy blooms within Gujaareh's great temple, Ehiru - the most famous of the city's Gatherers - must question everything he knows. Someone, or something, is murdering dreamers in the goddess' name, stalking its prey both in Gujaareh's alleys and the realm of dreams. Ehiru must now protect the woman he was sent to kill - or watch the city be devoured by war and forbidden magic." (Publisher's note)

Jen, Gish

The **love** wife. Knopf 2004 379p $24.95

ISBN 1-400-04213-5

LC 2004-40917

"A meddlesome Chinese-American mother bequeaths a Chinese nanny to her ambivalent son and his big blonde wife in this darkly comic fairy tale about cultural assimilation, biological destiny and domestic warfare." Publ Wkly

"In a story told from multiple points of view, Jen turns stereotypes upside down by giving each character an issue, label or characteristic you might not expect." USA Today

Jen, Gish

Mona in the promised land. Knopf 1996 303p

ISBN 978-0679445890

LC 95-44447

This work "has a wide-ranging exuberance that's unusual in what is still—to its credit—a realistic novel. Ms. Jen doesn't sacrifice her characters to satire. And her story can take the broad view even while it focuses on smaller, more personal matters because she works in so many voices and because she includes so many perfectly timed set pieces." N Y Times Book Rev

Jen, Gish

Typical American. Plume 1992 296p (Plume contemporary fiction) pa $13.95

ISBN 0-452-26774-9

LC 91-33814

First published 1991 by Houghton Mifflin

"Yefing Chang becomes Ralph Chang in America and begins a hard struggle to achieve the American dream—a career, a family and a home of his own. In poverty, he succeeds finally to win a doctoral degree, a college position, a happy marriage to Helen, two delightful daughters and a close reunion with his older sister, Theresa. The dream becomes a nightmare when he meets Grover Ding whose corrupt influence over Ralph and Helen begins to unravel all

that the Changs have managed to achieve. This is an honest novel that does not promise happy endings and recognizes the human weaknesses that can destroy a family's stability." Shapiro. Fic for Youth. 3d edition

Followed by Mona in the promised land (1996)

Jen, Gish

Who's Irish? stories. Knopf 1999 207p

ISBN 0-375-40621-2

LC 98-42801

"Jen's characters, Chinese immigrants and their American-born children, find themselves commuting between two cultures, between familial expectations and their own yearnings for self-definition, between remembered traditions and shiny, new dreams." N Y Times Book Rev

Jen, Gish

★ **World** and town; a novel. Alfred A. Knopf 2010 386p $26.95

ISBN 978-0-307-27219-5; 0-307-27219-2

LC 2010-07057

Gish sets this novel in "an idyllic New England town, the kind of place we like to carelessly fetishize as the real America. At the center is 68-year-old Hattie Kong, a descendant of Confucius who's still reeling from the back-to-back deaths of her husband and her best friend. Her life, flattened by grief, is shaken up when a former lover moves to town and a family of Cambodian immigrants takes up in the trailer down the hill. Everybody in these pages, it seems, is in desperate need of a fresh start and a sense of belonging. It's into this mix that Jen gracefully introduces some of the great issues of our time: how the shock of 9/11 reverberated from city to town; how lost souls can cling meanly to fundamentalism; how it feels when a chain store bulldozes into a mom-and-pop community, or a family farm finally collapses." Entertainment Wkly

Jenkins, Victoria

An **unattended** death; Victoria Jenkins. The Permanent Press 2012 214 p. $28

ISBN 1579622844; 9781579622848

LC 2012016405

In this mystery novel by Victoria Jenkins "Anne Paris is found dead, her body floating in the slough at the bottom of her family's remote summer property on an island in Puget Sound, the apparent victim of a sailing accident. Irene Chavez, the lone female detective in a rural Washington State sheriff's department, is assigned to investigate the death of this privileged young psychiatrist." (Publisher's note)

Jennings, Gary

Aztec. Atheneum Pubs. 1980 754p

LC 80-55608

"Mixtli (Dark Cloud), the book's hero, is a Mexicatl who is born on the outskirts of the capital city of Tenochtitlan a half-century before the arrival of Cortés. He becomes, in turn, a student, a scribe, a soldier, a merchant, a cultural anthropologist, an adviser to noble rulers, and finally an involuntary chronicler of his people's past for the victorious Spaniards. The book is presented as the verbatim transcript of the reminiscences of this 'elderly male Indian,' recorded at the command of Emperor Charles I, who is eager to learn more about his recently acquired colony of New Spain." N Y Times Book Rev

Jennings, Gary

Aztec blood. Forge 2001 525p

ISBN 0-312-86251-2

LC 2001-40130

An adventure tale set in "17th-century Mexico as seen through the eyes of a teenage boy. . . . Cristo is a lepero, a scorned mestizo beggar who lives by his wits, conniving and scheming merely to stay alive. He is taught to read, write, and converse in foreign tongues by Fray Antonio, a Catholic friar. When the friar is murdered, Cristo must flee for his life, although he doesn't know why. On the way to discovering the truth about himself, he encounters many colorful characters and adventures." Libr J

"Injustice has seldom been so keenly sketched nor valor so compellingly portrayed as in this swashbuckling adventure." Publ Wkly

Jennings, Gary

Raptor. Doubleday 1992 980p

LC 92-9433

"Like Michener, Jennings fills his boldly sketched historical canvas with lively action and dense, well-researched detail; in the works of both, a strong plot and interesting characters often camouflage an absence of style. But readers will enjoy this trip to an exotic world." Booklist

Jenoff, Pam

★ The Ambassador's Daughter; by Pam Jenoff. Harlequin Books 2013 336 p. (paperback) $14.95

ISBN 0778315096; 9780778315094

In this historical romance by Pam Jenoff, "conflicted Margot accompanies her German diplomat father to Paris for the treaty negotiations following WWI. . . . Margot deliberately delays . . . the impending union with her injured fiancé Stefan. . . . Her world changes when she meets Krysia--a pianist from Poland with radical political affiliations, an ethereal appearance, and an affinity for forthright speech--and then Georg, the striking but troubled German naval officer." (Publishers Weekly)

Jensen, Jane

Dante's equation; Jane Jensen. Ballantine Books 2003 484p ill. $15.95

ISBN 0345430379; 9780345430373

LC 2003273636

In this book, "physics professor Jill Talcott is experimenting with energy waves that somehow directly influence matter and living things. Journalist Denton Wyle . . . track[s] down the scattered fragments of a manuscript written in 1944 in Auschwitz by Yosef Kobinski. A kabbalist and physicist of genius, Kobinski mathematically described a dimension of good and evil. . . . In Jerusalem, rigid, self-absorbed Rabbi Aharon Handalman studies the Bible for coded messages supposedly buried in the text. Astonishingly, he finds dozens of menacing references to Kobinski and weapons. . . . Jill's experiment . . . causes an explosion that kills dozens of innocents. This attracts Handalman's attention—and also that of Calder Farris, part of a secret Defense Department group whose purpose is to acquire possible new weapons

technology and either co-opt or silence the inventors. Ambitious Jill is minded to accept Farris's job offer, until Handalman shows up and tells her about Kobinski." (Kirkus)

Jensen, Liz

The uninvited; Liz Jensen. Bloomsbury Publishing PLC 2012 307 p. (hardcover) $25

ISBN 1608199924; 9781608199921

LC 2012451595

In this horror novel, by Liz Jensen, "across the world, children are killing their families. . . . As chilling murders by children grip the country, anthropologist Hesketh Lock has his own mystery to solve: a bizarre scandal in the Taiwan timber industry. . . . Nothing obvious connects Hesketh's Asian case with the atrocities back home. . . . But when Hesketh's Taiwan contact dies shockingly . . . he is forced to acknowledge possibilities that defy . . . rational principles." (Publisher's note)

Jensen, Nancy

The sisters; Nancy Jensen. 1st ed. St. Martin's Press 2011 viii, 324 p.p

ISBN 9780312542702; 0312542704

LC 2011025854

This book is set in "hardscrabble Kentucky in the 1920s, . . . [and tells the story of] Bertie Fischer and her older sister Mabel [who] have no one but each other--with perhaps a sweetheart for Bertie waiting in the wings. But on the day that Bertie receives her eighth-grade diploma, good intentions go terribly wrong. A choice made in desperate haste sets off a chain of misunderstandings that will divide the sisters and reverberate through three generations of women. . . From the Depression through World War II and Vietnam, and smaller events both tragic and joyful, Bertie and Mabel forge unexpected identities that are shaped by unspeakable secrets. As the sisters have daughters and granddaughters of their own, they discover that both love and betrayal are even more complicated than they seem." (Publisher's note)

Includes bibliographical references

Jerkins, Grant

The ninth step; Grant Jerkins. 1st ed. Berkley Prime Crime 2012 p. cm. (paperback) $15.00

ISBN 9780425255988

LC 2012014770

This novel, by Grant Jerkins, follows "Helen, . . . a recovering alcoholic struggling through a twelve-step program. Now it's time to make amends for . . . a hit and run accident that killed the wife of school teacher Edgar Woolrich. . . . [T]he ninth step begins with a lie--the first of many as their relationship grows, and Helen knows it's far too late to reveal the truth to a man she's come to love. Then one day, she receives an anonymous note: Does he know you killed his wife?" (Publisher's note)

Jewell, Lisa

The making of us; a novel. by Lisa Jewell. 1st Atria paperback ed. Atria Books 2012 403 p. (paperback) $16.00

ISBN 9781451609110; 9781451609134

LC 2012009042

This novel, by Lisa Jewell, is "about three strangers who are brought together by the father they never knew. . . . Lydia, Dean and Robyn live very different lives, but each of them . . . has always felt that something was missing. . . . [A] letter is about to arrive that will turn their lives upside down. It is a letter containing a secret . . . that will bind them together and show them what love and family and friendship really mean." (Publisher's note)

Jewett, Sarah Orne
The **best** stories of Sarah Orne Jewett; selected and arranged with a preface by Willa Cather. Houghton Mifflin 1925 2v

Jewett, Sarah Orne
★ The **country** of the pointed firs. Houghton Mifflin 1896 213p

"Highly regarded for its sympathetic yet unsentimental portrayal of the town of Dunnet Landing and its residents, this episodic book is narrated by a nameless summer visitor who relates the life stories of various inhabitants, capturing the idiomatic language, customs, mannerisms, and humor peculiar to Down-Easters." Merriam-Webster's Ency of Lit

Jewett, Sarah Orne
The **country** of the pointed firs and other stories. Modern Lib. 1995 247p

ISBN 0-679-60173-2

LC 95-2831

Jhabvala, Ruth Prawer
East into Upper East; plain tales from New York and New Delhi. Counterpoint 1998 314p

ISBN 1-88717-850-3

LC 98-34881

"Jhabvala is a connoisseur of divided souls, conceiving characters whose inner longings are at odds with their outer protective coloration—Indians who covet and achieve more tidy, 'modernized' existences, then feel as if someone had stolen their life force; Westerners who eagerly hand themselves over to India's chaotic bliss, then find it too rigorous to endure." N Y Times Book Rev

Jhabvala, Ruth Prawer
★ **Heat** and dust. Harper & Row 1976 181p

First published 1975 in the United Kingdom

"The juxtaposition of past and present India is explored in this novel. The 1923 storyline tells of Olivia, who, though married to a British officer stationed in India, falls madly in love with an Indian prince. It is also about Olivia's husband's granddaughter by a second marriage, who has come to India to discover the details of Olivia's life but finds that, although India and women have become modernized, she must face many of the same choices as Olivia. The intrusion of British culture on India's own traditions and values is a second theme in the novel." Shapiro. Fic for Youth. 3d edition

Jhabvala, Ruth Prawer
My nine lives. Shoemaker & Hoard 2004 277p $25

ISBN 1-59376-028-0

"Jhabvala name-drops Chekhov, and this is no pretension given the grace of her spiraling plots, the depth of her psychology, the elegance of her humor, the subtly of her eroticism, and her masterfully concise descriptions of imperiled households, eccentric personalities, sexual enthrallment, unexpected alliances, and transcendent love." Booklist

Jhabvala, Ruth Prawer
Out of India; selected stories. Morrow 1986 288p

LC 85-25961

"Out of a web of subtle but not precious ironies, couched in a limpid style, arises a sense of the author's obvious love-hate attitude toward this land that is so difficult to live in, for foreigner and native alike. Jhabvala sensitively explores the tense juncture between Western and Indian cultures; plots and characters glow with realism and energy." Booklist

Jhabvala, Ruth Prawer
Shards of memory. Doubleday 1995 221p

LC 94-45311

"Jhabvala's understanding of character is shrewd, and her language is controlled and lucid. . . . {Her} technical fluency and poise are admirable; combined with Jhabvala's sensitivity, and her understanding of characters, they make the novel feel startlingly realistic, so that the vagueness of the central themes, and the sometimes slow development of plot seem almost irrelevant." Times Lit Suppl

Jiang Rong
Wolf totem; a novel. translated by Howard Goldblatt. Penguin Press 2008 527p $26.95

ISBN 978-1-59420-156-1; 1-59420-156-0

LC 2007-37554

Original Chinese edition, 2004

"The novel's literary claims are shaky; and Jiang Rong's apparent wish to transform China's national character through a benign conservationism is compromised by his boy-scoutish arguments for toughness. Yet few books about today's China can match Wolf Totem as a guide to the troubled self-images of so many of its people as they stumble, grappling with some inconvenient truths of their own, into modernity." N Y Times Book Rev

Jiles, Paulette
The **color** of lightning; a novel. William Morrow 2009 349p $25.99

ISBN 978-0-06-169044-0; 0-06-169044-9

LC 2008-46339

"It is 1863, and Britt Johnson saddles up with a few other men from his North Texas settlement to ride to a nearby town for supplies. Johnson, a free African American, has brought his beautiful wife and three small children to this desolate, dangerous country to build a life he hopes will be freer of racism than it would have been in Kentucky. While he is gone, a war party of 700 Comanche and Kiowa descend into the valley, killing the men and kidnapping women and children. His wife and two younger children are taken as captives. . . . Based on the true story of an African American who was legendary for his ability to bargain with Native Americans for the return of captives, the novel also tells the fictional tale of a well-meaning, but naive young

Quaker from Philadelphia, Samuel Hammond, who is sent to run a regional Bureau of Indian Affairs. The contrast between Johnson, a pragmatic man of action, and Hammond, an idealist who struggles with the ambiguities of reality, echoes the history of a period when government programs and westward expansion collided, ruinously, with Native cultures. Jiles' spare and melancholy prose is the perfect language for this tale in which survival necessitates brutality." Seattle Times

Jiles, Paulette
    Enemy women. Morrow 2002 321p
        ISBN 0-06-621444-0
                                                                LC 2001-40200
    "For Adair Randolph Colley, at 18 the eldest daughter of a widowed Missouri Ozarks schoolmaster and justice of the peace, the Civil War becomes personal when her father, who has remained neutral in the conflict, is arrested by the Union militia, their home is nearly burned and their possessions stolen. At the start of this . . . novel, Adair and her two younger sisters try to follow their father's captors, but Adair is falsely denounced as a Confederate spy. At the prison in St. Louis, upright commandant Maj. William Neumann is . . . touched by Adair's beauty and spirit and asks her to give him some information so she can be released. Instead, she writes the story of her life, augmented by folk tales and fables, and he finds himself falling in love. When he gets his reassignment orders, he proposes marriage and asks her to escape, promising to find her after the war. Thus begins a long and terrible journey for each of them." Publ Wkly

Jin, Ha, 1956-
    A **good** fall. Pantheon Books 2009 240p
        ISBN 0-307-37868-3; 978-0-307-37868-2
                                                                LC 2009-08638
    This is a collection of twelve stories by the author of Waiting (1999), The Bridegroom (2000), and A Free Life (2007).
    "It's an uneven collection in the best sense of the word, combining superfluous vignettes with moments of stark insight into an amalgamation that itself resembles a melting pot. . . . A few missteps don't spoil a collection of sublime moments, not the least of which occurs in the title story, its plot capturing the entire arc of the immigrant experience." Denver Post

Jin, Ha, 1956-
    Nanjing requiem. Pantheon Books 2011 303p $26.95
        ISBN 978-0-307-37976-4; 0-307-37976-0
                                                                LC 2010-47608
    This novel "focuses on the atrocities committed by the Japanese occupiers in 1937 Nanjing. Jin describes horrible acts in a style bordering on reportage, lending bitter realism to his chronicle of violence and privation. While much will be familiar to readers of Iris Chang's The Rape of Nanjing, Jin anchors his tale on two characters: the middle-aged narrator, Anling Gao, and real-life American missionary Minnie Vautrin, dean of Jinling Women's College. Anling assists Minnie, and through her eyes we follow the missionary's heroic decision to open the college to homeless refugees, creating a safety zone that the Japanese can't penetrate. . . .

Jin paints a convincing, harrowing portrait of heroism in the face of brutality." Publ Wkly

Jio, Sarah
    The **last** camellia; a novel. Sarah Jio. Plume 2013 320 p. $15
        ISBN 0452298393; 9780452298392
                                                                LC 2012049474
    In this novel by Sarah Jio set "on the eve of the Second World War, the last surviving specimen of a camellia plant known as the Middlebury Pink lies secreted away on an English country estate. Flora, an amateur American botanist, is contracted by an international ring of flower thieves to infiltrate the household and acquire the coveted bloom. Her search is at once brightened by new love and threatened by her discovery of a series of ghastly crimes." (Publisher's note)

Jio, Sarah
    The **violets** of March; Sarah Jio. Plume 2011 296p.
        ISBN 9780452297036 pa; 0452297036
                                                                LC 2010037282
    This book tells the "story of a woman rebuilding after romantic and professional setbacks. A few years ago, Emily Wilson was a bestselling writer married to a loving and handsome man. Now her husband has ditched her and she's unable to string four words together. Looking for rejuvenation and inspiration, Emily leaves New York City for a month at her great-aunt Bee's Bainbridge Island home, but soon after she arrives, she discovers a mysterious diary from 1943 and becomes fascinated by the love story captured by the unknown diarist. Emily's attempts to ferret out the story behind the diary bring her into contact with the island's . . . locals; as Emily enjoys a simmering romance with an artist, answers prove hard to come by, and even Bee is reluctant to share the truth." (Publishers Weekly)

Joe, Yolanda
    My fine lady. Dutton 2004 221p $23.95
        ISBN 0-525-94808-2
                                                                LC 2003-17788
    "A fantastic update of Pygmalion and hip Americanization of My Fair Lady . . . , Joe's compelling tale about one woman's coming into her own and the dichotomy between educated African Americans and those living in poverty may well become a popular classic in its own right." Booklist

Johansen, Iris
    And then you die-- Bantam Bks. 1998 344p
        ISBN 0-553-10616-3
                                                                LC 97-40073
    "When photojournalist Bess Grady is sent on assignment to a small town in Mexico, she unwittingly finds herself in the midst of a horrific nightmare. Every citizen of the town has died of anthrax poisoning as a result of a terrorist germ-warfare attack. Because she survived, Bess is sought by both the terrorists and a hard-hearted CIA man. The plot is filled with clever detours that twist and turn and cast suspicion on all of the main players until Bess doesn't know who to trust." Booklist

Johansen, Iris

  Blind alley. Bantam Books 2004 344p $25

  ISBN 0-553-80341-7

LC 2004-54410

In this thriller featuring "Atlanta detective Joe Quinn and the love of his life, forensic sculptor Eve Duncan, Joe gives Eve a skull to reconstruct. Eerily enough, the face resembles 17-year-old Jane MacGuire, who has been offered sanctuary by Eve and Joe after surviving a rough-and-tumble life on the streets. . . . Several look-alikes have already been killed in Europe, and Scotland Yard sends in hunky Mark Trevor to help. Eve mistrusts him, but Jane, who has had recurring nightmares related to the killings, believes that he's there to help her. Eve and Joe want to protect Jane, but the intrepid teenager knows that unless she confronts the killer, she will live the rest of her life in fear. Johansen has become adept at mixing supernatural elements with intriguing suspense." Booklist

Johansen, Iris

  Eight days to live. St. Martin's Press 2010 408p $27.99

    ISBN 978-0-312-36815-9; 0-312-36815-1

LC 2009-41533

The focus of this novel is on forensic sculptor Eve Duncan's "adopted daughter, Jane MacGuire, who has a successful art show at a Parisian gallery. But a painting titled Guilt has drawn some unwanted attention: the religious cult Sang Noir wants Jane dead. When the cult starts going after those closest to Jane, she turns to two strong, dangerous men: Jock, a trained assassin, and Seth, a hunter with psychic powers. Friction ensues between these two strapping guys as they fight to protect the globe-trotting Jane while she travels from Paris to Switzerland to Jerusalem in an attempt to find out why Sang Noir is so determined to kill her. She's fighting an intense attraction to Caleb, even as she disapproves of his methods of extracting information, and when Eve's life hangs in the balance, Jane finds herself crossing lines she never thought she would. Readers interested in hard forensic science will want to look elsewhere, but those receptive to paranormal abilities and religious mysteries will find much to enjoy in this page-turner." Booklist

Johansen, Iris

  The **face** of deception. Bantam Bks. 1998 354p

  ISBN 0-553-10623-6

LC 98-24713

Forensic sculptor Eve Duncan "is swept into a maelstrom of murder, deception, and political intrigue when she is coerced into rebuilding the face of an adult whose remains consist of a burned skull. Obsessed with establishing the identities of the skeletal remains of murdered children ever since her daughter was killed and the body was never found. Eve resists the request of billionaire John Logan to work on this mysterious case until her lab is destroyed and her mother threatened." Booklist

"With the help of well-timed, steady disclosures and surprising revelations, the book's twists and turns manage to hold the reader hostage until the denouement." Publ Wkly

Johansen, Iris

  Final target. Bantam Bks. 2001 340p $24.95

  ISBN 0-553-80094-9

LC 00-65124

At the center of this thriller "is the Wind Dancer, a priceless gold statue of the winged horse Pegasus. The statue has been in the Andreas family since the fall of Troy and now, centuries later, U.S. President Jonathan Andreas is in Paris to lend the family heirloom to a museum. On the night of the ceremony, his daughter, seven-year-old Cassie, is awakened at the family's farmhouse in the south of France by masked men who murder her nanny and her nurse, intent on kidnapping Cassie and ransoming her in exchange for the Wind Dancer. Cassie is saved in the nick of time by the arrival of Michael Travis, international underworld information dealer, but eight months later, the child is being treated in the Virginia home of psychiatrist Dr. Jessica Riley and Jessica's psychically extrasensitive sister, Melissa, for severe catatonic trauma. . . . Michael Travis then reappears and lures Cassie and the Riley sisters into a web of intrigue." Publ Wkly

Johansen, Iris

  The **killing** game. Bantam Bks. 1999 355p

  ISBN 0-553-10624-4

LC 99-20999

Following the abduction and murder of her daughter in The face of deception, forensic sculptor Eve Duncan "has abandoned the day-to-day world for life on a Tahitian island. Eve's tropical exile is interrupted, however, when Joe {Quinn} shows up to tell her that a pile of bodies has been discovered in the Georgia woods, including that of a young girl he believes may be Eve's daughter. Determined to reconstruct the skull and hoping to lay her daughter to rest, Eve returns to the U.S. Her arrival draws the attention of Dom, the psychotic serial killer responsible for the Georgia murders. Random attacks on social outcasts don't produce the rush they once did for Dom, and now he needs to up the ante, by stalking and murdering more prominent people and interacting with his victims before he attacks. Eve, whose story he has long followed in newspaper accounts, becomes his next target." Publ Wkly

"Johansen's novel of psychological suspense features a hair-raising plot, a fiendish killer, a brave heroine, and dozens of heartstopping plot twists." Booklist

Johansen, Iris

  Long after midnight. Bantam Bks. 1997 371p

  ISBN 978-0553097153

LC 96-24957

"Johansen knows how to take the formula and run with it, and readers will be won over by her flesh-and-blood characters, crackling dialogue and lean, suspenseful plotting." Publ Wkly

Johansen, Iris

  Taking eve; Iris Johansen. St. Martin's Press 2013 352 p. (hardcover) $27.99

    ISBN 1250019982; 9781250019981

LC 2013002635

This is Iris Johansen's 15th novel featuring forensic sculptor Eve Duncan and begins a new trilogy. "A gunman taking a shot at Eve's adopted daughter, Jane, interrupts the quiet life that Eve and her longtime lover, police detective Joe Quinn, have been leading at their lakeside cottage outside Atlanta, Ga. To add to their woes, a madman, Jim Doane, kidnaps Eve and orders her to reconstruct the face of his late son, Kevin, from what he claims is Kevin's skull." (Publishers Weekly)

Johansen, Iris

The **ugly** duckling. Bantam Bks. 1996 378p
ISBN 978-0553097146

LC 95-36175

"Nell Carter is plain and plump—and, for some mysterious reason, the target of a drug cartel hit that maims her but wipes out her husband and young daughter. Her world destroyed, Nell wills herself to die, until a stranger gives her a purpose to live: revenge. The mysterious Nicholas Tanek, once master of his own criminal network, will do anything and use anyone to destroy the drug cartel that, he tells Nell, murdered a 'very close' friend. . . . Given a new face and identity, Nell throws herself into guerrilla and martial arts training with Nicholas." Publ Wkly

Johnson, Adam, 1967-

★ The **orphan** master's son; Adam Johnson. Random House 2012 443p. hbk $26
ISBN 9780679643999 ebook; 9780812992793

LC 2011013410

Pulitzer Prize: Fiction (2013)

The novel is "set within the highest levels of the North Korean dictatorship. . . . The orphan master's son is Pak Jun Do, and he has perhaps the most valuable skill possible for advancement in North Korea -- the gift of saying a lie while speaking the truth. His bravery and fearlessness leading Army orphan brigades through dangerous mines is quickly noted, and Jun Do is selected for even more difficult missions - kidnapping Japanese citizens and repatriating them to North Korea, then language school and back to a fishing boat to spy on American submarines. . . . The Americans have confused Jun Do with a government minister who often is at dangerous odds with Kim Jong Il. . . . So the . . . Leader simply replaces the commander with Jun Do -- sending the once-powerful man into the mines and Do to live with his beautiful actress-wife and kids." (USA Today)

Johnson, Adam, 1967-

Parasites like us; a novel. Viking 2003 341p $24.95
ISBN 0-670-03240-9

LC 2002-41181

"Johnson relates all of this with great ingenuity and bravado—as well as a good deal of unfocused energy. . . . The most daring element in this heterogeneous mix, however, may well be the vein of earnest solemnity that Johnson adds to it. Unlike most satirists, he's not afraid to let the mask of irony fall occasionally." N Y Times Book Rev

Johnson, Alaya Dawn

Moonshine; [by] Alaya Johnson. Thomas Dunne Books/St. Martin's Press 2010 278p pa $14.99
ISBN 978-0-312-56547-3; 0-312-64806-5

LC 2009-39261

"The author imagines jazz-age New York as a city in which vampires and other supernatural denizens stalk the same streets as entertainers like Josephine Baker or the corrupt politicians of Tammany Hall. Our narrator is feisty Zephyr Hollis, daughter of a famous monster-hunter, who has reinvented herself in the city as a social organizer and teacher. Zephyr preaches tolerance of nonhumans but carries a silver switchblade to protect herself from the nightlife, despite a natural immunity to vampires. Among her interesting companions are ambitious tabloid reporter Lily Harding, progressive activist Iris Tomkins and, most dangerously, Amir the Djinn. . . . A bit jumbled, but entertaining and potentially a good start for a series offering a different take on the undead craze." Kirkus

Johnson, B. S.

The **unfortunates**; [with an introduction by Jonathan Coe] New Directions Pub. 2007 [134] $24.95
ISBN 978-0-8112-1743-9; 0-8112-1743-4

LC 2007-23007

First published 1969; this edition 1999, in the United Kingdom

"Johnson insisted that his randomly sorted sections were better at 'conveying the mind's randomness' than any other technique. But this novelty provides little in the way of mimesis, it only draws attention to itself. And yet it proves to be a great deal of fun. . . . For its honest depiction of how young men deal with cancer, 'The Unfortunates' can be widely recommended. . . Johnson's own dogged seriousness, and his concomitant boyishness, make a fascinating medium for his occasional bursts of pity and shy friendliness." N Y Sun

Johnson, Barb

More of this world or maybe another; Barb Johnson. Harper Perennial 2009 188, 12p (pbk.) $13.99
ISBN 9780061732270

LC 2010277106

Stonewall Book Awards: Barbara Gittings Literature Award (2011)

In this collection of interconnected short stories, author Barb "Johnson maps the lives of several New Orleanians who orbit Delia Delahoussaye's Laundromat on Palmyra Street, where 'saying hello and fighting can sound just alike.' The title story finds a stoned teenage Delia longing to kiss a girl named Chuck in the belly of an empty oil tank, a makeshift sense-deprivation chamber that Delia thinks 'shakes you loose from yourself.' By the end of the second story, 'Keeping Her Difficult Balance,' it's unclear whether Delia will ever escape her childhood identity. 'If the Holy Spirit Comes for You' finds her brother, Dooley, nursing a pig his uncles want to slaughter, and the story's moral nuance and consequences echo through 'Killer Heart,' where an older Dooley's good deeds lead to tragedy." (Publishers Weekly)

Johnson, Charles Richard

Dr. King's refrigerator and other bedtime stories; [by] Charles Johnson. Scribner 2005 123p $20
ISBN 0-7432-6453-3

LC 2004-56642

"Johnson is once again at the ready with his quirky, professorial writing style and his melange of Buddhism, Western philosophy and African magic realism." N Y Times Book Rev

Johnson, Charles Richard

Dreamer; a novel. [by] Charles Johnson. Scribner 1998 236p

ISBN 0-684-81224-X

LC 98-10201

"It's a joy to read fiction in which there is a cultivated vision at work. Among the accomplishments of 'Dreamer' is an overarching argument that the Truth is an amalgamation, a messy mosaic full of contradictions . . . and that the best way to get at it is to include a lot." N Y Times Book Rev

Johnson, Charles Richard

★ **Middle** passage; [by] Charles Johnson. Atheneum Pubs. 1990 209p

LC 90-32713

"Johnson's exciting sea narrative provides an unusual historical look at the horrifying Middle Passage experience. . . . Like Moby-Dick's Ahab, the captain of the Republic is on his own special quest (in this case, the capture of the African trickster god). . . . Above all, the book is valuable in offering a rare perspective of the shocking experience of the slave trade and the consequences of that event for American blacks." Choice

Johnson, Craig, 1961-

Another man's moccasins; Craig Johnson. Viking 2008 290 p.

ISBN 0670018619; 9780670018611

LC 2007029979

Spur Awards: Best Western Novel, Short Novel (2009)

In Craig Johnson's "fourth mystery to feature Wyoming sheriff Walt Longmire, . . . Walt responds to a call that leads to the discovery of the body of a young Vietnamese woman, Ho Thi Paquet, along an Absaroka County highway. Squatting nearby with Paquet's purse is a massive Crow Indian later identified as Virgil White Buffalo. When Walt finds a photograph of himself and a Vietnamese barmaid taken in 1968 among the victim's belongings, Walt realizes that the murder isn't as clear-cut as it appears. With the help of his longtime friend, Cheyenne Indian Henry Standing Bear, Walt retraces Paquet's steps and uncovers disturbing links to a California human trafficking ring as well as to his own past as a military inspector in Vietnam." (Publishers Weekly)

Johnson, Craig, 1961-

The **dark** horse. Viking 2009 318p

ISBN 0-670-02087-7; 978-0-670-02087-4

LC 2008-54093

In this outing, "Sheriff Walt Longmire goes undercover to prove that Mary Barsad, confessed murderer, did not kill her husband after he shot her horses and set the barn on fire. Walt finds that there is a lot more going on in Wyoming's remote Powder River area, as he meets a cast of characters with much to hide. . . . Johnson's deft, twisty storytelling immediately grips the reader. His latest has a heart as big as a Wyoming sky." Libr J

Johnson, Craig

Death without company; Craig Johnson. Viking 2006 xii, 271 p.p

ISBN 9780670034673; 0670034673

LC 2005042357

In this book, part of the Walt Longmire mystery series, "Mari Baroja is found poisoned at the Durant Home for Assisted Living" so "Sheriff Longmire is drawn into an investigation that reaches fifty years into the mysterious woman's dramatic Basque past. Aided by his friend Henry Standing Bear, Deputy Victoria Moretti, and newcomer Santiago Saizarbitoria, Sheriff Longmire must connect the specter of the past to the present to find the killer among them." (Amazon.com)

"Johnson combines a vivid sense of the dailiness of life--and the way human relationships take root in that dailiness--with a sure--handed touch for jolting both his characters and his readers out of their comfort zones and deep into harm's way." Booklist

Johnson, Craig, 1961-

Hell is empty. Viking 2011 viii, 312p

ISBN 9780670022779; 0670022772

LC 2010048021

This book tells the story of "Sheriff Walt Longmire of Absaroka County, Wyo., a self-deprecating and experienced lawman . . . [whose assignment to] a seemingly simple prisoner transport evolves into a grueling physical and mental trial where Walt doggedly pursues an escaped psychotic murderer." (denverpost.com)

Johnson, Dana

Elsewhere, California; Dana Johnson. Counterpoint 2012 276 p. $15.95

ISBN 158243784X; 9781582437842

This novel tells the story of Avery Arlington, an African-American girl who "is nine when her family escapes L.A.'s gang violence and moves to the suburbs, becoming the only black people in the neighborhood. Feeling alienated, but impressionable, Avery adjusts . . . . At 40, Avery has become a visual artist, her rich and sensual Italian boyfriend clearly instrumental in helping her find the self-acceptance that eluded her for so long." The story shifts between Avery's past and present. (Publishers Weekly)

Johnson, Denis, 1949-

Jesus' son; stories. Farrar, Straus & Giroux 1992 160p $19

ISBN 0-374-17892-5

LC 92-16880

This is a collection of eleven short stories "linked by a common narrator—a young, nameless substance abuser of unspecified background and education. Like the other marginal and directionless individuals who populate these tales, he is locked into a downward spiral of booze, drugs, and petty crime, the squalor of his life emblematic of a more profound spiritual malaise." (Libr J)

In this is "masterfully bleak sequence of short stories narrated by a young heartland lowlife, brutality is unpredictable and unremarkable: shootings, stabbings, guns held to heads, heroin overdoses, gruesome car wrecks—and confrontations that don't turn violent only because the antagonists can't stay focused. . . . As grunge sociology, 'Jesus' Son' is claustrophobic; as art, it's exhilarating." Newsweek

Johnson, Denis

Nobody move; a novel. Farrar, Straus and Giroux 2009 196p $23

ISBN 978-0-374-22290-1; 0-374-22290-8

LC 2008-43420

Originally serialized, in slightly different form, in Playboy

"Johnson's sympathies seem to be with Gambol, a bad man who isn't so much seeking redemption as having redemption thrust on him. When offered an exit out of this seedy underworld, he takes it with Mary, a 'heavyset blonde' and former Army medic who brings him back to health. Gambol may deal in death, and sometimes even take pleasure in it, but he is distinguished by a lack of human hatred for others and himself. In the brutal world of Nobody Move, that makes all the difference." Pittsburgh City Paper

Johnson, Denis, 1949-

★ **Train** dreams. Farrar, Straus and Giroux 2011 116p $18

ISBN 978-0-374-28114-4; 0-374-28114-9

LC 2011007505

First published, in slightly different form, 2002 in The Paris Review

"The story concerns the life of Robert Grainier, a fictional orphan shipped by train in 1893 into the woods of the Idaho panhandle. He grows up, works on logging gangs, falls in love, and loses his wife and baby daughter to a particularly pernicious wildfire. What Johnson builds from the ashes of Grainier's life is a tender, lonesome and riveting story, an American epic writ small, in which Grainier drives a horse cart, flies in a biplane, takes part in occasionally hilarious exchanges and goes maybe 42 percent crazy. It's a love story, a hermit's story and a refashioning of age-old wolf-based folklore like 'Little Red Cap.' It's also a small masterpiece. You look up from the thing dazed, slightly changed." N Y Times Book Rev

Johnson, Denis

Tree of smoke. Farrar, Straus & Giroux 2007 614p $27

ISBN 978-0-374-27912-7; 0-374-27912-8

LC 2007-06562

"Mr. Johnson not only succeeds in conjuring the anomalous, hallucinatory aura of the Vietnam War as authoritatively as Stephen Wright or Francis Ford Coppola, but he also shows its fallout on his characters with harrowing emotional precision. He has written a flawed but deeply resonant novel that is bound to become one of the classic works of literature produced by that tragic and uncannily familiar war." N Y Times (Late N Y Ed)

Johnson, Diane

L'affaire. Dutton 2003 340p

ISBN 0-525-94740-X

LC 2003-13725

"Amy Hawkins, a beautiful, naive, suddenly very rich Califonian dot-com entrepreneur, comes to a posh ski resort in the French Alps as part of her plan for cultural self-improvement. When she generously pays for transporting the dying Adrian Venn, a publisher crushed in a landslide, back to his native England, her humanitarian gesture backfires with exquisite irony. Venn's two grown English children, his illegitimate French daughter, his new much younger American wife and their toddler son become embroiled in a classic scenario of quarreling heirs, each seething with expectations at the expense of the others." Publ Wkly

"Much of the wit comes from Johnson's shrewd view of her characters' cultural assumptions, which are both simplistic and devilishly on target." N Y Times Book Rev

Johnson, Diane

Le divorce. Dutton 1997 309p

ISBN 978-0452277335

LC 96-9644

"The author pokes fun at the Americans for moralizing, and at the French for being amoral; and she manages to be even-handed because she displays admiration for French elegance of behavior, and affection for American earnest good will." N Y Rev Books

Johnson, Diane

Le mariage; a novel. Dutton 2000 322p $23.95

ISBN 0-525-94518-0

LC 99-89849

This companion to Le divorce is "set again in Paris with a few overlapping characters, the plot revolves around two couples—Tim Nolinger, a Belgian American journalist engaged to the very French Anne-Sophie, a dealer in equine collectibles; and the very beautiful American Clara, a former actress married to the reclusive film director Serge Clay. Thrown into the entertaining mix is a stolen illuminated manuscript, a murdered flea market dealer, Y2K cults, an adulterous liaison, and of course Johnson's perceptive and witty insights on love, marriage, and Anglo-French relations." Libr J

Johnson, Diane

Lulu in Marrakech. Dutton 2008 307p $25.95

ISBN 978-0-525-95037-0

LC 2008-07700

"The love story fizzles and pops and then seems to fizzle out, but as with any great mystery, the answers are not always what they seem, and Johnson rivets the story with romantic intrigue no matter how Lulu's luck is going." N Y Post

Johnson, Mat

Pym; a novel. Spiegel & Grau 2010 322p $24

ISBN 978-0-8129-8158-2; 0-8129-8158-8

LC 2010-29331

"Recently canned professor of American literature Chris Jaynes is obsessed with The Narrative of Arthur Gordon Pym of Nantucket, Edgar Allan Poe's strange and only novel. When he discovers the manuscript of a crude slave narrative that seems to confirm the reality of Poe's fiction, he resolves to seek out Tsalal, the remote island of pure and utter blackness that Poe describes with horror. Jaynes imagines it to be the last untouched bastion of the African Diaspora and the key to his personal salvation. He convenes an all-black crew of six to follow Pym's trail to the South Pole in search of adventure, natural resources to exploit, and, for Jaynes at least, the mythical world of the novel." Publisher's note

Johnson, Stephanie

The **sailmaker's** daughter. St. Martin's Press 2003 255p il map $23.95

ISBN 0-312-30693-8

LC 2003-40639

First published 1996 in the United Kingdom with title: The heart's wild surf

"The book follows 12-year-old Olive McNab during the month she is sent to her aunt and uncle's plantation while her mother is dying of influenza. Olive is haunted by ghosts of the family dead, appalled by her uncle's coarse brutality, fascinated by two free-spirited British lady travelers who are passing through, and, most of all, anguished by her mother's approaching death. In Johnson's poetic hands Olive and her eccentric family come to life." Libr J

Johnson, Wayne

The **devil** you know; a novel. Shaye Areheart Books 2004 381p

ISBN 0-609-60964-5

LC 2003011616

"Johnson surrounds a mythic, Deliverance-like confrontation with evil . . . with a subtly realsitic coming-of-age story about a teenager's conflict with his abusive father. Rising above cliché at every seemily predictable turn, the novel works on both levels: a literary thriller with an abundance of heart." Booklist

Johnston, Terry C.

Dance on the wind. Bantam Bks. 1995 517p

LC 95-7558

The author "is a deservedly popular western author whose appeal lies not so much in the adventures he dramatizes as in the depth of his characters. They love, grieve, laugh, and feel guilt, anger, and jealousy. They're real people, not just providers of vicarious thrills." Booklist

Johnston, Terry C.

Lay the mountains low; the flight of the Nez Perce from Idaho and the Battle of the Big Hole, August 9-10, 1877. St. Martin's Press 2000 xxii, 495p il

ISBN 0-312-26189-6

LC 00-24201

"In this tale of five Nez Perce tribal leaders who choose to resist the encroaching white settlers and who refuse to make treaties with the U.S. government, Johnston provides gripping, authentic details of historically accurate events; readers see the Nez Perce wars through the eyes of those involved and read actual letters and newspaper clippings of the day. Besides the historical details, the novel presents a compelling, action-packed story." Libr J

Includes bibliographical references

Johnston, Terry C.

Wind walker. Bantam Bks. 2001 461p map $24.95

ISBN 0-553-09090-9

LC 00-48570

This final installment in the Titus Bass series "covers six years (1847-1853) and sees the scarred, aging, one-eyed mountain man struggling to find peace and sanctuary in a changing world. The fur trade is finished, free mountain men are few and white immigrants are flooding the pristine and untamed wilderness. Bass knows his independent way of life is over, so he takes his Indian family north, hoping to settle with his wife's Crow relatives. Bass's final journey, however, will not be easy. . . . Titus Bass is a believable, enduring character, a solitary man who lives by his wits, believes in mountain justice and is willing to use rifle or tomahawk to settle a score when he knows right is on his side." Publ Wkly

Johnston, Wayne

The **colony** of unrequited dreams. Anchor Bks. (NY) 1999 562p

ISBN 0-385-49542-0

LC 99-19144

"The very human story of Smallwood and Fielding and its historical counterpoint may both appear inauspicious, even contrived, at first, but as the book proceeds they and their pairing gather momentum to achieve a mesmerizing inevitability." N Y Times Book Rev

Johnston, Wayne

The **custodian** of paradise. W. W. Norton & Co. 2007 510p $25.95

ISBN 978-0-393-06491-9; 0-393-06491-3

LC 2006-102234

First published 2006 in Canada

"If, as critics have suggested, Fielding is like Newfoundland itself—huge, beautiful, with an unknown heart (and an alcohol problem)—the trope here extends to her ancestry, which is irregular and also larger than life. In the manner of Lawrence Durrell's Alexandria Quartet, events in this book don't necessarily line up with those in the first. . . . By the book's end, many mysteries have been laid to rest, only to be replaced with new ones. This raises the happy possibility that Johnston intends to return to the scene again." Quill & Quire

Johnston, Wayne

The **navigator** of New York; a novel. Doubleday 2002 483p $27.95

ISBN 0-385-50767-4

LC 2002-71418

"Polar exploration—with its incredible hardships, its months of freezing isolation, darkness and despair—makes an irresistable metaphor for a lonely and uncertain childhood. The story itself is told through Devlin's deliberately understated narration and Cook's long expository letters and monologues, which can be tedious at times but which echo the straightforward humble-heroic tone of a Victorian explorer." N Y Times Book Rev

Joinson, Suzanne

A **lady** cyclist's guide to Kashgar; Suzanne Joinson. Bloomsbury 2012 374 p.

ISBN 9781608198115

LC 2011046720

Part of this book is set in "1923 . . . [as] Evangeline English, keen lady cyclist, arrives with her sister Lizzie at the ancient Silk Route city of Kashgar to help establish a Christian mission. Lizzie is in thrall to their forceful and unyielding leader Millicent, but Eva's motivations for leaving her bourgeois life back at home are less clear-cut. . . . In present-day London, . . . Frieda, a young woman adrift in her own life, opens her front door one night to find a man sleeping on the landing. . . . Tayeb, who has fled to England from Yemen, has arrived on Frieda's doorstep just as she learns that she is the next-of-kin to a dead woman she has never heard of. . . . The two wanderers begin an unlikely friendship as their worlds collide." (Publisher's note)

Jonasson, Jonas

The **100**-year-old man who climbed out the window and disappeared; Jonas Jonasson; translated from the Swedish by Rod Bradbury. Hyperion 2012 384 p. (paperback) $15.99; (ebook) $15.99; (lib. bdg.) $36.95

ISBN 1401324649; 9781401324643; 9781401304393; 9781611735949

LC 2012016448

This book by Jonas Jonasson follows "Allan Karlsson, the centenarian who sneaks out of his nursing home. . . . In his travels, he has not only met just about every famous and infamous world leader but has inadvertently played a significant role in many world events. . . . Chapters alternate between Allan's big adventures in the past and in the present, where he gets mixed up with a zany bunch of Swedes and a former circus elephant as they try to avoid both cops and gangsters." (Library Journal)

Jones, Chris Morgan

★ The **silent** oligarch; Chris Morgan Jones. Penguin Press 2012 312 p.

ISBN 9781594203190

LC 2011044536

In this book "[m]ysterious men, cryptic of speech and beautifully tailored, move through glittery settings-seacoasts, grand hotels, swank neighborhoods. . . . Rows of massive buildings 'bullied all the leaves off the bare limes and left the trees cowering in the middle of the road.' Ben Webster is a snoop employed by a London corporate espionage firm. His boss' client has hired the company to bring down a Kremlin functionary, the toadlike Malin, whose manipulation of Russia's oil industry is making him a trillionaire. Webster attempts to get at the toad through his dithering money launderer, Richard Lock. . . . Men are betrayed. Drugged. Kidnapped. Tossed off buildings. Downed by snipers. If the good guys win, it's at such a cost they're left wondering if they accomplished anything. They did." (Booklist)

Jones, Darynda

Second grave on the left. St. Martin's Press 2011 307p $21.99

ISBN 978-0-312-36081-8

LC 2011-11243

Sequel to First grave on the right (2011)

"The fiery relationship between Charley and Reyes will satisfy paranormal romance fans, but it's the distinctive characters, dead and alive, and the almost constant laughs that will leave readers eager for the next installment." Publ Wkly

Jones, Diana Wynne

A **sudden** wild magic. Morrow 1992 412p

LC 92-10860

"Jones's sly sense of humor and her accurate, affectionate depiction of relations between women and men give an extra kick to this effervescent tale." Publ Wkly

Jones, Douglas C.

Arrest Sitting Bull. Scribner 1977 249p

LC 77-7645

In this second volume of a western historical trilogy, the author tells it "as it really did happen when the order went out: 'Arrest Sitting Bull.' We begin with the Ghost Dance, when that confusion of Indian mythology and missionary-brought Christianity has fired the Plain Indians to a belief in the coming of an Indian Messiah. Sitting Bull, already the conqueror of Custer, the veteran of Buffalo Bill's Wild West Show, is back on the reservation, but at the center of a growing revolt against the white man. . . . Jones makes us understand the torment of a minority of decent white men and women who really cared about the Indians and of the Indians, trapped between a fight to the death (the novel closes with Wounded Knee three days off), and a willingness to try to assimilate themselves to the white man's ways." Publ Wkly

Followed by A creek called Wounded Knee

Jones, Douglas C.

★ The **court**-martial of George Armstrong Custer. Scribner 1976 291p

"Slowly building the cases for the prosecution and defense, Jones does well by mixing the drama of courtroom proceedings with the color of a controversial incident." Booklist

Followed by Arrest Sitting Bull

Jones, Douglas C.

A **creek** called Wounded Knee. Scribner 1978 236p

LC 78-16660

In the concluding volume of the trilogy, the author "tells the story of the Wounded Knee tragedy through the eyes of the principals: the Indians, the Federal troops, and the Press. Each chapter of the novel begins with a verbatim lead from an 1890 newspaper that if not finding the war inevitable at least found it irresistable. The Press did much to make the day." Best Sellers

Jones, Edward, 1951-

All Aunt Hagar's children. Amistad 2006 399p $25.95

ISBN 0060557567; 9780060557560

LC 2006-42746

"This collection of 14 short stories" by Edward P. Jones depicts "black life in America. His stories span the 20th century in Washington, DC. Jones's Washington is not as much the center of international power as a place offering hope for rural descendants of slaves. Several characters have made it to the middle class, often through government employment, but economic success doesn't exempt one from suffering." (Library Journal)

"In 14 short stories, Jones . . . demonstrates his skill at drawing complex and nuanced characters and predicaments.

Washington, D.C., is the setting for this collection of stories in assorted time frames with assorted characters, most of whom come from the rural South, and all of whom are coping with the transformation of their lives and their adjustments to a new way of life. . . . Jones' stories are rich in detail and emotions as he plumbs the intricacies of people's relationships with one another and with spiritual forces at work in urban as well as natural environments." Booklist

Jones, Edward P., 1951-

The **known** world. Amistad 2003 388p $24.95

ISBN 0-06-055754-0

LC 2003-40389

This work of historical fiction explores "the world of blacks who owned blacks in the antebellum South." The book "starts with the dying 31-year-old Henry Townsend, a former slave -- now master of 33 slaves of his own and more than 50 acres of land . . . worried about the fate of his holdings upon his early death." (Publishers Weekly)

"Henry Townsend, born a slave, is purchased and freed by his father, yet he remains attached to his former owner, even taking lessons in slave owning when he eventually buys his own slaves. Townsend is part of a small enclave of free blacks who own slaves, thus offering another angle on the complexities of slavery and social relations in a Virginia town just before the Civil War." Booklist

Jones, J. Sydney

The **silence**; J. Sydney Jones. Severn House 2011 240p.

ISBN 9780727880840

This book tells the story of "[y]oung lawyer Karl Werthen [who] loves taking on private investigations . . . [and] is eager to pursue the disappearance of a member of the illustrious Wittgenstein family. Concurrently, a Vienna councilman is found shot in his office, an apparent suicide. Working his missing-person case, Werthen interviews a gay freelance journalist who knows young Wittgenstein and, interestingly, has also been writing inflammatory articles about council activities. The missing man is soon found, but the journalist is murdered. Afraid that his interview triggered the man's death, Werthen feels morally compelled to identify the killer." (Libr J)

Jones, James, 1921-1977

★ **From** here to eternity. Scribner 1951 861p

This book by James Jones follows two American soldiers in the months before the bonbing of Pearl Harbor, Hawaii. " Pvt. Robert E. Lee Prewitt is a champion welterweight and a fine bugler. But when he refuses to join the company's boxing team, he gets "the treatment" that may break him or kill him. First Sgt. Milton Anthony Warden knows how to soldier better than almost anyone, yet he's risking his career to have an affair with the commanding officer's wife." (Publisher's note)

"Mr. Jones has grappled with a variety of materials and handles some of them less successfully than others. There is a good deal of weak stuff in the two love affairs and the characterizations of the women, and the sorties into the field of general ideas are unimpressive. The book as a whole, however, is a spectacular achievement; it has tremendous vitality and driving power and graphic authenticity." Atlantic

Jones, James, 1921-1977

★ The **thin** red line. Scribner 1962 495p

"This novel will surely offend some readers, lavishly bespattered as it is with Anglo-Saxon words and physiological detail. Nevertheless, it bears the Jones stamp of authenticity and is a major combat novel of World War II." Ont Libr Rev

Followed by Whistle

Jones, James

Whistle. Delacorte Press 1978 457p

LC 77-11980

This is the final installment of Jones' war trilogy, which also includes From here to eternity and The thin red line. This book begins in 1943, when "four soldiers from an infantry company in the Pacific are sent by boat and train to an army hospital in Tennessee. . . . These men, who have known no security except what the company provided, are quickly unhinged by faithless wives and intolerable families, by their rage and despair at the human condition. . . . To stave off disintegration, these out-of-work warriors resort to . . . drink and brawls, politics and sex. . . . The outline for the conclusion of the book . . . has been pieced together {following his death} from Jones's notes and conversations by his friend and fellow writer Willie Morris." Newsweek

Jones, Lloyd

Mister Pip. Dial Press 2007 256p hardcover o.p. pa $15

ISBN 978-0-385-34106-6; 0-385-34106-7; 978-0-385-34107-3 pa; 0-385-34107-5 pa

LC 2007-5224

First published 2006 in Australia

"The novel is a paean to the transformative power of literature, particularly its ability to occlude an unpleasant reality with a fictional alternative and to expand an individual's sense of possibility." N Y Sun

Jones, Luanne

The **Dixie** Belle's Guide to Love; Luanne Jones. Avon Books 2002 374p (pbk.) $5.99

ISBN 9780380819348

In this book, "when her two-timing husband leaves her with nothing but ownership of the local Pig Rib Palace, Rita Stark decides to get her life back into high gear and turn the rib joint into a cash cow. But her best girlfriends are sure the former Miss Dixie Belle Duchess needs help getting the eatery -- and her recently broken heart -- back into shape. So they've hired the sexiest man ever to hit Hellon, Tennessee, Will 'Wild Billy' West, to lend a hand. Will's suddenly relighting a fire that Rita was sure went out long ago. What could a sexy prize like him possibly see in a small-town gal like her, especially when he's planning to skip town at summer's end?" (Publisher's note)

Jones, Sadie

Outcast. Harper 2008 347p $24.95

ISBN 978-0-06-137403-6; 0-06-137403-2

"An explosive drama, fuelled by the repression of 1950s Britain. Troubled 19-year-old Lewis Aldridge has never recovered from the death of his mother. After a stint in prison, he heads home and attempts to convince his father of his worth. But his good intentions crumble in the face of his father's disapproval, and Lewis reveals the horrifying realities that lie under the seemingly sedate rural community. Devastatingly good." Marie Claire

Jones, Sadie

Small wars; a novel. Harper 2010 376p $24.99
ISBN 978-0-06-192988-5; 0-06-192988-3
LC 2009-45485
First published 2009 in the United Kingdom

"Hal Treherne graduated from the Royal Military Academy Sandhurst six months too late to see action in World War II. So the third-generation Army scion, now a popular major with a reputation for fair play, is rather chuffed when he gets his chance on British-occupied Cyprus 10 years later. His wife, Clara, and two baby daughters follow him out to the rocky island, where Clara is faced with the unenviable task of trying to maintain the home front in the face of guerrilla warfare. . . . Jones toggles back and forth between Clara's fear and boredom at home, and Hal's days of house-to-house searches for terrorists and firefights in the mountains. Jones is excellent at evoking fraught moments in both halves of the Trehernes' lives." Christ Sci Monit

Jones, Sadie

The **uninvited** guests; Sadie Jones. HarperCollins 2012 262 p.
ISBN 0062116509; 9780062116505
LC 2012372210
This novel by Sadie Jones begins "[o]ne late spring evening in 1912, in the kitchens at Sterne, preparations begin for an elegant supper party in honor of Emerald Torrington's twentieth birthday. But only a few miles away, a dreadful accident propels a crowd of mysterious and not altogether savory survivors to seek shelter at the ramshackle manor—and the household is thrown into confusion and mischief. . . . As the passengers wearily search for rest, the house undergoes a strange transformation. One of their number (who is most definitely not a gentleman) makes it his business to join the birthday revels. Evening turns to stormy night, and a most unpleasant parlor game threatens to blow respectability to smithereens." (Publisher's note)

Jones, Sherry

Four sisters, all queens; Sherry Jones. 1st Gallery Books trade pbk ed Gallery Books 2012 434 p. ill., map (paperback) $15.99
ISBN 1451633246; 9781451633245; 9781451633252
LC 2011044484
In this historical novel, by Sherry Jones, "[a]mid the lush valleys and fragrant wildflowers of Provence, . . . Marguerite's illustrious match with the young King Louis IX makes her Queen of France. Soon Eleonore . . . is betrothed to Henry III of England. In turn, . . . Sanchia and . . . Beatrice wed noblemen who will also make them queens. . . . [L]oyalty succumbs to bitter sibling rivalry, and sister is pitted against sister for . . . Provence itself." (Publisher's note)

Jones, Tayari

Silver sparrow; a novel. Algonquin Books of Chapel Hill 2011 340p
ISBN 1-56512-990-3; 978-1-56512-990-0
LC 2010-48098

"A tense, layered and evocative tale. . . , Jones explores the rivalry and connection of siblings, the meaning of beauty, the perils of young womanhood, the complexities of romantic relationships and the contemporary African-American experience." Minneapolis Star Trib

Jong, Erica

★ **Fear** of flying; a novel. Holt, Rinehart & Winston 1973 340p

"At times, Jong gets caught in clichés about women, men, sex, and Jewish mothers, all {of} which she could do without. However, when she takes herself more seriously, the language is penetrating, paying tribute to her worth as a poet." Libr J

Followed by How to save your own life (1977) and Parachutes and kisses (1984 paper only)

Jong, Erica

Sappho's leap; a novel. Norton 2003 316p $24.95
ISBN 0-393-05761-5
LC 2002-155113
Jong's "effort to bring to life an ancient writer engrossed in politics, family and the creation of poety is a relief from the relentlessly everyday sincerity of much current 'women-oriented' writing." N Y Times Book Rev

Jonsson, Reidar

My life as a dog; translated by Eivor Martinus. Farrar, Straus & Giroux 1990 219p
LC 89-46390
Original Swedish edition, 1983; this translation first published 1989 in the United Kingdom

"The novel's anecdotal style accommodates a boy's confabulation. Occasionally wayward and a bit too long in their descriptions, his comedic exploits cast Ingemar as schlemiel, underdog and, yes, dog. . . . It is Sickan's fate that finally helps Ingemar come to terms with his dead mother." N Y Times Book Rev

Jordan, Hillary, 1963-

Mudbound; a novel. Algonquin Books of Chapel Hill 2008 328p $22.95
ISBN 978-1-56512-569-8; 1-56512-569-X
LC 2007-44471
"With authentic, earthy prose . . . Jordan picks at the scabs of racial inequality that will perhaps never fully heal and brings just enough heartbreak to this intimate, universal tale, just enough suspense, to leave us contemplating how the lives and motives of these vivid characters might have been different." San Antonio Express-News

Jordan, Hillary, 1963-

When she woke; a novel. Algonquin Books of Chapel Hill 2011 344p
ISBN 1565126297; 9781565126299; 1-56512-629-7; 978-1-56512-629-9
LC 201122799
This book tells the story of "Hannah Payne . . . [whose] life has been devoted to church and family, but after her arrest, she awakens to a nightmare: she is lying on a table in a bare room, covered only by a paper gown, and cameras

are broadcasting her every move to millions at home, for home observing new Chromes--criminals whose skin color has been genetically altered to match the class of their crime--is a new and sinister form of entertainment. Hannah is a Red; her crime is murder. The victim, says the state of Texas, was her unborn child, and Hannah is determined to protect the identity of the father—a public figure with whom she's shared a fierce and forbidden love." (Publisher's note)

"Jordan manages to open up powerful feminist and political themes without becoming overly preachy—and the parallels with Hawthorne are fun to trace." Kirkus

Jordan, Robert, 1948-2007
A **memory** of light; Robert Jordan and Brandon Sanderson. 1st ed. Tor 2013 909 p. ill., col. maps (The wheel of time) (hardcover) $34.99

ISBN 0765325950; 9780765325952

LC 2012037361

In this book by Robert Jordan and Brandon Sanderson, "[i]t is time for Rand al'Thor to face the Dark One in the Last Battle for humanity, but he can't do it alone; he must also gather all of the forces of the world together and turn them, united, against the Trolloc armies that threaten to overwhelm." (Publishers Weekly)

Joseph, Manu
★ **Serious** men. W.W. Norton & Co. 2010 310p pa $14.95

ISBN 978-0-393-33859-1; 0-393-33859-2

LC 2010-09298

Joseph's "novel elegantly describes collisions with an unyielding status quo, ably counterpointing the frustrations of the powerless with the unfulfilling realities of power. With this astute comedy of manners he makes a convincing bid for his own recognition as a novelist of serious talent, the latest addition to a roster of Indian writers who are creating fine literary art from their country's fearsome contradictions." Independent

Joshi, S. T.
The **white** people and other weird stories; edited with an introduction and notes by S.T. Joshi; foreword by Guillermo del Toro. Penguin Books 2011 xxviii, 377p (Penguin classics)

ISBN 0143105590; 9780143105596

LC 2011027590

This book presents a collection of fantasy stories. "In 'The Inmost Light' . . . a scientist constructs a gem that can contain a human soul, leaving the soul's owner a demonic empty husk. . . . In the gory 'Novel of the White Powder'. . . a woman watches as her husband slowly turns into a malevolent creature from the ingestion of a curative prescribed for depression." (Times Literary Supplement)

"At the turn of the 20th century, Welsh author Machen (The Hill of Dreams) wrote tales about evil and 'ecstasy' (his term for supernatural experience) that made a significant impact on horror fiction. For this volume, weird fiction scholar S.T. Joshi collects 11 key works that typify Machen's vision of the uncanny and the veil that keeps 'the Beyond' mercifully concealed from mortal eyes. Included are his masterpieces 'The White People,' about an innocent's unwitting indoctrination into foul rites of sorcery; 'Novel of the Black

Seal,' which uncovers the survival of a malignant race of 'little people' in present times; and 'Novel of the White Powder,' in which a drug brings on a terrifying transformation in a victim who abuses it. Though the volume doesn't include Machen's best-known tale, 'The Great God Pan,' it features an insightful foreword by horror movie director Guillermo del Toro." Publ Wkly

Includes bibliographical references.

Joss, Morag
Among the missing; a novel. Delacorte Press 2011 255p $25

ISBN 978-0-385-34274-2; 0-385-34274-8

LC 2010-52989

"Ron, Annabel and Silva are all in their different ways among the missing. Ron, who's just completed a prison term for inadvertently causing the disastrous bus accident that killed a pregnant teacher and six schoolchildren, is working a job for which he has no credentials. Annabel ran away from her 50-year-old bridegroom Colin after he refused to accept any responsibility for the baby she was carrying. Silva has always felt that she was merely the substitute for the baby of her mother's friend, who died while Silva's mother was pregnant. Now, in the aftermath of the catastrophic wreck of the bridge near Netherloch that brought them together to make an ad hoc household in an out-of-the-way trailer, each of them is keeping a secret. . . . [Joss] builds the relationships among her sad trio slowly, through excruciatingly subtle modulations of tone. But the ending fully justifies every intimation of imminent doom." Kirkus

Joss, Morag
Half broken things; Morag Joss. Delacorte Press 2005 303 p. (pbk.) $15.00; (hbk.) o.p.

ISBN 9780440242444; 0385339402

LC 2005048487

Dagger Awards: Silver Dagger (2003)

This book offers "a novel that peers into the lives of three dangerously lost people . . . and the ominous haven they find when they find each other. Jean is a house sitter at the end of a dreary career. Steph is nine months pregnant and on the run. And Michael is a thief. Through a mixture of deceit, good luck, and misfortune, these three damaged loners have come together at a secluded country home called Walden Manor. Now all three have found what they needed most: a new beginning, a little kindness, a little love. Living off the manor's riches, tending its grounds and gardens, they leave the outside world far behind and build a happiness so long denied them. That is, until the first unexpected visitor arrives." (Publisher's note)

Joss, Morag
The **night** following. Delacorte Press 2008 354p $22

ISBN 978-0-385-34118-9; 0-385-34118-0

LC 2007034711

"While shopping for groceries, a middle-aged woman discovers her husband's infidelity — there's a condom wrapper in the glove compartment of their car. Driving home minutes later, she strikes and kills a bicyclist, then leaves the body by the side of the road. In The Night Following, a bleak, exquisitely written novel, Morag Joss braids together three stories of shattering loneliness that intersect in surprising, haunting ways." Entertainment Wkly

Joyce, Graham, 1954-

The **limits** of enchantment. Atria 2005 263p $22

ISBN 0-575-07231-8

"Although it's 1966, Mammy Cullen, a beloved midwife in rural Hallaton, still dispenses a kind of herbal medicine that women have practiced since time immemorial. But times are changing and prejudices are building. When one of her remedies appears to kill a patient, the locals turn on Mammy. Her practice falls to Fern, her adopted daughter and apprentice, who soon finds herself confronting contemporary reality in several forms: Arthur, an amorous biker with marriage on his mind; an intrusive commune of feckless hippies who settle next door; and a devious landlord who schemes to evict her from her cottage." Publ Wkly

"Generally the prose is economical, hurrying along a plot which engages as a whole, despite the weight of Fern's introspection." Times Lit Suppl

Joyce, Graham, 1954-

The **silent** land. Doubleday 2011 262p $23.95
ISBN 978-0-385-53380-5; 0-385-53380-2
First published 2010 in the United Kingdom
"A young British couple, Jake and Zoe Bennett, are skiing in the French Alps, when they're swallowed by an avalanche. . . . Somehow Jake digs his wife out. After descending the mountain, they find that the whole village is deserted. They have the hotel and its wine cellar and its delicately marbled beef to themselves, which, by the way, they totally don't appreciate as much as they should. Something's not right. For one thing, the candles never seem to burn down. Soon Jake and Zoe are accosted by threatening visions and their senses malfunction. As the weirdness piles up, so does the dread that this is all going to be explained as some dream. Luckily for the reader, in the end Mr. Joyce delivers relief along with satisfaction and wonder." N Y Times Book Rev

Joyce, Graham, 1954-

Some kind of fairy tale; a novel. Graham Joyce. 1st ed. Doubleday 2012 310 p. (hardcover) $24.95; (paperback) $15.95; (downloadable audio) $47.95

ISBN 0385535783; 9780385535786; 9780307949073; 9781455162642

LC 2012001946

In this novel by Graham Joyce, "[w]hen 35-year-old Tara Martin shows up on her parents' doorstep two decades after she disappeared, unkempt and looking oddly as if she's barely aged, her older brother, Peter, a farrier married with four kids, can't hide his hurt, angry feelings -- but they grow even stronger when Tara offers a preposterous story about riding away with a man on a white horse as an explanation for her disappearance." (Publishers Weekly)

Joyce, James

★ **Dubliners**. Knopf 1991 lxvii, 287p $19
ISBN 0-679-40574-7

LC 91-53001

First published 1914 in the United Kingdom; first United States edition published 1916 by Huebsch

"This collection of 15 stories provides an introduction to the style and motifs found in Joyce's writing. The stories stand alone as individual scenes of Dublin society and are intertwined by the use of autobiography and symbolism." Shapiro. Fic for Youth. 3d edition

Joyce, James

★ **Finnegans** wake. Viking 1939 628p
This novel is "written in a unique and extremely difficult style, making use of puns and portmanteau words, (using at least 40 languages besides English) and a very wide range of allusion. The central theme of the work is a cyclical pattern of history, of fall and resurrection inspired by Vico's Scienza nuova. This is presented in the story of Humphrey Chimpden Earwicker, a Dublin tavern-keeper, and the book is apparently a dream-sequence representing the stream of his unconscious mind through the course of one night. Other characters are his wife Anna Livia Plurabelle, their sons Shem and Shaun, and their daughter Isabel." Oxford Companion to Engl Lit. 6th edition

Joyce, James

★ A **portrait** of the artist as a young man; with an introduction by Richard Brown. Knopf 1991 xli, 318p $18
ISBN 0-679-40575-5

LC 91-52979

First appeared serially, 1914-1915 in the United Kingdom; first United States edition published 1916 by Huebsch

This autobiographical novel "portrays the childhood, school days, adolescence, and early manhood of Stephen Dedalus, later one of the leading characters in Ulysses. Stephen's growing self-awareness as an artist forces him to reject the whole narrow world in which he has been brought up, including family ties, nationalism, and the Catholic religion. The novel ends when, having decided to become a writer, he is about to leave Dublin for Paris. Rather than following a clear narrative progression, the book revolves around experiences that are crucial to Stephen's development as an artist; at the end of each chapter Stephen makes some assertion of identity. Through his use of the stream-of-consciousness technique, Joyce reveals the actual materials of his hero's world, the components of his thought processes." Reader's Ency. 4th edition

Joyce, James

★ **Ulysses**; with an introduction by Craig Raine. Knopf 1997 xlv, 1076p $25
ISBN 0-679-45513-2
First published 1922
"The novel is constructed as a modern parallel to Homer's Odyssey. All of the action of the novel takes place in Dublin on a single day (June 16, 1904). The three central characters—Stephen Dedalus (the hero of Joyce's earlier Portrait of the Artist as a Young Man), Leopold Bloom, a Jewish advertising canvasser, and his wife Molly Bloom— are intended to be modern counterparts of Telemachus, Ulysses, and Penelope, and the events of the novel parallel the major events in Odysseus' journey home. The main stream of Ulysses lies in its depth of character portrayal and its breadth of humor." Merriam-Webster's Ency of Lit

Joyce, Rachel, 1962-

The **unlikely** pilgrimage of Harold Fry; a novel. Rachel Joyce. 1st ed. Random House 2012 320 p. map (ebook) $25.00; (hardcover: acid-free paper) $25.00; (downloadable audiobook) $30.32

ISBN 0812993292; 9780679645115; 9780812993295; 9781448123148

LC 2011052581

In this book by Rachel Joyce, "Harold Fry receives a surprising letter . . . from beloved friend and colleague Queenie Hennessy, whom he hasn't heard from in 20 years, writing from a distant terminal cancer ward to say good-bye. This letter returns Harold to a . . . painful part of his past, [and] threatens his already troubled marriage. . . . He decides to embark on a 600-mile walk to say goodbye to Queenie in person." (Library Journal)

Judd, Alan

Legacy. Knopf 2002 245p $24

ISBN 0-375-41484-3

LC 2002-16262

First published 2001 in the United Kingdom

"Comparisons with John le Carre are inevitable, but Judd's style is more straightforward and his worldview far more benign. While fans of explosive action may find it slow going, this elegant and understated literary thriller is a worthy addition to the growing genre of historical espionage fiction." Libr J

Julavits, Heidi

The **uses** of enchantment; a novel. Doubleday 2006 356p $24.95

ISBN 0-385-51323-2

LC 2006-45434

"A spooky coming-of-age tale set in West Salem, Massachusetts, a town whose witch-hanging history both captivates and circumscribes the lives of the teenage girls who reside there. One afternoon in 1985, sixteen-year-old Mary Veal disappears from field-hockey practice at the austere Semmering Academy; she reappears a few weeks later claiming to have been abducted. The truth of what happened is only hinted at in Mary's sexually charged experiences with her supposed captor and in her provocative exchanges with the therapist assigned to her case. He decides that Mary is lying—aspects of her story seem taken from a previous student's faked abduction, itself inspired by a centuries-old fable involving a kidnapped girl and witchcraft—but, it turns out, he is not without his own agenda. Julavits expertly keeps the reader baffled until the end, but beneath the mystery is a sophisticated meditation on truth and bias." New Yorker

July, Miranda

No one belongs here more than you; stories. Scribner 2007 205p $23

ISBN 978-0-7432-9939-8; 0-7432-9939-6

LC 2006-51156

"July writes about desire — to be understood, to be part of another person. . . . The engine that drives these stories is July's voice — the book is full of wistful, wonderful observations about the limits of connection, about the hopes and disappointments of intimacy." Los Angeles Times

Jungstedt, Mari

The **inner** circle; English translation by Tiina Nunnally. St. Martin's Minotaur 2008 280p map $24.95

ISBN 978-0-312-36378-9; 0-312-36378-8

LC 2008-24761

Original Swedish edition, 2005

"In summer the Baltic island of Gotland, Beowulf's old stomping ground, offers stunning scenery for tourists and white nights for love and lust, all of which shape the backdrop of Det. Supt. Anders Knutas's investigation into one horrifying crime after another. . . . The decapitation of a harmless pony is followed by the 'threefold' Viking ritual murder of a female archeology student, who's been carrying on a torrid affair with a secret lover, then two more grisly executions, all punctuated by chilling glimpses into a psychopathic mind. The fluid translation evokes the stark economy of the ancient sagas, where all that mattered was how one fought and died. A little of that old warrior spirit still inhabits Jungstedt's tired, frustrated Swedish policemen and journalists, facing monsters within and without and, like Beowulf, never giving in." Publ Wkly

Just, Ward S.

Exiles in the garden; [by] Ward Just. Houghton Mifflin Harcourt 2009 279p $25

ISBN 978-0-547-19558-2; 0-547-19558-3

LC 2008-49572

"Wars and their consequences make exiles of all involved. The commando, the senator and Alec the observer form an triangle, but not an equilateral triangle. Ward Just is too astute for that. And he leaves us pondering that ageless question of where the personal becomes the political or if it is possible to maintain a distinction at all." Miami Herald

Just, Ward S.

Forgetfulness; [by] Ward Just. Houghton Mifflin Co. 2006 258p $25

ISBN 978-0-618-63463-7; 0-618-63463-0

LC 2006-13906

"Just makes no easy declarations in this often arduously analytical novel. . . . Thomas knows that forgetfulness is not a reasonable response to assault, either personal or national. But he also knows the utter futility of vengeance. This is the paradox that wrenches him in this mature meditation on the personal, private grief that's cultivated in a global war on terror, the search for subtle moral truths in a climate of slogans and curses." Washington Post Book World

Just, Ward S.

Rodin's debutante; [by] Ward Just. Houghton Mifflin Harcourt 2011 263p $26

ISBN 978-0-547-50419-3; 0-547-50419-5

LC 2010-42695

This novel "begins early in the 20th century with Tommy Ogden, a rich, enigmatic Chicagoan who drunkenly decides one day to endow a boys' prep school. Flash forward a few decades to Lee Goodell, who attends Ogden Hall School for Boys and privately wants to become a sculptor. We follow his life, witnessing the two acts of violence that change him. Rodin's Debutante is a surprising story, never going where you expect it to, and Just's spare prose packs a solid emotional punch." Entertainment Wkly

Just, Ward S.

★ An **unfinished** season; [by] Ward Just. Houghton Mifflin 2004 256p $24

ISBN 0-618-03669-5

LC 2004-42722

"Set in 1950's Chicago during a single summer, this novel recounts the story of the owner of a printing company, the narrator's father, who is on the management side of a vicious union dispute and begins to carry a gun. Wilson Raven, his son, takes a summer job at a scandal rag, where no amount of ink on his sleeves lives down the day he arrives at work wearing his bowed dancing shoes from debutante balls on the ritzy North Shore." Economist

Just, Ward S.

The **weather** in Berlin; {by} Ward Just. Houghton Mifflin 2002 305p $24

ISBN 0-618-03668-7

LC 2001-51885

This novel "follows a burned-out American movie director on a three-month stay at an artists-and-intellectuals institute in the capital of the new Germany. At 64, Dix Greenwood is remembered for a film made decades ago, an art-house favorite set in a German lake village just after World War I. . . . Ailing physically, tantalized by a fading memory of artistic inspiration, resenting his actress wife for her still-active career, Greenwood repairs to the city Willy Brandt once called Germany's Schicksalstadt, city of destiny. Berlin is experiencing a rebirth; perhaps Dix will too." N Y Times Book Rev

K

K'wan

Animal; K'wan. Cash Money Content 2012 407 p. (trade paper) $14.99

ISBN 1936399253; 9781936399253; 9781936399260

LC 2011943461

This book, part of author K'wan's "Hood Rat" series, focuses on "Animal, a rapper-turned-killer whom everyone thought had been murdered. The streets are tense as the crews of King James and Shai Clark sense a major gang war is set to erupt. Cruising on the perimeter is Animal, the vicious killer who is waiting to take revenge on the shooter who tried to kill his woman, Gucci." (Library Journal)

K'wan

Section 8; a hood rat novel. K'wan. St. Martin's Griffin 2009 ix, 358 p.p

ISBN 0312536968; 9780312536961

LC 2009012530

In this ninth novel of K'wan's 'Hood Rat' series, the author depicts "action, murder, betrayal, sex, more action, familiar faces and a few surprises. Readers are first introduced to Tionna, a single mom of two, desperate to recover her footing after her man gets arrested for his involvement in drug and gun dealing. Moving back to her old neighborhood in shame, Tionna devises a plan with her girlfriends-

-Gucci, Boots and Tracy--to con local record label mogul Don B. Meanwhile, Gucci meets and falls for Animal, a notorious criminal who's on the fence about going legitimate as a rapper. As their pursuits intertwine, Tionna and friends find much to learn about unintended consequences." (Publishers Weekly)

K'wan

Welfare wifeys; K'wan. St. Martin's Griffin 2010 337 p. (Hood rat novel.) (paperback) $14.99

ISBN 0312536976; 9780312536978

LC 2010030122

Street Literature Book Award Medal Honoree (2011)

In this novel by K'wan, part of the Hood Rat series, "the man known on the streets as Animal relocates to Texas and finds fame and stardom as the newest act signed to the notorious Big Dawg Entertainment. His girlfriend, Gucci, is thrilled when she gets the news that he's coming back to New York on a promotional tour, but when she discovers the hidden agenda behind his homecoming nothing can prepare her for the life-altering consequences that will come of it." (Publisher's note)

Kadare, Ismail

The **accident**; a novel. translated from the Albanian by John Hodgson. Grove Press 2010 265p $24

ISBN 978-0-8021-2995-6; 0-8021-2995-1

"When a taxi runs off the road in Vienna under suspicious circumstances, killing an Albanian couple in the back seat, a lonely researcher attempts to solve the case by reconstructing their final weeks. Through a series of vignettes and flashbacks spanning a decade of trysts in hotels across Europe, he assembles a portrait of a heated affair coming apart in a haze of mutual distrust, from the perspective of both lovers: Rovena, a volatile archaeology intern, and Besfort Y., a stoic analyst for the Council of Europe. As with Kadare's novels about real assassinations, the circumstances of the lovers' deaths are shrouded in a thick fog of uncertainty that only grows as the novel progresses." N Y Times Book Rev

Kadare, Ismail

The **general** of the dead army; a novel. [translated from the French of Jusuf Vrioni by Derek Coltman] Arcade Pub. 2008 264p $24.95

ISBN 978-1-55970-790-9

LC 2008-06946

Original Albanian edition, 1963; this translation first published 1971 in the United Kingdom and 1991 in the United States by New Amsterdam Books

"The book's protagonist is an Italian army officer who has come to Albania to recover the bodies of soldiers who died twenty years earlier in World War II. The General and his team carry crudely drawn maps and directions to burial sites supplied by aging war veterans. At first, the General fantasizes about returning home in triumph with his army of dead soldiers, but his optimism quickly fades. Rain and cold weather make recovery difficult, and the sullen Albanians continue to treat the Italians as invaders. . . . Before long, the General is haunted by terrifying dreams and hallucinations. He starts to see living people as skeletal remains and, fatally, begins to feel sympathy for the Albanians. This gloomy but powerful antiwar novel provides an excellent introduction to Albania's best-known author." Libr J

Kadare, Ismail

The **ghost** rider; translated from the French of Jusuf Vrioni by Jon Rothschild; updated, with new sections added, by Ismail Kadare and David Bellos; introduction by David Bellos. Canongate 2010 208p pa $13.95

ISBN 978-1-84767-341-1

Originally published in Albanian; this edition translated from French

The author "takes an ancient Albanian tale, 'The Ballad of Constantine and Doruntine,' as the starting point for this compelling if enigmatic novel set in medieval Albania. The deaths of the nine Vranaj brothers, all soldiers, many felled by a plague carried by their battlefield adversaries, have devastated a small Albanian community. Their mother's loss is only compounded by the absence at the time of her daughter, Doruntine, who was married three years earlier and moved far away from home. When Doruntine suddenly appears at her mother's door, claiming that one of her brothers, Kostandin, was her traveling companion, the news that Kostandin has been dead for years sends both mother and daughter to their deathbeds, leaving the local police captain to try to explain the inexplicable. Kadare excels at depicting the ever-expanding repercussions of what could have been a tragedy limited just to the Vranaj family." Publ Wkly

Kadare, Ismail

Spring flowers, spring frost; a novel. translated from the French of Jusuf Vrioni by David Belos. Arcade Pub. 2002 182p $23.95

ISBN 1-55970-635-X

LC 2002-20877

Original Albanian edition 2000

"Mark Gurabardhi, an artist in his late twenties, experiences the unfamiliarity of life after Communism in the provincial Albanian town where he was posted by the former regime. It feels almost like a loss not to be spied on, and he and his girlfriend thrill to words like 'heist,' so modern and Western do they seem. The couple discover, however, that dictatorship is replaced not so much by modernity as by old, crippling superstitions and family feuds. Throughout the book, images of icebergs, the Titanic, and enchanted snakes recur. . . . The result is like a dream-seemingly full of stirring meanings whose interpretations remain tantalizingly out of reach." New Yorker

Kadare, Ismail

The **Successor**; a novel. translated from the French of Tedi Papavrami by David Bellos. Arcade Publishing 2005 207p $24

ISBN 1-55970-773-9

LC 2005-10311

Original Albanian edition, 2003

This novel "depicts an Albania governed by the whim and vanity of the aging Guide when the Successor, second in command, is found dead in his bedroom. The international intelligence community and the citizens of Albania contemplate the questions of how the Successor fell from grace and whether he died through murder or suicide. From day to day, the official word varies as the Guide decides whether the Successor is an enemy of the state or a martyr for the party. Drawing on real events–Mehmet Shehu was poised to succeed Albanian dictator Enver Hoxha in 1981 when he mysteriously died–Kadare successfully builds suspense by portraying multiple suspects with the motivation to commit murder; all believe they are guilty of the crime in some small or large way." Libr J

Kadare, Ismail

★ The **three**-arched bridge; translated from the Albanian by John Hodgson. Arcade Pub. 1997 184p

ISBN 1-55970-368-7

LC 96-41236

Originally written 1976-1978; published in French translation 1993

In this "matter-of-fact parable, a fourteenth-century Albanian monk attempts to 'record the lie we saw and the truth we did not see' about the building of a stone bridge that is a threatening wonder to the local people. The lie is the myths and legends exploited by the foreign builders to destroy their competitors; the truth is the mercenary nature of their crime. Kadare manages to appeal to a sense of outrage and hunger for evidence even as he suggests the outlines of today's Balkans." New Yorker

Kadrey, Richard

Kill the dead. Eos 2010 434p $22.99

ISBN 978-0-06-171431-3

"James Stark, antihero of 2009's Sandman Slim, returns in this gritty, over-the-top tale of supernatural mayhem. Having taken his revenge on the rival magician who got him sent to Hell, Stark settles in sorcery-infested Los Angeles and gets a part-time gig with the Golden Vigil, an angelic hit squad of dubious morality that's somehow allied with Homeland Security. . . . When Lucifer comes to Earth, supposedly to oversee a Hollywood biopic of his life, he hires Stark to be his bodyguard, but something isn't quite right and soon the city is awash in murderous zombies. Stark has to get to the bottom of the mystery or risk being sent back to Hell, along with everyone he cares about. Profane, intensely metaphoric language somehow makes self-tortured monster Stark sympathetic and turns a simple story into a powerful noir thriller." Publ Wkly

Kafka, Franz, 1883-1924

★ **Amerika**; the man who disappeared. translated and with an introduction by Michael Hofmann. New Directions 2002 216p $23.95

ISBN 0-8118-1513-X

Original German edition, 1927; this translation first published 1996 in the United Kingdom

The narrative of this unfinished novel "concerns the efforts of young Karl Rossmann, newly arrived in America, to find his place in an enigmatic and hostile society."

"Kafka left six completed chapters and a number of additional scenes, two of which appear in English for the first time in this new translation. . . . Anything by Kafka is worth reading again, especially in the hands of such a gifted translator as Hofmann." N Y Times Book Rev

Kafka, Franz, 1883-1924

★ The **castle**. Knopf 1992 xxxviii, 378p $17
ISBN 0-679-41735-4

LC 92-52904

Original German edition, 1926; this translation first published 1930

In this unfinished novel, the hero, "known only as K., is constantly frustrated in his efforts to gain entrance into a mysterious castle to which he believes he has been summoned to work as a land surveyor. The castle is administered by an extraordinarily complicated and incompetent bureaucratic hierarchy that refuses to either recognize or reject K.'s claim. He is put to work instead as a school janitor and is denied his right to practice his craft. According to Brod, Kafka intended K., an ailing man throughout the novel, to die of exhaustion at the end of the novel." Reader's Ency. 4th edition

Kafka, Franz, 1883-1924

★ **Collected** stories; edited and introduced by Gabriel Josipvici. Knopf 1993 lv, 503p $21
ISBN 0-679-42303-6

LC 93-1858

Kafka, Franz, 1883-1924

The **complete** stories; edited by Nahum N. Glatzer; with a new foreword by John Updike. Centennial ed; Schocken Bks. 1983 xxi, 486p il hardcover o.p.
ISBN 9780805238631; 9780805210552

LC 83003233

First published 1971

"All of Kafka's writing, with the exception of his three novels, is collected here and includes a number of fairly long stories followed by a group of shorter pieces varying in length from several pages to a single paragraph." Booklist

Kafka, Franz, 1883-1924

★ **Metamorphosis**. Vanguard Press 1945 98p il
Written in 1915 this is "often regarded as Kafka's most perfectly finished work. 'The Metamorphosis' begins as its hero, Gregor Samsa, awakens one morning to find himself changed into a huge insect; the story proceeds to develop the effects of this change upon Samsa's business and family life and ends with his death. It has been read as everything from a religious allegory to a psychoanalytic case history; it is notable for its clarity of depiction and attention to significant detail, which give its completely fantastic occurrences an aura of indisputable truth, so that no allegorical interpretation is necessary to demonstrate its greatness." Reader's Ency. 4th edition

Kafka, Franz, 1883-1924

The **metamorphosis** and other stories; translated by Joachim Neugroschel. Scribner 1993 xxiii, 227p hardcover o.p. pa $13
ISBN 0-684-19426-0; 0-684-80070-5 pa

LC 92-43912

This is a collection of thirty stories, some of which are quite short. The stories are arranged in order of their original publication dates.

Kafka, Franz, 1883-1924

The **penal** colony: stories and short pieces; translated by Willa and Edwin Muir. Schocken Bks. 1948 320p il

Kafka, Franz, 1883-1924

Selected short stories of Franz Kafka; translated by Willa and Edwin Muir; introduction by Philip Rahv. Modern Lib. 1993 xxv, 346p
ISBN 0-679-60061-2

LC 93-14747

First Modern Library edition published 1952

Kafka, Franz, 1883-1924

★ The **trial**; translated from the German by Willa and Edwin Muir; revised, with additional notes, by E. M. Butler. Knopf 1992 299p $19
ISBN 0-679-40994-7

Original edition 1924; first Everyman's Library edition, 1922

"Joseph K., a respected bank assessor, is arrested and spends his remaining years fighting charges about which he has no knowledge. The helplessness of an insignificant individual within a mysterious bureaucracy where answers are never accessible is described in this provocative and disturbing book." Shapiro. Fic for Youth. 3d edition

Kafka, Kimberly

Miranda's vines. Dutton 2004 258p $23.95
ISBN 0-525-94763-9

"Since college, Miranda and Bridie's relationship has been that of sisters, surpassing any friendship by the depth of their commitment. It was Bridie Miranda relied upon when her husband died before their son could be born, and it was Bridie Miranda called again when her father died, bequeathing her the struggling Oregon vineyard to which he'd devoted his life. Now it's Miranda's turn. When Bridie, a champion Idatarod sledder, is critically injured, legs paralyzed and dangerously depressed, Miranda brings Bridie back to the vineyard she is reluctantly calling home again. In this lustrous tale of loyalty and devotion, Kafka limns the depths of intimacy and explores the nature of relationships, from mother to son, father to daughter, neighbor to stranger, and friend to friend." Booklist

Kalfus, Ken

The **commissariat** of enlightenment; a novel. Ecco Press 2003 295p $24.95
ISBN 0-06-050136-7

LC 2002-69308

"For Comrad Astapov of the Agitprop Section of the Commissariat of Enlightenment, the filmmaker protagonist of this début novel, 'life's struggle was not to control events, but the way in which they were remembered.' His story begins in 1910, at the press-besieged deathbed of Tolstoy, where his talent for manipulating film to satisfy events earns the notice of Stalin. Astapov's distortions are the perfect metaphor for Kalfus's own special effects: Stalin, of course, wasn't there when Tolstoy died. Preoccupied with truth, media, history, and politics, this novel shows its mechanisms proudly." New Yorker

Includes bibliographical references

Kalfus, Ken

A **disorder** peculiar to the country; a novel. Ecco 2006 237p $24.95

ISBN 978-0-06-050140-2

LC 2005-52697

"Like their country, Marshall and Joyce Harriman, a Brooklyn Heights couple, are at war. They are one year into an impossibly bitter divorce, and their hatred for one another has 'acquired the intensity of something historic, tribal, and ethnic.' When Joyce watches the destruction of the World Trade Center she is seized by a 'great gladness,' because Marshall works on the eighty-sixth floor of the south tower. But he escapes to fight another day in the apartment that neither will relinquish, home to their two young children—'their divorce's civilian casualties.' Kalfus skewers the pieties surrounding 9/11, but, having set his black comedy in the shadow of that national trauma, he reverently charts the powerful sway that world events briefly held over the lives of individual Americans." New Yorker

Kallos, Stephanie

Broken for you. Grove Press 2004 371p $24

ISBN 0-8021-1779-1

LC 2004-40631

"The novel itself is a mosaic of eccentric characters and their interlocking storylines, which sometimes border on the fantastic. . . . So lovely is the world Kallos has created that it seems more reparative to curl up on the couch with this book and suspend belief than to deconstruct the plot." Washington Post Book World

Kallos, Stephanie

Sing them home. Atlantic Monthly Press 2009 542p $25

ISBN 978-0-87113-963-4

"The Jones family would seem to have no luck. Aneira Hope Jones, already terminally ill, was swept away by a tornado in 1978. Now her husband has been felled by lightning, and his longtime mistress, Viney—best friend to his wife and virtually the stepmother of his three children—must rally alientated, overweight art scholar Larken; sex-obsessed Gaelen, a famed weatherman mostly because of his family history; and their slightly nutty little sister, Bonnie. The Jones siblings have had far from perfect lives. But they're also rooted in the warm and sensible little town of Emlyn, NE, proud of its Welsh heritage, and this fresh, invigorating novel fingers carefully through their pain." Libr J

Kalotay, Daphne

Sight Reading; Daphne Kalotay. HarperCollins 2013 336 p. (hardcover) $25.99

ISBN 0062246933; 9780062246936

This novel, by Daphne Kalotay, begins "on a warm spring day after a long New England winter, Hazel and Remy spot each other for the first time in years. . . . Remy, a gifted violinist, is married to the Scottish composer Nicholas Elko--once the love of Hazel's life. . . . In the twenty years since Hazel's world was tipped on its axis, these three artists have faced unexpected joys, mysterious afflictions and other puzzles of life, their fates irrevocably interlaced." (Publisher's note)

Kamensky, Jane

Blindspot; by a gentleman in exile and a lady in disguise. [by] Jane Kamensky and Jill Lepore. Spiegel & Grau 2008 500p $24.95

ISBN 978-0-385-52619-7; 0-385-52619-9

LC 2008-3111

"Set in 1760s Boston, Blindspot evokes the rollicking bawdiness, humor, and wit of that turbulent era. The story concerns Stewart Jameson, a Scottish portrait painter who flees to Boston to escape debts at home. Seeking an apprentice, he takes on Fanny Easton, a disowned daughter from a prominent Boston family who is masquerading as a boy — a ruse that makes for some hilarious scenes. The narrative is propelled forward by a budding romance and a murder mystery, which plays out as the first stirrings of the looming revolution grip colonial Boston." Chron of Higher Educ

Kaminsky, Stuart M.

★ The **big** silence; an Abe Lieberman mystery. Forge 2000 268p $23.95

ISBN 0-312-86926-6

LC 00-31811

Chicago cop Lieberman and "his morose partner, Bill Hanrahan, find themselves backed into a corner by a blackmailer who kills a mob informant's ex-wife, kidnaps his 17-year-old son and threatens to do away with the boy unless the informer pledges ultimate silence—by committing suicide. And that's only the first labor of the day for this herculean cop. Heaping one calamity on top of another, Kaminsky piles up a whole stack of woe to try his hero's soul." N Y Times Book Rev

Kaminsky, Stuart M.

Blood and rubles; a Porfiry Petrovich Rostnikov novel. Fawcett Columbine 1996 257p

ISBN 0-449-90949-2

LC 95-23885

"Rubles are scarce in Moscow, but Chief Inspector Porfiry Rostnikov and his subordinates are up to their shoe tops in blood: a shootout apparently involving a Mafia scheme to sell fissionable material to the highest bidder; three nearly feral small boys who kill passerbys for whatever they carry; and the kidnapping of a wealthy businessman that turns into multiple murders. . . . It's hard not to feel compassion for the cops and the Moscovites in general, and Kaminsky is deft at creating this feeling with small, telling details of ordinary life." Booklist

Kaminsky, Stuart M.

A **cold** red sunrise; an Inspector Porfiry Rostnikov mystery. Scribner 1988 210p

LC 88-15359

"Inspector Porfiry Rostnikov of the Moscow police . . . is assigned to Tumsk in deepest Siberia. . . . Two people have died mysteriously—the young and beautiful daughter of a famed dissident father who is scheduled, in the new climate of 'glasnost,' to depart for the West, and the police Commisar from Moscow who was sent to Tumsk to investigate her death. With him on this mission is his trusted associate, Emil Karpo." West Coast Rev Books

"The author has fine-tuned Porfiry and Karpo into a delightful sleuthing team and a fascinating study in odd contrasts." Booklist

Kaminsky, Stuart M.
Dancing in the dark. Mysterious Press 1996 228p

LC 95-13095

"In 1943, Arthur Forbes is a respected California businessman, but not too many years earlier he lived in Detroit and was known as Fingers Intaglia because he liked to remove the fingers of his victims. Luna, his mistress, wants to learn to dance, and she wants Fred Astaire to teach her. . . . To get Luna and her lover off his back, Astaire hires Toby Peters, private eye to the stars. When Luna drops dead at Toby's feet, Fingers is ready to resume his former profession but doesn't want a scandal. A deal is cut: If Toby can find the killer, he can live." Booklist

The author "effortlessly choreographs Hollywood history, colorful cast and dirty doings." Publ Wkly

Kaminsky, Stuart M.
Death of a Russian priest. Fawcett Columbine 1992 223p

LC 91-58638

In this Inspector Porfiry Rostnikov mystery "two crimes need solving: the disappearance of a Syrian diplomat's daughter and the ax murder of a prominently outspoken priest. The missing girl becomes the preoccupation of Rostnikov's emotionally messed-up young assistant Sasha, while Rostnikov himself, working with the vampiric Karpo, uncovers the priest's secret life, hindered by silent friends who seem to be dying for their loyalty." Booklist

Kaminsky, Stuart M.
★ The **dog** who bit a policeman. Mysterious Press 1998 275p
ISBN 0-89296-667-X

LC 98-13385

"Kaminsky takes care not to rob the beleaguered cops of their human core—a courtesy he also extends to Moscow, which comes across as a character in its own right: rough and dangerous and somehow tragic." N Y Times Book Rev

Kaminsky, Stuart M.
A **fatal** glass of beer. Mysterious Press 1997 246p

LC 96-49494

The author "balances one-liners from Fields with headlines about the war effort in this amiable adventure that delivers a nicely twisted plot with fully dimensioned characters, including the usually caricatured misanthropic comedian." Publ Wkly

Kaminsky, Stuart M.
Hard currency. Fawcett Columbine 1995 247p

LC 94-28273

This Inspector Porfiry Rostnikov mystery takes the "Moscow detective to Havana, where he investigates the murder of a Cuban woman who was apparently killed by a minor intelligence officer in the Russian embassy. . . . Meanwhile, back in Moscow, Rostnikov's associate Emil Karpo

is tracking down a vicious serial killer whose single-minded precision chillingly matches Karpo's own thought processes. Kaminsky, one of the genre's finest storytellers, is at the peak of his powers here." Booklist

Kaminsky, Stuart M.
Lieberman's choice; {by} Stuart Kaminsky. St. Martin's Press 1993 216p

LC 92-40797

"Abe's conversation—whether with his old Jewish buddies, some small-time cons or his family—is pure pleasure, with never a false, extraneous note." Publ Wkly

Kaminsky, Stuart M.
Lieberman's day; [by] Stuart Kaminsky. Holt & Co. 1994 260p
ISBN 0-8050-2575-8

LC 93-22910

Chicago homicide detective Abe Lieberman's "nephew, David, and David's pregnant wife are shot in a late night mugging. David dies; his wife and unborn child survive, barely. Lieberman gets the case and in the following 24 hours deals with the grief of his brother and sister-in-law, the aftereffects of the collapse of his daughter's marriage, the desperate deal he cuts with a violent drug-dealer called El Perro to catch the killers and the busting of two con artists." Publ Wkly

The author is "extraordinarily attuned to the domestic minutiae of his detectives' lives." N Y Times Book Rev

Kaminsky, Stuart M.
Lieberman's folly; {by} Stuart Kaminsky. St. Martin's Press 1991 216p

LC 90-49309

This mystery "features the partnership of Chicago cops Abe 'Rabbi' Lieberman and Bill 'Father Murphy' Hanrahan. When prostitute Estralda Valdez, a past informer, asks the pair for protection, tippler Hanrahan agrees to watch her apartment from a Chinese restaurant across the street. After Valdez is murdered during Hanrahan's watch, he and Lieberman investigate her death, despite the objections of their captain, who is unhappy about negative publicity." Publ Wkly

Kaminsky, Stuart M.
Lieberman's thief; [by] Stuart Kaminsky. Holt & Co. 1995 238p
ISBN 0-8050-2576-6

LC 94-27304

"George Patniks is a professional burglar and a good one. Unfortunately, the day he has chosen to burgle the Rozier home turns out to be the same day Mr. Rozier has chosen to kill Mrs. Rozier. . . . Chicago homicide detective Abe Lieberman and his partner Bill Hanrahan immediately suspect Rozier, but they have nothing on which to build a case. Kaminsky captures the sights and sounds of his Chicago setting most convincingly." Booklist

Kaminsky, Stuart M.
The **man** who walked like a bear; an Inspector Porfiry Rostnikov novel. Scribner 1990 261p

LC 89-29082

"Beset by the usual demons (including the plumbing in his apartment), visited by a few new ones, and still a thorn in the side of the Soviet bureaucracy, Rostnikov must deal with a host of problems: . . . a plot to kill a Politburo member, shady deals in a Moscow shoe factory, and several demented nationalists who mastermind a scheme to destroy Lenin's tomb. Then there's the inspector's sick wife to visit in the hospital and the matter of getting his son out of the military." Booklist

"Kaminsky masterfully balances stories of family life, humorous anecdotes and riveting suspense involving his distinctive characters." Publ Wkly

Kaminsky, Stuart M.

Murder on the Trans-Siberian Express. Mysterious Press 2001 277p

ISBN 0-89296-747-1

LC 2001-26218

"The action reaches back to Siberia in 1894, when one man in a band of starving, disease-ridden convicts, sentenced to work on constructing the great rail line from Moscow to Vladivostok, buries his treasure—a leather pouch containing a tiny gold box with a letter inside. More than a century later, Inspector Porfiry of the Moscow Police is sent on the 6,000-mile rail line to find this box. Porfiry leaves behind two other investigations: the kidnapping of a skinhead rock star and a series of murders in the Moscow Metro. How Kaminsky weaves these tangled plot lines into a taut suspense fabric, while providing fascinating, sad-funny commentary on his characters and the tensions inherent in the new Russian social order, is a matter of wonder." Booklist

Kaminsky, Stuart M.

Not quite kosher; an Abe Lieberman mystery. Forge 2002 254p $23.95

ISBN 0-312-87453-7

This installment "finds Lieberman trying to cope with a jewelry heist gone bad, a potential gang war, two corpses washed up from Lake Michigan and his grandson's bar mitzvah." N Y Times Book Rev

"Although Kaminsky can plot with the best of them, his characters are the real delights of the book." Publ Wkly

Kaminsky, Stuart M.

Retribution; a Lew Fonesca novel. Forge 2001 272p

ISBN 0-312-87452-9

LC 2001-40483

Lew Fonesca "rescued a teenage prostitute named Adele in 'Vengeance' and left her in the care of a rich and vulgar (but really sweet and lonely) widow who promised to put the girl through high school. Adele is in trouble again . . . and Lew has been charged with finding out why she skipped town with a cache of manuscripts, the unpublished life's work of the reclusive, Salingeresque author who was tutoring her." N Y Times Book Rev

Kaminsky, Stuart M.

Rostnikov's vacation; an Inspector Porfiry Rostnikov novel. Scribner 1991 244p

LC 91-13874

"While on forced vacation in Yalta, Rostnikov chances upon the murder of an acquaintance from military intelligence. He also befriends an American policeman, who points out the man tailing Rostnikov. Back in Moscow, meanwhile, Rostnikov's subordinates track a beautiful young woman and two accomplices connected with the murder of a German businessman. Kaminsky solidly and ably controls all these complications, but not without offering certain political vagaries, a cold-blooded atmosphere, and a certain dry humor." Libr J

Kaminsky, Stuart M.

To catch a spy; a Toby Peters mystery. Carroll & Graf Pubs. 2002 230p $24

ISBN 0-7867-1023-3

LC 2002-67254

In this installment the author supposes Cary Grant "to have been a British intelligence agent, his job to detect the activities of Nazi sympathizers in Hollywood. Married to Woolworth heiress Barbara Hutton at the time, he finds more pro-Nazis among his wife's rich friends than among the acting community. Grant hires Toby, who packs a .38 with which he's unable to hit the broad side of a sound stage, to deliver a satchel of money in the dark of night to a man who'll give him an envelope in return." Publ Wkly

Kaminsky, Stuart M.

Tomorrow is another day. Mysterious Press 1995 201p

LC 94-18987

"Set during World War II, when Hollywood was at its most glamorous, the plot involves the mysterious stabbing death of an extra on the set of Selznick International's Gone with the Wind. Five years after the murder, the debonair Clark Gable approaches Toby {Peters} to ask for help—seems Gable's been receiving bizarre death threats in the form of poems. . . . Nostalgic readers with a yen for the good old days—when men were men and movies were movies—will find Kaminsky's story entertaining, clever, eminently readable, and chock-full of snippets from Hollywood's Golden Age." Booklist

Kaminsky, Stuart M.

Vengeance; a Lew Fonesca mystery. Forge 1999 328p

ISBN 0-312-86927-4

LC 99-38393

"Fonesca is a middle-aged, widowed process server, a transplanted Chicagoan who has made a new home in Sarasota, Fla. . . . Occasionally he uses the investigative skills he developed while employed by the state attorney's office in Chicago to do a little ad hoc sleuthing. In {this novel} his skills and fortitude get stretched to the limit as he tries to locate two missing persons: a teenage girl whose sexually abusive and violent father has lured her away from her poverty-stricken mother, and a woman who has run away from her wealthy husband." Publ Wkly

Kane, Ben

★ **Spartacus**; the gladiator. Ben Kane. 1st U.S. ed. St. Martins Press 2012 466 p. maps (trade)

$26.99; (paperback) $15.99; (downloadable audio) $34.42

ISBN 1250001161; 9781250001160; 9781250021564; 9781466802667; 9781448115976

LC 2011279125

Author Ben Kane tells the story of Spartacus and the Roman Army. "Betrayed to the Romans by his jealous king, Spartacus--and with him Ariadne--are taken in captivity to the gladiator school at Capua. It is from here--against the unbelievable brutality of gladiatorial life--that Spartacus and Crixus the Gaul plan their escape to Vesuvius, where they recruit and train a huge slave army. An army which will keep the might of Rome at bay for two years." (benkane.net)

Kanon, Joseph

The **good** German; a novel. Holt & Co. 2001 482p

ISBN 0-8050-6422-2

LC 2001-16968

"Jake Geismar, a U.S. reporter assigned to cover the Potsdam Conference for Collier's magazine, stumbles upon a story that is intertwined with his own life. Though he has returned to Berlin primarily to reunite with his prewar lover, Geismar confronts a Germany he no longer recognizes. Further, he is compelled to solve the murder of an American soldier found with a money belt stuffed with black market cash." Libr J

Kanon, Joseph

Istanbul passage; a novel. Joseph Kanon. Atria Books 2012 404 p.

ISBN 1439156417; 9781439156414

LC 2011045510

This espionage novel is set in "1945 Istanbul, [as] Allied veteran Leon Bauer is running spy missions under the cover of a U.S. tobacco-importing business. With the war over, U.S. operations are closing up shop in the neutral capital, but Leon has one last big job: to take possession of a Romanian defector in possession of important Russian secrets and get him flown to safety. The rub is the defector, Alexei, was involved in a heinous massacre of Jews four years earlier." (Kirkus)

Kanon, Joseph

Los Alamos; a novel. Broadway Bks. 1997 403p

LC 96-44055

This book's plot involves the murder of a security officer of the Manhattan Project, which developed the atomic bomb. "Michael Connolly, a civilian intelligence expert called to New Mexico to investigate the murder, soon finds himself entangled in the insular, secretive world of Los Alamos: first he falls in love with one of the scientist's wives, and then he comes under the . . . spell of Oppenheimer himself." Booklist

"'Los Alamos,' besides being a terrific mystery, wonderfully evokes the Southwest in the '40s, reminding us in a dozen subtle ways that life goes on even while history is being made." Newsweek

Kantner, Seth

Ordinary wolves; Seth Kantner. 1st ed; Milkweed Editions 2004 324p hardcover o.p. pa $14.95

ISBN 1-571-31044-4; 1-571-31047-9 pa

LC 2003-24025

"Growing up in the unforgiving wilderness with his back-to-the-land artist father and siblings, Cutuk learns all the traditional skills necessary for living off the tundra and develops an abiding love for wolves. But Cutuk is white, and although he reveres traditional native Alaskan ways and wants to be a great hunter, he remains an outsider. Then when the 1970s bring radical change even to this distant realm and his indigenous neighbors trade in their dogsleds for snowmobiles, he becomes even more of an anachronism. So he tries his luck in Anchorage, discovers an alien form of wilderness, and hastily acquires a whole new set of survival skills. At every turn, Kantner fearlessly orchestrates dramatic communions between humans and the wild, hilarious incidents of culture shock." Booklist

Kantor, MacKinlay

★ **Andersonville**. World Pub. 1955 767p il

"After twenty-five years of research Kantor wrote this novel, which realistically portrays the atrocities of Andersonville Prison, home of many Yankee soldiers during the Civil War. Ira Claffey, Georgia planter and owner of the property on which Andersonville is built, serves as a humane central character whose sorrows and frustrations serve to point up the brutality of war. The primitive, indeed horrible, existence of the prisoners is described in detail." Shapiro. Fic for Youth. 3d edition

Kaplow, Robert

Me and Orson Welles; a novel. MacAdam/Cage Pub. 2003 269p $18.50

ISBN 1-931561-49-4

LC 2003-14982

"A comic coming-of-age novel set against the background of the twenty-two-year-old Orson Welles's debut production at the Mercury Theatre on Broadway. Richard Samuels is the stage struck seventeen-year-old from New Jersey who wanders onto the set one day and gets a small role in Welles's Julius Caesar. His life will never be the same." Publisher's note

This is "a delightful escape into a pre-war coming-of-age, and coming-of-stage, story—perfect for a quick and totally entertaining read." Booklist

Karbo, Karen

Motherhood made a man out of me. Bloomsbury Pub. 2000 212p $23.95

ISBN 1-58234-083-8

"Karbo writes about the intricacies of human nature and relationships with insight and humor, and her characters are realistic yet wonderfully over-the-top. The result is a fast-paced and delightful novel." Publ Wkly

Kardos, Michael

The **Three**-Day Affair; Michael Kardos. Pgw 2012 256 p. $24.00

ISBN 0802120261; 9780802120267

This crime novel by Michael Kardos follows a group of reunited college friends. "While the three are out for a drive, just after Will has persuaded the other two to invest in his plan to start a record label, Jeffrey emerges from a convenience store with a hostage in tow–for no good reason." (Publishers Weekly)

Karinthy, Ferenc

Metropole; translated from the Hungarian by George Szirtes. Telegram 2008 236p pa $14.95

ISBN 978-1-84659-034-4; 1-84659-034-5

Original Hungarian edition, 1970

"Budai, a linguist en route to a conference, steps off of a plane and finds himself not in Helsinki but in a land with an impenetrable language and a massive population swarming the streets and sidewalks. Every morning, he sets out to find his way home, or at least to find someone who speaks Hungarian, and every night, he finds himself back at the hotel with his dwindling supply of money, bewildered by the world in which he is trapped. Karinthy's story is anxious and claustrophobic, but it's shot through with humor and surprising believability. Budai is relentless and resourceful, and Karinthy is a skilled enough writer that his protagonist's failed attempts to make headway never become monotonous. Metropole invites comparisons to Kafka, and manages to live up to them." NPR

Karnezis, Panos

The maze. Farrar, Straus and Giroux 2004 376p $24

ISBN 0-374-20480-2

LC 2003-60261

"As with many an imperial expedition, the soldiers seem to be lost without honor; they massacre civilians on their fool's errand undertaken for worthless ends. Karnezis dramatizes their plight with remorseless clarity and dry humor." N Y Times Book Rev

Karon, Jan

A common life; the wedding story. Viking 2001 186p il $24.95

ISBN 0-670-89437-0

LC 00-31984

This novel in the author's Mitford series focuses "on a key event in the life of Father Tim Kavanaugh—his marriage. The book begins with Father Tim's proposal to next-door-neighbor Cynthia and ends with their honeymoon at the bishop's summer cottage in Maine. In between, Mitford's various residents prepare for the big day, each in his or her own way." Booklist

Karon, Jan

In this mountain. Viking 2002 382p $24.95

ISBN 0-670-03104-6

LC 2002-16877

In this Mitford novel "three years have passed since Father Tim Kavanagh and his wife, Cynthia, returned to Mitford from Whitecap Island, and depression and discontent are gnawing away at the good cleric as he faces the big '7-0.' As Cynthia's career reaches new heights, Father Tim makes some personal decisions that lead to tragedy. . . . Homespun dialogue, fresh and lively descriptions, laugh-out-loud mo-

ments and poignant scenes mark the heartfelt book, which is a happy reunion form Mitford devotees." Publ Wkly

Karon, Jan

A new song. Viking 1999 400p $24.95

ISBN 0-670-87810-3

LC 98-55141

In this episode in the Mitford series "Father Tim Kavanagh heads for the islands to serve as an interim priest. Although most of the book takes place in his new parish, fans of Mitford's eccentric citizens are not left bereft. Frequent bulletins keep Father Tim up-to-date as well as worried about his former flock. While juggling news of mysterious thefts, the arrest of his adopted son, Dooley, and fights over historic properties, he also must deal with congregational squabbles, being a foster parent to an active three-year-old, surviving a terrible storm, and bringing a lonely man out of decades of solitude." Libr J

Karon, Jan

Out to Canaan. Viking 1997 342p $23.95

ISBN 0-670-87485-X

LC 97-5867

"Racing from one good deed to another, Father Timothy takes in stray sick folk, finds an abandoned child, and helps his favorite baker write a winning jingle. A mayoral race pitting the long-time mayor Esther Cunningham against the possibly corrupt Mack Stroupe makes for some colorful sparring. Father Timothy applies his own unique, time-honored method of intuition, prayer, or dietary indulgence to a multitude of problems big and small. His late-in-life marriage to Cynthia continues to be a blessing readers will feel privileged to share." Libr J

Karp, Larry

A perilous conception. Poisoned Pen Press 2011 250p.

ISBN 1590589734; 9781590589731; 9781590589748; 9781590589755

LC 2011926981

This book takes place in "1976. Despite fierce international controversy over whether in vitro fertilization should ever be performed in humans, doctors around the world race to be first to produce a baby by this procedure. Dr. Colin Sanford, a[n] . . . obstetrician in the Pacific Northwest city of Emerald, has a plan. He recruits Dr. Giselle Hearn, an experienced laboratory geneticist-embryologist at the University. . . . Several months later, Dr. Sanford's patient, Joyce Kennett, gives birth to a healthy boy, and Sanford prepares to make an announcement at a press conference. But before it convenes, Ms. Kennett's schizophrenic husband kills Dr. Hearn and then himself. Police Detective Bernie Baumgartner's investigation is hampered by pressure from influential people at the University who want to control sensationalism that might harm the institution. Tenacious Baumgartner suspects more at play." (Publisher's note)

Karunatilaka, Shehan

The **legend** of Pradeep Mathew; a novel. Shehan Karunatilaka. Graywolf Press 2011 397 p. (pbk.) $16

ISBN 1555976115; 9781555976118

LC 2012931911

This novel follows "Sri Lankan . . . sportswriter Wijedasa Gamini Karunasena (Wije to his friends) [who] fits in well with the American stereotype of the journalist as a cigarette-smoking boozer. . . . After years of abusing his liver, and after the Cricket World Cup matches in 1996, he begins to track down the enigmatic Pradeep Mathew, a 'spinner' and the best Sri Lankan cricketer ever." (Kirkus Reviews)

Kashua, Sayed

Dancing Arabs; translated from the Hebrew by Miriam Shlesinger. Grove Press 2004 227p $24

ISBN 0-8021-4126-9

LC 2003-67765

Original Hebrew edition, 2002

"After solving a quiz-show riddle, the young Palestinian protagonist earns the rare opportunity to study at a Jewish university in Jerusalem. There is hope for him, so we suspect, and for his village and people. In Jerusalem, though, he feels the truth of his father's pessimism ('once an Arab, always an Arab, and you don't stand a chance') and finds and forfeits forbidden love with Naomi. Yet nationalism, optimism, and his family's hope that his intelligence will lead to the first Arab atom bomb fizzle out and leave a headachy and resentful middle-aged man, unhappily married to an Arab wife back in the borderlands." Booklist

Kashua, Sayed

Second person singular; Sayed Kashua; translated from the Hebrew by Mitch Ginsburg. Grove Press 2012 346 p.

ISBN 0802120199; 9780802120199

2011 Bernstein Award

This Bernstein Award-winning Israeli psychological novel by Sayed Kashua, "centers on an ambitious lawyer who is considered one of the best Arab criminal attorneys in Jerusalem. He has a thriving practice in the Jewish part of town, a large house, speaks perfect Hebrew, and is in love with his wife and two young children. One day at a used bookstore, he picks up a copy of Tolstoy's The Kreutzer Sonata, and inside finds a love letter, in Arabic, in his wife's handwriting. Consumed with suspicion and jealousy, the lawyer hunts for the book's previous owner—a man named Yonatan—pulling at the strings that hold all their lives together. . . . Kashua spins a tale of love and betrayal, honesty and artifice, and questions whether it is possible to truly reinvent ourselves." (Publisher's note)

Kasischke, Laura, 1961-

Eden Springs; a novella. Wayne State University Press 2010 145p il (Made in Michigan writers series) pa $18.95

ISBN 978-0-8143-3464-5; 0-8143-3464-4

LC 2009-41884

"The Eden Springs of the title sprung up in Benton Harbor, Michigan, when Kentucky-born turn of the century self-proclaimed preacher Benjamin Purnell turned up with a handful of followers to spread the word of his cult of immortality—and establish an internationally known amusement park near the shores of Lake Michigan. In little more than a hundred and forty pages Laura Kasischke narrates the progress and decline of Purnell's project, the so-called House of David. . . . Working from the historical record Kasischke dramatizes the conversion of a number of . . . Midwesterners, especially the young girls and women, to Purnell's vision of intercourse and eternity." Chicago Trib

"Kasischke explores the sensuous message of this paradisiacal cult, depicting gorgeously a web of irresistible impressions taken as God's truth." Publ Wkly

Kasischke, Laura

In a perfect world; a novel. Harper Perennial 2009 309, 14p pa $13.99

ISBN 978-0-06-176611-4; 0-06-176611-9

LC 2008-49378

"As end-of-the-world scenarios go, Kasischke's is frightening almost because of her willingness to avoid the usual scare tactics. . . . This is a doomsday book in the form of a finely observed domestic drama, showing how dysfunctional relationships shift and soften in response to the looming menace." Los Angeles Times

Kasischke, Laura

The **life** before her eyes. Harcourt 2002 273p $24

ISBN 0-15-100888-4

LC 2001-24311

"Diana and her best friend are confronted by a schoolmate killer, but only Diana is spared. Fast-forward 20 years: Diana, now middle-aged and still beautiful, is a housewife and artist living in the same idyllic university town with a handsome professor-husband and a young daughter. She has seemingly repressed her memory of the event as well as her survivor's guilt, but her perfect world and her grip on reality are both starting to crack." Libr J

This novel "evokes terror and redemption, shadows and light. Kasischke treads a delicate line with the precision and confidence of a tightrope walker." N Y Times Book Rev

Kasischke, Laura, 1961-

The **raising**; a novel. Harper Perennial 2011 461p pa $14.99

ISBN 978-0-06-200478-9; 0-06-204478-6

LC 2010-21605

"Kasischke excels at depicting the psychology of the young and the traumatized even as she delivers a scathing indictment of the siege mentality of college administrators. In this literary page-turner, reminiscent of Donna Tartt's Secret History (1992), the talented author inlays her academic novel with a touch of the supernatural and a deep sense of foreboding." Booklist

Katkov, Norman

Blood & orchids. St. Martin's Press 1983 503p

LC 83-2889

"Set in Hawaii in the early '30s, {this} crime novel is based on an actual case. The story begins when a quartet of beach boys play Good Samaritan and end up accused of beating and raping the U.S. naval officer's wife they rescued,

Hester Murdock. The trial brings to a boil the simmering racial tensions in the islands, and when it ends in a hung jury, vigilante justice takes over. Three of the boys are kidnapped and flogged by sailors, while the other is shot to death. A flamboyant trial lawyer named Bergman is imported from the States to defend the accused: Hester's husband, Gerald; Doris Ashby, her mother; and a hapless gob who was in the wrong place at the wrong time. As Honolulu detective Curt Maddox digs deeper into the matter, the situation is revealed to be even more sordid and scandalous than originally supposed. Studded with vivid characterizations, the story rolls inexorably to an awesome, tragic conclusion." Publ Wkly

Katzenbach, John

The **analyst**. Ballantine Bks. 2002 424p
ISBN 0-345-42626-6

LC 2001-43841

The author has "potently chronicled a long journey of revenge and redemption. Some of his psychological plot points . . . are a stretch, but the novel's fine sense of pacing, sudden switchbacks and chilling characterizations far overshadow its minor faults." Publ Wkly

Katzenbach, John

Hart's war; a novel. Ballantine Pub. Group 1999 490p
ISBN 0-345-42624-X

LC 98-29890

"Katzenbach's setting is flawlessly grim, and his characters chillingly reveal the divisive bigotry of soldiers ostensibly fighting for the same values, as well as some unexpected sources of redemption." Publ Wkly

Katzenbach, John

Just cause. Putnam 1992 431p
ISBN 0-399-13626-6

LC 91-15135

"Matthew Cowart is at the top of his profession—a member of the editorial page staff of a major Miami newspaper. Cowart thinks his days as a crime reporter are behind him until he receives a letter from death row inmate Robert Ferguson, who not only proclaims his innocence, but also to have learned the identity of the real murderer. Cowart, his personal life a mess, takes the bait, hits the crime beat again, and writes a series of articles that lead to Ferguson's release and win the journalist a Pulitzer Prize. But Cowart has opened a Pandora's box of events which leads him to a showdown with the killer." Libr J

"Despite some extraneous subplots, the story generally proceeds at a breakneck pace, enhanced by ear-perfect dialogue and complex characterization." Publ Wkly

Katzenbach, John

The **madman's** tale. Ballantine Bks. 2004 438p $24.95
ISBN 0-345-46481-8

The author "delivers an uplifting story of justice, friendship, mystery and, above all, the courage of certain men and women who rise up, no matter the circumstances, to defeat evil, no matter the consequences." Publ Wkly

Katzenbach, John

State of mind. Ballantine Bks. 1997 409p
ISBN 0-345-38631-0

LC 97-1415

"The U.S. has become more horrible than anyone could imagine; crime is rampant, and all citizens carry semiautomatic or even automatic weapons. When a teenage girl is found dead in a supposedly crime-free area controlled by the government, called the Fifty-first State, the murder appears to be one of a series that began a number of years prior. The Fifty-first authorities turn to criminal-mind expert Jeffrey Clayton, who has little choice but to help out, even though it means he will meet with personal demons he didn't want to resurrect." Booklist

"Katzenbach is a master at creating believable people caught up in horrific situations." Libr J

Katzenbach, John

★ **What** comes next; John Katzenbach. Mysterious Press 2012 448 p. $27.00
ISBN 0802126111; 9780802126115

In this book, "Adrian Thomas, a retired professor," recently diagnosed with degenerative dementia, "witnesses a man and a woman in an unmarked van kidnap 16-year-old Jennifer Riggins, who's running away from home. The couple have seized Jennifer to star in Whatcomesnext.com, a Web site where viewers watch the girl's torture in real time. Despite his failing mind, Adrian is able to use the psychological insights he gleaned as a professor to hunt for Jennifer." (Publishers Weekly)

Katzenbach, John

The **wrong** man; a novel. Ballantine Books 2006 461p $25.95
ISBN 978-0-345-46483-5; 0-345-46483-4

LC 2006-48254

"This haunting story will linger in your mind. . . . Katzenbach's wonderful, tense narrative flows effortlessly, drawing you deeper and deeper into a chilling atmosphere of evil, darkness, and shadows." Miami Herald

Kaufman, Bel

★ **Up** the down staircase. Prentice-Hall 1964 340p il

"Fresh from graduate study in English and crammed with pedagogy courses, young Sylvia Barrett begins her first year as a teacher in Calvin Coolidge High School. The experiences of this first year teacher, determined to remain true to her ideals despite the administrative confusion and organizational chaos of a New York City high school, form the core of Up the Down Staircase. . . . It tells its story through a series of letters, administrative memoranda, student compositions, suggestion box contributions, and intraschool communications." Best Sellers

Kaufman, Millard

Bowl of cherries; a novel. McSweeney's Books 2007 326p $22
ISBN 9781932416831; 1-932416-83-8

"Judd Breslau is a child prodigy who leaves Yale at the age of 14 at his doctoral adviser's urging, only to fall in with Phillip Chatterton, a retired Egyptologist with poor hygiene who is working on his opus in a dilapidated mansion. Soon, Judd falls in love with Chatterton's daughter, develops a deep hatred for her boyfriend, befriends an international student, and eventually ends up arrested in Iraq, awaiting his own execution. These events, however unrelated they seem, are tied together by Kaufman's narration following no set time line, with the narrative alternating between the jail cell and the events leading Judd there." Libr J

"Kaufman's rapier-sharp prose and keen instinct for finding the absurd in everyday life makes this a social satire of the first order." LA Wkly

Kaufman, Millard

★ **Misadventure**; a novel. McSweeney's Books 2010 218p $22

ISBN 978-1-934781-54-8

"Real-estate agent, impromptu detective and aspiring assassin, Jack Hopkins is a noir antihero waiting to happen—all he needs is a crooked scheme and a femme fatale. He finds both early in Millard Kaufman's aptly titled novel Misadventure. During a random house appraisal, he meets the beautiful, seductive and emotionally volatile Darlene, who wants to hire Jack to sell her cliffside Malibu mansion—and, it turns out, to kill her husband. The only problem: Darlene's husband, real-estate mogul Tod, is Jack's new boss and has taken him in as a confidant. Among other morally dubious assignments, Tod wants Jack to off Darlene. As if the situation weren't shady enough, people keep dying, and the only thing that links their deaths is Jack. Though it shares plot points with film-noir classics like Double Indemnity and Strangers on a Train, Kaufman's novel distinguishes itself with strong comic overtones." Time Out NY

Kaufman, Sue

★ **Diary** of a mad housewife. Random House 1967 311p

"Bettina Balser, in her mid-thirties, with a husband, two daughters ages nine and seven, and a bright apartment on Central Park West, (New York City), has arrived at a point in her life where she has completely lost her way, her purpose, her identity. She is literally terrified of so many things . . . that she is also afraid she is losing her mind. She decides to write out the things that so alarm her, as a form of therapy." Best Sellers

Kava, Alex

Hotwire. Doubleday 2011 291p $25.95

ISBN 978-0-385-53201-3

LC 2010-52991

"Detoured from a conference in Denver to investigate mutilated cows in isolated western Nebraska, FBI profiler Maggie O'Dell is nearby when teenagers having a drug party in a national forest are mysteriously attacked, leaving two of them dead. The attack seems right out of science fiction and becomes even more suspicious when the surviving teens start dying. Meanwhile, Maggie's boyfriend, Colonel Benjamin Platt, director of the Army Medical Research Institute of Infectious Diseases, is called in to investigate suspicious food-poisoning outbreaks at schools in Virginia and Washington, D.C. Inevitably, the two cases interwine, revolving around the ultrasecret development of mutating bacteria for biological warfare." Booklist

"A sizzling plot, achingly real characters, and government officials working their backsides off to save their backsides, all strike as lethally as lightning." Publ Wkly

Kavenna, Joanna

The **birth** of love; a novel. Metropolitan Books 2010 304p pa $15

ISBN 978-0-8050-9154-0; 0-8050-9154-8

LC 2009-30680

In this "novel of ideas, Kavenna shifts between time periods and genres, juxtaposing four thematically related tales. In nineteenth-century Vienna, an obstetrician confined to an insane asylum raves about the women he's killed; in contemporary London, a reclusive middle-aged writer finally publishes his first book, about a nineteenth-century obstetrician confined to an insane asylum; across the city a pregnant woman experiences the first pangs of labor; and in a totalitarian society of the future, in which women's eggs are forcibly harvested and children are bred in laboratories, a nameless prisoner is accused of conspiracy against the human species. At times, Kavenna's thesis, on the struggle of the individual versus the collective, is too overt. Still, the book's provocations are fascinating, and few writers have matched her ruthlessly naturalistic depiction of modern childbirth as half farce, half horror story." New Yorker

Kavenna, Joanna

Inglorious; a novel. Metropolitan Books 2007 286p $25

ISBN 978-0-8050-8189-3; 0-8050-8189-5

LC 2006-46868

Kavenna pursues the causes and trajectory of a nervous breakdown with a relentlessness that comes close to overwhelming the minimal plot; still, her understanding of the complexity of depression and her evocation of her heroine's bewilderment are precise, and Rosa, for all her misery, has an appealing and often funny voice. New Yorker

Kawabata, Yasunari

Snow country, and Thousand cranes; the Nobel Prize edition of two novels. translated from the Japanese by Edward G. Seidensticker. Knopf 1969 2v in 1

First United States editions published 1957 and 1959, respectively

Snow country "describes the three visits of Shimamura, a rich Tokyo dilettante, to a hotspring in the west of Japan, the snowiest region in the world. Here a young geisha, Komako, becomes his mistress and falls in love with him. . . . Komako's sparkling freshness stirs him, and he is touched by the 'irresistible sadness' she makes him feel, a sense of beauty going to waste and of immanent decay. But he cannot return her love; and their strange relationship, to which she gives so much, is doomed from the start." Atlantic

Kawabata, Yasunari

The **sound** of the mountain; translated from the Japanese by Edward M. Seidensticker. Knopf 1970 276p

"The language is delicate, allusive, intensely Japanese; and, since plot and character development count for little, the style is all-important. We are fortunate that it should have been a writer with Mr. Seidensticker's gifts who ventured to convey {Kawabata's} rarefied novels into English." N Y Times Book Rev

Kawabata, Yasunari

★ **Thousand** cranes; translated by Edward G. Seidensticker. Knopf 1959 147p

Original Japanese edition, 1949

"This melancholy tale uses the classical tea ceremony as a background for the story of a young man's relationships to two women, his father's former mistress and her daughter. Although it has been praised for the beauty of its spare and elegant style, the novel has also been criticized for its coldness and its suggestion of nihilism." Merriam-Webster's Ency of Lit

Kay, Guy Gavriel

The **last** light of the sun. Roc 2004 504p $24.95

ISBN 0-451-45965-2

"Kay's novel is an ambitious entertainment that transcends the historical record, offering cogent observations on fathers and sons, on the power of grief, on faith, courage, loyalty and the inevitability of change." Quill Quire

Kay, Guy Gavriel

★ **River** of Stars; Guy Gavriel Kay. Penguin Group USA 2013 656 p. (hardcover) $26.95

ISBN 0451464974; 9780451464972

LC 2013002317

This is the second in Guy Gavriel Kay's alternate historical fantasy series about the fictional country of Kitai. "Several hundred years after the events of 'Under Heaven' (which was set in the equivalent of the Tang Dynasty), teen Ren Daiyan demonstrates legend-level archery prowess and becomes a marsh outlaw. Years later, when a cloistered emperor's hobby begins destroying lives, Daiyan tries to redeem his honor by joining the imperial army to halt the empire's decline." (Publishers Weekly)

"An elegant, imaginative inhabitation of Song-dynasty China of 1,000 years ago." Kirkus

Kay, Guy Gavriel

The **summer** tree. ROC 2001 383p map (The Fionavar tapestry) pa $16

ISBN 0-451-45822-2

LC 00-45803

First published 1984 in Canada

In this first book in the Fionavar tapestry series, "five university students embark on a journey of self-discovery when they enter a realm of wizards and warriors, gods and mythical creatures—and good and evil." Publisher's note

Followed by The wandering fire (1986) and The darkest road (1986)

Kay, Guy Gavriel

Tigana. Penguin Bks. 1990 687p il map

ISBN 0-670-83333-9

LC 90-34423

"In a desperate attempt to revive the memory of a land banished from existence and to restore freedom to a battered world, a wandering musician and his small band of compatriots traverse a countryside bowed under the weight of its

sorcerer-conquerors. . . . Memorable characters and cultures add depth to a gracefully plotted story." Libr J

Kay, Guy Gavriel

Under heaven. Roc-New American Library 2010 573p $26.95

ISBN 978-0-451-46330-2

LC 2010-4833

"Virtually everything a reader could want in a book: a thrilling adventure, a love story, a coming-of-age tale, a military chronicle, a court-intrigue drama, a tragedy and on and on. It is a sumptuous feast of storytelling." Globe and Mail

Kay, Guy Gavriel

★ **Ysabel**. Roc 2007 421p

ISBN 978-0-451-46129-2; 0-451-46129-0

LC 2006-28326

This novel is set in "Aix-en-Provence. Fifteen-year-old Ned is staying with his father, a renowned photographer, who is working on a book. While exploring the Saint-Sauveur Cathedral, he meets Kate, an exchange student from New York, and together they encounter a mysterious man rising from a grate in the baptistry." Quill Quire

"The author's historical detail, evocative writing and fascinating characters—both ancient and modern—will enthrall mainstream as well as fantasy readers." Publ Wkly

Kay, Terry

The **runaway**. Morrow 1997 406p

ISBN 0-688-15033-0

LC 97-16737

"Naively defying the mores of their small Georgia hometown, 12-year-olds Tom Winter, white, and Son Jesus Martin, black, have been friends their whole lives. But their twelfth summer brings change. Their accidental discovery of a human bone buried in a sawdust pile at an abandoned mill they pass while running away from home and the vicious rape of Son Jesus' sister by the family's white landlord set in motion events that forever change the boys' relationship and the way they see the world." Booklist

"The dialog is authentic and the storytelling has a homespun Southern texture." Libr J

Kay, Terry

Shadow song. Pocket Bks. 1994 388p

LC 94-15369

"Naive and gentlemanly Madison Lee ('Bobo') Murphy is 17 when, in 1955, he leaves rural Georgia to work at a resort in the Catskills, where he experiences instant culture shock among the inn's Jewish clientele. He comes under the influence of Avrum Feldman, an elderly eccentric who has devoted his life to the memory of Amelita Galli-Curci, the legendary soprano. . . . Avrum encourages Bobo when he falls chastely in love with Amy Lourie, a rich Jewish girl from New York visiting the resort with her protective parents. . . . Now, 38 years later, Bobo has returned to the Catskills to bury Avrum—and discovers that Amy is there too." Publ Wkly

"An absolutely enchanted and lyrical testimonial to the indomitable spirit of friendship and the tenacity of true love." Booklist

Kaye, M. M.

The **far** pavilions. St. Martin's Press 1978 957p
LC 78-3975

This historical novel of India between the Mutiny of 1857 and the second Afghan war focuses on "the early life, loves, and military career of Ashton Pelham-Martyn, an impetuous Englishman born in mid-Victorian India, reared by a Hindu serving-woman, and educated in the stuffiest of British schools. Considered an odd duck by his fellow Englishmen for his liberal view on race, and held at arm's length by his Indian friends, Pelham-Martyn resolves undivided loyalties by serving as a secret agent for the British Guides. . . . A romantic subplot concerns his quest for an Indian princess he has loved all his life, and lost to a Rajah." Libr J

"It's a leisurely, panoramic, enjoyable tale, convincing and varied in characterization, rich in adventure, heroism, cruelty and love, rich in India." Publ Wkly

Kaye, M. M.

Shadow of the moon. St. Martin's Press 1979 614p
LC 79-5033

First published 1957 in the United Kingdom; an abridged version of this novel was published 1957, in the United States by Messner

The author exhibits "an intimate knowledge of Indian history, a deep feel for the land, unflagging vitality and an unfailing instinct for suspense. These qualities make her story delightfully readable." Publ Wkly

Kazantzakis, Nikos

The **last** temptation of Christ; translated from the Greek by P. A. Bien. Simon & Schuster 1960 506p

"The Christ created here by Kazantzakis is definitely not the Christ of the Gospels. . . . Far from it. Kazantzakis has composed a fictional biography of Jesus that is written with passion, a colorful, lyric testimony of his, Kazantzakis' own anguished search for God." Best Sellers

Kazantzakis, Nikos

★ **Zorba** the Greek; translated by Carl Wildman. Simon & Schuster 1952 311p

"The spirit of Zorba, full of energy and peasant philosophy, is contrasted with that of the narrator, a learned but staid Englishman who comes to Crete for adventure. The relationship between the two men deepens despite Zorba's mismanagement of the narrator's mining business, and despite Zorba's attempts to change his friend's behavior to a more zestful one. Kazantzakis creates in Zorba a character that represents the vitality sapped by the inhibitions civilization has created." Shapiro. Fic for Youth. 3d edition

Kazinski, A. J.

The **last** good man; a novel. by A.J. Kazinski; translated from the Danish by Tiina Nunnally. Scribner 2012 469 p. (hardcover) $26.99
ISBN 9781451640755; 9781451640762; 9781451640779
LC 2011044179

In this book, "[t]he Jewish legend that the world is kept from destruction by 36 just people, who are unaware of their status, underpins . . . [the plot by author A. J.] Kazinski, the

pseudonym of filmmaker Anders Rønnow Klarlund and Jacob Weinreich. When Italian police officer Tommaso di Barbara becomes aware that good people have been dying all over the world, he concludes that the victims are 34 of the 36, and contacts a Danish colleague, hostage negotiator Niels Bentzon, to assist him in saving the last two members of the group. Bentzon, in turn, finds unexpected help in the form of scientist Hannah Lund, who uses the inquiry to re-engage with the world after her son's suicide." (Publishers Weekly)

Kearsley, Susanna

The **Firebird**; Susanna Kearsley. Sourcebooks Inc 2013 544 p. (paperback) $16.99
ISBN 140227663X; 9781402276637
LC 2013010359

In this book by Susanna Kearsley, protagonist "Nicola Marter works for a London gallery. . . . She also has the secret ability to hold an object and see past events. When a woman comes in with a small carved bird, Nicola has a vision of the Empress Catherine giving it to a young woman named Anna. With no documented provenance, the carving is worthless to collectors, and Nicola feels impelled to authenticate it." (Booklist)

Kearsley, Susanna

Mariana; by Susanna Kearsley. Sourcebooks Landmark 2012 373 p. (alk. paper) $16.99
ISBN 1402258674; 9781402258671
LC 2011050596

The book "Mariana," by Susanna Kearsley, the winner of the 1993 Catherine Cookson Fiction Prize, tells the story of "Julia Beckett, [who] finds herself transported into seventeenth-century England, becoming Mariana, a young woman struggling against danger and treachery, and battling a forbidden love. . . . [She] realizes Mariana's life is threatening to eclipse her own, and she must find a way to lay the past to rest or lose the chance for happiness in her own time." (susannakearsley.com)

Keating, Celine

Layla. Plain View Press 2011 245p pa $18.95
ISBN 978-1-935514-77-0; 1-935514-77-6

This is a "novel built around a series of slow revelations, a book that asks the reader to be as patient as the titular main character in undertsanding the precise nature of the enigmas involved. It's also that most quintessentially American of genres, the road trip story. Whether the novel proves to be an engaging journey of discovery or a tedious series of deferred surprises will hinge directly on the reader's willingness to delay gratification, to accept that there is a perfectly logical explanation for all this secrecy and misdirection. . . . Neither a masterpiece nor a car wreck, then, Layla will prove to be a diverting enough ride, especially for the reader with an attachment to the era of the '60s." PopMatters

Keating, H. R. F.

The **bad** detective. St. Martin's Minotaur 1999 279p
ISBN 0-312-24371-5
LC 99-33531

First published 1996 in the United Kingdom

"Keating's low-key sense of humor and his dexterity at making a crooked protagonist sympathetic are firmly in place, as is the story's satirical edge, which explores the disparity between the financial rewards received by criminals and police and the symbiotic relationship between cops and robbers." Publ Wkly

Keating, H. R. F.
    Bribery, corruption also. St. Martin's Press 1999 282p $23.95
        ISBN 0-312-20502-3
            LC 99-15494

"Inspector Ghote, of the Bombay police, accompanies his wife to Calcutta in order to take possession of an inherited house. The hassles they encounter reveal corruption, conspiracy, and more." Libr J

Keating, H. R. F.
    Cheating death. Mysterious Press 1994 172p
            LC 94-9502

This "Inspector Ghote novel finds the lovable Indian detective embroiled in an academic cheating scandal, under pressure from his superiors and vexed by pressing domestic business. When a final exam paper is circulated throughout Bombay's Oceanic College prior to the test, Ghote is sent to investigate, only to find his prime suspect in a coma, having tried to commit suicide (Or was it a murder attempt?)." Publ Wkly

Keating, H. R. F.
    Doing wrong; an Inspector Ghote novel. Penzler Bks. 1994 218p
            LC 94-9287

"From Bombay, the exquisitely courteous, ever persistent police detective, Inspector Ghote, travels to the holy city of Banaras to find the murderer of the much loved Mrs. Popatkar, 'veteran freedom fighter, former Minister, upholder of a hundred good causes'. . . . In spite of a leisurely pace befitting a country where foot-sore pilgrims, sacred cattle and auto rickshaws clog the roads, this is an absorbing tale and an illuminating tour of Banaras." Publ Wkly

Keating, H. R. F.
    The **good** detective; a mystery. Scribner 1995 199p
            LC 95-9078

"Detective Ned French is smooth talking, ambitious, talented, and sure to move up quickly in the Norchester police. . . . Trouble is, Ned's so obsessed with keeping Norchester free of crime that he completely loses his good judgment. First, there's an illicit and ill-advised affair with attractive barrister Deborah Brooke, and then he foolishly covers up a damning incident from his past. Finally Ned makes his biggest mistake—a unilateral and extremely unwise decision about how to deal with a gang of 'London thugs' who are threatening Norchester. Deeply affecting and superbly written, this is an outstanding police procedural and a moving human drama." Booklist

Keating, H. R. F.
    ★ **Inspector** Ghote trusts the heart. Doubleday 1973 201p

First published 1972 in the United Kingdom
The author "writes with wonderful ease and energy—his understanding of the individuality of human beings is profound." New Yorker

Keating, H. R. F.
    The **soft** detective. St. Martin's Press 1998 268p
        ISBN 0-312-19335-1
            LC 98-8817

First published 1997 in the United Kingdom
"When Detective Chief Inspector Phil Benholme begins investigating the murder of a Nobel Prize-winning physiologist, he can scarcely believe what he discovers: his own teenage son may be involved. Keating's latest is a gripping examination of one of a police officer's worst nightmares—a portrait of a man faced with the choice between defending his son and helping to prove he's a killer." Booklist

Keegan, Nicola
    Swimming. Alfred A. Knopf 2009 305p $25.95
        ISBN 978-0-307-26997-3
            LC 2009-14051

"World-class swimming isn't all breathing and technique: for Philomena . . . it is a necessity. Haunted by a litany of childhood tragedy—an agoraphobic mother, a lost father, a drug-addled sister, and a Catholic education dominated by nuns—Pip escapes into the racing lane. . . . Swimming is the story of Pip's rise from the star of her small Midwestern swim team to her first state meets, her brutal professional training, and her eventual gold medals as an Olympic champion." (Publisher's note)

"Keegan's energy jumps off the page. . . . Swimming is a wonderful coming-of-age story, a richly detailed account of a young woman channeling her rage, grief and insecurity into a passion to win. The voice Keegan has invented for Pip is sarcastic, thoughtful, elegant, irreverent." Boston Globe

Keesey, Anna
    ★ **Little** century; a novel. Anna Keesey. 1st ed. Farrar, Straus and Giroux 2012 322 p. (hardcover) $26
        ISBN 0374192049; 9780374192044
            LC 2011046308

In this historical novel, "newly orphaned Esther Chambers leaves Chicago for the high desert of Oregon," and claims "a homestead adjoining" the land of her cattle rancher cousin Pick. Slowly Esther learns to feel at home in the small town, learning "to ride a horse and tak[ing] up typewriting and typesetting." Pick wants to marry her, but she loves a sheep farmer. "Then a murder turns the town inside out." (Library Journal)

Kehlmann, Daniel
    Fame; a novel in nine episodes. translated from the German by Carol Brown Janeway. Pantheon Books 2010 175p $24
        ISBN 978-0-307-37871-2; 0-307-37871-3
            LC 2009-52380

Original German edition, 2009
"The sly humor of this book is indebted to an excellent translation by Carol Brown Janeway. . . . Clearly divided and purposefully connected, the stories in 'Fame' make a terrific

case for the way fiction enables us to lead double lives — and then, at the stories' end, to go home." Boston Globe

Kehlmann, Daniel

Measuring the world; translated from the German by Carol Brown Janeway. Pantheon Books 2006 259p $23

ISBN 0-375-42446-6

LC 2006-40480

Original German edition, 2005

The "author plays his fiction game with great refinement and sparkling wit. The plot is strong and its dialogue totally hilarious." Frankfurter Rundschau

Keillor, Garrison

Happy to be here. Atheneum Pubs. 1982 210p

LC 81-66033

Keillor, Garrison

Lake Wobegon days. Viking 1985 337p

ISBN 0-670-80514-9

LC 85-40029

"Much of this is satirical, but Keillor's subtle humor is gentle, rather than biting or mocking, as he exposes the foibles and faults of Lake Wobegonians with affection and sympathy." Publ Wkly

Keillor, Garrison

Lake Wobegon summer 1956. Viking 2001 291p

ISBN 0-670-03003-1

LC 2001-26312

"It is summer, and as the denizens of Lake Wobegon sit on their front porches, listening to the radio and to the swish of sprinklers on their lawns, 14-year-old Gary struggles to find his own place within the community. . . . Gary has, by his own admission, been a good boy, but he is now exploring what it means to be bad—as @bad' is defined in 1950s Lake Wobegon. Keillor's wry vignettes of Gary's summer of change and turmoil are laced with his trademark self-deprecating humor." Libr J

Includes bibliographical references (p. 359-392) and index

Keillor, Garrison

Leaving home. Viking 1987 xxiii, 244p

LC 87-40219

"These radio monologues {from A Prairie Home Companion} read easily, and listeners to the weekly radio show will find the flow of Keillor's distinctive flat rendition ringing in their ears." Wilson Libr Bull

Keillor, Garrison

Love me. Viking 2003 272p $24.95

ISBN 0-670-03246-8

LC 2003-52540

The author "blends humor and compassion with just a touch of cynicism, cooking up a funny, insightful, and touching story of ambition, sacrifice, and love." Booklist

Keillor, Garrison

WLT; a radio romance. Viking 1991 401p

ISBN 0-670-81857-7

LC 91-50160

"Garrison Keillor's mythical America, unlike the faded and inoffensive Midwest of Sandburg, is dreamed with an unblinking eye. His characters are idiosyncratic. They are culled from who knows where—from our collective past, certainly, but also from the demotic oral tradition of a rich and very real community that is gone and now exists only in recollection." Nation

Keilson, Hans

★ Comedy in a minor key; translated from the German by Damion Searls. Farrar, Straus and Giroux 2010 135p $22

ISBN 978-0-374-12675-9; 0-374-12675-5

LC 2010-01482

Original German edition, 1947

"Not once does the author mention Hitler. Not once does he mention death camps. Not once does he put the word Nazi on paper. Rather, in 'Comedy in a Minor Key,' author Hans Keilson reveals the horrors of the Holocaust in an eerie, intense way. He takes readers inside the minds of three main characters and provides a gripping psychoanalysis of what it was like both for a Jew in hiding and the couple who gave him sanctuary. . . . The novel, a dark comedy, is semi-autobiographical. A Dutch couple, Marie and Wim, agree to hide a Jewish man during World War II. The fugitive, who gives his name as Nico rather than his Jewish-sounding name, dies after a prolonged illness. Dead, the man is more dangerous to the couple than alive." Boston Globe

Keilson, Hans

Life goes on; Hans Keilson; translated from the German by Damion Searls. Farrar, Straus and Giroux 2012 272 p.

ISBN 0374191956; 9780374191955

LC 2012012326

Originally published as Leben geht weiter: Berlin: S. Fischer, 1933.

This book by Hans Keilson is "an autobiographical novel that paints a dark yet illuminating portrait of Germany between the world wars. It is the story of Herr Seldersen -- a Jewish store owner modeled on Keilson's father, a textile merchant and decorated World War I veteran -- along with his wife and son, Albrecht, and the troubles they encounter as the German economy collapses and politics turn rancid." (Publisher's note)

Kelby, N. M.

White truffles in winter; a novel. [by] N. M. Kelby. W. W. Norton & Co. 2012 334p

ISBN 0-393-07999-6; 978-0-393-07999-9

LC 2011-29292

This novel "imagines the world of the remarkable French chef Auguste Escoffier (1846-1935). . . . A man of contradictions—kind yet imperious, food-obsessed yet rarely hungry—Escoffier was also torn between two women: the famous, beautiful, and reckless actress Sarah Bernhardt and his wife, the independent and sublime poet Delphine Daffis, who refused ever to leave Monte Carlo. In the last year of

Escoffier's life, in the middle of writing his memoirs, he has returned to Delphine, who requests a dish in her name as he has honored Bernhardt, Queen Victoria, and many others."

This novel "imagines the world of the remarkable French chef Auguste Escoffier (1846-1935). . . . A man of contradictions—kind yet imperious, food-obsessed yet rarely hungry—Escoffier was also torn between two women: the famous, beautiful, and reckless actress Sarah Bernhardt and his wife, the independent and sublime poet Delphine Daffis, who refused ever to leave Monte Carlo. In the last year of Escoffier's life, in the middle of writing his memoirs, he has returned to Delphine, who requests a dish in her name as he has honored Bernhardt, Queen Victoria, and many others." Publisher's note

Kellerman, Faye

Day of atonement; a Peter Decker\Rina Lazarus mystery. Morrow 1991 359p

LC 90-22682

"When Los Angeles detective Peter Decker and new wife Rina Lazarus visit her Jewish kinfolks in Brooklyn, startling events disturb their honeymoon. Quite unexpectedly and with great antipathy, Decker—an adoptee—recognizes his natural mother at a holiday gathering. Before he can confront her, though, her troubled 14-year-old grandson goes missing and Decker, fortuitously on hand, begins the search. . . . Hard-hitting details, vignettes of Jewish life, and uncomfortably close glimpses of a cold-hearted psycho make this an entrancing page turner." Libr J

Kellerman, Faye

The forgotten. Morrow 2001 374p
ISBN 0-688-15614-2

"The depiction of how teens and parents push and pull at one another's emotions is dead on." Booklist

Kellerman, Faye

Grievous sin; a Peter Decker/Rina Lazarus mystery. Morrow 1993 368p

LC 93-12344

"While the plot comes dangerously close to being overly saccharine and annoyingly artificial, Kellerman does know how to hook her readers. First, she tantalizes them with ambiguous clues and ominous glimpses of an unbalanced villain's psyche, then she teases them with a blend of pulse-quickening suspense and heartwarming family tableaux. Only then does she deliver the shocking climax." Booklist

Kellerman, Faye

Jupiter's bones; a novel. Morrow 1999 375p
ISBN 0-688-15612-6

LC 99-33356

"Kellerman has pulled together elements of suspense, violence, humor, pathos, and love and wrapped them into a potent plot certain to captivate genre fans." Booklist

Kellerman, Faye

★ Justice. Morrow 1995 388p

LC 95-14268

In this mystery "a high school prom queen is strangled to death after a wild night of drugs, drink and boisterous group sex. Peter Decker, a Los Angeles homicide detective, who

lies awake nights worrying about his own children, coaxes a confession from the dead girl's date. 'He's cold, he's calculating, he's eerie,' Decker says of this preternaturally self-contained youth, the nephew of a Mafia crime boss. . . . Rina Lazarus, Decker's wife and helpmate in this series, is uncharacteristically subdued here, which gives this sympathetic cop a rare chance to work independently on a case that raises touchy issues like ethnic stereotyping and religious prejudice." N Y Times Book Rev

Kellerman, Faye

Milk and honey; a novel. Morrow 1990 384p

LC 89-39592

"On a summer night in a housing development near Los Angeles, police sergeant Peter Decker finds a winsome two-year-old girl playing on a swing set—and wearing blood-soaked pajamas. Unclaimed, 'Sally' is placed in a foster home while Decker and partner Marge Dunn try to learn her identity. Bee stings on her arms lead them days later to the scene of a bloody multiple murder at a honey farm. While piecing together a bizarre puzzle of betrayal and revenge . . . Peter is also investigating rape and assault charges brought against an old army buddy from Vietnam. The pressures of the murder case and doubts about his friend's innocence compound Peter's anxiety as he waits for young Orthodox Jewish widow Rina Lazarus to decide if she will marry him." Publ Wkly

Kellerman, Faye

Moon music; a novel. Morrow 1998 424p

LC 98-6735

Las Vegas homicide cop Romulus Poe finds himself "in charge of investigating the gruesome death of a showgirl turned hooker. The case reminds Poe of a brutal, unsolved murder 25 years in his own past and brings up his unresolved feelings for his partner's troubled wife. When a second, similarly mutilated body is found, Poe and his team must uncover the truth, even if it involves confronting a powerful, corrupt casino owner. Kellerman's characters have complex interrelationships that often seem more important than the murder investigation itself." Libr J

Kellerman, Faye

Prayers for the dead. Morrow 1996 406p
ISBN 0688143679; 9780688143671

LC 96-7494

This novel "continues the story of Peter Decker and Rina Lazarus, an L.A. detective and his beautiful wife. Someone has murdered Azor Sparks, noted heart surgeon, and Peter must discover the motive and the murderer. Was the motive greed, ambition, random violence, or love gone wrong? Was the murderer one of Spark's colleagues, or one of his family? And what is the connection between Rina and Sparks's son Abram?" (Libr J)

This "mystery begins with the brutal murder and mutilation of renowned heart surgeon, researcher and fundamentalist Christian Azor Sparks. LAPD Lieutenant Decker gets the call. He also gets an abundance of suspects. . . . Religion and morality are integral to Kellerman's mysteries—built on the bedrock of the Deckers' orthodox Judaism. Here she deftly casts her net around the commanding victim, whose shadow lay equally over family and colleagues, and his son, the theologian Father Abram, whose past connection with Rina may force Decker off the case." Publ Wkly

Kellerman, Faye

The **quality** of mercy; a novel. Morrow 1989 607p

LC 88-29275

"Deft characterization and dazzling prose evoke the ambiance of the period. More than just a mystery, the novel is a spectacular epic—romantic, bawdy, witty and abounding with adventure." Publ Wkly

Kellerman, Faye

Sanctuary; a Peter Decker/Rina Lazarus mystery. Morrow 1994 396p

LC 94-11350

"L.A.P.D. sergeant Pete Decker and his Orthodox Jewish wife, Rina Lazarus, the parents of a baby daughter, are caught up in a case involving Rina's old school chum, Honey Klein, who comes to stay with the Deckers after leaving her diamond-merchant husband. When Honey and her children mysteriously disappear, Rina is first puzzled and then alarmed, especially considering that Pete is working on a double homicide involving another Jewish diamond merchant and his family. To solve the case, the Deckers travel to Israel and find themselves risking their lives to track down the disturbing truth." Booklist

Kellerman, Faye

Serpent's tooth; a Peter Decker/Rina Lazarus novel. Morrow 1997 400p

ISBN 0-688-14368-7

LC 97-10685

"The scope of the investigation is broad and the moralizing is kept to a minimum, giving Decker a rare chance to do some solid police work." N Y Times Book Rev

Kellerman, Faye

Stone kiss; a Peter Decker/Rina Lazarus novel. Warner Bks. 2002 390p $25.95

ISBN 0-446-53038-7

LC 2002-16886

"Whether Kellerman is depicting the ultra-Orthodox Jewish community or a pornographer's studio she is utterly convincing. Amid the wreckage of lives taken or thrown away, Kellerman's heroes find glimmers of hope and enough moral ambiguity to make even her most evil villain look less than totally black." Publ Wkly

Kellerman, Faye

Street dreams. Warner Bks. 2003 420p $25.95

ISBN 0-446-53131-6

LC 2003-45079

"Cindy, a rookie cop and Peter's 28-year-old daughter by his first marriage, takes center stage here. Both her rocky history with the department and with her dad come to the fore as she digs into the case of a developmentally disabled teenager who abandoned her baby, insists she was raped, and may have witnessed a murder. Following the strangely coincidental hit-and-run of another disabled teen from the same area, the case blossoms into a mystery that requires help from Peter." Booklist

Kellerman, Jesse

The **genius**. G.P. Putnam's Sons 2008 374p $24.95

ISBN 978-0-399-15459-1; 0-399-15459-0

LC 2008-5810

"When Manhattan art dealer Ethan Muller is shown a dingy rent-controlled apartment bursting with fabulous work, he jumps on it, soon mounting a show — even though the artist, Victor Cracke, has vanished. Who was Cracke, and why do some of the faces in his drawings look like young boys murdered years ago, the crimes unsolved? Prodded by a retired cop, Ethan begins to investigate — first unwillingly, then compulsively — and it becomes clear that Cracke's story is intertwined with that of Ethan's own family. Despite some cumbersome flashbacks, Jesse Kellerman's The Genius boasts a masterful plot and dead-on pacing." Entertainment Wkly

Kellerman, Jesse

Sunstroke; a novel. G.P. Putnam's Sons 2006 370p $24.95

ISBN 0-399-15330-6

LC 2005-51459

"L.A. novelty-company secretary Gloria Mendez, in love with her boss, is heartbroken when he dies while on vacation in Mexico. No family comes forward, so she heads south to claim the body. In sun-bleached Aguas Vivas, a dead town whose only industry is its graveyard, she finds ashes and a suspicious-acting cop. As Kellerman teasingly plays pieces of the puzzle, Gloria soon learns that nearly everything about the man she longed for has been a mirage— and she learns a few things about herself, too. This tightly focused thriller features expertly drawn characters, vivid scenes, and simmering tension." Booklist

Kellerman, Jonathan

Bad love. Bantam Bks. 1994 386p

LC 93-26678

The author "spins a tight, complicated plot and is careful to balance his grisly murder scenes with substantive shop-talk about childhood trauma and the devastating effects of authoritarian discipline." N Y Times Book Rev

Kellerman, Jonathan

Billy Straight; a novel. Random House 1999 467p

ISBN 0-679-45959-6

LC 98-19583

Hollywood homicide detective Petra Connor "frantically scours the city in search of a runaway 12-year-old boy who witnessed the vicious stabbing of a woman in Griffith Park. This case quickly draws the media carrion crows when it comes out that the victim was recently divorced from the popular star of a television series. Like Connor, the investigation is competent but strictly by the book—and not the reason you're turning the pages so fast. That distinction goes to the winsome title character and frequent narrator, a self-taught street kid with an artless affection for books." N Y Times Book Rev

Kellerman, Jonathan

Bones; an Alex Delaware novel. Ballantine Books 2008 353p $27

ISBN 978-0-345-49513-6; 0-345-49513-6

LC 2008-35125

"Kellerman's strength is that he can set up an intriguing situation and keep things moving at a breakneck pace. He can also, when he wants to, write well. He's good at short, vivid descriptions. . . . I don't think the plot of "Bones" will withstand scrutiny, but most readers probably won't care. The story sweeps them along, offering plenty of snappy dialogue and cheap thrills, plus a fair amount of suspense that is relieved by the final unveiling of the killer." Washington Post Book World

Kellerman, Jonathan

The **clinic**. Bantam Bks. 1997 370p

LC 96-24626

The author "has crafted another masterly, darkly psychological tale, drawing upon timely issues ranging from abortion to organ harvesting." Libr J

Kellerman, Jonathan

Devil's waltz. Bantam Bks. 1993 416p

LC 92-18089

"Alex Delaware, the child psychologist and amateur sleuth . . . returns to the beleaguered Los Angeles pediatrics hospital where he was trained. Called in to consult on the baffling case of a 2-year-old girl with phantom ailments, Alex performs his clinical chores with his customary tenderness, while bearing the details of the child's extraordinary medical history. Despite Mr. Kellerman's overelaborate approach, he maintains the harrowing suspense of a medical mystery too horrid to be anything but real." N Y Times Book Rev

Kellerman, Jonathan

Dr. Death; a novel. Random House 2000 352p

ISBN 0-679-45961-8

LC 00-29065

In this mystery Dr. Alex Delaware works "with old LAPD buddy Detective Milo Sturgis on a particularly gruesome murder. Dr. Eldon Mate, a Kervokian-like 'Dr. Death,' is found vivisected in the back of an Econoline van, hooked up to his 'humanitron' suicide machine. A crass farewell note is stapled to his chest. It's obviously the work of an extremely intelligent and bold killer, and suspects abound." Libr J

Kellerman, Jonathan

Gone; an Alex Delaware novel. Ballantine Books 2006 365p $26.95

ISBN 0-345-45261-5

LC 2006-296289

"Delaware joins forces with his sometimes official partner in crime, LAPD detective Milo Sturgis, and together they pursue an investigative trail littered with corpses leading to an unconventional acting school and the family of the eccentric woman who runs it. While the murderer's identity may not be that surprising, the author's ability to convey the unrelenting sadness of his characters' lives and his deep psy-

chological insights will satisfy those looking for more than mere thrills." Publ Wkly

Kellerman, Jonathan

Monster; a novel. Random House 1999 396p

ISBN 0-679-45960-X

LC 99-20098

"A handsome young actor is found murdered and mutilated, a female psychologist meets a similar fate, and twin brothers are gruesomely dispatched—all in separate events, on the same evening. The murders, though different, seem to be the work of the same killer. As Dr. Alex Delaware, psychologist and consultant to the LAPD, and detective Milo Sturgis unravel the mystery of the killer's identity, it becomes clear that Ardis Peake (a.k.a. 'Monster'), incarcerated in a psychiatric hospital for the criminally insane for the past 16 years, is somehow involved." Libr J

Kellerman, Jonathan

The **murder** book. Ballantine Bks. 2002 408p

ISBN 0-345-45253-4

LC 2002-74733

In this "caper starring Delaware and his mentor in police work, homicide detective Milo Sturgis, Delaware receives a package in the mail. It contains an official police case file, known as a '@murder book,' filled with stark crime scene photos and terse reports of some 40 cases. What Delaware finds most shocking, however, is the horrified reaction his hard-bitten detective pal Milo has upon seeing one particular scene. Kellerman departs from his standard focus on Delaware to a telling of Sturgis' story, going back to his struggles as a young black, gay cop and showing how his first victim, the girl depicted in the murder book, still haunts him." Booklist

Kellerman, Jonathan

Private eyes. Bantam Bks. 1992 475p

LC 91-17314

"Harvard-bound, 18-year-old heiress Melissa Dickinson, whom child psychologist Alex Delaware had successfully treated for anxiety 10 years earlier, calls him with concerns about leaving her wealthy mother, an agoraphobe. Years before Melissa's birth, Gina Dickinson Ramp had been disfigured by acid thrown for never-revealed reasons by a former lover, now out of prison and back in town. Widowed for many years, recently remarried and making progress in her own intensive therapy with a noted husband-and-wife team of behaviorial psychologists, Gina is still fragile. When she disappears, Melissa enlists Delaware's help and that of his friend, Milo Sturgis, on leave from the LAPD. . . . Kellerman deftly handles the strings of his plot." Publ Wkly

Kellerman, Jonathan

Self-defense. Bantam Bks. 1995 390p

LC 94-26175

Psychologist Alex Delaware "is treating 25-year-old Lucy Lowell for a recurring nightmare that she has been having ever since serving on the hanging jury that convicted a serial killer. . . . When Lucy's terrifying dream is complicated by incidents of sleepwalking, bed-wetting, narcolepsy and a possible suicide attempt, Alex suspects a repressed childhood memory. After putting his patient through hypnotic regression, he is convinced that she witnessed a murder and he sets out to prove it. . . . An exciting story that is loaded with tension and packed with titillating insights into abnormal psychology." N Y Times Book Rev

Kellerman, Jonathan

Survival of the fittest; a novel. Bantam Bks. 1998 401p

LC 97-3182

"Kellerman has things down to a science now, knowing instinctively what his fans want: suspense, adventure, romance, and a leading man to die for." Booklist

Kellerman, Jonathan

★ **Therapy**. Ballantine Bks. 2004 387p $26.95

ISBN 0-345-45259-3

The author "manages to take the story of a lovers' lane double murder near Mulholland Drive to the point where it involves human rights atrocities in Rwanda. Along the way Mr. Kellerman packs in the descriptive detail that is one of his hallmarks and one of the incidental attractions in his fiction." N Y Times (Late N Y Ed)

Kellerman, Jonathan

Time bomb; a novel. Bantam Bks. 1990 468p

LC 90-349

This novel featuring "child psychologist and private detective Alex Delaware begins when Delaware is called upon to deal with the potential trauma to elementary-school children of a sniper killed in their midst during lunch recess. He quickly learns that the sniper's target may not have been the children at all, but either a right-wing politician holding a news conference at the school or his liberal counterpart, a publicity-hungry, former 1960's radical who had appeared unexpectedly for an impromptu debate and whose bodyguard shot the sniper to death." N Y Times Book Rev

Kellerman, Jonathan

The **web**. Bantam Bks. 1996 342p

LC 95-32161

"An intriguing, keep-'em-guessing plot, Kellerman's usual mix of psychologically fascinating characters, a megadose of suspense, and that always reliable heartthrob, Dr. Alex Delaware, make this one a must-have for all mystery collections." Booklist

Kellerman, Jonathan

When the bough breaks. Atheneum Pubs. 1985 293p

LC 81-16805

Psychologist Alex Delaware "turns detective when he is called upon to interview a young girl who is the only living witness to a brutal dual murder. Whatever the girl may have seen, the actual crime veils an even more horrible contemporary phenomenon: a ring of child molesters at a school in Southern California. The psychologist is soon out of his professional depth in pursuing clues and leads, but he plods onward to solve the case, nearly at the expense of the girl's and his own life. Kellerman's story is long on sensational descriptions and short on believable disclosures—too many of the good turns of fortune seem coincidentally opportune—but as a suspenseful drama, the novel does rack up its points." Booklist

Kellogg, Marjorie

★ **Tell** me that you love me, Junie Moon. Farrar, Straus & Giroux 1968 216p

ISBN 9780871293244; 9780374475109 out of print

"Junie Moon, in a rehabilitation center after a crazy boyfriend threw acid in her face, meets Warren, a paraplegic who has been shot in the spine on a hunting trip, and Arthur, who is slowly dying of a degenerative nerve disease. Amid the protests of the hospital staff the three decide to leave the center to set up a household. The reaction of their new neighbors is anything but encouraging, but one of them, an Italian fish merchant, befriends them and sends them on a vacation in his truck. It is a wonderful interlude until Arthur, recognizing that he is in the last stages of his illness, asks to be taken home to die." Shapiro. Fic for Youth. 3d edition

Kelly, Erin

★ The **burning** air; a novel. Erin Kelly. Pamela Dorman Books 2013 336p. (hardback) $26.95

ISBN 0670026727; 9780670026722

LC 2012029302

In this suspense novel, the MacBride family gather to lay matriarch Lydia to rest, and "it becomes clear that all is not well. The usually sober father—retired headmaster Rowan—is unaccountably drunk; daughter Sophie and son-in-law Will may have reached an impasse because of an affair and a breakdown; mixed-race grandson Jake has been in trouble with the law; and disfigured son Felix has a beautiful new girlfriend whose initial silence unsettles everyone." (Publishers Weekly)

Kelly, Erin

The **poison** tree; a novel. Pamela Dorman Books/Viking 2011 322p $26.95

ISBN 978-0-670-02240-3

LC 2010-24260

First published 2009 in the United Kingdom

"Veteran mystery fans looking for nail-biting thrills will find plenty that is fresh and surprising about The Poison Tree, and Kelly's masterful plotting and intricately crafted story make the comparisons to Tana French and Donna Tartt well-deserved." BookPage

Kelly, James Patrick

The **wreck** of the Godspeed; with a foreword by Bob Eggleton. Golden Gryphon Press 2008 358p $24.95

ISBN 978-1-930846-51-7

LC 2007-48662

"Kelly's stories depend on future technologies based on physics, information theory, genetics, and other au courant disciplines, but they're about love, friendship, and loyalty." Booklist

Kelly, Jim

The **coldest** blood. St. Martin's Minotaur 2007 341p $24.95

ISBN 978-0-312-36478-6; 0-312-36478-4

LC 2006-52203

"This is another winner in what has become one of the best British crime series on the market. Kelly should be read as much for his Dickensian atmosphere (his descriptions of the abandoned orphanage and the Victorian workhouse-turned-hospital are achingly bleak) and his full-throttle characterizations as for his masterful plotting." Booklist

Kelly, Jim

The **fire** baby; Jim Kelly. St. Martin's Minotaur 2004 322 p. $26

ISBN 0312321457; 9780312321451

LC 2004048691

This book is a sequel to Jim Kelly's novel, "The Water Clock." "When his mother's old caretaker makes a startling deathbed confession, Cambridgeshire reporter Philip Dryden finds himself revisiting a decades-old tragedy—a fatal U.S. Air Force crash that claimed many lives, including a weeks-old infant. That probe may be intertwined with several others—into an illegal immigrant smuggling ring, a pornography and date-rape racket, and several murders. Assisted by a motley assortment of friends and allies, and, surprisingly, by his wife, who's been in a coma but has begun to communicate haltingly by spelling out words letter by letter, Dryden . . . uncovers the dark truths behind the crimes." (Publishers Weekly)

Kelly, Jim

The **moon** tunnel; Jim Kelly. St. Martin's Minotaur 2005 viii, 322 p.p

ISBN 031234922X; 9780312349226

LC 2005049449

In Jim Kelly's "third mystery to feature Cambridgeshire journalist Philip Dryden . . . an archeological team discovers human remains in the remnants of what appears to have been an escape tunnel from a WWII-era POW camp in England's fen country. That the victim was shot heading toward the camp piques Philip's interest. When forensic evidence dates the victim's death to well after the war, Philip sets out to find the corpse's identity. His search leads to the local Italian community, academics at Cambridge University, the proprietress of a nearby landfill--and to his intellectual and emotional reawakening after a period of feeling half alive." (Publishers Weekly)

Kelly, Thomas

Empire rising. Farrar, Straus and Giroux 2005 390p $25

ISBN 0-374-14781-7

LC 2004-8580

"The canvas is epic in scale, peopled with numerous arresting characters, recognizable in both senses: 'real' persons like Jimmy Walker, Babe Ruth, Primo Camera, the famously 'missing' Judge Crater and the many engaging but no less real inventions of his own. [Kelly's] special gift as a novelist is his ability to maintain a galloping tilt of narrative suspense, despite countless shifts in plot development, without overwhelming or confusing the reader. Unusual in an epic, to say the least, this novel is a page-turner; there is no plot-padding or authorial longueurs slackening the pace." America

Kelman, James

How late it was, how late. Norton 1995 373p

ISBN 0-393-03817-3

"Sammy, the novel's central figure, is an ex-convict who wakes on a Glasgow street after a two-day binge. . . . He gets himself into a fight with some soldiers. They beat him up, and then he is arrested and beaten some more by the police. The beatings cause him to lose his sight. He's released, blind, into the Glasgow streets, and must try to find his way home." N Y Times Book Rev

The novel "is a tour de force, both in its convincingly claustrophobic rendering of what it's like to be newly sightless and in its rhythmic prose." Newsweek

Kelman, James

Kieron Smith, boy. Harcourt 2008 422p $26

ISBN 978-0-15-101348-7; 0-15-101348-9

The author's "books tend to be written in a Scottish working-class vernacular, and part of the pleasure is untangling some of the thornier brambles out loud. Kieron Smith, boy is crafted with a gentler tongue, so readers should have no fear of taking it on the subway. Kelman excels at serving up the psyches of marginalized people, and young Kieron's narrative of being ignored by his parents and punished by his older brother and moving away from the grandparents who love him is heartwarming without being cheesy. The writing is also piercing and observant without feeling inauthentically wise. By the time you follow Kieron from snakes, snails and puppy dog tails to the first fluttering of his adolescence, the boy will feel like part of the family." NPR

Kelman, James

Mo said she was quirky; by James Kelman. Other Press 2013 303 p. (pbk.) $15.95

ISBN 1590516001; 9781590516003; 9781590516010

LC 2012036336

This novel by James Kelman "tells the story of Helen . . . a very ordinary young woman. Her boyfriend said she was quirky but she is much more than that. Trust, love, relationships; parents, children: these are the ordinary parts of the everyday that become extraordinary when you think of them as Helen does. On Helen's way home from work . . . man crosses the road [who] appears to be her lost brother. What follows [the] story of twenty-four hours in the life of a young woman." (Publisher's note)

Kelman, Judith

Summer of storms. Putnam 2001 288p $24.95

ISBN 0-399-14674-1

LC 00-45728

This thriller "chronicles the rekindling of a long-dormant murder investigation and the return of a ruthless killer. Thirty years after her young sister's death, Anna Jameson is haunted by memories of what was dubbed the Sleeping Beauty Murder. On a stormy summer night, five-year-old Julie Jameson was killed in her bedroom while her family slept. . . . Fast-forward to Anna, now 33 and an aspiring photographer, who returns to New York to work as a photojournalist for a high-powered media conglomerate and to confront family demons." Publ Wkly

Kelton, Elmer

Badger boy. Forge 2001 286p

ISBN 0-312-87319-0

LC 00-48457

Sequel to The buckskin line

As the Texas Rangers disband, Badger Boy, a white boy whose parents were murdered by Comanches and who was himself captured and raised by a Comanche warrior, falls prisoner to David "Rusty" Shannon

Kelton, Elmer
    Long way to Texas; three novels. Forge 2011 496p $25.99
    ISBN 978-0-7653-2976-9

                         LC 2011-21562
    Omnibus volume of three novels by Elmer Kelton writing as Lee McElroy, first published 1975, 1976 and 1981 respectively
    "In Joe Pepper, while awaiting a hangman's noose, the title character tells the story of how he discovered a propensity for violence while seeking revenge. The irony is that Joe's keen sense of justice puts him on he wrong side of the law. Long Way to Texas, taking place just after the Civil War battle of Glorieta Pass in New Mexico, is the story of Lt. David Buckalew, whose remnant of Confederate riflemen is under siege and low on rations and water. Complicating matters is the young officer's self-doubt and fear of failure. Thomas Canfield of Eyes of the Hawk, known to the Mexican citizens of his town of Stonehill, Texas, as 'El Gavilán' — the Hawk — is not a man to forgive a wrong. He sets out to prove this to an insolent ranchman rival who intends building a fortune at Canfield's expense." Publisher's note

Kelton, Elmer
    The **rebels**; sons of Texas. Forge 2007 302p $24.95
    ISBN 978-0-7653-1526-7; 0-7653-1526-2

                         LC 2007-28850
    First published 1990 under the pseudonym Tom Early with title: Sons of Texas: the rebels
    Kelton "concludes the Sons of Texas trilogy [previous titles: Sons of Texas and The raiders] with the strongest entry, set in the mid 1830s. The Lewis family—brothers Andrew, Michael and James, and sister Annie—are foreigners in a strange land, raising their families and farming while Mexican and American cultures, politics, racism and tempers simmer over the possibilities of rebellion and independence from Mexico. During these years, the Lewises must deal with outlaws, the Mexican army, troublemaking American politicians, a slick smuggler and their continuing feud with the thieving and back-shooting Blackwood brothers. When war does come, the Lewis boys and one Blackwood go off to fight in bloody battles at Velasco, the Alamo and San Jacinto, and not all come home. Historical figures—Sam Houston, General Santa Anna, Jim Bowie and Davy Crockett—have cameos and add depth and color to this superb saga of the Lone Star State." Publ Wkly

Kelton, Elmer
    Slaughter. Doubleday 1992 369p

                         LC 92-10317
    "Well written and fast-paced, this powerful, moving novel proceeds inexorably toward the extinction of the great herds and of the indigenous peoples' way of life." Publ Wkly
    Followed by The far canyon (1994)

Kelton, Elmer
    Texas sunrise; two novels of the Texas Republic. Forge 2008 363p $24.95
    ISBN 978-0-7653-2064-3; 0-7653-2064-9

                         LC 2008-34735
    "Two novels, both concerning the Texas revolution against Mexico as witnessed by two young brothers, Joshua and Thomas Buckalew. In the first book, 'Massacre at Goliad,' the Buckalews' dream of adventure and free land is dispelled by the harsh reality of the West: hard work, Indians, bandits and the simmering cultural, racial and political animosity between Americans and Mexicans. When violence finally breaks out, the boys miss the slaughter at the Alamo only to be caught up in the massacre of Texan prisoners at Goliad. Only one brother survives, going on to avenge Goliad at the Battle of San Jacinto. In 'After the Bugles,' the surviving brother returns home to rebuild his ranch and his life, but must contend with cheating opportunists, murderous outlaws and deadly Comanche attacks, as well as growing Texan racism against his Mexican friends and neighbors. As with all of Kelton's westerns, characters are colorful and well drawn, the action is fast and bloody, and the plotting carefully thought out." Publ Wkly

Kelton, Elmer
    Texas vendetta. Forge 2004 301p $24.95
    ISBN 0-7653-0572-0

                         LC 2003-17352
    "Within the exciting context of a western adventure, [Kelton] explores paternal relationships-good and bad-and the crippling consequences of hanging on too tightly to a painful past." Booklist

Kelton, Elmer
    ★ The **way** of the coyote. Forge 2001 283p
    ISBN 0-312-87318-2

                         LC 2001-40482
    "Kelton covers a wide swath of history with aplomb, illuminating a little-known period in Western history. California is still Mexican, Indians are a real threat and outlaws rule the land in this rough-riding adventure tale." Publ Wkly

Kemelman, Harry
    The **day** the rabbi resigned. Fawcett Columbine 1992 273p

                         LC 91-72891
    "Mr. Kemelman's fans will be mollified by his clever resolution of Rabbi Small's career crisis, which is woven into a deft murder mystery involving several characters of different faiths." N Y Times Book Rev

Kemelman, Harry
    Friday the rabbi slept late. Crown 1964 224p
    "Here are conflict and suspense, understanding and conversation, and a remarkable Biblical explanation of the differences between priests, ministers and rabbis." Libr J

Kemelman, Harry
    Monday the rabbi took off. Putnam 1972 316p
    "The rabbi and his family set out for Israel. The action alternates between Massachusetts, where Rabbi Small may or may not be losing his congregation to the rabbi substi-

tuting for him, and Jerusalem, where he soon becomes embroiled in troubles involving a TV commentator, the commentator's son, and plotting Arab militants." Saturday Rev

"This is not so much a novel of mystery and detection as it is a beautifully conceived and executed novel of conditions in Israel and a rabbi's dilemma." Best Sellers

Kemelman, Harry

One fine day the rabbi bought a cross. Morrow 1987 234p

LC 86-23571

"Central to the plot is a Palestine Liberation Organization arms cache that Druse fighters would dearly love to steal. An American professor unwittingly delivers a letter with a map of the cache to a Druse agent in Jerusalem. The American is promptly murdered. Rabbi Small is in Jerusalem and solves the case." N Y Times Book Rev

Kemelman, Harry

Saturday the rabbi went hungry. Crown 1966 249p

"The absent-minded knowledgeable young Rabbi, leader of a Conservative congregation, collaborates with his friend the Irish Catholic police chief in solving a mystery, this time deciding whether a death is murder or suicide and, if it is murder, who did it. The story is a good mixture of Jewish folk wisdom with modern community problems and with a murder mystery all nicely seasoned with humor." Publ Wkly

Kemelman, Harry

Sunday the rabbi stayed home. Putnam 1969 253p

"After six years at the Temple in Barnard's Crossing, Rabbi David Small is a little weary of the politics, dissention and factionalism of his congregation, and slightly disconcerted by the idea of a 'swinging Passover Service.' The weekend visit to Massachusetts College doesn't provide the release he expects, but neither does it prepare him for dealing with the rash of modern urban problems that confront him on Sunday when the body of Moose Carter is found in the empty house on the beach after a college student cookout." Libr J

Kemelman, Harry

Thursday the rabbi walked out. Morrow 1978 250p

LC 78-8466

"Kemelman's famous town, Barnard's Crossing, is in a turmoil after the murder of mean, anti-Semitic Ellsworth Jordan. Again Police Chief Lanigan asks Rabbi Small for help with the case, complicated by too many suspects. Those with motive and opportunity include members of Small's flock. Maltzman, president of the Temple, is one. So are the head of the local bank and his secretary as well as the dead man's illegitimate son by a Jewish mother." Publ Wkly

Kemelman, Harry

Wednesday the rabbi got wet. Morrow 1976 312p

In this story Rabbi Small "champions a young hippie, Akiva, suspected of causing a death. He has filled two prescriptions at his father's pharmacy. On the wet Wednesday,

a wheeler-dealer member of Small's congregation, Safferstein, picks up the pills—a vial for his ailing wife and one for crotchety old Kestler. Kestler dies. His prescription is not what the doctor ordered. Dissension within the Temple's membership, with Small at odds with powerful men among them, adds to the excitement as the Rabbi applies Talmudic 'pilpul' (logical reasoning) to solve the problem of the switched dosage and exonerate the boy." Publ Wkly

Keneally, Thomas, 1935-

★ The **Daughters** of Mars; Tom Keneally. Pocket Books 2013 544 p. (hardcover) $28
ISBN 1476734615; 9781476734613

LC 2012427270

In this book by Thomas Keneally, "[d]uring World War I, sisters Naomi and Sally Durance leave Australia to serve as nurses, first at Gallipoli and then on the western front, where their training hardly prepares them for the carnage they witness. In a French hospital, they both have the chance at love they never thought they'd take." (Library Journal)

"Keneally must have done copious research, but historical details and information about wartime medical treatment are presented organically, without the weight of historical retrospection... Highly recommended." LJ

Includes bibliographical references

Keneally, Thomas, 1935-

A **family** madness. Simon & Schuster 1986 336p

LC 85-26121

"Approximately half of the chapters of 'A Family Madness' are set in the present and concern a young workingclass Australian, Terry Delaney, who becomes involved with a family of Byelorussian origin, the Kabbels (originally Kabbelski), who immigrated to Sydney in the late 1940's. The other half deals with the terrible modern history of that family, a history reaching back to the early days of World War II." N Y Times Book Rev

"Keneally brilliantly combines three diverse narrative techniques, and while the book is not light or easy reading, it is enormously rewarding." Publ Wkly

Keneally, Thomas

Flying hero class. Warner Bks. 1991 289p
ISBN 0-446-51582-5

LC 90-50524

This is "despite some problems, a good book. Unlike many suspense novels, it never deadens our sensibilities with predictable characters, simpleminded politics or slick prose. Mr. Keneally's people are always fascinating, and so are the ideas his plot generates, making the hijacking a metaphor for the complex relationship between the West and third world peoples deprived of land and dignity." N Y Times Book Rev

Keneally, Thomas

Office of innocence. Doubleday 2003 319p $25
ISBN 0-385-50763-1

LC 2002-73653

Keneally moves his "protagonist, as confessor, from the banal to the transcendent: from insipid negotiations with schoolchildren to a primal reckoning in a war-ravaged landscape; from an innocence barely aware of its own spiritual vanity to a disillusioned acceptance of the ubiquity of sin and the stubborn mystery of fate." N Y Times Book Rev

Keneally, Thomas
River town. Talese 1995 324p
LC 94-48664

"There are times when Keneally's lapsed-Catholic sensibility and his not-at-all-lapsed Irish sensibility turn mawkish. . . . Nevertheless, Keneally's lapses are redeemed and overshadowed by his meticulous attention to psychological details which have nothing to do with his political agendas and which in fact subvert them." London Rev Books

Keneally, Thomas
★ **Schindler's** list. Simon & Schuster 1982 400p $25; pa $14
ISBN 0-671-51688-4; 0-671-88031-4 pa
LC 82-10489

"An actual occurrence during the Nazi regime in Germany forms the basis for this story. Oskar Schindler, a Catholic German industrialist, chose to act differently from those Germans who closed their eyes to what was happening to the Jews. By spending enormous sums on bribes to the SS and on food and drugs for the Jewish prisoners whom he housed in his own camp-factory in Cracow, he succeeded in sheltering thousands of Jews, finally transferring them to a safe place in Czechoslovakia. Fifty Schindler survivors from seven nations helped the author with information." Shapiro. Fic for Youth. 3d edition

Keneally, Thomas
To Asmara. Warner Bks. 1989 290p
LC 89-40035

This novel "is a rare entity in contemporary fiction, a work of advocacy and engagement that unhesitatingly takes sides in one of the world's longest-running and least understood wars." N Y Times Book Rev

Keneally, Thomas
The **tyrant's** novel. Nan A. Talese 2004 235p $25
ISBN 0-385-51146-9
LC 2003-59670

The protagonist of this "novel is a successful author in a country that bears more than a passing resemblance to Iraq. One day, he is ordered to write a novel to be published under the name of the country's dictator—and given only a month for the task. As luck would have it, he has recently completed a novel that, with slight modification, will fit the bill. However, he has buried the novel with his late wife. Can he bear to disinter the manuscript in order to save himself? Though concerned with current events, Keneally takes care to give his tale wider resonance. The Middle Eastern characters go by English names, a technique that makes them less foreign to the reader and draws parallels between the subtle self-censorship of Western commercialism and the blunter kind practiced by the arts community in a dictatorship." New Yorker

Keneally, Thomas
★ **Woman** of the inner sea. Doubleday 1993 277p
LC 92-28554
First published 1992 in the United Kingdom

This novel "succeeds on many fronts. It is a picaresque and often hilarious adventure story, recounting one woman's unforgettable if improbable travels. It is a series of love stories, as Kate meets the man who is appropriate for her at each stage of her life, and it is a mystery story as well. But the novel is also very much an exploration of ethics." N Y Times Book Rev

Kenin, Eve
Driven; Eve Kenin. Dorchester Pub. 2007 321p (pbk.) o.p.; (pbk.) o.p.
ISBN 9780505527097; 050552709X
LC 2008571727

Romantic Times Reviewers' Choice Award: Best Science Fiction & Fantasy (2007)

This science fiction romance novel takes place in the "aftermath of the Second Noble War, which killed off a third of the Earth's population, [and features] attractive but deadly trucker Raina Bowen [who] is determined to bring down powerful businessman and presidential adviser Duncan Bane, who brutalized Raina in her youth. Aided by a handsome but emotionless mercenary known simply as Wizard, Bowen hauls her rig up to the Northern Waste in search of her target; meanwhile, Bane is setting traps and sending agents of his own, imperiling the duo but intensifying their feelings for each other." (Publishers Weekly)

Kennedy, A. L.
What becomes; stories. Alfred A. Knopf 2010 208p $24.95
ISBN 978-0-307-27354-3; 0-307-27354-7
LC 2009-46507
First published 2009 in the United Kingdom

In this collection "Kennedy is familiarly off-kilter ('Story of My Life' revolves around the protagonist's deadpan, excruciating recounting of her successive dental traumas); unwelcoming ('Sympathy,' a tour de force that could easily be a disaster, recounts entirely in dialogue an episode of anonymous sex in a hotel room); and desolate (most of these stories involve marriages unhappy or unraveling; violence animates several and lurks in most). A preternaturally refined stylist, Kennedy leaves the reader shaken but not depressed: these are stories of endurance, not despair. And humor, albeit of a particularly hard-won variety, suggests Kennedy (a sometime stand-up comic), is vital to fortitude, even if that humor is sidelong and, though humane, unrelentingly cheerless." Atlantic

Kennedy, Douglas
The **big** picture. Hyperion 1997 374p
ISBN 0-7868-6298-X
LC 96-44446

"The book is more than just a compelling read: it also has poignant and moving things to say about lost opportunities and wasted lives in America, the cynical quality of sudden fame, the awfulness of willed seperation from deeply loved children." Publ Wkly

Kennedy, Douglas

Leaving the world; a novel. Atria Paperback 2010 480p pa $16

ISBN 978-1-4391-8078-5; 1-4391-8078-4

LC 2009-42377

First published 2009 in the United Kingdom

"Jane is a quintessential heroine who never makes excuses or wallows in self-pity, despite her grief. Episodically structured yet with a strong narrative drive, this is a book with lasting impact: powerful, provocative, and tender." Publ Wkly

Kennedy, Douglas

The **moment**; a novel. Atria Books 2011 535p $26.99

ISBN 978-1-4391-8079-2; 1-4391-8079-2

LC 2010-48577

"A newly divorced American novelist living alone in Maine, Thomas Nesbitt reflects on a distant relationship he's never quite recovered from. As he looks back on his life in Germany, he must confront his unforgotten passion for Petra Dussmann, the betrayal that ended their relationship and the sorrowful regret that has haunted him since. Thomas' story begins as the launch of his writing career leads him to Cold War Berlin, where everyone is filled with suspicion and uncertainty. He finds himself living in a flat with an emotionally erratic, yet talented painter from Ireland and secures a job that not only pays his rent, but also introduces him to a beautiful translator named Petra. Their relationship quickly evolves into something serious, only to be challenged by her unbearable situation with the German police. In a moment of distrust and forgotten loyalty, the two lovers part ways, leaving Thomas' life forever altered by his missed opportunity with Petra." Yakima Herald

"Despite his rambling pace, Kennedy's evocative prose makes the eventual spellbinding finish worth the trip." Kirkus

Kennedy, Kathryne

The **lord** of illusion; Kathryne Kennedy. Sourcebooks Casablanca 2012 437 p.

ISBN 1402236549; 9781402236549

This book is the last volume of Kathryne "Kennedy's Elven Lords romantic fantasy series. In a medieval England invaded by elves, the human rebellion has gained in strength thanks to the efforts of the elf/human half-breeds, and rebels have managed to steal several of the scepters that channel the lords' magic. Drystan Hawkes is an unexpected hero, a curator and historian of magical artifacts. The scepters send him visions of Camille Ashton, one of the elves' human slaves, and hint that she is the key to the rebellion's success. In love with Camille from his visions, Drystan is overjoyed when he finally finds her, but daunted by the twin challenges of uncovering Camille's powers and teaching her about loyalty, trust, and love." (Publishers Weekly)

"The hero and heroine are also out of the ordinary, and while this novel remains true to romance-genre mores, Kennedy infuses it with unexpected plot twists that will keep fantasy readers enthralled, too." Booklist

Kennedy, Thomas E.

In the company of angels. Bloomsbury USA 2010 276p $25

ISBN 9781608190164; 1-608-19016-1

LC 2009-16968

"Imprisoned for teaching political poetry to his students, Bernardo Greene has been tortured for months in Pinochet's Chile when he is visited by two angels who promise that he will survive to experience beauty and love once again. Months later, in Copenhagen, where he has come for treatment, the Chilean exile befriends Michela Ibsen, herself a survivor of domestic abuse." Publisher's note

Kennedy, William

Chango's beads and two-tone shoes. Viking 2011 328p $26.95

ISBN 978-0-670-02297-7; 0-670-02297-7

LC 2011-19764

The book "is a two-part invention. In the first part, newspaper reporter Daniel Quinn travels to Havana in March 1957 to meet two of his heroes—Ernest Hemingway and Fidel Castro. In the second part, Quinn is back home in Albany 11 years later to cover the race riots that break out after Robert F. Kennedy is gunned down in Los Angeles. What holds the two parts together is the figure of Quinn, the author's alter ego. As a journalist he is a 'failed witness to history.' And so, at the end of the novel, he turns to fiction as the more effective method to 'reveal history in language graceful but hip, simple but sly, exfoliating with the essential stories he had tracked down and wanted to tell the world.'" (Commentary)

"Kennedy's prose hangs on every deft noirish turn, never succumbing to lazy pastiche. Best of all is his Castro, an impressively human rendering of the Commandante who falls halfway between Brando and Marcus Aurelius." Bookforum

Kennedy, William

★ **Ironweed**. Viking 1983 227p hardcover o.p. pa $14

ISBN 0-14-007020-6 pa

LC 82-40370

With this "tale of skid-row life in the Depression, Kennedy adds another chapter to his 'Albany cycle'—a group of novels set in the Albany, New York, underworld from the 1920s onward. Following 'Legs' and 'Billy Phelan's Greatest Game,' 'Ironweed' tells the story of Francis Phelan, a 58-year-old bum with muscatel on his breath and hallucinations on his mind. Chief among the latter is a vision of his infant son, who died after falling out of Francis' arms. It is the desire to reconcile himself to the memory of his dead son that brings Francis home to Albany, ultimately opening the door to a possible reconciliation with his family." Booklist

Kennedy, William

Roscoe. Viking 2002 291p $24.95

ISBN 0-670-03029-5

LC 2001-33237

"As in all of Kennedy's Albany novels, the town is rendered with a hallucinatory, three-dimensional density. . . . This is an engrossing, comic vision of the dark side of politics." Publ Wkly

Kennedy, William

Very old bones. Viking 1992 292p

LC 91-40723

"Orson is wounded, pompous, a bit pedantic in his initial attempt at family history. What transpires in {the book} is the growth and increasing authenticity of his voice. . . . Beneath the mete and just end of this closely worked novel lie bitter bones of estrangement, of love hidden or misplaced, lives wasted by jealousy and fear." N Y Times Book Rev

Kenney, John

★ **Truth** in advertising; John Kenney. Simon & Schuster 2013 308 p. (hardcover) $24.99

ISBN 1451675542; 9781451675542

LC 2012009173

This book by John Kenney follows "Finbar Dolan, [who] has a successful career in commercials. . . . Fin's life is a mess: he broke up with his fiancée a month before their wedding, is infatuated with his office assistant, Phoebe, and is estranged from his entire family. When his workaholic boss drags him into the office over Christmas to craft a Super Bowl commercial . . . and his abusive, long-lost father turns up in the hospital Fin's universe is tipped on its ear." (Publishers Weekly)

Kent, Kathleen

The **heretic's** daughter; a novel. Little, Brown and Co. 2008 332p $24.99

ISBN 978-0-316-02448-8; 0-316-02448-1

LC 2008-01887

"After a bout of smallpox, 10-year-old Sarah Carrier resumes life with her mother on their family farm in Andover, Mass., dimly aware of a festering dispute between her mother, Martha, and her uncle about the plot of land where they live. The fight takes on a terrifying dimension when reports of supernatural activity in nearby Salem give way to mass hysteria, and Sarah's uncle is the first person to point the finger at Martha. Soon, neighbors struggling to eke out a living and a former indentured servant step forward to name Martha as the source of their woes. Sarah is forced to shoulder an even heavier burden as her mother and brothers are taken to prison to face a jury of young women who claim to have felt their bewitching presence. Sarah's front-row view of the trials and the mayhem that sweeps the close-knit community provides a fresh, bracing and unconventional take on a much-covered episode." Publ Wkly

Kepler, Lars

The **hypnotist**; translated from the Swedish by Ann Long. Farrar, Straus and Giroux 2011 503p $27

ISBN 978-0-374-17395-1; 0-374-17395-8

LC 2010-44603

Original Swedish edition, 2009

As this novel opens, "a schoolteacher and his librarian wife, pillars of their small Stockholm-area community, have been savagely butchered, and their young daughter, too, with a teenage son sliced to ribbons and left for dead. Enter Erik Maria Bark, a therapist and hypnotist called onto the scene by the supervising physician and a world-weary (naturally) police investigator, Joona Linna, who theorizes that the killer had waited for the father, a soccer referee in his off hours,

hacked him into pieces, then headed to his house to dispatch the rest of the family, suggesting at least some acquaintance. . . .Linna and Bark make a great crime-solving pair precisely because they puzzle each other so thoroughly—says Bark, for instance, 'The patient always speaks the truth under hypnosis. But it's only a matter of what he himself perceives as the truth.' To which Linna responds, 'What is it you're trying to say?' Indeed. What Bark is trying to say is that there are monsters hiding everywhere beneath the reasonable and rational, and Kepler's book makes for a satisfying and scary testimonial." Kirkus

Kerley, Jack

★ The **death** collectors; Jack Kerley. Dutton 2005 320p.

ISBN 0525948775

LC 2004028816

This book is "the second [volume] in the series featuring Mobile, Ala., PD detectives Carson Ryder and Harry Nautilus. Carson and Harry are the department's psychopathological and sociopathological investigative team. . . . When a naked female body buried beneath flowers and surrounded by candles is found in a seedy motel, the crime is weird enough to be assigned to them. More bodies turn up, each accompanied by a tiny but beautiful oil painting. Retired police detective Jacob C. Willow hears of the murder/painting connection and tells Carson he thinks it has something to do with a serial killer case he worked early in his career." (Publishers Weekly)

Kerley, Jack

The **hundredth** man. Dutton 2004 307p $23.95

ISBN 0-525-94821-X

LC 2004-696

"Kerley jacks up the tension effectively with nicely placed jumps between Carson's narration and the tortured thoughts of the killer, building to an all-stops-out climax involving a raging river and a supremely horrific home movie." Booklist

Kerouac, Jack, 1922-1969

And the hippos were boiled in their tanks; [by] William S. Burroughs and Jack Kerouac. Grove Press 2008 214p $24

ISBN 978-0-8021-1876-9; 0-8021-1876-3

This novel "was co-written in 1945 by the Beat writers William S. Burroughs and Kerouac, when the two were just beginning their friendship in New York, as mentor and acolyte respectively, and years before Kerouac had even coined the term Beat Generation. Based on a real murder in 1944 involving two early members of the proto-Beat gang, Lucien Carr and David Kammerer, 'Hippos' recounts the so-called 'honor slaying' of the older, homosexual Kammerer by the young, blond and incredibly handsome Columbia University student Carr dubbed Rimbaud by Kerouac and their other Beat friend, Allen Ginsberg. . . . 'Hippos,' which by Kerouac's own account was 'hidden under the floorboards' for decades, is an essential document of the Beat Generation filled with precise details and precisely recorded dialogue from a place and period, pre-Atomic Age America, now almost irretrievably lost to us." San Francisco Chron

Kerouac, Jack

The **Dharma** bums. Viking 1958 244p

"This novel deals with Zen Buddhism. It's about two young men who are seeking to find themselves through meditation, voluntary poverty, separation from society, and intimate contact with nature, especially the Western mountains. . . . Sometimes Kerouac seems a little foolish, often he is extreme, but he is genuine, he is alive, and he is native." Libr J

Kerouac, Jack, 1922-1969

★ **On** the road. Viking 1957 310p

"Sal Paradise (a self-portrait of Kerouac), a struggling author in his mid-twenties, tells of his meeting Dean Moriarty (based on Neal Cassady), a fast-living teenager just out of a New Mexico reform school, whose soul is 'wrapped up in a fast car, a coast to reach, and a woman at the end of the road.' During the next five years they travel coast to coast, either with each other or to each other. Five trips are described." Oxford Companion to Am Lit. 6th edition

Kerouac, Jack

On the road: the original scroll; edited by Howard Cunnell; introductions by Howard Cunnell, Penny Vlagopoulos, George Mouratidis, and Joshua Kupetz. Viking 2007 408p $25.95

ISBN 978-0-670-06355-0; 0-670-06355-X

LC 2007-5306

"The biggest immediate difference between the first draft and the finished product . . . is that while we know On the Road as a novel—the great novel of the Beat Generation—the scroll is essentially nonfiction, a memoir that uses real names and is far less self-consciously literary. It is a dazzling piece of writing for all of its rough edges, and, stripped of affectations that in the novel can sometimes verge on bathos, as well as of gratuitous punctuation supplied by editors more devoted to rules than to music, it seems much more immediate and even contemporary. The scroll clarifies the book's connection to the past—to Mark Twain and tramp narratives and Woody Guthrie and cowboy sagas—and underlines the features it shares with its nearest contemporaneous cultural relative, Robert Frank's great photographic road book The Americans." N Y Times Book Rev

Kerouac, Jack

★ **Road** novels 1957-1960; [edited by Douglas Brinkley] Library of America 2007 864p $35

ISBN 978-1-59853-012-4

LC 2007-924522

Kerouac's work "marked the articulation of a new voice far more interesting for what the author had to say and the way in which he said it than for the technical breakthroughs that it was heralded—and scorned—for at the time." San Francisco Chron

Kerouac, Jack, 1922-1969

The **sea** is my brother; Jack Kerouac; introduction by Dawn Ward. Penguin Books 2012 216 p. $23

ISBN 9780306821257

LC 2011278343

This book tells the story of "Wesley Martin, an itinerant merchant seaman on leave, stumbles around New York, from jazz clubs to the bars near Columbia University, where he meets Everhart, a young assistant professor "with the pasty pallor of a teacher of life." Over a drunken night, Everhart and his circle of hangers-on fall under the spell of Wesley's "brooding presence," after which Everhart takes leave from teaching and enlists with Wesley on his next sea voyage. . . . Wesley and Everhart bum their way to Boston to join the crew of a freighter bound for Greenland." (Publisher's Wkly)

Kerr, Katharine

Snare; a novel of the far future. TOR Bks. 2003 591p $27.95

ISBN 0-312-89045-1

LC 2002-40947

"Three very different groups of human settlers go, not all willingly, to the planet Snare: a band of Islamic fundamentalists, a group of horse tribes and the pragmatic Cantons people. All descend on Snare's indigenous repitilian species the ChaMeech, and eight centuries of territorial and social turmoil follow." Publ Wkly

"Compelling male and female characters and a thoughtful premise make this epic adventure a strong addition to most sf collections." Libr J

Kerr, Philip

Dark matter; the private life of Sir Isaac Newton. Crown 2002 345p

ISBN 0-609-60981-5

LC 2002-24155

"Plot devices such as secret coded documents, the pseudoscience of alchemy, and a string of strange murders make for an exciting read. Using as backdrop the Tower of London, the Royal Mint, Bedlam madhouse, and Newgate Prison. . . {The author} weaves a rich tapestry of interesting characters and period details." Libr J

Kerr, Philip

Field gray. G. P. Putnam's Sons 2011 435p

ISBN 978-0-399-15741-7

LC 2010-45006

Bernie Gunther "is living the lazy life in Cuba in 1954, doing this and that for the gangster Meyer Lansky, when a chance run-in with the American Navy sends him first to Guantánamo and then to Landsberg Prison in West Germany, where he's roughed up by American interrogators and grilled about his wartime relationship with Erich Mielke, soon to take charge of the East German Stasi. Anxious to distance himself from the war criminals stockpiled at Landsberg, Bernie takes his interrogators back to 1930, when a humanitarian impulse led him to save Mielke's life in Berlin. But the young Communist repaid the favor by killing two policemen, sending Bernie on a vengeance mission that lasted throughout the war. Thanks to his examiners, Bernie is forced to reflect on horrific events that Kerr seems to have culled from historical sources. But Bernie's cynical, completely twisted idea of payback is brilliantly in character." N Y Times Book Rev

Kerr, Philip

Hitler's peace; a novel of the Second World War. Philip Kerr. G.P. Putnam's Sons 2005 448p (pbk.) $15.00; (acid-free paper) o.p.

ISBN 9780143036951; 0399152695

LC 2004043170

This book takes place in "Autumn 1943. Since Stalingrad, Hitler has known that Germany cannot win the war. . . . Realizing that the unconditional surrender FDR has demanded will leave Germany in ruins, Hitler has put out peace feelers. . . . FDR and Stalin are willing to negotiate. Only Churchill refuses to listen. At the center . . . is Willard Mayer, an OSS operative who has been chosen by FDR to serve as his envoy. He is the perfect foil for the steamy world of deception, betrayals, and assassinations that make up the moral universe of realpolitik. . . . Mayer has embraced the stylish philosophy of the day, in which no values are fixed. In the course of the novel, his beliefs will be put to the ultimate test." (Publisher's note)

Kerr, Philip

If the dead rise not; a Bernie Gunther novel. Philip Kerr. G.P. Putnam's Sons 2010 437 p. (hc) $26.95

ISBN 9780399156151; 0399156151

LC 2009036134

Dagger Awards: CWA Ellis Peters Historical Award (2009)

In this book, "British author [Philip] Kerr sets the action of his sixth Bernie Gunther series in two distinct epochs—prewar Berlin (1934) and Havana 20 years later. Forced off the Berlin police force because of his allegiance to the old Weimar Republic, Bernie is now the Adlon Hotel's house detective. . . . Bernie, one-fourth Jewish himself, gets embroiled in a conflict between corrupt businessmen who aim to profit from the 1936 Olympiad and a beautiful American (and Jewish) journalist, Noreen Charalambides, who hopes to derail U.S. participation. By the time the dust settles, Bernie is locked in a stalemate with American mobster Max Reles. In 1954, Bernie is living in Havana and runs across Noreen, now a successful author living in Hemingway's Finca Vigía, where she consorts with Communists. To Bernie's surprise, Noreen's daughter is palling around with Max Reles, now in cahoots with Meyer Lansky and other mobsters." (Library Journal)

Kerr, Philip

A Man Without Breath; a Bernie Gunther novel. Philip Kerr. Penguin Group USA 2013 448 p. (hardcover) $26.95

ISBN 0399160795; 9780399160790

LC 2012050227

In this latest "in [Philip] Kerr's Bernie Gunther series, set during World War II and featuring a German police detective, Bernie is asked to investigate a mass grave site in the Katyn Forest that contains the bodies of Polish army officers." The book's authenticity was boosted by Kerr's discovery, while researching the book, of "a map of Smolensk made by SS cartographers in 1942, with all the streets renamed by Germany after it conquered Poland." (Library Journal)

Kerr, Philip

★ The one from the other; a Bernie Gunther novel. Philip Kerr. G.P. Putnam's Sons 2006 372 p.

ISBN 0399152997; 9780399152993

LC 2006044817

Working as a private detective in Munich in 1949, Bernie Gunther copes with the chaos of postwar Germany when a woman hires him to find out the fate of her missing husband, a war criminal whose death she wants to confirm.

"Kerr's stylish noir writing makes every page a joy to read... Perfectly plotted, the book builds to a satisfying conclusion." Pub Wkly

Kerr, Philip

Prague fatale; Philip Kerr. Marian Wood Books 2012 401 p. (Bernie Gunther novel)

ISBN 9780399159022

LC 2011051632

This book is "[Philip] Kerr's . . . eighth Bernie Gunther novel" and "takes the Berlin cop to Prague in October 1941, to investigate the murder of an adjutant of feared SS Gen. Reinhard Heydrich, who's just become the Protector of Bohemia and Moravia. The morning after a drunken party attended by SS officers at Heydrich's country estate outside Prague, the adjutant, who was shaken by what he witnessed as part of a Nazi death squad in Latvia, is found dead in a locked guestroom. Heydrich wants Gunther, suicidal himself after similar experiences in Russia, to find the adjutant's killer fast, but how is one to identify the culprit amid a house full of professional murderers? A subplot involving the death of a foreigner run over by a train and Czech nationalists' is included. (Publishers Wkly)

Kerr, Philip

A quiet flame; a Bernie Gunther novel. G. P. Putnam's Sons 2009 389p $26.95

ISBN 978-0-399-15530-7; 0-399-15530-7

LC 2008-033847

"A Berlin homicide cop conscripted into the SS during the course of the novels known as the Berlin Noir Trilogy, Bernie [Gunther] resurfaces in 1950 — on the same boat as Adolf Eichmann — in Buenos Aires, a vibrant city as depraved and dangerous as the one he left behind. Unlike other fugitive Nazi officers Juan Perón welcomed into Argentina, Bernie isn't allowed to slip into some anonymous job. Instead, he's pressed to solve the grisly mutilation murders of young girls, cases so similar to those he had to leave unsolved in Berlin when Hitler came to power that he suspects the same killer may now be on the loose in Argentina. Pursuing that lead, Bernie builds up contempt for government mendacity, expressing his reckless views in the wisecracking idiom of the hardboiled detective, rather than the suave tones of the undercover agent the Peronists would like him to be. But while his attitude is fashionably cynical, he cares too much about the future of civilized societies to pass himself off as a pessimist." N Y Times Book Rev

Kerstan, Lynn

The golden leopard; Lynn Kerstan. Onyx 2002 370p.

ISBN 0451410572

LC 2003611039

Romantic Times Reviewers' Choice Award: Historical (2002)

In this book, "[i]n 1821 India, charming con artist Lord Hugo Duran stands trial for stealing the Heart of Alanbad. Needing a lie when he knows the truth of innocence will not work, Hugo insists a dream brought him here and that he is to go home to England to find the Golden Leopard and return it to its rightful owner. The court rules if he fails to restore the jewel within a year, he will die. Hugo needs help to succeed and at the same time he sees this as an opportunity to finish his business with Jessica Carville, who he once hurt badly. . . . Jessie, tempted by his quest, agrees to accompany him, but does not relish the idea of marrying him to keep her reputation intact. As the excursion turns dangerous, both realizes they still love one another." (thebestreviews.com)

Kerstan, Lynn

Heart of the tiger; Lynn Kerstan. New American Library 2003 375 p. (pbk.) o.p.

ISBN 0451410858

LC 2004573017

This book, chosen by "Library Journal" as a Top Ten Best Romance Novel of 2003, follows the story of "Michael Keynes, mercenary adventurer, [who] returns to England to destroy his evil brother. . . . But someone else gets there first. Suspicion falls on Michael, the duke's own daughter, and a soft-voiced young woman with a heart of steel. Now he must find a way to exonerate both of them, even if it means confessing to a crime he didn't commit. . . . Then the real murderer and an enemy from Michael's past resurface, and survival itself becomes the only game in town." (lynnkerstan.com)

Kertesz, Imre

Detective story; translated from the Hungarian by Tim Wilkinson. Alfred A. Knopf 2008 112p $21

ISBN 978-0-307-26644-6; 0-307-26644-3

LC 2007-40216

Original Hungarian edition, 1977

"The story is constructed with a delicate, scientific objectivity. . . . Physical description is kept to a minimum, but the feel for characters' psychology, even or perhaps especially those of the policemen, is acute. Much happens between the lines, increasing a sense of claustrophobic intensity." Los Angeles Times Book Rev

Kesey, Ken

★ **One** flew over the cuckoo's nest; a novel. Viking 1962 311p hardcover o.p. pa $7.99

ISBN 0-670-03058-9; 0-451-16396-6 pa

"Life in a mental institution is predictable and suffocating under the iron rule of Nurse Ratched, who tolerates no disruption of routine on her all-male ward. Half-Indian Chief Bromden, almost invisible on the ward because he is thought to be deaf and dumb, describes the arrival of rowdy Randle Patrick McMurphy. McMurphy takes on the nurse as an adversary in his attempt to organize his fellow inmates and breathe some self-esteem and joy into their lives. The battle is vicious on the part of the nurse, who is relentless in her efforts to break McMurphy, but a spark of human will brings an element of hope to counter the despotic institutional power." Shapiro. Fic for Youth. 3d edition

Kesey, Ken

Sailor song. Viking 1992 535p

LC 92-5406

The author "includes a great deal of purposeful foolery, flooding the narrative with farcical incongruities, crude asides, wacky in-jokes, and countless allusions to literary classics and popular culture. . . . In sum, Sailor Song is vintage Ken Kesey: not for the faint-hearted, perhaps, but certainly instructive, and never boring." New Leader

Kesey, Ken

★ **Sometimes** a great notion. Viking 1964 628p

"This novel focuses on the person of Hank Stamper, raw and aggressive scion of an Oregon lumber empire. The struggle is . . . with a society unwilling to accommodate a strong individualist, but the issues are deepened and complicated by the fact that Hank's principal antagonist turns out to be his cerebral, introspective half-brother, Lee, and by Kesey's development of Lee as an equally appealing character, Kesey manipulates the clash of fraternal egos to a powerful climax, before reconciling the brothers to a tragic understanding of their own vulnerability to an indifferent fate and to a group of townspeople who have been made intolerably uncomfortable by the sight of the Stampers' strength." Ency of World Lit in the 20th Century

Kessel, John

The **Baum** plan for financial independence and other stories. Small Beer Press 2008 315p $24; pa $16

ISBN 978-1-931520-51-5; 1-931520-51-8; 978-1-931520-50-8 pa; 1-931520-50-X pa

LC 2007-52319

"What makes Kessel the sort of writer we should pay more attention to is not a particular quality of style. Like many fine writers he adapts his style to the story he has to tell. Nor is it that he is an especially innovative writer. You do find fresh ideas in his work, but rarely of the kind or scale that blow you away. Kessel is not a writer you turn to if you are looking for the old fashioned astonishments of science fiction. No, what makes John Kessel so interesting is that he is one of the most reflexive, one of the most self-aware writers around. He is acutely conscious of the fictionality of the genre, and plays with it." SF Site

Keyes, Daniel

★ **Flowers** for Algernon. Harcourt Brace Jovanovich 1966 274p

"Charlie Gordon, aged thirty-two, is mentally retarded and enrolls in a class to 'become smart.' He keeps a journal of his progress after an experimental operation that increases his I.Q. Although Charlie becomes brilliant, he is unhappy because he cannot shed his former personality and is tormented by his memories. In the end he begins to lose the mental powers he has gained." Shapiro. Fic for Youth. 3d edition

Keyes, Marian

Last Chance Saloon. Morrow 2001 370p $25

ISBN 0-688-18072-8

LC 00-67891

First published 1999 in the United Kingdom

This novel's "protagonists are two London women who grew up together in the small, repressive Irish town of Knockavoy. Tara, a computer analyst, lives with Thomas, a bitter and miserly high school geography teacher. . . . Katherine Casey, an accountant for an advertising agency, wears boring suits, has a hyperorganized underwear drawer and brushes off all advances, including those of attractive advertising account executive Joe Roth. As they turn 31, each woman is full of suggestions for improving the other's life and full of excuses for doing nothing about her own. That begins to change when Fintan O'Grady, their gay pal and fellow Knockavoy refugee, falls ill with a mysterious disease." Publ Wkly

Keyes, Marian

The **other** side of the story. W. Morrow 2004 516p $24.95

ISBN 0-06-052051-5

LC 2003-64939

This novel "follows the lives of three dynamic women—jilted Gemma Hogan; literary agent Jojo Harvey; and bestselling English author Lily Wright, who 'stole' Gemma's boyfriend Anton. Gemma, hurt and betrayed by her best friend's actions, must put her emotions on hold to care for her mam after her dad takes off with a younger woman." Publ Wkly

"Packing every page with her trademark one-liners, the insightful Keyes has the ability to examine life, love, and work issues with great wit and aplomb." Booklist

Khair, Tabish

The **thing** about thugs; Tabish Khair. Houghton Mifflin Harcourt 2012 256 p. (hardback) $24.00

ISBN 8172239785 HarperCollins India; 9780547731605 Houghton Mifflin Harcourt; 0547731604 Houghton Mifflin Harcourt; 9788172239787 HarperCollins India

LC 2010308952

This book, "[s]et largely in 1830s London, . . . centers on Amir Ali. Ali has come to England as a combination of refugee, research subject and mascot. He serves his condescending sponsor, Capt. William Meadows, by pretending to be a reformed member of the infamous Thugees. . . . A mystery emerges," where "someone is decapitating--and stealing the heads of--victims, many of them immigrants. Suspicion falls on Amir." (Kirkus Reviews)

Khemir, Sabiha

The **blue** manuscript. Verso 2008 307p $24.95

ISBN 978-1-84467-308-7; 1-84467-308-1

LC 2009-275213

The "account of the dig, and the truths excavated for the archeologists and the villagers, is interspersed with scenes from the court of the Fatimid Caliph al-Muizz as he conquers Egypt and marches to Cairo in 972, and as his calligrapher Ibn al-Warraq produces the beautiful blue manuscript for the Caliph's mother. Al Khemir seduces readers with the manuscript's mythical beauty and the philosophy of its art form. . . . Her cast of archeologists is led by the avaricious Mark, accompanied by Zohra, their Tunisian-English translator. Their intrigues dominate the novel: thwarted professional aspirations, comic and complicated romantic geometries, and their interactions with villagers like their

go-betweens Mustapha and Rayyed Ahmed, the cheeky little boy Mahmoud, the beautiful Zinab, and the blind sage Amm Gaber." Independent

Khoury, Elias

Gate of the sun; translated from the Arabic by Humphrey Davies. Archipelago Books 2006 539p (Rainmaker translations) $26

ISBN 0-976395-02-9

LC 2005-21036

Original Arabic edition, 1998

"This is a challenging novel that demands from us an imagination potent enough to link its many loose threads. The good news is that Khoury's language is derived from everyday colloquial Arabic, rather than the formal language of intellectuals and the media. Humphrey Davies's translation is masterful, allowing us to appreciate Gate of the Sun's short, clear sentences and crisp metaphors afresh." New Statesman

Kibler, Julie

Calling Me Home; a novel. Julie Kibler. 1st ed. St Martins Pr 2013 325 p. (hardcover) $24.99

ISBN 1250014522; 9781250014528

LC 2012041949

This novel, set in 1930s Kentucky, centers on a forbidden romance between a teenage white girl, Isabelle McAllister, and Robert Prewitt, the black son of the McAllister's maid. Chafing under her mother's restrictive notions of female propriety, Isabelle finds a kindred spirit in Robert. The two begin to meet clandestinely, but any hope of a future together is threatened by the overwhelming racism of the era. Against impossible odds, the pair elopes to neighboring Cincinnati." (Booklist)

Kidd, Sue Monk

The **mermaid** chair. Viking 2005 352p $24.95

ISBN 0-670-03394-4

"Forty-three-year old Jessie Sullivan is pulled out of her staid life in Atlanta with her husband and daughter, back to her childhood home on Egret Island after her mother, Nelle, cuts off one of her own fingers. Jessie has been uneasy with the island since her beloved father died when she was nine in a boating accident, a tragedy Jessie has always felt partially responsible for. At the behest of her mother's best friend, Jessie journeys back to the island to try to reconnect with the mother she's never been close to. Jessie wants to know what drove her obviously disturbed mother to sever her finger, and she thinks Father Dominic, one of the Benedictine monks who resides in a nearby monastery, might know more about her mother's state of mind. But it is another monk who claims Jessie's attention—handsome Brother Thomas, who ignites in Jessie a passion so intense it overwhelms her, leading her to question her marriage and rediscover her artistic drive." Booklist

This is an "emotionally rich novel, full of sultry, magical descriptions of life in the South." Publ Wkly

Kidd, Sue Monk

★ The **secret** life of bees. Viking 2002 301p hardcover o.p. pa $14

ISBN 0-670-89460-5; 0-14-200174-0 pa

LC 2001-26310

This is the "tale of a 14-year-old white girl named Lily Owen who is raised by the elderly African American Rosaleen after the accidental death of Lily's mother. Following a racial brawl in 1960s Tiburon, S.C, Lily and Rosaleen find shelter in a distant town with three black bee-keeping sisters." Libr J

"Lily is a wonderfully petulant and self-absorbed adolescent, and Kidd deftly portrays her sense of injustice as it expands to accommodate broader social evils." N Y Times Book Rev

Kiefer, Christian

★ The **infinite** tides; a novel. Christian Kiefer. Bloomsbury USA 2012 393 p. $26.00

ISBN 1608198103; 9781608198108

LC 2011045534

This book by Christian Kiefer follows "Keith Corcoran . . . an astronaut . . . [who] receives word that his sixteen-year-old daughter has died in a car accident, and that his wife has left him. Returning to earth, and to his now empty suburban home, he is alone with . . . feelings he can barely acknowledge, let alone process. . . . But healing begins through new relationships . . . first as a torrid affair with one neighbor, and then as an unlikely friendship with another." (Publisher's note)

Kienzle, William X.

★ **Assault** with intent. Andrews & McMeel 1982 273p

LC 82-1628

"The action takes place in a seminary in Detroit and it involves an apparent plot to kill some or all of the priests in seminaries. It is a perfect setting for one of the instructors at the seminary, Father Koesler, a priest-detective. . . . The attempts at murdering the priests are continuously foiled either by circumstances or the ineptitude of the assailant. We are led from one seminary to the other as the would-be murderers change their targets. The plot attracts such media attention that a TV movie is filmed at the major seminary to document the plot against the priests. In the process of the investigation attention is focused on a group of ultraconservative Catholics and their leader, Roman Kirkus." Best Sellers

Kienzle, William X.

Body count. Andrews & McMeel 1992 266p

LC 92-3266

This mystery involves Father Koesler, "Detroit detective-priest in conflicts between old and new Catholic theology. Hitman Guido Vespa loudly confesses to Koesler that he has bumped off Father Keating, the spiritual leader of a nearby parish, and buried the body in the grave of the long-dead, much beloved Monsignor Kern. Overhearing the confession, exuberant new resident priest Nick Dunn is delighted: one of the reasons he came to St. Joseph's was to be near its sleuthing pastor. Nick's enthusiasm increases when the police ask Koesler for help with Keating's disappearance." Publ Wkly

Kienzle, William X.

The **gathering**. Andrews McMeel Pub. 2002 280p $22.95

ISBN 0-7407-2229-8

LC 2001-55969

Father Koesler "reaches back in time and memory to clarify the ambiguous details surrounding the death of an old friend and fellow priest. Father Stan Benson is declared accidentally dead by carbon monoxide poisoning. Nursing his own doubts, Koesler convenes a reunion with the five remaining members of a close-knit group of friends who all initially chose religious vocations as a way of life. . . . Koesler's natural flair for detection is surpassed only by his deep and abiding compassion for the human condition." Booklist

Kienzle, William X.

The **greatest** evil. Andrews McMeel Pub. 1998 278p

ISBN 978-0836252064

LC 97-37738

"Father Robert Koesler is excited at the prospect of having Father Zachary Tully join his parish. Unfortunately, Bishop Vincent Delvecchio has misgivings about Tully's appointment. As Koesler and Tully discuss the matter, Koesler discovers a long-hidden mystery, which takes a back seat to numerous discussions that give fascinating insight into the working of the Catholic Church before Vatican II." Libr J

Kienzle, William X.

The **man** who loved God. Andrews & McMeel 1997 274p

ISBN 978-0836227543

LC 96-34604

"Father Bob Koesler, the popular amateur sleuth and Detroit priest, takes a vacation literally and figuratively away from the action. Taking his place is Father Zachary Tully, who comes to Detroit (from Dallas) to present an award to banker and philanthropist Thomas A. Adams. Father Tully is also eager to meet the half-brother he never knew he had, Detroit police lieutenant Alonzo 'Zoo' Tully. When one of Adam's vice-presidents is murdered just after being named to head a new inner-city bank branch, Father Tully and his brother find themselves working together." Publ Wkly

Kienzle, William X.

The **rosary** murders. Andrews & McMeel 1979 257p

LC 78-31833

"From Ash Wednesday, when the murderer first struck Detroit's Catholic community, the police seemed helpless to solve the string of senseless murders. The weeks that followed became a nightmare for the crack homicide team of investigators headed by Lieutenant Walter Koznicki, until Father Koesler broke the madman's code." Publisher's note

Kiernan, Caitlin R.

The **red** tree. Roc 2009 385p pa $16

ISBN 978-0-451-46276-3; 0-451-46276-9

LC 2009-15105

"Author Sarah Crowe leaves Atlanta after her girlfriend commits suicide, settling at a homestead in rural Rhode Island in order to finish her latest book, which is well past deadline. There's something sinister about the house, and Sarah quickly learns that the previous tenant, a professor and folklorist named Charles Harvey, killed himself while researching a book about the supernatural folklore of New England. Exploring the basement, Sarah discovers Harvey's manuscript, and she quickly finds herself in the middle of a living nightmare centered on a mysterious red oak tree in the house's yard. . . . [An] intelligent blend of folklore, horror, and dark fantasy." Libr J

Kiernan, Caitlín R.

Blood oranges; Caitlín R. Kiernan. Roc 2013 288 p. (pbk.) $16

ISBN 0451465016; 9780451465016

LC 2012032442

This book is the first in Kathleen Tierney's supernatural horror series featuring Siobhan Quinn. Here, heroin-addicted Quinn has "a steady supply of good dope and an apartment thanks to her benefactor, the mysterious fixer and manipulator she calls Mean Mr. B. . . . She goes werewolf hunting in Rhode Island. Instead of staying alert, however, Quinn shoots up and gets bitten by the werewolf—just as a vampire shows up! When she regains consciousness, . . . she finds she's now a werewolf and a vampire." (Kirkus)

Kiernan, Caitlín R.

The **drowning** girl; a memoir. Caitlín R. Kiernan. Roc 2012 336 p. ill. (pbk.) $16.00

ISBN 0451464168; 9780451464163

LC 2011044675

In this book, protagonist "India ('Imp') Morgan Phelps attempts to write a memoir as a way of exorcising the ghosts of her past: her mother and grandmother, both suicides; the lover who left her; and, most important, a young woman named Eva who might be a mermaid or a feral woman raised by wolves. Struggling with her perceptions of the world as filtered through the lenses of her acute schizophrenia and obsessive-compulsive disorder, Imp writes and rewrites her story." (Library Journal)

Kiernan, Stephen P.

The **Curiosity**; by Stephen Kiernan. HarperCollins 2013 320 p. $25.99

ISBN 006222106X; 9780062221063

In this novel by Stephen Kiernan "Dr. Kate Philo and her scientific exploration team make a . . . discovery in the Arctic: the body of a man buried deep in the ice. Remarkably, the frozen man is brought back to the lab and successfully reanimated. The team learns that he was—is—a judge, Jeremiah Rice. Kate and Jeremiah grow closer. But the clock is ticking and Jeremiah's new life is slipping away...and . . . Kate must decide how far she is willing to go to protect the man she has come to love." (Publisher's note)

Kiesbye, Stefan

Your house is on fire, your children all gone; a novel. Stefan Kiesbye. Penguin Books 2012 198 p.

ISBN 0143121464; 9780143121466

LC 2012023841

This horror story, by Stefan Kiesbye, takes place in "[a] village on the Devil's Moor. . . . There is the grand manor house whose occupants despise the villagers, the small pub whose regulars talk of revenants, the old mill no one dares to mention. This is where four young friends come of age--in an atmosphere thick with fear and suspicion. Their innocent games soon bring them face-to-face with the village's darkest secrets." (Publisher's note)

Kijewski, Karen

Alley Kat blues. Doubleday 1995 342p

LC 94-35200

In this mystery, Kat Colorado, "investigator and girlfriend of Las Vegas cop Hank Parker, becomes embroiled in a family controversy and murder investigation when she discovers a young girl's mangled body, an apparent hit-and-run victim. The girl's mother begs Kat to look into her daughter's death but her religious husband refuses to cooperate. To add to Kat's problem, Hank is involved with a murder investigation of his own." SLJ

The author "has written a solid narrative in a snappy style that fits Kat's clear-eyed intelligence and unpretentious methods of dealing with difficult people." N Y Times Book Rev

Kijewski, Karen

Copy Kat. Doubleday 1992 261p

LC 92-14482

"Hard-boiled female private eye Kat Colorado . . . takes on a new identity as Kate, the dyed-blonde bartender, to try to discover who murdered Diedre Durkin, the local bartender's wife. As she investigates motives, suspects, and alibis, Kat encounters blackmail and infidelity, a deep-seated and dangerous sibling rivalry, twisted family jealousies, and a web of bitter deceit and hatred." Booklist

Kijewski, Karen

Honky tonk Kat. Putnam 1996 323p

LC 95-49335

"Country-western singing star Dakota Jones, a friend of Kat's since childhood, is worried. Like most stars, she has enemies, but someone has been sending her unusually unnerving letters and really nasty gifts. Dakota, afraid that her one out-of-control fan might do something stupid, asks Kat to join her entourage and find out who's up to what." Booklist

The author "captures the sweaty thrills of road life while taking a clear-eyed view of the boozy dives and greasy food and the scary adoration of desperate fans." N Y Times Book Rev

Kijewski, Karen

Kat scratch fever. Putnam 1997 323p

ISBN 978-0399142451

LC 96-51141

"Taking the direct approach here, Kat marches up to the charity's most generous givers and demands to know if they were being blackmailed. When that doesn't work, she tries bullying, wheedling, groveling and breaking and entering. And when all her muscle and charm run out, she uses her brain." N Y Times Book Rev

Kijewski, Karen

Kat's cradle. Doubleday 1992 244p

LC 91-32218

"Outstanding among today's female detectives, PI Kat Colorado exhibits conscience and compassion, muscle and wisecracking savvy in an appealing and believable combination." Publ Wkly

Kijewski, Karen

★ **Stray** Kat waltz. Putnam 1998 311p

ISBN 0-399-14368-8

LC 97-46986

Sacramento P.I. Kat Colorado is recovering from the murder of her fiancé Hank Parker. "Although the heartache that makes Kat weep into her pillow sensitizes her to the plight of a battered wife who comes to her for help, it also blunts the P.I.'s normally sharp instincts for deceit and danger. Sara Bernard might well be the stalking victim she claims to be. Her husband might also be the model-cop-gone-nuts she says he is. But both their stories seem fishy, and Kat's judgment is too clouded by emotional cobwebs for her to think clearly. She perks up, though, for some undercover scenes at a fancy rehab clinic, where the pretentiousness is enough to restore her mental equilibrium, not to mention her sense of humor." N Y Times Book Rev

Kim, Suki

The **interpreter**. Farrar, Straus & Giroux 2003 294p $24

ISBN 0-374-17713-9

LC 2002-72120

This novel introduces Korean American "Suzy Park, a 29-year-old interpreter whose work involves her in a bevy of agencies throughout the five boroughs, from the Immigration and Naturalization Service to the criminal courts. Park is blasé about her occupation until a routine translating job reveals that her greengrocer parents were not murdered by random violence, as the police had indicated, but instead had been shot by political enemies. These data provide fodder for Park, and the novel tracks her investigation into what really happened." Libr J

"This is an intriguing, tortured portrait of a second-generation Korean-American by a promising young writer." Publ Wkly

Kimmel, Haven

Iodine; a novel. Free Press 2008 223p $24

ISBN 978-1-4165-7284-8; 1-4165-7284-8

LC 2007-49565

"The writing in 'Iodine' is genius. Comic renderings of parties — pretentious college kids demonstrating their love and obnoxiousness and equally pretentious professors demonstrating their civility and tedium — are downright hilarious. . . . As Trace's memories come and go, so does the book's sophistication of language and insight. Whether in Trace's voice, her dream journal voice or the narrator's voice, the writing in 'Iodine' is, at turns, fraught and hectic, and translucent and shimmering in its stillness." News & Observer

Kimmel, Haven

Something rising (light and swift) Free Press 2004 273p $24

ISBN 0-7432-4775-2

LC 2003-49114

"Kimmel's idea of a plot is not very linear. It's more like a net that hauls in great scenes. But while things may look superficially languid, this is one author who will not waste your time." Newsweek

Kimmel, Haven

The **used** world; a novel. Free Press 2007 308p $25

ISBN 978-0-7432-4778-8; 0-7432-4778-7

LC 2006-53172

This final entry in the trilogy that began with The solace of leaving early (2002) and Something rising (light and swift) (2004), "revolves around three extraordinary women from fictional Jonah, Indiana. All work at the Used World Emporium, a sprawling store crammed floor to ceiling with the stuff of people's lives. Fortysomething Claudia, mannish and a staggering 6 foot 5, desperately tries to cope with the reality of her beloved mother's death; red-haired Rebekah escapes the clutches of her family's religious zealotry only to find herself pregnant with no place to go; 65-year-old Hazel, armed with her belief in astrology, runs the emporium and serves as a mother hen of sorts to the two younger women. Kimmel's take on spirituality is intriguing, though her more detailed passages about religion slow an otherwise swift plot. . . . . [She] covers an encyclopedic range of emotions in this tale of love, loss, and the irrevocable acts that define us." Booklist

Kincaid, Jamaica

★ **Annie** John. Farrar, Straus & Giroux 1985 148p hardcover o.p. pa $12

ISBN 0-374-10521-9; 0-374-52510-2 pa

"Episodes from the young life of Annie John, aged 10 to 17, as she grows up on the Caribbean island of Antigua. This is a magical coming-of-age tale, ripe with the special ambience of its tropical setting and sustained by Annie's far from naive awareness of the world around her. Death, illness, and poverty intrude on the narrator's perceptive sensibility from time to time, but even these experiences instruct her and expand her understanding of life and its shifting reality. . . . A poetic and intensely moving work." Booklist

Kincaid, Jamaica

Autobiography of my mother. Farrar, Straus & Giroux 1995 228p

ISBN 0-374-10731-9

LC 94-24580

In Kincaid's "poised and crystalline prose, precise and serene as a knife drawn through water, she now gives us this starkly memorable 'self-portrait' of a calm, thoughtful, utterly alienated woman who has learned to lead a life devoid of love, but not devoid of dignity." Christ Sci Monit

Kincaid, Jamaica

★ **Lucy**. Farrar, Straus & Giroux 1990 163p

LC 90-83987

The narrator, Lucy Potter, a nineteen year old from Antigua, tells of her experiences as an au pair for a wealthy family in a large North American city

"The great motifs of Western literature, like goodness and evil, innocence and experience, resonate in Kincaid's novel in a completely updated and unselfconscious way. In other hands, this story of a West Indian au pair would just be sociology. In Kincaid's recasting, it is both art and argument." Christ Sci Monit

Kincaid, Jamaica

Mr. Potter. Farrar, Straus & Giroux 2002 195p $20

ISBN 0-374-21494-8

"Kincaid has exquisite control over her narrator's deep-seated rage, which drives the story but never overpowers it and is tempered by a clear-eyed sympathy. Her prose here is more incantatory and hypnotic than ever." Publ Wkly

Kincaid, Jamaica

See now then; Jamaica Kincaid. Farrar, Straus and Giroux 2013 192 p. (hardcover: alk. paper) $23

ISBN 9780374180560; 0374180563

LC 2012029932

In this novel by Jamaica Kincaid "a marriage is revealed in all its joys and agonies. . . . Kincaid inhabits each of her characters, a mother and father and their two children living in a small village in New England, as they move, in their own minds, between the present, the past, and the future. . . . But their minds wander, trying to make linear sense of what is, in fact, nonlinear." (Publisher's note)

Kincaid, Nanci

Verbena; a novel. Algonquin Bks. 2002 338p $24.95

ISBN 1-56512-348-4

LC 2001-56531

Sixth-grade teacher Verbena Eckerd "was happily married to Bob, or so she thought, until he died in a car accident with another woman at his side. She thinks she has raised her five children well, until her two oldest daughters run off with no-account men, her third moves away with Bena's arch rival, and her eldest son chooses the one woman in the world whose very name causes Bena anguish. She can't believe that good-natured mailman Lucky McKale really loves her, since he is married to Sue Cox, the most beautiful and richest woman in Baxter County, Ala. But after Sue Cox herself agrees to a divorce and blesses their union, Bena finally feels she can accept Lucky's proposal. A new kind of domestic unit is formed, with exes and stepchildren integrated into one colorful family. Then disaster strikes—Lucky disappears. Kincaid is both warmhearted and clear-eyed about the compromises people make to find happiness." Publ Wkly

Kinder, Chuck

Honeymooners; a cautionary tale. Farrar, Straus & Giroux 2001 357p $24

ISBN 0-374-17258-7

LC 00-63616

"Both wives emerge as major characters, reflecting the humor and anguish of living with men who, despite their successes, seem headed for rock bottom. Kinder's speedy, wry prose transports the reader to a time when drug use and personal freedom were unquestioned." Libr J

Kinder, R. M.

An absolute gentleman; a novel. Counterpoint 2007 288p pa $14

ISBN 978-1-58243-388-2; 1-58243-388-7

LC 2007-17932

"Taciturn English professor Arthur Blume launches his narrative by boldly stating that he is believed to have murdered as many as 17 women. Yet what most outrages him, now that he has been incarcerated, is that journalists are depicting him as a monster. He pens a memoir to correct this impression. In it, he describes in lavish detail the outfitting of his newly rented rooms in the small university town of Mason, Missouri; demurs over particulars of his illicit love affair with a fellow professor; and shares self-deprecating anecdotes about his gallant championing of a maligned colleague. Tucked among these decorous tidbits, however, are tantalizing clues to the demon within, one Kinder allows to emerge as stealthily as a cobra sliding from its bamboo basket. The addition of a self-explanatory epilogue regarding her personal experience detracts only slightly from Kinder's otherwise spellbinding debut novel, a pitch-perfect rendition of the cunning malevolence that can lie hidden beneath the guise of refined civility." Booklist

King, Dave

The ha-ha; a novel. Little, Brown and Co 2005 340p $23.95

ISBN 0-316-15610-8

LC 2004-7398

"With Howard as a guide, a potentially corny situation develops into a complex exploration of loss and loneliness that packs a potently bittersweet punch." Washington Post Book World

King, Laurie R.

The beekeeper's apprentice, or, On the segregation of the queen. Bantam Books 2002 xxi, 341p pa $12

ISBN 0-553-38152-0

LC 2001-43926

First published 1994 by St. Martin's Press

"A wonderfully original and entertaining story that is funny, heartwarming, and full of intrigue. . . . Holmes fans, history buffs, lovers of humor and adventure, and mystery devotees will all find King's book absorbing from beginning to end." Booklist

King, Laurie R.

A darker place. Bantam Bks. 1999 384p

ISBN 0-553-10711-9

LC 98-29835

"King's solid research into alternative religious sects makes the desert commune feel like a real place, while her taut pacing insures that an air of menace hangs over the strange rituals that go on there. But the strongest appeal of the story lies in its superb characters, especially the children who become Anne's charges." N Y Times Book Rev

King, Laurie R.

★ The **game**; a Mary Russell novel. Bantam Books 2004 368p map $23.95

ISBN 0-553-80194-5

LC 2003-55684

"Whatever this grueling land journey lacks in urgency, it repays in scenes of vibrant local color, described by Russell in the droll tongue of a woman with the wit to realize that, while she may be dirty and tired and in constant danger, she is having the time of her life." N Y Times Book Rev

King, Laurie R.

Garment of shadows; a novel of suspense featuring Mary Russell and Sherlock Holmes. Laurie R. King. 1st ed. Bantam Books 2012 266 p. map (hardcover) $32.99; (acid-free paper) $26.00

ISBN 9781410450890 Large Print; 0553807994; 9780553807998; 9780553907551

LC 2011047287

This mystery novel, by Laurie R. King, features "Mary Russell and her husband, Sherlock Holmes. . . . Holmes is pulled . . . into the growing war between France, Spain, and the Rif Revolt. . . . Holmes badly wants the wisdom and courage of his wife, whom he's learned, to his horror, has gone missing. As Holmes searches for her, and Russell searches for herself, each tries to crack deadly parallel puzzles before it's too late for them, for Africa, and for the peace of Europe." (Publisher's note)

King, Laurie R.

The **god** of the hive; a novel of suspense featuring Mary Russell and Sherlock Holmes. Bantam Books 2010 354p $25

ISBN 978-0-553-80554-3; 0-553-80554-1

LC 2009-52807

"In her last Mary Russell/Sherlock Holmes mystery, The Language of Bees, Laurie R. King left us with a killer cliffhanger. Mary Russell, Sherlock Holmes, his son and his granddaughter were all in the thrall of the psychotic leader of a murderous cult. As The God of the Hive opens, Mary, grasping the child, is running through the woods, evading the police as well as possible cult members. Holmes, meanwhile, is in a boat, ministering to his wounded son and in search of a safe harbour. The person Holmes believes can salvage his reputation and save him from the police is his brother Mycroft. But unbeknownst to the travellers, Mycroft is imprisoned and the real leader of the killer cult is intent on using the Holmes clan for his own evil ends. This is a great gloriously gripping tale replete with derring-do and lots of action. In short, another first-rate pastiche from Laurie R. King, channelling the ghost of Sir Arthur Conan Doyle." Globe and Mail

King, Laurie R.

Justice Hall; a Mary Russell novel. Bantam Bks. 2002 331p

ISBN 0-553-11113-2

LC 2001-37945

"Mary Russell is Sherlock Holmes' partner and wife. In the England of the 1920s, the pair find themselves shocked by the appearance of Ali and Mahmoud Hazr, their mysterious Arab associates from O Jerusalem. Ali is Alistair, and

Mahmoud is Maurice (called Marsh). Who would have divined that this pair of cousins is actually British, and Marsh is about to be named duke to his family's ancestral manse, the Hall of the title? King breaks most of the rules of mystery narrative with voluptuous abandon, and we don't care." Booklist

King, Laurie R.

Keeping watch. Bantam Bks. 2003 383p $23.95

ISBN 0-553-80191-0

LC 2002-34266

"At its simplest, this is the story of a man who helps rescue women and/or children from dangerously abusive men. King's lengthy, brilliantly executed backstory of Allen Carmichael's experiences in Vietnam, his disastrously unhappy return home and his eventual discovery of his 'calling' showcase some of her finest writing. Now in his early 50s, Allen is ready to retire from his dangerous vocation, to settle on his remote island and perhaps serve as a consultant to those who continue the struggle. But his last rescue, that of a 12-year-old boy trapped in a horrible situation, continues to haunt him." Publ Wkly

King, Laurie R.

A **letter** of Mary; a Mary Russell novel. St. Martin's Press 1996 276p

ISBN 978-0312146702

LC 96-22424

"For all the disparity of their investigative techniques, the ultra-perceptive Holmes and the super-scholarly Russell make an engaging pair of sleuths. Their quick minds and quirky personalities insure a lively adventure in the very best of intellectual company." N Y Times Book Rev

King, Laurie R.

Locked rooms; a Mary Russell novel. Bantam Books 2005 402p $24

ISBN 0-553-80197-X

"In alternating sections, told in first person for Mary and third for Holmes, the unraveling of long-buried and terrifying memories also unwinds a skein of wonderful historical texture: the place of Chinese immigrants and the use of feng shui; the nightlife of a city during the age of jazz, Prohibition, and flappers; and the presence of Dash Hammett, who plays a fascinating role as a very different sort of Irregular." Booklist

King, Laurie R.

The **moor**; a Mary Russell novel. St. Martin's Press 1998 307p il

ISBN 0-312-16934-5

LC 97-31886

"Sherlockians have their choice of being amused or affronted by these artful embellishments on the Holmes canon, and few will appreciate the curiously wan characterization of the great detective. But there's no resisting the appeal of King's thrillingly moody scenes of Dartmoor and her lovely evocation of its legends." N Y Times Book Rev

King, Laurie R.

O Jerusalem. Bantam Bks. 1999 367p

ISBN 0-553-11093-4

LC 98-56124

In 1918, Sherlock Holmes and Mary Russell, "the 19-year-old Oxford student whom he takes under his wing as an apprentice and partner, are sent on a mission to Palestine by Mycroft, Sherlock's powerful older brother. When Russell and Holmes are deposited, under cover of darkness, on the shores of Palestine, the British, under General Allenby, have just wrested control of the area from the Turks. . . . Eventually they encounter Joshua, a British agent, and Allenby himself." Publ Wkly

"With the feminist heroine chronicling events and the cerebral detective stirring the pot, readers can't lose." Booklist

King, Laurie R.

Pirate king; a novel of suspense featuring Mary Russell and Sherlock Holmes. Bantam Books 2011 304p $25

ISBN 978-0-553-80798-1; 0-553-80798-6

LC 2010-53043

"In England's young silent-film industry, the megalomaniacal Randolph Fflytte is king. Nevertheless, at the request of Scotland Yard, Mary Russell is dispatched to investigate rumors of criminal activities that swirl around Fflytte's popular movie studio. So Russell is traveling undercover to Portugal, along with the film crew that is gearing up to shoot a cinematic extravaganza, Pirate King. . . . Nothing seems amiss until the enormous company starts rehearsals in Lisbon, where the thirteen blond-haired, blue-eyed actresses whom Mary is bemusedly chaperoning meet the swarm of real buccaneers Fflytte has recruited to provide authenticity. But when the crew embarks for Morocco and the actual filming, Russell feels a building storm of trouble: a derelict boat, a film crew with secrets, ominous currents between the pirates, decks awash with budding romance—and now the pirates are ignoring Fflytte and answering only to their dangerous outlaw leader." Publisher's note

King, Lily

★ The **father** of the rain. Atlantic Monthly Press 2010 354p $24

ISBN 978-0-8021-1949-0; 0-8021-1949-2

The novel "begins in the 1970s, when 11-year-old Daley endures the cruel and wildly sexualized behavior of her boorish, alcoholic father while trying to protect her mother. Daley has learned early how to walk the tightrope of misery that stretches between her battling divorcing parents. Fast-forward to Daley as a 29-year-old adult on the brink of living her dream: a professorship at Berkeley and a life with her beloved Jonathan. When her brother calls her home, expecting her to care for her father, who is drowning in the bottle when his second marriage implodes, Daley is faced with impossible choices: save herself or stay with her father while he settles into his shaky sobriety." Libr J

"There's something so raw and affecting about Daley's love for her damaged father that the book will linger in your mind long after you've finished it." Entertainment Wkly

King, Rachael

The **sound** of butterflies; a novel. William Morrow 2007 338p

ISBN 978-0-06-135764-0; 0-06-135764-2

LC 2007-37442

"In May of 1904, when Thomas Edgar returns to England from his butterfly-collecting expedition to Brazil, his young wife Sophie expects that their happy life together will resume its familiar contented course. Instead, she is faced with a different man altogether, one whose eyes are colder, and who hardly acknowledges her. . . . Thomas' almost sacred quest for a particularly beautiful and elusive butterfly sets up an unforgettably bittersweet story, with its elliptical search for meaning in a world where one kills the thing one loves, and the victim is silent. King's jungle descriptions are masterful. . . . Her rippling prose builds to a wave of intrigue and danger as the narrative unfolds long-hidden revelations of steamy encounters and power plays 'in this godforsaken place' of de facto slavery and disease." BookPage

King, Roger

A **girl** from Zanzibar. Books & Co./Helen Marx Bks. 2002 307p $14.95

ISBN 1-885586-60-4 pa

LC 2002-105487

A picaresque novel about a young East African woman's adventures and loves across a dozen years and three continents.

"Marcella is the author's mouthpiece, his stage manager, theorizing, summing up the action, signaling transitions, and at times these extra roles blur her outline. But the minor characters are just themselves, seen whole with tragic clarity." N Y Times Book Rev

King, Ross

Domino. Walker & Co. 2002 435p $26

ISBN 0-8027-3378-6

LC 2002-29620

"Replete with mystery and suspense and immersed in vivid historical details, this work is also a sharp, philosophical musing on the disguises of the world and the search for the truth that lies beneath." Libr J

King, Stephen, 1947-

★ **11** /22/63; a novel. Stephen King. Scribner 2011 ix, 849 p.p

ISBN 1442344288; 1442344296; 1451627289; 1451627297; 1451627300; 1451651643; 1451663854; 9781442344280; 9781442344297; 9781451627282; 9781451627299; 9781451627305; 9781451651645; 9781451663853

LC 2011025874

The book, a "novel . . . combines a variety of genres, being a JFK assassination thriller, a story of time travel, a variation on the grail quest, a novel of voyeurism, a love story, a historical novel, a counterfactual historical novel, and the chilling tale of a sinister animate universe . . . King's protagonists, Al Templeton, the owner of a diner, and Jake Epping, his loyal customer and friend, take a dispassionate and calculated view of the assassinadon. At the back of his pantry in a small town in present-day Maine, Al finds a wormhole which comes out in September 1958 . . . Al then decides to use his access to the portal to further the public good, and to stay in the past until 1963 so that he can prevent Oswald from killing Kennedy. But Al is not quite sure, from his observadon of Oswald, that he was acting alone when he unsuccessfully attempted to assassinate General Edwin Walker in April 1963." (London Review of Books)

"The title might be '11/22/63' the date of the Kennedy assassination, but Stephen King's newest tome isn't about John F. Kennedy. And though it's steeped in the story of, and theories about, the president's assassin, it isn't necessarily about Lee Harvey Oswald, either. King's novel is a love story, anchored in history. It's two books, knit together in 849 pages. One tells the story of a Maine high school teacher, Jake Epping, traveling back in time on a mission: to save a president and enable a better future. Maybe. The other tale follows a time-traveler sidetracked when he falls in love a decade before he was even born. Like many of King's recent works 'Lisey's Story' and 'Duma Key,' in particular '11/22/63' has a sweetness that will surprise readers who think of him as a horror scribe." Cleveland Plain Dealer

King, Stephen, 1947-

The **Bachman** books: four early novels by Stephen King. New Am. Lib. 1985 692p

LC 85-11411

An omnibus edition of four novels first published in paperback under the author's pseudonym Richard Bachman

"In Rage, a high-school student goes berserk in the classroom, killing the teacher and holding the class hostage. Set in a militaristic ultra-conservative America, The Long Walk pits 100 teenagers against each other in a grueling 450-mile marathon walk in which the penalty is death. Roadwork is a novel of societal conflict, man vs. progress. The first three thrillers, while entertaining and gripping, occasionally suffer from unfocused and uneven writing. Unresolved questions cause the books to be somewhat unsatisfying. However the fourth novel, The Running Man . . . is an action-packed futuristic romp. Protagonist Ben Richards bets his life on a TV show in order to win the money to save the life of his deathly ill daughter. The story combines social commentary, adventure and science fiction, set against the backdrop of a decaying society." SLJ

King, Stephen, 1947-

Bag of bones. Scribner 1998 529p

ISBN 0-684-85350-7

LC 98-23801

"The big surprise here is the emotional wallop the story packs, particularly in the scenes where Noonan grieves for his dead wife. These are among the most disconsolate moments King has ever created." Newsweek

King, Stephen, 1947-

Black house; a novel. [by] Stephen King [and] Peter Straub. Random House 2001 624p

ISBN 0-375-50439-7

LC 2001-31657

Sequel to The talisman (1984)

"In French Landing, Wis., a serial killer called the Fisherman is doing unspeakable things to local children. But a retired Los Angeles homicide detective named Jack Sawyer, who has done a mighty job of repressing his boyhood trials in an alternate world called the Territories, knows that

there's more to these crimes than mere banal human cruelty. . . . What elevates 'Black House' beyond ordinary horror novels is the richness of its cast, from a bunch of philosophy-reading bikers to a sleazy journalist to a grieving mother on the brink of madness." N Y Times Book Rev

King, Stephen, 1947-

Blaze; a novel. [by] Richard Bachman; foreword by Stephen King. Scribner 2007 285p $25

ISBN 978-1-4165-5484-4; 1-4165-5484-X

LC 2007-15354

A novel originally written 1973 by Stephen King writing as Richard Bachman. "The protagonist is Clayton Blaisdell Jr., a lonely, brain-damaged outcast blessed (or perhaps cursed) with unusual physical strength. His life has been a series of heartbreaking calamities. Standing 6 foot 7 and weighing almost 300 pounds, Clayton is a man-child left 'soft in the head' after being twice thrown down a flight of stairs as a child by his abusive father. Bounced around foster homes and institutions for much of his childhood, Clayton eventually finds himself running with George, a know-it-all criminal who becomes his constant companion and adviser, who continues to counsel Clayton from beyond the grave. Alternating between Clayton's past and the present, in which Clayton has kidnapped the infant son of wealthy parents and is holding him for ransom, Blaze is a suspenseful crime yarn as well as a moving, sympathetic portrait of a man yearning to find a place in a world that seems to have callously rejected him." PopMatters

King, Stephen, 1947-

Blockade Billy. Cemetery Dance Publications 2010 112p il $25

ISBN 978-1-58767-228-6

"Plenty of familiar greats dot the field in Blockade Billy's tale, from Ted Kluszewski and Ted Williams to Mickey Mantle and Hank Aaron. King knows his way around the dugout and makes fine sport of the game's rhythms and gallows humor, too. . . . All in all, 'Blockade Billy' merits a curtain call for the endlessly prolific, and inventive, King. His novella makes a perfect companion for scanning the summer box scores and, most impressive of all, even conjures a momentary twinge of empathy for that most scorned baseball species: the umpire." Christ Sci Monit

King, Stephen, 1947-

★ **Carrie**. Doubleday 1974 199p $32.50

ISBN 0-385-08695-4

"Carrie is 16, lonely, the butt of all her Maine classmates' tricks and jokes, an object of scorn even to her own mother, who is fanatically religious and believes anything remotely sexual is from the devil. Then one girl becomes ashamed of the cruelty being vented on Carrie and plans an act of kindness that will give her the first happiness in her young life. The only trouble is the act backfires horribly and Carrie is worse off than ever before. It is at this point, at the senior prom, that Carrie begins to put into effect her awesome telekinetic powers, powers with which she has only toyed before." Publ Wkly

"A terrifying treat for both horror and parapsychology fans." SLJ

King, Stephen, 1947-
Cell; a novel. Scribner 2006 355p $26.95
ISBN 0-743-29233-2

LC 2005-57531

"The zombies evolve in interesting ways. Midway through the book, Mr. King takes the story to a private school that has become a post-Pulse campground and reveals the telepathic patterns that have begun to shape collective behavior. It is the author's little joke that these messages are delivered via the worst easy-listening songs he can name, to the point where Lawrence Welk and 'You Light Up My Life' become part of the apocalypse." N Y Times (Late N Y Ed)

King, Stephen, 1947-
Christine. Viking 1983 526p $35
ISBN 0-670-22026-4

LC 82-20105

"As always, there is the sense of descriptive detail that is the author's trademark. Yet the strength of King's prose is best seen here in the remarkable accuracy of language and attitude that captures the spirit of the teenage characters." Libr J

King, Stephen, 1947-
Cujo. Viking 1981 319p
ISBN 0-670-45193-2

LC 81-50265

"A Saint Bernard gone berserk, Cujo is the 200-pound family pet who is bitten by a rabid bat one very hot summer in Castle Rock, Maine. Victims of his violence are two families—that of his owner, backwoods auto mechanic Joe Cambers, and of Vic Trenton, an ad man struggling to keep an important account while 'dealing with his wife's infidelity and his four year old's fears.' Counterpoint to the ad campaign's folksy slogan and the writer's lush reveries are . . . vigils in stalled Pintos where one awaits deadly assault." SLJ

"Carefully plotted, the novel throbs with the malignant evil that permeates all of King's fiction." Saturday Rev

King, Stephen, 1947-
The dark half. Viking 1989 431p

LC 88-40628

The author is "a very good storyteller. 'The Dark Half' mostly succeeds, as both parable and chiller, in spite of occasional clichés of thought and expression and bits of sophomoric humor." N Y Times Book Rev

King, Stephen, 1947-
★ The dead zone. Viking 1979 426p
ISBN 0-670-26077-0

LC 79-12785

"Following a car accident, New England high school English teacher Johnny Smith is unconscious for five years only to wake a bewildered psychic in post-Watergate America. He quickly runs afoul of a national scandal sheet that wants to exploit his power to see the future. He also catches a sex murderer and eventually takes an interest in presidential politics. In the end he turns assassin to save the country from a Hitler-like congressman with White House aspirations." Libr J

King, Stephen, 1947-
Desperation. Viking 1996 690p
ISBN 0-670-86836-1

LC 96-17259

This horror tale shares character's with The regulators, entered below. An "alien force is loose in Desperation, Nevada, and, having occupied the bodies of a succession of citizens . . . has gruesomely slaughtered everyone else in town. Now in the body of a patrolling cop, it is picking up people motoring by on U.S. 50. Foremost among those are burned-out novelist Johnny Marinville and 11-year-old David Carver, who barely a year ago underwent a serious religious conversion and occasionally hears the voice of God. It is God—the God of the Christian Bible, both Testaments—who eventually saves Johnny, David, and the rest of those who survive Desperation, but saves them only by means of their own free will and their own heroic and gory exertions. If King wants to show how to inject religion honestly and effectively into the normally crass horror genre, he succeeds beautifully." Booklist

King, Stephen, 1947-
Different seasons. Viking 1982 527p $37.95; pa $7.99
ISBN 0-670-27266-3; 0-451-16753-8 pa

LC 82-70145

This "is a collection of four novellas. . . . The first tale is about how one self-contained individual coped with life in a Maine jail. The second is not so much about Nazism today as it is about how victim and victimizer can develop a symbiotic relationship. In the third search by 12-year-olds for a body in the woods has implications for their innocence. The last is a good old-fashioned horror story." Libr J

King, Stephen, 1947-
★ Dolores Claiborne. Viking 1993 305p
ISBN 0-670-84452-7

LC 92-15467

"What drives Dolores Claiborne is a powerful characterization of the title figure, a cranky old Maine islander who takes no guff from life or death. . . . King's mimicry is startlingly good." Time

King, Stephen, 1947-
Dreamcatcher; a novel. Scribner 2001 620p $28
ISBN 0-7432-1138-3

LC 00-67990

"One November afternoon in the Maine woods, four men, friends since childhood are on their annual hunting trip that has become as much a time for catching up on one another's lives as it is a time for drinking beer and pursuing game. But this congenial respite ends quickly for Pete, Beaver, Henry, and Jonesy when a dazed and disheveled stranger wanders into their campsite. The hours and days that follow are filled with spaceships, evil gray aliens, a toxic parasite called byrus, and a military search-and-destroy mission. . . . {King} serves up a powerful work that examines the interconnections between memory and imagination and studies the influence of friendship on the human condition." Libr J

King, Stephen, 1947-

Duma Key. Scribner 2008 611p $28

ISBN 978-1-416-55251-2; 1-416-55251-0

LC 2007-38941

"King is at the height of his powers with Duma Key, allowing him to exploit such themes as family conflict, the mixed blessing of artistic talent, the nature of masculine friendship and loyalty, and the possibility of redemption for even those most broken in body and spirit. . . . That all this comes in a rousing reinvention of the ghost story diminishes King's achievement not a bit." Houston Chron

King, Stephen, 1947-

Everything's eventual: 14 dark tales. Scribner 2002 459p $28

ISBN 0-7432-3515-0

LC 2002-17738

"Fourteen stories, most of them gems, featuring an array of literary approaches, plus an opinionated intro from King about the '(Almost) Lost Art' of the short story." Publ Wkly

King, Stephen, 1947-

Firestarter. Viking 1980 428p hardcover o.p. pa $7.99

ISBN 0-670-31541-9; 0-451-16780-5 pa

LC 80-14793

"This is your advanced post-Watergate cynical American thriller with some eerie parapsychological twists, and it's been done so distinctively well that we'd better talk about genius rather than genre." Quill Quire

King, Stephen, 1947-

Four past midnight. Viking 1990 763p hardcover o.p. pa $7.99

ISBN 0-451-17038-5 pa

LC 90-50046

This volume contains four novellas: The Langoliers; Secret window, secret garden; The library policeman; The sun dog.

This book "is hard to put down, truly chilling, and sure to be enjoyed by YA horror afficionados everywhere." SLJ

King, Stephen, 1947-

★ **From** a Buick 8; a novel. Scribner 2002 356p $28

ISBN 0-7432-1137-5

LC 2001-55118

This is a "horror novel, but it's one that gnaws away at the very premises of the horror novel. It knows what you want and expect from it, but it deftly gives you something else instead, something equally worth having and all the more pleasing for being a surprise." N Y Times Book Rev

King, Stephen, 1947-

Full dark, no stars. Scribner 2010 368p $27.99

ISBN 978-1-4391-9256-6; 1-4391-9256-1

LC 2010-32866

"Returning to the novella—possibly his brightest canvas—King provides four raw looks at the limits of greed, revenge, and self-deception. The first, '1922,' is an outright masterpiece and takes the form of the written confession of one Wilf James. Back in 1922, see, Wilf killed his wife

to prevent her selling off part of the farm, but tossing her corpse down the well didn't exactly stop her. It's Poe meets Creepshow by way of Steinbeck and carries the bleak, nearly romantic doom of an old folk ballad about murderin' done wrong. A pair of the remaining tales feature female protagonists considering hiding others' crimes: 'Big Driver' is a rape-revenge tale about a writer of cozy mysteries who ends up in the uncoziest of situations, while 'A Good Marriage' stars a wife whose husband of 27 years turns out to be hiding an unimaginable secret. Though the shortest story by far, 'Fair Extension' is no slouch, submitting for your approval one Mr. Elvid (get it?), who is out to shine a little light on our blackest urges. Rarely has King gone this dark." Booklist

King, Stephen, 1947-

Gerald's game. Viking 1992 332p

LC 91-47628

"Jessie and Gerald Burlingame have been married for 20 years. Kinky sex is Gerald's game; lately he has taken to handcuffing his wife to the bedposts. During one such session, via a series of bizarre circumstances, Jessie accidentally kills her husband, and for the next 28 hours she is trapped." Publ Wkly

King, Stephen, 1947-

★ The **girl** who loved Tom Gordon; a novel. Scribner 1999 224p $16.95

ISBN 0-684-86762-1

LC 99-13109

"Nine-year-old Trisha McFarland is hopelessly lost in the woods. Out for a morning hike with her bickering mother and brother, she runs off to relieve herself and discovers she can't find her way back to the path. . . . Trisha wanders for a week in the mosquito-infested forest with nothing but her wits, her Walkman and the pitching prowess of her hero, the dreamy Red Sox reliever Tom Gordon, to guide her. As Trisha fights to stay alive, King demonstrates his empathy for the inner lives of children and an outdoorsman's knowledge of the edible wild flora of Maine." N Y Times Book Rev

King, Stephen, 1947-

Hearts in Atlantis. Scribner 1999 523p $28

ISBN 0-684-85351-5

LC 99-23889

Five interconnected fictions follow three friends from their sixth-grade year, 1960, to 1999. The war in Vietnam serves as a unifying theme

"The characters are compelling and well drawn, the action is ingeniously interwoven from story to story, and the feel of the 60s, and the baggage carried into later decades, is vivid, harsh, and absolutely true." SLJ

King, Stephen, 1947-

Insomnia. Viking 1994 787p

ISBN 0-670-85503-0

LC 94-784

"On one of the long, exhausting walks old Ralph Roberts starts taking as a brain tumor slowly kills his wife, he witnesses a friendly young neighbor, Ed Deepneau, behaving totally out of character—indeed, like someone possessed. About a year later and after his wife's death, Ralph begins waking early and then earlier and earlier. He also starts seeing things—intense colors streaming off people and animals.

Meanwhile, Ed has turned into an antiabortion fanatic and wife-beater. Ralph intervenes to help Helen Deepneau escape from Ed, for which Ed threatens him. Or is it Ed? Ralph senses that someone or something else is in control of the troubled man. Ralph's right, of course. Ed has been involuntarily recruited on one side, and, it develops, Ralph and his also-widowed neighbor, Lois Chasse, on the other, of a supercosmic struggle the import of which King reveals with deliciously tantalizing gradualness." Booklist

King, Stephen, 1947-

It. Viking 1986 1138p
ISBN 0-670-81302-8

LC 85-41062

"Six adults, living separately in a blessed fog of forgetfulness, are summoned back to their hometown to complete the destruction of a horrific, shape-changing entity who breakfasts on the city's children. This same group first encountered the menace more than a quarter century before, as schoolchildren in the 1950s. Their quest breeds some riveting chase scenes as adults and children alike flee from an assortment of menacing humans and slavering monsters—most of which are manifestations of an evil so vile its true nature can never be known. King's considerable talent for grounding this supernatural stuff in the minutiae of everyday life is evident." Booklist

King, Stephen, 1947-

Just after sunset; stories. Scribner 2008 367p $28
ISBN 978-1-4165-8408-7; 1-4165-8408-0

LC 2008-13683

King "presents 14 tales that range from the philosophically themed, to one in which the author gleefully admits to playing with the gross-out factor ('A Very Tight Place'), to 'The Cat from Hell,' which makes its hardcover debut some 30 years after its original publication as part of a contest in Cavalier , one of the gentleman's magazines that put food on the table in King's early years as a writer. In his introduction, King cites his recent stint as guest editor for the 2007 edition of Best American Short Stories as an impetus to return to the form in his own writing." Libr J

"Many of Sunset's stories have the aura of classic Twilight Zone episodes. And no matter your taste in frightful fantasies, there's something here for everybody." USA Today

King, Stephen, 1947-

Lisey's story; a novel. Scribner 2006 513p $28
ISBN 0-7432-8941-2

LC 2006-44382

"What King does that is so exceptional here is to get out of his comfort zone and dig deep into the skin of his main character until he's conjured up on the page a living, breathing human such as is rarely found in his pulpier creations. Lisey's narrative is an all-too-recognizable inner loop of private jokes and obsessive memories that moves the book forward only in fits and starts. She doesn't just mourn Scott, she repeatedly conjures him without even trying, using all his dumb slang and repeating his awful jokes for no reason other than that, after a quarter-century of connected lives, his ghost is imbedded so deep within her that she couldn't exorcise him with a priest and a gallon of holy water. He's there to stay, as is the sadness of his being gone, and it's

that inescapable reality that proves particularly terrifying here." PopMatters

King, Stephen, 1947-

★ Misery. Viking 1987 310p

LC 86-40504

"Even if 'Misery' is less terrifying than his usual work— no demons, no witchcraft, no nether-world horrors—it creates strengths out of its realities. Its excitements are more subtle. And, as such, it is an intriguing work." N Y Times Book Rev

King, Stephen, 1947-

Needful things. Viking 1991 690p
ISBN 0-670-83953-1

LC 91-50148

"As the dreams of each strikingly memorable character, major and minor, inexorably turn to nightmare, individuals and soon the community are overwhelmed, while the precise nature of Gaunt's evil thrillingly stays just out of focus. King, like Leland Gaunt, knows just what his customers want." Publ Wkly

King, Stephen, 1947-

Night shift. Doubleday 1978 xxii, 336p hardcover o.p. pa $7.99
ISBN 0-385-12991-2; 0-307-74364-0 pa

LC 77-75146

The stories "all begin in our normal world, where everything is safe and warm. But in almost every instance, something slips, and we find ourselves in the nightmare world of the not-quite-real. . . . Such stories require a willing suspension of disbelief, of course, but they also require an author who is an expert manipulator. . . . King is an expert." Best Sellers

King, Stephen, 1947-

Nightmares & dreamscapes. Viking 1993 816p

LC 92-46881

"There's certainly nothing skimpy about this collection of large, leisurely short stories. . . . Fans of Mr. King's work will find here his usual menu: wild conspiracies; repellent, zestful monsters; scenes speckled and splashed with gore." N Y Times Book Rev

King, Stephen, 1947-

Pet sematary. Doubleday 1983 373p
ISBN 0-385-18244-9

LC 82-45360

"King's characters are so solid and next-door neighborly that we are drawn quite naturally and trustingly into their lives. And then, a single note at a time, the eerie music begins and we are entranced." Best Sellers

King, Stephen, 1947-

The regulators; [by] Richard Bachman. Dutton 1996 466p
ISBN 0-525-94190-8

LC 96-8931

"The premise owes a big unacknowledged debt to the classic Twilight Zone episode 'It's a Good Life'; echoes of earlier Kings resound often as well. . . . But King makes hay in this story in which anything can happen, and does, including the warping of space-time and the savage deaths of much of his large cast. The narrative itself warps fantastically, from prose set in classic typeface to handwritten journals to drawings to typewritten playscript and so on." Publ Wkly

King, Stephen, 1947-
  Rose Madder. Viking 1995 420p
    ISBN 0-670-85869-2
                                        LC 95-14376
  "In the book's first scene, having beaten his cowed, pregnant wife badly enough to induce a miscarriage, Norman blithely makes himself a sandwich while waiting for the ambulance to arrive. And when Rose suddenly flees, after 14 years of abuse, Norman calmly begins trolling for her, leaving in his wake a string of mutilated corpses. Rose doesn't leave Norman because she's afraid he'll kill her—she's driven to escape by the fear that he won't, that his cruel torments will simply go on and on. Her despair, her gradual creation of a new life in a Midwestern city, her hesitant romance with a wry, gentle pawnbroker, are all convincingly rendered." N Y Times Book Rev

King, Stephen, 1947-
  ★ **Salem's** Lot. Doubleday 1975 439p $35
    ISBN 0-385-00751-5
  "It is to Stephen King's credit as a stylist that he has charmed us into such familiar territory. Sparing the endless atmospheric creaks and cobwebs and cupolas of this New England landscape, he thrusts us into the private terror of his characters." Best Sellers

King, Stephen, 1947-
  ★ The **shining**. Doubleday 1977 447p $35
    ISBN 0-385-12167-9
                                        LC 76-24212
  "In a fast-paced and gory denouement, the terror comes to a violent end. King is a masterful technician of suspense whose readers as well as characters are the victims of his relentless heightening of horror." Libr J

King, Stephen, 1947-
  Skeleton crew. Putnam 1985 512p hardcover o.p. pa $7.99
    ISBN 0-451-16861-5 pa
                                        LC 84-15947
  This "collection of King's shorter work is a hefty sampler from all stages of his career, and demonstrates the range of his abilities. . . . There are several stories here that must rank among King's best." Publ Wkly

King, Stephen, 1947-
  The **stand**. Doubleday 1978 823 p.
    ISBN 9780385199575; 9780307743688; 9780606256155
                                        LC 77016928
  "A flu-like plague escapes from an experimental lab. Within days it devastates the country, leaving only a few thousand immune people. Besides their immunity, the survivors have in common a terrible dream pitting a faceless man of evil against a woman of goodness. The survivors make their choices and head west, gathering for the confrontation

between the satanic Randall Flagg and the God-anointed Mother Abigail." Libr J

King, Stephen, 1947-
  Thinner; {by} Richard Bachman. New Am. Lib. 1984 309p
                                        LC 84-11462
  "Bachman blends extraordinary events so cleanly and credibly into the fabric of his characters' lives that we are compelled to read on to the story's chilling conclusion. A superbly crafted drama." Booklist

King, Stephen, 1947-
  ★ **Under** the dome. Scribner 2009 1074p $35
    ISBN 978-1-4391-4850-1; 1-4391-4850-3
                                        LC 2009018780
  "The action takes place in the oh-so-ordinary, neighborly town of Chester Mills, Maine, where on a crisp and beautiful fall day a clear dome slaps down over the town, sealing it off from the outside world. You can sometimes reach someone outside with your cell phone, depending on the reception. You can speak to those who stand on the outside. But you're not going anywhere. And that becomes wildly problematic. . . . As for the characters, there's a super-bad guy, corrupt politician and car dealer (yeah, King embraces boldly some cliches) Big Jim Rennie, and some lesser creeps. The good guys include Gulf War veteran Dale 'Barbie' Barbara, dog-loving physician's assistant Julia Shumway and some kids who are going to try to set things right." Deseret News

King, Stephen, 1947-
  The **wind** through the keyhole; a dark tower novel. by Stephen King. Scribner 2012 viii, 309 p.p
    ISBN 1451658907; 9781442346963; 9781442346970; 9781451658903; 9781451658910; 9781451658927
                                        LC 2011050590
  This volume of the Dark Tower series "draws inspiration from tales of knighthood and Old West gunslingers, as its story-within-a-story (within a story) details the rite-of-passage heroism of Roland Deschain, who saves a terrified boy in Mid-World from a shape-shifting marauder. 'These tales nest inside each other,' explains Roland at the outset, as he prepares to recount a story through which its characters drew courage and inspiration from a story." (Kirkus)

King, Tabitha
  Survivor. Dutton 1997 433p
    ISBN 0-525-94241-6
                                        LC 96-26347
  Maine college student Kissy Mellors "is the driver who stopped in time to avoid killing two young women—but the drunk who passed her did not. One woman dies, and the other goes into a coma that lasts for years. Kissy's life is changed forever by this event and by the relationships she forms because of it—with the comatose victim and her family, with the dead girl's boyfriend (a hockey player Kissy later marries), with the investigating officer, even with the drunk driver." Libr J
  "King's brutally frank 'warts and all' writing style and bizarre dissection of ordinary events lend a chilling, vaguely eerie element to this suspenseful, enjoyable novel." Booklist

Kingsolver, Barbara

Animal dreams; a novel. HarperCollins Pubs. 1990 342p

LC 89-46571

This novel is set in Grace, Arizona. The narrator is Cosima (Codi) Noline, who returns home after abandoning a career in medicine. Codi looks after her aging father, the local doctor, and teaches high school biology. Her sister Halimeda (Hallie) is an agronomist helping the Sandinistas in Nicaragua. In Grace, Codi becomes involved with a former boyfriend, Loyd Peregrina, a Native American. She struggles to come to terms with her past and works to save the town from an impending ecological disaster

"Like all good novels, Animal Dreams is a web of interlacing news. It is dense and vivid, and makes ever tighter circles around the question of what it means to be alive." Nation

Kingsolver, Barbara

★ The bean trees; a novel. 10th anniversary ed; HarperFlamingo 1997 261p $19.95; pa $7.99
ISBN 0-06-017579-6; 0-06-109731-4 pa

LC 97-2691

A reissue of the title first published 1988

This book "gives readers something that's increasingly hard to find today—a character to believe in and laugh with and admire." Christ Sci Monit

Followed by Pigs in heaven (1993)

Kingsolver, Barbara, 1955-

★ Flight behavior; a novel. by Barbara Kingsolver. HarperCollins 2012 448 p. (hardback) $28.99
ISBN 0062124269; 9780062124265

LC 2012025321

Author Barbara Kingsolver's book "tells the story of Dellarobia Turnbow, a petite, razor-sharp 29-year-old who nurtured worldly ambitions before becoming pregnant and marrying at seventeen. Now, after more than a decade of tending to small children on a failing farm, oppressed by poverty, isolation and her husband's antagonistic family, she has mitigated her boredom by surrendering to an obsessive flirtation with a handsome younger man." (Publisher's note)

Kingsolver, Barbara

The lacuna; a novel. Harper 2009 507p $26.99
ISBN 978-0-06-085257-3; 0-06-085257-7

LC 2009-33697

In this novel, "Harrison Shepherd, the son of a Mexican flirt and a stolid American bureaucrat, has a remarkable life: cook for Diego Rivera and Frida Kahlo, secretary to Trotsky, and acclaimed author denounced as a Communist by HUAC. The story is narrated mostly through Shepherd's journal entries, with occasional interpolations by his literary executor. There are some lapses into gum-cracking, slang-filled dialogue, and the latter half of the book, which takes place in North Carolina, suffers from the relative insipidity of the setting. The most compelling moments occur when Trotsky, in exile and fearing assassination, takes refuge with Rivera and is seduced by Kahlo. Kingsolver's descriptions of life in Mexico City burst with sensory detail—thick sweet breads, vividly painted walls, the lovely white feet of an unattainable love." New Yorker

Kingsolver, Barbara

Pigs in heaven; a novel. HarperCollins Pubs. 1993 343p
ISBN 9780060922535; 9780061436680

LC 92054739

This is a sequel to The Bean Trees (BRD 1988). Taylor Greer and her adopted Cherokee Indian daughter Turtle, "are on a trip to the Hoover Dam, where Turtle is the only person to see a man fall over the side. . . . The rescue makes Turtle a heroine. But becoming a heroine, which culminates in an appearance on 'Oprah,' engenders a new disaster. Annawake Fourkiller, an Indian-rights lawyer, sees the white mother with her Cherokee daughter on TV and decides the child must be returned to the Cherokee Nation. . . . But Taylor isn't about to let go of the little girl. . . . They pack up and run." (Newsweek)

In this sequel to The bean trees, Taylor Greer and her adopted Cherokee Indian daughter Turtle "are on a trip to the Hoover Dam, where Turtle is the only person to see a man fall over the side. . . . The rescue makes Turtle a heroine. But becoming a heroine, which culminates in an appearance on 'Oprah,' engenders a new disaster. Annawake Fourkiller, an Indian-rights lawyer, sees the white mother with her Cherokee daughter on TV and decides the child must be returned to the Cherokee Nation. . . . But Taylor isn't about to let go of the little girl. . . . They pack up and run." Newsweek

Kingsolver, Barbara

★ The poisonwood Bible; a novel. HarperFlamingo 1998 546p $26; pa $16.99
ISBN 0-06-017540-0; 0-06-157707-3 pa

LC 98-19901

"Buttressing her suspenseful chronicle with authentic background detail, Kingsolver's narrative is at once a compelling family saga and an astute look at Western imperialism in Africa." Publ Wkly

Kingsolver, Barbara

Prodigal summer; a novel. HarperCollins Pubs. 2000 444p $26
ISBN 0-06-019965-2

LC 00-61361

The novel is full of "tenderness, humor, and earthy spirituality. . . . As usual, Kingsolver's dialogue is absolutely natural, often funny, and sometimes heartbreaking." Chris Sci Monit

Kinsale, Laura

Lessons in French; Laura Kinsale. Sourcebooks Casablanca 2010 458p $7.99
ISBN 9781402237010; 1402237014

This romance novel, chosen as a "Library Journal" Best Book of 2010, tells the story of "Trevelyan and Callie [who] are childhood sweethearts with a taste for adventure, until the fateful day her father discovers them embracing in the carriage house and, in a furious frenzy, drives Trevelyan away in disgrace. Nine long, lonely years later, Trevelyan returns. Callie discovers that he can still make her blood race and fill her life with excitement, but he can't give her the one thing she wants more than anything—himself." (Publisher's note)

Kinsella, Sophie

I've got your number; Sophie Kinsella. Dial Press 2012 433 p.

ISBN 9780385342063; 9780679644682

LC 2011031146

In this book, "Poppy Wyatt . . . is about to marry her ideal man, Magnus Tavish, but in one afternoon . . . [n]ot only has she lost her engagement ring in a hotel fire drill but in the panic that follows, her phone is stolen. As she paces shakily around the lobby, she spots an abandoned phone in a trash can. . . . Now she can leave a number for the hotel to contact her when they find her ring. . . . [But] the phone's owner, businessman Sam Roxton, . . . wants his phone back and doesn't appreciate Poppy reading his messages and wading into his personal life. What ensues is a hilarious and unpredictable turn of events as Poppy and Sam increasingly upend each other's lives through emails and text messages." (Publisher's note)

Kipling, Rudyard, 1865-1936

★ **Collected** stories; selected and introduced by Robert Gottlieb. Knopf 1994 xxxvii, 911p $25

ISBN 0-679-43592-1

LC 94-5854

"There is an enormous range of subject matter, genre, styles, and tones in Kipling's prose work. . . . {He} is undoubtedly one of the great short-story writers in English and the subtlety of his early narrative technique has led some to claim him as a proto-Modernist." Oxford Companion to 20th Cent Lit in Engl

Includes bibliographical references

Kirshenbaum, Binnie

An **almost** perfect moment. Ecco 2004 321p $23.95

ISBN 0-06-052086-8

LC 2003-54961

The protagonist of this novel is Valentine Kessler. "A nice Jewish girl growing up in late-1970s Brooklyn, she becomes infatuated with her Polish American math teacher and with the Virgin Mary, for she mysteriously resembles the vision of Mary seen by Bernadette of Lourdes. Valentine's father left when she was a baby, and ever since her mother, Miriam, indulges her beautiful, newly withdrawn daughter while eating herself into obesity and playing mahjongg every afternoon with her buddies. The so-called Girls are like a Greek chorus, commenting on life around them and wondering at Valentine's inspired silence. . . . Bursting with hyperbole, this is a hilarious and uncanny snapshot of a bygone era." Libr J

Kirst, Hans Hellmut

Forward, Gunner Asch! translated from the German by Robert Kee. Little, Brown 1956 368p

Sequel to The revolt of Gunner Asch

Original German edition, 1954; published in the United Kingdom as part two of the trilogy: Zero eight fifteen, with title: Gunner Asch goes to war

"The action of the book alternates between a sector of the Russian front in late winter of 1941-2, and a base depot somewhere in Germany. Gunner Asch and his companions, whom we met in the first volume training at home, have now gone to war. . . . The characters move like Breughel peasants against a bleak winter landscape; unshaven, filthy, swaddled in greatcoats and sacking, their minds set only on self-preservation, food, and, where possible, women." New Statesman (1913)

Followed by The return of Gunner Asch

Kirst, Hans Hellmut

The **return** of Gunner Asch; translated from the German by Robert Kee. Little, Brown 1957 310p

Sequel to Forward, Gunner Asch!

Original German edition, 1955; published in the United Kingdom as third part of the trilogy: Zero eight fifteen

The third volume in the author's series about the adventures of a German army sergeant in World War II describes "the disintegration of the front-line units of the German Army as the Allies advanced in the closing days of combat in Europe in 1945. Asch becomes involved in an effort to track down two officers who left their men to needless slaughter to catch up with a black-market cache." Booklist

Followed by What became of Gunner Asch (1964)

Kirst, Hans Hellmut

The **revolt** of Gunner Asch; translated from the German by Robert Kee. Little, Brown 1955 311p

First in a series of four novels about Gunner Asch; Original German edition, 1954; published in the United Kingdom as part of the trilogy Zero eight fifteen, with title: The strange mutiny of Gunner Asch

"A tale in which elements of drama and suspense are skillfully fused with high comedy—a tale which the author brings to a startling and altogether delightful conclusion. . . . Kirst has succeeded in distilling robust fun out of brutal realities without ever suggesting that the realities were other than brutal." Atlantic

Followed by Forward, Gunner Asch!

Kitt, Sandra

Celluloid memories. Harlequin 2007 320p $6.99

ISBN 9780373830152 pa; 0373830157

In this book, "Savannah Shelton knows the City of Angels breaks hearts more often than it fulfills dreams. Her late father spent fruitless years trying to make it big as an actor. Among his possessions, Savannah finds papers that hint at an old Hollywood secret that she's positive would make a red-hot screenplay. But when a fender bender introduces her to McCoy Sutton, a charming, sexy attorney, Savannah wonders if it's time to put aside her jaded ideas about L.A. and figure out if real life can have a Hollywood ending." (Publisher's note)

Kittredge, William

The **Willow** Field. Knopf 2006 342p $25.95

ISBN 1-4000-4097-3

LC 2006-45157

This "multigenerational saga begins with a stunning set piece—a classic horse drive, more than 200 head, from Nevada to Calgary. Rossie, a veteran ranch hand but still barely 20, signs on for the drive as a way of breaking ties with a girl and winds up forging even stronger ties with another girl, Eliza Stevenson, the unmarried but pregnant daughter of a rancher in Montana's Bitterroot Mountains. 'We could be it, entirely it,' Eliza says shortly after she meets Rossie, and as we watch their lives unfold, from the Depression through World War II and on into the 1960s, we realize that this strong-willed woman was both right and wrong. . . . Rossie and Eliza are 'entirely it,' but—fiery individuals both—they are also in perpetual conflict, cherishing their union just as they struggle not to be consumed by the other. This transcendent love story is at the heart of Kittredge's novel, but it is set against not one but two imposing landscapes—the Bitterroot and the Nevada desert, both of which demand their own allegiance from the characters' minds and hearts." Booklist

Klaussmann, Liza

Tigers in red weather; a novel. Liza Klaussmann. Little, Brown & Co. 2012 356 p. (hardcover) $25.99; (paperback) $14.99

ISBN 0316211338; 9780316211338; 9780316211321

LC 2011050204

This book by Liza Klaussmann, "set in . . . post-WWII Martha's Vineyard . . . finds a family unmoored by an unsolved murder. . . . Once carefree girls, now jaded women . . . [Nick and Helena have] returned to Tiger House with their families, but their lives have lost much of the rosy glow they had before the murder. Selfish and aloof, Nick can't stay faithful to her husband. . . . Helena . . . prefers pills and booze to dealing with her poor excuse for a relationship." (Publishers Weekly)

Klavan, Andrew

Empire of lies. Harcourt 2008 383p $25

ISBN 978-0-15-101223-7; 0-15-101223-7

LC 2007-33052

"A wickedly satiric thriller with political overtones. Jason Harrow was cynically immoral before he found God and became a conservative Midwestern family man. Now his former lover summons him back to New York City with the news that his teenage daughter (one he never knew about) is in trouble, mixed up with terrorists who are plotting a major atrocity. To save his daughter and thousands of others, Jason must confront the buried fear that he's inherited his mother's insanity and can't control his own dark urges. As Jason's insecurity intensifies, so does the novel's nightmarish mood. Disgusted by the excesses of the liberal media, Jason discovers that he's not just paranoid, he really is a persecuted outsider. The action builds to an explosive climax at the screening of a 3D movie at a Manhattan theater." Publ Wkly

Klein, Joe

Primary colors; a novel of politics. [by] Anonymous. Random House 1996 366p

ISBN 0-679-44859-4

LC 95-39823

This is a "romance à clef about the 1992 Democratic Presidential primary campaign, featuring an ambitious . . . . Southern governor named Jack Stanton seen through the eyes of {Henry Burton}, a disillusioned aide." London Rev Books

"This is, in short, a quite outstanding novel of political process and motive that reads like a slightly hipper version of Gore Vidal." New Statesman (1913)

Klein, Matthew

Con ed. Warner Books 2007 285p $23.99

ISBN 978-0-446-57955-1; 0-446-57955-6

LC 2006-18438

"Once-rich con-man Kip Largo is going straight, living small, and making $10 per hour in a dry-cleaning store after doing eight years for wire fraud. Life is dull, but Kip wants it that way, until his son Toby shows up, on the run from the Russian Mob. Kip needs a big score to save Toby, and a timely proposal from the stunning young wife of a dangerous Las Vegas casino owner provides him with a target for a grand scam. Con Ed is a brisk, clever, and charming page-turner." Booklist

Klein, Matthew

Switchback. Severn House Publishers 2011 296p $28.95

ISBN 978-0-7278-8051-2; 0-7278-8051-9

This book "starts with a setup primed for trouble: a gazillionaire hedge funder, the kind of guy who has no need to work very hard to earn the fanged envy of his colleagues, thanks not only to his money but also to his classy wife and the hormonal receptionist who lusts after him. Then, . . . things go haywire. He mismanages clients' fortunes and loses them. Lawsuits loom. A trusted associate sells him out. His wife disappears after threatening suicide, and an astute homicide cop turns up at awkward moments. Baffled, our hero begins his own inquiry. It leads him, in a tense, twisty way, to a chance to get it all back. Mystery fans shouldn't be put off by the novel's brush with fantasy; this author knows what he's doing, and he does it in high-energy prose that all but glitters on the page." Booklist

Klein, Rachel

The **moth** diaries; a novel. Counterpoint 2002 249p $24

ISBN 1-58243-205-8

LC 2001-7226

"The unnamed narrator of Klein's first novel is a studious, thoughtful 16-year-old at an elite boarding school in the late '60s. Her closest friend is her sweet, friendly roommate, Lucy, who navigates the school's social system with ease. The arrival of quiet, mysterious Ernessa upsets the balance between the friends when Ernessa befriends and seemingly takes Lucy away from the narrator. . . . Thanks to reading LeFanu's vampire story 'Carmilla' and other tales, and to Ernessa's odd behavior and Lucy's mysterious wasting illness, the narrator begins to suspect that Ernessa is a vampire. . . . The diary format of Klein's story gives it immediacy, and a menacing atmosphere permeates it." Booklist

Kleypas, Lisa

Crystal Cove. St. Martin's Griffin 2013 316 p. (paperback) $14.99; (hardcover) $26.99

ISBN 1250011752; 1250032075; 9781250011756; 9781250032072

LC 2012532398

This book follows Justin Hoffman, "born shortly before her father died. Losing the great love of her life was so hard on Justine's mother, Marigold, that Marigold cast a spell on her daughter to protect her from the pain of finding and then losing that kind of love. What her mother did based on a loving desire to protect her child, grown-up Justine views as a curse that needs to be lifted." (Kirkus)

Kleypas, Lisa

Rainshadow road; a novel. Lisa Kleypas. 1st ed. St. Martin's Griffin 2012 viii, 324 p.p (hardcover) $34.99; (trade pbk.) $14.99

ISBN 9781410446640 large print; 0312605889; 9780312605889; 9781429938372

LC 2011041081

This book follows "Lucy Marinn . . . [who] is stunned and blindsided . . . [when she is left by] her fiance Kevin. . . . His new lover is Lucy's own sister. . . . Facing the severe disapproval of Lucy's parents, Kevin asks his friend Sam Nolan, a local vineyard owner . . . to 'romance' Lucy and hopefully loosen her up. . . . Complications ensue when Sam and Lucy begin to fall in love . . . and Lucy discovers that the new relationship in her life began under false pretenses." (Publisher's note)

Klima, Ivan

No saints or angels; translated by Gerald Turner. Grove Press 2001 267p $24

ISBN 0-8021-1695-7

LC 2001-33994

Original Czech edition, 1999

"In Klima's world bureaucracy is a metaphor for the human condition: our dearest allies now are those who gassed our grandmothers, the young of the past had more purpose under interrogation than those of today have on the Internet, and we long for a God grown wholly inadequate to his creatures in the 21st century. Against this cosmic mismatch, frail, flawed human beings play out their volatile longings and their inglorious heroisms." N Y Times Book Rev

Klosterman, Chuck

Downtown Owl; a novel. Scribner 2008 275p $24

ISBN 978-1-4165-4418-0; 1-4165-4418-6

LC 2007-47088

This novel focuses on the lives of "the football-playing teenager Mitch, the 20-something Julia, and the elderly Horace. The three have little in common—they all live in the small town of Owl, North Dakota, but otherwise have little interaction—but by weaving their three stories around each other, Klosterman constructs a touching, incisive, and (of course) funny snapshot of small-town America circa 1984. And if the story occasionally falters or takes off on tangents, who cares? It's all tremendously fun to read." PopMatters

Klosterman, Chuck

The **visible** man; a novel. Scribner 2011 230p $25

ISBN 978-1-4391-8446-2; 1-4391-8446-1

"Klosterman has conjured up a novel that manages to be both wildly experimental and accessible, while making

perceptive observations about privacy, human nature, and of course, the author's forte, pop culture." Entertainment Wkly

Kneale, Matthew

English passengers; Matthew Kneale. Nan A. Talese 2000 446 p. facsim. (pbk.) $9.99

ISBN 0385497431; 9780385497442

LC 99016402

Whitbread Award for Novel and Book of the Year (2000)

This book takes place "[i]n 1857 when Captain Illiam Quillian Kewley and his band of rum smugglers from the Isle of Man have most of their contraband confiscated by British Customs . . . [and] are forced to put their ship up for charter. The only takers are two eccentric Englishmen. . . . The Reverend Geoffrey Wilson believes the Garden of Eden was on the island of Tasmania. His traveling partner, Dr. Thomas Potter, unbeknownst to Wilson, is developing a sinister thesis about the races of men. Meanwhile, an aboriginal in Tasmania named Peevay recounts his people's struggles against the invading British, a story that begins in 1824, moves into the present with approach of the English passengers in 1857, and extends into the future in 1870." (Publisher's note)

Kneale, Matthew

★ **When** we were Romans; a novel. Nan A. Talese 2008 224p $23.95

ISBN 978-0-385-52625-8; 0-385-52625-3

LC 2007-45523

First published 2007 in the United Kingdom

"We, the adult readers of 'When We Were Romans,' learn to peer through the screen of Lawrence's limited point of view to see what's really going on even as our narrator begins to guess at what lies behind his mother's version of events and even to catch a glimpse of the mysteries of his own heart. In life as well as in books, there are some truths that it's much better to sneak up on." Salon.com

Knebel, Fletcher

Seven days in May; by Fletcher Knebel and Charles W. Bailey II. Harper & Row 1962 341p

"The story set against a . . . political Washington background, is about a military plot to take over the government. Its hero is a President of the U.S. in the 1970's, who with six men he trusts, sets out to prove the plot exists and to foil it." Publ Wkly

Knight, Damon Francis

The **best** of Damon Knight; with an introduction by Barry N. Malzberg. Taplinger 1978 307p

First published 1976 in paperback by Pocket Books

"A writer of estimable talent, as these twenty-two stories from 1948-73 prove. Knight's motifs are common—time travel, after-the-holocaust, cyborgs, alien visitors to earth—but the wit, penetrating social satire, and quick narrative twists are distinctly his own." Booklist

Knight, Michael

Goodnight, nobody. Atlantic Monthly Press 2002 160p $23

ISBN 0-87113-867-0

LC 2002-27944

"Stylistically, Knight slaloms through old-fashioned noir and snarky postmodernism, and from Barthelmean set pieces to a riff on Stonewall Jackson that evokes one of Barry Hannah's Civil War fever dreams." N Y Times Book Rev

Knight, Michael

The **typist**. Atlantic Monthly Press 2010 190p $20

ISBN 978-0-8021-1950-6; 0-8021-1950-6

"Throughout, the typist is a quietly eloquent observer, deeply touched but not directly involved in much of what he tells. When he brings his observations to bear on his own story, the effect is oddly distant but satisfying, a very credible measure of the space between the operatic and the more realistic portrayal of life's true dramas." Minneapolis Star Tribune

Knipfel, Jim

The **blow**-off. Simon & Schuster Paperbacks 2011 318p pa $15

ISBN 978-1-4391-5413-7; 1-4391-5413-9

LC 2010-50194

This novel "about a misanthropic crime reporter at a Brooklyn paper who accidentally sets off a wave of mass hysteria with an article about a local monster, is a weary, hilariously sardonic shake of the head at the media and the public's willingness, even outright desire, to get riled up over nothing in particular. There may or may not be a monster at the end of this book, but Knipfel's writing has quite a bite." Entertainment Wkly

Knode, Helen

The **ticket** out. Harcourt 2003 340p $24

ISBN 0-15-100184-7

LC 2002-7804

The morning after a party, film critic Ann Whitehead "discovers aspiring moviemaker Greta Stenholm in the bathtub, dead from knife wounds. Even though the knife used to kill Greta belongs to her, Ann's primary concern is using the story as her ticket out of the movie-reviewing business and into feature writing. Even as she patiently answers taciturn Detective Doug Lockwood's questions about the murder scene, she's busily hiding evidence. . . . Her increasingly intimate relationship with the complicated Lockwood is the high point in this very entertaining novel." Booklist

Knopf, Chris

Black swan. Permanent Press 2011 304p $28

ISBN 978-1-57962-216-9; 1-57962-216-X

LC 2011-03132

"Sam Acquillo, the likable beach bum hero in an erratic series by Chris Knopf, is nice to know when he's talking smart to his dog on the porch of his bayside cottage on the East End of Long Island or hanging with his fellow townies at a local bar in the off-season — and not taking himself too seriously as a hardboiled noir hero. But when heroism is thrust upon him . . . Sam is entitled to a bit of showing off. This he does when he and his girlfriend are delivering a sailboat to a friend and a fierce storm blows them to Fishers Island, where people are unfriendly and murder transpires. Knopf has mastered the verbal drill for tough guys in tight situations, and like Sam's nautical knowhow, his banter with

imperfect strangers is a cut above the norm. . . . This unexpected sail into danger makes for a stimulating story, providing Sam with a lot to tell the gang at the bar when he finally gets home." N Y Times Book Rev

Knopf, Chris

★ **Dead** anyway; Chris Knopf. The Permanent Press 2012 248 p. $28.00

ISBN 1579622836; 9781579622831

LC 2012016404

In this book, a hitman shoots Arthur Cathcart, leaving him for dead, after killing Mrs. Cathcart. When Cathcart awakes from the subsequent coma, he "succeeds, with the connivance of his physician sister, in having himself declared dead. As he begins the tortuous rehabilitation process and looks into establishing new identities, Cathcart realizes that it's almost impossible to go off the grid totally and still be able to function effectively, so he has to compromise in inventive ways." (Publishers Weekly)

Knopf, Chris

Hard stop. Permanent Press 2009 263p $28

ISBN 978-1-57962-183-4; 1-57962-183-X

LC 2008-51795

In this outing "corporate dropout-turned-carpenter/PI Sam Acquillo is forced to look for the missing girlfriend of his former boss, George Donovan. As Sam traces the successful young businesswoman to a house on Long Island shared with a bunch of Gen-Xers from Manhattan, he uncovers what looks like dirty business dealings. Knopf is very much a contemporary crime writer, revealing the dangers of the world of big deals, commercial espionage, and the barracudas hanging out for all they can get. For readers who enjoy hardboiled mysteries in the tradition of Raymond Chandler and Robert Parker." Libr J

Knopf, Chris

Head wounds. Permanent Press 2008 310p $28

ISBN 978-1-57962-165-0

LC 2008-2517

"Ex-boxer and former corporate exec Sam Acquillo, now a hard-drinking carpenter living in a rundown cottage on the shores of the Little Peconic Bay in Southampton, N.Y., becomes the prime suspect in the murder of local builder Robbie Milhouser. . . . With the evidence against him almost overwhelming, Acquillo enlists a misfit group of supporters to help him uncover the real killer's identity. As he digs into the dead man's troubled past, Acquillo discovers a disturbing link between Milhouser and Acquillo's current girlfriend, Amanda Battiston. Knopf excels in describing the rustic underpinnings of Long Island's east end, especially its vast array of eccentric characters." Publ Wkly

Knopf, Chris

The **last** refuge. Permanent Press 2005 287p $26

ISBN 1-57962-118-X

LC 2004-65314

"While [Sam's] low-key investigation is only minimally suspenseful, the characters he chats up are such original oddballs and their conversation so bracing that you want to kick off your shoes and spend some time on the porch with them, just taking in the view and enjoying the talk." N Y Times Book Rev

Knopf, Chris

Two time. Permanent Press 2006 261p $28; pa $18

ISBN 1-57962-129-5; 1-57962-164-3 pa

LC 2005-56564

At the start of this mystery, ex-boxer and retired engineer Sam Acquillo is "enjoying a drink with a lady friend at an East Hampton restaurant when a nearby car and its driver are firebombed out of existence. In the aftermath, Sam, assisted by his old buddy, retired cop Joe Sullivan, looks into who might have had it in for the victim, wealthy consultant Jonathan Eldridge. After talking to Eldridge's agoraphobic widow and suspicious-acting lawyer, Sam continues to investigate—and the more he pokes around the more data he turns up suggesting a complex deception involving financial transfers, angry clients who may or may not be Mafia-connected, the murdered man's estranged artist brother and out-of-it mother. A sly depiction of the east end of Long Island and the Hamptons as they really are, combined with strong plotting, solid characters and hardboiled dialogue worthy of Elmore Leonard or John D. MacDonald." Publ Wkly

Knowles, John

Peace breaks out. Holt, Rinehart & Winston 1981 193p

ISBN 0-03-056908-7

LC 80-19678

Set in the Devon School in New Hampshire, scene of A separate peace, this novel takes place during the 1945-46 term. "Pete Hallam—Class of '37—returning . . . as a teacher, hopes to recover there from wartime traumas. But the boys in the class of '46 are an edgy bunch, frustrated and guilty because they won't be graduating from the prep school to the armed forces like the classes before them. There's a simmering air of violence among them during the long winter as Pete in his low-keyed way tries to help them across the threshold to adulthood." Publ Wkly

Knowles, John

★ A **separate** peace; a novel. Macmillan 1960 186p

ISBN 0-02-564850-0

First published 1959 in the United Kingdom

"Gene Forrester looks back on his school days, spent in a New England town just before World War II. He both admires and envies his close friend and roommate, Finny, who is a natural athlete, in contrast to Gene's special competence as a scholar. When Finny suffers a crippling accident, Gene must face his own involvement in it." Shapiro. Fic for Youth. 3d edition

Knox, Elizabeth

Billie's kiss. Ballantine Bks. 2002 343p $24

ISBN 0-345-45052-3

A "romantic mystery set in 1903. Billie Paxton, an uneducated but perspicacious young woman, thinks the worst is over after a rough voyage on the Gustav Edda, a Swedish steamer that has taken her to the outer Scottish island of Kissack and Skilling, along with her pregnant sister, Edith, and her brother-in-law, Henry Maslen, a tutor who has accepted a position with the local squire, Lord Hallowhulme, at Kiss Castle. But just as the Gustav Edda is docking in port, an explosion shatters the hull, leaving Edith dead and Henry injured. An excellent swimmer, Billie immediately jumps off the stricken ship and scrambles to shore." Publ Wkly

Knox's "characters are unique and yet somehow familiar, in the sense that they are reminiscent of famous characters in Victorian literature." Booklist

Knox, Elizabeth

Daylight. Ballantine Bks. 2003 356p map $23.95

ISBN 0-345-45795-1

LC 2003-544868

"Saint or vampire? The identity of the Blessed Martine Raimondi, a French nun murdered by the Nazis in 1944 for her part in the daring cave escape of rebel partisans, is only one question answered in this illuminating tour-de-force set in the south of France. . . . Brian 'Bad' Phelan, a New South Wales bomb tech and expert 'caver' on paid injury leave, helps retrieve Martine's blistered corpse outside a cave near the Italian border and discovers she bears a shocking resemblance to a woman he'd encountered years before in another flooded cave. He's further struck by Martine's resemblance to Eve Moskelute, the subject of a painting by Jean Ares, her Picasso-esque deceased husband. The author constructs an impressive mystery that dissects the meaning of miracles while putting a fresh spin on the vampire archetype." Publ Wkly

Koch, Herman, 1953-

★ The **dinner**; a novel. Herman Koch; translated from the Dutch by Sam Garrett. Crown Publishers 2013 304 p. $24

ISBN 0770437850; 9780770437855

LC 2012025626

This book by Herman Koch, which won the Publieksprijs prize, "starts out as a witty look at contemporary manners . . . before turning into a take-no-prisoners psychological thriller. The Lohman brothers . . . meet at an expensive Amsterdam restaurant . . . to discuss a situation involving their respective 15-year-old sons, Michel and Rick. . . . During this five-course dinner, from aperitif to digestif, secrets come out that threaten relations between the two families." (Publishers Weekly)

"In a single setting, Koch successfully deploys multiple narratives of a single event to effectively show that our construction of history, and constant attempts at overdetermining the future, is problematic. A shocking, humorous, and entertaining novel." LJ

Koen, Karleen

Before Versailles. Crown 2011 xii, 460p

ISBN 9780307716576; 0307716570

LC 2010035562

The book offers a historical fiction of young King of France Louis XVI. "After the death of his prime minister, Cardinal Mazarin, twenty-two-year-old Louis steps into governing France. He's still a young man, but one who, as king, . . . takes everything he can get--including his brother's wife. As the love affair between Louis and Princess Henriette burns, it sets the kingdom on the road toward unmistakable scandal and conflict with the Vatican. . . . But there are other problems lurking outside the chateau of Fontainebleau: a boy in an iron mask has been seen in the woods, and the king's finance minister, Nicolas Fouquet, has proven to be more powerful than Louis ever thought--a man who could make a great ally or become a dangerous foe." (Publisher's note)

Koen, Karleen

Dark angels; a novel. Crown 2006 530p $25.95
ISBN 0-307-33991-2

LC 2005-30734

In this prequel to Through a glass darkly, the "central character is Alice Verney, former lady-in-waiting to Charles II's consort, Queen Catherine, then to the king's sister, Henrietta, married to the brother of France's Louis XIV. Upon Henrietta's mysterious death, Alice returns to England and begins her adventures, making certain not only to remain afloat but also to triumph in the commotion and excitement of the English royal court." Booklist

Koen, Karleen

Through a glass darkly. Random House 1986 743p

LC 86-422

"Expertly paced, the novel blends quaint historical romance with a sharp-edged, contemporary psychodramatic style. Its characters are memorable and full-bodied, maturing through a series of rapidly escalating tragedies that bring the sweetly naive heroine into full womanhood and force her to make a decision that will forever change her life. A sophisticated, atmospheric work." Booklist

Koestler, Arthur

★ **Darkness** at noon; translated by Daphne Hardy. Macmillan 1987 267p
ISBN 0-02-565210-9

LC 86-31273

First published 1940 in the United Kingdom; this is a reissue of the 1941 edition

This novel "deals with the arrest, imprisonment, trial, and execution of N. S. Rubashov in an unnamed dictatorship over which 'No. 1' presides. Koestler describes Rubashov as 'a synthesis of the lives of a number of men who were victims of the so-called Moscow trials,' and the novel did much to draw attention to the nature of Stalin's regime." Oxford Companion to Engl Lit. 6th edition

Kolpan, Gerald

Magic words; The Tale of a Jewish Boy-Interpreter, the Frontier's Most Estimable Magician, a Murderous Harlot, and America's Greatest Indian Chief. Gerald Kolpan. Pegasus Books 2012 400 p.
ISBN 1605983691; 9781605983691

In this novel, "young Julius Meyer comes to the New World to find himself acting as translator for the famed Indian chief Standing Bear. Young Jewish immigrant Julius comes of age surrounded by the wild world of 1867 Nebraska. He . . . [is] captured by the Ponca Indian tribe. . . . Julius meets the noble chief Standing Bear and his young daughter, Prairie Flower, with whom he falls in love. . . . [Then] his older cousin, Alexander—who, as the Great Herrmann, is

the most famous young magician in America [arrives]. . . . [Julius]does . . . [not] suspect the ultimate consequences of Alex's affair with Lady-Jane Little Feather. . . . [The book] is [an] . . . adventure about the nature of prejudice, the horror of genocide, and a courageous young man who straddles two worlds to fight for love and freedom." (Publisher's note)

Koontz, Dean R. (Dean Ray), 1945-

The **bad** place. Putnam 1990 382 p.
ISBN 9780399134982 out of print; 9780425195482

LC 89010861

"Married detectives Julie and Bobby Dakota agree to help frightened amnesiac Frank Pollard figure out what he does when he's asleep. . . . In due course, Frank and the Dakotas join forces against murderer Candy Pollard and his weird sisters, who want to kill Frank—evidently the sole human in the monstrous family. Candy extends psychic feelers toward potential victims, emanations that are sensed by Julie's younger brother Thomas. A Down's syndrome child, Thomas is telepathically gifted and able to warn Bobby of the demons who threaten Julie." Publ Wkly

Koontz, Dean R. (Dean Ray), 1945-

Brother Odd; [by] Dean Koontz. Bantam Books 2006 364p $27
ISBN 978-0-553-80480-5; 0-553-80480-4

LC 2006-32253

"Odd is the kind of instantly and persistently likable narrator that Fredric Brown used in such detective classics as the Ed and Am mysteries . . . though the pace of a Brown novel is relaxed in comparison. Also like Brown, Koontz employs dry, goofy humor, often in daring counterpoint to the story's spikes in tension and horror. Koontz also waxes as honorably sentimental as Ray Bradbury, and writes in breathy, two-line paragraphs, recalling the punchy manner of Robert Bloch. Obviously, then, this is a book worthy of any of the great three Bs of pop fiction." Booklist

Koontz, Dean R. (Dean Ray), 1945-

By the light of the moon; {by} Dean Koontz. Bantam Bks. 2002 431p $26.95
ISBN 0-553-80143-0

LC 2002-29902

The author "introduces readers to a twentysomething trio consisting of artist Dylan O'Conner, his autistic younger brother, Shep; and a stand-up comedienne named Jilly Jackson. One momentous evening, these threeunexpectedly find themselves coping with the bizarre effects of mysterious injections forced upon them by mad scientist Lincoln Proctor in an Arizona motel. With a generous helping of dark humor, Koontz quickly charges his characters with the task of harnessing their paranormal abilities as weapons against real-world violence and evil in a setting littered with present-day totems ranging from fast-food restaurants to sensation-mongering radio personalities." Libr J

Koontz, Dean R. (Dean Ray), 1945-

Dark rivers of the heart; a novel. {by} Dean Koontz. Knopf 1994 487p

LC 94-12090

"Koontz has succeeded where many genre writers have failed: he has switched gears, put the zombies and creepy crawlers aside, and written a believable high-tech thriller." N Y Times Book Rev

Koontz, Dean R. (Dean Ray), 1945-

The **darkest** evening of the year; [by] Dean Koontz. Bantam Books 2007 354p $27

ISBN 978-0-55380-482-9; 0-55380-482-0

LC 2007-40255

"Amy Redwing, the survivor of a horrifying marriage, establishes Golden Heart to rescue golden retrievers. . . . A supernatural chain of events ensues after Amy and her architect boyfriend, Brian McCarthy, rescue Nickie during a violent intervention in a family dispute. Soon the pair are on a mission that leads to a transformative confrontation with a number of ugly characters—Gunther Schloss, a frustrated aspiring novelist turned killer-for-hire; Moonglow, a psychobitch in the Mommie Dearest league; and Moonglow's lover, Harrow, a self-obsessed sicko. This is the perfect book for thriller addicts who know the darkest hour is just before dawn and for canine lovers who remember 'dog' spelled backwards is 'god.'" Publ Wkly

Koontz, Dean R. (Dean Ray), 1945-

The **face**; [by] Dean Koontz. Bantam Bks. 2003 608p $26.95

ISBN 0-553-80248-8

LC 2003-40354

"The eponymous Face is the world's biggest movie star; he doesn't appear in the novel, but his smart, geeky 10-year-old-son, Fric, takes center stage, as does Ethan Truman, cop-turned-security chief of the Face's elaborate estate and Fric's main human protector when one Corky Laputa, who's dedicated his life to anarchy, decides to sow further disorderby kidnapping this progeny of the world's idol. . . . Koontz's characters are memorable and his unique mix of suspense and humor absorbing." Publ Wkly

Koontz, Dean R. (Dean Ray), 1945-

False memory; [by] Dean Koontz. Bantam Bks. 2000 627p

ISBN 0-553-10666-X

LC 99-54782

"The heroes are Southern Californians Dusty and Martie Rhodes, he a housepainting contractor, she a computer game designer. . . . As Martie shepherds her terrified, agoraphobic friend, Susan, on a visit to Susan's shrink (Ahriman), Dusty deals with his drug-addled stepbrother/employee, Skeet, about to jump to his death from the roof of Dusty's latest project. Skeet leaps, taking Dusty with him, but both survive; as Dusty checks Skeet into rehab, Martie suffers her first of several horrific phobic episodes, in which she imagines mutilating Dusty with household items. Seeking help, she and Dusty turn to Ahriman, who, it's eventually revealed first to the reader, then to the couple, is responsible for all the trouble. . . . An expertly crafted, ornate suspenser." Publ Wkly

Koontz, Dean R. (Dean Ray), 1945-

Fear nothing; by Dean Koontz. Bantam Bks. 1998 391p

LC 97-41129

"Tale of one night in the California coastal town of Moonlight Bay as experienced by Chris Snow. Saddled with a genetic defect that makes direct sunlight toxic to him, Snow is a nocturnal creature whose father has just died. When he discovers that his father's corpse has been stolen, he begins pursuit. Koontz expertly illuminates Snow's nocturnal world and friends, and incrementally, cleverly, the crises erupting in Moonlight Bay take shape. The plot is wonderfully unpredictable, and though the surfer slang wears thin after a while, the narrative remains taut." Libr J

Followed by Seize the night

Koontz, Dean R. (Dean Ray), 1945-

From the corner of his eye; [by] Dean Koontz. Bantam Bks. 2001 622p

ISBN 0-553-80134-1

LC 00-48619

"The large cast of characters, particularly the fully developed main players, is richly imagined. The plot is suspenseful and complex. Informing the novel throughout is a fascinating theory that involves quantum mechanics, faith, and human relationships." Voice Youth Advocates

Koontz, Dean R. (Dean Ray), 1945-

The **husband**; [by] Dean Koontz. Bantam Books 2006 400p $27.95

ISBN 978-0-553-80479-9; 0-553-80479-0

LC 2006-42696

"Koontz focuses relentlessly on Mitch and, in chapters scattered judiciously throughout the latter 230 pages, Holly. Not for him the flirtation with evil thinking that an Elmore Leonard does so well or the temptation to sympathize with evildoers that an Alfred Hitchcock offers. And yet Koontz is no less an artist for his championing of the good and his determination to have readers identify with it, as this hair-raising thriller attests." Booklist

Koontz, Dean R. (Dean Ray), 1945-

★ **Intensity**; a novel. by Dean Koontz. Knopf 1995 307p

ISBN 0-679-42525-X

LC 95-33591

"The velocity of the plot is the book's true pleasure; the story does not move so much as rocket up the portentously gloomy highway with the reader in violent pursuit." N Y Times Book Rev

Koontz, Dean R. (Dean Ray), 1945-

Lightning. Putnam 1988 351p

ISBN 9780425192030; 9781442080324; 9780399133190 out of print

LC 87021649

"On the night of Laura Shane's birth, a stranger appears from the lightning to prevent her delivery's being botched by an alcoholic physician. Throughout Laura's childhood the stranger reappears at times of danger. He protects rather than threatens, yet menace seems to follow him. Thirty years later another storm flashes and the stranger collapses, shot, at Laura's door. Now Laura protects her erst-while guardian from mysterious hunters. He reveals that he and the hunters are time travelers. Laura, quick-witted and brave, leads the way to a bloody showdown." Libr J

Koontz, Dean R. (Dean Ray), 1945-
Odd apocalypse; an Odd Thomas novel. Dean Koontz. Bantam Books 2012 355 p.
ISBN 0553807749; 9780345533586; 9780553807745
LC 2012013275
In this novel by Dean Koontz "the magnificent West Coast property known as Roseland is now home to a reclusive billionaire financier and his faithful servants. And, at least for the moment, it's also a port in the storm for Odd Thomas and his traveling companion, the inscrutably charming Annamaria, the Lady of the Bell. . . . But there's far more to Roseland than meets even the extraordinary eye of Odd, who soon suspects it may be more hell than haven." (Publisher's note)

Koontz, Dean R. (Dean Ray), 1945-
One door away from heaven; [by] Dean Koontz. Bantam Bks. 2001 606p
ISBN 0-553-80137-6
LC 2001-49952
The "story coalesces from two converging subplots steeped in the weirdness of fringe ufology: in one, loser Michelina Bellsong struggles to save crippled nine-year-old Leilani Klonk from an evil stepdad planning to pass off her imminent disposal as a benevolent alien abduction; in the other, a strange boy who goes by the alias Curtis Hammond is the quarry of two cross-country manhunts, one led by the FBI and the other by mass murderers who, like the messianic Curtis, may not be what they seem. En route to a pyrotechnic finale in rural Idaho, Koontz shoots bull's-eyes at target issues that shape his theme, including assisted suicide, substance abuse, the irresponsibility of the counterculture and the goofiness of true-believer ET enthusiasts." Publ Wkly

Koontz, Dean R. (Dean Ray), 1945-
Relentless; a novel. [by] Dean Koontz. Bantam Books 2009 356p $27
ISBN 978-0-553-80714-1; 0-553-80714-5
LC 2009-09866
"'Cubby' Greenwich is a bestselling novelist with a new book out and reviews hitting the stands. When he's eviscerated by renowned critic Shearman Waxx in a review full of errors, he can't help but wonder at the man behind the critique, the inaccuracies, and the poor syntax. Following one relatively harmless run-in at a local restaurant, Cubby and his family (wife and fellow author Penny, six-year-old son and off-the-charts genius son 'Spooky' Milo, and similarly spooky dog Lassie) are exposed to terrors beyond metaphorical slaying. Shearman Waxx is a man bent on destroying not merely Cubby's book sales but the man and his family. . . . This is an exquisite crafting of the thrilling, the unexplainable, and the personal." Libr J

Koontz, Dean R. (Dean Ray), 1945-
Seize the night; by Dean Koontz. Bantam Bks. 1999 401p
ISBN 0-553-10665-1
LC 98-31410
In this second novel featuring Christopher Snow, "the horrifying tale of Chris's hometown, Moonlight Bay, continues to unfold. Chris and his tight band of friends take up the search for four missing children in this town, where experi-ments with a genetically engineered retrovirus have begun to turn several local residents into creatures that are less than human. Koontz successfully blends his special brand of suspense from generous measures of mystery, horror, sf, and the techno-thriller genre. But his greatest triumph in this series is the creation of Christopher Snow, a thought-provoking narrator with a facility for surfer-lingo and dark humor who, despite his extreme situation, is an undeniably believable character." Libr J

Koontz, Dean R. (Dean Ray), 1945-
Strangers. Putnam 1986 526p
LC 85-25677
"Eight characters—all strangers to each other—form the core of the novel. Each is plagued by suspiciously similar fears and anxieties. Ernie Block, who runs a Nevada motel, fears the dark. Ginger Weiss, a Boston cardiology resident, suffers from panic attacks. Southern California horror novelist Dom Corvaisis is vexed with somnambulism. These and other seemingly disparate characters share only one link aside from their bewildering array of related symptoms—all had spent three days during the previous July at Block's motel, not far from a secret military depository." Booklist

Koontz, Dean R. (Dean Ray), 1945-
The taking; [by] Dean Koontz. Bantam Bks. 2004 388p $27
ISBN 0-553-80250-X
"In a small California town, Molly and Neil Sloan wake in the night to find the world experiencing the communication breakdown and extreme weather phenomena that will presage an extraterrestrial annexation of Earth. Along with the assistance of some intelligent and intuitive dogs . . . , Molly and Neil try to save as many children as they can from being 'taken' or killed outright. In The Taking, Koontz continues his ongoing exploration of the capacity of human nature for hope, goodness, and innocence in the face of evil." Libr J

Koontz, Dean R. (Dean Ray), 1945-
Velocity; [by] Dean Koontz. Bantam Books 2005 400p $27
ISBN 0-55380-415-4
"Billy Wiles, a 30-something bartender and former writer, is content with his solitary Napa County existence listening to 'beer-based psychoanalysis' from tavern regulars; visiting his hospitalized, comatose fiancée, Barbara; and carving wood sculptures. But the simple life gets mighty complicated when he finds a note with a deadly, time-sensitive ultimatum: he must choose between the death of a young schoolteacher or an elderly humanitarian in six hours. Reluctant local sheriff Lanny Olsen dismisses it as a joke until a comely teacher is found strangled and another threatening note appears—offering even less time for Billy to decide the fate of two more people. Who would have guessed that one of those people would be Olsen? After his friend's murder, Billy finds that the cunning killer has gained access to every aspect of his life as the ultimatums grow increasingly more personal. . . . Graphic, fast-paced action, well-developed characters and relentless, nail-biting scenes show Koontz at the top of his game." Publ Wkly

Koontz, Dean R. (Dean Ray), 1945-

Watchers. Putnam 1987 352p hardcover o.p. pa $7.99

ISBN 0-399-13263-5; 0-425-18880-9 pa

LC 86-22687

"When the Russians sabotage a genetic research project in California, two mutated creatures escape from the lab. One is a golden retriever with high enough intelligence to think and communicate with humans; the other is the Outsider, a vicious monster created from a baboon and bred to kill. Both the man who befriends and adopts the dog and his new bride find themselves stalked by government agents anxious to find the dog, a particularly repulsive Mafia hit man intent on stealing him, and the Outsider, with whom the dog is linked telepathically." Libr J

Korda, Michael

Curtain; a novel. Summit Bks. 1991 378p

LC 90-23198

"Robert Vance is a superb Shakespearean actor. He falls in love with an actress, Felicia Lisle, whose fastidious beauty conceals fierce passion. Unable to escape their marriages, they become Britain's favorite adulterous celebrity couple, playing the role of lovers both on stage and in private. Korda opens this page-turner with a prologue set 40 years in the future and hinting at dark, long-hidden secrets. He then flashes back to the 1940s when Vance and Felicia are stranded in Hollywood, broke after a disastrous attempt at taking Romeo and Juliet on the road in the U.S. Felicia, drinking and pill-popping, is on the verge of a breakdown, and Robby is anxious to return to London and serve in the RAF. . . . Having set his novel on stage, Korda can pull out all the stops—nothing is too theatrical. And it's a hit." Booklist

Korda, Michael

The **fortune**. Summit Bks. 1989 481p

LC 88-37980

"The wealthy, snobbish Bannerman family is a fictional hybrid of the Rockefellers and the Binghams. It's bad enough that Arthur Bannerman has the poor taste to die in the bed of an attractive young woman. But when she declares herself his widow and delivers a will giving her control of the family fortune, his son Robert and the redoubtable matriarch Eleanor haul out the heavy artillery. Korda has a wonderful ear for bitchy, brittle society chatter, and he takes satirical swipes in every direction." Publ Wkly

Korda, Michael

The **immortals**; a novel. Poseidon Press 1992 559p

ISBN 0-671-74526-3

LC 92-22265

A "novel about the love affair between John F. Kennedy and Marilyn Monroe. The theme it rests on is this: as JFK's star ascended, MM's descended, and as their stars crossed, heat was definitely generated. Korda understands politics as well as fatal attraction, so his fiction is several notches above your basic steamy romance." Booklist

Korda, Michael

Worldly goods. Random House 1982 353p

LC 81-40213

"At once a Holocaust novel from a new point of view, and a look at love, hate, power, and sex in the stratosphere of the modern corporation, this book is tightly constructed." Libr J

Koryta, Michael

The **Cypress** House. Little, Brown and Co. 2011 426p $24.99

ISBN 978-0-316-05372-3; 0-316-05372-4

LC 2010-11405

"Though Koryta's evocation of the Depression could be stronger, the novel builds to a richly satisfying climax in which Arlen is guided by the spirit of his father and voices of the recently departed. A commanding performance in the field of supernatural noir." Kirkus

Includes bibliographical references

Koryta, Michael

★ The **prophet**; Michael Koryta. Little, Brown and Co. 2012 416 p. $25.99

ISBN 0316122610; 9780316122610

LC 2012014690

In this book, "Adam Austin, a . . . bail bondsman and sometime private investigator in the small town of Chambers, Ohio, has never gotten past the guilt of letting his little sister Marie walk home from a football game alone" which led to her murder. "After Adam unknowingly sends a 17-year-old client to her death by telling her where she can find a letter-writing ex-con she thinks is her father, the past eerily collides with the present." (Kirkus)

Koryta, Michael

The **ridge**; Michael Koryta. Little, Brown and Co. 2011 357p. $24.99

ISBN 978-0-316-05366-2; 031605366X

LC 201111377

"In an isolated stretch of eastern Kentucky, on a hilltop known as Blade Ridge, stands a lighthouse that illuminates nothing but the surrounding woods. For years the lighthouse has been considered no more than an eccentric local landmark—until its builder is found dead. . . . For deputy sheriff Kevin Kimble, the lighthouse-keeper's death is disturbing. . . . Audrey Clark is in the midst of moving her large-cat sanctuary onto land adjacent to the lighthouse. . . . Her husband, the sanctuary's founder, died scouting the new property. . . . As strange occurrences multiply at the Ridge, the animals grow ever more restless, and Kimble and Audrey try to understand what evil forces are moving through this ancient landscape." (Publisher's note)

"When local drunk Wyatt French, who inexplicably built a wooden lighthouse far from any large body of water, calls Kevin Kimble, the county's chief deputy, and asks whether he'd investigate a suicide, Kimble, who's driving in his car to visit a prison inmate, refers French to a suicide hotline. Soon after, reporter Roy Darmus, whose newspaper has just folded, receives an unsettling call from French that prompts Darmus to go to the lighthouse, where he finds the man has apparently shot himself in the mouth. French's death may be connected with an eerie blue light seen in the vicinity of Blade Ridge, a phenomenon that riles the big cats residing in a wildlife refuge that's just set up shop on property adjoining French's. Koryta . . . matches an original and complex plot line with prose full of understated menace." Publ Wkly

Koryta, Michael

The **silent** hour. Minotaur Books 2009 311p $24.95

ISBN 978-0-312-36157-0; 0-312-36157-2

LC 2009-10485

When Cleveland, Ohio, PI Lincoln Perry "starts receiving letters from convicted murder Parker Harrison, he ignores them until the man shows up in his office. Twelve years earlier, the then recently paroled Harrison worked for Alexandra and Joshua Cantrell, a couple who ran a rehabilitation program for violent offenders. Then they disappeared, and Harrison wants Perry's help in tracking down Alexandra. Suspicious why Perry waited so long, Perry discovers that Joshua's bones were recently unearthed in Pennsylvania. Ken Merriman, a Pittsburgh PI, soon arrives in Cleveland, asking Perry for help finding out who killed Joshua." Publ Wkly

"Koryta writes with maturity and grace, delivering clipped, crisp prose and crackling suspense." Booklist

Koryta, Michael

So cold the river. Little, Brown and Co. 2010 508p $24.99

ISBN 9780316053631; 0-316-05363-5

LC 2009-32414

"Koryta spins a spellbinding tale of an unholy lust for power that reaches from beyond the grave and suspends disbelief through the believable interactions of fully developed characters. A cataclysmic finale will put readers in mind of some of the best recent works of supernatural horror, among which this book ranks." Publ Wkly

Koryta, Michael

Tonight I said goodbye; Michael Koryta. 1st ed; Thomas Dunne Books\St. Martin's Minotaur 2004 290p $21.95

ISBN 0-312-33245-9

LC 2004-46781

"The Cleveland police would charge private investigator Wayne Weston with murdering his wife and daughter except that their bodies can't be found and he's dead, apparently a suicide. Weston's father isn't buying it, however, and he hires private investigators Lincoln Perry and Joe Pritchard to clear his son's name and find his family. Perry is a former cop whose cheating ex-fiancée set him off on a bender that cost him his job. Pritchard, his old partner, is ready to retire and become what all retired cops become, a P.I. The hardboiled cliché works beautifully here as these two men find themselves chasing Russian Mafiya, a real estate mogul, and an ex-Marine while dodging bullets, cops, and the FBI. The Cleveland setting is a nice change from the usual East Coast/West Coast locales." Libr J

Kosinski, Jerzy N.

★ Being there; [by] Jerzy Kosinski. Harcourt Brace Jovanovich 1971 142p

ISBN 0-15-111700-4

"An illiterate gardener, Chance, knows the world only through his gardening and by watching television, to which he is addicted. Without education or any identifiable background, he is evicted into the outside world when his employer dies. He makes horticultural analogies to current events, which give him a reputation for wisdom that he really does not have, and which catapult him into national prominence. Chance's simple statements are interpreted by his listeners to be profound observations, and we see him being considered for positions of great importance. This is a satire on human behavior in the worlds of power, government, and the media." Shapiro. Fic for Youth. 3d edition

Kosinski, Jerzy N.

The **devil** tree; {by} Jerzy Kosinski. Harcourt Brace Jovanovich 1973 208p

This novel "confronts the disintegration of the American dream as seen through the eyes of Jonathan James Whalen, the man-who-has-everything. For Whalen and many of the people who surround him, the American dream has become the American nightmare. Their efforts to escape their roots become a frenetic search to find their roots, until, like the devil tree, they get turned upside down and confirm the fact of their own extinction. Jonathan Whalen is as empty as the life he leads, although on the surface he is a man who can be and do anything he wants." Publ Wkly

Kosinski, Jerzy N.

★ The **painted** bird; [by] Jerzy Kosinski. 2nd Modern Library ed; Modern Lib. 1983 234p

ISBN 0-394-60433-4

LC 82-42869

First published 1965 by Houghton Mifflin

"In Eastern Europe during World War II a ten-year-old boy is separated from his parents and struggles to survive in primitive villages where he is viewed as an unwanted outsider. Dark-haired and dark-eyed, he is unlike the Polish villagers among whom he tries to find refuge. He is the gypsy, the 'painted bird,' and savage abuse is heaped upon him time after time. He has, nevertheless, the will to transcend the sadism and superstition of these ignorant people." Shapiro. Fic for Youth. 3d edition

Kosmatka, Ted

★ The **games**; Ted Kosmatka. Del Rey 2012 360 p. (hardback) $25

ISBN 9780345526618; 9780345526632

LC 2011042718

In this science fiction novel, a "new gladiatorial contest between genetically engineered monsters has proven to be a popular Olympic sport. For this year's games, the U.S. Olympic Committee (USOC) uses its most sophisticated AI computer to design the latest combatant. . . . Despite disturbing signs that the program's reclusive creator is losing touch with reality, the USOC clears Felix for competition. The stage is set for a catastrophic finale, with international repercussions." (Library Journal)

Kostova, Elizabeth

★ The **historian**; a novel. Little, Brown and Co 2005 642p $25.95

ISBN 0-316-01177-0

LC 2004-22563

"Kostova's vampire is no campy Lugosi knockoff but a blend of the cunning, powerful count who debuts in Bram Stoker's 1897 classic novel and the actual Dracula, Vlad the Impaler, a 15th-century Romanian prince who was both a nationalist hero and a sadistic torturer. Blending history and myth, Kostova has fashioned a version so fresh that when a stake is finally driven through a heart, it inspires the tragic shock of something happening for the very first time." Newsweek

Kostova, Elizabeth

The **swan** thieves; a novel. Little, Brown and Co. 2009 564p $26.99

    ISBN 978-0-316-06578-8; 0-316-06578-1

                                LC 2009-31954

"The troubled, enigmatic artist about whom [Kostova] writes in The Swan Thieves is Robert Oliver, whose story begins with his confinement at a sanitarium after he attempts to slash a 19th-century painting of Leda, the mortal ravished by Zeus, who comes to her in the form of a swan. Psychiatrist Andrew Marlow, himself a painter, can't get Oliver to talk about the incident or anything else. Determined to unlock the mystery of Oliver's motivations, Marlow seeks out Oliver's ex-wife, Kate, and his ex-lover Mary, and investigates a mysterious trove of 19th-century letters that Oliver reads repeatedly. Through these sources, Marlow pieces together Oliver's story. There's much to like in The Swan Thieves. Kostova's painterly descriptions of artwork are luscious. . . . And the 19th-century love story which runs parallel to Oliver's story is exquisitely told." USA Today

Kotzwinkle, William

The **bear** went over the mountain. Doubleday 1996 306p

    ISBN 0-385-48428-3

                                LC 96-2296

"Kotzwinkle has imagined a disconsolate Maine professor, Arthur Bramhall, who sets out to write a bestseller, only to have a bear steal it, thinking it's something to eat. This is no ordinary bear, however; he has aspirations to becoming a person. . . . What better way to establish an identity than by becoming a celebrity novelist? Soon, the bear has found a pseudonym, Hal Jam, an agent and a publisher. With his distinctively masculine presence, and a monosyllabic way of talking that reminds many of Hemingway, he's on his way to stardom with a novel that everyone agrees has its roots deep in the natural world." Publ Wkly

"This genuine parable for our time is as full of truth as it is of humor." Nation

Kotzwinkle, William

E.T. the extra-terrestrial; a novel. Putnam 1982 246p

    ISBN 9789501501025; 9780399127304

                                LC 82009078

"A ten million year old alien botanist is accidentally marooned on Earth. He is befriended by three children and in particular by Elliott, whose bedroom closet becomes his hideout. With their help he learns something of our planet's bewildering ways, puts together a beacon to call for rescue and thrives on a diet of M&Ms, Oreos and, even more important, the children's love. Of course, the government suspects his presence and is hunting him, but after he is captured Elliott helps him escape in time to rendezvous with his ship." Publ Wkly

Kowal, Mary Robinette

Shades of milk and honey. Tor 2010 304p $24.99

    ISBN 978-0-7653-2556-3; 0-7653-2556-X

                                LC 2010-32725

"A tale of romance in Regency England with just a sprinkling of fantasy. . . . In the Ellsworth family, it is pretty and flirtatious Melodie who attracts the most attention from would-be suitors, but her older sister Jane is the one who knows how to work magic. Able to pull 'glamour' out of the ether and create intricate tableaux that trick the eye and delight the mind, Jane yearns for true love but believes herself to be too old and too plain to catch any bachelor's eye. While two eligible young men, Captain Livingston and Mr. Dunkirk, hover around Melodie, Jane finds herself intrigued by the older, taciturn and somewhat sullen Mr. Vincent, a professional glamourist creating a complicated mural at a neighboring estate. When Melodie's dalliances threaten to stain the Ellsworths' honor, it is up to Jane to set things right, perhaps at the expense of her own happiness. . . . A low-key and witty debut novel, one that succeeds through understated humor and sprightly prose, rather than through absurd juxtapositions of the historical and the supernatural." San Francisco Chron

Kowal, Mary Robinette

Without a summer; Mary Robinette Kowal. 1st ed. Tor 2013 368 p. (hardcover) $24.99

    ISBN 0765334151; 9780765334152

                                LC 2012043342

This is the third book in Mary Robinette Kowal's Glamorist Histories. Here, Sir David and Lady Jane Vincent "invite Melody, Jane's younger sister, to join them [in London], hoping to brighten her mood and provide better opportunities for making a good match. But the couple must also fend off demands from Vincent's estranged family, protect misunderstood coldmongers, determine the truth from lies told, and still work their artistry." (Library Journal)

Kowalski, David

The **company** of the dead; David J. Kowalski. Titan Books 2012 752 p. map (pbk.) $15.95

    ISBN 0857686666; 9780857686664; 9780857686671

                                LC 2012376486

In this work of speculative fiction, set "[i]n a very different 2012, Joseph Kennedy, a major in the Confederate army, must play the German and Japanese empires off against each other, as well as the Union and Confederate governments, to save the world from meddling time travelers who could bring about humanity's extinction." (Publishers Weekly)

Kowalski, William

Something noble; William Kowalski. Orca Book Pub 2012 128 p. (paperback) $9.95; (ebook) $9.99; (ebook) $9.99

    ISBN 1459800133; 9781459800137; 9781459800144 (pdf); 9781459800151 (epub)

                                LC 2011943697

In this book, "Linda was a teenage mother, and now" her high school-age son Dre has kidney failure and "needs a donor." She is not a match, and his incarcerated biological father "cannot be a donor due to his habitual drug use.

Surprisingly enough, Linda discovers that Dre has a half-brother with the correct blood type for a donor kidney. Linda is able to reach out to Levon, and the two brothers discover in a short time the meaning of nobility." (Voice of Youth Advocates)

Krantz, Judith

Mistral's daughter. Crown 1983 531p
ISBN 0-517-54906-9

LC 82-17966

"Three generations of Lunel women are intimately involved with Julien Mistral, France's greatest artist. Maggy is his model, the inspiration for a series of remarkable nude paintings in 1925, and he is her first lover. Years later Teddy, star of her mother Maggy's New York modeling agency, meets Mistral on assignment and lightening strikes; she becomes his mistress and the mother of Fauve. And Mistral's daughter Fauve, though an 'enfante adulterine,' has some of his talent and brightens his life before their estrangement." Libr J

The author "possesses an undeniable talent for plot-weaving and descriptive detail." Best Sellers

Krauss, Nicole

Great house. W. W. Norton & Co. 2010 289p $24.95
ISBN 978-0-393-07998-2; 0-393-07998-8

LC 2010-29946

Connected solely by a desk of enormous dimension and many drawers that exerts a power over those who possess it or give it away, three people-a lonely American novelist clinging to the memory of a poet who has mysteriously vanished in Chile, an old man in Israel facing the imminent death of his wife of 51 years, and an esteemed antiques dealer tracking down the things stolen from his father by the Nazis-struggle to create a meaningful permanence in the face of inevitable loss.

"For most of the novel, it's unclear what the desk represents or whether the book's far-flung characters will ever meet. But Krauss has a unique way of assembling novels—baroque, complex, and with a stunning tidiness that isn't clear until the very last page. All the parts do fit together in the end. The shape they form is a ghostly Great House, and its walls are ideas that leave the reader reverberating." Atlantic

Krauss, Nicole

The **history** of love. Norton 2005 252p $23.95
ISBN 0-393-06034-9

LC 2005-00936

"Beyond the vigorous whiplash that keeps Ms. Krauss's [book] moving (and keeps its reader off-balance until a stunning finale), this novel is tightly packed with ingenious asides. They range from parodying various publications' characteristic obituaries of a very famous writer, a man who was best known for a single, ecstatic five-page paragraph (Ms. Krauss perfectly mimics the syntax of both The Times and The New Republic) to skewering the kind of editor whom all writers dread." N Y Times (Late N Y Ed)

Krauss, Nicole

Man walks into a room. Talese 2002 248p
ISBN 0-385-50399-7

LC 2001-53699

"When a tumor in his brain is discovered and removed, Samson Greene, an English professor in his thirties, finds himself afflicted by a peculiar kind of amnesia: he cannot remember anything that happened after he was twelve. Even as he struggles to connect with his wife, Anna, he thinks that he might prefer the blankness of his new life. Samson's loss takes place against a backdrop of secret experiments on human memory and the social implications of atomic testing, but it is his shadow-filled scrutiny of intimacy—as he wonders why he might have married this beautiful stranger, and whether he can love her—that is the book's real strength." New Yorker

Krentz, Jayne Ann

Dream eyes; Jayne Ann Krentz. G. P. Putnam's Sons 2013 336 p. $26.95
ISBN 0399158952; 9780399158957

LC 2012027313

This book is Jayne Ann Krentz's sequel to "Copper Beach." "When Gwen Frazier returns to Wilby, Ore., to investigate the death of her mentor, she knows she's opening up psychic wounds she'd rather forget, and when her best friend sends in investigator Judson Coppersmith to help, she realizes she's met her match, romantically and psychically. Will their attraction, skills and talent be enough, in time, to solve the mystery and save them both?" (Kirkus)

Krentz, Jayne Ann

Lost and found. Putnam 2001 341p
ISBN 0-399-14669-5

LC 00-44563

"Cady Briggs, a Santa Barbara-based art consultant specializing in decorative arts and antiques, has been doing some work for Mack Easton, who runs a company called Lost and Found that tracks the movement of art and antiquities. When her eccentric aunt Vesta, an excellent swimmer, drowns, Cady has a hunch that something isn't right, especially since Vesta left controlling shares of Chatelaine, her tony art gallery, to her instead of to cousin Sylvia, Chatelaine's much more business-oriented CEO.... Cady enlists Mack to help uncover the truth." Booklist

"This is romantic suspense at its most enjoyable, enhanced by Krentz's . . . trademark humor and quirky characters." Libr J

Krentz, Jayne Ann

Running hot. G.P. Putnam's Sons 2008 337p $25.95
ISBN 978-0-399-15521-5; 0-399-15521-X

LC 2008-28340

Reluctantly paired for a murder investigation by the paranormal Arcane Society, former cop Luther Malone and aura-reading librarian Grace Renquist find their mutual disgust dissolving into a powerful attraction, during a case that is further complicated by operatives for a ruthless underground psychic group.

"This arresting tale combines witty humor with clever plotting to weave an exceptionally memorable romance." Libr J

Krentz, Jayne Ann

Smoke in mirrors. Putnam 2002 320p $23.95

ISBN 0-399-14792-6

LC 2001-19361

"The politics of academe, eerie antique mirrors, secret passages, and psychic contact contribute a haunting quality to Krentz's enticing blend of suspense and top-notch romance." Booklist

Krentz, Jayne Ann

White lies; Jayne Ann Krentz. G. P. Putnam's Sons 2007 371p o.p.; o.p.; (pbk.) $9.99

ISBN 039915373X; 9780399153730; 9780515143997

LC 2006044829

This book follows "Clare Lancaster, . . . a member of the clandestine Arcane Society, an association of parasensitives who are dedicated to the study of the paranormal. Clare's . . . abilities as a human lie detector make even other paranormals uneasy, with the exception of her half-sister Elizabeth. Elizabeth's troubled marriage brings Clare to Arizona. . . . There, Clare finally meets Archer Glazebrook, her biological father, but she also meets Jake Salter, another highly talented parasensitive who turns out to be on assignment . . . to track down a possible plot to take over the society. The cabal he's after has some connection to the still-unsolved murder of Clare's . . . brother-in-law months before. More murders follow, and Jake and Clare have to work together to save themselves and the society." (Publishers Weekly)

Kress, Nancy

After the Fall, Before the Fall, During the Fall. Independent Pub Group 2012 189 p. (paperback) $14.95

ISBN 1616960655; 9781616960650

In this novel from Nebula- and Hugo-winner Nancy Kress, teenager "Pete makes brief runs back in time from the . . . year 2035, using alien technology that can only transport children, to pick up fresh supplies and recruits. Julie, a mathematician in 2013, finds a pattern in a series of kidnappings. They are . . . Pete's expeditions, and as the two head towards their inevitable collision, the clock ticks down on the catastrophe that will turn Julie's orderly world into Pete's devastated landscape." (Publishers Weekly)

Kress, Nancy

Beggars & choosers. TOR Bks. 1994 315p

ISBN 0-312-85749-7

LC 94-21753

Sequel to Beggars in Spain

"Kress's work remains strongly character driven, an approach that in her hands raises social-speculation sf to about as high a level as one can reasonably expect." Booklist

Followed by Beggars ride

Kress, Nancy

Beggars in Spain. Morrow 1993 438p

LC 92-25070

Based on a novella of the same title

"This book is an intellectual roller-coaster ride, supplying no simple conclusions about right and wrong, and racing along with its brisk prose, stimulating ideas, and a variety of challenging characters." SLJ

Followed by Beggars & choosers

Kress, Nancy

Beggars ride. TOR Bks. 1996 304p

ISBN 0-312-85817-5

LC 96-19956

In this concluding volume of the Beggars trilogy, "the near-utopia that the genetically altered Sleepless finally realized is . . . well on the way to crumbling under the onslaught of warfare waged with tailored viruses. Society is devolving into a host of subgroups, some of which are virtually abandoning technology and surviving or failing as much through luck as through resistance to the viruses. Gradually, communication among tribes is restored, lost knowledge regained, disused knowledge again put to use, and the survival of the race assured." Booklist

"The scale of Kress's vision is large as she lays out a drama that—convincingly if unsurprisingly—argues that moral quandaries can't be addressed by technology." Publ Wkly

Kress, Nancy

Dogs; a novel. Tachyon Publications 2008 280p pa $14.95

ISBN 978-1-892391-78-0; 1-892391-78-3

"Tired of being passed over for promotion and suspecting that her recently deceased Tunisian husband is the cause, Tessa Sanderson leaves the FBI and relocates to the small town of Tyler, MD. Trouble follows her, however, in the form of a mysterious and sudden canine plague that heightens the aggression of its victims, causing them to attack anyone in their path-even their beloved owners. A series of threatening emails implicating Tessa in a terrorist plot connected with the plague causes her to turn fugitive in order to track down the perpetrators of the illness and restore the good name of both herself and her husband." Libr J

"The best scenes . . . have a straight-ahead, disaster novel feel to them, full of suspense and creepy details." San Francisco Chron

Kress, Nancy

Probability moon. TOR Bks. 2000 334p $23.95

ISBN 0-312-87406-5

LC 00-27117

"The climax of the book is a four-way conflict among the scientists, the two alien races, and the scientists' military superiors, each charging from a different corner, so to speak. Kress' characterizations are as sound as ever, but many will be agreeably surprised at her proficiency with military hardware and action scenes. Very impressive." Booklist

Kress, Nancy

Probability sun. TOR Bks. 2001 348p $24.95

ISBN 0-312-87407-3

LC 2001-27119

This sequel to Probability moon "continues humanity's war against the alien Fallers, a war humanity is losing. It again shows scientists and the military at odds if not in outright conflict while portraying the strengths and limitations of both with admirable even-handedness. A shipload of scientists has come to study the alien artifact discovered on the planet World, and the ship's military crew is holding the only Faller POW as a secret captive." Booklist

LIST OF FICTIONAL WORKS

Kress, Nancy

Steal across the sky. Tor 2009 317p il $25.95

ISBN 978-0-7653-1986-9; 0-7653-1986-1

LC 2008-46432

"Aliens calling themselves the Atoners have confessed to committing crimes against the human race thousands of years ago and have recruited a few individuals to travel to select worlds to 'Witness' what they have done. Kress . . . . once again demonstrates her absolute mastery of alien-human encounters, fleshing out her characters as believable individuals while at the same time managing surprising plot twists and philosophical conundrums at every turn." Libr J

Kricorian, Nancy

All the Light There Was; A Novel. Nancy Kricorian. Houghton Mifflin Harcourt 2013 288 p. (hardcover) $24.00

ISBN 0547939949; 9780547939940

LC 2012040359

This book presents "the story of an Armenian family's struggle to survive the Nazi occupation of Paris in the 1940s. . . . Like many . . . who survived the genocide in their homeland, they have come to Paris to build a new life. The adults immediately set about gathering food and provisions, bracing for the deprivation they know all too well. But the children . . . are spurred to action of another sort, finding secret and not-so-secret ways to resist their oppressors." (Publisher's note)

Krilanovich, Grace

The **orange** eats creeps; a novel. introduction by Steve Erickson. Two Dollar Radio 2010 172p il pa $16

ISBN 978-0-9820151-8-6

In this novel "a nameless teenage vampire travels through Oregon in the early 1990s, doing drugs, searching for her missing foster sister, going to hardcore shows, and preying on men when they aren't preying on her. The narrator claims to have ESP and spends much of the novel channeling Patty Reed, the young Donner Party member who credited her survival to a wooden doll. . . . Trying to capture the experience of a character on the brink of insanity is daring and rarely successful. When it works—think William Burroughs at his best—readers must be able to encounter the narrator's skewed psychology without becoming lost amid the hallucinatory logic. The Orange Eats Creeps performs this tricky balancing act, which partly explains how Krilanovich can inhabit a ludicrous plot (hobo vampires?) without tumbling into horror kitsch." Bookforum

Kring, Sandra

Thank you for all things. Bantam Books 2008 432p pa $12

ISBN 978-0-385-34120-2

LC 2008-6979

"Lucy McGowan is a 12-year-old genius with a photographic memory, an even more brilliant brother, Milo (IQ: 180), and a single mother, Tess, living in Chicago. What Lucy has that her brother doesn't is curiosity and people smarts, a quality that propels her to unearth the hidden relationships and buried secrets of her family. An imaginative and headstrong girl, Lucy finds herself on a grim family visit

to her sickly, estranged grandfather in Timber Falls, Wis. Witnessing her mom's unshakable hatred for her dying father, Lucy begins to investigate her family's past; her love for the sick old patriarch she knows is challenged repeatedly by what she finds out about the angry, abusive man he used to be." Publ Wkly

The author's "delightful and nuanced take on Midwestern America . . . feels real and moving—perhaps because it is so unpretentious." Salon.com

Krist, Gary

Chaos theory; a novel. Random House 2000 347p

ISBN 0-375-50080-4

LC 99-13411

"On a whim, two middle-class high-school boys, one African American, the other white, venture into one of Washington, D.C.'s less savory neighborhoods to buy drugs. . . . A wacko with a gun greets them in an alley, and they break his arm in the course of escaping. Imagine their surprise when police question them regarding a dead undercover cop found in the same alley. A caring teacher enlists the aid of an FBI agent, who steps in to uncover a scam involving corruption at the highest level of city government." Booklist

"Spinning a plausible situation into an extraordinary story while training a marksman's eye on character, Krist has conceived a sleek and thoughtful thriller." Publ Wkly

Krivak, Andrew

The **sojourn**. Bellevue Literary Press 2011 191p pa $14.95

ISBN 978-1-934137-34-5; 1-934137-34-0

LC 2010-53027

"After Jozef Vinich's mother dies while saving his life as an infant, Jozef and his widowed father relocate from a small Colorado mining town back to their Austrian homeland. Though Jozef's boyhood is marred by lingering feelings of abandonment, resentment, ingrained sadness, and two bullying stepbrothers, his life is enhanced by frequent dreams of his mother and a close friendship with troubled distant cousin Zlee. Both boys revel in the family hunting trips, which hone their sharpshooting abilities, expertise put to use when both go off to fight in WWI as marksmen, over Jozef's father's objections. Krivak dexterously exposes the stark, brutal realities of trench warfare, the horror of a POW camp, and the months of violent bloodshed that stole the boys' innocence. Once home from war, the author's depiction of Jozef's arduous return to life, love, and family is charged with emotion and longing." Publ Wkly

Krueger, William Kent

Northwest angle. Atria Books 2011 357p $24.99

ISBN 978-1-4391-5395-6

LC 2011-15331

The author "sets his 11th Cork O'Connor thriller on an Ojibwa reservation in the remote Minnesota-Canadian border region. After his wife's tragic death, Cork, a sheriff-turned-PI, reunites with his daughter, Jenny, for a houseboat vacation on the Lake of the Woods, where a violent windstorm forces them to seek shelter on an island. Emerging from the devastation, they discover a murdered woman and a wailing infant, and, in the distance, they hear someone in pursuit." Libr J

This book "is part adventure, part mystery, and all knockout thriller. . . . Catch-your-breath suspense throughout." Booklist

Krueger, William Kent

Ordinary grace; a novel. by William Kent Krueger. Atria Books 2013 320 p. (hardcover) $24.99

ISBN 1451645821; 9781451645828; 9781451645859; 9781451645866

LC 2012034884

This novel, by William Kent Krueger, is set in "New Bremen, Minnesota, 1961. . . . Frank begins the season preoccupied with the concerns of any teenage boy, but when tragedy unexpectedly strikes his family . . . he finds himself thrust into an adult world full of secrets, lies, adultery, and betrayal, suddenly called upon to demonstrate a maturity and gumption beyond his years . . . discovering the terrible price of wisdom and the enduring grace of God." (Publisher's note)

Krueger, William Kent

Vermilion drift; a novel. Atria Books 2010 304p $25

ISBN 978-1-4391-5384-0

LC 2010-13258

At the start of this mystery featuring Tamarack County, Minn., PI Cork O'Connor, "mining heir Max Cavanagh hires Cork to trace his missing sister, Lauren, founder of an artists' retreat—and to try to identify the sender of threatening letters to various people connected with Vermilion One, a Cavanaugh family mine, which the U.S. Department of Energy is considering for long-term nuclear waste storage. When Cork and a mine official descend into Vermilion One, they discover six bodies, five of them skeletal, which may be connected with a decades-old unsolved series of crimes known as 'the Vanishings,' which Cork's father looked into when he was sheriff. The sixth corpse, that of a well-dressed woman, appears to have been in the mine about a week." Publ Wkly

"For someone who writes such muscular prose, Krueger has a light touch that humanizes his characters." N Y Times Book Rev

Krusoe, James

Toward you. Tin House Books 2011 224p pa $14.95

ISBN 978-0-9825691-1-5; 0-9825691-1-4

LC 2010-45863

"Bob, who studied Auralogy and Past Life Regressology at the Institute for Mind/Body Research before becoming an upholsterer in the town of St. Nils, knows something is up when a dog bearing Bob on its nameplate appears outside his house, is struck by a car and dies. After Bob buries Bob in the backyard, he encounters Yvonne, a fellow student from the institute with whom he had a thing before she abruptly left him for someone else. She shows up with her little girl Dee Dee, looking for information about the dog who bit her daughter. Bob doesn't tell her about his dead namesake, but devotes himself to her in the hopes of restoring their rela-

tionship. Nothing goes right: not with the policeman who befriends Bob and plans on moving to Nevada with Yvonne, not with a feuding next-door neighbor and not with poor Dee Dee, who joins Bob the dog on the other side and files reports from there. Using his Communicator, an unwieldy concoction of egg cartons, plastic inserts and a microphone, Bob searches for answers with mounting urgency. . . . A seriously strange, funny and affecting novel about imagining another life while being stuck in this one." Kirkus

Kundera, Milan

★ The **book** of laughter and forgetting; translated from the Czech by Michael Henry Heim. Knopf 1980 228p

LC 80-7657

First published 1979 in France

"The novel is written in seven parts with an interwoven structure that the author likened to polyphonic music. The repetition of incidents, characters, and themes provides The Book of Laughter and Forgetting with its formal shape. Memories, which the characters want to keep or to forget, are a recurring subject, as is laughter, which is as often ironic as joyous." Merriam-Webster's Ency of Lit

Kundera, Milan

Identity; a novel. translated from the French by Linda Asher. HarperFlamingo 1998 168p

ISBN 0-06-017564-8

LC 97-31907

"Recently divorced ad executive Chantal, on a vacation with her younger boyfriend, Jean-Marc, believes that she is too old to be considered attractive by other men. For Chantal, identity is defined by the perceptions of strangers. . . . When she returns from her vacation, she begins to receive letters from an anonymous admirer. She suspects each new man she encounters to be the mysterious scribe and fantasizes how each might perceive her. Gradually, these letters, along with a few dreams, affect how Chantal views herself and her relationship with Jean-Marc, until her feelings and identity become unrecognizable both to her lover and to herself." Publ Wkly

Kundera, Milan

Ignorance; a novel. translated from the French by Linda Asher. HarperCollins Pubs. 2002 195p

ISBN 0-06-000209-3

"Kundera knows how to keep us turning the pages. He cuts his scenes skillfully, withholding essential information. . . . His characters may not linger on in the mind. But he is able in Ignorance to turn his house of ideas into a believable and moving edifice." New Leader

Kundera, Milan

★ **Immortality**; translated from the Czech by Peter Kussi. Grove Weidenfeld 1991 345p

LC 90-28628

"Immortality swings easily, almost imperceptibly, from narrative to rumination and back again, collapsing the distinction between action and concepts. . . . Out of a story about contemporary neuroses, Kundera has fabricated a context in which everything, literally, can be claimed to matter. What is more, the author indulges this obsessiveness without ever droning or turning out a dull page. In its inventiveness and its dazzling display of what written words can convey, Immortality gives fiction back its good name." Time

Kundera, Milan

The **joke**; definitive version; HarperCollins Pubs. 1992 317p

LC 91-58349

Original Czech edition, 1967; first English translation published 1969 by Coward, McCann

"Kundera's brilliance resides in his ability to strip away the lies and disguises which Ludvik and the others need to survive, and which their society has institutionalized and sanctified." New Repub

Kundera, Milan

Laughable loves; translated from the Czech by Suzanne Rappaport. Knopf 1974 242p

Original Czech edition, 1970

"The stories in {this volume} are buoyantly energetic and virtuosic. . . . The politics here is sexual: male dominance and impotence, role-playing and fantasizing detonate with startling effect." Newsweek

Kundera, Milan

Slowness; translated from the French by Linda Asher. HarperCollins Pubs. 1996 156p

ISBN 0-06-017369-6

LC 96-6253

"Mr. Kundera comes closer to polemic here than in his other fiction, but he is fiercely defending the 'spirit of complexity' that the novel embodies. . . . So it seems almost churlish to point out shortcomings in a writer of his spirit of play, breadth of reach and perspicacity—all admirably at work once again in 'Slowness.'" N Y Times Book Rev

Kundera, Milan

★ The **unbearable** lightness of being; translated from the Czech by Michael Henry Heim. Harper & Row 1984 314p

LC 83-48363

"Set against the background of Czechoslovakia in the 1960s, the novel concerns a young Czech physician who substitutes a series of erotic adventures over which he thinks he can maintain control for becoming involved in his country's politics, where he feels he can have no power or freedom. Inevitably, he is drawn into Czechoslovakia's political unrest. In a parallel vein, he is forced to choose among the women with whom he is involved." Merriam-Webster's Ency of Lit

Kunkel, Benjamin

Indecision; a novel. Random House 2005 241p $21.95

ISBN 1-4000-6345-0

LC 2004-62894

"Ever the clever chef, Kunkel reduces the sprawling, indigestible postmodern novel to an amiable pop confection that goes down like a milkshake. The result is a stylistic triumph of sorts. The half-serious pastiche is the ideal vehicle for bright apercus, capers, riffs, and dreamy ruminations." New Leader

Kunzru, Hari

★ **Gods** without men. Alfred A. Knopf 2012 369 p.

ISBN 0-241-14311-X pa; 978-0-241-14311-7 pa; 0-307-95711-X Knopf, 2012; 978-0-307-95711-5 Knopf, 2012; 024114311X pa; 9780241143117 pa; 9780307957115 Knopf, 2012; 030795711X Knopf, 2012

LC 2011488728

"Jaz and Lisa Matharu, a young couple from New York City, are plunged into a surreal public hell after their autistic son, Raj, disappears during a vacation to the California desert. But the desert is inexplicable and miraculous, and the fates of the Matharus are bound up with those of others, all converging at an odd, remote town near a rock formation called The Pinnacles; among them are a debauched British rock star, a former member of an extraterrestrial-worshipping cult, and a teenage Iraqi refugee who befriends a young black Marine while playing the role of 'Iraqi villager' in a military simulation exercise." (Publisher's note)

Kunzru, Hari

The **impressionist**. Dutton 2002 383p

ISBN 0-525-94642-X

LC 2001-47137

This novel "includes a multitude of richly imagined characters. A bold, unfashionably omniscient voice narrates the story as it tackles such subjects as race, class, colonialism, and the roots of personal identity" New Leader

Kunzru, Hari

My revolutions. Dutton 2008 280p $25.95

ISBN 978-0-525-94932-9; 0-525-94932-1

LC 2007-39459

First published 2007 in the United Kingdom

This novel "is, as Virginia Woolf said of George Eliot's Middlemarch, a book for grownup people (although that shouldn't imply it is at all ponderous or worthy) and it is very much a book about the process of growing up. My Revolutions is impassioned, intelligent and profoundly serious literature." Sydney Morning Herald

Kunzru, Hari

Transmission. Dutton 2004 276p $24.95

ISBN 0-525-94760-4

LC 2004-3295

"This novel introduces a daydreaming Indian computer geek whose luxurious fantasies about life in America are shaken when he accepts a California job offer. Lonely and naive, Arjun Mehta bides his time as a lowly assistant virus tester, pining away for his free-spirited colleague Christine. Despite building digital creatures in a feeble attempt to enhance his job security, Arjun gets laid-off like so many of his Silicon Valley peers. In an act of desperation to keep his job, he releases a mischievous but destructive virus around the globe that has major unintended consequences." Publisher's note

Kureishi, Hanif

The **Buddha** of suburbia. Viking 1990 284p

ISBN 0-670-83342-8

LC 90-168346

This novel deals with "father-son relations, punk rock, bisexuality, and class and racial prejudices in England. The story is told through the eyes of Karim Amir, 'an Englishman born and bred, almost.'" (Libr J)

"Resembling a modern-day Tom Jones, this is an astonishing book, full of intelligence and elan." Publ Wkly

Kureishi, Hanif
Something to tell you; a novel. Scribner 2008 375p $26
ISBN 978-1-4165-7210-7; 1-4165-7210-4
LC 2008-13755

This is "the kind of book in which people do seriously bad things — murder, incest, copious sex — and then sit around talking about it. The work owes as much of a debt to Pedro Almodóvar as it does to Oscar Wilde. Yet melodrama aside, the best thing about Something to Tell You is that it reminds readers that there used to be a place for intelligent conversation. The anecdotes are brief and well sculpted. The jokes, subtle and sad." Esquire

Kurtz, Katherine
The harrowing of Gwynedd. Ballantine Bks. 1989 384p (Heirs of Saint Camber)
LC 88-7414

This is the first volume of The heirs of Saint Camber trilogy; other titles are: King Javan's year (1992) and The bastard prince (1994).

This is a "tale of the events immediately after Saint Camber's death. The persecution of the Deryni is widespread and brutal, their own leadership is beginning to descend from the high culture of Camber's time to the petty politics of a later era, and Camber's daughter must face death to continue her father's work. Kurtz also manages to be sufficiently graphic about the violence without being gratuitous, and in short has added another well-told tale to the Deryni canon." Booklist

Kurtz, Katherine
King Kelson's bride. Ace Bks. 2000 387p il (Histories of King Kelson)
ISBN 0-441-00732-5
LC 99-48047

A fantasy "set in a land analogous to medieval Wales and featuring the Deryni, a human minority with magical powers. It also resolves the longstanding question of when King Kelson Haldane of Gwynedd is going to get married. He has missed two opportunities, one due to a lady's death and the other to family treachery." Publ Wkly

Kurtz, Katherine
The quest for Saint Camber. Ballantine Bks. 1986 xxvi, 435p (Histories of King Kelson)
LC 86-8249

Earlier titles in the King Kelson series are The bishop's heir (1984) and The King's justice (1985)

"The reported death of King Kelson on a quest for the tomb of the Deryni Saint Camber throws the Kingdom of Gwynedd into turmoil. As Kelson's friends set out to search for the truth, a power struggle at court brings deceit and murder in its wake. {This installment in the author's} Deryni series . . . skillfully combines magic with the medieval in a novel that will appeal to fantasy readers and medievalists alike." Libr J

Kurtz, Katherine
St. Patrick's gargoyle. Ace Bks. 2001 233p $21.95
ISBN 0-441-00725-2
LC 00-36275

"When Dublin's St. Patrick's Cathedral becomes the target of an act of vandalism, the gargoyle guardian of the building enlists the aid of an aging Knight of Malta to assist him in his pursuit of the vandals. Combining an interest in Irish history with snatches of Templar lore, the author. . . creates a story of angelic powers and demonic forces locked in an eternal struggle." Libr J

Kurtz, Katherine
Two crowns for America. Bantam Bks. 1996 375p
LC 95-32372

"Vivid portrayals of Washington and Charles Edward Stuart ('Bonnie Prince Charlie') are at the core of the book, which is otherwise well up to Kurtz's historically well-informed standards." Booklist

Kurzweil, Allen
The grand complication. Hyperion 2001 359p
ISBN 0-7868-6603-9
LC 2001-16811

"Henry James Jesson III, the kind of wealthy eccentric who seems to exist only to send other men on wild-goose chases, hires Alexander Short, a down-on-his-luck librarian, to help solve the mystery of an eighteenth-century cabinet of wonders that is missing one of its objects. Eager to escape his problems with his wife, a French artist and pop-up-book designer, Short discovers that the missing item is a fantastically precise timepiece that allegedly belonged to Marie Antoinette, and he is soon consumed by the quest for the watch. Kurzweil's intricately constructed novel has no shortage of esoterica, and the author's fondness for sexual comedy supplies a welcome counterweight." New Yorker

Kushner, Dale M.
The conditions of love; Dale Kushner. Grand Central Pub. 2013 384 p. (hardcover) $24.99
ISBN 1455519758; 9781455519750
LC 2012040786

This novel, by Dale M. Kushner, "traces the journey of a girl from childhood to adulthood as she reckons with her parents' abandonment . . . and her overwhelming desire for spiritual and erotic love. . . . Eunice lives in the backwaters of Wisconsin. . . . A freak storm sends Eunice away from all things familiar. Rescued by the shaman-like Rose, Eunice's odyssey continues with a stay in a hermit's shack and ends with a passionate love affair with an older man." (Publisher's note)

Kushner, Rachel
★ The flamethrowers; a novel. Rachel Kushner. Scribner 2013 400 p. ill. (hardcover) $26.99
ISBN 1439142009; 9781439142004; 9781439142011;

9781439154175

LC 2012027350

National Book Award Finalist (2013)

This novel, by Rachel Kushner, begins in 1975 in New York. "Reno . . . begins an affair with an artist named Sandro Valera, the semi-estranged scion of an Italian tire and motorcycle empire. When they visit . . . Italy, Reno falls in with members of the radical movement that overtook Italy in the seventies. Betrayal sends her reeling into a clandestine undertow." (Publisher's note)

Includes bibliographical references

Kushner, Rachel

Telex from Cuba; a novel. Scribner 2008 336p $25

ISBN 978-1-41656-103-3; 1-41656-103-X

LC 2007-42893

Kushner's novel is a "work of great care and research, directed at recreating a place that history has erased from the map. . . . With impressive fluency, [she] speaks in the voices of a series of latter-day colonialists." Bookforum

Kwok, Jean

Girl in translation; Jean Kwok. Riverhead Books 2010 293 p. $25.95

ISBN 9781594487569; 1594487561

LC 2009041041

Alex Award (2011)

In this book, a winner of the 2011 ALA Alex Award, "[w]hen Kimberly Chang and her mother emigrate from Hong Kong to Brooklyn squalor, they speak no English and own nothing but debt. Kimberly's talent for school does not pay the bills, and she quickly begins a double life, carefully hidden from the outside world: an exceptional student by day, she is a Chinatown sweatshop worker by evening and weekend. Disguising the most difficult truths of her life—her staggering poverty, the weight of her family's expectations, her love for a factory boy who shares none of her talent or ambition—Kimberly learns to translate not just her language but herself back and forth between the two worlds she straddles." (Publisher's note)

"Along with her widowed mother, 11-year-old Kimberly (Ah-Kim) Chang is transported from the balmy familiarity of her native Hong Kong to the icy, inhospitable projects of 1980s Brooklyn — a girl with little grasp of the language and cultural mores of her newly adopted homeland, and even less financial means. How Kimberly fights through almost obscene marginalization to forge her own version of the American dream is consistently compelling, even if Girl's needlessly soapy conclusion seems unworthy of what came before." Entertainment Wkly

Kyle, Aryn

The god of animals; a novel. Aryn Kyle. Scribner 2007 305p (hbk.) $25; (pbk.) $15

ISBN 9781416533245; 9781416533252

LC 200650605

Alex Award (2008), Spur Awards: Best Novel of the West (2008)

This book follows "12-year-old Alice Winston, whose father, Jody, knows more about horses than he does about running a successful business. After Alice's older sister Nona . . . runs off to marry a cowboy, Jody is reduced to stabling boarders. . . . Alice's mother Marian is a bed-ridden depressive; Alice herself is preoccupied by the drowning of her schoolmate Polly Cain, who was in the habit of making phone calls to her English teacher, Mr. Delmar. Alice . . . starts to make secret calls to Delmar herself. . . . Fearful expectations are . . . realized as a sequence of disasters unfolds, starting with a horrific riding accident that leaves Jody's possible lover Patty Jo badly damaged. . . . family argument brings about further cruelty, this time leading to the agonizing destruction of a horse." (Kirkus)

This "turns out to be smarter than most [coming-of-age novels], as it moves through sexual stirrings, family disillusionment, issues of separation and deception. . . . Kyle can be overripe, but most of her prose is a joy, fluid on the page." Cleveland Plain Dealer

L

L'Amour, Louis

★ **Bendigo** Shafter. Dutton 1979 324p

LC 78-15280

"This book's hero is 18-year-old Bendigo Shafter. He is part of a small band of migrants that breaks off its westward trek and builds a small community. The group increases with the coming of other members. It has to fight off the dangers of the frontier both within and outside its confines. Among the main influences on Ben's life are the Widow Macken, who inspires him to read Locke, Rousseau, and Blackstone; Uruwishi, an old Indian brave; and Ethan Sackett, woodsman nonpareil. There are heroes and villains, both white and red, and shooting from the hip in old Western style as Ben demonstrates all the traditional values of courage, honesty, loyalty, and stamina." Shapiro. Fic for Youth. 3d edition

L'Amour, Louis

Beyond the Great Snow Mountains. Bantam Bks. 1999 282p

ISBN 0-553-10963-4

LC 99-11757

The stories in this collection were written in the 1940s and 1950s

L'Amour, Louis

The **Californios**. Saturday Review Press 1974 188p

"An expert blend of the fascinating settling of California in the 1840's; strong, self-reliant characters . . . and a plot of evil doings but triumphant good. The theme of mysticism and the legends of The Old Ones is what lifts this book above the typical western. Intriguing even for those who aren't westerns fans." Libr J

L'Amour, Louis

The **Cherokee** Trail. Bantam Bks. 1982 179p

LC 82-90288

"The leading character {of this novel} is a woman, Southern born and bred, who is left a widow with a small girl in Colorado of the 1860's. She is a tough lady who believes anything a man can do, she can do, and does. As the only woman operator of a station on the Cherokee Trail, Mary Breydon battles enemies with her guns, brains, and supportive friends, male and female. . . . As always, L'Amour respects the history and nature of the West: His characters and language are representative; his details of life on a station are accurate." Libr J

L'Amour, Louis

End of the drive. Bantam Bks. 1997 257p

LC 96-36872

Contents: Caprock rancher; Elisha comes to Red Horse; Desperate men; The courting of Griselda; End of the drive; The lonesome gods; Rustler roundup; The skull and the arrow

L'Amour, Louis

The **haunted** mesa. Bantam Bks. 1987 357p

LC 86-47576

This novel is a "combination of western and occult adventure, with the former given a decided edge. Mike Raglan, the hero, is an investigator of occult phenomena, but he is also a tough loner who knows how to use a six-gun. When he travels to a remote Southwest mesa to investigate the mystery of the Anasazi—a race of vanished cliff-dwellers—he manages to cross over to the Other Side, a fourth dimension that turns out to be very much another western frontier, replete with hidden gold, treacherous landscapes and plenty of Indians to shoot down." N Y Times Book Rev

"Although L'Amour's didactic approach and his needless repetition of details get in the way, this curious hybrid should satisfy fans of both genres." Booklist

L'Amour, Louis

Jubal Sackett. Bantam Bks. 1985 375p

LC 84-91724

"An absorbing story filled with adventure, romance, a hint of the occult, and information about Indian tribes and life in the mountains in the 17th century." Libr J

L'Amour, Louis

★ **Last** of the breed. Bantam Bks. 1986 358p

LC 86-3622

"Joe Mack is a classic American hero, thrown back into the wilderness and forced to rely on his wits and his ancestral skills to survive the deadly cold and elude his Soviet pursuers, including his nemesis, a Siberian tracker. L'Amour brings the same colorful realism to this sweeping adventure that has made his Westerns so beloved." Publ Wkly

L'Amour, Louis

The **lonesome** gods. Bantam Bks. 1983 450p

LC 82-45945

"In the early 1840s six-year-old Johannes Verne survives abandonment in the desert to spend his growing years dreaming of vengeance for the murder of his father and defending himself against enemies, including his grandfather, who are determined to kill him. The pace is almost leisurely, and the book is filled with splendid descriptions of the desert country, historical facts, and nature lore. An absorbing story of the early years of California with plenty of action, gun play, heroes, and villains." Libr J

L'Amour, Louis

May there be a road. Bantam Bks. 2001 276p

ISBN 0-553-80213-5

LC 2001-18127

In this collection of 10 previously uncollected stories with settings ranging from the coasts of Brazil to the border of Tibet to the very heartland of America . . . [the author] takes us into those sudden moments when lives and futures are altered forever, when men and women face a deadly enemy, meet a kindred spirit, or confront their own mortality." Publisher's note

L'Amour, Louis

The **Sacketts**: beginnings of a dynasty. Saturday Review Press 1976 3v in 1

Contains The daybreakers, Sackett, and Lando, originally published by Bantam Books in 1960, 1961 and 1962 respectively. The three novels included in this omnibus edition all concern members of the Sackett family during the great frontier heyday of the 1850s and 1860s

"The first tale takes Tyrel and Orrin from the Tennessee hills to Santa Fe. The second adventure is told by William Tell Sackett, the third by Lando. All are well-drawn portraits of a unique period, unmistakably L'Amour, unmistakably among his best." Booklist

Other titles about the Sacketts are: Mojave crossing (1964); Sackett brand (1965); Mustang man (1966); The lonely man (1966); The sky-liners (1967); Galloway (1970); Treasure Mountain (1972); Ride the dark trail (1972); Sackett's land; To the far blue mountains; The warrior's path (1980); Lonely on the mountain (1980); Ride the river (1983); and Jubal Sackett

L'Amour, Louis

To the far blue mountains. Saturday Review Press 1976 287p

In this Sackett novel Barnabas returns from America with a cargo of goods. He "is in Lincolnshire on business when he learns that there is a queen's warrant out for him because he is suspected of stealing the crown jewels. He is thrown in prison but manages to escape and make his way to Bristol and a ship back to Raleigh's Land. In Virginia, he recruits a band of brave settlers and strong women and they take boats up the James River in the direction of the blue mountains until they find rich land to farm. There Barnabas's children are born and the community flourishes even though there is ever-present danger from hostile Indians. This tale is much more leisurely and nonviolent than the usual L'Amour story, but it has its share of suspense and gives us a different kind of look at colonial America." Publ Wkly

L'Amour, Louis

The **trail** to Seven Pines; a Hopalong Cassidy novel. Bantam Bks. 1992 244p

LC 91-43760

First published 1951 with title: Hopalong Cassidy and the trail to Seven Pines, by the author writing as Tex Burns

"Hopalong was headed northeast toward open country when he crossed the path of six suspicious-looking men wearing silver-plated Colts. By the time he heard the gunshots, he was too far up the trail to do anything—riding back in time to find a robbed stagecoach and two bodies lying sprawled and bloody in the dust. The shipment of gold was the fourth to be hijacked in only three months, and appeared to be connected to the range war exploding around the Rocking R Ranch in the nearby town of Seven Pines. Hiring on at the Rocking R, Hopalong organizes a rough and ragtag outfit to save the ranch, only to find himself accused of murder and the target of a ruthless gunman." Publisher's note

L'Amour, Louis

The **walking** drum. Bantam Bks. 1984 423p

LC 83-25703

"In 12th century Brittany, young Mathurin Kerbouchard, escaping from the evil baron who has slain Mathurin's mother and plundered their estate, is forced into galley slavery. He gains control of the boat and lands in Moorish Spain, where he quickly makes powerful friends and enemies. Mathurin's quest is to rescue his corsair father, prisoner in the Persian stronghold of the Assassins. On the way the youth becomes a famed scholar . . . warrior, merchant, doctor and lover." Publ Wkly

L'Engle, Madeleine

Certain women. Farrar, Straus & Giroux 1992 351p

ISBN 0-374-12025-0

LC 91-34048

In this novel, "terminally ill David Wheaton, a prominent and much-married American actor, obsessively recalls an unfinished play about King David, a role he coveted. L'Engle explores Christian faith, love, and the nature of God by framing the delayed-maturation story of Emma, Wheaton's daughter, within three subplots: the Wheaton family saga, the story of King David, and the history of the play's development. The characterizations of both Davids are compelling, but the primary interest here is the community of women which surrounds each man. L'Engle describes complex truths very simply. . . . Because she also details the emotional cost of discovering and accepting such concepts, many readers will find these observations memorable but never simplistic." Libr J

L'Engle, Madeleine

A **live** coal in the sea. Farrar, Straus & Giroux 1996 323p

ISBN 978-0060652869

LC 96-4909

"The story is not always pretty; it involves desertion, infidelity, miscarriages, untimely death, a four-year-old torn from his parents, and an eight-year-old seeing his father sodomized. But neither is it explicit. In fact, in L'Engle's hands it is infused with the warmth of love and mercy. A complex, modern saga that is most of all genteel." Booklist

L'Engle, Madeleine

The **love** letters. Farrar, Straus & Giroux 1966 365p

A "counterpoint tale of two young women, three centuries apart in time, tormented by their experience of love, each needing to understand love in its deepest sense for her salvation. One is Mariana, long-ago Portuguese nun, won from her vow and soon deserted by a French soldier. The other is Charlotte Napier whose disintegrating marriage,

built on an emotionally insecure childhood, has sent her in flight to Beja, Portugal. Learning about Mariana, lingering over her published letters, and pondering her fate, Charlotte comes to understand what love demands of her." Booklist

L'Engle, Madeleine

The **other** side of the sun. Farrar, Straus & Giroux 1971 344p

"Set in the post-bellum era, {this Gothic novel} chronicles the experiences of a 19-year-old English girl, Stella, who shortly after her marriage is sent alone to the South while her husband embarks on a secret . . . mission to Africa. . . . Through a brace of aging, eccentric relatives and some violent encounters with the blacks who inhabit the nearby scrub, she comes to know something of the Renier family. Her curiosity grows until it plunges her into a cauldron of racial strife. . . . {Woven into the plot are} richly drawn characters, the scars and guilt of the Civil War, and scattered bits of brilliant insight into the human condition." Libr J

L'Engle, Madeleine

A **severed** wasp. Farrar, Straus & Giroux 1982 388p

LC 82-15694

In this sequel to The small rain, "international pianist Katherine Vigneras settles into her comfortable brownstone on Greenwich Village's 10th Street . . . {expecting} a music-dominated retirement, peaceful and restorative. Instead, she becomes involved, through friendship with one of her tenents, a Jewish doctor stationed at nearby St. Vincent's Hospital, with the Episcopal community of the great Cathedral of St. John the Divine. . . . At the cathedral she finds connections with her own tortuous past through her music, her friendship with a retired bishop and with the young family of the cathedral's present dean." Publ Wkly

La Farge, Oliver

★ **Laughing** Boy. Houghton Mifflin 1929 302p

"This novel takes place in the early years of the twentieth century in Navajo country in the American Southwest. It is the story of the ill-fated love of Laughing Boy, worker in silver and maker of songs, and Slim Girl, whose education in American schools has embittered her. The reader is immersed in their tender romance but also learns a great deal about the culture and philosophical outlook of the Native American." Shapiro. Fic for Youth. 3d edition

La Plante, Lynda

Blind fury. Touchstone 2011 512p pa $15

ISBN 978-1-4391-3930-1; 1-4391-3930-X

First published 2010 in the United Kingdom

"The quintessential police procedural, with a flawed heroine and enough dark twists to keep even the seasoned mystery fan off balance. A must for fans of British cop stories." Booklist

La Plante, Lynda

Cold blood. Random House 1997 402p

ISBN 978-0679441045

LC 98-107026

First published 1996 in the United Kingdom

"The mystery of what happened to Anna Louise is interesting, but the real suspense concerns whether Page—who finds herself drinking again and in bed with the missing girl's father—will fall apart." Publ Wkly

Labiner, Norah
Miniatures. Coffee House Press 2002 381p $23
ISBN 1-566-89136-1
LC 2002-71283

"This is a haunting novel, written in the first person and switching from past to present, from Fern's life to the other characters' lives. It slowly and achingly reveals secrets, evokes literary figures from the Brontë sisters to Marcel Proust, and explores biography as a literary form." Booklist

Lackberg, Camilla, 1974-
The **ice** princess; Camilla Läckberg; translated [from the Swedish] by Steven T. Murray. Free Press 2011 391 p.
ISBN 1451621744; 9781451621747; 9781451621754
LC 2010032941

This crime novel begins when a "grisly death exposes the dark heart of a Scandinavian seaside village. Erica Falck returns to her tiny, remote hometown of Fjällbacka, Sweden, after her parents' deaths only to encounter another tragedy: the suicide of her childhood best friend, Alex. It's Erica herself who finds Alex's body—suspended in a bathtub of frozen water, her wrists slashed. Erica is bewildered: Why would a beautiful woman who had it all take her own life? Teaming up with police detective Patrik Hedström, Erica begins to uncover shocking events from Alex's childhood. As one horrifying fact after another comes to light, Erica and Patrik's curiosity gives way to obsession—and their flirtation grows into uncontrollable attraction." (Publisher's note)

Lackberg, Camilla
The **preacher**; translated by Steven T. Murray. Pegasus Crime 2011 419p $25.95
ISBN 978-1-60598-173-4; 1-60598-173-7

Original Swedish edition, 2004; this translation first published 2008 in the United Kingdom

This mystery featuring detective Patrik Hedstrom "is again set in the small Swedish village of Fjällbacka. The story opens with the discovery of the skeletons of two women who disappeared more than 20 years ago, along with a fresh victim killed in a similar manner. In researching the decades-old murders, the police are led to the dysfunctional family of a religious fanatic, Ephraim Hult, who was known as a preacher and healer. Hedstrom must find the key to connect the old crimes with the new. In addition, Patrik's girlfriend, Erica, is about to give birth, and he must come to terms with his feelings about becoming a father. Erica, in turn, is deeply troubled by her sister's increasingly serious marriage problems. Läckberg's many-layered story features plot twists and turns galore." Libr J

Lackberg, Camilla
The **stonecutter**; Camilla Lackberg; translated by Steven T. Murray. Pegasus Books 2012 473 p.
ISBN 9781605983301 Pegasus; 9780007253982 Harpercollins; 1605983306 Pegasus; 0007253982 Harpercollins; 9780007305933 Harpercollins;

0007305931 Harpercollins
LC 2010533249

In this mystery novel, "Patrik Hedström['s] . . . sympathies as both father and cop are demanded by the murder of Sara Klinga. . . . [Camilla] Läckberg . . . parcels out hints of the tragedy's roots in the loveless marriage some 75 years ago between flirtatious heiress Agnes Stjernkvist and Anders Andersson, the stonecutter she'd captivated and planned to leave before her father discovered her pregnancy and forced the couple to wed. . . . Patrik and his . . . colleagues on the Tanumshede police force focus their suspicions on imperious Lilian . . . ; Kaj Wiberg, the neighbor with whom she's long feuded over every pretext she can find; and Kaj's son Morgan, a computer game designer with Asperger's Syndrome who'd be poorly equipped to take the air even in a much sunnier spot than Fjällbacka."(Kirkus)

"A perfectly plotted and paced mystery bolstered by strong, realistic characters." Booklist

Lackberg, Camilla, 1974-
The **Stranger**. W W Norton & Co Inc 2013 384 p. (hardcover) $25.95
ISBN 1605984256; 9781605984254

In this book by Camilla Lackberg, "[a] local woman is killed in a tragic car crash, but it isn't a clear-cut drunk driving case. The victim's blood contains high alcohol levels, but she rarely drank a drop. Meanwhile, a reality TV show begins shooting in the town, and as cameras shadow the stars' every move, tempers start to flare. When a drunken party ends with an unpopular contestant's murder, all eyes turn to the cast and crew." (Publisher's note)

Lackey, Mercedes
The **fairy** godmother. Harlequin 2004 432p $24.95
ISBN 0-373-80202-1

This fantasy is "set in a world where The Tradition tries its magical—and surreptitious-best to force the characters into their 'legendary' roles. But things sometimes go awry, and when Elena is denied her predestined Cinderella role because her kingdom's prince is too young, she is chosen as an apprentice by the local Fairy Godmother and ends up creating a legend of her own. A spirited, resourceful, though somewhat impulsive heroine, a prince who needs to learn a lesson in manners, humility, and compassion, and a host of magical creatures—including some delightful house elves and besotted unicorns—result in a lively, humorous fantasy romance." Libr J

Lackey, Mercedes
Firebird. TOR Bks. 1996 352p
ISBN 978-0312858124
LC 96-23841

In this coming-of-age fantasy, "the author transports readers to a medieval Russian world based on the folktale of 'The Firebird.' Ilya Ivanovitch is beaten and teased by his ruffian brothers and ignored by his father, a boyar or Russian prince, whose singular concern is his stolen cherries. While trying to catch the thief, Ilya Ivanovitch is unknowingly cursed just by glimpsing at the Firebird, which is half maiden and half bird. During his brother's prewedding boar hunt, the young man gets lost, but becomes much wiser as the enchanting adventures unfold." SLJ

Lackey, Mercedes

Joust. DAW Bks. 2003 373p il $24.95; pa $7.99

ISBN 0-7564-0122-4; 0-7564-0153-4 pa

LC 2003-544990

Vetch, an Altan serf, must learn the secret of the Tian jousters and their dragons in order to save his people

"This uplifting tale, which contains a valuable lesson or two on the virtues of hard work, is a must-read for dragon lovers in particular and for fantasy fans in general." Publ Wkly

Lackey, Mercedes

The **serpent's** shadow. DAW Bks. 2001 343p $24.95; pa $7.99

ISBN 0-88677-915-4; 0-7564-0061-9 pa

LC 2002-265143

"To an alternative Victorian London Dr. Maya Witherspoon, [daughter] of a Brahmin lady and an English physician, comes to practice. Besides standard Western medicine, Maya knows the magic of India, where she grew up. Maya's aunt Shivani has also come to England, but as a devotee of Kali, she hates her sister's marriage and is determined to wreak havoc on the English. Maya must seek the aid of British magical masters before the powers of Kali devastate London." Booklist

Lackey, Mercedes

Winds of fate. DAW Bks. 1991 385p il (Mage winds)

ISBN 0-88677-489-6

This first volume of a trilogy is set in the "imperiled land of Valdemar, encountered earlier in Lackey's Heralds of Valdemar series. The heir to the throne, Herald Elspeth, sets out with Gwena, her Companion (a Guardian Spirit embodied as a horse), to find an Adept who can teach her people both to use and to deflect the power of magic. . . . Lackey's delightful world of magic is inhabited by strong and believable men, women and creatures." Publ Wkly

Followed by Winds of change (1992)

Lackey, Mercedes

Winds of fury. DAW Bks. 1993 387p il (Mage winds)

ISBN 0-88677-562-0

LC 93-219013

"In this concluding book of the Mage Winds trilogy . . . Elspeth returns home via the Forest of Sorrows where the manifest spirit of Vanyel and his lover, the bard Stefan, pull her from her intended destination to explain the now diminished shields against magic and the interlocking mind-web he once placed on Valdemar and how Elspeth must prepare to fight the evil and voracious Ancar of Hardorn." Voice Youth Advocates

LaFarge, Paul

Luminous airplanes. Farrar, Straus and Giroux 2011 245p $25

ISBN 978-0-374-19431-4; 0-374-19431-9

LC 2011-08428

"Following the burst of the Internet bubble, an unnamed narrator returns to upstate New York to reconnect with his past. As he does, the simple plot is interrupted by digressions involving the family's deceased patriarchs, Adventist lore, Norman Mailer's car and the history of manned flight. The details La Farge stumbles onto seem disparate, but upon closer inspection they reveal a thematic unity. For example, the narrator attempts to simultaneously navigate his own adolescent tendencies and the world of computer programming. As he works to understand the precepts of artificial reality, he also contends with his own life; all the commands that should work don't, and the ones that do defy logic. La Farge tells his tale of homecoming compassionately but without sentimentality. He has a knack for delivering details as if the reader had already accepted them and was welcoming each discursion freely." Time Out N Y

Lafferty, Mur

The **shambling** guide to New York City; Mur Lafferty. Orbit 2013 368 p. (paperback) $14.99

ISBN 0316221171; 9780316221160; 9780316221177

LC 2012032172

In this novel, by Mur Lafferty, "a travel writer takes a job with a shady publishing company in New York, only to find that she must write a guide to the city--for the undead! . . . Not to be put off by anything . . . , Zoe delves deep into the monster world. But her job turns deadly when the careful balance between human and monsters starts to crumble." (Publisher's note)

Lagerkvist, Par

Barabbas; translated by Alan Blair; with a preface by Lucien Maury and a letter by André Gide. Random House 1951 180p

Original Swedish edition, 1950

This "is a psychological study of the spiritual journey of Barabbas, the criminal in the New Testament who was offered to the mob in place of Jesus but was spared from execution. The widely translated work was noted for its economical writing style, and it brought Lagerkvist international fame." Merriam-Webster's Ency of Lit

Lahiri, Jhumpa

Interpreter of maladies; stories. Houghton Mifflin 1999 198p $23

ISBN 0-618-10136-5

LC 98-50895

First published in paperback

"The rituals of traditional Indian domesticity—currymaking, hair-vermilioning—both buttress the characters of Lahiri's elegant first collection and mark the measure of these fragile people's dissolution. . . . Lahiri's touch in these nine tales is delicate, but her observations remain damningly accurate, and her bittersweet stories are unhampered by nostalgia." Publ Wkly

Lahiri, Jhumpa

The **namesake**. Houghton Mifflin 2003 291p $24; pa $14

ISBN 0-395-92721-8; 0-618-48522-8 pa

LC 2003-41718

"Its incorrigible mildness and its ungilded lilies aside, Lahiri's novel is unfailingly lovely in its treatment of Gogol's relationship with his father. This is the classic American parent-child bond." N Y Times Book Rev

Lahiri, Jhumpa

Unaccustomed earth. Alfred A. Knopf 2008 333p $25

ISBN 978-0-307-26573-9; 978-0-676-97934-3

LC 2007-17612

"In a collection of stories as limpid yet complex as her Pulitzer Prize-winning debut, Interpreter of Maladies (1999), [Lahiri] returns to familiar terrain—most of her Indians are highly educated, upper-middle-class suburbanites on the Boston-New York corridor—and to her well-honed role. Lahiri is an unillusioned anatomist of the greatest immigrant success story in the United States. But this time, she has captured more clearly than ever before a restless feeling of uprootedness that is as representative of America now, in the post-9/11 era, as the credo of wide-eyed openness ever was." Slate

Laird, Nick

Utterly monkey. Harper Perennial 2006 344p pa $13.95

ISBN 0-060-82836-6

LC 2005-44784

First published 2005 in the United Kingdom

"Part caper movie, part coming-of-age story, part urban satire, Monkey introduces a writer with a wonderfully original and limber voice – a writer who seems able to jump genres as easily as he shifts narrative gears. . . . Along the way, Mr. Laird also gives us a memorable and kinetic portrait of London as a city of dreamers and immigrants." N Y Times (Late N Y Ed)

Lake, Jay

Endurance. Tor 2011 319p $26.99

ISBN 978-0-7653-2676-8

LC 2011-21613

Sequel to Green (2009)

Courtesan and trained assassin Green returns to Copper Downs where she must defend the gods from the Godslayers, magicians dedicated to the destruction of all deities, by tracking them down and removing the threat.

"Lake deftly weaves complicated, stubborn characters into a plot that reaches the grandest and most personal scales without ever straining credulity." Publ Wkly

Lake, Jay

Escapement. Tor 2008 383p $25.95

ISBN 978-0-7653-1709-4; 0-7653-1709-5

LC 2008-5263

Sequel to: Mainspring

"Paolina Barthes is a teenage scientific prodigy born in a small Portuguese fishing village at the base of the massive equatorial gear-wall. Determined to learn from English engineering 'wizards' and understand the work of the great gears and wheels that move the universe, Paolina creates a home-brew chronometer, or 'gleam,' and sets off toward London. When she discovers the gleam has astonishing magical properties that only she can evoke, she becomes a target of various political and philosophical factions. . . . Lake effectively anneals steampunk with geo-mechanical magic in an allegorical matrix of empire building and Victorian natural science." Publ Wkly

Lake, Jay

Mainspring. Tor 2007 320p $25.95

ISBN 978-0-7653-1708-7; 0-7653-1708-7

LC 2007-7313

This is a "breathlessly exciting tale that takes the best old-school storytelling and the most vivid contemporary world-building sensibilities and spot-welds them together. Think Edgar Rice Burroughs or Philip José Farmer meets China Miéville or Ian R. MacLeod, by way of religious allegory. I'd call the book perfect were it not for Lake's regrettable tendency to activate the cheat codes whenever the going gets a little rough. Still, Mainspring is always gripping and often dazzling in its vision." SF Reviews.Net

Lake, Jay

Pinion. Tor 2010 348p $26.99

ISBN 978-0-7653-2186-2; 0-7653-2186-6

LC 2009-40730

Third volume in the author's Clockwork Earth series; previous titles: Mainspring (2007) and Escapement (2008)

"Young Paolina Barthes, the gear-minded prodigy who became a target for the empire-building ambitions of rival governments . . . , is on the run, heading south over the Wall that God built to divide the hemispheres and keep the Earth's gear turning through the heavens. As spies and ancient secret societies scramble to find her, Paolina struggles to learn how to control her world-shaking abilities, while her heart pulls her toward Boaz, a golemlike man of brass. Lake wields big themes—magic and religion versus science, free will, colonialism, and a bit of romance—with surprising elegance, and readers will enjoy cherishing the characters and pondering the concepts of this clockpunk world." Publ Wkly

Laken, Valerie

Dream house; a novel. HarperCollins Publishers 2008 336p $24.99

ISBN 978-0-06-084092-1; 0-06-084092-7

LC 2008-32946

"Laken has written the perfect haunted house story for these unnerving times. While the ghosts that come with this property don't rattle chains or shake the bed at night, they manifest themselves in subtler and crueler ways, by reminding us that the homes we love may not love us back." N Y Times Book Rev

Laker, Rosalind

Banners of silk. Doubleday 1981 469p

LC 80-1453

"A historical romance portraying the rags-to-riches climb of two likable and hard-working couturiers in the nineteenth-century Parisian fashion world. Fate brings Charles Worth and Louise Vernet together when they are young and poor. Although they separate and lose touch, they again meet as colleagues after both have gained reputations as innovative dress designers." Booklist

Laker, Rosalind

The golden tulip. Doubleday 1991 585p

LC 90-27591

"The suspense rarely slackens, for Francesca's spirited younger sisters, Aletta and Sybylla, enter into highly entertaining and surprising romances of their own. Laker's . . . tightly woven novel, swift-moving and filled with lusty characters, is weakened only by a convoluted, lengthy cloak-and-dagger finale." Publ Wkly

Laker, Rosalind

To dance with kings. Doubleday 1988 564p

LC 88-3698

"Set during the reigns of Louis XIV and Louis XVI, the sweeping saga takes place mainly in the Chateau of Versailles and the surrounding town from which the magnificent edifice took its name. . . . Spanning four generations, the protagonists are the women of one family, named, in turn, Marguerite, Jasmin, Violette and Rose, all of whose destinies are entwined with those of their monarchs as well as the dashing men who bring them love and heartache." Publ Wkly

Lam, Vincent

The **headmaster's** wager; a novel. Vincent Lam. 1st U.S. ed. Random House Inc. 2012 423 p. (hardcover) $25.00; (audiobook) $76.00; (ebook) $25.00

ISBN 0307986462; 9780307986467; 9780449808306; 9780307986474

LC 2012462250

This "novel centres on the life of Percival Chen, the titular headmaster whose father, like others before him, left China . . . [for] a small town just outside Saigon. . . . Once there, Chen becomes headmaster of the Percival Chen English Academy. . . . Despite his best attempts to achieve some measure of stability, his idea of family keeps fracturing, and his belief in his Chinese superiority results in unexpected repercussions for his son." (Quill & Quire)

Lamanda, Al

Sunset; Al Lamanda. Five Star 2012 275 p.

ISBN 1432825844; 9781432825843

LC 2011049914

This psychological mystery novel by Al Lamanda follows "Police Detective John Bekker [who] had it all: a beautiful wife" a five-year old daughter and a job he loved . . . but all of that changed in the blink of an eye. Assigned to a special task force investigating organized crime, Bekker got a little too close to mob boss Eddie Crist. . . . Bekker's home is invaded, his wife murdered and all this witnessed by his five-year-old daughter. A decade later Bekker, a drunk with an institutionalized daughter, comes face to face with Eddie Crist, now near death from cancer with a final wish--to go to his grave with a clear conscience. In an ironic twist of fate, the man Bekker believed responsible for his wife's death hires him to solve the decade-old murder." (Publisher's note)

Lamb, Wally

I know this much is true. HarperCollins Pubs. 1998 901p $27.50

ISBN 0-06-039162-6

LC 98-167337

"Lamb's narrator, Dominick Birdsey, has lost his mother, his wife, his infant daughter, his career. His identical twin brother, the gentle Thomas has lost his mind. A paranoid

schizophrenic . . . Thomas goes into the public library one morning during the early rumblings of Desert Storm and cuts off his hand in a biblically inspired protest against the impending war. What follows is the 40-year-old Dominick's meltdown. In his struggle to do right by Thomas, the brother he loves, resents and envies in equal measure, he is forced to face not just his own demons but the entire cavalcade of nightmares that have bedeviled the Birdsey clan." N Y Times Book Rev

"The novel explores the subjects of mental illness, dysfunctional families and domestic abuse, but it also rings with humor and tenderness." Publ Wkly

Lambdin, Dewey

Hostile Shores; An Alan Lewrie Naval Adventure. Dewey Lambdin. St Martins Pr 2013 368 p. $25.99

ISBN 0312595727; 9780312595722

This book is part of Dewey Lambdin's Capt. Sir Alan Lewrie series. After his ship Reliant is refitted, Lewrie sails to Cape Town. There, "Lewrie talks his way into a naval brigade sent ashore with the troops and sees some action on land. But once the British secure the Cape, the admiral in charge sends the entire fleet to South America for a poorly planned invasion of the Argentine. Lewrie has no choice but to follow orders and does his best to make the best of a potentially bad situation." (Kirkus)

Lambdin, Dewey

King's captain; an Alan Lewrie naval adventure. St. Martin's Press 2000 358p

ISBN 0-312-26885-8

LC 00-31764

Fresh from a stunning victory against the formidable Spanish Armada in the Battle of St. Vincent's Cape, Lewrie is promoted and rewarded with the command of an enviable new warship. Shortly after being installed as the captain of the H.M.S. Proteus, he must contend with a treasonable mass mutiny, a bitter enemy bent on revenge, and several rather complicated romantic entanglements. A rip-roaring sea yarn brimming with riveting action and lusty diversions." Booklist

Lamberson, Gregory

The **frenzy** way. Medallion 2010 356p pa $15.95

ISBN 978-1-605421-07-0; 1-605421-07-3

"Possessing spirited action scenes and distinctive dialogue, the novel penetrates the psyche of a terrorist and comprehends the psychology of terror. It's like taking a savagely wild walk—in animal form." Hellnotes.com

Lamott, Anne

Blue shoe. Riverhead Bks. 2002 291p

ISBN 1-57322-226-7

LC 2002-22824

"The acceptence of one's imperfections is a pillar of wisdom in Lamott's New Age Christianity. Mattie is an embodiment of that philosophy, but she's better written than that makes her sound. She and her family are hilariously specific." NY Times Book Rev

Lamott, Anne

Imperfect birds; a novel. Riverhead Books 2010 278p $25.95

ISBN 978-1-59448-751-4; 1-59448-751-0

LC 2009-36107

A novel "about Elizabeth and James, liberal do-gooders from Marin County, California (and the subjects of [Lamott's] previous novels Rosie and Crooked Little Heart), and their daughter Rosie. At 17, Rosie is 'black-haired, strapping and fabulous' and an academic high achiever, but she does every drug under the sun, including her peers' parentally dispensed Adderall. The book is a stark illustration of deception, denial and parents' desperate desire to stay loved." Time

Lanagan, Margo

The **brides** of Rollrock Island; Margo Lanagan. Alfred A. Knopf 2012 305 p. (hardback) $17.99

ISBN 0375869190; 9780375869198; 9780375969195; 9780375989308

LC 2011047466

This novel, by Margo Lenagan, takes place around "remote Rollrock Island, [where] men go to sea to make their livings--and to catch their wives. The witch Misskaella knows the way of drawing a girl from the heart of a seal . . . [a]nd for a price a man may buy himself a lovely sea-wife. . . . But from his first look into [her] . . . eyes, he will be just as transformed as she. He will be equally ensnared. And the witch will have her true payment." (Publisher's note)

Lancaster, Jen

Here I go again; Jen Lancaster. New American Library 2012 320 p. $25.95

ISBN 0451236726; 9780451236722

LC 2012021417

This book is the story of Lissy Ryder. A bully during high school, Lissy "may finally be getting her karmic payback: her husband asks for a divorce, and she loses her PR job and moves back in with her parents. Mix in one hellish 20th high school reunion and a New Age classmate with a special potion . . . , and suddenly Lissy's back to 1991," where she tries to right her wrongs. "But in so doing, will she . . . mess up the future—not only for herself but for others?" (Publishers Weekly)

Lanchester, John

The **debt** to pleasure; a novel. Holt & Co. 1996 251p il

ISBN 0-8050-4388-8

LC 95-34658

The author "has written a novel masquerading as an essay masquerading as a cookbook, and it somehow manages to combine the virtues of all three. The narrator, Tarquin Winot, is the brother of a famous sculptor, but his own talent—as emerges in the course of his endlessly digressive, enormously erudite disquisitions on food—is for the art of murder. Tarquin's marvellously perverse intelligence never falters, and, fortunately, neither do his lapidary sentences." New Yorker

Lanchester, John

Fragrant Harbor. Putnam 2002 342p

ISBN 0-399-14866-3

LC 2001-57876

This "is not an enormous novel, but it feels like one—it is bursting with ideas. Lanchester takes on almost every major theme and succeeds with most of them: race, class, love, war, the fall of rulers and the rise of the ruled." N Y Times Book Rev

Land, Brad

Pilgrims upon the earth; a novel. Random House 2007 227p $23.95

ISBN 978-1-4000-6380-2; 1-4000-6380-9

LC 2006-49264

Fifteen-year-old Terry Webber's "mom is gone, his millworker dad moves town to town, and his high-school existence is pure ennui. . . . Alice Washington, a classmate on her own lost highway, plots with Terry to escape to her sister's commune in Colorado. Only hours into the getaway journey, Alice dies in a car crash. The second half of this . . . novel recounts Terry's grief-stricken wobble through a high-school labyrinth of cigarettes, drugs, fistfights, petty crime and—just maybe—back to hope again. . . . Land owns a spot-on gift for rendering what it's like to be young and, all too frequently, absurdly miserable." Paste

Land, Jon

Strong at the break; Jon Land. Forge 2011 348p.

ISBN 9780765323378; 0765323370

LC 2011011542

This book tells the story of "fifth-generation Texas Ranger Caitlin Strong," set "two decades" after "her father shot down the cult-like leader of a separatist church . . . That man's son, Malcolm Arno, has become head of a militia movement bent on unleashing chaos and anarchy across the country. . . . Already mired in one investigation of drug smuggling over the U.S.-Canadian border and another involving an Iraqi war veteran who claims the army is trying to kill him, Caitlin finds herself embroiled in the search for the kidnapped son of former outlaw Cort Wesley Masters. When the missing boy's trail leads to Malcolm Arno's Texas compound, the three cases converge". (Publisher's note)

Landay, William

★ **Defending** Jacob; William Landay. Delacorte Books 2012 421p.

ISBN 9780345527592; 9780385344227

LC 2011011623

This book offers a novel about "Andy Barber [who] has been an assistant district attorney in his suburban Massachusetts county for more than twenty years. He is respected in his community, tenacious in the courtroom, and happy at home with his wife, Laurie, and son, Jacob. But when a shocking crime shatters their New England town, Andy is blindsided by what happens next: His fourteen-year-old son is charged with the murder of a fellow student. Every parental instinct Andy has rallies to protect his boy. . . . But as damning facts and shocking revelations surface, as a marriage threatens to crumble and the trial intensifies, as the crisis reveals how little a father knows about his son, Andy will face a trial of his own—between loyalty and justice, between truth and allegation, between a past he's tried to bury and a future he cannot conceive." (Publisher's note)

Landers, Scott

Coswell's guide to Tambralinga; a novel. Scott Landers. Farrar, Straus and Giroux 2004 338p $24
ISBN 0-374-13021-3
LC 2003-21116

A novel set on a fictional Southeast Asian island. "At the center is Conrad, a meek computer systems analyst on a desperate second honeymoon with Lucy, who's furious at him for losing her all-important guidebook. Fearing 'that he was missing it, that better half of existence, the throbbing center of what it meant to be alive,' Conrad heads to a brothel on another island, while Lucy finds the guidebook and embarks on her own adventure." Publ Wkly

"In this offbeat first novel, Landers puts a wry spin on the theme of self-discovery, suggesting that jealousy, hardship, and disillusionment are good for the soul." Booklist

Landis, Jill Marie

Heartbreak Hotel; a novel. Jill Marie Landis. Ballantine Books 2005 335 p. (pbk.) $6.99; o.p.; (MM: alk. paper) o.p.
ISBN 9780345453297; 0345453301 (alk. paper); 0345453298
LC 2004063654

This book tells the story of "widowed Tracy Potter and novelist Wade MacAllister. When Tracy's wheeler-dealer, real-estate-developer husband dies suddenly, Tracy is shocked to learn that their wealthy lifestyle was mortgaged to the hilt. The only way to provide for her college-age stepdaughter and young son is to make a go of the dilapidated historical hotel her late husband's father left in his name. Before the Heartbreak Hotel is even open for business, Wade rides in on his Harley, planning to end his life. But after drinking himself into oblivion, Wade has a strangely realistic dream and wakes up refreshed after the first decent night's sleep he's had in ages. The longer Wade stays, the more sense his eerie dreams begin to make." (thebestreviews.com)

Lane, Harriet

Alys, always; a novel. Harriet Lane. Scribner 2012 209 p. $24.00
ISBN 1451673167; 9781451673166; 9781451673180
LC 2011040905

In this book, "a young woman named Frances Thorpe comes upon an overturned car in a ditch. She calls for help and speaks to the dying driver, Alys, offering sympathy, comfort, and support. Later, the family requests a meeting with Frances to thank her . . . . On meeting the bereaved husband, a noted English novelist who enjoys a life of culture and privilege, Frances is struck with the glimmer of an idea that grows and flourishes as her connection with the family deepens." (Library Journal)

Lange, Richard

Angel baby; a novel. Richard Lange. Mulholland Books / Little, Brown and Co. 2013 304 p. (hardcover) $25.99
ISBN 0316219827; 9780316219822
LC 2012037350

In this novel, by Richard Lange, "to escape the awful life she has descended into, Luz plans carefully. She takes only the clothes on her back, a Colt .45, and all the money in her husband's safe. . . . Luz needs to find the daughter she left behind years earlier, but she knows she may die trying. Her husband is . . . a key player in a high-powered drug cartel, a business he runs with the same violence he has used to keep Luz his perfect, obedient wife." (Publisher's note)

Langer, Adam

The thieves of Manhattan; a novel. Spiegel & Grau Trade Paperbacks 2010 259p $15
ISBN 9781400068913; 1-4000-6891-6 pa
LC 2009-40011

"Narrator Ian Minot is a writer, one without the burden of publications, instead collecting mean-spirited rejection notices. Now he works in a coffeehouse and is on the downhill part of a relationship that seems to have been wrong from the beginning. In the background is a woman he works with, an oddball artist but also someone who truly listens to his stories. What makes this a Good Story is that in addition to the full-screen showing of certain agents and editors and publishers as gerbil-like dolts, it's also a swell — though slow-building — love story. Desperate for success, Ian finds himself teamed with a ruined editor, Jed Roth, in an elaborate scheme to hoodwink the publishing business. Essentially it involves creating a false memoir and then exploiting the consequences of its later exposure. It's cynical as all get out, but the book snarls at the publishing industry early and often." Chicago Sun-Times

Langton, Jane

★ **Dead** as a dodo; a Homer Kelly mystery. Viking 1996 339p il
ISBN 0-670-86221-5
LC 96-6724

In this adventure "Homer takes a leave from Harvard to lecture at the Oxford University Museum. Exposed to the natural history scholarship at this seat of learning, he discovers Charles Darwin and is 'flabbergasted' by 'The Origin of Species.' . . . Homer is floored by a number of other things, including the theft of a 17th-century painting of a dodo, the discovery of some long-lost crustacean specimens collected by Darwin and two suspicious deaths. Adopting the style of a famous Oxonian, Charles Dodgson, Ms. Langton makes a Mad Tea Party of Homer's investigation of these curious events, which strike him as a Jabberwockian version of natural selection." N Y Times Book Rev

Langton, Jane

The deserter; murder at Gettysburg. St. Martin's Minotaur 2003 322p il $23.95
ISBN 0-312-30186-3
LC 2002-191961

"The suspense builds as the author adroitly shifts between past and present. Period photos, an 1860 playbill for the Hasty Pudding show, quotations from Walt Whitman and loads of Harvard lore add historical weight." Publ Wkly

Langton, Jane

Emily Dickinson is dead; a novel of suspense. illustrations by the author. St. Martin's Press 1984 247p il

LC 83-24451

"In a mystery that pokes fun at the behavior of professors in the academic world, a famous poet is chosen as a theme for a literary conference. Stemming from a photograph that an undistinguished professor from a small midwestern college claims is an authentic photo of Emily Dickinson, the faculty of an elite university begin to fight among themselves—sometimes even physically—about who will star at the conference. Entangled in that is Winifred Gaw, an overweight graduate student, and the professor whom she worships, as well as beautiful Allison Groves who becomes the object of Winifred's jealousy and hatred. Emily Dickinson, quietly dead for so many years, becomes a motivation for arson, forgery, and murder." Shapiro. Fic for Youth. 3d edition

Langton, Jane

The **Escher** twist; a Homer Kelly mystery. Viking 2002 240p il

ISBN 0-670-03067-8

LC 2001-26806

This "Homer Kelly book follows crystallographer Leonard Sheldrake as he pursues the enigmatic Frieda, who disappears after they meet at an Escher exhibition at a Cambridge, Mass., art gallery. The mystery here is less about the murders that crop up occasionally in this whimsical narrative than about identity." Publ Wkly

Langton, Jane

The **face** on the wall. Viking 1998 291p il

ISBN 0-670-87674-7

LC 98-2832

"Overlaying her mythic design with a trim narrative of modern-day wickedness, {Langton} steps back to let us marvel at the patterns of evil that she traces from Mother Goose to the murderer next door." N Y Times Book Rev

Langton, Jane

Murder at Monticello; a Homer Kelly mystery. illustrations by the author. Viking 2001 256p il $22.95

ISBN 0-670-89462-1

LC 00-43369

"It's the bicentennial of Jefferson's election to the presidency, and Homer and his wife, Mary, are invited to a Fourth of July celebration at Monticello, Jefferson's Virginia home, where, incidentally, a serial killer has been murdering young women. Like the previous Kelly novels, this one features a smart mystery, delightful characters, and vastly entertaining dialogue." Booklist

Langton, Jane

The **thief** of Venice. Viking 1999 247p il

ISBN 0-670-88210-0

LC 98-54894

Homer Kelly, "a policeman-turned-scholar, and his professor wife, Mary, have ventured to Venice to attend a scholarly conference on rare books. Homer is intoxicated by the riches afforded in the Biblioteca Marciana, while

Mary prowls the streets of the Italian city, camera in hand. An expatriate English doctor, Richard Henchard, seeking an apartment for his demanding mistress, stumbles upon a cache of golden artifacts. He kills twice to protect his secret, and his path soon intersects Mary's. . . . With a master hand, Langton develops the various subplots into a sophisticated, elegantly constructed thriller." Publ Wkly

Lankford, Terrill

Earthquake weather. Ballantine Bks. 2004 293p $24.95

ISBN 0-345-46777-9

LC 2004-41068

This novel starts with the "L.A. earthquake of 1994. Suffering from post-quake shell shock, Mark Hayes, D-Boy (or script reader) for schlocky producer Dexter Morton, finds his career in tatters, just like his quake-damaged apartment in the Valley. Then he finds a body floating in Dexter's pool and becomes a murder suspect. Along with a motley crew of similarly dysfunctional cronies, including a washed-up writer who spouts cliches about 'killing creativity for a paycheck,' Mark slouches toward Armageddon or a jail cell, whichever comes first. Lankford nails the updated noir mood, and he fills the tale with juicy insider stuff about the 'industry'." Booklist

Lansdale, Joe R., 1951-

★ The **bottoms**. Mysterious Press 2000 328p $30

ISBN 0-89296-704-8

LC 00-32886

"An emotionally charged tale very reminiscent of To Kill a Mockingbird. Effectively combining mystery and family history, it offers a vivid, multifaceted glimpse back to a simpler, but not necessarily better, time." Booklist

Lansdale, Joe R.

The **complete** Drive-in; three novels of anarchy, aliens & the Popcorn King. Underland Press 2010 376p il pa $16.95

ISBN 978-0-9802260-4-1

"The festivities get started with The Drive-In, the story of Jack and his friends Bob, Willard, and Randy, and the trip they take to the All Night Horror Show at the Orbit, a drive-in movie theater with six screens full of murder, mayhem, and madness. One special Friday, a comet comes out of the sky, grins at the crowd, and takes the rest of the outside world away. Without an exit, the Orbit's audience turns into a small country of starving psychotics, and whoever's running the show keeps throwing in plot twists to keep life interesting. Twists like the Popcorn King, a crazed despot made of twisted flesh, lightning, and concession-stand treats. Lansdale followed the original novel with The Drive-In: Not Just One Of Them Sequels and The Drive-In: The Bus Tour. In both, things continue to go downhill. It's no surprise that Lansdale's story loses some steam by the end. Given how much power he's able to wring out of the premise's stark simplicity, the real wonder is that the sequels work as well as they do." A V Club

Lansdale, Joe R.
Devil red. Alfred A. Knopf 2011 206p $24
ISBN 978-0-307-27098-6

LC 2010-47476

This Hap and Leonard mystery "opens with the duo investigating a series of murders in their patch of east Texas. Each murder site is signed with a drawing of a red devil's head . . . , and suspects are as thick on the ground as pine needles before the adrenaline-stoked shoot-out of a conclusion. Nobody's better at smacking us with the look, feel, and smell of derring-do. Along the way, there is the usual camaraderie, banter, and sex." Libr J

Lansdale, Joe R., 1951-
Edge of dark water; Joe R. Lansdale. Mulholland Books/Little, Brown and Co. 2012 292 p.
ISBN 0316188433; 9780316188432

LC 2011030557

This book features characters, who "paddling a makeshift raft down the Sabine River, . . . flee East Texas, a New York minute ahead of their pursuers. There are four of them: tough-minded Sue Ellen Wilson . . . ; Jinx, Sue Ellen's lifelong black friend who . . . knows she's better than the bigotry she's endured all her life; angry, resentful Terry, not wholly reconciled to the fact that he's gay; and Sue Ellen's alcoholic mom Helen. . . . They've been brought together by a murder." (Kirkus Reviews)

Lansdale, Joe R.
A **fine** dark line. Mysterious Press 2003 307p $24.95
ISBN 0-89296-729-3

LC 2002-71387

A regional mystery "which harks back to 1958. Thirteen-year-old Stanley Mitchel, Jr., has enough on his hands just growing up in Dewmont, Tex., when he literally stumbles on a buried cache of love letters. Stanley pursues the identity of the two lovers with help from the projectionist at his family's drive-in, an aged black man who quotes Sherlock Holmes and doesn't mince words about the world's injustices. As the truth of a gruesome 20-year-old double murder comes to light in the sleepy town, so do the facts of life, death, men, women and race for young Stanley." Publ Wkly

"Stanley doesn't unravel everything, but race and power, and what people do to each other in the name of desire and religion, coalesce to a mighty climax." Booklist

Lansdale, Joe R.
Leather maiden. Alfred A. Knopf 2008 287p $23.95
ISBN 978-0-375-41452-7; 0-375-41452-5

LC 2007-51854

"At the beginning of David Lynch's film 'Blue Velvet,' you may remember that the camera presents a typical American neighborhood and then moves closer, right through the sod and down into the ground as a metaphor for the nasty secrets hiding behind the veil of societal correctness. Lansdale's novel is a trip into that same hidden shame. You may not enjoy the exposure, but you'll definitely enjoy the ride." Los Angeles Times Book Rev

Lansdale, Joe R.
★ **Sunset** and sawdust. Alfred A. Knopf 2004 321p $22
ISBN 0-375-41453-3

LC 2003-60478

"The mystery is only mildly engrossing here; the great pleasure of Lansdale's work lies in his pitch-perfect vernacular prose. . . . The book opens with a cyclone, ends with a plague of grasshoppers and in between there's insanity, extreme violence, sex, grotesques aplenty and an excellent dog. What's not to like?" Publ Wkly

Lansdale, Joe R.
Vanilla Ride. Alfred A. Knopf 2009 243p $24.95
ISBN 978-0-307-27097-9; 0-307-27097-1

LC 2009-08821

In this "outing, the unlikely partners—Hap's a white, horny heterosexual good ol' boy, and Leonard's a black homosexual Vietnam vet—rescue a friend's daughter from the clutches of drug dealers. Unbeknownst to our heroes, the dealers are part of the Dixie Mafia, which proceeds to send waves of assassins in retaliation, each worse than the last. Joking as they go, Hap and Leonard dispose of each with their usual brand of brutality. Then, the mafia sends its weapon of last resort, Vanilla Ride, a beautiful hit woman. . . . Lansdale's storytelling skills are as sharp as ever." Publ Wkly

Lansens, Lori
The **girls**; a novel. Little, Brown 2006 345p hardcover o.p. pa $13.99
ISBN 978-0-316-06903-8; 0-316-06903-5; 978-0-316-06634-1 pa; 0-316-06634-6 pa

LC 2005-24510

First published 2005 in Canada

This "novel is told from two viewpoints: that of Rose and that of Ruby Darlen, 29-year-old conjoined twins. Rose and Ruby are about to go down in history as the oldest surviving twins to be joined at the head. A recent medical diagnosis has spurred Rose to write her autobiography, and she encourages Ruby to do the same. Between the two sections, the story of their lives is revealed, beginning with their birth to an unwed teen mother and their adoption by Lovey Darlen, the nurse who was with their mother when she was in labor, and her strong, silent husband, Stash. The girls grow up on the Darlens' farm in rural Ontario, where Lovey refuses to accept the word of skeptical doctors who doubt the girls will ever be able to walk on their own." Booklist

Lansens, Lori
The **wife's** tale; a novel. Little, Brown 2010 356p $24.99
ISBN 978-0-316-06931-1; 0-316-06931-0

LC 2009-22062

The novel contains "loving reflections on marriage and family in small-town Ontario, hilarious travelogues about American obsessions like McMansions and vanity license plates, and a tender documentary of the improbable compassion of strangers for fellow travelers. Of course, there's plenty of self-discovery too. . . . Mary is no Wife of Bath, but Lansens has more than a few tales worth telling." N Y Times Book Rev

Lantz, K. A.

Apricot jam, and other stories; translated by Kenneth Lantz and Stephan Solzhenitsyn. Counterpoint 2011 375p $28

ISBN 978-1-58243-602-9; 1-58243-602-9

LC 2011-12332

The book presents a collection of short stories which are "interconnected and juxtaposed using an experimental method [the author] referred to as 'binary'" and which take "Soviet and post-Soviet life as their focus." (counterpointpress.com). Particular focus is given to "flawed character[s] who start out in life with . . . good intentions and idealistic hopes but, when confronted by obstacles or opposing forces, [are] blown off course by weakness, selfishness, and ambition." Topics discussed include "the Tambov Rebellion of 1920 . . . World War II . . . . [and] "the Angara River." (New York Review of Books)

"The two contradictory sides of Soviet life reveal themselves to us in 'Apricot Jam.' The title story opens with a letter to a famous Soviet writer from a peasant whose family was imprisoned during Stalin's brutal campaign against the so-called kulaks during the days of Russian's great famine. The writer grapples with the devastating implications of the letter, revealing what Solzhenitsyn in a later story calls the fracture of modern Russian life. We see this fracture demonstrated again and again in other stories, finding ourselves deeply ensconced in the struggles of such groups as the kulaks rebelling against Stalin's oppression and in the battles fought by heroic Soviet troops on the German front in World War II. . . . In the jargon of the old Soviet regime, Solzhenitsyn is a wrecker of epic proportions, revealing the soft intellectual underbelly of Soviet thought and shining bright light on the iron fist the Stalinists used on the ordinary heroes of the Soviet era." NPR

Lapierre, Alexandra

Between love and honor; Alexandra Lapierre; translated by Jane Lizop. AmazonCrossing 2012 xix, 514 p.p $14.95

ISBN 1611091454; 9781611091458

LC 2011963463

Author Alexandra Lapierre tells "a historical love story based on the facts of Czar Nicholas I of Russia's 25-year struggle to contain the Muslims of the Caucasus Mountains. The book follows Jamal Eddin, son of the Jihadist warrior Imam Shamil, as he's taken hostage by the Czar. . . . [After falling in love with a girl,] Jamal Eddin could have her hand only if he agreed to convert to Christianity. . . . 17 years after his kidnapping, Jamal's father makes his move [to rescue his son], but leaves the choice to his son: will he return to his village or remain with his love?" (Publisher's note)

Laplante, Alice

Turn of mind. Atlantic Monthly 2011 307p $24

ISBN 978-0-8021-1977-3; 0-8021-1977-8

"The story is told from the perspective of Dr. Jennifer White, once an intellectually commanding orthopedic surgeon, now . . . a fast-deteriorating Alzheimer's patient. . . . As she's narrating the story, White often has no idea what's going on, or she's buried in her past, carrying on dementia-muddled conversations with loved ones now departed. Turn of Mind is part mystery novel, part family drama, and it's no small feat that LaPlante manages to spin a coherent tale despite her main character's profound disorientation. White's best friend, Amanda, has been murdered, her fingers sliced off with suspiciously surgical precision. Did White kill Amanda? The cops think so, but she's continually betrayed by her decaying brain: She just can't remember. Her two grown kids, meanwhile, are alternately protective and manipulative as they grapple with their mother's degeneration and some difficult family history. LaPlante has a gift for rhythm, crafting rat-a-tat passages that are their own pleasures." Entertainment Wkly

Lardner, Ring

The **best** short stories of Ring Lardner. Scribner 1976 346p

ISBN 0-684-14743-2

A reprint of the 1957 edition

"A selection of twenty-five stories by one of the most original figures in American literature, the colorful personality who was noted as a sports writer, humorist and columnist, as well as short-story writer." N Y Her Trib Books

Lardner, Ring

Ring around the bases; the complete baseball stories of Ring Lardner. edited and with an introduction by Matthew J. Bruccoli; foreword by Ring Lardner, Jr. Scribner 1992 609p il $35

ISBN 0-684-19374-4

LC 91-38363

"This volume collects all {of Lardner's baseball} tales, including the famous Jack Keefe epistolary stories that made up the well-known volume You Know Me Al (1914), plus some prime journalistic pieces. . . . They all display the writer's excellence in capturing the idiom and nuances of baseball talk." Libr J

Includes bibliographic references

Larison, John

Holding lies; a novel. Skyhorse Pub. 2011 250p il $24.95

ISBN 978-1-61608-255-0

LC 2011-07834

"Larison pays homage to Norman Maclean's novella 'A River Runs Through It,' but he doesn't copy that text. Larison's characters are pragmatic. Unlike Maclean's characters, who see God in the beauty of their Montana river, Larison's are trying to live in a place the rest of the world wants to use up. Larison is Maclean two generations along, when what is wild and majestic seems to be slipping away and some men (flawed and inadequate they may be) keep clinging to it as hard as they can. 'Holding Lies' is a fine piece of work, unsentimental and thought-provoking. If there were a genre called 'coming-of-age' for the middle-aged, this would be a prime example." Oregonian

Larsen, Deborah

The **white**; a novel. Knopf 2002 219p $22

ISBN 0-375-41359-6

LC 2001-53977

This novel "has escaped many of the dangers that ensnare fiction with this sort of subject. Its is neither epic nor sentimental, nor does it bang any political or anthropological drum. Beneath the smooth beauty of its descriptive language, there is some terrific concision and lightness." N Y Times Book Rev

Larsen, Jeanne

Silk road; a novel of 8th century China. Holt & Co. 1989 434p il

LC 88-27286

This novel "maintains a wonderfully mellow tone, perhaps so even a tone as to subvert intensity. But it accommodates much merriment, and moments of sadness and joy, as this feminist fable of mother- and sister-bonding draws together." N Y Times Book Rev

Larsen, Nella

Passing; introduction by Ntozake Shange; critical foreword and notes by Mae Henderson. Modern Lib. 2002 lxxxv, 206p (Modern Library classics) pa $10.95

ISBN 0-375-75813-5

LC 2001-45037

First published 1929 by Knopf

This "is a shrewdly conceived and finely executed novella that raises questions not only of racial identity in a realistically rendered middle and upper-middle-class Negro society (in Harlem and Chicago, 1927) but of the murderous rage one woman might feel for another who has 'passed' beyond her." N Y Rev Books

Larsen, Reif

The **selected** works of T. S. Spivet. Penguin Press 2009 374p il map $27.95

ISBN 978-1-59420-217-9; 1-59420-217-6

LC 2009-06277

"Only at the end does Larsen lose control of the already outlandish plot, but that's to be forgiven. His debut is oddly affecting, and T.S. Spivet is a character to root for." Dallas Morning News

Larson, Nathan

The **Dewey** Decimal system; a novel. Akashic Books 2011 251p pa $15.95

ISBN 978-1-61775-010-6; 1-61775-010-7

"Terrorist outrages committed on Valentine's Day and a superflu epidemic have devastated New York City, whose population is now about 800,000. . . . [The] narrator, a hygiene freak who can't remember his given name, runs errands for Manhattan DA Daniel Rosenblatt, a crime lord rather than a law enforcement officer. Rosenblatt has nicknamed the narrator Dewey Decimal, because Decimal is obsessed with reorganizing the books in the main branch of the New York Public Library, which no longer has a working computer catalogue. The loathsome Rosenblatt dispatches Decimal on various unsavory errands, including 'quieting' Yakiv Shapsko, a Ukrainian community leader. But when Decimal arrives at Shapsko's home in Queens, he encounters instead the man's attractive Latvian wife, Iveta, with whom he begins a complex and twist-filled relationship." Publ Wkly

"Proof positive that the private detective will remain a serious and seriously enjoyable literary archetype." PopMatters

Larsson, Asa

Until thy wrath be past; translated by Laurie Thompson. Silver Oak 2011 250p $24.95

ISBN 978-1-4027-8716-4; 1-4027-8716-2

Original Swedish edition, 2008

"Corporate lawyer Rebecka Martinsson is working as a prosecutor in Kiruna when the spring thaw reveals the body of a woman in the river. Rebecka's sleep has been troubled by a threatening spectre: what do these dreams have to do with the dead woman? Rebecka becomes part of an investigation into the disappearance of a plane carrying supplies for the wartime Wehrmacht, but there are those who believe that aspects of the country's past must remain hidden – among them, a ruthless killer. The novel shows that Larsson is ready to confront unpalatable truths. Among the current batch of Nordic writers, the new Larsson is one to be followed with the most minute attention." Independent (UK)

Larsson, Stieg, 1954-2004

★ The **girl** who kicked the hornets' nest; translated from the Swedish by Reg Keeland. Alfred A. Knopf 2010 563p $27.95

ISBN 978-0-307-26999-7; 0-307-26999-X

LC 2010-06361

Original Swedish edition, 2007; this translation first published 2009 in the United Kingdom

"The Millennium Trilogy is a fantastically exciting and original set of books, admittedly with flaws, but with a great breadth and intelligence — of the characters as well as of the story — and with an ability to draw the reader into an exciting narrative so that one is lost in the book, not knowing whether to turn the pages rapidly to find out what happens next, or to turn them slowly to prolong the totally mesmerising read, so ably conveyed to English readers by the translator, Reg Keeland." Euro Crime

Larsson, Stieg

The **girl** who played with fire; translated from the Swedish by Reg Keeland. Alfred A. Knopf 2009 503p $25.95

ISBN 978-0-307-26998-0; 0-307-26998-1

LC 2009-14053

Original Swedish edition, 2006

"For all the complications of the melodramatic story, which advances at a brisk, violently cinematic clip in Reg Keeland's translation, it's clear where Larsson's strongest interests lie—in his heroine and the ill-concealed attitudes she brings out in men." N Y Times Book Rev

Larsson, Stieg, 1954-2004

The **girl** with the dragon tattoo; by Stieg Larsson; translated from the Swedish by Reg Keeland. Alfred A. Knopf 2008 532p $24.95

ISBN 978-0-307-26975-1; 0-307-26975-2

LC 20080411003

Origina Swedish edition, 2005

This novel is "about the disappearance forty years ago of Harriet Vanger, a young scion of one of the wealthiest families in Sweden . . . and about her octogenarian uncle, determined to know the truth about what he believes was her murder. It's about Mikael Nlomkvist, . . . hired to get to the bottom of Harriet's disappearance . . . and about Lisbeth Salander, a twenty-four-year-old . . . [hacker] who assists Blomkvist with the investigation." (Publisher's note)

First title in the author's Millennium trilogy. "Convicted of libeling a prominent businessman and awaiting imprisonment, financial journalist Mikael Blomkvist agrees to industrialist Henrik Vanger's request to investigate the 40-year-old disappearance of Vanger's 16-year-old niece, Harriet. In return, Vanger will help Blomkvist dig up dirt on the corrupt businessman. Assisting in Blomkvist's investigation is 24-year-old Lisbeth Salander, a brilliant but enigmatic computer hacker." Libr J

Lasdun, James
The **horned** man. Norton 2002 193p $24.95
ISBN 0-393-00336-1
LC 2002-539

"This arch, assured satire is a psychological thriller, too, and it races cleanly and hungrily to unexpected (and expected) revelations; the academic and sexual politics that ground it are familiar, but this almost doesn't matter, since Lasdun is interested in the inevitability of error when we mistake trendiness for truth." New Yorker

Lasdun, James
It's beginning to hurt. Farrar, Straus and Giroux 2009 227p $23
ISBN 978-0-374-29902-6; 0-374-29902-1
LC 2008-54251

"Reading Lasdun is like reading a sly collaboration between Kafka and Updike: elegant, acutely observed and utterly unflinching . . . . This is a collection that examines the most inward mechanisms of rage, fear and desire with astonishing skill and strangely lyric power." Times (London)

Lashner, William
A **killer's** kiss. William Morrow 2007 327p $24.95
ISBN 978-0-06-114346-5; 0-06-114346-4
LC 2007-61202

In this crime thriller featuring Philadelphia DA Victor Carl, "two police detectives pay Carl a late-night call to inform him that Dr. Wren Denniston, the husband of Carl's former fiancée, Julia, was found shot to death in his Chestnut Hill mansion earlier that evening. Since Carl, known for his malleable ethics, had been entertaining Julia at his apartment shortly before the detectives' arrival in an effort to revive their relationship, he becomes a prime suspect in the doctor's murder. Unsure whether his lover is setting him up, Carl must dodge a rogue's gallery of villains who had their own reasons for wanting Denniston out of the way before he can uncover the real culprit and figure out Julia's true feelings for him. Chandler and Hammett fans looking for a fix will be well rewarded." Publ Wkly

Lashner, William
Kockroach; [by] Tyler Knox. William Morrow 2007 356p il $23.95
ISBN 978-0-06-114333-5; 0-06-114333-2
LC 2006-48138

"Literary fiction is not often this wildly funny. . . . Knox shifts voices and perspective, from hard-boiled to modern-hip, dropping allusions to people as varied as Richard Nixon and the Ramones. You can tell when an author is having a good time, and Knox has a ball." Seattle Times

Laskas, Gretchen Moran
The **midwife's** tale. Dial Press (NY) 2003 243p $23.95
ISBN 0-385-33551-2
LC 2002-41010

"Set in pre-World War I West Virginia, this novel flows along like the tributaries that feed the book's Appalachian foothills, as narrator Elizabeth Whitely traces the arc of four generations of midwives in her family, she being the last of the line. Poverty, lack of clean water, unemployment, an influenza epidemic, and severe weather also figure in this often melancholy tale. Laskas has injected many period details into her first book and a lot of verve into her characters to make them come alive." Libr J

Laskowski, Tim
Every good boy does fine; a novel. Southern Methodist Univ. Press 2003 176p $23.95
ISBN 0-87074-477-1
LC 2003-40726

"Robert was a recent college graduate with a promising future as a pianist when he fell in a mountain-climbing accident. After weeks in a coma and years in a nursing home, he is placed in a rehabilitation program. At the novel's beginning, he is accepted into an accelerated program that might prepare him for relatively independent living—if he can adapt." Libr J

Lasser, Scott
Say nice things about Detroit; Scott Lasser. W.W. Norton & Co. 2012 267 p.
ISBN 0393082997; 9780393082999
LC 2012006784

In this book, it's 25 "years after his high school graduation, [and] David Halpert returns to a place that most people flee--his hometown of Detroit. But David is making his own escape--from his divorce and the death of his son. In Detroit, David learns about the double shooting of his high school girlfriend Natalie and her black half-brother, Dirk. As David becomes involved with Natalie's sister, he will discover that both he and his hometown have reasons to hope." (Publisher's note)

Latham, Aaron
Code of the West. Simon & Schuster 2001 494p $26
ISBN 0-7432-0117-5
LC 00-51618

"Latham is booth a lyrical and an economical writer, and his ability to bring Jimmy Goodnight fully to life even in the stolen chain mail of a much larger figure transforms this compulsively readable novel from a farce into a good western." Booklist

Lathen, Emma

Brewing up a storm; a John Thatcher mystery. St. Martin's Press 1996 248p

LC 96-22116

In this novel "a protest organization sues a local brewery, claiming that the firm's new nonalcoholic beer contributed to the alcohol-related death of a teenager. When someone murders the protest leader, the brewery calls on series sleuth John Thatcher, a Wall Street banker." Libr J

Lathen, Emma

Double, double, oil and trouble. Simon & Schuster 1978 255p

LC 78-5151

"The scene shifts from London to Istanbul and Houston to Switzerland, in a story that wouldn't work in the hands of a less skilled writer. Lathen knows how to keep her novels from becoming bogged down by excess verbiage and unnecessary violence." Booklist

Lathen, Emma

★ **East** is east. Simon & Schuster 1991 268p

LC 91-32789

This John Putnam Thatcher adventure "takes the senior banking executive from the Sloan Guaranty Trust building in Manhattan on evenly paced travels to Japan, Alaska and England. Lackawanna Electric Industries, rebounding from bankruptcy under the forceful leadership of Carl Kruger, is about to pull off a distribution coup with Yonezawa Trading, one of Japan's largest corporations. Thatcher is present at the Tokyo signing, which is delayed by the discovery of a murdered accountant in Japan's Ministry of International Trade and Investment and a note suggesting a $1-million bribe." Publ Wkly

Ms. Lathen "has a wonderful knack for turning the driest, most complicated corporate maneuvers into high drama, and occasionally burlesque." N Y Times Book Rev

Lathen, Emma

Going for the gold. Simon & Schuster 1981 251p

"Unprecedented banking demands in Lake Placid during the Winter Olympics have caused the Sloan to open a branch. But the man in charge is not what he seems and his doings are followed by two murders and a blizzard. Thatcher and Co. have 48 hours to straighten out the mess. As usual, the background—here athletic—is worked into the plot without seeming forced or padded." Barzun. Cat of Crime. Rev and enl edition

Lathen, Emma

Right on the money; a John Putnam Thatcher mystery. Simon & Schuster 1993 256p

LC 92-35673

A "Wall Street mystery featuring banker John Thatcher of Sloan Guaranty Trust. When a Princeton manufacturing firm represented by a sister bank targets a Sloan family-owned business client for takeover, Thatcher monitors the ensuing negotiations. Friction erupts into fracas, however, when rumors fly, financial records burn, and possible industrial sabotage culminates in murder." Libr J

Lathen, Emma

A **shark** out of water; a John Thatcher mystery. St. Martin's Press 1997 293p

ISBN 0-312-17018-1

LC 97-23036

"Without ruffling his fabled composure, Thatcher manages to clarify the intricacies of international finance for the Polish police officer investigating the crime, and for the rapt reader too." N Y Times Book Rev

Lathen, Emma

Something in the air. Simon & Schuster 1988 270p

LC 88-4491

This mystery featuring "John Thatcher of New York's Sloan Guaranty Trust is set mainly in Boston, headquarters of the commuter airline Sparrow Flyways. A product of airline deregulation, Sparrow is a nonunion operation surviving on horizontal management and project development teams. Mitchell Scovil, CEO and guiding figure of the founders, dreams of expansion, but a group of lower-level employees (and shareholders) is worried about their investment. When their arrogant spokesperson is murdered, the Sloan, holding 20% of unsalable Sparrow stock in a trust, becomes involved." Publ Wkly

Latour, Jose

The **Havana** World Series; José Latour. 1st ed; Grove Press 2003 320p $23

ISBN 0-8021-1754-6

LC 2003-60716

The author "tells the story of a gang of Cuban crooks, funded by New York Mob boss Joe Bonanno, who sets out to rob Meyer Lansky's Capri casino on the last day of the 1958 World Series (when the coffers are overflowing). The portraits of Lansky, Bonnano, and the other gangsters are full-bodied, but it's the fictional blue-collar crooks, led by mastermind Ox Contreras, who give the novel its appeal and afford the best view of Cuban life. Although the documentary style occasionally seems flat, it contrasts nicely with the richness of detail and quirkiness of character." Booklist

Laukkanen, Owen

Criminal enterprise; Owen Laukkanen. G. P. Putnam's Sons 2013 416 p. $26.95

ISBN 0399157905; 9780399157905

LC 2012028673

This book, by Owen Laukkanen, is the second in the "Stevens and Windermere" series. "Carter [Tomlin] . . . robs a bank. Then he robs another. As the red flags start to go up, FBI Special Agent Carla Windermere homes in on Tomlin from one direction, while Minnesota state investigator Kirk Stevens picks up the trail from another. The two cops haven't talked since their first case together, but that's all going to change very quickly." (Publisher's note)

Laukkanen, Owen

The **professionals**; a novel. Owen Laukkanen. Putnam 2012 372 p.

ISBN 9780399157899

LC 2012000907

In this crime novel, "[f]our college friends . . . decide to make money by kidnapping bankers and other extremely wealthy men around the U.S. . . . The group's luck runs out on a Michigan job when their target turns out to be connected to the Mafia, a mistake that starts an avalanche of violence. Their crime spree leads to the involvement of FBI agent Carla Windermere and Minnesota state investigator Kirk Stevens, who race the mob to catch the kidnappers." (Publishers Weekly)

Lauren, Jillian

Pretty; a novel. Plume 2011 275p pa $15

ISBN 978-0-452-29734-0; 0-452-29734-6

LC 2011-05058

"Lauren writes in a relentless semi-poetic style, keenly observing the small handholds that her characters grip to keep themselves from spinning into the void of addiction, or sobriety, whichever cycle they happen to be in. To keep the demons at bay Bebe bands together with other misfits, whether they're her roommates or her classmates, and sometimes both." PopMatters

LaValle, Victor D., 1972-

Big machine; a novel. [by] Victor LaValle. Spiegel & Grau 2009 352p $25

ISBN 978-0-385-52798-9; 0-385-52798-5

LC 2009-00381

"Despite its steady pulse of dark humor, its supernatural Voice and the presence of some creepy entities known as the Devils of the Marsh, Big Machine is a novel about faith and the ways in which religion can create monsters far more terrifying than anything dreamed up by H.P. Lovecraft." Washington Post Book World

LaValle, Victor D., 1972-

The **devil** in silver; a novel. Victor LaValle. 1st ed. Spiegel & Grau 2012 412 p. (ebook) $81.00; (hardcover: acid-free paper) $27.00

ISBN 0679604863; 1400069866; 9780679604860; 9781400069866

LC 2011034970

This horror novel, by Victor LaValle, follows "Pepper, . . . [a] minor-league troublemaker, working-class hero (in his own mind), and, suddenly, the surprised inmate of a . . . mental institution. . . . [H]e's visited by a terrifying creature with the body of an old man and the head of a bison who nearly kills him. . . . It's no delusion: The other patients confirm that a hungry devil roams the hallways. . . . Pepper rallies three other inmates in a plot to fight back." (Publisher's note)

LaValle, Victor D., 1972-

The **ecstatic**; or, Homunculus. {by} Victor LaValle. Crown 2002 272p $22.95

ISBN 0-609-61014-7

LC 2002-6766

The protagonist of this novel is "Anthony James, a 318-pound, 23-year-old, Cornell-educated schizophrenic. In order to keep a semblance of order in his unstable mind, he narrates his family's slow road to destruction. Stops along the way include a small-town beauty pageant in Virginia, a weight-loss clinic, and a McDonald's beseiged by protesting college students. Throughout, Anthony remains sarcastic, intelligent, and conscious of his condition, though control of it increasingly eludes him. His experience is brought to life by Lavelle's acute sensory details and hyperbolic wordplay." Libr J

Lavender, Will

Dominance. Simon & Schuster 2011 353p $25

ISBN 978-1-4516-1729-0; 978-1-4516-1731-3 ebook

LC 2010046118

"Back in 1994, Alex Shipley was one of the elite chosen for a special night class at Jasper College, 'Unraveling a Literary Mystery,' taught by genius professor Richard Aldiss from his prison cell where he was serving a life term for the brutal slayings of two of his female students. Alex became one of Aldiss's favorites and was able to prove his innocence. Seventeen years later, Alex is a literature professor at Harvard, but she is called back to her old stomping ground because someone is killing her former classmates. . . . Well-drawn characters, excellent plot, good use of flashbacks, and many red herrings will keep the pages turning to the very end." Libr J

Law, Susan Kay

The **paper** marriage; Susan Kay Law. Berkley Books 2008 362 p. (pbk.) $19

ISBN 9780425219355

LC 2007046576

This book tells the story of Ann McCrary, whose "marriage came to a standstill when a car crash nearly ended her husband's life and put him into a deep coma. That was 12 years ago, and ever since, her life has been on hold. . . . Then former baseball star Tom Nash moves in, clueless as to how to deal with his rebellious teenage daughter, and Ann's world expands in a totally unexpected way." (Library Journal) "[O]ne night a few days before Ann's wedding anniversary she . . . realiz[es] that after this anniversary she . . . would officially have spent more of [her] relationship with him in a coma than when he was really alive. Tom comes over to comfort her. . . . She ends up getting pregnant after this one night. . . . 5 years after the baby is born Ann's husband finally succumbs to an infection and passes away and the book ends with Ann and Tom getting married." (debbiesworldofbooks.com)

Lawhead, Stephen R.

The **skin** map; Stephen R. Lawhead. Thomas Nelson 2010 403 p. (hardcover) $24.99

ISBN 9781595548047

LC 2010017750

This book follows a young man named Kit Livingston, whose "life has been uneventful--until his great-grandfather appears to him in an alley and tells him a wondrous story about Britain's legendary ley lines. These lines are real roadways to alternate worlds and times. One traveler who explored more than any other tattooed an intricate map on his own skin so he would not get lost in the cosmos. The man and the map have long since vanished, and now the . . . race is on to find the map and the secrets it may reveal." (Library Journal)

Lawhead, Steve

Avalon; the return of King Arthur. by Stephen R. Lawhead. Avon Eos 1999 442p $25

ISBN 0-380-97702-8

LC 99-25048

"In revisiting nearly every romantic Arthurian cliché and playing off snappy contemporary derring-do against the powerful shining glimpses of the historical Arthur he created, Lawhead pulls off a genuinely moving parable of good and evil." Publ Wkly

Lawrence, Caroline

The **case** of the deadly desperados; Caroline Lawrence. G.P. Putnam's Sons 2011 279 p. (Western mysteries) $16.99

ISBN 9780399256332

LC 2011013305

In this book, Caroline "Lawrence shifts her sleuthing . . . [to] Virginia City, Montana in the 1860s. . . . Whittlin' Walt . . . has just scalped and slain the foster parents of twelve-year-old P. K. (Pinky) Pinkerton, . . . who holds a coveted deed to an entire region of silver mines. Pinky hightails it to Virginia City . . . to register his claim, . . . [then] to Chicago, where he wants to join the detective whom he believes to be his father." (Bulletin of the Center for Children's Books)

Lawrence, D. H.

Collected stories; with an introduction by Craig Raine. Knopf 1994 xxxv, 1397p

LC 94-2493

Lawrence, D. H.

★ **Lady** Chatterley's lover; the historic unexpurgated Grove Press edition. with Archibald MacLeish's letter to Barney Rosset, an introduction by Mark Schorer, and Judge Bryan's decision in the obscenity case. Modern Lib. 1993 liii, 491p

ISBN 0-679-60065-5

LC 93-15337

First published 1928 in a limited edition in Florence

A novel "presenting the author's mystical theories of sex in the story of Constance, or Connie, the wife of an English aristocrat, who runs away with her gamekeeper. Her husband, Sir Clifford, has been rendered impotent by a war wound and is also an emotional cripple. The gamekeeper, Mellors, is a forthright individualistic man, uncontaminated by industrial society." Reader's Ency. 4th edition

Lawrence, D. H.

The **rainbow**; with an introduction by Barbara Hardy. Knopf 1993 xxxv, 460p $20

ISBN 0-679-42305-2

LC 93-1860

First published 1915

"The story line traces three generations of the Brangwen family in the Midlands of England from 1840 to 1905. The marriage of farmer Tom Brangwen and foreigner Lydia Lensky eventually breaks down. Likewise, the marriage of Lydia's daughter Anna to Tom's nephew Will gradually fails. The novel is largely devoted to Will and Anna's oldest child, the schoolteacher Ursula, who stops short of marriage when she is unsatisfied by her love affair with the conventional soldier Anton Skrebensky. The appearance of a rainbow at the end of the novel is a sign of hope for Ursula, whose story is continued in Lawrence's Women in Love." Merriam-Webster's Ency of Lit

Followed by Women in love

Lawrence, D. H.

★ **Sons** and lovers. Knopf 1991 xxvii, 403p $17

ISBN 0-679-40572-0

LC 91-53002

First published 1913

"Paul Morel, adored youngest son of a middle-class mother who feels that her coal-miner husband was unworthy of her, has difficulty in breaking away from her. Mrs. Morel has given her son all her warmth and love for so long a time that Paul finds it impossible to establish a relationship with another women. Miriam is supportive and understanding of his artistic nature but appeals mainly to his higher nature; Clara Dawes becomes his mistress but she is married and will not divorce her husband. After the death of his mother, Paul arranges a reconciliation between Clara and her husband and, after months of grieving for his mother, at last finds the strength to strike out on his own." Shapiro. Fic For Youth. 3d edition

Lawrence, D. H.

★ **Women** in love. Knopf 1992 475p

ISBN 0-679-40995-5

LC 91-53191

Sequel to The rainbow

First published 1920

This novel "examines the ill effects of industrialization on the human psyche, resolving that individual and collective rebirth is possible only through human intensity and passion. Women in Love contrasts the love affair of Rupert Birkin and Ursula Brangwen with that of Gudrun, Ursula's artistic sister, and Gerald Crich, a domineering industrialist. Birkin, an introspective misanthrope, struggles to reconcile his metaphysical drive for self-fulfillment with Ursula's practical view of sentimental passion. Their love affair and eventual marriage are set as a positive antithesis to the destructive relationship of Gudrun and Crich." Merriam-Webster's Ency of Lit

Lawrence, David

The **dead** sit round in a ring. Thomas Dunne Books 2004 435p $24.95

ISBN 0-312-32710-2

LC 2004-41878

This mystery offers a "perspective on London that is darker and grittier than in conventional treatments. But the writing is the thing. Whether he's describing a bizarre death scene . . . or observing a group of streetwalkers plying their night trade . . . Lawrence, a published poet, writes with a delicacy and restraint rare in the genre." N Y Times Book Rev

Lawrence, Margaret K.

The **burning** bride; [by] Margaret Lawrence. Avon Bks. 1998 387p

ISBN 0-380-97620-X

LC 98-4491

This novel finds eighteenth-century midwife Hannah Trevor hesitating on the brink of marriage. Her tormented lover, town militia commander Daniel Josselyn, father of her daughter, Jennet, and of the child Hannah now carries, is finally free to wed. But will Daniel insist that she give up her fierce independence and assume the duties of a gentleman's lady? Before she has a chance to find out, a man is murdered and violence erupts in the small Maine community, testing both Hannah and Daniel's loyalties and opening a Pandora's box of dark secrets." Booklist

Lawrence, Margaret K.

Hearts and bones; {by} Margaret Lawrence. Avon Bks. 1996 307p il

ISBN 978-0380973514

LC 96-2394

"Through a combination of diary entries, trial records, autopsy reports, and engrossing narrative, Lawrence reveals the story of a witness and a participant in a brutal war crime and their decade-long silence." Booklist

Lawrence, Mark

Prince of thorns. Ace Books 2011 324p $25.95

ISBN 978-0-441-02032-4; 0-441-02032-1

LC 2010-53561

"The most intriguing part of Prince Of Thorns is the setting. Lawrence gradually drops hints that the book isn't set in some fantasy world or even an alternate medieval Europe, but in a new age of sword and sorcery that rose from the ashes of modern civilization. This is just the opening of the Broken Empire series, and it leaves much to explore on the book's big world map." AV Club

Lawrence, Starling

The **lightning** keeper; a novel. HarperCollins 2006 414p il $25.95

ISBN 0-06-082524-3

LC 2006-280882

"Beautifully written and richly detailed, Lawrence's story brings to life a colorful period in American history and provides a timely reminder that every generation expects too much from its modern marvels." Baltimore Sun

Lawrenson, Deborah

The **lantern**; a novel. Harper 2011 386p $25.99

ISBN 978-0-06-204969-8; 0-06-204969-0

In this novel, "a sensuous gothic novel set in Provence, the chapters alternate between the past and present of Les Genévriers, a possibly haunted hamlet with buildings and fortunes that have crumbled over time. Its current tenants are Eve and Dom, whose romance has whispers of Rebecca (What happened to his ex-wife?). Bénédicte, the previous inhabitant, is a farmer undone by family history and the loss of old ways. Lawrenson's poetic prose vibrantly conjures up both the beauty of southern France and the ghosts, real or imagined, from different eras." Entertainment Wkly

Lawson, Mary

Crow Lake. Dial Press (NY) 2002 291p hardcover o.p. pa $14

ISBN 0-385-33611-X; 0-385-33763-9 pa

LC 2001-53779

"Lawson achieves a breathless anticipatory quality in her surprisingly adept first novel, in which a child tells the story, but tells it very well indeed." Booklist

Lawton, John

Old flames. Atlantic Monthly Press 2003 416p $24

ISBN 0-87113-864-6

LC 2002-28025

"Lawton has created an effective genre-bending novel that is at once a cerebral thriller and an uproarious, deliciously English spoof." Publ Wkly

Layton, Edith

To wed a stranger; Edith Layton. Avon Books 2003 375 p. (pbk.) $5.99

ISBN 0060502177

LC 2003611531

This book tells the story of "Lady Annabelle Wylde, [who] has had many flirtations but has never found love. Nevertheless, she knows she must wed; resigned to a loveless relationship, she dutifully agrees to an arranged marriage with Miles Croft, Viscount Pelham, a man she hardly knows. Disaster strikes on the couple's honeymoon as virulent influenza robs Annabelle of her beauty and vitality, and their relationship takes on a deeper dimension as they learn to know each other and discover what is really important to them." (Library Journal)

Lazar, Zachary

★ **Sway**; a novel. Little, Brown and Co. 2008 255p $23.99

ISBN 978-0-316-11309-0; 0-316-11309-3

LC 2007-9920

"It is not the now-historic acts of violence that make Sway so riveting, but its vivid character portraits and decadent, muzzy atmosphere, all rendered with the heightened sensory awareness associated with drugs and paranoia. The near miniaturist precision with which he describes Keith Richards's attempts to master his guitar, Brian Jones's acid trips and Anger's obsessive desire for Beausoleil bring this large-scale tableau into stunning relief." Time Out N Y

Le Carré, John, 1931-

Absolute friends. Little, Brown 2004 455p $26.95

ISBN 0-316-00064-7

LC 2003-61196

"The central characters in this novel are Ted Mundy, an old-school Englishman, the misfit son of a disgraced British Army major and once a spy but now a tour guide at one of Mad King Ludwig's Bavarian castles; and Sasha, a 1960's German radical. . . . Sasha, whose father was a Lutheran minister with Nazi ties, is a double and possibly a triple agent. . . . Their lives as friends, secret agents and idealists have been intertwined for more than 40 years." N Y Times (Late N Y Ed)

"If le Carre's symbols are a little obvious and his rhetoric a little heated, his technical skill is pure joy." New Leader

Le Carre, John

★ The **constant** gardener; a novel. Scribner 2001 492p

ISBN 0-7432-1505-2

LC 00-53340

"Globalization in its uglier aspects . . . has replaced the Cold War as the moral backdrop in Le Carre's work. His Cold War novels did not spare the conscience even of citizens on the 'right' side, confronting them with crimes committed in their names, and the globalization novels do not spare the stockholder." Atl Mon

Le Carré, John, 1931-

★ A **Delicate** Truth; A Novel. by John Le Carre. Viking Adult 2013 309 p. (hardcover) $28.95

ISBN 0670014893; 9780670014897

LC 2013001536

In this book by John Le Carre, a "plot to capture an arms dealer in Gibraltar under the mantle of counterterrorism goes awry. . . . Toby Bell, who was kept out of the loop, has incriminating information about the mission and the chance to use it three years later when one of the soldiers involved ends up dead and a retired British diplomat, roped into participating against his will, tries to salve his conscience about some nasty pieces of collateral damage." (Publishers Weekly)

Le Carre, John

★ The **honourable** schoolboy. Knopf 1977 533p

LC 77-75001

Jerry Westerby is the honorable schoolboy of the title. He works with George Smiley of the British Secret Service, described by the author as The Circus, to discover why the Russian Secret Service is paying $25,000 a month into the bank account of the prosperous Hong Kong business man, Drake Ko. The action takes place in London and Southeast Asia. The story opens in the Hong Kong press club

This "is superbly well-organized, combining a grandiose sweep with an intricate pattern. It has hard-edged reality instead of fuzzy near-fantasy, a host of sharply etched characters instead of a few eccentric caricatures, and a style which, subtle and flexible . . . never obtrudes, yet never goes unnoticed." Times Lit Suppl

Le Carre, John

The **little** drummer girl. Knopf 1983 429p

LC 82-48733

"Mr. le Carré's novel is certainly the most mature, inventive and powerful book about terrorists-come-to-life this reader has experienced. It transcends the genre." NY Times Book Rev

Le Carre, John

The **looking** glass war. Coward-McCann 1965 320p

"A bitter, cruel, dispassionate—yet passionate—study of an unimportant piece of espionage and the unimportant little men who are involved in it." Book Week

Le Carre, John

The **mission** song. Little, Brown 2006 339p $26.99

ISBN 0-316-01674-8

LC 2006-20099

The "novel's resolutions, romantic and political, are achieved at an emotional distance, behind a thick protective layer of thriller-awareness and thriller expectations. Le Carre has researched his chosen venue diligently . . . and delivered an entertainment whose foremost passion is a commendable indignation over the sufferings of a large African population at the hands of berserk militias, corrupt if not altogether absent government, and, from the West, cold corporate greed. 'The Mission Song' illuminates with animated personifications a portion of the globe's daily misery that tends to be, in American news, at least, murky and abstract." New Yorker

Le Carre, John

A **most** wanted man; a novel. Scribner 2008 323p $28

ISBN 978-1-4165-9488-8; 1-4165-9488-4

LC 2008-30704

"Le Carré's dialogue has snap, rhythm and wit, particularly in those passages where intelligence chiefs maneuver to gain an edge on each other. Too, his immaculate timing helps him fold in different plot lines without smudging narrative pace and tone. Ever the spymaster, he also differentiates the challenges faced by spies today from those of their Cold War counterparts." St. Louis Post-Dispatch

Le Carre, John

The **night** manager; a novel. Knopf 1993 429p

LC 92-55070

Le Carré "brings to the world of the drug wars the same skilled characterization, perceptive detail, and dramatic storytelling that made him the undisputed master of the Cold War spy novel. This novel is precisely what we have come to expect from him: a work of high literary merit that's also great entertainment." Libr J

Le Carre, John

Our **game**; a novel. Knopf 1995 301p

ISBN 0-679-44181-6

LC 95-2666

"This is classic le Carré, spun out beautifully: the ex-spy treated shabbily by his two-bit successors, then besting them by virtue of his superior spycraft. Delicious. But as the plot grows more complex, both politically and psychologically, it becomes clear that even after 14 novels, le Carré has no intention of repeating himself." Newsweek

Le Carre, John

★ **Our** kind of traitor; a novel. Viking 2010 305p $27.95

ISBN 978-0-670-02224-3; 0-670-02224-1

LC 2010-19513

Le Carre "seems positively re-invigorated in a retro sort of way. The story carries on with an extra spring in the step that harkens back, both in the manner of plotting and the style, to le Carré's earliest and still greatest novels. That's due in large part to how he engages with current events: the teetering economy, Britain (and Europe's) austerity-oriented response, and the rise of state surveillance even as the events of September 11 grow more distant." Daily Beast

Le Carre, John
A **perfect** spy. Knopf 1986 475p
LC 85-45587

"Not a spy novel in the usual sense . . . but a skillfully manipulated, complex, and probingly written study spiced with lively anecdotes. To be savored." Libr J

Le Carre, John
The **Russia** house. Knopf 1989 353p
LC 88-46159

"With scarcely an intimation of sex, no violence and not a side arm visible, Le Carre has again managed to construct a plot of commanding suspense. . . . The Russia House is both afire and thought provoking, a thriller that demands a second reading as a treatise on our time." Time

Le Carre, John
The **secret** pilgrim. Knopf 1990 335p
LC 90-52944

"There's always been a didatic quality to le Carré's work that has been part of his novels' charm, but in no other book has he said so much about the ravages that the spying profession works upon the agent." Newsweek

Le Carre, John
Single & Single; a novel. Scribner 1999 345p $26
ISBN 0-684-85926-2
LC 98-47174

Le Carré "provides a fascinating journey through the new landscape of corruption. . . . The power of {this novel} stems from the author's portrait of a world in which individuals are no match for the organized mania of greed." Time

Le Carre, John
Smiley's people. Knopf 1980 374p
LC 79-2299

First published 1979 in the United Kingdom
This novel "is a complete winner, exciting, well-paced, and convincing. . . . There is a lot of the Le Carré gloom, but now it seems almost elegiac and touching. Absolutely not to be missed." Libr J

Le Carre, John
The **spy** who came in from the cold. Walker & Company 2005 223p $19
ISBN 0-8027-1454-4

First published 1963 in the United kingdom; first United States edition published 1964 by Coward-McCann
"The story of Alec Leamas, 50-year-old professional secret agent who has grown stale in espionage, who longs to 'come in from the cold' and how he undertakes one last assignment before that hoped-for retirement. Over the years Leamas has grown unsure where his workday carapace ends and his real self begins. . . . Recalled from Berlin after the death of his last East German contact at the Wall, Leamas lets himself be seduced into a pretended defection-thereby providing the East Germans with data from which they can

deduce that the head of their own spy apparatus is a double agent." N Y Times Book Rev

Le Carre, John
The **tailor** of Panama. Knopf 1996 331p
ISBN 0-679-45446-2
LC 96-34802

Le Carré "reveals in the contortions of British diplomats, aghast at the arriviste spy masters whom they pretend to accept, all the while struggling to extricate themselves from absurd but inevitable catastrophe. Readers who wonder whether Graham Greene was not here 40 years ago are right, and Mr le Carré acknowledges his debt to 'Our Man in Havana'. This tale, told with wit and ingenuity, is a splendid homage from one master of political thrillers to another." Economist

Le Carre, John
★ **Tinker,** tailor, soldier, spy. Knopf 1974 355p

Smiley "instinctively realises from the outset who the traitor is but refuses to confront the embarrassing truth. A perceptive reader will sense the secret too, but one goes on reading entranced not so much by the ramifications of the plot, beautifully engineered though it is, as by concern for the characters, a rare thing in thrillers." New Statesman (1913)

Le Clezio, J.-M. G.
Mondo and other stories; translated [from the French] by Alison Anderson. University of Nebraska Press 2011 236p $50; pa $19.95
ISBN 978-0-8032-2999-0; 0-8032-2999-2; 978-0-8032-3000-2 pa; 0-8032-3000-1 pa
LC 2010-32665

Original French edition, 1978
"Le Clezio's style is the collection's greatest attraction. Anderson's elegant translation conveys the detailed, physical, fluid, and complex lushness of the language, which may engage and satisfy readers of García Márquez and other master stylists." Booklist

Le Fanu, Joseph Sheridan, 1814-1873
Uncle Silas; a tale of Bartram-Haugh. Joseph Sheridan Le Fanu; edited with introduction and notes by Victor Sage. Penguin 2000 xli, 476 p.p (pbk.) $14
ISBN 0140437460
LC 2001276573

In this book "[f]rom the moment that Madame de la Rougierre is hired as governess to the young, naïve Maud Ruthyn, a dark cloud of foreboding hangs over the entire household. A liar, a bully and a spy, Madame eventually leaves, taking her dark secret with her. But unhappily for Maud, that is not the last of Madame de la Rougierre. For when Maud is orphaned she is sent to live with her Uncle Silas, her father's mysterious brother, a man with a scandalous - even murderous - past. Here she encounters Madame once more. This time her sinister role in Maud's destiny is all too clear." (Publisher's note)
Includes bibliographical references

Le Guin, Ursula K., 1929-

The **beginning** place. Harper & Row 1980 183p

LC 79-2653

"The style is fluent, concise and elegant, and the story that is told is easily understood by anyone who has ever found himself at a loss to deal with the realities of modern life." Best Sellers

Le Guin, Ursula K.

The **birthday** of the world and other stories. HarperCollins Pubs. 2002 362p $24.95

ISBN 0-06-621253-7

LC 2001-39508

"Le Guin appears to have the most fun with her investigations of sex and gender . . . but the costs of revolution, religious bliss, and technology are also provicatively explored, and one returns to the current headlines with a fresh awareness of the exotic providional nature of human arrangements." New Yorker

Le Guin, Ursula K.

★ The **dispossessed**; an ambiguous Utopia. Harper & Row 1974 341p il

ISBN 9780060512750; 9781451783964; 9780060504007

"Shevek, a brilliant physicist, is caught between the prejudices and hatreds of two worlds. His quest to bridge the gap between Ararres, an anarchist, egalitarian society, and Varas, a structured, capitalistic world, unleashes a storm of intrigue and drama. The two distinct cultures provide insights into the role of women in society, the issue of free will versus obligation to the state, human rights, and ecomonic systems." Shapiro. Fic for Youth. 3d edition

Le Guin, Ursula K.

Four ways to forgiveness. HarperPrism 1995 228p

LC 95-11459

"Four interrelated novellas deal with the Hainish culture on the twin planets of Werel and Yeowe and examine the relationship between love, freedom and forgiveness." Publ Wkly

Le Guin, Ursula K.

The **lathe** of heaven. Scribner 1971 184p

"The author has done some profound research in psychology, cerebro-physiology and biochemistry. . . . In addition, her perceptions of such matters as geopolitics, race, socialized medicine and the patient/shrink relationship are razor-sharp and more than a little cutting." Natl Rev

Le Guin, Ursula K.

★ The **left** hand of darkness; with a new afterword and appendixes by the author. 25th Anniversary ed; Walker & Co. 1994 345p

ISBN 0-8027-1302-5

LC 94-27147

A reissue of the title first published 1969 by Walker & Company

"This is a tale of political intrigue and danger on the world of Gethen, the Winter planet. Genly Ai, high official of the Eukeman—the commonwealth of worlds—is on Gethen to convince the royalty to join the Federation. He soon becomes a pawn in Gethen's power struggles, set against the elaborate mores of the Gethenians, a unisex hermaphroditic people whose intricate sexual physiology plays a key role in the conflict. Allied with Estraven, fallen lord, Genly is forced to cross the savage and impassable Gobrin Ice." Shapiro. Fic for Youth. 3d edition

Le Guin, Ursula K.

Orsinian tales. Harper & Row 1976 179p

This is a cycle of interrelated short stories. "Set in a vaguely Middle-European country, Le Guin's tales deal with love, freedom, and tyranny in a society which over a series of historical periods appears to be perpetually in the last stages preceding cataclysm." Booklist

Le Guin, Ursula K., 1929-

The **other** wind. Harcourt 2001 246p

ISBN 0151006849

LC 2001-24632

In this novel, Alder the sorcerer is troubled by dreams of the dead, who may gain enough strength to invade Earthsea.

"The Earthsea saga, begun in 1968 as a young adults' series, has evolved into one of Le Guin's, and modern science fiction's, signature achievements." N Y Times Book Rev

Le Guin, Ursula K.

The **telling**. Harcourt 2000 264p

ISBN 0-15-100567-2

LC 00-29574

A title in the authors Hainish cycle. "As a member of the Ekumen's embassy on the planet Aka, Sutty undertakes a delicate mission that leads her to a mountain village reported to contain the last remnants of a dying culture. Following a trail of subtle clues concealed in stories and folk sayings, Sutty discovers the suppressed history of a planet willing to abandon its old ways in the name of progress. . . . This parable of the modern world's headlong rush toward monocultural sterility exemplifies the author's elegant simplicity and keen insight." Libr J

Le, Thi Diem Thuy

The **gangster** we are all looking for. Knopf 2003 160p $18

ISBN 0-375-40018-4

LC 2002-33999

"The nameless first-person narrator is born in Vietnam, carried across the ocean by her father and 'washed to shore' in Linda Vista, a section of San Diego. Her 'Ba' finds work as a house painter, a welder and finally a gardener. It is two years before her mother joins them and her parents' tempestuous marriage moves to center stage, but the father is always a haunted, brooding presence in this drama of the narrator's coming-of-age." N Y Times Book Rev

"The story opens slowly but gathers strength, and though it remains somewhat muted, Le's lyrical writing and skill with the telling vigette will reward patient readers." Libr J

Leavitt, Caroline

Pictures of you; a novel. Algonquin Books of Chapel Hill 2010 335p pa $13.95

ISBN 978-1-56512-631-2; 1-56512-631-9

LC 2010-09362

This novel "opens with a car crash between two women on a foggy Connecticut highway. Each is driving away from her marriage, though for different reasons. Isabelle, 36 and childless, has left the Cape Cod town of Oakrose and the man she married as a teenager for a fresh start in New York. April, a young mother in a frilly, mysterious red dress, has also left Oakrose, heading who knows where with a backseat stowaway discovered moments before the two cars collide: her asthmatic, nine-year-old son, Sam. April is killed, the mystery of her destination dying (for the moment) with her. Sam and Isabelle survive. Isabelle isn't charged; even so, she's plagued by guilt and the overactive imaginations of small-town types. Isolated and depressed (her husband is having a baby with another woman), she finds herself spying on Sam and his grieving father, Charlie, who, it turns out, live just six blocks away. At his school playground, Sam is the first to see and recognize Isabelle standing nearby; he becomes convinced that she's an angel who will help him talk to his dead mother. Circumstances (not always believable) conspire to draw the fated triangle together. . . . There's a page-turning pull to Pictures of You that will no doubt please readers who have come to count on Leavitt for the satisfactions of a good domestic drama." Boston Phoenix

Leavitt, David

The **Indian** clerk; a novel. Bloomsbury 2007 485p $24.95

ISBN 978-1-59691-040-9; 1-59691-040-2

LC 2007-9061

"Mathematics and its paradoxes provide a deep vein of metaphor that Leavitt uses to superb effect, demonstrating how the most meaningful relationships can defy both logic and imagination." New Yorker

Leavitt, David

★ The **lost** language of cranes. Knopf 1986 319p

ISBN 0-394-53873-0

LC 86-45277

"Mr Leavitt's sense of pacing, his graceful sentences and his storytelling ability dovetail nicely. On the other hand, the book feels young—experientially thin, intellectually timid, contrived, erratic and, understandably, not yet wise. . . . 'The Lost Language of Cranes' lingers in the mind, greater than the sum of its problematic parts." N Y Times Book Rev

Leavitt, David

Martin Bauman; or, A sure thing. Houghton Mifflin 2000 387p $26

ISBN 0-395-90243-6

LC 00-27589

"Martin Bauman, the gay writer protagonist of Leavitt's self-referential novel, has not even come out to himself let alone his parents or friends when he enters college in 1980. Happiest in the company of lesbians and seemingly immune to lust or love, he assiduously cultivates his literary ambitions under the brutal tutelage of professor Stanley Flint, who warns him that his need for approval and preference for 'a sure thing' could turn him into a mere hack. Flint continues to be his nemesis even after Martin achieves instant fame by disclosing his homosexuality in the first 'gay' short story ever published in the New York literary magazine, and Martin, analyzing himself two decades later, acknowledges Flint's prescience as he relates, in detail both mesmerizing and maddening, the story of his early success and rapid comeuppance." Booklist

Leavitt, David

While England sleeps. Viking 1993 304p

LC 92-45878

"A narrative that for the most part rings true, though in a curiously mannered way. The reader ends up with a feeling of respect for the assiduous research that has been undertaken, rather than with any sense of deep involvement with the characters." N Y Times Book Rev

Lebbon, Tim

Fallen. Bantam Spectra 2008 413p il pa $12

ISBN 978-0-553-38467-3; 0-553-38467-8

LC 2008-10401

"Some 4,000 years before the events of Dusk (2006), the people of Noreela are just beginning an era of expansion, with explorers going constantly further into unknown territory for profit and glory. Blocking the voyagers' southward journeys, however, is the Great Divide, a cliff that reaches into the clouds. Ramus Rheel, an aging explorer battling cancer, and Nomi Hyden, whose wealth has not diminished her craving for adventure, are friendly enemies who set out to scale the Divide and earn recognition as the greatest voyagers of all. When they find the lair of one of the ancient Sleeping Gods, they get considerably more excitement—and terror—than they bargained for. Lebbon creates vivid and convincing major and minor characters, places and creatures, blending wonder and nightmare in this dark and memorable novel." Publ Wkly

Lebrecht, Norman

The **song** of names. Anchor Bks. 2004 311p pa $14

ISBN 1-4000-3489-2 pa

LC 2003-67451

"Lebrecht's story delves into the horrors of the Holocaust and the Blitz, as well as the quiet communities of Hasidic Judaism that developed in Britain after the flight of so many refugees. What emerges is a vivid and outstanding story that sings about artistry, genius, music, love, envy, friendship, and revenge." Booklist

LeCraw, Holly

The **swimming** pool. Doubleday 2010 307p $25.95

ISBN 978-0-385-53193-1; 0-385-53193-1

LC 2009-08314

"This novel about Cape Cod's social circles reveals the upper-middle-class miseries hiding beneath its sanitized and highly chlorinated surface. When Jed, a moody lawyer in his mid-20s, finds an old, crumpled bathing suit in a closet at the family vacation home, it leads him to Marcella, a divorcé who, years earlier, conducted an affair with his father.

Jed and Marcella then embark on their own liasion. In The Swimming Pool, Holly LeCraw wades slowly into her narrative instead of diving straight in, so the story takes a while to pick up. But once it does, the suburban afflictions that are drowning these characters make it difficult to put down." Entertainment Wkly

Ledgard, J. M.

Submergence; a novel. by J. M. Ledgard. Coffee House Press 2013 209 p. (pbk.) $15.95

ISBN 1566893194; 9781566893190

LC 2012036524

In this novel, "James More is held captive by jihadist fighters. Posing as a water expert to report on al-Qaeda activity in the area, he now faces extreme privation. . . . On the Greenland Sea, Danielle Flinders, a biomathematician, half-French, half-Australian, prepares to dive in a submersible to the ocean floor. Both are drawn back . . . to a French hotel on the Atlantic coast, where a chance encounter on the beach led to an intense and enduring romance." (Publisher's note)

Lee, C. Y.

The **flower** drum song. Farrar, Straus & Cudahy 1957 244p

A story of family life in San Francisco's Chinatown. The principal characters are the elderly Mr. Wang and his oldest son, Wang Ta, torn between Chinese tradition and western custom

"A first novel that is always fascinating, and by turns amusing and pathetic—a novel written with grace and decorum in the even, unimpassioned narrative style that is characteristic of classical Chinese fiction." Chicago Sunday Trib

Lee, Chang-rae, 1965-

Aloft. Riverhead Books 2004 343p $24.95

ISBN 1-573-22263-1

LC 2003-58630

Set on affluent Long Island, {this novel} follows the life of a suburban, upper-middle-class man during a time of family crisis. Jerry Battle's favorite diversion is to fly his small plane over the neighboring towns and villages. When his daughter and her fiance arrive from Oregon to announce their marriage plans, he looks back on his life and faces his disengagement with it . . . and the people he loves." Publisher's note

Lee, Chang-rae, 1965-

A gesture life. Riverhead Bks. 1999 356p

ISBN 1-573-22146-5

LC 99-28382

"This is a wise, humane, fully rounded story, deeply but unsentimentally moving, and permeated with insights about the nature of human relationships." Publ Wkly

Lee, Chang-rae, 1965-

★ The **surrendered**. Riverhead Books 2010 469p $26.95

ISBN 9781594489761; 1-59448-976-9

LC 2009-30887

This is a novel by the author of Aloft (2004) and The Drama of Consciousness (2006). "The lasting memory of the Korean War changes the lives of two of its survivors—a

Korean girl and an American vet—as well as the lives of those who come to know them. Hector Brennan was a handsome GI stationed in Korea during the war. June Han was a girl orphaned by the fighting. For a season of wartime existence, their lives overlapped at a missionary-run orphanage. Now, thirty years later, they are reunited in the United States in an unusual mission that will force them to come to terms with their individual experiences of that time, but also the secret they share." (Publisher's note)

"In its ineffably quiet way, there really is something Tolstoyan in this searching fiction's determination to understand the characters specifically as members of families and products of other people's influences. The characterizations of Hector and Sylvie are astonishingly rich and complex, and the risktaken in depicting the adult June as the woman readers will hope she would not become is triumphantly vindicated." Kirkus

Lee, Don

Country of origin. W.W. Norton & Co 2004 315p $24.95

ISBN 0-393-05812-3

LC 2004-4722

"Set in Tokyo in 1980, the book centers on the disappearance of Lisa Countryman, a half-Japanese, half-black Berkeley graduate student who goes to Japan to research the 'sad, brutal reign of conformity' for her dissertation and, perhaps more importantly, embark on an identity quest. . . . When she vanishes, it is first brought to the attention of Tom Hurley, a vain and careless junior diplomat at the U.S. Embassy who tells people he's Hawaiian, though he's really half-Korean and half-white. The case is turned over to Kenzo Ota, a glum, divorced police inspector, who spent three hard years of his adolescence in Missouri." Publ Wkly

"Issues of race, class, and national identity drive this clear-eyed story of closure, redemption, and carving out a place in the world." Booklist

Lee, Gus

China boy; a novel. Dutton 1991 322p hardcover o.p. pa $14

ISBN 0-525-24994-X; 0-452-27158-4 pa

LC 90-21687

"Based on events in his own childhood, Mr. Lee's depiction of Kai's efforts to reconcile his Chinese heritage with the several equally bewildering worlds of American culture he is simultaneously exposed to . . . is vivid and moving." N Y Times Book Rev

Followed by Honor & duty (1994)

Lee, Harper

★ To kill a mockingbird; Harper Lee. 50th anniversary ed; Harper 2010 323p $25.00

ISBN 9780061743528

A reissue of the title first published 1960 by Lippincott

"Scout, as Jean Louise is called, is a precocious child. She relates her impressions of the time when her lawyer father, Atticus Finch, is defending a black man accused of raping a white woman in a small Alabama town during the 1930's. Atticus's courageous act brings the violence and injustice that exists in their world sharply into focus as it intrudes into the lighthearted life that Scout and her brother

Jem have enjoyed until that time." Shapiro. Fic for Youth. 3d edition

Lee, Janice Y. K.

The **piano** teacher. Viking 2009 336p $25.95

ISBN 978-0-670-02048-5

LC 2008-27449

"This cinematic tale of two love affairs in mid-century Hong Kong shows colonial pretensions tainted by wartime truths. Will Truesdale, a rootless, handsome Briton, arrives in the colony in 1941, and is swept up by Trudy Liang, the blithe and glamorous daughter of a Shanghai millionaire and a Portuguese beauty. They quickly become inseparable, their days spent in a whirl of parties and champagne, but when the Japanese invade, Will is interned and Trudy resorts to increasingly Faustian methods to survive. After the war, Claire Pendleton, the naïve wife of a British civil servant, arrives. She begins giving piano lessons to the daughter of a rich Chinese couple, and falls in love with their wounded and inscrutable driver: Will. Lee unfolds each story, and flits between them, with the brisk grace and discretion of the society she describes—a world in which horrors are adumbrated but seldom told." New Yorker

Lee, Krys

★ **Drifting** house; Krys Lee. Viking 2012 210 p.

ISBN 9780670023257

LC 2011036188

This book presents short stories "about the conflicts between Korean and American culture. [Krys] Lee tends to focus on domestic relationships, the tensions--sometimes unbridgeable--between husband and wife, between parent and child. In the opening story, 'A Temporary Marriage,' Mrs. Shin saves money to travel from Seoul to southern California to find her daughter Yuri, who she feels has been 'kidnapped' and spirited away to America by her ex-husband." (Kirkus Reviews)

Lee, Marie Myung-Ok

Somebody's daughter; Marie Myung-Ok Lee. Beacon Press 2005 x, 264 p.p (cloth: acid-free paper) o.p.; (pbk.) $16

ISBN 0807083887; 0807083895

LC 2004025757

This novel tells the "story of Sarah Thorson, who discovers the truth about her birth when she is nineteen. Sarah's story begins when she drops out of the University of Minnesota and, more by happenstance than design, decides to study in Korea. As the summer progresses, Sarah becomes more and more intrigued by her Korean heritage, eventually discovering the truth about her adoption: her birth mother did not die in a car crash. With the help of two remarkable men, Jun-Ho Kim, a Korean hoping to befriend Americans, and Doug Henderson, a Korean American struggling with his mixed heritage, Sarah embarks on a crusade to find her birth mother that leads her to a deepening involvement with the culture, language, and people of Korea." (Publisher's note)

Lee, Mark

The **canal** house. Algonquin Bks. 2003 353p $23.95

ISBN 1-56512-379-4

LC 2003-40401

This is the "story of the life and death of war correspondent Daniel McFarland, who after a brush with death in Uganda develops a new sense of mission and responsibility toward those whose wracked lives he is covering. He is drawn into an affair with Julia Cadel, an English doctor who idealistically ministers to the suffering in war zones, and the book's title refers to a brief idyll they share in London before setting out again on dangerous missions. Their new one is in East Timor." Publ Wkly

"Lee is a foreign correspondent who creates a powerful aura of realism that will forever alter your perception of the news." Booklist

Lee, Tanith

White as snow. TOR Bks. 2000 319p hardcover o.p. pa $15.95

ISBN 0-312-86993-2; 0-312-87549-5 pa

LC 00-41160

In this reworking of Snow White "evil queen, Arpazia, first appears as an innocent princess of 14, who is terrified when Draco, a rising new leader, conquers her father's castle and rapes her. Soon after he has her sister, Lilca, hanged because Lilca betrayed the castle. Draco forces Arpazia to travel with him and his barbaric army. She later bears him a girl, Candacis, whom she immediately shuns as an incarnation of evil, mumbling death spells as the infant tries to suckle her." Publ Wkly

"Incorporating many traditional fairy-tale elements, Lee's Gothic story is set in a medieval world filled with castles, wars, dwarves, pagan lore, and Christian ritual." Libr J

Leebron, Fred G.

In the middle of all this. Harcourt 2002 251p $30

ISBN 0-15-100834-5

LC 2001-5955

"Leebron's exceptional skills as a storyteller and observer of humanity produce a novel both tremendously enjoyable and grandly poignant, a novel almost anthropological in its keen examination of man's fate." Publ Wkly

Legal fictions; short stories about lawyers and the law. edited by Jay Wishingrad. Overlook Press 1992 402p

LC 91-46664

Lehane, Dennis

The **given** day; a novel. William Morrow 2008 704p $27.95

ISBN 978-0-688-16318-1; 0-688-16318-1

LC 2008-35137

This novel is set at the "end of the First World War, as waves of immigration, uneasy race relations, and agitation over labor issues culminate in a police strike in Boston. Danny, a patrolman and the son of a powerful captain, pursues a pair of anarchists determined to create chaos but also finds himself drawn to the growing police union; Luther, a talented black baseball player, flees to Boston after killing a drug lord in Tulsa. Lehane laces his narrative with melodrama—two brothers in love with the same woman, who harbors a secret past; a viciously racist cop out to destroy Luther and frame the burgeoning N.A.A.C.P.—and a subplot, involving Babe Ruth, feels stale and unnecessary. But he brings vividly to life the struggles that the working classes faced in pursuit of decent working conditions and a fair wage." New Yorker

Lehane, Dennis

★ **Live** by night; Dennis Lehane. William Morrow 2012 401 p.

ISBN 0060004878; 9780060004873

LC 2012462328

This novel by Dennis Lehane tells the story of "Joe Coughlin, . . . [who has] graduated from a childhood of petty theft to a career in the pay of [Boston's] most fearsome mobsters. . . . Joe embarks on a dizzying journey up the ladder of organized crime that takes him from the flash of Jazz Age Boston to the sensual shimmer of Tampa's Latin Quarter to the sizzling streets of Cuba." (Publisher's note)

Lehane, Dennis

Moonlight mile. William Morrow 2010 324p $26.99

ISBN 978-0-06-183692-3

LC 2010-25883

"Unlike the usual sequel writer who simply puts old creations through new paces, Mr. Lehane registers a deep affection for the Kenzie-Gennaro team and a passionate involvement in their problems. And he treats each book in this series as an occasion for wondering what kind of world can produce the depravity that each new plotline describes." N Y Times (Late N Y Ed)

Lehane, Dennis

★ **Mystic** river. Morrow 2001 401p il $25

ISBN 0-688-16316-5

LC 2001-273012

"Lehane identifies that turning point in the life and spiritual death of a working-class Boston neighborhood as the day in 1975 when 11-year-old Dave Boyle climbed into a car with two strange men—and his best friends, Sean Devine and Jimmy Marcus, did not. A quarter-century later, when the murder of Jimmy's 19-year-old daughter forces the three of them into a heart-scorching reunion, they still carry the scars of that childhood trauma. 'Maybe they had gotten in that car. All three of them,' Sean thinks. 'And what they now thought of as their life was just a dream state.' Lehane spares nothing in his wrenching descriptions of how a crime in the neighborhood kills the neighborhood, taking it down house by house, family by family." N Y Times Book Rev

Lehane, Dennis

Prayers for rain; a novel. Morrow 1999 337p $25

ISBN 0-688-15333-X

LC 99-22048

"In what he thinks is an open-and-shut case, Boston private investigator Patrick Kenzie and his sidekick Bubba Rowgoski convince Cody Falk, a stalker with a nasty record of rape and sexual assault, to cease his harassment of Pat-

rick's client, Karen Nichols. But six months later, a naked Karen leaps to her death off the observation deck of the Custom House tower. . . . Aided by Bubba and ex-partner/ex-lover Angie Gennaro, Patrick decides to investigate Karen's death. . . . Lehane's love of Boston, its neighborhoods, and its people shines through his hard-edged prose." Libr J

Lehane, Dennis

Sacred. Morrow 1997 288p

ISBN 0-688-14381-4

LC 96-53115

"When detectives Patrick Kenzie and Angela Gennaro are kidnapped by dying billionaire Trevor Stone and forced to find his lost daughter, they become entwined in a vicious whodunit in which 'up is down and north is south.' The case takes them to Grief Release Inc., a Boston-area church/cult whose members purge their sins, secrets, and financial records; then, accompanied by Stone's henchmen, to Tampa, Florida, where a top-of-the-line sports car and all the money they can spend are put at their disposal. . . . When the detectives finally find their prize, the perfecto, leggy Desiree Stone, she turns out to be much more than they bargained for." Libr J

Lehane, Dennis

Shutter Island. Morrow 2003 325p $25.95

ISBN 0-688-16317-3

LC 2003-48744

"From the 1993 perspective of the prologue, Shutter Island is one of those unpopulated islands in Boston's outer harbor that always look so mysterious from a distance and so scruffy up close. But in 1954, when the United States marshall Teddy Daniels and his partner, Chuck Aule, alight on its rocky shores to hunt for an escaped murderess, this bleak spot is home to Ashecliffe Hospital, a maximum-security institution for the criminally insane. . . . The atmosphere is properly dark and moody, and so long as Teddy and Chuck stick to the manhunt and their investigation of Ashecliffe's creepy medical staff, they play their roles with muscle and grace." N Y Times Book Rev

Lehmann, Stephanie

Astor Place Vintage; Stephanie Lehmann. Simon & Schuster 2013 416 p. (paperback) $16

ISBN 1451682050; 9781451682052; 9781451682069

LC 2012031168

This novel "tells the stories of two New York women a century apart." The "present-day timeline involves Amanda Rosenbloom, who owns the eponymous Astor Place Vintage clothing store and has a strong attachment to the past. . . . Amanda discovers the 1907 diary of Olive Westcott, an upper-class woman who dreamed of becoming a department store buyer. The story switches to the past, with Olive, after her father's death, facing widespread prejudices" against women working. (Publishers Weekly)

Lehrer, Jim

Purple dots; a novel. Random House 1998 262p $23.95

ISBN 0-679-45237-0

LC 98-12962

"The bad guys in this comedy of errors are uniformly inept and arrogant. The good guys behave like overgrown kids. Lehrer . . . has produced a very funny novel of Washington politics, broad and subtle by turns, and sly throughout." Libr J

Lehrer, Jim

The **special** prisoner; a novel. Random House 2000 227p

ISBN 0-375-50371-4

LC 00-701284

"A chance airport encounter sends retired Methodist bishop John Quincy Watson to San Diego, following a man whose too-familiar eyes drag Watson 50 years into the past, to a Japanese prisoner of war camp, where the then youthful, red-haired B29 pilot became a 'special prisoner' when captured after parachuting from his dying plane. His pursuit of the interrogator he knew as Tashimoto, the Hyena, alternates with the minister's memories of the horrors of Camp Sengei 4." Booklist

Leiber, Fritz

The **Wanderer**. Walker & Co. 1970 318p

First published 1964 in paperback by Ballantine Books

A "novel telling of the havoc caused by the arrival of a strange planet in the Solar System. Its mosaic narrative technique, through which events are observed through a multiplicity of viewpoints, foreshadowed the profusion of such novels and films in the 1970s." Ency of Sci Fic

Leicht, Stina

Of blood and honey; a book of the fey and the fallen. Night Shade 2011 296p pa $14.99

ISBN 978-1-59780-213-0

"Liam Kelly grows up in the Catholic section of Derry, Northern Ireland, aware that the man who married his mother was not his father, and he hates him for it. What Liam doesn't know is that his true father is a member of the Fair Folk, who are at war with the Fallen, angels exiled from Heaven who now cause trouble on Earth. As the Troubles of the 1970s escalate, another battle rages behind the scenes and threatens everything Liam loves. . . . [This book] treats a complicated era with realism and sensitivity while infusing the violence of the times with dark magic and spiritual warfare." Libr J

Leimbach, Marti

Daniel isn't talking. Nan A. Talese 2006 275p $22.95

ISBN 0-385-51751-3

LC 2005-52890

"Watching a handicapped child rend the fragile seams of a woman's personality and her marriage exposes us to some of the more honest and guilty realities of being a parent, and with it a mother's very human pursuit of a livable, if not perfect, ending." N Y Times Book Rev

Leimbach, Marti

The **man** from Saigon; a novel. Nan A. Talese/Doubleday 2010 342p $25.95

ISBN 978-0385-52986-0; 0-385-52986-4

LC 2009-30332

First published 2009 in the United Kingdom

"Sent by a women's magazine to find human-interest stories in 1967 Saigon, journalist Susan Gifford forms a fateful alliance with Son, a Vietnamese photographer. Traveling with U.S. troops, Gifford and Son survive an ambush only to be captured by the Vietcong. What follows is harrowing, as Leimbach vividly recreates the chemical strafing of the countryside, the misery of the refugee camps and the suffocating humidity of the jungle. This impressive novel finds a new way of illuminating the horrors of an old war." People

Leithauser, Brad

The **art** student's war. Alfred A. Knopf 2009 495p il $28.95

ISBN 978-0-307-27111-2; 0-307-27111-0

LC 2009-19468

"Detroit, 1943. In a crowded streetcar, a young soldier on crutches gallantly insists on a pretty young woman taking the one vacant seat. It's a Norman Rockwell moment, and Bea Paradiso, an 18-year-old art student, will cherish it. Her family considers her overemotional; certainly she is ardent and impressionable. Soon she will find an outlet for her patriotism, visiting the hospital to sketch wounded soldiers, giving them back their 'prewar faces.' The visits provide an escape from home, in turmoil since Bea's deranged mother accused her sister, sweet Aunt Grace, of trying to steal her husband Vico, an immigrant building contractor. . . . Bea also finds respite in the company of fellow art student Ronny Olsson, handsome, talented, provocative and heir to the city's largest drugstore chain." Kirkus

This novel "is, at its core, a traditional American wartime love story. As such, it is timely and engrossing." Boston Globe

Leithauser, Brad

A **few** corrections; a novel. Knopf 2001 273p $24

ISBN 0-375-41149-6

LC 00-62010

"At first, this exploration of a small-town Midwestern Lothario's life is like something out of Dreiser: Wesley Sultan—Rotarian, Episcopalian, and aspiring businessman—seems emphatically ordinary. The relevant characters, however, are Wesley's second wife, the brilliant, self-deprecating Sally, in France, who speaks in the style of the novels that fuel her mental life; and his brother Conrad, in Miami, riddled with disease and quite definitely raging against the dying of the light. The novel is formally constructed, each chapter offering a correction to the obituary of Wesley that appears on the first page, and this sobriety of design contrasts with the inventiveness of Leithauser's portraits." New Yorker

Lelchuk, Alan

Ziff; a life?: a novel. Carroll & Graf Pubs. 2003 408p $25

ISBN 0-7867-1115-9

LC 2002-191184

"Dimming literary light Danny Levitan takes a last shot at glory by penning a biography of his onetime mentor and sometime friend, Arthur Ziff, a great American writer whom many Jews consider a traitor, and whose sex-charged novels have been overlooked by the Pulitzer and Nobel committees.

What gives this story frisson is author Lelchuk's similar relationship with Philip Roth." Booklist

Lelic, Simon

The **child** who; a novel. Simon Lelic. Penguin Books 2012 303 p.

ISBN 0143120913; 9780143120919

LC 2011045210

In this book, "Felicity was a bright, bouncy, much-liked preteen. Adults doted on her, schoolmates clustered around her, and her future seemed unlimited--until Daniel Blake, barely a year older, assaulted her, tortured her, bound her hands with wire and left her to drown. County solicitor Leo Curtice happens to answer the phone call requesting representation for Daniel. From the moment he agrees, his life spirals out of control. . . . Leo needs to understand why Daniel became Daniel. The boy has nothing to say. . . . But Leo keeps asking why: why did this happen, what's in Daniel's past? When menacing letters arrive threatening Leo's family, he downplays the danger. . . . Then Leo's daughter goes missing, and he and his wife suffer the anguish of Felicity's family." (Kirkus)

Lelic, Simon

The **facility**; [a novel] Simon Lelic. Penguin Books 2011 339 p. (paperback) $15.00

ISBN 0143120689; 9780143120681

LC 2012023398

In this novel, by Simon Lelic, set "[i]n a near-future dystopian Britain, . . . [e]mboldened by new anti-terrorism laws, police start to 'disappear' people from the streets. . . . But when . . . Arthur Priestley is . . . held prisoner at a top-secret facility, his estranged wife, Julia, and a brave but naive journalist named Tom Clarke embark on a harrowing quest for the truth. Following a trail that leads to the very top of government, they soon find themselves fighting for their lives." (Publisher's note)

Lem, Stanislaw

★ **Eden**; translated by Marc E. Heine. Harcourt Brace Jovanovich 1989 262p

LC 89-1963

This novel "details the adventures of the crew of a crash-landed spaceship on an alien planet. The crew, composed of Captain, Engineer, Physicist, Cyberneticist, Doctor and Chemist, and remaining mostly nameless . . . sets about repairing the ship and exploring the beautiful, unmapped planet. They encounter increasingly exotic creatures and phenomena which they assume they understand, but all-too-human errors lead them to misinterpret nearly everything. Finally, when a communication of sorts is initiated with one of the planet's natives, the crew learns the full extent of their illusions." Publ Wkly

"No one writes sf more intellectually challenging or of greater literary distinction than Lem." Booklist

Lem, Stanislaw

★ **Fiasco**; translated from the Polish by Michael Kandel. Harcourt Brace Jovanovich 1987 322p

LC 86-31816

Original Polish edition, 1986

"The crew's dense, challenging discussions—of physics, philosophy, military tactics, morality, cybernetics, psychology, game theory, etc.—are punctuated by bursts of action whose initial release only serves to increase the tension, as new data disproves old theses and one fiasco follows another. Brilliant and demanding, this is one of Lem's best novels, putting the reader through an intellectual and emotional wringer." Publ Wkly

Lem, Stanislaw

His Master's Voice; translated from the Polish by Michael Kandel. Harcourt Brace Jovanovich 1983 199p

LC 82-15765

Original Polish edition, 1968

"A stream of 'signals' from outer space is the subject of various attempted decodings and an excuse for all kinds of wild hypotheses about who might have sent the message and why, in which are reflected various human hopes and fears. Good satire." Anatomy of Wonder 4

Lem, Stanislaw

Memoirs of a space traveler; further reminiscences of Ijon Tichy. drawings by the author; translated by Joel Stern and Maria Swiecicka-Zirmionek. Harcourt Brace Jovanovich 1982 153p il

LC 81-47310

"These stories of Ijon Tichy appeared in the original 1971 Polish edition of 'The Star Diaries' but were omitted from the English language editions of 1976. Some of these space age tall tales are funny, some are serious, but all are pointed. The targets range from SF itself to politics and commercialism." Publ Wkly

Lem, Stanislaw

★ **Solaris**; translated from the French by Joanna Kilmartin and Steve Cox; afterword by Darko Suvin. Walker & Co. 1970 216p

LC 75-123267

Original Polish edition, 1962

"This novel combines profound philosophic speculation with the structure of action-adventure SF, embodied in a clear, vivid writing style that somehow survived two translations. A planet under study by Earth scientists is swathed in a world-girdling ocean, which the scientists conclude is sentient. For unknown reasons, the ocean 'reads' the deepest memories of the four men and sends each a double of a woman in his past. The mysterious world-ocean, constantly flinging up strange shapes that defy the savants' efforts at classification, may be the first, infantile phase of an emerging 'imperfect God.' A major work by any measure." Anatomy of Wonder 5

Lemann, Nancy

Malaise; a novel. Scribner 2002 253p $23

ISBN 0-7432-1548-6

LC 2002-17584

Lemann's "novel is full of her customary antic charm, but here she has come up with something more: a beautifully nuanced anti-'Lolita,' in which the object of desire, wandering around L.A. in a brocade dressing gown and alligator slippers, is the now vanished twentieth century." New Yorker

Lennon, J. Robert

Castle; a novel. Graywolf Press 2009 229p $22

ISBN 978-1-55597-522-7; 1-55597-522-4

LC 2008-935603

"Like two other powerful novels of recent years—James Lasdun's Horned Man and Peter Cameron's Andorra—Castle is told by an egomaniacal, unlikable man with a precarious grasp on reality, especially his own. . . . Castle tells a terrific story, dire and confusing and convincing." N Y Times Book Rev

Lennon, J. Robert

Familiar; J. Robert Lennon. Farrar Straus & Giroux 2012 224 p. $15.00

ISBN 1555976255; 9781555976255

LC 2012936386

Author J. Robert Lennon tells the story of "a parallel universe. At some random midtrip interval, with Elisa wending her way homeward from her annual pilgrimage to the grave of her son, Silas, dead in an auto accident at age 15, she morphs into a different version of the same person. No longer a spare, contained woman . . . Elisa becomes more voluptuous . . . [and] on her way home from a professional conference. And Silas isn't dead, which she'll soon learn. But there is this: All that has been a barrier to peace and contentment remains." (Kirkus)

Lent, Jeffrey

Lost nation. Atlantic Monthly Press 2002 370p $25

ISBN 0-87113-843-3

LC 2001-56495

"In 1838, a man called Blood opens a tavern and one-girl brothel in an ungoverned area on the New Hampshire—Canada border. His prostitute, Sally, is a teenager he won in a game of cards. While the territory is already home to a number of society's escapees, Blood's presence introduces a new volatility. Blood and Sally's relationship grows in unpredictable ways, the law threatens to descend, and Blood's secret past returns in a surprising manner. . . . The author has tremendous literary gifts: a fine ear for speech, a keen eye for period detail, the ability to craft a well-turned phrase and create rich interior lives for his characters." Booklist

Leon, Donna

About face. Atlantic Monthly Press 2009 278p $24

ISBN 978-0-8021-1896-7; 0-8021-1896-8

LC 2009-12211

"It would be easy to punch holes in a contrived subplot, thick with symbolism, about a beautiful young woman whose face was ruined by cosmetic surgery. But who would want to, when Leon is being so generous with the humanizing details that make this series special? There are long walks in Brunetti's warm company and lively talks with his clever wife and even more engaging father-inlaw. . . . As detective work goes, it's a tiny masterpiece of analysis." N Y Times Book Rev

Leon, Donna

Beastly Things; Donna Leon. Atlantic Monthly 304 p.

ISBN 9780802120236

This detective novel, a volume of the Guido Brunetti series, offers a "tale of the murder of a quiet veterinarian. . . . One painfully human mistake, a simple act of hubris, draws an ordinary man into an inescapable trap that leaves him dead in a Venetian canal, carrying no identification and wearing only one shoe. Gradually, Commissario Brunetti and his colleague Inspector Vianello follow the trail to the town of Mestre, on the mainland near Venice, and to a slaughterhouse, where the animals that provide the meat which adorns the plates of the finest Venetian restaurants (and Brunetti's own table) are killed and 'dressed' in . . . [a] barbaric manner." (Booklist)

Leon, Donna

★ Blood from a stone; Donna Leon. Atlantic Monthly Press 2005 276p. o.p.; (pbk.) $14.95; (hbk.) o.p.

ISBN 0871138875; 9780143117094; 9780871138873

LC 2005040961

This crime novel "brings Commissario Brunetti . . . [to] the [crime] scene: On a cold Venetian night shortly before Christmas, a street vendor is killed in a scuffle in Campo Santo Stefano. The closest witnesses to the event are the American tourists who had been browsing the man's wares . . . before his death. The dead man had been working as a 'vu cumpra,' one of the many African immigrants peddling goods outside normal shop hours and trading without work permits. . . . Because these workers have few social connections and little money, infighting seems to be the answer. And yet the killings have all the markings of a professional operation. Once Brunetti begins to investigate, . . . he discovers that matters of great value are at stake within the secretive society." (Publisher's note)

Leon, Donna

Doctored evidence; Donna Leon. Atlantic Monthly Press 2004 245p $22

ISBN 0-87113-918-9

LC 2003-63941

"The detective's humane police work is disarming, and his ambles through the city are a delight; but it is this peculiar insistence on turning every case into a morality tale that gives Leon's fiction its subtlety and substance and makes us follow Brunetti wherever we must even into the sea." N Y Times Book Rev

Leon, Donna

Drawing conclusions. Atlantic Monthly 2011 260p $24

ISBN 978-0-8021-1979-7; 0-8021-1979-4

This installment "epitomizes what we treasure most about this series: a feeling for the life of a sublimely beautiful city and a sensitivity to the forces that are reshaping it. Not to mention the pleasure of being in Brunetti's company when this shrewd but scrupulously honest man is having a crisis of ethics at the flower market or trying to pry information from a hostile nun." N Y Times Book Rev

Leon, Donna

The **girl** of his dreams. Atlantic Monthly Press 2008 276p $24

ISBN 978-0-87113-980-1; 0-87113-980-4

"Political reality prevails over justice, and a child's death goes unpunished despite the best efforts of Commissario Guido Brunetti in Leon's . . . Venetian mystery. When 11-year-old Ariana Rocich drowns in a canal and goes unidentified for days, she begins to haunt Brunetti's dreams. But Ariana is a Rom, or gypsy, found with stolen jewelry items secreted in and on her person, a discovery that makes Brunetti's investigation particularly sensitive in the face of new departmental directives regarding multicultural issues. The book opens with the funeral of Brunetti's mother before segueing into a subplot about a religious charlatan; so religion, as well as politics, becomes a topic around the family table for Brunetti, wife Paola, daughter Chiara, and son Raffi." Libr J

Leon, Donna

The **Golden** Egg. Pgw 2013 256 p. (hardcover) $26

ISBN 0802121012; 9780802121011

In this, the 22nd entry in Donna Leon's Guido Brunetti mystery series, Commissario Guido Brunetti "investigates the suspicious death of a disabled man, Davide Cavanella. . . . Davide's mother is unwilling to discuss his death. Worse, there's no official evidence of Davide's existence: he apparently was never born and never went to school, saw a doctor, or received a passport. The colorful locals are uncooperative." (Publishers Weekly)

Leon, Donna

A **question** of belief; a Commissario Guido Brunetti mystery. Donna Leon. Atlantic Monthly Press Distributed by Publishers Group West 2010 262 p. (Commissario Guido Brunetti mystery.)

ISBN 0802119425; 9780802119421

LC 2011281197

In this book, "[s]et during an oppressive Venetian August, [author Donna] Leon's . . . 19th Commisario Guido Brunetti mystery . . . presents Brunetti with two puzzles that impinge on his most intimate beliefs. Close associate Ispettore Vianello, who's worried about his elderly aunt's involvement with an astrologer, nudges Brunetti toward ruminations on the differences in male and female evidences of affection. Meanwhile, Toni Brusca, head of employment records at the Commune, who's perplexed by a female judge's erratic court case postponements, surprises Brunetti by implying that a woman could be more criminal than a man. Brunetti patiently untangles a sordid skein of desires warped, trusts abused, and loves distorted into depravity." (Publishers Weekly)

Leon, Donna

Uniform justice. Atlantic Monthly Press 2003 259p $24

ISBN 0-87113-903-0

LC 2003-44326

"As a thinking man, Brunetti reads Cicero for moral direction, looks to his wife for doses of cynical realism and humbly consults his secretary, the terrifyingly efficient Si-

gnorina Elettra, on practical matters. But it is as a man of sensibility that this endearing detective most engages us." N Y Times Book Rev

Leonard, Elmore, 1925-2013

Bandits. Arbor House 1987 345p

LC 86-14104

"At its heart, the novel is about taking sides, the politically charged background of Contra aid used as one more tool to pull the reader in and out of the moral quicksand. Leonard is no Graham Greene, but the ethical issues called into play here give the novel depth and immediacy. This, then, is not just another gritty adventure novel; it's a top-notch thriller with a real moral resonance." Publ Wkly

Leonard, Elmore

★ **Be** cool. Delacorte Press 1999 292p

ISBN 0-385-33391-9

LC 98-36601

Sequel to Get Shorty

"Aside from the wit, the fun and the colorful figures that populate Elmore Leonard's novels, the real magic of his work is in the language. . . . This is Elmore Leonard at his best, the sweeping synaptic prose effortlessly echoing the argot of the gutter." N Y Times Book Rev

Leonard, Elmore

Cat chaser. Arbor House 1982 283p

ISBN 0-87795-398-8

LC 81-71687

This "is a tidy little thriller with sufficient twists and turns (not to mention sex and violence) to keep you intrigued and entertained. The characters are well drawn, the plotting is complicated but clear, and the suspense is strong without being too painful." Best Sellers

Leonard, Elmore

★ The **complete** Western stories of Elmore Leonard. William Morrow 2004 528p $27.95

ISBN 0-06-072425-0

LC 2004-55969

Leonard, Elmore

Djibouti. William Morrow 2010 279p $26.99

ISBN 978-0-06-173517-2; 0-06-173517-5

LC 2010-02111

"Leonard, as his many readers will attest, writes a wonderfully effective straightforward sentence that pushes the drama along. But the heart of this deliciously made novel — which is, geographically a stretch for the usually U.S.-bound novelist — comes in the dialogue." San Francisco Chron

Leonard, Elmore

Elmore Leonard's Dutch treat: 3 novels; introduction by George F. Will. Arbor House 1985 568p

LC 85-11246

An omnibus edition of three of the author's mid-1970s novels

In "Mr. Majestyk, a California melon grower, is set upon by professional killers but manages to turn his predators into prey. In Swag, originally called Ryan's Rules, two small-time Detroit thieves prosper until they go for bigger loot.

Riveting though these two tales are, they will strike readers as mere curtain raisers for The Hunted. Set in Israel, it focuses on the perilous state of Al Rosen, an American who receives large sums of money regularly from his lawyer in Detroit. When news of Rosen's whereabouts gets back to his home city, a gang of paid hoods jets to Tel Aviv and goes gunning for him. Sgt. Davis of the U.S. Marines, perceiving their lethal intentions, drives Rosen to a desolate spot in hopes of getting the drop on the pursuers. The climax to this story is a stunning, unforgettable surprise." Publ Wkly

Leonard, Elmore
Freaky Deaky. Arbor House 1988 341p

LC 87-19466

Leonard "excels here with his trademark menace and his deadpan, throwaway humor. His superlative ear for the vernacular makes all the characters spring to life; Woody, 'always in low with his dims on,' is a brilliant creation." Publ Wkly

Leonard, Elmore
★ Get Shorty. Delacorte Press 1990 292p

LC 89-25816

"Leonard's strongest books make you stand up and sit down a lot during their tight moments, but 'Get Shorty,' despite its occasional white-knuckle passages, belongs to that vast vinegary canon known as the Hollywood novel. . . . Best of all is the portrait Leonard gives us of a seven-million-dollar-a-picture star named Michael Weir." New Yorker

Followed by Be cool

Leonard, Elmore
Glitz. Arbor House 1985 228p

LC 84-16794

"There is a steady flow of intrigue and action set just outside the law in a world both dirty and glamorous. Several characters develop into complex personalities, but Mora is never quite clear." Libr J

Leonard, Elmore
The hot kid. William Morrow 2005 312p $25.95

ISBN 00-6072422-6

"Where so much of Leonard's recent fiction has a sharp, almost hyperrealistic quality, 'The Hot Kid' is noirish and even a little pulpy at times, in the fashion of 30's movies and detective magazines. . . . Tony Antonelli isn't a portrait of the artist as young man, exactly, but rather a fond wink at the tradition of potboilers and genre writing that gave rise to Leonard himself and from which, for all his success, he has never cut himself off." N Y Times Book Rev

Leonard, Elmore
★ Killshot. Arbor House 1989 287p

LC 88-31532

"Mr. Leonard has either done his homework or he's been there—up on the high beams in Detroit, on the Mississippi towing barges from Baton Rouge to Hickman, Ky., looking into the flat stare of an irritated cop, and somehow, improbably, inside the head of a woman who has had it with being treated like 'the wife.' 'Killshot' is pure, distilled, vintage Leonard." N Y Times Book Rev

Leonard, Elmore
LaBrava. Arbor House 1983 283p
ISBN 0-87795-527-1

LC 83-72676

"What makes the author's work memorable is his uncompromisingly direct prose, his affectionately crafted yet very real characters, and, of course, the fact that Leonard knows that providing entertainment is the novelist's first commandment. Nobody brings the illogic of crime and criminals to life better." Christ Sci Monit

Leonard, Elmore
Maximum Bob. Delacorte Press 1991 295p
ISBN 0-385-30142-1

LC 91-6539

"Maximum Bob is a Florida judge famous for his tough sentencing and, among women who have to work with him, as a fairly crude lecher. Parole officer Kathy Diaz Baker is the book's protagonist, though. For a slight violation, her parolee Dale Crowe Junior gets one of Bob's stiff sentences, by which he's not too pleased. Moreover, Dale's uncle Elvin, just out after doing 10 years from Bob on a murder conviction, conceivably could be nursing a grudge. What's more, Elvin hooks up with rich Dr. Tommy Vasco, who's under house arrest for illegal drugs—a sentence given him by guess who. When a live and lively alligator shows up in the judge's backyard, swallowing his wife's dog and scaring its owner clean out of town, and then when shots are fired through hizzoner's windows, Kathy gets suspicious and suspiciouser. Leonard's trademark toughness, grit, and sleaze are on every page." Booklist

Leonard, Elmore
Mr. Paradise. Morrow 2004 291p $25.95
ISBN 0-06-008395-6

LC 2003-64867

"Leonard addresses those who think they hear the same music he does, but who are open to questioning the familiar, to listening carefully and seeing when something has a different emphasis. . . . 'Mr. Paradise' is about deception. People deceive through false identity (appropriating, dissembling), just as they, themselves, have been deceived whether by the implied promise of collapsed dot-coms or by positive, false assumptions about family." N Y Times Book Rev

Leonard, Elmore
Out of sight. Delacorte Press 1996 296p
ISBN 978-0385308489

LC 96-8030

"A few stitches in the plot don't quite mesh, like the big part played by Foley's ex-wife, a magician's assistant. But even the finest silk suit can develop an errant thread, and this one, as sexy and well-tapered as Leonard's two new principals, will fit the author's fans just right." Publ Wkly

Leonard, Elmore
Pagan babies. Delacorte Press 2000 263p
ISBN 0-385-33392-7

LC 00-29506

This "is one of Mr. Leonard's funniest books, with a typically colourful cast of oddballs. The dialogue, too, is snappy. . . . Mr. Leonard steers the reader effortlessly through a maze of plots and counterplots, then brings the whole thing in with a bravura flourish and stops on a dime." Economist

Leonard, Elmore

Pronto. Delacorte Press 1993 265p

ISBN 0-385-30846-9

LC 93-2999

"Leonard's spare language and propulsive plotting still leave room for expositions of Sicilian slang, gamblers' lingo and Ezra Pound's private life. His colorful characters work together splendidly." Publ Wkly

Leonard, Elmore, 1925-2013

★ **Raylan**; Elmore Leonard. William Morrow 2012 263 p.

ISBN 006211946X; 0062119478; 0062132326 (B&N ed.); 9780062119469; 9780062119476; 9780062132321 (B&N ed.)

LC 2011024392

In this novel, "Raylan Givens, the U.S. Marshal . . . is back in a series of three interlinked stories. . . . The first . . . . of the stories complicates Raylan's apprehension of marijuana trader Angel Arenas with the discovery that the dealers with whom Angel was meeting left with his money, his grass and his kidneys, which they propose to sell back to him. . . . Their encounter ends with a sizable body count. . . . Raylan's second adventure pits him against Carol Conlan, a law-school–trained vice president of M-T Mining, whose skills in dealing with the problems that beset her employer extend far beyond the courtroom. . . . The villain of th[e] third piece, Delroy Lewis, forces three of his female acquaintances to rob banks and then gets mighty annoyed when one of them ends up with an exploding dye packet." (Kirkus)

Leonard, Elmore

Riding the rap. Delacorte Press 1995 294p

ISBN 0-385-30847-7

LC 94-38211

"Leonard's brilliance consists in having matched his style to his subject perfectly. These are not characters who would bloom into life in the hands of a more sophisticated writer. They are complete, because they are shallow." Commonweal

Leonard, Elmore

Road dogs. William Morrow 2009 262p $26.99

ISBN 0-06-173314-8; 978-0-06-173314-7

LC 2008-39607

"Road dogs are prison buddies who watch each other's backs. Jack Foley and Cundo Rey are trying to maintain that loyalty after they get out and start anew in Venice, CA, where Rey's girl Dawn Navarro awaits. Leonard . . . . brings back old favorites Foley and Rey, Dawn, and Karen Sisco—smart, sexy women and clever con artists, a mix the author knows well. Foley is being dogged by a rogue FBI agent who's convinced the infamous gentleman bank robber will strike again, and Rey's financial partner, Little Jimmy, is secretly in love with Dawn. The grifters' game of moving parts is quietly intriguing." Libr J

Leonard, Elmore

Rum punch. Delacorte Press 1992 297p

ISBN 0-385-30143-X

LC 91-38738

"Mr. Leonard never tells you; he shows you. The story is all action, a scam within a scam. . . . His style is the absence of style, stripped of fancy baggage . . . the absence, as far as it's possible, of an authorial ego." NY Times Book Rev

Leonard, Elmore

Split images. Arbor House 1982 282p

LC 81-67524

"When millionaire Robbie Daniels hires a trigger-happy cop as bodyguard, reporter Angela Nolan, who's been doing a story on Daniels, becomes worried. Daniels has killed people—supposedly by accident and in self-defense— and seems to be getting a taste for it. She and policeman Bryan Hurd find themselves in a deadly race to thwart Daniels' plans, which include video taping his killings. This is a fast-paced suspense novel with interesting characters and a warm-hearted romance between Hurd and Nolan." Libr J

Leonard, Elmore

Stick. Arbor House 1983 304p

ISBN 0-87795-436-4

LC 82-72073

"After seven years in a Michigan prison for armed robbery, Ernest Stickley, Jr. heads for Florida and gets together with a friend who served a three-four year sentence at the same prison for possession with intent to deliver. Stick is soon in the center of Miami's underworld of big money and illegal drugs. He barely escapes from the scene of a slaying, which is more of a human sacrifice than a murder. Soon a couple of drug-pushing czars and their goons are on his trail. But Stick is not exactly hiding, and his trail leads across yachts, through mansions, and to a country club gala." Best Sellers

"Despite his violence, Stick is likeable, and the scam he pulls on the drug dealers has the reader firmly on his side. Escapist but not shallow." Libr J

Leonard, Elmore

Tishomingo blues; a novel. Morrow 2002 308p

ISBN 0-06-000872-5

LC 2001-44405

"Dennis Lenahan, an itinerant high diver setting up for a Mississippi casino show, watches a Dixie drug-ring murder from his eighty-foot diving platform. Various factions—a smooth-talking Detroit con man, a mob-backed explosives expert, redneck crank dealers, local police on either side of the law—try to badger or buy his silence or coöperation, but Lenahan stays cool and uncommitted, until a 'Shane'-like showdown at a local Civil War re-enactment. Lenahan's composure and his easy acrobatics feel like a stand-in for the author's; both seem to play it by ear even after the guns start firing. And the hurtling plot twists keep coming, right up to the perfect rip of a finish." New Yorker

Leonard, Elmore

Touch. Arbor House 1987 245p

ISBN 978-0877959052

LC 87-12624

"The hard-as-nails-and-twice-as-real dialogue and sharp characterizations make this weird nonviolent thriller . . . as absorbing as Leonard's usual, more menacing fare." Booklist

Leonard, Elmore

Up in Honey's room. William Morrow 2007 292p $25.95

ISBN 978-0-06-072424-5; 0-06-072424-2

LC 2006-47080

"There's violence eventually—nicely done, of course—but while it's crucial, it's not central. The pleasure of the tale comes from the telling of it. Leonard would probably think the comparison pretentious, but the way in which the voices of the characters and the threads of narrative are introduced and interwoven reminds one of nothing so much as a well-crafted fugue with its subject, countersubject, episodes, false entries, and stretto (where everything can seem to be happening at once). Most of the story unfolds in dialogue, but even the third-person narrative has a pungent drawl to it, which makes the transition from one to another seamless." PopMatters

Leonard, Elmore

When the women come out to dance, and other stories. Morrow 2003 228p $24.95

ISBN 0-06-008397-2

LC 2002-26426

"Reading the clipped, unfailingly accurate dialogue that comes out of the mouths of Leonard's characters can make you feel as if you're in the presence of a writer who is both ventriloquist and psychic. It's not just that Leonard captures the cadences and elisions of each character's speech, it's that he has an uncanny sense of knowing what each will say next." N Y Times Book Rev

Lerner, Ben

★ **Leaving** the Atocha Station; a novel. Coffee House Press 2011 181p il pa $15

ISBN 978-1-56689-274-2; 1-56689-274-0

LC 2011-24105

The novel "has a beguiling mixture of lightness and weight. There are wonderful sentences and jokes on almost every page. Lerner is attempting to capture something that most conventional novels, with their cumbersome caravans of plot and scene and 'conflict,' fail to do: the drift of thought, the unmomentous passage of undramatic life." New Yorker

Leroy, Margaret

Postcards from Berlin; a novel. Little, Brown 2003 391p $22.95

ISBN 0-316-73813-1

LC 2003-40069

"The resolution of Leroy's novel has a fairy-tale aspect, but fairy tales can nevertheless be very absorbing. Despite the occasional straining of her plot, Leroy succeeded in making me care about these characters; even at my most incredulous." N Y Times Book Rev

Lescroart, John T.

The **first** law; a novel. by John Lescroart. Dutton 2003 403p $25.95

ISBN 0-525-94705-1

LC 2002-37902

"The popular lawyer-cop team of Dismas 'Diz' Hardy (lawyer) and Abe Glitzky (cop) returns for another episode of legal maneuvering on the streets of San Francisco. The bullet wound sustained by Abe in Lescroart's last adventure. . . confines him to a desk job, so he's no help to Diz when he goes up against the Patrol Special, a private-enterprise neighborhood security system supervised by the SFPD. It seems that Diz's good friend, John Holliday, a bar owner in one of the patrolled areas, is fingered as a murder suspect; however, John contends the corrupt beat 'cops' framed him. . . . Lescroart's expert crafting turns this legal thriller into quite a wild ride." Booklist

Lescroart, John T.

Guilt; [by] John Lescroart. Delacorte Press 1997 462p

ISBN 0-385-31655-0

LC 96-43756

"Lescroart effectively dramatizes the many moral dilemmas that emerge in this case, not the least of which is posed by the role of the Catholic Church." Booklist

Lescroart, John T.

The **hearing**; {by} John Lescroart. Dutton 2001 451p $25.95

ISBN 0-525-94575-X

LC 00-34119

In this legal thriller "attorney Dismas Hardy not only defends confessed murderer Cole Burgess but is forced to confront the fallibility of his friend, Abe Glitsky, chief of the San Francis Police Department's homicide division. Burgess, a heroin addict, is found near the lifeless body of a prominent female attorney, unable to remember the events that brought him there. Lescroart tantalizes readers with a tightly constructed plot in which Hardy and Glitsky track crime and political corruption to an unexpected source." Libr J

Lescroart, John T.

The **mercy** rule; a novel. by John Lescroart. Delacorte Press 1998 466p

ISBN 0-385-31658-5

LC 98-16726

"Lescroart has the technical clues of the plot perfectly arranged, locking in the attention of mystery mavens until the connections are revealed, but it's his credible characters who cement this entertaining front-rank whodunit." Booklist

Lescroart, John T.

Nothing but the truth; [by] John Lescroart. Delacorte Press 1999 435p

ISBN 0-385-33353-6

LC 99-32584

"Lescroart orchestrates a cadre of multi-dimensional characters through a plot full of political subterfuge and action without losing track of the subtlety of modern personal relationships." Libr J

Lescroart, John T.

The **oath**; [by] John Lescroart. Dutton 2002 408p

ISBN 0-525-94576-8

LC 2001-47055

San Francisco attorney Dismas Hardy "finds himself representing Dr. Eric Kensing, who stands accused of murdering his boss, Tim Markham, the CEO of the Parnassus Medical Group, a struggling HMO providing health services to all the city's employees. An autopsy shows that Markham, hospitalized in critical condition following a hit-and-run, died not of his injuries but of a potassium overdose. . . . The author wisely steers clear of taking cheap shots at the HMO industry, yet manages to direct a sharp beam into some of its darker crevices." Publ Wkly

Lescroart, John T.

The **second** chair; [by] John Lescroart. Dutton 2004 390p $25.95

ISBN 0-525-94775-2

LC 2003-19782

An installment in the "San Francisco legal/detective series featuring lawyer Dismas Hardy and police detective Abe Glitzky. Amy Wu, a young attorney in the law firm now headed by Dismas, has a high-profile client in Andrew Bartlett, a high school student accused of shooting his girlfriend and drama coach. The evidence against Andrew is extremely damning, and Amy arranges a plea-bargain whereby Andrew would agree to admit guilt in exchange for the case remaining in the juvenile justice system. She's forced to antagonize the court and the district attorney, however, by reneging on the deal when Andrew continues to claim his innocence. Dismas appoints himself to the case as 'second chair' to salvage the reputation of his firm, just as it seems that Andrew might not be guilty after all." Libr J

Leshem, Ron

Beaufort; translated from the Hebrew by Evan Fallenberg. Delacorte Press 2008 360p $24

ISBN 978-0-553-80682-3

LC 2007-30292

Original Hebrew edition, 2006

"In order to limit Hezbollah's attacks on Israeli settlements, Israel maintained a security force in southern Lebanon for close to 20 years. Leshem's . . . novel chronicles the lives of the last group of Israeli soldiers to man the outpost at Beaufort, a crusader-castle ruin of questionable military significance. Written as the diary of Liraz 'Erez' Liberti, the hotheaded twentysomething leader of a 13-man commando unit stationed in an outpost prior to the Israeli withdrawal in 2000, the novel brings to life the situation of very young men on a dangerous mission. This is a picture of war from a soldier's point of view. Its language is crude, the body count rises, and yet the tenderness of the bonds among the men is extraordinary." Libr J

Leskov, N. S. (Nikolai Semenovich), 1831-1895

The **enchanted** wanderer and other stories; by Nikolai Leskov; translated by Richard Pevear and La-

rissa Volokhonsky. Alfred A. Knopf 2013 608 p. (hardcover) $35

ISBN 0307268829; 9780307268822

LC 2012025416

This book is a new translation of several short stories by Nikolai Leskov. The stories gathered here are "all lightly linked in the way that those of the 'Canterbury Tales' are." The "opener is a stern study in the dangers of adultery; then come other pieces set in 'Wooden Russia,' the old heartland south of Moscow, with all its elaborate prejudices against Gypsies, Jews, Ukrainians and the other outsiders who so often figure in Leskov's pages." (Kirkus Reviews)

Includes bibliographical references

Lessing, Doris May

African stories; {by} Doris Lessing. Simon & Schuster 1965 636p hardcover o.p.

A collection of "tales which taken together reflect myriad aspects of African existence. Vivid personality delineation, narrative integrity, and artistry dominate each story whatever its subject or theme." Booklist

Lessing, Doris May

Ben, in the world; the sequel to The fifth child. [by] Doris Lessing. HarperCollins Pubs. 2000 178p

ISBN 0-06-019628-9

LC 99-89804

Ben Lovatt's "abnormal appearance and strength distinguishes him from other people. Rejected by his older siblings, he is now homeless in London. He has been fed and sheltered by the sickly Mrs. Biggs, but when she enters the hospital, Ben ends up staying with a prostitute named Rita. Rita's boyfriend enlists Ben's unknowing assistance to transport drugs to Paris, where he meets Alex and is taken to Brazil to make a movie. There, Ben meets a scientist who wants to run genetic tests on him. Ben is treated inhumanely but is excited when he hears that he may meet more people like himself." Libr J

"Lessing's unsentimental yet excruciating moral fable forces us to accept the Lovatts' dilemma as our own." New Yorker

Lessing, Doris May

Children of violence; [by] Doris Lessing. v1-5

v1-4 published by Simon & Schuster; v5 published 1969 by Knopf with title: The four-gated city

This "is an account of the life of Martha Quest and of her search for self-definition, which for her is to be achieved through total commitment to a person or a cause. We follow her from her beginnings as a wayward but intelligent child on a Rhodesian farm, through two unsuccessful marriages and active involvement in the Communist party in Salisbury during World War II. After the war Martha goes to London and becomes an increasingly disenchanted observer of London life and behavior in the 1950s; the last volume of the sequence anticipates an apocalyptic, science-fiction future, as Martha dies in a devastated, radioactive world at the end of the twentieth century." Wakeman. World Authors, 1950-1970

Lessing, Doris May

★ The **fifth** child; [by] Doris Lessing. Knopf 1988 133p

ISBN 0-394-57105-3

LC 88-2680

"Acting as a social moralist, Lessing exposes the division between the warm and comfortable domestic scene and the harsh reality of the outside world, piercing the boundary between the two as human desires clash with a more brutal vision of existence. A psychologically probing and emotionally powerful performance." Booklist

Followed by Ben, in the world

Lessing, Doris May

★ The **golden** notebook; [by] Doris Lessing. Simon & Schuster 1962 567p

"Regarded as one of the key texts of the Women's movement of the 1960s, it opens in London in 1957 with a section ironically entitled 'Free Women', a realistic account of a conversation between two old friends, writer Anna Wulf, mother of Janet, and Molly, divorced from Richard, and mother of disturbed son Tommy, who will later attempt suicide. The novel then fragments into the four sections of Anna's 'Notebooks.' . . . This pattern of five non chronological overlapping sections is repeated four times, as it tracks both the past and the present, and although one of Lessing's concerns is to expose the dangers of fragmentation, she also builds up through pastiche and parody, and through many refractions and mergings, a remarkably coherent and detailed account of her protagonists and the world they inhabit." Oxford Companion to Engl Lit. 6th edition

Lessing, Doris May

The **good** terrorist; {by} Doris Lessing. Knopf 1985 375p

LC 85-40214

"Unsparingly, fiercely, often satirically, Lessing is writing a narrative about death: the death of the heart when ideology tyrannizes over just, kindly human relations, abstractions over common sense." Ms

Lessing, Doris May

The **grass** is singing; [by]Doris Lessing. Crowell 1950 245p

The novel begins with the newspaper notice of the death of Mary Turner, wife of an unsuccessful South African farmer. There seems to be some reluctance among the other whites about discussing the case. The author then turns back to the story of Mary Turner's life, showing her gradual disintegration as a person, and ending with her murder by a Kaffir houseboy

This novel "besides being very well-written is an extremely mature psychological study. It is full of those terrifying touches of truth, seldom mentioned but instantly recognized. By any standards, this book shows remarkable powers and imagination." New Statesman (1913)

Lessing, Doris May

Love, again; a novel. {by} Doris Lessing. HarperCollins Pubs. 1996 352p

ISBN 978-0060176877

LC 95-53317

"Sarah Durham was widowed young; now in her mid-60s, she is manager of and playwright for a London fringe theater group. A production of a play based on the journals and music of a 19th-century quadroon from Martinique, Julie Vairon, inflames Sarah's dormant sexual impulses. And she is not the only one: all of the actors, the director and a rich patron, Stephen Ellington-Smith, are also sublimely seduced by Julie's words, music and the few portraits of her that survive. . . . Although the book is long and rambling, asking much of a reader's patience and willingness to spend so much time inside Sarah's head, Lessing wields a formidable analytic intelligence that makes this work provocative and often astonishingly beautiful." Publ Wkly

Lessing, Doris May

Mara and Dann; an adventure. [by] Doris Lessing. HarperFlamingo 1999 407p

ISBN 0-06-018294-6

LC 98-30782

"In this futuristic novel, in Ifrik, a land savaged by war and environmental disaster, seven-year-old Mara and her little brother Dann are snatched from their home and severed from their pasts. The children grow up literally on the run, made to fight for their enemies one moment and left to starve the next. But their love for each other remains as fierce as their surroundings are terrifying, and it transfigures their brutal trials. On the surface a grand adventure, this novel at its heart makes a fascinating argument for the force of affection and the power of the questioning mind." New Yorker

Lessing, Doris May

★ The **memoirs** of a survivor; [by] Doris Lessing. Knopf 1975 213p

First published 1974 in the United Kingdom

This is "an extraordinary and compelling meditation about the enduring need for loyalty, love and responsibility in an unprecedented time that places unbearable demands upon people." Time

Lessing, Doris May

★ **Shikasta**; re: colonised planet 5; personal, psychological, historical documents relating to visit by Johor (George Sherban) emissary (grade 9) 87th of the period of the last days. [by] Doris Lessing. Knopf 1979 364p (Canopus in Argos: archives)

LC 79-11295

"First of the Canopus in Argos: Archives five-volume series. Shikasta is Earth, whose history—extending over millions of years—is here put into the cosmic perspective, observed by Canopeans who seem to be in charge of galactic history although responsible to some higher, impersonal authority. The sequels follow the exploits of various human cultures whose affairs are subtly influenced by the Canopeans; all share the remotely detached perspective that transforms the way in which individual endeavors are seen. Thoughtful and painstaking." Anatomy of Wonder 4

Followed by The marriages between zones three, four, and five (1980); The Sirian experiments (1981); The making of the representative for Planet 8 (1982); Documents relating to the sentimental agents in the Volyen Empire (1983)

Lessing, Doris May

Stories; {by} Doris Lessing. Knopf 1978 625p

LC 77-20709

"All of Lessing's non-African stories are brought together from three of her previous collections: 'The habit of Loving,' 'A Man and Two Women,' and 'The Temptation of Jack Orkney and other Stories'. In addition, 'The Other Woman,' a short novel, previously published only in Great Britain, is also included." Booklist

Lessing, Doris May

The **sweetest** dream; [by] Doris Lessing. HarperCollins Pubs. 2002 478p hardcover o.p. pa $13.95

ISBN 0-06-621334-7; 0-06-093755-6 pa

LC 2002-279950

"Lessing's understanding of relationships-both personal and political-has always been keen; now . . . it is unparalleled. This novel is warm and heartfelt, old-fashioned and ambitious in its historical sweep." New Statesman

Lester, Julius

★ **Do** Lord remember me; a novel. Holt & Co. 1985 210p

LC 84-3845

"Smith's memories link with those of older people in his past, whose stories take him back to slavery times. What emerges is a picture of black experience covering more than 150 years, with memory and storytelling providing continuity between present and past. A rich and moving reading experience." Booklist

Lethem, Jonathan

Chronic city. Doubleday 2009 467p $27.95

ISBN 978-0-385-51863-5; 0-385-51863-3

LC 2009-07587

"Set in Manhattan, the story focuses on an unusual friendship between Perkus [Tooth], a wayward cultural critic with a penchant for marijuana and conspiracies, and former child actor Chase Insteadman. Holed up in Perkus's clapboard apartment, the duo try to weave together the chaotic events occurring in the city by way of virtual worlds, ghostwriters, and Marlon Brando." Libr J

"Lethem's vision of New York can approach the Swiftian. It is impressively observant in its detail and scouring in its mocking satire." Boston Globe

Lethem, Jonathan

★ **Dissident** Gardens. Random House Inc. 2013 384 p. (hardcover) $27.95

ISBN 0385534930; 9780385534932

This book "begins with the case of Rose Zimmer, in Queens, New York, who was officially ousted from the [American Communist] party in 1955 for sleeping with a black cop. Rose's daughter, Miriam, is a teenager at the time, and she soon discovers the pull of Greenwich Village bohemians. Rose's and Miriam's stories are interwoven, as the narrative moves back and forth in time." (Publishers Weekly)

"...The cast makes for a heady, swirly mix of fascinating, lonely people. Lethem's writing, as always, packs a witty punch." Pub Wkly

Lethem, Jonathan

The **fortress** of solitude; a novel. Doubleday 2003 511p $26

ISBN 0-385-50069-6

LC 2003-43535

"Dylan Ebdus is a white kid on a black-and-brown street. As he struggles through public school in 1970s Brooklyn, he is 'yoked'-put in a headlock-and frisked for change on a daily basis. Testing into a good Manhattan school, he steps into a long-lasting role: vulnerable among street kids, he's street-smart compared to his new, privileged pals, and loathes himself as a poseur with both crowds. When he finds a ring that grants the power of flight, he's afraid to use it, but his black friend, Mingus, is not." Booklist

Lethem, Jonathan

Motherless Brooklyn. Doubleday 1999 311p

ISBN 0-385-49183-2

LC 99018194

In this novel, Lionel Essrog, a Brooklyn private detective with Tourette's syndrome, investigates the murder of his boss, Frank Minna.

"The short and shady life of Frank Minna ends in murder, shocking the four young men employed by his dysfunctional Brooklyn detective agency/limo service. The 'Minna Men' have centered their lives around Frank. . . . Tourette's-afflicted Lionel has found security as a Minna Man and is shattered by Frank's death. Lionel determines to become a genuine sleuth and find the killer. The ensuing plot twists are marked by clever wordplay, fast-paced dialog, and nonstop irony." Libr J

Lethem, Jonathan

You don't love me yet. Doubleday 2007 223p $24.95

ISBN 0-385-51218-X; 978-0-385-51218-3

LC 2006-11768

"Lucinda Hoekke spends eight hours a day at the Complaint Line, listening to anonymous callers air their random grievances. Most of the time, the work is excruciatingly tedious. But one frequent caller, who insists on speaking only to Lucinda, captivates her with his off-color ruminations and opaque self-reflections. In blatant defiance of the rules, Lucinda and the Complainer arrange a face-to-face meeting— and fall desperately in love. Consumed by passion, Lucinda manages only to tear herself away from the Complainer to practice with the alternative band in which she plays bass." (Publisher's note)

"There's quite a bit of surface in this novel, but there's also a sweet truthfulness in its investigation of how the songs we love express something we can never fully articulate. Lethem understands this paradox, even if his characters don't." Paste

Letts, Billie

Shoot the moon; Billie Letts. Warner Books 2004 333p $24

ISBN 0-446-52900-1

LC 2004-3447

"No one in sleepy DeClare, Oklahoma, has forgotten the 1972 murder of pretty Cherokee Gaylene Harjo and the abduction of her infant son, Nicky Jack. Hard-nosed deputy sheriff Oliver 'O Boy' Daniels pinned the blame on local preacher Joe Dawson, but few in town believed the kindly Joe was capable of such an act. Powerful emotions resurface 30 years later, when Nicky Jack, adopted and raised by a rich couple in Beverly Hills, mysteriously reappears, determined to learn about his mother and the circumstances surrounding her death. . . . Letts peppers her prose with a cast of quirky characters." Booklist

Leung, Brian

World famous love acts; stories. Sarabande Books 2004 202p $14.95

ISBN 1-88933-016-7

LC 2003-11923

"As diverse as they are similar, Leung's characters and their conditions run the gamut from elderly widower to precocious youngsters, porn star to AIDS victim, serial killer to estranged sisters, and all are lucidly portrayed in prose that is achingly lyrical and elegantly refined." Booklist

Levack, Simon

Demon of the air; Simon Levack. Thomas Dunne Books/St. Martin's Minotaur 2005 xiv, 296p maps o.p.; o.p.

ISBN 9780312348342; 0312348347

LC 2005043976

This book takes place in "Mexico, 1517. Emperor Montezuma rules the known world . . . [but he] is troubled. Mysterious strangers have appeared in the East. . . . The soothsayers he turns to for guidance give him only enigmatic answers, and he knows he cannot trust his advisers---especially his chief minister . . . Lord Feathered in Black. Yaotl, the chief minister's slave, is troubled, too. He was ordered to escort a sacrificial victim up the steps of the Great Pyramid, but the victim ran amok, uttering a bizarre and sinister prophecy and leaping to his death before the War-God's priests could cut out his heart. Then Yaotl learns that the emperor's soothsayers have vanished. The emperor senses a connection between these two events and orders Yaotl to find it." (Publisher's note)

Leveen, Lois

The **secrets** of Mary Bowser; a novel. Lois Leveen. William Morrow 2012 453 p. $15.99

ISBN 006210702X; 0062107909; 9780062107022; 9780062107909

LC 2011038111

This book follows "Mary . . . a slave. . . When [her master's daughter] decides to send Mary to Philadelphia to be educated, she must leave her family to seize her freedom. Life in the North brings . . . a far different education than Mary ever expected, one that leads her into the heart of the abolition movement. . . . Posing as a slave in the Confederate White House in order to spy on President Jefferson Davis, Mary deceives even those who are closest to her to aid the Union command." (Publisher's note)

"Deftly balancing history, romance and adventure, Leveen honors the life and historical importance of a brave, resourceful woman." Kirkus

Levenkron, Steven

The **best** little girl in the world. Contemporary Bks. 1978 196p

LC 78-9063

"Francesca is 15, an excellent student, a docile girl at home in her affluent parents' Manhattan apartment. But Francesca sets about killing her 'fat' self to become imaginary Kessa—slim and firm. Within weeks she starves herself, so that she drops from 98 to an alarming 84 pounds and is hospitalized, another young victim of anorexia nervosa. The reader is drawn into the arena where dedicated professionals battle to save Francesca's life and the lives of others like her. This book, fiction in name only, proves what an impassioned and skillful author can do to make a novel more powerful than dry facts." Publ Wkly

Levi, Primo

If not now, when? translated from the Italian by William Weaver; introduction by Irving Howe. Summit Bks. 1985 349p

LC 85-2526

Original Italian edition, 1982

"The author, himself a victim of Nazi atrocities, has based his novel on true events. A band of Jewish partisans makes its way from Russia to Italy waging their personal war against the Nazis. They blow up trains, rescue concentration camp inmates, and face incredible dangers in their efforts to strike back against a ruthless, seemingly invincible enemy. The story is a testament to human endurance and courage." Shapiro. Fic for Youth. 3d edition

Levi, Primo

The **monkey's** wrench; translated from the Italian by William Weaver. Summit Bks. 1986 171p

LC 86-5803

Original Italian edition, 1978

"Among other things, The Monkey's Wrench is a model of the interplay between storytellers and listeners. For their part, readers can envy Levi's sixth sense about building bridges between what can be seen and what must be imagined." Time

Levi, Primo

The **sixth** day, and other tales; translated by Raymond Rosenthal. Summit Bks. 1990 222p

LC 90-9734

"These bizarre stories from master storyteller Levi are full of shadowed meanings, conveying truths about our technological society and how our scientific appetites have outstripped our moral capacities." Libr J

Levien, David

City of the sun; a novel. Doubleday 2008 310p $24.95

ISBN 978-0-385-52366-0; 0-385-52366-1

LC 2007-28002

"While it deals with the practical mechanics of how a private detective tracks down a boy who has been missing for more than a year, this relentless novel is really about how parents suffer the loss of a child. As such, the story conveys a piercing sense of honesty, even when the investigation itself seems implausibly free of complications." N Y Times Book Rev

Levin, Ira

★ The **boys** from Brazil; a novel. Random House 1976 312p

"Ninety-four potential Hitlers are created through the technique of cloning by Dr. Mengele, infamous doctor of Auschwitz. Striving to re-create the early environment of the original Hitler, Mengele plots the murder of the fathers of these ninety-four children. Yakov Liebermann, a pursuer of Nazis, tries to stop the murders at the cost of great, almost mortal, danger to himself." Shapiro. Fic for Youth. 3d edition

Levin, Ira

A **kiss** before dying. Simon & Schuster 1953 244p

"The plot has to do with a remarkably ingenious, subtle, and relentless murderer, who does away with a pregnant college girl, goes on from there to kill her sister and a more or less innocent bystander, and is cheated of the fortune that has driven him to these desperate measures only by a couple of tiny oversights that might easily have escaped Sherlock Holmes. The book is a succession of solid and quite legitimate surprises, the suspense is admirably sustained, the detail is thorough and convincing, and the writing is considerably above the level usually associated with fictional crime and passion." New Yorker

Levin, Ira

★ **Rosemary's** baby; a novel. Random House 1967 245p

ISBN 9780451194008

LC 68136323

"Guy and Rosemary Woodhouse dismiss the warnings of friends and move into a luxurious Manhattan apartment building where, supposedly, rites of witchcraft and suicides have occurred. Rosemary's instincts warn her to beware of their neighbors, the Castevets, but her husband is not convinced and they become a dominant influence on Guy when Rosemary becomes pregnant. She is alone in her fear and becomes a helpless victim." Shapiro. Fic for Youth. 3d edition

Followed by: Son of Rosemary (1998)

Levin, Ira

The **Stepford** wives. Random House 1972 145p

ISBN 0-394-48199-2

"Attractive, talented Joanna moves with her husband and kids to a suburb, where she comes to suspect that the village housewives have all been murdered and replaced by robots, the suspected villain being a chauvinistic Men's Association . . . and so Joanna begins to fear for her life." Libr J

Levin, Meyer

Compulsion. Simon & Schuster 1956 495p

Using fictionalized names and probing deeply into the psychological aspects of the crime, this is a retelling of the Loeb-Leopold murder case

"The writing shows the hand of a master. Despite the fact that the reader who is familiar with the history of the case knows the outcome, Mr. Levin manages to fill this book with sustained suspense." N Y Times Book Rev

Levine, Peter

The **appearance** of a hero; the Tom Mahoney stories. Peter Levine. 1st ed. St. Martin's Press 2012 165 p. (hardcover) $22.99

ISBN 1250001226; 9781250001221; 9781250008336

LC 2012013912

This short story collection, by Peter Levine, follows the character of Tom Mahoney. He "is the golden boy everyone knew in school. . . . In [the book] . . . Tom navigates the passage into adulthood, . . . chronicled from every perspective but his own. . . . As the mythology surrounding Tom grows richer, Tom struggles to understand what exactly has eluded him, and . . . we begin to see that being an icon is not all it's cracked up to be." (Publisher's note)

Levine, Sara

Treasure Island!!! Europa Editions 2011 172 p. (paperback) $15.00

ISBN 1609450612; 9781609450618

This book offers a "comedy about a young woman obsessed with Robert Louis Stevenson's classic pirate tale. . . . The narrator . . . is an unnamed twenty-five-year-old living in her home town a few years after completing an English degree. We gather that her life since graduation has amounted to not much more than "a history of low-paying jobs and hapless boyfriends," and that she has no . . . plans to better herself. . . . The story begins motion when the narrator picks up her sister's copy of "Treasure Island" and becomes enraptured with its hero, Jim Hawkins. . . . So begins the quest to transform the dross of her everyday life into a carnival of derring-do. . . . In practice, this means a series of reckless decisions that lead to wounded feelings and property damage." (TLS)

Levithan, David

The **lover's** dictionary. Farrar, Straus, and Giroux 2011 240p. $18

ISBN 978-0-374-19368-3

LC 201014392

Alex Award (2012)

"Levithan takes a hoary narrative—sexual electricity, domesticity, familiarity, tensions, betrayal—and recasts it in a fresh, modern way. The first person narrative is so intimate as to make the reader feel voyeuristic, like reading the diary of a logophile stranger. Entries echo the roller coaster of love, by turns wry, insecure, funny, coy, poetical, philosophical, bitter and even mawkishly sentimental." Maclean's

Levitt, Paul M.

Come with me to Babylon. University of New Mexico Press 2008 232p $24.95

ISBN 978-0-8263-4178-5; 0-8263-4178-0

LC 2007-39410

This historical novel "follows the Cohen family from their village in Russia to the United States, led by strongwilled Esther Cohen. Under the auspices of the Baron de Hirsch Fund, an agency focused on emigration, the Cohens are supposed to become farmers in rural New Jersey. But the bucolic occupation doesn't interest her husband, the gently raised Meyer Cohen. . . . All too soon, the Cohens have become a tenement family. Daughter Fanny is disabled in the Triangle Shirtwaist Co. fire, which killed more than 100 garment workers in a locked building. Son Ben begins dating a whore and running errands for a strikebreaking criminal. . . . Levitt hooks and plays his readers well. One influential character never appears directly: Jacob, Meyer and Esther's estranged son. The story of how he left the family, and how it grieves both parents, is a subtle but unmistakable undercurrent to Babylon." Rocky Mountain News

Levy, Andrea

Fruit of the lemon. Picador 2007 352p pa $15
ISBN 978-0-312-42664-4; 0-312-42664-X
LC 2006-52481

First published 1999 in the United Kingdom

This novel depicts the lives of London-born children of Jamaican immigrants "circa 1970, who grapple with the knowledge that they are often still considered outsiders. Faith, working as a dresser for children's television, is a somewhat heedless young woman whose assumption that she lives in a colorblind world is quickly demolished. At work, she finds that the only actors she's allowed to touch are dolls; soon afterward, she helps a black woman who has been attacked by three youths. Her concerned parents send her to Jamaica, where she slowly recovers a sense of balance and uncovers her family's past. Faith's initial obliviousness to prejudice makes the first half of the book feel implausible; but, once the narrative moves to Jamaica, Levy's remarkable ability to weave a complex, engrossing family history takes over." New Yorker

Levy, Andrea

★ The **long** song. Farrar, Straus and Giroux 2010 313p $26
ISBN 978-0-374-19217-4; 0-374-19217-0
LC 2009-43181

"For all its power to disturb, this is a beautifully written and cleverly constructed novel that projects convincing personal relationships on to the feral backdrop of the Jamaican plantations." Times (London)

Levy, Andrea

Small island. Picador 2005 441p pa $14
ISBN 0-312-42467-1
LC 2005-298527

First published 2004 in the United Kingdom

"In the shabby remnants of post-blitz London, three near-strangers find themselves in a single house. Queenie Bligh is a spirited Yorkshirewoman waiting for her husband to return from the war and taking in tenants to make ends meet. Gilbert Joseph, a Jamaican R.A.F. veteran, is struggling to establish himself in England, a country that he'd been taught was his motherland but which regards him as an interloper; his bride, Hortense, has just arrived in London and is bewildered that her education and class can't transcend the color of her skin. The narrative voice jumps between the characters, a technique that embeds familiar cultural observations in closely observed and surprising lives. If the plot sometimes verges on the operatic, Levy's writing deftly illuminates the complex and contradictory motives behind each character's behavior." New Yorker

Levy, Deborah

Swimming home; a novel. Deborah Levy; with an introduction by Tom McCarthy. Bloomsbury USA 2012 157 p. (alk. paper) $14
ISBN 162040169X; 9781620401699

This novel, by Deborah Levy, begins at a "villa in the hills above Nice, [where] Joe sees a body in the swimming pool. But the girl is very much alive. She is Kitty Finch: a self-proclaimed botanist with green-painted fingernails, walking naked out of the water and into the heart of their holiday. Why is she there? What does she want from them all? And why does Joe's enigmatic wife allow her to remain?" (Publisher's note)

Includes bibliographical references

Lewin, Michael Z.

Oh Joe. Five Star 2008 237p $25.95
ISBN 978-1-59414-667-1; 1-59414-667-5
LC 2008-016795

"Joe Prince drives a truck, loves his girlfriend, Kelly, and their infant son, Little Joe. But that isn't enough to keep him from straying, and when Kelly catches him in the act, she leaves him. As a form of self-imposed house arrest, he agrees to house-sit shady old pal George Wayne's permanently anchored houseboat in the middle of a large Indianapolis reservoir. But the loneliness wears on Joe. He jumps ship and swims for shore. A day or so later Joe finds himself under arrest for Wayne's murder. Steph Steponski, the lead detective assigned to the case, is sure of Joe's guilt—until she learns that Joe was played for a patsy and may now be at risk himself. . . . [Lewin] is as gently humorous and ironic as ever, and readers will find a kindred soul in Joe, as likeably flawed as any recent protagonist in mystery fiction." Booklist

Lewis, Beverly

The **brethren**; Beverly Lewis. Bethany House 2006 349p.
ISBN 0764201077; 0764202316; 0764202324; 9780764201073; 9780764202315; 9780764202322
LC 2006019314

This book, winner of the 2007 Christy Award, tells "the story of an Amish girl torn between her family's way of life and her artistic dreams. Annie Zook has been wrestling with the decision of whether to commit her life to the church even though it would mean giving up her art for good. Also complicating her life is Ben Martin, the non-Amish boy she fell in love with but sent away. Ben's own life and identity are tested when he learns a secret that his parents have kept from him for his entire life." (Library Journal)

Lewis, Beverly

The **missing**; Beverly Lewis. Bethany House 2009 332p (pbk.) $14.99
ISBN 9780764205729
LC 2009025139

In this book, "Grace Byler longs to uncover the secret that drove her mother to leave the family weeks ago. When all hopes are dashed for such a search, an unlikely friendship leads to a surprising invitation. Meanwhile, the young Amishman Grace thought was courting her best friend takes a sudden interest in her, and Grace's decision to remain single is challenged." (Publisher's note)

Lewis, Beverly

The **preacher's** daughter; Beverly Lewis. Bethany House Publishers 2005 349p (Annie's people) $19.99

ISBN 0764201204 (alk. paper); 0764201050 (pbk.: alk. paper); 0764201212 (lg print pbk.: alk. paper)

LC 2005018581

This book follows 20-year-old Annie Zook, "a budding artist . . . [whose] conservative Amish community forbids its members to draw or paint pictures. . . . How will she choose between family and vocation? The disappearance of a small child years ago has left scars on various characters, and new developments in the case threaten to open old wounds. Annie's best friend in the community, Esther Hochstetler, finds that her marriage to an abusive man has become a nightmare, while Annie's pen pal, the wealthy Colorado 'Englisher' Louisa Stratford, . . . visits Annie in Paradise to heal from a broken engagement. Both women explore the possibilities of change." (Publishers Weekly)

Lewis, C. S.

The **dark** tower and other stories; edited by Walter Hooper. Harcourt Brace Jovanovich 1977 158p

Lewis, C. S.

★ **Out** of the silent planet. Scribner Classics 1996 158p $22; pa $13

ISBN 0-684-83364-6; 0-7432-3490-1 pa

LC 96-30110

A reissue of the title first published 1938 in the United Kingdom; first United States edition published 1943 by Macmillan

"The trilogy can be read on two levels: first for its exciting plot and second as a theological allegory, although Lewis denied this interpretation. The stories are about temptation. They concern the classic battle between good, as represented by Ransom, the philologist, and evil, as represented by Weston, the physicist. The battle is played out on the planets of Malacondra (Mars), Perelandra (Venus), and Earth." Shapiro. Fic for Youth. 3d edition

Followed by Perelandra (1943) and That hideous strength (1945)

Lewis, C. S.

Perelandra; a novel. Scribner Classics 1996 190p $22

ISBN 0-684-83365-4

LC 96-20724

A reissue of the title first published 1944 by Macmillan

In the second volume of the fantasy trilogy Dr. Ransom "is ordered to Perelandra (Venus) by the supreme being and finds there a paradise threatened by the villainous scientist Weston, who becomes the devil incarnate." Booklist

Followed by That hideous strength

Lewis, C. S.

That hideous strength; a modern fairy-tale for grown-ups. Scribner Classics 1996 380p $23

ISBN 0-684-83367-0

LC 96-20722

A reissue of the title first published 1946 by Macmillan

In the final volume of the fantasy trilogy Ransom and Weston again represent the struggle between good and evil, this time in a college community on Earth. Mark Studdock learns the error of his attempts to play faculty politics, and his wife discovers the footlessness of modern theories of love and life

Lewis, C. S.

Till we have faces; a myth retold. Harcourt Brace & Co. 1957 313p il

First published 1956 in the United Kingdom

"The religious allegory is plain to read. In Mr. Lewis's sensitive hands the ancient myth retains its fascination, while being endowed with new meanings, new depths, new terrors." Saturday Rev

Lewis, Jim

The **king** is dead. Knopf 2003 259p $24

ISBN 0-375-41417-7

LC 2002-43288

Walter Selbly "was born in 1925 and became a World War II hero, lawyer, and indispensable aide to the governor of Tennessee. His life seemed complete when he marrried beautiful Nicole Lattimore, whom he adored, and they had a son, Frank, and a daughter, Gail. Then, on a single day, Walter's professional and personal lives were destroyed, and his young children were left without parents. Thirty-five years later Frank Cartwright (with his adoptive parents' name), an attractive, womanizing actor whose career is languishing, is provoked by a film proposal from a fabled dowager to find his roots. . . . Even if the parts of this novel outshine the whole, Lewis' language often soars." Booklist

Lewis, M. G.

★ The **monk**; by Matthew Lewis, with an introduction by Stephen King. Oxford Univ. Press 2002 442p (Oxford world's classics) $20

ISBN 0-19-515136-4

LC 2002-25111

First published 1796 in the United Kingdom

"Ambrosio, the worthy superior of the Capuchins of Madrid, falls to the temptations of Matilda, a fiend-inspired wanton who, disguised as a boy, has entered his monastery as a novice. Now utterly depraved, Ambrosio falls in love with one of his penitents, pursues the girl with the help of magic and murder, and finally kills her in and effort to escape detection. But he is discovered, tortured by the Inquisition, and sentenced to death, finally compounding with the devil for escape from burning, only to be hurled by him to destruction and damnation. Although extravagant in its mixture of the supernatural, the terrible, and the indecent, the book contains scenes of great effect. It enjoyed a considerable contemporary vogue." Oxford Companion to Engl Lit. 6th edition

Lewis, Sinclair

★ **Arrowsmith**. Harcourt Brace & Co. 1925 448p

ISBN 0-15-108216-2

"Although he is most interested in bacteriology and research, Martin Arrowsmith turns from that area to general medicine and then to public health. He is unable, however, to deal with the political aspects of the public health field and returns to laboratory work and research. Martin develops an antitoxin that he believes will be effective against bubonic plague, but when he gets the chance to test the serum during an epidemic in the West Indies, he invalidates the results by not adhering to a control situation. Returning to the States, he feels that he is a failure and refuses the offer of a prestigious position in order to join an old friend at a rural laboratory in a search for a cure for pneumonia." Shapiro. Fic for Youth. 3d edition

Lewis, Sinclair

Arrowsmith; Elmer Gantry; Dodsworth. Library of America, Distributed to the trade in the U.S. by Penguin Putnam 2002 1346p $40

ISBN 1-931082-08-1

LC 2002-19451

Lewis, Sinclair

★ Babbitt; with an introduction and notes by James M. Hutchisson. Penguin Books 1996 xxxii, 365p il pa $9.95

ISBN 0-14-018902-5

LC 95-36188

First published 1922 by Harcourt, Brace

Satire on American middle-class life in a good-sized city. George F. Babbitt is a successful real estate man, a regular fellow, booster, Rotarian, Elk, Republican, who uses all the current catchwords, molds his opinions on those of the Zenith Advocate-Times and believes in "a sound business administration in Washington"

"The novel's scathing indictment of middle-class American values made Babbittry a synonym for adherence to a conformist, materialistic, anti-intellectual way of life." Merriam-Webster's Ency of Lit

Lewis, Sinclair

Dodsworth; a novel. Harcourt Brace & Co. 1929 377p

"The book's protagonist, Sam Dodsworth, is an American automobile manufacturer who sells his company and takes an extended European vacation with his wife, Fran. Dodsworth recounts their reactions to Europeans and European values, their various relationships with others, their estrangement, and their brief reconciliation." Merriam-Webster's Ency of Lit

Lewis, Sinclair

★ Elmer Gantry. Harcourt Brace 1927 432p

This novel "deals with a brazen ex-football player who enters the ministry and, through his half-plagiarized sermons, his physical attractiveness, and his unerring instinct for promotion, becomes a successful evangelist and later the leader of a large Middle Western church. Carefully researched, the novel was realistic enough to shock both the faithful and unfaithful." Reader's Ency. 3d edition

Lewis, Sinclair

It can't happen here; a novel. Doubleday, Doran 1935 458p

"Doremus Jessup, editor of a small New England newspaper, follows the rise to the presidency of the United States of a fascist demagogue, Berzelius Windrip. Doremus and his friends publish an underground newspaper that tells the truth about what is happening. Doremus is imprisoned, escapes to Canada, and joins the underground movement, which is headed by the man who had opposed Windrip in the election. The novel inveighs against some aspects of capitalism as well as fascism, and communists come in for their share of criticism also." Shapiro. Fic for Youth. 3d edition

Lewis, Sinclair

★ Main Street. Harcourt, Brace 1920 451p

"Carol Milford, a girl of quick intelligence but no particular talent, after graduation from college meets and marries Will Kennicott, a sober, kindly, unimaginative physician of Gopher Prairie, Minn., who tells her that the town needs her abilities. She finds the village to be a smug, intolerant, unimaginatively standardized place, where the people will not accept her efforts to create more sightly homes, organize a dramatic association, and otherwise improve the village life." Oxford Companion to Am Lit. 6th edition

Lewis, Sinclair

Main Street & Babbitt. Library of Am. 1992 898p $40

ISBN 0-940450-61-5

LC 91-58224

In addition to Main Street, this book also features Babbitt (1922), a satire on American middle-class conventions. Set in the Midwest, it focuses on the life of George Babbitt, a prosperous and self-satisfied real estate man.

Lewycka, Marina

A short history of tractors in Ukrainian. Penguin Press 2005 294p

ISBN 1-59420-044-0

LC 2004-56542

"The author's imaginary world lets her explore the sort of problems that other east European emigres in Britain often fear but seldom confront: chiefly, what to do with people we are supposed to like but don't trust or understand. Her dialogue, conducted between educated people who lack a common language, is a comic feast." Economist

Li Yiyun

A thousand years of good prayers; stories. Random House 2005 205p $21.95

ISBN 1-4000-6312-4

LC 2004-62891

This collection is a "reminder that, at its best, the short story is the most elegant of literary forms. Each tale has a keen poignancy of its own, and assembled in a collection they give an impressively coherent sense of modern China. All melancholy, the stories are by turns angry and whimsical, and each bears the ugly imprint of Mao's China." Times Lit Suppl

Lianke, Yan

★ Dream of Ding Village; translated by Cindy Carter. Grove 2011 341p $24

ISBN 978-0-8021-1932-2

"Ding Village, a town of 800 people located in the Henan province, finds a quick fix to its dire needs in the form of a plasma-selling scheme promoted by county officials. Money flows the way the Yellow River once did before changing course and leaving the village parched. But exposed to dirty syringes and tainted cotton, and eager to give blood more frequently than their bodies can tolerate, townspeople in increasing numbers come down with 'the fever' and face certain death. Told from the grave by a 12-year-old boy whose grandfather is the deposed town leader and conscience, and whose father buys blood and resells it for a profit, the novel details the contamination of the town's moral as well as physical being. . . . A sorrowful but captivating novel about the price of progress in modern China. The book, which was censored in that country, builds to an act of violence that resonates with the impact of Greek tragedy or Shakespearean drama." Kirkus

Lichtenstein, Alice

Lost; a novel. Scribner 2010 242p $24
ISBN 978-1-4391-5982-8; 1-4391-5982-3
LC 2009-37973
The "characters are believable and fully drawn by Lichtenstein and well matched to share the stage of 'Lost.' They deploy impassioned subject matter with balance and control, never allowing the material to become maudlin. . . . [The novel] is a remarkable feat in technical craftsmanship that is nonetheless shot through with much raw feeling." St. Louis Post-Dispatch

Liebmann-Smith, Richard

The **James** boys; a novel account of four desperate brothers. Random House 2008 261p $25
ISBN 978-0-345-47078-2; 0-345-47078-8
LC 2007-38423
"In his first novel, The James Boys, humorist Richard Liebmann-Smith posits what life would have been like if real-life brothers Henry and William James (the novelist and the philosopher) had been the brothers of Frank and Jesse James (the outlaws)." NPR

The author "includes enough plot, to keep this single-joke, creatively imagined biography chugging along." Publ Wkly

Lightman, Alan P.

The **diagnosis**; [by] Alan Lightman. Pantheon Bks. 2000 369p
ISBN 0-679-43615-4
LC 00-24543
"Bill Chalmers is an executive at an 'information company' in Boston who on his way to work one day forgets completely who he is, what he does or where he is supposed to be going. After a number of nightmarish experiences, in which he rapidly becomes a homeless bum, he awakens in a hospital, more or less his old self—except that his body is beginning to turn numb." Publ Wkly

Lightman, Alan P.

★ **Einstein's** dreams; [by] Alan Lightman. Pantheon Bks. 1993 179p il
LC 92-50465
"Lightman starts out with commonplaces, neurological conditions or abstractions of our personal experience of time. Then, with one or two exceptions, he embodies the

concept in brilliant, folkloric tales with extraordinary assurance." New Statesman Soc

Lightman, Alan P.

Ghost; [by] Alan Lightman. Pantheon Books 2007 243p $23
ISBN 978-0-375-42169-3; 0-375-42169-6
LC 2007-05298
"Satirical and compassionate, Lightman's brilliantly orchestrated and gripping tale dramatizes our marshaling of fear, fantasy, and faith as we confront the unknown and the inevitable. At base, all we can truly trust, Lightman suggests, is wonder and kindness." Booklist

Lightman, Alan P.

Reunion; [by] Alan Lightman. Pantheon Bks. 2003 231p $23
ISBN 0-375-42167-X
LC 2002-34575
"Charles, a 'small-college professor' in his early 50's, more or less amicably settled into domestic banality in a leafy suburb, decides to attend his 30th college reunion. Once back at his unnamed alma mater . . . he is struck with eidetic force by recollections of his first passionate love affair, with an aspiring ballerina, Juliana. A narrative of this love affair and reflections upon it form the bulk of the novel." N Y Times Book Rev

"Lightman infuses even the simplest scenes with quiet menace as he explores the cataclysmic power of both erotic love and shocking betrayal." Booklist

Limon, Martin

G.I. bones. Soho Press 2009 266p $24
ISBN 978-1-56947-6031; 1-56947-603-9
LC 2009-14766
"Sergeant Sueño of the Criminal Investigation Division of the Eighth U.S. Army in Seoul, South Korea, is asked to find the bones of a G.I. murdered at the end of the Korean War. Apparently, his ghost is haunting local fortune-tellers. But Sueño and his partner, Bascom, who are also probing the disappearace of an officer's daughter, find their lives are on the line when present-day criminals get into the action." Libr J

This mystery "combines a brash, righteous hero with gritty local color for a crackling good read." Kirkus

Limón, Martin

Mr. Kill; Martin Limón. Soho Crime 2011 375p.
ISBN 1569479348; 9781569479346
LC 2011024936
'This book offers a military mystery story in which "the brutal rape of a young mother sparks rage on the powder-keg peninsula of Korea, pitting Koreans against Americans and the 8th Army brass against the truth. Eyewitness accounts indicate the culprit was most likely a U.S. serviceman, but by the time Sergeants George Sueno and Ernie Bascom, U.S. Army investigators, are called in, the rapist has disappeared and anti-American fervor in this proud Asian country is threatening to explode. George and Ernie search in vain for the culprit, all the while becoming entangled in the web of military apologists who deny that any Americans were

involved, and the designs of a beautiful blonde musician who fronts an all-female country western band--a woman who is out to entertain the troops in more ways than one." (Publisher's note)

Lin Yutang

Moment in Peking; a novel of contemporary Chinese life. Day 1939 815p

A story of family life among the upper middle class of China, covering forty years from the time of the Boxer Rebellion to the Japanese invasion

"There are many scenes and passages of great beauty in the book, excerpts from the classics, poetry and philosophy. There are also incidents of humor, delicate and subtle. Equally skillful is the author in depicting scenes of dramatic intensity, stark tragedy of war and acts of heroism" Springfield Repub

Lin, Jeannie

The **Dragon** and the Pearl; Jeannie Lin. Harlequin Books 2011 288p.

ISBN 9780373296620 pa

This book tells the story of "Lady Ling Suyin, former consort of the late Emperor, [who] is grateful but wary when fierce warlord Li Tao saves her from the assassins of powerful military governor Gao Shiming. With the kingdom in turmoil, Suyin trusts no one, especially not Li Tao, whose loyalty to Emperor Shen is in question and the reason for her rescue unclear. Li Tao has no idea why Gao Shiming would want the legendary beauty dead, but he wasn't about to let that happen. Despite their mutual distrust, Tao and Suyin can't resist the attraction that arcs between them or the star-crossed love that develops." (Libr J)

Lin, Jeannie

My fair concubine; Jeannie Lin. Harlequin 2012 280 p.

ISBN 0373296940; 9780373296941

This romance novel by Jeannie Lin is a "take on "My Fair Lady." In ninth-century China, Fei Long is a soldier from a noble family whose sister, Pearl, runs away with her lover to avoid becoming an alliance bride. After Fei Long gives his sister all of his money and allows her to escape, he meets the orphan Yan Ling, who begs him for help. He proposes a plan to substitute her for Pearl to maintain his family's wealth and honor. As Fei Long and his friends undertake the magnificent transformation of the unlearned and outspoken servant into a well-bred noblewoman, fooling even the suspicious Inspector Tong, the teacher and the pupil soon fall in love—jeopardizing the whole scheme." (Publishers Weekly)

Lin, Tao

Richard Yates. Melville House 2010 206p pa $14.95

ISBN 978-1-935554-15-8; 1-935554-15-8

LC 2010-17972

"The romance between a 22-year-old writer living in New York and a 16-year-old girl living in a faceless New Jersey suburb — a couple whom, for whatever reasons, Lin has chosen to name Haley Joel Osment and Dakota Fanning. (Also unexplained is the book's title reference to the late,

great American novelist and short-story writer.) The characters — whose correspondence takes place primarily through email, Gmail chat, and text message — begin seeing one another in person. The obstacles they face in shielding their relationship from Dakota's half-witted mother pale in comparison to the demons inherent in their dysfunctional bond. . . . [This novel] probably couldn't have come into existence without the buzz-generating antics that have earned Tao Lin a reputation as a prankster. But it's also the novel that begs him to divorce his work from the sideshow." Boston Phoenix

Lindgren, Torgny

Hash; a novel. translated from the Swedish by Tom Geddes. Overlook Press 2004 236p $23.95

ISBN 1-585-67408-7

LC 2003-63976

Original Swedish edition, 2002

"In December 1947, for the newspaper to which he corresponds from northern Sweden, a middle-aged man is writing about two newcomers to the village of Avaback: a schoolteacher, just released as cured from the tuberculosis sanitarium in which he spent his youth, and a middle-aged clothing peddler, who the writer believes is missing Nazi leader Martin Bormann. Then a messenger arrives with a termination letter from the newspaper editor, who has researched the places the writer reports on, only to be told that they don't exist. The writer stops writing, for 53 years, resuming at age 107, only after he has outlived old age and is regaining lost powers and attributes." Booklist

"Lindgren delivers a story that's a clever sendup of the conceits of storytellers and a bittersweet meditation on life and the pleasures that bind us to it." N Y Times Book Rev

Lindqvist, John Ajvide

Little star; John Ajvide Lindqvist; translated by Marlaine Delargy. Thomas Dunne Books 2012 533 p.

ISBN 0312620519; 9780312620516; 9781250012821

LC 2012028223

This novel by John Ajvide Lindqvist is a "portrait of adolescence . . . for the age of internet bullies, offensive reality television, and overnight You Tube sensations. . . . A man finds a baby in the woods. . . . He brings the baby home, . . [but] [w]hen a shocking and catastrophic incident occurs, the couple's son Jerry whisks the girl away to Stockholm, . . . [where] he enters her in a nationwide singing competition. Another young girl who's never fit in sees the performance on TV, and a spark is struck." (Publisher's note)

Lindsay, Jeffry P.

Darkly dreaming Dexter. Doubleday 2004 288p $22.95

ISBN 0-385-51123-X

LC 2004-45460

Dexter Morgan is a "Miami police-department blood-spatter analyst with a weakness for bowling shirts and batidos, who, when the moon is full, carves up villains in a careful ritual, keeping a single drop of blood on a slide as a souvenir. (He's collected thirty-six so far.) When other victims start popping up, dispatched with the same creativity as Dexter's, he pursues the copycat murderer with acute professional self-interest. Like other charismatic killers—Hannibal Lecter, say, or Tom Ripley—Dexter has a set of motives that are tough to untangle. But his quest proves weirdly convincing as he ponders whether to turn his doppelgänger over to the cops or take care of the problem himself." New Yorker

Lindsay, Jeffry P.

Dearly devoted Dexter; [by] Jeff Lindsay. Doubleday 2005 292p

ISBN 0-385-51124-8

This is the second book in the Dexter series. "Dexter Morgan, a Miami P.D. blood splatter analyst and ethical serial killer, is in a funk: his police department arch-nemesis, Captain Doakes, who rightly believes that Dexter is guilty of illegal behavior, is shadowing him. . . . So when a new serial killer with Doakes on his list arrives in Miami, Dexter is excited. Not only does he get to hunt a fellow hunter, but he also sees the opportunity to be rid of Doakes. The only thing worrying him is the involvement of his sister, since she's the only person for whom Dexter has feelings. . . . There's plenty of graphic violence and dark humor, but Lindsay manages to retain a light edge." Libr J

Lindsay, Jeffry P.

Dexter in the dark; a novel. [by] Jeff Lindsay. Doubleday 2007 302p $23.95

ISBN 978-0-385-51833-8; 0-385-51833-1

LC 2007-20277

Dexter Morgan is a serial killer who works as a blood-splatter expert for the Miami police department. In this installment "Dexter is shocked, while working a crime scene, to discover that his Dark Passenger, the evil thing that makes him who he is, has abruptly vanished. Soon after that, and still reeling from the unfamiliar sense of solitude, he learns that he's being stalked by someone more evil than anyone he's encountered in the past." Booklist

"Lindsay gives Dexter a great voice and provides the reader with several laugh-out-loud scenes." Libr J

Lindsay, Jeffry P.

Dexter is delicious; a novel. [by] Jeff Lindsay. Doubleday 2010 350p $25.95

ISBN 9780385532358; 0385532350

LC 2010-13405

"Dexter is celebrating the birth of Lily Anne, his first child, and dealing with feeling as though he is almost human, and his need to hurt bad people having almost disappeared. Order is restored somewhat when a couple of teenage girls go missing, and Dex is drawn into a case involving murder and cannibalism. He has to help his sister Deborah with the case while dealing on the home front not only with his new daughter but also with the suspicious reappearance of his brother and fellow killer, Brian. Lindsay deftly handles Dexter's apparent transition toward becoming more human and prevents the book from being weighed down or dull." Libr J

Lindsey, David L.

The color of night; [by] David Lindsey. Warner Bks. 1999 480p $32

ISBN 0-446-52361-5

LC 98-30770

"Harry Strand, a retired U.S. intelligence officer, thinks he's finally put his life back together after the tragic death of his wife. He has become a successful art dealer, and he's fallen in love with Mara Song, a beautiful collector. But everything changes abruptly when Harry discovers a tape in Mara's VCR that clearly shows his wife being murdered. Finding out who is responsible for her death proves to be far more complicated than this former spy can imagine. This is a fast-paced and exciting thriller." Booklist

Lindsey, David L.

The rules of silence; [by] David Lindsey. Warner Bks. 2003 405p $24.95

ISBN 0-446-53163-4

LC 2002-33059

"Multimillionaire Titus Cain is approached with a strange proposition: if he doesn't give a certain man $64 million, this same man will kill off some (or perhaps all) of Cain's friends and loved ones. The money has to be given to the extortionist in such a way that no one suspects anything is going on. . . and if Cain even tries to seek help, the killings will start instantly. . . . Lindsey's novels sometimes suffer from lethargy, as though he's just sort of wandering through his story, but this one moves swiftly to its rousing finale." Booklist

Lindsey, Johanna

Gentle rogue. Avon Books 1990 426p (Avon historical romance) pa $7.99

ISBN 978-0-380-75302-4

LC 90-93175

"Heartsick and desperate to return home to America, Georgina Anderson boards the Maiden Anne disguised as a cabin boy, never dreaming she'll be forced into intimate servitude at the whim of the ship's irrepressible captain, James Mallory." Publisher's note

Link, Kelly

Magic for beginners; illustrated by Shelley Jackson. Small Beer Press 2005 272p il $24

ISBN 978-1-931520-15-7; 1-931520-15-1

LC 2005-5394

"Link's second collection has a McSweeney's-like tendency to digress, but does so without irony. Whether describing witches filled with ants that carry pieces of time, or an orange-juice-colored corduroy couch that looks as if it 'has just escaped from a maximum security prison for criminally insane furniture,' these stories examine American middle and lower-middle-class life from unexpected angles that mix fairy tale, science fiction, and zaniness. . . . Reading Link, one has a sense that sometimes a person needs to wander off for a better perspective, and sometimes a person simply needs to wander off." New Yorker

Link, Teresa

Denting the Bosch; a novel of marriage, friendship, and expensive household appliances. Teresa Link. 1st ed. Thomas Dunne Books 2012 276 p. (hardcover) $25.99

ISBN 0312643411; 9780312643416; 9781250010506

LC 2012011014

In author Teresa Link's book, "three couples in San Diego--best friends, empty nesters living the California dream--have reached a tipping point. With the blurry years of child rearing and corporate ladder-climbing over, each pair is finally free to enjoy the golden years together. Until two of the husbands suddenly announce they want a divorce. . . . Marriages and friendships unravel and the prosperity of the last few decades spins toward financial meltdown." (Publisher's note)

Linscott, Gillian

Blood on the wood; a Nell Bray mystery. Gillian Linscott. 1st St. Martin's Minotaur ed; St. Martin's Minotaur 2004 311p $24.95

ISBN 0-312-33148-7

LC 2003-69721

"Readers will soak up fascinating detail about the Fabians, the Scipians, and the Arts and Crafts Movement while following the action in this delightful romp through England at the turn of the century." Booklist

Lipman, Elinor

The **dearly** departed; a novel. Random House 2001 269p $23.95

ISBN 0-679-46312-7

LC 00-67368

The novel "entertains the reader with quirky details and amusing dialogue, but most nourishing is its picture of small-town life, in which everyone knows everyone else's business but they love one another just the same." Atl Mon

Lipman, Elinor

The **family** man. Houghton Mifflin Harcourt 2009 305p $25

ISBN 978-0-618-64466-7; 0-618-64466-0

LC 2008-46222

"Hilarious, literate and unnervingly accurate in its observations of the quirks of human nature, 'The Family Man' proclaims that whatever bizarre sort of family you have, you're better off with it than without it." PopMatters

Lipman, Elinor

The **Inn** at Lake Devine. Random House 1998 253p

ISBN 0-679-45693-7

LC 97-1307

"Skillfully interweaving the bittersweet narrative with threads of both tragedy and comedy, Lipman displays a healthy amount of empathy and affection for her flawed and slightly eccentric cast of characters." Booklist

Lipman, Elinor

The **ladies'** man; a novel. Random House 1999 260p

ISBN 0-679-45694-5

LC 98-56450

"'The Ladies' Man' never suggests that all men are like Nash Harvey. . . . This book isn't even angry with its villain; it just shakes its head in amused amazement and, a little wiser, walks away." N Y Times Book Rev

Lipman, Elinor

My latest grievance. Houghton Mifflin 2006 243p $24

ISBN 0-618-64465-2

LC 2005-22576

"In the late 1970s, Frederica Hatch is the enchantingly outspoken daughter of brilliant college professors at a minor all-girls college in Massachusetts. Her temperate, mildly eccentric, and lovely parents, also union activists for the faculty of Dewing College, serve as houseparents at one of the dorms, where Frederica has lived her whole life. Wise beyond her years, Frederica takes it in stride when she discovers that her father was married once before and that Laura Lee French, the smashingly solipsistic first wife of Dr. David Hatch, has just been hired as housemother of one of the other dorms. Within hours of her arrival, French seduces the new president of Dewing in a flagrant affair that provides rich fuel for Frederica's hilariously dry wit and searing analysis of adult foibles." Libr J

Lipman, Elinor

The **pursuit** of Alice Thrift; a novel. Random House 2003 269p $23.95

ISBN 0-679-46313-5

LC 2002-31864

"The eponymous Alice is a sleep-deprived surgical intern at a Boston hospital. A graduate of MIT and Harvard and a congenital workaholic, she's also devoid of social skills, a sense of humor or elementary tact. Though miserably unequipped with self-esteem, Alice is an intelligent, well-brought-up offspring of upper-middle-class parents. Why, then, does she fall prey to the romantic blandishments of Ray Russo, a vulgar loudmouth and con artist who—it turns out—lies every time he opens his mouth? That Lipman can make this story plausible, and tell it with humor, pschological insight and rising suspense, is a triumph." Publ Wkly

Lippman, Laura

★ **And** when she was good; by Laura Lippman. 1st ed. William Morrow 2012 314 p. (hardcover) $26.99; (ebook) $21.99; (paperback) $14.99

ISBN 0061706876; 9780061706875; 9780062201614; 9780062197733

LC 2011279905

Author Laura Lippman's protagonist "Heloise Lewis is a survivor who rose from the ashes of her past to run a profitable call-girl service, occasionally meeting special clients herself. To her neighbors, she's a young widow and a devoted mother . . . [and] to the IRS, she's a lobbyist with several women on her payroll and a medical plan . . . [Her] carefully constructed life is falling apart because Val Deluca, her son's father . . . may be released from prison . . . [without knowing that] he's Scott's father or that Heloise's betrayal put him behind bars for murder." (Publishers Weekiy)

Lippman, Laura

Hardly knew her; stories. William Morrow 2008 292p $23.95

ISBN 978-0-06-158499-2; 0-06-158499-1

Lippman "clearly agrees with Kipling that the female of the species is deadlier than the male. Women's victims here include a female friend, boyfriends (both current and ex), a husband, and one-night stands and strangers; their murders are all the more chilling. The novella 'Scratch A Woman,' featuring a single suburban Maryland soccer mom who works as a prostitute, and one of several stories featuring Tess [Monaghan] are the only entries not published previously. But those that have been published are scattered in a variety of anthologies over the last seven years, including Baltimore Noir. Here are nearly all of the short stories Lippman has ever written in one volume; read them fast, like a glutton, or slowly to savor each one. Either way, this is a treasure." Libr J

Lippman, Laura

I'd know you anywhere. Morrow 2010 374p $25.99

ISBN 978-0-06-170655-4; 0-06-170655-8

"Eliza Benedict is an easygoing wife and mother of two living in suburban Maryland. The family recently returned to America after five years in England, which would seem to account for Eliza's lack of friends. Her biggest problem appears to be her argumentative 13-year-old daughter, Iso, who traded in kindness for popularity when the family crossed the ocean. Then Eliza receives a letter from Walter Bowman, the man who kidnapped her and held her hostage for nearly six weeks when she was 15. Walter wants a favor: He wants to talk to Elizabeth (the name that she used in her life 'before'), and, despite his residency on death row, he still holds sway over her. I'd Know You Anywhere is a crime story, but it's not a whodunit. Rather, it's an exquisitely sensitive story about the psychological impact of crime on its victims. It's a story about shame, about anger, about survivor's guilt." Ft. Worth Star-Telegram

Lippman, Laura

The most dangerous thing. Morrow 2011 344p $25.99

ISBN 978-0-06-170651-6; 0-06-170651-5

"Gordon 'GoGo' Halloran drives his car into a wall after a night of drinking, even though he's been on the road to sobriety. On the brink of divorce, Gwen Robison returns home to care for her aging father and learns of GoGo's death from his older brother, Sean. With the eldest Halloran brother, Tim, and a scruffy, nature-loving neighborhood girl, Mickey Wickham, the five had come together in the spring of 1977. The group broke apart after a violent encounter in the woods, an event that was never spoken of again, but permeates each of their lives." Publ Wkly

"No one explores the delicate interplay between children and the adults they grow into better than Lippman." Kirkus

Lippman, Laura

No good deeds. William Morrow 2006 343p $24.95

ISBN 978-0-06-057072-9; 0-06-057072-5

LC 2005-58358

"Lippman has pulled off the near-impossible: writing a conventional procedural that still feels fresh. It's impossible not to like the complex, all-too-real Monaghan, a strong, wry detective prone to 'derailing my own gravy train.'" Washington Post Book World

Lippman, Laura

What the dead know. William Morrow 2007 376p $24.95

ISBN 978-0-06-112885-1; 0-06-112885-6

LC 2006-52495

"As artful as she is at interweaving disarming scenes of two spirited girls on the day they vanished with painful moments in the lives of their parents—maintaining all the while a thread of continuity in the current-day police investigation—Lippman pulls off something more ambitious than a high-wire act of technical virtuosity. With great thought and compassion, she uses her fractured narrative style to delve into the ways in which every serious crime tears to shreds the lives of its victims." N Y Times Book Rev

Lipsyte, Sam

★ The ask. Farrar, Straus and Giroux 2010 296p $25

ISBN 0-374-29891-2; 978-0-374-29891-3

LC 2009-29508

After he loses his job as a development officer at a university, family man Milo Burke is given a chance to regain his position, but only if he can reel in a potential donor, one who has requested his involvement and turns out to be his sinister college classmate.

"Milo Burke, a recently fired donations officer at a third-tier university, is a paragon of failure: a horny, bile-filled chunk of a man, veering into middle age with nothing to show for his youthful dreams of artistic glory. The Ask's narrative heft comes from the reappearance of a wealthy friend from Milo's college days and the tragicomic scenarios that follow — the plight of socialist daycare workers and legless Iraq-war vets among them. But the gift is Sam Lipsyte's writing: a chewy, corrosive, and syntactically dazzling prose style that doesn't so much run across the page as pick it up and throttle it. You may want to throttle Milo yourself frequently, but you won't stop reading." Entertainment Wkly

Lipsyte, Sam

Home land; a novel. Picador 2005 229p pa $13

ISBN 0-312-42418-3

LC 2004-57318

First published 2004 in the United Kingdom

"The hero of this comic novel, Lewis Miner, a.k.a. Teabag, was a high-school stoner, and now makes it his mission to write extremely candid letters to the alumni newsletter. His life, as he writes, 'did not pan out.' He works as a dishwasher in his father's cheesy catering business and spends his free time moping with his friend Gary, who sued his parents for molestation and then sued the shrink who conjured up these false memories. Teabag's letters detail his sexual fantasies (most of which involve the leg warmers of the school's jazz-dancing squad), his stalled ambition, and the misshapen pearls of wisdom he's garnered from his bottomed-out life. The story ends in an improbable shootout, but Lipsyte transfigures Teabag's self-loathing into a sensibility that is both hilarious and noble." New Yorker

Liss, David

The **ethical** assassin. Ballantine Books 2006 327p $24.95

ISBN 1-4000-6421-X

LC 2005-46446

An "ecoterrorist romp shot through with elements of the absurd. It begins with a 17-year-old Jewish encyclopedia salesman working door to door in a South Florida trailer park. . . . Lem Altick is saving money for college by tricking poor people into buying supermarket encyclopedias, but he gets more than he bargained for when an assassin with 'Warholishy' hair saunters into a trailer where Lem is about to close a deal and efficiently kills the two would-be encyclopedia readers and then engages Lem in a chat about his favorite Shakespeare play (Lem is partial to Twelfth Night). It only gets weirder from there, as Lem finds himself a sort of comrade-in-arms with the ethical assassin, whose real purpose seems to be raising havoc with some distinctly unethical pig farmers. There's also a sicko small-town sheriff lurking in the wings, having apparently wandered into the action straight out of Jim Thompson's Pop. 1280." Booklist

Liss, David

A **spectacle** of corruption. Random House 2004 381p $24.95

ISBN 0-375-50855-4

LC 2003-54806

Weaver "turns out to be the hard-outside, soft-inside private investigator of the noir thrillers inserted into 1720s London: Philip Marlowe done up in a wig and buckles." Washington Post Book World

Liss, David

The **whiskey** rebels; a novel. Random House 2008 525p $26

ISBN 1-4000-6420-1; 978-1-4000-6420-5

LC 2008-00075

"Ethan Saunders, once among George Washington's most valued spies, now lives in disgrace, haunting the taverns of Philadelphia. An accusation of treason has long since cost him his reputation and his beloved fiancee, Cynthia Pearson, but at his most desperate moment he is recruited for an unlikely task—finding Cynthia's missing husband. To help her, Saunders must serve his old enemy, Treasury Secretary Alexander Hamilton." (Publisher's note)

The author "delivers a portrait of postcolonial Philadelphia and New York, as well as the western frontier, that is convincing and acutely detailed." Houston Chron

Littell, Jonathan

The **kindly** ones; a novel. translated by Charlotte Mandell. Harper 2009 992p $29.99

ISBN 978-0-06-135345-1; 0-06-135345-0

LC 2008-30788

Original French edition, 2006

Littell "eagerly displays vast amounts of research. We are treated to several pages on the languages of the Caucasus as well as a remarkable description of Jawizowitz, a subcamp of Auschwitz about which virtually no one who didn't survive its lethal mines would know. . . . Throughout Aue's morbidly picaresque travels, the tone is leering. A phenomenon that can only be called death porn saturates 'The Kindly Ones.' Despite its many, potent set pieces that vividly render the misery and insanity of war, the effect is voyeuristic as Aue, Littell and the unfortunate reader rubberneck at the innumerable bodies—gassed, shot, hanged, strangled, burnt, bombed, eyes gouged, intestines unwound, limbs severed, brains spattered—heaped in piles by history's roadside." Washington Post Book World

Littell, Robert

★ The **company**; a novel of the CIA. Overlook Press 2002 894p $27.95

ISBN 1-58567-197-5

LC 2001-51383

"Mixing real events and real people with the story of four fictional spies, Littell presents the history of the CIA, from post-war Berlin to the present. As we follow the intersecting careers of three Company agents and one KGB operative, we see the major events and personalities of the cold war from the inside." Booklist

"There is plenty here to amuse anyone with even a network news interest in current events—and a gold mine for true conspiracy theorists." N Y Times Book Rev

Littell, Robert

The **Stalin** epigram; a novel. Simon & Schuster 2009 366p $26

ISBN 9781416598640; 1-4165-9864-2

LC 2008-52277

"This is a timeless story of courage and truth confronting the madness of absolute power. It's a brilliant work, always readable, sometimes funny and often heartbreaking. There are many books about Stalin's terror, but there cannot be many that bring its truths more vividly, painfully to life." Washington Post Book World

Littell, Robert

Vicious circle; a novel of complicity. Overlook 2006 300p $24.95

ISBN 1-58567-855-4

This novel "takes place in the volatile Holy Land of the near future. When the Arab leader of a terrorist faction kidnaps a rabbi who heads an ultraconservative settlers' group, Israeli security services go on red alert. In adding a smart-alecky American reporter to the mix, Littell . . . ratchets up the action to a heart-bursting sprint that stops only for big gulps of violence and torture. What makes this book unforgettable is the extraordinary relationship between kidnapper and victim. Extremists both, they joust with vehement hatred yet are strangely drawn together. Littell's acute portrayal of their inflamed psychological states illuminates an understanding that goes far beyond the day's headlines." Libr J

Littell, Robert

Walking back the cat. Overlook Press 1997 220p

ISBN 0-87951-764-6

LC 96-49507

"Sinister deeds and playful characterizations ricochet the reader through a complex plot, replacing the genre's usual hightech gizmos with the strengths and skills of lone-wolf heroes." Publ Wkly

Littell, Robert

Young Philby; [a novel] Robert Littell. Thomas Dunne Books 2012 ix, 268 p.p (hardcover) $24.99
ISBN 1250005167; 9781250005168; 9781250013651
LC 2012035373

This novel, by Robert Littell, is the winner of the 2012 Kirkus Best Fiction Book and Kansas City Star Top Book of the Year awards. "When Kim Philby fled to Moscow in 1963, he became the most notorious double agent in the history of espionage. . . . Robert Littell recounts the little-known story of the spy's early years. . . . We follow the evolution of a mysteriously beguiling man who kept his masters on both sides of the Iron Curtain guessing about his ultimate loyalties." (Publisher's note)

Little, Terra

Where there's smoke; Terra Little. Urban Books 2009 326 p.
ISBN 1933967781; 9781933967783
LC 2008924560

In this novel, "Father's Day is an occasion for celebration--unless, that is, you don't know you're a father. So it goes for Alec 'Smoke' Avery, who learns that he has a 16-year-old son. Now a respectable teacher, Alec . . . used to deal down in the 'hood, and one of his best customers, Breanne, now Anne, similarly reformed, is the mother. 'I'd sampled some of the ladies,' admits Alec, 'but I hadn't left any babies behind that I knew of. . . .' But young Isaiah looks like dad. . . . He's also headed down a path that may not have such a happy ending. . . . It's up to Alec to offer some role modeling and save the son he didn't know he had--easier said than done, since down at the projects, the competition is fierce and the temptations many." (Kirkus)

Lively, Penelope, 1933-

Cleopatra's sister. HarperCollins Pubs. 1993 281p
LC 92-54424

In alternating chapters, the author "depicts the lives of paleontologist Howard Beamish and crusading journalist Lucy Faulkner, both successful in their careers but unfulfilled because they have not established enduring relationships. They meet when the plane they are taking to Cairo makes a forced landing in Callimbia, a fictional country in the throes of a bloody revolution led by a lunatic dictator. Lively's . . . construction of Callimbia's history ranges from its establishment by Cleopatra's sister Berenice through the rise of the 'moral renegade' who orders the plane's British passengers taken hostage. Through the eyes of Howard and Lucy, and in counterpoint to their growing love for each other, Lively depicts the passengers' responses to their plight." Publ Wkly

Lively, Penelope

Consequences. Viking 2007 258p $24.95
ISBN 978-0-670-03856-5; 0-670-03856-3
LC 2007-297882

"A keen perception of the meanings of time and space joins the three generations of women . . . . as much as their shared blood does; it also allows author Penelope Lively to observe the worlds of change that occur during their life-times. She remains a heartbreakingly human and elegant writer." BookPage

Lively, Penelope

Family album. Viking 2009 224p $25.95
ISBN 978-0-670-02124-6; 0-670-02124-5
LC 2009-04081

"Alison wants the world to know that she presides over a large, happy, close-knit family. She and her distracted, uninvolved scholarly husband, Charles, have a brood of six who, along with Ingrid, the au pair, fill Allersmead, a somewhat worn, sprawling Edwardian English manse. Through the masterly use of emotional intricacies, Lively gradually reveals the simmer beneath the surface that belies the image of unity Alison has insisted on for decades, both within the family framework and without, to the world at large." Libr J

Lively, Penelope

Heat wave; a novel. HarperCollins Pubs. 1996 214p
ISBN 978-0060174767
LC 96-19893

"Outwardly, the mother herself seems cool, but she is still seething over her own husband's infidelities, many years earlier. Wisdom tends to substitute for drama here, yet you don't want to part company with these characters, who, time and again, elicit a sensation of intense familiarity." New Yorker

Lively, Penelope, 1933-

How it all began; Penelope Lively. Viking 2012 229p.
ISBN 9780143122647; 9780670023448
LC 2011032994

In this novel, "[w]hen Charlotte Rainsford, a retired schoolteacher, is accosted by a petty thief on a London street, the consequences ripple across the lives of acquaintances and strangers alike. A marriage unravels after an illicit love affair is revealed through an errant cell phone message; a posh yet financially strapped interior designer meets a business partner who might prove too good to be true; an old-guard historian tries to recapture his youthful vigor with an ill-conceived idea for a TV miniseries; and a middle-aged central European immigrant learns to speak English and reinvents his life with the assistance of some new friends." (Publisher's note)

Lively, Penelope

★ Moon tiger. Grove Press 1988 208p
ISBN 0-8021-3533-1
LC 87-23798

First published 1987 in the United Kingdom
"Moon Tiger is an extremely accomplished novel which tells an interesting story with an impressive variety of fictional techniques." Quill Quire

Lively, Penelope

Pack of cards and other stories. Grove Press 1989 323p
LC 89-1851

First published 1986 in the United Kingdom with title: Pack of cards: stories, 1978-1986

"These witty, profoundly civilized stories display Lively's compassion, intelligence, and versatility." Libr J

Lively, Penelope

★ **Passing** on. Grove Weidenfeld 1990 210p

ISBN 0-8021-1155-6

LC 89-7459

First published 1989 in the United Kingdom

"Penelope Lively is blessed with the gift of being able to render matters of great import with a breath, a barely audible sigh, a touch. The result is wonderful writing, and a marvelous book." N Y Times Book Rev

Lively, Penelope

The **photograph**. Viking 2003 231p $24.95

ISBN 0-670-03205-0

LC 2002-32420

"Lively's characters are shallow, their efforts at introspection often hilarious, but they are all obliged to confront their complicity in the premature death of a woman they each claim to have loved." N Y Times Book Rev

Lively, Penelope

The **road** to Lichfield. Grove Weidenfeld 1991 215p

LC 90-47673

First published 1977 in the United Kingdom

This novel "centers around British housewife Anne, whose father is dying in a nursing home. Anne goes to see him, in Lichfield, and in the process of cleaning out his house discovers that her father was someone she hadn't known well at all. 'I knew my father in one dimension only,' she realizes. Her relationships with her husband, brother, and lover might be similarly described. Lively's prose is clean and readable." Libr J

Lively, Penelope

Spiderweb; a novel. HarperFlamingo 1999 218p

ISBN 0-06-019233-X

LC 98-45696

First published 1998 in the United Kingdom

"Though the leisurely pace and purposefully digressive narrative are somewhat slow to build suspense, Lively's perceptive vision about the insularity of modern life rings true." Publ Wkly

Livesey, Margot

Banishing Verona; a novel. Henry Holt 2004 321p $24

ISBN 0-8050-7462-7

LC 2004-52383

"Both Zeke and Verona have just enough quirks to be endearing without being implausible; the supporting characters are similarly well realized. As Livesey . . . probes the depths of longing, betrayal and forgiveness, her gift for creating sublimely unexpected sentences is abundantly on display." Publ Wkly

Livesey, Margot

Criminals; a novel. Knopf 1996 271p

ISBN 0-679-44487-4

LC 95-31512

The reader becomes "enmeshed in the complex windings of Ms. Livesey's plot, a web of criminal circumstance and moral consequence that conveys the awful randomness of life even as it offers the abiding pleasures of artfully constructed fiction." N Y Times Book Rev

Livesey, Margot

Eva moves the furniture. Holt & Co. 2001 232p

ISBN 0-8050-6801-5

LC 00-143895

"Eva McEwen grows up engulfed by a vast and hopeful loneliness. She lives in a small Scottish town with her father and an overprotective aunt, her mother having died of the flu at her birth, in 1920. After Eva turns six, her solitary play is interrupted at unpredictable moments by a girl and a woman who, more than once, come to her aid. Only when she starts school does she realize that these two are invisible to everyone else-and, moreover, jealous of new acquaintances. At eighteen, Eva is desperate to escape the emotional tyrannies of her upbringing, but she eventually comes to feel the fullness of her love for both the real and the imaginary companions of her childhood. Livesey has written a ghost story, of sorts, minus the theremin musiclike 'Our Town,' with its speakers from the grave-and, if it moves you, the end will send you back to the beginning again." New Yorker

Livesey, Margot

The **flight** of Gemma Hardy; Margot Livesey. HarperCollins 2012 447p.

ISBN 9780062064226; 9780062064233

LC 2012371565

This book tells the story of "Gemma Hardy. Orphaned by the age of ten, neglected by a bitter and cruel aunt, sent to a boarding school where she is both servant and student, young Gemma seems destined for a life of hardship and loneliness. . . . Fiercely intelligent, singularly determined, Gemma overcomes each challenge and setback. . . . Now an independent young woman with dreams of the future, she accepts a position as an au pair on the remote and beautiful Orkney Islands. But Gemma's biggest trial is about to begin . . . a journey of passion and betrayal that will lead her to a life she's never dreamed of." (Publisher's note)

Livesey, Margot

The **house** on Fortune Street. Harper 2008 311p $24.95

ISBN 978-0-06-145152-2; 0-06-145152-5

LC 2007-29611

"That people with the closest of bonds—lovers, family members, best friends—can be strangers to one another is a familiar literary motif, but it has seldom been more affectingly dramatized than in this extraordinary book." Entertainment Wkly

Livesey, Margot

The **missing** world; a novel. Knopf 2000 325p

ISBN 0-375-40581-X

LC 99-35785

"Hazel loses three years of her past when a traffic accident wipes out her memory. She doesn't remember that she and Jonathan quarreled, and she moved out of their apartment. All she knows is that he has dropped everything to care for her. But she becomes a virtual prisoner when Jonathan decides he can't let her out of his sight for fear someone will 'remind' Hazel of what really happened." Booklist

"Adroitly paced, meticulously plotted and increasingly suspenseful, the novel transcends its genre as psychological thriller." Publ Wkly

The **living** dead; edited by John Joseph Adams. Night Shade Books 2008 487p pa $15.95
ISBN 978-1-59780-143-0; 1-59780-143-7

"These stories range from the truly disgusting (Poppy Z. Brite's 'Calcutta: Lord of Nerves') to the nearly wistful ('Followed' by Will McIntosh) and even one with no supernatural elements at all (Joe Hill's 'Bobby Conroy Comes Back from the Dead'). Included are pieces by big names in horror like Stephen King and Clive Barker but also contributions by less obvious suspects like Harlan Ellison, Sherman Alexie, and George R.R. Martin. The final treat is John Langan's 'How the Day Runs Down,' a nasty little play best described as Our Town with zombies. Highly recommended for all horror fiction collections." Libr J

Llewellyn, Richard

★ **How** green was my valley. Macmillan 1940 495p

"A remarkably beautiful novel of Wales. And although it follows stirringly in the romantic traditions, there is the resonance of a profound and noble realism in its evocation, its intensity and reach of truth." N Y Times Book Rev

Llywelyn, Morgan
1916. Forge 1998 447p
ISBN 0-312-86101-X
LC 97-29838

"Battle scenes are both accurate and compelling. The betrayals, slaughters and passions of the day are all splendidly depicted as Llywelyn delivers a blow-by-blow account of the rebellion and its immediate aftermath. The novel's abundant footnotes should satisfy history buffs; its easy, gripping style will enthrall casual readers." Publ Wkly

Llywelyn, Morgan
1921. Forge 2001 445p $25.95
ISBN 0-312-86754-9
LC 00-49021

Sequel to 1916

"Incessantly haunted by the rather passive role he played in the doomed Easter Rebellion, Henry Mooney, a journalist struggling for objectivity in the midst of controversy and mayhem, reevaluates his own convictions and commitment to the cause of a free Ireland. When Henry falls in love with an Anglo-Irish woman, simmering tensions wrought by centuries of domination and repression are reflected in a microcosm of passion and agony. The lucid narrative and the compelling subject matter will enthrall both Irish history buffs and fans of sweeping historical fiction." Booklist

Includes bibliographical references

Llywelyn, Morgan
1949; a novel of the Irish Free State. Forge 2003 414p $25.95
ISBN 0-312-86753-0
LC 2002-32525

Sequel to: 1921

"Llywelyn's great strength is her ability to communicate sweeping historical events through the eyes of both passive bystanders and active participants." Booklist

Includes bibliographical references

Llywelyn, Morgan
1972; a novel of Ireland's unfinished revolution. Forge 2005 365p $24.95
ISBN 0-312-87857-5
LC 2004-51246

Sequel to 1949

The author "tells the story of Ireland from 1950-1972 as seen through the eyes of young Barry Halloran, son and grandson of Irish revolutionaries. Northern Ireland has become a running sore, poisoning life on both sides of the Irish border. Following family tradition, at eighteen Barry joins the Irish Republican Army to help complete what he sees as 'the unfinished revolution.'" Publisher's note

Includes bibliographical references

Llywelyn, Morgan
After Rome; a novel of Celtic Britain. Morgan Llywelyn. 1st ed. Forge 2013 332 p. map (hardcover) $24.99
ISBN 0765331233; 9780765331236
LC 2012027562

This historical novel by Morgan Llywelyn, set in Great Britain, "focuses on two cousins, Dinas and Cadogan, who develop different survival strategies in the arduous time after the fall of the Roman Empire. Dinas is a schemer with dreams of political power who, it seems, will always land on his feet, while Cadogan is more of a drifter and dreamer who eventually begins to stake out a new community to escape the chaos swirling about." (Kirkus Reviews)

Includes bibliographical references

Llywelyn, Morgan
Druids. Morrow 1991 456p
LC 90-44292

"Llywelyn's skill at making ancient history come alive for a modern audience without sacrificing authenticity of fact or detail is nothing short of brilliant. A richly atmospheric tale filled with subtle flashes of humor, perceptive characterizations, and heart-stopping suspense." Booklist

Llywelyn, Morgan
The **elementals**. TOR Bks. 1993 303p
LC 93-12760

"Remnants of humanity escape the great flood and make their way to safety in prehistoric Ireland. A singer and his companions survive the volcanic eruption that destroys the palace of Minos in Crete. A farmer's wife in 19th-century New Hampshire discovers the secrets of a sacred stone, and in the 21st century, George Burning Feather seeks the wisdom of the past to combat the ultimate natural disaster—the death of the air. . . . Though the connections among the four stories comprising this volume emerge only in the final story, each tale bears its own compelling message." Libr J

Llywelyn, Morgan

The **horse** goddess. Houghton Mifflin 1982 417p

LC 82-6234

"The Celts of 700 B.C. were a variety of tribes spread over Central Europe. Epona, a teenage Celt has just been initiated into womanhood when four strange horsemen visit her community. She is drawn to the leader, Kazhak, and leaves with the Scythians to escape the lecherous Druid priest. Epona's affinity for animals is held in awe by her new tribe, as is her boldness in a world where women are seen in veils only and never heard. Epona is eventually forced to flee the Russian steppes and returns to her old home, where her acquired wisdom helps her become the new Druid priestess." Libr J

"The author emphasizes the independent status of Celtic women, a proto-feminist characteristic that should heighten the appeal of the book." Publ Wkly

Llywelyn, Morgan

The **last** prince of Ireland. Morrow 1992 368p

LC 91-42516

Published in the United Kingdom with title: O'Sullivan's march

This "novel takes place in 17th-century Ireland as Queen Elizabeth I of England seeks to obliterate 2000 years of Celtic tradition and religion. It begins on December 30, 1602, soon after the Battle of Kinsale sounded the death knell for Irish independence. Fugitive nobleman Donal Cam O'Sullivan, the 'prince' of the title, denounces the queen and seeks to march 1000 followers to safety across wintry, dangerous terrain. Death, desertion, and near-constant fighting with the enemy, both English and Irish, reduce his band to a starving and exhausted group of 35 survivors." Libr J

"This tale of courage, love, cruelty and treachery, one of the great legends of Ireland, receives vivid, evocative treatment here." Publ Wkly

Llywelyn, Morgan

Pride of lions. Forge 1996 351p il

ISBN 978-0312857004

LC 95-42566

"The perils of royal succession and a choice between love and glory form the dominant themes of Llywelyn's . . . sequel to Lion of Ireland (1979). That novel described the rise of High King Brian Boru, who became known as the 'Charlemagne of Ireland' after he managed to briefly unite the tribes of the Emerald Isle at the end of the 10th century. Here it's Brian's 15-year-old son, Donough, who aspires to the throne, made ambitious by a brief initial success in battle against the Vikings at Contarf, where Brian has met his death. But Donough's brother Teigue also claims the crown. . . . Llywelyn tells a strong story distinguished by its psychological depth and by his knowledge of ancient Irish history." Publ Wkly

Llywelyn, Morgan

Red Branch. Morrow 1989 558p

LC 88-13508

In this novel the author has created a legendary world "based on disparate tales of Ireland's mythical warrior-hero Cuchulain. . . . The story begins with a boy, Setanta, born in mysterious circumstances to Dectera, the King's half sister. Either Dectera's husband, the King, or a god is Setanta's father. But the truth is concealed from him, and in a land where status and privilege derive from birthright, his uncertain paternity is a painful mark of difference. Though still a youth, Setanta's ferocity while in combat with a monstrous wolfhound owned by a blacksmith, Cullen, earns him the name Cuchulain, or hound of Cullen. Soon after, he enters a warrior clan, the 'Red Branch' of the book's title." NY Times Book Rev

"Llywelyn works a massive canvas, peopling it with larger-than-life characters, yet shaping them with intimate insights." Publ Wkly

Llywelyn, Morgan

Silverlight; [by] Morgan Llywelyn, Michael Scott. Baen Pub. Enterprises 1996 406p

ISBN 0-671-87728-3

LC 96-7635

Sequel to Silverhand

Caeled "possesses two magical artifacts that allow him to affect events but cause him to age with every use. Joined by three companions who hate the despotic twins who rule the world, Caeled seeks the remaining two Arcana artifacts that he will use to restore order to the world. A morality tale about how much power one can have and whether to use it that belongs in most fantasy collections." Libr J

Lochen, Andrea

The **repeat** year; Andrea Lochen. Berkley Books 2013 vi, 393 p.p (paperback) $16

ISBN 0425263134; 9780425263136

LC 2012045918

In this novel, by Andrea Lochen, "after a year of hardships, . . . Olive is ready to start fresh. But when she wakes up in her ex-boyfriend's bed on New Year's Day 2011--a day she has already lived--Olive's world is turned upside down. . . . Olive learns that she has the chance to rewrite her future. Given the opportunity of a lifetime, Olive has to decide what she really wants." (Publisher's note)

Lock, Norman

Love among the particles & other stories; Norman Lock. Bellevue Literary Press 2013 224 p. (alk. paper) $14.95

ISBN 1934137642; 9781934137642

LC 2012046160

This short story collection, written by Norman Lock, is "at once a . . . critique of our romance with technology and a love letter to language. In a whirlwind tour of space, time, and history, Norman Lock creates worlds that veer wildly from the natural to the supernatural via the pre-modern, mechanical, and digital ages." (Publisher's note)

Includes bibliographical references

Locke, Attica

The **cutting** season. Harper 2012 374 p. $25.99

ISBN 0061802050; 9780061802058

2013 BCALA Literary Award: Honor Book for Fiction

In this novel, by Attica Locke, "Caren Gray manages . . . a[n] . . . antebellum plantation. . . . Outside the gates, a corporation . . . has been . . . replacing local employees with illegal laborers. . . . [T]he body of a female migrant worker is found . . . on the edge of the property. . . . [Caren] ventures into dangerous territory as she unearths startling new facts about . . . the long-ago disappearance of a former slave . . . that has unsettling ties to the current murder." (Publisher's note)

Lockridge, Ross
★ **Raintree** County. Houghton Mifflin 1948 1066p il

An epic novel describing a day, the Fourth of July of 1892, in the life of school teacher Johnny Shawnessy in which he participates in the holiday ceremonies of his small Indiana town and meets two old boyhood friends. These events set off a series of flashbacks in his mind and he relives his schooldays, his Civil war experiences, his brief political life, his two marriages, and a love affair that ends badly

"The book is full-blooded, it has gusto, ribaldry, vision, beauty, and narrative skill. It is also repetitious, overly 'organized,' reminiscent of a variety of predecessors, 'literary' in the wrong sense, and too dependent upon source material. But the breath of life sweeps through its voluminous pages." Saturday Rev

Lodato, Victor
Mathilda Savitch. Farrar, Straus and Giroux 2009 292p $24
ISBN 978-0-374-20400-6; 0-374-20400-4
LC 2009-04719

A novel about "a preteen whose older sister has died, pushed off a train platform. Logging in to her sister's e-mail, Mathilda eventually adopts her sister's life, contacting her old boyfriends and trying to retrace the footsteps of her last days. . . . Trying to provoke her parents, Mathilda dresses up in her dead sister's birthday dress. Numb, in search of deeper numbness, her mother downs the vodka, and crawls on the kitchen floor, howling, in search of another bottle. Mathilda's original observations carry these incidents—blending imagination, intelligence and kookily beautiful imagery. . . . For the most part, this is a delight and a devil of a book, a tale that fills you with despair and pleasure—often at the same time." Time Out N Y

Lodge, David
Deaf sentence. Viking 2008 294p $25.95
ISBN 978-0-670-01992-2; 0-670-01992-5
LC 2008-1772

"Sexagenarian Desmond Bates wears a hearing aid after being diagnosed some 20 years earlier with 'acquired deafness' and consistently misinterprets people's words (which Lodge milks to maximum comic effect). Bates longs for activities after his retirement from teaching applied linguistics, other than contemplating e-mail spam about erectile dysfunction and watching his wife, Winifred, enjoy her success as an interior designer. The novel takes the form of his newly begun daily diary. At a gallery event, Bates mistakenly agrees to help shapely, enigmatic American student Alex Loom with her Ph.D. thesis on suicide notes." Publ Wkly

"This is a brave novel, which puts a brave face on everything we'd rather not know about ageing, without ducking the atrocity of it all." London Rev Books

Lodge, David
★ **Nice** work. Viking 1989 277p
ISBN 0-670-82806-8
LC 88-40480

A satirical look at "Thatcher's England. Two representatives from different worlds–the groves of academe and the dark satanic mills–meet and fall in (a semblance of) love as they aim to satisfy their physical passions and also open their emotions to new experiences. The academic is a young female professor of literature, and her industrial counterpart is a middle-aged factory manager. Their initial meeting does set off sparks but only to fan the flames of mutual antagonism before an attraction of sorts takes place." Booklist

Lodge, David
★ **Paradise** news; a novel. Viking 1992 293p
ISBN 0-670-84228-1
LC 91-32128

First published 1991 in the United Kingdom

"Mr. Lodge is a serious author who bravely uses coincidence and contrivance to tie up loose ends. And just under the surface of the spirited and often comic adventures of his travelers he runs an undercurrent of understanding about their longings for the perfection of paradise. This comes to us in graceful and disciplined prose that offers vivid glimpses of what lies beyond the tourist hotels of Waikiki–the natural and imperfect world." N Y Times Book Rev

Lodge, David
Therapy; a novel. Viking 1995 320p
ISBN 0-670-86358-0
LC 95-16337

"Laurence 'Tubby' Passmore is a successful British TV sitcom writer. He has plenty of money, homes in London and Rummidge, a fast car, and all the therapists his calendar will hold. Yet Tubby is chronically unhappy. In fact, he is so wrapped up in dismal self-contemplation that he does not notice when his daughter's pregnancy is announced or his wife of 30 years demands a divorce. He discovers and obsesses about Kierkegaard, seeing many similarities between his own life and that of the philosopher. When his world begins to crumble around him, Tubby sets off on a pilgrimage to find Maureen Kavanaugh, his first girlfriend." Libr J

"The novel is almost Victorian in its earnest goodness, which shines through its humor straight to the enormously moving and exultant ending." New Yorker

Lodge, David
Thinks-- a novel. Viking 2001 341p
ISBN 0-670-89984-4
LC 2001-17555

"This is the first Lodge novel set in the world of science, and it paints an utterly persuasive portrait of it. The story is a cracking tale, but read it, too, for the ideas. It's obvious that Lodge has become fascinated by the science of thought. Reading this is, so will you." New Sci

Lofts, Norah
Gad's Hall. Doubleday 1978 282p
LC 77-92220

First published 1977 in the United Kingdom

"Dismissing Mrs. Spender's claims that Gad's Hall is haunted, her son Bob and daughter-in-law Jill buy the grand

English country estate. . . . With this setup, Lofts deserts her modern family to describe the lives of the Thorleys who founded Gad's Hall in the 1800s. The widowed Mrs. Thorley of that era exerts firm control over the affairs of her children and stepchildren. When unwed Lavinia becomes pregnant, Mrs. Thorley hides the girl until the baby is born. The tragedy that results creates the ghosts that haunt the manor, to affect the Spenders, more than 100 years later." Publ Wkly

Followed by The haunting of Gad's Hall

Logan, Chuck

South of Shiloh; a thriller. HarperCollins Publishers 2008 402p $24.95

ISBN 978-0-06-113669-6; 0-06-113669-7

LC 2007-25672

"When Minnesotan Paul Edin was killed during a re-enactment of the battle of Kirby Creek near Corinth, Miss., local law enforcement quickly declares his death a tragic accident. But when Paul's widow, Jenny, learns that the bullet may have been meant for deputy Kenny Beeman, she's determined to uncover the truth. Reconnecting with John Rane—her ex-lover and the biological father of the child she raised with Paul—Jenny persuades John to go to Corinth and investigate. A photographer and former cop known for taking risks, John joins forces with Kenny in Mississippi and attempts to unravel a complex web of family feuds. John soon realizes that the upcoming re-enactment of the battle of Shiloh could end up as bloody as the original. Despite a few plot holes, Logan skillfully immerses the reader in the traditions and eccentricities of the men who meticulously recreate every aspect of the Civil War." Publ Wkly

Loh, Vyvyane

Breaking the tongue; a novel. W.W. Norton 2004 407p map $24.95

ISBN 0-393-05792-5

LC 2003-15870

The author "explores such concepts as loyalty to one's family and country, the place of language in culture, and the roles of race, racism and ethnicity in how we perceive ourselves and others. In doing so, she has skillfully touched on questions at the very heart of politics, culture and global relations today." Washington Post Book World

Includes bibliographical references

Lombardo, Billy

★ The **man** with two arms. Overlook Press 2010 335p $24.95

ISBN 978-1-59020-307-1; 1-59020-307-0

"The man of the title, really a young man from Chicagoland, has two golden arms. His name is Denny Granville and his baseball-crazed father Henry raises him from infancy to play ball—and specifically to pitch both left-handed and right-handed. With 'coach's thoughts' in his head and Astroturf in his basement, Henry cultivates a champion, a 'switch-pitcher' who grows up to become a beautifully trained athlete with a great talent for baseball. Through high school and college we watch Denny grow, and when he hits the majors—playing for the Cubs—his first season looks as though it's going to be a triumph. Lombardo sets his sights on writing a lovely homage to the game, and to what is undoubtedly modern America's finest literary tribute to the baseball since Bernard Malamud's novel 'The Natural.'" Chicago Trib

London, Jack

★ The **call** of the wild; pictures by Wendell Minor. Atheneum Books for Young Readers 1999 112p il $24; pa $4.95

ISBN 0-689-81836-X; 1-4165-0019-7 pa

LC 97-45019

First published 1903 by Macmillan

"Buck, half-St. Bernard, half-Scottish sheepdog, is stolen from his comfortable home in California and pressed into service as a sledge dog in the Klondike. At first he is abused by both man and dog, but he learns to fight ruthlessly. He becomes lead dog on a sledge team, after bettering Spitz, the vicious old leader, in a brutal fight to the death. In John Thornton, he finally finds a master whom he can respect and love. When Thornton is killed by Indians, Buck breaks away to the wilds and becomes the leader of a wolf pack, returning each year to the site of Thornton's death." Reader's Ency. 4th edition

London, Jack

The **complete** short stories of Jack London; edited by Earle Labor, Robert C. Leitz, III, and I. Milo Shepard. Stanford Univ. Press 1993 3v $195

ISBN 0-8047-2058-4

LC 92-44856

"The London scholar and enthusiast will find this collection of Jack London's short fiction invaluable for the 5 previously unpublished stories it contains and for the 28 others it collects for the first time since their original publication in magazines." Choice

London, Jack

Martin Eden. Macmillan 1909 411p

A semi-autobiographical novel. "Eden has had a knockabout life as a sailor, and falling in love with a girl used to middle-class refinement and luxuries, tries to write. He is rejected by editors, and the girl jilts him. The abysmal contrast between the genius of this man, his vital ideals and the big realities of life, and on the other hand, the narrow, unintelligent mediocrity of the 'cultured classes' is brought out with characteristic force." Baker. Guide to Hist Fic

London, Jack

★ **Novels** & stories; Jack London. Literary Classics of the United States, Distributed to the trade by Viking Press 1982 1020p $35

ISBN 0-940450-05-4

LC 82-249

London, Jack

The **Sea-Wolf**; with illustrations by W.J. Aylward. Macmillan 1904 366p

"Wolf Larsen, ruthless captain of the tramp steamer 'Ghost,' receives an unexpected passenger on the high seas, Humphrey Van Weyden, a wealthy ne'er-do-well. In spite of his selfish brutality, Larsen becomes an instrument for good. The treatment he gives to the dilettante Van Weyden teaches the latter to stand on his own legs. He and the poet Maude Brewster, whom the 'Sea-Wolf' loves also, escape to an island as the 'Ghost' sinks and Larsen, mortally sick, is deserted. The lovers later return to civilization." Haydn. Thesaurus of Book Dig

London, Jack
Short stories of Jack London; authorized one-volume edition. edited by Earle Labor, Robert C. Leitz III, I. Milo Shepard. Macmillan 1990 xli, 738p
LC 90-6175

London, Jack
South Sea tales. Macmillan 1911 327p

London, Jack
The star rover. Macmillan 1915 329p
In this science fiction novel about transmigration of the soul, Darrell Standing is condemned to solitary confinement in a corrupt prison. He discovers how to free his soul from his body and escapes through time and space to relive the experiences of his past lives, which include being a caveman, a Danish soldier in the Roman legions, a French swordsman, and an American pioneer boy

London, Jack
★ White Fang; Jack London. Scholastic 2001 252p. hardcover o.p. rpt $5.99
ISBN 9780439236195 rpt
LC 98-19241
First published 1906
White Fang "is about a dog, a cross-breed, sold to Beauty Smith. This owner tortures the dog to increase his ferocity and value as a fighter. A new owner Weedom Scott, brings the dog to California, and, by kind treatment, domesticates him. White Fang later sacrifices his life to save Scott." Haydn. Thesaurus of Book Dig

London, Jack
White Fang, and other stories; with photographs of the author and his environment as well as illustrations from early editions, together with an introduction by A.K. Adams. Dodd, Mead 1963 308p il
The title novel (entered separately) and short stories are about dogs in Canada's Yukon Territory

London, Joan
The good parents. Black Cat 2009 349p pa $14.95
ISBN 978-0-8021-7057-6; 0-8021-7057-9
"A girl from the Australian outback heads to Melbourne and, in thrall to the idea of having a secret, grownup life, runs off with her older, married boss, a shady businessman who, she recognizes, has little genuine feeling for her. This is just an overture to the novel's central story, in which the girl's parents, in the wake of their daughter's disappearance, confront their own youthful rebellions—the mother's early romance with a gangster, the father's hippie wanderings—and the inchoate ideals that led them to bury themselves in a rural backwater. The author comes at her characters from every angle, laying bare their compromises and delusions." New Yorker

London, Kelli
Cali boys; a boyfriend season novel. Kelli London. Dafina KTeen Books 2012 241 p. $9.95
ISBN 0758261292; 9780758261298
LC 9780758261298
This urban teen novel, by Kelli London, follows "Kassidy Maddox . . . [who] knows what she wants: Shooby, Romero, and Carsen, three extremely fine, must-have boys. . . . Jacobi Swanson is a late bloomer with a major crush on her neighbor, Malone. . . . Determined to break out of her shell and into his heart, Jacobi turns to Kassidy for beauty and boy tips. But when Jacobi finally captures Malone's attention, she'll have to figure out whether he's for real." (Publisher's note)

Long, David
The inhabited world. Houghton 2006 277p $23
ISBN 0-618-54335-X
LC 2005-20061
This is a "tale of everyday, getting-by existence in America, where joys can be sudden and painfully intense, and sorrows can be, too, and the trick is not to let the blues get the better of you. . . . This is a terrific novel, and you can't help thinking, from time to time, that in a better world David Long would be a famous writer. But, as the book makes pretty clear, there is no better world; just this one. And when the words are right, even this world is sweet enough." N Y Times Book Rev

Long, Jeff
The reckoning. Atria Books 2004 278p $25
ISBN 0-7434-6300-5
LC 2004-43657
A "journey into the dark past-and present-of Cambodia's former killing fields. Molly Drake, a would-be photojournalist, accompanies a U.S. Army-led search for the bones of a pilot shot down during the war. She meets Duncan O'Brian, an archeologist at a local dig, and John Kleat, who has come back to the country repeatedly, seeking his brother's remains. When bones unexpectedly turn up, Molly photographs them, breaking her agreement with the army not to take pictures of bodies. The captain in charge dismisses her along with O'Brian and Kleat, and the trio make their way to an ancient, fog-enshrouded Angkor-like city where they have evidence an army patrol went missing years ago. . . . Long's considerable knowledge of Cambodian folklore and history is put to good use as he superbly depicts the war-scarred country, its people and its beautiful, hazardous landscape." Publ Wkly

Longworth, M. L. (Mary Lou), 1963-
Death at the Chateau Bremont; a Verlaque and Bonnet mystery. by M. L. Longworth. Penguin 2011 320p
ISBN 9780143119524
LC 2011007573
In author M. L. Longworth's book, Marine Bonnet "and best friend Sylvie console each other over their affairs, most recently Marine's breakup with Antoine Verlaque . . . So Marine has big butterflies in her stomach as she climbs the stairs to . . . Verlaque's apartment to help him in his latest case: the death of Étienne de Bremont, who supposedly fell from the

window of his family's chateau. Marine, a childhood friend of Etienne and his brother François, confirms that a fall by the sure-footed young count is unlikely . . . Verlaque and Bonnet want answers—but is that all they want?" (Kirkus)

Longworth, M. L. (Mary Lou), 1963-

Death in the Vines; a Verlaque and Bonnet Provencal mystery. M.L. Longworth. Penguin Books 2013 304 p. (paperback) $15

ISBN 0143122444; 9780143122449

LC 2012044302

This is M.L. Longworth's third Verlaque and Bonnet mystery. Here, a few hours "after Pauline d'Arras—an older woman who may be displaying the onset of Alzheimer's—disappears, her frantic husband shows up at police headquarters in Aix-en-Provence. In addition, an inventory of an always-locked wine cellar, part of a winery where a police official's wife works, reveals that someone has been looting the cellar of its most precious contents." (Publishers Weekly)

Longworth, M. L. (Mary Lou), 1963-

Murder in the Rue Dumas; a Verlaque and Bonnet provençal mystery. M.L. Longworth. Penguin Books 2012 296 p.

ISBN 0143121545; 9780143121541

LC 2012023725

This novel by M. L. Longworth "finds Verlaque stumped. The director of theology at the Université d'Aix was just about to name the recipient of an elite fellowship, as well as his own successor, when his lips were sealed permanently. Yet Verlaque isn't convinced that any of the academics are capable of murder. Aided by Bonnet, Verlaque turns Provence upside down, uncovering a world far more complicated than university politics." (Author's note)

Lopez, Barry Holstun

Resistance; [by] Barry Lopez. Alfred A. Knopf 2004 163p il $18

ISBN 1-400-04220-8

LC 2003-65986

"If it's true the author's erudite, well-meaning characters all sound very much alike, it's also true that one of his goals is to underscore the responsibility of artists to speak as one when speaking truth to power. To his credit, Lopez never sacrifices craft to politics." N Y Times Book Rev

Lord, Bette Bao

The **middle** heart; a novel. Knopf 1996 370p $25

ISBN 0-394-53432-8

LC 95-36165

The story begins in early 1930s China, "when three young people forge an unlikely alliance that survives five decades of loss and love. There's Steele Hope, the second son of the head of the once noble and powerful Li family; Mountain Pine, his 'bookmate' and retainer; and a destitute girl posing as a boy named Firecrackers. The novel's early sections sparkle with hope and joy as the three devoted friends romp and grow, but personal tragedy and war soon intrude." Booklist

Lord, Karen

Redemption in indigo; a novel. Small Beer Press 2010 188p pa $16

ISBN 9781931520669 pa; 1931520666 pa

LC 2009-54298

Based on a Senegalese folktale, Lord "recounts the fantastical adventures of Paama, who escapes her unfortunate marriage only to be placed in unwitting charge of awesome universal powers. An enchanted kitchen implement allows Paama to bring the slightest probabilities to pass. At first unconscious of this ability, she rescues a drowning boy and resurrects a plague victim from the dead. Gradually the 'undying ones' . . . teach her how the branching implications of her interference lead to consequences a mere human woman could never foresee. Full of sharp insights and humorous asides. . . , 'Redemption' extends the Caribbean Island storyteller's art into the 21st century and hopefully, beyond." Seattle Times

Lordan, Beth

But come ye back; a novel in stories. Morrow 2004 278p $23.95

ISBN 0-06-053036-7

LC 2003-56217

"Lordan's muted prose and fluting Irishisms ('Right, so,' 'Grand') are pleasant if rather selfconscious, and her characters are human, breathing people, forthrightly crafted. The novel-in-stories structure produces some inconsistencies and redundancies, but this is a quietly engaging effort." Publ Wkly

Lott, Bret

Ancient highway; a novel. Random House 2008 241p $25

ISBN 978-1-4000-6374-1; 1-4000-6374-4

LC 2007-38760

This novel "shows how one man's aspirations to become a famous Hollywood actor reverberate over three generations. In 1927, handsome Earl Holmes runs away from his Texas home at age 14 to Southern California. Some years later, after he has married budding, talented songstress Saralee Kennedy, his schemes to make it in the entertainment industry affect his young daughter, Joan. Years pass again, and Joan's twentysomething son, Brad, fresh off the boat after six years in the navy in Southeast Asia, arrives at Earl and Saralee's Southern California home to try to find direction in his life." Libr J

"Lott's language is poetic in its rhythm and rich in detail, lending equal humanity to a real-life Hollywood character and an imagined flea market vendor." San Francisco Chron

Lourie, Richard

A **hatred** for tulips. Thomas Dunne Books 2007 182p $22.95

ISBN 978-0-312-34933-2; 0-312-34933-5

LC 2006-48862

"Lourie's novel is more than a mystery: at its heart is not only Anne Frank's history, but all of Holland's. Joop derides the Dutch for indulging what, until recently, was a very real Anne Frank amnesia. . . . Ironically, the book is best where it has little to say about Anne Frank. The connection allows Lourie to pose interesting questions about collaboration and guilt during the war, but it rings truest as a story about a boy, in a difficult family, in a difficult time, and the unintended consequences of trying to do what looks like the right thing." Christ Sci Monit

Lovecraft, H. P.

At the mountains of madness, and other novels; selected by August Derleth; with texts edited by S.T. Joshi and introduction by James Turner. Arkham House Pubs. 1985 458p

ISBN 0-87054-038-6

LC 85-1254

A reissue of the title first published 1964 and analyzed in Short story index

Lovecraft, H. P.

The **Dunwich** horror, and others; selected by August Derleth, with texts edited by S.T. Joshi and an introduction by Robert Block. Arkham House Pubs. 1985 433p

ISBN 0-87054-037-8

A reissue of the title first published 1963 and analyzed in Short story index

Lovecraft, H. P.

★ H. P. Lovecraft; tales. edited by Peter Straub. Library of America 2005 838p $35

ISBN 1-93108-272-3

LC 2004-48979

"If you spend enough time in Lovecraft's lonely landscapes, fear really does develop: not the fear that you will come across unearthly creatures, but the fear that you will come across little else. And what first seems horridly overdone accumulates a creepy minimalism. Taken as a whole, Lovecraft's work exhibits a hopeless isolation not unlike that of Samuel Beckett: lonely man after lonely man, wandering aimlessly through a shadowy city or holing up in rural emptiness, pursuing unspeakable secrets or being pursued by secret unspeakables, all to little avail and to no comfort. There is something funny about this—in small doses. But by the end of this collection, one does not hear giggling so much as the echoes of those giggles as they vanish into the ether lonely, desperate and, yes, very, very scary." N Y Times Book Rev

Lovecraft, H. P.

The **horror** in the museum, and other revisions; with texts edited by S. T. Joshi, and an introduction by August Derleth. Arkham House Pubs. 1989 450p

LC 88-7921

"The volume is divided into 'Primary Revisions,' those stories that are all Lovecraft but for an idea, and 'Secondary Revisions,' clients' manuscripts heavily edited and revised." Publ Wkly

Lovecraft, H. P.

Tales of H.P. Lovecraft; major works selected and introduced by Joyce Carol Oates. Ecco Press 1997 328p

ISBN 0-88001-541-1

LC 96-47196

Lovesey, Peter

Bertie and the seven bodies. Mysterious Press 1990 196p

LC 89-12405

"Narrated by Bertie himself, the voice here is perfectly accurate; Lovesey gives his main character just the right tone of sophistication, charm, anti-intellectualism, and savoir faire—mixed in with ennui. A wonderfully put together puzzle." Booklist

Lovesey, Peter

Bloodhounds. Warner Bks. 1996 359p

LC 96-22244

In this takeoff on the traditional "locked room" mystery "Lovesey's wise but beleaguered hero Peter Diamond confronts a homicide case as perplexing as any he's faced. The perpetrator appears to be both brilliant and devious, composing a series of riddles designed to offer clues to upcoming crimes while effectively throwing the police off the scent, then stealing a priceless postage stamp while the coppers' collective backs are turned." Booklist

Lovesey "skillfully pays homage to the old style whodunit in this thoroughly modern mystery." Publ Wkly

Lovesey, Peter

The **detective** wore silk drawers. Dodd, Mead 1971 188p

"Three London detectives of the 1880s, all boxing fans, uncover a clandestine center of the sport while investigating several headless corpses." Booklist

"Although the mystery is nothing special, it suffices, and the kicks come from the 19th century atmosphere of Victorian sex and mild sadism." Publ Wkly

Lovesey, Peter

★ **Diamond** dust. Soho Press 2002 343p $24

ISBN 1-56947-291-2

LC 2002-17567

"In a bold display of virtuosity, Lovesey takes his hero to emotional places he's never been before while constructing a plot of infernal ingenuity." N Y Times Book Rev

Lovesey, Peter

Diamond solitaire. Mysterious Press 1993 343p

ISBN 0-89296-535-5

LC 92-50660

First published 1992 in the United Kingdom

"Peter Diamond is plagued by bad karma. Formerly detective superintendent of police in Bath, he's sunk to being a security guard at Harrod's—until a small Asian child is found in the area of the store Peter patrols. Out of a job once again (security breaches are no laughing matter at terrorist-obsessed Harrod's), Diamond becomes intrigued by the Asian child, who is autistic and who remains unclaimed despite massive publicity. What starts out as a kindly effort to restore the child to her parents turns into an international adventure as Diamond travels from London to New York to Japan and confronts millionaire sumo wrestlers, unethical drug researchers, and corrupt businessmen." Booklist

Lovesey, Peter

The **house** sitter. Soho Press 2003 346p $25
ISBN 1-56947-326-9

LC 2002-42626

"Initially brought in as an auxilliary police consultant, Bath's Inspector Peter Diamond soon proves himself indispensable to a missing person case turned murder investigation. A woman from Bath discovered dead on a Sussex beach turns out to have been strangled—apparently right there in the midst of a crowd. The main witnesses, a family of three, seem to be hiding something. The victim was a psychological offender profiler, apparently working on the case of a serial murderer." Libr J

"The identity of the killer, when finally revealed, is genuinely startling, and not because of authorial obfuscation. The writing is as smooth as polished steel." Publ Wkly

Lovesey, Peter

The **last** detective. Doubleday 1991 331p

LC 91-11859

"An intricate, many-tiered examination of police work, especially modern forensic technology, complete with computers and genetic fingerprinting. Everything meshes perfectly in this airtight tale." Booklist

Lovesey, Peter

On the edge. Mysterious Press 1989 204p

LC 88-13549

"Set in Britain immediately after World War II, this is a novel that balances wit and wickedness, ambitions and just desserts. Rosie married badly—to a penniless philanderer. Antonia married well—to a wealthy man—but her lover is going to the U.S. and she wants to join him there. Rosie and Antonia meet by chance, talk, and a plan is gradually hatched. With a helpful shove from Antonia, Rosie's hubby comes to a bad end beneath a tube train. The second half of the deal becomes more convoluted, as Antonia's past (she having murdered her husband's first wife) and several secret agendas throw a wrench in the works." Booklist

"Told mostly in racy, ear-perfect dialogue that magnifies the impact of events, the story dodges from one unguessable outcome to the next." Publ Wkly

Lovesey, Peter

Rough cider. Mysterious Press 1986 216p

LC 86-18212

"A tightly knit tale that has its roots in the hanging for murder in England of an American G.I. Twenty years later his daughter, who lives in the U.S., attempts to exonerate his name by enlisting the aid of an English professor whose childhood was marked by the crime. Readers incidentally learn about cider making and discover some grisly evidence of murder and guilt in the course of the demonstration." Barzun. Cat of Crime. Rev and enl edition

Lovesey, Peter

Skeleton Hill. Soho Press 2009 326p $24
ISBN 978-1-56947-598-0; 1-56947-598-9

LC 2009-11128

Another of Lovesey's "convoluted plots, layered with historical lore and teeming with comic characters up to their

necks in no good. Diamond is a classic—better catch him while you can." N Y Times Book Rev

Lovesey, Peter

The **tooth** tattoo; Peter Lovesey. Soho Press, Inc. 2013 348 p. (hardcover) $25.95
ISBN 161695230X; 9781616952303

LC 2012043412

This is Peter Lovesey's 13th Peter Diamond mystery. Violist Mel Farran is robbed of his viola. "Seven years later, an acclaimed string quartet, whose previous violist disappeared in Budapest in 2008, recruits Farran. Meanwhile, Bath CID's Diamond, who's having some trouble with his significant other, looks into the suspicious death of a woman found in a canal. The only clue to her identity is the tattoo of a musical note on one of her teeth." (Publishers Weekly)

Lovesey, Peter

Upon a dark night. Mysterious Press 1998 374p
ISBN 978-0892966691

LC 97-48922

First published 1997 in the United Kingdom

Peter Diamond, "head of the murder squad in Bath, England, annoys his peers by poking around in two seemingly clear-cut suicides—an unknown woman who leaped to her death and a farmer who blew his head off with a shotgun. His poking soon uncovers murder, and eventually the two deaths become linked to the disappearance of an amnesia victim." Booklist

A "triumph of plotting from this master of the classic puzzle form." N Y Times Book Rev

Lovesey, Peter

The **vault**. Soho Press 2000 331p $23
ISBN 1-56947-208-4

LC 00-41010

First published 1999 in the United Kingdom

"A wealth of good things fills this novel: Lovesey's deft plotting, his hilarious send-ups of the Brits through the perspective of the American professor, and his intriguing allusions to the architecture and literary history of Bath." Booklist

Lovesey, Peter

Waxwork. Pantheon Bks. 1978 239p

LC 77-90420

"There is certainly enough here to warrant the praise given this tale by more than one highly regarded colleague in crime. Set in the London and Kew of 1888, a case of KCN poisoning following upon blackmail taxes the abilities of the police, but in the end Sgt. Cribb really does distinguish himself. The title alludes to Tussaud's Waxwork Exhibition." Barzun. Cat of Crime. Rev and enl edition

Lovett, Charlie

The **bookman's** tale; a novel of obsession. Charlie Lovett. Viking 2013 352 p. (hardcover) $27.95
ISBN 0670026476; 9780670026470

LC 2013001559

In this novel, by Charlie Lovett, "nine months earlier, the death of his beloved wife, Amanda, had left him shattered. The young antiquarian bookseller relocated from North

Carolina to the English countryside. . . . But upon opening an eighteenth-century study of Shakespeare forgeries, . . . a portrait of Amanda tumbles out of its pages. Of course, it isn't really her. . . . Yet the resemblance is uncanny, and Peter becomes obsessed with learning the picture's origins." (Publisher's note)

Lovric, Michelle
The **floating** book; a novel. Regan Bks. 2004 480p $25.95
ISBN 0-06-057856-4
LC 2003-58400
A novel set in Venice in 1486. "Sosia Simeon, married to a Jewish doctor who is repulsed by her, finds comfort in the arms of many other men. German-born Wendelin von Speyer comes to Venice to capitalize on the invention of the printing press. Sosia bewitches handsome young Bruno, Wendelin's editor, but it is the cold, disinterested Felice, his scribe, who captivates her. Wendelin falls in love with Lussieta, the beautiful daughter of a bookseller, and marries her. All of them are drawn in by the amorous poems of the Latin poet Catullus, which Wendelin intends to print. . . . Meticulous historical detail and a splendid, complex story make this portrait of Venice and its denizens memorable and moving." Booklist

Lowell, Elizabeth
Die in plain sight. Morrow 2003 385p $24.95
ISBN 0-06-050412-9
LC 2003-40606
"Art buyer and struggling southern California artist Lacey Quinn shows a few of her grandfather's paintings to renowned artist Susa Donovan, in the area for a charity event. The paintings are mostly landscapes, but also include a few samples from his dark later work, including detailed depictions of murder and death by fire and drowning. Believing that the landcapes are really the work of famous California plein air painter Lewis Marten, Susa asks Lacey to have them professionally appraised. Lacey resists Susa's pleas, fearing that her grandfather may have been guilty of forgery, but she discovers something far more complicated and horrifying. The murders her grandfather depicted actually took place." Publ Wkly

Lowell, Elizabeth
Pearl Cove. Avon Bks. 1999 376p
ISBN 0-380-97404-5
LC 99-21639
This is the author's "third book featuring the Donovan clan. . . . Archer, the oldest son, is plunged into the past with a call for help from the only woman he has ever loved, Hannah McGarry, his half-brother Len's wife. After an injury paralyzes Len, he focuses on developing a unique strain of black pearls and mentally torturing his wife. When a cyclone hits their Australian pearl farm, Hannah finds her husband dead and the pearls missing. Archer comes to protect her and avenge Len's death. . . . This is a riveting mix of suspense and romance." Booklist

Lowenthal, Michael
Charity girl. Houghton Mifflin 2007 323p $24
ISBN 978-0-618-54629-9; 0-618-54629-4
LC 2005-37775

"Lowenthal's narrative style is perfect for a heroine who suffers but remains a survivor, striking just the right mix of dark and light, worldly and innocent. Providing Frieda with flickers of humor and joy, he guarantees her our sympathy." N Y Times Book Rev

Lowry, Malcolm
★ **Under** the volcano. Reynal & Hitchcock 1947 375p
This novel "presents in detail the events of {a} single day in a single place—the Day of the Dead in a town in Mexico, with Popocatepetl and Ixtaccihuatl looking down. It is the last day on earth of the British Consul, Geoffrey Firmin, and he is dying of alcoholism. Like any tragic hero, he is fully aware of the choice he has made: he clings to his sloth, he needs salvation through love but will not utter the word which will bring it, he lets his morbid lust for drink drag him from bar to bar. In other words, he has made a deliberate choice of damnation. . . . We don't despise or even dislike Firmin, despite his weaknesses and his self-destructive urge. As with all tragic heroes (and this novel is a genuine tragedy) he sums up the flaws which are latent or actual in all of us." Burgess. 99 Novels

Ludlum, Robert, 1927-2001
The **apocalypse** watch. Bantam Bks. 1995 645p
LC 95-1860
"A powerful, exploding novel that, frightening as it sounds, may not be so far reaching, for it touches on the issues of hate, ethnic cleansing, and racism that we read about every day." Booklist

Ludlum, Robert, 1927-2001
The **Aquitaine** progression. Random House 1984 647p
LC 83-19078
This novel "features five present or former generals from five different countries who mean to take over the world. They have decided to put an end to the quagmire of Western politics and set up a super-fascist state with themselves in control. The hub of this enterprise is Gen. George Marcus Delavane, a fanatic who makes Genghis Khan look like a Peace Corps volunteer. Joel Converse, an international lawyer, has reason to know and hate Delavane. It was Delavane who insisted on an Air Force mission in Vietnam that resulted in Converse's capture and subsequent agonies at the hands of the enemy. While in Geneva working on a case for his New York law firm, Converse is contacted by one A. Preston Halliday, who gives him information he finds hard to believe. But there follows a series of entanglements and murders that clearly prove Halliday's assertions." N Y Times Book Rev

Ludlum, Robert, 1927-2001
★ The **Bourne** identity. Marek, R. 1980 523p
ISBN 9780553593549; 9781417618101
LC 79023638
"Jason Bourne is shot and left for dead. He survives, but without a memory. Slowly, painstakingly, he retraces his past, only to find himself hunted by assassins of several governments, including his own. He fights against seemingly insurmountable odds—especially his very limited knowledge

of his past—to discover his identity and stop his enemies before it is too late." Libr J

Followed by The Bourne supremacy

Ludlum, Robert, 1927-2001

The **Bourne** supremacy. Random House 1986 597p

ISBN 9781442081284; 9780345538208

LC 85018318

"In this sequel to The Bourne Identity David Webb, still suffering flashbacks to his Jason Bourne persona, is forced to undertake a final, possibly fatal mission after his wife is kidnapped. He must find and capture an assassin who is posing as Bourne in Hong Kong. By so doing he'll foil a plot that could plunge the Far East and then the world into war." Libr J

Followed by The Bourne ultimatum

Ludlum, Robert, 1927-2001

The **Bourne** ultimatum. Random House 1990 611p

ISBN 9780345538215; 9780679400431

LC 89043201

"When the international terrorist known as Carlos the Jackal penetrates his civilian identity, Webb must again assume the Bourne persona to protect his wife and small children. In their renewed struggle, the two master assassins uncover the revived existence of Medusa, the sinister alliance that originally led to the establishment of the Bourne identity." Publ Wkly

Ludlum, Robert, 1927-2001

The **Gemini** contenders. Dial Press (NY) 1976 402p

"The twin sons of a former Italian government official search for a mysterious document he was forced to leave behind when fleeing his fascist-dominated homeland in 1939." Smith. Cloak and Dagger Fic

Ludlum is "at the top of his form here as he tells a suspenseful story that gives fresh slants to old themes." Publ Wkly

Ludlum, Robert, 1927-2001

The **Holcroft** covenant. Marek, R. 1978 542p

LC 77-95295

"Thirty years after Hitler, Noel Holcroft sees an astounding document, drawn up by three supposedly contrite Nazis (all now dead), one of them his own father. If he signs it and collects signatures from the sons of the other two men, the Holocaust victims' heirs should become the beneficiaries of a gigantic fund. The fund's 'real' purpose is to establish the Fourth Reich, not atone for the Third, but Holcroft doesn't realize this as he flings around the world in search of those signatures, precipitating . . . ruthless clashes between secret Nazi and anti-Nazi organizations." Publ Wkly

Ludlum, Robert, 1927-2001

The **Janson** directive. St. Martin's Press 2002 547p $27.95

ISBN 0-312-25348-6

LC 2002-5136

"The hero is Paul Janson, a private security consultant who retired a few years ago after a notorious career as the U.S. government's go-to guy for nasty jobs no one else was willing to take. Against his better judgment, Janson accepts an assignment to rescue Peter Novak, a Nobel Peace Prize-winning philanthropist and international troubleshooter held captive by Islamic extremists on an island in the Indian Ocean. . . . Extremely engaging and agonizingly suspenseful, Ludlum's plot bolts from scene to scene and locale to locale—Hungary, Amsterdam, London, New York City—never settling for one bombshell when it can drop four or five." Publ Wkly

Ludlum, Robert, 1927-2001

The **Matarese** Circle. Marek, R. 1979 601p

LC 78-31673

This novel of international intrigue "features the world's top secret agents: Scofield, American, and Taleniekov, Russian. They have sworn to kill each other—Scofield was responsible for the death of Taleniekov's brother, Taleniekov for that of Scofield's wife—yet they have much in common besides their brilliance: both are semiretired, held in suspicion by their respective governments and encumbered (occasionally) by the humane streak in their characters. And now they are drawn into cooperation, as the only men capable of destroying an international circle of killers, the Matarese, originally Corsican, which is dedicated to reducing the world to chaos via assassination and terror." Publ Wkly

Ludlum, Robert, 1927-2001

The **Matlock** paper. Dial Press (NY) 1973 312p

"James Matlock, instructor in Elizabethan literature at Carlyle University in Connecticut, formerly an Army officer in Vietnam, is drawn into the most personally dangerous and violent struggle of his life when he is requested to cooperate with a government narcotic agent in exploring Carlyle's connection with the expanding drug traffic in New England." Publ Wkly

Ludlum, Robert, 1927-2001

The **Parsifal** mosaic. Random House 1982 630p

LC 84-8925

"The tale has all the hallmarks of vintage Ludlum: nonstop action, precisely timed curtain-raisers, the darksome deeds of agent and double agent, a deadly secret ultimately revealed and an underlying theme of the whole world jeopardized by a few fanatics." Publ Wkly

Ludlum, Robert, 1927-2001

The **Prometheus** deception. St. Martin's Press 2000 509p

ISBN 0-312-25346-X

LC 00-62585

"Nick Bryson works for an ultrasecret intelligence organization; after making a mistake during a mission, he's put out to pasture. Later, he's brought back into the game by a different intelligence group, and he learns that everything he believed about his former bosses was a lie—until, that is, he discovers that everything the second organization has told him is also a lie. Bryson winds up trying single-handedly to save the world from a shadowy terrorist group, while simultaneously trying to figure out which of the various 'good guys' he should believe. . . . The pace is fast, the action plentiful, and the story confusing enough to keep us turning the pages." Booklist

Ludlum, Robert, 1927-2001

The **Rhinemann** exchange. Dial Press (NY) 1974 460p

"A World War II espionage novel detailing an attempted treasonous exchange between the Germans and the Americans—the technological secret of a gyroscopic guidance system in return for industrial diamonds. This is to be brought off by a disenfranchised German Jew in Buenos Aires, tracked by an American agent not quite in the know and thus in jeopardy." Booklist

Ludlum, Robert, 1927-2001

The **Scarlatti** inheritance; a novel. World Pub. 1970 358p

"An American agent becomes concerned about the decline in his family's fortune and looking into the matter finds that his relative, Ulster Scarlatti, is using the money to bankroll Hitler's World War II effort." Smith. Cloak and Dagger Fic

Ludlum, Robert, 1927-2001

The **scorpio** illusion. Bantam Bks. 1993 534p

LC 93-9272

In this thriller, "the beautiful, anarchistic Basque terrorist Amaya Bajaratt . . . modestly sets out to eliminate the leaders of the United States, Britain, France and Israel. The only person able to stop her and thus save civilization as we know it is Tyrell Nathaniel Hawthorne 3d, a disillusioned former United States Naval Intelligence officer, now going to seed in the Caribbean. The two adversaries circle warily, each desperate to eliminate the other, neither able to strike the fatal blow." N Y Times Book Rev

Ludlum, Robert, 1927-2001

The **Sigma** protocol. St. Martin's Press 2001 535p

ISBN 0-312-27688-5

LC 2001-48240

"Ludlum keeps things moving with plenty of gunplay and running about. Uncharacteristically, he also lets things slow down from time to time, long enough for us to get to know the players in this complicated story." Booklist

Lukas, Michael David

The **Oracle** of Stamboul; a novel. Harper 2011 294p $24.99

ISBN 978-0-06-201209-8; 0-06-201209-6

LC 2010-14810

"Lukas' book is an appealing blend of magical and historical realism. Its story line is as loosely drawn, and as purposeful, as that flock of hoopoes that accompany the protagonist everywhere she goes. Lukas, too, is a graceful and inventive writer, and reflects his travels across Turkey and his love especially for Istanbul in dozens of polished and elegant passages scattered through the narrative. . . . And while it might seem a novel for young readers, this is a polished literary work that will appeal to a wide readership." Cleveland Plain Dealer

Lundrigan, Nicole

Glass boys; a novel. Douglas & McIntyre 2011 300 p. (paperback) $18.95

ISBN 1553657977; 9781553657972

In this book by Nicole Lundrigan, "when Roy Trench is killed in a drunken prank gone wrong, his brother Lewis sees blood on the hands of the man responsible: the abusive alcoholic, Eli Fagan. Though the courts rule the death an accident, the event opens a seam of hate between the two families of Knife's Point, Newfoundland." (Publisher's note)

Lupica, Mike

Wild pitch. Putnam 2002 352p

ISBN 0-399-14927-9

LC 2002-21952

An "account of the comeback of Showtime Charlie Stoddard, a pitching phenom for the New York Mets forced into early retirement by a ruined arm. Five years after his final sorry major league appearance, Charlie encounters a mysterious therapist named Chang, whose treatments make his tortured arm feel so good he dreams of pitching again. . . . How Charlie ends up pitchings for the Red Sox as they try to hold off the Yankees in a tight pennant race and just possibly shake off the collective curses of the Bambino, Bill Buckner and Bucky Dent, is fast and funny and occasionally brings a tear to the eye." Publ Wkly

Lupton, Rosamund

Afterwards; a novel. Rosamund Lupton. Crown 2012 386 p.

ISBN 9780307716545

LC 2011041524

In this book, "Grace Covey and her teenaged daughter Jenny are badly injured in an arson fire, and both lie unconscious in the hospital. Despite outside appearances, both are well aware of what's going on around them and are taking steps to understand what happened. Grace, suffering from a head injury that leaves her in a coma, and Jenny, badly burned, are both able to leave their damaged bodies. They can speak to each other, hear all the conversations going on around them, and can even hitch rides in cars as police and family members inspect the scene and question those involved. . . . [T]hey realize the danger isn't over. They are the only ones who have all the pieces of the mystery but they can only communicate with each other." (Libr J)

Lupton, Rosamund

Sister; a novel. Crown Publishers 2011 319p $24

ISBN 978-0-307-71651-4

LC 2010-25327

"Written in the form of a letter from Beatrice, the older, more substantial sister, to her younger, bohemian sibling, Tess, the narrative reveals within the first few pages that Tess has gone missing and is found dead. Bea and Tess, even with a big age difference and an ocean between them, were incredibly close, so when Bea receives the 'phone call,' she drops everything and races from New York City to London. Although Tess's death is ruled a suicide, Bea knows her sister would never kill herself. As Bea frantically tries to find the murderer, in the process losing pieces of herself, the reader is catapulted into the search." Libr J

Lurie, Alison

Foreign affairs. Random House 1984 291p

LC 84-42657

This novel follows "the actions and reactions of two English professors, both Americans, both from the same university, who are on leave in London to do research: Virginia Miner, 54, unmarried, happy to be back in the city she adores, and Fred Turner, 28, separated from his wife and depressed over being more or less in exile. Both Vinnie and Fred indulge in, while there, affairs with unlikely persons, with the result that they learn more about themselves from the experiences." Booklist

"Lurie portrays these entanglements with her customary astute wit and deft characterization, but also with unexpected warmth and generosity. A wry, wonderful book." Libr J

Lurie, Alison

The **last** resort; a novel. Holt & Co. 1998 321p

ISBN 0-8050-5866-4

LC 97-42985

In this novel a "forbearing New England wife puts up with an overbearing nature-writer husband; he's twenty-four years her senior, famous, and secretly thinks he's dying. During a sojourn in the Florida Keys, opportunities for mixing and rematching abound: she is coveted by a celebrated poet and by a lush lesbian, while he is worshipped by a would-be savior of manatees. Lurie sets this gavotte in a Key West whose pastels take on a tasty acidity, and the novel goes down like Key-lime pie." New Yorker

Lurie, Alison

The **nowhere** city. Coward-McCann 1966 276p

First published 1965 in the United Kingdom

The author describes the Los Angeles "scene with such a cool and penetrating eye, such total disbelief in its existence, that she is able to portray it with a pristine freshness. . . . Transformed by her wicked wit, the most exhausted clichés come alive, galvanized into original revelation." Newsweek

Lurie, Alison

Only children. Random House 1979 259p

ISBN 0-394-50471-2

LC 78-21994

"The novel spans the Fourth of July weekend {of 1935}. Bill and Honey Hubbard and their eight-year-old daughter Mary Ann, and Dan and Celia Zimmern and their daughter Lolly (and Dan's sullen adolescent son from a previous marriage) abandon New York City and its suburb, Larchmont, for the Catskill farm owned by Anna King, headmistress of the progressive school the two girls attend. This innocent outing doesn't turn out to be a relaxing weekend. . . . Instead the grownups start romping in an unseemly way and end up fighting while the two little girls look on, bewildered." New Repub

"Lurie has a sharp, ironic eye for the man-woman game and a dramatic deftness for setting the scene. Her rendering of the children is particularly effective." Libr J

Lurie, Alison

The **war** between the Tates. Random House 1974 372p

"An outline of the plot does scant justice to the substance and wit of Lurie's novel. What makes the lines sing is her skill in catching the idiosyncracies of the mind and the tongue, the twists and turns of sophisticated sensibilities trapped in absurd situations." America

Lurie, Alison

Women and ghosts. Talese 1994 179p

LC 93-46332

"In each tale Lurie pits a female protagonist against an apparition of varied, often comical, spectral persuasions. . . . These entertaining and enchanting tales deliver far more than one might bargain for, with afterimages that reverberate long after the initial delight with Lurie's dexterous prose has worn off." Booklist

Lustbader, Eric Van

Black Blade; {by} Eric Lustbader. Fawcett Columbine 1993 518p

LC 91-72890

New York homicide cop "Wolf Matheson is assigned to investigate a chain of murders perpetrated by the furtive Black Blade Society. That's a nationalistic, militaristic, but intellectual cabal that, for centries, has been nurturing the 'Oracle,' an enhanced mental state in which practitioners are able to predict the future and attain long lifespans. Alas, the Black Blade is bent on world domination and has been maneuvering events in both the U.S. and Japan toward world war. Wolf, with his sexy-but-clairvoyant Japanese girl friend, Chika, at his side, is equal to the task of saving the world, but he wouldn't be if it weren't for his Shoshone childhood, where shamans knew the same kind of stuff the Black Blade know." Booklist

Lustbader, Eric Van

Dark homecoming; [by] Eric Lustbader. Pocket Bks. 1997 353p

ISBN 0-671-00329-1

LC 96-48909

"Seeking refuge from his former life as a cop, Lew Croaker finds his reverie on his fishing boat in Miami cut short when his estranged sister, Matty, reappears. Matty begs him to find a kidney donor for her daughter, Rachel, whose self-abusive lifestyle has left her near death. Suddenly, Croaker is catapulted into the nefarious world of the feral Bonita twins, who murder people to harvest their organs. In a race against time to save Rachel, he agrees to murder a Latin American drug lord in exchange for a kidney; and then his friends become his enemies." Libr J

"An accomplished crime novel from a writer whose work has grown in depth without sacrificing thrills." Booklist

Lustbader, Eric Van

Floating city; a Nicholas Linnear novel. by Eric Lustbader. Pocket Bks. 1994 404p

LC 93-49360

"Nicholas Linnear and his private-eye buddy, Lew Croaker, dash around the globe attempting to thwart the murder of the Yakuza boss of bosses and stop the development of a terrible new weapon and a supercartel bent on world domination." Booklist

Lustbader, Eric Van

Mistress of the pearl. Tor Bks. 2004 588p map $27.95

ISBN 0-312-87237-2

LC 2003-60698

This novel "builds powerfully upon its predecessors, thanks to characters of uncommon depth and complexity, lots of perplexing dilemmas for them to wrestle with, and plenty of exciting swordplay and gore." Booklist

Lustbader, Eric Van

Second skin; a Nicholas Linnear novel. Pocket Bks. 1995 454p

LC 95-14365

In this adventure Nicholas Linnear "heads a computer firm on the verge of a mega-breakthrough that here is threatened by: a crazed Nietzsche-spouting American gangster who is Nicholas's doppelganger; the gangster's equally crazed, California-based brother, who's trying to take over the Eastern U.S Mafia family run by a middle-aged suburban matron; an unholy mix of Japanese tycoons, pols and Yakuza; and a creepy, untrustworthy aide to Nicholas's ailing mentor." Publ Wkly

Lutz, John

Burn. Holt & Co. 1995 278p

ISBN 0-8050-3480-3

LC 94-32187

Florida private eye "Fred Carver's new client, an attractive, widowed housing developer with the 'guileless blue eyes' of a serial killer, claims he is being persecuted by a woman who has accused him of stalking her. Keeping an open mind, Carver sets out to determine whether the frantic businessman is your 'typical compulsive male sexual psychopath' or a much-maligned guy." N Y Times Book Rev

This mystery, "in which the motive isn't greed or passion but rather grief and loss, is one of the best in a fine series." Booklist

Lutz, John

Dancing with the dead. St. Martin's Press 1992 208p

LC 92-2997

"St. Louis realtor Mary Arlington, whose mother is alcoholic and whose lover is physically abusive, lives for her mambo, cha-cha and tango lessons with Mel Holt at the Romance Studio. After kicking her lover out of her life and checking her mother into a detox center, Mary agrees to dance with Mel in the Ohio Star Ball, a major competition. Meanwhile in Seattle and New Orleans, women dancers resembling Mary are murdered. Rene Verlane, the husband of the New Orleans victim, insists the crime is related to his wife's dancing. Mary follows the case on TV and one night calls Verlane to offer her help in finding the killer." Publ Wkly

Lutz, John

Death by jury. St. Martin's Press 1995 291p

LC 95-11363

St. Louis detective Alo Nudger "is hired by Lawrence Fleck, an odious and permanently small-time attorney, to investigate his client, banker Roger Dupont, who is about to stand trial for the murder of his wife. The twist is that Fleck wants Nudger to find incriminating evidence because he wants his client to accept a plea bargain. Lutz is a master storyteller, and this plot is an intricate masterpiece." Booklist

Lutz, John

Final seconds; by John Lutz and David August. Kensington Bks. 1998 316p

ISBN 1-57566-259-0

LC 97-75929

"The most welcome realism in the book comes from the authors' resistance to the far-fetched elements that creep into many thrillers. Their seamless collaboration is notable for the efficiency of the plotting and for the unusual credibility of the story, its characters and the methodical way they do their work." Publ Wkly

Lutz, John

Lightning. Holt & Co. 1996 296p

ISBN 0-8050-4379-9

LC 95-43273

"Behind the intransigent and hackneyed rhetoric of both sides, Carver finds venality aplenty as he and Beth attempt to come to terms with their loss. Veteran novelist Lutz ties some nifty twists into his plot, which moves quickly towards a final deadly confrontation." Publ Wkly

Lutz, John

Oops! a Nudger mystery. St. Martin's Press 1998 278p

ISBN 0-312-18152-3

LC 97-36529

"St. Louis private investigator Alo Nudger doesn't usually accept referrals from other PI's, but this time Lacey Tumulty does the referring. Her friendship and his dwindling bank account induce Nudger to attempt to find out if Betty Almer's death was an accident, as the police believe, or something else, as her father contends." Booklist

"Nudger's novice partner Lacey . . . provides sometimes humorous complications." Libr J

Lutz, Lisa

Curse of the Spellmans. Simon & Schuster 2008 409p $25

ISBN 978-1-4165-3241-5; 1-4165-3241-2

LC 2007-21152

"Licensed P.I. Isabel 'Izzy' Spellman has been arrested for the fourth time in two months, and no one from her oddball family of fellow investigators will bail her out. Her sister, Rae, has run over Izzy's 'fiancé,' Inspector Henry Stone, during a driving lesson. The senior Spellmans have staged a 'disappearance,' their term for a vacation where no one can reach them. To complicate Izzy's life further, a man with the suspiciously ordinary name of John Brown has moved next door, and she's absolutely positive he's up to no good. . . . Once again, Lutz treats readers to a madcap roller-coaster ride." Libr J

Lutz, Lisa

The **last** word; a Spellman novel. Lisa Lutz. Simon & Schuster 2013 352 p. $25

ISBN 1451686668; 9781451686661

LC 2013005096

This is Lisa Lutz's sixth Spellman novel. Here, everyone "in the Spellman clan is in an uproar because of Isabel's hostile takeover of the firm. . . . Meanwhile, Izzy is helping client Edward Slayter hide his Alzheimer's, but it's clear someone is determined to get him kicked out as CEO of a very profitable venture capital firm, and that someone is willing to sic the FBI on Izzy for embezzlement as part of the scheme." (Publishers Weekly)

Lutz, Lisa

Revenge of the Spellmans. Simon & Schuster 2009 375p $25

ISBN 978-1-4165-9338-6

LC 2009-2281

This "third installment of Lutz's series . . . opens with series protagonist Isabel 'Izzy' Spellman, the single, snarky middle Spellman child, in court-ordered therapy, where she spends her time avoiding personal questions. Despite her parents' desperate attempts to win her back, Izzy has sworn off investigating—but she's bored. Snooping and prying is a dominant family trait, and before long Izzy is lured away from her bartending job by a seemingly easy case of a possibly straying wife. But when her older brother, the straight-living David, goes missing, her instincts really kick in." Kirkus

"Those in the market for mayhem and mirth will revel in Lutz's irresistible blend of suspense, irony, and wit." Booklist

Lutz, Lisa

The **Spellman** files; a novel. Simon & Schuster 2007 352p $25

ISBN 978-1-4165-3239-2; 1-4165-3239-0

LC 2006-49161

"Isabel 'Izzy' Spellman, a San Francisco PI who began working for Spellman Investigations at age 12, could easily pass as Buffy or Veronica Mars's wiser but funnier older sister. Izzy digs TV, too, especially Get Smart (an ex-boyfriend's ownership of the complete bootlegged DVD set is his major selling point). Now 28, Izzy thinks she wants out, but elects to take on a cold case while dealing with 14-year-old sister Rae, a nightmarish Nancy Drew, and parents who have no qualms about bugging their children's bedrooms. At times the dialogue-heavy text reads like a script and the action flags, but these are quibbles. When Rae suddenly disappears, Izzy and her family must learn some serious lessons in order to find her." Publ Wkly

Lychack, William

The **architect** of flowers; stories. Houghton Mifflin Harcourt 2011 161p pa $14

ISBN 978-0-618-30243-7; 0-618-30243-3

LC 2010-24953

"Deceptively simple stories about 'ordinary' working class characters. Lychack brings them to life with tiny insights and dazzling images he seems to exhale into every line." Columbine

Lychack, William

The **wasp** eater. Houghton Mifflin 2004 164p $21

ISBN 0-618-30244-1

LC 2004-42728

"Just when the dysfunctional family drama seems entirely wrung out, along comes a book so freshly original that it seems to have invented the genre. What's so remarkable here is the understatedness, the quietly intense writing carefully containing more emotion than many louder novels have to show. Original, too, is the impulse to heal rather than break away-however mixed the outcome." Libr J

Lynch, Jim

Border songs. Alfred A. Knopf 2009 291p $25.95

ISBN 978-0-307-27117-4; 0-307-27117-X

LC 2008-53514

"Six foot eight and dyslexic, Brandon Vanderkool has trouble relating to people, but he's supremely knowledgeable about birds. His dad doesn't think he's cut out for dairy farming, so Brandon ends up in the Border Patrol ruling the divide between Washington and Canada. Though he spends most of his time bird watching, smugglers and illegals keep falling his way, and he soon has a reputation as the patrol's top man. Meanwhile, his father struggles with the farm, his mother struggles with incipient Alzheimer's, a Canadian girl that Brandon's sweet on struggles with her decision to cultivate pot to smuggle across the border, and a new neighbor delights in interviewing everyone." Libr J

Lynch, Jim

Truth like the sun; Jim Lynch. Alfred A. Knopf 2012 253 p. $25.95

ISBN 030795868X; 9780307958686; 9781408830314

LC 2011050564

This novel, set in Seattle, Washington, follows "Roger Morgan . . . the mastermind behind the fair that made the city famous and . . . a backstage power forty years later, when at the age of seventy he runs for mayor in hopes of restoring all of Seattle's former glory. Helen Gulanos, a reporter . . . sees her assignment to investigate the events of 1962 become front-page news with Morgan's candidacy, and resolves to find out who he really is and where his power comes from." (Publisher's note)

"A briskly paced novel that gives us an insider's view into both the politics of culture and the culture of politics." Kirkus

Lynch, Scott

The **lies** of Locke Lamora. Bantam 2006 499p map hardcover o.p. pa $7.99

ISBN 0-553-80467-7; 978-0-553-80467-6; 0-553-58894-x pa; 978-0-553-58894-x pa

LC 2006-42653

"Fans of lavishly appointed fantasy will be in seventh heaven here, but it will be nearly as popular with readers of literary crime fiction. This is a true genre bender, at home on almost any kind of fiction shelf." Booklist

Lyndon, Robert

Hawk quest; Robert Lyndon. 1st U.S. ed. Sphere 2012 658 p. map (hardcover) $25.99

ISBN 0316219568; 0748128441; 9780316219563; 9780748128440

LC 2012429363

This book is set in 1072, when "the known world is at war, hunger and disease are widespread, Viking raids are still common, and explorers are just beginning to investigate beyond the confines of Europe. Into this turbulence Vallon, a minor nobleman, escapes from a Moorish prison, becoming the leader of a motley crew of adventurers who travel thousands of miles from continental Europe to Iceland, across the steppes of Russia, to ransom Sir Walter, captive of the Turkish leader Süleyman." (Library Journal)

Lynn, Allison

Now you see it; a novel. Touchstone 2004 281p $13

ISBN 0-7432-5026-5 pa

LC 2003-70450

In this "novel, a Manhattan couple decides to infuse their lives with meaning by having a child. David hangs out in the middle of the masthead at a middlebrow magazine while Jessica teaches school, but after several failed fertility treatments, they focus on clearing hurdles in the adoption process. And then one day, Jessica vanishes, her keys left on the counter, a bedroom window ajar. . . . So without evidence of a crime, the detached David and Jessica's increasingly desperate mother must come to grips with the jarring disappearance in their own way and time. David does so by revisiting the story of a U.S. businessman gone missing in Peru—the one real scoop of his career, which he landed on his honeymoon. Although Jessica is more plot device than compelling character, Lynn deftly employs David's journey to explore how someone might rediscover his internal compass when he no longer has any reason to lie to himself." Booklist

Lyon, Annabel

The **sweet** girl; by Annabel Lyon. Alfred A. Knopf 2013 235 p. $24.95

ISBN 0307962555; 9780307962553

LC 2012049210

This novel by Annabel Lyon "follows Aristotle's . . . daughter as she shapes her own destiny. Aristotle has never been able to resist a keen mind, and Pythias is certainly her father's daughter. With the death of Alexander the Great, her fortunes suddenly change. Aristotle's family is forced to flee Athens for a small town, where the great philosopher soon dies. Pythias quickly discovers that the world is not a place of logic after all, but one of superstition." (Publisher's note)

Lytal, Benjamin

A **map** of Tulsa; Benjamin Lytal. Penguin Books 2013 272 p. (paperback) $15

ISBN 0142422592; 9780142422595

LC 2012036711

In this novel, by Benjamin Lytal, "Jim Praley is home from college, ready to unlock Tulsa's secrets. He drives the highways. . . . He's invited to a party. And . . . he meets Adrienne Booker; Adrienne rules Tulsa, in her way. A high-school dropout with a penthouse apartment, she takes a curious interest in Jim. Through her eyes, he will rediscover his hometown: its wasted sprawl, the beauty of its late nights, and . . . the unsleeping light of its skyscrapers." (Publisher's note)

"Although [Adrienne] is the focus of Jim's obsession, the strength of this debut novel is Lytal's evocation of place: Tulsa through Jim's eyes is tenderly revealed. There is magic here if the reader has experienced any such provincial city, for the prose provokes remembered images, acutely vivid." Pub Wkly

Lytton, Edward Bulwer Lytton

The **last** days of Pompeii. Harper 1834 2v

The setting is Pompeii just before and during the famous eruption of Vesuvius, A.D. 79. "The simple story relates principally to two young people of Grecian origin, Glaucus and Ione, who are deeply attached to each other. The former is a handsome young Athenian, impetuous, high-minded, and brilliant, while Ione is a pure and lofty-minded woman. Arbaces, her guardian, the villain of the story, under a cloak of sanctity and religion, indulges in low and criminal designs. His character is strongly drawn; and his passion for Ione, and the struggle between him and Glaucus, form the chief part of the plot. . . . The book, full of learning and spirit, is not only a charming novel, but contains many minute and interesting descriptions of ancient customs; among which, those relating to the gladiatorial combat, the banquet, the bath, are most noteworthy." Keller. Reader's Dig of Books

López Barrio, Cristina

The **House** of Impossible Loves; Cristina Lopez Barrio; translated from the Spanish by Lisa Carter. Houghton Mifflin Harcourt 2013 336 p. (hardcover) $25

ISBN 0547661193; 9780547661193

In this novel, by Cristina Lopez Barrio, "the Laguna women suffer from an odd affliction: each generation is condemned to tragic love affairs and to give birth only to girls who are unable to escape the cruel fate of their mothers. . . . Clara Laguna, the latest in the family line, . . . [is] pregnant with yet another daughter, but the seeds of change are sown. Eventually the long-awaited son--Santiago, the great-great grandson of Clara--is born." (Publisher's note)

M

Ma Jian

Beijing coma; translated from the Chinese by Flora Drew. Farrar, Straus & Giroux 2008 586p

ISBN 0374110174; 9780374110178

LC 2008-925628

Awakening after a decade in a coma, former Tiananmen Square protester Dai Wei learns that his mother had sold one of his kidneys to finance his care, and that the China he knew has undergone radical change.

"A valuable work. Ma's writing can be lively, and his use of dialogue that embraces everyday chitchat gives the book a sense of reality. The idealism of youth is ably captured. Indeed, the students' frequently lofty and at times naive emotions are touching." New Leader

Ma Jian

Stick out your tongue; translated from the Chinese by Flora Drew. Farrar, Straus and Giroux 2006 93p $16

ISBN 0-374-26988-2

LC 2006-4282

Original Chinese edition, 1998

In these five loosely connected stories "a Chinese writer whose marriage has fallen apart travels to Tibet. As he wanders through the countryside, he witnesses the sky burial of a Tibetan woman who died during childbirth, shares a tent with a nomad who is walking to a sacred mountain to seek forgiveness for sleeping with his daughter, meets a silversmith who has hung the wind-dried corpse of his lover on the wall of his cave, and hears the story of a young female incarnate lama who died during a Buddhist initiation rite. In the thin air of the high plateau, the divide between dream and reality becomes confused." Publisher's note

Maalouf, Amin

Balthasar's odyssey; a novel. translated from the French by Barbara Bray. Arcade Pub. 2002 391p $25.95

ISBN 1-55970-666-X

LC 2002-74630

Original French editon, 2000

The author " sets this historical novel mostly in the Mediterranean of the mid-1600s. Balthasar Embriaco, an exiled Italian merchant, becomes fixated on retrieving a mysterious religious text called The Hundreth Name that he mistakenly sold to a traveler who stopped in his shop in the Levant. He thus sets out on a long journey, accompanied by his two nearly grown nephews, his manservant, and a woman seeking her estranged husband." Libr J

Maalouf, Amin

Leo Africanus; translated by Peter Sluglett. New Amsterdam 1992 360p pa $16.95

ISBN 1-561-31022-0

LC 91-36145

Original French edition, 1986; this translation first published 1988 in England with title: Leo the African

This "historical novel recreates the era when the Moors were expelled from Spain, and much of North Africa and southern Europe was in turmoil. Hassan al-Wazzan was just a child the year Columbus sailed to the New World. . . . The gradual exile of Hassan's family from Spain is developed through recollections of his proud, erring father, his badly treated mother and her diplomat brother. As a merchant and emissary, Hassan travels from Fez to Cairo to Mecca and—by misadventure—to Rome and the Vatican, where he is later renamed Leo Africanus." Publ Wkly

Maazel, Fiona

Last last chance. Farrar, Straus and Giroux 2008 337p $25

ISBN 978-0-374-18385-1; 0-374-18385-6

LC 2007-19428

This is "one strange, beautiful novel. It's the most shattering fictionalization of addiction and recovery since David Foster Wallace's Infinite Jest—yet the narrator's story is set against the outbreak of a global superplague that threatens to decimate humanity. . . . [It] is overflowing with a gallow's humor that makes the impending end of the world almost palatable. Few modern novels have brought together brainy introspection and pure nail-biting entertainment so well." Anthem

MacAlister, Katie

A girl's guide to vampires. Love Spell 2003 374p pa $7.99

ISBN 0-505-52530-5

"All Joy Randall wants is a little old-fashioned romance, but when she participates in a 'Goddess evoking' ceremony with her friend, Roxy, Joy finds out her future true love is a man with the potential to put her immortal soul in danger. At first the ever-practical Joy is ready to dismiss her vision as a product of too much gin and too many vampire romances, but while traveling through the Czech Republic with Roxy, Joy begins to have some second thoughts about her mystery lover because she is suddenly plagued by visions of a lethally handsome stranger. . . . With its superb characterization and writing that manages to be both sexy and humorous, this contemporary paranormal love story is an absolute delight." Booklist

MacBride, Stuart

Blind eye; Stuart MacBride. 1st U.S. ed. Minotaur Books 2009 517 p. (hardcover) $26.99

ISBN 0312382642; 9780312382643

LC 2009021058

This is Stuart MacBride's fifth Logan McRae thriller. Here, "Aberdeen's growing Polish community is under attack from a serial offender who leaves mutilated victims to be discovered on building sites—eyes gouged out and the sockets burned. Detective Sergeant Logan McRae is assigned to the investigation, code-named Operation Oedipus, but with the victims too scared to talk, it's going nowhere fast." (Publisher's note)

MacBride, Stuart

Close to the Bone; Stuart Macbride. HarperCollins Publishers 2013 viii, 511 p.p (hardcover) $24.99

ISBN 0007344260; 9780007344260

In this installment of Stuart MacBride's Logan MacRae series, the detective inspector "is working under Acting Detective Chief Inspector Steel, who is dumping cases and more paperwork on Logan than he can handle. Among his cases are rival drug gangs fighting over the cannabis trade in Aberdeen, a pair of missing teens, and a jewelry store robbery. Logan also has a new detective sergeant assigned to him who is efficient but very ambitious and eager to make a name for herself." (Library Journal)

MacBride, Stuart

★ **Cold** granite; Stuart MacBride. St. Martin's Minotaur 2005 458p (pbk.) $6.99; o.p.; o.p.

ISBN 9780312940591; 9780312339951; 031233995X

LC 2005042780

This book is "set in Aberdeen, Scotland. Det. Sgt. Logan MacRae, back from a lengthy convalescence caused by a crazed suspect's knife attack, is plunged straightaway into the investigation of a brutally murdered child. To make matters worse, the victim's family learns of the death from a reporter before the police have a chance to inform them. Angered and embarrassed by the press leak, Logan, aided by WPC Jackie Watson, vows to expose the source within the precinct. . . . More children go missing, and soon the populace of Aberdeen is screaming for blood. Further inciting the rabble, a notorious defense attorney earns acquittal for a habitual child molester. As a result, a hapless, ruined scholar–turned–street sweeper becomes a scapegoat for the chilling fear that grips the community." (Publishers Weekly)

MacBride, Stuart

Dying Light; Stuart MacBride. 1st St. Martin's Minotaur ed. St. Martin's 2006 424 p. (hardcover) $24.95

ISBN 0312339976; 9780312339975

LC 2006043700

This is Stuart MacBride's second Logan MacRae novel. Here, "a madman has sealed up a squatter's apartment and set it—and the six people partying inside—afire. That same evening, a prostitute is found beaten to death, and Det. Sgt. Logan MacRae . . . is on the case. But his star has fallen; after a botched raid, MacRae has been demoted to the 'Screw-Up Squad,' led with a droll lack of enthusiasm by one Inspector Steel." (Publishers Weekly)

MacBride, Stuart

Flesh house. St. Martin's Minotaur 2008 467p il $24.95

ISBN 978-0-312-38263-6; 0-312-38263-4

LC 2008-23605

Det. Sgt. Logan McRae "is on the hunt for a serial killer called the Flesher who butchers his victims and then feeds their meat to their family members. The first murders occurred 20 years ago, and Ken Wiseman was convicted but later released on a technicality. Now the Flesher is again terrorizing Aberdeen, and McRae is working to find Wiseman and stop the murders. To add to the pressure, a BBC documentary on the Grampian police force is being filmed during the investigation, so every move the officers make is being recorded. McRae, a very human hero, is juggling the investigation along with his superior officers' eccentricities and a breakup with his girlfriend, even as he ferries around a visiting police chief who was involved in the investigation of the first murders." Libr J

MacBride, Stuart

Shatter the bones; Stuart MacBride. HarperCollins 2011 438 p. (hardcover) $24.95; (paperback) $16.95; (paperback) $12.99

ISBN 000734421X; 0007344228; 0007344244; 9780007344215; 9780007344222 reprint; 9780007344246 reprint

LC 2012371203

This is Stuart MacBride's seventh Logan McRae novel. Here, the Aberdeen, Scotland detective "finds himself working two kidnapping cases . . . . In the first, a mother-daughter singing duo, made famous on the TV show 'Britain's Next Big Star,' is being held for ransom . . . . In the other, a junkie has gone missing, presumably due to her boyfriend's role in a drug deal." (Booklist)

MacColl, Gail

To marry an English Lord; by Gail MacColl and Carol McD. Wallace. Workman Pub. 1989 x, 403 p.p ill. (pbk.) $15.95; o.p.

ISBN 9780761171959; 0894809393

LC 85040529

This book traces how "[f]rom the Gilded Age until 1914, more than 100 American heiresses invaded Britannia and swapped dollars for titles--just like Cora Crawley, Countess of Grantham, the first of the Downton Abbey characters Julian Fellowes was inspired to create [for the television program] after reading 'To Marry An English Lord.' Filled with . . . personalities, . . . anecdotes, grand houses, and . . . period details--plus photographs, illustrations, quotes, and the finer points of Victorian and Edwardian etiquette--'To Marry An English Lord' is [a] social history." (Publisher's note)

MacDonald, Ann-Marie

Fall on your knees; a novel. Simon & Schuster 1997 508p il

ISBN 0-684-83320-4

LC 96-34186

In this novel "James Piper and his Lebanese child bride raise their four daughters on Cape Breton Island in the early 1900s. Gorgeous, talented, and aloof, Kathleen finds her way to New York City, studying opera by day and sneaking into the smoky world of Harlem jazz by night. Her sister Mercedes, cursed with imperfect religious fervor, tries to keep the two youngest sisters safe from the dark forces that threaten the family left behind. Frances, with her own destructive secrets, seeks solace in sleazy back alleys and raunchy speakeasies. And little Lily, damaged by polio, whose ethereal innocence protects her from nothing, proves toughest of all." Libr J

MacDonald, Ann-Marie

The **way** the crow flies; a novel. HarperCollins Publishers 2003 722p $26.95

ISBN 0-06-057895-5

LC 2003-61076

This is "a brilliant portrayal of child abuse and its consequences, but it is much more than that. It is a fiercely intelligent look at childhood, marriage, families, the 1960s, the Cold War and the fear and isolation that are part of the human condition." Washington Post Book World

MacDonald, Gerard

The **prisoner's** wife; Gerard Macdonald. Thomas Dunne Books 2012 306 p.

ISBN 0312591802; 1250012430; 9780312591809; 9781250012432

LC 2011050641

This novel by Gerard Macdonald "is a political thriller ripped from [the] headlines--a . . . trip through the murky worlds of state-sponsored terrorism, nuclear politics, secret American jails and lawless rendition. Shawn Maguire, unemployed American spy, has been paid to find a young Iranian now being interrogated in one of the CIA's black prisons. The prisoner may be in Fes, in Cairo or in Peshawar, but Shawn has every confidence that he'll find his man. Based on his time as an agent, it's an assignment he knows he can handle. But he's not so sure he can handle . . . the prisoner's wife. (Publisher's note)

MacDonald, John D.

Cinnamon skin; the twentieth adventure of Travis McGee. Harper & Row 1982 275p

LC 81-48159

"Travis McGee and his friend Meyer search for Meyer's niece's new husband, who has killed his wife and faked his own death in an explosion. The search is plodding and long, but MacDonald makes it interesting through the diverse and lively characters involved. The showdown, on Mexico's Yucatán Peninsula, is a bit slow but colorful and original." Libr J

MacDonald, John D.

A **deadly** shade of gold. Lippincott 1974 336p

First published 1965 in paperback by Fawcett Books

An old friend of Travis McGee's is found dead, and an Aztec idol worth more than its weight in gold disappears. McGee's search for the perpetrator (or perpetrators) leads him to Florida, New York, California and Mexico

MacDonald, John D.

The **deep** blue good-by. Lippincott 1975 200p

First published 1964 in paperback by Fawcett Books

"Travis McGee, as usual helping out a damsel in distress, encounters a psycho ladykiller who makes most of the women he fancies soon wish they were dead. Plenty of action on the 'Busted Flush,' McGee's houseboat and on the deep seas off the Florida coast, but the deep blue of the title is that of a stolen sapphire. McGee's probings go back to the fly-boys of World War II, including some who came home from the China run with more gold than good conduct medals." Booklist

MacDonald, John D.

The **dreadful** lemon sky. Lippincott 1975 228p

"After successfully smuggling a huge quantity of Jamaican marijuana into Florida in a plane and boat operation, a team of felons fall victim to greed and treachery among themselves. A member of the team, a girl who had once been Travis's lover, entrusts him with her share of the loot for safekeeping (not specifying its origin, of course). Then she's murdered. As Travis investigates this death, with the aid of his philosophical friend Meyer, he finds himself investigating a whole series of related deaths, none of them accidental." Publ Wkly

MacDonald, John D.

Dress her in indigo. Lippincott 1971 255p

First published 1969 in a paperback edition

"Travis McGee and friend Meyer {go} to the Mexican village of Oaxaca, among the gay, the depraved, {the drug addicted} and the violent, to find out about the kind of life Bix Bowie led there before her tragic death." Libr J

MacDonald, John D.

Free fall in crimson. Harper & Row 1981 246p

LC 80-7871

"A jig-saw trail takes Trav to a small Iowa town where Peter Kesner is making 'Free Fall' a movie about balloon racing he hopes will salvage his career after several flops.

Financing the current flick is Josie Laurant, Kesner's lover. She has inherited a fortune from her former husband and daughter, both victims of unsolved murders McGee is investigating. Adding to the bank roll are porn flicks made by Desmin Grizzel, a real-life biker Kesner had featured in a film about motorcycle gangs. Grizzel has seduced local minors and forced them to take part in the scabrous movies, outraging the citizens. A mob attacks the film crew and a pitched battle leaves scores dead and injured." Publ Wkly

MacDonald, John D.

The **green** ripper. Lippincott 1979 221p

LC 79-12063

"MacDonald is unsurpassed at showing the American brand of loneliness. He catches foibles in a phrase and gives us many-sided, wounded but courageous, characters." Booklist

MacDonald, John D.

★ The **lonely** silver rain. Knopf 1985 232p

LC 84-23373

"Travis McGee is growing older, and here he has good reason to feel his age. Besides combating a drug-smuggling potentate out to kill him, he finds himself the father of a young woman, all of which make the sleuth-philosopher reflect even more somberly on his life, his friends, his lonely job. One of the last MacDonald stories, it is also one of the best." Barzun. Cat of Crime. Rev and enl edition

MacDonald, John D.

The **long** lavender look. Lippincott 1972 264p

First published in paperback 1970 by Fawcett Books

When McGee avoids running his Rolls Royce into a young girl, he finds himself embroiled in intrigue

MacDonald, John D.

One fearful yellow eye. Lippincott 1978 286p

LC 77-24165

First published 1966 in paperback by Fawcett Books

Travis McGee "answers an SOS from Glory Geis. She tells him that her late husband had secretly disposed of a fortune in cash before his death, money Geis's other heirs accuse the widow of stealing. Smelling blackmail, McGee digs into the dead man's past and finds evidence of a venomous plot. A gang of Nazi criminals, passing for respectable citizens, had extorted Geis's money by threatening the lives of his wife and children." Publ Wkly

MacDonald, John D.

One more Sunday. Knopf 1984 311p

LC 83-48858

The author "is far too wise to fall into any simplistic traps, nor does he dismiss all of the religious work as worthless. His descriptions of the church's organization and its power over ordinary mortals are brilliantly done, and the questions of conscience come vividly to life." NY Times Book Rev

MacDonald, John D.

A **purple** place for dying. Lippincott 1976 204p

First published 1964 in paperback by Fawcett Books

"Travis McGee is pondering whether to take on the beautiful Mona Yeoman as a client when someone decides for him by shooting her in the back and hiding the body. Mona's husband soon dies of poison, and the killers might have been in the clear if they had not tried to add McGee (and one of those lovely women he always attracts) to their list. The usual literate and fast-paced stuff expected from MacDonald." Booklist

MacDonald, John D.

The **scarlet** ruse. Lippincott 1980 262p
LC 79-24843
First published 1973 in paperback by Fawcett Books
Private detective Travis McGee, "who lives on a houseboat, is told that the owner is planning on cleaning up the waterfront so he's going to lose his mooring place. McGee is bothered by this but to take his mind off this impending disaster, he takes on a case wherein a dealer of rare stamps is being made the victim of a stamp collector who is substituting 'junk' stamps—worthless stamps for valuable one-of-a-kind stamps. MacDonald keeps the pot boiling as McGee conducts his investigation and, as tradition would have it, runs into all kinds of unforeseen difficulties in settling this case, up to and including murder." West Coast Rev Books

MacDonald, John D.

The **turquoise** lament. Lippincott 1973 287p
McGee goes to the rescue of the daughter of a man who saved his life
"One of the best McGee adventures." Publ Wkly

MacDonald, Philip

The **list** of Adrian Messenger. Doubleday 1959 224p
"If some readers find Mr. MacDonald's style a bit stiff and old-fashioned, they will also find that he provides such other old-fashioned elements as honest clues, characters who stick in the mind from page to page, an original idea, and, in Anthony Gethryn, a detective who inspires utter confidence." New Yorker

Macdonald, Ross

Archer in Hollywood; with a foreword by the author. Knopf 1967 528p

Macdonald, Ross

Archer in jeopardy; with a foreword by the author. Knopf 1979 757p
LC 79-63807
An omnibus volume of three titles published separately 1958, 1962 and 1968 respectively
Three mysteries featuring Lew Archer. In The doomsters the activities of an unscrupulous doctor occupy the sleuth; in The zebra-striped hearse the detective becomes involved in an ice pick murder, and in The instant enemy it is the high school runaway that is the focus of Archer's attention
"Three classic Lew Archer mysteries. . . . This stunning trilogy is a must for all mystery enthusiasts." Booklist

Macdonald, Ross

★ The **drowning** pool. Knopf 1950 244p

"Admirers of the later Ross Macdonald will detect in this early book the capacities subsequently so well exploited. Lew Archer started as he continued: tough and straight; clever and informed, but not omniscient; full of love and hostility toward Southern California. This story, of a woman who has made a bad marriage to a mother-dominated husband of ambivalent sexual character, has a bit too much violence, but the character-drawing shows a sure hand, and the tangle is so capably manipulated that it does not annoy." Barzun. Cat of Crime. Rev and enl edition

Macdonald, Ross

★ The **far** side of the dollar. Vintage Books 1996 247p pa $12
ISBN 0-679-76865-3
LC 97-120671
First published 1965 by Knopf
This mystery "begins with Lew Archer's visit to a school for troubled boys, in search of a lead on Tommy Hillman, who has just escaped. . . . It turns out that Hillman had borrowed and wrecked a neighbor's car, and was put in the school by his father to teach him a lesson. Next, Archer learns that a ransom of $25,000 has been demanded for the return of Tommy Hillman. The Hillmans are a typically horrifying wealthy couple whose life has become unmoored through too much lying. The investigation of their past at one point brings up a connection to Archer's, showing that he has more in common with these people than he at first supposed." Murphy. Ency of Murder and Mystery

Macdonald, Ross

★ The **Galton** case. Vintage Books 1996 242p pa $12
ISBN 0-679-76864-5
LC 97-118474
First published 1959 by Knopf
"Archer is hired by Lawyer Gordon Sable on a hopeless case: to search for the elderly Mrs. Galton's son and heir, Anthony Galton. What he quickly turns up is a decapitated corpse buried on the spot where Anthony had lived twenty years before, and a young man working in a gas station who looks exactly like Anthony and may be his son. . . . The Galton trail leads to a bleak provincial town in Canada, and Macdonald's wry and funny glance at the beatnik poetry scene in San Francisco enriches the early part of the novel, putting on display the strength and flexibility of Macdonald's mature style. With The Galton case, Macdonald had 'arrived' precisely by finding a mythical form for his own beginnings." Murphy. Ency of Murder and Mystery

Macdonald, Ross

The **goodbye** look. Knopf 1969 243p
Private detective Lew Archer is brought "into the affairs of the Chalmers family because their lawyer thinks they are worried about a theft from their safe. But the Chalmers have other problems, and Lew becomes involved with murders old and new." Libr J

Macdonald, Ross

Sleeping beauty. Knopf 1973 271p
The scene "is California and the concern is with what power and money can do to wreck a family. Lew {Archer}

befriends a lost lady who is running away from fears and responsibilities and from her young husband. Before very long word comes that the girl has been kidnapped and a ransom is demanded of her oil rich family. Bit by bit, as Archer probes deeper into the family relationships, he begins to see that nothing is what it seems and the key to the present lies deep in the past." Publ Wkly

Macdonald, Ross

★ The **underground** man. Knopf 1971 272p

"With his customary skill and economy of means, the author gets us, through Archer, into a tangle of passions about runaway spouses, disaffected and drug-taking children, amateur blackmail, and, of course, murder." Barzun. Cat of Crime. Rev and enl edition

Machart, Bruce

The **wake** of forgiveness. Houghton Mifflin Harcourt 2010 309p $26

ISBN 978-0-15-101443-9; 0-15-101443-4

LC 2009-47459

"A historical tale set at the end of the 19th century up to the mid-1920s, The Wake of Forgiveness is a tragic family saga in the Faulknerian tradition of sins long simmering and revenge gone wrong. Set in a mythical South Texas town, full of dark deeds and troubled townsfolk, it details a somber world marked by flashes of romance. At the outset, in 1895, the bitter figure of Vaclav Skala commands the stage, ruing the death of his wife in childbirth to his last son, Karel, and treating all three of his sons as either livestock or his curse and cross to bear. Karel emerges as the central figure of the novel, and although he inherits some of his father's tendencies, he's certainly more complex. It's his role to stand up to and stand by his difficult father, to inherit his curse of anger and see it through to the end. Into this mix of personalities ride the Knedlik twins, local orphans and ne'er-do-wells. Both eloquent and fast-paced, the novel only bogs down in extremely detailed action scenes." Dallas Morning News

MacInnes, Helen

Above suspicion. Harcourt Brace & Co. 1954 333p

ISBN 0-15-102707-2

A reprint of the title first published 1941 by Little, Brown

"An Oxford don and his pretty wife are chosen to perform a secret mission to Germany in late 1939. While using their vacation as a cover, they are to locate the whereabouts of an anti-Nazi agent. The plan seems foolproof—until someone betrays it and them." Smith. Cloak and Dagger Fic

MacInnes, Helen

Prelude to terror. Harcourt Brace Jovanovich 1978 368p

"Colin Grant, art consultant, is asked by a wealthy art collector to purchase a specific seventeenth-century painting at an art auction in Vienna. The owner of the painting needs money to escape from Hungary, and the transaction must be kept secret. When Colin arrives in Vienna, he finds that the auction conceals a conspiracy for laundering money that is used to buy weapons for terrorist groups. In spite of great personal danger Colin searches for the key piece of informa-

tion that will stop this source of financing." Shapiro. Fic for Youth. 2d edition

MacInnes, Helen

Ride a pale horse. Harcourt Brace Jovanovich 1984 355p

LC 84-9037

"Karen Cornell, journalist for an American world affairs magazine, is about to leave a peace convention in Prague disgruntled by her treatment and the lack of material when she is approached by a Czech intelligence officer who is about to defect. The papers he gives her to relay to a CIA expert on 'disinformation' start her on a harrowing course from Prague to Vienna, Rome, and Washington." Libr J

"The device of dual protagonists moves the plot along smartly, and the demonstration of the insidious uses of disinformation could hardly be more timely." Booklist

MacInnes, Helen

The **Venetian** affair. Harcourt, Brace & World 1963 405p

This "suspense novel is set in Paris and Venice in 1961. An American newspaperman on vacation picks up the wrong raincoat on arrival at Orly airport, and finds himself involved in a communist plot to assassinate De Gaulle and implicate the United States. American agents enlist his help to thwart the plotters and to unmask the mysterious and ruthless spymaster." Publ Wkly

Mackenzie, Jassy

Random violence. Soho 2010 326p $25

ISBN 978-1-56947-629-1; 1-56947-629-2

LC 2009-44015

First published 2008 in South Africa

"No sooner does Jade de Jong return home to South Africa, . . . than she heads for the bad side of town to buy a gun. Like most of Jade's activities in this tense thriller, the gun is unlicensed, illegal and dangerous. But this is Johannesburg, where car-jacking is a local sport, so a young woman on her own might need a little extra protection as she tries to settle the score with her father's killer. First things first, though. In a crime a local newspaper calls 'brutal, senseless and typical of the new South Africa,' a wealthy woman has been murdered outside her well-fortified home, and Jade, now a private investigator, has been asked to lend a hand by the detective in charge of the case, who happens to be a dear old friend. Even as Mackenzie captures Johannesburg's 'crazy boomtown energy,' she doesn't shy away from the rough stuff. None of which, it should be said, is quite rough enough to scare this remarkable new sleuth, whose future exploits should be worth watching." N Y Times Book Rev

MacKenzie, Sally

Bedding Lord Ned; Sally MacKenzie. Zebra Books 2012 426 p $7.99

ISBN 1420123211; 9781420123210

This historical romance novel by Sally MacKenzie follows "Nell Bowman, [who] can't remember when she fell in love with Ned Valentine. . . .[B]ut instead he proposes to their mutual friend, Cecily. . . . [S]he dies during childbirth, leaving Ned bitter and guilt-ridden. Some years later, . . . Lady "Venus" Valentine . . . hosts a party to celebrate Ned's thirtieth birthday. However, the clever duchess' real plans involve her most important matchmaking coup to date." (Booklist)

Mackey, Nathaniel

   Bass cathedral; with a preface by Wilson Harris. New Directions 2007 183p il pa $16.95

   ISBN 978-0-8112-1720-0; 0-8112-1720-5

LC 2007-34666

   This is the fourth volume of From a broken bottle traces of perfume still emanate, the author's ongoing novel with no beginning or end

   "Plot serves as a platform from which Mackey launches a volley of poetic and philosophical concerns. . . . That these idiosyncratic yet rigorously applied thought processes never become overly cerebral is testament to Mackey's tremendous musicality. Such is the exquisitely rhythmic lyricism of the novel that not once does the conceptual language dampen the sound of the music inhabiting the prose. With [this work], Mackey writes into being a fiction worthy of the songs he interrogates." Bookforum

MacLean, Alistair

   Floodgate. Doubleday 1984 369p

   ISBN 0-385-18263-5

LC 83-45013

   First published 1983 in the United Kingdom

   "The novel is set in and around Amsterdam, where a band of canny, sophisticated terrorists are threatening to flood the Netherlands by blowing up dikes and exploding offshore nuclear devices. The terrorists demand that Holland must negotiate with Great Britain for the withdrawal of all British troops from Northern Ireland. Peter van Effen, senior detective and explosives expert, eventually saves the nation, a task he carries out with cool, dispassionate efficiency." Booklist

   "Readers accustomed to thrillers of a more lurid hue may well appreciate MacLean's stylistic restraint, neat plotting and attention to characterization." Publ Wkly

MacLean, Alistair

   Force 10 from Navarone. Doubleday 1968 274p

   The three heroes of The guns of Navarone, Mallory, Miller and Stavros are assigned a new mission during World War II. "They are dropped into Yugoslavia to join the Partisans, prevent a German attack, blow up a dam, and provide a diversion to draw German troops out of Italy." Publ Wkly

MacLean, Alistair

   ★ The **guns** of Navarone. Doubleday 1957 320p

   "World War II is being fought, and the Germans control the island that guards the approaches to the eastern Mediterranean with big guns. After all other attempts have failed, a five-man British army team is chosen to silence the guns of Navarone. They land on the island, elude the Nazis, and scale a seemingly unclimbable cliff." Shapiro. Fic for Youth. 3d edition

   Followed by Force 10 from Navarone

MacLean, Alistair

   ★ **Ice** Station Zebra. Doubleday 1963 276p

A novel of suspense and intrigue that begins on "a bittercold morning in Holy Loch, Scotland, when a British doctor with top-level endorsements from the American and British military forces seeks admission to an American nuclear submarine. The submarine is slated for a perilous trip to rescue the starving, freezing British crew of a meteorological station situated on an ice floe in the Arctic." Publ Wkly

MacLean, Alistair

   Night without end. Doubleday 1960 287p

   "An airliner crash lands on the Greenland icecap near a small I.G.Y. observation station. It soon becomes clear that the landing was planned and certain of the passengers and crew murdered for reasons unknown, while at least eight of the 10 survivors were drugged into insensibility—the other two of course, being the killers. But which two? . . . A sometimes barely credible, but always absorbing, thriller that combines elements of the espionage story and murder mystery with those of the 'castaway' adventure tale." Libr J

MacLean, Alistair

   When eight bells toll. Doubleday 1966 288p

   "Sure and deadly with guns and knives, an expert at underwater work, Philip Calvert, British secret service agent, polishes his skills to a high gloss in this tense adventure story set in the western Scottish Highlands. Calvert and his friends oppose a gang of killers who operate at sea and in harbors. What the killers are doing, why they are busy in this cold, rainy, windy part of Scotland, and whether Calvert will survive his fight against them are questions that provide suspense." Publ Wkly

MacLean, Alistair

   Where eagles dare. Doubleday 1967 312p

   "Secrecy and stealth are essential to the mission of an assorted crew from MI 6 who must rescue an American general, the coordinator of Overlord, from Schloss Adler, a castle built by a mad Bavarian prince, which is the combined HQ of the German Secret Service and the Gestapo of South Germany in the bitter winter of 1943-44. And if that isn't enough, there is Major Smith's second assignment to bring out the pyrotechnic display of excitement and suspense." Libr J

MacLean, Sarah

   One Good Earl Deserves a Lover; Sarah MacLean. HarperCollins 2013 384 p. $7.99

   ISBN 0062068539; 9780062068538

   Sequel to: A rogue by any other name (2012)

   In this novel by Sarah MacLean, Pippa Marbury is "looking forward to marrying her simple fiancé and living out her days quietly with her dogs and her scientific experiments. But before that, Pippa has two weeks to experience all the rest -- fourteen days to research the exciting parts of life. . . .She needs Cross, the clever, controlled partner in London's most exclusive gaming hell, with a carefully crafted reputation for wickedness." (Publisher's note)

MacLean, Sarah

A **rogue** by any other name; edited by Henriette Sinding Aasen, Uichol Kim, Geir Helgesen. Avon 2012 400p.

ISBN 9780062068521

In this romance novel set before Victorian England, "Michael Lawler, the marquess of Bourne, lost everything in an ill-considered wager with a scheming neighbor. He spends 10 years recreating his fortune three times over by running the Fallen Angel, London's notorious gaming hell. Wealth hasn't stopped him from wanting to regain his family estate, and when the opportunity presents itself, Michael jumps at the chance, regardless of the strings attached—namely, marriage to his childhood friend Miss Penelope Marbury, the villain's daughter. Perpetuating a farce of a marriage for London society isn't difficult, but Bourne's all-consuming need for revenge endangers the possibility for real love between the two." (Publishers Weekly)

MacLeod, Alexander

Light lifting; (stories) Alexander MacLeod. Biblioasis 2010 219p.

ISBN 978-1-89723-194-4 pa

LC 2010533764

Atlantic Book Awards (Canada): Margaret and John Savage First Book Award (2011)

'This book is a "collection of seven stories by Alexander MacLeod, which has been short-listed for the Giller Prize. . . . Light Lifting's characters live mostly in gritty industrial Windsor, Ontario, their lives occasionally threatened by violence. . . . One of these, "Miracle Mile," concerns a distance runner named Burns and is narrated by a friend of his. For Burns, importance has become mania—as it can for 'scholars of Renaissance poetry, car buffs, sexual perverts, collectors of all kinds.' Winning means everything to him. . . . In other stories one discovers a twelve-year old drugstore delivery boy has frightening or repulsive experiences with disconcerting sexual connotations; a family befriends a neighbour boy whose mild reaction to being severely beaten by one of the boys in the family indicates his desperation to belong; a group of driveway brick-layers fail to take enough care of the seventeen-year-old boy hired on the summer and, as a consequence, his life prospects are implicitly diminished." (Notre Dame Review)

MacLeod, Alistair

Island; the complete stories. Norton 2001 434p. $25.95

ISBN 0-393-05035-1

LC 00-51524

"The author, an expatriate from Cape Breton, Nova Scotia, writes about his homeland and its dying traditions, in tales that marry the elemental themes of Gaelic song (loneliness, sorrow, work, death) with a simple but deceptively modern narrative style. In the course of the sixteen stories (presented in order of publication, from 1968 to 1999), MacLeod's spare style grows more artful, but the ache of loss is constant as he captures the direct eloquence of the islanders-the coal miners, lobstermen, farmers, and lighthouse keepers who know they are the last of their kind." New Yorker

MacLeod, Charlotte

Exit the milkman. Mysterious Press 1996 311p

ISBN 978-0892965724

LC 96-18337

In this mystery Balacava Agricultural College's "Peter Shandy is the last person to see fellow professor Jim Feldster—a man who welcomes any excuse to get away from his wife—before he disappears. When Feldster's wife accuses the Shandys of hiding her husband, they begin sleuthing. Another series charmer." Libr J

MacLeod, Charlotte

The **Gladstone** bag. Mysterious Press 1990 218p

LC 89-43143

"Six feisty and contentious characters with inventive names surround aging-but-active Emma Kelling during her stay at a friend's Maine retreat. Strange events, attempted theft, and a sodden body propel her to consult niece and nephew-in-law/detectives Sarah and Max Bittersohn . . . , as well as cousin-in-law Theonie. Tongue-in-cheek eccentricities, the usual casual but astute deductions, and a certain luxuriousness of language make this a most welcome addition to the MacLeod canon." Libr J

MacLeod, Charlotte

Rest you merry. Doubleday 1978 182p

LC 77-27713

"Christmas time at Balaclava Agricultural College is the background for this academic mystery tale. Professor Peter Shandy capitulates to the badgering of a resident busy-body Jemima Ames and shows his Christmas spirit—by decorating his house with plastic reindeer, flashing lights, and leering Santas. . . . He then flees, but driven back by his conscience, he returns to find the body of Jemima in his living room. Helen Marsh, the new librarian, joins the professor in the investigation of the murder." Publisher's note

MacLeod, Charlotte

Vane pursuit; a Peter Shandy mystery. Mysterious Press 1989 185p

LC 88-25595

"Detective Peter Shandy, and his redoubtable wife, Helen the librarian, are swept up in the diabolical theft of antique weather vanes by crooks who use arson as their mode d'accomplis. . . . Endless puns punctuate MacLeod's delightfully absurd tale, which, beneath all the frivolity, is masterfully executed." Booklist

MacLeod, Charlotte

The **withdrawing** room. Doubleday 1980 186p

"Widowed Sarah Kelling takes boarders into her stately home on Boston's Beacon Hill to pay the heavy mortgage, a move that means trouble. Mr. Quiffen, who settles into the former 'withdrawing room,' is killed and so is Mr. Hartler, who rents the vacated premises. Sarah appeals to her brainy, attractive friend Max Bittersohn for help but begins to investigate her guests personally, afraid that one may be the murderer." Publ Wkly

MacMahon, Kathleen

This is how it ends; Kathleen MacMahon. Grand Central Pub. 2012 346 p.

ISBN 1455511315; 9781455511310

LC 2011942017

This novel, by Kathleen MacMahon, begins in "Fall, 2008 . . . [on] [t]he coast of Dublin, Ireland. . . . Bruno, an American, has come to Ireland to search for his roots. Addie, an out-of-work architect, is recovering from heartbreak while taking care of her infirm father. When their worlds collide, they experience a connection unlike any they've previously felt, but soon a tragedy will test them-and their newfound love-in ways they never imagined possible." (Publisher's note)

MacNeil, Robert

Breaking news; a novel. Doubleday 1998 371p $24.95

ISBN 0-385-42020-X

LC 98-19562

"By the novel's end, MacNeil has delivered some extremely disheartening news about the state of our national news media wrapped neatly in a shiny literary package: Jim Lehrer's loss is fiction's gain." N Y Times Book Rev

MacNeil, Robert

Burden of desire. Doubleday 1992 466p

LC 91-28919

This novel "is at once a wonderful romance involving one of the more appealing triangles in recent fiction and a thoughtful dissection of the glacial pace of social change." N Y Times Book Rev

Magary, Drew

The **postmortal**; a novel. Penguin Books 2011 369p pa $15

ISBN 978-0-14-311982-1; 0-14-311982-6

LC 2011-14531

"As the novel progresses, it turns from a snappy morality tale, to a noir-ish revenge fable, to an action movie; complete with guns, rogue religious cults and government-sanctioned hit men. The narrative comes to us through John's blog entries and collections of news bytes and pundit commentary. Through his sixty years as a 29-year-old, he experiences all the love, pain, grief, and terror of a standard lifetime and is still in good enough shape to kick some ass at the end. Like much good dystopian fiction, The Postmortal is an at-times unflattering commentary on human beings, present, past and future, that hits the mark in many ways." Nervous Breakdown

Magnin, Joyce

The **prayers** of Agnes Sparrow; by Joyce Magnin. Abingdon Press 2009 398 p. (pbk.) $13.99

ISBN 1426701640; 9781426701641

LC 2009014854

This book tells the story of "two sisters, Agnes and Griselda Sparrow. The titular Agnes forswears leaving home when she tips the scale at 600 pounds, and stays put and prays. When what seem to be miracles--healings from serious illnesses--occur, the residents of the small Pennsylvania town of Bright's Pond naturally attribute them to Agnes.

Agnes's putative power attracts a stranger in need of an unstated miracle." (Publishers Weekly)

Maguire, Gregory

Confessions of an ugly stepsister; illustrations by Bill Sanderson. ReganBooks 1999 368p il $25.95

ISBN 0-06-039282-7

LC 00-59085

"Adult and sophisticated, . . . [the author's] musings on beauty, ugliness, magic, reality, and imagination explore how our past follows us always and shapes our self-perception." Chicago Trib

Maguire, Gregory

A **lion** among men; with illustrations by Douglas Smith. William Morrow 2008 312p il $26.95

ISBN 978-0-06-054892-6

LC 2008-16694

"Most of this is superbly entertaining, but Maguire has bitten off more complex interactions than he can chew, and his story's seams frequently show. No matter. Brrr and his acquaintances are irresistible company, and issues of legitimate and responsible rule are herein really rather subtly grafted onto the venerable free will vs. predestination conundrum. . . . Maguire's inspired world-building strides from strength to strength." Kirkus

Maguire, Gregory

Mirror mirror; a novel. Regan Books 2003 280p $24.99

ISBN 0-06-039384-X

LC 2003-46774

This novel "unearths our buried fascination with the primal fears and truths fairy tales contain. Through this forest of wry, sometimes bawdy humor, Maguire leaves a trail of profound reflections on the nature of identity, the persistence of love, the self-destruction of evil." Christ Sci Monit

Maguire, Gregory

Son of a witch; a novel. ReganBooks 2005 337p il $26.95

ISBN 0-06-054893-2

LC 2005-46232

"This sequel to the adult fairy tale Wicked (1995) . . . begins ten years after the destruction of Elphaba, a.k.a. the Wicked Witch of the West. In Maguire's dark version of the Land of Oz, there's not much to ring the bells for in the Emerald City, despite the tyrannical Wizard's departure. Corruption is rife, political factions compete for power, and radicals proclaim 'Elphaba lives!' Elsewhere, a horribly injured young man called Liir wakes in the religious House of Saint Glinda to many puzzles. . . . Above all, was Elphaba his mother? These and other questions drive a tale that adroitly mixes drama, humor, and political satire into a well-knit examination of good and evil-and leaves several doors open for future journeys over the rainbow into this cleverly constructed dystopia." Libr J

Maguire, Gregory

★ **Wicked**; the life and times of the wicked witch of the West: a novel. Gregory Maguire; illustrations by Douglas Smith. ReganBooks 1995 406 p. ill. $26.99

ISBN 0060391448

LC 950669

This book tells the story of "Elphaba, the future Wicked Witch of the West. . . . Her mother is embarrassed and repulsed by her bright-green baby with shark's teeth and an aversion to water. At college, the coed experiences disapproval and rejection by her roommate, Glinda, a silly girl interested only in clothes, money, and popularity. Elphaba is a serious and inquisitive student. When she learns that the Wizard of Oz is politically corrupt and causing economic ruin, Elphaba finds a sense of purpose to her life -- to stop him and to restore harmony and prosperity to the land. . . . The conclusion, however, is the same as L. Frank Baum's." (School Library Journal)

"Born with green skin and huge teeth, like a dragon, the free-spirited Elphaba grows up to be an anti-totalitarian agitator, an animal-rights activist, a nun, then a nurse who tends the dying—and, ultimately, the headstrong Wicked Witch of the West in the land of Oz. Maguire's strange and imaginative postmodernist fable uses L. Frank Baum's Wonderful Wizard of Oz as a springboard to create a tense realm inhabited by humans, talking animals (a rhino librarian, a goat physician), Munchkinlanders, dwarves and various tribes." Publ Wkly

Mahfouz, Naguib, 1911-2006

Children of the alley; by Naguib Mahfouz; translated by Peter Theroux. Doubleday 1996 448 p.

ISBN 9780385264730; 9780385420945

LC 95015510

Original Arabic version serialized 1959 in Cairo newspaper; previous English translation with title: Children of Gebelaawi, published 1981 in paperback by Three Continents Press

"Gabalawi's mansion sits at the desert's edge, surrounded by high-walled gardens. His sons, however, quarrel over his estate, and the omnipotent gangster banishes them from his earthly paradise. Their descendants settle outside the wall, desperately poor but always praying to Gabalawi for salvation. As each succeeding generation spawns its messiah, the people rise up against the ruling gangsters, seizing their portion of the estate, but greed and ignorance prove their ultimate undoing, poverty and suffering their inescapable fate." Libr J

Mahfouz, Naguib, 1911-2006

Midaq Alley; {by} Naguib Mahfouz; translated by Trevor Le Gassick. Anchor Bks. (NY) 1992 286p

LC 91-27459

"Written in the 1940s, this novel . . . deals with the plight of impoverished classes in an old quarter of Cairo. The lives and situations depicted create an atmosphere of sadness and tragic realism. Indeed, few of the characters are happy or successful. Protagonist Hamida, an orphan raised by a foster mother, is drawn into prostitution. Kirsha, the owner of a café in the alley, is a drug addict and a lustful homosexual. Zaita makes a living by disfiguring people so that they can become successful beggars. Transcending time and place, the social issues treated here are relevant to many Arab countries today." Libr J

Mahfouz, Naguib, 1911-2006

★ **Palace** of desire; translated by William M. Hutchins and Olive E. Kenny. Doubleday 1991 422p

LC 90-3753

Original Arabic edition, 1957

"Mr. Mahfouz excels at fusing deep emotion and soap opera. Fortunately, the translators . . . are equal to the task of animating rather than embalming Mr. Mahfouz's elegant and often explosive text." N Y Times Book Rev

Followed by Sugar Street

Mahfouz, Naguib, 1911-2006

★ **Palace** walk; translated from the Arabic by William M. Hutchins with Olive E. Kenny. Doubleday 1990 498p

LC 89-23348

Originally published in Arabic

This is the first volume in the author's trilogy "dealing with three generations of a Cairo family in the first half of the twentieth century. The emotional and physical struggles of these middle-class people are depicted with a great deal of sympathy and honesty, from the torments of adolescent love through the banked passions of an established marriage. The novel begins with a series of domestic scenes featuring the five children of a merchant and his wife; later, the setting shifts to Cairo nightclubs, coffee shops, and stores as Mahfouz re-creates the everyday existence of his characters in almost Dickensian detail." Booklist

Followed by Palace of desire

Mahfouz, Naguib, 1911-2006

★ **Sugar** Street; translated by William Maynard Hutchins and Angele Botros Samaan. Doubleday 1992 308p

LC 91-12938

Original Arabic edition, 1957

"The ordinary nature of Mr. Mahfouz's world, with its willingness to confront the complexities of human intentions, makes it an extraordinary exception in a marketplace of manufactured ideas and is, for that, all the more admirable." N Y Times Book Rev

Mailer, Norman

Ancient evenings. Little, Brown 1983 709p

LC 82-22839

"Set in the span between the reigns of Ramses II and Ramses IX, Mailer's . . . novel is narrated by the remnant spirits of Menenhetet I and his great-grandson as they join mutuality to survive the land of the Dead and to ascend to Ra. The story is largely the account of Menenhetet's first life (he has had four) as he rises from peasant stock to become first charioteer to Ramses II, then general, then overseer of the harem." Libr J

Mailer, Norman

The **castle** in the forest; a novel. Random House 2007 477p $27.95

ISBN 978-0-394-53649-1; 0-394-53649-5

LC 2006-49389

"Over the course of the novel a complex demonology is posited, clearly based on Dante and medieval scholasticism, and the narrator's chatty tone and Jesuitical logic are strangely reminiscent of C.S. Lewis' persuasive devil, Screwtape. All of this takes Hitler's life out of the realm of moral choice and into that of the supernatural, making it irrelevant to the novel's stated theme-unless one is an Augustinian Catholic, which as everyone knows the author is not. . . . . Occasionally a real insight slips in, almost by accident." New Leader

Mailer, Norman

★ The **executioner's** song. Modern Lib. 1993 1002p

ISBN 0-679-42471-7

LC 92-51066

A reissue of the title first published 1979 by Little, Brown

"In this study of a condemned murderer Mailer not only vividly portrays the character in a real-life drama but also invokes the whole history of westward migration of the Mormons of Utah." Reader's Ency. 3d edition

Mailer, Norman

The **Gospel** according to the Son. Random House 1997 242p

LC 96-48018

This is a "novel that purports to be a first-person memoir written by Jesus." Time

Mailer's "gospel is written in a direct, rather relaxed English that yet has an eerie, neo-Biblical dignity." New Yorker

Mailer, Norman

Harlot's ghost. Random House 1991 1310p

ISBN 0-394-58832-0

LC 90-53152

"Harry Hubbard is a bright young man whose father and whose mentor, Hugh Montague (also known as Harlot), are both senior CIA figures and induct him into the Agency. Most of the book . . . is one long flashback, Harry's autobiographical account of his early career—partly in his own words, partly in an exchange of letters with Harlot's beautiful, brilliant wife, Kittredge, whom Harry admires from afar and will one day steal." Publ Wkly

"An immensely long but never laborious book, one where Mailer works compelling variations on his quintessential themes." Libr J

Mailer, Norman

★ The **naked** and the dead. Holt & Co. 1948 721p

ISBN 9781439571606; 9780312265052

"In 1944 an American platoon takes part in the invasion and occupation of a Japanese-held island. The action is divided into three parts: the landing on the island, the counterattack by night, and a daring patrol by the platoon behind enemy lines. The style is simple realism and therefore the language is rough, in keeping with the army setting." Shapiro. Fic for Youth. 3d edition

Mailer, Norman

Tough guys don't dance. Random House 1984 229p

LC 84-42514

"Tim Madden is a writer who lives in Provincetown, where the action takes place one dreary November. . . . After

a night of monumental drinking, Madden awakens with a mysterious tatoo on his arm, blood all over the passenger seat of his Porsche, and no memory of his actions. Later he discovers one, then another decapitated head buried with his stash of marijuana. Madden is obviously the prime suspect in the murders, and his task is to find which of the many unsavory characters of his acquaintance is responsible." Publ Wkly

"This genre is not exactly Mailer's forte, but the nononsense prose and the hard-as-nails style . . . may attract readers." Booklist

Maillard, Keith

The **clarinet** polka. Thomas Dunne Bks. 2003 406p $24.95

ISBN 0-312-30889-2

LC 2002-32511

"Jimmy is a wry, down-to-earth, irresistable narrator, and Maillard draws all the characters in the working-class community with compassion and obvious affection. This moving, well-drawn story of sin and redemption in a fading industry town may remind readers of Richard Russo." Publ Wkly

Maine, David

The **book** of Samson. St. Martin's Press 2006 229p $23.95

ISBN 978-0-312-35339-1; 0-312-35339-1

LC 2006-45803

A "first-person account of the life of Samson, the Israelite judge remembered for his voluminous hair, Herculean strength and ill-advised relationship with Delilah. Samson delivers his monologue from the Philistine temple of Dagon where, shorn and shackled and awaiting execution, he reflects upon a life of 'frustration and pain plus a fair bit of sex and lots of killing and broken bones.' Hatred of the Philistines is the narrative's central theme, and Samson delights in recalling his violent exploits." Publ Wkly

"Here is a beguiling, original writer who is determined to reinterpret the Bible's humanity in ways that make sense in the modern world." N Y Times (Late N Y Ed)

Maine, David

Fallen. St. Martin's Press 2005 244p $23.95

ISBN 0-312-32849-4

LC 2005-46588

"The first recorded murder takes barely 26 lines in Genesis. What Maine does with those few facts is masterfully creative. The story is told in reverse, beginning with Cain as an old man waiting to die and mourning the fact that the ghost of his murdered brother has left him. It deftly moves backward to the murder and God's punishment, where the point of view shifts to Abel just a few days before the murder. Finally, the point of view is shared by Adam and Eve alternately as they deal with aging and their burgeoning family, back to their first moments outside of the garden. Maine's explanations of Cain's hatred, God's dismissal of his sacrifice, and the real forbidden fruit are fascinating and often wildly funny. Once again he has turned his focus on the family dynamics and come away with a divinely passionate tale." Booklist

Maine, David

★ The **preservationist**. St. Martin's Press 2004 230p $24.95

ISBN 0-312-32847-8

LC 2003-70881

This is an "elegant, inventive book and in no way a cynical one, despite the author's keen appreciation of the incongruous. . . . The book resounds with the gravity of Noe's mission even as it invents the quotidian details of his story." N Y Times Book Rev

Majmudar, Amit

Partitions; Amit Majmudar. 1st ed.; Metropolitan Books 2011 xii, 211p.p

ISBN 9780805093957; 0805093958; 9781250007629

LC 2010045159

This book takes place "[a]s India is rent into two nations, [and] communal violence breaks out on both sides of the new border and streaming hordes of refugees flee from blood and chaos. At an overrun train station, Shankar and Keshav, twin Hindu boys, lose sight of their mother and join the human mass to go in search of her. A young Sikh girl, Simran Kaur, has run away from her father, who would rather poison his daughter than see her defiled. And Ibrahim Masud, an elderly Muslim doctor driven from the town of his birth, limps toward the new Muslim state of Pakistan, rediscovering on the way his role as a healer." (Publisher's note)

Majors, Inman

Love's winning plays; Inman Majors. 1st ed. W. W. Norton & Company 2012 256 p. (hardcover) $25.95

ISBN 0393062805; 9780393062809

LC 2012020171

This novel by Inman Majors is "about the sublimely ridiculous world of college football. . . . Raymond Love, a young coach unfamiliar with the banquet circuit of big-shot boosters and chat-room gurus, will go along as . . . head coach Von Driver's . . . wide-eyed errand boy . . . on a Pigskin Cavalcade to the small towns in the state. . . . Also on the trip is the athletic director's daughter, whom Love has tried to win by joining her book club -- a dubious strategy at best." (Publisher's note)

Makine, Andrei, 1957-

★ **Dreams** of my Russian summers. Arcade Pub. 1997 241p

ISBN 1-55970-383-0

LC 97-2720

Original French edition, 1995

This is the story "of Charlotte Lemonnier, born in France at the turn of the century, who as a child moved to Russia, where her father practiced medicine. Traveling back and forth over the years, she found herself in France on the eve of World War I, only to return to Russia with a Red Cross mission during the Revolution. There she remained to see the horrors of civil war and famine, and later witnessed the Stalinist purges, the war with Germany, the dehumanizing industrialization of the country and ultimately the fall of Communism's idols. By the time her grandson, the novel's narrator, begins visiting her for his summer holidays, she has

been long settled in the sleepy Siberian town where her Russian husband lies buried." N Y Times Book Rev

Makine, Andrei, 1957-

The **life** of an unknown man; Andrei Makine; translated by Geoffrey Strachan. Sceptre 2010 vi, 250 p.p (hardcover) $29.80; (paperback) $15.00

ISBN 155597614X; 9780340998786; 9781555976149

LC 2010467995

This novel, by Andrei Makine, tells of how "a disenchanted writer, revisits St. Petersburg after twenty years. . . . Instead, he meets Volsky, an old man who tells him . . . of surviving the siege of Leningrad, the march on Berlin, and Stalin's purges, and of a transcendent love affair. Volsky's life is an inspiration to Shutov. . . . This depth of feeling stands in sharp contrast to the empty lives Shutov encounters in the new Russia, and to his own life." (Publisher's note)

Makine, Andrei, 1957-

Music of a life; translated from the French by Geoffrey Strachan. Arcade Pub. 2002 109p $21.95

ISBN 1-55970-637-6

LC 2002-25854

Original French edition, 2001. Published in the United Kingdom with title: A life's music

"It is 1941, and Alexei, a budding concert pianist, is returning to his Moscow apartment two days before his first public recital when a neighbor warns his off: his parents are being arrested. Knowing that he will be sent to the Gulag, too, Alexei flees to the home of relatives in the countryside. Then the Germans invade, decimating his family's village but providing a plethora of bodies from which he can pillage an identity. . . . Stalin's atrocities are made visceral in this wisp of a book." New Yorker

Makine, Andrei, 1957-

The **woman** who waited; translated from the French by Geoffrey Strachan. Arcade Publishing 2006 182p $24

ISBN 1-559-70774-7

LC 2005-10314

Original French edition, 2004

"The Woman Who Waited quite deliberately avoids breaking your heart. It just comes very, very close. Vera is perceived only through the eyes of the narrator, but she is clearly more than just the woman who waits: only a fool would fail to understand that she's also the kind of woman worth waiting for, and far kinder and wiser than any romantic fiction." Washington Post Book World

Makkai, Rebecca

The **borrower**; a novel. Viking 2011 324p $25.95

ISBN 978-0-670-02281-6; 0-670-02281-0

LC 2010-52432

A "crime farce about a hapless librarian–cum–accidental kidnapper. Lucy Hull is a 26-year-old whose rebellion against her wealthy Russian mafia parents has taken the form of her accepting a children's librarian job in smalltown Missouri. After an unnecessarily long-winded first act, the novel picks up when Lucy discovers her favorite library regular, 10-year-old Ian Drake, hiding out in the stacks one morning after having run away from his evangelical Christian parents, who censor his book choices and are pre-emptively sending him to SSAD (Same-Sex Attraction Disorder) rehab, and Lucy soon aids and abets his escape. The tale of their subsequent jaunt across several state lines dodging cops, a persistent suitor of Lucy's, and a suspicious black-haired pursuer is fast-paced, suspenseful, and thoroughly enjoyable." Publ Wkly

Maksik, Alexander

A **marker** to measure drift; by Alexander Maksik. Alfred A. Knopf 2013 240 p. (hardcover) $24.95; (ebook) $74.85

ISBN 0307962571; 9780307962577; 9780307962584; 9780345803863

LC 2012038249

This novel, written by Alexander Maksik, focuses on Jacquelin, a young Liberian woman living alone in a cave on a remote island in the Aegean Sea. She experiences "the euphoric obliteration of memory and, with it, the unspeakable violence she has seen and from which she has miraculously escaped. Slowly, irrepressibly, images from a life before this violence begin to resurface. Jacqueline must find the strength to contend with what she has survived or tip forward into . . . madness. (Publisher's note)

Malae, Peter Nathaniel

What we are. Grove Press 2010 383p $24

ISBN 978-0-8021-1907-0; 0-8021-1907-7

"Predictably, Paul doesn't take to conformity all that well, and gives it up. But he does grow more empathetic for the exercise. Even so, in testament to how hostile this novel is to empathy, much of its climactic dialogue is in Spanish. You can get the gist of it without knowing the language, but you miss out on the exact voice of our hero at his most generous and self-affirming. It's a wasted moment that makes it hard for us to care about Paul's future. And yet we have to care, since his is the voice of the Me Generation, which needs a lot of help." N Y Times Book Rev

Malamud, Bernard

★ The **assistant**; a novel. Farrar, Straus & Giroux 1957 246p hardcover o.p. pa $13

ISBN 0-374-50484-9 pa

This novel is "set in the prison of a failing grocery store, where Morris Bober, its elderly, long-suffering Jewish owner, teaches his assistant, Frankie Alpine, what it means to be a Jew, and what it means to be a man. After decades in which Jewish protagonists struggled to assimilate to the non-Jewish world around them, The Assistant is a tale about reverse assimilation, one in which Frankie takes over the store on Morris's death and undergoes a painful conversion to Judaism." Benet's Reader's Ency of Am Lit

Malamud, Bernard

★ The **complete** stories; introduction by Robert Giroux. Farrar, Straus & Giroux 1997 634p hardcover o.p. pa $18

ISBN 0-374-12639-9; 0-374-52575-7 pa

LC 97-12394

"Whether, stark, comic or fanciful, Malamud's stories give us immigrant Jews and their descendants pondering moral questions and experiencing moments of magical intervention while enduring life's ridiculous situations. Yet the stories transcend their ethnic settings and achieve a universal resonance." Publ Wkly

Malamud, Bernard

★ The **fixer**. Farrar, Straus & Giroux 1966 355p hardcover o.p. pa $14

ISBN 0-374-52938-8 pa

"Yakov Bok, a handyman, is arrested and charged with the killing of a Christian boy. Innocent of the crime, he is only guilty of being a Jew in Czarist Russia. In jail he is mentally and physically tortured as a scapegoat for a crime he insists he did not commit. Although his suffering and degradation are unrelenting, Bok emerges a hero as he maintains his innocence. Malamud has fashioned a powerful story of injustice and endurance based on a true incident." Shapiro. Fic for Youth. 3d edition

Malamud, Bernard

A **Malamud** reader. Farrar, Straus & Giroux 1967 528p

Malamud, Bernard

★ The **natural**. Harcourt Brace & Co. 1952 237p

ISBN 9780374502003

LC 93241037

"The fanaticism and seriousness of baseball to both players and fans are vividly pictured in this novel about a man whose sole ambition was to be 'the greatest ever.' Roy Hobbs, who has made his own bat, Wonderboy, starts off at nineteen years of age to a possible spot on a big team. That promising beginning is blasted when he has an encounter with an erratic, seductive woman. When we next meet Roy fifteen years later, he is trying again to realize his dream as the best baseball player. His wrong-headed decisions and the exciting descriptions of the games played by his team, The Knights, make this a tense story up to the last out." Shapiro. Fic for Youth. 3d edition

Malamud, Bernard

The **tenants**. Farrar, Straus & Giroux 1971 230p

ISBN 0-374-27290-5

LC 71-165400

A novel "about Harry Lesser, a Jewish writer whose third novel is not completed after nearly ten years of incessant work. Lesser lives alone, the last occupant of an apartment building located in a dying neighborhood. The clash between Lesser and Willie Spearmint, an aspiring but as yet unpublished black writer who takes over one of the empty apartments, serves as the focus of the novel." Libr J

"A magnificent story is told with grieving insight into some of life's more damaging conflicts and betrayals." Saturday Rev

Malliet, G. M.

A **fatal** winter; a Max Tudor novel. G.M. Malliet. Minotaur Books 2012 384 p. (hardcover) $24.99

ISBN 0312647972; 9780312647971; 9781250018250

LC 2012035879

Sequel to: Wicked Autumn (2011)

Author G.M. Malliet features a murder mystery. "Traveling back to his home in Nether Monkslip, Anglican priest Max Tudor . . . [is] summoned to Chedrow Castle by DCI Cotton, of the Monkslip-super-Mare police, who eagerly seeks Max's MI5 experience to investigate at the castle when Lady Baynard's brother and titleholder, Lord Footrustle, is murdered . . . Soon after his arrival, Lady Baynard's body is found. Now, the pressure is on Max to determine who most profited from the deaths of the brother and sister." (Kirkus)

Malliet, G. M.

Wicked autumn; a Max Tudor novel. Minotaur Books 2011 297p map $23.99

ISBN 978-0-312-64697-4

LC 2011-19523

His tranquility as the established vicar of a New Age village shattered by the murder of an unpopular woman, former MI5 agent Max Tudor struggles with past demons while trying to identify a killer in his peaceful community.

"Malliet has mastered the delights of the cozy mystery so completely that she seems to be channeling Agatha Christie, albeit with a hero who adds sex appeal to the mix. She also includes snippets of ironic humor that contribute a little spice to the village charm, making the story even more delicious. Religion, espionage, tea, and crumpets: a winning menu." Booklist

Mallinson, Allan

A **close** run thing; a novel of Wellington's army of 1815. Bantam Bks. 1999 306p

ISBN 0-553-11114-0

LC 98-52512

"Hervey's story begins in 1814, with Napoleon's defeat. Hervey narrowly escapes a court martial for impetuous, albeit brave, action in the Peninsular Campaign against the French, and is invited to purchase his lieutenancy. He returns to Britain, rekindles his affections for his childhood sweetheart, and is posted to Ireland: there he explores the country's religious strife, rides horses and reads Pride and Prejudice. But when Bonaparte escapes from Elba and raises a new army for a rematch with Wellington, Hervey's dragoons must return to war." Publ Wkly

"An exciting historical adventure steeped in authentic military detail." Booklist

Mallon, Thomas

Bandbox. Pantheon Books 2004 305p $24.95

ISBN 0-375-42116-5

LC 2003-54861

"Mallon, in his other books, has gravitated toward previous eras out of an affinity for something like reticence. 'Bandbox,' then, is a real departure: antic, stylized, and up-tempo. The dialogue has a Kaufman-and-Hart crackle, and the story boasts more lotharios, floozies, mobsters, and wised-up dames than an MG-M double feature." New Yorker

Mallon, Thomas

★ **Dewey** defeats Truman; a novel. Pantheon Bks. 1997 355p

ISBN 0-679-44425-4

LC 96-26812

"Owosso, Michigan, was Dewey's birthplace, and in the summer and fall of 1948 the townspeople are basking in the national attention that brushes the town. Anne Macmurray, a bookstore clerk and aspiring novelist, is being courted by two men, one a U.A.W. organizer, the other a smug Republican lawyer running for state senator. That romantic rivalry is shaped not only by the political passions of 1948 but also by the skeletons buried (and in one case unburied) in the pasts of other Owossoans. This work is so tightly constructed that it sometimes feels contrived, but Mallon's gift for the telling detail, whether of place or of character, quickly banishes such reservations." New Yorker

Mallon, Thomas

Fellow travelers. Pantheon Books 2007 353p $25

ISBN 978-0-375-42348-2; 0-375-42348-6

LC 2006-24586

"The author keeps his own political convictions to himself. . . . Mallon is not an ideologically driven writer; political issues are his springboard for questions of individual integrity. We might take Mary, the novel's most adult character, as his stand-in. She quietly uses her affluent father's connections to help a State Department coworker fired for "lavender" inclinations and works behind the scenes in Congress to stymie McCarthyite legislation. . . . . Rueful maturity and large-minded sympathy are not qualities that help you navigate a city gripped by political hysteria. They are, however, among the salient qualities of 'Fellow Travelers,' a work of art that tempers judgment with compassion." Los Angeles Times Book Rev

Mallon, Thomas

Two moons; a novel. Pantheon Bks. 2000 303p

ISBN 0-375-40025-7

LC 99-34235

"Mallon refracts questions of war, woman's rights, and the ordering of the cosmos through the perfect prism of her heroine's mind, adeptly mixing keen social commentary with sheer entertainment." Booklist

Mallon, Thomas

Watergate. Pantheon Books 2012 x, 432 p.p

ISBN 0307378721; 9780307378729

LC 2011017393

This book offers a "retelling of the Watergate scandal, as seen through a kaleidoscope of its . . . perpetrators and investigators. . . . [It covers] the Nixon presidency through the . . . perspectives of seven characters, . . . moving readers from the private cabins of Camp David to the klieg lights of the Senate Caucus Room, from the District of Columbia jail to the Dupont Circle mansion of Theodore Roosevelt's sharp-tongued ninety-year-old daughter, . . . and into the hive of the Watergate complex itself, home not only to the Democratic National Committee but also to the president's attorney general, his . . . loyal secretary, and the shadowy man from Mississippi who pays out hush money to the burglars." (Publisher's note)

Malone, Michael

The **four** corners of the sky; a novel. Source-books Landmark 2009 560p $24.99

  ISBN 978-1-570717-44-4; 1-570717-44-3

LC 2008-38938

"Malone delivers a tale that takes a little long to tell but that pays off nicely in the end. Secrets and intrigues among the honeysuckle: a sun-washed yarn of the New South, affectionately told." Kirkus

Malouf, David

The **complete** stories. Pantheon Books 2007 508p $27.50

  ISBN 978-0-375-42497-7; 0-375-42497-0

LC 2006-37694

"Malouf is a master of the art of the short story in its most elusive, Chekhovian form, and he uses the genre, it seems to me, for three delicate purposes in particular: the exploration of the ordinary; the evocation of moments of change, often seemingly slight; and the interrogation of loss." Slate

Malouf, David

Ransom. Pantheon Books 2010 224p $24

  ISBN 978-0-307-37877-4; 0-307-37877-2

LC 2009-20669

First published 2009 in Australia

A "retelling of Achilles' desecration of Hector's corpse and his capitulation to Priam's appeal for proper rites and burial for the Trojan hero. Malouf's prose is triumphantly sure, and his characterizations of the subtle and complex bonds between Priam and Achilles, gods and mortals, wives and husbands, parents and children, nobles and commoners, and beasts and men resonate with authority." Libr J

Malouf, David

★ **Remembering** Babylon. Pantheon Bks. 1993 200p

LC 93-7888

"The book is more reflective than polemic. Without excusing the actions of the townsfolk, . . . Malouf shows how difficult original thought is for members of a community that perceives itself as surrounded by danger. The book is a joy to read: richly layered, complex, and dense." Christ Sci Monit

Maloy, Kate

Every last cuckoo; a novel. Algonquin Books of Chapel Hill 2008 277p $22.95

  ISBN 978-1-56512-541-4; 1-56512-541-X

LC 2007-16641

Maloy "has created a truly engrossing novel, with situations at times both joyful and horribly sad and an entirely likable protagonist surrounded by an eclectic cast of friends and family. An excellent book club selection." Libr J

Malraux, Andre

★ **Man's** fate (La condition humaine) translated by Haakon M. Chevalier. Smith & Hass 1934 360p

  Original French edition, 1933; published in the United Kingdom with title: Storm in Shanghai

"The time is 1927, during the unsuccessful Communist uprising in China. The author focuses on three types of revolutionaries. Ch'en, a Chinese terrorist, believes that Chiang Kai-shek must be killed to start a revolution and is willing to sacrifice himself to bring this about. Kyo, half-French, half-Japanese, is drawn to the revolution because of his belief in human dignity. He finds it difficult to reconcile the idealistic theories of Marx with the political realities of the revolution. Katov, a Russian who has had experience in the revolution in his own country, feels there is strength in the solidarity of his comrades. Though their attempts at revolution fail, each man dies feeling he has given meaning to his life trying to bring change to China." Shapiro. Fic for Youth. 3d edition

Malraux, Andre

★ **Man's** hope; translated from the French by Stuart Gilbert and Alastair Macdonald. Random House 1938 511p

  Original French edition, 1937; published in the United Kingdom with title: Days of hope

The story of the first eight months of the Civil War in Spain based on the author's experiences as commander of the Loyalist government's international air force

"Vividly realistic as it is, the book is remarkably free from the senseless dwelling upon physical injuries which often weakens the effect of war novels. M. Malraux has concentrated upon the essential rather than the incidental horrors of war, of civil war in particular." Manchester Guardian

The **mammoth** book of steampunk; edited by Sean Wallace. Perseus Books Group 2012 vii, 498 p.p

  ISBN 0762444681; 9780762444687

LC 2011930509

This anthology of steampunk short stories edited by Sean Wallace "focus[es] on newer elements of steampunk, one which deconstructs the staples of the genre and expands on them, rather than simply repeating them, with a greater spread both in terms of location and character. This is steampunk with a modern, post-colonial sensibility." (Publisher's note)

Manchette, Jean-Patrick

Fatale; translated from the French by Donald Nicholson-Smith; afterword by Jean Echenoz. New York Review Books 2011 98p pa $12.95

  ISBN 1590173813; 9781590173817

LC 2010-34848

Original French edition, 1977

The MO of the murderer Aimée Joubert "involves insinuating herself into the financial elite of a new locale, most recently the obscure coastal industrial town of Bléville." (Bookforum)

"'For her stay in Bléville, the young woman had chosen to call herself Aimée Joubert, and that is what I shall call her from now on,' Manchette says of his female assassin, who 'aside from her husband,' as French author Jean Echenoz mentions in the afterword, 'has already killed seven men, among them a factory owner, a stock breeder, and a doctor.' Told in tight behaviorist language and laced with deadly black humor, this compact neo-noir follows Joubert as she steps much too far into her self-made career toward a showdown worthy of any action film." Publ Wkly

Manfredi, Valerio Massimo

A **Winter's** Night; by Valerio Manfredi. Penguin Group USA 2012 368 p. (paperback) $18.00

ISBN 1609450760; 9781609450762

Author Valerio Manfredi tells "the story of the Brunis, a family of farmers from the Italian Padan Plain who have worked the land since time immemorial. And it is a story about the homeless multitudes, travelers, and tinkers, roaming Europe during the hardscrabble nineteen-twenties and thirties . . . [T]hese two worlds meet when the Brunis open their great barn and offer it as a refuge for those in need of a warm, dry, and safe place to sleep and eat, [and] the barn becomes font and inspiration for a series of vivid stories involving sundry strangers." (Amazon)

Manfredo, Lou

Rizzo's daughter; Lou Manfredo. Minotaur Books 2012 292 p. (hardback) $25.99

ISBN 0312538073; 9780312538071; 9781429940764

LC 2011041004

This book follows "a burned-out cop [who] can't quit because he's also a devoted dad. NYPD Det. Sgt. Joe Rizzo . . . suspects he's been on the job too long. It's not that he's lost effectiveness. . . . It's just that time and bitter experience have rubbed off the gloss since the days when he loved being a cop, replacing it with a pervasive existential heaviness . . . For a while now Rizzo has been promising his wife Jen that resignation is just around the corner, a plan that seems eminently feasible until suddenly it isn't. Carol Rizzo, their youngest daughter, announces . . . she too has opted for blue. . . . Carol's choice, however, means that seasoned, savvy Rizzo must stay on in order to protect his beloved child as much as possible. But how much will that be?" (Kirkus Reviews)

Manfredo, Lou

Rizzo's fire; Lou Manfredo. Minotaur Books 2011 292p.

ISBN 9780312538064; 9781250001641

LC 2010040693

This book tells the story of "Brooklyn Det. Sgt. Joe Rizzo, . . . a battle-hardened veteran nearing retirement with a zen approach to his work . . . [who] has a new detective partner, Priscilla Jackson, a lesbian African-American. . . . The pair start investigating the strangling homicide of ex-shoe clerk Robert Lauria. Lauria's death may be connected with a similar killing of a Pulitzer Prize-winning playwright." The book also chronicles the detectives' personal troubles: "Jackson's estranged from her mother, who cut her off over her sexual preference, while one of Rizzo's daughters wants to join the force against his wishes." (Publishers Weekly)

Manicka, Rani

The **rice** mother. Viking 2003 432p $24.95

ISBN 0-670-03192-5

LC 2002-32421

"When 14-year-old Lakshmi marries a widower of 37, she believes that she is leaving her Sri Lankan village for a life of luxury in Malaysia. Instead, she endures hardship and poverty, giving birth to six children in the years before the Japanese invasion of World War II. In this gripping multigenerational saga, the tumultuous history of Malaysia becomes the backdrop for Lakshmi's indomitable spirit. The barbarity of the Japanese, postwar prosperity, the bursting of the Southeast Asian financial bubble, the vice trades of opium, gambling, and sex—all take their toll on Lakshmi's children and grandchildren." Libr J

Mankell, Henning, 1948-

Dogs of Riga; a Kurt Wallander mystery. translated by Laurie Thompson. Norton 2003 326p $24.95

ISBN 1-56584-787-2

LC 2002-30503

Original Swedish edition, 1992

"Set against the chaotic backdrop of eastern Europe after the fall of the Berlin Wall, Mankell's intense, accomplished mystery, the last in his Kurt Wallander series. . . explores one man's struggle to find truth and justice in a society increasingly bereft of either. Here the provincial Swedish detective takes on a probably fruitless task: investigating the murders of two unidentified men washed up on the Swedish coast in an inflatable dinghy." Publ Wkly

Mankell, Henning

The **eye** of the leopard; translated from the Swedish by Steven T. Murray. New Press 2008 315p $26.95

ISBN 978-1-59558-077-1; 1-59558-077-8

LC 2008-299522

Original Swedish edition, 1990

"The story revolves around a young Swede, Hans Olofson, who flies to Zambia in the 1970s in search of himself and to fulfil the quest of a dead friend. For lack of anything better to do, Olofson finds himself taking over the running of an upcountry egg farm. Intending to stay weeks, 20 years pass before he finally manages to extricate himself. . . . Where his white farmer neighbours only speak to blacks when giving orders, he tries to befriend them, provides materials to improve their homes, builds a school, takes a woman called Joyce and her daughters under his care and tries a number of other ways to break down the barriers that stand between himself and the people around him. But in a tense tale whose violence and uneasiness contrast to great effect with Olofson's deadpan narrative tone and Mankell's spare prose, it is made clear that there are no easy fixes, no quick ways to remedy the situation. Olofson escapes the gruesome fate of his neighbours, whose butchered corpses he finds, but he cannot escape his own despair." Spectator

Mankell, Henning

Firewall; translated by Ebba Segerberg. New Press (NY) 2002 405p $25.95

ISBN 1-56584-767-9

LC 2002-25543

Original Swedish editon, 1998

A mystery featuring Swedish police inspector Kurt Wallander. A "criminal mastermind is about to press the button and send the global financial network into free fall when his partner is murdered, giving Wallander a window of opportunity to scotch this mischief and let us use our A.T.M.'s again. Although things get pretty tense at the end in Ebba Segerberg's well-paced translation, this a thinking man's thriller bearing the messsage that no infernal machine is a match for a decent man with a sense of good and evil." N Y Times Book Rev

Mankell, Henning, 1948-

The **man** from Beijing; translated from the Swedish by Laurie Thompson. Alfred A. Knopf 2010 366p $25.95

ISBN 0-307-27186-2; 978-0-307-27186-0

LC 2009-45198

Original Swedish edition, 2008

This novel "opens with the discovery of 19 dead and disfigured bodies in the fictional town of Hesjovallen. . . . The local police uncover exactly two clues: The victims appear to be distantly related, and someone dropped a red ribbon in the adjoining woods." (N Y Times Book Rev)

"A sweepingly ambitious tale of corruption, injustice and revenge that ranges over three continents and 140 years. . . . Breathtakingly bold in its scope. If Mankell never links his far-flung, multigenerational horrors closely together, that's an important part of his point." Kirkus

Mankell, Henning

The **man** who smiled; a Kurt Wallander mystery. translated from the Swedish by Laurie Thompson. New Press 2006 325p $24.95

ISBN 978-1-56584-993-8; 1-56584-993-0

LC 2006-21925

Original Swedish edition, 1994; this translation first published 2005 in the United Kingdom

"When the bleak landscapes of Henning Mankell's Swedish police procedurals start to look like home, it's time to head for the hills. Either that, or confront the grim truths about modern society that give weight to this author's absorbing but disquieting existential mysteries." N Y Times Book Rev

Mankell, Henning, 1948-

★ **One** step behind; translated by Ebba Segerberg. New Press (NY) 2002 408p $24.95

ISBN 1-56584-652-4

LC 2001-34254

Original Swedish edition, 1997

This is a "Swedish police prodedural which features a conscience-driven detective named Kurt Wallander who works out of the port city of Ystad. . . . {The case is} the meticulously staged homicide of three friends who costumed themselves as 18th-century bacchants and went into the woods on Midsummer's Eve to party. When a murdered police officer is implicated in the widening investigation, Wallander suspects internal corruption." (N Y Times Book Rev)

This mystery, featuring chief Inspector Kurt Wallander of the Ystad, Sweden police turns on the "meticulously staged homicide of three friends who costumed themselves as 18th-century bacchants and went into the woods on Midsummer's Eve to party. When a murdered police officer is implicated in the widening investigation, Wallander suspects internal corruption. . . . The sweep and complexity of Mankell's plot are reason enough for tackling this dense book, thoughtfully translated by Ebba Segerberg. But his meditations on surprising subjects like time travel and 'man's relationship to monsters' make him something special." N Y Times Book Rev

Mankell, Henning

★ The **return** of the dancing master; translated by Laurie Thompson. New Press 2004 391p $24.95

ISBN 1-56584-860-8

Original Swedish edition, 2000

"With its expansive time frame and meticulous procedural details, the story (as translated by Laurie Thompson) has a density that demands–and rewards–intellectual involvement." N Y Times Book Rev

Mankell, Henning

The **troubled** man; translated from the Swedish by Laurie Thompson. Knopf 2011 367p $26.95

ISBN 978-0-307-59349-8; 0-307-59349-5

LC 2010-49169

Original Swedish edition, 2009

Not only does this novel "widen the scope of the detective's investigations into the world of international geopolitics and the relationship of Sweden to the United States and Russia, it is a work of genuine heft and substance, a melancholy, elegiac book that is thoughtful and perceptive about memory, regret and the unfathomability of human nature." PopMatters

Mann, Thomas, 1875-1955

The **black** swan; translated from the German by Willard R. Trask. Knopf 1954 141p

LC 90-38617

Original German edition, 1953; this is a reissue of the 1954 Knopf edition

Tragic psychological tale of a middle-aged German widow's passion for the young American tutor of her son

In this novelette Mann "returns to the compact dimensions and to the subject matter of Death in Venice (transposed into heterosexual terms)—the infatuation of an aging person for a young one. The current novella—though it is not nearly as memorable a piece of storytelling as the masterpiece of 1913—is a provocative addition to Mann's writings." Atlantic

Mann, Thomas

★ **Buddenbrooks**; the decline of a family. translated from the German by John E. Woods. Knopf 1993 648p

ISBN 0-679-41994-2

LC 92-18990

Original German edition, 1901. First United States edition translated by H. T. Lowe-Potter published 1924 in two volumes

"Mann's first novel, it expressed the ambivalence of his feelings about the value of the life of the artist as opposed to ordinary, bourgeois life. The novel is the saga of the fall of the Buddenbrooks, a family of merchants, from the pinnacle of their material wealth in 1835 to their extinction in 1877." Merriam-Webster's Ency of Lit

Mann, Thomas

Confessions of Felix Krull, confidence man; the early years. translated from the German by Denver Lindley. Knopf 1955 384p

Originally written as a short story in 1921; this novel was first published 1954 in Germany

"Krull, a charming young man with absolutely no moral awareness, avoids military service and takes a job in a hotel. This begins a series of erotic and criminal escapades that eventually lead the young man to prison, from where he purportedly writes his confessions. Like many of Mann's characters, Krull represents the artist, and his profession indicates the symbolic connection in Mann's mind between the artist and the actor, or charlatan." Reader's Ency. 3d edition

Mann, Thomas

★ **Death** in Venice; translated from the German by Kenneth Burke. Knopf 1965 118p

Original German edition, 1913; this translation first published 1925 as the title novella of a collection

"Gustav von Aschenbach, the hero, is a successful author, proud of the self-discipline with which he has ordered his life and work. On a trip to Venice, however, he becomes aware of mysterious decadent potentialities in himself, and he finally succumbs to a consuming love for a frail but beautiful Polish boy named Tadzio. Though he learns that there is danger of a cholera epidemic in Venice, he finds he cannot leave the city, and eventually dies of the disease. The story is permeated by a rich and varied symbolism with frequent overtones from Greek literature and mythology." Reader's Ency. 4th edition

Mann, Thomas

Death in Venice and other tales; translated from German by Joachim Neugroschel. Viking 1998 366p

ISBN 0-670-87424-8

LC 98-2803

Mann, Thomas, 1875-1955

Doctor Faustus; translated from the German by John E. Woods. Knopf 1997 534p

ISBN 0-375-40054-0

LC 97-2818

A new translation of the novel originally published 1947 in German; first English translation by H. T. Lowe-Parker published 1948

In this novel "the intense and tragic career of the hero Adrian Leverkühn, a composer, is made to parallel the collapse of Germany in World War II. To achieve this end, Mann employs the device of having another character, Serenus Zeitblom, narrate Leverkühn's story from memory, while the war is going on, and intersperse his narrative with remarks about the present situation. In this way, it is implied that it is the same demonic and always potentially destructive energy inherent in Leverkühn's music that is also, on a larger scale, behind the outburst of Nazism. Mann thus suggests that the violent 'Faustian' drive, when it is not diverted into art, or when there is no single artistic genius to harness it into creative process, will be perverted and result in grossly sub-human degradation." Reader's Ency. 4th edition

Mann, Thomas

Joseph and his brothers; translated from the German by H. T. Lowe-Porter; with a new introduction by the author. Knopf 1948 xxi, 1207p $65

ISBN 0-394-43132-4

An omnibus edition of the author's tetralogy based on the Biblical story of Joseph

The tales of Jacob (1933; first United States edition 1934 with title: Joseph and his brothers) is mainly the story of Jacob. It describes his long service with Laban, the deception by which Leah was palmed off on Jacob in place of Rachel, the birth of Leah's sons, and of Rachel's death in childbirth

In these tales Mann has expanded upon "the original story tremendously, but most of the added episodes contribute not so much to the tale itself as to the characters' depth and symbolic significance. In its overall attitude, the 'Joseph' tetralogy is neither ambiguous like 'The Magic Mountain' nor tragic like 'Doktor Faustus,' but unqualifiedly redemptive." Reader's Ency. 4th edition

Mann, Thomas

★ The **magic** mountain; a novel. translated from the German by John E. Woods. Knopf 1995 706p

ISBN 0-679-44183-2

LC 94-42885

Original German edition, 1924

This novel "tells the story of Hans Castorp, a young German engineer, who goes to visit a cousin in a tuberculosis sanatorium in the mountains of Davos, Switz. Castorp discovers that he has symptoms of the disease and remains at the sanatorium for seven years, until the outbreak of World War I. During this time, he abandons his normal life to submit to the rich seductions of disease, introspection, and death. Through talking with other patients, he gradually becomes aware of and absorbs the predominant political, cultural, and scientific ideas of 20th-century Europe. The sanatorium comes to be the spiritual reflection of the possibilities and dangers of the actual world away from the magic mountain" Merriam-Webster's Ency of Lit

Mann, Thomas

Six early stories; translated from the German with a note by Peter Constantine; edited with an introduction by Burton Pike. Sun & Moon Press 1997 128p

ISBN 1-55713-298-4

"These newly translated stories give insight into the still-forming mind of the Nobel laureate, revealing his philosophical and literary influences as well as demonstrating the uninhibited experimentation of a young, romantic writer." Publ Wkly

Mann, Thomas

Stories of three decades; translated from the German by H. T. Lowe-Porter. Knopf 1936 567p

The novellas are psychological studies. Tonio Kröger is concerned with the struggle between the artist and normal citizen. Tristan's concern deals with music's irrational and frequently destructive powers. Death in Venice is entered separately

Mansbach, Adam

The **end** of the Jews; a novel. Spiegel & Grau 2008 310p $23.95

ISBN 978-0-385-52044-7; 0-385-52044-1

LC 2007-19465

"Mansbach narrates in a syncopated style, moving back and forth among Tristan, Nina and Tris until the three stories finally merge at the novel's conclusion. His writing is adjective-happy and sometimes ungainly, but it charms with an almost goofy persistence." N Y Times Book Rev

Mansbach, Adam

Rage is back; Adam Mansbach. Viking 2012 304 p. $26.95

ISBN 0670026123; 9780670026128

LC 2012019123

In this novel by Adam Mansbach "Dondi Vance is the son of two famous graffiti artists from New York City's 'golden era' of subway bombing. . . . [and is] immune to rumors that his long-lost father, Billy Rage, has returned after sixteen years on the lam. . . . Anastacio Bracken, the transit cop who ruined Billy's life and shattered his crew back in 1987, is running for mayor. Only by rallying the forgotten writers of the eighties . . . can Billy and Dondi bring Bracken down." (Publisher's note)

Mansbach, Adam

Shackling water. Doubleday 2002 232p

ISBN 0-385-50205-2

LC 2001-47398

This novel "about an aspiring saxophonist in Harlem . . . introduces us to Latif James-Pearson, an 18-year-old from Boston who moves to New York to hone his chops and, ultimately, to meet his idol, the jazz aristocrat Albert Van Horn. Along the way, Latif faces a series of tests through a relationship with an older white woman, a jazz-club job dealing drugs and eventually an addiction to them; he loses touch with both his music and himself before a tragedy shocks him back to life." N Y Times Book Rev

"This bold, resonant portrait of the artist as a young man isn't flawless, but Mansbach's eloquence and energy are unwavering." Booklist

Manseau, Peter

Songs for the butcher's daughter; a novel. Free Press 2008 370p $25

ISBN 978-1-4165-3870-7; 1-4165-3870-4

LC 2007-49787

This is "the story of fictional Yiddish poet Itsik Malpesh, born in the Moldovan city of Kishinev in 1903. Itsik's story is told through his Yiddish memoirs, which he helps a young American Catholic . . . translate. Inspired by the image of Sasha, the brave butcher's daughter who was present at his birth, Itsik reaches America in young adulthood through haphazard luck, a taste for troublemaking and the inventiveness of a printer. Sasha continually inspires and confounds Itsik throughout his life, becoming an apt symbol for Yiddish humor, sorrow and idealism. As Itsik's darkly picaresque immigrant narrative unfolds, it competes with the translator's modern romance and with insights into the art of translation and the history of Yiddish. Occasional narrative missteps are not enough to undercut this rich, often ironic homage to Yiddish culture and language." Publ Wkly

Mansfield, Katherine

The garden party and other stories. Knopf 1991 xxxv, 267p

LC 91-53004

Mansfield, Katherine

★ The short stories of Katherine Mansfield. Knopf 1937 688p $22.95

ISBN 0-394-44532-5

"In this comprehensive edition Katherine Mansfield's stories are arranged approximately in chronological order." Introduction

Mantel, Hilary, 1952-

Beyond black. Henry Holt & Co. 2005 365p $26

ISBN 0-00-715775-4

LC 2004-63589

"A paragon of efficiency, well-schooled in the mundane tasks of an average existence, Colette took the next natural step after finishing secretarial school–marrying a man who would do just fine. After a sobering do-it-yourself divorce, Colette, for the first time, is at a loss as to what to do next. Convinced that she deserves a life-affirming revelation, she strays into the world of psychics and clairvoyants. . . . At a psychic fair in Windsor she sneaks into Alison's show. Alison, beleaguered by spirits since early childhood, lives in a different kind of solitude. She can never escape the dead who speak to her, and the physical pain of their broken bodies–least of all the constance presence of Morris, her low-life spiritual guide." Publisher's note

"This is, I think, a great comic novel. Hilary Mantel's humor, like Flannery O'Connor's, is so far beyond black it becomes a kind of light." N Y Times Book Rev

Mantel, Hilary, 1952-

★ Bring up the bodies; a novel. Hilary Mantel. Henry Holt and Co. 2012 xvii, 410 p.p $28

ISBN 0805090037; 9780805090031

LC 2012006335

Sequel to: Wolf Hall
Costa Novel Award Winner 2012

This biographical historical novel by Hilary Mantel, winner of the 2012 Man Booker Prize, tells how "[Thomas] Cromwell helped Henry annul his marriage to his wife of 20 years, Catherine, so he could marry the younger Anne Boleyn. But three years later, Anne has committed two fatal errors: she hasn't given the king a son, and she has become outspoken. Henry's eyes are on a younger, more placid woman, Jane Seymour. He wants to be rid of Anne, and it is up to Cromwell to see that Henry gets what he wants." (Library Journal)

Mantel, Hilary, 1952-

Wolf Hall; a novel. Henry Holt and Co. 2009 532p $27

ISBN 978-0-8050-8068-1; 0-8050-8068-6

LC 2009-19912

This novel depicts the world of Henry VIII. "England in the 1520s is a heartbeat from disaster. If the king dies without a male heir, the country could be destroyed by civil war. Henry VIII wants to annul his marriage of twenty years, and marry Anne Boleyn. The pope and most of Europe opposes him. The quest for the king's freedom destroys his adviser, the brilliant Cardinal Wolsey, and leaves a power vacuum. Into this impasse steps Thomas Cromwell. Cromwell is a . . . consummate politician, hardened by his personal losses, implacable in his ambition. But Henry is volatile: one day tender, one day murderous. Cromwell helps him break the opposition, but what will be the price of his triumph?" (Publisher's note)

"Set in 16th-century Tudor England, Wolf Hall thrusts the reader into Henry VIII's seething court, where the players include Anne Boleyn, her sister Mary, Cardinal Wolsey, Thomas More and Jane Seymour. At the book's center: Thomas Cromwell, the ruthless blacksmith's son who rose to power under Henry VIII because of his intelligence, cunning and work ethic. . . . Mantel's novel is less about Henry's sex life and more about power: how to get it, wield it, keep it, particularly if you — like the lowborn Cromwell — lived in a merciless world ruled by the rich and titled. Cromwell usually is presented as a bully utterly lacking scruples, but Mantel's Cromwell is a sympathetic character modern readers will understand." USA Today

Mapson, Jo-Ann

Bad Girl Creek; a novel. Simon & Schuster 2001 381p

ISBN 0-7432-0256-2

LC 2001-27006

"Phoebe DeThomas has lived carefully all her life. Thirty-eight years old and in a wheelchair because of a bad heart, she's always felt dwarfed by her flamboyant aunt Sadie and her successful brother James. Now Sadie has died, bequeathing her a flower farm on California's Central Coast. In order to make a go of it, Phoebe takes in three women as boarder/farmhands. Each of the three is 'homeless,' having recently undergone traumatic life changes: Ness, a black cowgirl with a horse and a secret fear that she has AIDS, has lost her job; Nance, a down-on-her-luck Southern belle, has broken up with her boyfriend; and Beryl, a former kindergarten aide with a prison record, has been evicted from her apartment. . . . Mapson combines poignancy with the good-natured banter of girlfriends in her tale of women in transition, waiting to be reborn." Publ Wkly

Mapson, Jo-Ann

Loving Chloe; a novel. HarperCollins Pubs. 1998 347p

ISBN 0-06-017217-7

LC 97-20578

"Mapson knows her territory intimately, and she populates it with memorable characters who readily engage our emotions. Her dialogue is earthy and funny, her setting evocative, her portrayal of good people facing difficult choices compassionate." N Y Times Book Rev

Mapson, Jo-Ann

Solomon's oak; a novel. Bloomsbury 2010 374p $25

ISBN 978-1-608-19330-1; 1-608-19330-6

LC 2010-09792

"Mapson's three damaged souls, and the ghosts in their lives, are able to find in each other just the thing to make life worth living. A tender portrayal of those left behind in the wake of tragedy." Kirkus

Marcantel, Pamela

An **army** of angels; a novel of Joan of Arc. St. Martin's Press 1997 578p

ISBN 0-312-15030-X

LC 96-31791

"In this historical novel, Marcantel resurrects the mysterious Jehanne, the Maid of Orleans, whose devotion to God led her to be burned at the stake for witchcraft before she is 20. Jehanne's visions and voices influenced her at an early age to leave her village and fulfill God's will. Guided to the future King of France, Charles VII, the peasant Jehanne persuades him to give her an army to recapture French lands from Henry VI's England." Libr J

March, William

The **bad** seed. Rinehart 1954 247p

"Rhoda Penmark at 8 years of age had a mind of her own and a will to match. Aged people doted on her splendid manners, but rogues knew her as one of themselves while older children were afraid of her. Christine, her mother suddenly discovers her daughter's horrible tendencies and also finds out that she is the murderess of two people who stood in her way. Christine resolves to check back and finds that she had been adopted and that the mother she had never known had also been a successful killer. Christine tries to stop the pattern in her daughter, but in the process dies herself." Libr J

Marcus, Ben

The **flame** alphabet; Ben Marcus. Alfred A. Knopf 2012 289 p. $25.95

ISBN 9780307739971; 030737937X; 9780307379375

LC 2011936249

In this book, "a terrible epidemic has descended: whenever children speak, adults sicken and eventually die. At first, only Jewish families are stricken, stirring echoes of history's uglier sentiments. But soon every adult is affected. Near death . . . Claire still longs for daughter Esther, a standard-issue obnoxious teenager who's hardened with the knowledge of her power. . . . But what terrifies Esther's . . . father, Sam, is that soon Esther will be an adult." (Library Journal)

Margolin, Phillip

After dark. Doubleday 1995 340p

ISBN 0-385-47548-9

LC 94-41997

"The reversals and revelations are many and diabolically clever. . . . No legal-triller fan, once hooked, will wiggle free of the story line of this hammy but exciting yarn before reaching its utterly surprising, and surprisingly dark, conclusion." Publ Wkly

Margolin, Phillip

The **burning** man. Doubleday 1996 344p

ISBN 0-385-48053-9

LC 96-12093

This novel "is set in Eastern Oregon, where a mildly retarded man is charged with the brutal slaying of a young woman. His lawyer, having never tried a capital crime case before, fumbles badly, but a glimmer of native wit gets him back on track. Working the genre with a discipline some popular authors have begun to ignore, Margolin relies on a few crafty stereotypes to keep up the pace and simplify

LIST OF FICTIONAL WORKS

the action. The dialogs in the jailhouse and the interrogation scenes, though, are intense and fierce. The moral zigzags of desperate people are laid out to contrast with the lawyer and his client as they feint and weave to avoid the ultimate penalty." Libr J

Margolin, Phillip

Fugitive; a novel. HarperCollins 2009 344p $26.99

ISBN 978-0-06-123623-5; 0-06-123623-3

LC 2008-50713

"When the editor-in-chief of World News magazine offers Amanda Jaffe a $500,000 retainer to defend Charlie Marsh, an ex-con turned bestselling spiritual guru, in . . . [this] fourth thriller to feature the Portland, Ore., lawyer . . . ., Amanda can't say no. Marsh, who fled the country in 1997 after being accused of murdering Congressman Arnold Pope Jr., has spent the 12 years since in the African country of Batanga 'under the protection of its benevolent ruler,' Jean-Claude Baptiste, whose threat to kill Marsh for sleeping with his favorite wife has prompted Marsh to return to the U.S. to stand trial." Publ Wkly

"The pages fly in this violent, twisty tale of one man's journey through the legal system." Libr J

Margolin, Phillip

Wild justice. HarperCollins Pubs. 2000 332p

ISBN 0-06-019624-6

LC 00-24351

"The plot is straightforward enough: a serial killer is torturing and murdering people seemingly at random, and investigators scramble to stop the psychopath. . . . There are not one but two prime suspects—Dr. Vincent Cardoni, a prominent surgeon, and Dr. Justine Castle, Cardoni's estranged wife. Each accuses the other of a frame-up, and Amanda Jaffe, a rather inexperienced young attorney, has to figure out which of her clients may be a murderer. A very clever thriller indeed." Booklist

Marias, Javier

All souls; translated by Margaret Jull Costa. New Directions 2000 210p pa $14.95

ISBN 978-0-8112-1453-7; 0-8112-1453-2

LC 00-55026

Original Spanish edition, 1989; this translation first published 1992 by HarperCollins

"'Oxford is, without a doubt, one of the cities of the world where the least work gets done.' So opens this arch portrait of a university town, marked by languid ennui and gossipy, semifossilized dons. The point of view is that of an unnamed visiting Spaniard scholar, whose memory flits among several eccentric people and events. Thus the recollection doesn't unfold chronologically. The reader learns early on that the Spaniard carried on a desultory affair with a don's wife, whom he met at 'High Table,' a stylized Oxfordian dinner that Marias spoofs to good effect. The personality of that wife, Clare, emerges in a discrete fashion, with dots of conversations and digressions of personal revelations that say, verily, this will not be an affair to remember. The Spaniard seems better acquainted with Cromer-Blake, a sickly professor, closet gay, and guide to Oxford's picayune atmosphere of bored superiority. Though nothing eventful occurs,

Marias' refined prose achieves an appealing characterization of place." Booklist

Marias, Javier

Dark back of time; translated from the Spanish by Esther Allen. New Directions 2001 336p il map $27.95; pa $16.95

ISBN 978-0-8112-1466-7; 0-8112-1466-4; 978-0-8112-1570-1 pa; 0-8112-1570-9 pa

LC 00-69565

Original Spanish edition, 1998

This is "by far the brainiest, most emblematic book by Marias, as well as the most demanding. . . . I'm inclined to describe the book as a meditative essay. But to pigeonhole it seems preposterous anyway, for its strength lies precisely in its amphibious, if not anarchistic, structure. This, after all, is a nonlinear opera aperta that functions as a circuitous rendezvous through the realms of knowledge and imagination. It mixes autobiography with fiction, truth with lies, so as to show the extent to which an author—Javier Marias himself—is enriched and also cursed by his oeuvre." Nation

Marias, Javier

A **heart** so white; translated from the Spanish by Margaret Jull Costa. New Directions 2000 278p $24.95; pa $14.95

ISBN 978-0-8112-1505-9; 0-8112-1452-4; 978-0-8112-1505-3 pa; 0-8112-1505-9 pa

LC 00-55021

Original Spanish edition, 1992; this translation first published 1995 in the United Kingdom

Marias is "the most subtle and gifted writer in contemporary Spanish literature." Boston Globe

Marias, Javier

★ The **man** of feeling; translated from the Spanish by Margaret Jull Costa. New Directions 2003 182p $22.95

ISBN 0-8112-1531-8

LC 2002-153935

Original Spanish edition, 1986

"While in Madrid to perform the role of Cassio in Verdi's 'Otello,' a Spanish tenor meets a man whose job is to amuse the neglected wife of a powerful Brussels banker. The paid companion invites the singer on his outings with the woman, setting the stage for an affair. . . . (This). . . would seem to offer little more than banal melodrama. Everything depends, however, on how the plot unfolds. Marias avoids a straightforward delivery in favor of a digressive narrative that moves back and forth in time. . . . This suggestive indirection perfectly suits Marias's preoccupation: the erotic imagination." N Y Times Book Rev

Marias, Javier

Voyage along the horizon; translated from the Spanish by Kristina Cordero. Believer Books 2006 182p pa $16

ISBN 1-9324164-0-4

Original Spanish edition, 1988

"An unnamed narrator ruminates on the intentions of a man (variously called Holden Branshaw and Hordern Bragshawe) who decides not to publish a novel written by an un-

651

named author who died penniless pursuing the life of that novel's subject: Victor Arledge, an author who died a recluse at age 38. The plot is pure Borges; the elongated sentences reflect nested perspectives in a manner that recalls Conrad's Heart of Darkness. The bulk of the book is devoted to the reading aloud of the novel, titled Voyage Along the Horizon; it's set around 1900 and concerns a voyage of French and English writers, Arledge among them, to Antarctica headed by an American patrician and former steamboat captain named Kerrigan. The goal—a collaborative work based on their travels—gets derailed by a variety of stock fictive plot points. The reserved 19th-century diction is flawlessly translated throughout, and Marías's joy in folly is everywhere evident." Publ Wkly

Marias, Javier

Your face tomorrow: volume one: Fever and spear; translated from the Spanish by Margaret Jull Costa. New Directions 2005 387p $24.95

ISBN 0-8112-1612-8

LC 2005-992

Original Spanish edition, 2002

The book uses "spy novel elements in order to frame certain far-ranging meditations on history, memory, and identity. The resultant effect is reminiscent of the cerebral play of Borges, the dark humor of Pynchon, and the meditative lyricism of Proust." Review of Contemporary Fiction

Marias, Javier

★ **Your** face tomorrow: volume three: Poison, shadow and farewell; translated from the Spanish by Margaret Jull Costa. New Directions 2009 546p $24.95

ISBN 978-0-8112-1812-2; 0-811-21812-0

Original Spanish edition, 2007

"Marías has concluded one of the most striking works in recent memory, giving us the cap to a philosophical espionage trilogy that could have been written by Henry James or Marcel Proust. . . . [He] weaves multi-page disquisitions on the Nationalist takeover of Spain, the collapse of the Cold War spy state and 16th century Italian art with moments of revelry involving Ian Fleming, hairnets, armpits, sex and swordplay. With an elegant, nimble translation by Margaret Jull Costa, the trilogy's 1,273 pages move right along." Los Angeles Times Book Rev

Marias, Javier

Your face tomorrow: volume two: Dance and dream; translated from the Spanish by Margaret Jull Costa. New Directions 2006 341p $24.95

ISBN 0-8112-1656-x

LC 2006-15589

Oiginal Spanish edition, 2004

"Marias's is a style of thinking more than writing. In 'Your Face Tomorrow' it is faithfully rendered by Margaret Jull Costa, his principal English translator, who achieves a rare feat: presence and near invisibility." N Y Times Book Rev

Marillier, Juliet

Daughter of the forest. TOR Bks. 2000 400p (Sevenwaters trilogy) hardcover o.p. pa $15.95

ISBN 0-312-84879-X; 0-312-87530-4 pa

LC 00-25216

"As the only daughter and youngest child of Lord Colum of Sevenwaters, Sorcha grows up protected and pampered by her six older brothers. When a sorceress's evil magic ensorcels Colum's sons, transforming them into swans, only Sorcha's efforts can break the curse. . . . The author's keen understanding of Celtic paganism and early Irish Christianity adds texture to a rich and vibrant novel that belongs in most fantasy collections." Libr J

Other titles in the Sevenwaters trilogy are:
Child of the prophecy (2002)
Son of the shadows (2001)

Marillier, Juliet

Foxmask. Tor Bks. 2004 464p $27.95

ISBN 0-7653-0674-3

LC 2003-71154

"The Norseman Eyvind becomes a Wolfskin a Viking dedicated to Thor and travels to the mystical Orkney Islands, where he meets the Princess Nessa, a seer who becomes his soul mate. As Vikings and Orkney residents work out a peace, a new generation arises to forge strong ties. A question of paternity throws the delicate balance between the two peoples in jeopardy, and some young folk set out on a journey to discover the truth. The author . . . continues her exploration of the fusion of two cultures with strong family ties and great trust in powers beyond the merely human." Libr J

Marinick, Richard

Boyos; a novel. Kate's Mystery Books 2004 274p $24.95

ISBN 1-932112-32-4

LC 2004-54843

"Set in and around 'Southie,' the South Boston working-class Irish-American enclave . . . , the story focuses on Jack 'Wacko' Curran, a rising young player in the criminal underworld. Local 'boyos' like Curran resent the steady influx of young working professionals, who are gentrifying the area and pricing the old-time residents out. Curran and his coked-out brother, Kevin, work for mob boss Marty Fallon, wholesaling drugs to a network of area dealers. Tired of giving Fallon a cut of every score, Jack dreams of replacing Fallon and figures that the bankroll from the armored-car heist he's planning will put him on his way." Publ Wkly

"The writing is gritty and serious, the action intense, and the characters well drawn and compelling despite their imperfections." Libr J

Marion, Isaac

Warm bodies; a novel. Atria Books 2011 241p pa $15

ISBN 978-1-4391-9231-3; 1-4391-9232-6

LC 2010-48583

"R, as he calls himself (the rest of his name has rotted away), is a zombie. He can't remember his former existence, can't read, can't speak more than four syllables at a time. . . Life among the undead is meaningless for him until he kills a suicidal teen leading a scavenging party and eats his brain. Zombies, in Marion's gruesome yet poetic vision, eat brains to get high on memories like those they've lost. When R consumes the teen's gray matter, he becomes infused with that boy's love for Julie Grigio, the feisty blonde accompanying him. R saves Julie from being killed by the rest of his pack and takes her back with him to their airport lair. . . . Absurd as its premise could be called, 'Warm Bodies' works on lots of levels. It's a moving romance that makes obvious allusions to Shakespeare: R is a stand-in for Romeo, and Julie for Juliet. It's a metaphor for the battle between the forces of hope and despair. And it's a paean to the power of storytelling." Seattle Times

Mark, David

The **dark** winter; David Mark. Blue Rider Press 2012 304 p. (alk. paper) $25.95

ISBN 0399158642; 9780399158643

LC 2012024256

In this book by David Mark, "a series of suspicious deaths has rocked Hull, a port city in England. . . . Detective Sergeant Aector McAvoy is sure there is a connection between these crimes, but his fellow officers are not convinced -- they would rather get a quick arrest than bother themselves with finding the true killer. . . . Compelled by his keen sense of justice, McAvoy decides to strike out alone."(Publisher's note)

Includes bibliographical references

Mark, David

Original skin; David Mark. Blue Rider Press 2013 448 p. (DS Aector McAvoy) (hardcover) $26.95

ISBN 0399158650; 9780399158650

LC 2013001237

In this book, part of author David Mark's Aector McAvoy series, "Det. Supt. Trish Pharaoh and her detectives look into the escalating attacks on Vietnamese cannabis farmers by brutal rival gangs. Meanwhile, McAvoy is distracted by the year-old apparent suicide of Simon Appleyard, a gay man who had been frequenting sex parties with his self-loathing best friend, Suzie Devlin. McAvoy believes that Suzie may be a murderer's next target, and her unique tattoos are a clue." (Publishers Weekly)

Markandaya, Kamala

Nectar in a sieve; with a new introduction by Indira Ganesan. Signet Classic 2002 190p pa $6.95

ISBN 0-451-52823-9

LC 2001-49544

First published 1954 in the United Kingdom; first United States edition published 1955 by Day

"This realistic novel of peasant life in a southern Indian village portrays the struggle that Nathan and Rukmani must make to survive. Their first child is a daughter, Irawaddy, and there follow five other children, all sons, after an interval of seven years. Hardships are innumerable and insurmountable, whether they are disasters of nature such as drought, or such manmade catastrophes as the coming of a tannery to their village and a subsequent labor conflict. After many crises, Nathan and Rukmani come to the city to seek help from one of their sons, but he has disappeared. Nathan, finally destroyed by privation, dies, believing to the end that

his life with Rukmani has been a happy one." Shapiro. Fic for Youth. 3d edition

Markovits, Anouk

I am forbidden; a novel. Anouk Markovits. Hogarth 2012 302 p.

ISBN 9780307984739

LC 2011041305

2013 Sophie Brody Medal Honor Book

In this book, "[o]rphaned during the Holocaust, two ultra-orthodox Jews bound by love and faith are driven apart by the same forces. . . . French-raised [Anouk] Markovits' . . . debut opens in Manhattan in 2005 with the meeting of two women: Atara, who . . . fled her Hasidic family to avoid an arranged marriage; and Judith, the granddaughter of Atara's adopted sister, burdened by a cataclysmic secret. Then the clock turns back to Transylvania in 1939" to trace Atara's family history. (Kirkus)

Marks, John

Fangland. Penguin Press 2007 385p $25.95

ISBN 1-59420-117-X; 978-1-59420-117-2

LC 2006-49809

Marks has "written an electrifying modern tale of horror that pays homage to Bram Stoker's Dracula. He goes much further, however, creating a hideous vampire more horrifying than anything that ever came from Stoker's imagination." Libr J

Marks, Laurie J.

Fire logic. Tor Bks. 2002 335p $25.95

ISBN 0-312-87887-7

LC 2001-58352

"Marks is an absolute master of fantasy in this book. Her characters are beautifully drawn, showing tremendous emotional depth and strength as they endure the unendurable and strive always to do the right thing." Booklist

Markson, David

The **last** novel. Shoemaker & Hoard 2007 190p pa $15

ISBN 978-1-59376-143-1; 1-59376-143-0

LC 2006-38793

"Just when one had started mourning the demise of avant-garde and postmodern fiction, buried under the avalanche of historical novels, chick lit and just plain old traditional stories, here comes David Markson's latest 'novel,' 'The Last Novel,' which is anything but a novel in any conventional sense of the term. Yet it manages to keep us enthralled during the length of its short 190-page span, and even moved to tears at the end. And what a thrill it is to witness the performance, a real tour de force." N Y Times Book Rev

Markson, David

Vanishing point; a novel. Shoemaker & Hoard 2004 191p pa $15

ISBN 1-59376-010-8 pa

"The premise is that 'The Author' as the narrator refers to himself, is assembling a box of note cards full of information he has gathered over the years with the hope of forging a novel. Life then imitates art as Markson literally accomplishes what his narrator hopes to: he creates a novel out of fragments of ideas and information. Vanishing Point feels a little like a literary Trivial Pursuit, or the associative stream of consciousness produced by a surrealist party game, and it's just as entertaining." Booklist

Markson, David

Wittgenstein's mistress. Dalkey Archive Press 1988 240p

ISBN 0-916583-25-2

LC 87-73068

"In this unsettling, shimmering novel, the reader is immediately drawn into the world of a woman who has gone mad because she is the last surviving creature on earth. Sitting at a typewriter in a beach house day after uncharted day—she keeps no calendar or clocks—she pours out her thoughts on music, art and ancient Greek legends, and remembrances of her travels across the globe in abandoned cars, looking for other living beings. But after a while, some discrepancies creep into her rambling, compelling monologue. . . . By the end of this seamless stream of consciousness, there is no distinction between fantasy and reality, past and present." Publ Wkly

Marlantes, Karl

★ **Matterhorn**; a novel of the Vietnam War. Atlantic Monthly Press; El Len Literary Arts 2010 598p il map $24.95

ISBN 978-0-8021-1928-5; 0-8021-1928-X

"Matterhorn is one of those countless hills in Vietnam that makes young men's lives so cheap. In this case, it's the Marines of Bravo Company and the hardened NVA (North Vietnamese Army) soldiers. The story revolves around a young Marine lieutenant, Waino Mellas, who must quickly learn the difference between officer candidate school and the reality of life in the bush. Lt. Mellas tries to straddle the line between being one of the guys and a platoon commander. This division between the troops and a low-ranking officer like Mellas (who is only a few years older than his men) can become too vague if he is overly friendly. In combat, that can be disastrous. The delicate balance between life and death resonates throughout Matterhorn, as it does in real combat. What is so fresh and fascinating about this novel is Marlantes' depiction of the specific activities and conflicting motivations that take place in a war zone." BookPage

Marlette, Doug

Magic time. Farrar, Straus and Giroux 2006 480p $25

ISBN 978-0-374-20001-5; 0-374-20001-7

LC 2005-36396

"Magic Time presents a realistic portrait of the collective amnesia of the South and the generational tensions that the civil rights movement stirred up, then and now. It's a real Mississippi story, not merely a faded imitation." Washington Post Book World

Marley, Louise

The **child** goddess; Louise Marley. Ace Books 2004 324p $23.95

ISBN 0441011365

LC 2003063836

This book is "set on 23rd-century Earth and the oceanic world Virimund. . . . The Magdalenes, a celibate Roman Catholic order of women priests known as Enquirers, travel the galaxy as anthropological investigators. . . . Assigned to probe Oa, a mysterious child discovered on Virimund, empathetic Isabel soon learns that Oa represents one of humanity's deepest yearnings, for the fountain of eternal youth. Torn between her forbidden love for Dr. Simon Edwards, like herself a healer, and her sacred vow of celibacy, Isabel asks Simon to help Oa escape the megaworld Extra-Solar Corporation, whose general administrator, Gretchen Boreson, has her own devious reasons to claim Oa and her few fellow 'anchens,' the abandoned children of Virimund." (Publishers Weekly)

Maron, Margaret

Bootlegger's daughter. Mysterious Press 1992 261p

LC 91-58021

This mystery takes place in "Cotton Grove, N.C., a close-knit rural community on the outskirts of Raleigh, and introduces savvy Deborah Knott, a lawyer whose singular upbringing as a child of a bootlegging power broker has prepared her well for the county race for district court judge. But just as she begins her campaign . . . Deborah is asked to turn over the dead leaves of an 18-year-old murder case. It seems that the daughter of an old flame can't start her life until she finds out who killed her mother as she watched with uncomprehending infant eyes." N Y Times Book Rev

Maron, Margaret

The **buzzard** table; Margaret Maron. Grand Central Pub. 2012 305 p. (hardcover) $25.99

ISBN 0446555827; 9780446555821

LC 2012939350

This novel, by Margaret Maron, is part of the "Deborah Knott Mystery" series. When "Lt. Sigrid Harald and her mother, Anne . . . [gather] for dinner at Mrs. Lattimore's Victorian home, they meet the enigmatic Martin Crawford. . . . When a string of suspicious murders sets Colleton County on edge, Deborah, Dwight, and Sigrid once again work together to catch a killer, uncovering long-buried family secrets along the way." (Publisher's note)

Maron, Margaret

Fugitive colors. Mysterious Press 1995 260p

LC 95-1703

"Maron adeptly establishes a coolly thematic and deceptive link among the deaths as she constructs her affecting mystery out of distinctive blend of art-world politics, past crimes and present grief." Publ Wkly

Maron, Margaret

★ **High** country fall. Mysterious Press 2004 303p $24

ISBN 0-89296-808-7

LC 2004-1953

"Deborah's narrative voice, with its engaging tone of amusement at the human foibles she witnesses in her travels, is just the ticket for this dramatic view of the spectacular Blue Ridge Mountains." N Y Times Book Rev

Maron, Margaret

Home fires burning. Mysterious Press 1998 243p $32

ISBN 0-89296-655-6

LC 98-6632

North Carolina Circuit Court Judge Deborah Knott, "who narrates, is at the start of a reelection campaign when a nephew is arrested, with two friends, for desecrating a cemetery. When the same spraypainted graffiti appears at an African American church that's been torched, the young men are suspected of arson. Two more black churches are burned and two bodies uncovered before Deborah fingers the culprit." Publ Wkly

Maron, Margaret

Killer market. Mysterious Press 1997 273p $21.50

ISBN 0-89296-654-8

LC 97-20835

"North Carolina district court judge Deborah Knott unintentionally 'crashes' several manufacturer's receptions at the internationally known Southeastern Furniture Market in High Point, where she becomes involved in murder. Initially befriended by a mysterious and elusive woman with bogus name tags, series protagonist Knott soon runs into an old woman friend from law school as well as a hunky ex-beau now in the furniture business. When Deborah later discovers the man dead, she and police begin investigating." Libr J

Maron, Margaret

Shooting at loons. Mysterious Press 1994 229p

LC 93-47141

"District Court Judge Deborah Knott, a native North Carolinian, looks forward to filling in for a sick colleague at the Harker's Island courthouse. But on her first fishing trip after arriving on the island, she discovers the body of an old fisherman known to her since childhood. . . . The down-home prose flows well, spiced by Judge Knott's wit, charm, and extended family as well as by references to the local food and drink." Libr J

Maron, Margaret

Slow dollar. Mysterious Press 2002 276p

ISBN 0-89296-764-1

LC 2002-20098

"It's opening night at Dobbs' Annual Harvest Festival, and Deborah, along with half of Colleton County North Carolina, is intent on riding the Ferris wheel, eating elephant ears, and, finally, throwing quarters at the Dozer game. When Deborah runs out of change, she steps into the interior of the game wagon, where she finds the proprietor dead on the floor, his mouth overflowing with quarters. . . . As always, the mystery takes a backseat to the engaging characters and the charming southern setting." Booklist

Maron, Margaret

Southern discomfort. Mysterious Press 1993 241p

LC 92-56770

"Maron's written a thriller that simply oozes southern charm and atmosphere. The clever plot is full of surprises— a good blend of menace, poignancy, and humor. But perhaps Maron's real strength is her refreshing heroine, who doesn't mind admitting she wears a size fourteen dress and who approaches life with humor, determination, and good sense." Booklist

Maron, Margaret

Storm track. Mysterious Press 2000 260p $28

ISBN 0-89296-656-4

LC 99-51761

"Deborah Knott, the district court judge who presides over this enchanting regional series, guides us through these crises with her customary good sense. . . . Deborah is the voice of sanity and the soul of wit." N Y Times Book Rev

Maron, Margaret

Uncommon clay. Warner Bks. 2001 288p $28

ISBN 0-89296-720-X

LC 00-66266

This mystery "does more than honor local folk art and the generations of artisans who carry on the regional heritage. It shows us how deeply these homespun crafts are rooted in the collective artistry of individual families—and what a devastating loss it is when these families die out." N Y Times Book Rev

Maron, Margaret

Up jumps the Devil. Mysterious Press 1996 278p

ISBN 978-0892965687

LC 96-7715

"As the pecan trees of the beautiful North Carolina countryside give way to tract housing, land values are escalating rapidly, and all over Colleton County, longtime neighbors and family members are engaged in acrimonious disputes over whether to sell their family land. In this . . . entry in the Deborah Knott series, the straight-talking, down-to-earth district court judge is drawn into two murders tied to greed over land-development money." Booklist

"The droll characters and their lilting regional humor seem ever more endearing because we sense their days are numbered." N Y Times Book Rev

Marr, Melissa

Graveminder. William Morrow 2011 324p $22.99

ISBN 978-0-06-182687-0; 0-06-182687-1

LC 2010-37261

"For years, Rebekkah has bounced from city to city. But when her grandmother Maylene passes away, she's drawn back to tiny Claysville and finds she's inherited more than just the family home. She's responsible for seeing that the dead stay dead. Claysville isn't a regular little hamlet. It's tied just a little too tightly to the land of the dead. To manage that connection, previous generations made a compact with the lord of the underworld, and Rebekkah returns home to find herself intimately involved in upholding that bargain. Like Maylene, she's actually the town's Graveminder, responsible for working with the Undertaker to ensure the dead stay in their tombs. Making matters even more complicated is the identity of her new partner: It's Byron Montgomery, her sometime lover and the man she just can't seem to get over, no matter how hard she tries. . . . [The author] has the rare talent of making deeply weird things seem perfectly normal, and making perfectly normal things seem deeply weird." io.9

Marra, Anthony
★ A **constellation** of vital phenomena; a novel. Anthony Marra. Hogarth 2013 400 p. $26

ISBN 0770436404; 9780770436407

LC 2012017444

This novel "intertwines the stories of a handful of characters at the end of the second, war in bleak, apocalyptic Chechnya. Though the novel spans 11 years, the story traces five days in 2004 following the arrest of Dokka, a villager from the small Muslim village of Eldar. His eight-year-old daughter escapes, and is rescued by Dokka's friend Akhmed, the village doctor, who entrusts her to the care of Sonja, the lone remaining doctor at a nearby hospital." (Publishers Weekly)

Marsh, Ngaio
Dead water. Little, Brown 1963 244p

Scotland Yard's Superintendent "Roderick Alleyn finds himself involved unofficially in magic and faith healing when his former French teacher, now a formidable lady of 80, inherits an island off the coast of Cornwall which has, as its chief claim to fame and source of income, a Pixie Well supposed to cure warts, asthma and other ills. . . . Skillful writing, convincing atmosphere, and sharply etched characterization will please Ngaio Marsh fans, but the plot is less complex than some of her others." Publ Wkly

Marsh, Ngaio
False scent. Little, Brown 1959 273p

This mystery "takes place in the opulent London home of a famous—and temperamental—actress on her 50th birthday anniversary. The flamboyant people surrounding Mary Bellamy are properly subdued only when the polished Roderick Alleyn of Scotland Yard and his capable assistant, Inspector Fox, enter the scene and uncover the ugly secrets that led to murder." Libr J

Marsh, Ngaio
Grave mistake. Little, Brown 1978 252p

LC 78-16910

"When a rich eccentric old lady in a rest home suddenly dies, friends and the police suspect murder. {Inspector} Alleyn's trail leads him to the old lady's daughter, her fiance, his father, a close friend, and a few assorted others including a Scots gardener—named Gardener! When a will turns up leaving all her money to the doctor who runs the rest home, the supposed case of suicide really becomes murder." West Coast Rev Books

Marsh, Ngaio
Last ditch. Little, Brown 1977 265p

LC 76-52287

The novel takes place on one of the Channel Islands, to which Ricky, Superintendent Roderick Alleyn's son, "has come during the Easter vacation to write a novel. Here he meets Jasper and Julia Pharamond, friends of his parents, and falls in love with the magnolia-skinned Julia. . . . A riding expedition ends in a fatal accident, attended by suspicious circumstances; at the same time Ricky stumbles, he thinks, across the tracks of a gang of drug smugglers. But Scotland Yard's attention has already been called to the island, and Chief Superintendent Alleyn and Inspector Fox are soon on their way there." Times Lit Suppl

Marsh, Ngaio
Light thickens. Little, Brown 1982 232p

LC 82-13085

"A production of Macbeth, directed by Peregrine Jay at the Dolphin Theatre, is beset with macabre incidents. During rehearsals, realistic-looking dummy heads turn up in dark corners and on banquet trays, and a rat's head is found in the witch's effects. But the incidents cease, and reviews call the production 'the flawless Macbeth'—until the night when the actor playing Macbeth is decapitated during the play. Roderick Alleyn is, of course, in the audience." Libr J

Marsh, Ngaio
When in Rome. Little, Brown 1971 260p

First published 1970 in the United Kingdom

Set in Italy, "much of the action takes place in an ancient church which reproduces three levels of civilization. . . . The mystery centers on a sinister blackmailing tour entrepreneur who gathers together a motley group of people, some innocent, some with good reason to want him out of the way. Drugs, sex orgies, even more delicate scandals are all grist to his mill and when he meets a very nasty demise the field of suspects is wide open. Not the least of the pleasures here is a charming love affair, and the slightly comic opera encounters between English Inspector Roderick Alleyn and the Rome police." Publ Wkly

Marshall, Catherine
★ **Christy**. Avon Books 2006 576p pa $6.99

ISBN 0-380-00141-1

A reissue of the title first published 1967 by McGraw-Hill

"A spirited young woman leaves the security of her home to become a teacher in Cutter Gap, Kentucky. It is 1912 and the needs of the Appalachian people are great. Christy learns much from the poverty and superstition of the mountain folk. Marshall's Christian faith and ideals are intertwined in the plot, which includes a love story." Shapiro. Fic for Youth. 3d edition

Marshall, Paule
Brown girl, brownstones; with a foreword by Edwidge Danticat; afterword by Mary Helen Washington. 2nd Feminist Press ed.; Feminist Press at the City University of New York 2006 319p pa $16.95

ISBN 1-55861-498-2; 978-1-55861-498-7

LC 2005-29191

First published 1959 by Random House

"Set in Depression-era Brooklyn, NY, this 1959 coming-of-age novel finds Selina Boyce caught in the middle of her immigrant parents. Mom wants Selina to get an American education, while dad dreams of returning to Barbados. Along with her parental woes, our heroine must deal with the poverty and racism that surrounds her." Libr J

Marshall, Paule

The **fisher** king; a novel. Scribner 2000 222p $23

ISBN 0-684-87283-8

LC 00-28470

"Story of a family in turmoil over the memory of Sonny-Rett Payne, a jazz pianist who fled the racism of New York for Paris in 1949. The action is set in the present, as Sonny's brother, Edgar, now a successful businessman in Brooklyn, organizes a memorial concert for his brother and lures Hattie Carmichael, Sonny's former lover, who lives in Paris with Sonny's grandchild, back to the States for the event. The narrative jumps from the present, as Edgar subtly attempts to gain custody of young Sonny, and the past, as Hattie remembers Sonny-Rett, his music, his wife, and their unconventional life in Paris." Booklist

"Marshall's prose is full of expert dialogue, mellifluous rhythms and sharply drawn portraits of Sonny-Rett's loved ones." N Y Times Book Rev

Marshall, Paule

Praisesong for the widow. Putnam 1983 256p

LC 82-13215

This novel "tells of a sixtyish widow, Avey Johnson, refined, well-to-do, and complacent. Troubled by strange dreams and symptoms, she cuts short her annual Caribbean cruise and disembarks on a small island. An old man recognizes her as one of the 'people who can't call their nation,' and persuades her to join him and others on their yearly ritual visit to a neighboring island they call home. There, purged of her old self, Avey rediscovers her roots." Libr J

Marston, Edward

The **Bawdy** basket. St. Martin's Minotaur 2002 262p

ISBN 0-312-28501-9

LC 2002-2510944

An Elizabethan mystery featuring "Nicholas Bracewell, stage manager of Lord Westfield's Men. . . . When a young actor's father is tried, convicted, and hung for a brutal murder he claims he did not commit, his sins are unfortunately visited upon his loyal son. Nicholas agrees to investigate the matter in an effort to clear the unlucky man's name and to restore a promising young thespian to the ranks of his beloved theater company." Booklist

Marston, Edward

The **Devil's** apprentice; a novel. St. Martin's Minotaur 2001 273p

ISBN 0-312-26574-3

LC 2001-19259

Elizabethan stage manager Nicholas Bracewell "fends off accusations of witchcraft and worse after the troupe performs at a manor house in Essex. A new apprentice taken on there seems to be at the root of the trouble. Lively and entertaining: for fans of Elizabethan historicals." Libr J

Marston, Edward

The **roaring** boy; a novel. St. Martin's Press 1995 260p

LC 95-8568

"Marston's colorful (and convincing) characterizations shine as Nicholas chases the secrets of the murder in order to save the company. The plot, except for one transparently finagled episode, is expertly wrought, with the suspense building steadily to breathtaking climax and some surprises saved for the very end." Publ Wkly

Marston, Edward

The **stallions** of Woodstock. St. Martin's Press 1999 275p

ISBN 0-312-20021-8

LC 98-50733

First published 1997 in the United Kingdom

In this installment in the author's Domesday series "Gervase Bret and Ralph Delchard, commissioners to King William the Conqueror, are sent to Oxford, England, to settle a land dispute and soon find themselves embroiled in a murder investigation." Publ Wkly

Marston, Edward

The **vagabond** clown. St. Martin's Minotaur 2003 292p $24.95

ISBN 0-312-30789-6

LC 2002-191950

"Lord Westfield's Men, the actors' troupe for which Bracewell works as stage manager, are forced to leave their theater after a violent act of sabotage trashes the place. Worse, someone has killed one of Westfield's friends during the melee. Bracewell struggles to save the troupe and its reputation. An outstanding historical." Libr J

Marston, Edward

The **wanton** angel; a novel. St. Martin's Press 1999 279p

ISBN 0-312-20391-8

LC 99-22062

This mystery, set in Elizabethan England, finds Nicholas Bracewell's "acting troupe ejected from its theater at the Queen's Head when one of the actors impregnates the landlord's daughter and is then murdered." N Y Times Book Rev

Marston, Edward

The **wildcats** of Exeter; volume VIII of the Doomesday Books. St. Martin's Minotaur 2001 275p il

ISBN 0-312-25355-9

First published 1998 in the United Kingdom

In this installment tax collectors Gervase Bret and Ralph Delchard travel to Exeter in Devon. "A land dispute, already complicated by many claimants, grows ever more so when the current owner, one Nicolas Picard, meets a grisly death. He's clawed by a wildcat but also has his throat cut. The wildcats of the title also refer to several women wronged by Nicolas, all of whom have claims to his property. Monks peevish and saintly, a jester wise in his foolery, another murder, and some marital mayhem complete the entertaining picture." Booklist

Martel, Yann

Beatrice and Virgil; a novel. Spiegel & Grau 2010 197p $24

ISBN 978-1-4000-6926-2; 1-4000-6926-2

LC 2009-48995

"The protagonist here is Henry L'Hte, an author who, having earned worldwide fame with his second novel, bears more than a passing resemblance to Martel himself. When Henry's publishers reject his convoluted idea for a book on the Holocaust, he gives up writing and passes the time answering fan mail. One letter leads him to a local taxidermist, an octogenarian who has spent decades toiling over a play about a donkey (Beatrice) and a howler monkey (Virgil) that suffer ghastly persecution by humans. Now he needs Henry's help to finish the work. Henry agrees, and soon discovers that this gruff, emotionless preserver of dead animals is attempting the very thing his publishers told him he could not: represent the Holocaust through means other than historical realism." Entertainment Wkly

"Whimsy takes a deadly serious turn in a novel that will enchant some readers and exasperate others." Kirkus

Martel, Yann

★ Life of Pi; a novel. Harcourt 2001 319p $25

ISBN 0-15-100811-6

LC 2001-39737

"An impassioned defense of zoos, a death-defying trans-Pacific sea adventure à la 'Kon-Tiki,' and a hilarious shaggy-dog story starring a four-hundred-and-fifty-pound Bengal tiger named Richard Parker: this audacious novel manages to be all of these. . . . This breezily aphoristic, unapologetically twee saga of man and cat is a convincing hands-on, how-to guide for dealing with what Pi calls, with typically understated brio, 'major lifeboat pests.'" New Yorker

Martin, Charles

Where the river ends. Broadway Books 2008 375p $19.95

ISBN 978-0-7679-2698-0; 0-7679-2698-6

LC 2007-42819

"Doss Michaels, a fishing guide and part-time artist in Charleston, SC, is willing to face possible kidnapping and other serious charges generated by his disapproving father-inlaw to fulfill his wife Abbie's last wishes for one more adventure together—a 130-mile trip down the St. Mary's River." Libr J

"This tale is a pleasure to read because it eloquently pictures unquestioning, steadfast love." Fayetteville Observer

Martin, Clancy W.

How to sell; [by] Clancy Martin. Farrar, Straus & Giroux 2009 296p $24

ISBN 978-0-374-17335-7; 0-374-17335-4

LC 2008-55450

This novel is, "with memorably dark comedy, a virtual handbook on fraud. The world the Clark boys build for themselves and teeter precariously upon . . . is a compelling setting for Martin's propulsive storytelling. His narration feels cinematic, the sets and scenery popping off the page. With remarkable skill as the story spools out, Martin omits just enough exposition and interior insights to keep his characters shrouded in mystery, as if constantly reminding us that we'll always be the customer, never the insider." Elle

Martin, George R. R.

A clash of kings. Bantam Bks. 1999 761p (Song of ice and fire) $26.95

ISBN 0-553-10803-4

LC 98-37954

"The novel is notable particularly for the lived-in quality of its world, created through abundant detail that dramatically increases narrative length even as it aids suspension of disbelief; for the comparatively modest role of magic . . . and for its magnificent action-filled climax." Publ Wkly

Martin, George R. R., 1948-

A dance with dragons. Bantam Books 2011 1016p map (Song of ice and fire) $35

ISBN 978-0-553-80147-7

LC 2011-15508

Sequel to A feast for crows (2005)

This is the fifth book in a series begun with A game of thrones (1996). New threats emerge to endanger the future of the Seven Kingdoms, as Daenerys Targaryen, ruling in the East, fights off a multitude of enemies, while Jon Snow, Lord Commander of the Night's Watch, faces his foes both in the Watch and beyond the great Wallof ice and stone.

"The heart-hammering conclusion hints that the next installment will see a return to the fiery battles and icy terror that earned the series its fanatic following. Even ostensibly disillusioned fans will be caught up in the interweaving stories, especially when Martin drops little hints around long-debated questions such as Jon's parentage." Publ Wkly

Martin, George R. R., 1948-

A feast for crows. Bantam Books 2005 753p maps (Song of ice and fire) $30

ISBN 0-553-80150-3

LC 2005-53034

The author introduces "plot twists and characters that continue to flesh out one of the genre's most detailed and intriguing worlds. A must-purchase for libraries owning the series, this panoramic fantasy adventure is highly recommended." Libr J

Martin, George R. R.

★ A game of thrones. Bantam Bks. 1996 694p il (Song of ice and fire)

LC 95-43936

The first volume in A Song of Ice and Fire saga, "combines intrigue, action, romance, and mystery in a family saga. The family is the Starks of Winterfell, a society in crisis due to climatic change that has created decades-long seasons, and a society almost without magic but with human perversity abundant and active. Martin reaches a new plateau in terms of narrative technique, action scenes, and integrating . . . his political views into the story." Booklist

Followed by A clash of kings

Martin, George R. R.

Hunter's run; [by] George R.R. Martin, Gardner Dozois, and Daniel Abraham. Eos 2008 303p $25.95

ISBN 978-0-06-137329-9; 0-06-137329-X

LC 2007-29817

"The first item of business to get out of the way is the tripartite authorship of this book. At first it seems a rather circuslike distraction that, however, has actually resulted in a superb fusion of talents. . . . The book reads like the work of one melded intelligence, seamless and organic. In Ramón, the authors have created an appallingly attractive antihero straight out of Leigh Brackett's canon. His rough-and-tumble progress from unknowingness to self-awareness is handled deftly all the way." SciFi Wkly

Martin, Lee

Break the skin; a novel. Crown 2011 275p $24

ISBN 978-0-307-71675-0; 0-307-71675-9

LC 2011-03329

Martin "gets the claustrophobia of small town life just right. With their oh-what-might-have-been voices, these women win our hearts, even as we long to give them a kick in the behind." Cleveland Plain Dealer

Martin, Lee

The bright forever; a novel. Lee Martin. Shaye Areheart Books 2005 269p. o.p.; (pbk.) $14.00

ISBN 1400097916; 9780307209863

LC 2004023758

In this book, "Katie Mackey is nine and lives with older brother Gilley and her parents in the small town of Tower Hill, Ind[iana]. . . . On the other side of the tracks is Henry Dees, a lonely bachelor and math teacher, who is Katie's private tutor this summer of 1972. His neighbor is the equally lonely widow, Clare Mains, who has taken up with the self-styled Raymond R., a new arrival and, like Dees, victim of a grim childhood. . . . Then, on a perfect summer evening, Katie disappears. . . . The searchers for Katie feel burdened by 'the weight of all their sins.' Small wonder, then, that in time Katie's murder will lead to vigilante justice and another missing body." (Kirkus)

Martin, Malachi

Vatican; a novel. Harper & Row 1986 657p

ISBN 0-06-015478-0

LC 85-42645

The author "compresses the history of the modern Roman Catholic church into . . . the 40 years since World War II. Its focus is the highly secret inner workings of the Vatican State in Rome, a religious and political bureaucracy that affects not only its members but also individuals and events around the world. The novel opens with the arrival in Rome of Richard Lansing, who at age 24 is the youngest ranking monsignor in the powerful archdiocese of Chicago. We watch as he develops from a politically naive but dedicated religious into a papal emissary and eventually into the highest ranking leader of the Catholic church. . . . This authentic depiction of the world's richest, most powerful religion will stun readers with its revelations and intrigue them with its multitextured plot." Booklist

Martin, Malachi

Windswept House; a Vatican novel. Doubleday 1996 646p

ISBN 978-0385484084

LC 95-26716

This novel about the Catholic Church in crisis focuses on the "conflict between two American brothers—one a priest, one a lawyer, both heirs to a fortune and to the family manse of Windswept House. . . . {As he develops his plot} . . . Martin's concern is what he sees as the erosion of the Church's moral authority, both from within and without. Here, a Slavic pope who's obviously John Paul II is being maneuvered into approving the Resignation Protocol, which, if enacted, will force him to resign in the name of Church unity. Martin attributes this erosion to a global conspiracy among world powers both East and West, fueled by Satanic influence and by the failure of John Paul XXIII to act upon the Third Prophecy of the Fatima Letter in 1960. The narrative is richly detailed with Church lore." Publ Wkly

Martin, Steve

An object of beauty; a novel. Grand Central Pub. 2010 295p il $26.99

ISBN 978-0-446-57364-1; 0-446-57364-7

LC 2010-07885

"For all her charisma, the ruthlessly self-serving Lacey is not inherently a creature of much emotional heft or warmth. Still, Martin has a gift for rendering an esoteric scene accessible, piercing its sillier pretensions while making a case for art's real aesthetic (if not monetary) value. It takes a certain nimbleness to play the dual roles of proxy art-history professor and compelling storyteller without falling off the literary balance beam. Martin, wry, wise, and keenly observant, rarely misses a step." Entertainment Wkly

Martin, Steve

The pleasure of my company; a novella. Hyperion 2003 163p $19.95

ISBN 0-7868-6921-6

LC 2003-49954

This work features "one of the odder yet more charming protagonists in recent fiction, Daniel Pecan Cambridge, a gentle soul suffering from a mild mix of autism and obsessive-compulsive disorder. Daniel, 33, lives in a rundown Santa Monica apartment, his life constricted by an armor of defensive habit. . . his dull days punctuated only by imagined romances and visits by his student social worker, lovely and kind Clarissa. Daniel's ways (a product of child abuse, Martin shows with subtlety) are challenged when Clarissa and her infant son, Teddy, move in to escape an abusive husband. . . . This novella is a delight, embodying a satisfying story arc, a jeweler's eye for detail, intelligent pacing and a clean, sturdy prose style." Publ Wkly

Martin, Steve

★ Shopgirl; a novella. Hyperion 2000 130p

ISBN 0-7868-6658-6

LC 00-38874

The main characters in this novella are Mirabelle Butterfield, "a 28-year-old woman behind the glove counter at the Neiman Marcus department store in Beverly Hills . . .

{and} Ray Porter, the fiftysomething man Mirabelle admits into her solitary life." Time

Martin, Valerie

The **confessions** of Edward Day; a novel. Nan A. Talese 2009 286p $25

ISBN 978-0-385-52584-8; 0-385-52584-2

LC 2008-44965

This novel recreates "the New York theater world of the 1970s and '80s. What seems quaint now — onstage nudity — was brand-new then, and the group of acting students in the novel is smack dab in the middle of the whole scene, which includes favorite bars and escapes to the Jersey Shore. On one such escapee, Edward, a young actor fresh from a successful seduction of the lovely Madeleine, goes for a late-night walk and falls into the sea. Guy Margate, a fellow actor, rescues him, setting up an everlasting debt which Edward can hardly repay. . . . After his dramatic rescue of Edward, Guy uses every opportunity to wrest payment from him, sometimes by asking for money, sometimes by appropriating Madeleine's wandering affections. She is the weakest link in the novel, having little will of her own. Guy and Edward pass her back and forth until matters escalate to a horrific and very theatrical climax." Seattle Times

Martin, Valerie

Italian fever; a novel. Knopf 1999 259p $22

ISBN 0-375-40542-9

LC 98-31824

"When Lucy Stark's employer falls inelegantly down a well in Tuscany, Lucy must travel there to see that he's given a decent burial. Not surprisingly, within a day she has contracted the kind of gruesome fever that makes you revel in your own health, and she has encountered the kind of Italian lover that makes you book the next flight over. What lingers in the mind, though, is the novel's final touching twist, which slyly dismantles its own satire and casts a long and mysterious shadow over everything that has come before." New Yorker

Martin, Valerie

★ **Mary** Reilly. Doubleday 1990 263p

LC 89-38313

"Whereas the atmosphere of Robert Louis Stevenson's tale was all foggy nights and sinister uncertainties, Mary Reilly weaves a somewhat more ambiguous but equally gripping web of mystery around the same riveting events. In both cases the end product is a fascinating story." Quill Quire

Martin, Valerie

Property. Talese 2003 196p $23.95

ISBN 0-385-50408-X

LC 2002-66846

This work "presents itself as a novel about the abuse of power within the loveless marriage between an antebellum plantation owner and his wife, their private suffering amplified by the social context of slavery. Bondage and its invitation to brutality are not unexplored terrain, but embedded within what might be mistaken as a morality play is a more subtle and compelling story—a contest of wills between two women, Manon Gaudet and Sarah, the slave she received from her aunt as a wedding gift." N Y Times Book Rev

Martin, Valerie

Trespass; a novel. Nan A. Talese/Doubleday 2007 288p $25

ISBN 0-385-51545-6; 978-0-385-51545-0

LC 2006-101676

"Chloe Dale's life is in good order. Her only child, Toby, has started his junior year at New York University; her husband, an academic on sabbatical, is working at home on his book about the Crusades; and Chloe is busy creating illustrations for a special edition of Emily Brontë's Wuthering Heights. Yet Chloe is disturbed—by the aggression of her government's foreign policy, by the poacher who roams the land behind her studio punctuating her solitude with rifle fire, and finally, by Toby's new girlfriend, a Croatian refugee named Salome Drago." (Publisher's note)

The novel "provides a searing commentary on the human desire to set boundary lines against threats, perceived and real. It's a testament to Martin's skill as both storyteller and writer that her complex characters defy separation into two camps those who accept and those who judge. Nothing in 'Trespass' is quite as it seems, and that is precisely the point." San Francisco Chronicle

Martin, William

Annapolis. Warner Bks. 1996 685p

ISBN 978-0446515115

LC 96-1021

"A storyteller whose smoothness equals his ambition, Martin has written a panoramic entertainment that brings to vivid life the history of the American struggle to control the high seas." Publ Wkly

Martin, William

Cape Cod. Warner Bks. 1991 652p

LC 90-50534

"Martin embraces the entire sweep of American history with unflagging relish for authentic detail and private moments. He creates generation after generation of feisty Hilyards and cruel Bigelows, pitting them against one another in religious and political skirmishes and joining them in risky love. They endure hardships and shipwrecks, scandal and imprisonment, shame and anger, and contribute their bit to the making of America." Booklist

Martin, William

Harvard Yard. Warner Bks. 2003 580p map $25.95

ISBN 0-446-53084-0

LC 2003-12329

"When antiquarian bookseller Peter Fallon follows the clues he hopes will lead him to recover a lost Shakespeare play written in the bard's own hand, he himself becomes the target of both underworld thugs and unscrupulous academics. The most compelling action takes place in the past as he traces the utterly fascinating evolution of Harvard University by interweaving it with the intimate history of one of New England's first families. . . . The unexpected twists and turns through history will keep readers guessing and the pages turning." Booklist

Martinez, A. Lee

The **automatic** detective. Tor 2008 317p pa $14.95

ISBN 978-0-7653-1834-3; 0-7653-1834-2

LC 2007-37645

This is "a hardboiled, hardwired, hard-riveted, hard-hitting blend of classic detective stories and science fiction, giving off a distinctly retro-futuristic vibe as it plays up the conventions of old school science fiction and mystery." SF Site

Martinez, A. Lee

Gil's All Fright Diner; A. Lee Martinez. Tor 2005 268p o.p.; (pbk.) $6.99

ISBN 9780765311436; 0765311437; 9780765350015

LC 2004063791

In this book, author A. Lee "Martinez leads us into the lives of Earl the Vampire and Duke the Wolf Man, who met on the night that Duke first changed from human to werewolf, attacked Earl in the woods and began eating his guts. We meet these two . . . in their ratty pickup truck as they pull into Gil's All Night Diner in Rockwood County in the middle of nowhere. . . . Loretta . . . run[s the] . . . diner. Over the years she's shotgunned about 185 zombies, but they continue to attack the eatery in small groups. Duke and Earl decide to stick around and help Loretta ward off these unwelcome walking dead. It turns out that Rockwood County has been pestered in recent years by various occult disturbances, thanks to Tammy, a high-schooler intent on becoming Lilith, Queen of the Universe." (Kirkus)

Martinez, Nina Marie

Caramba! a tale told in turns of the card. Knopf, distributed by Random House 2004 359p il $24.95

ISBN 0-375-41375-8

LC 2003-56192

"At times, ¡Caramba! transcends kitschiness and absurdity to evoke something more authentic. Natalie and Consuelo's relationship, for instance, conveys genuine intimacy, particularly in their unique brand of shorthand-speak." Washington Post Book World

Martini, Steven Paul

The **attorney**; [by] Steve Martini. Putnam 2000 429p $25.95

ISBN 0-399-14536-2

LC 99-44260

In this suspense novel featuring San Diego attorney Paul Madriani "lottery winner Jonah Hale's drug-addicted daughter demands a big payoff when he won't relinquish the granddaughter she left in his care, then accuses him of sexual abuse when he refuses to deliver. A famed feminist activist helps spirit away mother and daughter and then gets bumped off." Libr J

"Tense courtroom drama, plenty of action, and a deviously twisted plot." Booklist

Martini, Steven Paul

Compelling evidence; [by] Steve Martini. Putnam 1992 379p

LC 91-30253

"Besides giving us the scoop on ballistics analysis and post-mortem blood distribution, the author answers just about every cynical question you've ever had about the games lawyers play." N Y Times Book Rev

Martini, Steven Paul

Critical mass; [by] Steve Martini. Putnam 1998 436p

ISBN 0-399-14362-9

LC 98-24327

"A first-rate, post-Cold War espionage thriller that touches on many hot-button themes from today's headlines: distrust of the government, public apathy, high-tech crime, and antigovernment militias." Booklist

Martini, Steven Paul

The **judge**; [by] Steve Martini. Putnam 1996 389p

ISBN 978-0399140433

LC 95-41835

"Judge Armando Acosta has been summarily dismissed from the bench after being arrested on what he maintains is a trumped-up charge of soliciting a prostitute. When the key witness in the case against Acosta is found murdered and all the evidence points to Acosta as the killer, the former judge suddenly finds himself in desperate need of a tough, savvy lawyer to handle his case. An ironic set of circumstances eventually leads him to his longtime enemy Paul Madriani." Booklist

"Legal thrillers don't get much better than this." Publ Wkly

Martini, Steven Paul

The **jury**; [by] Steve Martini. Putnam 2001 291p

ISBN 0-399-14672-5

LC 2001-19834

Madriani, "still struggling to establish his law practice in San Diego, is defending Dr. David Crone, a brilliant genetic researcher accused of killing colleague Kalista Jordan: her strangled and dismembered body was found washed up on a beach. Not only does all the evidence point to Crone, but his lies and deceptions are starting to test the patience of Madriani and his partner, the quick-tempered Harry Hinds. . . .[Martini] takes the moving parts of a standard plot and spins them for maximum effect." Publ Wkly

Martini, Steven Paul

The **list**; [by] Steve Martini. Putnam 1997 438p

ISBN 978-0399142611

LC 96-46410

The author "clearly had a good time writing this fanciful book, in which he manages to incorporate multiple settings, invent gossamer disguises for important publishing personalities and skewer the machinery that produces blockbuster books." Publ Wkly

Martini, Steven Paul

Prime witness; [by] Steve Martini. Putnam 1993 384p

LC 93-16908

"When attorney Paul Madriani offers to assist a friend—the county's ailing district attorney, who subsequently dies—in investigating six brutal killings, he becomes entangled in a series of machinations that threaten his career and even his private life." Publ Wkly

"The novel effectively relays the great demands of being a district attorney and also depicts the behind-the-scenes maneuverings of a trial." Booklist

Martini, Steven Paul

Undue influence; {by} Steve Martini. Putnam 1994 462p

LC 94-10144

"The action builds to a rousing climax through a brilliant series of trial scenes with several surprises. The characters are sharply drawn, the facts of the case are presented simply and the courtroom psychology is laid out vividly." Publ Wkly

Martinusen-Coloma, Cindy

The **salt** garden; Cindy McCormick Martinusen. Tyndale House Publishers 2004 313p o.p.; (pbk.) $14.99

ISBN 0842373640; 9781595542922

LC 2003024485

In this book, set in "a small town on the Pacific coast, a shipwreck is being salvaged that will disclose secrets from the past. [Cindy] Martinusen . . . tells her story from the viewpoints of three women. Claire O'Rourke is a San Francisco reporter recently returned to her small hometown. . . . Her path soon intersects with that of Sophia Fleming, a 70-something reclusive author whom Claire has admired since childhood. When a salt-damaged book washes ashore, some long-buried secrets are illuminated through the journal entries of Josephine Vanderook, a passenger on an ill-fated ship." (Publishers Weekly)

Marusek, David

Counting heads. Tor 2005 336p $24.95

ISBN 0-7653-1267-0

LC 2005-05316

"Life on Earth in 2134 ought to be perfect: nanotechnology can manufacture anything humans need; medical science can control the human body's shape or age; and AIs, robots and contented clones do most of the work. If only there were a way to get rid of the surplus people. When Eleanor Starke, one of the major power brokers, is assassinated, her daughter's cryogenically frozen head becomes the object of a quest by representatives of several factions, including Eleanor's aged and outcast husband, a dense zealot for interstellar colonization, a decades-old little boy and husband and wife clones who are straining at the limitations of their natures. Marusek's writing is ferociously smart, simultaneously horrific and funny, as he forces readers to stretch their imaginations and sympathies." Publ Wkly

Followed by: Mind over ship (2008)

Marías, Javier, 1951-

While the women are sleeping; translated by Margaret Jull Costa. New Directions 2010 128p

ISBN 978-0-8112-1663-0; 0-8112-1663-2;

9780811219143

LC 2010-21110

Original Spanish edition, 1990

This collection of short stories, by Javier Marías, translated by Margaret Jull Costa, features "slippery figures in anomalous situations -- ghosts, spies, bodyguards, criminals. . . . The characters come bearing their strange and special secrets. . . . In one story, a man obsessed with his much younger lover endlessly videotapes her every move, and then confides his surprising plans for her; in another, a ghost can't stop resigning from his job." (Publisher's note)

"Having sneaked out of the hotel bed where his wife is sleeping to sit by a pool where a stranger relates a plan to kill his girlfriend before she grows old, the narrator of the title story in Marías's collection glances nervously back to his own balcony, as if half-suspecting himself of murder. In another story, a soldier returns from war to see his wife strangled by a man who looks exactly like him. Like many of Marías's narrators, these men are observers whose instinct when confronted with mortal danger is to stand and ruminate. In much of his short fiction, Marías . . . relies on occult devices like doppelgängers and ghosts to remind us of the life-or-death stakes. Other stories, including one in which a butler must dispose of an infant's corpse, cast their own spells. Few of these tales rise to the level of Marías's longer works (most of them also adeptly translated by Costa), which build up suspense by punctuating long passages of erudition with moments of brutal violence. But some are quite good on their own terms." N Y Times Book Rev

Masello, Robert

The **Romanov** cross; a novel. Robert Masello. Bantam Books 2013 512 p. (acid-free paper) $26

ISBN 0553807803; 9780345533593; 9780553807806

LC 2012015943

In this supernatural thriller, Robert Masello "weaves together the story of the deaths of the Russian royal family with the possibility of a new worldwide influenza pandemic. St. Peter's, a small island . . . , was once the home of a tiny community of followers of Rasputin, the notorious Russian monk. St. Peter's sole living inhabitant, if living is the right word, is a Romanov—the recipient of a blessing from Rasputin, or maybe it was a curse." (Publishers Weekly)

Mason, Bobbie Ann

Feather crowns. HarperCollins Pubs. 1993 454p

ISBN 0-06-016780-7

LC 92-56227

This novel "tells the story of Chrissie Wheeler, a tobacco farmer's wife in Hopewell, Kentucky, who, in 1900, gives birth to America's first recorded quintuplets. Curiosity seekers pass in a steady stream through the Wheeler's small farmhouse. When the babies take ill and die, Chrissie and her husband are persuaded to go on tour, displaying the grotesquely painted bodies of the dead infants to the idly curious." Libr J

"Mason's triumph here is to make her uneducated, bewildered heroine as vivid as the country life she describes." Publ Wkly

Mason, Bobbie Ann

The **girl** in the blue beret; a novel. Random House 2011 352p $26

ISBN 978-1-4000-6718-3; 1-4000-6718-9

LC 2010-36861

This novel "tells the story of a B-17 co-pilot shot down over Belgium in 1944, then helped by the French Resistance network to escape across the Pyrenees to Spain, and then to England. This drama, however, is recounted from a distance, as the co-pilot, Marshall, widowed and forced into retirement from his job as an airline pilot in 1980, goes to France to seek out those who helped him evade the Nazis in occupied France. In particular, Marshall is interested in finding Annette, the girl in the blue beret who guided him and whose family hid him for weeks while the network of conspirators arranged his escape. When he locates this girl, now a woman of 50 and a widow herself, a connection is made between the two, with their buried pasts, and the stories that neither has ever told finally emerge." Minneapolis Star Tribune

"Like Marshall himself, the novel maintains a reserved, laconic, even pedantic tone—offputting at times yet often moving." Kirkus

Mason, Bobbie Ann

In country; a novel. Harper Perennial 2005 245, 16p pa $14.99

ISBN 978-0-06-083517-0; 0-06-083517-6

LC 2006-273518

First published 1985

"Sam, 17, is obsessed with the Vietnam War and the effect it has had on her life—losing a father she never knew and now living with Uncle Emmett, who seems to be suffering from the effects of Agent Orange. In her own forthright way, she tries to sort out why and how Vietnam has altered the lives of the vets of Hopewell, Kentucky. . . . A harshly realistic, well-written look at the Vietnam War as well as the story of a young woman maturing." SLJ

Mason, Bobbie Ann

Love life; stories. Harper & Row 1989 241p

LC 88-45535

"Moments of insight emerge in Mason's stories as her Kentuckian characters encounter life's twists and turns. . . . The immediacy of these stories comes not just from Mason's frequent use of the present tense, or her often-criticized references to Wal-Mart and MTV, but, most of all, from her impressive ability to cut to the innermost emotions of a wide range of characters." SLJ

Mason, Bobbie Ann

Midnight magic; selected stories of Bobbie Ann Mason. selected & introduced by the author. Ecco Press 1998 301p

ISBN 0-88001-595-0

LC 97-36369

This "is a selection of 17 stories drawn from 'Shiloh and Other Stories,' the 1982 debut collection . . . and it's 1989 successor, 'Love life.' The book's characters live in the brave new world of strip malls and franchised food that is the New—or, rather, the New New—South. Most of them are Baptists, and they take the old strictures seriously, even though they're hardly able to live by them." N Y Times Book Rev

Mason, Bobbie Ann

Nancy Culpepper; stories. Random House 2006 224p

ISBN 0-375-50718-3

LC 2005-541241

This volume "collects all of Mason's fiction about its title character, but a single novella takes up almost half the book. 'Spence + Lila,' published on its own in 1988, showcases Nancy's return home after her mother, Lila, is hospitalized for a mastectomy. . . . Even in its lighter moments, Mason's fiction can inspire a yearning for something lost — whether it's a person, a place or a moment. That ache animates Nancy in the later stories as she moves through her middle years, always feeling slightly out of place, always searching for connections that just barely elude her." N Y Times Book Rev

Mason, Bobbie Ann

Shiloh and other stories; with a foreword by George Ella Lyon. University Press of Ky. 1995 247p $19.95

ISBN 0-8131-1948-0

LC 95-16581

A reissue of the title first published 1982 by Harper & Row

"Capturing in vivid detail the emotional frustrations of her characters and the unsettling ambience of her small-town Kentucky settings, Mason portrays the uneasy feelings of people who don't know what they want out of life but who do know that what they have isn't it." Booklist

Mason, Bobbie Ann

Zigzagging down a wild trail; stories. Random House 2001 209p $22.95

ISBN 0-679-44924-8

LC 00-66480

The author's terrain is "the Kentucky she's famous for writing about, but she has succeeded in making rural America seem exotic, strange, and mysterious, a looking-glass world. This lends a shimmering aura to each expertly rendered, boldly open-ended tale." Booklist

Mason, Daniel

A **far** country. Alfred A. Knopf 2007 267p $24

ISBN 978-0-375-41466-4; 0-375-41466-5

LC 2006-46530

The author "doesn't try to make things easy-once Isabel makes it to the city, the plot gets so vague that readers may struggle to retain a purchase. But those who persevere will be rewarded by the climax, when Isabel at last discovers what has become of Isaias. While the novel doesn't attain the level of modern myth one senses Mason was striving for, it does achieve a certain power as an imperfectly realized, yet moving, fable." Christ Sci Monit

Mason, Daniel

The **piano** tuner. Knopf 2002 317p $24

ISBN 0-375-41465-7

LC 2002-19069

"Mason proves himself equally adept at scenes of wry humor and moments of rapture; most remarkable, he has written a profound adventure story with an unexpected climax, as the mild piano tuner finally becomes the hero of his own life." New Yorker

Massey, Sujata

The **pearl** diver. HarperCollins 2004 335p $23.95

ISBN 0-06-621296-0

LC 2003-67614

Japanese American antiques dealer Rei Shimura's "assignment to furnish a new Japanese restaurant in Washington yields wonderful detail about Asian cuisines and the multicultural kitchen workers who prepare them. The narrative dovetails nicely with a moving subplot about a war bride who in her native Japan had been an ama-san, a female shellfish diver, until both stories are swamped by blow-by-blow updates on the heroine's personal life and a smelly red herring about Washington politics. There are still lessons to be learned from the uncluttered and serene lines of Japanese art." N Y Times Book Rev

Massie, Allan, 1938-

Caesar. Carroll & Graf Pubs. 1994 228p

LC 94-26430

One of the author's novels set in ancient Rome; previous titles Let the emperor speak (1987) and Tiberius (1993)

First published 1993 in the United Kingdom

This work "offers an evocative portrait of ancient Rome as well as a gripping and suspenseful analysis of the most intriguing conspiracy of all time. Superb historical fiction." Booklist

Master's choice [v1]-2: mystery stories by today's top writers and the masters who inspired them; edited by Lawrence Block. Berkley Prime Crime 1999 2v v1 $21.95; pa $5.99; v2 pa $7.50

ISBN 0-425-17031-4 v1; 0-425-17803-X v1 pa; 0-425-18225-8 v2 pa

LC 99-30270

These volumes pair stories chosen as personal favorites by some of the genre's top crime-fiction writers with a story of their own. Among the authors represented are Joe Gores, Sharyn McCrumb, Stuart Kaminsky, Stanley Ellin, and Joyce Carol Oates

"Block has assembled this anthology, which pairs stories chosen as personal favorites by some of the genre's top crime-fiction writers with a story of their own. Brit Peter Lovesey's sharp wit shines in a story about two eccentric twins. Lovesey picks Donald Westlake's hilarious tale of a bank robbery gone awry as his companion piece. . . . In all, nine principal writers are included, who select the 18 diverse and diverting stories. A well-conceived and entertaining anthology." Booklist

Masters, Hilary

Post; a fable. BkMk Press, University of Missouri-Kansas City 2011 274p pa $16.95

ISBN 978-1-886157-75-0; 1-886157-75-8

LC 2011-03157

"In a whirl of historic fact, erotic mayhem, and comic suspense, Masters ingeniously connects the bloodlust that drove the once sky-filling passenger pigeon into extinction with endangered forms of culture and love in an uproarious and wise inquiry into why we destroy what awes and sustains us." Booklist

Matar, Hisham

Anatomy of a disappearance; a novel. Dial Press 2011 224p $22

ISBN 978-0-385-34044-1; 0-385-34044-3

LC 2011-01561

"Part of what makes 'Anatomy of a Disappearance' worth reading is that its ambiguous and slightly cruel ending does not yield easy transcendence. In fact, it entirely recasts the meaning of the title. There are many disappearances that haunt the narrator not least his own. Though politics take a back seat, they shadow its margins, like the unknown men who kidnap Kamal. . . . For Americans attempting to understand the Middle East, this book provides a poignant picture of grief at the hands of political forces much larger than the individual lives they rupture." Cleveland Plain Dealer

Matar, Hisham

★ **In** the country of men. Dial Press 2007 246p $22

ISBN 978-0-385-34042-7; 0-385-34042-7

LC 2006-50649

First published 2006 in the United Kingdom

"A remarkably perceptive and affecting portrait of a young boy's premature political awakening. . . . [Matar] expertly builds an atmosphere of palpable tension, and though this novel never delves directly into politics, the menacing pall cast by political tyranny looms over the proceedings." Miami Herald

Matheson, Richard

Hunted past reason. Forge 2002 335p $24.95

ISBN 0-7653-0271-3

LC 2001-50768

"Two old friends, Bob (a novelist) and Doug (an actor), head off into the woods for a short hiking trip. Bob wants some hands-on experience for a novel he's working on; Doug is an expert in woodsmanship. From the get-go, there is tension between them: Doug seems excessively demanding; Bob reacts a little too sharply to his friend's criticisms of his stamina and abilities. Soon the mood turns dark, transforming the story into a psychological thriller." Booklist

Matheson, Richard

★ **I** am legend. Tom Doherty Associates 2007 317p pa $14.95

ISBN 0-7653-1874-1; 978-0-7653-1874-9

First published 1954

A pandemic devastates the human population, turning its victims into vampires. Robert Neville, the only man who escapes from the disease, must try to survive in a world in which he is now considered the monster.

Mathews, Francine

Death in a cold hard light. Bantam Bks. 1998 323p

ISBN 978-0553104646

LC 97-44253

"While visiting her future in-laws, Nantucket police detective Meredith ('Merry') Folger gets an urgent call from John Folger, her father and Nantucket chief of police. He needs help investigating the apparent drowning of Jay Santorski, a young scalloper. Santorski's death sets off a nor'easter of emotion and crime. . . . Mathews sustains a nail-biting pace to the finale, which takes place in a mansion on a stormy December night. Dialogue crackles, and most of the characters are well rounded." Booklist

Mathews, Francine

Death in a mood indigo. Bantam Bks. 1997 294p

ISBN 978-0553104639

LC 96-48324

"Detective Meredith Folger of the Nantucket police relishes the thought of solving an eight-year-old murder, especially since the initial missing person's investigation was flubbed by an incompetent. Meredith feels that she 'owes' the dead woman, a prominent female psychiatrist, some kind of resolution, regardless of their impact on her children." Libr J

Mathews, Harry

My life in CIA; a chronicle of 1973. Dalkey Archive Press 2005 203p pa $13.95

ISBN 1-56478-392-8

LC 2004-63478

"Novelist Mathews, an American living in Paris circa 1973, can't convince his French artistic friends he is not a CIA agent, so he resolves to fake the part—it beats soaking up idle time by learning ancient Greek, he thinks. Knowing a spy needs cover, Mathews sets up as 'international travel counsel,' and the audience attending his seminar yields several recruiting prospects. 'Patrick,' also in the consultancy 'business,' develops into Mathews' boon companion to whom he confides his charade. A second prospect from that seminar (a Russian) becomes the plot's vehicle for eliding Mathews from a world of fantasy espionage into something more real, and menacing. Strangers contact him; he accepts a courier mission; Patrick vanishes; the Soviet embassy summons him, as does French counterintelligence, which warns Mathews a Stasi assassin is pursuing him. Evolving in mood from ludicrous to serious, the yarn's inventive literary elements elegantly mesh into a stylish amusement." Booklist

Mathis, Ayana

The twelve tribes of Hattie; by Ayana Mathis. Alfred A. Knopf 2013 p. cm.

ISBN 9780307959423

LC 2012010779

2013 BCALA Literary Award: 1st Novelist Award

In this book, "Ayana Mathis tells the story of the children of the Great Migration through the trials of one . . . family. In 1923, fifteen-year-old Hattie Shepherd flees Georgia and settles in Philadelphia, hoping for a chance at a better life. . . . Hattie gives birth to nine . . . children. . . . Captured here

in twelve . . . narrative threads, their lives tell the story of a mother's . . . courage and the journey of a nation." (Publisher's note)

Matthews, Jason

Red sparrow; a novel. Jason Matthews. 1st Scribner hardcover ed. Scribner 2013 448 p. (hardcover) $26.99

ISBN 1476706123; 1476706131; 147670614X; 9781476706122; 9781476706139; 9781476706146

LC 2012031933

In this book, the "malicious injuring of a ballerina starts a train wreck that ends in the unmasking of highly placed moles in the United States and Russia. The dancer is inveigled into service as an agent but must first attend a graphically described 'Sparrow School' where recruits are taught the art of sexual seduction. Her target is an American agent whose defeat obsesses Russian leader Vladimir Putin himself." (Library Journal)

Matthiessen, Peter

Bone by bone. Random House 1999 410p $26.95

ISBN 0-375-50102-9

LC 98-46180

In this final volume in the trilogy about E.J. Watson, "Matthiessen has given us Watson's own story in Watson's own words. . . . That story goes right back to Civil War days in South Carolina, and the terrible childhood E.J. endured at the hands of his drunken, brutal and rascally father and his remote and vindictive mother. Thus were laid the seeds of the later outbursts of violence and rage that so frequently punctuated what should have been a promising life. For Watson, as he portrays himself, is ambitious, hardworking and ever ingenious at figuring ways to make the remote Florida Everglades shores yield riches—a true pioneer spirit." Publ Wkly

Matthiessen, Peter

★ Far Tortuga. Random House 1975 408p il

"Almost casually, we have been given a full measure of suspense, adventure, and first-rate descriptive writing; and along with and underneath these things, a group of characters who come fully alive with a complexity and even depth that the usual, traditional story of men at sea never gives us." Choice

Matthiessen, Peter

★ Killing Mister Watson. Random House 1990 372p

LC 89-43424

"By the time he was murdered, Watson was one of the most successful sugar-cane farmers between Tampa and Key West. Everyone liked and admired him, but no one trusted him. Proof was always scant but people wound up dead when Watson was around. . . . Matthiessen tells his story through the voice of Watson's family and neighbors in a series of oral histories, diary entries and old newspaper accounts, all of it fiction. By turns droll, rambunctious, foolish and wise, this collective narration mounts into a carefully orchestrated cacophony of contradictory testimony in which suspicion and mistrust are gradually revealed as the base elements of mystery." Newsweek

Followed by Lost Man's River

Matthiessen, Peter

Lost Man's River. Random House 1997 539p

ISBN 0-679-40377-9

LC 97-10124

In this sequel to Killing Mister Watson, "Lucius Watson, who has spent most of his life on the move, returns home to try to separate the truths from the myths of his father's killing, forty years earlier. A good part of Mathiessen's sprawling, uneven, novel comes straight from the characters' own mouths, but his ample skills as a naturalist and a journalist are in evidence, too. The Watson story is bound up in the landscape and the bloody history of the region, where gator poaching has given way to gunrunning, and where, nearly a hundred years after Reconstruction, racism is still as firmly rooted and as common as mangroves." New Yorker

Followed by Bone by bone

Matthiessen, Peter

On the river Styx and other stories. Random House 1989 208p

LC 86-3206

Six of the stories included in this collection originally appeared in book form in Midnight turning gray, published 1984 in paperback by Ampersand Press

Matthiessen's "stories delve into brutal facets of humankind and show the often hapless responses of well-intentioned individuals. Bitter scenes of racism are portrayed in several stories, including the title piece, in which a white couple on an innocuous fishing vacation sparks a violent racial backlash." Booklist

Matthiessen, Peter

★ **Shadow** country; a new rendering of the Watson legend. Modern Library 2008 892p $40; pa $16

ISBN 978-0-679-64019-6; 0-679-64019-3; 978-0-8129-8062-2 pa; 0-8129-8062-X pa

LC 2007-25117

"Matthiessen is meticulous in creating characters, lyrical in describing landscapes, and resolute in dissecting the values and costs that accompanied the development of this nation." Seattle Times

Mattison, Alice

In case we're separated; connected stories. Alice Mattison. William Morrow 2005 viii, 226p $23.95

ISBN 9780066213774; 0066213770

LC 2005043422

This book "us[es] a poetic form as the organizing principle. In a note on the last page, . . . [author Alice Mattison] explains: 'This book's 13 stories imitate in prose the 13 stanzas of a double sestina, using repeated topics or tropes in something like the way a sestina . . . uses repeated words. In the changing order prescribed by the sestina pattern, each story includes a glass of water, a sharp point, a cord, a mouth, an exchange and a map that may be wrong.' . . . The title story trades on a little irony: it and the other 12 pieces in the collection are about a family whose members couldn't

lose one another if they tried - which, for the most part, they don't. They're Jewish, originally from Eastern Europe, immigrants who settled in Chicago and Brooklyn and then dispersed farther, to Wisconsin, to New Haven, to Boston." (New York Times)

Mattison, Alice

The **wedding** of the two-headed woman. Morrow 2004 275p $23.95

ISBN 0-06-621378-9

"Mattison's voice is intelligent, spare and without pretense. She lays out Daisy's story in a way that makes it seem as if not much is happening, while quietly weaving in four or five intriguing subplots, including a murder mystery, a rent strike and, toward the end, Sept. 11. All these stories press in on Daisy in some meaningful way, each playing a role in her quest to come to terms with herself." Washington Post

Maturin, Charles Robert

★ **Melmoth** the wanderer; edited with and introduction and notes by Victor Sage. Penguin Books 2000 xxxi, 659p pa $12

ISBN 0-14-044761-x

LC 2001-265474

First published 1820 in the United Kingdom

This novel "was in effect the last, and also one of the most effective, of the 'Gothic' school. The tale rushes energetically through every kind of horror and iniquity, and has moments of genuine power. Melmoth, who has sold his soul for the promise of prolonged life, offers relief from suffering to each of the characters, whose terrible stories succeed one another, if they will take over his bargain with the Devil. But Stanton, imprisoned in the cell of a raving lunatic; Moncada in the hands of the Inquisition; Walberg, who sees his children dying of hunger; and many other sufferers, all reject the proposed bargain." Oxford Companion to Engl Lit. 6th edition

Maugham, W. Somerset

The **best** short stories of W. Somerset Maugham; selected, and with an introduction by John Beecroft. Modern Lib. 1957 489p

Maugham, W. Somerset

Cakes and ale; or, The skeleton in the cupboard. Doubleday, Doran 1930 308p

This novel, Maugham's "most genial book, is a comedy about the good-natured Rosie Driffield, the wife of a Grand Old Man of Letters; whom most took to be based on Hardy; Alroy Kear, a self-promoting writer, was recognized as Hugh Walpole." Oxford Companion to Engl Lit. 5th edition

Maugham, W. Somerset

★ **Complete** short stories. Doubleday 1952 2v

Maugham, W. Somerset

The **moon** and sixpence. Doran, G.H. 1919 314p

"Based closely on the life of Paul Gauguin it tells of Charles Strickland, a conventional London stockbroker, who in middle life suddenly decides to desert his wife, family, and business in order to become a painter. He goes to paint in Tahiti, where he takes a native mistress. Eventually Strickland dies of leprosy." Reader's Ency. 4th edition

Maugham, W. Somerset

★ **Of** human bondage; introduction by Gore Vidal. Modern Library 1999 xxxix, 611p pa $11.95
    ISBN 0-375-75315-X

                          LC 98-46169
    First published 1915

This novel's "hero is Philip Carey, a sensitive, talented, club-footed orphan who is brought up by an unsympathetic aunt and uncle. It is a study of his struggle for independence, his intellectual development, and his attempt to become an artist. Philip gets entangled and obsessed by his love affair with Mildred, a waitress. After years of struggle as a medical student, he marries a nice woman, gives up his aspirations, and becomes a country doctor. The first part of the novel is partly autobiographical, and the book is regarded as Maugham's best work." Reader's Ency. 4th edition

Maugham, W. Somerset

★ The **razor's** edge. Doubleday 1944 343p hardcover o.p. pa $14
    ISBN 1-4000-3420-5 pa

"The novel is concerned in large part with the search for the meaning of life and with the dichotomy between materialism and spirituality. The main focus of the story is on Larry Darrell, who has returned from service as an aviator in World War I utterly rejecting his prewar values. He is concerned chiefly with discovering the meaning of human existence and eliminating evil in the world. To that end, he spends five years in India seeking—but not finding—answers." Merriam-Webster's Ency of Lit

Maupin, Armistead

Mary Ann in autumn; a Tales of the city novel. Harper 2010 287p $25.99
    ISBN 978-0-06-147088-2; 0-06-147088-0

                         LC 2010-24322

"Twenty years have passed since Mary Ann Singleton left her husband and child in San Francisco to pursue her dream of a television career in New York. Now a pair of personal calamities has driven her back to the city of her youth and into the arms of her oldest friend, Michael 'Mouse' Tolliver, a gardener happily ensconced with his much-younger husband. Mary Ann finds temporary refuge in the couple's backyard cottage, where, at the unnerving age of fifty-seven, she licks her wounds and takes stock of her mistakes. Soon, with the help of Facebook and a few old friends, she begins to reengage with life, only to confront fresh terrors when her checkered past comes back to haunt her in a way she could never have imagined." Publisher's note

Maupin, Armistead

Michael Tolliver lives. HarperCollins Publishers 2007 277p $25.95
    ISBN 978-0-06-076135-6; 0-06-076135-0

                         LC 2006-52979

This is a "novel only in the loosest sense of the term. The chapters are independent yet interdependent, flowing into one another gracefully while remaining very much sin-

gular entities. . . . The book is great fun to read. Maupin is a master at sustained and sustaining comic turns." N Y Times Book Rev

Maurois, André, 1885-1967

Climates; by André Maurois; translated by Adriana Hunter. Other Press 2012 400 p. (trade pbk.) $15.95
    ISBN 1590515382; 9781590515389; 9781590515396
                         LC 2012008856

In a new translation of the 20th-century French classic, wealthy Philippe Marcenat makes two attempts to find the perfect partner and fails both times. . . . Stripped of its period shading, this is a sad and timeless tale of women on pedestals and the pain of loving not wisely, but too well." Kirkus

Maurois, André, 1885-1967

★ The **collected** stories of Andre Maurois; translated by Adrienne Foulke. Washington Sq. Press 1967 396p

Mawer, Simon

The **fall**; a novel. Little, Brown 2002 370p $24.95
    ISBN 0-316-09780-2

                         LC 2002-73193

"Intricately weaving time and place, from the bombed-out ruins of World War II London to isolated Alpine mountain peaks, Mawer crafts a sinuously devastating tale of foridden love and faithless betrayal. A haunting and mesmerizing novel from an expert storyteller." Booklist

Mawer, Simon

The **glass** room. Other Press 2009 405p il pa $14.95
    ISBN 978-1-59051-396-5; 1-59051-396-7
                         LC 2009-39912

Mawer "has written this novel as though it were a translation, endowing his prose with a patina of Old World formality that sounds all the more romantic. He claims he doesn't know Czech or German, but his characters speak both fluently, and his attention to foreign languages enriches every episode." Washington Post Book World

Maxwell, Robin

Jane; the woman who loved Tarzan. Robin Maxwell. 1st ed. Tor 2012 320 p. ill.
    ISBN 0765333589; 9780765333582; 9780765333599; 9781466803213
                         LC 2012019452

This novel by Robin Maxwell is a "version of the Tarzan story. . . . When dashing American explorer Ral Conrath invites . . . budding paleoanthropologist . . . Jane and her father to join an expedition deep into West Africa, she can hardly believe her luck. . . . [B]ut Jane quickly learns that the lush jungle is full of secrets -- and so is Ral Conrath. When danger strikes, Jane finds her hero, the key to humanity's past, and an all-consuming love in one extraordinary man: Tarzan of the Apes." (Publisher's note)

Maxwell, Robin

The **Queen's** bastard; a novel. Arcade Pub.
1999 436p $24.95

    ISBN 1-55970-475-6

                              LC 98-50502

    Sequel to The secret diary of Anne Boleyn

    "Arthur's first person narration is cleverly juxtaposed
with third-person dramatization of significant events in the
queen's life. . . . Maxwell's research examines the biographical gaps in, and documented facts about, the queen's life,
making this incredible tale plausible, and the author aptly
embellishes her story with rich period details and the epic
dramas of the late 16th century." Publ Wkly

Maxwell, Robin

The **secret** diary of Anne Boleyn. Arcade Pub.
1997 281p

    ISBN 1-55970-375-X

                              LC 96-49275

    This "novel supposes that Anne Boleyn, second wife of
King Henry VIII of England, kept a secret diary that was delivered to her daughter, Elizabeth, upon her succession to the
throne. Elizabeth was only three when Anne was renounced
by Henry, tried for treason, and sentenced to death. Now,
despite her queenly schedule, juggling affairs of state and
heart, Elizabeth finds time to read her mother's story avidly
and learns lessons that will secure her reign." Libr J

    "Painting vicious court intrigue, national and interna-
tional politics and the role of the Reformation, Maxwell
brings not only the two queens but all of bloody Tudor England vividly to life." Publ Wkly

    Followed by The Queen's bastard

Maxwell, Robin

The **wild** Irish. William Morrow 2003 393p
$24.95

    ISBN 0-06-009142-8

                            LC 2003-42184

    "When Grace O'Mally, passionate clan chieftain and
legendary Irish pirate, visits the court of Elizabeth I to
plead for the release of her imprisoned son, the two most
extraordinary women of their time find they have much in
common. As Grace relates her incredible life and times to
Elizabeth, the aging Bess also revisits her own often tragic
past. Caught between these two powerful and magnetic females, Elizabeth's favorite courtier and onetime lover, Robert Devereaux, earl of Essex, is inexorably drawn into the
tangled web of the Irish rebellion. . . . Superbly crafted, this
dynamic tale brings a host of historical characters vividly to
life." Booklist

Maxwell, William

All the days and nights; the collected stories of
William Maxwell. Knopf 1995 415p

                            LC 94-27509

Maxwell, William

Early novels and stories; [edited by Christopher
Carduff] Library of America 2008 997p

    ISBN 978-1-59853-016-2; 1-59853-016-X

                        LC 2007-934857

    The bright corner of heaven (1934) is a comic novel set
in an artist's colony. They came like swallows (1937) is an
autobigraphical novel set in the Midwest. In it a devoted
wife and mother succombs to the Spanish flu during the epidemic of 1918. The folded leaf (1846), set in Chicago and a
Middle Western college, is the story of an intense friendship
between two adolescent boys. In Time will darken it (1948),
set in a straitlaced Illinois community of 1912, gossip ruins the lives of a respected married lawyer and an ambitious
young woman.

    "At last—at last!—The Library of America brings out
the first in a pair of volumes devoted to the writings of the
New Yorker editor who in his spare time produced some of
America's most lyrical and poignant fiction." Arts J

Maxwell, William

Later novels and stories; [edited by Christopher
Carduff] Library of America 2008 994p $35

    ISBN 978-1-59853-026-1; 1-59853-026-7

    The setting of The chateau (1961) "is France in 1948,
the place and its people still recovering from the German
occupation. A newlywed American couple spends two
weeks in the Loire Valley at the château of Mme Viénnot,
an impoverished aristocrat whose actions and motivations
are inscrutable to her paying guests. . . . So Long, See You
Tomorrow (1980) is an Old Testament tragedy played out
on the Illinois prairie. It is told by a witness to this tragedy's
devastation–an old man much like Maxwell who, some 60
years after the murderous events he describes, struggles to
forgive his failure to reach out to the survivors. . . . [Among
the short stories included are] 'Over by the River' and 'The
Thistles in Sweden,' two classic evocations of New York
City life, and the complete contents of Billie Dyer (1992), a
companion volume to So Long, See You Tomorrow collecting seven fictionalized portraits of figures from Maxwell's
youth. The volume concludes with 40 . . . 'improvisations'–
fairy tales that Maxwell wrote mainly to entertain his wife."
Publisher's note

May, Julian

The **adversary**. Houghton Mifflin 1984 xxxviii,
470p il (Saga of Pliocene exile)

    ISBN 0-395-36516-3

                              LC 83-49065

    Intervention, a novel linking the Saga of Pliocene exile
with the Galactic Milieu trilogy was published in 1987

    "In this concluding volume of the quartet, King Aiken
and the children of the telepathic rebels, exiled from the future Milieu, must fight against Marc Remillard and his allies,
the Firvulag. This book will be barely intelligible to those
unfamiliar with the rest of the saga—despite May's extensive synopsis—but it should keep the author's regular readers turning pages." Booklist

May, Julian

Blood Trillium. Bantam Bks. 1992 391p (Trillium)

    ISBN 0-553-08851-3

                              LC 92-2888

    Second in a fantasy series that started with Black Trillium
by Marion Zimmer Bradley, Julian May, and Andre Norton

"A superior tale, giving life, character and emotion to the three Petals of the Living Trillium as they continue their adventures." Publ Wkly

Followed by Golden Trillium by Andre Norton

May, Julian
Diamond mask; a novel. Knopf 1994 461p
LC 93-37802

The author "maintains a personal focus on her luminary characters, opening their private lives to intense scrutiny while at the same time expanding the boundaries of an imaginative future world. Rich in intrigue and vibrating with creative energy, this is a superb addition to sf collections." Libr J

Followed by Magnificat

May, Julian
The **golden** torc. Houghton Mifflin 1982 xxv, 381p il (Saga of Pliocene exile)
ISBN 0-395-31261-2
LC 81-4126

"In this second volume of the saga, May continues the story of the diverse group of time-exiles we met in the first book and shows how they help to bring about the overthrow of the Tanu and the closing of the time gate. . . . May develops her premises seriously and gives her large cast of characters a surprising amount of life." Publ Wkly

Followed by The nonborn king

May, Julian
Jack the bodiless; a novel. Knopf 1992 463p
LC 91-53176

This is the first volume of the Galactic Milieu trilogy describing events that precipitated the action of the author's Saga of Pliocene exile tetralogy. "As a consortium of five alien races stands ready to accept Earth as a full partner in the Galactic Milieu, the birth of a very special child heralds a new stage in human evolution. . . . May combines a compelling vision of humanity's future with the drama and political intrigue surrounding the Remillard family, whose metapsychic powers and personal ambitions shape the destiny of the world." Libr J

Followed by Diamond mask

May, Julian
Magnificat; a novel. Knopf 1996 427p
ISBN 978-0679441779
LC 95-35088

Concluding volume of the author's Galactic Milieu trilogy. "As human rebellion against the unified mind of the Galactic Milieu intensifies, the psychically powerful Remillard family races against time to find and destroy the murderous Fury. Fascinating characters enhance an intricate and thoughtfully executed plot. {A} satisfying end to a remarkable feat of the imagination." Libr J

May, Julian
The **many**-colored land. Houghton Mifflin 1981 415p (Saga of Pliocene exile)
ISBN 0-395-30230-7

In this first volume of a four part saga "a one-way, fixed-focus time portal to Europe in the Pliocene epoch allows the prehistoric past to become a last frontier and a refuge for misfits fed up with the well-ordered world of the 22nd century. This novel follows the adventures of a group newly arrived in Exile. They are prepared for almost anything but what they actually find, a world ruled by humanoid aliens who can control them with artificially augmented psionic powers. The arrogant, beautiful Tanu are opposed, however, by the ugly, outcast Firvulag. Allied with them the humans may hope to overthrow the Tanu and win the freedom they came for. Deftly combining SF and the Celtic myths of the Tuatha de Danaan, Julian May has made a most enjoyable entertainment that will have readers eagerly turning pages." Publ Wkly

Followed by The golden torc

May, Julian
The **nonborn** king. Houghton Mifflin 1983 xli, 394p il (Saga of Pliocene exile)
ISBN 0-395-32211-1
LC 82-11950

"There is a new balance of power among the 22nd century's voluntary exiles to the Europe of 6-million years ago and the two factions of aliens (Tanu and Firvulag) they found waiting for them there. The humans are no longer slaves, and one of them, a trickster upstart named Aiken Drum, becomes the Tanu king. A new element is introduced in the form of yet another group of (involuntary) exiles, the remnants of the Metapsychic Rebellion of 2083. Beams of mental force clash spectacularly as Aiken seeks their help against Felice, the mad psychic prodigy, and in defending his throne against Tanu traditionalists." Publ Wkly

Followed by The adversary

May, Peter
The **Blackhouse**; Peter May. SilverOak 2012 432 p. (hardcover) $24.95
ISBN 1454901276; 9781454901273; 9781454901280
LC 2012016939

In this book by Peter May, "Edinburgh-based DI Fin Macleod is dispatched to Scotland's remote Isle of Lewis to compare two deaths. Two hangings, one in Edinburgh and one in Fin's childhood home of Crobost, share the same traits. Is a serial killer or a copycat at work? Since the Crobost victim was the village bully, Fin must sift through multiple motives and his own memories to tease out the killer." (Library Journal)

Mayle, Peter
Anything considered. Knopf 1996 303p $23
ISBN 0-679-44123-9
LC 96-5761

Mayle has "written an entertaining thriller that moves along apace, but his loyal readers need not worry. Much of his raw material is familiar: wonderful meals decribed in succulent detail; vintage wines, all named to stimulate fantasy; and a rich assortment of French 'characters.'" NY Times Book Rev

Mayle, Peter
Chasing Cezanne. Knopf 1997 295p $23
ISBN 0-679-45511-6
LC 97-71925

"The trail to the lost Cézanne becomes a comedy of errors. Along the way, there are vibrant descriptions of Paris, Provence, Cap Ferrat, and of course mouth-watering French meals and wine. Part travelog and part art mystery caper, this . . . is a thoroughly enjoyable romp through the international art world." Libr J

Mayle, Peter

A **good** year. Knopf 2004 287p $24

ISBN 0-375-40591-7

LC 2003-65674

"On the very day his boss steals his biggest account and maneuvers him out of his job in London's financial district, Max Skinner learns that he's inherited his uncle's vineyard in Provence. Unfortunately, the place is rundown and–worse–the wine it produces is awful. But what about the small plot at the edge of the vineyard that his caretaker bad-mouths and the private-label 'garage wine' being sold oh-so-discreetly in Bordeaux for $40,000 a case? Then there's the unexpected visit of Californian Christie Roberts, who knows a thing or two about wine herself and may have a valid claim to the estate. Though his plot is predictable, Mayle juggles complications, chicanery, and romance with entertaining and informative tidbits about wine-and his Provence never fails to charm." Libr J

Mayle, Peter

Hotel Pastis; a novel of Provence. Knopf 1993 389p

LC 93-14641

The author "displays his satiric eye for social foibles by skewering advertising execs in England and the U.S.; he is equally adept at evoking typical Provencal villagers. Wickedly sharp and sympathetic at the same time, his characterizations are accurate down to nuances of class differences, voice, accent and vocabulary." Publ Wkly

Maynard, Joyce

Labor Day; a novel. William Morrow 2009 244p $24.99

ISBN 978-0-06-184340-2; 0-06-184340-7

LC 2009-13167

"During a trip to the local discount department store, 13-year-old Henry, worldly well beyond the limits of his New Hampshire town, meets the mysterious, middle-aged Frank. Bleeding and limping, Frank asks Henry's lonely, single mom, Adele, to take him to their house. She wordlessly assents. Soon, over coffee, Frank reveals the root of his injury: an escape from the state penitentiary. What follows is the tale of a mid-1980s weekend that's physically imprisoning (with Frank on the lam, the house becomes a hideout) but emotionally freeing, for everyone. Frank and Adele, both broken in multiple ways, find comfort in each other, and Adele and Henry quickly turn from Frank's captives to his confidants. . . . Maynard writes from the point of view of the angsty adolescent, and compellingly so." USA Today

Maynard, Joyce

The **usual** rules. St. Martin's Press 2003 390p $24.95

ISBN 0-312-24261-1

LC 2002-36754

"The novel is about a thirteen-year-old girl whose mother dies in the World Trade Center on September 11. . . . Not long after that, {her} ne'er-do-well biological dad (Peter Pan) shows up and whisks Wendy off with him to California." Women's Rev Books

Mayor, Archer

The **catch**; a Joe Gunther novel. St. Martin's Minotaur 2008 274p $24.95

ISBN 978-0-312-38191-2; 0-312-38191-3

LC 2008-23437

"Archer Mayor doesn't do quaint. He might use poetic imagery to describe the austere beauty of New England's rugged mountains and snowbound villages, but as far as their crime content is concerned, his police procedurals are about as authentic as it gets." N Y Times Book Rev

Mayor, Archer

Chat. Grand Central Pub. 2007 326p $24.99

ISBN 978-0-446-58258-2; 0-446-58258-1

LC 2007-15310

"On the same night that an unidentified body of a man is found floating in a lake near Brattleboro, VT, detective Joe Gunther must leave his investigative team at the scene and return to his hometown, where his mother and brother have been seriously injured in an automobile accident. . . . [This case] is one of the hardest for Gunther because it becomes apparent that someone is trying to kill his loved ones. Torn between his loyalty to his coworkers and his commitment to his family, he discovers that people rise to the occasion and offer help in unexpected ways. All the ingredients for a great mystery are here: fast pacing, a believable plot, a plausible solution, and characters so real they walk off the pages. Mayor's books just get better and better." Libr J

Mayor, Archer

★ **Occam's** razor. Mysterious Press 1999 339p $30

ISBN 0-89296-682-3

LC 99-26221

"As a stylist, Mayor is one of those meticulous construction workers who are fascinated by the way things function. He's the boss man on procedures, and he loves to poke around in whatever complicated mechanism is making all the wheels turn." N Y Times Book Rev

Mayor, Archer

Red herring; a Joe Gunther novel. Minotaur Books 2010 291p $24.99

ISBN 978-0-312-38193-6; 0-312-38193-X

LC 2010-30458

"Three people are dead in Vermont. There is a dearth of clues, except for a single drop of blood left at the scene of each death. The Vermont Bureau of Investigation is called in, and Joe Gunther's . . . team must use every new investigation technique available (this even involves a trip to Long Island's Brookhaven National Laboratory) as well plain, old-fashioned legwork to catch the guilty. With cool forensic details for CSI fans, Mayor's heart-racing tale ends in a dramatic finish that will leave readers gasping." Libr J

Mayor, Archer

★ The **sniper's** wife. Mysterious Press 2002 312p $23.95

ISBN 0-89296-767-6

LC 2002-67183

"Mayor writes a tough story for his tortured protagonist, and the unfamiliar setting brings out a new, edge-of-the-knife side of his incisive descriptive powers." N Y Times Book Rev

Mayor, Archer

Tag man; a Joe Gunther novel. Minotaur Books 2011 290p

ISBN 9780312681944; 978-0-312-68194-4

LC 2011018779

A mystery featuring Joe Gunther, "head of the Vermont Bureau of Investigation, and VBI staffers Willy Kunkle, Sammie Martens, and Lester Spinney as well as their Brattleboro police colleague, Ron Klesczewski. The action centers on the person known as 'Tag Man,' who breaks into supposedly secure, occupied houses, explores them, takes nothing of value, but leaves a Post-it as his calling card. The Tag Man enjoys the challenge and the risk, until he makes a grisly discovery and is identified by one of his victims, who sends a hit man after him. Gunther, though on medical leave following a grievous personal loss, volunteers to help Klesczewski unmask the Tag Man. Multiple games of cat-and-mouse ensue as the Tag Man tries to elude both police and a determined killer. Vermont's history and geography again serve Mayor well in this deadly and highly entertaining entry."

Mazzarella, Nicole

This heavy silence; a novel. Nicole Mazzarella. Paraclete Press 2005 255 p. o.p.; (pbk.) $14.95

ISBN 1557254257; 9781557255082

LC 69248687

Christy Award: First Novel (2006)

This book, a finalist for the Paraclete Press Fiction Award of 2004, tells the story of "[s]tubborn, independent Dottie Connell, [whose] greatest desire is to won the 300 acres of farmland that her family has worked all her life. Then childhood friend Zela Brubaker dies unexpectedly, naming Dottie as the guardian of her young daughter, Mattie. Although Dottie is not sure she wants to raise the girl, she finally has her chance to purchase her beloved land, but the cost requires Mattie's total inheritance, which is more than the property will ever be worth." (Library Journal)

McAfee, Annalena

The **spoiler**; a novel. Annalena McAfee. Alfred A. Knopf 2012 287 p. (hardcover) $25.95

ISBN 1846554357 Harvill Secker; 9780307957344 Knopf; 0307957349 Knopf; 9781846554353 Harvill Secker

LC 2011043742

This book follows "Pulitzer prize-winning journalist Honor Tait. . . . She has had a distinguished career and won the Pulitzer for her reporting from Buchenwald in April of 1945. But 1997, the year in which the novel is set, discloses a different type of reporting when Tamara Sim is asked to do an interview of the crusty, reclusive and highly intelli-

gent older woman for S*nday, a journal whose clientele is more interested in scandal than in truth or integrity. . . . Tamara's initial interview goes badly because she feels Tait's contempt for what she's doing, but Tamara keeps pursuing the story. . . . [I]t becomes clear that Tait has been stringing Tamara along until truth has gotten swallowed in speculation." (Kirkus Reviews)

McAllister, Bruce

The **girl** who loved animals and other stories; with an introduction by Harry Harrison and an afterword by Barry N. Malzberg. Golden Gryphon Press 2007 306p $24.95

ISBN 978-1-930846-49-4; 1-930846-49-5

LC 2007-9623

"How far would a person go to protect a loved one? That question is at the heart of many of the 17 stories in McAllister's career-spanning collection. . . . [His] haunting work will enthrall any reader who appreciates thoughtful, evocative science fiction." Publ Wkly

McAuley, Paul J.

White devils. Tor Bks. 2004 464p $25.95

ISBN 0-7653-0761-8

LC 2003-57067

"The African continent suffers from plague, civil war, and unchecked genetic experimentation. Sent to investigate a particularly heinous crime in the Congo, Nicholas Hyde and his team come under attack by a group of apelike creatures and find themselves in the middle of a government conspiracy to hide its actions from the common people." Libr J

"Though more complex than necessary, this novel serves as a powerful warning about the sinister possibilities inherent in genetic engineering." Publ Wkly

McBain, Ed

Alice in jeopardy. Simon & Schuster 2005 292p $25

ISBN 0-7432-6250-6

LC 2004-52478

"Alice Glendenning has been surviving, just barely. When her husband, Eddie, died in a boating accident nearly a year ago, she was left a widow with two very young children and a life insurance policy with a fly-by-night company that has delayed payment because the body was lost at sea. But things can always get worse, much worse. The ransom call comes not long after her two kids don't return home on the bus after school. The instructions are simple: the money from the insurance policy or the kids are dead–plus the standard 'Don't call the cops.' Alice doesn't call the cops, but the baby-sitter does, and soon Alice is mired in a jurisdictional jihad among local, state, and federal law-enforcement agencies of varying levels of competence." Booklist

McBain, Ed

The **big** bad city; a novel of the 87th Precinct. Simon & Schuster 1999 271p

ISBN 0-684-85512-7

LC 98-40890

"A young woman is murdered in a city park across town from her home. She has no identification except a wedding ring with the inscription IHS. Detetctive Steve Carella of the

NYPD's 87th Precinct recognizes the inscription from his Catholic schoolboy days as a Latin monogram for 'Jesus, Savior of Men.' Jane Doe is a nun, Sister Mary Vincent, once known as Kate Cochrane. . . . Meanwhile, the man who killed Carella's father and walked because of an incompetent prosecution, Samson Wilber 'Sonny' Cole, has revenge on his mind." Booklist

McBain, Ed

Eight black horses; an 87th Precinct novel. Arbor House 1985 250p il

LC 85-7348

"The Deaf Man, scourge of McBain's famed 87th precinct, returns to plot his biggest coup in this . . . thriller. While Carella, Hawes, Brown, Kling and the other detectives investigate the murder of a woman bank teller, their legendary adversary sends them clues to his operation. . . . By switching the narrative from activities at the precinct to a description of the psychotic's fail-safe plan, the author keeps the tension at white heat from the first word to the shattering conclusion of the drama." Publ Wkly

McBain, Ed

★ Fat Ollie's book; a novel of the 87th Precinct. Simon & Schuster 2002 271p $25

ISBN 0-7432-0270-8

LC 2002-75830

This installment features "Det. Oliver Wendell Weeks of the 88th Precinct. Fat Ollie, of the gross appetite and the even grosser ignorance of political correctness. . . . Two major crimes occur at almost the same time: the shooting of Councilman (and possible mayoral candidate) Lester Henderson as he is getting ready for a rally and the theft of the just completed manuscript of Ollie's first novel, Report to the Commissioner. Ollie enlists Carella's help (Henderson lived in the 87th) and pursues both the murderer and the thief." Publ Wkly

"In McBain's howlingly funny sendup, the novel is pure drivel; but Ollie loved it, and darned if we don't like him for that." N Y Times Book Rev

McBain, Ed

Fiddlers; a novel of the 87th Precinct. Harcourt 2005 259p $25

ISBN 0-15-101216-4

LC 2005-4255

"A blind violinist is shot in the alley behind the restaurant where he works. A sales rep is gunned down in her apartment while cooking dinner. They are both killed with the same gun. Detective Steve Carella and his 87th Precinct team investigate. The case grows more confusing when an elderly priest and an old woman walking her dog are also murdered with the same gun. The killer, a seemingly ordinary man, is on a last fling with a call girl, who doesn't understand the darkness residing within the man she hopes will pull her out of the life. . . . This one will have readers waking in the middle of the night wondering if they, too, have killers inside themselves." Booklist

McBain, Ed

The frumious Bandersnatch; a novel of the 87th Precinct. Simon & Schuster 2004 287p $25

ISBN 0-7432-5034-6

LC 2003-57258

"Tamar Valparaiso, a hot young singer on the verge of superstardom, is set to launch her debut CD and video Bandersnatch when she is kidnapped in the middle of a performance for a record industry party and the press. The whole episode is caught on camera, but the masked abductors flee, leaving behind few clues. Steve Carella and Cotton Hawes of the 87th Precinct are called in and are soon joined by a Joint Task Force and FBI agents. Detective Ollie Weeks, resident racist, homophobe, and misogynist, is also back on the scene, this time romancing a fellow officer. McBain displays his usual mastery of the police procedural along with an astute grasp of the music industry, the news media, and publicity, as well as political ramifications within the force." Libr J

McBain, Ed

Hark! a novel of the 87th Precinct. Simon & Schuster 2004 293p il $24.95

ISBN 0-7432-5035-4

LC 2004-49102

"Vintage McBain, complete with pitch-perfect dialogue, subplots that thrust various precinct cops into the spotlight, a pace that encourages the reader to forget about dinner or a good night's rest, and a plot that teases and tantalizes from start to finish." Publ Wkly

McBain, Ed

Heat; an 87th Precinct novel. Viking 1981 227p

LC 81-65263

"Jeremiah Newman's death was almost definitely suicide, but certain details—for instance, the air conditioning was off on a 99 degree day—bother Detective Steve Carella. His partner, Bert Kling, has other problems—his wife may be cheating on him and someone's taking shots at him." Libr J

McBain, Ed

Ice; a major new novel about the world of the 87th Precinct. Arbor House 1983 317p

LC 82-74061

A "vivid, often brutal, description of life in the ghetto with its subculture of hookers, pushers, addicts, burglars, muggers, rapists and even savage killers. Yet despite this, it is not without its moments of humor, tenderness, compassion and occasional optimism." Best Sellers

McBain, Ed

Kiss; a novel of the 87th Precinct. Morrow 1991 351p

LC 91-15908

"With its interwoven threads of violence, tenderness and world-weary ruminations on the breakdown of urban life, this is hardboiled mystery in the tradition of Chandler and Hammett. And the ending features the best kind of twist: it's both surprising and satisfying." Publ Wkly

McBain, Ed

The **last** dance; a novel of the 87th Precinct. Simon & Schuster 2000 269p il
  ISBN 0-684-85513-5

                LC 99-53534

"Detectives Meyer Meyer and Steve Carella are questioning Cynthia Keating, whose father lies lifeless in a nearby bed. Cynthia claims she hasn't touched Andrew Hale since she discovered his body, but the cops suspect she's lying: for one thing, the corpse's feet are blue from postmortem lividity, a sign of death by hanging." Publ Wkly

An "accomplished mix of police procedure, characterization, social commentary and tight plotting that has long distinguished this landmark series." Booklist

McBain, Ed

Learning to kill; stories. Harcourt 2006 478p
  ISBN 978-0-15-101222-0; 0-15-101222-9

                LC 2005-27059

McBain "wrote short fiction, paid by the word, for 1950s pulp magazines such as Manhunt and Argosy under the names of Richard Marsten, Hunt Collins, and Evan Hunter. This collection presents 25 of those crime stories, published between 1952 and 1957 . . . . Grouped thematically under such headings as 'Women in Jeopardy,' 'Private Eyes,' and 'Cops and Robbers,' the stories are definitely of the period, long on hardboiled tone, short on subtlety. More interesting than the stories themselves are McBain's general introduction, which presents both comic details about his career and valuable insights into his writing, and the short prefaces he gives each section, which provide a window into the times and his own development as a writer." Booklist

McBain, Ed

Lightning; an 87th Precinct novel. Arbor House 1984 304p

                LC 84-3030

"A grotesque series of crimes confronts the officers of the 87th Precinct. First, two women college track stars are found hanging, lynch-mob style, from the lampposts of brilliantly lit city streets; and then a rapist who harbors wild psycho-sexual/religious hang-ups stalks an ever-increasing number of victims, torturing them through repeated attacks. A key role in catching the maniac is played by gutsy Eileen Burke, an undercover officer in Special Forces whose aggressive work puts her own life in peril. Filled with realistic police procedure, cop humor, and eerie action." Booklist

McBain, Ed

Lullaby; an 87th Precinct novel. Morrow 1989 350p

                LC 88-13709

"Returning from a party, a couple find their adopted baby and her teenaged sitter murdered. There are so many ramifications, including the later death of the biological mother, that the case seems hopelessly muddled. But Carella and Meyer, outraged by the crime, stick to the wearying routine and finally bring the guilty to book. . . . McBain's staccato dialogue and authentic characters, as always, make . . . {this} a page turner." Publ Wkly

McBain, Ed

Mischief; a novel of the 87th Precinct. Morrow 1993 346p

                LC 93-10404

"The Deaf Man, nemesis of the beleaguered 87th Precinct, is back, and he's scattering cryptic clues all over town, which only serves to multiply the frustrations of Detective Steve Carella and his coworkers. Not that their usual potpourri of crime doesn't offer its own fair share of frustration: graffiti writers are turning up dead in a series of seemingly random killings; mentally impaired senior citizens are being 'dumped' on local hospitals; and, in a city on the edge of racial violence, a free outdoor concert is expected to attract a quarter-million rap fans. . . . McBain tackles social issues . . . tells a good joke, reveals small details of his regular characters' personalities, and provides subplots that add depth and humanity to all the crime in the foreground." Booklist

McBain, Ed

The **mugger**. Armchair Detective Lib. 1990 150p

                LC 90-32352

First published 1956 in paperback

In this 87th Precinct mystery the police "must contend with a plethora of eccentric criminals, including a guy who steals household cats and a mugger who attacks women, then bows debonairly and offers a polite farewell. . . . McBain fans will instantly recognize the crisp dialogue that the series would soon become famous for: a hypnotic mix of terse truths, perpetual perplexities, and crude coptalk." Booklist

McBain, Ed

★ **Nocturne**. Warner Bks. 1997 291p
  ISBN 978-0446518055

                LC 96-42030

In this 87th precinct novel "detectives Carella and Hawes catch the first call on the night shift: the shooting death of a destitute woman who was once a renowned concert pianist. . . . Right away we're hooked, because these cops not only know their procedures, they also value a human life. Before this long, dark night is through, Mr. McBain will make us care abot a 19-year-old hooker who is savagely killed in a gang rape, a pimp and a drug dealer who also die hard and 25 roosters torn up in a cockfight." N Y Times Book Rev

McBain, Ed

Poison; an 87th Precinct novel. Arbor House 1987 264p

                LC 86-17342

"Detectives Steve Carella and Hal Wallis interrogate beautiful, wealthy Marilyn Hollis when one of her swains dies of poison, possibly a suicide. Marilyn becomes a murder suspect later, as two more men she has been socially and sexually involved with are killed in a development that creates a serious problem for the investigators. Wallis is now the woman's lover, living with her despite Carella's protest. Both detectives continue to track Marilyn's former male companions, looking for a jealous killer. But Wallis, heartsick, begins to believe that Marilyn is guilty. The taut, gripping story closes with a knockout surprise." Publ Wkly

McBain, Ed

There was a little girl. Warner Bks. 1994 323p
LC 94-29145

In this Matthew Hope novel "the hero spends most of his time in a semi-coma after being shot outside a bar on the seedy side of Calusa, Fla. . . . Meanwhile, Hope's PI pals Warren Chambers and Toots Kiley, as well as police detective Morris Bloom, try to reconstruct Hope's previous week, probings that are intercut with flashbacks to Hope's own investigation of the years-old suicide of a circus star. What emerges is an intricate, lurid tale of sex, blackmail and murder fueled by greed." Publ Wkly

McBain, Ed

★ **Three** blind mice; a novel. Arcade Pub. 1990 293p
LC 89-18543

"Mr. McBain's square-jawed dialogue and stout grip on detection procedures give his narrative the muscularity characteristic of the whole Hope series. But the real strength to flex those muscles comes from the perfectly constructed plot." N Y Times Book Rev

McBain, Ed

Tricks; an 87th Precinct novel. Arbor House 1987 247p
LC 87-11350

This novel "begins on a Halloween eve, and with the most unlikely of events. Four kids, wearing costumes and garish masks, hold up a series of liquor stores and kill the proprietors before escaping with their plunder. Detectives Brown and Genero make a grisly discovery in a garbage can—a headless torso. A professional magician, Sebastian the Great, puts on a disappearing act that confounds his attractive wife. She appeals to the police for help. Meanwhile, Detective First Class Eileen Burke draws the unenviable assignment of playing a hooker at a notorious bar in hopes of engaging a serial killer who is heavily armed and has a fondness for ladies of the evening." West Coast Rev Books

McBain, Ed

Vespers; a novel of the 87th Precinct. Morrow 1990 331p
LC 89-13124

"A priest is killed in his church, which is the scene of a standoff between a drug dealer and his assailants. Meanwhile, four blocks away, devil worshippers hold their own religious meetings. The men of the precinct must find the killer, extract the truth from myriad conflicting accounts, and explore the link with the demonic church." Booklist

McBain, Ed

Widows; a novel. Morrow 1991 332p
LC 90-49861

"On the same summer night that a young blond woman, the mistress of a wealthy, older, married man, is stabbed to death, detective Steve Carella's father is killed in his bakery by two thieves. Distracted by grief, Carella, with colleague Arthur Brown, investigates the woman's murder, which is followed by the wealthy man's death and those of his first and second wives." Publ Wkly

McBride, James

Miracle at St. Anna. Riverhead Bks. 2002 271p
ISBN 1-573-22212-7
LC 2001-48778

"Through his sharply drawn characters, McBride exposes racism, guilt, courage, revenge and forgiveness, with the soldiers confronting their own fear and rage in surprisingly personal ways at the decisive moment in their lives." Publ Wkly

McBride, James

Song yet sung. Riverhead Books 2008 359p $25.95
ISBN 978-1-59448-972-3; 1-59448-972-6
LC 2007-35969

"McBride borrows liberally from actual historical events and figures to fabricate this engrossing tale, and then emphasizes the implications of past actions by interspersing them with Liz's recurring nightmares of the future. . . . [His] characters evoke an extraordinary time that spawned ghosts that haunt us still." Seattle Times

McCabe, Patrick

★ The **butcher** boy. Fromm Int. 1993 215p
ISBN 0-88064-147-9
LC 93-2831

First published 1992 in the United Kingdom

"'The Butcher Boy' is the side of the murder story never revealed in the newspapers: a map of a murderer's mind, a revelation of a murderer's reason. It is the story of the heritage of madness and loneliness, a stunning picture of the desperation of the unloved." N Y Times Book Rev

McCabe, Patrick

Winterwood; a novel. Bloomsbury Pub. 2007 242p $23.95
ISBN 978-1-59691-163-5; 1-59691-163-8
LC 2006-15837

First published 2006 in the United Kingdom

"This is grim stuff, but no grimmer than your average Stephen King novel. Like King, McCabe knows how to invest pop culture with a sinister bathos. . . . McCabe is also more intense than King (or just about anyone else), and his characters are so trapped inside their own skulls that his novels can feel hermetically sealed. In the past, he's balanced that with an appealing dark humor, but in Winterwood he settles for urgent, sustained apprehension." N Y Times Book Rev

McCaffrey, Anne

★ **Acorna**; the unicorn girl. [by] Anne McCaffrey and Margaret Ball. HarperPrism 1997 291p
ISBN 978-0061052965
LC 97-11099

"Found in a survival pod in space by prospectors, the infant Acorna soon exhibits the ability to analyze deficiencies in plants by taste, purify water and air, and heal. Taken to the planet Kezdet to avoid scientists who want to study her, Acorna discovers barbaric child-labor practices and vows to rescue the children. McCaffrey and Ball have created a magical alien in this fantasy/science fiction story." Libr J

Followed by Acorna's quest

McCaffrey, Anne

Acorna's people; [by] Anne McCaffrey and Elizabeth Ann Scarborough. HarperPrism 1999 314p
ISBN 0-06-105094-6
LC 99-12850

In the third title in the series "Acorna is at last among her own. The beautiful healing horn in the center of her forehead and the 'funny' feet and hands that once set her apart now make her one with the telepathic Linyaari who live on as lush agrarian planet where they pursue their peaceful dreams. Acorna's people welcome her with a lavish costume ball—and an already-chosen mate! But Acorna still has much to do before she can enjoy the peaceful home she is offered. The legendary resting place of the lost Linyaari ancestors has yet to be found. With the help of the rogue spacetrader Becker and his cat, RK (RoadKill), Acorna must strive to right an unspeakable wrong and defeat an enemy even more cruel than the Khleevi themselves." Publisher's note

Followed by Acorna's world

McCaffrey, Anne

Acorna's quest; [by] Anne McCaffrey and Margaret Ball. HarperPrism 1998 292p
ISBN 0-06-105297-3
LC 97-51201

"Acorna has grown into a lovely adolescent humanoid whose physical appearance is reminiscent of the fabled unicorn. Her human protectors plan to help her seek her home world, but she and Calum leave prematurely and follow an unpredictable path on their mission to search the sector of space where her survival pod has launched from. Subsequent events intervene with her quest for home. . . . McCaffrey and Acorna fans will delight in this." Voice Youth Advocates

McCaffrey, Anne

Acorna's rebels; {by} Anne McCaffrey and Elizabeth Ann Scarborough. Eos 2003 p. cm
ISBN 0-380-97899-7; 0-380-81847-7 (alk. paper)
LC 2002-73873

McCaffrey, Anne

Acorna's search; [by] Anne McCaffrey and Elizabeth Ann Scarborough. Eos 2001 292p
ISBN 0-380-97898-9
LC 2001-33562

In this fifth installment in the series "Acorna helps her people, the Linyaari, try to restore their beloved home world, which was literally laid waste by the vicious Khleevi. Aari, the young man so brutally tortured by the Khleevi, is now Acorna's life mate and at work on a survey team trying to locate mountains and rivers in all the rubble." Booklist

McCaffrey, Anne

Acorna's triumph; [by] Anne McCaffrey and Elizabeth Ann Scarborough. 1st ed; Eos 2004 308p $24.95
ISBN 0-380-97900-4
LC 2003-59622

"The Linyaari home world of Vhiliinyar has been reclaimed, and Acorna, the unicorn-horned girl, has found her life-mate, Aari, who had once suffered at the hands of the Khleevi invaders. However, all is not right, since Aari has changed drastically, and Acorna discovers a new threat of an invasion by the Linyaari's ancient enemies. . . . [The authors] combine their talents in this conclusion to a series about a young woman's growth into maturity and her determined search for her missing people and her vanished mate." Libr J

McCaffrey, Anne

Acorna's world; [by] Anne McCaffrey and Elizabeth Ann Scarborough. HarperCollins Pubs. 2000 320p
ISBN 0-06-105095-4
LC 00-28830

In the fourth installment in the series Acorna "finds herself unable to adjust to her native culture because of her upbringing by her human 'uncles' and her involvement in so many space adventures. So she ships out with the salvager Becker; his ship's cat, Roadkill; and Aari, a young man of Acorna's race whose torture at the hands of the vicious, buglike aliens, the Khleevi, has left him hornless and vulnerable." Booklist

McCaffrey, Anne

All the Weyrs of Pern. Ballantine Bks. 1991 404p (Dragonriders of Pern)
LC 91-91910

"This is an exciting, full-bodied, richly detailed . . . chapter in the Pern chronicle as the knowledge of the first settlers is united with the wisdom of the descendants. . . . Once again McCaffrey's narrative flows smoothly, maintaining the world and characters she has so lovingly created and setting new challenges for them to meet." Booklist

McCaffrey, Anne

The chronicles of Pern; first fall. Ballantine Bks. 1993 306p
LC 93-10079

"These five original stories . . . offer a glimpse into the early history of the world of 'thread' and Dragonriders. McCaffrey's unadorned prose allows characters and plot to take center stage." Libr J

McCaffrey, Anne

Crystal line. Ballantine Bks. 1992 294p
LC 92-53219

Sequel to Killashandra

In this conclusion of the trilogy, "crystal singer of the Heptite Guild, Killashandra Ree enjoys the benefits of increased longevity and the status of an elite artisan at a terrible price: the slow erosion of her memory. When the Guild faces a crisis that could result in its demise, Killashandra faces a battle to overcome her own fears and learn to trust in someone other than herself." Libr J

McCaffrey, Anne

Crystal singer. Ballantine Bks. 1982 311p
LC 82-4009

"This is a well-constructed story with a strong-willed and courageous young heroine who finds her niche in the workplace." Voice Youth Advocates

Followed by Killashandra

McCaffrey, Anne

Dragon's Kin; [by] Anne McCaffrey [and] Todd McCaffrey. Del Rey/Ballantine Bks. 2003 304p $24.95

ISBN 0-345-46198-3

The action in this Dragonriders of Pern tale "takes place during an unexplored period in the history of Pern, before the coming of the Thread. The watch-whers are already playing a prominent role, however, keeping watch at night at the holds and weyrs and helping in the mines. The protagonists are Kindin and Nuella, young people living in a mining camp. A cave-in wipes out Kindin's father and brothers as well as the old watch-wher, and Kindin moves in with camp Harper. There he learns the skills of being a Harper, including discretion and mediation. Eventually, he and Nuella learn the secret of how watch-whers see in the dark, and about their communication with dragons, which opens a wholly new range of capabilities for the dragonriders." Booklist

McCaffrey, Anne

Dragon's time; [by] Anne McCaffrey and Todd McCaffrey. Del Rey/Ballantine Books 2011 $26

ISBN 978-0-345-50089-2; 0-345-50089-X

LC 2010-47869

"Illness and accident has robbed Pern of many of the planet's people and dragons. Fiona, Weyrwoman of Telgar, her lovers, Weyrleader T'Mar and Harper Kindan, and Kindan's other lover, the ex-dragonrider Lorana, seek desperately for a way to get the Weyrs up to fighting strength against the threat of Thread, the devouring alien spores that periodically invade the planet. The solution involves riding the dragons backward and forward in time." Kirkus

McCaffrey, Anne

★ **Dragonflight**; volume 1 of The Dragonriders of Pern. Ballantine Bks. 1978 337p il (Dragonriders of Pern) hardcover o.p. pa $12.95

ISBN 0-345-27749-X; 0-345-48426-6 pa

LC 78-16707

First published 1968 in paperback. Based on two award winning stories entitled: Weyr search and Dragonrider. Many titles co-written by Todd McCaffrey

ALA YALSA Margaret A. Edwards Award (1999)

The planet Pern, originally colonized from Earth but long out of contact with it, has been periodically threatened by the deadly silver Threads which fall from the wandering Red Star. To combat them a life form on the planet was developed into winged, fire-breathing dragons. Humans with a high degree of empathy and telepathic power are needed to train and preserve these creatures. As the story begins, Pern has fallen into decay, the threat of the Red Star has been forgotten, the Dragonriders and dragons are reduced in number and in disrepute, and the evil Lord Fax has begun conquering neighboring holds.

McCaffrey, Anne

Dragonquest; volume 2 of The Dragonriders of Pern. Ballantine Bks. 1979 351p il (Dragonriders of Pern)

LC 78-19721

Sequel to Dragonflight

First published 1971 in paperback

The inhabitants of Pern begin to resent the attitudes of the oldtime Dragonriders who were brought forward in time to aid their modern counterparts in defeating the deadly Thread from the Red Star and now feel that their new world owes them a living. The Weyrleader F'lar and his consort Lessa try to mediate between the Dragonriders and the landbound people they had protected, but new forces upset Pern's delicate social structure and threaten to destroy not only the unique privileges of the Dragonriders, but their very reason for existence

Followed by The white dragon

McCaffrey, Anne

Dragonsdawn. Ballantine Bks. 1988 431p (Dragonriders of Pern)

LC 88-9307

Chronologically the first novel in the Dragonriders of Pern series "it tells of the colonizing of the uninhabited planet Pern by a few thousand carefully selected humans, of the colonists' first encounter with the life-threatening spores known as Thread and of the creation (by genetic engineering) of the winged, telepathic, fire-breathing 'dragons' who become the colonists' first line of defense against the periodic falls of Thread." Booklist

McCaffrey, Anne

Dragonseye. Ballantine Bks. 1997 353p (Dragonriders of Pern)

ISBN 978-0613134712

LC 96-44206

In this title, in the Dragonriders of Pern series "the Dragonriders finally get to protect their world from the danger they've been anticipating for 200 years. When signs appear that Thread, the deadly silver strands that devour everything organic, will soon make an appearance, Dragonrider Chalkin's failure to believe in the danger of Threadfall threatens to destroy the entire civilization." Libr J

The author "brings us another diverse cast of responsible, heroic good guys and dragons in a novel that's going to please fans old and new." Publ Wkly

McCaffrey, Anne

★ **Freedom's** landing. Putnam 1995 342p

LC 94-43820

"With her customary talent for imaginative storytelling, the author skillfully portrays the environmental and personal challenges faced by the new colonists." Libr J

Followed by Freedom's choice (1997) and Freedom's challenge (1998)

McCaffrey, Anne

Freedom's ransom. Putnam 2002 288p $23.95

ISBN 0-399-14889-2

LC 2001-56669

Fourth title in the author's Cattani/Freedom series. "In Freedom's Challenge (1998), the colonists on the planet Botany, who were initially dropped there as slaves, freed themselves from the Eosi-dominated Cattani overlords. Now it is time to reestablish contact with Earth and 'ransom' Earth's stolen technological materials, which are in warehouses on the Cattani planet Barevi. Zainal and Kris head an expedition to a decimated and devastated but slowly recovering Earth to trade for items to use in bartering with shifty Barevi merchants." Booklist

"The visit to a bleak Manhattan after the Eosian looting is as disturbing, touching and humorous as the trading in the Barevian market." Publ Wkly

McCaffrey, Anne
The **girl** who heard dragons. TOR Bks. 1994 352p il

LC 94-118

This is a "diverse assortment of 15 short fiction pieces never before gathered in one volume. The heroine of the engaging title story, a new Pern novella and the only Pern tale in the collection, is somewhat akin to Menolly in Dragonsong in that she, too, eventually rises above her birthright to follow the destiny that her particular talent dictates. Perhaps the strongest inclusion here is 'The Greatest Love,' also a novella, which predicted in 1977 (when McCaffrey wrote it) the extrauterine fertilization of a human ovum to produce a healthy baby. . . . Other stories focus on everything from spaceship adventure, shifting time-storms, and the unwitting near-destruction of sentient life-forms by human colonists on a distant planet (and the fitting, if gruesome consequences)—to ghosts and romance." Booklist

McCaffrey, Anne
Killashandra. Ballantine Bks. 1985 303p

LC 85-6193

"This suspenseful and romantic story exhibits McCaffrey's usual verve in building convincing societies, developing vital characters, and sustaining mood." Booklist
Followed by Crystal line

McCaffrey, Anne
The **Masterharper** of Pern. Ballantine Bks. 1998 431p (Dragonriders of Pern)
ISBN 0-345-38823-2

LC 97-30896

This installment in the Dragonriders of Pern series "details the life, loves, and heartbreaks of Robinton, Pern's most beloved harper. Readers follow him through a childhood filled with rejection and neglect by his Mastercomposer father, the loss of his wife, the death of his best friend, to his becoming Masterharper of Pern. This is McCaffrey at her best, combining excellent writing with vivid settings and detailed, fully fleshed-out characters." SLJ

McCaffrey, Anne
Pegasus in space. Ballantine Bks. 2000 373p
ISBN 0-345-43466-8

LC 99-53225

"Following To Ride Pegasus (1973) and Pegasus in Flight (1990), this is a third prequel to the Rowan series. . . . Here, the first space station becomes a reality, and quadriplegic teenager Peter Reidinger, whose telekinetic Talent proved amazing in Pegasus in Flight, is the protagonist. Peter tests and hones his ability not only to move his body naturally but also to teleport large objects instantaneously through space. Peter helps other Talents, as such gifted youngsters are called, thwart a mutiny aboard the nearly finished space station." Booklist

McCaffrey, Anne
The **renegades** of Pern. Ballantine Bks. 1989 384p il (Dragonriders of Pern)

LC 89-6694

This tale "begins during the time of Dragonquest and continues beyond the closing of The White Dragon, focusing on some of the commoners, and how they cope with the return of the life-consuming Thread. A number of lives intertwine, such as that of the trader boy Jayge Lilcamp, whose family is almost destroyed when his father refuses to believe the first Thread warning." Publ Wkly

McCaffrey, Anne
The **skies** of Pern. Ballantine Pub. Group 2001 434p (Dragonriders of Pern)
ISBN 0-345-43468-4

LC 00-51859

A Dragonriders of Pern novel. "With the discovery of Aivas, the artificial intelligence hidden for centuries in Pern's southern continent, the residents of the third planet of the sun called Rukbat have learned how to end the threat posed by the periodic fall of Thread from the erratic red star that orbits the planet. Despite the abundance of rediscovered knowledge, new dangers and old fears surface, forcing Dragonriders, Holders, and Craftmasters all to reconsider their purpose and functions in society." Libr J

"As all her Pern novels amply demonstrate, McCaffrey's sexy and cunning dragons carry the day—and the novel—with impeccable, irresistible panache." Publ Wkly

McCaffrey, Anne
The **white** dragon; volume 3 of The Dragonriders of Pern. Ballantine Bks. 1978 497p il (Dragonriders of Pern)

LC 77-18913

Sequel to Dragonquest
"A prologue summarizes the first two volumes of the saga. . . . Young Jaxom and his white dragon Ruth (a male), previously encountered, mature, fight the deadly Threads from the Red Planet, help open the largely unexplored continent and discover in an ancient spaceship a map, key to major changes for Pern. Once all the necessary background is assimilated, it's a rousing adventure and colorful portrayal of a unique and carefully-worked-out culture." Publ Wkly

McCaffrey, Todd
Dragonsblood; Todd McCaffrey. Ballantine Books 2005 viii, 438p map (hbk.) o.p.; (hbk.) o.p.; (pbk.) $7.99
ISBN 0345441249; 9780345441249; 9780345441256

LC 2004051086

This fantasy novel of the Pern saga follows "Wind Blossom, one of the original colonists of Pern, who's struggling to create a legacy for future generations before she dies, and Lorana, a young dragonrider born 450 years later with unusual talents for healing and telepathy. A . . . set of time travel puzzles and paradoxes is set against the . . . backdrop of two populations struggling to survive: the children of the colonists, learning to live in a new world as they lose the technology of the old one, and the dragons of Lorana's time, who are dying of a mysterious plague just when they're needed to protect Pern. The strength of the two women and the mysterious connection between them is gradually revealed through a number of . . . parallel occurrences." (Publishers Weekly)

McCaffrey, Vincent

A **slepyng** hound to wake; a mystery. Small Beer Press 2011 277p $24

ISBN 978-1-931520-26-3; 1-931520-26-7

LC 2011-04627

"Henry Sullivan's old flame Barbara runs the failing Alcott & Poe bookstore, where he used to work before he realized he wasn't cut out for dealing with the public. Now he sells the fine volumes he collects on his website. Barbara's icy partner Sharon, looking for money to keep the store going, tells Henry that popular author George Duggan plagiarized his last bestseller from Sharon's lover, a murdered history professor. Henry ends up with a murder of his own when reformed junkie Eddy Perry, who sold him a book, is killed, apparently for the money Henry paid him, and his estate includes a manuscript of his own that Henry feels is worthy of publication. Meanwhile, Henry's current girlfriend, Della, gets involved in the mess Sharon's accusations have created. . . . The strong mystery is woven into a slow-paced, philosophical discussion of the painful demise of those special bookstores whose nooks and crannies once yielded fabulous finds." Kirkus

McCaig, Donald

Jacob's ladder; a story of Virginia during the war. Norton 1998 525p

ISBN 0-393-04629-X

LC 97-31165

"Delving into letters, diaries and memoirs for period detail, McCaig follows Jesse, Maggie and a large cast of characters through the battlefields, hospitals, prisons and slave wharves of the crumbling Confederacy. Throughout, he binds his narrative with a meticulous respect for authenticity." N Y Times Book Rev

McCall Smith, Alexander, 1948-

Blue shoes and happiness. Pantheon Books 2006 227p $21.95

ISBN 0-375-42272-2

LC 2005-52122

In this installment "Botswana detective Precious Ramotswe faces one of her toughest challenges: losing weight. Luckily, there are plenty of dilemmas to keep her mind off her girth: a nearby village that seems under the influence of witchcraft, a cook suspected of filching food for her increasingly portly spouse, and a newspaper advice columnist who's doing more damage than good. Readers become better acquainted with assistant detective Mma Grace Makutsi, best known for earning a stellar 97 percent grade at the Botswana Secretarial College. . . . McCall Smith renders brisk, seamless tales that are both wry and profound. Amidst the mayhem (like the cobra that slithers its way into the detective agency's headquarters) are eloquent descriptions of the serene African country that holds a special place in his heart." Booklist

McCall Smith, Alexander

The **comforts** of a muddy Saturday. Pantheon Books 2008 240p $23.95

ISBN 978-0-375-42513-4; 0-375-42513-6

LC 2008-18573

Philosophical sleuth Isabel Dalhousie, "who's recently assumed ownership of the obscure journal she's edited for many years, the Review of Applied Ethics, applies her deductive gifts to the case of a disgraced doctor. When a patient dies after taking a new antibiotic that Marcus Moncrieff deemed safe in clinical trials, the doctor's original report turns out to contain falsified data. Did Moncrieff skew the data to please the drug manufacturers? Moncrieff's wife turns to Isabel for help in lifting her husband out of his despondency. While the truth isn't straightforward, the motives of the guilty party prove to be both plausible and rational. The strengths of the book . . . lie in its protagonist's determination to treat others without judgment—and in the author's revealing glimpses into the human soul." Publ Wkly

McCall Smith, Alexander, 1948-

A **conspiracy** of friends; Alexander McCall Smith. Pantheon Books 2011 261 p $24.95

ISBN 0307907236; 9780307907233

LC 2011051041

This novel "visits the self-contained fictional world encompassing the residents of Corduroy Mansions in London's Pimlico neighborhood. The book opens by introducing an immense ensemble cast, which includes Oedipus Snark, 'the only truly nasty Liberal Democrat Member of Parliament'; his mother, Berthea, at work on a 'hostile biography' of her son; . . . as well as the hapless, affable wine merchant William French and his dog, Freddie de la Hay. Each has his or her own tale: a conflict at work, a longing for love, the search for new smells." (Publishers Weekly)

McCall Smith, Alexander

Corduroy mansions; illustrations by Iain McIntosh. Pantheon Books 2010 353p il $24.95

ISBN 978-0-307-37908-5; 0-307-37908-6

LC 2009-47155

First published 2009 in the United Kingdom

First title in a "new series set among a collection of flats in London's lively Pimlico neighborhood. Residents here run the gamut from the very likable to the much loathed. There's William, a well-meaning, widowed wine merchant determined to oust his lazy twentysomething son from his house. . . . Then there's the thoroughly despicable Oedipus Snark, a Parliament member devoid of scruples, conscience, and class. Even his own mother despises him; she's writing his biography, with the aim of exposing every one of his faults. Four young women share a flat as well. Among them is Dee, a health-food devotee who can't understand a male coworker's resistance to her offer of a high-colonic, and art history student Caroline, who has designs on a friend unsure whether he wants to date women or men. Also afoot throughout the book is the astonishingly astute Freddie de la Hay, a canine inclined to paws and reflect." Booklist

McCall Smith, Alexander

The **Double** Comfort Safari Club. Pantheon Books 2010 211p $24.95

ISBN 978-0-375-42450-2; 0-375-42450-4

LC 2009-49060

"It's not in the stories themselves, but in the telling of them, that the secret of McCall Smith's appeal lies. His Botswana may indeed be a kindly place, but he has an ability – a very rare one – to write with kindness too. This world, he says, is only ours for a short time, and we realise that more and more with age. And when we cry, he'll point out, how odd it is that we rock forward and back, as our mothers comforted us, as if we were trying to comfort ourselves. Such aperçus are, of themselves, not original. What is, is the way McCall Smith effortlessly weaves them into stories of fun and laughter and heartfelt love of place and character." Scotsman

McCall Smith, Alexander, 1948-

The **full** cupboard of life; Alexander McCall Smith. Pantheon Books 2003 198 p.

ISBN 0375422188; 9780375422188

LC 2003062379

In this book, "Mma Ramotswe and Mr. J.L.B. Matekoni are still engaged, but with no immediate plans to get married. . . . For indeed he has other things on his mind--particularly a frightening request (involving a parachute jump) made by Mma Potokwani, the persuasive matron of the orphan farm. Mma Ramotswe herself has weighty matters on her mind, including a case in which a wealthy woman wonders whether her suitors are interested in her or just her money. Meanwhile, Mma Makutsi--plucky assistant detective and deputy manager of the Tlokweng Road Speedy Motors garage--is moving. Her entrepreneurial venture, the Kalahari Typing School for Men, is thriving and with this new income she has rented two rooms in a house." (Publisher's note)

McCall Smith, Alexander

The **good** husband of Zebra Drive. Pantheon Books 2007 213p (No. 1 Ladies Detective Agency) $21.95

ISBN 978-0-375-42273-7; 0-375-42273-0

LC 2006-39047

In this mystery, set in Botswana, "Dr. Cronje, who's half Xhosa and half Afrikaner, consults . . . Precious Ramotswe, because patients at his hospital who have occupied a particular bed have been dying mysteriously at the same time of day. Meanwhile, Mma Ramotswe's recently engaged assistant, Grace Makutsi, threatens to break their longstanding association. Mma Ramotswe must adjust their relationship in order to retain Mma Makutsi's services. The author's subtlety of touch and humane portrayal of figures at all levels of society will continue to win him new readers even as his deepening of the ties binding the main figures will satisfy those who have followed the lady detectives from their first recorded case." Publ Wkly

McCall Smith, Alexander

★ **In** the company of cheerful ladies. Pantheon Books 2005 233p $19.95

ISBN 0-375-42271-4

LC 2004-56827

In this installment, "Botswana detective Precious Ramotswe, the traditionally built-and newly married-owner of the No. 1 Ladies' Detective Agency, is saddled with a surfeit of challenging cases and personal crises. There has been an intruder in her home (he managed to escape, but left a telltale pair of trousers in his wake). And the levelheaded sleuth is flustered by an encounter with a man from her past. Meanwhile, Mma Ramotswe's husband, master mechanic Mr. J.L.B. Matekoni, is neck-deep in work after the resignation of one of his apprentices, who has become romantically entangled with a married woman (Mma Ramotswe and assistant detective Grace Makutsi slyly gather the scurrilous details). . . . [The author] renders colorful characters with names that trip off the tongue." Publ Wkly

McCall Smith, Alexander, 1948-

The **Kalahari** typing school for men; Alexander McCall Smith. Pantheon Books 2003 186 p.

ISBN 037542217X; 9780375422171

LC 2002030709

In this book, "Mma Precious Ramotswe is content. Her business is well established with many satisfied customers, and in her mid-thirties . . . she has a house, two adopted children, a fine fiancé. But, as always, there are troubles. Mr. J.L.B. Matekoni has not set the date for their marriage. Her able assistant, Mma Makutsi, wants a husband. And worse, a rival detective agency has opened in town--an agency that does not have the gentle approach to business that Mma Ramotswe's does." (Publisher's note)

McCall Smith, Alexander, 1948-

The **Limpopo** Academy of Private Detection; Alexander McCall Smith. Pantheon Books 2012 257 p. (No. 1 Ladies Detective Agency)

ISBN 9780307378408

LC 2011050788

This book is the 13th in Alexander McCall Smith's No. 1 Ladies' Detective Agency series featuring detective Precious Ramotswe. In it, "an unknown tall man appears in a dream to Mma Ramotswe, and before long, one shows up for real, in the person of American Clovis Andersen. . . . Anderson ends up assisting his biggest fan in looking into the dirty laundry of a businessman whose plans to make the local orphanage more efficient threaten the role of its matron and its successful operation." (Publishers Weekly)

McCall Smith, Alexander

The **lost** art of gratitude. Pantheon Books 2009 262p $23.95

ISBN 978-0-375-42514-1; 0-375-42514-4

LC 2009-22618

A mystery featuring Scottish philosopher Isabel Dalhousie. "Minty Auchterlonie, who once alerted Isabel to some insider trading, fears someone is out to get her. The tax authorities have suddenly investigated Minty, and an unknown party has sent her a funeral wreath. When Isabel looks into these provocative acts, she draws on lessons learned from the journal she edits, the Review of Applied Ethics, to arrive at the complex truth behind them. Meanwhile, the father of Isabel's young son proposes marriage, and a defeated academic rival accuses her of knowingly publishing plagiarism.

Smith's trademark humor and telling observations about people heighten the appeal." Publ Wkly

McCall Smith, Alexander

Love over Scotland. Anchor Books 2007 357p pa $13.95

ISBN 978-0-307-27598-1

LC 2007-22072

First published 2006 in the United Kingdom; originally serialized in The Scotsman

In this installment "anthropologist Domenica has flown off to the Straits of Malacca to study modern-day pirates. Back in Edinburgh, Pat moves from 44 Scotland Street and develops a crush on fellow art student Wolf, whose strange ways hint at a darker subplot that involves Pat's flatmate. Pat moves in with gallery owner Matthew, who struggles with both a sudden fortune and a yearning for Pat. Meanwhile, child prodigy saxophonist Bertie becomes a reluctant member of the Edinburgh Teenage Orchestra at age six and later, on a trip to Paris, finds himself wonderfully unsupervised. Poet/portrait painter Angus is tormented by the theft of his beloved dog Cyrus. The proceedings sparkle with McCall Smith's trademark wit (It was not always fun being a child, just as it had not always been fun being a medieval Scottish saint), proving once again, he's a true treasure. Illustrations by Iain McIntosh enliven the text." Publ Wkly

McCall Smith, Alexander, 1948-

The **No.** 1 Ladies' Detective Agency; Alexander McCall Smith. Pantheon Books 2005 235 p.

ISBN 0375423877; 9780375423871

LC 2005047587

"This first novel in Alexander McCall Smith's . . . The No. 1 Ladies Detective Agency series[, which was voted one of the International Books of the Year and the Millennium by the 'Times Literary Supplement,'] tells the story of . . . Precious Ramotswe, who is drawn to her profession to 'help people with problems in their lives.' Immediately upon setting up shop in a small storefront in Gaborone, she is hired to track down a missing husband, uncover a con man, and follow a wayward daughter. But the case that tugs at her heart, and lands her in danger, is a missing eleven-year-old boy, who may have been snatched by witchdoctors." (Publisher's note)

McCall Smith, Alexander, 1948-

The **Saturday** big tent wedding party; The New No. 1 Ladies' Detective Agency Novel. Alexander McCall Smith. Recorded Books 2011 213 p. $24.95

ISBN 9781456116224 lib bdg

LC 2010054099

In this book, "Mma Precious Ramotswe's latest client, Botsalo Moeti, made no enemies working for a mining company, and he's hardly had the opportunity to make any as a farmer. So why has someone killed two of his cattle by cutting their Achilles tendons? Although a trip to his farm persuades Mma Ramotswe that he may have more enemies than he realizes, it doesn't tell her which of them is responsible. . . . Charlie, the eternal apprentice mechanic at Tlokweng Road Speedy Motors, the establishment owned by Mma Ramotswe's husband, Mr. J.L.B. Matekoni, seems so determined to avoid Prudence Ramkhwane after she bears

his twins that he runs away when he's taxed with his responsibilities." (Kirkus)

McCall Smith, Alexander, 1948-

Tea time for the traditionally built; Alexander McCall Smith. Pantheon Books 2009 212 p.

ISBN 9780375424496

LC 2009000774

This book is the 10th in Alexander McCall Smith's series featuring detective Precious Ramotswe. Here, she is asked by "Leungo Molofololo, the owner of the Kalahari Swoopers, a local soccer team with a lot of athletic talent," to explore a possible "traitor on the squad [who] is deliberately sabotaging games for an unknown reason. Despite her complete ignorance of the sport, Mma Ramotswe agrees to look into the matter. She and her prickly assistant, Grace Makutsi, attend a match and begin interviewing the players in an effort to solve what amounts to the book's main mystery. The soccer inquiry, though, is secondary to a major event in Mma Ramotswe's life--the impending demise of the little white van she's used for many years that's much more than a machine to her." (Publishers Wkly)

McCall Smith, Alexander, 1948-

Trains and Lovers; Alexander McCall Smith. Pantheon Books 2013 256 p. $22

ISBN 0307908542; 9780307908544

LC 2012042073

In this novel by Alexander McCall Smith "four travelers pass the time by sharing tales of trains that have changed their lives. A . . . Scotsman recounts how he turned a friendship with a female coworker into a romance. An Australian woman shares how her parents . . . spent their life together running a railroad siding. A[n] . . . American . . . recalls his own youthful crush on another man. A young Englishman describes how exiting his train at the wrong station [le] him to meet [a] . . . woman." (Publisher's note)

McCall Smith, Alexander

The **world** according to Bertie. Anchor Books 2008 343p il pa $13.95

ISBN 978-0-307-38706-6; 0-307-38706-2

LC 2008-28140

First published 2007 in the United Kingdom

"It is clear even to an outsider that someone who knows Edinburgh would recognize many people and places in '44 Scotland Street.' But an outsider can still relish McCall Smith's depiction of this place 'of angled streets and northern light,' and enjoy his tolerant, good-humored company." N Y Times Book Rev

McCall, Dinah

Dreamcatcher; Dinah McCall. HarperPaperbacks 1996 292 p. (pbk.) $5

ISBN 0061083259; 9780061083259

LC 2011656139

In this book, "[u]nable to free herself from her husband's obsession, beautiful Amanda Potter retreats into her own dream world where a comforting lover adores her. But Jefferson Dupree, a man searching for the woman he knows is his destiny, is determined to create for Amanda a reality more fulfilling than any dream." (Publisher's note)

McCammon, Robert R.

★ **Boy's** life. Pocket Bks. 1991 440p

LC 91-2813

"In 1964, 12-year-old Cory Mackenson lives with his parents in Zephyr, Alabama. It is a sleepy, comfortable town. Cory is helping with his father's milk route one morning when a car plunges into the lake before their eyes. His father dives in after the car and finds a dead man handcuffed to the steering wheel. Their world no longer seems so innocent: a vicious killer hides among apparently friendly neighbors." Libr J

McCammon, Robert R.

Gone south. Pocket Bks. 1992 359p

ISBN 0-671-74306-6

LC 92-28062

"The plot flows well and quickly. The extreme characters only point up McCammon's theme: everybody has a hidden deformity and can only become free and happy by facing it. An engrossing read." Booklist

McCammon, Robert R.

The **Queen** of Bedlam; [by] Robert McCammon. Pocket Books 2007 645p pa $16

ISBN 978-1-416-55111-9; 1-416-55111-5

"Set in Manhattan in 1703, this . . . sequel to Speaks the Nightbird (2002) . . . finds Matthew Corbett, a 23-year-old magistrate's clerk, on the trail of the Masker, a killer who stalks prominent businessmen. Matthew stumbles on the bodies of two of the Masker's victims, including pederast Eben Ausley, the headmaster of the orphanage Matthew once reluctantly called home. Plucky Matthew, who becomes a junior associate of the New York branch of a London problem-solving firm called the Herrald Agency, discovers a possible link to the crimes in the person of an elderly amnesiac patient in a mental asylum who's known as the Queen of Bedlam. Matthew and his cohorts later make a dangerous foray to the headquarters that the villainous Professor Fell maintains for young-criminals-in-training. McCammon brilliantly captures colonial New York and closes with a tantalizing cliffhanger that suggests more exciting sleuthing to come." Publ Wkly

McCann, Colum

Dancer; a novel. Metropolitan Bks. 2003 336p $26

ISBN 0-8050-6792-2

LC 2002-71879

"It's hard to tell what a reader unfamiliar with the outlines of Nureyev's life might make of 'Dancer.' Much, deliberately, is left unsaid. Reduced to words, the dance evaporates—only passion and the personal can make it move again." N Y Times Book Rev

McCann, Colum

Let the great world spin; a novel. Random House 2009 349p $25

ISBN 978-1-4000-6373-4; 1-4000-6373-6

LC 2008-46963

This "begins on August 7, 1974, when New Yorkers are stopped in their tracks by the sight of a man walking between the towers of the World Trade Center. Yes, it's Philippe Petit, the subject of the Academy Award–winning documentary Man on Wire and one of McCann's many intense and valiant characters. The cast also includes two Irish brothers: Corrigan, a radical monk, and Ciaran, who follows him to the blasted Bronx, where he encounters resilient prostitute Tillie and her spirited daughter Jazzlyn. Gloria lives in the same housing project, and she befriends Claire of Park Avenue as they mourn the deaths of their sons in Vietnam. McCann's hallucinatory descriptions of a great city tattooed and besmirched with graffiti, blood, and drugs in the midst of a financial freefall are eerie in their edgy beauty, chilling reminders of how quickly civilization unravels. Here, too, are portals onto war, the justice system, and the dawning of the cyber age." Booklist

McCann, Colum

Zoli; a novel. Random House 2007 333p $24.95

ISBN 978-1-4000-6372-7; 1-400-06372-8

LC 2006-42922

First published 2006 in the United Kingdom

"Zoli becomes a flash point for her tribe while raising an important question: In a world driven by conformity and (more lately) consumerism, how can the outsider survive? . . . . McCann's story feels like an important reminder of one dimension that has gladly been left behind: the soul-deadening totalitarianism that snuffs out dissent and difference with the force of its bureaucracy." Seattle Times

McCarry, Charles

★ **Old** boys. Overlook Press 2004 476p $25.95

ISBN 1-58567-545-8

LC 2004-48320

American spy novelist "McCarry returns to the world of his character Paul Christopher--who has mysteriously disappeared. Led by Christopher's cousin Horace, a group of his retired colleagues--the 'Old Boys' from the Outfit--embark on a . . . worldwide search for the master spy and an ancient scroll that may reveal an unspeakably dangerous truth." (Publisher's note)

"When Paul Christopher, the enigmatic hero of several earlier McCarry novels, disappears while on a quest for his nonagenarian mother, Lori, his black-sheep cousin, Horace Hubbard, convenes a discreet cadre of over-the-hill spies to find his confrere-and to save the world from Ib'n Awad, an aging Islamic terrorist in possession of 12 nuclear suitcase bombs. In a beguiling twist . . . . , all parties also seek a fabled ancient scroll that unmasks Jesus as an agent provocateur, handled by Judas for Roman spymaster Paul. The nonstop peregrinations of this league of extraordinary spooks take them to a score of exotic locales, pitting them against Chechen thugs, Chinese secret police, Nazi doctors, and a case of acute myocardial fibrillation. McCarry's commitment to this fanciful premise is absolute, and the resulting yarn combines the intrepid exploits of John Buchan, the cagey intrigue of Eric Ambler, and the clipped cadences of Dashiell Hammett. Tremendous fun." Booklist

McCarthy, Cormac, 1933-

★ **All** the pretty horses. Knopf 1992 301p $27.50; pa $14.95

ISBN 0-394-57474-5; 0-679-74439-8 pa

LC 91-58560

In the spring of 1950, after the death of his grandfather, sixteen-year-old John Grady Cole "is evicted from the Texas ranch where he grew up. He and another boy Lacey Rawlins, head for Mexico on horseback, riding south until they finally turn up at a vast ranch in mountainous Coahuila, the Hacienda de la Purisima, where they sign on as vaqueros. . . . John Grady's unusual talent for breaking, training and understanding horses becomes crucial to the hacendado Don Hector's ambitious breeding program. For John Grady, La Purisima is a paradise, complete with its Eve, Don Hector's daughter, Alejandra." N Y Times Book Rev

"Though some readers may grow impatient with the wild prairie rhythms of McCarthy's language, others will find his voice completely transporting." Publ Wkly

McCarthy, Cormac

★ **Blood** meridian; or, The evening redness in the West. Random House 1985 337p

ISBN 0-394-40027-5

"This book is set in the south-west borderland between the United States and Mexico, and follows the experiences of the (unnamed) kid, as he gets involved with a gang of mercenaries called the Glantons, and meets one of the most menacing figures in modern literature, Judge Holden, a huge, pale, manic individual who seems to know every aspect of human culture and to conduct a single-handed and satanic campaign to destroy it all. This is a savage book, full of rape and pillage, with more scalpings described in more detail–the Indians are just as savage as the whites–than (surely) in any other book. It is also beautifully written, a great poetic exploration of nature and the myth of the West." Good Fiction Guide

McCarthy, Cormac

Cities of the plain. Knopf 1998 291p $27.50

ISBN 0-679-42390-7

LC 98-11583

"McCarthy's language carries a brooding, evolutionary sense of time and labor—in his hands the changing of a tire on an old truck becomes a mythic deed. The weight of history rests on the shoulders of John Grady, too, and he's doomed to learn that 'when things are gone they're gone. They aint comin back.'" New Yorker

McCarthy, Cormac

The **crossing**. Knopf 1994 425p

ISBN 0-394-57475-3

LC 94-4281

The author "is a great and inventive storyteller, and he writes brilliantly and knowledgeably about animals and landscapes—but . . . the power and delight of the book derive from the fact that he seems incapable of writing a boring sentence. Reading him, one is very much in the hands of a stylist. . . . The style comes from Joyce and Hemingway out of Gertrude Stein. It is a matter of straight-on writing, a veering accumulation of compound sentences, stinginess with commas and a witching repetition of words." N Y Times Book Rev

McCarthy, Cormac

No country for old men. Knopf 2005 309p $24.95

ISBN 0-37540-677-8

"As devised and refined by James M. Cain, Jim Thompson and their gloomy paperback peers, the crime novel aimed its cheap handgun at the heart of America's most prized beliefs about its destiny: that the loot we've scooped up will belong to us forever and that history allows clean getaways. Cormac McCarthy's 'No Country for Old Men' is as bracing a variation on these noir orthodoxies as any fan of the genre could expect." N Y Times Book Rev

McCarthy, Cormac, 1933-

The **road**. Knopf 2006 241p $24.00

ISBN 0307265439; 9780307265432

LC 2006-23629

"A father and his son walk alone through burned America. Nothing moves in the ravaged landscape save the ash on the wind. It is cold enough to crack stones, and when the snow falls it is gray. They sky is dark. Their destination is the coast, although they don't know what, if anything, awaits them there. They have nothing; just a pistol to defend themselves against the lawless bands that stalk the road, the clothes they are wearing, a cart of scavenged food—and each other." (Publisher's note)

"A nuclear holocaust has reduced everything to ash, mummifying all but a few unlucky souls, who must kill or be killed (and eaten). The main characters are a father and his son, who was born a few nights after the bombs fell. 'We're still the good guys,' the man repeatedly assures the boy as they scavenge their way south for the winter, trying to avoid 'bad guy' survival techniques. . . . The horrors here—an infant 'headless and gutted and blackening on the spit'—are extreme, and, deprived of historical context, . . . [the author's] brutality can seem willful. But McCarthy's prose retains its ability to seduce . . . and there are nods to the gentler aspects of the human spirit." New Yorker

McCarthy, Mary

★ **Birds** of America. Harcourt Brace Jovanovich 1971 344p

"Miss McCarthy is astringent and sharp in all the right places, gentle where she should be. What she has written is an honest and appropriate love letter to an essentially decent young American." Publ Wkly

McCarthy, Mary

A **charmed** life. Harcourt Brace & Co. 1955 313p

"John and Martha Sinnott encounter an amazing assortment of would-be bohemians when, in the hope of gaining a new lease on their marriage, they move to the artistic community of New Leeds. They long for privacy but cocktail parties, drama groups, and Martha's first husband Miles keep breaking in. Even Martha's pregnancy brings unforeseen problems for due to one after-the-party interlude the question of fatherhood broadens to two possibilities: John or Miles. The author is at her brilliant best in this comic tragedy of modern man's dilemma: the fluctuation between belief and unbelief, courage and despair." Booklist

McCarthy, Mary

★ The **group**. Harcourt Brace & Co. 1963 378p

"It is perhaps as social history that the novel will chiefly be remembered; but over and above its sensitive observations it has a quality that one has not come to expect from this particular author, and that is compassion." Saturday Rev

McCarthy, Mary

The **groves** of Academe. Harcourt Brace & Co. 1952 302p

"An intelligent and sophisticated dissection of faculty life at Jocelyn, a small progressive college in Pennsylvania. The impending dismissal of self-styled liberal, Henry Mulcahy, Joycean scholar and instructor in literature, and the spring Poetry Conference are the main incidents in the narrative; but woven around them and even tying them together quite neatly is the probing, satirical and often deadly accurate account of college administration and personalities. A few of America's leading poets seem to appear pseudonymously during the conference." Libr J

McCarthy, Morgan

The **other** half of me; a novel. by Morgan McCarthy. Free Press 2012 316 p.

ISBN 1451668236; 9781451668230

LC 2012001082

In this novel, by Morgan McCarthy, "Jonathan Anthony and his little sister, Theo, are inseparable. Together they explore the wild acres of Evendon, [Wales]. . . . When a family tragedy brings their . . . grandmother . . . home, . . . [they] are initially elated by the attention. . . . But . . . there is more to the Anthony family history than either Eve or Alicia will acknowledge, trapping . . . [them] in a web of dark secrets that have haunted Evendon for generations." (Publisher's note)

McCarthy, Tom

★ **C**. Alfred A. Knopf 2010 310p $25.95

ISBN 978-0-307-59333-7; 0-307-59333-9

LC 2010-04071

"Opening in England at the turn of the twentieth century, C is the story of a boy named Serge Carrefax, whose father spends his time experimenting with wireless communication while running a school for deaf children. Serge grows up amid the noise and silence with his brilliant but troubled older sister, Sophie: an intense sibling relationship that stays with him as he heads off into an equally troubled larger world. After a fling with a nurse at a Bohemian spa, Serge serves in World War I as a radio operator for reconnaissance planes. When his plane is shot down, Serge is taken to a German prison camp, from which he escapes. Back in London, he's recruited for a mission to Cairo on behalf of the shadowy Empire Wireless Chain." Publisher's note

McCarthy, Tom

Remainder. Vintage Books 2007 308p pa $13.95

ISBN 978-0-307-27835-7; 0-307-27835-2

LC 2006-50565

First published 2005 in France

"In a very subtle way, McCarthy is saying something about our attitude toward pleasure. Fleeting moments no longer count; we require the best all the time. Then we dis-

cover the pursuit of this goal turns fetishistic." Cleveland Plain Dealer

McCauley, Stephen

Alternatives to sex. Simon & Schuster 2006 289p $24

ISBN 978-0-7432-2473-4; 0-7432-2473-6

LC 2005-54121

"With his self-effacing wit and disarming compassion for even the most unlikely characters, McCauley proves once again that he's a master of the modern comedy of manners." USA Today

McCauley, Stephen

True enough. Simon & Schuster 2001 314p $24

ISBN 0-684-81054-9

LC 00-66177

McCauley is "uncannily good at illuminating character through speech. . . . {He} wants nothing more than to entertain us, and if that's become an old-fashioned thing to do, it may be because few writers do it so well." N Y Times Book Rev

McClellan, Brian

Promise of blood; Brian McClellan. Orbit 2013 548 p. maps (The powder mage) (hardcover) $23.99; (paperback) $16.00

ISBN 0316219037; 9780316219037; 9780316219044

LC 2012032171

This novel, by Brian McClellan, is the first entry in "The Powder Mage" Trilogy. "Field Marshal Tamas' coup against his king . . . brought bread to the starving. But it also provoked war . . . , internal attacks by royalist fanatics, and the greedy to scramble for money and power by Tamas's supposed allies. . . . Tamas is relying heavily on his few remaining powder mages, including . . . his estranged son, and . . . a retired police inspector whose loyalty is being tested by blackmail." (Publisher's note)

McClure, James

The **steam** pig. Harper & Row 1972 247p

First published 1971 in the United Kingdom

White Lieutenant Kramer and his Zulu sergeant Zondi investigate the grisly murder of a beautiful white girl in a small South African town

"An absolutely scathing look at contemporary South Africa is provided in {this} . . . novel that is uncanny in its multi-leveled perceptions. It is a grostesquely vivid picture of life under apartheid. But it is also a first-rate mystery with a solution that is a shocker." Saturday Rev

McCorkle, Jill, 1958-

Carolina moon; a novel. Algonquin Bks. 1996 260p $18.95

ISBN 1-56512-136-8

LC 96-16115

"We sense that the author, like a modern-day phrenologist, has her hands on the head of Fulton to study its psychological profile. Seemingly plotless, the novel's final revelation shows how much of a craftswoman McCorkle really is." America

McCorkle, Jill

★ **Ferris** Beach; a novel. Algonquin Bks. 1990 343p

ISBN 0-945575-39-4

LC 90-37089

"The central metaphor is the place that gives the novel its name—a place associated with ideas of sex, freedom, and broken dreams. . . . Here, Katie will get a powerful dose of reality and suffering rendered so wistfully and obliquely, with multiple forewarnings designed to heighten the sense of foreboding, and a commendable balance of tragedy and mirth, that the full texture of a child's wonder and terror is preserved." Booklist

McCorkle, Jill, 1958-

Life after life; a novel. by Jill McCorkle. 1st ed. Algonquin Books of Chapel Hill 2013 352 p. (hardcover) $24.95

ISBN 1565122550; 9781565122550

LC 2012023445

In this novel, "single mother C.J. is desperate not to repeat her mother's cycle of prostitution and suicide but knows she faces long odds. Stanley enters a nursing home and feigns dementia to keep his son Ned at a distance . . . . Mired in a hopeless marriage, Ben tries to reach out to his daughter Abby with magic tricks. . . . Hospice volunteer Joanna, Ben's childhood friend and former assistant, is the point of connection among many storylines." (Publishers Weekly)

McCracken, Elizabeth

★ The **giant's** house; a romance. Dial Press (NY) 1996 259p

ISBN 0-385-31433-7

LC 95-52433

"The reader is mesmerized by this low-key narrative, first lured by Peggy's alternately acerbic and tender voice, then captivated by James's situation and intrigued by his family, later engulfed by pathos as James's body begins to fail and, finally, amazed by a turn of events that ends the novel with a major surprise. McCracken also invests the narrative with humor, sometimes through Peggy's astringent comments and more often through the use of minor characters who add vivid color and their own distinctive voices." Publ Wkly

McCracken, Elizabeth

Niagara Falls all over again. Dial Press (NY) 2001 308p

ISBN 0-385-31837-5

LC 2001-28314

This novel chronicles the ups and downs in the relationship between two vaudeville entertainers. It is narrated by an aging Moses Sharensky, who as Mose Sharp was the straight man to his more exuberant partner Rocky Carter

"McCracken understands the ambiguous relationship between comedy and tragedy as well as she understands the relationship between these two funny men. Even a fictional celebrity memoir risks being maudlin, but McCracken knows when to pull back. . . . {She} has a wonderful ear for the way a line or a friendship breaks." Christ Sci Monit

McCrumb, Sharyn

★ The **ballad** of Frankie Silver. Dutton 1998 386p

ISBN 0-525-93969-5

LC 97-24867

"By working in two time frames and alternating the narrative voice, McCrumb threads both stories into a single pattern, a dense and lovely but very dark design that illustrates the social hypocrisy of the legal system as much as the harshness of mountain justice—then and now." N Y Times Book Rev

Includes bibliographical references

McCrumb, Sharyn

The **ballad** of Tom Dooley; a ballad novel. Thomas Dunne Books 2011 311p

ISBN 0-312-55817-1; 978-0-312-55817-8

LC 2011-19929

A novel "based on actual events that happened in Wilkes County, N.C. in 1866, the year after the end of the Civil War. The real Tom Dula (Dooley was the local pronunciation of his name) was the prime suspect when Laura Foster, a young girl, was found murdered and buried in a shallow grave. Dula was her lover, and as the prime suspect, was hanged for the crime. He was also involved in a longtime affair with a married woman, Ann Melton, who was jailed as a possible accomplice after her cousin, Pauline Foster, reported that Ann had showed her where Laura's body was buried. . . . The sensational elements in this love-triangle case attracted national attention. Even former North Carolina Governor Zeb Vance boosted his political career by leading the defense team. Add to this mix Dula's confession on the eve of his execution, saving Ann Melton, the woman he really loved. . . . McCrumb has written a compelling work of fiction, coming up with a new version of the intricacies of relationships that led to murder. In the process of sorting out the mystery, she may have developed the most villainous Appalachian woman character ever written." A! Magazine for the arts

McCrumb, Sharyn

Foggy Mountain breakdown and other stories. Ballantine Bks. 1997 326p

ISBN 0-345-41493-4

LC 97-18787

The author "has an uncanny knack for picking up the subtle nuances of dialogue, place, and personality that make her characters and settings sparkle with life. She can perfectly mimic the hillbilly twang of an Appalachian healer or the dulcet, pearshaped tones of an upper-class Briton; she can create the excitement of teenagers in lust, mirror the evil that lurks in a serial killer's heart, or convey the quiet desperation of a woman trapped in a miserable marriage. But most of all, McCrumb can make her readers believe what she writes." Booklist

McCrumb, Sharyn

The **hangman's** beautiful daughter. Scribner 1992 306p

ISBN 0-684-19407-4

LC 91-46057

"Revisiting some of the characters from If Ever I Return, Pretty Peggy-O . . . McCrumb weaves Appalachian folklore and death, in natural and unnatural forms, into a story that meanders like a mountain stream through the hills of east Tennessee. . . . Wake County Sheriff Spencer Arrowood asks Laura Bruce, wife of the local Baptist minister, who is now an Army chaplain stationed overseas, to comfort the bereaved at the scene of a bloody murder. Ret. Maj. Paul Underhill, his wife and two of his four children are dead, shot apparently by one of the sons, who took his own life after killing the others. Laura serves as advocate for the surviving children. . . . But when deputy Joe LeDonne discovers that the two have disinterred their father's body from its grave, he wants to know what really happened on the night of the shooting." Publ Wkly

McCrumb, Sharyn
★ **If** ever I return, pretty Peggy-O. Scribner 1990 312p
ISBN 0-684-19104-0
LC 89-24337
The author's "strongly individualized characters give serious and intelligent thought to the ghosts raised by the reunion—including the tangible spector of a murderer." N Y Times Book Rev

McCrumb, Sharyn
If I'd killed him when I met him; an Elizabeth MacPherson novel. Ballantine Bks. 1995 277p
LC 94-23701
"Buoyed by intriguing characters, a wry—sometimes macabre—wit, and lush Virginia atmosphere, McCrumb's mystery spins merrily along on its own momentum, concluding that justice will triumph . . . but in surprising ways." Publ Wkly

McCrumb, Sharyn
MacPherson's lament; an Elizabeth MacPherson mystery. Ballantine Bks. 1992 260p
LC 92-52661
In this mystery Elizabeth MacPherson's "brother, Bill, a new lawyer, sets up shop in Danville, Va., with Amy Powell (A.P.) Hill, descendant of the southern general known by the same initials. The firm's first few cases aren't auspicious. . . . The pace picks up when the body of a young woman is found in the trunk of A.P.'s client's car and a wealthy businessman from New York wants to buy the house very quickly. Elizabeth, who has been represented in letters sent from Scotland, finally flies home to help the fledgling attorneys. Interspersed is the tale of Civil War soldier Gabriel Hawks, who with a friend confiscates a part of the Confederate treasury." Publ Wkly
A "witty story that will beguile both mystery buffs and Civil War enthusiasts." Booklist

McCrumb, Sharyn
Missing Susan; an Elizabeth MacPherson mystery. Ballantine Bks. 1991 295p
LC 91-91887
The author "spins the British cozy formula on its ear, slipping in the expected sly one-liner or two and driving her plot so far up a narrative one-way street that only a writer with her nerve and ever-ready wit would have a snowball's chance in hell of pulling the whole tricky caper off." Booklist

McCrumb, Sharyn
The **rosewood** casket. Dutton 1996 303p
ISBN 0-525-94011-1
LC 96-11135
"Ms. McCrumb spins out the Stargill family secret in the hypnotic tones of a storyteller who knows she has a warming fire at her back and rapt listeners at her feet. Longstanding conflicts and quarrels within this ornery clan give substance to the characters; and some anxiety, if not suspense, is built up when a predatory real estate speculator starts sniffing around the farm. But the author reserves her most persuasive voice for the old stories that she digs out of these ancient hills." N Y Times Book Rev

McCrumb, Sharyn
She walks these hills. Scribner 1994 336p
ISBN 0-684-19556-9
LC 94-9458
"In 1779, Katie Wyler, 18, was captured by the Shawnee in North Carolina. The story of her escape and arduous journey home through hundreds of miles of Appalachian wilderness is the topic of ethno-historian Jeremy Cobb's thesis. . . . As Cobb begins to retrace Katie's return journey, 63-year-old convicted murderer Hiram (Harm) Sorley escapes from a nearby prison. Suffering from Korsakoff's syndrome, he has no recent memory. . . . Hamelin, Tenn., police dispatcher Martha Ayers uses the opportunity to convince the sheriff to assign her as a deputy. . . . Deftly building suspense, McCrumb weaves these colorful elements into her satisfying conclusion." Publ Wkly

McCrumb, Sharyn
The **songcatcher**; a ballad novel. Dutton 2001 321p
ISBN 0-525-94488-5
LC 00-50831
"McCrumb follows a single ballad through seven generations of the McCourry family, beginning with Malcolm McCourry, kidnapped as a child from the Scottish Isle of Islay in 1751 and brought to the American frontier. The 'songcatcher' is Lark McCourry, a contemporary country-western singer, haunted by her memory of fragments of this ballad from her childhood. Past collides with present when Lark is called home to care for her dying father, from whom she has long been estranged. . . . Investing surprising suspense into Lark's search for the words to the ballad and for the tune of her own life, McCrumb gives the reader intriguing characters, great insight into the landscape and folkways of the South, and rich bits of comedy." Booklist

McCrumb, Sharyn
St. Dale. Kensington 2004 311p $25
ISBN 0-7582-0776-X
"A group of stock car racing fans embarks on a bus tour of Southern speedways—seven states in eight days—as a tribute to legendary NASCAR champion Dale Earnhardt in this meandering road novel modeled after the Canterbury Tales. Harley Claymore, a down-and-out race car driver who yearns to be reinstated, is a tour guide with an encyclopedic knowledge of spectacular races and risk-loving drivers. His 'Where are you folks from?' introduces a diverse group of tour participants: Karen and Shane plan to be married at the first stop, where the bride's Wiccan mother will be wait-

ing, and the groom will try to come to terms with his grief over the death of his hero, Dale, in the 2001 Daytona 500; longtime fan Jim, married 47 years to Arlene, hopes her incipient Alzheimer's won't spoil their enjoyment of the tour; Bill Knight, an Episcopalian priest in smalltown Canterbury, N.H., is chaperone for a dying orphan who was selected for a Last Wish trip; Nebraska resident Ray has proudly plowed his alfalfa field with a giant three (Dale's racing number). Veteran McCrumb provides a lively illustration of the cult of celebrity and offers instructive speculation about the human need for heroes." Publ Wkly

McCrumb, Sharyn

The **Windsor** knot; an Elizabeth MacPherson mystery. Ballantine Bks. 1990 281p

LC 90-34168

"Back in Chandler Grove for her nuptials, forensic anthropologist Elizabeth MacPherson finds herself involved in a local police investigation when she is called upon to identify some cremated remains." Booklist

"Elizabeth is less centrally involved in the crime and detection than usual, but this doesn't diminish the appeal of McCrumb's sparkling spoof." Publ Wkly

McCullers, Carson

Collected stories; including The member of the wedding and The ballad of the sad cafe. introduction by Virginia Spencer Carr. Houghton Mifflin 1987 392p

LC 87-3944

"McCullers often wrote about grotesques, people afflicted physically and emotionally. Her themes include loneliness and the mental anguish that stems from love gone awry. Her style is unadorned, quietly rigorous. She's both charming and disquieting—an absorbing challenge to readers of serious fiction." Booklist

McCullers, Carson

★ **Complete** novels. Library of America, Distributed to the trade in the United States by Penguin Putnam 2001 827p $35

ISBN 1-931082-03-0

LC 2001-29049

Includes bibliographical references

Contents: The heart is a lonely hunter; Reflections in a golden eye; The ballad of the sad café; The member of the wedding; Clock without hands

McCullers, Carson

The **heart** is a lonely hunter. Modern Lib. 1993 430p $14.95

ISBN 0-679-42474-1

LC 92-51062

A reissue of the title first published 1940 by Houghton Mifflin

"After his friend is committed to a hospital for the insane, John Singer, a deaf mute, finds himself alone. He becomes the pivotal figure in a strange circle of four other lonely individuals: Biff Brannon, the owner of a cafe; Mick Kelly, a young girl; Jake Blount, a radical; and Benedict Copeland, the town's black doctor. Although Singer provides

companionship for others, he remains outside the warmth of close relationships." Shapiro. Fic for Youth. 3d edition

McCullers, Carson

The **member** of the wedding. Houghton Mifflin 1946 195p hardcover o.p. pa $7.95

ISBN 0-395-07981-0; 0-618-49239-9 pa

"Twelve-year-old Frankie is experiencing a boring summer until news arrives that her older brother will soon be returning to Georgia from his Alaska home in order to marry. Plotting to accompany the newlyweds on their honeymoon occupies much of Frankie's waking hours, while at the same time she is coping with the pressures of puberty and its effects on her body and mind. Particularly revealing are her conversations with her six-year-old cousin and the nurturing black family cook, Bernice." Shapiro. Fic for Youth. 3d edition

McCullers, Carson

Reflections in a golden eye. Houghton Mifflin 1941 182p

"Set in the 1930s on a Southern army base, the novel concerns the relationships between self-destructive misfits whose lives end in tragedy and murder. The cast of characters includes Captain Penderton, a sado-masochistic, latent homosexual officer; his wife, who is having an affair with Major Langdon; the major's wife, who responds to the trauma of her son's death with self-mutilation; Anacleto, a homosexual servant who is befriended by the major's wife, and an army private who engages in voyeurism." Merriam-Webster's Ency of Lit

McCullough, Colleen

Caesar; let the dice fly. Morrow 1997 664p il

ISBN 0-688-09372-8

LC 97-24391

"Caesar is essentially the same character one recalls from his admittedly self-promoting memoirs—brilliant, ambitious, ruthless and fascinating. The real tragic hero here is Pompey, whose military triumphs are over-shadowed by his rival's, whose political fortunes are undermined by Cato and the boni, and whose assassination in Alexandria closes this thoroughly Romanized epic novel." N Y Times Book Rev

McCullough, Colleen

Caesar's women. Morrow 1996 696p

ISBN 0-688-09371-X

LC 95-34498

"With great brio, and ample attention to Roman customs and rites, as well as to the religious, sexual and social institutions of the day, including slavery, McCullough captures the driven, passionate soul of ancient Rome." Publ Wkly

Followed by Caesar

McCullough, Colleen

★ The **first** man in Rome. Morrow 1990 896p il

LC 90-37080

The first installment in the Masters of Rome series "outlining the demise of the Roman republic and tracing the origins of the Roman Empire, this volume commences in 110 B.C.E. and revolves around the smoldering political ambitions of two seemingly unsuitable statesmen. Lacking the requisite patrician pedigree, stolid and wealthy Gaius Marius, a brilliant general, acquires respectability by marrying into the irreproachable Julian dynasty. Deprived of his noble birthright by a dissolute and profligate father, the impoverished and curiously amoral Lucius Cornelius Sulla resorts to murder in order to claim an inheritance and purchase his way into the senate. Branded as outsiders, Marius and Sulla forge a formidable alliance, culminating in a succession of unparalled military and political triumphs." Booklist

Followed by The grass crown

McCullough, Colleen
  Fortune's favorites. Morrow 1993 878p il
      LC 93-534
  "Painstakingly researched, McCullough's Roman saga is like a trip through time. Her characters come to life as do their surroundings. While giving us rollicking good fiction, McCullough has also made clear the bribery and chicanery that made up Roman politics. She has given us clear insight into how Rome found itself changing from a republic to an empire." Libr J

Followed by Caesar's women

McCullough, Colleen
  The **grass** crown. Morrow 1991 894p il
      LC 91-17009
  In the second novel in the author's series about the Roman Empire "the action hinges on the rivalry between arrogant, paunchy general Marius, eager to fulfill a prophecy and become consul of Rome for a seventh time, and Sulla, a monster who has turned to war-making out of either sexual frustration or boredom. . . . In recreating the Social War between Rome and the rebellious Italian nations (90-88 B.C.), Sulla's crushing of King Mithridates of Pontus and the ensuing bloody Roman civil war, McCullough sustains a keen sense of urgency, framing precarious personal lives against an empire in flux. A quietly magnificent tour de force." Publ Wkly

Followed by Fortune's favorites

McCullough, Colleen
  ★ An **indecent** obsession. Harper & Row 1981 317p
      LC 81-47547
  This novel is "set in the psychiatric ward of a small military hospital in the South Pacific soon after the end of the Second World War. A novel about duty (the 'indecent obsession'), it has the prescribed mix of best-selling ingredients, romance, sex, violence and paranoia." Oxford Companion to Australian Lit

McCullough, Colleen
  Morgan's run. Simon & Schuster 2000 604p il
  ISBN 0-684-85329-9
      LC 00-41006
  A historical saga about Richard Morgan, "a man who falls afoul of villains and suffers the degradation of the 18th-century British penal system. But, as even he admits, he has great luck as a convict. His resourceful cousin, a druggist, fixes him up with survival necessities, and wherever the beautiful, strong, educated Richard goes—overcrowded jails or the hulks of convict transports, suffering the appall-

ing conditions of passage to an unknown continent—he becomes a leader of men. The novel displays fine, informative period details." N Y Times Book Rev

McCullough, Colleen
  The **October** horse; a novel about Caesar and Cleopatra. Simon & Schuster 2002 792p $28
  ISBN 0-684-85331-0
      LC 2002-32753
  This sixth and final volume in the Masters of Rome series "traces the last days of the Roman Republic, including the events leading up to the assassination of Julius Caesar and the aftermath of that famous murder. Here, that most renowned of Romans, at the height of his power, and Cleopatra, his illustrious mistress, are at center stage." Booklist
  "Though some readers may find the sheer wealth of detail occasionally tedious, the book will find a niche among those who can appreciate the scholarship and research that contributed to recreating Caesar's remarkable career." Libr J

McCullough, Colleen
  The **song** of Troy. Orion 2001 404p maps
  ISBN 0-7528-1705-1
      LC 98-215810
  First published 1998 in the United Kingdom
  "McCullough's version of the 10-year siege of Troy by the armies of Greece unfolds slowly and dramatically, with each chapter narrated by one of the conflict's major players. . . . This vivid portrayal of the people and events of the Trojan War is actually a rewritten version of McCullough's first novel, which was never published." Booklist

McCullough, Colleen
  ★ The **thorn** birds. Harper & Row 1977 533p
  "The backdrop to this congested, sensational and often bizarre plot, is the Australian outback, with its dramatic landscapes, vast distances, isolation, bush camaraderie, and natural hazards. The novel aroused lively literary controversy. It was labelled by its critics as a 'potboiler': crudely crafted, sensationally exaggerated, devised to cater to the florid expectations of the mass of undiscriminating readers of modern popular fiction. Its supporters see it as a vigorously-written and racy narrative." Oxford Companion to Australian Lit

McCutchan, Philip
  Apprentice to the sea. St. Martin's Press 1995 183p
      LC 94-45091
  First published 1994 in the United Kingdom with title: Tom Chatto
  "McCutchan effectively and economically limns bustling Liverpool, the daunting mission of beating around the Horn and Victorian England's rigid caste system. Despite its sometimes excessive jargon . . . this spankingly paced novel augurs well for Tom's further voyages." Publ Wkly

Followed by The second mate

McCutchan, Philip
  Cameron's crossing. St. Martin's Press 1993 171p
      LC 93-24284

"Commander Cameron along with a small crew of enlisted men take passage on the escort carrier HMS Charger, which is sailing from Belfast to Norfolk, Virginia, for an overhaul. On passage across the Atlantic HMS Charger is beset by a severe North Atlantic storm that not only damages her beyond recovery but reveals the inadequacy of the commanding officer, Captain Mason-Goodson. Cameron takes command in an effort to save both ship and crew from a watery grave." Libr J

"As usual, the stolid, intrepid Cameron soldiers along very ably, while McCutchan's spare prose smartly re-creates the lore and real lives of the British navy." Publ Wkly

McCutchan, Philip

The **last** farewell; a novel. St. Martin's Press 1991 308p

LC 90-49227

"McCutchan weaves a tapestry of stories about the passengers and crew aboard the Laurentia as it makes its final voyage from New York to England in 1915. Without a protective escort, Captain Pacey must guide his ship through waters and times more treacherous than he can possibly believe. The U-boat commander has his problems, too, as the action moves from the liner to the submarine to the offices of the British ministers, who, in noncommittal ways, have sentenced the Laurentia to its dismal fate. A mesmerizing tale of the sea and the men who pit their lives against nature and politics." Booklist

McCutchan, Philip

The **new** lieutenant. St. Martin's Press 1997 181p

ISBN 0-312-15604-9

LC 97-10026

First published 1996 in the United Kingdom with title: Tom Chatto, RNR

This "installment of the Tom Chatto military series finds our hero out of the merchant marine and into the Royal Navy Volunteer Reserve in the first year of WWI. Chatto is navigator and third officer (and eventually master) of Geelong, an armed decoy battling German U-boats in the Mediterranean, and must face not only hostile submarines but also the personal problems of various shipmates. . . . Though the writing occasionally lapses into generic passages about war disillusionment, readers who have followed Tom Chatto will be interested in the challenges—both epic and personal—posed by The Great War." Publ Wkly

McCutchan, Philip

The **second** mate. St. Martin's Press 1996 186p

ISBN 978-0312144104

LC 96-1189

First published 1995 in the United Kingdom with title: Tom Chatto, second mate

"It is now some years after the events of Apprentice, to the Sea and Chatto is second mate of a liner on the South American run. After a trouble-plagued voyage, he plays a heroic role in trying to save a derelict sailing ship, with the unexpected help of Patience, the bucko mate from the Pass of Drumochter. . . . Second Mate is that rare thing today, a book that could easily have been twice as long without boring the sea-loving reader." Booklist

Followed by The new lieutenant

McDermid, Val

The **distant** echo. St. Martin's Minotaur 2003 404p $24.95

ISBN 0-312-30199-5

LC 2003-52902

"Individually, the characters are sensitively drawn. Collectively, they present the inscrutable face of closed-off communities so terrified of change they would kill for peace." N Y Times Book Rev

McDermid, Val

Grave tattoo. St. Martin's Minotaur 2007 390p $24.95

ISBN 978-0-312-33921-0; 0-312-3392-6

LC 2007-295846

First published 2006 in the United Kingdom

Once all the "narrative balls are tossed in the air, McDermid provides enough violence to add real urgency to her intriguing premise, which the late curator of the Wordsworth Trust declared 'improbable, but charmingly plausible.' Even without the melodramatic plot twists, the novel's scholarship is exciting on its own terms, and entirely appropriate for a district so wildly beautiful that it attracts both poets and pirates." N Y Times Book Rev

McDermid, Val

A **place** of execution. St. Martin's Minotaur 2000 403p

ISBN 0-312-26632-4

LC 00-59145

First published 1999 in the United Kingdom

"When a 13-year-old English schoolgirl goes missing from her Derbyshire village in the winter of 1963, George Bennett, the police inspector in charge of the case, quickly realizes that the secrets of the child's life and possible death are locked in the collective mind of Scardale, an isolated hamlet of inbred families united by their common surnames and their hostility to strangers. Through Bennett's exhaustive efforts, the likely villain is caught and hanged—or so it seems, until the story reaches 35 years into the future for its chilling resolution." N Y Times Book Rev

McDermott, Alice

After this. Farrar, Straus and Giroux 2006 279p $24

ISBN 978-0-374-16809-4; 0-374-16809-1

LC 2006-5598

McDermott's "easy authority with this material, combined with her clear-eyed sympathy for her characters, results in a moving, old-fashioned story about longing and loss and sorrow." N Y Times (Late N Y Ed)

McDermott, Alice

At weddings and wakes. Farrar, Straus & Giroux 1992 213p

LC 91-42070

Set in Brooklyn during the sixties, this novel "tells the story of an extended Irish-American family observed primarily through the eyes of the children, son and two daughters. Time circles backwards and forwards around a variety of family rituals: holiday meals, vacations at the shore, the wedding of a favorite aunt. The poignant middle-aged romance that develops between the aunt, a former nun, and her suitor, a shy mailman, exacerbates already pronounced family tensions. As they listen to oft-repeated stories about poverty, disease, and early deaths, the children are solemn witnesses to the Irish immigrant experience in America." Libr J

McDermott, Alice

★ **Charming** Billy; a novel. Farrar, Straus & Giroux 1998 280p

ISBN 0-374-12080-3

LC 97-77089

This "novel opens at the wake of the debonair Billy Lynch—gifted talker, abandoned suitor, faithful husband, devout Catholic, raging alcoholic. It then ranges back and forth through dozens of family theories and anecdotes to answer the question of what did or didn't make him who he was. At once a love story, a portrait of Irish Catholic Queens, and an ode to an edenic postwar East Hampton, this novel honors the consequences of everyday decisions, both sacred and profane, burnishing them in the retelling to a high shine." New Yorker

McDermott, Alice

Child of my heart. Farrar, Straus & Giroux 2002 242p $23

ISBN 0-374-12123-0

LC 2002-69764

This is a "summer idyll in which a cat is hit by a car, a dog is shot, the heroine loses her virginity, and her fairy-like cousin succumbs to a fatal disease and want of parental love. All this loss—of innocence, of dearly loved creatures—and yet, there is not a word of sentimentality or taste of treacle. On the contrary, Child of My Heart is a golden and luminous memory retrieved by a narrator who has achieved a cool and slightly ironic distance from one of those summers in the late fifties or early sixties." Commonweal

McDermott, Alice

Someone; A Novel. Alice McDermott. 1st ed. Farrar, Straus and Giroux 2013 224 p. (hardcover) $25

ISBN 0374281092; 9780374281090

LC 2013014938

This historical novel, by Alice McDermott, follows "Marie's first heartbreak and her eventual marriage; her brother's brief stint as a Catholic priest, subsequent loss of faith, and eventual breakdown; the Second World War; her parents' deaths; the births and lives of Marie's children; [and] the changing world of her Irish-American enclave in Brooklyn." (Publisher's note)

McDermott, Alice

★ **That** night. Farrar, Straus & Giroux 1987 183p $14.95

ISBN 0-374-27361-8

LC 84-45765

"In spite of its brevity, 'That Night' is a wonderfully unfettered, ample novel, one that celebrates voice, personality and feeling when so much fiction avoids those rewarding characteristics. Ms. McDermott has invested her novel with a strong sense of historical authority, rendering with sure clarity a time and place marked by both a cultural inno-

cence and the premonition of its inevitable loss." N Y Times Book Rev

McDermott, J. M.

Last dragon. Wizards of the Coast Discoveries 2008 390p pa $14.95

ISBN 978-0-786948-57-4; 0-786948-57-4

LC 2007-18085

"A journey focused on revenge becomes an odyssey of self-discovery and of the founding of an empire in blood and sacrifice. As Zhan searches for her grandfather, a creature no longer human that has killed his entire village, she travels in the company of Seth, a fire-breathing shaman; Korinyes, a gypsy who is more than she seems; and Adel, a paladin present at the slaying of the last dragon. McDermott's debut novel requires careful reading to piece together a story told in nonlinear form, as mercurial as memories and as visceral as death. This fantasy adventure belongs in libraries where literary fantasy in the tradition of Gene Wolf, A.A. Attanasio, and Gabriel García Márquez is popular." Libr J

McDevitt, Jack

★ The **Cassandra** project; Jack McDevitt and Mike Resnick. Ace Books 2012 387 p. (hardcover) $25.95

ISBN 1937008711; 9781937008710

LC 2012021236

This book by Jack McDevitt and Mike Resnick follows "Jerry Culpepper, a NASA press agent, [who] is caught between his hopes for a better future for the space program and puzzling clues that suggest Neil Armstrong was the fifth man to walk on the Moon. Adding in a libertarian entrepreneur with his own Moon rocket and a president anxious to learn what may be hiding on the far side of the moon, Jerry is caught in a race to discover [the] truth." (Publishers Weekly)

McDevitt, Jack

Deepsix; Jack McDevitt. EOS 2001 432p. map $6.99; o.p.; (hbk.) o.p.

ISBN 9780061020063; 9780061051241; 0061051241

LC 00046587

This science fiction novel takes place "[i]n the 23rd century [when] Deepsix is a planet in deep trouble. In about three weeks a Jovian-sized world will collide with it. Although Deepsix is a treasure trove of life, it has been left unexplored for the last 20 years because hostile animals slaughtered most of the first human landing party. Now, with the discovery of traces of an advanced civilization on the planet, a new expedition hastily sets out to rescue bits and pieces of the culture before they are lost forever. To find the lander that was abandoned two decades earlier, the disgraced commander of the original expedition must make a deadly trek across Deepsix with (among others) two feisty women and a misogynistic celebrity writer who once pilloried the team leader in the press. Goaded by their off-planet superiors, they also have to solve the mystery inherent in the disappearance of Deepsix's civilization." (Publishers Weekly)

McDevitt, Jack

Infinity beach. HarperCollins Pubs. 2000 435p $25

ISBN 0-06-105123-3

LC 99-40569

McDevitt "has created a future that is technologically sound and filled with hubristic, foolish people who make choices based more on how they will look to history than on what's best for it. Though his aliens are insubstantial . . . the mystery of what happened to Kim's sister and her fellow celestial seekers unfolds as precisely as an origami flower, and will hold readers in thrall." Publ Wkly

McDevitt, Jack

✓ **Odyssey**; Jack McDevitt. Ace Books 2006 410p. o.p.; (pbk.) $7.99; o.p.

ISBN 044101433X; 9780441015405; 9780441014330

LC 2006019259

This science fiction book is "[s]et in the 23rd century . . . [and] explores the immorality of big business and the short-sightedness of the American government in minimizing support for space travel. These destructive forces are held off by . . . Gregory MacAllister, editor of a non-partisan journal, The Nation, and Priscilla 'Hutch' Hutchins, manager of a government-sponsored space-research agency, the Academy. While often on opposite sides of support for the Academy's research budget, MacAllister and Hutch together uncover and react to evidence that Orion Tours' CEO, Charles Dryden, is engaged in a massive conspiracy to jump-start his intergalactic tour business. MacAllister unmasks the others supporting Dryden's faked alien attacks, targeting a physicist who colluded in the hoax. His skepticism about space travel, however, prevents him from seeing the existence of real aliens, something Hutch must pursue at risk to her career." (Publishers Weekly)

Mcdonald, Gregory

★ **Fletch**. Bobbs-Merrill 1974 179p

"A rich young California industrialist, Stanwyck, who is apparently dying of cancer, offers someone he takes to be a beach bum a rich reward if he'll murder him on a particular date. The 'bum' chosen is Fletch, ace journalist, ace philanderer, who accepts the proposition. However, Fletch, who is already investigating the beach drug scene for his newspaper, now investigates Stanwyck—his marital and extramarital life, his relationship with his parents, his obsession with piloting experimental planes. The two strands of the story come together in one deft twist as Fletch . . . both gets the drop on the doublecrossing Stanwyck and uncovers the source of the beach's drugs." Publ Wkly

Mcdonald, Gregory

The **Fletch** chronicles. Hill & Co. Pubs. 1987 3v

LC 87-8742

A three-volume omnibus collection of nine award-winning Fletch novels, some of which first appeared in paperback

Mcdonald, Gregory

Son of Fletch. Putnam 1993 236p

LC 93-684

"Good-natured hero Irwin Maurice ('Fletch') Fletcher discovers he has a heretofore unknown son from a friendly one-night stand 20 years earlier. Somehow son Jack has become involved with a bunch of neo-Nazi thugs fresh out of prison, but Fletch has trouble believing that the fruit of his loins could really be a bad guy at heart. . . . Good pacing, good humor, and good writing make Mcdonald's latest another fan pleaser in a predictable but comfortable series." Booklist

McDonald, Ian

Ares express. Pyr 2010 389p pa $16

ISBN 978-1-61614-197-4; 1-61614-197-2

LC 2009-50115

Sequel to: Desolation Road (1988)

First published 2001 in the United Kingdom

"In an unimaginably distant future Mars has been terraformed by machines so powerful that they're understood as (and might as well be) angels. Across the Martian deserts, enormous trains carry passengers, resources, and factories. These trains are so huge that they're effectively societies of their own, with their own peculiar customs and rigidly distinct social strata – the locomotive functionaries, like Engineers and Stuards and Deep-Fusion tenders, are more like tribes than they are like jobs. From the great train Catherine of Tarsis, Sweetness Octave Glorious Honey-bun Asiim Engineer 12th flees an arranged marriage and stumbles into a mad adventure on which the future of Martian civilization depends. . . . MacDonald eschews the limitations that hard-SF imposes, to instead construct a paean to all possible red planets, a story that follows a gloriously tricky path through the many conceptions of Mars that literature has woven over the years. It is a Mars that is, above all, a Mars of the imagination." io9

McDonald, Ian

✓ **Brasyl**; a novel. Pyr 2007 357p $25

ISBN 978-1-59102-543-6; 1-59102-543-5

LC 2007-1563

"McDonald sets up three separate characters in different eras—a cynical contemporary reality-TV producer, a near-future bisexual entrepreneur and a tormented 18th-century Jesuit agent. He then slams them together with the revelation that their worlds are strands of an immense quantum multiverse, and each of them is threatened by the Order, a vast conspiracy devoted to maintaining the status quo until the end of time." Publ Wkly

"Much more often than not, McDonald's prose is a wonder, from a hundred vivid and witty details . . . to sustained passages of perfectly judged atmosphere. . . . McDonald finds the poetry and the energy of the outcast, the refuse of society." Strange Horizons

McDonald, Ian

✓ The **Dervish** House. Pyr 2010 357p $26

ISBN 978-1-61614-204-9

LC 2010-12843

McDonald "brilliantly [imagines] what a world of functional, consumer nano would mean for business, culture, faith, play and terrorism; painting a vivid picture of Istanbul as a gem of human society; and delighting with details of the marvels to be found there." Boing Boing

McDonald, Ian

★ **River** of gods. Pyr 2006 597p $25

ISBN 1-59102-436-6; 978-1-59102-436-1

LC 2005-35110

"It's 2047, and the centennial of India's nationhood approaches. Amid the turmoil and vigor of a nation teeming with people and clogged with information, the lives of nine individuals, including a policeman, a journalist, a scientist, a politician, and a standup comic, intersect in an unanticipated union with the fate of their country at stake. . . . [The author] provides a kaleidoscopic, freewheeling encounter with the near future in one of the most exotic—and impoverished—parts of the world. . . . Every library should purchase this multitextured tale of future perils and possibilities in the land of a thousand gods." Libr J

McDonald, L. J.

The **battle** sylph; L.J. McDonald. Leisure Books 2010 323p. (pbk.) $7.99

ISBN 9780843963007; 084396300X

LC 2010414521

In this fantasy book, "[h]e is one of many: a creature of magic, unrelentingly male. He is lured through the portal by pure female beauty, a virgin sacrifice. She is killed, and he is silenced and enslaved. Such a dark ritual is necessary. Unlike their elemental cousins--those gentler sylphs of wind and fire--battlers find no joy in everyday labor. Their magic can destroy an army or demolish a castle, and each has but one goal: find his queen, then protect and pleasure her at any cost." (Publisher's note)

McDonald, Roger

Mr. Darwin's shooter. Atlantic Monthly Press 1999 365p

ISBN 0-87113-733-X

LC 98-36819

"Mr. MacDonald is a generous, leisurely author who gives the reader a large cast of quirky characters, much peripheral detail, lively action, and a view of nineteenth-century social patterns. Covington, moreover, is no plaster saint, and the Beagle's long voyage offers opportunities for adventure. One need not be pro or anti either Darwin or Genesis to enjoy this well-written tale." Atl Mon

McDonell, Nick

An **expensive** education; a novel. Atlantic Monthly Press 2009 294p $24

ISBN 978-0-8021-1893-6; 0-8021-1893-3

"McDonell is stingy with the action sequences, but when they come, they're swift and hot, showing us how Teak strikes, kills and subdues with awesome precision. It would seem silly if McDonell didn't write with such disciplined restraint, and fortunately he's far more interested in showing Teak wrestling with his conscience than with his enemies." San Jose Mercury News

McElroy, Joseph

Actress in the house; a novel. Overlook Press 2003 432p $26.95

ISBN 1-58567-350-1

LC 2002-34555

"McElroy's prose, especially his dialogue, is enigmatic and layered with meaning, and the mood he creates is both subtly threatening and achingly wistful. Over a 40-year career, McElroy has been compared to William Gaddis, Don DeLillo, and Thomas Pynchon. This absorbing and unsettling novel, his first in 14 years, may finally bring him the wider recognition he deserves." Booklist

McEuen, Paul

Spiral; a novel. Dial Press 2011 312p $25

ISBN 978-0-385-34211-7; 0-385-34211-X

LC 2010-09768

McEuen "makes the early part of 'Spiral' a galloping read. The pace stays frisky most of the way through. Neat tricks abound, from the modification of lichen with jellyfish genes to the use of genetics as a form of vanity publishing. With particular ingenuity Mr. McEuen allows the same story elements to be used for either malicious or miraculous purposes, depending on who controls them." N Y Times (Late N Y Ed)

McEwan, Ian, 1942-

Amsterdam. Doubleday 1999 193p

ISBN 0-385-49423-8

LC 98-41401

"Two longtime friends meet at the cremation of the woman they shared, beautiful restaurant critic and photographer Molly Lane. Clive Linley, a celebrated composer, and Vernon Halliday, the editor of a financially troubled London tabloid, could never understand Molly's third liaison—with conservative Foreign Secretary Julian Garmony, who is angling to be prime minister, or her marriage to dour but rich publisher George Lane. . . . Immediately afterwards, both Clive and Vernon are enmeshed in a crisis: Clive must finish his commissioned Millennium Symphony so it can premiere in Amsterdam, and Vernon must grapple with the moral issue of publishing photos of Julian Garmony in drag that George has discovered with Molly's effects." Publ Wkly

McEwan "has written a tastily vicious tale in his usual polished prose." Libr J

McEwan, Ian

Atonement; a novel. Doubleday 2002 351p $26

ISBN 0-385-50395-4

LC 2001-44291

First published 2001 in the United Kingdom

This is a "work of astonishing depth and humanity. . . . The upper-class milieu, the sense of place and time, are rendered with an exactitude worthy of Elizabeth Bowen. . . . Mr McEwan has achieved the difficult task of combining literary sophistication with moral gravity." Economist

McEwan, Ian

★ **Black** dogs. Putnam 1992 xxii, 149p

LC 92-7418

This novel is "compassionate without resorting to sentimentality, clever without ever losing its honesty, an undisguised novel of ideas which is also Ian McEwan's most human work." Times Lit Suppl

McEwan, Ian

★ The **child** in time. Houghton Mifflin 1987 263p

ISBN 0-395-42912-9

LC 87-8603

"Many of the plot turns in the novel may seem improbable and even fanciful, but the feelings expressed by the characters and their sense of time (running up, running down and running out) are, without exception, genuine. . . . [This is an] astonishing book." Time

McEwan, Ian

Enduring love; a novel. Talese 1998 252p

ISBN 0-385-49112-3

LC 97-23029

First published 1997 in the United Kingdom

McEwan is a "maestro at creating suspense: the particular, sickening, see-sawing kind that demands a kind of physical courage from the reader to continue reading." New Statesman (1913)

Includes bibliographical references

McEwan, Ian

★ The **innocent**. Doubleday 1990 270p

LC 89-25669

"There is . . . a point to all this, which is to display the astonishing deeds that human beings can perpetrate and yet retain a measure of innocence. . . . In spite of what has happened, Leonard is able to live with himself. This is far and away Ian McEwan's most mature work." New Statesman Soc

McEwan, Ian

On Chesil Beach. Nan A. Talese/Doubleday 2007 176p $22.95

ISBN 978-0-385-52240-3; 0-385-52240-1

LC 2006-100720

McEwan's brief novel is as "tautly constructed as anything he has written, though sprawling in imagination. It's emblematic of a generation, a semi-scornful elegy for a repressed age, sarcastic about mores and unrelentingly honest about psychological and sexual intimacy. It's a big book in a little space. You can feel the author at times wishing to burst the bounds of his limited span, to go crashing past these tightly constrained boundaries and begin sweeping up the host of other generational topics available to him. McEwan resists the urge, which is for the best, this is a book better suited for the sprint than the marathon." PopMatters

McEwan, Ian

Saturday. Nan A. Talese/Doubleday 2005 289p $26

ISBN 0-385-51180-9

"It's clear that with this volume, Mr. McEwan has not only produced one of the most powerful pieces of post-9/11 fiction yet published, but also fulfilled that very primal mission of the novel: to show how we—a privileged few of us, anyway—live today." NY Times (Late NY Ed)

McEwan, Ian, 1942-

Solar; a novel. Nan A. Talese/Doubleday 2010 287p $26.95

ISBN 978-0-385-53341-6; 0-385-53341-1

LC 2009-46508

"The novel's hero is an aging Nobel Prize-winning physicist named Michael Beard. In truth, no one would call Beard a hero, apart from Beard himself: He's vain and vulgar, a glutton for food, sex, and praise. He runs a blue-ribbon government initiative to reverse climate change, but in actuality it's a paycheck job to keep him busy while he screws up women's lives. Though his novel tackles some heady science, McEwan is making a simple point here: The planet must be saved, even if some of the people on it are just awful. . . . The plot of Solar — a jerk builds such a tower of lies that it seems certain to fall on him — is not the cleverest thing McEwan has ever dreamed up. But it's a surprising book in other ways. Decades ago, McEwan wrote about the violence we do to others. Solar is about the violence we do to ourselves." Entertainment Wkly

McEwan, Ian, 1942-

★ **Sweet** tooth; a novel. Ian McEwan. Nan A. Talese/Doubleday 2012 301 p. (hbk.: alk. paper) $26.95

ISBN 0385536828; 9780385536820

LC 2012013932

In this novel by Ian McEwan "Serena Frome's beauty and intelligence make her the ideal recruit for MI5. The year is 1972. The Cold War is far from over. England's legendary intelligence agency is determined to manipulate the cultural conversation by funding writers whose politics align with those of the government. . . . [Serena is assigned to] infiltrate the literary circle of a promising young writer named Tom Haley. At first, she loves his stories. Then she begins to love the man." (Publisher's note)

McFadden, Bernice L.

Gathering of waters; by Bernice L. McFadden. Akashic Books 2012 252 p. (pbk.) $15.95

ISBN 161775031X; 9781617750311; 9781617750328

LC 2011923109

In this book, NAACP Image Award and Hurston/Wright Legacy Award finalist Bernice McFadden "reimagines the summer Emmett Till spent in Mississippi in 1955 and the events leading up to his murder. The story chronicles the young love between Emmett and Tass Hilton, which finally transcends death. Having left Mississippi for Detroit after Emmett dies, Tass returns 40 years later as a widow to reawaken his spirit, trapped in the dank waters of the Tallahatchie River." (Library Journal)

McFadden, Bernice L.

Sugar; a novel. Dutton 2000 229p

ISBN 0-525-94531-8

LC 99-35589

"A small Arkansas town in the 1950s provides the setting for a story of redemption and forgiveness. Sugar, a dark, beautiful black woman with a bitter past and a life of prostitution, arrives in Bigelow and disrupts the social order. For her neighbor, Pearl, Sugar bears a disturbing resemblance to her daughter, who was sexually assaulted and killed 15 years earlier. Pearl, virtually withdrawn since her daughter's death, is slowly revived by the saucy, uninhibited Sugar." Booklist

"McFadden captures the full character of small-town life and the strengths and weaknesses of its people." Libr J

McFarland, Dennis

A **face** at the window. Doubleday 1997 309p

ISBN 978-0553066944

LC 96-31232

The author "has a most beguiling narrative style: he is sometimes funny and sometimes moving; in descriptions of the hauntings he is so exact that it is easy to suspend disbelief, and in his ulterior purposes he is persuasive. Behind the haunting of Cookson Selway by the ghosts of the hotel and the ghosts of his own past lurks the haunting of the author by the idea of the dysfunctional American family. The whole makes for a thoroughly satisfying novel." N Y Times Book Rev

McFarland, Dennis

Letter from Point Clear; a novel. Henry Holt and Company 2007 290p $25

ISBN 978-0-8050-7766-7; 0-8050-7766-9

LC 2006-52574

"With its finely evoked tableaus from Wellfleet to the Alabama coast, 'Letter From Point Clear' is a gratifying, emotionally resonant novel—its heart and longing steeped in the Old South, its sensibility years and miles beyond." Boston Globe

McFarland, Dennis

★ The **music** room. Broadway Bks. 1990 275p

LC 89-71721

"In one startling realistic scene after another, with evocative description and a fluid, natural language, 'The Music Room' itself builds to a comprehensive vision, remarkable from its beginning to its surprising, satisfying end." N Y Times Book Rev

McFarland, Dennis

School for the blind. Houghton Mifflin 1994 287p

ISBN 0-395-64497-6

LC 93-49831

"Readers of 'School for the Blind' may find their attention held less by the plot than by everything that supports it. This is an inversion of expectations, but not finally a disappointing one." N Y Times Book Rev

McFarland, Dennis

Singing boy; a novel. Holt & Co. 2001 309p $25

ISBN 0-8050-6608-X

LC 00-32051

"The language here is always apt, and always in tune with the characters' thoughts. McFarland has a gift for selecting details, so that we see this novel's world with remarkable intimacy." N Y Times Book Rev

McGahan, Andrew

The **white** earth. Soho 2006 376p $25

ISBN 1-56947-417-6

LC 2005-50415

"Set in Australia's Queensland province, the novel begins with the blaze of 70 acres of wheat, a conflagration that consumes nine-year-old William's father and sends the boy and his mother packing to his great-uncle John McIvor's rotting mansion on the arid plains of what was once a vast sheep ranch. Chapters alternate between William settling into his new existence (action set in the early 1990s), and the story of John's youth on the ranch, where as the son of the ranch manager he nurtured ambitions to one day own the estate. John recruits William's help in organizing a rally for his right-wing group, which opposes the proposed Native Title laws that would return Aboriginal-claimed land to the original inhabitants. The novel's first half is a slow build, the second half, a well-wrought, meditative reflection on Australia's colonialist demons, brings the book's gothic intimations home to roost." Publ Wkly

McGahern, John

★ **By** the lake; a novel. Knopf 2002 335p

ISBN 0-679-41914-4

LC 2001-50258

"The story is an old one: in search of a quieter way of life, Joe and Kate Ruttledge have traded their careers in London for a farm near a small Irish village, where they learn how to raise sheep and are steadily drawn into the lives of their neighbors. There's the Shah, a rich bachelor in search of an heir for his business; John Quinn, a weaselly sexual predator, and a danger to women throughout the county; and Jimmy Joe McKiernan, an I.R.A. leader whose exploits periodically stir up high feeling. McGahern is never sentimental, and the novel's greatest pleasures come from the unflinching probity of his observations." New Yorker

McGarrity, Michael

The **big** gamble; a Kevin Kerney novel. Dutton 2002 272p $23.95

ISBN 0-525-94656-X

LC 2002-20755

"When two murder victims turn up after a fire in an abandoned fruit stand on a rural highway, Kerney, now the police chief of Sante Fe, N. Mex., takes a personal interest in the case. One blackened corpse is a John Doe. The other remains belong to a 29-year-old college student, Anna Marie Montoya, who disappeared 11 years before. As it happens, Kerney was involved in the search for the missing Anna Marie. Investigating the John Doe is Kerney's estranged son, Clayton Istee, now a deputy sheriff for the Lincoln County (N. Mex.) police." Publ Wkly

McGarrity, Michael

Death song; a Kevin Kerney novel. Dutton 2008 293p $24.95

ISBN 978-0-525-95036-3

LC 2007-26642

"Written in the terse staccato of law enforcement, Death Song sets a police procedural with plenty of action in Albuquerque, Santa Fe and northern New Mexico. The double homicide of a Lincoln County sheriff's deputy and his wife bring together Santa Fe Police Chief Kevin Kerney and his Mescalero Apache son, a Lincoln County officer. Their investigation uncovers a major international drug ring, but the killers and the real reason for the crimes elude police as more murders ensue." Rocky Mountain News

McGarrity, Michael

★ **Everyone** dies; a Kevin Kerney novel. Dutton 2003 273p $23.95

ISBN 0-525-94761-2

LC 2003-9208

"Michael McGarrity is one of those low-key pros who keep the genre honest with realistic crime stories and plain-talking cops who know the procedures." N Y Times Book Rev

McGarrity, Michael

★ The **Judas** judge; a Kevin Kerney novel. Dutton 2000 274p

ISBN 0-525-94547-4

LC 99-89181

"McGarrity is no nature writer, and his sketches of dusty desert towns like Alamogordo and Ruidoso are as blunt as his unsentimental character studies. Still, his portrait of the region is a strong one, built on meticulously detailed intelligence gathered, sifted and analyzed for unspoken secrets and lies by the author's own deeply cunning mind." N Y Times Book Rev

McGarrity, Michael

Nothing but trouble; a Kevin Kerney novel. Dutton 2006 305p $24.95

ISBN 0-525-94916-X

LC 2005-25660

In this Kevin Kearney mystery "readers are treated to moviemaking in New Mexico and, in a real departure for the series, a venture to Ireland featuring the Santa Fe police chief's wife, Sara, an army officer. McGarrity dedicates a third of the book to Sara, homing in on her covert operation in Ireland as she tries to capture a fugitive whose schemes have ties to important U.S. government officials. Her operation upsets a superior officer who immediately deploys her to Iraq. Although Kevin and Sara are accustomed to a long-distance marriage, they now have just a few days to make arrangements for Kevin to assume the care of their five-year-old son. In the meantime, Kevin gets involved with the filming of a movie along the Mexican border, thus allowing McGarrity to once again exhibit his remarkable ability to make the landscape and people of the Southwest a vital character in his story." Libr J

McGarrity, Michael

Under the color of law; a Kevin Kearney novel. Dutton 2001 272p $23.95

ISBN 0-525-94604-7

LC 00-69406

Kevin Kerney "is settling into his new job as police chief of Santa Fe, N. Mex., and his new subordinates are of two minds whether they should trust him or not. They have ample opportunity to observe him in action, because as the book opens, Phyllis Terrell, the estranged wife of an ambassador and ex-military honcho, is found stabbed to death in the kitchen of her hilltop mansion, and Father Joseph Mitchell, an ex-soldier turned priest researching the government's covert operations, turns up dead in the Christian Brothers Residence at the College of Santa Fe." Publ Wkly

McGarry, Terry

Illumination; Terry McGarry. Tor 2001 494 p. map $1.99; o.p.

ISBN 9780812540031; 0312873891

LC 2001027476

In this book, which takes place on an "island world, Eiden Myr, are illiterate but protected from storm and disease by the Ennead, nine powerful mages hidden in the bowels of the enigmatic Holding and supported by lesser magic makers functioning in 'triads.' The thinking wordsmiths shape spells, while the feeling binders wordlessly sign them into being and the sensing illuminators elaborately decorate the vellums the binders strip from the flesh of sheep and goats. When Liath, daughter of a humble publican, petitions the Ennead for help in regaining her gift of the magelight, they set her a daunting task: to ensnare Torrin, the elusive Darkmage unsettling the realm by teaching its children to read and think for themselves, and return him to the Holding for 'coring and sealing.' Before the resolution of Liath's quest, her world is . . . turned inside out, and she falls in . . . love with the man she's supposed to hate." (Publishers Weekly)

McGill, Bernie

The **butterfly** cabinet; a novel. Free Press 2011 227p $22.99

ISBN 978-1-4516-1159-5

LC 2010-51294

First published 2010 in the United Kingdom

92 year-old "Maddie tells her tales of coming to work at Oranmore House in Northern Ireland in the early 1900s, of the gentle folk she worked with and their trials with love and class. Through the diary that Maddie found by accident, the tale of Harriet Ormond, the harsh, emotionless mistress of the house, is also told. Harriet relates her childhood mistreatment, her marriage troubles, and her puzzlement over everyone's criticism of her punishments of her eight children, even after said punishment caused the death of her youngest daughter. The intertwining of the family's woes and those of the staff, leading to a future neither could have foreseen, is played out against a backdrop of political and cultural upheaval. Chilling and gripping." Booklist

McGilloway, Brian

Bleed a river deep. Minotaur Books 2010 297p il $24.99

ISBN 978-0-312-59947-8; 0-312-59947-1

LC 2010-22129

"McGilloway is definitely a writer to watch. Dark but not as pessimistic as Ken Bruen and Declan Hughes, his action-packed stories feature great characters and evoke a strong sense of modern Ireland." Libr J

McGinniss, Joe

The **delivery** man; [by] Joe McGinniss Jr. Black Cat 2008 276p pa $14

ISBN 978-0-8021-7042-2; 0-8021-7042-0

"A harrowing journey set in the suburbs and exurbs of Las Vegas, this debut novel . . . provides a snapshot from hell of a contemporary youth culture in full cardiac arrest, children forced to become adults all too soon, compelled to absorb childhood traumas and adolescent catastrophes in a quiet and understated way until the whole bloody mess comes boiling to the surface in anarchic, antisocial behavior." PopMatters

McGowan, Heather
Duchess of nothing; a novel. Bloomsbury Pub. 2006 215p $23.95
  ISBN 1-59691-066-6
                                        LC 2005-18197
  McGowan reveals her "narrator's character slowly, with delicacy and precision. 'Duchess of Nothing' is the kind of book that relies entirely on the power of its voice. McGowan is no ironist, smirking at the world and going for cheap laughs. There's plenty of comedy here, but its function turns out to be solace." N Y Times Book Rev

McGowan, Heather
Schooling. Doubleday 2001 314p $24.95
  ISBN 0-385-50138-2
                                        LC 00-47452
  "McGowan works in an experimental mode. At once lush and harsh, and inventive in form, the novel reads like an extended sensory exercise. Readers who prefer a straightforward narrative may be bemused, but those willing to accept the challenge will be rewarded with a beautifully written coming-of-age tale." Publ Wkly

McGowan, Kathleen
The expected one. Simon & Schuster 2006 449p (Magdalene line) $25.95
  ISBN 978-0-7432-9942-8; 0-7432-9942-6
  This novel "introduces readers to Maureen Pascal, a journalist unprepared for the visions that haunt her as she researches her new book on misunderstood heroines of the past. In France, Maureen uncovers a family secret and a document that many have died to protect (both linked to Mary Magdalene) and becomes entwined with two secret societies whose rivalry has extended over centuries. McGowan's ability to create dimensional characters while sustaining multiple, fast-paced story lines is sure to win her many readers. This work, based on 20 years of research, may prove to be . . . controversial . . . , as it addresses not only the possibility that Jesus and Mary Magdalene produced offspring but also that other biblical relationships may have differed from what the Catholic Church had ordained to be true." Libr J

McGown, Jill
Murder at the old vicarage. St. Martin's Press 1989 256p
                                        LC 88-30603
  "While snow blankets the small village of Byford, the vicar, George Wheeler, is in a hopeless muddle. . . . He finds himself attracted to a young widow—a fact that has not escaped his wife's notice. In addition, his daughter has moved back to the vicarage in order to escape an abusive husband. When the husband is discovered dead, the three members of the Wheeler family are the prime suspects. What appears

to be a simple case of domestic murder to Chief Inspector Lloyd and Sergeant Judy instead becomes a complicated plot to love and revenge." Booklist
  First published 1988 in the United Kingdom with title: Redemption
  "McGown's complex plot is masterful and her sleuths and their predicament are enthralling." Publ Wkly

McGown, Jill
Picture of innocence. Ballantine Pub. Group 1998 325p
  ISBN 0-449-00250-0
                                        LC 97-45816
  "Inspectors Lloyd and Hill study a bizarre case of murder. Someone has finally killed the obnoxious, abusive man who ruined two marriages in his financially motivated quest to produce a male heir." Libr J
  This "mystery possesses a wealth of psychological nuance and narrative depth, all the way through to the resolution, a masterpiece of controlled complexity." Publ Wkly

McGown, Jill
Plots and errors. Ballantine Bks. 1999 375p $22.95
  ISBN 0-345-43313-0
                                        LC 99-14226
  First published 1998 in the United Kingdom
  "When Andy Cope and his wife, Kathy, owners of a struggling detective agency, are found dead in their car . . . Detective Chief Inspector Lloyd rejects the majority opinion that they committed suicide. His theory, that the Copes were murdered, receives serious consideration when their one client, wealthy Mrs. Angela Esterbrook, is shot to death. Why would someone with her sort of money employ an untried agency to carry out an investigation? That's just one of many puzzles that Lloyd and his partner, Judy Hill, confront in a case that defies reason." Publisher's note

McGown, Jill
The stalking horse. St. Martin's Press 1988 186p
                                        LC 88-15834
  "Businessman Bill Holt fails to convince anyone that he did not commit the two murders of which he is accused: that of his lifelong friend, Alison Bryant, and of a private detective he never even met, Michael Allsopp, who had been assigned to trail Alison. Holt spends 16 years in prison pondering the link between the crimes and becomes obsessed with discovering the identity of the murderer, belatedly realizing that it had to be one of his acquaintances. When he is paroled, he returns home to the English countryside in quest of the truth and the person who framed him." Publ Wkly
  "McGown has constructed a taut, enthralling mystery, borrowing from the hard-boiled and the British procedural styles to write in a way all her own." Booklist

McGown, Jill
Verdict unsafe. Fawcett Columbine 1997 327p
  ISBN 978-0449910672
                                        LC 97-4949
  "In an English Midlands town, Colin Drummond, known as 'the stealth bomber,' is in prison for rape. Forty-year-old

Detective Inspector Judy Hill took his confession. Now, after three years in prison, Drummond has been released to be tried again. He harasses Hill with phone calls and threats, and she fears that he will add to his total of four rapes. Judy's lover, Detective Chief Inspector Lloyd . . . is also involved in the case." Libr J

"The pace is methodical and the cast cheerless, but McGown wraps her grim tale in a complex, satisfying solution." Publ Wkly

McGrath, Patrick, 1950-
Asylum. Random House 1997 254p
ISBN 0-679-45228-1
LC 96-24849

"It is part of McGrath's bemusing artfulness in Asylum that he can make the reader suffer the fate of all his characters. Everyone in the novel, that is to say, is deranged by their own, and other people's, plausibility. When anyone speaks in Asylum–and McGrath has an extraordinary ear for the hollows in conversation, for the lurking soliloquies–we seem to see through them in the full knowledge that they never see through themselves." London Rev Books

McGrath, Patrick, 1950-
Constance; a novel. Patrick McGrath. Bloomsbury 2013 240 p. (hardcover: alk. paper) $25
ISBN 1608199436; 9781608199433
LC 2012025657

In this novel, by Patrick McGrath, "Constance Schuyler . . . [is] tortured by memories of the bitterly unhappy childhood she spent with her father in a dilapidated house upstate. When she learns devastating new information about that past, Constance's fragile psyche suffers a profound shock. Her marriage, already tottering, threatens to collapse completely. Frightened, desperate and alone, Constance makes a disastrous decision, then looks on as her world rapidly falls apart." (Publisher's note)

Includes bibliographical references and index

McGrath, Patrick
★ The grotesque. Poseidon Press 1989 186p
ISBN 0-671-66509-X
LC 89-3486

"Part of the fun of reading 'The Grotesque' is recognizing the literary allusions and watching as one after another the subgenres of murder mystery, Gothic horror, social satire, black comedy and stories of the double are invoked and skillfully woven together." N Y Times Book Rev

McGrath, Patrick
Martha Peake; a novel of the Revolution. Random House 2000 367p
ISBN 0-375-50081-2
LC 00-29064

"A Young man named Ambrose is summoned by his dying Uncle William to an ancient pile called Drogo Hall, there to hear the story that the uncle, with the last of his strength, is driven to tell. It is the story of Harry Peake—smuggler, poet, freak, madman, tormented soul—and of his splendid red-haired daughter, Martha, who emigrates to America and becomes an early martyr of the Revolution. But Uncle William is erratic in his delivery and wandering in his mind. .

. . So it is Ambrose who by means of sympathy, imagination, intuition, must fashion a coherent account." N Y Times Book Rev

"McGrath is a vivid writer, and his detailed evocations of the atmosphere and settings of its various times and places are among the pleasures of the book." Times Lit Suppl

McGrath, Patrick
★ Spider. Poseidon Press 1990 221p
ISBN 0-671-66510-3
LC 90-7492

"Despite a less pungent second half, Spider confirms McGrath's mastery of the terrain he's staked out for himself: a twisted place where the most rank, hideous experiences are conveyed in a prose so tight, assured, and essentially self-mocking that he maintains a fine balance between high gothic horror and fussy stylization." Voice Lit Suppl

McGrath, Patrick
Trauma. Alfred A. Knopf 2008 209p $24.95
ISBN 978-1-4000-4166-4; 1-4000-4166-X
LC 2007-31071

"Beautifully crafted and paced, Trauma can be viewed as either a superb psychological thriller or as a masterly evocation of modern alienation and despair—assuming, of course, there is any difference. The contemporary novel of terror typically focuses on the breakdown of personality, the return of the repressed, the untimely mixing of memory and desire. Happily for us wimps, McGrath eschews splatter or gruesomeness, instead relating Charlie Weir's story in clear, quick-flowing prose, as if Dick Francis had rewritten Ford Madox Ford's The Good Soldier. . . . Trauma is, in short, a terrific literary entertainment." Washington Post Book World

McGregor, Elizabeth
The ice child. Dutton 2001 372p
ISBN 0-525-94567-9
LC 00-67703

"McGregor introduces perhaps one dramatic twist too many, but her novel otherwise artfully mixes historical background, up-to-date medical information about a rare disease, a bit of pop psychologizing and some upbeat lessons about the survival of the human spirit." Publ Wkly

McGregor, Jon
Even the dogs; a novel. Bloomsbury USA 2010 195p pa $14
ISBN 978-1-59691-348-6; 1-59691-348-7
LC 2009-49556

"The book is narrated by a group of urban ghosts, victims of drug overdoses who look on as someone they know, Robert Radcliffe, is found dead in his shabby apartment. Other friends, family members and acquaintances, most of whom were part of Robert's life, come in and out of focus as they move around the city looking for their next fixes and, along with the police and investigators, respond to Robert's death. As a novel about the consequences of addiction—particularly heroin addiction—'Even the Dogs' is harrowing. .
. . But McGregor's devotion to craft comes at a significant cost to a reader's emotional engagement with his characters and story. His technique intrudes, becomes showy." N Y Times Book Rev

McGuane, Thomas

★ The **cadence** of grass. Knopf 2002 238p

ISBN 0-679-44674-5

LC 2001-50623

"The real engine of the book is not plot . . . but language: McGuane's sentences are like no one else's, crisp and spare, yet some how baroque, and he perpetually balances the picaresque against the sublime." New Yorker

McGuane, Thomas

★ **Driving** on the rim. Alfred A. Knopf 2010 305p $26.95

ISBN 978-1-4000-4155-8; 1-4000-4155-4

LC 2010-01255

This novel is "reminiscent of the author's earlier, funnier work, like his second, picaresque novel, 'The Bushwhacked Piano,' from 1971. And yet, this is in no way a novel that could have been written in an author's 20s or even 30s (or maybe even 40s). The archaeology of Berl Pickett, the complex layering of memories, the behavioral ruts and yes, the full understanding of how difficult it can be to get one's wheels up and out require a bit of living — no shortcuts. This is a novel in which events matter so much less than the spirit in which we conduct ourselves and the lessons we learn." L A Times Book Rev

McGuane, Thomas

Gallatin Canyon; stories. Knopf 2006 220p $24

ISBN 1-4000-4156-2

LC 2005-44680

"McGuane has become our poet-philosopher of the arm's length, of the prudently aborted intimacy that keeps both isolation and commitment equally at bay." N Y Times Book Rev

McGuane, Thomas

★ **Keep** the change. Houghton Mifflin 1989 230p

ISBN 0-395-48887-7; 0-7710-5517-X

LC 89-30996

"Thomas McGuane is the pool shark of our prose. His sentences click with imperious precision. Masse and carom and draw shots follow each other with elan. McGuane puts English on his English so the words swerve with fatal charm. . . . What singles out this novel is the honesty with which McGuane has tested his version of Huck Finn. The final pages have overwhelming authority." Christ Sci Monit

McGuane, Thomas

★ **Ninety**-two in the shade. Farrar Straus and Giroux 1973 197p

ISBN 0-374-22259-2

LC 73-76222

Despite "unexpected, complex ironies, the relation of Skelton and Dance is too laconic and abstract to achieve quite the classic fatality McGuane aims for. . . . What keeps [the novel] exciting to read is McGuane's feeling for the rambunctious oddities, forlorn vulgarity and green beauty of Key West. . . . [This] is, with its faults, a very fine book." Newsweek

McGuane, Thomas

Nobody's angel. Random House 1981 227p

ISBN 0-394-52264-8

LC 81-13885

"What stamps this as a McGuane novel are the bizarre episodes he invents for his character and the wit with which he reports them; what is new . . . is a depth of feeling." N Y Times Book Rev

McGuane, Thomas

Nothing but blue skies. Houghton Mifflin 1992 349p

ISBN 0-395-54540-4

LC 92-23623

"The author's underlying theme is the unimportance of money by comparison with love, an old point that he makes with novel means and without sentimental sugar." Christ Sci Monit

McGuane, Thomas

Panama. Farrar Straus and Giroux 1978 175p

ISBN 0-374-22942-2

LC 78-12344

"The plot finds drugged-out and washed-up rock star Chet Pomeroy trying to get his act together in wild and wonderful Key West, Florida." Libr J

"Thomas McGuane is the pool shark of our prose. His sentences click with imperious precision. . . . The words swerve with fatal charm." Christ Sci Monit

McHugh, Maureen F.

After the apocalypse; Maureen F. McHugh. Small Beer Press 2011 188p.

ISBN 9781931520294 (trade pbk.: alk. paper); 9781931520355 (ebook); 978-1-931520-29-4; 978-1-931520-35-5

LC 20116769

Each short story in this collection "takes place in the near future, and usually in the aftermath of some global disaster." (Washington Post) It was the author's intent to explore "what the fall of civilization might actually feel like. The cataclysms . . . range from flu epidemics to dirty bombs to water shortages to good old-fashioned economic depression. . . . One of the persistent themes in this book is that when the world as we know it collapses, certain groups are far more likely to end up crushed in the rubble." (salon.com)

McHugh, Maureen F.

Nekropolis. Eos 2001 257p

ISBN 0-380-97457-6

LC 2001-33525

"As a 'jessed' or bonded servant, Hariba possesses a chemically induced sense of loyalty to her master until her growing affection for an artificial construct drives her to an act of desperation and changes her life forever. . . . This luminous tale of forbidden love in a near-future Morocco explores the evolution of human nature in a world where technology has redefined the meaning of the word human." Libr J

McInerney, Jay

Bright lights, big city; a novel. Vintage Bks. 1984 182p pa $15

ISBN 0-394-72641-3

LC 84-40074

This "is a very funny, oddly touching book, and something of a tour de force as well. McInerney employs an unusual and challenging narrative device; he tells his tale through the second person in the historical present tense and fashions a coherent and engaging voice with it, one that is totally believable at almost every moment in the novel." New Repub

McInerney, Jay

The good life. Knopf 2006 353p $25

ISBN 0-375-41140-2

LC 2005-44370

This is a novel "about 9/11's effects on four privileged Manhattanites: a retired corporate raider, a would-be screenwriter, a former model, and a book editor. . . . This is really the story of two of the above, part of a cast meaningfully reassembled from Brightness Falls (1992), who meet as volunteers at a soup kitchen for rescue workers at Ground Zero. Both of them are in miserable marriages, and they're left shaken when the nation's worst day leads to the best days of their lives. McInerney probes the human response to tragedy, and the complexity of human desire, with both precision and empathy." Booklist

McInerney, Jay

How it ended; new and collected stories. Alfred A. Knopf 2009 331p $25.95

ISBN 978-0-307-26805-1; 0-307-26805-5

LC 2008-53518

"Mr. McInerney was a callow, facile and extremely entertaining writer from the very first. He had a smart student's command of technical virtues and an eagerness to show them off. He also had such a tiresome infatuation with 1980s-style decadence that it lingers sentimentally even now. But his stories have grown more elegant, subtle, shapely and reflective over time, to the point where some of the recent works are perfect specimens. He has quietly achieved the literary stature to which he once so noisily laid claim." N Y Times (Late N Y Ed)

McInerney, Monica

Upside down, inside out; a novel. Ballantine Books 2008 419p pa $14

ISBN 978-0-345-50624-5; 0-345-50624-3

LC 2008-274694

First published 2002 in Australia

"There is a huge 'aaahh' factor in Monica McInerney's second novel. . . The book is great fun (but) laughter aside, there's also a serious aspect regarding communication, truth and honesty and how vital these are in close relationships." Irish Examiner

McInerny, Ralph M.

Bishop as pawn; a Father Dowling mystery. {by} Ralph McInerny. Vanguard Press 1978 219p

LC 78-54978

"Father Dowling's housekeeper's husband returns after a desertion of 15 years, only to be killed. Involved in this odd collection of bits and pieces is a good Catholic girl who wants to marry an irreligous man, leading to a singularly bleak affair, a young undogmatic and fundamentalist priest much disliked by Father Dowling, and an incomprehensible kidnapping of the remarkably smooth bishop." Libr J

McInerny, Ralph M.

Body and soil; an Andrew Broom mystery. {by} Ralph McInerny. Atheneum Pubs. 1989 245p

LC 88-38209

In this mystery Indiana attorney Andrew Broom, "represents some very unpopular clients, including a strange young man who has confessed to the murder of a local boy. In the midst of that trial, the town's wealthiest couple brawls in public, loudly insists on a divorce, and hires Broom and his partner/nephew as opposing attorneys. Then murder interrupts the proceedings. In a departure from the traditional whodunit, McInerny offers readers front-row seats to observe the villain's activities." Booklist

McInerny, Ralph M.

The book of kills; a mystery set at the University of Notre Dame. {by} Ralph McInerny. St. Martin's Minotaur 2000 275p $23.95

ISBN 0-312-20346-2

LC 00-40257

"A series of pranks, including the kidnapping of the chancellor, has alarmed the Notre Dame administration, and the Knight brothers get the call to investigate. The various shenanigans seem somehow related to the claim by a group of Native Americans that the land on which the famed university stands was stolen from them and should be returned. . . . Another deft and mordantly witty excursion into the rarefied atmosphere of Notre Dame." Publ Wkly

McInerny, Ralph M.

A cardinal offense; {by} Ralph McInerny. St. Martin's Press 1994 372p

LC 94-3481

"A man, pursuing an annulment, and his wife, who is opposed, meet separately with Fr. Dowling in St. Hilary's rectory on the same day that the priest receives two surprise tickets to the next Notre Dame-Southern California football game. The husband says his wife was never really a Catholic; she insists that the 30-year marriage and the couple's grown children remain valid. After the man is murdered, Dowling and his cop friend Phil Keegan consider possible suspects." Publ Wkly

McInerny, Ralph M.

Celt and pepper; {by} Ralph McInerny. St. Martin's Minotaur 2002 210p $22.95

ISBN 0-312-29117-5

LC 2002-69938

"After a young Notre Dame professor/Poet dies unexpectedly, Professor Roger Knight. . . suspects murder. His erudition, coupled with assistance from his brother Philip, a private investigator, ultimately leads to a killer. Solid plotting from a practiced hand." Libr J

McInerny, Ralph M.

★ **Grave** undertakings; a Father Dowling mystery. [by] Ralph McInerny. St. Martin's Minotaur 2000 374p

ISBN 0-312-20309-8

LC 99-54817

"Mimi O'Toole is hoping for a miracle when she asks Father Dowling in the hospital for absolution for her dying husband, a shooting victim. Vincent O'Toole was known to be an associate of the Pianone crime family, and his funeral draws every notable in the local underworld to St. Hilary's church in Fox River, Ill. The cops don't seem all that anxious to find O'Toole's killer, until someone tries to dig up his grave on Halloween and his casket is later discovered to be empty. In his effort to figure out what happened to O'Toole both before and after death, Father Dowling remains the calm center in a swirl of events." Publ Wkly

McInerny, Ralph M.

Irish coffee; [by] Ralph McInerny. St. Martin's Minotaur 2003 247p $23.95

ISBN 0-312-30901-5

LC 2003-50620

"Everybody likes Fred Neville, who works in Notre Dame's sports information office. Everybody but one person-the person who killed him. A different side of unassuming Fred surfaces when two women arrive at his funeral, each claiming Fred as their fiance. Because South Bend, home of Notre Dame, is always deferential to the university, the locals have no objection when the Knight brothers become unofficial consultants on the case. Phillip Knight is a streetwise PI, and his immensely rotund brother, Roger, is an amateur sleuth and a revered professor of Catholic studies. . . . A fine effort by a deservedly respected genre veteran." Booklist

McInerny, Ralph M.

★ **Irish** tenure; a mystery set at the University of Notre Dame. [by] Ralph McInerny. St. Martin's Minotaur 1999 246p

ISBN 0-312-20345-4

LC 99-16992

"Two young philosophy professors, Amanda Pick and Hans Wiener, are vying for the single tenured spot open in their department. . . . Pick has become the object of obsession of a Chesterton expert on the English faculty, Prof. Sean Pottery. So when her body is found in a lake on campus, Pottery seems like a good suspect. . . . A second murder clouds the issue momentarily, but sleuth Roger Knight, a mountain of a man who holds a chair in Catholic Studies at Notre Dame, uncovers the truth." Publ Wkly

McInerny, Ralph M.

Judas Priest; a Father Dowling mystery. {by} Ralph McInerny. St. Martin's Press 1991 184p

LC 91-21819

"A seminary friend of Dowling's, former priest Chris Bourke, and his ex-nun wife now promote sexual liberation as televangelists of Enlightened Hedonism (EH). Meeting Dowling one day after Mass, Bourke asks the parish priest to talk about the hard facts of religious life with his daughter, Sonya, who wants to enter the convent. Before Dowling can do that, Sonya is reported kidnapped and then found stabbed to death. . . . Dowling, worldly-wise and armed with ready references to St. Paul and other Church fathers, is at his vintage best." Publ Wkly

McInerny, Ralph M.

Last things; a Father Dowling mystery. {by} Ralph McInerny. St. Martin's Minotaur 2003 307p $24.95

ISBN 0-312-30899-X

LC 2003-40641

"Father Dowling first becomes involved with the Bernardo family when Eleanor Wygant asks him to try to persuade her niece, Jessica Bernardo , to stop writing a novel based on the Bernardo family. Eleanor is afraid of the resultant scandal if her long-buried secret is revealed. . . . There is a murder for Father Dowling to solve, of course, but this time McInerny seems more interested in exploring the motivations and entwined family relationships of his characters. There's also plenty of the Catholic minutiae that Father Dowling fans enjoy." Booklist

McInerny, Ralph M.

Requiem for a realtor; a Father Dowling mystery. [by] Ralph McInerny. St. Martin's Minotaur 2004 263p $23.95

ISBN 0-312-32417-0

LC 2004-41858

"Stanley Collins is Fox River's most notorious philandering realtor. His wife, Phyllis, wants to divorce him but is afraid to lose her claim on an impending inheritance. She is stringing along her dentist, love-struck Dave Jameson, who's also a devout Catholic. Jameson is a prominent member of St. Hilary's parish and, as an emissary for Phyllis Collins, asks Father Dowling's advice regarding a divorce and her standing in the church. Circumstances change when Stanley Collins is run down by his own car a couple of blocks from the apartment of a local nightclub torch singer, with whom he is having an affair. Dowling closely watches as the investigation–directed by his closest friend, Phil Keegan, of the Fox River PD–unfolds. . . . McInerny adds a moral catch-22 for Dowling as he struggles to choose between helping solve a murder and betraying the sanctity of a parishioner's confidences." Booklist

McInerny, Ralph M.

Second vespers; a Father Dowling mystery. {by} Ralph McInerny. Vanguard Press 1980 224p

LC 79-56379

Father Dowling "moves in on the criminals uncovering their various attempts to cheat collectors of O'Rourke memorabilia. Among the characters are two people who have a bookshop located in the old O'Rourke mansion, the local librarian who has a collection of letters, and another who is trying to get his hands on all the available O'Rourke papers. When a body is discovered, it throws doubt on the state of the 'estate' and also on the murder of O'Rourke." West Coast Rev Books

McInerny, Ralph M.

Still life; a novel. {by} Ralph McInerny. Five Star 2000 255p $21.95

ISBN 0-7862-2895-4

LC 00-61724

This mystery features "Captain Egidio Manfredi of the Fort Elbow, Ohio, police force. Manfredi is staring at mandatory retirement when he and his young assistant are ordered to reopen a 30-year-old case involving the disappearance of the poet-wife of a now-retired professor." Booklist

"Clever repartee, hidden alliances both present and past, false claims of guilt, pointed observations on aging, and surprising marriage plans underscore the author's talents." Libr J

McInerny, Ralph M.

Thicker than water; a Father Dowling mystery. {by} Ralph McInerny. Vanguard Press 1981 255p

LC 81-10432

This "Father Dowling mystery takes off from a couple of petty crimes . . . to a series of bizarre murders. Father Dowling . . . discovers a dead body in a pickup truck parked in front of the rectory. Murders start piling up around the quiet little town." Booklist

McIntosh, Will

Hitchers; Will McIntosh. Night Shade Books 2012 283 p.

ISBN 1597803359; 9781597803359

The author, Hugo Award winner Will McIntosh, "delivers a . . . tale of individual grief and recovery against the backdrop of a devastated world. When an anthrax attack on Atlanta devastates the population, widower Finn Darby loses two of his few remaining friends . . . [and] finds himself . . . uttering sentences that have no meaning to him. They seem to be connected to his late grandfather, . . . who created the comic strip that Darby now writes against his grandfather's dying wishes. . . . Darby discovers other sufferers, including . . . a waitress who might be possessed by Darby's dead wife. Darby, with his . . . grief serving as synecdoche for the entire city, is forced to confront his guilt over his wife's death and his co-opting of his grandfather's work." (Publishers Weekly)

McIntyre, Vonda N.

Dreamsnake. Houghton Mifflin 1978 313p

LC 77-18891

"This is based on McIntyre's Nebula Award-winning novelette, 'Of Mist, and Grass, and Sand,' which is also the first chapter of the book. Snake, the healer, and her three healing serpents attend a young boy ill with a tumor. His fearful parents kill Grass, the dreamsnake, who can ease the dying by removing their pain. Without Grass, Snake is incomplete as a healer, and since the dreamsnakes come from off-world, she cannot get a replacement. To atone for her carelessness in losing Grass, Snake sets off for the city where off-worlders trade, hoping to get more dreamsnakes. She has many heart-stopping adventures, and the reader is engrossed every step of the way." Libr J

McKenzie, Sophie

Close My Eyes; by Sophie McKenzie. 1st U.S. ed. St. Martin's Press 2013 391 p. (hardcover) $25.99

ISBN 1250033896; 9781250033895

LC 2013011566

This novel, written by Sophie McKenzie, is about Geniver Loxley, "a grieving mother who finds out years after her daughter's death that her child may still be alive [when] a stranger shows up . . . telling Gen . . . that her daughter Beth was not stillborn, but was taken away as a healthy infant and is still out there, somewhere, waiting to be found. Gen begins to [search] her past, hopeful she'll find a clue to her daughter's whereabouts." (Publisher's note)

McKillip, Patricia A., 1948-

Alphabet of thorn. Ace Books 2004 314p $22.95

ISBN 0-441-01130-6

LC 2003-62912

"The day that the new queen of Raine is crowned, a translator working in the palace receives a book written in a strange language of thornlike characters. As Nepenthe, the translator, unlocks the language's secret, she learns of a legend from the ancient past that involves her and the queen in an intrigue that threatens the kingdom itself. McKillip . . . creates the atmosphere of a fairy tale with her elegantly lyrical prose and attention to nuance. Her characters are at once intimately personal and larger than life." Libr J

McKillip, Patricia A., 1948-

Ombria in shadow; Patricia A. McKillip. Ace Books 2002 298p. (pbk.) $16

ISBN 044100895X; 9780441010165

LC 2001046388

Mythopoeic Award: Adult Literature (2003), World Fantasy Awards: Novel (2003)

In this fantasy novel, the winner of the 2003 World Fantasy Award and Mythopoeic Award, "[g]reed, despair, grief and avarice have all taken their toll on the once-beautiful city of Ombria, but it is the death of its prince that pushes it over the edge into darkness and shadow. Several key players participate in this particular procession of dying and rebirth: Kyel Greve, the new prince-to-be who is too young to rule but old enough to feel the despair of those around him; Lydea, the dying prince's lover who feels the weight of the city resting on her shoulders; Ducon Greve, the bastard prince who sees and feels the change happening but is in no position to alter the coming darkness; Domina Pearl, the sorceress who is pushing the city even further on its path of destruction; and Mag and Faey, two mysterious women who hold some of the past, present and future of Ombria inside them." (Publishers Weekly)

McKillip, Patricia A.

The **sorceress** and the Cygnet. Ace Bks. 1991 231p

LC 90-44103

This fantasy "features imaginative worldbuilding, strong male and female characters, and an intense (though sometimes esoteric) style." Libr J

Followed by The Cygnet and the firebird (1993)

McKinney-Whetstone, Diane
  Blues dancing; a novel. Morrow 1999 307p
  ISBN 0-688-14995-2

"This love story is set in Philadelphia. Verdi is the naive, pampered only child of a prominent Southern preacher who has come north for college, while black student leader Johnson is brash, energetic, and sometimes angry. . . . Caught between the desire for success and the fast life of the streets, Johnson experiments with drugs, ultimately becoming addicted to heroin and getting Verdi addicted as well. Upright, conservative professor Rowe, who believes that it is his duty to guide Verdi in the right direction, falls in love with her and eventually leaves his wife for her. They live together comfortably for 20 years, until Johnson returns and forces Verdi to make a decision that will change her life forever. A captivating read." Libr J

McKinney-Whetstone, Diane
  Leaving Cecil Street; a novel. Diane McKinney-Whetstone. 1st ed; Morrow 2004 297p $24.95
  ISBN 0-688-16385-8
                              LC 2003-55845

"Cecil Street is a quiet, tree-lined haven in West Philadelphia, a place where everyone knows everyone else, a place removed from the turmoil and violence of the late 1960s. Yet the residents of Cecil Street have their problems. Joe and Louise's marriage is strained; Johnetta's sexy niece has arrived, ripe for trouble; and teenaged Shay tries to help best friend Neet deal with an unwanted pregnancy. When Neet's abortion goes tragically wrong, everyone on the street must rally around her, while Joe, Louise, and Neet's mother, Alberta, discover how their pasts have now drawn them together. McKinney-Whetstone's portrayal of African American family life is sensitive and compassionate, with characters who love, work, live, and die without veering into soap opera." Libr J

McKinney-Whetstone, Diane
  Tempest rising; a novel. Morrow 1998 280p
  ISBN 978-0688149949
                              LC 97-40942

This "novel is set in Philadephia during the sixties. Three sisters, Bliss, Victoria, and Shern, are raised as privileged middle-class children until tragedy unravels their lives. . . . The death of the family's 'rock' causes the mother to suffer a nervous breakdown, and the girls are removed from her care. The novel focuses on the attention they receive and the relationship that develops between each girl and their caregivers, Mae and Ramona. Mae is a politically connected foster-care provider, but she shows little concern for her own daughter, Ramona. Ramona struggles to accept her role as secondary child-care provider, yet she resents the children and her mother's abuse. Each character is unforgettable." Booklist

McKinty, Adrian
  The **cold** cold ground; a Detective Sean Duffy novel / by Adrian McKinty. Seventh Street Books 2012 p. cm.
  ISBN 9781616147167
                              LC 2012023528

In this book by Adrian McKinty, book one of the Troubles Trilogy, "a Catholic cop tracks a killer operating amidst the sectarian violence of the conflict in Northern Ireland. The Thatcher government has flooded the area with soldiers but nightly there are riots, bombings, and sectarian attacks. In the midst of the chaos, Sean Duffy, a young, witty, Catholic detective in the almost entirely Protestant Royal Ulster Constabulary, is trying to track down a serial killer who is targeting gay men." (Publisher's note)

McKinzie, Clinton
  Crossing the line; Clinton McKinzie. Delacorte Press 2004 373p $23
  ISBN 0-385-33637-3
                              LC 2003-64602

"When the Burns brothers are high up on a rock face or hunting down evil banditos, the pace and intensity shoot skyward. Readers will find themselves hanging on by their fingernails as they wait to see who will fall and who will live to climb again." Publ Wkly

McLain, Paula
  The **Paris** wife; a novel. Ballantine Books 2011 320p $25
  ISBN 978-0-345-52130-9; 0-345-52130-7
                              LC 2010-37878

"McLain's vivid, clear-voiced novel is a conjecture, an act of imaginary autobiography on the part of the author. Yet her biographical and geographical research is so deep, and her empathy for the real Hadley Richardson so forthright (without being intrusively femme partisan), that the account reads as very real indeed. Big things happen: Hadley is there as Hemingway meets Gertrude Stein and Scott Fitzgerald, as he writes The Sun Also Rises, as he falls in love with bullfighting. But a thousand less glamorous, more quotidian things happen too, as Hadley tries to find a way to live her own life (she's a fine pianist) and support her moody husband, and keep up with hard-drinking company, and run a household in a country not her own. By making the ordinary come to life, McLain has written a beautiful portrait of being in Paris in the glittering 1920s — as a wife and one's own woman." Entertainment Wkly

McLarty, Ron
  Art in America. Viking 2008 366p $25.95
  ISBN 978-0-670-01895-6; 0-670-01895-3
                              LC 2007-40454

"In Creedemore, Colo., a land-rights dispute pitches locals against one another and attracts national media attention. Into the fray arrives Steven Kearney, a prolific New York author of unpublished novels, poems and plays, who has been invited by the Creedemore Historical Society to write and direct a play dramatizing the town's history. Steven's relocation sparks a colorful fish-out-of-water story populated with cowboys, environmental activists, hordes of reporters, performance artists, ecoterrorists and bona fide outlaws. Keeping the peace is sheriff Petey Myers, whose recollections of (and occasional conversations with) his slain partner provide some of the novel's finest moments." Publ Wkly

McLarty, Ron

Traveler. Viking 2007 280p $24.95
ISBN 978-0-670-03474-1; 0-670-03474-6
LC 2006-46763

"When Jono Riley, an aging NYC actor and bartender, receives word that his first love, Marie D'Agostino, has died, he immediately returns to his hometown of East Providence, Rhode Island. Marie died when a bullet, lodged in her back some 40 years ago, traveled, causing her heart to stop. Jono was present on the winter day in 1961 when the shooting occurred, but the shock of Marie's death has caused him to remember the event in more detail. He seeks the aid of a retired cop who is still bothered that he never solved the case. McLarty gives us a real sense of place here, evoking both East Providence's past as an immigrant enclave for dockworkers and its newly gentrified present." Booklist

McLaughlin, Emma

The **nanny** diaries; a novel. [by] Emma McLaughlin and Nicola Kraus. St. Martin's Press 2002 305p
ISBN 0-312-27858-6
LC 2001-48652

This is "a diabolically funny New York story. . . . [Nanny] is a vastly entertaining narrator and impromptu social critic. . . . Not surprisingly, 'The Nanny Diaries' fades slightly when the X's are out of sight, despite the boyfriend and family matters that are meant to fill out Nanny's story. The heart of the matter remains perfectly pitched social satire. . . . This book is saved from self-righteousness not only by the authors' cleverness but also by their compassion. For oblivious parents, lonely offspring and overworked, underpaid employees alike, they're out to fix something that's broken." N Y Times (Late N Y Ed)

McLaughlin, Emma

Nanny returns; a novel. by Emma McLaughlin and Nicola Kraus. Atria Books 2009 320p $25
ISBN 978-1-4165-8567-1; 1-4165-8567-2
LC 2009-28118

Sequel to: The nanny diaries

"Narrator Nan is now 33, a world-traveled, master's-degreed consultant well past her dark Park Avenue days with the spectacularly dysfunctional 'X' family. . . . Returned to New York with her U.N.-employed husband (Diaries' Harvard Hottie) after years abroad, Nan finds a job in the cashmere-clad overachievement Olympics that is the city's private-school system — and is reunited, too, with the erratic X family, who are more unhinged than ever. The authors' breezy wit . . . carries an often cartoonish plot, and their surprisingly affecting portrayal of childhood hurts pierces the world of monstrous privilege the book springs from." Entertainment Wkly

McMahon, Jennifer

Dismantled; a novel. Harper 2009 422p $24.99; pa $13.99
ISBN 978-0-06-168933-8; 0-06-168933-5; 978-0-06-168934-5 pa; 0-06-168934-3 pa
LC 2009-18308

"Ten years ago, five students went into the Vermont woods to live and breathe their art in a cabin by a lake; only four came back. The survivors—Tess, Henry, Winnie, and Spencer—have tried to forget that summer, but they are forced to confront it by a mysterious postcard that quotes Suz, the missing member and charismatic ringleader. Spencer kills himself, an act that sets in motion an investigation that will test Tess and Henry's rocky marriage and endanger their nine-year-old daughter, Emma." Libr J

"While some of the characters may seem a tad unsuspecting, the book provides more than enough thrills and chills to compensate and is an engaging read." PopMatters

McMahon, Jennifer

Don't breathe a word; a novel. Harper 2011 447p pa $14.99
ISBN 978-0-06-168937-6; 0-06-168937-8

"A compelling yet disturbing contemporary tale where dreams and nightmares breathe in shadows and the veil between reality and fantasy is gossamer thin. Hauntingly enigmatic." Book'd Out

McMahon, Jennifer

The **One** I Left Behind; Jennifer McMahon. HarperCollins 2013 432 p. $14.99
ISBN 006212255X; 9780062122551

In this book by Jennifer McMahon, "a serial killer called Neptune begins kidnapping women. He leaves their severed hands on the police department steps and . . . displays their bodies around town. Just when Reggie needs her mother, Vera, the most, Vera's hand is found on the steps. But after five days, there's no body and Neptune disappears. Now, twenty-five years later, Reggie . . . gets a call revealing that her mother has been found alive." (Publisher's note)

McMahon, Thomas A.

Ira Foxglove. Brook Street Press 2004 169p $21.95
ISBN 0-9724295-3-0
LC 2003-21792

This is a "darkly genial novella discovered among McMahon's papers a year or so after his death. . . . This may be an early work, set aside for who knows what reason, but it has the same loopy charm and rueful insight as McMahon's previously published fiction." N Y Times Book Rev

McMahon, Thomas A.

★ **Principles** of American nuclear chemistry; a novel. University of Chicago Press 2003 246p (Phoenix fiction) pa $15
ISBN 0-226-56110-0
LC 2003-48355

First published 1970 by Little, Brown

"One of the rewarding things about [this] novel . . . is the total absence of any predictable generation-gap bitterness. Beyond lost innocence the book is about a problem that troubles the age—a sense of having pursued wrong priorities too hotly, an awareness of the neglect of life and love that results." Time

McMillan, Rosalyn

Blue collar blues. Warner Bks. 1998 359p $30
ISBN 0-446-52243-0
LC 98-19553

"Thyme Tyler is an African American plant manager for Champion Motors (a hybrid of Ford, GM and Chrysler) who has hit the glass ceiling even though she holds a Ph.D. Khan Davis is a handsomely paid factory worker who faces the threat of layoff and daily struggles for overtime in the plant. The two women maintain a . . . friendship despite their class differences and despite Khan's refusal to forgive Thyme's marriage to a sterotypically lily-white Champion exec." Publ Wkly

McMillan, Terry

A **day** late and a dollar short. Viking 2001 448p
ISBN 0-670-89676-4

LC 00-46232

McMillan "takes a multiperspective view of dysfunctional families with each member of the Price clan giving his or her own version of how screwed up they all are. . . . Their heavy load—incest, substance abuse, poverty, infidelity, death—makes this a soap opera, but it is leavened with a big dollop of sass." Time

McMillan, Terry

Disappearing acts. Viking 1989 384p
ISBN 0-670-82461-5

LC 88-40412

"What raises this work above a mere sentimental love story is the finely tuned humor, which McMillan uses effectively to subtly alter the meaning of a scene or to draw the reader into her circle of characters." Booklist

McMillan, Terry

★ **How** Stella got her groove back. Viking 1996 368p
ISBN 978-0670869909

LC 96-15374

"Readers who have been yearning for a Judith Krantz of the black bourgeoisie—albeit one with a dirty mouth and a more ebullient spirit—will be pleased with this fantasy of sexual fulfillment." Publ Wkly

McMillan, Terry

The **interruption** of everything. Viking 2005 365p $25.95
ISBN 0-670-03144-5

LC 2005-42207

"With twists on familiar themes, irreverent humor, and a heroine who has more backbone than we initially thought, . . . [this book] brings it all back home. This is life-affirming women's fiction delivered by one of the best in the field." Libr J

McMillan, Terry

★ **Waiting** to exhale. Viking 1992 409p $22.95
ISBN 0-670-83980-9

LC 91-46564

"Terry McMillan's heroines are so well drawn that by the end of the novel, the reader is completely at home with the four of them. They observe men—and contemporary America—with bawdy humor, occasional melancholy and great affection. But the novel is about more than four lives; the bonds among the women are so alive and so appealing

they almost seem a character in their own right." N Y Times Book Rev

McMullen, Sean

Glass dragons. Tor Bks. 2004 495p map $27.95
ISBN 0-7653-0797-9

LC 2003-60677

In this sequel to Voyage of the Shadowmoon (2002), "the honorable vampire Laren, the priestess Terikel, and the voluptuous Lady Velander continue their journey aboard the exploratory ship Shadowmoon. Their search for a doomsday weapon known as the Dragonwall leads them to an encounter with a fugitive bard, a runaway sailor, and a widowed princess. Australian author McMullen depicts a world filled with intrigue and strange magic, where the borders between the living and the dead are thin and where mystical weapons have the power to destroy the world. His sometimes whimsical, always literate style brings a gentle touch of wry humor to a tale of courage and cowardice, love and death, mystery and magic." Libr J

McMullen, Sean

Souls in the great machine. Tor Bks. 1999 448p
ISBN 0-312-87055-8

LC 99-21934

"In the fortieth century, librarians rule the world. Through a byzantine system of political favor, mathematical expertise, civil service testing, and dueling, the librarians strive for power in the 'mayoralty' of Rochester, the most powerful of several Australian fiefdoms that emerged long ago from a nuclear winter. The highliber is the scheming yet honorable Zarvora. She has ruthlessly assembled scores of mathematicians, who make the Calculor, a bizarre flesh-and-machine supercomputer that Zarvora needs to unify this quasi-medieval world and save it from the impending doom implicit in the Call. . . . Decidedly original, sometimes whimsical, and captivating, this is a genuine tour de force." Booklist

McMurtry, Larry

★ **Anything** for Billy. Simon & Schuster 1988 382p
LC 88-22732

"McMurtry's prose is as readable as ever, served up in short, episodic chapters that effectively capture time and place, conjure up authentic images of pathetic heroes and villains, and yet pull the reins in on action. The tale's strength lies in Sippy's commanding first-person delivery and the less-than-admirable profile of the title character." Booklist

McMurtry, Larry

Boone's Lick; a novel. Simon & Schuster 2000 287p
ISBN 0-684-86886-5

LC 00-56342

"McMurtry's historical novel, told with humor and candor from the perspective of Mary Margaret's oldest son, Shay, is highly recommended for adults and adolescents alike." Libr J

McMurtry, Larry

Buffalo girls; a novel. Simon & Schuster 1990 351p

LC 90-42486

"This is a nostalgic, funny, and sad novel about the Old West when cowboys and Buffalo girls whooped it up. Their behavior was amoral rather than immoral, and they lived by their own special code of behavior. Friendship was often life-saving as well as comforting, and the women of the bawdy houses called their clients 'sweethearts' even if their encounter was only for one night. Jim Ragg and Bartle Bone had become almost a dying breed and Custer, in their opinion, was a stupid old man at Little Big Horn to think that he could fight 3,000 Indians with 200 of his men. Highlights of the book are Bill Cody's (Buffalo Bill's) Wild West show and Calamity Jane's (whose drunkenness was calamitous) letters to a daughter. Fact and fiction are entwined in an enjoyable story that is mythic and memorable." Shapiro. Fic for Youth. 3d edition

McMurtry, Larry

By sorrow's river; a novel. Simon & Schuster 2003 347p (Berrybender narratives) $26

ISBN 0-7432-3304-2

LC 2003-53892

"In this third volume of McMurtry's Berrybender Narratives, Lord Berrybender and his obnoxious, sniveling brood are, surprisingly, still alive on the dangerous Great Plains of Wyoming and Colorado. The wry story of mountainman adventure and European stupidity, set in the 1830s, is just as wacky and gruesome as its predecessors." Publ Wkly

McMurtry, Larry

Cadillac Jack; a novel. Simon & Schuster 1982 395p

ISBN 0-671-45445-5

LC 82-5962

"Jack was a rodeo bulldogger before he graduated to roaming America 'in a pearl-colored Cadillac with peach velour interior,' scouting for antiques he can resell to collectors. . . . But now Jack is undergoing a midlife crisis, juggling old wives and new girl friends as he flounders in the amiable venality and lechery of Washington, D.C." Libr J

"The sheer exuberance of McMurtry's imagination makes this book well worth reading." West Coast Rev Books

McMurtry, Larry

Comanche moon; a novel. Simon & Schuster 1997 752p

ISBN 0-684-80754-8

LC 97-29609

"McMurtry has created a sprawling, picaresque novel that, like the history of the West itself, leaves more than a few loose ends. . . . The characters are the novel's strength. McMurtry's rangers are heroic because of their vulnerabilities, not despite them." N Y Times Book Rev

McMurtry, Larry

Dead man's walk; a novel. Simon & Schuster 1995 477p

ISBN 0-684-80753-X

LC 95-21011

"If Dead Man's Walk were not a prequel, it would be worth only glancing notice. As things are, it is a satisfactory foothill, with the grand old mountain in view. There are no heroics, though there is plenty of calamity. . . . McMurty has a fine time with youthful damnfoolishness, and so does the reader." Time

McMurtry, Larry

The **desert** rose; a novel. Simon & Schuster 1983 254p

LC 83-4687

"A topless dancer in a casino, Harmony 'had been said by some to have the best legs in Las Vegas and maybe the best bust too.' But now Harmony is approaching her 39th birthday, and her teenage daughter Pepper has become a contender for those honors. . . . {The} novel charts good-natured Harmony's sudden decline and Pepper's . . . well, peppery rise." Libr J

McMurtry, Larry

Duane's depressed; a novel. Simon & Schuster 1999 431p

ISBN 0-684-85497-X

LC 98-45712

"Duane is no intellectual, but he isn't stupid. Abandoning the ordinary ways of making do, he moves to a crude cabin on the prairie and starts trying to figure out where his life stalled. Before long he is seeing a psychiatrist, who has him reading Proust as part of his therapy. Novelistically, some of this seems too, um, made up, but Duane himself is always achingly affecting and real. . . . He is one of McMurtry's greatest characters." Newsweek

McMurtry, Larry

The **evening** star. Simon & Schuster 1992 637p

LC 92-2596

Sequel to Terms of endearment

"The success of a book like this one depends on the tone the author manages to muster up. Mr. McMurtry's is sentimentality laced with comic irony, and it works very well. . . . And if, in the end, Aurora Greenway and her extended and highly dysfunctional family turn out to be more entertaining than genuinely moving, it's reassuring to know that they—and the reader—are in the hands of a real pro." N Y Times Book Rev

McMurtry, Larry

Folly and glory. Simon & Schuster 2004 236p (Berrybender narratives) $25

ISBN 0-7432-3305-0

LC 2003-64173

"While McMurtry doesn't stint on frantic action, violence or seemingly round-the-clock gropings, Folly and Glory marks a somber and satisfying end to a long, rambunctious trip." N Y Times Book Rev

McMurtry, Larry

★ **Lonesome** dove; a novel. Simon & Schuster 1985 843p hardcover o.p. pa $18

ISBN 0-671-50420-7; 1-4391-9526-9 pa

LC 85-2192

"'Lonesome Dove' shows, early on, just about every symptom of American Epic except pretentiousness. McMurtry has laconic Texas talk and leathery, slim-hipped machismo down pat, and he's able to refresh heroic clichés with exact observations about cowboy prudery, ignorance and fear of losing face." Newsweek

Other titles in the Lonesome dove trilogy are:

Dead man's walk (1995)

Streets of Laredo (1993)

McMurtry, Larry

Loop group. Simon & Schuster 2004 242p $25

ISBN 0-7432-5079-6

LC 2004-52216

"Clearly, more sincere praise of the mature woman is overdue. And McMurtry's adulation is more than sincere, it's heated. He doesn't shy away from the pleasures of sexagenarian flesh." N Y Times Book Rev

McMurtry, Larry

Rhino Ranch; a novel. Simon & Schuster 2009 278p $26

ISBN 978-1-4391-5639-1; 1-4391-5639-5

LC 2009-19648

With this novel "McMurtry ends the west Texas saga of Duane Moore, begun in 1966 with The Last Picture Show. . . . Duane, now in his late 60s, is a prosperous and retired widower, lonely in his hometown of Thalia, Tex. Then billionaire heiress K.K. Slater moves in and opens the Rhino Ranch, a sanctuary intended to rescue the nearly extinct African black rhinoceros. Slater is a strong-willed, independent woman whose mere presence upsets parochial Thalia, and Duane can't quite figure her out. His two best buddies, Boyd Cotton and Bobby Lee Baxter, both work for Slater, and the three friends schmooze with the rich, talk about geezer sex, rat out local meth heads and try to keep track of a herd of rhinos." Publ Wkly

McMurtry, Larry

Sin killer. Simon & Schuster 2002 300p (Berrybender narratives) $25

ISBN 0-7432-3302-6

LC 2002-17616

"The first of four tales of the Berrybender family. It's 1832, and Lord and Lady Berrybender—wealthy Brits incongruously venturing into the Wild West—make their way up the Missouri River. . . . Among those in the sizable entourage are 6 of the 14 Berrybender children, including Tasmin, a gutsy, industrious young woman who generally takes charge of the hapless group. . . . But Tasmin's independence brings strife, too, especially when she hooks up with frontiersman Jim Snow, an Indian fighter and wanna-be preacher." Booklist

"McMurtry's prose is plain and exact, exhibiting the kind of clarity that appears simple yet is anything but." N Y Times Book Rev

McMurtry, Larry

★ **Streets** of Laredo; a novel. Simon & Schuster 1993 589p

LC 93-19279

"As in some great 19th-century saga, the story has more than its share of improbable coincidences—but these seem only mild contrivances to shape a story packed with action, terror, humor and pathos. Laredo is a fitting conclusion to a remarkable feat of reconstruction and sheer storytelling genius." Publ Wkly

McMurtry, Larry

Telegraph days; a novel. Simon & Schuster 2006 289p $25

ISBN 978-0-7432-5078-8; 0-7432-5078-8

LC 2005-57458

"Few male writers can match McMurtry for his ability to understand and conjure strong female characters. . . . Some of the novel's most entertaining moments involve Nellie's long-running relationship with Cody, a restless publicity hound and entrepreneur. . . . The wistful closing chapters—which center on Cody's death and Nellie's affluent decades in southern California at the dawn of the movie age—speak to McMurtry's fascination with mythmaking." Christ Sci Monit

McMurtry, Larry

★ **Terms** of endearment; a novel. Simon & Schuster 1975 410p

"Suddenly, just when we are enjoying ourselves the most, McMurtry changes his style, and we are plunged into a moving but agonizing realistic account of daughter Emma's death from cancer at 37 and the way in which her family and old friends react. . . . The shift of pace may throw some readers off stride badly. McMurtry certainly remains, however, one of our most exciting novelists." Publ Wkly

Followed by The evening star

McMurtry, Larry

Texasville; a novel. Simon & Schuster 1987 542p

ISBN 0-671-62533-0

LC 86-31520

"What's funniest, and most lifelike, about McMurtry's . . . book is that his people, having enjoyed a brief but exhilarating run of American abundance (both financial and sexual), don't mind indulging in a little harmless romanticizing of their frontier history, but they're not about to give up what they've got and go back to their arid, windswept beginnings without some kicking and screaming. . . . In its affable, offhand way, McMurtry's novel, which ends with a joke about repetition . . . really is about history, at least as Americans live it." New Yorker

Followed by Duane's depressed

McMurtry, Larry

The **wandering** hill; a novel. Simon & Schuster 2003 302p (Berrybender narratives) $26

ISBN 0-7432-3303-4

LC 2002-30595

"The landscape is stunningly beautiful, but the beauty is often disrupted by spasmodic, gruesome violence. Nonetheless, this novel is an engrossing, exciting, and sometimes heart-rending saga of the American West that shows McMurtry at his best." Booklist

McMurtry, Larry

Zeke and Ned; a novel. by Larry McMurtry and Diana Ossana. Simon & Schuster 1997 478p

ISBN 978-0684811529

LC 96-44906

"In the years just after the Civil War, life in the Indian Territory west of Arkansas—Cherokee land since the Trail of Tears—is more than a bit rugged, particularly for the Indians. Guns blaze with minimal provocation. Women are at the mercy of wandering marauders. And when the white man's justice does come, it's usually meted out by thugs from Arkansas, temporarily deputized as Federal marshals. Against this backdrop, a Cherokee named Zeke Proctor accidentally shoots the woman he had planned to bring home as his second wife—a killing that sets in motion a chain of events that destroys several families, nearly leads to war and concludes with a mountaintop standoff between Federal marshals and Zeke's friend and son-in-law, Ned Christie." N Y Times Book Rev

"What gives this well-wrought tale its depth is how McMurtry and Ossana convey the era's various moral shades of gray." Publ Wkly

McNally, T. M.

The **goat** bridge; a novel. T. M. McNally. University of Michigan Press 2005 310p $29

ISBN 0472115111; 9780472115112

LC 2005008513

This book "follows Stephen Brings, a burnt-out American photographer who is reeling from the unexplained disappearance of his son in Rome, and who finds an unlikely measure of understanding and acceptance in the wartorn Sarajevo of the early '90s. Brings, pointedly not 'covering' the war in any conventional sense, drifts through the city, helping where he can, taking the occasional photograph and forming attachments with a . . . group of locals, diplomats and journalists, including the German journalist Elise, with whom he begins a tentative affair." (Publishers Weekly)

McNamer, Deirdre

Red rover; a novel. Viking 2007 264p $24.95

ISBN 978-0-670-06350-5

LC 2006-36075

"McNamer depends on a complex web of coincidence to tell her story, and some readers may resist threads that connect so neatly. Arranging for so many people to be assembled in the same room 75 years down the road might be a difficult assignment even for hale survivors on the high plains of Montana. Nevertheless, it would be hard to argue against the wholly satisfying ending this reunion produces. We can be grateful that, in McNamer's world, it is never too late for a redemptive act; never too late for a life to matter." Houston Chron

McNaught, Judith

Paradise. Pocket Bks. 1991 489p

ISBN 0-671-60129-6

LC 91-12897

"Heiress to a famous department store fortune, Meredith Bancroft chafes under the strict supervision of her interfering father. When she meets ambitious, handsome steelworker Matt Farrell, Meredith is ripe for the picking, and trouble brews on both sides of the tracks when she becomes pregnant at 18. Mcnaught's skillful treatment of Meredith, the self-styled ugly duckling and poor little rich girl, will pique readers' interest and engage their sympathy." Libr J

McNeal, Tom

To be sung underwater; 1st ed.; Little, Brown and Company 2011 436 p.

ISBN 9780316127394; 0316127396

LC 2010041554

In this novel, "Judith Whitman, a film editor in California, doesn't seem to like her life, which includes teenage daughter, Camilla, and husband, Malcolm, and so, as she says, she came up with a swerve. 'My life had utterly settled into itself and then this little swerve occurred, or maybe I meant it to occur, maybe I'd actually plotted it out in one of those corners of your brain or heart you access only in dreams.' That swerve took her back to Nebraska and her first love, Willie Blunt. . . . One of them is really in love, and one of them just thinks so. That tempers the underlying structure." (JournalStar.com)

McNicholl, Damian

A **son** called Gabriel. CDC Books 2004 343p $22.95

ISBN 1-59315-018-0

"A coming-of-age story set in Northern Ireland during the years 1964-78 . . . . Catholic schoolboy Gabriel Harkin faces formidable obstacles to fitting into his family and community. In the background lurks the threat of religious prejudice; in the foreground is his increasing awareness that he may be homosexual. Subjected to brutal hazing by his more athletic classmates, Gabriel feigns an interest in football and seeks to repress his sexuality. He becomes almost hyperaware of all the characteristics that mark him as different and channels his energy into studying for the exams that will become his ticket out of his insular, increasingly violent hometown. A secret involving his uncle, a conflicted priest, also haunts the family. Perhaps the most poignant aspect of this novel, though, is the way his parents and siblings, although severely limited in their knowledge of how to help him, seek to comfort him in his struggle to conform." Booklist

McOmber, Adam

The **white** forest; Adam McOmber. Simon & Schuster 2012 303 p.

ISBN 1451664257; 9781451664256; 9781451664263; 9781451664270

LC 2011048720

In this novel, by Adam McOmber, "Jane Silverlake . . . [can] see the souls of man-made objects. . . . Her greatest joy is wandering the wild heath with her neighbors, Madeline and Nathan. . . . A year later, Nathan has vanished, and the famed Inspector Vidocq arrives in London to untangle the events. . . . As a sinister truth emerges, Jane realizes she must discover the origins of her talent, and use it to find Nathan herself." (Publisher's note)

McPhee, Jenny

A **man** of no moon; a novel. Counterpoint Books 2007 271p $24

ISBN 978-1-58243-375-2; 1-58243-375-5

LC 2007017929

"In post-World War II Italy, Dante Sabato, the country's most famous living poet, is alternately planning his suicide and his next sexual encounter. At a star-studded party, he meets the Godfrey sisters, Gladys and Prudence, B-level American actresses who have found film work in Italy. Captivated by their alluring scents, their brashness, and their mystery, Dante embarks on a perverse sexual affair with Gladys and falls obsessively in love with Prudence. . . . Focusing primarily on the film world, McPhee . . . expertly depicts 1940s movie glamour; in fact, the beginning of the novel reads like a film noir." Libr J

McPhee, Jenny

No ordinary matter; a novel. Free Press 2004 259p $23

ISBN 0-7432-6072-4

LC 2004-43246

"For more than a decade, thirtysomething sisters Lillian and Veronica have met at a Manhattan Hungarian bakery the first Monday of the month. Stunningly beautiful but ice-cold Lillian is a brilliant neurologist. Her lovely younger sister, warmhearted, insecure Veronica, is a scriptwriter for the wildly popular soap opera Ordinary Matters. Veronica has spent a lifetime worshiping her older sister, who unfailingly swats back at Veronica's overtures. In a series of coincidences that would give Victor Hugo pause, the sisters' already complicated and deeply entwined lives become even more so. A dysfunctional childhood (a dead father and a neglectful mother), a pregnancy, a new lover, a psychiatrist with Tourette's syndrome, several independent private investigations into secret second families, a long-lost brother, and other delicious surprises draw the reader in for the fun." Libr J

McPhee, Martha

Dear money. Houghton Mifflin Harcourt 2010 346p $25

ISBN 978-0-15-101165-0; 0-15-101165-6

LC 2009-29923

The novel "especially rich in social satire. McPhee knows what brand of chocolate truffles (Teuscher's) someone like Win would bring the girls as a present, and precisely how Emma might go about winning over the aging academic couple who own the Maine beach house she covets. McPhee gives perfect descriptions to even minor – or less than minor – characters." Dallas Morning News

McPhee, Martha

Gorgeous lies. Harcourt 2002 326p $31

ISBN 0-15-100613-X

LC 2002-7213

Sequel to Bright angel time (1997)

"In 20 years, many things have changed in the lives of the large Furey-Cooper clan. Once the members were widely known as exemplars of a new kind of blended family, living out the utopian visions of patriarch Anton. Now Anton lies virtually helpless, dying slowly with many dreams unreal-

ized and his magnum opus on human sexuality unwritten. The siblings gather at the family farm, linked painfully not only by grief but also by longtime resentments, disappointments, and misunderstandings that fester as Anton's end approaches." Libr J

McPhee, Martha

L'America. Harcourt 2006 294p $25

ISBN 0-15-101171-1

LC 2005-20986

McPhee "is a brilliant stylist, and here she creates characters so palpably real, they seem to ache on the page. . . . L'America is dizzyingly hypnotic, roaming back and forth across time, telling the story through Cesare, Beth and, later, through Beth's grown daughter, Valeria. The shadow of 9/11 is subtly referenced throughout the story, and its power becomes almost unbearable." Washington Post Book World

Mda, Zakes

★ The **Madonna** of Excelsior. Farrar, Straus and Giroux 2004 258p $23

ISBN 0-374-20008-4

LC 2003-54728

"The voice that emerges suggests not just a writer who can seduce us through beautiful language and unfailing humor. We also encounter a writer who has the power to shock and frighten us, to astound and anger and unsettle us. The Madonna of Excelsior suggests, in short, that his is a voice for which one should feel not only affection but admiration." N Y Times Book Rev

Mda, Zakes

The **whale** caller. Farrar, Straus and Giroux 2005 230p $23

ISBN 0-374-28785-6

LC 2005-14196

"Despite the lighthearted and often hilarious antics, this love triangle, like so many others, is tragically unsustainable. Perhaps this is where The Whale Caller defies expectation: If it is a morality play, these are unusually funny, richly developed characters. If it is a quirky, romantic comedy, it's dispensed with a heaping helping of human frailty, tragic behavior and self-destruction. With an offhanded mastery of lyrical language, this gifted storyteller's prose shimmers without extravagance." Washington Post Book World

Meacham, Leila

Roses. Grand Central Pub 2010 609p $24.99

ISBN 978-0-446-55000-0

LC 2009-07026

"Meacham's multigenerational family saga, set in East Texas circa 1914–1985, charts the transformation of Mary Toliver, a wide-eyed 16-year-old heiress, into a calculating cotton plantation queen as hardheaded as Scarlett O'Hara. Her brother, Miles, goes off to WWI, returns home, but then goes back to France to marry Marietta, a French Communist, leaving Mary to deal with their plantation, Somerset, and Darla, their alcoholic mother (who later hangs herself). Many years later, Mary, now an elderly, terminally ill widow, resolves to defeat the 'Toliver Curse' and regrets 'selling her soul for Somerset' and giving up her true love, Percy Warwick, the father of their secret child, to marry their friend Ollie DuMont, who helped her save Somerset when Percy refused." Publ Wkly

"A suitably long and intermittently engaging descendant of such Southern-fried epics as Gone with the Wind and Giant-just the thing for genre fans with time to spare." Kirkus

Means, David
The **secret** goldfish; stories. Fourth Estate 2004 211p
ISBN 0-00-716489-0
LC 2004-50617
"With stunning simplicity, Means offers 15 stirring portraits of tragedy, loss, and love." Esquire

Medeiros, Teresa
The **Temptation** of Your Touch. Pocket Books 2013 432 p. (paperback) $7.99
ISBN 1439157901; 9781439157909
In this book, "after his fiancée abandons him at the altar to marry his brother, Max Burke flees London for the isolation of a ramshackle, reputedly haunted castle in Cornwall, where he'll contend with a surly, secretive staff, a mesmerizing portrait of a woman-turned-ghost and a housekeeper he's tempted to strangle—or seduce." (Kirkus)

Medlicott, Joan A.
Gardens of Covington; a novel. [by] Joan Medlicott. Thomas Dunne Bks. 2001 326p $23.95
ISBN 0-312-27555-2
LC 2001-19149
Sequel to The ladies of Covington send their love
"Amelia, Grace and Hannah are now happily ensconced in their beautiful old farmhouse in the foothills of North Carolina, but when developers threaten to turn their Eden into a condo haven, Hannah at least is up in arms. Grace and her lover, Bob, are busy preparing to open a tearoom and Amelia's photography talent continues to bloom. She falls for a man she meets in a fender-bender, but the new romance isn't all sweetness and light." Publ Wkly

Medlicott, Joan A.
The **ladies** of Covington send their love; [by] Joan Medlicott. St. Martin's Press 2000 326p
ISBN 0-312-25329-X
LC 99-89922
"The women grow in self-confidence until one publishes a book, one finds love, and one runs a physically demanding business. The ending is pure fantasy, but readers will enjoy the ride." Libr J

Meek, James
The **heart** broke in; James Meek. Farrar, Straus and Giroux 2012 401 p. (hardcover: alk. paper) $28.00
ISBN 0374168717; 9780374168711
LC 2012012377
This novel, by James Meek, is "about everything that matters to us now: children, celebrity, secrets and shame, the quest for youth, loyalty and betrayal, falls from grace, acts of terror, and the wonderful, terrible inescapability of family." It follows the family dynamics of "an aging pop star and a producer of a reality show for teen talent, . . . the editor of a

powerful tabloid newspaper, . . . a gene therapist, . . ." and a just-released prison convict." (Publisher's note)

Meek, James
The **people's** act of love. Canongate 2005 391p $24
ISBN 1-841-95706-2
LC 2005-363497
"Thrown together in a remote Siberian village during the civil war that followed the Russian Revolution, the leader of a sect of Christian castrates and an escaped convict who aspires to be a terrorist revolutionary play out the fatal logic of, respectively, religious and political extremism. Meek expertly renders each man's devotion to the task of securing paradise on earth, and exposes the unsettling affinity between the devout servant of God and the cold, calculating murderer. The higher purpose assumed by Meek's tormented believers is mocked by the novel's subsidiary characters, a lusty village woman and the Jewish lieutenant of an occupying Czech legion." New Yorker

Meek, James
We are now beginning our descent. Canongate Books 2008 295p $24
ISBN 978-1-84195-988-7; 1-84195-988-X
"Meek, himself a former war correspondent, writes with authority about the physical and psychological landscapes of war, especially wars that unfold through the reporting of modern media. . . . He fills We Are Now Beginning Our Descent to the brim with ideas. And while the plot slackens and occasionally staggers under the weight of its concepts, Meek holds onto our attention by writing some of the most breathtaking and provocative sentences in contemporary English." BookPage

Mehta, Gita
Raj; a novel. Simon & Schuster 1989 479p
LC 88-38504
"Grounded in details of ancient royal tradition and Hindu ritual, Jaya's story counterpoints a vanished way of life against the complex political realities involved in the passing of the Raj and the birth of the modern nations of India and Pakistan." Publ Wkly

Mehta, Gita
A **river** Sutra. Doubleday 1993 291p
LC 92-35779
"This is an idealized India, free of political and religious violence. 'A River Sutra' takes place in a fabled land of the romantic imagination, drawing on timeless literary traditions. Told with skill and sensitivity, Gita Mehta's tales are a delight to read, bringing to Western readers the mystery and drama of a rich cultural heritage." N Y Times Book Rev

Mehta, Rahul
Quarantine; stories. Rahul Mehta. Harper Perennial 2011 214 p.
ISBN 0062020455; 9780062020451
LC 2010053604
This collection of "stories . . . revolve[s] around artsy, educated protagonists trying to navigate young adulthood as gay Indian-American men. In the title story, a young

Indian-American man takes his boyfriend, Jeremy, home to West Virginia to meet his parents. . . . The narrator resents having to hide the fact that he is in a gay relationship from his grandfather, and has conflicted feelings when the old man hits it off with Jeremy. . . . While the older generation struggles to adjust to life in the States, the first- or second-generation protagonists encounter their own identity crises as well. In 'Floating,' Darnell and his boyfriend, Sid, take a trip to India, where they juggle the pain of homophobia and the guilt of privilege after having been scammed." (Publishers Weekly)

Meidav, Edie
   Lola, California. Farrar, Straus and Giroux 2011 433p $28
   ISBN 978-0-374-10926-4; 0-374-10926-5

LC 2010-46275
   "Lana and Rose grew up in Berkeley, California in the 1980s, and the book is as much about that town and the millennial Northern California zeitgeist as any character. Meidav is harrowingly precise in her descriptions of the place . . . . Lola, California is a startling novel, as prodigiously smart as it is technically proficient. Her characters may be narcissistic zeligs, but Meidav is an American original." Daily Beast

Melman, Peter Charles
   Landsman; a novel. Counterpoint Press 2006 323p $24.95
   ISBN 978-1-58243-367-7; 1-58243-367-4

LC 2006-33305
   "A barely literate hard-bitten gambler and petty criminal, Elias Abrams, the 20-year-old cardsharp hero of Melman's . . . debut, flees hometown New Orleans (and a bogus murder charge), joins the Confederate Army and realizes "every circumstance of his life now conspires to kill him." He survives the infantry as he had the city—using his wiles, card skills and fists—until his colonel hands over an envelope containing a charming missive from Nora Bloom, a young New Orleans maiden who wrote a support-the-troops letter at the urging of her rabbi. Unexpectedly stirred, Elias begins a correspondence and finds himself obsessively fantasizing about her. A battlefield injury leads to a furlough during which he returns to the city to meet both Nora (he falls in love) and cronies from his seedy past, who use his new flame as leverage to draw him into a sinister plot." Publ Wkly
   "At times ribald and always real, Melman creates a rich and authentic story." Booklist

Melnyczuk, Askold
   The **house** of widows; an oral history. Graywolf Press 2008 255p pa $16
   ISBN 978-1-55597-491-6 pa; 1-55597-491-0 pa
   "A superbly written tale of intrigue, contemporary history, mystery and illicit international trade. . . . Literary, cerebral, elegant, almost every sentence perfect." Milwaukee Journal Sentinel

Meloy, Maile
   A **family** daughter; a novel. Scribner 2006 325p $24
   ISBN 0-7432-7766-X

LC 2005-51574
   "Continuing the family saga of her first novel, 'Liars and Saints.' Meloy's second follows Abby Collins from the age of seven, when her feckless mother and sober father separate, to her success as a young novelist. The kernel of the story is a melodrama involving her uncle Jamie, who rescues her first from the boredom of her childhood illness and then, later, from grief after the sudden death of her father. When a mutual sexual attraction develops, though, Abby must learn to rescue herself, which she does mainly by recasting the dilemmas of her extended family as a work of fiction. All this might easily come off as soap opera were Meloy not a wise and astonishing conjurer of convincing realities." New Yorker

Meloy, Maile
   Liars and saints; a novel. Scribner 2003 260p $24
   ISBN 0-7432-4435-4

LC 2002-30852
   "Meloy's unerring mastery of narrative is remarkable. The disciplined economy and resonant clarity of her prose allow her to present a complex story in swift, lean chapters. The alternating points of view of eight main characters shine with authenticity and illuminate the moral complexities felt by each generation." Publ Wkly

Meltzer, Brad
   The **book** of lies. Grand Central Pub. 2008 336p il $25.99
   ISBN 978-0-446-57788-5; 0-446-57788-X

LC 2008-13692
   A "conspiracy mystery inspired by the Biblical tale of Cain and Abel and real-life story of comics scribe Jerry Siegel, who co-created Superman with artist Joe Shuster in 1932. In his book — which concerns a Florida activist with a family secret linked to Siegel and a centuries-spanning conspiracy involving Nazis, secret societies, and a cryptic tome called The Book of Lies Meltzer advances the theory that the death of Siegel's father (who may or may not have been murdered in a robbery gone wrong) inspired his son to make the ultimate wish fulfillment fantasy of 20th-century pop culture." Entertainment Wkly

Meltzer, Brad
   Dead even. Weisbach Bks. 1998 401p
   ISBN 0-688-15090-X

LC 98-5935
   New Yorkers "Sara Tate and Jared Lynch are married to each other and to their legal careers: he's a rising star for the defense in a big firm; she's just starting as an assistant district attorney after six months of job seeking. On her first day, Sara hears that a budget cut could put her back on the unemployment lines, so she swipes a burglary case earmarked for a top man in the pecking order. But this is more than a routine burglary, and a powerful villain named Oscar Rafferty wants it to go away. He hires Jared to defend the

accused, a sadistic monster called Tony Kozlow, telling him that unless Kozlow walks, Sara dies." Publ Wkly

The author "gives the reader well-rounded characters; demonizing neither prosecution nor defense, he shows both as human beings doing a job." Libr J

Meltzer, Brad

The **first** counsel. Warner Bks. 2001 479p $25.95

ISBN 0-446-52728-9

LC 00-28963

Meltzer "relies on some heavy-handed techniques to generate suspense . . . and the plot has a familiar Hollywood ring to it. But Meltzer's relentless narrative finally digs its hooks in, and even skeptical readers will want to continue through the twists and turns, if only to confirm their own predictions." Publ Wkly

Meltzer, Brad

The **inner** circle. Grand Central Pub. 2011 449p $26.99

ISBN 978-0-446-57789-2

LC 2010-36506

"Beecher White is an archivist with the National Archives, who stumbles upon an old book hidden away in a room used exclusively by the president. But did the president know that the book (a spelling dictionary that once belonged to George Washington) was there? And—almost impossible for Beecher to imagine—could it be that the president or someone close to him is willing to kill to regain possession of the book? . . . Meltzer expertly develops the story, throwing in twists and turns at appropriate intervals, and he does an excellent job of putting us in Beecher's corner and making us care about what happens to him." Booklist

Meltzer, Brad

The **tenth** justice. Morrow 1997 389p

ISBN 0-688-15089-6

LC 96-44815

"Hotshot young lawyer Ben Addison is on top of the world. Just out of Yale Law School, he's already landed the highly desirable top job of clerk to a Supreme Court justice, experiences instant chemistry with his new co-clerk Lisa, and shares an apartment with three lifelong friends. Then a misplaced trust leads Ben to reveal a confidential court decision, and his world begins to crash. With Ben's career in jeopardy and a blackmailer on his trail, his friends use their job connections at the State Department, a Washington newspaper, and a senator's office to aid Ben and Lisa in a plot to apprehend Ben's blackmailer." Libr J

"Meltzer moves the story along at a crisp pace, spicing the action and legalese with lively banter and intriguing D.C. arcana." Publ Wkly

Meltzer, Brad

The **zero** game. Warner Bks. 2004 460p $25.95

ISBN 0-446-53098-0

LC 2003-15157

"Bored congressional staffer Harris Sandler plays something called the zero game with his coworkers, but it turns deadly when a vote concerning an abandoned gold mine in South Dakota is brought to the floor. Together with

a 16-year-old Senate page named Viv Parker, Harris finds himself being chased by a ruthless killer in the halls of the Capitol as well as in the bowels of the mine." Libr J"Bored congressional staffer Harris Sandler plays something called the zero game with his coworkers, but it turns deadly when a vote concerning an abandoned gold mine in South Dakota is brought to the floor. Together with a 16-year-old Senate page named Viv Parker, Harris finds himself being chased by a ruthless killer in the halls of the Capitol as well as in the bowels of the mine." Libr J

This thriller is "packed with plenty of backroom D.C. ambience and lots of action." Booklist

Melville, James

The **chrysanthemum** chain. St. Martin's Press 1982 181p

LC 82-5546

"An English subject living in Japan is murdered and the British consul and the local police want to know why. David Murrow was a distinguished educator but he moved in a rather peculiar, though prominent, circle of friends, which included many political luminaries. There is great concern among them about the case and its possible effect on the outcome of an impending election. . . . Although Melville keeps the action moving in this fast paced novel, he still pays close attention to characterization and background." Best Sellers

Memminger, Charles

Aloha, lady blue; a mystery. Charles Memminger. Minotaur Books 2013 320 p. (hardback) $24.99

ISBN 125000778X; 9781250007780

LC 2012038368

In this novel, "former investigative journalist Stryker McBride maintains a . . . secluded lifestyle aboard his luxurious houseboat . . . . One phone call from his high school crush Amber . . . changes everything. Amber wants Stryker to do a little digging into the suspicious death of her grandfather." When he "looks into the case, . . . secrets of the past combined with the local mafia lead Stryker into Hawaii's dangerous criminal underground." (Publishers Weekly)

Mendelsohn, Jane

American music. Alfred A. Knopf 2010 237p $23.95

ISBN 978-0-307-27266-9; 0-307-27266-4

LC 2009-37382

"Unpretentious, moving, intelligent, and fresh . . . An inventive, passionate, pithy novel whose major theme is love itself and whose minor theme, music, is an emotional, meaningful counterpoint. Like Count Basie and His Orchestra, this book swings." Elle

Mendelson, Cheryl

Morningside Heights; a novel. Random House 2003 326p $24.95

ISBN 0-375-50836-8

LC 2002-31760

The first title of a projected trilogy. The "intersecting lives of a group of Manhattanites living in the staid but rapidly changing Upper West Side neighborhood of Morningside Heights near Columbia University are the focus of this {novel}. . . . Opera singer Charles Braithwaite; his wife, Anne, a pianist; and their three (soon to be four) childen are the novel's ostensible protagonists. The books's real hero, however, is their beloved neighborhood, which they fear they will soon have to leave, unable to afford their cramped apartment." Publ Wkly

"With her motley cast, Mendelson paints an accurate, often comical portrait of the Upper West Side." N Y Times Book Rev

Menendez, Ana

The **last** war; a novel. HarperCollins 2009 225p $24.99

ISBN 978-0-06-172476-3; 0-06-172476-9

LC 2008-40919

The author focuses on "life in Istanbul, Afghanistan, and Iraq in a novel narrated by a freelance photographer known as 'Flash.' Her husband, Brando, a journalist reporting from the war in Baghdad, waits for her to join him there; Flash, however, chooses to remain in Istanbul, their base for several years. The reasons for this consume most of Menendez's impressionistic and introspective tale, as Flash grapples with a vague feeling that 'something essential' is giving way in their marriage—a feeling compounded by an anonymous letter alluding to Brando's ongoing affair. . . . Flash is weary of their constant migration from one war zone to the next, while Brando seems slavishly devoted to war for his very existence. Menendez offers astute and perceptive commentary on both the hidden and obvious effects of war and its aftermath." Booklist

Mengestu, Dinaw

The **beautiful** things that heaven bears. Riverhead Books 2006 228p $22.95

ISBN 978-1-59448-940-2; 1-59448-940-8

LC 2006-25058

"In his rundown store in a gentrifying neighborhood of Washington, D.C., Ethiopian immigrant Stepha Stephanos regularly meets with fellow African immigrants Ken the Kenyan and Joe from the Congo. Their favorite game is matching African nations to coups and dictators, as they consider how their new immigrant expectations measure up to the reality of life in America after 17 years. . . . When Judith, a white woman, and Naomi, her mixed-race daughter, move into the neighborhood, Stephanos finds tentative prospects for friendship beyond his African compatriots." Booklist

"A tender, thoughtful novel that quietly takes on serious themes: the meaning of home and family, of nationality and exile, of isolation and connection." People

Mengestu, Dinaw

How to read the air. Riverhead Books 2010 305p $25.95

ISBN 978-1-59448-770-5; 1-59448-770-7

LC 2010-03045

"Mengestu's lyrical prose makes each layer upon layer of story a satisfying read, despite the book's sometimes unbearable sense of foreboding. It's hard not to root for Jonas, even during his most misguided attempts to engage. It's hard not to ache for Jonas, wondering if he'll ever find his place." Seattle Times

Mengiste, Maaza

★ **Beneath** the lion's gaze; a novel. W. W. Norton & Co. 2010 384p $24.95

ISBN 978-0-393-07176-4; 0-393-07176-6

LC 2009-34759

"This novel of the Ethiopian revolution charts the fortunes of a doctor, his family, and their middle-class neighborhood in Addis Ababa from the fall of Haile Selassie, in 1974, to the beginning of the Red Terror, two years later. Mengiste's social intelligence and historical research allow her to write compassionately about emotions denatured by a brutal regime or calcified by conviction. But the real marvel of this tender novel is its coiled plotting, in which coincidence manages to evoke the colossal emotional toll of the revolution." New Yorker

Meno, Joe

Bluebirds used to croon in the choir. Northwestern University Press 2005 180p $21.95; pa $12.95

ISBN 0-8101-5167-7; 0-8101-2424-6 pa

LC 2005-19766

"In Meno's offbeat universe, a horse predicts the future by crying into a bucket, and the Astronaut of the Year gets memorialized on ceramic garlic holders. The author . . . narrates his tales of awkward interpersonal relationships unfolding amid semisurreal situations in a cool, half-adolescent deadpan. . . . Though these stories don't always end as well as they begin, they're edgy and interesting, with a fine blend of the dark and the absurd." Publ Wkly

Meno, Joe

The **boy** detective fails. Akashic 2006 320p pa $14.95

ISBN 1-933354-10-0

LC 2006-923114

"In their youth, Billy Argo, his kid sister Caroline, and their friend Fenton solved a series of puzzling crimes with only a cheap detective kit and their imaginations. After Billy goes to college to study criminology, Caroline commits suicide and guilt-ridden Billy attempts it, ending up heavily sedated in a mental hospital. Ten years later, he connects with two other outcast, nerdy sorts to help solve the mysteries going on in their lives and in that of a kleptomaniac widow who is as fragile and traumatized as he is. The one mystery he can't solve is Caroline's death. This is postmodern fiction with a head and a heart, addressing such depressing issues as suicide, death, loneliness, failure, anomie, and guilt with compassion, humor, and even whimsy." Libr J

Meno, Joe

The **great** perhaps; a novel. W. W. Norton & Company 2009 414p $24.95

ISBN 978-0-393-06796-5; 0-393-06796-3

LC 2008-54280

"Meno's plain style is set off nicely by his taste for modernist formal daring: the novel makes room for drawings, long transcripts of old radio serials, declassified government documents and several chapters consisting of exactly 26 short sections, each headed by a letter of the alphabet. There is an occasional streak of fancy to events as well." N Y Times Book Rev

Meno, Joe

Office girl; Or Bohemians, or Young People on Bicycles Doing Troubling Things. Joe Meno, Cody Hudson, Todd Baxter. Akashic Books 2012 288 p. $24.95

ISBN 1617750751; 9781617750755

In this novel, "art school dropout Odile Neff and amateur sound artist Jack Blevins work deadening office jobs; gush about indie rock, French film, and obscure comic book artists; and gradually start a relationship that doubles as an art movement. . . . [T]heir tale of promiscuous roommates, on-again/off-again exes, and awkward sex is punctuated on the page by . . . doodles, black and white photographs, . . . and monologues." (Publishers Weekly)

Mercier, Pascal

Perlmann's silence; Pascal Mercier; translated by Shaun Whiteside. Grove 2012 624p.

ISBN 9781848877177; 9780802119575

This book presents a "psychological portrait of a man striving to get his life back on track in the wake of his beloved wife's death. Philipp Perlmann, prominent linguist and speaker at a gathering of renowned international academics in a picturesque seaside town near Genoa, is struggling to maintain his grip on reality. Derailed by grief and no longer confident of his professional standing, writing his keynote address seems like an insurmountable task, and, as the deadline approaches, Perlmann realizes that he will have nothing to present. Terror-stricken, he decides to plagiarize the work of Leskov, a Russian colleague. But when Leskov's imminent arrival is announced and threatens to expose Perlmann as a fraud, Perlmann's mounting desperation leads him to contemplate drastic measures." (Publisher's note)

Meredith, George

★ The **ordeal** of Richard Feverel; a history of father and son. edited with an introduction and notes by Edward Mendelson. Penguin Books 1998 xxxi, 522p (Penguin classics)

ISBN 978-0-14-043483-5; 0-14-043483-6

LC 99-461805

First published 1859

This novel is representative of Meredith's "best work, full of allusion and metaphor, lyrical prose and witty dialogue, with a deep exploration of the psychology of motive and rationalization. The novel's subject is the relationship between a cruelly manipulative father and a son who loves a girl of a lower social class. Both men are self-deluded and proud, and the story's ending is tragic." Merriam-Webster's Ency of Lit

Merey, Ilike

A + E 4ever; a graphic novel. Lethe Press 2011 214 p.

ISBN 1590213904; 9781590213902

This book tells the story of "Asher Machnik [who] is a teenage boy cursed with a beautiful androgynous face. Guys punch him, girls slag him and by high school he's developed an intense fear of being touched. Art remains his only escape from an otherwise emotionally empty life. Eulalie Mason is the lonely, tough-talking . . . [lesbian] from school who befriends Ash. The only one to see and accept all of his sides

as a loner, a fellow artist and a best friend, she's starting to wonder if ash is ever going to see all of her. . . . [The book] is a graphic novel set in that ambiguous crossroads where love and friendship, boy and girl, straight and gay meet." (Publisher's note)

Merimee, Prosper

★ **Carmen**; translated from the French and illustrated by Edmund H. Garrett, with a memoir of the author by Louise Imogen Guiney. Little, Brown 1896 xxx, 117p il

Original French edition, 1845

"Georges Bizet's opera Carmen is based on the story. As a hot-blooded young corporal in the Spanish cavalry stationed near Seville, Don José is ordered to arrest Carmen, a young, flirtatious Gypsy woman, for assaulting a coworker. Greatly charmed by her, José allows her to escape. He deserts the army, kills two men on Carmen's account, and takes up a life as a robber and smuggler. He is insanely jealous of Carmen, who is unfaithful to him, and when she refuses to change on his behalf, he kills her and surrenders himself to the authorities." Merriam-Webster's Ency of Lit

Merullo, Roland

Breakfast with Buddha; a novel. Algonquin Books of Chapel Hill 2007 323p $23.95

ISBN 978-1-56512-552-0; 1-56512-552-5

LC 2007-7978

"Somewhere between bowling and yoga class, Rinpoche teaches Otto to examine himself, and readers will be rooting for the success of this unlikely pair. Merullo's clear writing ensures that readers will master Rinpoche's sometimes cryptic reflections as well." BookPage

Merullo, Roland

The **talk**-funny girl; Roland Merullo. Crown Publishers 2011 x, 304p.p

ISBN 9780307452924; 0307452921

LC 2011003328

Alex Award (2012)

This book tells the story of "seventeen-year-old- Marjorie Richards . . . [who] has been raised by parents so intentionally isolated from normal society that they have developed their own dialect . . . as the nearby factory town sinks deeper into economic ruin and as her parents fall more completely under the influence of a sadistic cult leader, her options for escape dwindle. But then, thanks to a loving aunt, Marjorie is hired by a man . . . who is building what he calls 'a cathedral,' right in the center of town. . . . Gradually, through exposure to the world beyond her parents' wood cabin thanks to the kindness of her aunt and her boss, and an almost superhuman determination, she discovers what is loveable within herself." (Publisher's note)

Messud, Claire

The **emperor's** children. Alfred A. Knopf 2006 431p $25

ISBN 0-307-26419-X

LC 2005-57783

The author "writes with the archness of a Muriel Spark, only more subtly and sympathetically wielded. . . . Ultimately, most impressive is the way Messud relates 9/11 to her characters' lives: The public tragedy doesn't eclipse but rather seeps into and amplifies their private sorrows." Nation

Messud, Claire

The **hunters**; two short novels. Harcourt 2001 181p $29

ISBN 0-15-100588-5

LC 00-50571

"These novellas both have displaced protagonists who cannot decide whether to seek a deathlike stillness or to embrace life's mess. In the first, a Toronto cleaning woman finds that the ritualized relationship she enjoys with a long-term employer has provided more continuity than anything else in her life, which has included famine in rural Ukraine, slave labor in Germany, love in a displaced-persons camp, emigration, and a cozy family existence. In widowhood, however, her sense of order is in danger of taking over and annihilating all that is left. Being almost too fastidious to live is also the dilemma of the narrator of the second tale, an American academic in London who loathes the friendly woman who lives downstairs. The tone is Jamesian, but the ending holds a beast in the jungle only for the hapless fellow-tenant." New Yorker

Messud, Claire

★ The **woman** upstairs; a novel. Claire Messud. 1st ed. Alfred A. Knopf 2013 253 p. (hardcover) $25.95; (ebook) $77.85

ISBN 0307596907; 9780307596901; 9780307962409

LC 2012017806

In this book by Claire Messud, "elementary school teacher Nora Eldridge . . . [has] sold out her artistic dreams for success and stability, and become angry and full of self-loathing somewhere along the way. But when a young student, Reza Shahid, and his family enter her life, Nora finds herself changing as she is drawn into the Shahids' world." (Publishers Weekly)

Mestre-Reed, Ernesto

The **second** death of Unica Aveyano; a novel. Vintage Contemporaries 2004 259p $13

ISBN 1-400-03316-0 pa

LC 2003-52544

"A Miami nursing home is no place for Unica Aveyano, as she vociferously reminds her daughter-inlaw at every opportunity. Although she is ill with terminal cancer and terribly frail, she cannot bear the thought of spending one more night wandering the halls or sitting by the cracked windows. Miraculously, she finds her way out the door, across a four-lane highway, and into the ocean. When she is rescued by her male nurse, she gravely tells him that she was led there by a pack of wild angels. Her past is suddenly more alive to her than the present, and she spends hours immersed in memories of her Cuban childhood, her marriage, and her son, a bisexual artist who refused to emigrate with them. She has no time for her mournful husband, who is sick at the thought of being left behind. Mestre-Reed . . . is a lyric novelist of uncommon power, creating a memorable portrait of a woman wracked by longing and memory yet fearlessly embracing her impending death." Booklist

Mewshaw, Michael

Shelter from the storm; a novel. Putnam 2003 280p $23.95

ISBN 0-399-14988-0

LC 2002-74640

In this thriller "a feral child from the steppes of Central Asia becomes the bargaining chip in a hostage negotiation. Scarred hero Zack McClintock, a private-sector intelligence agent, travels to ex-Soviet territory in search of his kidnapped son-in-law and finds plenty of people with plenty to hide. . . .This is the sort of intelligent and morally ambitious thriller—like those of Craig Nova or Paul Watkins—that offers a welcome change from typical fare." Libr J

Meyer, Carolyn

Brown eyes blue; a novel. Bridge Works 2003 228p $23.95

ISBN 1-88259-368-5

LC 2002-12674

"Little do these women guess how much they have in common—shared passions, losses and secrets that lead them to question the choices they have made in their lives. Meyer weaves the story of three generations of women who, with their distinctive voices, will endear themselves to readers." Publ Wkly

Meyer, Deon

Devil's peak; a novel. translated by K.L. Seegers. Little, Brown 2008 409p $24.99

ISBN 0-316-01785-X; 978-0-316-01785-5

LC 2007-30129

Original Afrikaans edition, 2004; this translation first published 2007 in the United Kingdom

"Former mercenary Thobela Mpayipheli is trying to live a peaceful life, but these plans are shattered when his eight-year-old son, Pakamile, is shot dead. The two gunmen responsible escape before sentencing, and the grieving father decides to take matters into his own hands. As he pursues his son's killers, Mpayipheli begins to target pedophiles and other perpetrators of violence against children, meting out justice with a Xhosa tribal sword called an assegai. Dubbed 'Artemis' by the papers as the killings increase, Mpayipheli becomes a kind of folk hero to the people of Capetown. Insp. Benny Griessel, an aging alcoholic whose struggles with the bottle have all but cost him his family and his life, works the case with a desperate intensity." Publ Wkly

Meyer, Deon

Heart of the hunter; translated by K. L. Seegers. Little, Brown 2004 374p $23.95

ISBN 0-316-93549-2

LC 2003-25683

"Despite the complexity of its tightly woven plot-skillfully revealed through newspaper articles and intelligence reports-Meyer's U.S. debut moves at a breathtaking pace that will carry readers away. A sympathetic protagonist and the landscape of South Africa add color to the story." Libr J

Meyer, Deon

★ **Trackers**; translated from Afrikaans by K.L. Seegers. Atlantic Monthly Press 2011 488 p. map

ISBN 080211993X; 9780802119933; 9781444723656

LC 2012358359

In this book, "Lemmer, a freelance bodyguard, goes against his rule to not get involved when a wealthy farmer asks for his help smuggling a pair of rare black rhinos out of Zimbabwe, where the animals are murdered for their horns. Before he knows it, Lemmer is in a small airplane, zipping across the border with an airsickness bag in his hand and a military-grade shotgun at his feet. . . . Back in Cape Town, Milla Strachan, the emotionally abused wife of a philandering husband and the mother of a cruel teenage son, . . . start[s] a new life . . . [and] find[s] work as a journalist and Milla takes what she can get--in this case, a classified job writing intelligence reports. . . . Connecting Milla and Lemmer is Mat Joubert, a former detective working on his first case as a private eye." (Publisher's note)

Meyer, Nicholas

★ The **seven**-per-cent solution; being a reprint from the reminiscences of John H. Watson, M.D., as edited by Nicholas Meyer. Dutton 1974 253p

"In a field replete with pastiche Meyer succeeds because of a superior ear for Conan Doyle's style, a gentle sense of fun, and a talent for plot that few of the imitators have possessed." Libr J

Meyer, Nicholas

The **West** End horror; a posthumous memoir of John H. Watson, M.D., as edited by Nicholas Meyer. Dutton 1976 222p

This novel "is set in London's theatre district in 1895. A much disliked theatre critic has been murdered, and Sherlock Holmes is engaged to find the murderer. His client is another critic of the day whose years of fame are ahead of him: George Bernard Shaw. Inspector Lestrade, Holmes's old foil, is on the scene, but, as always, his efforts are misdirected and before long he has managed to incarcerate an obvious innocent. Clues abound and so too do real but suspicious characters." Best Sellers

Meyer, Philipp

American rust. Spiegel & Grau 2009 368p $24.95

ISBN 978-0-385-52751-4; 0-385-52751-9

LC 2008-22461

The author "conjures up this blue-collar Rust Belt town with the same sort of social detail and emotional verisimilitude that Richard Russo has brought to his depictions of upstate New York and Russell Banks has brought to downstate New Hampshire. He writes about his characters' lives in Buell with sympathy and unsentimental clarity." N Y Times (Late N Y Ed)

Meyer, Philipp

★ The **Son**; Philipp Meyer. HarperCollins 2013 viii, 561 p.p (hardcover) $27.99

ISBN 0062120395; 9780062120397

This historical family novel, by Philipp Meyer, presents "an epic of the American West and a multigenerational saga of power, blood, land, and oil that follows the rise of one [prominent] . . . Texas family, from the Comanche raids of the 1800s to the to the oil booms of the 20th century." (Publisher's note)

Meyer, Stephenie

The **host**; a novel. Little, Brown and Co. 2008 619p $25.99

ISBN 978-0-316-06804-8; 0-316-06804-7

LC 2007-33060

"While the straightforward narrative is short on detail about the invasion and its stunning aftermath, it shines with romantic intrigue, especially when a love triangle (or quadrangle?!) develops for Wanda/Melanie." Publ Wkly

Meyers, Kent

The **work** of wolves. Harcourt 2004 416p $24

ISBN 0-15-101057-9

LC 2003-26365

Meyer's "spare dialogue is brilliantly and often comically expressive, and Carson, his taciturn, rational hero, is an original and compelling character. Strong themes of generational responsibility and family history add resonance to this gratifying, very American novel." Publ Wkly

Miasha, 1981-

Chaser; Miasha. Simon & Schuster 2009 211 p.

ISBN 1416589864; 9781416589860

LC 2009011380

In this novel, "Leah Baker is in trouble. Her boyfriend, Kenny, is . . . determined to kill her . . . [then] the novel flashes back five months earlier as Leah, whose toxic relationship with Kenny is all about being draped in money, is angry at Kenny's lack of attention. She [meets] one of Kenny's helpers, Nasir, who is a chaser running a scam on accident victims by towing their cars to a shady repair shop." (Libr J) "[Leah and Nasir] quickly become lovers and soon business partners. She helps him discover his inner hustler and he shows her the way to independence. Together they work every angle and scheme of the wreck-chasing business, regardless of the law, until they find themselves at the top. But they've angered many on their way up and there are many who want to see them fall." (Publisher's note)

Michael, Judith

Acts of love. Crown 1997 376p

ISBN 0-517-70324-6

In this novel "theater director Lucas Cameron discovers a box of letters left behind by his deceased grandmother, the famous stage actress Constance Bernhardt. The letters were written by her protégée Jessica Fontaine, who disappeared from the stage years before. Even in the midst of his busy world . . . Luke finds himself returning again and again to the letters, recognizing in them a deeply passionate young woman discovering herself and the magic of the theater. Luke begins to realize that he has fallen in love with the woman who wrote them. Finally he can bear it no longer—and tracks down the elusive Jessica Fontaine. But when he travels to her hideaway on Lopez Island off the coast of Washington, nothing is as he expected it." Publisher's note

Michael, Judith

A **certain** smile. Crown 1999 301p
ISBN 0-517-70325-4

LC 98-52333

"Miranda Grant, a 40-year-old widow with two adolescent children, travels from her home in Boulder, Colo., to Beijing. . . . The story focuses on Miranda's relationship with Yuan Li, a successful builder/construction engineer. The son of a Chinese mother and an American soldier, he becomes her soulful guide to China, romance and personal growth. Danger intrudes after Miranda innocently acts as courier for a letter from a former dissident, now in America; the authorities put Miranda and Yuan Li under round-the-clock surveillance." Publ Wkly

Michael, Judith

Deceptions. Pocket Bks. 1982 472p

"When twin sisters, who have been mistaken for each other all their lives, are on vacation together in China, they decide on a whim to switch roles for a week, thus beginning a deception that has far-reaching effects. The aristocratic Lady Sabrina, assuming the suburban housewife's duties of her sister Stephanie Anderson, is surprised to find she scarcely misses her former high life, reveling instead in the acceptance and security of being part of a family. Stephanie, leaving her humdrum life behind to assume Sabrina's jet-set life of partying and dealing in antiques, so much enjoys her liberation that she is reluctant to come home. Sabrina has fallen in love with Stephanie's husband; she postpones ending the deception until a freak accident leaves her unsure of her identity at all." Publ Wkly

Followed by A tangled web

Michael, Judith

Sleeping beauty; a novel. Poseidon Press 1991 539p

LC 91-31298

"The wealthy, influential Chatham family, founders of a Chicago-based realty empire, present a wholesome image to the outside world. But 30-year-old financial whiz Vince Chatham has raped his 13-year-old niece, Anne, and continues to abuse her sexually. When Anne overcomes her fear and guilt to accuse Vince at a family gathering, she is met with skepticism from her relatives and denial from Vince. After Anne runs away from home, however, Vince is stripped of his position at the corporation; enraged, he vows to destroy the rest of the Chatham clan." Publ Wkly

"Michael does this sort of thing much better than most of the competition: the characters, naturally larger than life, are still believable." Booklist

Michaels, Anne

★ **Fugitive** pieces. Knopf 1997 294p
ISBN 0-679-45439-X

LC 96-36678

First publishd 1996 in Canada

Michaels "offers a richly imagined portrait of Jakob's slow progress from reticence to poetic eloquence and of the complex blend of memories, feelings, insights, and experiences that makes him the man he becomes. She even tackles the perpetually troubling question of how so many seemingly ordinary, 'civilized' people could have eagerly committed such monstrous crimes against defenseless children and civilians." Christ Sci Monit

Michaels, Barbara

The **dancing** floor. HarperCollins Pubs. 1997 326p
ISBN 978-0060177645

LC 96-39331

"Frumpy but spunky American tourist Heather Tradescant's vacation in Britain is blighted by her parents' recent death. Hoping to fulfill her late father's dream, she tries to visit the 17th-century garden of Troytan House, home of businessman Frank Karim and his taciturn son, Jordan. Rebuffed, Heather finds a hidden entrance to the estate, but as she wanders through a bramble-thickened maze, she falls at the feet of the Karims enjoying an al fresco breakfast. At first hostile, the Karims soon prove more than hospitable, begging her to stay because they believe she's an horticultural expert. . . . An unlikely object of desire, Heather attracts the men around her through her strong personality, lively wit and huge appetite. She and other well-delineated characters make this tale everything a romance reader can ask for." Publ Wkly

Michaels, Barbara

Houses of stone. Simon & Schuster 1993 334p

LC 93-27926

"Michaels sets her heroine, Professor Karen Holloway, to the task of discovering the provenance of a remnant from an old manuscript. Holloway is convinced that it is a thinly disguised autobiographical novel by an obscure feminist poet whose verses have already helped Holloway carve a niche in the cutthroat business of academia. The professor's archenemies, two fellow literature experts, are equally convinced of the work's value and attempt desperate measures to gain access of the manuscript. Michaels has composed a mystery that is brimming with suspense yet revolves around authorial research rather than money and multiple murders." Booklist

Michaels, Barbara

Shattered silk. Atheneum Pubs. 1986 369p
ISBN 0-689-11620-9

LC 86-47658

Karen Nevitt "begins a new life in Georgetown after her unhappy marriage crumbles. She plans to open an antique-clothing shop with the encouragement of old and new friends. But a series of seemingly unrelated yet terrifying events begins to unfold, and Karen is caught up in a web of deadly suspense." Libr J

Michaels, Barbara

Stitches in time. HarperCollins Pubs. 1995 307p
ISBN 0-06-017763-2

LC 95-4286

A "mystery based on a haunted quilt. Rachel Grant is a doctoral student working on her thesis—an investigation of women's garments designed for important rites of passage—when she takes a part-time job at a chic vintage clothing shop run by two women, Kara and her sister-in-law Cheryl. When Cheryl's police officer husband is shot, Rachel is drawn into the family because she moves into Cheryl's home, which is connected to the shop. Meanwhile, the message from the quilt lures Rachel into dangerous misdeeds. The unraveling of the mystery proves fascinating." Booklist

Michaels, Fern

Celebration. Kensington Pub. Corp. 1999 358p

ISBN 1-57566-402-X

LC 98-67474

"When her husband retires and disappears with their savings, Kristine's whole family structure disintegrates as her children express their disgust with her continuing faith in a man they've known for years as a self-centered womanizer. With the help of friends and, eventually, a new love interest, Kristine focuses on work and rebuilds her family's toy business but keeps her new love at arm's length." Booklist

Michaels, Fern

Finders keepers. Kensington Bks. 1998 396p

ISBN 1-57566-323-6

"Adorable toddler Hannah Larson, only child of poor but decent Grace and Ben, is sitting in her stroller outside a Tennessee gas station when baby-starved Thea and Barnes Roland pull in for a cream soda. Thea snatches the child, Barnes puts pedal to metal and Hannah becomes 'adopted' Jessie, doomed to a life of smothering love and material overabundance in Charleston, S.C., while her birth parents suffer and hope. On her way to NYU . . . Jessie detours through Washington and talks herself into a job as secretary to powerful Texas Senator Angus Kingsley, who has an icy wife, Alexis; a dying mistress, Irene; and a gorgeous son, Tanner. Jessie, of course, marries Tanner, and the trouble really begins." Publ Wkly

Michaels, Leonard

★ The collected stories. Farrar, Straus and Giroux 2007 403p $26

ISBN 978-0-374-12654-4; 0-374-12654-2

LC 2006-102556

"Michaels never stopped reflecting on the condition of being Jewish. Now that he is gone, it is easier to place him in a broader context, as part of that astonishing flowering of American Jewish writing that included Bellow, Malamud, Mailer and Roth, toward which he can be seen as both filial heir and mischievous critic." Nation

Michaud, Jon

When Tito loved Clara; a novel. Algonquin Books of Chapel Hill 2011 338p $23.95

ISBN 978-1-56512-949-8; 1-56512-949-0

LC 2010-37075

"Clara Lugo — born in the Dominican Republic, raised in New York City's Inwood, 'the neighborhood of parks and bodegas, of rivers and bridges' — escaped a painful childhood when Cornell offered her a full scholarship. Now a librarian, married and living in the New Jersey suburbs, she finds she cannot scrub herself clean of the past. Her sister, her pregnant 16-year-old niece, and her old high school sweetheart Tito, who's suddenly reappeared after 15 years, see to that. It's entertaining to watch the smart, piquantly funny Clara desperately try to impose a library-like order on her life." Entertainment Wkly

Michener, James A.

Alaska. Random House 1988 868p

LC 87-43232

This novel begins with the prehistory of Alaska before concentrating on the history of the region since the 18th century

"Besides multiple heroes and heroines, there are knaves and opportunists who have depleted Alaska's resources and contributed to the high rates of alcoholism and suicide. One of Michener's favorite words is noble, but after mushing through his Arctic saga of persistence and greed, one is not surprised that he uses it mainly to describe grizzly bears, salmon and whales." Time

Michener, James A.

★ The bridges at Toko-ri. Random House 1953 146p

"In this hard-hitting novel of the Korean conflict, Admiral George Tarrant commands the Naval Task Force, whose carrier-based jets are to knock out strategic points throughout Korea. The focal point of the novel is Harry Brubaker, a lawyer who goes reluctantly to war after being called up as a jet pilot. The reader will remember also Beer Barrel, the landing officer who can get the jets back on the carrier's decks, no matter how rough the seas; and Mike Forney, helicopter rescue pilot who gets pilots out of the freezing waters if they are downed." Shapiro. Fic for Youth. 3d edition

Michener, James A.

Caravans; a novel. Random House 1963 341p

The story, set in Afghanistan in the year 1946, "focuses on Ellen Jasper, an American bored with her native land, who flees to Afghanistan to become the second wife of a man named Nazrullah. Her parents haven't heard from her in 13 months and Mark Miller, of the U.S. Embassy in that country, is sent to investigate. The search takes Miller into unknown territory. He joins a nomad tribe and experiences a love affair of rare beauty with Mira, daughter of the Great Zulfiqar, chieftain of all the nomadic peoples scattered around Afghanistan. {The novel describes} Ellen's degeneration into a sensualist, {and} the encounter of Miller (a Jew) with an ex-Nazi who tortured Jews." America

Michener, James A.

Caribbean. Random House 1989 672p

LC 89-42785

A novel about the "Caribbean islands from the days when the peace-loving Arawak Indians were overpowered by cannibalistic Caribs, to a ship's tour of today's still lush, but troubled, paradise. Sir Francis Drake, pirate Henry Morgan, Horatio Nelson, Haitian General Toussaint L'Ouverture, Fidel Castro march across the pages, and while the pace is sometimes achingly slow, the dialogue stilted and the characterization skimpy, Michener laces the whole with fiery Caribbean drama." Publ Wkly

Michener, James A.

★ Centennial. Random House 1974 909p

"Written to celebrate the United States centennial, the book centers on a fictional town in Colorado. It begins with an examination of the geological formation of the land and a discussion of the first animals to live there. It continues with the arrival of the Indians, the coming of the first settlers, the traders, the search for gold, the building of the railroads, and the start of cattle ranching—virtually all the activities that made this country develop as it did. The conclusion brings us to the social and ecological problems of the 1970s." Shapiro. Fic for Youth. 3d edition

Michener, James A.
Chesapeake. Random House 1978 865p
LC 78-2892
"Through the interwoven stories of three families and the Indians, Blacks, and Irish immigrants with whom they interact, Michener chronicles four centuries of life on Maryland's Eastern Shore. . . . Michener elaborates . . . variations on his themes of personal accountability for social change, man's self-expulsion from paradise, and the interrelated ecological network of all things." Libr J

Michener, James A.
The covenant. Random House 1980 887p
LC 80-5315
This novel spans 500 years of South African history. Three families mingle "with the outstanding historic figures of their times. They are the Nxumalos, the Van Doorns, and the Saltwoods, representing respectively the African, Afrikaans, and English. . . . Over several hundred years their descendants make contact, and thrive through the contact, only to become adversaries as contact subsequently gives way to conflict. Finally they find themselves irretrievably stuck in the hard concrete of South Africa's racial policies." Christ Sci Monit

Michener, James A.
Creatures of the kingdom; stories of animals and nature. illustrations by Karen Jacobsen. Random House 1993 281p il
LC 92-46075
"Gathered in this delightful 'anthology' . . . are sections from Michener's novels that deal with animals and other less animate aspects of the natural world. . . . These selections represent nature writing as its most fluid and involving." Booklist

Michener, James A.
The drifters; a novel. Random House 1971 751p
"The Drifters is something of a guidebook loosely dressed up as fiction; a guide to quaint and colorful places, especially on the Iberian peninsula, and to the life-styles of the rebellious young." Saturday Rev

Michener, James A.
★ Hawaii. Random House 1959 937p
"High-domed, long-haired littérateurs may argue that Michener's characters are often as paper-thin as the colored image in which Hawaii is held by mainland tourists, but 'Hawaii,' is still a masterful job of research, an absorbing performance of storytelling, and a monumental account of the islands from geologic birth to sociological emergence as the newest, and perhaps the most interesting of the United States." Saturday Rev

Michener, James A.
Mexico. Random House 1992 625p
LC 92-50151
"There are splendid and authentic scenes in the plaza de toros that are as dramatic as any written by Ernest Hemingway or Barnaby Conrad, and one chapter, where the bulls' horns are shaved by the father of a torero, is James Michener the storyteller and parabolist at his finest." N Y Times Book Rev

Michener, James A.
The novel. Random House 1991 446p
ISBN 0-679-40133-4
LC 90-53489
"To his credit, Michener tries to be fair to both sides of the literary vs. popular fiction debate. The elitist Streibert is presented as an honest, well-intentioned man who genuinely loves literature and worries about the dangers of commercialism. The position Michener seems to be advocating in 'The Novel' is that experimental, elitist fiction and old-fashioned storytelling are both legitimate forms for the novel." Christ Sci Monit

Michener, James A.
Poland. Random House 1983 556p
LC 83-4477
"The author's description of the devastating invasions of Poland by Tartars, Germans, Swedes, Turks, Russians and Soviets is historically accurate as well as highly vivid. . . . But the most unforgettable and deeply moving pages of the book are those in which Michener narrates the horrid experiences of the inmates of the Polish concentration camp of Majdanek, where 140,000 Jewish and 220,000 Christian prisoners died. . . . Michener's Poland is an engrossing and fast moving novel by a superb storyteller." America

Michener, James A.
Recessional. Random House 1994 484p
ISBN 0-679-43612-X
LC 94-17414
"Opening with obstetrician Andy Zorn taking a job as manager of one of the nation's poshest retirement and final-care facilities, the novel weaves through the challenges Zorn faces and the experiences of many of the residents of the Palms in Florida. . . . The fine line between euthanasia and the excessive use of mechanical life supports is drawn with poignant scenes of aging and AIDS patients. Despite the dreary subject, this novel is full of life and romance." Booklist

Michener, James A.
Sayonara. Random House 1954 243p
The love story of an American Air Corps major and a beautiful Japanese girl. When Major Gruver sets up housekeeping with Hanaogi there is consternation among the Americans, for Gruver is engaged to an American general's daughter. Contrary to the course of Madam Butterfly, in this instance it is the Japanese girl who says Sayonara (farewell) to the American

Michener, James A.
Space. Random House 1982 622p
LC 82-40127

"Michener has caught the essence of what motivated and then enfeebled our space program. . . . As usual, Michener has done his homework, this time with affection and excitement as well—his pro-space enthusiasm is the book's driving force, and he has deftly woven an incredible amount of information into the tale." Natl Rev

Michener, James A.

Texas. Random House 1985 1096p

LC 85-8248

"As a novel, this book is remarkably good. . . . Michener, however, has given us here something even more: a marvelous and sympathetic analysis of historical and social relations." Best Sellers

Mieville, China

The **city** & the city. Del Rey Ballantine Books 2009 312p $26

ISBN 978-0-345-49751-2; 0-345-49751-1

LC 2009-13775

"A murder mystery set in two cities, Ul Qoma and Beszel, one rich and one poor, where residents have been trained to 'unsee' each other in order to coexist. . . . The story takes the form of a police procedural as the protagonist, Inspector Tyador Borlú of the Extreme Crime Squad, tries to crack the murder case. There are no elves or UFOs. Instead, the story focuses on the lengths to which people will go to enforce borders and maintain separate cultural identities. Evoking such writers as Franz Kafka and Mikhail Bulgakov, Mr. Miéville asks readers to make conceptual leaps and not to simply take flights of fancy." Wall Street J

Mieville, China

Embassytown. Ballantine Books 2011 345p $26

ISBN 978-0-345-52449-2

LC 2011-02854

"It's a joy to find this young author coming into his own, and bringing the craft of science fiction out of the backwaters where it's been caught lately between the regressive drag of publishers marketing to a 'safe' readership and the bewildering promises of change and growth offered by postmodernism in all its forms and formlessness. Embassytown is a fully achieved work of art. Only the trash forms of science fiction are undemanding and predictable; the good stuff, like all good fiction, is not for lazy minds. Where the complexity of realistic novels is moral and psychological, in science fiction it's moral and intellectual; individual character is seldom the key. But Miéville's characters are deftly sketched, and his narrator-protagonist, Avice, is a subtler portrait than she seems at first." Guardian (UK)

Mieville, China

Iron council. Del Rey/Ballantine Books 2004 564p $24.95

ISBN 0-345-46402-8

LC 2004-49394

"In myriad ways, China Miéville's New Crobuzon is an unweeded garden of unearthly delights, and Iron Council a work of both passionate conviction and the highest artistry." Washington Post Book World

Mieville, China

★ **Kraken**; an anatomy. Del Rey/Ballantine Books 2010 509p $26

ISBN 978-0-345-49749-9; 0-345-49749-X

LC 2010-13893

"With his tale of a giant-squid corpse, Miéville, never predictable, lobs a grenade into the urban-fantasy genre, remaking it into wild comedy. To wit: A perfectly preserved Architeuthis dux specimen — percolating in the bowels of London's Natural History Museum — vanishes, plunging curator Billy Harrow into a bizarre shadow world of vampires, criminals, and cults. Miéville tears through the story with an almost manic energy, bulldozing past the few places where the plot falters. (It's saying something about his imagination that the gigantic tentacled creature is one of the least odd things in Kraken.) Anyone who reads this is never going to think about natural-history museums — or aquariums — in the same way again." Entertainment Wkly

Mieville, China

Perdido Street Station. Del Rey 2001 710p map pa $18.95

ISBN 0-345-44302-0

LC 00-67474

"Scientist Isaac Dan der Grimnebulin and his lover, an insectlike creature named Lin, discover the risks of meddling in the affairs of mobsters, renegades, and revolutionaries when they fall afoul of the powers that rule the sprawling city of New Crobuzon. The author . . . delivers a powerful tale about the power of love and the will to survive in a dystopian universe that combines Victorian elements with a fantasy version of cyberpunk." Libr J

Mieville, China

The **scar**. Ballantine Books 2002 638p pa $18.95

ISBN 0-345-44438-8

"This complicated fantasy seemingly could go in any number of directions and doesn't end up in quite the places a reader expects it to. Armada, a vibrant creation, with the uncertainties of its press-ganged residents and the machinations of its politics, makes this compelling reading." Booklist

Miles, Jonathan

Dear American Airlines. Houghton Mifflin 2008 180p $22

ISBN 978-0-54705-401-8; 0-54705-401-7

LC 2007-52150

In this novel, "Benny Ford, a 53-year-old recovering alcoholic and failed poet, has been stranded at Chicago's O'Hare International Airport for most of a day. He is about to miss his long-lost daughter's wedding. While he waits, Benny decides to give the airline a piece of his mind in writing. The letter he writes turns into his life story. Rage and a rambling self-narrative is a brutal barroom combination, best avoided on the page, too. But Miles is such a clever, amusing writer that he turns what should be a shtick into a terrifically fun read." Boston Globe

Miller, A. D.

Snowdrops; a novel. [by] A.D. Miller. Double-day 2011 273p $24.95

ISBN 978-0-385-53344-7; 0-385-53344-6

LC 2010-10310

"The wonderfully evoked corrupt atmosphere of modern Moscow, a dangerous mix of extreme poverty and decadent wealth, of simple old-fashioned values and unrestrained debauchery reads like Graham Greene on steroids. . . .Tightly written, with fascinating insider detail gained in three years as The Economist magazine's Moscow correspondent, Miller's complex, gripping debut novel is undoubtedly the real thing." Daily Mail

Miller, Alyce L.

Water; nine stories. Sarabande Books 2007 217p $15.95

ISBN 978-1-932511-56-7

LC 2007-10152

"These stories, which feature interracial relationships in small-town Ohio and Oakland, CA, mirror the ebb and flow of personal struggles and project the reader, believably, into a future that makes sense for the characters we come to know. Miller's skill at manipulating point of view is admirable. The relaxed fluidity of these stories makes their dénouements all the more surprising." Libr J

Miller, Andrew

Oxygen. Harcourt 2002 323p $30

ISBN 0-15-100721-7

LC 2001-51459

First published 2001 in the United Kingdom

"Written in elegant, resonant prose, this book breathes with compassion and honesty, and with the rare quality called hope." Publ Wkly

Miller, Andrew

Pure. Europa Editions 2012 331 p.

ISBN 1609450671; 9781609450670

Costa Book of the Year (2011); Costa Novel Award Winner (2011).

In this book, the 2012 winner of the Costa Book of the Year, a "young man of humble background, Jean-Baptiste Baratte is ordered to exhume the vast and ancient cemetery of Les Innocents in the poor Parisian quarter of Les Halles and demolish its church. No one knows how many bodies are buried there . . . but it has recently begun to burst its banks, poisoning the city and spreading 'moral disturbance.' . . .As Baratte's story unfolds, the impending [French] revolution hangs over the narrative. . . . Jean-Baptiste Baratte, or John the Baptist the Churn, is in Paris to prepare the people for the coming of the true messiah. It is his duty to rip away the filth of the past, to lay the foundations for a new, better world." (The Guardian)

Miller, Arthur

Homely girl, a life, and other stories. Viking 1995 115p

LC 95-14267

These three stories "evoke the pre- and postwar New York City of the author's best-known plays. After being dominated for years by her Communist first husband, the homely girl of the title story finds happiness and fulfillment with a blind musician. In 'Fame,' a newly acclaimed playwright fears he won't be able to write another play. And in 'Fitter's Night,' a cynical Italian metalworker risks his life on a freezing January evening to repair a destroyer headed out to protect a World War II convoy. . . . The ability to sum up in clear, unequivocal prose the essence of an emotion, a situation, a theme—characteristic of Mr. Miller's best writing—makes the reader wish that these stories were longer, and that there were more of them." N Y Times Book Rev

Miller, Derek B.

Norwegian by night; a novel. Derek B. Miller. Houghton Mifflin Harcourt 2013 304 p. $26

ISBN 0547934874; 9780547934877

LC 2012018089

In this novel by Derek Miller "Sheldon Horowitz . . . a former Marine . . . who failed his only son by sending him to Vietnam to die . . . move[s] in with his granddaughter . . . in Norway. Sheldon witnesses a dispute between [a] woman . . . and a . . . stranger. When events turn dire, Sheldon . . . shields the neighbor's young son from the violence, and they flee the scene. As Sheldon and the boy look for a haven . . . reality and fantasy, past and present, weave together." (Publisher's note)

Miller, Henry

★ Tropic of Cancer. Grove Press 1961 318p

First published 1934 in France

Miller "uses themes—cadging for food, shelter, and sex; attacks on such bourgeois values as work and marriage; denunciations of traditional art and literature—and imagery—wild, exuberant, often shockingly frank—that together represent a savage, nihilistic (and at times enormously funny) revulsion against a world of stupidity and ugliness." Ency of World Lit in the 20th Century

Followed by Tropic of Capricorn

Miller, Henry

★ Tropic of Capricorn. Grove Press 1962 348p

First published 1939 in France

"In a form like that of Tropic of Cancer the autobiographical account describes the writer's boyhood in Brooklyn, his quest to discover himself by sexual experiences and by other means, and his fury at the faults he finds in many of the values and ways of life in the U.S." Oxford Companion to Am Lit. 6th edition

Miller, Jennifer

The year of the gadfly; a novel. Jennifer Miller. Houghton Mifflin Harcourt 2012 374 p.

ISBN 0547548591; 9780547548593

LC 2011042369

This novel by Jennifer Miller takes place in "Mariana Academy . . . founded with a serious honor code; its reputation has been unsullied for decades. Now a long-dormant secret society, Prisom's Party, threatens its . . . halls with vigilante justice, exposing students and teachers alike. . . . Iris Dupont, a budding journalist whose only confidant is the chain-smoking specter of Edward R. Murrow, feels sure she can break into the ranks of . . . the Party's underground newspaper, and there uncover the source of its blackmail schemes and vilifying rumors. . . . And everything connects to a rare book called "Marvelous Species." But the truth comes with its own dangers, and Iris is torn between her allegiances, her reporter's instinct, and her own troubled past." (Publisher's note)

Miller, Karen E. Quinones

An **angry**-ass black woman; Karen E. Quinones Miller. Gallery Books Karen Hunter Publishing 2012 272 p. $15

ISBN 1451607822; 9781451607826; 9781451608991

LC 2011047077

In this autobiographical novel by Karen E. Quinones Miller, Ke-Ke Quinones "grew up poorer than poor in Harlem in the 1960s and '70s, a place of unrelenting violence, racism, crime, rape, scamming, drinking, and drugging. . . . [But she] was whip smart and sassy, a voracious reader of everything from poetry to the classics. . . . Decades later, comatose in a hospital bed after a medical crisis, she reflects on her life." (Publisher's note)

Miller, Madeline

★ The **song** of Achilles; Madeline Miller. Ecco 2012 378 p. $25.99

ISBN 0062060619; 0062060627; 9780062060617; 9780062060624

LC 2011275637

Orange Prize for Fiction (2012)

This novel, which was featured on "the New York Times best-seller list and is in the running for the U.K.'s . . . Orange Prize, is a . . . romantic retelling of the Trojan War as a story of longtime companions narrated by Patroclus. . . . The future lovers meet as 5-year-olds at a footrace and are reunited when Patroclus is banished to Achilles' father's kingdom. By the time they are 13, there are the first of many 'stirrings' . . . followed some years later by couplings." (Time)

"With language both evocative of her predecessors and fresh, and through familiar scenes that explore new territory, this first-time novelist masterfully brings to life an imaginative yet informed vision of ancient Greece featuring divinely human gods and larger-than-life mortals." Pub Wkly

Miller, MaryAnn G.

Stalking season; a seasons series mystery. Maryann Miller. Five Star 2012 280 p. (hardcover) $25.95

ISBN 1432825984; 9781432825980

LC 2012019916

In this mystery novel, by Maryann Miller, "Dallas detectives Sarah Kingsly and Angel Johnson . . . return to confront a case almost as gnarly as their relationship. Newly assigned to each other, the women just don't feel as comfortable as partners should. . . . When a young woman is strangled, nothing about her suggests a connection to the sleazy motel in which she's found, and once she's identified, her actual connections start the Dallas PD hopping." (Kirkus Reviews)

Miller, Rebecca

★ **Jacob's** folly; a novel. Rebecca Miller. 1st ed. Farrar, Straus and Giroux 2013 384 p. (hardcover) $26

ISBN 0374178542; 9780374178543

LC 2012022882

The protagonist of this book is "an 18th-century Jewish peddler reincarnated as a fly on contemporary Long Island, NY. At first devastated to discover that he is not an angel, as he first presumed, Jacob Cerf nonetheless exerts a mysterious influence on two individuals: Leslie Senzatimore, a saintly boat remodeler, and Masha, a young Orthodox Jewish woman. Jacob feels compelled to pull Masha away from her religion and to knock Leslie off his do-gooder pedestal." (Library Journal)

Miller, Rebecca

The **private** lives of Pippa Lee. Farrar, Straus and Giroux 2008 239p $23

ISBN 978-0-374-23742-4; 0-374-23742-5

LC 2007-47321

"This is a book about do-overs and, as suggested by the title, about the different possibilities contained in each human life span. It's a beautifully written novel, choppy and delicate and true, as unique as Pippa herself. Miller shows that the sum of a person's life is not what she has accomplished but what she has experienced, not her legacy but her memories." San Francisco Chron

Miller, Risa

Welcome to Heavenly Heights. St. Martin's Press 2003 230p $23.95

ISBN 0-312-30180-4

LC 2002-31876

The author "has peered inside Tova's life to show us the search for joy that lies at the heart of her religious ritual and the beauty of people like her who devote themselves to that search. And then Miller has broken our hearts—with Tova's—by showing us how horrible it is when the poetic liturgical metaphors of Judaism become the terrible realities of nationalism, when holiness tries to reconcile itself with the inevitable human corruption of statehood." N Y Times Book Rev

Miller, Sue

The **distinguished** guest. HarperCollins Pubs. 1995 282p

LC 95-2951

"The guest of the title is a woman who in her seventies wrote a celebrated memoir about being the wife of the radical minister of an integrated church in Chicago, and who eventually split with her husband over issues of black separatism and militancy. Now in her Parkinson's-afflicted eighties, she is visiting her architect son, whose view of his mother is necessarily different from her public image. This novel, as full of rich domestic detail as Miller's previous books, is, like them, a work of consolation informed by a psychotherapeutic perspective—very literal, yet also highly readable." New Yorker

Miller, Sue

Family pictures; a novel. Harper & Row 1990
389p

LC 89-46109

"'Family Pictures' is a novel that might have intrigued
and startled Woolf—profoundly honest, shapely, ambitious,
engrossing, original and true, an important example of a new
American tradition that explores what it means, not to light
out for the territories but to make a home, live at home and
learn what home is." N Y Times Book Rev

Miller, Sue

For love. HarperCollins Pubs. 1993 301p

LC 92-54422

"Fortyish freelance writer Lottie leaves her new husband in Chicago to spend part of the summer in Cambridge,
Massachusetts, getting the family house ready to sell now
that her brother Cameron has placed their alcoholic mother
in a nursing home. While she and her son Ryan paint and
clean, Lottie examines the concept of love in an article she
is writing, studying her own troubled marriage and Cameron's resumption of a love affair with childhood sweetheart
Elizabeth. For Elizabeth, who is staying with her mother after leaving her philandering husband, this romance is just a
fling. But Cameron's obsessive love for the golden girl of his
youth leads to {an accident}." Libr J

Miller, Sue

★ The **good** mother. Harper & Row 1986 310p

LC 85-45475

"The fulcrum on which the novel's plot pivots is the allegation by Anna's ex-husband that Anna's lover has molested
Molly, and the ensuing custody trial. Miller's treatment of
this high point of tension in the novel is dramatic, discreet,
compassionate. Each development in the legal process increases the tension. The drama heightens, the suspense
builds, character is further developed, and the latitude for
choice logically narrowed. Like a final judgment, the custody decision breaks over reader and character alike." Christ
Sci Monit

Miller, Sue

Inventing the Abbotts and other stories. Harper
& Row 1987 180p

LC 86-46089

"These stories report from a frontier, from the discontented and guilty world of divorce and the single parent, of
marriage as a threatened institution, and if the landscape is
a bleak and dispiriting one, that is not the author's fault; she
is merely giving evidence. As stories they vary—some effective, others less so—but as testimonies of our times they
seem highly apposite." NY Times Book Rev

Miller, Sue

The **Lake** Shore Limited. Alfred A. Knopf 2010
269p $25.95

ISBN 978-0-307-26421-3; 0-307-26421-1

LC 2009-46504

The novel is "craftily plotted, too good for a reviewer
to give much of it away. Also, as with her previous novels, Miller resists allowing her characters the resources of
eloquence; nor does she — in Henry James's words — 'go

behind' them to offer us deeper truths about their behavior."
Boston Globe

Miller, Sue

Lost in the forest. Knopf 2005 247p $24.95
ISBN 1-400-04226-7

LC 2004-48963

"Miller has always been adept at rendering the complexities of family life, the way even well-intentioned, decent
people can't walk across a room without wounding at least
one person they love. But while some of her plots . . . can
be cluttered and occasionally clumsy, Lost in the Forest has
a seemingly effortless grace; Miller quickly captures and
never loses our attention." N Y Times Book Rev

Miller, Sue

The **senator's** wife. Alfred A. Knopf 2008 306p
$24.95

ISBN 978-0-307-26420-6

LC 2007-14659

"No one captures the domestic landscape with language
as lush as Miller's. She is the Martha Stewart of fictional
space. From peeling an orange to laying out Christmas dinner to arranging lilies on a table, her prose is almost erotic.
Moreover, her writerly gift extends beyond graceful imagery. She describes sexual encounters with graphic intensity
and brings to Meri's labor and delivery a verisimilitude that
will flatten you." Houston Chron

Miller, Sue

While I was gone. Knopf 1999 265p
ISBN 0-375-40112-1

LC 98-14211

In this novel, Joey Becker, a veterinarian married to a
minister, "is just beginning to feel dissatisfied with her predictable life when Eli Mayhew, a housemate from her hippie
past, moves to town. His presence both reawaken's questions
about an old, unsolved murder and kindles in Joey what she
has been hungering for: a youthful 'sense of a surprise, that
heady feeling of not knowing' what life will bring." Time

"Miller's narrative is a beautifully textured picture of the
psychological tug of war between finding integrity as an individual and satisfying the demands of spouse, children and
community." Publ Wkly

Miller, Sue

The **world** below; a novel. Knopf 2001 275p
$25

ISBN 0-375-41094-5

LC 2001-33731

"As Catherine sorts through her grandmother's life, she
also sorts through her own: her mother's death, her two marriages, her boyfriends and her children. . . . As readers have
come to expect, Miller limns contemporary life in deft, sure
strokes, with an unerring ear for the way parents and children talk; no one can parse a modern marriage as well as she
can. But in this novel Miller's special gift to readers is her
rendering of Georgia's life, particularly the two love stories
that mark it." Publ Wkly

Miller, Walter M.

★ A **canticle** for Leibowitz; a novel. by Walter M. Miller, Jr. Lippincott 1960 320p hardcover o.p. pa $13.95

ISBN 0-06-089299-4

"Here is science fiction of the highest literary excellence and thematic intelligence. A monastery founded by the scientist Leibowitz is discovered decades after an atomic war. In the first part of the book a young novice in the monastery is the protagonist; in the second part we see scholars in a new period of enlightenment; and in the final section we observe man's proclivity for repeating mistakes and the apparent inevitability of history's repeating itself." Shapiro. Fic for Youth. 3d edition

Millet, Lydia

Ghost lights; a novel. Lydia Millet. W. W. Norton & Co. 2011 255p $24.95

ISBN 978-0-393-08171-8; 0-393-08171-0

LC 2011026502

"Picking up in the vicinity of where her last novel, How the Dead Dream, left off, Ghost Lights finds new protagonist Hal flying to Belize to find the previous novel's main man T., who disappeared there months before. Hal's wife is T.'s executive assistant, and when she contemplates hiring a private investigator to root out her boss, Hal volunteers, claiming his experience at the IRS qualifies him to track a person down. The truth is Hal suspects his wife of cheating on him, and his decision to embark on a hero's quest is as much fueled by booze and insecurity as it is by any sense of righteousness. . . . A much more contemplative novel—where T. is led by action and bravado, Hal prefers to ruminate and be led—Ghost Lights puts together a clearer vision of the previous book's themes of the way identity is tied up with social purpose." Time Out Chicago

Millet, Lydia

How the dead dream; a novel. Counterpoint 2008 244p $24

ISBN 978-1-59376-184-4; 1-59376-184-8

LC 2007-35242

"For the reader, T.'s adventures with animals carry more emotional impact than any of the human encounters. They prompt the serious , sometimes convoluted but always moving meditations that are the spine if this strange, lovely novel." Chicago Sun-Times

Millet, Lydia

★ **Magnificence**; a novel. Lydia Millet. W.W. Norton & Co. 2012 255 p. $25.95

ISBN 0393081702; 9780393081701

LC 2012015145

This novel by Lydia Millet "introduces Susan Lindley, a woman adrift after her husband's death. Suddenly gifted her great uncle's Pasadena mansion, Susan decides to restore his extensive collection of preserved animals. . . . Meanwhile, a menagerie of uniquely damaged humans--including a cheating husband and a chorus of eccentric elderly women--joins her in residence." (Publisher's note)

Millet, Lydia

Oh pure and radiant heart; Lydia Millet. Soft Skull Press 2005 489p (hbk.) $25

ISBN 1932360859; 9781932360851

LC 2005001028

This novel is framed around the questions "What if Robert Oppenheimer, Enrico Fermi and Leo Szilard, the primary physicists from the Manhattan Project, returned to contemporary America to survey their atomic legacy? . . . [In this book,] the souls of the three take earthly form in the present-day Southwest. Ann, a New Mexico librarian, spots the reincarnated Oppenheimer and Fermi at a restaurant near her home; Szilard soon joins them; Ann persuades her garden-designer husband, Ben, to take them all in. Subsequent trips to Los Alamos and . . . Japan to view the monuments at Hiroshima persuade the three to work for disarmament. Army surveillance ensues; at one rally, shots are fired; and Christian Fundamentalists" also find their way into the narrative. (Publishers Weekly)

Millhauser, Steven

★ **Dangerous** laughter; thirteen stories. Alfred A. Knopf 2008 244p $24

ISBN 978-0-307-26756-6; 0-307-26756-3

LC 2007-22929

"While most short-story writers in the past three decades joined the realist rebellion against the fabulism of the '70s, Steven Millhauser has stayed true to the fantastic tradition that extends from Scheherazade to Poe, to Kafka and Barth. He rejects the ordinary world of the merely real, and playfully and powerfully explores the incredible world of purely aesthetic creation. . . . Millhauser's stories are not mere ingenuity, although they are devilishly clever. Millhauser is motivated by the desire to see a world in a grain of sand, to affirm that the road of excess leads to the palace of wisdom. He is our most brilliant practicing romantic, for whom surface reality is merely an uninteresting illusion." San Francisco Chron

Millhauser, Steven

★ The **king** in the tree: three novellas. Knopf 2003 241p $23

ISBN 0-375-41540-8

LC 2002-72956

"An excitable widow leads the reader on a tour of her house—apparently being offered for sale—in the harrowing 'Revenge'. . . . 'An adventure of Don Juan' finds the famous philanderer, bored with a lifetime of easy conquests, leaving the Continent for a change of scenery on his friend's English estate, where he will experience unrequited desire for the first time. Millhauser retells the tragedy of Tristan and Isolde in the title story. . . . Millhauser's precision, coupled with his brave imagination, makes these stories as smart and fresh as they are grim." Publ Wkly

Millhauser, Steven

The **knife** thrower and other stories. Crown 1998 256p

ISBN 0-609-60070-2

LC 97-45796

"In these darkly magical stories, Millhauser turns town squares, backyards, and department stores into strange and luminous realms." New Yorker

Millhauser, Steven

★ **Martin** Dressler; the tale of an American dreamer. Crown 1996 294p

ISBN 0-517-70319-X

LC 96-683

The author "again examines the American imagination in terms of cosmology. This time, his world-creator is young Martin Dressler, an entrepreneurial wunderkind who starts out at his father's cigar store. What ensues is an expertly woven fable of Victorian Manhattan, as Martin transforms his hunger for 'something else' into a series of colossal hotels. Martin's sights are firmly set on tomorrow, but he's cursed to be forever premodern: the skyscraper always seems to lurk around the next turn of the page, but he can envision only period eclecticism. As the new century dawns, Martin's crowning achievement, the Grand Cosmo, begins to look like the ultimate castle in the air, and he ponders—without regret—the consequences of having 'dreamed the wrong dream.'" New Yorker

Millhauser, Steven

We others; new and selected stories. Alfred A. Knopf 2011 387p $27.95

ISBN 978-0-307-59590-4; 0-307-59590-0

LC 2011-00078

This short story collection, by Pulitzer Prize-winning author Steven Millhauser, part of the "Vintage Contemporaries" series, is placed "in settings as disparate as nineteenth-century Vienna, a contemporary Connecticut town, the corridors of a monstrous museum, and Thomas Edison's laboratory, and they are inhabited by a wide-ranging cast of characters, including a knife thrower and teenage boys, ghosts and a cartoon cat and mouse." (Publisher's note)

"These tales teem with wild and original ideas, some incidental, some central to the plot, but all hinting that any apparent narrative simplicity should not be taken at face value. . . . Six of these stories are new (the rest are selected from previous collections), but all have more than mere hints of darkness." Washington City Paper

Milligan, J.

Jack Fish; a novel. Soho Press 2005 217p il $23

ISBN 1-569-47382-X

LC 2004-48190

"Moving from Brooklyn diner to Midtown architecture firm to New Jersey theme park, the novel has the stealthy and web-toed Jack tangling with New York demimondaines and corporate wonks as he dodges a violent gang called the Maltese. The book brims throughout with hyperspecific detail and hipster patois; it's like a Mark Leyner novel, but with a plot, and harpoons." N Y Times Book Rev

Mills, Mark

Amagansett; Mark Mills. Putnam 2004 394p $24.95

ISBN 0-399-15184-2

LC 2004-44394

"The novel combines a touching love story, told in flashback, with a nicely detailed procedural starring an unlikely investigative duo: the taciturn Basque and the Amagansett assistant police chief, who hopes to resurrect his career in the wake of scandal. . . . This is a novel to savor, both for its portrait of roughhewn individuals finding selfhood beyond the breakers and for its snapshot of the postwar world not yet locked in the death grip of modernity." Booklist

Mills, Mark

The **information** officer; a novel. Random House 2010 276p map $25

ISBN 978-1-4000-6818-0; 1-4000-6818-5

LC 2009-20047

The author "skillfully combines grim historical reality with murder in this tautly gripping mystery. . . . Most memorably, his historical research offers a reminder of an often-forgotten fragment of a war." Washington Times

Milton, Giles

Edward Trencom's nose; a novel of history, dark intrigue, and cheese. Thomas Dunne Books/St. Martin's Press 2007 310p $23.95

ISBN 978-0-312-36217-1; 0-312-36217-X

LC 2006102652

"The eponymous Trencom owns the finest cheese shop in London, one that has been in the possession of his family since the 17th century. He also owns the finest nose in generations, one that can distinguish the provenance of a cheese down to the cow from which it originated. . . . When the story opens in 1969, he appears to have never questioned the strange fates that befell his ancestors—particularly odd since most of them met grisly ends. . . . So when Edward Trencom is warned by a mysterious stranger that he is being watched, his first reaction is to be completely baffled. After all, the world of cheese isn't exactly the world of high espionage and Trencom is no 007. So his second reaction is that of the mild-mannered introvert—to start researching his family history, from which he uncovers many surprises. . . . What it all adds up to is a highly entertaining novel." PopMatters

Min, Anchee

Becoming Madame Mao. Houghton Mifflin 2000 337p $25

ISBN 0-618-00407-6

LC 99-58520

"Min reveals the complexities of love, betrayal, and ambition in this lyrical and thrilling depiction of a once-powerless woman in the jaws of power, giving us an all-too-rare glimpse into the life of a woman within the machine." Ms

Includes bibliographical references

Min, Anchee

Empress Orchid. Hougton Mifflin 2004 336p $24

ISBN 0-618-06887-2

LC 2003-56891

The author "has done a prodigious amount of on-site research to capture the glorious, hopeless last days of the Ching dynasty. . . . Readers will be enthralled by the gorgeously woven cultural tapestry and the psychologically astute portrait of the empress a talented girl from the provinces who married (way) up." Publ Wkly

Min, Anchee

The **last** empress. Houghton Mifflin 2007 308p $25

ISBN 978-0-618-53146-2; 0-618-53146-7

LC 2006-030466

A sequel to Empress Orchid about the life of Lady Yehonala, a.k.a. the Dowager Empress, or the last empress of China. The author "picks up Orchid's story from the time of her mother's death and takes readers through the empress's own death in 1908. Departing from the stereotype of Orchid as the 'dragon lady' empress, Min uses first-person narration to portray her as a caring mother to Emperor Tung Chih and her nephew, Emperor Guang-hsu. The softness of Orchid's persona is revealed in her relations with her eunuchs, Antehai and Li-Lien-ying, while her strength is played out in the politics of the period and in her ability to survive the hardships of the Boxer Rebellion." Libr J

Mina, Denise, 1966-

The **dead** hour; a novel. Little, Brown and Co. 2006 341p $24.99

ISBN 978-0-316-73594-0; 0-316-73594-9

LC 2006-01610

"On her rounds as a crime reporter for the Scottish Daily News, Paddy Meehan visits the scene of a disturbance at a home in Beardsden, a wealthy suburb of Glasgow. There she finds an attractive couple who appear to be in the midst of a domestic dispute. The police give the couple a warning and, as they are leaving, the man presses a 50-pound note into Paddy's hand and asks her to keep the matter out of the paper. The next morning Paddy reads in the paper that the woman, a lawyer and political activist, has been murdered. The man was not her husband. Suddenly, Paddy has to confront the class prejudices that allowed her to leave another woman in a dangerous situation and decide what to do about the money she accepted from the murderer." Libr J

"Surely Paddy Meehan is the most unlikely, and most relistic, investigator in recent crime fiction. . . . The Dead Hour is some kind of magnificent." Wall Street Journal

Mina, Denise

Deception; a novel. Little, Brown 2004 311p $23.95

ISBN 0-316-73592-2

LC 2003-65861

"Mina's novel is a smart example of the crime novel as postmodern puzzle, a work that coolly offers to match wits with the unwary reader and is not likely to lose the game." Washington Post Book World

Mina, Denise, 1966-

The **end** of the wasp season; a novel. Little, Brown and Company 2011 390p $25.99

ISBN 978-0-316-06933-5; 0-316-06933-7

LC 2011-18242

A procedural "set in Glasgow and featuring a gutsy cop named Alex Morrow. Since Morrow is pregnant with twins, her mates on the Strathclyde police force try to shield her from the savagery done to the victim of a home invasion in the exclusive suburb of Thorntonhall. But when she realizes the prudish cops are actually revolted by the dead woman's provocatively exposed body, Morrow feels 'sheer, suffocating pity' for the victim, whose battered face and half naked corpse have nullified both her identity and her dignity. This is the sort of insightful observation that makes Mina's novels so extraordinarily rich and unpredictable. There are the usual rewards in following the evidence that leads the police to the teenage sons of Kay Murray, who cleaned house for the murdered woman and the invalid mother she had only recently buried. But there's greater satisfaction in watching Mina transform this seemingly simple cleaning woman into a complex character, possessed of great depths of feeling." N Y Times Book Rev

Mina, Denise, 1966-

Field of blood; a novel. Denise Mina. Little, Brown 2005 360p (pbk.) $7.50; (hbk.) $35

ISBN 0316735930; 9780316154581; 9780316735933

LC 2004023408

In this novel, "Patricia 'Paddy' Meehan, a copygirl at Glasgow's 'Daily News,' has struggled with issues of goodness since childhood. 'I knew I was lying when I made my first communion,' she confesses to fiancé Sean Ogilvy the night she delivers other shockers. She won't marry him. And she wants his help interviewing his 10-year-old cousin, Callum, who's been charged with murdering a toddler. . . . Paddy, who shares a nickname with a career criminal wrongfully imprisoned for murder, can't tolerate injustice. At the heart of the plot is her decision pose as colleague Heather Allen when she makes dangerous inquiries, a choice that spells death for the real Heather, who's everything Paddy isn't: slim blonde whistle bait—and ambitious enough to steal a story from Paddy." (Publishers Weekly)

Mina, Denise, 1966-

Gods and beasts; a novel. Denise Mina. Reagan Arthur Books/Little, Brown and Co. 2013 320 p. (hardback) $25.99

ISBN 0316188522; 9780316188524

LC 2012022241

This book is the third in Denise Mina's Det. Sgt. Alex Morrow series. Here, Morrow tries to figure out why a bank robber guns down an elderly gentleman who apparently tried to assist during his robbery. "Meanwhile, looming budget cuts and police layoffs lure two of Morrow's subordinates into stealing a pile of dirty drug money. Finally, a former labor hero turned politician is caught up in a sex scandal with a 17-year-old female staffer." (Publishers Weekly)

Mina, Denise

Slip of the knife; a novel. Little, Brown and Co. 2008 340p $24.99

ISBN 978-0-316-01558-5; 0-316-01558-X

LC 2007-42881

First published 2007 in the United Kingdom

"Mina excels at this kind of writing, the back-and-forth of competitors and colleagues, the way tension and love bind people uneasily. She's a leisurely writer; although Terry's murder opens the book, the action plays out slowly, and she lets us soak up the abundant ambience and personality." Boston Globe

Mina, Denise

Still midnight; a novel. Little, Brown and Co. 2010 342p $24.99

ISBN 9780-316015639; 0316015636

LC 2009-22061

First published 2009 in the United Kingdom

"Mina's strength has always been her depiction of her characters' inner lives. With a background in health care, law, and criminology, she knows — and can show readers — the small choices, the subtle moral nuances that make one sibling a cop, another a gangster. In 'Still Midnight,' she concentrates on such character studies, keeping the action — the home invasion and kidnapping, their cause and resolution — on a smaller scale than in previous works." Boston Globe

Minot, Eliza

The **Brambles**. Knopf 2006 243p $23.95

ISBN 1-4000-4269-0

LC 2005-44421

This "novel follows three siblings as they cope with their father's impending death from cancer, not long after their mother was killed in an airplane accident. The siblings' main preoccupations, though, are more individual. Margaret, a harried mother of three, has difficulty accepting that her children are growing up. Max can't bring himself to tell his wife that he quit his job in a moment of frustration, and he resents the burden that she and their baby son represent. The youngest, Edie, has fewer responsibilities, but is the most adrift, deeply lonely and plagued by an eating disorder. These quotidian problems sometimes seem overwrought, and the book's end brings an unnecessary plot twist, but the precision of Minot's descriptions succeeds in making her characters seem real and sympathetic." New Yorker

Minot, Susan

★ **Evening**. Knopf 1998 264p

ISBN 0-375-40037-0

LC 98-15437

"Ann Lord's life has been shaped by the men who have married her. As she lies on her deathbed, trying to make some sense of that life, a rediscovered balsam pillow evokes a Maine wedding, in 1954, where she fell in love for the first—and perhaps the last—time. This almost crude conceit produces a narrative of considerable ambition and complexity. . . . For heroine and reader alike, death's painful confusions are tempered by the spirited directness of Ann's younger self, as yet unscathed by time and experience." New Yorker

Minot, Susan

Folly. Houghton Mifflin 1992 278p

ISBN 0-395-60339-0

LC 92-21035

The author's "carefully thought out depiction of Lilian's inner world and of the difficulty of finding an accommodation between desire and reality, silence and self-expression, has a universal resonance." Christ Sci Monit

Minot, Susan

Lust & other stories. Houghton Mifflin 1989 147p

LC 89-1677

"Men remain emotionally distant and unwilling to commit throughout these 12 short stories, while women attempt to hold back. Alas, love insinuates itself and the man disappears. Minot's writing is sparse and poetic, painfully close to the surface." Libr J

Minot, Susan

★ **Monkeys**. Dutton 1986 159p

ISBN 0-525-24342-9

LC 85-30775

Interconnected episodes "trace the fortunes of a large boisterous New England family. Arranged into rough chronological order, the stories dramatize the growing up of the seven Vincent siblings. Their everyday world of family gatherings, teenage parties, and vacations seems frivolous on the surface but is underlaid with tension and ultimately leads to tragedy. The episodic nature of the book leaves a few questions unanswered about the engaging clan, while occasionally some events are reiterated. Yet there is a wonderful sense of slipping into the private, important moments of the Vincents, sharing their fun and their sadness." Booklist

Minot, Susan

Rapture. Knopf 2002 115p $18

ISBN 0-375-41327-8

LC 2001-38377

"This novella takes place during a single act of oral sex. . . . Benjamin is a handsome and hapless film director with a moneyed and supportive fiancée; Kay is his former production designer, with whom he had a fling on a shoot in Mexico. After three years of agonized liaisons and enforced partings, Benjamin and Kay fall into bed once more, but they seem to bring the rest of their lives along with them, and Minot's saucy conceit evolves into a disconcerting examination of love and war between the sexes." New Yorker

Mirvis, Tova

The **outside** world. Alfred A. Knopf 2004 283p $24

ISBN 1-400-04161-9

LC 2003-58923

"Beneath the women's wigs and the men's black fedoras, Mirvis finds reservoirs of belief, doubt, ambition, folly, lust and the rest of the human equation." Washington Post Book World

Mishima, Yukio, 1925-1970

★ The **decay** of the angel; translated from the Japanese by Edward G. Seidensticker. Knopf 1974 236p (Sea of fertility)

ISBN 0-394-46613-6

Original Japanese edition, 1971

"The novel concludes with a superbly written scene that casts doubt on the reality of the events described in the four volumes. In the end we discover that the 'sea of fertility' may be as arid as the region of that name on the moon, although it seems to suggest infinite richness." Ency of World Lit in the 20th Century

Mishima, Yukio, 1925-1970

Runaway horses; translated from the Japanese by Michael Gallagher. Knopf 1973 421p (Sea of fertility)

ISBN 0-394-46618-7

Original Japanese edition, 1969

"Mishima uses the same literary artistry in this novel as in the first but changes the gently romantic tone to one of martial ideology with a weirdly beautiful emphasis on ritual suicide. In the interplay of entanglements between the two novels, each self-contained, the author experiments with the Buddhist doctrine of reincarnation." Booklist

Followed by The Temple of Dawn

Mishima, Yukio, 1925-1970

The **sound** of waves; translated by Meredith Weatherby; drawings by Yoshinori Kinoshita. Knopf 1956 182p il

ISBN 9781448733767; 9780679752684

LC 56008911

"Returning to his village after a day on the fishing boats, Shinji, 18 years old, comes upon a beautiful stranger, Hatsue, who is the daughter of the wealthiest man in the village. After several unplanned encounters the two realize that they are in love, but many obstacles must be overcome before they can be married." Shapiro. Fic for Youth. 3d edition

Mishima, Yukio, 1925-1970

★ **Spring** snow; translated from the Japanese by Michael Gallagher. Knopf 1972 389p (Sea of fertility)

ISBN 0-394-44239-3

Original Japanese edition, 1968

"Kiyoaki Matsugae, a young Japanese, comes from a wealthy family whose attention to the most formal aspects of Japanese life has changed because of their attraction to Western culture. His best friend, Shigekuna Honda, is not so handsome or affluent but is a more serious scholar. The story emphasizes the difference in the character of the two young men as the plot describes the passionate, although ambivalent, love that Kiyoaki feels for the beautiful Satoko. When she concludes that Kiyoaki does not return her love, despite the fact that their affair has been serious and intimate, she allows herself to be betrothed to someone else. As always, what is forbidden becomes more desirable and Kiyoaki tries desperately to regain his loved one. Japanese customs and rituals intervene to bring a tragic ending to this love story." Shapiro. Fic for Youth. 3d edition

Followed by Runaway horses

Mishima, Yukio, 1925-1970

★ The **Temple** of Dawn; translated from the Japanese by E. Dale Saunders and Cecilia Segawa Seigle. Knopf 1973 334p (Sea of fertility)

ISBN 0-394-46614-4

Original Japanese edition, 1970

The third volume in the Sea of fertility series is "divided into two parts: the first is set in southeast Asia, where we first see the Thai princess who is the reincarnation of Isao; the second takes place in Japan after World War II, when the old values of society have been corrupted." Ency of World Lit in the 20th Century

Followed by The decay of the angel

Mishima, Yukio, 1925-1970

The **temple** of the golden pavilion; translated by Ivan Morris; introduction by Nancy Wilson Ross; drawings by Fumi Komatsu. Knopf 1959 262p il

"Based on an actual incident in 1950, when a Zen Buddhist acolyte burned down a temple which was a national shrine. Like the real arsonist, the fictional Mizoguchi is ugly and a pathological stutterer, and long before his hostility becomes overt, has developed a compulsion to destroy whatever is morally or physically beautiful. As told by the young acolyte, this is a masterly description of the growth of an obsession and an acute interpretation of the deliberate symbolism underlying Mizoguchi's irrational, perverse behavior." Booklist

Mistry, Rohinton

Family matters. Knopf 2002 431p

ISBN 0-375-40373-6

First published 2001 in the United Kingdom

"Mistry is not just a fiction writer; he's a philosopher who finds meaning—indeed, perhaps a divine plan—in small human interactions. This beautifully paced, elegantly expressed novel is notable for the breadth of its vision as well as its immensely appealing characters and enticing plot." Publ Wkly

Mistry, Rohinton

A **fine** balance; a novel. Knopf 1996 603p

ISBN 0-679-44608-7

LC 95-49317

"It is impossible not to seethe at the injustices of the police state, and impossible not to take these characters passionately to heart: this is a novel that can stand with the best of Dickens." New Yorker

Mitcham, Judson

★ **Sabbath** Creek; a novel. University of Georgia Press 2004 169p $22.95

ISBN 0-8203-2577-5

LC 2003-15704

"Lewis observes everything with the alertness of someone who does not yet take common experiences, such as kissing and drunkenness, for granted; he never resorts to shorthand to convey them, but describes them with a scrupulous fidelity to his own perceptions." N Y Times Book Rev

Mitchard, Jacquelyn

The **breakdown** lane; Jacquelyn Mitchard. HarperCollins Publishers 2005 382p o.p.; (pbk.) $12.95

ISBN 0060587245 (alk. paper); 9780061374524

LC 2004042375

This book tells the story of "[a]n advice columnist for a local newspaper, Julieanne Gillis. . . . Devoted to being a good mother and keeping her twenty-year marriage fresh and exciting, she is shocked by her husband's surprise announcement that he needs a 'sabbatical' from their life together—and devastated when he disappears, leaving Julie with no funds to raise two teenagers and a small daughter alone. But it is the discovery that Julieanne suffers from a serious illness that truly crumbles her family's foundation—setting her children on a . . . journey to locate their missing father before it's too late." (Publisher's note)

Mitchard, Jacquelyn

★ The **deep** end of the ocean. Viking 1996 434p

ISBN 0-670-86579-6

LC 95-26234

"One of the most remarkable things about this rich, moving and altogether stunning first novel is Mitchard's assured command of narrative structure and stylistic resources. Her story about a child's kidnapping and its enduring effects upon his parents, siblings, and extended family is a block-buster read." Publ Wkly

Mitchard, Jacquelyn

No time to wave goodbye; a novel. Random House 2009 228p $25

ISBN 978-1-4000-6774-9; 1-4000-6774-X

LC 2009-12905

"In this sequel to The Deep End of the Ocean, Mitchard returns to the Cappadora family. It's been 13 years since Ben was returned to his family after being abducted at age three. Now, the family is gathered to watch the premiere of oldest son Vincent's documentary about abducted children. As they watch the film, his parents are hurled back into their troubled past. As much as they would like to leave all the turmoil behind, the family is thrust once again into the spotlight as the documentary earns an Oscar nomination. And then another child is abducted." Libr J

"Mitchard charts a tormented family dynamic with shocking ease. This action-packed and emotionally rich drama is every bit as satisfying as its predecessor." Publ Wkly

Mitchard, Jacquelyn

Still summer. Warner Books 2007 307p $24.99

ISBN 978-0-446-57876-9; 0-446-57876-2

LC 2006-33941

"This fast-paced novel borrows qualities from several genres—suspense, survival epic, coming-of-age—and mostly succeeds in melding the better aspects of each, though Mitchard has a surer hand in creating women characters than men." Publ Wkly

Mitchard, Jacquelyn

A **theory** of relativity. HarperCollins Pubs. 2001 351p $26

ISBN 0-06-621023-2

LC 00-54261

"Keefer Nye, only a year old when her parents die in a car crash near Madison, Wis., is the focal point of a bitter, protracted and precedent-setting custody battle. Keefer's bachelor uncle, 24-year-old science teacher Gordon McKenna, seems the most appropriate custodian for his tiny niece, since he helped his elderly parents care for Keefer while his sister (Keefer's mother, Georgia) battled cancer. Challenging his claim, the affluent Nye grandparents, country-club Floridians, believe that their niece and her husband, born-again Christians, should get custody. Mitchard's nuanced character portrayals are her strong suit; no one is without frailties." Publ Wkly

Mitchard, Jacquelyn

Twelve times blessed. HarperCollins Pubs. 2003 532p $25.95

ISBN 0-06-621475-0

LC 2002-31781

"True Dickinson has everything: a loving 10-year-old son, Guy; a successsful business; and a cadre of friends who mostly fill the empty places in her life—until she falls for Hank Bannister, a restaurateur 10 years her junior." Booklist

"Mitchard infuses the courtship and domestic life with gentle humor." Publ Wkly

Mitchell, David

Black swan green; a novel. Random House 2006 294p hardcover o.p.

ISBN 0-8129-7401-8 pa; 1-4000-6379-5; 978-0-8129-7401-0 pa; 978-1-4000-6379-6

LC 2005052914

This is a novel by the author of Cloud Atlas (2004). "Black Swan Green tracks a single year in what is, for thirteen-year-old Jason Taylor, the sleepiest village in muddiest Worcestershire in a dying Cold War England, 1982." (Publisher's note)

This is a "portrait of a thirteen-year-old boy, growing up in Worcestershire in 1982, who is afflicted with a stammer, unhappy parents, and a snide older sister. Mitchell hasn't abandoned his fascination with the chapter: his meditation on being thirteen has thirteen sections, each featuring a self-contained story. This time, however, his approach has the subtlety of a watermark. . . . By settling into a single narrative voice, and skipping the pyrotechnics, Mitchell has come by something that eluded him before: a sense of earned emotion." New Yorker

Mitchell, David

★ **Cloud** atlas; a novel. Random House Trade Paperbacks 2004 509p pa $14.95

ISBN 0-375-50725-6 pa

LC 2003-69314

The author "presents six narratives that evoke an array of genres, from Melvillean high-seas drama to California noir and dystopian fantasy. There is a naïve clerk on a nineteenth-century Polynesian voyage; an aspiring composer who insinuates himself into the home of a syphilitic genius; a journalist investigating a nuclear plant; a publisher with a dangerous bestseller on his hands; and a cloned human being created for slave labor. These five stories are bisected and arranged around a sixth, the oral history of a post-apocalyptic island, which forms the heart of the novel. Only after this do the second halves of the stories fall into place, pulling the novel's themes into focus: the ease with which one group enslaves another, and the constant rewriting of the past by those who control the present. Against such forces, Mitchell's characters reveal a quiet tenacity." New Yorker

Mitchell, David

Number9dream; a novel. Random House 2002 400p

ISBN 0-375-50726-4

LC 2001-41910

First published 2001 in the United Kingdom

"Eiji Miyake, the young protagonist, leaves his rural Japanese home and travels to Tokyo to find the father who abandoned him years before. What begins as a fairly straightforward filial quest soon devolves into a kaleidoscopic adventure filled with Japanese mobsters and increasingly baroque futuristic scenarios. What is even more alarming, Eiji does not always maintain a firm grasp on reality. Mitchell's pyrotechnics are never less than interesting." New Yorker

Mitchell, David

★ The **thousand** autumns of Jacob de Zoet; a novel. Random House 2010 479p il $26

ISBN 978-1-4000-6545-5; 1-4000-6545-3

LC 2009-47296

"Mitchell's meticulously reconstructed the lost world of Edo-era Japan, and in doing so he's created his most conventional but most emotionally engaging novel yet: it's as if an acrobatic but show-offy performance artist, adept at mimicry, ventriloquism and cerebral literary gymnastics, had decided to do an old-fashioned play and, in the process, proved his chops as an actor." N Y Times (Late N Y Ed)

Mitchell, James C.

Lovers crossing. St. Martin's Minotaur 2003 294p $23.95

ISBN 0-312-31530-9

LC 2003-41350

"Roscoe Brinker, a Tucson-based private detective and former INS agent, left the service after being shot in the line of duty by, he suspects, a fellow agent. A local business mogul, Mo Crain, hires him to look into the murder of Crain's wife, Sandra, who worked along the border as a nurse helping abandoned and battered children. Sandra seems to have had few enemies, but as Brinker's investigation proceeds, it seems that her death might be linked to a smuggling operation, and to Henry Sanchez, the corrupt INS agent that Brinker believes shot him." Publ Wkly

"The instantly likable Brinker is full of surprises, and the secondary characters who surround him also have great depth." Booklist

Mitchell, Margaret

★ **Gone** with the wind; with a new preface by Pat Conroy and an introduction by James A. Michener. 60th Anniversary ed; Scribner 1996 959p il

ISBN 0-684-82625-9

LC 95-52609

A reissue of the title first published 1936 by Macmillan

"The proud people of the South have been subjugated in the Civil War, the dreadful period of Reconstruction has followed, and Scarlett O'Hara, beautiful and headstrong, has been reduced to poverty and near-starvation. No longer the belle of the ball, she must do whatever possible to feed herself and her family, and she does not hesitate to use feminine wiles to accomplish her ends. When she finds a man she can respect, she discovers her real feelings too late and loses him. Scarlett and her plantation home, Tara, are among the most memorable names in fiction." Shapiro. Fic for Youth. 3d edition

Mitford, Nancy

★ The **pursuit** of love & Love in a cold climate; two novels. Modern Lib. 1994 617p $19.95

ISBN 0-679-60090-6

LC 93-43632

A combined edition of two titles about the Radlett family originally published 1945 and 1949 respectively. Subsequent works about the family and its associates are The blessing (1951) and Don't tell Alfred (1960)

These quasi-autobiographical novels take a satiric look at the various social and amatory trials and triumphs of an eccentric upper-class English family following World War I

Miyamoto, Teru

Kinshu: Autumn brocade. New Directions 2005 196p $22.95

ISBN 0-8112-1633-0

LC 2005-20111

Original Japanese edition, 1982

This novel "features letters exchanged over the course of about a year between Aki Katsunuma and her ex-husband, Yasuaki Arima. Aki's initial letter stems from a chance encounter with Yasuaki over a decade after their divorce. Through their correspondence, readers discover Aki's grief in having to raise her eight-year-old mentally challenged son with her unfaithful second husband, Soichiro Katsunuma. Aki herself learns the true motives behind the suicide/murder that Yasuaki's then lover attempted, which, in an ironic twist of fate, ends her life only to save his. After Yasuaki recovers from his attack, his life is no picnic either as he learns to confront his own share of demons while striving to forge ahead. As the story progresses, the former husband and wife come to realize the cathartic properties of their letters; by learning to forgive and respect each other, they bring about a sense of closure to their relationship once and for all. Though brief, this novel features a distinctly compelling narrative; credit Thomas's effective translation." Libr J

Mizner, David

Political animal; a novel. Soho Press 2004 293p $24

ISBN 1-569-47386-2

LC 2004-11250

"Arnie Schecter ("Shecter the Protector") is running for the New York senate with the help of Director of Communications Ben Bergin. As dedicated as Bergin is to Schecter's liberal causes, he's even more zealous in his pursuit of fellow staffer Calliope Berkowitz. His concern with winning Calli's affection vastly outweighs his zeal for winning the election, and Ben idolizes Calli with a sweetly bumbling fervor that exhibits all the angst of a prepubescent youth. Not since Bridget Jones has a character parsed contemporary dating rituals with such a fine degree of anxiety and self-doubt, as Mizner uproariously captures the incipient insanity inherent in both courting and campaigning. An endearing and irreverent love story." Booklist

Mo Yan, 1955-

Life and death are wearing me out; translated from the Chinese by Howard Goldblatt. Arcade Pub. 2008 540p $29.95

ISBN 978-1-55970-853-1; 1-55970-853-0

LC 2007-22843

Original Chinese edition, 2006

This novel's protagonist is "Ximen Nao, a landowner known for his generosity and kindness and benevolence to his peasants, but who in Mao's Land Reform Movement of 1948 was . . . cruelly executed, despite his protestations of innocence. The novel opens in Hell, where Lord Yama, king of the underworld, has Ximen Nao tortured endlessly. . . . He is reborn not, alas, as a human but first as a donkey, then a horse, a pig, a monkey, and finally the big-headed boy Lan Qiansui." (Publisher's note)

"Yan's hero and chief narrator, Ximen Nao, is a former rich landowner who falls victim to Mao Zedong's Land Reform Movement. Although known as a fair and decent man, Nao loses both his land and his life to the Communist regime. Relegated to Hell, Nao is forced by Lord Yama, King of the Underworld, to be reborn, again and again, until his anger with his perceived injustice is purged from his soul. First, he reenters the world as a donkey, then, in succession, as an ox, pig, dog, and monkey, until he finally returns as a human. From the unique vantage point as an animal with some lingering human thoughts, Nao relates the life of his peasant village and its people through 50 years of economic and personal struggle. Inventing a large cast of believable people is one thing. (Yan's list of principle characters numbers 17.) To bring them vividly to mind while simultaneously fashioning a counter world of animal intelligence—the smells, sights, fears and violence implicit in the daily life of creatures—is a spectacular achievement." Seattle Times

Moberg, Vilhelm

★ The **emigrants**; a novel. translated from the Swedish by Gustaf Lannestock. Simon & Schuster 1951 366p

Original Swedish edition, 1949

This is the first volume of a cycle which tells the story of a band of Swedish emigrants to the United States. This volume tells the story in particular of one family, Karl Oskar Nilsson, his wife and children, and his young brother Robert; of their life in Sweden; and of the long, arduous journey across the Atlantic in the summer of 1850

"A novel of peasant life, drawn to the last homely and superstitious detail. It is a story of poverty and heartbreak over which human faith has its will. And it is filled with an earthly humor, the unpredictable flash of human malice and emotion which bring Mr. Moberg's characters sharply into focus." N Y Times Book Rev

Followed by Unto a good land

Moberg, Vilhelm

The **last** letter home; a novel. translated from the Swedish by Gustaf Lannestock. Simon & Schuster 1961 383p

Originally published in Sweden 1956 and 1959. Parts 3 and 4 of the author's cycle, the first of which is The emigrants and the second, Unto a good land

"It is solemn, rather slow and quietly moving. Mr. Moberg is at least as much concerned with the thoughts and emotions of his stolid characters as with the historical events of their time." Publ Wkly

Moberg, Vilhelm

Unto a good land; a novel. translated from the Swedish by Gustaf Lannestock. Simon & Schuster 1954 371p

Sequel to The emigrants

Original Swedish edition, 1952

The book "tells how farmer Karl Oskar Nilsson, his wife and children, and ten other peasants from his own parish in the province of Smaland, sailed in the brig Charlotta in the spring of 1850 to North America, landing ten weeks later at the East River Pier in New York on a sweltering June day and how, by river-boat and steam-wagon, on foot and in an ox-drawn cart, Karl Oskar and his family reach at last the shore of the Minnesota lake where out of the great trees he finds there he hews himself a home." N Y Her Trib Books

Followed by The last letter home

Modesitt, L. E.

Antiagon fire; L. E. Modesitt, Jr. 1st ed. Tor 2013 464 p. map (hardcover) $27.99

ISBN 0765334577; 9780765334572

LC 2012043364

This is the seventh book in L.E. Modesitt Jr.'s Imager Portfolio series. Here, having "nearly single-handedly annihilated the vast armies of Bovaria, . . . scholar, imager and now soldier Quaeryt receives a promotion from Lord Bhayar of Telaryn—and a new mission. Bovaria is subdued, if not entirely pacified, and Bhayar next intends to bring Khel under his dominion. . . . But to win Khel over, Quaeryt must persuade the Pharsi High Council to become a client state." (Kirkus)

Modesitt, L. E.

Archform; beauty. TOR Bks. 2002 330p $25.95

ISBN 0-7653-0433-3

LC 2001-59655

"Set against a background of biological terrorism, Modesitt's tale explores social issues . . . sure to resonate with many readers. This brilliant novel is as thought provoking as it is entertaining." Publ Wkly

Modesitt, L. E.

Imager; the first book of the imager portfolio. L.E. Modesitt, Jr. 1st ed. Tor 2009 432 p. map (Imager portfolio) (hardcover) $25.95

ISBN 0765320347; 9780765320346

LC 2008046429

This is the first book in L.E. Modesitt Jr.'s Imager series. Here, "apprentice portraitist Rhennthyl finds out the hard way that he has the magical ability called Imaging: an explosion kills his master right after Rhenn wishes for just such an event. Rhenn's ability, which allows him to form objects from thin air and slay with a glance, appears to be quite strong, and he begins training as a covert operative. Just when he starts to relax into his new career, an unknown assassin tries to kill him." (Publishers Weekly)

Modesitt, L. E.

Imager's battalion; L.E. Modesitt, Jr. 1st ed. Tor 2013 512 p. (hardcover) $27.99

ISBN 0765332833; 9780765332837

LC 2012027589

This book is the "third part of a prequel fantasy series . . . wherein wizards are known as 'imagers,' since the work involves the intense, precise and accurate visualization of the magic's objective. Previously, scholar, imager and now soldier Quaeryt almost single-handedly defeated the invasion of Telaryn by the megalomaniac Rex Kharst of Bovaria. Recognizing that the only way to bring peace is to annihilate Rex Kharst, Lord Bhayar of Telaryn orders his armies to invade Bovaria." (Kirkus)

Modesitt, L. E.

Imager's challenge; the second book of the Imager portfolio. by L.E. Modesitt, Jr. 1st ed. Tor 2009 460 p. (hardcover) $27.99

ISBN 0765321262; 9780765321268

LC 2009019454

This is the second book in L.E. Modesitt's Imager Portfolio series. Here, "still recovering from injuries received in foiling the plots of the Ferran envoy, Rhenn is preparing to take up his new duties as imager liaison to the Civic Patrol of L'Excelsis." He finds that "the Commander of the Civic Patrol doesn't want a liaison from the infamous Collegium." Further, "Rhenn receives formal notice that one of the High Holders . . . has declared his intention to destroy Rhenn and his family." (Publisher's note)

Modesitt, L. E.

Imager's intrigue; L.E. Modesitt, Jr. 1st ed. Tor 2010 495 p. map (hardcover) $27.99

ISBN 0765325624; 9780765325624

LC 2010030209

In this third installment of J.R. Modesitt's Imager series, "Rhennthyl, a powerful 'imager' (as wizards are known here) and security operative is also a captain of police, and only a little distracted by his beautiful wife Seliora and their three-year-old daughter Diestrya. But several ominous developments are stirring great unease at the Collegium Imago and among the Civil Patrol and the Council of Solidar." (Kirkus Reviews)

Modesitt, L. E.

Princeps; a novel in the Imager portfolio. by L.E. Modesitt, Jr. 1st ed. Tor 2012 496 p. map (Imager portfolio.) (hardcover) $27.99

ISBN 0765330954; 9780765330956

LC 2012001829

This fantasy novel, by L. E. Modesitt, Jr., is book 5 in "The Imager Portfolio" series. "Now second only to the governor, and still hiding his powers as an Imager, Quaeryt is enjoying his new position, as well as his marriage to Lord Bhayar's youngest sister, Vaelora, when a volcanic eruption devastates the old capital of Telaryn. He and his wife . . . must restore order to a city filled with chaos and corruption, and do so quickly." (Publisher's note)

Modesitt, L. E.

Scholar; L.E. Modesitt, Jr. Tor 2011 508p. map

ISBN 9780765329554; 0765329557

LC 2011021610

This book is "set on the world of Terahnar . . . where a handful of people have the power to create objects through visualization. . . . Telaryn's young, talented ruler, Bhayar . . . suggests to Quaeryt, a young scholar whose advice he values, that troops might be withdrawn from the occupation of Tilbor for redeployment. . . . Quaeryt allows Bhayar to persuade him to travel to Tilbor and report. Quaeryt is secretly an imager, or wizard, as well as a scholar. . . . Quaeryt arrives in Tilbor, where he finds that the governor, Rescalyn, has quietly accreted and trained an army vastly larger than anybody suspected. . . . After combing through the records, Quaeryt realizes he might need to risk his own life to uncover the truth." (Kirkus)

Modesitt, L. E.

Viewpoints critical; selected stories. [by] L.E. Modesitt, Jr. Tor 2008 350p $25.95

ISBN 978-0-7653-1857-2; 0-7653-1857-1

LC 2007-42148

This "collection of reprints dating back to 1973 and a handful of new stories displays Modesitt's breadth of experience and knowledge to great effect. . . . As in Modesitt's novels, eloquent prose and skilled characterization are evident, only slightly diminished by occasional outbreaks of slow pacing. Readers will find this an excellent showcase of a very fine writer's highest quality work." Publ Wkly

Moehringer, J. R.

Sutton; J. R. Moehringer. Hyperion 2012 334 p.

ISBN 1401323146; 9781401323141

LC 2011052473

This biographical novel, by J. R. Moehringer, tells the story of the bank robber Willie Sutton. "[I]n the first year of the twentieth century, Willie Sutton came of age at a time when banks were out of control. . . . Sutton saw only one way out, only one way to win the girl of his dreams. So began the career of America's most successful bank robber. . . . In Moehringer's retelling, it was more than need or rage at society that drove Sutton. It was one unforgettable woman." (Publisher's note)

Mofina, Rick

Every fear. Pinnacle Books/Kensington Pub. 2006 381p $6.99

ISBN 0-7860-1746-5 pa

This novel begins with a "baby's kidnapping and his mother's near-fatal hit-and-run. . . . Seattle Mirror reporter Jason Wade is on the story—pressured by an unscrupulous editor to get the story, even embellish it, if necessary. . . . Despite his digging, Jason can't find out why the hardworking, nice couple who were high school sweethearts were targeted. As the case becomes more bizarre, Jason draws on all his journalistic skills. An unusual break comes from his father, with whom Jason hasn't always had the best relationship. A recovering alcoholic and a former cop, his father also is trying to reinvent himself as a private detective. Mofina shows his strength at creating gripping plots enhanced by realistic characters and social awareness." PopMatters

Mofina, Rick

They disappeared; Rick Mofina. Harlequin 2012 379 p. $7.99

ISBN 0778313816; 9780778313816

In this novel, by Rick Mofina, "Jeff Griffin . . . and his wife, Sarah, . . . give their nine-year-old son, Cole, his dream vacation. . . . While sightseeing near Times Square, Jeff steps into a store to buy batteries for their camera--but upon returning to the street he finds that Sarah and Cole have vanished. . . . Jeff fights to rescue Sarah and Cole, . . . amid growing fears that they have become entangled in an unfolding plot that could have global consequences." (Publisher's note)

Mogford, Thomas

Shadow of the rock; Thomas Mogford. Walker & Co. 2012 261 p. (hardcover) $25

ISBN 0802779999; 9780802779991

LC 2011038765

This is the first in Thomas Mogford's series with "Spike Sanguinetti, a tax lawyer turned detective. One night in Gibraltar's Old Town, Spike runs into an old school friend, Sephardic Jew Solomon Hassan, who needs his help . . . fighting extradition to Morocco, where Solomon is wanted for the murder of Esperanza Castillo, the tattooed, multi-pierced, promiscuous stepdaughter of Ángel Castillo, co-founder of a new solar energy venture that promises billions of euros in potential revenues." (Publishers Weekly)

Mogford, Thomas

Sign of the cross; Thomas Mogford. 1st U.S. ed. Bloomsbury USA 2013 240 p. (hardcover) $25

ISBN 1620402009; 9781620402009

LC 2012049779

This is Thomas Mogford's second Spike Sanguinetti mystery. Here, "the Gibraltar lawyer scours Malta in an attempt to solve the apparent—and unexpected—murder-suicide of his uncle and aunt, David and Teresa Mifsud. Why would an aging art historian kill his wife, who devoted her life to helping African refugees?" (Publishers Weekly)

Moggach, Deborah

Tulip fever. Delacorte Press 2000 281p

ISBN 0-385-33489-3

LC 99-42048

First published 1999 in the United Kingdom

A novel set in 17th-century Amsterdam. "Moggach introduces us to the elderly Cornelis Sandvoort; his beautiful young bride, Sophia, . . . her lover, Jan, who is hired to paint the Sandvoorts' portrait; and Sophia's maid, Maria. As 'Tulip Fever' unfolds, Sophia's tentative romance with Jan gradually becomes so reckless that it is analogous to Amsterdam's obsession with tulips. Made ruthless by love, the couple plan to escape the city. . . . Moggach's book reads like a thriller: it's a novel that ponders what it means to push things too far, and keenly examines what the consequences might be." N Y Times Book Rev

Mohr, Joshua

Damascus; a novel. Two Dollar Radio 2011 206p pa $16

ISBN 978-0-9826848-9-4

LC 2011-925179

"It's 2003, and Mohr's Damascus is not the Syrian capital but a dingy Mission District bar decorated with shards of broken glass and cotton-ball clouds. Its lovable and lonely owner, Owen, feels less proud of his bar than imprisoned by it. After 18 years, he's still barely scraping by, partly because he's too generous toward his patrons. Haunting Damascus is a man called No Eyebrows, who is dying of cancer, his skin 'gray like toxic oatmeal,' and Shambles, a commitment-phobic woman who eschews intimacy by performing sexual favors in the bar's bathroom. Joining them is Byron Settles, a bitter Iraq veteran 'missing in inaction' after a parachute accident forced him to come home the moment he touched down in Bashur. Driving the story to its violent but cathartic climax is Syl, an artist who honors the fallen soldiers of the wars in Iraq and Afghanistan with an exhibition in Damascus that involves a fish slaughter." San Francisco Chron

Moloney, Susie

The **dwelling**; a novel. Atria Bks. 2003 408p $25

ISBN 0-7434-5662-9

LC 2003-276274

The house "is a character in its own right, but Moloney . . . has thankfully peopled the narrative with other well-developed characters as well, ones with such recognizable strengths and weaknesses that the reader actually cares about their outcomes. The ending is horrible but poignant and exactly fitting." Libr J

Momaday, N. Scott

The **ancient** child; a novel. Doubleday 1989 313p

LC 89-31304

"Locke Setman, a highly successful Bay Area painter, fears that he has lost touch with his 'inner child' in the process of making it big. Then, during a brief trip to Oklahoma, he meets a beautiful American Indian woman named Grey who dresses in beaded buckskin, speaks Kiowa and Nanajo like one of the elders, and has elaborate visionary conversations with the ghost of Billy the Kid. Armed with a medicine bundle and a bag of peyote buttons, Grey slowly draws Setman into a magical world of ritual that both revitalizes and transforms him. . . . A fascinating and hypnotically beautiful book that belongs in every collection of Western Americana." Libr J

Momaday, N. Scott

House made of dawn. Harper & Row 1968 212p

"Abel, a young American Indian, lives with his grandfather, observing Indian customs, until he is drafted into the army. The story covers the years 1945 to 1952, during which time Abel seems unable to find his place either in the white world, where he is driven to violence, or on the Indian reservation where he was born. The pain of being caught between two cultures is keenly felt and can be comprehended as a problem that has affected other ethnic groups." Shapiro. Fic for Youth. 3d edition

A **moment** on the edge; 100 years of crime stories by women. edited by Elizabeth George. HarperCollins 2004 540p $24.95

ISBN 0-06-058821-7

LC 2003-67608

"George here collects short mysteries by women, bracketing the 26 entries with two tales about the death of abusive husbands, written more than 80 years apart. Between them springs an entertaining assortment of locked-room murders, theatrical whodunits, white-collar-crime and detective stories, and psychological puzzlers, each headed by revealing author notes." Booklist

Monaghan, Nicola

The **killing** jar; a novel. Scribner 2007 288p $24

ISBN 978-0-7432-9968-8; 0-7432-9968-X

LC 2006-48679

First published 2006 in the United Kingdom

"The violence of The Killing Jar is often difficult, the inhumanity often unbearable, but the book rewards a reader who wants an unsparing-really, really unsparing-account of a disastrous childhood, an account that is nonetheless sensitively rendered and deceptively simple." City Paper (Baltimore)

Monette, Paul

Afterlife. Crown 1990 278p

LC 89-48754

"Despite its comic flourishes, this is a tough, painful book about gay sex and love, pursued in the valley of the shadow of AIDS. And its unrelenting descriptions of the ravages of the disease, along with its sexual details and 'talking dirty,' are surely going to make some readers uncomfortable." N Y Times Book Rev

Monfredo, Miriam Grace

Blackwater spirits. St. Martin's Press 1995 328p

LC 94-40980

A "historical mystery featuring Glynis Tryon, librarian in Seneca Falls, N.Y., in the mid-18th century. Glynis and the newly arrived doctor, a young Jewish woman from New York City, overhear a farmer voice fears for his life to Constable Cullen Stuart. Soon the farmer is fatally poisoned, and Cullen enlists Glynis's aid in talking to the farmer's angry widow, who suggests her husband's murder will be followed by others." Publ Wkly

Monfredo, Miriam Grace

The **stalking** horse. Berkley Prime Crime 1998 340p

ISBN 0-425-15783-0

LC 97-21547

This historical mystery is "set just after Lincoln's presidential election. The Southern states are calling for secession and there is talk of war. Bronwyn Llyr, the niece of Seneca Falls, NY, librarian Glynis Tryon, has left school and taken a job as an operative with the Pinkerton Detective Agency. Her first assignment is to accompany a railroad owner to Alabama and learn about possible plans to confiscate the train line. Bronwyn accidentally overhears a conversation about

a secret plan called Equus, which she correctly fears is an assassination plot." SLJ

The author "ably mixes real-life figures with her own creations into an engaging brew that combines solid historical research with a fast-moving plot." Publ Wkly

Moning, Karen Marie

The **immortal** highlander. Delacorte Press 2004 267p $15

ISBN 0-385-33825-2

LC 2004-40764

"For eons Adam Black has aided humanity and meddled in its affairs, much to the chagrin of the queen of the Seelie Court. He has finally pushed her too far and finds himself, a once powerful Fae, invisible and very human. But he is still as resourceful as ever, and finds a way to reach the queen and plea to have his curse lifted with the help of a young lawyer, Gabrielle O'Callaghan, a human born with the ability to see his kind. As old enemies yearn to take advantage of his weakened state, threatening his life and all existence, Adam discovers that Gabrielle threatens a heart he never thought he had." Booklist

Monsarrat, Nicholas

★ The **cruel** sea. Knopf 1951 509p

"The Compass Rose is a British corvette commissioned to convoy duty and to the hunting of German U-boats during World War II. First Mate Lockhart and Skipper Erikson develop a close relationship. When their ship is sunk and few of the crew survive, Lockhart and Erikson team up again on a new ship, undaunted by the experiences visited upon them by the cruel sea." Shapiro. Fic for Youth. 3d edition

Moody, Bill

Looking for Chet Baker; an Evan Horne mystery. Walker & Co. 2002 253p $23.95

ISBN 0-8027-3368-9

LC 2001-56772

In London, jazz pianist and amateur sleuth Evan Horne "meets an old friend, Ace Buffington. An English professor who needs to publish one more book to achieve tenure, Ace wants Horne to help him research real-life jazz great Chet Baker. . . . Horne has no interest in more detective work, but when he gets to Amsterdam, he discovers that Ace has disappeared. Since the police express little interest in finding the missing professor, Horne is obliged to go looking for his buddy himself. Ace's trail parallels that of Chet Baker's last days, so Horne has to learn a lot more about Baker, his legendary talent, his tragic addiction to drugs. Moody does a wonderful job of re-creating the man and his times." Publ Wkly

Chet Baker selected discography

Moody, David

Hater. Thomas Dunne Books 2009 281p $21.95

ISBN 978-0-312-38483-8; 0-312-38483-1

LC 2008-36519

First published 2006 in the United Kingdom

"The novel moves at a deliberate, relentless pace, feeding readers just enough information to keep them perplexed and paranoid, and the depiction of a society being rent at the seams by violence rings true. Moody creates some truly chilling scenes, but there are also flashes of black comedy. At times savagely brutal—the moments of outrageous violence may be considered over-the-top by some readers—but engrossing and effective." Kirkus

Moody, Rick

The **diviners**; a novel. Rick Moody. Little, Brown 2005 567 p. (hbk.) o.p.; (pbk.) $14.99
ISBN 0316085391; 9780316013277
LC 2005003823
This book traces "the exploits of Vanessa 'Minivan' Meandro, an overweight, pathologically cruel film-and-television producer, and her attempts to produce a 13-part miniseries about diviners . . . [and] follows the tangentially connected stories of at least a dozen characters around the time of the 2000 [U.S. Presidential] election recount. Vanessa has no idea who authored the treatment or the novel the miniseries is supposedly based on; her accountant absconds with her production company's funds; her mother suffers delusions brought on by nonstop drinking. Meanwhile, a second-rate action film star is making demands, a television executive has a perversion for young, handicapped girls and a bike messenger may have murdered the gallery curator who touted his art as genius." (Publishers Weekly)

Moody, Rick

The **four** fingers of death; a novel. Little, Brown and Co. 2010 672p $25.99
ISBN 978-0-316-11891-0; 0-316-11891-5
LC 2009-40756
"Moody dedicates this sprawling novel, about a detached human arm infected with a killer bacteria incubated on Mars, to the memory of Kurt Vonnegut, and Vonnegut's influence is visible throughout—in the metafictional narrative, sci-fi touchstones, and depiction of a dystopian future characterized by enfeebling consumerism. Purporting to be the novelization of the remake of a 1963 B movie, 'The Crawling Hand,' written by a fictional author, Montese Crandall, the novel gives voice to various characters: a lovelorn astronaut, a Korean stem-cell scientist, and a Marxism-spouting chimpanzee. Postmodern gymnastics aside, the book is entertaining and often poignant, probing the limits of technology, consciousness, and language in the face of grief." New Yorker

Moody, Rick

Right livelihoods; three novellas. Little, Brown 2007 223p $23.99
ISBN 978-0-316-16634-8; 0-316-16634-0
LC 2006-26937
"In 'The Omega Force,' a tale rife with satirical meaning, the patriotic doctor defending the security of his domain against people who are 'dark-complected' turns out to be a lunatic. Paranoia is also evident in 'K&K' as an office manager finds some dissident messages in the company's suggestion box and suspects a conspiracy. The third, 'The Albertine Notes,' introduces an amateur journalist who, while researching the drug issue for a porno magazine, falls victim to drug culture and suffers from hallucinations that New York City is being obliterated. The unreliable and eccentric characters that so often populate Moody's novels again effectively remind us of the nation's collective hysteria. His

convoluted narrative may challenge the patience of some readers, but those who persist will find it rewarding." Libr J

Moon, Elizabeth

Moon flights; with an introduction by Anne McCaffrey. Night Shade Books 2007 272p $24.95
ISBN 978-1-59780-109-6; 978-1-59780-108-9
"Fans of the Chicks in Chainmail anthology series will enjoy 'And Ladies of the Club' and three other tales of the intrepid females of the Ladies' Aid and Armor Society. . . . The heart of the collection is 'Politics,' a story of young soldiers serving a questionable authority; it sums up many of Moon's themes, from honor and family to being true to oneself. Readers who only know Moon's novels will be thrilled to learn that her short stories are equally entertaining and thoughtful." Publ Wkly

Moon, Elizabeth

Once a hero. Baen Pub. Enterprises 1997 400p
ISBN 0-671-87769-0
LC 96-48176
"Moon's mastery of contemporary science fiction is evident in every line. The characters spring to life on the page, the intricacies of societies are astutely explored, and the pace never flags." Booklist

Moon, Elizabeth

The **speed** of dark. Del Rey Bks. 2002 340p $23.95
ISBN 0-345-44755-7
LC 2002-20771
"Moon is effective at putting the reader inside Lou's mind, and it is both fascinating and painful to see the behavior and qualities of so-called normals through his eyes." Booklist

Mooney, Ted

The **same** river twice. Alfred A. Knopf 2010 361p $24.95
ISBN 978-0-307-27273-7; 0-307-27273-7
LC 2009-41691
The novel "succeeds on a number of different levels: as a page-turning mystery in which conceptual art meets the scientific vanguard of stem-cell research and as a meditation on the trusts and betrayals of marriage, on truth and illusion and the relation of each to artistic creativity." Kirkus

Moor, Margriet de

The **storm**; a novel. translated by Carol Brown Janeway. Alfred A. Knopf 2010 257p $25.95
ISBN 978-0-307-26494-7
LC 2009-37578
Original Dutch edition, 2005
"In the winter of 1953, hurricane-driven flood waters rushing in from the North Sea destroyed dikes and obliterated an entire province in the southwestern Netherlands. . . . De Moor observes this disaster from the juxtaposed viewpoints of two sisters—young wife and mother Lidy and her virginal younger sibling Armanda. When Armanda offers to take Lidy's two-year-old daughter Nadja to a party, in exchange for Lidy's appearance at a similar event held for Armanda's godchild—for the sisters resemble each other so

closely, few people can tell them apart—they also exchange destinies. Lidy travels to the imminently endangered seaside town of Zierkezee, while Armanda becomes companion for the day to Nadja and her father (and Lidy's husband) Sjoerd. . . . It's hard to resist using the word 'symphonic' to describe this exquisitely composed, piercingly moving story. De Moor continues to scale increasingly impressive heights." Kirkus

Moorcock, Michael

★ An **alien** heat; volume one of a trilogy The dancers at the end of time. Harper & Row 1973 158p (Dancers at the end of time)

First published 1972 in the United Kingdom

This novel "is set near the end of the world, when Earth is populated by hedonistic immortals who restructure continents and their own bodies at whim. A young man named Jhereck becomes unfashionably obsessed with Mrs. Amelia Underwood, a time traveler from the 19th century, his favorite period. He follows her to London of 1896, where he is tried for murder and hanged, which somehow returns him to the future, sans Amelia but with insights into love and the true human condition. This tale could be called an Art Nouveau morality play or a science fiction comedy of manners. The humor is genuine, the style lush but controlled." Libr J

Followed by The hollow lands

Moorcock, Michael

The **best** of Michael Moorcock; edited by John Davey with Ann & Jeff VanderMeer. Tachyon Publications 2009 403p pa $14.95

ISBN 978-1-892391-86-5; 1-892391-86-4

"One of the progenitors of the sword-and-sorcery genre as well as the New Wave literary sf movement, Moorcock crosses genres, bends boundaries, and breaks rules as only a master storyteller can. This important contribution to the author's oeuvre contains variant versions and some previously uncollected stories." Libr J

Moorcock, Michael

The **dreamthief's** daughter; a tale of the albino. Warner Bks. 2001 343p $35

ISBN 0-446-52618-5

LC 00-43836

"In this latest installment in his multivolume saga of the Eternal Champion, Moorcock . . . teams his favorite hero, the melancholy albino swordsman Elric of Melniboné, with Count Ulric von Bek, the last in a line of German noblemen. . . . War is in the offing, and Hitler, having learned that the von Bek family may own both an enchanted sword and the Holy Grail itself, sends SS Major Gaynor von Minct to take possession of these mystical relics so they may be used to further the cause of the Third Reich. Von Bek and Gaynor, however, are merely the current earthly avatars of the Eternal Champion and one of his greatest foes; they are knights fighting in the causes, respectively, of Chaos and Law, in innumerable, gorgeously described, alternate realities." Publ Wkly

Moorcock, Michael

The **end** of all songs; volume three of a trilogy The dancers at the end of time. Harper & Row 1976 271p (Dancers at the end of time)

"Moorcock wraps up his Dancers at the End of Time trilogy with a volume that . . . brings together the two central characters—Jhereck Carnelian, one of the hedonistic immortals who dwell at the End of Time, and Mrs. Amelia Underwood, a reluctant time traveler from Victorian England. Although their reunion is a cause for celebration, the fabric of time has been ruptured, threatening to plunge all into disordered chronological gulfs. Even the inhabitants at the End of Time—an amoral, whimsical, all-but-thoughtless, utterly powerful, and thoroughly likable lot—know concern for the first time in their immortal lives." Booklist

Moorcock, Michael

The **hollow** lands; volume two of a trilogy The dancers at the end of time. Harper & Row 1974 182p (Dancers at the end of time)

In this volume "jaded Jhereck Carnelian is back in his futuristic world after narrowly escaping being hanged in 1896 London while on a time trip with Mrs. Amelia Underwood. He's bored with his life of instant gratification and wants to return to his Victorian lady, but he can't find a working time machine anywhere. Until he falls into a pit full of never-aging children and a robot nurse shoots him back to 1896. Lost in London, he luckily stumbles on Frank Harris and H. G. Wells at the Cafe Royale, and they help reunite him with Amelia." Publ Wkly

Followed by The end of all songs

Moorcock, Michael

The **skrayling** tree; the albino in America. Warner Bks. 2003 330p $24.95

ISBN 0-446-53104-9

LC 2002-27247

"The tale's power stems largely from the astounding lyricism of the author's prose, the only flaw being the sometimes stilted and overly expository dialogue about the nature of the Multiverse." Publ Wkly

Moore, Alison

The **Lighthouse**; Alison Moore. Salt Publishing 2012 183 p. (paperback) $9.17; (ebook) $15.82

ISBN 1907773177; 9781907773174; 9780857869968

Man Booker Prize Shortlist (2012)

This book by Alison Moore was longlisted for the Man Booker prize. "Its Anglo-German protagonist, Futh, takes a walking holiday on the continent to recover from the break-up of his marriage. But as his story unfolds -- a series of memories nested like Russian dolls -- we soon see that what's really under his skin is his mother's decision to leave him and his father some 30 years earlier." (Guardian)

Moore, Brian

★ **Black** robe; a novel. Dutton 1985 246p

LC 84-21222

"Each culture is seen whole, with intelligence and sympathy, and considering the clichés that prevail about both Indians and priests, that alone makes 'Black Robe' special." N Y Times Book Rev

Moore, Brian

★ **Cold** heaven; a novel. Holt, Rinehart & Winston 1983 265p

LC 82-18720

"What begins as an extravagant thriller becomes a metaphysical story of a woman's struggle to regain control of her life. . . . The religious view that Moore expresses here is rarely found in fiction; it has the same kind of freshness that Alaric brought to Rome. 'Cold Heaven's' spell derives from its author's skill at preparing a most meticulously realistic field in which he plants two uncanny seeds—just to see what the effect will be." Newsweek

Moore, Brian

★ The **lonely** passion of Judith Hearne. Little, Brown 1956 223p

First published 1955 in the United Kingdom with title: Judith Hearne

"Judith Hearne is a middle-aged spinster whose plain looks and loneliness make her depressed and increasingly isolated from any social contact. The other renters in her Belfast boarding house disdain her. Only Mrs. O'Neill, an old school friend, treats her kindly. When her landlady's brother, Jim Madden, returns from America, he pays some attention to Judith, thinking she has money. Jim's bad character is revealed in many ways, including a sexual attack on a young housemaid, and Judith finds more and more solace in drinking. Her pathetic world falls apart completely when even her religious faith deserts her. This sad novel presents a portrait of despair that is almost unbearable." Shapiro. Fic for Youth. 3d edition

Moore, Brian

The **statement**. Dutton 1996 250p

ISBN 0-525-94128-2

LC 95-43885

"'The Statement' is a book to be read in one sitting. A straightforward shocker, a psychological thriller, a chase and travelogue through France, a religio-political conundrum—any way you take it, this is first-class fare." N Y Times Book Rev

Moore, Christopher

A **dirty** job; a novel. Morrow 2006 387p il $24.95

ISBN 0-06-059027-0

LC 2005-57501

"Much of the pleasure of Moore's tale resides not only in the ingeniously unpredictable events but also in the prickly vitality of his language. Striking figures of speech . . . and aphorisms grace the text." Washington Post Book World

Moore, Christopher

Fluke; or, I know why the winged whale sings. Morrow 2003 321p $23.95; pa $13.95

ISBN 0-380-97841-5; 0-06-056668-X pa

LC 2002-43231

"Nate Quinn spends his time in the waters off Maui researching whales. . . . One day, when photographing the tail of one particular whale to determine its size, Nate spies foot-high letters on the underside spelling out, 'Bite Me.' . . . When Nate finds the group's offices plundered and all of the data either stolen or ruined, the scientists are thrown into the beginning of a bizarre plot complete with . . . scientific explanations, potential alien conspiracies, and well-rounded, hilarious characters." Voice Youth Advocates

Moore, Christopher, 1957-

Sacre bleu; a comedy d'art. Christopher Moore. HarperCollins 2012

ISBN 006177975X; 0061779741; 9780061779756; 9780061779749

LC 2012009804

In this novel, "[a]n aspiring painter and unabashed romantic joins the greatest artists of the age in chasing his muse across fin de siècle-era France. . . . The story surrounds the mysterious suicide of Vincent van Gogh, who famously shot himself in a French wheat field only to walk a mile to a doctor's house. The mystery . . . is blue: specifically the exclusive ultramarine pigment that accents pictures created by the likes of Michelangelo and van Gogh. To find the origin of the hue, [Christopher] Moore brings on Lucien Lessard, a baker, aspiring artist and lover of Juliette, the brunette beauty who breaks his heart. After van Gogh's death, Lucien joins up with the diminutive force of nature Henri Toulouse-Lautrec to track down the inspiration behind the Sacré Bleu." (Kirkus)

Moore, Christopher

You suck; a love story. Morrow 2007 208p $21.95

ISBN 978-0-06-059029-1; 0-06-059029-7

Moore "manages, despite figures like a blue-painted prostitute who prompts visions of sex with a Smurf, to keep the book's eccentricity in check and its screwball antics from becoming insufferable. As with his best work, there's a fundamental sweetness beneath the antics." N Y Times (Late N Y Ed)

Moore, Edward Kelsey

The **Supremes** at Earl's all-you-can-eat; by Edward Kelsey Moore. 1st ed. Alfred A. Knopf 2013 320 p. (hardcover) $24.95

ISBN 0307959929; 9780307959928

LC 2012028743

This debut novel from Edward Kelsey Moore tells the "story of a trio of women nicknamed the Supremes in small-town Indiana—Odette, Clarice, and Barbara Jean. . . . From high school on, through marriages and children, the three friends regularly get together with their husbands at Earl's All-You-Can-Eat (the first black-owned business in Plainview) to see and be seen, share gossip, and help each other through bad times." (Library Journal)

Moore, Graham

★ The **Sherlockian**. Twelve 2010 350p $24.95

ISBN 978-0-446-57259-0; 0-446-57259-4

LC 2010-09554

"Thanks to the sly self-awareness that keeps "The Sherlockian" smart and agile, it's possible to enjoy this book's laughable affectations and still be seduced by them. This is a novel by, for and about Holmes-quoting mystery nuts, and it understands what makes them happy." N Y Times (Late N Y Ed)

Moore, Jeffrey

The **extinction** club; by Jeffrey Moore. Arcade Publishing 2013 372 p. (alk. paper) $23.95

ISBN 1611458374; 9781611458374

LC 2013003100

In this novel by Jefferey Moore "Nile Nightingale is on the run [after] he has just witnessed a body drop. [It] turns out to be fifteen-year-old Céleste Jonquères, who has been beaten and slashed. Animal rights activists, Céleste and her beloved grandmother have taken on a vicious poaching ring . . . with the collusion of corrupt rangers and police. Now that Nile has saved Céleste . . ., the poachers . . . have taken notice and are cautiously, but inexorably, closing in." (Publisher's note)

Moore, Kate

Sexy Lexy; Kate Moore. Love Spell/Dorchester Pub. Co. 2005 324p. (pbk.) o.p.

ISBN 0505526239

LC 2005574671

In this book, "[w]hen her married friends complain to athletic Lexy Clark that they no longer have the time or energy to exercise or make love, she writes a book about how to get a good workout on the marriage bed, killing two birds with one stone, so to speak. 'Workout Sex: A Girl's Guide to Home Fitness' succeeds beyond her wildest dreams. Known across the country as Sexy Lexy, she is the focus of rampant media attention. Determined to stay out of the limelight, she purchases an inn in a Brigadoon-like setting: no more cable, cell phone, or Internet, and no more workout clothes. When she meets Sam Worth, fine physical specimen and handyman, they begin a no-strings affair against her better judgment, each keeping secrets from the other." (Booklist)

Moore, Kate

To seduce an angel. Berkley Sensation 2011 304 p.

ISBN 9780425243695 pa

This book tells the story of "the vindictive Duke of Wenlocke's heir, Kit Jones, Marquess Daventry, [who] is still on guard against his grandfather, the Duke, and hasn't forgotten the abandoned boys he has taken under his wing. But when he hires Emma Portland to tutor the lads, Kit has no idea that she has been blackmailed by his embittered grandfather into spying on him." (Libr J)

Moore, Lisa

February. Black Cat 2010 310p pa $14.95

ISBN 978-0-8021-7070-5; 0-8021-7070-6

First published 2009 in Canada

This is the account "account of how one ordinary Newfoundland family carries on after the Ocean Ranger disaster, the infamous sinking of the offshore oil rig on Valentine's Day, 1982, that killed all 84 men aboard, including the fictional Cal O'Mara. Cal leaves behind his wife, Helen, and four children, one of whom is just a twinkle in her dead father's eye that night. (Not even Helen knows she's pregnant yet.) How Helen manages on her own, and doesn't, and the effect the loss of his father has on John, Cal and Helen's firstborn, 10 in 1982, amounts to a meditation on grief. . . . Moore offers us, elegantly, exultantly, the very consciousness of her characters." Globe and Mail

Moore, Lorrie

Birds of America. Knopf 1998 291p

ISBN 0-679-44597-8

LC 98-6144

"These stories chart the intersection of the ridiculous and the tragic. . . . Moore peers into America's loneliest perches, but her delicate touch turns absurdity into a warming vitality." New Yorker

Moore, Lorrie

A **gate** at the stairs; a novel. Alfred A. Knopf 2009 321p $25.95

ISBN 978-0-375-40928-8; 0-375-40928-9

LC 2009-03091

"The novel concludes in a tone of wan hope, with Tassie wiser and stronger, though forever sadder. . . . This book is—not above all, but in the service of all—funny. Moore is not shy about the bad joke, and never pushes a great one too far. Her humor, always pointed at insight and elaboration, strikes the perfect balance between taste and feeling." PopMatters

Moore, Meg Mitchell

So far away; a novel. Meg Mitchell Moore. Reagan Arthur Books 2012 322 p.

ISBN 0316097691; 9780316097697

LC 2011051322

This novel by Meg Mitchell Moore follows "thirteen-year-old Natalie Gallagher [who] is trying to escape. . . . Adrift, confused, she is a girl trying to find her way in a world that seems to either neglect or despise her. Her salvation arrives in an unlikely form: Bridget O'Connell, an Irish maid working for a wealthy Boston family. The catch? Bridget lives only in the pages of a dusty old 1920s diary Natalie unearthed in her mother's basement." (Publisher's note)

Moore, Susanna, 1948-

The **big** girls. Alfred A. Knopf 2007 224p $24

ISBN 978-1-4000-4190-9; 1-4000-4190-2

LC 2006-48819

"Set in a women's prison on the Hudson River, Moore's sixth novel chronicles the aftermath of a highly publicized murder and its impact on four intertwined lives. The story is told in the alternating voices of Helen, who has long suffered terrifying schizophrenic hallucinations and is serving a life sentence for killing her two small children; Helen's psychiatrist, a single mother who came to work at the prison out of guilt over a patient's suicide; a corrections officer who becomes involved with the psychiatrist; and an ambitious Hollywood star whom Helen believes to be her sister. Moore gradually probes Helen's psychosis to its horrifying origins, while also delivering a nuanced and devastating account of the fights, rapes, and alliances built from necessity that constitute prison life." New Yorker

Moore, Susanna, 1948-

The **life** of objects; Susanna Moore. Alfred A. Knopf 2012 239 p.

ISBN 0307268438; 9780307268433

LC 2012019890

This novel, by Susanna Moore, takes place "in 1938. . . . Seventeen-year-old Beatrice, . . . finds herself . . . whisked away . . . to join the Berlin household of Felix and Dorothea Metzenburg. . . . But Germany has launched its campaign of aggression across Europe, and . . . the conflict reaches the Metzenburgs' threshold. . . . Beatrice, . . . bears heart-rending witness to the atrocities of the age and to the human capacity for strength in the face of irrevocable loss." (Publisher's note)

Morais, Richard C.

The **hundred**-foot journey; a novel. Scribner 2010 245p $23

ISBN 978-1-4391-6564-5; 1-4391-6564-5

LC 2009-50619

An earlier edition of this work was originally published in India in 2008

"A lovely little book, something sweet, savory, if not dense, agreeable to all, ambitious about food, if not necessarily about plot or character. Sometimes readers yearn for a feast of a book. Other times, a tasty morsel will do." Philadelphia Inquirer

Moran, Michelle

Madame Tussaud; Michelle Moran. Crown Publishers 2011 xii, 448p.p map

ISBN 9780307588654; 9780307588661

LC 2010035785

This work of historical fiction follows Marie Tussaud, who "has learned the secrets of wax sculpting by working alongside her uncle in their celebrated wax museum, the Salon de Cire. . . . Her customers hail from every walk of life, yet her greatest dream is to attract the attention of Marie Antoinette and Louis XVI. . . . After months of anticipation, Marie learns that the royal family is willing to come and see their likenesses. When they finally arrive, the king's sister is so impressed that she requests Marie's presence at Versailles as a royal tutor in wax sculpting. It is a request Marie knows she cannot refuse—even if it means time away from her beloved Salon and her increasingly dear friend, Henri Charles. . . . Meanwhile, many resent the vast separation between rich and poor. In salons and cafés across Paris, people like . . . Maximilien Robespierre are lashing out against the monarchy. Soon, there's whispered talk of revolution. . . . Will Marie be able to hold on to both the love of her life and her friendship with the royal family as France approaches civil war?" (Publisher's note)

Moran, Michelle

The **second** empress; a novel of Napoleon's court. Michelle Moran. Crown Publishers 2012 312 p. $25.00

ISBN 0307953033; 9780307953032; 9780307953056

LC 2012017691

This historical novel, by Michelle Moran, is set "under the rule of Emperor Napoleon Bonaparte as he casts aside his . . . wife to marry a Hapsburg princess he hopes will bear him a royal heir. . . . When Marie-Louise . . . is told that the Emperor has demanded her hand in marriage, . . . [she faces] a terrible choice: marry the cruel, capricious Napoleon, leaving the man she loves and her home forever, or say no, and plunge her country into war." (Publisher's note)

Moravia, Alberto

Two friends; I due amici. translated by Marina Harss; edited by Simone Casini; introduction by Thomas Erling Peterson. Other Press 2011 327p pa $18.95

ISBN 978-1-59051-336-1; 1-59051-336-3

LC 2011-13258

Original Italian edition, 2007

"Readers are offered an extraordinary view of [Moravia's] unique literary process as his characters come to life and he builds a disturbing story of politics, romance, and passion gone terribly wrong." Italian Tribune

Moravia, Alberto

★ **Two** women; translated from the Italian by Angus Davidson. Farrar, Straus & Giroux 1958 339p

"Through his description of the brutal, dehumanizing forces of war we see Moravia's belief that man is man because he suffers most cogently illustrated. This novel is also probably the most poignant expression of Moravia's view of the human condition." Ency of World Lit in the 20th century

Morgan, C. E.

All the living. Farrar, Straus and Giroux 2008 208p $23

ISBN 978-0-374-10362-0; 0-374-10362-3

LC 2008-13854

"Aloma, the 21-year-old protagonist of C.E. Morgan's debut novel, doesn't appear to have a whole lot going for her. An orphan whose guardians farmed her out to a mission school before her 12th birthday, she's never lived in a house, is poorly educated and has no family to speak of. Romanced by a young tobacco farmer from Kentucky hill country, Aloma falls in love as only a young woman with so little life experience can. When Orren invites her to quit her job teaching piano at the mission school and live with him on his family's broken-down farm after his widowed mother and brother are killed in a car accident, she packs up what little she has and moves in. Thus sets the stage for a quiet but undeniably moving story about loss and desire, and how to reconcile the two." Edmonton J

Morgan, Richard K.

Altered carbon. Del Rey Bks. 2003 375p pa $13.95

ISBN 0-345-45768-4

LC 2002-31165

"In the 25th century, it's difficult to die a final death. Humans are issued a cortical stack, implanted into their bodies, into which consciousness is 'digitized' and from which—unless the stack is hopelessly damaged—their consciousness can be downloaded ('resleeved') with its memory intact, into a new body. While the Vatican is trying to make resleeving (at least of Catholics) illegal, centuries-old aristocrat Laurens Bancroft brings Takeshi Kovacs (an Envoy, a specially trained soldier used to being resleeved and trained to soak up clues from new environments) to Earth, where Kovacs is resleeved into a cop's body to investigate Bancroft's first mysterious, stack-damaging death." Publ Wkly

First published 2002 in the United Kingdom

A "seamless marriage of hardcore cyberpunk and hard-boiled detective tale." Times (London, England)

Morgan, Richard K.

Broken angels. Del Rey Bks. 2004 366p pa $14.95

ISBN 0-345-45771-4 pa

LC 2003-62515

This novel "is clearly the work of a gifted, ambitious storyteller. Morgan's prose is clean and direct, his characters almost uniformly hard-edged, his future convincing, well conceived and decked out with an almost limitless array of technological marvels." Washington Post Book World

Morgan, Richard K.

Thirteen. Del Rey 2007 544p $24.95

ISBN 978-0-345-48525-0; 0-345-48525-4

LC 2007-10617

Published in the United Kingdom with title: Black man

"For all that Morgan steps outside some of the usual conventions he is still recognisably working in the format and [Thirteen] comes with some of its bad habits. . . . Morgan's approach is problematic but at the same time it is so utterly different to anything else ou there that it is almost impossible not to admire it." Strange Horizons

Morgan-Jones, Chris

★ The **jackal's** share; Chris Morgan Jones. The Penguin Press 2013 336 p. $25.95

ISBN 1594205353; 9781594205354

LC 2012039511

Sequel to: The silent oligarch (2012)

This book is part of Chris Morgan Jones's Ben Webster series. Here, Webster works for the corporate investigation company, Ikertu Consulting. Darius Qazai, London-based refugee Iranian owner of Tabriz Asset Management, needs their services" to determine why a business deal fell through. "A . . . phone call unearths the rat: rumors circulate that Qazai was responsible for the theft of the Sargon relief, a half-ton eighth-century Assyrian stone art object looted from Baghdad post-invasion." (Kirkus)

Morgenstern, Erin

The **night** circus. Doubleday 2010 387 p. $26.95

ISBN 978-0-385-53463-5; 0-385-53463-9; 9780385534635

LC 2010050546

Alex Award (2012), RUSA Reading List: Fantasy (2012)

In this book "two magicians of indefinite but certainly magically long lifespan - one a public performer named Prospero the Enchanter, aka Hector Bowen; the other known only as 'the man in the grey suit' or 'Mr. A. H---' - are engaged in a profound rivalry, played out over many generations by appointed pupils. In the late 19th century, Bowen elects his six-year-old daughter Celia, while his counterpart chooses a nameless nine-year-old orphan who will be called Marco Alisdair. These two are bound into a lifelong challenge, the parameters of which are never fully explained to them; and for years they do not know their adversaries. The circus . . . is also the creation of Marco and Celia, both of who, over the years, become passionately embroiled in its performances and acts, as well as, inevitably, with each other." (The Guardian)

"The plot follows the separate and then intertwining lives of Celia and Marco, both forced to spend their lives pitting their unusual talents against each other in a cruel competition. But their world is Morgenstern's most vivid creation, a fantastical circus featuring illusionists whose powers transcend mere sleight of hand; like those performers, the author entices her audience to suspend disbelief and rewards its members with captivating pleasure." People

Moriarty, Laura

The **center** of everything. Hyperion 2003 291p $22.95; pa $14

ISBN 1-401-30031-6; 0-7868-8845-8 pa

LC 2002-32898

"Any map clearly shows that Kansas is the center of everything. Ten-year-old Evelyn Bucknow notices it on every map that she sees and truly believes that is where she belongs—in the center. Unfortunately, Evelyn is forced to parent her mother, a flighty, unrealistically romantic woman who is having an affair with her married boss. . . . Fortunately, Evelyn takes the events of her life and her mother's life and learns her lessons, with a few glitches along the way. Young people will find Evelyn appealing and real despite the book's setting in the age of Ronald Reagan and big hair, and they will respond positively to her determination." Voice Youth Advocates

Moriarty, Liane

What Alice forgot. Amy Einhorn Books 2011 426p $24.95

ISBN 978-0-399-15718-9; 0-399-15718-2

LC 2011002904

First published 2009 in Australia

"Alice's journey of reconciling herself to how her life came to be what it is, and her slowly building understanding of how the threads of her marriage began to unravel, is moving, well-paced, and thoroughly pleasurable." Publ Wkly

Morley, Isla

Come Sunday. Sarah Crichton Books/Farrar, Straus and Giroux 2008 322p $25

ISBN 978-0-374-12687-2; 0-374-12687-9

LC 2008-38829

"Although true resolution is far from sure, Come Sunday, organized by portions of the liturgical year, ends with Ascension Day. It's a hopeful note that promises redemption." Christianity Today

Morrell, David, 1943-

The **brotherhood** of the rose; a novel. St. Martin's Press 1984 353p

LC 83-21324

"Though Morrell's tale is thoroughly incredible, its engaging protagonists, whirlwind pace, and heartstopping action scenes make it an adventure of great cinematic appeal." Booklist

Morrell, David, 1943-

Murder as a fine art; David Morrell. Mulholland Books/Little, Brown and Co. 2013 368 p. $25.99

ISBN 0316216798; 9780316216791

LC 2012020034

Author David Morrell tells a mystery story about a serial killer in London, England. "Thomas De Quincey . . . is the prime suspect in a series of horrific murders that paralyze London. The killer seems to be imitating De Quincey's true-crime essay 'On Murder Considered as One of the Fine Arts.' Desperate to prevent more atrocities but crippled by opium addiction, De Quincey is aided by his brilliant daughter, Emily, as well as two determined Scotland Yard detectives." (Publisher's note)

Morrell, David, 1943-
Scavenger. Vanguard Press 2007 349p
ISBN 1-593154-41-0; 978-1-593154-41-7
LC 2006-37662
This thriller features ex-cop Frank Balenger, who was first introduced in Creepers (2005). Frank and his lover Amanda, "the only survivors of an incident at the Paragon Hotel, are swept into a deadly situation by a devious video game designer. Amanda is kidnapped, and while Frank searches for her, she is forced to search for a geocached time capsule in a Roanoke-like town in Wyoming. Told in near real time, the novel is fraught with tension and ever-ratcheting suspense." Libr J

Morris, Bob
Baja Florida. Minotaur Books 2010 242p $24.99
ISBN 978-0-312-37726-7; 0-312-37726-6
LC 2009-34522
"Morris' affection for the Bahamas shines as he showcases the islands' history and scenery and gives an insider's view of the hidden Bahamas — and its residents — that tourists never see. . . . Zack is an appealing hero, an all-around nice guy until those he cares about are threatened. 'Baja Florida' works as a nail-biting thriller as well as a novel about loyalty and friendship." South Florida Sun-Sentinel

Morris, Keith Lee
The dart league king. Tin House Books 2008 270p pa $14.95
ISBN 978-0-9794198-8-1; 0-9794198-8-3
LC 2008-20391
This novel "follows five characters through a handful of hours culminating in a dart contest on a Thursday night in Garnet Lake, Idaho: Russell Harmon, who lives for the dart league and his cocaine habit; teammate Tristan Mackey, who is haunted by having not prevented the drowning of a classmate; Kelly Ashton, who wants desperately for someone to rescue her and her young daughter from this small town; Russell's darts rival Brice Habersham, a DEA agent posing as the owner of a gas station; and drug dealer Vince Thompson, who, tonight, is carrying a 9mm Beretta to his meeting with Russell." Publ Wkly

"A dark and deeply involving novel with a haunting moment on just about every page. Suspenseful, gritty, great." McSweeney's

Morris, Mary McGarry
A dangerous woman. Viking 1991 358p
ISBN 0-670-83699-0
LC 90-50405
"Martha Horgan, the emotionally disabled protagonist, was gang-raped as a teenager; now, 15 years later, her life is finally flowing smoothly. She has moved away from her cold, domineering aunt and has a job at the cleaners, a room in a boarding house, even a worshipful admirer in Wesley Mount, the town mortician. But someone has been stealing from the till and 'Marthorgan' as her taunters call her, gets canned. Back at her aunt's place she is seduced by the caretaker, a frustrated, manipulative writer, and then must suffer through his affair with her aunt." Libr J

"Morris performs one of the most difficult writing tasks, creating a character crazy enough to be interesting but sane enough to describe her own dilemma." Time

Morris, Mary McGarry
Fiona Range. Viking 2000 418p
ISBN 0-670-89156-8
LC 99-87724
"The characters have weirdly varying powers of perception, and that keeps the juggled plots in the air, but it doesn't matter if you guess the gothic family secrets: this author is the literary equivalent of Spanish fly." New Yorker

Morris, Mary McGarry
The lost mother. Viking 2005 274p $23.95
ISBN 0-670-03389-8
LC 2004-57170
This novel tells the "story of 12-year-old Thomas and eight-year-old Margaret. . . . Reduced to living in a tent in Vermont during the Depression, the children and their father, Henry Talcott, a butcher who must travel daily seeking work, are barely surviving their abandonment by the children's reluctant mother. The shattered family aches with the desire to bring home beautiful, troubled Irene while Henry crumbles into a 'whipped man... worn down and grim,' and Thomas takes on the role of caretaker. Henry's longtime friend Gladys shows the family rare kindness, but a long-standing animosity between her crotchety father and Henry makes it impossible for the Talcotts to accept her charity. In typical Morris fashion, the author paints a brutal landscape and authentic characters with delicacy and precision: from the chaotic household of Irene's alcoholic sister to the creepy relationship between a sick boy and his doting mother, who wants to adopt Thomas and Margaret." Publ Wkly

Morris, Mary McGarry
Songs in ordinary time. Viking 1995 740p
ISBN 0-670-87907-X
LC 94-44071
"The novel is frequently perceptive about the bitter pathos bred by the feeling that you've always lived on someone else's leftovers. . . . The novel is also insightful and frightening on the unshakable resilience of family grudges." N Y Times Book Rev

Morris, Michael
Man in the blue moon; Michael Morris. Tyndale 2012 400 p. (hc) $19.99
ISBN 1414373309; 9781414368429; 9781414373300
LC 2012016147
"Single mother Ella Wallace fights to keep a banker from buying the Florida land that has been in her family for generations when a mysterious stranger shows up and convices Ella he can help her, until his past comes to light." (Publisher's note)

"A magical and mesmerizing page-turner..." Pub Wkly

Morris, R. N.

The **gentle** axe. Penguin 2007 305p $24.95

ISBN 978-1-594-20112-7; 1-594-20112-9

LC 2006-49543

The author's "use of a generic form does not dilute the idea of human suffering that Dostoyevsky wished to explore. Morris' twist is investigating the suffering of the investigator, not the criminal. In identifying with the killers he chases, Petrovich bears the terrible weight of suffering in the world. His profession forces him to perpetually wander the Siberia of his own soul. Morris' novel is a book not about the metaphysics of murder, but rather the metaphysics of the investigation of murders." PopMatters

Morris, Willie

★ **Taps**; a novel. Houghton Mifflin 2001 340p $26

ISBN 0-618-09859-3

LC 00-68250

"Over the course of a year, in intervals framed by a dozen graveside ceremonies for men shipped back from Korea to the summer-baked or winter-frozen cemetery outside town, Swayze tells the story of a passing Southern world and his own troubled growing up. . . . Funerals are its talismans and 'Taps' is at it strongest when it describes them." N Y Times Book Rev

Morris, Wright

★ **Collected** stories, 1948-1986. Harper & Row 1986 274p

LC 86-45334

"Spanning close to 40 years of Morris's work and ranging in settings throughout the U.S. and in many cities abroad, this collection deals with wartime experiences, race relations in the South and displacement, both cultural and temporal. Through his eyes we glimpse the mysteries of life and the small epiphanies that render them a little more comprehensible." Publ Wkly

Morrison, Toni, 1931-

★ The **bluest** eye; with a new afterword by the author. Knopf 1993 215p

ISBN 0-679-43373-2

LC 93-43124

A reissue of the title first published 1970 by Holt, Rinehart & Winston

"This tragic study of a black adolescent girl's struggle to achieve white ideals of beauty and her consequent descent into madness was acclaimed as an eloquent indictment of some of the more subtle forms of racism in American society. Pecola Breedlove longs to have 'the bluest eye'and thus to be acceptable to her family, schoolmates, and neighbors, all of whom have convinced her that she is ugly." Merriam-Webster's Ency of Lit

Morrison, Toni, 1931-

★ **Home**; Toni Morrison. Random House Inc 2013 145 p. (pbk.) $14

ISBN 0307740919; 9780307740915

LC 2012462661

In this book, the "Korean conflict is over, and soldier Frank Money has returned to the States with a disturbed psyche that sends him beyond anger into actually acting out his rage. From the mental ward in which he has been incarcerated for an incident he can't even remember, he determines that he must escape. He needs to get to Atlanta to attend to his gravely ill sister and take her back to their Georgia hometown of Lotus." (Booklist)

Morrison, Toni

Jazz. Knopf 1992 229p $26.95

ISBN 0-679-41167-4

LC 91-58555

"As the story unfolds, we come to understand, if not excuse, what happened. The characters themselves cannot excuse their own behavior, which baffles them. Violet is obsessed by the memory of the dead girl whose face she slashed: What was it about her that Joe found so special? She is driven to visit the girl's aunt Alice, who is understandably frightened. . . . Some of the most interesting scenes in the book are the subsequent meetings of these two very different women who come to respect each other, even before they learn to understand each other." Christ Sci Monit

Morrison, Toni

Love. Knopf 2003 201p $23.95

ISBN 0-375-40944-0

LC 2003-52737

"Like all of Morrison's best fiction, this is a village novel. Race and racism, ancillary concerns in 'Love' for the most part, throw the small groups she writes about upon one another, steeping their passions. Even when the setting is contemporary, Morrison's books feel old fashioned, set in a world where the perpetual distraction of the media hasn't diluted people's fascination with their neighbors." N Y Times Book Rev

Morrison, Toni

A **mercy**; a novel. Knopf 2008 167p $23.95

ISBN 978-0-307-26423-7; 0-307-26423-8

LC 2008-21067

The fate of a slave child abandoned by her mother animates this allusive novel part Faulknerian puzzle, part dream-song about orphaned women who form an eccentric household in late-17th-century America. Morrison's farmers and rum traders, masters and slaves, indentured whites and captive Native Americans live side by side, often in violent conflict, in a lawless, ripe American Eden that is both a haven and a prison an emerging nation whose identity is rooted equally in Old World superstitions and New World appetites and fears. N Y Times Book Rev

Morrison, Toni

Paradise. Knopf 1998 318p $25

ISBN 0-679-43374-0

LC 97-80913

"In 1950, a core group of nine old families leaves the increasingly corrupted African American community of Haven, Okla., to found in that same state a new, purer community they call Ruby. But in the early 1970s, the outside world begins to intrude on Ruby's isolation, forcing a tragic confrontation. It's about this time, too, that the first of five damaged women finds solace in a decrepit former convent near Ruby. . . . The individual stories of both the women and the townspeople reveal Morrison at her best." Publ Wkly

Morrison, Toni

★ **Song** of Solomon. Knopf 1977 337p $27.50
ISBN 0-394-49784-8

LC 77-874

"Chaos marked the world into which Macon (known as Milkman) Dead was born. Each member of his family was haunted by some wild obsession—his father's desire for money, land, and social status, his mother's need for love, his sisters' silence, and his Aunt Pilate's madness. To these was added Macon's desire to unearth the family's buried past. This is a novel of mystery and revelation as it unfolds the lives of four generations of blacks in America." Shapiro. Fic for Youth. 3d edition

Morrison, Toni

Sula. Knopf 1974 174p hardcover o.p. pa $14
ISBN 0-394-48044-9; 1-4000-3343-8 pa

This "is the story of two black women friends and of their community of Medallion, Ohio. The community has been stunted and turned inward by the racism of the larger society. The rage and disordered lives of the townspeople are seen as a reaction to their stifled hopes. The novel follows the lives of Sula and Nel from childhood to maturity to death." Merriam-Webster's Ency of Lit

Morrison, Toni

★ **Tar** baby. Knopf 1981 305p $26.95
ISBN 0-394-42329-1

LC 80-22821

"Each of the characters in Toni Morrison's Tar Baby comes with a history, quite a complete history that is given to us in a series of stunning performances." New Repub

Morrow, Bradford

The **diviner's** tale; a novel. Houghton Mifflin Harcourt 2011 311p $26
ISBN 978-0-547-38263-0; 0-547-38263-4

LC 2009-47462

"Morrow couples evocative prose . . . with steadily increasing momentum as we learn what lies at the root of Cassandra's divinations (A 'beetle-branched tree' Cassandra spots 'looked for all the world like a photographic negative of a lightning mass, St. Elmo's Fire done up in black') and what really happened to the injured girl and her visionary dead doppelgänger. With 'The Diviner's Tale,' Morrow demonstrates, as many others have and ought to, that one need not sacrifice literary chops for more commercial leanings when the two are easily and readily combined." Los Angeles Times Book Rev

Morrow, James

The **last** witchfinder; a novel. William Morrow 2006 526p il $25.95
ISBN 0-06-082179-5

LC 2005-47177

"Although steeped in period language and scholarship, the narrative never falters. Morrow's panoramic vision of the Enlightenment encompasses the ideology of that turbulent, transformative era, and his wry commentary–related through the sprightly voice of Newton's Principia Mathematica, speaking for itself–lightens the novel's tone without soften-

ing its message. This impeccably researched, highly ambitious novel. . . is a triumph of historical fiction." Booklist

Morrow, James

The **philosopher's** apprentice. William Morrow 2008 411p $25.95
ISBN 978-0-06-135144-0; 0-06-135144-X

LC 2007-29815

This novel " begins with Mason Ambrose walking out on his Ph.D. defense, disgusted by what he perceives as the innate hypocrisy in the process. He stumbles into a job for which he seems ideal. Edwina Sabacthani, world-renowned geneticist, hires him to teach her 17-year-old daughter, Londa, about morality. According to Edwina, Londa suffered an accident that caused not only profound amnesia but a complete loss of her moral sense. . . . A satirist of the first water, Morrow gives us a novel by turns poignant, piquant and potent. From his initial premise — part 'Frankenstein,' part 'Emile,' with a dash of 'The Island of Dr. Moreau' thrown in—he backs away from none of the implications of the technology or the ideologies of the main characters, taking us down a rabbit hole that is both haunting and exhilarating. He confronts the reader with the ramifications of choice and action, offering a harrowing tour of cause and consequence." St. Louis Post-Dispatch

Morsi, Pamela

The **love** charm; Pamela Morsi. Avon Books 1996 376 p. (pbk.) o.p.; (pbk.) o.p.
ISBN 0380786419; 9780380786411

LC 96096759

This book is a "heartland romance . . . about insular societies--the rules they follow and the rules they get around. In 19th century Louisiana, five Acadians and a German search for love: Armand Sonnier fears he's not cute enough for Aida Gaudet, the prettiest girl on the Vermilion River; Laron Boudreau is pledged to Aida but in love with Helga Shotz, almost 10 years his senior and still married; and Jean Baptiste Sonnier and his wife Felicite are young and saddled with three children and a fourth on the way." (Publishers Weekly)

Mortimer, John

Felix in the underworld. Viking 1997 246p
ISBN 978-0670860791

LC 97-16562

"This novel is actually about the characters of literary and legal London, and we soon realize that the point is not just to allow these people to circulate in the pages of narrative but, more importantly, to turn character into caricature. . . . John Mortimer's writing is fluent, gently humorous, and possesses the comic's virtue, tact." Times Lit Suppl

Mortimer, John

★ **Paradise** postponed. Viking 1986 373p
ISBN 0-670-80094-5

LC 85-40712

First published 1985 in the United Kingdom
"A realistic novel of manners in the grand nineteenth-century British tradition, this sweeping look at postwar England focuses on a group of villagers from the London suburb of Rapstone Fanner. From the upwardly mobile conservative politician through the activist vicar to the jazz-playing coun-

try doctor, these characters reflect the comic follies of the modern age as they try to come to grips with an overwhelming sense of expectations unfulfilled." Am Libr

Mortimer, John

Quite honestly. Viking 2006 206p $24.95

ISBN 0-670-03483-5

LC 2005-53157

First published 2005 in the United Kingdom

"Good intentions pave Lucy Purefoy's way into all kinds of misadventures in this engaging satire.... Mortimer clearly enjoys poking fun at middle-class do-gooders-especially Lucy's dad, a bishop so tolerant that he probably puts a 'pretty please' at the end of the Sixth Commandment. The end result is a tad slight, but fine for readers who enjoy light satire with a little larceny on the side." Christ Sci Monit

Mortimer, John

Rumpole a la carte. Viking 1990 245p

LC 91-161338

Contents: Rumpole à la carte; Rumpole and the summer of discontent; Rumpole and the right to silence; Rumpole at sea; Rumpole and the quacks; Rumpole for the prosecution

Mortimer, John

Rumpole and the angel of death. Viking 1996 260p

LC 95-41851

Contents: Rumpole and the model prisoner; Rumpole and the way through the woods; Hilda's story; Rumpole and the little boy lost; Rumpole and the rights of man; Rumpole and the angel of death

Mortimer, John

Rumpole misbehaves. Viking 2007 196p $23.95

ISBN 978-0-670-01830-7; 0-670-01830-9

LC 2007-37323

Published in the United Kingdom with title: The antisocial behaviour of Horace Rumpole

"Rumpole has for many volumes now ... remained fixed in our imaginations at about age 70. Perhaps it's because of the author's age, but this novel, which is rather intricately plotted and propulsively rich in incident for so short a narrative, has the feeling of a summation. Over its course, the incorrigible Horace will meet and surmount not only a variety of novel challenges — political correctness and human trafficking, for example — but also old temptations, particularly the pressure to sacrifice his generally undeserving clients on the expedient altar of long unrealized ambition." Los Angeles Times Book Rev

Mortimer, John

Rumpole on trial. Viking 1992 243p

ISBN 978-6708445947

Contents: Rumpole and the children of the devil; Rumpole and the eternal triangle; Rumpole and the miscarriage of justice; Rumpole and the family pride; Rumpole and the soothsayer; Rumpole and the reform of Joby Jonson; Rumpole on trial

Mortimer, John

Rumpole rests his case. Viking 2002 210p $24.95

ISBN 0-670-03139-9

LC 2002-19046

Contents: Rumpole and the old familiar faces; Rumpole and the rememberance of things past; Rumpole and the asylum seekers; Rumpole and the Camberwell carrot; Rumpole and the actor Laddie; Rumpole and the teenage werewolf; Rumpole rests his case

"With Mortimer's greatly felicitous style and careful plotting, these stories are sheer, absolute reading pleasure." Booklist

Mortimer, John

Rumpole's return. Armchair Detective Lib. 1992 159p

LC 91-29415

First published 1980 in paperback in the United Kingdom

"After losing in Judge Bullingham's court for the tenth straight time, Rumpole finds the beaches of Florida a welcome change from the dampness of home. Basking in the sun, he comes across an account of the Notting Hill Gate murder in a back copy of The Times which sparks a nerve. This is the sort of case he enjoyed. The evidence is stacked against the accused. . . . Rumpole's uncanny assessment of the situation is that the facts are out of synch." Publisher's note

Mortimer, John

★ The **second** Rumpole omnibus. Viking 1987 667p

Companion volume to The first Rumpole omnibus (1983)

Mortimer, John

The **sound** of trumpets. Viking 1999 272p

ISBN 0-670-87861-8

LC 98-38968

First published 1998 in the United Kingdom

This novel "chronicles the bewildering career of the young Labour candidate Terry Flitton, who madly accepts Titmuss's offer of aid when the local Conservative M.P. is found face down in a swimming pool and the seat Flitton covets becomes vacant." New Yorker

Mortimer, John

Summer's lease. Viking 1988 288p

"The advertisement that Molly Pargenter answered made the Tuscany villa to let sound like the ideal place—suspiciously too ideal—for her family to spend its summer vacation. Arriving in Italy with her husband, three daughters, and father, she finds an unusual assortment of locals and English expatriates for neighbors, as well as detailed notes on the proper use of the house left by her absentee landlord, one S. Kettering. Molly's obsession with learning as much as possible about the Kettering household leads her to some ominous conclusions." Libr J

"Mortimer puts in a graceful performance as he untangles a whole bundle of liaisons and portrays a whole array of human emotions with skill and subtlety." Booklist

Mortimer, John

Titmuss regained. Viking 1990 280p

ISBN 0-670-82333-3

LC 89-40801

"Mortimer's touch remains as light as ever, and the novel is full of beautifully-poised social comedy–but there can be no denying the bitterness with which he views contemporary Britain." New Statesman Soc

Mortman, Doris

The **lucky** ones. Kensington Bks. 1997 407p

ISBN 1-57566-204-3

LC 96-80069

"When rising politician Benjamin Knight gets married on a perfect summer day, the four women watching don't realize how prophetic the best man's toast for success is. And over the next 20 years, the women all forge their own ambitious careers: Zoë becomes a foreign affairs analyst, a career choice made in order to get as far from Ben as possible; Celia, Ben's sister-in-law, uses her beauty and talent to build a career in national television; Georgie, Ben's childhood friend, becomes a congresswoman; and Kate, Ben's college classmate, founds a national child protection organization following the murder of her daughter. When a dangerous hostage situation arises overseas in an election year, the current president announces he will not run again. A heated political race erupts, and Ben throws his hat in the ring." Booklist

"In the midst of a well-paced thriller, Mortman takes a bubbly peek into the drawing rooms and back rooms where history is brokered." Publ Wkly

Mortman, Doris

True colors; a novel. Crown 1995 553p

LC 94-13068

"The internationally renowned artist Isabelle de Luna, born into the aristocracy of Barcelona, Spain, lost a life of privilege when her mother was brutally raped and murdered. For Isabelle's protection she is sent to New Mexico to live with the Durans, friends of the family who raise her together with their adopted daughter, Nina. As adults, the two young women become successful but lose their bonds of sisterhood." Libr J

"Mortman sets out quite a feast: alluring and sophisticated characters, steamy sex, and a captivating plot involving murder, great wealth and power, international intrigue, art, ambition, and redemption." Booklist

Morton, Carson

Stealing Mona Lisa; Carson Morton. 1st ed.; Minotaur Books 2011 340p.

ISBN 9780312621711; 9781250015730

LC 2011009099

This book, which was named Library Journal's Best Mystery of 2011, tells the story of Eduardo de Valfierno, an art forger who "makes a very respectable living in Argentina fleecing the nouveau rich. . . . But when Eduardo meets the beautiful Mrs. Hart on his latest con, he takes a risk that forces him back to the city he loved and left behind—Paris. There he assembles his team of con artists for their final and most ambitious theft, one that will enable them to leave the game forever: The Mona Lisa. But when a member of the team turns up missing, and Mr. Hart shows up in Paris, Val-

fierno and his crew must stay one step ahead of a relentless police inspector, endure a devastating flood, and conquer their own doubts to keep the priceless painting in play—and survive." (Publisher's note)

Includes bibliographical references

Morton, Kate

The **distant** hours; a novel. Kate Morton. Atria Books 2010 562 p. $26

ISBN 1439152780; 9781439152782

LC 2010033472

This book by Kate Morton is an "intergenerational story . . . centering on two families: the Blythes of Milderhurst Castle and the Burchills, from working-class London. While researching a children's novel, Edie Burchill is led to the idiosyncratic Blythe sisters, now quite elderly, who had resided at Milderhurst when her mother, Meredith, was sent there to escape the blitz during World War II." (Library Journal)

Morton, Kate

The **house** at Riverton; a novel. Atria Books 2008 473p $24.95

ISBN 978-1-4165-5051-8; 1-4165-5051-8

LC 2008-7023

First published 2006 in Australia with title: The shifting fog

"For decades, Grace Reeves has kept secret the truth of a poet's violent death by the lake at Riverton House in Oxfordshire. Now at the end of her life, 98-year-old Grace's memory is swept back, after interviews for a film about the tragic incident, to those years of her service for the Hartford family. At 15, Grace begins her adult life as a housemaid in the grand Riverton House, quickly learning her place in the servant hierarchy. Her loyalty and attachment to Hannah and Emmeline Hartford grow over the years, as the Hartford family is affected by war, death, financial failings, and illicit love. . . . A suspenseful and beautifully atmospheric novel capturing the transitional time from the end of the Edwardian era through World War I into the Roaring Twenties." Libr J

Moses, Kate

Wintering; a novel of Sylvia Plath. St. Martin's Press 2003 292p $23.95

ISBN 0-312-28375-X

LC 2002-36753

"A fictionalization of the grueling months following the dissolution of Plath's marriage to Ted Hughes and leading up to her suicide at the age of 30 in 1963. 'Wintering' is beautiful and moving. The narrative voice is a distillation of Plath's diaries, letters and poems; with lyrical dexterity and great economy, Moses portrays a demanding, pitiless woman struggling against the stark fact of her husband's infidelity and her own inner demons." N Y Times Book Rev

Mosher, Howard Frank

On Kingdom Mountain. Houghton Mifflin Co. 2007 276p $24

ISBN 978-0-618-19723-1; 0-618-19723-0

LC 2006-23568

"Jane Hubbell Kinneson is the sole owner and last resident of Kingdom Mountain, Vermont, a wild and unspoiled place on the U.S.–Canadian border in 1930. Outside forces led by her cousin Eben are trying to get the Connector, a new highway that will run through the mountain, pushed through. Miss Jane says, 'Over my dead body,' and means it. On her fiftieth birthday, stunt pilot and rainmaker Henry Satterfield crashes his biplane on her lake. Miss Jane offers him shelter and Henry joins her fight against the Connector. Henry is in Vermont to solve the riddle his Confederate grandfather left him about the location of stolen federal gold." Booklist

"Mosher's passionate geographical hyperbole is both justifiable and charming, producing a wonderfully intriguing sense of place." Washington Post Book World

Mosley, Walter

All I did was shoot my man; Walter Mosley. Riverhead Books/Penguin Group 2012 326p $26.95
ISBN 9781594488245

LC 2011046844

In this book, "author Walter Mosley takes readers back into the world of private investigator Leonid McGill. The novel is Mosley's fourth thriller featuring the New York City PI, and this time, he's wrapped up with the case of a woman named Zella Grisham. Grisham has just served eight years on a 16-year prison term for grand larceny. Though McGill played a key role in her arrest, he is convinced that Grisham is innocent. . . . The novel follows McGill's journey to atone for his corrupt past, as he helps Grisham get her life back on track." (NPR)

Mosley, Walter

Always outnumbered, always outgunned. Norton 1997 208p
ISBN 0-393-04539-0

LC 96-54870

"In these interconnected short stories about an aging black man, Socrates Fortlow, living in a makeshift two-room apartment in an abandoned Watts building, Mosley turns on its head the fundamental fantasy of the detective story. . . . These are often difficult stories to read; never sentimental, they are finally, one and all, about pain and how we live with it. Perhaps that's why those brief moments when Socrates eases someone else's pain deliver such a powerful sense of catharsis." Booklist

Mosley, Walter

Bad Boy Brawly Brown. Little, Brown 2002 311p
ISBN 0-316-07301-6

LC 2002-16232

"As Easy persists in his investigation, he is dismissed by black radicals and rousted by racist cops. . . . So he can't really be blamed for spending more time than he should in places like Sam's Hambones soul food diner, engaging in invigorating of often aimless conversations with characters who have little to offer on Brawly's whereabouts but lots to say about whatever is on their minds. Aside from their appealing hero, Mosley's crime novels take their vitality from the racy language and boisterous humanity of his characters, so these neighborhood encounters provide their own joy." N Y Times Book Rev

Mosley, Walter

Black Betty. Norton 1994 255p
ISBN 0-393-03644-8

LC 94-6839

"Mosley gives us a recognizable moment in American history viewed through the eyes of a single black man. This perspective, rare in crime fiction, vivifies not only the black experience but the larger event as well. Here we feel the hot winds that would eventually ignite the Watts riots not as abstract issues in race relations, but as emotions in the hearts of individuals we have come to know and care about." Booklist

Mosley, Walter

Cinnamon kiss. Little Brown 2005 312p $24.95
ISBN 0-316-07302-4

LC 2005-5739

"As ever, Mosley is able to capture the era–hippies, Watts, communes–in brief strokes that provide a brilliant background to Easy's search for solutions to both a convoluted mystery and complex personal problems." Publ Wkly

Mosley, Walter

★ **Devil** in a blue dress. Norton 1990 219p $19.95
ISBN 0-393-02854-2

LC 89-25503

In this novel "Ezekiel 'Easy' Rawlins, a young, tough black veteran living in 1948 Los Angeles, only wants respect and enough money to pay his mortgage. When fired from his factory job, however, he undertakes some paid errands for a shady white mobster who wishes to locate a light-haired, blue-eyed beauty. As Easy plumbs his usual hangouts for clues, he relays information to the mobster, runs afoul of the police, meets the mysterious woman, discovers a murder, then investigates in self-defense." Libr J

"Mosley's prose is a little stiff and his plot is far too complicated. But he has a keen eye for period details. . . . And his lowdown humor never deserts him." Newsweek

Mosley, Walter

Fear itself; a mystery. Little, Brown 2003 316p $24.95
ISBN 0-316-59112-2

LC 2003-46092

"Set in 1955 Los Angeles, this . . . thriller finds Fearless and compatriot Paris Minton, the story's narrator, searching for a friend's missing husband. That seemingly simple task rapidly escalates into a case of multiple murders, blackmail, and a quest for a priceless heirloom that makes this Mosley's answer to the Maltese Falcon." Libr J

Mosley, Walter

Fear of the dark. Little, Brown and Co. 2006 308p $25.99
ISBN 978-0-316-73458-5; 0316734586

LC 2006-12741

A mystery featuring bookseller Paris Minton set in Watts, 1956. "Trouble comes to Paris's door in the form of his cousin Ulysses 'Useless' S. Grant IV, who needs help after getting mixed up in a scheme that has gotten totally out of hand. Despite refusing to even let Useless cross his threshold, Paris is drawn, violently, into the fray." Publ Wkly

Mosley, Walter

★ **Fearless** Jones; a novel. Little, Brown 2001 312p

ISBN 0-316-59238-2

LC 00-53502

This "mystery is narrated by Paris Minton, a black man who sells used books in nineteen-fifties L.A. Paris's life is perfect—he reads all day without interruption—until a be-witching young woman named Elana Love walks through his door. She's looking for a religious group called the Mes-senger of the Divine, but the thug who bursts in after her is looking for a bond worth thousands of dollars. Mayhem and seduction ensue, and when Paris's bookstore is burned to the ground, he knows it's time to seek the aid of the incompa-rable Fearless Jones. The unlikely friendship of these men—Fearless is all fists and testosterone, Paris is a gun-shy truth-seeker—is the source of the novel's humor, and propels the reader through the plot's knottier moments." New Yorker

Mosley, Walter

Fortunate son. Little, Brown and Co. 2006 313p hardcover o.p. pa $13.99

ISBN 978-0-316-11471-4; 0-316-11471-5; 978-0-316-06628-0 pa; 0-316-06628-1 pa

LC 2005-24477

"Tommy was born out of wedlock with a hole in his heart; he's also lame and black. Eric, on the other hand, glows with health; he is so beautiful that people want to touch him—and he's white. For a few years, the boys live together after Tommy's mother and Eric's widowed doctor father fall in love after meeting in the hospital ward. Then Tommy's mother dies, and Tommy is wrested from the only family he's known. Eric grows up leading a life that appears blessed, but with Tommy gone, he's lost all that is important to him. Tommy, meanwhile, ends up on the street but feels lucky simply to be alive. . . . The writing is crisp and the plotting impeccable." Libr J

Mosley, Walter

Gone fishin' an Easy Rawlins novel. Black Clas-sic Press 1997 244p

ISBN 978-1574780253

LC 97-124077

This novel marks the first appearance of Mosley's de-tective-hero, Easy Rawlins. "Written before the other Raw-lins novels but never published, it takes Easy and his lethal friend Mouse back to Texas before World War II and their subsequent move to Los Angeles. The 19-year-old Easy . . . knows little of the larger world. His journey to awareness begins with a soul-changing road trip to the bayous of Pa-riah, Texas, where Mouse hopes to settle a score with his hated stepfather." Booklist

Mosley, Walter

Known to evil. Riverhead Books 2010 325p $25.95

ISBN 978-1-59448-752-1; 1-59448-752-9

LC 2009-42643

"This second installment of Walter Mosley's new detec-tive series opens at the dinner table. He gives you a quick look around the room — walnut cabinet, Blue Danube china, old quart pickle jar doing duty as a flower vase — then takes you inside the protagonist's head. That's how a great por-tion of the story unfolds: through private detective Leonid McGill's inner musings. If you thought Easy Rawlins was a complicated character, spend a little time with McGill as he tries to find a missing woman, avoid police determined to jail him, deal with his imploding marriage, protect his sons from themselves, fend off a move to evict him from his offices and heal from a broken heart administered by an ex-lover." NPR

Mosley, Walter

The **last** days of Ptolemy Grey. Riverhead Books 2010 277p $25.95

ISBN 978-1-59448-772-9; 1-59448-772-3

LC 2010-12317

"Physically fragile and mentally lost, 91-year-old Ptol-emy Grey . . . [is] dependent on his great-grandnephew Reg-gie for the basic necessities of life. . . . When Reggie is killed in a drive-by shooting, his caregiver duties are assumed by 17-year-old Robyn Small." (N Y Times Book Rev)

"Narrated in an intimate whisper, the story draws us deep into the mind of an old man wandering through the remnants of his memories, searching for the key to an old mystery. Physically fragile and mentally lost, 91-year-old Ptolemy Grey lives alone in shocking squalor, dependent on his great-grandnephew Reggie for the basic necessities of life. Ptolemy is still capable of holding a conversation — but mostly with people from long ago, like Coy McCann, the charismatic friend and mentor who entrusted the young Ptolemy with a stolen fortune. . . . When Reggie is killed in a drive-by shooting, his caregiver duties are assumed by 17-year-old Robyn Small, a 'wild and violent' but 'sweet and loving' family friend who cleans and fumigates Ptol-emy's pestilential apartment and takes him to a clinic where the old man's dementia is temporarily reversed with a mi-raculous but toxic experimental drug. . . . His wits restored, Ptolemy takes action, in the short time he has left to live, to unearth Coy's lost 'pirate's treasure,' avenge Reggie's mur-der and ensure the future well-being of his family. The tale of an aged superhero who performs valiant deeds with the aid of a devoted young sidekick (pointedly named Robyn) may sound like the charming stuff of myth. But Mosley in-vests his wish-fulfillment fantasy with deeper meaning and higher purpose." N Y Times Book Rev

Mosley, Walter

Little green; an Easy Rawlins mystery. Walter Mosley. Doubleday 2013 304 p. (hardcover) $25.95

ISBN 0385535988; 9780385535984; 9780385535991

LC 2012036464

This novel, by Walter Mosley, is part of the "Easy Raw-lins Mystery" series. "We last saw Easy . . . fighting for his life after his car plunges over a cliff. True to form, the tough WWII veteran survives, and soon his murderous sidekick Mouse has him back cruising the mean streets of L.A., in all their psychedelic 1967 glory, to look for a young black man, Evander 'Little Green' Noon, who disappeared during an acid trip." (Publisher's note)

Mosley, Walter

★ **Little** Scarlet; Walter Mosley. 1st ed. Little, Brown and Co. 2004 306 p. (hardcover) $24.95

ISBN 0316073032; 9780316073035

LC 2003023002

In this book by Walter Mosley, private investigator "Easy Rawlins returns to solve a mystery. . . . Just after devastating riots tear through Los Angeles in 1965 . . . the police turn up at Easy Rawlins's doorstep. . . . [T]hey've come to ask for his help. A man was wrenched from his car by a mob at the riots' peak and escaped into a nearby apartment building. Soon afterward, a woman known as Little Scarlet was found dead in that building . . . but the man has vanished." (Publisher's note)

"This is Mosley's best novel to date: the plot is streamlined and the language simple yet strong, allowing the serpentine story line to support Easy's amazingly complex character and hypnotic narration as Mosley plunges us into his world and, by extension, the world of all blacks in white-run America. Fierce, provocative, expertly entertaining, this is genre writing at its finest." Pub Wkly

Mosley, Walter

A **little** yellow dog; an Easy Rawlins mystery. Norton 1996 300p

ISBN 0-393-03924-2

LC 96-4231

This mystery, set in the early 1960s, finds Easy Rawlins "working in a high school as head custodian for the Board of Education two years after giving up drinking and the 'street life.' When a corpse turns up on school grounds, Easy finds himself reluctantly caught up in the investigation—between the rock and the hard place of the cops and the killers. Mosley writes in the grand tradition of the American hard-boiled private investigator. His dialog is sharp and his characters vivid—the reader can almost feel the mean L.A. streets." Libr J

Mosley, Walter

The **long** fall. Riverhead Books 2009 305p $25.95

ISBN 978-1-59448-858-0; 1-59448-858-4

LC 2008-46238

The novel "accomplishes most of what an inaugural installment of a mystery series should. The three major plot strands are solidly developed and neatly resolved. McGill's quest for redemption, however, is far from over, but it will be interesting to watch it play out across a number of subsequent volumes. If 'The Long Fall' is overstuffed with incidental characters whose importance may not be obvious until later installments, that's a minor flaw. Having retired Easy Rawlins, Mosley has devised a worthy successor in Leonid McGill." San Francisco Chron

Mosley, Walter

The **man** in my basement; a novel. Little, Brown 2004 249p $22.95

ISBN 0-316-57082-6

LC 2003-56317

"In this successful and intriguing departure from his usual work, Mr. Mosley creates a substantial subplot about heritage and history. . . . In the end this audacious novel is about facing up to such brutal realities. But it is also about seeking refuge." N Y Times (Late N Y Ed)

Mosley, Walter

A **red** death. Norton 1991 284p

ISBN 0-393-02998-0

LC 90-23660

"In this second installment in the series, the calendar has moved ahead to the early 1950s, and the good-natured (and aptly named) Easy is in a pickle. The IRS is after him for hiding income from the apartment buildings he secretly owns; a Red-hating FBI agent strong-arms him into investigating a labor agitator; and the local police suspect him in two murders." Booklist

Mosley, Walter

RL's dream. Norton 1995 267p

ISBN 0-393-03802-5

LC 95-8695

"A mesmerizing and redemptive tale of friendship, love, and forgiveness. . . . {This} is, without doubt, the author's finest achievement to date, a rich literary gumbo with blue-stinged rhythms that make it a joy to read and a book to remember." San Francisco Rev Books

Mosley, Walter

Six easy pieces. Atria Bks. 2003 278p $24

ISBN 0-7434-4252-0

"Mosley is as fine as ever, offering compelling commentary on black-white relations in 1964, writing in a style so simple that it deceives us into thinking wwriting great fiction is as easy as putting one foot in front of the other. It's not, but turning these pages is." Booklist

Mosley, Walter

Walkin' the dog. Little, Brown 1999 260p $35

ISBN 0-316-96620-7

LC 99-16407

In this "volume of interconnected short stories, Mosley gives his hero, 59-year-old ex-con Socrates Fortlow, a new job, a new home, and a new commitment to ridding his Watts neighborhood of a rogue cop. Overtly political fiction is difficult to pull off, but Mosley makes it work by grounding his issues in the felt life of his characters." Booklist

Mosley, Walter

When the thrill is gone. Riverhead Books 2011 359p $26.95

ISBN 978-1-59448-781-1; 1-59448-781-2

LC 2010-39098

This installment finds Leonid McGill still "unable to shake his underworld connections — as a personal favor he['s undertaking a search for the lost friend of a powerful crime boss. But there are other pressing matters to be taken care of: a man who has been like a father to him lies dying in McGill's apartment, McGill's wife is sleeping with a man half her age and if McGill doesn't get a paying job he won't be able to pay the rent on his office. . . . For a healthy retainer, McGill takes the case of a nervous wife who suspects her billionaire husband of having an affair and planning to murder her to avoid a messy divorce. . . . Unlike the flamboyant criminals who swagger through Mosley's Easy Rawlins novels, the characters who catch your eye here are people who are normally invisible: old folks living on the edges of society and young black men with 'no notion of their history and no hope for a future except what they were told by the TV.' The qualities that make McGill fit to be their hero are the same ones that make him the quintessential New Yorker: he sees it all and knows it all and somehow feels responsible for it all." N Y Times Book Rev

Mosley, Walter

White butterfly. Norton 1992 272p $19.95

ISBN 0-393-03366-X

LC 91-44700

"Standard stuff, to be sure—the makings of your typical made-for-television movie. But what elevates it is the character. It is not just that Rawlins is such an engaging fellow. He is a man who both ages and evolves." N Y Times Book Rev

Mosse, Kate

Labyrinth. G. P. Putnam's Sons 2006 515p hardcover o.p. pa $15

ISBN 0-399-15344-6; 0-425-21397-8 pa

LC 2005-50985

First published 2005 in the United Kingdom

"Medieval life in the Languedoc region is brought vividly to life, and Mosse manages to integrate her research smoothly into the tale. Fans of fantasy and historical romance are the most likely to enjoy the tale, which relies on reincarnation, ancient spells, and other genre conventions." Christ Sci Monit

Motion, Andrew

Silver; return to Treasure Island. Andrew Motion. Crown 2012 viii, 403 p.p (alk. paper) $24

ISBN 0307884872; 9780307884879; 9780307884893

LC 2012023773

This book by Andrew Motion is a sequel to Robert Louis Stevenson's book "Treasure Island." "Jim Hawkins now runs an inn . . . with his son, Jim, and Long John Silver has returned to England to live in obscurity with his daughter, Natty. . . . But for Jim and Natty, the adventure is just beginning. One night, Natty approaches young Jim with a proposition: return to Treasure Island and find the remaining treasure that their fathers left behind so many years before." (Publisher's note)

Mott, Jason

★ The **Returned**. Harlequin Books 2013 400 p. $24.95

ISBN 0778315339; 9780778315339

In this book, all "are confused and disconcerted when people who have died inexplicably come back, including [an elderly] couple's 8-year-old son, whom they lost nearly 50 years ago. No one understands why people who died are coming back. . . . Considered by some the work of the devil, by others a miracle, the confounding reality is that an already struggling planet must abruptly support a staggering influx of beings who have typical human needs: food, water, shelter, sanitation." (Publishers Weekly)

Moulessehoul, Mohammed

The **swallows** of Kabul; translated from the French by John Cullen. Nan A. Talese\Doubleday 2004 195p $18.95

ISBN 0-385-51001-2

LC 2003-50769

The author is "intimately familiar with the consequences that war and religious extremism have on people's daily lives, and in this book he gives the reader a tactile sense of what life under the Taliban might have been like." N Y Times (Late N Y Ed)

Mowat, Farley

★ The **Snow** Walker. Little, Brown 1975 222p

The stories range "from the ancient to the overwhelmingly modern. . . . There are tales of starvation, cannibalism out of love, the giving of one body to another with the poignancy of the Eucharist. There are tales so simple and strong you read them again to make sure you haven't been tricked into feeling a story in your stomach for a change." N Y Times Book Rev

Moyes, Jojo

The **last** letter from your lover; a novel. Pamela Dorman Books/Viking 2011 390p $26.95

ISBN 978-0-670-02280-9

LC 2011-02023

"Jennifer Stirling awakens with no memory from a terrible accident. Then she finds a letter fervently begging her to abandon her husband and run away with the writer, identified only as 'B.' Decades later, a journalist named Ellie discovers the letter in her newspaper's file and determines to solve the mystery and bring together the long-lost lovers—all while landing a front-page story." Libr J

Mrazek, Robert J.

Unholy fire; a novel of the Civil War. Thomas Dunne Bks. 2003 299p $24.95

ISBN 0-312-30673-3

LC 2002-32512

"Mrazek's portrayal of Civil War battle is stark, graphic, bloody and exciting, and is only exceeded by his memorable description of Washington, D. C. as a Gomorrah on the Potomac." Publ Wkly

Mueenuddin, Daniyal

In other rooms, other wonders. W. W. Norton & Company 2009 247p $23.95

ISBN 0-393-06800-5; 978-0-393-06800-9

LC 2008-40632

This collection of linked stories describes the lives of landowners and their retainers on the Gurmani family farm in Pakistan.

"In eight beautifully crafted, interconnected stories, Mueenuddin explores the cutthroat feudal society in which a rich Lahore landowner is entrenched. . . . An elegant stylist with a light touch, Mueenuddin invites the reader to a richly human, wondrous experience." Publ Wkly

Mukherjee, Bharati

Miss New India. Houghton Mifflin Harcourt 2011 328p $25

ISBN 978-0-618-64653-1; 0-618-64653-1

LC 2010-25569

"Mukherjee subtly continues the stories of the sisters from Desirable Daughters (2002) and The Tree Bride (2004) as she introduces Anjali Bose, a smart, rebellious 19-year-old who flees her provincial town after her father's attempt to arrange her marriage goes catastrophically wrong. With the help of her scholarly, covertly gay, expat American teacher, Anjali finds refuge in a decaying mansion, a remnant of the Raj, in Bangalore, the booming capital of call centers and electronic startups. There the brave country girl undergoes a crash course in urban life and the fizzing world of outsourcing, avatars, and social networks. Each character fascinates, and every detail glints with irony and intent, as Mukherjee brilliantly choreographs her compelling protagonist's struggles against betrayal, violence, and corruption in a dazzling plot that cunningly considers forms of tyranny blatant and insidious in a metamorphosing society." Booklist

Mullen, Thomas

The **last** town on earth; a novel. Random House 2006 394p $23.95

ISBN 1-4000-6520-8

LC 2005-46687

The author "patiently unfolds the plot, using historical facts as a springboard. His long and absorbing novel is a timely and sobering look back at a nation during a deadly war involving a human enemy far away, a disease at home, fear, and political and cultural forces." Libr J

Mullen, Thomas

The **many** deaths of the Firefly Brothers; a novel. Random House 2010 397p $26

ISBN 978-1-4000-6753-4; 1-4000-6753-7

LC 2009-19712

A novel about "the Fireson Brothers, popularly known as the Firefly Brothers, who roam the Midwest robbing banks during the Great Depression. The Fireflies have a habit of getting killed during their capers but, like characters from a Flann O'Brien work, they refuse to stay dead. They wake up in morgues or in the beds of vehicles on the way to hospitals and make their getaways. Mullen writes with great brio, and the world he conjures can be hilarious, hideous and hearkening—much here feels like the American underbelly in our current economic downturn." Paste

Muller, Marcia

Both ends of the night. Mysterious Press 1997 353p

ISBN 978-0892966226

LC 97-10129

Sharon McCone "sets out to help a friend and former flying instructor find her missing lover, but soon the friend has been murdered, and a missing-persons case has been transformed into a grudge match. With the help of her own lover and fellow flyer Hy Ripinsky, McCone ventures into the depths of the federal witness protection program, finding first the missing lover and then the killer in the wilds of Minnesota. There's plenty of nicely paced action here, and

the flying lore provides effective ballast. Best of all, though, there is McCone at work, both as day-to-day professional detective and as aggrieved friend out for justice." Booklist

Muller, Marcia

The **broken** promise land. Mysterious Press 1996 388p

LC 95-52187

"Leading Sharon into the rocky psychological terrain of families, Muller gives her meticulously plotted story, with its absorbing picture of the music industry, a commanding emotional authenticity." Publ Wkly

Muller, Marcia

Burn out. Grand Central Pub. 2008 309p $24.99

ISBN 978-0-446-58107-3; 0-446-58107-0

LC 2008-4500

"Traumatized by a recent life-or-death investigation, Sharon McCone flees to her ranch in California's high desert country to contemplate her future. Deep depression shadows her days and nights, and a chance encounter with a troubled, highly secretive Native American woman begins to haunt her dreams. Even though she is determined not to investigate anything during her stay—and perhaps not ever again—McCone is drawn into the plight of the young woman and her dysfunctional family." Publisher's note

"By the upbeat ending, McCone has learned that with judicious use of both her investigative and executive skills she can reshape her life." Publ Wkly

Muller, Marcia

City of whispers. Grand Central Pub. 2011 262p $25.99

ISBN 978-0-446-57333-7

LC 2010051674

Private eye Sharon McCone receives an e-mail asking for help from her emotionally disturbed half-brother, Darcy Blackhawk, but he fails to reply to her response. As her search widens, Sharon uncovers a connection to an unsolved murder of a young woman who was heiress to a multimillion dollar fortune.

"Alternating chapters narrated by different characters add to the suspense of the intricate plot, which propels readers through a San Francisco few tourists see—from Colma, the city's necropolis, to the exclusive mansions of Sea Cliff—and to a harrowing, haunting denouement." Publ Wkly

Muller, Marcia

Cyanide Wells. Mysterious Press 2003 292p map $24.95

ISBN 0-89296-781-1

LC 2002-45516

"Matt Lindstrom leaves the life he has rebuilt in British Columbia to search for his ex-wife, Gwen. After she vanished from their California home, innuendo that he had murdered her ruined him, forcing his relocation. He discovers that she's in a Soledad County town called Cyanide Wells, living with a lesbian lover and an adopted child. When he goes there—For revenge? for solace?—he discovers she has taken off again, this time with the child. He and Carly McGuire, publisher of the county newspaper and Gwen's partner, perform an uneasy dance as they try to bring her back." Booklist

Muller, Marcia

The **dangerous** hour. Mysterious Press 2004 290p $25

ISBN 0-89296-804-4

LC 2003-24625

"Muller's plotting isn't quite as tidy as usual . . . , but once again she gives us a solid slice of a San Francisco community and a protagonist with character. Fans of the sturdy, ongoing series will be especially pleased with the final scene, which opens the way for a new chapter in McCone's personal life." Booklist

Muller, Marcia

★ **Dead** midnight. Mysterious Press 2002 289p

ISBN 0-89296-765-X

LC 2002-20097

This mystery has Sharon McCone "gathering evidence for a wrongful-death suit brought by the family of a sensitive young man driven to kill himself by the deplorable working conditions at a trendy online magazine. But events never advance in a straight line in Muller's complicated narratives, and the job that McCone took on because she thought it would help her come to grips with her own brother's suicide turns into a lethal game of industrial sabotage." N Y Times Book Rev

Muller, Marcia

Listen to the silence. Mysterious Press 2000 289p $28

ISBN 0-89296-689-0

LC 99-87734

"When Detective Sharon McCone's father dies suddenly, she is startled to learn that he has requested that she, not her four siblings, go through his personal effects. In a box marked 'Legal Papers,' Sharon discovers a long-secret document that shatters her very identity and threatens to tear her family apart. As she begins to investigate, a Shoshone lawyer who may be the key to the mystery is nearly killed, and Sharon becomes tangled in a land dispute between Native Americans and white developers that involves greed, environmental corruption, racism, and a 40-year-old murder." Libr J

Muller "delivers an emotion-packed tale that adds new depth to her heroine." Publ Wkly

Muller, Marcia

Pennies on a dead woman's eyes; a Sharon McCone mystery. Mysterious Press 1992 297p

LC 91-58025

"Muller is perhaps the least showy crime author around. Her protagonist, driven always into dangerous and emotional culs-de-sac, emerges as a pleasing composite of toughness and vulnerability without seeming to be either overstated or overwritten." Booklist

Muller, Marcia

The **shape** of dread. Mysterious Press 1989 218p

LC 89-42606

"Solid plots, sound procedures and enlightening views of San Francisco's diversified neighborhoods are characteristic of the author's sensible style, which makes up in technical skill what it lacks in esthetics." N Y Times Book Rev

Muller, Marcia

There's something in a Sunday; a Sharon McCone mystery. Mysterious Press 1989 213p

LC 88-22005

"San Francisco investigator Sharon McCone is hired to watch a man on his day off as he drives from flower garden to flower shop. Then the shirtmaker who has employed her is murdered, the man she follows disappears, a Mission District bum goes into hiding . . . and dark deeds are uncovered at the ranch where the missing man works." Booklist

"This is a provocative work, infused with compassion and sensitivity, that explores the complexities of human relationships and the plight of the homeless." Publ Wkly

Muller, Marcia

Till the butchers cut him down; a Sharon McCone mystery. Mysterious Press 1994 339p

LC 93-42306

Sharon "McCone has just left the All-Souls Legal Cooperative and opened her own business when an eccentric friend from her UC-Berkeley days, who now specializes in rescuing failing corporations, asks her to find out who is sabotaging his efforts to save a San Francisco shipping firm and threatening his life." Publ Wkly

Muller, Marcia

Trophies and dead things. Mysterious Press 1990 266p

LC 90-33448

"Like her heroine, Ms. Muller works in a style more admirable for its clarity and efficiency than for boldness or brilliance. Her dense plots are models of construction, and if her characters lack spark, they are observed in a manner both sensible and rational." N Y Times Book Rev

Muller, Marcia

A **walk** through the fire. Mysterious Press 1999 293p $23

ISBN 0-89296-688-2

LC 98-51314

In this adventure, "Sharon McCone is seduced by the legends of Hawaii and nearly by one particular Hawaiian. Brought to Kauai initially to investigate 'accidents' on the set of her filmmaker friend's documentary, McCone finds herself dealing with murder, Hawaiian militants, and drug dealers." Libr J

Muller, Marcia

Where echoes live. Mysterious Press 1991 326p

LC 90-84898

"Private eye Sharon McCone is on the ecological beat, as a renovated gold mine that could lead to environment destruction also leads to several deaths. A good mystery as fresh as today's headlines." Booklist

Muller, Marcia

While other people sleep. Mysterious Press 1998 344p

ISBN 0-89296-650-5

LC 98-13394

"The renowned Sharon McCone finds life and livelihood threatened by a malicious look-alike. When police detain Sharon for a crime committed by the imposter, anger spurs her to find her double." Libr J

"Muller's straightforward, no-nonsense writing and fully dimensioned characterizations lend credibility and color to her deftly plotted tale." Publ Wkly

Muller, Marcia

A **wild** and lonely place. Mysterious Press 1995 386p

LC 94-48255

Sharon McCone's "precious Mission District is looking mean and dirty, and colleagues at her legal collective have turned into greedy bureaucrats. Tossing caution over her shoulder, McCone signs on with a secret security agency to go after the Diplo-bomber, a terrorist who attacks embassies and consulates. The mission takes McCone to a heavily guarded hideaway in the Leeward Islands, where she executes a daring ocean swim in the dead of night to rescue an Arab diplomat's granddaughter from kidnappers." N Y Times Book Rev

"A mellow, engaging and determined Sharon here heads a diverse and intriguing supporting cast." Publ Wkly

Muller, Marcia

Wolf in the shadows. Mysterious Press 1993 356p

ISBN 978-0892965250

LC 92-50536

"San Francisco private eye Sharon McCone is understandably concerned about the disappearance of her mysterious lover, Hy Ripinsky. When she finds out that he had gone to Mexico to deliver $2 million in ransom, she really gets worried." Libr J

Munoz Molina, Antonio

In her absence; translated by Esther Allen. Other Press 2007 134p $13.95

ISBN 978-1-59051-253-1; 1-59051-253-7 pa

LC 2006-38139

Original Spanish edition, 2001

"Mario's limited yet intensely focused world does not let the reader take a breath for even a paragraph. Perhaps that is why the novel is so short. Neither the writer nor the reader could sustain such a pitch of living inside the head of an increasingly disturbed human being. But how can a short novel, a mere 134 pages, with little action and a mystery left unsolved, take hold of the reader in this way? The power is in the writing—preserved masterfully in Esther Allen's translation—the ability to slice away the exterior of a character like Mario and to offer a simple, naked view of his small joys and great sufferings." Washington Post Book World

Munoz Molina, Antonio

A **manuscript** of ashes; translated from the Spanish by Edith Grossman. Harcourt 2008 305p $25

ISBN 978-0-15-101410-1; 0-15-101410-8

LC 2007-36557

Original Spanish edition, 1986

"The most piercing moments arrive as the narrative edges toward Minaya's own voice. It may be that the author was still discovering how to experiment with the limitations and possibilities of third-person narration. Regardless, the release of this first novel not only provides insight into Munoz Molina's development as a writer but also ably introduces readers to one of his favorite themes: that the essence of a story lies in the mechanics of its telling." Bookforum

Munro, Alice, 1931-

Carried away; a selection of stories. with an introduction by Margaret Atwood. Alfred A. Knopf 2006 xxxv, 559p (Everyman's library) $25

ISBN 0-307-26486-6

LC 2006-43585

"Munro's stories are composed with a clarity and economy that make novel-writing look downright superfluous and self-indulgent." N Y Times Book Rev

Munro, Alice, 1931-

★ **Dear** life; stories. Alice Munro. Alfred A. Knopf 2012 319 p. (hardcover) $26.95

ISBN 0307596885; 9780307596888

LC 2012020455

This collection of short stories by Alice Munro "illumines the moment a life is forever altered by a chance encounter or an action not taken, or by a simple twist of fate that turns a person out of his or her accustomed path and into a new way of being or thinking. While most of these stories take place in Munro's home territory--the small Canadian towns around Lake Huron--the characters sometimes venture to the cities." (Publisher's note)

Munro, Alice

Friend of my youth; stories. Knopf 1990 273p

LC 89-43295

"Ms. Munro, who has deepened the channels of realism, is a writer of extraordinarily rich texture; her imagery stuns or wounds and her sentences stick to the rough surfaces of our world." N Y Times Book Rev

Munro, Alice

Hateship, friendship, courtship, loveship, marriage; stories. Knopf 2001 320p

ISBN 0-375-41300-6

LC 2001-29870

"Opulent in their beauty and gem-bright psychology, the extraordinary stories in {this} collection span the spectrum from romance to tales of manners to deep meditations on love and mortality, and all evince Munro's profound understanding of the power of memories and the stories we tell ourselves." Booklist

Munro, Alice

Lives of girls & women. McGraw-Hill 1971 250p

ISBN 0-07-044043-3

"Although the locale is Canada, Del Jordan's story could take place in the United States as well. She lives among hard-working, lower-middle-class people in a family that includes her parents and a brother, Owen. The mother seeks independence from the traditional role of women and even goes 'out on the road,' as her disapproving sisters-in-law term it, to sell encyclopedias. For Del's mother the pursuit of knowledge is an ideal. For Del and her best friend Naomi more interest lies in their maturing and curiosity about sex as a vital part of growing up. There is humor and recognizable adolescent self-questioning. While sexual scenes are explicit, they are also sensitive and real and avoid both vulgarity and titillation. In spite of the experiences that Naomi and Del have, it becomes clear that the paths they will follow will diverge greatly." Shapiro. Fic for Youth. 3d edition

Munro, Alice

The love of a good woman; stories. Knopf 1998 339p

ISBN 0-375-40395-7

LC 98-36721

"Munro knows her characters intimately, yet she is at peace with the fact that their lives will, and should, retain a fundamental mysterious quality. This paradox, which originates in a knowledge of life, is not often so knowledgeably conveyed in fiction." Yale Rev

Munro, Alice

The moons of Jupiter; stories. Knopf 1983 233p

LC 82-48734

First published 1982 in Canada

"These stories expose the conundrums of love and mortality. At the least they are engaging, and at their luminous best, reveal precision as the highest wisdom." Saturday Rev

Munro, Alice

Open secrets; stories. Knopf 1994 293p

ISBN 0-679-43575-1

LC 94-2099

The author "peoples these exquisite tales with sad, lonely eccentrics leading lives of quiet self-deception. Her heroines are often troubled souls with the unforgiving task of fitting into the rigorously confining community that spawned them. . . . Munro expertly captures the vagaries of history and geography in this satisfying and immensely pleasurable collection." Booklist

Munro, Alice

Runaway; stories. Knopf 2004 337p $25

ISBN 1-400-04281-X

LC 2004-46539

"Munro's spare style belies the psychological depth of the stories, which feature characters running away from someone or something (often representative of the past) or telling a lie by commission or omission (another form of running away)." Libr J

Munro, Alice

Selected stories. Knopf 1996 545p $30

ISBN 0-679-44627-3

LC 96-4145

"Little gems from one of Canada's best writers, drawn from seven collections." Libr J

Munro, Alice

★ Too much happiness; stories. Alfred A. Knopf 2009 303p $25.95

ISBN 978-0-307-26976-8

LC 2009-200010

"The collection's 10 stories take on some sensational subjects. In fact, a quick tally yields all the elements of pulp fiction: violence, adultery, extreme cruelty, duplicity, theft, suicide, murder. But while in pulp fiction the emotional climax coincides with the height of external drama, a Munro story works according to a different scheme. Here the nominally momentous event is little more than an anteroom to an echo chamber filled with subtle and far-reaching thematic reverberations." N Y Times Book Rev

Munro, Alice

The view from Castle Rock; stories. Knopf 2006 349p

ISBN 1-4000-4282-8

LC 2006-45261

This collection differs from Munro's "usual examinations of women in rural Canada leaving home to remake their possibilities. She draws instead on family documents, historical records, and what feels like memoir to piece together, in 12 parts, a fictionalized chronicle of how her tough-minded clan got from the Ettrick Valley near Edinburgh, Scotland, to America. The book shows how much can be done in a simple short story but breaks every rule ever taught in a writing seminar, setting up a writing master class along the way." Time

Munson, Sam

The November criminals; a novel. Doubleday 2010 258p $24.95

ISBN 978-0-385-53227-3; 0-385-53227-X

LC 2009-16750

This novel "follows high school senior Addison Schacht as he stumbles through the Washington, D.C., teenage underworld to investigate a classmate's unsolved murder. Schacht—a small-time pot dealer, consummate anti-social, and Jewish collector of Holocaust jokes—makes for a poor but entertaining detective, and when he places a stoned phone call to his prime suspect, Addison and his friends become caught up in the mystery he set out to solve. . . . Munson keeps things lightly dark, though his weakness for wandering asides—Addison is just as likely to riff on the Aeneid, Latin syntax, or his favorite movies as he is to discuss his investigation and efforts to outsmart the police—trips up the pace, even if they are what one would expect from a self-absorbed adolescent. The plotting could use some work, but Munson nails the voice." Publ Wkly

Murakami, Haruki, 1949-

★ 1Q84; translated from the Japanese by Jay Rubin and Philip Gabriel. Alfred A. Knopf 2011 924p $30.50

ISBN 978-0-307-59331-3; 0-307-59331-2

LC 2011-14274

Original Japanese edition, 2009

This novel "follows two people who find themselves in an alternate world (dubbed 1Q84 by one character) where dual moons hang in the sky and small differences start to have big implications. Several characters spend extended periods sitting by themselves in small rooms. A mysterious band of 'Little People' crawl out of a dead goat's mouth. Religious cults, menacing bill collectors, expert assassins, and questions about the nature of time and space all figure prominently. 'It's like the rules that govern the world have begun to loosen up around us,' says one of the book's lost souls. In typical Murakami fashion, the result is deeply weird—and surprisingly convincing." Entertainment Wkly

Murakami, Haruki

After dark; translated from the Japanese by Jay Rubin. Knopf 2007 191p $22.95

ISBN 978-0-307-26583-8; 0-307-26583-8

LC 2007-4828

"The narrative flows like a jazz ballad, excruciatingly slow yet hypnotically entrancing . . . . Each character is unique in his or her form of loneliness, yet each possesses a capacity for momentary empathy that is both sweet and heartbreaking. Murakami's genius, on both large and small canvases, is to create worlds both utterly alien and disconcertingly familiar." Booklist

Murakami, Haruki

After the earthquake; stories. translated from the Japanese by Jay Rubin. Knopf 2002 181p $22

ISBN 0-375-41390-1

LC 2001-38829

Original Japanese edition, 2000

"These six stories, all loosely connected to the disastrous 1995 earthquake in Kobe, are Murakami. . . at his best. The writer, who returned to live in Japan after the Kobe earthquake, measures his country's suffering and finds reassurance in the inevitability that love will surmount tragedy, mustering his casually elegant prose and keen sense of the absurd in the service of healing." Publ Wkly

Murakami, Haruki

Blind willow, sleeping woman; twenty-four stories. translated from the Japanese by Philip Gabriel and Jay Rubin. Knopf 2006 333p

ISBN 1-4000-4461-8

LC 2005-44544

"Murakami's first collection of short stories in more than a decade again demonstrates his fabulous talent for transporting readers and making 'the world fade away' with a few short strokes of his pen. . . . Murakami's characters are as alienated as any in Albert Camus, and as lost as any in J.D. Salinger. . . . What shines in all of [the stories] is Murakami's love for the open-ended mystery at the core of existence and his willingness to give himself up 'to the flow' in order to capture some of the magic in the mundane." Christ Sci Monit

Murakami, Haruki, 1949-

Kafka on the shore; Haruki Murakami; translated from the Japanese by Philip Gabriel. Alfred A. Knopf 2005 436 p. (pbk.) $15.95; o.p.

ISBN 9781400079278; 1400043662

LC 2004048907

World Fantasy Awards: Novel (2006)

This book tells the story of "Kafka Tamura [who] is a 15-year-old boy . . . [and] runs away from home to escape an Oedipal curse: he will murder his father, a famed sculptor with whom he lives alone, and sleep with both his sister and his mother, who abandoned him as a small boy. He runs off to a city where no one will know him and finds work and shelter at a library under the watchful tutelage of a hermaphroditic librarian, Oshima, and his mysterious and elegant employer, Miss Saeki, a middle-aged woman that may be Kafka's mother, and who lives in mourning following the death of her lover years before. No sooner does Kafka leave than his father is found murdered, and Kafka wakes up in a city miles away, covered in blood." (January Magazine)

"Like his characters' quests, Murakami's expeditions off the worn path of literature can be both rewarding and terrifying. Finishing 'Kafka on the Shore' is like waking from a great dream. Nothing has changed, but everything about the world looks different." Newsweek

Murakami, Haruki

South of the border, west of the sun; translated from the Japanese by Philip Gabriel. Knopf 1999 213p

ISBN 0-375-40251-9

LC 97-49459

"The narrative unfolds as an introspective ghost story in which Hajime must exorcise his past in the person of the enigmatic Shimamoto before he can affirm the new direction of his life. The ending, at once tender and hopeful, shows Murakami in a more mellow aspect than his work has exhibited before." Publ Wkly

Murakami, Haruki

★ The wind-up bird chronicle; translated from the Japanese by Jay Rubin. Knopf 1997 610p

ISBN 0-679-44669-9

LC 97-2813

Original Japanese edition, 1995

Murakami's "protagonist is a harmless fellow who merely wants to recover his cat and his wife. The troubles, real and delusional, that he encounters can be seen as extravagant metaphors for every ill from personal isolation to mass murder. The novel is a deliberately confusing, illogical image of a confusing, illogical world. It is not easy reading, but it is never less than absorbing." Atl Mon

Murakami, Ryu

In the miso soup; translated by Ralph McCarthy. Kodansha International 2004 180p $22.95

ISBN 4-7700-2957-8

Original Japanese edition, 1997

"Beyond one terribly shocking scene, Miso is a thoughtful novel about loneliness, lack of identity and cultural and moral corruption. Through simple yet chilling language, Murakami doesn't condemn his characters. Instead he takes aim at rampant consumerism and the dumbing-down of Japanese and American culture. No one, Murakami seems to say, is completely guilty because we are shaped by the world around us." USA Today

Murasaki Shikibu

The **tale** of Genji; a novel in six parts. {by} Lady Murasaki; translated from the Japanese by Arthur Waley. Modern Lib. 1960 1135p

"A Japanese romance of the Heian period (794-1185). . . . This vast chronicle, often considered the world's first novel for its psychological depth, centers on the career of Prince Genji, his progeny, and the women with whom they associate. While delineating the elaborate rituals of courtly life, this work reflects the melancholy beauty of a world in constant flux and the vulnerability of women dependent upon the instability of human affection. Rich in poetry and elaborate wordplay, this work has had tremendous impact on the subsequent literary tradition." Reader's Ency. 4th edition

Murdoch, Iris

★ An **accidental** man. Viking 1971 442p
ISBN 0-670-10208-3
"The central figure of this novel is one of those accident-prone figures whose . . . misfortune becomes a substitute source of strength. . . . Ever since his brother injured his hand in a childhood incident, the world owes Austin a blank cheque to cover subsequent reverses—which do not fail to arrive. But someone is always sorry for him, always getting him out of trouble even at the price of their own. His self-pity destroys others in accordance with what Miss Murdoch . . . calls 'whatever deep mythological forces control the destinies of men.'" New Statesman (1913)

Murdoch, Iris

The **bell**; a novel. Viking 1958 342p
"The setting is an Anglican lay community attached to an abbey on one of the great estates of England. . . . The members of this community and its temporary residents are on the whole an odd, and certainly an oddly assorted, bunch. And their high-minded leader is a homosexual who was once involved in a scandal that ended his plans for entering the church. The story concerns itself with the relationships between various members of this hothouse world, with the arrival of a new bell for the abbey and the simultaneous discovery in the lake of the lost fourteenth-century bell about which there is a sinister legend. The climax is an eruption of scandal and disaster." Atlantic

Murdoch, Iris

The **book** and the brotherhood. Viking 1988 607p

LC 87-40294
First published 1987 in the United Kingdom
"Despite its excessive length and passages that can seem almost as self-indulgent as the characters they represent, The Book and The Brotherhood demonstrates again and again that Iris Murdoch is among the most gifted descriptive and

narrative writers in English—and certainly one of the most consistently entertaining." NY Rev Books

Murdoch, Iris

A **fairly** honourable defeat. Viking 1970 436p
"As is usual with a Murdoch novel, the action in summary seems preposterous. But given her inventiveness, her Gothic imagination, her gift for melodrama and suspense, she creates a world that becomes an effective vehicle for her moral vision." Choice

Murdoch, Iris

The **good** apprentice. Viking 1986 522p
LC 85-40635
"The esthetic puzzle is whether the comic story and the spiritual kernel can be held together by Miss Murdoch's archaic stance as an authorial will. And yet no other contemporary British novelist seems to me of her eminence." N Y Times Book Rev

Murdoch, Iris

★ The **green** knight. Viking 1994 472p
LC 93-30618
First published 1993 in the United Kingdom
"That a cold, dark, evil act should open up a gap through which warmth and light can flood into the world is a paradox characteristic of Iris Murdoch's deeply meditated insight into the nature of the good." London Rev Books

Murdoch, Iris

Jackson's dilemma. Viking 1996 249p
ISBN 978-0670868155
LC 95-39986
First published 1995 in the United Kingdom
"The peripheries of 'Jackson's Dilemma' are lush with anecdotal material; Murdoch has a way, with her minor or even offstage characters, of suggesting a wealth of motivation, a repletion of interior life." N Y Times Book Rev

Murdoch, Iris

The **nice** and the good. Viking 1968 378p
The action "begins with a violent death in the chambers of Whitehall faintly suggestive of a Le Carré thriller. . . . At times hilariously funny, slightly shivery (intimations of blackmail, suicide, dabblings in black magic) 'The Nice and the Good' is first and foremost a delightful love story. The friends, relatives, hanger-ons, whose lives revolve around the happily married Octavian and Kate Gray are all seeking after love in their own ways. They find it, too, and sometimes in the most amazing places. The characterizations are superb, the mood that of a happy fairy tale crossed with highly sophisticated sexual comedy." Publ Wkly

Murdoch, Iris

Nuns and soldiers. Viking 1981 505p
LC 80-16935
First published 1980 in the United Kingdom
This novel explores the tangled lives of recently widowed Gertrude; Tim, a painter; Anne, a former nun; and "Count" Peter who is in love with Gertrude
"The glory of Iris Murdoch at her best—as she almost always is in Nuns and Soldiers—is that she can convey with

total respect the awareness, readjusting and hunger, and at the same time 'place' it, with a severe but not savage irony, in a world which hints at quite different forces and priorities." New Statesman (1913)

Murdoch, Iris
★ The **philosopher's** pupil. Viking 1983 576p
LC 82-45901

This "collaboration between Murdoch and her imagination is both challenging and irresistible: a combination of gossip and profundity, modern times and ancient edicts." Time

Murdoch, Iris
The **sea,** the sea. Viking 1978 502p
LC 78-13516

The narrator of this "novel is Charles Arrowby, a former actor and director who has retired from the theater to take up solitary residence in a remote house on a northern coast. His tale begins as a mixture of diary and memoir: alternately he records his first impressions of his new home and reviews his past life as though the better to understand the man he has become. . . . His recollections largely concern a succession of love-affairs with actresses; but before all these, and dwarfing them in its importance to his development, was an unconsummated but passionate childhood relationship with a girl named Hartley, who disappeared abruptly and woundingly from his life before he was twenty and married another man." Times Lit Suppl

Murdoch, Iris
Something special; a story. illustrated by Michael McCurdy. Norton 2000 55p $15.95
ISBN 0-393-05007-6
LC 00-40212

First published in Winter's Tale, no.3, 1957

Set in the 1950's this story "concerns one epiphanic evening in the life of Yvonne Geary, a spirited Dublin shopgirl who seeks to flee her oppressive life. Though 24, she still shares a bed with her mother and can only dream of escape on the mail boat to England, the place where 'every Irish person with a soul in them' wants to travel. Even the arrival of a suitor fails to provide release—Sam may be a responsible, doting man, but he is still 'nothing special.' Pressure from her mother persuades Yvonne to go out with him anyway. . . . Murdoch's story can be subtle and heartfelt, most notably as it charts the melancholy, meandering voyage the young couple take toward compromised lives." N Y Times Book Rev

Murphy, Margaret
Darkness falls. St. Martin's Minotaur 2004 355p $24.95
ISBN 0-312-32851-6
LC 2003-70098

"The critical task, as sleekly presented in the form of a police procedural, is to identify the kidnapper and trace him through his underworld associates. Meanwhile, in alternating chapters written in the skin-chilling style of a thriller, Murphy places the reader in the cellar where Clara has been blindfolded, beaten and shackled to the wall by a man who challenges her to defend her values and plead for her life.

The objective is still to identify the stranger and determine his motive. But in Murphy's bold treatment, the victim is made to acknowledge her own intimate acquaintance with evil." N Y Times Book Rev

Murphy, Yannick
The **call**; Yannick Murphy. Harper Perennial 2011 220p. pa $14.99
ISBN 0-06-202314-4; 978-0-06-202314-8
LC 2010051661

L. L. Winship/PEN New England Award: Fiction category (2012)

"An extraneous plot twist at the end tests the family and the reader's suspension of disbelief, and the emotional resonance seems to recede. But throughout, the most delicate and satisfying snippets answer questions like what the house says at night—'I'm closing you in, and buttoning you tight,' which quietly and brilliantly speaks to both comfort and threat. In the quotidian details of farm life, Murphy demonstrates how crucial it is to focus on the small, real tasks in the face of something too big and too dark to understand." Time Out N Y

Murphy, Yannick
Signed, Mata Hari; a novel. Little, Brown 2007 278p $23.99
ISBN 978-0-316-11264-2; 0-316-11264-X
LC 2006-102966

"Weaving back and forth in time between Mata Hari's prison cell in Paris and her prior life in its many manifestations, the seductive narrative spins an irresistible tale of a woman whose legendary exploits are still a matter of historical debate. Was she or was she not a victim of time and circumstance? Did she really deserve to be executed as a spy? In the end, it doesn't really matter, but what does matter is that Murphy has fashioned a mesmerizing novel that creatively reimagines the life of one of the most notorious, and perhaps overvilified, women of all time." Booklist

Murr, Naeem
★ The **perfect** man; a novel. Random House Trade Paperbacks 2007 451p pa $13.95
ISBN 978-0-8129-7701-1; 0-8129-7701-7
LC 2006-43088

This novel "succeeds in recreating an entire world with a full spectrum of human emotions in a small Missouri town, as Faulkner did in the imaginary Yoknapatawpha County in Mississippi." Times Lit Suppl

Murray, Paul
Skippy dies. Faber & Faber 2010 661p $28; pa 3v boxed set $30
ISBN 978-0-86547-943-2; 0-8654-7943-7; 978-0-8654-7948-7 pa; 0-8654-7948-8 pa
LC 2010-926173

"First off, the title of Skippy Dies should come with a spoiler alert, because Skippy does in fact die. And oh, the humanity! He dies like a fish on the floor of Ed's Doughnut House, where he's been locked in a doughnut-eating contest with his tubby, brilliant, but unhinged prep-school buddy Ruprecht. . . . Essentially, though, the novel's about a fusty old Catholic school trying to cope and connive after the Skippy Doughnut Tragedy, while dealing with the more commonplace tragedy that being an adolescent sucks, as do being middle-aged and being old. Murray's humor and inventiveness never flag. And despite a serious theme — what happens to boys and men when they realize the world isn't the sparkly planetarium they had hoped for — Skippy Dies leaves you feeling hopeful and hungry for life. Just not for doughnuts." Entertainment Wkly

Murray, Sabina

Forgery. Grove Press 2007 248p $24
ISBN 978-0-8021-1844-8; 0-8021-1844-5
LC 2006-52645

The author "juxtaposes the subject of fake antiquities with both fake and real portraits of characters. Lacking rhythm, the restrained prose does not effectively create flowing dialog, but with just a few words Murray conjures images that stay with the reader for days." Libr J

Musil, Robert

★ The **man** without qualities; translated from the German by Sophie Wilkins. Knopf 1995 1774p 2v
ISBN 0-394-51052-6
LC 92-37943

"The first two volumes of this monumental work were published in 1930 and 1932; a fragmentary third was published posthumously in 1942, and in 1952 the novel appeared, with additional chapters, in one volume. Apart from providing a brilliant, existential portrait of Ulrich, the scholarly, purposeless 'man without qualities' the book is a vivid depiction of Austrian decadence before the outbreak of World War I. This single remarkable work established Musil as one of the most influential German-language novelists in the first half of the 20th century." Reader's Ency. 4th edition

My mistress's sparrow is dead; great love stories, from Chekhov to Munro. edited by Jeffrey Eugenides. HarperCollins 2008 587p $24.95; pa $15.99
ISBN 978-0-06-124037-9; 0-06-124037-0; 978-0-06-124038-6 pa; 0-06-124038-9 pa
LC 2007-35989

Eugenides "has assembled something quite extraordinary here: a fascinating, consistently compelling, and superbly edited collection of short stories about romantic love. Part of the collection's appeal is its range and depth: at 600 pages, it offers gems and new discoveries at every turn." Libr J

The **Mysterious** West; edited by Tony Hillerman. HarperCollins Pubs. 1994 392p
LC 94-25842

"This stunning collection . . . offers readers some wonderful choices in fiction. Each story is strikingly different in tempo, plot, and setting, yet each is part of and contributes to the diversified world of the mysterious West." SLJ

Myśliwski, Wiesław

Stone upon stone; Wiesław Myśliwski; translated from the Polish by Bill Johnston. Archipelago Books

Distributed by Consortium Book Sales and Distribution 2010 534 p.
ISBN 098262462X; 9780982624623
LC 2010038451

This book, a winner of Three Percent's 2012 Best Translated Book Award, offers an "epic in the rural tradition—a . . . stream of memory cutting through the rich and varied terrain of one man's connection to the land, to his family and community, to women, to tradition, to God, to death, and to what it means to be alive. Wise and impetuous, plain-spoken and compassionate Szymek, recalls his youth in their village, his time as a guerrilla soldier, as a wedding official, barber, policeman, lover, drinker, and caretaker for his invalid brother. Filled with interwoven stories and voices, . . . Szymek's narrative . . . [presents the] wisdom of one who has suffered, yet who loves life to the very core." (Publisher's note)

Müller, Herta, 1955-

The **hunger** angel; a novel. Herta Müller; translated by Philip Boehm. Henry Holt and Co. 2012 p. cm. $26
ISBN 9780805093018
LC 2011050952

"This novel of the Gulag" follows "17-year-old Leo Auberg, [who] has just started having sex with men in the park, fearfully, risking jail; when the soldiers come calling, he's glad to escape his watchful small town. That gladness disappears on the cattle cars. . . . What follows are dozens of short sections as Leo riffs on conditions in the camp." (Kirkus Reviews)

"Under Müller's influence, the subject matter not only begs a reader's sympathy, but deftly illuminates the complex psychological state of starvation and displacement." Pub Wkly

N

Nabb, Magdalen

Some bitter taste. Soho Press 2002 247p $24
ISBN 1-569-47317-X
LC 2002-70579

The author "has Simenon's knack of unlocking the deeper mysteries of ordinary people's pedestrian lives. . . . In Nabb's world, nothing is simple and no life, after all, is ordinary." N Y Times Book Rev

Nabokov, Vladimir Vladimirovich

★ **Ada**; or, Ardor: a family chronicle. [by] Vladimir Nabokov. McGraw-Hill 1969 589p

"In its prodigious length and with the family tree on its frontispiece the book recalls the great 19th-century novels of the author's native Russia, but Ada boldly turns its predecessors on their heads. For his rich, sweeping saga of the Veen-Durmanov clan, Nabokov invented an incestuous pair of 'cousins' (actually siblings, Van and Ada), a hybrid country (Amerussia), a familiar but strange planet (Antiterra), and a dimension of malleable time. The novel follows the lovers from their childhood idylls through impassioned estrangements and reunions to a tenderly shared old age. The work's rich narrative style incorporates untranslated foreign phrases, esoteric data, and countless literary allusions." Merriam-Webster's Ency of Lit

Nabokov, Vladimir Vladimirovich

★ **King,** queen, knave; a novel. [by] Vladimir Nabokov; translated by Dmitri Nabokov in collaboration with the author. McGraw-Hill 1968 272p

Original Russian edition, 1928

"The image of a deck of playing cards is used throughout the novel. Franz, an unsophisticated young man, works in the department store of his rich uncle Dreyer. Out of boredom Martha, the uncle's young wife, seduces Franz. The lovers subsequently plot to drown Dreyer and marry each other. Martha changes her mind abruptly when she learns that an invention by Dreyer stands to increase his wealth, but she then dies suddenly from pneumonia. Her husband never discovers his wife's duplicity." Merriam-Webster's Ency of Lit

Nabokov, Vladimir Vladimirovich

★ **Lolita**; [by] Vladimir Nabokov. Knopf 1992 335p $19

ISBN 0-679-41043-0

LC 92-52931

First published 1955 in France

"Humbert Humbert is a middle-aged intellectual who has a passion for girls between the ages of nine and fourteen. He falls in love with the twelve-year-old Dolores Haze, whom he calls Lolita. In his plot to seduce her, he marries Dolores's mother, whose accidental death then allows Lolita and Humbert to take off on an odyssey across the U.S. Humbert is surprised when, contrary to his schemes, Lolita seduces him and again when she leaves him for Clare Quilty, whom Humbert later murders. Lolita eventually marries Richard F. Schiller. The book presents a quest for eternal innocence, albeit in satirical terms. . . . It combines parody, fanciful imaginative flights, literary puzzles, and a brilliant satirical overview of American culture." Reader's Ency. 4th edition

Nabokov, Vladimir Vladimirovich

Look at the harlequins! {by} Vladimir Nabokov. McGraw-Hill 1974 253p

In this pseudo-autobiographical novel, the narrator, a Russian émigré novelist and college professor who has lived in London, Paris and the United States, recalls his life, loves (including four marriages) and work in a manner which often parodies Nabokov's own life and writings

This is a book "to enchant Nabokov fans and irritate everybody else. . . . {It} is part roman a clef, part fantasy, a tale of 'wives and books interlaced monogrammatically.' It is full of erudite allusions, Russian words in various stages of translation and absurd mistranslation, puns, anagrams, acronyms. Also opinions. . . . Comic, polished, international, {Nabokov} offers sophisticated entertainment, a concoction of romantic and literary matters." Christ Sci Monit

Nabokov, Vladimir Vladimirovich

Novels and memoirs, 1941-1951; . Literary Classics of the U.S. 1996 710p il (Library of America) $35

ISBN 1-883011-18-3

LC 96-15257

The real life of Sebastian Knight (1941) is about a Russian living in Paris who learns about his half-brother, a famous English novelist, by writing his biography. Bend sinister (1947) is about a professor's attempts to maintain his integrity in a totalitarian state.

Nabokov, Vladimir Vladimirovich

Novels, 1955-1962. Library of Am. 1996 904p $35

ISBN 1-883011-19-1

LC 96-15256

Contents: Lolita; Pnin; Pale fire; Lolita, a screenplay

Nabokov, Vladimir Vladimirovich

Novels, 1969-1974. Library of Am. 1996 824p il $35

ISBN 1-883011-20-5

LC 96-15255

Contents: Ada; Transparent things; Look at the harlequins!

Transparent things (1972) is a novella about a rootless American who murders his wife

Nabokov, Vladimir Vladimirovich

★ **Pale** fire; a novel. [by] Vladimir Nabokov. Putnam 1962 315p

This novel is "both pedantry and a satire on pedantry. The core of the novel is a 999-line poem by an American author, John Shade—a sort of Robert Frost—which consists mainly of a rather moving meditation on the tragic end of the poet's daughter. After Shade's death, a foolish scholar named Kinbote—an exile from the mythical country of Zembla and a visiting professor of Zemblan at Wordsmith College, New Wye, Appalachia—edits this work, providing a preface and a detailed corpus of notes. But Kinbote has an 'idée fixe'—the history of his own country—and he believes that Shade's poem is an allegory of this history, with Kinbote himself—fantasized into the deposed King Charles Xavier II—as the hero. The humour—and Nabokov's humour is subtle as well as occasionally brutal—lies in the disparity between the simple truth of the poem and the gross self-exalting hallucinations of its editor." Burgess. 99 Novels

Nabokov, Vladimir Vladimirovich

Pnin; {by} Vladimir Nabokov. Doubleday 1957 191p

"Not a novel, not really a collection of short stories, but rather a series of sketches, all of them dealing with Timofey Pnin, professor of Russian in a small American university. Each one finds Pnin valiantly trying to cope with the daily crises of American society—Pnin on the wrong train, Pnin learning to drive, Pnin giving a party, Pnin and the washing machine. They are all gently amusing, affectionate portraits of a Russian expatriate of the old school caught up in the inexplicable complexities of daily life." Libr J

Nabokov, Vladimir Vladimirovich

The **stories** of Vladimir Nabokov. Knopf 1996 659p

ISBN 0-394-58615-8

LC 95-23466

For this chronologically-arranged collection, "Nabokov's son Dmitri has assembled the 52 stories published in English before Nabokov died in 1977, and translated another 13 written in Russian between 1920 or '21 and 1924." Newsweek

Nadas, Peter

Parallel stories; a novel. translated from the Hungarian by Imre Goldstein. Farrar, Straus, and Giroux 2011 1133p $40

ISBN 978-0-374-22976-4; 0-374-22976-7

LC 2010-39688

Original Hungarian edition, 2005

This book by Péter Nádas is "the tale of a family, the Lippay-Lehrs, living in Budapest in the mid-twentieth century. . . . Each of these characters occupies center stage for a while--a few pages or a few hundred. Stories are nested within stories, time frames shift back and forth without warning. . . . The body, the condition of embodiment, is . . . Nádas's . . . subject. . . . [T]he first half of the novel is anchored by two . . . long sex scenes." (New Republic)

"Three unusual men are at the heart of Parallel Stories: Hans von Wolkenstein, whose German mother is linked to secrets of fascist-Nazi collaboration during the 1940s; Ágost Lippay Lehr, whose influential father has served Hungary's different political regimes for decades; and András Rott, who has his own dark record of mysterious activities abroad. The web of extended and interconnected dramas reaches from 1989 back to the spring of 1939, when Europe trembled on the edge of war, and extends to the bestial times of 1944-45, when Budapest was besieged, the Final Solution devastated Hungary's Jews, and the war came to an end, and on to the cataclysmic Hungarian Revolution of October 1956. We follow these men from Berlin and Moscow to Switzerland and Holland, from the Mediterranean to the North Sea, and of course, from village to city in Hungary. The social and political circumstances of their lives may vary greatly, their sexual and spiritual longings may seem to each of them entirely unique, yet . . . [the novel] unveils uncanny reverberating parallels that link them across time and space." Publisher's note

Nadel, Barbara

The **Ottoman** cage; a novel of Istanbul. Barbara Nadel. Thomas Dunne Books/St. Martins Minotaur 2005 312 p. $14.95

ISBN 0312337698; 9781933397849

LC 2004061875

In this book, "[w]hen a brutal murder shocks Istanbul's rundown Jewish quarter, the Turkish police force unleashes their best weapon - the chain-smoking, brandy-swilling Inspector Cetin Ikmen, husband to a strict Muslim woman (who disapproves of his drinking) and loving father of eight (with another on the way)." (Publisher's note)

Nadler, Stuart

Wise men; a novel. Stuart Nadler. Reagan Arthur Book 2013 335 p. (hardcover) $25.99

ISBN 0316126489; 9780316126489

LC 2012020020

This novel, by Stuart Nadler, begins in Cape Cod "during the summer of 1952. . . . Arthur's teenage son, Hilly, makes friends with Lem Dawson, a black man whose job it is to take care of the house. . . . When Hilly finds himself falling for Lem's niece, Savannah, . . . the results shatter his family, and hers. Years later, haunted by his memories of that summer, Hilly sets out to find Savannah, in an attempt to right the wrongs he helped set in motion." (Publisher's note)

Nadzam, Bonnie

Lamb; a novel. Other Press 2011 275p pa $15.95

ISBN 978-1-59051-437-5; 1-59051-437-8

"People can tell about Lamb, a man whose wife has left him and who finds so little control left in his own life he decides to exert some on Tommie, a seventh-grade girl. Tommie's friends put her up to bumming a cigarette off Lamb just after his dad's funeral. Lamb takes it as an opportunity to teach her and her friends a lesson, pretending to kidnap her (in a manner convincing enough that Tommie's not sure if it's real). The two strike up what could charitably be called an uneasy friendship, with Lamb convincing himself he's finally doing right by guiding Tommie, and Tommie happy for the attention and the wealthier Lamb's gifts. They both make the very bad decision to road trip to the Rockies together, where pretty much everything goes wrong. Nadzam oversaturates every inch of Lamb's pages. The title character's unacknowledged grief for his father and his own misdirected life floods the subtext, and the writing is both beautiful and unabashedly indulgent. . . . But Nadzam earns that excess. As Lamb always sits on the flinty side of combustion, so does the reader." Time Out Chicago

Naipaul, V. S.

★ A **bend** in the river. Knopf 1979 278p

LC 78-21591

"This is a beautifully composed book, with an almost Conradian power of description. Aesthetically most satisfying, it is also profoundly depressing. But depression is sometimes a stone on the road to literary exaltation." Burgess. 99 Novels

Naipaul, V. S.

★ **Guerrillas**. Knopf 1975 248p

"This is a novel without a villain, and there is not a character for whom the reader does not at some point feel deep sympathy and keen understanding, no matter how villainous or futile he may seem." N Y Times Book Rev

Naipaul, V. S.

Half a life. Knopf 2001 211p $24

ISBN 0-375-40737-5

LC 2001-33730

"In the book's last moments a narrative that has seemed to meander pulls suddenly tight, giving 'Half a Life' an interest that lies beyond its relation to Naipaul's other work. . . . The very fissures in its structure, its change from voice to voice, transform 'Half a Life' into a meditation on the difficulties of building a coherent self." N Y Times Book Rev

Naipaul, V. S.

★ A **house** for Mr. Biswas; with an introduction by Karl Miller. Knopf 1995 xxi, 564p $20

ISBN 0-679-44458-0

A reissue of the title first published 1961 by McGraw-Hill

"Trinidad, West Indies, is the setting for the story of lonely Mr. Mohun Biswas, a Hindu of high caste but low economic status. Throughout the book he longs for independence from his wife's large family and a house of his own. In a portrait that is both funny and compassionate, West Indian life is vividly described, especially the relationships among members of Mr. Biswas's family." Shapiro. Fic for Youth. 3d edition

Naipaul, V. S.

Magic seeds. Knopf 2004 280p $25

ISBN 0-375-40736-7

LC 2004-48964

The author "has written a calculated polemic. . . . Naipaul is suggesting that our racial and ethnic fate is sealed; we can never escape who we are, and must learn to live with our unchosen identities whether we like them or not. It's not a consoling vision; neither is it despairing. It simply is." N Y Times Book Rev

Naipaul, V. S.

A **way** in the world; a novel. Knopf 1994 380p

ISBN 0-394-56478-2

LC 93-44680

In this autobiographical fiction, Naipaul examines "feelings of rootlessness, the realities of the colonial experience, the impact of cultural displacement, and our need to belong. He does so through a series of linked historical narratives. Among them is an imagined vision of Raleigh's desperate but futile search for El Dorado. We are also introduced to Francisco de Miranda, one of the precursors to Bolivar's revolution. We are witness to the irony inherent in the life of Lebrun, a Trinidadian/Panamanian Communist of the 1930s. And then there is Blair, a former co-worker of the narrator in Trinidad, whose African roots prove no help when he becomes an adviser to an East African despot. These are tales of lost souls desperate to find a place at the table but who never quite succeed, leaving them doomed to remain on the fringes of history." Libr J

Nance, John J.

Fire flight. Simon & Schuster 2003 353p map $25

ISBN 0-7432-5050-8

LC 2003-59095

"Fires are raging out of control in Yellowstone National Park, and planes from the aging fleet of water tankers are crashing. Veteran pilot Clark Maxwell has returned from retirement to help out—not only in his official capacity but also as an investigator in light of the recurring crashes. Where have the planes been over the preceding winter instead of having lifesaving maintenance performed on them? Maxwell suspects a major cover-up. Despite a rushed and contrived ending, Nance has crafted an exciting and compelling story." Libr J

Nance, John J.

The **last** hostage. Doubleday 1998 373p

ISBN 0-385-49055-0

LC 97-44861

"Airbridge Airlines pilot Ken Wolfe fakes engine trouble to force a landing; then, having tricked his co-pilot off the plane, he takes off. His plan: to extort a confession from a surprise passenger, U.S. Attorney General nominee Rudolph Bostitch. It seems that, as a Connecticut DA, Bostitch covered up for the man who Wolfe believes tortured and killed his 11-year-old daughter. Wolfe rolls the plane to convince the crew that a hijacker with a bomb shares the cockpit, a Flitephone call alerts the FBI and novice female negotiator Kat Bronsky is put on the case." Publ Wkly

"Nance is a master of suspense, and his fast-moving plot has more twists than a corkscrew." Libr J

Nance, John J.

Medusa's child. Doubleday 1997 388p

ISBN 978-0385483438

LC 96-27656

"For his livelihood, pilot and small businessman Scott McKay leases a converted Boeing 727 and ferries cargo across the country, much like a truck driver. On one particular flight, however, he comes to realize that his cargo hold contains a thermonuclear bomb: a modern instrument of destruction dubbed the Medusa device and capable of an incredible act of terrorism—destroying every computer chip within a very wide radius. The effort to incapacitate the bomb before it can detonate is the warp and woof of an exciting plot that offers hours of pure diversion." Booklist

Nance, John J.

Pandora's clock. Doubleday 1995 357p

ISBN 978-0385479448

LC 95-8409

"Shortly after Quantum Airlines Flight 66 departs Frankfurt, Germany, for New York, one of the passengers succumbs to an apparent heart attack. It may be, however, that Professor Ernest Helms was exposed to a doomsday virus just before boarding his flight; if so, more than 200 passengers and crew members could be dead within a matter of hours. Word of this imminent disaster leaks to governments and media organizations around the world, of course, and the jumbo jet is refused landing clearance everywhere." Publ Wkly

"A uniquely suspenseful and terrifying story." Booklist

Narayan, R. K.

The **grandmother's** tale and selected stories. Viking 1994 312p

LC 94-4581

Set in India these stories "emphasize perceptively drawn characters and situations rather than their colorful foreign backdrops. All the tales display a wry, gentle humor." Publ Wkly

Narayan, R. K.

★ **Malgudi** days. Viking 1982 246p

LC 81-52204

"This selection distills, magically, Malgudi's vibrancy, its mythological-animistic throb, the large and small corruptions of its citizens—from bureaucrats to back-street people—and the reassuring backdrop of its cyclical rhythms. Distinguished writing; rewarding reading." Booklist

Narayan, R. K.
Mr. Sampath--the printer of Malgudi, The financial expert, Waiting for the Mahatma; with an introduction by Alexander McCall Smith. Everyman's Library 2006 xxxviii, 578p $25

ISBN 0-4000-4477-4

LC 2006-279228

An omnibus edition of three novels first published 1949, 1952 and 1955, respectively

"Mr. Sampath—The Printer of Malgudi is the story of a businessman who adapts to the collapse of his weekly newspaper by shifting to screenplays, only to have the glamour of it all go to his head. In The Financial Expert, a man of many hopes but few resources spends his time under a banyan tree dispensing financial advice to those willing to pay for his knowledge. In Waiting for the Mahatma, a young drifter meets the most beautiful girl he has ever seen—an adherent of Mahatma Gandhi—and commits himself to Gandhi's Quit India campaign, a decision that will test the integrity of his ideals against the strength of his passions." Publisher's note

Narayan, R. K.
Swami and friends, The bachelor of arts, The dark room, The English teacher; with an introduction by Alexander McCall Smith. Everyman's Library 2006 xxxvii, 609p $25

ISBN 1-4000-4476-6

LC 2006-279229

An omnibus edition of four titles first published 1935, 1937, 1938 and 1945, respectively

"Swami and Friends introduces us to Narayan's beloved fictional town of Malgudi, where ten-year-old Swaminathan's excitement about his country's initial stirrings for independence competes with his ardor for cricket and all other things British. The Bachelor of Arts is a poignant coming-of-age novel about a young man flush with first love, but whose freedom to pursue it is hindered by the fixed ideas of his traditional Hindu family. In The Dark Room, Narayan's portrait of aggrieved domesticity, the docile and obedient Savitri, like many Malgudi women, is torn between submitting to her husband's humiliations and trying to escape them. The title character in The English Teacher, Narayan's most autobiographical novel, searches for meaning when the death of his young wife deprives him of his greatest source of happiness." Publisher's note

Narayan, R. K.
Under the banyan tree and other stories. Viking 1985 193p

LC 85-3234

"Narayan's clarity, his mastery of technique, his respect for the spectrum of human predicament, his absence of malice and his freedom from a single philosophy that explains everything away put him in the unique position of being able to turn a teeming cultural life into lucid and enjoyable stories." New Statesman

Nasaw, Jonathan Lewis
Twenty-seven bones; a thriller. [by] Jonathan Nasaw. Atria Books 2004 360p $25

ISBN 0-7434-4653-4

LC 2003-69637

"Former FBI agent E.L. Pender heads to St. Luke, one of the Virgin Islands, to help hunt for a murderer whose modus operandi is to torture his victims, cut off their right hands, and leave them to bleed slowly to death. The authorities, fearful of bad publicity, want to keep the killer's existence quiet. Pender, clearly from the mainland and unaccustomed to the speech patterns and social customs of the island, is at a disadvantage as he tries to familiarize himself with the community and its inhabitants. . . . Although the reader knows who is behind the killings, tension arises from not knowing whether Pender will figure it out in time to save other people while putting himself at grave risk." Libr J

Naslund, Sena Jeter
Abundance; a novel of Marie Antoinette. William Morrow 2006 545p $26.95

ISBN 978-0-06-082539-3; 0-06-082539-1

LC 2006-43817

"With vivid detail and exquisite narrative technique, Naslund exemplifies the best of historical fiction, finding the woman beneath the pose, a queen facing history as it rises up against her." Publ Wkly

Naslund, Sena Jeter
Ahab's wife; or, The star-gazer; a novel. Morrow 1999 668p $28

ISBN 0-688-17187-7

LC 99-22135

"At age 12, Una escapes her religiously obsessed father in rural Kentucky to live with relatives in a lighthouse off New Bedford, Mass. When she is 16—disguised as a boy—she runs off to sea aboard a whaler, which sinks after being rammed by its quarry. Una and two young men who love her are the only survivors of a group set adrift in an open boat, but the dark secret of their cannibalism will leave its mark. Rescued, Una is wed to one of the young men by the captain of the Pequod, handsome, commanding Ahab, who has not as yet met the white whale that will be his destiny. . . . Una's later marriage to Ahab—a passionate and intellectually satisfying relationship—the loss of her mother and her newborn son in one night, and her life as a rich woman in Nantucket are further developments in a plot teeming with arresting events and provocative ideas." Publ Wkly

Naslund, Sena Jeter
Four spirits; a novel. Morrow 2003 524p $26.95

ISBN 0-06-621238-3

LC 2003-51170

"Naslund has done something unusually fine—she's written a drifting collective portrait of a city in distress. The characters of 'Four Spirits' are deeply entwined, sometimes without knowing it." N Y Times Book Rev

Nathan, Robert
Portrait of Jennie. Knopf 1940 212p

"Eban Adams, a struggling artist who is unable to sell his art work, meets an unusual child named Jennie in the park and immediately begins to prosper. He knows little about her except that she belongs in the past and that every few months, when their paths cross, she has aged by years. His finest painting is a portrait of her, a token of his love, which ends in predestined tragedy." Shapiro. Fic for Youth. 3d edition

Nathanson, E. M.

The **dirty** dozen. Random House 1965 498p

This "is not an ordinary war book. The fight here is not so much against the Wehrmacht as it is against self, society, and 'the system.' . . . If the situation seems impossible, if Reisman seems a superman, no matter, for the insights into good and evil are richly rewarding in this exciting and highly compelling novel." Libr J

Naylor, Gloria

Bailey's Cafe. Harcourt Brace Jovanovich 1992 229p

LC 91-42089

The author "takes us many keys down, and sometimes back up, in this virtuoso orchestration of survival, suffering, courage and humor, sounding through the stories of these lives." N Y Times Book Rev

Naylor, Gloria

Linden Hills. Ticknor & Fields 1985 304 p.
ISBN 9780140088298; 9780899193571 out of print

LC 84016222

The author "sketches the development of the community of Linden Hills through its founder, Luther Nedeed, and successive generations of Nedeeds, showing in the decline of the family the corrosive effect of ambition, arrogance and the abuse of power. The residents of Linden Hills are similarly subverted by the accommodations, sacrifices and perversions of soul blacks must endure to live in an affluent community, even, as in this case, an all-black one." Publ Wkly

Naylor, Gloria

★ **Mama** Day. Ticknor & Fields 1988 311p

LC 87-18157

"When she is not didactically fostering our spiritual instruction, Gloria Naylor serves another worthy purpose beautifully: she invites us to imagine the lives of complex characters at work and play, and gives us a faithfully rendered community in all its seasons." Ms

Naylor, Gloria

The **men** of Brewster Place. Hyperion 1998 173p
ISBN 0-7868-6421-4

LC 97-45987

"Ben, a neighborhood janitor (and chorus) resurrected from the previous Brewster Place novel, narrates seven tales of neighborhood men and the women who love them. Their travails feature the familiar ills of the inner city, yet Naylor lends these archetypal situations complexity and depth: Basil yearns to be the kind of father he never had but chooses a path that leads to heartbreak; Eugene's restlessness in his marriage and friendship with a transsexual force him to face a difficult fact about himself; Reverend Moreland T. Woods rehearses his political aspirations with maneuvers on his church's board; and C.C. Baker, involved in local drug trafficking, keeps a startling truth from the police." Publ Wkly

Naylor, Gloria

The **women** of Brewster Place. Viking 1982 192p

LC 81-69969

This "novel is set, as the title indicates, in Brewster Place, a block-long dead-end street of run-down apartment buildings in a northern city. In an interrelated series of vignettes, Naylor focuses on seven black women, residents of Brewster Place. She is concerned with the distance between their dreams and realities, problems and solutions; these women are of different ages, come from different backgrounds, react differently to their blackness and to men, and have different notions of personal accomplishment, but all are burdened by being both black and female. Naylor is not angry; she writes with conviction and beautiful language, but spares the reader any bitterness. Characters are not puppets but exist and function as well-rounded personalities." Booklist

Naylor, Phyllis Reynolds

After; Phyllis Reynolds Naylor. Soho Press 2003 371p $25
ISBN 1-569-47354-4

LC 2003-50695

"Especially in its early sections, the novel will remind many readers of Anne Tyler, with its slightly off-center characters and its sympathetic but wry and somewhat distanced point of view...After is popular fiction for intelligent readers, something always in short supply and always welcome." Washington Post

Nayman, Shira

The **listener**; a novel. Scribner 2010 305p $27
ISBN 978-0-7432-9282-5; 0-7432-9282-0

LC 2009-27289

"Featuring a plot as rich as the characters, this is a thought-provoking and psychological exploration of love, war, and human identity. . . . Readers who enjoyed Ian McEwan's Atonement will enjoy the introspective tone of Nayman's work." Libr J

Ndiaye, Marie

Three strong women; a novel. by Marie NDiaye; translated by John Fletcher. Alfred A. Knopf 2012 293 p.
ISBN 0307594696; 9780307594693

LC 2012003533

This novel, by Marie NDiaye winner of the Prix Concourt award, "is the story of three women: . . . Norah, a French-born lawyer who finds herself in Senegal, summoned by her estranged, tyrannical father; . . . Fanta, who leaves a modest but contented life as a teacher in Dakar to follow her white boyfriend back to France; . . . and Khady, a penniless widow put out by her husband's family with nothing but the name of a distant cousin . . . who lives in France." (Publisher's note)

★ **Nebula** Awards Showcase 2013; The Year's Best Science Fiction and Fantasy Selected by the Science Fiction and Fantasy Writers of America. edited by Catherine Asaro. Pyr 2013 380 p. $18
ISBN 1616147830; 9781616147839

This book, edited by Catherine Asaro, "includes [science fiction and fantasy] stories and excerpts by Connie Willis, Jo Walton, Kij Johnson, Geoff Ryman, John Clute, Carolyn Ives Gilman, Ferrett Steinmetz, Ken Liu, Nancy Fulda, Delia Sherman, Amal El-Mohtar, C. S. E. Cooney, David Goldman, Katherine Sparrow, E. Lily Yu, and Brad R. Torgersen." (Publisher's note)

Neel, Janet

To die for. St. Martin's Press 1999 240p
ISBN 0-312-20598-8

LC 99-18077

A mystery featuring Chief Superintendent John McLeish and his wife Francesca. "The investors in Judith Delves's London cafe, including her co-owner, want to sell, but Judith is obstinately against the transaction. Shortly after her friend and partner, Selina, comes around to her way of thinking, Selina's body is found stuffed into an unused freezer." Publ Wkly

Neely, Barbara

Blanche cleans up. Viking 1998 258p
ISBN 0-670-87626-7

LC 97-39834

"Blanche's caustic comments, streetwise attitude and lusty approach to life cast an illuminating light on both ends of the social spectrum and add sparks to an already sizzling mystery." Publ Wkly

Nelscott, Kris

Stone cribs. St. Martin's Minotaur 2004 323p $24.95
ISBN 0-312-28784-4

LC 2003-50604

"One year after the assassination of Martin Luther King Jr., Smokey Dalton has moved from Memphis to Chicago with an 11-year-old witness to the shooting. There, he investigates rental housing owned by white girlfriend Laura Hathaway. Adding to the unsettled political climate is the fight for the right to abortion, crystallized by Smokey and Laura's involvement in saving a young black woman, pregnant as the result of rape, from death-by-botched-abortion. Smokey subsequently hunts down the rapist, as well as the clumsy abortionist. . . . Nelscott skillfullly recreates a troubled 1960s Chicago, complete with sympathetic protagonists who fight its racial inequalities, widespread ignorance, and political ineptness." Libr J

Nelson, Antonya

Bound; a novel. Bloomsbury 2010 231p $25
ISBN 978-1-59691-575-6; 1-59691-575-7

LC 2010-09791

"Nelson wields words with breathtaking precision. . . . This is no heartwarming makeshift-family-bonding story; Nelson has something truer in mind. Turning tiny moments into revelations, she brilliantly exposes the fears and delusions that drive people to rationalize destructive choices. . . . [A] wise exploration of the war between our worst impulses and our better selves." O Magazine

Nelson, Peter

I thought you were dead: a love story; a novel. [by] Pete Nelson. Algonquin Books of Chapel Hill 2010 264p $23.95
ISBN 978-1-56512-597-1; 1-56512-597-5

LC 2009-47626

"Narrator Paul Gustavson is recently divorced, holed up in his Northampton, Mass., apartment, drinking too much, shakily employed as a writer for the series '[Subject] for Morons' and distancing himself from everyone, including his family back in Minneapolis. He feels like a failure as a husband, lover, brother, son, friend, writer. The only creature he can talk to honestly is his old dog, Stella. And Stella talks back." Minneapolis Star Tribune

"Like a big, friendly mutt-a bit too eager to please, but sweet-souled and companionable." Kirkus

Nemirovsky, Irene, 1903-1942

Fire in the blood; translated by Sandra Smith. Alfred A. Knopf 2007 137p $22
ISBN 978-0-307-26748-1; 0-307-26748-2

LC 2007-28730

"In a book fuelled with images of fire and embers, Némirovsky brilliantly depicts a closed-in, inward-looking community, then gives what happens in it universal resonance by exhibiting not only what people do to each other but what the passing of time does to us all." London Times

Nemirovsky, Irene, 1903-1942

Suite Francaise. Knopf 2006 401p $25
ISBN 1-4000-4473-1

LC 2006-3461

Original French edition, 2004

"Nemirovsky, a young Russian Jewish emigre, became a celebrated novelist in Paris at age 26 in 1929. She wrote eight more novels; then, even though she was certain that she wouldn't survive Germany's occupation of France, she embarked on a . . . work about France's collaboration with the Nazis. She completed two of five planned movements before she was sent to Auschwitz, a heart-wrenching story meticulously documented in a supplemental section. As for Nemirovsky's masterpiece, it begins with the tumultuous 'Storm in June,' in which diverse Parisians frantically evacuate Paris during the June 1940 German invasion. Nemirovsky's gift for combining the panoramic with the intimate, high emotion with stinging wit, is reminiscent of Turgenev, Babel, and Berberova. Acutely sensitive to class differences, and mordantly scornful of hypocrisy, she orchestrates a veritable carnival of cowardice, lies, larceny, and murder as a panicked populace drops all pretense of civilization. The second movement, 'Dolce,' evokes the eye of the storm in the village of Bussy, where German officers are billeted in French homes, and life and love resume. Suite Francaise is a magnificent novel of the insidious devastation of occupation, and Nemirovsky is brilliant and heroic, summoning up profound empathy for all, including regretful German soldiers." Booklist

Nersesian, Arthur

The **swing** voter of Staten Island; a novel.
Akashic Books 2007 271p $22.95

ISBN 978-1-933354-34-7; 1-933354-34-8

LC 2007-926051

"Though sometimes uncomfortably similar to the B-movie classic Escape From New York, Swing Voter aspires to be more than just a genre thriller. This isn't always a good thing: The central mystery is solved on the last page, as though it were an afterthought; for long stretches, Nersesian ditches the plot and focuses on the Armenian genocide. But the book succeeds as a teasing love letter to the dirtier city of yesteryear—downtown stalwarts like P.S.122, Tompkins Square Park, and CBGB appear in disguise. La MaMa materializes, rendered as Mamasita's Blah Blah Theater. Of course, in Nersesian's world, it's a place for both political drama and a gruesome double murder by means of sharpened broomstick. That's entertainment." Village Voice

Nesbo, Jo, 1960-

The **devil's** star; translated from the Norwegian by Don Bartlett. Harper 2010 452p $25.99

ISBN 978-0-06-113397-8; 0-06-113397-3

LC 2009-17819

Original Norwegian edition, 2003

"Devastated by his inability to convince his superiors that fellow detective Tom Waaler is both guilty of his former partner Ellen's murder . . . . and an arms dealer, Harry Hole goes on a four-week bender. Dragged back to work by his loyal boss, Harry is partnered with Waaler to investigate what quickly looks like a serial killer on the loose in Oslo who leaves star-shaped red diamonds with his victims. . . . Scandinavian noir is alive and well, and Nesbø is one of its best authors." Libr J

Nesbo, Jo, 1960-

The **headhunters**; translated from the Norwegian by Don Bartlett. Vintage Crime/Black Lizard 2011 265, 21p pa $14.95

ISBN 978-0-307-94868-7; 0-307-94868-4

Original Norwegian edition, 2008

"Roger Brown, a British expat comfortably ensconced in Oslo, has developed a reputation as one of the best corporate headhunters in the business, but money problems lead him to use information he gleans from job applicants about valuable art they own. Brown arranges to steal their art works and replace them with clever fakes. When Clas Greve, the former CEO of a major European GPS company, lets slip that he accidentally discovered a long-lost Rubens painting in the apartment he inherited from his aunt, Brown anticipates making his biggest score. Of course, the heist doesn't go smoothly, and the dizzying reversals of fortune and situations that would be over-the-top in lesser hands make for a delightful roller-coaster ride." Publ Wkly

Nesbo, Jo, 1960-

★ The **leopard**; Jo Nesbo; translated from the Norwegian by Don Bartlett. Alfred A. Knopf 2012 517 p. map (alk. paper) $26.95

ISBN 0307595870; 9780307595874

LC 2011041049

In this book by Jo Nesbo, "Inspector Harry Hole has literally and figuratively run away from home. Harry hides in Hong Kong's underbelly, drowning his sorrows and painful memories. He only reluctantly returns home to Oslo after two women are violently killed and his father lay on his deathbed, both events demanding Harry's attention and singular expertise." (Library Journal)

Nesbø, Jo

★ **Phantom**; Jo Nesbo; translated from the Norwegian by Don Bartlett. Alfred A. Knopf 2012 377 p.

ISBN 0307960471; 9780307960474

LC 2012019892

In this novel by Jo Nesbo "Former Police Detective Harry Hole returns to Oslo after three years abroad. . . . to request permission to investigate a homicide. But the case is already closed; a young junkie, Gusto, was in all likelihood shot by a pal in a conflict over drugs. Harry is granted permission to visit the accused boy in prison. There, he meets himself and his own history. It's the start of a solitary investigation of the most impossible case in Harry Hole's life." (Author's note)

Nesbo, Jo, 1960-

The **redbreast**; translated from the Norwegian by Don Bartlett. HarperCollins 2007 521p $24.95

ISBN 978-0-06-113399-2; 0-06-113399-X

Original Norwegian edition, 2006

"This is a fine novel, ambitious in concept, skillful in execution and grownup in its view of people and events. In important ways it's also a political novel, one concerned with the threat of fascism, in Norway and by implication everywhere. All in all, The Redbreast certainly ranks with the best of current American crime fiction." Washington Post Book World

Nesbø, Jo

The **redeemer**; 1st U.S. ed. Alfred A. Knopf 2013 416 p. (hardcover) $25.95

ISBN 0307595854; 9780307595850

This book, the sixth in author Jo Nesbo's Harry Hole series, "introduces 17-year-old Robert Karlsen and his year older brother, Jon, who in 1991 are cadets at a Salvation Army retreat in the Norwegian countryside, where a 14-year-old girl is sexually assaulted. . . . 22 years later, detective Hole is winding up the investigation of a drug-related murder in Oslo. The main action begins when a Serbian hit man, Cristo Stankic, shoots Robert on a crowded city street." (Publishers Weekly)

Nesbø, Jo

The **snowman**; translated from the Norwegian by Don Bartlett. Alfred A. Knopf 2011 383p $25.95

ISBN 978-0-307-59586-7; 0-307-59586-2

LC 2010049170

Original Norwegian edition, 2007; this translation originally published 2010 in the United Kingdom

This book follows "antihero police investigator, Harry Hole, . . . [through a murder investigation] that will take Hole to the brink of insanity. . . . A boy named Jonas wakes in the night to find his mother gone. Out his window, in the cold moonlight, he sees the snowman that inexplicably appeared in the yard earlier in the day. Around its neck is his mother's pink scarf. Hole suspects a link between a menacing letter he's received and the disappearance of Jonas's mother—and of perhaps a dozen other women, all of whom went missing on the day of a first snowfall. As his investigation deepens, something else emerges: he is becoming a pawn in an increasingly terrifying game whose rules are devised—and constantly revised—by the killer." (Publisher's note)

This mystery featuring Oslo's Inspector Harry Hole is "about a psychopath who waits for the year's first snowfall to build menacing snowmen outside the homes of his victims, all married women cheating on their spouses. Nesbo has a horrormeister's flair for transforming natural scenes into ominous situations, so those recurring images of beady-eyed snowmen can ruin a walk in the woods or a stolen hour of sexual pleasure. The atmosphere of guilt and gloom is also a reflection of Harry's moody thoughts about his own troubled relationships, his obsessive work ethic and his unhealthy preoccupation with the nature of evil. . . . Harry is a cool hero, but whenever his musings get a bit sticky it's worth remembering that he's afraid of the dark" N Y Times Book Rev

Netzer, Lydia

Shine shine shine; Lydia Netzer. 1st ed. St. Martin's Press 2012 312 p.

ISBN 1250007070; 9781250007070; 9781250015075

LC 2012007426

In this novel by Lydia Netzer "[Sunny has] got the housewife thing down perfectly, but Maxon, a genius engineer, is on a NASA mission to the moon. . . . Once they were two outcasts who found unlikely love in each other . . . now they're parents to an autistic son . . . [and] [t]heir marriage is on the brink of imploding. . . . When an accident in space puts the mission in peril . . . [d]ark secrets, long-forgotten murders, and a blond wig all come tumbling to the light." (Publisher's note)

Neugeboren, Jay

★ **1940**; a novel. Two Dollar Radio 2008 274p pa $15

ISBN 978-0-9763895-6-9

LC 2008-900720

"Neugeboren traverses the Hitlerian tightrope with all the skill and formal daring that have made him one of our most honored writers of literary fiction and masterful nonfiction. This new book is, at once, a beautifully realized work of imagined history, a rich and varied character study and a subtly layered novel of ideas, all wrapped in a propulsively readable story." Los Angeles Times Book Rev

Neugeboren, Jay

Other side of the world; Jay Neugeboren. Two Dollar Radio 2012 267 p. (paperback) $16.50

ISBN 1937512029; 9781937512026

LC 2012950610

In this novel, by Jay Neugeboren, "Charlie is a journeyman whose friend Nick convinces him to move to Singapore. . . . One night, during a fight at a cocktail party in Singapore, Nick dies . . . , prompting Charlie to return to New England where he discovers that a former student has moved in with his father, Max. . . . Seana is a . . . writer who

is equally wild and provocative in life. Together, she and Charlie . . ." form a complex relationship. (Publisher's note)

Neugeboren, Jay

You are my heart and other stories. Two Dollar Radio 2011 180p pa $16

ISBN 978-0-9826848-8-7; 0-9826848-8-6

LC 2011-925178

The author "might not be as famous as some of his compeers, like Philip Roth or John Updike, but it's becoming increasingly harder to argue that he's any less talented. Neugeboren's new short story collection serves as a convincing piece of evidence of the author's rare talent. . . . Dazzlingly smart and deeply felt." Kirkus

Neuhaus, Nele

Snow White must die; Nele Neuhaus; translated by Steven T. Murray. Minotaur Books 2013 384 p. (hardback) $24.99

ISBN 0312604254; 9780312604257

LC 2012038365

In this mystery novel, by Nele Neuhaus, "A woman has fallen from a pedestrian bridge onto a car driving underneath. . . . The investigation leads [detectives] Pia and Oliver to a small village, and the home of the victim, Rita Cramer. . . . In the village, Pia and Oliver encounter a wall of silence. When another young girl disappears, the events of the past seem to be repeating themselves in a disastrous manner." (Publisher's note)

Neuman, Andres, 1977-

Traveler of the century; Andrés Neuman; translated from the Spanish by Nick Caistor and Lorenza Garcia. Farrar, Straus and Giroux 2012 564 p.

ISBN 0374119392; 9780374119393

LC 2011047016

This Alfaguara Prize and National Critics Prize-winning Spanish novel by Andrés Neuman begins when "the enigmatic traveler Hans stops in a small city on the border between Saxony and Prussia. . . . [H]e begins to meet the various characters who populate the town, including a young freethinker named Sophie. Though she is engaged to be married, Sophie and Hans begin a relationship that defies contemporary mores about female sexuality and what can and cannot be said about it." (Publisher's note)

Nevill, Adam

The ritual; Adam Nevill. St. Martin's Griffin 2012 432p.

ISBN 9780312641849

LC 2011036132

This book tells the story of "four old University friends [who] set off into the Scandinavian wilderness of the Arctic Circle . . . to briefly escape the problems of their lives and reconnect with one another. But when Luke . . . finds he has little left in common with his well-heeled friends, tensions rise. With limited experience between them, a shortcut meant to ease their hike turns into a nightmare scenario. . . . But then they stumble across an old habitation. Ancient artefacts decorate the walls and there are bones scattered upon the dry floors. The residue of old rites and pagan sacrifice for something that still exists in the forest. Something responsible for the bestial presence that follows their every step." (Publisher's note)

Neville, Katherine

The **eight**; a novel. Ballantine Bks. 1989 550p

LC 87-91363

"Involving Napoleon, Talleyrand, Casanova, Voltaire, Rousseau, Robespierre and Catherine the Great in the quest, Neville has great fun rewriting history and making it all ring true." Publ Wkly

Neville, Katherine

The **fire**; a novel. Ballantine Books 2008 451p il $26

ISBN 978-0-345-50067-0; 0-345-50067-9

LC 2008-26624

"Alexandra Solarin, child chess prodigy now grown, finds herself immersed in the Game, searching for a legendary chess set, the Montglane Service, which when assembled spells out the formula for the secret of immortality. The quest for the set ranges from the harem of Ali Pasha in 19th-century Albania to present-day Baghdad and Washington, D.C., and involves such historic figures as Charlemagne, Isaac Newton, Lord Byron and Napoleon. Despite the staggering amount and quality of the research, nothing feels shoehorned or extraneous. The story's relentless pace is matched by characters both sympathetic and real." Publ Wkly

Neville, Stuart

The **ghosts** of Belfast. Soho 2009 326p $25

ISBN 978-1-56947-600-0; 1-56947-600-4

LC 2009-11312

Published in the United Kingdom with title: The twelve

"Neville's debut is as unrelenting as Fegan's ghosts, pulling no punches as it describes the brutality of Ireland's 'troubles' and the crime that has followed, as violent men find new outlets for their skills. Sharp prose places readers in this pitiless place and holds them there. Harsh and unrelenting crime fiction, masterfully done." Kirkus

New Cthulhu; edited by Paula Guran. Prime Books 2011 520p.

ISBN 9781607012894

This book collects short speculative fiction inspired by the creations of horror writer H. P. Lovecraft. "Both Laird Barron in 'Old Virginia' and Charles Stross in 'A Colder War' speculate on the horrors that might ensue if government research teams were allowed to explore Lovecraftian monsters as potential weapons. In Cherie Priest's 'Bad Sushi,' a chef uncovers a cosmic conspiracy involving supernaturally corrupted seafood. Sherlock Holmes foils worshipers of Lovecraft's Great Old Ones in Neil Gaiman's 'A Study in Emerald,' while in Elizabeth Bear's 'Shoggoths in Bloom,' an African-American scientist finds himself sympathizing with enslaved creations of those eldritch entities." (Publishers Weekly)

The **new** space opera; edited by Gardner Dozois and Jonathan Strahan. Eos 2007 517p pa $15.95

ISBN 978-0-06-084675-6; 0-06-084675-5

"An exceedingly fine set of stories written specifically for this collection by some of the best sf authors writing today. These 18 tales run the gamut from technologically centered hard science (think exploding comets and artificial intelligence) to character-driven soft science (settling on new worlds). Alien perspectives are balanced by humanistic introspection. Many of the stories mine the genre's favorite nuggets by exploring political and ethical questions from varied and unusual points of view." Libr J

New stories from the South: the year's best [date] edited by Shannon Ravenel. Algonquin Books of Chapel Hill

Annual. First published 1986

An annual collection of short stories culled from a wide variety of magazines. Among the authors represented are Frederick Barthelme, George Singleton, Chris Offutt, Tony Earley, Janice Daugharty, and Elizabeth Spencer

The **New** treasury of great racing stories; Dick Francis and John Welcome, editors. Norton 1992 211p $42

ISBN 0-393-03102-0

LC 92-9647

First published 1991 in the United Kingdom with title: Classic lines: more great racing stories

Newman, Janis Cooke

Mary; a novel. MacAdam/Cage Pub. 2006 707p $26

ISBN 978-1-93156-163-1; 1-93156-163-X

LC 2006-15591

A "portrait of Mary Todd Lincoln. Writing in her journal while confined to Bellvue asylum, Mary alternates between recalling her past life as First Lady and detailing her current experiences in that institution. The first-person narrative and liberal use of descriptive details, perfected perhaps by Newman's extensive experience writing nonfiction, enlist the reader's sympathy for the mentally unstable Mrs. Lincoln. At the same time, we can become dismayed at her seeming lack of common sense. Her obsessions are chronicled, from compulsive shopping and fears for the safety of her loved ones, to her sexual needs. Mary's hopes, dreams, feelings, and thoughts are conveyed with depth and subtlety." Libr J

Newman, Sharan

Strong as death. Forge 1996 384p

LC 96-1410

A "medieval mystery featuring the indefatigable Catherine Le Vendeur. En route to Santiago de Compostela, Spain, in order to petition for a child at the holy shrine of the apostle Saint James, Catherine and her beloved husband, Edgar, join forces with a curious band of pilgrims. Their fellow wayfarers include four aging knights, a couple of wandering musicians, an imperious gentlewoman, a bitter prostitute, and two zealous monks. As their journey progresses, a series of fatal misfortunes plagues various members of their company, prompting Catherine and Edgar to undertake a quiet investigation." Booklist

"Colorful characters and thoroughly researched culture add up to wonderful historical fiction." Libr J

Newton, Charlie

Calumet City. Touchstone/Simon & Schuster 2008 388p pa $14

ISBN 978-1-4165-3322-1; 1-4165-3322-2

LC 2007-16112

"An atmospheric shocker. . . . Newton certainly has all the hallmarks and above all the classic noir tone — urban and nocturnal, stealthy and smoky, grim determination doing its two-step with gallows humor." Chicago Sun Times

Newton, Charlie

Start shooting; Charlie Newton. Doubleday 2012 305 p.

ISBN 9780385534697; 9780385534703

LC 2011002844

In this book, set "thirty years after the rape-murder of his childhood girlfriend Coleen Brennan in his West Side Chicago neighborhood—a crime for which a retarded African-American man was executed—young Latino cop Bobby Vargas finds himself accused of the killing. Meanwhile, Coleen's twin sister Arleen, an actress, is targeted by criminal elements after fatally shooting a member of the Korean mafia on a police sting she was forced into by Bobby's older brother Ruben, also a cop. . . . Chicago is re-bidding for the 2016 Olympics . . . meaning the City Hall will do anything to protect its image. With star crime reporter Tracy Moens on the prowl for juicy exposes for the fictional Chicago Herald, that's going to take some doing." (Kirkus)

Newton, Mark Charan

Nights of Villjamur; Mark Charan Newton. Spectra/Ballantine Books 2009 437 p. (alk. paper) o.p.; (pbk.) $16; (alk. paper) o.p.

ISBN 9780345520845; 9780345520852; 034552084X

LC 2010009845

This fantasy novel, the first volume of the Legends of the Red Sun series, takes place in "Villjamur [which] is under siege from the encroaching ice age. Refugees threaten to overwhelm the city and stability is undermined from within by scheming chancellors. After the suicide of the emperor, Captain Brynd Lathraea is charged with bringing back the emperor's daughter from self-imposed exile, to be installed as a puppet empress. Meanwhile Randur Estevu, a country lad with vaunting ambitions, comes to Villjamur seeking immortality." (The Guardian)

Followed by: City of ruin (2011)

Ng, Fae Myenne

Bone. Hyperion 1993 193p

ISBN 1-56282-944-0

LC 92-6028

The novel concerns "two generations of Chinese Americans in San Francisco's Chinatown. Mah, who has worked hard all her life in garment sweatshops, finally is able to own her baby-clothing store. Her husband, Leon, who used to be a merchant seaman, worked two shifts in ships' laundry rooms to provide for his family. Nevertheless, the family is torn apart after Ona, the middle daughter, jumps from the tallest building in Chinatown. . . . Nina, the youngest daughter, leaves Chinatown for New York City and then Leila, the oldest, marries and moves out to the suburbs. Leon, the

'paper son' to old Leung, fails to keep his promise to take Leung's bones back to China." Libr J

"Ng is a master storyteller. Her gift for observation and language make Bone truly extraordinary." Women's Rev Books

Nicholas, Douglas

Something red; a novel. Douglas Nicholas. Atria Books 2012 336 p.

ISBN 1451660073; 9781451660074; 9781451660227; 9781451660234

LC 2011044435

This book is set "[d]uring the thirteenth century in northwest England." An "Irish healer, Molly, and the troupe she leads are driving their three wagons, hoping to cross the Pennine Mountains before the heavy snows set in." The group becomes "aware that they are being stalked by something terrible. As danger continues to rise, it becomes clear that the creature must be faced and defeated—or else they will all surely die." (Publisher's note)

Includes bibliographical references and index

Nicholls, David

One day. Vintage Books 2010 437p pa $14.95

ISBN 978-0-307-47471-1; 0-307-47471-2

First published 2009 in the United Kingdom

"On July 15, 1988, the night they graduate from the University of Edinburgh, brainy, working-class Emma Morley and posh hottie Dexter Mayhew share a bed, and almost recognize the powerful chemistry in their unlikely pairing. Almost. The point is they don't, because Emma and Dexter haven't lived enough yet to know who they really are, as opposed to who they fancy themselves to be. That part takes time — 20 years — during which Dex wastes most of the opportunities the universe showers on him (the women who desire him, the shallow TV career) and Emma, a writer in the making, clings to her belief that she deserves only the universe's castoffs (the dingy waitressing jobs, the dull boyfriend). Nicholls charts the maturing of these two Gen-X specimens by the calendar, marking July 15 as the day to check in on Emma and Dex, year after year. Along the way, the author is alert not only to how it feels to be in one's twenties and thirties in the '80s and '90s, but in a larger sense, of how it feels to age. Loss lurks in the wings — don't expect sunshine and cute quirks. But even as he explores sadness, Nicholls creates new poignancy from the old truth that a life is just a stack of days, one after another, stretching into years. One day can truly make a difference." Entertainment Wkly

Nicholls, David

A question of attraction. Villard Books 2004 338p $23.95; pa $13.95

ISBN 1-400-06181-4; 0-8129-7140-X pa

LC 2003-59627

This book "centers around British scholarship student Brian through his struggles to mix with his posh peers, and triumph with his school team on a TV quiz show." Booklist

"Recounted in the first person with good-natured, self-deprecating humor, this first novel tells a delightful coming-of-age story." Libr J

Nichols, John

On top of Spoon Mountain; John Nichols. University of New Mexico Press 2012 223 p.

ISBN 0826352707; 9780826352705; 9780826352729

LC 2012012396

In this novel by John Nichols "Jonathan Kepler wants to climb Spoon Mountain with his grown son and daughter on his sixty-fifth birthday. . . . Still reeling from his third, nearly fatal, divorce, he has a rotten heart, serious asthma, and a fed-up girlfriend. . . .Once a celebrated novelist, Hollywood screenwriter, and environmental activist, Jonathan is now tottering at the ragged end of his career and yearning to make amends to his children for his past sins." (Publisher's note)

Nichols, John Treadwell

★ The **Milagro** beanfield war; by John Nichols; illus. by Rini Templeton. Holt, Rinehart & Winston 1974 445p

"Nichols has written a bawdy, slangy, modern proletarian novel that is—if finally perhaps excessively sentimental—still a consistently entertaining film scenario while at the same time it manages to make funny-serious sense out of a contemporary situation enduring injustice and imminent violence." Choice

Nichols, John Treadwell

The **sterile** cuckoo; by John Nichols. McKay, D. 1965 210p

When the heroine, Pookie Adams "first stumbles on the hero, Jerry Payne, waiting at a cross-country bus stop, he sees only a skinny, scrubby-haired girl, balancing a toothpick on her tongue. Then she bursts into speech and Jerry . . . remains bewitched until the last syllable. Her pursuit of Jerry is launched with . . . determination. . . . When fate places the couple at neighboring Eastern colleges, Jerry succumbs to his first frantic affair. . . . As their romance plunges into its second year, they make a final attempt to slow to a more normal pace, but on a New York weekend, somewhat the worse for an over indulgence in Tiki Puka Pukas, their affair staggers to a close." Publisher's note

Nichols, Peter

Voyage to the North Star; a novel. Carroll & Graf Pubs. 1999 342p $24

ISBN 0-7867-0664-3

This novel's "protagonist is Will Boden, a skilled seaman down on his luck in depression-era New York. In a moment of ill judgment, he once abandoned the ship he was captaining, and is now reduced to scraping a living, literally, on the waterfront. Along comes Carl Schenck, a wealthy industrialist who wants to ape his idol, Teddy Roosevelt, as a big game hunter, but fears it's all been done. He hits upon the notion to take the beautiful luxury yacht he has just acquired up into the Arctic to hunt for seal, bear, whatever he can find, and among the motley crew he assembles, including a skipper who is a fake British naval officer, is poor Will." Publ Wkly

"A gripping novel of blood lust, human folly, and desperate hope in the tradition of Melville, Conrad, and Jack London." Libr J

Nicholson, Christopher

The **elephant** keeper. William Morrow 2009 298p $24.99

ISBN 978-0-06-165160-1; 0-06-165160-5

LC 2009-00852

"Tom Page is the plain-spoken narrator who begins his working life as a stable boy to Mr. John Harrington, sugar merchant of Bristol, and who later finds his vocation as the elephant keeper to Lord Bidborough of Sussex. In 1773, Tom's master, in the cause of science, instructs Tom to write a full description of the elephant in his care. The elephant's story, as related by Tom, is of course his own story. In Nicholson's hands, however, it is also a lively portrait of 18th-century manners and ideas." Boston Globe

Nicholson, William

The **secret** intensity of everyday life. Soho Press 2010 346p $24

ISBN 978-1-56947-647-5; 1-56947-647-0

LC 2010-07769

First published 2008 in the United Kingdom

"Hugely funny. . . . But beneath the Wodehousian surface, it is a serious book about men, women and children with complex inner lives trying to find happiness and coping with disappointment." Daily Telegraph

Nickson, Chris, 1954-

Cold cruel winter. Creme de la Crime 2011 224p

ISBN 9781780290058

In this crime fiction novel, "[s]et in 1732, . . . [the reader] finds Richard Nottingham, constable of the city of Leeds, fearful that he will lose more loved ones after his older daughter falls ill and dies. An especially hard winter is making things tough for the entire community. Then a savage murder—that of wool merchant Samuel Graves, whose throat was cut and the skin flayed from his back—tests Nottingham and his men to their utmost. While the motive for the mutilation murder of the respectable Graves isn't obvious, the constable soon learns the grisly reason for the trophy taking. Other victims will follow, he realizes, if he doesn't manage to stop the butcher first." (Publishers Weekly)

Nicolson, Juliet

Abdication; a novel. by Juliet Nicolson. Atria Books 2012 344 p. $25

ISBN 1451658834; 9781451658835; 9781451658842; 9781451664799

LC 2012006993

This historical novel by Juliet Nicolson takes place in "England, 1936. The year began with the death of a beloved king and the ascension of a charismatic young monarch, sympathetic to the needs of the working class, glamorous and single. By year's end, the world would be stunned as it witnessed that new leader give up his throne in the name of love, just as the unrest and violence that would result in a Second World War were becoming impossible to ignore." (Publisher's note)

"Anyone requiring a post-Downton Abbey fix could do worse than this beguiling, Thirties-era, class-conscious soap opera, written by the granddaughter of Harold Nicolson and Vita Sackville-West. Enthusiastically recommended." LJ

Includes bibliographical references

Niffenegger, Audrey

Her fearful symmetry; a novel. Scribner 2009 406p il $26.99

ISBN 978-1-4391-6539-3; 1-4391-6539-4

LC 2009018771

The novel is "at its best in its early pages, when Niffenegger gives herself room to present her cast of characters; there are some charming descriptions, particularly of these odd, wan mirror twins. The author's love for and deep research into Highgate is also apparent. . . . Not a deep meditation, the novel requires its readers to thoroughly suspend their disbelief and to go along for the haunted ride." Chicago Trib

Niffenegger, Audrey

The time traveler's wife; a novel. MacAdam\ Cage 2003 518p $25

ISBN 1-931561-64-8

LC 2003-10159

Niffenegger "writes with the unflinching yet detached clarity of a war correspondent standing at the sidelines of an unfolding battle. She possesses a historian's eye for contextual detail. This is no romantic idyll." USA Today

Nin, Anais

Cities of the interior; introduction by Sharon Spencer. Swallow Press 1974 xx, 589p

First one-volume version published 1959 by the author. Although intended as a connected work exploring the lives of women, it was originally published as five separate novelettes. This edition contains the expanded and retitled version of the fifth novelette

In Ladders to fire (1946), which concerns a largely American group of characters in Paris, Lillian's hunger for life and love leave her unsatisfied with her seemingly changeless marriage to Larry. She develops an increasingly possessive relationship with Djuna, whose inner clarity and control, concealed beneath a delicate feminine exterior, offer a comforting contrast to her own emotional turbulence. Lillian's love affair with the painter Jay is complicated by the love-hate relationship which they both establish with Sabina

Nissenson, Hugh

The pilgrim. Sourcebooks Landmark 2011 356p $24.99

ISBN 978-1-4022-0924-6

LC 2011-17815

"A marvelously intimate look back through time. Charles' fears and desires are made quite believable as he recalls the everyday horrors of the time—and the bits of Scripture that both justified and aggravated them. And while the young protagonist earnestly seeks salvation, his all-too-human failings—such as when he and the pretty Abigail Winslow flirt on the Sabbath—make him as sympathetic as any young striver since Holden Caulfield. The author's return to historical fiction raises human questions with immediacy and flair." Kirkus

Niven, Larry

The Best of Larry Niven; edited by Jonathan Strahan. Subterranean 2010 616p $40

ISBN 978-1-59606-331-0; 1-59606-331-9

"These 27 short stories, originally published from 1965 to 2000, demonstrate Niven's tremendous range and literary prowess in the fields of SF (Hugo winners 'Neutron Star' and 'The Borderland of Sol,' featuring clever pilot Beowulf Shaeffer), fantasy ('Not Long Before the End'), nonfiction (the famously footnote-heavy 'Man of Steel, Woman of Kleenex'), and mystery ('The Deadlier Weapon'). . . . An introduction by frequent Niven collaborator Jerry Pournelle (Escape from Hell) focuses on Niven's attraction to hard SF, and brief headnotes by Niven himself provide context and color. This spellbinding collection is a must for fans of classic SF." Publ Wkly

Niven, Larry

The burning city; {by} Larry Niven & Jerry Pournelle. Pocket Bks. 2000 486p

ISBN 0-671-03660-2

LC 99-57479

"In a world where magic is dying and the gods are slowly becoming myth, Whandall Placehold passes from boyhood to manhood in a city beset by devastating Burnings. To save his family and his home from the ravages of the dying god Yangin-Atep, Whandall leaves his familiar surroundings and embarks on a journey of self-discovery that leads to a greater destiny. Set in the world first described in Niven's classic The Magic Goes Away, the latest effort by coauthors Niven and Pournelle blends the grim background of a post-apocalyptic world with the mystic intensity of a vision quest." Libr J

Niven, Larry

Lucifer's hammer; by Larry Niven & Jerry Pournelle. Playboy Press 1977 494p

LC 77-8074

"The hammer of the title is an eons-old comet that strikes earth with devastating physical and psychological consequences that are meticulously dramatized in the lives of dozens of major and minor characters. The second and more powerful part details the immense task of rebuilding civilization or preserving what remains of it. The authors excel in their suspenseful and thought-provoking hypothesis about the nature of civilized man and the ethics of survival when the future of their fragile community is at stake." Booklist

Niven, Larry

★ The Mote in God's Eye; by Larry Niven & Jerry Pournelle. Simon & Schuster 1974 537p hardcover o.p. pa $7.99

ISBN 0-671-74192-6

"Superior space opera in which Earth's interstellar navy contacts and does battle with an enormously hostile alien race. The scenes of space warfare are well handled, and the alien Moties are fascinating." Anatomy of Wonder 4

Another title about the war between humans and the Moties is:

The gripping hand (1993)

Niven, Larry

★ Ringworld. Ballantine Bks. 1970 342p pa $7.99

ISBN 0-345-33392-6

"The Ringworld, a world shaped like a wheel so huge that it surrounds a sun, is almost too fantastic to conceive of. With a radius of 90 million miles and a length of 600 million miles, the Ringworld's mystery is compounded by the discovery that it is artificial. What phenomenal intelligence can be behind such a creation? Four unlikely explorers, two humans and two aliens, set out for the Ringworld, bound by mutual distrust and unsure of each other's motives." Shapiro. Fic for Youth. 3d edition

Other available titles in this series are:
The Ringworld engineers (1980)
The Ringworld throne (1996)
Ringworld's children (2004)

Niven, Larry
The **Ringworld** engineers. Holt & Co. 1980

"Twenty-three years after their original journey, Louis Wu and Speaker-to-Animals once more find themselves kidnapped companions of a mad Puppeteer who returns with them to Ringworld to steal a transmutation device. The Puppeteer encounters unexpected obstacles to this goal, however: Louis has become a wirehead addicted to the electric current fed almost constantly to his brain; Speaker-to-Animals is now a kzinti Patriarch and resents his enforced participation in the venture; the Ringworld has developed an unstable orbit and is about to desintegrate into its sun." SLJ

"This is a good example of the kind of novel where the basic idea—the Ringworld itself—is the true 'hero.'" Booklist

Followed by The Ringworld throne

Niven, Larry
The **Ringworld** throne. Ballantine Bks. 1996 424p
ISBN 978-0345358615
LC 95-47882

The third title in the author's Ringworld series "offers two stories crowded into one. A motley array of hominid inhabitants are seeking to defeat a plague of vampires. Meanwhile, returning hero Louis Wu is battling what effectively is a plague of Protectors . . . whose rivalries threaten Ringworld's existence. The battle against the vampires is the more exciting of the two stories, filled with action, scenes of the Ringworld and explorations of ritualistic interspecies sex. Wu's pursuit of the Protectors displays Niven's deft hand at portraying aliens." Publ Wkly

Niven, Larry
Ringworld's children. Tor Bks. 2004 $24.95
ISBN 0-7653-0167-9
LC 2003-26581

In this fourth title in the series, "the Ringworld, an artificially engineered realm resembling a ribbon or ring that is home to over a trillion people of wildly different species, faces threats from outsider ships from the inhabited worlds and its own aging superstructure. Newly restored in mind and body, Louis Wu, a member of the first expedition to Ringworld, joins three individuals of different species to prevent the destruction of Ringworld." Libr J

"Action and clever world building should captivate newcomers to Ringworld, while returners will appreciate picking up loose ends from previous Ringworld volumes." Booklist

Niven, Larry
Saturn's race; [by] Larry Niven & Steven Barnes. TOR Bks. 2000 317p
ISBN 0-312-86726-3
LC 00-28646

"Brilliantly weaving high-tech internets, augmentation technologies and social issues into a fast-paced cloak-and-dagger action adventure, this novel effortlessly moves from the depths of the ocean to the heights of VR to create a dazzling, seamless whole." Publ Wkly

Noel, Katharine
Halfway house. Atlantic Monthly Press 2006 367p $23
ISBN 0-871-13934-0
LC 2005-53636

"There are moments when the author could have allowed feel-good plot turns to transform the story into a sentimental domestic drama, but instead she tenaciously adheres to the realistic trajectory of mental illness. While reading [the novel], a reader can't help considering the classic protagonist of this literary genre: Esther Greenwood in 'The Bell Jar,' by Sylvia Plath. . . . Thankfully, Ms. Noel doesn't attempt to reinvent Plath's masterpiece; she steers clear of the first-person voice and instead relies on her third-person tapestry. That said, Ms. Noel offers her own contemporary, insightful chronicle of a young woman trying to define herself through the miasma of mental illness." N Y Times (Late N Y Ed)

Noire (Author)
Natural born liar; Misadventures of Mink LaRue. Noire. Dafina Books/Kensington Pub. Corp. 2012 275 p. (pbk.) $15.00
ISBN 0758266081; 9780758266088
LC 2011279554

This novel, by Noire, follows "what happens when beautiful, twenty-year-old petty thief and ex-stripper Mink LaRue finds out she's a dead ringer for the age-progressed photo of the missing oil heiress Sable Dominion. Harlem-born Mink LaRue makes a beeline to Dallas, Texas, pretending to be the Dominion's long-lost daughter, Sable. . . . But it's not long before Mink's newfound siblings grow suspicious of the ghetto princess, who has a rap sheet a mile long." (Publisher's note)

Noon, Jeff
Vurt. Crown 1995 342p
LC 94-25544

First published 1993 in the United Kingdom

This "fluorescent and phantasmagorical novel . . . isn't quite the equal of Anthony Burgess's A Clockwork Orange, with which it is being compared, but in some ways it comes close. It's good enough in its first 50 or 60 pages of atmosphere setting, all smoke machines and flashing strobes, that the reader blinks, shakes his head and wonders whether Noon can sustain the weirdness." Time

Nooteboom, Cees
★ **All** souls' day; translated from the Dutch by Susan Massotty. Harcourt 2001 338p $31
ISBN 0-15-100566-4
LC 2001-24310

Original Dutch editions, 1998

"Not the least of the novel's satisfactions is the deftness with which Nooteboom incorporates signposts of Western high culture into his densely observant narrative." New Yorker

Nooteboom, Cees

★ **Lost** paradise; translated from the Dutch by Susan Massotty. Grove Press 2007 151p $23

ISBN 978-0-8021-1855-4; 0-8021-1855-0

Original Dutch edition, 2004

"After surviving a gang rape in São Paulo, a young, affluent Brazilian woman, Alma, takes off for Australia with her best friend, Almut: the two plan to train as masseuses. Nooteboom then cuts to an embittered middle-aged critic, Erik Zondag, who is cast out of his home in Amsterdam by his fed-up younger girlfriend and sent to an Alpine spa in order to dry out and become a different man. The first part of the novel tracks the two Brazilians as they travel though Australia with hope of stopping at the legendary Aboriginal Sickness Dreaming Place. Their Australian adventures take a turn involving the Angel Project, a multisite piece of participatory art in Perth. For the second part, Eric endures a punishingly ascetic stay at the Alpine spa, where he recognizes his masseuse." Publ Wkly

Nordan, Lewis

★ **Wolf** whistle; a novel. Algonquin Bks. 1993 290p

ISBN 1-56512-028-0

LC 93-1011

"The wolf whistle of the title comes from Bobo, a black teenager from Chicago visiting in Arrow Catcher, Mississippi. Directed at the wife of the town's most prominent white resident, this whistle soon leads to Bobo's murder. Based on the Emmett Till lynching, . . . {this novel} examines the intertwined fates of blacks and poor whites in the Mississippi delta." Libr J

"Propelled by Nordan's musical prose, much of this narrative soars above the commonplace into the realm of myth." Publ Wkly

Nordhoff, Charles, 1887-1947

Botany Bay; by Charles Nordhoff and James Norman Hall. Little, Brown 1941 374p

"The story of the Australian penal colony at Botany Bay, and especially of Hugh Tallant, an American, who had been stranded in England, turned highwayman, and was one of the first criminals shipped to Botany Bay, where life was bitterly hard and adventurous." Ont Libr Rev

Nordhoff, Charles, 1887-1947

The **Bounty** trilogy; by Charles Nordhoff and James Norman Hall; illustrated by N. C. Wyeth. Little, Brown 1982 691p il hardcover o.p.

A reissue of the combined volume first published 1936

Based on actual events stemming from a mutiny on a British war vessel in 1787, "this great trilogy begins with the story of the men who mutinied against the now famous Captain Bligh—'Mutiny on the Bounty.' In 'Men Against the Sea' Bligh and his supporters, set adrift in a small boat, made an incredible journey to safety. 'Pitcairn's Island' is

the story of the mutineers who found refuge on a remote Pacific island." Books for you

Nordhoff, Charles, 1887-1947

Men against the sea; by Charles Nordhoff and James Norman Hall. Little, Brown 1934 251p

ISBN 9780316738880; 9780891905646

Sequel to Mutiny on the Bounty

This volume tells the story of Captain Bligh and the eighteen loyal men, who under his leadership sailed in an open boat thirty-six hundred miles from the Friendly Islands in the South Pacific to the Dutch colony of Timor in the East Indies. The story is told as if by Ledward, the surgeon, but the events, the wind and the weather of the narrative are those recorded in Captain Bligh's log

Followed by Pitcairn's Island

Nordhoff, Charles, 1887-1947

Mutiny on the Bounty; by Charles Nordhoff and James Norman Hall. Little, Brown 1932 396p hardcover o.p. pa $13.95

ISBN 0-316-61157-3; 0-316-61168-9 pa

Also available from other publishers

This narrative is "based on the famous mutiny that members of the crew of the 'Bounty', a British war vessel, carried out in 1787 against their cruel commander, Captain William Bligh. The authors kept the actual historical characters and background, using as narrator an elderly man, Captain Roger Byam, who had been a midshipman on the 'Bounty.' The story tells how the mate of the ship, Fletcher Christian, and a number of the crew rebel and set Captain Bligh adrift in an open boat with the loyal members of the crew." Reader's Ency. 4th edition

Other titles in the Bounty trilogy are:
Men against the sea (1934)
Pitcairn's Island (1934)

Nordhoff, Charles, 1887-1947

Pitcairn's Island; by Charles Nordhoff and James Norman Hall. Little, Brown 1934 333p

ISBN 9780316611602 out of print; 9780316738873

LC 88008520

Sequel to Men against the sea

"This final volume {of the trilogy} is the history of those mutineers who, with eighteen Polynesian men and women, reached Pitcairn's Island and there destroyed the 'Bounty.' Unvisited for eighteen years, the community fought over women and possession, and all but one of the men died violent deaths. A blood-curdling story, not for the squeamish reader." Booklist

Norfolk, Lawrence

John Saturnall's feast; Lawrence Norfolk. Grove Press 2012 416 p. (hardcover) $26.00

ISBN 0802120512; 9780802120519

This novel by Lawrence Norfolk is "the story of a cook and his eponymous cookbook and an allegory of service and human purpose. . . . [When] the Reformation asserts itself, . . . John [Saturnall] and his mother are victimized. Their lives appear heretical. Exiled from home, John . . . grows into his calling as a cook in the clattering kitchens of Master Scovell; into his consciousness of class and the wages of factional warfare; and into his awareness of the importance of his mother's holy book." (Kirkus Reviews)

Norman, Howard
★ The **bird** artist. Farrar, Straus & Giroux 1994 289p

LC 94-70542

"Fabian, son of Alaric and Orkney Vas, has spent his entire life in remote Witless Bay, Newfoundland. Looking back on his life, he decides that he has distinguished himself in only two ways: as a modestly successful artist whose illustrations graced the covers of Bird Lore magazine and as the murderer of the local lighthouse keeper, Botho August. The murder was the result of excessive coffee consumption combined with the stress brought on by his parents' plan to force him into an arranged marriage with a cousin he had never seen; this in turn would keep him from his hard-drinking girlfriend." Libr J

This work evokes "a way of life, a distinctive community and a fatalistic view of human behavior. The novel sings with tension and sparkles with antic humor." Publ Wkly

Norman, Howard
The **haunting** of L. Farrar, Straus & Giroux 2002 326p $24
ISBN 0-374-16825-3

LC 2001-51120

"This is a mesmerizing melodrama rendered magical thanks to lyrical evocations of fog and storm, sexual bliss and fear, a conflation of atmospheric conditions and states of mind that makes of the human heart a realm as treacherous and exquisite as the Arctic." Booklist

Norman, Howard
The **museum** guard; a novel. Farrar, Straus & Giroux 1998 310p
ISBN 0-374-21649-5

LC 98-8413

The author "fills this enigmatic novel with elements of fable and fairy tale blended with memorable characterizations and subtle narrative probings into the nature of self and the consequences of actions." Libr J

Norman, Howard
What is left the daughter. Houghton Mifflin Harcourt 2010 243p $25
ISBN 978-0-618-73543-3; 0-618-73543-7

LC 2009-44460

A novel "set in the gray majesty of Nova Scotia, where 17-year-old orphan Wyatt Hillyer moves in with his devoted aunt and uncle and their adopted daughter, Tilda, the love of stoic Wyatt's life. The ravages of Hitler and his dastardly German U-boats lurking beneath Canadian waters hit their home hard. . . . Norman writes with spare elegance and dry humor, and the extraordinary emotional power of his slim new novel is earned with authentic grace." Entertainment Wkly

Norris, Frank
★ **McTeague**; a story of San Francisco. edited with an introduction by Kevin Starr. Penguin Books 1994 xlviii, 442p pa $10.95
ISBN 0-14-018769-3

First published 1899 by Doubleday

"A prime example of the American naturalistic novel, McTeague treats the gradual degeneration of a stupid, but initially harmless, giant of a man whose instincts are nearer brute than human. McTeague practices dentistry without a license in a poor section of San Francisco's Polk Street and marries Trina, who has just won $5,000 in a lottery. He soon loses his job and takes to drink. Trina becomes a miser, and McTeague murders her in a fit of rage and steals her money but is tracked down and killed by her cousin." Benet's Reader's Ency of Am Lit

Norris, Frank
Novels and essays. Library of America 1986 1232p $40
ISBN 0-940450-40-2

Vandover and the brute (1914) depicts the degeneration of a once affable and talented young man after he is afflicted with the psychological condition lycanthropy. McTeague and The octopus are entered separately.

Norris, Frank
★ The **octopus**; a story of California. Doubleday 1901 652p

First volume of an unfinished trilogy The epic of wheat

"The battle waged between the wheat growers and the railroad men in California is the theme of this novel. Concerned with social injustice, man's inhumanity to man, and the relentlessness of power struggles, Norris is able to combine these themes with a love interest." Shapiro. Fic for Youth. 3d edition

Followed by The pit

Norris, Frank
★ The **pit**; a story of Chicago. Doubleday 1903

The second volume of the author's unfinished The epic of wheat trilogy "is a story of manipulations in the Chicago Exchange. Curtis Jadwin, a stock speculator, is so absorbed in making money that he neglects his emotionally starved wife Laura. Into this situation steps Sheldon Corthell, dilettante artist, to console her. Laura loves her husband, and postpones for awhile going away with the aesthete. Meanwhile, Jadwin engages in a struggle with the Crookes gang of speculators. He beats them, but is crushed by fluctuations in wheat production. He and Laura effect a reconciliation." Haydn. Thesaurus of Book Dig

The **Norton** book of science fiction; North American science fiction, 1960-1990. edited by Ursula K. Le Guin and Brian Attebery; Karen Joy Fowler, consultant. Norton 1993 869p hardcover o.p. pa $38.13
ISBN 0-393-03546-8; 0-393-97241-0 pa

LC 93-16130

Damon Knight, Robert Silverberg, Connie Willis and Harlan Ellison are among the authors represented in this anthology of more than 60 stories.

A "compilation of intelligent and entertaining sf that belongs in virtually every fiction collection." Booklist

Norton, Andre

Beast Master's ark; [by] Andre Norton and Lyn McConchie. TOR Bks. 2002 318p

ISBN 0-7653-0041-9

LC 2002-67249

Third volume in the author's Beast Master series begun with the Beast Master (1959) and Lord of Thunder (1962)

"A mysterious killer, referred to as 'Death-which-come-in-the-night' by the planet Arzor's indigenous inhabitants, threatens to eradicate sentient life on the desertlike world. Beast Master Storm Hosteen discovers that the only chance of saving his adopted home lies with a young woman name Tani, who has learned to deny her own Beast Master heritage." Libr J

Norton, Andre

The **elvenbane**; an epic high fantasy of the Halfblood chronicles. [by] Andre Norton, Mercedes Lackey. Doherty Assocs. 1991 390p (Halfblood chronicles)

LC 91-21177

"In a world ruled by some of the most brutal and tyrannical elves ever encountered, the most persecuted are the part-human, part-elven halfbloods. After her human mother is cast into the desert, {Shana} the bastard daughter of the powerful Lord Dyran survives and is raised by dragons to seek her destiny as the Elvenbane." Booklist

Followed by Elvenblood

Norton, Andre

Elvenblood; an epic high fantasy. [by] Andre Norton and Mercedes Lackey. Doherty Assocs. 1995 348p (Halfblood chronicles)

LC 95-5797

"Following rumors of the existence of a tribe of humans immune to the enslaving magics of the land's elven overlords, halfelven rebel Shana and her dragon companion encounter unexpected complications in their struggle for freedom. The talents of collaborators Norton and Lackey blend seamlessly as they expand the background to their epic fantasy to include an exotic desert culture, which provides a rich contrast to the stifling atmosphere of elven society." Libr J

Norton, Andre

Golden Trillium. Bantam Bks. 1993 296p (Trillium)

ISBN 0-553-09507-2

LC 92-43875

Third in the fantasy series that includes Black Trillium by Marion Zimmer Bradley, Julian May, and Andre Norton, and Blood Trillium by Julian May

"Having aided her sisters in establishing peace in the land of Ruwenda, the warrior-maiden Kadiya journeys through the swamps to return the Three-Orbed Sword to the place of its origin only to find that her fight against evil is not yet done. The grande dame of sf and fantasy returns to a favorite theme—the discovery of an ancient and highly advanced lost civilization—in this heroic adventure." Libr J

Norton, Andre

Redline the stars; [by] Andre Norton, P.M. Griffin. Tor Bks. 1993 304p

LC 92-43708

The authors "recreate the flavor of Norton's four Solar Queen books . . . while updating some concepts and quite a bit of technology. The crew of the Free Trader vessel Solar Queen, flying under Capt. Miceál Jellico, has mixed reactions to new crewmate Rael Cofort, who is plying the space lanes as a jack-of-all-trades despite her position as a physician and status as sister of the successful rival Free Trader, Teague Cofort. Upon arriving at Canuche of Halio, the most advanced planet of the sector, the Queen's crew is endangered when Rael picks up the odor of man-eating rodents used in a gruesome gem-stealing scheme." Publ Wkly

Nothomb, Amelie

Tokyo fiancee; translated from the French by Alison Anderson. Europa Editions 2009 152p pa $15

ISBN 978-1-933372-64-8; 1-933372-64-8

Original French edition, 2007

"Nothomb exoticizes Japanese culture without succumbing to Orientalist stereotypes. The situations she refreshingly depicts reveal Amelie's education in the Japanese art of living. . . . [A] spare, elegant novel." N Y Times Book Rev

Nova, Craig

★ The **informer**; a novel. Shaye Areheart Books 2010 306p $26

ISBN 978-0-307-23693-7; 0-307-23693-5

LC 2009-23689

"Nova's main concern is the complex interplay among his characters, but he develops the suspense nicely, too, flashing forward to Berlin in 1945 for a peculiar but effective finale, the city's post-Armageddon rubble providing the inevitable flip side to Weimar's forced gaiety. An entrancing mood piece." Booklist

Novack, Sandra

Everyone but you; stories. Random House 2011 272p $26

ISBN 978-1-4000-6681-0; 1-4000-6681-6

LC 2010-53002

"Trouble simmers beneath the surface of a bucolic Pennsylvania town in Novack's dramatic, elegantly rendered debut. . . . [She] writes tellingly of the complex relationships among families, lovers, and friends." Booklist

Novak, Chase

Breed; Chase Novak. Mulholland Books 2012 310 p. $25.99

ISBN 0316198560; 9780316198561

LC 2012014689

In author Chase Novak's book, "Alex and Leslie have everything--luxurious Manhattan domicile, fine jobs, each other--except a baby. Leslie seems more willing to adopt, but Alex is desperate to try anything. If he weren't, he might have had second thoughts after they traveled to see the mysterious doctor in Slovenia . . . Bad choice . . . [T]hey proceed at Alex's insistence, subsequently indulge in some spectacularly animalistic sex, have twins . . . and develop a taste for rodents, household pets, fellow human beings and perhaps even their offspring." (Kirkus)

Novakovich, Josip

   April Fool's Day; a novel. HarperCollins Publishers 2004 226p map $23.95

    ISBN 0-06-058397-5; 0-06-058398-3

                    LC 2003-67656

   "Politics turn personal for Ivan Dolinar, born April 1, 1948, in Croatia, as the ricocheting course of his life reflects the tumult of his home country. His medical studies are cut short when he's imprisoned after a classmate jokes about assassinating Tito, who-along with Indira Gandhi-visits the labor camp and offers Ivan a Cuban cigar and a longer sentence. Released but barred from medicine, Ivan is drafted into the Yugoslav army just before the Croats organize their own defense force, putting him into an absurd and horrific war with his own countrymen. Finding his captain raping his former classmate Selma, Ivan rescues and later marries her, raising her daughter as his own. But marriage, fatherhood, hypochondria, and adultery fail to bring the peace Ivan finds in life after death." Booklist

   "A heartfelt novel about the war-torn Balkans that's actually quite funny. . .and touching." GQ

Novik, Naomi

   His majesty's dragon. Del Rey 2006 356p (Temeraire series) pa $7.50

    ISBN 0-345-48128-3

                    LC 2005-46342

   Published in Great Britain with title: Temeraire

   In this novel, the opening salvo of the Temeraire series, Novik "blends fantasy into the history of the Napoleonic wars. Here be dragons, beasts that can speak and reason, bred for strength and speed and used for aerial support in battle. Each nation has its own breeds, but none are so jealously guarded as the mysterious dragons of China. Veteran Capt. Will Laurence of the British Navy is therefore taken aback after his crew captures an egg from a French ship and it hatches a Chinese dragon, which Laurence names Temeraire. When Temeraire bonds with the captain, the two leave the navy to sign on with His Majesty's sadly understaffed Aerial Corps." Publ Wkly

   Followed by: Throne of jade (2006), Black powder wars (2006), Empire of ivory (2007), Victory of eagles (2009)

Noyes, Deborah

   Captivity. Unbridled Books 2010 340p $25.95

    ISBN 978-1-93607-163-0

                    LC 2009-53813

   "In general, Noyes' narration is low-key and evocative, eschewing both ornate linguistic tricks and stripped-down austerity. Chapters alternate between Clara and Maggie, adhering to a close third person and the immediacy of the present tense. . . . The trajectories of their two lives create an effective double-strand, a sort of literary double-helix that uses as its raw material both faith-based spiritualism and scientific naturalism. Readers with a sympathy toward either philosophy will find much to ponder here." PopMatters

Nunez, Elizabeth

   Anna in-between. Akashic Books 2009 347p $22.95

    ISBN 978-1-933354-84-2; 1-933354-84-4

                    LC 2009-922936

   "The title of her latest novel suggests a sitcom, or the upbeat identity lit marketed to teenagers. But Elizabeth Nunez layers Anna In-Between, a psychologically and emotionally astute family portrait, with dark themes like racism, cancer and the bittersweet longing of the immigrant. Foremost, she explores the late innings of a successful marriage, in which husband and wife cling together in the shadow of mortality." N Y Times Book Rev

Nunez, Elizabeth

   Grace. Ballantine Bks. 2003 294p $23.95

    ISBN 0-345-45533-9

                    LC 2002-26260

   "Trinidad-born Justin Peters seemingly has it all: a beautiful, accomplished wife named Sally; a precocious four-year-old daughter; a fabulous brownstone in the hip Fort Greene section of Brooklyn; and a professorship at a public university. Everything is picture perfect until his mate blindsides him by confessing that she is unhappy and planning to move out, taking their child with her." Libr J

   "This is a tender, graceful novel of personal amd material struggle that also explores the power of literature and poetry in everyday life." Booklist

Nunez, Sigrid

   The **last** of her kind. Farrar, Straus and Giroux 2006 375p $25

    ISBN 0-374-18381-3

                    LC 2005-40098

   This "portrait of countercultural America in the sixties and seventies opens in 1968, when two girls meet as roommates at Barnard College. Ann is rich and white and wants to be neither, confiding, 'I wish I had been born poor'; Georgette has no illusions about poverty, having just escaped her depressed home town, where 'whole families drank themselves to disgrace.' Georgette finds Ann at once despicable and mesmerizing, and she's stunned—if not entirely surprised—when, years after the end of their friendship, Ann is arrested for killing a cop. In previous works, Nunez has proved herself a master of psychological acuity. Here her ambitions are grander, and the result is a remarkable and disconcerting vision of a troubled time in American history, and of its repercussions for national and individual identity." New Yorker

Nunez, Sigrid

   Salvation city. Riverhead Books 2010 280p $25.95

    ISBN 978-1-59448-766-8; 1-59448-766-9

                    LC 2010-01989

   "The great success of Nunez's book is that the end of the world is filtered through Cole's imperfect perspective, so that the collapse of society is no more devastating than first love, and deeply felt conflict rages as a young man tries to find something worth preserving in a place determined to obliterate the past." Publ Wkly

Nye, Robert

The **late** Mr. Shakespeare; a novel. Arcade Pub. 1999 398p $25.95

ISBN 1-55970-469-1

LC 98-50763

First published 1998 in the United Kingdom

"Nye brilliantly weaves together almost all the known facts about Shakespeare, a great many of the spurious anecdotes which have been attached to his life, and a tissue of rare inventions of his own." Times Lit Suppl

O

O'Brian, Patrick

Blue at the mizzen. Norton 1999 261p il $24

ISBN 0-393-04844-6

LC 99-42043

"There is nothing in this century that rivals Patrick O'Brian's achievement in his chosen genre. His novels embrace with loving clarity the full richness of the 18th-century world." N Y Times Book Rev

O'Brian, Patrick

★ The **commodore**. Norton 1995 281p $22.50

ISBN 0-393-03760-6

LC 95-2653

First published 1994 in the United Kingdom

Another "novel in O'Brian's series following Captain (now Commodore) Jack Aubrey and his surgeon friend, Stephen Maturin, through the naval side of the Napoleonic Wars. Although O'Brian is ingenious at devising new adventures, it is the richness of his characters which justifies his readers' continuing enthusiasm. The most arresting moments in this installment come not in battle but in dramas of parenthood and marriage far from the sea. O'Brian acknowledges Jane Austen as one of his inspirations, and she need not be ashamed of the affiliation." New Yorker

O'Brian, Patrick

The **golden** ocean; a novel. Day, J. 1957 316p il

First published 1956 in the United Kingdom

"This novel is based on the exploits of Commodore George Anson, who set out in 1740 with five men-of-war to circle the globe and returned four years later with one ship and a small but very wealthy crew. The expedition is seen through the eyes of Peter Palafox, a young midshipman who blossoms into an able-bodied seaman. . . . As always, the author's erudition and humor are on display. . . . The attention to period speech and detail is uncompromising, and while the cascades of nautical lore can be dizzying, both aficionados and newcomers will be swept up by the richness of Mr. O'Brian's prodigious imagination." N Y Times Book Rev

O'Brian, Patrick

The **hundred** days. Norton 1998 280p $24

ISBN 0-393-04674-5

LC 98-35866

"Battles there are aplenty, and O'Brian matches Forester in the excitement, detail and bloody realism of his reconstructions. But these naval tales are blended into a larger panorama of Georgian society and politics, science, medicine, botany and the whole conspectus of contemporary Enlightenment knowledge about the natural world." N Y Times Book Rev

O'Brian, Patrick

The **unknown** shore. Norton 1995 313p $23

ISBN 0-393-03859-9

LC 95-32887

First published 1959 in the United Kingdom

"Based on British Commodore Anson's 1740 circumnavigation of the world . . . this is the story of HMS Wager, a ship separated from Anson's squadron while sailing around Cape Horn. The Wager is shipwrecked off Patagonia, and the largest part of the narrative details the hardships of the diminishing band of survivors on that inhospitable shore. . . . Though this novel isn't quite as polished or stylish as the author's later work, it's a most honorable ancestor." Publ Wkly

O'Brian, Patrick

★ The **wine**-dark sea. Norton 1993 261p $22.50

ISBN 0-393-03558-1

LC 93-1521

"The naval actions are bang-on and bang-up—fast, furious and bloody—and the Andean milieu is as vivid as the shipboard scenes." Publ Wkly

O'Brian, Patrick

The **yellow** admiral. Norton 1996 261p $24

ISBN 0-393-04044-5

LC 96-24149

"As their careers have advanced and their children have grown, Captain Jack Aubrey and Stephen Maturin have battered Napoleon's ships and thwarted his spies, but here, at last, the Emperor is Elba-bound, and our heroes are left high and dry. Aubrey, ashore at half pay and with scant hope of promotion, prays that peace may not last long—a sentiment doubtless shared by O'Brian's readers. Still, Elba is not St. Helena, so war will surely return, if only for a short finale." New Yorker

O'Brien, Dan

The **contract** surgeon; a novel. Lyons Press 1999 316p $24.95

ISBN 1-55821-932-3

LC 99-35243

This novel is "based on the true story of the unusual friendship between Crazy Horse and Dr. Valentine McGillicuddy, a civilian surgeon contracted to serve with the army during the Indian wars on the Great Plains. McGillicuddy relates the tale as an old man. . . . He faces his greatest moral test when Crazy Horse is bayoneted in the back by a soldier, and McGillicuddy is pressured by the army to keep the famous warrior alive, because his death would spur on the Indians to renewed battle. . . . This powerful story is a thinking man's western, in which action is secondary to O'Brien's nuanced exploration of character and the tragic dimensions of a morally fraught conflict." Publ Wkly

O'Brien, Edna

★ The **country** girls trilogy and epilogue. Farrar, Straus & Giroux 1986 531p

ISBN 978-0374130275

LC 85-32113

Omnibus edition of three titles originally published separately in 1960, 1962 and 1964 respectively, with an epilogue added by the author

The country girls portrays two friends, Kate and Baba, growing up in Ireland. They are sent to a convent school they despise and they contrive to get expelled and move to Dublin. In The lonely girl, Kate, now 21, becomes involved first with an older married man, then with a filmmaker. Eugene encourages and pampers her, but she is unresponsive. The relationship disintegrates and she moves to London. In Girls in their married bliss, Kate has married Eugene and has a son, but the marriage is destroyed when Eugene's indifference pushes Kate into a love affair. Meanwhile, Baba settles into marriage and financial security with an architect, and pulls through the crisis of a pregnancy brought on by a one-night stand. The Epilogue contains Baba's reflections, twenty years later

"O'Brien's particular appeal is that she can be tender yet merciless, romantic yet grittily sexual. She resides admirably where quality and popular writing intersect." Booklist

O'Brien, Edna

A **fanatic** heart; selected stories of Edna O'Brien. Farrar, Straus & Giroux 1984 461p

LC 84-13762

"Each story is superbly written and, despite the overall seriousness, graced by humor." Publ Wkly

O'Brien, Edna

House of splendid isolation. Farrar, Straus & Giroux 1994 232p $21

ISBN 0-374-17309-5

LC 93-42602

The author "manages to sum up a century of Irish sorrow in this taut, lyrical novel, filled with scenes so vividly rendered they seem captured in a flash of lightning. Not the least of O'Brien's accomplishments is her ability to present both sides of the Irish problem in all their complexity without settling heavily on either side." Libr J

O'Brien, Edna

In the forest. Houghton Mifflin 2002 262p $24

ISBN 0-618-19730-3

LC 2001-51883

From an early age, Michen O'Kane "displays spontaneous unsociability, for which he is punished with unremitting cruelty, first by his wife-beating father, then by the villagers of Cloosh, his small Irish village, and then by the Irish juvenile detention system, where he is sodomized and psychologically tortured. O'Kane comes back to Cloosh a ticking bomb, hearing voices in his head. After he sets up a camp in the woods, he sets his sights on a relative stranger in the village, a free spirit named Eily Ryan who, with her son, Maddie, is living a modern, single mother's lifestyle obscurely disapproved of by the conservative villagers. One morning O'Kane kidnaps her and the boy. She's forced to drive O'Kane to his woods, passing through the village in full view of several frightened bystanders, who do nothing to help her. After murdering his two victims, O'Kane kidnaps a priest and repeats the act." Publ Wkly

A novel about "how a community can be collectively paralyzed by fear. The result is a brilliant illumination of human nature." Booklist

O'Brien, Edna

Lantern slides; stories. Farrar, Straus & Giroux 1990 223p

ISBN 0-374-18332-5

LC 90-33594

"O'Brien's short stories expand on the anguish and brutality endemic to modern Irish lives, and her characters have more than their own secret problems to brood and moon about. . . . O'Brien mines her home territory to splendid effect with her glinting looks at what the Irish have made of their struggle and what Ireland has made of their unhappy lives." Booklist

O'Brien, Edna

Saints and sinners; stories. Back Bay Books/ Little, Brown and Co. 2011 245p pa $13.99

ISBN 978-0-316-12272-6; 0-316-12272-6

LC 2010-31577

"The world, if viewed in clichéd terms, is indeed populated by the two types of individuals cited in the title of this new collection of short stories by the doyenne of contemporary Irish literature, an acknowledged master of the form. But that is all that is clichéd about this splendid book. . . . Eleven stories in total bring literary lovers' rapt attention to this author's clear, immaculate style and her brilliant selection of detail, nimble plot construction, and astute character delineation. Recommend O'Brien along with William Trevor and Alice Munro." Booklist

O'Brien, Edna

★ **Time** and tide. Farrar, Straus & Giroux 1992 325p

LC 92-3962

This novel is O'Brien's "harshest yet most beautiful work. She has a touchy, rich theme: the sexuality of the bond between mothers and sons. . . . O'Brien brings together the earthy and the delicately poetic: she has the soul of Molly Bloom and the skills of Virginia Woolf." Newsweek

O'Brien, Edna

Wild Decembers. Houghton Mifflin 2000 259p $24

ISBN 0-618-04567-8

LC 99-56110

First published 1999 in the United Kingdom

"The novel is a dirge that keens and lulls by turns. The entrancing rhythms and refrains, the density and chant-like, drumming fragmentation work on the reader like magic. . . . O'Brien combines this lyricism with a masterly storytelling instinct, so that {the novel} reads at once like an intricate poem and a taut, suspenseful page-turner." Commonweal

O'Brien, Flann

★ The **complete** novels; with an introduction by Keith Donohue. Everyman's Library 2007 xxxiii, 787p $25

ISBN 978-0-307-26749-8; 0-307-26749-0

"Truth is an odd number, even numerals are the province of the devil class, and there is safety in a triad. These are some of the essential wisdoms in the world of Flann O'Brien, the Irish writer who is often said to form, along with Samuel Beckett and James Joyce, 'the holy trinity of modern Irish literature.' . . . There may be safety in a triad, but to lump O'Brien with Joyce and Beckett is to miss the playfulness, black humor, and deranged whimsy that characterize his style." Slate

O'Brien, Tim

★ **Going** after Cacciato; a novel. Lawrence, S. 1978 338p hardcover o.p. pa $14.95

ISBN 0-440-02948-1; 0-7679-0442-7 pa

LC 77-11723

"Paul Berlin's squad is sent to retrieve Cacciato, a young deserter from the Vietnam War. Fantasy colors the progress of the squad as a dream of peace and the possibility of forsaking war follow them through many adventures. The horror and destruction of war is vividly conveyed and the language is rough, as would be expected. Cacciato becomes a kind of symbol for resisting bureaucratic militarism and an enviable model for Berlin himself." Shapiro. Fic for Youth. 3d edition

O'Brien, Tim

In the Lake of the Woods. Houghton Mifflin 1994 306p

ISBN 0-395-48889-3

LC 94-5395

"What O'Brien really offers is a portrait of one man and woman at the most critical juncture of their relationship. It's a dark portrait, taking issue with a stock notion of commercial fiction: that after suffering comes redemption. Maybe not. Maybe there's only oblivion. A beautifully written, haunting novel that evokes lives in deep crisis." Booklist

O'Brien, Tim

★ The **things** they carried; a work of fiction. Houghton Mifflin 1990 273p

LC 89-39871

This is a collection of stories about American soldiers in Vietnam. . . . All of the stories "deal with a single platoon, one of whose members is a character named Tim O'Brien." N Y Times Book Rev

"This book may be self-conscious . . . but through its determination to treat these men with dignity and decency it proves immensely affecting." Newsweek

O'Brien, Timothy L.

The **Lincoln** conspiracy; a novel. Timothy L. O'Brien. Ballantine Books 2012 349 p. (hardcover) $26.00

ISBN 0345496779; 9780345496775; 9780345535597

LC 2012022133

This historical thriller novel, by Timothy L. O'Brien, asks, "What if the plot to assassinate President Lincoln was wider and more sinister? . . . In late spring of 1865, . . . Washington, D.C., police detective Temple McFadden makes a startling discovery: . . . [T]wo diaries . . . that together reveal the true depth of the Lincoln conspiracy. Securing the diaries will put Temple's life in jeopardy--and will endanger the fragile peace of a nation still torn by war." (Publisher's note)

O'Connell, Carol

The **chalk** girl; Carol O'Connell. G. P. Putnam's Sons 2012 384p.

ISBN 9780399157745

LC 2011027853

This murder mystery book tells the story of a "little girl [who] appeared in Central Park: red-haired, blue-eyed, smiling, perfect-except for the blood on her shoulder. It fell from the sky, she said, while she was looking for her uncle, who turned into a tree. . . . For Mallory, newly returned to the Special Crimes Unit after three months' lost time, there is something about the girl that she understands. Mallory is damaged, they say, but she can tell a kindred spirit. And this one will lead her to a story of extraordinary crimes: murders stretching back fifteen years, blackmail and complicity and a particular cruelty that only someone with Mallory's history could fully recognize." (Publisher's note)

O'Connell, Carol

Crime school. Putnam 2002 352p

ISBN 0-399-14928-7

LC 2002-22860

Detective Kathy Mallory, "of the Special Crimes Unit, comes face to face with her past when she and her partner are called to a crime scene in which a call girl has been ritualistically murdered. The call girl, Sparrow, offered Mallory protection when she was a child but later betrayed her. Before Mallory has time to call up her knowledge of Sparrow's past in finding the killer, she and her partner are thrown into a morass of spree killings on the streets of New York. O'Connell's crime-scene investigations techniques ring true, her plotting is breathtaking, and her psychology acute. Searing suspense." Booklist

O'Connell, Carol

Judas child. Putnam 1998 340p $24.95

ISBN 0-399-14380-7

LC 97-46504

"O'Connell thoughtfully tackles material that in other hands would be merely sensational. Dark in tone, gripping suspense, and tempered with the hope of redemption, this is highly recommended." Libr J

O'Connell, Carol

Killing critics. Putnam 1996 308p

ISBN 978-0399141683

LC 95-43894

"As mesmerizing as the murder case is, it's heartless, soulless Mallory herself—computer genius, street fighter, provocative waif, peerless investigator, manipulative beauty—who's absolutely the star of this brilliant thriller." Booklist

O'Connell, Carol

Mallory's oracle. Putnam 1994 286p

LC 94-2234

The author's "writing is stunning in its luminosity, originality, simplicity, and power. Her plot is ingenious, inventive, and enigmatic, and her characters sparkle with originality and charm." Booklist

O'Connell, Carol

The **man** who cast two shadows. Putnam 1995 278p

LC 94-43797

This mystery features New York cop Kathleen Mallory. "Taken off suspension to cover the murder of a woman at first identified as Mallory herself, she pits her uncanny intelligence and formidable computer skills against a compulsive and evasive adversary. Moments of wry humor invade the author's incisive prose, tempering an admirable female protagonist sure to gather a following." Libr J

O'Connell, Carol

Stone angel. Putnam 1997 341p

LC 96-44504

How the author "manages to imbue what's basically a who-was-that-masked-man tall tale of revenge with Molierian elegance is as great a mystery as who killed Mallory's mother nearly two decades ago." New Yorker

O'Connell, Jack

The **resurrectionist**; a novel. Algonquin Books Of Chapel Hill 2008 304p $24.95

ISBN 978-1-56512-576-6

LC 2007-49423

"In the first storyline, Sweeney appears at the Peck Clinic, a monstrosity of a family-run hospital for coma patients, hoping that they'll take better care of his comatose young boy, Danny. . . . While Sweeney just seems to want the best for Danny, there are demons chasing him, and apparently a whole batch of new ones waiting at the Clinic, which seems to have plans for Danny that don't involve making him better. In the second storyline, O'Connell inserts installments from the epic, tragic story of a band of traveling circus freaks in Old Bohemia (an invented Balkan/Eastern Europe country from earlier O'Connell novels); this turns out to actually be stories from the comic Limbo, a hugely popular series Danny had loved and which Sweeney still reads to him as often as possible. The story of Limbo seems shockingly gothic for a hit comic (with requisite film, TV, and merchandise spin-offs, of course), but given that the supposedly real storyline quickly involves biker gangs, a nurse with witchlike powers, and a salamander who just might be magic, the line does seem to be a thin one." PopMatters

O'Connor, Edwin

All in the family. Little, Brown 1966 434p

"The plot though rather melodramatic is outweighed by the felicitous childhood recollections of Jack, the authenticity of dialog, and the skillful establishment of political atmosphere." Booklist

O'Connor, Edwin

★ The **last** hurrah. Little, Brown 1956 427p

"A revealing study of a benevolent dictator at work. More, it is a genuine portrait of all the ebullience and rascality, loyalty and duplicity that enliven the typical Irish-American community." Christ Sci Monit

O'Connor, Flannery

★ **Collected** works. Library of Am. 1988 1281p $35

ISBN 0-940450-37-2

LC 87-37829

Contents: Wise blood; A good man is hard to find; The violent bear it away; Everything that rises must converge; Stories and occasional prose; Letters

O'Connor, Flannery

The **complete** stories. Farrar, Straus & Giroux 1971 555p hardcover o.p. pa $17

ISBN 0-374-51536-0

This collection is "arranged in chronological order from the story she wrote for her master's thesis at the University of Iowa to 'Judgement Day.' . . . The stories here include the original openings and other chapters of her two novels 'Wise Blood' and 'The Violent Bear It Away.'" N Y Times Book Rev

O'Connor, Flannery

Everything that rises must converge. Farrar, Straus & Giroux 1965 xxxiv, 269p

Contents: Everything that rises must converge; Greenleaf; A view of the woods; The enduring chill; The comforts of home; The lame shall enter first; Revelation; Parker's back; Judgement Day

O'Connor, Flannery

A **good** man is hard to find and other stories. Harcourt Brace & Co. 1955 251p

O'Connor, Flannery

The **violent** bear it away. Farrar, Straus & Cudahy 1960 243p

"A macabre tale set in the backwoods of Georgia and presenting the fanatical mission of a boy intent on baptizing a still younger boy." Oxford Companion to Am Lit. 6th edition

O'Connor, Flannery

Wise blood. Harcourt Brace & Co. 1952 232p

This novel "centers on Hazel Motes, a discharged serviceman who abandons his fundamentalist faith to become a preacher of anti-religion in a Tennessee city, establishing the 'Church Without Christ.' Motes is a ludicrous and tragic hero who meets a collection of equally grotesque characters. One of his young followers, Enoch Emery, worships a museum mummy. Hoover Shoats is a competing evangelist who creates the 'Holy Church of Christ Without Christ.' Asa Hawks is an itinerant preacher who pretends to have blinded himself to show his faith in redemption." Merriam-Webster's Ency of Lit

O'Connor, Frank

Collected stories; introduction by Richard Ell-mann. Knopf 1981 701p hardcover o.p.

    ISBN 0-394-51602-8

                               LC 81-1253

The author "grew up with 'the troubles,' but the Ireland he evokes in these 72 stories . . . is the provincial life of his Cork boyhood." Libr J

O'Connor, Joseph

Ghost light. Farrar, Straus and Giroux 2011 246p $25

    ISBN 978-0-374-16187-3; 0-374-16187-9

                            LC 2010-22672

First published 2010 in the United Kingdom

"O'Connor's impressionistic, intense style delivers a mismatched love story and a social landscape dominated by forceful characters such as W.B. Yeats and Synge's formidable mother, but it is Molly's perspective which prevails, the voice of a comical, intuitive, irrepressible life force. An empathetic act of literary homage offering nuggets of emotional intensity." Kirkus

O'Connor, Robert

Buffalo soldiers. Knopf 1993 323p

                            LC 92-54278

"O'Connor writes bitter, funny prose and creates bureaucratic snafus of the first order. Alternating scenes of Army idiocy and clinically realistic drug addiction are far more compelling than O'Connor's attempt to attribute his hero's bracing nihilism to his tragic past. Toward its end the book falters, as Elwood flirts with maudlin self-pity. But O'Connor misfires now and then only because he aims high." Publ Wkly

O'Dell, Tawni

Back roads. Viking 1999 338p $24.95

    ISBN 0-670-88760-9

                            LC 99-20649

"Harley's first-person account of the deterioration of his family and his own slow-motion meltdown is harrowing. O'Dell, a native of western Pennsylvania, renders finely detailed characters and settings in a desperate and failed mining town. This is a riveting first novel of violence, incest, murder, and madness." Booklist

O'Dell, Tawni

Coal Run. Viking 2004 354p $24.95

    ISBN 0-670-89995-X

                            LC 2003-62645

"After more than 15 years living in Florida, Ivan Zoschenko returns to his home in western Pennsylvania, his arrival coinciding with the release from prison of his high-school alter ego, Reese Raynor. Ivan is not thrilled to return home: he had gladly left behind memories of the explosion at the mine that killed his father and nearly 100 other miners when he was six, and he doesn't look forward to hearing the locals' reaction to the bizarre injury that brought his career as a pro football player to an abrupt end. But here he is, sleeping on his sister's couch and working temporarily as deputy for the sheriff's office. The novel takes place over the course of only one week, yet O'Dell manages to give the story an epic dimension through masterful intercutting of past and present. Reese's pending release drives the plot, and as the day nears, Ivan confronts his own demons and secrets with true-to-life reluctance." Booklist

O'Dell, Tawni

Fragile beasts; a novel. Shaye Areheart Books 2010 401p $25

    ISBN 978-0-307-35168-5; 0-307-35168-8

                            LC 2009-34352

"O'Dell's eye for class conflict remains as sharp as ever, but she's broadened the reach of her sympathies, tamed her taste for lurid plotting and found new depths in her subject matter and her human understanding." Kirkus

O'Dell, Tawni

Sister mine; a novel. Shaye Areheart Books 2007 416p $23

    ISBN 978-0-307-35126-5; 0-307-35126-2

                            LC 2006-15355

"At 40, Shae-Lynn Penrose has overcome a mostly motherless, abusive childhood and a teenage pregnancy to finish college, work for the D.C. Capitol Police, raise her son alone, and return to her coal-mining hometown of Jolly Mount, Pennsylvania. Here she runs a one-vehicle cab company; her father died in a mine; her best friend, E. J., was one of the Jolly Mount 5, whose survival after a mine explosion made headlines; and her son, Clay, is a deputy for Sheriff Ivan Zoschenko . . . . Then Shannon, the younger sister Shae-Lynn thought long dead, shows up and reveals an unorthodox means of making money that's causing a ruckus. Dealing with a burgeoning love affair and revelation of parentage, plus the surviving miners' intent to sue the coal company, O'Dell also examines such issues as abuse, betrayal, abandonment, perseverance, and reconciliation, with love at the heart of it all, in crisp, insightful prose that sweeps the reader along. A knockout." Booklist

O'Donnell, Lillian

Blue death. Putnam 1998 215p $22.95

    ISBN 0-399-14367-X

                            LC 97-47589

"The proud mother of an adopted toddler as well as the head of her own homicide division, NYPD Lieutenant Norah Mulcahaney learns how difficult it is to balance home life and work. . . . Just when her live-in sitter suddenly quits, she's confronted with a case that has left some NYPD higher-ups a little nervous. It seems there's been a rash of suicides among police officers. . . . A clever, low-key puzzler, this is a nice break from the usual violent, high-octane police procedural." Booklist

O'Donnell, Lillian

Pushover. Putnam 1992 239p

                            LC 91-30205

Norah Mulcahaney "is called in to investigate the murder of an aging screen star, only to find, in addition, that the woman's grandson is missing. While sorting through suspects and evidence for a kidnapping charge, Norah is also asked to assist the New York City transit authority police in finding the 'perp' who pushes young women to their deaths from subway platforms. O'Donnell's snappy style sets the pace here, as Mulcahaney races to solve the mysteries before another death occurs." Booklist

O'Donnell, Lillian

The **raggedy** man. Putnam 1995 232p

LC 95-3925

"When NYPD sergeant Ray Dixon nudges PI Gwenn Ramadge into hiring a suspended rookie detective for help in an investigation, the Brooklyn investigator . . . is drawn into a bitter—but for readers, delicious—brew of murder and police corruption." Publ Wkly

O'Donnell, Lisa

The **death** of bees; a novel. Lisa O'Donnell. Harper 2013 311 p. $25.99

ISBN 0062209841; 9780062209849

LC 2012031882

This novel, by Lisa O'Donnell, is "a coming-of-age story in which two young sisters attempt to hold the world at bay after the mysterious death of their parents. Marnie and Nelly, left on their own in Glasgow's Hazlehurst housing estate, attempt to avoid suspicion until Marnie can become a legal guardian for her younger sister." (Publisher's note)

O'Donovan, Gerard

Dublin dead; a novel. Gerard O'Donovan. Scribner 2012 280 p.

ISBN 9781451610635

LC 2011031170

In this book, "it seems eminently logical that Cormac Horgan, the millionaire head of his family's chain of estate agents, would have completed his financial ruin by topping himself at a spot favored by dozens of other suicides. Nor is anyone shedding tears over the demise of Declan (Bingo) Begley in sunny Spain--except for accountant Gemma Kearney's mother. . . . Gemma was Begley's girlfriend, she tells . . . reporter Siobhan Fallon . . . [DI Mike] Mulcahy follows a tip from veteran informant Eddie McTiernan that seems to link still another death . . . to an epic consignment of drugs by sea and a well-traveled Colombian assassin. . . . Siobhan and Mulcahy realize that they're pulling opposite ends of the same tangled skein and reluctantly join forces." (Kirkus)

O'Donovan, Gerard

The **priest**; a novel. Scribner 2011 323p $25

ISBN 978-1-4516-1060-4; 1-4516-1060-2

LC 2010-33448

"Although it's clear early on who the psycho is . . . Mr. O'Donovan builds suspense carefully and cleverly, leading us to a pulse-raising climax at a huge cross in a Dublin park." Pittsburgh Post-Gazette

O'Faolain, Sean

★ The **collected** stories of Sean O'Faolain. Little, Brown 1983 1304p il

LC 83-205346

O'Farrell, Maggie

The **hand** that first held mine. Houghton Mifflin Harcourt 2010 341p $25

ISBN 978-0-547-33079-2; 0-547-33079-0

LC 2009-42058

"Lexie Sinclair moves from the Cornwall area to post-World War II London and begins a thrilling new life under the tutelage of her lover, Innes Kent, an editor and art collector. Even the eventual knowledge that he is legally married doesn't alter her allegiance to him, and she becomes the mother of his son, as well as a respected art critic. In between chapters about Lexie and Innes, readers meet contemporary London artist Elina, who lives with her boyfriend Ted. They have just had a son together, and Elina, who almost died in childbirth, is housebound during her recovery. Growing into his new role as a father, Ted suffers confusing flashbacks about his own childhood." Libr J

O'Farrell, Maggie

The **vanishing** act of Esme Lennox. Harcourt 2007 245p $23

ISBN 978-0-15-101411-8; 0-15-101411-6

LC 2007-6079

First published 2006 in the United Kingdom

"At the heart of this fantastic new novel is a mystery you want to solve until you start to suspect the truth, and then you read on in a panic, horrified that you may be right." Washington Post Book World

O'Flynn, Catherine

The **news** where you are; a novel. Henry Holt and Co. 2010 252p pa $15

ISBN 978-0-8050-9180-9; 0-8050-9180-7

LC 2009-45217

This is "a funny, moving, acutely observed story about family and loss, getting old and being alone. That it also manages to take in British architecture and urban space and the problems of celebrity culture, while being disarmingly easy to read, is testament to Catherine O'Flynn's comic timing and lightness of touch." Scotland on Sunday

O'Hagan, Andrew

Be near me. Harcourt, Inc. 2007 305p $24

ISBN 978-0-15-101303-6; 0-15-101303-9

LC 2006-30402

First published 2006 in the United Kingdom

"A distinctive voice resonates clearly through the first-person narrative, clerically portentous at times, a shade trite or unabashedly sentimental at others, yet in all its registers convincing. What it tells us is a story compounded from passion and resurrection as opposed to professional failure or spiritual collapse." Times Lit Suppl

O'Hara, John, 1905-1970

★ **Appointment** in Samarra. Modern Lib. 1994 xxi, 269p $14.95

ISBN 0679601104

LC 94-4340

A reissue of the title first published 1934 by Harcourt Brace & Co.

"The novel is written episodically, but achieves integration by its hard-boiled theme of the destructive effects of fast living." Haydn. Thesaurus of Book Dig

O'Hara, John, 1905-1970

★ **Butterfield** 8; a novel. Harcourt Brace & Co. 1935 310p

"A novelization of the sensational lives of the night-club set involved in an actual New York murder case. Young Gloria Wandrous is found drowned on a beach near New York. The problem is to find the murderer and his motive. The investigation, described in machine-gun reportage, reveals that Gloria had had a good education, but owing to an adolescent sexual experience had become a 'party girl' in the unsavory life of New York speakeasies and luxurious Long Island clubs. Under the sleekness of Park Avenue sophistication, O'Hara reveals New York's hard soullessness." Haydn. Thesaurus of Book Dig

O'Hara, John

Collected stories of John O'Hara; selected and with an introduction by Frank MacShane. Random House 1984 414p

LC 84-42661

O'Hara, John

From the terrace; a novel. Random House 1958 897p

"Alfred Eaton, the younger son of Samuel Eaton, steel magnate of Port Johnson, Pennsylvania, had a tolerably happy childhood until the death of his older brother William, when Alfred was twelve. After the death of his favorite son, Samuel Eaton retreated into an obsessive grief. Alfred's mother, neglected, turned elsewhere for affection and Alfred was left to grow up as best as he could, closer to the servants than to his parents. The rest of his life though rewarded with business success and filled with a variety of amorous adventures, was basically barren and loveless." Booklist

O'Hara, John

Ten North Frederick. Random House 1955 408p

A character study of one of the 'first citizens' of a Pennsylvania town, Gibbsville. "In the first quarter of a crowded, eventful narrative, Joe Chapin is seen only through the eyes of some of those at {his} funeral. Then {O'Hara} . . . switches back to Joe's parents, who established the home at Ten North Frederick Street, where Joe lived all his life. He tells Joe's story from the beginning, and the stories of those whose lives have touched Joe's at some significant point." N Y Times Book Rev

O'Malley, Daniel

The **rook**; a novel. Daniel O'Malley. Little, Brown and Co. 2012 486p.

ISBN 9780316098793

LC 2011019741

In this book, "Myfanwy Thomas wakes in a London park surrounded by bodies, unable to remember her identity. However, she quickly learns she's a Rook: a mid-level member of the Chequy, an intelligence agency of superpowered operatives. So Myfanwy begins investigating clues to fill in the gaps of her lost memory and determine the cause of her amnesia." (Publishers Weekly)

"O'Malley's narrative is peppered with sly humor, referential social commentary and the ironic, double-layered self-awareness that will have genre fans believing Buffy the Vampire Slayer has joined Ghostbusters." Kirkus

O'Malley, Thomas

This magnificent desolation; a novel. Thomas O'Malley. Bloomsbury 2013 416 p. (hardcover) $26

ISBN 1608192792; 9781608192793

LC 2012025659

In this novel, by Thomas O'Malley, "Duncan's entire world is the orphanage where he lives. . . . Aged ten in 1980, he has no memories of his life before now. . . . Duncan is sure that his mother is dead until the day she turns up to claim him. . . . Thrown into [a] mysterious adult world, Duncan finds comfort in an ancient radio, from which tumble the voices of Apollo mission astronauts who never came home, and dreams of finding his real father." (Publisher's note)

O'Nan, Stewart, 1961-

Emily, alone. Viking 2011 255p $25.95

ISBN 978-0-670-02235-9; 0-670-02237-7

LC 2010-35333

This "novel revisits the Emily Maxwell of Wish You Were Here [2002] as a widow and traces the course of three-quarters of a year near the end—but decidedly not at the end—of her long life. Born in small-town Appalachia to a building inspector and a teacher, Emily achieved the cultured and refined life for which she yearned by marrying into a gracious Pittsburgh family. She appreciates classical music, visits the library regularly, reserves a table at 'the club' for special occasions, pines for the heyday of Masterpiece Theatre and Mystery! (although not the gritty, Helen Mirren era, much as she admires the actress herself). O'Nan cannot write without nuance, and Emily contains the contradictions and failings of a real person. Her second-guessing of, frustration with, and love for her adult children and grandchildren; her observations concerning her comparatively young neighbors; her dependence on and resentment toward her sister-in-law are all a voyeuristic pleasure." Atlantic

O'Nan, Stewart

The **good** wife. Farrar, Straus and Giroux 2005 312p $24

ISBN 0-374-28139-4

LC 2004-53247

"From the trial, through the various appeals process, the visits to the prison, the waiting, the hoping, the struggle to make ends meet, and the gradual resilience and self-sufficiency, O'Nan, with seldom a false beat, perceptively and compassionately depicts the bureaucratic insanities of the penal system and the hardships, fears, and frustrations of those left behind." Booklist

O'Nan, Stewart, 1961-

Last night at the Lobster; a novel. Viking 2007 146p

ISBN 0-670-01827-9; 978-0-670-01827-7

LC 2006-102825

Managing a failed seafood restaurant in a New England mall just before Christmas, Manny DeLeon coordinates a final shift of mutinous staff members, an effort that is complicated by his love for a waitress.

"O'Nan's empathy for his characters is one of his great gifts as a novelist, and it is an impressive achievement that

Manny's misplaced affection for Red Lobster is not risible, but tragic." N Y Times Book Rev

O'Nan, Stewart

★ The **names** of the dead. Doubleday 1996 399p

ISBN 978-0385481922

LC 95-36745

"O'Nan's language is powerfully restrained; his word pictures of the war and its effect on the men who fought there are fresh and vivid. He rightfully refuses to pander to our desire for easy answers and happy endings." Booklist

O'Nan, Stewart

The **night** country; or, The darkness on the edge of town. Farrar, Straus & Giroux 2003 229p $23

ISBN 0-374-22215-0

LC 2002-44765

"O'Nan is wonderful at describing teenage ritual, the simultaneous desire for the comforting familiarity of friends and the lust for speed and novelty and excitement that will lift teenagers out of the confines of their suburban town, the routine of school, out of their own restless bodies." N Y Times Book Rev

O'Nan, Stewart, 1961-

The **odds**; a love story. Stewart O'Nan. Viking 2012 179p.

ISBN 9780670023165; 0670023167

LC 2011033330

The novel "examines the quotidian sore spots and the comforting core of a realistic 30-year marriage against the . . . background of Niagara Falls. Marion and Art Fowler, middle-class victims of the 2008 crash, revisit the site of their honeymoon to gamble what remains of their liquid assets in a last-ditch attempt to skirt bankruptcy. Even more than solvency is at stake, however, since their marriage is foundering along with their finances, and the weekend, at least from Art's point of view, is also a chance to win big in love and reclaim his wife." (Atlantic Monthly)

O'Nan, Stewart

★ **Snow** angels. Doubleday 1994 305p

ISBN 0-385-47574-8

LC 94-12037

The author "weaves together these seemingly disparate small-town tragedies–one narrated in the first person, the other in the third–with consummate skill, seamlessly shifting the focus among characters he wishes to make the reader care about." Libr J

O'Nan, Stewart

Songs for the missing. Viking 2008 287p $25.95

ISBN 978-0-670-02032-4; 0-670-02032-X

LC 2008-22274

The author's "greatest literary talent lies with his characters. It's as if he has lived each of the lives he creates, and nothing is too mundane nor too overblown. . . . O'Nan has honed his ability to tap into the most basic components of small town life and ordinary people. His latest is both an intriguing page-turner and a sometimes agonizing look

at human emotion in the face of inexplicable loss." Rocky Mountain News

O'Neill, Anthony

The **lamplighter**; a novel. Scribner 2003 308p

ISBN 0-7432-4349-8

LC 2002-36453

"It is 1886. Although the new electric lamp has conquered Paris and London, it has yet to make its way to Edinburgh, whose medieval streets and modern boulevards are still illuminated at dusk by the 'leeries,' the traditional lamplighters. But someone—or something—is also coming out in the evenings, leaving a trail of horribly mutilated bodies: those of a professor, a lighthouse keeper, and a shady businessman. Assigned to the case is acting Chief Inspector Carus Groves." Libr J

O'Neill, Jamie

At swim, two boys; a novel. Scribner 2002 572p $27

ISBN 0-7432-2294-6

LC 2001-57694

First published 2001 in the United Kingdom

"In this novel the cause of Ireland and the cause of gay people fuse with a complete lack of apology or embarrassment. . . . O'Neill is not, however, being patly outrageous; the closeness and exactness of his vision prove that." N Y Times Book Rev

O'Neill, Jamie

Kilbrack; or, Who is Nancy Valentine? Scribner 2004 305p pa $14

ISBN 0-7432-5595-X pa

LC 2003-65911

"O'Leary Montague, a facially scarred amnesiac as the result of a car accident, travels to the Irish village of Kilbrack because it is the setting of his favorite novel, Ill Fares the Land, by Nancy Valentine. The small-town residents prove to be deeply eccentric, with habits ranging from button hoarding to cocaine addiction, so O'Leary, a veritable bundle of nervous tics and obsessions, fits right in. His desire to write a biography of the revered Nancy Valentine leads him to a hapless meeting with reclusive Valentine Brack, a still raffish if aging member of the landed gentry who harbors a terrible secret. O'Neill sends up the rural Irish to a fare-thee-well, devoting paragraph after paragraph to the hidebound villagers' convoluted conversations, so cryptic in tone that they inevitably lead to absurdly comic misunderstandings." Booklist

O'Neill, Joseph

Netherland. Pantheon Books 2008 256p $23.95

ISBN 978-0-307-37704-3; 0-307-37704-0

LC 2007033711

This novel is "narrated by a Dutch financier whose privileged Manhattan existence is upended by the events of Sept. 11, 2001. When his wife departs for London with their small son, he stays behind, finding camaraderie in the unexpectedly buoyant world of immigrant cricket players, most of them West Indians and South Asians, including an entrepreneur with Gatsby-size aspirations." N Y Times Book Rev

O'Reilly, Brian

Angelina's bachelors; a novel, with food. recipes by Virginia O'Reilly. Gallery Books 2011 359p pa $15

ISBN 978-1-4516-2056-6; 1-4516-2056-X

LC 2011-13170

Managing sudden widowhood and joblessness by cooking bounteous and sumptuous feasts that she shares with her neighbors, Angelina D'Angelo is offered a job as cook for a retiree and his elderly sister and finds her culinary talents winning her a circle of friends and protectors.

"Filled with more than 20 (fairly complicated) recipes for Angelina's gourmet fare, the food is only half of the novel's winning ingredient—O'Reilly's keen ear for the neighborhood swells lends a charming, timeless quality to the tale. Light comedy and good food make a winning combination." Kirkus

O'Shaughnessy, Perri

Breach of promise. Delacorte Press 1998 435p $23.95

ISBN 0-385-31872-3

LC 98-5519

"O'Shaughnessy offers up a gripping courtroom drama, throws in pithy ethical and moral dilemmas and some surprising plot twists, and adds plenty of heart-stopping action." Booklist

O'Shaughnessy, Perri

Invasion of privacy. Delacorte Press 1996 419p

ISBN 978-0385314138

LC 96-1251

"Tahoe-area attorney Nina Reilly was shot at the end of Motion to Suppress. As the increasingly alarming facts of her latest case pile up, she is haunted by memories of that wounding. No less haunting are certain details of her personal past, which Nina's new client, Terry London, an energetically spiteful documentary filmmaker, seems to know as much about as Nina does. Out of that past and into Tahoe comes Kurt Scott, the father of Nina's son, Bob. Almost immediately, Terry is murdered, Kurt is accused of the crime and Nina must assemble his murder defense. . . . Fans of the genre will luxuriate in this deft, multileveled tale of legal and criminal treachery, whose pleasures include elegant courtroom sleight-of-hand and the eerily wintry backdrop of Lake Tahoe." Publ Wkly

O'Shaughnessy, Perri

Motion to suppress. Delacorte Press 1995 420p

LC 95-5615

"Although the characterizations are a bit uncertain (the luscious Misty is unbelievably prim and proper), the plot is a real puzzler, with twists diabolical enough to take to court." N Y Times Book Rev

O'Shaughnessy, Perri

Obstruction of justice. Delacorte Press 1997 392p

LC 96-48585

In this thriller, attorney Nina Reilly is "a witness to the death by lightning of a construction mogul in the Tahoe Mountains. When his father returns from a business trip, he wants Nina to have the body exhumed and autopsied for signs of murder, setting off a family furor. Suddenly, the grave is empty, the bodies of both father and son turn up in a smoldering mountain cabin, and the grandson is charged with murder. Nina is then asked to clear the grandson amid an increasingly complex series of interrelationships involving the D.A., his dead wife, a not-so-grieving widow, and, of course, the gardener. . . . A compelling story with some great courtroom drama and a likable heroine." Libr J

O'Shaughnessy, Perri

Unlucky in law. Delacorte Press 2004 376p $25

ISBN 0-385-33646-2

LC 2004-47840

In this legal thriller California lawyer Nina Reilly has "moved herself and 14-year-old son Bob from their usual Tahoe turf to the Monterey Peninsula to spend time with her lover, PI Paul van Wagoner. Paul has asked Nina to marry him, offering a big diamond to seal the deal. Nina puts him off while she prepares for a big trial: she's newly employed at Pohlmann, Cunningham, and Turk, and her first case, working with Klaus Pohlmann, is defending 28-year-old Stefan Wyatt, charged with murder and grave robbing. O'Shaughnessy has been accused of sloppy plotting in the past, but not so here." Publ Wkly

O'Shaughnessy, Perri

Writ of execution. Delacorte Press 2001 403p

ISBN 0-385-33483-4

LC 2001-28468

"Readers will relish the myriad plot details and the procedural drama, and enjoy the cast of offbeat characters." Publ Wkly

The **O. Henry** prize stories 2007. Anchor Books 2007 pa $14.95

ISBN 0-307-27688-0; 978-0-307-27688-9

Annual. First published 2003 as a continuation of Prize stories: The O. Henry Awards; first collection, published in 1919 with title: O. Henry Memorial Award prize stories, was edited by Blanche C. Williams

This annual anthology of outstanding short stories by American authors includes contributions by such authors as John Updike, Joyce Carol Oates, Alice Adams, Alice Munro, Louise Erdrich, Andrea Barrett, and T. Coraghessan Boyle.

Oates, Joyce Carol, 1938-

★ The **Accursed**. HarperCollins 2013 688 p. $27.99

ISBN 0062231707; 9780062231703

In this book by Joyce Carol Oates, "strange things start happening in peaceful, polished Princeton, NJ. Folks dream about vampires, the daughters of the town's classiest families start vanishing, and a bride-to-be runs away with a vaguely menacing European, presumably a prince and possibly the Devil. As her brother gives chase, he encounters characters from former President Grover Cleveland and future President Woodrow Wilson to authors like Upton Sinclair." (Library Journal)

Oates, Joyce Carol, 1938-
American appetites. Dutton 1989 340p
LC 88-18904

"Ian McCullough, 50 years old, is editor of a prestigious journal and a research fellow. His wife, Glynnis, writes cookbooks. Their marriage is not perfect but far from unfulfilling. Then an incident from the past—Ian loaned money to a friend of Glynnis' for an abortion—resurfaces and provokes a horrible row between husband and wife. Glynnis ends up falling through a pane of glass and being killed." Booklist

"A zippy story about successful lives dramatically altered by one sudden and inexplicable lapse of judgment." Publ Wkly

Oates, Joyce Carol
★ Because it is bitter, and because it is my heart. Dutton 1990 405p
LC 89-25965

This novel "is set in a small town in western New York from the early 1950s to the early 1960s, and follows the . . . fortunes of two families, one white (the Courtneys) and one black (the Fairchilds). When Jinx Fairchild, at 16, gets in a fight with a white kid who has menaced Iris Courtney, 14, and ends up killing him, the secret they share is . . . both a bond and a barrier between the two." Nation

"At its best, the novel awakens the reader to something like the unexpected new comprehensions of the universe that Iris experiences." N Y Rev Books

Oates, Joyce Carol
★ Bellefleur. Dutton 1980 558p
ISBN 0-525-06302-1
LC 79-28193

"In this Gothic novel, Oates weaves a shimmering tapestry made of odd and contradictory threads: a hermaphroditic birth, a vulture that devours an infant, a dwarf with 'powers,' a vampire, a cannibal, religious mystics and clairvoyants. Such are the Gothic trappings of this epic about the Bellefleurs, an old and powerful American family whose estate is located in the Adirondacks and whose history is an interpretation of American history from pioneer days to the present." Benet's Reader's Ency of Am Lit

Oates, Joyce Carol, 1938-
Black dahlia & white rose; stories. Joyce Carol Oates. Ecco 2012 274 p. $24.99
ISBN 0062195697; 9780062195692
LC 2012462476

This collection of short stories by Joyce Carol Oates "explores the menace that lurks at the edges of and intrudes upon even the seemingly safest of lives. . . . Oates takes readers deep into dangerous territory, from a maximum-security prison . . . to the inner landscapes of two beautiful and mysteriously doomed young women in 1940s Los Angeles: Elizabeth Short, otherwise known as the Black Dahlia, . . . and her roommate Norma Jeane Baker, soon to become Marilyn Monroe." (Publisher's note)

Oates, Joyce Carol
Black girl/White girl. Ecco 2006 272p $25.95
ISBN 0-06-112564-4
LC 2006-48306

"Oates has never been shy about peering into the darkest corners of American culture. Her best books . . . showcase her fascination with violence, her almost vampiric ability to tap into the subconscious of her troubled characters and her taste for appropriating real-life tragedy. Oates's latest offering is no exception." N Y Times Book Rev

Oates, Joyce Carol
Black water. Dutton 1992 154p
LC 91-40463

"Those who remember Chappaquiddick can predict Kelly's ultimate fate, but certainly not the horrors she must have suffered strapped to the seat of a car that would become an aqueous death chamber. Immense courage shines through the tangled streams of her thoughts, memories, and hallucinations. As witnesses to her plight, we can only keep vigil as she drifts in and out of consciousness, waiting for the reprieve that surely must be hers. Oates brilliantly redefines the meanings of guilt and innocence, vengeance and reward in this thought-provoking allegory of our life and times." Libr J

Oates, Joyce Carol
Blonde. Ecco Press 2000 738p
ISBN 0-06-019607-6

"Joyce Carol Oates takes the boldest path to comprehending 'the riddle, the curse of Monroe' by proceeding directly and frankly to fiction. Her novel 'Blonde' is fat, messy and fierce. It's part Gothic, part kaleidoscopic novel of ideas, part lurid celebrity potboiler, and it is seldom less than engrossing." N Y Times Book Rev

Oates, Joyce Carol
A Bloodsmoor romance. Dutton 1982 615p
LC 82-2416

The novel "details the bizarre goings-on in a 19th-century inventor's family. One daughter becomes a medium, another an actress and Mark Twain's mistress, a third runs away on her wedding night. Even Octavia, the perfect wife, is secretly subversive. . . . The narrator misunderstands and misinterprets much that happens; the reader, therefore, enters into collusion with the characters who use the period's conventions to subvert prescribed female roles." Libr J

Oates, Joyce Carol
Broke heart blues. Dutton 1999 369p $24.95
ISBN 0-525-94451-6
LC 98-51570

Oates "dramatizes how wanting and memory compete. It's about how lonely, unhappy people mythologize their adolescence. . . . This is not a bashful or subtle book. It doesn't woo you so much as run you down." N Y Times Book Rev

Oates, Joyce Carol
The collector of hearts; new tales of the grotesque. Dutton 1998 321p
ISBN 0-525-94445-1
LC 98-17508

Oates, Joyce Carol, 1938-

Daddy Love; Joyce Carol Oates. Pgw 2013 240 p. $24

ISBN 0802120997; 9780802120991

In Joyce Carol Oates' book, "Dinah Whitcomb is playing . . . with her five-year-old son, Robbie . . . when a stranger seizes the boy. . . . Robbie is renamed Gideon by Daddy Love, his abductor, who has kidnapped several little boys through the years, killing them when they're adolescents. . . . Spanning six years, the action shifts between Gideon and Daddy Love, who's quick to mete out cruel punishments, and Dinah and her husband, bonded by guilt in a crumbling marriage." (Publishers Weekly)

Oates, Joyce Carol

Dear husband, Ecco 2009 326p $24.99

ISBN 978-0-06-170431-4; 0-06-170431-8

"Oates' characters are masterfully rendered, but she is particularly gifted at creating a certain type: The appallingly egocentric, sometimes to the point of (usually) unwitting hostility. . . . Oates' characters are all self-absorbed to some extent. They all regard themselves as more real than their bystanders, with needs that always take precedence. They appear to exist for their own benefit, certainly not the reader's. While it may seem obvious that any worthwhile fiction will feature such characters, some authors are more skilled at delivering them than others. In this regard, Oates is one of the best." Idaho Statesman

Oates, Joyce Carol

Faithless; tales of transgression. Ecco Press 2001 386p

ISBN 0-06-018525-2

LC 00-60007

"As the subtitle suggests, the book's preoccupation is sin, but otherwise the stories are richly various. They range from quiet, intimate tales—such as the chilling opening effort, 'Au Sable,' about a man let in on a suicide he cannot prevent—to the satiric fantasia on TV journalism and police brutality that closes the volume." Publ Wkly

Oates, Joyce Carol

★ The **falls**; a novel. Ecco 2004 481p $26.95

ISBN 0-06-072228-2

LC 2004-43310

"Set around Niagara, the story reflects all the romance, mystery, and terror of that spectacular waterfall. It's a great confluence of tones-grotesque and domestic, tragic and comic. The currents of various styles and points of view blend together in a way that can't possibly work, but does." Christ Sci Monit

Oates, Joyce Carol

Foxfire; confessions of a girl gang. Dutton 1993 328p

ISBN 0-525-93632-7

LC 92-43858

"Legs Sadovsky is a brilliant creation—wholly heroic, wholly convincing, racing for her tragic consummation impelled by a finer sensibility and a more thoughtful daring than is usually granted to the tragic male outlaws we love

and need. . . . 'Foxfire' burns brightly; it is completely assured and occasionally exhilarating." N Y Times Book Rev

Oates, Joyce Carol

A **garden** of earthly delights. Vanguard Press 1967 440p

The book describes the early life of Clara Walpole, the daughter of a migrant farm worker; her life after she leaves her father; her romance with a rum-runner; and her marriage to a rich man, whom she convinces is the father of her illegitimate baby. The final part of the novel deals with the childhood and adolescence of Swan, the son

"The book has much to say of society's indifference to the plight of the disadvantaged, and of the shallowness of a way of life based entirely on getting and spending." Libr J

Oates, Joyce Carol

The **gravedigger's** daughter; a novel. Ecco 2007 582p $26.95

ISBN 978-0-06-123682-2; 0-061-23682-9

LC 2006-48546

"This is neither a depressing story nor an uplifting one. Oates succeeds here, as she often does, in making such judgments feel simpleminded. What it all seems is true and therefore moving and somewhat terrible, but in an exhilarating way. Every aspect of the ungainly plot feels right, including its ungainliness." Washington Post Book World

Oates, Joyce Carol

Haunted; tales of the grotesque. Dutton 1994 310p

LC 93-25223

"All the pieces here have a redeeming literary bent, although some are transparent in their motives. Undoubtedly a master of this form, Oates plies her craft like a skilled seducer, setting the mood and moving in for the conquest night after night after night." Publ Wkly

Oates, Joyce Carol

Heat, and other stories. Dutton 1991 397p

LC 91-8007

Oates, Joyce Carol

High lonesome; new & selected stories, 1966-2006. Ecco 2006 664p $34.95

ISBN 0-06-050119-7; 978-0-06-050119-8

LC 2005-51147

This "collection, which includes classic stories like "In the Region of Ice," which won the O. Henry prize in 1967, and the much anthologized "Where Are You Going, Where Have You Been?" as well as 11 new stories, spans Oates's career and gives a remarkably coherent picture of her work." N Y Times Book Rev

Oates, Joyce Carol

I am no one you know; stories. Ecco 2004 290p $24.95

ISBN 0-06-059288-5

LC 2003-61283

"Oates is vitally concerned, even obsessed, with the most primal and disturbing encounters between females and males, and her new searing short stories explore the malevolent aspects of human sexuality with unflinching authenticity and a cathartic fascination." Booklist

Oates, Joyce Carol

★ I lock my door upon myself. Ecco Press 1990 98p

    ISBN 0-88001-260-9

                            LC 90-31878

    Is this "all a parable of the artist's position as an observer and interpreter of society? Is it an illustration of how a writer constructs a coherent story out of disjointed events? Either way, it provokes thought." Atlantic

Oates, Joyce Carol

    Little bird of heaven; a novel. Ecco Press 2009 442p $25.99

    ISBN 978-0-06-182983-3; 0-06-182983-8

    The narrators of this novel, set in upstate New York, are "an angry young man whose mother is murdered and a shy, introspective young woman whose father is a suspect. But the character who leaps most off the page is the victim, Zoe Kruller. . . . She abandons her son, Aaron, and her husband, Delray. She has an affair with Eddy Diehl, whose daughter Krista finds life in their small town of Sparta almost impossible to bear. And singing with her band, the Black River Breakdown, she wears spangly outfits, enchants the townspeople and belts out the song that gives the novel its title. . . . Krista and Aaron meet as teenagers. He's a gruff, rough, half-Indian guy with tattoos and little use for school. She is a blond waif, trying to tough it out on the basketball court to win the affection of her daddy and the respect of her peers. But it is her longing for Aaron that rules her life, particularly after Zoe Kruller is found murdered. Her death seals their connection forever, even though they rarely speak and, when they are together, the conditions are as far from romantic as you can get. . . . Oates deftly merges the personalities of Zoe, Eddy, Krista and Aaron into what is essentially a mystery." St. Louis Post-Dispatch

Oates, Joyce Carol

    Marriages and infidelities; short stories. Vanguard Press 1972 497p

Oates, Joyce Carol

    Marya; a life. Dutton 1986 310p

                            LC 85-16283

    "Marya's development and her innermost fears and insecurities are revealed in a very personal, almost autobiographical manner. A major work by an important writer." Libr J

Oates, Joyce Carol

    Middle age; a romance. Ecco Press 2001 464p
    ISBN 0-06-620946-3

                            LC 2001-23062

    "Adam Berendt, an eccentric sculptor, goes sailing on the Hudson River one Fourth of July. A nearby boat capsizes, and Adam leaps in to save a drowning child. He gets to her in time, but is struck by a heart attack as he holds her afloat, and dies. Adam's death is the engendering mistake, the accidental firecracker that sets off the rest of the book. In 'Middle Age,' the people affected are those left behind:

Adam Berendt's neighbors in Salthill-on-Hudson." N Y Times Book Rev

Oates, Joyce Carol

    Missing mom. Ecco 2005 434p $25.95
    ISBN 0-06-081621-X

                            LC 2005-40002

    "Oates's grip on crime, violence and the long-buried is sure, but Missing Mom is actually more disturbing in its relentless, dead-on accretion of small-time, small-town, middle-class details. Oates piles them on with pitiless virtuosity." N Y Times Book Rev

Oates, Joyce Carol, 1938-

    Mudwoman; Joyce Carol Oates. Ecco 2012 448 p.

    ISBN 9780062095626

                            LC 2012376456

    In this book, "Mudgirl is a child abandoned by her mother." After being adopted she grows up to be the "first woman president of an Ivy League university. . . . Involved with a secret lover whose feelings for her are teasingly undefined, and concerned with the intensifying crisis of the American political climate as the United States edges toward war with Iraq, M.R. is confronted with challenges to her leadership that test her in ways she could not have anticipated." (Publisher's note)

Oates, Joyce Carol

    Rape; a love story. Carroll & Graf 2004 154p $16

    ISBN 0-7867-1294-5

    A novel "about the nearly fatal beating and gang rape of Teena MacGuire on the Fourth of July in the small town of Niagara Falls. Teena and her 12-year-old daughter, Bethel, are walking home from a party when the vicious attack takes place, and Bethel only narrowly escapes her mother's terrible fate. Terrorized but valiant, Bethel identifies their assailants and is determined to testify, but the townspeople close ranks behind the indicted brutes, their sons and brothers, and Teena is assaulted all over again in court. But there is one man on the case who possesses a clear and unshakable sense of justice, and his empathic connection with Bethel is at the heart of this lean and potent tale." Booklist

Oates, Joyce Carol

    Sourland; stories. Ecco/HarperCollins 2010 373p $25.99

    ISBN 978-0-06-199652-8; 0-06-199652-1

    "This collection could be used as a master class in the art of pure, suspenseful storytelling. There are real plots here, fascinating psychological and domestic mysteries we need to solve, portraying people we want to understand...Oates is a dangerous writer in the best sense of the word, one who takes risks almost obsessively, with energy and relish. For a writer in her early 70s, she continues to be wonderfully, unnervingly anarchic, experimental, angry. As if her aim were not to satisfy or entertain—though she always does both—but to do the vandalistic prose equivalent of spray-painting or setting fire to bins in public parks." N Y Times Book Rev

Oates, Joyce Carol

Them; introduction by Greg Johnson; afterword by the author. 2000 Modern Library ed; Modern Lib. 2000 xxiv, 546p $21.95

ISBN 0-679-64025-8

LC 99-54471

A reissue of the title first published 1969 by Vanguard Press

"Violent and explosive in both incident and tone, the work is set in urban Detroit from 1937 to 1967 and chronicles the efforts of the Wendell family to break away from their destructive, crime-ridden background. Critics praised the novel for its detailed social observation and its bitter indictment of American society." Merriam-Webster's Ency of Lit

Oates, Joyce Carol

We were the Mulvaneys. Dutton 1996 454p

ISBN 0-525-94223-8

LC 96-17267

"Oates has written an uncharacteristically cathartic book with a provocatively happy ending. . . . Oates eloquently employs daily details, cataloguing Corinne's antiques, mapping Patrick's Ithaca jogging route, calculating the number of paint gallons required to spruce up High Point Farm. She is a vivid storyteller, and the occupations, names and places are rich in allusive imagery. . . . Oates is fascinated by the markings of kinship. Particularly impressive is her shaping of siblings' passions, allegiances and resentments." Nation

Oates, Joyce Carol

Where are you going, where have you been? selected early stories. Ontario Review Press 1993 522p

LC 92-44899

Oates, Joyce Carol

Where is here? stories. Ecco Press 1992 193p

LC 92-3634

Oates, Joyce Carol

Wild nights! stories about the last days of Poe, Dickinson, Twain, James, and Hemingway. Ecco 2008 238p $24.95

ISBN 978-0-06-143479-2; 0-06-143479-5

LC 2008-273051

"The classic authors who appear as fictionalized characters in 'Wild Nights!' aren't the ones most of us met in Intro to American Literature. Edgar Allan Poe copulating with a one-eyed amphibian? Mark Twain pursuing pubescent girls? Henry James clubbing a cat to death? Joyce Carol Oates may cause a few elderly professors to keel over, but the rest of us can take perverse delight in her five surreal tales. In each, Oates imagines the final days of a famous author, drawing from biographical fact but freely embroidering with Gothic excess. " Buffalo News

Oates, Joyce Carol

Will you always love me? and other stories. Dutton 1996 326p

ISBN 978-0525939726

LC 94-43865

"Joyce Carol Oates's readers have come to expect from her a sensationalistic terrain of accident, suicide, rape, murder and madness, all of which are well represented in this collection, which includes none of the small, too-precious moments that can vitiate the short story." N Y Times Book Rev

Object lessons; the Paris Review presents the art of the short story. edited by Lorin Stein and Sadie Stein. Picador 2012 358 p. (trade pbk.) $16

ISBN 1250005981; 9781250005984; 9781250016188

LC 2012026322

In this book, edited by Lorin Stein and Sadie Stein, "twenty contemporary authors introduce twenty . . . examples of the short story from the pages of 'The Paris Review.' Over the course of the last half century, the Review has launched hundreds of careers while publishing some of the most inventive and best-loved stories of our time. This anthology. . . [is a] resource for writers, students, and anyone else who wants to understand fiction from a writer's point of view." (Publisher's note)

Obreht, Tea

The **tiger's** wife; a novel. The Dial Press 2011 337p $25

ISBN 0385343833; 9780385343831; 978-0-385-34383-1; 0-385-34383-3

LC 2010-09612

Orange Broadband Prize for Fiction (2011)

The novel's "narrator is a doctor named Natalia Stefanovi, a young Serb living in Belgrade a dozen years after the wars that dissolved Yugoslavia in 1995. She and a friend, Zóra, are sent by her university to a Croatian orphanage to set up a free clinic. On the way, Natalia learns that her beloved grandfather—a doctor of reputation and the person most responsible for rearing her—has died. For reasons neither she nor her horrorstruck grandmother comprehend, he fled his home and met his end in a remote Croatian shantytown called Zdrevkov. His body has been returned but not his possessions. Some of his belongings, though, are needed for Eastern Orthodox mourning rituals, so Natalia decides to continue her journey to the orphanage, hoping eventually to find the shantytown, learn why her grandfather was there and locate his things. . . . To Natalia, the key to understanding her grandfather can be found in the stories that he held closely. Imbued with the magic of fables, they ran 'like secret rivers through all the other stories of his life.' And so she begins to relate the stories as a sort of eulogy. Ms. Obreht skillfully entwines these tales—there are two main ones—with Natalia's description of her mission to the orphanage and the shantytown." Wall Street J

Ochsner, Gina

Russian dreambook of color and flight. Houghton Mifflin Harcourt 2010 370p $25

ISBN 978-0-618-56373-9; 0-618-56373-3

LC 2009-51595

First published 2009 in the United Kingdom

"Satirical yet never losing touch with deep emotion, Ochsner illuminates her forlorn characters with . . . loving care." Boston Globe

Odell, Jonathan

The **healing**; Jonathan Odell. 1st ed. Nan A. Talese/Doubleday 2012 340p.

ISBN 978-0-385-53467-3; 0385534671

LC 2011005998

This book tells the story of "Mississippi plantation mistress Amanda Satterfield [who] loses her daughter to cholera after her husband refuses to treat her for what he considers a 'slave disease.' Insane with grief, Amanda takes a newborn slave child as her own and names her Granada, much to the outrage of her husband and the amusement of their white neighbors. Troubled by his wife's disturbing mental state and concerned about a mysterious plague sweeping through his slave population, Master Satterfield purchases Polly Shine, a slavewoman reputed to be a healer. But Polly's sharp tongue and troubling predictions cause unrest across the plantation. Complicating matters further, Polly recognizes "the gift" in Granada, the Mistress's pet, and a domestic battle of wills ensues." (Publisher's note)

Odom, Mel

The **destruction** of the books. Tor 2004 381p $25.95

ISBN 0-7653-0723-5

LC 2003-27368

"Almost 100 years after the events of The Rover (2002), Edgewick Lamplighter is grandmagister at the Vault of All Known Knowledge, a secret repository of books rescued from destruction by the dreaded goblinkin. This time the protagonist is Jugh, another halfling, whom Wick rescued from goblin slavers and made his apprentice. Feeling an outsider on the island, Jugh ships out as a crew member on one of the ships that service and help protect the island. But when he discovers that a book is aboard a goblin ship, he manages with great difficulty and danger to retrieve it and take it back to the island. The book turns out to be designed to open a path for dark forces to invade the island and destroy the library." Booklist

"The narrative moves along at a snappy pace, with much good humor, zest and color." Publ Wkly

Oe, Kenzaburo

★ The **changeling**; translated from the Japanese by Deborah Boliver Boehm. Grove Press 2010 468p $26

ISBN 978-0-8021-1936-0; 0-8021-1936-0

Original Japanese edition, 2000

"Oe's deft mix of high intellectual reflection and absurd slapstick scenarios is polished to a high gloss, giving this book a tone that may remind American readers of Saul Bellow's Humboldt's Gift." Publ Wkly

Oe, Kenzaburo

★ An **echo** of heaven; translated by Margaret Mitsutani. Kodansha Am. 1996 204p $25

ISBN 4-7700-1986-6

Original Japanese edition, 1989

"This profound novel is . . . as concerned with common humanity as with art and ideas. Indeed, it constitutes an argument that art is greatest when it is concerned with the essentially human, with death, suffering, fellowship, and sex—each of which figures prominently in it." Booklist

Oe, Kenzaburo

Nip the buds, shoot the kids; translated and introduced by Paul St. John Mackintosh and Maki Sugiyama. Boyars, M. 1995 189p $22.95

ISBN 0-7145-2997-4

LC 94-40897

Original Japanese edition, 1958

"In the waning days of WW II, a group of Japanese reformschool boys are evacuated to a remote village in a densely wooded valley. The villagers treat the teenagers horribly, making them bury a mountain of animal corpses, locking them into a shed for the night and feeding them raw potatoes. The unnamed narrator—one of the group's leaders—discovers that a plague is ravaging the valley. When a couple of people are infected by the disease, the villagers panic. Believing the boys to be infected, the villagers remove themselves to the other side of the valley and block the only road out of town. At first, the boys can think only of escape, but then . . . they start to make the village their own. . . . But each pleasant turn, every apparently liberating step away from unremitting brutality, serves to make the characters' inevitable future suffering even more painful." Publ Wkly

Oe, Kenzaburo

The **pinch** runner memorandum; translated by Michiko N. Wilson and Michael K. Wilson. Sharpe, M.E. 1994 251p $59.95

ISBN 1-56324-183-8

LC 93-26114

Original Japanese edition, 1976

"Based on the metaphor of a sandlot baseball pinch runner, the novel centers around the exchange of identities of a father and a son who venture out together to confront the kingpin of the political underworld. "Oe unfolds the adventure through the complex narrative structure of the protagonist's words, which sometimes resonate and sometimes clash with the narrative voice of his ghost-writer, who initiates the tale. These two layers of the text are further enriched by a third voice, that of the idiot son Mori who speaks to his 'switched-over' father through the conduit of their clasped hands. Simultaneously, the reader is treated to a smorgasbord of satire, black humor, manga-like slapstick, Mikhail Bakhtin's grotesque realism, and various socio-political phenomena such as marginalization, factionalism, and terrorism." Introduction

Oe, Kenzaburo

★ A **quiet** life; translated from the Japanese by Kunioki Yanagishita with William Wetherall. Grove Press 1996 240p

ISBN 978-0802115973

LC 96-25795

Original Japanese edition, 1990

"A famous Japanese writer whose first name begins with K takes off with his wife for a year to become writer in residence at 'one of the several campuses of the University of Carolina,' leaving their almost equally famous son, an idiot savant who is a remarkable composer, in the care of their daughter, Ma-chan. It is Ma-chan, a conscientious young woman acutely aware of the responsibility that devolves on her during her parents' absence, who tells the story related in Kenzaburo Oe's novel 'A Quiet Life,' and the translators, Kunioki Yanagishita and William Wetherall, admirably succeed in conveying a certian archness of style that infuses the work with Ma-chan's personality." N Y Times Book Rev

Oe, Kenzaburo

Somersault; a novel. translated from the Japanese by Philip Gabriel. Grove Press 2003 570p $29.95

ISBN 0-8021-1738-4

LC 2002-29746

Original Japanese edition, 1999

This novel "takes place against the background of a religious cult's terrorist plan (even more drastic than Aum Shinrikyo's 1995 gas attack on the Tokyo subway), which is thwarted when the cult's leaders appear on television to renounce their creed—the 'somersault' of the title. Now, ten years later, the cult's charismatic guru is planning to reestablish his church. . . . Through the believers' motivations for joining the cult, Oe explores the struggle of contemporary Japanese to situate themselves between a traditional culture and the bullet-train pace of the boom years." New Yorker

Ogawa, Yoko

The **housekeeper** and the professor; translated by Stephen Snyder. Picador 2009 180p pa $14

ISBN 978-0-312-42780-1 pa; 0-312-42780-8 pa

LC 2006-41568

"A mysterious, suspenseful, and radiant fable. . . . The smart and resourceful housekeeper, the single mother of a baseball-crazy 10-year-old boy the Professor adores, falls under the spell of the beautiful mathematical phenomena the Professor elucidates, as will the reader, and the three create an indivisible formula for love." Booklist

Ogilvie, Elisabeth

When the music stopped. McGraw-Hill 1989 326p

ISBN 0-07-047792-2

LC 88-28636

"Author Eden Winters, finds herself in the midst of local scandal and terrifying deaths. Set in a small town along the Maine coast, the plot turns on the return to town of two aging sisters who had left on the wings of scandal decades earlier. While there are plenty of people with reason to despise the returning ladies—who audaciously take up residence in the area's most elegant house—there are just as many people, such as Eden and her family, who are delighted to see them. When the women are found brutally murdered, suspects abound, including a stranger who alternately captures Eden's suspicions and heart. Well-crafted fiction that holds the reader's attention and avoids contrivance." Booklist

Ohlsson, Kristina

Silenced; a novel. by Kristina Ohlsson. Emily Bestler Books/Atria 2013 352 p. (hardcover) $25

ISBN 143919890X; 9781439198902

LC 2012049745

In this thriller novel, by Kristina Ohlsson, "A teenage girl is viciously assaulted . . . one night in midsummer. The crime is never reported. . . . A man with no identification . . . is killed in a hit-and-run. He is never reported missing. . . . A priest and his wife are found dead in an apparent suicide. Fredrika Bergman is assigned to the case. What she and her colleagues discover is that a sinister evil . . . is the link behind these seemingly unrelated crimes." (Publisher's note)

Ohlsson, Kristina

Unwanted; a novel. Kristina Ohlsson. Atria Books 2012 357 p.

ISBN 9781439198896; 9781439198919; 9781439198933

LC 2011031787

Stabilo Prize for Best Crime Writer of Southern Sweden (2010)

"When a young girl is abducted off a train in Stockholm, it seems like a classic custody crime, as the parents are divorced and hostile. But Frederika Bergman isn't willing to accept the easy answer, even though she's only a civilian researcher working for one of the most revered detectives in Sweden, Alex Recht. Then the girl's body appears in a remote town in the north with the word "Unwanted" written across it. Bergman is the only one who isn't surprised, but that still doesn't make the investigation any easier. Realizing that he is up against a highly intelligent serial killer, Recht acknowledges that it's going to take a combination of his experience and Bergman's research skills to track down the sociopath." (Booklist)

Okorafor, Nnedi

Who fears death; Nnedi Okorafor. Daw Books Inc. 2010 386 p. $24.95

ISBN 9780756406172

LC 2011389634

Romantic Times Reviewers' Choice Award: Best Science Fiction & Fantasy (2010), World Fantasy Awards: Novel (2011)

This book is set in "a desolate, postapocalyptic Africa of endless desert, failing technology, superstition, and magic. . . . Prophesy speaks of a sorcerer who will change the future, end the wars and slavery, and reunite the people. Onyesonwu is a child of rare talent. Conceived by rape, physically different from her peers, Onyesonwu has the light skin, fair hair, and freckles that traditionally mark her as unworthy, frightening, ugly, and evil. But rather than accepting her outcast role, a defiant Onyesonwu uses her magic to prove herself, avenge her mother's rape, and lead her people." (Library Journal)

"There's a lot of grim, painful stuff in this book: it starts with an horrific gang rape scene (be forewarned), then progresses through violence, torture, prejudice, bullying, female genital cutting, colorism, child soldiering, and more. Yet these are all treated in a nuanced fashion. . . . This is a horrifying, inspiring, painful, joyous book." io9

Okuizumi, Hikaru

The **stones** cry out; translated from the Japanese by James Westerhoven. Harcourt Brace & Co. 1999 138p $20

    ISBN 0-15-100365-3

                           LC 98-14434

    Original Japanese edition, 1993

    "A monstrous tale, The Stones Cry Out is written with a lyrical beauty that only underscores the horror Manase's life becomes. As Okuizumi elegantly plays Manase's nightmare out, Manase is compelled to reenact the real atrocities he has tried so desperately to forget." Booklist

Olafur Johann Olafsson

    ★ The **journey** home; [by] Olaf Olafsson. Pantheon Bks. 2000 296p $24

    ISBN 0-375-42061-4

                           LC 00-39186

    Original Icelandic edition, 1999

    "This is not a morose novel, but one lifted by love, friendship and cooking, an art Disa has spent much of her life perfecting at an English country inn. Hers is a hard, unflinching life, and one skillfully revealed in a steady stream of memories that accompanies Disa on a last migration back to her Arctic nest." Time

Oldham, Nick

    Fighting for the dead. Severn House 2012 216 p. $28.95

    ISBN 0727882139; 9780727882134

    This is the 18th in Nick Oldham's Henry Christie mystery series. Here, "the Lancashire detective superintendent pursues two cases: the murder of an unidentified Eastern European teenage girl; and the disappearance of Jennifer Sunderland, a businessman's wife, who later turns up floating in the River Conder." (Publishers Weekly)

Oliver, Chad

    ★ **From** other shores; an omnibus. NESFA Press 2007 403p $26

    ISBN 978-1-886778-66-3; 1-886778-66-5

    In Shadows in the sun, Paul Ellery discovers a colony of aliens while making an anthropological study of a small Texas town. Subsequently, he must decide whether he wants to be educated to take his place in the alien society. In Unearthly neighbors, investigators from a future Earth undertake an anthropological study of planet Sirius Nine's humanoid civilization. In The shores of another sea, an anthropologist makes first contact with aliens while conducting a study of baboons in Kenya.

    Oliver was "a pioneer in the application of competent anthropological thought to sf themes. . . . He is a careful author whose speculative thought deserves to be more widely known and appreciated." Clute and Nicholls. Ency of Sci Fi

Olmstead, Robert

    ★ **Coal** black horse. Algonquin Books of Chapel Hill 2007 218p $23.95

    ISBN 978-1-56512-521-6; 1-56512-521-5

                         LC 2006-42914

    This novel "is mostly memorable as an exquisite corpse, a fictive vision of war so vivid and gruesome that it remains in the memory—grotesque, stiff and gape-mouthed—after every other detail of Olmstead's tale fades away." Paste

Olmstead, Robert

    The **coldest** night; a novel. by Robert Olmstead. Algonquin Books 2012

    ISBN 9781616200435

                        LC 2011045515

    In this book, "Henry Childs grew up in the mountains of West Virginia, raised by his grandfather and his sweet-natured mother Clemmie. . . . He helps out at some stables where he meets Mercy. She comes from money and is university-bound, while Henry seems headed for a factory. . . . Henry is warned off by her father and brother. The lovers elope to New Orleans, where an apartment is waiting for them, courtesy of Mercy's accommodating aunt. They make it their Eden. Father and brother come to expel them, abducting Mercy, giving Henry a final warning. Though underage, he enlists as a Marine and is sent to Korea. He does recon with Lew, a gruff World War II vet. . . . The cold is arctic. The Chinese come at night, waves of them. It's kill or be killed; answer atrocity with atrocity." (Kirkus)

Olmstead, Robert

    Far bright star; a novel. Algonquin Books of Chapel Hill 2009 207p $23.95; pa $13.95

    ISBN 978-1-56512-592-6; 1-56512-592-4; 978-156512-980-1 pa; 1-56512-980-6 pa

                        LC 2008-41858

    "Gleaming, spellbinding fiction . . . . Terrifying and abruptly beautiful, the new novel gleams with a masculine intensity; it is hard to read and hard to put down." Cleveland Plain Dealer

Olsen, Tillie

    Tell me a riddle; a collection. Lippincott 1961 156p

    "In writing which is individualized but not eccentric, experimental but not obscure, Mrs. Olsen has created imagined experience which has the authenticity of autobiography or memoir. With a faultless accuracy, her stories treat the very young, the mature, the dying—poor people without the means to buy or invent lies about their situations—and yet her writing never succumbs to mere naturalism." Commonweal

Olsson, Linda

    Astrid & Veronika. Penguin Books 2007 259p pa $14

    ISBN 978-0-14-303807-8; 0-14-303807-9

                        LC 2006-50660

    First published 2005 in New Zealand with title: Let me sing you gentle songs

    "Unlike the voice of the novel's omniscient narrator, [Veronika and Astrid's] are natural and vivid, utterly convincing. And unlike the nove's flatly depicted present, the physical world of the past, in which their stories take place, generously opens to admit us." N Y Times Book Rev

Omarsdottir, Kristin

    Children in Reindeer Woods; Kristín Ómarsdóttir; translated from the Icelandic by Lytton Smith.

Open Letter 2012 198 p. (pbk.: acid-free paper) $14.95

ISBN 1934824356; 9781934824351

LC 2011043995

In this book, "[t]hree soldiers arrive at a farm that is also a 'temporary home for children' named Children in Reindeer Woods. Without apparent motive, they murder everyone except an 11-year-old girl, Billie. Then the soldier named Rafael murders his comrades. Now he wants to stop killing and become a farmer. Billie is oddly unmoved by the killings and becomes his (platonic) companion as he tries to remake himself into a peaceful human being." (Kirkus Reviews)

Ondaatje, Michael, 1943-

Anil's ghost. Knopf 2000 307p $25

ISBN 0-375-41053-8

LC 99-59208

"Anil comes with Western-bred investigative passion: the certainty that facts are there to be unearthed and that truth is to be constructed out of them. Sarath, a polymorphous spirit and the book's most memorable figure, cautions that the real truth of his country is ambiguous and unobtainable. . . . It is Ondaatje's extraordinary achievement to use magic in order to make the blood of his own country real." N Y Times Book Rev

Includes bibliographical references

Ondaatje, Michael, 1943-

★ The **cat's** table. Alfred A. Knopf 2011 269p $26

ISBN 978-0-307-70011-7; 0-307-70011-9

LC 2011-20820

This novel takes place on "a cruise ship sailing from Ceylon to England in 1954. The tale opens with the narrator, who shares with the author the name Michael, recalling how, as an 11-year-old, he left his aunt and uncle for a 21-day ocean voyage to be reunited with his mother, who had left the family home some years previously. . . . [Michael] Ondaatje presents . . . the daily shipboard lives of the 11-yearold boy, his cousin Emily and his two companions, Cassius and Ramadhin. . . . Years after his arrival in England, the narrator returns to the voyage as he retells the story to his own children. . . . He also wrestles with mid-life questions as to whether . . . he has a cold heart, whether he loved his friends enough and whether he has become a distracted, superficial person." (America)

"The book tells the tale of an 11-year-old boy named Michael who is on a boat trip from Colombo, Sri Lanka, to England in 1954. In the sections that take place on the boat, we are entirely in a boy's head and feverish point of view. It is also told by a Michael 50 years later, when he has become a celebrated writer and lives in Canada. His long past is behind him, but emigration has marked him. He has never truly felt at home anywhere in the world. . . . [The novel] expertly strums these cords of autobiography without overdoing it. As a result this small, and beautifully minor book, vibrates with the borrowed intimacy of real life. It also never force-feeds its young hero with wisdom he could not have acquired or stolen at such an age." Boston Globe

Ondaatje, Michael, 1943-

★ The **English** patient; a novel. Knopf 1992 307p

ISBN 0-679-41678-1

LC 92053089

This novel "begins in 1945, in a bomb-damaged Italian villa near Florence, recently used as a war hospital. Abandoned as the Allied front moved north, it now shelters one last casualty, an Englishman slowly dying of burns. . . . Hana, a young Canadian nurse, stays on devotedly, supplying him with morphine and foraged food. They are joined by David Caravaggio, a friend of Hana's family from Toronto who is a professional thief turned military spy, and by Kirpal Singh {Kip}, a Sikh soldier, charged with defusing bombs and mines in the area." (N Y Times Book Rev)

"This is a poetic and solemn narrative of the horrible process of war, the discipline, displacement, loss, and sudden, desperate love. Ondaatje seems to whisper, even confess each scene to his readers, handling them gingerly like shards of shattered glass." Booklist

Ondaatje, Michael

In the skin of a lion; a novel. Knopf 1987 243p

LC 87-45340

Ondaatje is a "beautiful writer. What he writes about most beautifully is work. Mr. Ondaatje is passionate about process, the way work, particularly construction of all kinds, is done and how it feels to do it. This is, of course, a rarity in fiction at any time, and one can only be grateful for a man who is not focused on the classroom, the bedroom and the bar." N Y Times Book Rev

Orczy, Emmuska

Adventures of the Scarlet Pimpernel. Double-day, Doran 1929 302p

Further "exploits of the Scarlet Pimpernel, Sir Percy Blakeney, the daring Englishman, who, with his loyal friends and helpers, rescues aristocrats from the guillotine during the French Revolution. Each chapter records a separate adventure." Cleveland Public Libr

Orczy, Emmuska

The **elusive** Pimpernel. Dodd, Mead 1908 344p

Another chapter in the adventurous life of The Scarlet Pimpernel, that thorn in the side of the terrorists of the French Revolution, and a delivering angel to condemned aristocrats. In an increasingly tense situation, this languid, Englishman deliberately enters the French trap in an attempt to rescue his wife, the beautiful Marguerite Blakeney

Orczy, Emmuska

★ The **Scarlet** Pimpernel; [by] Baroness Orczy. Alfred A. Knopf 1999 299p (Everyman's library children's classics) $14.95

ISBN 0-375-40658-1

LC 2001-272396

First published 1905 by Putnam

"An adventure story of the French Revolution. The apparently foppish young Englishman, Sir Percy Blakeney, is found to be the daring Scarlet Pimpernel, rescuer of distressed aristocrats." Reader's Ency. 4th edition

Orner, Peter

Love and shame and love; a novel. Little, Brown and Co. 2011 439p il $24.99

ISBN 978-0-316-12939-8

LC 2011-22547

"Orner anatomizes family relationships with precision in a novel that spans three—and touches on four—generations. At the center of the author's examination is Alexander Popper, a fiction writer manqué (he tries in vain to write a 'good, sad story') and reluctant law-school graduate who winds up handling misdemeanor cases for the Cook County Public Defender. . . . [This] is a masterful, multifaceted novel. Readers will find both love and shame in abundance in Orner's teeming fictional world." Kirkus

Orozco, Daniel

Orientation; and other stories. Faber and Faber 2011 162p $23

ISBN 978-0-86547-853-4; 0-86547-853-8

LC 2010-38531

"These nine darkly funny, profoundly compassionate stories take as their subject the loneliness particular to contemporary culture. . . . 'You can't know anybody, not really, not in the brief overlaps of flimsy acquaintance, nor in the tenuous and fleeting opportunities for connection that we are afforded,' thinks a man about to be shot for the $60 in his wallet. But the real genius here is the subtle accumulation of evidence to the contrary—the insistence that even in the office cubicle, or between the lines of the police blotter, human contact is sought after and made." More

Orringer, Julie

★ The **invisible** bridge. Alfred A. Knopf 2010 602p $26.95

ISBN 978-1-4000-4116-9; 1-4000-4116-3

LC 2009-46498

"Andras is a Hungarian Jew studying in Paris as Hitler's influence begins to spread across a continent already riddled with anti-Semitism and bloodlust. He falls for fellow émigré Klara, and their world is soon rocked by war. Other characters weave in and out of the story line, but it's the love tethering Andras and Klara that powers the narrative's massive machinery. The Invisible Bridge is without a doubt an ambitious slice of literature, but Orringer fulfills her ambitions with crisp writing that never wanders far from the story's path. World War II is hardly undiscovered literary territory. Still, this stunning work manages to feel both original and part and parcel of the well-blazed tradition of historical novels that came before it." Entertainment Wkly

Orullian, Peter Vance

The **unremembered**; Peter Orullian. Tor 2011 669p.

ISBN 9780765325716

LC 2010036105

This book tells the story of "Tahn, Wendra, and Sutter," orphans who are recruited for "a perilous and mysterious quest . . . by a wizardly stranger and an elven Far." (Publishers Weekly) The danger which threatens their world is "the god Quietus" who has been "bound behind a magical barrier, along with the horrific monsters of his making . . . [and now] seeks to escape his prison." (Libr J) As the barrier begins to weaken, and "the most remote cities are laid waste by fell, nightmarish troops . . . some people dismiss the attacks as mere rumor. Instead of standing against the real threat, they persecute those with the knowledge, magic and power to fight these abominations, denying the inevitability of war and annihilation." (Publisher's note)

Orwell, George, 1903-1950

★ **Animal** farm; with an introduction by Julian Symons. Knopf 1993 xl, 113p $16

ISBN 0-679-42039-8

LC 92-54299

First published 1945 in the United Kingdom; first United States edition 1946

"The animals on Farmer Jones's farm revolt in a move led by the pigs, and drive out the humans. The pigs become the leaders, in spite of the fact that their government was meant to be 'classless.' The other animals soon find that they are suffering varying degrees of slavery. A totalitarian state slowly evolves in which 'all animals are equal but some animals are more equal than others.' This is a biting satire aimed at communism." Shapiro. Fic for Youth. 3d edition

Orwell, George, 1903-1950

Burmese days; Keep the aspidistra flying; Coming up for air; with an introduction by John Carey. Alfred A. Knopf 2011 xxxiii, 677p (Everyman's Library) $28

ISBN 978-0-307-59504-1; 0-307-59504-8

Burmese days (1934) is an indictment of British colonial rule, based on Orwell's own experience while serving in the Indian Imperial Police. Keep the aspidistra flying (1936) recounts the literary aspirations, financial humiliations, and shot-gun wedding of a bookseller's assistant. Coming up for air (1939) is about the suburban frustration and Edwardian nostalgia of an insurance agent on the eve of the Second World War.

Orwell, George, 1903-1950

★ **Nineteen** eighty-four; with an introduction by Julian Symonds. Knopf 1992 xlii, 325p $19

ISBN 0-679-41739-7

LC 92-52906

First published 1949 by Harcourt, Brace

"A dictatorship called Big Brother rules the people in a collectivist society where Winston Smith works in the Ministry of Truth. The Thought Police persuade the people that ignorance is strength and war is peace. Winston becomes involved in a forbidden love affair and joins the underground to resist this mind control." Shapiro. Fic for Youth. 3d edition

Osborne, Lawrence

The **forgiven**; a novel. Lawrence Osborne. 1st ed. Hogarth 2012 272 p. (hardcover) $25.00; (ebook) $25.00

ISBN 0307889033; 9780307889034; 9780307889058

LC 2011025942

This book by Lawrence Osborne "follows British couple David and Jo Henniger into the Moroccan desert for a debauched weekend at their friends' palatial ksar. Driving to the estate, David is distracted while arguing with Jo, and consequently hits and kills a young Moroccan. . . . The next morning, the dead boy's father, Abdellah, arrives and demands that David return with him to help bury his son." (Publishers Weekly)

Osondu, E. C.

Voice of America; stories. HarperCollins Publishers 2010 215p $19.99

ISBN 9780061990861; 0-06-199086-8

LC 2010-05729

"Osondu's excellent short stories, set in both Nigeria and the U.S., reveal the vast cultural chasm that persists between our countries. . . . These richly shaded tales explore old ways and new, wealth and poverty, myth and misapprehension. Though there is sadness here, the tone is deadpan, and the reader can imagine the storyteller's eyes crinkled in a smile." Booklist

Oster, Christian

My big apartment; translated and with an introduction by Jordan Stump. University of Neb. Press 2002 155p pa $20

ISBN 0-8032-3567-4; 0-8032-8612-0 pa

LC 2002-17977

Original French edition published, 1999

"In a nutshell, {this is} the story of a man who loses his keys and finds a life, sort of, maybe. That's all that really happens—well, that and a few laps in a pool and a driving lesson and an episiotomy. The specifics don't much matter anyway. This is simply the course the man, a Parisian called Gavarine, follows, and he has no more control over his fate than the leaf in the stream has over the eddy." N Y Times Book Rev

Ostermiller, Dori

Outside the ordinary world. Mira 2010 374p pa $14.95

ISBN 978-0-7783-2889-6; 0-7783-2889-9

"Traumatized as a child by her mother's affair, Sylvia Sandon has vowed never to repeat her mother's infidelities. But at 42, Sylvia is facing a moment of uncomfortable truth. Her marriage to Nate, a kind city planner obsessed with renovating their antique farmhouse, is faltering, and her own creative life as a painter is stalled. Her two daughters, 4-year-old Emmie and sulky, teenage Hannah, are exhaustively demanding and she's fraying at the seams. When she meets Tai, an affable landscape artist whose son is one of her art students, passion sparks in a way that's frighteningly familiar. . . . Partly set against the fire-shocked California coast in the 1970s, the age of 'The Joy of Sex' and Helen Reddy songs about female empowerment, Ostermiller captures what it's like to be a child caught in a sticky web of family drama." Boston Globe

Othmer, James P.

The **futurist**; a novel. Doubleday 2006 257p $23.95

ISBN 0-385-51722-X

LC 2005-51871

The author's "voice echoes other, well-established ones: Max Barry's for outrageously deft business satire, Christopher Buckley's for geopolitical comedy of errors, Bruce Wagner's for free-floating malice. That he can even dimly be equated with any of them makes 'The Futurist' an impressive foray into satirical fiction." N Y Times (Late N Y Ed)

Otsuka, Julie, 1962-

The **Buddha** in the attic. Alfred A. Knopf 2011 129p

ISBN 0307700003 Alfred A. Knopf; 9780307700001 Alfred A. Knopf; 9781905490875 Fig Tree

LC 20110013568

"The novel revolves around a group of mail-order brides who leave Japan in the early 1900s. They're on their way to meet husbands in San Francisco who emigrated years earlier and have written of their many successes in America. When the travelers — some as young as 14 — disembark, they discover that the photographs the men sent are outdated, their successes are a fantasy, and a hard life awaits. We also know the snare that history has set for them. Decades after they establish themselves, they will be sent to internment camps. . . . . [The tale unfolds in a] daring first-person plural narrative. Even as the women step off the boat and their paths diverge, the novel proceeds in a flow of we and us, with the occasional individual voice raised from the whole. Knowing what will come, plot is not what urges the reader on. Rather, it is the details of the women's lives that fascinate as they spread throughout California like fireflies released from a jar." Cleveland Plain Dealer

Otsuka, Julie, 1962-

When the emperor was divine; a novel. Knopf 2002 141p hardcover o.p. pa $10.95

ISBN 0-375-41429-0; 0-385-72181-1 pa

LC 2002-20814

This novel traces the "fortunes of a Japanese-American family from the spring of 1942—when President Roosevelt's evacuation order came through—to the spring of 1946. In four brief chapters, we follow a mother, daughter and son from their comfortable home in Berkeley through their five months in a temporary 'assembly center' (a converted stable at a racetrack south of San Francisco) to an internment camp in Topaz, Utah, where they spend three years." N Y Times Book Rev

Otsuka "demonstrates a breathtaking restraint and delicacy throughout this supple and devastating first novel." Booklist

Otto, Whitney

Eight girls taking pictures; a novel. Whitney Otto. Scribner 2012 342 p. (hardback) $25

ISBN 1451682697; 9781451682694; 9781451682724; 9781451682731

LC 2012009167

Author Whitney Otto "explores the ambitions, passions, conflicts and desires of eight female photographers throughout the twentieth century. . . . From San Francisco to New York, London, Berlin, Buenos Aires, and Rome, Otto . . . [offers a] portrait of the history of feminism and of photography. While their circumstances may differ, the tensions these women experience--from wanting a private life or a public life; passion or security; art or domesticity; children or creative freedom--are universal." (Publisher's note)

Includes bibliographical references.

Otto, Whitney

How to make an American quilt. Villard Bks. 1991 179p $20

ISBN 0-679-40070-2

LC 90-48233

"Otto has tremendous insight and compassion, understanding the rareness of a perfect marriage, the anger of thwarted lives, and the vagaries of love and motherhood." Booklist

Overholser, Wayne D.

Death of a cattle king; a western story. Five Star 2011 188p $25.95

ISBN 978-1-43282-517-1; 1-43282-517-8

LC 2011-15379

"The Holt family traveled the Oregon Trail from Pennsylvania to the Northwest, where they established the modest Rainbow Ranch. Even after Sam's wife, Helen, dies, leaving him with two kids, Mary and Bruce, the ranch continues to prosper. But trouble arrives in the form of Morgan Drew, son of Sam's late best friend. Drew's ambition and greed become plain as he allies himself with the valley's biggest rancher. Now he intends to absorb the Holt ranch as well as all the other small claims in the valley. If Sam doesn't accept Drew's offer, the implied threat is that the Rainbow will be taken by force. An Indian uprising puts a temporary hold on the land grab as the ranchers form an uneasy alliance to ward off the threat . . . . Like most of [Overholser's] work, this novel is driven less by violence and more by the timeless human emotions of greed, jealousy, and love." Booklist

Overholser, Wayne D.

Law at Angel's Landing; a western story. Five Star 2010 164p $25.95

ISBN 978-1-59414-907-8; 1-59414-907-0

LC 2010-08448

"Mark Girard moved to Angel's Landing in the Colorado foothills as a young boy with his mother and father, who was a chase-the-rainbow gold miner. When the strike played out and the town was destined to be abandoned, the elder Girard wanted to pick up stakes and move to the next big strike. Mark's mother refused, opting for stability in the soon to be very tiny village. Mother, son, and the town all survived, with Mark becoming county sheriff. Overholser tells two stories here: the melancholy saga of a broken family reunited too late and the pendulum-swinging life of a boom-and-bust gold town. . . . Overholser, a consummate western storyteller with an eye for character and dialogue, delivers another solid effort." Booklist

Owens, Robin D.

Heart thief; Robin D. Owens. Berkley Sensation 2003 343p (pbk.) $7.99

ISBN 0425190722; 9780425190722

LC 2003611828

This fantasy novel, a 2004 PRISM Winner for Best Futuristic novel, takes place "[o]n the planet Celta, founded by adherents of a Wiccan-like religion whose followers have 'psionic,' or psychic, talents, [where] Ruis Elder is an outcast on trial for his life. Not only doesn't he possess psionic talent but his mere presence nullifies the powers of others. Ailim Silver Fir, a judge and a strong empath, finds peace .

. . when Ruis' null field gives her respite. . . . Sentenced to exile, Ruis sneaks back into Druida to hide in the spaceship that first brought humans to the planet, and he endears himself to the ship's artificial intelligence. As Ailim and Ruis fall more in love, they uncover the dirty deeds that stripped him of his inheritance and rightful place." (Booklist)

The **Oxford** book of American detective stories; edited by Tony Hillerman, Rosemary Herbert. Oxford Univ. Press 1996 686p $35; pa $18.95

ISBN 0-19-508581-7; 0-19-511792-1 pa

LC 95-4504

This collection includes stories by B. Pronzini, E. A. Poe, E. S. Gardner, E. Queen and M. Muller

The **Oxford** book of American short stories; edited by Joyce Carol Oates. Oxford Univ. Press 1992 768p $40; pa $18.95

ISBN 0-19-507065-8; 0-19-509262-7 pa

LC 92-1353

"Fifty-six short stories showcase this ever-vital and challenging art form's suppleness and power from Washington Irving's classic, 'Rip Van Winkle,' to the work of Sandra Cisneros. While Oates couldn't resist masterpieces such as Ernest Hemingway's 'A Clean, Well-Lighted Place,' her goal was 'familiar names, unfamiliar titles,' and her intention was to call our attention to works by the likes of Edgar Allan Poe, Harriet Beecher Stowe, Henry James, Kate Chopin, William Carlos Williams, and Saul Bellow that aren't anthologized to death. . . . Her standards of excellence are consistent throughout." Booklist

The **Oxford** book of English ghost stories; chosen by Michael Cox and R. A. Gilbert. Oxford Univ. Press 1987 xvii, 504 p.p hardcover o.p.

ISBN 9780199556304; 9780192141637 out of print

LC 86008690

First published 1986 in the United Kingdom

Arranged chronologically, the forty-two stories gathered here "date from the 1820s . . . to the 1980s. . . . In addition to featuring those writers one would expect to find here— Sheridan Le Fanu, M. R. James, and Walter de la Mare, for example—there is also a bounty of wonderful authors with whom U.S. audiences may not be familiar." Booklist

The **Oxford** book of English love stories; edited by John Sutherland. Oxford Univ. Press 1997 452p $30

ISBN 0-19-214237-2

LC 96-38252

The **Oxford** book of English short stories; edited by A.S. Byatt. Oxford Univ. Press 1998 xxx, 439p hardcover o.p. pa $19.95

ISBN 0-19-214238-0; 0-19-956160-5 pa

LC 97-44998

In this anthology Byatt "includes necessary masters— Rudyard Kipling, Saki, D. H. Lawrence, and V. S. Pritchett, to name a few. But . . . she draws into the fold the work of several extremely talented writers of which few readers on this side of the Atlantic will have heard. Falling into this category are such writers as Malachi Whitaker, H. E. Bates, Sylvia Townsend Warner, and Charlotte Mew." Booklist

The **Oxford** book of gothic tales; edited by Chris Baldick. Oxford Univ. Press 1992 xxiii, 533p hardcover o.p. pa $19.95
ISBN 0-19-286219-7 pa

LC 91-27290

This chronologically arranged anthology contains thirty-seven stories dating from the 18th to 20th century. Among the authors are Hawthorne, Poe, Stevenson, Hardy, Faulkner, Welty, Borges, Angela Carter and Isabel Allende.

The **Oxford** book of Irish short stories; edited by William Trevor. Oxford Univ. Press 1989 567p $40; pa $17.95
ISBN 0-19-214180-5; 0-19-280193-7 pa

LC 88-28147

"The great Irish writers—from Oliver Goldsmith and Oscar Wilde to James Joyce and Edna O'Brien—are represented in a collection for older advanced readers." Booklist

The **Oxford** book of Jewish stories; edited by Ilan Stavans. Oxford Univ. Press 1998 493p $30
ISBN 0-19-511019-6

LC 98-16631

Includes index

The **Oxford** book of Latin American short stories; edited by Roberto González Echevarria. Oxford Univ. Press 1997 xiv, 481 p.p
ISBN 9780195095906 out of print; 9780195130850

LC 97005395

"The 53 stories in {this anthology} are grouped together in three chapters—the 'Colonial Period,' 'New Nations,' and the 'Contemporary Period.' . . . Classic writers such as Gabriel García Márquez, Carlos Fuentes, and Jorge Luis Borges are included, as well as lesser-known authors like José Balza and Horacio Quiroga." (Libr J) Index.

The **Oxford** book of modern fairy tales; edited by Alison Lurie. Oxford Univ. Press 1993 455p $30; pa $14.95
ISBN 0-19-214218-6; 0-19-282385-X pa

LC 92-28007

This volume is "full of old favorites and some priceless new gems, with a wonderful chronological arrangement that allows readers to absorb information on literary developments and trends, or simply to enjoy the well-told tales. . . . The whole collection is first rate and demonstrates beautifully that modern fairy tales are not just for kids." SLJ

The **Oxford** book of science fiction stories; edited by Tom Shippey. Oxford Univ. Press 1992 xxvi, 587p (paperback) $19.95
ISBN 9780192142047 out of print; 9780192803818

LC 92009512

The **Oxford** book of short stories; chosen by V.S. Pritchett. Oxford Univ. Press 1981 547p hardcover o.p. pa $19.95
ISBN 0-19-214116-3; 0-19-958313-7 pa

LC 81-156872

In addition to one of his own short stories, Pritchett has selected 40 others, written in English during the 19th and 20th centuries. Most of the authors are English, Irish or American and include Somerset Maugham, D. H. Lawrence, Faulkner, Twain, and Eudora Welty.

The **Oxford** book of spy stories; edited by Michael Cox. Oxford Univ. Press 1996 356p $30
ISBN 0-19-214242-9

LC 95-15519

The **Oxford** book of twentieth-century ghost stories; edited by Michael Cox. Oxford Univ. Press 1996 xix, 425 p
ISBN 9780192142603 out of print

LC 96004913

Oyeyemi, Helen
  Mr. Fox. Riverhead Books 2011 324p $25.95
  ISBN 978-1-59448-807-8; 1-59448-807-X

LC 2011-13747

"St. John Fox is a writer famous for killing off women in his stories; Mary Fox is a creation he uses as a tool to scold and inform himself of his motivations and to act as moxie gatekeeper of his most closely held secrets. His wife, Daphne Fox, is the writer's loving, lighthearted companion — until she wises up to the existence of Mary Fox, whom she at first believes to be her husband's mistress. She finds out otherwise, and then both Fox women go out to lunch. Each character is so superbly formed, and they are believable people whose habits of thought and language are so perfectly pitched and entertaining that they become instantly lovable, that is until we learn more about them. The combination of intensity and changeability in all three characters reflect many of the archetypal baddies from myth and batty old fairy-fables, the most prominent of which is Bluebeard, with his many bloodbaths, and the Furies, with their readiness to punish crime." Chicago Sun-Times

Oyeyemi, Helen
  The **opposite** house. Nan A. Talese/Doubleday 2007 257p $23.95
  ISBN 978-0-385-51384-5; 0-385-51384-4

LC 2006-36812

The novel is "insightful, urgently and sometimes painfully so. What Oyeyemi shows us about cultural alienation, about what makes and marks a migrant, needs to be seen. . . . At times, it's true, Maja's skin feels thin, stretched, raw. We can feel Oyeyemi writing through her character. But those times are rare; on most of the pages in this novel Maja lives, and it matters that she lives. This is her life." Strange Horizons

Oz, Amos

Don't call it night; translated from the Hebrew by Nicholas de Lange. Harcourt Brace & Co. 1996 199p

ISBN 978-0151001521

LC 96-14587

Original Hebrew edition, 1994

"This novel is a piece of sweet but melancholy chamber music—light but not necessarily insubstantial. It belongs to a genre of restful novel that is ruled by an esthetic of peace and a yearning for peace. If one is looking for politics, there is that—clearly, if quietly." N Y Times Book Rev

Oz, Amos

★ **Fima**; translated from the Hebrew by Nicholas de Lange. Harcourt Brace & Co. 1993 322p

LC 92-44200

Original Hebrew edition, 1991

"Not only does Mr. Oz strive toward a Chekhovian compassion for his characters, but his novel depends . . . on making us believe in the possibility of last-minute grace. When tragedy strikes, we watch Fima rise to the occasion and begin to tap his own resources of generosity, humility, common sense, and his sense of purpose." N Y Times Book Rev

Oz, Amos

Panther in the basement; translated from the Hebrew by Nicholas de Lange. Harcourt Brace & Co. 1997 147p $21

ISBN 0-15-100287-8

LC 97-20577

Original Hebrew edition, 1995

"It is Jerusalem in 1947, during the final days of the British mandate in Palestine, and Proffy, a twelve-and-a-quarter-year-old Jewish boy, is leading a double life. In his parents' eyes, Proffy (short for Professor) is a word savant. By his own definition, he is second-in-command of the underground organization F. O. D. (Freedom or Death), for whose noble cause he scatters bent nails and composes war slogans like 'Perfidious Albion, hands off Zion!' Proffy's identity as an eloquent militant is threatened, however, when his compatriots charge him with treason for befriending a British policeman, and he is forced to reevaluate the implications of word 'enemy.'" New Yorker

Oz, Amos

The **same** sea; translated from the Hebrew by Nicholas de Lange in collaboration with the author. Harcourt 2001 201p $30

ISBN 0-15-100572-9

LC 2001-24121

Original Hebrew edition, 1999

This novel depicts "the lives of four people brought together by death: Albert, an aging tax lawyer whose wife recently died of ovarian cancer; his son Enrico, who flees to Tibet; Enrico's girlfriend, Dita, a voluptuous screenwriter; and Bettine, a widowed accountant who is drawn into an uncomfortable intimacy with Albert." New Yorker

"Never has the author's writing been more controlled and polished. . . . His depictions of his characters' lives are tableaux vivants, succint and visual." Times Lit Suppl

Oz, Amos

Scenes from village life; [translated from the Hebrew by Nicholas de Lange] Houghton Mifflin Harcourt 2011 182p.

ISBN 978-0-547-48336-8 Houghton Mifflin Harcourt; 978-0-701-18550-3 Chatto and Windus; 9780547483368; 0547483368

LC 2011016055

"This . . . volume of eight stories with recurring characters (which Mr Oz has referred to as a novel) is alive with individuals who are less preoccupied with 'The Situation'--as Israelis call the regional conflict--than with other more universal concerns. In one chapter Kobi, a 17-year-old with a crush on the 30-year-old postmistress and librarian of the town, decides to act on his feelings, which leads to an awkward confrontation. In another a middle-aged doctor reflects on her relationship with a nephew, who has failed to materialise from the bus he was meant to have arrived on. . . . Tel Ilan is the small fictional town where these stories take place." (Economist)

Ozeki, Ruth L., 1956-

★ A **tale** for the time being; Ruth Ozeki. Viking 2013 432 p. (hardcover) $28.95

ISBN 0670026638; 9780670026630

LC 2012039878

Man Booker Prize Shortlist (2013)

This novel, by Ruth Ozeki, begins in "Tokyo, [where] sixteen-year-old . . . Nao . . . plans to document the life of her great grandmother. . . . A diary is Nao's only solace. . . . Across the Pacific, we meet Ruth, a novelist living on a remote island who discovers a collection of artifacts washed ashore in a Hello Kitty lunchbox. . . . As the mystery of its contents unfolds, Ruth is pulled into the past, into Nao's drama and her unknown fate, and forward into her own future." (Publisher's note)

"The novel's seamless web of language, metaphor and meaning can't be disentangled from its powerful emotional impact: These are characters we care for deeply, imparting vital life lessons through the magic of storytelling. A masterpiece, pure and simple." (Kirkus)

Includes bibliographical references

Ozick, Cynthia

Dictation; a quartet. Houghton Mifflin 2008 179p $24

ISBN 978-0-547-05400-1; 0-547-05400-9

LC 2007-52331

"In the wonderfully witty and biting opening novella, 'Dictation,' Miss Bosanquet and Miss Hallowes, the respective amanuenses of Henry James and Jospeh Conrad at the height of their careers, concoct a marvelous scheme to write themselves into posterity. . . . 'Actors' follows the fortunes of Matt Sorley as he searches for work in New York and eventually is tapped to play Lear in an adaptation of the play that features Lear as a Jewish emigrant. Sorley's production is interrupted by a real Lear—an elderly and quite mad Jewish actor who had performed this role originally many years ago. In 'At Fumicaro,' an art critic attempts to marry his Italian maid only to realize that she has strung him along to rob him. Finally, in 'What Happened to the Baby?' a young girl rehearses the story of her uncle's infidelity and her aunt's

Medea-like revenge. Ozick is at the top of her form in these splendid stories." Libr J

Ozick, Cynthia

★ **Foreign** bodies. Houghton Mifflin Harcourt 2010 255p $26

ISBN 978-0-547-43557-2; 0-547-43557-6

LC 2010-05757

"Ozick is a craggy writer, with strenuous climbs, momentary slides and startling views. Some of Bea's confrontations, feeling out her new independence back in the United States, seem contrived, even stagy. But her vision of Europe and its tragic history is profound; and Lili is a creation of stunning depth. It is not Jamesian, it is Ozickian." Boston Globe

Ozick, Cynthia

★ **Heir** to the glimmering world. Houghton Mifflin 2004 310p $24

ISBN 0-618-47049-2

LC 2004-42723

"In 1933, the Mitwissers, a family of German Jews, arrive in America after a narrow and eccentric escape from Berlin. . . . After landing somewhat haphazardly in New York, they place an ad for help in a local paper. The only applicant for the job is an eighteen-year-old orphan, Rose Meadows, who narrates the story, and who observes the Mitwissers with the dry neutrality of an invisible servant. Her duties are vaguely defined—part nanny, part secretary—and her salary comes intermittently, the family's sole source of income being the whimsy of a troubled benefactor. Ozick portrays this ramshackle household to dazzling effect, as it adjusts to its many states of exile—from a sense of security, from cherished ideas, and from the consolations of each other." New Yorker

Ozick, Cynthia

The **Messiah** of Stockholm; a novel. Knopf 1987 141p $15.95

ISBN 0-394-54701-2

LC 86-46014

This "novel is a complex and fascinating meditation on the nature of writing and the responsibilities of those who choose to create—or judge—tales. Yet on a purely realistic level, it manages to capture the atmosphere of Stockholm and to be, at times, very funny indeed about the daily operations of one of the city's newspapers and Lars's peculiar detachment from everyday work and life." N Y Times Book Rev

Ozick, Cynthia

★ The **Puttermesser** papers. Knopf 1997 235p $23

ISBN 0-679-45476-4

LC 96-39155

This book presents "five previously published episodes from the imagined life of Ruth Puttermesser. . . . The first paper, 'Puttermesser: Her Work History, Her Ancestry, Her Afterlife,' introduces the protagonist, age 34, as a New York Jew who has quit the 'blue-blood Wall Street' law firm where she was going nowhere fast. She is now working in the Department of Receipts and Disbursements of the City

of New York, where she is going nowhere even faster." N Y Times Book Rev

"This entertaining fable is a social commentary as well as a comic tour de force, and it bristles with Ozick's formidable intelligence and wit." Publ Wkly

Ozick, Cynthia

The **shawl**. Knopf 1989 69p $12.95

ISBN 0-394-57976-3

LC 89-2652

"Rosa is brilliantly realized. Her dark night of the soul is lit by flashes of insight about memory, culture, old age, a welcome meditation on the euphemistic inadequacy of the word 'survivor.'" N Y Times Book Rev

P

Paasilinna, Arto

The **howling** miller; translated by Will Hobson from the French of Anne Colin de Terrail. Canongate 2007 284p pa $14

ISBN 978-1-84767-181-3; 1-84767-181-0

Original Finnish edition, 1981

"Paasilinna describes the frenetic inner workings of his characters' minds with an expert touch. . . . It is Paasilinna's gift in this gem of a novel (in Will Hobson's pellucid translation from the French of Anne Colin du Terrail) to wring humor from the most desperate of circumstances." N Y Times Book Rev

Packer, Ann

★ The **dive** from Clausen's pier; a novel. Knopf 2002 369p hardcover o.p. pa $14

ISBN 0-375-41282-4; 0-375-72713-2 pa

LC 2001-42522

"A reckless attempt to impress Carrie, Mike's dive off Clausen's Pier rendered him paralyzed. Now Carrie finds herself torn between the loyalty she's expected to feel toward Mike and her need to transform herself. She takes a dive of her own—into adulthood—when she escapes to New York." Booklist

Packer, Ann

Songs without words. Knopf 2007 321p $24.95

ISBN 978-0-375-41281-3

LC 2006-100512

This "novel examines the bonds of female friendship and how the connections formed by a childhood tragedy develop with age. Liz, married to a Bay Area technology executive and the mother of two teenagers, is preoccupied with yoga and creating a pleasurable environment for her children. Sarabeth, who was absorbed into Liz's family when her mother committed suicide, lives a makeshift existence in Berkeley. When Liz's daughter attempts to kill herself, a rift opens between the two women. . . . [Packer] shows a deft touch in framing emotional dilemmas, such as whether it is the duty of those who have been raised with affection to compensate those who have gone without." New Yorker

Packer, Ann

Swim back to me. Alfred A. Knopf 2011 225p $24.95

ISBN 978-1-4000-4404-7; 1-4000-4404-9

LC 2010-51792

This book is a collection of short stories by Ann Packer. "In the opener, 'Walk for Mankind,' teenager Richard Appleby describes his bittersweet relationship with Sasha Horowitz, a rebellious, risk-taking 14-year-old, who has a clandestine affair with a drug dealer. . . . 'Molten' conveys a mother's grief over her adolescent son's senseless death; 'Dwell Time' features a protagonist's happy second marriage—until her husband disappears." (Publisher's note)

"Packer's sterling collection is framed by two novellas. In the opener, 'Walk for Mankind,' teenager Richard Appleby describes his bittersweet relationship with Sasha Horowitz, a rebellious, risk-taking 14-year-old, who has a clandestine affair with a drug dealer. . . . 'Things Said or Done' is set three decades later, when Sasha, now 51 and divorced, has become Richard's caretaker, forced to deal with his self-destructive, narcissistic personality while recognizing the ways in which they are alike. Packer's talents are evident in these psychologically astute novellas, and also in the stories in between. . . . [She] presents complex human relationships with unsentimental compassion." Publ Wkly

Packer, ZZ

Drinking coffee elsewhere. Riverhead Bks. 2003 238p hardcover o.p. pa $14

ISBN 1-57322-378-6 pa; 1-57322-234-8

LC 2002-73971

"The predominantly African American characters in Packer's first collection of short fiction struggle to maintain their sense of self while they confront unexpected life events." Booklist

Paddock, Jennifer

A **secret** word; a novel. Jennifer Paddock. Simon & Schuster 2004 206p $13

ISBN 0-7432-4707-8 pa

LC 2003-57343

This is the "story of three girls from Fort Smith, Ark., linked for life by a high school tragedy. In 1986, tennis and country club pals Sarah and Chandler hitch a ride to lunch from the less privileged Leigh; they're pursued by footballer Trey, who crashes his car and dies. Flash forward to 1990: Chandler and Sarah have gone to college; Leigh stays behind to work at a dry cleaner's. But their paths continue to intersect, and Paddock follows her characters through 15 years as they peel apart and reunite, capturing each of the young women in separate first-person chapters." Publ Wkly

"Filled with many moving and sometimes devastating moments and observations, Paddock's first novel is three coming-of-age stories for the price of one." Booklist

Page, Katherine Hall

The **body** in the Big Apple. Morrow 1999 239p $22

ISBN 0-688-15748-3

LC 99-33511

This prequel to the Faith Fairchild series "catches the amateur sleuth at the start of her career. . . . It's winter in Manhattan and 23-year-old Faith is darting from one holiday party to the next, bearing hearty comfort foods to a chic clientele of East Side socialites and yuppies. . . . At one of these soirees Faith runs into an old school chum, now married to an up-and-coming politician, who confides that she is being blackmailed." N Y Times Book Rev

Page, Katherine Hall

The **body** in the bog. Morrow 1996 276p

ISBN 978-0688145736

LC 96-3468

"Sleuth Faith Fairchild occupies her time in small-town Massachusetts with her husband, Tom, a preacher; their two small children; Have Faith, her catering business; and an occasional murder. When wetlands are converted into a chi-chi housing development, poison pen letters fly, one of the houses burns, and police discover murder. Faith's persistent quest for clues exposes many secrets, but the ultimate confrontation occurs in Have Faith's kitchen. Well-delineated action and characters mix easily with Faith's attendant domesticity." Libr J

Page, Katherine Hall

The **body** in the bookcase. Morrow 1998 244p $22

ISBN 0-688-15747-5

LC 98-36708

A mystery featuring Faith Fairchild, "the Aleford, Mass., caterer, wife and mother of two. Faith, like everybody else in town, is appalled when 80-year-old Sarah Winslow is found dead after her house is burglarized. After her own home is broken into, Faith decides to solve the crimes. . . . Page's tale is tightly written, with strong characterizations and delightful descriptions of its New England setting." Publ Wkly

Page, Katherine Hall

The **body** in the vestibule. St. Martin's Press 1992 211p

LC 92-18455

This Faith Fairchild mystery is "set in Lyons, France. Faith, four months pregnant, her husband Tom, a minister who is finishing research for his dissertation, and their three-year-old Ben live in a huge fifth-floor apartment. Taking out the garbage one evening, Faith finds the body of a homeless man from the neighborhood in the trash bin. When the police arrive, however, the body is gone and Faith's credibility is in question. At a party she meets Chief Inspector Michel Ravier, who asks about the body and tells her to call if she witnesses anything else unusual. . . . With beautifully detailed descriptions of Lyons added to Faith's intelligent observations, Page . . . continues to hit the mark with this charming series." Publ Wkly

Pajer, Bernadette

Capacity for murder; Bernadette Pajer. 1st ed. Poisoned Pen Press 2013 250 p. (hardcover) $24.95; (paperback) $14.95

ISBN 1464201285; 9781464201264; 9781464201288

LC 2012952569

This is Bernadette Pajer's third Professor Bradshaw mystery. This installment takes the professor-detective "to the Healing Sands Sanitarium in the remote coastal town of

Ocean Springs, Wash. Dr. Arnold Hornsby, Healing Sands' owner, wants Bradshaw to investigate the electrocution death of his son-in-law, David Hollister, in an electrotherapy machine." The professor quickly determines the death was not accidental. (Publishers Weekly)

Pajer, Bernadette
   Fatal induction; Bernadette Pajer. 1st ed. Poisoned Pen Press 2012 225 p. (hardcover) $24.95; (paperback) $14.95
   ISBN 1590586123; 9781590586129; 9781590586143
                                                 LC 2011942724
   This is Bernadette Pajer's second Professor Bradshaw mystery. Here, "people in 1901 Seattle are quick to dismiss the death of a gypsy peddler as not important, but Professor Bradshaw knows the dead man's young daughter is desperately in need of protection. At the same time, Bradshaw has entered a 'musical telephone' contest that just might generate a tool (wiretapping comes to mind) he and the police can use for spying on the suspected bad guys." (Library Journal)

Pajer, Bernadette
   A **spark** of death. Poisoned Pen 2011 210p pa $14.95
   ISBN 978-1-59058-907-6
   "Ever since his mentally unstable wife committed suicide at a dinner party, Prof. Benjamin Bradshaw has devoted himself to bringing up his son Justin. He's moved to Seattle, settled at the University of Washington and hired the competent Mrs. Prouty as a housekeeper. Now his life may be ruined by the murder of his colleague Prof. Oglethorpe, a man he had no cause to like. Oglethorpe was found electrocuted, apparently by a machine built in a university lab that was soon to be used in a demonstration for President McKinley. Bradshaw is certain that he must solve the murder to save his own life. . . . [This book] presents a good mystery, a clever detective and a fascinating look at the early days of electrical power." Kirkus

Palahniuk, Chuck
   Choke; a novel. Chuck Palahniuk. Doubleday 2001 293p (pbk.) $15; o.p.; o.p.
   ISBN 9780385720922; 9780307388926; 0385501560; 9780385501569
                                                 LC 00063905
   This book tells the story of "Victor Mancini [who] plays a colonial servant by day and reveals his true sex-addicted con artist self by night. All for the purpose of trying to cope with and fix a withered relationship with his ailing mother. Mancini purposely chokes on food at restaurants to gain the attention of other diners and force someone to save his life. . . . As if Victor couldn't get any more pathetic, his raging sex addiction sends him to sex addicts anonymous meetings to troll for sexual partners. Although his Alzheimer's-suffering mother has no idea who he is, she tells him--through a diary written completely in Italian—that he is a direct descendent of Jesus Christ himself." (Publisher's note)

Palahniuk, Chuck
   Diary; a novel. Doubleday 2003 260p $24.95
   ISBN 0-385-50947-2
                                                 LC 2003-43900

"Catchy, jarring prose, cryptic pronouncements and baroque flights of imagination are instantly recognizable, and {the author's} sharp, bizarre meditations on the artistic process make this twisted tale one of his most memorable works to date." Publ Wkly

Palahniuk, Chuck
   Fight Club; by Chuck Palahniuk. W. W. Norton & Company 1996 208p $25.95
   ISBN 0393039765; 9780393039764
                                                 LC 95047591
   Oregon Book Awards: Ken Kesey Award for Fiction (1997)
   In this book, "[e]very weekend, in the basements and parking lots of bars across the country, young men with white-collar jobs and failed lives take off their shoes and shirts and fight each other barehanded just as long as they have to. Then they go back to those jobs with blackened eyes and loosened teeth and the sense that they can handle anything. Fight club is the invention of Tyler Durden, projectionist, waiter, and dark, anarchic genius, and it's only the beginning of his plans for violent revenge on an empty consumer-culture world." (Publisher's note)

Palahniuk, Chuck
   Lullaby; a novel. Doubleday 2002 260p
   ISBN 0-385-50447-0
                                                 LC 2001-52979
   "Middle-aged journalist Carl Streator discovers that all children who died of SIDS are read the same poem the night before their deaths. . .. Once he discovers that simply reciting the poem in someone's direction is invariably fatal, Streator can't stop murdering. Then he finds out that Helen Hoover Boyle, a real-estate agent who sells the same haunted houses over and over again, knows the secret, too. They set out on a grand literary road trip to destroy all extant copies of the song." Booklist
   "This is vintage Palahniuk: weird, creepy, twisted, upsetting, and ultimately a great read for anyone who wants to be scared for pleasure." Libr J

Palahniuk, Chuck
   Pygmy. Doubleday 2009 241p $24.95
   ISBN 978-0-385-52634-0; 0-385-52634-2
                                                 LC 2009-06507
   A "novel about an unlikely terrorist cell: foreign-exchange students who arrive at a midwestern city, bent on unleashing 'Operation Havoc.' The story unfolds in a series of dispatches from an unnamed 13-year-old agent, dubbed 'Pygmy' by the locals. . . . Despite Pygmy's command of the deadly arts, he is still a 13-year-old, prone to unwanted erections, and he is not the coolest kid in the cadre, either. The frisson around his internal, target-acquiring narrative, the locals' unwitting perception of him, and his outsider's view of the routine humiliations inflicted upon high-school youth is so spot-on it produces a sense of déjà vu: surely someone would have thought of this before." Booklist

Palahniuk, Chuck

Rant; an oral biography of Buster Casey. Doubleday 2007 320p $24.95

ISBN 978-0-385-51787-4; 0-385-51787-4

LC 2006-28918

"In telling this utterly bizarre tale, a story that only gets heavier as it goes on, Rant's friends and family give their recollections of the twisted things he did as a kid and young adult before his violent death, stories as improbable as the all-American tall tale, only really gross. Gross, but fiercely smart, and in Palahniuk's signature way of raging against the deadening sterility of modern life." PopMatters

Paley, Grace

★ The **collected** stories. Farrar, Straus & Giroux 1994 386p $27.50

ISBN 0-374-12636-4

LC 93-42230

This volume includes stories from three previously published collections

Palliser, Charles

★ The **quincunx**. Ballantine Bks. 1990 788p

LC 89-91787

"This is not an ironic parody à la Barth, not an echo of Eco, but a genuine reproduction of a full-bodied 19th-century page-turner of a novel, set in late Regency England, thick with characters of all classes, with plots, counterplots, fore-bodings, reversals and interpolated tales. . . . Mr. Palliser's re-creation of this period is absolutely convincing, his dialogue never jars, his command of details never falters." N Y Times Book Rev

Palliser, Charles

The **unburied**. Farrar, Straus & Giroux 1999 403p $25

ISBN 0-374-28035-5

LC 99-14740

"All the murders are puzzles, and Palliser constructs his plot like a maze and lures his readers into it. The book's ruthless consistency of style and the somewhat bleak view of humankind set it apart from the usual thriller." New Yorker

Palma, Felix J.

The **map** of the sky; a novel. by Felix J. Palma. 1st Atria Books hardcover ed. Atria Books 2012 594 p. (hardcover: alk. paper) $26.00; (paperback) $16.00; (ebook) $24.99

ISBN 1451660316; 9781451660319; 9781451660326; 9781921942907

LC 2012028794

Sequel to: The map of time

In this book by Felix J. Palma, "H. G. Wells . . . meet[s] . . . Garrett Serviss, the man who dared write a sequel to his 'War of the Worlds.'. . . An alcohol-infused sense of camaraderie and adventure inspire the two men to set off to view a hidden secret -- a Martian kept in a locked room in the Natural History Museum. As alien forces converge on London, a group of citizens struggle to preserve the once-proud city against destruction." (Library Journal)

Palmer, Daniel

Helpless; Daniel Palmer. Kensington 2012 409 p.

ISBN 9780758246653

LC 2011937865

In this novel, "[f]ollowing his ex-wife's murder, things go from terrible to worse for New Hampshire high-school soccer coach Tom Hawkins, who is falsely implicated in a child-pornography ring, accused of sleeping with his 16-year-old daughter Jill's best friend and targeted by an old military pal who was involved in smuggling heroin from Germany with the dead wife. . . . [Tom's] daughter was already mad enough at him thanks to all the terrible things her mother told her about him. . . . Now their long-unheard-from third wheel overseas appears on the scene. . . . [Tom's] old high school nemesis [is] the cop assigned to the case and other town folk [want] bad things to happen to this good person." (Kirkus)

Palmer, Dexter Clarence

The **dream** of perpetual motion; [by] Dexter Palmer. St. Martin's Press 2010 340p $24.99

ISBN 978-0-312-55815-4; 0-312-55815-5

LC 2009-40231

"Palmer takes elements from Nabokov, Neal Stephenson, Steven Millhauser and 'The Tempest,' tosses them into a retro-futuristic blender and hits 'purée.' The result is a singular riff on steampunk—sophisticated, subversive entertainment that never settles for escapism." N Y Times Book Rev

Palmer, Liza

Nowhere but home; Liza Palmer. HarperCollins 2013 384 p. (paperback) $14.99

ISBN 0062007475; 9780062007476

In this novel, by Liza Palmer, "after Queenie Wake is dismissed from her restaurant job, she returns to North Star. . . . Hopeful that the bad memories of her late mother and promiscuous sister . . . have been forgotten by the locals, Queenie discovers that some people can't be forgotten--heartbreaker Everett Coburn--her old high-school sweetheart. When secrets from the past emerge, will Queenie be able to stick by her family or will she leave home again?" (Publisher's note)

Palmer, Michael

The **fifth** vial. St. Martin's Press 2007 372p $25.95

ISBN 0-312-34351-5; 978-0-312-34351-4

LC 2006-50971

"Palmer is adept at tapping into people's natural fear of disease, doctors, and hospitals and converting that fear into unnerving suspense. In this . . . medical thriller, Palmer plays with the phenomenon of organ donation, forcing the reader to ask nervously, 'Where do donated organs come from?' The answer comes slowly, in the best medical-thriller tradition." Booklist

Palmer, Michael

The **last** surgeon. St. Martin's Press 2010 373p $26.99

ISBN 978-0-312-58749-9; 0-312-58749-X

LC 2009-39234

In this medical thriller, "former trauma surgeon Dr. Nick Garrity, who suffers from PTSD as the result of a suicide attack on his field hospital in Afghanistan, is now in charge of the Helping Hands RV, a mobile clinic that plies the streets of Baltimore offering medical aid to the homeless. Meanwhile, a high-priced hit man starts to commit a series of murders, his first victim being Belle Coates, a nurse in Charlotte, N.C. When Belle's sister, Jillian, who lives in Virginia, searches for her sister's killer, she finds a connection to Nick. Several missing homeless men lead everyone to a massive plot involving high-level politicians and a secret CIA program." Publ Wkly

"Palmer's latest has an appealing couple at its center, plus good pacing and gritty action to keep the pages turning." Libr J

Palmer, Michael

Miracle cure. Bantam Bks. 1998 399p $23.95

ISBN 0-553-10523-X

LC 98-4884

A medical thriller revolving around a new drug "called Vasclear, a heart medication being developed at the Boston Heart Institute by Newbury Pharmaceuticals. The FDA is being pressured by a Massachusetts senator (who, it turns out, is secretly taking Vasclear himself) to approve the release of the drug. And Vasclear may be the magic wand that can save the life of Jack 'Coach' Holbrook, whose health is declining after a quintuple bypass. Coach's son, Brian . . . not only faces the ethical dilemma of stealing the drug if he can't place his father as a test patient but also finds evidence of potentially dangerous side effects—evidence that could derail the drug's release to the public." Publ Wkly

Palmer, Michael

The **patient**. Bantam Bks. 2000 324p $24.95

ISBN 0-553-10983-9

LC 99-57838

This medical thriller features "Dr. Jessie Copeland, a neurosurgeon in her 40s with a combined under-graduate degree in biology and mechanical engineering. Now working under egomaniacal chief surgeon Carl Gilbride at a top Boston hospital, Jessie gets to try out ARTIE (Assisted Robotic Tissue Incision and Extraction) on cadavers, while Gilbride coaxes foundations to cough up millions for the revolutionary new procedure. Attracted by the media attention, . . . shadowy terrorist Claude Malloche, known as 'the Mist,' who also has a brain tumor, comes to the hospital for treatment—and winds up holding patients and staff hostage in case the operation fails. It's finally up to Jessie and a rogue CIA agent to keep everyone healthy." Publ Wkly

Includes bibliographical references

Palmer, Michael

The **society**. Bantam Bks. 2004 351p $25

ISBN 0-553-90057-9

LC 2004-303038

This thriller begins "with the murder of several loathsome CEOs of HMOs in Massachusetts. Dr. Will Grant is a talented and caring physician in the Boston area who works long hours and hates the unfair and obstructive practices of the big insurance companies. Patty Moriarity is a rookie state cop whose first big case is investigating the deaths of the health care vultures. After some early research, Patty suspects Will, but soon enough that's all straightened out and they're smooching on the couch. After Will is drugged and collapses during a delicate operation, things get rough: he's kicked out of his hospital for drug abuse and sued. Next he's being tortured, while Patty, shot after attempting to save the boorish chauvinist detective who has taken over her case, lies in a coma. The action is a bit preachy in the beginning, but once Palmer gets all his characters in place, the suspense builds." Publ Wkly

Palwick, Susan

Mending the moon; Susan Palwick. Tor 2013 336 p. (hardcover) $24.99

ISBN 0765327589; 9780765327581

LC 2012043362

In this novel by Susan Palwick, "Melinda Soto . . ., vacationing in Mexico, is murdered by a fellow American tourist. She leaves behind her adopted son, Jeremy [and] a circle of friends: Veronique, the academic stuck in a teaching job from which she can't retire; Rosemary, who's losing her husband to Alzheimer's; Henrietta, the priest at Rosemary's and Melinda's church. An invitation to them all, from the murderer's mother, to come to Seattle for his memorial [brings] a chance to heal." (Publisher's note)

Palwick, Susan,

★ The **necessary** beggar; Susan Palwick. Tor 2005 316p $24.95

ISBN 076531097X; 9780765310972

LC 2005041919

Alex Award (2006)

This book follows a family from "Gandiffri, a world of peace and abundance," who are exiled to Earth. "Twenty-something Darroti and a devout young noblewoman, Gallicina, fall in love. . . . Darroti comes to be accused of murdering her and his sentenced to exile in another dimension. . . . Darroti's father, brothers, and the latter's wives and children accompany him. Taking only what they can carry, they walk through a strange blue door and into a refugee camp in Nevada. There Darroti . . . commits suicide, which marks each remaining family member differently. . . . Yet the magic of Gandiffri isn't lost to them. It lives in a tiny, undying pet beetle; in the unbreakable bond of Darroti and Gallicina; in a ghost seeking redemption; and in the healing power of love." (Booklist)

Palwick, Susan

Shelter. Tor 2007 576p pa $15.95

ISBN 978-0-312-86602-0; 0-312-86602-X

LC 2007-7316

"Palwick has built a rich and complex possible future, complete with political and religious systems, rapid and extraordinary technological advancement, and all the moral polarization that naturally follows such developments." Strange Horizons

Pamuk, Orhan, 1952-

The **museum** of innocence; translated from the Turkish by Maureen Freely. Alfred A. Knopf 2009 535p il map $28.95

ISBN 978-0-307-26676-7; 0-307-26676-1

LC 2009-19475

Original Turkish edition, 2008

Readers "view Istanbul in the tumultuous 1970s and '80s through the lens of a doomed love affair. Kemal is happily engaged to a beautiful, intelligent woman of his own social class, Sibel—and yet, he falls deeply, irrevocably in love with a poor, distant relation, Füsun. When Kemal refuses to leave Sibel, Füsun disappears. Inconsolable, he returns almost daily to the scene of their lovemaking, cradling the objects she once touched as though they still contain some trace of her. He descends deeper into despair, alienating everyone around him except Sibel, now bound to him as much by love as by the shame that she will face should they break off their engagement. But Kemal cannot forget Füsun, and will dedicate his life to possessing her—or at least, the objects that remind him of her—even to the point of destroying himself, and those he loves most." BookPage

"Pamuk is brilliant at the human parade, and especially at humiliation in its masculine forms, frequently played out in Istanbul along East-West tensions." Cleveland Plain Dealer

Pamuk, Orhan, 1952-

★ **My** name is Red; translated from the Turkish by Erdağ Göknar. Knopf 2001 417p

ISBN 0-375-40695-6

LC 2001-29866

Original Turkish edition, 1998

This is a novel by the author of The Black Book, The New Life and The White Castle. It "is set in the late 16th century, during the reign of {the Turkish} Sultan Murat III, a patron of the miniaturists whose art had come over from Persia. . . . {The story} tells of two murders among Murat's court artists; one of Elegant, a master miniaturist, the other of Enishte, a . . . figure commissioned by the sultan to produce a book by his four finest artists. . . . The style the sultan's artists are surreptitiously instructed to adopt . . . is that of the Italian Renaissance." (N Y Times Book Rev)

"The Ottoman Istanbul, which Mr. Pahmuk depicts with skill and linguistic energy, is a rich, cruel and claustrophobic world where art leads, through dark alleyways to murder. The novel is also about the conflicts of Turkishness, about . . . a society caught between religious zealotry and an authoritarian state—themes as relevant to Turkey now as they were 400 years ago." Economist

Pamuk, Orhan, 1952-

Silent house; by Orhan Pamuk; translated from the Turkish by Robert Finn. Alfred A. Knopf 2012 334 p. $26.95

ISBN 0307700283; 9780307700285

LC 2012005468

This novel by Orhan Pamuk, translated by Robert Finn, "is the story of a Turkish family gathering in the shadow of the impending military coup of 1980. . . . A widow, Fatma, awaits the annual summer visit of her grandchildren. . . . The eldest, Faruk, a dissipated historian, wallows in alcohol. . . . His sensitive leftist sister, Nilgün, has yet to discover the real-life consequences of highminded politics; and Metin, a high school nerd . . . fantasizes about going to America." (Publisher's note)

Pamuk, Orhan, 1952-

★ **Snow**; translated by Maureen Freely. Knopf 2004 426p

ISBN 0375406972

Original Turkish edition, 2002

This novel concerns the conflict between Islamism and secularism (the legacy of Ataturk) in contemporary Turkey. Ka, the protagonist, "a blocked poet and one time radical, . . . returns from Germany after 12 years' exile to get back in touch with his country. A newspaper assignment takes him to {Kars}, a town near the Georgian border, to investigate a rumor . . . about a wave of schoolgirls who killed themselves when ordered to remove their head scarves. . . . There is an old Communist who tolerates a daughter's head scarf as a rebellion against the establishment, and a newspaper editor who publishes as past events those that are still to take place. . . . {Ka} is chilled and infuriated by Blue, a lethal yet childlike underground activist. . . . He becomes involved with Sunay, a theater impresario and former leftist who . . . glories in having achieved a supreme work of art, one whose dramatic culmination will be his own death onstage." (N Y Times (Late N Y Ed))

"Upon returning to his home in secular Turkey, a poet named Ka discovers two things that will change his life: Ipek, the girl he loved as a child, still lives in the city of Kars, and the community has been stunned by a rash of suicides of zealously religious girls who refused to remove their head scarves while in public. With an investigator's eye, Ka seeks out information about the tragedies from all sources, eventually leading to the man at the eye of the storm "Blue," a charismatic Islamite who will not let the message that these girls carried be silenced." Libr J

Pancake, Ann

Strange as this weather has been; a novel. Shoemaker & Hoard 2007 360p pa $15.95

ISBN 978-1-59376-166-0; 1-59376-166-X

LC 2007-11838

"With her beloved West Virginia hollows and valleys under constant onslaught by a savage coal-mining industry whose raping of the land threatens her home with devastating floods, Lace Ricker finds herself battling callous forces both without and within her own family. As thunderous blasts weaken their home's foundation and poisoned wastewater infiltrates their well, Lace and her daughter, Bant, secretly become more determined to find a way to stop the mines, while Lace's husband pragmatically refuses to fight the union bosses, and her sons tentatively, then calamitously, accept the challenges and adventure of life lived in the shadow of imminent danger. By tracing the devastating impact of coal mining through the eyes of Lace and her four children, Pancake's powerful debut novel evinces a poetic pathos and authentic respect for the land and the people who love it." Booklist

Parameswaran, Rajesh

I am an executioner; love stories. Rajesh Parameswaran. Knopf 2012 259 p.

ISBN 0307595927; 9780307595928

LC 2011033754

The infamous Bengal Ming -- The strange career of Dr. Raju Gopalarajan -- Four Rajeshes -- I am an executioner -- Demons -- Narrative of Agent 97-4702 -- Bebhutibhushhan Mallik's final storyboard -- Elephants in captivity (part one) -- On the banks of the Table River (Planet Lucinda, Andromeda Galaxy, AD 2319).

This book is a collection of love stories from author Rajesh Parameswaran. In one story, "although the executioner takes pride in doing his job well, he hid the true nature of his work from his new, now deeply depressed wife and is, therefore, exiled to the couch. . . . A thoughtful zoo tiger is only trying to express love when he inadvertently goes on a killing spree. . . . [Another is a] story about an aging art director helplessly in love with the wife of a world-famous filmmaker." (Booklist)

Paretsky, Sara

Bitter medicine. Morrow 1987 321p

LC 86-33238

"A young Hispanic woman and her premature infant die in a wealthy suburban hospital. Her doctor is found beaten to death the next day. As a favor to Lottie Herschel, her longtime friend and mentor, Chicago private investigator and lawyer V. I. Warshawski agrees to look into the case. Abortion and medical ethics are the backdrop for this powerful and moving novel." Libr J

Paretsky, Sara

Blacklist; a V.I. Warshawski novel. Putnam 2003 415p $24.95

ISBN 0-399-15085-4

LC 2003-43157

"A dead reporter, a missing Egyptian boy wanted in connection with terrorist activities, and an elderly woman convinced that an intruder is in her family manse are all elements of Paretsky's . . . novel featuring Chicago private investigator V. I. Warshawski. As V. I. looks into these peoples' lives, she discovers connections among them. She uncovers a story of betrayal and secrets that spans several generations and involves Chicago's wealthiest families, the Red Scare, and the House Un-American Activities Committee hearings of the 1950s. As always, V. I.'s determined pursuit of the truth ensures at least a few heart-stopping moments." Libr J

Paretsky, Sara

Bleeding Kansas. G.P. Putnam's Sons 2008 431p $25.95; pa $9.99

ISBN 978-0-399-15405-8; 978-0-451-22448-4 pa

LC 2007-35962

"Set in the rural Kaw River Valley, where the author grew up, and sparked by a feud between two families that pioneered this farm region during the 1850s, the multigenerational narrative bristles with the kind of prickly social issues that give substance to Paretsky's detective stories. . . . The blood-boiling issue in Bleeding Kansas is religious intolerance. Bigotry comes naturally to the members of the Schapen clan, who worship at the Salvation Through the Blood of Jesus Full Bible Church and become apoplectic when Gina Haring, a New York lesbian and New Age Wiccan, moves into an old farmhouse and attempts to practice her beliefs. . . . Any inclination on the part of the reader to sympathize with the Schapens (for being born and bred stupid) in this barnyard feud are wiped out when Chip Grellier, who joins the Army after being suspended from school for a fight started by his Schapen tormentors, is killed in Iraq. But the Schapens do provide much black humor by breeding the 'perfect red heifer' referred to in the Old Testament, creating an international storm that ensnares both fundamentalist Christians and ultraorthodox Jews." N Y Times Book Rev

Paretsky, Sara

Blood shot; a novel. Delacorte Press 1988 328p

LC 88-3861

"Blood Shot takes {the detective-heroine V.I. Warshawski} back to the working-class Chicago neighbourhoods of her youth, where a callous industrialist lurks at the centre of a deadly web of violence and intrigue." Quill Quire

Paretsky, Sara

★ **Breakdown**; Sara Paretsky. G. P. Putnam's Sons 2012 431p

ISBN 9780399157837

LC 2011047676

This book tells the fictional story of "pre-teens who are crazy about a series of books featuring 'Carmilla,' a shapeshifter who can turn into a raven. In the Carmilla books, there's a lot of werewolf and vampire activity too. . . . In 'Breakdown,' V.I. (which is short for Victoria Iphigenia . . .), stumbles across the girls doing some sort of initiation ceremony in a dark cemetery in the rain. All the girls are out after curfew and V.I.'s cousin Petra has been frantic to know where they are. After V.I. rounds them up, they turn to leave, only to find that a man has been laid out on a tomb perilously close to where the girls were frolicking, and he's been pierced through the heart with a large hunk of steel. Instead of leaving in the orderly way planned, everyone goes screaming through the night, and it's V.I. who has to explain everything to the police. . . . V.I. (or Vic, as some call her) dashes from the homes of the rich girls' parents to the bleak mental hospital to the right-wing news station, all trying to make the facts fit together." (Technorati.com)

Paretsky, Sara

★ **Burn** marks. Delacorte Press 1990 340p

LC 89-23418

"The 'whydunit' in Ms. Paretsky's books is often embedded in the fabric of problems that confront us all—the poisoned environment, for example, or urban blight. This extra dimension adds an immediacy to 'Burn Marks' that is not found in many private-eye novels." N Y Times Book Rev

Paretsky, Sara

Fire sale. Putnam 2005 402p $25.95

ISBN 0-399-15279-2

LC 2005-47601

This entry draws V. I. Warshawski "back to her South Chicago roots when she reluctantly agrees to coach the girls basketball team at her former high school, which is struggling with poverty, teen pregnancy, a lack of equipment, and gang influence. The old neighborhood has declined, too, and when a small local factory is sabotaged, V.I. is persuaded to investigate. Meanwhile, she hopes to gain financial support for the basketball team from By-Smart, a megadiscount chain whose founder also grew up in South Chicago. In a series of events that includes an explosion at the local factory, a horrifying murder, and the disappearance of a basketball player, V.I. is drawn into a deadly conflict between By-Smart and South Chicago's residents. Fast-paced and as entertaining." Libr J

Paretsky, Sara

Ghost country. Delacorte Press 1998 386p $24.95

ISBN 0-385-29933-8

LC 98-12294

Chicagoans "Harriet and Mara Stonds have been raised in luxuary by their grandfather, famous neurosurgeon Abraham Stonds. Harriet is the apple of her grandfather's eye—tall, blond, successful at everything she does, always the good girl. Mara plays the role of ugly stepsister, at least to her grandfather, who has told her for years that she's lazy, stupid, and ungrateful. But things are about to change for the Stonds family. A drunken opera singer, a softhearted psychotherapist, a group of homeless women, and a mysterious visitor who performs miracles will each play a key role in opening the eyes of Harriet and Mara to a world they've never imagined. This book is rich, astonishing, and affecting." Booklist

Paretsky, Sara

Guardian angel. Delacorte Press 1992 370p

LC 91-24976

While investigating a local manufacturer Chicago private eye V.I. Warshawski uncovers a bond-parking scheme that reaches into her ex-husband's law firm and ties into the bizarre behavior of her neighbors

"The plot serves nicely to bring V.I. into contact with tough, down-and-out types, whom Ms. Paretsky draws extremely well. . . . Bits and pieces of V.I.'s background are worked into the narrative unobtrusively, so that we come to know her as the story progresses, the way we come to know people in real life." N Y Times Book Rev

Paretsky, Sara

Hard time; a V.I. Warshawski novel. Delacorte Press 1999 384p $24.95

ISBN 0-385-31363-2

LC 99-22214

When V. I. Warshawski "swerves to avoid a body lying in the middle of the road, she never imagines that her search for the reasons behind the vicious beating death of Nicola Aguinaldo will take her from the upper classes of Chicago society to a long stint behind bars at a private women's prison overrun with sadistic guards and almost equally threatening inmates." Libr J

Paretsky, Sara

Hardball. G.P. Putnam's Sons 2009 446p $26.95

ISBN 978-0-399-15593-2; 0-399-15593-7

LC 2009-20700

"The thing about Sara Paretsky is, she's tough—not because she observes the bonebreaker conventions of the

private-eye genre but because she doesn't flinch from examining old social injustices others might find too shameful (and too painful) to dig up." N Y Times Book Rev

Paretsky, Sara

Indemnity only; a novel. Dial Press (NY) 1982 244p

LC 81-5452

"Chicago private eye V. I. Warshawski is hired to locate a young woman and instead comes across the body of her boyfriend, a crooked union, and an insurance scam. Thugs beat V. I. up, and another man is murdered. This is all standard hard-boiled detective stuff, except that V. I. is a woman—tough, independent, good looking, and believable. Paretsky has done an excellent job of presenting a real female private eye, without falling into parody." Libr J

Paretsky, Sara

★ **Total** recall; a V.I. Warshawski novel. Delacorte Press 2001 414p

ISBN 0-385-31366-7

LC 2001-28801

"At a Chicago conference on Jews and Christians, an unassuming man calling himself Paul Radbuka makes some startling assertions. Claiming that a recovered memory therapist has recently helped him to regain memories of a childhood destroyed by the Holocaust, he seeks to find his true family. Before she knows it, private detective V.I. Warshawski is drawn into the turmoil unleashed by these claims and watches helplessly as her dearest friend and mentor, Lotty Hershel, is consumed by a past she wishes to forget." Libr J

This mystery "is written with the stylistic verve and intellectual energy of a writer just coming into her own." N Y Times Book Rev

Paretsky, Sara

Tunnel vision. Delacorte Press 1994 432p

LC 94-6050

Chicago private detective V.I. Warshawski uncovers a "cynical swindle when she tries to help a wretched family she finds living in the basement of her office building. After getting the bum's rush from an advocacy group for the homeless and from feminist friends protecting their own grants, V.I. sticks out her jaw and goes it alone on this dirty, complicated fraud case. Mustn't feel sorry for V.I., though, because her outrage gives her the strength to take on the whole corrupt establishment. This principled private eye intimidates people because she doesn't know the meaning of compromise and won't tolerate moral slackers." N Y Times Book Rev

Paretsky, Sara

Windy City blues; V. I. Warshawski stories. Delacorte Press 1995 258p

LC 95-8302

"Although V.I.'s just as feisty and tough-talking as ever, she presents a somewhat softer side in this series of stories that gives a nostalgic nod to Vic's friends, family, and past." Booklist

Parini, Jay

The **apprentice** lover; a novel. HarperCollins Pubs. 2002 307p $24.95

ISBN 0-06-621071-2

LC 2001-39675

"Derailed by his brother's death in Vietnam, Alex Massolini, Parini's immensely likable, jejune hero, has dropped out of Columbia and secured the position of secretary for the renowned Scots writer Rupert Grant, currently ensconced in a villa on Capri with his astute yet longsuffering wife and two lovely and worshipful 'research assistants.' . . . Parini's lucent and sensuous tale nimbly dissects the confluence of ego and art and ponders the unending wounds of war, ultimately affirming the consoling power of literature, however disappointing writers themselves may be. Wittily drawn cameos of W. H. Auden, Graham Greene, and Gore Vidal add to the deep pleasures of this smart, graceful novel." Booklist

Parini, Jay

The **passages** of H.M. a novel of Herman Melville. Doubleday 2010 454p $26.95

ISBN 978-0-385-52277-9; 0-385-52277-0

LC 2010-06291

"Most intriguing . . . is the way Parini weaves elements from Melville's writings into his account of the author's life and travels. . . . Even if you've read none of Melville, or remember only echoes from readings long ago, the narrative is complete, the literary facts clear enough to sustain its powerful drama. And for those who know Melville well, 'The Passages of H.M.' is a labor of love and inspiration." Cleveland Plain Dealer

Park, Ed

Personal days; a novel. Random House Trade Paperbacks 2008 241p pa $13

ISBN 978-0-8129-7857-5; 0-8129-7857-9

LC 2007-40834

This novel is "narrated by a collective 'we' of youngish Manhattan office grunts who watch in helpless horror as their company keeps shrinking, taking their private world of in-jokes and nicknames along with it. . . . As office survivors Lizzie, Jonah, Pru, Crease, Lars and Jason II try to figure out who's next to get the axe, mysterious clues point to a conspiracy that may involve one or more of the survivors." Publ Wkly

Park, Samuel

This burns my heart; Samuel Park. Simon & Schuster 2011 288p.

ISBN 9781439199619

LC 2010043441

This book presents a "love story set in the . . . landscape of postwar South Korea. On the eve of marriage to her weak, timid fiancé, Soo-Ja falls in love with a young medical student. But out of duty to her family and her culture she turns him away, choosing instead a world that leaves her trapped by suffocating customs. In a country torn between past and present, Soo-Ja struggles to find happiness in a loveless marriage and to carve out a successful future for her only daughter. Forced by tradition to move in with her in-laws, she must navigate the dangers of a cruel household and pay the price of choosing the wrong husband." (Publisher's note)

Parker, Barbara

Blood relations. Dutton 1996 374p

ISBN 978-0525939764

LC 95-32085

"Prosecutor Sam Hagen is known for being a straight arrow, so he's the perfect choice to investigate a potentially explosive case and dismiss it for lack of evidence. Or so think both his boss, the Miami DA, who has his eye on national office and doesn't want controversy, and the city manager, who's courting the tourist industry. The plaintiff is a young model who claims that several men, including a well-connected local businessman and a football player turned actor, raped her. Hagen believes the girl and, despite political pressure, pursues the case." Publ Wkly

"Stylish writing, glamorous characters, a glitzy setting, and an intricately constructed plot—there's a formula for success in any genre of popular fiction." Booklist

Parker, Barbara

Criminal justice. Dutton 1997 304p

ISBN 978-0525939771

LC 96-44143

"Dan Galindo was a Boy Scout among the Federal prosecutors in Miami. Because he refused to put a flawed and sleazy witness on the stand, a drug kingpin walked. His virtue was rewarded by the loss of his job, forcing him to take up private legal scut work. Now, defending a beautiful but scary rock musician on a minor criminal charge, Dan finds himself in a web of money launderers, suspected bigtime drug lords, informants and ruthless narcs who may even have murdered to cover their tracks." N Y Times Book Rev

The author "has written a brutal commentary on the Miami music scene, offering unforgettable characters and some hilarious potshots at suburbia." Libr J

Parker, Barbara

Suspicion of betrayal; a novel. Dutton 1999 347p $23.95

ISBN 0-525-94468-0

LC 98-52080

This suspense novel features Miami "attorney Gail Connon, whose love affair with high-powered defense attorney Anthony Quintana is going full-speed ahead. Gail's plate is way too full as she tries to save her struggling solo practice while addressing a custody dispute with her ex over their 10-year-old daughter, Karen. Just when Gail thinks everything's under control, the bottom falls out when Karen starts receiving anonymous death threats." Booklist

Parker, Barbara

Suspicion of deceit. Dutton 1998 358p $23.95

ISBN 0-525-94401-X

LC 97-38429

A novel featuring attorneys Gail Connor and Anthony Quintana. "To build business for her new solo practice, Gail takes on the Miami Opera as a client, only to learn of a pending crisis: the rising young bass-baritone scheduled to play Don Giovanni in Mozart's opera sang recently in Castro's Cuba. The singer may be in danger, as may several of Gail's opera contacts who have ties to puzzling aspects of Anthony's past, ties that lead back to Nicaragua in the late 1970s." Booklist

"The narrative triumphs, . . . thanks to Parker's rich mix of tropical politics, edgy romance and secrets from the past." Publ Wkly

Parker, Barbara

Suspicion of vengeance. Dutton 2001 359p $23.95

ISBN 0-525-94601-2

LC 2001-33521

Gail Connor "is asked to take on the case of an old family friend's grandson, Kenny Ray Clark, who was convicted of the stabbing death of a housewife over a decade earlier, indirectly causing the death of her infant son. Now, after 11 years on death row, his appeals are about to run out. Anthony, Gail's on-again, off-again fiancé, himself a high-powered Florida attorney, warns her of the futility of trying to save Clark. But Gail digs into the records and finds, among other things, a drunk defense attorney, a bogus confession and a witness who would have provided an alibi but was threatened by police." Publ Wkly

Parker, Dorothy

★ **Here** lies; the collected stories of Dorothy Parker. Viking 1939 362p

Parker, K. J.

The **company**. Orbit 2008 419p $24.99

ISBN 978-0-316-03853-9; 0-316-03853-9

LC 2008-35282

The author "blends gritty military fantasy with the 18th-century 'island story' tradition. Seven years after the end of a war between unnamed countries, four friends who fought together have settled back into civilian life. Then their former leader, Kunessin, now a celebrated and embittered general, turns up and reminds them of their old pledge to retire together to a peaceful island. Better yet, he's found a suitable place and will fund the venture. A local matchmaker finds women smart and desperate enough to be colonists, and they marry the ex-soldiers in a group wedding that sets the tone of the book: humorous, grim and utterly unromantic. The would-be republicans soon reach the island and settle in, but the discovery of gold in a stream changes everything." Publ Wkly

Parker, K. J.

Devices and desires. Little, Brown 2007 635p (Engineer trilogy) pa $12.99

ISBN 978-0-316-00338-4; 0-316-00338-7

LC 2007-9926

First published 2005 in the United Kingdom

"When engineer Ziani Vaatzes is sentenced to death for building a device that differs from the official standards, he manages to flee from his home in the Guild-controlled Republic of Mezentia and find refuge in the enemy country of Eremia. To ensure his safety, he offers to teach Mezentine engineering techniques to the technologically ignorant Eremians, so that they can build weapons equal to those of their Mezentine enemies. Eremia's Duke Orsea reluctantly gives his approval, unwittingly laying himself and those he loves open to the machinations of a man out for vengeance against the country that condemned his work as well as the

enemy who gave him succor. . . . [A] richly textured and emotionally complex fantasy." Libr J

Parker, K. J.

Sharps; K.J. Parker. Orbit 2012 471 p. (paperback) $15.99

ISBN 031617775X; 9780316177757

LC 2011944517

In this novel by K. J. Parker "an uneasy truce has been called between two neighbouring kingdoms. The war has been long and brutal, fought over the usual things: resources, land, money. . . . Now, there is a chance for peace. Diplomatic talks have begun and with them, the games. Two teams of fencers represent their nations at this pivotal moment. When the future of the world lies balanced on the point of a rapier, one misstep could mean ruin for all." (Publisher's note)

Parker, Robert B.

★ **Appaloosa**. Putnam 2005 276p $24.95

ISBN 0-399-15277-6

LC 2004-58745

In this western, "deputy Everett Hitch recounts the struggle between lawman Virgil Cole and outlaw rancher Randall Bragg for control of the little town of Appaloosa. Modeled on Wyatt Earp, Cole is the kind of man who never loses a fight, and he comes close to taking down the murderous Bragg with ease, until Bragg's hired guns rescue him by abducting Cole's romantic interest and using her as a hostage. This precipitates a long chase, a struggle with wandering Kiowa, and a gunfight reminiscent of the OK Corral. The story gallops along to a surprise ending, but beneath the trappings of this gunfighter novel, Parker really has something to say about the nature of men and women in the Old West." Libr J

Parker, Robert B.

Back story. Putnam 2003 291p $24.95

ISBN 0-399-14977-5

LC 2002-36901

"The repartee between Spenser and Hawk is fast and funny; the sentiment between Spenser and Susan and the musings about Spenser's code are only occasionally cloying; and there's a scattering of remarkable action scenes including a tense shootout in Harvard Stadium." Publ Wkly

Parker, Robert B.

Blue-eyed devil. G.P. Putnam's Sons 2010 276p $25.95

ISBN 978-0-399-15648-9; 0-399-15648-8

LC 2010-03109

"More shifting allegiances, moral dilemmas and characters capable of change than Virgil and Everett's fans may be used to. It's a shame that this youngest of the late Parker's franchises has to end so soon." Kirkus

Parker, Robert B.

Brimstone. G.P. Putnam's Sons 2009 293p $25.95

ISBN 978-0-399-15571-0; 0-399-15571-6

LC 2009-08107

"Parker's gunslinging saddle pals Virgil Cole and Everett Hitch return for their third adventure. . . . Here, Virgil and Everett rescue Allie French, Virgil's former sweetie who ran off to become a prostitute, and head to Brimstone, where the two gunmen sign on as deputy sheriffs. Brimstone, however, doesn't exactly provide a quiet respite for this trio. Virgil and Allie have a hard time getting over his hurt and her shame, a mysterious Indian is killing local folks and leaving taunting messages, and brutal saloon owner Pike and corrupt preacher Brother Percival are headed for a showdown. . . . The result is classic Parker—exciting, suspenseful, fast-moving and entertaining." Publ Wkly

Parker, Robert B.

A **Catskill** eagle; a Spenser novel. Delacorte Press/Seymour Lawrence 1985 311p

LC 84-28617

After Spenser "receives a plea for help from true love Susan Silverman (who is being restrained by the son of a shadowy armaments manufacturer), Spenser travels from Boston to California to Chicago to Connecticut to Idaho, taking Hawk, his favorite colleague, with him on the rescue quest. All this is mainly an excuse for derring-do and violence. At one point the FBI and CIA contract with Spenser to kill the armaments manufacturer. The plot may be ridiculous, but the dialogue is snappy as usual, and the characters are fascinating." Libr J

Parker, Robert B.

Chance. Putnam 1996 307p

ISBN 978-0399141348

LC 95-49950

"Parker's stouthearted hero proves that he is still as tough and manly as they come, and more principled than ever in this punchy private-eye caper." N Y Times Book Rev

Parker, Robert B.

Cold service. Putnam 2005 305p $24.95

ISBN 0-399-15240-7

LC 2004-56608

"As the tale begins, the heretofore-indestructible Hawk is recovering from a near-death experience: shot in the back while protecting a bookie from the upstart Ukrainian Mob. It's payback time, of course, but not before Hawk nurses himself back to psychic and physical health. Meanwhile, Spenser does a bit of sleuthing on his own, determining that Hawk's assailants are the tip of a Ukrainian iceberg that has stuck its tentacles deep into Boston's underworld. Payback, Hawk style, requires eliminating not just the shooters but also the entire Mob. The action comes in a rush near the end, but the satisfying part here is watching Parker dig deeply into the remarkable friendship between two tough guys constitutionally averse to the whole touchy-feely side of life." Booklist

Parker, Robert B.

Crimson joy. Delacorte Press 1988 211p

LC 87-33043

"When Police Lieutenant Marty Quirk is faced with an insane serial killer, who threatens to ignite all of Boston into a racial bonfire, he turns to Spenser for help. There aren't many clues to point the way, until the killer makes it personal by first going after Spenser and then his lady, psychologist Susan Silverman. Never one to take such an affront lightly, Spenser and his pal Hawk set out to put an end to these brutal murders." West Coast Rev Books

Parker, Robert B.

Death in paradise. Putnam 2001 294p

ISBN 0-399-14779-9

LC 2001-31874

"Given his raw nerves, bursts of violence and unhealthy devotion to his ex-wife, Jesse is still unpredictable and a little scary. Let's trust Parker to keep him on the edge." N Y Times Book Rev

Parker, Robert B.

Double Deuce. Putnam 1992 224p

LC 91-29594

In this novel Spenser "finds himself, at the behest of his pal Hawk, defending the residents of a gang-terrorized Boston housing project known as Double Deuce. The drive-by shooting of a teenage mother and her child brings the duo into a confrontation with gangleader Major Johnson and his posse." Publ Wkly

Parker, Robert B.

Double play. Putnam 2004 288p $24.95

ISBN 0-399-15188-5

LC 2004-40029

"Parker pretty much defies category altogether in this deeply felt and intimately told memory tale, which takes place during the historic baseball season of 1947, when Jackie Robinson broke the color bar in major-league baseball by playing first base for the Brooklyn Dodgers. Fusing this chapter of sports history with a hardboiled gangster plot and haunting recollections of his own Boston boyhood, Parker fashions a hugely entertaining fiction that also serves as a blueprint for the themes that preoccupy him as a writer and the code of values that sustains his work." N Y Times Book Rev

Parker, Robert B.

Family honor. Putnam 1999 322p $22.95

ISBN 0-399-14566-4

LC 99-27488

Private detective Sunny Randall "is hired by a powerful family to find their runaway daughter, Millicent, who, it transpires, is hooking and needs rescuing. . . . Millicent, it happens, witnessed a conspiracy to murder arising from her cold, ambitious parents—her father aims to be governor—and the Italian mobsters who control them. The mobsters now want her dead, and Sunny, too, if need be. . . . The high suspense is equaled by the emotional power of Sunny's bonding with the damaged girl. A bravura performance." Publ Wkly

Parker, Robert B.

Gunman's rhapsody. Putnam 2001 289p

ISBN 0-399-14762-4

LC 00-53327

The novel "shows surprising fidelity to most of the known facts without letting them get in the way of a good story. Parker's strengths here, as in his crime novels, are plot and dialogue." N Y Times Book Rev

Parker, Robert B.

Hugger mugger. Putnam 2000 307p

ISBN 0-399-14587-7

LC 99-56105

"Culture shock brings out a certain waggishness in Spenser, who is fascinated by the elaborately staged lives of the horsy set and more amused than appalled by the character flaws he uncovers beneath all the polite gentility. Without compromising his expert sleuthing techniques . . . he manages to pick up enough regional skills to communicate with the devious natives in their own idiom—and catch them at their own wicked games." N Y Times Book Rev

Parker, Robert B.

Hush money. Putnam 1999 309p $22.95

ISBN 0-399-14458-7

LC 98-37344

In this mystery Boston private eye Spenser "is thrown by the lethal combination of sex (straight, gay, kinky) and politics (racial, sexual, academic) that erupts at a certain university in Cambridge when an African-American professor is implicated in the suicide of a militantly gay graduate student. In a situation that adds to his discomposure, Spenser finds himself being sexually hounded by a woman whom he has just rescued from the similarly unhealthy attentions of a former boyfriend." NY Times Book Rev

Parker, Robert B.

Melancholy baby. Putnam 2004 296p $24.95

ISBN 0-399-15218-0

LC 2004-50377

"Boston P.I. Sunny Randall is unhappy to learn that the ex-husband she still loves is getting married to someone else. Her life seemingly a mess, Sunny seeks the help of psychiatrist Susan Silverman. In between sessions that probe her relationship with her insufferable mother and beloved father, Sunny works on the case of Sarah Markham, a distraught 21-year-old woman who wants to track down her biological parents. The only trouble is that the couple who raised her claim she's theirs but refuse to take a DNA test to prove it. Sunny soon learns that Sarah's parents have lied about their past. . . . Parker, as always, leavens his story with sly wit while relying on dialog to advance the plot and develop character." Libr J

Parker, Robert B.

Night passage. Putnam 1997 322p $21.95

ISBN 0-399-14304-1

LC 97-6901

This mystery features "complex, expertly shaded relationships, especially romantic, as Jesse flails and fails at loving both his ex-wife and his new girlfriend. The most powerful romance here, though, is between Parker and the written word." Publ Wkly

Parker, Robert B.

Now and then. G. P. Putnam's Sons 2007 296p $25.95

ISBN 978-0-399-15441-6; 0-399-15441-8

LC 2007-23056

In this "addition to the series, the troubled client is a husband who feels his wife has been behaving bizarrely.

Spenser thinks she's probably having an affair, and through the magic of a planted listening device, he presents the worried husband with the damning evidence. The device has also picked up that the wife's lover is involved in a group called Last Hope, which turns out to be a kind of brokerage outlet for terrorists looking for equipment and other terrorists. The case has moved from the kind of private-eye work that Spenser finds sleazy to one with horrific ramifications. The story itself makes compelling reading on its own, but Parker, as usual, spikes it with caustic wit and the interplay between Spenser and his longtime love, Susan. And here he ups the ante by calling on Spenser to use all his brain and brawn to protect Susan. Terrific." Booklist

Parker, Robert B.

Painted ladies. G.P. Putnam's Sons 2010 291p $26.95

ISBN 978-0-399-15685-4; 0-399-15685-2

LC 2010-20027

"The focus on Susan comes at the expense of the plot, which, as Spenser novels go, is fairly pedestrian. . . . The story gives us extended looks at two of the most-beloved Spenser side characters, homicide Capt. Martin Quirk and Sgt. Frank Belson, as well as brief nods to many of the others who have stood at Spenser's side in the past — Hawk, Vinnie, Chollo, Lee Farrell, Epstein, Tedy Sapp, the Grey Man. Mostly, though, what Painted Ladies gives us is Spenser being Spenser. And he couldn't do that without Susan." Chicago Sun-Times

Parker, Robert B.

Paper doll. Putnam 1993 223p

LC 92-30528

"Mr. Parker has trimmed his language and characterizations right down to the knuckle to tell this poignant story about the false fronts that people put up to shield themselves from shame. There's no flab on Spenser, either." N Y Times Book Rev

Parker, Robert B.

Perchance to dream; Robert B. Parker's sequel to Raymond Chandler's The big sleep. Putnam 1991 271p

LC 90-47004

"Parker plots with little more scope and linear logic than Chandler ever managed, and he fires off enough smart-ass one-liners to keep most readers happy. It's true, he never ventures near the subterranean emotional depths that Chandler would occasionally explore, but, after all, sequels—even when, they're written by the same person—rarely match the originals." Booklist

Parker, Robert B.

Potshot. Putnam 2001 294p

ISBN 0-399-14710-1

LC 00-68342

"Spenser takes on the job of clearing out a gang of 'mountain trash' who are intimidating the residents of Potshot, Arizona. Even the supremely resourceful Spenser needs a little help with this one, so he drafts six of his compadres from previous adventures." Booklist

Parker, Robert B.
Resolution. G.P. Putnam's Sons 2008 292p $25.95

ISBN 978-0-399-15504-8; 0-399-15504-X

LC 2008-6589

In this sequel to Appaloosa "narrator and hired gun Everitt Hitch takes a job as lookout in Amos Wolfson's Blackfoot Saloon and, in short order, guns down local upstart Koy Wickman and stands up for the town's beleaguered prostitutes. Without fully intending it, he creates a haven of orderliness amid the chaos of sheriff-less Resolution. But larger forces are at work as Eamon O'Malley, competing with Wolfson for control of Resolution, hires freelance thugs Cato and Rose to replace Wickman. Lest Everitt end up outnumbered, his old friend Virgil Cole turns up just as Wolfson and O'Malley amass armies for a decisive battle. . . . Though the plot meanders its way to a too-fast climax, Parker's dialogue is snappy and his not-a-word-wasted scenes suit this Spartan western." Publ Wkly

Parker, Robert B.
Rough weather. G.P. Putnam's Sons 2008 294p $26.95

ISBN 978-0-399-15519-2; 0-399-15519-8

LC 2008-33702

"The familiar elements here include the child in distress, the wealthy with their own agenda, the killer with a code of honour, and an almost interminable repetition of the Spenser-Susan-Hawk mutual self-appreciation society. I'm not sure if Parker figures he's got to reprise the psychology between this triangle, . . . but he does and they do at great length here, to the detriment of what is otherwise a pretty interestingly plotted book. . . . Parker remains the master of the easy-reading, compelling, thriller." Crime Time

Parker, Robert B.
School days. Putnam 2005 295p $24.95

ISBN 0-399-15323-3

LC 2005-74690

"A wealthy grandmother hires Spenser to clear her 17-year-old grandson of being the coconspirator and co-killer in a school shooting at a private school that has left five students, a teacher, and an administrator dead. The boy's buddy has named him, and he has confessed to the crime. Everyone–police, school officials, the defense lawyer, and the immediate family–has given up on the kid, but Spenser has never seen a slammed door he didn't long to break down. Soon he's questioning everyone in the kid's circle, looking for the chink in that slammed door. Along the way, he rummages through all sorts of closets in the privileged world of the private school, turning up links to the underworld." Booklist

Parker, Robert B.
Sea change. Putnam 2006 295p $24.95

ISBN 0-399-15267-9

LC 2004-43150

"The body of an unidentified woman is found in a cove off the Massachusetts village of Paradise, where Jesse Stone, former L.A. homicide detective, is now chief of police. With no clues and a bevy of nonlocals in town for the annual sailboat competition, Stone must use every resource at his disposal to find out who the woman was, what happened to her, and why no one has reported her missing. . . . Parker is a master at creating memorable characters and crime stories that are inevitably tied to social issues of some importance." Libr J

Parker, Robert B.
Shrink rap. Putnam 2002 304p $24.95

ISBN 0-399-14930-9

LC 2002-24826

The Sunny Randall novel "has the Boston private eye on a national book tour with a best-selling author who is being stalked by her former husband, an unethical and possibly unhinged psychiatrist. The situation proves ideal for Parker's patented brand of knowing humor, yielding glossary snapshots of dithering book dealers, dollar-driven publishers and awe-struck fans." N Y Times Book Rev

Parker, Robert B.
Sixkill. G. P. Putnam's Sons 2011 293p map $26.95

ISBN 978-0-399-15726-4; 0-399-15726-3

LC 2010-48041

In this mystery, "a young woman is found dead in a Hollywood star's Boston hotel room. Looks like murder, smells like murder, but something doesn't sit right with police captain Quirk — he prefers surety, so he asks Spenser to nose around. The star, Jumbo Nelson, a self-absorbed pig, rubs everyone the wrong way but insists he didn't kill her. Jumbo's bodyguard, a Cree Indian named Zebulon Sixkill, first gets thumped by Spenser and then adopted by him like a big puppy. Spenser helps him turn his life around and gets a new temporary sidekick. . . . The ending is typical A-Grade Parker. Things gleaned earlier in the book coalesce when another piece of info triggers a connection, and when that happens, Spenser sets into motion a trap that nets the truth. Plus he has a word or two with the story's true villain. The story has the depth of a puddle, but it's a well-designed puddle, so when it ripples, the clean, steady rolling of the waves is like a shimmering poem." Chicago Sun-Times

Parker, Robert B.
Small vices. Putnam 1997 308p $21.95

ISBN 0-399-14244-4

LC 96-9827

"Mr. Parker has written a powerful piece about the defeat and reclamation of a hero, but I wouldn't say that Spenser's dance with death teaches the old knight to act his age. . . . By virtue of his mythic death and rebirth, he has defied mortality altogether and become like some fertility god who lowers himself into the ground each winter and comes roaring back to life each spring." N Y Times Book Rev

Parker, Robert B.
★ **Taming** a sea-horse; a Spenser novel. Delacorte Press/Seymour Lawrence 1986 250p

LC 85-29297

Spenser is "in grave danger on an all but unpaid quest to avenge the deaths of a prostitute he met briefly and a pimp he disliked. He confronts slick mob bosses, two-bit thugs and corrupt financiers, relying on his wits but not fearing to apply a little muscle." Time

Parker, Robert B.

Thin air. Putnam 1995 293p

LC 94-39046

Spenser's "friend and ultradeadly ally, Hawk, is off in Burma, leaving Spenser on his own when longtime pal Frank Belson of Boston Homicide needs help. Belson's beautiful young bride, Lisa St. Claire, has disappeared. When Belson is wounded in an ambush that may be related to Lisa's disappearance, Spenser undertakes the search." Booklist

Parker, Robert B.

Trouble in Paradise. Putnam 1998 324p $22.95

ISBN 0-399-14433-1

LC 98-7354

This novel finds Jesse Stone, "the chief of police of modest Paradise, Mass., battling a ruthless gang of thieves even as he jousts with personal demons. Two parallel plotlines tell the story. One follows career criminal James Macklin and his moll, Faye, and their planning and subsequent execution of the heist of all the money and valuables on superrich Stiles Island, which is connected by bridge to Paradise. Meanwhile, there's Stone, a cool customer who's not afraid to step on wealthy toes but who can't get his love life in order and can barely control his taste for booze. . . . Stone's romantic entanglements, particularly his troubled relationship with his ex-wife, add texture to the novel." Publ Wkly

Parker, Robert B.

Walking shadow. Putnam 1994 270p

LC 94-5127

Boston PI Spenser "encounters danger, venality and plenty of comic material in this . . . tale spanning the worlds of experimental theater and illegal immigration. While he'd rather be at work renovating the old farmhouse that he and his lover, psychiatrist Susan, have bought in nearby Concord, Spenser agrees to find out who is following the Artistic Director of the Port City Theater Company, on whose board of directors Susan sits." Publ Wkly

Parker, Robert B.

Widow's walk. Putnam 2002 294p

ISBN 0-399-14845-0

LC 2001-48771

"Attorney Rita Fiore, who's worked with the Boston PI before, hires Spenser to find out if her new client, Mary Smith, . . . indeed shot to death her husband, banker and Mayflower descendant Nathan Smith, as the evidence indicates. . . . The writing is as clean as fresh ice, and from the opening sentence ('I think she's probably guilty,' Rita Fiore said to me), it's clear that readers are in the hands of a vet who knows what he's doing." Publ Wkly

Parker, T. Jefferson

Black water. Hyperion 2002 338p

ISBN 0-7868-6804-X

LC 2001-51903

"Merci Rayborn, homicide detective for the Orange County, California, sheriff's department, has a crime scene that's a puzzler. And it's going to be very high profile—it's in an upscale enclave of million-dollar estates, and one of the victims is a cop. Gwen Wildcraft is dead, and her husband, Archie, is unconscious with a severe head wound. Wildcraft is a patrol officer with the department, and his gun appears to be the murder weapon. Merci's superiors would prefer a quick call of murder-suicide, but her instincts tell her that's the wrong conclusion. . . . A thoughtful, multilayered tale in which crime is a catalyst rather than the centerpiece." Booklist

Parker, T. Jefferson

The **blue** hour. Hyperion 1999 359p $23.95

ISBN 0-7868-6288-2

LC 98-43135

"Solid police work, beefed up with some ingenious devices from Parker's bottomless bag of tricks, makes it all come out right—but not before the wondrously weird characters have taken this lurid plot to its outer limits." N Y Times Book Rev

Parker, T. Jefferson

California girl. Morrow 2004 370p $24.95

ISBN 0-060-56236-6

A mystery set in 1960s Southern California. "The Becker boys (Andy the homicide reporter, Nick the cop, and David the minister; Clay was killed in Vietnam) grew up near the Vonns, a troubled, abusive family burdened with more than its share of tragedy. When 19-year-old beauty queen Janell Vonn, the essence of a California girl, is found beheaded in the abandoned SunBlesst packing house, the Becker brothers begin their separate quests to find her killer, finally bringing him to justice while realizing redemption for themselves. But 40 years after a conviction, it becomes apparent that the Beckers were wrong, very wrong. Drenched in lust, love, betrayal, and unfulfilled promise, California Girl features masterly plotting, smart prose, and memorable characters." Libr J

Parker, T. Jefferson

Cold pursuit. Hyperion 2003 360p $23.95

ISBN 0-7868-6805-8

LC 2002-32940

"The murder of retired San Diego Port Commissioner and local politician Pete Braga falls in the lap of homicide detective Tom McMichael, whose family has a multigenerational feud going with the Bragas. Parker makes the most of a standard mystery device here—murder driven by a motive from the distant past—but the real joy of the novel is its remarkably evocative prose, which flows seamlessly from lyrical descriptions of rainy San Diego to crisp, no-nonsense dialogue." Booklist

Parker, T. Jefferson

The **fallen**; a novel. William Morrow 2006 323p $24.95

ISBN 0060562382

LC 2005047934

"This stand-alone classic police procedural, replete with its portrait of big-city crime and power-hungry politicians, follows a recognizable storyline. However, its lively writing, well-paced plot, rounded characters (from call girls to shady politicians), and twists stand out." Bookmarks Magazine

Parker, T. Jefferson

L.A. outlaws; a novel. Dutton 2008 372p $25.95

ISBN 978-0-525-95055-4; 0-525-95055-9

LC 2007-33722

"Parker writes with an understanding of the West's essential character: in Outlaws, he casts Los Angeles as an eternally sprawling, brawling camp town, populated by bandits and bigots, the quick and the dead, where the poor who once rendered tallow now work the deep fryer at KFC. . . . His concise prose, at once low-key and lyrical, plays almost like cowboy poetry." Los Angeles Times

Parker, T. Jefferson

Laguna heat. St. Martin's Press 1985 342p

LC 85-10055

"The hero is Tom Shephard, 'the new and sole member of the Laguna Beach Police Homicide Division.' Normally, one man would be all that is needed; there are not many homicides in Laguna Beach. But suddenly a sadistic murderer is loose, burning bodies after mutilating them. Shephard, an experienced cop, gets a lead very fast, is attacked and hurt, finds his home vandalized and goes through other harrowing experiences, many psychological." N Y Times Book Rev

"Parker's narrative is a bit heavy-handed, but his ultimately satisfying novel delivers deep and sensitive characterizations." Booklist

Parker, T. Jefferson

Little Saigon. St. Martin's Press 1988 354p

LC 88-11586

"Chuck Frye, a surf bum who has recently failed at journalism, business and marriage, lives in the shadow of his war-hero brother Bennett, and their father, a wealthy real-estate tycoon. Bennett's Vietnamese wife is a singer whose protest music has made her a heroine among anticommunists and Asian expatriates. When she is kidnapped during a performance, Chuck joins the search for her, hoping to end his estrangement from the Frye clan. But the more he learns about the crime's motive—politics, gang warfare or revenge are all possibilities—the more intently his family tries to shut him out of the investigation." Publ Wkly

Parker, T. Jefferson

Pacific beat. St. Martin's Press 1991 364p

LC 90-27411

"John Weir, an ex-sheriff's department employee, and brother-in-law Raymond battle corrupt police, development-at-all-cost advocates, and a known sex offender when they try to find the murderer of John's beloved sister. Splayed against the coastal community of Newport Beach, California, where oldtime residents hope to elect a 'slow-growth' candidate, their investigation reveals ever-deeper layers of deception. This exciting, multidimensional plot should grab even the most demanding mystery reader." Libr J

Parker, T. Jefferson

Silent Joe. Hyperion 2001 341p

ISBN 0-7868-6728-0

LC 00-53938

"Joe Trona is a dutiful son, but horrible facial scars have made him an outcast. He lived in an orphanage until he was

adopted at five by Will Trona, a powerful politician in Southern California's Orange County. As a hulking teenager and later as a young man, Joe became Will's right-hand man—running errands, extracting revenge on enemies, protecting his flank—all the while living a lonely life because of his disfigurement. One night, Joe drops his guard for a moment, and Will is gunned down. Despite aggressive investigations by the FBI and sheriff's department, Joe seeks his own vengeance." Publ Wkly

"A complex mix of seemingly unconnected plot lines, vivid characterization, and real mystery merge to form a truly satisfying thriller." Libr J

Parker, T. Jefferson

Storm runners. HarperCollins 2007 370p $25.95

ISBN 978-0-06-085423-2; 0-06-085423-2

"In Southern California, as San Diego weather lady Frankie Hatfield puts it, 'Rain is life!' Rain is also raw power in the land of avocadoes and sod farms. When Hatfield stumbles upon a family secret that allows her to control the rain, that discovery brings her unfathomable power with potentially deadly consequences. P.I. Matt Stromsoe is battling with his own demons—his wife and child have been murdered, and he's seeking redemption—and he willingly accepts an assignment to protect Hatfield. The case takes him from fragrant orange groves in the San Diego hills to the cold cement of Pelican Bay State Prison. Parker's trademark is the ability to create real characters—tangible, flawed, and heroic—and Stromsoe follows the tradition." Libr J

Parker, T. Jefferson

Where serpents lie. Hyperion 1998 432p $23.95

ISBN 0-7868-6287-4

LC 97-2633

A thriller set in "Orange County, California, where cop Terry Naughton, head of Crimes Against Youth, a division he helped create, is fiercely trying to track down a creepy pedophile who calls himself Horridus . . . before he kills one of the young girls that he has kidnapped. It seems that besides child pornography and rape, Horridus is also into snakes—really big, hungry snakes—and there's evidence that he has used these 'pets' to dispose of victims in the past. . . . This taut police procedural mixes high suspense with believable characters; it's a real page-turner." Libr J

Parkhurst, Carolyn

★ The dogs of Babel. Little, Brown 2003 264p $21.95

ISBN 0-316-16868-8

LC 2002-43644

"As Paul slips into ever more desperate behavior, we hear an account of his and Lexy's courtship and marriage—the tender, tentative union of two damaged people. But then Paul contacts a man convicted of operating on dogs to install vocal chords, and what had been a poignant, affecting tale turns truly frightening . . . . Parkhurst delivers a remarkable debut in quiet, authoritative prose." Libr J

Parkhurst, Carolyn

Lost and found. Little, Brown and Co. 2006 292p hardcover o.p. pa $13.99

ISBN 978-0-316-15638-7; 0-316-15638-8; 978-0-316-06639-6 pa; 0-316-06639-7 pa

LC 2005-029741

This "novel focuses on several characters competing on an Amazing Race-like reality show called Lost and Found, where teams of two travel from destination to destination following enigmatic clues and collecting various items in hopes of winning the game. Laura wants to connect with her sullen teenage daughter, Cassie, after a traumatic experience highlighted the distance between them. Justin and Abby believe they have cast off their homosexual urges in favor of a traditional Christian marriage, but the game offers unexpected tests for their resolution. Carl and Jeff are two middle-aged, recently divorced brothers looking for adventure. Juliet and Dallas are former child stars seeking to recapture fame and willing to do just about anything to achieve that end." Booklist

"Older teens may find that this book presses just the right buttons." SLJ

Parkhurst, Carolyn

The **nobodies** album; a novel. Doubleday 2010 313p $25.95

ISBN 978-0-385-52769-9; 0-385-52769-1

LC 2009-41886

"Novelist Octavia Frost is used to inventing unlikely plots, but when her famous rocker son is accused of bludgeoning his girlfriend to death, she finds her life is turning into one of her own books. A previously dormant maternal instinct drives her to attempt to prove her son's innocence and, in the process, close the wounds that have kept them from speaking to each other for four years. Excerpts from Frost's novels punctuate the low-key, introspective murder-mystery narrative, offering a pinhole glimpse into the mind of a fascinating woman for whom life and fiction are stitched tightly together." Entertainment Wkly

Parkinson, Heather

Across open ground; a novel. Bloomsbury Pub. 2002 248p $23.95

ISBN 1-58234-243-1

LC 2001-56527

"The narrative is often powerful, . . . with a concern for female characters and a tenderness generally absent from more conventional books about this era in the American West." Publ Wkly

Parks, Brad

The **girl** next door; a mystery. Brad Parks. Minotaur Books 2012 326 p. (hbk.) $24.99

ISBN 1429949996; 031266768X; 9780312667689; 9781429949996

LC 2011040880

Carter Ross mysteries

In this book by Brad Parks, "Carter Ross's insignificant decision to write a feature obit about hit-and-run victim Nancy Marino, a hard-working waitress and deliverer of the very newspaper for which he works, plunges him into a far more sinister . . . story. . . . Quickly discovering there was more to the middle-aged everywoman than met the eye, including her role as a leader in her union's acrimonious labor dispute at the paper, Ross starts to suspect her death was no accident." (Publishers Weekly)

Parks, Gordon

★ The **learning** tree. Harper & Row 1963 303p

"At 12 years of age Newt is awakening to the world around him in his small town of Cherokee Flats, Kansas, in the 1920s. There is the impact of a first sexual experience and a first love, and because he is a Negro, special responsibility of behavior when one individual may represent an entire group in the eyes of the community." Shapiro. Fic for Youth. 3d edition

Parks, Suzan-Lori

Getting mother's body; a novel. {by} Suzanne Lori. Random House 2003 257p $23.95

ISBN 1-400-06022-2

LC 2002-31762

"Set in the summer of 1963, and recounted in a slow, Southern drawl befitting the mood, the story unravels from a myriad of viewpoints, including the no-good custom coffin salesman who's fathered Billy's unborn baby, the one-legged neighbor in love with Billy, and her deceased mother's feisty lesbian lover." Publ Wkly

Parks, Tim

Cleaver; a novel. Arcade Publishing 2008 316p $25

ISBN 978-1-55970-855-5

LC 2007-22844

First published 2006 in the United Kingdom

"British journalist Harold Cleaver—egotist, incurable philanderer, unapologetic gourmand—scores a career high by humiliating the U.S. president in a televised interview. But his son has just published a scene-stealing roman à clef. Retreating to an isolated cabin in the Alps without TV or cell-phone reception, Cleaver engages his son, the president, and a doll (yes, a doll) named Olga in intense, imaginary debates. It's much saner than it sounds, as Tim Parks draws a lively critique of modern media out of Cleaver's soul-searching rants and a surprisingly affectionate portrait of self-reflection and forgiveness in Cleaver." Entertainment Wkly

Parks, Tim

Destiny. Arcade Pub. 2000 248p $24.95

ISBN 1-559-70517-5

LC 00-130423

First published 1999 in the United Kingdom

"As Burton's stream of consciousness approaches disintegration, he finally admits truths about himself and his behavior in what becomes a deeply affecting portrait of a man in mental anguish." Publ Wkly

Parks, Tim

Rapids; a novel. Arcade Pub. 2006 246p $24

ISBN 1-55970-811-5

LC 2005-29292

First published 2005 in the United Kingdom

"Parks is prolific, and his books are written with a compelling urgency and energy. In Rapids this urgency—and the varied cast—sometimes lead to narratorial splashiness: big ideas and themes are introduced only for some of them to be left underdeveloped. Yet the book has great strengths. It is thrillingly paced. Vince is a monumental character, difficult and rewarding. And Parks is constantly alert to the nuances of everyday patter, a clever and magnanimous describer of ordinary people." London Rev Books

Parris, S. J.

Sacrilege; a novel. S.J. Parris. Doubleday 2012 423 p.

ISBN 0385535473; 9780385535472

LC 2011047763

This historical thriller by S. J. Parris is "set in sixteenth-century England and centered on the highly secretive cult of Saint Thomas Becket. . . . London, summer of 1584: Radical philosopher, ex-monk, and spy Giordano Bruno suspects he is being followed by an old enemy. He is shocked to discover that his pursuer is in fact Sophia Underhill, a young woman with whom he was once in love. When Bruno learns that Sophia has been accused of murdering her husband, a prominent magistrate in Canterbury, he agrees to do anything he can to help clear her name. . . . Bruno begins to uncover unsuspected secrets that point to the dead man being part of a larger and more dangerous plot in the making." (Publisher's note)

Parry, Richard

The **winter** wolf; Wyatt Earp in Alaska. Forge 1996 380p $24.95

ISBN 0-312-86017-X

LC 96-18269

"It's 1897, and the days of the OK Corral are a memory, but notoriety is still a burden for hard-up Wyatt Earp. He and his second wife, Josie, are heading north to Alaska to make their fortune in the gold rush. Circumstances conspire against him, however, and he must settle for law-related jobs. At every turn, he's wary that an old nemesis may be coming up behind him, but the greatest danger zeroing in on Earp is the son he didn't know he had." Booklist

"The inevitable confrontation between father and son packs genuine emotional wallop. Parry, who lives in Alaska, skillfully evokes both era and place." Publ Wkly

Parshall, Sandra

Bleeding through; Sandra Parshall. 1st ed. Poisoned Pen Press 2012 250 p. (ebook) $6.99; (hardcover: alk. paper) $24.95; (trade pbk.: alk. paper) $14.95

ISBN 9781615954124; 1464200297; 9781464200274; 9781464200298

LC 2012936476

Author Sandra Parshall tells the story of Rachel Goddard, "the northern Virginia veterinarian living with her beau, Deputy Sheriff Tom Bridger, and dealing with a case that literally hits too close to home. Shortly before her sister, Michelle, [comes to visit] . . . Rachel and Tom come across the body of missing law school student Shelley Beecher along a highway in rural Mason County . . . Meanwhile, Rachel struggles to rescue Michelle from a breakdown brought on by . . . a stalker who appears to have followed her from her Maryland home." (Publishers Weekly)

Parsons, Julie

Mary, Mary; a novel. Simon & Schuster 1999 299p $22.50

ISBN 0-684-85324-8

LC 98-33753

First published 1998 in the United Kingdom

"Parsons writes short, quickly paced scenes that raise the suspense level in taut increments, and her story is full of genuine surprises and fresh plot twists. While shocking, the novel's conclusion is powerful and convincing." Publ Wkly

Pasternak, Boris Leonidovich

★ **Doctor** Zhivago; [by] Boris Pasternak. Pantheon Bks. 1958 558p hardcover o.p.

First published 1957 in Italy

"The account of the life of a Russian intellectual, Yurii Zhivago, a doctor and a poet, during the first three decades of the 20th c. A broad epic picture of Russia is developed as the background to Zhivago's family life, his creative ecstasies, his love for Lara (another man's wife), his emotional upheavals, wanderings, and moments of happiness. Though the novel ends with Zhivago's decline and death as a result of what the author saw as the dehumanization of life that prevailed in the postrevolution years, the epilogue is full of expectations of the freedom that is to come." Ency of World Lit in the 20th Century

Patchett, Ann

Bel canto; a novel. HarperCollins Pubs. 2001 318p $25

ISBN 0-06-018873-1

LC 00-53671

Loosely based on the 1996 events in Lima, Peru, when members of the guerrilla group Tupac Amaru seized hostages at the residence of the Japanese ambassador, "Patchett's fourth novel is set in the vice-presidential mansion of an unnamed South American capital, where some 200 foreign diplomats, government officials and businessmen have gathered to celebrate the birthday of a Japanese electronics mogul and opera buff named Katsumi Hosokawa." (N Y Times Book Rev)

"An impoverished South American country hosts a birthday extravaganza for a Japanese industrialist in the hope of securing new foreign investment. The lure? An internationally renowned lyric soprano. Indeed, when Roxane Coss sings, even the ragtag terrorists who are about to flood through the air-conditioning vents and take the guests hostage hold their breath, transported by the beauty of her voice. Patchett's tragicomic novel—a fantasia of guns and Puccini and Red Cross negotiations—invokes the glorious, unreliable promises of art, politics, and love." New Yorker

Patchett, Ann

Run. HarperCollins Publishers 2007 295p $25.95

ISBN 978-0-06-134063-5; 0-06-134063-4

LC 2006-41297

"Ms. Patchett gives her readers much to contemplate when genetics, privilege, opportunity and nurture come into play. And to her credit she is neither vague nor reductive about any of these things; she creates a genuinely rich landscape of human possibility." N Y Times (Late N Y Ed)

Patchett, Ann

★ **State** of wonder. Harper 2011 353p $26.99
ISBN 978-0-06-204980-3; 0-06-204980-1
LC 2010-29229

"Dr. Marina Singh, a scientist with a Minnesota pharmaceutical company, is dispatched to the Amazon to investigate a colleague's death. Anders Eckman had been her research partner charged with finally confronting the elderly and elusive head of the Amazonian project, Dr. Annick Swenson. The women of the Lakashi tribe can bear babies throughout their lives. By scraping the bark from a grove of isolated trees with their teeth they are fertile unto death. Families of five generations are the norm. If a viable fertility drug can be synthesized and marketed, billions are to be made. But Swenson is so secretive as to make a paranoid seem transparent. An abrupt note informs the head office that Eck man died of a fever. That's all she wrote, not bothering to fill in any details of the enterprise in which the company is so heavily invested." N Y Daily News

Paton, Alan

Ah, but your land is beautiful. Scribner 1982 271p
ISBN 0-684-17336-0
LC 81-13547

First published 1981 in the United Kingdom

"Alan Paton's considerable practical life in South Africa aside, his place in the literature of social protest has been secured by his steady devotion to the ideal of the empathetic imagination in fiction." N Y Times Book Rev

Paton, Alan

★ **Cry,** the beloved country. Scribner Classics 2003 316p $28; pa $15
ISBN 0-7432-6195-X; 0-7432-6217-4 pa
First published 1948

"Reverend Kumalo, a black South African preacher, is called to Johannesburg to rescue his sister. There he learns that his son Absalom has been accused of murdering a young white attorney whose interests and sympathies had been with the natives. Despite this, the attorney's father comes to the aid of the minister to help the natives in their struggle to survive a drought." Shapiro. Fic for Youth. 3d edition

Paton, Alan

Tales from a troubled land. Scribner 1961 128p

"Most of the tales are told from the point of view of a compassionate white director of a boy's reformatory; however, one of the most moving concerns a native shepherd who, though innocent, becomes a victim when his employer is robbed." Booklist

Paton, Alan

Too late the phalarope. Scribner 1953 276p

"The book is written with superb simplicity. It is cadenced but unaffected; it will inevitably be called Biblical and yet there is no conscious parodying of scriptual prose. It flows relentlessly to its crisis, and sometimes we cry out at its power. The people are all clear and real, the South African backgrounds are colorfully and deeply etched. The conflicts are diverse but they all contribute to the basic struggle; father and son, races, languages, prejudices." Christ Sci Monit

Patterson, James

1st to die; a novel. Little, Brown 2001 424p $32
ISBN 0-316-66600-9
LC 00-61123

"The story opens in San Francisco with the gruesome murder of a bride and groom on their wedding night. Detective Lindsay Boxer is called to the scene, just after learning she is suffering from a rare and potentially life-threatening blood disease. For help with the case, she calls on her best friend, Claire, a medical examiner, and, reluctantly at first, Cindy, a newspaper reporter who is covering the story. . . . Patterson keeps up the suspense until the very last page." Booklist

Patterson, James

★ **Along** came a spider; a novel. Little, Brown 1993 435p
ISBN 0-316-69364-2
LC 92-24581

"Alex Cross, a black Washington, D.C., police detective with a Ph.D. in psychology, and Jezzie Flanagan, a white motorcycling Secret Service agent, become lovers as they work together to apprehend a chilling psychopath who has kidnapped two children from a posh private school. . . . Patterson's storytelling talent is in top form in this grisly escapist yarn." Libr J

Patterson, James

★ **Cat** & mouse; a novel. Little, Brown 1997 399p
ISBN 0-316-69329-4
LC 97-20277

Black Washington, D.C. detective/psychologist Alex Cross' "old nemesis, psychopath Gary Soneji, is dead set on killing Alex in the ugliest, most terrifying way he can devise, but first, he's decided to play a game of cat and mouse with his intended victim. In Europe, a sadistic torturer dubbed 'Mr. Smith' is on the loose, and if Soneji is the king of cat and mouse, Mr. Smith is the grand high emperor. Elusive and terrifying, he performs autopsies on his living victims. FBI Agent Thomas Pierce has been assigned to the Smith case, but he's come back to America especially to help Alex track down Soneji." Booklist

Patterson, James

Cross. Little, Brown and Co. 2006 393p $27.99
ISBN 978-0-316-15979-1; 0-316-15979-4
LC 2006-12929

"Even as the story whips by with incredible speed, Patterson manages to pack it full of suspense, emotion, and a resolution that, while perfectly satisfying, carries the author's trademark teaser hinting at the 'more' that surely will come." Booklist

Patterson, James

Four blind mice; a novel. Little, Brown 2002 387p $27.95
ISBN 0-316-69300-6
LC 2002-67540

"The action leads, as is Patterson's custom, to a firecracker string of climaxes; the finale finds Cross handcuffed and stripped naked in deep woods, about to be killed. Throughout, Patterson expertly balances the conspiratorial action with intriguing developments in Cross's domestic life." Publ Wkly

Patterson, James

Hide & seek; a novel. Little, Brown 1996 356p
ISBN 978-0316693868

LC 95-35928

"Beautiful Maggie Bradford seems to have it all: a successful career as a singer/songwriter, fame, money, and two precious children. However, she killed her first husband in self-defense and now she's in jail awaiting trial for the murder of her second husband, Will Shepherd, a charming, psychotic professional soccer player. At first, Maggie's marriage seems fine, but soon Will begins to act irrationally. The increasing tension comes to a head when Maggie comes to believe that Will has been sexually abusing her daughter, the resulting confrontation ends in Will's death and Maggie's arrest. Climaxing in Maggie's celebrity trial, this page-turner delivers a solid punch, complete with a surprise ending." Libr J

Patterson, James

I, Alex Cross. Little, Brown and Co. 2009 374p
$27.99
ISBN 978-0-316-01878-4; 0-316-01878-3

LC 2009-15513

In this installment Alex Cross takes on a serial killer known as Zeus. "Word that an estranged 24-year-old niece, Caroline Cross, has been murdered disturbs Cross's birthday party. To make that horror even worse, the killer fed Caroline's body through a wood chipper. Cross soon discovers that Caroline supported herself as a high-price escort for Washington, D.C.'s elite, and that other women who served similar clients have turned up missing. Cross's investigation soon attracts the attention of the feds, and he concludes that Zeus is better connected than most of the psychopaths he's brought to justice." Publ Wkly

Patterson, James

Jack and Jill; a novel. Little, Brown 1996 432p
ISBN 0-316-69371-5

LC 96-8037

This novel features "African American psychologist-turned-detective Alex Cross. . . . Alex is troubled when a young child is murdered near the school his son attends and frightened when the murderer strikes again. On the other side of town, away from the scary inner-city D.C. streets, a pair of killers who call themselves Jack and Jill are terrorizing the movers and shakers by murdering a series of high-profile people. . . . A fast-paced, electric story that is utterly believable." Booklist

Patterson, James

Kiss the girls; a novel. Little, Brown 1995 451p
ISBN 0-316-69370-7

LC 94-14177

"'Casanova' works the East Coast, 'The Gentleman Caller' works the West Coast, and these two serial killers might just be working together. Washed-up Washington, D.C., police detective Alex Cross gets involved when his niece is abducted." Libr J

Patterson, James

London bridges; a novel. Little, Brown and Co 2004 391p $27.95
ISBN 0-316-71059-8

LC 2004-16752

"Terrorists have seized the worlds largest cities. London, Washington, DC, New York, and Frankfurt will be destroyed, unless their demands are met. . . . Heading up the investigation by the FBI, CIA, and Interpol, Alex Cross is stunned when surveillance photos show Geoffrey Shafer, the Weasel, near one of the bombing sites. He senses the presence of the Wolf as well, the most vicious predator he has ever battled." Publisher's note

"The book is a model of economy, delivering a full package of suspense, emotion and characterization in a minimum number of words." Publ Wkly

Patterson, James

Pop! goes the weasel; a novel. Little, Brown 1999 423p $26.95
ISBN 0-316-69328-6

LC 99-21473

"If Shafer is almost too good to be true—another fictional psychopath with infinite resources—Patterson is shrewd enough to show him making mistakes . . . as he comes apart at the seams. The killer is caught in the middle of the narrative, setting the scene for a bold courtroom drama." Publ Wkly

Patterson, James

Roses are red; a novel. Little, Brown 2000 400p
ISBN 0-316-69325-1

LC 00-28192

In this Alex Cross thriller set in Washington, D.C. a sociopath calling himself "the Mastermind" orchestrates a series of bank robberies, but he "isn't content to relieve the banks of their cash. He also has to torment the bankers by massacring their families when the mood strikes him. Having captured people's attention with these acts of cunning cruelty, the Mastermind pulls off a coup de théâtre when he hijacks a tour bus carrying the wives and children of insurance company executives and demands $30 million in ransom." N Y Times Book Rev

Patterson, James

Suzanne's diary for Nicholas; a novel. Little, Brown 2001 266p $28
ISBN 0-316-96944-3

LC 00-50707

"The story alternates between diary entries, written by a young wife and mother named Suzanne to her newborn son, Nicholas, and the present, as the diary is read by Kate, who has just been abandoned by her new love—who happens to be Matthew, the young husband in the diary. . . . How Kate, Matthew, and Suzanne connect in the beginning of the novel and what happens by the pretty predictable ending will entertain and please most readers." Libr J

Patterson, Kevin

Consumption; a novel. Nan A. Talese 2007 384p $25

ISBN 978-0-385-52074-4

LC 2006-36573

First published 2006 in Canada

"In the early sixties, the 'anachronistic malady' of tuberculosis haunts a small Inuit community in the Canadian Arctic. A child is taken from her family for treatment in Montreal and returns six years later, forever marked as unique by her hunger for the outside world and the scars of a brutal surgery. Meanwhile, an influx of white men—and modernity—has estranged the natives from the land and the traditions that enabled them to survive there. Sweeping in scale but microscopic in its portrait of dislocated lives, this début novel finds its most compelling voice in the rueful meditations of a blundering, morphine-addicted American doctor, marooned by his own volition at the edge of the world." New Yorker

Patterson, Richard North

Balance of power. Ballantine Bks. 2003 611p $27.95

ISBN 0-345-45017-5

LC 2003-51848

"This complex novel has a fascinating debate at its heart. To his credit, Patterson has done his research, and though it's clear which side he's on, he does a good job of presenting all the arguments." Booklist

Patterson, Richard North

Conviction; a novel. Random House 2005 465p $25.95

ISBN 0-345-45019-1

LC 2004-51175

"Fifteen years ago, brothers Rennell and Payton Price were sentenced to death for the brutal murder of nine-year-old Thuy Sen. Now, as Rennell's scheduled execution approaches, pro bono lawyer Theresa Peralta Page (also seen in Eyes of a Child), along with her attorney husband and attorney stepson, takes his final appeal all the way to the Supreme Court. At the same time, Theresa deals with her troubled teenage daughter and her own guilt. While it is apparent that the author opposes the death penalty, Patterson nevertheless provides compelling evidence for both sides of the argument." Libr J

Patterson, Richard North

Dark lady; a novel. Knopf 1999 384p $25.95

ISBN 0-679-45043-2

LC 99-23565

"Patterson is familiar with the civic shenanigans that can destroy a community, and he draws wisely on the history and geography of Cleveland to portray a city struggling to escape its bondage to organized crime, racial conflict and the entrenched corruption of its elected officials." N Y Times Book Rev

Patterson, Richard North

★ **Degree** of guilt. Knopf 1993 547p

LC 92-54446

"TV journalist Mary Carelli shoots and kills famous writer Mark Ransom in his hotel room, claiming that Ransom tried to rape her. The man she asks to defend her is Christopher Paget, with whom she has had a complicated relationship: Paget is the father of Mary's son, who lives with Paget and whom Mary has not seen for eight years. Paget agrees to defend Mary to protect his son." Libr J

"For those not put off by the sudsy plotting and the People magazine cast, the legal machinations are satisfactorily intricate." Time

Patterson, Richard North

Eclipse; a novel. Henry Holt and Company 2009 369p $26

ISBN 978-0-8050-8772-7; 0-8050-8772-9

LC 2008-17386

"Eclipse aspires to be any number of books: a novel of political intrigue, an international conspiracy thriller, a courtroom drama, a romance, even a straightforward murder mystery. . . . To Patterson's credit, the novel succeeds on all counts." Washington Post Book World

Patterson, Richard North

Eyes of a child. Knopf 1995 593p

LC 94-28630

"Local San Francisco politics and an accusation of child molestation against Paget's teenage son contribute to this complex brew, in which . . . narrative skill and legal know-how take precedence over characterization and credibility." Publ Wkly

Patterson, Richard North

The final judgment. Knopf 1995 437p

ISBN 0-679-42989-1

LC 95-35083

"San Francisco lawyer Carolyn Masters, featured in Eyes of a Child returns as this story's central character, drawn back to her New England home on the eve of her presidential appointment to the Court of Appeals. Her young niece Brett is accused of brutally murdering the boy she loves, and Caroline comes to her defense. Caroline has had no contact with her family in years and now must confront the sister and father who fatally betrayed Caroline's own young love 20 years before." Libr J

"Filled with surprises, 'The Final Judgment' uses a backdrop of courtroom fireworks to tell a tightly wound story of loss and betrayal." N Y Times Book Rev

Patterson, Richard North

No safe place. Knopf 1998 497p

ISBN 978-0679450429

LC 98-14573

"The main character, Kerry Kilcannon, is an Irish Catholic U.S. senator, reminiscent of the Kennedy brothers. Embroiled in a close campaign with the vice president for the Democratic presidential nomination, Kilcannon struggles to maintain his honesty and upright values in a sleazy world where everything depends on image and the proper spin. At the same time, a militant right-to-lifer vows to kill Kilcannon for his pro-choice stance on abortion. Throughout the constant twists and turns of the plot, Patterson builds realistic supporting characters and brings to life the surrealistic world of a presidential campaign." Libr J

Patterson, Richard North

Protect and defend; a novel. Knopf 2000 549p il

ISBN 0-679-45044-0

LC 00-712975

"When the Chief Justice drops dead at the inauguration of Kerry Kilcannon, the charismatic new president appoints federal judge Caroline Masters to the high court and begins assembling a strategy to get her approved by a contentious Congress. Meanwhile, a pregnant teen with a damaged fetus goes to court to challenge her parents, who helped to pass a new parental-consent law that prevents her from having an abortion. The two events become intertwined. . . . Patterson skillfully juggles a large cast of characters and controversies." SLJ

Patterson, Richard North

Silent witness. Knopf 1997 493p

ISBN 0-679-45040-8

LC 96-36672

"Silent Witness is more than a typical legal thriller; it is a story about the growth of two men and how each one deals with and subsequently changes after experiencing the anguish and the introspection that come from being accused of murder." Booklist

Patterson, Victoria

This vacant paradise; a novel. Counterpoint 2011 309p $25

ISBN 978-1-58243-645-6; 1-58243-645-2

"In debt and unmarried, Esther Wilson works at a clothing boutique and lives with her wealthy grandmother, Eileen, whose financial generosity is orchestrated to 'encourage dependence.' Terrified of poverty, Esther is in the midst of securing a proposal from an unattractive but wealthy heir, but she blows it. Enter ex-boyfriend Charlie Murphy, who, though from a well-off family, is a liberal-minded sociology professor at the local community college, and therefore an object of Eileen's derision. Charlie takes it upon himself to emancipate Esther from the chains of vapid privilege. . . . As an acerbic commentary on mid-'90s Southern Californian excess, the novel walks a fine line between critic and unintentional participant—commentaries on the retrograde position of Orange County women jostle against overindulgent physical description—though Patterson's Southern California has echoes of Nathanael West and early Bruce Wagner." Publ Wkly

Pattison, Eliot

The lord of death; Eliot Pattison. Soho 2009 314 p. (alk. paper) $24

ISBN 1569475792; 9781569475799

LC 2009005421

In this book by Eliot Pattison, part of the Inspector Shan series, "two women -- a Chinese minister and an outspoken American hiker -- have been shot and left for dead at the side of the road. . . . Shan questions revered soothsayers and surly colonels in search of answers, ever aware that the survival of his son Ko -- currently imprisoned in a Chinese asylum -- depends on his success." (Booklist)

Pattison, Eliot

The skull mantra. St. Martin's Minotaur 1999 403p $24.95

ISBN 0-312-20478-7

LC 99-23847

"Sentenced to penal servitude in Tibet, Shan, a disgraced prosecutor, is assigned instead to complete a pro forma investigation of the gruesome murder of a Chinese official. The party line is that dissident Tibetan monks are to blame, but Shan quickly realizes that the truth lies in other directions." Libr J

"Set against a background that is alternately bleak and blazingly beautiful, this is at once a topnotch thriller and a substantive look at Tibet under siege." Publ Wkly

Patton, Frances Gray

Good morning, Miss Dove; illustrated by Garrett Price. Dodd, Mead 1954 218p

Miss Dove had taught geography in the same school for thirty-five years; some people in town thought that was too long. Miss Dove was a stern disciplinarian with old-fashioned ideas and ideals, but on the April day when she was stricken in the classroom the whole town came to realize how much Miss Dove had meant in their lives

"Leavened with wit and sound common sense, written with an unerring rightness of touch, the whole book rings with the truth about human nature in its nicer aspects." N Y Her Trib Books

Paul, Bart

Under Tower Peak; by Bart Paul. 1st ed. Arcade Publishing 2013 288 p. (hardcover) $23.95

ISBN 1611458366; 9781611458367

LC 2012043982

In this novel, by Bart Paul, "Tommy Smith has returned to his former life as a cowboy and wilderness guide in California's Sierra Nevada, hoping to reclaim the simplicity of his youth and heal the wounds the world can't see. When, high on a mountain pass, he and his partner find the wrecked plane of a billionaire adventurer who disappeared months earlier, a seemingly innocent act triggers a breathtaking cycle of violence that threatens Tommy's world." (Publisher's note)

Paul, Jim

Elsewhere in the land of parrots. Harcourt 2003 405p $24

ISBN 0-15-100495-1

LC 2003-7918

When reclusive poet David Huntington "receives an exotic parrot from his father, his preferred life of airless solitude is turned upside down, and in frustration David soon tosses it out his apartment window. Little does he know that through that open window his carefully controlled and spiritless existence has begun its exit as well. David's guilty search for the bird serendipitously leads him into an adventure outside his quiet apartment and all the way to the swamplands of Ecuador, where a young researcher named Fern happens to be studying the same type of parrot in its native habitat." Libr J

"Paul's story successfully weds an odd theme —the ethology of parrots—to the perennial fascinations of human courtship behavior." Publ Wkly

Pausch, Jai

Dream new dreams; reimagining my life after loss. Jai Pausch. Crown Archetype 2012 xi, 228 p.p $24.00

ISBN 0307888509; 9780307888501

LC 2011046264

This book presents a memoir by "the widow of Randy Pausch, who wrote the bestseller 'The Last Lecture' and died of pancreatic cancer in 2008. . . . [Jai] Pausch begins by recounting the beginnings of her relationship with her husband . . . They married, started a family and were living a normal life when Randy was diagnosed with cancer. Despite surgery and chemotherapy, the cancer recurred, and his case was deemed terminal. 'The Last Lecture' made Randy's final months unusual, but the publication of the book and the activity regarding it are largely in the background of the overall story. With her husband's death, the author was left to parent three young children and to find new direction in her life while in her early 40s." (Kirkus Reviews)

Pavone, Chris

★ The **expats**; a novel. Chris Pavone. Crown Publishers 2012 327 p. (hardback) $26

ISBN 0307956350; 9780307956354; 9780307956378

LC 2011046207

This book tells the story of "Kate Moore [who] is a working mother, struggling to make ends meet, to raise children, to keep a spark in her marriage . . . and to maintain an increasingly unbearable life-defining secret. So when her husband is offered a lucrative job in Luxembourg, she jumps at the chance to leave behind her double-life, to start anew. She begins to reinvent herself as an expat." (Publisher's note)

Pawel, Rebecca

Death of a nationalist. Soho Press 2003 262p $24

ISBN 1-56947-304-8

LC 2002-26921

"Madrid in 1939 is filled with bomb craters, desecrated churches and nearly abandoned streets, while black markets are just about the only markets with anything to sell. The hatreds and atrocities shared by the Nationalists (supported by the Communists) still simmer and erupt in sporadic violence. The Guardia Civil has the responsibility to maintain authority—and their enthusiasm and ruthlessnesss for enforcing order terrorizes the citizens. The intertwined fates of Sergeant Tejada Alonzo Leon of the Guardia Civil and that of Gonzalo Llorente, a wounded Republican in hiding are handled with unusual skill and subtlety." Publ Wkly

Peace, David

Occupied city. Alfred A. Knopf 2010 275p $25.95

ISBN 978-0-307-23675-9; 0-307-26375-4

LC 2009-43254

First published 2009 in the United Kingdom

"Powerful and ambitious, this British import is deepened by a multiperspective, Rashomon-like approach. But reader be warned: The immensely talented Peace . . . is not in the business of making his work easy." Kirkus

Peace, David

Tokyo year zero. Alfred A. Knopf 2007 $24

ISBN 978-0-307-26374-2; 0-307-26374-6

LC 2007-23813

This novel is based "on a real-life serial-killer case in post-WWII Japan. When the nude body of a young woman turns up in a local park, Inspector Minami of the Tokyo police and his squad of detectives investigate. At the crime scene, Minami finds another woman's body nearby and begins to suspect there will be more to come. Minami, married and a father of two, is smart, tenacious and experienced; he's also addicted to sedatives, keeps a mistress, is in the pocket of a local crime lord and not above sampling the wares of prostitutes he encounters while roaming the city at night. . . . Peace, whose complex style feels like a cross between Haruki Murakami and James Ellroy, delivers an expressionistic portrait of a harrowing, devastated time and place." Publ Wkly

Peacock, Justin

Blind man's alley. Doubleday 2010 465p $26.95

ISBN 978-0-385-53106-1; 0-385-53106-0

LC 2010-02640

"An angry portrait of Big Apple corruption and the efforts of two young people, a lawyer and a journalist, to resist its embrace. . . . A superior legal thriller by a writer with talent to burn." Washington Post

Pearce, Mary Emily

Apple tree lean down; [by] Mary E. Pearce. St. Martin's Press 1976 494p

This volume contains Apple tree lean down, Jack Mercybright and The sorrowing wind, originally published separately in the United Kingdom in 1973, 1974 and 1975 respectively

"Many novels have depicted the upper classes of this era; few have delved so deeply into the lives of the common laborers and the lower middle class." Libr J

Followed by The land endures (1978) and Seedtime and harvest (1982)

Pearce, Mary Emily

Cast a long shadow; {by} Mary E. Pearce. St. Martin's Press 1983 246p

LC 83-2953

First published 1977 in the United Kingdom

"The blissful early years of Richard Lancy and Ellen Wainwright's marriage in the small English village of Dingham are shattered after Richard is accidentally trapped in the cellar of a burned-out mill for 16 days. Richard's horrifying experience distorts his entire life and disrupts his family as well. After throwing his wife and son out of their house (and forcing them to find refuge with the compassionate village blacksmith), the disturbed Richard lurks about as a specter. His haunting presence torments Ellen and John and threatens the new lives they try to forge for themselves in this closed, watchful English village." Booklist

"Old-fashioned story-telling, people one cares about and low-key charm add up to solid reading pleasure." Publ Wkly

Pearl, Matthew

The **Dante** Club; a novel. Random House 2003 372p $24.95

ISBN 0-375-50529-6

LC 2002-17886

A literary thriller about a "serial murderer who draws gory inspiration from the torments of Dante's Inferno. . . . The author sets this novel in Boston in 1865, when Henry Wadsworth Longfellow, James Russell Lowell, and Oliver Wendell Holmes were translating Dante into English. As they work through the cantos, the Dante-inspired corpses arrive on cue, and the versifiers must turn detective." New Yorker

Pearl, Matthew

The **last** Dickens; a novel. Random House 2009 386p $25

ISBN 978-1-4000-6656-8; 1-4000-6656-5

LC 2008-46962

"Pearl is too smart to hinge his plot on mere publishing rights. Like Dickens, he finds compelling stories in every social stratum, viewing the downtrodden with sympathy and the upper crust with a gimlet eye." N Y Daily News

Pearl, Matthew

The **Poe** shadow; a novel. Matthew Pearl. Random House 2006 370p o.p.; (pbk.) $15

ISBN 1400061032; 9780812970128

LC 2005057998

This book follows "[y]oung Baltimore lawyer Quentin Clark, [who,] already obsessed with his favorite writer, Edgar Allan Poe, becomes outraged when newspapers write off Poe's mysterious death as an alcoholic breakdown. So outraged in fact that he abandons his practice and fiancée to visit France to locate the detective whom Poe's character Auguste Dupin is based upon, in an attempt to solve the mystery and clear Poe's name. Instead, Clark finds two such men--one a flamboyant charlatan, the other an eccentric genius--both of whom come to Baltimore and compete to explain Poe's demise." (Library Journal)

Pearl, Matthew

The **technologists**; Matthew Pearl. 1st ed. Random House 2012 480 p. ill.

ISBN 9780679605072; 9781400066575

LC 2011014628

This book takes place in "Spring 1868, and the population of Boston is being terrorised by technological attacks: first a magnetic storm causes ships in the harbour to collide in flames, then in another bizarre catastrophe every piece of glass in the financial district spontaneously melts - clocks, windows, eyeglasses. Nothing in nature can do this: these are man-made disasters. . . . The city's fate relies on four young students of the recently founded Massachusetts Institute of Technology: Marcus Mansfield, a Civil War veteran determined to repay MIT's founder for taking a chance on him, brash Bob Richards, meticulous Edwin Hoyt and the eccentric but brilliant Ellen Swallow, the first woman at MIT, who experiments secretly in a basement laboratory. . . . In a climate of rising hysteria, these four courageous individuals must unite against the forces of darkness to uncover

the mastermind before he can stage his greatest outrage." (Publisher's note)

Pearlman, Edith

Binocular vision; new & selected stories. Edith Pearlman. Lookout Books/University of North Carolina Wilmington 2011 xiii, 373p

ISBN 0-9823382-9-5; 978-0-9823382-9-2

LC 2010033376

National Book Critics Circle Award for Fiction (2011)

Edward Lewis Wallant Award (2011)

This is a collection of 34 stories by the author of Vaquita and Other Stories (1996), Love Among the Greats and Other Stories (2002), and How to Fall (2005).

"Short stories are like miniatures: A delicate touch makes all the difference. In Edith Pearlman's world, that light hand means choosing the perfect phrase to capture a moment or a mood. Often it leaves the reader breathless. In 'Binocular Vision,' a hefty collection of 34 stories, including 13 new ones, . . . Pearlman shows her unerring sense for the right words. . . . Set all over the world, in different times during the last hundred years, and involving characters of all ages, these tales focus on the precise pivotal moments when life changes — often for the worse. Death and dying are common themes, while ill-fated liaisons, frequently involving incest, occur with regularity." Boston Globe

Pears, Iain

Death and restoration; a Jonathan Argyll mystery. Scribner 1998 223p $22

ISBN 0-684-81461-7

LC 97-39932

This mystery features "esthete-sleuth, Jonathan Argyll, and his companion, Flavia di Stefano, a senior, investigator for Italy's Art Theft Squad. Most of the legwork falls to Flavia when an icon is stolen from a rundown monastery in Rome and a French dealer is discovered floating in the Tiber. This frees up Jonathan to sprinkle his acidic wit on art experts and thieves like Dan Menzies, . . . who has been engaged by the monastery to apply his savage artistry to its dubious Caravaggio." N Y Times Book Rev

Pears, Iain

The **dream** of Scipio. Riverhead Bks. 2002 398p

ISBN 1-57322-202-X

LC 2001-58916

"Pears builds a multilayered tale of moral choice, love, danger and loss. Like an archaeologist, he uncovers worlds beneath worlds in a few square miles of Provencal earth." N Y Times Book Rev

Pears, Iain

The **immaculate** deception. Scribner 2000 221p

ISBN 0-7432-1257-6

LC 2001-267391

In this Jonathan Argyll "mystery, set in Rome and Tuscany, the police investigator Flavia di Stefano is called in to find a painting that has been stolen by a radical performance artist; meanwhile, her husband, an art historian, is trying to track down the provenance of a beguiling little fifteenth-century Virgin that belongs to Flavia's former boss. Like those classic Nick and Nora whodunits, this book is really a comedy in disguise: the plot twists are finely turned, our heroes flirt harmlessly with danger, and in the end everyone gets what he may not have known he wanted all along." New Yorker

Pears, Iain

An **instance** of the fingerpost. Riverhead Bks. 1998 691p $27

ISBN 1-57322-082-5

LC 97-23899

First published 1997 in the United Kingdom

"Robert Boyle, the devout chemist, and John Thurloe, Cromwell's inscrutable spymaster, are among the historical characters who figure in this richly imagined mystery set in Oxford in the sixteen-sixties, after Charles II has been restored to the throne. A Fellow of New College is found dead, and a woman accused of whoring and witchcraft is sentenced to hang for the murder. Three narrators—all unreliable and all self-interested—tell their versions of the story, which unfolds in a turbulent atmosphere of scientific, political, and religious dissent. Not until a fourth, and final, narrator speaks are the mysteries, including the meaning of the book's title, revealed." New Yorker

Pears, Iain

The **last** judgment. Scribner 1996 224p

ISBN 978-0684814599

LC 95-38120

First published 1993 in the United Kingdom

"Jonathan Argyll, British art dealer, and his amour, Flavia de Stefano, a member of Rome's art-theft squad, have decided to marry after happy months of living together. But first, there's business to tend to. On a buying trip to Paris, Jonathan is asked by a colleague to deliver a valuable painting to a client in Rome. He soon discovers that whoever is interested in this picture seems to wind up dead. . . . A sophisticated, adventurous, and gripping story that is sure to hold wide appeal." Booklist

Pears, Iain

The **portrait**; Iain Pears. Riverhead Books 2005 211 p. (alk. paper) o.p.; (pbk.) $15

ISBN 1573222984; 9781594481758

LC 2004051204

This book presents a "monolog, delivered by an unnamed artist painting the portrait of an old friend . . . [which] reveals . . . the characters' shared past and the sitter's irredeemable sins. As a callow Scottish boy, the artist had been in thrall to his sitter, a monstrously powerful critic who helped his career. At its height, however, the artist fled early 20th-century London for a rough and rocky little island off the coast of France, and the critic has evidently come to discover why, with the request to have his portrait painted serving as pretext. As the artist unleashes his ever-darker discourse, we learn just how carelessly the critic has treated others, including the artist's model Jacky and a colleague named Evelyn." (Library Journal)

Pears, Iain

Stone's fall; a novel. Spiegel & Grau 2009 594p $27.95

ISBN 978-0-385-52284-7; 0-385-52284-3

LC 2009-00472

"Pears manages his complicated structure with a confidence and dexterity possible only to a master of the craft of fiction. It is a novel which frequently and daringly challenges credibility, skating on the thinnest of ice, and yet meets that challenge successfully every time." Scotsman

Pearson, Allison

I think I love you. Alfred A. Knopf 2011 331p $24.95

ISBN 978-1-4000-4235-7; 1-4000-4235-6

LC 2010-36710

The author "does a winning job of making Petra and Bill, and Petra's best friend and fellow David worshipper — the sunny, goodhearted and slightly ditsy Sharon — as funny and incisive as characters created by, say, Nick Hornby or Stephen Fry, though with considerably more tenderness and felt emotion. Her portraits somehow manage to combine effervescence with earnestness, a finely tuned sense of absurdity with nostalgia, satiric wit with genuine warmth. . . . Ms. Pearson has written a groovy little novel whose charms easily erase any objections the reader might have to the prepackaged and heavily borrowed plot." N Y Times (Late N Y Ed)

Pearson, Ridley

The **angel** maker; a novel. Delacorte Press 1993 341p

LC 92-36573

In this crime thriller someone is "running around with a scalpel removing a kidney here, a lung there, then selling the organs to desperate patients willing to pay upward of $15,000. This grisly brand of 'harvesting' comes to light in Seattle when victims begin turning up minus a part or two. It's the job of a police psychologist named Daphne Matthews, aided by her piano-playing ex-lover, Lou Boldt, to try to bring the perpetrator of these ghastly crimes to justice." N Y Times Book Rev

"Pearson's engaging forensic detail . . . and brisk prose will have readers racing to the cliffhanger climax." Publ Wkly

Pearson, Ridley

The **art** of deception. Hyperion 2002 451p

ISBN 0-7868-6724-8

LC 2002-69055

This Lou Boldt-Daphne Matthews suspense novel "finds the Seattle police lieutenant and his forensic psychologist colleague investigating two cases that ultimately become one. Boldt is tracking a serial killer, and Matthews is investigating the death of a woman who was thrown from Seattle's Aurora Bridge. . . . Pearson makes particularly good use of his Seattle setting this time; the legendary Underground (created when the city was rebuilt after its great fire of 1889) has often appeared in mysteries, but Pearson's detail-rich treatment goes well beyond the typical clichés of dark passages and abandoned storefronts. On every level, this series remains one of the mystery genre's great pleasures." Booklist

Pearson, Ridley
  Beyond recognition. Hyperion 1997 480p
  ISBN 978-0786862405

LC 96-21125

"A rag and a bone are literally all the Seattle PD has to work with after a violent fire consumes a home and its helpless female occupant, a divorced mother. When a second victim dies the same way, detective Lou Boldt and police psychologist Daphne Matthews begin the process of profiling a serial killer who uses rocket fuel to torch women because they resemble his mother. Elsewhere, a young boy named Ben, whose abusive stepfather has all but driven him into the street, has been befriended by a fraudulent 'psychic' named Emily Richland, who hires Ben to scout her clients' vehicles while they're meeting with her. This task leads, . . . to Ben witnessing an exchange of cash for rocket fuel, a sighting that in turn eventually takes the police to their killer." Publ Wkly

Pearson, Ridley
  ★ The **body** of David Hayes. Hyperion 2004 344p $23.95
  ISBN 0-7868-6725-6

LC 2003-56575

In this "Detective Lou Boldt thriller, computer whiz David Hayes has embezzled $17 million from the bank where he worked and hidden it within the computer system. Now paroled for the crime, he wants to get the money and be free of all competing parties, including some utterly ruthless Russian Mafia types who will stop at nothing to get the loot. Years before, Hayes had an affair with Boldt's wife—now VP of systems at the bank—and he blackmails her into helping him recover the money. Though dedicated and skilled, Boldt and his team are human and fallible; Boldt must balance his jealousy as a husband with his professionalism as a detective. Pearson's novels are always well written, and he takes special care with richly drawn subordinate characters." Libr J

Pearson, Ridley
  Chain of evidence. Hyperion 1995 348p
  LC 95-32320

"Police Lieutenant Joe 'Dart' Bartelli is called to one suicide after another of various psychopaths (a vicious child molester, a hard-core pornographer) in the Hartford, Connecticut, area. The deaths seem more like murders to Dart, who was well trained in police investigation by his mentor, former police sergeant Walter Zeller. Dart carefully, plausibly tracks down the killer with the help of former love, Ginny, fellow lieutenant Abby Lang, and various three-dimensional characters who add believably to his painstaking search. Bad guys, burnouts, and screwups—all the characters are well delineated." Libr J

Pearson, Ridley
  The **first** victim. Hyperion 1999 381p $23.95
  ISBN 0-7868-6440-0

LC 98-49992

"Boldt's usual partner, forensic psychologist Daphne Matthews, plays a lesser role this time, but in her place Pearson substitutes television news anchor Stevie McNeal, who mounts her own investigation, thus introducing a meaty subplot involving media excesses. As always, Pearson builds suspense incrementally, brilliantly amassing details until his plot reaches critical mass at just the right moment." Booklist

Pearson, Ridley
  Killer summer. G. P. Putnam's Sons 2009 367p $24.95
  ISBN 978-0-399-15572-7; 0-399-15572-4

LC 2009-12998

"Although his ending is a bit flat, seasoned thriller writer Pearson serves up steady suspense and a compelling setting in which members of society's underbelly prey on those living above it all." Booklist

Pearson, Ridley
  Middle of nowhere; a novel. Hyperion 2000 375p
  ISBN 0-7868-6563-6

LC 99-51670

This thriller "boasts simmering suspense, a plot with a level of detail that comes only from painstaking research, and dynamic chemistry between Boldt and his colleagues and family." Publ Wkly

Pearson, Ridley
  No witnesses; a novel. Hyperion 1994 365p
  LC 94-11158

"Wealthy food industry mogul Owen Adler receives a series of FAXes demanding that he liquidate his business and commit suicide within a month. The alternative is that consumers of Adler Foods will begin to die. After the deadline passes and two children are hospitalized with a mysterious infection, Adler lets his girlfriend, Seattle forensic psychologist Daphne Matthews, contact detective Lou Boldt. Boldt's empathy for the rising number of victims compels him to put his life at risk as he coordinates an extended investigation while trying to prevent mass panic." Libr J

Pearson, Ridley
  Undercurrents. St. Martin's Press 1988 386p
  LC 88-1014

"A killer is on the loose—a brutal, terrifying murderer who was himself supposed to be dead. Seattle Police Sergeant Lou Boldt, haunted by the deaths of the man he believed to have been the Cross Killer (so called because of the crosses he slashes onto his victims) and of the real criminal's new victims, is in charge of the case and determined to solve it. . . . Undercurrents is not for the squeamish; it is grittily detailed and no punches pulled. But Pearson clearly understands what makes a good mystery move, and this one sprints breathlessly along, taking the reader with it to a surprising, and satisfying, conclusion." West Coast Rev Books

Pearson, T. R.
  Blue Ridge. Viking 2000 243p $24.95
  ISBN 0-670-89269-6

LC 00-25826

"Pearson has never been timid about pushing form to its limits, and his splendid prose is also artifical, stunningly so—high-pitched, evocative, decorative and closer to the human heart than the rictus-grinned pseudo-realism of many modern mysteries." N Y Times Book Rev

Pearson, T. R.

Cry me a river; a novel. Holt & Co. 1993 258p

ISBN 0-8050-2200-7

LC 92-13860

"A police officer is found brutally murdered in a small southern town, his head so disfigured by bullet wounds that he can only be identified by the distinctive smell of his hair tonic. A fellow officer vows to find the killer. Accompanied by a whiskey-addled sidekick who functions as a backwoods Dr. Watson, the investigator assembles clues, interviews suspects, proposes and discards theories, and in the process paints the portrait of an entire community." Libr J

Pearson, T. R.

A short history of a small place; a novel. Linden Press/Simon & Schuster 1985 381p

ISBN 0-671-54352-0

LC 84-29720

"Narrated by young Louis Benfield {this} is the story of Miss Myra Angelique Pettigrew, sister of the late mayor of a small Southern town, who is elegant and beautiful and has gone quite mad. After many years of seclusion, she finally emerges from her home to jump to her death from the water tower. In the process of telling his tale, Louis offers vignettes about other residents of Neely, N.C., and their strange habits and activities." Publ Wkly

"Pearson handles the interlinked strands of these stories with a truly wonderful offhand comic style that doesn't dismiss the reality of his characters' lives." Booklist

Peck, Robert Newton

★ A day no pigs would die. Knopf 1973 150p $25; pa $5.50

ISBN 0-394-48235-2; 0-679-85306-5 pa

"Rob lives a rigorous life on a Shaker farm in Vermont in the 1920s. Since farm life is earthy, this book is filled with Yankee humor and explicit descriptions of animals mating. A painful incident that involves the slaughter of Rob's beloved pet pig is instrumental in urging him toward adulthood. The death of his father completes the process of his accepting responsibility." Shapiro. Fic for Youth. 3d edition

Peebles, Frances de Pontes

The seamstress; a novel. HarperCollins 2008 646p map $25.95

ISBN 978-0-06-073887-7; 0-06-073887-1

This "historical saga of Brazil in the 1920s and 1930s follows sisters Emília and Luzia dos Santos from their impoverished childhoods as village seamstresses to their unimaginable futures: Emília marries the scion of an upper-class family in Recife, while Luzia marries The Hawk, an infamous bandit-cum-Robin Hood who terrorizes provincial landowners. Using as backdrop the populist revolt of 1930 and the push to develop Brazil's enormous resources at the expense of the subsistence farmers, Peebles creates a vast and diverse cast of characters. . . . However, the novel's true beauty is the exquisitely realized relationship between Emília and Luzia, two strong women who, despite the separate paths their lives take, remain connected and committed to each other." Libr J

Pekearo, Nicholas T.

The wolfman; [by] Nicholas Pekearo. Tor 2008 286p $23.95

ISBN 978-0-7653-2026-1; 0-7653-2026-6

LC 2008-3984

"At first glance, Marlowe Higgins seems like a typically flawed noir protagonist: He's an ill-tempered Vietnam War veteran who has drifted from job to job since returning to the U.S. a changed man. He has a propensity for razor-sharp sarcasm, jaw-dropping profanity, binge drinking and sudden outbursts of psychotic violence . . . . Although he has never had a lasting relationship (he's currently involved with a prostitute named Alice), Higgins is a diehard romantic with a heroic code of honor. He also happens to be a werewolf, and when transformed into the beast he is nothing short of 'the wrath of God.' Having slaughtered more than 300 people since returning from the war, and now settled down in the small town of Evelyn, Higgins, who retains the memories and mannerisms of all those he has killed, has vowed to use his torturous affliction for the greater good. Every full moon when he becomes a primeval 'boogeyman,' he tracks down criminals in the region with the help of information from Danny Pearce, a detective with the local police who is the closest thing Higgins has to a friend. . . . Crime-fiction, paranormal-fantasy and horror fans alike should cherish this outstanding debut." Chicago Tribune

Pelecanos, George

The cut; a novel. Little, Brown and Co. 2011 292p $25.99

ISBN 978-0-316-07842-9; 0-316-07842-5

LC 2010-44937

"At 29, Spero Lucas, an unlicensed investigator for a criminal defense attorney (and anyone else who'll give him a cut of the action), is considerably younger and friskier than the heavy-lidded private eyes who have imprinted their world-weary stamp on this genre. His values are also different, shaped by the street culture of his tough neighborhood and by his experiences as a Marine in Iraq. . . . Moonlighting for an imprisoned mobster who agrees to his hefty cut for retrieving some stolen shipments of marijuana, Lucas becomes trapped in a gang war that quickly turns brutal and bloody. Before he knows it, he's aiming to kill. The novel's story is O.K., but nowhere near as heart-racing as the storytelling." N Y Times Book Rev

Pelecanos, George P.

★ The big blowdown. St. Martin's Press 1996 313p

ISBN 0-312-14284-6

LC 95-53148

"Pelecanos lovingly recreates old Washington with small details about soft-drink brands, finned cars and cherished smokes. The ending is a haze of gunsmoke that drifts away to leave a mixed tableau of heroism and futility. With stylistic panache and forceful conviction, Pelecanos delivers a darkly powerful story of the American city." Publ Wkly

Pelecanos, George P.

Drama city; a novel. [by] George Pelecanos. Little, Brown and Co 2005 291p $24.95

ISBN 0-316-60821-1

LC 2004-16757

"There is a fierce inevitability to the way George Pelecanos's new book unfolds. Drama City is unleashed, not simply set in motion. In the tough, imperiled parts of Washington, where his earlier books have been set, Mr. Pelecanos puts the forces of good and evil on a collision course, igniting the kind of suspense that hinges on heartbreak. As this lean, stirring, knife-edged novel escalates, the question is not whether one of its principals will become a casualty. The question is when." N Y Times (Late N Y Ed)

Pelecanos, George P.

Hard revolution; a novel. [by] George Pelecanos. Little, Brown 2004 376p $24.95

ISBN 0-316-60897-1

LC 2003-54501

"Pelecanos's foray into Strange's past does not in the end diminish, but rather adds to, our sense of his complexity and humanity. In narrating Derek's buried crime story, Pelecanos has further tapped into an archetypal vein of family experience in the black community since the 1950's, as drugs, murder and prison cut a swath through three generations of young men." N Y Times Book Rev

Pelecanos, George P.

Hell to pay; a novel. Little, Brown 2002 344p $24.95

ISBN 0-316-69506-8

LC 2001-38111

This mystery, set in Washington, D.C., features ex-cop detectives Derek Strange and Terry Quinn. "As a black man with plenty of miles behind him, Strange has access to neighborhoods where his Irish partner would be handed his head; but both of them take big chances when they cross Worldwide Wilson, a menacing pimp who breaks in teenage runaways, and then go after the wild street kids who shot the 9-year-old quarterback of the Petworth Panthers, the Pee-Wee team Strange coaches. Pelecanos's style is one of total-shock immersion in the sights, sounds and cultural codes of the dangerous world he roams." N Y Times Book Rev

Pelecanos, George P.

The **night** gardener; a novel. Little, Brown 2006 377p $24.99

ISBN 978-0-316-15650-9; 0-316-15650-7

LC 2006-1286

"In 1985, the body of a 14-year-old girl turns up in a Washington, D.C., park, the latest in a series of murders by a killer the media dub 'The Night Gardener.' T.C. Cook, the aging detective on the case, works with a quiet, almost monomaniacal, focus. Also involved are two young uniformed cops, Gus Ramone, who's diligent, conscientious and unimpressed by heroics, and Dan 'Doc' Holiday, an adrenaline junkie who's decidedly less straight. Fast forward 20 years. Detective Ramone, now married with kids of his own, investigates the murder of one of his teenage son's friends. The homicide closely resembles the earlier unsolved Night Gardener murders. Holiday, now an alcoholic chauffeur and bodyguard, follows the case on his own and tracks down Cook, long retired but still obsessed with the original murders." Publ Wkly

A "disturbingly gritty excavation of racism and social politics in modern Washington." Christ Sci Monit

Pelecanos, George P.

Right as rain; a novel. Little, Brown 2001 332p

ISBN 0-316-69526-2

LC 00-34886

"What is perhaps most remarkable about this outstanding novel . . . is the way his plot-rich, extremely violent stories parallel the turbulence of his characters' inner lives. We care about these characters passionately, and we savor their tentative moments of tranquility as we do our own." Booklist

Pelecanos, George P.

Shame the devil; a novel. Little, Brown 2000 299p $24.95

ISBN 0-316-69523-8

LC 99-29854

"Pelecanos is one of those dangerous writers who aren't afraid to take risks, so there's a merciless reality to his characters and a cold clarity about the way they talk, think and feel. Whatever their flaws, none of the people in this writer's world are ashamed to tell the truth." N Y Times Book Rev

Pelecanos, George P.

Soul circus; a novel. Little, Brown 2003 341p $24.95

ISBN 0-316-60843-2

LC 2002-16207

"Pelecanos is fascinated with the way things work, and he takes apart the gun trade like an urban anthropologist, fitting the pieces into the drug business and the gang culture with an exactness that is breathtaking—and depressing. At the same time, he treats his criminals like human beings, talking their talk, driving their cars, listening to their music, getting into their world with something that can only be called sympathy." N Y Times Book Rev

Pelecanos, George P.

★ The **sweet** forever; a novel. Little, Brown 1998 298p $23.95

ISBN 0-316-69109-7

LC 97-41963

Sequel to King Suckerman (1997)

"Pelecanos's kickback style works just as well when his characters put down their weapons to watch a ball game or to hit the music clubs on a Friday night. This may be a battleground, but it's also Pelecanos's home ground, and he knows the territory as well as any crime writer alive." N Y Times Book Rev

Followed by Shame the devil

Pelecanos, George P.

The **turnaround**; a novel. [by] George Pelecanos. Little, Brown, and Co. 2008 294p $24.99

ISBN 978-0-316-15647-9; 0-316-15647-7

LC 2007-33276

"Pelecanos does what few, if any, American writers do: He tells the truth. Twain told the truth; Faulkner toyed with the truth; Hemingway told his version of the truth and Chandler certainly told a cold, cynical truth. Pelecanos' truth is from deep in the heart, from places where red blood cells know more than all the sweet, heady words truth usually hides behind." Chicago Sun-Times

Pelecanos, George P.

The **way** home; a novel. [by] George Pelecanos. Little, Brown and Co. 2009 323p $24.99

ISBN 978-0-316-15649-3

LC 2008-54837

This novel "examines a generational battle between working-class Thomas Flynn, owner of a Washington, D.C., carpet business, and his son Chris, who is more concerned with the rules of the urban streets than with his future. . . . [Chris eventually lands] in the Pine Ridge facility for juveniles, where punishment, not redemption, is the order of the day. Chris survives the system, but the jailhouse code of standing tall, staring down authority and avenging wrongs dogs him as he tries to build a new, adult life in the face of temptation. In a sense, 'The Way Home' is a coming-of-age story, as Chris tries to find his place in the world. More fortunate than most of the boys who share his past, he can succeed, Pelecanos tells us — but not everybody is quite so lucky." PopMatters

Pelevin, Victor

The **hall** of singing caryatids; translated by Andrew Bromfield. New Directions 2011 pa $9.95

ISBN 978-0-8112-1942-6 pa

"After auditioning for the part as a singing geisha at a dubious bar, Lena and eleven other 'lucky' girls are sent to work at a posh underground nightclub reserved exclusively for Russias upper-crust elite. They are to be a sideshow attraction to the rest of the club's entertainment, and are billed as the 'famous singing caryatids.' Things only get weirder from there. Secret ointments, praying mantises, sexual escapades, and grotesque murder are quickly ushered into the plot." Publisher's note

Pelevin, Victor

The **sacred** book of the werewolf; translated by Andrew Bromfield. Viking 2008 304p $25.95

ISBN 978-0-670-01988-5; 0-670-01988-7

Original Russian edition, 2004

"It's a joy to read Pelevin's phantasmagoria so brilliantly translated by Andrew Bromfield, a crowning achievement of the pair's longtime association. Complex ideas are rendered simply and organically, never disturbing the narrative flow. Bromfield's English text is fleet and magical." N Y Times Book Rev

Penguin book of gay short fiction; edited by David Leavitt and Mark Mitchell; introduction by David Leavitt. Viking 1994 655p

LC 93-1390

The **Penguin** book of lesbian short stories; edited by Margaret Reynolds. Viking 1994 429p

LC 93-34061

First published 1993 in the United Kingdom

Penkov, Miroslav

East of the West; a country in stories. Farrar, Straus and Giroux 2011 226p $24

ISBN 978-0-374-11733-7; 0-374-11733-0

LC 2010-47602

"In representing the history of Bulgaria, the eight stories cover the end of Ottoman rule in the late 19th century, moving through the Communist state of the mid-20th century to the contemporary period where many young Bulgarians enter green-card lotteries to immigrate elsewhere. There are tiny bright spots in each step in Bulgaria's story, centered on small moments of families being happy together. Each one is a pause in the surge forward in the name of progress and the betterment of society, which never seems to bring peace or satisfaction to anyone. . . . Penkov's imagination creates a country with loose historical borders, a people stranded across the world, trying to preserve some kind of cohesive personal history in contrast to the back-and-forth, ever-changing story of their homeland." AV Club

Penman, Sharon Kay

Cruel as the grave; a medieval mystery. Holt & Co. 1998 242p $22

ISBN 0-8050-5608-4

LC 98-13085

"Penman's clear prose and engrossing plot, the skill with which she brings the politics, people, and ambience of medieval England alive, and her engaging characters make this a must-read, must-have mystery." Booklist

Penman, Sharon Kay

Devil's brood. G. P. Putnam's Sons 2008 734p $28.95

ISBN 978-0-399-15526-0

LC 2008-29451

Final volume in the author's trilogy based on the lives of Henry II and Eleanor of Aquitaine; earlier titles: When Christ and his saints slept; Time and chance

"As the novel opens, [Eleanor and Henry's] four sons are beginning to chafe under the heavy hand of their father, who has crowned the eldest, Hal, as a coregent but gives him little authority or power. Egged on by their mother, the young king and his brothers mount a decadelong crusade of rebellion and treachery against their father and each other as they vie for land, money, and power. The empathetic reader can't help but be both horrified by the machinations of this grievously dysfunctional family and filled with pity for the pain they inflict upon one another. Penman does a remarkable job of depicting passionate, dramatic characters and the perilous times in which they live. For those who like their historical fiction as complex and tightly woven as a medieval tapestry, this book cannot fail to please." Libr J

Penman, Sharon Kay

Dragon's lair; a medieval mystery. Sharon Kay Penman. G.P. Putnam's Sons 2003 322p $23.95

ISBN 0-399-15077-3

LC 2003-46745

In this mystery, "Justin de Quincy, tries to recover, quite literally, a king's ransom in coffers of precious metals and bales of wool, which are as valuable as gold, that have been stolen in northern Wales. It's 1193, and Queen Eleanor of

Aquitaine fervently needs to ransom her eldest son, Richard Lionheart, from the Holy Roman Emperor before King Philippe of France can interfere and her younger son, John, can seize the crown. Justin proceeds into the thickets and wild forests of Wales, where he's deeply mistrusted both as an Englishman and an outsider. He must penetrate abundant Welsh intrigues and deceptions in order to discover the treasure as well as solve murders and comfort bereaved lovers. Despite a large cast of characters from every social class, Penman keeps them all clearly distinguishable." Publ Wkly

Penman, Sharon Kay

Falls the shadow. Holt & Co. 1988 580p

LC 87-32255

In this second volume of the trilogy begun with Here be dragons "Penman focuses on the mid-13th-century reign of England's Henry III and stories of those who opposed that inept king. A main detractor is French-born Simon de Montfort, Earl of Leicester, who leads the fight for parliamentary restrictions on the monarch, and later becomes Henry's brother-in-law through marriage to Eleanor, Countess of Pembroke. She emerges as a major figure, as does a distant relative by marriage, Llewelyn ap Gruffydd, who fights for supremacy in Wales." Libr J

Followed by The reckoning

Penman, Sharon Kay

Here be dragons. Holt, Rinehart & Winston 1985 704p

LC 84-23480

This first title in the author's historical trilogy about 13th century England "is the story of one man, a Welsh prince called Llewelyn the Great, who dares to dream of peace and who will spend a lifetime trying to wrest his country away from feudal England. Standing in his way is King John, who marries his daughter, Joanna, to Llewelyn in hopes of taming the rebellious prince. Penman focuses her novel on the tempestuous emotional and political battles that Joanna is forced to endure as both the daughter and wife of warring kings." Booklist

Followed by Falls the shadow

Penman, Sharon Kay

Lionheart. G. P. Putnam's Sons 2011 594p map $28.95

ISBN 978-0-399-15785-1

LC 2011-13731

Richard, the second surviving son of Henry Plantagenet and Eleanor of Aquitaine, inherits the throne from his brother, before embarking on the Third Crusade, a conflict that is complicated by the schemes of his usurping brother, John.

"Penman expertly weaves well-researched historical events into her fast-paced revisionist story. Certain to appeal to historical fiction fans interested in the medieval era." Libr J

Penman, Sharon Kay

The **queen's** man; a medical mystery. H. Holt 1996 291p $20

ISBN 0-8050-3885-X

LC 96-15027

"In the troubled time of King Richard, his mother, Eleanor of Aquitaine, commissions Justin de Quincey, the bastard son of the bishop of Chester, to find the murderer of a goldsmith in her employ. Thus dunked into the dangerous waters of royal conspiracy, Justin defies one treachrous current after another." Libr J

"Penman's authentic period details, larger-than-life characters, and fast-paced plot add up to great reading for both mystery fans and history buffs." Booklist

Penman, Sharon Kay

The **reckoning**. Holt & Co. 1991 592p

LC 90-27099

"The action involves religious and political intrigue, battles and plots. The players include well-researched historical personages and fictional characters. As with Penman's other historical novels, this one is both informative and enjoyable. Settings, events, and individuals are well drawn." Libr J

Penman, Sharon Kay

The **sunne** in splendour. Holt, Rinehart & Winston 1982 936p

LC 81-20149

"The novel covers a great deal of ground, tracing the shifting alliances and the battles between the noble houses of York and Lancaster from 1459, when Richard was seven to 1492, seven years after his death on Bosworth Field. . . . A historical novel of the first rank." Publ Wkly

Penman, Sharon Kay

Time and chance. Putnam 2002 515p

ISBN 0-399-14785-3

LC 2001-48255

Sequel to: When Christ and his saints slept

This second volume of the author's medieval trilogy "re-creates the drama, the intrigue, and the passion that distinguished the lives of Henry Plantagenet, Eleanor of Aquitaine, and Thomas Becket. Though the subject has been exhaustively chronicled in both history and literature, this fictionalized account of the trials and tribulations of this prominent trio of historical figures manages to breathe new life into a familiar story." Booklist

Penman, Sharon Kay

When Christ and his saints slept. Holt & Co. 1995 746p il

LC 94-22593

The author "showcases her mastery of the historical novel in this long and thoroughly engrossing study of pragmatic politics, idealism, and the role of women during the 12th century. She brings to life a vast array of unforgettable characters, both historical and invented, all of whose loyalties are being constantly tested by the chaos of the times." Libr J

Penney, Stef

The **invisible** ones; by Stef Penney. G.P. Putnam's Sons 2012 400p

ISBN 9780399157714; 9780425253212

LC 2011046797

This book tells the story of "private eye Ray Lovell [who] wakes up in an English hospital with little memory and partial paralysis. . . . Ray, who is half-Gypsy himself, is offered a job by a fellow Gypsy, Leon Wood, who wants Ray to find his daughter, Rose, who he hasn't seen or spoken to in seven years, ever since she married Ivo Janko, another Gypsy. . . . Why Leon wants to find Rose after so much time begins the mystery. He tells Ray it's because her mother has died and she should know, but Leon suspects foul play." (Publishers Weekly)

Penney, Stef

The **tenderness** of wolves; a novel. Simon & Schuster 2007 371p $25

ISBN 978-1-4165-4074-8; 1-4165-4074-1

LC 2006-100796

First published 2006 in the United Kingdom

A "confident and complex portrait of 1860s Ontario. . . . Between twists and turns of plot, Penney evokes the land—its shades of light and changes of weather, its marshes and treacherous waters. Rarely has winter seemed so febrile." Books of Canada

Penny, Louise

★ The **beautiful** mystery; a Chief Inspector Gamache novel. Louise Penny. St. Martin's Minotaur 2012 373 p. (hardcover: alk. paper) $25.99

ISBN 0312655460; 9780312655464; 9781250015273

LC 2012024186

This book by Louise Penny presents "a locked-room mystery set in a remote monastery deep in the wilderness of northern Québec. There are 24 cloistered monks. One is dead. There are only 23 suspects. The monks have taken a vow of silence, except that they made the most beautiful recording of Gregorian chant ever heard. And it caused a schism. And then a murder. Chief Inspector Gamache and Jean-Guy Beauvoir of the Sûreté du Québec come to investigate." (Library Journal)

Includes bibliographical references and index

Penny, Louise

Bury your dead. Minotaur Books 2010 371p $24.99

ISBN 978-0-312-37704-5; 0-312-37704-5

LC 2010-26415

"Front and center are the travails of Gamache, chief inspector of the Sûreté du Quebec, who is visiting an old friend in Quebec City and hoping to recover from a case gone wrong. Soon, however, he is involved with a new case: the murder of an archaeologist who was devoted to finding the missing remains of Samuel de Champlain, founder of Quebec. As Gamache is drawn into this history-drenched investigation—the victim's body was found in an English-language library, calling up the full range of animosity between Quebec's French majority and dwindling English minority—he is also concerned that he might have jailed the wrong man in his last case (The Brutal Telling, 2009) and orders his colleague, Jean Guy Beauvoir, back to the village of Three Pines to find what they missed the first time. Hovering over both these present investigations is the case gone wrong in the past, the details of which are gradually revealed in perfectly placed flashbacks. Penny brilliantly juggles the three stories, which are connected only by a kind of psychological membrane." Booklist

Penny, Louise

The **cruelest** month; a Three Pines mystery. St. Martin's Minotaur 2008 311p $23.95

ISBN 978-0-312-35257-8; 0-312-35257-3

LC 2007-42422

Chief Inspector Armand Gamache of the Surete du Quebec is called to investigate the death of a villager at an Easter seance that was held at the Old Hadley House.

"Penny paints a vivid picture of the French-Canadian village, its inhabitants and a determined detective who will strike many Agatha Christie fans as a 21st-century version of Hercule Poirot." Publ Wkly

Penny, Louise

How the light gets in; Chief Inspector Gamache novel. Louise Penny. 1st Minotaur Books ed. Minotaur Books 2013 416 p. (hardcover) $25.99

ISBN 0312655479; 9780312655471

LC 2013013622

This book is part of Louise Penny's Chief Inspector Armand Gamache series. Here, Inspector Gamache heads to "Three Pines to help therapist-turned-bookseller Myrna find out why her friend Constance Pineault didn't turn up for Christmas. . . . En route to Three Pines, Gamache happens upon a fatality at the Champlain Bridge and agrees to handle the details. But this case takes a back seat to the disappearance of Constance when she turns up dead in her home." (Kirkus)

Penny, Louise

Still life. St. Martin's Minotaur 2006 312p $22.95

ISBN 978-0-312-35255-4; 0-312-35255-7

LC 2006-41992

First published 2005 in the United Kingdom

"The residents of a tiny Canadian village called Three Pines are shocked when the body of Miss Jane Neal is found in the woods. Miss Neal, the village's retired schoolteacher and a talented amateur artist, has been a good friend to most of the townsfolk, so her loss is keenly felt. At first, her death appears to be a tragic accident—it's deer-hunting season, and it looks a stray hunter's arrow killed her. But some folks are suspicious, and Chief Inspector Armand Gamache of the Montreal Surete is called in to investigate." Booklist

Penny, Louise

A **trick** of the light. Minotaur Boooks 2011 339p $25.99

ISBN 978-0-312-65545-7; 0-312-65545-2

LC 2011020256

"Penny, elevating herself to the pantheon that houses P.D. James, Ruth Rendell and Minette Walters, demonstrates an exquisite touch with characterization, plotting and artistic sensitivity. And there could be no better explanation of A.A. than you will find here." Kirkus

Percy, Benjamin

Red moon; Benjamin Percy. Grand Central Pub. 2013 544 p. (hardcover) $25.99

ISBN 1455501662; 9781455501663

LC 2012016127

In this werewolf novel, a "lycan rights group launches a terrorist attack on an airliner that shocks the nation, and the main characters deal with the aftereffects. Claire is a lycan who lives an uneventful suburban life with her parents when a post-attack government raid sends her on the run. The lone passenger who survived the attack is Patrick, whose father's National Guard unit has just shipped out as part of the U.S. peacekeeping mission in the werewolf homeland." (Library Journal)

Percy, Benjamin

The **wilding**; a novel. Graywolf Press 2010 258p $23

ISBN 978-1-55597-569-2; 1-55597-569-0

LC 2010-922923

"The plot concerns a hunting trip taken by Justin Caves and his sixth-grade son, Graham, with Justin's bullying father, Paul, a passionate outdoorsman in failing health who's determined to spend one last weekend in the Echo Canyon before real estate developer Bobby Fremont turns the sublime pocket of wilderness into a golfing resort. Justin, a high school English teacher, has hit an almost terminally rough patch in his marriage to Karen, who, while the boys camp, contemplates an affair with Bobby, though she may have bigger problems with wounded Iraq war vet Brian, a case study in creepy stalker. The men, meanwhile, are being tracked by a beast and must contend with a vengeful roughneck roaming the woods. A taut plot and cast of deeply flawed characters—Justin is a masterwork of pitiable wretchedness—will keep readers rapt as peril descends and split-second decisions come to have lifelong repercussions. It's as close as you can get to a contemporary Deliverance." Publ Wkly

Percy, Walker

★ **Lancelot**. Farrar, Straus & Giroux 1977 257p

In this novel the author "knowledgeably fingers what he perceives as the rotting fabric of Southern aristocratic life, and describes it with vividness and a kind of affection, even as he starts to shred it." Christ Sci Monit

Percy, Walker

★ The **last** gentleman. Modern Lib. 1997 442p $18.50

ISBN 0-679-60272-0

LC 97-15381

"The plot is less important than the delineation of character, the preoccupation with the way people speak and define themselves geographically and historically . . . and the rendering of a composite South." Burgess. 99 Novels

Followed by The second coming

Percy, Walker

Love in the ruins; the adventures of a bad Catholic at a time near the end of the world. Farrar, Straus & Giroux 1971 403p

"A beautifully comic and humane work, the satirist's projection of a grotesque future world based on the realities of the present and stimulus to thought and evaluation and, hopefully, to improvement. Percy's style shows mastery of language." Choice

Percy, Walker

★ The **moviegoer**. Knopf 1961 241p $26

ISBN 0-394-43703-9

"A philosophical exploration of the problem of personal identity, the story is narrated by Binx Bolling, a successful but alienated businessman. Bolling undertakes a search for meaning in his life, first through an obsession with the movies and later through an affair." Merriam-Webster's Ency of Lit

Percy, Walker

The **second** coming. Farrar, Straus & Giroux 1980 359p

ISBN 0-374-25674-8

LC 80-12899

In this sequel to The last gentleman, Will Barrett "has become a widowed, middle-aged millionaire. He didn't marry Kitty, who he loved in the earlier book, but a crippled heiress. He has had an unforeseen success as a Wall Street lawyer, fathered a {daughter} . . . and now, retired, suffers undiagnosed fall-downs on the golf course. Released from the amnesia that used to afflict him, he remembers . . . his suicidal father's attempt to kill him before taking his own life. Will meets and falls in love with a schizophrenic girl escaped from an asylum, who speaks in rhymes and is gradually revealed to be Kitty's daughter." Newsweek

"A beautiful . . . exploration of Percy's recurrent theme—an individual man's search for the hand of God in the meaningless muddle of contemporary life." Booklist

Perdue, Lewis

Slatewiper. Forge 2003 367p $24.95

ISBN 0-7653-0111-3

LC 2002-45496

"In Tokyo, a particularly violent and deadly plague has broken out. Inexplicably, it seems as if the virus only uses Koreans as its carrier. Enter Lara Blackwood, a genetic engineer recruited to fight this virus that somehow piggybacks itself on people with specific genetic characteristics. Ejected from her own company, Lara sees in this investigation her chance to get herself back in the research game, but she doesn't count on uncovering a genetic weapon of unimaginable power. . . . Perdue unflinchingly treads on Crichton's turf but emerges with a novel that feels fresh and original." Booklist

Perec, Georges

★ **Life**; a user's manual. translated by David Bellos. Godine 1987 581p

ISBN 0-87923-700-7

LC 87-8782

Original French edition, 1978

The author of this novel set in a Paris apartment house on a single day describes the building's 100 rooms and the life stories of past and present occupants as a painting in progress, the work of one of the tenants

"The inextricable incoherence of things is presumably the basic theme of the late Georges Perec's work, but this pessimistic view of life is dramatized with inventiveness, audacity, and even humor." Atlantic

Perec, Georges

★ A **void**; translated by Gilbert Adair. Harper-Collins Pubs. 1994 285p

ISBN 0-00-271119-2

Original French edition, 1969

"Gilbert Adair has now shown quite brilliantly that a lipogrammatic text in one language can be more than adequately done into another, retaining not only the alphabetical constraint but much of the virtuosity of the original." London Rev Books

Perez Galdos, Benito

Dona Perfecta; translated by Mary J. Serrano; introduction by William Dean Howells. Harper & Row 1896 319p

Original Spanish edition, 1876

"The social problem which engrosses so much of the author's interest, the struggle between scientific and social enlightenment and the tyrannous obscurantism of the church, is here set forth in the domestic conflict of a group of characters and the political strife agitating a provincial town. Dona Perfecta is a devout lady whose daughter is sought by a promising young man, a representative of modernism. A wily priest is her chief ally, and eventually the rival intrigues drag in a host of forces on either side." Baker. Guide to the Best Fic

Perez Galdos, Benito

Torquemada; translated from the Spanish by Frances M. López-Morillas. Columbia Univ. Press 1986 569p

LC 85-19560

Omnibus edition of the author's Torquemada tetralogy portraying middle-class Madrid society, and focusing on the miserly Francisco de Torquemada from the time he is 50 years old to his deathbed ten years later. The novels were originally published separately in the late nineteenth century

Perez-Reverte, Arturo

★ **Captain** Alatriste; translated from the Spanish by Margaret Sayers Peden. Putnam 2005 253p $23.95

ISBN 0-399-15275-X

LC 2004-60210

"Equipped with a quick-witted, charismatic hero and much to provoke and goad him, Mr. Pérez-Reverte has the makings of a flamboyantly entertaining series. Captain Alatriste ends with a wicked flourish, an evil laugh and a strong likelihood that the best is yet to come." N Y Times (Late N Y Ed)

Perez-Reverte, Arturo

★ The **Club** Dumas; translated from the Spanish by Sonia Soto. Harcourt Brace & Co. 1996 362p il $23

ISBN 0-15-100182-0

LC 96-11962

Original Spanish edition, 1993

"Corso, a tough-guy bibliophile living in Madrid, is hired by a wealthy client to track down a rare seventeenth-century book on how to summon the Devil. He soon finds himself in noir metafiction in which he's been cast as D'Artagnan and is threatened by characters suspiciously like Richelieu's agents—a menacing man with a scar and a blonde with a fleur-de-lis tattoo. Even a reader armed with a Latin dictionary and a copy of 'The Three Musketeers' cannot anticipate the thrilling twists of this stylish, Escher-like mystery." New Yorker

Perez-Reverte, Arturo

The **fencing** master; translated from the Spanish by Margaret Jull Costa. Harcourt Brace & Co. 1999 245p $24

ISBN 0-15-100181-2

LC 98-35536

Original Spanish edition, 1988

"In lieu of snappy pater, Pérez-Reverte provides artful, intricate conversation. Rather than send his characters on a relentless search, he provides them with an inexorable unfolding of revelation, increasingly ghastly. And instead of the clever puzzle that lies at the heart of many a lesser crime novel, he substitutes a subtle meditation on the deeper mysteries of fate and choice." N Y Times Book Rev

Perez-Reverte, Arturo

The **nautical** chart; translated from the Spanish by Margaret Sayers Peden. Harcourt 2001 466p

ISBN 0-15-100534-6

LC 2001-39446

Original Spanish edition, 2000

"This is the story of a down-and-out sailor ('We could call him Ishmael, but in truth his name is Coy') who washes up in modern-day Barcelona, where he is recruited to join in the treasure hunt for a cargo of emeralds . . . that went down with a merchant ship that sank off the Spanish coast in 1767." N Y Times Book Rev

Perez-Reverte, Arturo

The **painter** of battles; a novel. translated from the Spanish by Margaret Sayers Peden. Random House 2008 211p $25

ISBN 978-1-4000-6598-1; 1-4000-6598-4

LC 2007-16997

Original Spanish edition, 2006

"The character of the title is Andrés Faulques, a hermit who spends his time painting a colossal battle scene on the interior of a watchtower. Faulques was once a war photographer, famed for his ability to capture in a single image horror, beauty and geometry. One day he has a visitor, the subject of one of Faulques's most celebrated shots: a weary Croatian soldier in the hour of dejected defeat. The photograph helped to change Faulques's life, winning an award. It also changed the soldier's: its publication and his identification as the husband of a young woman sheltering in a Serbian village saw her raped and then, along with his son, tortured and murdered. Now he has come to pay Faulques back. What follows is a game of mental chess, an excursion into art, history and imagination, and both men's lives as Faulques realises that only the continuation of their discourse, and his painting, is keeping him alive." London Times

Perez-Reverte, Arturo

Purity of blood; translated from the Spanish by Margaret Sayers Peden. G.P. Putnam's Sons 2006 267p $23.95

ISBN 0-399-15320-9

LC 2005-50984

Original Spanish edition, 1997

In this installment featuring the 17th-century swordsman, Alatriste "is contracted to help a man from a Jewish-turned-Catholic family rescue his daughter from behind the thick walls of a Madrid convent, which the chaplain 'has turned . . . into his private seraglio.' This novel is written in the mold of Dumas' musketeer novels and excitingly upholds the tradition." Booklist

Perillo, Lucia, 1958-

★ **Happiness** is a chemical in the brain; stories. Lucia Perillo. W.W. Norton & Co. 2012 211 p.

ISBN 0393083535; 9780393083538

LC 2012001613

This book, by the Kingsley Tufts Prize-winning author Lucia Perillo, presents a series of short stories in "a small town in the Pacific Northwest. . . . An addict trapped in a country house becomes obsessed with vacuum cleaners. . . . An accidental mother struggles to answer her daughter's badgering about her paternity. And . . . a woman with Down syndrome . . . serves as an accomplice to her younger sister's sexual exploits and her aging mother's fantasies of revenge." (Publisher's note)

Perlman, Elliot

Seven types of ambiguity. Riverhead Books 2004 628p $27.95

ISBN 0-571-20717-0

LC 2004-45348

"This is an exciting gamble of a novel, one willing to lose its shirt in its bid to hold you. Be prepared to give it time. Be prepared to skim when you come to a particularly annoying digression. But most of all be prepared to stay with it for the long haul. It's worth it." N Y Times (Late N Y Ed)

Perlman, Elliot

★ The **street** sweeper; Elliot Perlman. Riverhead Books 2012 600p.

ISBN 9781594488474

LC 2011046366

This book is "is a . . . tale that spans decades and bridges generations while chronicling the predominant chapters of racial persecution perpetrated in the darkest hours of the 20th century. . . . Lamont Williams, a janitor on probationary period at New York's Memorial Sloan-Kettering Cancer Center, wants to start afresh after a spell in prison, and locate the estranged daughter he hasn't seen for years. Adam Zignelik, a Columbia history professor, is raw after casting off his girlfriend, a feeling exacerbated when the university denies him tenure for his lack of ambition. Both characters get their second chances from unimagined collisions with history [and the Holocaust in particular]." (SFGate)

Perrotta, Tom

★ The **abstinence** teacher. St. Martin's Press 2007 358p $24.95

ISBN 978-0-312-35833-4; 0-312-35833-4

LC 2007-21961

"Perrotta, an accomplished satirist who has made the suburbs his personal stomping ground, turns Stonewood Heights . . . into a battleground for the hearts and minds (and, need I add, souls) of his characters. While Perrotta does do more than give lip service to both sides, it's pretty clear where his allegiance lies. . . . What keeps the book from getting too heavy-handed, besides the sharply written humor, is the fact that Perrotta makes his evangelical Christian protagonist less of a zealot than the atheist." Christ Sci Monit

Perrotta, Tom

Joe College. St. Martin's Press 2000 306p

ISBN 0-312-26184-5

LC 00-31722

"Danny, a New Jersey working-class boy at Yale, circa 1980, finds himself both enchanted by a schoolmate and dodging calls from a hometown girlfriend. Spring break, and the inevitable crisis, loom." Newsweek

"Perrotta's genius is his ability to depict student culture with dead-on accuracy. His satiric touch is like a light, but killing frost." Christ Sci Monit

Perrotta, Tom

The **leftovers**. St. Martin's Press 2011 355p $25.99

ISBN 978-0-312-35834-1; 0-312-35834-2

LC 2011-19509

In this novel, "the catalyst to the plot is the Sudden Departure, a 'Rapture-like event' in which millions of people suddenly vanished from the face of the earth. . . . The nuclear family that [Tom] Perrotta takes as his focus survives the Sudden Departure intact, only to splinter under the weight of its implications. It is left to the father, Kevin, the mayor of their small town . . . and the daughter, Jill, to keep calm and carry on." (Times Literary Supplement)

"When the 'Sudden Departure' occurs, millions of people around the world—true believers and nonbelievers alike—simply disappear in an 'indiscriminate Rapture.' In the town of Mapleton, the young and old struggle through their daily lives as they come to grips with losing family members and childhood friends, while cults such as the Healing Hug Movement, the Barefoot People and the Guilty Remnant (also known as the Watchers) prey upon the vulnerable and the grieving survivors. . . . Kevin Garvey's wife, Laurie, leaves him for the Guilty Remnant, while his son chooses to seek a father figure in the charismatic leader of the Healing Hug Movement. Kevin's teenage daughter lives at home, but spends her time drinking and playing a more adventurous version of 'Spin the Bottle' with other bored teenagers. Meanwhile, Kevin takes on the role of Mapleton's new mayor, with no real agenda except to try to bring together a town that is about to fall apart. Perrotta has a gifted ear for dialogue and a distinct appreciation for the particularities of suburban life." Minneapolis Star Tribune

Perrotta, Tom

★ **Little** children. St. Martin's Press 2004 355p $24.95

ISBN 0-312-31571-6

LC 2003-15947

"The eponymous children in this satirical novel are actually adults who, chafing at the burdens of parenthood, try to recreate their unencumbered youth. Sarah, an overeducated young homemaker, likens her tantrum-prone daughter to a 'brooding Russian epileptic' out of Dostoevsky, and pines for lost college days of feminism and bisexuality. While her husband orders used panties online, she has furtive sex with a stay-at-home dad whose repeated failure to pass the bar has earned him the contempt of his gorgeous wife. The humor is sometimes cruel, but Perrotta never betrays the complexity of his characters." New Yorker

Perry, Anne, 1938-

Bedford Square. Fawcett Columbine 1999 330p $24.95

ISBN 0-449-90633-7

LC 98-29854

"Through a campaign of 'whisper, suspicion and innuendo,' someone is slandering men of high position in 1891 London society, and it is up to Thomas Pitt, commander of the Bow Street police station, to scotch these poisonous rumors of dishonorable behavior before reputations are destroyed and lives ruined. Through his discreet investigations, the sympathetic Pitt exposes the subtle cruelty of the anonymous letters that bring disgrace to one man and death to another." N Y Times Book Rev

Perry, Anne

Belgrave Square. Fawcett Columbine 1992 361p

LC 91-73144

The author "paints handsome portraits of . . . {Victorian} aristocratic society and provides luxurious details of the gala balls and garden parties, the fashionable outings at Covent Garden and the Royal Academy of Arts, where they congregate to preen themselves. But it isn't all done for show. The author has the eyes of a hawk for character nuance and her claws out for signs of the criminal injustices rampant among the privileged classes during this gilded historical period." N Y Times Book Rev

Perry, Anne

Bluegate Fields. St. Martin's Press 1984 308p

LC 84-11769

"Inspector Pitt and his splendid wife, Charlotte, pursue {a} murder investigation that takes them from the squalor of the slums to the hypocrisy of high-society drawing rooms in Victorian London. Pitt is uncomfortable with a case built against a humorless tutor by a zealous young policeman who possesses a potentially obstructive reverence for the upper class. However the witnesses appear irrefutable . . . and Pitt's superior is adamant about not reopening so embarrassing a case—a teenager from a wealthy family was murdered in a bathtub and shoved down a London sewer. Charlotte, impelled by the tutor's wife, launches her own campaign to prove that the wrong man has been arrested." Booklist

Perry, Anne

A breach of promise. Fawcett Columbine 1998 374p $25

ISBN 0-449-90849-6

LC 98-21212

"Gifted architect Killian Melville begs barrister Sir Oliver Rathbone to defend him in what is certain to be an ugly breach-of-promise suit. Melville claims he never asked lovely young Zillah Lambert, the daughter of his mentor and patron Barton Lambert, to marry him. Unfortunately, the young lady and her mother think otherwise. . . . Days later, Melville is dead, an apparent suicide. Rathbone can't get the unfortunate young man out of his mind and determines to get to the bottom of the case." Booklist

"Aside from the jarring coincidence that sets up the resolution, the story is full of feeling and weighted with intelligent thought about the status of women in mid-Victorian society." N Y Times Book Rev

Perry, Anne

Buckingham Palace gardens; a novel. Ballantine Books 2008 312p $26

ISBN 978-0-345-46931-1; 0-345-46931-3

LC 2007-42767

A mystery featuring Perry's 19th-century police inspector, Thomas Pitt. "Unlike so many detective series gliding on cruise control, this mature work provides a fine introduction to Perry's alluring world of Victorian crime and intrigue. Ever the master of her milieu, she delivers sumptuous descriptions of life among the gentry when England still basked in its imperial glory. And in an intricate plot about a murder at the palace while the Prince and Princess of Wales are in residence, she also marshals the series's major themes: the way crime reverberates throughout the social classes; the precarious status of women of every rank; and the need for honorable heroes to preserve and protect the Empire, sometimes from itself." N Y Times Book Rev

Perry, Anne

Cain his brother. Fawcett Columbine 1995 390p

LC 95-8680

Genevieve Stonefield comes to Victorian detective William Monk "for help, believing that her missing husband, the upright Angus Stonefield, has been murdered by his depraved twin brother, Caleb. When Monk finds evidence of Angus's death, he also comes upon a makeshift typhoid hospital staffed by his two friends, Lady Callandra Daviot and Hester Latterly." Publ Wkly

"This one deserves high marks for superb plotting, fine writing, intriguing characters, and outstanding historical detail." Booklist

Perry, Anne

Cardington Crescent. St. Martin's Press 1987 314p

LC 86-27942

A Victorian "mystery featuring the stalwart Inspector Thomas Pitt of Scotland Yard and his inquisitive wife, Charlotte. When Charlotte's beloved sister is suspected of poisoning her philandering husband, the Pitts undertake the investigation of the unfortunate victim's seemingly irreproachable, upper-crust family. Amid the luxurious splendor of an elegant town house and the hideous squalor of a London slum, they uncover a scandalous web of depravity and corruption that has inevitably culminated in the murder. A detailed period puzzler suffused with atmosphere, emotion, and suspense." Booklist

Perry, Anne

A **dangerous** mourning. Fawcett Columbine 1991 330p

LC 91-70655

"Murder in an aristocratic London household pits Inspector William Monk . . . against the Victorian sense of propriety, a bootlicking superior officer and a family's fierce determination to protect its reputation. Octavia Haslett, widowed daughter of Sir Basil Moidore, is found stabbed to death in her bedroom dressed only in nightclothes; when Monk proves no outsider could have entered the house that night, the family and servants remain sole suspects. As tension mounts in the household and a handsome and disliked footman becomes a scapegoat, Monk covertly arranges to introduce Hester Latterly, who served with Florence Nightingale in the Crimea and has helped Monk before, as a nurse in the Moidore home." Publ Wkly

Perry, Anne

Death of a stranger. Ballantine Bks. 2002 337p
ISBN 0-345-44005-6

LC 2002-66735

This Monk mystery "opens with the murder of a wealthy railroad businessman in a brothel. Outraged by the crime, high society pressures the police into cracking down on prostitution. But a police presence is bad for business, and the pimps take out their frustration on the call girls. These battered women seek medical assistance at a Coldbath Square clinic rum by Monk's wife, Hester. . . . Meanwhile, a mysterious young socialite asks Monk to investigate her fiancé, a partner in a successful railroad company that, she fears, is involved in fraud and corruption." Libr J

Perry, Anne

Defend and betray. Fawcett Columbine 1992 385p

LC 92-52665

"The climactic trial, and its ugly disclosures, are well wrought. . . . Throughout, the plight of the intelligent, educated woman who is not rich—her need for a meaningful independence, her culture's resistance to her fulfillment—is, while not deeply explored, frequently touched upon." N Y Times Book Rev

Perry, Anne

The **face** of a stranger. Fawcett Columbine 1990 328p

LC 90-34169

The author "understands her amnesiac sleuth so intimately that she knows he can rediscover himself only in moments of inspiration along the trail of his quarry. This, and the fact that Monk has more to learn about himself even as the story concludes, are brilliant touches that effectively blend contemporary understanding of character with a Victorian sensibility." N Y Times Book Rev

Perry, Anne

Farriers' Lane. Fawcett Columbine 1993 374p

LC 92-54390

"In the wave of anti-Semitic hysteria in 1884 that follows the crucifixion of an English gentleman, a young Jewish actor is hastily tried and executed for the crime. Five years later, a justice of the appeals court is murdered when he attempts to reopen the sensational case. Only a man of discretion, intelligence and integrity—a man like Inspector Thomas Pitt of the Bow Street police division—can solve the devious affair of passion and political intrigue in Victorian London." N Y Times Book Rev

Perry, Anne

Funeral in blue. Ballantine Bks. 2001 344p
ISBN 0-345-44001-3

LC 2001-37481

A mystery featuring Hester and William Monk. "In the studio of a London artist, two women have been murdered, one of them the wife of Dr. Kristian Beck, a physician from Vienna with whom Hester's dear friend, Lady Callandra, is secretly in love. When Beck is charged with the murder, Callandra enlists the aid of Hester and William. . . . The author excels at re-creating the ambience of 1860s London streets." Publ Wkly

Perry, Anne

Half Moon Street. Ballantine Bks. 2000 312p
ISBN 0-449-00655-7

LC 99-55232

"Perry sinks inspector Pitt knee-deep in the morally suspect world of the theater and the completely subterranean culture of pornography. . . . Cameos from Oscar Wilde and W.B. Yeats add to the sense of artistic turmoil set against middle-class timidity." Booklist

Perry, Anne

Highgate rise. Fawcett Columbine 1991 330p

LC 90-85131

"Inspector Thomas Pitt, is appalled by the callousness of an arsonist who torches a physician's town house, burning his wife to death. Pitt's highborn wife, Charlotte, shares his horror when she learns that the dead woman was a quiet crusader on behalf of poor slum tenants. . . . Ms. Perry gives Pitt a breather from his customary gutter research by confining his investigation to the victim's upper-class social circle. Following her own conscience, Charlotte insinuates her way into elegant drawing rooms where the author's satirical wit is free to spread its rather showy skirts." N Y Times Book Rev

Perry, Anne

The **Hyde** Park headsman. Fawcett Columbine 1994 392p

LC 93-22124

Inspector Thomas Pitt "struggles to solve the brutal and confounding murder of Captain the Honorable Oakley Winthrop, R.N., who's been found beheaded in Hyde Park. Pitt suspects the victim knew his killer, but it's only after three more deadly murders take place that enough evidence can be mustered to accuse the real killer." Booklist

Perry, Anne

No graves as yet; a novel of World War I. Ballantine Bks. 2003 642p $25.95

ISBN 0-345-45652-1

LC 2003-52233

"This is the debut novel in Perry's projected five-book series about a British family during World War I. The family in question includes brothers Matthew and Joseph Reavley and sisters Judith and Hannah, whose parents are killed in a car accident when the book opens. Reavley pere had been on his way to deliver a document that purports to be of national importance. Matthew, a trusted employee in the Intelligence Service, can't quite believe that the document could really threaten Britain's honor. Meanwhile, Joseph, an ordained minister and teacher of classical languages at Cambridge, struggles with the senseless murder of his brilliant protege." Libr J

"Perry's melancholy evocation of the 'eternal afternoon' that would soon turn to night all over England is lovely." N Y Times Book Rev

Perry, Anne

Paragon Walk. St. Martin's Press 1981 204p

"A psychopathic killer stalks the fashionable London neighborhood called Paragon Walk—the rapist's atrocities are as incredible, and terrifying to the Paragon Walk aristocrats as a sudden outbreak of the bubonic plague. Inspector Pitt's investigation of one brutal slaying, that of 17-year-old Fanny Nash, leads him to his own family—and himself." Booklist

Perry, Anne

Pentecost Alley. Fawcett Columbine 1996 405p

ISBN 978-0449906354

LC 95-43557

"Perry has created a superbly plotted, grippingly suspenseful period piece filled with intriguing characters and fascinating descriptions of the manners and customs of Victorian London." Booklist

Perry, Anne

Resurrection row. St. Martin's Press 1981 204p

LC 81-8846

"For no discernible reason, someone digs up the corpses of recently buried citizens and sets them up in public places. With these crimes demanding Pitt's concentration, he also has to investigate the murder of Godolphin Jones—an artist, pornographer and blackmailer. The detective's efforts to gather evidence against Jones's clients, obvious suspects, are fruitless until (as always) his quick-witted wife Charlotte drops a startling hint." Publ Wkly

Perry, Anne

Seven dials. Ballantine Bks. 2003 345p $25.95

ISBN 0-345-44007-2

LC 2002-35605

"When the Egyptian mistress of a senior cabinet minister is discovered in her garden in the middle of the night, using a wheelbarrow to dispose of the body of a junior diplomat, the apparent crime of passion turns into an international incident. Thomas Pitt. . . chafes at the order from Special Branch to extricate the government official, Saville Ryerson, from

the affair; but he sees the gravity of the political situation. . . . Although the focus of the plot tends to drift, the visual panorama is voluptuous to behold." N Y Times Book Rev

Perry, Anne

Shoulder the sky. Ballantine Bks. 2004 338p $25.95

ISBN 0-345-45654-8

"Questions about the morality of war resonate throughout this harrowing novel, which Perry has constructed with hallmark attention to period detail and sense of place. Her vivid evocations of the battlefield . . . are unforgettable." Booklist

Perry, Anne

The **silent** cry. Fawcett Columbine 1997 361p $24.95

ISBN 0-449-90848-8

LC 97-16848

"With her grimly detailed descriptions of the match factories, sweatshops, paupers hospitals and tenement 'rookeries' crowded into these slums, Perry brings a rank sense of reality to the wretched living conditions of the working poor." N Y Times Book Rev

Perry, Anne

The **sins** of the wolf. Fawcett Columbine 1994 374p

LC 94-12099

"Nurse Hester Latterly, who served courageously in the Crimean War and has assisted former policeman William Monk in many of his investigations . . . is charged with murdering a patient for personal gain. Hester hires on to accompany aging but lively Mary Farraline by train from Edinburgh to London and to administer the proper dose of heart medication. But Mary dies enroute—and her pearl brooch is discovered in Hester's bag. The dead woman's family, the police and most of Edinburgh are convinced that Hester killed her to obtain the pin. Coming to her aid are former policeman Monk, barrister Oliver Rathbone and Lady Callandra Daviot." Publ Wkly

Perry, Anne

Slaves of obsession. Ballantine Bks. 2000 344p

ISBN 0-345-43326-2

LC 00-40375

"William Monk, agent of enquiry, is employed to discover who is blackmailing respectable merchant and arms dealer Daniel Alberton. Monk soon finds himself investigating Alberton's murder, however, and looking for the murderer on the battlefield at Bull Run." Libr J

"Perry's images of the carnage and confusion of battle are relentless in their intensity, unflinching in their truth-telling detail." N Y Times Book Rev

Perry, Anne

★ **Southampton** Row. Ballantine Bks. 2002 326p

ISBN 0-345-44003-X

LC 2001-52664

Thomas Pitt "ventures into the world of spiritualism when, on the eve of a critical parliamentary election, the wife of the Liberal candidate is implicated in the murder of a clairvoyant. As she has done increasingly in recent books, Perry links the crime to a secret political cabal known as the Inner Circle and draws everyone into its machinations. . . . Perry's proto-feminists have the kind of intellectual radiance that eludes their spouses." N Y Times Book Rev

Perry, Anne, 1938-

A **sunless** sea; a William Monk novel. Anne Perry. Ballantine Books 2012 372 p. (hardcover: alk. paper) $26.00

ISBN 034551064X; 9780345510648; 9780345535931
LC 2012022484

This book is part of the William Monk Victorian mystery series. Here, Monk investigates the death of Zenia Gadney, found mutilated on Limehouse Pier. "While the public cries out for blood, Monk, his spirited wife, Hester, and their brilliant barrister friend, Oliver Rathbone, search for answers. From dank waterfront alleys to London's fabulously wealthy West End, the three trail an ice-blooded murderer." (Publisher's note)

Perry, Anne

Traitor's gate. Fawcett Columbine 1995 411p
LC 94-27624

"In combination with her meticulous research, Ms. Perry's infallible feeling for the historical moment yields animated political debate over the colonization of Africa, glittering views of Victorian society at play and tantalizing glimpses of a confident, assertive creature known as the 'new woman.'" N Y Times Book Rev

Perry, Anne

The **twisted** root. Ballantine Bks. 1999 346p $25

ISBN 0-345-43325-4
LC 99-34689

"A beautiful widow named Miriam Gardiner has disappeared, leaving behind a distraught fiancé and a dead coachman. Monk is called in to find Gardiner and then must uncover the truth when she is charged with murdering the coachman." Libr J

Perry, Anne

★ **Weighed** in the balance. Fawcett Columbine 1996 355p

ISBN 978-0345514059
LC 96-34824

William Monk "a Victorian-era 'agent of inquiry,' is still haunted by a baffling amnesia, and he feels that his associates—the rigidly proper barrister Sir Oliver Rathbone and the uncompromising and outspoken nurse Hester Latterly—have taken on more than they can handle when Sir Oliver decides to defend Countess Zorah Rostova against a slander charge. The patriotic Zorah has accused Princess Gisela of Felzburg of murdering her husband, Prince Friedrich, heir to the throne, who presumably had died as a result of a fall from a horse. Gisela is suing. " Publ Wkly

Perry, Anne

The **Whitechapel** conspiracy. Ballantine Bks. 2001 341p

ISBN 0-345-43328-9
LC 00-64206

"When Pitt delivers the testimony that condemns a prominent man for murder, he is 'rewarded' by being shuffled off to the Special Branch, which operates in London's risky East End." Libr J

Perry, Drew

This is just exactly like you. Viking 2010 320p $25.95

ISBN 978-0-670-02154-3; 0-670-02154-7
LC 2009-42562

"If the novel's world sounds a little circumspect, Perry brings it all to life in such remarkably pinpoint, hilarious, and convincing fashion that you revel in spending more than 300 pages here. It's difficult to come across a sentence, let alone a word, that doesn't smack tone-perfect and also refreshingly colloquial, candid, real. His quietly comic touch is equally consistent." Boston Globe

Perry, Thomas

Blood money; a novel. Random House 2000 351p $24.95

ISBN 0-679-45304-0
LC 99-18340

"Perry's inventive ways of keeping Jane and her charges one step ahead of the mob squad are downright dazzling—all the more so because they pass up coldblooded technology and go for good old human wit and ingenuity." N Y Times Book Rev

Perry, Thomas

The **boyfriend**. Grove Press 2013 288 p. (hardcover) $25

ISBN 0802126065; 9780802126061

In this mystery, "private investigator Jack Till is hired by the parents of Catherine Hamilton to find her killer. . . . He relentlessly pursues leads to find Catherine's killer, stepping into the sordid territory of high--priced call girls . . . . Before long, he discovers that it isn't just a case of call girls being murdered by their clients. The pattern is in the girls' looks, all beautiful strawberry blondes, and in a custom-made necklace and anklet each of the dead girls was wearing." (Library Journal)

Perry, Thomas

Dance for the dead. Random House 1996 324p

ISBN 0-679-44911-6
LC 95-32716

In this thriller, Native American private agent Jane Whitefield, "appoints herself the guardian angel of Timmy Phillips, a little boy with a big trust fund. The master criminal who had Timmy's foster parents murdered has an ingenious scheme for plundering his inheritance; but, since 'none of this works if the heir is alive,' Jane takes aggressive action to save his life." N Y Times Book Rev

Perry, Thomas

Death benefits; a novel. Random House 2001 383p $24.95

ISBN 0-679-45305-9

LC 00-41476

San Francisco insurance data analyst John Walker is "sleepwalking through his young life when the boss assigns him to assist a private detective on an inside job involving Walker's ex-girlfriend, a claims adjuster who disappeared after being implicated in a $12 million scheme to defraud the company. Judicious applications of Perry's knowing wit energize the tutor-pupil dynamics between Walker and Max Stillman, the crafty and somewhat sinister P.I. who calls the shots on this case." N Y Times Book Rev

Perry, Thomas

The **face**-changers; a novel. Random House 1998 372p $24

ISBN 0-679-45303-2

LC 97-34078

Seneca Indian guide Jane Whitefield "is asked by her surgeon husband to help her old mentor, Dr. Richard Dahlman, who has been accused of murdering his research partner. In her attempts to keep Dahlman out of the hands of the law and far away from the two men who want to kill him, she finds that someone is using her name to make people disappear permanently, and Dahlman has gotten caught in the backlash. . . . The plot is full of heart-stopping suspense, Native American lore, and engaging characters, but the real pull is how Jane will surmount adversity and still keep her honor and ethics intact." Libr J

Perry, Thomas

Fidelity. Harcourt 2008 357p $25

ISBN 978-0-15-101292-3; 0-15-101292-X

LC 2007-26507

Perry's "characters are uncannily good at sizing one another up and anticipating what the next moves will be. Though he briefly equates Hobart's tactics to the ways a coyote slinks through a neighborhood, Mr. Perry need not even articulate this. It's always built into his storytelling, and it's already on the page." N Y Times (Late N Y Ed)

Perry, Thomas

The **informant**. Houghton Mifflin Harcourt 2011 325p $27

ISBN 978-0-547-56933-8; 0-547-56933-5

LC 2010-43566

"Perry's immaculate style—clean, polished, uncluttered by messy emotions—suits the Butcher's Boy, who executes his kills with the same cool, dispassionate skill." N Y Times Book Rev

Perry, Thomas

Nightlife; a novel. Random House 2006 373p $24.95

ISBN 1-4000-6004-4

LC 2005-46449

"This novel's intensity comes from the skillful way in which Perry lets readers in on the secrets of the serial killer: we see her change disguises and identities; we see her pick up and destroy men. We see more than the police and the private eye do, as they try to find the woman they suspect killed the Portland man, and as we see her leave that old identity far, far behind. Perry also offers a complex character in detective Catherine Hobbes as she races against the private eye to catch a protean killer." Booklist

Perry, Thomas

Poison flower; a Jane Whitefield novel. Thomas Perry. Mysterious Pr: Grove/Atlantic 2012 274 p. $24

ISBN 9780802126054

In this book, "Jane Whitefield's latest attempt to hide someone other people are looking for puts her in even more danger than usual, and that's not easy. Jane has . . . little trouble breaking James Shelby, framed for murdering his wife, out of police custody at the Clara Shortridge Foltz Criminal Courts Building in Los Angeles. . . . Three hard types who've been tracking Shelby go after Jane instead. Driving her to a remote desert location, they . . . seek . . . information about her client, then realize that they can make a queen's ransom by auctioning her off to one of the many criminals she's outwitted. . . . Jane manages to escape and takes refuge in a battered women's shelter in Las Vegas, where she acquires yet another fugitive who must be hidden away." (Kirkus)

Perry, Thomas

Pursuit; a novel. Random House 2002 370p $24.95

ISBN 0-679-45306-7

LC 2001-40365

The key players in this thriller "are James Varney, a sociopathic hit man whose handiwork has left 13 people dead in a Louisville, Ky., restaurant, and Roy Prescott, the professional manhunter hired to track him down by the father of one of the victims. . . . Although Prescott initiates most of the fiendish maneuvers, he is checkmated at every turn by his opponent's ability to anticipate or recover from each trap. When this brilliant game is finally called, it isn't advanced weaponary or high-tech skills that determine the victor; it's one player's greater insights into the other's twisted mind— a mind very much like his own." N Y Times Book Rev

Perry, Thomas

Runner. Houghton Mifflin Harcourt 2009 441p $26

ISBN 978-0-15-101528-3; 0-15-101528-7

LC 2008-7119

"Never melodramatic and always masterful at creating conflicted characters . . . , Perry offers a highly enjoyable tale in which the roles of hunter and hunted are reversed with devastating effect." Libr J

Perry, Thomas

Shadow woman. Random House 1997 350p $22

ISBN 0-679-45302-4

"Although the frantic pace allows no time for sight-seeing, Perry lingers long enough over Pete's amiable character to make him worth all this excruciating suspense." N Y Times Book Rev

Perry, Thomas

Vanishing act. Random House 1995 289p
ISBN 0-679-43536-0

LC 94-17413

"Jane Whitefield is a Seneca Indian from upstate New York who has set herself up as a one-woman underground railroad to help worthy fugitives disappear. . . . A desperate man like John Felker is right up her alley. A burned-out cop who quit the job to become an accountant, Felker was set up on an embezzlement rap. But he grabbed the dough anyway, and now he has a contract on his head. Drawing on her clan contacts, Jane guides Felker on a trip into oblivion, via a rugged route across the Canadian border. This is all very satisfying and quite scenic—until certain deadly reversals tip off Jane that her operation has been compromised." N Y Times Book Rev

Persson, Leif G. W.

Another time, another life; the story of a crime. Leif GW Persson; translated from the Swedish by Paul Norlen. Pantheon Books 2011 404 p.
ISBN 9780307377463

LC 2011017394

In this book, "[t]he story, based on real events linked to the still-unsolved assassination of Swedish prime minister Olof Palme, picks up in 1989, as the seemingly unrelated stabbing death of a civil servant is investigated by officers Bo Jarnebring and Anna Holt. . . . [T]he case gets surreptitiously swept under the rug, and the victim is tied to a string of sex-related crimes, despite evidence to the contrary. Another ten years pass before the confounding truth about the murder victim is unearthed. Just as Lars Martin Johansson, a friend of Jarnebring's, begins his tenure as the head of the Swedish Security Police, . . . [r]evealed . . . are not only the identities of the other collaborators but also the identity of the murderer: an intelligent, capable lawyer a heartbeat away from the top position in Sweden's Ministry of Defense." (Publisher's note)

Persson, Leif G. W.

Between summer's longing and winter's end; the story of a crime. Leif G.W. Persson; translated from the Swedish by Paul Norlen. Pantheon Books 2010 551 p.
ISBN 0307377458; 9780307377456

LC 2010004678

This book begins when a "young man falls to his death from a window in a student dorm in Stockholm, his loose shoe striking and killing the little dog being taken for his evening walk by an old man. . . . [T]he young man is American, not Swedish, and there are a couple of odd things about his room when . . . [the police] search it. . . . [Author] Leif GW Persson . . . begins to unravel . . . a web of international espionage, backroom politics, greed, sheer incompetence, and the shoddy work of Sweden's intelligence force that leads to the murder of the prime minister. [This book is t]he first novel in a . . . trilogy . . . [that offers a] fictional account of the unsolved 1986 assassination of Swedish Prime Minister Olof Palme." (Publisher's note)

Pesci, David

Amistad; the thunder of freedom. Marlowe & Co. 1997 292p hardcover o.p. pa $12.95
ISBN 1-56924-748-X; 1-56924-703-X pa

LC 96-54050

"In August 1839, Singbe-Pleh, a Mende tribesman, led his fellow African captives aboard the Spanish ship Amistad in successful revolt. The Africans took over the ship but could not sail it back to Africa. They were captured and put on trial in Connecticut. . . . The case was politically charged, with pro-slavery President Van Buren's administration wanting to give the Africans to Spain, abolitionists rallying for their freedom, and former President John Quincy Adams eventually defending them before the Supreme Court. Pesci deftly blends the facts of this fascinating historical episode with story." SLJ

Pessl, Marisha

Special topics in calamity physics. Viking 2006 514p il $25.95
ISBN 0-670-03777-X

LC 2005-58474

"Even the physics equation on the book's back cover has outsized verve. And what begins as a dubious proposition, in a world wholly without need for additions to its Prep School Confidential bibliography, becomes a whirling, glittering, multifaceted marvel, delivered in an irrepressibly smart and flamboyant new voice." N Y Times (Late N Y Ed)

Peters, Elizabeth

Children of the storm. Morrow 2003 400p $25.95
ISBN 0-06-621476-9

LC 2002-41083

This installment, set in 1919, finds Amelia Peabody "back in Egypt, reunited with her extended brood of family and friends (a helpful preface sorts them all out) and anticipating an enriching season at the archaeological dig being excavated by her husband. In some respects, the story follows the formula of the 14 earlier books in this spirited series—precious tomb artifacts go missing and the logical suspect turns up dead, necessitating adventures filled with romance and fraught with peril." N Y Times Book Rev

Peters, Elizabeth

The **deeds** of the disturber; an Amelia Peabody mystery. Atheneum Pubs. 1988 289p

LC 87-33457

"Determined Victorian feminist Peabody refuses to be intimidated by a phenomenon reported at the British Museum, where a sem priest is supposedly working a curse in revenge for the desecration of an ancient mummy. The priest's supernatural figure is momentarily glimpsed at the exhibit, before a murderer strikes. Disobeying Emerson, of course, Peabody lays her life on the line and unmasks the decidedly human villain." Publ Wkly

Peters, Elizabeth

The **golden** one. Morrow 2002 429p
ISBN 0-380-97885-7

LC 2001-52169

"On arriving in Luxor for a season of archaeological investigation, Amelia {Peabody Emerson} and her family discover that war (it's 1917) has taken its toll on their beloved Egypt. Before too long, the conflict intrudes on their plans and embroils them in an adventure, complete with double agents, Turkish spies, derring-do, and the ever-puzzling Sethos. At the same time, they must reckon with tomb robbers, killers, and antiquities fraud." Booklist

Peters, Elizabeth
★ **Guardian** of the horizon. Morrow 2004 416p $24.95
ISBN 0-06-621471-8
LC 2003-67665

"Peters' writing works on several levels. She maintains a fast-paced mystery story, her characters are complex, and the fictional cast interacts with historical figures convincingly." Archaeology

Peters, Elizabeth
He shall thunder in the sky; an Amelia Peabody mystery. Morrow 2000 400p
ISBN 0-380-97659-5
LC 00-25807

In this episode, set in 1915, Amelia Peabody's family's "annual excavations in Egypt are overshadowed by the specter of world war. An invasion of Egypt by the Turks seems imminent, the climate is ripe for spies, and it isn't long before the Emerson clan is up to its eyebrows in intrigue. Then there's Emerson's discovery of a beautiful gold statue: Has the ardent archvillain Sethos returned with more tricks? Peters works in drama galore, plus the usual shots of wry humor and local color." Booklist

Peters, Elizabeth
The **hippopotamus** pool. Warner Bks. 1996 384p
ISBN 978-0446518338
LC 95-31886

In this mystery set in 19th century Egypt, Amelia Peabody "is celebrating the turn of the century at a New Year's Eve ball at Shepheard's Hotel in Cairo when she and her husband, the sexy Egyptologist Radcliffe Emerson, are approached by a mysterious stranger who hands over a scarab ring that he claims was recovered from the lost tomb of Queen Tetisheri. 'Oh, good Gad!' Emerson explodes. 'Are we to have another of these melodramatic distractions?' Indeed we are—and it's a dandy one too. Such romantic nonsense. Such fun." N Y Times Book Rev

Peters, Elizabeth
The **last** camel died at noon. Warner Bks. 1991 352p il
LC 90-26759

"The Emersons are decidedly unstodgy Victorians—feminist, democratic, egalitarian, respectful of other cultures—and charming, witty, entertaining sleuths." Booklist

Peters, Elizabeth
Lion in the valley; an Amelia Peabody mystery. Atheneum Pubs. 1986 291p
LC 85-48126

"The stouthearted Victorian Englishwoman, Amelia Peabody Emerson, and her lusty, irascible husband are back in Egypt (with their precocious eight-year-old son, Ramses in tow). . . . The master criminal whom they thwarted but did not bring to justice in 'The Mummy Case' is once again up to nefarious deeds, which include kidnapping Amelia in order to woo her. Murder, mayhem . . . and a pair of distressed young lovers, not to mention a modicum of archaeological pursuits, round out a decided treat for fans of the indomitable duo—or, perhaps, with Ramses, it is now a trio." Booklist

Peters, Elizabeth
The **mummy** case. Congdon & Weed 1985 313p
LC 84-21500

"Victorian Amelia Peabody with her virile husband Emerson and precocious son Ramses embarks on a . . . archaeological dig in Egypt—but not before the death of a dealer in stolen antiquities. A disappearing mummy case and missing Coptic Papyri are the clues in this slapstick comedy-mystery. The ample archaeological detail is vivid, albeit a bit confusing. The irresistable attraction of this story: the heroine's droll tone and intrepid spirit." Libr J

Peters, Elizabeth
Night train to Memphis. Warner Bks. 1994 353p
LC 94-3967

Vicky Bliss, "a curator at Munich's National Museum, is asked to go undercover on a cruise down the Nile. Her mission: to spot who among her fellow passengers might be the master criminal about to carry out a major theft of valuable antiquities. Vicky has a sneaking suspicion that the thief the police are after is the mysterious man she knows as John, who's perfectly capable of illegal activities and who's been both her sworn enemy and her sometime lover. When John shows up on the cruise and a crew member is murdered, Vicky begins to fear her suspicions are correct—but she doesn't have enough evidence to rule out the other passengers. This one is vintage Peters at her entertaining best." Booklist

Peters, Elizabeth
Seeing a large cat. Warner Bks. 1997 386p il
ISBN 978-0446518345
LC 96-37998

"Amelia's unquenchable joie de l'aventure continues to define the exuberant style of these mysteries, but Peters doesn't leave it at that. There are always grand views of Egyptian antiquities in her stories, as well as acidic caricatures of globe-trotting tourists and the endlessly entertaining spectacle of busy professional parents confounded by their own progeny." N Y Times Book Rev

Peters, Elizabeth
The **snake,** the crocodile, and the dog. Warner Bks. 1992 340p
LC 92-54096

In this mystery novel, archaeologist Amelia Peabody Emerson and her husband leave their son Ramses in England to excavate in Egypt. "Amelia anticipates time alone with Emerson, but the Master Criminal devises otherwise:

In his quest for directions to the . . . Lost Oasis, he attempts abduction, subterfuge, and espionage." Libr J

Peters, Elizabeth

Trojan gold; a Vicky Bliss mystery. Atheneum Pubs. 1987

LC 86-26486

Art historian Vicky Bliss "receives a photograph of a modern woman dressed in the gold jewelry that Schliemann discovered in his archaeological excavation of Troy. The gold has been missing since the night the Soviet Army marched into Munich in 1945. The usual assortment of male admirers gather round, all trying to out-maneuver Vicky; but she manages to side-step nicely and come out the winner in this scintillating, captivating tale." Libr J

Peters, Ellis

The **benediction** of Brother Cadfael. Mysterious Press 1992 348p il maps

LC 91-50965

A combined edition of A morbid taste for bones and One corpse too many, both entered separately. This volume also includes a description of Cadfael country by Rob Talbot and Robin Whiteman

Peters, Ellis

Brother Cadfael's penance; the twentieth chronicle of Brother Cadfael. Mysterious Press 1994 292p

LC 94-27140

This Brother Cadfael mystery "has the gentle monk leaving his cloister on a journey that will prove both dangerous and wrenching. In twelfth-century Britain, a rebellion has arisen, with factional fighting between the knights supporting Empress Maud and those swearing allegiance to her cousin Stephen. Philip FitzRobert, a traitor to the empress, has taken 30 hostages, among them a young man named Olivier de Bretagne, who is Cadfael's son from a chance encounter years earlier. Although Cadfael has lost tract of the boy's mother, he's never forgotten his son, and once he finds out that Olivier has been spirited away and imprisoned, nothing . . . can keep him from setting out to find the young man who has never known his true father." Booklist

Peters, Ellis

Dead man's ransom; the ninth chronicle of Brother Cadfael. Morrow 1985 189p

LC 84-22668

First published 1984 in the United Kingdom

This "novel focuses on the brutality of civil war between England and Wales in the early twelfth century, as the Benedictine monk is pulled into a hostage drama that turns into a politically repercussive murder. A young Welshman is exchanged for the sheriff of Shropshire and taken to Cadfael's abbey, where he falls in love with the sheriff's daughter. The sheriff's subsequent murder leaves rampant speculation that the young lovers are the perpetrators of the crime. Cadfael, as ever, is patient and insightful. A wonderfully atmospheric whodunit." Booklist

Peters, Ellis

Death to the landlords! Morrow 1972 221p

The setting is "southern India, and the landlords are wealthy landholders who are the objectives of a terrorist murder gang. Dominic Felse . . . is at the center of the action, touring with a casual American acquaintance. The two young men meet up again and again with some of the same people as they travel India's Cape Comorin, among them a very intense English girl and a shy Indian nurse. Although the setting seems idyllic and the young people most attractive there is an undercurrent of brutal violence that hits home hard. The deaths are achieved by bombing. . . . Most effective of all is the interesting, perceptive, intuitive portrait of . . . problem-ridden India that emerges." Publ Wkly

Peters, Ellis

Fallen into the pit. Mysterious Press 1994 324p

LC 92-50656

First published 1951 in the United Kingdom

"This mystery launched Peters's Inspector Felse series. Set in Britain just after WW II, the main sleuth here is not actually George Felse but his 13-year-old son Dominic. He and his best friend, Pussy Hart, are playing when Dom finds the body of Helmut Schauffler, an ex-P.O.W. who had stayed on after the war in the Comerford area. An autopsy indicates that Schauffler's skull was fractured by blows that were 'precise, neat and of murderous intention.' Helmut, a loathsome blend of cruelty, cowardice and anti-Semitism, is hardly mourned, but his death so rends the village's social fabric that solving the case is imperative. In his first murder investigation, George has difficulty viewing his neighbors as suspects." Publ Wkly

Peters, Ellis

★ The **hermit** of Eyton Forest. Mysterious Press 1988 224p

LC 87-40398

"A 10-year-old boy in school at the abbey suddenly finds himself Lord of Eaton when his father dies. His grandmother has plans for him; she wants him to marry a neighboring heiress. The abbot refuses to let him go. The grandmother takes steps to get him back. During all this, a mysterious monk living as a hermit and an equally mysterious young man who runs errands for him make their presence strongly felt. A nobleman is murdered, and the sharp eyes of Brother Cadfael notice things that are not apparent to all." N Y Times Book Rev

Peters, Ellis

The **holy** thief. Mysterious Press 1992 246p

LC 92-50451

"Twelfth-century Shropshire comes vividly alive when peopled with Peter's aristocratic ladies, sturdy lawmen, eager squires and, above all, devout—and devious—monks." Publ Wkly

Peters, Ellis

Monk's-hood; the third chronicle of Brother Cadfael. Morrow 1981 223p il

LC 80-26326

First published 1980 in United Kingdom

In this novel Brother "Cadfael investigates the murder by monkshood of Gervase Bonel, a wealthy man who was about to donate his lands to the monastery. Along the way,

Cadfael becomes swept up in the monastery's internecine power plays. Peters' language has a full, rich cadence, and her story is wonderfully vivid." Booklist

Peters, Ellis

The **pilgrim** of hate; the tenth chronicle of Brother Cadfael. Morrow 1985 190p

LC 85-62509

First published 1984 in the United Kingdom

"It is A.D. 1141, a year that brings a tide of pilgrims to the Benedictine Abbey at Shrewsbury. The occasion is a joyous one—a celebration in honor of St. Winifred, whose sacred relics were transferred to the abbey from Wales four years earlier. . . . Meanwhile, far away in embattled Winchester, a knight, supporter of the Empress Maud (who is campaigning against Stephen for the throne of England), is mysteriously murdered. But this seemingly disparate event, Cadfael begins to suspect, may be connected to the arrival at the shrine of a pair of pilgrims." Publisher's note

Peters, Ellis

The **potter's** field; the seventeenth chronicle of Brother Cadfael, of the Benedictine Abbey of Saint Peter and Saint Paul, at Shrewsbury. Mysterious Press 1990 230p

LC 90-6340

"In place of the pretty romances with which the author often lightens her historically plausible fictions, Ms. Peters provides darker characters and a more somber view of Shrewsbury life. More than the brilliant detection of a crime, the true subject of her wintry tale is human misery, as it extends from the meanest peasant cottage to the grandest manor house." N Y Times Book Rev

Peters, Ellis

A **rare** Benedictine. Mysterious Press 1989 118p il $19.95

ISBN 0-89296-397-2

LC 89-42603

First published 1988 in the United Kingdom

The author "reveals for the first time how her medieval sleuth, Brother Cadfael, came to his calling at Shrewsbury Abbey. . . . For all his spirituality, mild Brother Cadfael once again impresses us with his practical grasp of the criminal side of human nature." N Y Times Book Rev

Peters, Ellis

The **rose** rent; the thirteenth chronicle of Brother Cadfael. Morrow 1986 190p

LC 87-5733

"When Judith Perle, a most generous benefactor of the abbey, vanishes without a trace, Cadfael immediately connects her disappearance with the vicious murder of a pious young monk and the seemingly senseless destruction of a rose bush. An accomplished whodunit meticulously wrought with a wealth of medieval detail." Booklist

Peters, Ellis

Saint Peter's Fair; the fourth chronicle of Brother Cadfael. Morrow 1981 219p il

LC 81-11020

Brother Cadfael, "who led an adventurous life in the world before becoming a monk, is on the side of young love, honor and truth as he investigates deaths taking place while a local fair is in full swing. A well-respected merchant is found murdered, and his lovely daughter takes it upon herself to keep secrets so she involves two young men, both of whom fancy her. Another death occurs. Peters has an authentic eye and ear for her 12th century way of life and death, and engages our interest all the way." Publ Wkly

Peters, Ellis

The **sanctuary** sparrow; the seventh chronicle of Brother Cadfael. Morrow 1983 221p

LC 83-5389

Brother Cadfael "undertakes the problems of young Liliwin, a juggler and acrobat of Shrewsbury who stands accused of pilfering the valuables of one Master Walter Aurifaber, the townships's goldsmith, while Liliwin was amusing Aurifaber and the assembled patrons who were at the wedding feast of Aurifaber's son, Daniel." West Coast Rev Books

Peters, Ellis

The **summer** of the Danes. Mysterious Press 1991 251p

LC 91-11621

In this novel Brother Cadfael "must pilgrimage deep into Wales on an errand of Church diplomacy. He is accompanied by young Brother Mark and the passionate Heledd, a young woman fleeing an arranged marriage. The three become pawns in the battle between two Welsh princes and the mercenary Danes whom one prince has hired to help vanquish his brother. There is a murder to be considered when Bledri ap Rhys—who has offended everyone from Heledd's father, Canon Meirion, to countless common soldiers—is found in his bed, stabbed through the heart." Publ Wkly

Peters, Ellis

The **virgin** in the ice; the sixth chronicle of Brother Cadfael. Morrow 1983 220p il

LC 82-14500

First published 1982 in the United Kingdom

"The setting is England during the winter of 1139, A.D. Brother Cadfael, who has taken a vow against war and arms, finds himself in a country torn by civil war. Brother Elyas, a fellow monk of a nearby town, is sent to deliver two orphans, Ermina and Yves Hugonin, and their chaperone Sister Hilaria, to Laurence d'Angers, the childrens' uncle. During the journey Ermina sees her chance to escape and marry her lover. . . . Brother Elyas is attacked by a brutal band of marauders and left for dead. Brother Cadfael, sent on a medical errand to look after Brother Elyas, takes over his responsibility to bring the three safely to Laurence d'Angers. During his journey, Brother Cadfael discovers a murder and feels morally obliged to solve it." Best Sellers

Peterson, Paula W.

Women in the grove. Beacon Press 2004 205p $20

ISBN 0-8070-8352-6

LC 2003-14314

"Each of the stories in this beautiful collection focuses on a woman living with HIV/AIDS. . . . [Peterson] clearly knows her subject, and she challenges the reader to put an individual face and story on the HIV/AIDS epidemic. Rich with emotion, this book is too good to be categorized as any one genre of fiction but should be celebrated and read widely." Libr J

Petrushevskaya, Ludmila

There once lived a woman who tried to kill her neighbor's baby; scary fairy tales. selected and translated with an introduction by Keith Gessen and Anna Summers. Penguin Books 2009 206p pa $15

ISBN 978-0-14-311466-6; 0-14-311466-2

LC 2009-29419

Petrushevskaya "is so disquieting that long after Solzhenitsyn had been published in the Soviet Union, her fiction was banned—even though nothing about it screams 'political' or 'dissident' or anything else. It just screams. These stories work the boundary states of consciousness—between sleep and waking, hallucination and realization, life and death—like a tongue works an aching tooth. You never know where you are or where you're going, because the ground beneath the narratives is constantly shifting. You know only that the world you are in is as bleak as Beckett, as astringent as witch hazel, as poetic as your finest private passing moments." Elle

Petry, Ann Lane

★ The **street**; [by] Ann Petry. Houghton Mifflin 1946 435p

"Set in Long Island, New York, in suburban Connecticut, and in Harlem, The Street is the story of intelligent, ambitious Lutie Johnson, who strives to make a better life for herself and her son despite a constant struggle with sexual brutality and racism." Merriam-Webster's Ency of Lit

Petterson, Per

I curse the river of time; translated from the Norwegian by Charlotte Barslund with Per Petterson. Graywolf 2010 233p (Lannan translation series) $23

ISBN 978-1-55597-556-2; 1-55597-556-9

LC 2010-920770

Original Norwegian edition, 2008

This novel "concerns thirtysomething Arvid Jansen, who's reeling from a divorce just as his mother is dying of stomach cancer. Needless to say, it's a sad book, and at times it'll feel alien to readers who've never been young Communists or hung out in, say, Nittedal or Eidsvoll. (The translation can also be quite a rickety bridge.) But there's no denying the novel's Raymond Carver-like power as Arvid and his mother come to terms with how life hands you hope just before it hands you disappointment and tragedy." Entertainment Wkly

Petterson, Per

In the wake; translated from the Norwegian by Anne Born. Thomas Dunne Books 2006 202p $22.95

ISBN 0-312-34383-3

LC 2006-40196

Original Norwegian edition, 2002

This novel is, "among other things, a story about literature itself. . . . Arvid, amid his struggles, reads and rereads the works of favorite writers and poets. Ultimately, moving between literature, with its ability to confer meaning on life, and his growing willingness to re-engage with life, Arvid cautiously rejoins the world. In 'In the Wake' Mr. Petterson demonstrates, through his own commanding art, the solace of the written word as well as the necessity of human connection. It is understandable why European readers have long admired his work." N Y Times Book Rev

Petterson, Per

★ **Out** stealing horses; translated by Anne Born. Graywolf Press 2007 258p (Lannen translation series selection) $22

ISBN 978-1-55597-470-1; 1-55597-470-8

LC 2006-938263

Original Norwegian edition, 2003; this translation first published 2005 in the United Kingdom

In this "novel, Trond Sander, a widower nearing seventy, moves to a bare house in remote eastern Norway, seeking the life of quiet contemplation that he has always longed for. A chance encounter with a neighbor—the brother, as it happens, of his childhood friend Jon—causes him to ruminate on the summer of 1948, the last he spent with his adored father, who abandoned the family soon afterward. Trond's recollections center on a single afternoon, when he and Jon set out to take some horses from a nearby farm; what began as an exhilarating adventure ended abruptly and traumatically in an act of unexpected cruelty. Petterson's spare and deliberate prose has astonishing force, and the narrative gains further power from the artful interplay of Trond's childhood and adult perspectives." New Yorker

Pettersson, Vicki

The **taken**; Vicki Pettersson. Harpercollins 2012 417 p.

ISBN 0062064649; 9780062064646

This supernatural suspense romance novel by Vicki Petterson follows "Griffin Shaw [who] used to be a PI, . . . Fifty years later, he's an angel. . . . One small mistake has altered fate, and now he's been dumped back onto the mortal mudflat to collect another soul—Katherine 'Kit' Craig, a journalist whose latest investigation is about to get her clipped. . . . Grif refuses to let [her] come to harm. Besides, protecting her offers a chance to solve the mystery of his own unsolved murder. . . . But a ruthless killer determined to destroy them isn't Grif's biggest threat. His growing attraction to Kit could cost them both their lives, along with the answer to the haunting question of his long afterlife." (Publisher's note)

Phillips, Arthur, 1969-

Prague; a novel. Random House 2002 367p

ISBN 0-375-50787-6

LC 2001-48975

"In Phillips's wry and skillful telling, a sexual tryst or the renting of an apartment can become a tragicomic pantomime about East and West. . . . As 'Prague' progresses, each of the five foreigners at the cafe table becomes less and less attractive, and the satiric edge to Phillips's portrayal sharpens into something close to anger: at their solipsism, their savage cynicism, their detachment from their surrounding and from one another." N Y Times Book Rev

Phillips, Arthur, 1969-

The **song** is you; a novel. Random House 2009 254p $25

ISBN 978-1-4000-6646-9; 1-4000-6646-8

LC 2008-28845

This novel "takes on loneliness, alienation, middle age and what it means to feel passé and weighted down by your past. . . . Yet despite these sober concerns, Phillips' sparkling prose makes for a seriously fun read." San Francisco Chron

Phillips, Arthur, 1969-

★ The **tragedy** of Arthur. Random House 2011 368p $25.95

ISBN 978-1-4000-6647-6

LC 2010-21192

This novel "turns on the discovery of a lost Shakespearean drama, 'The Most Excellent and Tragical Historie of Arthur, King of Britain,' purportedly written in 1596. The play spreads across the final 107 pages of this book in strict iambic pentameter and five acts. The drama centers on King Arthur, without his famous sword in the stone, mired in 5th century lust, doubt and battle. The novel's narrator, Arthur Phillips, believes the play a hideous fraud, perpetrated by his con-artist father, a forger also called Arthur Phillips. If you are counting, we're up to five Arthurs — the mythical king, the pivotal character in the new play, the writer of this novel, the narrator of the book (himself a novelist) and the narrator's father. But instead of sinking into an annoying bog of meta-fiction; the story is light, the tone often diabolically merry. Random House, the publisher of both actual novelist and fictional narrator, is hungry to capitalize, drawing up contracts and recruiting a vetting panel of scholars." Cleveland Plain Dealer

Phillips, Caryl

★ **Crossing** the river. Knopf 1994 237p

LC 93-35933

First published 1993 in the United Kingdom

"One of the values of fiction is that it can tell the story anew, can go back and include a neglected truth. 'Crossing the River' does this and is therefore a book with an agenda. Mr. Phillips proposes that the diaspora is permanent, and that blacks throughout the world who look to Africa as a benevolent fatherland tell themselves a stunted story. They need not to trace but to put down roots. The message, however, is neither simply nor stridently conveyed." N Y Times Book Rev

Phillips, Caryl

Dancing in the dark. Knopf 2005 209p $23.95

ISBN 1-4000-4396-4

LC 2005-44106

"As subjects for historical novels go, Bert Williams is an inspired choice; his strange career exemplified all the ironies and paradoxes that confronted the African-American performers of his time. . . . Dancing in the Dark is riveting when it recreates mores and social conventions our culture has done its best to forget." N Y Times Book Rev

Phillips, Caryl

A **distant** shore. Knopf 2003 277p $23.95

ISBN 1-400-04109-0

"This muted, sad novel breaks down the distinction between the placed and the displaced, dissolving our sense of security, if we had one, about safely belonging in the world, dispelling our illusion of being at home. We are all adrift, Phillips says, whether we know it or not: a fact not of race or nationality, but of the human condition." N Y Times Book Rev

Phillips, Caryl

Foreigners. Alfred A. Knopf 2007 235p $24.95

ISBN 978-1-4000-4397-2

LC 2007-29219

"With great empathy, and through a collage of voices, Phillips has created three distinct portraits. All are superbly crafted and utterly absorbing . . . . As Phillips suggests, Englishness, like foreignness, is a complex and changeable thing. An important and sobering book, highly relevant today." Daily Mail

Phillips, Caryl

The **nature** of blood. Knopf 1997 212p $23

ISBN 0-679-45470-5

LC 96-49641

"Phillips's object in creating a work in which dialogue, description and characterization are of no real significance has been, laudably enough, to protect the universality of his themes." Times Lit Suppl

Phillips, Jayne Anne

Lark and Termite; a novel. Alfred A. Knopf 2009 254p $24

ISBN 978-0-375-40195-4; 0-375-40195-4

LC 2008-33453

Phillips "has done in Lark and Termite what she did in previous novels such as Machine Dreams (1984) and Shelter (1994), which is to take a relatively simple, straightforward tale and twist it into something luminous and haunting and singular. This is Phillips' first novel in almost a decade, but it doesn't feel tardy or excessively fussed over. It feels fresh. It feels as if it has been taken straight from the griddle and is still too hot to touch. And because it deals with issues over which people have been arguing for centuries—family and war—the novel's raw immediacy is really quite spectacular." PopMatters

Phillips, Jayne Anne

MotherKind; a novel. Knopf 2000 295p $24

ISBN 0-375-40194-6

LC 99-49256

"Over the course of a year, Kate, a resolutely independent poet and editor, becomes enmeshed in domesticity: she has a baby, acquires two stepchildren, and discovers that her mother is dying of cancer. Kate has always resisted her mother's desire to care for others perfectly, but she's now preoccupied with making crisp French fries, turning down beds, ironing out problems; frequently overwhelmed, she must also rely on nurses and efficient neighbors. Phillips, an abundantly talented writer, never lapses into sentimentality while describing this woman." New Yorker

Phillips, Marie

Gods behaving badly; a novel. Little, Brown and Co. 2007 293p $23.99

ISBN 978-0-316-06762-1; 0-316-06762-8

LC 2007-9919

This first novel, " hovers somewhere between Pride and Prejudice and an episode of 'Bewitched.' I'm not complaining; I have an unusually high regard for Elizabeth Montgomery's oeuvre. And Austen got off some good lines, too. . . . The tension doesn't ratchet too high; it's a romantic comedy, after all. The key is to fly through a book like this very fast—on Hermes' wings. But Phillips has an Olympian sense of absurdity, and there's enough ambrosial wit here to seduce most mortals for an afternoon or two on the divan." Washington Post Book World

Phillips, Susan Elizabeth

Ain't she sweet. Morrow 2004 383p $24.95

ISBN 0-06-621124-7

LC 2003-59297

"Fifteen years ago, Sugar Beth Carey reigned supreme over the small Mississippi town of Parrish, but now she's returning home a little bit shabby around the edges to claim a valuable painting left to her by her disapproving aunt. Fifteen years ago, Colin Byrne arrived in Parrish from England as a new teacher only to have his career destroyed by a spiteful young Sugar Beth. Fifteen years ago, Sugar Beth had everything Winnie Davis ever wanted, but because Winnie had the one thing Sugar Beth could never have, she turned Winnie's life into a perpetual hell. So now Colin, a bestselling author, and Winnie, Parrish's richest citizen, are determined to exact revenge for Sugar Beth's past sins, but much to their surprise, neither one finds revenge to taste quite as sweet as they expected once they get to know the new Sugar Beth." Booklist

This "light, contemporary, and enjoyable love story is filled with alluring plot lines." Libr J

Phillips, Susan Elizabeth

Call me irresistible. Morrow 2011 400p

ISBN 9780061351525; 0061351520; 0062064215; 9780062064219

LC 2010526285

This book tells the story of a young woman named Meg Koranda, whose best friend "is about to Marry Mr. Irresistible -- Ted Beaudine -- the favorite son of Wynette, Texas. . . . [Meg] is determined to save her friend from a mess of heartache. Even though Meg knows that breaking up her best friend's wedding is the right thing to do, no one else seems to agree. . . . [S]tuck . . . with a dead car, an empty wallet, and a very angry bridegroom," (Publisher's note) "Meg earns the animosity of the town, and gradually she and Ted fall in love." (Publishers Weekly)

Phillips, Susan Elizabeth

First lady; Susan Elizabeth Phil[l]ips. Avon Books 2000 376 p. (pbk.) $7.99

ISBN 0380808072; 9780380808076

LC 99095329

In this novel, "[t]he beautiful young widow of the President of the United States thought she was free of the White House, but circumstances have forced her back into the role of First Lady. Not for long, however, because she's made up her mind to escape -- if only for a few days -- so she can live the life of an ordinary person. All she needs is the perfect disguise . . . and she's just found it. An entire nation is searching for her, but the First Lady is in the last place anybody would think to look: in the company of a man, an infuriatingly secretive and quietly seductive stranger whose charm, good looks, and sensuous appeal are awakening the forgotten woman within the dignitary." (Publisher's note)

Phillips, Susan Elizabeth

The great escape; Susan Elizabeth Phillips. 1st ed. HarperCollins 2012 432 p. (hardcover) $25.99; (paperback) $14.99; (ebook) $20.99

ISBN 0062106066; 9780062106063; 9780062106186; 9780062106100

This book by Susan Elizabeth Phillips follows "Lucy Jorik . . . saved as a young teen by the woman who would become the first female President of the United States, Lucy has spent her life . . . [in] the perfect First Family. But on the day she's supposed to marry . . . she bolts from a life she feels she has fallen into, rather than one she really wants. Accepting a ride from the church on the back of a motorcycle . . . Lucy embarks on a journey of self-discovery." (Kirkus Reviews)

Phillips, Susan Elizabeth

It had to be you. Avon 2008 381p pa $12.95

ISBN 978-0-06-155581-7; 0-06-155581-9

First published 1994

"The Windy City isn't quite ready for Phoebe Somerville — the outrageous, curvaceous New York knockout who has just inherited the Chicago Stars football team. And Phoebe is definitely not prepared for the Stars' head coach Dan Celebow, a sexist jock taskmaster with a one-track mind. Celebow is everything Phoebe abhors. And the sexy new boss is everything Dan despises — a meddling bimbo who doesn't know a pigskin from a pitcher's mound." Publisher's note

Phillips, Susan Elizabeth

Match me if you can; Susan Elizabeth Phillips. William Morrow 2005 386p (pbk.) $7.99; o.p.

ISBN 9780060734565; 0060734558

LC 2004065644

This book tells the story of sports "agent, Heath Champion, and Annabelle Granger, the girl least likely to succeed. Annabelle's endured dead-end jobs, a broken engagement . . . even her hair's a mess! But that's going to change now that she's taken over her late grandmother's matchmaking business. All Annabelle has to do is land the Windy City's hottest bachelor as her client, and she'll be the most sought-after matchmaker in town. Why does the wealthy, driven, and gorgeous sports agent Heath Champion need a matchmaker, especially a red-haired screw-up like Annabelle Granger? True, she's entertaining, and she does have a certain quirky appeal. But Heath is searching for the ultimate symbol of success -- the perfect wife." (Publisher's note)

Phillips, Susan Elizabeth

Natural born charmer. William Morrow 2007 394p $24.95

ISBN 978-0-06-073457-2; 0-06-073457-4

LC 2006-49173

"After her ex-boyfriend Monty insists that she is the only person he ever loved, Blue Bailey packs up everything she has (which isn't much) and moves from Seattle to Colorado to be with him. But once Blue arrives, she discovers Monty has found love again with a younger, blonder new girlfriend. With few job options and practically no money, Blue thought she might be stuck in Colorado for a long time, until Dean Robillard drives through on his way to Tennessee. The last person Blue wants to ask for a favor is a way-too-gorgeous-for-his-own-good stranger who annoys her to no end. And who turns out to be the quarterback for the Chicago Stars. But Dean is Blue's only ticket out, even if it means she is stuck with him all the way to Tennessee." Booklist

"While the verbal sparring in this textbook case of opposites attracting feels stagy at first, the rough edges come together in an alluring way." Publ Wkly

Piazza, Tom

City of refuge; a novel. HarperCollins Publishers 2008 403p $24.95

ISBN 978-0-06-123861-1; 0-06-123861-9

LC 2008-13673

"Piazza describes the families' experience with a journalist's eye for detail and a New Orleanian's fury over the mismanagement that led to the breach of the levees and the government's lackadaisical approach to helping the survivors. . . . Righteous anger propels 'City of Refuge' forward, but occasionally it can overwhelm the story line." Christ Sci Monit

Piccirilli, Tom

The **Last** Whisper in the Dark; a novel. Tom Piccirilli. Bantam Books 2013 336 p. (acid-free paper) $26

ISBN 0345529006; 9780345529008

LC 2012043223

In this novel by Tom Piccirilli "thief Terrier Rand has come home to the family that has lawbreaking in its blood. With generations of Rands keeping secrets from the outside world—not to mention from one another—Terry is sure of one thing: He owes it to the woman he loved and lost to make sure her husband stays alive. Terry [dodges] mobsters, moguls, and murderers and the truth about one crime of his own." (Publisher's note)

Pickard, Nancy

The **27** ingredient chili con carne murders. Delacorte Press 1993 296p

LC 92-17498

"In her home in New England, the widowed Mrs. Potter receives a call from Ricardo Ortega, manager of her Arizona ranch, who hints at trouble. Alarmed, she flies out to find that Ricardo and his granddaughter have disappeared. As neighboring ranchers and friends conduct a search, Mrs. Potter tries to determine the cause of Ricardo's unease. . . . Suspense with dollops of romance and gossip makes this offering irresistible." Publ Wkly

Pickard, Nancy

Blue corn murders; a Eugenia Potter mystery. Delacorte Press 1998 257p $21.95

ISBN 0-385-31224-5

LC 98-11354

In this mystery based on Virginia Rich's notes, Pickard "continues the adventures of 64-year-old Arizona rancher Eugenia Potter, taking her to an archaeological hiking camp in Colorado. There, amid splendid scenery and mystical ancient cities, Eugenia encounters idiosyncratic characters, a camp management under stress, and savage murder. Among the suspects are a spiteful old woman on the camp's board of directors, a pair of selective teachers, and a spacey blonde Indian wannabe. Delightful plot, colorful surroundings, and solid prose makes this a winner." Libr J

Includes bibliographical references

Pickard, Nancy

★ **Bum** steer; a Jenny Cain mystery. Knopf 1990 240p

LC 89-49198

"Although Jenny gets perkier, her companions more eccentric and their adventures more hair-raising as the hunt goes on, Ms. Pickard maintains her control over the derring-do and delivers an exciting climax." N Y Times Book Rev

Pickard, Nancy

But I wouldn't want to die there; a Jenny Cain mystery. Pocket Bks. 1993 243p

LC 93-15772

"Pickard's in fine form here, combining a wonderfully acerbic, wickedly humorous commentary on the 'joys' of big-city life with a keep-'em-guessing plot and a smart, sexy, sensible . . . heroine." Booklist

Pickard, Nancy

Confession; a Jenny Cain mystery. Pocket Bks. 1994 307p

LC 93-87794

"Fortunately, Geof and Jenny have a strong sense of humor, a sturdy marriage, plenty of common sense, and enough love to get them through one of the toughest tests they've faced together. Fine reading from an outstanding mystery writer." Booklist

Pickard, Nancy

Dead crazy; a Jenny Cain mystery. Pocket Bks. 1988 276p

LC 88-15324

"Pickard nicely balances Jenny's wit and likability against her tough-minded, realistic examination of mental illness and its treatment. An outstanding mystery series." Booklist

Pickard, Nancy

Generous death. Scribner 1993 239p

First published 1984 in paperback

This is the "first Jenny Cain story that Pickard wrote and serves as an introduction to the attractive and vivacious director of the Port Frederick Civic Foundation as well as to other characters who figure prominently in the series. The plot concerns the murders of several wealthy donors to the foundation. If the nasty little poems left with each of the bodies are any indication, Jenny herself may be the next victim." Booklist

Pickard, Nancy

Marriage is murder; a Jenny Cain mystery. Dark Harvest 1987 210p

LC 87-4911

"Three homicides in two weeks: each victim the husband of a battered wife, each family beset by drinking problems, poverty, and too many children to feed. Either the wives are fighting back with a vengeance, or someone is doing their fighting for them. This is Pickard's fourth mystery starring wealthy young philanthropist Jenny Cain and her lover, policeman Geof Bushfield." Booklist

"An energetic array of Jenny's friends and co-workers keep this novel—a fine mix of romance, violence, and sleuthing—moving at a fast clip." Publ Wkly

Pickard, Nancy

No body; a Jenny Cain mystery. Scribner 1986 227p

LC 86-13118

Jenny Cain, "serving as the head of the Port Frederick Civic Foundation, relates events that stun the population in her New England town when a mud slide reveals the disappearance of 133 bodies, supposedly interred during the 19th century in the old cemetery. At the same time, the corpse of Sylvia Davis is found in the casket with John Rudolph just before he's due to be buried in the new cemetery. The next day, Rudolph's widow is murdered, and Jenny sets out to gather evidence on possible killers." Publ Wkly

Pickard, Nancy

The **scent** of rain and lightning; a novel. Ballantine Books 2010 319p $25

ISBN 978-0-345-47101-7; 0-345-47101-6

LC 2010-02092

"Well-plotted, clearly written mystery novels are always welcome. A novel that simultaneously qualifies as a gripping read, a master character study and as literary is more than welcome — it is exceedingly rare." Kansas City Star

Pickard, Nancy

The **truth** hurts. Simon & Schuster 2002 328p $24

ISBN 0-7434-1203-6

LC 2002-510452

In this Marie Lightfoot mystery, "the Florida-based true crime writer is working on a book about her parents, civil rights activists in Alabama who disappeared in 1963 when Lightfoot was a toddler. She's suddenly threatened by a mysterious fan, who signs his emails Paulie Barnes and demands that she collaborate with him on a book about her own murder, or he'll start killing her friends, including her lover, Franklin DeWeese." Publ Wkly

"The campaign of terror against Lightfoot, involving psychological torture through devices like e-mail and FedEX, is wickkedly well constructed and convincing." Booklist

Pickard, Nancy

The **whole** truth. Pocket Bks. 2000 264p $22.95

ISBN 0-671-88795-5

LC 99-46816

"By alternating chapters from Lightfoot's book about the case with coverage of the trial and the sleuth's search for information, Pickard effectively uses her character's work in progress as a narrative device." Booklist

Pickens, Cathy

Southern fried. St. Martin's Minotaur 2004 277p $23.95

ISBN 0-312-32492-8

LC 2003-58548

"After losing her job in Columbia, attorney Avery Andrews returns home to Dacus, SC, where everybody knows everybody else's business. She soon lands a corporate client, Garnet Mills, which is due for an inspection by government environmental authorities. Not surprisingly, the plant blows up, and vital documents are destroyed. Meanwhile, Avery becomes involved in a 15-year-old missing-persons case. Police have just recovered the body of the woman, a former Garnet employee, and are suspicious of her husband, who has just returned to town. Pickens's lively first mystery . . . features tidy plotting rounded out with gossipy humor, colorful characters, and Southern ethos." Libr J

Picoult, Jodi, 1966-

Change of heart; a novel. Atria Books 2008 447p $26.95; pa $16

ISBN 978-0-7434-9674-2; 0-7434-9674-4; 978-0-7434-9675-9 pa; 0-7434-9675-2 pa

LC 2007-35721

"Freelance carpenter Shay Bourne was sentenced to death for killing a little girl, Elizabeth Nealon, and her cop stepfather. Eleven years after the murders, Elizabeth's sister, Claire, needs a heart transplant, and Shay volunteers, which complicates the state's execution plans. Meanwhile, death row has been the scene of some odd events since Shay's arrival—an AIDS victim goes into remission, an inmate's pet bird dies and is brought back to life, wine flows from the water faucets. The author brings other compelling elements to an already complex plot line: the priest who serves as Shay's spiritual adviser was on the jury that sentenced him; Shay's ACLU representative, Maggie Bloom, balances her professional moxie with her negative self-image and difficult relationship with her mother. Picoult moves the story along with lively debates about prisoner rights and religion." Publ Wkly

Picoult, Jodi

House rules; a novel. Atria Books 2010 529p $28

ISBN 978-0-7432-9643-4; 0-7432-9643-5

LC 2009-26381

"Emma, a single mother, copes just fine with her teenage sons — until the day Jacob is arrested for the murder of his tutor. Jacob has Asperger's, and the cops confuse his symptoms — such as avoiding eye contact — with guilt. Jodi Picoult loses points for ruining what could have been a riveting mystery by establishing Jacob's innocence at the outset. (The real story behind the tutor's death is obvious to the careful reader.) The author has delivered a sweet family drama that doubles as a handbook on Asperger's — not exactly a thrill, but hardly a bad thing." Entertainment Wkly

Picoult, Jodi

Keeping Faith; a novel. Morrow 1999 422p $24

ISBN 0-688-16825-6

LC 98-43953

"When seven-year-old Faith White and her mother, Mariah, swing by the house on the way to ballet class, they find that Daddy is home and he's brought a playmate. This is not the first time he's been caught cheating. After the fuss and feathers have settled and Dad has moved out, Faith begins talking to an imaginary friend who, it seems, is God. And God is not male but female. Faith is able to effect miraculous cures and is also occasionally afflicted with stigmata. When the media gets wind of this, the circus begins... . If you can suspend disbelief on one or two points, this is an entrancing novel." Libr J

Picoult, Jodi, 1966-

Lone wolf; a novel. Jodi Picoult. 1st Atria Books hardcover ed. Atria Books 2012 vi, 421 p.p ill. (paperback) $16.00; (hardcover) $28.00

ISBN 9781439149690; 9781439102756; 1439102740; 9781439102749

LC 2011039017

This book is the story of "Luke Warren [who] has spent decades learning the inner workings of wolf packs. Yet his relationship with his own family is strained. Divorced from his wife and estranged from his son, Edward, Luke remains close to his daughter, Cara. When the two are involved in a car accident that leaves Luke in a coma, Edward must return home to make important medical decisions regarding life-sustaining measures." (Library Journal)

Picoult, Jodi

My sister's keeper; a novel. Atria 2004 423p $25; pa $15

ISBN 0-7434-5452-9; 0-7434-5453-7 pa

LC 2004-300043

"Picoult's timely and compelling novel will appeal to anyone who has thought about the morality of medical decision making and any parent who must balance the needs of different children." Libr J

Picoult, Jodi

Nineteen minutes; a novel. Atria Books 2007 455p $26.95; pa $15

ISBN 978-0-7434-9672-8; 0-7434-9672-8; 978-0-7434-9673-5 pa; 0-7434-9673-6 pa

LC 2006-49276

"Picoult's adept character development and intelligent plot twists make for a story that runs deeper than mere voyeurism of tititillation. [The novel] is both a page turner and a thoughtful exploration of popularity, power, and the social ruts that can define us in ways we may not wish to be defined." Rocky Mountain News

Picoult, Jodi

Sing you home; a novel. Atria Books 2011 466p $28

ISBN 978-1-4391-0272-5; 1-4391-0273-4

LC 2010-41180

"After years of infertility, it looks as if Zoe and Max Baxter are finally going to have the baby they've longed for. But when their hopes are dashed by a miscarriage and their marriage collapses, Max escapes, first into alcoholism then into religion, while Zoe concentrates on her career as a music therapist. While working with a troubled teen at a local high school, Zoe begins a friendship with Vanessa, the school guidance counselor, which unexpectedly blossoms into love. Zoe again begins thinking of starting a family, specifically with the three embryos she and Max have in cold storage at the fertility clinic." Libr J

Picoult "may have an agenda, but she has written an immensely entertaining melodrama with crackerjack dialogue." USA Today

Picoult, Jodi, 1966-

The **Storyteller**; a novel. Jodi Picoult. 1st Emily Bestler/Atria hc.ed. Atria/Emily Bestler Books 2013 ix, 460 p.p (hardcover) $28.99

ISBN 1439102767; 9781439102763

LC 2012048982

In this book, "twenty-five-year-old reclusive baker Sage Singer befriends the elderly Josef Weber, who shares something shocking from his past and asks her to help him die, a request that pins Sage between morality and retribution. Sage, a Jew who now considers herself an atheist, begins to think more deeply about faith. [Author Jodi] Picoult examines the links between family identity, religion, humanity, and how it all figures in difficult decisions." (Publishers Weekly)

Picoult, Jodi

Vanishing acts; a novel. Atria Books 2005 418p $25

ISBN 0-7434-5454-5

LC 2004-59454

"Picoult weaves together plot and characterization in a landscape that is fleshed out in rich, journalistic detail, so that readers will come away with intriguing questions rather than pat answers." Publ Wkly

Piercy, Marge

Braided lives; a novel. Summit Bks. 1982 443p

ISBN 0-671-43834-4

LC 81-16695

"As with most of Piercy's work, this is very political, and a major theme here is abortion—the dire need for safe, legal abortion. But while abortion is the visible theme, what lies beneath it is a rich, complex and thoroughly satisfying examination of life." Publ Wkly

Piercy, Marge

Gone to soldiers; a novel. Summit Bks. 1987 703p

LC 86-30118

"In many male war novels character development is sacrificed; the 'woman's touch' here is excellent. The battlefront is not all blood and guts—there is also the grief of separation from family and the mitigating solace of friendship. On the home front there are race riots as well as ration books, and the heartbreak of shattered families." N Y Times Book Rev

Piercy, Marge

The **longings** of women; a novel. Fawcett Columbine 1994 455p

ISBN 0-449-90907-7

LC 93-34125

"As Piercy draws us into the alarming predicaments of each of these women, she traces the progress of their struggles to earn respect and love with unerring accuracy and discernment. Magnetic from start to finish." Booklist

Piercy, Marge

Sex wars; a novel of the turbulent post-Civil War period. Morrow 2005 411p $24.95

ISBN 0-06-078983-3

LC 2005-41499

This novel, "set in post-Civil War New York stars a true-life cast of characters that includes Victoria Woodhull, the spiritualist turned first woman to run for the U.S. presidency; passionate suffragette Elizabeth Cady Stanton; the aged Cornelius Vanderbilt, who sits atop a $100-million fortune as he tries to make contact with his dead son; and Anthony Comstock, a crusading moralist who dedicates his life to outlawing pornography and 'obscene objects made of rubber.' . . . Most poignant among the invented characters is Freydeh Leibowitz, a young Russian-Jewish widow, who, far from the scandalous headlines and saloon gossip of the times, makes a living for herself and her adopted children, penny by penny, as a manufacturer of reliable condoms." Publ Wkly

Piercy, Marge

Summer people; a novel. Summit Bks. 1989 380p

LC 89-30007

"Piercy eschews sensationalism in portraying her unorthodox trio; her characterizations are solid and believable. Some readers may find the story's pace too deliberate, but those who like to ponder the ways in which character influences fate will welcome this solidly satisfying novel." Publ Wkly

Piercy, Marge

Three women. Morrow 1999 309p $25

ISBN 0-688-17106-0

LC 99-13324

"Piercy keeps the plot humming with issues of motherhood, Judaism, generational tensions, sexuality, and independence. Her pacing is confident, as usual, and she interweaves the three narrative threads with aplomb. Apart from Jake, who remains an elusive sketch, Piercy's insight into her characters' emotional lives is an accurate reflection of intergenerational tensions." Publ Wkly

Piercy, Marge

★ **Vida**. Summit Bks. 1979 412p

ISBN 0-671-40110-6

LC 79-19298

This novel "is not 'simply' a novel but a political brief. I have my differences with 'Vida,' but I think they are substantive rather than literary. It is an interesting—and challenging—book. . . . Marge Piercy has written about movement people before but never, I think, as lovingly as here." N Y Times Book Rev

Piercy, Marge

★ **Woman** on the edge of time. Knopf 1976 369p

"A Hispanic-American mother undergoes experimental psychosurgery. She makes psychic contact with the 22nd-century world that has resulted from a feminist revolution whose success may depend on the subversion of the experiments in which she is involved. Outstanding for the elaborate description of the future utopia and the graphic representation of the inhumanity inherent in the way that contemporary people can and do treat one another." Anatomy of Wonder 4

Pierre, D. B. C.

Lights out in Wonderland. W.W. Norton & Co. 2011 350p $25.95

ISBN 978-0-393-08123-7; 0-393-08123-0

LC 2011-20688

First published 2010 in the United Kingdom

"If Gabriel is reminiscent of anyone, it's Ignatius J. Reilly, the picaresque antihero of John Kennedy Toole's 'A Confederacy of Dunces,' or Eddie Coffin, the philosopher-turned-bank robber at the center of Tibor Fischer's 'The Thought Gang.' Like them, he is an outsider who not so much reflects the world as he remakes it, spinning with such absurdist force that he transforms the lives of anyone who draws close to his gravitational field. And like them he is a bit of a bumbler — or not a bumbler exactly but more of a holy fool." L A Times Book Rev

Pierson, D. C.

The **boy** who couldn't sleep and never had to; a novel. DC Pierson. Vintage Books 2010 226 p. ill. $14.95

ISBN 9780307474612

LC 2009021984

Alex Award (2011)

In this book, the recipient of a 2010 ALA Alex Award, "[w]hen [high-school student] Darren Bennett meets [classmate] Eric Lederer, there's an instant connection. They share a love of drawing, the bottom rung on the cruel high school social ladder and a pathological fear of girls. Then Eric reveals a secret: He doesn't sleep. Ever. When word leaks out about Eric's condition, he and Darren find themselves on the run. Is it the government trying to tap into Eric's mind, or something far darker? It could be that not sleeping is only part of what Eric's capable of, and the truth is both better and worse than they could ever imagine." (Publisher's note)

Pietroni, Anna Lawrence

Ruby's spoon; a novel. Spiegel & Grau 2010 366p $26

ISBN 978-1-4000-6868-5; 1-4000-6868-1

LC 2009-34841

The author "knows her territory as thoroughly as Ruby, and she has created an evocative fairy tale that slowly pulls a reader under as surely as one of the mermaids the locals tell legends about. . . . The Black Country English dialect her characters speak takes some getting used to, but it's more than showboating. Lawrence Pietroni is able to conjure an entire lost world through their words, and the writing of 'Ruby's Spoon' is one of its chief pleasures." Christ Sci Monit

Pilch, Jerzy

My first suicide; Jerzy Pilch; translated from the Polish by David Frick. Open Letter 2012 276 p.

ISBN 1934824402; 9781934824405

LC 2011043996

This book offers "a set of loosely concatenated stories that . . . [offer an] exploration of contemporary urban life in Poland. In the title story a man reminisces about a time 40 years before, when at the age of 12 he first had the impulse to take his life. He's heard from Pastor Kalinowski (one of the recurring characters) about the 'other world' and has some curiosity. . . . In 'The Double of Tolstoy's Son-in-Law,' the narrator develops an obsession about an old photograph of Tolstoy playing chess." (Kirkus Reviews)

Pilch, Jerzy

A **thousand** peaceful cities; translated from the Polish by David Frick. Open Letter 2010 143p pa $14.95

ISBN 978-1-934824-27-6; 1-934824-27-5

LC 2010-12026

Original Polish edition, 1997

The action "takes place in 1963, in the latter days of the Polish post-Stalinist 'thaw.' The narrator, Jerzyk ('little Jerzy'), is a teenager who is keenly interested in his father, a retired postal administrator, and his father's closest friend, Mr. Traba, a failed Lutheran clergyman, alcoholic, would-be Polish insurrectionist. . . . One drunken afternoon, Mr. Traba and the narrator's nameless father decide to take charge of their lives and do one final good turn for humanity: travel to distant Warsaw and assassinate the de facto Polish head of state, First Secretary of the Polish United Workers' Party, Wladyslaw Gomulka—assassinating Mao Tse-tung, after all, would be impractical. And they decide to involve Jerzyk in their scheme." Publisher's note

Pilcher, Robin

A **risk** worth taking. Thomas Dunne Bks. 2004 308p $24.95

ISBN 0-312-27002-X

LC 2003-58564

"Dan Porter had it all: the nice house in suburban London, three children, a beautiful wife, and a great job in finance until the dot-com crash and 9/11 changed his outlook about life and making money. Dan lost a good friend in the tragedy, and is now content being a househusband focusing on his family, while his wife, Jackie, pursues her high-level job with a fashion designer, but changes in income have caused strife. His wife and daughters want their old life back, and Jackie perceives Dan and their son, Josh, as loafers because they seem content with less. Recognizing his wife's discontent, Dan takes action after reading an article in a women's magazine about a woman who started a clothing company in a remote area of Scotland and now wants to sell. Dan travels to Scotland with the hope of buy-

ing the company and expanding the business, but he finds something much more valuable. Pilcher offers a charming story about life in the new millennium and one man's pursuit of happiness." Booklist

Pilcher, Rosamunde

Coming home. St. Martin's Press 1995 728p $25.95

ISBN 0-312-13451-7

LC 95-21656

"The book's heroine is Judith Dunbar, who is a schoolgirl of 13 when the tale begins in 1935. Sent to boarding school in Cornwall because her parents are posted to Singapore, Judith becomes friends with Loveday Carey-Lewis, who introduces her to a family and an estate, Nancherrow, that is to influence her for the rest of her life. Pilcher does a marvelous job of describing life in England before World War II." Booklist

Pilcher, Rosamunde

Flowers in the rain & other stories. St. Martin's Press 1991 277p

LC 91-18237

"Throughout this collection of stories, Pilcher maintains a pervasive gentility along with an abiding wisdom. Filled with poignant scenes, romantic and bittersweet, these stories, many written earlier in the author's career, will appeal to readers of Pilcher's very successful novels." Booklist

Pilcher, Rosamunde

September. St. Martin's Press 1990 536p

ISBN 0-312-04419-4

LC 89-70340

"A lavish coming-out party for the daughter of one of the leading families of a town in the Scottish Highlands brings together characters whose lives change in various ways during the novel's four-month span. The Airds and the Balmerinos of Strathcroy and their friends and relatives in London, Majorca and the States are the focal point of the love affairs, domestic complications, estrangements, reconciliations and other gently momentous events." Publ Wkly

"Character is at the heart of a story, and this fine tale has plenty of that." N Y Times Book Rev

Pilcher, Rosamunde

★ The **shell** seekers. St. Martin's Press 1987 530p

LC 87-28345

"It is a measure of this story's strength and success that a reader can be carried for more than 500 pages in total involvement with Penelope, her children, her past and the painting that hangs in her country cottage. 'The Shell Seekers' is a deeply satisfying story, written with love and confidence." N Y Times Book Rev

Pilcher, Rosamunde

Voices in summer. St. Martin's Press 1984 215p

LC 83-22998

"Laura, married to Alec, an older divorcé, feels alienated from the people and events of her husband's past, especially his daughter and longtime friends. A recuperative stay with

Alec's aunt and uncle in a lovely Cornwall mansion finally forces these and many other issues into the open." Booklist

The author "evokes the sense of contentment that flows from affection grounded in a comfortable lifestyle, all of which makes for gently entertaining reading." Publ Wkly

Pilcher, Rosamunde

Winter solstice. Thomas Dunne Bks. 2000 454p $27.95

ISBN 0-312-24426-6

LC 00-31713

A novel set in "northern Scotland, where five vaguely connected people find themselves together at Christmas in a large Victorian house. . . . Elfrida, a lonely retired actress, befriends Oscar, who is barely surviving the grief of the deaths of his wife and daughter in a car crash. Carrie, bereft after an aborted love affair, takes over the holiday care of her 14-year-old niece, Lucy, who is unwanted by her mother, grandmother, and indifferent father, Sam, in town to take charge of the old woolen mill, is reeling because his wife left him for another man. What lifts this saga above melodrama is the author's skill at creating believable, multifaceted characters." Libr J

Pinborough, Sarah

A **matter** of blood; Sarah Pinborough. Ace Books 2013 352 p. (The forgotten gods) (paperback) $16

ISBN 0425258467; 9780425258460

LC 2012049588

This novel, by Sarah Pinborough, is the first entry in "The Forgotten Gods" trilogy. "London's ruined economy has pushed everyone to the breaking point. . . . Detective Inspector Cass Jones struggles to keep integrity in the police force, but now, two gory cases will test his mettle. A gang hit goes wrong, leaving two schoolboys dead, and a serial killer calling himself the Man of Flies leaves a message on his victims saying 'nothing is sacred.'" (Publisher's note)

"Nuanced characters, evocative settings, tricky plot connections and a spin on genre conventions mark what appears to be the start of a distinctive series." Kirkus

Pintoff, Stefanie

In the shadow of Gotham. Minotaur Books 2009 385p $24.99; pa $14.99

ISBN 978-0-312-54490-4; 0-312-54490-1; 978-0-312-62812-3 pa; 0-312-62812-9 pa

LC 2008-45676

"Detective Simon Ziele lost his fiancée in the General Slocum ferry disaster—a thousand perished on that summer day in 1904 when an onboard fire burned the boat down in the waters of the East River. Still reeling from the tragedy, Ziele transferred to a police department north of New York, to escape the city and all the memories it conjured. But only a few months into his new life in a quiet country town, he's faced with the most shocking homicide of his career to date: Young Sarah Wingate has been brutally murdered in her own bedroom in the middle of an otherwise calm and quiet winter afternoon. After just one day of investigation, Simon's contacted by Columbia University's noted criminologist Alistair Sinclair, who offers a startling claim about one of his patients, Michael Fromley—that the facts of the murder bear

an uncanny resemblance to Fromley's deranged mutterings." Publisher's note

Pipkin, John

Woodsburner; a novel. Nan A. Talese 2009 365p $24.95

ISBN 978-0-385-52865-8; 0-385-52865-5

LC 2008-33233

"Pipkin doesn't underplay Thoreau's horror at what he's done (or overplay the inherent irony of the author of 'Walden' burning down the woods). Instead, he concentrates on the ability of a natural disaster to act as a catalyst in people's minds and lives. The result is, well, transcendent." Christ Sci Monit

Pirandello, Luigi

The **outcast**; authorized translation from the Italian by Leo Ongley. Dutton 1925 334p

Condemned and cast out by husband and father for a crime she has not committed, Marta makes a brave attempt to build life over again. She goes with her mother and sister to a town where she is unknown and there supports them by teaching. After a time happiness comes back to the three. Then the man for whose sake Marta was persecuted comes to their village. He finds Marta lovelier and more desirable than ever. The result is inevitable. The outcry against her breaks forth afresh, and she is forced into the situation she has tried to escape. Too late her chastened husband sues for forgiveness. This drama of Italian life draws to a close in a moving scene of reconciliation

The novel is "significant thematically for its unconventional treatment of adultery and historically for its subtle undermining of the assumptions of naturalism on which it appears to be based." Ency of World Lit in the 20th Century

Pirandello, Luigi

Short stories; selected, translated and introduced by Frederick May. Oxford Univ. Press 1965 xxxvi, 260p

Pirie, David

The **patient's** eyes; the dark beginnings of Sherlock Holmes. St. Martin's Minotaur 2002 244p il

ISBN 0-312-29095-0

"A 'fictional' account of Arthur Conan Doyle's early life that relates how his association with Edinburgh physician Joseph Bell was the inspiration for his Holmes character. Pirie vividly evokes the dark ambience of Victorian England, his prose is elegant, and his gift for mimicking the slightly haughty tone of Doyle's writing is uncanny." Booklist

Pittard, Hannah

The **fates** will find their way; a novel. Ecco 2011 243p $22.99

ISBN 978-0-06-199605-4; 0-06-199605-X

LC 2010-09129

"Nora Lindell, a 16-year-old private schoolgirl in a suburban town, disappears one Halloween night. The boys in the town collectively narrate this haunted tale of Nora's imagined fate and their own lives, from their teens until they are adults with families. Nora lives on in their imagination—there are sightings and multiple theories about where she ended up, the boys fantasize about and date her younger sister, and they continue to think of her when they are with their own wives and children." Libr J

Pitts, Leonard

Freeman; a novel. Leonard Pitts. Agate 2012 404 p. (paperback) $16

ISBN 1932841644; 9781572846999; 9781932841640
LC 2012009592

Pulitzer Prize winner Leonard Pitts, Jr.'s second novel "begins in the first few months after President Lincoln has died. By that time Philadelphian Sam Freeman has already taken to the road to return to the brutal Mississippi plantation he fled 15 years earlier. His mission: to find Tilda, the wife he left behind. Unbeknownst to Sam, Tilda is traveling west with a gun pointed at her head by her former master, who has a scheme to start plantations in territories that will uphold enslavement." (Essence)

Plaidy, Jean

The **captive** Queen of Scots. Putnam 1970 410p

Sequel to Royal road to Fotheringay (1968)

First published 1963 in the United Kingdom

"The story of the last 18 years of Queen Mary's life, during which she was first a prisoner of her Scottish enemies and later, after a dramatic escape and flight to England, the captive of her archenemy, Queen Elizabeth. Treated with at least some respect due a queen, Mary is pictured with her retinue of loyal friends and servants, living in varying degrees of discomfort and confinement as she moved from one castle to another at the whim of Elizabeth. She emerges as a generous, overly trustful, emotional victim, attractive even as she grew older though not wise, who met her tragic fate because she could not cope with the treachery and intrigue of both friends and enemies." Booklist

Plaidy, Jean

Murder most royal. Putnam 1972 542p

First published 1949 in the United Kingdom

"Concentrating on Anne Boleyn and her younger cousin Catherine Howard, the author follows the two from childhood to death on the block, with her usual thoroughness, sentimentality, and overdramatization, sparing the reader few details of torture, violence, intrigue, or thwarted love affairs." Booklist

Plaidy, Jean

The **pleasures** of love; the story of Catherine of Braganza. Putnam 1992 329p

ISBN 0-399-13731-9
LC 91-34593

First published 1991 in the United Kingdom

When Catherine, daughter of King John IV of Portugal, finally married Charles II her "happiness as the new Queen of England was short-lived. The Merry Monarch's notorious affairs amused the public but devastated Catherine, who longed for the love only a husband and children could provide. When it became clear that Catherine was barren, the people verged on rebellion and court intimates intrigued against her, hoping that Charles would divorce his queen, marry one of his mistresses, and beget an heir. But while Charles would never be faithful to Catherine, he loved her

and was her fiercest protector. And in the end, their struggle against their enemies only drew the king and queen closer together." Publisher's note

Plaidy, Jean

William's wife. Putnam 1993 276p
LC 92-32588

In this historical novel about the "struggle for power between Catholic and Protestant, England's heir to the throne, the lovely and bright Princess Mary, is forced to marry William of Orange in order to prevent the kingdom from falling under Catholic rule. Despite Mary's attempts to win her husband's love, the dour, power-hungry William won't even feign affection for her; instead, he continues a blatant affair with Elizabeth Villiers. As the inevitable power struggle ensues between her husband and her father, James II, Mary finds herself torn between marital and filial loyalties. But with the crown of England the ultimate prize, Mary discovers that while she is James's daughter, she is first and foremost William's wife." Publisher's note

Plain, Belva

Blessings. Delacorte Press 1989 340p
LC 89-1565

"The author stretches an awkward subplot concerning mob-connected real estate developers far too thin, but her mixture of romance, suspense, and deeply felt familial conflicts should leave her fans well entertained." Publ Wkly

Plain, Belva

Crescent City; a novel. Delacorte Press 1984 429p
LC 84-5045

A novel "set against the backdrop of America's South during the Civil War. At the story's center is Miriam Raphael, a European Jew transplanted as a child to New Orleans, the 'Crescent City' nestled at the mouth of the Mississippi. Both she and her older brother, David, must adjust to what seems a bright, promising new land filled with languid days and lavish feasts. But all too quickly their eyes are opened to the grimmer features of their landscape—the slaves whom David vows to set free and the southern tradition of youthful marriage, which Miriam, herself no better off than a slave, must gracefully endure." Booklist

Plain, Belva

Evergreen; a novel. Delacorte Press 1978 593p
LC 77-20778

"The young orphan Anna shows her spunk by leaving Poland to make a way for herself in the turn-of-the-century U.S.A. Opting for domestic service rather than the sweatshops of lower Manhattan, she becomes infatuated with the master's son, Paul Werner. His marriage to another woman puts a damper on Anna's longing, and she settles for poor but loyal Joseph Friedman. Joseph is hard working and has a vision of fulfilling the American Dream. He persuades his wife to borrow some money from the Werners, and Anna finds herself asking Paul for the money. He gladly obliges, but the old flame is fanned into heedless passion and Anna leaves with the money and a secret she will carry with her for the rest of her life." Best Sellers

"This warm and sympathetic family saga gives life and meaning to the commonplace events of unspectacular lives." Publ Wkly

Followed by The golden cup

Plain, Belva

The **golden** cup. Doubleday 1986 399p

LC 86-8851

Evergreen "told the story of immigrant Anna Friedman and her love for Paul Werner. Here the focus shifts to Paul's aunt, Hennie DeRivera, from age 18 in 1891 through World War I. As a volunteer, Hennie teaches English at a settlement house where she meets Daniel Roth. Their relationship is frowned upon by her family, but they marry when she becomes pregnant. Her uncertainty over whether Dan would have married her otherwise is aggravated by his roving eye. The grown-up Paul, Hennie's son Fred, and Leah, an orphan she raises, are also featured." Libr J

The author "invests her story with dignity and historical relevance while insightfully depicting the class consciousness of Progressive Era Americans." Publ Wkly

Followed by Tapestry

Plain, Belva

Harvest. Delacorte Press 1990 409p

LC 90-34417

This novel continues the "saga of the Werners and their extended clan as they reaffirm their Jewish heritage during the stormy 1960s. Dark, sensitive Iris, daughter of the glowing, russet-haired Anna (by urbane banker Paul Werner—unbeknownst to Iris) is married to wealthy, improvident Dr. Theo Stern, whose European glamour excites other women. Iris's jealousy goads her to play at her own romance with a sinister partner. Her four children are growing up, but rebel Steve balks at his bar mitzvah, already anticipating the anarchist/bomb expert he will be at college, radicalized by cynical professor Tim Powers, whom he doesn't know is his distant cousin. When Paul's wife dies and his mistress leaves to fulfill her mission as a doctor in Israel, Paul hovers protectively over Iris's, troubled family." Publ Wkly

Plain, Belva

Looking back. Delacorte Press 2001 340p $25.95

ISBN 0-385-33471-0

LC 00-65691

A "story about three college roommates—brainy Norma, lovely Amanda, preppy Cecile. . . . When the three women graduate, Amanda, desperate to escape her lower-class background, marries Larry Balsan, Norma's brother, who is in the family real estate business. As Mrs. Balsan, she can shop to her heart's content, but she soon realizes she is not as happy as Cecile, who marries her college sweetheart, or even Norma, who is biding her time until she meets Mr. Right." Publ Wkly

Plain, Belva

Random winds. Delacorte Press 1980 496p

LC 79-26845

The author "knows how to sweep from one dramatic scene to another, often evoking poignancy, and the irony underlying Martin's daughter's romance with Fern's stepson produces a bittersweet ending." Publ Wkly

Plain, Belva

Tapestry. Delacorte Press 1988 440p

LC 87-22346

"Paul Werner, the key figure of a powerful New York banking family, is the protagonist in this saga of one man's concerns with the impending doom of World War II and the plight of his German-Jewish relatives and friends. Paul is caught in a passionless, childless marriage, and he struggles for years with the memory and reality of his first love and subsequent affairs of the heart." Libr J

Followed by Harvest

Plath, Sylvia

★ The **bell** jar; with an introduction by Diane Wood Middlebrook. Knopf 1998 xxv, 229p $17

ISBN 0-375-40463-5

LC 98-27309

First published 1963 in the United Kingdom; first United States edition published 1971 by Harper & Row

"Esther Greenwood, having spent what should have been a glorious summer as guest editor for a young woman's magazine, came home from New York, had a nervous breakdown, and tried to commit suicide. Through months of therapy, Esther kept her rationality, if not her sanity. In telling the story of Esther, Plath thinly disguised her own experience with attempted suicide and time spent in an institution. Like Esther, she was rehabilitated and finished college. She went to London, married poet Ted Hughes, had three children and published some poetry and this novel. When she felt the world slipping away from her again, she did commit suicide." Shapiro. Fic for Youth. 3d edition

Includes bibliographical references

Pletzinger, Thomas

Funeral for a dog; a novel. translated by Ross Benjamin. W.W. Norton 2011 322p il pa $14.95

ISBN 978-0-393-33725-9; 0-393-33725-1

LC 2010-39784

Original German edition, 2008

This novel "intertwines three storylines: First, there's Daniel Mandelkern, an ethnologist turned journalist who works for his wife, Elisabeth, a woman whose first child died at birth and wants to try again. Now. He's not necessarily comfortable with this, or himself, but regardless of Daniel's insecurities, his wife sends him off on assignment to Italy to write a profile of . . . Dirk Svensson, a recluse who authored The Story of Leo and the Notmuch, an illustrated children's book that's become a surprising success. Svensson has a bit of a sordid backstory—one that gets pieced together over the course of the novel, mainly through interstitial pieces that are from Svensson's Astroland, a collection of stories about his unique ménage a trois relationship with Tuuli and Felix. This relationship ends, someone is the father of Tuuli's son, and Svensson escapes first into post-9/11 New York where he meets the artist Kiki Kaufman, and then to Italy, where he lives on a secluded late with . . . Lua, the three-legged dog of the title who, yes, does die, and who serves as the third 'ring' that holds this narrative together. . . . In addition to being compelling on structural and philosophical levels, Funeral for a Dog is damn good on a line-byline basis. Pletzinger's writing (and Ross Benjamin's translation) is graceful and evocative." Quarterly Conversation

Poe's children; the new horror: an anthology. [edited by] Peter Straub. Doubleday 2008 534p $24.95

ISBN 978-0-385-52283-0; 0-385-52283-5

LC 2008-3013

"An impressive, highly personal assortment of perspectives and techniques. The result is a remarkably consistent, frequently unsettling book that does as much to blur the artificial boundary between genre fiction and 'literature' as any anthology in living memory. . . . [The anthology] transcends genre labels and deserves to be recognized for what it is: first-rate fiction." Washington Post Book World

Poe, Edgar Allan
The **collected** tales and poems of Edgar Allan Poe. Modern Lib. 1992 1026p $20

ISBN 0-679-60007-8

LC 92-50231

A reissue of The complete tales and poems of Edgar Allan Poe published 1938

This volume contains short stories, poems, and a sampling of Poe's essays, criticism and journalistic writings

Poe, Edgar Allan
★ **Complete** stories and poems of Edgar Allan Poe. Doubleday 1966 819p $21.95

ISBN 0-385-07407-7

Poe, Edgar Allan
The **imaginary** voyages: The narrative of Arthur Gordon Pym; The unparalleled adventure of one Hans Pfaall; The journal of Julius Rodman. Twayne Pubs. 1981 667p

LC 81-2915

Omnibus edition of three titles, the first of which is entered separately under variant form: The narrative of Arthur Gordon Pym of Nantucket, The unparalleled adventure of one Hans Pfaall, first published 1835 describes a voyage to the moon and The journal of Julius Rodman, an unfinished novel first published anonymously in 1840 deals with exploration of the Missouri River Basin

Pohl, Frederik
All the lives he led. Tor 2011 347p $25.99

ISBN 978-0-7653-2176-3; 0-7653-2176-9

LC 2010-36667

"In a tired, terrorist-plagued 2079 still reeling from the aftereffects of a massive Yellowstone eruption, Brad Sheridan escapes from America's refugee camps by signing up for an overseas indenture. Chance earns him a spot working in Italy's lavish commemoration of the 2,000th anniversary of the destruction of Pompeii. Beneath quiescent Vesuvius, tourists enjoy entertainments real and virtual. Brad's ambition is limited to minor scams and romance, but fate places him near the epicenter of a terrorist plot of unprecedented scale." Publ Wkly

"An entertaining futuristic thriller with several thought-provoking threads ranging from the ethics of biotechnology to the fragility of the global economy." Libr J

Pohl, Frederik
The **annals** of the Heechee. Ballantine Bks. 1987 388p

LC 86-26584

Sequel to Heechee rendezvous

In this episode "the human-Heechee cooperation that first materialized in 'Heechee Rendezvous' has solidified as the two races unite against a common enemy. Once again Robinette Broadhead—alive after death as a machine-stored personality, compliments of Heechee technology—is called upon to face a dangerous challenge. He is the only one able to meet eyeball to eyeball with the deadly Foe, aliens determined to mold the universe to their own needs. . . . The novel is gripping, both in story line and in the colorful depiction of the alien Heechee." Booklist

Pohl, Frederik
Beyond the blue event horizon. Ballantine Bks. 1980 327p

LC 79-21757

Sequel to Gateway

"Multimillionaire Robinette Broadhead, still mourning the loss of his great love from the first book, backs an expedition to investigate one of the alien Heechee's 'food factories.' Earth is overpopulated, and the ship's resources are desperately needed to prevent mass starvation. The members of the expedition are all from the same family: Lurvey, a veteran space pilot and her engineer husband; Lurvey's money hungry father, and her precocious 14-year-old sister. Despite the tensions which surface during their three and a half year voyage, the family manages to successfully make contact with the factory and its innocent, human occupant. They begin to explore the marvels of the alien technology, but events on Earth and the inhabitants of another Heechee spaceship threatens to end the expedition in disaster." Voice Youth Advocates

Followed by Heechee rendezvous

Pohl, Frederik
The **boy** who would live forever; a novel of Gateway. Tor Bks. 2004 380p $25.95

ISBN 0-7653-1049-X

LC 2004-49579

A title set in the author's Heechee universe. "When recently orphaned Stan Avery inherits enough money to buy a trip to Gateway, the alien Heechee waystation that allows travel to all parts of space, he doesn't realize that his voyage has effectively cut him off forever from the world he left behind. Pohl's first Gateway novel in 15 years (the 1977 original Gateway won the Hugo and Nebula Awards) revitalizes a favorite far-future setting as it tells the tale of a young man's journey to self-realization amid the stars." Libr J

Pohl, Frederik
Chernobyl; a novel. Bantam Bks. 1987 355p

ISBN 0-553-05210-1

LC 86-47896

The author "re-creates in fiction the massive 1986 Ukrainian nuclear power plant disaster. The book opens during normal days just before the accident; suspense builds, as the reader expects the worst. Characters that would actually have been on the scene are seen being overwhelmed by berserk technology, their lives shattered. The tale is gripping, and the locale well established." Libr J

Pohl, Frederik
★ **Gateway**. St. Martin's Press 1977 313p
First volume in the author's Heechee saga
"The novel's protagonist, Robinette Broadhead, suffers from tremendous feelings of guilt: for the death of his parents, for his wealth (a stroke of luck he feels he does not deserve), and for the living death of his girl friend and fellow crew members. Gateway presents Broadhead's story in chapters that alternately describe his life before the novel opens and record present conversations between Broadhead and his computer psychiatrist, Sigfrid von Shrink. With a sensitive mixture of humor and sympathy, Pohl explores Broadhead's condition and ends with one of the finest affirmations of humanity in any literary work." New Ency of Sci Fic
Followed by Beyond the blue event horizon

Pohl, Frederik
Heechee rendezvous; a novel. Ballantine Bks. 1984 311p
LC 83-15637
Sequel to Beyond the blue event horizon
In this novel "the elusive, benevolent aliens called Heechee are forced to come out of hiding because the future not only of humankind but of the universe itself is at stake. Compelled by personal reasons, tycoon Robinette Broadhead takes part in another dangerous venture into space, moving inexorably toward his surprising yet fitting destiny." Booklist
Followed by The annals of the Heechee

Pohl, Frederik
Homegoing. Ballantine Bks. 1989 279p
LC 88-7413
"An alien spaceship lands on Earth for a double purpose: to give the people of Earth the benefit of their advanced technology and to return to them a human rescued in infancy and raised by the kangaroo-like Hakh'hli to be as 'human' as possible—under the circumstances. Pohl's unerring gift for satire delivers a splendidly skewed alien-eye-view of human culture while spinning a touching, slightly quirky story of a young man's coming of age." Libr J

Pohl, Frederik
★ **Man** Plus. Random House 1976 215p
"The novel describes the transformation of a human astronaut into a cyborg capable of living on Mars and confronts the question of human dignity: as the central character, Roger Torraway, becomes less 'human,' the people who were once so important to him are unable to cope with what he is, and Roger must also learn to handle the new thing he has become. Moreover, Roger's reflections on his growing inability to control his own life parallel the thoughts of people throughout the country who believe the world has gone out of control. The result is a remarkably readable novel that succeeds in presenting a fully rounded character in an SF setting." New Ency of Sci Fic

Pohl, Frederik
Mars Plus; {by} Frederik Pohl, Thomas T. Thomas. Baen Pub. Enterprises 1994 342p $20
ISBN 0-671-87605-8
LC 93-44782
Fifty years after the events in Man Plus, "man is, or seems to be, on Mars to stay, but things have become . . . strange, even compared to the population of cyborgs, half-cyborgs and just plain humans who now occupy the Red Planet. The computer net on which all Martian life depends has long seemed to have 'a mind of its own,' and now that mind seems to be in a very bad mood." Publisher's note

Pohl, Frederik
★ The **space** merchants; by Frederik Pohl and C. M. Kornbluth. Ballantine Bks. 1953 179p
"Kornbluth later stated that he and Pohl packed into this story everything they hated about advertising, and it came out with Swiftian savagery. One of the first novels by writers with primary roots in the pulps to make an impact in mainstream circles." Anatomy of Wonder 4
Followed by The merchants' war (1984)

Pohl, Frederik
The **world** at the end of time. Ballantine Bks. 1990 393p
LC 89-18462
"As vast intelligences play deadly power games using stars for pawns, the fledgling colonists on the planet Home fight to maintain their existence while 'unknown forces' wreak havoc with the laws of physics and the universe. Pohl's sparkling wit attaches itself to macro- and micro-cosmic themes in a novel which pits a luckless human hero against a childlike being of inordinate power and extraordinary paranoia. Grand in scope, poignant in delivery." Libr J

Polansky, Daniel
Low Town; a novel. Doubleday 2011 341p $25.95
ISBN 978-0-385-53446-8; 0-385-53446-9
LC 2010-49587
"Polansky's writing is confident and punchy from the offset. The action rips along at a brilliant pace allowing us to experience this gritty world through the eyes of a thrilling, dangerous, flawed, yet strangely endearing protagonist. This is modern, dark fantasy at its best and a debut to be envied." British Fantasy Society

Pollen, Bella
The **summer** of the bear. Atlantic Monthly 2011 441p $24
ISBN 978-0-8021-1974-2; 0-8021-1974-3
First published 2010 in the United Kingdom
"When Nicky Fleming, a British diplomat working in East Germany in 1979 dies, he leaves behind his wife, Letty, and children, Georgie, 17, Alba, 14, and Jamie, 8. Jamie has some kind of learning disability and some kind of gift. On the way to the family's summer house in the Outer Hebrides after his father's death, Jamie leaves hand-drawn maps to the house so that his father can find him. He remembers a grizzly bear he and his father saw at the zoo; he knows that bear has something to do with his father's death and something

to do with his young life. The 800-pound bear, in the meantime, has escaped from a cargo boat in the North Atlantic and swum to shore. It lives in a cave in the Outer Hebrides. The novel has a bit of the style of Lemony Snicket and a smidgeon of 'The Secret of Roan Inish.' Pollen's writing is clean and clear enough that you can really smell the peat smoke and feel the wind. As for the question of Jamie's father's unexpected death — was it truly suicide? Was he a traitor?" L A Times Book Rev

Pollock, Donald Ray

The **devil** all the time; a novel. Doubleday 2011 261p $26.95

ISBN 978-0-385-53504-5; 0-385-53504-X

LC 2010-53322

Set in "in rural, impoverished Knockemstiff [Ohio] and nearby Mead, the novel opens with the relationship of young Arvin Russell and his father, Willard, a haunted World War II vet who marries a beautiful woman and then watches her die from cancer. He alternates between praying and drinking, neither of which do much to alleviate his pain. In fact, his son 'didn't know which was worse, the drinking or the praying.' The tragic ways of the world (in a novel that sometimes aims at dark comedy) leave Arvin an orphan. As he's maturing into young adulthood, raised by his grandmother, the plot shifts include a huckster pair of religious revivalists, a preacher who preys on young girls and a husband-and-wife pair of serial killers (she seduces their victims, whom they call 'models,' and he photographs and kills them)." Kirkus

"The flawless cadence of Pollock's gorgeous shadow-and-light prose plays against the heinous acts of his sorrowful and sometimes just sorry characters." Elle

Pollock, Donald Ray

Knockemstiff. Doubleday 2008 206p

ISBN 978-0-385-52382-0

LC 2007-39806

"Knockemstiff — real name, real town — is full of the sorriest group of people imaginable, a bunch of damaged souls with crass manners, greasy hair, sour breath, addictions galore and savage tendencies. Some can sense the possibilities of a better life, but their longing for escape just might lead them to do something crazy. Others are simply rotting away, trapped by self-defeating habits impossible to shake. Pollock underscores their struggles with vivid imagery and, at times, a tender touch. . . . Pollock's writing has been compared to that of Flannery O'Connor, Raymond Carver and Cormac McCarthy. He draws his readers in slowly, tangling them in the mundane toil of small-town life, before smacking them upside the head with something unexpected and primal. Small moments yield big surprises." Oregonian

Pomerantz, Sharon

★ **Rich** boy. Twelve 2010 517p $24.99

ISBN 978-0-446-56318-5; 0-446-56318-8

LC 2009-32386

The novel's protagonist is "Robert Vishniak, the golden-boy progeny of a working-class Jewish family in 1950s Philadelphia whose singular drive to transcend his circumstances is — almost — matched by his abilities. As a boy, he craves the security and social acceptance that comes with money; as a young man, he is ushered into the rarefied, sweet-smelling world of those who possess it in staggering amounts. There's more than a little of Saul Bellow's Augie March in Robert, too, especially in Rich Boy's opening chapters, populated by a colorful cast of neighbors, extended family, and schoolmates (his romantic education begins early). Soon enough, though, he finds escape via admission to a top-tier Northeastern University, where his charm and good looks garner him a new class of friends. . . . It would spoil Pomerantz's pleasingly soapy narrative to detail too much of Robert's subsequent journey, first in 1960s Boston and then in the go-go Manhattan of the '70s and '80s. But while his tale often feels allegorical . . . Rich Boy is told with such page-turning skill that its pleasures, if not deep, feel rich indeed." Entertainment Wkly

Poole, Sara

The **Borgia** mistress; a novel. Sara Poole. St. Martin's Press 2012 406 p. $14.99

ISBN 031260985X; 9780312609856; 9781250010926

LC 2012007569

In this book, part of the Poisoner Mysteries series, "Francesca Giordano -- court poisoner to the House of Borgia -- returns to confront an ancient atrocity that threatens to extinguish the light of the Renaissance. . . . As the enemies of Pope Alexander VI close in and the papal court is forced to flee from Rome, Francesca joins forces with her lover, the brilliant and ruthless Cesare Borgia to unravel a conspiracy that strikes at the heart of Christendom." (Publisher's note)

"True to its characters and historical facts, Poole's novel immerses readers in a seductive Renaissance environment, full of danger and passion." Pub Wkly

Pope, Barbara Corrado

The **blood** of Lorraine. Pegasus Books 2010 367p $25

ISBN 978-1-60598-098-0; 1-60598-098-6

A "look at the rise of anti-Semitism in France after the arrest of Capt. Alfred Dreyfus for treason in 1894. Now transferred to Nancy, the capital of Alsace, [magistrate Bernard]Martin doesn't relish investigating a politically sensitive case—the murder of seven-month-old Marc-Antoine Thomas, whose parents claim that a Jew killed and mutilated their son—that Martin's Jewish colleague, David Singer, insists that Martin take over. When a prominent member of the Jewish community, Victor Ullmann, is later bludgeoned to death, the magistrate fears that it was a revenge killing. Martin must also deal with a devastating personal tragedy as pressure to solve the Ullmann case mounts. Pope, a historian, more than compensates for a not fully satisfying ending with a complex lead and the skill with which she makes the anti-Semitic atmosphere of the times both palpable and tragically prophetic." Publ Wkly

Includes bibliographical references

Porter, Henry

The **bell** ringers. Atlantic Monthly Press 2010 402p $24

ISBN 978-0-8021-1931-5; 0-8021-1931-X

"The tale is set in England, where cameras identify license plates and faces, computers catalog phone and financial records, and submitting an incomplete form can be a felony. What's to prevent a prime minister from abusing these powers? Just a few committed (if sometimes cliched) characters, some intricately complex plotting and gobs of local color. The world of 'The Bell Ringers' isn't as dystopian as '1984,' but it's not that far off." Cleveland Plain Dealer

Porter, Joseph Ashby

★ **All** aboard; stories. [by] Joe Ashby Porter. Turtle Point Press 2008 187p pa $15.95

ISBN 978-1-933527-17-8; 1-933527-17-X

LC 2007-910440

"Beyond disregarding literary fashion, Joe Ashby Porter seems to inhabit his own world, producing compelling short fiction exclusively on his own terms. His latest collection contains six valuable and unique studies of connection and detachment as mediated by age, sexuality, and proximity. Though more grounded in the familiar than his previous collection, Touch Wood, an initial strangeness, both of content and style, still threatens to alienate the casual reader. Consideration, however, is rewarded." Bookslut

Porter, Joseph Ashby

The **near** future; [by] Joe Ashby Porter. Turtle Point Press 2006 248p pa $15.95

ISBN 1-88558-641-8

LC 2005-926845

"Porter's narrative style is vaguely cubist, with words often turned at slight angles to one another. But what the occasional sentence loses in textbook syntax it gains in color and sheer playfulness. . . . 'The Near Future' is an exceedingly odd book yet also, despite the gunplay, a genuinely endearing one." N Y Times Book Rev

Porter, Katherine Anne

Collected stories and other writings. Library of America 2008 1093p $40

ISBN 978-1-59853-029-2

LC 2008-927625

In addition to short prose (reviews, criticism, essays, travel pieces, and more), this volume contains three collections of short stories: Flowering Judas and other stories (1935); Pale horse, pale rider: three short novels (1939); The leaning tower and other stories (1944)

Porter, Katherine Anne

★ The **collected** stories of Katherine Anne Porter. Harcourt Brace & World 1965 495p hardcover o.p. pa $16

ISBN 0-15-618876-7

Contains three collections of short stories: Flowering Judas, and other stories (1935); The leaning tower, and other stories (1944); Pale horse, pale rider (1939); and four additional short stories: Virgin Violeta; The martyr; The fig tree; and Holiday.

"These are perfect examples of the short story and are representative not only of the best American writing but of the best in the world." SLJ

Porter, Katherine Anne

Flowering Judas and other stories. Harcourt Brace Jovanovich 1935 285p

First published 1930. This edition adds four additional stories

Contents: María Concepción; Magic; Rope; He; Theft; That tree; The jilting of Granny Weatherall; Flowering Judas; The cracked looking-glass; Hacienda

Porter, Katherine Anne

The **leaning** tower, and other stories. Harcourt Brace & Co. 1944 246p

Contents: The source; The witness; The circus; The old order; The last leaf; The grave; The downward path to wisdom; A day's work; The leaning tower

Porter, Katherine Anne

★ **Pale** horse, pale rider: three short novels; Modern Library ed; Modern Lib. 1998 205p $18.95

ISBN 0-679-60303-4

LC 98-12008

A reissue of the title first published 1939 by Harcourt, Brace

In the title story "Miranda, a young journalist, is caught in a personal dilemma. She must choose between a career and a commitment to Adam, a soldier on leave during World War I. Porter's simple tale becomes more complex as Miranda's anxieties and fears about war, death, and personal loss are revealed. She hovers close to death during the terrbile flu epidemic of 1918. Miranda survives and the war ends, but it brings her no happiness because the epidemic has claimed Adam as a victim." Shapiro. Fic for Youth. 3d edition

Porter, Katherine Anne

Ship of fools. Little, Brown 1962 497p

"A satire in which the world is likened to a ship whose passengers, fools and deranged people all, are sailing toward eternity. Porter's novel is set in 1931 aboard a German passenger ship returning to Bremerhaven, Germany, from Veracruz, Mexico. The ship carries a microcosm of peoples, including Germans, Americans, Spaniards, Gypsies, and Mexicans, Jews, anti-Semites, political reactionaries, revolutionaries, and neutrals coexist aboard ship, at the same time that jeaolusy, cruelty and duplicity pervade their lives." Merriam-Webster's Ency of Lit

Portes, Andrea

Hick. Unbridled Books 2007 245p pa $14.95

ISBN 978-1-932961-32-4; 1-932961-32-1

LC 2007-105

"The 13-year-old narrator of Hick is headed down the wrong path in life, but it's not one she has chosen. . . . After a particularly bad episode involving her drunken father and estranged mother, Luli opts out, she leaves Nebraska to begin anew in Vegas. . . . Luli's journey begins as a series of rides. Her street smarts come in handy immediately when goggle-eyed cowboy Eddie picks her up. He's not a good guy, but tough Luli takes care of herself—something she's been doing her whole life. Her next ride comes from Glenda, a Patsy Cline fan with smeared red lips and a cocaine habit. Luli immediately finds herself entranced by Glenda's straight-shooting personality and seemingly glamorous life on the road. A surreal quality emerges when Luli discovers that Glenda knows Eddie. From here, Luli becomes inextricably linked to this particular group of societal outcasts. Throughout her experiences with Glenda, including a botched robbery job, it's easy to forget Luli is just 13. She's the antithesis of the modern American teenager; she has grit. Her story is especially interesting as it is based on the real-life experiences of Hick's author, Portes." PopMatters

Portis, Charles

★ The **dog** of the South. Knopf 1979 245p

ISBN 0-394-4506146

LC 78-65780

"Simultaneously hilarious and heart breakingly odd. . . you find yourself laughing so hard in sections that tears run down your face." Baltimore Sun

Portis, Charles

★ **Gringos**; a novel. Simon & Schuster 1991 269p

ISBN 0-671-72457-6

LC 90-42476

"'Gringos,' by far, is Portis's most inward-turning book, a story of a grownup trying to grow up, to keep it together with some dignity. Watching him pull it off is one of the finest pleasures afforded by any novel in a long time." Newsweek

Portis, Charles

★ **Masters** of Atlantis; a novel. Knopf 1985 247p

ISBN 0-394-54683-0

LC 85-40212

This novel "concerns the establishment of the order of Gnomons, a secret society purporting to teach the hidden knowledge of Atlantis. The action begins in 1917, when soldier Lamar is relieved of $200 by a fast-talking stranger in exchange for the key to Gnomonism. The plot spins dizzily along as sly Sydney Hen and antic Austin Popper are drawn into the society, engineer a farcical schism, and espouse assorted crackpot causes. . . . Those who enjoy deadpan comedy should get a good laugh here." Libr J

Portis, Charles

Norwood. Simon & Schuster 1966 190p

LC 66-21822

"An artlessness and simplicity in style and plot skillfully projects Norwood and his problems quite convincingly. For those readers more interested in characterization than action." Libr J

Portis, Charles

True grit; a novel. Simon & Schuster 1968 215p

"Mattie Ross, a fourteen-year-old living in Yell County, Arkansas, is determined to get justice when her father is killed by a hired hand. She is joined in her quest by Rooster Cogburn, a U.S. marshal, and by a Texas Ranger. This strange trio faces a series of perilous encounters requiring true grit to confront them." Shapiro. Fic for Youth. 3d edition

Potok, Chaim

★ The **chosen**; a novel. Simon & Schuster 1967 284p

"Living only five blocks apart in the Williamsburg section of Brooklyn, New York, Danny and Reuven meet as opponents in a softball game. Out of this encounter evolves a strong bond of friendship between a brilliant Hasidic Jew and a scholar who is Orthodox in his religious thinking.

During the course of their relationship Reuven becomes the means by which Danny's father, a rabbi, can communicate with his son, who has been reared under a code of silence." Shapiro. Fic for Youth. 2d edition

Followed by The promise

Potok, Chaim

The **gift** of Asher Lev. Knopf 1990 369p

LC 89-43401

Sequel to My name is Asher Lev

"Following the death of his beloved uncle, Asher, who is now middle-aged and settled in France, finds he must return with his family to the Brooklyn Hasidic Jewish community from which he has been exiled 20 years. Greeted there with suspicion and anger by many who still insist that his art is anathema to Hasidim—a sentiment that continues to haunt his relationship with his father, a tireless, well-respected ambassador for the religious community's Rebbe—Asher finds himself struggling once again to balance art and faith, this time in a difficult emotional coming-to-terms that involves the future of his five-year-old son, Avrumel." Booklist

Potok, Chaim

★ **My** name is Asher Lev. Knopf 1972 369p

"Young Asher Lev is an obedient son of strict Jewish parents. When his artistic endeavors are discovered, he is sent to a religious leader for consultation because artists are not viewed favorably by the Hasidim. Asher's struggle for fulfillment and his ultimate rejection by his parents are poignantly drawn." Shapiro. Fic for Youth. 3d edition

Followed by The gift of Asher Lev

Potok, Chaim

Old men at midnight. Knopf 2001 273p $23

ISBN 0-375-41071-6

LC 2001-33861

"A collection of three novellas that share a character, Ilana Davita Dinn, and the theme of the effects of war on men's lives. In 'The Ark Builder,' which takes place the summer before she begins college, Ilana begins to teach English to a young boy, Noah, who has survived the Holocaust. . . . In the second story {The war doctor} Ilana is hardly present at all; a former KGB officer leaves her the story of his life in written form. . . . Finally, in 'The Troupe Teacher,' Ilana, now a writer, coaxes a disturbing story out of Benjamin Walter, a professor of warfare. A moving and powerful book." Booklist

Potok, Chaim

The **promise**. Knopf 1969 358p

Sequel to The chosen

"Reuven Malter and Danny Saunders, two Jewish friends living in Brooklyn, choose to alter the destinies chosen for them by their fathers. Reuven, studying to be a rabbi, finds his vocation blocked by a challenge to his scholarship and his father's book. Danny, who is studying clinical psychology, risks his career by a decision, based on intuition, that he feels can save a young boy's sanity." Shapiro. Fic for Youth. 3d edition

Pottinger, Stanley

The **fourth** procedure. Ballantine Bks. 1995 550p

ISBN 0-345-38400-8

LC 94-34282

In this novel "corpses of antiabortionists keep turning up in Washington, D.C., in unlikely spots, but even more unlikely is their condition—all have fresh incisions and a toy doll with a message stuffed inside it. Drawn into this web of murder and mystery is a wide variety of characters whose seemingly random connections turn out to be not so random after all. Each one has a past that sheds light on the current abortion controversy." Libr J

"Pottinger handily proves the adage that politics makes strange bedfellows, adding ironic twists that skewer long-accepted assumptions." Publ Wkly

Pottinger, Stanley

The **last** Nazi. St. Martin's Press 2003 324p $24.95

ISBN 0-312-27676-1

LC 2003-53852

"Melissa Gale, a lawyer and agent with an investigative unit of the FBI, is on the trail of the mysterious Adalwolf, a former assistant to Joseph Mengele, who aided in experiments on concentration camp prisoners. For Melissa it's not just a job, it's a personal mission because her grandmother died in a concentration camp. When she and her partner botch the swat team operation, their careers are put in jeopardy, and the elusive Nazi is emboldened to continue with his plot to develop a killer virus." Booklist

"Be prepared to feel horror for a villain who is not only the last Nazi but also one of the most terrifying." Libr J

Pouncey, Peter R.

Rules for old men waiting; a novel. [by] Peter Pouncey. Random House 2005 210p $21.95

ISBN 1-400-06370-1

LC 2004-54174

"As MacIver's book-within-a-book takes shape, Pouncey reminds us how the smallest choices can make a dramatic difference in the breadth and scope not just of a story but of a life." N Y Times Book Rev

Powell, Anthony

★ A **dance** to the music of time. University of Chicago Press 1995 12v in 4 pa set $72.80

ISBN 0-226-67719-2

LC 94-47228

An omnibus reissue of the twelve titles comprising The Music of time series, which were originally published separately

"The novels, spanning a period of over fifty years, from the early 1920s, describe the school days, youth, and maturity of the narrator-hero, Nicholas Jenkins, and his upper-class cohorts, especially the egregious Widmerpool. Though primarily satiric in tone, they express an underlying melancholy about life and time reminiscent of Marcel Proust." Reader's Ency. 4th edition

Powell, Dawn

Novels, 1930-1942. Library of Am. 2001 1068p $35

ISBN 1-931082-01-4

LC 00-54595

Dance night is about obsessive longing set in a 1920s Ohio factory town. Come back to Sorrento depicts a woman's friendship with a music teacher. Turn, magic wheel is a satirical look at New York's literary world. Angel on toast is a comic treatment of New York businessmen on the make. A time to be born portrays a monstrously egotistical woman just before America's entry into World War II

Includes bibliographical references

Powell, Dawn

Novels, 1944-1962. Library of Am. 2001 969p $35

ISBN 1-931082-02-2

LC 00-54596

My home is far away is the fictionalized memoir of Powell's life in small town Ohio. The locusts have no king is a satirical look at a scholar's brush with celebrity. The wicked pavilion portrays the habitués of a Greenwich Village cafe. The golden spur is a satirical look at the Manhattan art world of the late 1950s

Includes bibliographical references

Powell, Jim

The **breaking** of eggs. Penguin Books 2010 342p pa $15

ISBN 978-0-14-311726-1; 0-14-311726-2

LC 2010-07716

"That Powell succeeds in placing the conflicted and evolving Feliks at the center of a profound tale encapsulating Europe's 20th-century travails makes 'The Breaking of Eggs' that rare and remarkable achievement: a novel that meshes storytelling potency with historical erudition." Boston Globe

Powell, Padgett

★ **Edisto**; a novel. Farrar, Straus & Giroux 1984 183p

ISBN 0-374-14651-9

LC 83-25334

This is "distinctly a tour de force. . . . Powell's ear is acute: one of the pleasures of the book is his ability to catch the nuances of Southern speech, whether it is the malicious conversation of the Doctor's academic colleagues at a cocktail party or the genial banter of country Negroes at the fishing pier." N Y Times Book Rev

Powell, Padgett

Edisto revisited; a novel. Holt & Co. 1996 145p

ISBN 0-8050-4237-7

LC 95-34071

"'Edisto Revisited' is a puzzling work of high style, a rendering of haplessness that seems to poeticize passivity. While his novel may make you wonder if it has much of what is called meaning, Mr. Powell finally overpowers such doubts with his countless quotable passages, his humor and his seductive evocation of the romance of giving up." N Y Times Book Rev

Powell, Padgett

The **interrogative** mood; a novel? Ecco 2009
176p $21.99

ISBN 978-0-06-185941-0; 0-06-185941-9

"Our inquisitor, by turns cantankerous and plaintive, mourns the decline of butter churns and wonders under what circumstances—impending death, perhaps—it might be acceptable to molest a candy striper. There's not a whisper of a plot, but the torrent of queries is hypnotic, and the cumulative effect is of a latter-day Scheherazade, desperately staving off the final answer." New Yorker

Powell, Sophie

The **Mushroom** Man. Putnam 2003 196p
$23.95

ISBN 0-399-14963-5

LC 2002-21355

At the heart of this novel is a "child's invented fairy tale, set in a Welsh forest, about an amiable hermit who fashions umbrellas from wild mushrooms to protect the local fairy population from the rain. . . . Eleven-year-old Amy—a triplet who lives on a farm in the Welsh countryside with her identical sisters; her older brother, Joseph; and her widowed mother, Beth—is the creator of the tale. One night she tells it to her 6-year-old cousin, Lily, who's so enchanted that she sets out to find the mushroom man and goes missing in the process, thus setting the novel's plot in motion. . . . The Welsh countryside has never seemed so alluring, or the existence of simple magic, despite the nasty disappointments of adult life, so probable." N Y Times Book Rev

Power, Susan

The **grass** dancer. Putnam 1994 300p hardcover o.p. pa $7.99

ISBN 0-399-13911-7; 0-425-14962-5 pa

LC 93-47199

"Set on a North Dakota reservation, 'The Grass Dancer' tells the story of Harley Wind Soldier, a young Sioux trying to understand his place among people whose intertwined lives and shared heritage move backward in time in the narrative from the 1980's to the middle of the last century." N Y Times Book Rev

This "is a passionate portrayal of universal human emotions and a vivid account of Native American history and culture." SLJ

Powers, J. F.

★ **Morte** d'Urban. Doubleday 1962 336p

"Father Urban, member of a Catholic order that is financially impoverished, spends his time in two worlds, the religious and the secular. He must try to gain friends and funds for the Clementine order and yet make decisions that may cost him the friendship of his wealthy benefactors, among them eccentric and willful Billy Cosgrove and Mrs. Thwaites. The wide cast of characters within the church and the world outside makes for both a sad and amusing portrait." Shapiro. Fic for Youth. 3d edition

Powers, J. F.

★ **Wheat** that springeth green. Knopf 1988
335p

LC 87-46104

"The beauty of Mr. Powers's writing lies in its art's being almost invisible. The craft and balance of the novel's literary achievement are discernible in every sentence, but only on second thought, so thoroughly has the author subordinated form to function." N Y Times Book Rev

Powers, John R.

★ **Do** black patent-leather shoes really reflect up? a fictionalized memoir. Regnery Bks. 1975 227p

Sequel to The last Catholic in America

Powers "reproduces the insulated milieu of the big-city Catholic school where harsh discipline and religious fervor molded students for an alternatively naive and cynical survival. The interludes of sentimentality don't detract as Powers' episodic structure and genuine affection carry the day." Booklist

Powers, John R.

★ The **last** Catholic in America; a fictionalized memoir. Saturday Review Press 1973 228p

"Bittersweet variations on the familiar U.S. literary theme of growing up Catholic . . . strike funny, trite, sometimes overlong, and inevitably sensitive chords. The nostalgic entertainment, occasionally bordering on the mawkish, rings true with seriocomic overtones and honest dialog." Booklist

Followed by Do black patent-leather shoes really reflect up?

Powers, Kevin

★ The **yellow** birds; a novel. Kevin Powers. 1st ed. Little, Brown & Company 2012 226 p. (hardcover) $32.99; (paperback) $14.99; (hardcover) $24.99

ISBN 9781410452566 large print; 9780316219341; 0316219363; 9780316219365

LC 2012019435

New York Times Notable Books - Fiction and Poetry: 2012

Guardian First Book Award (2012)

National Book Awards Finalist: (2012)

This book by Kevin Powers follows "twenty-one-year old Private Bartle and eighteen-year-old Private Murphy. . . . Bound together since basic training when Bartle makes a promise to bring Murphy safely home, the two have been dropped into a war neither is prepared for. . . . The two young soldiers do everything to protect each other. . . . Murphy becomes increasingly unmoored from the world around him and Bartle takes actions he could never have imagined." (Publisher's note)

Powers, Kim

Capote in Kansas; a ghost story. Carroll & Graf 2007 254p $25

ISBN 978-0-7867-2033-0; 0-7867-2033-6

In the last year of his life Truman Capote is "plagued by the ghosts of the people whose deaths he chronicled in his greatest book, In Cold Blood. The now-old Harper Lee, or Nelle as she calls herself, is the only one who has a shot at understanding Truman—his childhood friend, she served as companion and researcher on the trip to Kansas that produced In Cold Blood. But Nelle has her own ghosts to exorcise having to do with why she never wrote a second book. In Kansas, Powers speculates, Truman exposed Nelle to her own sexuality, which she continues to suppress. And at his famous 1966 Black and White Ball, green with envy over Nelle's having won the Pulitzer Prize for fiction, Truman spreads the rumor that it was he who wrote To Kill a Mockingbird, not she. Powers . . . succeeds brilliantly in blending fact and fiction to produce a sensitive portrait of two lost souls." Libr J

Powers, Richard

The **echo** maker. Farrar, Straus and Giroux 2006 451p $25

    ISBN 978-0-374-14635-1; 0-374-14635-7

                      LC 2006-00093

This "novel—a kind of neuro-cosmological adventure—is an exhilarating narrative feat. The ease with which the author controls his frequently complex material is sometimes as thrilling to watch as the unfolding of the story itself." Washington Post Book World

Powers, Richard

★ **Galatea** 2.2. Farrar, Straus & Giroux 1995 329p

    ISBN 0-374-19948-5

                      LC 94-44319

In this novel, protagonist Richard Powers is a "humanist-in-residence at the Center for the Study of Advanced Science, where he uses his literary expertise to help Dr. Philip Lentz, a cognitive neurologist, win a bet that he can create a thinking machine capable of passing a comprehensive master's exam in English. As the computer, Helen, learns the fundamentals of language and literature, she develops a sense of her own identity and self-worth. Paralleling Powers' growing attachment to Helen is a reassessment of the year he spent living in Holland writing his novels and the demise of his longtime relationship with a former student." Booklist

Powers, Richard

Generosity; an enhancement. Farrar, Straus and Giroux 2009 296p $25

    ISBN 978-0-374-16114-9; 0-374-16114-3

                      LC 2008-54249

"Depending on personal philosophy, readers will disagree as to whether Generosity has a happy ending. But few will fail to be moved by Thassadit's joyful vision of human life." Dallas Morning News

Powers, Richard

The **gold** bug variations. Morrow 1991 639p

    ISBN 0-688-09891-6

                      LC 90-20267

"The novel jumps back and forth between the late '50s, when brilliant scientists Stuart Ressler is involved with an Illinois research team trying to break the mysteries of DNA coding, and the '80s, when librarian Jan O'Deigh and computer programmer Franklin Todd get to know Ressler, now holding an insignificant night job at a massive computer database operation in Brooklyn, N.Y., and try to figure what derailed his promising career." Publ Wkly

Powers, Richard

Operation wandering soul; a novel. Morrow 1993 352p

    ISBN 0-688-11548-9

                      LC 92-43860

This novel, set in the pediatric ward of a large metropolitan hospital is "about the plight of the world's children in a time of cynicism, corruption and easy destruction of life. The only recognizable adults are surgical resident Richard Kraft, desperately weary of trying to patch up the shattered lives and bodies of innocents, and therapist Linda Espera, who tries to instill hope through storytelling and play-acting. The two are deeply involved with a band of patients led by a precociously wise but hopelessly crippled Thai girl and a cynical, commanding boy whose rare disease has withered his body into that of an old man." Publ Wkly

Powers, Richard

★ **Plowing** the dark. Farrar, Straus & Giroux 2000 415p $25

    ISBN 0-374-23461-2

                      LC 99-45084

"In Seattle, a woman painter joins a team of software engineers who are devising a virtual-reality module; at the same time, an American hostage, moldering in a bare cell in Beirut, tries to mentally reconstruct his Stateside existence. Powers's intellectual dexterity is dazzling, especially in the descriptions of virtual-realty programming, and he has plenty to say about the intersections of art, war, commerce, and literature." New Yorker

Powers, Richard

Prisoner's dilemma. Beech Tree Bks. 1988 348p

    ISBN 0-688-07350-6

                      LC 87-31824

"Prisoner's Dilemma is a paradigm for the nuclear game, the only door left ajar by Hobbes's enlightened self-preservation, the dictates of right reason. Or, is Artie's last oracular pronouncement on his father's legacy the hard answer: 'What we can't bring about in no way releases us from what we must.' We finish this novel, as we do all grand fiction, ready to figure on. Prisoner's Dilemma is magnificent." Nation

Powers, Richard

★ The **time** of our singing. Farrar, Straus & Giroux 2002 631p $28

    ISBN 0-374-27782-6

                      LC 2002-22397

"Powers's blending of unlikely tones in order to probe the problems of a society that continues to insist, all grays to the contrary, on seeing everything in terms of black and white is, more often than not, a fascinating, stimulating and moving artistic imagining of a harmony that continues to elude us in life." N Y Times Book Rev

Powers, Tim, 1952-

Declare; Tim Powers. William Morrow 2001 517p (alk. paper) o.p.

    ISBN 0380976528

                      LC 2001267560

International Horror Guild Awards: Best Novel (2000); World Fantasy Awards: Novel (2001)

This book offers a "spy story involving rivalries between . . . four intelligence services: British, French, Russian and American. In 1963, Andrew Hale is summoned to reenter the secret service. He has a past [which includes] . . . a[n] . . . unsuccessful mission on Mount Ararat in 1948. . . . [Author Tim] Powers posits that the mountain . . . is . . . the dwelling place of many djinns, supernatural beings that often take the form of rocks in the Arabian deserts. . . . [I]t seems that a supernatural power, manifesting itself as an old woman, is safeguarding the Soviet Union, and if fragments of a destroyed djinn can be introduced into Moscow, they could destroy her protection and make the Soviet Union susceptible to normal human laws. This is Hale's mission." (Publishers Weekly)

Powers, Tim

Hide me among the graves; Tim Powers. William Morrow 2012

ISBN 9780061231544

LC 2011049629

This book takes place in "London, winter of 1862, [when] Adelaide McKee, a former prostitute, arrives on the doorstep of veterinarian John Crawford, a man she met once seven years earlier. Their brief meeting produced a child who, until now, had been presumed dead. McKee has learned that the girl lives--but that her life and soul are in mortal peril from a vampiric ghost. But this is no ordinary spirit; the bloodthirsty wraith is none other than John Polidori, the onetime physician to the mad, bad, and dangerous Romantic poet Lord Byron. . . . Determined to save their daughter, McKee and Crawford join forces . . . and soon . . . are plunged into a supernatural London underworld whose existence goes beyond their wildest imaginings." (Publisher's note)

Powers, Tim

Three days to never; a novel. William Morrow 2006 420p $25.95

ISBN 978-0-380-97653-9

LC 2006-41900

"Imagine a world where time travel is possible. Now imagine a world where the mummified head of an Einstein clone is helping a secret sect, led by a quasi-hermaphroditic ghost who speaks in iambic pentameter, track down and locate the time machine, an integral component of which is Charlie Chaplin's footprints in a cement slab, and you'll begin to get a grasp on just how bizarrely populated Powers' world is. Almost despite its wonderful weirdness, this thriller maneuvers at a frantic clip as Frank Marrity, Einstein's great-grandson, must pit his wits against not only the malicious secret society bent on attaining immortality but also a specialized paranormal branch of Israel's Mossad, who'd like to use the time machine to avert the Six Days' War of 1967, a stunning psychic assassin who can only see out of other people's eyes, and none other than his own bitter, alcoholic future Frank Marrity self to save his daughter, Daphne, from not merely death but from never having been." Booklist

Powning, Beth

The **sea** captain's wife; Beth Powning. Plume 2011 374p map (pbk.) $15

ISBN 9780452296954

LC 2010030032

This book tells the "19th-century tale of a young woman desperate to live at sea with her captain husband. . . . When Azuba married Nathaniel, she thought that as husband and wife they would exploring the world together on his boat. . . . But when Carrie is born, Nathaniel insists Azuba stay safely ashore at home in Whelan's Cove, New Brunswick, Canada, to raise their daughter. During Nathaniel's long absences, Azuba befriends Rev. Simon Walton, and their companionship sparks rumors of an affair that even reach Nathaniel, who returns to Whelan's Cove in a jealous rage. But Azuba persuades him to finally bring her and Carrie aboard ship, turning a long-held dream into bittersweet reality." (Publishers Weekly)

Poyer, David

Black storm. St. Martin's Press 2002 292p

ISBN 0-312-26969-2

LC 2001-58562

In this "Dan Lenson adventure, Poyer injects the special ops ace into the heart of Operation Desert Storm and confrontation with the menace of Iraqi biological warfare. Attached, along with Major Maddox, a female army doctor, to a marine recon team aiming to infiltrate Baghdad and target a suspected bioweapons site, Lenson survives claustrophobic rides in a milk truck's tank, mad SAS men, and capture and torture by the Iraqis. . . . The remarkably vivid portraits he draws of the variety of men and women drawn to serve their country merit high praise, too." Booklist

Poyer, David

China Sea. St. Martin's Press 2000 337p il

ISBN 0-312-20287-3

LC 99-55067

Lenson and his crew "engage the Chinese in a climactic battle that ranks high among single-ship actions in maritime fiction. Readers who can meet Poyer halfway with knowledge of modern seafaring stand to be especially richly rewarded." Booklist

Poyer, David

The **circle**. St. Martin's Press 1992 432p

LC 92-2980

"The individual events convincingly present the gritty details of life aboard a pre-computer-age destroyer, and Poyer provides a compelling sense of the Cold War Navy's operational dynamics." Publ Wkly

Poyer, David

The **command**. St. Martin's Press 2004 386p map $24.95

ISBN 0-312-31836-7

LC 2003-28058

"After receiving the Congressional Medal of Honor for action in Iraq, Commander Daniel V. Lenson is given new orders: 'Take over as skipper of USS Thomas W. Horn.' His mission: Prepare the Tomahawk-equipped strike destroyer and her crew for the Red Sea, where she'll join an international task force searching for weapons of mass destruction." Publisher's note

Poyer, David

A **country** of our own; a novel of the Civil War at sea. Simon & Schuster 2003 429p $24

ISBN 0-684-87134-3

LC 2003-45435

"Lt. Ker Claiborne has reluctantly relinquished his commission in the U.S. Navy and joined the Confederacy. He's an anomaly—a Virginian who opposes slavery. The plot follows Claiborne throughout the South and then across the Atlantic as captain of a highly successful and feared rebel commerce raider. There are enough spies, plots, battles, storms, and shipwrecks to satisfy any reader." Libr J

Poyer, David

Down to a sunless sea; a Tiller Galloway thriller. St. Martin's Press 1996 306p

ISBN 0-312-14589-6

LC 96-3120

"The cave-diving scenes are riveting, claustrophobic, terrifying, and beautiful, and Tiller has grown into one of the most spectacularly flawed and failed characters ever to seek redemption in popular fiction." Booklist

Poyer, David

Fire on the waters; a novel of the Civil War at sea. Simon & Schuster 2001 445p

ISBN 0-684-87133-5

LC 2001-20307

This novel "introduces naval officer Elisha Eaker. The pampered son of a successful shipping magnate, Eli enlists to take a stand for his country and against his overbearing father. Commissioned to protect the Union forces at Fort Sumter, Eli and Captain Parker Bucyrus Tresevant, a Southerner torn between allegiances, sail into the danger, intrigue, and indecision necessarily engendered by a nation at war with itself." Booklist

"An interesting character study of a young man's coming of age as well as an accurate historical novel." Libr J

Poyer, David

The **gulf**. St. Martin's Press 1990 xx, 442p

LC 90-36140

"Dan Lenson, is the executive officer on a frigate in the Persian Gulf, assigned to convoy a succession of oil tankers through perilous waters. Lenson's shipmates include hard-living helicopter pilots, minor crooks, and idealistic young officers. Not far away, a group of divers, naval reservists, must battle the hostility of 'real' sailors as they undertake a dangerous mission of their own. Lenson's physical and mental courage are sorely tried in the climactic scenes, where he battles enemies and the ocean itself." Libr J

Poyer, David

Thunder on the mountain. Forge 1999 382p $25.95

ISBN 0-312-86494-9

LC 98-43454

Poyer's "pitch-perfect dialogue and explosive imagery capture both sides of the bloody battle that gave birth to

the unions. This is a stunning period tale in which the oft-forgotten essence of the American dream is visible in every chapter." Publ Wkly

Poyer, David

The **Whiteness** of the Whale; David Poyer. St Martins Pr 2013 336 p. (hardcover) $26.99

ISBN 1250020565; 9781250020567

LC 2013002630

In this novel, "Dr. Sara Pollard joins the antiwhaling activists aboard the Black Anemone, a high-tech yacht. ... The crew battles snow, ice, frigid temperatures, storms, and each other before encountering the whalers in the midst of slaughtering hundreds of whales. The appearance of a mysterious rogue whale, however, introduces an even more deadly hazard than the crew's human enemies." (Publishers Weekly)

Pratchett, Terry

★ The **color** of magic; a novel of Discworld. Harper 2005 224p pa $13.95

ISBN 0-06-085592-4

LC 2005-46289

First published 1983 by St. Martin's Press with title: The colour of magic

This first book of Discworld features the tourist Twoflower, the wizard Rincewind, and several other unusual characters as they travel together on a flat planet.

Pratchett, Terry

The **fifth** elephant; a novel of Discworld. HarperPrism 2000 321p

ISBN 0-06-105157-8

LC 99-43960

"Pratchett cheerfully takes readers on an exuberant tale of mystery and invention. ... Along the way, he skewers everything from monarchy to fascism, as well as communism and capitalism, oil wealth and ethnic identities, Russian plays, immigration, condoms and evangelical Christianity—in short, most everything worth talking about." Publ Wkly

Pratchett, Terry

Going postal; a novel of Discworld. HarperCollins 2004 377p $24.95

ISBN 0-06-001313-3

LC 2004-47391

"When petty con man Moist von Lipwig is hung for his crimes ... it appears to be the end. But this is Discworld after all, a world 'a lot like our own but different.' Moist awakes from the shock of his hanging to find that the city's Patrician, Lord Vetinari, has assigned him a government job (a fate worse than death?) restoring the defunct postal system. Of course, there is much more to restore than the flow of letters and packages. Justice as well as communication has been poorly served by a hostile takeover of the 'clacks' a unique messaging system that is part semaphore, part digital, and under the monopoly of the Grand Trunk Company. Before Moist can get very far into the job, he encounters ghosts, the voices of unsent letters, and a ruthless corporate conspiracy. ... The author's inventiveness seems to know no end, his playful and irreverent use of language is a delight, and there is food for thought in his parody of fantasyland." SLJ

Pratchett, Terry

Monstrous regiment; a novel of Discworld. HarperCollins Pubs. 2003 353p hardcover o.p. pa $7.99

ISBN 0-06-001315-X; 0-06-001316-8 pa

LC 2003-50800

"Pratchett revels in pricking pomp and assurance, but it isn't going too far to say that of late his real subject, like Wilfred Owen's, is the pit of war. Pratchett's approach may be less lyrical, but he can move from farce to sadness in seconds." N Y Times Book Rev

Pratchett, Terry

Thief of time; a novel of Discworld. HarperCollins Pubs. 2001 324p

ISBN 0-06-019956-3

LC 00-65347

"This is Discworld, an adolescent Oz in which far fewer folks are immortal, but long life doesn't entail decrepitude; magic works; and politics and culture are fluid, far off, and mostly for old guys. Spun out of words and wit, it is as light and curiously tasty as cotton candy." Booklist

Pratchett, Terry

Thud! a novel of Discworld. HarperCollins 2005 384p $24.95

ISBN 0-06-081522-6

LC 2005-46271

"Commander Sam Vines of Ankh-Morpork's City Watch finds a 'perfect day' going downhill quickly. Not only is there a murderer loose in the city but Sam also faces pressure to add a vampire to a police force that already contains trolls and werewolves and an old rivalry that threatens to break out into overt warfare. It's all in a day's work for the City Watch in the latest novel set in the author's hilariously surreal Disc World." Libr J

Pratchett, Terry

The **truth**; a novel of Discworld. HarperCollins Pubs. 2000 324p il

ISBN 0-380-97895-4

LC 00-31928

"When he stumbles upon the dwarven secret of movable type, young scribe William de Word discovers a new career and starts a newspaper—the first of its kind in the city of Ankh-Morpork. Pratchett's . . . 'Discworld' novel takes on the press and investigative journalism in a hilarious romp that examines the fleeting nature of truth and lies." Libr J

Prcic, Ismet

Shards. Black Cat 2011 392p pa $14.95

ISBN 978-0-8021-7081-1

The author's "debut is about a young Bosnian, also named Ismet Prcic, who has fled his wartorn homeland and is now struggling to reconcile his past with his present life in California. He is advised that in order to make peace with the corrosive guilt he harbors over leaving behind his family behind, he must 'write everything.' The result is a great rattlebag of memories, confessions, and fictions: sweetly humorous recollections of Ismet's childhood in Tuzla appear alongside anguished letters to his mother about the challenges of life in this new world. As Ismet's foothold in the present falls away, his writings are further complicated by stories from the point of view of another young man real or imagined named Mustafa, who joined a troop of elite soldiers and stayed in Bosnia to fight. When Mustafa's story begins to overshadow Ismet's new-world identity, the reader is charged with piecing together the fragments of a life that has become eerily unrecognizable, even to the one living it." Bookreporter

Preston, Caroline

The **scrapbook** of Frankie Pratt; Caroline Preston. Ecco Press 2011 228p. ill. (some col.)

ISBN 0061966908; 9780061966903

LC 2012372952

Alex Award (2012)

In this book, "Frankie receives a blank scrapbook and her deceased father's typewriter as high-school graduation gifts and begins to record her adventures with the keepsakes she collects. Although Vassar offers Frankie a scholarship, Frankie still can't afford to attend college. Instead she takes a job caring for elderly Mrs. Pingree. . . . The dowager's visiting nephew Jamie, a dashing, emotionally damaged World War I vet in his 30s, emotionally seduces 17-year-old Frankie. . . . When the not-yet-sexual affair is discovered, Mrs. Pingree gives Frankie a $1,000 check. . . . Soon Frankie heads off to Vassar. . . . After graduation, Frankie moves to Greenwich Village and finds a job at 'True Story.' . . . When Frankie realizes why [her boyfriend doesn't propose], she goes to Paris, . . . where the past catches up with her and a whole new chapter of life starts." (Kirkus)

Preston, Douglas

Blasphemy; [by] Douglas J. Preston. Forge Books 2008 414p il $25.95

ISBN 978-0-7653-1105-4; 0-7653-1105-4

LC 2007-31811

This suspense novel centers around "Isabella, a giant superconducting supercollider particle accelerator. . . . The ostensible goal of Isabella's creator, physicist Gregory North Hazelius, is to discover new forms of energy, but what he really wants is to talk to God. The project, located inside Red Mesa (a five-hundred-square-mile tableland on the Navajo Indian Reservation), is behind schedule, so presidential science adviser Stanton Lockwood hires ex-CIA man Wyman Ford to go to Red Mesa and find out what's causing the holdup. Meanwhile, a Navajo medicine man, a televangelist and a pastor who runs a failed mission on the reservation are gearing up to pull the plug on Isabella before she destroys the earth. Science has often tangled with religion in this genre, but Preston puts his own philosophical spin on the usual proceedings, and when he gets his irate villagers with their burning torches headed for the castle, the pages simply fly." Publ Wkly

Preston, Douglas

Brimstone; [by] Douglas Preston and Lincoln Child. Warner Bks. 2004 497p $25.95

ISBN 0-446-53143-X

LC 2004-1968

A mystery featuring FBI agent Pendergast. "In an exotic mansion, Jeremy Grove's charred remains are discovered in an otherwise locked and barricaded room. The area smells of brimstone, and singed into the floorboard appears to be a cloven hoofprint. According to rumor, Jeremy made a Faustian pact with Satan in his youth. Did the Dark Lord finally demand payment? Pendergast can't resist a mystery, and he incorporates the help of police officers from the authors' previous novels. In addition, a major character appears courtesy of Wilkie Collins's The Woman in White." Libr J

"Erudite, swiftly paced, brimming (occasionally over-brimming) with memorable personae and tense set pieces, this is the perfect thriller." Publ Wkly

Preston, Douglas

The **cabinet** of curiosities; {by} Douglas Preston and Lincoln Child. Warner Bks. 2002 466p

ISBN 0-446-53022-0

LC 2001-39580

This novel features "fabulous locales, colorful characters, pointed riffs on city and museum politics, cool forensic and paleontological speculation and several gripping set pieces including an extended white-knuckle climax." Publ Wkly

Preston, Douglas

The **codex**. Forge 2004 396p $24.95

ISBN 0-7653-0700-6

LC 2003-49427

"A treasure hunter and tomb raider, Maxwell Broadbent is one of the wealthiest men on the planet owing to his extensive art collection. Dying of cancer, he decides to force his three estranged sons to work together for their inheritance. Leaving them a videotape of his plan, Max takes everything of value and buries himself and the goods somewhere in the world. To claim their inheritance, his sons have to find the tomb. Others are watching and rooting them on so that they can claim the rewards for themselves. One item of significance is a Mayan codex that contains the secret instructions to create medicine from the native jungle plants. This discovery would revolutionize the pharmaceutical industry. Fascinating characters, exotic jungle scenery, and surprising twists make this nonstop thrill ride well worth deciphering." Libr J

Preston, Douglas

Impact. Forge 2010 364p $25.99

ISBN 978-0-7653-1768-1; 0-7653-1768-0

Near the start of this thriller, "the U.S. president's science adviser asks former CIA operative Wyman Ford, last seen in 2008's Blasphemy, to look into the sudden appearance of radioactive gemstones, in particular to identify the precise location of their origin in Cambodia. Meanwhile, college dropout and frustrated astronomer Abbey Straw, who believes she witnessed a meteor's fall, embarks on a search of small islands near her Maine home to locate pieces of the meteorite to sell on eBay. In California, soon-to-be murdered professor Jason Freeman sends Mark Corso, a Mars mission technician at the National Propulsion Facility, a classified hard drive with evidence of gamma rays emanating from the red planet." Publ Wkly

"The thriller elements mix well with the science aspects of the story, and the author makes even the hard-to-grasp concepts easy to understand." Libr J

Preston, Douglas

Reliquary; [by] Douglas Preston, Lincoln Child. Forge 1997 382p $24.95

ISBN 0-312-86095-1

LC 96-53533

"Although Reliquary is a sequel, its exposition carries us easily into the new plot and excites interest in seeing what Preston and Child come up with next, after this yarn's all-loose-ends-tied finale." Booklist

Preston, Douglas

Riptide; {by} Douglas Preston and Lincoln Child. Warner Bks. 1998 417p $25

ISBN 0-446-52336-4

LC 97-23907

"Dr. Malin Hatch is at first reluctant to let the Thalassa Group plunder his Ragged Island, off the coast of Maine, in yet another attempt to reclaim pirate Red Ned Ockham's 17th-century treasure. But its leaders assure him that they have the technology and skill to breach the deadly Water Pit that has claimed the lives of countless treasure hunters. They also have the encrypted diary of the Pit's designer, which, they claim, holds the key to the treasure's reclamation." Libr J

"Machine-gun pacing, startling plot twists and smart use of legend, scientific lore (including cyptanalysis) and the evocative setting carry the day." Publ Wkly

Preston, Douglas

Still life with crows; {by} Douglas Preston and Lincoln Child. Warner Bks. 2003 435p $24.95

ISBN 0-446-53142-1

LC 2002-192401

FBI Agent Pendergast arrives "in tiny Medicine Creek, KS, just in time to investigate a series of gruesome murders. Life in rural Medicine Creek usually revolves around the local turkey-processing plant and growing corn, but all hell breaks loose when a female corpse is found in a clearing in a cornfield, surrounded by a ring of dead crows impaled on arrows." Libr J

Preston, Douglas

Tyrannosaur Canyon. Forge 2005 368p $24.95

ISBN 0-765-31104-6

LC 2005-5171

"A prospector discovers the treasure of his lifetime and takes bullets in the back for his effort. With his dying breath, he gives a journal to innocent bystander Tom Broadbent (the hero of Preston's . . . The Codex) and asks Tom to deliver the information to his daughter. The prospector's killer, of course, wants the ledger, so now Tom and his wife are in mortal danger. Why is the journal so valuable? It contains information leading to the fossilized remains of a complete Tyrannosaurus rex, a scientific discovery worth millions and a lifetime of accolades to the finder. In addition, a mysterious black ops agency wants the skeleton to hide a deadly secret originally discovered on the moon over 30 years ago by the crew of Apollo 17. The truth will shake the foundation of paleontology to its core. Preston's exhilarating and absorbing science-based effort will thrill readers from the first page to the last." Libr J

Preston, Douglas

The **wheel** of darkness; [by] Douglas Preston & Lincoln Child. Warner Books 2007 388p $25.99

ISBN 978-0-446-58028-1; 0-446-58028-7

LC 2007-20551

In this supernatural thriller, "FBI agent Aloysius Pendergast and his ward, Constance Greene, seek peace of mind at a remote Tibetan monastery, only to fall into yet another perilous, potentially earthshaking assignment. The monastery's abbot asks them to recover a stolen relic, the cryptic Agozyen, which could, in the wrong hands, wipe out humanity. The pair follow the trail to a luxury cruise ship, where a series of brutal murders suggests the relic's evil spirit might already have been invoked. . . . While not as frightening as others in the series, this entry still shows why the authors stand head and shoulders above their rivals in this subgenre." Publ Wkly

Preston, Richard

The **Cobra** event; a novel. Random House 1997 404p $25.95

ISBN 0-679-45714-3

LC 98-106915

"When two completely unrelated people die horrifically in New York City, Alice Austen, a young doctor working for the Centers for Disease Control in Washington, D.C., is called in to investigate. What Austen finds in New York is like nothing she has ever seen; two victims whose symptoms include self-cannibalism and brains that have turned to mush. More victims follow, and soon she realizes that the mystery illness was caused by a man-made virus that spreads as easily as the common cold. Drawing on her findings, a team of government scientists is formed and set up on Governor's Island in the middle of New York Harbor. Their job is to find the person behind the virus and to stop him before he causes a worldwide outbreak." Libr J

"Preston marshals his narrative with sufficient precision to persuade and terrify readers." Publ Wkly

Price, Eugenia

Savannah. Doubleday 1983 595p

LC 82-45572

The first volume in the author's Savannah quartet; other titles To see your face again (1985); Before darkness falls (1987) and Stranger in Savannah (1989)

This "novel tells the story of a handsome young Yankee, Mark Browning, who finds a secure place for himself in the gracious society of Savannah, Georgia, in the early 19th century. Browning, befriended by a merchant named Robert Mackay, is taken into the man's mercantile firm, and soon finds himself in love with Mackay's virtuous wife. The situation is further complicated by Mark's growing attraction to his first cousin, Caroline Cameron, and his relationship with a blackguard uncle, Osmund Kott, who may or may not be on the edge of true repentance and conversion to Christianity." Publ Wkly

Price, Nancy

Night woman. Pocket Bks. 1992 314p

ISBN 0-671-74993-5

LC 92-50164

"Gritty, wry characterization, chilling images of insanity, and a long, ultimately satisfying tease which ends with Mary at last getting her due will keep readers flipping pages." Publ Wkly

Price, Nancy

Sleeping with the enemy. Simon & Schuster 1987 332p

LC 86-29778

"Battered women don't usually have the courage of Sara Burney. Desperate and bruised physically and emotionally, she evolves a plan to flee her obsessive husband. She knows he will come after her and kill her eventually, so that mere flight will offer only temporary reprieve. So she decides to 'get lost.' She assumes a new identity, a new look, and seeks respite and a new life hundreds of miles from their home in Massachusetts. . . . Price has written an absorbing tale and her language has a sensual quality that transports the reader into her panoramas that affect all the senses." West Coast Rev Books

Price, Reynolds

Blue Calhoun. Atheneum Pubs. 1992 373p $23

ISBN 0-689-12146-6

LC 91-22877

"Price is in top form here, forcing us to wrestle with Blue even as he wrestles with himself, portraying his anguish in painfully clear, clean prose that captures perfectly the rhythms of the South and of the human heart." Libr J

Price, Reynolds

★ The **collected** stories. Atheneum Pubs. 1993 625p $25

ISBN 0-689-12147-4

LC 92-36807

"Many of the characters in these magical, quietly revelatory, death-obsessed tales are transformed by chance encounters, in settings that include Price's native south but also range throughout the world." Publ Wkly

Price, Reynolds

The **foreseeable** future. Atheneum Pubs. 1991 253p $21.95

ISBN 0-689-12110-5

LC 90-45463

"In his eloquent and distinctive voice, Price reveals in each of these stories how love and memory, loss and redemption, and essential human goodness 'prop' us up and allow us to move forward into an uncertain future." Libr J

Price, Reynolds

★ The **good** priest's son. Scribner 2005 278p $26

ISBN 0-7432-5400-7

LC 2004-65383

This novel is "thematically rich—indeed, it is rather bowed by its meanings—and features many pleasing Southern voices, along with an impeccable depiction of the region's deep-rooted traditions." N Y Times Book Rev

Price, Reynolds

★ **Kate** Vaiden. Atheneum Pubs. 1986 306p
ISBN 0-689-11787-6

LC 85-48143

"Mr. Price's successful creation of a female voice may be a tour de force, but it never feels like a showy ventriloquial act. Instead, Kate is a wholly convincing girl and a not improbable woman." N Y Times Book Rev

Price, Reynolds

The **promise** of rest. Scribner 1995 353p
ISBN 0-684-80149-3

LC 94-48086

Conclusion of the author's Mayfield family trilogy begun with The surface of earth (1975) and The source of light (1981). "Wade Mayfield, great-grandson of the woman whose runaway marriage in 1903 set the family's tragic 20th-century history in motion, is dying of AIDS. Long estranged from his parents (his black lover, Wyatt Bondurant, hated them as complicit beneficiaries of the South's racist past), Wade comes home to North Carolina in April 1993, after Wyatt's death. His mother, Ann, has left his father, Hutchins, claiming that her husband has shut her out of his life for years. Meanwhile, Hutchins's lifelong friend and onetime lover, Strawson Stuart, makes his own reproaches about Hutchins's inability to fully accept love. Extended family and friends gather around the dying Wade, grappling with matters as general as America's poisoned racial heritage and as intimate as the Mayfield legacy." Publ Wkly

Price, Reynolds

Roxanna Slade. Scribner 1998 301p $25
ISBN 0-684-83292-5

LC 97-39167

"Many of the virtues that have endeared Price . . . to readers are present in this story of a North Carolina woman and several generations of her family. Price's musically cadenced, nostalgia-washed prose, plangent with portent and loss and vibrant with imagery, is as beguiling as ever. His picture of life in the South a century ago is imbued with candor about customs and attitudes—especially those concerning women and race." Publ Wkly

Price, Reynolds

The **tongues** of angels. Atheneum Pubs. 1990 192p $17.95
ISBN 0-689-12093-1

LC 89-37427

"As much prey to mutual irritation as to esteem, they worry and argue their way—the 14-year-old boy and the 21-year-old man—through the 10-week intimacy of the camp, cut of from so-called civilization and therefore free, in terms they hold in common, to aim beyond the commonplace: into myth, art, ritual and pain." N Y Times Book Rev

Price, Richard

★ **Clockers**. Houghton Mifflin 1992 599p
ISBN 0-395-53761-4

LC 91-43318

The author "divides his narrative between two main characters: Strike (a k a Ronald Dunham), the black crew leader of a small-time group of cocaine dealers—the 'clock-ers' of the title—in the slums of northern New Jersey, and Rocco Klein, an experienced but disillusioned white homicide detective who's about to take early retirement. The stories of Rocco and Strike are pulled together when Strike's by-all-accounts paragon brother, Victor, confesses to an apparently routine drug murder and Rocco, refusing to believe Victor guilty, becomes convinced that he's taking the heat for his brother." N Y Times Book Rev

This is "an incredible course in urban street life, particularly the crack culture." Booklist

Price, Richard

Freedomland. Broadway Bks. 1998 546p $25
ISBN 0-7679-0024-3

LC 98-10527

A novel set in an inner-city neighborhood in northern New Jersey. "Through a haze of shock and exhaustion, a young white woman manages to tell a disjointed story of being carjacked by a black man outside the Henry T. Armstrong housing projects; she claims her four-year-old son was asleep in the backseat. Asthmatic black policeman Lorenzo 'Big Daddy' Council catches the case and can sense the political firestorm brewing in the background. . . . As the frantic search for the boy ensues, the media, project residents, a neighboring majority white police district, black activists, and a zealous missing-children's group all converge on the scene, each with their own agendas." Booklist

"Price's characters are, as usual, dead-on, and his eye for unflinchingly capturing humans at their very best—and very worst—is unrivaled." Libr J

Price, Richard

Lush life. Farrar, Straus & Giroux 2008 455p $26
ISBN 978-0-374-29925-5; 0-374-29925-0; 0374299250; 9780374299255

LC 200808437

This novel is set in New York City. Eric Cash is "thirty-five years old and he's still living on the Lower East Side, still in the restaurant business, still serving the people he wanted to be. What does Eric do? He manages. Not like Ike Marcus. Ike was young, good-looking, people liked him. Ask him what he did, he wouldn't say tending bar. He was going places—until two street kids stepped up to him and Eric one night and pulled a gun. At least, that's Eric's version." (Publisher's note)

"Price has been around for what seems like forever, but there's a reason we still read him. Because every sentence is a pleasure. Because he never puts a foot wrong, and never lingers. He takes just enough time to make you care." Esquire

Price, Richard

Samaritan. Knopf 2003 377p $25
ISBN 0-375-41115-1

"Ray Mitchell, an Emmy-nominated TV writer who returned to teach pro bono at his old high school amid the projects of Dempsy, New Jersey, has had his head bashed in. Nerese Ammons, a cop 10 weeks from retirement, takes the case personally because of a good turn Ray did her when they were children. But Ray, deteriorating in the hospital, doesn't want to tell her who attacked him." Booklist

Priest, Cherie

Boneshaker. Tor 2009 416p pa $15.99
ISBN 978-0-7653-1841-1

LC 2009-18700

"Intelligent, exceptionally well written and showcasing a phenomenal strong female protagonist who embodies the complexities inherent in motherhood, this yarn is a must-read for the discerning steampunk fan." Publ Wkly

Priest, Cherie

Clementine; Cherie Priest. Subterranean Press 2010 201 p. $25
ISBN 1596063084; 9781596063082

"In this steampunk thriller" by Cherie Priest "Maria Isabella Boyd, a notorious former actress and Confederate spy, is on her first mission for the renowned Pinkerton Detective Agency. The airship Clementine must deliver its cargo unimpeded, but its former owner, escaped slave-turned-air pirate Croggon Hainey, is determined to recover the ship he stole fair and square. A simple pursuit quickly evolves, and soon Maria and Croggon are forced to fight on the same side." (Publishers Weekly)

Priest, Cherie

Dreadnought; Cherie Priest. Tor 2010 400 p. (pbk.) $14.99
ISBN 0765325780; 9780765325785

LC 2010032571

In this "Civil War steampunk thriller"by Cherie Priest, "Mercy Lynch, recently widowed and taxed to exhaustion by caring for Confederate wounded in Richmond, must cross the war-torn nation to reach her estranged father, who lies dying in the Washington territories. After her dirigible is shot out of the air, Mercy joins Horatio Korman, a Texas Ranger with an agenda, on the Union's famous steam engine, the Dreadnought." (Publishers Weekly)

Priest, Cherie

Ganymede; Cherie Priest. Tor Books 2011 349 p. $14.99
ISBN 0765329468 pa; 9780765329462 pa

LC 2011021569

In the book by author Cherie Priest, "the air pirate Andan Cly is going straight. Well, straighter. Although he's happy to run alcohol guns wherever the money's good, he doesn't think the world needs more sap, or its increasingly ugly side-effects. But becoming legit is easier said than done, and Cly's first legal gig--a supply run for the Seattle Underground--will be paid for by sap money." (Publisher's note)

Priest, Cherie

The inexplicables; Cherie Priest. Tor 2012 366 p. (trade pbk.) $14.99
ISBN 0765329476; 9780765329479; 9781429944922

LC 2012024853

In this novel by Cherie Priest "Rector 'Wreck 'em' Sherman . . . sneaks . . . inside the walled city of Seattle. . . . [The city is] chock-full of the hungry undead and utterly choked by the poisonous, inescapable yellow gas. . . . Rector comes across another incursion through the wall--just as bizarre but entirely attributable to human greed. It seems some outsiders have decided there's gold to be found in the city and

they're willing to do whatever it takes to get a piece of the pie unless Rector and his posse have anything to do with it." (Publisher's note)

Priest, Christopher

The islanders; Christopher Priest. Gollancz 2011 339 p.
ISBN 0575070048; 9780575070042

LC 2012379979

This book "presents itself as a [fictional] gazetteer for the Dream Archipelago, a vast array of islands situated between two warring continents to the north and south, [but] becomes, instead, a study of some of the islands' most interesting inhabitants. As the stories of a reclusive novelist, a simple young man accused of murder, a social theorist and author, a celebrated mime, and other significant individuals unfold, another tale—of a very public murder . . . --evolves." (Library Journal)

Pritchett, V. S.

★ **Complete** collected stories. Random House 1991 1219p

LC 90-47478

First published 1990 in the United Kingdom

Pronzini, Bill

Blue lonesome. Walker & Co. 1995 207p

LC 95-13049

"Two quotes that connect hell, the devil, and loneliness foreshadow the suicide of a woman known as Ms. Lonesome. The often-solitary James Messenger sets out in search of the aloof woman's identity even though he spoke to her only once. He finds himself in Beulah, Nevada, a harsh countryside dominated by embittered people, violent murder, and mulish sensibilities. Pronzini skillfully handles Messenger's quest. He uses jazz to accompany changes in mood, but is not verbose." Libr J

Pronzini, Bill

Bones. St. Martin's Press 1985 196p

LC 85-1708

"The 'Nameless Detective' is hired by Michael Kiskadon to find out why his father, pulp writer Harmon Crane, committed suicide 35 years ago. This proves to be a locked room puzzle. The twisting plot eventually turns up three murders. This is a crisply written mystery with perfect pacing; new clues are cunningly placed so that reader interest is constantly piqued." Libr J

Pronzini, Bill

★ **Crazybone**; a nameless detective novel. Carroll & Graf Pubs. 2000 197p
ISBN 0-7867-0730-5

Pronzini's nameless detective "lumbers down the San Francisco Peninsula to a private enclave of wooded estates and walled country clubs to find out why a grieving widow has refused a $50,000 insurance settlement for the accidental death of her husband. The look of 'raw terror' on the woman's face when he confronts her . . . suggests that she might have something to hide, and the nameless hero does a good job of ferreting out her secret. But the real fun comes from watching the old war horse plod through a hostile social environment, observing the swells at their selfish pursuits and making them regret every condescending sneer they threw in his face." N Y Times Book Rev

Pronzini, Bill

The **crimes** of Jordan Wise. Walker & Co. 2006 233p $23.95

ISBN 0-8027-1493-5

LC 2006-46115

"Like an expert fisherman, Pronzini spins out his yarn to its inevitable conclusion; there's only one way to end the old story of a lovesick sap and a dame whose appetites can never be satisfied. The Crimes of Jordan Wise is a neat piece of writing: James M. Cain by way of Jimmy Buffett." Washington Post Book World

Pronzini, Bill

Fever; a Nameless Detective novel. Forge 2008 288p $24.95

ISBN 978-0-7653-1818-3; 0-7653-1818-0

LC 2008-5228

"Mitchell Krochek, who's worried about the gambling addiction of his wife, Janice, hires Nameless to trace Janice, who's disappeared for the fourth time in four years. When Jake Runyon, Nameless's associate, traces Janice to an apartment hotel near their San Francisco office, Nameless and Jake decide to honor Janice's request not to reveal her location to her husband. Later, a battered Janice shows up at the detective agency's office, where she agrees to go home, only to vanish again amid circumstances strongly indicating foul play. . . . This insightful novel will appeal to those who like the mean streets portrayed with understatement and subtlety rather than gory violence." Publ Wkly

Pronzini, Bill

Hardcase; a Nameless Detective mystery. Delacorte Press 1995 215p

LC 95-5723

This mystery "opens as the California PI, approaching 60, marries his longtime girlfriend, Kerry. After a civil ceremony marked by his nervous clumsiness, Nameless takes on a client who wants him to find her birthparents. Melanie Ann Aldrich has just discovered that she was adopted and is sure there's a reason her adoptive parents, who are deceased, kept this information from her. Nameless fairly quickly identifies the woman's birthparents, but that's just the beginning." Publ Wkly

Pronzini, Bill

Hellbox; a nameless detective novel. Bill Pronzini. 1st ed. Forge 2012 302 p. ("Nameless Detective" mysteries) (hardcover) $24.99

ISBN 9781429947237; 0765325659; 9780765325655

LC 2012011650

In this suspense mystery novel, by Bill Pronzini, "Bill, the 'Nameless Detective,' and his wife Kerry were in the Sierra foothills . . . until Kerry went missing. . . . In a small town with limited resources, . . . a private investigator demanding action wasn't very popular. . . . With the help of his longtime associate Jake Runyon, . . . Bill and Jake follow the few leads they have, and come face to face with the Hellbox." (Publisher's note)

Pronzini, Bill

The **hidden**; a novel of suspense. Walker & Co. 2010 210p $24

ISBN 978-0-8027-1800-6; 0-8027-1800-0

LC 2010-30153

This "is a fairly short novel in these days of bloated best sellers, tightly written and tightly plotted, but never mechanical or obvious. It is strongly cinematic, but the pleasures, as always with Pronzini, are in the writing and not merely his visual sense. His characters are recognizable people, not merely pawns to the suspense element." Mystery Scene

Pronzini, Bill

Illusions; a Nameless Detective novel. Carroll & Graf Pubs. 1997 243p

LC 97-4274

"Shaken by the suicide of his former partner and onetime best friend, a pathetic figure whose life had shrunk to 'drinking, brooding, building his own private gallows day by day,' Nameless throws himself into a job for a Santa Fe businessman who wants to contact his former wife. The woman is easily found; but before the shamus can cash his check, a second suicide delivers another body blow to his code of ethics and deposits another load of guilt on his conscience. . . . The parallel investigations offer prime examples of Pronzini's ace plotting techniques . . . and if you can take the mood swings, Nameless is a good man to walk you through the noir landscape." N Y Times Book Rev

Pronzini, Bill

In an evil time. Walker & Co. 2001 266p $23.95

ISBN 0-8027-3353-0

LC 00-49996

"Jack Hollis, a family man and law-abiding citizen, is ready to cross the line. His daughter, Angela, is being stalked by her abusive second husband, David Rakubian, a successful personal-injury lawyer in San Francisco. In fact, it's Rakubian's knowledge of the law's limitations that makes him so dangerous to Angela and her toddler son. Jack has weighed the options and sees Rakubian's death as the only way out for his daughter. . . . {Pronzini} has fashioned a nail-biter out of the issue of domestic abuse and the law's inability to deal with it effectively." Booklist

Pronzini, Bill

Mourners; a nameless detective novel. Forge 2006 285p $24.95

ISBN 0-7653-0932-7

LC 2005-43510

"When Nameless made his assistant, Tamara, a partner in his detective agency and hired Jake, a new operative, he genuinely felt he was moving toward retirement. But business has increased, and Nameless finds himself reluctant to give up the work that has defined him for so long, even though he has recently become a husband and father. His current case involves a wealthy financial planner who attends the funerals of strangers, walks deserted beaches at night, and makes solitary visits to a secret rental apartment. His wife is worried and hires the firm to investigate. . . . Pronzini's series becomes more layered and complex with each entry. This time the primary characters are all in one stage or another of mourning, but the only one who recognizes it is the initial subject of the investigation. He is also the only one who understands the timeless omnipresence of grief. . . . A dark, foreboding entry in a classic series." Booklist

Pronzini, Bill

Nightcrawlers; a nameless detective novel. Forge 2005 301p $24.95

ISBN 0-7653-0931-9

LC 2004-56323

"The 'Nameless' detective is doing his best to settle into semiretirement after making his longtime assistant, Tamara Corbin, a partner in the agency and adding Jake Runyon, a former cop, as a field operative. However, some cases require Nameless' attention. Thugs are roaming the streets of San Francisco's Castro district, attacking gay men. Runyon's son's lover is one of the thug's victims, prompting Runyon and Nameless to investigate. Meanwhile Tamara, on a routine surveillance of a credit deadbeat, sees her subject carry something into his house that raises the hair on the back of her neck. The long-running Nameless series continues to evolve. With the novels no longer exclusively first-person narratives by Nameless, parallel plotlines have been introduced from multiple points of view, giving readers a chance to view Nameless as others see him. And, as always, the novels are never just about crime." Booklist

Pronzini, Bill

The **other** side of silence; a novel of suspense. Walker and Co. 2008 216p $24

ISBN 978-0-8027-1713-9; 0-8027-1713-6

A "suspense novel set in Las Vegas and California's Mohave Desert. While camping in the desert, Rick Fallon, a corporate security officer whose marriage has finally crumbled in the wake of his son's accidental death, comes across Casey Dunbar, who's tried and failed to kill herself after months of fruitlessly searching for her young son, who's been abducted by her ex-husband. Fallon empathizes with the woman, and what follows is a good old-fashioned search-and-capture mission with all the usual Pronzini virtues: a simple yet disciplined prose style; a strong, multilayered central character; and a compelling plot that builds to a nice little closing twist." Publ Wkly

Pronzini, Bill

★ **Quarry**; a Nameless Detective mystery. Delacorte Press 1992 216p

LC 91-15284

"Pronzini can get a shade overwrought . . . but his detective is a welcome journey into yesterday, where a shamus could bend the law and not have to agonize about it for too long afterwards." Booklist

Pronzini, Bill

Savages; a nameless detective novel. Forge 2007 300p $24.95

ISBN 978-7653-0933-4; 0-7653-0933-5

"San Francisco detective Nameless is asked by a former client to look into the death of her sister, who was trapped in an unhappy marriage. Although the death had been ruled an accident, Nameless soon finds himself stymied by ethical questions and lack of evidence. Meanwhile, Jake Runyon, a partner in Nameless's agency, is trying to serve a subpoena

and gets caught in a case of serial arson and murder. It is hard to find a better crime writer than Pronzini, and his understanding of feminine angst as well as male motivations has made this one of the best detective series ever." Libr J

Pronzini, Bill

Spook; a nameless detective novel. Carroll & Graf Pubs. 2003 233p $25

ISBN 0-7867-1086-1

"The case seems simple enough. Spook, a homeless street person, becomes a fixture at a local business; its employees provide assistance as needed for the obviously mentally disturbed individual. He is murdered in an especially heinous assault. His unofficial 'family' wants San Francisco private investigator 'Nameless' to learn his real identity. Nameless hands the case over to his newly hired field operative, Jake Runyon, a former Seattle cop. . . . A fascinating entry in a series that continues to redefine noir fiction even as it honors its roots." Booklist

Pronzini, Bill

★ **Step** to the graveyard easy. Walker & Co. 2002 165p $21.95

ISBN 0-8027-3375-1

LC 2001-55914

"Matt Cape is 35 and stuck in a rut: when his wife catches him in bed with another woman, he quits his job and takes to the road, leaving his old life (or lack thereof) behind. He heads south, then west, eventually landing in San Francisco, where he is fleeced in a card game by Boone Judson and his sidekick, Tanya. Cape gets his and the other players' money back, along with some mysterious photographs. He returns the money to its owners and follows the cardsharps to Lake Tahoe, where he also tracks down the people in the photos and warns them that they may be in danger." Publ Wkly

"Compelling modern noir with a thought-provoking conclusion." Booklist

Pronzini, Bill

A **wasteland** of strangers. Walker & Co. 1997 257p $22.95

ISBN 0-8027-3301-8

LC 96-50927

"The story fairly tears along to the jolting climax. Even after everyone has his or her say in the epilogue, readers still don't know John Faith's secrets. But that mystery is more haunting than maddening. Pronzini's . . . story is a gem." Publ Wkly

Prose, Francine

★ **Blue** angel; a novel. HarperCollins Pubs. 2000 314p $25

ISBN 0-06-019541-X

LC 99-40564

An "ironic gloss on Von Sternberg's tragedy of erotic abasement. . . . Prose's retelling focuses less on the ridiculous and self-destructive behavior of the professor . . . than on the far more laughable (and hazardous) rigidity of the politically correct behavior codes governing his tiny Vermont campus." New Yorker

Prose, Francine

A **changed** man; a novel. Francine Prose. HarperCollins Publishers 2005 421p $24.95
ISBN 0-06-019674-2

LC 2004-47448

A "satire of liberal pieties, the radical right and the fund-raising world. The 'changed man' of the title is Vincent Nolan, a 32-year-old tattooed ex-skinhead who appears one morning in the New York offices of World Brotherhood Watch, a foundation headed by Meyer Maslow, a Holocaust survivor. Vincent declares that he has had a personal conversion (never mind that it was triggered by a heavy dose of Ecstasy) and wants to work with the foundation to 'save guys like me from becoming guys like me.' Meyer takes Vincent on faith—and convinces Bonnie Kalen, the foundation's fundraiser, to put Vincent up in the suburban home she shares with her two sons, Max, 12, and Danny, 16. Prose tears into this unusual premise with the piercing wit that has become her trademark." Publ Wkly

Prose, Francine

Goldengrove; a novel. HarperCollins Publishers 2008 275p $24.95
ISBN 978-0-06-621411-5; 0-06-621411-4

LC 2008-02112

A young girl faces the consequences of sudden loss after the death of her sister. As her parents drift toward their own risky consolations, thirteen-year-old Nico is left alone to grope toward understanding and clarity, falling into a seductive, dangerous relationship with her sister's enigmatic boyfriend. Over one haunted summer, Nico must face that life-changing moment when children realize their parents can no longer help them. She learns about the power of art, of time and place, the mystery of loss and recovery. But for all the darkness at the novel's heart, the narrative itself is radiant with the lightness of summer and charged by the restless sexual tension of teenage life.

"Nico's introduction into adult situations is accelerated and scary, and Prose doesn't handle the topic with kid gloves. As Nico's relationship with Aaron progresses, her thoughts about physical intimacy run rampant. Prose expertly conveys the newfound sexual desires teenagers experience as they grow into adults." Deseret News

Prose, Francine

Household saints. St. Martin's Press 1981 227p
LC 80-29116

"When Joseph Santangelo, the sausagemaker, wins the bride, Catherine, in a pinochle game, he sets in motion a pattern of events laced with ancient Mediterranean customs, superstition and religion that affect the women in his life. In addition to Catherine, there is his mother, a nonstop oracle of doom, and his Americanized daughter who seeks and perhaps finds Jesus in obsessive domesticity. A skillful fabulist, {the author} . . . not only captures the domestic scenes and smells of Little Italy but allows her 'naifs' to unfold in recognizable earthiness and warmth as they confront life's mysteries." Publ Wkly

Prose, Francine

Hunters and gatherers. Farrar, Straus & Giroux 1995 247p

LC 95-3569

This is a "delightful satire, . . . irreverent, funny, critical, compassionate. . . . Prose brilliantly captures the absurdities and hypocrisies inherent in such groups. The women obsess about wombs, menstrual periods and the glories of being female. Yet separatism does not remove the worst dynamics between women." Women's Rev Books

Prose, Francine

My new American life. Harper 2011 306p $25.99
ISBN 978-0-06-171376-7

LC 2010-43012

"Lula is 26 and restless, an Albanian immigrant whiling away her days in suburban New Jersey as a spectacularly lax caretaker to sullen teenager Zeke (her "nannying' largely consists of mixing up afterschool mojitos and heating frozen pizzas) while his single father works long hours in finance. Soon enough, intrigue arrives in the form of three leather-jacketed comrades from the old country on her doorstep, asking Lula — though, really, it's not a request — to stash a gun for them, and Prose . . . is in her sweet spot as a nimble chronicler of contemporary culture. Though satirical fiction can often leave a sour aftertaste, her deft comic touch rarely falters." Entertainment Wkly

Prose, Francine

★ **Primitive** people. Farrar, Straus & Giroux 1992 227p
ISBN 0-374-23722-0

LC 91-28692

This "comedy of manners has a serious purpose but it is never earnest and provides a lot of shrewd and malicious fun. . . . The author finds it hard to write a dull sentence. Her gargoyles are sometimes gruesome. They are also witty and she has a perfect ear for the chatter of this particular set of rich Americans." Economist

Proulx, Annie

Accordion crimes; [by] E. Annie Proulx. Scribner 1996 381p
ISBN 0-684-19548-8

LC 96-16299

"Following successive owners of an accordion—from its creator, an Italian immigrant, who was lynched in Louisiana in 1891, to some fatherless black children living on the edge of a noxious landfill in 1991—this twelve-car pileup of a book brims with the sort of disasters you read about on the inside pages of the paper." New Yorker

Proulx, Annie

Bad dirt; Wyoming stories 2. Scribner 2004 219p $25
ISBN 0-7432-5799-5

LC 2004-56530

"This poignant and often humorous collection is packed with well-drawn characters that linger in the mind and heart. As expected, the Wyoming landscape is the enduring character in each story, silently wielding its magical and brutal power." Libr J

Proulx, Annie

Close range; Wyoming stories. watercolors by William Matthews. Scribner 1999 283p il $23.50

ISBN 0-684-85221-7

LC 98-56066

"Geography, splendid and terrible, is a tutelary deity to the characters in 'Close Range': hardpan ranchers, battered cowpokes and bull riders, bar girls and bar brawlers. Their lives are a futile uphill struggle conducted as a downhill, out-of-control tearaway. Proulx writes of them in a prose that is violent and impacted and mastered just at the point where, having gone all the way to the edge, it is about to go over." N Y Times Book Rev

Proulx, Annie

Fine just the way it is; Wyoming stories 3. Scribner 2008 221p $25

ISBN 978-1-4165-7166-7; 1-4165-7166-3

LC 2008-13682

This "collection of Wyoming tales, continues [Proulx's] Dickensian delight in memorable nomenclature. So, prepare to meet: Duck Slaver, Harp Daft, the Grainblewer twins, Wacky Lipe, Fenk Fipps, Tug Diceheart and more. Like Dickens, Proulx has a keen eye for the eccentricity of the individual, admitting that 'everyone in the sparsely settled country' is noted for a 'salty dog quirk or talent' that their names might suggest. . . . Proulx's writing can be as fine as anything being produced in America today." Times Lit Suppl

Proulx, Annie

Postcards; by E. Annie Proulx. Scribner 1992 308p il

ISBN 0-684-18718-3

LC 91-25089

"Ms. Proulx's expansion of the concept of postcards is what transforms a rambling tale into a minimalist saga. . . . Story makes this novel compelling; technique makes it beautiful. What makes 'Postcards' significant is that Ms. Proulx uses both story and technique to make real the history of post-World War II America." N Y Times Book Rev

Proulx, Annie

★ The shipping news. Scribner 1993 337p

LC 92-30315

The author "blends Newfoundland argot, savage history, impressively diverse characters, fine descriptions of weather and scenery, and comic horseplay without ever lessening the reader's interest in Quoyle's progress from bumbling outsider to capable journalist." Atlantic

Proulx, Annie

That old ace in the hole; a novel. Scribner 2002 361p $26

ISBN 0-684-81307-6

LC 2002-30462

This novel's "hero, Bob Dollar, a decent sort who was abandoned at 8, is sent by his company to Woolybucket, Tex., to scout locations for factory hog farms, but is soon smitten with the high, flat country, the locals and their tales

of stubborn ranchers, plagues of locusts and family farms undone by corporate greed." N Y Times Book Rev

Proust, Marcel

The captive [and] The fugitive; translated by C.K. Scott Moncrieff & Terence Kilmartin; revised by D.J. Enright. Modern Lib. 1993 957p (In search of lost time) $24.95

ISBN 0-679-42477-6

LC 93-15168

Sequel to Sodom and Gomorrah

Original French edition, 1923

In The captive "Albertine is living in the narrator's Paris home, where he attempts to keep complete watch on her activities. The Verdurins provoke a scandalous rupture between Morel and Charlus. Albertine suddenly flees, just as the narrator is ready to dismiss her. {In the fugitive} the narrator seeks the return of Albertine, but after her death he observes the gradual encroachment of oblivion on grief until, on a trip to Venice, he finds his pain completely cured. Gilberte has become the social-climbing Mlle de Forcheville; she marries Saint-Loup, who is now Morel's lover." Merriam-Webster's Ency of Lit

Followed by Time regained

Proust, Marcel

The complete short stories of Marcel Proust; compiled and translated by Joachim Neugroschel; foreword by Roger Shattuck. Cooper Sq. Pubs. 2001 201p $25.95

ISBN 0-8154-1136-7

LC 00-65739

This collection contains Proust's "first literary endeavor, 'Pleasures and Days,' translated into English for the first time in 50 years, along with six additional stories, never before seen in English. . . . Delicately translated by Neugroschel . . . these early musings are priceless, insightful venturing into the mind of a maturing virtuoso." Booklist

Proust, Marcel

The Guermantes way; translated by C.K. Scott Moncrieff and Terence Kilmartin; revised by D.J. Enright. Modern Lib. 1993 834p (In search of lost time) $23.95

ISBN 0-679-60028-0

LC 92-33975

Sequel to Within a budding grove

Original French edition published 1920-1921

"The narrator, whose family have been tenants in the large Guermantes home in Paris, conducts his laborious ascent to the summit of high society, finally attending the duchesse de Guermantes's reception. He also describes Saint-Loup's passion for the actress and prostitute Rachel, and the death of his own beloved grandmother." Reader's Ency. 4th edition

Followed by Sodom and Gomorrah

Proust, Marcel

★ **Remembrance** of things past. Random House 1981 3v

ISBN 0-394-50643-X set

LC 79-5542

Includes the seven volumes, published separately and entered in this catalog. Volume one and two translated by C. K. Scott Moncrieff and Terence Kilmartin; volume three by C. K. Scott Moncrieff, Terence Kilmartin and Andreas Mayor

This "is the first complete English version of Proust's masterpiece, translated from the definitive 1954 Pléiade edition, Terence Kilmartin has checked the Scott Moncrieff translation (which comprised the first 11 volumes of the English language version and was made from the uneven first French edition) against the impeccable Clarac-Ferre Pléiade edition. The 12th volume, Andreas Mayor's 1970 translation of 'Time Regained' was the only English translation based on the Pléiade edition prior to this one and has been incorporated into it with only minor changes." Libr J

Proust, Marcel

Sodom and Gomorrah; translated by C.K. Scott Moncrieff and Terence Kilmartin; revised by D.J. Enright. Modern Lib. 1993 747p (In search of lost time) $22.95

ISBN 0-679-60029-9

LC 92-27272

Sequel to The Guermantes way

Original French edition published 1921-1922. Variant title: Cities of the plain

"Marcel again meets Swann at a reception given by the Princesse de Guermantes, a cousin of the Duchesse. Swann is now suffering from a deadly ailment. He is an ardent adherent of Alfred Dreyfus. Swann urges Marcel to write to Gilberte, since she speaks of him frequently. But Gilberte, no longer has any enchantment for Marcel; Albertine again holds his affections. She offers herself to him, but distracted by physical attachments for other owmen, he desires her company only at intervals to titillate his jaded senses. Eventually he is drawn closer to her, but now his suspicion that she is a Lesbian causes him jealousy and endless torment." Haydn. Thesaurus of Book Dig

Followed by The captive

Proust, Marcel

Swann's way; translated by C.K. Scott Moncrieff and Terence Kilmartin; revised by D.J. Enright. Modern Lib. 1992 xx, 615p (In search of lost time) $21.95

ISBN 0-679-60005-1

LC 92-25657

Original French edition, 1913

The first volume of the In search of lost time series "describes in an involved parenthetical style, with a multitude of details, the brilliant society in which the author moved. The 'Marcel' of the story is Proust's own counterpart, and it is through his hypersensitive and critical eye that we examine the tastes, feelings, motives and actions of the characters, most of whom can be identified as real people." Enoch Pratt Free Libr

Followed by Within a budding grove

Proust, Marcel

Time regained; translated by Andreas Mayor and Terence Kilmartin; revised by D.J. Enright. Modern Lib. 1993 749p (In search of lost time) $24.95

ISBN 0-679-42476-8

LC 93-3628

Sequel to The fugitive

Original French edition, 1927

In this final volume of the series "World War I accelerates the kaleidoscopic changes in society. The narrator attends a reception of the new princesse de Guermantes, actually the former Mme Verdurin, and finds most of his acquaintances almost unrecognizable. He has enjoyed three 'privileged moments' of memory, and in contemplating them discovers that his vocation is to be the shaping of his experiences into a literary work of art." Reader's Ency. 4th edition

Proust, Marcel

Within a budding grove; translated by C.K. Scott Moncrieff and Terence Kilmartin; revised by D.J. Enright. Modern Lib. 1992 749p (In search of lost time) $24

ISBN 0-679-60006-X

LC 92-25656

Sequel to Swann's way

Original French edition, 1918

"As he grows up, Marcel falls in love with Swann's daughter, Gilberte. It is a deep and poetic attachment, but she gradually tires of him; his ardent nature and his attentions begin to irritate her. Out of wounded pride he avoids her, although he continues his friendly relations with the Swanns. Two years later he feels he is thoroughly cured of his hopeless passion, when he becomes involved with Albertine, a beautiful brunette he meets in Balbec. But he eventually discovers that she is interested only in platonic relations with men, and so he suffers another disappointment." Haydn. Thesaurus of Book Dig

Followed by The Guermantes way

Puchner, Eric

Model home; a novel. Scribner 2010 360p $26

ISBN 978-0-7432-7048-9; 0-7432-7049-7

LC 2009-38051

"Warren Ziller has bankrupted himself and his family in an unsuccessful real estate development in the California desert. When he confesses what he has done, his perfect nuclear family spirals out of control. A gas explosion at their own home forces the Zillers to live in one of the development's unsold houses, and family relations deteriorate until Jonas, the youngest son, runs away." Libr J

"Family love flickers capriciously throughout this fine domestic drama, which runs the gamut from hilarious to harrowing." Kirkus

Puenzo, Lucía, 1973-

The **fish** child; Lucía Puenzo; translated by David William Foster. Texas Tech University Press 2010 161 p.

ISBN 0896727149; 9780896727144

LC 2010024465

In this novel, "[a]ffluent Lala and impoverished Guayi, her Paraguayan maid, are determined to pursue their romance despite overwhelming disparities in class and status. Although they have plotted a future together near Paraguay's Ypacaraí Lake, Guayi's native region, a shocking discovery and an even more shocking reaction lead Lala to depart without her disappeared lover. As she ventures by bus far from her privileged Buenos Aires home, Lala delves into Guayi's past, in due time encountering the disturbing legend of the fish boy who is said to guide drowning victims to the bottom of the lake. . . . [Lucia] Puenzo's debut novel explores the character and choices of two strong-willed young women through the vehicle of the economic and social circumstances of two South American nations where archaic elements coexist with shrill modernity." (Publisher's note)

Puig, Manuel

★ **Kiss** of the spider woman; translated from the Spanish by Thomas Colchie. Knopf 1979 281p
LC 78-14307

Original Spanish edition, 1976

"Mostly consisting of dialogue between two men in an Argentine jail cell, the novel traces the development of their unlikely friendship. Molina is a middle-aged homosexual who passes the long hours in prison by acting out scenes from his favorite movies. Valentin is a young socialist revolutionary, who initially berates Molina for his effeminacy and his lack of political conviction. Sharing the hardships of a six-month prison term, the two eventually forge a strong relationship that becomes sexual. In an ironic role reversal at the end of the novel, Molina dies as a result of his involvement in politics while Valentin escapes the pain of torture by retreating into a dream world." Merriam-Webster's Ency of Lit

Pullman, Philip, 1946-

★ **Fairy** tales from the Brothers Grimm; a new English version. [edited by] Philip Pullman. Viking 2012 405 p. $27.95
ISBN 067002497X; 9780670024971
LC 2012027181

In this book "[Philip] Pullman retells [fairy tales by Jacob and Wilhelm Grimm], . . . from much-loved stories like 'Cinderella' and 'Rumpelstiltskin,' 'Rapunzel' and 'Hansel and Gretel' to lesser-known treasures like 'The Three Snake Leaves,' 'Godfather Death' and 'The Girl with No Hands.' At the end of each tale he offers a brief personal commentary, opening a window on the sources of the tales, the various forms they've taken over the centuries and their everlasting appeal." (Publisher's note)

Includes bibliographical references

Purdy, James

★ **In** a shallow grave. Arbor House 1975 140p
ISBN 0-87795-124-4
LC 75-30399

"Garnet Montrose is a man severely disfigured in the war, a modern leper, an often drugged prophet of the disintegration of values. Unwilling to hide in a veteran's hospital, Montrose returns to his home in Virginia. Obsessed with a childhood sweetheart, now the widow Georgina Rance, he devises an elaborate system of correspondence to woo her, depending on his 'applicants' to carry letters to the lady. The relationship with these applicants forms the basis of the book. Quintus Pearch is quiet and mysterious, a wraithlike

character who reads to Montrose from abstract tomes and rubs his master's feet with cynical adoration. Potter Daventry is a wild young man with twisted values and a go-for-broke attitude. Daventry courts Georgina for Montrose, then for himself. He marries her and is carried away by a freak storm. The implications are biblical in proportion; Purdy utilizes every subtlety and shading of language to enhance the demented howlings of these three lost souls. Purdy's skill consists of taking the familiar and distorting it; the results are often eerie." Independent Publisher

Purdy, James

★ The **nephew**. Farrar Straus and Cudahy 1960 210p
LC 60-15672

This novel "tells of the revelations following the death in war of the nephew of a doting spinster, a retired schoolteacher, in a small Midwest town, who decides to write a memorial booklet. She thereby learns more than she wants to about him and about life as she discovers he was a homosexual." Oxford Companion to Am Lit. 6th edition

Pushcart prize XXXVII; Best of the small presses. edited by Bill Henderson. Pushcart Prize Fellowships 2012 651 p. $35
ISBN 1888889667; 9781888889666

This book is an anthology of writing published in 2012 by small presses, edited by Bill Henderson. It includes "Marilynne Robinson's . . . essay 'On "Beauty."' Other . . . essays include Robin Hemley's piece on rain forests, . . . and Andrew Hudgins' on telling jokes. Guest poetry editors Bob Hicok and Maxine Kumin select poems . . . by Sommer Browning, Christian Flores Garcia, and Diane Wakoski," among others. (Booklist)

Pushkin, Aleksandr Sergeevich

★ **Alexander** Pushkin: complete prose fiction; translated with an introduction and notes, by Paul Debreczeny; verse passages translated by Walter Arndt. Stanford Univ. Press 1983 545p $60
ISBN 0-8047-1142-9
LC 81-85450

This collection also contains the non-fictional History of Pugachev (which furnishes historical background for The captain's daughter) and Appendices which contain minor fictional fragments and outlines

"The translations are accurate and graceful and well supported by an ample array of footnotes." Libr J

Putney, Mary Jo

The **burning** point; Mary Jo Putney. Berkley Books 2000 335 p.
ISBN 042517428X
LC 2003576658

In this book, "Kate Corsi and Patrick Donovan, divorced 10 years ago, are reunited by the death of Kate's father, Sam, who was killed in an explosion at work. The Corsi family company, Phoenix Demolition, takes pride in its spotless accident record, and Sam's death is suspicious. His will leaves the business to his former son-in-law, on the condition that Donovan and Kate live under the same roof for one year. If Kate refuses, the company will be sold. Forbidden by her father to work for the company, Kate now has her chance to work at Phoenix. But can she work and live in such close proximity to the ex-husband she seems to both love and fear?" (Publishers Weekly)

Putney, Mary Jo

A **kiss** of fate. Ballantine Bks. 2004 340p $23.95

ISBN 0-345-44916-9

"Born into a legendary family of mages known as the Guardians, Gwyneth Owens believes that she has little inherited power. She does, however, have a destiny to fulfill. When the Guardian elders seek to forestall a coming disaster by invoking her Guardian oath and asking her to marry Duncan Macrae, Lord Ballister, the most powerful weather mage in the realm, she cannot honorably refuse. Although they are already attracted to each other, Gwyneth can't forget the single kiss from him that sent alarming visions of destruction flaming through her mind—or the sword that he held in his hand. Intelligent, compelling characters that appeal to both heart and mind, a brilliant blending of history and fantasy, and a beautifully unfolding love relationship combine to produce a magical tale." Libr J

Putney, Mary Jo

Loving a lost lord; Mary Jo Putney. Kensington Publishing Corp. 2009 340 p.

ISBN 1420103288; 9781420103281

LC 2010398215

Romantic Times Reviewers' Choice Awards: Best Historical (2009)

This historical romance novel, the first volume of the Lost Lords series, is set in "[t]he year . . . 1812. Westerfield [Academy]'s first student, Adam Lawford, Duke of Ashton, who is now a respected member of the peerage despite his Anglo-Indian heritage, has lost his memory in a steamboat accident. When Adam awakes he is relieved to find that he was dragged ashore near his own home, in Cumberland, and is safe in the delectable arms of his wife. There is just one problem: Mariah Clarke falsely claimed her injured guest as her husband in order to rid herself of an obnoxious suitor. Mariah wishes to end the deception but fears that, if she acknowledges the truth, her patient may never recover his wits." (Historical Novel Series)

Putney, Mary Jo

The **marriage** spell; a novel. Mary Jo Putney.. Ballantine Books 2006 322p o.p.; (pbk.) $6.99

ISBN 0345449185 (acid-free paper); 9780345449191

LC 2005057087

This book is set "in an alternate Regency England, where magic flourishes but is despised, and practicing it may lead to death. . . . As a daredevil officer in Wellington's army, Jack [Langdon] breaks his neck and is treated by Abigail Barton, a talented healer, who states that her price will be marriage. After a grueling healing process, Abby discovers that Jack possesses untapped magical powers. . . . Jack marries Abby, even though his injuries prevent him from consummating the marriage. Abby suspects that Jack's reckless ways and reluctance to return to his home may be the result of an evil spell. Together they must discover the cause of the blight and use their love to save their lands and tenants." (Booklist)

Putney, Mary Jo

No longer a gentleman; Mary Jo Putney. Zebra Books 2012 368 p.

ISBN 1420117238; 9781420117233

This romance novel is the fourth in Mary Jo Putney's 'Lost Lords Regency' series. "Experienced secret agent Cassie Fox is sent to France at the height of the Napoleonic wars in search of the long-missing Grey Sommers, Lord Wyndham, illegally imprisoned by the corrupt and vengeful official Claude Durand after a tryst with Durand's wife. Even a successful rescue and the pair's passionate encounters cannot heal the trauma of Grey's decade-long ordeal or bridge the social gap between the dedicated spy with a mysterious past and the heir to an earldom." (Publishers Weekly)

Putney, Mary Jo

Nowhere near respectable; Mary Jo Putney. Zebra Books 2011 352p.

ISBN 9781420117226 pa; 9781611730760

LC 2011008371

This book tells the story of "Anglo-Hindu Lady Kiri Lawford, [who] is about to accept a proposal from an English gentleman when she learns that his racist, fortune-hunting relatives secretly despise her. Stealing a horse, Kiri rides for Dover and right into a den of smugglers. Gambling club owner Damian Mackenzie aids her escape and passion instantly flares between them, but they resist, knowing the daughter of a duke and an Indian princess could never wed an actress's bastard son. When Kiri visits Damian's club, foils a kidnapping, and gets involved in a covert investigation, their romance sizzles out of control." (Publishers Weekly)

Putney, Mary Jo

Stolen magic; M.J. Putney. Del Rey Books 2005 337p (pbk.) $7.99

ISBN 0345476891; 9780345476906

LC 2004063400

This fantasy novel tells the story of "Earl of Falconer, Simon Malmain, chief enforcer of the Guardian Council, which oversees the use of magic in 18th-century Britain, [who] has been turned into a unicorn by Lord Drayton, a renegade mage whom Simon charges with encouraging the Jacobite uprising; only a virgin can transform Simon back into human form. Luckily for Simon, animal-loving 'Mad Meggie,' Drayton's 'servant,' succeeds in doing so, while Simon breaks the spell that's kept Meg in the dark sorcerer's thrall. Allied in a 'pretend' marriage, the pair pool their unusual talents in an effort to ruin Lord Drayton's plan to prevent the Industrial Age from revolutionizing England." (Publishers Weekly)

Puzo, Mario

The **family**; a novel. completed by Carol Gino. ReganBooks 2001 373p il

ISBN 0-06-039445-5

LC 2001-31876

"In his final novel, 'The Family'—Puzo died in 1999, and this book was completed by his companion, the novelist Carol Gino—he has dipped back into 15th-century Italy to tell the tale of the Borgia family, led by Cardinal Rodrigo Borgia, who became Pope Alexander VI." N Y Times Book Rev

Puzo, Mario
★ The **godfather**. Putnam 1969 446p $24.95
ISBN 0-399-10342-2

This novel focuses on "Vito (Don) Corleone, boss of an important New York City Mafia family. Names, places, crimes have been changed, but the Mafia world remains true to fact. Here is Cosa Nostra: the wars of the competing families; their changing 'business enterprises'; their struggle for power and money; their weapons—graft, guns, spies, violence, murder. A wide variety of characters are colorfully drawn. The Don comes though as a person you will remember." Libr J

Puzo, Mario
The **last** Don. Random House 1996 482p
978-0679401438

LC 96-3401

"The story opens in 1965, with Don Clericuzio, head of the most powerful Mafia family in the country, deciding to make his enterprises legit. He is looking ahead to his grandchildren's lives, wanting them to enjoy his largesse without the danger inherent in life in the criminal underworld. Zoom—we're transported to the present day and involved in how the don's plans for his family's future are playing out. Hollywood and Las Vegas provide venues for one grandson's attempts, at the expense of another grandson, to undermine the master plan." Booklist

"Mr. Puzo wraps up his intricate plot with the same ingenuity he exhibits throughout this satisfying novel." N Y Times Book Rev

Puzo, Mario
The **Sicilian**. Linden Press 1984 410p

LC 84-17087

"Perhaps only an American writer with deep Sicilian roots and passions could have succeeded as Mr. Puzo has in symbolizing a desperate society through the deeds of a desperado, and in revealing how thin is the line that often separates a freedom-fighter from a terrorist." N Y Times Book Rev

Pye, Michael
The **pieces** from Berlin. Knopf 2002 335p $24
ISBN 0-375-41436-3

LC 2002-20524

"Pye writes well, and this is a mature novel. It must also be said that it is not an easy novel, in its themes or its structure. A lot of assembling and clue-tracking is required to make sense of the narrative. It's a page-turner, but often one is turning the pages backward to find some lost, or tenuous, connection. Yet this hard work seems appropriate, even necessary." N Y Times Book Rev

Pym, Barbara
Civil to strangers and other writings. Dutton 1988 388p

LC 87-30341

First published 1987 in the United Kingdom

This is a volume of selections from Pym's unpublished writings. It contains a complete novel, Civil to strangers, written in 1936, sections of three others: Gervase and Flora, Home front novel, and So very secret, written between 1937

and 1941, four short stories (So, some tempestuous morn; Goodbye Balkan capital; The Christmas visit; Across a crowded room) and a radio talk

"We are not often given the chance to witness a writer's struggle to find a voice. But this 'last sheaf,' blemishes and all, shows us how very hard Barbara Pym worked for the voice she eventually found." N Y Times Book Rev

Pym, Barbara
Excellent women. Dutton 1978 256p

LC 78-19877

First published 1952 in the United Kingdom

"Mildred Lathbury, 30ish, a spinster, a clergyman's daughter, is an excellent woman, one who, with no life of her own to speak of, finds herself somewhat unwillingly a part of the lives of others. Her days are made up of small things—church, flowers, dinner with the bachelor vicar and his sister, brief encounters with neighbors. . . . Pym's singular world is a lonely, bittersweet familiar place. She travels it with rueful wit, views the human landscape with a wise, sharp, compassionate eye." Publ Wkly

Pym, Barbara
Jane and Prudence. Dutton 1981 222p

LC 81-68399

First published 1953 in the United Kingdom

"Jane is the somewhat scatterbrained wife of a country vicar; Prudence, once her student at Oxford, works at a 'vague cultural organization' in London, where she alternately revels in and despairs over her unrequited passion for the rather dreary little man who is her employer. As she goes about doing 'those tasks in the parish that seem within her powers,' Jane knows she really is unsuited to be a clergyman's wife—she somehow never seems to have the right money for the collection plate—but she does love Nicholas. And in her good-hearted, if usually ineffectual, way she tries to look after Prudence too, hoping to supply a suitable man for her younger friend." Libr J

Pym, Barbara
Quartet in autumn. Dutton 1978 218p

LC 78-58498

First published 1977 in the United Kingdom

This novel "follows the lives and thoughts of four elderly single people on the verge of retirement, in a society that has no time for them but relegates them to the impersonal care of the Welfare State. Here Pym achieves something of a tour de force, showing, with wit and compassion, how ordinary quirky acts of impulsive kindness and human feeling make the difference between despair and hope." Libr J

Pym, Barbara
The **sweet** dove died. Dutton 1979 208p

LC 78-74024

First published 1978 in the United Kingdom

"Pym's extraordinary vision of an ordinary world wherein she details the intricacies of loneliness, the ditherings of hesitating souls, the comedies of errors, sexual and asexual makes this a little masterpiece." Publ Wkly

Pym, Barbara

★ An **unsuitable** attachment. Dutton 1982 256p

ISBN 0-525-24117-5

LC 82-70741

"The bygone mysteries of the Church of England and the lost snobberies of empire return as ghostly and gently comic echoes of themselves in the habits and pretensions of Barbara Pym's people, who, like the good antiques that furnish their rented bed-sitters . . . are no longer quite appropriate to the present day." N Y Times Book Rev

Pynchon, Thomas

Against the day. Penguin Press 2006 1085p $35

ISBN 1-59420-120-X

LC 2006-50714

"For all its brilliant passages, this is the book that makes you wonder whether even Pynchon knows what lies behind all those veils he's always urging us to part. But wouldn't you know it? Even when he jumps the shark, he does it with an agility that can take your breath away." Time

Pynchon, Thomas

★ The **crying** of lot 49. Lippincott 1966 183p

"Oedipa Maas becomes a coexecutor of the estate of her former multi-millionaire lover, Pierce Inverarity. She becomes involved in tracking down the significance of a geometric symbol that appears to have some connection with the existence of an ancient, revolutionary mail service. In this search, she meets a strange assortment of characters, loses her husband, her psychiatrist (named Hilarious!), and her lover. The author aims his arrows at many of those phenomena that have turned people into things. Among his targets are rock 'n' roll (a group called 'The Paranoids'), right-wing extremists, and a strange group called Inamorati Anonymous." Shapiro. Fic for Youth. 3d edition

Pynchon, Thomas

★ **Gravity's** rainbow. Viking 1973 760p

ISBN 0-670-34832-5

"Fiction allows at last what was forbidden to the original suffering poets and novelists of 1914-18—the utmost in obscene description, the limit of masochistic pornography. If 'Gravity's Rainbow' is often nauseating it is in a good cause. This is the war book to end them all." Burgess. 99 Novels

Pynchon, Thomas

Inherent vice. Penguin Press 2009 369p $27.95

ISBN 978-1-59420-224-7; 1-59420-224-9

LC 2009-07705

"An account of the adventures of a hippie private eye pursuing assorted nonlucrative commissions in a Southern California beach town around 1970, 'Inherent Vice' is a sun-struck, pot-addled shaggy dog story that fuses the sulky skepticism of Raymond Chandler with the good-natured scrappiness of 'The Big Lebowski.' It's an inspired formula; the mystery plot supplies the novel with a minimum of structure (as well as confidence that there's some point to the enterprise) and the genre provides ample cover for Pynchon's literary weaknesses." Salon

Pynchon, Thomas

Mason & Dixon. Holt & Co. 1997 773p $27.50

ISBN 0-8050-3758-6

LC 97-6467

"From historical odds and ends and the Field Journal they left behind, Pynchon re-imagines Mason and Dixon before, during and after the four-plus years, 1763-1767, they took to draw their 244-mile-long line through the American wilderness, dividing the proprietorships of the Penns of Pennsylvania and the Calverts of Maryland, ordaining our North and South. From his omnivorous reading, with his diabolical genius for mimicry, he also re-creates their tumultuous era." Nation

Pynchon, Thomas

★ **V.** a novel. Lippincott 1963 492p

This novel is a "parody of the 'Black Humor' techniques it employs. The multiple plots involve the schlemiel Benny Profane, a hunter of alligators in New York's sewers, and Herbert Stencil, who becomes obsessed by his pursuit of V., an initial he found in his dead father's notebooks. V.'s various manifestations include a femme fatale, a spy, and a hag who happened to be present at every significant event in Europe from 1890 to World War II." Reader's Ency. 4th edition

Pynchon, Thomas

Vineland. Little, Brown 1990 385p

LC 89-13025

This is "manifestly the work of a man of quick intelligence and quirky invention. Many of its episodes flicker with an appealingly far-flung humor. And Pynchon displays throughout Vineland what might be called an internal loyalty: he keeps the faith with the generally feckless and almost invariably inarticulate misfits he assembles, tracking their looping thoughts and indecisive actions with a patience that seems grounded in affection." N Y Rev Books

Pyne, Daniel

★ **Twentynine** Palms; a novel. Counterpoint 2010 229p pa $14.95

ISBN 978-1-58243-573-2; 1-58243-573-1

LC 2010-05454

"Marginal Hollywood actor Jack Baylor ends an affair with the wife of his best friend, Tory, and knowing Tory's anger-management issues, he retreats to the California desert town of Twentynine Palms to let the metaphorical dust settle. There he promptly begins an affair with Mona, a young mother of two. But Tory arrives in the town bent on revenge, Mona and her kids disappear, and Jack's motel room is awash with blood. Jack is promptly arrested and must escape to clear himself. Character is everything in this desert-noir debut, and Jack is the embodiment of fecklessness; without a script, he's simply lost. Rachel, a clever 14-year-old runaway, saves him repeatedly. . . . Great fun" Booklist

Pyper, Andrew

The **killing** circle. St. Martin's Minotaur 2008 321p $24.95

ISBN 978-0-312-38476-0; 0-312-38476-9

LC 2008-20635

The novel is "gorgeously written and thoroughly unnerving. . . . Taken as either a classy ghost story or the chronicle of one man's mental breakdown, this is a terrific yarn." N Y Times Book Rev

Pywell, Sharon L.

What happened to Henry; [by] Sharon Pywell. G.P. Putnam's Sons 2004 292p $19.95

ISBN 0-399-15168-0

LC 2003-62239

The plot of this novel revolves around a "tightly knit family. Henry, Lauren, and Winston Cooper are 10, 7, and 5 in 1960, when their newborn sister dies of SIDS. Henry pulls his younger siblings through their grief while their mother is barely functioning and their father is lost in his work. But four years later, Henry begins to crack, becoming obsessed with a picture of a man near Hiroshima's firestorm. . . . A powerful novel full of surprises, unbreakable sibling bonds, and insightful reflection on the power of love to overcome grief." Booklist

Pötzsch, Oliver

The **beggar** king; a hangman's daughter tale. Oliver Pötzsch; translated by Lee Chadeayne. 1st Mariner Books ed. Houghton Mifflin Harcourt 2013 512 p. (paperback) $18.00

ISBN 054799219X; 9780547992198

LC 2012038023

This book is the third historical mystery in Oliver Pötzsch's Hangman's Daughter Tale series. Here, hangman and garbage collector Jakob Kuisl is "accused of murder in the Free City of Regensburg, where he has gone to visit his ailing sister. Meanwhile, Kuisl's fiercely independent daughter, Magdalena, an apprentice midwife, accuses master baker Michael Berchtholdt of both impregnating his maid and fatally poisoning her with ergot in an attempt to induce an abortion." (Publishers Weekly)

Pötzsch, Oliver

The **Poisoned** Pilgrim; A Hangman's Daughter Tale. Oliver Pötzsch; translated by Lee Chadeayne. Houghton Mifflin Harcourt 2013 512 p. $18

ISBN 0544114604; 9780544114609

LC 2013026783

This book is part of Oliver Pötzsch's Hangman's Daughter series. Here, "Magdalena Kuisl and her husband, Simon, have embarked on a religious pilgrimage to the Bavarian Holy Mountain. . . . This trip goes awry when the duo encounters violence, including a bell tower attack on Magdalena, and three apparent murders. When a monk is wrongfully jailed for the murders, he confides in Magdalena that he's a former hangman and begs her to get her father, Jakob, to come help." (Library Journal)

Q

Qiu Xiaolong

Red mandarin dress. St. Martin's Minotaur 2007 320p

ISBN 978-0-312-37107-4; 0-312-37107-1

LC 2007-44109

In this mystery featuring Shanghai's Chief Inspector Chen, "young women, clad in torn, red mandarin dresses—hose with slits on the sides to show attractive legs—start turning up dead in public places. Chen is away, pursuing his love of literature, and the case bumps along, murder victim after murder victim, and the Shanghai police department looks incompetent in its duty of protecting the public. Then Chen becomes re-engaged halfway through the book, and the story takes off at a brisk pace. The suspense, and the way Qiu weaves in the human wreckage caused by Mao Zedong's Cultural Revolution, gives one of contemporary fiction's best pictures yet of the wrenching changes facing China as it struggles with its recent, wretched past." St. Louis Post-Dispatch

Qiu Xiaolong

When red is black. Soho Press 2004 309p $25

ISBN 1-569-47369-2

LC 2003-23436

"When Yin Lige, the author of a banned book, is found murdered in her Shanghai apartment, detective Yu Guangming and his boss, Chief Inspector Chen Cao, must solve a case that may have far-reaching political and social implications." Publ Wkly

This mystery "offers a complex and riveting portrait of Shanghai, a city in transition from a proletarian dictatorship to a capitalist playground." Washington Post Book World

Qiu Xiaolong

Years of Red Dust; stories of Shanghai. St. Martin's Press 2010 227p $24.99

ISBN 978-0-312-62809-3; 0-312-62809-9

LC 2010-29209

"Qiu's witty, evocative book of interrelated short stories . . . focuses more on the moral compromises wrought by China's growing materialism than on the government's resistance to political change. He portrays—without sentimentality—the ordinary man adrift in a freer market, not the hero fighting for free expression." Washington Post Book Rev

Quartey, Kwei J.

Children of the street; a novel. [by] Kwei Quartey. Random House Trade Paperbacks 2011 335p pa $15

ISBN 978-0-8129-8167-4

LC 2010-26476

This book "centers on the mean streets of Accra, Ghana, where a street child is found brutally murdered and dumped in a bog. When a second child's body is found, [Inspector Darko] Dawson is convinced he's chasing a serial killer, but the deaths of unwanted street children don't command much interest, especially after an oil executive is murdered. Helped only by his assistant, Chikata, and his driver, Baiboo, Dawson digs into the brutal lot of the thousands of children who live, eat, and work in Accra's streets. . . . A must-read for anyone who follows African crime fiction." Booklist

Queen, Ellery

The **best** of Ellery Queen; four decades of stories from The mystery masters. edited by Francis M.

Nevins, Jr. and Martin H. Greenberg. Beaufort Bks. 1985 238p

LC 84-21572

Queen, Ellery

A **fine** and private place. World Pub. 1971 214p

"The 'padrone,' Nino Importuna, heads a huge conglomerate. He catches one of his executives embezzling, and as the price of freedom, demands that he hand over his young daughter as the aging Nino's bride. Of course, this is the perfect setup for murder. First Nino's two brothers, who share in the conglomerate, die, then Nino himself. For the solution, Ellery Queen returns to his (their) original style of detection—a stream of bizarre clues that confuse the detective Queen no end." Publ Wkly

Queen, Ellery

The **Roman** hat mystery; a problem in deduction. Stokes, F.A. 1929 325p

"Inspector Richard Queen and his son Ellery tackle a puzzling murder with immense thoroughness and almost fatiguing pertinacity. Though the egregious bonhomie of the Queens and Ellery's pseudo bookishness occasionally irritate, the neatness of the plot involving a missing hat in a theater murder cannot be denied. But the police procedure is not what it would be now, and the criminal's luck in carrying out his complex plan strains the believables." Barzun. Cat of Crime. Rev and enl edition

Queen, Ellery

The **XYZ** murders; three mysteries in one volume complete and unabridged: The tragedy of X; The tragedy of Y; The tragedy of Z. Lippincott 1961 575p

These books were originally published under the name of Barnaby Ross in 1932, 1932 and 1933 respectively

Drury Lane, retired Shakespearean actor and brilliant connoisseur of crime, helps New York City's District Attorney Bruno and Inspector Thumm solve the mysteries

Quick, Amanda

I thee wed. Bantam Bks. 1999 341p $23.95

ISBN 0-553-10084-X

LC 98-37168

"Strong-willed, and with a redhead's combustible temper, paid companion Emma Greyson finds herself embroiled in a dangerous adventure with the dashing Edison Stokes. A wealthy member of Regency England's 'Polite World,' Stokes follows the clue in a dying man's last words to arrive at Ware Castle, where he suspects a dark plot is underway. At the castle he encounters Emma, who stands out among the era's decadent and depraved society as a woman of sharp intelligence. . . . Attractive protagonists, loose bodices, thwarted love and odds overcome prove themselves once again the ingredients for success in this genre." Publ Wkly

Quick, Amanda

Late for the wedding. Bantam Bks. 2003 322p $24.95

ISBN 0-553-80271-2

LC 2002-34254

""The killer, an insider with easy access to the opulent homes of Regency England's elite, has left his calling card, a memento-mori ringa jeweled, coffin-topped band with a white skull inside. He's clever, but not nearly clever enough to fool the fearless team of Lavinia Lake and Tobias March." Booklist

As this engaging effort demonstrates, Quick has the Regency-murder mystery mix down to a fine science." Publ Wkly

Quick, Amanda

The **paid** companion. Putnam 2004 418p $24.95

ISBN 0-399-15174-5

LC 2003-62348

"Elenora Lodge is in quite a fix. Her stepfather lost her farm and all of her possessions in a mining venture, and her fiance dumps her faster than the proverbial hot potato. But Elenora is practical and pragmatic. So when Arthur Lancaster, earl of St. Merryn, offers her a position as a paid companion, she accepts. St. Merryn is in a bit of a fix himself. His favorite uncle has been murdered, and he's sworn vengeance on the killer, a mad alchemist intent on perfecting the ultimate weapon of mass destruction. Unfortunately, St. Merryn's fiancee has also dumped him, and his renewed status as one of London's most eligible bachelors is interfering with his quest for justice, hence his paying Elenora to pose as his new fiancee. . . . {Quick} mixes humor, suspense, and tantalizing historical detail with all the savory ingredients her fans have come to expect: a feisty, resourceful heroine; a hero with a decidedly dangerous edge; witty repartee; and strongly appealing secondary characters." Booklist

Quick, Amanda

Slightly shady. Bantam Bks. 2001 343p

ISBN 0-553-80188-0

LC 00-58528

"Londoner Lavinia Lake had made a comfortable home for herself and her niece, running an antique store in Rome. Little did she know, however, that a band of thieves was using her quaint little shop for their illegal purposes. This bit of information was made perfectly clear to Lavinia when one Tobias March barged in and began tearing the antique shop—junk shop, to be more precise—apart, searching for incriminating evidence." Booklist

"Arch humor and the expert removal of bodices are Quick's stock in trade, and the old formula still works splendidly." Publ Wkly

Quick, Amanda

Wicked widow. Bantam Bks. 2000 297p

ISBN 0-553-10087-4

LC 99-59194

"Regency-era historical romance features Madeline Deveridge, a misunderstood London widow with a reputation for murder, and the strapping Artemis Hunt, a secret owner of the Dream Pavilions, a popular pleasure garden. When one of Madeline's maids is abducted outside the Dream Pavilions, she blackmails Artemis into helping her in the rescue. . . . A delicious combination of adventure and romance, this lively tale keeps the reader enthralled from start to finish." Booklist

Quindlen, Anna

Black and blue. Random House 1998 293p $23

ISBN 0-679-43539-5

LC 97-25208

"Following fault lines of power, dependence, and love, Quindlen takes her heroine to a bereaved country where there are no answers, only choices; in Brooklyn-born Frannie, she has created an utterly believable, flinty character." New Yorker

Quindlen, Anna

Blessings; a novel. Random House 2002 226p

ISBN 0-375-50223-8

LC 2002-24802

"Quindlen's fine-tuned ear for the class distinctions of speech results in convincing dialogue. Evoking a bygone patrician world, she endows Blessings with an almost magical aura. While it skirts sentimentality by a hairbreadth, the narrative is old-fashioned in a positive way." Publ Wkly

Quindlen, Anna

Every last one; a novel. Random House 2010 299p $26

ISBN 978-1-4000-6574-5; 1-4000-6574-7

LC 2010-292390

Quindlen "has a talent for gently, almost imperceptibly, setting the stage for what happens. The narrative of life with the Lathams is subtly prophetic regarding the impending doom. All the while, we come to love this family, because Quindlen makes their ordinary lives so fascinating, their mundane interactions engaging and important. Every Last One is about excruciating grief. It's about how people treat victims of violence, survivors' guilt, random blame and figuring out how to go on living." USA Today

Quindlen, Anna

Object lessons. Random House 1991 262p

ISBN 0-394-56965-2

LC 90-48656

This novel describes a summer in the life of an Irish American family in suburban New York in the 1960s. The central figure is twelve-year-old Maggie, daughter of Tommy Scanlan and Connie, an Italian American whose father is a cemetery caretaker in the Bronx. Tommy's father John, who made a fortune in religious goods and construction, is dying after a stroke, but still seeks to control the lives of his children and grandchildren, especially Tommy, the rebel

"Quindlen's social antennae are acute: she conveys the fierce ethnic pride that distinguishes Irish and Italian communities, their rivalry and mutual disdain. Her character portrayal is empathetic and beautifully dimensional, not only of Maggie but of her mother, who experiences her own wrenching rite of passage." Publ Wkly

Quindlen, Anna

One true thing. Random House 1994 289p

ISBN 0-679-40712-X

LC 94-22238

This novel "follows the psychological travails of Ellen Gulden, who against all personal inclinations returns home to care for her dying mother, Kate, and eventually finds herself accused of mercy-killing. Ellen, an intelligent though

not particularly warm person, has spent her life earning her professor father's approval. After achieving high school valedictorian and Harvard honors, she aspires to advance her New York career. At her father's insistence, however, she leaves her job and takes on the role of nurse and homemaker. Through long hours as companion to Kate, she discovers the real value of her mother's life." Libr J

"Quindlen's story sustains an emotional momentum, and she addresses difficult issues with compassion." Publ Wkly

Quinn, Julia

An **offer** from a gentleman; Julia Quinn. Avon Books 2001 377 p. (pbk.) $7.99

ISBN 0380815583; 9780380815586

LC 2002568860

This book tells the story of "Sophie Beckett [who] never dreamed she'd be able to sneak into Lady Bridgerton's famed masquerade ball - or that 'Prince Charming' would be waiting there for her! Though the daughter of an earl, Sophie has been relegated to the role of servant by her disdainful stepmother. But now, spinning in the strong arms of . . . Benedict Bridgerton, she feels like royalty. Alas, she knows all enchantments must end when the clock strikes midnight. Who was that extraordinary woman? Ever since that magical night . . . [h]e has sworn to find and wed his mystery miss, but this breathtaking maid makes him weak with wanting her. Yet, if he offers her his heart, will Benedict sacrifice his only chance for a fairy tale love?" (Publisher's note)

R

Raban, Jonathan

Surveillance. Pantheon Books 2007 257p $24

ISBN 978-0-375-42244-7; 0-375-42244-7

LC 2006-50332

"In a near-future Seattle, a police state, replete with imagined disaster scenarios, spy cameras, and intelligence gathering, is in effect, and everyone is under a surveillance of some kind. Aspiring actor Tad Zachary performs in emergency drills while his friend Lucy Bengstrom, a freelance journalist and single mom, tries to support her 11-year-old daughter. Lucy hits pay dirt when GQ hires her to write about August Vanags, a reclusive author of a memoir describing his World War II childhood. But as she delves into his life, Lucy starts to suspect literary fraud," Bookmarks

Raban, Jonathan

Waxwings; a novel. Pantheon Bks. 2003 281p $24

ISBN 0-375-41008-2

LC 2003-42997

"Tom Janeway is a professor of writing, a novelist and a public radio commentator; his wife, Beth, works for GetaShack.Com, a startup providing virtual neighborhood tours for prospective house buyers. They have a four-year-old son named Finn, and they appear content. Behind the happy facade, though, Beth has grown deeply unhappy with her self-absorbed husband. . . . Unfolding in counterpoint to Raban's chronicle of the rather civilized collapse of their marriage is the story of a shady Chinese immigrant called Chick; he survives a horrific journey to America and becomes an off-the-books contractor who bullies Tom into employing him to renovate their gloomy old house after Beth moves out." Publ Wkly

This novel "succeeds as a sharply observed satire of the Internet boom and as a bittersweet meditation the American dream." Libr J

Rabb, Jonathan

The **book** of Q; a novel. Crown 2001 375p

ISBN 0-609-60483-X

LC 00-47550

"Father Ian Pearse, a researcher at the Vatican Library, stumbles upon an ancient conspiracy that could destroy the Catholic Church. Long thought dead, a dangerous sect called the Manichaeans has resurfaced, and Pearse must decipher an enigmatic prayer if he is to stop their plan. His life in jeopardy, Pearse finds that the closer he gets to the truth, the closer he gets to the Pope himself." Libr J

"A solid, hard-edged tale set in a climate of Catholic intrigue and social controversy." Publ Wkly

Racculia, Kate

This must be the place; a novel. Henry Holt and Co. 2010 350p $25

ISBN 978-0-8050-9230-1; 0-8050-9230-7

LC 2010-01434

"The story opens with Arthur Rook, a Hollywood photographer besotted by love for his quirky wife, Amy, who then dies—electrocuted at her job, building monsters for movies. Armed with a box of her baffling memorabilia and her enormous, cranky cat, Arthur makes his way back East to Amy's hometown, where he rents a room in a boardinghouse run by her high school friend Mona. And the book simply explodes from there. Plot, characters, secrets, back story, subplots and sub-subplots there's much to keep track of in this rich and overstuffed book, but it's all well worth it." Minneapolis Star Tribune

Rachman, Tom

★ The **imperfectionists**. Dial Press 2010 272p

ISBN 0-385-34366-3; 978-0-385-34366-4

LC 2009-33148

This novel traces the history of a struggling English-language newspaper in Rome. Each of the eleven chapters is devoted to one of the newspaper's staff members.

"A flagging international newspaper in Rome is about to fold. Unsurprising, considering the 1950s-founded paper doesn't even have a website. Circulation, like the readership, is slowly dying off. But the staff are so caught up in their own lives that they barely notice. Rachman takes us by the hand and introduces us to the paper's staff, with each chapter of the book dedicated to one character. Lloyd Burko, the ageing and down-on-his luck reporter in France who doesn't own a computer and still sends pitches by fax is desperate and without work. Ruby Zaga, the spinster copy editor whose office chair is always amiss, has a life that is both amusing and heartbreaking. Rachman's strength lies in his rendering of the characters – all 11 are believable, flawed and loveable. The narrative works and forms a coherent whole." Scotsman

Radcliffe, Ann Ward

★ The **mysteries** of Udolpho; [by] Ann Radcliffe; edited with an introduction and notes by Jacqueline Howard. Penguin Books 2001 xxxix, 653p (Penguin classics) pa $13

ISBN 0-14-043759-2

LC 2001-277143

First published 1794 in the United Kingdom

"The orphaned Emily St Aubert is carried off by her aunt's villanous husband Montoni to a remote castle in the Apennines, where her life, honour, and fortune are threatened and she is surrounded by apparently supernatural terrors. These are later explained as due to human agency and Emily escapes, returns to France and, after further mysteries and misunderstandings, is reuinted with her lover Valancourt." Oxford Companion to Engl Lit. 6th edition

Rahimi, Atiq

A **thousand** rooms of dream and fear; a novel. translated from Dari by Sarah Maguire and Yama Yari. Other Press 2011 155p $15.95

ISBN 978-1-59051-361-3

LC 2010-38973

First edition in English published 2006 in the United Kingdom

"In prose that is spare and incisive, poetic and searing, prizewinning Afghani author Rahimi, who fled his native land in 1984, captures the distress of his people." Booklist

Raimondo, Lynne

Dante's wood; a Mark Angelotti novel. by Lynne Raimondo. Seventh Street Books 2012 350 p. (pbk.) $15.95

ISBN 1616147180; 9781616147181

LC 2012031725

In this book by Lynne Raimondo, "Chicago psychiatrist Mark Angelotti receives a visit from the parents of 18-year-old Charlie Dickerson, who has the mental age of a grade schooler and has been crying in the middle of the night at his care facility, the New Horizons Center. . . . The psychiatrist . . . doubts abuse, but he soon faces a bigger problem after Charlie confesses to the murder of the center's art teacher, Shannon Sparrow." (Publishers Weekly)

Rajaniemi, Hannu

The **fractal** prince; Hannu Rajaniemi. Tor 2012 320 p. $25.99

ISBN 0765329506; 9780765329509

LC 2012037360

In this book by Hannu Rajaniemi, "when Mieli, the winged Hunter . . . encounters quantum thief Jean de Flambeur for the second time, the thief is in the process of experimenting with Schrödinger's box for his current patron. . . . At the same time, two sisters in the haunted city of Sirr, one of the last cities on a broken Earth, plan a revolution to free their city from the might of the Sobornost's virtual control of the solar system." (Library Journal)

Rajaniemi, Hannu

The **quantum** thief. Tor 2011 329p $24.99

ISBN 978-0-7653-2949-3

LC 2011-07399

"Liberated from the infamous Dilemma Prison run by the Archons of the Sobernost collective of the Inner Solar System, master thief Jean le Flambeur agrees to accompany his rescuer, a mysterious woman named Mieli who owns a sentient spaceship with a taste for flirtation, to the Oubliette, a moving city of Mars that traffics in time as currency. Flambeur's tale intersects with that of detective Isidore Beautrelet in an intricately woven, highly charged pas de deux that brings both men to a startling discovery that reinvents the story of their experiences." Libr J

Ramirez Mercado, Sergio

A **thousand** deaths plus one; a novel. by Sergio Ramirez; translated from the Spanish by Leland H. Chambers. McPherson & Co. 2009 295p $25

ISBN 978-0-929701-87-5

LC 2009-02415

Original Spanish edition, 2004

"In 1987 Warsaw, an unnamed narrator becomes obsessed with a photographer named Castellón when he stumbles upon an exhibit showing the same scenes before and during the Nazi occupation. He learns that Castellón was Nicaraguan and took the photos while traveling with the Nazis, who had murdered his daughter and son-inlaw. From here, the book shifts to Castellón's own voice as the story moves back and forth in time, connecting Castellón to luminaries such as Chopin, George Sand, Turgenev and Flaubert." Publ Wkly

Ramsland, Morten

Doghead; translated from the Danish by Tiina Nunnally. St. Martin's Press 2009 383p $24.95

ISBN 978-0-312-37654-3; 0-312-37654-5

LC 2008-35410

Original Danish edition, 2005; this translation first published 2007 in the United Kingdom

This "quirky novel follows three generations of a Scandinavian family with enough dysfunction to make Augusten Burroughs squirm: There's Askild, the alcoholic grandfather who survived a Nazi concentration camp; Jug Ears, the father forced to wear an armor-plated corset as a youngster so that he'd stop touching his ears; and narrator Asger, who as a child felt a certain satisfaction in wrestling his obese, mentally challenged aunt. Sound bizarre? It is, but the absurd scenes are infused with enough playful emotion to make their outlandishness forgivable, and even enjoyable. Though intricate shifts in time make for a complex read, Doghead — which has plenty of bite — is definitely worth the effort." Entertainment Wkly

Rand, Ayn

Anthem; 50th anniversary ed; Dutton 1995 253p $23.95

ISBN 0-525-94015-4

LC 95-9854

First published 1946 by Pamphleteers

"A short novel about a heroic dissenter in a future monolithic and collectivized state." Oxford Companion to Am Lit. 6th edition

Rand, Ayn

★ **Atlas** shrugged. Random House 1957 1168p

"In a technological civilization Rand's characters remain insecure and look to the government for protection. In exchange they sacrifice their creativity and independence. The heroes, a copper tycoon and an inventor, reject this philosophy and fight for the individualist." Shapiro. Fic for Youth. 3d edition

Rand, Ayn

★ The **fountainhead**. Macmillan 1943 754p

First published by Bobbs-Merrill

This novel "celebrates the achievements of an architect (presumably suggested by Frank Lloyd Wright) who is fiercely independent in pursuing his own ideas of design and who is therefore an example of the author's concept of Objectivism, which lauds individualism and 'rational self-interest.'" Oxford Companion to Am Lit. 5th edition

Rand, Ayn

We the living. Random House 1959 433p

Originally published in 1936 by Macmillan, this edition of Rand's first novel contains a foreword describing the plight of the individual in the Soviet Union since then. It is the story of post-revolutionary Russia, and of a woman torn between two men who love her, one a Communist, the other an aristocrat

Randall, Alice

The **wind** done gone. Houghton Mifflin 2001 210p $23

ISBN 0-618-10450-X

LC 00-46544

"Cynara's voice and character are, in fits and starts, inspired and inspiring. Newly emancipated and literate, she acquires, by virtue of what she calls her 'crazy quilt' education, an arresting fictional presence." Time

Rankin, Ian

★ **Black** and blue; an Inspector Rebus mystery. St. Martin's Press 1997 394p

ISBN 978-0312167837

LC 97-25381

"Rankin has a point to make about the corrosive effects of human wickedness that, if left unchecked, seeps into the bloodstream and poisons the national body—a point well made in his blunt and bruising style." N Y Times Book Rev

Rankin, Ian

The **black** book; an Inspector Rebus novel. Penzler Bks. 1994 278p

LC 94-8929

Frist published 1993 in the United Kingdom

In this mystery novel, Inspector Rebus of Edinburgh "has alienated his girlfriend, his ne'er-do-well brother has deposited himself in Rebus' apartment with every appearance of staying for good, his promising new sergeant has been mugged, and his most unfavorite colleague is again out to discredit Rebus. But Rebus' personal troubles pale when a local butcher is stabbed, and the investigation leads Rebus to conclude that the attack is somehow connected to a years-old unsolved arson-homicide case. . . . Rankin's compelling and original plot is almost as intriguing as the gruff, tough, rebellious Rebus, whose rough exterior hides a charming, funny, tenderhearted human being we'd all like to know." Booklist

Rankin, Ian

The **complaints**. Little, Brown and Company 2011 438p $24.99

ISBN 978-0-316-03974-1; 0-316-03974-8

LC 2010-12792

First published 2009 in the United Kingdom

Edinburgh DI Malcom Fox "works in Complaints and Conduct, which means he investigates other cops. His boss assigns him to sniff around DS Jamie Breck for possible child porn trafficking. Meanwhile, Fox's sister is in an abusive relationship with a man who turns up brutally murdered, and Fox himself is a prime suspect. As he and Breck become acquainted, both realize they are being framed in a complicated plot that involves mobsters, wealthy developers in trouble, and possible police treachery." Libr J

This novel is "part mystery, part buddy story, part morality essay. Mr. Rankin never lets the reader down for a single page." Pittsburgh Post-Gazette

Rankin, Ian

Dead souls; an Inspector Rebus novel. St. Martin's Minotaur 1999 406p $24.95

ISBN 0-312-20293-8

LC 99-44276

In this novel "Inspector John Rebus, is in another of his black moods. A colleague commits suicide; the teenage son of his high school sweetheart goes missing; a pedophile crawls onto his turf; and a mad-dog killer arrives from America to play a sadistic game of chicken with him. An irreligious man who harbors a perverse streak of spirituality, Rebus blames blind fate (or an uncaring God) for conjoining these seemingly random circumstances into a force field of evil so strong that it sweeps aside his sense of decency and pulls him in." N Y Times Book Rev

Rankin, Ian

Doors open. Little, Brown and Co. 2010 364p $24.99

ISBN 978-0-316-02478-5; 0-316-02478-3

LC 2009-22283

First published 2008 in the United Kingdom

"The heist is meticulously planned and carried out with impressive efficiency, but it's when the thieves fall out that the fun begins. Not up to Rankin's best—Rebus, we miss you—but certainly entertaining." Kirkus

Rankin, Ian

Exit music. Little, Brown and Co. 2008 421p $24.99

ISBN 978-0-316-05758-5; 0-316-05758-4

LC 2008-1888

First published 2007 in the United Kingdom

The "final novel in Rankin's Inspector Rebus series is set during the Edinburgh detective's final week at work. (He

is nearing the mandatory retirement age of sixty.) The novel begins with a dissident Russian poet beaten to death, and expands to take in smalltime drug dealers, cloak-wearing women who act in walking mystery tours of the city, international oligarchs, and Scottish bank executives. A contemporary artist who makes sound installations may be in league with politicians agitating for Scotland's independence. Rebus is as gruffly mischievous as ever, and the novel ends in a cliffhanger scene with his archenemy that will have readers gasping into the blank space that follows. Rankin's work is crime fiction at its most consuming, cerebral best." New Yorker

Rankin, Ian

The **falls**; an Inspector Rebus novel. St. Martin's Minotaur 2001 399p $24.95

ISBN 0-312-20610-0

LC 2001-41946

First published 2000 in the United Kingdom

Inspector Rebus "needs all his interviewing skills to get a handle on Philippa Balfour, a 20-year-old art student at the University of Edinburgh who has gone missing. It's like extracting molars to get information from Philippa's father, mother, boyfriend or friends, who are in turn too controlling, browbeaten, calculating or clueless to be anything but obstructive. The plot opens up when a nasty little doll in a creepy little coffin directs Rebus to an interactive game that Philippa has been playing on the Internet." N Y Times Book Rev

Rankin combines "complicated multiple plot lines with finely drawn characters and fascinating Scottish lore and settings." Libr J

Rankin, Ian

The **impossible** dead. Little, Brown and Company 2011 391p $25.99

ISBN 978-0-316-03977-2

LC 2011-34256

Edinburgh Internal Affairs cop Malcolm Fox and his "two colleagues receive a frosty reception in Kirkcaldy, where they must decide whether a disgraced officer's three fellow cops helped cover up his misdeeds. Det. Constable Paul Carter, found guilty of sexual misconduct, intrigues Fox because it was Carter's ex-copper uncle, Alan, who turned him in. Since interviewing the belligerent Carter and his mates leads nowhere, Fox turns to Alan for insight. He discovers the elder Carter was hired by a prestigious lawyer to look into the 1985 'suicide'—or possible murder—of Francis Vernal, a fellow attorney, well-known orator, and vocal supporter of the fringe Scottish separatist movement. Soon Fox's attention is divided between following up scant leads in the Carter investigation and unearthing decades-old secrets about Vernal's life and associates. Rankin elegantly weaves together the two story lines without forcing a connection." Publ Wkly

Rankin, Ian

The **naming** of the dead; an Inspector Rebus novel. Little, Brown and Co. 2007 425p $24.99

ISBN 978-0-316-05757-8; 0-316-05757-6

LC 2006-31495

First published 2006 in the United Kingdom

"In his backhanded, reluctant way Rebus winds up uniting all the book's loose ends, and seeing how he accomplishes this is a pleasure. Besides, 'The Naming of the Dead' isn't really about its detective plot. It's about Rebus's taking stock, not only of his own past but also of the world around him." N Y Times (Late N Y Ed)

Rankin, Ian

★ A **question** of blood; an Inspector Rebus novel. Little, Brown and Co. 2004 406p $22.95

ISBN 0-316-09564-8

LC 2003-59549

First published 2003 in the United Kingdom

"This series's strength starts with Rebus himself, who . . . has emerged as the baddest of the bad boys of modern crime fiction. He is fiftyish, overweight, alcoholic, a chain smoker, surly, short-tempered, divorced, estranged from his family, a loner, a nut about obscure rock-and-roll groups, hostile to all authority and possibly psychotic. Needless to say, women love him—ladies love outlaws—and his police colleagues tolerate him because he's an ace detective." Washington Post Book World

Rankin, Ian

Resurrection men; an Inspector Rebus novel. Little, Brown 2003 436p $23.95

ISBN 0-316-76684-4

LC 2002-16271

"It's the perfect cover. Edinburgh Detective Inspector John Rebus, the maverick's maverick, guilty of throwing a coffee cup at his superior officer, is sent to a remedial 'career counseling' course on being a better team player. But the fix is in; Rebus' real assignment is to investigate four Glasgow renegade coppers also forced to take the course." Booklist

"We are well and truly in Rankin country—a shady world where good and evil are relative terms and truth is an arbitrary concept." N Y Times Book Rev

Rankin, Ian

Set in darkness. St. Martin's Press 2000 415p

ISBN 0-312-20609-7

"Rebus has been assigned to a bogus task force called the Policing of Parliament Liaison Committee. Things liven up, though, when a body is found inside a bricked-up fireplace in one of the buildings under construction for the new Scottish Parliament. That's a tantalizing enough mystery, but when a top politico is found dead at the construction site, Rebus has something he can sink his teeth into—a decades-old crime whose tentacles touch the present and lead to a new confrontation with Rebus' longtime nemesis, Edinburgh crime boss Big Ger Cafferty. . . . Nobody writes darker than Rankin." Booklist

Rankin, Ian

Watchman. Little, Brown and Co. 2007 258p $24.99

ISBN 978-0-316-00913-3; 0-316-00913-X

LC 2007-19761

First published 1988 in the United Kingdom; first American edition published 1991 for the Crime Club by Doubleday

This thriller "features British spy Miles Flint, a markedly different sort of agent than, say, James Bond. Flint is a

watcher from behind darkened windows, a listener to tapped phone lines. When a lapse in judgment results in the death of a valued source, his shot at redemption comes in the form of a seemingly routine mission to Belfast. . . . The mission quickly turns deadly, and Flint realizes that he has been set up by someone in his organization. Watchman keeps the reader on pins and needles from page one." BookPage

Rash, Ron

Burning bright; stories. Ecco 2010 205p $22.99

ISBN 978-0-06-180411-3; 0-06-180411-8; 0061804118; 9780061804113

The stories in this collection "are set in the rural, meth-addled hills of North Carolina. Pervaded with desperation — pawn shops, gravediggers, arson and a sense of impending death — these are not uplifting stories. . . . 'Burning Bright' is a collection to be read for the quality of the prose, which reflects Rash's intimate knowledge of this region and its history. His heart is clearly in this place—the dialect is pitch-perfect and he is a skillful translator of the inner worlds and difficult lifestyles of the unique, hardened-by-necessity breed of people who have populated the area, past and present." Portland Oregonian

Rash, Ron

★ The **cove**; Ron Rash. Ecco Press 2012 255p.

ISBN 9780061804199; 9780061804205; 9781410448583

This book, set in "North Carolina during WWI—tells the story of "the alienated Laurel Shelton [who] lives with her wounded war veteran brother in an isolated cabin. While out doing laundry by the creek one day, Laurel discovers Walter Smith, an illiterate, mute flutist en route to New York City, who has been incapacitated by hornet stings. As she nurses the mysterious Walter back to health, Laurel begins to fall in love. . . . However, local Army recruiter Chauncey Feith threatens to ruin all that Laurel and Walter hope for. A rabid anti-German agitator, he begins to suspect that Walter is not who he claims to be. Driven by fear, patriotism, and bloodlust, Chauncey progresses from arrogant drunk to a craven yet dangerous force." (Publishers Weekly)

Rash, Ron

Saints at the river. Henry Holt 2004 239p $24

ISBN 0-8050-7487-2

LC 2003-67630

"When the 12-year-old daughter of a wealthy banker drowns in South Carolina's Tamassee River, her death sets off an emotionally charged battle between the grieving parents, who want to put up a dam to recover her body, and the local environmentalists, who will risk everything to defend the pristine state of their river. . . . The book is rich with nuance, mostly because Rash selects Maggie Glenn as his first-person narrator. A Tamassee native who now works as a news photographer in the state capital, Columbia, Maggie has deep ties to the town, but she's detached from the main fray. As a result, her news angles and her romantic attachments keep shifting. Maggie's rage against her father isn't sufficiently explored to carry the weight it bears in the plot, but Rash compensates for this weakness by creating detailed, highly particular characters." Publ Wkly

Rash, Ron

    Serena; a novel. Ecco 2008 371p $24.95

      ISBN 978-0-06-147085-1; 0-06-147085-6

                          LC 2008-00712

    "Set in 1929, in the rugged mountains of North Carolina, Rash's novel is a tightly knit tale of industrial development, greed, and betrayal. George Pemberton and his new bride, Serena, maintain a close watch over a burgeoning logging empire, dealing with their workers while fighting off the efforts of environmental activists to expand the country's network of national parks. As the title character—a Depression-era Lady Macbeth wholly comfortable in the wilderness—drives her husband to commit increasingly malevolent acts, he must also contend with the reemergence of a woman with whom he had an illegitimate child years earlier. Rash's evocative rendering of the blighted landscape and the tough characters who inhabit it recalls both John Steinbeck and Cormac McCarthy, while the malignant character of Serena, who projects a 'stark unflinching certainty' about her actions, propels his finely paced story." New Yorker

Rathbone, Julian

    The **last** English king. St. Martin's Press 1999 381p $24.95

      ISBN 0-312-24213-1

                          LC 99-55913

    "Rathbone takes considerable historical liberties, writing in contemporary vernacular modern prose and painting King Edward as a man more interested in Harold's fetching brother Tostig than in the sister, whom he is slated to marry. However, Rathbone defends his decisions convincingly in an author's note, and his narrative presents an interesting interpretation of a tumultuous period in English history." Publ Wkly

Ratner, Vaddey

    In the shadow of the banyan; Vaddey Ratner. Simon & Schuster 2012 336 p.

      ISBN 1451657706; 9781451657708; 9781451657715; 9781451657722

                          LC 2011033320

    This novel explores "the atrocities committed by the Khmer Rouge regime in Cambodia between 1975 and 1979, when an estimated two million people lost their lives. . . . For seven-year-old Raami, the shattering end of childhood begins with the footsteps of her father returning home in the early dawn hours, bringing details of the civil war that has overwhelmed the streets of Phnom Penh, Cambodia's capital. Soon the family's world of carefully guarded royal privilege is swept up in the chaos of revolution and forced exodus. Over the next four years, as the Khmer Rouge attempts to strip the population of every shred of individual identity, Raami clings to the only remaining vestige of her childhood the mythical legends and poems told to her by her father." (Publisher's note)

Raucher, Herman

    Summer of '42. Putnam 1971 251p

    This is a novel "describing with great accuracy what it was like to be a 15-year-old boy just entering the obsessed-with-sex stage of life in the wartime summer of 1942. Hermie and Oscy and Benji are three tough, foul-mouthed but innocent Brooklyn boys spending the summer on Packett Island off the coast of Maine. The central story revolves around Hermie's tender and believable relationship with a war widow who initiates him into sex at the end of the novel." Publ Wkly

    "There is hilarity here and vulgarity, warmth and humanity—and so much detail and nostalgia that the work seems almost like a historical novel." Libr J

Rawles, Nancy

    My Jim; a novel. Nancy Rawles. Crown Publishers 2005 174p hardcover o.p. (paperback) $12.95; (hardcover) $19.95

      ISBN 9781400054015; 1400054001

                          LC 2004011606

    Alex Award (2006)

    This book "is the story of Sadie Watson, the wife of 'N##ger Jim,' as he was referred to in the Mark Twain classic 'Huckleberry Finn.' Jim was the escaped slave who took the journey down the Mississippi . . . with runaway Huck. [Author Nancy] Rawles says that Jim mentions his family at least twice in Twain's book, but that the classic divulges no details about who this woman was. Starting from that point, Rawles created Sadie, a woman who never resigned herself to involuntary servitude, and who was Jim's lifelong love. Rawles relied upon new research revealing more about the daily lives of slaves to show how Jim and Sadie—like real-life slaves in the South—created family in the midst of chaos, and, . . . sought stability in an environment that offered none." (National Public Radio)

Rawlings, Marjorie Kinnan

    Short stories; edited by Rodger L. Tarr. University Press of Fla. 1994 376p $49.95

      ISBN 0-8130-1252-X

                          LC 93-30649

Rawn, Melanie

    The **diviner**. DAW Books 2011 374p $25.95

      ISBN 978-0-7564-0681-3; 0-7564-0681-1

      Prequel to: The golden key (1996)

    "The Sheyqa Nizzira, despotic ruler of a Middle East–flavored land in the year 611, has meticulously planned to wipe out a large family of her rivals, murdering them down to the smallest child. When young wastrel Azzad alMa'alique misses his date with doom and flees, he sets in motion a complex revenge plot that will change the future of many lands and generations of both families. . . . Rawn at her best remains a mesmerizing writer, and there is some of her best here." Publ Wkly

Rawn, Melanie

    Touchstone; Melanie Rawn. Tor 2012 363 p. $25.99

      ISBN 9780765323620

                          LC 2011025175

    In this fantasy novel, "Cayden Silversun, a blend of Elven, Fae, and Wizard bloodlines, defies his noble family to pursue a life in the theater, forming the four-person troupe Touchstone with the goal of making it to the highest echelons of the performing circuit. Given the talents of troupe member Mieka Windthistle, a brilliant glisker' whose job is to enhance with magic both the crowd's emotions and the performances' special effects, their goal seems reachable. Yet Cayden's prophetic dreams indicate something sinister about Mieka's presence and tempt him to try to change fate without incurring a larger doom." (Libr J)

Ray, Shann

American masculine; stories. Graywolf 2011 185p pa $15

ISBN 978-1-55597-588-3; 1-55597-588-7

LC 2011-923187

"Set almost exclusively in Montana, Ray's stories depict broken families from every possible angle. A dead brother, abusive or absent fathers, unfaithful spouses, separating parents: The collection runs the whole gamut. This isn't the American West of Annie Proulx or Cormac McCarthy; it's less centered on landscapes and overarching narrative, and more closely focused on relatives drawing blood with words, fists, or mere looks." AV Club

Raymond, Jonathan

The **half**-life; a novel. Bloomsbury 2004 355p $23.95

ISBN 1-582-34448-5

LC 2003-22602

"In the early nineteenth century, a half-starved band of fur trappers struggles through the Oregon woods. Their young, diffident cook is intimidated by the rougher members of the group. When another young man, fleeing from some vengeful Russians, stumbles into camp, a friendship blossoms. Move ahead to the Reagan era. A teenager is dragged by her mother to live in an Oregon commune. Lonely and resentful while living among slightly absurd, aging counterculturists, she is drawn to the only other young woman in the settlement, and as their bond grows, they work together on a film project. The discovery of a pair of skeletons buried on the commune provides the link between these pairs of friendships. Raymond, in his first novel, seamlessly links the two narratives with elegant and often haunting prose. The characters are finely drawn, and Raymond poses them against a seductively beautiful landscape." Booklist

Rayne, Sarah

Property of a lady. Severn House 2011 252p $28.95

ISBN 978-0-7278-8028-4

"Rayne's crisp and fast-paced writing deftly combines sharp characters, obscure legend, the panorama of 20th-century history, subtle romance, and even subtler melancholy, turning the picked-over bones of the haunted house story into something fresh and frequently terrifying." Publ Wkly

Rayner, Richard

The **cloud** sketcher; a novel. HarperCollins Pubs. 2001 435p

ISBN 0-06-019634-3

LC 00-56695

The author "vividly captures details of Finnish culture, history and landscape and the developing architectural aesthetic of the age. This is an old-fashioned novel in the best sense: full of incident and passion, presenting a slice of history and relating a gripping story." Publ Wkly

Read, Miss

Affairs at Thrush Green; illustrations by J. S. Goodall. Houghton Mifflin 1984 256p il

LC 84-6702

First published 1983 in the United Kingdom

"The catastrophic fire that destroyed Thrush Green rectory in Gossip from Thrush Green, has caused Charles Henstock and his wife, Dimity, to move into the luxurious, large rectory in Lulling, thus drawing the adventures of the residents of these two towns even closer. . . . Henstock tends to his new duties with gracious vigor despite his own doubts and those expressed by several parishioners." Booklist

Read, Miss

At home in Thrush Green; illustrated by J.S. Goodall. Houghton Mifflin 1986 261p il

LC 86-20864

First published 1985 in the United Kingdom

The author describes "a year of bustling and visiting at Thrush Green. The creation of eight homes for elderly residents on the site of the old vicarage takes up much of the novel's action, absorbing the interests of the villagers as the recipients must be decided upon and settled in. School life under the stern Miss Watson and the more amiable Miss Fogarty also receives a share of attention. Readers familiar with Thrush Green's inhabitants will be delighted to note the changes in the lives of their favorite characters and will be pleased as always by the book's emphasis on familiar annual patterns." Booklist

Read, Miss

Chronicles of Fairacre; comprising: Village school, Village diary and Storm in the village. illustrated by J. S. Goodall. Houghton Mifflin 1977 534p il

First published 1964 in the United Kingdom. A combined edition of three titles first published separately in 1956 (1955 in the United Kingdom), 1957, and 1959 (1958 in the United Kingdom) respectively

Village school describes one year in the life of an English schoolmistress in a two-room church-governed school in the rural English village of Fairacre. Through her eyes we see the whole of village life with its fetes, sales, outings, festivals, quarrels and friendships. Village diary continues the account of school and village life. When a retired male school teacher settles in the village, the villagers hope for a romance for their schoolmistress until a wife appears. In Storm in the village, the "storm" is caused by fear that the British Atomic Research Authority is going to take over Harold Miller's "Hundred Acre Field" to make room for a new housing development and that the village school will be closed

Read, Miss

Farewell to Fairacre; illustrations by John S. Goodall. Houghton Mifflin 1994 213p il

LC 94-25628

"With an influx of new students, Miss Read's worries about the future of her beloved school can finally be set aside. In their wake, however, come concerns about the head mistress' own health. Two small strokes spur her decision to retire, and she spends her final months in her usual busy fashion, tending to her students at Fairacre, fending off the surprising attentions of two suitors, and becoming ever more comfortable with thoughts of a new life ahead. Nostalgic without being sentimental, this is a fitting conclusion to a delightful series, recalling old friends and pleasant times in a tranquil English village." Booklist

Read, Miss

Friends at Thrush Green; illustrations by John S. Goodall. Houghton Mifflin 1991 244p il

LC 91-10857

First published 1990 in the United Kingdom

In this novel "we meet a crazy-quilt collection of delightfully eccentric characters who eagerly await and gossip endlessly about their old friends' return visit. The town's attention is also riveted to the pending sale of the much-loved residence abutting the schoolhouse at Thrush Green, speculation about which gives rise to a cornucopia of interesting tales and rumors surrounding various townspeople. While some readers might deem Miss Read's novel sluggish for its seeming uneventfulness, many others will be drawn to this throwback to an easier, slower-paced life." Booklist

Read, Miss

Mrs. Pringle; illustrations by John S. Goodall. Houghton Mifflin 1990 165p il

LC 90-4669

First published 1989 in the United Kingdom

This novel focuses on the exploits of Mrs. Pringle, the custodian of the school in the village of Fairacre

Read, Miss

Return to Thrush Green; illustrated by J.S. Goodall. Houghton Mifflin 1979 255p il

LC 79-858

First published 1978 in the United Kingdom

In this chronicle of Thrush Green "Albert Piggott, the sexton, is his usual irascible self despite the efforts of his wandering wife and his loyal daughter. On the other hand, the return of Joan Young's ailing father works out much better than expected. Miss Fogarty handles the school crises capably and finds that some clouds do have silver linings. As flowers bloom and birds do nest, neighbors chat away as usual, and Dotty Harmer cares for her stray animals and offers acorn coffee to friends. Best of all is the village's newest romance, one that takes just about everyone by surprise." Publ Wkly

Read, Miss

Thrush Green; illustrated by J.S. Goodall. Houghton Mifflin 1960 226p il

First published 1959 in the United Kingdom

"Confined to the events of May 1, the day when Mrs. Curdle's traveling carnival brings its special magic to Thrush Green, the story tells what takes place in the lives of a small boy, a lonely girl, an elderly doctor and his young assistant, and various other people, including the redoubtable Mrs. Curdle herself." Booklist

Read, Cornelia

Invisible boy. Grand Central Pub. 2010 418p $24.99

ISBN 978-0-446-51134-6; 0-446-51134-X

LC 2009-17205

"Read expertly evokes the New York City of the period, from the nearly palpable grime of Chelsea to disturbing undertones of racism and classism in the justice system. Equal parts toughness and vulnerability, Madeline is always a bracing heroine." Publ Wkly

Read, Piers Paul

Alice in exile. St. Martin's Press 2002 344p $24.95

ISBN 0-312-30398-X

"As striking in her beauty as she is shocking in her behavior, Alice Fry has an uninhibited sexuality that makes her attractive to two very different men. Pregnant with fiance Edward Cobb's child, Alice is abandoned by him when her father becomes embroiled in a sexual scandal that threatens Cobb's political ambition. With no one to turn to and nowher to go, Alice is rescued by Baron von Rettenberg, a womanizing Russian nobleman who hires her as his children's governess. . . .To read Read is to be caught up in an epic wonder of passion, scandal, adn international intrigue." Booklist

Read, Piers Paul

The **professor's** daughter. Lippincott 1971 276p

Henry Rutledge, "the professor is a middle-aged old-line liberal who has dabbled in politics behind the scenes in the Kennedy era. In . . . flashbacks we learn how and why he and his wife have become the kind of people they are, and what has gone wrong with their marriage. The professor's daughter is something else again, desperate, attempting suicide, all but destroyed sexually and every other way by traps she has drifted into without ever understanding what was happening to her. When father and daughter strike up an incongruous but ultimately quite believable alliance with a group of campus radical activists who believe assassination is a valid revolutionary tool, tension mounts to a keen pitch." Publ Wkly

Read, Piers Paul

A **season** in the West. Random House 1989 238p

LC 88-29682

"Read engages his audience with biting pictures of British publishing and banking circles, while the romance is played up for all its blazing erotic qualities. Witty commentary on sedate lives moved by unruly passions." Booklist

Reasoner, James

Antietam. Cumberland House 2000 383p $22.95

ISBN 1-58182-084-4

LC 00-22578

This novel focuses on "the Brannon clan of Culpepper County, Virginia. As the hostilities move ever closer and finally threaten the security of the family farm in northern Virginia, each of the six Brannon siblings is faced with an inevitable crisis of either the heart or the conscience. . . . Fraught with passion, tension, and tenderness, this enthralling family saga will appeal to fans of epic well-researched historical fiction." Booklist

Rebeck, Theresa

Three girls and their brother; a novel. Shaye Areheart Books 2008 341p $23.95

ISBN 978-0-307-39414-9; 0-307-39414-X

LC 2007-036711

A "satire of celeb-obsessed NYC about flame-haired teenage sisters who get photographed for The New Yorker and soon become megastars. Rebeck relies on four narrators, cannily beginning with the girls' brother (who retains our sympathy even as he tosses barbs like 'I've been over here on the Planet of Total Morons, someplace you apparently own property'). If the ending strains believability, well, by then we'll buy anything — even supermodels scarfing burgers." Entertainment Wkly

Red Spectres; Russian Gothic tales from the twentieth century. selected, translated from the Russian, and with an introduction by Muireann Maguire. Penguin Group USA 2013 224 p. $25.95

ISBN 1468303481; 9781468303483

This collection of 20th century Russian gothic fiction "includes eleven vintage tales by seven writers of the period: Valery Bryusov, Mikhail Bulgakov, Aleksandr Grin and Sigizmund Krzhizhanovsky;. . . Aleksandr Chayanov, . . . and the emigres Georgy Peskov and Pavel Perov. Through the traditional gothic repertoire of ghosts, insanity, obsession, retribution and terror, Red Spectres conveys the turbulence and dissonance of life in Russia in these years." (Publisher's note)

Redfern, Elizabeth

Auriel rising. G.P. Putnam's Sons 2004 386p $24.95

ISBN 0-399-15105-2

LC 2003-58507

"Redfern sets a blistering pace and never breaks stride or tone. Resisting the standard static historical tableau, she gives us a troubled city constantly reinventing itself, peopled by souls no less changeable." N Y Times Book Rev

Redfield, James

The **celestine** prophecy; an adventure. Warner Bks. 1994 246p $19.95

ISBN 0-446-51862-X

LC 93-61754

"The saga begins when the unnamed middle-aged male narrator whimsically quits his nondescript life to track down an ancient Peruvian manuscript (pretentiously called the Manuscript) containing nine Insights that supposedly prophesy the modern emergence of New Age spirituality. South of the border, he encounters resistance from the Peruvian government and church authorities, who believe the document will undermine traditional family values. While dodging evil soldiers, paranoid priests and pseudoscientific researchers, our hero sequentially discovers all nine Insights during a series of chance encounters. Redfield has a real talent for page-turning action." Publ Wkly

Followed by The tenth insight (1996)

Redhill, Michael

Consolation; a novel. Little, Brown and Co. 2007 340p $24.99

ISBN 978-0-316-73498-1; 0-316-73498-5

LC 2006-934104

First published 2006 in the Canada

"A gentle but unfaltering cadence, a well-tempered voice, and a highly resolved sense of detail bring readers back and forth smoothly between these two eras." Quill & Quire

Reed, Barry

The **choice**. Crown 1991 358p

ISBN 0-517-58124-8

LC 90-48217

"Frank Galvin is at the peak of his legal career with a blue-chip Boston law firm. As chronicled in The Verdict {1980} he has risen to the height of Boston's legal set through a brilliant performance in a highly publicized hospital case. When he is approached by a young and inexperienced attorney with evidence that a highly touted new wonder drug may cause birth defects, he sees it as an opportunity to exert his firm's sense of humanity. However, the firm is the principal legal counsel for the drug's manufacturer. What seems at first to be a simple matter of potential conflict of interest rapidly escalates into an intricate web of intrigue involving both U.S. and British law as well as medical ethics." Libr J

Reed, Barry

The **indictment**. Crown 1994 370p

ISBN 0-517-59433-1

LC 94-8346

"Reed surrounds the mystery plot with an intriguing, behind-the-scenes look at the historically fascinating sociopolitical world of Boston, and he offers plenty of detail on the decision-making, strategy, and processes that go into preparing a criminal case." Booklist

Reed, Ishmael

★ **Japanese** by spring. Atheneum Pubs. 1993 225p

LC 92-36280

"Borrowing from vivid African-American slang and turning academic jargon inside out, Mr. Reed constructs brilliant verbal fusillades that reduce his targets to their most ridiculous components." N Y Times Book Rev

Reed, Kit

The **baby** merchant. Tor 2006 334p $24.95

ISBN 978-0-7653-1550-2; 0-7653-1550-5

LC 2006-40385

"In Reedland—the fantasy world where the author's characters live, breathe, and inevitably screw up—half the fun is viewing how surreal events send her anti-heroes bumping into each other like so many demented dominoes." Hartford Courant

Reed, Kit

Enclave. Tor 2009 366p $25.95

ISBN 978-0-7653-2161-9; 0-7653-2161-0

LC 2008-46433

Reed's "characters may be flawed and immoral, but they are also fascinating and believable. The carefully crafted plot and multiple points of view engage readers immediately." Romantic Times

Reeman, Douglas
A **ship** must die. Morrow 1979 284p
LC 79-66009

"In January 1944 Captain Richard Blake, Royal Navy, is preparing to hand over his battle-scarred cruiser 'Andromeda' to the Australian navy. Before he can do so, a German commerce raider appears in the Indian Ocean, and Blake is ordered to destroy him." Libr J

"Reeman gives dimension to his characters and imparts his usual sense of realism in vivid scenes of battle action." Booklist

Reich, Christopher
Rules of deception. Doubleday 2008 390p $24.95
ISBN 978-0-385-52406-3; 0-385-52406-4
LC 2007-36368

"Reich's everyman hero, Jonathan Ransom, is plunged into a world of intrigue when his wife dies in an accident. Growing questions about her true identity dig him deeper into trouble. Ransom is unaware that he is interrupting the endgame of an enormous and long-running conspiracy that he—and the Swiss cop tracking him—could derail. Reich . . . throws readers off the scent but never loses control of the plot. He skillfully handles the pacing, and this results in a suspenseful story balanced by cinematic action scenes. . . . Fans of early Ludlum will particularly enjoy it." Libr J

Reich, Tova
My Holocaust; a novel. HarperCollins 2007 326p $24.95
ISBN 978-0-06-117345-5; 0-06-117345-2
LC 2007-297195

"Tova Reich is fearless, in the best possible way, and her take on the culture of victimization spares no captives in the gulag of self-anointed martyrdom. Reich's gift for satire is impeccable, her ear for absurdity pitch perfect." Philadelphia Inquirer

Reichs, Kathleen J.
★ **Bare** bones; [by[Kathy Reichs. Scribner 2003 306p $23.95
ISBN 0-7432-3346-8
LC 2003-40725

"Tempe, a forensic anthropologist, is back home in Charlotte, N.C., anticipating a nice, long vacation from the county medical examiner's office, when a series of unnatural disasters drags her back to the lab. . . . Whether she's examining the pulverized remains of the victims of a suspicious plane crash or reassembling the bones of an illegally slaughtered bear, Tempe is a pro's pro at her job, but also a compassionate woman who isn't afraid to show her outrage at the cruelty done to man and beast for the sake of a dirty dollar." N Y Times Book Rev

Reichs, Kathleen J.
Break no bones; [by] Kathy Reichs. Scribner 2006 339p $25.95
ISBN 978-0-7432-3349-1; 0-7432-3349-2
LC 2006-45038

"While supervising a dig of Native American burial grounds in Charleston, S.C., Brennan finds more recent remains. Soon, her ex-husband, who's a lawyer, appears in town, pursuing leads in a missing persons case connected with a local church. Bodies start piling up at an alarming rate, and Brennan begins to suspect that the deaths are linked to each other—and her ex-husband's inquiry. Reichs's down-to-earth heroine is an appealing creation, who deftly juggles personal problems with professional challenges." Publ Wkly

Reichs, Kathleen J.
★ **Deadly** decisions; [by] Kathy Reichs. Scribner 2000 333p $25
ISBN 0-684-85971-8
LC 00-22220

"The author doesn't dumb down the scientific stuff, delivering the full textbook version of subjects like hydrocephalus, blood-spatter analysis, ground-penetrating radar devices and the history of outlaw motorcycle clubs in North America." N Y Times Book Rev

Reichs, Kathleen J.
Death du jour; {by} Kathy Reichs. Scribner 1999 379p $25
ISBN 0-684-84118-5
LC 98-48763

This mystery opens with forensic anthropologist Temperance Brennan "digging up the body of a nun buried more than a century ago in a convent graveyard in Quebec. While her job is to identify the corpse as a possible saint, Tempe's attention is drawn to the grisly killings of four-month-old twin boys and their parents. At the same time, Tempe's troubled sister Harry comes to Montreal to take a self-help workshop. Investigating these deaths leads Tempe back to the Carolinas, where more bodies are discovered on an island monkey preserve, and clues point to a mysterious cult." Libr J

Reichs, Kathleen J.
Deja dead; [by] Kathy Reichs. Scribner 1997 411p
ISBN 978-0684841175
LC 97-2990

"Dr. Tempe Brennan, a trowel-packing forensic anthropologist from North Carolina, works in Montreal's Laboratoire de Médecine Légale examining recovered bodies to help police solve missing-persons cases and murders. It's clear to Tempe that the remains of several women killed and savagely mutilated point to a sadistic serial killer, but she can't convince the police. Determined to prevent more brutal deaths, she sleuths solo, tracking her quarry through Montreal's seedy underworld of hookers, where her anthropologist friend Gabby, doing her own scary research, is being stalked by a creep. . . . Except for imparting an excess of lab information, Reichs, also a forensic anthropologist, drives the pace at a heady clip. A first-class writer, she dazzles readers with sensory imagery that is apt, fresh, and funny." Libr J

Reichs, Kathleen J.

Grave secrets; [by] Kathy Reichs. Scribner 2002 317p $25

ISBN 0-684-85973-4

LC 2002-22695

"While in Guatemala to assist in the exhumation of an old mass grave, forensic specialist Temperance Brennan is called upon to determine whether a body found in a septic tank is that of the missing daughter of the Canadian ambassador to Guatemala. The gruesome search, vividly described, leaves even the toughened Tempe aghast." Booklist

Reichs, Kathleen J.

Monday mourning; [by] Kathy Reichs. Scribner 2004 305p $25

ISBN 0-7432-3347-6

LC 2004-45263

This Temperance Brennan mystery "finds the forensic anthropologist in Montreal to testify in a murder case. Arriving a day early to prepare, she becomes caught up in a new investigation when three sets of human bones are discovered in the basement of a pizza parlor. Examining the remains, she discovers that the victims were Caucasian and female. Antique buttons found near the bodies lead Homicide Detective Claudel to believe that the remains are over a century old, but Tempe is not so convinced and investigates with the help of her friend Anne, who has come to visit while contemplating her marriage. Readers of the series will be pleased to see the relationship between Tempe and Detective Andrew Ryan develop further." Libr J

Reid, Taylor Jenkins

Forever, interrupted; a novel. by Taylor Jenkins Reid. 1st Washington Square pbk ed. Washington Square Press 2013 352 p. (paperback) $15

ISBN 1476712824; 9781476712826; 9781476712833

LC 2012035073

In this book, written by Taylor Jenkins Reid, "Elsie Porter is an average twentysomething [who meets] the adorable and charming Ben Ross. Within weeks, the two are head over heels in love. By May, they've eloped. Only nine days later, Ben is out riding his bike when he is hit by a truck and killed on impact. At the hospital, she must face Susan, the mother-in-law she has never met—and who doesn't even know Elsie exists." It Interweav[es] Elsie and Ben's . . . romance with Elsie and Susan's healing process." (Publisher's note)

Reiken, Frederick

Day for night. Little, Brown and Co. 2010 326p $24.99

ISBN 978-0-316-07756-9

LC 2009-38597

"During a 1984 trip to Florida, a widowed marine biologist swims among tolerant manatees with her pediatrician girlfriend, a Polish Jew who fled the Nazis. Their young-dude guide, Tim, of German descent, accompanies his bandmate Dee, whose wealthy Utah family is part of a violent cult, on a clandestine visit to see her brother, who is in a coma after surviving a motorcycle accident in Israel. On the plane, Tim sits next to a tall, reserved woman, who may be a 1960s radical turned fugitive from justice with mystical powers. A Massachusetts veterinarian suffering from severe allergies ends up in Israel, where a man working at a nature reserve . . . . Well, it's an entrancing and profoundly complicated tale Reiken tells as he slowly reveals the submerged connections among his intriguing characters while sustaining psychological sophistication, suspense, shrewd humor, and many-tiered compassion." Booklist

Reimringer, John

★ Vestments. Milkweed Editions 2010 407 p.

ISBN 1-57131-080-0; 1571310800; 978-1-57131-080-4; 9781571310804

LC 2010007143

"Just a few years after his ordination and his first assignment as a parish priest, James Dressler is placed on leave. His housekeeper found some letters from a woman and turned them into the archdiocese. For little more than a kiss, he is relegated to a parish in a backwater burg. He opts instead to live back home with his mother in St. Paul until he can come up with a better game plan. But his gritty hometown has its own temptations, and, broke and in need of work, James finds himself renovating apartments and butting heads with his tough, bad-tempered father and attracted once again to his old highschool lover, Betty Garcia. Through his thoughtful themes and lyrical prose, Reimringer effortlessly restores a measure of dignity to the priesthood even as he pays tender homage to the working-class roots of St. Paul." Booklist

Reisman, Nancy

The first desire. Pantheon Books 2004 310p $24

ISBN 0-375-42308-7

LC 2004-44665

"The catalyst for this narrative about the hidden dramas of a Jewish family living in Buffalo from the late 1920s to 1950 occurs offstage. Rebecca Cohen, wife of jewelry store owner Abe, has died, leaving five adult children. Goldie, the eldest, on whom the responsibility for caring for her siblings has fallen, suddenly disappears without a word. Her departure leaves Sadie Cohen Feldstein, the only married sister, to cope with her tyrannical father and difficult siblings, who live together in the family home." Publ Wkly

The novel is "both lovely and heartbreaking in its vision of family ties at their most inevitable." N Y Times (Late N Y Ed)

Remarque, Erich Maria

★ All quiet on the western front; translated from the German by A. W. Wheen. Little, Brown 1929 291p $24.95

ISBN 0-316-73992-8

"Four German youths are pulled abruptly from school to serve at the front as soldiers in World War I. Only Paul survives, and he contemplates the needless violation of the human body by weapons of war. No longer innocent or light-hearted, he is repelled by the slaughter of soldiers and questions the usefulness of war as a means of adjudication. Although the young men in this novel are German, the message is universal in its delineation of the feelings of the common soldier." Shapiro. Fic for Youth. 3d edition

Followed by The road back

Remarque, Erich Maria

Arch of triumph; translated from the German by Walter Sorell and Denver Lindley. Appleton-Century 1945 455p

"A story of Paris in the period preceding the {Second World} war. The central character is a German doctor who, having escaped from the Nazis, is living illegally in France, subject to deportation if the police discover his presence. Without a passport and identification papers he is not allowed to practice, but in secret performs difficult operations for a well-known society doctor. Other refugees, figures from the underworld, outcasts and derelicts are the characters in a book which pictures a society nearing its doom." Wis Libr Bull

Remarque, Erich Maria

The **night** in Lisbon; translated by Ralph Manheim. Harcourt, Brace & World 1964 244p

Original German edition, 1962

"One night in Lisbon in 1942 a German refugee offers passage to the U.S. and his passport to another refugee on condition that he be kept company through the night and that he be permitted to tell his story. The narration reveals the first refugee's flight from Germany in the 1930's, his hazardous return after five years to see his wife, his second escape in which his wife joins him, and their subsequent flight from place to place in Europe during which, in spite of dangers, they achieved moments of intense happiness because of their mutual love and understanding." Booklist

Remarque, Erich Maria

The **road** back; translated from the German by A. W. Wheen. Little, Brown 1931 343p

Sequel to All quiet on the western front

"A profoundly moving, a painfully moving, document. Unlike tragedy, it has no katharsis, but, like a tragedy, it has to be looked at open-eyed, honestly, courageously." Spectator

Remarque, Erich Maria

A **time** to love and a time to die; translated from the German by Denver Lindley. Harcourt Brace & Co. 1954 378p

"Ernst, a young German soldier, gets a furlough in the closing days of World War II. He marries Elizabeth, a neighbor girl, who grew up while he was away. Their brief but touching honeymoon helps them to discover love and each other—a time to love. Upon his return from a furlough, Ernst is sent to guard four Russian prisoners. In a generous gesture, he releases them, but one of them, turns on him and kills him—a time to die." Wis Libr Bull

"The whole story is told with great restraint, with little sentimentality for those in misery and with little open rage at those who caused it." Chicago Sunday Trib

Renault, Mary

★ The **bull** from the sea. Pantheon Bks. 1962 343p

"A sequel to The King Must Die, this mythological novel begins with Theseus, King of Athens, returning in triumph from Crete, where he has killed the Minotaur. On a subsequent adventure he captures and falls in love with the warrior princess, Hippolyta. Although married to Phaedra of Crete, Theseus continues his relationship with Hippolyta and both women bear him sons. Tragedy occurs when Phaedra is attracted to and spurned by Hippolyta's youthful son." Shapiro. Fic for Youth. 3d edition

Renault, Mary

Funeral games. Pantheon Bks. 1981 335p

ISBN 9780394520681 out of print; 9780375714191

LC 81047273

This concludes the story of Alexander the Great that began in Fire from heaven and The Persian boy. "At 32 Alexander is dying in Babylon. The generals, two pregnant wives and a covey of conspirators keep a jackal-like vigil, anticipating the fight for possession of the empire, extending from Europe to India, that will break out when the godlike leader dies. At his death, the murderous power struggle ensues—Alexander's mother and his brain-injured half-brother, Philip, vie with the Regent and other extrafamilial seekers of the throne." Publ Wkly

Renault, Mary

The **king** must die. Pantheon Bks. 1958 338p hardcover o.p. pa $14

ISBN 0-394-75104-3

"Retold by its hero, the legend of Theseus becomes a logical sequence of adventures that befell a slight, wiry, quick-witted youth impelled to prove his manhood in a semi-barbaric society that put a premium on size and brawn. Although, at seventeen, he was already a king and a seasoned warrior, Theseus obeyed his patron god's prompting and voluntarily joined a company of young people conscripted for the bull-dances in Crete, became a renowned bull-leaper, and took advantage of an earthquake to overthrow the Cretan kingdom." Booklist

Followed by The bull from the sea (1962)

Renault, Mary

★ The **last** of the wine. Pantheon Bks. 1956 389p

"This is a fictionalized account of Athens during the years of the Peloponnesian War told by Alexias, a young Athenian of good family background. We learn the details of daily life within the Greek city state, including the literary, cultural, recreational, and political texture of the time. One very memorable account is that of a wrestling match at the Isthmian Games." Shapiro. Fic for Youth. 3d edition

Renault, Mary

The **Persian** boy. Pantheon Bks. 1972 432p

This sequel to Fire from heaven continues the "story of Alexander the Great, focusing upon his momentous expedition into Asia. This time we observe events through the eyes of Bagoas, a beautiful Persian eunuch who was loved by King Darius and then by Alexander himself. The multiple facets of Renault's art, familiar to a host of admirer's, are once again apparent: a particularly sensitive depiction of boyhood and youth; an astounding grasp of the facts and the spirit of the ancient world; an unerring sense of the dramatic which, along with her superb descriptive powers, brings to life a great historical period." Libr J

Followed by Funeral games

Rendell, Ruth

Adam and Eve and Pinch me; a novel. Crown 2002 356p pa $13.95

ISBN 0-609-61025-2; 1-4000-3118-4 pa

LC 2001-32539

First published 2001 in the United Kingdom

"Part ghost story, part serial-killer hunt, part excoriation of the wicked ways of Westminster and Fleet Street, this tale tightens the noose of suspense through the build-up of vivid domestic and social detail." Booklist

Rendell, Ruth

Blood lines; long and short stories. Crown 1996 215p

ISBN 978-0517703236

LC 96-852

"In this collection of short stories, Rendell is at her best, using her own quixotic brand of dark humor and an often heartwrenching poignancy to produce 11 minimasterpieces." Booklist

Rendell, Ruth

★ The **bridesmaid**. Mysterious Press 1989 259p

ISBN 0-89296-388-3

LC 88-43471

"Ms. Rendell is a diabolically subtle writer. For much of this claustrophobic study of mutual obsession, she has us peering into Senta's mind through Philip's eyes, suspiciously analyzing her bizarre statements and mysterious behavior. But, like a cunning old spider, the author has caught two flies in her web; and in the end, Philip proves the more interesting study, with his phobia about violence and his fanaticism for propriety." N Y Times Book Rev

Rendell, Ruth

★ **Collected** stories. Pantheon Bks. 1988 536p

LC 87-35949

First published 1987 in the United Kingdom

Rendell, Ruth

★ The **crocodile** bird. Crown 1993 361p

LC 93-14734

"A kind of fairy-tale unreality informs this narrative, for all its present-day accoutrements; it is written in careful, straightforward, almost childlike prose; and it keeps you on tenterhooks, once you've surrendered to the atmosphere." Times Lit Suppl

Rendell, Ruth

The **face** of trespass. Doubleday 1974 184p

The author "conveys the derelict half-dream, half-nightmare life Gray is leading in an Essex hovel far better than a crime-writer need, and through this . . . makes credible the blindness that allows him to be led to total disaster." Times Lit Suppl

Rendell, Ruth

Going wrong. Mysterious Press 1990 260p

LC 90-40421

"Guy Curran—remarkably handsome, rich, the product of London's underworld, at once ill educated and quite

bright—is obsessed with Leonora Chisholm, a childhood sweetheart who has drawn away from him, indeed plans to marry another man, but who oddly and somewhat irresolutely continues to have a rital lunch with Curran every Saturday. Curran repeatedly convinces himself that she is still in love with him but has been turned away by a college roommate, or her mother, stepfather or some other evil figure." N Y Times Book Rev

"Rendell is a master of depicting the long, slow slide into madness, making each tiny step toward the abyss resound with chilling logic." Publ Wkly

Rendell, Ruth

Harm done; an Inspector Wexford mystery. Crown 1999 346p $24

ISBN 0-609-60547-X

LC 99-20432

Three of the cases Wexford is involved in "have to do with the abuse of women or children. The crimes range from the ridiculous (a petulant university girl and a mentally challenged girl from a low-income housing project are each kidnapped to do housework and returned for ineptitude) to the monstrous (Wexford and his men must protect a child molester who was released from prison while a rich man tortures his wife in the comfort of his spacious home." Publ Wkly

Rendell, Ruth

Heartstones; illustrations by George Underwood. Harper & Row 1987 80p il

LC 86-46098

"Adolescent Elvira is in intense spiritual communion with her father; she plans to devote all the rest of her life to him. Elvira's mother is dead, and her sister is outside the orbit that Elvira and her father have created for themselves. This arrangement works fine, as long as it lasts, but trouble arrives in the form of a woman Elvira's father wants to marry. Elvira is determined the marriage will not take place. And, alas, the fiancée dies—violently!" Booklist

"Such is Rendell's mastery of psychological suspense that throughout we remain unsure of the seriousness of Elvira's intentions." Libr J

Rendell, Ruth

★ A **judgment** in stone. Doubleday 1978 188p

LC 77-76961

"Despite our knowing on p.2 who will die, and at whose hand, we are carried along by the powerful suspense of events in one upper-middle-class English family. The sense of impending doom amply takes the place of detective work, of which there is a little in the last three short chapters. The depiction of the 'perfect servant' is masterly and the whole thing a tour de force." Barzun. Cat of Crime. Rev and enl edition

Rendell, Ruth

The **keys** to the street; a novel of suspense. Crown 1996 326p $24

ISBN 0-517-70685-7

LC 96-3114

A novel about the "homeless denizens who haunt Regent's Park in London. Residents of the exclusive neighborhoods abutting the park make a point of not even noticing wretches like Effie and Dill and Pharaoh and Roman. Only Mary Jago, a frail, sensitive young woman who has recently moved into the neighborhood as a housesitter, pays any attention to these street people—until someone starts killing them and impaling their bodies on the spiked railings that surround the park. . . . All the characters are drawn with psychological insight, but it takes a visionary author to see the bonds that connect them all." N Y Times Book Rev

Rendell, Ruth

Kissing the gunner's daughter. Mysterious Press 1992 378p

LC 91-50615

This is an "intricate story that hinges on vanity and self-deception, a story in which the most minor and seemingly innocent relationships are charged with meaning and malice." N Y Times Book Rev

Rendell, Ruth

Live flesh. Pantheon Bks. 1986 272p

LC 86-4922

"The obvious way to write this novel would have been to tell it through the eyes of the crippled policeman; Rendell takes the bolder path of getting inside the mind of Jenner. . . . {This} is a frightening, resonant novel—an extraordinary achievement." New Statesman (1913)

Rendell, Ruth

Not in the flesh; a Wexford novel. Crown 2008 303p $25.95

ISBN 978-0-307-40681-1; 0-307-40681-4

LC 2007-40945

First published 2007 in the United Kingdom

"Rendell has been documenting change in her imaginary Kingsmarkham for 44 years; 'Not in the Flesh' continues to hold a mirror to British society. . . . [She] also weaves into the story Wexford's heartbreaking attempts to address the tradition of female genital mutilation within the Somali community of Kingsmarkham." Los Angeles Times Book Rev

Rendell, Ruth

Road rage. Crown 1997 344p

ISBN 978-0609600566

LC 97-1200

"Taking what he vows will be his last walk in the deep woods that border his Sussex village, Chief Inspector Reginald Wexford contemplates with dread the new superhighway that will soon plow it all under. . . . But whatever sympathy he feels for the militant conservationists who pitch camp in Framhurst Great Wood to protest the highway is lost when a radical splinter group calling itself Sacred Globe kidnaps five innocent people—including Wexford's wife—and threatens to kill them unless the road is stopped." N Y Times Book Rev

Rendell, Ruth

A sight for sore eyes. Crown 1999 327p $24

ISBN 0-609-60417-1

LC 98-27654

"Rendell charts a harrowing collision course for two preternaturally beautiful teen-agers: Teddy Brex, an unloved child who grows up to be a sociopath, and Francine Hill, an overprotected child who grows up to be his ideal victim. . . . Reaching back a generation to get more traction for her macabre love story, Rendell takes a ruthless probe to every person (from Teddy's emotionally arrested parents to the faceless stranger who murdered Francine's mother) who had a hand in shaping the psyches of this ill-met pair. Spare and unforgiving, these incisive character studies illuminate the darker corners of Teddy's and Francine's family histories without dimming the originality of their bizarre lives." N Y Times Book Rev

Rendell, Ruth

Simisola. Crown 1995 327p

LC 95-8428

"Rendell's long acquaintance with her characters has not diminished the freshness of her work, nor her consummate storytelling. Rather, in Simisola, she offers a finely tuned moral tale that raises questions as it solves crimes." Times Lit Suppl

Rendell, Ruth

A sleeping life. Doubleday 1978 180p

LC 77-27716

When Chief Inspector Wexford is "called in to investigate the murder of one Rhoda Comfrey he is baffled to be unable to learn anything at all about her private life, friends, or means of supporting herself. His only clue, an expensive leather wallet, leads him up and down blind alleys until a chance remark by his own daughter, whose marriage is in jeopardy, leads him to Webster's International Dictionary and a brilliant deduction about the motive of the murderer." Shapiro. Fic for Youth. 3d edition

Rendell, Ruth

Thirteen steps down; a novel. Crown 2005 340p $25

ISBN 1-4000-9842-4

LC 2005-750

First published 2004 in the United Kingdom

"Fitness-equipment repairman Mix Cellini lodges in a crumbling London mansion presided over by octogenarian Gwendolen Chawcer. Mix and Gwendolen have little in common except a lack of nurturing as children that has impaired their ability to develop meaningful relationships. The decay of the house mirrors the disintegration of Mix's personality as his obsessions with fame, murder, and beautiful model Nerissa Nash (a fellow lodger) eat his mind like a cancer. The creepiness of the mansion and its occupants is so pronounced that it is, at times, difficult to maintain interest in their fate. However, Rendell . . . veers away from the expected in her characters and in her plot, which saves the novel and makes for riveting reading." Libr J

Rendell, Ruth

Tigerlily's orchids; a novel. Scribner 2011 257p $26

ISBN 978-1-4391-5034-4; 1-4391-5034-6

LC 2011-18103

First published 2010 in the United Kingdom

"Aside from the wretched woman in Flat No. 6 who is systematically drinking herself to death, the residents of Lichfield House take their sweet time in revealing themselves through the secret vices and obsessions that will bring several of them to grief. But that doesn't inhibit Duncan Yeardon, the lonely widower and self-acknowledged 'people watcher' who lives across the street, from speculating wildly (and mistakenly) on the intimate details of their lives. Stuart Font, the conspicuously beautiful narcissist who has recently moved into the building, gives everyone something to gossip about when the raging bull husband of his mistress crashes his housewarming party. And both Stuart and Duncan spin romantic fantasies about an elusive Asian woman they call Tigerlily. But it takes a murder to accelerate the destructive actions of ostensibly civilized strangers when they're suddenly involved in their neighbors' private lives. Rendell builds her characters with such subtle strokes that it's impossible to catch the moment when she begins to tear them down." N Y Times Book Rev

Rendell, Ruth

The **tree** of hands. Pantheon Bks. 1985 271p

LC 84-19002

First published 1984 in the United Kingdom

"Benet, successful author and unwed mother, is visited by her mentally unstable mother, Mopsa. When the baby dies, Mopsa snatches another child to give to Benet. Substitute-baby Jason is the offspring of child abuser, larcenous Carol. The child's putative father is a gigolo intent on defrauding his current patroness. The story explores spectrum of parental feeling against a background of pervasive anxiety and impending doom. This is not a mystery, really, but rather an engrossing psychological thriller." Libr J

Rendell, Ruth

The **water's** lovely; a novel. Crown Publishers 2007 340p $25.95

ISBN 978-0-307-38136-1; 0-307-738136-6

LC 2006-29492

First published 2006 in the United Kingdom

"Rendell is in absolute top form here. The Water's Lovely is as suspenseful as any crime novel she has written, but it also has the generous humanity of her best Inspector Wexford cases. . . . Rendell provides the reader with many pleasures: her intelligence and humanity, her sculpted sentences, her jokeless wit, her refusal to join her colleagues in the torture-porn business to spice up her plots. Oh, yes—those plots. What a sneaky mind the woman has." Washington Post Book Rev

Resnick, Mike

The **return** of Santiago. TOR Bks. 2003 464p $25.95

ISBN 0-7653-0224-1

LC 2002-75660

Sequel to: Santiago (1986)

"A century after the alleged demise of the legendary Santiago, the greatest outlaw of the Inner Frontier, a petty thief named Danny Briggs stumbles upon a lost collection of poems by Black Orpheus, the interstellar bard whose verses immortalized Santiago. Inspired by his discovery, Briggs—now renamed Dante—sets off across the galaxy in search of someone to re-create the legend of Santiago and start a rebellion against the enemies of freedom." Libr J

"An eminently satisfying space western, with just the right mixture of fast-drawing gunmen and talented women to keep the action going." Booklist

Restrepo, Laura

No place for heroes; a novel. translated from the Spanish by Ernesto Mestre-Reed. Nan A. Talese/ Doubleday 2010 272p $25.95

ISBN 978-0-385-51991-5

LC 2009-47858

Original Spanish edition, 2009

"Lorenza, a Colombian woman who spent her youth as a leftist activist under the Argentine dictatorship of the '70s and '80s, has returned to Buenos Aires with her 18-year-old son, Mateo. They have come in search of Mateo's father, Ramón, whom Lorenza met when they were both clandestine organizers against the regime. Locating this mysterious, lost father is almost absurdly easy: After much conjecture about what sophisticated guerrilla tactics they might have to use, they find his name in the phone book. He is not, after all, one of the 'disappeared.' He split up with Lorenza after a harrowing incident she calls the 'dark episode,' during which he abducted their infant son across national borders. The more complicated challenge lies in deciding how to approach Ramón, and, even more important, coming to understand him by shedding light on the convoluted past. It is this quixotic endeavor that occupies the protagonists for most of the book. . . . Ultimately, this coming-of-age dance, the winding stories of Lorenza's past and the search for Ramón all converge in a climax as unexpected as it is moving." San Francisco Chron

Reuland, Rob

Semiautomatic; a novel. Random House 2004 242p $24.95

ISBN 0-375-50502-4

LC 2003-46806

"Brooklyn prosecutor Andrew Giobberti has been exiled to the Appeals Bureau for so long he's almost forgotten that putting away murderers is in his DNA. Almost. When he's pulled out of purgatory to rescue a politically sensitive homicide trial prepped by a green, painfully ethical prosecutor, Giobberti's soon ready for his courtroom comeback. But even as he shows his unwilling partner the ropes they'll use to encircle the defendant's neck, disturbing holes start appearing in the case" Booklist

This thriller is "notable not for violence but for subtle characterizations, moral ambiguities and exceptional writing." Washington Post Book World

Reuss, Frederick

Henry of Atlantic City. MacMurray & Beck 1999 249p

ISBN 1-87844-889-7

LC 99-26946

"Reuss's manner—a spare third-person narrative, sticking largely to terms and phrases Henry knows—becomes a courageously concentrated show of authorial control and tonal fidelity." Publ Wkly

Reuss, Frederick
★ **Horace** afoot. MacMurray & Beck 1997 278p
ISBN 1-878448-79-X
LC 97-21601

This novel "combines two strands of plot: a sly satire of Midwestern life and a restrained account of how a closed heart comes to be unlocked. . . . combines two strands of plot: a sly satire of Midwestern life and a restrained account of how a closed heart comes to be unlocked." N Y Times Book Rev

Reuss, Frederick
Mohr; a novel. Unbridled Books 2006 312p il $25.95
ISBN 1-932961-17-8
LC 2005-37958

"Reuss's prose rarely if ever impresses through sheer imagery or wordplay or beauty, but it's concise and solidly-constructed, and it conveys his meaning well. The strength of Reuss's writing is more in his observations, the way he builds emotions out of little details like the objects in the clutter of a room or the way a certain person moves. The writing and the photographs play off of one another, illustrating each other. And the images seem to perfectly capture the mood of the story as it goes on." PopMatters

Reuss, Frederick
The **wasties**. Pantheon Bks. 2002 229p $23
ISBN 0-375-42071-1
LC 2001-55450

"English professor Michael 'Caruso' Taylor has lost the ability to speak and embarks on a journey of infantilization that progressively strips him of his autonomy—a condition he labels 'the wasties.' He grows entirely dependent on others: his pregnant wife, Gina; his nurse, Theresa; and a host of health-care professionals who attempt to rein in his childish impulses. Taylor communicates via scribbled messages, IBM ThinkPad and hand gestures." Publ Wkly

"This should appeal to sophisticated readers who like darkly humorous, cerebral fiction." Booklist

Revoyr, Nina
Wingshooters. Akashic Books 2011 250p
ISBN 978-1-936070-71-8 pa; 978-1-936070-86-2
LC 2010-928792

"The racism [Revoyr] depicts is disheartening; the loss of innocence she chronicles is shattering; the love shared between a fallible man and his granddaughter is remarkable, and the best thing about this novel." Milkwaukee J Sentinel

Reyn, Irina
What happened to Anna K. a novel. Simon & Schuster 2008 244p $24
ISBN 978-1-4165-5893-4; 1-4165-5893-4
LC 2007-39332

"It takes a lot of self-confidence to suggest that your first novel is a modern-day retelling of Anna Karenina. But once you're finished marveling at Reyn's audacity, her formidable storytelling gift sweeps you along and keeps you turning the pages in rapt anticipation, even as you're aware

that the sound in the distance is the rumble of that inevitable approaching train." N Y Times Book Rev

Reynolds, Alastair
The **prefect**. Ace Books 2008 410p $25.95
ISBN 978-0-441-01591-7; 0-441-01591-3
LC 2008-60017

"As a prefect working for the Panoply, Tom Dreyfus enforces the law in the utopian society of the Glitter Band, a collection of space habitats that orbit the planet Yellowstone. When an attack on one of the habitats leaves nearly 1000 people dead, Dreyfus uncovers a plot that threatens the freedom of the entire Glitter Band. Reynolds . . . returns to the universe of Revelation Space as he demonstrates his powerful ability to blend futuristic suspense/intrigue with personal drama in a tale of one man's search for truth, however unpleasant or demanding it may be. . . . Action-packed hard sf." Libr J

Reynolds, Marjorie
The **Starlite** Drive-in; a novel. Morrow 1997 282p $23
ISBN 0-688-15389-5
LC 97-728

"When developers find a body in a well at the old Starlite Drive-In, Callie Ann Benton knows whose body it is. It takes her back to when she was 12; her father ran the drive-in, and her mother, Teal, had become completely trapped inside her house by agoraphobia. It traps her father, too, forcing him to give up dreams, and his resentment comes out in nasty sniping, continuous put-downs that drain her—until a drifter named Charlie Memphis arrives, falls in love with Teal, and plans to take her and Callie away. This stunning novel is told by 12-year-old Callie, torn between her crush on Memphis, her love for her father, and her resentment of her mother's sexuality and personhood." Libr J

Reynolds, Sheri
A **gracious** plenty; a novel. Harmony Bks. 1997 205p $21
ISBN 0-609-60225-X
LC 97-21544

"Lyricism and the gentle voice of her heroine carry this poignant but redemptive story of an emotionally and physically scarred woman who finds her way out of the land of the dead and into the land of the living." Publ Wkly

Reznikoff, Charles
By the waters of Manhattan; introduction by Philip Lopate. David R. Godine 2009 170p pa $17.95
ISBN 978-1-57423-214-1; 1-57423-214-2
LC 2009-03263

First published 1930 by C. Boni

Reznikoff "writes prose like a poet, indeed he is one, with his rock-hard choice of words styled into deceptively simple sentences. Deceptive because when juxtaposed, each sentence accelerating into the next, they relay condensed lives, jammed with emotion, kin, and striving. Lopate's tender and eloquent introduction sets the record straight for this under-acknowledged literary master." BOMB

Rhodes, David

Driftless. Milkweed Editions 2008 429p $24

ISBN 978-1-57131-059-0; 1-57131-059-2

LC 2008-20881

"Set in a rural Wisconsin town, the book presents a series of portraits that resemble Edgar Lee Masters's 'Spoon River Anthology' in their vividness and in the cumulative picture they create of village life. There's a drifter trying to put down roots, a hardworking dairy farmer being taken advantage of by a corrupt milk coöperative, a female pastor who hears heavenly voices, and a cranky retiree who discovers a cougar living in his haymow." New Yorker

Rhodes, David

Jewelweed; a novel. David Rhodes. Milkweed Editions 2013 448 p. (hardcover: acid-free paper) $26

ISBN 1571311009; 9781571311009; 9781571311061; 9781571318831

LC 2012027827

This book by David Rhodes "introduces a cast of characters who must overcome the burdens left by the past. After serving time for a dubious conviction, Blake Bookchester is paroled. As Blake attempts to adjust, he reconnects with Danielle Workhouse, a single mother whose son, Ivan, explores the woods with his precocious friend, August. Ivan and August befriend Lester Mortal, a recluse who lives in a melon field. These characters . . .approach the future with . . . hope and trepidation." (Publisher's note)

Rhodes, Jewell Parker

Voodoo dreams; a novel of Marie Laveau. St. Martin's Press 1993 436p

LC 93-24283

This novel is about "Marie Laveau, New Orleans' legendary nineteenth-century voodoo queen. Although few biographical facts are known about Marie, Rhodes has parlayed them into a character of vast dimension and feminine power. Like her grandmother and mother before her, Marie is a voodooienne, a woman visited and possessed by the African god Damballah, and the third Marie Laveau to suffer the consequences of this terrifying blessing in a world poisoned by the sin of slavery. As Rhodes imagines Marie's strange and painful life, from her protected childhood deep in the bayou to her reign as healer in New Orleans, she evokes all the lust, tumult, and cruelty of that race-obsessed city." Booklist

Rhodes, Jewell Parker

Yellow moon. Atria Books 2008 293p $24

ISBN 978-1-4165-3710-6; 1-4165-3710-4

LC 2008-15221

This sequel to Voodoo season (2006) is the second title in the author's New Orleans trilogy

In this thriller, "a wazimamoto, or African vampire, stalks Dr. Marie Laveau, a 21st-century doctor, modern voodoo practitioner and descendant of the legendary Voodoo Queen of New Orleans. Haunted by the unquiet spirits of people killed by the wazimamoto, the young doctor vows to stop it with the help of new boyfriend NOPD Det. Daniel Parks; her Creole boss, Dr. Louis DuLac; and others devoted to Marie and her young adopted daughter, Marie-Claire. . . . Rhodes includes an informative author's note about the evo-

lution of the African vampire as a 'response and a warning about racist brutality' and 'cultural vampirism,' giving some cultural weight to this hypnotic thriller." Publ Wkly

Rhys, Jean

The **collected** short stories; introduction by Diana Athill. Norton 1987 403p

LC 88-138678

Rhys, Jean

Quartet. Simon & Schuster 1929 228p

First published 1928 in the United Kingdom with title Postures

"The ingredients: an English girl in Paris, married to a Polish adventurer, who is imprisoned for theft and leaves her penniless, a stranger except for casual acquaintances in the foreign colony, to become the guest of an English couple, a man who desires her and can arouse her passion, and his wife, who keeps the girl in the home where she has her always under observation, always at a disadvantage, until she can finally crush her. The attitudes of the three are exposed with pitiless precision—the utter helplessness of the victim, the diabolic ingenuity of the wife, the social cowardice of the husband which makes a peculiarly disgusting setting for his lust. The background of Paris, in its cold hostility, with its tedious round of mechanical pleasures, throws the episode into harsh relief." Bookman (NY)

Rhys, Jean

★ **Wide** Sargasso Sea; introduction by Francis Wyndham. Norton 1967 189p

First published 1966 in the United Kingdom

This novel, "set in Dominica and Jamaica during the 1830s, presents the life of the mad Mrs. Rochester from 'Jane Eyre,' a Creole heiress here called Antoinette Cosway; in the brief last section she is imprisoned in the attic in Thornfield Hall." Oxford Companion to Engl Lit. 6th edition

Ricci, Nino

The **origin** of species; a novel. Other Press 2010 472p pa $16.95

ISBN 978-1-59051-349-1; 1-59051-349-5

LC 2009-41070

First published 2008 in Canada

"Set in Montreal in the 1980s, [this] is the tale of Alex Fratarcangeli, a graduate student struggling with his dissertation, which seeks to link Charles Darwin's theory of evolution to human narrative. Alex's inability to make progress on his dissertation mirrors his inability to move forward in life. Though he effortlessly draws in a cast of colorful characters, he is unable to commit himself to anyone, in particular a five-year-old son about whose existence he has only recently learned. Two relationships among many, however, help him on his journey of self-discovery. One is with Esther, a young neighbor with multiple sclerosis; the other is with Desmond, an arrogant researcher whom Alex accompanied years before in the Galápagos Islands." Libr J

"A profoundly moving novel that lovingly creates a world of flawed but very real characters." Winnipeg Free Press

Rice, Anne

Angel time; a novel. Alfred A. Knopf 2009 267p (The songs of the seraphim) $25.95

ISBN 978-1-4000-4353-8; 1-4000-4353-0

LC 2009-15470

In this first volume of "a new series, 'The Songs of the Seraphim,' Rice sets up an intriguing premise: A hit man named Toby O'Dare, who finances a personal life of spiritual exploration and lute-playing through his success as an assassin, comes face to face with his guardian angel, Malchiah. As Malchiah explains Toby's life to him, he urges him to accept God's forgiveness and to take up the work of life rather than of death. Toby seizes his second chance at life, and Malchiah spirits him through the realm of 'Angel Time,' outside the world of 'Natural Time' and back to the past, to the Christmas season of 1257 in the little town of Norwich, where a Jewish family is under siege from an angry mob. It is Toby's task to bring peace to the town, and to Meir the poet and his wife, Fluria; his adventures in medieval England and France, in the guise of a Dominican friar, are a race against religious prejudice to save lives." New Orleans Times-Picayune

"Angelically inspiring. Devilishly clever." Kirkus

Rice, Anne

Blackwood Farm. Knopf 2002 527p (Vampire chronicles) $26.95

ISBN 0-375-41199-2

LC 2003-272519

In this ninth volume in the author's vampire chronicles "fledgling vampire Quinn Blackwood makes a desperate appeal to the older, stronger Lestat to save his loved ones from Goblin, a doppelganger out to destroy them. Since Quinn entered the dark world of the undead, the once caring and protective Goblin has amassed tremendous strength and a ruthlessness that cannot be controlled. Lestat is intrigued but refuses to make a decision until Quinn tells his life story. Slowly, the dark, Gothic settings and eccentric characters that make Rice's fiction so fascinating emerge." Libr J

Rice, Anne

Blood and gold; or, The story of Marius. Knopf 2001 471p (Vampire chronicles) $26.95

ISBN 0-679-45449-7

LC 2001-94703

This eighth volume of the Vampire chronicles features Marius, a mentor to Lestat, the creator of Armand, and the lover of Pandora. "The intellectual and artistic 'Child of the Millennia' meets ice-age Thorne, another vampire, who's just waking up after a very long sleep and is eager to hear his history. Marius grants Thorne's wish, taking him and the reader on a rollicking vampire adventure through time." Booklist

Rice, Anne

Blood canticle. Knopf 2003 305p (Vampire chronicles) $25.95

ISBN 0-375-41200-X

LC 2002-192475

This tenth volume of the Vampire chronicles takes up where "Blackwood Farm ended, the now-doppelganger-free Quinn Blackwood and Lestat save Quinn's true love, the witch Mona Mayfair, from certain death by making her an immortal. In his effort to attain sainthood, Lestat must deal with a lot of metaphysical angst. The opulent Blackwood estate and its spooky swamps, as well as New Orleans and a Caribbean isle, provide the settings for many elegant costume changes as the exquisite vampiric triumvirate gleefully suck several deserving victims dry and lay waste to dozens of a drug lord's minions." Publ Wkly

Rice, Anne

Christ the Lord: out of Egypt. Knopf 2005 336p $25.95

ISBN 0-375-41201-8

LC 2005-44077

"Rice is a first-rate writer. There are no purple patches in this narrative, and no attempts to sermonize. There is a story to tell, and since we know the story on which it is based, Rice adroitly forces us to think about how she is going to weave in the gospel stories without sounding contrived or forced." Commonweal

Rice, Anne

Christ the Lord: the road to Cana. Knopf 2008 242p $25.95

ISBN 978-1-4000-4352-1; 1-400-04352-2

The second title in the author's projected four-volume life of Christ "opens with Jesus, known as Yeshua, as a young man, now more than 30, living with his extended family in the village of Nazareth. He knows who he is, or rather what he is, to be sure, but the path of this book takes him through his 40 days in the desert to the first great miracle of his ministry, the changing of water into wine. The story of Christ is the most famous story in the world; what revelations are there for the novelist? One of the great achievements of Rice's undertaking, thus far, is to reveal Christ's Jewish roots in all their strength and complexity. . . . Rice has achieved a prose style that is much simpler, much more straightforward, than that of her earlier works. Yet, in moments of revelation, her old breathless rapture serves her well." New Orleans Times-Picayune

Rice, Anne

The **Feast** of All Saints. Simon & Schuster 1979 571p

LC 79-16680

"The world of the Free People of Color (the 'gens de couleur libre') in antebellum New Orleans (the old French city) is the background for this romantic historical novel that brings to life an era and a place. . . . Quadroon Marcel Ste. Maria and his lovely sister Marie, children of a white plantation owner, and the lovely Cecile, his dusky mistress, grow up in the demimonde, housed and supported and educated as gentility by their father, but destined to be separated from his world by virtue of their mixed blood. . . . {The story} pits passion and principle and love against the hard realities of class and color in old New Orleans." Publ Wkly

Rice, Anne

★ **Interview** with the vampire; Reset for anniversary ed; Knopf 1996 340p $27.95; pa $7.99

ISBN 0-394-49821-6; 0-345-33766-2 pa

LC 96-232882

First published 1976

"In contemporary New Orleans a young reporter listens as Louis, a vampire, unfolds his tale. His story spans several hundred years . . . of a Faustian search for some meaning to his life-in-death existence, an existence complicated by his relationship to three other vampires. Lestat, the vampire who made him, is hated by Claudia, the five-year-old extraordinarily beautiful child-vampire Louis loves. . . . After Claudia attempts to kill Lestat she and Louis go to Europe in search of other vampires. In Paris they find Armand, Master Vampire, and he and Louis fall in love, remaining together for a time after Claudia's death in a state of meaningless immortality." Libr J

Followed by The vampire Lestat (1985); The queen of the damned (1988); The tale of the body thief (1992); Memnoch the Devil (1995); The vampire Armand (1998); Merrick (2000); Blood and gold; or, The story of Marius (2001)

Rice, Anne

Lasher; a novel. Knopf 1993 577p $30

ISBN 0-679-41295-6

LC 93-12246

"Returning to the Mayfair clan she introduced in The Witching Hour Rice offers another vast, transcontinental saga of witchcraft and demonism in the tradition of Gothic melodrama. . . . Embedded in this antique demonism is a contemporary tale of incest and family abuse that achieves resonance. It is maintained through the character of Lasher, both child and man at the same time, who manipulates his victims with his own pain. At their best, Rice's characters rise above the more wooden plot machinations with an ironic and modern complexity." Publ Wkly

Followed by Taltos

Rice, Anne

Memnoch the Devil. Knopf 1995 353p (Vampire chronicles) $25

ISBN 0-679-44101-8

LC 95-77866

The fifth volume of the Vampire chronicles "finds vampire Lestat de Lioncourt being courted by fallen archangel Memnoch, a.k.a. Satan, to be his lieutenant in Hell, but not for the purpose of pursuing evil. Memnoch instead desires Lestat's help in redeeming souls." Libr J

The author "boldly probes the significance of death, belief in the afterlife and other spiritual matters." Publ Wkly

Followed by The vampire Armand

Rice, Anne

Merrick; a novel. Knopf 2000 307p $26.95

ISBN 0-679-45448-9

LC 99-88556

"This volume merges several long-running plots. . . . Merrick must revisit the Guatemalan rainforest, where she traveled as a young girl, to locate a secret treasure trove of ominous ancient runes. Displaying her imaginative talents for atmosphere and suspense, Rice creates a riveting scene that shows Merrick's awesome magic at work." Publ Wkly

Rice, Anne

Of love and evil; the songs of the seraphim: a novel. Alfred A. Knopf 2010 171p $24.95

ISBN 978-1-4000-4354-5; 1-4000-4354-9

LC 2010-28267

"If this kinder, gentler Rice has you rattled, fear not, for the scenes in the seething cesspool of sin that typify Pope Leo X's Rome prove the author hasn't lost her verve for the seamier side of life." Minneapolis Star Tribune

Rice, Anne

★ The **queen** of the damned; the third book in the vampire chronicles. Knopf 1988 448p (Vampire chronicles) $27.50

ISBN 0-394-55823-5

LC 88-45311

"Don't let the title or the subject matter fool you; this is quality fiction written with care and intelligence. There are no false steps or wasted words in the multilayered plot, and the many characters each have a distinct voice. It's not absolutely necessary to have read the other 'Chronicles' to understand this one, but it would add greatly to the richness of the whole." Libr J

Followed by The tale of the body thief

Rice, Anne

The **tale** of the body thief. Knopf 1992 430p (Vampire chronicles) $30

ISBN 0-679-40528-3

LC 92-53085

"Readers who crave a happy ending, a justice and a moral coherence that transcend the muddle they really live in, may feel {the author} has broken faith with them. After all, isn't that what escapist fiction is supposed to provide? Grown-ups, on the other hand, will be intelligently entertained, and no more disquieted than usual." Newsweek

Followed by Memnoch the Devil

Rice, Anne

Taltos; lives of the Mayfair witches. Knopf 1994 467p $25

ISBN 0-679-42573-X

LC 93-35693

"This third book in the Mayfair Witches series tells the story of Ash, a centuries-old Taltos who resides in New york City. The Taltos grow to a height of seven feet, carry an extra set of chromosomes, and have a superior intelligence that enables them to digest dictionaries and encyclopedias in moments. There is something rotten in the state of the Talamasca, an order of scholars who study the supernatural and keep records of the Mayfair witches. When one such scholar is murdered, Rowan Mayfair, the mother of the two late Taltos in Lasher, and husband Michael Curry investigate. . . . Although this novel is a suspenseful and sometimes thought-provoking page-turner, it does not stand on its own; the first two books in the series must be read first." Libr J

Rice, Anne

The **vampire** Armand. Knopf 1998 387p (Vampire chronicles) $26.95

ISBN 0-679-45447-0

LC 98-14579

The sixth volume of the Vampire chronicles follows the vampire Armand "from his boyhood in Kiev Rus, a conquered city under the rule of the Mongols, to ancient Constantinople, where he is sold into slavery by vicious Tartars, to the palazzo in Renaissance Venice, where he meets the great vampire Marius, who gives him the gift of the vampire blood and shows him how to be an 'ethical' vampire. . . . As always, Rice paints a fascinating and dazzling historical tapestry, providing a beautifully written and incredibly absorbing tale." Booklist

Rice, Anne

The **vampire** Lestat; the second book in the chronicles of the vampires. Knopf 1985 481p (Vampire chronicles) $27.50

ISBN 0-394-53443-3

LC 85-40123

This novel "is ornate and pungently witty. In the classic tradition of Gothic fiction, it teases and tantalizes us into accepting its kaleidoscopic world. Even when they annoy us or tell us more than we want to know, its undead characters are utterly alive. Their adventures and frustrations are funny, frightening and surprising at once." N Y Times Book Rev

Followed by The queen of the damned

Rice, Anne

Vittorio the vampire; new tales of the vampires. Knopf 1999 292p $19.95

ISBN 0-375-40160-1

LC 98-14209

In this novel, "Vittorio tells of his human life and the dramatic events that led him to join the ranks of the undead. He is 16, living the privileged life of the nobility in Renaissance Italy, when a host of vampires savagely attacks his family. His parents, brother, and sister are ruthlessly murdered, but Vittorio has caught the eye of the beautiful vampiress Ursula and is spared. Eventually, Vittorio has his revenge on the demons who have destroyed his loved ones, but he pays a terrible price." Libr J

Rice, Anne

★ The **witching** hour; a novel. Knopf 1990 965p $29.95

ISBN 0-394-58786-3

LC 90-53103

Rice "tells the story of the prominent and wealthy Mayfair family who, for five centuries, has cavorted with a supernatural entity that has brought them both great bounty as well as abject misery. Neurosurgeon Rowan Mayfair inherits the family fortune, along with the sinister attentions of this entity. When Rowan saves the life of Michael Curry their fates become entwined, and together they seek to understand and destroy the terrible force that holds her family in its power. Helping them in this dangerous task is occult investigator Aaron Lightner. . . . Although a bit long-winded at times, this is still a compelling novel." Libr J

Followed by Lasher

Rice, Luanne

★ **Blue** moon. Viking 1993 305p

LC 92-50732

"Such a rare combination of realism and romance comes along well, once in a blue moon. You don't have to be a sucker for happy endings to love this book, but it helps." N Y Times Book Rev

Rice, Luanne

The **deep** blue sea for beginners; a novel. Bantam Books 2009 302p $26

ISBN 978-0-553-80514-7; 0-553-80514-2

LC 2009-13277

This sequel to Geometry of sisters is "about a reunion of a mother and her two daughters who've been separated for 10 years due to a disturbing secret. Set on the picturesque isle of Capri, Rice's touching tale reflects on how families can survive and thrive despite tragedies. Lyra Nicholson is a lonely heiress living in Italy while her equally lonely daughters, 16-year-old Pell and Lucy, a 14-year-old math whiz, live in Newport, R.I. with their grandmother. Lucy's already tried to contact (via equations) the ghost of her dead father with Beck, her BFF and the sister of Pell's boyfriend, Travis. Pell travels to Italy, wanting Lyra, who abandoned her and Lucy, to finally take responsibility for them. . . . Rice gives Pell an old-beyond-her-years stability that Lyra lacks in this beguiling beach read." Publ Wkly

Rice, Luanne

The **geometry** of sisters. Bantam Books 2009 319p $25

ISBN 978-0-553-80513-0; 0-553-80513-4

LC 2008-55703

"Maggie Shaw second-guesses herself all the way from Columbus, Ohio, to Newport, Rhode Island, after two tragedies threaten to tear her family apart. While on vacation, her husband drowned, and her oldest daughter Carrie ran away after surviving the accident. Maggie is uprooting her son Travis, the football star, and her fragile daughter Beck, who mourns the loss of her beloved sister, so she can support the family as a teacher at a unique private high school. Maggie's past is anchored to Newport, with her estranged sister and J. D., the man who drove a wedge between them, living nearby. . . . The always insightful and engaging Rice explores the mystical bond between sisters as she portrays families learning what it means to love and forgive." Booklist

Rice, Luanne

Home fires. Bantam Bks. 1995 312p

LC 94-23911

In this novel, "privileged New Yorker Anne Davis returns to her New England island childhood home after the death of her four-year-old daughter and the breakup of her marriage. Seeking solitude from her sister, who has never left the island, she finds kinship—and love—with a scarred fireman who understands tragedy, having survived it himself. At the same time she reconnects with her teenaged niece, whose high school days are in danger of becoming a haze of alcohol and lust. . . . A strikingly real story of family feelings and grief." Libr J

Rice, Luanne

Last kiss. Bantam Books 2008 339p $25

ISBN 978-0-553-80512-3; 0-553-80512-6

LC 2007-52179

"Rice makes a . . . return visit to the Hubbard's Point, Conn., setting of Beach Girls (2004). As the book opens, a year soaked in Wild Turkey has passed since singer/songwriter Sheridan Rosslare lost her son, Charlie, in a random New York mugging. While Sheridan drowns her sorrows, Charlie's girlfriend, Nell Kilvert, is more assiduous; she hires private investigator Gavin Dawson to prove there was nothing random about Charlie's death. For his part, Hubbard's Point native Gavin, a New York transplant, had pretty much written off Hubbard's Point after Sheridan, once the love of his life, dumped him for his wild and reckless ways years before. Now, older and wiser, he's still in love with Sheridan and wants to start over, but Sheridan's grief soon proves a formidable obstacle. An element of supernatural whimsy, a dark secret involving a trust fund and a disturbing question related to Charlie's estranged father, Randy, add complexity, while cameos from other Beach Girls characters contribute an engaging, homey touch." Publ Wkly

Rice, Luanne

The **letters**; [by] Luanne Rice & Joseph Monninger. Bantam Books 2008 199p $22

ISBN 978-0-553-80741-7; 0-553-80741-2

LC 2008-25627

"With each character–and each author–providing vivid descriptions of his and her surroundings and intense emotions, it's hard for the reader to remember that she is reading fiction and not eavesdropping on personal correspondence saturated with sadness and love." Booklist

Rice, Luanne

Little night; Luanne Rice. Pamela Dorman Books/Viking 2012 321 p.

ISBN 0670023566; 9780670023561

LC 2011049237

In this novel, "Clare Burke's life took a devastating turn when she tried to protect her sister, Anne, from an abusive and controlling husband and ended up serving prison time for assault. The verdict largely hinged on Anne's defense of her spouse—all lies—and the sisters have been estranged ever since. Nearly twenty years later, Clare is living a quiet life in Manhattan as an urban birder and nature blogger, when her niece, Grit, turns up on her doorstep. . . . Together they face the wounds inflicted by Anne and find in their new connection a place of healing. When Clare begins to suspect her sister might be in New York, she and her niece hold out hope for a long-awaited reunion with her." (Publisher's note)

Rice, Luanne

Safe harbor. Bantam Bks. 2002 337p

ISBN 0-553-80218-6

LC 2001-49954

A novel set in the seaside town of Black Hall, Connecticut. "Grief-stricken Dana Underhill returns home to care for her two nieces, Quinn and Allie, following the death of her sister, Lily, and Lily's husband, Mike, in a sailing accident. Dana, a professional painter, had intended to whisk her nieces back to France with her, but her plans are put on hold when she realizes that change may not be what's best for Quinn and Allie. Indeed, Quinn, a cigarette-smoking 12-year-old with a chip on her shoulder, is dead set against leaving, particularly since she's determined to uncover the circumstances surrounding her parents' deaths. . . . Dana's childhood acquaintance, oceanographer and Yale professor Sam Trevor, arrives to provide Dana with a shoulder to lean on and to help Quinn find the answers she seeks." Publ Wkly

Rice, Luanne

Summer light. Bantam Bks. 2001 372p

ISBN 0-553-80122-8

LC 2001-25475

A novel about wedding planner May Taylor and her "daughter, Kylie, a special child who seems to feel things more deeply than others and who sees angels. It's Kylie who brings her mother and Bruins hockey star, Martin Cartier, together. For Martin, its love at first sight, but May is leery of relationships. She finally agrees to marriage, but life is complicated as their careers require that they live alternately in Connecticut, Canada, and Boston. . . . With her gift, Kylie tries to unite the family in the face of tragedy, and the prolific Rice skillfully blends romance with magic." Booklist

Rich, David

Caravan of thieves; David Rich. Dutton 2012 295 p. $25.95

ISBN 0525952888; 9780525952886

LC 2012001870

In author David Rich's book, Rollie is "assigned undercover in Afghanistan to stop black-market weapons thefts . . . Recalled to Camp Pendleton when his undercover connection is killed, Rollie learns he's being tailed . . . Rollie soon learns he's being followed because the feds are tracing [stolen] military caskets full of money . . . Now word is circulating that [his con man father] Dan dug up one casket from a veteran's gravesite, and with Dan nowhere to be found, good guys and bad suspect devious Dan has the millions, and they want Rollie to find him." (Kirkus)

Rich, Nathaniel

The **mayor's** tongue. Riverhead Books 2008 310p $24.95

ISBN 978-1-594-48990-7; 1-594-48990-4

LC 2008-06832

"Both Eugene Brentani and Mr. Schmitz are on quests to the enchanted hinterlands of Italy's mountainous North—one for his disappeared lady love, the other for his inexplicably deteriorating best friend. Their journeys are distinct but complementary, not overlapping so much as being similarly mired in a fantastical domain ruled by the words and rumored presence of Constance Eakins, a celebrated lothario, philosopher king and profligate poet. The novel's foremost delight is its measured, nearly imperceptible descent into the realm of fairy-tale. There is no rabbit hole to fall through—reality and fairy-tale coexist, sharing the same borders, the same characters, and the same heartbreak for jilted lovers." Paste

Rich, Nathaniel

Odds against tomorrow; [a novel] Nathaniel Rich. 1st ed. Farrar, Straus and Giroux 2013 320 p. ill. (hardcover) $26

ISBN 0374224242; 9780374224240

LC 2012028928

In this novel, by Nathaniel Rich, "Mitchell Zukor, a gifted young mathematician, is hired by a mysterious new financial consulting firm, FutureWorld. . . . He is asked to calculate worst-case scenarios in the most intricate detail. . . . As Mitchell immerses himself in the mathematics of catastrophe. . . . Then, . . . an actual worst-case scenario overtakes Manhattan. Mitchell realizes he is uniquely prepared to profit. But at what cost?" (Publisher's note)

Rich, Virginia

The **baked** bean supper murders. Dutton 1983 267p

LC 83-70156

"Eugenia Potter arrives at her sometime home in Northcutt Harbor, Me., just in time for the annual baked-bean dinner. She is also just in time to see her dearest friends carried off, first by accident and then by natural causes. She begins to feel uneasy, and when her beloved weimaraner is electrocuted in an accident that saves her own life, she takes another look at the earlier deaths. While Mrs. Potter goes about discovering who is responsible for what she determines to be murder, we get to sample Maine cooking, complete with recipes." Publ Wkly

"Colorful and chatty, with a fleet of diverse, realistic characters, this novel presents the rich tapestry of small-town life." Libr J

Rich, Virginia

The **cooking** school murders. Dutton 1982 207p

LC 81-22162

"Harrington, Iowa, has its own 'beautiful people' and 12 of them gather for the first session of a gourmet cooking class. James Redmond, chef 'extraordinaire,' instructs his students in the versatility of a thin, sharp boning knife. The next day, the enrollment is minus three. One lies dead, stabbed with a boning knife. One is an apparent suicide and murderer. One is drowned accidentally. Eugenia Potter, home on a visit, knows the town and suspects that not all is what it seems." Publ Wkly

Rich, Virginia

The **Nantucket** diet murders. Delacorte Press 1985 276p

LC 84-21501

"It is the middle of winter in Nantucket, and a group of year-round residents, more or less well-to-do widows who call themselves 'Les Girls,' gather to welcome home an old friend, Eugenia Potter, an erstwhile member of the group who now resides in Arizona and Maine. Their latest subject for talk is the arrival of a charismatic diet doctor, the mysterious Count Tony Ferencz, who has Les Girls all in a flutter and looking better than they have in years. No sooner has Eugenia arrived however, than strange events begin to occur. . . . Eugenia finally manages to find the answers in a dangerous and suspense-filled conclusion. Fans of Nantucket and haute cuisine will find and enjoy both in this somewhat overlong, but well-written book." Publ Wkly

Richards, David Adams

The **bay** of love and sorrows; a novel. Arcade Pub. 2003 307p $24.95

ISBN 1-55970-650-3

LC 2002-38348

"Michael is as naive as the other downtrodden individuals Everette has chosen as pawns to carry out his darkly laid plans, and the tragic events that ensue will forever be ingrained in the minds of the townpeople residing in The Bay of Love and Sorrows. Richards' story falls into place with the ease of a domino rally, providing all of the elements for a riveting story." Booklist

Richardson, C. S.

The **end** of the alphabet. Doubleday 2007 119p $16.95

ISBN 978-0-385-52255-7; 0-385-52255-X

LC 2006-36823

"The surprise of this little book is not that it is poignant but that it is delightful: graceful, stylish, humorous, intelligent and lacking even the faintest whiff of sanctimony." Washington Post Book World

Richardson, Kat

Greywalker. Roc 2006 341p pa $14

ISBN 0-451-46107-X

LC 2006-11233

"Recovering from a brutal assault that had left her clinically dead for two minutes, private investigator Harper Blaine finds her perceptions have changed. Now she sees people that others can't and often struggles against a grayish mist that seems to permeate her world. A friendly couple with experience in the paranormal explain to her that she is a Greywalker, someone with the ability to cross between the living and the ghostly worlds. Suddenly, her life—and her business—grow a lot more interesting and much more dangerous. Richardson's first novel features a genuinely likable and independent heroine with a unique view of reality." Libr J

Richardson, Samuel

★ **Clarissa**; or, The history of a young lady. edited with an introd. and notes by Angus Ross. Penguin Books 1985 1533p

ISBN 0-14-043215-9

First published 1749

In this epistolary novel Clarissa Harlowe "has been coldly commanded by her tyrannical family to marry Mr. Solmes, a man she despises. She refuses, even though it pains her to defy her parents. Locked in her room, isolated from family and friends, Clarissa corresponds secretly with Robert Lovelace, a suitor disapproved of by her family; she finally throws herself upon his protection and flees with him. It soon becomes clear to her, however, that Lovelace's sole aim is to seduce her. Her virtue is so great that Lovelace becomes obsessively absorbed in breaking it down." Reader's Ency. 4th edition

Richardson, Samuel

★ **Pamela**; or, Virtue rewarded. edited with explanatory notes by Thomas Keymer and Alice Wakely; with an introduction by Thomas Keymer. 2008 xxlv, 546p (Oxford world's classics) pa $9.95

ISBN 978-0-19-953649-8; 0-19-953649-X

First published 1740-1741

"On the death of Pamela Andrews' mistress, her mistress's son, Mr. B, begins a series of mild stratagems designed to end in Pamela's seduction. These failing, he abducts her and renews his siege in earnest. Pamela spurns his advances, and halfway through the novel Mr. B offers marriage. In the second half of the novel, Pamela wins over those who had disapproved of the misalliance." Merriam-Webster's Ency of Lit

Richler, Mordecai

★ **Barney's** version; a novel, with footnotes and an afterword by Michael Panofsky. Knopf 1997 355p $25

    ISBN 0-679-40418-X

                      LC 97-37033

"What entertains and affects us in 'Barney's Version' is the headlong, spendthrift passage of a life, redeemed from oblivion in the unbridled telling. The edge of the grave makes a lively point vantage." New Yorker

Richler, Mordecai

★ **Solomon** Gursky was here; a novel. Knopf 1990 413p

                      LC 89-43393

Richler is a "ringmaster, making his performers do dazzling backflips without missing a beat. At the same time he is a moralist, recoiling from those who would sentimentalize the Holocaust or make power a sacrament." Time

Richler, Nancy

Your mouth is lovely; a novel. Ecco Press 2002 357p $25.95

    ISBN 0-06-009677-2

                    LC 2002-23521

This "novel summons up the lost world of the Russian shtetls around the Pripet marshes in Ukraine, and shows how those communities were first changed and then annihilated by the events that led, ultimately, to the Russian Revolution. At the center of Richler's tale is Miriam Lev, whose mother drowned herself when she was a day old, and who at age six is taken in hand by her father's new wife, Tsila, a harsh, beautiful seamstress who teaches Miriam the alphabet and dreams of another life. After an ill-starred and and painful series of events, Miriam ends up, at nineteen, in Siberia, having shot an officer of the Tsar at point-blank range. Miriam's hegira is told here as a letter to her own daughter, whom she hasn't seen since she gave birth to her, in prison. Richler's work recalls the stories of Isaac Babel, in which the knowable is charged with mystery." New Yorker

Richmond, Michelle

No one you know; a novel. Delacorte Press 2008 306p pa $15

    ISBN 978-0-385-34013-7; 0-385-34013-3; 978-0-385-34014-4 pa; 0-385-34014-1 pa

                    LC 2008-13508

"Twenty years ago, Ellie Enderlin's sister, Lila, a mathematical prodigy, was murdered, and Andrew Thorpe, Ellie's English professor and a friend, exploited the family's grief with a true-crime bestseller that claimed Peter McConnell, Lila's married lover and colleague, was the killer. On a coffee-buying trip to Nicaragua, Ellie encounters McConnell, whose life was destroyed by Thorpe's conjecture. Sparked by this meeting, Ellie traces her way back through

Lila's life and work, pursuing leads that the manipulative Thorpe abandoned when they did not fit his literary ambitions." Publ Wkly

"As complex and beautiful as a mathematical proof, this gripping, thought-provoking novel will keep you thinking long after the last page has been turned." Family Circle

Richter, Conrad

★ The **awakening** land. Knopf 1966 3v in 1

This trilogy depicts " a pioneer family and settlement's slow evolution from virgin wilderness to an organized community." Reader's Ency. 4th edition

Richter, Conrad

★ The **light** in the forest. Knopf 1953 179p

Companion volume to A country of strangers (1966)

"John Butler is kidnapped at the age of four and raised by Delaware Indians. Eleven years later, under a truce agreement between the Indians and the colonials, he is forcibly returned to his family. Irrevocably divided in his heart, he escapes and goes back to the Indians but is sent away after the failure of an Indian ambush." Shapiro. Fic for Youth. 3d edition

Richter, Conrad

★ The **sea** of grass. Knopf 1937 149p

"Set in New Mexico in the late 19th century, the novel concerns the often violent clashes between the pioneering ranchers, whose cattle range freely through the vast sea of grass, and the farmers, or 'nesters,' who build fences and turn the sod. Against this background is set the triangle of rancher Colonel Jim Brewton, his unstable Eastern wife Lutie, and the ambitious Brice Chamberlain. Richter casts the story in Homeric terms, with the children caught up in the conflicts of their parents." Merriam-Webster's Ency of Lit

Rickards, John

Winter's end; John Rickards. 1st U.S. ed; Thomas Dunne Books 2003 297p $23.95

    ISBN 0-312-31097-8

                    LC 2003-46874

"Sheriff Dale Townsend asks for an old friend's help in interrogating a very slippery and clever murder suspect in small-town Maine. Dale himself found the suspect standing over the victim clutching the alleged murder weapon, but the guy refuses to give his name or answer any questions. When Dale's PI friend Alex Rourke, an ex-FBI agent good at interrogation, appears, he bores a few chinks in the guy's armor. Strangely, the suspect knows about Alex and seemed to expect him. An attention-getting plot, riveting prose, calculated suspense, and tense, human-interest subplotting mark this noteworthy first novel." Libr J

Ricks, Thomas E.

A **soldier's** duty; a novel. Random House 2000 250p $24.95

    ISBN 0-375-50544-X

                    LC 2001-18601

"When a peacekeeping mission in Afghanistan goes tragically wrong, officers led by Gen. B.Z. Ames form a treasonous group called the 'Sons of Liberty' to unravel American foreign policy and further General Ames's position. Army majors Cindy Sherman and Bud Lewis are newly assigned to the Pentagon, where they become involved in both sides of the developing problem." Libr J

"One would have to look far for a novel that touches so deftly on the complexities and challenges of leadership of military organizations at the highest levels." Parameters

Ridley, John
A **conversation** with the Mann; a novel. Warner Bks. 2002 433p
ISBN 0-446-52836-6
LC 2001-52605

This "roman a clef is set against the backdrop of 19501960s Hollywood, Rat Pack Las Vegas and the Civil Rights movement, The fictional narrator is a mordant, world-weary Harlem-raised black comic, Jackie Mann, who irreverently recounts a journey from poverty to his symbol of success, an appearance on The Ed Sullivan Show, a path strewn with compromise and degradation. . . . Ridley vividly brings to life noirish panoramas of high-stakes show business, as well as the myriad humiliations endured by a black man trying to win fame in segregated America. The novel is a veritable 'who's who' of well-known showbiz personalities." Publ Wkly

Rigosi, Giampiero
Night bus; translated from the Italian by Ann Goldstein. Bitter Lemon Press 2006 348p pa $14.95
ISBN 1-904738-11-7
LC 2006-386274

Original Italian edition, 2000

"Francesco is a gambling-addicted bus driver in Bologna, with a thuggish debt collector on his trail; Leila is a smart dame with a great pair of legs, who each night looks for a man to bed, drug, and rob. In perfect noir fashion, the two become uneasy allies, trying to escape a pair of vicious intelligence agents after Leila unknowingly swipes a mysterious document from a victim's apartment. Rigosi somewhat overdoes character quirks—one agent has a condition that leads him to constantly leak tears as he slices apart his victims—but an ever-expanding cast of creeps and criminals keeps the plot accelerating, and he describes the dripping of blood and the angle of a broken neck as lovingly as the preparation of a nice eggplant parmigiana." New Yorker

Riley, Judith Merkle
In pursuit of the green lion. Delacorte Press 1990 440p
LC 90-32498

"In this non-stop picaresque adventure quips fly as thickly as a barrage of arrows; a steady stream of drunken noblemen, corrupt priests, scheming ladies and truculent ghosts keep the action white-hot." Booklist

Riley, Judith Merkle
The **serpent** garden. Viking 1996 467p
ISBN 978-0670866618
LC 95-36067

"Susanna Dallet is determined to support herself after the untimely death of her spouse and turns to the art of miniature portraiture, a profession she learned from her enlightened father. After Susanna becomes enmeshed in the politi-

cal intrigue of the court of Henry VIII, she is sought after by a heretical religious sect, a minor demon, and a free-spririted archangel, all of whom believe she is the key to their success. Riley . . . creates a stunning period fantasy that combines historical detail with magical realism." Libr J

Riley, Judith Merkle
A **vision** of light. Delacorte Press 1989 442p
LC 88-17514

This "is a chronicle rich with the ambience and flavor of the Middle Ages, but it is a 14th-century story told with a 20th-century sensibility." N Y Times Book Rev

Followed by In pursuit of the green lion

Riley, Lucinda
The **girl** on the cliff; a novel. Lucinda Riley. Atria Books 2012 407 p. (trade paper) $15
ISBN 1451655827; 9781451655827; 9781451655858
LC 2012027861

In this book by Lucinda Riley, "after a heartbreaking miscarriage, Grania Ryan abandons New York . . . to return to her rural Irish roots in a wind-swept coastal village. There, she befriends a motherless red-haired child, despite her own mother's cryptic warnings, and becomes involved with the rich, reclusive Lisle family. Only after she has given her heart to the girl, Aurora, does Grania's mother hand over a packet of letters that explains the long-standing family feud." (Kirkus Reviews)

Rinaldi, Nicholas
Between two rivers. HarperCollins 2004 448p $24.95
ISBN 0-06-057876-9

"Though the timeline of Between Two Rivers steers inevitably toward the horrors of 9/11, there is nothing overdetermined or reductive about the stories themselves. Rinaldi . . . indulges his characters in their untidy lives, and readers who do the same will find their patience rewarded." N Y Times Book Rev

Rindell, Suzanne
The **Other** Typist; Suzanne Rindell. Amy Einhorn Books/Putnam 2013 368 p. (hardcover) $25.95
ISBN 0399161465; 9780399161469
LC 2013000995

In this novel, by Suzanne Rindell, "Rose Baker [is] . . . a typist in a New York City Police Department precinct. . . . It is 1923, . . . a new era for women, and New York is a confusing place for Rose. . . . Prudish Rose is stuck in the fading light of yesteryear. . . . When glamorous Odalie, a new girl, joins the typing pool, . . . the two women navigate between the sparkling underworld of speakeasies by night and their work at the station by day." (Publisher's note)

Rinehart, Mary Roberts
The **circular** staircase; with illustrations by Lester Ralph. Bobbs-Merrill 1908 362p il

Featuring the detective talents of Mr. Jamieson, this novel concerns a maiden aunt and her nephew and niece who take a country house for the summer and are plunged into a series of mysterious crimes

Rinehart, Mary Roberts

Miss Pinkerton: adventures of a nurse detective. Rinehart 1959 403p

Two short stories and two novels featuring the exploits of nurse Hilda Adams

Rinehart, Steven

Built in a day; a novel. Doubleday 2003 241p $23.95

ISBN 0-385-49855-1

LC 2003-41968

"The charm of the protagonist, clearly, is not the primary appeal of this novel. The charms of Rinehart's writing, however, more than countervail; though stripped-down and deadpan, his sentences pack a lot of raw, juicy comic power." N Y Times Book Rev

Riordan, Rick

Cold Springs. Bantam Bks. 2003 340p $23.95

ISBN 0-553-80236-4

LC 2003-40365

"Cold Springs is an east Texas wilderness boarding school for troubled teens. Haunted by his own unresolved guilt over his daughter's death from a heroin overdose nine years earlier, ex-teacher Chadwick now makes his living escorting children into this boot camp for losers, giving them a second chance whether they want it or not. When an ex-lover asks him to locate her self-destructive 15-year-old daughter and take her to Cold Springs, Chadwick finds himself involved in a case of blackmail, murder, and financial skullduggery." Libr J

Riordan's "voice is fresh yet sure, with insights so trenchant they nearly provoke tears. And Riordan's characters, even the minor ones, are achingly believable." Booklist

Rivas, Manuel

In the wilderness; Manuel Rivas; translated from the Galician by Jonathan Dunne. Overlook Press 2005 170 p.

ISBN 1585674672; 9781585674671

LC 2005040603

This book is set in "the village of Aran, in Galicia, [where] a young girl (Rosa) notices a fresco that has suddenly appeared on a church wall, depicting gorgeously arrayed females whom she presumes to be saints. Aran's priest, Don Xil, however, assures his parishioners that the figures are embodiments of the Seven Deadly Sins. This accusation was perhaps unwise, for Don Xil dies—and is reincarnated as a mouse . . . . As years pass, Rosa grows up and marries, bears her brutal husband Cholo three children, befriends the wealthy old woman (Misia) . . . , and takes a lover: 'Spider-man,' recently returned from working on a construction gang in New York City. These events" and others are observed by several people, including Don Xil, who have transmigrated into the bodies of animals after dying. (Kirkus)

Robards, Karen

Ghost moon. Delacorte Press 2000 313p $24.95

ISBN 0-385-31972-X

LC 99-47420

"Summoned home at the request of a dying stepaunt, single mom Olivia Morrison returns to LaAngelle Plantation in the steamy swamps of Louisiana with her eight-year-old daughter, Sara. . . . What she discovers is that her closest cousin, Seth, is also divorced and the father of an eight-year-old daughter, who suffers mightily from spoiled rich-kid syndrome. Meanwhile, alternate chapters detail the stalkings of a serial killer who preys on girls the same age as Sara. . . . As Olivia works toward reconciliation with her stepfamily, she is haunted by dreams of her mother's supposed suicide. She also finds herself romantically drawn to Seth." Booklist

Robards "has crafted a mossy modern gothic drenched in gore. . . . {She} conveys the dusty heat of the Louisiana summer, and has an ear for the nuances of dialogue." Publ Wkly

Robards, Karen

Shiver; Karen Robards. Gallery Books 2012 400 p. (hardcover: alk. paper) $25

ISBN 1451678673; 9781451678673; 9781451678680; 9781451678697

LC 2012037437

In this suspense romance novel, by Karen Robards, Daniel Panterro is rescued by tow truck driver Samantha. "Danny knows he hasn't seen the last of the vicious drug runners who kidnapped him from protective custody. His only recourse is to take his pretty savior hostage and force her to help him. . . . With ruthless killers stalking their trail, Sam's only choice is to trust this handsome, menacing stranger. But as she relinquishes control, Sam feels an unmistakable desire." (Publisher's note)

Includes bibliographical references

Robards, Karen

To trust a stranger. Pocket Bks. 2001 341p

ISBN 0-671-78653-9

LC 2001-52056

"Julie Carlson, once a poor girl from the wrong side of the tracks but now the beautiful owner of a successful boutique in Charleston, S.C., seems to have it all. As the novel begins, however, a hit man circles her suburban mansion: Julie's rich husband, Sid, has hired thugs to kill her. Unaware of the danger she is in but convinced that Sid is cheating on her, Julie slips out of the house just in time and follows her husband to the red-light district, where she serendipitously—and literally—runs into private detective Mac McQuarry, dressed up in drag to spy on a client's husband. . . . Soon she and Mac are working together to get the goods on Julie's crooked husband." Publ Wkly

Robb, Candace M.

The cross-legged knight; an Owen Archer mystery. {by} Candace Robb. Mysterious Press 2003 321p $23.95

ISBN 0-89296-772-2

LC 2002-27248

"When William of Wykeman, bishop of Winchester, fears reprisal after being blamed for the death of a local knight by his irate family, Owen Archer. . . must protect him. In the meantime, Owen copes with wife Lucie's overwhelming sorrow upon losing the child she was carrying." Libr J

"Once again, Robb provides the reader with an evocative and suspenseful whodunit thoroughly bolstered by a wealth of authentic historical detail." Booklist

Includes bibliographical references

Robb, Candace M.

A **gift** of sanctuary; an Owen Archer mystery. {by} Candace Robb. St. Martin's Press 1998 195p $22.95

ISBN 0-312-19266-5

LC 98-41394

In this medieval mystery Owen Archer returns "to his native Wales to inspect the duke's Welsh fortifications and to recruit two companies of archers in anticipation of a threatened French invasion of the British Isles. Joined on his journey by poet and author Geoffrey Chaucer, the two must solve a perplexing murder and investigate a possible case of treason against the crown." Booklist

"Robb deftly interweaves a complex story of love, passion and murder into the troubled and tangled fabric of Welsh history, fashioning a rich and satisfying novel." Publ Wkly

Robb, Candace M.

The **riddle** of St. Leonard's; a medieval mystery. [by] Candace Robb. St. Martin's Press 1997 303p

ISBN 978-0312169831

LC 97-16231

"The plague is taking its toll in 14th-century York, and all the one-eyed former royal spy wants is to weather it without losing any family members. However, Owen is called to detective duty by the master of St. Leonard's Hospital when its pensioners start dying in rapid succession." Publ Wkly

"An evocative historical mystery steeped in authentically gritty period detail." Booklist

Robb, J. D.

Naked in death. G.P. Putnam's Sons 2004 294p

ISBN 0-399-15157-5

LC 2003-54813

This is the first volume in the author's futursitic police procedural At death series. Over thirty titles have followed

"Naked in Death features Lt. Eve Dallas of the NYPD as she searches for a serial killer of prostitutes. It hints at the isolation, neglect, and sexual abuse that Eve suffered as a child, memories that she tries to suppress. The adult Eve is slow to trust and awkward when faced with affection and kindness. Yet over the course of this series, she acquires a husband, Roark; a partner, Peabody; and a varied host of friends—hardboiled reporter Nadine, humanitarian doctor Louise, and worldly wise, bursting with life, rock star Mavis." Libr J

Robbins, Charles

The **accomplice**; a novel. Charles Robbins. 1st ed. Thomas Dunne Books 2012 viii, 356 p.p (hardcover) $24.99

ISBN 1250010519; 9781250010513; 9781250018359

LC 2012026602

This book by Charles Robbins presents a "look at how love, lust, and murder can derail a presidential campaign. Press secretary Henry Hatten . . . accepts a top spot in the presidential campaign of Sen. Tom Peele, a moderate Nebraska Republican. . . . Peele has a decent shot at the upcoming nomination. Unfortunately, he also has . . . a tendency to skirt and often cross lines that are at least unethical and sometimes illegal." (Publishers Weekly)

Robbins, David L.

The **last** citadel; a novel of the Battle of Kursk. Bantam Bks. 2003 421p $24.95

ISBN 0-553-80177-5

LC 2003-44304

"The battle for the Soviet city of Kursk in July 1943 during World War II involved two million soldiers. Code-named Citadel, it was Hitler's frenzied—and final—attempt to defeat Russia on the eastern front and was the largest buildup of German armed power of the war. Robbins re-creates the battle in this rousing novel: its characters being Hitler; his generals and advisers; Russian, German, and Spanish foot soldiers and tank drivers; fighter pilots (both men and women); partisans; and even elderly men and women digging trenches." Booklist

Includes bibliographical references

Robbins, David L.

War of the rats; a novel. Bantam Bks. 1999 392p $23.95

ISBN 0-553-10817-4

LC 98-43918

"The final confrontation takes a while to play out, but once Robbins . . . gets to the heart of the matter, he presents a riveting account of a battle within a battle, and the sniper motif proves an ideal vehicle to analyze the strengths and weaknesses of both sides." Publ Wkly

Includes bibliographical references

Robbins, Harold

Sin city. Forge 2002 383p $25.95

ISBN 0-7653-0001-X

LC 2002-69257

"Though questions linger about just how much Robbins contributed to later books published under his name, this posthumous novel moves quickly and is great fun, a roman à clef reminiscent of his early bestselling bildungsroman." Publ Wkly

Robbins, Tom

Fierce invalids home from hot climates. Bantam Bks. 2000 415p

ISBN 0-553-10775-5

LC 99-51683

"Switters, the protagonist, is an errand boy for the CIA, a secret lover of Broadway show tunes and a pedophile. On assignment in Peru . . . Switters encounters a Kandakandero medicine man who gives him mind-altering drugs and wisdom, but in exchange inflicts a curse: if Switters's feet ever touch the ground, he will be struck dead instantly. So Switters spends the rest of the novel in a wheelchair, although this in no way slows him down. He returns to Seattle, chases after his 16-year-old stepsister and numerous art students, then embarks on a mission to Syria to sell gas masks to Kurds; there, he beds a nun who even so remains a virgin. In true Robbins style, the writing throughout is lush and sexy, containing a great deal of witty social and political commentary." Publ Wkly

Robbins, Tom

Half asleep in frog pajamas. Bantam Bks. 1994 386p

LC 94-11549

In this novel "Gwen, an endangered stockbroker, is involved with straitlaced Belford and his born-again monkey. When she is attracted to Larry—who has cancer and is currently between trips to Timbuktu—she must choose among the American dream, the Timbuktu alternate, and something else." Libr J

"The yarn has a genuineness, a warmth, a humor, and an incredibly compelling plot, which hold our attention to the end." Booklist

Robbins, Tom

Jitterbug perfume. Bantam Bks. 1984 342p

LC 84-45233

"Priscilla Partido, a Seattle member of Daughters of the Daily Special (waitresses with college degrees), gets a beet tossed in her window; Madame Devalier and V'lu Jackson, New Orleans purveyors of fine perfume, get a beet too; so do the owners of LeFever Odeurs in Paris. What does it all mean? . . . The real theme here is immortality, in the person of Alobar, a 1000-year-old Nordic imp who sports across the globe (ending up as Einstein's janitor) with the secrets to olfactory wisdom and eternal life and love. Also at large is a Leary-esque philanderer, Wiggs Dannyboy, who as founder of an immortalist sect, the Last Laugh Foundation, accompanies Priscilla on her quest for happiness and the perfect (beet-based) scent. Robbins is still in top form, still mixing the lunatic and the thoughtful—or rather, doing a literary watusi up every page and jitterbugging back down." Publ Wkly

Robbins, Tom

Skinny legs and all. Bantam Bks. 1990 422p il

LC 89-18309

"A painter's struggle with her art, a restaurant opened as an experiment in brotherhood, the journey of several inanimate objects to Jerusalem, a preacher's scheme to hasten Armageddon, and a performance of a legendary dance: these are the diverse elements around which Robbins has built this wild, controversial novel. Ellen Cherry Charles, one of the 'Daughters of the Daily Special' in Jitterbug Perfume, takes center stage. She has married Boomer Petway and moved to New York, hoping to make it as a painter. Instead, she winds up a waitress at the Isaac and Ishmael, a restaurant co-owned by an Arab and a Jew. . . . Few contemporary novelists mix tomfoolery and philosophy so well." Libr J

Robbins, Tom

★ **Still** life with Woodpecker. Bantam Bks. 1980 277p

LC 81-103498

This novel "relates the meeting (at an ecological 'Care Fest') and subsequent love affair between Leigh-Cheri, an all-American princess of a deposed royal line, and Bernard Mickey Wrangle, alias The Woodpecker, an anarchistic bomber and self-styled 'outlaw.' He is captured and imprisoned; she . . . tries to remain close to him by mimicking his experience, living as a recluse in her parents' attic. When he rejects this as a futile gesture, she agrees to marry a fabulously wealthy oil-sheik and, having been introduced by her solitary incarceration with [a] packet of Camels to the mysteries of pyramid-power, demands a new, full-sized pyramid as a wedding gift. The story's climax is her reunion with Bernard in the inner sanctum of this pyramid." Times Lit Suppl

The author's "prose, as spasmodic as his heroine's sex life, is marbled with limping puns heavily splattered with recurrent motifs and a boyish zeal for the scatalogical." SLJ

Robbins, Tom

Villa incognito. Bantam Bks. 2003 241p $27.50

ISBN 0-553-80332-8

LC 2003-40353

"The novel begins with the story of Tanuki, a badgerlike Asian creature with a reputation as a changeling and trickster and a fondness for sake. Also part of the cast is a beautiful young woman who may or may not have Tanuki's blood in her veins. . . and three American MIAs who have chosen to remain in Laos long after the Vietnam War. Events are set in motion when one of the MIAs, dressed as a priest, is arrested with a cache of heroin taped to his body. In vintage Robbins style, the plot whirls every which way, as the author, writing with unrestrained glee, takes potshots at societal pillars: the military, big business and religions of all ilks. The language is eccentric, electrifying and true to the mark." Publ Wkly

Roberts, Gillian

The **bluest** blood; an Amanda Pepper mystery. Ballantine Bks. 1998 230p $22

ISBN 0-345-40326-6

LC 97-26868

"Something isn't quite right with Philadelphia bluebloods Neddy and Tea Roederer, benefactors of the Philadelphia Prep School library. Philly Prep teacher and amateur sleuth Amanda Pepper sees the first signs in the Roederers' son's glum manner. Then a more urgent problem appears: the crusade of the Reverend Harvey Spiers' book-burning Moral Ecologists—the same Reverend Spiers whose stepson, Jake, is best friends with the Roederers' son. As Amanda talks with both boys, she realizes there are much deeper problems, and when the crusading Reverend Spiers is murdered, she knows things have spun out of control." Booklist

A "swift and intriguing spin through the sometimes murderous precincts of Philadelphia." Publ Wkly

Roberts, Gillian

★ **Helen** hath no fury; an Amanda Pepper mystery. Ballantine Bks. 2000 228p $23

ISBN 0-345-42933-8

LC 00-40360

"Roberts skillfully negotiates some rather tricky emotional waters in this . . . addition to a series notable for its smooth mix of traditional mystery conventions with the darker underpinnings of modern crime fiction." Publ Wkly

Roberts, Gillian

The **mummers'** curse; an Amanda Pepper mystery. Ballantine Bks. 1996 231p $21

ISBN 0-345-40323-1

LC 96-3472

"Philadelphia schoolteacher Amanda Pepper . . . . witnesses the murder of a clown in the Mummer's Parade. When a fellow teacher (and principal suspect) falsely names Amanda as his alibi, she begins sleuthing. Fascinating plot and wit-filled prose." Libr J

Roberts, Kenneth Lewis

Arundel; by Kenneth Roberts. Doubleday, Doran 1930 618p

"An historical novel of the Revolutionary period, the setting of which is the garrison house at Arundel in southern Maine. Steven Nason, the hero of the story, goes with his friend Benedict Arnold on a hazardous expedition against Quebec. Young Nason has a very personal interest in the success of the enterprise, since Mary Mallinson, the girl he loves, has been taken by the Indians and is a captive in Quebec. Steven's recollections of the hardship and dangers of the expedition, and its blunders and failure in spite of individual acts of heroism, make up the bulk of the narrative." Freeport Journal-Standard

Followed by Rabble in arms

Roberts, Kenneth Lewis

Lydia Bailey; by Kenneth Roberts. Doubleday 1947 488p

"A susceptible young Maine lawyer who has fallen in love with the portrait of a girl he believes to be in Haiti reaches the island just as Napoleon's attempt to take over the government sets off the bloody . . . uprising under Toussaint. The hero finds the girl, and from that point the extremely elaborate plot carries them through an encounter with Tobias Lear, the pig-headed evil genius of Jefferson's State Department; spirited engagements against the French; capture by Barbary pirates and slavery in Tripoli; and, finally, the Tripolitan War and its intrigues and political jealousies." New Yorker

Roberts, Kenneth Lewis

Northwest Passage; by Kenneth Roberts. Doubleday, Doran 1937 709p

"This sprawling novel describes Major Robert Rogers' expedition in 1759 to destroy the Indian town of St. Francis and then his idea of finding an overland route to the Northwest. . . . In preparing his novel, Roberts made extensive research and unearthed documents that historians had believed were lost. The book is one of Roberts' best works." Benet's Reader's Ency of Am Lit

Roberts, Kenneth Lewis

Oliver Wiswell; {by} Kenneth Roberts. Doubleday, Doran 1940 836p

"The American revolution as seen by Oliver Wiswell, a young American who remained loyal to the English government, and was therefore the victim of fanatics, bent not only on fighting for liberty but also on destroying the liberty of others. Hounded out of his home in Milton, he fled to Boston with his father and a constantly devoted friend. He experienced there the privations of war and observed the tactical stupidities of the English. Then on to Halifax, England, France and finally back to America, where he fought with the Loyalists. The war over, Oliver found again his childhood sweetheart and turned with new hope to Nova Scotia." Booklist

Roberts, Kenneth Lewis

Rabble in arms; a chronicle of Arundel and the Burgoyne invasion. by Kenneth Roberts. Doubleday, Doran 1933 870p

Sequel to Arundel

The principal villain of this realistic, unromantic tale of the American Revolution is the American Congress, the real hero is Benedict Arnold. The story relates the adventures of a group of men from Arundel, Maine, who fight with the American forces in the campaign ending with the battle of Saratoga. Men and events, politics and battles are seen through the eyes of one Peter Merrill, mariner, who tells the story

Followed by The Lively Lady (1931) and Captain Caution (1934)

Roberts, Michele

Ignorance; Michèle Roberts. Bloomsbury USA 2012 240 p.

ISBN 9781608197712

LC 2011042283

This novel from Michele Roberts tells the "story of poverty and prejudice: two girls, one Catholic and the other a convert, grow up in a small town in Catholic France in the period before World War II. The war divides them from each other and their values. . . . Jeanne and Marie-Angèle attend the convent school in Ste. Madeleine. Marie-Angèle is Catholic and daughter of a local shopkeeper. Jeanne is Jewish and poor." (Kirkus)

Roberts, Michele

Reader, I married him. Pegasus Books 2006 229p pa $13.95

ISBN 1-933648-02-3

First published 2004 in the United Kingdom

"To say that Aurora has been unlucky in love is an understatement. Husbands one, two, and three all met untimely deaths, but now Aurora is ready to move on with her life. A trip to the Italian countryside, ostensibly to scout out new tempting tidbits for her London delicatessen and visit with her old friend, the feisty feminist turned convent abbess Leonora, seems just the ticket, and would have been, had not Aurora's domineering stepmother, Maude, arrived along with her parish priest, the oh-so-attractive and oh-so-mysterious Father Michael. Unable to stay at the convent for more than one night, Aurora is offered lodging in the museum apartment owned by another old friend, Frederico, a man whose sexual orientation Aurora has evidently mistaken. As Aurora succumbs to her passion for the erstwhile priest, Frederico expresses more than just friendship for the vulnerable Aurora. Roberts whimsically indulges her passion for favored themes of religion, sex, and food in this riotous and ribald tale that packs a didn't-see-that-one-coming ending." Booklist

Roberts, Nora, 1950-

Angel's fall. G. P. Putnam's Sons 2006 439p $25.95

ISBN 0-399-15372-1

LC 2006-40902

"After suffering a horrific shock, Reece Gilmore is slowly starting to put her life back together. Leaving her home in Boston, Reece travels around the country, but when she arrives in Angel's Fist, Wyoming, her car refuses to go any further. Planning on staying only until she earns enough money to fix her car, Reece takes a job as a cook in the Angel Food Cafe. Then, as she gets to know her new boss, her co-workers, and the other residents of the little town, including Brody, an annoyingly stubborn yet mysteriously sexy writer, she starts to believe that for the first time in a very long time, she may have found a place she might actually want to call home. Reece's hard-won happiness and sense of security is threatened, however, when she becomes not only the sole witness to a murder but also the next target of the killer, who is determined to drive her crazy. . . . Roberts deftly imbues a deliciously subtle sense of menace into a chilling and thrilling plot." Booklist

Roberts, Nora, 1950-

Dance upon the air; Nora Roberts. Jove Books 2001 386p (pbk.) $7.99

ISBN 0515131229; 9780515131222

LC 2002554345

In this book, "[w]hen Nell Channing arrives on charming Three Sisters Island, she believes that she's finally found refuge from her abusive husband—and from the terrifying life she fled so desperately eight months ago. . . . [I]n this quiet, peaceful place, Nell never feels entirely at ease. Careful to conceal her true identity, she takes a job as a cook at the local bookstore café—and begins to explore her feelings for the island sheriff, Zack Todd. . . . Just as Nell starts to wonder if she'll ever be able to break free of her fear, she realizes that the island suffers under a terrible curse—one that can only be broken by the descendants of the Three Sisters, the witches who settled the island back in 1692." (Publisher's note)

Sequel: Heaven and earth.

Roberts, Nora

Honest illusions. Putnam 1992 383p

ISBN 0-399-13761-0

LC 92-277

"Max Nouvelle is the patriarch of a family of magicians and jewel thieves made up of Lily, his partner in love; Roxanne, his headstrong, beautiful daughter; and Luke, the abused runaway Max had taken in years ago, now a charming young man. They join Max in elaborate performances onstage and in equally elaborate robberies. For years Roxanne and Luke battle constantly, but as young adults they finally realize they are deeply in love. Luke, haunted by the fear that his past will hurt his adopted family, is the target of coldblooded Sam Wyatt, driven by a vow of revenge on the Nouvelles." Publ Wkly

Roberts, Nora

Midnight Bayou. Putnam 2001 352p

ISBN 0-399-14824-8

LC 2001-41643

"When wealthy Boston attorney Declan Fitzgerald discovers that Manet Hall, a dilapidated mansion on the bayou just outside New Orleans, is for sale, he leaves his practice and moves in to renovate, restore, and redecorate. Independent and tough, bar owner Lena fascinates him from the minute he lays eyes on her. Believing that he's incapable of romance, he's amazed by how quickly and overwhelmingly he falls head over heels in love with her. But he worries about his own sanity when he experiences fugue states that leave him with memories of events and people who lived in the mansion more than 100 years earlier. . . . Roberts has cleverly crafted an enticing tangle of times and relationship." Booklist

Roberts, Nora

River's end. Putnam 1999 420p $23.95

ISBN 0-399-14470-6

LC 98-36160

"One summer night in 1979, four-year-old Olivia Tanner finds her doped-up father, Sam, bloodied shears in hand, poised over the dead body of her movie-star mom. Haunted by the image of 'the monster' pursuing her, Olivia is sent to live with her grandparents in the Pacific Northwest, where she is sheltered from her memories by towering Douglas firs. Two decades later, the specter of the 'monster' returns. From prison, her father urges young investigative reporter Noah Brady—son of the police detective who discovered Olivia after the murder—to research the crime." Publ Wkly

Roberts, Nora, 1950-

Whiskey Beach; Nora Roberts. G. P. Putnam's Sons 2013 496 p. (hardcover) $27.95

ISBN 0399159894; 9780399159893

LC 2012047883

In this novel, by Nora Roberts, "a Boston lawyer, Eli has weathered an intense year . . . after being accused of . . . the murder of his soon-to-be-ex wife. He finds sanctuary at Bluff House. . . . Abra Walsh is always there, though. Whiskey Beach's resident housekeeper, yoga instructor, jewelry maker, and massage therapist, Abra is a woman of many talents--including helping Eli take control of his life and clear his name." (Publisher's note)

Roberts, Nora, 1950-

The witness; Nora Roberts. G.P. Putnam's Sons 2012 488 p.

ISBN 0399159126; 9780399159121

LC 2011049445

In this suspense romance novel by Nora Roberts, "[a] young woman in hiding from the Russian mob faces a difficult decision when she falls in love with a cop. . . . Gifted with an eidetic memory, an IQ over 200 and an affinity for cool, calculated mayhem, Liz/Abigail is a skilled hacker and a highly paid security consultant. In her spare time she investigates the Russian mob and the crooked federal agents who are responsible for her current predicament; whenever possible, she throws virtual monkey wrenches into the mob's Internet scams. When she witnesses an altercation between

LIST OF FICTIONAL WORKS

Brooks and the wastrel son of a local magnate, she's thrust back into the horror of the last time she witnessed a crime. . . . Before they can marry, Brooks must help Liz come in from the cold." (Kirkus)

Roberts, Victoria

After the fall; an illustrated novel. by Victoria Roberts. W. W. Norton & Company 2012 184 p. (hardcover) $24.95

ISBN 0393073556; 9780393073553

LC 2012023516

This novel by Victoria Roberts "introduces us to a brilliantly eccentric family from New York's Upper East Side. . . . One fateful day, Alan returns home to find that the family has gone bust, not even a penny to be found. The next morning, to the children's surprise, the family wakes up in Central Park along with the entire contents of their penthouse arranged just as before--art, furniture, pugs, and all. . . . the family makes Central Park into a comfortable and creative home." (Publisher's note)

Robertson, Imogen

Anatomy of murder; Pamela Dorman Books 2012 382 p.

ISBN 9780670023172

LC 2011036291

In this novel, "[s]pies, corpses, tarot cards and countertenors combine in this . . . adventure featuring a pair of amateur sleuths in 18th-century London. . . . Mrs. Harriet Westerman, one half of the detective duo, is preoccupied with the mental health of her naval captain husband James, wounded after capturing a French ship carrying a spy during the war with the American Rebels. Now Harriet and her forensic scientist friend Gabriel Crowther are invited by the British authorities to help trace the espionage links to London, starting with the examination of a body found floating in the Thames. These investigations, and the dark fears of a slum-dwelling fortune-teller[, are depicted]." (Kirkus)

Robertson, Imogen

Circle of shadows; Imogen Robertson. Viking 2013 384 p. (hardcover) $27.95

ISBN 9780670026289

LC 2013009688

This book by Jenny Robertson "takes widow Harriet Westerman and her investigative partner, anatomist Gabriel Crowther, to Germany's Duchy of Maulberg, where her brother-in-law, Daniel Clode, has been charged with murder. Clode, disoriented and bleeding from an apparent suicide attempt, was found behind a locked door near the smothered corpse of Maria Martesen. . . . Westerman and Crowther, having doubts about Clode's guilt, soon find evidence suggesting someone else was the killer." (Publishers Weekly)

Robertson, Imogen

Instruments of darkness. Pamela Dorman Books/Viking 2011 373p $26.95

ISBN 978-0-670-02242-7; 0-670-02242-X

LC 2010-33777

First published 2009 in the United Kingdom

"The plot is a little loopy, but the dialogue crackles along, and Robertson's enjoyment of the period and her characters

is infectious. One begins not to mind the incongruity of it all — in the 18th century, could Harriet really befriend a single gentleman like Crowther without scandal? — not to mention Harriet's surprisingly modern ruminations on subjects like breastfeeding. Even the appearance of characters who seem to have been recycled from other books — the enigmatic manservant, the kindly guardian — becomes part of the fun." N Y Times Book Rev

Robertson, Imogen

Island of bones; Imogen Robertson. Pamela Dorman Books 2012 384 p.

ISBN 0670026271; 9780670026272

LC 2012003378

Sequel to: Anatomy of murder (2012) and Instruments of darkness (2011)

This novel by Imogen Robertson features "the forthright Mrs. Harriet Westerman and reclusive anatomist Gabriel Crowther. . . . In 'Island of Bones,' Crowther's haunting past is at last revealed. For years he has pursued his forensic studies -- and the occasional murder investigation -- far from his family estate. But an ancient tomb there will reveal a wealth of secrets. When laborers discover an extra body inside, the lure of the mystery brings Crowther home at last." (Publisher's note)

Robertson, Michael

The brothers of Baker Street. Minotaur Books 2011 274p $24.99

ISBN 978-0-312-53813-2; 0-312-53813-8

LC 2010-42020

"According to the terms of their lease, . . . Reggie and Nigel Heath were able to set up their modern-day law practice in the desirable 200 block of Baker Street by agreeing to answer all correspondence addressed to Sherlock Holmes at 221B. Reggie, the less whimsical of the pair, has been neglecting that responsibility, so . . . that task falls to Nigel, freeing up Reggie to concentrate on defending a young cab driver accused of robbing and killing two American tourists. An anonymous letter to Holmes gives Reggie a valuable tip, but the communications from a certain Professor Moriarty add a more sinister twist to this breezy and entertaining legal mystery." N Y Times Book Rev

Robinson, Elisabeth

The true and outstanding adventures of the Hunt sisters; a novel. Little, Brown 2004 327p $23.95

ISBN 0-316-73502-7

LC 2003-47713

"Over the course of about 200 letters (and a few e-mails), Robinson succinctly shows the full range of Olivia's emotions and relationships, from the optimism she tries to instill in her shocked family to the admiration she holds for Maddie's spouse. She poignantly portrays the frustration of trying to sustain a relationship while engaged in a consuming profession." USA Today

Robinson, Jeremy

Island 731; Jeremy Robinson. Thomas Dunne Books 2013 352 p. (hardcover) $25.99

ISBN 0312617879; 9780312617875

LC 2012042087

In this adventure novel, by Jeremy Robinson, "Mark Hawkins . . . is . . . working on board . . . a research vessel. . . . But his work is interrupted when . . . the ship . . . malfunctions and the crew is battered by a raging storm. When the storm fades . . . the beaten crew awakens to find themselves anchored . . . [at] a tropical island . . . and no one knows how they got there. Even worse, the ship has been sabotaged, two crewman are dead and a third is missing." (Publisher's note)

Robinson, Kim Stanley

2312; Kim Stanley Robinson. Orbit 2012 561 p.
ISBN 9780316098120

LC 2011044805

This science fiction novel takes place "In the year 2312, [when] humans have developed the technology to colonize most of the solar system, including Mercury, which boasts a single city that travels on rails around the planet just ahead of the rising sun. When Swan Er Hong arrives to mourn her recently deceased grandmother Alex, one of Mercury's movers and shakers, Swan realizes how little she knew about the woman who raised her. Meeting some of Alex's scientific friends reveals to Swan that mysterious projects were in the works and that she must uncover her grandmother's secrets before they destroy not only Mercury but the entire solar system." Kim Stanley Robinson presents a "portrait of a solar system economy based on the mining of the asteroid belt." (Libr J)

Robinson, Kim Stanley

★ **Antarctica**. Bantam Bks. 1998 511p $24.95
ISBN 0-553-10063-7

LC 97-41701

This is "an exhilarating addition to a body of work distinguished by two elements all too rare in modern science fiction: a sense of character and a sense of place. Robinson brings the two together by writing about people who are in love with where they are." N Y Times Book Rev

Robinson, Kim Stanley

Blue Mars. Bantam Bks. 1996 609p
ISBN 9780553101447 out of print; 9780553573350; 9780553898293

LC 95046700

In this concluding volume of the trilogy "colonists almost succeed in terraforming Mars. While they fight for independence from Earth and attempt to avert a civil war, they find their new civilization threatened by an ice age." Libr J

Robinson, Kim Stanley

Galileo's dream. Ballantine Books 2010 532p $26
ISBN 978-0-553-80659-5; 0-553-80659-9

LC 2009-42729

"Kim Stanley Robinson is one of the great 'hard science fiction' authors and this novel is no exception, with fantastic theories of the evolution of science, quantum theory and the true nature of time. Galileo's Dream is a little slow paced in the beginning but unfolds to a very thought-provoking and fresh science fiction novel with a very engrossing story challenging preconceptions about time, reality and history itself." Sciencefictionandfantasy.co.uk

Robinson, Kim Stanley

The **Martians**. Bantam Bks. 1999 336p hardcover o.p. pa $7.50
ISBN 0-553-80117-1; 0-553-57401-9 pa

LC 99-13115

Set in the universe of the author's Mars trilogy this volume includes vignettes, essays, fables, poems, and the following short stories: Michel in Antarctica; Exploring Fossil Canyon; Maya and Desmond; Four teleological trails; Coyote makes trouble; Michel in provence; Arthur Sternbach brings the curveball to Mars; Jackie on Zo; Keeping the flame; Big Man in love; Sexual dimorphism; What matters; Sax moments; A Martian romance; Purple Mars

"Also included is 'Green Mars,' a previously published novella about climbing Olympus Mons, the highest mountain in the solar system. . . . Some of the pieces here will be of interest only to those who have already read the trilogy, but the finest of the short fiction stands firmly on its own. As is the norm with Robinson's work, the stories are beautifully written, the characters are well developed and the author's passion for ecology manifests on every page." Publ Wkly

Robinson, Kim Stanley

★ **Red** Mars. Bantam Books 1993 519p il hardcover o.p. pa $7.99
ISBN 0-553-09204-9; 0-553-56073-5 pa

LC 92-21607

The story "concerns the first permanent settlement on Mars, a multinational band of 100 hardy experts, and their mission {of terraforming it}—to begin making Mars habitable for humans by releasing underground water and oxygen into the atmosphere. Unfortunately, they are divided over whether this is a desirable step in human evolution or an ecological crime." (Booklist)

"A novel fully inhabited both by detailed technical processes and by people whose careers those processes are; it is also a novel with a complex sense of political reality. . . . This is one of the finest works of American SF because it is one of the few that aspire to the dignity of the genuinely tragic." Times Lit Suppl

Other titles in the Mars trilogy are:
Blue Mars (1996)
Green Mars (1994)

Robinson, Kim Stanley

★ The **years** of rice and salt. Bantam Bks. 2002 658p
ISBN 0-553-10920-0

LC 2001-43492

"Because this alternate history is set in the same lawful universe as ours, its science must be the same. Because its people have the same basic human needs, their societies resemble ours. However, as events march toward the alternative year of 2002, some of his characters come to believe, despite much evidence to the contrary, that they can change the way they live. The reader is left to ponder whether this is an illusion." N Y Times Book Rev

Robinson, Lewis

Water dogs; a novel. Random House 2009 244p $25

ISBN 978-1-4000-6217-1; 1-4000-6217-9

LC 2008-16564

"Bennie knows that the details of his life don't show well. A twenty-seven-year-old college dropout with stalled ambitions, he works at an animal shelter and lives with his bullheaded older brother, Littlefield, in their old family home on Meadow Island, Maine... When a massive blizzard hits the state one Saturday afternoon, Bennie, Littlefield, and a crew of roughneck war-game enthusiasts decide to play paintball at the local granite quarry. Bennie accidentally falls into a gully, landing in the hospital, and wonders if his life can get any worse. But when one of the players disappears during the storm and Littlefield becomes the main suspect in the disappearance, Bennie realizes that the game might have had much higher stakes. Then Littlefield takes off without a word of explanation, forcing Bennie to seriously question his loyalty to his enigmatic brother. With the guidance of his intrepid girlfriend, Helen, and his twin sister, Gwen, Bennie goes looking for answers. . . . Written in prose as arresting and spare as the novel's rural Maine setting, Lewis Robinson's Water Dogs is a marvel of modern fiction, a book rich in empathy that follows one man's path through the uncertainties of youth and loss toward self-discovery." Bookmarks

Robinson, Lynda Suzanne

Murder at the feast of rejoicing; a Lord Meren mystery. {by} Lynda S. Robinson. Walker & Co. 1996 229p $20.95

ISBN 0-8027-3274-7

LC 95-33190

This novel is set in "the sun-seared landscape of the Egyptian Nile in the days of Tutankhamun. One of the young Pharoah's close confidants, Lord Meren, visits his family estate for a brief rest but finds, instead, that his sister has invited a tedious group of friends and relatives for a family celebration. One of these unwelcome guests has the bad taste to be murdered." SLJ

"Good scholarship authenticates the historical setting; imagination provides the sense of danger and romance to make it come alive." N Y Times Book Rev

Robinson, Lynda Suzanne

Murder at the God's gate; a Lord Meren mystery. {by} Lynda S. Robinson. Walker & Co. 1995 236p $19.95

ISBN 0-8027-3198-8

LC 94-28806

"Young King Tutankhamun's chief adviser/agent Lord Meren, known to some as the Falcon, investigates the murder of a priest in a temple dedicated to the teenaged Tut. Robinson . . . surrounds Meren with palace and temple intrigue, authentic details of daily life, and frequent mention of a wide assortment of indigenous animals." Libr J

Robinson, Marilynne

★ **Gilead**. Farrar, Straus and Giroux 2004 247p $23

ISBN 0-374-15389-2

LC 2004-47063

"Gilead possesses the quiet ineluctable perfection of Flaubert's A Simple Heart as well as the moral and emotional complexity of Robert Frost's deepest poetry. There's nothing flashy in these pages, and yet one regularly pauses to reread sentences, sometimes for their beauty, sometimes for their truth." Washington Post Book World

Robinson, Marilynne

Home. Farrar, Straus & Giroux 2008 325p $25

ISBN 978-0-374-29910-1; 0-374-29910-2

LC 2008-18301

"There is almost no first-rate American fiction about what happens in a household where religion is the family business, but if you ever wondered what it's like to be a preacher's kid, you can't do better than 'Home.' Robinson's greatest achievement is that she manages to introduce the notions of belief and religious mystery without ever seeming vague. She never shies from uncomfortable truths." Newsweek

Robinson, Patrick

Kilo class. HarperCollins Pubs. 1998 442p $25

ISBN 0-06-019129-5

LC 97-51172

In this sequel to Nimitz class, "the plot concerns 10 formidable Soviet-built Kilo Class patrol submarines, which can run submerged at speeds up to 17 knots without being detected, travel 6,000 miles before refueling, and fire nuclear-tipped torpedoes. An insolvent Russian military has agreed to sell them to China. With the subs, China could control the Taiwan Strait, blocking Western trade routes. The Chinese could then attack and conquer Taiwan. The U.S. Navy must stop delivery of the subs without starting World War III." Booklist

Robinson, Patrick

Nimitz class. HarperCollins Pubs. 1997 411p il

ISBN 978-0060187552

LC 96-46872

"Military fiction fans will admire {the author's} authoritative exploitation of weaponry and tactics, however, and most readers will be engaged, despite some sluggish passages, by his persuasive cautionary tale about the perils of military downsizing at a time when rogue nations are amassing weapons of great and terrible destructiveness." Publ Wkly

Followed by Kilo class

Robinson, Peter

Caedmon's song The first cut. Dark Alley 2004 310p $13.95

ISBN 0-06-073535-X pa

LC 2003-67660

"Recent university graduate Kirsten survives a brutal Jack the Ripper-style attack of which she has no memory. As Kirsten recovers, she becomes fixated on finding the man who nearly killed her. Miles away, Martha has come to the coastal town of Whitby, where she is doing research for a book. Or is she? Carefully surveying her surroundings, Martha grows more obsessed with the object of her trip. The women's stories are told in alternate chapters until the unsettling end. This atmospheric tale of suspense will keep readers wondering what's really going on." Libr J

Robinson, Peter

Cold is the grave. Morrow 2000 369p

ISBN 0-380-97808-3

LC 00-37231

"Banks discovers the precariousness of Emily's position in her new life and, more disturbingly, the grotesque truth behind a facade of perfect family life. A cunningly constructed plot, enhanced by Robinson's engaging descriptions and insights." Booklist

Robinson, Peter

★ Innocent grave; an Inspector Banks mystery. Berkley Prime Crime 1996 346p

ISBN 978-0670869039

LC 95-38218

"Although the story follows the classical form of a whodunit, the characters have complexity and the issues range broad and deep, raising interesting moral questions about bigotry, class privilege and the terrible crime of being different." N Y Times Book Rev

Robinson, Peter

Piece of my heart. William Morrow 2006 336p $24.95

ISBN 978-0-06-054435-5; 0-06-054435-X

LC 2005-58363

The author "invokes the most disturbing aspects of the 60's—to the point at which even the Manson murders have repercussions in Yorkshire—to sustain the book's ominous mood. There is pathos too, as Banks winds up revisiting characters who were young and energetic in 1969 but are now tea-sipping retirees." N Y Times (Late N Y Ed)

Robinson, Roxana

Cost. Farrar, Straus & Giroux 2008 420p $25

ISBN 978-0-374-27187-9; 0-374-27187-9

LC 2007-47954

"It's a nice touch that no one much likes Carpenter, the bossy and authoritative purveyor of unwelcome information. One of Robinson's most impressive achievements is to show that even in extreme situations, individual personalities come into play, and people respond in characteristic ways. . . . Bleak though it undeniably is, 'Cost' is also a warmly human and deeply satisfying book, marking a new level of ambition and achievement for this talented author." Chicago Tribune

Robinson, Roxana

A perfect stranger; and other stories. Random House 2005 235p $23.95

ISBN 0-375-50918-6

LC 2004-59537

Robinson's "finely tuned realism, as well as her settings and characters—New York, its bedroom communities, the Eastern seaboard and the comfortable upper-middle-class living there—recall Cheever and Updike. . . . The collection's most affecting stories touch on the chasm between parents and children, husbands and wives. Robinson's ear is wonderful, her graceful prose a real pleasure." Publ Wkly

Robinson, Roxana

Sparta; Roxana Robinson. Sarah Crichton Books/Farrar, Straus and Giroux 2013 400 p. (hardcover: alk. paper) $27

ISBN 0374267707; 9780374267704

LC 2012034611

In this novel, "Conrad entered the Marines shortly before 9/11 with an ambition to do something big: He studied Greek military history in college, admiring the discipline of city-states like Sparta (hence the title) but neglecting that place's undercurrent of hubris. Returning home after two tours in Iraq to his sturdily middle-class family outside New York, Conrad is incapable of shaking off his experience." (Kirkus Reviews)

Robinson, Roxana

Sweetwater; a novel. Random House 2003 319p $24.95

ISBN 0-375-50916-X

LC 2002-31830

"Robinson writes big solid scenes bubbling with tension, that hold the reader's interest. She has always shown her characters' flaws, and the dark emotions stirred up by divorce and parenthood; here she has reached farther to relate her characteristic predicaments to the larger world outside." N Y Times Book Rev

Robinson, Spider

Callahan's con. Tor Bks. 2003 286p $23.95

ISBN 0-7653-0270-5

LC 2003-40285

"When Jake Stonebender and his wife, Zoey, move to Florida and open up the Place, the latest incarnation of the unusual bar once known as Callahan's Place, he acquires a collection of strange friends, including a talking German shepherd, a merman, and a foul-mouthed parrot. An encounter with the Florida bureaucracy over the homeschooling of his hyperintelligent daughter, Erin, and the intrusion of the local Mafia result in a grand scheme to outwit both intrusions and rescue Jake's missing wife in the process. Robinson's latest entry in his Callahan series features more zaniness, good humor, and bad jokes." Libr J

Robison, Mary

One D.O.A., one on the way; a novel. Counterpoint 2009 166p $23

ISBN 978-1-58243-305-9; 1-58243-305-4

LC 2008-35700

"Constructed of miniature, numbered packets of terse observations, darkly comic dialogues, lists dashed off in anger or despair, this novel by Mary Robison viscerally evokes the physical and emotional exhaustion of living in post-Katrina New Orleans, that erstwhile good-time city drowning in neglect. Decadence has always been the local specialty, and Robison evokes that as well in the monologue her frazzled narrator, Eve, unfolds in bits and pieces. Eve is married to Adam, a sardonic conceit, for what they are witnessing is clearly the destruction of something, not the creation. Eve has been struggling among the ruins to revive her business while attending with rather less determination to her husband. Afflicted with hepatitis and ennui, Adam has moved back in with his genteel parents and his drug-addicted twin brother. So tenuous is the marriage that Eve has trouble telling the two men apart. From time to time the narrative breaks the fourth wall of fictional illusion and bursts into a diatribe enumerating the woes of New Orleans, kicked to the curb like a used-up floozy. But the story has an appointment with destiny, and Robison makes sure it gets there." Boston Globe

Robotham, Michael

Say you're sorry; Michael Robotham. Mulholland Books 2012 433 p. $24.99

ISBN 0316221244; 9780316221245

LC 2012020772

In this novel by Michael Robotham, part of the Joe O'Loughlin series, "pretty and popular teenagers Piper Hadley and Tash McBain disappear one Sunday morning. . . . Three years later, during the worst blizzard in a century, a husband and wife are brutally killed in the farmhouse where Tash McBain once lived. A suspect is in custody, a troubled young man who can hear voices and claims that he saw a girl that night being chased by a snowman." (Publisher's note)

Robotham, Michael

★ **Suspect**; Michael Robotham. Doubleday 2005 360p. $24.95; (pbk.) $13.95

ISBN 0385508611; 9788496940277

LC 2004050156

This mystery thriller tells the story of "Joe O'Loughlin, a London psychologist, [who] loves his job and loves his family. . . . O'Loughlin's life takes two disastrous turns: first, he's diagnosed with Parkinson's disease; second, while helping Det. Insp. Vincent Ruiz on the case of a murdered nurse, Catherine Mary McBride, he becomes the primary suspect in the killing. The crime occurred close to O'Loughlin's London home, giving him opportunity, and it turns out that McBride had been his patient and had accused him of harassment, giving him plenty of motive." (Publishers Weekly)

Robotham, Michael

The **wreckage**. Mulholland Books/Little, Brown and Co. 2011 439p $24.99

ISBN 978-0-316-12640-3; 0-316-12640-3

LC 2011-12657

After being robbed of his briefcase, ex-cop Vincent Ruiz tracks down the thieves, who had mistaken him for someone else, and becomes unwittingly involved in unraveling plots surrounding bank bombings in Baghdad and a missing VP at an international finance powerhouse.

"This fast-paced, gritty, and violent tale of international crime and investigation, with a sharp political edge, will appeal to readers seeking summer fiction with depth." Libr J

Robson, Justina

Keeping it real. Pyr 2007 337p pa $15

ISBN 978-1-59102-539-9; 1-59102-539-7

LC 2007-483

First title in the author's Quantam gravity series

First published 2006 in the United Kingdom

"Life is anything but real in this entertaining fusion of SF and fantasy spiced with sex, rockin' elves and drunk faeries. . . . Deft prose helps the reader accept what in lesser hands would be merely absurd." Publ Wkly

Robson, Justina

Living next door to the god of love. Bantam Books 2006 453p pa $13

ISBN 0-553-58742-0

LC 2005-56271

Robson "handles her characters' voices with confidence and wit, weaving together multiple stories to produce an elaborate whole that's somehow, finally, compacted into a simple seed, a timeless myth of death and resurrection." Strange Horizons.com

Rock, Peter

My abandonment. Houghton Mifflin Harcourt 2008 240p $22

ISBN 978-0-15-101414-9; 0-15-101414-0

LC 2007-44412

"The narrative unfolds as a meditative interior monologue, with some of the plot developing beyond Caroline's immature comprehension, leaving tantalizing gaps for the reader to fill. Gaps that may be filled with crime and sex. Yet bit by bit steady as water dripping on limestone reality carves a groove in Caroline's consciousness, turning her childhood trust into a sense of betrayal. . . . If this is a Bildungsroman, it's one for grownups. Caroline comes of age in circumstances so harsh yet so tender that her redemption will be tempered by loss and uncommon learning." Newsday

Rock, Peter

The **Shelter** Cycle; Peter Rock. Houghton Mifflin Harcourt 2013 224 p. (hardcover) $23

ISBN 0547859082; 9780547859088

LC 2012040363

In this book, "Francine and Colville are friends who grew up in the Church Universal and Triumphant, adherents of the Violet Flame. Members believed in the coming apocalypse and the possibility of Soviet air strikes, building underground bunkers to protect themselves. But nothing happened, and the community broke up, leaving the two friends to negotiate the larger world on their own. Now married and pregnant, Francine is searching for a girl gone missing from her Idaho town when Colville shows up." (Library Journal)

Rodriguez, Linda

Every broken trust; Linda Rodriguez. 1st ed. Thomas Dunne Books/Minotaur Books 2013 304 p. (hardcover) $25.99

ISBN 1250030358; 9781250030351

LC 2013006992

In this novel, by Linda Rodriguez, "a party to celebrate the arrival of George 'Mel' Melvin, a Kansas City politician . . . , rapidly turns into disaster when Skeet's best friend, Karen Wise, stumbles on a body in Chouteau University's storage caves and is attacked herself. . . . Skeet . . . serving as chief of campus police . . . must struggle against the clock to solve a series of linked murders before . . . her best friend winds up in jail--or worse." (Publisher's note)

Rodriguez, Linda

Every last secret; a mystery. Linda Rodriguez. Minotaur Books 2012 289 p. (hardcover) $24.99

ISBN 1250005450; 9781250005458; 9781466802285

LC 2012005484

In this book, "former Kansas City police officer Marquitta 'Skeet' Bannion now heads a small college's police force in a nearby Missouri town. Things fire up pretty quickly when the college newspaper's student editor, Andrew, is murdered at his desk. Not well liked, the victim had a number of enemies on campus. . . . When Skeet figures out that Andrew was blackmailing several individuals," she realizes the murderer isn't done yet. (Library Journal)

Roger Caras' Treasury of great cat stories. Dutton 1987 495p $19.95

ISBN 0-525-24398-4

LC 86-2200

An anthology featuring feline tales by Kipling, Wodehouse, Saki, Gallico, Twain, and others

Roger Caras' Treasury of great dog stories. Dutton 1987 497p $19.95

ISBN 0-525-24399-2

LC 86-6264

Among the authors represented in this collection are Turgenev, Narayan, Bradbury, Terhune and O. Henry

Rogers, Jane

★ **Mr.** Wroe's virgins. Overlook Press 1999 276p

ISBN 0-87951-702-6

LC 99-10232

First published 1992 in the United Kingdom

This novel, "based on historical events and set in Lancashire in 1830, begins when John Wroe, 'prophet' of a Judeo-Christian sect, claims that God has instructed him to comfort himself by taking seven virgins into his home. The story spans the nine months the women spend under Wroe's roof before he is ousted by his congregation following charges of indecency." Booklist

Rogers, Rob

Devil's Cape. Wizards of the Coast Discoveries 2008 409p il pa $14.95

ISBN 978-0-786949-01-4; 0-786949-01-5

LC 2007-21311

"Devil's Cape is a town in Louisiana, just a few miles away from New Orleans. The town was founded by pirates and, today, the bad guys rule in Devil's Cape. Pity any superhero who dares try to fight them. If they can't kill you, they'll kill your family. If you don't have a family, they'll find someone close to you to kill, whatever it takes for them to keep their power over you – and the city. Rogers creates a vivid and vibrant world from whole cloth which seems like it truly can exist right outside your window. And that is what makes this book so successful. Devil's Cape is a quick read in the best sense of the word. It is truly difficult to put down. It proudly deserves a place next to Tom Clancy and Stephen King as a sterling example of the best of genre fiction. Even if you don't like superheroes, you are bound to be captivated by Devil's Cape." PopMatters

Rogan, Charlotte

The **lifeboat**; a novel. Charlotte Rogan. Little, Brown and Co. 2012 278 p.

ISBN 0316185906; 9780316185905

LC 2011032492

This book, "[s]et at the beginning of WWI," is "[Charlotte] Rogan's debut" and "follows 22-year-old Grace Winter, a newlywed, newly minted heiress who survives . . . three weeks at sea following the sinking of her ocean liner and the disappearance of her husband, Henry. Safe at home in the U.S., Grace and two other survivors are put on trial for their actions aboard the under-built, overloaded lifeboat. At sea, as food and water ran out, and passengers realized that some among them would die, questions of sacrifice and duty arose. Rogan interweaves the trial with a . . . day-by-day story of Grace's time aboard the lifeboat, and circles around society's ideas about what it means to be human, what responsibilities we have to each other, and whether we can be blamed for choices made in order to survive." (Publishers Wkly)

Roiphe, Anne Richardson

An **imperfect** lens; a novel. [by] Anne Roiphe. Shaye Areheart Books 2006 296p $25

ISBN 1-4000-8211-0

LC 2005-11250

"Commissioned by an aging Louis Pasteur to identify and isolate the cholera microbe and 'bring glory to France,' an eclectic band of young researchers arrive in plague-stricken Alexandria in 1883. Set loose in this exotic locale, these novice scientists face a daunting task as pestilence and disease ravage the city. In addition to racing against time and famed German scientist Dr. Robert Koch, the team members face multiple political, cultural, and romantic distractions. Roiphe does an incredible job of painting paradoxical portraits of collective fear and coolheaded reason as she painstakingly reconstructs the life cycle of a deadly epidemic. This authentically detailed blend of fact and fiction gift wraps the history of an astonishing medical and scientific breakthrough inside an irresistible love story, providing a little something for everyone across a wide spectrum of readers." Booklist

Roiphe, Anne Richardson

★ **Lovingkindness**; a novel. by Anne Roiphe. Summit Bks. 1987 279p

LC 87-6448

"Annie Johnson, widowed before the birth of her daughter Andrea, is a modern, successful, professional woman. Her relations with Andrea has been marked with alienation on her daughter's part, as she appears to be intent on destroying her life as a drop-out from schools, an abuser of drugs, and a young woman who has already experienced three abortions. Annie Johnson seeks psychiatric help for Andrea with no success. It is not until Andrea, finding herself a visitor in Israel, is taken into a yeshiva community that some change in her behavior comes about. The rigorous, although warm, Jewish orthodox discipline appears to change Andrea into a submissive young woman living a life completely foreign to anything her mother understands. The destruction inherent in some parent-child conflicts is painfully described here." Shapiro. Fic for Youth. 3d edition

Rollins, James

The **devil** colony. William Morrow 2011 480p map $27.99

ISBN 978-0-06-178478-1

LC 2011-15981

This is the seventh novel in the author's Sigma Force series. "While exploring a mysterious cavern full of desiccated human bodies in the Rocky Mountains of Utah, two teenage boys discover the gold-coated skull of a saber-toothed tiger atop a granite plinth. Later, after others bring this prehistoric artifact to the surface, it triggers a blast that creates a strange force that dissolves rock and eats its way into the ground, eventually unleashing a volcano. When the members of the special forces unit known as Sigma, led by Painter Crowe, investigate, they uncover a massive conspiracy that has its roots in Mormonism, Native American legends, Thomas Jefferson, and explorer Meriwether Lewis, to name just a few of the fascinating characters and scientific threads that stitch this intricate action thriller together." Publ Wkly

Rolvaag, Ole Edvart

★ **Giants** in the earth; a saga of the prairie. by O. E. Rölvaag; translated from the Norwegian. Harper 1927 465p

This novel "chronicles the struggles of Norwegian immigrant settlers in the Dakota territory in the 1870s. . . . The book's indomitable protagonist, Per Hansa, his wife Beret, their children, and three other Norwegian immigrant families settle at Spring Creek, living in makeshift sod huts. Surviving the winters' fierce blizzards, they see their crops destroyed by locusts in summer. They nonetheless persist; new settlers arrive, and the community grows." Merriam-Webster's Ency of Lit

Followed by Peder Victorious

Rolvaag, Ole Edvart

Peder Victorious; a novel. by O. E. Rölvaag; translated from the Norwegian; English text by Nora O. Solum and the author. Harper 1929 350p

"Carries on the characters of 'Giants in the earth,' the interest centering in Peder Victorious and Beret, the boy's mother, against the background of a community no longer intensely struggling with the soil, but adapting itself to the ways of the new country, or resisting adaptation as Beret continues to do. The boy Peder, with his changing ideas and his ardent pursuit of girls is a foil for the character of Beret, perhaps the most finely conceived personality in the book." N Y Libr

Followed by Their father's God (1931)

Romano, Stephen

Resurrection Express; Stephen Romano. 1st Gallery Books hc. ed. Gallery Books 2012 437 p. (hardcover) $25.00; (trade paperback) $7.99

ISBN 1451668643; 9781451668643; 9781451668650; 9781451668667

LC 2012015053

In this mystery novel, "[t]wo years after . . . Elroy Coffin survived a gunshot to the head that's affected his memory," he's in prison. "Wealthy and well-connected Jayne Jenison [visits and] tells him his . . . wife, Toni, whom he believed dead, is still alive. Jenison promises to get Coffin released . . .

. if he'll agree to help track down her grown daughter, who's being held . . . along with Toni." (Publishers Weekly)

Romano, Tony

When the world was young. HarperCollins 2007 309p $24.95

ISBN 978-0-06-085792-9; 0-06-085792-7

LC 2006-43312

"The complexities and mysteries of familial bonds are brought into sharp, agonizing focus. . . . Romano's tale emerges into surprising and satisfying territory." Chicago Sun-Times

Romano-Lax, Andromeda

The **Spanish** bow. Harcourt 2007 554p $25

ISBN 978-0-15-101542-9; 0-15-101542-2

LC 2006-100937

"Expertly woven throughout the book are cameo appearances by Pablo Picasso, Adolf Hitler, Francisco Franco, Bertolt Brecht, and others, but it is the fictional Feliu, Justo, and Aviva who will keep you mesmerized to the last page." Christ Sci Monit

Roncagliolo, Santiago

Red April; translated from Spanish by Edith Grossman. Pantheon Books 2009 271p $24.95

ISBN 978-0-375-42544-8; 0-375-42544-6

LC 2008-36654

Original Spanish edition, 2006

"A latter-day Candide gets a crash course in Peruvian terrorism and counter-terrorism in Roncagliolo's precocious debut. . . . An angry, despairing dispatch, punctuated with illiterate notes from a killer and equally meaningless reports in bureaucratic doublespeak, from a land torn apart by civil war and official denial." Kirkus

Roorbach, Bill

Life among giants; a novel. by Bill Roorbach. Algonquin Books of Chapel Hill 2012 331 p. $24.95

ISBN 1616200766; 9781616200763

LC 2012016965

In this novel by Bill Roorbach "David 'Lizard' Hochmeyer is nearly seven feet tall, a star quarterback, and Princeton-bound. His future seems all but assured until his parents are mysteriously murdered, leaving Lizard and his older sister, Kate, adrift and alone. Sylphide, the world's greatest ballerina, lives across the pond from their Connecticut home, . . . and it turns out that her rock star husband's own disasters have intersected with Lizard's--and Kate's." (Publisher's note)

Roosevelt, Elliott

The **Hyde** Park murder. St. Martin's Press 1985 231p

LC 85-1752

"A stock swindle threatens to keep two young lovers apart. Bob Hannah is the son of the indicted financier, and his fiancée's father wants no part of a family marked by scandal. Mrs. Roosevelt's matchmaking for the two sweethearts is further complicated when the elder Hannah dies in what is claimed to be a suicide. Bob Hannah and Eleanor suspect murder." Wilson Libr Bull

"The author's fascinating glimpses into history, into the Roosevelts at home, and into corrupt politics are delivered in a measured and surefooted manner." Booklist

Roosevelt, Elliott

Murder and the First Lady. St. Martin's Press 1984 227p

LC 83-24659

"This historical mystery is set just before World War II, when international tensions are at a peak. Philip Garber, a lowly bookkeeper and assistant to the chief usher at the White House, is found murdered. Eleanor Roosevelt turns sleuth when it's discovered that Garber was found dead in the room of her British secretary, Pamela Rush-Hodgeborne." Booklist

Roosevelt, Elliott

Murder at midnight; an Eleanor Roosevelt mystery. St. Martin's Press 1997 216p $20.95

ISBN 0-312-15596-4

LC 96-53530

"Judge Horace Blackwell, friend and adviser to the president, is stabbed to death in his White House suite, and Sara Carter, a black maid, is arrested after finding the body. After promising the girl a fair hearing and gaining the confidence of lead investigator Lawrence Pickering, Eleanor takes an active role. Her doubts about Sara's guilt lead to some disturbing discoveries, not least of which is that the judge appears to have been a sadistic womanizer. . . . Peopled with famous lights of 1933, including Babe Ruth, William Faulkner and Gertrude Stein, Washington, D.C., is bought to life in the mirror of the White House." Publ Wkly

Roosevelt, Elliott

Murder at the palace. St. Martin's Press 1987 232p

LC 87-27961

This novel "is set at Buckingham Palace in wartime London. On a visit to British and American troops (including son Elliott), Mrs. Roosevelt greets the king and queen, princesses Margaret and Elizabeth, and Sir Alan Burton. . . . When Burton becomes a suspect in a top-secret and terribly embarrassing murder case, Mrs. Roosevelt comes to his aid." Booklist

Roosevelt, Elliott

Murder in the Blue Room. St. Martin's Press 1990 215p

LC 89-77677

"Set in 1942 during Soviet Foreign Minister Molotov's secret visit to FDR, {this} mystery . . . finds the author's mother, Eleanor Roosevelt, solving a double murder and combating racial discrimination in the armed forces. A droll, yet affectionate, portrait that is standard but intriguing fare." Booklist

Roosevelt, Elliott

Murder in the map room; an Eleanor Roosevelt mystery. St. Martin's Press 1998 251p il $21.95

ISBN 0-312-18168-X

LC 97-37243

"When Mrs. Roosevelt discovers a murder in the White House during the state visit of Madame Chiang Kai-shek in 1943, her investigation is hampered by both diplomatic protocol and the fact that the U.S. is deeply involved in a war raging on two fronts. . . . As usual, Elliot Roosevelt's respectfully playful portrayal of his down-to-earth mother as a clever sleuth is enough to keep the pages turning." Booklist

Roosevelt, Elliott

Murder in the Oval Office; an Eleanor Roosevelt mystery. St. Martin's Press 1989 247p

LC 88-18848

"Her sense of justice (not to mention her curiosity) sparked by the murder of a Southern Congressman during a White House soiree, the resourceful First Lady shows spunk and wit, and also considerable charm, in her investigation of the locked room puzzle." N Y Times Book Rev

Roosevelt, Elliott

Murder in the Rose Garden. St. Martin's Press 1989 232p

LC 89-35326

"During the summer of 1936, popular Washington hostess Vivian Taliafero is strangled in the White House Rose Garden. . . . The First Lady helps the Secret Service and the D.C. police gather information about the murdered woman who was, it turns out, an extortionist. . . . Vivian's partner in blackmail, photographer Joe Bob Skaggs, is killed, as is one of their victims, while Mrs. Roosevelt strives to solve the mystery." Publ Wkly

Roosevelt, Elliott

The **White** House pantry murder; an Eleanor Roosevelt mystery. St. Martin's Press 1987 231p

LC 86-26249

"It is December, 1941, and Winston Churchill is a guest at the White House. The body of an unidentified man is found in the White House freezer. When weapons are found in a storm sewer leading to the White House, espionage or an assassination attempt is suspected. Mrs. Roosevelt, ably assisted by Secret Service agent Deconcini and British Lieutenant-Commander Leach, must find the person responsible before something terrible happens." Libr J

Roosevelt, Kermit

In the shadow of the law. Farrar, Straus and Giroux 2005 370p $24

ISBN 0-374-26187-3

LC 2004-24222

This novel "portrays life inside a cutthroat corporate firm in Washington." (N Y Times Book Rev)

This novel "goes behind the scenes at Morgan Siler, one of Washington, D.C.'s most powerful K Street law firms, as several lawyers become embroiled in two difficult cases: a pro bono death penalty case in Virginia and a class action suit brought against a Texas chemical corporation after an explosion kills dozens of workers. . . . Though the novel features plenty of satisfying twists and turns, the book transcends the legal thriller genre. Roosevelt . . . offers a fascinating insider's look into the culture of a high-stakes firm, while also presenting a considered meditation on the law itself and its potential to compromise those driven to practice it." Publ Wkly

Rosales, Guillermo

The **halfway** house; introduction by Jose Manuel Prieto; translated by Anna Kushner. New Directions 2009 121p pa $14.95

ISBN 978-0-8112-1802-3

LC 2009-05947

Written 1987; original Spanish edition, 2003

A "story set in a Miami home for the mentally ill. William Figueras, a 38-year-old [exiled schizophrenic Cuban writer] . . . , is deposited in a boarding house by his aunt, because nothing more can be done. His writing was deemed morose, pornographic, and also irrelevant by the Cuban government, and now he has grown as hopeless and abandoned as the other desperate outcasts who inhabit the shabby home owned by the miserly Mr. Curbelo and run by a beer-guzzling flunky named Arsenio. Figueras despises the other residents and clearly recognizes how they are being exploited by Mr. Curbelo and Arsenio, yet out of his own state of self-debasement, he joins in the cruelty. Briefly, hope inspires him in the form of a new female inmate, and together they plan an escape. However, life outside promises to be more treacherous than staying in the ward. It's a frightening, nihilistic cousin of One Flew Over the Cuckoo's Nest." Publ Wkly

Rose, Joel

Blackest bird; a novel of murder in nineteenth-century New York. W.W. Norton 2007 479p $24.95

ISBN 978-0-393-06231-1; 0-393-06231-7

LC 2006-31703

"Sixty-nine-year-old High Constable Jacob Hays is facing a long, hot summer in 1841. The soaring temperatures are nothing compared to the heat being generated by the sensation-seeking newspapers and the vicious gangs that rule the New York neighborhoods known as the Five Points. When Mary Rogers, a pretty clerk at a tobacco shop, is found brutally murdered in the Hudson River, Hays is charged with the search for her killer. A long-respected lawman known for creating a new interrogation technique called the third degree, Hays is starting to feel the full weight of his position, caught between public outrage and political red tape. High on his list of suspects is the eccentric poet Edgar Allan Poe, who freely admits that he was in love with the 'cigar girl.'" Booklist

"Rose does a scrupulous and impressive job of mustering the pace and mood of the rapidly expanding city, its still pastoral fringes and its customs." PopMatters

Rose, M. J.

Seduction; a novel of suspense. by M.J. Rose. Atria Books 2013 372 p. (hardcover) $24.00

ISBN 1451621507; 9781451621501

LC 2013005582

This book follows "Jac L'Etoile . . . a mythologist by trade and perfumer by pedigree. . . . Jac has been dodging her painful past for years. . . . [M. J.] Rose's time-shifting narrative recounts French novelist Victor Hugo's exile on the Isle of Jersey and his participation in hundreds of séances. In the present day, Jac is lured by the island's Celtic

history and becomes enmeshed in a family drama that seems to stem back to ancient times." (Library Journal)

Includes bibliographical references

Rosen, Jonathan

Joy comes in the morning. Farrar, Straus and Giroux 2004 389p $25

ISBN 0-374-18026-1

LC 2004-1742

"In her work as a hospital volunteer, Deborah Green, a Manhattan rabbi, encounters an ailing Holocaust survivor—recovering from a debilitating stroke and a suicide attempt—and his skeptical son. To complicate matters, she is beautiful and single, while the skeptical son is a shy bachelor; the romance causes crises of faith for both, as they negotiate their divergent attitudes toward their religion. As the story moves from wedding to funeral and back again, and Deborah officiates at the momentous changes in other people's lives, she increasingly finds her own life empty of the things that she has always counselled her congregation to treasure. Served with the merest teaspoon of schmaltz, Rosen's touching novel of Jewish manners thoughtfully addresses the question of whether piety can teach us faith." New Yorker

Includes bibliographical references

Rosenberg, Joel C.

Damascus Countdown; Joel C. Rosenberg. Tyndale House Publishers, Inc. 2013 470 p. (hardcover) $26.99

ISBN 1414319703; 9781414319704

LC 2012040475

This is Joel C. Rosenberg's third David Shirazi novel. Here, the Iranian-born agent "has infiltrated the jihadist regime in Iran. Although Israel has successfully launched a first strike, destroying Iran's nuclear sites, two Iranian warheads have survived. David moves quickly to find the surviving warheads before the Twelfth Imam can launch a retaliation and bring about full-scale war." (Library Journal)

Rosenberg, Joel C.

The **Tehran** initiative; Joel C. Rosenberg. Tyndale House Publishers, Inc. 2011 xiii, 462 p.p (hardcover) $26.99

ISBN 1414319355; 9781414319353

LC 2011026051

This book is in Joel C. Rosenberg's David Shirazi series. Here, he "continues to work undercover to glean information about Iran's plan to eradicate Israel and the United States through a nuclear attack. In Tehran, the Twelfth Imam has emerged, attracting those Muslims who believe him to be the messiah and call for the destruction of those who would oppose them." (Library Journal)

Rosenberg, Joel C.

The **twelfth** Imam; Joel C. Rosenberg. Tyndale House Publishers 2010 viii, 490p o.p.; o.p.; (pbk.) $14.99

ISBN 141431163X; 9781414311630; 9781414311647

LC 2010030082

In this book, the 2011 Retailers Choice Award winner, "[a]s the apocalyptic leaders of Iran call for the annihilation of Israel and the U.S., CIA operative David Shirazi is sent into Tehran with one objective: use all means neces- sary to disrupt Iran's nuclear weapons program—without . . . triggering a regional war. . . . [N]one of his training has prepared Shirazi for what will happen next. An obscure reli- gious cleric is suddenly hailed throughout the region as the Islamic messiah known as the Mahdi or the Twelfth Imam. News of his miracles, healings, signs, and wonders, spread like wildfire, as do rumors of a new and horrific war. With the prophecy of the Twelfth Imam seemingly fulfilled, Iran's leaders prepare to strike Israel and bring about the End of Days." (Publisher's note)

Rosenberg, Nancy Taylor
Abuse of power. Dutton 1997 326p $23.95
ISBN 0-525-93768-4
LC 96-44141

In this novel, "policewoman Rachel Simmons takes on a corruption-riddled police force. Molested as a child, she is filled with a fiery purpose and uncompromising honesty. These scruples act against her when she witnesses an abuse of police authority and reports it. The duel between Rachel's conscience and her own family's safety forms the basis of the plot line. The novel moves rapidly to a powerful conclu- sion." Libr J

Rosenberg, Nancy Taylor
Buried evidence. Hyperion 2000 359p
ISBN 0-7868-6619-5
LC 00-35073

Sequel to Mitigating circumstances
"Lily Forrester, formerly of the Ventura DA's office, is now DA in Santa Barbara. Her ex-husband, John Forrester, who has been living with their 18-year-old daughter, Shana, is losing his battle with the bottle and has been arrested for vehicular manslaughter. . . . John blackmails Lily into bail- ing him out of jail, bartering Lily's secret in an effort to escape prosecution. (Six years before, Shana was brutally raped while Lily was forced to look on, and Lily shot and killed the wrong man in retaliation.) The real rapist has re- cently been released on parole and is once again stalking the two women." Publ Wkly

Rosenberg, Nancy Taylor
First offense. Dutton 1994 338p
LC 94-550

"Probation officer Ann Carlisle's husband, a highway patrolman, disappeared mysteriously four years ago, and it's been tough for Ann and her 12-year-old son to put their lives back together. A new love interest plus a heavy caseload at work are just beginning to help heal Ann's wounds when she becomes involved in a narcotics trial that will unravel her life all over again." Booklist
"Just when readers will have figured all the angles, savvy Rosenberg unveils the villain and flips the plot into an excit- ing manhunt, with Ann as bait." Publ Wkly

Rosenberg, Nancy Taylor
Interest of justice; a novel. Dutton 1993 368p
LC 93-13005

"Lara Sanderstone, a California judge, finds her life turned upside down when her house is burglarized, her sister and brother-in-law are brutally murdered, and she's left with a sullen 14-year-old nephew to care for. With the help of

police sergeant Ted Rickerson, Lara tries to determine if the crimes were the random work of some sicko or if one of the deadbeats she's sent to prison is out for revenge." Booklist
"Lara Sanderstone is such an intelligent, finely detailed character that even the unlikeliest plot twists work in this absorbing legal thriller." Publ Wkly

Rosenberg, Nancy Taylor
Mitigating circumstances. Dutton 1993 362p
LC 92-23035

"For all the adrenaline that the author pumps into her story, her writing is far more persuasive when it isn't so fe- verish—during intimate mother-daughter exchanges, for ex- ample, and in the realistically mundane procedures of ordi- nary, hard-working cops and lawyers." N Y Times Book Rev

Rosenberg, Nancy Taylor
Sullivan's law. Kensington Bks. 2004 314p $24
ISBN 0-7582-0618-6

Carolyn Sullivan is a "probation officer attending night school to become an attorney. Juggling her coursework and her job is hard enough, let alone having to worry about how she'll handle single parenthood with her preteen daughter and college-bound son. Carolyn's pressures only mount when one of her probationary charges, convicted killer and paranoid schizophrenic Daniel Metroix, is arrested for rape. . . . Rosenberg puts it all together here with another thor- oughly believable heroine dealing with corruption, greed, deceit, and danger." Booklist

Rosenberg, Robert
This is not civilization. Houghton Mifflin 2004 293p $24
ISBN 0-618-38601-7

"This is risky comedy that in less deft hands would clunk into condescension, but Rosenberg keeps it aloft with a sweet sense of appreciation. . . . What a generous, bighearted book this is, perceptive enough to catch the goodness in all these well-intentioned people." Christ Sci Monit

Rosenblatt, Roger
Lapham rising. Ecco 2006 243p $23.95
ISBN 0-06-083361-0
LC 2005-48835

"This is a zany tale. It is a comic novel perfectly con- jugated, moving the reader with delight through a three-act plot featuring a hero who is slightly mad, not quite prevail- ing over the antagonist, who is slightly mad; all of this with appropriate commentary from Hector, a talking dog who is pious and insolent." National Rev

Rosenfeld, Lucinda
I'm so happy for you; a novel about best friends. Little, Brown 2009 268p pa $13.99
ISBN 978-0-316-04450-9 pa; 0-316-04450-4 pa
LC 2008-45124

"The hapless, too-eager-to-please heroine of Rosenfeld's new novel is an ill-paid editor at an obscure leftist journal who secretly resents her husband for abandoning his job to write a sci-fi screenplay and for failing to get her pregnant. No wonder she thrills to the travails of her best friend, a suicidal beauty who has always overshadowed her but is now languishing in a dead-end affair. Then, to her chagrin, her friend meets Mr. Right. The book's confectionery veneer belies a heart of poison, as Rosenfeld tartly dispels the cherished chick-lit notion that female friendship conquers all. Equally ruthless is her sendup of overachieving New York women in feral pursuit of have-it-all motherhood without having first ascertained if they even like children." New Yorker

Rosenfelt, David

Don't tell a soul. St. Martin's Minotaur 2008 306p $24.95

ISBN 978-0-312-37395-5; 0-312-37395-3

LC 2008-14777

"Rosenfelt keeps the plot hopping and popping as he reveals a complex frameup of major proportions with profound political ramifications both terrifying and enlightening." Publ Wkly

Rosenthal, Pam

The **bookseller's** daughter; Pam Rosenthal. Brava 2004 328p pa $14

ISBN 0758204450

LC 2004558159

This book is set "[i]n 1793 . . . [and tells the story of] Marie-Laurie [Vernet who] is probably better at eluding the men than she is at serving tea. Her only exception happens to be book smuggler Viscount Joseph d'Auvers-Raimond whom she met when he became ill in her late father's bookstore. Joseph shares Marie-Laurie's passion for books and has gone so far as to draft an erotic tale that stars the woman who haunts his dreams, Marie-Laurie. When Joseph learns that his odious father has chosen Marie-Laurie to warm his bed, he makes her his mistress to keep her safe. Instead of sex, they discuss books and soon they fall in love. However, anything beyond being his mistress is forbidden for this duo and betrayal looms on the horizon." (thebestreviews.com)

Rosero Diago, Evelio

★ The **armies**; [by] Evelio Rosero; translated from the Spanish by Anne McLean. New Directions 2009 199p pa $14.95

ISBN 978-0-8112-1864-1; 0-8112-1864-3

LC 2009-19620

Original Spanish edition, 2007

"The novel begins idyllically with a rural scene saturated in color and lust: Ismail, retired teacher, spends his days picking oranges and stealing glimpses of his neighbor's naked, sunbathing wife. Mortified, Otilia, Ismail's wife of 40 years, urges her husband to confess his misdeed. But Ismail never seeks out the priest. Instead, he wanders through San Jose, meeting up with old friends. Through their beautifully written conversations, San Jose's troubled past emerges: kidnappings, murders and violent incursions that rocked the town only four years ago and threaten it once more. When Ismail returns home, Otilia is missing, and as he searches for her, armed forces begin to sack the town." Time Out N Y

Rosero, Evelio

Good offices. New Directions 2011 119p pa $13.95

ISBN 978-0-8112-1930-3

LC 2011-12524

Original Spanish edition, 2009

"Tancredo, a young hunchback, observes and participates in the rites at the Catholic church where he lives under the care of Father Almida. Also in residence are the sexton Celeste Machado, his goddaughter Sabina Cruz, and three widows known collectively as the Lilias, who do the cooking and cleaning and provide charity meals for the local poor and needy. One Thursday, Father Almida and the sexton must rush off to meet the parish's principal benefactor, Don Justiniano. It will be the first time in forty years Father Almida has not said mass. Eventually they find a replacement: Father Matamoros, a drunkard with a beautiful voice whose sung mass is spellbinding to all. The Lilias prepare a sumptuous meal for Father Matamoros, who persuades them to drink with him. Over the course of the long night the women and Tancredo lose their inhibitions and confess their sins and stories to this strange priest, and in the process reveal lives crippled by hypocrisy." Publisher's note

Ross, Adam

Mr. Peanut; Adam Ross. Alfred A. Knopf 2010 335 p. $25.95

ISBN 978-0-307-27070-2; 0-307-27070-X; 030727070X; 9780307270702

LC 2009041693

"This story of a marriage, played out in flashbacks, . . . is told in alternating chapters by David Pepin and by Ward Hastroll, the police detective assigned to investigate Pepin after his wife, Alice, is found slumped on the kitchen floor, dead of anaphylactic shock (an offending peanut still wedged in her throat). Though Pepin argues that Alice who long battled obesity and depression took her own life, Hastroll isn't buying it, especially once he finds a link to a notorious hitman." Entertainment Wkly

Ross, Adam

Ladies and gentlemen. Alfred A. Knopf 2011 243p

ISBN 0-307-27071-8; 978-0-307-27071-9

LC 2011-6960

This book presents a "short-story collection [entitled] 'Ladies and Gentlemen,' . . . by [author Adam] Ross. . . . 'Futures,' the first and longest of the set, follows David Applebow . . . as he tries to find employment after losing his job as manager of a theater company. . . . 'When in Rome,' [is] about the disastrous relationship between two boys grown to manhood. . . . In another story, 'The Suicide Room,' Ross presents a college sophomore in a foursome slowly getting stoned in a dorm room, ending in a game of 'Can you top that?' and its repercussions. . . .The title story, 'Ladies and Gentlemen,' . . . packs the . . . life of Sara, a successful freelance writer on an interview assignment in Nashville when the past catches up to her, or she catches up with it." (Yale Review)

"Truly funny, original, acerbic [and] surprising. . . . Ross deftly dissects how our best efforts to establish intimacy or better ourselves in the economy can result in excruciating, if hilarious, humiliations. Amusing morality at its compulsive, can't-wait-to-pick-it-up-again best." AM N Y

Ross, Ann B.

Miss Julia throws a wedding. Viking 2002 308p

ISBN 0-670-03105-4

LC 2001-56798

"The inimitable Miss Julia pushes an indecisive couple toward matrimong in this Southern comedy-of-manners, . . . which begins with the protagonist frustrated at the inability of her friend, Miss Hazel, to get her beau to propose. But another opportunity surfaces when Sheriff Coleman Bates proposes to his lawyer girlfriend Binkie Enloe. . . . Ross gets a bit carried away with wedding details, but her cheeky style works flawlessly once Miss Julia digs into the romantic intrigue and begins to ply her unique combination of common sense and old-fashioned, smalltown wisdom." Publ Wkly

Ross-Macdonald, Malcolm

For they shall inherit; a novel. {by} Malcolm Macdonald. St. Martin's Press 1985 591p

LC 84-52352

First published 1984 in the United Kingdom with title: In love and war

"MacDonald skillfully depicts the English class system and the struggles inherent in it. The characters are multifaceted and solidly drawn, and the writing is smooth. An absorbing portrayal of human emotion and an individual's will to prevail." Libr J

Ross-Macdonald, Malcolm

The rich are with you always; [by] Malcolm Macdonald. Knopf 1976 483p

"In this sequel to 'The World From Rough Stones' Macdonald continues the interlocking family dramas of John and Nora Stevenson, born dirt poor, driving hard for money and power in Victorian England, and Walter and Arabella Thornton, aristocratic, unhappy, the Stevensons' opposites in every way. It is Nora and John who dominate this part of the saga in the fierce get-rich-quick era of railroad schemes and bonanzas and bankruptcies." Publ Wkly

Followed by Sons of fortune (1978)

Ross-Macdonald, Malcolm

Tamsin Harte; [by] Malcolm Macdonald. St. Martin's Press 2000 345p il $24.95

ISBN 0-312-20628-3

LC 99-88104

"Set in a Cornish fishing village at the turn of the last century. . . . Tamsin Harte and her mother, Harriet, fall from the upper echelon of society when Tamsin's father dies and his shipping firm goes bankrupt. They open a boarding house to get by. Energetic, enterprising and ambitious, Tamsin discovers that she has a mind suited to business enterprises. (Her secret ambition is to build 'the best hotel in Cornwall.') When it comes to romance, however, she is still bound by tradition." Publ Wkly

Ross-Macdonald, Malcolm

The Trevarton inheritance; {by} Malcolm Macdonald. St. Martin's Press 1996 395p $24.95

ISBN 0-312-14748-1

LC 96-20035

This novel's protagonist, Crissy Moore, "loses both parents and her grandfather within a few days. Determined to keep her orphaned family of six together, she puts herself at the mercy of the grandmother who years ago disowned Crissy's mother. The old woman offers Crissy the position of lady's maid while secretly arranging to break up the family by having all the other children placed in agencies throughout Cornwall. A secondary plot concerns the attempt of Crissy and Jim, the young man she eventually marries, to establish a business photographing tourists at the seaside." Libr J

"Macdonald always maintains a brisk narrative pace, and his sound social commentary adds to the reader's enjoyment." Publ Wkly

Ross-Macdonald, Malcolm

The world from rough stones; [by] Malcolm Macdonald. Knopf 1975 535p il

"This saga of England in 1839-40 and the start of a great railroad building dynasty opens fast and never once lets up its pace and drama. Above all, its people are believable human beings, caught up in the tumultuous movement of beginning social change." Publ Wkly

Followed by The rich are with you always

Rossner, Judith

August. Houghton Mifflin 1983 376p

ISBN 0-395-33970-7

LC 83-6191

"Rossner writes about the technical side of analysis and simultaneously shows it at work. In spite of a few awkward passages that tell rather than show how analysis works and an unavoidable lack of completeness resulting from the nature of her topic, Rossner has written a fascinating study of the human mind growing." Best Sellers

Rossner, Judith

Emmeline. Simon & Schuster 1980 331p

LC 80-15553

The author "handles her material so meticulously that she inspires a renewed respect for the complexities of skillful story-telling. Instead of propagandizing, she evinces complete respect for the period and setting of her story." Books of the Times

Rossner, Judith

★ **Looking** for Mr. Goodbar. Simon & Schuster 1975 284p

"The tale is stark, capably told, believable; Rossner's prose is a delight, and her sense of the inner life of her characters, all tortured, is deft and sure. This is a very good novel." Booklist

Rossner, Judith

Perfidia; a novel. Talese 1997 308p

ISBN 978-0385484275

LC 97-10882

"Rossner reveals a gritty new style, stripped down to the clean bones of feeling. 'Perfidia' is an unsparing close-up of the seductive attachment and growing repulsion of a mother and daughter who mean far too much to each other." N Y Times Book Rev

Rosten, Leo

Captain Newman, M.D. Harper 1962 331p

First published 1961 in the United Kingdom

"A book of great insight, warmth and humor. . . . It is a tremendously impressive piece of verbal tight-rope walking. There are the expected flashes of GI humor, the much-documented war of rank, there are also moments of great tenderness and understanding in this chronicle of that most delicate of explorations, the exploration into the shattered minds that are the common responsibilities of all of us." N Y Her Trib Books

Roth, Henry

★ **Call** it sleep. Ballou, R.O. 1934 599p

"The years between the sixth and ninth birthdays of a young boy are described in this vivid, sensitive portrayal of a Jewish childhood in the ghettos of Brownsville, and the Lower East Side in New York. Because David's father is a violent and bitter man, the child always turns to his mother, with whom he is very close. Her love protects him from the terrors of street gangs, poverty, the sexual conflicts between his parents, and his own initiation into sex by a lame girl. A literary technique that distinguishes between the language used by members of this family when they are speaking their native tongue (Yiddish) and when they speak broken English they have learned as immigrants in the United States is an unusual feature in this remarkable book." Shapiro. Fic for Youth. 3d edition

Roth, Henry

A **diving** rock on the Hudson. St. Martin's Press 1995 418p (Mercy of a rude stream)

ISBN 0-312-11777-9

This second volume of the author's autobiographical cycle "continues the saga of Ira Stigman, teenage son of Orthodox Jewish immigrant parents, as he struggles to find his way in the larger world. Narrated by the now elderly Ira, it effectively evokes both life in 1920s New York and the angst of adolescent existence. In Ira's case, this angst results not only from the growing distance that separates his and his parents' views of the world but from uncontrollable urges that drive him to violate one of society's strongest taboos." Libr J

"Simultaneously, we are inside the mind of a troubled adolescent and that of an aged but still mentally vital man, a man engaged with words, with concepts, obsessively reconsidering the role of the artist and in particular his own responsibility in portraying events truthfully." Booklist

Followed by From bondage

Roth, Henry

From bondage. St. Martin's Press 1996 397p (Mercy of a rude stream) $25.95

ISBN 0-312-14341-9

This third volume of Roth's autobiographical cycle "continues the story of Ira Stigman, son of East European

Jewish immigrant parents and now college aged, as he struggles to find his way in 1920s New York. But, like the previous volumes, it is also the story of Ira the octogenarian writer who, nearing the end of his life, is trying to come to terms with both the forces and the choices that shaped it. Paralleling Roth's own experience, this volume focuses on the beginnings of what was to become a decade-long affair between Ira and NYU professor Edith Welles." Libr J

Followed by Requiem for Harlem

Roth, Henry

Requiem for Harlem. St. Martin's Press 1997 291p il (Mercy of a rude stream) $24.95

ISBN 0-312-16980-9

LC 97-17824

"Even as we see the older writer commenting ruefully on all that has come to pass, we see the young artist taking in every detail of the world. . . . And if it is hard to sympathize with either the egocentric youth or the rueful old man, taken together they meld into a living whole. This is Roth's achievement, this double vision of the artist as both young and old man, hungry and regretful, flawed and penitent." N Y Times Book Rev

Roth, Henry

★ A **star** shines over Mt. Morris Park. St. Martin's Press 1994 290p (Mercy of a rude stream)

LC 93-37270

"Mr. Roth remains an admirable craftsman, and the scenes of immigrant life in the second decade of the century are evoked with persuasive concreteness." N Y Times Book Rev

Followed by A diving rock on the Hudson

Roth, Joseph

★ The **collected** stories of Joseph Roth; translated with an introduction by Michael Hofmann. Norton 2002 400p $27.95

ISBN 0-393-04320-7

LC 2001-44747

The triumph of beauty explores the impact of a fickle hypochondriac on her husband. In the bust of the emperor an elderly nobleman continues to perform dutifully even after the state renders his commitment obsolete. The leviathan portrays a coral merchant preoccupied with the mystery of the exotic life forms that provide his livelihood

"Combining a shrewd reportorial eye with a taste for the fantastic and droll, Roth portrays characters living materially and spiritually impoverished lives in isolated Eastern European villages and those left homeless in their own homes in the tumultuous aftermath of World War I." Booklist

Roth, Philip, 1933-

★ **American** pastoral. Houghton Mifflin 1997 423p

ISBN 0-395-86021-0

LC 96-49368

"This cultural horror story is deepened by Roth's genius for blending humor, pathos, sympathy and rage. . . . You will search the shelf of contemporary fiction long and hard to find a parental nightmare projected with the emotional force and verbal energy that Roth brings to American Pastoral." Time

Roth, Philip

The **American** trilogy, 1997-2000. Library of America 2011 1094p $40

ISBN 978-1-59853-103-9; 1-59853-103-4

LC 2011-923051

"The tragic hero of American Pastoral (1997) is Seymour 'Swede' Levov—a legendary high school athlete, a devoted family man, a hard worker, the prosperous inheritor of his father's Newark glove factory—who comes of age in thriving, triumphant postwar America. But everything he loves is lost when the country goes to war in Vietnam, and the family of this strong, confident master of social equilibrium is overwhelmed by the forces of disorder unleashed by the turbulent 1960s. I Married a Communist (1998) is set in America's anti-Communist 1940s. Radio actor Iron Rinn (born Ira Ringold) is a big Newark roughneck blighted by a brutal personal secret from which he is perpetually in flight. A self-educated ditchdigger turned popular performer, a six-foot six-inch Abe Lincoln look-alike, he emerges from serving in World War II a clandestine and formidable Communist. His passionate commitment to Marxist revolution in America will lead him to ruin in the era of the blacklist. The Human Stain (2000) concludes Roth's . . . trilogy of postwar American lives. . . . The time is 1998, the year of the presidential impeachment; the location is a small New England town, where an aging classics professor, Coleman Silk, is forced to retire when his colleagues declare him a racist. The charge is a lie, but the real truth about Silk would astonish his most virulent accuser." Publisher's note

Roth, Philip

★ The **anatomy** lesson. Farrar, Straus & Giroux 1983 291p

LC 83-11645

"A ferocious, heartfelt book. . . . One might venture to say that, like a goodly number of Roth's previous works, 'The Anatomy Lesson' revolves around the paradox of incarnation—the astonishing coexistence in one life of infantilism and intelligence, of selfishness and altruism, of sexual appetite and social conscience—and has the form and manner of a monologue conducted under psychoanalysis." New Yorker

Roth, Philip

The **dying** animal. Houghton Mifflin 2001 156p $22

ISBN 0-618-13587-1

LC 00-54225

"Like many works of modern literature, The Dying Animal ends on a note of radical ambiguity and indeterminacy. What is rather unusual about it is the way it challenges the reader at every point to define and defend his own ethical position toward the issues raised by the story. It is a small, disturbing masterpiece." N Y Rev Books

Roth, Philip

Everyman. Houghton Mifflin 2006 182p $24

ISBN 0-618-73516-X

LC 2005-31538

"From a distance, Everyman looks like a shaggy dog story—a long, quotidian story whose meaning resides in its final pointlessness. Up close, though, it is a parable that captures, as few works of fiction have, the pathos of Being, as it's manifested even in the favored precincts of affluent America." Washington Post Book World

Roth, Philip

Exit ghost. Houghton Mifflin 2007 292p $26

ISBN 978-0-618-91547-7; 0-618-91547-8

LC 2006-102467

"Mr. Roth has created a melancholy, if occasionally funny, meditation on aging, mortality, loneliness and the losses that come with the passage of time. . . . For fans of the Zuckerman books, it provides a poignant coda to Nathan's story, putting a punctuation point to his journey from youthful idealism and passion through midlife confusion and angst toward elderly renunciation." N Y Times (Late N Y Ed)

Roth, Philip

The **ghost** writer. Farrar, Straus & Giroux 1979 179p

LC 79-13146

"A brief but intricate tale about a young writer {Nathan Zuckerman} who, when accused of travestying his fellow Jews, seeks counsel from a respected older Jewish author and finds this distinguished figure ambiguously involved with a girl whom the young writer fantasizes to be Anne Frank." Oxford Companion to Am Lit. 6th edition

Followed by Zuckerman unbound

Roth, Philip

★ **Goodbye,** Columbus, and five short stories. Modern Lib. 1995 298p hardcover o.p. pa $14

ISBN 0-679-60159-7; 0-679-74826-1 pa

LC 94-44528

A reissue of the title first published 1959 by Houghton Mifflin

"The title story in this collection is about a young Radcliffe girl and a Rutgers boy who learn that there is more to love than exuberance and passion. All of the stories dramatize the dilemma of modern American Jews, torn between two worlds." Publ Wkly

Roth, Philip

The **great** American novel. Holt, Rinehart & Winston 1973 382p

ISBN 0-8050-1734-8

This novel is "at once a burlesque and an allegory, its telling of the downfall of a great baseball team serving as a satirical parallel to contemporary American political and social events." Oxford Companion to Am Lit. 6th edition

Roth, Philip

The **human** stain. Houghton Mifflin 2000 361p $26

ISBN 0-618-05945-8

LC 99-89867

"Roth is clearly enjoyed himself. The Human Stain is as fresh, as angry and as bitterly amused as his early fiction. It vibrates with mockery, disapproval, poetry, and a healthy dose of personal vindictiveness that one would be tempted to dismiss as unworthy if it weren't so funny." New Leader

Roth, Philip

The **humbling**. Houghton Mifflin Harcourt 2009 140p $26

ISBN 978-0-547-23969-9; 0-547-23969-6

LC 2009013742

"In this searing novel, Roth adds dark shadings to the austere vision he has explored in recent works like Everyman and Exit Ghost; there are precious few shafts of light that break through his clinical examination of one man's catastrophic fall from grace. But in recounting with unrelenting precision the grim story of Simon—not a bad man, simply a tragically human one—Roth offers another unflinching assessment of the essence of our mortality." BookPage

Roth, Philip

I married a communist. Houghton Mifflin 1998 323p $26

ISBN 0-395-93346-3

LC 98-16797

"What Zuckerman/Roth does with this imagined material is constantly mesmerizing. Library shelves groan under the weight of books published about the witch hunts and blacklistings during the Truman and Eisenhower presidencies, but it would be hard to find one among them that presents as nuanced, as humanly complex an account of those years as I Married a Communist." Time

Roth, Philip

Indignation. Houghton Mifflin Company 2008 233p $26

ISBN 978-0-54705-484-1; 0-54705-484-X

LC 2008-11431

"We are back in nineteen-fifties Newark, and nineteen-year-old Marcus Messner, the son of a kosher butcher, attempts to escape his father's stifling influence by enrolling at a college in Ohio farm country. Messner is a scholarly type, while his new classmates are an unfriendly bunch of churchgoing, beer-swilling louts. Stubbornly disregarding overtures of friendship from members of the school's only Jewish fraternity, Messner devotes his attentions to a troubled Gentile named Olivia Hutton. There's something of Portnoy in the masturbation-filled high jinks that follow, but Messner, fearful that he might 'wind up a rifleman in Korea,' is a far darker creation." New Yorker

Roth, Philip

Letting go. Random House 1962 630p $12.50

ISBN 0-394-43305-X

Gabe Wallach is "a young university instructor who is literally unable to let go in his personal relationships. This is true with his father, a well-to-do Jewish dentist who suffers because his wife is dead and his only child lives in Chicago instead of New York; with Martha Reganhart, a divorcée, mother of two small children, a woman Gabe loves enough to make his mistress but not his wife; and with Paul and Libby Herz, a young couple suffering the difficulties arising from a mixed marriage, no money, inability to have children, and a host of other problems real and imagined." Libr J

Roth, Philip

My life as a man. Holt, Rinehart & Winston 1974 330p

The "novel consists of three stories: a long autobiographical narrative told by the novelist Peter Tarnopol, preceded by two of Peter's stories, 'useful fictions' in which elements of his 'true story' are metamorphosed. Peter's alter ego, Nathan Zuckerman, is, like his author, a highly self-conscious intellectual urban Jew, adept at eliciting astonishing sexual performances from teen-age girls, but fatally drawn into a disastrous marriage with an older, damaged woman who is incapable of sexual response." Newsweek

Roth, Philip, 1933-

★ **Nemesis**. Houghton Mifflin Harcourt 2010 280p

ISBN 978-0-547-31835-6

LC 2010026217

"In a book set in 1944 Newark, devoted playground director Bucky Cantor, sidelined from the war due to his poor eyesight, watches in horror as the city's polio epidemic begins to ravage the children on his playground." (Publisher's note)

In this novel Roth "evokes his native Newark amid a raging [polio] epidemic in 1944. . . . Popular young athlete and high school physical education teacher Eugene 'Bucky' Cantor has been hired to manage a playground for the summer in the city's Jewish Weequahic section. Soon, some of the adolescent boys who spend the long summer days playing baseball there are stricken, and panic spreads in the community as parents blame the outbreak on everything from Italian toughs spitting on the sidewalk to overly vigorous physical activity. Despairing of any hope of stemming the outbreak, Bucky flees . . . to a place of apparent safety: a summer camp in Pennsylvania's Pocono Mountains where his fiancée works as a counselor." BookPage

Roth, Philip

★ **Novels** & stories, 1959-1962; Philip Roth. Library of America 2005 913p $35

ISBN 1-931082-79-0

LC 2005-40916

Includes bibliographical references

Contents: Goodbye, Columbus; Five short stories; Letting go

Roth, Philip

Novels and other narratives 1986-1991. Library of America 2008 767p

ISBN 978-1-598530-30-8

The focus in The counterlife (1986) is how people enact "their dreams of renewal and escape, some going so far as to risk their lives to alter seemingly irreversible destinies. Illuminating these lives in transition is the skeptical, enveloping intelligence of the writer Nathan Zuckerman. . . . At the center of . . . Deception (1990), are a married American named Philip, living in London, and the married Englishwoman—trapped with a little child in a loveless upper-middle-class household—who eloquently and minutely reveals herself to her lover as they talk before and after making love." Publisher's note

Roth, Philip

★ **Novels,** 1967-1972. Library of America 2005 671p $35

ISBN 1-931082-80-4

LC 2005-40917

When she was good and Portnoy's complaint are entered separately. Our gang (1971) is a satire of the Nixon administration, featuring a president named Trick E. Dixon. The breast (1972) is "a novella about a male professor of literature who suffers a Kafka-like transformation into a gigantic breast." Oxford Companion to Am Lit. 6th edition

Includes bibliographical references

Roth, Philip

Novels, 1973-1977. Library of America 2006 912p $35

ISBN 978-1-931082-96-9; 1-931082-96-0

LC 2006-41030

In The Great American novel (1973), "Roth lifts the lid on the suppressed history of the homeless Ruppert Mundys of baseball's despised and vanquished third major league, turning the national pastime into unfettered picaresque farce. . . . My Life as a Man (1974) is Roth's . . . lurid account of the all-out battle waged between the young writer Peter Tarnopol and the wife who is his nemesis, his demon, and his muse. . . . The Professor of Desire (1977) charts the second sexual metamorphosis of David Kepesh, protagonist of The Breast. Roth follows Kepesh, an adventurous man of intelligence and feeling, into a vast wilderness of erotic possibility." Publisher's note

Roth, Philip

Novels, 1993-1995. Library of America 2010 842p $35

ISBN 978-1-59853-078-0; 1-59853-078-X

Operation Shylock (1993) "presents the author in face-to-face confrontation with his double, a look-alike impostor—and perfect stranger—who has usurped his biography and whose self-appointed task is to lead the Jews out of Israel and back to Europe, a Moses in reverse and a monstrous nemesis to the real Philip Roth. . . . [The novel] is at once spy story, political thriller, meditation on identity, confession, and unfathomable journey through a volatile, frightening Middle East. Sabbath's Theater (1995) is a comic creation of epic proportions. . . . Once a scandalously inventive puppeteer, [Mickey] Sabbath at sixty-four is still defiantly antagonistic and exceedingly libidinous. But ghost-ridden and grief-stricken after the death of his longtime Croatian mistress, the unsurpassable Drenka, he contrives a succession of farcical disasters that take him to the brink of madness and extinction." Publisher's note

Roth, Philip

The **plot** against America. Houghton Mifflin 2004 391p $26

ISBN 0-618-50928-3

LC 2004-47490

"When the renowned aviation hero . . . Charles A. Lindbergh defeated Franklin Roosevelt by a landslide in the 1940 presidential election, fear invaded every Jewish household in America. Not only had Lindbergh, in a nationwide radio address, publicly blamed the Jews for selfishly pushing America toward a pointless war with Nazi Germany, he negotiated a cordial 'understanding' with Adolf Hitler, whose conquest of Europe and virulent antiSemitic policies he appeared to accept with difficulty. . . . [The protagonist Philip Roth] recounts what it was like for his Newark family . . . during the menacing years of the Lindbergh presidency." Publisher's note

Roth, Philip

★ **Portnoy's** complaint. Random House 1969 274p

"Roth has the courage to wish to show things as he has experienced them, but the exaggerations of Portnoy's Complaint have a shrillness which could be considered unwholesome if the book were not so funny. It is very funny." Burgess. 99 Novels

Roth, Philip

The **professor** of desire. Farrar, Straus & Giroux 1977 263p

ISBN 0-374-23756-5

LC 77-24032

This novel concerns "David Kepesh, professor of comparative literature. . . . Kepesh becomes involved with a series of women: the coeds at Syracuse University, whom he affronts with his outrageous candor; two Swedish girls in London, who join him, one with self-loathing and the other with zest, in various sexual adventures; a disorganized California beauty, with whom he takes up at the end of his graduate studies at Stanford University; and a well-organized New York beauty, who rescues him from the wreckage of his marriage to the Californian." New Yorker

Roth, Philip

Sabbath's theater. Houghton Mifflin 1995 451p

LC 95-914

"There is plenty of the nasty in this virtuoso performance by our best literary stand-up comic. . . . The verbal play is almost tactile, like slaps, as the narrative moves from third-person comic to first-person perverse confession, but there is a polemical energy that lifts it beyond verbal playfulness; at times the message is painful." N Y Times Book Rev

Roth, Philip

When she was good. Random House 1967 306p

"Roth knows exactly what he's doing. With unerring fidelity, he records the flat surface of provincial American life, the look and feel and sound of it—and then penetrates it to the cesspool of its invisible dynamisms. Beneath the 'good,' and impelling it, he says, lies the horrid." Newsweek

Roth, Philip

Zuckerman bound; a trilogy and epilogue, 1979-1985. Library of America 645p $35

ISBN 978-1-59853-011-7; 1-59853-011-9

LC 2007-926533

"The Ghost Writer (1979) introduces Nathan Zuckerman in the 1950s, a budding writer infatuated with the Great Books, discovering the contradictory claims of literature and experience while an overnight guest in the secluded New England farmhouse of his literary idol, E. I. Lonoff. Zuckerman Unbound (1981) finds him far from Lonoff's domain—the scene is Manhattan as the sensationalizing 1960s are coming to an end. Zuckerman, in his mid-thirties, is suffering the immediate aftershock of literary celebrity. The high-minded protégé of E. I. Lonoff has become a notorious superstar. The Anatomy Lesson (1984) takes place largely in the hospital isolation ward that Zuckerman has made of his Upper East Side apartment. It is Watergate time, 1973, and to Zuckerman the only other American who seems to be in as much trouble as himself is Richard Nixon. Zuckerman, at forty, is beset with crippling and unexplained physical pain; he wonders if the cause might not be his own inflammatory work. In The Prague Orgy (1985), entries from Zuckerman's notebooks describing his 1976 sojourn among the outcast artists of Soviet-occupied Czechoslovakia." Publisher's note

Roth, Philip

★ **Zuckerman** unbound. Farrar, Straus & Giroux 1981 225p

LC 81-4640

"After three marriages and a respected body of fiction, Nathan Zuckerman has suddenly struck free with the scandalous and subversive success of a book about a Portnoyish complainer called Carnovsky. The promising apprentice of The Ghost Writer who engaged in biographical fantasy, has himself become a creature of public fantasy who cannot cope comfortably even with material success. The consequences range from bizarre comedy (the plague of a ruined quiz show contestant who claims his life has been plagiarized) to the distortion of family relations." Libr J

Followed by The anatomy lesson

Rothfuss, Pat

The **name** of the wind; the Kingkiller chronicle, day one. by Patrick Rothfuss. DAW Books 2007 661p $24.95

ISBN 978-0-7564-0407-9; 0-7564-0407-X

This is "quite simply the best fantasy novel of the past 10 years, although attaching a genre qualification threatens to damn it with faint praise. Say instead that The Name of the Wind is one of the best stories told in any medium in a decade." Onion

Rothfuss, Pat

The **wise** man's fear; the Kingkiller chronicle, day two. [by] Patrick Rothfuss. DAW Books 2011 993p $29.95

ISBN 978-0-75640-473-4; 0-75640-473-8

Sequel to: The name of the wind

"As Kvothe, now the unassuming keeper of the Waystone Inn, continues to share his astounding life story—a history that includes saving an influential lord from treachery, defeating a band of dangerous bandits, and surviving an encounter with a legendary Fae seductress—he also offers glimpses into his life's true pursuit: figuring out how to vanquish the mythical Chandrian, a group of seven godlike destroyers that brutally murdered his family and left him an orphan. But while Kvothe recalls the events of his past, his future is conspiring just outside the inn's doors. This breathtakingly epic story is heartrending in its intimacy and masterful in its narrative essence, and will leave fans waiting on tenterhooks for the final installment." Publ Wkly

Rourke, Lee

★ The **canal**. Melville House 2010 199p pa $14.95

ISBN 978-1-935554-01-1; 1-935554-01-8

LC 2010-11960

"You have to salute Rourke — he has written a novel about boredom and how it saturates modernity, which is a ballsy thing to do. But The Canal also takes in urban renewal, technology and violence as it questions the manner in which we live our lives in the 21st century. . . . For a book about urban ennui it's one hell of a page-turner." GQ (UK)

Rowell, Rainbow

★ **Eleanor** & Park; Rainbow Rowell. St. Martin's Griffin 2013 320 p. (hardcover) $18.99

ISBN 1250012570; 9781250012579; 9781250031211

LC 2012042136

Boston Globe-Horn Book Award: Fiction (2013).

This book tells the story of the friendship between half-Korean sophomore Park Sheridan and the new girl Eleanor. "Tall, with bright red hair and a dress code all her own, [Eleanor is] an instant target. Too nice not to let her sit next to him, Park is alternately resentful and guilty for not being kinder to her. When he realizes she's reading his comics over his shoulder, a silent friendship is born" that will become something more. (Publishers Weekly)

"Through Eleanor and Park's alternating voices, readers glimpse the swoon-inducing, often hilarious aspects of first love... Funny, hopeful, foulmouthed, sexy and tear-jerking, this winning romance will captivate teen and adult readers alike." Kirkus

Rowling, J. K., 1965-

The **casual** vacancy; J.K. Rowling. Little, Brown and Co. 2012 503 p. $35

ISBN 1451696191; 9780316228534; 9780316228541

LC 2012943788

In this novel by J. K. Rowling "Barry Fairbrother dies unexpectedly in his early forties, [and] the little town of Pagford is left in shock. Pagford is, seemingly, an English idyll, with a cobbled market square and an ancient abbey, but what lies behind the pretty façade is a town at war. And the empty seat left by Barry on the town's council soon becomes the catalyst for the biggest war the town has yet seen." (Publisher's note)

Rowling, J. K., 1965-

The **cuckoo's** calling; Robert Galbraith. 1st north American ed. Mulholland Books / Little, Brown and Co. 2013 464 p. (hardcover) $25.99

ISBN 0316206849; 9780316206846

LC 2013933193

In this mystery novel, by Robert Galbraith, "Cormoran Strike is barely scraping by as a private investigator. . . . He has also just broken up with his longtime girlfriend and is living in his office. Then John Bristow walks through his door with an amazing story: His sister, the legendary supermodel Lula Landry, known to her friends as the Cuckoo, famously fell to her death a few months earlier. The police ruled it a suicide, but John refuses to believe that." (Publisher's note)

Roy, Anuradha

An **atlas** of impossible longing. Free Press 2010
319p

ISBN 1-4516-0862-4; 978-1-4516-0862-5

LC 2010-19362

First published 2008 in the United Kingdom

This novel "covers multiple generations of an Indian
family from the turn of the 20th century to India's partition.
Three distinct sections revolve around Amulya, who runs
an herbal medicine and fragrance business; his mentally ill
wife, Kananbala, who spies on the goings-on of her English
neighbors from the room Amulya keeps her locked in; their
sons, Kamal and Nirmal; their wives; Nirmal's daughter
Bakul, whose mother died in childbirth; and finally Mukunda, an orphan that Amulya helps support, at which point
Nirmal brings Mukunda home as a companion for Bakul."
Pub Wkly

"Roy's prose is luscious yet economical. Capturing the
rhythms of life in rural backwater and big city alike, she
strings together jewellike episodes, skipping across decades
and defining historical events in mere sentences, and giving
her story the quality of something remembered. Incidental
characters are conjured with an almost Dickensian alacrity."
National Newspaper

Roy, Arundhati

The **god** of small things. Random House 1997
321p

ISBN 978-1606865613

LC 96-39190

A novel "set in the tiny river town of Ayemenem in
Kerala, India. The story revolves around a pair of twins,
brother and sister, whose mother has left her violent husband to live with her blind mother and kind, if ineffectual,
brother, Chacko. Chacko's ex-wife, an Englishwoman, has
returned to Ayemenem after a long absence, bringing along
her and Chacko's lovely young daughter. Their arrival not
only unsettles the already tenuous balance of the divisive
household, it also coincides with political unrest." Booklist

"If the symbolism is a trifle overdone, the lush local col-
or and the incisive characterizations give the narrative power
and drama." Publ Wkly

Roy, Lori

Bent Road. Dutton 2011 355p $25.95

ISBN 978-0-525-95183-4; 0-525-95183-0

LC 2010-37239

"Like Michael Chabon's work, which sometimes crosses
genres, Roy's novel could be called literary fiction or mystery. Whatever the label, 'Bent Road' is written with the care
and craft of standout storytelling. There's inevitability to the
novel's crisis and denouement but plenty of surprise. Psychological acuity, tight plot and in-depth character development keep the reader trying to resist the urge to read ahead."
Kansas City Star

Roy, Lori

Until she comes home; Lori Roy. Dutton 2013
352 p. (hardcover) $26.95

ISBN 0525953965; 9780525953968

LC 2012031919

In this book, "the placid lives of Malina Herze, Julia
Wagner, Grace Richardson, and the other women of Alder Avenue are upended, first by the murder of a 'colored'
woman near the factory where their husbands work, then by
the disappearance of Elizabeth Symanski, a mentally challenged young adult who lives with her widowed father."
(Publishers Weekly)

Roy-Bhattacharya, Joydeep

The **watch**; a novel. Joydeep Roy-Bhattacharya.
Hogarth 2012 290 p.

ISBN 0307955893; 9780307955890

LC 2011037317

This novel by Joydeep Roy-Bhattacharya takes place in
the U.S.-led Afghan War. "Following a desperate night-long
battle, a group of beleaguered soldiers in an isolated base
in Kandahar are faced with a lone woman demanding the
return of her brother's body. Is she a spy, a black widow,
a lunatic, or is she what she claims to be: a grieving young
sister intent on burying her brother according to local rites?
Single-minded in her mission, she refuses to move from her
spot on the field in full view of every soldier in the stark outpost. Her presence quickly proves dangerous as the camp's
tense, claustrophobic atmosphere comes to a boil when the
men begin arguing about what to do next." (Publisher's note)

Rozan, S. J.

Winter and night. St. Martin's Minotaur 2002
338p $24.95

ISBN 0-312-24555-6

LC 2001-48659

In this mystery featuring New York PIs Lydia Chin and
Bill Smith it is "Smith's turn to tell the story, which here
concerns his teenage nephew, Gary Russell, the athlete son
of his estranged sister Helen. When Gary is arrested for
pickpocketing in Manhattan, the boy asks for his uncle's
help. Gary denies running away from his Warrenstown, N.
J. home; he was doing something important. Then the boy
vanishes, drawing Smith and Chin into a nightmarish case
in which a small town's obsession with its high school football team overwhelms standards of justice and morality."
Publ Wkly

Ruark, Robert

Uhuru; a novel of Africa today. McGraw-Hill
1962 555p

This novel "tells of the Kenya of 1960—eight years after
the Mau-Mau rebellion—a Kenya where native Africans are
heard in the House of Parliament and the UN, where modern-day sophistication is blended with ancient tribal customs
to produce a new form of cannibalism, where one nauseating
throat-cutting ceremony follows another nauseating betrayal
of ethics and morals." Libr J

Rubenfeld, Jed

The **death** instinct. Riverhead Books 2011 464p
$26.95

ISBN 978-1-59448-782-8; 1-59448-782-0

LC 2010-16609

"The novel has many stellar set pieces: life in post-World
War I America as it roars into the 1920s, shady Washington
politics, the radium craze in which the element was credited

with everything from reviving male virility to curing cancer, and the early days of Prohibition. Rubenfeld's novel is brilliantly concocted and more than just a little eerie. The fictional and actual events surrounding the 1920 bombing are as relevant today as they were nearly a century ago." USA Today

Ruby, Ilie

The **salt** god's daughter; Ilie Ruby. Soft Skull Press 2012 338 p. (hard cover) $25

ISBN 1619020025; 9781619020023

LC 2012040919

This novel, by Ilie Ruby, uses the folk mythology of selkies, or Celtic mermaids. "Young Naida yearns for her mysterious father. But to understand his role in her life, she must first understand the stories of the women who came before her. The story swirls back to begin with her mother's tale... . [Later,] Ruthie meets Graham, a Scottish fisherman whose soul calls to hers. Graham's love for Ruthie is intense, yet his presence ebbs and flows like the tide." (Publisher's note)

Rucka, Greg

Batwoman; elegy. Greg Rucka, writer; J.H. Williams III, artist; Dave Stewart, colorist; Todd Klein, letters. Deluxe ed. DC Comics 2010 1 v. chiefly col. ill. $24.99

ISBN 9781401226923; 1401226922

LC 2010283560

In this graphic novel, "Batwoman battles a madwoman known only as Alice, inspired by Alice in Wonderland, who sees her life as a fairy tale and everyone around her as expendable! Batwoman must stop Alice from unleashing a toxic death cloud over all of Gotham City—but Alice has more up her sleeve than just poison, and Batwoman's life will never ever be the same." (Publisher's note)

Rucker, Rudy von Bitter

Hylozoic; [by] Rudy Rucker. Tor 2009 334p $25.95

ISBN 978-0-765-32074-2; 0-765-32074-6

LC 2008-53399

This sequel to Postsingular "chronicles the fight to keep Earth 'gnarly' in the face of aliens who want to steal the quantum chaos that makes the planet interesting. Metanovelist Thuy and her husband, JayJay, who's addicted to the global groupmind called Gaia, maneuver between worlds to fend off chaos-diverting Peng real estate developers and flying manta-ray Hrull. Math prodigy Chu, who mitigates his autism with telepathy, and a parallel universe Hieronymus Bosch join Thuy and JayJay as they escape from modern-day fundamentalists and Renaissance witch-hunters and try to keep Gaia from going volcanic." Publ Wkly

"Serious, uproarious fun, with brain-teasers and brilliant ideas tossed about like confetti." Kirkus

Rucker, Rudy von Bitter

★ **Mathematicians** in love; [by] Rudy Rucker. Tor 2006 364p $24.95

ISBN 978-0-7653-1584-7; 0-7653-1584-X

LC 2006-5725

Rucker "is palpably and quiveringly tuned in to the zeitgeist and can offer cultural and scientific commentary and

satire better than almost any other SF author practicing today.... But aside from all the glories of the speculative science and math and interdimensional jaunts..., what we have here is a rollicking, roisterous, (ir-)reverent campus novel." Sci Fi Wkly

Rucker, Rudy von Bitter

Postsingular; [by] Rudy Rucker. Tor 2007 320p $25.95

ISBN 978-0-7653-1741-4; 0-7653-1741-9

LC 2007-20210

"In the very near future, two influential and maladjusted individuals initiate a radical transformation of the world through the use of sentient nanotechnology-only to have their plans foiled by Chu, the autistic son of two scientists engaged in nanotechnology research. The persistence of money and politics, however, creates a strange new world in which humans become telepaths and can travel to other worlds in the quantum universe; finally, gigantic visitors from another place entirely arrive to sort things out. Rucker... excels in mind-bending premises and thought-stretching stories peopled with appealingly flawed characters that resonate with familiarity despite their eccentricities." Libr J

Ruff, Matt

Bad monkeys. Harper Collins Publishers 2007 230p $20

ISBN 978-0-06-124041-6; 0-06-124041-9

LC 2006-52184

"At times the twists are enough to give the reader whiplash. Ruff's expert characterization of Jane and agile manipulation of layers of reality ground the novel and make it more than just a Philip K. Dick ripoff." Publ Wkly

Ruiz Zafon, Carlos, 1964-

The **angel's** game; translated into English by Lucia Graves. Doubleday 2009 531p $26.95

ISBN 978-0-385-52870-2; 0-385-52870-1

LC 2008-53650

A prequel to: The shadow of the wind

Original Spanish edition, 2008

"As the book opens in 1917, David Martín is 17, a down-on-his-luck Barcelona writer and budding journalist. An orphan since his father was murdered, David is forced by necessity to subvert his lofty literary ambitions in the service of writing a series of pulp novels in the macabre Grand Guignol tradition. Then a mysterious stranger named Andreas Corelli, a close relative of the stranger in Mark Twain's book of the same name and every other deal-with-the-devil tale you've ever read, presents a proposal to Martín — write a book that will create a perfect narrative for a religion. In essence, his assignment is to create a mythical story that will seduce the masses into belief. The mortal medical condition Martín suffers from goes into remission, and a fortune is placed in his bank account. And off we go. This novel operates on so many levels, a brief review can't quite do justice to its many layers." Seattle Times

Ruiz Zafon, Carlos, 1964-

The **prisoner** of heaven; a novel. Harper 2012 288 p. (hardcover) $25.99

ISBN 0062206281; 9780062206282; 0062207261

Large Print; 9780062207265 Large Print

This novel, by Carlos Ruiz Zafon, is set in "Barcelona, 1957. . . . Daniel Sempere and his wife . . . have a beautiful new baby son, . . . and their close friend Fermin Romero de Torres is about to be wed. But their joy is eclipsed when a mysterious stranger visits the Sempere bookshop and threatens to divulge a terrible secret that has been buried for two decades in the city's dark past." (Publisher's note)

Ruiz Zafon, Carlos, 1964-

The **shadow** of the wind; translated by Lucia Graves. Penguin Press 2004 486p $24.95

ISBN 1-59420-010-6

LC 2003-062376

Original Spanish edition, 2001

"In post-World War II Barcelona, young Daniel is taken by his bookseller father to the Cemetery of Forgotten Books, a massive sanctuary where books are guarded from oblivion. Told to choose one book to protect, he selects The Shadow of the Wind, by Julian Carax. He reads it, loves it, and soon learns it is both very valuable and very much in danger because someone is determinedly burning every copy of every book written by the obscure Carax. . . . Daniel's initiation into the mysteries of adulthood is given the same weight as the mystery of the book-burner. And the setting—Spain under Franco—injects an air of sobriety into some plot elements that might otherwise seem soap operatic. Part detective story, part boy's adventure, part romance, fantasy, and gothic horror, the intricate plot is urged on by extravagant foreshadowing and nail-nibbling tension." Booklist

Ruiz, Luis Manuel

Only one thing missing; translated from the Spanish by Alfred Mac Adam. Grove Press 2003 308p $24

ISBN 0-8021-1730-9

LC 2002-29723

Original Spanish edition, 2000

"A distraught young woman living in Seville, Spain, Alicia has just lost her husband and only child in a horrible accident. She suffers from terrifying nightmares of wandering through a nameless city whose monuments and inhabitants begin appearing to her during waking moments. Carmen Barroso, the most sought-after psychotherapist in Seville. . . treats her with hynosis and medication but is strangely dismissive of her harrowing dreams. . . . Aided by her brother-in-law, Esteban, who loves her deeply, Alicia comes to realize that she is the victim of a sinister conspiracy with roots in devil worship." Libr J

"As translated by Adam, Ruiz's prose is ornate and word-drunk. Ruiz sometimes falls in love with the sound of his narrator's voice, but it is easy to forgive him." Booklist

Runcie, James

Canvey Island; a novel. Other Press 2008 301p pa $13.95

ISBN 978-1-59051-293-7; 1-59051-293-6

LC 2007-52431

First published 2006 in the United Kingdom

"In 1953 Canvey Island, off the coast of Britain, suffered the ill effects of a storm surge, which flooded the island. In this fictionalized account of the tragedy, nine-year-old Mar-

tin and his mother, Lily, fight to stay above water, but Lily is unable to free herself from the debris, and she is swept under. Her death becomes the defining moment of Martin's life; he grows up obsessed with water and becomes an engineer, forever trying to figure out the best way to hold back the sea. He never quite forgives his father, Len, for failing to save his wife and for taking up with her sister, the flamboyant Violet. Martin himself gives up his free-spirited girlfriend, in part because he loves her too much, opting instead to marry Claire, a vicar's daughter with a rebellious streak. In highly readable chapters narrated by each family member, the book manages to address class and generational conflict as it travels through the decades." Booklist

Runyon, Damon

Guys and dolls. Lippincott 1950 505p

Contents: Guys and dolls: Bloodhounds of Broadway; Social error; Lily of St. Pierre; Butch minds the baby; Lillian; Romance in the roaring forties; Very honorable guy; Madame La Gimp; Dark Dolores; ¿Gentlemen, the King!¿; Hottest guy in the world; Brain goes home; Blood pressure ; Blue plate special: Hold 'em Yale!; That ever-loving wife of Hymie's; What, no butler?; Brakeman's daughter; Snatching of Bookie Bob; Dream Street Rose; Little Miss Marker; Dancing Dan's Christmas; Old doll's house; Lemon drop kid; Three wise guys; Princess O'Hara; For a pal ; Money from home: Earthquake; Bred for battle; Breach of promise; Story goes with it; Sense of humor; Broadway financier; Broadway complex; It comes up mud; Nice price; Pick the winner; Undertaker song; Tobias the terrible

An omnibus volume of three titles first published by F.A. Stokes in 1931, 1935 and 1934 respectively and analyzed in Short story index

Rush, Norman

★ **Mating**. Knopf 1991 480p

LC 90-25752

"Mr. Rush has created one of the wiser and wittier fictive meditations on the subject of mating. His novel illuminates why we yield when we don't have to. It seeks to illuminate the nature of true intimacy—how to define it, how to know when one has achieved it. And few books evoke so eloquently that state of love at its apogee." N Y Times Book Rev

Rush, Norman

Mortals; a novel. Knopf 2003 715p $26.95

ISBN 0-679-40622-0

LC 2002-43289

This "novel is about middle-class Americans in Botswana, Africa. . . . The protagonist is a minor secret CIA agent in the early 1990s with the region in turmoil as Mandela struggles to come to power across the border. Ray's not quite sure how he landed in his spy job, but he quite likes it. He's sure he's never been involved with anything really bad. What matters to him is his beautiful wife, Iris. After 17 years, he's still totally obsessed with every part of her body, every glance, every funny word. But is she having an affair with Morel, the black American doctor who believes the way to fix broken Africa is to get rid of Christianity? When Ray is sent on a bungled mission and lands up with the brutal apartheid paramilitary, Morel comes to the rescue, and the two bond in a prison cell." Booklist

"The richness of Rush's vision, and its stringent moral clarity, sweep the reader into his brilliantly observed world." Publ Wkly

Rushdie, Salman, 1947-

East, west; stories. Pantheon Bks. 1995 214p
LC 94-28277

First publishd 1994 in the United Kingdom

"Rushdie's brilliant style reinforces his stories' marvelous combination of dignity and poignancy. Though these stories were originally published in such periodicals as the New Yorker and the Atlantic, the collection will serve for many readers as an introduction to Rushdie's talent in the short story form." Booklist

Rushdie, Salman

The **enchantress** of Florence; a novel. Random House 2008 355p $26
ISBN 978-0-375-50433-4; 0-375-50433-8
LC 2008-70

"A tall, yellow-haired, young European traveler calling himself 'Mogor dell'Amore,' the Mughal of Love, arrives at the court of the Emperor Akbar, lord of the great Mughal empire, with a tale to tell that begins to obsess the imperial capital, a tale about a mysterious woman, a great beauty believed to possess powers of enchantment and sorcery, and her impossible journey to the far-off city of Florence." Publisher's note

Rushdie, Salman

The **ground** beneath her feet; a novel. Holt & Co. 1999 575p $26
ISBN 0-8050-5308-5
LC 98-42407

"A distraught young woman living in Seville, Spain, Alicia has just lost her husband and only child in a horrible accident. She suffers from terrifying nightmares of wandering through a nameless city whose monuments and inhabitants begin appearing to her during waking moments. Carmen Barroso, the most sought-after psychotherapist in Seville. . . treats her with hynosis and medication but is strangely dismissive of her harrowing dreams. . . . Aided by her brother-in-law, Esteban, who loves her deeply, Alicia comes to realize that she is the victim of a sinister conspiracy with roots in devil worship." Libr J

"Vina and Ormus are icons, not fully formed characters. But that's the point. And Rai . . . is the most moving character Rushdie's ever created." Newsweek

Rushdie, Salman

Haroun and the sea of stories. Granta Books in association with Viking 1990 219p hardcover o.p. pa $14
ISBN 0-14-015737-9 pa
LC 90-45496

"This delightful fantasy is filled with adventures, amusing characters with names like Iff and Butt, and villains to fight against and defeat. Rushdie's puns and rhymes will be enjoyed by young and old—the catchy tunes by the younger readers and the political allegory by the adults. Rashid is a professional story-teller whose son, Haroun, delights in hearing them. When Rashid's source of stories seems to have disappeared Haroun faces many dangerous opponents to help his father regain his Gift of Gab." Shapiro. Fic for Youth. 3d edition

Rushdie, Salman

★ **Midnight's** children; with an introduction by Anita Desai. Knopf 1995 xxxi, 589p $20
ISBN 0-679-44462-9
LC 90-38447

A reissue of the title first published 1980 in the United Kingdom; 1981 in the United States

"The novel is about Shiva and Saleem, two of the 1,001 babies born in the hour following independence at midnight on August 15, 1947. It is notable as much for its portrayal of contemporary politics in India as for the brilliance of its style and insights into human nature and mind." Reader's Ency. 4th edition

Rushdie, Salman

The **Moor's** last sigh. Pantheon Bks. 1996 435p
ISBN 978-0679420491
LC 95-24392

First published 1995 in the United Kingdom

This is a "marvellously inventive display of verbal dexterity; an exuberant, entertaining, zestful novel which proves, if proof were needed, that Mr Rushdie's spirit remains undiminshed." Economist

Rushdie, Salman, 1947-

★ The **satanic** verses. Viking 1989 546p $27.95
ISBN 0670825379
LC 88-40266

"When a terrorist's bomb destroys a jumbo jet high above the English Channel, two passengers fall safely to earth: Gibreel {Farishta}, an Indian movie actor, and Saladin {Chamcha}, star of the controversial British television program, The Alien Show. The near-death experience changes them into living symbols of good and evil—Saladin grows horns, Gibreel a halo." (Libr J)

A "panoramic novel which moves with dizzying speed from the streets and film studios of Bombay to multicultural Britain, from Argentina to Mount Everest, as Rushdie questions illusion, reality, and the power of faith and tradition in a world of hijackers, religious pilgrimages and warfare, and celluloid fantasy." Oxford Companion to Engl Lit. 6th edition

Rushdie, Salman

Shalimar the clown. Random House 2005 398p $25.95
ISBN 0-679-46335-6
LC 2005-42796

"Rushdie has written an intensely political novel, infused with recent events, but its emotional scope reaches so far beyond our current crisis and its vision into the vagaries of the heart is so perceptive that one can imagine Shalimar the Clown being read long after this age of sacred terror has faded into history." Washington Post Book World

Russell, Karen

St. Lucy's home for girls raised by wolves. Knopf 2006 246p

ISBN 0-307-26398-3

LC 2006-45156

"A series of upbeat, sentimental fables, the 10 stories of Russell's debut are set in an enchanted version of North America and narrated by articulate, emotionally precocious children from dysfunctional households. Each merges the satirical spirit of George Saunders with the sophisticated whimsy of recent animated Hollywood film." Publ Wkly

Russell, Karen

★ Swamplandia! Karen Russell. Alfred A. Knopf 2011 315p. $24.95

ISBN 0307263991; 9780307263995

LC 201036708

This book tells the story of "Swamplandia!, [which] is a shabby tourist attraction deep in the Everglades, owned by the Bigtree clan of alligator wrestlers. When Hilola, their star performer, dies, her husband and children lose their moorings, and Swamplandia! itself is endangered as audiences dwindle. The Chief leaves. Brother Kiwi, 17, sneaks off to work at the World of Darkness, a new mainland amusement park featuring the 'rings of hell.' Otherworldly sister Osceola, 16, vanishes after falling in love with the ghost of a young man who died while working for the ill-fated Dredge and Fill Campaign in the 1930s. It's up to Ava, 13, to find her sister." (Booklist)

"When Hilola Bigtree, professional alligator wrestler and star attraction at a Florida venue that calls itself "the Number One Gator-Themed Park and Swamp Café in the area," dies in the vise grip not of some prehistoric behemoth but of unglamorous cancer, the family-owned tourist destination shrivels into insolvency. Likewise, the remaining Bigtree clan unspools in her absence, and Ava, the youngest of three children, can only watch as they drift apart. Her sister, Ossie, obsessed with the afterlife, carries out furtive relationships with the spirits of dead boys she claims possess her. Her brother, Kiwi, runs off to work for the World of Darkness, an amusement park designed to resemble hell. The plot of Swamplandia! tilts toward the odd. Kiwi toils in his ersatz inferno; Ava goes on a quest to save Ossie after she elopes into the otherworldly wetlands with one of her phantom paramours. But Russell isn't a magic realist. In fact, the only truly magical things about this book are its effortless prose and its small, beautifully drawn cast of characters." Entertainment Wkly

Russell, Karen

★ Vampires in the lemon grove; stories. by Karen Russell. Alfred A. Knopf 2013 243 p. (paperback) $15.00; (hardcover) $24.95; (ebook) $74.85

ISBN 0307957233; 9780307947475; 9780307957238; 9780307961082

LC 2012027415

Author Karen Russell presents a collection of short stories, with plots including a "teenager [who] discovers that the universe is communicating with him through talismanic objects left behind in a seagull's nest. A community of girls held captive in a silk factory slowly transmute into human silkworms, . . . a massage therapist discovers she has the power to heal by manipulating the tattoos on a war veteran [and] a group of boys [find a] scarecrow [resembling a] missing classmate." (Publisher's note)

Russell, Mary Doria

Children of God; a novel. Villard Bks. 1998 438p $23.95

ISBN 0-679-45635-X

LC 97-42160

"Having returned from a disastrous, 21st-century expedition to the planet Rakhat, Jesuit Father Emilio Sandoz, the sole survivor of the mission, faces public rage over the order's part in the war between the gentle Runa and the predatory Jana'ata—fury more than matched by the priest's own self-hatred and religious disillusionment. . . . He is forced to return to Rakhat with a new expedition more interested in profits than prophets. When they discover the planet in turmoil and the Runa precariously in power, the temptation to interfere is more than they can withstand." Publ Wkly

"Russell succeeds in painting an alien culture with remarkably detailed verisimilitude." N Y Times Book Rev

Russell, Mary Doria

★ Doc. Random House 2011 394p $26

ISBN 978-1-4000-6804-3; 1-4000-6804-5

LC 2010-15062

"An engaging bit of de-mythology, a vivid re-imagining of a more authentic, slightly less 'wild' West than the one we've come to know through dime-store novels." Cleveland Plain Dealer

Russell, Mary Doria

Dreamers of the day; a novel. Random House 2008 251p il

ISBN 978-1-40006471-7; 1-400-06471-6

LC 2007-24665

"Russell perfectly captures the political and social milieus of the 1920s, driving home how important it is to consider history when dealing with present-day issues. . . . The fact that Agnes is telling her story after she has—yes—already died does not come across as a literary conceit but as perfectly fitting for this perfectly enchanting tale." BookPage

Russell, Mary Doria

★ The sparrow. Villard Bks. 1996 408p

ISBN 978-0679451501

LC 96-11180

This novel about first contact with an extraterrestrial civilization features "Father Emilio Sandoz, a Jesuit linguist whose messianic virtues hide his occasional doubt about his calling. . . . The narrative ping-pongs between the years 2016, when Sandoz begins assembling the team that first detects signs of intelligent extraterrestrial life, and 2060, when a Vatican inquest is convened to coax an explanation from the physically mutilated and emotionally devastated priest." Publ Wkly

Followed by Children of God

Russell, Mary Doria

A **thread** of grace; a novel. Mary Doria Russell. 1st ed; Random House 2005 430p $25.95

ISBN 0-375-50184-3

LC 2004-50942

"This is a morality play that at times uses black humor, and then shifts to solemn reflection or moving portraiture. A Thread of Grace is deft, sensate, ruthless in its moral incisiveness, and affirming in that even in the worst of times, the lamp of humanity cannot be completely extinguished." Hudson Rev

Russell, Sheldon

This insane train. Minotaur Books 2010 312p $25.99

ISBN 978-0-312-56671-5; 0-312-56671-9

LC 2010-32672

The author "imbues even bit characters with personality, and presents a rough-edged view of the world that will be familiar to fans of classic hardboiled writers such as Chandler and Hammett." Publ Wkly

Russo, Richard

Bridge of sighs. Alfred A. Knopf 2007 528p $26.95

ISBN 978-0-375-41495-4

LC 2007-27970

"Whatever the scale of their lives, Russo's characters—the stars and the walk-ons are gorgeously drawn. The writing is always in service of illuminating them—with one exception. The black characters speak in a corny-sounding dialect, which can make the reader stop to decode sentences. In this case, the reach for authenticity doesn't work. But everything else works brilliantly. . . . That Russo manages to juggle so many characters, themes, places, and time periods through 528 delicious pages is an astounding achievement. From its lovely beginning to its exquisite, perfect end, Russo has written a masterpiece." Boston Globe

Russo, Richard

★ **Empire** Falls. Knopf 2001 483p $29.95

ISBN 0-679-43247-7

LC 2001-88568

"Miles Roby is a typical Russo hero: wry, unlucky in love and money; and just a little bit smarter than the people who populate his run-down industrial town. In this case, the town is Empire Falls, Maine, where Miles manages a restaurant that serves as a kind of meeting hall for the novel's large cast of characters. There's David, Miles's recovering-alcoholic brother; Walt, the health-club entrepreneur who has stolen Miles's estranged wife; Tick, Miles's precocious, befuddled teen-age daughter; and Francine Whiting, the rich widow who runs everything. Russo is preoccupied with the death of a certain version of the American dream, but his belief in the power of comedy—sometimes low, sometimes high—rescues his work from bathos and elvates it into the realm of literature." New Yorker

Russo, Richard

★ **Nobody's** fool. Random House 1993 549p

ISBN 0-394-57778-7

LC 92-56844

"A grand read sparkling with witty dialogue and memorable characters, Russo's novel is a rollicking tale of a born loser on a downward slide. An economically depressed upper New York State community is the setting, and its lower-middle-class and blue-collar inhabitants are portrayed with empathy and a shrewd understanding of human nature." Publ Wkly

Russo, Richard

The **risk** pool. Random House 1988 479p

ISBN 0-394-56527-4

LC 88-42666

"A superbly original, maliciously funny book, peopled by characters that most of us would back away from plenty fast if they ever lurched toward our barstool. It is Mr. Russo's brilliant, deadpan writing that gives their wasted lives and miserable little town such haunting power and insidious charm." N Y Times Book Rev

Russo, Richard

The **straight** man. Random House 1997 391p

ISBN 0-679-43246-9

LC 96-48578

"The novel's greatest pleasures derive not from any blazing impatience to see what happens next, but from pitch-perfect dialogue, persuasive characterization and a rich progression of scenes, most of them crackling with an impudent, screwball energy reminiscent of Howard Hawks's movies." N Y Times Book Rev

Russo, Richard

That old Cape magic; a novel. Alfred A. Knopf 2009 261p $25.95

ISBN 978-0-375-41496-1; 0-375-41496-7

LC 2009-20311

"Joy and Jack Griffin head to Cape Cod to attend a friend's wedding, where their daughter Laura announces her own engagement. Sensing the malaise in their 30-year marriage, the Griffins decide to reconnect by visiting the B & B where they once honeymooned. Their arrival in separate vehicles seems symbolic of the discord in their hearts and minds. Jack, still coming to terms with his father's death and bristling at his mother's constant criticism, feels restless in his career as a college professor, wondering whether he should have left a lucrative screenwriting gig in L.A. Joy, chafing at Jack's implicit displeasure with her sunny disposition and maddening family, longs for an empathetic listener." Libr J

"Suffused with Russo's signature comic sensibility, and with insights, by turns tender and tough, about human frailty, forbearance, fortitude, and fervor." Boston Globe

Russo, Richard

The **whore's** child; and other stories. Knopf 2002 225p

ISBN 0-375-41168-2

LC 2002-19023

"Russo's rueful understanding of the twisted skein of human relationships is as sharp as ever, and the dialogue throughout is barbed, pointed and wryly humorous." Publ Wkly

Rutherford, Ethan

The **Peripatetic** Coffin and other stories; by Ethan Rutherford. HarperCollins 2013 240 p. $13.99

ISBN 0062203835; 9780062203830

This collection of short stories by Ethan Rutherford offers "eight tales that ponder the methods in which humans achieve isolation. While many of these methods take the form of physical vessels—the Civil War-era submarine in the title story, the Russian ship headed toward the North Pole in 'The Saint Anna,' a futuristic shipper-tank named Halcyon roaming the desert for dying prey in 'Dirwhals!'—the author also fashions narratives focusing on psychological, corporeal seclusion." (Publishers Weekly)

Rutherfurd, Edward

The **forest**; a novel. Crown 2000 598p il

ISBN 0-609-60382-5

LC 00-22219

This historical saga focuses on "the New Forest, part of the southern coast of England bounded by the English Channel. Rutherfurd traces the lives of peasants, smugglers, churchmen, woodsmen, and upper-class families from the 11th to the 20th centuries. These assorted men and women take part in the events surrounding the death of King Rufus (William the Conqueror's son), the failure of the Spanish Armada, England's Civil War, and more." Libr J

Rutherfurd, Edward

London. Crown 1997 829p $25.95

ISBN 0-517-59181-2

LC 97-10176

First published 1995 in the United Kingdom

This "fictional history of London is told through the experiences of a group of diverse families who, over the generations, meet, mingle, intermarry, and feud. Beginning with prehistory and continuing to the present, Rutherfurd combines geological details, historical events, real people, and his fictional characters to bring London to life." Libr J

Rutherfurd, Edward

Paris; the novel. Edward Rutherfurd. 1st ed. Random House Inc 2013 x, 809 p.p (hardcover) $32.50

ISBN 0385535309; 9780385535304

LC 2013005884

This novel by Edward Rutherfurd explores the history of Paris, "recounting all the most significant transformative events as the City of Light evolves from its humble origins as a Roman trading post to the cultural epicenter of Western civilization. Utilizing . . . real-life and fictional characters, he stitches their individual stories and experiences together in order to humanize and personalize the emergence of a mighty metropolis over a period of 2,000 years." (Booklist)

Rutherfurd, Edward

★ The **princes** of Ireland; the Dublin saga. Doubleday 2004 776p $27.95

ISBN 0-385-50286-9

LC 2003-70005

"Beginning in the tribal, pre-Christian times of the warrior kings at Tara, this first book in a two-part novelized history of Ireland sweeps readers through the early centuries of Druids, chieftains, monks, Vikings, noblemen, merchants, and mercenaries, ending with the disastrous invasion of England that tragically changed the course of Irish history. Through the eyes of the men and women who built the mighty city that became Dublin, the unfolding of a colorful and turbulent history is told with energy and a meticulous attention to historical detail." Libr J

Rutherfurd, Edward

The **rebels** of Ireland; the Dublin Saga. Doubleday 2006 xxv, 863p $28.95

ISBN 0-385-51289-9

LC 2006-273953

"Beginning with Elizabeth's ascendancy to the English throne and the 'plantation' period of the English conquest of Ireland and ending with the founding of the Irish republic in 1922, this sequel to Princes of Ireland vividly tells the history of Irish suppression through the lives of ordinary people on both sides of the turmoil. It is a story of bitter and tragic contrast. Rutherfurd casts the Irish, thought to be savages by England's Protestant elite, against a backdrop of a vibrant, intellectual Dublin, deeply divided by religion and politics yet aglow with the literary renaissance of Yeats, Shaw, and Joyce." Libr J

Rutherfurd, Edward

Russka; the novel of Russia. Crown 1991 760p

LC 90-34457

"Tells the story of a Ukrainian village . . . and some of the families who lived there from A.D. 180 to the 1917 Revolution and, anecdotally, almost to the present." N Y Times Book Rev

The book "does provide a sweeping overview of the land whose very vastness and complexity make it overwhelming and fascinating." Christ Sci Monit

Rutherfurd, Edward

Sarum; the novel of England. Crown 1987 897p

LC 87-6710

This novel, set in Salisbury, England, aims to trace English history from the last Ice Age to the present through the lives of five fictional families

"Rutherfurd is strong on the explication of trends and the narration of events. But he relies heavily on the repetition of character types. Nevertheless, 'Sarum' is fascinating and will appeal to Anglophiles, history buffs, and fans of epic-style novels." Christ Sci Monit

Rutland, Eva

No crystal stair; Eva Rutland. Mira 2000 474p.

ISBN 9781551666624; 9781551665191; 1551665190

LC 2003576586

The story follows "the lives of privileged Ann Elizabeth Carter and Army Air Corps pilot Robert Metcalf--their romance, their struggles, and their ultimate happiness--as it sweeps its characters from the genteel, segregated world of Atlanta's black elite through the rough realities of war, prejudice, and civil rights activism and into the present." (Libr J)

Ryan, Hank Phillippi

The **other** woman; Hank Phillippi Ryan. 1st ed. Forge 2012 416 p. (hardcover) $24.99

ISBN 0765332574; 9780765332578; 9781466800861

LC 2012019932

In this novel, by Hank Phillippi Ryan, "Jane Ryland, . . . a disgraced newspaper reporter, . . . finds herself tracking down a candidate's secret mistress just days before a pivotal Senate election. Detective Jake Brogan is investigating a possible serial killer. . . . It becomes clear to Jane and Jake that their cases are connected . . . and that they may be facing a ruthless killer who will stop at nothing to silence a scandal." (Publisher's note)

Ryman, Geoff

Paradise tales. Small Beer Press 2011 313p pa $9.99

ISBN 978-1-931520-64-5; 1-931520-64-X

LC 2010-48947

"Often contemplative and subtly ironic, the 16 stories in this outstanding collection work imaginative riffs on a variety of fantasy and SF themes. 'Pol Pot's Beautiful Daughter,' a Cambodian ghost story, and 'The Last Ten Years in the Life of Hero Kai,' a samurai-style narrative, have the delicacy of Asian folktales or lyrical fantasies. By contrast, 'V.A.O.,' about a future society destabilized by prohibitively expensive health care, and 'The Film-makers of Mars,' which suggests that Edgar Rice Burroughs's John Carter stories were drawn from life, are set in futures that credibly extrapolate current scientific and cultural trends. Ryman . . . frequently explores human emotional needs in heartless environments, as in 'Warmth,' which poignantly portrays a young boy's bond with his robot surrogate mother. Readers of all stripes will appreciate these thoughtful tales." Publ Wkly

S

Sabatini, Rafael

Captain Blood; his odyssey. Houghton Mifflin 1922 356p

"Peter Blood was many things in his time—soldier, country doctor, slave, pirate, and finally Governor of Jamaica. Incidentally, he was an Irishman. Round his humorous-heroic figure Mr. Sabatini has written an exciting romance of the Spanish Main, the facts of which he alleges to have been found in the diary and log books of one Jeremiah Pitt, a follower of Monmouth in 1685 and Blood's faithful companion in adventure." Times Lit Suppl

Sabatini, Rafael

Scaramouche; a romance of the French revolution. Houghton Mifflin 1921 392p

"The story, primarily of love and adventure, is woven around a hero who devoted himself to furthering the republican cause during the first years of the French Revolution (1788-1792). The title character, successively a lawyer, politician, swordsman, and buffoon, crosses paths repeatedly with his sworn enemy, in the end attaining love and happiness." Lenrow. Reader's Guide to Prose Fic

Followed by Scaramouche, the king-maker (1931)

Saberhagen, Fred

Berserker fury. TOR Bks. 1997 383p $23.95

ISBN 0-312-85939-2

LC 97-1157

This adventure "finds the intelligent, deadly Berserker machines infiltrating human colonies to destroy them. The humans have cracked the Berserkers' codes and plan a battle defense. Although it helps to be familiar with the series, this novel can stand alone." Libr J

Saberhagen, Fred

Berserker's star. TOR Bks. 2003 368p $24.95

ISBN 0-7653-0423-6

LC 2003-41016

"Wanted in parts of the galaxy for his theft of a powerful space cannon, pilot Harry Silver accepts a business proposition from a mysterious woman who claims she wants to rescue her husband from cultists on Maracanda, a pseudo-planet wedged between a black hole and a neutron star. En route, Silver discovers that his passenger's agenda is not quite what it seems and, after making planefall, he finds that Maracanda holds secrets and terrors beyond his worst fears. . . . Witty dialog, clever plot twists, and a likeably roguish protagonist make this a good selection for most sf collections." Libr J

Saberhagen, Fred

The **fifth** book of lost swords: Coinspinner's story. Doherty Assocs. 1989 244p

LC 89-39878

"When the legendary sword Woundheale disappears from its resting place in the White Temple of Sarykam, investigations reveal that the Sword of Chance, Coinspinner, is once again loose in the world." Libr J

Saberhagen, Fred

The **first** book of lost swords: Woundhealer's story. Doherty Assocs. 1986 281p

LC 86-50319

This book begins a new sequence in the author's fantasy series about mythical swords

A "pleasant adventure that benefits greatly from Saberhagen's narrative gifts as the various strands leapfrog forward, keeping the reader off balance but constantly intrigued." Publ Wkly

Saberhagen, Fred

The **fourth** book of lost swords: Farslayer's story. Doherty Assocs. 1989 252p

LC 89-11638

"Two rival families wage a war of attrition and vengeance for possession of 'Farslayer,' one of the 12 Lost Swords made by the gods and imbued with unearthly powers. A grim sense of fatality underlies the deceptive simplicity of the author's style." Libr J

Saberhagen, Fred

The **last** book of swords: Shieldbreaker's story. TOR Bks. 1994 255p

LC 93-43232

In this concluding book of the saga, "battle extends from palace to peasant hut—indeed, all the way to the moon—and is loaded with remnants of premagical technology as well as the secret of why the Old World fell and magic came to rule. Key to the battle against Vikata the Dark King is Prince Mark's second son, Prince Stephen, who turns out to be a formidable wielder of swords. By the time journeys and battles are done, the only one of the twelve swords that survives is Woundhealer, for even the terrifying Shieldbreaker has perished." Booklist

Saberhagen, Fred

The **second** book of lost swords: Sightblinder's story. Doherty Assocs. 1987 248p

LC 87-50477

"The present story limits itself to a single locale, the island castle of the wizard Honan-Fu, where Prince Mark is imprisoned in ice alongside the wizard by the usurper called the Ancient One. Mark's friends find themselves the temporary allies of Honan-Fu's traitorous daughter, Ninazu, and of the magician emperor, currently incognito with a traveling show. . . . An entertainment of high order." Publ Wkly

Saberhagen, Fred

The **seventh** book of lost swords: Wayfinder's story. TOR Bks. 1992 251p

LC 92-858

"One of 12 magical swords forged by the Gods, Wayfinder has the power to guide its possessor to whatever the seeker wants. Chance brings Wayfinder to Ben of Purkinje, who uses it to find Woundhealer, the sword with powers to cure the injured wife of Prince Mar of Sarykam. The evil magician Wood also wants the swords; his attack on Ben brings Mark, and even more swords, into the fray. . . . Saberhagen keeps the plot moving, providing a pleasurable light reading experience." Publ Wkly

Saberhagen, Fred

The **sixth** book of lost swords: Mindsword's story. TOR Bks. 1990 250p

LC 90-38899

"Intended as a peace offering from Prince Murat to the Princess Kristin, the Mindsword—one of the legendary weapons used in the war that brought about the death of the gods—plunges two countries into near-war as the well-meaning Murat falls victim to the sword's seductive powers. Saberhagen treads a fine line between fantasy and moral fable in his latest addition to a popular series." Libr J

Saberhagen, Fred

The **third** book of lost swords: Stonecutter's story. Doherty Assocs. 1988 247p

LC 87-51397

This novel "deals with the search of Prince al-Farabi and Magistrate Wen Chang for the lost sword Stonecutter. The book's virtues include a cast of well-drawn characters and some vividly realized societies, as well as Saberhagen's usual spare prose and sound narrative technique." Booklist

Sackville-West, V.

All passion spent. Doubleday, Doran 1931 294p

"When Lady Slane, after the death of her famous husband, shocks her family by going to live by herself in a little house in Hempstead, she is for the first time in her eighty-eight years asserting her right to live her own life. The year

of quiet reminiscences there is not without exciting moments, for a man who has loved her silently for sixty years renews his friendship, tells her of his love, then suddenly dies, and leaves her his enormous fortune. What she does with this fortune is another instance of her self-assertion. Gentle, charming Lady Slane, her family, and her friends, drawn with wit and skill in this tale of graceful old age, create an impression of subtlety and beauty." Booklist

Sackville-West, V.

The **Edwardians**. Doubleday, Doran 1930 314p

The setting of this story of Edwardian England is the beautiful old manor-house of Chevron. The characters are grouped around Sebastian, the young heir to the dukedom, and his mother, a famous hostess of the day. Individuals count for less in the novel—a decadent but decorative society. The close of the story, marked by King George's coronation, finds the young duke breaking with the traditions that have bound him, not unwillingly, and starting a new era for himself

"'The Edwardians' is of undoubted excellence from two points of view. First, it is a magnificent portrait of a class and an era. Secondly, it is remarkable for its excellent prose style." Springfield Repub

Sada, Daniel

Almost never; Daniel Sada; translated by Katherine Silver. Graywolf Press 2012 330 p. (alk. paper) $16

ISBN 1555976093; 9781555976095

LC 2011944859

This book by Daniel Sada presents a "Rabelaisian tale of lust and longing in the drier precincts of postwar Mexico. . . . One day, more bored than usual, Demetrio visits a bordello. . . . There he begins an all-consuming . . . relationship with a prostitute named Mireya. . . . He meets the beautiful and virginal Renata and quickly falls in love. . . . Naturally he tries to maintain both relationships." (Publisher's note)

Saer, Juan Jose

The **sixty**-five years of Washington; translated from the Spanish by Steve Dolph. Open Letter 2010 203p pa $14.95

ISBN 978-1-934824-20-7; 1-934824-20-8

LC 2010-29041

Original Spanish edition, 1986

In this novel, "the Argentine writer Saer packs several decades of his country's history into a single hour. The premise is deceptively simple. On a fall morning in 1961 a pair of young men take a stroll in the city of Santa Fe. Ángel Leto, a skinny man who lives with his mother, skips work and runs into a tall, white-clad acquaintance known among friends as 'the Mathematician,' a chemical engineer distributing press releases about a recent trip to Europe. In three sections covering seven blocks each, Saer flits between his protagonists' minds, relating their fleeting sensations, memories, epiphanies and distractions in exquisite detail. As they speculate about the events of a recent party that neither attended (for the 65th birthday of Jorge Washington Noriega, the 'Washington' of the title) the reader begins to grasp the web of relationships that bind their circle of intellectuals and activists. . . . With meticulous prose, rendered by Dolph's translation into propulsive English, Saer's novel captures the wilderness of human experience in all its variety." N Y Times Book Rev

Safire, William
   Freedom. Doubleday 1987 xxl, 1,125p
LC 86-29254
"The book is a triumph of historical imagination. . . . Safire uses the trained eye of a Washington insider to show us the characters' tentative political and military gropings based on limited information and sketchy precedents. . . . Our scribe tells this monumental and heartbreaking tale in a way one won't soon forget." Christ Sci Monit

Safire, William
   Scandalmonger. Simon & Schuster 2000 496p il
   ISBN 0-684-86719-2
LC 99-58831
This historical novel is set in the new American republic during the 1790s. The cast of characters includes Alexander Hamilton, Aaron Burr, Thomas Jefferson, and James Monroe, as well as two journalists. "William Cobbett is a pompous English import who bloviated in his Porcupine's Gazette on behalf of Hamilton and his law-and-order Federalists. His rival in vitriol is James Thomson Callender, wanted for sedition in his native Scotland. He was Jefferson's hit man who, when slighted, . . . spread informed innuendo about his arrangement with slave and lover Sally Hemings." Time
   Includes bibliographical references

Sagan, Carl
   Contact; a novel. Simon & Schuster 1985 432p
LC 85-14645
"A serious blend of science fact and speculation with a fast-paced and well-crafted story . . . suggesting that Sagan is more interested in illustrating human relations and human response than depicting alien creatures. . . . Sagan has provided a novel of ideas, and finds drama in how people interact with them in a situation of challenge and discovery." Christ Sci Monit

Sagan, Francoise
   ★ **Bonjour** tristesse; translated from the French by Irene Ash. Dutton 1955 128p
   Original French edition, 1954
"The story of a jealous, sophisticated 17-year-old girl whose meddling in her father's impending remarriage leads to tragic consequences, it was written with 'classical' restraint and a tone of cynical disillusionment. The book showed the persistence of traditional form during a period of experimentation in French fiction." Merriam-Webster's Ency of Lit

Saint James, Simone
   The **haunting** of Maddy Clare; Simone St. James. New American Library 2012 330 p.
   ISBN 0451235681; 9780451235688
LC 2011033391
This novel, by Simone St. James, begins when "Sarah Piper's . . . temporary agency sends her to assist a ghost hunter. Alistair Gellis . . . has been summoned to investigate

the spirit of nineteen-year-old maid Maddy Clare, who is haunting the barn where she committed suicide. . . . Maddy's ghost is real [and] she's angry. . . . Can Sarah and Alistair's assistant . . . discover who Maddy was, where she came from, and what is driving her desire for vengeance-before she destroys them all?" (Publisher's note)

Saint, H. F.
   Memoirs of an invisible man. Atheneum Pubs. 1987 396p
   ISBN 0-689-11735-3
LC 85-48144
"The CIA agents, always just one step behind, are deliciously funny Keystone Cops, ridiculous in their attempts to capture a non-entity. This delightful first novel updates a common childhood fantasy with the excitement of a spy story and a hilarious adult portrayal of life and love under the most peculiar conditions." Libr J

Saint-Exupery, Antoine de
   ★ The **little** prince; written and illustrated by Antoine de Saint-Exupery; translated from the French by Richard Howard. Harcourt 2000 83p il $18; pa $12
   ISBN 0-15-202398-4; 0-15-601219-7 pa
LC 99-50439
A new translation of the title first published 1943 by Reynal & Hitchcock
"This many-dimensional fable of an airplane pilot who has crashed in the desert is for readers of all ages. The pilot comes upon the little prince soon after the crash. The prince tells of his adventures on different planets and on Earth as he attempts to learn about the universe in order to live peacefully on his own small planet. A spiritual quality enhances the seemingly simple observations of the little prince." Shapiro. Fic for Youth. 3d edition

Saint-Exupery, Antoine de
   Night flight; preface by André Gide; translated by Stuart Gilbert. Century 1932 198p
   "In a story that captures the adventures of early aviation, Rivière, chief of the airport at Buenos Aires, supervises the night flights of airmail in South America. He challenges his crew to meet any and all obstacles. When one of his three mail planes crashes over the Andes, he dispatches the European mail plane on schedule anyway." Shapiro. Fic for Youth. 3d edition

Sakamoto, Kerri
   One hundred million hearts. Harcourt 2003 279p $23
   ISBN 0-15-101037-4
LC 2003-57064
"Set in Toronto, the novel opens with 32-year-old Miyo narrating the story of her life with her Canadian-born Japanese father, Masao, who singlehandedly raised her. When he suddenly falls ill, Miyo is surprisingly reunited with Setsuko, her father's former live-in girlfriend. Miyo then learns that she has a half-sister, Hana, living in Japan. In the rest of the story, Sakamoto focuses on Miyo's emotional journey to Japan to meet her sister, which also leads to the unraveling of her father's past as a kamikaze pilot." Libr J

Sakey, Marcus

The **blade** itself. St. Martin's Minotaur 2007 307p $22.95

ISBN 978-0-312-36031-3; 0-312-36031-2

LC 2006-50562

As the author "takes Danny apart and looks to see what the man is really worth, the novel delivers some implicit social commentary about the shaky foundation on which Danny's new life has been built. . . . Not until the very end of the story is it clear who Danny is or where he stands. His ability to churn these questions so vigorously will bring Mr. Sakey attention." N Y Times (Late N Y Ed)

Sakey, Marcus

Brilliance; by Marcus Sakey. Amazon Pub 2013 452 p. (paperback) $14.95

ISBN 1611099692; 9781611099690

In his novel, author Macus Sakey focuses his plot on individuals with extraordinary psychological abilities "called 'brilliants,' and since 1980, one percent of people have been born this way. Nick Cooper is among them; a federal agent, Cooper has gifts rendering him exceptional at hunting terrorists. His latest target may be the most dangerous man alive, a brilliant drenched in blood and intent on provoking civil war. But to catch him, Cooper will have to violate everything he believes in—and betray his own kind."

Sakey, Marcus

The **two** deaths of Daniel Hayes; a novel. Dutton 2011 390p $25.95

ISBN 978-0-525-95211-4

LC 2011-04280

This book "begins with Daniel Hayes, naked and nearly drowned, lying in the surf off the coast of Maine. Suffering from amnesia and a vague feeling of guilt, he believes the answers to his current state lie in Los Angeles and heads there trying to find his identity. He discovers that he is a successful screenwriter and that his glamorous TV star wife has just been murdered in a car accident. The cops are after him as a suspect, and a blackmailing hard guy is also pursuing him. . . . The action is fast-paced, the tension is nearly constant, and there are more twists in the plot than in a double helix." Libr

Saki

★ The **short** stories of Saki; with an introduction by Christopher Morley. Modern Lib. 1983 $12.95

ISBN 0-394-60428-8

LC 83-5468

First published 1930 by Viking; first Modern Library edition 1951

Salak, Kira

The **white** Mary; a novel. Henry Holt and Co. 2008 351p $25

ISBN 978-0-8050-8847-2; 0-8050-8847-4

LC 2008-7278

"Salak's descriptions of the jungle passage are compelling and dreamlike. Even stronger are flashbacks of Marika in Bodo and a wrenching, horrific account of Lewis's capture and torture in East Timor. Salak's own journalistic experiences—she covered the Rwandan genocide and the 2003

war in the Congo, among other conflicts—have armed her with heartfelt, if indelibly grim, insights into man's capacity for 'an endless stream of the worst, most inconceivable acts of inhumanity'. . . . In The White Mary, Salak shows the courage of facing down that darkness and the inescapable price it exacts upon one's soul." Washington Post Book World

Salinger, J. D.

★ The **catcher** in the rye. Little, Brown 1951 277p $24.95; pa $5.99

ISBN 0-316-76953-3; 0-316-76948-7 pa

"The story of adolescent Holden Caulfield who runs away from boarding-school in Pennsylvania to New York where he preserves his innocence despite various attempts to lose it. The colloquial, lively, first-person narration, with its attacks on the 'phoniness' of the adult world and its clinging to family sentiment in the form of Holden's affection for his sister Phoebe, made the novel accessible to and popular with a wide readership, particularly with the young." Oxford Companion to Engl Lit. 5th edition

Salinger, J. D.

★ **Franny** & Zooey. Little, Brown 1961 201p $24.95; pa $5.99

ISBN 0-316-76954-1; 0-316-76949-5 pa

"At 20, Franny Glass is experiencing desperate dissatisfaction with her life and seems to be looking for help via a religious awakening. Her brother Zooey tries to help her out of this depression. He recalls the influence on their growth and development of their appearance as young radio performers on a network program called 'It's a Wise Child.' An older brother, Buddy, is also an important component of the interrelationships in the Glass family." Shapiro. Fic for Youth. 3d edition

Salinger, J. D.

★ **Nine** stories. Little, Brown 1953 302p $24.95; pa $5.99

ISBN 0-316-76956-8; 0-316-76950-9 pa

This collection "introduced various members of the Glass family who would dominate the remainder of Salinger's work. Critical response divided itself between high praise and cult worship. Most of the stories deal with precocious, troubled children, whose religious yearnings—often tilting toward the East—are in vivid contrast to the materialistic and spiritually empty world of their parents. The result was a perfect literary formula for the 1950s." Benet's Reader's Ency of Am Lit

Salinger, J. D.

★ **Raise** high the roof beam, carpenters, and Seymour: an introduction. Little, Brown 1963 248p $24.95

ISBN 0-316-76957-6

This volume "reprints stories from The New Yorker (1955, 1959), in which Buddy Glass tells, first, of his return to New York during the war to attend his brother Seymour's wedding and of Seymour's jilting of the bride and then of their later elopement; and, second, after Seymour's suicide, of Buddy's own brooding, to the point of breakdown, upon

Seymour's virtues, human and literary." Oxford Companion to Am Lit. 6th edition

Sallis, James

    Cripple Creek; a novel. Walker & Co. 2006 193p $23

    ISBN 978-0-8027-3382-5; 0-8027-3382-4

LC 2005-28095

"As this tale opens, Turner, ex-cop, ex-con, and ex-psychotherapist, remains on the lam in rural Cypress Grove, Tennessee, escaping the demons of past lives in Memphis, but he is starting to mend. There's a developing relationship with Val Bjorn, teacher and country musician; there's the appearance of his daughter from Seattle; and there's the fact that he has come out of hibernation to accept the job as deputy sheriff of Cypress Grove. Then his boss, the kindly sheriff, is assaulted by a gang of mobbed-up toughs in the act of breaking one of their own out of the small-town jail. Turner pursues the thugs to Memphis, confronting his past and giving vent to his suppressed blood lust. Every action prompts a reaction, however, and soon the thugs return to Cypress Grove looking for some blood of their own. Sallis tells the violent tale quietly, effectively using jump cuts, flashbacks, and flashforwards to generate both suspense and, simultaneously, a sense of inevitability. The stunning finale makes clear that Turner has a lot more healing to do." Booklist

Sallis, James

    Cypress Grove. Walker & Co. 2003 255p $24

    ISBN 0-8027-3380-8

LC 2002-41480

"Turner ('just Turner'), a former Memphis cop who went to prison for something he'd like to forget, has dropped out of human circulation and buried himself in a cabin in the deep woods. Because Turner's communication skills are rusty, Sallis gives him a constrained narrative voice, the guarded speech of a man so wary of emotion that the very act of speaking seems to leave his throat raw. When the sheriff of this rural backwater asks for his help with a murdered drifter who was found with a wooden stake in his chest, Turner crawls out of hibernation." N Y Times Book Rev

Sallis, James

    Drive. Poisoned Pen Press 2005 Book $18.95

    ISBN 1590581814; 9781590581902

LC 2005925325

This noir fiction novel, adapted into a 2011 motion picture, centers on "amoral Driver, who is what he does – a man who drives stunt cars in Hollywood for a day job, and getaway cars in his spare time. The novel opens with the aftermath of a shoot-out, the result of the gang Driver is with robbing someone too powerful for them. Driver continues to kill in order to stay alive and, as he does so, the novel asks just how much we are tied to our fates; whether we can ever escape our backgrounds." (The Independent)

"Sallis gives us his most tightly written mystery to date, worthy of comparison to the compact, exciting oeuvre of French noir giant Jean-Patrick Manchette." Pub Wkly

Sallis, James

    ★ **Driven.** Poisoned Pen Press 2012 158p

    ISBN 9781464200113; 9781464200120

LC 2011944604

This noir fiction novel, a sequel to the author's novel "Drive," continues with "[t]he enigmatic loner known as Driver, introduced in 2005's Drive, [who] takes to the road again after two thugs assault him and his fiancée on a Phoenix, Ariz., street. . . . Maybe Driver is paranoid, but is it really paranoia when one team of hit men after another track you down and try to put you on ice? 'Two cars this time, and they'd waited for an isolated stretch of road. Chevy Caprice and a high-end Toyota.'" (Publishers Weekly)

"The language is plain, the action is brutal, and the characters are memorably and briefly etched... This gritty, gristly tale will rivet Sallis's growing audience.—" LJ

Sallis, James

    The **killer** is dying; a novel. Walker Pub. Co. 2011 232p $24

    ISBN 978-0-8027-7945-8; 0-8027-7945-X

LC 2010-38548

Sallis "takes his time weaving together the lives of these lost souls, each apparently as aimless as the bugs and birds they can't help noticing. The payoff is a moment of well-nigh miraculous consolation." Kirkus

Sallis, James

    Salt River; a novel. Walker & Company 2007 146p $21.95

    ISBN 978-0-8027-1617-0; 0-8027-1617-2

In this mystery featuring John "Turner—Vietnam veteran, former cop, ex-con, retired psychiatrist, and interim sheriff of a rural county south of Memphis—Sallis's story meanders through a summer and fall, chronicling Turner's professional and private lives as they merge into one. Turner's tranquillity is shattered when the son of his predecessor drives what might be a stolen car through the front of the city hall, seriously injuring himself and launching a case that escalates into breaking and entering, elder abuse, kidnapping, and murder. Meanwhile, Turner deals with the return of a friend who is wanted by the police in Texas and a less-than-welcome report from his physician. Sallis has created a laid-back, small-town setting in which understanding motives sometimes takes precedence over punishing crimes." Libr J

Salter, James

    All that is; a novel. James Salter. 1st ed. Alfred A. Knopf 2013 304 p. (ebook) $80.85; (hardcover) $26.95

    ISBN 1400043131; 9780307961099; 9781400043132

LC 2012020914

In this book, World War II veteran "Philip Bowman returns to America and finds a position as a book editor" while struggling with his love life. "One marriage goes bad; another fails to happen; and, finally, he meets a woman who enthralls, then betrays him, setting him on a course he could never have imagined for himself." (Publisher's note)

Salter, James

    Last night. Knopf 2005 132p $20

    ISBN 1-4000-4312-3

LC 2004-57793

"All of the stories in 'Last Night' are superb, but the title story is the tautest and most memorable. . . . This story about the consequences of adultery gives new meaning to the phrase 'the morning after.' Despite its shocking plot twist, the story maintains the exacting, calm narrative voice that has distinguished all of Salter's work. His characters may be haunted by death and disappointment, but Salter never judges them, never even pretends to have them neatly pegged. He lets them stay elliptical, in shadow." N Y Times Book Rev

Salvatore, R. A.

Immortalis. Ballantine Bks. 2003 487p il map $26.95

ISBN 0-345-44122-2

LC 2002-33046

"A satisfying tale of personal responsibility, forgiveness, and redemption, this conclusion to the second 'DemonWars' trilogy features strong, memorable characters and superb plotting and storytelling." Libr J

Salzman, Mark

Lying awake. Knopf 2000 181p $21

ISBN 0-375-40632-8

LC 99-89890

"Salzman, who doesn't claim to be a believer, handles the religious setting amazingly well. His artistic intuition helps him avoid the sermonizing that might tempt a more religious (or antireligious) writer. He clearly loves his characters." Christ Century

Samarasan, Preeta

Evening is the whole day. Houghton Mifflin 2008 340p $24

ISBN 978-0-618-87447-7; 0-618-87447-X

LC 2008-4729

This "novel revolves around a wealthy Indian family living in modern-day Malaysia. What seems like a simple act—the firing of the servant girl—has greater implications for the family than it could ever have imagined, especially for six-year-old Aasha. Aasha has a secret, one that could devastate not only her family but also the entire community. Samarasan wisely withholds this secret and others, pulling readers in. Because the description of Malaysia and its diverse population is so achingly lyrical, readers will want to slow down to absorb each word; at other times, as when they get caught up in the family drama, they will want to quicken their pace." Libr J

Sams, Ferrol

Down town; the journal of James Aloysius Holcombe, Jr. for Ephraim Holcombe Mookinfoos. Mercer University Press 2007 309p $25

ISBN 978-0-8814-6072-8; 0-8814-6072-9

LC 2007-12030

"For poetry-spouting bachelor lawyer James 'Buster' Aloysius Holcombe Jr., even the finest Southern woman is no competition for his beloved Georgia hometown. . . . [This novel is] crafted as a folksy journal tracing the paths of the good people of Fayette County, Georgia, from the Civil War right up to the prosperous present. . . . Despite Buster's penchant for quoting Edna St. Vincent Millay as a means of seduction, in advancing years he ambles on blissfully single. After all, who needs romance when the folks in your hometown are so utterly charming—the wise doctor, the wealthy and eccentrically frugal banker and his blithering albeit loveable wife all keep Buster plenty busy with their conceits and confidences. Like the best road trips, Down Town is not intent upon reaching any particular destination, but rather savoring the journey along the way." BookPage

Samson, Lisa

Embrace me; Lisa Samson. Thomas Nelson 2007 314p (pbk.) $15.99

ISBN 1595542108; 9781595542106

LC 2007048456

This book "starts out in two different years to explain events that at first seem totally disconnected. In 2002, fallen pastor Drew alternates between punishing himself through self-mutilation and confessing his sins in a written account to a sympathetic priest. In 2008, 'lizard woman' Valentine and her friends have just finished their freak show tour and it's time to winter in Mount Oak, North Carolina." (Christian Fiction Review) "When [the] . . . 'lizard woman,' [the] . . . self-mutilating preacher, a tattooed monk, and a sleazy lobbyist find themselves in the same North Carolina town one winter, their lives are edging precariously close to disaster . . . and improbably close to grace." (Publisher's note)

Samuel, Barbara

No place like home; Barbara Samuel. Ballantine Books 2002 298p (pbk.) $19

ISBN 0345445651 (alk. paper); 9780345460370

LC 2001052666

RITA Awards: Best Contemporary Single Title (2002), Romantic Time Reviewers' Choice Award: Mainstream (2002)

This book tells the story of "Jewel Sabatino [who] lives in New York and has a gay best friend dying of AIDS, rancid memories of a nonmarriage to a nonstarter, a teen musician son, an estrangement from her father, . . . and an unrelieved case of low self-esteem. When she learns . . . that she's inherited her great-aunt's house and that her apartment building in Greenwich Village is going condo, Sabatino knows it's time to go home. She, 17-year-old son Shane and ill best friend Michael Shaunnessey head for her third-generation Italian-American enclave in Pueblo, Colo. There she comes to terms with who she is, helped considerably by Malachi Shaunnessey, a 'big, alligator-blood-drinking tough guy' who shows up to ease his dying brother Michael's last days, bringing more than just comfort to Jewel in the process." (Publishers Weekly)

Sanchez, Thomas

King Bongo; a novel of Havana. Knopf 2003 309p $25

ISBN 0-679-40696-4

LC 2002-40770

"The byzantine plot is neatly constructed and thoroughly involving but never an end in itself. Sanchez shows us a city and a people on the eve of revolution but filters it all through the emotions of a conflicted hero, sympathetic to the cause but loyal only to himself and those he loves. Havana is both setting and soul in this pulsing bolero of a novel." Booklist

Sand, George

★ **Lelia**; translated, with an introduction by Maria Espinosa. Indiana Univ. Press 1978 xxi, 234p

LC 77-23639

Original French edition, 1833

"Independent and sensual Lélia has had many lovers. Now repelled by physical passion, which represents the means by which men dominate women, Lélia tells her sister Pulchérie, a courtesan, that neither celibacy nor love affairs satisfy her. Pulchérie suggests that Lélia become a courtesan; she may find fulfillment by giving pleasure to others. Lélia tries to seduce Sténio, a young poet who is in love with her; she cannot continue, however, and sends Pulchérie in her stead. As a result of this betrayal, Sténio falls into utter debauchery, and despite attempts to rescue him, he comes to a tragic end." Merriam-Webster's Ency of Lit

Sand, George

Marianne. Carroll & Graf Pubs. 1988 171p

LC 88-7308

Original French edition, 1876

"Marianne Chevreuse, the 25-year-old heroine of this romantic tale set in 1825 . . . is independent yet intensely female, and she breaks many conventions of society while living by her own deeply held moral beliefs. Pierre André is an older man who has known her since her childhood. When asked to introduce her to a prospective suitor, he discovers his own love for Marianne. The plot twists and turns until the unsuitable Philippe Gaucher—who is indeed gauche—is sent packing and Pierre and Marianne are betrothed. While very much a period piece, this last scrap of Sand's tremendous oeuvre is a charming bit of entertainment." Publ Wkly

Sandburg, Carl

Remembrance Rock. Harcourt Brace & Co. 1948 1067p

"Sandburg's only novel, the work is a massive chronicle that uses historical facts and both historical and fictional characters to depict American history from 1607 to 1945 in a mythic, passionate tribute to the American people." Merriam-Webster's Ency of Lit

Sanders, Dori

★ **Clover**; a novel. Algonquin Bks. 1990 183p $17.95

ISBN 0-945575-26-2

LC 89-39072

After her father dies within hours of being married to a white woman, Clover Hill, a ten-year-old black girl, learns with her new stepmother to overcome grief and to adjust to a new place in their rural Black South Carolina community

The author "has staked out an impressive new territory here, replete with peach farmers, textile workers, drunks and crazy people, with the newly middle class as well as the terminally poor. As a specimen of the new realism in regional fiction, 'Clover' is very much the genuine item." N Y Times Book Rev

Sanders, Lawrence

★ The **first** deadly sin. Putnam 1973 566p

This novel "pits a psychopathic killer loose in New York against a tough, dedicated police officer who is not with-

out his own hangups. Telling his story alternately from the psychopath's point of view and that of the detective, Mr. Sanders draws the two men closer and closer together on an inevitable collision course. Probing the dark side of the killer's mind, his sexual conflicts and involvement with a strange trio of brother, sister and valet who are as kinky as they come, he shows the man's accelerating descent into total madness. Meanwhile, Captain Edward X. Delaney, in whose upper East Side precinct a series of random murders is taking place, accepts an undercover assignment to track down the man responsible." Publ Wkly

Sanders, Lawrence

The **fourth** deadly sin. Putnam 1985 380p

LC 84-24789

"Delaney displays that combination of computerlike efficiency and human touch that make him such an appealing detective. It's a masterly performace, not only chilling, but thought-provoking and often touching." Publ Wkly

Sanders, Lawrence

Guilty pleasures. Putnam 1998 310p $24.95

ISBN 0-399-14365-3

LC 97-32937

Scandal rocks a wealthy South Florida publishing family as brother and sister "battle for future control of the empire—never guessing that a trusted family friend with a hidden agenda is quietly manipulating them all." Publisher's note

Sanders, Lawrence

McNally's dilemma. Putnam 1999 309p $24.95

ISBN 0-399-14490-0

LC 99-20988

"McNally is a Palm Beach gumshoe who, with his attorney father, makes up the firm of McNally and Son's Department of Discreet Inquiries. . . . This time, the action begins with a late-night call from wealthy Melva Ashton Manning Williams, who has just blown away her second husband, Geoff Williams, née Wolinsky, after finding him in the arms of another woman. Things quickly shift from murder to blackmail and puzzles within puzzles, all of which Archy sorts out in his usual stylish fashion." Booklist

Sanders, Lawrence

★ **McNally's** gamble. Putnam 1997 307p $24.95

ISBN 0-399-14248-7

LC 96-50369

A "comic whodunit featuring Archy McNally, the foppish but likable head of 'discreet inquiries' at his father's law firm in Palm Beach, Fla. This time Archy's task is to investigate the credentials of a suspicious investment adviser, Frederick Clemens, and his secretary, Felix Katz. . . . Mr. Sanders clearly delights in playing up the bumbling, spoof aspects of this detective yarn, especially during its climactic but unavoidably funny denouement." NY Times Book Rev

Sanders, Lawrence

McNally's luck. Putnam 1992 319p

LC 92-1394

"Hot on the trail of a stolen cat on behalf of a client of his family's law firm, McNally and Son, Archy enters Palm Beach's seamy nether-world of psychics, charlatans, and thieves. His seemingly innocuous search for the missing cat leads him to the heart of a grisly and intricate plot. As the body count climbs, Archy must resolve the links between several violent local murders and the disappearance of the ill-tempered feline." Publisher's note

Sanders, Lawrence

McNally's puzzle. Putnam 1996 311p

ISBN 978-0399141355

LC 95-45703

In this mystery, playboy/sleuth Archy McNally "must dig into the gruesome death of a millionaire parrot-shop owner named Hiram Gottschalk in an attempt to unravel the circumstances of his passing and the tangled mess of the family he leaves behind. . . . The real focus is on Archy's prancing and preening and so-called life of the mind as he tools around south Florida entertaining the millionaire's twin daughters, fencing with his housekeeper and tracking the bizarre activities—parrot smuggling is one, perhaps—of Gottschalk's troubled stepson." N Y Times Book Rev

Sanders, Lawrence

McNally's secret. Putnam 1992 317p

LC 91-9803

"Four priceless U.S. airmail stamps issued in 1918 and known as 'inverted Jennies' have been stolen from a wealthy matron's mansion in Palm Beach. . . . McNally's task is to find the thief 'without the barest hint of scandal coming to light.' There are lots of suspects, a couple of deaths, and a fine romance." Booklist

Sanders, Lawrence

McNally's trial. Putnam 1995 309p

LC 94-33943

Palm Beach's Archy McNally, "an occasional investigator for his stuffy lawyer father, here agrees to look into the sudden 'uptick' in business that is worrying a pretty exec at the exclusive Whitcomb Funeral Homes. Too many people are dying, observes the woman, and being shipped up north in coffins." Publ Wkly

The novel "boasts a delightful assembly of supporting characters, especially Archy's pal, the totally dissolute, utterly inept would-be detective Binky Watrous. A pleasant diversion." Booklist

Sanders, Lawrence

The **second** deadly sin. Putnam 1977 412p

LC 77-3652

A "police procedural in which Edward X. Delaney, recently retired as Manhattan's chief of detectives, returns by invitation of the department to work on the mystery-murder of a thoroughly unlikable genius, painter Victor Maitland. Delaney, a curious mixture of force and sensitivity, is teamed with a young sergeant, whose drinking has brought him to the edge of dismissal. The two, with an accidentally added starter, Jason T. Jason (black, smart, and very big), by a combination of hard work, intuition, and some luck finally track down the killer." Booklist

Sanders, Lawrence

The **sixth** commandment; a novel. Putnam 1979 350p

ISBN 0-399-12305-9

LC 78-13158

"This gloomy escapade about a hard-drinking, chain-smoking, world-pitying investigator . . . is brimful of juice and excitement, with some insight and much foolishness—a genuinely riveting diversion." New Yorker

Sanders, Lawrence

Sullivan's sting. Putnam 1990 348p

ISBN 0-399-13542-1

LC 89-70046

This novel "profiles the slimy underbelly of south Florida, where con men posing as financial wizards bilk greedy, unsuspecting investors out of their money (aging widows are a prime mark). The main player here is sexy David Rathbone, a man who apparently could sell igloos to Eskimos. Equally sexy undercover cop Rita Angela Sullivan is on a mission from the SEC to 'sting' Rathbone. She traps her prey, starts to play house, and moves in for the kill—then finds herself falling in love with the guy." Booklist

Sanders, Lawrence

The **tenth** commandment; a novel. Putnam 1980 385p

ISBN 0-399-12500-6

LC 80-13002

Joshua Bigg, "chief investigator for a New York law firm, gets two tough assignments from his bosses. One is a missing person case: a crotchety professor whose family want an estate settlement. The other is an apparent suicide: an aging textile manufacturer whose merry young widow has suddenly become religiously attracted to a churchless clergyman. Bigg plows his way through mountains of clues, allies himself with a black police detective and unearths evidence to indicate that the suicide was murder and that the missing man is dead." Publ Wkly

Sanders, Lawrence

The **third** deadly sin. Putnam 1981 444p

LC 80-26325

"Sergeant Boone of Manhattan's Homicide Squad persuades former Chief of Detectives Delaney to help find what police fear most, a random killer. The two men . . . begin the slow, almost hopeless, scrupulously painstaking chore of tracking down and piecing together the tiniest clues. The detecting account alternates with vivid, step-by-step descriptions of drab Zoe Kohler, who tarts herself up periodically and ritually murders men she picks up in convention-crowded hotels. In the telling, Sander's characters discuss facets of feminism and crime provocatively, and not at all simplistically, adding to the dimensions of a superior mystery." Publ Wkly

Sanders, Lawrence

The **Timothy** files. Putnam 1987 380p

LC 86-25496

Three novella-length episodes "feature Timothy Cone, 'the Wall Street dick,' who works for an investigative agency. . . . The files deal respectively with a murderous real-estate conglomerate, a fertility clinic devoted to considerably more than 'original biotechnological research' and an investment house involved in drugs—though only detective work of the highest caliber can discover the seamy details." Publ Wkly

Sanders, Lawrence
   Timothy's game. Putnam 1988 382p
LC 87-29073
   This novel is "set on Wall Street, where clever detective Timothy Cone dresses in Salvation Army chic, chainsmokes Camels, and drinks too much. Cone has a cat named Cleo who eats ham hocks, potato salad, and garlic salami, and a girlfriend named Samantha who sports long, auburn hair. Throw in a foul-mouthed woman who owns a garbagehauling firm controlled by the mob, an insider-trading leak, murder, and a tong war in Chinatown, and you have the usual brand of Sanders' readable fiction." Booklist

Sanderson, Brandon
   Elantris. Tor 2005 492p il $27.95
   ISBN 978-0-765-31177-1
LC 2004-63765
   This fantasy is "refreshingly complete unto itself and free of the usual genre clichés, offers something for everyone: mystery, magic, romance, political wrangling, religious conflict, fights for equality, sharp writing and wonderful, robust characters." Publ Wkly

Sanderson, Brandon
   Mistborn: the final empire. Tor 2006 541p il $27.95
   ISBN 978-0-765-31178-8; 0-765-31178-X
LC 2005-34496
   First volume of the author's epic fantasy trilogy
   "The Sliver of Infinity, the Lord Ruler, is the locus of religious and temporal order in a world in which the skaa are slaves or worse. Half-skaa erstwhile thief Kelsior is the only person to survive and escape the Lord Ruler's most brutal prison, in which, however, he discovered he has the powers of the Mistborn, which are based on the internal 'burning' of certain metals, all of which the Mistborn can use, while most others can burn only one. Now Kelsior plans his most daring raid ever, into the center of the palace to discover the secret of the Lord Ruler's power. . . . Intrigue, politics, and conspiracies mesh complexly in a world Sanderson realizes in satisfying depth and peoples with impressive characters." Booklist
   Followed by: The well of ascension (2007) and The hero of ages (2008)

Sandford, John, 1944-
   Broken prey. Putnam 2005 390p $26.95
   ISBN 0-399-15272-5
LC 2005-42981
   Lucas Davenport, a "Minnesota State Bureau of Criminal Apprehension investigator, had lately been doing political fix-it jobs for the governor, but this time he's got a psychopathic serial killer on his hands. . . . The first victim, a young woman, was 'scourged' with a wire whip; number two, a young man, had his penis cut off. Evidence first points to recently released sex offender Charlie Pope. Though Charlie is pretty dumb and the killer is extremely smart, it

takes Davenport and his series partner, Detective Sloan, a while to realize they're chasing the wrong guy. Sandford introduces some lighter moments, the most entertaining about Davenport's new iPod and his quest to compile a list of the 100 best rock songs ever recorded, which every cop on the force gives him suggestions for. These moments allow readers to catch their breath amid the otherwise nonstop tension." Publ Wkly

Sandford, John
   Buried prey. G. P. Putnam's Sons 2011 390p $27.95
   ISBN 978-0-399-15738-7
LC 2011-04990
   "The bodies of two teenage sisters are discovered in a plastic bag beneath the concrete-floor basement of a house being razed in Minneapolis. City police are called, but Davenport, an investigator with a state law enforcement agency, also arrives quickly at the scene. To his anguish, Davenport readily recognizes their clothing. Two and a half decades earlier, he had been the lead investigator on the Minneapolis police force that probed their 1985 disappearance. Sandford . . . flashes back to 1985, when a suspect died during a manhunt. Davenport never believed the suspect killed the girls because the homeless drifter didn't seem mentally capable. Also, Minneapolis police were never able to identify the caller of two tips that made the drifter the top suspect. Flashing forward to the present, Davenport takes on the reopened case." San Antonio Express-News

Sandford, John
   Certain prey. Putnam 1999 339p $24.95
   ISBN 0-399-14496-X
LC 99-19048
   "Trying to avoid facing his empty personal life, enigmatic Minneapolis Deputy Police Chief Lucas Davenport is jolted out of the doldrums by the handiwork of professional hitwoman Clara Rinker, in town to do what she does best. Adding to his problems is glamorous defense attorney Carmel Loan, a clever and intimidating lawyer. When Davenport suspects an alliance between the two women, he soon faces two deadly enemies. Sandford keeps the level of suspense dizzyingly high as he shifts viewpoints between the women and Davenport." Booklist

Sandford, John
   Chosen prey. Putnam 2001 357p
   ISBN 0-399-14728-4
LC 2001-18594
   "Troubled by both city politics and his relationship with his fiancee, Minneapolis Deputy Police Chief Lucas Davenport finds the comfortable routines of a murder investigation as soothing as a worn pair of jeans. The discovery of a young woman's body, missing 18 months, leads to a local pornographic photography ring that posts its handiwork on the Internet." Booklist

Sandford, John
   Easy prey. Putnam 2000 407p
   ISBN 0-399-14613-X
LC 00-23962
   "Minnesota-born supermodel Alie'e Maison is back in Minneapolis for a photo shoot. At the raucous wrap party,

she turns up dead. Lucas Davenport, the millionaire homicide specialist who often corrals serial killers, is called to the scene." Booklist

Sandford, John

    Hidden prey. Putnam 2004 393p $26.95

    ISBN 0-399-15180-X

                      LC 2004-44351

"When a Russian man is found murdered on the shores of Lake Superior, Lucas Davenport must join forces with a cop from Moscow to track down the culprit." Libr J

Sandford, John

    Mind prey. Putnam 1995 323p

                      LC 95-3790

"When psychiatrist Andi Manette and her two young daughters are kidnapped, {Davenport} must discover whether it's a ransom snatch, the work of one of Andi's ex-patients or the ruse of someone in her life who might benefit from her death. . . . Readers know the kidnapper is John Mail, a scary ex-patient who's entertained nasty dreams of Andi for years. . . . Sandford expertly ratchets up the suspense from beginning to the brutal finish." Publ Wkly

Sandford, John

    Mortal prey. Putnam 2002 354p

    ISBN 0-399-14863-9

                    LC 2002-19051

Assassin Clara Rinker, an old nemesis of Lucas Davenport's "is now back on the prowl, looking for revenge against old enemies from Kansas City who killed her fiancé and shot her in the gut. The bullet spared her life, but not that of her baby. The FBI, knowing she's headed to Missouri, assembles a huge team of shirt-and-tie, laptop-carrying agents, but also taps Davenport to make the trip. . . . Longtime fans should take note that changes are ahead for Davenport. He's marrying his sweetie, Dr. Weather Karkinnen, and they're having a kid. He's also about to leave the city police force, following his boss, Rose Marie Roux, to a job with the state police." Publ Wkly

Sandford, John

    ★ **Naked** prey. Putnam 2003 359p $26.95

    ISBN 0-399-15043-9

                    LC 2003-41364

Lucas Davenport "is now Director of Regional Studies in the Minnesota Bureau of Criminal Apprehension, which is a fancy name for the job of investigating difficult crimes as quickly as possible and answering to the governor of the state. Known for his ability to solve the unsolvable, he goes to a remote area of the state to discover why a black man and a white woman were hanged in a groove of trees. . . . Fast paced and full of surprises, this may be Sandford's best novel yet." Libr J

Sandford, John

    Night prey. Putnam 1994 336p

                    LC 94-7564

"Despite its length, Night Prey is a tight, fast-moving thriller with appealing good guys and a suitably evil villain. Especially fascinating among the characters is Policewoman Connell." Libr J

Sandford, John

    Rules of prey. Putnam 1989 316p

                    LC 89-4040

"A killer who calls himself the 'maddog' has been murdering Minneapolis women, seemingly without pattern or motive. The crimes are linked only by their brutality and by the slayer's 'signature': at each scene, he leaves a written rule of crime, such as 'Never kill anyone you know,' or, 'Never carry a weapon after it has been used.' Into the case comes Lucas Davenport, a policeman with five kills in the line of duty, a surefire sense of how to handle the thirsty media and strong instincts about the killer's psyche." Publ Wkly

Sandford, John

    Shock wave. G.P. Putnam's Sons 2011 388p $27.95

    ISBN 978-0-399-15769-1; 0-399-15769-7

                    LC 2011-27848

"Virgil Flowers is a pretty mellow guy. If he isn't casting off in some quiet trout stream, John Sandford's Minnesota crime-stopper might be found behind Bob's Bad Boy Barbeque & Bar, watching some well-nourished farm girls playing a cutthroat game of beach volleyball. But when Virgil's troubleshooting skills are called for, as they are . . . when a bomb-maker initiates a wave of industrial terrorism against the small-town incursions of a big-box chain store, he can move as fast as the next action hero. For someone who casually saunters onto a crime scene in a pink T-shirt, jeans and cowboy boots, Virgil can think on his feet, a valuable asset when the bomber steps up his deadly campaign against Willard Pye's PyeMart empire, which threatens to destroy the small-town character of Butternut Falls." N Y Times Book Rev

Sandford, John

    Silent prey. Putnam 1992 320p

                    LC 91-43696

"Mad pathologist Bekker's face is battered and broken after his encounter with unorthodox Minneapolis cop Lucas Davenport in Eyes of Prey. Now Bekker's on the loose again, having escaped during his trial and landed in New York City. Even more nutso than ever, he's determined to exact revenge on Lucas and to continue his evil experiments, in which he searches the eyes of his victims in the few, pain-creased seconds before death." Booklist

Sandford, John, 1944-

    Silken prey; John Sandford. G.P. Putnam's Sons 2013 416 p. (Prey) (hardcover) $27.95

    ISBN 0399159312; 9780399159312

                    LC 2013003703

This novel, by John Sandford, is an episode in the author's "Prey" thriller series. "Murder, scandal, political espionage, and an extremely dangerous woman. Lucas Davenport's going to be lucky to get out of this one alive. . . . Davenport is investigating another case when the trail leads to the man's disappearance, then . . . to the Minneapolis police department, then . . . to a woman who could give Machiavelli lessons." (Publisher's note)

Sandford, John

Sudden prey. Putnam 1996 360p
ISBN 978-0399141386

LC 96-4598

This Lucas Davenport adventure "opens with the Candy LaChaise gang's robbery of a Minnesota credit union. When Candy is ambushed and killed by Davenport and his men, Candy's husband, Dick LaChaise, swears vengeance on the spouses and families of all officers involved. A series of attacks ensue in which spouses are killed at work. With the lives of Davenport's own daughter and his fiancée threatened, he quickly metamorphoses into a hunting machine himself." Libr J

Sandford, John

★ Winter prey. Putnam 1993 336p

LC 92-42072

"Davenport, a cool, cynical man of action, is entirely in his element in this harsh terrain—so bitter that it turns animals against men, so brutal that it turns men into beasts." N Y Times Book Rev

Sankaran, Lavanya

The hope factory; a novel. Lavanya Sankaran. 1st ed. Dial Press 2013 384 p. (hardcover) $26
ISBN 0385338198; 9780385338196; 9780812984620

LC 2012023483

This novel, "set in Bangalore, traces the disparate yet intersecting lives of Anand Murthy, principal at Cauvery Auto, and Kamala, his family's maid, who is struggling to provide for her 12-year-old son. . . . While Anand and Kamala are both desperately working for what they want, the distance between their worlds is further emphasized by the chasm between their goals." (Publishers Weekly)

Sansom, C. J.

Winter in Madrid. Viking 2008 537p $25.95
ISBN 978-0-670-01848-2; 0-670-01848-1

LC 2007-42552

First published 2006 in the United Kingdom

"Sansom deftly plots his politically charged tale for maximal suspense, all the way up to its stunning conclusion. . . . This moving opus leaves the reader mourning for the Spain that might have been—and the England that maybe never was." Publ Wkly

Sansom, Ian

The case of the missing books. HarperCollins 2006 336p pa $12.95
ISBN 978-0-06-082250-7; 0-06-082250-3

This title launches a "new series set in Tumdrum, Northern Ireland, the small village that transplanted Londoner Israel Armstrong reluctantly makes his home. The nebbishy Jewish vegetarian shows up at the Tumdrum and District Public Library eager to assume his post as the new librarian, only to find the place boarded up and that it's his job to steward the beat-up mobile library instead. When he finally gets inside the library building, he discovers its 15,000 books are missing. Less astute than the detective characters in the novels he has devoured, Israel blunders through an investigation, making startling discoveries while suffering some hard knocks along the way." Publ Wkly

Santiago, Esmeralda

Conquistadora; a novel. Alfred A. Knopf 2011 416p
ISBN 9780307268327

LC 2010051324

"The book's greatest strength lies in its dissection of the systematic enslavement and oppression of people without which the large-scale planting, harvesting, processing, and transporting of sugar was impossible. Santiago's language is most animated in her depiction of slavery. . . . In Ana, Santiago creates a woman consciously at odds with her culture, chafing at her own oppression, and reluctant but willing to oppress others in order to achieve her own freedom. Though the plot of 'Conquistadora' is thin and the characterizations are flat, in Ana's uneasy rationalization of the brutal, unsustainable system on which these dreams depend, Santiago fleetingly achieves the hallmark of great historical fiction — she makes her protagonist a woman of her times." Boston Globe

Santmyer, Helen Hooven

--and ladies of the club. Ohio State Univ. Press 1982 1344p

LC 81-22401

The author's "perceptive saga is steeped not just in the changing political, religious, and social mores of the period covered, but also in the personal joys, sorrows, and scandals that beat the cadence of life in a midwestern town. This novel has an old-fashioned dignity and seriousness that will win some readers and lose others, and although its girth is perhaps its most notable quality, its literary scope and depth of feeling are equally impressive." Booklist

Saramago, José, 1922-2010

All the names; translated by Margaret Jull Costa. Harcourt 2000 238p $24
ISBN 0-15-100421-8

Original Portuguese edition 1997; this translation first published 1999 in the United Kingdom

"Modest, self-mocking, mildly ironic, yet magisterial, Saramago's gentle voice rings with the unmistakable authority of the true artist." Christ Sci Monit

Saramago, Jose

★ Blindness; a novel. translated from the Portuguese by Giovanni Pontiero. Harcourt Brace & Co. 1998 294p $22
ISBN 0-15-100251-7

LC 98-12009

Original Portuguese edition, 1995; this translation first published 1997 in the United Kingdom

"A man waiting in his car for a red light to turn green is the first of an entire city's population—with one exception—to be blinded by a 'milky sea' of dazzling whiteness. The inexplicably disabled victims grope and stumble their way through nightmarish landscapes—first an asylum where those initially afflicted are quarantined, and then the chaotic, squalid streets to which they return. Saramago's surreal allegory explores the ability of the human spirit to prevail in even the most absurdly unjust of conditions, yet he reinvents this familiar struggle with the stylistic eccentricity of a master." New Yorker

Saramago, José, 1922-2010

Cain; translated from the Portuguese by Margaret Jull Costa. Houghton Mifflin Harcourt 2011 159p

ISBN 978-0-547-41989-3

LC 2011-28600

Original Portuguese edition, 2009

This book follows "Cain, the firstborn son of Adam and Eve . . . Cain's travels across a barren landscape lead him to a lusty tryst with Lilith and the witnessing, or altering, of many key events of the Old Testament (the building of the Tower of Babel; the destruction of Sodom and Gomorrah). God appears often and is defined less by his perfection than his faults; He is morally ambiguous . . . and doesn't understand his powerlessness in preventing Cain's meddling. Rounding out the narrative are angels who circumvent God's will, visions of the urban modernity that the future holds, an ironic description of Darwinian evolution, and God himself touting the heliocentric theory that will cause something of a ruckus five centuries on." (Publishers Weekly)

This is the author's "final novel, but the story it tells is among the world's first. In this version of several biblical tales, characters lose their initial capitals, and readers follow the adventures and misadventures of adam and eve, cain and abel, lilith and joshua and job — plus those of 'the lord, also known as god' with new eyes. Typographical diminution is the first of many wonderful acts of estrangement. Like a postmodern Creator of sorts, Saramago crafts a new world by recycling a series of well-known episodes and interpreting them from the viewpoint of a common reader." San francisco Chron

Saramago, Jose

★ The **cave**; translated from the Portuguese by Margaret Jull Costa. Harcourt 2002 307p $25

ISBN 0-15-100414-5

LC 2002-2355

Original Portuguese edition, 2000

"As a further warning against the urge to seek safety on common ground—moving to the center, as it were—the writer highlights the menaces of cliche by parodying the worldly-wise narrative interventions of an earlier era. . . . Such deft manipulations in Saramago's style are brilliantly rendered in Margaret Jull Costa's agile English version of his Portuguese." N Y Times Book Rev

Saramago, Jose

Death with interruptions; translated from the Portuguese by Margaret Jull Costa. Harcourt 2008 238p $24

ISBN 978-0-15-101274-9; 0-15-101274-1

LC 2008-10088

Original Portuguese edition, 2005

"Starting at the stroke of midnight on New Year's, in an unidentified country in an undetermined year, in Jose Saramago's new novel, death goes on strike. Nobody dies from illness or suicide or, Mr. Saramago writes, 'from a car accident, so frequent on festive occasions, when blithe irresponsibility and an excess of alcohol jockey for position on the roads to decide who will reach death first.' Thus the Saramago sentence: conversational but a conversation with oneself; portentous yet ludicrous, like a solemn address delivered by someone who has forgotten to wear pants. Thus

too the Saramago plot: an impossible event like universal blindness, or Portugal's history altered because of a proofreader's error in a history book. Or, as here, death feeling unappreciated and refusing to oblige. . . . Mr. Saramago, one of the last of the old-line Communists, has written an atheist's religious parable; a story abounding in sentiment and purged of it." N Y Times (Late NY Ed)

Saramago, José, 1922-2010

★ The **elephant's** journey; translated from the Portuguese by Margaret Jull Costa. Houghton Mifflin Harcourt 2010 205p $24

ISBN 978-0-547-35258-9; 0-547-35258-1

LC 2010-19044

Original Portuguese edition, 2008

This novel "begins in 1551, when Portugal's Catholic King João III and his wife, Caterina of Austria, send the elephant Solomon as a wedding gift to her cousin, the Lutheran-sympathetic Archduke Maximilian of Austria. Saramago conjures up a cast of fictional characters to flesh out those based on historic record. First among them is Subhro, Solomon's mahout or keeper. . . . Subhro is a canny man who would be near the bottom of the rigid hierarchy were he not outside it. To keep his job and preserve Solomon's health and safety, he must be prepared to match wits with everyone he encounters, including the Portuguese captain leading the retinue and the Austrian archduke. . . . [This] is a tale rich in irony and empathy, regularly interrupted by witty reflections on human nature and arch commentary on the powerful who insult human dignity." Los Angeles Times

Saramago, Jose

The **history** of the siege of Lisbon; translated from the Portuguese by Giovanni Pontiero. Harcourt Brace & Co. 1997 314p

ISBN 978-0151002382

LC 96-46826

Original Portuguese edition 1989; this translation first published 1996 in the United Kingdom

"Although the novel's stream-of-consciousness technique, baroque prose and paragraphs that run on for pages may daunt some readers, this hypnotic tale is a great comic romp through history, language and the imagination." Publ Wkly

Saramago, José, 1922-2010

Manual of painting & calligraphy; a novel. Jose Saramago; translated from the Portuguese by Giovanni Pontiero. Mariner Books/Houghton Mifflin Harcourt 2012 243 p. $13.95

ISBN 1857540433 Carcanet Press; 1994; 0547640226 Houghton Mifflin; 2012; 9780547640228 Houghton Mifflin; 2012

LC 2012005375

This novel is the story of "a portrait painter . . . known only as 'H.' While H. is introspective and speculative, he's also self-critically aware of his limitations as an artist. At the moment he's working on a portrait of 'S.,' a successful industrialist." He has an affair with S.'s "secretary, Olga. . . . Dissatisfied with his original portrait, H. works on a second portrait and, still dissatisfied, tries to capture a 'portrait' of S. in words." Additionally, "H. makes a brief but serene visit to Italy, where he embarks on a pilgrimage to see the works of truly great artists like Cimabue and Piero della Francesca, but he's quickly pulled back to life in Portugal, where his friend Antonio has been arrested by the secret police in Salazar's regime." (Kirkus)

Saramago, Jose
Seeing; translated from the Portuguese by Margaret Jull Costa. Harcourt 2006 307p $25
ISBN 0-15-101238-5
LC 2005-32688
Original Portuguese edition, 2004
"With run-on paragraphs and dialogue, the author challenges readers to pay close attention; the appreciators of literary fiction who do so will find a clever, even sly, but also sobering exploration of when governments do and when they do not have reason to be paranoid." Booklist

Sargent, Colin
Museum of human beings. McBooks Press 2008 337p map $23.95
ISBN 978-1-59013-167-1; 1-59013-167-3
LC 2008-37492
"Sargent sends the youthful Baptiste on a multi-leveled grand tour of discovery that never lets up or disappoints . . . With wit, humor, detailed understanding of the time, imagination and uncomplicated storytelling, Sargent opens a door on an era." Maine Sunday Telegram

Saroyan, William
★ The **human** comedy; Rev by the author; Dell 1971 192p pa $7.50
ISBN 0-440-33933-2
First published 1944 by Harcourt, Brace and Company
"Homer, the narrator, identifies himself in this novel as a night messenger for the Postal Telegraph office. He creates a view of family life in the 1940s in a small town in California. His mother, Ma Macauley, presides over the family and takes care of four children after her husband dies. Besides Homer, there is Marcus, the oldest, who is in the army; Bess; and Ulysses, the youngest, who describes the world from his perspective as a solemn four-year-old." Shapiro. Fic for Youth. 3d edition

Sarton, May
Anger; a novel. Norton 1982 223p
ISBN 0-393-01643-9
LC 82-7843
"Successful Boston banker Ned Fraser finds himself captivated by an unexpected encounter with mezzo-soprano Anna Lindstrom. He pursues the gifted, determined-to-be-famous performer without success until, at a chance meeting, he wins her—somewhat to the surprise of them both. They marry within a short time, no starry-eyed youngsters, but two mature adults. Both are settled in their emotional patterns: she given to outspoken and tempestuous outbursts of joy and despair, he to internalizing his feelings and maintaining the proper facade. This results in a lack of communication that threatens their marriage until Anna penetrates Ned's reserve. A romantic, yet realistic portrait." Libr J

Sarton, May
As we are now; a novel. Norton 1973 133p $10.95
ISBN 0-393-08372-1
"It is a bitter book, more a tract than a novel, and an utterly desolating experience, as it is meant to be. There are complexities that unwind themselves now and then, which preserve the concerns of the novel; but on the whole, the work is a piece of rhetoric, and very good rhetoric, too. . . . For the book satisfies in the way that cold anger can when it is pure, despairing, and written with no aim but the impulse to record the way things are." Saturday Rev/World

Sarton, May
Kinds of love; a novel. Norton 1970 464p
ISBN 0-393-08620-8
"The touching friendship of two elderly women, the love/hate relationship of the permanent residents and the summer people, and a young girl's discovery of the magic and the pain of love are some of the threads in this quiet tale." Booklist

Sarton, May
★ A **reckoning**; a novel. Norton 1978 254p
LC 78-9691
"Laura Spelman, genteel Boston widow, has just learned that she is dying of cancer. Determined to take a candid look at herself as a means of tying up loose ends, she is surprised to find her thoughts turning mostly to women. Confiding in strangers, avoiding her family, Laura speaks of discovering herself as a woman. In particular, she examines her relationships with her domineering mother and with a dearly loved friend, the two people who, she feels, have shaped her life most profoundly. Ironically, as her body becomes increasingly unfamiliar, her old, unexamined passions begin to resolve themselves." Atlantic
"Sarton incorporates . . . the issues of mother/daughter relationships, what it is to be a woman (and a man), and the conflict of art and life." Libr J

Sarton, May
A **small** room; a novel. Norton 1961 249p
Sarton "presents her cast of faculty types with scrupulous respect. There is no villain among them. . . . The essence of this novel is not so much in the conflict of characters as in the conflict in ideas—and ideas about teaching." N Y Her Trib Books

Sartre, Jean Paul
★ The **age** of reason; translated from the French by Eric Sutton. Knopf 1947 397p (Roads to freedom)
Original French edition, 1945
First of a series of three novels by the French philosopher, exponent of existentialism. The scene of this novel is Paris in 1938. A fourth title was never completed
"The central character is Mathieu, a professor of philosophy who writes one short story a year. . . . The problem that obsesses Mathieu, that of freedom, how to remain free, is worked out in the story and exemplified in the lives of the characters. . . . Mathieu differs from your ordinary character of fiction in that he is motivated by this abstract ethical ideal

to keep his freedom. It is assailed as soon as the novel opens, for he learns that his mistress is pregnant; the action consists largely of his attempts to raise by borrowing—in the end, by stealing—the five thousand francs required to procure an abortion; unnecessarily, as it turns out, for Marcelle decides to marry someone else and have the child." Spectator

Followed by The reprieve

Sartre, Jean Paul

Intimacy, and other stories; translated by Lloyd Alexander. New Directions 1952 270p

First published 1948 in a limited edition with title: The wall, and other stories

"The most impressive thing about the book, rising from it like a stench, is a disgust for life, a sense of universal defilement. The insistence on the physical in the stories is indistinguishable from an aversion to it." New Repub

Sartre, Jean Paul

★ **Nausea**; translated from the French by Lloyd Alexander. New Directions 1949 238p

Original French edition, 1938

"Nausea is written in the form of a diary that narrates the recurring feelings of revulsion that overcome Roquentin, a young historian, as he comes to realize the banality and emptiness of existence. As the attacks of nausea occur more frequently, Roquentin abandons his research and loses his few friends. In an indifferent world, without work, love, or friendship to sustain him, he must discover value and meaning within himself." Merriam-Webster's Ency of Lit

Sartre, Jean Paul

The **reprieve**; translated from the French by Eric Sutton. Knopf 1947 445p (Roads to freedom)

Original French edition, 1945

This sequel to The age of reason "confines itself to the eight frenetic days that led to the Munich Pact and the rape of Czechoslovakia. The original characters reappear merging now with many others as a shocked France mobilizes for war. Sartre, the leading exponent of Existentialism manages in this kaleidoscope novel to re-create the confusion, even the odor of the fear that gripped Europe in September, 1938." Libr J

Followed by Troubled sleep

Sartre, Jean Paul

Troubled sleep; translated from the French by Gerald Hopkins. Knopf 1950 421p (Roads to freedom)

Sequel to The reprieve

Original French edition, 1949; published in the United Kingdom with title: Iron in the soul

"No other book gives such insight into the anguished feelings of the French as they passed from apathy to consciousness of their dignity as men revolting against fate, accepting their solidarity with other men—wretched, but lucid and free fighters." Saturday Rev

Saul, John

Darkness. Bantam Bks. 1991 341p

ISBN 0-553-07373-7

LC 90-25842

This is the "tale of a little town in the Florida swamps where a lot of old guys are remarkably youthful and a lot of kids rather soulless. 'Dead in the eyes' is how folks see these children, a new one of whom, Kelly Anderson, has just come to town with her adoptive parents. She hooks up with another teenager, also an adoptee, Michael Sheffield. Together they find out about, and are irresistibly drawn to, a mysterious circle of children controlled by the Dark Man that meets deep in the swamp." Booklist

Saul, John

The **homing**. Fawcett Columbine 1994 389p $21.50

ISBN 0-449-90863-1

LC 93-50606

"Karen Spellman and her daughters Julie, 16, and Molly, 9, move from L.A. back to the bucolic community in which Karen grew up. For with the girls' father years dead, Karen has remet and decided to marry farmer Russell Owen. Things start going awry right away: at Karen and Russell's home wedding, Molly is stung by a bee, and although it's happened before with no untoward results, this time she nearly dies. More accidents with bees and other insects occur—not least to Julie—and while local entomologist Carl Henderson, who works for the agricultural branch of a huge chemical company, is able to provide seemingly effective antivenins when folks react badly to bites, he also occasionally behaves most peculiarly." Booklist

The author provides "splendidly creepy bug-infested house of horrors and a fitting revenge for the villain." Libr J

Saul, John

Midnight voices. Ballantine Bks. 2002 341p

ISBN 0-345-43331-9

LC 2002-283839

"Mother of two and widow of a murdered Central Park jogger, Caroline Evans thinks she has found the answer to her prayers in her new husband, Anthony Fleming. The family moves into his apartment in the Rockwell, a storied old Upper West Side building. Ryan and Laurie, the children, quickly begin to have nightmares in which they are haunted by menacing voices, while Ryan realizes that he doesn't like his creepy stepfather." Publ Wkly

"This is good, drafty atmospheric horror stuff unafraid to indulge in not-at-all subtle gory bits." Booklist

Saul, John

The **presence**. Fawcett Columbine 1997 338p $25

ISBN 0-449-91055-5

LC 97-14756

Anthropologist Katharine Sundquist has recently moved to Hawaii with her teenage son Michael. "Katharine has come to the islands to study anomalies of early human development found in the lava beds of Maui. She is quickly distracted from her work by Michael's suddenly worsening asthma attacks and by the inexplicable disappearance and death of several boys with whom he went on a secret nighttime scuba dive. It's only a matter of time before she discovers that her research and Michael's problems are interrelated through the Serinus Project, a covert scientific experiment funded by her employer for the purpose of investigating the genetic origins of human life. . . . Although he breaks no new ground, Saul distills familiar elements of horror, science fiction and the cyberthriller into a potent brew." Publ Wkly

Saul, John

The **right** hand of evil. Ballantine Bks. 1999 344p $25

ISBN 0-345-43316-5

LC 98-51980

In this psychological thriller a "family moves into an old house, intending to refurbish it as a hotel, but, soon, both the father and his son begin to act rather oddly. . . . Saul makes Ted, the father, a raving alcoholic who becomes, under the influence of whatever's possessing him, a model dad. In several places, the story seems to be going in one way, until Saul wrenches it in a different direction, keeping his readers on their toes. Although the novel is sometimes drastically overwritten . . . the author clearly succeeds in his primary mission: to give readers a serious case of the willies." Booklist

Saul, John

Second child. Bantam Bks. 1990 341p

LC 89-77149

Melissa "doesn't fit into the snooty social life of the exclusive East Coast beach community of Secret Cove, and her cruel mother hates her for this failing. The arrival of Melissa's beautiful half-sister, Teri, exacerbates the situation. Melissa escapes her mother's punishments by entering a trance state where her imaginary friend D'Arcy protects her. And who is D'Arcy? Apparently, the ghost of a spurned servant girl who returned an engagement ring still attached to her severed hand. Murderous Teri tries to manipulate Melissa's apparent psychosis, but D'Arcy intercedes. Mother and half-sister are evil incarnate." Booklist

Saul, John

Shadows. Bantam Bks. 1992 390p

LC 92-1317

"Ten-year-old genius Josh MacCallum is bored, lonely and almost always angry at his older, teasing classmates. After he attempts suicide, his frantic single mother jumps at the chance to enroll him in the Academy, a school for very gifted kids in Northern California. Run by aloof Dr. Engersol and matronly housemother Hildie, the school, which occupies an old mansion, offers Josh a friend in another genius, Amy Carlson. . . . Engersol and Hildie are revealed as nasty and the mad-scientist plot hurtles to a violent conclusion featuring dueling brains connected to a mainframe computer." Publ Wkly

Saunders, George

In persuasion nation; stories. Riverhead Books 2006 228p $23.95

ISBN 1-59448-922-X

LC 2005-57715

"The most unnerving fiction boldly envisions the dire consequences of our most hubristic tendencies: our bottomless greed, maniacal competitiveness, hyper-materialism, environmental obliviousness, spiritual callousness, and fear of being different. Following in the footsteps of Orwell, Bradbury, and Atwood, Saunders writes shrewd, off-the-charts speculative fiction. . . . In his third savagely imaginative collection, his most riveting to date, he considers various forms of diabolical persuasion in a techno-colonized world in which advertising governs every aspect of life." Booklist

Saunders, George

★ **Tenth** of December; stories. George Saunders. Random House 2013 272 p. $26

ISBN 0812993802; 9780812993806 (acid-free paper); 9780812993813

LC 2012013782

This fiction collection, by George Saunders, presents multiple short stories. "In 'Victory Lap,' a boy witnesses the attempted abduction of the girl next door. . . . In 'Home,' a . . . soldier moves back in with his mother and struggles to reconcile the world . . . to which he has returned. And in the title story, . . . a . . . cancer patient walks into the woods to commit suicide, only to encounter a troubled young boy who . . . gives the dying man a final chance." (Publisher's note)

Savage, Sam

The **cry** of the sloth; the mostly tragic story of Andrew Whittaker being his collected, final, and absolutely complete writings. Coffee House Press 2009 224p pa $14.95

ISBN 978-1-56689-231-5; 1-56689-231-7

LC 2009-20904

"Success, sex and sense all elude Whittaker as he half-heartedly tries to keep his life together . . . . Savage's sense of humor is true to his name, but The Cry of the Sloth reminds us of the great Russian satirist Ivan Goncharov, who also saw the tragedy in pretending to be productive." Time Out Chicago

Savage, Sam

Firmin; adventures of a metropolitan lowlife: a novel. Coffee House Press 2006 151p pa $14.95

ISBN 978-1-566-89181-3; 1-566-89181-7

LC 2005-35803

In this dark comedy, "the titular metropolitan lowlife is a rat, albeit one with lofty literary ambitions. The runt of 13 siblings spawned in the basement of a shambolic Boston bookshop, Firmin survives his lean first weeks by munching on the edges of books. He quickly develops a predilection for actually reading them, too. Soon he's perusing everything from Joyce to compendiums of dirty jokes and even developing a secret fondness for the bookshop's owner, Norman. Tutored by a sign-language book, Firmin tries to communicate with Norman and his human brethren with predictably disastrous results until an obscure science fiction author, who writes about rats and lives above the bookshop, takes him in as a pet. There Firmin enjoys a brief respite of security, writing odes in his head and dreaming of glory, until the wrecking ball threatens the decaying neighborhood. Blending philosophy and abundant literary references with originality, Savage crafts a small comic gem about the costs and rewards of literary illusions." Booklist

Savage, Sam

Glass; a novel. Coffee House Press 2011 223p pa $15

ISBN 978-1-56689-273-5; 1-56689-273-2

LC 2011-24104

This novel, by Sam Savage, "should be a tedious read and the first pages feel like the beginning of a long, high-fiber slog, but Savage's uncanny control over his material soon has the story pulling the reader in." Minneapolis Star Tribune

Savage, Sam

The **way** of the dog; a novel. by Sam Savage. Coffee House Press 2013 153 p. (paperback) $14.95

ISBN 1566893127; 9781566893121

LC 2011046604

This novel, by Sam Savage, "follows Harold Nivenson, a decrepit, aging man who was once a painter and arts patron. The death of . . . his friend turned romantic and intellectual rival, prompts him to ruminate on his own career as a minor artist and collector and make sense of a lifetime of gnawing doubt. Over time, his bitterness toward his family, his gentrifying neighborhood, and the decline of intelligent artistic discourse gives way to a kind of peace within himself." (Publisher's note)

Sayers, Dorothy L.

★ **Busman's** honeymoon; a love story with detective interruptions. Harper & Row 1986 381p $17.95

ISBN 0-06-055021-X

LC 86-45139

First published 1937 by Harcourt, Brace

"Not near the top of her form, but remarkable as a treatment of the newly wedded and bedded pair of eccentrics, Peter Wimsey and Harriet Vane, with Bunter in the offing and three local characters, chiefly comic. Peter's mother—dowager duchess of Denver—Peter's sister, John Donne, a case of vintage port, and the handling of 'corroded sut' provide plenty of garnishing for an indifferent murder, even if we weren't also given an idea of Lord Peter's sexual tastes and powers under trying circumstances." Barzun. Cat of Crime. Rev and enl edition

Sayers, Dorothy L.

Clouds of witnesses. Dial Press (NY) 1927 288p

Variant title: Clouds of witness

The unpleasant duty of clearing his brother, the Duke of Denver, of a murder charge devolves upon Lord Peter Wimsey. Even when his only sister is involved—the dead man was her unregretted fiancé—Lord Peter does not lose his head

Sayers, Dorothy L.

The **Dawson** pedigree. Dial Press (NY) 1928 299p

First published 1927 in the United Kingdom; reissued 1987 by Harper & Row with title: Unnatural death

A chance remark overheard in a restaurant starts a long inquiry and an apparently natural death is proved to have been a murder. But Lord Peter Wimsey, aided by his friends, Parker from Headquarters, and that garrulous and delightful maiden lady, Miss Climpson, has a very difficult time to catch the murderer

Sayers, Dorothy L.

★ The **documents** in the case; by Dorothy L. Sayers and Robert Eustace. Brewer & Warren 1930 304p

A reissue of the title first published 1930 by Brewer & Warren

An "account, largely in letter form, of a case of poisoning by synthetic muscarine alkaloid made to look like mushroom poisoning. Evidence of optical activity and what it means beautifully handled, although the authors are said to have made a mistake in their choice of the particular mushroom to which the 'accidental' death should be attributed. Characters outstanding." Barzun. Cat of Crime. Rev and enl edition

Sayers, Dorothy L.

★ The **five** red herrings; (Suspicious characters) Harper & Row 1958 306p il

First published 1931. Variant title: Suspicious characters

Lord Peter Wimsey had always found himself welcome in the proud Scottish village of Kirkcudbright, although the villagers were not ordinarily tolerant of outsiders. But one day the body of an artist was found on the pointed rocks. The artist might have fallen, but there were too many suspicious elements in his death, especially when six suspects had wished him dead. Lord Peter uses all his ingenuity to unravel the tangles of this crime

"A work that grows on rereading and remains in the mind as one of the richest, most colorful of her group studies. The Scottish setting, the artists in the colony, the train-ticket puzzle, and the final chase place this triumph among the four or five chefs d'oeuvre from her hand." Barzun. Cat of Crime. Rev and enl edition

Sayers, Dorothy L.

Gaudy Night. Harcourt Brace & Co. 1936 469p

First published 1935 in the United Kingdom

Harriet's return to Oxford for the Gaudy Dinner is welcomed by poison-pen letters and attempted blackmail. Lord Peter, of course, summons all his skill to detect the blackmailer and win Harriet

"Harriet Vance and the grown-up nephew of Lord Peter help give variety, and the college scene justifies good intellectual talk. The motive is magnificently orated on by the culprit, a scene that in itself is a unique bit of work. And though the don-esses are sometimes hard to keep apart, the architecture is very good." Barzun. Cat of Crime. Rev and enl edition

Sayers, Dorothy L.

Hangman's holiday. Harper & Row 1987 191p $21.95

ISBN 0-06-055033-3

LC 86-45691

A reissue of the title first published 1933 by Harcourt, Brace and analyzed in Short story index

Sayers, Dorothy L.

Have his carcase. Brewer, Warren & Putnam 1932 448p

Harriet Vane finds a body on the beach and Lord Peter Wimsey has a case to solve. Other ingredients of the mystery are an ivory-handled razor, three hundred pounds in gold coins and a coded message

"A great achievement, despite some critics' carping. The people, the motive, the cipher, and the detection are all top-notch. Here, too, is the first (and definitive) use of hemophilia as a misleading fact. And surely the son, the mother, and her self-deluded gigolo are definitive types." Barzun. Cat of Crime. Rev and enl edition

Sayers, Dorothy L.
In the teeth of the evidence and other stories. Harcourt Brace & Co. 1940 311p
First published 1939 in the United Kingdom

Sayers, Dorothy L.
Lord Peter; a collection of all the Lord Peter Wimsey stories. compiled and with an introduction by James Sandoe; coda by Carolyn Heilburn; codetta by E.C. Bentley. Harper & Row 1972 464p
Analyzed in Short story index

Sayers, Dorothy L.
Murder must advertise; a detective story. Harcourt Brace & Co. 1933 344p
Lord Peter Wimsey, less whimsical and more interesting than usual, enters the advertising profession in order to solve the possible murder by catapult of an advertising copywriter
"A superb example of Sayers' ability to set a group of people going. The advertising agency is inimitable, and hence better than the De Momerie crowd that goes with it." Barzun. Cat of Crime. Rev and enl edition

Sayers, Dorothy L.
The **nine** tailors. Harcourt Brace Jovanovich 1989 397p il $15.95
ISBN 0-15-165897-8
LC 89-38102
A reissue of the title first published 1934
"One New Year's Eve, Lord Peter Wimsey, driving through a snowstorm, goes off the road near Fenchurch, St Paul, and is the chance guest of the rector. A providential visit all around, for Peter, acquainted with the ancient art of bellringing, acts that night as a substitute, but further than that, he finds use for his versatile mind later, upon the shocking discovery of a mutilated corpse in another man's grave. The unusual plot is developed with dexterity and ingenuity." N Y Libr

Sayers, Dorothy L.
Strong poison. Brewer & Warren 1930 344p
Because Harriet Vane's lover died of arsenic poisoning, and because Harriet was writing a book on the subject of poisons, everybody—except Lord Peter Wimsey—was convinced of her guilt. Lord Peter, with the aid of the inimitable Miss Climpson, gets to work on the business of clearing Harriet

Sayers, Dorothy L.
Thrones, dominations; {by} Dorothy L. Sayers and Jill Paton Walsh. St. Martin's Press 1998 312p $23.95
ISBN 0-312-18196-5
LC 97-42585
Paton Walsh "has made a valiant and resourceful stab at mimicry. No devotee of Lord Peter and his novelist wife Harriet Vane will want to miss it." New Stateman (Engl)

Sayers, Dorothy L.
The **unpleasantness** at the Bellona Club. Harper & Row 1986 345p $17.95
ISBN 0-06-055026-0
LC 86-45145
A reissue of the title first published 1928 by Payson & Clarke
Lord Peter Wimsey investigates the murder of an elderly member of a staid men's club

Sayers, Dorothy L.
Whose body? Boni & Liveright 1923 278p
When a nude corpse, wearing a golden pince-nez only, is found in the bathtub of the flat of a timid little architect, and the discovery coincides with the disappearance of a wealthy financier, Sir Reuben Levy, whom the body resembled, Sir Peter's sporting blood is aroused. Together with a friend from Scotland Yard he unofficially, playfully, as it were, conducts a roundabout inquiry under the jealous eye of the bungling official Scotland Yard investigators and finally tracks down the murderer

Sayers, Valerie
The **powers**; a novel. Valerie Sayers. Northwestern University Press 2013 ix, 297 p.p ill. (hardcover) $24.95
ISBN 0810152290; 9780810152298
LC 2012036262
This novel, by Valerie Sayers, Is set in "1941 . . . , Joe DiMaggio's record-breaking hitting streak enlivens the summer, and winter begins with the shock and horror of the Japanese attack on Pearl Harbor. . . . Joltin' Joe, possessing a sweet swing and range in center, also has another gift: he can see the future. And he sees dark times ahead. . . . At once magical and familiar, [the novel] is a story of witness and moral responsibility." (Publisher's note)

Sayles, John
A **moment** in the sun; a novel. McSweeney's 2011 955p $29
ISBN 978-1-936365-18-0; 1-936365-18-9
"At times, Sayles' research for A Moment in the Sun makes the writing absolutely vivid: His description of a difficult childbirth is so precise that it will have you flinching. But at other times, the historical trivia overcrowds the book: The novel's world can be so cluttered with exterior detail that it feels as though there is insufficient space for its characters' interior lives. This might seem a natural pitfall for a filmmaker writing a novel. Persnickety fans and critics point out any accidental anachronism that slips into a film's frames, and, so, perhaps, he transfers this anxiety to his fiction. But it is wrongheaded to look at Sayles as just a

filmmaker writing a book. If anything, his career has been so interesting because it has demonstrated the opposite: how a novelist would think about and make films." Daily Beast

Saylor, Steven

The **house** of the Vestals; the investigations of Gordianus the Finder. St. Martin's Press 1997 260p $22.95

ISBN 0-312-15444-5

LC 97-7597

"Saylor serves up a collection of short stories designed to fill in some of the gaps that have piqued the curiosity of devoted fans of his popular Roma Sub Rosa series. Set between the years 80 and 72 B.C., these nine tales document some of the early adventures of Gordianus the Finder. . . . While each brief mystery presented is a gem in and of itself, readers will delight in the informational overview provided by the collection as a whole. As usual, Saylor does a superb job of seamlessly incorporating the tumultuous history of the Roman Republic into the narrative flow." Booklist

Saylor, Steven

The **judgment** of Caesar; a novel of Ancient Rome. St. Martin's Minotaur 2004 290p maps $24.95

ISBN 0-312-27119-0

LC 2003-69548

"Readers will be equally absorbed by the bloody history unfolding (Saylor's description of the beheading of Pompey is both suspenseful and wrenching); by the historical figures depicted (Ptolemy listening to his flute player with the head of Pompey in a clay jar at his feet is a miniature study in royal pathology); and by the mysteries Gordianus must solve to keep his own head. Wonderful reading." Booklist

Saylor, Steven

A **mist** of prophecies. St. Martin's Press 2002 270p

ISBN 0-312-27121-2

LC 2001-58901

A mystery set in "Rome during the Civil War. A beautiful young woman, given the street name Cassandra for her habit of delivering prophesies, is found murdered. Gordianus is disturbed that no one claims her body—even though, he reflects, someone cared enough to murder her. Yet, at Cassandra's funeral pyre, seven of the most powerful women in Rome, including the wives of Caesar, Cicero, and Marc Antony, attend. Gordianus sorts out the tangled motives of the women who watched Cassandra burn, believing one of them to be her murderer. Saylor brings a wealth of historical information lightly to bear on a chilling mystery." Booklist

Saylor, Steven

Roma; the novel of ancient Rome. St. Martin's Press 2007 555p map $25.95

ISBN 978-0-312-32831-3; 0-312-32831-1

LC 2006-51179

"Livy's Early History of Rome offers fertile material for a crime writer. The body count is high, and Saylor adds plenty more along the way. Even Livy smelt a 'whodunit' in the sudden apotheosis of Romulus in a thunderclap in the middle of a Senatorial meeting. Saylor illuminates the

mystery in gory detail as, with unfailing efficiency, he unravels the enigmas. There is plenty of instruction here for students of classical civilization but sometimes the period detail founders in bathos when characters explain to each other facts they must already know, for the reader's benefit. Sometimes, though, with the scalpel-like deftness of a Hollywood director, Saylor puts his finger on the very essence of Roman history." Times Lit Suppl

Saylor, Steven

Rubicon; a novel of ancient Rome. St. Martin's Press 1999 276p $23.95

ISBN 0-312-20576-7

LC 99-18090

In this mystery "Gordianus the Finder attempts to solve the murder of Pompey's cousin Numerius. The civilized world of 49 B.C.E. is in turmoil at the onset of the Roman Civil War. Julius Caesar has crossed the Rubicon River into Italy with his hand-picked troops. Pompey, his chief rival for control of Rome, has fled Rome with his followers from the Senate, and all is chaos as the people leave the city. . . . This novel is an excellent blending of mystery and history." Libr J

Saylor, Steven

The **seven** wonders; a novel of the ancient world. Steven Saylor. Minotaur Books 2012 321 p.

ISBN 0312359845; 9781466801967; 9780312359843

LC 2012005475

This historical adventure novel by Steven Saylor is set in "92 B.C. Gordianus has just turned eighteen and is about to embark on the adventure of a lifetime: a far-flung journey to see the Seven Wonders of the World. . . . Accompanying Gordianus on his travels is his tutor, Antipater of Sidon, the world's most celebrated poet. . . . Teacher and pupil journey to the fabled cities of Greece and Asia Minor, and then to Babylon and Egypt. . . . Along the way they encounter murder, witchcraft and ghostly hauntings. . . . Gordianus discovers that amorous exploration goes hand-in-hand with crime-solving. . . . and at the end of the journey, an Eighth Wonder awaits him in Alexandria. Her name is Bethesda." (Publisher's note)

Saylor, Steven

The **triumph** of Caesar; a novel of ancient Rome. St. Martin's Minotaur 2008 311p $24.95

ISBN 978-0-312-35983-6; 0-312-35983-7

LC 2008-3668

"Julius Caesar, the dictator of Rome, and Cleopatra, the queen of Egypt, have followed the Gordianus clan back to Rome, and Caesar is planning to celebrate not one but four triumphs in recognition of his many military victories around the Mediterranean. Hieronymus, an old friend of Gordianus . . . has become a spy for Calpurnia, Caesar's wife, and gotten himself stabbed in the heart for his pains. Calpurnia is obsessed with the idea that Caesar's life is in danger, and Gordianus reluctantly agrees to investigate Hieronymus' death. . . . Saylor's vivid character sketches of historical figures are just as strong as always, with bright cameos by Arsinoë (Cleopatra's younger sister) and, for the first time in this series, the aloof, reserved Octavius (the future emperor Augustus). But Saylor's acute historical sensibility is aware that his readers already know how the story ends." January

Scalzi, John

The **android's** dream. Tor 2006 396p $24.95

ISBN 978-0-765-30941-9; 0-765-30941-6

LC 2006-10480

"When a human diplomat causes the death of an alien counterpart, the aliens threaten war unless Earth's government can present them with a particular kind of sheep used in their race's coronation ceremony. War hero and superhacker Harry Creek, along with his friend Brian Javna (now an artificial intelligence), tracks down the sheep, only to discover that it is, in fact, Robin Baker, a pet store owner whose DNA contains remnants of sheep genetic material. While Creek and Javna attempt to find a way around their dilemma, other forces are searching for Baker—and they don't care whether she's dead or alive. . . . . A tongue-in-cheek sf adventure that delivers serious action and intrigue as well as clever comedic barbs aimed at diplomatic airs, sf cults, and other foibles of the modern era." Libr J

Scalzi, John

The **ghost** brigades. Tor 2006 317p $23.95

ISBN 0-765-31502-5

LC 2005-27330

"The premise of a schizophrenic soldier allows Scalzi to explore the essence of conciousness and the ways in which it is shaped and influenced by memory, experience, and the individual's intrinsic personality. Combine that with good battle scenes, clever storytelling, and the ability to juggle abstruse scientific principles without breaking a sweat, and it makes for an impressive piece of work." Philadelphia Inquirer

Scalzi, John

The **human** division; John Scalzi. 1st ed. Tor 2013 432 p. (hardcover) $25.99

ISBN 0765333511; 9780765333513

LC 2012049551

This science fiction novel, by John Scalzi, "tells the story of the fight to maintain the unity of the human race. The people of Earth now know that the human Colonial Union has kept them ignorant of the dangerous universe around them. . . . Now the CU's secrets are known to all. Other alien races have come on the scene and formed a new alliance. . . . And they've invited the people of Earth to join them. For a shaken and betrayed Earth, the choice isn't obvious or easy." (Publisher's note)

Scalzi, John

Old man's war. Tor 2005 316p

ISBN 0-765-30940-8

LC 2004-57953

"The story obviously resembles such novels as Starship Trooper and Time Enough for Love, but Scalzi is not just recycling classic Heinlein. He's working out new twists, variations that startle even as they satisfy. The novel's tone is right on target, too—sentimentality balanced by hardheaded calculation, know-it-all smugness moderated by innocent wonder." Publ Wkly

Scalzi, John

Redshirts; John Scalzi. Tor 2012 317 p.

ISBN 0765316994; 1429963603; 9780765316998;

9781429963602

LC 2012009383

This science fiction novel by John Scalzi follows "Ensign Andrew Dahl [as he] has just been assigned to the Universal Union Capital Ship Intrepid, flagship of the Universal Union since the year 2456. . . . Life couldn't be better . . . until Andrew begins to pick up on the fact that (1) every Away Mission involves some kind of lethal confrontation with alien forces, (2) the ship's captain, its chief science officer, and the handsome Lieutenant Kerensky always survive these confrontations, and (3) at least one low-ranked crew member is, sadly, always killed." (Publisher's note)

Schaefer, Jack Warner

The **collected** stories of Jack Schaefer; with an introduction by Winfield Townley Scott. Houghton Mifflin 1966 520p

"The author's mastery of narrative technique, his excellent character development, and his consistently concise description combine in avoiding the unfortunate aspects of typical 'Western' fiction and melodrama." Libr J

Schaefer, Jack Warner

Monte Walsh. Houghton Mifflin 1963 501p

This novel of the old West follows Monte from runaway boy to trail hand, to topnotch cowhand and bronc buster, to aging saddle bum and encompasses the rise, the peak and the eventual collapse of the open range

"His characters seem real, and, according to the author, the characters and the episodes are based upon historical accounts. This is not just another 'Western.' It is worthy of a place alongside the writing of Will James and Eugene Manlove Rhodes." Libr J

Schaefer, Jack Warner

★ **Shane**; [by] Jack Schaefer; illustrated by John McCormack. Houghton Mifflin 1954 214p il $18

ISBN 0-395-07090-2

Illustrated edition of the title first published 1949

"Wyoming in 1889 is the scene of conflict between cattlemen and homesteaders when Shane mysteriously disappears. He works hard as a hired hand for the Starrett family, and young Bob Starrett grows to love him, unaware that he is a feared gunfighter escaping his past." Shapiro. Fic for Youth. 3d edition

Schaffert, Timothy

The **coffins** of Little Hope; a novel. Unbridled Books 2011 262p

ISBN 1609530403; 9781609530402

LC 2010043201

This novel's narrator, Essie, is an eighty-three-year-old obituary writer for a small-town Nebraska newspaper. When Lenore, "a young country girl, is reported to be missing, perhaps whisked away by an itinerant aerial photographer, Essie stumbles onto the story of her life. Or, it all could be simply a hoax, or a delusion, the child and child-thief invented from the desperate imagination of a lonely, lovelorn woman. Either way, the story of the girl reaches far and wide, igniting controversy, attracting curiosity-seekers and cult worshippers from all over the country to this dying rural town. And then it is revealed that the long awaited final book of a . . . series of YA gothic novels, [the Miranda-and-Desiree books], is being secretly printed on the newspaper's presses." (Publisher's note)

"Schaffert's protagonist is Esther Myles, an 83-year-old obituary writer for the County Paragraph, a small Nebraska newspaper. . . . Myles does not normally specialize in scoops, but when she hears that an 11-year-old girl named Lenore might have been abducted, she cannot ignore the story, for personal and professional reasons. As Myles investigates, however, the truth becomes more, not less, murky. Was the abduction real, or a hoax perpetrated by Daisy, the alleged mother? Does Lenore even exist in the flesh, or is she a figment of Daisy's imagination? In a parallel narrative, Schaffert spins a sendup of book publishing. The newspaper employing Myles has been chosen as a contract printer by a New York City publisher for the final book of a bestselling young adult series. The printing is supposed to be confidential, because the publisher wants to avoid leaks before the official release date of the book. The confidentiality disintegrates, though, when somebody reveals portions of the manuscript. The formerly lazy, peaceful Nebraska town is now a center of attention, with amusing and not-so-amusing consequences." Minneapolis Star Trib

Schanbacher, Gary

Crossing Purgatory; by Gary Schanbacher. 1st ed. W W Norton & Co Inc 2013 336 p. (hardcover) $25.95

ISBN 1605984434; 9781605984438

In this novel by Gary Schanbacher, Thompson Grey, a young farmer, travels to his father's estate seeking funds to expand his holdings. He returns home to find that his absence has contributed to a devastating family tragedy. Thompson abandons his farm and begins a westward exile in the attempt to outpace his grief. Set against the backdrop of the frontier during the years just preceding the Civil War, [it] tells a story of unprincipled ambition, guilt, and the price one man is willing to pay for atonement." (Publisher's note)

Schappell, Elissa

Blueprints for building better girls; fiction. Simon & Schuster 2011 288p $24

ISBN 978-0-7432-7670-2; 0-7432-7670-1

LC 2011-28068

"A sequence of eight darkly comic, interlinked tales explores the common experiences that shape early adulthood, marriage and motherhood and features an eclectic cast of archetypal female characters who navigate the pitfalls of the cultural landscape between the 1970s and the present." (Publisher's note)

"Schappell's stories read like snapshots—capturing precise moments from a woman's life from a distinct perspective. Considered together, Blueprints for Building Better Girls is a treasured photo album." BookPage

Schickler, David

Sweet and vicious. Dial Press 2004 242p $23

ISBN 0-385-33568-7

LC 2004-47830

"Schickler is a rare find; with straightforward and yet deeply insightful writing, he mixes love, violence, ardor, and humor in this funny and heartbreaking modern-day fable." Booklist

Schine, Cathleen

The **love** letter. Houghton Mifflin 1995 257p

LC 95-5202

"As light, and as risky, as a soufflé, The Love Letter indulges an enchanting fantasy, while invoking the powerful interplay of language and love. Literature, Schine suggests, can make booksellers glamorous, can ignite passion in the most unlikely of settings, and can even allow doomed love to live on." N Y Rev Books

Schine, Cathleen

The **New** Yorkers; with drawings by Leanne Shapton. Farrar, Straus and Giroux 2007 290p il $24

ISBN 978-0-374-22183-6; 0-374-22183-9

LC 2006-32711

"A swift-moving, gently poignant romantic comedy of manners. . . . The breezy storytelling in The New Yorkers is deceptive: the novel offers more than a sweet story of puppy love. Schine strikes a rare, deeply personal, and very loving chord as she portrays the way these devoted pets elicit joy from the depressed (except once, when it's already too late) and humanity from the merciless, and inspire flirtations and encounters between the shy and monastic." Village Voice

Schine, Cathleen

The **three** Weissmanns of Westport. Farrar, Straus & Giroux 2010 292p $25

ISBN 978-0-374-29904-0; 0-374-29904-8

LC 2009-25425

"When Joseph Weissmann divorces Betty, his wife of forty-eight years, she takes refuge in her cousin's cottage in Connecticut, with her two daughters. Annie, the elder, is a sober worrywart, while Miranda, the younger, is self-involved, inclined to melodrama, and on the verge of bankruptcy after her literary agency represented too many fraudulent memoirs. The sisters become involved in a shifting game of romantic entanglements that include a celebrated reclusive writer, a semi-retired lawyer, a Hollywood-bound schemer, an epidemiologist, and a couple of vacuous hangers-on. The ironic title—the three are anything but wise men—does little justice to Schine's real wit, which playfully probes the lies, self-deceptions, and honorable hearts of her characters." New Yorker

Schlink, Bernhard

Homecoming; translated from the German by Michael Henry Heim. Pantheon Books 2008 260p $24; pa $14.95

ISBN 978-0-375-42091-7; 0-375-42091-6; 978-0-375-72557-9 pa; 0-375-72557-1 pa

LC 2007-16121

Original German edition, 2006

This is "an exceedingly delicate meditation on the German past that refuses to moralize. Decent people can be driven to do the devil's work, just as truly moral verdicts can result in unimaginable collateral damage: Debauer witnesses both of these." N Y Sun

Schlink, Bernhard

★ The **reader**; translated from the German by Carol Brown Janeway. Pantheon Bks. 1997 218p $20

ISBN 0-679-44279-0

LC 97-1511

Original German edition, 1995

"In post WW II Germany, a teenage boy is seduced by a streetcar conductor twice his age who insists that he read to her before they make love. Years later, when he is a law student, she appears as a defendant on trial for war crimes during the Nazi era. This novel raises provocative questions about guilt and responsibility, as well as the power of literature to heal and bind." Publ Wkly

Schlink, Bernhard

Self's punishment; [by] Bernhard Schlink and Walter Popp; translated from the German by Rebecca Morrison. Vintage Books 2005 248p pa $14

ISBN 0-375-70907-X

LC 2004-57166

This mystery features former Nazi prosecutor turned investigator Gerhard Self. "It's the early 1980s, and Self has been hired by a boyhood friend to smoke out a hacker who's playing havoc with the computers at Rhineland Chemical Works. But after Self springs a trap that gets the troublemaker murdered, he gradually faces the guilt he still carries for his youthful embrace of National Socialism. His simple refusal to let himself off the hook and step back into his old public prosecutor's role after the war doesn't seem like penance enough anymore. . . . Self's unwitting participation in the new crime drives him to pursue the path of justice wherever it may lead. A fascinating exploration of how people often manage to carve out normal lives even after being complicit in terrible acts." Booklist

Schlink, Bernhard

Summer lies; stories. Bernhard Schlink; translated from the German by Carol Brown Janeway. Pantheon Books 2012 229 p. (hardcover) $25.95

ISBN 0307907260; 9780307907264

LC 2012005994

This fiction collection, by Bernhard Schlink, translated by Carol Janeway, features seven short stories "brim[ming] with the delusions, the passions, the outbursts, and the sometimes irrational justifications people make within a melange of . . . relationships." Stories include "After the Season," "Johann Sebastian Bach on Ruegen," and "The Night in Baden-Baden." (Publisher's note)

Schlink, Bernhard

The **weekend**; translated from the German by Shaun Whiteside. Pantheon Books 2010 215p $24.95

ISBN 978-0-307-37815-6; 0-307-37815-2

LC 2010-05396

Original German edition, 2008

"The narrative style can sometimes be confusing. We spend a little time inside each guest's head — learning how they feel about Jorg and why they think they were invited for the weekend. Credit must be given to the English translator, Shaun Whiteside, who distills the often-difficult German

into relatively simple sentences that add to the pace of Schlink's plot." Deseret News

Schneider, Bart

Beautiful Inez; a novel. Bart Schneider. 1st ed; Shaye Areheart Books 2005 353p (pbk.) $14; (hbk.) $24

ISBN 9781400054428; 9781400054435; 1400054427

LC 2004016227

This book takes place in 1962 and tells the story of Inez Roseman who "is a talented if moody violinist for the San Francisco Symphony; it doesn't help that she's turning 40 and that her husband, a flashy attorney, has become an accomplished philanderer and now speaks to her mostly when he wants to criticize her. . . . Enter Sylvia Bran, a plain but beguiling woman ten years Inez's junior, who introduces herself as a writer for the 'San Francisco Chronicle' wanting to do a profile of Inez. Her would-be subject has never seen her byline. . . . [The plot involves a romance between] Inez and Sylvia, . . . [and] there's also the nodding understanding between the two that though this sort of thing isn't supposed to happen in their day and age, . . . it does. And so do many other things that, in the end, tear the Rosemans' house apart." (Kirkus)

Scholes, Ken

Antiphon; by Ken Scholes. 1st ed. Tor Books 2010 380 p. ill. (hardcover) $25.99

ISBN 0765321297; 9780765321299

LC 2010032567

In this novel by Ken Scholes "the hand of the Wizard Kings still reaches out to challenge the Androfrancine Order, to control the magick and technology that they sought to understand and claim for their own. Nebios, the boy who watched the destruction of the city of Windwir, now runs the vast deserts of the world, far from his beloved Marsh Queen. He is being hunted by strange women warriors, while his dreams are invaded by warnings from his dead father." (Publisher's note)

Scholes, Ken

Canticle; by Ken Scholes. 1st ed. Tor Books 2009 384 p. ill. (hardcover) $25.99

ISBN 0765321289; 9780765321282

LC 2009016764

In this novel by Ken Scholes, the sequel to "Lamentation," "it is nine months after the end of the previous book. Many noble allies have come to the Ninefold Forest for a Feast in honor of General Rudolfo's first-born child. As the feast begins . . . invisible assassins begin attacking. All of Rudolfo's noble guests are slain. On the Keeper's Gate, which guards the Named Lands from the Churning Waste, a strange figure appears, with a message for Petronus, the Hidden Pope." (Publisher's note)

Scholes, Ken

Lamentation. Tor 2009 366p map (Psalms of Isaak saga) $25.95

ISBN 9780765321275; 0765321270

LC 2008-38024

As an ancient weapon destroys the city of Windwir, a young apprentice watches from a nearby hilltop, mourning the death of the city and his father. When Rudolfo, Lord of the Nine Forest Houses, realizes what has happened, he knows for certain that the land will soon be plunged into a devastating war.

Scholes, Ken

Requiem; by Ken Scholes. Tor Books 2013 398 p. (hardcover: v. 4) $27.99

ISBN 0765321300; 9780765321305

LC 2012043814

This novel by Ken Scholes is the fourth book in the Psalms of Isaak series. It asks "who is the Crimson Empress, and what does her conquest of the Named Lands really mean? Who holds the keys to the Moon Wizard's Tower? The plots within plots are expanding as the characters seek their way out of the maze of intrigue. The world is expanding as they discover lands beyond their previous . . . knowledge. Hidden truths reveal even deeper truths, and nothing is as it seemed to be." (Publisher's note)

Scholz, Carter

The **amount** to carry; stories. Picador 2003 208p $23

ISBN 0-312-26901-3

LC 2002-192667

"In each keenly meta-physical fable Scholz, a connoisseur of the imagination, parses the language of science, literature, art, and music as he ponders the quintessentially human habit of telling stories, a valiant attempt to render sense out of the delirium of existence." Booklist

Scholz, Carter

★ **Radiance**. Picador 2002 388p $24

ISBN 0-312-26893-9

LC 2001-56018

"It is the mid-1990s, and the press has just learned that a recent demonstration of a missile interception system was rigged. Leo Highet, the Machiavellian director of a California defense lab, is forced from his position and replaced by his rival Philip Quine, a closet peacenik." Libr J

"Wickedly satiric and eggheaded in its level of scientific detail, 'Radiance' is a serious, engrossing novel." N Y Times Book Rev

Schulberg, Budd

★ **Waterfront**; a novel. Random House 1955 320p

"The prize-winning screen play 'On the waterfront' has been expanded into a novel which differs on several counts from the film. It remains an angry indictment of racketeering in the labor unions along the New Jersey waterfront, but the happy ending of the screen play has been supplanted by a tragic one, in which the hero Terry Malloy is murdered by the henchmen of Johnny Friendly, the labor racketeer, and the terrorism along the waterfront continues. The more leisurely framework of the novel form permits the author to document to the full the abuses in longshoremen's unions, without sacrificing the explosive force of the film." Booklist

Schulberg, Budd

★ **What** makes Sammy run? Modern Lib. 1941 303p

"The protagonist, Sammy Glick, is a tough New York youth who works his way into a position of power in the motion-picture industry, where his harshness and crude manners are not out of place." Benet's Reader's Ency of Am Lit

Schulman, Helen

This beautiful life; a novel. HarperCollins 2011 222p $24.99

ISBN 978-0-06-202438-1; 0-06-202438-8

This novel tells the story "of the four Bergamots, who have moved from a college town . . . to the Upper West Side of Manhattan." (N Y Times (Late N Y Ed))

In this novel "15-year-old Jake Bergamot is newly arrived at a competitive private school on the Upper East Side when a younger girl, hoping to be taken seriously as girlfriend material, emails him a video of herself stripping for the camera in her messy bedroom. . . . Shocked, confused, and unsure whether he finds the video sexy or horrifying, Jake forwards the email to his best friend for advice. Overnight, [the video] has made Gawker and the teens and families involved are devastated. . . . Because this is a story about kids, sex, and the Internet, we expect it also to be a story about the irreconcilable generation gap between today's teens and their parents. Instead, This Beautiful Life illuminates the common ground, or maybe more aptly, the common void between the generations. Shulman knows her characters well, and her prose comes alive when she's rendering a character's thorniest, most intimate moments." Slate

Schulze, Ingo

New lives; the youth of Enrico Turmer in letters and prose. edited and with commentary and foreword by Ingo Schulze; translated from the German by John E. Woods. Alfred A. Knopf 2008 570p $28.95

ISBN 978-0-307-26559-3; 0-307-26559-5

LC 2008-19615

Original German edition, 2005

"All his life Türmer has wanted nothing so much as to write a novel, to pour experience onto the page and make it ripple. . . . But he never manages to create a shaped and formed work. The only writing he produces is a series of long letters about his agonies to his sister, friends, and love interests. As it happens, all of Türmer's letters are all composed in the first half of 1990, in the months between the fall of the Berlin Wall and the reunification of East and West Germany – a strange era, at once a kind of twilight and a dawn. Despite his failure to write a novel, when Türmer re-reads these letters, he finds his literary aspirations renewed. . . . He believes he now has the material for an epistolary novel in his hands, a work that will 'essentially write itself.' It is these letters, with their mixture of ambition and naiveté, that are presented to us in 'New Lives' as collected and annotated by a skeptical but fastidious literary scholar named Ingo Schulze." Christ Sci Monit

Schupack, Deborah

The **boy** on the bus; a novel. Free Press 2003 215p $23

ISBN 0-7432-4220-3

LC 2002-32179

"Motherhood with all its contradictions has rarely been shown so nakedly. Schupack gives us Meg's view and everyone else's in overlapping layers. . . . From beginning to end in this novel, nothing is ordinary, while at the same time everything is." N Y Times Book Rev

Schwartz, John Burnham

The **commoner**; a novel. Nan A. Talese 2008 351p $24.95

ISBN 978-0-385-51571-9; 0-385-51571-5

LC 2007-15391

"An American taking on a fictional memoir about a living Japanese empress is a gutsy move, but Schwartz makes it work. . . . While the external details of life in the palace remain stunning, it's Schwartz's grasp of [Haruko's] internal struggle that resonates after the last page is turned." Denver Post

Schwartz, John Burnham

Northwest corner; a novel. Random House 2011 285p $26.00

ISBN 1400068452; 9781400068456

LC 2010045784

"Twelve years after a tragic accident and a cover-up that led to prison time, Dwight Arno, now fifty, is a man who has started over. . . . Dwight manages a sporting goods store and dates a woman to whom he hasn't revealed the truth about his past." (Publisher's note)

In Reservation Road (1998), Dwight Arno "accidentally hit and killed a child while driving; now, his prison time served, he plods through his days as manager of a dreary sporting-goods store, haunted by memories of his past life. . . . Then his son Sam, whom he has not seen in 12 years, lands on Dwight's doorstep, on the run after clobbering someone with a metal bat in a bar fight. 'I wanted to hurt him," Sam admits to his dad. And that is the bitter, awful truth that father and son must work through as they struggle to patch their tattered relationship: Deep down, they harbor the same dark impulses. They can succumb to them, or they can take a shot at redemption. The choice is theirs. The story emerges, slowly at first, not just from their viewpoints but from those of their girlfriends as well as Sam's mother. Multiple viewpoints are usually jarring, interrupting the flow of a novel, but not here: In Schwartz's hands, the narrative unfolds delicately, each chapter a puzzle piece that fits seamlessly into the whole. It's painful to watch the two men confront their lives—but it's also exhilarating." Entertainment Wkly

Schwartz, John Burnham

Reservation Road; a novel. Knopf 1998 292p

ISBN 978-0375402630

LC 98-14580

This novel focuses on "two unhappy Connecticut families linked by one violent moment. The Learners are the victims of tragedy: an ordinary stop at a country gas station turns to horror when their oldest child is killed by a hit-and-run driver in full view of his father, Ethan. As his wife and small daughter suffer through grief, depression, and guilt, Ethan is consumed by his compulsion to find and punish his son's murderer after the police give up. Nearby, . . . Dwight Arno tortures himself with his memories of speeding away from the accident." Libr J

"The story is told in the alternating voices of father, mother and murderer, which overlap and swell to a crescendo in an operatic chorus of pain." Economist

Schwartz, Leslie

Angels Crest; a novel. Doubleday 2004 303p $23.95

ISBN 0-385-51185-X

LC 2003-64635

"Ethan Denton is out for a drive with his three-year-old son, Nate, in the woods of Northern California, when he decides to stop to follow several bucks he spots just off the road. When he returns 15 minutes later, his son is gone, and his own personal hell, as well as that of the small town of Angels Crest, is just beginning. Ethan's alcoholic ex-wife, Cindy, who lost custody of Nate; his former best friend, Glick, who slept with Cindy; Rocksan and Jane, a settled lesbian couple; and Jack, a lonely judge from outside the town are among those who help Ethan search for his son. . . . This beautiful, moving novel works brilliantly as a study of a tragedy and the various characters' reactions to the tragedy itself, as well as how it causes them to reexamine their own lives." Booklist

Schwartz, Lynne Sharon

★ **Disturbances** in the field. Harper & Row 1983 371p

LC 83-47555

"There are weighty passages and themes here, not for the casual reader. However, the journey from resignation to a grudging reaffirmation of living, of returning to the field, disturbs the reader's own field with its unmistakable ring of truth." Libr J

Schwartz, Lynne Sharon

The **fatigue** artist; a novel. Scribner 1995 320p il $23

ISBN 0-684-80247-3

LC 94-48009

"Like Laura, Schwartz is a writer's writer, indulging in lavish description, then subverting clichés with succinct turns of phrase. Her dialogue is arrestingly urbane." Women's Rev Books

Schwartz, Lynne Sharon

In the family way; an urban comedy. Morrow 1999 325p $24

ISBN 0-688-17071-4

LC 99-22134

"The story takes place in an apartment building on New York's Upper West Side and centers on Roy, a psychotherapist; his first wife, Bea, a caterer; and their quest to preserve family. Bea's mother is the landlady of the building, and the tenants include Bea's lesbian sister, Bea's Russian lover, the superintendent, and Roy's second and current wife. In an attempt to keep her four children and their father together, Bea convinces Roy and his new wife to reside in her mother's building." Libr J

"A fast-paced, hugely entertaining novel about a group of people unwilling to compromise on their hopes for happiness." Booklist

Schwartz, Lynne Sharon

The **writing** on the wall; a novel. Counterpoint 2005 297p $24

ISBN 1-582-43299-6

LC 2004-24877

This novel "would have been excellent already without its 9/11 ballast. It is full of intuitive dread, as if Joan Didion had written Play It As It Lays in the same Brooklyn boarding house where Norman Mailer was writing Barbary Shore." Harper's

Schwartzman, Adam

Eddie Signwriter. Pantheon Books 2010 293p $25.95

ISBN 978-0-307-37873-6; 0-307-37873-X

LC 2009-19509

"Themes and scenes from multiple other works poke through the lattice of Schwartzman's prose, including the Book of Genesis itself. . . . Resonating with allusions, this book features literary rediscovery too. If 'Eddie Signwriter' is about the struggle to recover from the flip-flops of fate, it's also about the problem of recovering oneself, about remaining who one is in a world prone to terrifying transformation." Los Angeles Times

Schwarz, Christina

All is vanity; a novel. Doubleday 2002 368p $24.95

ISBN 0-385-49972-8

LC 2002-67583

"Schwarz's portrait of the talentless, self-absorbed Margaret is surgically accurate. . . . Anyone who has ever tried to write and been blocked will howl with recognition at the indignities that befall the novelist. . . . The novel is both a page turner and a cautionary tale of consumerism run amok." N Y Times Book Rev

Schwarz, Christina

Drowning Ruth. Doubleday 2000 338p $23.95

ISBN 0-385-50253-2

LC 00-29523

"The vivid realism of the novel's setting adds depth to an already gripping plot. . . . Schwarz maintains her mystery with an expert hand, arriving at far more than a simple determination of guilt." N Y Times Book Rev

Schwarz, Christina

The **Edge** of the Earth; a novel. by Christina Schwarz. 1st Atria Books hardcover ed. Pocket Books 2013 275 p. (hardcover) $25

ISBN 1451683677; 9781451683677

LC 2013000480

In this novel by Christina Schwarz "[Trudy] falls in love with enigmatic and ambitious Oskar, [and] she believes she's found her escape from the banality of her pre-ordained life. . . . The couple moves across the country to take a job at a lighthouse in the eerily isolated Point Lucia, California. Upon arriving they meet the light station's only inhabitants--the Crawleys, a family whose plain appearance is no indication of what lies below the surface." (Publisher's note)

Schwarz-Bart, Andre

The **last** of the just; translated from the French by Stephen Becker. Atheneum Pubs. 1960 374p

Original French edition, 1959

"The thread that runs through the narration is the ancient Jewish tradition of the Lamed-Vov, according to which the world reposes upon 36 Just Men, who often are not aware themselves of the position they hold. . . . Harrowing as the book is, it is a valuable addition to the titles on the Holocaust, lest we forget how inhumane man can be." Shapiro. Fic for Youth. 3d edition

Schwegel, Theresa

Person of interest. St. Martin's Minotaur 2007 372p $24.95

ISBN 978-0-312-36426-7; 0-312-36426-1

LC 2007-33535

"Chicago PD detective Craig McHugh is deep into an undercover investigation of a deadly batch of heroin allegedly being peddled by the Fuxi Spiders, a powerful Chinese gang. Hoping to gain their trust, Craig burns through his department allowance and his own funds playing at a Fuxi card game. Meanwhile, Craig's sullen teenage daughter, Ivy, is dragged home from a party by his police colleagues after being caught with ecstasy. Unaware of her husband's undercover assignment, Craig's wife, Leslie, is convinced he's having an affair, and she soon begins flirting with Ivy's handsome jazz-playing boyfriend." Publ Wkly

Scoppettone, Sandra

Everything you have is mine. Little, Brown 1991 261p

LC 90-48889

"Lauren Laurano, a bighearted, wisecracking lesbian who makes her debut here as a Manhattan private eye, brings cunning as well as caring to her investigation of the murder of a young rape victim who might have met her killer by hooking into a dating service on her personal computer." N Y Times Book Rev

Scoppettone, Sandra

Gonna take a homicidal journey. Little, Brown 1998 229p $22.95

ISBN 0-316-77665-3

LC 97-44247

"While helping her life partner and friends renovate a beach place in a small Long Island town, private investigator Lauren Laurano becomes sidetracked by murder. Hired by the old-money cousin of a supposed suicide, Lauren soon detects a pattern that may include the deaths of several women and children. Each suspect she questions withholds crucial information; meanwhile, the idea of a police conspiracy grows. The wide-ranging, all-encompassing case may seem shallow or far-fetched, but Scoppettone's tongue-in-cheek attitude makes the book work." Libr J

Scoppettone, Sandra

My sweet untraceable you. Little, Brown 1994 275p

LC 93-47426

"Scoppettone is a highly entertaining writer with her fingers on current political and commercial pulses. So she ably transmits the modish urban-grit feel of Laurano's encounters with Manhattan's winos, weirdos, and wise guys as she counterpoints the complex case her sleuth is solving with the deterioration from AIDS of the brother of Laurano's lesbian partner of 14 years." Booklist

Scott, A. D.

Beneath the abbey wall; a novel. by A. D. Scott. Atria Books 2012 340 p. (trade paper) $15
ISBN 1451665776; 9781451665772; 9781451665789
LC 2012030071

Author A. D. Scott presents a murder mystery. "In the Highlands in the late 1950s, much of the local newspaper's success was due to Mrs. Smart, the no-nonsense office manager who kept everything and everyone in line. Her murder leaves her colleagues in shock and the 'Highland Gazette' office in chaos. Joanne Ross, a budding reporter and shamefully separated mother, assumes Mrs. Smart's duties, but an intriguing stranger provides a distraction not only from the job and the investigation but from everything Joanne believes in." (Publisher's note)

Scott, A. D.

A **double** death on the Black Isle; a novel. Atria Paperback 2011 357p pa $15
ISBN 978-1-4391-5494-6
LC 2011-13152

"Set against the bleak beauty of the Highlands, . . . [this book explores] the slow transformation of Scotland from a highly ordered society while presenting a fine mystery with engaging characters." Kirkus

Scott, Anne

Calpurnia. Knopf 2003 293p $24
ISBN 0-375-41380-4
LC 2002-30096

"Scott sets the book in the 1980's, before online antique auctions and the advent of dot-com billionaires who might have competed fiercely to buy a flashy old pile like Calpurnia. Her central theme, however, the impulse to make and live with art, is timeless." N Y Times Book Rev

Scott, Joanna

Everybody loves somebody; stories. Back Bay Books/Little, Brown and Co. 2006 260p $13.99
ISBN 978-0-316-01345-1; 0-316-01345-5
LC 2006-12310

A "collection of 10 stories that stalk across the 20th century to document love and its consequences. . . . Scott's craft can be breathtaking—and her perceptions uncanny." Publ Wkly

Scott, Joanna

Follow me; a novel. Little, Brown and Company 2009 420p $24.99
ISBN 978-0-316-05165-1; 0-316-05165-9
LC 2008-42643

Scott "traces the meandering path of a runaway girl from place to place, name to name, starting as 16-year-old Sally Werner in 1947 rural Pennsylvania. Her saga begins with an innocent motorcycle ride with an older cousin at a church picnic, which results in a baby son and rejection by her fun-

damentalist parents. She decides her only option is escape, following the Tuskee River that snakes across the Werners' back fields. . . . Over the next four decades, she washes up in towns farther along the Tuskee, surviving on the kindness of strangers. . . . Her many reincarnations are pieced together years later by her granddaughter and a man who believes he is the infant that Sally abandoned. Scott . . . excels in her stream-of-consciousness descriptions of the mysterious Tuskee that provides Sally's true north." Washington Post Book World

Scott, Joanna

★ **Tourmaline**; a novel. Little, Brown 2002 279p $23.95
ISBN 0-316-77618-1
LC 2002-67111

"Book reviewers are fond of calling belletristic novels 'poetic.' 'Tourmaline' isn't poetic because of its pretty writing but because of its sympathetic ordering and reordering of ideas, its philosophical probing." N Y Times Book Rev

Scott, Justin

The **wrecker**; [by] Clive Cussler and Justin Scott. G.P. Putnam's Sons 2009 470 p. (hardcover) $27.95
ISBN 0399155996; 9780399155994
LC 2009017216

This adventure story, by Clive Cussler and Justin Scott, is the second "Isaac Bell" novel by the author. "It is 1907, . . . wrecks, fires, and explosions sabotage the Southern Pacific Railroad's Cascades express line and . . . the railroad hires the fabled Van Dorn Detective Agency. . . . [Isaac] Bell quickly discovers that a mysterious saboteur haunts the hobo jungles of the West, a man known as the Wrecker. . . . Whoever he is, . . . Bell senses that he is far from done." (Publisher's note)

Scott, Kim

That deadman dance; Kim Scott. 1st U.S. ed; Bloomsbury 2011 368p.
ISBN 9781608197057; 1608197050
LC 2011014163

Australian Literature Society Gold Medal (2011)
Miles Franklin Award (Australia) (2011)
Commonwealth Writers' Prize: Regional Award: South East Asia & Pacific: Best Book (2011)
Adelaide Festival Awards (Australia): Fiction (2012)
Adelaide Festival Awards (Australia): Premier's Award (2012)

This book, which won the Miles Franklin Award in 2011, tells the story of "the early contact between the Aboriginal Noongar people and the first European settlers [of Western Australia]. . . . Clever, resourceful and eager to please, Bobby [Wabalaginy, a young Aborigine] befriends the new arrivals . . . [and] is even welcomed into a prosperous local white family. . . . But slowly – by design and by accident – things begin to change. . . . Stock mysteriously start to disappear; crops are destroyed; there are 'accidents' and injuries on both sides. As the Europeans impose ever stricter rules and regulations in order to keep the peace, Bobby's Elders decide they must respond in kind. . . . Bobby is forced to take sides: he must choose between the old world and the new." (Publisher's note)

Scott, Kirstin

Motherlunge; Kirstin Scott; [edited by] William Olsen, Kimberly Kolbe. 1st American ed. New Issues Poetry & Prose 2013 252 p. (Awp award series in the novel) (paperback) $15

    ISBN 1936970112; 9781936970117

LC 2012936333

In this debut novel from Kirstin Scott, winner of the 2011 Association of Writers & Writing Programs Prize, motherhood, sisterhood, and making decisions is explored. Readers hear "Thea tell her unborn daughter about sex and love and sorrow, and what happened when she left her small Montana town to go to the big city and help out the pregnant Pavia." (Publishers Weekly)

Scott, Paul

The **day** of the scorpion; a novel. Morrow 1968 483p

This second volume of the Raj quartet tells the lives of Sarah and Susan Layton, Lady Manners and Parvati; Kasim and his two sons and Captain Merrick, all caught up in the violence and strife that engulfed India when the Congress Party adopted a resolution calling for a nationwide insurrection

The author's "ability in characterization and in realization of the love-hate relationship of Indian and Englishman are again amply demonstrated in a poignant story constantly interest-holding." Booklist

Followed by The towers of silence

Scott, Paul

A **division** of the spoils; a novel. Morrow 1975 597p

"Scott makes nothing simple; thus his work bears a disturbing resemblance to life. He mixes up lovers, friends, enemies, families, servants, strangers, soldiers, businessmen, murders, suicides, illnesses in five or six interrelated stories. . . . And all have one focus: corrupted British morality in India." N Y Times Book Rev

Scott, Paul

★ The **jewel** in the crown; a novel. Morrow 1966 462p

This is the first volume of The Raj quartet

"Around a central incident of the rape of a young Englishwoman in an Indian garden in August, 1942, the author has woven a . . . picture of India before independence. The two main threads of plot are the fate of the raped girl and the tragic end of an elderly English school-teacher who is a very brave woman. There are other stories within the story. . . . This is a masterly narrative, a leisurely and skillful depiction of a wide Indian landscape and a large canvas showing people who are made very real. It is also a dissection of Anglo-British animosities." Publ Wkly

Followed by The day of the scorpion

Scott, Paul

The **Raj** quartet; introduction by Hilary Spurling. Alfred A. Knopf 2007 1032p 2v ea $32.50

    ISBN 978-0-307-26396-4 v1; 0-307-26396-7 v1; 978-0-307-26397-1 v2; 0-307-26397-5 v2

LC 2007-277260

Contents: v. 1 The jewel in the crown; The day of the scorpion v2 The towers of silence; A division of the spoils

Scott, Paul

★ **Staying** on; a novel. Morrow 1977 215p

LC 77-1491

"After India succeeds in obtaining independence from Britain, Tusker and Lucy Smalley, part of the British colonial army, stay on in the country where almost all their married life has been spent. The book describes their relationships with the Indians who, at this point, constitute all of their daily and social contacts. . . . There is humor in the informative portrayals of the relationships between the British and the Indians, and the final scene is as simple and moving a description of loss as has ever been written." Shapiro. Fic for Youth. 3d edition

Scott, Paul

The **towers** of silence; a novel. Morrow 1972 392p

First published 1971 in the United Kingdom

"This elegy on the decline and fall of the Indian empire sounds harsh notes, but is moving as well. Mr. Scott has the trick of being sympathetic without ever losing his clear sightedness." Times Lit Suppl

Followed by A division of the spoils

Scott, Walter

The **bride** of Lammermoor; edited by J.H. Alexander. Columbia Univ. Press 1995 398p $44.50

    ISBN 0-231-10572-X

LC 96-143055

First published 1819

"The most tragic of Scott's romances, on which Donizetti's opera 'Lucia di Lammermoor' is based. The last scion of a ruined family and the daughter of his ancestral enemy in possession of the estates fall in love. For a while there is a glimpse of hope and happiness; but the ambitious mother opposes the match, prophecies and apparitions prognosticate tragedy, and the romance closes in death and sorrow. . . . Caleb Balderstone, the faithful retainer, is one of Scott's humorous creations, whose obstinate care for his unhappy master relieves the overpowering tragedy." Baker. Guide to the Best Fic

Scott, Walter

★ **Ivanhoe**; a romance. Modern Lib. 1997 xxxvii, 535p $16

    ISBN 0-679-60263-1

LC 96-48579

First published 1819

"The action occurs in the period following the Norman Conquest. The titular hero is Wilfred, knight of Ivanhoe, the son of Cedric the Saxon, in love with his father's ward Rowena. Cedric, however, wishes her to marry Athelstane, who is descended from the Saxon royal line and may restore the Saxon supremacy. The real heroine is Rebecca the Jewess, daughter of the wealthy Isaac of York, and a person of much more character and charm than the mild Rowena. Richard the Lion-Hearted in the guise of the Black Knight and Robin Hood as Locksley play prominent roles." Reader's Ency. 4th edition

Scott, Walter

★ **Rob** Roy; with an introduction by Eric Anderson. Knopf 1995 xliii, 494p $20

ISBN 0-679-44362-2

First published 1817; first Everyman's library edition 1906

"Full of intrigue with political overtones, it is set in northern England just before the Jacobite rebellion of 1715, and it is considered one of the author's masterpieces. Francis Obaldistone, the novel's hero, contends with his jealous, unscrupulous cousin Rashleigh for the hand of the beautiful Diana Vernon. Aided by the Scottish outlaw Rob Roy (based on a historical Jacobite outlaw), Francis succeeds in exposing Rashleigh's villainy." Merriam-Webster's Ency of Lit

Scottoline, Lisa

★ **Come** home; Lisa Scottoline. St. Martin's Press 2012 371 p.

ISBN 9780312380823; 9781429942324

LC 2011046492

This book tells the story of "Jill Farrow [who] is a typical suburban mom . . . [and] has finally gotten her and her daughter's lives back on track after a divorce. She is about to remarry, her job as a pediatrician fulfills her . . . and her daughter, Megan, is . . . happily . . . juggling homework and the swim team. But Jill's life is turned upside down when her ex-stepdaughter, Abby, shows up on her doorstep . . . and delivers shocking news: Jill's ex-husband is dead. Abby insists that he was murdered and pleads with Jill to help find his killer. Jill reluctantly agrees to make a few inquiries and discovers that things don't add up. As she digs deeper, her actions threaten to rip apart her new family, destroy their hard-earned happiness, and even endanger her own life." (Publisher's note)

Scottoline, Lisa

Dead ringer. HarperCollins Pubs. 2003 339p $25.95

ISBN 0-06-051493-0

LC 2002-191931

A "legal caper featuring the lady lawyers of series heroine Bennie Rosato's Philadelphia law firm Rosato and Associates. This time out it's Bennie playing the lead role, as she fights to save her financially sinking firm; mother her lovable partners, Mary DiNunzio and Judy Carrier; solve the murder of a valuable client; and battle her evil twin, Alice. . . . Bennie grows on you, and soon enough you're rooting for the home team and laughing at her corny jokes." Publ Wkly

Scottoline, Lisa

Don't Go; Lisa Scottoline. 1st ed. St Martins Pr 2013 384 p. (hardcover) $27.99

ISBN 1250010071; 9781250010070

LC 2013002622

In this mystery novel, "Mike Scanlon, a reservist in the Army Medical Corps serving in Afghanistan, is allowed to return for one week to his suburban Philadelphia home to bury his wife, Chloe, who apparently died in an odd household accident. Overcome with grief, Mike realizes that . . . Chloe was hiding a shocking secret." He "begins an out-of-control campaign to uncover Chloe's secret life, risking the loss of custody of his daughter, his health, and his own freedom." (Publishers Weekly)

Scottoline, Lisa

Killer smile. HarperCollins 2004 358p $25.95

ISBN 0-06-051495-7

LC 2003-67650

In this installment in the "series starring the all-female Philadelphia law firm of Rosato & Associates, young Mary DiNunzio takes center stage. Mary has taken on a pro bono case representing her 'peeps' an Italian American business group (the circolo) working on behalf of the estate of Amadeo Brandolini, who committed suicide while interned during World War II. The estate seeks reparations, and Mary feels drawn to the case, so much so that others fear she's obsessed with it. Under the guise of taking a vacation, Mary visits the site of the internment camp in Montana where Amadeo killed himself and finds herself with still more unanswered questions. Interesting author's notes at the end of this engaging drama disclose Scottoline's own discovery of her grandparents' internment, lending this unusual story a welcome authenticity." Booklist

Scottoline, Lisa

Legal tender. HarperCollins Pubs. 1996 291p

ISBN 978-0060176587

LC 96-7165

The protagonist of this legal thriller is Philadelphian Bennie Rosato "a ravishing six-foot blonde, one of two partners in a thriving law firm. In quick order, the foundations of her world come crashing down. Her partner and ex-lover, Mark, turns up murdered shortly after he tells Bennie that he is planning to dissolve the partnership. It's not surprising that she then becomes the cops' prime suspect. When the murder weapon is found in her apartment, Bennie goes underground. Then a drug company CEO is killed, and she is falsely accused of that death, too." Publ Wkly

Scottoline, Lisa

Mistaken identity. HarperCollins Pubs. 1999 480p $24

ISBN 0-06-018747-6

LC 98-43200

Scottoline "succeeds in creating a brisk, multilayered thriller that plunges Rosato & Associates into a maelstrom of legal, ethical and familial conundrums, culminating in an intricate, dramatic and intense courtroom finale." Publ Wkly

Scottoline, Lisa

Moment of truth. HarperCollins Pubs. 2000 358p

ISBN 0-06-019609-2

LC 99-89325

"Sharp, funny characters, crafty plot twists, and a flavorful depiction of high- and lower-middle Philadelphia society will keep readers riveted to this tense, often mischievous page-turner." Publ Wkly

Scottoline, Lisa

Rough justice. HarperCollins Pubs. 1997 344p

ISBN 978-0060187460

LC 97-5810

"Scottoline deftly balances the varied personalities of the women and manages a large cast, including judge and jury, with precision. She skillfully depicts personal quirks that give her characters dimension." Publ Wkly

Scottoline, Lisa

The **vendetta** defense. HarperCollins Pubs. 2001 390p

ISBN 0-06-018507-4

LC 00-50556

A legal yarn featuring Judy Carrier of Philadelphia's all-female firm of Rosato & Associates. The plot "revolves around Anthony 'Pigeon Tony' Lucia, a lovable septuagenarian who killed his longtime rival, Angelo Coluzzi, who murdered Lucia's wife in their native Italy 60 years ago. Coluzzi, the wealthy, mob-connected owner of a big construction firm, always seems to get the upperhand-until Pigeon Tony breaks his neck during a showdown at the pigeon-racing club where they're both members. Pigeon Tony freely admits he killed Coluzzi, but maintains he was justified because of the longstanding Italian tradition of vendetta; Carrier knows it will be a big stretch to make that argument fly before a 21st-century American jury." Publ Wkly

Searles, John

Boy still missing. Morrow 2001 292p

ISBN 0-688-17570-8

LC 00-40758

"Searles builds suspense and excitement with surprising turns of plot weaving back into one another, and while many of the secondary characters lack depth, Dominic Pindle will resonate with readers." Booklist

Sears, Michael

Black Fridays; Michael Sears. G. P. Putnam's Sons 2012 341 p. (hardcover) $25.95

ISBN 0399158669; 9780399158667

LC 2012011085

Author Michael Sears's protagonist "disgraced executive Jason Stafford lands a new job in record time . . . fresh from two years in jail . . . He's called in to tidy up records that were left in disarray after junior trader Brian Sanders died in an apparent boating accident. It doesn't take long to figure out that the death wasn't accidental . . . [and] the trail leads Sanders through the Wall Street world he once frequented and leads to a colorful FBI showdown." (Kirkus)

Sebald, Winfried Georg, 1944-2001

★ **Austerlitz**; [by] W.G. Sebald; translated by Anthea Bell. Random House 2001 298p il $25.95

ISBN 0-375-50483-4

LC 2001-19785

"As so often in Sebald's fiction, direct connections are never highlighted in the vast loops and sudden knottings of his rhetoric, but the reader cannot escape the inference that in the long sweep of history the Nazis were not alone, but that an inquirer searching for meaning is." NY Times Book Rev

Sebald, Winfried Georg, 1944-2001

★ The **emigrants**; [by] W.G. Sebald; translated by Michael Hulse. New Directions 1996 237p il $22.95

ISBN 0-8112-1338-2

LC 96-22223

Original German edition, 1995

The four fictional "accounts/reports/reminiscences tell of . . . people who left Germany in the 20th century. Three are about Jews who went to England or Switzerland—either in the 1930s or before WW I—die or commit suicide long after WW II, but who, nonetheless, are victims of the Holocaust. One is about the narrator's non-Jewish great uncle, who went to America at the turn of the century, led an adventuresome life, and died a horrible death in the 1950s." (Choice)

"A profound and original work . . . . W. G. Sebald has created an end-of-century meditation that explores the most delicate, most painful, most nervously repressed and carefully concealed lesions of the last hundred years. Illuminatingly engaged with the history and literature of the modern era, Mr. Sebald's book gains power through its poetic obsessions with the past." N Y Times Book Rev

Sebald, Winfried Georg, 1944-2001

★ **Vertigo**; [by] W.G. Sebald; translated by Michael Hulse. New Directions 2000 263p il $23.95

ISBN 0-8112-1430-3

LC 99-58955

Original German edition published 1990; this translation first published 1999 in the United Kingdom

"W.G. Sebald is unusual for a literary star. He fuses genres (travelogue, biography, the novel, meditation, myth), confounding the categories most readers are used to. The narrator of 'Vertigo' offers a fair account of Mr. Sebald's intricate methods. . . . This is poetic or philosophical fiction for readers content to follow the path of a remarkable author's thoughts without the guard-rail of an overarching story." Economist

Sebold, Alice

The **almost** moon; a novel. Little, Brown and Co. 2007 291p $24.99

ISBN 978-0-316-67746-2; 0-316-67746-9

LC 2007-09917

This novel is "brilliantly paced, it's brutally honest, and the Gordian knot at its core— an abusive mother and her traumatically attached daughter — is depicted with such generous intelligence that the fineness of the novel more than surpasses its own horror show of circumstance. Sebold has managed to give us a sympathetic protagonist who smothers her mother in the opening pages, and yet the decades that led up to this black moment are delivered without a shred of sentimentality or melodramatic overkill. It's a tightrope walk of character building." Boston Globe

Sebold, Alice

★ The **lovely** bones. Little, Brown 2002 328p $21.95; pa $13.95

ISBN 0-316-66634-3; 0-316-16881-5 pa

LC 2001-50622

"As pleasant as Susie's heaven is, there's no God there, and certainly no Jesus. This is spirituality for an age that's ecumenical to a fault. But emotionally, it's faultless. Sebold never slips as she follows this family. The risks she walks are enough to give you vertigo." Christ Sci Monit

Sedia, Ekaterina

Alchemy of stone. Prime 301p pa $12.95

ISBN 978-0-8095-7284-7; 0-8095-7284-2

This "steampunk fable about the price of industrial development, follows Mattie, an emancipated automaton, as her home city is rent by conflict between alchemists and the mechanics whose clanking, steaming inventions are changing society. Though created by a leader of the mechanics, Mattie chose to join the alchemists, but her creator still holds the key that winds her up. When a terrorist bombing and an assassination touch off all-out war between the two factions, she discovers the ugly secrets and exploitation that keep the city supplied with food and coal. Sedia's exquisitely bleak vision deliberately skewers familiar ideas from know-it-all computers to talking statues desperate for souls." Publ Wkly

See, Carolyn

★ The **handyman**. Random House 1999 220p $22.95

ISBN 0-375-50155-X

LC 98-21098

"Bob Hampton, a future great artist, leads a quintessentially California life as a freelance handyman before he answers his true calling; in the course of a hot Los Angeles summer, he worries about his lack of aesthetic sophistication, comforts lonely housewives in the time-honored way, and rescues a drowning child and an AIDS patient. Despite a confusing start, the novel quickly takes on the brightness of a sun-dazzled swimming pool and makes a case for shadowless living—a state its hero achieves through an unlikely combination of application and hedonism." New Yorker

See, Carolyn

There will never be another you; a novel. Random 2006 242p $24.95

ISBN 0-679-46317-8

LC 2005-44932

"Among the most potent and poignant new novels to address post-9/11 America. . . . It is potent because the sense of dread and unease that mark almost every moment in the book is palpable; it is poignant because See, who in previous books has proven eminently capable of skewering her characters when they misbehave, has such compassion for the largely villain-less ensemble that populates this tale." Washington Post Book World

See, Lisa

Dragon bones; a novel. Random House 2003 348p $24.95

ISBN 0-679-46320-8

LC 2002-24871

"Hulan and David must overcome their estrangement and work together to solve the crimes. In a land where bribery and corruption are the norm, there are many suspects. The novel flows beautifully, engaging readers in the mystery while gently introducing them to China's rich cultural history." Libr J

See, Lisa

Dreams of joy; a novel. Random House 2011 354p $26

ISBN 978-1-4000-6712-1; 1-4000-6712-X

LC 2011-03891

Sequel to: Shanghai girls

"In 1957, Pearl's 19-year-old daughter Joy learns that her mother and aunt have kept secrets from her about her parentage. She is stunned. Rash and naïve, she immediately sets off for Shanghai in search of her birth father, the artist Z.G. Li, with whom Pearl and May were in love before they fled the city after the Japanese bombing in 1937. Idealistic Joy, who, with one year of university under her belt, has come to be enamored with the idea of China's reforms, easily finds her famous father in Shanghai and then jumps headfirst into the New Society. She heads off with him to the countryside, where his mandate is to teach peasants to paint. Pearl, meanwhile, fearing for her daughter's safety in the communist regime, leaves her modern life behind and pursues her daughter to the city she once loved so much, hoping to talk some sense into the young woman and bring her home. Through clandestine means, May, still in Los Angeles, becomes Pearl's financial and emotional lifeline to home." Miami Herald

"Although the ending betrays See's roots in genre fiction, this is a riveting, meticulously researched depiction of one of the world's worst human-engineered catastrophes." Kirkus

See, Lisa

Peony in love; a novel. Random House 2007 284p $23.95

ISBN 978-1-4000-6466-3; 1-4000-6466-X

LC 2007-01623

This novel, "is—for the reader willing to venture a crucial suspension of disbelief—a complex period tapestry inscribed with the age-old tragedy of love and death and bordered round with vignettes from Chinese metaphysics, dynastic history and the intimate chamber tales of women's friendship and rivalry. . . . See is gifted with a lucid, graceful style and a solid command of her many motifs." N Y Times Book Rev

See, Lisa

Shanghai girls; a novel. Random House 2009 314p $25

ISBN 978-1-4000-6711-4; 1-4000-6711-1

LC 2008-49245

"Pearl and May Chin are 'Beautiful Girls,' models in 1930s Shanghai whose images grace calendars and ads and who party with the young and restless in the Paris of Asia. But the party is soon over. . . . Their father sells them into arranged marriages with the sons of a Chinese family that emigrated to Los Angeles. The daughters rebel and literally miss the boat — until the Japanese attack on Shanghai in 1937 forces them on an Odyssean journey to America. In this moving historical novel, Lisa See explores her Chinese-American roots and those of the Chinese who headed to California in the early 20th century in hopes of a better life, only to find hardship and discrimination." USA Today

Segal, Erich

★ **Love** story. Harper & Row 1970 131p

"A very professionally crafted short first novel. The author makes no great claims of insight for his work. Indeed, the story is all on the surface. But it is funny and sad and generally recommended." Libr J

Followed by Oliver's story (1977)

Segal, Lore Groszmann

Shakespeare's kitchen; stories. [by] Lore Segal. The New Press 2007 225p $22.95

ISBN 978-1-59558-151-8; 1-59558-151-0

LC 2006-30107

"In Segal's world, a world where domestic tragedies occur against the backdrop of historic human cruelties, people tend to behave badly not out of a perverted sense of ambition or power but from a deep need for attachment and belonging. And so it's crucial that the book doesn't move in a straight line. The same people who are good are not good. The bad guys sometimes do decent things. The truth—surprise!—is nuanced, and so is the story, which doesn't end the way it seems to be heading." N Y Times Book Rev

Seiffert, Rachel

Field study. Pantheon Books 2004 215p $19.95

ISBN 0-375-42259-5

LC 2003-66364

In this collection of stories, "all set primarily in Europe, we meet a variety of characters, among them an architect losing his grip on his profession and on reality, a British soldier AWOL in World War II Italy, a teenaged couple struggling with the reality of becoming parents, and an American woman driving her elderly father-in-law to his former street in East Berlin. . . . This is a fine collection from a young writer who displays a modern Europe with its particular social and political issues amid universal human themes." Libr J

Seitz, Nicole

Trouble the water; Nicole Seitz. Thomas Nelson 2007 v, 296 p.p (softcover) $15.99

ISBN 1595544003; 9781595544001

LC 2007051520

This book follows a woman named "Honor, in her mid-40s, [who] escapes to St. Anne's Isle off the South Carolina coast with her life in tatters. She's unemployed and broke, and feels unworthy of love after a divorce and a failed relationship. Her attempted suicide is thwarted by a group of Gullah nannies who rescue her and love her back to health, introducing her to Duchess, a quirky woman with a penchant for nudity. Honor lives with Duchess for a while as they help each other heal, and eventually Honor reclaims her love for life and painting, and reconnects with her sister Alice. The narration switches regularly among the three women (Honor, Duchess and Alice) and the story jumps back and forth over an eight-year span." (Publishers Weekly)

Self, Will

The **Book** of Dave; a revelation of the recent past and the distant future. Bloomsbury Pub. 2006 495p $24.95

ISBN 0-670-91443-6

LC 2006-4750

"In this tale of an embittered taxi-driver whose psychotic rantings become the creed of a blighted people hundreds of years after his death, Self unleashes his apparently boundless misanthropy on modern London, the origins of religion, and the postapocalyptic future. Dave Rudman, driven mad by divorce and ill-prescribed antidepressants, thinks he is God and writes a vitriolic screed, which he has printed on metal plates and buries in a garden. Discovered by the survivors of a catastrophic flood and adopted as a gospel, it demands the complete separation of mothers and fathers (children to spend exactly half the week with each). Switching between a narrative of Dave's unlucky life and the phonetically rendered 'Mokni' speech of his wretched followers, Self achieves an elaborate vision of vicious superstition and hopeless struggle." New Yorker

Self, Will

Dorian; an imitation. Grove Press 2002 277p $23

ISBN 0-8021-1729-5

LC 2002-29962

"In this retelling of Oscar Wilde's The Picture of Dorian Gray, most of the original's characters are cleverly transmuted into their late-20th-century counterparts: dissolute Henry Wotton, now openly homosexual with a nasty heroin habit; his protege, eager young video artist 'Baz' Hallward; and the title character, the quintessential amoral narcissist. . . . Self uses Wilde's plot to examine post-Stonewall gay life, from its drug-fueled hedonistic excesses to the reckoning of the AIDs epidemic. The novel skewers every layer of British society—street hustlers, members of Parliament and the idle rich." Publ Wkly

Self, Will

Umbrella; Will Self. Pgw 2013 397 p. $25

ISBN 0802120725; 9780802120724

Man Booker Prize Shortlist (2012)

This novel, by Will Self, follows "maverick psychiatrist Zachary Busner" and his encounters with his patient "Audrey Dearth," an elderly woman born in the slums of West London in 1890. Audrey's memories of a bygone Edwardian London, her lovers, involvement with early feminist and socialist movements, and, in particular, her time working in an umbrella shop, alternate with Busner's attempts to treat her condition and bring light to her clouded world." (Publisher's note)

Self, Will

The **undivided** self; selected stories. introduction by Rick Moody. Bloomsbury 2010 461p $30

ISBN 978-1-59691-297-7; 1-59691-297-9

LC 2010-17365

"Spanning several earlier books (and including some recent uncollected stories), this collection provides the perfect introduction to the gamut of Self's darkly comic, verbally dexterous shorter prose." Libr J

Selgin, Peter

Drowning lessons; stories. University of Georgia Press 2008 235p (Flannery O'Connor Award for Short Fiction) $24.95

ISBN 978-0-8203-3210-9; 0-8203-3210-0

LC 2008-20377

"Whether as a force for life or one of destruction, water in all its forms is the unifying theme in writer and artist Peter Selgin's powerful collection, Drowning Lessons. Selgin is never heavyhanded in his use of metaphor, and it's rewarding to trace the skill with which he employs it in many of these 13 stories." BookPage

Semple, Maria

Where'd you go, Bernadette; a novel. Maria Semple. Little, Brown and Company 2012 336 p. $25.99

ISBN 0316204277; 9780316204279

LC 2011040639

Alex Award (2013)

This novel, by Maria Semple, is an "Internet-age domestic comedy about a wife/mother/genius architect who goes a little nuts from living in . . . Seattle." Bernadette lives with her genius husband Elgie and her daughter Bee in Seattle, where she "hates everything" and everyone, "especially the other mothers at Bee's" school. She disappears days before a "planned family trip to Antarctica," leaving Elgie and Bee to search for her. (Kirkus Reviews)

Senate, Melissa

The **love** goddess' cooking school. Gallery Books 2010 326p pa $15

ISBN 978-1-4391-0723-2; 1-4391-0723-8

LC 2010-21190

"When Holly Maguire was little, she spent long summers with her Italian fortunetelling grandmother, Camilla, absorbing how to cook in a very special way: dishes needed wishes, hopes, and dreams to come out right. Now that Holly's life has come out anything but right, she retreats to the safety of Camilla's Cucinotta and Cooking School on Blue Crab Island, ME. But she is allowed only a few brief weeks with her grandmother before Camilla gently passes away, leaving Holly with a cooking school and shop—and not the least idea of how to really cook, much less tell fortunes. Chick-lit fans will delight as Holly slowly finds her way, gathering new friends, connecting with childhood pals, and navigating both love and the island's mean girls who have grown into catty women." Libr J

Sendker, Jan-Philipp

The **art** of hearing heartbeats; a novel. Jan-Philipp Sendker; translated from the German by Kevin Wiliarty. Other Press 2012 325 p. (paperback) $14.95; (ebook) $14.95

ISBN 1590514637; 9781590514634; 9781590514641

LC 2011030638

"This tearful, circuitous German bestseller traces the lost romance between a blind young monk and a poor crippled girl in pre-WWII Burma." Pub Wkly

Serber, Natalie

Shout her lovely name; Natalie Serber. Houghton Mifflin Harcourt 2012 226 p.

ISBN 0547634528; 9780547634524

LC 2011036904

This book is a collection of short stories by Natalie Serber. "Mothers and daughters ride the familial tide of joy, regret, loathing, and love in these stories of resilient and flawed women. In a battle between a teenage daughter and her mother, wheat bread and plain yogurt become weapons. An aimless college student, married to her much older professor, sneaks cigarettes while caring for their newborn son. On the eve of her husband's fiftieth birthday, a pilfered fifth of rum, an unexpected tattoo, and rogue teenagers leave a woman questioning her place. And in a suite of stories, we follow capricious, ambitious single mother Ruby and her cautious, steadfast daughter Nora through their tumultuous life, stray men, stray cats, and psychedelic drugs, in 1970s California." (Publisher's note)

Seth, Vikram

An **equal** music. Broadway Bks. 1999 380p $25

ISBN 0-7679-0291-2

LC 99-20421

Seth's "writing is a throwback, freely romantic, wondrously out of date, totally unhedged. His book attempts no cool, contains not a single pose. He can be playful with language, though not distractingly so. . . . The book is also stocked with humor, which appears when it is most needed, as the story grows almost suffocatingly sad." Natl Rev

Seth, Vikram

★ A **suitable** boy; a novel. HarperCollins Pubs. 1993 1349p

LC 92-54744

This novel is, "at its heart an elegy as well as a comedy of manners, about a traditional society in a time of change, and about a leisurely world of graces giving way to a new, more democratic time." Times Lit Suppl

Seton, Anya

Avalon. Houghton Mifflin 1965 440p

"Late tenth- and early eleventh-century life in England and in the lands colonized by the Norsemen {i.e. Iceland} is re-created from early Anglo-Saxon chronicles, French manuscripts, and secondary sources. . . . The action and milieu are vivid and though the characterization is not strong the psychological and historical motivations are believable. An honest historical novel for enthusiasts of the genre." Booklist

Seton, Anya

★ **Dragonwyck**. Houghton Mifflin 1944 336p

An American "Gothic" novel. The time is the 1830's and 1840's; the place, New York City and the great Van Ryn estate, Dragonwyck, on the Hudson. A young farm girl, a distant cousin of the Van Ryn's goes to live at Dragonwyck as governess to the Van Ryns' small daughter. At the death of the child's mother, Miranda becomes the second Mrs. Van Ryn. The story of Miranda's gradual horrified awakening follows

"For all its trappings and devices—and they are good, spine-chilling trappings, handled with considerable skill—the novel manages to have life and substance." NY Her Trib Books

Seton, Anya

Green darkness. Houghton Mifflin 1973 591p

First published 1972 in the United Kingdom

"Reincarnation is the theme of {this} . . . novel. A 16th-century Benedictine monk, Stephen Marsdon, falls prey to a consuming passion for alluring Celia de Bohun and forsakes his vows. The tragic end of the lovers, involving murder and suicide, brings, nearly 400 years later, madness and near death to their reincarnations, newlyweds Celia and Richard Marsdon. Fortunately, a Hindu doctor (himself a reincarnated Italian physician in Tudor England who longed for warmer climates) hovers nearby to monitor the proceedings and brings the souls to rest." Libr J

Seton, Anya

Katherine. Houghton Mifflin 1954 588p

Historical romance about the life of Katherine Swynford, sister-in-law of Geoffrey Chaucer, and mistress and later wife of John Gaunt

"It is a story that demands no intellectual or emotional effort from the reader. . . . But Miss Seton presents her facts accurately. Her research extends as far as visiting what remains of any of John of Gaunt's 30 castles and her zest for her subject communicates itself to the reader." San Francisco Chron

Seton, Anya

★ The **Winthrop** woman. Houghton Mifflin 1958 586p

In this biographical novel the author rallies to the defense of a maligned historical figure. "The young widow Elizabeth Winthrop was perhaps the most unwilling Puritan who ever came to New England, for she detested and feared Governor John Winthrop, who was her uncle as well as her father-in-law. A second marriage to Robert Feake, the governor's choice, dragged through years of Robert's increasing insanity; when he deserted her Elizabeth secured a divorce in New Amsterdam, contracted a common-law marriage with virile William Hallet, and found with him a love that was adequate recompense for exile and persecution." Booklist

"The novel is noteworthy for its insights into the Puritan 'Bible Commonwealth.'" Saturday Rev

Settle, Mary Lee

★ **Charley** Bland. Farrar, Straus & Giroux 1989 207p il

ISBN 0-374-12078-1

LC 89-207125

"Having fled the suffocating small-town environment of her West Virginia home and recreated herself as a writer in postwar Paris, the heroine of this condensed, lyric novel returns to discover that having dreams come true is sometimes disastrous. For there she again meets Charley Bland, the golden boy she worshiped as a child, now the town's most eligible–and elusive–bachelor. . . . The affair they begin quickly demolishes everything this woman had made of herself in the years she had been away." Libr J

Settle, Mary Lee

★ The **killing** ground. Farrar, Straus & Giroux 1982 385p

ISBN 0-374-18107-1

LC 82-2477

"In this novel, the last of the Beulah Quintet, Settle describes the various homecomings of Hannah McKarkle, a woman from an affluent West Virginia coal-mining family who has pursued a writing career in New York. In 1960, Hannah returns to find that her brother Johnny has been killed by a man who turns out to be a poor distant relative. The brother's death, the intricate interplay among classes in the closed rural society of West Virginia, and the inevitable pull of one's native home on the heart and soul are central to her subsequent visits in 1978 and 1980." Libr J

Settle, Mary Lee

★ **O** Beulah Land; a novel. Viking 1956 368p

First published volume of the author's Beulah Quintet, set in rural West Virginia. Chronologically follows Prisons (1973). Subsequent titles in the series: Know nothing (1960); The scapegoat (1980) and The killing ground

Historical novel of the Virginia frontier from 1754 to 1775. "Jonathan Lacey is a strong man, as only a gentleman is strong. And he is a gentleman, by the standards of the Virginia wilderness country in the years preceding the American Revolution. After his service at the Battle of Little Meadows in 1775, Johnny scouts and surveys far into the mountains, and leads a heterogeneous group of early Americans westward with him, to claim and clear his bounty land in the undefended King's Part of the colony, beyond the Proclamation Line. It is on this land, called Beulah by Jeremiah the New Light preacher, that Johnny proves his strength." N Y Times Book Rev

Seymour, Gerald

A **Deniable** Death; Gerald Seymour. Thomas Dunne Books 2013 448 p. $25.99

ISBN 1250018803; 1444705857; 9781250018809; 9781444705850

This mystery is from Gerald Seymour. Here, the "Engineer, a brilliant Iranian bombmaker, may be responsible for 80 percent of the coalition casualties in the Iraq War." If British intelligence can confirm the Engineer's identification, "an Israeli assassin will perform the kill—a deniable death." But things aren't that easy. (Booklist)

Seymour, Gerald

The **heart** of danger. HarperCollins Pubs. 1995 358p

ISBN 0-06-100968-7

LC 95-4808

"Using this wheels-within-wheels frame, Seymour constructs a harshly detailed novel about a dirty little war, peopled with a wide variety of deeply etched characters and suffused with a nearly palpable sense of despair and weariness." Publ Wkly

Seymour, Gerald

Killing ground. HarperCollins Pubs. 1997 390p

ISBN 978-0061011955

LC 96-51178

"Twenty-three-year-old Charlotte 'Charlie' Parsons is suffocating. Living at home with her parents in a small village in Cornwall, she sees no future except teaching snotty first-formers in the village primary. But excitement enters her life twice in one day. First, she receives a letter from Giuseppe and Angela Ruggerio, the Italian family Charlie worked for one wonderful summer. Will she come back to Italy and take care of the three Ruggerio children? To Charlie, it's a heaven-sent opportunity to escape. Later that day, she's visited by a coldly sinister American DEA agent named Axel Moen, who plans to use Charlie to reel in Mario Ruggerio, brother of Giuseppe and capo of the Sicilian Mafia. . . . A gripping thriller that leads to a shattering climax." Booklist

Seymour, Gerald

Rat run. Overlook Press 2007 240p $24.95

ISBN 978-1-58567-894-5; 1-58567-894-5

LC 2006-51533

"Seymour gives us two stories to follow: Malachy's pursuit of drug lord Ricky Capel and the saga of his gradual personal redemption. The pursuit story is intricate and suspenseful, as Seymour's many fans have come to expect; in the redemption story, he nimbly avoids most of the cliches associated with the type (it's probably not possible to avoid them all). A thriller with a human side." Booklist

Shaara, Jeff

★ A **blaze** of glory; a novel of the Battle of Shiloh. Jeff Shaara. Ballantine Books 2012 xxiv, 435 p.p maps (acid-free paper) $28.00

ISBN 0345527356; 9780345527356; 9780345527370

LC 2012010107

This historical Civil War novel by Jeff Shaara offers a "re-creation of one of the war's bloodiest and most iconic engagements--the Battle of Shiloh. . . . [H]e dramatizes the key actions and decisions of the commanders on both sides: Johnston, Grant, Sherman, Beauregard, and . . . Colonel Nathan Bedford Forrest. Here too are the thoughts and voices of the junior officers, conscripts, and enlisted men who gave their all for the cause." (Publisher's note)

Shaara, Jeff

A **Chain** of Thunder; A Novel of the Siege of Vicksburg. 1st ed. Random House Inc. 2013 xxvi, 562 p.p maps (hardcover) $28

ISBN 0345527380; 9780345527387

LC 2013009360

This historical novel by Jeff Shaara presents "an account of the siege of Vicksburg. Analyzing what historians call the 'brilliant and innovative' campaign to secure the Mississippi River for the Union, Shaara rides into the camps of Grant and Sherman and lurks with Pemberton, the general charged with the Confederate's linchpin defense. Shaara also follows Lucy Spence, young resident of besieged Vicksburg, and Fritz Bauer, Wisconsin infantryman and Shiloh veteran." (Kirkus Reviews)

Includes bibliographical references.

Shaara, Jeff

The **glorious** cause; a novel of the American Revolution. Ballantine Bks. 2003 638p $26.95

ISBN 0-345-42756-4

LC 2002-34240

Sequel to Rise to rebellion

"This is vivid and compelling historical fiction, but also a primer on leadership and the arts of war and diplomacy. Shaara reaches new heights here, with a narrative that's impossible to put down." Publ Wkly

Shaara, Jeff

Gods and generals. Ballantine Bks. 1996 498p $25

ISBN 0-345-40492-0

LC 95-53360

This novel "focuses simultaneously on the lives of four men who played significant roles in the military side of the Civil War in battles leading up to the great one at Gettysburg. The novel follows Stonewall Jackson, Winfield Scott Hancock, Joshua Chamberlain, and Robert E. Lee from 1858 to 1863, giving the reader splendidly detailed witness to how the war drew them into commanding positions. As should be the case with good historical fiction, Shaara, in taking actual figures from the past, rekindles them; he uses the personal experiences of these four men to meaningfully explore the political and military issues of the day." Booklist

Shaara, Jeff

Gone for soldiers. Ballantine Bks. 2000 424p il

ISBN 0-345-42750-5

LC 00-22745

"The book is simply wonderful, populated with eminently human heroes who are called upon to perform Herculean tasks in a war muddied beyond redemption by the ambitions of back-home and battlefield politicians." Libr J

Shaara, Jeff

The **last** full measure. Ballantine Bks. 1998 560p map $25

ISBN 0-345-40491-2

LC 97-49383

This volume follows "the course of the war in Virginia from Lee's retreat from Gettysburg to his surrender at Appomattox Court House. Ulysses S. Grant has come East to assume command of all Federal forces and to confront Lee, and the war they make is marked by such horrendous battles as The Wilderness and Spotsylvania. As characters, Grant and Lee dominate this book. . . . Civil War buffs will find Shaara nodding on some small details, but they generally will be delighted with this book." Libr J

Shaara, Jeff

Rise to rebellion. Ballantine Bks. 2001 492p $26.95

ISBN 0-345-42753-X

LC 2001-18448

"Making excellent use of a you-are-there approach, Shaara focuses on a handful of prominent historical figures, including Benjamin Franklin, George Washington, John and Abigail Adams, and British general Thomas Gage.

. . . Shaara's novel gives historical figures flesh-and-blood viability." Booklist

Shaara, Jeff

The **rising** tide; a novel of the World War II. Ballantine Books 2006 xxxvi, 536p $27.95

ISBN 978-0-345-46141-4; 0-345-46141-X

LC 2006-42936

Shaara opens this first volume of a projected trilogy "in the deserts of North Africa, where Allied troops attempt to match wits and forces with the Desert Fox, wily German commander Field Marshall Erwin Rommel, and his formidable Afrika Korps. After Hitler overruns France, solidifying his position in Western Europe, he turns his attention eastward toward the vast Russian expanse. With the German focus split, the Allies sense the time is right to launch a united second front in North Africa, setting their sights on an eventual invasion of southern Italy. As plans for Operation Torch become a reality, Shaara vividly recreates a cast of military and political heroes and villains, including General Dwight D. Eisenhower, General George Marshall, General George Patton, British general Bernard Montgomery, German field marshal Erwin Rommel, Adolf Hitler, Winston Churchill, and Franklin Roosevelt." Booklist

Shaara, Jeff

The **steel** wave; a novel of World War II. Ballantine Books 2008 xxvi, 493p map $28

ISBN 978-0-345-46142-1; 0-345-46142-8

LC 2008-4813

Sequel to The rising tide; this is the second volume of Shaara's World War II trilogy

This "epic-scale novel opens on January 25, 1944, with British commandos gathering soil samples on Omaha Beach to assess landing sites. Shaara gives the Americans, called the great waves of steel by the Germans, their due portion in the grisly, brutal Allied invasion, and the experiences of the grunt soldiers—most notably the indefatigable U.S. Army Sgt. Jesse Adams—offers a field-level view of D-Day and afterward, generating more suspenseful reading than the matter-of-fact accounts of the big-brass dealings of Eisenhower and Churchill. The Allied leaders' personalities emerge with agile clarity, while German Field Marshal Erwin Rommel embodies the good soldier laboring under a delusional Hitler and German High Command ensconced in cozy Berlin. Rommel's ambivalent complicity in the assassination plot on Hitler is convincingly rendered and paves the way for the final act. The muscular prose, deft sense of military drama and relentless pacing are well suited for this crackerjack saga." Publ Wkly

Shaara, Michael

★ The **killer** angels; a novel. Random House 1993 374p il $24

ISBN 0-679-42541-1

LC 92-38365

This is a fictionalized account of four days in July, 1863 at the Battle of Gettysburg. The point of view of the Southern forces is represented by Generals Robert E. Lee and James Longstreet, while Colonel Joshua Chamberlain and General John Buford are the focus for the North

"Shaara's version of private reflections and conversations are based on his reading of documents and letters. Al-

though some of his judgments are not necessarily substantiated by historians, he demonstrates a knowledge of both the battle and the area. The writing is vivid and fast moving." Libr J

Shabtai, Yaakov

Uncle Peretz takes off; short stories. translated from the Hebrew by Dalya Bilu. Overlook Press 2004 239p $24.95

ISBN 1-585-67340-4

LC 2004-58316

"At their best, the stories in this collection . . . are masterful, ironically drawn character studies evoking the Israeli frontier spirit under the British mandate while capturing the shift from old world religiosity to new world secularism. Originally published in Hebrew in 1972, the collection is bookended by two linked stories chronicling the deaths of the narrator's grandparents and with them the loss of Jewish traditions." Publ Wkly

Shade, Eric

Eyesores; stories. University of Ga. Press 2003 205p $24.95

ISBN 0-8203-2432-9

LC 2002-7151

A collection of stories set in a small Pennsylvania town. "Windfall, recently bypassed by a freeway, is losing its blue-collar jobs and shuddering toward new life as a destination for golfers. Residents are torn between the desire for and the fear of change. . . . Shade captures perfectly the way in which it's hard to leave your mistakes behind when you're surrounded by people who remember when you made them." Booklist

Shafak, Elif

The **bastard** of Istanbul. Viking 2007 360p $24.95

ISBN 978-0-670-03834-3; 0-670-03834-2

LC 2006-42116

"Shafak's writing is seductive; each chapter of her novel is named for a food, and the warmth of the Turkish kitchen lies at the center of its wide-ranging plot. The Bastard of Istanbul portrays family as more than merely a function of genetics and fate, folding together history and fiction, the personal and the political into a thing of beauty." Elle

Shafak, Elif

Honor; Elif Shafak. Viking 2013 352 p. (hardcover) $26.95

ISBN 0670784834; 9780670784837

LC 2012039761

In this novel, by Elif Shafak, "an honor killing shatters and transforms the lives of Turkish immigrants in 1970s London. . . . While Jamila stays to become a midwife, Pembe follows her Turkish husband, Adem, to London, where they hope to make new lives for themselves and their children. . . . When Pembe begins a chaste affair with a man named Elias, Iskender, [the eldest son,] . . . will discover that you could love someone with all your heart and yet be ready to hurt them." (Publisher's note)

Shaffer, Mary Ann

The **Guernsey** Literary and Potato Peel Pie Society; [by] Mary Ann Shaffer & Annie Barrows. The Dial Press 2008 277p $22

ISBN 978-0-385-34099-1; 0-385-34099-0

LC 2008-15477

"Juliet's ready wit is enchanting, as are the discussion of authors from Catullus to Shakespeare. . . . There is the occasional false note. . . . However, 'The Guernsey Literary and Potato Peel Pie Society' is a labor of love, and it shows on almost every page." Christ Sci Monit

Shakar, Alex

Luminarium; a novel. Soho Press 2011 432p il $25

ISBN 978-1-56947-975-9; 1-56947-975-5

LC 2011013331

The novel's "most impressive aspect is that it always seems to be grounded. It's about the possibility of life after death, spiritualism through technology, Lord Of The Rings, 9/11, and the societal potential of videogames, and yet it mostly doesn't feel like it's overreaching." A.V. Club

Shakespeare, Nicholas

Secrets of the sea. HarperPerennial 2008 402, 25p pa $14.95

ISBN 978-0-06-147470-5; 0-06-147470-3

LC 2007-41924

First published 2007 in the United Kingdom

This is a "novel fundamentally interested in marriage that long-term investment in that capricious thing love. There will be gossip, there will be harvest, the weather will affect the bounty now and again, surprises will upset the whole enterprise and there will be the slog and beauty of routine, but, at bottom, the static commitment remains, and while reading 'Secrets of the Sea,' one wants to believe in it." San Francisco Chron

Shakespeare, Nicholas

Snowleg. Harcourt 2004 386p $25

ISBN 0-15-101146-X

LC 2004-47543

"British student Peter Hithersay learns on his sixteenth birthday that his real father was an East German political prisoner, and his life is never the same. Developing an obsession with all things German, he opts to attend medical school in Hamburg. Lured to Leipzig by a theatrical troupe and his own desire to see the scene of his mother and father's brief tryst, he ends up falling in love with a willful, passionate young woman nicknamed Snowleg. But at a crucial moment in their relationship, he fails her. For the next 20 years, he struggles on all fronts, succumbing to drug addiction and a series of empty affairs. Shakespeare paints an especially chilling picture of the repressed lives of East Germans, one in which a young girl's straightforward declaration of love takes on near-heroic stature. A beautifully written, utterly compelling story of love and politics." Booklist

Shalev, Meir

A **pigeon** and a boy; translated from the Hebrew by Evan Fallenberg. Schocken Books 2007 311p $25

ISBN 978-0-8052-4251-5; 0-8052-4251-1

LC 2007-843

Original Hebrew edition, 2006

"Yair Mendelsohn, a middle-aged Israeli tour guide favored with bird watchers, learns that one of his new American clients fought in the Palmach, a clandestine military force in Israel's 1948 war of independence. The American recounts a day when a homing pigeon handler, nicknamed the Baby for his childlike features, was killed in that war and, in his final moments, sent off one last pigeon. Yair is familiar with the American's story and listens with wistfulness. As Yair slowly tells of his present and his past, Shalev patiently builds tension around the Baby's final dispatch, giving vivid detail on homing pigeons and conveying the unique relationship between the birds and their keepers—which echoes the touching care with which the Baby and his true love, the Girl, treat one another. The dark, stocky Yair, whose marriage is threatened by his burgeoning relationship with childhood friend Tirzah, makes a sympathetic protagonist. This gem of a story about the power of love, which won Israel's Brenner Prize, brims with luminous originality." Publ Wkly

Shalev, Tseruyah

Husband and wife; {by} Zeruya Shalev; translated from the Hebrew by Dalya Bilu. Grove Press 2002 311p $24

ISBN 0-8021-1718-X

LC 2001-58479

"Na'ama is a social worker who heals ailing young mothers and their children, though she is unable to turn an observant eye on the lives of her own husband and child, or herself. When her husband, Udi, a healthy hiking guide who periodically leaves the family for long, solitary jaunts into nature, wakes up one morning unable to move his legs, Na'ama begins an inner monologue, wrestling over whether to take him to a hospital. . . or whether to keep him at home, where she and their nine-year-old daughter Noga can finally have a constant relationship with him." Publ Wkly

Shames, Laurence

Mangrove squeeze. Hyperion 1998 309p $22.95

ISBN 0-7868-6301-3

LC 97-35880

"The Russian mafia is alive and well in Key West, operating a string of T-shirt shops as a cover for their more nefarious activities. Selling advertising space for the local newspaper, Suki Sperakis meets Lazslo Kalynin, who in a fit of lust reveals too much about the real business he and his Russian cohorts are conducting. Because Suki knows too much Lazslo is ordered to kill her. On the other side of town, Suki has met Aaron Katz, a former New Yorker renovating a guest house while taking care of his aging father. . . . {Shames} has included his signature cast of geriatric zanies and organized-crime types doing what they do best—causing mayhem and hilarity in the seemingly calm, sun-drenched streets of Florida." Libr J

Shames, Laurence

Virgin heat; a novel. Hyperion 1997 274p $21.95

ISBN 0-7868-6203-3

LC 96-26804

"The plot of this slapstick caper, a gravity-defying structure of impossible coincidences, has been built for fun, not analysis. But into this raucous hilarity Mr. Shames sneaks some nice observations on fading mobsters." N Y Times Book Rev

Shames, Laurence

Welcome to paradise; a novel. Villard Bks. 1999 220p $22.95

ISBN 0-375-50252-1

LC 98-50785

This "caper novel finds Big Al Marracotta, a low-level mobster, vacationing in Key West while his rival, an equally inept thug, plots to have him bumped off. Stumbling into the fray is a nerdy furniture salesman from New Jersey who happens to have the same 'Big Al' license plate as his mobster namesake. The hitmen naturally confuse their Als, and the chaos begins." Booklist

Shames "is both hilariously funny as well as insightful in his handling of his characters." Libr J

Shamsie, Kamila

Kartography. Harcourt 2002 305p $24

ISBN 0-15-101010-2

LC 2003-4989

"Karachi, Pakistan's largest city, is a place under constant siege: ethnic, factional, sectarian and simply random acts of violence are the order of the day. This violence— and the lingering legacy of the civil war of 1971—is the backdrop for the story of Raheen and Karim, a girl and boy raised together in the 1970s and '80s, whose lives are shattered when a family secret is revealed. . . . This is a complex novel, deftly executed and rich in emotional coloratura and wordplay." Publ Wkly

Shan Sa

The **girl** who played go; translated from the French by Adriana Hunter. Knopf 2003 312p $22.95

ISBN 0-4000-4025-6

Original French edition, 2001

"When a young Japanese soldier meets a lovely 16-year-old Chinese girl playing Go in the Square of a Thousand Winds, they form a silent bond, meeting daily to play the game. As a fragmented China battles for her dignity, the 1930 Japanese occupation of Manchuria is in full force. The girl and the soldier are opponents in more than just a game of Go; they are on opposite sides of a deadly war in which their muted love receives a crushing blow." Booklist

"The alternating parallel tales add an extra spark of energy to this swift-moving novel, as Sa portrays tenderness and brutality with equal clarity." Publ Wkly

Shange, Ntozake

Betsey Brown; a novel. St. Martin's Press 1985 207p

LC 85-2663

"Miss Shange is a superb storyteller who keeps her eye on what brings her characters together rather than what separates them: courage and love, innocence and the loss of it, home and homelessness. Miss Shange understands backyards, houses, schools and churches. {This novel} rejoices in—but never sentimentalizes—those places on earth where you are accepted, where you are comfortable with yourself." N Y Times Book Rev

Shange, Ntozake

Sassafrass, Cypress & Indigo; a novel. St. Martin's Press 1982 224p

LC 82-5565

"Poetry, magical spells, recipes, and choreographs are woven into the narrative providing a vital interplay between the sisters and their creations. The setting of much of the story, Charleston, South Carolina, becomes a place of magic and joy for the reader." Libr J

Shannon, Dell

Chaos of crime. Morrow 1985 190p

LC 84-22624

"A maniac is loose on the streets of Los Angeles, tying prostitutes to their beds, beheading them, disemboweling them, and then surgically dissecting them like laboratory animals. Detective Luis Mendoza and the Los Angeles Police Department are sufficiently stumped in trying to locate this madman who never leaves a clue—until finally the discovery of a rare French wristwatch helps to reveal a seemingly unlikely killer." Booklist

Shannon, Dell

The **Manson** curse. Morrow 1990 262p

LC 90-36989

An American reporter based in London visits his novelist friend in Cornwall and becomes curious about the writer's obsession with the occult

Shannon, Samantha

The **bone** season; Samantha Shannon. Bloomsbury Press 2013 480 p. (alk. paper) $24

ISBN 1620401398; 9781620401392

LC 2012038358

In this novel by Samantha Shannon "it is the year 2059. Cities are under the control of a security force called Scion. Paige Mahoney works [for] secret cell known as the Seven Seals. Paige is a dreamwalker, a rare kind of clairvoyant. When Paige is captured and arrested . . . the voyant prison is a separate city. Paige is assigned to . . ., Warden, who will be in charge of her. If she wants to regain her freedom, Paige will have to learn something of his mind and his own mysterious motives." (Publisher's note)

Shapiro, Dani

Black & white. Alfred A. Knopf 2007 255p $24

ISBN 978-0-375-41548-7; 0-375-41548-3

LC 2006-30424

"As the novel opens, Clara Brodeur returns to Manhattan to face her dying mother, Ruth Dunne, whom she has not seen in 14 years. Clara dropped out of high school, fled New York at 18 and finally made herself a home all the way up in Maine, on Mount Desert Island. . . . Clara had fled, all those years ago, because her mother's fame as a photographer arose out of the images she took of her daughter, images Clara has needed to leave behind." N Y Times Book Rev

Shapton, Leanne

Important artifacts and personal property from the collection of Lenore Doolan and Harold Morris, including books, street fashion, and jewelry. Farrar, Straus & Giroux 2009 129p il

ISBN 0374175306; 9780374175306

LC 2008-43417

"Auction catalogs can tell you a lot about a person— their passions and vanities, peccadilloes and aesthetics; their flush years and lean. . . . [In this] invented auction catalog, the 325 lots up for auction are what remain from the relationship between Lenore Doolan and Harold Morris. . . . Through photographs of the couple's personal effects—the usual auction items (jewelry, fine art, and rare furniture) and the seemingly worthless (pajamas, Post-it notes, worn paperbacks)—the story of a failed love affair . . . emerges. From first meeting to final separation, the progress and rituals of intimacy are revealed through the couple's accumulated relics and memorabilia." (Publisher's note)

This is a "faux auction catalog consisting of sediment — love letters, vintage clothes, paperbacks, etc. — left in the wake of a couple's breakup. As the highs and lows of Lenore and Harold's relationship (2002–06) slowly reveal themselves in Important Artifacts and Personal Property from the Collection of Lenore Doolan and Harold Morris, Including Books, Street Fashion, and Jewelry, you're likely to find yourself swooning and cursing along with the lovers. Of course, there's something suffocating about their privileged and meticulously curated lives — their cleverly inscribed first editions, vintage designer clothes, stationery from the Chateau Marmont, postcards of Nan Goldin photos, tastefully hip mix CDs — and so you may also find that you hate them." Entertainment Wkly

Sharfeddin, Heather

Mineral spirits; a novel. Bridge Works 2006 250p $21.95

ISBN 978-1-882593-98-9; 1-882593-98-7

LC 2006-762

"Freshly elected as the sheriff in a one-lawman town in Montana, Kip Edelson is immediately put to task when 10-year-old Gray Dausman discovers a rotting corpse down by the river. As Edelson attempts to discern the identity of the victim, he becomes increasingly convinced that it is none other than the boy's missing mother, and he reluctantly takes Gray under his wing even as his own marriage evaporates before him. When Edelson stumbles upon an illicit drug ring involving the local tavern owner and various other shady locals, the identity of the corpse takes on a new, unexpected significance." Booklist

The author "blends Western and mystery genres into a fine, heady concoction." Libr J

Sharp, Adrienne

The **true** memoirs of Little K. Farrar, Straus and Giroux 2010 378p $25

ISBN 978-0-374-20730-4; 0-374-20730-5

LC 2010-10289

The novel " is rich with historical detail, describing the decadent excesses of the Russian nobility, the intrigue of the theater, and the paralysis of Russia's rulers in their waning days of power. Sharp sweeps us into another place and time, blending fact and fiction into an engrossing tale of love, loss and history." Wichita Eagle

Sharp, Zoë

Die easy; A Charlie Fox Thriller. W W Norton & Co Inc 2013 336 p. $25.95

ISBN 1605984000; 9781605984001

This is Zoë Sharp's 10th Charlie Fox thriller. Here, professional bodyguard Charlie takes on an assignment in post-Katrina New Orleans—the first job with her lover and partner, Sean Meyer, since he recovered from being shot in the head. . . . Tasked with protecting wealthy businessman Blake Dyer during the After Katrina Foundation fundraising event, Charlie is grateful for what appears to be a straight-forward task." Things inevitably go wrong. (Publishers Weekly)

Sharp, Zoë

Fifth victim; Zoe Sharp. Pegasus 2012 448 p. (hardcover) $25.95

ISBN 1605982768; 9781605982762

In Zoë Sharp's ninth Charlie Fox mystery, Fox is "tasked with protecting Dina, the daughter of a wealthy Long Island family and the target of a kidnapping ring preying on rich kids. As the list of kidnapping victims steadily grows longer, Charlie begins to realize that Dina and her friends may not all be innocent victims. As she struggles to figure out who is behind these crimes, she receives shocking news about her lover, Sean." (Library Journal)

Sharp, Zoë

Fourth Day. Pegasus 2011 447 p. (hardcover) $25

ISBN 1605981214; 9781605981215

In this, Zoë Sharp's fourth Charlie Fox novel, Charlie, "now working for a Manhattan company, seeks to extricate schoolteacher Thomas Witney from Fourth Day, a cult in the desert near Los Angeles. . . . While Charlie and her lover, Sean Meyer, manage to get Thomas out, they're unprepared for either his complete about-face on [cult leader] Bane or the intense interest that Homeland Security suddenly has in the cult and Thomas's insider knowledge." (Publishers Weekly)

Sharp, Zoë

Third strike; a Charlie Fox thriller. Zoë Sharp. 1st ed. Thomas Dunne Books 2008 viii, 327 p.p (hardcover) $24.95

ISBN 0312358970; 9780312358976

LC 2008023441

This is Zoë Sharp's third Charlie Fox thriller. Here, "the British soldier-turned-bodyguard, now settled in New York City and working for an exclusive close-protection agency, is shocked to see an interview with her father on the morning TV news. A prominent U.K. orthopedic surgeon, he is under investigation after the death of one of his patients." She unearths "a coverup involving a shadowy government agency and the testing of a controversial new medical treatment." (Publishers Weekly)

Sharpe, Matthew

The **sleeping** father; a novel. Soft Skull Press 2003 291p pa $14

ISBN 1-932360-00-X pa

LC 2003-13840

"Sharpe's arch tone is charmingly at odds with the sprawling, inclusive structure of 'The Sleeping Father.' His raised-eyebrow formality suggests a host surveying unwanted guests, yet he keeps waving more and more characters in the front door. He's a rare find: an ironist who actually seems to like other people." N Y Times Book Rev

Sharratt, Mary

Daughters of the Witching Hill. Houghton Mifflin Harcourt 2009 333p $24

ISBN 978-0-547-06967-8; 0-547-06967-7

LC 2009-42057

"Based on the infamous 1612 Lancashire witch trials, Sharratt's . . . novel vividly portrays the religious turmoil and hardscrabble life of 17th-century rural England. It's a familiar premise: an old beggar woman accused of witchcraft is sentenced to hang, along with others of her ilk. What makes this story stand out are the strong voices of the two main characters, stalwart Bess Southerns (aka Demdike) and her feisty granddaughter Alizon Device. Demdike is a cunning woman, able to heal animals and people with herbal folk magic. She strives to do only good, but when she teaches her dear friend the craft, she releases a Pandora's box of resentment, revenge, and evil." Libr J

Sharratt, Mary

Illuminations; a novel of Hildegard von Bingen. Mary Sharratt. Houghton Mifflin Harcourt 2012 xiv, 274 p.p (hardcover) $25

ISBN 0547567847; 9780547567846

LC 2012014252

This novel by Mary Sharratt "reveals the . . . story of how . . . [Benedictine abbess and polymath] Hildegard [of Bingen], offered as a tithe to the Church at the age of eight, triumphed against impossible odds to become the greatest woman of her age." The book presents a "portrait of a woman of faith and power -- a visionary in every sense of the word." (marysharratt.com)

Shattuck, Jessica

Perfect life; a novel. W.W. Norton & Co. 2009 315p $24.95

ISBN 978-0-393-06950-1; 0-393-06950-8

LC 2009-15080

"Jenny, a former prom queen climbing the corporate ladder in the pharmaceutical industry, has gone to great lengths to keep her ex, the underachieving Neil, at a distance. When he returns to Boston after a long L.A. exile, however, he quickly draws in another old friend, the vulnerable Laura, just as the sharp-minded scientist Elise gets tangled in the ropes of familial obligation. The four main characters are pulled together and spun apart by various dramas (sperm-donor babies, corporate espionage) that could come off as soap-opera-ish in lesser hands, but Perfect is too nuanced to slide into broad archetypes or easy resolutions. With her elegant prose, Shattuck manages to make her characters' stories feel both engrossing and utterly real." Entertainment Wkly

Shaw, Ali

The **girl** with glass feet; a novel. Henry Holt and Co. 2010 287p $24

ISBN 978-0-8050-9114-4; 0-8050-9114-9

LC 2009-21780

First published 2009 in the United Kingdom

"Written in the tradition of magical realists like Haruki Murakami and Gabriel García Márquez, The Girl with Glass Feet is a singular, slippery narrative that defies easy categorization. Shaw writes finely honed prose and knows how to wring maximum suspense out of a tightly woven plot." BookPage

Shaw, Irwin

Beggarman, thief. Delacorte Press 1977 436p

ISBN 0-440-00673-2

LC 77-24523

Sequel to Rich man, poor man

"Wayward brother Tom Jordache has been murdered, leaving his son Wesley with a legacy of violence and revenge that is echoed in his nephew Billy, who becomes involved in a terrorist group in Brussels while serving in the U.S. Army. The story does not focus entirely on the second generation—the tangled lives of the older Jordaches are also featured. . . . Scenes from the earlier novel are interwoven allowing the unfamiliar reader to complete enjoyment and understanding." Booklist

Shaw, Irwin

Bread upon the waters. Delacorte Press 1981 438p

ISBN 0-440-00911-1

LC 81-3106

This novel "concerns the effects of misdirected philanthropy on a middle-class New York family—the Strands. Allen Strand is a history teacher at a public (state) school. His wife Leslie gives piano lessons to bring in extra money. Jimmy, their son, has ambitions to be a rock singer. The elder daughter, Eleanor, is an executive in a large corporation, and the younger daughter, Caroline is a sporty schoolgirl. One night Caroline . . . saves a millionaire called Russell Hazen from attack by a gang of muggers. She takes him home to have a wound dressed and Hazen is swiftly entranced by the warmth and harmony of the Strand family. His gratitude prompts him to set about making their dreams come true." Times Lit Suppl

Shaw, Irwin

Evening in Byzantium. Delacorte Press 1973 368p

The author writes of "a once-famous Hollywood producer, now 48, something of a has-been, who is reliving the past and preparing a final conquest of the future at the Cannes Film Festival. Jesse Craig is in trouble and he knows it. His marriage has been a failure, he is desperately fond of his daughter but cannot help her at a crisis moment in her own life, his attractive mistress is making demands he no longer cares to meet, and a shrewd, tough-minded young woman interviewer has him just where she wants him." Publ Wkly

Shaw, Irwin

★ **Rich** man, poor man. Delacorte Press 1970 723p

"Each member of the clan is doomed in one way or another. They fight, love, live hard and their fortunes are inevitably intertwined. Mr. Shaw has juxtaposed their rise and fall against a panoramic picture of the times. . . . This may not be great literature but it certainly has popular appeal." Publ Wkly

Followed by Beggarman, thief

Shaw, Irwin

Short stories: five decades. Delacorte Press 1978 756p

LC 78-16020

Shaw, Irwin

The **young** lions. Random House 1948 689p

"World War II changes the lives of Christian, ex-Communist and Nazi; Michael, a Broadway stage manager; and Noah, an American Jew married to a Christian woman. We follow their lives during the years 1938 to 1945 as they experience frustrations, hardships, and the dangers of the war. The three fight, and two are killed." Shapiro. Fic for Youth. 3d edition

Shearn, Amy

How far is the ocean from here; a novel. Shaye Areheart Books 2008 307p $23

ISBN 978-0-307-40534-0

LC 2007-33956

"Ms. Shearn's shifting points of view are a bit tricky. The book is told mostly through Susannah's eyes, but every now and then we're suddenly in Frankie's head or Tim's or Kit's for a paragraph or two. She also has a glorious way with description, conjuring vivid images with brevity and wit." Dallas News

Sheck, Laurie

A **monster's** notes. Alfred A. Knopf 2009 544p $30

ISBN 978-0-307-27105-1; 0-307-27105-6

LC 2008-55081

"The book's conceit is high-concept: that Shelley's literary monster was inspired by a mysterious being who visited her as a young girl during visits to her mother's grave. (That would be author and proto-feminist Mary Wollstonecraft, who died days after giving birth to Shelley.) But this 'real' creature, who has survived into the 21st century, is gripped by a profound identity crisis; his understanding of self is limited to the backstory Shelley devised. He attempts to glean further enlightenment by — and here's where this gets tricky — envisioning correspondence written by Shelley, her stepsisters, and Wollstonecraft, as well as (and here's where it gets really tricky) two fictional characters, Henry Clerval from Frankenstein and a leper dying in an Italian sanitarium. These letters are presented as part of the monster's journal, which also contains articles on subjects — robotics, genetic privacy, the nature of time, John Zorn's experimental music, medieval philosophers — that speak to the creature's existential plight. Yep: This is a heady, hard read, at times repetitive and ponderous. Nonetheless, A Monster's Notes is a thrilling feat of literary scholarship, beautiful wordsmithing, and deep empathy." Entertaiment Wkly

Includes bibliographical references.

Sheehan, Aurelie

The **anxiety** of everyday objects; a novel. Penguin Books 2004 278p pa $14

ISBN 0-14-200370-0 pa

LC 2003-49873

This novel is "set at the law firm of Grecko Mauster Crill, where Winona Bartlett toils as a secretary. She has the potential to be much more and, indeed, aspires to be a filmmaker. Her would-be film, entitled The Anxiety of Everyday Objects, centers on the theme of how people misreading something as simple as a street sign can gain significant insight into their lives. The only one who seems to see Winona's potential (other than Rex, the cute lawyer who has a crush on her) is the firm's new associate, Sandy Spires, who has been hired in conjunction with a case involving the beauty makeover consulting firm Lisa Box. Sandy–beautiful, glamorous, and blind–befriends Winona, treating her to a day at a spa and introducing her to a filmmaker. But as Winona becomes interested in Sandy as a subject for her film, she gradually realizes Sandy may be as manipulative as she is charming. A quirky, introspective novel about a creative woman finding her footing in a very corporate world." Booklist

Sheehy, Hugh

The **invisibles**; stories. by Hugh Sheehy. University of Georgia Press 2012 208 p. (cloth: alk. paper) $24.95

ISBN 0820343293; 9780820343297

LC 2011050391

This collection of short stories by Hugh Sheehy, which won the Flannery O'Connor Award for Short Fiction, "shine[s] a spotlight on the bleak fringes of America. . . . A dismal assistant teacher spiking her coffee after school is suddenly locked in a basement with a student who has just witnessed his father's murder. A seventeen-year-old girl at a skate rink whose name no one can remember is motherless, friendless, and sure she will be the next to go." (Publisher's note)

Sheers, Owen

Resistance; a novel. Nan A. Talese/Doubleday 2008 306p $23.95

ISBN 978-0-385-52210-6; 0-385-52210-X

LC 2007-15068

First published 2007 in the United Kingdom

"Sheers is at his best describing the everyday rituals of rural life amid the rocky and unforgiving Welsh countryside, and in particular the tenderness exerted by the women in caring for their livestock in a strangely childless community. The novel's most memorable image is of an orphaned lamb sewn into the skin of a larger, dead lamb to lure the bereaved ewe into accepting the orphan as her own. That mixture of brutality and kindness—the bloody exigencies carried out not only in wartime, but in everyday rural life—is the great insight of Resistance." N Y Times Book Rev

Shelby, Philip

   Days of drums; a novel. Simon & Schuster 1996 318p

   ISBN 0-684-80177-9

LC 95-31045

   "Rookie Secret Service agent Holland Tylo, daughter of the late Senator Beaumont, has a plum assignment in guarding Senator Westbourne during a meeting of Washington moguls at his estate. As she escorts the senator to his guest house for a late night tryst, he's suddenly shot dead, and her career with him. As the investigation progresses, more bodies fall while a professional assassin stalks Washington. Holland becomes both hunter and hunted as she fights to vindicate herself and sort out the good guys from the bad." Libr J

   "Shelby delivers an edge-of-the-seat page-turner with a likable cool-headed heroine." Booklist

Shelby, Philip

   Gatekeeper. Simon & Schuster 1998 331p $25

   ISBN 0-684-84260-2

LC 97-39934

   "Hollis Fremont, a functionary at the American embassy in Paris, is duped by her superior and boyfriend, Paul Mc-Gann, into accompanying a man she believes to be a small-fry criminal back to the States for country-club prison incarceration. In fact, the rumpled expat turns out to be 'the Handyman,' a freelance assassin on a mission. At Kennedy Airport the Handyman bolts and disappears, and Hollis falls under the protective wing of Sam Crawford (the Gatekeeper of the title), who is an agent for the mysterious Omega group. While the Handyman stalks his quarry around the Statue of Liberty, Hollis and her 'friends' . . . try to track him down." Publ Wkly

   "Well-defined characters, compelling intrigue, and a crisp-paced plot whisk the reader along. And Hollis Fremont is no wimpy damsel in distress." Libr J

Sheldon, Sidney

   The **doomsday** conspiracy. Morrow 1991 412p $22

   ISBN 0-688-08489-3

LC 91-12109

   "Navy Commander Robert Bellamy is assigned to investigate the crash of a weather balloon in the Swiss Alps. All witnesses to the accident must be found and questioned. However, for Bellamy it is the beginning of a journey of terror into the incomprehensible. From Washington to London, Zurich, Rome, and Paris the story unfolds to reveal Bellamy's past—why the woman he loves most cannot return his love, why his friends become his deadly enemies, and why the world must never learn an incredible secret shielded by an unknown lethal force." Publisher's note

Sheldon, Sidney

   Master of the game. Morrow 1982 495p

   ISBN 0-688-01365-1

LC 82-60920

   "Kate Blackwell, born of a loveless marriage, striving through will, intelligence, and charm to control one of the richest conglomerates in the world, uses her power in wonderfully fiendish ways, which almost result in the destruction of those she loves most. The South African diamond mines provide vivid adventure; when the scene shifts to the United States, we encounter the more political maneuverings of business, but the pace never slackens." Libr J

Sheldon, Sidney

   Rage of angels. Morrow 1980 504p

   ISBN 0-688-03687-2

LC 80-13328

   "Young lawyer Jennifer Parker makes an incredible blunder in her first day as assistant D.A. Fired and in disgrace, she is reduced to serving writs to earn a living. Smart and stubborn, she perseveres, taking on unpromising clients. By inspired strategies of courtroom drama, she wins a few spectacular cases. Soon the world is taking notice, especially the Mafia. Their attractive offers are refused, but one day Parker must ask them for help in a desperate situation. In return, she becomes a Mafia mouthpiece, tempered somewhat by her love affair with the Mafioso." Libr J

Sheldon, Sidney

   Windmills of the gods. Morrow 1987 384p

LC 86-23593

   The heroine of this novel is a "college lecturer from Kansas elevated to the politically volatile position of ambassador to Romania. Mary Ashley is plunged unaware into a cauldron of intrigue. Her surprise appointment, coming after the mysterious death of her husband, is the first stage in a newly elected president's plans to cement East-West relations. Up against Mary and the president are a secret alliance of political extremists and a ruthless international assassin known as Angel." Booklist

   "The story speeds along and the epilogue is a chiller." Libr J

Shelley, Mary Wollstonecraft

   ★ **Frankenstein;** or, The modern Prometheus; with an introduction by Wendy Lesser. Knopf 1992 xxxiii, 231p $15

   ISBN 0-679-40999-8

LC 91-53195

   First published 1818

   "The tale relates the exploits of Frankenstein, an idealistic Genevan student of natural philosophy, who discovers at the university of Ingolstadt the secret of imparting life to inanimate matter. Collecting bones from charnel-houses, he constructs the semblance of a human being and gives it life. The creature, endowed with supernatural strength and size and terrible in appearance, inspires loathing in whoever sees it." Oxford Companion to Engl Lit. 5th edition

Shelley, Mary Wollstonecraft

   Maurice; or, The fisher's cot; a tale. edited with an introduction by Claire Tomalin. Knopf 1998 179p il $20

   ISBN 0-375-40473-2

LC 98-88124

   The manuscript of this previously unpublished story was discovered in Italy in 1997. It "is the tale of a lost child and opens with a small boy in tears following a coffin. It is set on the coast in Devonshire. . . . It was written in Pisa in 1820, about a year after Mary Shelley had lost her own child, little William Shelley, to a lethal fever. . . . The child in the story, Maurice, is befriended by a kindly old fisherman and is eventually found by his loving father." N Y Rev Books

Includes bibliographical references

Shepard, Jim

Like you'd understand, anyway; stories. Alfred A. Knopf 2007 211p $23

ISBN 978-0-307-26521-0

LC 2007-3639

"Each of the 11 stories is presided over by a different narrator, and they're as diverse as can be: Chernobyl engineers, Roman centurions, high school football stars, Victorian Australian explorers, Russian cosmonauts and the chief executioner of Paris' age of terror all tell their tales, shoving the reader from continent to continent, and from past to present like a pinball. . . . Despite the variety of voices in these stories, they are sewn deftly together with a dark and ominous thread; in all their diversity, the characters share troubled fates, with many of the pieces ending either on the very edge of impending disaster or with a foreboding abruptness that hits the reader like a power outage." St. Louis Post-Dispatch

Shepard, Jim

You think that's bad; stories. Alfred A. Knopf 2011 225p $24.95

ISBN 978-0-307-59482-2; 0-307-59482-3

LC 2010-35998

This collection "focuses on characters whose love for a wild, demanding task leads to some very messy relationships. Selfishness is the centripetal force at work in these eleven stories. A woman explores uncharted terrain by following a map Marco Polo left behind in 'The Track of the Assassins.' In 'Poland Is Watching,' winter mountaineers embrace risk. Other pieces feature 15th-century French cultists, 'black ops' spies and beleaguered Dutch engineers. Throughout, a common element is extruded: an addictive impulse to isolate and sacrifice closeness with other people. . . . Shepard has plenty of technique he makes sharp, tightly constructed stories. Their sharp and shiny edges, which may attract some, will warn away others. It's hard to find a way inside or to reach a comfortable place. Which may be the point, if you find humanity that way." Cleveland Plain Dealer

Shepard, Karen

The **Celestials**; a novel. by Karen Shepard. Tin House Books 2013 320 p. $15.95

ISBN 1935639552; 9781935639558

LC 2012050808

In this book, industrialist "Calvin Sampson manages a successful shoe factory in North Adams, MA, in 1870 but is troubled by union demands. To break a strike, he takes the unusual step of importing workers from San Francisco—young Chinese men, most of them teenagers. Thus begins North Adams's decade-long experiment with the Celestials, as the workers are called, since China was then known as the Celestial Kingdom." (Library Journal)

Shepard, Lucius

The **best** of Lucius Shepard. Subterranean Press 2008 623p $40

ISBN 978-1-59606-133-0; 1-59606-133-2

Contents: The man who painted the dragon griaule; Salvador; A Spanish lesson; The jaguar hunter; R & R; The arcevoalo; Shades; Delta Sly honey; Life of Buddha; White trains; Jack's decline; Beast of the heartland; Radiant green star; Only partly here; Jailwise; Hands up! who wants to die?; Dead money; Stars seen through stone

"Shepard is fantasy literature's Joseph Conrad or perhaps its Saul Bellow, a writer who never tires of staring directly into the abyss." Booklist

Shepard, Lucius

Softspoken. Night Shade Books 2007 179p $23.95

ISBN 978-1-59780-073-0; 1-59780-073-2

"Sanie's tale is, ultimately, after the final page is turned, a little slight. . . . But while you're immersed in its ectoplasmic toils, you get the full measure of domestic creepiness and occult horror." Sci Fi Wkly

Shepard, Sam

Day out of days; stories. Alfred A. Knopf 2010 282p $25.95; pa $15

ISBN 978-0-307-26540-1; 0-307-26540-4; 978-0-307-27782-4 pa; 0-307-27782-8 pa

LC 2009-19578

"Highways, rundown motels, Muzak-plagued franchises, bars, and beaches, snowstorms and blistering heat, these are the settings and circumstances in Shepard's hypnotic new book of entwined short stories. . . . Strands of autobiography infuse Shepard's magnetic and beautifully tooled stories with their potent intimacy, wry humor, and tightrope tension. Shepard's central narrator is a restless man with a thousand-mile stare who prowls America's interstates and back roads with no particular purpose except to catch the buzz of forward motion through scrolling landscapes. As much as he roams, he can't escape his past, even as age plays havoc with his memories, and the ordinary collides with the inexplicable." Booklist

Shepard, Sam

Great dream of heaven; stories. Knopf 2002 142p $20

ISBN 0-375-40505-4

LC 2002-70054

"Each involving story is psychologically loaded, but what lassoes the reader is the tension between Shephard's acuity and tenderness, his high regard for the recklessness of life." Booklist

Shepherd, Lynn

★ A **fatal** likeness; a novel. by Lynn Shepherd. 1st ed. Delacorte Press 2013 384 p. (hardcover) $26.00; (ebook) $78.00

ISBN 0345532449; 9780345532442; 9780345538673

LC 2012038988

In this book, a "note from Sir Percy Shelley, son of the late Romantic poet, causes elderly Charles Maddox to have a fit of apoplexy," so "Maddox's great-nephew and namesake, who's a private detective, responds to Sir Percy instead. The Shelley family hires the younger Maddox to prevent the poet's former lover, Claire Clairmont, from tarnishing his posthumous reputation." (Publishers Weekly)

Shepherd, Lynn

★ The **solitary** house; a novel. Lynn Shepherd. Delacorte Press 2012 340 p.

ISBN 0345532422; 9780345532428; 9780345533555
LC 2011029728

This novel by Lynn Shepherd presents a "detective story . . . that borrows characters from Charles Dickens' 'Bleak House' and Wilkie Collins' 'The Woman in White'. Ever since Metropolitan police officer Charles Maddox was dismissed for insubordination, he's eked out a living as a private detective. He currently has two cases. The first is finding the grandchild of a man who had cast out his pregnant daughter years before. The second is identifying the writer of threatening scrawls for Edward Tulkinghorn, a powerful attorney who represents the interests of the wealthy and high-born. . . . At length he realizes that his work for Tulkinghorn is leaving in its wake a string of corpses, many of them evidently connected to the horrific murder of several women." (Kirkus Reviews)

Sher, Ira

Gentlemen of space. Free Press 2003 291p $23
ISBN 0-7432-4218-1
LC 2002-192807

"Sher's affection for his characters is clear, and they shine with softly absurd humor. . .and a DeLillo-like nostalgia for Americana and belief. This is beautiful, eloquent first novel." Booklist

Sherman, Jory

The **Baron** war. Forge 2002 318p
ISBN 0-7653-0255-1
LC 2001-54750

"Set in the lawless Texas landscape, this latest installment in Sherman's Baron series . . . reaches a watershed on the eve of the Civil War. Grieving the shameful death of his wife, Caroline, estranged patriarch Martin Baron must mend fences with his son, Anson—the new owner of the family's Box B Ranch—in order to face a deadly threat from a fractious neighbor, Matteo Aguilar. . . . Strong female characters and plenty of romance could help this title bridge the western gender gap." Publ Wkly

Sherman, Susan

The **little** Russian; Susan Sherman. Counterpoint 2012 384 p.
ISBN 9781582437729
LC 2011037731

This "novel opens with a . . . description of an 1897 pogrom in Little Russia (modern-day Ukraine). The 14-year-old boy who numbly watches a peasant beat his father to death, we learn, is Hershel Alshonsky. Seven years later, he catches the eye of Berta Lorkis, a restless grocer's daughter who thinks Hershel will give her back the comfortable life she enjoyed as companion to a wealthy Moscow family. Berta doesn't know that Hershel's travels as a wheat merchant disguise his activities smuggling guns for the Bund, which aims to arm Jews against pogroms. They have nine happily married years before a gun raid gone wrong sends Hershel fleeing to America in early 1914. Berta refuses to join him, thinking she and her two children can remain secure in the affluence Hershel's trade created; by the time she realizes her mistake, World War I has begun, and they are trapped." (Kirkus)

Sherrill, Martha

My last movie star; a novel of Hollywood. Random House 2003 349p $23.95
ISBN 0-375-50769-8
LC 2002-69707

"Fed up with her manipulative editor, entertainment journalist Clementine James is packing up to move to her boyfriend's Virginia farm when Flame magazine asks her to write an in-depth profile of captivating actress Allegra Coleman. When their interview ends in a car crash, Clementine awakes to find herself a celebrity. Allegra has vanished, and Clementine was the last person to see her. Allegra's disappearance catapults her into instant superstardom." Booklist

Sherwood, Frances

The **book** of splendor. Norton 2002 348p $25.95
ISBN 0-393-02138-6
LC 2002-520

"A young, illiterate Jewess of dubious birth, given to fanciful stories, Rochel is able to escape poverty through an arranged marriage to Zev, a widowed tailor. This domestic scene is played out in the shadow of 17th-century imperial Prague alongside oppression and poverty during the reign of Habsburg Emperor Rudolph. . . . The characters include the famous Rabbi Loew, who fashions the man of mud, the Golom of Prague; astromomers Tycho Brahe and Johannes Kepler; the alchemists John Dee and Edward Kelley; and an assortment of spies, lepers, monks, and mountebanks." Libr J

This is a "provocative, gripping novel that's part farce, historical adventure, theological meditation, and bodice-ripping romance. Fans of magic realism will love this." Booklist

Sherwood, Frances

Night of sorrows. Norton 2006 425p map $24.95
ISBN 978-0-393-05825-3; 0-393-05825-5
LC 2006-420

"An account of conquest and dehumanization, [this novel] is also a story of survival in the midst of a harsh cultural clash. The linguistic and narrative riches of the book enhance its moral complexity: Sherwood has refused to settle for the black-and-white thinking that so often mars this sort of historical fiction." N Y Times Book Rev

Shields, Carol

The **republic** of love. Viking 1992 366p
LC 91-16154

"Not only are Fay and Tom exceptionally likable and capable of arresting insights, their worlds are complete and organic. Secondary characters are respectfully but economically drawn via short monologues, and the city of Winnipeg bustles in the background." Publ Wkly

Shields, Carol

★ The **stone** diaries. Viking 1994 361p il
LC 93-30239

This "novel provides, glancingly, a panorama of 20th-century life in North America. Written in a diary format, it traces the life of one seemingly unremarkable woman: Daisy Goodwill Flett, who is born in 1905 and lives into the 1990's." N Y Times Book Rev

Shields, Carol

Unless; a novel. Fourth Estate/HarperCollins Pubs. 2002 213p

ISBN 0-00-714107-6

LC 2002-19923

Reta Winters—loving helpmate "to a doctor, mother of three cheerful daughters, and author of a successful comic novel—has always considered herself happy, even blessed. Then her eldest child, nineteen-year-old Norah, briefly disappears and resurfaces as a panhandling mute on a Toronto street corner, holding up a homemade placard that says 'Goodness.' Shields's ability to use Reta's darkest fears to reveal the order lurking in chaos, without ever losing her light touch . . . is nothing short of astonishing." New Yorker

Shields, David

★ **Dead** languages; a novel. Knopf 1989 245p

LC 88-13444

"As touching and funny a rendering of adolescence as The Catcher in the Rye. Those recently emerged from adolescence will readily see its truth; the well read will delight at Shields's ability with narrative. But Dead Languages speaks to everyone who has ever struggled to articulate an emotion and failed to find the words." Libr J

Shields, Kieran

A **Study** in Revenge; Kieran Shields. Random House Inc 2013 384 p. $25

ISBN 0307985768; 9780307985767

Sequel to: The truth of all things (2012)

This book is the second to feature detectives Archie Lean and Perceval Grey. Burglar Frankie Cosgrove is shot during a deal, but then his "burned corpse turns up after its burial in an abandoned house adorned with drawings of Satan and the message 'Hell Awaits.' Meanwhile, a wealthy dying man hires Grey to look for his long-lost granddaughter, though the dying man's family is more interested in a recently stolen heirloom." (Publishers Weekly)

Shiner, Lewis

Dark tangos; a novel. Subterranean Press 2011 213p $35

ISBN 978-1-59606-396-9; 1-59606-396-3

"Rob Cavenaugh, an American computer programmer, has sought solace in Buenos Aires after the breakup of his marriage. While tangoing one night in a dance club, Rob meets Elena, a beautiful but troubled woman who's been followed for the past several weeks by a tall, gaunt man who stays in the shadows. Under pressure from Rob, Elena finally reveals that the stranger may be a hit man sent by her stepfather, whom she recently discovered was a leading figure in the murder of thousands of political dissenters in the mid-1970s. Finding himself now a target, Rob must scramble not only to protect Elena but to elude danger himself. Shiner gracefully and efficiently tells his moving tale

within a tight frame. Along the way are short tutorials on tango, Argentine history, and torture techniques." Publ Wkly

Shinn, Sharon

Jenna Starborn; Sharon Shinn. Ace Books 2002 381 p. (pbk.) $25.00

ISBN 044100900X; 9780441009008

LC 2001056051

This book tells the story of "Jenna Starborn [who] was created out of frozen embryonic tissue, a child unloved and unwanted." (Publisher's note) "Jenna accepts a job as a nuclear reactor maintenance technician at remote Thorrastone Park, owned by the wealthy Everett Ravenbeck. She becomes indispensable to the household—and to Everett. Despite their difference in stations—Jenna is only a half-citizen—they fall in love. After a long, difficult courtship, . . . the two plan to marry. But at the wedding, Jenna receives a terrible shock: Everett has another wife. Unable to live with him as his wife without being married, Jenna flees to a remote planet, where she falls in with a family that provides help and aid to travelers. She's on the verge of deciding whether to marry another and go with him to colonize a new planet when she hears Everett's voice, impossibly calling from afar." (Publishers Weekly)

Shinn, Sharon

The **shape** of desire; Sharon Shinn. Ace Books 2012 324 p.

ISBN 1937007170; 9781937007171

LC 2011041164

This fantasy romance novel by Sharon Shinn follows "Maria Devane . . . passionately in love with Dante Romano. But . . . Maria knows that Dante can never give all of himself back-at least not all the time. Every month, Dante shifts shape, becoming a wild animal. During those times, he wanders far and wide, leaving Maria alone. . . . But Maria, who loves him without hesitation, wouldn't trade their unusual relationship for anything. Since the beginning, she has kept his secret, knowing that their love is worth the danger. But when a string of brutal attacks occur in local parks during the times when Dante is in animal form, Maria is forced to consider whether the lies she's been telling about her life have turned into lies she's telling herself." (Publisher's note)

Shirley, John

Demons. Ballantine Pub. Group 2002 372p $25

ISBN 0-345-44647-X

LC 2001-43478

This "apocalyptic tale, redolent with the terror of inexplicable carnage, is two novels in one: a first-person account of an initial advent of demons in everyday reality, followed by the story of their later return. Ira, narrator of the first, plays a significant role in the second, and Shirley links the two episodes nearly seamlessly. Ira reports a world gone mad with demonic possession, its people clinging to normalcy for dear life." Booklist

Shoemaker, Bill

Stalking horse. Fawcett Columbine 1994 311p

LC 93-22125

"The plot is big, complicated and thoroughbred-fast as Coley's hard-boiled, first-person chapters alternate with a third-person focus on Starbuck. Shoemaker's characters provide the most fun." Publ Wkly

Sholem Aleichem

The **adventures** of Menahem-Mendl; translated from the Yiddish by Tamara Kahana. Putnam 1969 222p

> Original Yiddish edition published 1909 in Russia
>
> This book "consists of an exchange of letters between the hero and his . . . wife Sheineh-Sheindl, whom he has left behind looking after the children in their . . . native town of Kasrilevka while he tries to make his fortune in the big city—first Odessa, then Kiev. Menaham-Mendl is . . . {an} over-optimistic schemer who somehow contrives to make a living out of thin air; at one moment he is a currency speculator . . . then next a dabbler in commodities, after that a would-be broker, a journalist, a matchmaker, an insurance agent." N Y Rev of Books

Sholem Aleichem

The **adventures** of Mottel, the cantor's son; translated by Tamara Kahana; illustrated by Ilya Schor. Abelard-Schuman 1953 342p il

> "The lighthearted humor of young Mottel, the narrator, adds a touch of pathos to the stories of an impoverished Jewish family in a European village, its wanderings in Europe en route to America, and finally its arrival and settlement in the U.S." Booklist

Sholem Aleichem

The **best** of Sholom Aleichem; edited by Irving Howe and Ruth R. Wisse. New Republic Bks. 1979 276p

> Contents: The haunted tailor; A Yom Kippur scandal; Eternal life; Station Baranovich; The pot; The clock that struck thirteen; Home for Passover; On account of a hat; Dreyfus in Kasrilevke; Two anti-semites; A Passover expropriation; If I were Rothschild; Tevye strikes it rich; The bubble bursts; Chava; Get thee out; From Mottel the cantor's son; Bandits; The guest; The Krushniker delegation; One in a million; Once there were four

Sholem Aleichem

The **further** adventures of Menachem-Mendl; New York--Warsaw--Vienna--Yehupetz. translated by Aliza Shevrin. Syracuse Univ. Press 2001 172p $26.95

> ISBN 0-8156-0677-X
>
> LC 00-55701
>
> "Written in Yiddish in 1913 and only now translated into English, it's a sequel to The Adventures of Menachem-Mendl, which was first translated and published in the U.S. in 1969. Loosely based on Aleichem's experience, the story is told in the form of letters between Menachem-Mendl (who now has a job as a writer on a Warsaw newspaper) and his wife, Sheyne-Sheyndl, left behind with the children in a Kasrilevka village, where she faces crushing poverty and persecution." Booklist

Sholem Aleichem

The **nightingale**; or, The Saga of Yosele Solovey the cantor. translated by Aliza Shevrin. Putnam 1985 240p

> LC 85-12073
>
> Originally written in Yiddish and copyrighted 1917
>
> This "is more than a popular novel; it is a social document, a study of a failed artist and, in its way, an early feminist work." N Y Times Book Rev

Sholem Aleichem

Tevye the dairyman and The railroad stories; [by] Sholom Aleichem; translated from the Yiddish and with an introduction by Hillel Halkin. Schocken Bks. 1987 xli, 309p hardcover o.p. pa $15

> ISBN 0-8052-1069-5 pa
>
> LC 86-24835
>
> "In the first eight stories of this collection, Tevye, the Russian Jew so familiar from Fiddler on the Roof, bemoans his fate. In these as well as the following 21 tales, the author displays his splendid storytelling skills." Booklist

Sholem Aleichem

★ **Tevye's** daughters; translated by Frances Butwin. Crown 1949 302p

> Translated from the Yiddish, many of these stories are "about the seven daughters of Tevye the Dairyman and the life each chooses as she comes of age in Russia during the years preceding the first World War." Publ Wkly

Sholokhov, Mikhail Aleksandrovich

★ **And** quiet flows the Don; [by] Mikhail Sholokhov; translated from the Russian by Stephen Garry. Knopf 1934 755p

> "Set in the Don River basin of southwestern Russia at the end of the czarist period, the novel traces the progress of the Cossack Gregor Melekhov from youthful lover to Red Army soldier and finally to Cossack nationalist. War—in the form of both international conflict and civil revolution—provides the epic backdrop for the narrative and determines its tone of moral ambiguity." Merriam-Webster's Ency of Lit
>
> Followed by The Don flows home to the sea

Sholokhov, Mikhail Aleksandrovich

The **Don** flows home to the sea; {by} Mikhail Sholokhov; translated from the Russian by Stephen Garry. Knopf 1941 777p

> This translation first published 1940 in the United Kingdom
>
> This sequel to And quiet flows the Don, covers the period following the Revolution of 1917 to the end of the civil war in 1921. The narrative traces the fortunes of a group of Cossacks as they fight alternately with the Reds and the Whites
>
> "It is a tale of misfortunes multiplied, yet a broad and earthy humor and the hearty Cossack gaiety break continuously over the grim surface. At the end the Cossack, with his intense individualism, his passionate love of the land, and his primitive pride, stands revealed." Nation
>
> Followed by Seeds of tomorrow (1959)

Shomer, Enid

The **twelve** rooms of the Nile; Enid Shomer. Simon & Schuster 2012 449 p. (paperback) $16.00; (hardcover) $26.00

ISBN 9781451642971; 1451642962; 9781451642964
LC 2011037151

This book by Enid Shomer "imagines Gustave Flaubert and Florence Nightingale meeting in Egypt, among the crowds cruising the Nile. . . . Sharing itineraries, the two discover they both possess unquenchable ambition, and they both suffer from depression over the gap between dreams and reality. Mutual respect begets attraction, and soon Nightingale is teaching Flaubert how women think, while Flaubert teaches Nightingale how men feel." (Publishers Weekly)

Shonk, Katherine

Happy now? Farrar, Straus and Giroux 2010 262p $25

ISBN 978-0-374-28143-4; 0-374-28143-2
LC 2009-29509

"On the surface, such a story might seem like fodder for a Lifetime television network drama or a women's magazine story. But Shonk (the sort of writer Saul Bellow might have dubbed 'a first-class noticer') makes gold of it — invariably stripping away sentimentality and replacing it with the mix of caustic intelligence and biting wit of someone who feels things deeply but never loses the ability to step back a bit and see the dysfunctional theater of it all." Chicago Sun-Times

Shonk, Katherine

The **red** passport. Farrar, Straus & Giroux 2003 209p $22

ISBN 0-374-24847-8
LC 2003-7680

In this "collection set primarily in post-Communist Russia, expatriates and natives alike endeavor to make their way in a new social and economic landscape, often sharing an intense desire for whatever the other possesses: money, freedom, love, family. . . . Shonk is at her best examining the lives of Americans whom the natives revere as potential saviors at the same time they dismiss them as frivolous tourists who could never hope to understand life in the former Soviet republic. That tension lends these stories an impressive vitality." Publ Wkly

Shreve, Anita

★ **All** he ever wanted. Little, Brown 2003 310p $25.95

ISBN 0-316-78226-2
LC 2002-36847

"Aside from an exchange of letters between his wife and his rival, everything is seen from the point of view of Nicholas, who grows increasingly jealous and pathetic, his motives couched in formal, self-justifying language that almost always sounds like a form of evasion. In the end, he admits, he's telling 'the story of a faintly ridiculous man,' but luckily it's a tale that also flirts with full-scale tragedy as well as the darkest kind of comedy." N Y Times Book Rev

Shreve, Anita

Body surfing; a novel. Little, Brown and Co. 2007 295p $25.99

ISBN 978-0-316-05985-5; 0-316-05985-4
LC 2006-31133

"Shreve's devastating depiction of the family's dissolution—the culmination of sublimated jealousies suddenly exploding into the open—is wrenching. Shreve's omniscience is asserted with such ease that it often feels like she's toying with her characters, but her control is masterful, particularly in the sure-handed and compassionate aftermath." Publ Wkly

Shreve, Anita

★ **Eden** Close; a novel. Harcourt Brace Jovanovich 1989 265p $17.95

ISBN 0-15-127582-3
LC 89-34712

"'Eden Close' is not a novel of suspense but one of sensibility. Its insights are keen, its language measured and haunting. In it, a sense of loss and then of rupture is everywhere." N Y Times Book Rev

Shreve, Anita

Fortune's Rocks; a novel. Little, Brown 2000 453p $24.95

ISBN 0-316-78101-0
LC 99-42665

"The level of suspense never falters, but becomes breathtaking during a custody court battle. . . . The astounding denouement of cascading events will leave no reader unmoved." Publ Wkly

Shreve, Anita

★ The **last** time they met; a novel. Little, Brown 2001 313p $28

ISBN 0-316-78114-2
LC 00-53496

In this novel featuring Thomas Janes, first introduced in the author's The weight of water, "we learn the history of Thomas's great love with fellow poet Linda Fallon. The novel is told in reverse time, starting with the present, when Linda and Thomas, now in their fifties, reconnect at a literary festival. The middle section takes place in Africa, where the couple, then age 26, had a disastrous affair that horribly affected a number of loved ones and changed their own lives forever." Libr J

"Romantic regret is Anita Shreve's subject in this instantly captivating novel. . . . Fiction writers could go to school on Shreve's command of scene." Atl Mon

Shreve, Anita

Light on snow; a novel. Little, Brown and Co 2004 305p $24.95

ISBN 0-316-78148-7
LC 2004-8907

"The story shifts brilliantly between childlike visions of a simple world and the growing realization of its cruel ambiguities. Aside from a few saccharine moments and a rather pat ending, Shreve does a skilled job of portraying grief, conflict and anger while leaving room for hope, redemption and renewal." Pub Wkly

Shreve, Anita

The **pilot's** wife; a novel. Little, Brown 1998
293p $23.95

ISBN 0-316-78908-9

LC 97-51647

"The climax, less dramatic than meditative, may strike
some readers as too muted: understatement is one of this
novel's strengths. What haunts us is the way Jack's secret
life gradually weakens its hold on Kathryn's imagination
and ours." Publ Wkly

Shreve, Anita

Rescue; a novel. Little, Brown and Co. 2010
288p $26.99

ISBN 978-0-316-02072-5; 0-316-02072-9

LC 2010-26165

"Paramedic Pete Webster is worried sick about his
daughter, Rowan, a high-school senior whom he has raised
single-handedly ever since she was two. Rowan has adopted
very untypical behavior, ignoring her studies and drinking
heavily. It brings back bad memories of his ex-wife, Sheila.
He pulled her from a car wreck while on the job and soon fell
madly in love with her both for her beauty and her irreverent
sense of humor. When she became pregnant, he married her
though he was only 21. They were very happy until Sheila
began drinking all day, every day. Now Pete is worried that
their daughter believes she is doomed to repeat her mother's
mistakes; he decides to contact Sheila, whom he has not seen
or heard from for 16 years." Booklist

Shreve, Anita

Resistance; a novel. Little, Brown 1995 222p

LC 94-39269

The author "adds subtle gray shadings to a familiar morality tale of good and evil, bravery and betrayal. In her vivid
story, . . . Ms. Shreve questions the very nature of courage."
N Y Times Book Rev

Shreve, Anita

Sea glass; a novel. Little, Brown 2002 378p

ISBN 0-316-78081-2

LC 2002-20897

"Shreve does not use her characters frivolously. They
reveal who they are through their actions, with the author—
who writes with admirable economy—rarely having to point
a finger or underline the obvious. The true power of her novel comes from the appalling social conditions she describes
so vividly, the grim but heroic lives her characters live." N
Y Times Book Rev

Shreve, Anita

Strange fits of passion; a novel. Harcourt Brace
Jovanovich 1991 336p

ISBN 0-15-185760-1

LC 90-23874

This novel opens "with oblique hints of a violent event—
here a murder committed by a woman in response to domestic abuse—then segues to flashbacks that slowly reveal the
circumstances leading up to it. A reporter who wrote a book
about the crime shares her notes, presented in alternating
versions and voices. Most affecting is the voice of the accused woman, who flees Manhattan with her six-month-old

daughter to seek sanctuary in a coastal Maine village where
she is protected by the clannish but sympathetic townspeople. She finds temporary solace in an affair with a sensitive
lobsterman, but is betrayed to her husband by another man
out of jealousy." Publ Wkly

Shreve, Anita

Testimony; a novel. Little, Brown 2008 307p
$25.99

ISBN 9780316059862; 0-316-05986-2

LC 2008-5027

"Shreve arrows in on many targets—underage drinking, instant exposure via the Internet, familial expectations,
youthful insecurities, and peer pressure, among them—as
she flawlessly weaves a tale that is mesmerizing, hypnotic,
and compulsive." Libr J

Shreve, Anita

The **weight** of water. Little, Brown 1997 246p
$22.95

ISBN 0-316-78997-6

LC 96-21326

"Deftly moving among almost as many plot lines as
there are islands and employing at least two distinct voices,
Ms. Shreve unravels themes of adultery, jealousy, crimes of
passion, incest, negligence, loss and guilt, and then manages
somehow to knit them all together into an engrossing tale."
N Y Times Book Rev

Shreve, Anita

Where or when; a novel. Harcourt Brace & Co.
1993 240p

LC 92-39392

The "two main characters are not presented in isolation, enveloped by a cloud of concupiscence. Instead, they
are placed against a richly drawn background that encompasses everything from the grim reality of a deteriorating
economy to the thin black dirt of the Richards farm." N Y
Times Book Rev

Shreve, Susan Richards

★ A **country** of strangers. Simon & Schuster
1989 239p

ISBN 0-671-64409-2

LC 88-28735

This is an "ambitious novel that attempts to create a
parable of how racial harmony may be achieved. And, because of their youthful exuberance and quirkiness, Pruden-
tial and Kate are finally memorable characters." N Y Times
Book Rev

Shreve, Susan Richards

Daughters of the new world. Doubleday 1992
471p

LC 91-8146

"As the novel unfolds and daughters become mothers,
mothers grandmothers, grandmothers great-grandmothers,
Shreve explores the wonder of personalities and genetics,
the astonishing accommodation and resiliency of wom-
en, the courage and dignity of true love, and the surge of
change that has driven this unlikely century. An enveloping,

Shreve, Susan Richards

★ **Plum** & Jaggers; a novel. Farrar, Straus & Giroux 2000 228p

    ISBN 0-374-23462-0

                  LC 99-47619

"Sam is the only one of the four McWilliams kids who can remember exactly what happened on the day their parents were killed in the terrorist bombing of a Rome-bound train. Their Scottish-born father and American mother had led the family on a carefree tour of the world, but after the tragedy, the kids–all under seven–are shipped off to their nice but vague grandparents in Grand Rapids. Years later, Sam turns his orphan family unit into a comedy team inspired by the missing parents, whose nicknames for each other were Plum and Jaggers. They are a big hit on late-night television." Booklist

Shreve "writes eloquently, painting a story of tragedy, obsession, love, and loss with a broad brush." Libr J

Shreve, Susan Richards

A **student** of living things. Viking 2006 246p $24.95

    ISBN 0-670-03758-3

                LC 2005-57473

"Her affinity for biology prompted her mother to call her a 'student of living things,' although Claire Frayn had no qualms about scrutinizing the dead. Not that this enables her to cope with her brother's death, especially since she was standing beside him on the library steps when he was shot. Claire and Steven had been living at home in a Washington, D.C., suburb while attending graduate school. Bombings and other terrorist acts have become commonplace in a grim near-future, and it is against this malevolent backdrop that the politically outspoken Steven is assassinated. The Frayns—an eccentric extended family of survivors of many atrocities and sorrows sensitively and charmingly portrayed—are unaware of the danger Claire is in as she is drawn to an enigmatic man who claims to have been Steven's friend. Shreve's novels are always elegant in their blend of restraint and intensity, and this is an exquisite hybrid, a poetic and resonant story of grief, family bonds, risk, and love that is as propulsive and unpredictable as a first-class thriller." Booklist

Shreve, Susan Richards

The **visiting** physician. Talese 1996 288p

    ISBN 0-385-47701-5

                LC 95-23877

"Twenty-odd years ago, Helen Fielding suffered severe trauma on a visit to her aunt in small-town Ohio when her toddler sister disappeared while in Helen's care. Now a doctor, Helen returns to Meridian as an outbreak of legionella threatens the town's children. One child is dead, another has disappeared, and so has the town doctor. Meridian itself has lost its collective innocence after being the subject of an unscrupulous TV director's documentary on the perfect small town. . . . A well-structured method of revealing the past adds to the story's appeal." Libr J

Shrier, Howard

Boston cream. Vintage Canada 2012 xv, 303 p.p

    ISBN 0307359565; 9780307359568

                LC 2012358546

Sequel to: High Chicago

This book follows "Jonah Geller, a Toronto PI with a penchant for cases south of the border. When the Brookline, Mass., police are unable to find David Fine, a 'transplant fellow' and devout Jew who's disappeared from Boston's Sinai Hospital, Fine's parents hire Geller to investigate. Aided by partner Jenn Raudsepp, Geller follows a twisted trail that involves Fine's distinguished transplant surgeon boss; a mob guy with a new scam; Fine's rabbi; a Boston lawyer whose wife needs a kidney; and an Indian grocer who vanished the week before Fine. When Raudsepp's life is on the line, Geller calls in reinforcements, including a friend who's a former contract killer, and prepares for war." (Publishers Weekly)

Shriver, Lionel

★ **Big** Brother. HarperCollins 2013 384 p. (hardcover) $26.99

    ISBN 0061458570; 9780061458576

In this book by Lionel Shriver, "Pandora Halfdanarson . . . lives an apparently tranquil life as a successful businesswoman in Iowa with her 'nutritional Nazi' husband and stepchildren, until the arrival of her glamorous jazz pianist brother Edison. Edison has grown fat: appallingly, stinkingly, suicidally, repellently so. . . . [Pandora] decide whether she is prepared to sacrifice her family to save her brother." (Times Literary Supplement)

"Brilliantly imagined, beautifully written, and superbly entertaining." LJ

Shriver, Lionel

The **post**-birthday world. HarperCollins Publishers 2007 517p $25.95

    ISBN 978-0-06-118784-1; 0-06-118784-4

                LC 2006-49233

"Lawrence often verges on being a parody of a judgmental, snobbish prig, while Ramsey often verges on being a parody of a hard-living, irresponsible celebrity. . . . That we're able to overlook the flaws of Ramsey and Lawrence is, in the end, a testament to Ms. Shriver's ability to make Irina into a thoroughly compelling character, an idiosyncratic yet recognizable heroine about whom it's impossible not to care." N Y Times (Late N Y Ed)

Shriver, Lionel

So much for that; a novel. Harper 2010 436p $25.99

    ISBN 978-0-06-145858-3; 0-06-145858-9

                LC 2009-28815

"Though there is one farcical plot development that is poorly woven into the emotional fabric of the story, and though some of the asides about health care feel shoehorned into the narrative, the author's understanding of her people is so intimate, so unsentimental that it lofts the novel over such bumpy passages, insinuating these characters permanently into the reader's imagination." N Y Times (Late N Y Ed)

Shriver, Lionel

We need to talk about Kevin. Counterpoint 2003 400p

ISBN 1-58243-267-8

LC 20020152753

This is a novel by the author of The Bleeding Heart (1990). "That neither nature nor nurture bears exclusive responsibility for a child's character is self-evident. But such generalizations provide cold comfort when it's your own son who's just opened fire on his fellow students and whose class photograph—with its unseemly grin—is blown up on the national news. The question of who's to blame for teenage atrocity tortures our narrator, Eva Khatchadourian. Two years ago, her son, Kevin, murdered seven of his fellow highschool students, a cafeteria worker, and a popular algebra teacher. Because he was only fifteen at the time of the killings, he received a lenient sentence and is now in a prison for young offenders in upstate New York. Telling the story of Kevin's upbringing, Eva addresses herself to her estranged husband through a series of letters." (Publisher's note)

"It's a harrowing, psychologically astute, sometimes even darkly humorous novel, with a clear-eyed, hard-won ending and a tough-minded sense of the difficult, often painful human enterprise." Publ Wkly

Shteyngart, Gary

Absurdistan; a novel. Random House 2006 333p $24.95

ISBN 1-4000-6196-2

LC 2005-54308

This is "a satire that is profoundly funny, genuinely moving and wholly lovable. . . . The same way Gatsby chased Daisy, Misha chases his imagined America–with perfect, pure good faith, going further and further out on a limb until he's the only true believer in sight. He is, of course, doomed to be disillusioned and heartbroken–the novel ends hopefully, but the dateline is early morning, Sept. 11, 2001. Still, there's no doubt that he will reillusion himself again, repeatedly, as many times as necessary." Time

Shteyngart, Gary

The Russian debutante's handbook. Riverhead Bks. 2002 452p

ISBN 1-57322-213-5

LC 2001-47676

"Failurchka-Mother's Little Failure-is what Vladimir Girshkin's overweening Russian immigrant mother calls her 25-year-old son at the beginning of this picaresque . . . first novel. Vladimir is stuck in a dead-end job and saddled with girlfriend Challah, 'queen of everything musky and mammal-like.' Then through a series of chance encounters, he is catapulted to the eastern European city of 'Prava' to find himself welcomed into the fold of powerful Mafiosi." Libr J

Shteyngart, Gary

★ Super sad true love story; a novel. Random House 2010 334p

ISBN 1-4000-6640-9; 978-1-4000-6640-7

LC 2009-37971

On his last night of a year's stay in Rome, Lenny meets Eunice Park, a Korean American "who traveled to Europe to escape her abusive father. Soon, she follows Lenny to New York." (Bookforum)

"Full-tilt and fulminating satirist Shteyngart . . . is mordant, gleeful, and embracive as he funnels today's follies and atrocities into a devilishly hilarious, soul-shriveling, and all-too plausible vision of a ruthless and crass digital dystopia in which techno-addled humans are still humbled by love and death." Booklist

Shulman, Alix Kates

Memoirs of an ex-prom queen; a novel. Knopf 1972 274p

"In the third grade, tomboy Sasha realizes that 'there's only one thing worth bothering about: becoming beautiful,' and begins to apply herself to that end. At 15 she has succeeded: she is elected queen of the high school prom and loses her virginity the same evening, an occurrence not at all coincidental, since she measures beauty in terms of sex appeal. By her 25th birthday, she's had 25 lovers. Although she's intelligent (a Columbia Ph.D. candidate) and ambitious, she is unable to escape the trap she has set for herself. Her identity is determined only in terms of her femininity and her relationships with men. Her ideas and ambitions must be sacrificed to theirs, if necessary, and it always seems to 'be' necessary. Her decline from potential philosopher to typical housewife appears completed by the birth of her children, but age and fading looks finally prove to be her salvation." Publ Wkly

Shulman, Max

The many loves of Dobie Gillis; eleven campus stories. Doubleday 1951 223p

"Here are 11 short stories dealing with Dobie Gillis, of the crew cut set, and his adventures and misadventures on the Golden Gopher's campus. The stories appeared individually in the Saturday Evening Post, American Magazine and other periodicals. Most of the time Dobie is becoming infatuated or disinfatuated with one fair coed or another, and the woes and worries which these damsels bring with them supply obstacles for the nimble-witted freckled Casanova." San Francisco Chron

Shulman, Max

Rally round the flag, boys! Doubleday 1957 278p

"A bit of lusty fun at the expense of commuters, exurbian manners and mores, teen-age cults, Army red tape, progressive education, and whatever else catches the author's satiric eye." Booklist

Shumway, Charity

Ten girls to watch; a novel. Charity Shumway. 1st ed. Washington Square Press 2012 356 p. (paperback) $15.00

ISBN 1451673418; 9781451673418; 9781451673425

LC 2011048888

In this book by Charity Shumway, "recent graduate Dawn West . . . lands a job tracking down the past winners of 'Charm' magazine's 'Ten Girls to Watch' contest. . . . As Dawn gets to know their life stories, she'll discover that success, love, and friendship can be found in the most unexpected of places. Most importantly, she'll learn that while those who came before us can be role models, ultimately, we each have to create our own happy ending." (Publishers Weekly)

Shute, Nevil

★ **On** the beach. Morrow 1957 320p

"A nuclear war annihilates the world's Northern Hemisphere, and as atomic wastes are spreading southward, residents of Australia try to come to grips with their mortality. In spite of the inevitability of death, these people face their end with courage and live from day to day. They even plant trees they may never see mature." Shapiro. Fic for Youth. 3d edition

Siddons, Anne Rivers

Heartbreak Hotel. Simon & Schuster 1976 252p

ISBN 0-671-22315-1

"Maggie Deloach, a Southern beauty of the 50s, seems well on the way to success Dixie-style. Sorority girl, well-born, a leader, she is pinned to Boots Claiborne, scion of an old land-owning Delta family. It would seem that marriage and a happy-ever-after life are ahead of her. But Randolph University exposes her to more that frat parties and frivolity. A professor, a reporter and a student from New Jersey sow the seeds of questions. A visit to Boot's family and an ugly incident there make Maggie's questions more insistent and, for her, unnerving since they not only challenge her carefully planned future, but reveal stirring in the South she had never anticipated." Publ Wkly

Siddons, Anne Rivers

Islands. HarperCollins 2004 374p $24.95

ISBN 0-06-621111-5

LC 2003-51139

"When Charleston protagonist Anny Butler marries Dr. Lewis Aiken, she becomes a member of the 'Scrubs' a long-time group of friends who all have medical connections. For years, they share their free time together at a communal beach house. Then misfortune begins to plague the group, resulting in three deaths. . . . Gaynelle Toomer, a Harley-riding, freckle-faced, enormous-breasted librarian, is hired to do odd jobs for the Scrubs. She and her seven-year-old daughter, Britney, a beauty pageant contestant regular, become constant companions to Anny's frail friend, Camilla. Camilla, the stabilizing force of this group, turns out to be not at all what she appears, making the story's end a shocker." Libr J

Siddons, Anne Rivers

Nora, Nora; a novel. HarperCollins Pubs. 2000 263p $25

ISBN 0-06-017613-X

LC 00-40996

"In 1961, Nora, an outrageous, exotic, outspoken woman who smokes cigarettes and drives a pink Thunderbird, arrives in the sleepy, segregated town of Lytton, GA. While some residents are ruffled by her 'unsouthern' behavior, the effect Nora has on her adolescent and impressionable cousin Peyton is electric, opening Peyton's senses to the world around her." Libr J

"In addition to her impeccable re-creation of Southern speech and atmosphere, Siddons captures the angst of adolescence with practiced skill." Publ Wkly

Siddons, Anne Rivers

Outer banks; a novel. HarperCollins Pubs. 1991 400p

ISBN 0-06-016249-X

LC 90-56370

"Kate Abrams hasn't spoken to three of her sorority sisters for 28 years. But now Ginger, the eager rich girl who stole and married Kate's brilliant boyfriend, is hosting a reunion at her home in Nags Head, N.C. And Cecie, the orphan whose wit and cynical reserve attracted Kate, and Fig Newton, the unsightly and bumbling outcast, will both attend. . . . The narrative flows smoothly, journeying seamlessly between places and eras. While the pseudo-thriller ending seems pat, Siddons displays real strength in her subtle characterizations and delineation of emotional nuances." Publ Wkly

Siddons, Anne Rivers

Sweetwater Creek; a novel. HarperCollins 2005 356p $24.95

ISBN 0-06-621335-5

LC 2005-46279

"Twelve-year-old Emily Parmenter helps in the family business of raising hunting spaniels at their Charleston area plantation, Sweetwater Farm. Her only pals are her own dog, Elvis, and her deceased older brother, Buddy (who speaks to her from the grave). But her life is about to change radically with the arrival of rich, sophisticated 20-year-old Lulu Foxworth. During her visit to the plantation, she falls in love with the dogs and Emily's family before moving in. . . . Under Lulu's tutelage, Emily leaves her child's world and enters one for which she's not quite ready. As usual, Siddons never lets you forget where you are–the essence of South Carolina's Low Country is prominently featured and intricately . . . described." Libr J

Sidor, Steven

The **mirror's** edge. St. Martin's Minotaur 2008 287p $24.95

ISBN 978-0-312-35413-8; 0-312-35413-4

LC 2007-51830

"As the first anniversary of the kidnapping of two-year-old twins Liam and Shane Boyle approaches . . . Chicago freelance journalist Jase Deering decides to investigate with his partner and girlfriend, the blind Robyn Matchfrost. Jase has his own demons: his 12-year-old brother, Matthias, was abducted and murdered when they were children. With the help of police detectives, Jase traces the palindrome mirror-rorrim, which the twin's abductor carved into their nanny's living flesh, to cult leader Aubrey Hart Morick, who advocated human sacrifice. Though Morick is long dead, Jase discovers that his son, Graham, lives in the area and isn't as harmless as he first appears. . . . Sidor is a master of the unsettling, and each twist is more grisly and unexpected than the last." Publ Wkly

Sidor, Steven

Pitch dark. St. Martin's Griffin 2011 305p pa $14.99

ISBN 978-0-312-35414-5; 0-312-35414-2

LC 2010-43574

"It's Christmas Eve, and what should be a peaceful night in the small town of American Rapids, Minn., turns out to be a living hell when satanic followers and their leader, The Pitch, invade the town in search of the Tartarus Stone, described in the book as the fallen angel's equivalent of the Holy Grail. A small town is the perfect setting for such a story, an arena that germinates suspicion, where people point fingers and oddities are the norm. Sidor has a gift for blending misfit characters and perverse situations with the right dose of intrigue and suspense that will keep readers glued until the book's end." Chicago Sun-times

Sidor, Steven

Skin River. St. Martin's Minotaur 2004 241p $23.95

ISBN 0-312-32949-0

LC 2004-46784

"When a psychotic almost kills the single-mother/waitress who lives above his rural Wisconsin tavern, Buddy Bayes goes ballistic. Buddy recently found the severed hand of a different victim, and because of his own former criminal life in Chicago, he feels both attacks may be a message for him. So he secretly returns to the Windy City to see if there's still a contract on him, while back in Wisconsin the serial killer continues to operate with chilling immunity. Deft descriptions, slick prose, and growing tension mark this first novel." Libr J

Siegel, James

Deceit. Warner Books 2006 369p

ISBN 978-0-446-53186-3; 0-446-53186-3

LC 2006-08610

Siegel's "inventive plotting and delicious humor are in the forefront, while his fluid writing masks a multitude of sins in characterization and dialogue, resulting in first-rate entertainment." Booklist

Siegel, James

Derailed. Warner Bks. 2003 339p $23.95

ISBN 0-446-53158-8

LC 2002-73572

Charles Schine "writes advertising copy and worries a lot about his stressed-out wife and diabetic daughter. Charles makes his fatal mistake one morning on the 9:05 commuter train from Babylon to Penn Station, when he looks up from his newspaper. . . and makes eye contact with a beautiful stockbroker named Lucinda. One thing leads to another, but their hotel tryst is interrupted by an armed intruder who rapes Lucinda, pistol-whips Charles and proceeds to blackmail them. Desperate, Charles resorts to criminal measures to stop this sadistic torment." N Y Times Book Rev

"With its clean prose, high-velocity plotting and just the right amount of emotional shading darkening its sharply drawn characters, this novel is the bomb." Publ Wkly

Siegel, James

Detour; James Siegel. Warner Books 2005 341p (pbk.) $21.99; o.p.; o.p.

ISBN 9780446617062; 0446531855; 9780446531856

LC 2004016749

This novel tells the story of "Paul and Joanna Breibard, childless Manhattan professionals, [who] travel to Colombia to adopt a baby, but are kidnapped by left-wing militia who make an offer they can't refuse: Paul must swallow 36 condoms stuffed with cocaine and deliver the contraband to a contact in New Jersey within 18 hours; if he fails, Joanna and the baby will die. But in New Jersey, Paul finds a burned-out shell of a house at the contact's address. For help, he contacts Miles Goldstein, the Orthodox Jewish lawyer who arranged the adoption, and when a further delivery attempt ends in gunplay, Paul and Miles turn to Moshe Skolnick, a Russian mobster; later, a DEA agent steps in. Meanwhile, Joanna is held hostage in a country house whose walls are stained with blood." (Publisher Weekly)

Siegel, Jan

Prospero's children; Jan Siegel. Ballantine Pub. Group 2000 xviii, 350p (pbk.) $6.99; o.p.

ISBN 9780345441430; 0345439015

LC 000190160

In this fantasy novel, "[t]he sunken island is the former homeland of the mystically minded kind that 16-year-old Fern Capel and her younger brother, Will, encounter when they move to an inherited family house in the Yorkshire countryside. . . . [T]hey soon discover that their home is a magnet for sorceresses, shapeshifters, unicorns and god-possessed vessels, all of whom survived the island's cataclysmic collapse into the sea eons before and are drawn by a potent Atlantean talisman--a magic key that unlocks the door between life and death--kept hidden on the premises. When a scheming opportunist misuses the key and accidentally ruptures the barrier separating past and present, feisty Fern . . . must retrieve it from the antediluvian past it has disappeared into." (Publishers Weekly)

Siegel, Sheldon

Final verdict. Putnam 2003 391p $25.95

ISBN 0-399-15042-0

LC 2002-37189

This legal procedural features "law partners Mike Daley and ex-wife Rosie Fernandez working together in their San Francisco firm, Fernandez, Daley and O'Malley. . . . Skid row resident Leon Walker, successfully represented by Michael and Rosie in a murder case 10 years earlier, reappears and seeks legal help once again. Leon is charged with the murder of Tower Grayson, a Silicon Valley venture capitalist found stabbed to death in a Dumpster behind a liquor store. Publ Wkly

"An ending that's full of surprises—both professional and personal—provides the perfect finale to a supremely entertaining legal thriller." Booklist

Sienkiewicz, Henryk

The **deluge**; in modern translation by W. S. Kuniczak. Copernicus Soc. of Am. 1991 2v

LC 91-5047

Original Polish edition, 1886

In this second volume of the trilogy "a mere five years have passed since the knights of the Polish-Lithuanian Commonwealth threw back the Cossack invasion from the East, yet a new and far more dangerous threat appears: Swedish troops are pouring across the Northern border. . . . Central to the story is Andrei Kmita, a young Lithuanian noble whose ruthlessness obscures his military sagacity and bravery, branding him an outlaw. But for the love of the beautiful Olenka, he undertakes to reshape his character in the forge of battle, and in so doing helps save king, country, and church from the heretic invaders." Libr J

Followed by Fire in the steppe

Sienkiewicz, Henryk

Fire in the steppe; in modern translation by W. S. Kuniczak. Copernicus Soc. of Am. 1992 717p $24.95

ISBN 0-7818-0025-0

LC 92-218600

Original Polish edition, 1887

This "is an unabashed, extravagant celebration of romance and patriotism, but with a difference: the novel ends with wrenching scenes of Polish nobility, courage and hope in the face of defeat—showing why Sienkiewicz's trilogy is so beloved in his native country." N Y Times Book Rev

Sienkiewicz, Henryk

★ **Quo** Vadis; a narrative of the time of Nero. translated from the Polish by Jeremiah Curtin. Little, Brown 1896 541p

A historical novel dealing with the "Rome of Nero and the early Christian martyrs. The Roman noble, Petronius, a worthy representative of the dying paganism, is perhaps the most interesting figure, and the struggle between Christianity and paganism supplies the central plot, but the canvas is large. A succession of characters and episodes and, above all, the richly colorful, decadent life of ancient Rome give the novel its chief interest. The beautiful Christian Lygia is the object of unwelcome attentions from Vinicius, one of the Emperor's guards, and when she refuses to yield to his importunities, she is denounced and thrown to the wild beasts of the arena. She escapes and eventually marries Vinicius, whom Peter and Paul have converted to Christianity." Reader's Ency. 4th edition

Sienkiewicz, Henryk

With fire and sword; in modern translation by W.S. Kuniczak; foreword by James A. Michener. Copernicus Soc. of Am. 1991 1135p

LC 91-161

Original Polish edition, 1883

This novel "should have taken place in the general literary repertory long ago, alongside the works of the elder Dumas, Walter Scott, Margaret Mitchell." N Y Times Book Rev

Followed by The deluge

Sigler, Scott

Contagious. Crown Publishers 2008 438p $24.95

ISBN 978-0-307-40631-6; 0-307-40631-8

LC 2008-39985

Sequel to: Infected

"In the near future, U.S. president John Gutierrez goes straight from his inauguration to crisis management when his national security team informs him that he must focus his attention on Project Tangram, a secret government program to stave off an epidemic caused by alien parasites, which form itchy blue triangular patches on the skin. Victims eventually become paranoid and violent. As the infestation spreads, Gutierrez must decide whether the outbreak can be contained without the use of tactical nukes on American soil. Meanwhile, the creatures responsible for the parasites get a foothold in Michigan through a seven-year-old girl, who manifests possession by drawing blue triangles on her dolls. . . . This page-turner builds inexorably to an explosive ending." Publ Wkly

Sigler, Scott

Infected; a novel. Crown Publishers 2008 342p il $24.95

ISBN 978-0-307-40610-1; 0-307-40610-5

LC 2007-41037

Originally released as a podcast in 2006

In this "horror thriller, alien seeds from outer space infect a number of unlucky humans, who develop some unusual symptoms—itchy, blue triangular growths on their skin—that eventually result in the carriers becoming screaming, homicidal maniacs. CIA agent Dew Phillips must find out why these formerly docile citizens are running amok, aided by Margaret Montoya, a Centers for Disease Control epidemiologist, who reported the first of the strange cases. One of the infected, former football player Perry Dawsey, doesn't take any crap from anybody, not even the aliens residing in his body. Sigler . . . leads the reader from one startling detail to the next . . . until even hardened genre fans will find themselves whimpering at each new revelation." Publ Wkly

Sigurosson, Sigurjon Birgir

The **blue** fox; Sjón; translated from the Icelandic by Victoria Cribb. Farrar Straus & Giroux 2013 128 p. $10

ISBN 0374114455; 9780374114459

LC 2012039701

In this novel by Sjón, winner of the 2005 Nordic council Literature Prize, "set against the . . . backdrop of the Icelandic winter, an elusive, enigmatic fox leads a hunter on a transformative quest. At the edge of the hunter's territory, a naturalist struggles to build a life for his charge, a young woman with Down syndrome . By the end . . . none of their lives will be the same." (Publisher's note)

Silber, Joan

Ideas of heaven; a ring of stories. W.W. Norton 2004 250p $23.95

ISBN 0-393-05908-1

LC 2003-24324

"Six elegantly connected stories explore, through first-person narratives, the conflicts and commonalities of love, faith and sex. A minor character in the first story becomes the narrator in the second, and so on, with each story building on its predecessor until they come full circle. . . . Silber uses the device of interwoven narratives beautifully; these lengthy stories can stand alone, but the subtle connections and emotional resonances help create a satisfying structural unity." Publ Wkly

Silber, Joan

The **size** of the world; a novel. W.W. Norton 2008 288p $23.95

ISBN 978-0-393-05909-0; 0-393-05909-X

LC 2008-01342

This "work of fiction consists of interlinked stories where minor or passing characters in one piece become the narrators of others, roaming from WWII Sicily to roaring '20s Siam, and from Vietnam-era Mexico to 9/11-era Bloomington, Ind. All six stories turn on the tensions between home, exile and otherness, but to follow any of the threads would be to give away the subtle connections among the characters, from a male Sicilian-American postcolonialist professor from Hoboken to a Florida woman named Kit who can sum up an old boyfriend as the sort of boy who seemed startled when having sex. At the time his awe and confusion were endearing. The frankness of Silber's characters is deliciously at odds with the delicacy of their observations as they absorb children, affairs, fractured and repaired families and early death in environments familiar and alien to them." Publ Wkly

Silko, Leslie

Gardens in the dunes; a novel. {by} Leslie Marmon Silko. Simon & Schuster 1999 479p $25

ISBN 0-684-81154-5

LC 98-51987

Set in the 19th century this is the "tale of two sisters, the last remaining members of the ancient Sand Lizard tribe. Sister Salt, so called for her light skin, and her younger sister, Indigo, learn all about the hidden, life-sustaining plants of the desert from Grandma Fleet, who teaches them how to live happily with a minimum of material goods and a wealth of knowledge. Such self-sufficiency is essential if they are to stay free from the misery of reservation life, but even so their liberty is put at risk when they travel to the mean little town of Needles, Arizona, where hundreds of Indians gather to dance in anticipation of the arrival of the Messiah. In the chaotic aftermath of the miraculous visitation, the girls lose their mother and grandmother and then are cruelly separated by the authorities." Booklist

Sillitoe, Alan

★ The **loneliness** of the long-distance runner. Knopf 1960 176p

First published 1959 in the United Kingdom

"This collection of short stories portrays life from the point of view of the English working class. The unnamed narrator in the title story, which is probably the best known in the book, is a roguish young man who has been in trouble with authority all his life. He is told by the head of a Borstal institution where he is an inmate that he can reform himself by training to be a long-distance runner. He enters into training, and during practice runs, his thoughts go back to the circumstances that led to his detention. The climax of the story is in a track meet between his penal institution and a private school. The boy easily outruns his competitors but pulls up at the finish line and refuses to cross it, thus revenging himself against the head of the institution and spoiling the victory of the other school." Shapiro. Fic for Youth. 3d edition

Sillitoe, Alan

★ **Saturday** night and Sunday morning. Knopf 1959 239p

First published 1958 in the United Kingdom

This novel's "protagonist, anarchic young Arthur Seaton, lathe operator in a Nottingham bicycle factory, provided a new prototype of the working class Angry Young Man; rebellious, contemptuous towards authority in the form of management, government, the army, and neighbourhood spies, he unleashes his energy on drink and women, with quieter interludes spent fishing in the canal. . . . A landmark in the development of the post-war novel." Oxford Companion to Engl Lit. 6th edition

Silone, Ignazio

★ **Bread** and wine; a new version translated from the Italian by Harvey Fergusson II; with a new preface by the author. Atheneum Pubs. 1962 331p

First published 1937 in the United States by Harper

"The hero, Pietro Spina, returns to his native Abruzzi after fifteen years of exile to continue his antifascist agitation. As he travels through the country, disguised as a priest, he sees the inroads made upon the Italian character by Mussolini's rule. Finding that the underground movement is in chaos and doubting the validity of his old revolutionary slogans, he eventually flees to avoid certain arrest." Reader's Ency. 4d edition

Followed by The seed beneath the snow (1942)

Silva, Daniel

The **mark** of the assassin; a novel. Villard Bks. 1998 465p $25

ISBN 0-679-45563-9

LC 98-5268

"When an airliner is shot down after taking off from New York's Kennedy Airport, an Islamic terrorist group called the Sword of Gaza is immediately blamed for the crime. But CIA operative Michael Osbourne suspects a different perpetrator, a lone assassin with the code name October who, years earlier, took the life of Osbourne's girlfriend in a London confrontation." Publ Wkly

"With concise, vivid character sketches, Silva weaves a swiftly paced, internationally tangled plot." Libr J

Silva, Daniel

The **messenger**. Putnam 2006 388p $25.95

ISBN 0-399-15335-7

LC 2006-367534

A "thriller starring Israeli art restorer and spymaster Gabriel Allon. Ahmed bin Shafiq, a former chief of a clandestine Saudi intelligence unit, targets the Vatican for attack, in particular Pope Paul VII and his top aide, Monsignor Luigi Donati. . . . Shafiq, who now heads his own terrorist network, is allied with a militant Islamic Saudi businessman known as Zizi, a true believer committed to the destruction of all infidels. Gabriel's challenge is to infiltrate Zizi's organization, a task he assigns to a beautiful American art expert, Sarah Bancroft." Publ Wkly

"An engrossing and beautifully written contemporary spy thriller." Booklist

Silva, Daniel

Moscow rules. G.P. Putnam's Sons 2008 433p $26.95

ISBN 978-0-399-15501-7; 0-399-15501-5

LC 2008-18318

"A Russian journalist dies and once more Gabriel Allon, the mysterious Israeli agent/fine picture restorer, ends up back in Moscow. . . . It seems a second Russian journalist wants to tell Allon and only Allon why the first journalist, his coworker, was killed. This meeting never takes place – the second journalist is killed right before Allon can get to him – and in short order, Allon has a full-fledged case on his hands. . . . Allon summons up an Israeli investigative team and he and his fellow agents eventually turn up the name of one Ivan Kharkov, a former KGB colonel. Kharkov has carried over his previous covert training into his new career as an international arms dealer, and one willing to sell to Al-Qaeda. To collect information on him, Allon must persuade Kharkov's wife to betray her husband. . . . Silva's latest is both fast-past thriller with all the appropriate twists and turns and a fascinating look at the inner workings of Russian society today." Houston Press

Silva, Daniel

Portrait of a spy. HarperCollins 2011 455p $26.99

ISBN 978-0-06-207218-4

After failing to stop a suicide bomber attack in London, master art restorer and assassin Gabriel Allon is summoned by the CIA and is faced with an organization riddled with dissent—and ill-equipped to deal with the deadly new face of global jihadist terror.

"Gadgets, back-stabbing machinations and political duplicities lend an aura of realism to the intricate plot." Kirkus

Silva, Daniel

Prince of Fire. Putnam 2005 369p $25.95

ISBN 0-399-15243-1

LC 2004-60066

"Not long after an explosion in Rome destroys the Israeli embassy compound, a file linked to the terrorists behind the bombing surfaces; it contains a remarkably comprehensive account of the career of Gabriel Allon, including the date of his recruitment by the Israeli secret service. Living in Venice and about to embark upon the restoration of a priceless Rubens painting, Gabriel, a talented art restorer and a reluctant spy, must return to Israel and the auspices of the agency bureaucrats. He is assigned the task of identifying the bombers, which eventually results in a face-to-face meeting with Yassar Arafat, the man responsible for the death of Gabriel's child and the maiming of his wife some 10 years earlier. He suspects that Arafat is deeply connected to the Rome bomber, whom Gabriel believes is a third-generation terrorist who has been protected and schooled as a mastermind by Arafat himself. Along with the meticulously detailed plot, Silva . . . provides a clear-eyed chronicle of the endless warfare between the Israelis and the Palestinians." Booklist

Silva, Daniel

The **secret** servant. G.P. Putnam's Sons 2007 385p $25.95

ISBN 978-0-399-15422-5; 0-399-15422-1

LC 2007-17548

"Daniel Silva is a craftsmanlike writer of international thrillers. He has a nice, no-nonsense style; he plots simply, directly and suspensefully; and in Gabriel Allon he has a reliable protagonist." Los Angeles Times Book Rev

Silver, Marisa

The **god** of war. Simon & Schuster 2008 271p $23

ISBN 978-1-4165-6316-7; 1-4165-6316-4

LC 2007-25424

"Twelve-year-old Ares Ramirez has a life as unique as his name. His mother, who has a taste for men who don't stick around, raises Ares and his mentally handicapped brother, Malcolm, on the shores of the isolated Salton Sea in the California desert. Ares is saddled with far too much responsibility while his mother flits through life as a free spirit, leaving him to watch over the brother Ares thinks he damaged by dropping him accidentally as a baby. Ares looks elsewhere for the attention and acceptance he's not getting at home, finally finding it in the kindly librarian who tutors Malcolm and her dangerous foster son, Kevin. Ares's new friend leads him on a path of destruction with a tragic end." Libr J

"Finely wrought characters and an illuminating portrait of the secret world of autism makes for a powerful, often tragic tale." Kirkus

Silver, Marisa

★ **Mary** Coin; A Novel. Marisa Silver. Blue Rider Press 2013 336 p. $26.95

ISBN 0399160701; 9780399160707

LC 2012039861

This novel from Marisa Silver is "inspired by Dorothea Lange's most emblematic Depression-era photo. Her characters are Mary Coin, a struggling migrant mother; Vera Dare, an ambitious young photographer compelled to abandon her own children to work; and Walker Dodge, a contemporary professor of cultural history with a surprising personal connection to Vera's photo of Mary." (Library Journal)

Includes bibliographical references

Silverberg, Robert

The **collected** stories of Robert Silverberg. v1 Bantam Bks. 1992 546p v1 pa $25

ISBN 978-0-553-37068-3; 0-553-37068-5

LC 92-9958

Followed by: v2 The secret sharer (1993); v3 Beyond the safe zone (1994); v4 Road to nightfall (1995); v5 Ringing the changes (1997); v6 Lion time in Timbuctoo (2000)

Silverberg, Robert

The **longest** way home. Eos 2002 294p $25.95

ISBN 0-380-97858-X

LC 2001-55601

"While neither the protagonist of this bildungsroman nor his transformation is remarkable, the land that our young hero journeys through and the exotic creatures that inhabit it testify to the author's rich imagination." Publ Wkly

Silverberg, Robert
★ **Lord** Valentine's castle. Harper & Row 1980 449p

ISBN 9780060780456; 9780451464613; 9780060140267 out of print

LC 79002658

"Majipoor is an enormous planet inhabited by intelligent beings and ruled by a benevolent lord. . . . The story begins as Valentine, a young amnesiac, wanders into the city of Pidruid in time for a festival celebrating a once-in-a-lifetime visit of another Valentine, Lord Valentine, the supreme ruler of the planet. Early in the book readers know what Valentine is slow to understand; he is the real Lord Valentine and the one in power is an imposter. On a coming-of-age journey to Lord Valentine's Castle, gathering friends, supporters, and ultimately troops en route, Valentine discovers his true identity and gains a better understanding of the people and place he is destined to rule. A good story, inventively told, which abounds with adventure and curious characters." SLJ

Followed by Majipoor chronicles

Silverberg, Robert
A **Robert** Silverberg omnibus; The man in the maze; Nightwings; Downward to the Earth. Harper & Row 1981 544p

LC 80-8232

An omnibus edition of three titles first published separately 1969, 1969, and 1970 respectively

In the novel Nightwings Earth is taken over by aliens; the man in the maze dramatizes aspects of alienation and Downward to the Earth employs religious imagery in a story of repentence and rebirth

All three novels in this collection "feature strong but psychologically wounded male protagonists, descriptions of bizarre beings and far-away worlds and imaginative, if sometimes unrealistic plots. . . . For readers who appreciate swiftly-paced action." Voice Youth Advocates

Silverberg, Robert
★ **Roma** eterna. Eos 2003 396p $25.95

ISBN 0-380-97859-8

LC 2002-35416

This is "a what-if history of the world, starting from the premise that the Roman Empire never fell. Spaning 1,500 years, the narrative unfolds in a world without Christianity. It seems that the failure of the ancient Hebrews to escape Pharaonic oppression prevented the rise of mystical religious cults in the province of Syria Palaestina, thereby guaranteeing the survival of Roman hegemony down to the beginning of space travel. Silverberg, who has written numerous popular works of history and archaeology, brings his alternate Rome to life by blending invention with a dazzling array of details borrowed from the annals of the real Rome." N Y Times Book Rev

Simenon, Georges
Inspector Maigret and the killers; translated from the French by Louise Varèse. Doubleday 1954 187p

Original French edition, 1952. Variant title: Maigret and the gangsters

"Inspector Lognon, widely known as 'the most dismal man in the Paris police,' is always trying to solve some spectacular case that will land him with Maigret's Crime Squad on the Quai des Orfevres. Lognon's latest exploit involves a drug stakeout during which he sees a car pull up to the curb and a body dumped out on the pavement. By the time Lognon makes his call, another car has pulled up to retrieve the corpse. Maigret joins Lognon in finding the disappearing body, while events become more outlandish and dangerous. The witty pace featuring kidnappings and shootings, is effectively sustained throughout." Booklist

Simenon, Georges
Maigret and the black sheep; translated from the French by Helen Thomson. Harcourt Brace Jovanovich 1976 158p

Original French edition, 1972

"The victim is a retired carton manufacturer who has been shot, without apparent motive, while sitting at home in his favorite armchair. To {Chief Inspector Maigret's} chagrin, he can find no crack or crevice in the utter respectability of the dead man's life. . . . The season is the end of summer. Parisians are drifting back to the city from their vacations, there is a nip in the air. . . . Maigret sips his beer in several cafés, confers with his faithful colleague Lapointe, and ponders the many facts of this . . . case." New Yorker

Simenon, Georges
Maigret and the fortune-teller; translated by Geoffrey Sainsbury. Harcourt Brace Jovanovich 1989 140p

LC 88-16301

Original French edition, 1944

Maigret "is forewarned of a murder but fails to prevent it. He tracks down the villain by exercising his famous 'capacity for putting himself in other people's shoes.' In this case, the shoes belong to a woebegone old man, apparently senile, who was found at the scene of the crime. Obviously more terrified of his wife and daughter than he is of the thunderous Maigret, the old man piques the policeman's interest and so leads him to the solution." Booklist

Simenon, Georges
★ **Maigret** and the madwoman; translated from the French by Eileen Ellenbogen. Harcourt Brace Jovanovich 1972 176p

Original French edition, 1970

"Maigret exerts himself to make up for his failure to prevent the murder of a nice old lady who had told him of her fears. He goes to Toulon to interview a suspect and generally behaves as a chief superintendent should. Madame Maigret plays a larger part than usual." Barzun. Cat of Crime. Rev and enl edition

Simenon, Georges
Maigret and the Saturday caller; translated by Tony White. Harcourt Brace Jovanovich 1991 124p

LC 90-46032

Original French edition, 1962

"Maigret is visited by a harelipped man who confesses that he wants to murder his wife and her lover but hasn't yet done so. Needless to say, Maigret cannot dismiss the man's plans as the fantasy of a harmless lunatic and begins to probe around the edges, irritated by the handicaps imposed by the public prosecutor's recent restrictions on police powers." Booklist

Simenon, Georges

Maigret and the toy village; translated by Eileen Ellenbogen. Harcourt Brace Jovanovich 1979 139p

LC 79-1843

Original French edition, 1944

In this novel "Maigret, the solemn, slow-moving, yet brilliant Chief Superintendent of the Police Judiciare, is entangled in the most exasperating murder case of his career. A man is slain in a new suburban housing development (the 'toy village' of the title). The prime suspect is his housekeeper, a young woman who has the motive for murder (she stands to inherit the old man's money), plenty of opportunities to execute the crime, and a maddening propensity for keeping Maigret at bay." Booklist

Simenon, Georges

★ **Maigret** and the wine merchants; translated from the French by Eileen Ellenbogen. Harcourt Brace Jovanovich 1971 187p

Original French edition, 1970

"A wealthy wine merchant {in Paris} is shot down. His wife takes the news with complete unsurprise and a shrug of the shoulders. His business associates discuss him as some sort of artifact coolly, unemotionally. His mistresses neither liked nor disliked him. Eventually the murderer comes into Maigret's sight." N Y Times Book Rev

Simenon, Georges

Maigret bides his time; translated by Alastair Hamilton. Harcourt Brace Jovanovich 1985 165p

LC 84-25134

Original French edition, 1965; this translation first published 1966 in the United Kingdom

This novel "combines a delight in the sensual world with an exploration of the horrors of human cruelty. The plot revolves around the murder of master jewel thief and gang leader Manuel Palmari, a criminal Maigret has known for many years and whose death he half-guiltily mourns. The chief suspect is Palmari's young mistress, though Maigret finds many more suspects and motives crowded into the deceased man's life. Maigret's investigation does not end until a welter of vice has been uncovered—and more murder is committed. Vintage Simenon." Booklist

Simenon, Georges

Maigret goes home; translated by Robert Baldick. Harcourt Brace Jovanovich 1989 139p

LC 89-2011

Original French edition, 1931; this translation first published 1940 in the United Kingdom

"The countess of the estate where Maigret grew up drops dead during early mass on All Souls' Day, shocked to death by a fake newspaper report falsely reporting the suicide of her son. Although the estate had been heavily mortgaged to pay for the son's debts and the countess' young lovers, the inheritance is still not inconsiderable, and, of course, there are at least three likely suspects." Booklist

Simenon, Georges

Maigret in Holland; translated by Geoffrey Sainsbury. 2nd ed; Harcourt Brace & Co. 1993 165p

LC 92-30504

Original French edition, 1931; first English translation with title Crime in Holland, published 1940 in the collection Maigret abroad

"Although Maigret speaks no Dutch, he is called to Holland to assist a compatriot, Jean Duclos. Unfortunately, Duclos was present when Conrad Popinga, a former captain in the merchant marine, was murdered, and the Dutch police think Duclos, along with Popinga's wife and sister-in-law, a young sailor, and a local farm girl, is a prime suspect. Once the capable but long-suffering Maigret arrives, he methodically reviews the evidence and questions suspects. . . , Readers will marvel at the inspector's brilliant logic." Booklist

Simenon, Georges

Maigret's memoirs; translated from the French by Jean Stewart. Harcourt Brace Jovanovich 1985 134p

LC 85-8591

Original French edition, 1951; this translation first published 1963 in the United Kingdom

"Inspector Maigret, upset by writer Georges Simenon's 'caricature' of him, decides to correct the world's misconception of his personality and his cases by writing his memoirs. . . . Maigret outlines a few criminal cases, digresses about the Parisian weather, explains his dislike for Simenon, and presents his views on the criminal mind and on life in general in this odd but marvelous 'autobiographical' account." Booklist

Simenon, Georges

The **man** who watched trains go by; a new translation by Marc Romano, D. Thin; introduction by Luc Sante. New York Review Books 2005 203p (New York Review Books classics) pa $12.95

ISBN 978-1-59017-149-3; 1-59017-149-7

LC 2005-8102

Original French edition, 1938

"Kees Popinga is a solid Dutch burgher whose idea of a night on the town is a game of chess at his club. Or so it has always appeared. But one night this model husband and devoted father discovers his boss is bankrupt and that his own carefully tended life is in ruins. Before, he had looked on impassively as the trains to the outside world swept by; now he catches the first train he can to Amsterdam. Not long after that, he commits murder." Publisher's note

Simenon, Georges

A **man's** head; translated by Geoffrey Sainsbury. Penguin Books 2006 170p pa $12

ISBN 0-14-303728-5; 978-0-14-303728-6

LC 2006-41670

Original French edition, 1931; first United States edition published 1940 with title: The patience of Maigret. Also previously published under title: Maigret's war of nerves

Maigret is convinced that Heurtin, a condemned prisoner is innocent. The Inspector persuades officials to allow Heurtin to escape hoping that he will lead Maigret to the real killer.

Simenon, Georges

My friend Maigret; [an Inspector Maigret mystery] translated by Nigel Ryan. Penguin Books 2007 195p pa $13

ISBN 978-0-14-311284-6

LC 2007-25931

Original French edition 1949

"This 1949 outing in Simenon's wonderful Inspector Maigret mystery series finds the sleuth leaving Paris to investigate the murder of a small-time crook who was talking loudly about him just before being killed." Libr J

Simenon, Georges

Strangers in the house; ttanslated by Geoffrey Sainsbury; with revisions by David Watson & others; introduction by P.D. James. New York Review Books 2006 194p (New York Review Books classics) pa $14

ISBN 978-1-59017-194-3; 1-59017-194-2

LC 2005-36189

Original French edition, 1940; this translation first published 1951 in the United Kingdom

"Dirty, drunk, unloved, and unloving, Hector Loursat has been a bitter recluse for eighteen long years—ever since his wife abandoned him and their newborn child to run off with another man. Once a successful lawyer, Loursat now guzzles burgundy and buries himself in books, taking little notice of his teenage daughter or the odd things going on in his vast and evermore-dilapidated mansion. But one night the sound of a gunshot penetrates the padded walls of Loursat's study, and he is forced to investigate. What he stumbles on is a murder. Soon Loursat discovers that his daughter and her friends have been leading a dangerous secret life. He finds himself strangely drawn to this group of young people, and when one of them is accused of the murder, he astonishes the world by taking up the young man's defense." Publisher's note

Simmons, Dan

Black Hills. Reagan Arthur Books 2010 487p $25.99

ISBN 978-0-316-00698-9; 0-316-00698-X

LC 2009-31827

"When we meet Paha Sapa (that's 'Black Hills' in the language of the Lakota Sioux) in 1934, he's just another old Indian powder man toiling beneath architect Gutzon Borglum at Mount Rushmore, helping carve the faces of four Wasicun ('white') presidents into his forefathers' sacred mountain. But Paha Sapa is no septuagenarian Tonto. . . . . [He hatches] a plan to seed Borglum's monument with dynamite and destroy it during a visit from FDR, reclaiming Six Grandfathers for his people. This mission is political and personal – as a young brave, Paha Sapa touched the body of George Armstrong Custer after he perished at Little Big Horn, and has carried the soldier's ghost with him ever since. . . . [He] hopes to reassert his native American identity with one mighty explosion." Christ Sci Monit

"In his ability to create complex characters and pair them with suspenseful situations, Simmons stands almost unmatched among his contemporaries." Publ Wkly

Simmons, Dan

Drood; a novel. Little, Brown and Co. 2009 775p $26.99

ISBN 978-0-316-00702-3; 0-316-00702-1

LC 2008-24501

"In this creepy intertextual tale of professional jealousy and possible madness, Wilkie Collins tells of his friendship and rivalry with Charles Dickens, and of the mysterious phantasm named Edwin Drood, who pursues them both. Drood, cadaverous and pale, first appears at the scene of a railway accident in which Dickens was one of the few survivors; later, Dickens and Collins descend into London's sewer in search of his lair. Meanwhile, a retired police detective warns Collins that Drood is responsible for more than three hundred murders, and that he will destroy Dickens in his quest for immortality. Collins is peevish, vain, and cruel, and the most unreliable of narrators: an opium addict, prone to nightmarish visions. The narrative is overlong, with discarded subplots and red herrings, but Simmons, a master of otherworldly suspense, cleverly explores envy's corrosive effects." New Yorker

Simmons, Dan

★ **Endymion**. Bantam Bks. 1996 486p

ISBN 9780553572940; 9780553100204 out of print

LC 95033191

"The protagonist, a good-hearted soldier named Raul Endymion, sets off on a quest with historic consequences: he must keep from harm a young girl who holds the key to a rebirth of human civilization. Arrayed against him is the power of the Pax, a militarized Catholic Church that offers its adherents a literal resurrection of the body. It is Mr. Simmons's inspiration to embody the Pax in the person of Father Captain Federico de Soya, a starship commander who pursues Endymion and the young girl from one exotic planet to the next." N Y Times Book Rev

Followed by The rise of Endymion (1997)

Simmons, Dan

The **fall** of Hyperion. Doubleday 1990 517p

ISBN 0-385-24950-0

LC 89-37438

"While the worlds of the Hegemony fight a desperate war in space against the Ouster rebels who threaten galactic unity, a group of seven pilgrims on the planet Hyperion wage their own war within the Tombs of Time, a mysterious artifact which conceals a hideous creature whose freedom means death for humanity. In this sequel to Hyperion, Simmons weaves together many strands of a complex plot with lucidity and poetic imagination." Libr J

Simmons, Dan

Flashback; a novel. Little, Brown 2011 554p $27.99

ISBN 978-0-316-00696-5; 0-316-00696-3

LC 2010-48842

"Flashback is at its strongest when its lurking societal doomsday treatise is kept in the background and Bottom's effort to solve the mystery—and survive solving it—is kept to the fore. Fortunately, that accounts for most of the novel, making Flashback worth the read the first time around." BookPage

Simmons, Dan

   Hyperion. Doubleday 1989 481p

   ISBN 0-385-24949-7

LC 88-33407

"On the world called Hyperion, beyond the law of the Hegemony of Man, there waits the creature called the Shrike. There are those who worship it. There are those who fear it. And there are those who have vowed to destroy it. In the Valley of the Time Tombs, where huge, brooding structures move backward through time, the Shrike waits for them all. On the eve of Armageddon, with the entire galaxy at war, seven pilgrims set forth on a final voyage to Hyperion seeking the answers to the unsolved riddles of their lives. Each carries a desperate hope-and a terrible secret. And one may hold the fate of humanity in his hands." Publisher's note

   Followed by The fall of Hyperion

Simmons, Dan

   ★ **Ilium**. Eos 2003 576p $25.95

   ISBN 0-380-97893-8

LC 2002-44791

"For answers to the mysteries laid out in 'Ilium'—from the true identity of the Olympian gods to the fate of robots and humans and of the 'little green men' on Mars for whom communication means death—you will have to wait for the promised sequel. For now, matching wits with Simmons and his lively creations should be reward enough." N Y Times Book Rev

   Followed by Olympos (2005)

Simmons, Dan

   Muse of fire. Subterranean Press 2008 105p $35

   ISBN 978-1-59606-181-1; 1-59606-181-2

In the "far future, Earth is a mausoleum and the far-flung human race occupies the lowest level of a complex interstellar hierarchy. The Earth's Men travel to distant worlds and perform Shakespeare before human servants and slaves, bringing them some moments of pleasure and notions of Earth's lost glory. When aliens take an interest, the Earth's Men find themselves giving command performances of King Lear, Hamlet and 'the Scottish play' for a series of increasingly important alien species, with evidence that the fate of all humanity may rest on the quality of their work. This finely crafted novella is a perfect example of Simmons's many strengths." Publ Wkly

Simmons, Dan

   Olympos. HarperCollins 2005 690p hardcover o.p. pa $7.99

   ISBN 0-380-97894-6; 0-380-81793-4 pa

LC 2005-40024

   Sequel to Ilium (2003)

In this sequel to Ilium, "posthumans masquerading as the Greek gods and living on Mars travel back and forth through time and alternate universes to interfere in the real Trojan War, employing a resurrected late 20th-century classics professor, Thomas Hockenberry, as their tool. Meanwhile, the last remaining old-style human beings on a far-future Earth must struggle for survival against a variety of hostile forces. Superhuman entities with names like Prospero, Caliban and Ariel lay complex plots, using human beings as game pieces. From the outer solar system, an advanced race of semiorganic Artificial Intelligences, called moravecs, observe Earth and Mars in consternation, trying to make sense of the situation, hoping to shift the balance of power before out-of-control quantum forces destroy everything. This is powerful stuff, rich in both high-tech sense of wonder and literary allusions, but Simmons is in complete control of his material as half a dozen baroque plot lines smoothly converge on a rousing and highly satisfying conclusion." Publ Wkly

Simmons, Dan

   ★ The **rise** of Endymion; a novel. Bantam Bks. 1997 579p

   ISBN 9780553106527 out of print; 9780553572988

LC 97005658

   Sequel to Endymion (1996)

   "In 3131, most of the galaxy is populated by born-again Christians and ruled by the Catholic pope. Nonbelievers are persecuted and forced to accept the cruciform parasite, which allows people to be resurrected. The biggest threat to the establishment is Aenea, a young female architectural apprentice who teaches peace and the way to immense knowledge of the heart and mind. Aided by her lover, Raul Endymion, Aenea exposes organized religion as a parasite of the Core—the sentient evolution of the World Wide Web." (Libr J)

   In this concluding volume of the author's series about a far-future interstellar society, "most of the galaxy is populated by born-again Christians and ruled by the Catholic pope. Nonbelievers are persecuted and forced to accept the cruciform parasite, which allows people to be resurrected. The biggest threat to the establishment is Aenea, a young female architectural apprentice who teaches peace and the way to immense knowledge of the heart and mind. Aided by her lover, Raul Endymion, Aenea exposes organized religion as a parasite of the Core—the sentient evolution of the World Wide Web." Libr J

Simmons, Dan

   ★ The **terror**; a novel. Little, Brown and Co. 2007 769p $25.99

   ISBN 978-0-316-01744-2; 0-316-01744-2

LC 2006-14608

   This historical suspense novel follows the "difficulties of the dwindling remains of Sir John Franklin's failed 1840s mission to find the Northwest Passage. However, in addition to scurvy, frostbite, botulism, snow-blindness, and threats of mutiny, the crews of HMS Terror and HMS Erebus are harried by some enormous Thing out on the ice. The story is told from the viewpoints of several members of the ships' crews, with emphasis on Terror captain Francis Crozier and Erebus surgeon Harry Goodsir." Libr J

   "A deeply absorbing story that combines awe-inspiring myth, grinding horror and historically accurate adventure." Seattle Times

Simon, Claude

The **trolley**; translated from the French by Richard Howard. New Press (NY) 2002 112p

ISBN 1-56584-734-2

LC 2002-19026

Original French edition, 2001

This "slim but dense new novel is indebted to Proust in everything from its labyrinthine, parentheses-laden sentences to its meditations on memory and painstaking representations of a bygone time." N Y Times Book Rev

Simone, Alina

Note to self; Alina Simone. 1st ed. Faber and Faber, Inc. 2013 256 p. (hardcover) $25

ISBN 0865478996; 9780865478992

LC 2012048024

In this novel, by Alina Simone, "Anna Krestler is adrift. . . . Despite the exhortations of Leslie, her friend and volunteer life coach, Anna seeks refuge in the back alleys of Craigslist, where she connects with . . . an adherent of a nebulous movement known as Nowism that occupies the most self-absorbed fringes of the art world. . . . But when Anna's twenty-seven-year-old roommate . . . announces her pregnancy, it forces Anna to confront reality." (Publisher's note)

Simonson, Helen

Major Pettigrew's last stand; a novel. Random House 2010 358p

ISBN 1-4000-6893-2; 978-1-4000-6893-7

LC 2009-22231

This novel is set in an English village. Major Pettigrew, a widower, "leads a quiet life valuing the proper things that Englishmen have lived by for generations: honor, duty, decorum, and a properly brewed cup of tea. But then his brother's death sparks an unexpected friendship with Mrs. Jasmina Ali, the . . . shopkeeper from the village. Drawn together by their shared love of literature and the loss of their respective spouses, the Major and Mrs. Ali soon find their friendship blossoming into something more. But village society insists on embracing him as the quintessential local and her as the permanent foreigner. Can their relationship survive the risks one takes when pursuing happiness in the face of culture and tradition?" (Publisher's note)

"As with the polished work of Alexander McCall Smith, there is never a dull moment but never a discordant note either. Still, this book feels fresh despite its conventional blueprint. Its main characters are especially well drawn, and Ms. Simonson makes them as admirable as they are entertaining." N Y Times (Late N Y Ed)

Simpson, Dorothy

Dead and gone; an inspector Luke Thanet novel. Scribner 2000 247p

ISBN 0-684-86336-7

LC 99-39091

First published 1999 in the United Kingdom

"Inspector Thanet is the very model of the paternalistic English detective, offering comfort to the relatives of a woman who was pushed down a well to her death, while shrewdly picking apart every detail of their alibis until he lays bare every dirty little secret in this affluent, complacent household. Tactful and discreet, Thanet is also relentless as he guides the investigation backward in time. . . . A perfect puzzle, perfectly solved." N Y Times Book Rev

Simpson, Dorothy

Dead by morning. Scribner 1989 277p

LC 89-6270

"Inspector Thanet is faced with a murder at a luxurious English country inn and an overzealous superintendent who is busily reorganizing with all the annoying haste of the newly promoted." Booklist

Simpson, Dorothy

Doomed to die. Scribner 1991 245p

LC 91-4185

"Inspector Thanet's mother-in-law has had a heart attack; Sergeant Lineham's wife is clinically depressed; and Superintendent Draco has just learned that his beloved wife, Angharad, has leukemia. Among the civilian populace of this suddenly blighted Kentish town, a young nanny is stricken with a ruptured appendix, and the woman who takes her place, a tormented artist with an abusive husband and a dying mother, is found murdered." N Y Times Book Rev

"Confirmed clue-sniffers should be ready for a surprise here: both the solution and the sinner are shockers, though eminently fair ones." Booklist

Simpson, Dorothy

★ **Last** seen alive; a Luke Thanet mystery. Scribner 1985 220p

LC 85-14530

The author "invites us to reflect on the murder by strangling of a lovely woman, widowed, who is spending one night only in a small Kentish village, ostensibly to hear a violin recital. What could possibly account for a killing under such conditions? The congenial pair of Thanet and Lineham uncovers several 'pasts,' 20 years distant, when all parties were teen-agers in school. Dramatic surprises punctuate a piece of detection in which the ratiocination is neither static nor obvious." Barzun. Cat of Crime. Rev and enl edition

Simpson, Dorothy

No laughing matter. Scribner 1993 262p

LC 93-19799

"Simpson turns out her usual high-caliber tale and gives the reader more to ponder than a simple mystery. Her shrewd understanding of what makes humans tick results in a story that is both entertaining and thought-provoking." Booklist

Simpson, Dorothy

Once too often; an Inspector Luke Thanet novel. Scribner 1998 223p

ISBN 978-0061011955

LC 97-32513

In this Thanet mystery, an "unlikable woman named Jessica Dander, a reporter for a newspaper in Kent, is found lying at the foot of the stairs in her home, her neck broken. Even though the death appears to be an accident, any number of people might have killed her: the husband she humiliated, the lover she annoyed, the teen-age admirer she fascinated. With the exception of Thanet, a thoughtful man with a rich emotional history, the characters are well observed without being especially complex." N Y Times Book Rev

Simpson, Helen

In the driver's seat; stories. Alfred A. Knopf 2007 177p $22

ISBN 978-0-307-26522-7; 0-307-26522-6

LC 2006-37215

"Helen Simpson is mordantly funny and unafraid of life's big issues, such as love, aging, and war . . . . Vigorously written." Atlantic

Simpson, Mona

Anywhere but here. Knopf 1987 406p

LC 86-45282

The "novel opens with its two heroines, Adele and her daughter Ann, fleeing their provincial home-town in Wisconsin for a fresh start in California. . . . Adele is both protector and manipulator, encouraging Ann's success as a child star but also displaying her own unrealistic expectations and selfish motives. Ann tolerates her mother's lying and eccentricity, but she longs for a rootedness her mother cannot give her. The . . . flashbacks to stories told by Adele's Wisconsin relatives give us a sense of the home they have left behind, and the disparity between it and their new home." Libr J

"Any single episode could stand on its own, but Simpson keeps piling them on, building with strength and grace." Booklist

Simpson, Mona

Off Keck Road. Knopf 2000 167p

ISBN 0-375-41010-4

LC 00-40569

"When Bea Maxwell returns to her small home town, in 1964, after college and a stint at a big-city ad agency, she wants to believe that this is not the end of her story—that the chapter including 'the startling redemption' is still to come. But what follows is less a story than a catalogue of fragile moments that never crystallize into actual events. Bea wrestles with the propriety of a woman telephoning a man, flirts awkwardly with a priest, and deflects a sexual advance from her married boss, to her regret. It's not easy to write a novel in which the central tragedy is that nothing happens, but the author uses the cumulative power of small details to convince us that Bea's stalled life is a life worth knowing." New Yorker

Simsion, Graeme

The Rosie project; a novel. Graeme Simsion. Simon & Schuster 2013 304 p. (hardcover) $24

ISBN 1476729085; 9781476729084; 9781476729091

LC 2013000364

This book focuses on genetics professor Don Tillman's search for a wife. His "devised solution is the Wife Project: dating only those who 'match' his idiosyncratic standards as determined by an exacting questionnaire. His plans take a backseat when he meets Rosie, a bartender who wants him to help her determine her birth father's identity. His rigidity and myopic worldview prevents him from seeing her as a possible love interest, but he nonetheless agrees to help." (Publishers Weekly)

Sinclair, April

Coffee will make you black. Hyperion 1994 239p hardcover o.p.

LC 93-13271

This novel's protagonist "is Jean ('Stevie') Stevenson, a spunky 11-year-old when the story begins; a high-school student when it concludes. The setting is Chicago, circa 1965-70. . . . Raised by a strict, if well-meaning, mother and an affectionate, if vague, father, Stevie soon finds herself caught up in one of the many riddles of youth: to be cool or be square. . . . Meanwhile, she is listening to Dr. Martin Luther King and Malcolm X and liberating herself from the confines of her upbringing and her fear of being 'different.'" Booklist

"Sinclair gives a realistic portrayal of personal awakening during a politically tumultuous time." Publ Wkly

Sinclair, Upton

★ The jungle; introduction by Jane Jacobs; afterword by Anthony Arthur. Modern Library pbk. ed., Centennial ed.; Modern Library 2006 xxii, 388p pa $9.95

ISBN 978-0-8129-7623-6; 0-8129-7623-1

LC 2007-279794

First published 1906 by Doubleday, Page

"Jurgis Rudkus, an immigrant from Lithuania, arrives in Chicago with his father, his fiancée, and her family. He is determined to make a life for his bride in the new country. The deplorable conditions in the stockyards and the harrowing experiences of impoverished workers are vividly described by the author." Shapiro. Fic for Youth. 3d edition

Includes bibliographical references

Singer, Isaac Bashevis

★ Collected stories: A friend of Kafka to Passions. Library of America 2004 856p $35

ISBN 1-931082-62-6

LC 2003-66057

The sixty-five short stories in this volume have appeared in the three books: A friend of Kafka and other stories (1970); A crown of feathers and other stories (1973); Passions and other stories (1975).

Singer, Isaac Bashevis

★ Collected stories: Gimpel the fool to The letter writer; [Ilan Stavans is the editor of this volume] Library of America 2004 789p $35

ISBN 1-931082-61-8

LC 2003-66055

The fifty-four short stories in this volume have appeared in the four books: Gimpel the fool & other stories (1955); The Spinoza of Market Street (1966); Short Friday & other stories (1964); and The séance & other stories (1968). Gimpel the fool & other stories is entered separately.

Singer, Isaac Bashevis

Collected stories: One night in Brazil to The death of Methuselah. Library of America 2004 899p $35

ISBN 1-931082-63-4

LC 2003-66081

Most of the short stories in this volume have appeared in the six books: Old love (1979); The collected stories of Isaac Bashevis Singer (1982); Image & other stories (1985); Gifts (1985); and The death of Methuselah & other stories (1988). Also included are thirteen uncollected stories at the end of the volume. The collected stories of Isaac Bashevis Singer and The death of Methuselah are entered separately.

Singer, Isaac Bashevis
 Enemies, a love story. Farrar, Straus & Giroux 1972 280p
  ISBN 0-374-14830-9
  Originally written in Yiddish, 1966
 "The book has the surface gaiety, ribaldry and surprise of a medieval fabliau. Yet the New York subways, telephone calls, Bronx Zoo, bus trip to the Adirondacks are solidly, meticulously real. Herman's three women expand into mythic dimension. . . . Whether or not you accept its ending, {this} is a brilliant, unsettling novel." Newsweek

Singer, Isaac Bashevis
 The **estate**. Farrar, Straus & Giroux 1969 374p
  Sequel to The manor (1967)
 This novel covers the last years of the nineteenth century. It explores the lives of a Polish Jewish family who have emerged from the ghettos to seek a new life in a country that is itself struggling to emerge from a feudal past.
 "Even in their manner of dying, Singer's characters seem to be literally swept away by storms of passion. Indeed, the only thing that keeps the book from disintegrating into an anthology of melodramatic episodes is Singer's unfaltering stylistic control." N Y Times Book Rev

Singer, Isaac Bashevis
 The **family** Moskat; translated from the Yiddish by A.H. Gross. Knopf 1950 611p
 "Panoramic in sweep, the novel follows many characters and story lines in depicting Jewish life in Warsaw from 1911 to the late 1930s. Singer examines Hasidism, Orthodoxy, the rise of secularism, the breakdown of 19th-century traditions, assimilation, Marxism, and Zionism." Merriam-Webster's Ency of Lit

Singer, Isaac Bashevis
 An **Isaac** Bashevis Singer reader. Farrar, Straus & Giroux 1971 560p
 This anthology "contains among works previously published in journals and other collections, 15 short stories, a novel 'The magician of Lublin,' and four episodes not included in the English translation of 'In my father's court.'" Booklist

Singer, Isaac Bashevis
 ★ The **magician** of Lublin; translated from the Yiddish by Elaine Gottlieb and Joseph Singer. Farrar, Straus & Giroux 2010 246p
  ISBN 978-0-374-53254-3; 0-374-53254-0
  Originally serialized 1959 in Yiddish newspaper; first published in book form 1960 by Noonday Press
 "The novel is set in late 19th-century Poland. It concerns Yasha Mazur, an itinerant professional conjurer, tightrope walker, and hypnotist. He loves five women, including his barren and pious wife. To support himself, his assorted women, and his future plans to escape to Italy, he attempts a robbery and fails. Yasha has a crisis of conscience and returns to his wife, becoming a recluse. People begin to refer to him as Jacob the Penitent, and they flock to him as if to a holy man." Merriam-Webster's Ency of Lit

Singer, Isaac Bashevis
 Shadows on the Hudson; translated by Joseph Sherman. Farrar, Straus & Giroux 1998 548p $28
  ISBN 0-374-26186-5
            LC 97-18677
  Originally serialized 1957-1958 in Yiddish newspaper
 A novel "about a postwar circle of emigres who gather for Sabbath dinners in the Upper West Side apartment of the wealthy Boris Makaver. The events are unceasingly tempestuous: Grein, an investor with a passionate streak, runs off to Miami with Anna, Makaver's daughter (both are married); Luria, whom Anna abandoned, begins to have visions of his first wife, Sonia, who died in the camps; Solomon, Makaver's oldest friend, re-establishes contact with his first wife, who left him for a Nazi; and so on. Nothing that happens, however, is so pressing that it cannot be interrupted for fierce argument—about sin, the dead, lost pieties, God's betrayals." New Yorker

Singer, Israel Joshua
 ★ The **brothers** Ashkenazi; [by] I. J. Singer; translated from the Yiddish by Maurice Samuel. Knopf 1936 642p
 "Deals with the rise and decay of the textile city of Lodz, Poland, and with the fortunes of the Polish-Jewish brothers, Max and Jacob Ashkenazi, whose personalities gradually come to dominate the life of the town. . . . What gives the book its significance is not the picture of nineteenth-century Jewish family life, and not the characterizations of the two brothers, but the clear exposition of the class struggle of which Max and Jacob form unconscious parts." New Yorker

Sinha, Indra
 ★ **Animal's** people. Simon & Schuster 2008 374p $25
  ISBN 978-1-4165-7878-9; 1-4165-7878-1
           LC 2007-42118
 "Animal is a teenage boy who lives on the streets of the Indian city of Khaufpur. He goes around on all fours since his spine is badly damaged; he cannot walk normally. As an infant, he was one of the thousands of victims of a poison gas leak at an American-owned company, here just called 'the Kampani.' Animal also lost his parents 'that night' (as the local people refer to the horrible event). Animal has a lively mind and a way with words, some of them angry and profane, some of them bitterly funny, as he gets caught up in the struggle of those in Khaufpur who seek long-delayed justice from the Kampani. Sinha . . . has clearly based his story on the human and environmental disaster at the Union Carbide factory in Bhopal in 1984. The result is a gripping novel that also reminds us of a continuing real-life tragedy." Libr J

Sinisalo, Johanna

Troll; a love story. translated from the Finnish by Herbert Lomas. Grove Press 2004 278p pa $12

ISBN 0-8021-4129-3 pa

LC 2003-69113

Original French edition 2000; this translation first published 2003 in the United Kingdom with title: Not before sundown

"Sinisalo handles all this mythic conflict in an admirably matter-of-fact way; her main innovations have to do with the novel's narrative structure. She has all the players drawn into Angel's dark fairy-tale intrigue relate their part in short first-person snippets, which are then intercut with reference materials, of both online and print vintage, recounting the Finnish history of troll-sightings and the symbolic significance of the forest creatures in the nation's myth and folklore." Washington Post Book World

Sittenfeld, Curtis

The **man** of my dreams; a novel. Random House 2006 272p $22.95

ISBN 1-400-06476-7

LC 2005-52910

"The exciting thing about Sittenfeld, aside from her remarkably lucid, incisive prose is thet she has the potential to carve out a new place, based largely on the strength of that prose, for every woman who wants to write (or read) good fiction about growing up and messing up—just the way the boys do—without being issued a stigma and a cutesy cover." San Francisco Chronicle

Sittenfeld, Curtis

Prep; a novel. Random House 2005 406p hardcover o.p. pa $13.95

ISBN 1-4000-6231-4; 0-8129-7235-X pa

LC 2004-46858

During the late 1980s, a fourteen-year-old leaves her middle-class Indiana family to enroll in an elite New England boarding school, becoming a shrewd observer of the rituals and mores of upper-class Easterners.

"Lee Fiora, a scholarship student at the prestigious Ault School (not Ault Academy, as her parents embarrassingly refer to it), negotiates her days there in a blaze of self-consciousness that is, by turns, hilarious and excruciating: 'I believed then that if you had a good encounter with a person, it was best not to see them again for as long as possible.' And yet she becomes an expert on the rituals that govern the rarefied microenvironment in which she finds herself: the students' fondness for catchphrases like 'therein lies the paradox' and 'LMC' (lower middle class); the taboo against enthusiasm for anything other than sports; the fact that the school always sings 'God be with you till we meet again' at chapel before breaks. In the end, Lee's incisive vision of herself and others is her downfall but also—as this richly textured narrative suggests—her greatest gift." New Yorker

Sittenfeld, Curtis

★ **Sisterland**; a novel. Curtis Sittenfeld. 1st ed. Random House Inc. 2013 416 p. (hardcover) $27

ISBN 1400068312; 9781400068319

LC 2012043726

In this novel, by Curtis Sittenfeld, "Kate and her identical twin sister, Violet, knew that they were unlike everyone else. Kate and Vi were born with . . . innate psychic abilities concerning future events and other people's secrets. Though Vi embraced her visions, Kate did her best to hide them. Now, years later, their different paths have led them both back to their hometown of St. Louis." (Publisher's note)

"The author turns conventions on their collective head and creates a world that is familiar, maddening, alluring, and, ultimately, guardedly hopeful." LJ

Sjowall, Maj

Cop killer; the story of a crime. {by} Maj Sjöwall and Per Wahlöö; translated from the Swedish by Thomas Teal. Pantheon Bks. 1975 296p

Original Swedish edition, 1974

"A divorced woman is murdered, has 'disappeared,' but Martin Beck, Chief Detective Inspector, is called in from Stockholm to investigate. Prime suspect is a former convict who lived near the victim, Sigbrit; and her ex-husband, ex-ship captain, may also be guilty. It takes a midnight shoot-out between three cops and two teenagers to help speed the identification of the real killer." Best Sellers

Sjowall, Maj

★ The **laughing** policeman; [by] Maj Sjöwall and Per Wahlöö; translated from the Swedish by Alan Blair. Pantheon Bks. 1970 211p

Original Swedish edition, 1968

In this Martin Beck mystery "a Stockholm city bus is found one rainy night with a cargo of bullet-riddled corpses. Nothing unites the passengers that could explain the mass murder, but one of the victims is a young colleague from the homicide division. . . . The gloomy weather of the Swedish winter, the commercialization of Christmas, Vietnam War protests, and the low morale of the much-criticized police leave Beck and his harassed colleagues with not much to laugh about. The atmosphere and ingenious plotting of the novel make it one of the best in the series." Murphy. Ency of Murder and Mystery

Sjowall, Maj

The **locked** room; {by} Maj Sjöwall and Per Wahlöö: translated from the Swedish by Paul Britten Austin. Pantheon Bks. 1973 311p

Original Swedish edition, 1972

"A man commits suicide or is murdered in a completely locked room {in Stockholm}. He is shot but there is no weapon. Martin Beck rises from his sick bed to handle this situation." Best Sellers

Sjowall, Maj

The **man** on the balcony; the story of a crime. {by} Maj Sjöwall and Per Wahlöö; translated from the Swedish by Alan Blair. Pantheon Bks. 1968 180p

Original Swedish edition, 1967

"The chief problem is child murder in Stockholm, and it is a macabre race with death when the only clues are disturbing and intangible for Beck and for the 75-man force assigned to help him." Libr J

Sjowall, Maj

Murder at the Savoy; {by} Maj Sjöwall and Per Wahlöö; translated from the Swedish by Amy and Ken Knoespel. Pantheon Bks. 1971 216p

Original Swedish edition, 1970

"In the dining room of the posh Savoy hotel in Malmö, Viktor Palmgren's address is interrupted when a killer guns him down, then escapes through a window. Was the wealthy industrialist murdered for personal reasons—or for political motives related to his arms shipments to Africa? Once again Chief Inspector Martin Beck of Swedish National Police goes into action." Saturday Rev

Skarmeta, Antonio

The **dancer** and the thief; a novel. translated from the Spanish by Katherine Silver. W. W. Norton 2008 300p $24.95

ISBN 978-0-393-06494-0; 0-393-06494-8

LC 2007-33340

Original Spanish edition, 2003

"Though Skarmeta scarcely ranks at the very top of Latin America's remarkably distinguished and varied literary elite, he is a serious writer to whom the death and rebirth of democracy in his native Chile is an endlessly compelling subject.... Though the ending that Skarmeta gives his characters falls well short of happy, the Chile that he portrays herein is vibrant and strong." Washington Post Book World

Skibell, Joseph

A **curable** romantic; a novel. Algonquin Books of Chapel Hill 2010 593p $26.95

ISBN 978-1-56512-929-0

LC 2010-18605

Skibell "Skibell plays fast and loose with the intermingling of historical fact and fiction, giving Sigmund Freud his own resurrection, as well as Esperanto founder Dr. L.L. Zamenhof, and others. The past here is bathed in a soft-focus filter, cloaked in gaslights and cigar smoke, brought to life with stylistic flair and linguistic pizazz, complete with multilingual translations and breathless enthusiasm. Sammelsohn, like Zelig, is there to see it all." Dallas Morning News

Skinner, B. F.

★ **Walden** two. Macmillan 1948 266p

"Unlike most post-World War II science fiction, which considered social control by psychological conditioning to be a form of hell on Earth, Skinner presented it grandly as utopian. The structure of the story (which, as a story, doesn't amount to much) is a debate between an advocate of human free choice and a champion of behavioral manipulation, which is offered as the answer to all of society's ills." Anatomy of Wonder 4

Skvorecky, Josef

When Eve was naked; stories of a life's journey. Farrar, Straus & Giroux 2002 352p

ISBN 0-374-14975-5 $25

LC 2002-20652

"Like memory, the collection is kaleidoscopic, shifting perspectives, hurtling jerkily through time, filtering its narrative through the author's momentary preoccupations. Written over a period of 50 years, the stories read to some

extent like a diary, capturing an emotional landscape in lucid detail." N Y Times Book Rev

Skyhorse, Brando

The **Madonnas** of Echo Park; a novel. Free Press 2010 199p $23

ISBN 978-1-4391-7080-9; 1-4391-7080-0

LC 2009-34403

"By having each chapter introduce a fresh story and a new perspective, Skyhorse propels the reader through the novel at a breakneck pace. And in each section, readers are rewarded with a deeper layer, and a new connection, that enriches the plot. While the novel pivots around Mexican-Americans in L.A., Skyhorse uses elegant prose and vivid storytelling to tackle questions surrounding culture, belonging, and identity that haunt every immigrant community." Christ Sci Monit

Slattery, Brian Francis

Liberation; being the adventures of the Slick Six after the collapse of the United States of America. Tor 2008 299p pa $14.95

ISBN 978-0-7653-2046-9; 0-7653-2046-0

LC 2008-31020

Slattery's novel "has many brilliant ideas, but its depiction of a 21st century revival of slavery is really what burns it into your memory.... It's a book that rewards attention, and you'll find yourself flipping back after you finish it to find the best parts of its off-kilter odyssey and piece together new connections between its huge and memorable cast of characters. It's also a book that gets even better on the second read." io9

Slattery, Brian Francis

Spaceman blues; a love song. Tor 2007 219p $22.95; pa $12.95

ISBN 978-0-7653-1610-3; 0-7653-1610-2; 978-0-7653-1614-1 pa; 0-7653-1614-5 pa

LC 2007-9543

This novel is a "welcome Band-Aid for those still mourning the loss of Kurt Vonnegut and his uniquely wacky, satirical brand of sci-fi. There's also a touch of Paul Auster's flair for genre blending and New York mythologizing... A strange and whimsical mash note to the city, Slattery's apocalyptome proves that this newcomer is as thoughtful and irreverent as doomsayers come." Time Out New York

Slaughter, Karin

Beyond reach. Delacorte Press 2007 404p $25

ISBN 978-0-385-33947-6; 0-385-33947-X

LC 2007-9359

"Slaughter's latest page-turner offers both wrenching emotional highs and lows and a gripping plot, but what gives it emotional heft is its unwavering focus on the grim social ills of the rural South." Booklist

Slaughter, Karin

Fallen; a novel. Delacorte Books 2011 387p $26

ISBN 978-0-345-52820-9; 0-345-52820-4

LC 2011-04941

"Georgia Bureau of Investigation agent Faith Mitchell arrives at the Atlanta house of her widowed mother, Evelyn, to find serious trouble: her mother, a retired police captain, is missing; a dead man is lying on the laundry room floor; and an Asian man is holding her mother's pistol to a Hispanic man's head in Evelyn's bedroom. More violence follows. Faith's partner, Will Trent, tries to gather clues without stepping on any jurisdictional toes in the ensuing investigation, but Will fears that Evelyn's kidnapping is tied to a corruption scandal involving Evelyn's past as a narcotics officer, an angle he knows Faith doesn't want to consider. Will's deepening friendship with Dr. Sara Linton, currently working in an Atlanta E.R. and one of the few people able to crack his protective shell, adds depth. Family-biological, professional, and everything in between-plays a key role in a thriller sure to please Slaughter's many fans." Publ Wkly

Slavnikova, Olga
2017; translated from the Russian by Marian Schwartz. Overlook/Duckworth 2010 414p $27.95
ISBN 9781590203095
Original Russian edition, 2006
"Slavnikova is a thoroughly modern writer; her cutting humor and over-the-top descriptions of classic Russian characters and nouveau-riche thugs recall Russian-born American writer Gary Shteyngart. . . . Though the plot twists can be outlandish, Slavnikova's sensitivity to detail, character, and the human condition keeps 2017 clear in the reader's mind, long after the excursion is over." ForeWord

Sledge, Michael
The **more** I owe you; a novel. Counterpoint 2010 328p pa $15.95
ISBN 978-1-58243-576-3; 1-58243-576-6
LC 2010-03258
This "cinematic novel is as lush and fecund as the jungle itself, with its innumerable fruits, ferns, and hidden dangers, leaving readers with the indelible image of a brilliant, tormented woman writing tirelessly through the tropic night by the light of a kerosene lamp. . . . Strong and intoxicating." Booklist

The **Sleeper** wakes; Harlem Renaissance stories by women. edited and with an introduction by Marcy Knopf; foreword by Nellie Y. McKay. Rutgers Univ. Press 1993 xxxix, 277p
LC 92-30446
"This anthology rescues short stories written by the women writers of the Harlem Renaissance from archival obscurity. . . . While these writers share some common themes . . . each has her own distinctive voice, and none sacrifices the art of storytelling for polemics. A passionate, dynamic, and invaluable collection." Booklist

Sloan, Robin, 1979-
Mr. Penumbra's 24-hour bookstore; Robin Sloan. Farrar, Straus and Giroux 2012 288 p.
ISBN 0374214913; 9780374214913
LC 2012012357
Alex Award (2013)
This novel by Robin Sloan "follows Clay Jannon, a young San Franciscan with a background in the tech indus-

try, as he starts work at the titular bookstore . . . Most of the store's customers don't buy books at all; they borrow a series of beautiful, cryptic volumes that contain nothing but grids of numbers. Clay recruits some fellow high-tech friends to try to figure out the secret behind the store and its curious proprietor." (NPR)

Slouka, Mark
God's fool. Knopf 2002 271p $24
ISBN 0-375-40216-0
LC 2001-53975
"Slouka, a gifted stylist, eschews much of the freakshow energy that thrust Chang and Eng onto the stage of world history, in favor of an alluring balance between the elegiac and the ironic." Publ Wkly

Slouka, Mark
The **visible** world. Houghton Mifflin 2007 242p $24
ISBN 978-0-618-75643-8; 0-618-75643-4
LC 2006-23705
"It is a rare thing for a novel to split open the illusion of narrative . . . to reveal the underlying mechanics of creation, memory and desire. It is even rarer for a tricky book like this to hit you in the heart." Washington Post Book World

Smiley, Jane
The **age** of grief; a novella and stories. Knopf 1987 213p
LC 87-45120
"These short pieces are about male-female relations—the high points and the pitfalls (more of the latter than the former). Smiley knows her characters inside out and lets the reader in on everything she knows." Booklist

Smiley, Jane
Good faith. Knopf 2003 417p $26
ISBN 0-375-41217-4
LC 2002-73096
"Everyone trusts Joe Stratford, the affable Pennsylvania real-estate agent who narrates Smiley's ninth novel—his clients, his bankers, his boss, his boss's sexy married daughter, and even the irascible contractor who builds the most beautiful houses in the country. But when Marcus Burns, a charismatic I.R.S. agent turned developer, comes to town, Joe feels that no one else understands his potential the way Marcus does. With Joe as his partner, Marcus soon seduces half the county into investing in a development venture that he says will make everyone rich. It is hard to imagine a novelist better suited to taking on the S.& L. scandals of the nineteen-eighties than Smiley." New Yorker

Smiley, Jane
The **Greenlanders**. Knopf 1988 555p
LC 88-2758
"Vivid, even stunning descriptions of the land and customs of these 'lost settlements' are the book's strong points. Characterizations are less successful; many personalities remain wooden throughout the lengthy action. Nevertheless, the exotic subject matter will appeal to historical novel fans." Libr J

Smiley, Jane

Horse heaven. Knopf 2000 561p
ISBN 0-375-40600-X

LC 99-52728

In this novel about thoroughbred horse racing Smiley introduces "new characters in nearly every chapter, from rich and troubled owners to eccentric and troubled trainers; nervous fillies and scampish stallions; a boy with the gift for picking winners; an articulate, horse-crazy 11 year-old girl; a gorgeous store clerk who catches the eye of a wealthy rap star then goes horse-crazy; horse-crazy Irish cousins; an animal communicator who can tune into a horse's stream of consciousness; a kind horse masseur; a calm and creative veterinarian; and a young mother trying valiantly to run her grandfather's stud farm." Booklist

"What's remarkable about Smiley's handling of horses as characters is that she manages to bring it off at all—and more, she does it brilliantly." N Y Times Book Rev

Smiley, Jane

Moo. Knopf 1995 414p

LC 94-12840

"This metafiction, set in a sprawling Midwestern university known as Moo, concerns an economics professor who's cozy with corrupt Latin-American governments and rapacious corporations, a seven-hundred-pound hog named Earl Butz, many couples in and out of love, and a secretary who quietly runs the whole place. As usual, Smiley knows more than seems likely about everything from equine management and the niceties of butchering to—of course—the nuances of how people feel and behave toward animals of their own species." New Yorker

Smiley, Jane

Private life; a novel. Alfred A. Knopf 2010 317p $26.95
ISBN 978-1-4000-4060-5; 1-4000-4060-4

LC 2009-37000

"The novel closes with Margaret at last asserting herself, but that hardly makes up for a lifetime of emotions suppressed and chances missed. Rage and bitterness may not be the most comfortable human emotions, but depicting them takes Smiley's formidable artistry to its highest pitch. Her most ferocious novel since the Pulitzer Prize-winning A Thousand Acres (1991) and every bit as good." Kirkus

Smiley, Jane

Ten days in the hills. Knopf 2007 449p $26
ISBN 978-1-4000-4061-2; 1-400-04061-2

LC 2006-46579

"Each chapter is roughly half talk and half sex. The sexual descriptions set a new mark for explicitness in a work of non-pornographic intent. . . . The twists of libido are wound into a cultural exchange, and the anatomy of our inward hollows is illuminated to surprising and comic effect." New Yorker

Smiley, Jane

★ **A thousand** acres. Knopf 1991 371p $25
ISBN 0-394-57773-6

LC 91-52720

"What makes this novel such a triumph is Smiley's brilliant twist on the Lear story: she tells it not from Larry's point of view but from his eldest daughter's. . . . In the end Smiley does what Shakespeare himself never did: she creates a female heroine who grows through her own anguish until she towers over the hero and conquers him." Newsweek

Smith, Ali

The **accidental**. Pantheon Bks. 2006 305p $22.95
ISBN 0-375-42225-0

LC 2005-51031

First published 2005 in the United Kingdom

Smith "is a wonderful ventriloquist, adept at throwing her voice into an astonishing array of characters. . . . [She] can do suicidal teenage angst and middle-aged ennui, a 12-year-old's sardonic innocence and an aging Lothario's randy daydreams with equal aplomb. And in riffing on the stream of consciousness form, pioneered by such highbrow litterateurs as Joyce and Woolf, she manages to make it as accessible and up to the minute (if vastly more entertaining) as talk radio or an Internet chat room." N Y Times (Late N Y Ed)

Smith, Ali

There but for the. Pantheon Books 2011 236p $25
ISBN 978-0-375-42409-0; 0-375-42409-1

LC 2010-51377

The novel is "ostensibly about a dinner-party guest who locks himself in a spare bedroom and refuses to come out, inadvertently sparking a media frenzy. But the book — packed with jokes and random facts — is really about small stuff like life and death and the meaning of human existence, all told with sharp humor and real insight. The novel itself is a riddle with no solution, which is exactly the point: When you reluctantly come to the end, you can't help going back to the beginning, trying to unravel this beautifully elusive book's mysterious spell." Entertainment Wkly

Smith, Anne Easter

Royal mistress; Anne Easter Smith. 1st Touchstone trade pbk. ed. A Touchstone Book, published by Simon & Schuster 2013 xiv, 489 p.p (paperback) $16
ISBN 1451648626; 9781451648621

LC 2013005218

This historical novel looks at "Jane Lambert, the quick-witted and alluring daughter of a silk merchant." Jane's father has married her to a silk merchant, but when "the king's chamberlain, Will Hastings, comes to her husband's shop, Will knows King Edward will find her irresistible." She becomes the mistress of Edward IV. "But when his hedonistic tendencies get in the way of being the strong leader England needs, his life, as well as those of Jane and Will Hastings, hangs in the balance." (Publisher's note)

Smith, April

Good morning, killer. Knopf 2003 356p $24
ISBN 0-375-41240-9

LC 2002-35917

"This kidapping thriller starts off like most kidnapping thrillers, with the abduction of a pampered teenager, 15-year-old Juliana Meyer-Murphy, that has the local cops running around in circles. But we know we're in uncharted territory here when Juliana returns home, raped, battered and deeply traumatized, and Ana Grey, the F.B.I. agent assigned to the case, is so distressed by the girl's condition that she ignores procedures and starts acting on impulse. . . . A risk taker herself, Smith writes in the forceful style of a true literary maverick, someone who has earned the right to break a few rules." N Y Times Book Rev

Smith, April

Judas horse; an FBI special agent Ana Grey mystery. Alfred A. Knopf 2008 318p $23.95

ISBN 978-1-4000-4205-0; 1-4000-4205-4

LC 2007-42863

Smith "writes too well to settle for the mindless shootouts of a plot geared to summon armed-to-the-teeth SWAT teams at the least provocation. With every dynamic scene, including a wild mustang roundup that thunders right off the page, the reader, like Ana, is reminded of the lost ideals and divided loyalties that make these mortal conflicts so bloody—and so sad." N Y Times Book Rev

Smith, April

North of Montana; a novel. Knopf 1994 295p $23

ISBN 0-679-43197-7

LC 94-12311

As this mystery opens, "success-hungry L.A.-based FBI agent Ana Grey is just waiting for the case that will catapult her from the humdrum Bank Robbery Squad into the exalted Kidnapping and Extortion Division. The hoped-for promotion is Ana's first step to her ultimate goal: a plum job as Special Agent in Charge. But department politics, a jealous supervisor, and Ana's abrasive impatience detour her to a case that's a real hot potato. Glamorous movie star Jayne Mason, past her prime but still adored by her fans, claims a local M.D. hooked her on painkillers. She wants his head on a platter courtesy of the FBI, even though the doctor appears to be clean as a whistle." Booklist

This is "an LA novel in the tradition of some of the best writers of detective fiction. . . . There are swift, vivid portraits of scene and characters." Times Lit Suppl

Smith, Betty

★ **Joy** in the morning. Harper & Row 1963 308p

LC 62-14560

"When their families find out that Annie McGairy and Carl Brown have married, the two are cut off without a cent. Carl, a law student, takes a full-time job and goes to law school at night. Annie, who had dropped out of school to help her family, longs to be at college. She is given a chance to audit a course in literature because of her abiding interest in it. Her pregnancy, however, increases the pressure on their lives, and only their deep love sees them through their difficulties." Shapiro. Fic for Youth. 3d edition

Smith, Betty

★ A **tree** grows in Brooklyn; with a foreward by Anna Quindlen. HarperCollins Pubs. 2001 493p $23.95; pa $16.95

ISBN 0-06-000194-1; 0-06-112007-3 pa

LC 2001-39509

A reissue of the title first published 1943

"Life in the Williamsburg section of Brooklyn during the early 1900s is rough, but the childhood and youth of Francie Nolan is far from somber. Nurtured by a loving mother, Francie blossoms and reaches out for happiness despite poverty and the alcoholism of a father whose weakness is somewhat compensated for by his lovable disposition." Shapiro. Fic for Youth 3d edition

Smith, Brad

All hat; a novel. Holt & Co. 2003 308p $24

ISBN 0-8050-7217-9

LC 2002-27307

"His attempt to live 'a half-ass normal life' doomed out of the starting gate, ex-con Ray Dokes hatches a plot to swap racehorses before a race. Set in rural Onario and featuring an ensemble cast of delightfully eccentric, even downright loopy, characters, this big-hearted caper novel mixes laugh-out-loud-comedy with streaks of country noir that call to mind Daniel Woodrell." Booklist

Smith, Charlie

★ **Three** delays; a novel. Harper Perennial 2010 352p pa $14.99

ISBN 978-0-06-185945-8; 0-06-185945-1

Smith's "startling, rhapsodic descriptions are mind-blowing, as are his feral, weirdly smart, self-destructive characters, their lashing dialogue, and their insane, heartbreaking predicaments. This isn't Smith's first tale of toxic and nihilistic obsession, but it is his most ravishing, painfully funny, and wildly mythic." Booklist

Smith, Dan

The **Child** Thief; Dan Smith. W.W. Norton & Co Inc. 2013 352 p. (hardcover) $25

ISBN 160598440X; 9781605984407

This novel, by Dan Smith, follows "a troubled First World War veteran [who] races across the frozen steppe of 1930s Ukraine to save a child from a shadowy killer with unthinkable plans. . . . And though his toughest enemy is the man he tracks, his strongest bond is a promise to his family back home." (Publisher's note)

Smith, Deborah

The **Crossroads** Cafe; Deborah Smith. Belle-Books 2006 378p $16.95

ISBN 0976876051 pa

LC 2007295420

This book follows Cathy Deen, who "is Hollywood's 'it girl' until a paparazzi car chase ends in a car fire that horrifically scars Cathy. . . . News of the accident soon reaches her hometown in the mountains of North Carolina, where Cathy's cousin, Crossroads Café proprietress Delta Whittlespoon, sees the news on CNN and resolves to get in touch with Cathy. She enlists the help of Thomas Mitternich . . . who appeared in town four years ago to drink himself through the grief of losing his wife and son in 9/11. Thomas, using his New York contacts, helps Delta get through to Cathy. . . . Cathy returns to her ancestral home, where she falls in love with Thomas as they both try to rebuild their lives." (Publishers Weekly)

Smith, Diane

Pictures from an expedition. Viking 2002 277p
ISBN 0-670-03129-1

"Set in the Montana badlands a decade after the Civil War, the novel begins with fossil hunters stumbling upon the remains of possibly the largest dinosaur ever uncovered. Thrown in with a peripatetic crew of scientists and settlers, explorers and exploiters, Eleanor Peterson, a scientific illustrator hired to document their discoveries, recounts those daring days through her remembrances of the circumstances that inspired a series of paintings done by her traveling companion and mentor, Augustus Starwood, an eccentric artist." Booklist

Smith's "precise evocation of the stark western landscape matches her exacting portrayal of scientific debate and the assimilation of new theories." Publ Wkly

Smith, Dodie

I capture the castle. Little, Brown 1948 343p il
LC 48-4880

"From its memorable opening line, 'I write this sitting in the kitchen sink', the 17-year-old narrator, Cassandra Mortmain, captivates the reader as she describes a life of penury in a gloomy Gothic castle with her oddball family. Wise beyond her years, romantic and lyrical, yet beadily perceptive . . . , Cassandra is wonderfully engaging and believable." Good Fiction Guide

Smith, Dominic

The **beautiful** miscellaneous; a novel. Atria Books 2007 329p $24
ISBN 978-0-7432-7123-3; 0-7432-7123-8
LC 2007-297066

"This unusual, gorgeously written novel is filled with pleasures: among them are richly imagined supporting characters. . . . Best of all, though, is the book's invitation to wonder—about the imponderables of life and death, the nature of intelligence, and the ultimately inexplicable relationships of fathers and sons." Booklist

Smith, Dominic

Bright and distant shores. Washington Square 2011 470p map
ISBN 9781439198865

Chicago, 1897. An obsessive collector and insurance magnate commissions the world's tallest building. Determined to compete with Marshall Field's recent donation of $1 million to found the Field Museum, the tycoon funds a private collecting voyage into the Pacific.

"Beautifully researched and ripe with symbolism—an enthralling narrative peopled by characters both exotic and real." Kirkus

Smith, Julie

82 Desire; a Skip Langdon novel. Ballantine Pub. Group 1998 309p $24
ISBN 0-449-00060-5
LC 98-22259

"Russell Fortier, a prominent businessman, has vanished. His wife asks Langdon, a New Orleans detective, to look into his disappearance. Later, a private detective who was investigating Fortier turns up dead, and one of his employees, a poet and freelance computer expert, wants to know how Fortier's disappearance is connected with the murder. . . . The novel is intricately constructed, and while Smith keeps nothing important unfairly hidden from her readers, she manages to spring some nice little surprises." Booklist

Smith, Julie

Crescent city kill; a Skip Langdon novel. Fawcett Columbine 1997 326p $23.50
ISBN 0-449-91000-8
LC 97-22099

"New Orleans police detective Skip Langdon pits her skills against a vigilante group known as The Jury. Skip suspects her old nemesis, the con man and killer Errol Jacomine." Libr J

Smith, Julie

House of blues; a Skip Langdon novel. Fawcett Columbine 1995 343p
LC 94-48823

"Arthur Hebert, a prominent restaurateur and domineering patriarch hated by his children, doesn't attend the opening of his restaurant in New Orleans' first casino—because he's been gunned down at home while enjoying his usual Monday evening meal of red beans and rice. Hebert's daughter, his son-in-law and his baby granddaughter have vanished. In the race to find the killer and the missing family, Skip calls on the denizens of the New Orleans underworld. . . . Smith carries off a tricky balancing act, rendering Skip heroic while imbuing her with a credibly textured emotional life. But the real star of this superb effort is New Orleans, which has never seemed more dangerous or alluring." Publ Wkly

Smith, Julie

★ **Jazz** funeral; a Skip Langdon novel. Fawcett Columbine 1993 365p
LC 92-54997

This mystery featuring New Orleans cop Skip Langdon is "about the murder of a local jazz entrepreneur and the disappearance of his 16-year-old sister. . . . Even though she wears her badge like a piece of jewelry, Skip has the social skills to pump information from her uptown friends, and her amateur detection methods pay off with solid insights into an emotionally bankrupt family. Ms. Smith takes special pains to be gentle with a musically gifted teen-ager who runs away from the horrors of home to join a family band very much like the Neville Brothers. The kid is a bit of a brat, but the portrayal has such integrity that it makes up for Skip's lax procedures." N Y Times Book Rev

Smith, Julie

The **kindness** of strangers; a Skip Langdon novel. Fawcett Columbine 1996 338p $21

ISBN 0-449-90937-9

LC 95-52460

Langdon "takes on the Big Easy's corrupt political machine, as three 'pick the best of the worst' candidates line up for the mayoral race. New Orleans voters, tired of years of corruption and scandal, are leaning toward Errol Jacomine, a Christian right-winger who appears to have the right stuff. But Skip senses evil lurking behind Jacomine's jovial facade, and she figures to discredit him before he gains control of the city. . . . Smith serves up a gritty, gripping story along with a big helping of action and a pinch of humor." Booklist

Smith, Julie

Louisiana hotshot. Forge 2001 335p $24.95

ISBN 0-7653-0058-3

LC 2001-18958

A mystery set in New Orleans featuring "Talba Wallis (aka Baroness de Pontalba), the black poet/computer expert and would-be investigator. . . . Answering an unlikely ad with her customary bravado lands her a job as assistant to aging PI Eddie Valentino. The young black female and 65-year-old Italian male have striking similarities that offset their obvious differences. Both are stubborn and strongly attached to, if somewhat alienated from, their families. Throw in a vulnerable young girl, Cassandra, being preyed on by a rap star's hanger-on identified only by the nickname 'Toes,' and you have a story that spans generations, races and lifestyles." Publ Wkly

Smith, Julie

Mean woman blues. Forge 2003 304p $24.95

ISBN 0-7653-0552-6

LC 2003-40018

"The Formosan termites that infest new Orleans every May haunt police detective Skip Langdon's dreams, an apt image for the gnawing fear that her happiness will collapse. That happiness is based on the fact that her long distance lover, a documentary filmmaker, has moved to New Orleans. Her fear is that her enemy, an evangelical fanatic who aspires to the mind control of Jim Jones, is coming back to kill her, after a disappearance of two years." Booklist

Smith, Julie

New Orleans beat; a Skip Langdon novel. Fawcett Columbine 1994 359p

LC 93-46506

"Smith is a skilled writer who can evoke the steamy, mysterious ambience of New Orleans while simultaneously proving that computer jargon can be comprehensible even to the 'computer-challenged.' This is a humorous, suspenseful mystery." Booklist

Smith, Lee

The **devil's** dream. Putnam 1992 315p

LC 92-1027

"It is ultimately the writer's sensibility that gives 'The Devil's Dream' its charm and power. If there's weeping to be done, Ms. Smith allows her reader to weep, but she never descends to sentimentality." N Y Times Book Rev

Smith, Lee

★ **Fair** and tender ladies. Putnam 1988 316p

ISBN 0-399-13382-8

LC 88-10915

An "exquisite novel. . . . Through Ivy's curiously spelled and situated letters, we see the growth not only of her own family, but also of wider Appalachia." Christ Sci Monit

Smith, Lee

Family linen. Putnam 1985 272p

ISBN 0-399-13080-2

LC 85-3664

"The Hess clan gather in their hometown of Booker Creek, Virginia, upon the death of their matriarch, Miss Elizabeth. There are some serious skeletons in the family closet—sexual abuse, an illegitimate child, a murder. The family history is recounted in turn by relatives spanning four generations, and their narratives reveal both comical attempts to seek solace and bewilderment at the complexity of their lives." Booklist

"This is a companionable, chatty book populated by people who tell us about themselves in a rambling style and with good humor." N Y Times Book Rev

Smith, Lee

The **last** girls; a novel. Algonquin Bks. 2002 384p

ISBN 1-565-12363-8

LC 2002-18671

Smith is "perhaps best known for her nuanced portraits of gritty, often dirt-poor Appalachian women. It's a pleasure to see her directing her talents to a different class of women with a different set of concerns." N Y Times Book Rev

Smith, Lee

Mrs. Darcy and the blue-eyed stranger; new and selected stories. Algonquin Books of Chapel Hill 2010 352p $23.95

ISBN 978-1-56512-915-3; 1-56512-915-6

LC 2009-27915

"A Southern writer with characteristic wry wit and a keen eye for tragic humor, Smith is often compared to Katherine Anne Porter, Eudora Welty, and Flannery O'Connor. . . . As the characters face the changes that upend them, Smith turns ordinary struggles of love, health, and faith into believable and entertaining moments of meaning — even, occasionally, transcendence." Providence J

Smith, Lee

On Agate Hill; a novel. Algonquin Books of Chapel Hill 2006 367p $24.95

ISBN 1-56512-452-9

LC 2006-45859

"Molly is like a grown-up, Southern version of Louisa May Alcott's Jo, only she is thrown into circumstances that test her essentially wholesome nature. For the most part, she battles back not with sass—which modern novels seem to think is universally charming—but pluck. As this is Smith's first historical novel, she deserves credit for understanding this subtle, but essential period point." Denver Post

Smith, Lee

★ **Oral** history. Putnam 1983 286p

ISBN 0-399-12794-1

LC 82-18081

"Smith is excellent at making the separate voices distinctive. . . . Serious fiction readers will be interested in Smith's techniques and will appreciate her decision to utilize this 'oral history' format to best achieve her intentions." Booklist

Smith, Lee

★ **Saving** Grace. Putnam 1995 273p

ISBN 0-399-14050-6

LC 94-43904

"Florida Grace is the daughter of Virgil Shepherd, a snake-handling self-appointed preacher who starves and sometimes abandons his many children. Of all these, Gracie is the 'contentious and ornery' one who will not embrace Jesus—though she does, along the way (between the ages of seven and thirty-eight), embrace a half brother, a kindly minister, and middle-class luxury. Grace narrates, in irresistible Southern mountain tones." New Yorker

Smith, Lillian Eugenia

★ **Strange** fruit; a novel. [by] Lillian Smith. Reynal & Hitchcock 1944 371p

This novel, set in a small town in Georgia, is about the love of an educated black girl for a white man. The reaction to this affair results in murder and a lynching

This is a "regional novel, in the finest sense. As such, it offers a magnificently detailed picture of the small-town South, lashed by an urge for self-destruction as old as time. The author has suggested no cure for that urge: you will find no black messiahs here, no white devils." N Y Times Book Rev

Smith, Mark Allen

★ The **Inquisitor**; Mark Allen Smith. 1st ed. Henry Holt and Co. 2012 336 p. $27

ISBN 0805094261; 9780805094268; 9780805095920

LC 2011026552

This book tells the story of "Geiger, [who] . . . knows a lie the instant he hears it. . . . [W]hen his partner, former journalist Harry Boddicker, unwittingly brings in a client who demands that Geiger interrogate a twelve-year-old boy, Geiger . . . rescues the boy from his captor. . . . But if Geiger and Harry cannot quickly discover why the client is so desperate to learn the boy's secret, they themselves will become the victims of an utterly ruthless adversary." (Publisher's note)

Smith, Mark Haskell

Baked. Black Cat 2010 336p pa $14

ISBN 978-0-8021-7076-7; 0-8021-7076-5

"L.A. botanist Miro Basinas prides himself on the quality of his latest batch of homegrown marijuana, Elephant Crush, a wickedly strong pot that tastes like mangoes. When he wins the prized Cannabis Cup competition in Amsterdam, he feels like he has finally hit the big time and is on his way to breaking into the top echelon of cannabis breeders, able to sell his seeds to growers everywhere. His cerebral approach to farming in no way prepares him for the warfare heading his way when the greedy owner of a chain of medical marijuana dispensaries decides to steal Miro's plants and take him out." Booklist

"As cockeyed and riotous as Carl Hiaasen on really good dope." Kirkus

Smith, Martin Cruz

December 6; a novel. Simon & Schuster 2002 339p

ISBN 0-684-87253-6

LC 2002-29437

This "thriller is set in Tokyo in the last days of 1941, just before the bombing of Pearl Harbor; its central character, the American Harry Niles, grew up in Japan, where his missionary parents were preaching the Word. Harry isn't very holy, however: he owns a night club called the Happy Paris, dabbles in assorted short cons, and spends much of his time with various mistresses. . . . As the rumors of war heat up, Harry finds that he has become too Japanese, and the Japanese suspect him of being a spy. Smith's plot is more than slightly reminiscent of 'Casablanca' and the spectre of the Second World War seems, at this distance, almost quaint, but the characters are so well drawn and the local color so colorful that these quibbles hardly interfere with the novel's pleasures." New Yorker

Smith, Martin Cruz

★ **Gorky** Park. Random House 1981 365p

LC 80-6022

The author "has succeeded in rendering very believable, realistic, and gripping portrayals of certain segments of Soviet society and of one man's search for meaning." Christ Sci Monit

Smith, Martin Cruz

Havana Bay; a novel. Random House 1999 329p $25.95

ISBN 0-679-42662-0

LC 99-235977

"His earnest unsentimentality and calm tenaciousness on the hunt are what make Renko one of the most interesting detectives in modern fiction. What a clever stroke for Smith to dispatch him to Havana, where sentimentality and passion are in rare abundance." N Y Times Book Rev

Smith, Martin Cruz

Polar Star. Random House 1989 386p il

LC 88-43232

"Rich in humor, generous in spirit, endlessly entertaining and deeply serious, 'Polar Star' is not merely the work of our best writer of suspense, but of one of our best writers, period." N Y Times Book Rev

Smith, Martin Cruz

Red Square. Random House 1992 418p

LC 92-50166

"Just prior to the 1991 attempted coup, {Arkady Renko} finds himself reestablished as an investigator with the Moscow police and struggling to contain a flourishing underworld in the newly democratic Soviet Union. . . . A seemingly straightforward murder investigation leads Arkady first to corruption in high places, then to official censure, and finally to Munich, where he is reunited with Irina, the lover who got him in . . . trouble back in the early 1980s." Booklist

Smith, Martin Cruz
   Rose. Random House 1996 364p
   ISBN 978-0679426615
                                          LC 95-37914
   "Rose has everthing a compelling novel needs: Blair is a fascinating protagonist, by turns a hero and a boor; other significant characters are complex and as multifaceted as a chunk of coal; the mystery is gripping. But it is the horrific, mesmerizing portrayal of the dark, hellish Wigan, the mines themselves, and the lives of miners that makes this novel much more than a good read." Booklist

Smith, Martin Cruz
   Stalin's ghost; an Arkady Renko novel. Simon & Schuster 2007 333p $26.95
   ISBN 978-0-07432-7672-6; 0-7432-7672-8
                                          LC 2006-100963
   "Every page reeks of Moscow: dirty snow, the stink of cigarette and vodka fumes, the cynicism and tasteless opulence of the mafia, the all-pervasive corruption. . . . Like the Red Army facing the Nazis, Renko refuses to give up, surrendering neither his investigation nor those he loves. In this subtle, moving book, he is an everyman, whose loyalty and courage speak to all of us." Economist

Smith, Martin Cruz
   ★ Stallion Gate. Random House 1986 321p
                                          LC 85-24444
   "Obviously Stallion Gate is not meant to be taken too literally. There is a touch of the folk hero about Peña as he moves across the New Mexican landscape. A conscious stylist, Smith relies strongly on emotional echoes and calibrated suspense." Time

Smith, Martin Cruz
   Tatiana; An Arkady Renko Novel. by Martin Cruz Smith. Simon & Schuster 2013 304 p. $25.99
   ISBN 1439140219; 9781439140215
   In this novel by Martin Cruz Smith "Tatiana Petrovna falls to her death from a sixth-floor window in Moscow the same week that a mob billionaire, Grisha Grigorenko, is shot. No one makes the connection, but Arkady [Renko] is transfixed by the tapes he discovers of Tatiana's voice. His only link is a notebook written in the personal code of a translator whose body is found in the dunes. Arkady's only hope of decoding the symbols lies in Zhenya, a teenage chess hustler." (Publisher's note)

Smith, Martin Cruz
   Three stations; an Arkady Renko novel. Simon & Schuster 2010 243p $25.99
   ISBN 978-0-7432-7674-0; 0-7432-7674-4
                                          LC 2010-19996
   "The main investigation underpinning 'Three Stations' doesn't carry the full force of past adventures. . . . The denouement, in particular, feels rushed and half-hearted. Smith does, however, nail the key to the structure of a detective novel, when Renko thinks 'there was still time for [him] to walk away from a case he did not fathom and a woman he

did not understand.' One can trace that very essence back to Hammett and Chandler, who imbued their respective gumshoes with dogged determination no matter what price they paid later. So too must Arkady, who is doomed to repeat this existential cycle in book after book." L A Times Book Rev

Smith, Martin Cruz
   Wolves eat dogs; a novel. Simon & Schuster 2004 337p $25.95
   ISBN 0-684-87254-4
                                          LC 2004-52585
   Senior Investigator Arkady Renko "must determine whether the defenestration death of a Russian tycoon was suicide or murder. The discovery of radioactive salt in the dead man's apartment leads Renko to the abandoned Ukrainian towns of Chernobyl and Pripyat, still dangerously contaminated 18 years after the world's deadliest nuclear accident. There he finds a ghostly world inhabited by scavengers, elderly villagers, and a small group of Russian militia and scientists. As Renko pursues his investigation, he uncovers a greater crime, the sad legacy of Soviet ineptitude and corruption." Libr J

Smith, Michael Marshall
   The intruders; [by] Michael Marshall. William Morrow 2007 392p $24.95
   ISBN 978-0-06-123502-3; 0-06-123502-4
                                          LC 2006-47087
   "Mr. Marshall recalls Stephen King's ability to set a story in the world of the commonplace, then suddenly jolt it into a more hellish realm. He also has some of Mr. King's ability to rivet attention with eerie surprises. It's not necessary to believe this book's spooky underlying premise to be caught up in the campfire-tale power of its action." N Y Times (Late N Y Ed)

Smith, Robert Kimmel
   Jane's house. Morrow 1982 344p
                                          LC 82-2277
   "This book is about how one family deals with the loss of a parent. Paul Klein's wife of 18 years, Jane, died suddenly, leaving him to raise their two children, Hilary and Bobby. The first part of the book deals with Paul's slow adjustment to single parenthood, emphasizing the day-to-day problems. Then he meets Ruth, a lively and intelligent advertising woman. They fall in love and marry. The second part of the story is seen mostly through Ruth's eyes, as she tries to gain the children's friendship." Libr J

Smith, Roger
   Wake up dead; a thriller. Henry Holt and Co. 2010 290p $26
   ISBN 978-0-8050-8876-2; 0-8050-8876-8
                                          LC 2009-21779
   "The backdrop for Smith's urban nightmare is both fantastic and hyperrealistic, somewhat in the manner of graphic novels or urban fantasy. . . . [His] Cape Town slums are as grim as any steampunk Victorian hellhole, and none of his characters rich, poor, colored, white, or black has anything better than a bleak present and an infernal past. The novel's flashbacks, narrative asides, and occasional political jabs,

even the inflection of the characters' speech, contribute to a vivid sense of place. " Philadelphia Inquirer

Smith, Scott, 1965-

★ A **simple** plan; a novel. Knopf 1993 335p

ISBN 0-679-41985-3

LC 92-42478

This novel is so "cunningly imagined that for the most part Mr. Smith drags us willingly through what in less deft hands could be a morally repugnant story." N Y Times Book Rev

Smith, Stevie

★ **Novel** on yellow paper; or, Work it out for yourself. New Directions 1994 252p il (A revived modern classic) pa $10.95

ISBN 0-8112-1239-4

LC 93-49827

First published 1936 in the United Kingdom

This novel is "narrated in the first person by Pompey Casmilus, who lives with her darling Auntie Lion, and is an outpouring of her thoughts and feelings about the world around her–about fear, love, death, marriage, religion, sex, anti-Semitism; about her friends and lovers and her childhood. To list the topics cannot begin to capture the delicious flavour, which is whimsical, poetic, self-deprecatingly (or at times, mercilessly) humorous , and often absurd." Good Fiction Guide

Smith, Tom Rob

★ **Agent** 6. Grand Central Pub. 2012 448p

ISBN 978-1-84737-567-4; 1-84737-567-7; 9781847375681; 9780446550765

LC 2011505662

"Leo Demidov is no longer a member of Moscow's secret police. But when his wife, Raisa, and daughters Zoya and Elena are invited on a 'Peace Tour' to New York City, he is immediately suspicious." (Publisher's note)

Smith, Tom Rob

Child 44. Grand Central Pub. 2008 439p $24.99

ISBN 978-0-446-40238-5; 0-446-40238-9

LC 2007-28272

"Smith captures the rhythm of day-today paranoia in Stalinist Russia and the ways that personal jealousies can balloon into ruthless vendettas. It's hard to fathom which is more grisly, the descriptions of the serial murders or the scenes of torture perpetrated by Leo's colleagues in the MGB. Throughout, Smith's prose is propulsive but plain; his real genius is his careful plotting." Entertainment Wkly

Smith, Tom Rob

The **secret** speech. Grand Central Pub. 2009 407p $24.99

ISBN 978-0-446-40240-8; 0-446-40240-0

LC 2008-48329

"Former state security officer Leo Demidov, eyes now wide open to Soviet excess, is struggling to forge a new life. His heroism in 'Child 44' earned him a job in the newly formed Moscow homicide bureau, but his efforts to create a family with his wife Raisa and two orphaned girls are a struggle, mainly because the elder, Zoya, rightly blames Leo

for her parents' deaths. Other things have changed as well: Stalin is dead, and a widely distributed, once-secret letter denouncing his actions — from his successor Khrushchev — acts as a catalyst for those seeking revenge against Stalin's oppressors. Like Leo. Based on real events, 'The Secret Speech' is jam-packed with action — the near-sinking of a prison ship, a violent takeover at a Kolyma gulag, and a rebellion in Hungary — and Smith explores pertinent questions of revenge, morality and responsibility." PopMatters

Smith, Wilbur A.

Birds of prey; a novel. {by} Wilbur Smith. St. Martin's Press 1997 554p

ISBN 978-0312157913

LC 97-8192

"Smith's depiction of the African coast, and of life aboard ship, is vivid and believable. He handles the action sequences well, opting for short, trenchant paragraphs to sustain momentum. . . . Smith knows what his readers want, and once again he delivers the goods." Publ Wkly

Followed by Monsoon

Smith, Wilbur A.

Golden fox; {by} Wilbur Smith. Random House 1991 433p

ISBN 0-394-58971-8

LC 90-39062

First published 1990 in the United Kingdom

"Smith excels at creating finely drawn characters; descriptive settings in London, Europe, and Africa; and a masterful development of an action-packed thriller that gets better as each new predicament unfolds." SLJ

Smith, Wilbur A.

Monsoon; {by} Wilbur Smith. St. Martin's Press 1999 613p $26.95

ISBN 0-312-20339-X

LC 99-24554

This sequel to Birds of Prey "finds Sir Hal Courtney and his sons up to their bloody sword arms in piracy, intrigue, treachery and civil war in late 17th and early 18th century East Africa and Arabia. . . . Wealthy English landowner Sir Hal earned his fortune as a sea captain with the East India Company. To protect his overseas investments, he becomes a privateer to combat Arab pirates attacking company ships from bases in Zanzibar and Madagascar. Accompanied by three of his four sons, Sir Hal embarks on a desperate voyage that will bring either glory and treasure or ruin. . . . Clever plot twists and lavish historical detail attend the siblings' adventures." Publ Wkly

Smith, Wilbur A.

Power of the sword; [by] Wilbur Smith. Little, Brown 1986 618p

ISBN 0-316-80171-2

LC 86-10279

"The central characters in this robust tale of politics, adventure and romance set in South Africa are step-brothers Manfred and Shasa, sons of Centaine Courtney (from 'The Burning Shore'), owner of a diamond mine. As representatives, respectively, of the Afrikaner cause and that of the more liberal, English-speaking whites, headed in the early days by Jan Smuts, they are, however, destined to be enemies. . . . What Smith may lack in subtlety, he makes up for in raw vigor." Publ Wkly

Followed by Rage

Smith, Wilbur A.

Rage; by Wilbur Smith. Little, Brown 1987 627p

LC 87-3078

"The interlocking stories of these and many others, set against the authentic African historical and cultural background that Smith so effectively provides, produces both a compelling tale and some real insights into South Africa." Libr J

Followed by A time to die

Smith, Wilbur A.

River god; {by} Wilbur Smith. St. Martin's Press 1994 530p

LC 93-45249

First published 1993 in the United Kingdom

This novel, set in Egypt ca.1780 B.C., "tells the story of Taita the eunuch, slave to a noble's daughter. Taita narrates the dramatic events of which he was either witness or participant as his mistress receives the dubious honor of marriage to the pharaoh. The brutality of life in ancient times is everywhere evident in Taita's tale, which involves fatal intrigue at every turn. It's clear Smith knows his subject: his graphic depiction of lust, bloodletting, politics, and, in Taita's case, honor is firmly grounded in rich details that evoke the period." Booklist

Followed by The seventh scroll

Smith, Wilbur A.

The **seventh** scroll; {by} Wilbur Smith. St. Martin's Press 1995 486p

LC 95-768

"Smith excels at action sequences, getting his attractive heroes and despicable villains into and out of hugely entertaining predicaments, all the while tossing off vivid descriptions, bits of historical detail, and classic low-key British banter." Booklist

Smith, Wilbur A.

Those in peril. Thomas Dunne Books/St. Martin's Press 2011 385p il $27.99

ISBN 978-0-312-56725-5; 0-312-56725-1

LC 2010-54434

This novel "consists for the most part of one scalp-cooling set piece after another. . . . If Smith handles action better than any writer since Ian Fleming the same goes doubly for the more steamy part of the book." Daily Express

Smith, Wilbur A.

A **time** to die; [by] Wilbur Smith. Random House 1990 448p

ISBN 0-394-58475-9

LC 89-27360

First published 1989 in the United Kingdom

This novel in the Courtney family saga, focuses on "Sean Courtney, Rhodesian African Rifles officer turned big-game hunter. Leading a safari on his licensed land in

Africa, Courtney is lured over the Mozambique border in pursuit of a long-sought elephant trophy, for which his client promises him half a million dollars. Courtney turns into the quarry, however, when a Mozambiquan guerrilla leader kidnaps the client's daughter, Claudia, and forces Courtney into abetting the rebel cause. A few stolen American-made missiles and the devastation of a Soviet-equipped helicopter base later, Courtney and Claudia are fleeing for their lives through the African wilderness." Booklist

Followed by Golden fox

Smith, Zadie, 1975-

The **autograph** man; a novel. Random House 2002 347p

ISBN 0-375-50186-X

LC 2002-69705

"Smith's pen portraits of the shabby, yobbish autograph trading circle are intermittently funny, but her prose is so busy being clever that the laughter never builds. This is disappointing but, even with its faults, the novel points to a literary talent of a high order." Publ Wkly

Smith, Zadie, 1975-

★ **NW**; a novel. Zadie Smith. Penguin Press 2012 401 p. $26.95

ISBN 1594203970; 9781594203978

LC 2012015114

This novel by Zadie Smith "is the story of a city. . . .[The] novel follows four Londoners--Leah, Natalie, Felix and Nathan--as they try to make adult lives outside of Caldwell, the council estate of their childhood. From private houses to public parks, at work and at play, their London is a complicated place, as beautiful as it is brutal, where the thoroughfares hide the back alleys and taking the high road can sometimes lead you to a dead end." (Publisher's note)

Smith, Zadie, 1975-

On beauty. Penguin Press 2005 445p $25.95

ISBN 1-59420-0637

"Ms Smith has her shortcomings. The novel's first half is under-edited; surely we do not need to meet every guest at an anniversary party. . . . Nevertheless, the book gathers momentum, and the second half gallops along." Economist

Smith, Zadie, 1975-

★ **White** teeth; a novel. Random House 2000 448p $24.95

ISBN 0-375-50185-1

LC 99-43658

"Hopscotching through several continents and 150 years of history, 'White Teeth' encompasses a teeming family saga, a sly inquiry into race and identity and a tender-hearted satire on religious antagonism and cultural bemusement. . . . Smith holds it all together with a raucous energy and confidence." N Y Times Book Rev

Smollett, Tobias George

★ The **expedition** of Humphry Clinker; introduction and notes by Thomas R. Preston; the text edited by O M Brack, Jr. University of Georgia Press 1990 lx, 500p

ISBN 0-8203-1203-7

LC 89-36020

First published 1771

In this epistolary novel "the letters are written by Matthew Bramble, his sister Tabitha, their niece, their nephew, and their maid, Winifred Jenkins. Each correspondent has a highly individual style and caricatures himself unwittingly. The titular hero of this comic masterpiece, who plays a lesser role than the Brambles, is a workhouse lad who enters into their service by chance and who later becomes a Methodist preacher. He falls in love with Winifred, and is eventually found to be the natural son of Mr. Bramble. The 'expedition' of the title is a family tour through England and Scotland, during which the correspondents express surprisingly varied reactions to the same events. Of particular note is the picture of Hot Wells (a sobriquet for the city of Bath), a fashionable watering place." Reader's Ency. 4th edition

Snow white, blood red; edited by Ellen Datlow & Terri Windling. Morrow 1992 411p

LC 92-24899

"The dark and shadowed aspects of well-known folk stories and fairy tales are explored in updated retellings. . . . Some of these tales are enchanting; some are horrifying; most, like the originals, offer insight into human nature." Publ Wkly

Snow, C. P.

The **conscience** of the rich. Scribner 1958 342p (Strangers and brothers)

"As a result of his friendship with Charles March, Lewis Eliot is taken into the private world of one of England's wealthiest and most influential Jewish families and through his eyes the March drama is slowly unfolded; the close bond between Charles, his father, and his sister, Charles's marriage to a gentle Communist, and the ensuing political scandal which estranges father and son, brother and sister. . . . Set in London during the late 1920's and the 1930's." Booklist

Snow, C. P.

Corridors of power. Scribner 1964 403p (Strangers and brothers)

"The workings of inner power in the British government—with key administrators, politicians, and the wealthy manipulators, male and female—{are} traced in a novel of the period 1955-1958. . . . Since the power in this fictional case is concerned with the use of nuclear arms, the fate of the world can easily hang on the fate of one minister, Roger Quaife." Publ Wkly

"We see the corridors of political power illuminated with a fine and discriminating light." Libr J

Snow, C. P.

Homecoming. Scribner 1956 399p (Strangers and brothers)

Published in the United Kingdom with title: Homecomings

"An introspective, subtly shaded novel which again stars Lewis Eliot. . . . Eliot's unhappy marriage to a neurotic woman, her death, and his affair with and eventual marriage

to a woman more worthy of his love comprise the chief incidents in a story that accents not the events themselves but their psychological effect upon the persons involved. Crisp, carefully fashioned prose; for the discriminating." Booklist

Snow, C. P.

Last things. Scribner 1970 435p (Strangers and brothers)

"Student protest, Lewis Eliot's decision on whether or not to enter the Labor government's ministry, his serious eye operation during which a cardiac arrest brings him near to death—these are some of the essential plot elements {of this novel}." Publ Wkly

Snow, C. P.

★ The **light** and the dark. Scribner 1961 406p (Strangers and brothers)

First published 1947 in the United Kingdom

Cambridge University is the scene of the greater part of this character study of a young Cambridge don. In an attempt to curb his dark moods Roy tries promiscuity, drink, concentration on his studies, and religion. With the out-break of the war he joins the RAF and is killed in action

"A painstaking and readable account of university life seen from high table." Times Lit Suppl

Snow, C. P.

The **masters**. Macmillan 1951 374p (Strangers and brothers)

"Lewis Eliot, a Cambridge Fellow, tells about the election of a new Master of his college, and uses the rivalry and jealousy attendant on the election to illuminate the lives and hearts of the candidates and their friends and enemies. The book begins with notice of the impending death of the old Master, Vernon Royce, continues at a leisurely rate as Royce waits to die and finally dies, and ends with the election of the new Master." New Yorker

"For a quiet novel of subtle characterization this one contains a surprising element of suspense." Ont Libr Rev

Snow, C. P.

★ The **new** men. Scribner 1954 311p (Strangers and brothers)

The novel describes a group of nuclear scientists and high government officials working together in England during the war. As usual Lewis Eliot is the narrator

The author "handles a fateful new theme with challenging insight and impressive moral sensitivity. . . . {This is a} novel which searchingly explores the moral dilemmas created by the atom bomb." Atlantic

Snow, C. P.

★ **Strangers** and brothers. Scribner 1960 309p (Strangers and brothers)

First published 1940 in the United Kingdom

George Passant, a solicitor in an English provincial town, exerts a crucial influence on his group of young protegés, Lewis Eliot among them. An idealist, courageous and high-principled Passant seems destined for great things yet the story ends in his trial for fraud. The reasons for this are revealed

"Essentially the tragedy of a good man defeated by the mediocrity of his world, the story of George Passant is completed in the novel 'Homecoming.' . . . Like all the novels in the series, 'Strangers and Brothers' is distinguished by virtue of its analysis of motive and character and its anatomization of a world in which a smooth mediocrity is the greatest virtue." Libr J

Snow, C. P.

Time of hope. Macmillan 1950 416p (Strangers and brothers)

"Here, as in 'Light and the Dark' (1948) Lewis Eliot is the main character that typifies middle class English life, and as in the earlier work, Mr. Snow shows the impact of spiritual values on individuals. The 1930s are the background here and the years are brilliantly drawn. Moral problems are vivid and the characters are varied in their reactions." Libr J

Snyder, Don J.

Night crossing; a novel. Knopf 2001 277p $24
ISBN 0-375-40906-8

LC 00-62008

"This competent—albeit derivative and inflammatory—thriller delivers some exciting moments as well as insights into the mind of a woman who slowly realizes her own complicity in the wreck of her marriage." Publ Wkly

Sofer, Dalia

The Septembers of Shiraz. Ecco/HarperCollins Publishers 2007 340p $24.95
ISBN 978-0-06-113040-3; 0-06-113040-0

LC 2007-299587

"Sofer paints a complicated picture of postrevolutionary Iran: The Amins (and especially their relatives) aren't entirely innocent, having shut their eyes to brutality and corruption under the shah, but [the author] recoils from the idea of justice by 'collective retribution' voiced by Farnaz's formerly docile housekeeper. While the dialogue can feel overly formal at times, the impression the reader is left with at the end is that of a powerful story honestly told." Christ Sci Monit

Soli, Tatjana

The forgetting tree; Tatjana Soli. St. Martin's Press 2012 406 p. (hardcover) $25.99
ISBN 1250001048; 9781250001047; 9781250019349

LC 2012028236

This book by Tatjana Soli "centers on Claire, the matriarch of an orchard that's been the source of plenty of financial and emotional heartbreak. Her young son was killed there, and the aftermath of his death drove a wedge between her and her husband and two daughters. Years later, when Claire is diagnosed with breast cancer, she begins to search for live-in help and is introduced to Minna, a young woman low on housekeeping experience but high on charm." (Kirkus)

Soli, Tatjana

The lotus eaters. St. Martin's Press 2010 389p $24.99
ISBN 978-0-312-61157-6; 0-312-61157-9

LC 2009045697

This is Soli's debut novel. "On a stifling day in 1975, the North Vietnamese army is poised to roll into Saigon. As the fall of the city begins, two lovers make their way through the streets to escape to a new life. Helen Adams, an American photojournalist, must take leave of a war she is addicted to and a devastated country she has come to love. Linh, the Vietnamese man who loves her, must grapple with his own conflicted loyalties of heart and homeland. As they race to leave, they play out a drama of devotion and betrayal that spins them back through twelve war-torn years, beginning in the splendor of Angkor Wat, with their mentor, larger-than-life war correspondent Sam Darrow, once Helen's infuriating love and fiercest competitor, and Linh's secret keeper, boss and truest friend." (Publisher's note)

"Soli is at her best in conveying the day-to-day mix of adventure, tedium, and violence in wartime. Her descriptions are visceral, almost cinematic. . . . And she captures the camaraderie and tension among soldiers in a way that seems authentic." Boston Globe

Solomita, Stephen

Damaged goods. Scribner 1996 380p
ISBN 978-0684815848

LC 95-33277

"Jilly Sappone truly is 'damaged goods.' The gunshot that wrecked his brain years before also made him into a vicious killer. Released from prison by family connections, he takes revenge on everyone responsible for his prison term. Beginning with his ex-wife, Ann, Jilly and his brainless psychotic partner, Jackson-Davis, commence a spree of kidnapping and violent murders. Ex-cop Stanley Moodrow is hired, as is detective cum-computer-whiz Ginny Gadd, to track down Jilly." Libr J

"The pace is energetic, and with Ginny at his side to blunt his cynicism, Moodrow seems less morose and more alert than we've seen him in a long time." N Y Times Book Rev

Solomita, Stephen

A good day to die. Penzler Bks. 1993 297p

LC 93-19400

"As Means researches the profiled backgrounds of serial killers, he recognizes his own abused childhood; his search for the killer becomes a search for himself. This multiethnic thriller vividly depicts the gritty streets of the city, the dark and feral forest, and the danger lurking in both." Libr J

Solomita, Stephen

Last chance for glory. Penzler Bks. 1994 310p

LC 93-38616

"Blake and Kosinski initially form an uneasy alliance that inevitably turns to friendship, but it happens easily and believably. It's the old mismatched-partner plot, but seldom has it been handled better." Booklist

Solomon, Anna

The little bride; Anna Solomon. 1st Riverhead trade pbk. ed. Riverhead Books 2011 314p. pa $15
ISBN 978-1-59448-535-0; 1-59448-535-6

LC 201054194

This book tells the story of "Minna Losk, [who] flees an unhappy life as a servant in Odessa to become the mail-order bride of a Jewish man in South Dakota in the late nineteenth century. . . . [S]he's disappointed to discover that her intended, Max, is 40 years old and has two teenage sons, one of them older than Minna. It is this older son, Samuel, who captures Minna's attention and awakens desires in her that his father is incapable of stirring. An unfulfilling marriage is hardly the only challenge Minna faces. Frontier life is difficult and isolating, and Minna's inability to become pregnant weighs on her. A neighbor's carelessness costs Minna and her family their house, and as soon as the house is rebuilt, South Dakota is hit with a brutal winter that puts them in jeopardy again." (Booklist)

In this debut novel, the author, "draws on an 1880s U.S. homesteading movement called Am Olam. Jewish newcomers were encouraged to settle out west as pioneers. The result wasn't some cheerful 'little shtetl on the prairie,' as Solomon's heroine discovers. Impoverished Minna Losk is a 16-year-old Jewish mail order bride from Odessa and one of the more realistic pioneers depicted in recent historical fiction. Suffering hasn't hewn her into a plucky stereotype. Instead, she is someone the reader instantly empathizes with. She wants love, and ends up with a husband twice her age. She craves comfort, and ends up in a South Dakota one-room sod hut. A fascinating if sometimes bleak page turner." USA Today

Solomon, Nina

Single wife; a novel. Algonquin Bks. 2003 307p $23.95

ISBN 1-56512-382-4

LC 2003-40406

"Solomon tells a funny and bizarre story that is both hard to believe and hard to put down, with characters who are real, almost tangible. She captures the essence of the struggle for self." Libr J

Solzhenitsyn, Aleksandr

★ **Cancer** ward; translated from the Russian by Nicholas Bethell and David Burg. Farrar, Straus & Giroux 1969 560p

"Set mostly in a provincial cancer ward, the novel traces the ways in which a number of moribund patients come to terms with their death, centering on an investigation of the moral and psychological development of the exiled hero, Kostoglotov. This novel, in which the cancer ward has been widely interpreted as symbolizing the Soviet state, was typeset for publication in the Soviet Union but never published there until after Perestroika began." Reader's Ency. 4th edition

Solzhenitsyn, Aleksandr

★ **In** the first circle; a novel. [by] Aleksandr I. Solzhenitsyn; translated by Harry T. Willetts. the restored text; Harper Perennial 2009 xxx,741 pa $18.99

ISBN 978-0-06-147901-4 pa

LC 2008-39336

First English version, translated by Thomas P. Whitney, published 1968 by Harper & Row with title: The first circle

"It has taken a half-century for English-language readers to receive the definitive text of 'In the First Circle,' the best novel by one of the greatest authors of our time. Such is the fate of art created under a totalitarian regime. But now it is finally available in the West as the author envisioned it. The

English translator is Harry T. Willetts, renowned for combining fidelity to Aleksandr Solzhenitsyn's rich, complex Russian with supple equivalents in English prose and the only person Solzhenitsyn fully trusted to render his fiction into English." Wall Street J

Solzhenitsyn, Aleksandr

★ **One** day in the life of Ivan Denisovich; translated from the Russian by H. T. Willets; with an introduction by John Bayley. Knopf 1995 xxvii, 159p $15

ISBN 0-679-44464-5

Original Russian edition, 1962; this is a reissue of the translation published 1991 by Farrar, Straus & Giroux

"Drawing on his own experiences, the author writes of one day, from reveille to lights-out, in the prison existence of Ivan Denisovich Shukhov. Innocent of any crime, he has been convicted of treason and sentenced to ten years in one of Stalin's notorious slave-labor compounds. The protagonist is a simple man trying to survive the brutality of a totalitarian system." Shapiro. Fic for Youth. 3d edition

Somerville, Patrick

The **cradle**; a novel. Little, Brown 2009 203p $23.99

ISBN 978-0-316-03612-2; 0-316-03612-9

LC 2008-25148

"Somerville's Midwesterners . . . must often be forced into honest self-examination, preferring to hide behind work and duty to prevent the ice-crusted layers of memory from melting into the present. . . . Matt finds the cradle. In fact, that happens more easily than he — or the reader — expects, and the detours and false leads he follows en route feel superfluous, even in this slim novel. The post-cradle journey — and what he discovers — becomes the life-rattling trip." N Y Times Book Rev

Somerville, Patrick

This bright river; a novel. Patrick Somerville. Reagan Arthur Books/Little, Brown and Co. 2012 453 p. (hardback) $24.99

ISBN 0316129313; 9780316129312

LC 2011046159

In this book by Patrick Somerville, "Ben returns to his hometown to prepare his late uncle's home for sale. A recovering addict and ex-felon, Ben feels adrift, but he seeks to rebuild some sort of relationship with his family and find direction for his life. He encounters Lauren, a high school classmate, who has escaped an abusive marriage. They find solace in each other, but dark secrets put both of them in peril." (Library Journal)

Somerville, Rowan

The **end** of sleep. W. W. Norton & Co. 2008 246p $23.95

ISBN 978-0-393-06660-9; 0-393-06660-6

LC 2008-18240

"In this madcap picaresque, we follow Fin, an Irish journalist, as he spends a day in the streets of Cairo pursuing a story of buried treasure that he believes will restore his floundering career at an English-language newspaper there. Fin seeks a 'pacy linear narrative with obvious and satisfying climaxes,' but Somerville leads us, instead, down numerous back alleys and side streets, with frequent breaks for mint tea. The best moments are those of unbridled irreverence, such as when Fin, who is conversant only in 'gastronomical Arabic,' becomes 'inappropriately passionate' on the subject of the perfect kebab (the secret ingredient is thyme), or when we are told that the desert air is 'so pure you can smell the farts of the camels.' Fin's surreal experiences amid Cairo's chaos are a vivid reminder of the challenges inherent in encountering the foreign, and the rewards of 'not only learning to accept, but inhabit' difference." New Yorker

Somoza, Jose Carlos

Zig Zag; a novel. translated from Spanish by Lisa Dillman. Rayo 2007 504p $24.95
  ISBN 978-0-06-119371-2; 0-06-119371-2
                                    LC 2006-50406
  Original Spanish edition, 2006

This novel "could've been a bad Crichton tech-thriller knockoff, but José Carlos Somoza displays an unhurried style and a refreshing appreciation for advanced science." Entertainment Wkly

Sontag, Susan

★ **In** America; a novel. Farrar, Straus & Giroux 2000 387p $26
  ISBN 0-374-17540-3
                                    LC 99-54641

This novel "displays Sontag in a relaxed, pleasure-seeking mode, guiding her characters through a long travelogue in time, specifically the beginnings of the gilded age in the brave new world." Time

Sontag, Susan

The **volcano** lover; a romance. Farrar, Straus & Giroux 1992 419p il $22
  ISBN 0-374-28516-0
                                    LC 92-71738

Sontag's "narrative deftly blends the magnetism of personality and the suspense of event with shrewd commentary and sly mockery as she contrasts the habits of thought in that age with ours and reflects on the meaning of mercy and vengeance, self-invention and praise, love and obsession. In all, a memorable group portrait and a brilliant, fresh improvisation on classically grand themes." Booklist

Sorokin, Vladimir, 1955-

Day of the oprichnik; translated from the Russian by Jamey Gambrell. Farrar, Straus and Giroux 2011 191p $23
  ISBN 978-0-374-13475-4
                                    LC 2010039060
  Original Russian edition, 2006

This novel is "set . . . [in] Moscow in 2028. 'Holy Russia' has been reborn out of the 'Gray Ashes' of its history into a new era of 'Orthodoxy, Autocracy, and Nationality.' A Great Western Wall cuts Russia off from a decayed Europe. The people have long since ritually burned their foreign-travel passports on Red Square. . . . On Lubianka Square . . . stands a . . . statue of Malyuta Skuratov, the most powerful and cruelest of Ivan the Terrible's oprichniks [or untouchables]. . . . [The plot follows] a high-ranking, middle-aged oprich-

nik, Andrei Komiaga, as he goes about his Monday round of state business. Through Komiaga's present-tense stream of consciousness, . . . [author Vladimir] Sorokin opens up the myth of the Russian state." (N Y Review of Books)

"In the year 2028, 16 years into Holy Russia's revival, a new and bloody dictatorship holds sway. The Oprichnina, an elite squadron of thugs, carries out the tsar's directive to 'keep order and exterminate rebellion.' The reader is invited to job shadow one of the oprichniks for a day, as he and his colleagues assassinate a treasonous nobleman, censor and intimidate authors and artists, protect the borders from the Chinese and cyberpunks, and partake in a bit of illicit pleasure in between assignments. Sorokin's creations are at once fantastically strange and all too familiar. His pen drips with imaginative fury as he skewers a wide range of targets, not least of which is an intellectual class whose increasing irrelevance makes them easy prey." Libr J

Sorokin, Vladimir, 1955-

Ice; translated from the Russian by Jamey Gambrell. New York Review Books 2007 321p $23.95
  ISBN 978-1-59017-195-0
                                    LC 2006-21077
  Original Russian edition, 2002

"The ice of the title is from a giant comet that landed in Tungus, Siberia, in 1908 and transformed 23,000 alien beings of light into human form, all blue-eyed blonds. Only a few are aware of their true selves, and they must locate the others to awaken their hearts by bashing them in the chest with axes made from the cosmic ice. For every new Brother or Sister of Light so transformed, many humans must die. Sorokin builds the suspense by incrementally telling the story from the perspectives of three beings in the process of reawakening, their spiritual leader, and a variety of beings who are transformed in their version of the Rapture. Ice succeeds brilliantly as both a thriller and a cautionary tale about totalitarianism, bigotry, elitism, and fundamentalism." Libr J

Sorrentino, Gilbert

The **abyss** of human illusion; a novel. with a preface by Christopher Sorrentino. Coffee House Press 2010 151p pa $14.95
  ISBN 978-1-56689-233-9; 1-56689-233-3
                                    LC 2009-28064

This novel consists of "a series of vignettes with a mildly experimental structure (they are followed by explanatory endnotes). . . . Abyss (which borrows its title from Henry James) finds Sorrentino in familiar territory: Brooklyn artists, writers, alcoholics, adulterers and former military men agonize over failed marriages, futile manuscripts and faulty bodies. Sorrentino hits inventive and unsentimental high notes with these vignettes." Time Out N Y

Sorrentino, Gilbert

The **moon** in its flight; stories. Coffee House Press 2004 266p $16
  ISBN 1-56689-152-3 pa
                                    LC 2004-665

"A sort of grim nostalgia pervades his stories, many of the best of which are set in a perfectly evoked mid-20th century New York of shabby cocktail lounges and afternoon papers." N Y Times Book Rev

Sorrentino, Gilbert

A **strange** commonplace. Coffee House Press 2006 154p pa $14.95

ISBN 1-56689-182-5

LC 2005-35804

This novel "portrays a circle of struggling New Yorkers living back in the sexist, alcohol-sodden, and hypocritical 1950s on into the egomaniacal present. Ugly sex, adultery, and vicious domestic battles make a misery of marriage and family life, and old age is nothing to aspire to. Memories fizzle and morph into fantasies, and one elderly fellow courts death with solitary card games. The book itself resembles a deck of cards, what with its 52 tales imprinted with repeating patterns and emblems, and sly Sorrentino shuffling the cards, cutting the deck, and dealing some tough hands." Booklist

Sosin, Danielle

The **long**-shining waters. Milkweed Editions 2011 270p $24

ISBN 978-1-57131-083-5

LC 2011-02077

"Lake Superior proves to be more than a bucolic backdrop for Sosin's debut novel. It swallows fishing nets, boats, and even men, and shapes the lives of three women from different eras: Grey Rabbit, an Ojibwe woman following seasonal routes with her family in 1622 and struggling to feed her children; Berit Kleiven, who lives in a lonely cove with her husband, Gunnar, in 1902; and Nora Truneau, a Duluth bar owner who explores the lake in 2000 after a crisis. . . . Sosin writes sensuously detailed prose and distills the emotions of her characters into a profound and universal need for acceptance and love." Publ Wkly

Southgate, Martha

The **fall** of Rome; a novel. Scribner 2002 223p hardcover o.p. pa $13

ISBN 0-684-86500-9; 0-7432-2721-2 pa

LC 2001-34225

The author "delves deeply into the social and emotional elements that unite and divide us. Issues of race, identity, and integrity are intensely explored through a tragic human triangle." Booklist

Southgate, Martha

The **taste** of salt; a novel. Algonquin Books of Chapel Hill 2011 281p pa $13.95

ISBN 978-1-56512-925-2; 1-56512-925-3

LC 2011-24615

"Growing up in shabby, landlocked Cleveland in a household ravaged by alcoholism, Josie Henderson finds escape in 'the pure blue pleasure' of water. Her fascination with the life aquatic eventually leads to an esteemed position as a research scientist, making her one of few black women in the cloistered field of marine biology. Still, the tidal pull of her troubled family — and the sad legacy of her father's addiction, revisited upon her beloved baby brother, Tick — laps at the edges of her orderly life. . . . Southgate writes with a minor-key melancholy that comes on softly, but lingers long after." Entertainment Wkly

Spanidou, Irini

Before. Alfred A. Knopf 2007 211p $23

ISBN 978-0-375-41381-0; 0-375-41381-2

LC 2007-5265

"Spanidou's beautiful writing almost perfectly evokes the 1970s in New York, its fascinating characters, its low rents and withheld ambitions—her sentences have just the right measure of elegant lassitude, of quiet, humming sexiness, and of a singular devotion to seeing things deeply, no matter what the cost." Oprah Magazine

Spark, Muriel

The **Abbess** of Crewe. Viking 1974 116p

"The Abbess of Crewe has the closely woven texture and the structural coherence of good poetry: it is executed with a subtlety and intelligence that safeguard against the tones of complacent moralizing that might very easily have spoiled the articulation of the book's themes." Saturday Rev/World

Spark, Muriel

Aiding and abetting. Doubleday 2000 166p

ISBN 0-385-50153-6

LC 00-55559

"The unsettling wit of 'Aiding and Abetting' hits the funny bone as hard it pricks the conscience. . . . It's kiln-dried wit that never cracks, with a smile that dares you to laugh. As always {Spark is} breathtakingly deft with the anxieties of well-bred people, people who know how to dress, where to eat, and how to commit the most heinous cruelty. If satire is your cup of tea, . . . {this is a} perfectly seeped book to be savored." Christ Sci Monit

Spark, Muriel

The **bachelors**. New Directions 1999 186p pa $12.95

ISBN 0-8112-1424-9

LC 99-30688

First published 1960 in the United Kingdom; first published in the United States 1961 by Lippincott

This "novel follows a group of British bachelors whose cozy little world is shattered when they suddenly find themselves the target of blackmail, fraud, and other bits of nastiness courtesy of one of the lads. Spark is always a great read." Libr J

Spark, Muriel

The **ballad** of Peckham Rye. Lippincott 1960 160p

"A fresh comic style does not appear every day, and that is what Muriel Spark has developed in this expert fantasy. . . . The wackiness is cumulative, the style dead-pan and blow-by-blow, and above all no overt attempt is ever made to get a laugh." N Y Times Book Rev

Spark, Muriel

The **driver's** seat. Knopf 1970 117p

"The author's perspective is cosmically cool and fantastic: she knows no more about her protagonist, Lise, than does the reader. . . . She follows this woman, another of her slightly bizarre lunatics, through a day's grotesque project, narrating only its circumstances, leaving all motive, all emotion, all inner plan to be inferred. The result is a long, elusive joke that casts as deep an irony on life's arbitrariness as do the more 'compassionate' ironies of, say, E. M. Forster." Nation

Spark, Muriel

★ A **far** cry from Kensington. Houghton Mifflin 1988 189p

ISBN 0-395-47694-1

LC 88-5904

"Spark balances devastatingly eccentric characters and funny situations with darker elements, even pathos. Her well-constructed novel has no loose ends and few contrived situations." Libr J

Spark, Muriel

The **finishing** school; Muriel Spark. 1st ed; Doubleday 2004 181p $16.95

ISBN 0-385-51282-1

LC 2004-45533

The author "satirically assails, among other subjects, the culture of spectacle that has grown up around novel writing, particularly novel writing by attractive young people." Atl Mon (1993)

Spark, Muriel

★ The **girls** of slender means. Knopf 1963 176p

"The novel, set primarily in London during World War II, focuses on the inhabitants of a residential club for unmarried women and on the friendship of several of them with a young man named Nicholas Farringdon. When tragedy strikes and 13 of the women are killed, Nicholas realizes that there is no safety anywhere, especially for those on whom fortune had once seemed to smile. This epiphany stimulates his conversion to Roman Catholicism. Years later, he dies in Haiti, where he has gone as a missionary." Merriam-Webster's Ency of Lit

Spark, Muriel

Loitering with intent. Coward, McCann & Geoghegan 1981 217p

ISBN 0-698-11047-1

LC 80-26049

"Would-be novelist Fleur Talbot works for the snooty, irascible Sir Quentin Oliver at the Autobiographical Association, whose members are all at work on their memoirs. When her employer gets his hands on Fleur's novel-in-progress, mayhem ensues when its scenes begin coming true. Generating hilarious turns of phrase and larger-than-life characters (especially Sir Quentin's batty mother), Sparks's inimitable style make this literary joyride thoroughly appealing." Publ Wkly

Spark, Muriel

★ The **Mandelbaum** Gate. Knopf 1965 369p

"The changing shape of any identity, be it of person or of situation, is the theme of this novel, typified by the Mandelbaum Gate of the title, 'hardly a gate at all, but a piece of street between Jerusalem and Jerusalem'. . . The narrative goes and returns piecemeal between the two parts of the Holy Land, focusing on two English characters–Barbara Vaughan, a spinster, half Jewish by birth and Roman Catho-

lic by conviction, come to Israel to be near her archeologist fiance (and lover) in Jordan and to make a pilgrimage to the Holy sites; and Freddy Hamilton, proper foreign officer, moved by an unexpected impulse to change his personal pattern of responsibility and by kindness to keep Barbara from the danger of being apprehended by Jordan authorities because of her background." Libr J

Spark, Muriel

★ **Memento** mori. Lippincott 1959 224p

"Several elderly London friends receive anonymous telephone calls with a single message: 'Remember you must die.' Each hears and interprets the words differently. Old rivalries and romances still color the friends' relations, and Spark makes clear that their personalities in old age are but a continuation of their earlier lives." Merriam-Webster's Ency of Lit

Spark, Muriel

A **Muriel** Spark trio; The comforters; The ballad of Peckham Rye; Memento mori. Lippincott 1962 608p

The three complete novels reprinted here were first published 1957, 1960 and 1959 respectively. The comforters is a novel in experimental form. It is a book within a book, in which many of the characters are neurotics or oddities of some sort. The most normal character is Louisa Jepp, aged seventy-eight, whose experiments with smuggling diamonds provide much of the action. The scene is England, and Roman Catholic life is part of the background

Spark, Muriel

★ **Open** to the public; new & collected stories. New Directions 1997 376p $24.95

ISBN 0-8112-1367-6

LC 97-20607

"With 10 tales new to American readers, Open to the Public brings Spark's stories up to date with the rest of her prolific output." Publ Wkly

Spark, Muriel

★ The **prime** of Miss Jean Brodie. Lippincott 1962 187p

First published 1961 in the United Kingdom

"Miss Jean Brodie, teacher at the Marcia Blaine School for Girls in Edinburgh in the 1930s, gathers around herself a group of young girls who are set apart from other students as the Brodie set: Monica Douglas, who will be famous for her mathematical ability; Rose Stanley, who will be famous for her sex appeal; Eunice Gardiner, of great swimming and gymnastic ability; Sandy Stranger, of the small eyes and outstanding vowel sounds; and Mary MacGregor, who is considered a silent lump. Miss Brodie will make these girls the 'crème de la crème,' especially if they will follow her advice to recognize their prime. Her teaching is unorthodox and her relationship with the students most informal, so that they are privy to her affair with the school's music teacher. We get glimpses into the future of these young girls and are made aware that students are capable of treachery as well as teacher-worship." Shapiro. Fic for Youth. 3d edition

Spark, Muriel

Reality and dreams. Houghton Mifflin 1997 160p

ISBN 0-395-83811-8

LC 96-52913

First published 1996 in the United Kingdom

"A glimpse of a girl selling hamburgers at a French campground ignites film director Tom Richard's imagination, and around it he builds his latest movie. When the film is still in production, he suffers a serious accident and awakens to find his vision being threatened as others try to take over the story. He also awakens to disruptions in his 'real' life-many of those around him are losing their jobs, his daughters' marriages are in the process of breaking up, and long held resentments/jealousies, both personal and professional, are coming to the surface." Libr J

Sparks, Nicholas, 1965-

A **bend** in the road. Warner Bks. 2001 341p

ISBN 0-446-52778-5

LC 2001-26419

Deputy sheriff Miles Ryan's "high school sweetheart, Missy, was killed in an unsolved hit and run accident, leaving him to raise their son, Jonah, in New Bern, N.C. [Sarah Andrews'] politically ambitious husband, Michael, dumped her when her ovaries proved inactive, and she fled to New Bern to teach, and love, other people's kids. Miles and Sarah meet at a parent-teacher conference, and the sparks fly. But there's a fly in the ointment as well." Publ Wkly

"Sparks brings a powerful tale of true love to fruition, proving that love stories can be sweet without being cloying." Booklist

Sparks, Nicholas

Dear John. Warner Books 2006 276p $24.99

ISBN 978-0-446-52805-4; 0-446-52805-6

LC 2006-020714

"John Tyree is on the fast track to nowhere. At 20 he has no real relationship with his strange and dispassionate father, no attachments to anyone else, and no job, so after breaking up with his girlfriend, he decides to join the army. Military life does alter him, yet he remains disconnected. While home visiting his father in Wilmington, North Carolina, however, he meets Savannah Curtis, a college coed who is everything he is not. A warm, morally straight-ahead woman with a commitment to special education, she captures John's heart and he hers. In the short time they spend together, he opens up to Savannah and true love develops as they plan for a future. Then September 11 changes everything. John feels that it is his duty to renew his commitment to the army, while Savannah wants him home with her. The good soldier now lives in dread of receiving a 'Dear John' letter. Sparks . . . lives up to his reputation with his latest novel, a tribute to courageous and self-sacrificing soldiers." Booklist

Sparks, Nicholas

The **guardian**. Warner Bks. 2003 384p $24.95

ISBN 0-446-52779-3

LC 2002-192411

"On Christmas Eve, Julie Barenson, 25 years old and newly widowed, finds an unexpected present—a Great Dane pup that her late husband, Jim, had arranged for her to receive after her died from a brain tumor. . . . Julie's new dog,

Singer, turns out to be a better judge of character than she, which is unfortunate because the dog nearly gives away the book's ending when he growls warily at Richard Franklin, the new man in Julie's life." Publ Wkly

Sparks, Nicholas

The **last** song. Grand Central Pub. 2009 413p $24.99; pa $14.99

ISBN 978-0-446-54756-7; 0-446-54756-6; 978-0-446-54755-0 pa; 0-446-54755-7 pa

LC 2009-24801

In this novel "17-year-old Ronnie is forced to abandon her club-hopping Manhattan ways for a summer with her estranged father in a North Carolina beach town. The story that follows is typically Sparksian, an engaging if heavily telegraphed stew of romance, betrayal, and youthful discovery, garnished with a healthy dollop of Christianity. Fans of The Notebook, Message in a Bottle, etc., will gobble it up with glee." Entertainment Wkly

Sparks, Nicholas

Message in a bottle. Warner Bks. 1998 322p $20

ISBN 0-446-52356-9

LC 97-39158

"Boston parenting columnist Theresa Osborne has lost faith in the dream of everlasting love. Three years after divorcing her cheating husband, the single mother is vacationing on Cape Cod when she finds a bottle washed up on the shore. Inside, a message begins: 'My Dearest Catherine, I miss you.' Subsequent publication of the poignant missive in her column turns up two more letters, found by others, from the same mysterious writer, Garrett Blake. Piqued by his epistolary constancy, Theresa follows the trail to North Carolina, where she discovers that Garrett has been mourning his late wife for three years; writing the seaborne messages is his only solace. Theresa also finds that Garrett just might be ready to love again . . . and that she might be the woman for him." Publ Wkly

Sparks, Nicholas

Nights in Rodanthe. Warner Bks. 2002 212p

ISBN 0-446-53133-2

LC 2002-66189

"Adrienne Wills is a 45-year-old mother of three whose husband recently abandoned her for a younger woman. When she visits the small coastal town of Rodanthe, North Carolina, seeking a bit of respite from her problems, she meets Paul Flanner, a 54-year-old doctor who has sold his thriving medical practice and come to Rodanthe to escape his own tortured past." Booklist

"Sparks builds a taut, plausible relationship between his protagonists." Publ Wkly

Sparks, Nicholas, 1965-

★ The **notebook**. Warner Bks. 1996 214p

ISBN 0446520802

LC 96-33815

"At 80, Noah Calhoun reads daily from a notebook containing the love story of Noah and Allie. We learn of the teenaged lovers, their 14-year separation and reunion in New Bern, North Carolina, just weeks before Allie is to marry another man. Back in the present, we learn that Noah and Allie did marry and were happy for more than 40 years. Now, they are residents of a nursing home, separated both by rooms and, more profoundly, by Allie's Alzheimer's. Noah's daily reading from the notebook is not to himself; he reads aloud to Allie, hoping that the power of their love story will reach her." Libr J

Sparks, Nicholas

A **walk** to remember. Warner Bks. 1999 240p $19.95

ISBN 0-446-52553-7

LC 99-12079

In Beaufort, North Carolina in 1958, 17-year-old high school senior Landon Carter takes Jamie Sullivan, the minister's daughter, to the homecoming dance, stars with her in the Christmas play, and falls in love with her, only to discover her sad secret

The author "is a master at pulling heartstrings and bringing a tear to his readers' eyes. . . . Told in Landon's down-home voice, this bittersweet tale will enthrall Sparks' numerous fans." Booklist

Spatz, Gregory

Inukshuk; Gregory Spatz. Bellevue Literary Press 2012 220 p. (paperback) $14.95

ISBN 1934137421; 9781934137420

LC 2012008326

This novel by Gregory Spatz focuses on a modern family. "John Franklin has moved his fifteen-year-old son to the remote northern Canadian town of Houndstitch to make a new life together after his wife, Thomas' mother, left them. Mourning her disappearance, John, a high school English teacher, writes poetry and escapes into an affair, while Thomas withdraws into a fantasy recreation of the infamous Victorian-era arctic expedition led by British explorer Sir John Franklin." (Publisher's note)

Speller, Elizabeth

The **return** of Captain John Emmett. Houghton Mifflin Harcourt 2011 442p $26

ISBN 978-0-547-51169-6

LC 2010052590

First published 2010 in the United Kingdom

"Laurence Bartram is a young widower grappling not only with the loss of his young wife and infant son but also with a return to normalcy after his service in World War I when he receives a letter from Mary Emmett, the sister of a boyhood friend, asking him to look into her brother's supposed suicide. He is as intrigued by Mary herself as he is by her letter, and his investigations uncover a series of crimes and help Laurence confront his own horrendous memories of the war. An absorbing mystery set in postwar London, . . . [this book] is brimming with historical details of the period and doesn't shy away from war's atrocities." Libr J

Speller, Elizabeth

The **strange** fate of Kitty Easton; Elizabeth Speller. Houghton Mifflin Harcourt 2012 407 p.

ISBN 0547547528; 9780547547527

LC 2011036972

This historical mystery novel by Elizabeth Speller begins "[w]hen Great War veteran Laurence Bartram arrives in Easton Deadall. . . . Now peace prevails, and the rest of England is newly alight with hope, but Easton Deadall remains haunted by tragedy - as does the Easton family. In 1911, five-year-old Kitty disappeared from her bed and has not been seen in thirteen years; only her fragile mother still believes she is alive. While Laurence is a guest of the manor, a young maid vanishes in a sinister echo of Kitty's disappearance. And when a body is discovered in the manor's ancient church, Laurence is drawn into the grounds' forgotten places, where deadly secrets lie in wait". (Publisher's note)

Spencer, Elizabeth

★ The **southern** woman; new and selected fiction. Modern Lib. 2001 448p $23.95

ISBN 0-679-64218-8

LC 00-54612

"This collection offers selections from the Mississippi native's earlier short fiction together with several new stories. Best known of the earlier fiction is her stunning novella, The Light in the Piazza (1960), the deceptively simple tale of an American mother and daughter in Florence." Libr J

Spencer, Elizabeth

The **stories** of Elizabeth Spencer; with a foreword by Eudora Welty. Doubleday 1981 429p

ISBN 0-385-15697-9

LC 79-6601

The stories included in this collection were written between 1944 and 1977 and were originally published in various periodicals. The novelette Knights & dragons was published separately in 1965 by McGraw-Hill. It concerns an American divorcee living in Rome. Other stories in the collection are: The little brown child; The eclipse; First dark; A southern landscape; Moon rocket; The white azalea; The visit; Ship Island; The fishing lake; The adult holiday; The Pincian gate; The absence; The day before; The Bufords; Judith Kane; Wisteria; A bad cold; Presents; On the Gulf; Sharon; The finder; Instrument of destruction; Go South in the winter; A kiss at the door; A Christian education; Mr. McMillan; I, Maureen; Prelude to a parking lot; Indian summer; The search; Port of embarkation: The girl who loved horses

Spencer, LaVyrle

Bitter sweet. Putnam 1990 382p

ISBN 0-399-13508-1

LC 89-38089

"The untimely death of her husband leaves Maggie Pearson wealthy but emotionally bereft. Two decades after she has left home, Maggie returns to Wisconsin to fortify her spirits and decides to open a bed-and-breakfast despite dire warnings from her tight-lipped mother and the hurt fury of her college-age daughter. Her first love, Eric Severson, is also back in town, running a family-owned charter fishing boat to the great displeasure of his beautiful, ambitious wife." Publ Wkly

"Readers who can accept the plausibility of Maggie's original separation from Eric will enjoy following her journey of self-discovery and reawakening." Booklist

Spencer, LaVyrle
Forgiving. Putnam 1991 382p

LC 90-42821

"Bowing to the formulaic demands of historical romance without descending into parody or cliché, Spencer gives us an interesting, titillating story peopled by intriguingly human characters." Booklist

Spencer, LaVyrle
Morning glory. Putnam 1989 384p

ISBN 0-399-13413-1

LC 88-28166

"Tall, dark and handsome Will Parker has served time for the killing of a Texas prostitute, but keeps losing jobs as his reputation becomes known. In the small town of Whitney, Ga., at the beginning of WW II, he answers the advertisement of a pregnant widow and mother of two, the abused and reclusive Eleanor Dinsmore, who is looking for a husband. Soon in love with ostensibly plain, bedraggled Ellie, Parker dotes on her two boys, and works to support the family. Fittingly for this sort of bucolic idyll, Will and Ellie, despite their rudimentary educations, love books and develop a special friendship with wise old Miss Beasley, the local librarian. Alas, brazen and rapacious Lula Peak, the town floozie, sets her sights on Will, waylaying him in the library; meantimes, Lula is blackmailing her lover, the cowardly Harley Overmire, who is no friend of Will. The clearly drawn characters fulfill their imperatives—including Will, who becomes a war hero—and all is neatly and pleasingly resolved." Publ Wkly

Spencer, LaVyrle
Small town girl. Putnam 1997 364p

ISBN 0-399-14249-5

LC 96-24317

"When small-town girl Tess McPhail followed the pull of Nashville's glittering lights, she placed her dreams on becoming a country singer. Eighteen years later, she is a megastar and is caught in a whirlwind of tours, recording sessions, and financial meetings—a whirlwind that crashes to a stop when her sister demands her help in caring for their mother. Angered at her sister's orders, Tess breezes in to town for a month and crashes straight into the past in the form of Kenny Kronek, the boy-next-door 'dork' from high school who has been helping her mother." Booklist

Spencer, LaVyrle
That Camden summer. Putnam 1996 368p

ISBN 0-399-14120-0

LC 95-20055

In 1916, divorceé Roberta Jewett, "returns to her provincial hometown of Camden, Maine, in order to build a new life for herself and her three daughters. Braving adversaries such as her lecherous brother-in-law, condemning mother, and a community that considers a divorced woman little better than a prostitute, Roberta Jewett behaves 'scandalously,' securing a job as a country nurse to support her children, learning to drive, and buying a 'Model-T car.' Roberta is embittered by her humiliating marriage to an outrageous philanderer, but not surprisingly she 'finds love' with Gabriel Farley, the gruff yet inwardly sensitive widowed carpenter retained to renovate her home. Although predictable

and somewhat belabored, Spencer's latest novel is overall an enjoyable read." Libr J

Spencer, Sally
Backlash; A Monica Paniatowski mystery. Sally Spencer. Severn House Pub Ltd 2011 216 p. (Monika Paniatowski mysteries) $28.95

ISBN 0727880551; 9780727880550

In this fourth police procedural featuring Det. Chief Insp. Monica Paniatowski, former "Chief Supt. Tom Kershaw, is involved in an auto accident and informs the responding officers in a panic that his wife, Elaine, is missing." The case "appears to be a kidnapping and could be a career maker or a career breaker. When prostitute Grace Meade also disappears, Monika finds enough similarities to widen the investigation, though she's warned to concentrate on finding Elaine." (Publishers Weekly)

Spencer, Sally
★ Echoes of the dead. Severn House Pub Ltd 2011 224 p. (Monika Paniatowski mysteries) $28.95

ISBN 0727869809; 9780727869807

In this DCI Monika Paniatowski mystery, a "dying man who served 20 years for a young girl's murder reveals that he was coerced by the police to confess. DCI Monika Paniatowski is ordered to lead an unofficial investigation, but the man in charge of the original case was her old mentor, Scotland Yard DI Charlie Woodend. Moving between the two time periods," the reader sees both Woodend's and Paniatowski's investigations. (Library Journal)

Spencer, Sally
The ring of death; a DCI Monikay Paniatowski mystery. Severn House Pub Ltd 2010 233 p. (hardcover) $28.95

ISBN 0727868683; 9780727868688

This is Sally Spencer's "second mystery featuring Det. Chief Insp. Monika Paniatowski set in 1970s Lancashire. Early one morning in the woods outside Whitebridge, a dog breeder discovers the naked, mutilated body of a man in his mid-30s. . . . Monika and her team get to work on the case and soon learn the victim is Andrew Adair—a recently discharged army officer who was one of the paras involved in the notorious 1972 Bloody Sunday killings in Northern Ireland." (Publishers Weekly)

Spencer, Sally
A walk with the dead; a Monica Paniatowski mystery. Severn House Pub Ltd 2013 218 p. (hardcover) $27.95

ISBN 0727882422; 9780727882424

This book is Sally Spencer's "sixth 1970s Lancashire mystery featuring Det. Chief Insp. Monika Paniatowski. . . . When 13-year-old Jill Harris disappears after a family wedding in Whitebridge that Monika attended, the girl's mother phones Monika to ask for her help. The next day, furtive young lovers discover Jill's corpse hidden in the bushes of a town park, and Monika and her team go into action." (Publishers Weekly)

Spencer, Scott

★ **Endless** love. Knopf 1979 417p

LC 79-2089

The author "has achieved something quite remarkable in this unabashedly romantic and often harrowing novel. He has created an adolescent love that is believably endless. . . . Mr. Spencer has an acute grasp of character and situation. He gives us details that make these often tormented people uncommonly convincing." N Y Times Book Rev

Spencer, Scott

★ **Man** in the woods; a novel. Ecco 2010 307p $24.99

ISBN 978-0-06-146655-7; 0-06-146655-7

A "novel about what happens to a couple when the man, Paul Phillips, impulsively decides to stop a stranger from beating his dog. . . . Paul's partner, Kate Ellis, is successful, sober and blissfully happy in love, a hard-won trifecta. Her collection of essays, 'Prays Well With Others,' chronicling her years as an alcoholic and wayward mother, has become a best seller; Kate's brand of honesty, humor and religion has found a wide audience. She and her young daughter Ruby (both characters from Spencer's novel, 'A Ship Made of Paper') are living with Paul, a carpenter. . . . After a stressful meeting with a Manhattan client one day, Paul stops off at a state park to clear his head before driving on to Kate's home in rural New York. He spots the man and the dog. One life-altering moment isn't new in fiction, of course, but Spencer makes it fresh, and compelling." Cleveland Plain Dealer

Spencer, Scott

Willing. Ecco 2008 244p $24.95

ISBN 978-0-06-076015-1; 0-06-076015-X

LC 2007-28230

"Spencer's sumptuous prose adds much to the pleasure of this novel's provocative, and often disturbing, story. His elaborate and hilarious verbal riffs recall some of Philip Roth's writing at its best. Willing doesn't flinch in exposing one seamy corner of a world where everything can be bought and sold—for the right price." BookPage

Spencer-Fleming, Julia

All mortal flesh. St. Martin's 2006 336p $22.95

ISBN 0-312-31264-4

While the "setup might sound conventional, Spencer-Fleming's handling of it is far from mechanical. Her unusual heroine has brains and wit and the fearless spirit of an ex-Army chaplain and helicopter pilot who saw action in Kuwait. If anyone can clear Russ and find the real murderer, Clare can do it — if she can only escape from Elizabeth de Groot, the 'frighteningly competent deacon' who has been sent by the bishop to monitor her unorthodox behavior. In a story as unpredictable as its characters, the resolution takes this series in a direction that should give the good bishop heart palpitations." N Y Times Book Rev

Spencer-Fleming, Julia

In the bleak midwinter. Thomas Dunne Bks. 2002 308p $23.95

ISBN 0-312-28847-6

LC 2001-51303

A mystery set in the "upstate New York town of Millers Kill. As the new (and first female) priest of St. Alban's Episcopal Church, Clare {Fergusson} faces her first test when an infant is left on the rectory doorstep by an unwed teenage mother who is found frozen to death by the river. More crises follow in this freshly conceived and meticulously plotted whodunit when a police investigation raises suspicions about two parishioners who are frantic to adopt the child, and when Clare's own inquiries within her conservative flock turn up troubling evidence of domestic abuse." N Y Times Book Rev

Spiegelman, Ian

Everyone's burning; a novel. Villard Bks. 2003 164p $18.95

ISBN 1-400-06056-7

LC 2002-33191

"A nightmarish tour of the drug-fueled subculture of Queens. Leon Koch, a recent high-school graduate, leads a streamlined existence: his goals are to avoid getting killed by any of the neighborhood psychopaths who might have any grievance (real or imagined) against him and to make sure he has enough cocaine and alcohol to cushion his bleak existence. He bounces from one dead-end job to another and seeks out sadomasochistic relationships with the equally damaged women who make up his world." Booklist

"Spiegelman's characters talk to one another like David Mamet's: in staccato bursts, with verve and irony." N Y Times Book Rev

Spiegelman, Peter

Black maps. Knopf 2003 285p $22.95

ISBN 1-4000-4075-2

LC 2003-273218

This mystery introduces John March, "a Manhattan P.I. who walks the mean streets of Beaver and Broad. As the rebel son in four generations of merchant bankers, who turned his back on the family business to become a cop . . . he's quick enough to grasp the byzantine forensic accounting procedures that fire up this technically accomplished financial mystery." N Y Times Book Rev

Spiegelman, Peter

Red cat. Alfred A. Knopf 2007 285p $22.95

ISBN 0-307-26316-9; 978-0-307-26316-2

LC 2006-49529

"Spiegelman has a genuine understanding of what we are capable of doing for love and the cruel cost of settling for anything else. Mystery fans will love his nifty guess-again plot, fuel-injected prose and deeply complex characters, but what shines is the way the author makes the murky psychological secrets of relationships just as thrilling as the crime itself." People

Spiegelman, Peter

Thick as thieves. Alfred A. Knopf 2011 295p $24.95

ISBN 978-0-307-26317-9; 0-307-26317-7

LC 2011-17855

"When a self-professed robber ('cash and highly liquid items only') asks former CIA agent Carr to assume the leadership of a group of highly skilled thieves, Carr, who's been using his gifts to anticipate problems and organize sophisticated schemes for criminal purposes in Houston, reluctantly accepts. The group is aiming at its richest prize yet—tens of millions of dollars belonging to a disgraced financier, Curtis Prager, who evaded conviction for money laundering and conspiracy after the key witness against him fortunately died and now runs a financial services company for organized criminals in the Caymans. To loot Prager, the team must penetrate multiple layers of security-both physical and cyber." Publ Wkly

"Though the end has perhaps one too many surprise! moments, Spiegelman's sharp prose and deft plotting elevate this Ocean's Eleven-style caper story." Entertainment Wkly

Spielberg, Christoph

The **Russian** Donation. AmazonCrossing 2013 318 p. (paperback) $14.95

ISBN 1612184308; 9781612184302

This novel, first in a series from Christoph Spielberg, won Germany's Friedrich Glauser prize for best debut crime novel. It "introduces reluctant detective Felix Hoffmann, . . . who's been an attending ER physician for eight years at a Berlin teaching hospital. Half a year earlier, soon after Hoffman treated Misha Chenkov, a Russian on the hospital's cleaning staff, apparently successfully, Chenkov disappeared. Now, Hoffmann" must treat Chenkov's suspicious case on short notice. (Publishers Weekly)

Spillane, Mickey

The **Consummata**; by Mickey Spillane and Max Allan Collins. Hard Case Crime 2011 255p pa $9.95

ISBN 978-0-85768-288-8; 0-85768-288-1

Spillane "decided to introduce a new series featuring a master criminal called Morgan the Raider. The first entry, The Delta Factor, came out in '67. So far, so good. Then the business intervened in the form of Hollywood, which decided to make a movie out of the first Morgan book. But the experience left Spillane so upset that he stopped work on the already announced second installment. . . . Collins finishes this project seamlessly. It is impossible to tell where one great writer left off and another begins." Bookreporter

Spillane, Mickey

The **Goliath** bone; [by] Mickey Spillane with Max Allan Collins. Harcourt 2008 274p $23

ISBN 978-0-15-101454-5; 0-15-101454-X

LC 2008-10091

"Much of the jargon is vintage, as is the indomitable Hammer as he strives to protect the kids and prevent the Goliath bone from setting off the next big war. While not on a par with early Spillane classics, this is a fitting capstone to Hammer's career." Publ Wkly

Spillane, Mickey

★ The **Mike** Hammer collection [v1] [introduction by Max Allan Collins] New Am. Lib. 2001 513p pa $16

ISBN 0-451-20352-6

LC 00-52728

Omnibus edition of the author's first three Mike Hammer mysteries. Includes I, the jury (1947), My gun is quick

(1950), and Vengeance is mine (1950). "Hammer is a foul-mouthed, violent vigilante and a sucker for beautiful damsels in distress, some of whom pull the wool over his eyes. With his trusty, sexy assistant Velda keeping him honest (sort of), he exacts revenge on racketeers, cheats and murderers." Publ Wkly

Spillane, Mickey

★ The **Mike** Hammer collection [v2] [introduction by Lawrence Block] New Am. Lib. 2001 517p pa $17

ISBN 0-451-20425-5

Omnibus edition of three Mike Hammer mysteries. Includes One lonely night (1951), The big kill (1951), and Kiss me, deadly (1952).

Spiotta, Dana

Eat the document. Scribner 2006 291p $24

ISBN 0-7432-7298-6

LC 2005-54050

"Spiotta has written a glorious sendup of contemporary social and ecological activists with all their preening idealism and absurdity—especially the intelligent—sounding nonsense people spew at one another, even as they rarely connect on any meaningful level." N Y Times Book Rev

Spiotta, Dana

Stone Arabia; a novel. Scribner 2011 239p $24

ISBN 978-1-4516-1796-2; 1-4516-1796-8

LC 2011-17816

The "story of rock musician Nik Worth, a fictional almost-pop star in the '80s. He has withdrawn from public life but continues to make music, releasing handcrafted CDs only to those closest to him and writing fake, intricate reviews and self-interviews. Is he a genius madman, or a sane artist unsullied by 21st-century American idolatry? The tale is told by his sister, who is equal parts ambivalent enabler and ultimate fan. . . . [A] movingly fab narrative; it's as though Nabokov had written a rock novel." Entertainment Wkly

Spragg, Mark

Bone fire. Alfred A. Knopf 2010 243p $25.95

ISBN 978-0-307-27275-1; 0-307-27275-3

LC 2009-29645

"Reuniting readers with some characters from two previous novels, 'The Fruit of Stone' and 'Unfinished Life,' . . . Spragg again lands us on the prairie-grass-covered ranchlands of Ishawooa, Wyo. . . . Here, a frontier ethic of self-reliance butts heads with a deep need for human connection, igniting tensions among a cast of characters who are as stoic as they come. Among them is the local sheriff, Crane, who's struggling with his manhood and a potential health crisis. There's his wife Jean, who drinks away her frustrations about their marriage. Jean's college-age-daughter Griff is torn between her aspirations to study and do sculpture and an urge to stay home to help care for her ailing grandfather, Einar. People are tugged to and fro in 'Bone Fire' by impulses they scarcely understand. Spragg uses a precision-writing skill that borders on poetry to dissect these interior worlds, and it's a wonder to experience." Seattle Times

Sprott, Duncan

The **Ptolemies**. Knopf 2004 xxii, 462p map $25.95

ISBN 1-400-04154-6

LC 2004-5305

"Sprott chronicles the calamitous, ill-fated reign of the first Greek pharaoh of Egypt. . . . The initial chapters chart Ptolemy's ascension from soldier to leader in Egypt, where he becomes a satrap, keeping the body of the late Alexander the Great around as a good luck charm. After consolidating his power, Ptolemy agonizes over the decision to declare himself pharaoh while facing military challenges from a parade of enemies; he also must overcome emotional fallout from his exhausting relationship with his two wives, Berenike and Eurydice. . . . Sprott's scholarship and his command of the material is formidable and impressive, and structurally the novel hangs together despite the author's insistence on documenting much of the historical minutiae of Ptolemy's reign." Publ Wkly

St. Aubyn, Edward, 1960-

At last; Edward St. Aubyn. Farrar, Straus and Giroux 2012 266 p. $15

ISBN 0374298890; 1250023904; 9780374298890; 9781250023902

LC 2011034964

This book follows "Patrick Melrose as he . . . attends the funeral of his mother, who died after a lingering illness—and after giving her home and fortune not to Patrick but to a New Age spiritual center. Eleanor was often absent in Patrick's life, somehow oblivious as he was raped by his sadistic father. Highly intelligent Patrick, now divorced with two sons and sober after years of drug and alcohol abuse, is always analyzing those around him but never fully participates in life." (Library Journal)

St. John Mandel, Emily

★ The **singer's** gun. Unbridled Books 2010 287p $24.95

ISBN 978-1-93607-164-7; 1-93607-164-9

LC 2009-53826

"This is a gripping story, full of moral ambiguities, where deception and betrayal become the norm, and where the expression, 'a riddle wrapped in a mystery, inside an enigma,' is lifted to new heights." St. Louis Post-Dispatch

Stabenow, Dana

A **deeper** sleep. St. Martin's 2007 256p

ISBN 0-312-34322-1; 978-0-312-34322-4

LC 2006-52221

"Private investigator Kate Shugak is determined to find the evidence to convict Louis Deem, who has been arrested and tried for several serious crimes but never convicted. When a double homicide occurs after his latest acquittal, Kate investigates. A witness places Deem at the scene, but Kate wants additional evidence to convince the jury. Deem is a dangerous character who intimidates witnesses, and Kate and her family won't be safe until he is in jail." Booklist

Stabenow, Dana

A **fine** and bitter snow. St. Martin's Minotaur 2002 211p $24.95

ISBN 0-312-20548-1

LC 2002-22863

The "Alaskan P.I. finds herself in the middle of a volatile situation involving proposed drilling for oil in a wildlife preserve. A ranger there is fired for political reasons, and then an important conservationist is poisoned." Libr J

"Rich with details about life in this snowbound culture, the story moves at a steady pace to a classic ending." Publ Wkly

Stabenow, Dana

★ **Hunter's** moon; a Kate Shugak mystery. Putnam 1999 260p $23.95

ISBN 0-399-14468-4

LC 98-33465

Aleut sleuth Kate Shugak "and her boyfriend sign on here as wilderness guides for the management team of a German software company whose arrogant C.E.O. fancies himself a big-game hunter. . . . His cowed employees would have been better advised to bone up on 'The Most Dangerous Game,' because the first big catch is one moose, a few salmon and two junior executives." NY Times Book Rev

Stabenow, Dana

Killing grounds. Putnam 1998 273p $22.95

ISBN 0-399-14356-4

LC 97-23900

"Alaskan private investigator Kate Shugak . . . who practically wallows in the surrounding wild beauty of nature, spars with an abusive, strikebreaking fisherman who later winds up dead. Kate's recently returned lover, enigmatic kin, and eccentric acquaintances make this a delightful read." Libr J

Stabenow, Dana

Restless in the grave; Dana Stabenow. Minotaur Books 2012 371 p. (Kate Shugak series.)

ISBN 9780312559137; 9781429950381

LC 2011037662

In this book, "Finn Grant's death in the crash of his small plane in an apparent act of sabotage raises the question: who would want the self-made billionaire dead? About half the population of southwest Alaska, as Kate Shugak discovers when she goes undercover as a barmaid. . . . Kate's . . . prying reveals that the unsavory Grant was involved in blackmail, mail fraud, and embezzlement, all connected to Alaska's many small airlines. Kate has a casual approach to evidence gathering, and her skill at breaking and entering finds her eventually thrown into a chest freezer, tossed into a Dumpster, and locked inside a freight container while her stalwart and highly intelligent companion, Mutt, who's half-wolf, half-husky, provides assistance." (Publishers Weekly)

Stabenow, Dana

The **singing** of the dead. St. Martin's Minotaur 2001 254p map $23.95

ISBN 0-312-20957-6

LC 2001-19146

"Anne Gordaoff, candidate for the Alaska state senate, is receiving threatening letters. Though sharp, fiesty Aleutian PI Kate Shugak is still recovering from her last job, she allows herself to be talked into protecting Anne." Libr J

"With well-drawn characters, splendid scenery and an insider's knowledge of Alaskan history and politics, this fine novel ranks as one of Stabenow's best." Publ Wkly

Stabenow, Dana

So sure of death; a Liam Campbell mystery. Dutton 1999 275p $23.95

ISBN 0-525-94519-9

LC 99-25121

"Alaska state trooper Liam Campbell begins to investigate the murders of a family on a fishing boat and an archaeologist on a dig. Meanwhile, on a personal level, he entertains two very different visitors: his overbearing, perfectionist father and his great love Wyanet Chouinard. Personal and professional come together when Wyanet helps with the investigations and when the murders appear to be linked to Liam's father." Booklist

Stabenow, Dana

Though not dead; Dana Stabenow. Minotaur Books 2011 446 p. (Kate Shugak series.)

ISBN 0312559119; 9780312559113

LC 2010039080

This book tells the story of "Alaskan native Kate Shugak, ... former investigator for the Anchorage DA, [who] investigates her own family's past. When he dies, Kate's uncle and foster father, Old Sam, leaves everything to Kate. . . . While packing up Sam's extensive book collection, she finds an old diary. But before she's read very much of it, someone bashes her in the head and steals it. The theft is only the first in a series of dangerous encounters. After she's run off the road, attacked and shot at while checking out Sam's property in the remote Canyon Hot Springs area, she realizes that Sam had something someone badly wants, and that Sam's life must hold the clues to what she needs to know. So she travels around Alaska digging up information." (Kirkus)

Stabenow, Dana

Whisper to the blood. Minotaur Books 2009 354p map $24.95

ISBN 978-0-312-36974-3; 0-312-36974-3

LC 2008-33959

Between two suspicious murders and a series of attacks on snow mobilers up the Kanuyaq River, part-time P.I. and newly elected chairman of the Niniltna Native Association Kate Shugak has her hands full.

"A dynamite combination of atmosphere, action, and character." Booklist

Stace, Wesley

By George; a novel. Wesley Stace. Back Bay Books 2008 383p. (pbk.) $14.99; o.p.; o.p.

ISBN 9780316018685; 0316830321; 9780316830324

LC 2006038194

In this book a "young ventriloquist and his wooden alterego trace the story of four generations of a family of entertainers, in a tale that follows the eleven-year-old protagonist's search for answers to secrets about his grandfather's

World War II-era traveling act." (National Public Radio)

"[W]hen his great-grandmother Evie dies, George begins to pore over the books left to him in her bequest, books written by his grandfather Joe that hint at the powers of ventriloquism and reveal family secrets that George starts to wish he'd never learnt. Joe, it seems, fled from his marriage to Queenie and into Ensa, the second world war troop-entertainment organisation, performing his act on the frontlines and dying a hero in Italy, though not before falling in love with someone entirely surprising." (The Guardian)

"Every novel is a ventriloquist act, in which the writer throws his or her voice into the mouths of characters and narrators. In some books you can see the author's lips move; in others the actual speaker seems to vanish altogether. Stace occasionally alerts the reader of his presence—he's something of a showoff. But these intrusions don't sour the spectacle. Some illusions delight even when you know how they're performed." Village Voice

Stachniak, Eva

The Winter Palace; Eva Stachniak. Bantam Books 2011 444p.

ISBN 9780553808124; 9780553908046 ebook

LC 2011004928

This book takes place "[i]n 1745, [when] 16-year-old Vavara, the orphaned daughter of a bookbinder, enters the Russian court as a servant. She soon catches the attention of the Chancellor, who teaches her to spy for him. Trained to listen and report, Vavara is tasked to befriend the young Princess Sophia, who is to marry the Empress Elizabeth's nephew, and then disclose all her secrets to the Chancellor and the Empress. But Sophia and Vavara become confidants and friends and Vavara switches sides, assisting Sophia in her transformation into Catherine and her subsequent rise to power. Narrated by Vavara, this historical novel takes readers on a grand tour of the 18th-century Russian Court. . . . Catherine and Vavara each navigate the palace intrigue in their own way according to their stations, but Vavara, loyal to Catherine, uses her influence . . . to help Catherine gain power." (School Libr J)

Stade, George

Love is war. Turtle Point Press 2006 300p pa $16.95

ISBN 1-885586-47-7

LC 2005-926846

This satirical novel "features an English professor who teaches at Columbia University. Acerbic George Lockhart channels his 'wiseassisms' into his literary criticism when he isn't directing them at his wife, Jane—their relationship seems to consist of one long argument about conservative radio host Dr. Lena and various lines-in-the-sand drawn over household chores. Deciding that he has felt sexually deprived for too long, he enters into a joyful affair with a married redheaded poet. Soon the two are reciting poetry to each other and plotting to murder their respective spouses. Stade leaves a few seams showing in stitching such disparate story lines together—the poignancy of Lockhart's quest for meaning at midlife doesn't quite mesh with his (not entirely credible) homicidal streak. Still, Stade offers a pleasing prose style, with many subtle literary allusions . . . and a nice touch of the absurd." Booklist

Stafford, Jean

The **collected** stories of Jean Stafford. Farrar, Straus & Giroux 1969 463p

Stahlberg, Lance

★ **Billy** Budd, sailor; supplementary material written by Kathleen Helal. Pocket Books 2006 xxi, 166p pa $4.99

ISBN 978-1-416-52372-7; 1-416-52372-3

LC 2006-299200

Written in 1891 but in a still 'unfinished' manuscript stage when Melville died. First publication 1924 in the United Kingdom, as part of the Standard edition of Melville's complete works

"Narrates the hatred of petty officer Claggart by Billy, handsome Spanish sailor. Billy strikes and kills Claggart, and is condemned by Captain Vere even though the latter senses Billy's spiritual innocence." Haydn. Thesaurus of Book Dig

Includes bibliographical references

Stahlberg, Lance

The **complete** shorter fiction; with an introduction by John Updike. Knopf 1997 478p $20

ISBN 0-375-40068-0

Contents: The piazza; Bartleby, the scrivener; Benito Cereno; The lightning-rod man; The encantadas; or, Enchanted isles; The bell-tower; Fragments from a writing desk; Authentic anecdotes of ¿Old Zack¿; Hawthorne and his mosses; The happy failure; The fiddler; Cock-a-doodle-doo!; Poor man's pudding; Rich man's crumbs; The two temples: Temple second; The paradise of bachelors; The tartarus of maids; Jimmy Rose; The 'gees; I and my chimney; The apple-tree table; Billy Budd, sailor; The two temples: Temple first

Stahlberg, Lance

The **confidence**-man: his masquerade; edited, with an introduction and notes by John Bryant. Modern Library 2003 xlix, 331p pa $11.95

ISBN 0-375-75802-X

LC 2003-44561

First published 1857

"The scene is a Mississippi River boat, ironically named the 'Fidele.' A plotless satire taking place on April Fool's Day, the book is filled with characters difficult to distinguish from one another; most of them are different manifestations of the confidence man. A sign hanging on the door of the 'Fidele's' barbershop expresses the theme: 'No Trust.' The confidence man, king of a world without principle, succeeds in gulling men by capitalizing on false hopes and offering false pity. At the end of the book, the flickering light hanging above the table where an old man reads the Bible goes out completely." Reader's Ency. 4th edition

Stahlberg, Lance

★ **Moby**-Dick; or, The whale; illustrated by Rockwell Kent. Modern Library 1992 xxxv, 822p il $21

ISBN 0-679-60010-8

LC 92-50222

First published 1851

"'Moby-Dick' had some initial critical appreciation, particularly in Britain, but only since the 1920s has it been recognized as a masterpiece, an epic tragedy of tremendous dramatic power and narrative drive." Oxford Companion to Engl Lit. 5th edition

Stahlberg, Lance

★ **Omoo**: a narrative of adventures in the South Seas; edited by Harrison Hayford, Hershel Parker, G. Thomas Tanselle. Northwestern University Press 1999 316p pa $16.95

ISBN 0-8101-1765-7

LC 99-41391

First published 1847 by Harper

"Based on Melville's own experiences in the South Pacific, this episodic novel, in a more comical vein than that of Typee, tells of the narrator's participation in a mutiny on a whale ship and his subsequent wanderings in Tahiti with the former doctor of the ship." Merriam-Webster's Ency of Lit

Stahlberg, Lance

Pierre; or, The ambiguities, Israel Potter: his fifty years of exile, The piazza tales, The confidence-man: his masquerade, Uncollected prose, Billy Budd, Sailor: (an inside narrative) Library of America 1984 1478p $45

ISBN 0-940450-24-0

LC 84-11249

Pierre; or, The Ambiguities (1852) "moves between the idyllic Berkshire countryside and the nightmare landscape of early New York City. Its hero, a young American patrician trying to redeem the secret sins of his father, elopes to the city, discovers Bohemian life, attempts a literary epic, and struggles his way through incest, murder, and madness. . . . Israel Potter [1855, is] the story of a veteran of the Revolution, victim of a thousand mischances, and a long-suffering exile in England. . . . The Piazza Tales [1856, is a collection of six stories], including 'The Encantadas,' about nature's two faces—enchanting and horrific; the famous 'Bartleby the Scrivener,' about a Wall Street copyist who 'would prefer not to'; and the enigmatic 'Benito Cereno,' about a credulous Yankee sea captain who stumbles into an intricately plotted mutiny aboard a disabled slave ship. The Confidence-Man [1857], Melville's last published novel, is in many ways a forerunner of modernist American fiction. . . . Many pieces never before collected are also included. . . . Finally, there is the posthumously published masterpiece Billy Budd, Sailor, the haunting story of a beautiful, innocent sailor who is pressed into naval service, slandered, provoked to murder, and sacrificed to military justice." Publisher's note

Stahlberg, Lance

Redburn, his first voyage; White-jacket, or, The world in a man-of-war; Moby-Dick, or, The whale. Literary Classics of the United States, Inc, Distributed to the trade by the Viking Press 1983 1437p $35

ISBN 0-940450-09-7

LC 82-18677

Redburn (1849) is a semiautobiographical novel about a young man's ill-fortuned trip across the Atlantic. White-jacket (1850), another semiautobiographical novel, centers around a young sailor nicknamed for the white jacket that he buys in Peru and wears throughout the novel. It also features an appearance by Jack Chase, a character who appears in several of Melville's works and who is here the first captain of the top, and a vivid description of the floggings and other punishments suffered by the crew for often minor infractions. Moby-Dick is entered separately.

Includes bibliographical references

Stahlberg, Lance

Typee: a peep at Polynesian life. Northwestern Univ. Press 1968 374p il $75

ISBN 0-8101-0161-0

First published 1846

"Based on Melville's own experiences, the story tells of the hero and his friend Toby, who jump ship in the Marquesas Islands and wander mistakenly into the valley of Typee, which is inhabited by cannibals. The Typees become their benevolent captors, refusing to allow them to leave. Toby escapes, while the hero, suffering from a leg wound, remains to be nursed by the lovely Fayaway. Tempted to enjoy a somnolent, vegetative existence, the moral American chooses, with regret, to return to civilization." Reader's Ency. 4th edition

Stahlberg, Lance

★ **Typee**: a peep at Polynesian life; Omoo: a narrative of adventures in the South Seas; Mardi: and a voyager thither. Library of Am. 1982 1333p $40

ISBN 0-940450-00-3

LC 81-18600

Omnibus edition of the author's first three novels. The first two titles are entered separately. In Mardi, first published 1849, Melville "entertained questions of ethics and metaphysics, politics and culture, sin and guilt, innocence and experience. The complexity of the novel's content, in fact, destroys all pretensions to literary form. Originally a narrative of adventure, 'Mardi' became an allegory of mind." Benet's Reader's Ency of Am Lit

Stamm, Peter

On a day like this; a novel. translated by Michael Hofmann. Other Press 2007 229p $23.95

ISBN 978-1-59051-279-1; 1-59051-279-0

LC 2007-35108

Original German edition, 2006

"Andreas is a forty-something German teacher in Paris whose life consists of monotonous routines and impersonal encounters. 'Emptiness was the normal state of things,' Stamm writes. Yet when he develops a bad cough he decides not to wait for his biopsy results; he quits his job and sells his apartment to seek out a girl from his youth, with whom he thinks he may still be in love. Stamm's affectless tone belies the richness of his psychological portraiture; in spite of attempts to shrug off connections ('He had always been careful not to be loved too much himself'), Andreas is driven to revisit primal scenes of loss and mourning." New Yorker

Stamm, Peter

Seven years; a novel. translated from the German by Michael Hofmann. Other Press 2010 264p pa $15.95

ISBN 978-1-59051-394-1

LC 2010-40658

Original German edition, 2009

In this novel, "set in Germany during the 1980s, Alex, an aspiring architect, decides to marry a beautiful and ambitious fellow architect named Sonia because she seems to be the kind of woman who would raise 'two or three children . . . just as well behaved and presentable as she was.' But after he and Sonia have embarked on what he expects to be a comfortable domestic life, Alex begins to fixate on Ivona, a homely and slightly delusional former bookstore clerk with whom he once had an affair. As 'Seven Years' follows Alex's romantic struggle, Stamm explores the way obsession can lead to emotional and physical bankruptcy, but he also examines one of his favorite themes: alienation. Ultimately, Alex doesn't feel at home with any woman — or anyone." N Y Times Book Rev

Stamm, Peter

We're flying; stories. Peter Stamm; translated from the German by Michael Hofmann. Other Press 2012 vi, 370 p.p (pbk.: acid-free paper) $15.95

ISBN 159051324X; 9781590513248; 9781590514191

LC 2012001180

This book presents a short story collection by Peter Stamm. "Some of these stories deal with the awkwardness of adolescence and sexual initiation, but the protagonists of many more are innocents as well. In 'Children of God' . . . a minister navigates between sin and divinity as he falls in love with a young girl who insists that her pregnancy is an immaculate conception. . . . Another protagonist, a young girl who lives 'In the Forest,' survives through 'alert indifference.'" (Kirkus Reviews)

Standiford, Les

Black Mountain; a novel. Putnam 2000 320p

ISBN 0-399-14584-2

LC 99-32943

"Even the most contrived scenes . . . capture the treacherous beauty of the wilderness, defined here in the crisp lines and clear detail of an assured author's strong prose style." N Y Times Book Rev

Standiford, Les

Bone Key. Putnam 2002 319p

ISBN 0-399-14874-4

LC 2002-19052

"The labyrinthine plot, involving a case of rare wine worth $100,000, will delight oenophiles. Thriller buffs in general and readers of South Florida mysteries in particular should find this one well up to Standiford's standard." Publ Wkly

Standiford, Les

Deal on ice; a novel. HarperCollins Pubs. 1997 239p

ISBN 978-0060176204

LC 96-8431

Miami sleuth John Deal "sets out to find the murderer of a bookstore-owning friend, who dies holding a religious tract. Deal finds himself struggling against dangerously ultraconservative preacher James Ray Willis, whose megalithic organization plots to control all area media. A solid crime novel." Libr J

Standiford, Les

Deal with the dead; a novel. Putnam 2001 302p
ISBN 0-399-14704-7

LC 00-55938

In this John Deal novel, "the independent building contractor working in South Florida is still marinating in his guilt over how his wife was nearly killed during his last caper and his agony over the splintering apart of their marriage. A blast from Deal's late father's checkered past, in the form of a visit from one of Dad's cronies just after Deal has been awarded a lucrative waterfront project, theatens to annihilate his carefully pieced together recovery. . . . The action is nonstop, the setting of volatile South Florida from the 1950s to the present is fascinating, and the characterization of a man forced to defend what he loves because of the greed of others is compelling." Booklist

Standiford, Les

Havana run. Putnam 2003 304p $24.95
ISBN 0-399-15059-5

LC 2002-37021

"Standiford does a superb job of setting up his complex plot, using the color-drenched, ever-threatening Havana landscape both to ratchet up the tension and to emphasize the otherworldly nature of this latest and most baffling call from the grave." Booklist

Stanisic, Sasa

How the soldier repairs the gramophone; translated from the German by Anthea Bell. Grove Press 2008 304p $24
ISBN 978-0-8021-1866-0; 0-8021-1866-6

"Through the eyes of the fourteen-year-old narrator, Aleksandar Krsmanovi, we witness a massacre perpetrated by Bosnian Serbs against their Muslim neighbors in the town of Visegrad in 1992. The outlines of the plot are autobiographical: The protagonist's escape to Germany from the attack on Visegrad parallels the author's own at the same age. But rather than rendering a direct account, Stanisic refracts these events through his young narrator's wildly imaginative storytelling. A hyperactive fabulist, Aleksandar embarks on madcap flights of invention and comic exaggeration, which clash movingly with the painfully real chronicle of terror, loss, and exile at the story's heart." Bookforum

Stanley, Kelli

City of secrets. Minotaur Books 2011 290p $24.99
ISBN 978-0-312-60361-8

LC 2011-18777

"Pandora Blake, a performer at the 1940 World's Fair on San Francisco's Treasure Island, has been murdered. An anti-Semitic slur marks her body. Miranda, working security at the fair, is fired to prevent her from investigating the crime. Of course, that doesn't stop her. Between cigarettes and shots of bourbon, Miranda and a reporter friend uncover a layer of anti-Semitism and Fascist sympathy in local society that links to some shocking events at the Calistoga spas. Miranda continues to fight the good fight in Hammett's San Francisco, making Sam Spade proud and giving readers a treat." Booklist

Stanley, Michael

A **carrion** death; introducing Detective Kubu. HarperCollins 2008 467p map $23.95
ISBN 978-0-06-125240-2; 0-06-125240-9

LC 2008-299326

"A skeleton is found in the Kalahari Desert in modern-day Africa. It is unclothed, one of its arms is missing, and its teeth have been knocked out, making identification difficult. It falls to Det. David Bengu (aka Kubu) of the Botswana police to figure out what happened; in the meantime, more deaths follow." Libr J

"Readers may be lured to Africa by the landscape, but it takes a great character like Kubu to win our loyalty." N Y Times Book Rev

Stanley, Michael

Deadly Harvest. HarperCollins 2013 xiv, 477 p.p (paperback) $14.99
ISBN 0062221523; 9780062221520

This is the fourth in Michael Stanley's Detective Kubu series. Here, "newcomer Det. Samantha Khama helps Det. David 'Kubu' Bengu when a serial killer targets girls in Botswana, possibly to use their bodies in a potion called muti. A father, devastated by loss, seeks revenge by murdering a politician in this complicated case." (Library Journal)

Stanley, Michael

Death of the mantis; Michael Stanley. 1st ed.; Harper Paperbacks 2011 448p map
ISBN 9780062000378 pa

LC 2011022154

This book tells the story of "A dedicated Botswana detective [who] finds himself in the middle of simmering tensions between police and nomadic Bushmen." (Kirkus) "A fractious ranger named Monzo is found dying from a severe head wound in a dry ravine. . . . Detective David 'Kubu' Bengu is on the case, an investigation that his old school friend Khumanego claims is motivated by racist antagonism on the part of local police. But when a second bizarre murder, and then a third, seem to point also to the nomadic tribe, the intrepid Kubu must journey into the depths of the Kalahari to uncover the truth." (Publisher's note)

Stansberry, Domenic

The **ancient** rain. St. Martin's Minotaur 2008 293p $24.95
ISBN 978-0-312-36453-3; 0-312-36453-9

LC 2007-49768

In this Dante Mancuso mystery "the former San Francisco cop becomes entangled in a cold case surrounding the unintentional shooting death of a woman during a bank robbery involving a group of militant political anarchists in 1976. In a paranoia-fueled post 9/11 America with new antiterror laws, a federal prosecutor with a deep-rooted grudge arrests Bill Owens, an acquaintance of Mancuso's who was

the prime suspect in the 1976 murder. Hired to help exonerate Owens, Mancuso tracks down individuals linked to the
original case. . . . Equal parts contemporary crime fiction and
dark, existential poetry, this novel should win Stansberry
new fans." Publ Wkly

Stark, Richard

Ask the parrot. Mysterious Press 2006 279p
$23.99

ISBN 0-89296-068-X

LC 2006-927625

"Unconscious in front of the TV is the fate awaiting most
in this corner of purgatory, and Parker's assistance in helping Tom Lindahl escape its confines with a decent stash is
the closest he's come to an act of mercy in his entire bullet-
ridden career. As for what happens to the parrot—don't ask."
N Y Times Book Rev

Stark, Richard

Breakout. Mysterious Press 2002 299p $23.95
ISBN 0-89296-779-X

LC 2002-23492

"Richard Stark (the name that Donald E. Westlake uses
when he lets Parker off the leash) writes with ruthless efficiency. His bad guys are polished pros who think hard, move
fast and turn on a dime in moments of crisis. And because
talk doesn't come cheap, every bit of dialogue counts." N Y
Times Book Rev

Stark, Richard

Comeback. Mysterious Press 1997 292p
ISBN 978-0892966615

LC 97-7019

"The plot for this caper is a cunningly engineered sequence of catastrophes, each one set in motion by some
seemingly minor miscalculation that escalates into disaster.
Oiling the machinery is the author's biting irony toward
characters who talk the big talk about love and trust and
loyalty but ditch their Christian values for a hot babe or a
cool buck. In a world of warped values, an honest crook like
Parker is a true treasure." N Y Times Book Rev

Stark, Richard

Dirty money. Grand Central Pub. 2008 276p
$23.99

ISBN 978-0-446-17858-7; 0-446-17858-6

LC 2007-931314

"Lots went wrong after Parker and two partners robbed
an armored car in rural Massachusetts of $2.2 million in
2004's Nobody Runs Forever. The money was 'poisoned'
(i.e., marked); one of his partners was captured before killing
a marshal and escaping; and bounty-hunter Sandra Loscalzo
wants to cut herself in on the take. The pragmatic, quick-
thinking Parker must find a way to retrieve the stashed haul
he and his confederates left in Massachusetts without getting caught by the law or nibbled to death by other crooks."
Publ Wkly

Stark, Richard

The **hunter**; University of Chicago Press ed.;
University of Chicago Press 2008 198p
ISBN 0-226-77099-0; 978-0-226-77099-4

LC 2008-11226

First published 1963 by Pocket Bks.
In this first novel of the author's Parker series, "Parker
roars into New York City, seeking revenge on the woman
who betrayed him and on the man who took his money, stealing and scamming his way to redemption." Publisher's note

Stark, Richard

The **jugger**; with a new foreword by John Banville. The University of Chicago Press 2009 211p
pa $14

ISBN 978-0-226-77102-1; 0-226-77102-4

LC 2008-42432

First published 1965 by Pocket Bks.
This novel in the author's Parker series has the main
character in Sagamore, Nebraska, at the request of Joe
Sheer, a retired safe cracker who carries many of Parker's
criminal secrets.

Starr, Jason

Lights out. St. Martin's Minotaur 2006 296p
$22.95

ISBN 978-0-312-35972-0; 0-312-35972-1

LC 2006-45057

"High school baseball stars Jake Thomas and Ryan
Rossetti were destined to make it out of the mean streets of
Brooklyn and into the major leagues, but a career-ending injury to Ryan's pitching arm sends him back to living with his
parents and making $10 an hour as a house painter. Charmed
Jake becomes one of the most promising young players,
earning a $10 million signing bonus—and an ego to match.
Jake returns home for a celebration weekend, mainly to announce his engagement to high school sweetheart Christina
Mercado, not out of love but to negate the bad publicity from
a sex scandal lurking in his past. Meanwhile, Christina has
fallen in love with Ryan and must choose between living in
Brooklyn with a house painter or a loveless future on Easy
Street. . . . [This novel] sizzles with streetwise dialog and
furious emotional energy." Libr J

Starr, Jason

Panic attack. Minotaur Books 2009 324p
$24.99

ISBN 978-0-312-38706-8; 0-312-38706-7

LC 2009-10486

"Carlos Sanchez wasn't expecting anyone to be home,
much less have an entire clip emptied into him as he reached
the top of the stairs of the brownstone he breaks into in Forest Hills Gardens, Queens. The gun-wielding psychologist,
Adam Bloom, is almost equally surprised-instead of being
hailed as a hero for defending his wife and daughter in his
own home, the media vilify him as a crazed vigilante for using all 10 bullets. Even worse, the sociopathic Johnny Long,
going along with his pal Carlos for an easy score, decides to
make the Blooms pay in more blood for the incident after he
escapes into the night." Publ Wkly
"Baleful and scorching. No one in the suspense field today does nasty as well as Starr." Kirkus

Stead, Christina

★ The **man** who loved children; with an introduction by Doris Lessing. Knopf 1995 xxxvii, 529p $22

ISBN 0-679-44364-9

A reissue of the title first published 1940 by Simon & Schuster

"Unfolding a harrowing portrait of a disintegrating family, Stead examines the hostility between a husband and wife: Sam Pollit, revealed to be a tyrannical crank far removed from the civilized man he thinks he is, whose claim to love his children lends the ironic title; and Henny, who has become a bitter virago." Merriam-Webster's Ency of Lit

Stedman, M. L.

★ The **light** between oceans; a novel. M.L. Stedman. Scribner 2012 352 p. (hardback) $25.00

ISBN 9781451681734; 9781451681758; 9781451681765

LC 2011050244

In this debut novel, WWI veteran "Tom Sherbourne . . . takes a lighthouse keeper's post on an Australian island," and marries a woman named Isabel. Their "love grows, [b]ut four years on the island and several miscarriages" dampen their spirits "until a boat washes ashore with a dead man and a living child. Isabel convinces herself--and Tom--that the baby is a gift from God." Two years later, they must confront the child's still-alive real mother. (Publishers Weekly)

Steel, Danielle, 1947-

Amazing grace. Delacorte Press 2007 324p $27

ISBN 978-0-385-34023-6

LC 2007-7523

"Sarah Sloane, 30-something wife of Seth, a wildly successful hedge fund entrepreneur, and mother of two, has planned to perfection a high-ticket charity auction. The only thing she hasn't counted on is the biggest seismic event to hit San Francisco since 1906 and the aftershocks it will cause in her marriage. Meanwhile, hot Grammy-winning 19-year-old singer Melanie Free, flown in to perform at the benefit, likewise finds her life overturned. . . . Sarah and Melanie face change with support from the 40-ish Sister Maggie Kent, a California nun whose good deeds draw the interest of recovering alcoholic and former AP photojournalist Everett Carson, who captures her in pictures. As marriage, faith and vows of chastity are tested, there's nothing complicated to spoil the romance. Steel delivers a sparkly story with an uplifting spiritual twist." Publ Wkly

Steel, Danielle, 1947-

First sight; by Danielle Steel. Delacorte Press 2006 373 p. (hardcover) $28.00

ISBN 0385338309; 9780385338301

LC 2006042666

This novel by Danielle Steel focuses on "Timmie O'Neill, whose renowned [fashion] line, Timmie O, is the embodiment of casual chic, in fashion and for the home. She has created a business that . . . consumes her life. During Paris Fashion Week, [a] Frenchman comes into her life. First, Timmie and Jean-Charles Vernier are only patient and physician. They become confidants. But neither can deny their growing friendship and the electricity that sparks whenever they meet." (Publisher's note)

Steel, Danielle

The **house** on Hope Street. Delacorte Press 2000 231p $19.95

ISBN 0-385-33306-4

LC 00-25688

"Married legal team Liz and Jack Sutherland have a successful family law practice and a house on Hope Street near San Francisco, where they live with their five happy children (one with special needs). Liz and her children's lives are changed forever when Jack is murdered on Christmas Day. In the year following the murder, Liz struggles to come to terms with the loss of her husband, both personally and professionally, and is dealt another devastating blow when her eldest son has a near-fatal accident. Divorced doctor Bill Webster saves her son and becomes close to Liz, much to the chagrin of her daughters, who accuse her of betraying their dead father." Libr J

Steel, Danielle

Johnny Angel. Delacorte Press 2002 181p $19.95

ISBN 0-385-33549-0

LC 2001-37188

"Killed in a car crash after his senior prom, 17-year-old Johnny Peterson is sent back to earth as an angel. His mission: to fix certain troubles left unresolved at the time of his death involving his girlfriend, Becky, her impoverished mother and his dysfunctional family. . . . Steele's heartfelt depiction of the central relationship between Johnny and his mother is touching, and few readers will get through the revelation of Johnny's final gift with dry eyes." Publ Wkly

Steel, Danielle

Journey. Delacorte Press 2000 323p $26.95

ISBN 0-385-31687-9

LC 00-31512

"To the outside world, Washington, D.C., television coanchor Maddy Hunter appears to have an enviable life. . . . Yet Maddy—whose current husband saved her from a physically abusive former spouse—is trapped in another relationship that's as devastating and destructive as her first. Jack doesn't hit Maddy, but he subjects her to mind games, putdowns and constant undermining; it's obvious psychological abuse to observers, though not to Maddy. Using Maddy's participation in a commission on violence against women chaired by the nation's First Lady, Steel explicates the various forms of spousal abuse." Publ Wkly

Steel, Danielle

The **kiss**. Delacorte Press 2001 347p $26.95

ISBN 0-385-33540-7

LC 00-66009

"Isabelle Forrester is the unhappy wife of a coldhearted and distant Parisian banker. . . . Unable to bear the strain of her lonely, unhappy life, Isabelle strikes up an innocent friendship—conversing mostly by phone or mail—with American Bill Robinson. A Washington power broker, Robinson is also trapped in an unhappy marriage. The pair's relationship intensifies steadily until they finally agree to meet in London for a few passionate days. There they are involved in a serious car accident, which leaves them both in a coma, fighting for their lives." Booklist

Steel, Danielle

No greater love. Delacorte Press 1991 392p $23

ISBN 0-385-29909-5

LC 90-29106

As this novel "opens, the boisterous Winfield family is boarding the ill-fated ocean liner Titanic for their return to America from England. Kate Winfield, mistress of the perfect family, nobly stays behind with her beloved husband and thrusts her children into the lifeboats under the care of 20-year-old daughter Edwina. After the disaster, Edwina takes seriously her mother's entreaty to care for her five siblings, who range in age from 2 to 16. For the next 12 years, Edwina, aided by a substantial inheritance, dutifully cares for the kids, even to the point of pursuing her runaway teenage sister back to England (by boat) and wresting her out of the arms of a cad. Steel's tale eventually takes an interesting turn into the early days of Hollywood." Booklist

Steel, Danielle

Sunset in St. Tropez. Delacorte Press 2002 230p $19.95

ISBN 0-385-33546-6

LC 2001-47517

Three pairs of friends in their 50s and 60s decide to vacation together in St. Tropez

"Shortly before the vacation begins, one of the women dies of a heart attack, and the other women are scandalized when her supposedly grieving husband brings along a hot, young movie star in his wife's stead. Another scandal soon unfolds as another husband is revealed to be having an affair with a much younger woman. In addition, the house the group has rented (sight unseen) turns out to be a dump and comes complete with two very strange caretakers, who lend a bit of comic relief to the high drama all around them." Booklist

Steele, Allen M.

Coyote; a novel of interstellar exploration. Ace Bks. 2002 390p $23.95

ISBN 0-441-00974-3

LC 2002-74517

"A much-foreshadowed 'surprise' ending is by far the least of the surprises in Steele's bag of tricks. But each page of this novel bears evidence of fresh thought about the opportunities inherent in science fiction to take the familiar and make it new." N Y Times Book Rev

Steele, Jon

Angel City; Part two of the Angelus trilogy. by Jon Steele. Blue Rider Press, A member of Penguin Group, USA 2013 528 p. (hardcover) $27.95

ISBN 9780399158759; 0399158758

LC 2013009626

This novel, written by Jon Steele, is part two of the Angelus Trilogy and occurs "almost three years since . . . Detective Jay Harper and high-priced escort Katherine Taylor['s] biblical showdown with the Nephilim. Baby Max has . . . stirred the interest of vengeful spirits—and only a world-

wide (and cosmic) effort to save his life will bring Harper and Katherine together. Meanwhile, . . .a defrocked priest named Astruc . . . [and] his brilliant young ward, Goose, have discovered something . . . that will confirm that 'the time of the prophecy' is at hand. (Publisher's note)

Steele, Jon

The **watchers**; Jon Steele. Blue Rider Press 2012 592 p. $26.95

ISBN 039915874X; 9780399158742

LC 2012001267

This book, set at the Lausanne cathedral in Switzerland, tells the story of "Marc Rochat, who's served for years as the cathedral's 'watcher,'" "American expatriate Katherine Taylor, who through her work as a highly paid escort has recently run afoul of vicious Russian criminals," and "Jay Harper, an amnesiac operative for the International Olympic Committee who's been investigating a former Olympian's bizarre death." Events bring the three together to defend the cathedral. (Publishers Weekly)

Stefaniak, Mary Helen

The **Turk** and my mother; a novel. W.W. Norton 2004 316p $24.95

ISBN 0-393-05924-3

LC 2004-1102

This novel explores the "history of a Croatian-American family settled in Milwaukee after World War I. The book's Decameron-esque framework is set from the beginning as George, the first-generation American son of Josef and Agnes, is on his deathbed, surrounded by his adult children. The stories he tells about life in Milwaukee in the 1930s lead to stories-within-stories told by his grandmother Staramajka, the family matriarch, who steals the show. . . . Stefaniak's easy familiarity with the vernacular idioms of the old country and the new, and her zestful, respectful ear for different voices, create a world whose past, present and story-loving afterlife are at once magical and grounded in reality." Publ Wkly

Stegner, Wallace Earle

All the little live things; [by] Wallace Stegner. Viking 1967 345p

"Mr. Stegner's narrative skill and his talent for imaginative recreation is evident throughout the book. His choice of words, the turn of a phrase, evoking a scene, an emotion, or a personality are to be savored. His writing, leisurely as it may appear, can be dramatic and moving." Best Sellers

Followed by The spectator bird

Stegner, Wallace Earle

Angle of repose; {by} Wallace Stegner. Doubleday 1971 569p

This novel "is set mainly in the West in the late 1800's; but the central characters cannot be confined to the West nor to the 19th Century. They have a healing effect on the narrator, their grandson and biographer. . . . The beautiful, talented, charming Susan and her inarticulate engineer husband Oliver Ward rough it in mining camps and desolate, unfinished irrigation project camps. Their lives are hard and their marriage is strained past redemption. Yet their suffering and their strength do redeem." Libr J

Stegner, Wallace Earle

★ The **Big** Rock Candy Mountain; [by] Wallace Stegner. Duell, Sloan & Pearce 1943 515p

"A well-written study of the footloose family. . . . The life of the household is a misery of continual cruelty and often crushing poverty, alternating with occasional scenes of simple family happiness which stand out beautifully and unforgettably." New Yorker

Stegner, Wallace Earle

★ **Collected** stories of Wallace Stegner. Random House 1990 525p

LC 89-37342

"This retrospective . . . exhibits a mastery of the effortlessly beautiful metaphor, an abiding interest in the American West, and an ability to create quick but complete portraits and concise but fully engrossing narratives." Booklist

Stegner, Wallace Earle

★ **Crossing** to safety; [by] Wallace Stegner. Random House 1987 277p

LC 87-20482

"The Langs and the Morgans, young couples who meet when their husbands begin teaching at a Wisconsin university, forge bonds of wonderful, lasting friendship. Charity Lang and Sally Morgan are unlike in personality but see each other through devastating crises because of that friendship. Sid Lang is a frustrated poet whose life is over-directed by his wife; Larry Morgan, much less financially secure than Sid, realizes a slow but successful climb to a position of noted writer. This novel has no violence, explicit sex or ugliness. Instead it is a hymn to solid marriages and loyalty in friendship. The dramatic events are those that occur in the lives of ordinary people." Shapiro. Fic for Youth. 3d edition

Stein, Garth

The **art** of racing in the rain; a novel. Harper 2008 321p $23.95

ISBN 978-0-06-153793-6; 0-06-153793-4

LC 2007-33890

"Enzo narrates his life story, beginning with his impending death. Enzo's not afraid of dying, as he's seen a television documentary on the Mongolian belief that a good dog will reincarnate as a man. Yes, Enzo is a dog. And he belongs to Denny: husband, father, customer service technician. Denny's dream is to be a professional race-car driver, and Enzo recounts the triumphs and tragedies-medical, financial, and legal-they share in this quest, the dangers of the race-track being the least of their obstacles. . . . [Stein] creates a patient, wise, and doggish narrator that is more than just fluff and collar." Libr J

Stein, Gertrude

★ **Three** lives; stories of the good Anna, Melanctha, and the gentle Lena. Grafton Press 1909 279p

"Written in a clear and masterly style, free from any of its author's later stylistic mannerisms, this book consists of three character studies of women. 'The Good Anna' deals with a kindly but domineering German servingwoman; 'Melanctha' is concerned with an uneducated but sensitive black girl; and 'The Gentle Lena' is about a pathetically feebleminded young German maid." Reader's Ency. 4th edition

Steinbeck, John, 1902-1968

★ **Cannery** Row. Viking 1945 208p hardcover o.p.

"In this episodic work Steinbeck returned to the manner of Tortilla Flat (1935) and produced a rambling account of the adventures and misadventures of workers in a California cannery and their friends." Herzberg. Reader's Ency of Am Lit

Followed by Sweet Thursday (1954)

Steinbeck, John

★ **East** of Eden. Viking 1952 602p

Steinbeck's "most ambitious post-war novel is . . . a parable of the fall of man, of Cain and Abel, and of human possibility, showing many of the virtues of his best books, but touched with sentimentality, melodrama and intrusive commentary." Penguin Companion to Am Lit

Steinbeck, John

★ The **grapes** of wrath. Viking 1939 619p

"In this moving book, Steinbeck wrote a classic novel of a family's battle with starvation and economic desperation. The story also tells in vivid terms the story of the westward movement and the frontier. The Joads, Steinbeck's central figures, are 'Okies,' farmers moving west from a land of drought and bankruptcy to seek work as migrant fruit-pickers in California. They are beset by the police, participate in strike violence, and are harried by death." Benet's Reader's Ency of Am Lit

Steinbeck, John

In dubious battle. Covici-Friede 1936 349p

"One of the more important books to come out of the proletarian movement. This was Steinbeck's first successful novel. 'In Dubious Battle' deals with a fruit strike in a California valley and the attempts of the radical leaders to organize, lead, and provide for the striking pickers. Perhaps the most important, although not the central, character is Doc Burton, who helps the strikers and is concerned with seeing things as they exist, without labels of good and bad attached. The strike fails, and Jim, one of the two leaders, is senselessly killed." Benet's Reader's Ency of Am Lit

Steinbeck, John

The **long** valley. Viking 1938 304p

This volume "includes the four magnificent 'Red Pony' stories, and could serve as an admirable introduction to Steinbeck, showing his characteristic interests—the tensions of the town and country, of past and present, of labour and ownership, as well as the objectivity of biological observation and a sort of Lawrencean mystic concept of personal power." Penguin Companion to Am Lit

Steinbeck, John

The **moon** is down; a novel. Viking 1942 188p

This novel describes the occupation of a small mining town, presumably in Norway, by an unidentified army, evidently German. The villagers resort to sabotage and completely ignore the invaders whenever possible. In the end the courageous village mayor is shot to bring the people to terms. The mayor goes to his death reciting Socrates's dying message, knowing full well that his people will understand his death, and will continue their resistance

Steinbeck, John

Novels and stories, 1932-1937; John Steinbeck. Library of America, Distributed to the trade in the U.S. by Penguin Books USA 1994 909p $35

    ISBN 1-88301-101-9

                          LC 94-2943

The pastures of heaven (1932) is a linked collection of short stories, all of which deal with the inhabitants of the California farm community of the same name. To a god unknown (1933) tells the story of a California farmer who performs pagan fertility rites to ensure good crops. After a long drought, the farmer commits suicide at his own altar of worship. Tortilla Flat, In dubious battle, and Of mice and men are entered separately.

    Includes bibliographical references

Steinbeck, John

Novels, 1942-1952. Library of America, Distributed to the trade in the United States by Penguin Putnam 2001 983p il $35

    ISBN 1-931082-07-3

                     LC 2001-38119

    Contents: The moon is down; Cannery Row; The pearl; East of Eden

    Includes bibliographical references

Steinbeck, John

★ **Of** mice and men. Covici-Friede 1937 186p

"Two uneducated laborers dream of a time when they can share the ownership of a rabbit farm in California. George is a plotter and a schemer, while Lennie is a mentally deficient hulk of a man who has no concept of his physical strength. As a team they are not particularly successful, but their friendship is enduring." Shapiro. Fic for Youth. 3d edition

Steinbeck, John

The **pearl**; with drawings by José Clemente Orozco. Viking 1947 122p il

"Kino, a poor pearl-fisher, lives a happy albeit spartan life with his wife and their child. When he finds a magnificent pearl, the Pearl of the World, he is besieged by dishonest pearl merchants and envious neighbors. Even a greedy doctor ties his professional treatment of their baby when it is bitten by a scorpion to the possible acquisition of the pearl. After a series of disasters, Kino throws the pearl away since it has brought him only unhappiness." Shapiro. Fic for Youth. 3d edition

Steinbeck, John

The **short** reign of Pippin IV; a fabrication. drawings by William Péne du Bois. Viking 1957 188p il

A satire on French politics. Having run out of governments the French decide to revive the monarchy and settle on Pippin, a quiet amateur astronomer who happens to be a descendant of Charlemagne. Bored with the whole situation

Pippin is instrumental in starting a revolution, and finally wanders off home

Steinbeck, John

Sweet Thursday. Viking 1954 273p

    Sequel to Cannery Row

After World War II the "Palace Flophouse passed into new hands, the Bear Flag Café got a new madam named Fauna (nee Flora), and Doc lost his old pleasure in women, liturgical music, and the Western Biological Laboratories. Then Suzy came to Cannery Row . . . {and} egged on by the others, she brought Doc back to his prewar contentment." Booklist

Steinbeck, John

Tortilla Flat; illustrated by Ruth Gannett. Covici-Friede 1935 316p

"This episodic tale concerns the poor but carefree 'paisano' Danny and his friends Pillon, Pablo, Big Joe Portagee, Jesus Maria Corcoran, and the old Pirate, all of whom gather in Danny's house, which Steinbeck tells us 'was not unlike the Round Table.' The novel (accepted after nine publishers had turned it down) contrasts the complexities of modern civilization with the simple life of the 'paisanos.'" Benet's Reader's Ency of Am Lit

Steinbeck, John

Travels with Charley and later novels, 1947-1962. Library of America 2007 990p $40

    ISBN 978-1-59853-004-9; 1-59853-004-6

                    LC 2006-48757

First published 1950, Burning bright, "an allegory set against shifting backgrounds (circus, sea, farm) and revolving around the fear of sterility and the desire for self-perpetuation, marks Steinbeck's involvement with the drama in its fusion of the forms of novel and play." Publisher's note

Steinbeck, John

The **wayward** bus. Viking 1947 312p

"A novel in which the passengers on a stranded bus in California become a microcosm of contemporary American frustrations." Camb Guide to Lit in Engl

Steinbeck, John

The **winter** of our discontent. Viking 1961 311p

Ethan Allen Hawley, the impoverished heir to an upright New England tradition is the focus of this story. Ethan, under pressure from his restless wife and discontented children who want more of this world's goods than his grocery store job provides, decides to take a holiday from his scrupulous standards to achieve wealth and success. What happens as he compromises with his integrity makes up this story

In this novel Steinbeck "continues his exploration of the moral dilemmas involved in being fully human, this time in contemporary America, where choices between genteel poverty and corrupt comfort press in upon the protagonist with a force and reality that suggest no easy resolution." Ency of World Lit in the 20th Century

Steinbeck, Thomas

Down to a soundless sea. Ballantine Bks. 2002 283p

ISBN 0-345-45576-2

This "collection draws on folklore, historical research, and tales that Steinbeck (son of John) heard growing up. The stories celebrate the early lore of Monterey County, CA. . . . Set in the dusky past of horse trails, grizzly bears, and small fishing villages and ranging forward to the early 1930s, they portray humble people living in a beautiful but often unforgiving environment." Libr J

Steinbeck, Thomas

In the shadow of the cypress. Gallery Books 2010 246p $25

ISBN 978-1-4391-6825-7; 1-4391-6825-3

LC 2009-33355

This novel is "set on the rugged California coast of Monterey and Big Sur. It's both a history lesson and a mystery novel, revolving around a 1906 discovery — and subsequent disappearance — of two ancient jade Chinese artifacts, buried for centuries under a majestic cypress and unearthed through a natural disaster. Almost 100 years later, a quirky young American scientist unearths new evidence of this incredible discovery and its mysterious disappearance, assembling a group of explorers to resume the search, this time in the ocean's depths. The story is intriguing and well-told — the artifacts are believed to have been buried in the early 1400s, almost a century before Columbus arrived on our shores — but it's Steinbeck's respect for turn-of-the-century Chinese immigrants that shines through." USA Today

Steiner, Peter

The **resistance**; a thriller. Peter Steiner. 1st ed. Minotaur Books 2012 p. cm. (hardcover) $26.99

ISBN 9781250003713; 9781250011305

LC 2012013572

This mystery thriller novel, by Peter Steiner, is part of his ex-CIA operative Louis Morgon series. "When Louis purchases a rundown house in Saint-Leon-sur-Deme, . . . he discovers evidence of a long forgotten crime hidden beneath the floorboards. Unable to leave a good mystery unsolved, he enlists the help of his friend Renard, a French cop, and sets out to discover exactly what happened in this small French village during the Nazi occupation." (Publisher's note)

Steiner, Peter

The **terrorist**. Minotaur Books 2010 216p $23.99

ISBN 978-0-312-37344-3; 0-312-37344-9

LC 2009-47489

Louis Morgon, "the hero of this improbable and charming spy novel, the third in a series, is a kind of septuagenarian Jason Bourne: a former intelligence operative, he was drummed out of the C.I.A. decades ago, and is now lying low in a sleepy French village. When the agency comes calling, wanting him to reactivate his contacts in the Middle East as part of the war on terror, he refuses. Only when an Algerian boy he has taken under his wing is arrested does he decide to plunge back into his old life. Few men of any age could so nimbly chase down Taliban leaders and Al Qaeda sleepers—all while undergoing chemotherapy for prostate cancer. Steiner has a light touch, and what the story may lack in verisimilitude it makes up for in wit and an appreciation, amid the action, for the gentler pleasures." New Yorker

Steinhauer, Olen

An **American** spy; Olen Steinhauer. Minotaur Books 2012 416 p

ISBN 9780312622909; 9780312622893; 9781429950442

LC 2011040874

This book tells the story of "Milo Weaver . . . [who is] no longer a member of the CIA's deeply clandestine Department of Tourism, which was shut down after Chinese spy Xin Zhu, motivated more by personal vengeance than allegiance to his government, orchestrated the assassination of 33 of its agents one by one around the world. When Alan Drummond, Weaver's boss at the now defunct department, disappears from his London hotel. Weaver gets on his trail -a matter that becomes much more urgent after Drummond's wife and daughter are kidnapped." (Publishers Weekly)

Steinhauer, Olen

The **Bridge** of Sighs. St. Martin's Minotaur 2003 278p $23.95

ISBN 0-312-30245-2

LC 2002-68127

"This is an intelligent, finely polished debut, loaded with atmospheric detail that effortlessly re-creates the rubble-strewn streets of the postwar period in an Eastern state 'liberated' from German occupation by the Russians." Libr J

Steinhauer, Olen

The **nearest** exit. Minotaur Books 2010 404p $25.99

ISBN 978-0-312-62287-9; 0-312-62287-2

LC 2009-47486

Sequel to: The tourist (2009)

"Like le Carré's George Smiley, Weaver is a richly imagined creation with a scarred psyche and a complex back story that elevates him above the status of run-of-the-mill world-weary spook." N Y Times Book Rev

Steinhauer, Olen

The **tourist**. Minotaur Books 2009 408p $24.95

ISBN 978-0-312-36972-9; 0-312-36972-7

LC 2008-33958

"As rich and intriguing as the best of Le Carré, Deighton or Graham Greene, Steinhauer's complex, moving spy novel is perfect for our uncertain, emotionally fraught times." Los Angeles Times Book Rev

Steinke, Rene

Holy skirts. Morrow 2005 360p $24.95

ISBN 0-688-17694-1

LC 2004-52783

"Steinke's writing is vivid and wonderful, and she can make even a sorrowful story entertaining because she never allows the character's melancholy to infect the prose. The baroness might have been sad, but not tragic. The heroism of her spirit is expressed in a way that transcends the shroud of misfortune." Hudson Rev

Stemple, Adam

Singer of souls; Adam Stemple. Tor 2005 237p $22.95

ISBN 9780765311702; 0765311704

LC 2004063758

This novel tells the story of Douglas, who, "[l]eaving his life of petty crime and drug abuse behind, . . . flees from Minneapolis to Edinburgh, Scotland, to his stern but fair-minded Grandma McLaren. . . . [S]oon Douglas is making a decent living as the busker who can write a song about you on the spot. But Edinburgh has its dangers for the unwary, . . . and when a mysterious but alluring young girl offers him drugs, Douglas's resolve fails him. What follows isn't what he expects. Suddenly, Douglas can see, in all their beauty and terrifying cruelty, the fey folk who invisibly share Edinburgh's ancient streets. Worse, they can see him, and they're determined to draw him into their own internecine wars--wars that are fought to the death." (Publisher's note)

Stendhal

★ The **charterhouse** of Parma; translated from the French by Richard Howard; illustrations by Robert Andrew Parker. Modern Lib. 1999 507p il maps $24.95

ISBN 0-679-60245-3

LC 98-36417

Original French edition, 1839. Variant title: The chartreuse of Parma

"The scene is a little Italian Court, whither the young adventurer Fabrice has found his way, and in dramatic importance plays second fiddle to the fascinating Duchess Sanseverina and her jealous lover, the astute minister, Count Mosca. The book opens with a famous narrative of the battle of Waterloo. It is a novel that set a standard of flawless technique, of the lucid unfolding of character and motive, of accurate comprehension of the inherent disorder of life, that has rarely been approached in dramatic narration." Baker. Guide to the Best Fic

Stendhal

★ The **red** and the black; a chronicle of 1830. a new translation by Burton Raffel; introduction by Diane Johnson; notes by James Madden. Modern Library 2003 xxii, 524p

ISBN 0-679-64284-6

LC 2002-40798

Original French edition, 1830; first United States edition published 1898 by G.H. Richmond

"The author's most celebrated work, it is equally acclaimed for its psychological study of its protagonist—the provincial young romantic Julien Sorel—and as a satiric analysis of the French social order under the Bourbon restoration. Its intensely dramatic plot is purposively romantic in nature, while Stendhal's careful portraiture of Sorel's inner states is the work of a master realist, foreshadowing new developments in the form of the novel." Reader's Ency. 4th edition

Stephenson, Neal

Anathem. William Morrow 2008 937p $29.95

ISBN 978-0-06-147409-5; 0-06-147409-6

LC 2008-13175

"Set on an Earthlike planet called Arbre and narrated by Fraa Erasmus, a young scholar, the story begins within the walls of Saunt Edhar, a 3,400-year-old monastery. A home to cloistered philosophers, scientists and mathematicians, Edhar opens its gates to the 'saecular' world at Apert, a celebration that happens every one, ten, hundred or thousand years. This rite allows visitors to enter and residents to experience a taste of an 'extramuros' society steeped in religion, obsessed with technology and diverted by movies, shopping and legalized gambling. While he does provide a glossary and a timeline, Stephenson isn't interested in quickly explicating Arbre's history and language for the casual reader. . . . Readers who persevere, however, will be rewarded by a slight acceleration in the plot when Erasmus, along with some of his peers and teachers, is expelled from Saunt Edhar and sent on a mission in which the fate of the entire planet hangs in the balance." San Francisco Chron

Stephenson, Neal

Cryptonomicon. Avon Bks. 1999 918p $27.50

ISBN 0-380-97346-4

LC 99-11685

"This fast-paced, genre-transcending novel is full of absorbing action, witty dialogue and well-drawn characters. Amazingly, it is also, even at its tremendous length, only the first volume in what promises to be one of the most extravagant literary creations of the turn of the millennium—and beyond." Publ Wkly

Stephenson, Neal

The **diamond** age; or, Young lady's illustrated primer. Bantam Bks. 1995 455p

ISBN 0-553-09609-5

LC 94-30486

"With breathtaking vision and insight, Stephenson establishes himself as not only a major voice in contemporary sf but also a prophet of technology's future." Booklist

Stephenson, Neal

Reamde. Morrow 2011 1044p $35

ISBN 978-0-06-197796-1; 0-06-197796-9

LC 2011-20573

"Stephenson's novels have always been a little nuts, but thoughtfully nuts. That he is even able to keep this big, careening, recreational-vehicular novel on the road during its hairpin narrative turns says a lot about him as a plot juggler and information wrangler." N Y Times Book Rev

Sterling, Bruce

The **caryatids**. Del Rey/Ballantine Books 2009 295p $25

ISBN 978-0-345-46062-2; 0-345-46062-6

LC 2008-51828

"Whether tackling ubiquitous computing, biotechnology, natural disasters, failed states, celebrity, or the social dynamics of family, Sterling unites astute powers of observation, sharp wit, and powerful imagination to astound the reader with infinite possibilities." Booklist

Sterling, Bruce

Holy fire; a novel. Viking 1996 326p

LC 96-15139

The author "understands that salvation in a posthuman world can only be a process, not a prize. He has written a book in praise of ambiguity that manages to find consoling moments of joy in the most unlikely places." N Y Times Book Rev

Sterling, Bruce

Schismatrix plus. Ace Books 1996 319p pa $16

ISBN 0-441-00370-2

LC 97-106127

This compilation of short stories in the author's Shapers-Mechanists universe includes Schismatrix (1985), which focuses on the life and political struggles of Shaper-trained renegade Abélard Lindsay.

Stern, Steve

The **angel** of forgetfulness. Viking 2005 403p $24.95

ISBN 0-670-03387-1

LC 2004-57155

The author "has little interest in reworking Yiddish literature's social realist strains, or in excavating the political events that helped shape the world he loves. What he offers instead is a rollicking compendium of myth and historical tidbits, of dybbuks, wonder-working rebbes and clandestine prayer houses where lapsed Talmud students meditate on the holy letters of God's name until they levitate." N Y Times Book Rev

Stern, Steve

The **frozen** rabbi; a novel. Algonquin Books of Chapel Hill 2010 370p $24.95

ISBN 978-1-56512-619-0; 1-56512-619-X

LC 2009-47396

"A family of long-suffering eastern European Jews protects a frozen rabbi from pogroms, revolution, and racketeers in this intermittently fabulous multigenerational saga. Stern . . . uses two narrative threads, one beginning in 1999 when 15-year-old Bernie Karp discovers a body in his family's freezer, the other beginning in 1889 when the rabbi is frozen during a winter storm. With a ferocious grasp of history and Yiddish humor, Stern follows the family of misfits and geniuses as they flee the Lodz ghetto in Poland with their icy cargo, eventually making their way to New York, Palestine, and Memphis, where, in 1999, the rabbi reawakens." Publ Wkly

Sterne, Laurence

★ The **life** and opinions of Tristram Shandy, gentleman and A sentimental journey through France and Italy. Modern Lib. 1995 832p $19.50

ISBN 0-679-60091-4

A combined edition of two titles first published 1759-67 and 1768 respectively

A sentimental journey is a "combination of autobiography, fiction, and observations made by Sterne on his own travels, chronicles the journey through France of a charming and sensitive young man named Yorick and his servant LaFleur. (Though the title mentions Italy, the book ends before they reach that country.)" Merriam-Webster's Ency of Lit

Stevens, Chevy

Always watching; Chevy Stevens. St. Martin's Press 2013 352 p. (hardcover) $25.99

ISBN 0312595697; 9780312595692

LC 2013011251

In this thriller, psychiatrist Nadine Lavoie "has largely managed to repress traumatic memories of the time she spent as a teen in a commune . . . led by charismatic self-styled guru Aaron Quinn. Then she hears his name for the first time in years--from new patient Heather Simeon, a suicidal, terrified young woman who has just left Quinn's River of Life Spiritual Center." Her investigation into Quinn, for Heather's sake, leads to strange events and distressing flashbacks. (Publishers Weekly)

Stevens, Chevy

Still missing. St. Martin's Press 2010 342p $24.99

ISBN 978-0-312-59567-8; 0-312-59567-0

LC 2009-47037

"As Annie's experience as an abductee prompts her to explore hidden corners of her former life and dredge up old secrets, 'Still Missing' risks sounding extremely generic. This, after all, is the template for countless current novels in which a single shattering event leads to shocking revelations about the past. But 'Still Missing' runs deeper than that in the chills it delivers, the surprises it holds and the resilience of its main character." N Y Times (Late N Y Ed)

Stevens, Marcus

The **curve** of the world; a novel. Algonquin Bks. 2002 302p $23.95

ISBN 1-56512-336-0

LC 2001-56530

"Lewis Burke is aboard a plane forced to make an emergency landing in the Congo. Once on the ground, the passengers become the hostages of rebels. Lewis sees an opportunity to escape and plunges into the rain forest. Meanwhile, Lewis' wife, Helen, learns that his plane is down and departs immediately for Kinshasa with their seven-year-old son, blind since birth. The diffident Lewis lurches through the wilderness with no idea of how to survive, while the tenacious Helen defies U.S. diplomats and sets out for the rebel-held interior. Their stories are told in parallel." Booklist

Stevens summons the African "landscape and atmosphere with vividly descriptive detail, and captures the terror of a man reduced to life's essentials." Publ Wkly

Stevens, Marcus

Useful girl; a novel. Algonquin Books of Chapel Hill 2004 306p $24.95

ISBN 1-565-12366-2

LC 2003-70808

"The descriptions of late 19th-century battles and living conditions are unsettling in their vivid and authentic detail, riveting even the least historically minded reader, and the account of Erin's plight is clear-eyed and uncompromising. Writing with compassion and grace, Stevens delivers a timeless story of brutality and forgiveness." Publ Wkly

Stevens, Taylor

The **informationist**; a novel. Taylor Stevens. 1st ed. Shaye Areheart Books 2011 307 p. (paperback) $23.00

ISBN 0307717097; 9780307717092

LC 2009045523

In this novel, by Taylor Stevens, "Vanessa 'Michael' Munroe deals in information. . . . Born . . . in lawless central Africa, Munroe took up with an infamous gunrunner and his mercenary crew when she was just fourteen. . . . A Texas oil billionaire has hired her to find his daughter who vanished in Africa four years ago. . . . Munroe finds herself back in the lands of her childhood, betrayed, cut off from civilization, and left for dead." (Publisher's note)

Stevenson, Jane

The **shadow** king. Houghton Mifflin 2003 304p $24

ISBN 0-618-14913-9

LC 2003-47899

"Stevenson has immersed herself in the literature of the period, and one can sense the heady zest with which she details Balthasar's medical treatments or spins off a line of dialogue." N Y Times Book Rev

Stevenson, Jane

The **winter** queen. Houghton Mifflin 2002 307p $25

ISBN 0-618-14912-0

First published 2001 in the United Kingdom with title: Astraea

"Without apparent strain, Stevenson extends her reach to Calvinist doctrine, Yoruba divination, 17th-century European politics and the details of daily life in the Low Countries. In her hands, the clandestine love story is inseparable from the political and spiritual preoccupations of the time, making vivd a world no less complex and capricious than our own." N Y Times Book Rev

Stevenson, Robert Louis

★ The **complete** short stories; edited and introduced by Ian Bell. Holt & Co. 1994 2v set $50

ISBN 0-8050-3203-7

LC 93-79628

Stevenson, Robert Louis

The **complete** short stories of Robert Louis Stevenson; with a selection of the best novels. edited and with an introduction by Charles Neider. Viking 1969 xxx, 678p

The strange case of Dr. Jekyll and Mr. Hyde is entered separately. In The story of a lie (first published 1879 in New Quarterly magazine, 1882 in book form) Dick Naseby, a young Englishman, becomes estranged from his father due to a misunderstanding and from the girl he loves due to his concealment of the true character of her father—an untalented, parasitical but likable painter, whom the girl hasn't seen since childhood and romantically idolizes. The Merry Men (1887) is set on an island off the coast of Scotland. It deals with a man of dour religious temperament who kills the survivor of a shipwreck in a fit of drunken madness and

is driven to death by his guilt after another shipwreck. The beach of Falesá (first published 1893 in Island nights' entertainments) concerns a trader on a South Seas island whose marriage to a native woman is promoted by a business rival who knows that she is the object of a native taboo which will pass on to her husband

Stevenson, Robert Louis

★ The **strange** case of Dr. Jekyll and Mr. Hyde; with an introduction by Joyce Carol Oates. Vintage Books 1991 97p pa $8.95

ISBN 0-679-73476-7

LC 90-50600

First published 1886. Variant title: Dr. Jekyll and Mr. Hyde

"The work is known for its vivid portrayal of the psychopathology of a 'split personality.' The calm, respectable Dr. Jekyll develops a potion that will allow him to separate his good and evil aspects for scientific study. At first Jekyll has no difficulty abandoning the drug induced persona of the repulsive Mr. Hyde, but as the experiments continue the evil personality wrests control from Jekyll and commits murder. Afraid of being discovered, he takes his life; Hyde's body is found, together with a confession written in Jekyll's hand." Merriam-Webster's Ency of Lit

Stevenson, Robert Louis

The **strange** case of Dr. Jekyll and Mr. Hyde, and other famous tales; with photographs of the author and his environment as well as illustrations from early editions of the stories, together with an introduction by W. M. Hills. Dodd, Mead 1961 339p il

The title novelette is entered separately, and the novelette: The beach of Falesá is described under: The complete short stories of Robert Louis Stevenson. The three-part story: The suicide club, which originally appeared in The New Arabian Nights (1882) is a partly satirical fantasy-adventure story about a sinister London club which exploits the nihilistic tendencies of its members, and the mysterious Prince Florizel who opposes it

Stewart, Edward

Deadly rich. Bantam Bks. 1991 566p

LC 91-17638

A "thriller about a serial murderer who calls himself 'Society Son of Sam.' His first victim is a wealthy socialite found unpleasantly done in on a dressing room floor of an exclusive department store, and after a few more high society types are similarly dispatched, Lieutenant Vince Cardozo of the NYPD finds himself deeply involved in Yuppie scandal." Libr J

Stewart, Fred Mustard

Ellis Island; a novel. Delacorte Press 1983 396p

ISBN 0-688-01622-7

LC 82-14301

"In 1907 five young immigrants arrive at the legendary Ellis Island, the gateway to the American Dream. There's Jacob Rubenstein, fortunate to escape the pogrom that destroyed his family; Tom Banicek, who fled conscription into the Austro-Hungarian Army; Marco Santorelli, possessed of magnificent looks and driving ambition; and the beautiful O'Donnell sisters, escaping the Irish troubles." Libr J

"Stewart is a wonderful storyteller, and his novel—sentimental and even corny in spots—is nevertheless thoroughly satisfying." Publ Wkly

Stewart, George Rippey

Earth abides. Random House 1949 373p

LC 49-11267

"In a near future, a plague devastates humankind, leaving isolated pockets of survivors. . . . One group in the San Francisco Bay area subsists for some time on the bounties of civilization that have remained intact. But the subtler social fabric, formerly held together by the cooperation of large numbers of people, is too much for this handful to sustain. With a mournful backward look at the millions of now-doomed volumes in the University of California library, the protagonist teaches the new children how to make bows and arrows. He lives long enough to see society forming itself anew at the tribal level. He himself is fated to be misremembered as a legendary culture hero. A major work." Anatomy of Wonder. 5th edition

Stewart, Mary

Airs above the ground. Mill, M.S. 1965 286p

Vanessa, a young English veterinarian, "after inadvertently discovering that her husband is not just a traveling salesman but doubles as a secret agent, helps him solve a case involving the Lipizzan horses, a medieval Austrian castle, a circus, a murder, and a narcotics ring." Booklist

Stewart, Mary

★ The **crystal** cave. Morrow 1970 521p

First title in the author's Merlin trilogy. "Presumed to be the offspring of the daughter of the King of Wales and the devil himself, Merlin spends a difficult childhood in the court of the king. He learns much that is mystical under the tutelage of a learned wizard and gains a knowledge of several languages. Escaping to 'Less Britain,' Merlin becomes an important element in the struggle to unite all Britain. The book is rich in descriptions of fifth-century Britain and Brittany, the Druids and their fearful rites, and the superstitions surrounding pagan worship." Shapiro. Fic for Youth. 3d edition

Followed by The hollow hills

Stewart, Mary

The **Gabriel** hounds. Forge 1967 320p

"Traveling in the Middle East Christy Mansel runs into her second cousin Charles in Damascus and the pair decide to visit their great aunt, an eccentric recluse who lives in a crumbling palace in Lebanon. Odd even for their aunt's household the situation at the castle arouses the cousins' suspicions, and their investigation turns up a startling secret in the underground passages." Booklist

Stewart, Mary

★ The **hollow** hills. Morrow 1973 499p

This second novel in the author's Merlin trilogy begins with "Merlin's dismissal by Uther, Arthur's father, who has nonetheless promised to deliver the babe, when born, to Merlin's care. The book traces Merlin's travels to the east, during which time he monitors, through his second sight,

Arthur's growth in Brittany and in England. Merlin returns to finish Arthur's education, and the book concludes with Arthur being proclaimed king. With this Merlin epic Mary Stewart has rightly won an honorable place among the modern writers of Arthurian legend." Tymn. Fantasy Lit

Followed by The last enchantment

Stewart, Mary

The **ivy** tree. Mill, M.S. 1961 320p

A Canadian girl visiting England is mistaken for a missing and supposedly dead heiress to an estate "by handsome Connor Winslow, a cousin of the runaway, and now manager of Whitescar. Finally convinced that she is Mary Grey, he and his dour sister Lisa persuade her to masquerade as the long-gone Annabel, promising her the opportunity to claim the considerable legacy left to Annabel by her mother on condition that she surrender her share in Whitescar to Connor upon the death of Uncle Matthew. Reluctantly, Mary enters into the scheme, but soon repents but finds herself too deeply involved." Best Sellers

Stewart, Mary

The **last** enchantment. Morrow 1979 538p

LC 79-12937

This is the concluding volume of a trilogy about "Merlin the Enchanter, set amidst the turbulent events of fifth-century Britain when Arthur became High King. . . . This novel tells of the early years of Arthur's reign: the battles with the Saxons, building of Camelot, marriages with two successive Guiniveres, and birth of Mordred" Libr J

Stewart, Mary

Mary Stewart's Merlin trilogy. Morrow 1980 919p maps $29.95

ISBN 0-688-00347-8

LC 80-21019

The first novel in this trilogy based on Arthurian legends concerns the difficult childhood and youth of the magician Merlin who grows up as a bastard at the court of the King of Wales where he is believed to be the offspring of the King's daughter and the devil. He gains much knowledge from a learned wizard and escapes to "Less Britain" where he becomes involved in efforts to unite all of Britain. The second novel tells of Merlin's involvement with the childhood of Arthur and Arthur's search for the magical sword, Caliburn. The last novel deals with Merlin's death and Arthur's turbulent reign.

The author's "skill in creating colorful characters, suspense, and a brooding atmosphere serves her well in portraying England's Dark Ages, where witches, sorcerers, and tragic kings moved heroically through an enchanted land. Though Arthur's rise to power is the subject, the true star and narrator of the tale is Merlin the magician." Husband. Sequels

Includes bibliographical references

Stewart, Mary

The **moon**-spinners. Mill, M.S. 1963 303p

First published 1962 in the United Kingdom

"Nicola Ferris, an English girl on vacation in Crete, decides to walk the last mile over a rough track to the tiny village where she is expected the next day. She walks into a mystery. She stumbles upon a shepherd's hut guarded by a

Greek who threatens to kill her if she makes a sound. Inside the hut, she finds a young Englishman seriously wounded and much upset by her intrusion. In her determination to help him, she is drawn into his dangerous situation." Horn Book

Stewart, Mary

My brother Michael. Mill, M.S. 1960 313p

This suspense story has "a modern Greek setting enriched by classical antiquities and haunted by the shades of Hellenic tragedy. Camilla Haven, the heroine-narrator, is on her way to Delphi when she encounters Simon Lester, an English schoolmaster who has come to investigate the death of his brother Michael, supposedly killed fighting during World War II. A strange letter written just before his death leads Camilla, along with Simon, through a terrifying maze of danger and violence to an amazing discovery on the slopes of Mount Parnassus." Booklist

Stewart, Mary

Nine coaches waiting. Mill, M.S. 1959 342p

First published 1958 in the United Kingdom

"Intelligent, spirited Linda Martin comes to Valmy, an isolated château in the French Alps, as English governess to nine-year-old Philippe, the orphaned Comte de Valmy. After several frightening 'accidents' Linda discovers that her pupil is the object of a murder plot which apparently involves his crippled uncle and the latter's handsome son Raoul, with whom she is in love." Booklist

Stewart, Mary

The stormy petrel. Morrow 1991 189p

LC 91-14509

"The visitors are jumpy, evasive and mutually antagonistic, and Rose's suspicions are aroused. The mystery of their relationship and real purpose, never menacing, is quickly solved, and takes second place to Stewart's vivid rendering of Moila's lochs, glens and wild birds, especially the graceful stormy petrels who nest there." Publ Wkly

Stewart, Mary

Thunder on the right. Mill, M.S. 1958 284p

First published 1957 in the United Kingdom

"Jennifer answers her cousin Gillian's plea to visit a French convent in the Pyrenees where Gillian hopes to become a nun. On her arrival from England, Jennifer discovers that her cousin has supposedly died after a mysterious auto accident. She does some sleuthing and unveils smuggling and murder. All the ingredients for a mystery-love story with authentic background." Libr J

Stewart, Mary

Touch not the cat. Morrow 1976 336p

A "tale set on a family estate in England. Garbled words of warning uttered by her dying father lead Bryony Ashley into danger as she investigates the intricacies of past and present intrigues within the Ashley family. Bryony's inherited extrasensory abilities add to the suspenseful story." Booklist

Stewart, Mary

The wicked day. Morrow 1983 453p

LC 83-12091

The author "returns to the Arthurian world she portrayed . . . in her Merlin trilogy. The principal character is Mordred, born of the incestuous liaison between Arthur the High King and his half-sister, the evil sorceress and northern queen Morgause. Mordred is summoned to Camelot by the formidable warrior king, along with Morgause and her four legitimate but ungovernable sons, and told of his true parentage. After growing to manhood in Arthur's court . . . Mordred is left in charge of the kingdom, and of Queen Guinevere, while Arthur is off fighting the Romans in Brittany. Reported dead, the king returns to Britain and there ensues the fulfillment of the 'wicked day' that has been prophesied by Merlin." Publ Wkly

Stewart, Mary

Wildfire at midnight. Appleton-Century-Crofts 1956 214p

Gianetta Brooke comes to the Isle of Skye to forget the husband she has painfully divorced and finds herself in danger as a series of murders takes place

Stirling, Jessica

The island wife. St. Martin's Press 1998 410p $24.95

ISBN 0-312-19289-4

LC 98-35162

First published 1997 in the United Kingdom

"The characters are well drawn, with realistic motivations, and the atmosphere is 'like the island itself, two-faced and moody.' Some of the Scottish words will be unfamiliar to Americans, but this does not detract from the enjoyment." Libr J

Followed by The wind from the hills

Stirling, Jessica

The marrying kind. St. Martin's Press 1996 359p

ISBN 978-0312143664

LC 96-1191

First published 1995 in the United Kingdom

Set in pre-WWII Glasgow, This sequel to the The penny wedding "coming-of-age novel centers around third-year medical student Alison Burnside as she struggles toward the realization that having it all is impossible. At the same time, all the characters, one way or another, illustrate just how naïve the world was on the eve of Hitler's reign of terror. . . . Exposing her characters to feminism, class conflict and the stormclouds of war, Stirling expertly guides them through the growing pains of the heart into genuine maturity." Publ Wkly

Stirling, Jessica

The penny wedding. St. Martin's Press 1995 394p

LC 95-1732

First published 1994 in the United Kingdom

"A working-class Scottish family strives to survive personal tragedy and financial devastation during the Great Depression. When her mother unexpectedly dies and her father loses his job, gifted and intelligent 17-year-old Alison Burnside expects to forgo her dreams of obtaining a medical degree in order to help support her struggling family.

Before she has a chance to leave school, however, her favorite teacher and her four older brothers intervene on her behalf. . . . A bittersweet portrait of a realistically flawed family banding together out of a sense of love, loyalty, and necessity in a heartfelt effort to overcome poverty and misfortune." Booklist

Followed by The marrying kind

Stirling, Jessica

The **piper's** tune. St. Martin's Press 2002 486p $26.95

ISBN 0-312-28870-0

LC 2001-57854

"Eighteen-year-old Lindsay Franklin gets an unexpected jolt when her shipbuilding magnate grandfather gives her a share of the family business. At the same time, her all-too-charming Irish cousin, the womanizing Forbes McCulloch, comes to Glasgow to learn the family business from the bottom up and sets his sights on marrying Lindsay. The style and design of the cover give the impression that this is a historical romance, but the tale is much more than a formulaic love story. Stirling does a bang-up job of illustrating how character shapes a person's life." Publ Wkly

Stirling, Jessica

The **wind** from the hills. St. Martin's Press 1999 442p $25.95

ISBN 0-312-24433-9

LC 99-50171

First published 1998 in the United Kingdom

This novel, the second in the Isle of Mull trilogy begun with The island wife, finds Innis married to Michael Tarrant and Biddy a wealthy widow with few ties to her past

Stirling, Jessica

The **workhouse** girl. St. Martin's Press 1997 472p

ISBN 978-0312156985

LC 97-5500

First published 1996 in the United Kingdom

Set in Victorian Scotland, "Stirling's tale follows Cassie Armitage into an unfortunate marriage to the evil, deceitful, and abusive Reverend Robert Montague. Cassie's servant, Nancy Winfield, is the workhouse girl of the book's title. Nancy shares the story's center stage and is as engaging and likable as her wealthy counterpart. But it is Nancy's station in life to carry the weight of an illegitimate child on her very capable and resourceful shoulders. . . . A thoroughly entertaining and satisfying read." Booklist

Stirling, S. M.

The **city** who fought; [by] Anne McCaffrey, S.M. Stirling. Baen Pub. Enterprises 1993 435p

ISBN 0-671-72166-6

LC 93-2651

Previous titles in this series published in paperback are: The ship who sang (1969); Partnership (1992); and The ship who searched (1992)

"Within the fabric of McCaffrey's universe, she and Stirling merge seamlessly, sporting wit, action galore, superior characterization, and plausible hardware." Booklist

Followed by The ship who won (1994)

Stirling, S. M.

Dies the fire; S.M. Stirling. New American Library 2004 483p (hbk.) o.p.; (pbk.) $7.99

ISBN 0451459792; 9780451460417

LC 2004004363

This book takes place after "a mysterious event that caused electricity, internal combustion engines, and gunpowder to fail, [and takes place in] the Pacific Northwest [which] furnishes enough land to support subsistence existence in a future that belongs . . . to people who know older ways. Musician Juniper takes refuge on her family's land with a growing group of friends that becomes 'Clan MacKenzie.' Reenactors know useful things, . . . such as how to build log houses and craft bows for hunting. Meanwhile, Mike Havel, a pilot who was flying when the Change happened, and his passengers, having survived . . . [and t]hanks to a former Society for Creative Anachronism . . . fencer, and after hard work and the accident that gives their group the name 'Bearkillers,' they have the knowledge to sell their protective services." (Booklist)

Stockett, Kathryn

★ The **help**. Amy Einhorn Books 2009 451p $24.95

ISBN 978-0-399-15534-5; 0-399-15534-1

LC 2008-30185

Twenty-two-year-old Skeeter has just returned home after graduating from Ole Miss. She may have a degree, but it is 1962, Mississippi, and her mother will not be happy till Skeeter has a ring on her finger. Skeeter would normally find solace with her beloved maid Constantine, the woman who raised her, but Constantine has disappeared and no one will tell Skeeter where she has gone.

Stoker, Bram

The **Bram** Stoker bedside companion; 10 stories by the author of Dracula. edited and with an introduction by Charles Osborne. Taplinger 1973 224p

Stoker, Bram

★ **Dracula**; edited with an introduction and notes by Maurice Hindle; preface by Christopher Frayling. Penguin Books 2003 xlvii, 454p pa $11

ISBN 0-14-143984-X

LC 2003-269578

First published 1897

"Count Dracula, an 'undead' villain from Transylvania, uses his supernatural powers to lure and prey upon innocent victims from whom he gains the blood on which he lives. The novel is written chiefly in the form of journals kept by the principal characters—Jonathan Harker, who contacts the vampire in his Transylvanian castle; Harker's fiancee (later his wife), Mina, adored by the Count; the well-meaning Dr. Seward; and Lucy Westenra, a victim who herself becomes a vampire. The doctor and friends destroy Dracula in the end, but only after they drive a stake through Lucy's heart to save her soul." Merriam-Webster's Ency of Lit

Stoker, Bram

Midnight tales; edited and with an introduction by Peter Haining. Owen, P. 1990 182p il

Stone, Irving

★ The **agony** and the ecstasy. New American Library 2004 776p pa $16

ISBN 0-451-21323-8

First published 1961 by Doubleday

"Stone's Michelangelo is an idealized version, purged not only of ambisexuality, but of the egotism, faultfinding, harsh irony, and ill temper that we know were characteristic of Michelangelo." Saturday Rev

Stone, Irving

Love is eternal; a novel about Mary Todd and Abraham Lincoln. Doubleday 1954 468p

This novel presents a sympathetic portrait of Mary Todd Lincoln. The author absolves her from the shrewishness with which many historians have clothed her and pictures her marriage to Abraham Lincoln as a great love story

"Recommended in spite of the controversial nature of its interpretation of Mary Todd Lincoln." Booklist

Stone, Irving

★ **Lust** for life; a novel of Vincent van Gogh. illustrated with 150 reproductions of Vincent van Gogh's pictures arranged by J. B. Neumann. Twentieth anniversary ed.; Doubleday 1954 507p il

First published 1934 by Longmans, Green and Co.

"Vincent Van Gogh lived a turbulent life but throughout it he was loved and supported by his brother, Theo. Sons of a Dutch Protestant minister, Vincent and Theo were raised rather strictly, but Vincent's love of color and movement led him into the life of an artist. He always felt challenged to fill a blank canvas with light and color. Vincent's search for meaning and fulfillment in his life took him over Europe but only toward the end of his life did he meet other artists who shared his artistic views, and it was not until after his death that his work began to be appreciated." Shapiro. Fic for Youth. 3d edition

Stone, Katherine

Happy endings. Kensington Pub. Corp. 1994 362p

"Raven Winter is the best entertainment attorney in the business. She is handling the reclusive, best-selling author Holly, who fears that Jason Cole, an Academy Award-winning filmmaker, is going to change the happy ending in the film version of her book. Nick is introduced to this group when Raven distractedly jogs in front of his nursery truck. . . . Most romance readers expect a happy ending, but the pleasure comes in the journey to reach it, and Stone does not disappoint." Libr J

Stone, Nick

The **king** of swords; a novel. Harper 2008 559p $24.95; pa $14.99

ISBN 978-0-06-089731-4; 0-06-089731-7; 978-0-06-089732-1 pa; 0-06-089732-5 pa

LC 2008-33704

"The Miami of the early 1980s has become an almost mythical place, an era steeped in the lore of Miami Vice and Scarface and seen as the epicenter for drugs and the glamour of a new South Beach. Nick Stone captures that reality in his gritty, brutal and expertly plotted The King of Swords, offer-

ing an authentic vision of South Florida along with plenty of hardboiled action." Miami Herald

Stone, Robert

★ **Bay** of souls. Houghton Mifflin 2003 249p $25

ISBN 0-395-96349-4

LC 2002-192171

"Unusual (for Stone) in is brevity, this is a highly concentrated work, probably the least violent yet most unnerving of his novels. And the philosophical conflict dramatized in it ends surprisingly, in a way that provokes new questions about what Stone is up to in his writing." N Y Times Book Rev

Stone, Robert

Damascus Gate. Houghton Mifflin 1998 500p $26

ISBN 0-395-66569-8

LC 97-49615

Stone "is so comprehending of Israel's convoluted workings and its bifurcated culture—where the Biblical fervor of Jerusalem coexists with the disco fever of Tel Aviv—that he makes other writers on the subject seem like the breeziest of literary tourists." New Yorker

Stone, Robert

★ **Dog** soldiers; a novel. Houghton Mifflin 1974 342p

"Part melodrama, part morality play, 'Dog Soldiers' offers a vision of a predatory, insensate society from which all moral authority has fled. It is a world in which innocence or vestigial remnants of decent behavior prove fatal to their owners; Hicks . . . is nearly violent enough to survive, but he is done in by his own loyalty to Marge. All of this corruption and vulnerability, this savagery and stoned withdrawal, this combination of passion and cynicism works convincingly, for Stone is a very good storyteller indeed." Newsweek

Stone, Robert

★ A **flag** for sunrise; a novel. Knopf 1981 439p

ISBN 0-394-40757-1

LC 81-47507

This "book is at once a high-tension adventure tale, a densely plotted political novel and, at its heart, a meditation on the inavailability of God. Stone writes as if announcements of the death of the novel had not reached him: 'A Flag for Sunrise' shows narrative confidence, crisscrossed motives, a moral sense and sustained inventiveness of an amplitude we have almost given up expecting from fiction." Newsweek

Stone, Robert

Fun with problems; stories. Houghton Mifflin Harcourt 2010 195p $24

ISBN 978-0-618-38625-3; 0-618-38625-4

LC 2009-13748

"The stories in Fun With Problems, Stone's 11th book of fiction and his second collection of short stories, are as spare and razor-edged as any of Stone's early work, and for the uninitiated reader, every bit as unnerving. Stone's title comes from a 1999 rehab video: 'Overcoming difficulties can present spiritual opportunities. It is actually possible to have fun with problems.' Used as an epigraph, it defines Stone's temperament and his approach: in its derived meaning earned from hard experience, in its balance of elements sacred and profane, and in its sly, deadpan humor." Dallas Morning News

Stone, Robert

★ **Outerbridge** Reach. Ticknor & Fields 1992 409p

LC 91-34875

"Robert Stone's blend of heroic aspiration and mordantly deflationary irony results in something like tragicomedy. . . . But whatever you call it, 'Outerbridge Reach' seems to me a triumph—a beautifully and painstakingly composed piece of literary art." N Y Times Book Rev

Stonich, Sarah

Vacationland; a novel. Sarah Stonich. University of Minnesota Press 2013 288 p. (pb: acid-free paper) $16.95

ISBN 0816687668; 9780816687664

LC 2012048343

In this novel by Sarah Stonich "on a lake in northernmost Minnesota, you might find Naledi Lodge—only two cabins still standing. And there you might meet Meg, or the ghost of the girl she was, growing up under her grandfather's care in a world apart and a lifetime ago. Now an artist, Meg paints images 'reflected across the mirrors of memory and water,' much as the linked stories of 'Vacationland.' Those whose paths have crossed at Naledi inhabit 'Vacationland.' (Publisher's note)

Stories; all - new tales. edited by Neil Gaiman and Al Sarrantonio. William Morrow 2010 428p $27.99

ISBN 978-0-06-123092-9; 0-06-123092-8

LC 2010-20363

"An ambitious anthology with a pleasing mix of modes and moods. 'Stories' has a little something for everyone who appreciates the possibilities of short fiction." San Francisco Chron

Stott, Rebecca

The **coral** thief; a novel. Spiegel & Grau 2009 286p il map $25

ISBN 978-0-385-53146-7; 0-385-53146-X

LC 2009-12846

"Aside from her graceful writing style and believable characters, Stott also delights with her grasp of history. Romantic, full of twists and turns and glimpses of the past, The Coral Thief is an unlikely page-turner." BookPage

Stott, Rebecca

Ghostwalk; a novel. Spiegel & Grau 2007 304p il $24.95

ISBN 978-0-385-52106-2; 0-385-52106-5

LC 2006-22326

"A Cambridge historian dies under suspicious circumstances, leaving behind the nearly completed manuscript of a book on the alchemical experiments of Isaac Newton. Her

son, a research scientist, hires his former lover, Lydia, to finish the book. Meanwhile, a shadowy group of animal-rights activists escalate their violent attacks. As Lydia is drawn further into Newton's seventeenth-century world, she begins to believe that his ghost is haunting her and, perhaps, directing the murderous events of the present." New Yorker

"Stott brings a nervy intelligence to her work, skillfully linking the war on terror, quantum physics, alchemy, serial murder, ghosts, and thwarted romance." Miami Herald

Stout, Rex

Black orchids; &, the silent speaker; introduction to Black orchids by Lawrence Block; introduction to The silent speaker by Walter Mosley. Bantam Books 2009 various paging il pa $16

ISBN 978-0-553-38655-4; 0-553-38655-7

LC 2009-464755

Black orchids first published 1942 by Farrar & Reinhart; The silent speaker first published 1946 by Viking Press

Contains two titles in the author's Nero Wolfe series. In The black orchids, Wolfe goes to a flower show to see a rare black orchid; "unfortunately, the much-anticipated event is soon overshadowed by a murder as daring as it is sudden. . . . [In The silent speaker,] a government power broker scheduled to speak before an influential group of millionaires turns up dead. . . . Soon a second victim is discovered, a missing stenographer's tape causes a panic, and a dead man speaks, after a fashion." Publisher's note

Stout, Rex

The **doorbell** rang; a Nero Wolfe novel. Viking 1965 186p

"Nero Wolfe tangles with the FBI, on behalf of a wealthy woman who has sent as gifts to prominent people 10,000 copies of Fred Cook's book criticizing the FBI. . . . She is being shadowed and spied on by the FBI. To the surprise of Wolfe and of Archie Goodwin, they have the good will of the New York Police Department. The New York Police believe that FBI agents have murdered a magazine writer who was doing an article on the FBI. The police are powerless to prove anything or to prosecute. Clever and ingenious, this ranks among the best Rex Stout mysteries." Publ Wkly

Stout, Rex

Fer-de-lance; &, The league of frightened men; introduction to Fer-de-lance by Loren D. Estleman; introduction to The league of frightened men by Robert Goldsborough. Bantam Books 2008 285, 302p il pa $16

ISBN 978-0-553-38545-8; 0-553-38545-3

LC 2008-299738

Combined edition of two titles first published 1934 and 1935 respectively by Farrar & Rinehart

Contains two titles in the author's Nero Wolfe series. "The fer-de-lance is among the most deadly snakes known to man. When someone makes a present of one to Nero Wolfe, his partner, Archie Goodwin, suspects it means Wolfe is getting close to solving the devilishly clever murders of an immigrant and a college president. . . . [In The league of frightened men,] Paul Chapin's Harvard cronies never forgave themselves for the hazing prank that left their friend a cripple. Yet they believed that Paul himself had forgiven them—until a class reunion ends in death and a series of poems promising more of the same. Now this league of frightened men is desperate for Nero Wolfe's help." Publisher's note

Stout, Rex
★ **Gambit**; a Nero Wolfe novel. Viking 1962 188p

"There is more detection in this story than in any other of the mulling-and-quizzing sort; here we really see N.W.'s thoughts whirring. Moreover, Archie is in excellent form, and although a chess tournament is a feature, the game itself is not. The great scene is that in which Nero reads and burns the pages of Webster's Dictionary, Third Edition." Barzun. Cat of Crime. Rev and enl edition

Stout, Rex
The **rubber** band & The red box; introduction to The red box by Carolyn G. Hart. Bantam Books 2009 189, 257p pa $15
ISBN 978-0-553-38603-5; 0-553-38603-4
LC 2009-455172

Combined edition of two titles first published 1936 and 1937 respectively by Farrar & Rinehart

Contains two titles in the author's Nero Wolfe series. In The rubber band, "a forty-year-old pact, a five-thousand-mile search, and a million-dollar murder are all linked to an international scandal that could rebound on the great detective and his partner, Archie, with fatal abruptness. . . . [In The red box] a beautiful woman is poisoned after indulging in a box of candy." Publisher's note

Stout, Rex
Some buried Caesar & The golden spiders; introduction to Some Buried Caesar by Diane Mott Davidson; introduction to the Golden Spiders by Linda Barnes. Bantam Books 2008 206p pa $15
ISBN 978-0-553-38567-0
LC 2008-301309

Some buried Caesar first published 1939 by Farrar & Rinehart; The golden spiders first published 1953 by Viking Press

Contains two titles in the author's Nero Wolfe series. In Some buried Caesar "a prize bull destined for the barbecue is found pawing the corpse of a late restaurateur. Wolfe is certain that Hickory Caesar Grindon, the soon-to-be-beefsteak bull, isn't the murderer. But who among a veritable stampede of suspects—including a young woman who's caught Archie's eye—turned the tables on Hickory's would-be butcher? . . . [In The golden spiders] a twelve-year-old boy shows up at Wolfe's brownstone with an incredible story. Soon the great detective finds himself hired for the grand sum of $4.30 and faced with the question of why the last two people to hire him were murdered. To keep it from becoming three, Wolfe must discover the unlikely connection between a gray Cadillac, a mysterious woman, and a pair of earrings shaped like spiders dipped in gold." Publisher's note

Stout, Rex
Too many cooks; & champagne for one; introduction to Champagne for One by Lena Horne. Bantam Dell/Random House, Inc. 2009 179, 205p pa $15
ISBN 978-0-553-38629-5; 0-553-38629-8
LC 2009-464724

Too many cooks first published 1938 by Farrar & Rinehart; Champagne for one first published 1958 by Viking Press

Contains two titles in the author's Nero Wolfe series. Too many cooks involves a poisoning at a gathering of great chefs in which Wolfe is a guest of honor. In Champagne for one, "Faith Usher talked about taking her own life and even kept cyanide in her purse. So when she died from a lethal champagne cocktail in the middle of a high society dinner party, everyone called it suicide—including the police. But Nero Wolfe isn't convinced—and neither is Archie. Especially when Wolfe is warned by four men against taking the case." Publisher's note

Stowe, Harriet Beecher
★ **Uncle** Tom's cabin; with an introduction by Alfred Kazin. Knopf 1995 xxix, 494p $20
ISBN 0-679-44365-7

"The book relates the trials, suffering, and human dignity of Uncle Tom, an old slave. Cruelly treated by a Yankee plantation owner, Simon Legree, Tom dies as the result of a beating. Uncle Tom is devoted to Little Eva, the daughter of his white owner, Augustine St. Clare. Other important characters are the mulatto girl Eliza; the impish black child Topsy; Miss Ophelia St. Clare, a New England spinster; and Marks, the slave catcher. The setting is Kentucky and Louisiana." Reader's Ency. 4th edition

Stowe, Harriet Beecher
Uncle Tom's cabin: or, Life among the lowly; The minister's wooing; Oldtown folks. Library of Am. 1982 1477p il $47.50
ISBN 0-940450-01-1
LC 81-18629

Omnibus edition of three titles first published 1852, 1859 and 1869 respectively

In the minister's wooing, a young woman rejects her suitor because he has no religious faith. Oldtown folks concerns the everyday life of a small Massachusetts town

Straight, Susan
Between heaven and here; Susan Straight. McSweeney's Books 2012 234 p. $24
ISBN 1936365758; 9781936365753

In this novel by Susan Straight "Glorette Picard is dead, and across the canal, out in the orange groves, they'll gather shovels and pickaxes and soak the dirt until they can lay her coffin down. As the residents of [Rio Seco, California] prepare to bury their own, it becomes clear that Glorette's life and death are deeply entangled with the dark history of the city and the untouchable beauty that, finally, killed her." (Publisher's note)

Straight, Susan
The **gettin** place. Hyperion 1996 488p $22.95
ISBN 0-7868-6086-3
LC 95-50065

"Against the backdrop of the under-acknowledged race riots of 1920s Tulsa and the contrastingly media-saturated 1992 L.A. riots, Straight realizes the chillingly natural, almost blithe cynicism and violence of teenagers, the profound weight of hard history on the old, and the bewilderment of those in-between. A lyrical and unflinching stunner." Libr J

Straight, Susan

Highwire moon; a novel. Houghton Mifflin 2001 306p map $24

ISBN 0-618-05614-9

LC 00-53878

"Susan Straight's Rio Seco is a microcosm of suspicious, segregated America, a place where racism often boils down to fear, ignorance and willful obliviousness." N Y Times Book Rev

Straight, Susan

I been in sorrow's kitchen and licked out all the pots; a novel. Hyperion 1992 355p

ISBN 1-56282-963-7

LC 92-3566

"Time and place . . . are evoked with stirring accuracy. But it is Marietta's intricate constitution, and the Gullah rhythms streaming through her mind, that give the novel its special edge and distinction." N Y Times Book Rev

Followed by Blacker than a thousand midnights (1994)

Straight, Susan

A **million** nightingales. Pantheon Books 2006 340p $24.95

ISBN 0-375-42364-8

LC 2005-50052

"Straight's book is a deep consideration of the servitude all women experienced then—and, in some ways and some places, continue to experience even now. . . . But her novel is, besides, a powerful and moving story, written in language so beautiful you can almost believe the words themselves are capable of salving history's wounds." N Y Times Book Rev

Straight, Susan

Take one candle light a room; Susan Straight. Pantheon Books 2010 320 p. $25.95

ISBN 0307379140; 9780307379146

LC 2010012683

This novel, by Susan Straight, follows the charater of "Fantine Antoine. . . . When she returns to mark the fifth anniversary of the murder of her . . . friend, Glorette, she finds herself pulled into the tumultuous life of Glorette's twenty-two-year-old son . . . Victor. After getting involved in a shooting, Victor has fled to New Orleans. Together with her father, Fantine follows Victor, determined to help him avoid the criminal future that he suddenly seems destined for." (Publisher's note)

Straub, Peter

★ A **dark** matter; a novel. Doubleday 2010 397p $26.95

ISBN 978-0-385-51638-9; 0-385-51638-X

LC 2009-20028

A "multiple-perspective take on a murky collegiate misadventure in 1966. Spencer Mallon, campus-flitting intellec-

tual and seducer of coeds, is compared in the early pages to a host of flattering figures: a god, a hero, a guru. What Mallon feels most like to us, though, is a Manson-like charmer who lures several young people out to a field, where one of them dies. How, though? Straub expertly weaves a Rashômon-crazy quilt of varying and sometimes conflicting recollections of the incident, left purposefully vague, as we shuttle through the intervening years—unkind ones in which his characters are struck by blindness, become criminals and, in an especially sad case, go insane. A slight slackness in the story's middle game will have some readers exhorting, 'Get over it already!'—whatever it is. But ambitiously, the author mounts his referendum on a wild, unpredictable moment of the 1960s, saluting the era's competing urges of decadence and justice." Time Out N Y

Straub, Peter

★ **Ghost** story. Coward, McCann & Geoghegan 1979 483p

ISBN 0-698-10959-7

LC 78-27120

"With considerable technical skill, Peter Straub has constructed an extravagant entertainment which, though flawed, achieves in its second half some awesome effects." Newsweek

Straub, Peter

The **Hellfire** Club. Random House 1995 462p

LC 95-21773

"A former nurse in Vietnam, Nora Chancel lives in Westerholm, Connecticut, with her ineffectual husband, Davey. While visiting the local police station to identify the most recent victim of a serial killer, Nora is kidnapped by the accused killer, the satirical villain Dick Dart. Intertwined with the kidnapping plot is an account of the terrifying events that followed the writing of a horror story at the Shorelands writers' colony in 1938. Fighting her own demons from Vietnam, Nora becomes stronger and braver as the story progresses. The climax brings the two stories together, as Dart and Nora visit Shorelands. Horror meets horror in this bizarre, enigmatic tale, which reveals itself in onion-like layers." Libr J

Straub, Peter

In the night room; a novel. Random House 2004 330p $21.95

ISBN 1-400-06252-7

LC 2004-51425

In this sequel to Lost boy lost girl, horror novelist Tim Underhill receives "an e-mail sent to him by the spirit of an ancient Byzantine, who explains that the daughter of one of the serial killers in Lost boy lost girl wasn't murdered by her father, as Tim supposed; that the exceedingly strange fan who cornered Tim in his local breakfast hangout is an embodiment of the wronged murderer's spirit; and that, yes, that was an angel Tim saw fly away over Manhattan while he walked home. Meanwhile, over in New Jersey, YA novelist Willy Patrick is about to marry mysterious Mitchell Faber when she comes upon evidence that he is responsible for her husband's violent, gangland-like killing. She flees Faber's estate, pursued by his minions, to New York and into a reading-signing appearance by Tim. There is a catch to this, for Willy's plot is that of the new novel Tim has been writing;

that is, a character Tim created has emerged in his reality. As Tim and Willy repair to their hometown, Millhaven, Illinois, to slake the murderer's spirit, his real and her fictive worlds converge toward an ending that promises, like that of Lost boy lost girl, the transcendent redemption of violated souls. Inventive and moving." Booklist

Straub, Peter

Lost boy lost girl; a novel. Farrar, Straus & Giroux 2003 281p $24.95

ISBN 1-4000-6092-3

LC 2003-046689

"Inquisitive and open-minded as Tim is, he makes it easy for Mr. Straub to move from conventionally hair-raising effects . . . to the more happening teenage world of cyberscares. Strongly visual without resorting to secondhand cinematic imagery, the book is equally well equipped to play both kinds of tricks." N Y Times (Late N Y Ed)

Straub, Peter

Magic terror; seven tales. Random House 2000 335p

ISBN 0-375-50393-5

LC 99-53216

"Straub is not called a master of horror for nothing. In this collection of seven tales, ranging from the story of a grade school teacher with an evil secret to a Vietnam War grunt whose reality is 'melting at the edges,' Straub shows that horror comes in numerous forms—many of which are not so much frightening as deeply disturbing." Libr J

Straub, Peter

Mr. X; a novel. Random House 1999 482p $25.95

ISBN 0-679-40138-5

LC 98-47688

"From childhood, Ned Dunstan has experienced precognitive visions. . . . Summoned home to Edgerton, Ill., by a premonition of his mother's death on the eve of his 35th birthday, Ned finds himself implicated in a tangle of felonies and murders, all of which point to someone strenuously manipulating events to frame him. Digging into local history, he finds reason to believe that the mysterious father he never knew, or possibly a malignant doppelgänger, are pulling the strings. . . . {Straub's} evocative prose, a seamless splice of clipped hard-boiled banter and poetic reflection, contributes to the thick atmosphere of apprehension that makes this one of the most invigorating horror reads of the year." Publ Wkly

Straub, Peter

★ **Mystery**. Dutton 1990 548p il

LC 89-7734

Second title in the author's Blue rose trilogy. "When a traffic accident nearly ends his young life, Tom Pasmore experiences all the usual near-death sensations: warm lights at the end of tunnels and friendly faces beckoning him onward. But by cheating death, his life is forever changed. Tom becomes obsessed with murder, with detection, and especially with a recent killing on Mill Walk, the fictional Caribbean island where his family lives. Tom's sleuthing mania is fed by an eccentric neighbor, Lamont von Heilitz, a famous retired detective. . . . The remarkable depth of characterization

make apparent the fact that Mystery is meant to be much more than a conventional shocker. For the most part, Straub delivers the goods." Booklist

Straub, Peter

★ A **special** place; the heart of a dark matter. Pegasus 2010 136p pa $12.95

ISBN 978-1-60598-102-4; 1-60598-102-8

"Young Keith Hayward idolizes his charming, charismatic Uncle Till. When Keith's mother asks Till to talk to Keith after the boy is found dismembering a dead cat, Till recognizes a kindred spirit and begins to instruct Keith on smart, secret ways to pursue his evil endeavors. As the years pass, Keith grows older and bolder in his sadistic pleasures, and when Till comes back into town, Keith finds the perfect way to impress him. Vivid but never overly graphic or grotesque, Straub's words paint horrific pictures of two depraved men." Publ Wkly

Strauss, Darin

More than it hurts you; a novel. Dutton 2008 401p $24.95

ISBN 978-0-525-95070-7; 0-525-95070-2

LC 2007-43742

The "novel is most effective not in its sweeping, occasionally grandiloquent observations about society as a whole, but in its mastery of personal, domestic issues, the disturbing, soul-searching, what-if questions Strauss raises about marriage, parenthood, loyalty and responsibility." Chicago Tribune

Strauss, Darin

The **real** McCoy; a novel. Dutton 2002 326p

ISBN 0-525-94651-9

LC 2002-23545

The author has "taken the tale of an all-but-forgotten boxer and used it as his jumping-off point to worry questions of identity and the thin, often nonexistent lines between filmflamming and lying and storytelling itself." N Y Times Book Rev

Strauss, Jacques

The **dubious** salvation of Jack V. Farrar, Straus and Giroux 2011 240p

ISBN 978-0-374-14412-8

LC 2011-08456

"Strauss's often-hilarious debut captures a remarkable period of time without resorting to any heavy-handed political messaging. And in Jack he has created an unlikely, and utterly believable, voice of a generation. [A] profane, brutally honest portrait of tween angst." Kirkus

Strayed, Cheryl

Torch. Houghton 2005 322p $24

ISBN 0-618-47217-7

LC 2005-10333

"A beautiful book, expansive in its treatment of tragedy and grief, but equally attentive to all of the most telling details. The language is lovely, offering delicious, compelling imagery without being heavy-handed." Providence Journal

LIST OF FICTIONAL WORKS

Strieber, Whitley

2012: the war for souls. Tor 2007 319p $24.95

ISBN 978-0-7653-1896-1; 0-7653-1896-2

LC 2007-17374

This sequel to The Grays "blends equal parts science fiction thriller, supernatural horror and provocative spiritual speculation. As struggling author Wylie Dale works on his latest novel, which revolves around an upcoming date when the earth crosses both the galactic equator and the solar ecliptic—a time that the Maya predicted would mark the cataclysmic end of this age—he begins to uncover evidence that what he's writing about is actually happening on a parallel earth. If nothing is done, on December 21, 2012, gateways will open into this world and reptilian invaders will not only enslave humanity but feast on their succulent souls as well. While Strieber's exploration into the existence and import of the soul isn't exactly profound, it is wildly entertaining." Publ Wkly

Strieber, Whitley

The **forbidden** zone. Dutton 1993 309p

ISBN 0-525-93683-1

LC 93-6726

"The action and danger in this novel are exciting, and while the physics and the explanation for the horrific events are rather muddy, the story works well as a Lovecraft-style tale brought into modern times." Libr J

Strieber, Whitley

The **Grays**. Tor 2006 335p $24.95

ISBN 0-765-31389-8

LC 2005-34494

"Danny and Katelyn Callaghan are a happily married couple oblivious that both took a saucer ride as kids—until a UFO sighting in their Indiana town awakens subliminal memories and excites their genius teenage son, Conner. Meanwhile, in a secret facility in Colorado, Air Force Lt. Lauren Glass learns that the Roswell incident really happened, and that for decades the surviving ETs have been sharing their advanced science with us. In exchange, these 'Grays' have sought to rejuvenate their dying species by genetically manipulating human receptacles for their DNA. But some military hard-liners see this as a betrayal of humanity, and they launch a manhunt that brings them to Indiana and the Callaghans' doorstep. . . . [The author's] depiction of black ops intrigue and military espionage is a first-rate exercise in literary paranoia." Publ Wkly

Strieber, Whitley

The **hunger**. Pocket Books 1981 357p pa $24.95

ISBN 978-1-416-58374-5

First published 1981 by Morrow

Miriam Blaylock, an ancient vampire, sets out to find a new human companion when her current one begins to age rapidly.

Followed by The last vampire

Strieber, Whitley

The **last** vampire. Pocket Bks. 2001 303p $24.95

ISBN 0-7434-1720-8

LC 2001-21013

Sequel to The hunger (1981)

"There's much here to admire, not least Strieber's expert modulation of tone and dialogue as POV shifts from Miriam (fluid, refined) to Paul (muscular, slangy)." Publ Wkly

Strieber, Whitley

Majestic. Putnam 1989 317p

LC 89-8495

"Strieber has managed to weave two major themes in ufology (crashes and abductions) into an intriguing and unconventional tale that has both the dialogue and flavor of postwar America as well as the surrealistic aura of contemporary fiction." Booklist

Strieber, Whitley

Warday; and the journey onward. {by} Whitley Strieber and James W. Kunetka. Holt, Rinehart & Winston 1984 374p

LC 83-18678

"On Oct. 28, 1988, the Soviet Union launches a surprise attack on the United States. Ten-megaton atomic bombs detonate over Washington, San Antonio and the eastern edge of Queens. Smaller bombs strike the Minuteman and MX missile fields spread out across the northern plains. Washington and San Antonio are 'instantly vaporized.' Manhattan escapes destruction but is abandoned. Five years later, two writers brave the hazards of post-Warday travel to report back to us on how surviving America 'feels and tastes and smells.'" NY Times Book Rev

Strieber, Whitley

★ The **Wolfen**. Morrow 1978 252p

LC 78-7482

"Two cops are brutally killed and their guts are devoured by what appears to be a pack of wild animals. The police in charge, a middle-aged slob and a newly fledged woman detective, bicker endlessly through the killings of a blind man, a couple of junkies, and more, while the pack, mutant wolves, kill for food and to keep their secret from being discovered. This is a very specialized form of animal disaster novel, but much more suspenseful and imaginative than most. The windup is total thrill." Libr J

Stringer, Vickie M.

Low down & dirty; a novel. Vickie M. Stringer. Atria Books 2012 312 p. (hardback) $23.99

ISBN 1451660863; 9781451660869; 9781451660876; 9781451660890

LC 2011046471

This book is part of Vicki M. Stringer's Dirty Red series. "Having apparently wounded all of her enemies, . . . Red finds herself . . . living the life of luxury in Arizona. She's become a successful home broker with a bestselling book, and . . . all of her dirty tricks have finally paid off . . . . Unfortunately for Red, she's made more enemies than she can count, and she soon finds herself running across the

country in fear of them all while still being in love with Q."
(Publisher's note)

Stroby, Wallace

The **barbed**-wire kiss. St. Martin's Minotaur
2003 340p $24.95

ISBN 0-312-30034-4

LC 2002-35879

"Although the story advances predictably. . . Stroby does
wonders with his blue-collar characters, the hard-working
fishermen and mechanics and bar waitresses who put their
hand to petty crime the way they play the lottery—to try
their luck and get a thrill, the way they did when the seashore
was a kinder place to live." N Y Times Book Rev

Stroby, Wallace

Cold shot to the heart. Minotaur Books 2011
289p $24.99

ISBN 978-0-312-56025-6; 0-312-56025-7

LC 2010-37538

"Crissa Stone is a robber for hire, now employed by a
mobster who wants her and two cronies to break into a Fort
Lauderdale hotel and bust up a card game that has a million
bucks on the table. The three miscreants decide to rappel
down the side of the building. The scenes of preparation and
execution are chilling. But the heist goes wrong. A man is
killed because, we're told, one of the gunmen spooked. But
maybe not. Could the caper be disguised murder for hire?
Why else does Crissa suddenly find herself pursued by a
reptile called Eddie the Saint? Their clashes are cinematic:
hurtling cars and bloodstained snow. Stroby has been called
a nascent Crumley or Pelecanos. He shares their sense that
cynicism is the last pose left to a romantic." Booklist

Stroby, Wallace

Kings of midnight; Wallace Stroby. Minotaur
Books 2012 272 p. (hardcover) $24.99

ISBN 1250000378; 9781250000378; 9781429951166

LC 2011045371

In this book, "chasing her retirement number, superthief
Crissa Stone . . . fills bunches of money bags. And body
bags. Crissa Stone is a one-woman larceny machine--smart,
resourceful and, above all, careful, which explains an enviable success rate. But she's reached the point where it makes
sense for her to leave the life behind. Her exit will require
a really big final score. . . . The aging racketeer and the
slick young highway person form an unlikely partnership."
(Kirkus Reviews)

Stross, Charles

Accelerando. Ace Books 2005 390p

ISBN 0-441-01284-1

LC 2005-42815

"Expanded from several stories originally published in
Asimov's Science Fiction, . . . [this] novel follows several
generations of the Macx family through the rapidly transforming, Internet-enabled global economy of the early
twenty-first century to the human and transhuman populated
worlds of the outer solar system a half century later. . . .
Stross has his thumb squarely on the pulse of technology's
leading edge and exults in extrapolating mere glimmers of
ideas out to their mind-bending limits." Booklist

Stross, Charles

The **apocalypse** codex; Charles Stross. Ace
Books 2012 326 p. (hardback) $25.95

ISBN 1937007464; 9781937007461

LC 2012008569

In this book, "supernatural nasties are real, so naturally
the British government has a department to deal with them.
. . . Applied computational demonologist Bob Howard has
been fast-tracked into management, having survived a series
of dangerous and unpleasant encounters. His boss, James
Angleton, an Eater of Souls . . . , worries about . . . Raymond
Schiller, a supernaturally charismatic American televangelist, [who] has grown uncomfortably chummy with the
Prime Minister." (Kirkus Reviews)

Stross, Charles

The **Fuller** memorandum. Ace Books 2010
312p $24.95

ISBN 978-0-441-01867-3; 0-441-01867-X

LC 2010-13534

Stross "returns to Bob Howard and the other spooks employed by The Laundry, Britain's occult intelligence agency.
The titular document is given to Bob by his boss, Angleton,
just before the older man disappears. Bob is left on his own
to contend with the potential awakening of the ancient entity
known as the Eater of Souls. Previous entries in the series
took their cues from the espionage novels of Len Deighton
and Ian Fleming. This time the model seems to be Adam
Hall and his 'Quiller' series. Rather than worrying about
sleeper agents who might be working for the KGB, Bob
plays a cat-and-mouse game with a mole in his department
and cultists who want to awaken the Elder Gods early and
precipitate the apocalypse. Stross has perfected the deadpan
tone that gives these horror/spy mashups their satirical energy." San Francisco Chron

Stross, Charles

Glasshouse. Ace Books 2006 335p $24.95

ISBN 0-44101-403-8

LC 2006-4358

The novel "gives in a little to convention near the end, as
the story inevitably progresses toward a rebellion plot, but
even here, Stross keeps the sweet little surprises coming. .
. . Mostly, Glasshouse is an incisive look into societies that
allow themselves, for whatever reason, to be guided not by
cooperation and the greater good but by fear and mistrust."
SF Reviews.net

Stross, Charles

Halting state. Ace Books 2007 351p $24.95

ISBN 978-0-441-01498-9; 0-441-01498-4

LC 2007-15872

"Brimming with suspense and awash in contemporary
references — evidently, iPods and Starbucks will still be
popular in 2018 — Stross' storytelling is not only edgy and
smart but grounded in human concerns, making State perfect
fodder for n00bs and old-timers alike." Wired

Stross, Charles

Iron sunrise. Ace Bks. 2004 355p $23.95

ISBN 0-441-01159-4

"Stross skillfully balances suspense and humor throughout, offering readers—especially fans of Iain M. Banks and Ken MacLeod—a fascinating future that seems more than possible." Publ Wkly

Stross, Charles

The **Jennifer** morgue; plus bonus story Pimpf and afterword: The golden age of spying. Golden Gryphon Press 2006 313p $25.95

ISBN 1-930846-45-2

LC 2006-11154

"Bob Howard is a computer übergeek employed by the Laundry, a secret British agency assigned to clean up incursions from other realities caused by the inadvertent manipulation of complex mathematical equations: in other words, magic. In 1975, the CIA used Howard Hughes's Glomar Explorer in a bungled attempt to raise a sunken Soviet submarine in order to access the Jennifer Morgue, an occult device that allows communication with the dead. Now a ruthless billionaire intends to try again, even if by doing so he awakens the Great Old Ones, who thwarted the earlier expedition. It's up to Bob and a collection of British eccentrics even Monty Python would consider odd to stop the bad guy and save the world, while getting receipts for all expenditures or else face the most dreaded menace of all: the Laundry's own auditors. Stross has a marvelous time making eldritch horror appear commonplace in the face of bureaucracy." Publ Wkly

Stross, Charles

Neptune's brood; by Charles Stross. Ace Hardcover 2013 336 p. (hardcover) $25.95

ISBN 9780425256770; 0425256774

LC 2013002384

In this novel by Charles Stross "the year is AD 7000. The human species is extinct—for the fourth time—due to its fragile nature. Krina Alizond-114 is metahuman, descended from the robots that once served humanity. She's on a journey to the water-world of Shin-Tethys to find her sister Ana. But her trip is interrupted when pirates capture her ship. Their leader, the enigmatic Count Rudi, suspects that there's more to Krina's search than meets the eye." (Publisher's note)

Stross, Charles

Rule 34. Ace Books 2011 358p $25.95

ISBN 978-0-441-02034-8; 0-441-02034-8

LC 2011-08662

"Murder is rare in Edinburgh, and the case of an ex-con spammer murdered apparently by bad drugs and a defective machine seems bizarre in the extreme, but DI Liz Kavanaugh soon notices similarities with other equally weird cases in Germany and Italy. And soon Euro-cop Kemal Aslan arrives with other examples. A second Edinburgh victim turns up, a shady accountant shrink-wrapped to a bed of obsolete currency. Meanwhile, the Toymaker, a (literally) psychotic enforcer and facilitator for a criminal network, the Organization, arrives to houseclean the current incompetent staff and recruit some fresh talent." Kirkus

Stross, Charles

Saturn's children; a space opera. Ace Books 2008 323p $24.95

ISBN 978-0-441-01594-8

LC 2008-8228

"Stross tosses out ideas aplenty. Since his robots know they were created by humans, for example, they consider evolution heretical. It isn't a relaxing bedtime read, but it is the sort of mind-expanding adventure that made 'hard' science fiction famous." New Scientist

Strout, Elizabeth

Abide with me; a novel. Random 2006 294p $24.95

ISBN 1-4000-6207-1

LC 2005-50380

"The handsome minister Tyler Caskey, of West Annett, Maine, is beloved by his parishioners because he really does think they're all God's children. But in the bleak autumn of 1959, more than a year after the death of his wife, Tyler is still awash in grief. The man who once held them rapt from the pulpit now appears ridiculous up there—'like a big tractor being driven by a teenage kid, slipping in and out of gear'—and his daughter has started screaming and spitting in kindergarten. How can he lead them if he himself is lost? Just as she did in her first novel, 'Amy and Isabelle,' Strout has created an absorbing world peopled by characters who argue the merits of canned cranberry sauce and using one's turn signal; meanwhile, dark fears about Freud and Khrushchev run beneath the surface of their lives like water under ice. With superlative skill, Strout challenges us to examine what makes a good story—and what makes a good life." New Yorker

Strout, Elizabeth

Amy and Isabelle. Random House 1999 303p $22.95

ISBN 0-375-50134-7

LC 98-19995

"As the cacophony of disaster grows ever louder in contemporary culture, Strout has written an excellent novel about enduring the banalities of ordinary life." New Yorker

Strout, Elizabeth

★ The **burgess** boys; a novel. Elizabeth Strout. 1st ed. Random House Inc. 2013 336 p. (ebook) $78.00; (hardcover) $26.00

ISBN 1400067685; 9780812984613; 9781400067688

LC 2012035132

In this book, "haunted by the freak accident that killed their father when they were children, Jim and Bob Burgess escaped from their Maine hometown . . . . as soon as they possibly could. . . . Their long-standing dynamic is upended when their sister, Susan . . . urgently calls them home. Her lonely teenage son, Zach, has gotten himself into a world of trouble, and Susan desperately needs their help. And so the Burgess brothers return to the landscape of their childhood." (Publisher's note)

Strout, Elizabeth

Olive Kitteridge. Random House 2008 270p $25

ISBN 1-4000-6208-X; 978-1-4000-6208-9

LC 2007-16999

Olive Kitteridge, a retired schoolteacher, deplores the changes in her little town [in Maine] and in the world at large, but she doesn't always recognize the changes in those around her. (Publisher's note)

These linked stories introduce the inhabitants of Crosby, Maine, where the pull of domestic tragedy is stronger for rarely being spoken of. Angela doesn't mention the bruises shes noticed on her mother's arm at the nursing home; Marlene learns of her husband's infidelity only after his funeral; Kevin plans to shoot himself, like his mother before him. And there in every story, like a tree thats been blackened by lightning but still leafs in the spring, stands Olive Kitteridge, a retired math teacher who loves her tulips, bullies her husband, and barks at anyone foolish enough to irritate her. You loathe this woman at the book's beginning; you long for her at its finish. Strout makes us experience not only the terrors of change but also the terrifying hope that change can bring: she plunges us into these churning waters and we come up gasping for air. New Yorker

Strugatsky, Arkady Natanovich, 1925-1991

Roadside picnic; Arkady and Boris Strugatsky; translated by Olena Bormashenko. Chicago Review Press 2012 ix, 209 pages

ISBN 1613743416; 9781613743416

LC 2012001294

This book is a re-release of a 1972 Russian science fiction novel by Arkady Natanovich Strugatsky and Boris Natanovich Strugatsky. "Red Schuhart is a stalker, one of those young rebels who are compelled, in spite of extreme danger, to venture illegally into the Zone to collect the mysterious artifacts that the alien visitors left scattered around. His life is dominated by the place and the thriving black market in the alien products." (Publisher's note)

Stuart, Julia

The **tower,** the zoo, and the tortoise. Doubleday 2010 304p $24.95

ISBN 978-0-385-53328-7; 0-385-53328-4

LC 2009-46840

"Set on the grounds of famed tourist attraction the Tower of London, the story follows Balthazar Jones, a Beefeater grieving for his 11-year-old son. Jones suddenly finds himself in charge of a menagerie of exotic animals, whose various eccentricities rival those of the delightful cast of human characters. . . . [Stuart] crafts a subculture that is so sweet and enchanting that the whole affair would be terribly twee were it not for the sense of heartbreak and longing that holds it all together." Entertainment Wkly

Stubbs, Jean

Family games. St. Martin's Press 1994 294p

LC 93-44054

The Malpas family assembles for Christmas at their Cornwall farmhouse: "headstrong daughter Blanche, an unwed mother, brings her infant son and temporarily abandons her feud with her father, the brilliant and irascible Anthony;

recently separated son Edward, still reeling from his wife's departure, arrives with his two children; and beautiful, dependent daughter Lydia surprises the others by bringing a likable woman friend instead of another one of a parade of 'moneyed and moronic' male beaux. At the close of the Malpases' impromptu Christmas Eve open house, three unexpected visitors appear, Magi-like, at the door. One is Natalie, Anthony's imperious twin sister; another is Katrina, Edward's estranged wife; the third is Daniel Kidd, the father of Blanche's child." Publ Wkly

"The writer appears fully in control of this entertaining romp concerning one very dysfunctional, if provocative, family." Booklist

Stubbs, Jean

Like we used to be. St. Martin's Press 1990 387p

LC 89-27133

First published 1989 in the United Kingdom

"This is the story of Leila and Zoe Gideon, sisters who are in every way different, yet who love each other and their marvelous British family unreservedly. The story begins with Zoe's wedding and Leila's first love affair in the summer of 1953, and spans the next 15 years. Zoe struggles to create a loving home with her difficult husband, Matthew. Leila, the rebellious sister, makes an independent life for herself as an artist in London. Told alternately by Leila and Zoe, the book has leisurely pace filled with emotional detail. This will appeal to lovers of old-fashioned family novels." Libr J

"Social ferment and family history are vigorously blended in a dramatic style characteristic of a master storyteller." Publ Wkly

Stuckey-French, Elizabeth

Revenge of the radioactive lady; a novel. Doubleday 2010 333p $25.95

ISBN 978-0-385-51064-6; 0-385-51064-0

LC 2010-14724

"Stuckey-French's desire to keep the action moving makes some connections feel hastily drawn. Characters occasionally come to realizations that seem delivered by the author rather than organic to who they are. But the author's insistence on rendering her characters as complex human beings with conflicting desires keeps the novel from reading like mere farce. While the plot may hinge on revenge, the unpredictability of love is the true subject. It turns out to be the best kind of page-turner — one with heart ." Boston Globe

Stumpf, Douglas

Confessions of a Wall Street shoeshine boy; [by] Doug Stumpf. HarperCollins Publishers 2007 290p $24.95

ISBN 978-0-06-088953-1; 0-06-088953-5

LC 2006-53546

This satirical "novel views corruption at Wall Street's highest levels through the eyes of two outsiders. Gil, who immigrated to New York from São Paulo as a child and retains a Portuguese-flavored grammar, overhears tales of life on the trading floor while shining some of the nicest shoes in business. He absorbs the particulars of a world where jockeying banter about sex, drugs, and pushup contests is interspersed with long hours of watching numbers on a screen, and where the appeal of insider trading as a way to break the tedium becomes unignorable. Stumpf switches between Gil's voice and that of a magazine writer in need of a big story who fastens onto him as a source. As they become entangled in mounting financial and sexual scandals, Stumpf exposes the sordidness in both the financial and the journalistic worlds." New Yorker

Styles, Toy

Miss Wayne & the queen of DC; T. Styles. Cartel Publications 2010 281 p.

ISBN 098239134X; 9780982391341

LC 2010928716

This book is a spin-off from the novels "Black and Ugly" and "Black & Ugly as Ever" featuring the character of Miss Wayne. "When Miss Daffany's mother's risky lifestyle finally catches up with her, they all come back from LA, to Washington DC for her funeral. Once in town, Miss Wayne hooks up with his fabulous male friends and decides he misses home. . . . With the Queens of DC, he can wear flashy clothes, live the glamorous and be around people like him. But when the novelty wears off, he realizes that there is a reason he never fully embraced his alternative lifestyle. But it's too late and he becomes a victim of the company he keeps. . . . [S]oon the life of those he cares about become endangered." (Publisher's note)

Styron, Alexandra

All the finest girls; a novel. Little, Brown 2001 259p $23.95

ISBN 0-316-89080-4

LC 00-50051

Styron "beautifully juxtaposes Addy's past and the present on St. Claire, dealing deftly with a series of ironies. Although some readers may find Addy slow to catch on, Styron's gift is to make the reader feel real grief for her characters and real relief for Addy when she begins to make a peace with herself and her parents." Publ Wkly

Styron, William

★ The **confessions** of Nat Turner. Modern Lib. 1994 xliv, 428p hardcover o.p. pa $14

ISBN 0-679-60101-5; 0-679-73663-8 pa

LC 94-9393

A reissue of the title first published 1967 by Random House

This "account of an actual person and event is based on the brief contemporary pamphlet of the same title presented to a trial court as evidence and published in Virginia a year after the revolt of fellow slaves led by Turner in 1831. Imagining much of Turner's youth and early manhood before the rebellion that he headed at the age of 31, Styron in frequently rhetorical and pseudo-Biblical style has Turner recall his religious faith and his power of preaching to other slaves." Oxford Companion to Am Lit. 5th edition

Styron, William

Lie down in darkness. Bobbs-Merrill 1951 400p

"The book is not bleakly written. On the contrary, it is richly and even (in the best sense) poetically written. . . . If the parts seem to succeed each other with no apparent logic or dialectic, each part is brilliantly made and lovingly accomplished." Atlantic

Styron, William

Set this house on fire. Random House 1960 507p

"The narrator, Peter Leverett, a government employee returning to the U.S., stops in the little Italian village of Sambuco to see his old schoolmate Mason Flagg. The next morning the satyrical Flagg is found dead at the base of a cliff, a peasant girl has been raped and beaten until she dies, and Cass Kinsolving, a drunken, psychoneurotic American painter and the butt of Flagg's devilish humor, has temporarily disappeared. Though the case is written off as one of murder and suicide, the remainder of the novel probes minutely the past lives of the main characters, focusing through Peter's concern and his desire to know the whole truth. A large part of the action takes place in the Mediterranean village, but the novel is also one of contemporary America and Americans; of a world of conflict, too much wealth, too much sex and commercialism, too prevalent shallowness and lack of values." Libr J

Styron, William

★ **Sophie's** choice. Modern Lib. 1998 599p $22; pa $14

ISBN 0-679-60289-5; 0-679-73637-9 pa

LC 97-36895

A reissue of the title first published 1979

"It was a daring act for Styron, whose sensibilities are wholly Southern, to venture into the territory of the American Jew, to say nothing of his plunge into European history. The book is powerfully moving." Burgess. 99 Novels

Sullivan, J. Courtney

Maine; a novel. Alfred A. Knopf 2011 388p

ISBN 0307595129; 9780307595126

LC 2011-03396

In this novel, "three generations of women converge on the [Kelleher] family beach house." (Publisher's note)

"Sullivan spins a leisurely yarn that looks into why people do the things they do—particularly when it comes to drinking and churchgoing—and why the best-laid plans are always the ones the devil monkeys with the most thoroughly. The story will be particularly meaningful to Catholic women, though there are no barriers to entry for those who are not of that faith. Mature, thoughtful, even meditative at times—but also quite entertaining." Kirkus

Sullivan, Michael J.

Necessary heartbreak; a novel of faith and forgiveness. Michael J. Sullivan. Gallery Books 2010 246, [4] p.p (trade paper: alk. paper) $15

ISBN 1439184232; 9781439184233

LC 2009044471

This book tells the story of a "journey back in time show[ing] a struggling single dad that the faith he's lost is still alive. . . . Michael Stewart has weathered his share of hardships: a troubled childhood, the loss of his mother, even the degradation of living on the city streets. . . . [One] morning Michael and [his daughter] Elizabeth volunteer for a food pantry at their local church. While storing boxes, . . . they step through a mysterious door . . . and find themselves in first-century Jerusalem during the . . . last week of Jesus Christ's life. . . . [W]hen they come face-to-face with Judas Iscariot and the condemned Christ himself, Michael realizes that before they can escape Jerusalem, he must experience history's most necessary and shattering heartbreak." (Publisher's note)

Sullivan, Michael J.

Theft of swords; Michael J. Sullivan. 1st ed. Orbit 2011 691p.

ISBN 9780316187749

LC 2011008814

In this fantasy book, "Royce Melborn, a skilled thief, and his mercenary partner, Hadrian Blackwater, make a profitable living carrying out dangerous assignments for conspiring nobles--until they are hired to pilfer a famed sword. What appears to be just a simple job finds them framed for the murder of the king and trapped in a conspiracy that uncovers a plot far greater than the mere overthrow of a tiny kingdom. Can a self-serving thief and an idealistic swordsman survive long enough to unravel the first part of an ancient mystery that has toppled kings and destroyed empires in order to keep a secret too terrible for the world to know? And so begins the first tale of treachery and adventure, sword fighting and magic, myth and legend." (Publisher's note)

Sundaresan, Indu

In the Convent of Little Flowers; stories. Atria Books 2008 216p $22

ISBN 978-1-4165-8609-8; 1-4165-8609-1

LC 2008-34437

Sundaresan "bluntly questions how evolved the globalized world truly is in these stories of individuals trapped between India's archaic traditions and blitz into modernity. . . . Sundaresan (The Twentieth Wife) bluntly questions how evolved the globalized world truly is in these stories of individuals trapped between India's archaic traditions and blitz into modernity." Publ Wkly

Sundaresan, Indu

The splendor of silence; a novel. Atria Books 2006 403p $25

ISBN 978-0-7432-8367-0; 0-7432-8367-8

LC 2006-48364

"Flashbacks to 1940s India occur when Olivia receives a mysterious trunk that promises to explain who she is. The trunk arrives on the same day that her father, Sam, dies and contains information about her biological mother, Mila. Through a letter hidden among the keepsakes in the box, Olivia learns that her father spent time in India searching for his missing brother. While there, he fell in love with Mila, the daughter of the local political agent and fiancée of a prince. It was also there that he got to know Mila's brothers, who knew the whereabouts of his own brother. A series of events leads to the arrival of the trunk for Olivia years later. Sundaresan's descriptive writing style makes for a colorful, engrossing read, and while the story does hop between time periods and locations, the reader is never lost along the way." Libr J

Suri, Manil

The age of Shiva; a novel. W. W. Norton 2008 455p $24.95

ISBN 978-0-393-06569-5; 0-393-06569-3

LC 2007-37322

"Coming of age in Delhi in the fifties, Meera takes her father's atheism and progressive attitudes for granted, but she keenly resents the tyrannies of her favored older sister, who forces Meera to play the go-between in her romance with the handsome Dev. When Dev is dumped for a more suitable fiancé, Meera rashly attempts to console him; soon she is stuck with yet another of her sister's hand-me-downs—this time, forever. Dev drinks too much, and his family lives in a one-bedroom flat by the railroad tracks. Only when Meera conceives a child will she truly have something to call her own. Suri's . . . novel is a sensuous, nuanced portrait of motherhood, but it also sparks with the frictions of being female in an India where television soaps and political slogans compete noisily with Hindu myth." New Yorker

Suri, Manil

The death of Vishnu. Norton 2001 295p $24.95

ISBN 0-393-05042-4

LC 00-58414

"Its clever structure allows {this book} to display a manageable cross-section of contemporary Indian life, including class and religious frictions. But Suri . . . has more to offer here than gentle social comedy. During the course of the novel, Vishnu's soul disentangles itself from his earthly remains and begins ascending the apartment house stairs. As this spirit looks back on the life just ending, Suri's novel achieves an eerie and memorable transcendence." Time

Suskind, Patrick

★ **Perfume**: the story of a murderer; translated from the German by John E. Woods. Knopf 1986 255p

LC 86-45419

Original German edition, 1985

"Those readers who feel they are wasting their time with novels unless they are picking up facts will welcome Süskind's encyclopedic overview of the methods of making perfume. Like the best scents, there is something fundamentally formulaic about this novel, but its effects will linger long after it has been stoppered." Time

Sussman, Ellen

French lessons; a novel. Ballantine Books 2011 242p il pa $15

ISBN 978-0-345-52277-1; 0-345-52277-X

LC 2010-42458

"Three couples, each composed of a hot young French tutor and an attractive, emotionally bruised American student, spend a day strolling, café-ing, and conjugating through the streets of Paris. And since they're in the City of Love, chatting in the language of love, secrets of the heart are revealed and beds are fallen into. Sussman certainly knows her way around a boudoir scene — and when those boudoirs are in Paris, well, you end up with some sizzling escapist reading." Entertainment Wkly

Sutcliff, Rosemary

Sword at sunset. Coward-McCann 1963 495p

A novel based on historical facts about the legendary Arthur. "The time is the century after the last Roman legions leave Britain, and Arthur is desperately striving to hold Britain against the Saxons, Picts, and other invading savage tribes. {This is} the story of his tragic fate, his good times and bad." Publ Wkly

Svevo, Italo

★ **Zeno's** conscience; translated from the Italian by William Weaver with an introduction by Elizabeth Hardwick. Knopf 2001 xlix, 437p $20

ISBN 0-375-41330-8

LC 2001-40821

Original Italian edition, 1923; previous English translations had title: The confessions of Zeno

This is "a highly human story and its material is fundamentally as sound as its method. . . . The work of a man who wrote to please himself, it has an individuality and originality you cannot escape noticing, and it has, too, a fine and comprehensive knowledge of its character." N Y Times Book Rev

Swain, James

Midnight rambler; a novel of suspense. Ballantine Books 2007 350p $24.95

ISBN 978-0-345-47546-6; 0-345-47546-1

LC 2007-28324

"No one would accuse James Swain of writing mandarin prose; in fact, he uses language with such blunt force he could be hammering in nails." N Y Times Book Rev

Swann, Maxine

Flower children. Riverhead Books 2007 211p $21.95

ISBN 978-1-594-48945-7; 1-594-48945-9

LC 2006-39269

This novel is "made up of vignettes about four sibling 'flower children' whose parents are Pennsylvania farm country back-to-the-land hippies. Swann portrays the free-floating '70s coming-of-age of these four siblings—Lu, Maeve (who narrates much of the novel), Tuck and Clyde—who delight in running freely in the countryside, but grow embarrassed by the unconventional practices of their politically active, casual-dressing parents. Their parents, Sam, a Harvard graduate, and Dee, a gardener and artist, built their own house, and though they aim to raise their children in an ideal world 'in which nothing is lied about, whispered about, and nothing is ever concealed,' the parents separate, and subsequent storylike chapters delineate their children's sometimes rocky confrontation with the world of TVs, junk food and schoolyard cliques." Publ Wkly

"Swann evokes the wonder of childhood with an almost hallucinatory precision." Vogue

Swann, Maxine

The **foreigners**. Riverhead Books 2011 258p $25.95

ISBN 978-1-59448-830-6; 1-59448-830-4

"Daisy, 35, arrives in Argentina from the United States in 2002, just a year after her nine-year marriage has dis-solved and disenchantment with her work in the theater has led her to explore other job possibilities. A bout with a mysterious illness has left her frustrated, confused, and very disillusioned — estranged, in fact, from her own life. . . . A friend decides what Daisy needs is to travel and offers her an urban studies grant to study public water works in Buenos Aires. Though the project is out of her comfort zone, Daisy jumps at the trip as a kind of 'renegade expedition.' The fashionable Isolde, also 35, is from a small village in Austria. Good-natured, innocent, hopeful, she is 'someone to whom life happened, one thing led to the next, with minimal forethought on her part.' Her one surprising move is to quit her safe, predictable job at a bank and set off with her savings to travel, reinventing herself as a darling of the cocktail party crowd in Buenos Aires, where being European conveys instant status. She dreams of becoming an ambassador to the European art world, but constantly skirts the edges of desperation with dwindling finances, no real job, and a pervasive loneliness. . . . [Swann] vividly evokes the city and its lively, diverse, and conflicted social landscape, from the denizens of posh hotels to the unfortunate poor living in the city's slums." Boston Globe

Swanwick, Michael

The **best** of Michael Swanwick. Subterranean Press 2008 469p $38

ISBN 978-1-59606-178-1; 1-59606-178-2

"More than a quarter century's worth of short fiction is gathered in this comprehensive collection of stories. . . . The tales run the gamut from strict space adventures like 'The Very Pulse of the Machine' to deceptively complex ghost stories like 'Radio Waves.' . . . Swanwick's blend of savvy science fiction, Freudian fantasy and topnotch storytelling both chills and charms." Publ Wkly

Swanwick, Michael

Bones of the earth. HarperCollins Pubs. 2002 335p

ISBN 0-380-97836-9

LC 2001-40196

"Swanwick writes about paleontologists who travel back to the Mesozoic to study dinosaurs firsthand, with a technology supplied by enigmatic aliens. . . . His focus never strays far from the two reluctant collaborators, Griffin and the Old Man, who have transformed paleontology into an experimental science. The air of competence they adopt in their day-to-day operations cannot mask their anxiety over who ultimately are the experimenters and who are the subjects." N Y Times Book Rev

Swanwick, Michael

Dancing with bears; the postutopian adventures of Darger & Surplus. Night Shade Books 2011 268p $24.99

ISBN 978-1-59780-235-2

In this novel "a couple of charming con men set out for post-apocalyptic Moscow, only to blunder into a revolutionary mess. Darger and Surplus are on their way from Byzantium to Moscow, to deliver a caravan of beautiful concubines (known as the Pearls Beyond Price) to wed the Duke of Muscovy. They're not entirely on the up-and-up, though. On their way, they meet a strannik, a religious pilgrim, who wants to get to sin city to help bring about the Eschaton, along with a silly boy who just wants to get in one of the Pearls' pants. And when they finally get to Moscow, handing off the lovelies isn't as simpie as it seemed. Plus, there are nefarious forces stoking the fires of civil unrest (for their own purposes, naturally). Swanwick has a light touch, and therefore manages to pull off something unlikely: a buddy comedy set in post-apocalyptic Russia. Dancing with Bears resembles nothing so much as one of those old 'Road To...' movies with Bob Hope and Bing Crosby." io9

Swanwick, Michael

The **dog** said bow-wow. Tachyon Publications 2007 296p pa $14.95

ISBN 978-1-892391-52-0; 1-892391-52-X

"There is a camaraderie about the stories Michael Swanwick has assembled in The Dog Said Bow-Wow, a willingness to share their deepest ingenuities with the reader, that makes the book almost tingle in the mind: wagging its tale to tell more. What the stories in this collection are so good at doing, to put it another way, is being stories. They wear their hearts on their sleeves. This is not exactly to say that Michael Swanwick does the same. The other side of the exuberance of The Dog Said Bow-Wow is a severe chastity of reticence. Michael Swanwick is a teller, but he does not tell himself. But we cannot fault a writer for selecting his remit. And the polished variousness of Swanwick's gift is in itself gift enough." Sci Fi Wkly

Swarthout, Glendon Fred

★ **Bless** the beasts and children; [by] Glendon Swarthout. Doubleday 1970 205p

"Six rich teenagers, rejected by their parents and avoided by their peers, group together at Box Canyon Summer Boys' Camp. Fragile egos and self-destructive personalities begin to heal under the leadership of Cotton, who gently pokes fun at their soft spots while building up their self-esteem. An effort on the part of the group to stop the wanton slaughter of buffalo provides a high point of suspense." Shapiro. Fic for Youth. 3d edition

Swarthout, Glendon Fred

The **shootist**; {by} Glendon Swarthout. Doubleday 1975 186p

"J. B. Books, last of the West's big-time gunfighters and stoic sufferer of terminal cancer, plays out his death rites. Ensconced in a boarding house in El Paso, Books is approached by a host of exploiters who desire to use his impending death to enhance their own reputations and monetary status; the shootist, however, plans otherwise. He maneuvers his adversaries' self-aggrandizing behavior to his advantage, engineering them to carry out his desire; a quick and respectable death by bullet." Booklist

"This is definitely more than a Western; the characterization is flawless, the plot absorbing and convincing." Libr J

Swerling, Beverly

City of promise; a novel of New York's Gilded Age. Simon & Schuster 2011 422p $26

ISBN 978-1-4391-3694-2; 1-4391-3694-7

LC 2011-10782

"A vivid tableau of 1870s Manhattan. The Civil War has finally ended, and the island is practically aglow with its citizens' renewed schemes. Everyone from the Vanderbilts . . . to just-arrived tenement dwellers is out to stake a claim. The central characters in City of Promise — a one-legged war vet with progressive plans to house the burgeoning middle class, and the brothel-raised Macy's seamstress he falls for — drive the multipronged plot. But the star is really grasping, filthy, glorious New York, which was as much a lure for the wildly ambitious and the real-estate-obsessed back then as it is today." Entertainment Wkly

Swerling, Beverly

Shadowbrook; a novel of love and war. Beverly Swerling. Simon & Schuster 2004 490p il $24.95

ISBN 0-7432-2812-X

LC 2003-64127

"Covering the years 1754-1760, with the British, French and Indians slaughtering each other for king and empire, Swerling tells of two men who straddle the white and red man's worlds, desperate to preserve the best of each culture, but fearful they will lose everything they love. Quentin Hale is a gentleman turned scout whose family owns a prosperous New York plantation called Shadowbrook. He is white, but also follows the Indian ways of his adopted tribe, the Potawatomi. Cormac Shea is part-Irish and part-Indian, nearly a brother to Hale, but he wants all whites driven from Canada. Together these men find themselves caught up in a bloody war neither wants, but they must fight to save the plantation and create a homeland for the Indians. . . . Surrounding them are colorful historical figures like the young George Washington, the hapless General Braddock and the powerful Ottawa chief, Pontiac." Publ Wkly

Swierczynski, Duane

Expiration date. Minotaur Books 2010 245p il pa $13.99

ISBN 978-0-312-36340-6; 0-312-36340-0

LC 2009-39947

"Originally conceived as a serial for the New York Times Magazine, this short novel provides plenty of plot twists and turns in a deftly realized Philadelphia setting. Out of a job and at loose ends, journalist Mickey Wade moves into the apartment of his comatose grandfather. After he takes what he believes to be aspirin from a bottle in the bathroom, he wakes up to find himself back in 1972. With a few notable exceptions, the people he meets in the past don't seem able to see him, but those who do are especially dangerous. One of them, in fact, might grow up to kill Mickey's musician father. . . . Plausibility may not be the book's virtue, but Mickey's tour through his family's long-buried secrets is ultimately affecting, suspenseful and satisfying." San Francisco Chron

Swierczynski, Duane

Fun and games. Mulholland Books 2011 286p pa $14.99

ISBN 978-0-316-13328-9; 0-316-13328-0

LC 2010-44951

"After second-tier movie actress Lane Madden survives multiple attempts by aggressive fellow drivers to run her off some treacherous Los Angeles roads, she has the good fortune to meet Charlie Hardie, a peripatetic house-sitter with a violent past, at the house in the Hollywood Hills where she takes refuge. Hardie, a former police consultant who's haunted by the deaths of several innocents, is skeptical of the actress's claim that she's being pursued by the Accident People, a shadowy group of killers who stage their homicides to appear as accidents. An escalating series of violent encounters builds to an unforgettable climax." Publ Wkly

Swift, Graham, 1949-

★ **Last** orders. Knopf 1996 294p

ISBN 978-0330345590

LC 96-13726

"On a bleak spring day, four men meet in their favorite pub in a working-class London neighborhood. They are about to begin a pilgrimage to scatter the ashes of a fifth man, Jack Dodds, friend since WWII of three of them, adoptive father to the fourth. By the time they reach the seaside town where Jack's 'last orders' have sent them, the tangled relationship among the men, their wives and their children has obliquely been revealed." Publ Wkly

Swift, Graham, 1949-

Tomorrow. Alfred A. Knopf 2007 255p $23.95

ISBN 978-0-307-26690-3

LC 2007-18684

"The need to hold our interest is more than adequately covered by Paula's poignant account of what was required of her and Mike when she resolved to become pregnant, and the psychological adjustments subsequently required of both of them; this is Graham Swift at his impressive best in entering the minds of people with whom he can have little genuine connection or affinity." Times Lit Suppl

Swift, Graham, 1949-

★ **Waterland**. Poseidon Press 1984 309p il

ISBN 0-671-49863-0

LC 83-21248

This novel concerns "Tom Crick, an English history teacher in his mid-50s who, as the novel opens, has just been forced to accept early retirement. In response to his students' belief that history is a 'fairy-tale' and only the 'here and now' matters, Crick has abandoned the formal curriculum to tell stories about his childhood in East England's Fens. The headmaster, a physicist, shares the students' opinion of the past, and Crick's 'trying to put himself into history' is the last straw. But Crick won't go—his students are for once interested in his 'crazy yarns'—until one day his wife goes mad and steals a baby from a supermarket shopping cart. The prospect of retirement gives Crick the freedom to tell his pupils the lurid story that lies behind his wife's theft." (Nation)

"The novel exceeds credibility and attenuates our tolerance in exactly the same degree as it creates, through [Swift's] own words, the portrait of a man who is deeply disturbed, and who is vainly attempting to build a structure from these words which will protect him from his childlessness, from his failure to create the future." Times Lit Suppl

Swift, Graham, 1949-

Wish you were here; Graham Swift. Alfred A. Knopf 2012 319p.

ISBN 0307700127; 9780307700124

LC 2011050296

"This . . . novel is about longing for the people in our lives who have died. Taking place over just a few days, it focuses on Jack Luxton's journey to retrieve the remains of his brother Tom, a soldier who died in Iraq. The brothers grew up on a farm in the British countryside, and hovering over the story is the specter of mad cow disease on one end and terror (both political and personal) on the other." (Library Journal)

Swift, Jonathan

★ **Gulliver's** travels; with an introduction by Pat Rogers. Knopf 1991 xlv, 318p map $20

ISBN 0-679-40545-3

LC 91-53011

First published 1726

"In the account of his four wonder-countries Swift satirizes contemporary manners and morals, art and politics—in fact the whole social scheme—from four different points of view. The huge Brobdingnagians reduce man to his natural insignificance, the little people of Lilliput parody Europe and its petty broils, in Laputa philosophers are ridiculed, and finally all Swift's hatred and contempt find their satisfaction in degrading humanity to a bestial condition." Baker. Guide to the Best Fic

Swinson, Kiki

Playing dirty; Kiki Swinson. Dafina Books 2009 281 p.

ISBN 075822835X; 9780758228352

In this novel, "Miami defense attorney Yoshi Lomax bribes, manipulates, blackmails and uses her body to win cases and a promotion at her firm, but her physical assets and flexible morals end up doing her more harm than good. . . . Yoshi's singular . . . motivation is money, and it drives her to, among other things, sleep with her boss, betray her DEA agent best friend and make some questionable calls about what clients she takes on. Then her lucky streak ends: she gets demoted at work, loses her bid to get a case dismissed, gets arrested for drug possession, gets abandoned by her best friend and is framed for murder." (Publishers Weekly)

Syjuco, Miguel

Ilustrado. Farrar, Straus and Giroux 2010 306p $26

ISBN 978-374-17478-1; 0-374-17478-4

LC 2009-43083

"This début novel begins as a murder mystery and develops into an ambitious exploration of cultural identity, ambition, and artistic purpose. When the Filipino writer Crispin Salvador is found dead, his protégé, Miguel, resolves to investigate and to resurrect Salvador's precarious reputation as the Philippines' quintessential intellectual export. The narrative of Miguel's quest is intercut with e-mails, fragments of manuscripts, interviews, poems, and blog entries; real people mingle with fictional characters. The result is a self-referential collage encompassing both sociopolitical polemic and lighter fare, such as a memorable thread of bawdy jokes." New Yorker

Symons, Julian

The **Kentish** manor murders. Viking 1988 191p

LC 87-40460

"The detective in this book is an actor famous for his Sherlock Holmes readings. A reclusive billionaire engages him for a private reading. It seems that the man is a Conan Doyle enthusiast and a collector of Holmesiana. It seems also that an unknown Sherlock Holmes story has just turned up and the actor is asked to be a go-between in a sale to the billionaire. But is he really the billionaire? Or is he an impersonator? Fun and games, in Mr. Symons' best style." N Y Times Book Rev

Symons, Julian

Something like a love affair. Mysterious Press 1992 199p

LC 92-5980

"Symons' tale is chillingly and compellingly told. Exploring the dark underside of the human spirit, it's story of a desperate woman who can no longer cope." Booklist

Szado, Ania

Studio saint-ex; a novel. Ania Szado. Alfred A. Knopf 2013 368 p. $25.95

ISBN 0307962792; 9780307962799

LC 2012032018

This novel by Ania Szado, set in 1940s New York, is "about a wartime triangle involving {Mignonne Lachapelle,]a twenty-two-year-old fashion designer poised to launch her promising career, the acclaimed French expatriate writer/war pilot, Antoine de Saint-Exupéry, who's fled his Nazi-occupied country and come to Manhattan for a month, only to stay for two years, and his . . . wife . . . Consuelo." (Publisher's note)

T

Tabucchi, Antonio

It's getting later all the time; a novel in the form of letters. translated from the Italian by Alastair McEwen. New Directions 2006 232p pa $15.95

ISBN 978-0-8112-1546-6; 0-8112-1546-6

LC 2006-7369

Original Italian edition, 2001

"This epistolary novel is composed of 18 love letters; the fictional authors are 17 men and one woman, whose sweeping, summative voice closes the collection abruptly. . . . Written from places all over Europe, the letters are intimate and often exquisite, lingering over transcendent details of landscape, or ruefully soliloquizing on memory. One rancorous letter, 'A Good Man Like You,' recalls a betrayal seven years in the past, while another contemplates a journey never taken: 'Do you remember when we didn't go to Samarkand?' The whole makes for delicious voyeurism, leavened with pointed bafflement at these partially rendered relationships: just as the reader wishes for all the gaps to be filled in, the letter writers wish to recompose fractured relationships." Publ Wkly

Tademy, Lalita

Cane River. Warner Bks. 2001 418p il

ISBN 0-446-53052-2

LC 00-43682

"Five generations and a hundred years in the life of a matriarchal black Louisiana family are encapsulated in this . . . novel that is based in part upon the lives, as preserved in both historical record and oral tradition, of the author's ancestors. . . . Her frank observations about black racism add depth to the tale, and she demonstrates that although the practice of slavery fell most harshly upon blacks, and especially women, it also constricted the lives and choices of white men. Photos of and documents relating to Tademy's ancestors add authenticity to a fascinating story." Publ Wkly

Talarigo, Jeff

The ginseng hunter. Nan A. Talese 2007 177p $21.95

ISBN 978-0-385-51739-3; 0-385-51739-4

LC 2007-11395

"From the smallest flowers to the majestic mountain landscape, Talarigo unobtrusively pays homage to the expansive beauty that still exists all around, as if gently buffering the pain of the landscape's inhabitants. . . . While Talarigo is an expert at luring us out of our comfort zones to bear witness with him, he also gives us quiet heroes who do not give in, who do not give up." Christ Sci Monit

Tallis, Frank

Death and the maiden; a Max Liebermann mystery. Frank Tallis. Random House Trade Paperbacks 2012 373 p. (paperback) $15.00

ISBN 0812983343; 9780679644866; 9780812983340

LC 2012001662

Author Frank Tallis presents a murder mystery. "When DI Oskar Rheinhardt investigates the suspicious death of an opera diva in early-20th-century Vienna, he finds a nest of vipers and a closet full of skeletons. Tensions simmer at an elegant gathering that includes the Emperor Franz Josef, Prince Rudolph Liechtenstein, Mayor Lueger and members of the Court Opera, led by Gustav Mahler . . . [where singer] Ida Rosenkrantz, who recently supplanted a bitter [singer] Arianne] Amsel as the opera's foremost soprano . . . is found dead under suspicious circumstances." (Kirkus)

Tallis, Frank

A death in Vienna. Grove Press 2006 458p $22

ISBN 0-8021-1815-1

LC 2005-50318

First published 2005 in the United Kingdom with title: Mortal mischief

"Tallis deftly brings to life a city of contrasts, caught between polite manners and virulent antiSemitism. This first volume in a new historical series should appeal to Sherlock Holmes fans as well as those of John Dixon Carr's locked-room puzzlers." Libr J

Tallis, Frank

Fatal lies; a novel. Frank Tallis. Random House Trade Paperbacks 2009 439 p. (trade pbk.) $15.00

ISBN 0812977777; 9780812977776

LC 2008023474

In this book by Frank Tallis, "a dogged police inspector and an insightful young psychiatrist match wits with depraved criminal minds," investigating "the mysterious and savage death of a young cadet in the most elite of military academies." Psychiatrist Max Liebermann is also dealing with "a crisis of his own: handling his conflicted and forbidden feelings for two different women, one a former patient." (Publisher's note)

Tallis, Frank

★ **Vienna** blood; a novel. Frank Tallis. Random House Trade Paperbacks 2007 485 p. ill.
ISBN 0812977769; 9780812977769
LC 2007019605
Sequel to: A death in Vienna (2006)
In the sequel to "A Death in Vienna," 1902 Vienna is terrorized by a serial killer targeting prostitutes and leaving strange crosslike symbols in his wake, and Detective Oscar Rheinhardt and Dr. Max Liebermann reunite to find a murderer. (Publisher's note)
Includes bibliographical references

Tallis, Frank

Vienna Twilight; Frank Tallis. Random 2011 368 p. $15.00
ISBN 0812981006; 9780812981001
LC 2011284360
In this novel, by Frank Tallis, set "[i]n . . . Vienna of 1903, a brilliant psychoanalyst and a brave detective battle to catch criminals. . . . Detective Inspector Oskar Reinhardt finds that young women are being slain . . . with a small, almost undetectable, hat pin. . . . [T]he killer . . . murders in the midst of consensual love. . . . As danger mounts, Liebermann must find the answer while struggling with his own forbidden desire for a female patient." (Publisher's note)

Talty, Stephan

Black Irish. Random House Inc 2013 368 p. $26
ISBN 0345538064; 9780345538062
This book by Stephan Talty "centers on a working-class Irish enclave in contemporary Buffalo, N.Y. The macabre killing of gas-meter reader Jimmy Ryan brings Det. Absalom 'Abbie' Kearney to South Buffalo. . . . More gruesome, carefully staged deaths occur, pointing to members of the secretive, powerful Clan na Gael as targets. Hampered by community distrust, Abbie must dig deeply into long-buried secrets that could endanger her father's life and reputation as well as her own life." (Publishers Weekly)

Tan, Amy

The **bonesetter's** daughter. Putnam 2001 353p
ISBN 0-399-14643-1
LC 00-62673
"A fine and highly readable novel, The Bonesetter's Daughter is essentially about writing and the act of writing, what fuels it and how it is created. More specifically still, it is about how we, as women creatively express ourselves via language." Women's Rev Books

Tan, Amy

The **hundred** secret senses. Putnam 1995 358p
LC 95-31791
"Nearing divorce from her husband, Simon, Olivia Yee is guided by her elder half-sister, the irrepressible Kwan, into the heart of China. Olivia was five when 18-year-old

Kwan first joined her family in the United States, and though always irritated by Kwan's oddities, Olivia was entranced by her eerie dreams of the ghost World of Yin. Only when visiting Kwan's home in Changmian does Olivia realize the dreams are, in Kwan's mind, memories from past lives. . . . Tan tells a mysterious, believable story and delivers Kwan's clipped, immigrant voice and engaging personality with charming clarity." Libr J

Tan, Amy

★ The **Joy** Luck Club. Putnam 1989 288p $24.95
ISBN 0-399-13420-4
LC 88-26492
"Four aging Chinese women who knew life in China before 1949 and now live in San Francisco meet regularly to play mah-jongg and share thoughts about their American-born children. In alternating sections we learn about the cultural differences between the elderly 'aunties' and the younger generation. When one of the older women dies, her daughter is pressed to take her place in the Joy Luck Club. Her feeling of being out of place gradually gives way to an understanding of the need to retain cultural continuity and an appreciation for the strength and endurance of the older women." Shapiro. Fic for Youth. 3d edition

Tan, Amy

★ The **kitchen** god's wife. Putnam 1991 415p
LC 91-7828
"Within the peculiar construction of Amy Tan's second novel is a harrowing, compelling and at times bitterly humorous tale in which an entire world unfolds in a Tolstoyan tide of event and detail." N Y Times Book Rev

Tan, Amy

Saving fish from drowning. Putnam 2005 474p $26.95
ISBN 0-399-15301-2
LC 2005-48724
"Amy Tan has created a meta-fable of Orwellian stature, where Americans abroad think they know best, yet follow others blindly; where illusions and assumptions meet self-righteousness and arrogance." Ms.

Tan, Twan Eng, 1972-

The **Garden** of Evening Mists; a novel. Tan Twan Eng. 1st U.S. ed. Weinstein Books 2012 335 p. (paperback) $15.99; (ebook) $15.99
ISBN 1602861803; 9781602861800; 9781602861817
LC 2012462473
Man Booker Prize Shortlist (2012)
This novel, by Tan Twan Eng, short list nominee of the 2012 Man Booker Prize, is set in "Malaya, 1949. . . . Yun Ling Teoh, herself the scarred lone survivor of a brutal Japanese wartime camp, seeks solace among the jungle fringed plantations of Northern Malaya. . . . There she discovers . . . the only Japanese garden in Malaya, and its owner and creator, the enigmatic Aritomo, exiled former gardener of the Emperor of Japan." (Publisher's note)
Includes bibliographical references

Tanenbaum, Robert

Act of revenge; a novel. [by] Robert K. Tannenbaum. HarperCollins Pubs. 1999 402p $25

ISBN 0-06-019218-6

LC 98-54268

"Tanenbaum has crafted a believably twisted gem of a gangster tale with visceral action and smooth comic relief in a technicolor, Big Apple setting that waxes nostalgic for the 'gentleman' killers of yesteryear." Publ Wkly

Tanenbaum, Robert

★ Corruption of blood; [by] Robert K. Tanenbaum. Dutton 1995 347p

ISBN 0-525-93870-2

LC 95-12803

When Butch Karp "is lured from his unhappy berth in the Manhattan District Attorney's office to assist in the recently reopened Kennedy investigation, he must wade through conspiracy theories, stale evidence and the perennial Washington quagmire. . . . Karp's wife, the formidable Marlene Ciampi . . . joins her husband in the capital. Marlene, reluctant to join the 'wife-of' set, soon takes up an avenue of inquiry seemingly unrelated to the Kennedy conundrum when she sets out to clear the besmirched name of Richard Dobbs, the father of Karp's Congressional sponsor, who died in 1963. As in all good thrillers, everything that rises must converge, and so it is with Marlene's sleuthing and her husband's." N Y Times Book Rev

Tanenbaum, Robert

Falsely accused; [by] Robert K. Tanenbaum. Dutton 1996 304p

ISBN 0-525-94168-1

LC 96-17305

A legal thriller featuring married lawyers Butch Karp and Marlene Ciampi. In this episode "Bruce has spent over a year as the well-compensated pit bull litigator for a downtown law firm, and Marlene is getting antsy after a year-plus as a full-time mom. Soon Marlene partners with cop Harry Bello in a PI firm, and Karp sues New York City for former Chief Medical Examiner Murray Selig, fired at the urging of Manhattan DA (and Karp/Ciampi nemesis) Sanford Bloom. Tanenbaum draws together subplots involving political and police corruption, domestic violence, and illegal immigration in an involving tale that also illuminates Karp's and Ciampi's romantic and parental challenges." Booklist

Tanenbaum, Robert

Hoax; a novel. [by] Robert K. Tanenbaum. 1st Atria Books hardcover ed; Atria Books 2004 490p $25.95

ISBN 0-7434-5288-7

LC 2004-47941

A suspense novel featuring New York District Attorney Butch Karp. "The vicious murder of a West Coast rapper sets things in motion, unleashing a white-hot cascade of events that expose violence, greed, and corruption not only at the NYPD and the DA's office but also at the city's Catholic archdiocese. Tanenbaum . . . rentlessly builds suspense and gets ever closer to the hearts and minds of his singular characters." Booklist

Tanenbaum, Robert

Immoral certainty; [by] Robert K. Tanenbaum. Dutton 1991 282p

ISBN 0-525-24941-9

LC 90-13841

"The action is set mainly in the wilds of New York City's East Village, where a serial killer who brutalizes children is on the rampage. There's also a messy Mob hit in Little Italy to complicate the lives of no-nonsense D.A. Butch Karp and his colleague and 'occasional main squeeze,' Marlene. Are the cases related? And just how involved is one Felix Tighe, an ambitious yet minor-league criminal with a major-league mother fixation. The novel boasts a wealth of well-developed characters (the principals as well as the minor players); a slew of gallows humor; and a visceral prose style ideally suited to dealing with the sickening brutality of child abuse." Booklist

Tanenbaum, Robert

Irresistible impulse; [by] Robert K. Tanenbaum. Dutton 1997 346p

ISBN 0-525-94310-2

LC 97-16331

A legal thriller featuring NYDA Butch Karp and his wife Marlene Ciampi, the head of her own PI firm. "Against the advice of everyone from his boss to his secretary, Karp takes on the prosecution of a high-visibility defendant: a young white man charged with the brutal murders of elderly black women. Meanwhile, Marlene's cases win more publicity than she needs, as well as threats to her safety and that of her family." Booklist

Tanenbaum's "authentic background detail and his likable characters provide irresistible entertainment." Publ Wkly

Tanenbaum, Robert

Reckless endangerment; [by] Robert K. Tanenbaum. Dutton 1998 324p $23.95

ISBN 0-525-94347-1

LC 98-4902

This thriller "pits Deputy DA Karp, his detective cronies Raney and Fulton and his security-expert wife, Marlene, against an amorphous army of Palestinians terrorizing New York." Publ Wkly

"Tanenbaum controls the strands of his complex plot and maintains readers' interest in the growing Karp-Ciampi clan." Booklist

Tanenbaum, Robert

Reversible error; [by] Robert K. Tanenbaum. Dutton 1992 294p

ISBN 0-525-93423-5

LC 91-34464

New York "assistant D.A. Butch Karp faces a dilemma. A rogue cop is on the streets, taking out drug dealers, but Karp's investigation is brought to a halt when he is asked to suppress evidence. Sharing center stage with Karp's case is that of the D.A.'s colleague and lover, Marlene, who is on the trail of a rapist who wraps a pair of panty hose around each victim. With some unexpected help, Marlene spots a similarity in the victims. . . . With twin plots sizzling and exploding, the novel takes us inside the psyches of its characters, revealing the crime fighters' dark humor, rigid notions of right and wrong, and righteous anger." Booklist

Tanenbaum, Robert

True justice; [by] Robert K. Tanenbaum. Pocket Bks. 2000 374p il

ISBN 0-7434-0589-7

LC 00-708721

"Each of the deftly drawn characters wrestles with the moral dilemmas raised by the intertwined plots in a believable way, and readers will close True Justice's final page satisfied they've wrestled with those dilemmas a bit themselves." Booklist

Tanizaki, Jun'ichiro

★ The Makioka sisters; translated and introduced by Edward G. Seidensticker. Knopf 1993 xxxv,498 $20

ISBN 0-679-943452-0

LC 92-55051

Original Japanese edition, 1949; this translation first published 1957

"The narrative is very quiet, very leisurely. At times it seems interminable, but it is like the pigment used by a Renaissance painter to build up his picture. It is done with utmost skill and results in a dignified masterpiece of great beauty and quality." Chicago Sunday Trib

Tanner, Haley

Vaclav and Lena; a novel. Dial Press 2011 292p $25

ISBN 978-1-4000-6931-6; 1-4000-6931-9

LC 2010023907

"This debut starts off cute but slight, with 10-year-olds Vaclav and Lena exploring a proto-romance to the odor of borscht and the lilt of mangled syntax in Russian-immigrant Brooklyn. Then Lena suddenly leaves under murky circumstances and the book heads for something darker and deeper, especially after the story jumps forward seven years and the couple reunite to grapple with the past and, possibly, feel their way toward a future. Vaclav and especially Lena never quite cohere into threedimensional characters, but Tanner is a gifted-enough storyteller to bring some real emotional heft to Vaclav & Lena." Entertainment Wkly

Tapply, William G.

Bitch Creek; a novel. Lyon's Press 2004 292p $22.95

ISBN 1-592-28435-3

LC 2004-48954

"Stoney Calhoun works in Kate Balaban's bait/tackle shop in small-town Maine but has gaps in his memory after five years in an institution. When mutual friend and fishing guide Lyle goes missing, Stoney searches, finding the man's 'secret' trout stream and the man himself suspiciously drowned. Lyle's client, meanwhile, has disappeared. Aided by determination, logic, a psychic vision or two, and Kate's love, Stoney discovers that he was the intended target and that he's really an experienced investigator." Libr J

The author "mixes crisp plotting and character development with a subtle sense of time and place." Booklist

Tapply, William G.

Client privilege. Delacorte Press 1990 260p

LC 89-23729

"Acting on behalf of his client and best friend, Judge Popowski (Pops) {Boston attorney} Coyne meets a TV reporter, Wayne Churchill, who threatens the judge's virtually certain appointment to the federal courts. Implicitly trusting the judge's statement that the newsman has no real grounds for blackmail, Coyne refuses Churchill's demand of $10,000 for his silence. The reporter's murder that same night brings the police to question the attorney, who, standing on client privilege, withholds Pops's name and therefore risks his own arrest as the killer. The circumstances force Coyne to search for the guilty party in order to clear himself." Publ Wkly

Tapply, William G.

Close to the bone. St. Martin's Press 1996 208p

ISBN 978-0312145675

LC 96-18990

Boston lawyer Brady Coyne "recommends Paul Cizek, a fishing buddy and a defense attorney with a reputation as a miracle worker, to defend a client's son involved in a fatal DUI rap. Cizek takes and wins the case, but privately explains to Coyne how his victories are eating at him. He detests the people he is defending—the child molester, the Mafia hit man and now an unremorseful alcoholic. When Cizek, depressed and separated from his wife, disappears and his empty boat is found drifting in a storm, the police assume accident or suicide. But Coyne's investigation, undertaken at the behest of Cizek's wife, and accruing dead bodies suggest more sinister possibilities. . . . Tapply treats his characters and his readers with respect." Publ Wkly

Tapply, William G.

Cutter's run; a Brady Coyne novel. St. Martin's Press 1998 274p $23.95

ISBN 0-312-18561-8

LC 98-5331

"Boston lawyer Brady Coyne, in rural Maine for the weekend to visit his 'virtual spouse' Alex, stops and offers Charlotte Gillespie, a middle-aged black woman, a ride. In short order, someone poisons her dog and paints swastikas on her cabin door. Then Charlotte disappears. Brady explores the obvious: wanna-be klansmen and skinheads. Brady eventually realizes it may have been Carlotte's past and not her present—as an unwelcome resident in an unfriendly town—that resulted in her disappearance. Brady also realizes his relationship with Alex may not be as rock solid as he thought. . . . {This} mystery reaffirms Tapply's reputation for sound plotting, sterling dialogue, and poignant glimpses into the heart of a lonely man." Booklist

Tapply, William G.

Dead meat; a Brady Coyne mystery. Scribner 1987 213p

LC 86-26143

"Heeding the call of one of his eccentric, well-to-do clients, Brady packs rod and reel and journeys to Raven Lake Lodge in the wilds of Maine, where his friend Tiny Wheeler, the lodge's owner, is trying to cope with the disappearance of a guest and a takeover bid by a group of Indian activists, who contend that the lodge is situated on sacred tribal ground. It doesn't take Brady long to realize that the situations are inextricably linked in a web of intrigue that points toward organized crime." Booklist

Tapply, William G.
Dead winter; a Brady Coyne novel. Delacorte Press 1989 230p
LC 88-13867

"The plot takes some gothic turns—bastardy, incest, and earlier violent death—but Tapply never neglects his nicely defined characterizations or loses his cool control over narrative tension in this very satisfying caper." Publ Wkly

Tapply, William G.
First light; the first ever Brady Coyne\J.W. Jackson novel. {by} William G. Tapply and Philip R. Craig. Scribner 2002 351p $24
ISBN 0-7432-2208-3
LC 2001-49053

This mystery, set on Martha's Vineyard, features "Boston lawyer Brady Coyne and former cop J.W. Jackson. . . . When tough businessman Jack Bannerman's wife goes missing, he hires private detective Jackson to find her. A parallel missing person's case develops when Coyne, Jackson's buddy, arrives for a fishing derby, only to see his elderly client Sarah Fairchild's private nurse vanish mysteriously in the midst of a nasty dispute over the future of ailing Mrs. Fairchild's sizable beachfront property." Publ Wkly

Tapply, William G.
Muscle memory; a Brady Coyne novel. St. Martin's Press 1999 257p $23.95
ISBN 0-312-20563-5
LC 99-22042

Tapply "integrates Coyne's personal travails and his professional obligations, marking this novel as a model addition in a mature series: smoothly written, accessible to new readers and solidly plotted." Publ Wkly

Tapply, William G.
Past tense; a Brady Coyne novel. St. Martin's Minotaur 2001 292p
ISBN 0-312-28442-X
LC 2001-41943

"Brady Coyne and girlfriend Evie . . . become prime suspects when a stalker from Evie's past winds up dead outside the couple's rented Cape Cod cottage. Evie's subsequent disappearance sends the Boston attorney into investigative mode." Libr J

Tapply, William G.
★ Scar tissue. St. Martin's Minotaur 2000 276p $24.95
ISBN 0-312-26679-0
LC 00-40229

Once Boston attorney Brady Coyne's "suspicions are aroused about a tragic road accident that swept two teenagers to their deaths in an icy river, he handles the sleazy business of small-town rot with the commitment and discretion that distinguish him as a sleuth. Tapply's understated style may forever condemn Coyne to a dull love life; but it serves

the sordid nature of the story and well suits the hero." N Y Times Book Rev

Tapply, William G.
Tight lines; a Brady Coyne novel. Delacorte Press 1992 277p
LC 91-31880

Brady Coyne, "a Boston lawyer whose client base is profoundly rich if not famous, is called to the side of Susan Ames, a wealthy widow dying of cancer. Using the pretense of establishing ground rules for the disposition of the historically significant family estate, she asks Brady to find the daughter she hasn't seen in 11 years." Booklist

Tapply, William G.
A **void** in hearts; a Brady Coyne mystery. Scribner 1988 198p
LC 88-12203

"A marginally unscrupulous private eye, Les Katz, gets himself killed after blackmailing a client. Brady is called to the sleuth's deathbed but arrives too late, leaving him no choice but to figure out what happened." Booklist

Tarkington, Booth
★ Alice Adams; illustrated by Arthur William Brown. Doubleday, Page 1921 434p il

"A social climber, the title character is ashamed of her unsuccessful family. Hoping to attract a wealthy husband, she lies about her background, but she is found out and is shunned by those whom she sought to attract. At the novel's end, she knows her chances for happiness and a successful marriage are bleak, but she remains unbowed." Merriam-Webster's Ency of Lit

Tarkington, Booth
★ The **magnificent** Ambersons. Modern Library 1998 268p pa $12.95
ISBN 0-375-75250-1
LC 98-19552

First published 1918 by Doubleday, Page

"The novel traces the growth of the United States through the decline of the once-powerful, socially prominent Amberson family. Their fall is contrasted with the rise of new industrial tycoons and land developers, whose power comes not through family connections but through financial dealings and modern manufacturing." Merriam-Webster's Ency of Lit

Tarr, Judith
Lady of horses. Forge 2000 415p $25.95
ISBN 0-312-86114-1
LC 00-27653

This prehistoric epic's "heroine, Sparrow, possesses the gift of divination, but as a girl in a culture that only values males, she is compelled to conceal it. She must also hide her forbidden passion for horses. When she and her sister-in-law, Keen, are discovered with the horse herd, they flee taking the king stallion with them. They end up in a land where females are not stigmatized, and where they are free to worship the Horse Goddess. . . . Tarr blends mythology and fantasy to make an unrecorded era of time vibrant and alive while brilliantly depicting nomadic cultures." Booklist

Tarr, Judith

Pillar of fire. Forge 1995 448p

LC 95-6315

"Tarr makes of this intriguing speculation an exhilarating ride, powerfully written, through a lost world of chariot races, royalty, revolt, and enduring loyalty that is sure to please many readers." Booklist

Tarr, Judith

Queen of swords. Forge 1997 464p

ISBN 978-0553801491

LC 96-33220

This historical novel "focuses on the reign of Melisende, the oldest daughter of Baldwin II, King of Jerusalem. She ruled from 1129 to 1153, first as queen to Fulk of Anjou, who succeeded her father, then as regent to her son. When he reached his majority, she refused to relinquish her power until he forced her from the throne. The story is told from the viewpoints of her son and a lady-in-waiting, Richildis, and her family. Richildis came to the Holy Land on the ship with Fulk searching for her brother. She stayed on to serve the queen." Libr J

"A richly textured tapestry steeped in history and fraught with romance, adventure, and intrigue." Booklist

Tartt, Donna

The **little** friend. Knopf 2002 555p $26

ISBN 0-679-43938-2

LC 2002-66878

Tartt's "book is a ruthlessly precise reckoning of the world as it is—drab, ugly, scary, inconclusive—filtered through the bright colors and impossible demands of childhood perception. It grips you like a fairy tale, but denies you the consoling assurance that it's all just make-believe." N Y Times Book Rev

Tartt, Donna

★ The **secret** history. Knopf 1992 523p

ISBN 0-679-41032-5

LC 92-53053

This novel "is set on a small college campus in Vermont. Dissatisfied with the crass values of their fellow students, a small corps of undergraduates groups itself around a favored professor of classics, who nurtures both their sense of moral elevation and an insularity from conventional college life that ultimately proves fatal. Among Prof. Julian Morrow's followers are Henry Winter, a tall scion of a wealthy St. Louis family, . . . the twins Charles and Camilla Macaulay, both intellectually gifted and eccentric only in their excessive mutual devotion; Francis Abernathy, a dandyish homosexual slowly awakening to his sexuality; and Edmund (Bunny) Corcoran, . . . [who] becomes the group's victim." N Y Times Book Rev

Tatlock, Ann

Things we once held dear; Ann Tatlock. Bethany House 2006 396p o.p.

ISBN 0764200046 (pbk.)

LC 2005028048

In this book, "artist Neil Sadler's wife dies suddenly in New York City, [and] he is drawn back to Mason, Ohio, the hometown that he fled almost three decades before. He spends the summer helping remodel an old 'Gothic Horror' farmhouse into a bed-and-breakfast, trying to reconnect with his past and his cousin Mary Beeken. After a childhood spent caring for an invalid mother, Mary is trapped in a 23-year-old marriage to a troubled, alcoholic cop and feels her life has never quite gotten started. Mary's mother's murder years earlier . . . cast shadows on the lives of several Mason families. As Neil and Mary try to make sense of what has happened to their lives, they both discover that '[y]ou don't have to understand something completely to know it's true.'" (Publishers Weekly)

Tax, Meredith

Rivington Street. Morrow 1982 431p

LC 81-22587

"This is the story of Russian immigrant men and women caught up in the social upheavals at the beginning of this century. Set on the Lower East Side of New York, the book concerns strong-willed Hannah Levy, her daughters, Sarah, a social activist, and Ruby, a creative designer of clothes, and their beautiful and romantic friend, Rachel Cohen. It is the women who dominate this book. Their struggle to survive the terrible working conditions and low pay of jobs in the garment industry and the violence that comes when they demand a better life make an absorbing story. Tax has used real incidents—the fire at the Triangle Waist factory, a strike of garment workers, and the jailing of suffragists—to add color and authenticity to the story." Libr J

Followed by Union Square

Taylor, Benjamin

The **book** of getting even; a novel. Steerforth Press 2008 166p $23.95

ISBN 978-1-58642-143-4

LC 2008-5834

Gabriel Geismar "is the son of a domineering rabbi growing up in nineteen-fifties New Orleans. Homosexual, suffering from a physical deformity (he has a supernumerary thumb), and enthralled by mathematics—'calculability, sweet detachment from the corporeal universe'—Gabriel has 'a furious craving for other, nobler origins.' In college, he meets Marghie and Danny Hundert, whose famous physicist father is one of his heroes, and adopts the family as his own. The book explores the tortured and often misguided process by which children attempt to define themselves in relation to their parents (one iteration of the 'getting even' of the title), a process from which Danny and Marghie, as Gabriel slowly discovers, are not exempt. Taylor captures their quests for identity in pitch-perfect dialogue and lengthy meditative passages; his elegant plotting feels at once deliberate and improvised." New Yorker

Taylor, D. J.

Ask Alice; a novel. Pegasus 2010 342p $24.95

ISBN 978-1-605980-86-7; 1-605980-86-2

First published 2009 in the United Kingdom

"Set in the first third of the 20th century, Ask Alice traces the rise of an orphaned Kansas girl from pretty young thing on the prairie to bright young thing in 1920s London to society hostess in the '30s. Taylor . . . alternates point of view between the woman and a boy of uncertain parentage. The book has all the makings of Victorian high drama—a slew of colorful characters, vivid and varied scenes, precipitous changes in fortune, and inescapable revelations of long-buried secrets." Atlantic

Taylor, Elizabeth
★ **Mrs.** Palfrey at the Claremont. Viking 1971 178p

"A tale about an elderly British widow who takes up residence in one of those shabby, genteel hotels along London's Cromwell Road. She is at a desperate loss for what to do with herself to fill in the time and try to make her fellow lodgers believe she still has some semblance of a personal life. The portraits of the elderly and crotchety residents are drawn with a pen only lightly tipped in acid, and Mrs. Palfrey herself is very human and endearing. She finds her real hope for the future in pretending that a rather callow but not unkind casual acquaintance is really her grandson." Publ Wkly

Taylor, M. Glenn
The **ballad** of Trenchmouth Taggart. Vandalia Press 2008 276p pa $16.50
ISBN 978-1-933202-31-0; 1-933202-31-9
LC 2008-927388

"Taylor's prose is so fluid and seemingly effortless that The Ballad of Trenchmouth Taggart bridges the usually irreconcilable gap between popular fiction and literary fiction. It's that rare creature — a literary page-turner — and it will please both the casual reader and the college professor . . . . [This] is a stunning, fully realized, unique and ambitious book that proves there's still passion, fire and brilliance in the American novel." Houston Chron

Taylor, M. Glenn
The **Marrowbone** Marble Company; a novel. [by] Glenn Taylor. Ecco 2010 360p $24.99
ISBN 978-0-06-192393-7; 0-06-192393-1

"Each chapter of 'The Marrowbone Marble Company' stands as a self-contained bit. Each could be taken, individually, as a short story; puzzled together as a whole, they paint a picture composed of sideways glances. The resulting work is nuanced, with characters and conflicts emerging as three-dimensional creations. It's a rich stew, one well-worth savoring." Denver Post

Taylor, Peter Hillsman
★ A **summons** to Memphis; [by] Peter Taylor. Knopf 1986 209p
LC 86-45417

"A son, now a grown man, recounts the family's subservience to a strong-willed father. Against a background of Southern manners in Memphis and Nashville, the Carver daughters and sons experience frustration of their hopes to marry and enjoy family lives of their own. The mother, soon after her marriage to George Carver, withdraws from resisting his authority. The daughters never find suitors who suit their father. One brother, escaping to war, is killed and the narrator, Philip, a bachelor still at 49, is summoned home by his sisters to prevent their father, at 81, from remarrying. The seemingly selfless care given by the daughters might stem from self-interest rather than filial devotion." Shapiro. Fic for Youth. 3d edition

Taylor, Robert Lewis
The **travels** of Jaimie McPheeters. Doubleday 1958 544p

"The piquant combination of solid historical content, satisfying adventure, good literary style, sophisticated wit and humor will give this book wide appeal." Libr J

Tea, Michelle
Rose of no man's land; a novel. MacAdam/Cage Pub. 2006 306p $22
ISBN 1-59692-160-9
LC 2005-224876

This novel is "both a riotously funny coming-of-age story and a poignant cautionary tale that smacks of 'there but for the grace of God' heartbreak. . . . But Trisha's cynical, wisecracking descriptions are almost too brilliantly evocative, too clever as she illuminates the story's small cast of characters with vivid, telling details." Boston Globe

Tearne, Roma
Mosquito. Europa Editions 2008 299p pa $16.95
ISBN 978-1-933372-57-0; 1-933372-57-5
First published 2007 in the United Kingdom

"Flashes of true beauty, along with an impressively sustained forward drive, are enough to make Mosquito an engaging and thought-provoking novel." Times Lit Suppl

Temple, Peter
The **broken** shore. Farrar, Straus and Giroux 2007 357p $25
ISBN 978-0-374-11693-4; 0-374-11693-8
LC 2006-32983
First published 2005 in Australia

"Flinty, funny, subtle, and smart, The Broken Shore sags under the burden of a few too many narrative complications and, like many a top-drawer mystery, collapses toward the end, as the haunting questions, so elegantly posed, are suddenly and a little awkwardly answered. But this is a hazard of the genre, and Temple ranks among its very best practitioners." Entertainment Wkly

Templeton, Edith
Gordon. Pantheon Bks. 2001 226p $22
ISBN 0-375-42194-7
LC 2002-70427
First published 1966 in the United Kingdom under the pseudonym Louise Walbrook

"This eerie tale of sexual obsession is narrated by a young woman adrift in London just after the Second World War. She meets a 'frightening, sinister, implacable' psychiatrist who, over all protest, invades her, body and mind, arousing previously unsuspected tastes for submission and humiliation. One part 'Story of O' to two parts Muriel Spark, the book beautifully evokes the tightened belts and loose morals of postwar London." New Yorker

Tennant, Emma
★ **Pemberley**; or Pride and prejudice continued. St. Martin's Press 1993 184p $18.95
ISBN 0-312-10793-5
LC 94-171082

The author's "narrative is made uncomfortably compelling by her utter mastery of Austen's style. In its pace and sensibility, the text virtually breathes Jane Austen; the malaise that Ms. Tennant so powerfully exploits is solidly rooted in her model." N Y Times Book Rev

Followed by An unequal marriage

Tennant, Emma

An **unequal** marriage; or, Pride and prejudice twenty years later. St. Martin's Press 1994 186p

ISBN 0-312-11533-4

LC 94-26108

"In this sequel-to-the-sequel, {Elizabeth and Darcy} experience the mixed blessings children can bring. At 17, Miranda is lovely, competent, and her father's pride and joy, but heir-apparent Edward, a student at Eton, has long been a problem. As guests gather for the wedding of close friend Colonel Fitzwilliam, reports come that Edward has fallen under bad influences in London and gambled away part of the family estate. Cold disciplinarian Darcy acts, while compassionate chatelaine Elizabeth is distraught and susceptible to the admiring glances of handsome Mr. Gresham." Libr J

Tepper, Sheri S.

★ The **gate** to Women's Country. Doubleday 1988 278p

LC 88-387

"A feminist fable set somewhere in the Pacific Northwest 300 years after a nuclear holocaust. Men and women now live in separate but adjacent communities. Although the men are organized into military garrisons, the women appear to have the upper hand in government, deciding matters of trade and law and, most important, reproduction. . . . The elaborate society that the author takes such pains to describe is based on a big lie; the story she tells is part of the deception. Some will find this narrative strategy as distasteful as the secret it conceals. But Ms. Tepper is not afraid to ask hard questions, beginning with this: If biology is destiny, how can society hope to control its self-destructive tendencies without controlling biology as well?" N Y Times Book Rev

Tepper, Sheri S.

★ **Grass**. Doubleday 1989 426p

LC 89-30105

In this first volume of a trilogy "diplomats are dispatched to the planet Grass in search of the cure for a deadly disease that is spreading throughout inhabited space. The human settlers, xenophobic and conservative landed gentry, lead an existence tightly structured around the Hunt, a complex and violent ritual involving the use of alien mounts that seem nearly demonic in their malevolence. The presence of a number of not particularly sympathetic religious groups adds complexity to the situation. This is a beautifully written novel with well-developed characters and a number of very interesting aliens." Anatomy of Wonder 4

Followed by Raising the stones

Tepper, Sheri S.

The **Margarets**. Eos 2007 508p il $26.95

ISBN 978-0-06-117065-2; 0-06-117065-8

LC 2006-47079

"Margaret is the only kid on a research colony orbiting Mars. Smart, bored and profoundly lonely, she begins to create alter egos for fun. . . . As Margaret grows into a smart and lonely teenager her family must return to the grim, environmentally ravished Earth, where the only economically viable product for interplanetary export is human slaves. Facing a series of blind choices that pull her in two directions, she begins to shed the imaginary Margarets. The Margarets scatter off to other settled worlds, unaware of their other selves. Each Margaret struggles to survive by her (or his) wits, and to understand the growing threats to Earth and humanity. . . . [This novel] incorporates a grab bag of creatures, cultures, psychological metaphors, characters, commentaries and predicaments. The result is a delightful variation on the kind of novel with disparate characters and plot threads that somehow come together at the end. In this tale, they are together in the mind of a child at the beginning." Salon.com

Tepper, Sheri S.

Raising the stones. Doubleday 1990 453p

LC 90-30191

This is a "complicated, exciting narrative that explores central questions of religion and faith, and of the dangers and usefulness of technology." Women's Rev Books

Followed by Sideshow

Tepper, Sheri S.

Sideshow. Bantam Bks. 1992 467p

LC 91-40420

In this concluding volume of the trilogy begun with Grass, "a sentient fungus has infested most of the galaxy, reworking the life forms it inhabits to enhance their physical and spiritual comfort. The people of the planet Elsewhere, however, see the fungus's contented hosts as slaves; to preserve free will on Elsewhere, the rulers have imposed absolute cultural relativity within which pleasant and unsavory societies coexist, their integrity rigidly maintained by Enforcers. But powers have arisen to challenge the status quo." Publ Wkly

"Tepper's imaginative vision holds forth and delivers one of her most challenging works." Libr J

Tepper, Sheri S.

Singer from the sea. Avon Eos 1999 426p $24

ISBN 0-380-97480-0

LC 99-10231

"Despite her status as a young noblewoman of the planet Haven, Genevieve rebels against the strict regulations concerning highborn women. Defying her father's wishes, she seeks her own forbidden destiny and discovers the dark secrets that lie at the heart of her world and its forgotten history. Tepper . . . continues to explore the intricacies of human societal structures and the complex connections between humans and their environment, combining stylistic grace with imaginative insight." Libr J

Tepper, Sheri S.

The **visitor**; a novel. Eos 2002 407p

ISBN 0-380-97905-5

LC 2001-40197

"Dismé Latimer is an orphan, tyrannized by an evil stepmother and stepsister who deprive her of her heritage. Her rigid, corrupt society is ruled by a bureaucracy that keeps its people in line through a systematic and legally sanctioned use of torture, as its leaders pursue the black arts in their quest for power. Dismé secretly possesses a forbidden book, the memoir of her ancestor, Nell Latimer, who was a scientist at the time of The Happening. A thousand years earlier, an asteroid (the 'Visitor') hit Earth, nearly wiping out the human race and causing huge changes in geography and climate." SLJ

"Tepper has created a mesmerizing story full of intriguing characters, resonant images and powerful themes." Publ Wkly

Terrell, Whitney

The **huntsman**. Viking 2001 358p il

ISBN 0-670-89465-6

Terrell provides a "Dreiseresque study of Kansas City in the nineties, in all its complicated manners and minutiae. An unsung corner of the American landscape, the city is the real hero here, as white and black, rich and poor, old and young collide." New Yorker

Tevis, Walter S.

★ The **queen's** gambit; [by] Walter Tevis. Random House 1983 243p

LC 82-15058

"Familiarity with chess is not needed in order to enjoy this book though aficionados will delight in its evocation of their esoteric freemasonry." Times Lit Suppl

Texier, Catherine

Victorine. Pantheon Books 2004 324p $24

ISBN 0-375-42124-6

LC 2003-54860

The author "imagines the life of her great-grandmother, who left her husband and two children in a French provincial town in the late 1890's and supposedly ran off to Indochina with a customs officer. The affair might have lasted a year and a half; in 1900, Victorine returned to her husband in France and gave birth to a third child." N Y Times Book Rev

"With lush, vivid description, Texier brings to life both the world around Victorine and the woman herself." Libr J

Tey, Josephine

Brat Farrar. Macmillan 1950 219p

First published 1949 in the United Kingdom

"The scene is an English country home owned by the orphaned Ashby children and managed for them by their aunt, who has made a success of the horses she bred and exhibited. Simon, charming and spoiled, is about to take over as he comes of age, when a well-coached imposter arrives and claims to be the elder brother who had disappeared eight years before, leaving a suicide note." Booklist

Tey, Josephine

The **daughter** of time. Macmillan 1952 204p

First published 1951 in England

The author "not only reconstructs the probably historical truth, she re-creates the intense dramatic excitement of the scholarly research necessary to unveil it." N Y Times Book Rev

Tey, Josephine

Four, five and six by Tey. Macmillan 1958 3v in 1

An omnibus edition of three complete Scotland Yard mysteries in which Inspector Alan Grant solves the crimes. Includes The singing sands (1952) and The daughter of time (1951) and A shilling for candles (1936), about a film star whose death by strangulation is the focus of Grant's investigation

Tey, Josephine

The **Franchise** affair. Macmillan 1948 238p

"A lawyer in an English country town answers an appeal for help from two women who, having only recently inherited a home, were still outsiders to the townspeople and, being independent, reserved, and unusual, were called witches. When a girl in another town accused them of imprisoning, starving, and beating her in their attic, they were helpless, for the circumstantial evidence seemed indisputable. Good characterization, good writing, and to the lawyer's surprise, an emotional involvement for him." Booklist

Tey, Josephine

The **man** in the queue. Macmillan 1953 213p

First published 1929 by Dutton under the pseudonym Gordon Daviot

A man is stabbed to death waiting in the ticket line of a popular London musical, and Inspector Grant of the C.I.D. is assigned to the case

"Every detail of the discovery of first the identity and then the murderer of the knifed man is admirably invented, and the story, at first sight a simple build-up . . . turns out to be a serious inductive exercise." Springfield Repub

Tey, Josephine

Miss Pym disposes. Macmillan 1948 213p

First published 1946 in the United Kingdom

An English woman psychologist delivers a lecture at a physical training college and decides to stay a little longer. She becomes very friendly with some of the seniors, and eventually finds herself involved in an "accident" which turns out to be a murder

Tey, Josephine

The **singing** sands. Macmillan 1953 221p

First published 1952 in the United Kindgom. Variant title: Grant's last case

A cryptic fragment of verse, found near a dead man on a train en route to Scotland is Inspector Grant's only clue to the identity of the man's murderer

Tey, Josephine

Three by Tey; Miss Pym disposes; The Franchise affair {and} Brat Farrar. with an introduction by James Sandoe. Macmillan 1954 3v in 1

An omnibus edition of three titles entered separately

Thackeray, William Makepeace

★ **Vanity** fair; [by] W.M. Thackeray; edited with an introduction by John Sutherland; with 193 illustrations by the author. Oxford University Press 2008 lviii, 949p il (Oxford world's classics) pa $8.95

ISBN 978-0-19-953762-4; 0-19-953762-3

First published 1848

"The book is a densely populated, multi-layered panorama of manners and human frailties. . . . The novel deals mainly with the interwoven fortunes of two women, the wellborn, passive Amelia Sedley and the ambitious, essentially amoral Becky Sharp, the latter perhaps the most memorable character Thackeray created. The adventuress Becky is the character around whom all the men play their parts." Merriam-Webster's Ency of Lit

Thackeray, William Makepeace

The **Virginians**; introduction by M. R. Ridley. Dutton 1965 2v

First published 1857; first United States edition published 1869 by Fields, Osgood & Co.

"A sequel to 'Henry Esmond', it relates the story of George and Harry Warrington, the twin grandsons of Colonel Henry Esmond. The novel follows the brothers from boyhood in America, through various experiences in England, and finally through the American Revolution, in which George fights on the British side and Harry on the side of his friend George Washington." Reader's Ency. 4th edition

Thayer, Nancy

An **act** of love. St. Martin's Press 1997 245p $22.95

ISBN 0-312-15471-2

LC 97-14404

"Owen and Linda McFarland, both novelists, have been married for seven years and reside on a Massachusetts farm with Bruce and Emily, the children from each of their respective first marriages. Their uneventful existence is disrupted, however, when Emily, now a teenager attending the same boarding school as Bruce, attempts suicide. After voluntarily staying on at the psychiatric hospital, Emily whose recent behavioral changes include sudden weight gain and newfound religious devotion, reveals in therapy that the reason behind her despair is that her stepbrother raped her, a charge that Bruce vehemently denies." Publ Wkly

"Thayer's prose is fluid and concise, her characters rich and human, her dialogue easy and believable." Booklist

Thayer, Nancy

Belonging. St. Martin's Press 1995 341p

LC 95-15457

"The story surely captivates at moments and mostly satisfies. Except for the overattention to material and social superficiality, Thayer's story of a woman's quest for self-identity and self-affirmation does inspire." Booklist

Thayer, Nancy

Between husbands and friends; a novel. St. Martin's Press 1999 241p $22.95

ISBN 0-312-20613-5

LC 99-27233

"Narrator Lucy West, 37, is a self-employed mother of two; her husband, Max, edits the local newspaper in Sussex, a Boston suburb. Suave, irreverent Kate Cunningham and her husband, Chip, an attorney, move to Sussex in 1987; Kate

and Lucy meet at their children's preschool and become fast friends. Soon the couples summer together on Nantucket, and their lives grow ever more entwined. Thayer's narrative jumps back and forth between the couples' present and their shared past. . . . Readers prepared for the slow pace of Thayer's plot will appreciate her detailed, realistic records of motherhood, child-rearing and domestic routine in Sussex and Nantucket." Publ Wkly

Thayer, Nancy

Everlasting. Viking 1991 322p

LC 90-50462

"Catherine Eliot, at 18, is aimless until she falls into a job in a flower shop and realizes that this is the business she was born for. Though her social register family has cut her off, she uses her own social connections to build her business into a giant. This rejected daughter does all she can to rescue her family from financial and emotional distress. Though her help is neither understood nor appreciated, Catherine eventually finds contentment in herself, her marriage, and her business. An absorbing story and heroine." Libr J

Thayer, Nancy

Family secrets. Viking 1993 338p

LC 92-50746

At the center of this novel is "Diane, driven, successful, and suffering the disillusionment of mid-life crisis. The FBI contacts her in an attempt to locate her recently widowed mother, who they believe possesses top-secret information. At the same time, Julia, her unhappily college-bound daughter who's desperately in love with the boy next door and more desperately in need of breaking away from her mother's expectations, runs off to be married. Meanwhile, Diane's mother, Jean, captures the foregone dream of her youth: traveling through Europe with no itinerary, enjoying only quiet, anonymous days of her very own. Gradually, gently, the lives of these women unfold before us and Jean's mysterious secret is revealed." Booklist

Thayer, Nancy

Island girls; a novel. Nancy Thayer. 1st ed. Random House Inc. 2013 320 p. (hardcover) $26.00

ISBN 0345528735; 9780345528735

LC 2013010417

In this novel, "thrice-married Rory Randall dies and in his will leaves his expensive home in Nantucket to his three daughters on the condition that they all live in it together for a summer. Arden and Meg are half sisters. Jenny is the daughter of Rory's third wife, Justine, whom Rory legally adopted." The formerly estranged women "embark upon the requisite summer together. After a rocky start, the reunion results in a life-changing summer for all." (Kirkus Reviews)

Thayer, Nancy

My dearest friend. Scribner 1989 342p

LC 89-6276

"Divorcée Daphne Miller is the mother of a 16-year-old daughter who takes off abruptly for California to live with a father she has not heard from for 14 years. Deprived of child support payments, Daphne moves into a country shack. Once a college professor like her ex-husband and two married swains, she is now a lowly but plucky department secretary. Flashbacks reveal her best friend's betrayal and its impact on Daphne's marriage, and counterpoint her slow recovery during which Daphne again allows friends to play key roles in her life." Publ Wkly

Thayer, Steve

The **leper**. North Star 2008 389p map $24.95

ISBN 978-0-87839-266-7

This is the story of "the life of soldier turned schoolteacher John Eric Severson, from World War I to the mid-1970s. . . . Severson, soon after his return to the U.S. from the war, is diagnosed with leprosy and sent to a Louisiana leper colony. He never sees his home, his family, or the woman he loves again. . . . The book is filled with engaging, memorable supporting players, and Severson himself is such a vividly drawn character that readers may have to remind themselves that he is a fictional character." Booklist

Thayer, Steve

The **weatherman**; a novel. Viking 1995 452p $21.95

ISBN 0-670-84958-8

LC 94-20142

"Dixon Bell is a television meteorologist with an eerie gift for reading the weather. Rick Beanblossom is a news producer who hides his disfigured face behind a mask. Andrea Labore is the beautiful cop turned reporter whom they both love. Meanwhile, the Calendar Killer is strangling a woman each season during a significant weather event. When Bell is arrested and accused of the murders, Beanblossom and Labore join forces to prove his innocence. The novel's characters are deeply developed, and the riveting plot is cloaked in descriptive episodes of weather. Additionally, readers will receive a fascinating view of the intense machinations of television news productions." Libr J

Thelen, Albert Vigoleis, 1903-1989

★ The **island** of second sight; from the applied recollections of Vigoleis. Albert Vigoleis Thelen; translated from the German by Donald O. White. Penguin Group USA 2012 816 p. $29.95

ISBN 1468301160; 1903385067; 9781468301168; 9781903385067

LC 2011379493

First published in German as Die Insel des zweiten Gesichts: Dusseldorf: Diederichs, 1953.

This novel by Albert Vigoleis Thelen is "set on Mallorca in the 1930s in the years leading up to World War II. . . . Pursued by both the Nazis and Spanish Francoists, Vigoleis and Beatrice embark on a series of the most unpredictable and surreal adventures in order to survive. Low on money, the couple seeks shelter in a brothel for the military, serves as tour guides to groups of German tourists, and befriends such literary figures as Robert Graves and Harry Kessler." (Publisher's note)

Theorin, Johan

Echoes from the dead. Delacorte Press 2008 388p pa $12

ISBN 978-0-385-34221-6; 0-385-34221-7

LC 2008-6631

Original Swedish edition, 2007

This novel "set on the desolate Baltic island of Öland, a 'summer place' which is almost uninhabited for the rest of the year. Julia Davidsson has never come to terms with the disappearance of her five-year-old son 20 years previously. No trace of the child has ever been found; until Julia's father, a retired sea captain who lives on the island, receives one of the boy's shoes in the post. Together, father and daughter begin to piece together fragments of the past. Yes, there's plenty of etiolated Nordic gloom, but Theorin's prose is wonderfully descriptive and he writes so well about the natural world that the island is as much a character as the people who live there. The exposition of history and the nature of memory is haunting and lyrical, but never impedes a cracking good plot." Guardian

Theroux, Alexander

★ **Darconville's** cat. Doubleday 1981 704p

ISBN 0-385-15951-X

LC 80-00629

"The hero works as English lecturer in an American Southern women's college and falls in love with a student. Marriage is proposed and arranged, but the false hilding falls for another man. Revenge is planned and curses are articulated, but Darconville meets natural death in Venice. This simple tale easily fills 704 pages, for, in the Rabelaisian manner, it is decorated with monstrous catalogues, liturgies, baroque pastiches, diaries–anything, in fact, to prevent the story from moving fast" Burgess. 99 Novels

Theroux, Alexander

Laura Warholic; or, The sexual intellectual. Fantagraphics 2007 878p $29.95

ISBN 978-1-56097-798-8; 1-56097-798-1

"A remarkable achievement, a bombastic, squirm-inducing, and belief-rattling satire on political correctness shown through the lens of a sexless love story between two of the most unlovable (if not repulsive) characters in recent American letters. It takes an author like Theroux, who is as established as he is antiestablishment, to pull off a novel that for many other authors would be career suicide." Believer

Theroux, Marcel

Far north. Farrar, Straus and Giroux 2009 314p $25

ISBN 978-0-374-15353-3; 0-374-15353-1

LC 2008-49224

"In a postapocalyptic world where civilization is a thing barely remembered, one man in Siberia sees a plane overhead and sets off in search of the place where planes still have the fuel to fly. Theroux's haunting meditation on annihilation gives his novel the power of grief-stricken mourning." Booklist

Theroux, Paul

★ The **collected** stories. Viking 1997 660p

ISBN 978-0670861279

LC 96-52417

Theroux, Paul

A **dead** hand; a crime in Calcutta. Houghton Mifflin Harcourt 2010 279p $26

ISBN 978-0-547-26024-2; 0-547-26024-5

LC 2009-14083

In this novel, "Theroux brings his best gifts as a travel writer to one of his walk-on-the-dark-side fables of masked identity and psychosexual quest. The book's detail on Calcutta — from its genteel hotel lobbies to its back street 'underworld' — couldn't be more vivid." Seattle Times

Theroux, Paul

The **Elephanta** suite. Houghton Mifflin 2007 274p $25

ISBN 978-0-618-94332-6; 0-618-94332-3

LC 2007-13978

"Together, the three novellas of 'The Elephanta Suite' render India as a mass of contradictions: both a testing ground for patience and a training ground for serenity, if you're an American. The stories also recall the best of the author's earlier psychosexual parables ('Doctor Slaughter,' 'Chicago Loop'), blending Theroux the traveler and Theroux the connoisseur of our most wanton instincts into one." Seattle Times

Theroux, Paul

Half Moon Street; two short novels. Houghton Mifflin 1984 219p

LC 84-10495

This work "contains two novellas on a single theme: the terrors of leading a double life. In 'Doctor DeMarr,' the shorter work, a man who believes his twin brother to be dead steps into his brother's life. . . . {In 'Doctor Slaughter,' an} American woman on a study grant in London finds nothing working well for her until she sells her talents to an 'escort service.'" Newsweek

"Theroux endows these two cautionary tales with a palpable sense of danger and a trenchant wit that are both disturbing and enticing." Booklist

Theroux, Paul

Hotel Honolulu. Houghton Mifflin 2001 424p $26

ISBN 0-618-09501-2

LC 00-54125

"The episodic narrative is presided over by two protagonists: the unnamed narrator, a has-been writer who leaves the mainland to manage the seedy Hotel Honolulu, and raucous millionaire Buddy Hamstra, the hotel's owner and former manager, who fired himself to give the narrator his job." Publ Wkly

"The book brims with eccentric characters and their wild, usually morbid tales." Atl Mon

Theroux, Paul

Kowloon Tong. Houghton Mifflin 1997 243p

ISBN 978-0395860298

LC 96-29717

"Neville 'Bunt' Mullard is a quintessential Englishman: he likes eating at Fatty's Chophouse, going to the races, and having tea and oaties with Mum. Only Bunt was born and bred in Hong Kong, where he now runs a factory that his father established with Mr. Chuck, who has just died and left his shares to the Mullard family. Bunt is trying to ignore the imminent Chinese takeover of Hong Kong, but then Mr. Hung arrives from the mainland, demanding to buy the well-situated factory—and backing up his demands with some ugly tactics." Libr J

Theroux, Paul

★ The **lower** river; Paul Theroux. Houghton Mifflin Harcourt 2012 323 p.

ISBN 0547746504; 9780547746500

LC 2011036975

In this novel, "Ellis Hock decides to return to the one place he was really happy: the remote Lower River in Malawi, where he served in the Peace Corps until called home prematurely to take over the family business. . . . As Ellis wonders what he's got himself into, [author Paul] Theroux asks . . . questions . . . about the fate of contemporary Africa and the consequences of the West's do-gooding efforts worldwide." (Library Journal)

Theroux, Paul

★ The **Mosquito** Coast; a novel. with woodcuts by David Frampton. Houghton Mifflin 1982 374p

LC 81-6787

"The physical impact of the style, the exact observation, the occasional intrusion of the hallucinatory make this a remarkable work of art; its philosophical content is profound." Burgess. 99 Novels

Theroux, Paul

★ **My** secret history. Putnam 1989 511p

LC 88-32182

"'My secret history' is about the permanence of marriage in the face of mistrust and infidelity; it's about the wisdom of women and the foolishness of men; and it's about mature love as the necessary and sometimes successful antidote to youthful selfishness." N Y Times Book Rev

Theroux, Paul

★ **Picture** palace; a novel. Houghton Mifflin 1978 359p

ISBN 0-395-26475-8

LC 77-18725

Picture palace "is an elaborate visual conceit, a sublime meditation on seeing and knowing. Confident and commanding, the author displays his narrative gifts which range from the laconic to the lyrical, the telescopic to the microscopic. This is a novel which, like a photograph, one will return to again and again." Christ Sci Monit

Thilliez, Franck

Syndrome E; Franck Thilliez; translated by Mark Polizzotti. Viking 2012 384 p. $26.95

ISBN 9780670025787

LC 2012004718

In this "French thriller, a veteran Paris profiler struggling with paranoid schizophrenia and a lonely female police detective are brought together by a series of . . . murders" related to "an old experimental film containing disturbing subliminal images." Detective Lucie Hennebelle and Chief Inspector Franck Sharko meet in Canada, where they "learn about the . . . phenomenon of Syndrome E--the inducement of hysteria and violence through sensory control--and its possible role in mass killings." (Kirkus Reviews)

Thirlwell, Adam

The **escape**; a novel. Farrar, Straus and Giroux 2009 321p $25

ISBN 978-0-374-14878-2; 0-374-14878-3

LC 2009-42321

"Visiting an alpine spa town to reclaim the villa expropriated from his late wife's Jewish family in the 1930s, septuagenarian English banker Haffner muses over a lifetime of erotic self-absorption as he racks up a couple of new conquests in the debased, farcical mode that is an aging player's last resort. . . . At times arch and too clever, but so minutely perceptive that it all works." Kirkus

Thom, James Alexander

Panther in the sky. Ballantine Bks. 1989 655p il

LC 88-48012

The "portrait of Tecumseh, the renowned Shawnee chief and warrior who established a confederacy of tribes in order to resist U.S. encroachment into the Ohio valley, is suitably suffused with fascinating elements of native American lore, legend, and culture. . . . Action and reflection are juxtaposed in a riveting narrative that animates a remarkable cast of celebrated characters and vivifies recorded events. This respectful version of the life of a heroic and courageous native American represents historical fiction at its finest." Booklist

Thom, James Alexander

The **red** heart. Ballantine Bks. 1997 454p map $25

ISBN 0-345-41719-4

LC 97-18577

A "novel based on the well-known true life story of Frances Slocum. The five-year-old daughter of a Pennsylvania Quaker family, Slocum was kidnapped by Delaware Indians in 1778 and adopted by an Indian woman who raised the child as her own. In Thom's telling of her story, we see Slocum grow into a respected figure among the Miamis, becoming Maconakwa—Little Bear Woman—and raising a family on her own. The events of her life are set against the gradual destruction of Indian life on the early U.S. frontier. . . . Thom's research is exhaustive, his eye for detail impressive." Publ Wkly

Thomas, Craig

Firefox. Holt, Rinehart & Winston 1977 288p

ISBN 0-03-020791-6

LC 77-71356

"Suspenseful to the end, the psychological ups and downs are well handled, as are the flight sequences." Booklist

Followed by Firefox down (1983)

Thomas, D. M.

★ The **white** hotel. Viking 1981 274p

LC 80-52004

"Repetition, stunningly enacted in imagery that continually circles in on itself, is the method by which Thomas binds us to his prose. The white hotel is the leitmotif. . . .

The richness of this book is reminiscent of a painstakingly woven tapestry; one can focus on the details but must be absorbed by the whole." New Repub

Thomas, Dylan

★ The **collected** stories. New Directions 1984 362p

LC 84-6822

Thomas, Elizabeth Marshall

Reindeer Moon. Houghton Mifflin 1987 338p

LC 86-18530

"What makes the reader care for this young girl so far removed from us by time and distance is that in telling her story the author conveys sentiments and feelings not remote from our own today." N Y Times Book Rev

Thomas, Michael M.

Black money. Crown 1994 309p

LC 93-33813

This novel "tracks a criminal scam from its detection in a small California mall through its connections to South American drug cartels, the Mafia, and the highest reaches of the U.S. government. A middle-level federal bureaucrat and the socially well-connected editor of a muckraking magazine join forces to expose an enormously complicated scheme for laundering drug money." Booklist

Thomas "writes a very exciting and almost-too-believable tale of power politics and international crime." Libr J

Thomas, Michael M.

Hanover Place. Warner Bks. 1990 479p $19.45

ISBN 0-446-51330-X

LC 89-40038

"Hanover Place, in 1924, is the site of a moderately successful brokerage house owned by the Warringtons. Thomas' novel charts the triumphs, losses, and peccadilloes of the Warringtons and their kind, also serving up a portrait of the world of high finance, from the rudimentary days of stocks (and the Depression) to the modern age of junk bonds, forced mergers, unfriendly takeovers, and so on. One prominent theme here is anti-Semitism, symbolized by a bright young Jewish clerk who is upgraded into the partners' circle, yet must endure the bigotry of the WASPish men and women who dominate high-level New York society. Later, financial revenge is wrought. A big tale of Americans and their money certain to entertain." Booklist

Thomas, Rosie

All my sins remembered. Bantam Bks. 1992 548p

LC 92-8547

First published 1991 in the United Kingdom

This "tale revolves around interviews biographer Elizabeth Ainger records with her grandmother's elderly cousin, Clio, an accomplished novelist. Once three generations of family history are reconstructed, Elizabeth's project has revealed much more than girlish crushes and failed love affairs. This rousing, thoroughly engaging read moves from Victorian drawing rooms to bohemian Bloomsbury and Nazi Germany, with painful secrets and bittersweet betrayals revealed at every turn." Booklist

Thomas, Rosie

The **Kashmir** Shawl; Rosie Thomas. Penguin Group USA 2013 480 p. $26.95

ISBN 1468302469; 9781468302462

In this mystery novel, "while cleaning out her deceased father's house, Mair Ellis discovers an old shawl that belonged to her grandmother, along with a curious lock of hair. Mair, a single woman who has floated through life, is moved to find out more about the shawl, the hair, and her grandmother Nerys, who once lived as a Christian missionary in India. She travels to Kashmir, where Nerys's story unravels in extensive flashbacks." (Publishers Weekly)

Thomas, Rosie

Other people's marriages. Morrow 1994 425p

LC 93-8885

First published 1993 in the United Kingdom

"Effective, precise details vivify physical settings (various homes are as acutely rendered as the cathedral, the novel's central symbol), and the characters, some unappealing but all understandable, are well drawn." Libr J

Thomas, Ross

Ah, treachery! Mysterious Press 1994 274p

LC 94-15118

"In 1989, army major Edd 'Twodees' Partain took part in an illegal operation in El Salvador that his former comrades now want expunged from the record. Meanwhile, top political fund-raiser Millicent Altford needs to recover $1.2 million in stolen under-the-table contributions. These two scenarios dovetail as Altford engineers to have Partain, who was drummed out of the service for assaulting a superior officer, fired from his job in a Wyoming gun store in order to hire him to 'ride shotgun' as she goes after the loot. . . . Thomas's yarn reaffirms his expertise at the black-humored political thriller." Publ Wkly

Thomas, Ross

The **fourth** Durango. Mysterious Press 1989 312p

LC 89-3091

Durango, California is "the ideal hideout for a man with a price on his life. For a fee, the shrewd mayor and her loyal chief of police offer sanctuary to a judge who has just done time on a cooked-up bribery charge. The judge and his son-in-law, a disbarred lawyer, move into 'the only money-losing Holiday Inn west of Beirut' and devise a plan for smoking out the person with the vendetta against the judge. For an even bigger fee, the mayor and her top cop are game to conspire in the scheme—until an extremely ugly man comes to town and starts shooting up the citizenry." N Y Times Book Rev

Thomas, Ross

Voodoo, Ltd. Mysterious Press 1992 282p $19.95

ISBN 0-89296-451-0

LC 91-51185

"Ione Gamble, an actress 'with a face known throughout the world,' is in a real jam. The police think she murdered her former lover, Billy Rice, a dissolute publishing heir and independent movie producer, at his Malibu beach house.

Gamble isn't so sure about that, since she was blind drunk at the time. Desperate, she hires Enno Glimm, who will spare no expense in recruiting a discreet hypnotist to probe her alcoholic blackout for the truth without concurrently selling her story to the tabloids. Glimm's company, based in Germany, is a sort of global office-temp agency that fills unusual short-term employment requirements." N Y Times Book Rev

Thomas, Sherry

Beguiling the beauty; Sherry Thomas. Berkley Sensation 2012 296 p.

ISBN 0425246965; 9780425246962

In this late Victorian historical novel, "Venetia Easterbrook is blindsided when Christian de Montfort, the Duke of Lexington, recklessly states during a Harvard lecture that all beautiful women are untrustworthy and then twists the events of her past marriages to illustrate his point. The twice-widowed beauty gathers her wits and plots the perfect revenge--she will disguise herself during their transatlantic crossing, make him fall in love with her, and then drop him. But her bold plan has unexpected consequences when their passionate, soul-searing affair flares into something more. Venetia realizes too late that she has fallen in love and into her own trap--and Christian will never forgive her deception." (Libr J)

Thomas, Sherry

Delicious; Sherry Thomas. Bantam Books 2008 viii, 404p $6.99

ISBN 9780440244325; 0440244323

LC 2008577558

This romance novel tells the story of "Madame Verity Durant [who] works for Bertram 'Bertie' Somerset at his estate, Fairleigh Park—after serving as the mistress he failed to marry (due to a questionable background that includes an illegitimate child). When Bertie dies unexpectedly at 38, Verity worries as Bertie's 'bastard-born' brother, Stuart—now London's foremost barrister—takes over the estate. Verity had shared a secret, mouthwatering affair with Stuart 10 years earlier, and she doesn't expect him to keep her on, especially since he's affianced to the very proper Miss Lizzy Bessler." (Publishers Weekly)

Thomas, Sherry

Private arrangements. Bantam Books 2008 351p pa $6.99

ISBN 978-0-440-24431-8; 0-440-24431-5

LC 2008-577025

"Camden Saybrook, Lord Tremaine, returns to late 19th-century England to confront his wife, Gigi, about her petition for divorce. Still bitter from Gigi's machinations to snare him as her husband, Camden will grant the divorce under one condition—Gigi must give him an heir within a year. Sparks fly as the two embark on heated attempts to put the bun in the oven, despite Gigi's fear that her next conquest, the insipid Lord Frederick, will discover her duplicitously lusty reunion. A captivating subplot emerges when Gigi's mother, Mrs. Rowland, sets her own plan in motion for Gigi's next nuptials. Thomas propels the plot forward with revealing repartee and gives the leads real nuance." Publ Wkly

Thomas, Sherry

Ravishing the heiress; Sherry Thomas. Berkley Sensation 2012 304 p. $7.99

ISBN 0425250873; 9780425250877

This book is the "second in [Sherry] Thomas's Fitzhugh romance trilogy [and] is set against the realism of 19th-century English arranged marriages. To fill the empty coffers of his family's estate, Lord Fitzhugh must marry Millie Graves, a prosperous manufacturer's daughter" despite wanting to marry his childhood love Isabelle. "Millie . . . proposes a marriage of convenience for a term of eight years. . . . Fitz and Millie's romantic tension grows as they renegotiate their marriage terms." (Publishers Weekly)

Thomas, Sherry

Tempting the bride; Sherry Thomas. Berkley Sensation 2012 296 p.

ISBN 0425251020; 9780425251027

In this historical romance novel, by Sherry Thomas, "Helena Fitzhugh understands perfectly well that she would be ruined should her secret love affair be discovered. So . . . it is with the greatest reluctance that she accepts help from David Hillsborough, Viscount Hastings, and elopes with him to save her reputation. . . . Helena has despised David since they were children. . . . David, on the other hand, has always loved Helena, but his pride will never let him admit the secrets of his heart." (Publisher's note)

Thompson, James

Lucifer's tears; James Thompson. G.P. Putnam's Sons 2011 323p.

ISBN 9780399157004; 039915700X

LC 2010037041

This book tells the story of Inspector Kari Vaara, a detective who "is pushed into investigating a ninety-year-old national hero for war crimes committed during World War II. The Interior Minister demands a conclusion of innocence, preserving Finland's heroic perception about itself and its role in the war, but Germany wants extradition. In a seeming coincidence, Kari is drawn into the murder-by-torture case of Iisa Filippov, the philandering wife of a Russian businessman. Her lover is clearly being framed for the crime -- and Ivan Filippov's arrogance and nonchalance point the finger at him. But he's being protected from above, leading Kari to the corrupt corridors of power." (Publisher's note)

Thompson, Jean, 1950-

The **humanity** project; Jean Thompson. Blue Rider Press 2013 352 p. (hardcover) $26.95

ISBN 0399158715; 9780399158711

LC 2012028041

"This novel follows two single fathers and their teenage kids. Sean is struggling to find construction work as his house goes into foreclosure. His son, Conner, should be looking forward to college, but, instead, he, too, is scrambling for a job. Art, a pot-smoking, part-time college teacher smitten with his neighbor, Christie, a worldly-wise nurse . . . , has played no role in his now 15-year-old daughter's life," but must after she moves in with him following a school shooting. (Booklist)

Thompson, Jean, 1950-

Wide blue yonder; a novel. Simon & Schuster 2002 367p $24

ISBN 0-7432-0512-X

LC 2001-34157

"It's summer 1999 in Springfield, IL, and Harvey Sloan's sole interest in life continues to be the Weather Channel. His great-niece, Josie, possessed by a hopeless teenage love, confides in Abe Lincoln. Her divorced mother, Elaine, starts to believe that a good or bad day is indicated by her car's service engine light. Meanwhile, Rolando Gottschalk, armed with a gun and an unknown agenda, seems to be headed to Springfield from Los Angeles, leaving a wake of random destruction. Add Mitch, a gorgeous cop, and Rosa, a Mexican cleaning woman, to the mix and you have a novel with characters both memorable and believable." Libr J

Thompson, Jean, 1950-

★ The **year** we left home. Simon & Schuster 2011 325p $25

ISBN 978-1-4391-7588-0; 1-4391-7588-8

LC 2010-47553

"even minor characters receive the full attention of the author's prodigious talents; each one is drawn so vividly that they never feel less than utterly real. To say too much more would ruin the slow, lovely unfurling of Home, a string of largely unremarkable moments told with extraordinary grace." Entertainment Wkly

Thompson, Victoria

Murder in Chinatown; a gaslight mystery. Victoria Thompson. Berkley Prime Crime 2007 305 p. (hardcover) $23.95

ISBN 0425215318; 9780425215319

LC 2006052669

This book by Victoria Thompson is part of the Gaslight Mystery series "featuring midwife Sarah Brandt and Detective Sergeant Malloy in turn-of-the-century New York City. Sarah Brandt has made her uneasy way to Chinatown to deliver a baby. . . . When the new mother's half-Chinese, half-Irish niece goes missing, Sarah knows that alerting the police will accomplish nothing, and seeks the one person she can turn to--Detective Sergeant Malloy." (Publisher's note)

Thompson, Victoria

Murder on Fifth Avenue; Victoria Thompson. 1st ed. Berkley Prime Crime 2012 296 p. (A gaslight mystery) (hardcover) $24.95

ISBN 0425247414; 9780425247419

LC 2011052355

This novel, by Victoria Thompson, is part of the Edgar Award-nominated "Gaslight Mystery" series. "From the tenements to the town houses of nineteenth-century New York, midwife Sarah Brandt and Detective Sergeant Frank Malloy never waiver in their mission to aid the innocent and apprehend the guilty. Now, the latest novel . . . finds Sarah and Malloy investigating the murder of a Knickerbocker club member who was made to pay his dues." (Publisher's note)

Thompson, Victoria

Murder on Lenox Hill; a gaslight mystery. Victoria Thompson. 1st ed. Berkley Prime Crime 2005 291 p. (paperback) $23.95

ISBN 0425202607; 9780425202609

LC 2004062759

In this book, part of author Victoria Thompson's Gaslight Mystery series, "[w]hen the affluent Lintons of Lenox Hill summon Sarah Brandt to examine their teenage daughter, their worst fear is confirmed: she is with child. The pregnancy is a mystery, however, as the young woman--mentally still a child herself--is never left on her own. . . . It's a delicate situation, casting suspicion on those close to the Lintons, including their beloved minister." (Publisher's note)

Thompson, Victoria

Murder on Lexington Avenue; a gaslight mystery. Victoria Thompson. Berkley Prime Crime 2010 328 p. (hardcover) $24.95

ISBN 0425234371; 9780425234372

LC 2009050680

In this book, part of author Victoria Thompson's Gaslight Mystery series, "The murder of a wealthy, influential businessman has Det. Frank Malloy investigating the complications of the dead man's family life and rivalries between two schools for the deaf. The case has personal ramifications for Malloy as his own son attends one of the schools." Other plot lines involve "a secret pregnancy [and] the tense conflict among educators on how to teach the deaf." (Library Journal)

Thompson, Victoria

Murder on Waverly Place; a gaslight mystery. Victoria Thompson. 1st ed. Berkley Prime Crime 2009 296 p. (Gaslight mystery) (hardcover) $24.95

ISBN 0425227758; 9780425227756

LC 2008054338

In this book, part of author Victoria Thompson's Gaslight Mystery series, "[m]idwife and sleuth Sarah Brandt and Detective Sergeant Frank Malloy must protect Sarah's mother from scandal after . . . a séance that sends one of the attendees into the afterlife. But first, they have to determine how the woman was murdered in the pitch dark when all the suspects were holding hands." (Publisher's note)

Thon, Melanie Rae

In this light; new and selected stories. Graywolf Press 2011 270p pa $16

ISBN 978-1-55597-585-2

"Two of the book's nine stories center on men. In the other stories in this fine, edgy, often bleak collection, young women crash parties on Indian reservations, break into homes, or live in the woods or in broken-down trailers at the end of desolate Montana roads. Sexually and physically abused as children, the characters experience more in their frequent journeys from home than most adults experience in a lifetime. . . . The book's epigraph reads 'within the pain of living and the tragedy of dying there is ... a luminous mystery that redeems the human adventure in the world.' Luminous mysteries comfort the suffering in Thon's luminous book." Minneapolis Star Tribune

Thorne, Melanie

Hand me down; a novel. Melanie Thorne. Dutton 2012 311 p.

ISBN 9780525952688

LC 2011022362

Author "[Melanie] Thorne's debut is a . . . game of musical chairs wherein teenage sisters Elizabeth and Jamie Reid struggle to find their respective places in the world after their divorced parents' delinquencies--Dad's a drunk and Mom is remarried to a sexually predacious ex-con--force them to take life into their own hands. Liz initially goes to live with Aunt Tammy, though Uncle Sam isn't fond of the new houseguest, and Liz misses her sister. Jamie moves in with Dad and . . . starts skipping school and hanging around liquor stores. Both girls eventually wind up in the conservative Christian home of Aunt Deborah, where Jamie finds comfort and stability, but Liz is left yearning for Aunt Tammy." (Publishers Wkly)

Thornton, Tim

The **alternative** hero. Alfred A. Knopf 2009 403p $24.95

ISBN 978-0-307-27109-9

LC 2009-14054

"Clive's first-person melodramatics strike a deep and resonant chord, not because they revolve around any particular band, but because they're about those of us who live and die for music. . . . Those particular teenage heart-scars still pain us decades later, seething to a beat that goes on and on and on, even when our own lives seem to have come to a full stop. Thornton's peculiar genius is in marking those teenage tablatures and playing them all the way through, a music fan's grace note, a love song to what was and may yet still be." Austin Chron

Tie Ning, 1957-

The **bathing** women; a novel. Tie Ning; translated by Hongling Zhang and Jason Sommer. Scribner 2012 361 p. $26.99

ISBN 1451694849; 9781451694840

LC 2012372350

This book by Tie Ning "follows the lives of four women -- Tiao, a children's book editor; Fan, her sister, who thinks escaping to America might solve her problems; Fei, a hedonistic and self-destructive young woman; and Youyou, a chef -- from childhood during the Cultural Revolution to adulthood in the new market economy. This . . . novel charts the journey of these women as they grapple with love, sibling rivalry, and, ultimately, redemption." (Publisher's note)

Tilghman, Christopher

The **right**-hand shore; Christopher Tilghman. Farrar, Straus and Giroux 2012 358 p. (alk. paper) $27.00

ISBN 9780374203481

LC 2011041211

This novel is a prequel to Christopher Tilghman's book "Mason's Retreat," about the Masons, a family on Maryland's Eastern Shore. "In 1922, Edward Mason first visits the Retreat because its dedicated caretaker, Miss Mary, is dying and needs an heir. Before Edward can inherit, he must learn all of the family's, and the land's, dark history. . . .

After both her brothers are killed in the Civil War, Ophelia Mason must marry to inherit and save the Retreat. In Baltimore, she meets Wyatt Bayly, who becomes responsible for the land and house." (Library Journal)

Tillman, Lynne

American genius; a comedy. Soft Skull Press 2006 292p pa $15

    ISBN 1-933368-44-6

                         LC 2006-04047

   "Every book is an experiment. What emerges here is a bold showcase of a novel, a cabinet of curiosity, a proposal for what fiction could be—a statement of intent, perhaps, rather than a fully formed artifact." N Y Times Book Rev

Tillman, Lynne

Someday this will be funny. Red Lemonade/Cursor 2011 159p pa $14.95

    ISBN 978-1-935869-00-9; 1-935869-00-0

                         LC 2010-941274

   The book presents a "collection of . . . stories" consisting of "twenty-one discrete works in a sequence". The subjects include "Peter Dreher . . . a German painter who, since 1974, has made several thousand images of the same simple object . . . Tillman's people are mostly educated, middle-class men and women of the present . . . . [some] pieces in the collection . . . . dramatize episodes in the private lives of celebrities". Particular focus is given to "New York's circles of artists and intellectuals, people estranged from much of American culture, who are doing what they can to build a fragile working intimacy, a sense of common cause, among themselves." (Yale Review)

   "Clever intricate fictions that map both the complication and comedy of the moments that most writers miss." Times Lit Suppl

Tillyard, Stella K.

Tides of war; a novel. [by] Stella Tillyard. Henry Holt 2011 353p $27

    ISBN 978-0-8050-9457-2; 0-8050-9457-1

                         LC 2011-25731

   A novel "set during England's Peninsular War against Napoleon Bonaparte in 1812-15. The action opens with young Harriet, daughter of eccentric amateur scientist Sir William Guest, bidding farewell to her dashing husband, James Raven, who is about to set off for Spain to join the forces of Gen. Wellington. After these initial scenes, the narrative splits in two, following the adventures of Harriet (and her new friend Kitty, Lady Wellington) and the adventures of James (and his new friend Lord Wellington)." Wall Street J

Timm, Uwe

   ★ **Morenga**; translated from the German by Breon Mitchell. New Directions 2003 340p $25.95

    ISBN 0-8112-1514-8

                         LC 2002-15248

   Original German edition, 1978

   The "fragmentary approach has great cumulative moral power, making us consider all sides of the story without forgetting that there were victims who deserve some remembrance." N Y Times Book Rev

Tinti, Hannah

Animal crackers. Dial Press 2004 197p $22.95

    ISBN 0-385-33743-4

                         LC 2003-70125

   "Tinti boldly parses primal emotions in her stealthy short stories, which, like cats' paws, conceal weapons of great precision. Each tale posits interaction between animals and humans, which, rather than offering cuddly moments, lead to vicious or spooky confrontations. Zoos make perfect theaters for Tinti's creepy and caustic satires. . . . Tinti's fables are dark and wily, grim yet morbidly fascinating exposures of both our animal selves and our uniquely human psychoses." Booklist

Tinti, Hannah

The **good** thief. Dial Press 2008 327p $25

    ISBN 978-0-385-33745-8

                         LC 2008-13507

   This "novel is an homage to old-fashioned boy's-own adventure stories, and unfolds like a Robert Louis Stevenson tale retold amid the hardscrabble squalor of Colonial New England. The sheer strangeness of the story is beguiling: a one-handed boy, tainted by his upbringing in a Catholic orphanage and with little to offer but a head full of lice, is adopted by a con artist, and enters an underworld of ruthless mousetrap-manufacturing barons, feisty chimney-dwelling dwarves, and, perhaps most terrifying of all, black-market dentists. In keeping with the gothic tradition, Tinti writes with an arch, almost camp sensibility. While on a nocturnal grave-digging excursion to procure bodies for a crazy scientist, for instance, the pair encounter an assassin, who tells the twelve-year-old hero that he was 'made for killing.' Will the boy ever discover the truth of his past? It's good fun watching him find out." New Yorker

Tirone Smith, Mary-Ann

Love her madly; a novel. Holt & Co. 2002 307p $25

    ISBN 0-8050-6648-9

                         LC 2001-39306

   "Smith delivers a smart, irreverent heroine; pitch-perfect Texan dialogue; gasp-worthy plot twists; and quite a bit of substance along with the action. Poppy has some serious and scathing things to say about the death penalty, religion, and Texas politics." Booklist

Tirone Smith, Mary-Ann

She smiled sweetly; a Poppy Rice mystery. Mary-Ann Tirone Smith. 1st ed; Holt & Co. 2004 275p $25

    ISBN 0-8050-7224-1

                         LC 2003-55757

   FBI agent Poppy Rice "agrees to help a friend's mom find closure in the case of the death of a pregnant woman in her native Ireland during the 1970s, but before you can say 'Erin go bragh,' the body of another pregnant young woman with an Irish link washes up on a beach in Boston Harbor. Police detective and Hindu/Catholic Rocky Patel heads the Beantown investigation of the American victim, and his coolness and wisdom complement Poppy's no-nonsense professionalism." Publ Wkly

Tirone Smith, Mary-Ann

She's not there; a Poppy Rice novel. Holt & Co. 2003 317p map $25

ISBN 0-8050-7223-3

LC 2002-68592

"The ease with which Poppy gets technical support from Washington and manpower from the Rhode Island mainland is some stretch, but that doesn't take away from her shrewd analysis of the isolationist island mentality or her understanding of teenage behavior." N Y Times Book Rev

Tobar, Héctor

The **barbarian** nurseries. Farrar, Straus and Giroux 2011 422p il $27

ISBN 978-0-374-10899-1; 0-374-10899-4

LC 2011-10703

This book by Hétor Tobar, set in Orange County, California, follows the "Torres-Thompson household. . . . "Scott, a programmer, . . . lives in the shadow of his own faded glory as a start-up wizard. . . . Maureen is a creative and driven mother. . . . Araceli, the aloof housekeeper and cook . . . is thrust into serving as nanny when Scott dismisses the other Mexican employees because of finances." (World Literature Today)

"Maureen and Scott Torres-Thompson live with their children in upscale Laguna Rancho Estates. Despite Scott's income as a computer game company vice president, bad investments and extravagant spending have forced them to fire their Mexican gardener and nanny. Housekeeper Araceli Ramirez must now do double duty. Though she's a dazzling cook, she's not up for child care, but her undocumented status forces her to accept the situation. Meanwhile, a disconnect is growing between Scott and Maureen. Without communicating to each other or to Araceli, they separately escape the pressures at home, and neither returns for four days. Araceli, alone and worried, has to do something, so she takes off with the two boys to Grandpa John's, with only a vague idea where he lives in central Los Angeles." Libr J

Todd, Charles

A **duty** to the dead; Charles Todd. William Morrow 2009 329 p. (pbk.) $14.99; o.p.; (hbk.) o.p.

ISBN 9780061791772; 0061791768; 9780061791765

LC 2008055909

In this book, "[d]edicated to helping the many wounded during the Great War, Bess Crawford receives a desperate request from a dying lieutenant while serving as a nurse aboard a hospital ship. 'Tell my brother Jonathan that I lied,' the young man says. 'I did it for Mother's sake. But it has to be set right.' Back home in England, Bess receives an unexpected response from the dead soldier's family, for neither Jonathan Graham, his mother, nor his younger brother admit to understanding what the message means. But the Grahams are harboring a grim secret, and Bess must, somehow, get to the bottom of it." (Publisher's note)

Followed by: An impartial witness (2010).

Todd, Charles

The **red** door. William Morrow 2010 344p $24.99

ISBN 978-0-06-172616-3; 0-06-172616-8

LC 2009-24160

In post-World War I England, Scotland Yard detective Ian Rutledge faces a wall of silence as he attempts to bring a ruthless killer to justice for the bludgeoning death of a Lancashire woman and the murder of a man who never came home from the Great War

"Twelve books into a series of mysteries set in England in the aftermath of World War I, the mother and son who team-write under the name of Charles Todd keep finding new ways to gauge the emotional effects of war on the living and the half-dead." N Y Times Book Rev

Todd, Charles

An **unmarked** grave; a Bess Crawford mystery. by Charles Todd. William Morrow 2012 262 p. $24.99

ISBN 9780062015723

LC 2011050979

"Gripping, powerful, and evocative, this superb mystery masterwork unfolds during the deadly Spanish Influenza pandemic of 1918, as Bess [Crawford] discovers the body of a murdered British officer among the many dead and sets out to unmask a craven killer." (Publisher's note)

Toer, Pramoedya Ananta

All that is gone; translated from the Indonesian by Willem Samuels. Hyperion East 2004 255p $23.95

ISBN 1-401-36663-5

LC 2003-56675

"A sense of duty is perhaps natural for a writer who spent nearly two decades as a political prisoner under three different regimes. But the striking achievement of these stories is an unshakable innocence of voice and a willingness to leave judgment to the reader. Pramoedya's art is made more of sadness than of anger, and he is particularly adept at narrating from a child's perspective—as when a six-year-old boy sees his best friend, a girl of eight, married off, beaten by her husband, and, after she flees, made a social outcast." New Yorker

Toer, Pramoedya Ananta

The **girl** from the coast; translated by Willem Samuels. Hyperion 2002 280p $22.95

ISBN 0-7868-6820-1

LC 2002-69063

Original Indonesian edition, 1987

In this "tale of feudal Java, a beautiful young woman from a poor fishing village has the misfortune of catching the eye of a Muslim aristocrat who asks to marry her, but who, after a brief ceremony in which a dagger takes the place of the groom, merely installs her in his bleak residence as a lowly concubine. . . . As Toer unfurls this entrancing, indelible tale based on his grandmother's hard life, he deftly dissects the conventions that enable a brutal few to oppress the suffering many." Booklist

Toews, Miriam

A **complicated** kindness; a novel. Miriam Toews. Counterpoint 2004 246p $23

ISBN 1-582-43321-6

LC 2004-7960

"Nomi's hunger for life prevents the novel from being as bleak as her situation might suggest; her account of her trials is veined with a dark humor that glints with the glee of payback." N Y Times Book Rev

Toibin, Colm

The **blackwater** lightship; a novel. Scribner 2000 273p

ISBN 0-684-87389-3

LC 00-21036

First published 1999 in the United Kingdom

"The novel shows us discreetly what a practical, complicated matter dying is, how much logistics and paraphernalia it requires, and its unflinchingly exact style is a kind of respect paid to this. The commonplce and the catastropic lie cheek-by-jowl." London Rev Books

Toibin, Colm

Brooklyn; a novel. Scribner 2009 262p $25

ISBN 978-1-4391-3831-1

LC 2009-10753

"A diligent young woman with few opportunities in nineteen-fifties Ireland is packed off by her family to Brooklyn, where she works in a department store, goes to church and night school, and acquires a boyfriend, before a family crisis presents her with a stark choice between her new life and her old one. Within these confines, Tóibín creates a narrative of remarkable power, writing with a spareness and intensity that give the minutest shades of feeling immense emotional impact. Seen through his protagonist's cautious eyes, even hackneyed tropes of Brooklyn life, such as trips to Ebbets Field and Coney Island, take on a subtle strangeness. Purging the immigrant novel of all swagger and sentimentality, Tóibín leaves us with a renewed understanding that to emigrate is to become a foreigner in two places at once." New Yorker

Toibin, Colm

★ The **empty** family; stories. Scribner 2010 275p $24

ISBN 978-1-4391-3832-8; 1-4391-3832-X

LC 2010-32931

The "slow deletion of personal relationships is at the core of the nine stories in this collection, as Tóibín projects a slideshow of reclusive figures, many of whom have found that a life well-hid is a life sufficient. With a spare, eloquent style, he guides us through hotel lobbies and pensiónes from Dublin to Barcelona. He directs our attention to estranged family members, divorcées and Muslim immigrants, catching each of them at the moment in which they are forced to reckon with their pasts." Los Angeles Times Book Rev

Toibin, Colm

★ The **master**. Scribner 2004 338p $25

ISBN 0-7432-5040-0

LC 2003-67376

This novel depicts the writer Henry James during his middle years.

"What Tóibín has so boldly done-and so brilliantly and successfully-is forge a sympathetic imagining of James' interior life. . . . Even the reader who knows little about Henry James or his work can enjoy this marvelously intelligent and engaging novel, which presents not on a silver platter but in tender, opened hands a beautifully nuanced psychological portrait." Booklist

Toibin, Colm

Mothers and sons; stories. Scribner 2007 271p $24

ISBN 978-1-4165-3465-5; 1-4165-3465-2

LC 2006-47181

First published 2006 in the United Kingdom

"So flawless and unshowy is the language in Mothers and Sons that only on reflection does it sink in how varied the tone is among these stories. Yes, they're nearly all melancholic, but every shade in the rainbow of melancholy is represented, and the perspective shifts from mother to son to omniscient with no discernible change in authority." Montreal Gazette

Tolkien, J. R. R. (John Ronald Reuel), 1892-1973

The **book** of lost tales; part I-II. edited by Christopher Tolkien. Houghton Mifflin 1984 2v (History of Middle Earth)

LC 83-12782

Part one first published 1983 in the United Kingdom

"These fascinating stories of fairies and elves battling evil creatures shed considerable light on the evolution of Tolkien's elaborate fictional world." Booklist

Tolkien, J. R. R.

★ The **fellowship** of the ring; being the first part of The lord of the rings. 2nd ed.; Houghton Mifflin 1986 423p il $21.95

ISBN 0-395-48931-8

LC 88-120282

First published 1954

"Frodo, a home-loving young hobbit, inherits the magic ring which his uncle Bilbo brought back from the adventures described in the juvenile fantasy 'The hobbit'. This sequel, expressly addressed to adults, is the first of a three-part saga that tells of Frodo's valiant journey undertaken to prevent the ring from falling into the hands of the powers of darkness. Elves, dwarfs, hobbits, men, and sundry evil beings, each as real as the other, populate an allegorical tale that shows how power corrupts." Booklist

Followed by The two towers

Tolkien, J. R. R. (John Ronald Reuel), 1892-1973

★ The **hobbit**; or, There and back again. illustrated by Michael Hague. Houghton Mifflin 1984 290p il $29.95

ISBN 0-395-36290-3

LC 84-9023

First published 1937 in the United Kingdom; first United States edition 1938

Bilbo Baggins, a respectable, well-to-do hobbit, lives comfortably in his hobbit-hole until the day the wandering wizard Gandalf chooses him to share in an adventure from which he may never return. "Grades four to eight." (Bull Cent Child Books)

"It must be understood that this is a children's book only in the sense that the first of many readings can be undertaken in the nursery. . . . [The hobbit] will be funniest to its youngest readers, and only years later, at a tenth or twentieth reading, will they begin to realize what deft scholarship and profound reflection have gone to make everything in it so ripe, so friendly, and in its own way so true." Times Lit Suppl

Tolkien, J. R. R.

★ The **lord** of the rings; 2nd ed; Houghton Mifflin 1986 3v

The trilogy was first published 1954-55 in the United Kingdom. This revised edition first published 1966 in the United Kingdom

"This is a tale of imaginary gnomelike creatures who battle against evil. Led by Frodo, the hobbits embark on a journey to prevent a magic ring from falling into the grasp of the powers of darkness. The forces of good succeed in their fight against the Dark Lord of evil, and Frodo and Sam bring the Ring to Mount Doom, where it is destroyed." Shapiro. Fic for Youth. 3d edition

Tolkien, J. R. R.

Narn i chin Hurin; the tale of the children of Hurin. edited by Christopher Tolkien; illustrated by Alan Lee. Houghton Mifflin 2007 313p il map $26
ISBN 978-0-618-89464-2; 0-618-89464-0
LC 2007-1420
"If anyone still labors under the delusion that J. R. R. Tolkien was a writer of twee fantasies for children, this novel should set them straight. A bleak, darkly beautiful tale played out against the background of the First Age of Tolkien's Middle Earth, The Children of Hurin possesses the mythic resonance and grim sense of inexorable fate found in Greek tragedy." Washington Post Book World

Tolkien, J. R. R.

★ The **return** of the king; being the third part of The lord of the rings. 2nd ed; Houghton Mifflin 1986 440p $21.95
ISBN 0-395-48930-X
LC 88-195987
First published 1955 in the United Kingdom
In the concluding volume of the trilogy "The dark lord of evil is overthrown, the rightful king comes into his own, and the Age of Men begins." Booklist

Tolkien, J. R. R.

The **Silmarillion**; edited by Christopher Tolkien. Houghton Mifflin 1977 365p hardcover o.p.
LC 77-8025
"Tolkien began writing these introductory legends in 1917 and, sporadically throughout his life, continued adding to them; his son Christopher has edited and compiled the various versions into a single cohesive work. Two brief tales, which outline the origin of the world and describe the gods who create and rule, precede the title story about the Silmarils—three brilliant, jewel-like creatures who are desired and fought over, setting up a clash between good and evil." Booklist

Tolkien, J. R. R.

★ The **two** towers; being the second part of The lord of the rings. 2nd ed; Houghton Mifflin 1986 352p $21.95
ISBN 0-395-48933-4
LC 88-195969
First published 1954
"Here the Companions of the Ring, separated, meet Saruman the wizard, cross the Dead Marshes, and prepare for the Great War in which the power of the Ring will be undone." Libr J
Followed by The return of the king

Tolkien, Simon

The **king** of diamonds; Simon Tolkien. 1st ed.; Minotaur Books 2011 324p.
ISBN 9780312539085; 9781250002006; 0312539088
LC 2010040567
This book tells the story of "Oxford police inspector Bill Trave, [who] wasn't fully convinced that David Swain was guilty of murder" when his testimony led to Swain serving a life sentence for the murder of his ex-girlfriend Katya's lover. (Booklist) "Two years later, Trave's marriage has fallen apart. His wife, Vanessa, finds support in the unlikely person of Titus Osman, Katya's uncle, unaware that Titus is keeping Katya a virtual prisoner in her own home. Meanwhile, an embittered Swain plots an escape from prison to get his revenge on his former girlfriend, a plan that results in yet another murder." (Publishers Weekly) "Trave's suspicions lead him to . . . Osman . . . and his sinister brother-in-law, Franz Claes who will go to any lengths to conceal his past connections to the Nazis. . . . Once David is captured, Trave is willing to risk everything . . . to pursue his obsessive belief in Osman's guilt." (Publisher's note)

Tolkien, Simon

Orders from Berlin; Simon Tolkein. Minotaur Books 2012 320 p. $25.99
ISBN 0312632142; 9780312632144
In this World War II novel by Simon Tolkein, "Albert Morrison, ex-chief of MI6, is pushed over the banister outside his London apartment. . . .Scotland Yard detective . . . Trave discovers that Morrison was visited by Alec Thorn, deputy head of MI6, on the day of his death. Could Thorn . . . be involved in a plot to betray his country that Morrison tried to halt?" (Publisher's note)

Tolstaia, Tatiana, 1951 May 3-

The **slynx**; {by} Tatyana Tolstaya; translated by Jamey Gambrell. Houghton Mifflin 2003 278p $24
ISBN 0618124977
LC 2002-27627
Original Russian edition, 2000
This is a first novel by the author of the short story collections "On the Golden Porch" (1989) and "Sleepwalker in a Fog" (1992) and the nonfiction collection "Pushkin's Children: Writings on Russia and Russians." "The novel takes place some 200 years after 'the Blast'—an apparently catastrophic event that left many of the inhabitants of what was once known as Moscow with terrible physical mutations—and concerns the adventures of a numbskull named Benedikt: a foolish, self-centered dolt, thoroughly ignorant

of history and thoroughly devoid of moral intelligence." (N Y Times (Late N Y Ed))

"It takes some time for a plot to develop, but Tolstaya sketches a vivid picture of life in this permanent winter. . . . In this extended fable, she captures the Russian yearning for culture, even in desperate circumstances. Gambrell ably translates the mix of neologisms and plain speech with which Tolstaya describes this devastated world." Publ Wkly

Tolstaia, Tatiana, 1951 May 3-

White walls; collected stories. [by] Tatyana Tolstaya; translated by Antonina W. Bouis [and] Jamey Gambrell. New York Review Books 2007 404p (New York Review Books classics) pa $16.95

ISBN 978-1-59017-197-4; 1-59017-197-7

LC 2007-5450

"Angels, imaginary friends, near-saints, shades and über-ogres fall to Earth among ordinary Russians and routinely succeed in whetting the imagination in this sparkling collection from Tolstoy's great-grandniece. . . . It includes her two previous story collections, On the Golden Porch and Sleepwalker in a Fog, along with more recent work. . . . Beautiful, imaginative and disconcerting, Tolstaya's Russia is a labyrinth of treasures and horrors." Publ Wkly

Tolstoy, Leo, graf, 1828-1910

★ **Anna** Karenina; edited and introduced by Leonard J. Kent and Nina Berberova. Modern Lib. 1993 xxvii, 927p $22.95

ISBN 0-679-60079-5

LC 93-43634

Written in 1873-1876

This novel "is the story of a tragic, adulterous love. Anna meets and falls in love with Aleksei Vronski, a handsome young officer. She abandons her child and husband in order to be with Vronski. When she thinks Vronski has tired of her, she kills herself by leaping under a train. The idea for the story reputedly came to Tolstoy after he had viewed the body of a young woman who committed a similar suicide. A subplot concerns the contrasting happy marriage of Konstantin Levin and his young wife Kitty. Levin's search for meaning in his life and his love for a natural, simple existence on his estate are reflections of Tolstoy's own moods and thoughts of the time." Reader's Ency. 4th edition

Tolstoy, Leo

Childhood, Boyhood and Youth; translated from the Russian by C. J. Hogarth. Knopf 1991 314p $17

ISBN 0-679-40578-X

LC 91-52984

Originally published separately, 1852, 1854 and 1857 respectively; this edition first published 1912

"An autobiographical trilogy. . . . 'Childhood' was the first of Tolstoy's works to receive wide attention. The descriptions of life on a provincial estate are among the best depictions of nature in Russian literature." Reader's Ency. 4th edition

Tolstoy, Leo

The **death** of Ivan Ilyitch, and other stories; a new translation from the Russian by Constance Garnett. Dodd, Mead 1927 362p

Tolstoy, Leo

Divine and human and other stories; new translations by Peter Sekirin. Zondervan 2000 211p $19.99

ISBN 0-310-22367-9

LC 00-20791

"These 16 selections from Tolstoy's final eclectic collection of tales titled The Sunday Reading Stories represent the Russian novelist's turn away from the troubling human condition in Anna Karenina toward a growing preoccupation with moral issues." Publ Wkly

Tolstoy, Leo

The **Kreutzer** sonata, The Devil, and other tales; translation of Family happiness, by J. D. Duff, and of other stories by Aylmer Maude; with an introduction by Aylmer Maude. Oxford Univ. Press 1957 xxi, 375p

Tolstoy, Leo

Resurrection; a new translation, with an introduction, by Anthony Briggs. Penguin Books 2009 xxxiv, 520p (Penguin classics) pa $16

ISBN 978-0-14-042463-8; 0-14-042463-6

Original Russian edition, 1899

"The story deals with the spiritual regeneration of a young nobleman, Prince Nekhlyudov. In his earlier years, he seduced a young girl, Katyusha Maslova. She became a prostitute and later became involved with a man she is accused of poisoning. Nekhlyudov, serving on the jury, recognizes her and decides that he is morally guilty for her predicament. He decides to marry her, and when she is convicted he follows her to Siberia to accomplish his aim. Maslova is repelled by his reforming zeal. She marries another prisoner, but is finally convinced of Nekhlyudov's sincerity and accepts his friendship." Reader's Ency. 4th edition

Tolstoy, Leo

The **short** novels of Tolstoy; selected with an introduction by Philip Rahv; translated by Aylmer Maude. Dial Press 1946 xx, 716p

Tolstoy, Leo

Short stories; selected and introduced by Ernest J. Simmons. Modern Lib. 1964 2v

Tolstoy, Leo

War and peace; translated by Richard Pevear and Larissa Volokhonsky. Knopf 2007 1273p $37

ISBN 978-0-307-26693-4; 0-307-26693-1

LC 2007-15989

Original Russian edition, 1864-1869

"Stressing that their War and Peace sticks more closely to the Russian text than any other, including Louise and Aylmer Maude's semi-canonical 1923 version, Pevear and Volokhonsky retain the considerable amount of French used by Tolstoy's counts and princesses, preserve the author's penchant for word repetition and aim to match his tidy syntactic conciseness. The result certainly reads smoothly, its English being neither egregiously contemporary nor inappropriately old-fashioned." Washington Post Book World

Toole, F. X.

Pound for pound; a novel. Ecco 2006 366p $25.95

ISBN 978-0-06-088133-7

LC 2005-49508

This is the "story of Eduardo 'Chicky' Garza, a young San Antonio fighter and grandson of onetime contender Eloy 'Texas Wolf' Garza. When Chicky is cheated out of a shot at the Olympic team, his grandfather encourages him to move to Los Angeles and find trainer Dan Cooley, a former boxer who lost to the grandfather 40 years earlier in a fixed fight. Though struggling with a deep depression brought on by the accidental death of his young grandson, Cooley decides to take Chicky on, paving the way for him to face the fighter who cheated him. The result is powerful and very readable, if somewhat sentimental, and Toole's deep love of boxing's rituals, traditions, and code of honor shines through." Libr J

Toole, John Kennedy

★ A **confederacy** of dunces; foreword by Walker Percy. Louisiana State Univ. Press 1980 338p $24.95

ISBN 0-8071-0657-7

LC 79-20190

"At the heart of this splendid mock-heroic with its blundering and canniness, its falstaffian excesses and 'Alice in Wonderland' wit, lies a profound sense of solitude. Like everything else in Ignatuis J. Reilly's world, the absence of love is larger than life." Newsweek

Torday, Paul

Salmon fishing in the Yemen. Harcourt 2007 333p $24

ISBN 978-0-15-101276-3

LC 2006-33713

This is an "oddball piece of fiction that—despite being told through dry diary extracts, e-mails and reports—is an amusing satire on the tensions between the West and the Middle East, and a commentary on the value of belief to mankind. . . . The success of the book lies in the charm of Mr. Torday's storyline—his love of salmon fishing shines through his text—and his skill at portraying the petty officialdom and manipulativeness of modern government." Economist

Torres, Justin

★ **We** the animals. Houghton Mifflin Harcourt 2011 128p $18

ISBN 978-0-547-57672-5; 0-547-57672-2

LC 2011-09159

"An unnamed narrator—the youngest of three boys—grows up dirt poor in upstate New York with a fragile white mother and an unpredictable Puerto Rican father. From flying kites made of trash bags to pounding tomatoes with a mallet until juice runs down their kitchen walls, these boys are out of control and vividly alive. Though partially autobiographical, the novel evokes the exhilaration and violence of boyhood with such authenticity, the reader wonders how the author accessed his memories with such accuracy. Torres . . . brings a poet's attention to the placement and rhythm of words. His lyrical language sustains an almost trancelike reading experience—that is, until an abrupt chronological leap late in the novel finds the narrator transformed from boy to adolescent. Despite this jarring effect, the picture of the narrator's messy upbringing feels complete. His relationships with his brothers and his parents veer off in unexpected, often unwanted, directions, and the force of the book's final emotional punch surprises." Time Out N Y

Tournier, Michel

★ **Friday**; translated from the French by Norman Denny. Johns Hopkins University Press 1997 235p pa $25

ISBN 0-8018-5592-6

LC 96-45295

Original French edition, 1967; this translation first published 1969 by Doubleday

"M. Tournier is a cultivated and disciplined writer, and his Robinson, the son of a Yorkshire draper, is most likable. . . . The castaway has that quaint and peculiarly English stolidity that seems to exist only in the imagination of the French." New Yorker

Tournier, Michel

★ The **ogre**; translated from the French by Barbara Bray. Johns Hopkins University Press 1997 373p pa $19.95

ISBN 0-8018-5590-x

LC 96-46778

Original French edition, 1970; this translation first published 1972 by Doubleday and in the United Kingdom by Collins with title: The Erl-king

A work that "bears patently the marks of greatness. It relentlessly pushes individual idiosyncrasy to–and even beyond–the point of universality. It covers simultaneously the events inside one head and one continent. It uses documentary knowledge–minute and encyclopedic knowledge of photography, history, zoology, anthropometry, weaponry– to illustrate the otherwise undocumentable progress of a human obsession." New Yorker

Tower, Wells

Everything ravaged, everything burned. Farrar, Straus and Giroux 2009 238p $24

ISBN 978-0-374-29219-5; 0-374-29219-1

LC 2008-42757

"Holy hell! After enduring years of literary atrophy, mostly reading stories by authors so alienated from what the majority of actual human beings suffer, they compensate for a lack of authentic visceral insight with decorative, purple prose and quirky coincidences, now an author emerges who again dares to pierce the heart of modern realism, revealing the conflicted spirit of middle-America, a troubling yet real place populated by lonely divorcees, hormonal teens, Alzheimer-afflicted fathers and the sons who can't care for them, each person searching for the treasure chest of meaning in a landscape that's already been pillaged, the earth salted." PopMatters

Towles, Amor

Rules of civility; a novel. Viking 2011 335 p.

ISBN 9780670022694

LC 2011004118

This novel, which takes place in "1930s New York, . . . [opens with] Katey and her roommate Eve [who are] . . . too besotted with the dashing young banker Tinker to see any signs of trouble. . . . [The book pursues] this love triangle. . . . Katey winds up on Fifth Avenue at the end of her book." (Commonweal) The book features "New York's wealthy class . . . [with] an unmistakable sense of who belongs and who does not. . . . Towles . . . depict[s] . . . how the upper class can use its money and influence to manipulate others' lives in profoundly unsavory ways." (Publishers Weekly)

"On New Year's Eve 1937, at a jazz bar in New York's Greenwich Village, Katey and Eve are charmed by the handsome and successful Tinker Grey. The three become fast friends and spend early 1938 exploring the town together, until a car accident permanently injures Eve. Feeling guilty, Tinker, the driver, takes care of Eve and unsuccessfully tries to love her. Despite the presence and initial impact of Tinker and Eve, though, this first novel is about Katey's 1938." Libr J

Townsend, Sue
Adrian Mole; the Cappucino years. Soho Press 2000 390p
ISBN 1-56947-204-1
LC 99-87241

First published 1999 in the United Kingdom
"Adrian is a comic Job in a world gone mad with irony and greed. But his confused heart brims with love and good intentions, and Townsend skewers end-of-the millennium Britain with acumen and glee." Booklist

Townsend, Sue
★ The **Adrian** Mole diaries. Grove Press 1986 342p
ISBN 0-394-55298-9
LC 86-226

First published 1985 in the United Kingdom; A combined edition of two titles: The secret diary of Adrian Mole, age 13 ¾ (1982); and Growing pains (1984)
"The messy, inconsistent world of adulthood is seen through the eyes of a 14-year-old aspiring intellectual and poet. Adrian Mole begins his diary when spots appear on his face and his parents' marriage dissolves. By the diary's end he has been in love, become helpmate to a feisty 89-year-old, and held his mother's hand during the birth of his sister. Adrian's pithy commentary records the ludicrousness of school and state bureaucracy and the aberrations of the nuclear age." Booklist
Followed by Adrian Mole: the lost years

Townsend, Sue
Adrian Mole: the lost years. Soho Press 1994 309p $22
ISBN 1-56947-014-6
LC 94-11276

"Portions of this text appeared in The True Confessions of Adrian Albert Mole, while 'Adrian Mole and the Small Amphibians' appeared in Adrian Mole, From Minor to Major. Adrian Mole, The Wilderness Years appears in its entirety. All were first published in Great Britain." Verso of title page
"Adrian's latest diaries chronicle his mighty struggle to survive the adolescent and postpubescent years. His outra-

geous clothes and strong views about everything from the government to unwed mothers can't disguise the angst he suffers: he's still trying to find a niche for his unrecognized genius. . . . Townsend is a satirist of the first order, offering brilliantly witty humor peppered with sobering insights into the troubles and traumas of working-class Brits." Booklist

Townsend, Sue
Number 10; Sue Townsend. Soho 2003 277p $24
ISBN 1-569-47349-8
LC 2003-50562

This novel combines "social satire with an odd-couple road trip. The buddy team includes Jack, a policeman who grew up on the edge of squalor but manages to emerge a decent and levelheaded man. The other half is Edward, reared in privilege to take his all-but-predestined place as prime minister. Struck with the realization that he has no idea what life is like for ordinary citizens, Edward sets off, incognito, for a week-long safari into the land of the common folk, with Jack as his escort. Because it's hard for the prime minister to travel unnoticed, he does what any sensible man would do—slips into a wig and high heels and becomes 'Edwina.' The book doesn't lack for skewering observations of the upper and lower classes, but Edward and Jack are both such well-meaning characters, the book comes off ultimately as more affirming than biting." Booklist

Toyne, Simon
The **key**; Simon Toyne. 1st ed. HarperCollins 2012 436 p. map (hardcover) $25.99; (paperback) $9.99; (ebook) $20.99
ISBN 0062038338; 9780062038333; 9780062038340; 9780062038357; 9780062204660
LC 2012007666

This book is the second in the Sanctus trilogy by Simon Toyne. "When the Citadel, the original center of the Roman Catholic Church in Turkey, is compromised by a terrorist act, the revelation of ancient secrets and modern lies threatens to destroy the Church. At the center of this storm is Liv Adamsen, a woman who survived the attack, but lost her memory and finds her life in peril for reasons she cannot remember." (Publishers Weekly)

Toyne, Simon
Sanctus. William Morrow 2011 486p $25.99
ISBN 978-0-06-203830-2; 0-06-203830-3
LC 2010-47233

In this first volume of a projected trilogy, "an ancient sect of monks who live in the Citadel, a church carved out of a mountain near the fictional Turkish city of Ruin, have been protecting a secret, 'the Sacrament,' since before the Christian era. A monk who knows the secret, Brother Samuel, escapes from the Citadel and throws himself off the mountain in full view of spectators and news crews. Later, American newspaper reporter Liv Adamsen learns that her phone number, carved into a small leather strap, has been found inside Samuel's stomach. The monk turns out to be her brother, whom she hasn't seen in years, so Liv travels to Ruin to try to solve the puzzle of his mysterious death. She and several other groups battle the deadly monks, who will stop at nothing to thwart their efforts to discover the Sacrament's secret. The truly mind-boggling revelation will leave astounded readers eager for the next installment." Publ Wkly

Toynton, Evelyn

The **Oriental** wife; a novel. Other Press 2011 289p pa $15.95

ISBN 978-1-59051-441-2

LC 2010-54143

This is "the story of Louisa and Rolf, childhood friends in Nuremberg who escape Hitler's Germany and eventually settle in New York. Louisa leaves as a young woman to study art history in London and travels to New York with her English boyfriend. Rolf works diligently to find sponsors and employment for Jewish refugees trying desperately to get to America. It seems that serious, almost melancholy Rolf and the modern, glamorous Louisa have little in common, but when she seeks out Rolf and their mutual friend Otto after her relationship ends and she has nowhere to go, Rolf and Louisa fall in love. They marry and settle into a happy life in their Jewish community of friends and old neighbors, and they have a daughter. Unfortunately, a disastrous event shatters their marriage, and their plans for the future are tragically altered. . . . At times very sad, this nonetheless enjoyable novel will certainly appeal to those with an interest in Jewish literature as well as to general readers." Libr J

Tracy, P. J.

Monkeewrench. Putnam 2003 373p $23.95

ISBN 0-399-14978-3

LC 2002-68139

"Unlike the conventionally dimwitted cops and hick sheriff's deputies, Grace and her four geek partners in the software company . . . add real flavor to the proceedings with their colorful jargon and quirky personas. These techno-nerds may be freaks—and one of them may even be a killer—but they have style." N Y Times Book Rev

★ **Transgressions**; edited by Ed McBain. Forge 2005 783 p. (hdbk.: acid-free paper) $27.95

ISBN 0765308517

LC 2004061960

This book presents an anthology of novellas in the "crime and suspense" genre. Donald E. Westlake's "Walking Around Money" follows a "humorous burglar hero." Anne Perry's "Hostages" is a "portrait of a woman caught up in the current Irish troubles who tries to keep her sanity by doing household chores." (Publishers Weekly) Other stories include "The Corn Maiden" by Joyce Carol Oates, a "tabloid thriller about a mean girl who abducts a slow classmate for ritual sacrifice" and Lawrence Block's "Keller's Adjustment," which tells the story of an "assassin [who] finds himself having existential thoughts about golf communities after 9/11." (Booklist)

Traven, B.

★ The **treasure** of the Sierra Madre. Knopf 1935 366p

Original German edition, 1927

This novel analyzes the "psychology of greed in telling of three Americans searching for a lost gold mine in Mexican mountains." Oxford Companion to Am Lit. 6th edition

Traver, Robert

★ **Anatomy** of a murder. St. Martin's Press 1958 437p

"Not the usual murder mystery but a review by the lawyer for the defense from the time he takes the case of an army lieutenant who admits to having killed the man who raped his wife, until the end of the trial. Much attention is given to establishing the fact of rape. Although the recital is wordy it maintains suspense in showing the legal and personal resources the lawyer calls on to build his defense and the way that rivalry between prosecution and defense shapes the trial." Booklist

Tregillis, Ian

The **coldest** war; Ian Tregillis. Tor 2012 349 p. (Milkweed triptych) (hardcover) $25.99

ISBN 0765321513; 9780765321510

LC 2012011657

Sequel to Bitter seeds, by Ian Tregillis

This book, the second in Ian Tregillis's Milkweed Triptych, "takes up years later, in an alternate 1963 in which the warlocks of the British Empire protect the land from the Soviet Union. Secret agent Raybould Marsh and mage Will Beauclerk again find themselves drawn into the conflict, as the plans of the precognitive Gretel -- newly escaped from Russia -- finally start to come to fruition." (Publishers Weekly)

Tregillis, Ian

Necessary evil; Ian Tregillis. Tor Books 2013 384 p. (The Milkweed triptych) (hardcover) $25.99

ISBN 0765321521; 9780765321527

LC 2012042627

This is the "third volume of [Ian] Tregillis's Milkwood Triptych. "Sociopathic clairvoyant Gretel hatches a plan to send secret agent Raybould Marsh back in time to protect humankind. Landing in 1940, an older, scarred Marsh manipulates his younger self, his young wife, and novice wizard Will Beauclerk into courses of action that often parallel those of the first book." (Publishers Weekly)

Tremain, Rose

The **color**. Farrar, Straus & Giroux 2003 382p $25

ISBN 0-374-12605-4

LC 2002-192528

"As the story gathers momentum, it widens . . . . Tremain's excursions into the minds of her Maori and Chinese characters are written with a blend of sympathy and irony that sabotages our expectations of things exotic and inscrutable." N Y Times Book Rev

Tremain, Rose

Music & silence. Farrar, Straus & Giroux 2000 485p

ISBN 0-374-19989-2

LC 99-42880

First published 1999 in the United Kingdom

"So hypnotic are Rose Tremain's seductive paragraphs that we are borne along without effort in a world which is neither fact nor fiction but has the strengths of both, with a uniquely sensitive imagination at work." N Y Rev Books

Tremain, Rose

The **road** home. Little, Brown 2008 432p $24.99

ISBN 978-0-316-00261-5; 0-316-00261-5

LC 2008-921700

First published 2007 in the United Kingdom

"Lev has left his mother and child in his village in Eastern Europe to seek work in London, bringing with him an E.U. passport, a handful of English phrases, and a small stash of cash and vodka. At first, he is repelled by what he finds: the shaved heads, the greasy food in disposable packaging, the women thrusting their breasts at him from the pages of the daily paper. But opportunities also push themselves forward in this cold new world; soon he is scheming for a way to unite his future and his past. At once timeless and bitingly contemporary, this novel explores the life now lived by millions—when one's hope lies in one country and one's heart in another." New Yorker

Tremain, Rose

Sacred country. Atheneum Pubs. 1993 323p $21

ISBN 0-689-12170-9

LC 92-21457

First published 1992 in the United Kingdom

The author "gives us a precisely imagined landscape and a complicated group of characters that we come to care deeply about." N Y Times Book Rev

Tremain, Rose

★ **Trespass**. W. W. Norton & Co. 2010 253p $24.95

ISBN 978-0-393-07956-2

LC 2010-20934

This novel's first chapter "delivers a minute study of the dissatisfactions of a young girl on a field trip on a hot day. The insights into psychology are penetrating; the aggressive quality of nature is forcefully and believably evoked; the prose itself is luminous. The reader finds much to admire and enjoy, even though the stakes don't seem terribly high. And then the girl starts screaming. Set in the Cévennes region of France (known for its relentless mistrals and wild mountains), written in an unfaltering style, and peopled by robust characters with shameful, life-altering secrets and unbreakable emotional bonds, this is both a page-turning thriller packed with betrayal, murder, and love, and a gorgeous, meaty literary novel. Perhaps real life cannot unfold as neatly as this plot, but in fiction, such clarity satisfies." Atlantic

Tremain, Rose

★ The **way** I found her. Farrar, Straus & Giroux 1998 358p $25

ISBN 0-374-28666-3

LC 97-32676

First published 1997 in the United Kingdom

"Thirteen-year-old Lewis Little—dog-lover, chess player, amateur detective—joins his mother on a summer translating job in Paris to see the city and improve his French. But when he meets their glamorous hostess, Valentina Gavrilovich, with her infectious laugh, her cerise lipstick, and her large white breasts, his life is changed forever. And when Valentina vanishes he dedicates himself, like a knight from one of the medieval romances she writes, to rescuing her. Lewis's own narrative of innocence and experience is curiously reminiscent of the nineteen-fifties, and the effect is one of pleasurable nostalgia." New Yorker

Tremayne, Peter

Chalice of blood; a mystery of ancient Ireland. Minotaur Books 2011 368p map $25.99

ISBN 978-0-312-55121-6

Investigating the murder of an eminent scholar who was robbed of mysterious manuscripts, Sister Fidelma and her companion, Brother Eadulf, are quickly targeted by the same killer in a case that is complicated by divisive personal problems.

"Tremayne delves deep beneath the surface puzzle, peeling back layer upon layer of fascinating medieval Irish history." Booklist

Trenhaile, John

The **gates** of exquisite view. Dutton 1988 374p

LC 87-13630

"Trenhaile craftily weaves a portentous web of political intrigue, masking until the final pages the exact nature of his characters' intentions and loyalties. . . . Neatly paced suspense from a master of the genre." Booklist

Treuer, David

The **translation** of Dr Apelles; a love story. Graywolf 2006 344p $23

ISBN 978-1-55597-451-0; 1-55597-451-1

LC 2006-924339

This "novel is a metaphysical blending of two love stories, one mythological, the other very much in the urban present. Dr Apelles is a Native American translator of ancient Native American texts—every other Friday. The rest of his time is spent in a vast library, sorting an endless succession of obscure books. He feels that no one would notice if he disappeared, and knows that he takes too much comfort in 'the bouquet of languages he holds so dear.' Then a new translation he is working on sends him into a tailspin. It's a mythological tale of two orphaned Native Americans from different tribes who fall in love, suffer hardships, and eventually marry. Dr Apelles becomes immersed in his translation, seeing his own life as pale and loveless in comparison. As he becomes romantically involved with a coworker, the translation becomes the story he tells her of his own life. Treuer's novel comprises an intricate and provocative labyrinth that challenges the reader at every turn." Booklist

Trevanian

★ The **Eiger** sanction. Crown 1972 316p

"American art professor-mountain climber Dr. Jonathan Hemlock moonlights as an assassin in the employ of the Search and Sanction Division of the mythical counter-assassination bureau known as C-11. In his last mission before retirement, he is sent along on a top-flight mountain climbing expedition in Switzerland with orders to liquidate one of three companions known to have killed an unlucky C-11 agent in Montreal. Not knowing the identity of the assassin Hemlock ruthlessly plans to bump off all three." Smith. Cloak and Dagger Fic

Trevanian

Incident at Twenty Mile. St. Martin's Press 1998
308p $24.95
ISBN 0-312-19233-9

LC 98-19401

"Matthew Dubcheck wanders into the dying silver-mining town of Twenty-Mile, Wyoming, and declares himself the Ringo Kid, after the hero of his favorite dime novels. The romanticized West clashes with the real West when an escaped con comes to town, befriends Matthew, and the wheels begin to turn toward an inevitably tragic conclusion. The anti-western is also a staple of the genre, and this tragicomic tale takes its place alongside such similar efforts as True Git and poet David Waggoner's delightful Where Is My Wandering Boy Tonight?" Booklist

Trevanian

The **Loo** sanction; a novel. Three Rivers Press
2005 294p pa $13.95
ISBN 1-4000-9828-9; 978-1-4000-9828-6

LC 2004-29743

First published 1973

"The plot, though fast-moving, is not the most sophisticated, yet there is a certain excitement in this descendant of James Bond, and it works despite one's better judgment." Libr J

Trevanian

Shibumi. Crown 1979 374p

LC 78-20950

This novel relates the "feats of Hel, the world's highest-paid assassin. Hel guns down political terrorists of the CIA, PLO, and various other organizations, then takes on the superpower of espionage agencies, the Mother Company." Publ Wkly

Trevanian

★ The **summer** of Katya. Crown 1983 242p

LC 83-1790

"The time is 1914 and the story takes place in a small French Basque village. Dr. Jean-Marc Montjean, young and newly graduated from medical school, meets and falls in love with Katya, a beautiful young girl. Their encounter comes by way of an accident that befalls Katya's brother Paul, to whom she is very attached. Jean-Marc becomes involved with their family and begins to pay court to Katya. He is warned that any romantic attachment is out of the question because of her delicate health. A mystery in the background of the family hangs over all their relationships, and in a final meeting there is a shocking climax that leaves the reader stunned." Shapiro. Fic for Youth. 3d edition

Trevor, William

A **bit** on the side. Viking 2004 244p $24.95
ISBN 0-670-91507-6

LC 2004-42035

The author "reveals his native Ireland as a world sandwiched between modernity and its accompanying wealth, secularism and vulgarity, and a past that was more soulful and pious but also more restrictive.... Trevor ... explores the many sources and shadings of regret with his usual delicate but brilliant psychological nuance, brightened occasion-

ally by nostalgia for the lost love that once impelled his characters forward. " Pub Wkly

Trevor, William

Cheating at canasta. Viking 2007 231p $24.95
ISBN 978-0-670-01837-6

LC 2007-13499

"While many story collections suffer from repetitiveness when read in rapid succession, Trevor's scope is sufficiently broad to avoid this pitfall. . . . His characters are filled with yearning but, stymied by forces beyond their control, must resign themselves to stasis. If this sounds less than chipper, it is offset by the beauty and solace to be found in the deep level of understanding Trevor brings to his characters." Christ Sci Monit

Trevor, William

★ The **collected** stories. Viking 1992 1261p

LC 92-54071

Trevor, William

★ **Death** in summer. Viking 1998 214p $23.95
ISBN 0-670-88202-X

LC 98-21569

"A sudden death brings together a rootless, shifty young woman named Pettie and the recently widowed Thaddeus Davenant, who is trying to find a nanny for his baby daughter. With a badly typed letter of reference and threadbare clothing, Pettie is quickly turned away, but not before she has formed an irresistible (if deceived) impression of the life she could share with Thaddeus. Trevor inhabits his characters so fully that they seem present before us, and his exploration of their accidental connections demonstrates, yet again, his ability to imbue the most casual actions with unsettling significance." New Yorker

Trevor, William

★ **Felicia's** journey. Viking 1995 212p
ISBN 0-670-85745-9

LC 94-32413

First published 1994 in the United Kingdom

"Trevor is chilling and precise in his evocation of the loss of innocence, loss of heart, while he highlights the dismal features of contemporary society. Felicia's journey proceeds in an inimical atmosphere in which disquiet and corruption are the order of the day." New Statesman Soc

Trevor, William

Fools of fortune. Viking 1983 238p
ISBN 0-670-32355-1

LC 83-47867

"Willie Quinton tells of an idyllic childhood on his family's small estate, an ordered life shattered by the uprising, by the division of Irish society and, finally, by murder and destruction of their home. Uprooted to Cork, Willie lives with his widowed, alcoholic mother; goes to school; and eventually meets Marianne, a distant cousin from England. Their brief love is eclipsed by Willie's vengeance on his family's destroyer, shattering all their lives until his gentle daughter, Imelda, resumes the thread." Libr J

Trevor, William

The **hill** bachelors. Viking 2000 244p

ISBN 0-670-89373-0

LC 00-32485

"All the stories deal with the major disappointments and small rewards that life brings, particularly within the arena of love. No story here is less that a bravura performance." Booklist

Trevor, William

Love and summer. Viking 2009 211p $25.95

ISBN 978-0-670-02123-9; 0-670-02123-7

LC 2009-18184

"The speech in this novel, bare and unvarnished, is a constant joy, partly because [Trevor's] characters tend to reticence, to a reluctance to reveal themselves in what they say, and yet do so time and again, even in conversations in which nothing is said openly, but only obliquely, indeed especially in such conversations. His sympathy extends, with rare art, to them all." Scotsman

Trevor, William

Selected stories. Viking 2010 567p

ISBN 978-0-670-02206-9

LC 2010-19583

"The title of this hefty volume is a little misleading. It doesn't select anything, strictly speaking, but merely assembles the stories from William Trevor's last four collections, so that in effect it's a sequel to the huge edition of his collected stories that came out in 1992. Together the two books add up to almost 2,000 pages of short fiction—an enormous, Kiplingesque quantity of work—and they are more than ample proof that Trevor is one of the two greatest short-story writers working in English right now. The other is Alice Munro, and no one else is even close." N Y Times Book Rev

Trevor, William

★ The **silence** in the garden. Viking 1988 204p

LC 87-40662

"While the subject might seem common, Trevor's treatment is a dazzling tour de force of epigrammatic detail and psychological insinuation as the writer reconstructs whole lives through the telling deployment of a single episode. Moreover, there is a tissue of lies, secrets, and deceptions that is gradually revealed in the progress of these people's stories. Trevor captures the contradictions and subtle ironies brilliantly." Booklist

Trial and error; an Oxford anthology of legal stories. edited by Fred R. Shapiro and Jane Garry. Oxford Univ. Press 1997 479p $35

ISBN 0-19-509547-2

LC 97-19789

"The stories treat the human dimension of the law, focusing on the institutions, legal rules, and legal actors. . . . The wide range of situations, predicaments, and interpretation make this a fascinating compilation." Libr J

Includes index

Trigiani, Adriana

Big Cherry Holler; a Big Stone Gap novel. Random House 2001 272p

ISBN 0-375-50617-9

LC 2001-18599

"Although readers of Big Stone Gap are going to find this novel more serious, they should rest assured that most of the old favorite small town characters are still there. Catching an earful, usually unsolicited, of their views and advice on life, marriage, and love is a part of the charm of both the predecessor and this follow-up." Booklist

Trigiani, Adriana

Big Stone Gap; a novel. Random House 2000 272p

ISBN 0-375-50403-6

LC 99-43306

"One chapter, which is based on a real-life campaign visit from John Warner and his then-wife Elizabeth Taylor is a hoot. And you don't want to miss Ave Maria's friend, the sexy Iva Lou Wade, one of the best fictional librarians to come along in years." Libr J

Trigiani, Adriana

Milk glass moon; a Big Stone Gap novel. Random House 2002 256p

ISBN 0-375-50618-7

LC 2002-17945

"The folksy dialogue and unabashed sentimentalism can be cloying, but Ave's astringent insights and critical self-appraisal sharpen the tale." Publ Wkly

Trigiani, Adriana

Very Valentine. HarperCollins Publishers 2009 371p $25.95

ISBN 978-0-06-125705-6; 0-06-125705-2

LC 2008-34314

In this first book in a projected trilogy, Valentine Roncalli struggles to save her decades-old family business, finding love and the life she wants along the way.

"Food, shoes and romance feature prominently in this zesty novel of an Italian-American family. . . . Rich descriptions of beautiful things—a Greenwich Village rooftop garden, the Blue Grotto of Capri, a bounty of well-made meals, sexy men in sweaters—create a (not quite) fairy tale of guilty pleasures." Kirkus

Trollope, Anthony

★ **Barchester** Towers. Knopf 1992 xxxiii, 277p (Chronicles of Barsetshire) $20

ISBN 0-679-40587-9

LC 91-53197

First published 1857. Second of the Chronicles of Barsetshire

"Continues the picture of clerical society with its peculiar humors and foibles. The chief incidents are connected with the appointment of a new bishop, the troubles and disappointments this involves, and the intrigues and jealousies of the clergy: the henpecked bishop, the ambitious archdeacon, and the dean, canons, and others, with their wives. The picture of the eccentric Stanhope family is particularly delicious." Lenrow. Reader's Guide to Prose Fic

Followed by Doctor Thorne

Trollope, Anthony
Can you forgive her? with an introduction by A.O.J. Cockshut. Knopf 1994 xxxiii, 447p $23
ISBN 0-679-43595-6
LC 94-6553
First published 1864-65
This first of the Palliser novels "tells the interwoven stories of two women, Alice Vavasor and Lady Glencora M'Cluskie, who struggle to come to terms with the choices available to them concerning marriage." Merriam-Webster's Ency of Lit

Trollope, Anthony
The **complete** shorter fiction; edited by Julian Thompson. Carroll & Graf Pubs. 1992 959p

Trollope, Anthony
Doctor Thorne; with an introduction by N. John Hall. Knopf 1993 xxxi, 319p (Chronicles of Barsetshire) $20
ISBN 0-679-42304-4
LC 93-1853
First published 1858. Third of the Chronicles of Barsetshire
"A story of quiet country life; and the interest of the book lies in the character studies rather than in the plot. The scene is laid in the west of England about 1854. The heroine, Mary Thorne, is a sweet, modest girl, living with her kind uncle Doctor Thorne, in the village of Greshambury, where Frank Gresham, the young heir of Greshambury Park, falls in love with her." Keller. Reader's Dig of Books
Followed by Framley parsonage

Trollope, Anthony
★ The **Eustace** diamonds. Knopf 1992 xxxi, 249p $20
ISBN 0-679-41745-1
LC 92-52910
First published 1872
The third Palliser novel. "The story follows two contrasting women and their courtships. Lizzie Eustace and Lucy Morris are both hampered in their love affairs by their lack of money. Lizzie's trickery and deceit, however, contrast with Lucy's constancy. Trollope was understood to be commenting on the malaise in Victorian England that allowed a character like Lizzie, who marries for money, steals the family diamonds, and behaves despicably throughout, to rise unscathed in society." Merriam-Webster's Ency of Lit

Trollope, Anthony
Framley parsonage; with an introduction by Graham Handley. Knopf 1994 xxxi, 587p (Chronicles of Barsetshire) $20
ISBN 0-679-43133-0
First published 1861. Fourth of the Chronicles of Barsetshire
"The vicar of Framley, a weak but honest young man, is led astray and into debt by a spendthrift M. P., and finds himself in a false position. The other branch of the story deals with his sister's chequered love affair and marriage to young Lord Lufton. A great crowd of characters are engaged in the social functions, the intrigues and the match making, the general effect of which is comic, though graver interest is never far off, and there are situations of deepest pathos." Baker. Guide to the Best Fic
Followed by The small house at Allington

Trollope, Anthony
The **last** chronicle of Barset; with an introduction by Graham Handley. Knopf 1995 xxix, 983p (Chronicles of Barsetshire) $24
ISBN 0-679-44366-5
LC 95-75205
First published 1867. Sixth in the Chronicles of Barsetshire
"The ecclesiastical society of 'The Warden,' Mr. Harding, Mrs. Proudie, and the rest make their last appearance. The dominant situation is one of intense anguish. A poor country clergyman, proud, learned, sternly conscientious is accused of a felony, and the pressure of family want makes his guilt seem only too probable." Baker. Guide to the Best Fic

Trollope, Anthony
The **Pallisers**; abridged and introduced by Michael Hardwick. Coward, McCann & Geoghegan 1975 436p
One volume abridgment of six "parliamentary novels"

Trollope, Anthony
★ The **prime** minister. Oxford University Press 2009 xxiv, 438p il (Oxford world's classics) pa $14.95
ISBN 978-0-19-953775-4; 0-19-953775-5
First published 1876
"Considered by modern critics to represent the apex of the 'Palliser novels', it is the fifth in the series and sustains two plot lines. One records the clash between the Duke of Omnium, now prime minister of a coalition government, and his high-spirited wife, Lady Glencora, whose drive to become the most brilliant hostess in society causes embarrassment for her husband and eventually contributes to his downfall. The second plot reveals the machinations of Ferdinand Lopez, an ambitious social climber who wins the support of Lady Glencora—but not her husband—for an election campaign. The novel brilliantly dissects the politics of both marriage and government." Merriam-Webster's Ency of Lit

Trollope, Anthony
The **small** house at Allington; with an introduction by A.O.J. Cockshut. Knopf 1997 xxix, 740p (Chronicles of Barsetshire) $23
ISBN 0-375-40067-2
"Country life, its quiet, its pleasures and troubles, monotony and dullness, and with digressions into boarding-house life in London and into high society. Many old friends appear in the usual concourse of characters, among whom stand out Mr. Crosbie, a snobbish and cowardly trifler. . . . Lily Dale, the jilted maiden, amiable and weak Johnny Eames, and the aristocratic doll, Lady Dumbello; all closely copied from life." Baker. Guide to the Best Fic

Followed by The last chronicle of Barset

Trollope, Anthony

The **warden**; introduction by Louis Auchincloss; notes by Andrew Maunder. Modern Library 2003 230p (Chronicles of Barsetshire) pa $11

    ISBN 0-8129-6704-6

                              LC 2002-24533

First published 1855. First of the Chronicles of Barsetshire

"The Reverend Septimus Harding, the conscientious warden of a charitable retirement home for men, resigns after being accused of making too much profit from the sinecure." Merriam-Webster's Ency of Lit

Includes bibliographical references

Followed by Barchester Towers

Trollope, Joanna

The **best** of friends. Viking 1998 293p $23.95

    ISBN 0-670-87973-8

                              LC 97-49162

First published 1995 in the United Kingdom

"Trollope's facility at spinning an intricate story is enhanced by light-fingered dialogue, and the lesson she spins in this tale of easy pleasure and its complicated aftermath is both sobering and hopeful." Publ Wkly

Trollope, Joanna

Brother and sister. Bloomsbury 2004 311p $23.95

    ISBN 1-582-34400-0

                              LC 2003-62649

"Trollope is a pointillist of domestic relationships, and she has built an impressive body of work addressing powerful tensions like those that animate Brother and Sister. With well-placed strokes, she brings to life all of her characters, including the complex lives of the birth mothers. She's especially accomplished in her portrayals of children by turns humorous, frustrating or heartbreaking, but never precious." Washington Post Book World

Trollope, Joanna

★ The **choir**. Random House 1995 261p

                              LC 95-11612

First published 1993 in the United Kingdom

"The all-boy choir at Aldminster Cathedral is blessed with a cheerfully ferocious choirmaster, a magnificent seventeenth-century organ, and a celestial new treble in the earthly guise of eleven-year-old Henry Ashworth. But the choir also costs the diocese more than fifty thousand pounds a year, which the dean thinks might be better spent elsewhere—on new lighting, perhaps—and a delicious cathedral-town battle about tradition and privilege ensues. Almost all the characters in this companionable novel are on speaking terms with God, but His will, while frequently consulted, is variously interpreted." New Yorker

Trollope, Joanna

Friday nights; a novel. Bloomsbury 2008 330p $24.99

    ISBN 978-1-59691-407-0; 1-59691-407-6

                              LC 2007-37579

"Retiree Eleanor often sees Paula and Lindsay, two harried young mothers, passing on the street and decides they should have time to relax. Paula and Lindsay, who have never met each other before, turn down Eleanor's offer of babysitting but are flustered enough to accept her invitation to visit her one Friday evening. The group soon expands to include Blaise, Eleanor's neighbor; Karen, Blaise's coworker; and Jules, Lindsay's younger sister. Trollope outlines each woman's history, deftly interweaving their individual stories with those of the new connections growing among them. When Paula begins dating Jackson Miller, the equilibrium of the group is altered, and as Jackson becomes a part of all of their lives, events occur that will change the group forever. Trollope's novel rings true, portraying the complexities of contemporary women's lives without sentimentality or melodrama." Libr J

Trollope, Joanna

Legacy of love; {by} Joanna Trollope writing as Caroline Harvey. Viking 2000 385p

    ISBN 0-670-89181-9

                              LC 00-36791

"A novel in three parts featuring three generations of daring Englishwomen from the same family who challenge societal mores to pursue love and passion. Although unexceptional in its writing and plot, the book reveals Harvey's vast knowledge of travel and history, from Victorian England and British-ruled Afghanistan to World War II." Libr J

Trollope, Joanna

Marrying the mistress. Viking 2000 293p

    ISBN 0-670-89150-9

                              LC 99-462175

"None of the themes here . . . are terribly unusual, but Trollope's proven ability to present them intelligently, as moral and emotional tangles faced by thinking, interesting people, satisfyingly combines the universally recognizable and the intellectually engaging." Publ Wkly

Trollope, Joanna

The **men** and the girls. Random House 1993 248p

                              LC 93-18421

First published 1992 in the United Kingdom

"One of the pleasures in good contemporary British fiction like 'The Men and the Girls' is the writing itself—deft, fluid, perceptive and concise. Another is the wonderfully wry humor, particularly when its objects are sacred cows. Like Muriel Spark, Joanna Trollope is hilarious about old people, for instance." N Y Times Book Rev

Trollope, Joanna

Next of kin. Viking 2001 289p $23.95

    ISBN 0-670-89999-2

                              LC 2001-17743

"In addition to crafting an absorbing narrative, Trollope charms with her depiction of several young children, whose speech and behavior are captured with clarity and endearing fidelity." Publ Wkly

Trollope, Joanna

The **other** family. Simon & Schuster 2010 321p pa $15

ISBN 978-1-4391-2983-8

LC 2010-00529

"Richie Rossiter is an aging crooner with a shrinking yet substantial fan base. He lives in London with Chrissie, his beautiful, common-law wife, 20 years his junior. Chrissie has been managing his career for 25 years, ever since they embarked on the affair that demolished his marriage. Only Richie never legally ended his marriage. Even after raising three daughters with Chrissie, he has refused to propose. Chrissie has been comforting herself with the knowledge that he hardly thinks of his wife and their son. But when Richie dies suddenly of a heart attack, she learns the truth. Richie has left his first family the lion's share of his musical estate, which includes a beautiful Steinway piano, his prized possession. The novel brilliantly explores the fallout of Richie's will." Globe and Mail

Trollope, Joanna

★ **Other** people's children. Viking 1999 294p $23.95

ISBN 0-670-88513-4

LC 98-40004

"Falling in love with a man does not mean falling in love with his children: that is the premise of this story of linked and sundered families. Josie's second marriage includes three stepchildren, whose loyalty to their inadequate mother makes them hate Josie for her very competence; Elizabeth's beloved fiancé comes with a son she adores and a grown daughter determined to oust her. Trollope may not aim high, but she aims for the heart, and she hits it." New Yorker

Trollope, Joanna

★ The **rector's** wife. Random House 1994 287p

LC 94-20625

First published 1991 in the United Kingdom

The provincial English "rector in The Rector's Wife, Peter Bouverie, has spent his life and defined his ministry according to what other people think, and he expects his family to do the same. . . . The turning point comes early in the story, when Peter is passed over for a much hoped-for appointment to the position of archdeacon. When his career hits dead end, it becomes bitterly clear that he has no inner resources or satisfying relationships to fall back on. In his marriage and ministry, Peter has dried up. Anna, too, is on the verge of either drying up or going mad. As her frustration deepens over Peter's disappointment and the estrangement between them, she decides to change her life. She begins to carve out small spaces of independence from the parish by transferring their daughter to a Catholic school, taking a job at a local supermarket and, finally, seeking the love absent in her marriage with the brother of the new archdeacon." Christ Century

Trollope, Joanna

Second honeymoon; a novel. Bloomsbury 2006 323p $23.95

ISBN 978-1-59691-038-6; 1-59691-038-0

LC 2005-57011

The author "excels at middle-class family dramas, and [this] is a welcome entry in her canon. Like an overzealous housewife who just can't step away from the vacuum, she succumbs to the impulse to tidy up all the subplots. But Edie, Russell, and their brood are winning enough that fans will want to move in right along with the kids." Christ Sci Monit

Trollope, Joanna

A **Spanish** lover. Random House 1996 334p

ISBN 978-0679425861

LC 96-24846

First published 1993 in the United Kingdom

"Lizzie has been rather smug about her thriving marriage, her four children, her successful shop, and her big house, but she becomes unconscionably jealous when Frances, her quiet, devoted twin, finds love with the sexy, supportive, but married—and foreign—Luis. This British author excels at setting up the stuff of female fantasy and, from those worn materials, making something that draws you in and slams you with a thud of emotion so authentic it becomes your own." New Yorker

Tropper, Jonathan

How to talk to a widower. Delacorte Press 2007 341p $20

ISBN 978-0-385-33890-5; 0-385-33890-2

LC 2006-28678

"Since magazine columnist Doug Parker's wife died in a plane crash one year ago, he's been caught in the whirlpool of his grief. The bigger world, though, is trying to pull him back out. Doug's teen stepson is getting into trouble at school, and his little sister is getting married soon. Meanwhile, his other sister is trying to set him up with every woman in town. What ensues is equal parts hilarity and despair—often, both at once. As always, Jonathan Tropper cares deeply for his characters, warts and all, and writes very sweetly about the fragile yet resilient world they inhabit." PopMatters

Tropper, Jonathan

One last thing before I go; a novel. Jonathan Tropper. Dutton 2012 324 p.

ISBN 0525952365; 9780525952367

LC 2012019370

In this novel by John Tropper "Drew Silver is dying in many ways: his marriage has been over for seven years, his ex-wife is getting remarried, his career as a rock drummer is long past, his 18-year-old daughter is pregnant, and he has a life-threatening heart condition. . . . [T]he awareness of his precarious health causes him to rethink his pathetic life, and he's able to come up with a to-do list. . . . By the end of the novel he's able to cross almost everything off." (Kirkus)

Trotter, William R.

The **sands** of pride; a novel of the Civil War. Carroll & Graf Pubs. 2002 754p $28

ISBN 0-7867-1013-6

LC 2002-22697

"Opening on New Year's Eve 1860, almost six months before North Carolina's grudging decision to secede from the Union of May 20, 1861, this sprawling account revolves around the bustling seaport of Wilmington, which serves as the lifeline of the Confederacy, Jefferson Davis; the architect of Fort Fisher, Col. William Lamb; Lafayette Baker, deputy director of the fledgling Secret Service; Gen. Robert E. Lee; Gen. Ambrose Burnside; and the naval commander William Barker Cushing are some of the real-life historic figures that are artfully integrated with an extensive dramatis personae of flamboyant and idiosyncratic fictional character." Publ Wkly

Trueblood, Valerie

Seven loves; a novel. Little, Brown and Co. 2006 232p $23.95

ISBN 978-0-316-05893-3

LC 2005-26604

This "novel follows the story of 74-year-old May Nilsson, a retired English teacher and widow, who finds herself belonging to the country of old women and reminiscing on a past defined by love. May remembers the difficult and pleasurable years of her marriage to a doctor as well as the excitement and pain of an extramarital affair. She reflects on a young coworker's elementary nature, her son's capriciousness, and her mother's political convictions. Each chapter presents an impressionistic view of May's family, friends, and lovers and their varying degrees of longing and happiness. Gently told, Trueblood's first work is poetic, contemplative, and tender." Booklist

Truman, Margaret

Murder at Ford's Theatre. Ballantine Bks. 2002 326p $24.95

ISBN 0-345-44489-2

LC 2002-74748

"When the body of congressional intern Nadia Zarinski turns up outside the stage door of Ford's Theatre, D.C. police detectives Mo Johnson and Rick Klayman, who happens to be a Lincoln buff, are assigned the case. Nadia worked in the office of Senator Bruce Lerner, ex-husband of Clarise Emerson, head of Ford's Theatre and nominee for chair of the National Endowment for the Arts. Once Clarise determines with Klayman's help that her son, Jeremiah, was the last to see Nadia alive, she appeals to former attorney Mackensie 'Mac' Smith to represent him." Publ Wkly

Truman, Margaret

Murder at the Library of Congress. Random House 1999 322p $25

ISBN 0-375-50068-5

LC 99-14953

"Pre-Columbian art expert Annabel Smith has been asked to write an article on a second diary of Columbus' voyage—if such an artifact really exists. Her research takes her into the inner workings of LC and leads to the discovery of illicit payoffs and the solutions to a pair of murders, one old, one new." Booklist

Truman, Margaret

Murder in the White House; a novel. Arbor House 1980 235p

LC 79-54004

"When Secretary of State Blaine is murdered in the Lincoln Sitting Room of the White House, President Webster orders Special Counsel Fairchild to coordinate efforts to solve the case with the authorities. The lawyer turned detective begins investigating everyone with access to the White House, including Webster, the First Lady and her daughter Lynne." Publ Wkly

Truman, Margaret

Murder on Capitol Hill; a novel. Arbor House 1981 255p

LC 80-70223

"Lawyer Lydia James agrees to the request of Veronica Caldwell to act as counsel for the senatorial committee investigating the killing of her husband, Senate Majority leader Cale Caldwell. He has been stabbed at a reception honoring him, where his black-sheep son Mark, member of a fanatical cult, is among the 200 or more guests. Mark is arrested for the murder, and also on suspicion of having killed Jimmye, Veronica's niece, years earlier, an unsolved crime. His mother and brother, Cale Jr., sorrowfully agree that Mark is guilty, but Lydia believes the charges are trumped up. She gets herself into dicey situations, chasing clues." Publ Wkly

Trumbo, Dalton

★ **Johnny** got his gun. Lippincott 1939 309p

"Far more than an antiwar polemic, this compassionate description of the effects of war on one soldier is a poignant tribute to the human instinct to survive. Badly mutilated, blind, and deaf, Johnny fights to communicate with an uncomprehending medical world debating his fate." Shapiro. Fic for Youth. 3d edition

Truong, Monique T. D.

Bitter in the mouth; a novel. [by] Monique Truong. Random House 2010 282p $25

ISBN 978-1-4000-6908-8; 1-4000-6908-4

LC 2009051674

A personal tragedy compels Linda to return to Boiling Springs, North Carolina, and spend time with her family.

"Linda, a young woman coming of age in small-town North Carolina, has a fascinating condition—one that causes her to 'taste' the words she hears. It forces her to struggle through a distracting bombardment of flavors like canned green beans, sour cream, parsnips and Fruit Stripe gum. But Linda's relationship with food and language soon becomes quirky background music when compared with the relationships she has with the people in her life, including her overweight childhood best friend, her doting gay uncle, her first secret affair and her oddly distant mother. . . . Truong's narrative yanks the reader through Linda's world swiftly and with impressive command." Time Out N Y

Truong, Monique T. D.

The **book** of salt; [by] Monique Truong. Houghton Mifflin 2003 261p $24

ISBN 0-618-30400-2

LC 2002-192152

"Truong is tapping some trendy territory here: the post-colonial perspective; the book derived from a minor character in another well-known book. . .; the gay novel; the novel of exile. And Truong's central character, the gay Asian houseboy, is something of a stereotype in itself. But nothing in this distinctive novel feels secondhand." N Y Times Book Rev

Truscott, Lucian K.

Heart of war. Dutton 1997 370p

ISBN 978-0525941170

LC 96-29876

"Despite some occasionally breathy prose, Truscott's novel provides a fascinating peek behind the olive drab curtain, blending a solid plot with a piercing critique of hypocrisy, power politics and sexual misconduct in today's armed forces." N Y Times Book Rev

Trussoni, Danielle

Angelology. Viking 2010 451p $27.95

ISBN 978-0-670-02147-5; 0-570-2147-4

LC 2009-41430

"Sister Evangeline, the secretary who handles all inquiries concerning the archives of angel arcana at an upstate New York convent, receives a letter from researcher V.A. Verlaine inquiring about an unknown link between the convent and philanthropist Abigail Rockefeller dating to 1943. It turns out that the Rockefellers were interested in a legendary artifact associated with an order of fallen angels. That priceless artifact is coveted by Verlaine's employer, Percival Grigori, a Nephilim—offspring of the union between mortal and angel parents—who will stop at nothing to retrieve it for the awesome power it will give his race over humanity." Publ Wkly

"An ambitious adventure story with enough literary heft and religious fervor to satisfy anyone able to embrace its imaginative conceits and Byzantine plot." Kirkus

Trussoni, Danielle

Angelopolis; Danielle Trussoni. Penguin Group USA 2013 320 p. (hardcover) $27.95

ISBN 0670025542; 9780670025541

LC 2013001515

In this novel, by Danielle Trussoni, "now an elite angel hunter for the Society of Angelology, [Verlaine] pursues his mission with single-minded devotion: to capture, imprison, and eliminate . . . [half-angels]. But when Evangeline suddenly appears on a twilit Paris street, Verlaine finds her nature to be unlike any of the other creatures he so mercilessly pursues, casting him into a spiral of doubt and confusion." (Publisher's note)

"Trussoni's unevenly paced second offering is not quite up to the standards set by her debut novel. Exciting skirmishes and conflicts are dragged down by extensive historical explanations, and the introduction of a new major character falls flat. Despite the inconsistencies, devotees of Trussoni's first novel will enjoy this continuation of the crusade to save humankind." LJ

Tryon, Thomas

In the fire of spring. Knopf 1991 609p

LC 91-414

In this sequel to The wings of the morning "a runaway slave, Rose Mills, is helped to safety by the abolitionist Appleton Talcott and two of his daughters as they return home to Pequot Landing. . . . The Talcotts and the slave-owning Grimes family are still feuding, but it's now 1841, and fuel has been added to the fire. First of all, the Talcotts open a school for young black women, which gives the Grimeses something new to holler about. Second, Appleton's wife, Mabel Talcott, is secretly dying. As she ponders her mortal-

ity and worries about her children, her dying wish is granted: daughter Aurora, abroad for years with husband and child, returns home. Mab's heart breaks as she learns of her daughter's travails and of her undying love for the true father of her child—none other than the swashbuckling, lady-killing Sinjin Grimes." Booklist

Tryon, Thomas

★ The **other**. Knopf 1971 280p

"Bizarre events occur in and around the once-prosperous Perry family in Connecticut during the 1930s. The men have all died mysteriously and brutally. Niles and Holland, 12-year-old twins, seem to be linked to the ghastly deaths and disasters. A compassionate Russian grandmother plays along with Niles's deception and tries to protect him." Shapiro. Fic for Youth. 3d edition

Tryon, Thomas

The **wings** of the morning. Knopf 1990 567p

LC 89-39513

"Unalloyed pleasure for fans of this genre, Tryon's literate 19th-century soap opera is steeped in the rhythms of Trollope and Scott." Publ Wkly

Followed by In the fire of spring

Tsan-hsueh

Blue light in the sky & other stories; [by] Can Xue; translated by Karen Gernant and Chen Zeping. New Directions 2006 212p pa $14.95

ISBN 978-0-8112-1648-7; 0-8112-1648-9

LC 2006-9091

Can Xue "writes in the artless prose of fairy tales and employs a curious dreamlike logic in her narratives. Characters witness grotesque illnesses, dodge natural catastrophes and endlessly wander through dark labyrinths of misunderstanding. . . . [One of her narrator's] says of fishing nets, 'Only a random string is needed-the less related, the better,' and it's a deft description of Can Xue's eccentric storytelling." Publ Wkly

Tsiolkas, Christos

The **slap**. Penguin Books 2010 482p $15

ISBN 9780143117148; 0-14-311714-9 pa

LC 2009-50139

"In The Slap we live for a few short weeks in suburban Australia, learning the language, becoming intimate with the characters and experiencing their customs. But finally the novel transcends both suburban Melbourne and the Australian continent, leaving us exhausted but gasping with admiration." Washington Post Book World

Tsukiyama, Gail

Dreaming water. St. Martin's Press 2002 288p $23.95

ISBN 0-312-20607-0

LC 2001-58896

"At 38, Hana Murayama is dying of Werner's syndrome, a genetic defect that causes premature aging. Hana is almost totally dependent on her mother, Cata, who at 62 is still recovering from the sudden death of her husband, Max. . . . Over the course of two days, Hana and Cate retrace in memory their lives and Max's. Their scattered and sometimes conflicting expectations are brought into sharp focus when Hana's best friend, Laura, now a successful East Coast lawyer, arrives with her two daughters, Hana's godchildren, allowing Hana and Cate to find a measure of the reconciliation that has eluded them." Publ Wkly

Tsukiyama, Gail

The **street** of a thousand blossoms. St. Martin's Press 2007 422p $24.95

ISBN 978-0-312-27482-5; 0-312-27482-3

LC 2007-21012

"Set in Japan and spanning over 25 years (1939-66), the novel unravels the hardships and triumphs of two brothers raised by their loving maternal grandparents following the loss of their parents in a tragic accident. The dreams of older brother Hiroshi of becoming a sumotori (a sumo wrestler) and younger brother Kenji of becoming a Noh theater mask artisan are quelled by the onset of World War II. Passages describing the devastation wrought by the atomic bombings upon their lives and of those close to them, particularly the family of sisters Haru and Aki, who later becomes Hiroshi's wife, are well written and emotionally gripping." Libr J

Tsypkin, Leonid

★ **Summer** in Baden-Baden; a novel. translated from the Russian by Roger and Angela Keys; introduction by Susan Sontag. New Directions 2001 xxi, 146p $23.95

ISBN 0-8112-1484-2

LC 2001-32658

Originally serialized 1982 in Russian emigré weekly; this translation first published 1987 in the United Kingdom

"Tsypkin's stream-of-consciousness prose style is associative, inclusive, allusive, detached and yet humane." N Y Times Book Rev

Tuck, Lily

I married you for happiness. Atlantic Monthly Press 2011 193p $24

ISBN 978-0-8021-1991-9; 0-8021-1991-3

"This slim, magnificent novel is rarefied by its heart-breaking immediacy, and the moving, aching stream of consciousness chronicles not only the psychology of shock and mourning, but also the minute-by-minute way in which Nine begins to put life as she knows it in the past tense." BookPage

Tucker, Todd

Over and under. Thomas Dunne Books/St. Martin's Press 2008 275p $23.95

ISBN 978-0-312-37990-2; 0-312-37990-0

LC 2008-12472

"A bitter 1979 labor strike at southern Indiana's Borden Casket Company serves as the volatile backdrop for this haunting coming-of-age novel. . . . With their fathers on opposite sides of the dispute, Andrew Jackson Gray and Thomas Jefferson Kruer, both 14, learn there is more to life than exploring caves, shooting targets with their prized M-6 Scout rifles and sneaking out on starry nights to run through the woods. . . . Tucker convincingly makes Andy's voice at once eloquent and gritty, and makes the rural Indiana landscape palpable." Publ Wkly

Tuomainen, Antti

The **healer**; Antti Tuomainen; translated from the Finnish by Lola Rogers. 1st ed. Henry Holt and Co. 2013 224 p. (hardcover) $26

ISBN 0802777511; 9780805095548

LC 2012027372

In this novel, by Antti Tuomainen, "Helsinki is battling a ruthless climate catastrophe. . . . The authorities have issued warnings about malaria, tuberculosis, Ebola, and the plague. . . . When Tapani's beloved wife, Johanna, a newspaper journalist, goes missing, he embarks on a frantic hunt for her. Johanna's disappearance seems to be connected to a story she was researching about a politically motivated serial killer known as 'The Healer.'" (Publisher's note)

Turgenev, Ivan Sergeevich

★ **Fathers** and sons; a new translation by Michael R. Katz. Norton 1994 157p $25

ISBN 0-393-03559-X

LC 92-40010

Original Russian edition, 1862. Variant title: Fathers and children

This novel "concerns the inevitable conflict between generations and between the values of traditionalists and intellectuals. The physician Bazarov, the novel's protagonist, is the most powerful of Turgenev's creations. He is a nihilist, denying the validity of all laws save those of the natural sciences. Uncouth and forthright in his opinions, he is nonetheless susceptible to love and by that fact doomed to unhappiness. In sociopolitical terms he represents the victory of the revolutionary nongentry intelligentsia over the gentry intelligentsia to which Turgenev belonged." Merriam-Webster's Ency of Lit

Turgenev, Ivan Sergeevich

First love and other stories; {by} Ivan Turgenev; translated by Isaiah Berlin and Leonard Schapiro; introduced by V.S. Pritcett. Knopf 1994 xxxvii, 253p $17

ISBN 0-679-43594-8

LC 94-6233

Turgenev, Ivan Sergeevich

★ The **torrents** of spring; [by] Ivan Turgenev; illustrated by Valentin Popov; translated by Ivy and Tatiana Litvonov. Grove Press 1996 174p il $25

ISBN 0-8021-1594-2

LC 96-14697

Original Russian edition, 1872. Variant title: Spring torrents

This classic Russian novel "is a love story beautifully and simply told: a young Russian nobleman, Dimitry Sanin, falls in love with a pure and sweet girl, Gemma, but through unforeseen circumstances and his own weakness he forsakes her for a sensual woman of the world, Maria Nikolayevna, for whom men are mere playthings of the moment. He does so in spite of being fully aware that this liaison will bring him nothing but ruin and humiliation. . . . This short novel has no political overtones and deals only with the emotional experiences of the characters." Libr J

Turner, Frederick W.

★ **1929**; [by] Frederick Turner. Counterpoint Bks. 2003 390p $25

ISBN 1-58243-265-1

LC 2002-154007

"Written in a period-appropriate overheated, romantic prose, and incorporating memorable appearances by Capone, Bing Crosby, Maurice Ravel, Paul Whiteman, and Clara Bow, the book is by turns corny, intoxicating, and ineffably sad, like the 'hot' music it is designed to evoke." New Yorker

Turner, Frederick W.

The **go**-between; a novel of the Kennedy years. [by] Frederick Turner. Houghton Mifflin Harcourt 2010 324p

ISBN 978-0-15-101509-2; 0-15-101509-0

LC 2009-36908

"No shortage of fireworks here, obviously. However, if Turner appears to have drawn his story line from the tabloid press, his approach in The Go-Between will defy any expectations that our author is interested in dishing the dirt. Instead of kiss-and-tell, we get a very acute psychological novel, one that probes deeply into motives and misgivings, and never settles for the merely tawdry." PopMatters

Turner, Frederick W.

Redemption. Harcourt 2006 348p $24

ISBN 978-0-15-101470-5; 0-15-101470-1

LC 2006-9241

"Turner's slow, humid tale, punctuated by indescribable violence, sexual and otherwise, unrolls in 1913, along the streets of Storyville, New Orleans. Every night, Francis Muldoon, a.k.a Fast-Mail, a former cop whose gunshot injury has put him out of commission, keeps an eye on business for Tom Anderson, whose fiefdom extends from swank saloons to two-bit whorehouses. Turner's subject is the way a district's history of poverty, defilement, and petty retribution can coexist with, and be elevated by, its trade in beauty and every kind of physical and spiritual release." New Yorker

Turner, Nancy E.

These is my words; the diary of Sarah Agnes Prine, 1881-1901. ReganBooks 1998 384p $23

ISBN 0-06-039225-8

LC 97-37622

"Based on the real-life exploits of the author's great-grandmother, this fictionalized diary . . . details one woman's struggles with life and love in frontier Arizona at the end of the last century. When she begins recording her life, Sarah Prine is an intelligent, headstrong 18-year-old capable of holding her own on her family's settlement near Tucson. Her skill with a rifle fends off a constant barrage of Indian attacks and outlaw assaults. it also attracts a handsome Army captain named Jack Elliot. By the time she's 21, Sarah has recorded her loveless marriage to a family friend, the establishment of a profitable ranch, the birth of her first child—and the death of her husband. The love between Jack and Sarah, which dominates the rest of the tale, has begun to blossom." Publ Wkly

"The language is rich and fine, sounding true to its time without being precious." Booklist

Turner, Nikki

Ghetto superstar; a novel. Nikki Turner. One World/Ballantine Books 2009 x, 262 p.p (pbk.) $14

ISBN 0345493893; 9780345493897

LC 2009279701

In this book, "Fabiola Mays was born to sing . . . , but one heartbreaking setback after another threatens to derail her dreams of a recording deal. To make matters worse, it's Christmastime, rent is past due, and the cops intend to kick her tight-knit family to the curb—until a small-town gangster comes to the rescue and offers them a place to stay. Years pass, and Fabiola continues to play gigs and travel around the country hoping for another shot at fame." (Publisher's note)

Turner, Nikki

Heartbreak of a hustler's wife; a novel. Nikki Turner. One World Trade Paperbacks 2011 x, 212 p.p

ISBN 0345511085; 9780345511089; 9780345526403

LC 2011001780

In his novel, "the fourth installment of [Nikki] Turner's . . . series (after 'Forever a Hustler's Wife'), hustler Desmond 'Des' Taylor has found a new gig raking in the money as head of the Good Life Ministry, to the dismay of his wife, Yarni. Not only does the once-wild hustler's wife have moral qualms, but as an attorney, she's gaining a new respect for the consequences of crime. Then masked men hold up a church service, gun down one of Des's closest associates, and force his accountant to wire them $10 million. Threats also mount against Yarni, their young daughter, and Des's mother, in violation of the gangsta code. Meanwhile, his previously unsuspected 18-year-old daughter turns up and announces she needs to move in with them." (Publishers Weekly)

Turner, Nikki

Natural born hustler; a novel. Nikki Turner. One World Trade Paperbacks/Ballantine Books 2010 xi, 114 p.p

ISBN 9780345523600

LC 2010022021

In this novel, "Desember Day is beautiful, confident, and smart. . . . But . . . her love for [her boyfriend] Fame can't stand in the way of Desember selling anything and everything . . . so that she never has to depend on a man. The only thing Desember feels she's lacking is a father to call her own. And her mother refuses to tell Desember who he is. When Fame finds himself at the wrong end of a gun . . . Desember wants nothing more than to stand by her man, but Fame warns her . . . that she isn't safe. Desember wonders if she was the real target. Her mother . . . arranges for her daughter to travel to Richmond, Virginia, to live with Desember's father and his wife. And when her father's identity is finally revealed, Desember learns that she is a Natural Born Hustler." (Publisher's note)

Turow, Scott

The **burden** of proof. Farrar, Straus & Giroux 1990 515p $22.95

ISBN 0-374-11734-9

LC 90-33593

"The plotting is clear and clean, spun out with Greek inevitability and the niceties of law and finance are lucidly, smoothly, explained. Stern's complex character is well-drawn . . . and the members of his family are individualized and believable. The Federal judges and prosecutors have unique backgrounds and prejudices. Even the minor characters are given faces and personalities." America

Turow, Scott

★ **Innocent**. Grand Central Pub. 2010 406p $27.99

ISBN 978-0-446-56242-3; 0-446-56242-4

LC 2009-49544

Sequel to: Presumed innocent (1987)

"The writing is elegant, the characters lived-in, and the legal and trial details expertly rendered. It's the suspense, though, that will keep you reading. The narrative perspective and timeline jump around — first person for Rusty, his mistress, and his adult son; third person for Molto. None is perfectly reliable. They all have their prejudices and agendas. Turow's neatest trick is to plant small inconsistencies or omissions in their accounts. These pockets of doubt allow readers the satisfaction of detecting weaknesses and contradictions in the case before the characters do." Philadelphia Inquirer

Turow, Scott

The **laws** of our fathers. Farrar, Straus & Giroux 1996 533p $26.95

ISBN 0-374-18423-2

LC 96-16104

In this legal thriller, "the wife of a state senator has been killed in a drive-by shooting, and Judge Sonia Klonsky is presiding over the trial of the victim's son, who has been accused of masterminding the murder. Most of the protagonists have crossed paths decades before, when they were campus radicals, and there are some distinctly unconvincing flashbacks to the apocalyptic days of '69. Still, as the novel gathers momentum it reveals a complex portrait, in which children are forced to live in the shadow of their parents, and chastened middle-aged idealists must reckon with the enthusiasms and sins of their youth." New Yorker

Turow, Scott

Limitations. Picador 2006 197p pa $13

ISBN 978-0-312-42645-3; 0-312-42645-3

LC 2006-50345

First published in serial form in the New York Times Magazine

"The action centers on the fictional Kindle County in Illinois, and [Turow] revives some familiar characters, including George Mason from Personal Injuries and Rusty Sabich, the hero of . . . . Presumed Innocent. Mason is now an appellate judge, faced with the challenge of crafting the decision in a high-profile case involving a sexual assault that reawakens his long-suppressed guilt over his role in a similar incident decades before. To compound his inner turmoil, Mason finds himself the object of threatening e-mails from an unknown source. . . . Turow's writing is assured as ever." Publ Wkly

Turow, Scott

Ordinary heroes. Farrar, Straus & Giroux 2005 384p $25

ISBN 0-374-18421-6

LC 2005-11824

"Stewart Dubinsky is not especially close to his father, David Dubin. Even their names are different, yet David's death prompts Stewart to try and find out more about this enigmatic man. He uncovers some startling information: that his father was engaged to another woman before his mother, and that he was court-martialed during the Battle of the Bulge. Dubinsky decides to write a family history, starts digging, and uncovers a manuscript his father wrote about his war experiences that is alternately moving and horrifying, vindicating, and vilifying and shines light on a side of his parents that he never knew. While some of the historical facts presented are not 100 percent accurate, the book's emotional wallop more than justifies the literary license and should secure its place in the canon of World War II literature." Libr J

Turow, Scott

Personal injuries. Farrar, Straus & Giroux 1999 403p $27

ISBN 0-374-28194-7

LC 99-30829

"U.S. Attorney Stan Sennett has set his sights on a powerful group of corrupt judges, vowing to prosecute them at any cost. With the help of the FBI, he devises a set of legal traps designed to produce the evidence he needs to convict. The centerpiece of this subversion is Robbie Feaver, a Kindle County personal injury lawyer nabbed for tax evasion by Sennett. . . . Densely packed and tightly constructed, this tangle of human relationships and legal machinations will have Turow fans burning the midnight oil." SLJ

Turow, Scott

★ **Presumed** innocent. Farrar, Straus & Giroux 1987 431p

ISBN 0-374-23713-1

LC 87-368

This is a "courtroom novel about a prosecuting attorney who is charged with the murder of a female colleague with whom he once had an affair." (Christ Sci Monit)

"Rusty Sabich, the chief deputy prosecuting attorney assigned to investigate the murder of his co-worker and former lover, Carolyn Polhemus, is the narrator who draws us into the world of big-city crime and law enforcement as seen through a lawyer's eyes. Because his boss, Raymond Horgan, the Prosecuting Attorney in this unnamed Midwestern city, is up for re-election, Carolyn's murder has become a political issue, and the heat is on Rusty to bring in the killer as soon as he can." N Y Times Book Rev

Turow, Scott

★ **Reversible** errors. Farrar, Straus & Giroux 2002 433p il $28

ISBN 0-374-28160-2

LC 2002-70891

"What Turow has done, in book after book, is to give us page turners that are also pleasing literary artifacts, mysteries that are also investigations into coomplex human emotions." N Y Times Book Rev

Tursten, Helene, 1954-

Night rounds; Helene Tursten; translation by Laura A. Wideburg. Soho Press 2012 326p.
ISBN 1616950064; 9781616950064
LC 2011034073

This "Scandinavian crime novel . . . [begins when] a nurse, Marianne Svärd, is found strangled at a small hospital in Göteborg after a blackout that also claimed the life of a patient who was on a respirator, [and] the night nurse on duty, Siv Persson, tells the police an incredible story. While the power was out, Persson claims she saw the ghost of a nurse who committed suicide in the hospital 50 years earlier after having an affair with a surgeon. While Huss and her team instantly dismiss a supernatural explanation, she becomes convinced that the motive for Svärd's slaying stems from the hospital's past." (Publishers Weekly)

Turtledove, Harry

The **big** switch. Del Rey/Ballantine Books 2011 418p (The war that came early) $27
ISBN 978-0-345-49186-2
LC 2011-02642

This "foray into alternate history is based on the premise that Chamberlain did not appease Hitler in 1938 and that World War II was thus launched a year early, before many of the Third Reich's superstructures were in place. As the war progresses slowly, the sudden death of a key player changes the game, and suddenly no one is certain where the lines of loyalty are drawn." Libr J

This "saga is not for the faint of heart or weak of stomach. It is for lovers of high-quality alternate history." Booklist

Turtledove, Harry

Into the darkness. Doherty Assocs. 1999 540p
ISBN 0-312-86895-2
LC 98-43610

First title in the author's Alternate world fantasy series. "In the beginning, militarily efficient Algarve occupies the Duchy of Bari . . . and is quickly followed by one of Algarve's traditional foes, Unkerlant. . . . Throughout, World War II buffs will search for further reflections in Turtledove's fantastic mirror, but they will also, like other readers, be quickly caught up in the sheer ingenuity of the tale, in which dragons provide airpower, behemoths (think rhinoceroses the size of elephants) are tanks, magic wands take the place of rifles, and submarine warfare is in the hands of leviathan-riders." Booklist

Turtledove, Harry

Rulers of the darkness. TOR Bks. 2002 576p il $27.95
ISBN 0-7653-0036-2
LC 2001-58465

Sequel to: Through the darkness

"The fourth volume of the alternate-history saga Darkness deals with the fourth year of a World War II. . . . Kuusamo's sorcerous Manhattan Project has the potential to generate destructive energy by drawing on the past and the future, which is the same way the Algarvians use the life energy of

murdered Kaunians. Meanwhile, more conventional counteroffensives against Algarve are in progress, with Unkerlant and Algarve reaching a gigantic confrontation in a battle recognizable as a re-imagining of the Battle of Kursk. One need not, however, be able to run down all of Turtledove's real-world parallels to appreciate how well he presents the human dilemmas of global warfare." Booklist

Tussing, Justin

The **best** people in the world. HarperCollins 2006 336p $24.95
ISBN 0-06-081533-7
LC 2005-46064

"The scenes between Alice and Thomas are almost absurdly lyrical and chaste. . . . But Tussing's indexes and inventories of Actual Things, circa 1972, are mercifully never more than a page or two away. At his best, Tussing is a kind of Wacko-Thoreau, and 'The Best People in the World' is one bright book of exuberant American life." N Y Times Book Rev

Twain, Mark, 1835-1910

★ The **adventures** of Huckleberry Finn. Modern Library 1993 xx, 433p $16.95
ISBN 0-679-42470-9
LC 92-51065

First published 1885. This is a companion volume to: The adventures of Tom Sawyer

This novel "begins with Huck's escape from his drunken, brutal father to the river, where he meets up with Jim, a runaway slave. The story of their journey downstream, with occasional forays into the society along the banks, is an American classic that captures the smells, rhythms, and sounds, the variety of dialects and the human activity of life on the great river. It is also a penetrating social commentary that reveals corruption, moral decay, and intellectual impoverishment through Huck and Jim's encounters with traveling actors and con men, lynch mobs, thieves, and Southern gentility." Reader's Ency. 4th edition

Twain, Mark

★ The **adventures** of Tom Sawyer; [illustrated by True W. Williams]; foreword and notes by John C. Gerber; text established by Paul Baender. University of California Press 2002 274p il pa $14.95
ISBN 0-520-23575-4
First published 1876. This is a companion volume to: The adventures of Huckleberry Finn

"Tom, a shrewd and adventurous boy, is at home in the respectable world of his Aunt Polly, as well as in the self-reliant, parentless world of Huck Finn. The two friends, out in the cemetery under a full moon, attempt to cure warts with a dead cat. They accidentally witness a murder, of which Muff Potter is later wrongly accused. Knowing that the true murderer is Injun Joe, the boys are helpless with fear; they decide to run away to Jackson's Island. After a few pleasant days of smoking and swearing, they realize that the townspeople believe them dead. Returning in time to hear their funeral eulogies, they become town heroes. At the trial of Muff Potter, Tom, unable to let an innocent person be condemned, reveals his knowledge. Injun Joe flees. Later Tom and his sweetheart, Becky Thatcher, get lost in the cave in which the murderer is hiding. They escape, and Tom and Huck return to find the treasure Joe has buried." Reader's Ency. 4th edition

Twain, Mark

The **adventures** of Tom Sawyer, Tom Sawyer abroad, Tom Sawyer, detective; edited by John C. Gerber, Paul Baender, and Terry Firkins. University of Calif. Press 1980 717p il

LC 76-47974

A combined edition of three Tom Sawyer titles first published 1876, 1894 and 1896, respectively

Twain, Mark

The **complete** novels of Mark Twain; edited with an introduction by Charles Neider. Doubleday 1964 2v

Twain, Mark

The **complete** short stories of Mark Twain; now collected for the first time. edited with an introduction by Charles Neider. Doubleday 1957 xxiv, 676p hardcover o.p. pa $6.95

ISBN 0-553-21195-1 pa

"The sixty pieces which are here hospitably called short stories illustrate both the weaknesses and the strengths of Mark Twain as a writer of fiction." N Y Times Book Rev

Twain, Mark

★ A **Connecticut** Yankee in King Arthur's court; edited by Bernard L. Stein; with an introd. by Henry Nash Smith. Published for the Iowa Center for Textual Studies by the University of California Press 1979 827p il $75

ISBN 0-520-03621-2

LC 77-91761

First published 1889; published in the United Kingdom with title: Yankee at the court of King Arthur

This satiric novel is a "tale of a commonsensical Yankee who is carried back in time to Britain in the Dark Ages, and it celebrates homespun ingenuity and democratic values in contrast to the superstitious ineptitude of a feudal monarchy." Merriam-Webster's Ency of Lit

Twain, Mark

The **gilded** age and later novels. Library of America 2002 1053p $40

ISBN 1-931082-10-3

LC 2001-38053

The gilded age (1873), written with Charles Dudley Warner, is a panorama of an age in which the nation's capital teemed with would-be power brokers and vast fortunes piled up amid thriving corruption. In The American claimant (1892), an English viscount travels to America in search of an heir to his father's earldom. There he meets the primary claimant to the title, an eccentric yet good natured inventor, Colonel Mulberry Sanders. In Tom Sawyer abroad (1994), Tom, Huck Finn, and Jim take a trip via balloon across the Atlantic to the Sahara desert. In Tom Sawyer, detective (1896), Tom and Huck solve a complex murder mystery involving a diamond theft and Tom's Uncle Silas. No. 44,

the mysterious stranger (1969) is a different version of the posthumously published The mysterious stranger, based on Twain's final manuscript. This version, set in Eseldorf, Austria in 1490, features "a likable young printer's devil, called only No. 44, who is possessed of satanic powers that allow him to master the craft of printing in a few hours. Single-handedly he speedily produces a Bible and magically summons up phantasmagoric people to print innumerable copies." Oxford Companion to Am Lit. 6th edition

Includes bibliographical references

Twain, Mark

Historical romances; The prince and the pauper, A Connecticut Yankee in King Arthur's court, Personal recollections of Joan of Arc. [notes by Susan K. Harris] Library of Am. 1994 1029p maps (Library of America) $35

ISBN 0-940450-82-8

LC 93-40246

In The prince and the pauper (1882), a prince, Edward VI, switches clothes with Tom Canty, a poor boy who looks exactly like him. When the two are discovered, Edward is mistakenly driven from the castle and forced to endure Tom's harsh, impoverished life while Tom experiences Edward's life as royalty. A Connecticut Yankee in King Arthur's court and Personal recollections of Joan of Arc are entered separately.

Twain, Mark

The **man** that corrupted Hadleyburg, and other stories and essays. Harper 1900 364p

Twain, Mark

Mississippi writings. Literary Classics of the United States 1982 1084p $30

ISBN 0-940450-07-0

LC 82-9917

The adventures of Tom Sawyer, The adventures of Huckleberry Finn, and Pudd'nhead Wilson are entered separately. Life on the Mississippi (1883) is an autobiographical narrative that focuses on the author's childhood near the river.

Twain, Mark

Mysterious stranger, and other stories. Harper 1922 324p il

Twain, Mark

Personal recollections of Joan of Arc; by the Sieur Louis de Conte (her page and secretary); illustrated by G. B. Cutts. Harper 1926 596p il

First published 1896

"De Conte, who tells the story in the first person, has been reared in the same village with its subject, has been her daily playmate there, and has followed her fortunes in later life, serving her to the end, his being the friendly hand that she touches last. After her death, he comes to understand her greatness; he calls hers 'the most noble life that was ever born into this world save only One.' Beginning with a scene in her childhood that shows her innate sense of justice, goodness of heart, and unselfishness, the story follows her throughout her stormy career. We have her audiences with the king; her marches with her army; her entry into Orleans; her fighting; her trial; her execution; all simply and naturally and yet vividly told. The historical facts are closely followed." Keller. Reader's Dig of Books

Twain, Mark

Pudd'nhead Wilson; and, Those extraordinary twins. introduction by Ron Powers; illustrations by F.M. Senior and C.H. Warren. Modern Library 2002 xvi, 263p il (Modern Library classics)

ISBN 0-81296-622-8

LC 2002-66002

Pudd'nhead Wilson was first published 1894 with title: The tragedy of Pudd'nhead Wilson. The short story Those extraordinary twins is about conjoined twins of completely opposite philosophy and temperament

"David Wilson is called 'Pudd'nhead' by the townspeople, who fail to understand his combination of wisdom and eccentricity. He redeems himself by simultaneously solving a murder mystery and a case of transposed identities. The mystery revolves around two children, a white boy and a mulatto, who are born on the same day. . . . The book is an implicit condemnation of a society that allows slavery. It also includes a series of brilliant epigrams which are distillations of Twain's wit and wisdom." Reader's Ency. 4th edition

Tyler, Anne

★ The **accidental** tourist. Knopf 1985 355p

LC 85-40161

"After 20 years of marriage, Macon and Sarah separate. Thus, a man used to intense order in his life finds his existence thrown into disorder; forced to create a new life for himself, Macon must overcome numerous obstacles—particularly his inability to communicate, to relate to other people's needs and problems." Booklist

"Thanks to her inimitable mix of an extraordinary inventiveness with characters and a profound humanity, Tyler makes this book a joy to read." Wilson Libr Bull

Tyler, Anne

★ The **amateur** marriage; a novel. Knopf 2004 306p $24.95

ISBN 1-400-04207-0

LC 2003-59536

This novel presents a portrait of the six-decade marriage of a Baltimore couple, Michael and Pauline Anton. Although acquaintances like to think of them as a perfect couple, Pauline and Michael are constantly bickering, sulking and fighting at home. . . . {Yet} Pauline and Michael are also tied to each other by their children, by shared adventures and, as the years pass, by bonds of memory and inertia. Caring for aging parents, witnessing the illnesses and travails of friends, adapting to a move to the suburbs-these are all experiences that bind Pauline and Michael to each other, even as their very different temperaments and interests increasingly pull them apart." N Y Times (Late N Y Ed)

Tyler, Anne

Back when we were grownups; a novel. Knopf 2001 273p $25

ISBN 0-375-41253-0

LC 2001-88107

This "is as perceptive, as full of gentle comedy and human warmth as any of Ms Tyler's previous novels. She manages her quirky, engagingly named characters (Patch, Biddy, NoNo, Jeep, Zeb) beautifully, spinning a web of family tensions with a wonderful lightness of touch—in this, Ms Tyler is matchless." Economist

Tyler, Anne

The **beginner's** goodbye; a novel. by Anne Tyler. Alfred A. Knopf 2012 197 p.

ISBN 9780307957276

LC 2011033507

This novel by Anne Tyler focuses on "Aaron, who works for a small-family publishing firm that specializes in its Beginners series. . . . Aaron is in the beginning stages of mourning, after a tree crashed through his house and crushed his slightly older wife. . . . Early on, Aaron receives visits from his dead wife, whom no one else can see, and whom he admits might well be a projection or an apparition. . . . Mourning is both a rite of passage and a process of discovery for Aaron." (Kirkus Reviews)

Tyler, Anne

★ **Breathing** lessons. Knopf 1988 327p

LC 88-45260

This novel has "irresistibly funny passages you want to read out loud and poignant insights that illuminate the serious business of sharing lives in an unsettling world." Publ Wkly

Tyler, Anne

Celestial navigation. Knopf 1974 273p

Set in Baltimore, this novel tells of artist Jeremy Pauling's attempts to overcome his comfortable isolation and make contact with others

The author "is especially gifted in the art of freeing her characters and then keeping track of them as they move in their unique and often solitary orbits. . . . She has a way of transcribing their peculiarities with such loving wholeness that when we examine them we keep finding more and more pieces of ourselves." N Y Times Book Rev

Tyler, Anne

The **clock** winder. Knopf 1972 312p

The author has a "remarkable understanding of the intricacies of family life, a sympathy for odd-ball characters who never become merely southern grotesques . . . but are observed so gently that the term 'neurotic' seems equally inappropriate for them." New Repub

Tyler, Anne

Digging to America; a novel. Knopf 2006 277p $24.95

ISBN 0-307-26394-0

LC 2005-52963

With this novel, "Tyler has delivered something startlingly fresh while retaining everything we love about her work . . . . Her success at portraying culture clash and the complex longings and resentments of those new to America confirms what we knew, or should have known, all along: There's nothing small about Tyler's world, nothing precious about her attention to the hopes and fears of ordinary people." Washington Post Book World

Tyler, Anne

★ **Dinner** at the Homesick Restaurant. Knopf 1982 303p hardcover o.p. pa $14.95

ISBN 0-394-52381-4; 0-449-91159-4 pa

LC 81-13694

"Pearl Tull, an angry woman who vacillates between excesses of maternal energy and spurts of terrifying rage, has been deserted by her husband and has brought up her three children alone. Cody, the eldest, is handsome, wild, and in a lifelong battle of jealousy with his young brother, the sweet-tempered and patient Ezra. Their sister Jenny tries, through three marriages, to find a stability which was never present in Pearl's home. Ezra also tries to achieve a permanence through his homey Homesick Restaurant in Baltimore, but he is cruelly tricked by his brother and is unable to establish any unity in the family." Shapiro. Fic for Youth. 3d edition

Tyler, Anne

Earthly possessions. Knopf 1977 197p

ISBN 0-394-4114-7

LC 76-41222

This "novel concerns Charlotte Emory, a 35-year-old woman who goes to her bank in Clarion, Md., one morning to withdraw enough cash to leave her husband. Instead, she is hustled off as hostage to a bank robber and peripatetic demolition-derby rider named Jake Simms. Simms needs funds to get to Florida and take his girlfriend out of a home for unwed mothers. All that he and Charlotte share, apart from the stolen car they are riding in, is a distrust of 'closed-in spaces'—for him, the prison he has just escaped; for her, a household that includes a gaunt preacher husband, two children, three brothers-in-law and a procession of itinerant sinners, soldiers and salesmen." Newsweek

Tyler, Anne

Ladder of years. Knopf 1995 325p $24

ISBN 0-679-43941-2

LC 94-38909

"'Ladder of Years' feels, indeed, like the story of a woman who thought she could prune her life down to a short story, only to find it blooming, unexpectedly, into an Anne Tyler novel. There can be few more delightful revelations." New Yorker

Tyler, Anne

Morgan's passing. Knopf 1980 311p

LC 79-20272

"A young girl-wife goes into labor while she and her boy-husband are putting on a puppet-show of Cinderella at a church fair in Baltimore in 1967. Her baby is delivered en route to the hospital by a member of the audience who claims to be a doctor. . . . The fake doctor—who lives in a tumultuous . . . cluttered house with an imperturbable wife, seven daughters, his half-senile mother, and crackpot sister—attaches himself to the young couple and their child, following them, popping up at odd moments. Later, after they have all become friends, this attachment, narrows, focusing upon the young wife, with unsettling consequences for everyone." New Repub

Tyler, Anne

Noah's compass; a novel. Alfred A. Knopf 2009 277p $25.95

ISBN 978-0-307-27240-9; 0-307-27240-0

LC 2009-14925

"When Liam Pennywell is nearly 61, he loses his job teaching fifth grade at St. Dyfrig, a 'second-rate' boys' school in Baltimore. He's been downsized, not fired, he's quick to point out to inquisitive family members, and he never really liked being a teacher anyway. . . . Within the week, Liam moves to a one-bedroom apartment near the Baltimore Beltway and begins his own systematic downsizing. . . . The first night in his sparse new home Liam is attacked by an intruder—an event he can't remember when he wakes up the next day in the hospital, bandaged and bruised. And so unfolds the next stage in Liam's quiet life, in which he reopens himself to the possibility of love, while finally accepting the fact that his relationships with his father and daughters are fixed, whatever their flaws may be. Tyler's acutely perceptive observations of family interactions are dead on." BookPage

Tyler, Anne

A **patchwork** planet. Knopf 1998 287p $24

ISBN 0-375-40256-X

LC 98-84431

This novel, set in Baltimore, "tells the story of a year in the life of 30-year-old Barnaby Gaitlin who, despite coming from a wealthy family, works as an odd-job man. Barnaby is an ordinary and somewhat bewildered man whose life turns on a chance encounter with a woman who may represent the angel that brings change and gives direction to his life." Libr J

Tyler, Anne

★ **Saint** maybe. Knopf 1991 337p $22

ISBN 0-679-40361-2

LC 91-52704

"Tyler's remarkable novel pulls at the heart strings and jogs the memories of forgotten youth. . . . While the majority of YA readers lack enough life experiences to appreciate the pure joy of Tyler's descriptions and thoughts, not to steer them in her direction would be a shame." SLJ

Tyler, Anne

Searching for Caleb. Knopf 1976 309p

ISBN 0-394-49848-8

"Anne Tyler's tone is understated, ironic, and elliptical, which suits her characters well. Searching for Caleb rarely gives us heights and depths of emotion or the excitement of discovery, but it does offer the very welcome old-fashioned virtues of a patient, thoughtful chronicle." Saturday Rev

Tyler, Anne

A **slipping**-down life. Knopf 1970 214p

"Evie Decker, unattractive and unpopular, and Drumsticks Casey, an unknown rock musician, are misfits living in a small Southern town. They are drawn together in a union which is more bizarre than romantic. It is a union, however, that seems to fulfill the needs of each and makes for a marriage that is marked by quiet desperation." Shapiro. Fic for Youth. 3d edition

Tyler, Anne

The **tin** can tree. Knopf 1965 273p

"Six-year-old Janie Rose Pike was killed in a fall from a tractor, an accident which shook but does not really change the little world in which she lived. Mrs. Pike, left stunned and silent by her daughter's death, is too apathetic to pay attention to her 10-year-old son, Simon. Her grown-up niece, who lives with the family, tries to take care of Simon and at the same time to cope with her own problems. It is Simon himself . . . who finally awakens his mother to the need for life to continue." Libr J

Tóibín, Colm, 1955-

★ The **heather** blazing. Viking 1993 245p

ISBN 0-670-84789-5

LC 92-50350

First published 1992 in the United Kingdom

The novel "explores the rigidly controlled mind and soul of a high court Dublin judge, Eamon Redmond. Tóibín . . . {presents the} particulars of Redmond's life: his devotion to the law, his daughter's out-of-wedlock pregnancy, his controversial decision in a case concerning the expulsion of a pregnant high school student, and his wrenching memories of his motherless childhood and his father's debilitation after a stroke." Booklist

Tóibín, Colm, 1955-

The **testament** of Mary; Colm Tóibín. Scribner 2012 81 p. $19.99

ISBN 1451688385; 9781442354944; 9781451688382; 9781451690750; 9781451692389

LC 2012007578

This novel, by Colm Tóibín, portrays the Virgin Mary "as a solitary older woman still seeking to understand the events that become the narrative of the New Testament and the foundation of Christianity. In the ancient town of Ephesus, Mary lives alone, years after her son's crucifixion. She has no interest in collaborating with the authors of the Gospel. . . . She does not agree that her son is the Son of God; nor that his death was 'worth it.'" (Publisher's note)

"A stunning interpretation that is as beautiful in its presentation as it is provocative in its intention." (Booklist)

U

Udall, Brady

The **lonely** polygamist; a novel. W. W. Norton 2010 602p $26.95

ISBN 978-0-393-06262-5; 0-393-06262-7

LC 2009-52226

"Udall's control over his complex plot, and his psychological insight into his characters, are admirable and impressive. But perhaps the most pleasing thing about 'The Lonely Polygamist' is the way it avoids giving in to the prurient interests that could easily have dominated a novel about polygamy." Chicago Tribune

Uhnak, Dorothy

Codes of betrayal. St. Martin's Press 1997 293p $23.95

ISBN 0-312-15582-4

LC 97-23598

"Nick O'Hara was raised by his uncle Frank, an Irish cop, but his mother was a Ventura, daughter of an underworld crime boss. Nick follows his uncle into the NYPD, juggling professional life and family ties, until his son is killed in a sour drug deal while hanging out with a Ventura cousin. Then he learns his own father was a victim of the Ventura crime family. Marriage on the skids, Nick turns to gambling, loses big, rips off a drug dealer to pay his debts, and winds up snared by the Feds, who offer a deal: exploit his family connection and help bring down the Venturas." Booklist

"This work effectively portrays one man's agony with life gone wrong and the decline of mobster power as the century ends." Libr J

Uhnak, Dorothy

★ The **investigation**; a novel. Simon & Schuster 1977 344p

LC 77-7981

Sgt. Joe Peters is "a detective on the Queens County district attorney's squad. He accompanies his partner one morning on a house call involving two missing children. The distraught parents are George and Kitty Keeler. George is 'an obese, balding, sloppy middle-aged man' who owns a bar. Kitty, more than twenty years his junior, is a 'very beautiful kid' who manages a health spa owned by a small-time gangster. The Keeler marriage is shaky, and Kitty accuses George of having taken the boys. But when their bodies are found in a nearby park and Kitty's account of her actions begins to sound suspicious, she is indicted for murder. . . . Out of curiosity and an attraction to Kitty, {Peters} sets out to investigate on his own." Newsweek

Uhnak, Dorothy

Victims; a novel. Simon & Schuster 1986 316p

LC 85-26246

"Young nurse Anna Grace is stabbed to death on a street in Queens in full view of scores of apartment dwellers who decide not to get involved. Tough, good-looking NYPD detective Miranda Torres investigates the crime in association with bigshot newspaper columnist Mike Stein, whose only goal is to show the insensitivities of modern society without caring who the criminal is or why poor Anna was his victim. Miranda stays honest in trying to do her job, but finds that the well-spring of corruption in law enforcement is so powerful that it even touches her friends in the highest levels of government." Booklist

Ulfelder, Steve

Purgatory chasm; Steve Ulfelder. Minotaur Books 2011 292p.

ISBN 9780312672928; 0312672926; 9781250007025

LC 2011001265

This book tells the story of "Conway Sax, a recovering alcoholic, ex-con, and car mechanic who lives in Massachusetts, fulfills his moral obligations to the Barnburners, the AA group that got him clean and sober, by doing odd jobs for them. Tander Phigg, a Barnburner whose 1980 Mercedes-Benz 450SEL Sax once worked on, persuades him to help retrieve the classic car--and the $3,500 deposit--from Das Motorenwerk, a garage in New Hampshire that's had the vehicle for 18 months and done nothing. When Sax visits the garage, someone he doesn't see coldcocks him. The assault heightens Sax's suspicions about Das Motorenwerk, and his later discovery of a dead body confirms them." (Publishers Weekly)

Ulinich, Anya

Petropolis. Viking 2007 324p $24.95
ISBN 978-0-670-03819-0; 0-670-03819-9
LC 2006-41356

"In the end, [the author] ties a neat bow around Sasha's serious coming-of-age problems, but bittersweetness lingers. Petropolis bursts with artful details of an immigrant's peripatetic youth and quest for home-the grappling for the strong woman inside of the lost girl." Ms.

Ullman, Ellen

By blood; Ellen Ullman. Farrar, Straus and Giroux 2012 378p.
ISBN 0374117551; 9780374117559
LC 2011041626

This book follows a "disgraced professor [who] takes an office in a downtown tower to plot his return. But the walls are thin and he's distracted by voices from next door—his neighbor is a psychologist, and one of her patients dislikes the hum of the white-noise machine. And so he begins to hear about the patient's troubles with her female lover, her conflicts with her adoptive, avowedly WASP family, and her quest to track down her birth mother. . . . Armed with the few details he's gleaned, the professor takes up the quest and quickly finds the patient's mother in records from a German displaced-persons camp. . . . His research leads them deep into the history of displaced-persons camps, of postwar Zionism, and—most troubling of all—of the Nazi Lebensborn program." (Publisher's note)

Umrigar, Thrity

The **world** we found; Thrity Umrigar. HarperCollins 2012 320 p.
ISBN 9780062107138; 0061938343; 9780061938344

This book tells the "story of four women and the unbreakable ties they share. As university students in late 1970s Bombay, Armaiti, Laleh, Kavita, and Nishta were inseparable. . . . But much has changed over the past thirty years. Following different paths, the quartet drifted apart. . . . Then comes devastating news: Armaiti, who moved to America, is gravely ill and wants to see the old friends she left behind. . . . In the course of their journey to reconnect, Armaiti, Laleh, Kavita, and Nishta must confront the truths of their lives--acknowledge long-held regrets, face painful secrets and hidden desires, and reconcile their idealistic past and their compromised present." (Publisher's note)

Umrigar, Thrity N.

The **space** between us; a novel. [by] Thrity Umrigar. William Morrow 2005 321p
ISBN 0-06-07915-5-1
LC 2005-50510

"The life of the privileged is harshly measured against the life of the powerless, but empathy and compassion are evoked by both strong women, each of whom is forced to make a separate choice. Umrigar is a skilled storyteller, and her memorable characters will live on for a long time." Washington Post Book World

Umrigar, Thrity N.

★ The **weight** of heaven; a novel. [by] Thrity Umrigar. Harper 2009 365p $25.99
ISBN 978-0-06-147254-1
LC 2008-32950

"Frank and Ellie Benton, grappling with the death of their seven-year-old son, move from Ann Arbor, Mich., to Girbaug, India, where Frank takes a job running a factory. While he tackles the barriers faced by an educated, wealthy American in charge of a Third World work force, Ellie, a psychologist, makes inroads with the impoverished locals at a health clinic. Frank has a difficult time adjusting at work, and at home he takes an interest in their housekeepers' son, Ramesh, and begins tutoring him. While Frank buries his grief by helping Ramesh, he ends up in competition with the boy's bitter father, Prakash, and further damaging his already troubled marriage." Publ Wkly

This is "is a bold, beautifully rendered tale of cultures that clash and coalesce." Booklist

Under African skies; modern African stories. edited and with an introduction by Charles R. Larson. Farrar, Straus & Giroux 1997 315p $25
ISBN 0-374-21178-7
LC 96-48601

An "impressive collection of short stories from sub-Saharan Africa. Published between 1952 and 1996, some translated from French, Portuguese, and Arabic, these stories share a common outrage against Africa's decay, whether from oppressive colonialism and corruption or the repression of tradition and ignorance. These are not folk tales about great chiefs but heart-rending stories about ordinary people . . . trying to make a life for their families, caught up in the political and spiritual struggle for Africa." Libr J

Undset, Sigrid

★ **Kristin** Lavransdatter; translated from the Norwegian. Knopf 1935 3v in 1 $50
ISBN 0-394-43262-2

Contains three novels originally published separately in Norway in 1920, 1921, and 1922 respectively; first United States publication with titles: The bridal wreath (1923); The mistress of Husaby (1925); The cross (1927)

Although the "action takes place in the fourteenth century, the lives of the characters are marked by almost the same problems depicted in modern novels: passion, adultery, premarital pregnancy, ambition, conflict. Kristin, daughter of Lavrans and Ragnfrid, is betrothed to Simon Andressön but falls in love with Erlend Nikulassön and finally wins her father's approval to marry him. Her father realizes on their wedding night that they are already lovers. The book follows Kristin's life as she tries to manage her estate and as her husband loses his lands and leaves her after a bitter quarrel. After several attempts at reconciliation, Erlend returns, only to be killed in a fight. The six sons of Kristin follow different paths. Two die during the Black Plague, which was so dreadful a scourge in that era. The portrayal of this Norwegian woman is vivid and human." Shapiro. Fic for Youth. 3d edition

Unferth, Deb Olin
  Vacation. McSweeney's 2008 215p $22
  ISBN 978-1-93478-109-8; 1-93478-109-6
  "The novel follows a woman who finds out her husband's deepest secret: he once jumped out of a window in pursuit of a bird who flew into the room. The deadpan humor continues as the woman decides to harbor her own secret: she has an affair, which consists entirely of trailing of a random man whom she never seeks to meet. The prose is highly stylized and full of devastating wit. Each sentence springs from an almost visual idiom. . . . Funny, bleak, often brilliant, Vacation once again proves that Unferth can preform a linguistic high-wire act all her own." Esquire

The **Unforgetting** heart: an anthology of short stories by African American women (1859-1993) edited by Asha Kanwar. Aunt Lute Bks. 1993 xxi, 292p
  ISBN 1-879960-31-1
                                        LC 93-3240

Unger, Lisa
  Heartbroken; a novel. Lisa Unger. Crown 2012 370 p.
  ISBN 0307465209; 9780307465207
                                        LC 2011050497
  In this psychological thriller, "[a]n island on an Adirondack lake becomes both a haven and a hell for three women. . . . Kate Burke's annual visits to Heart Island, owned by her wealthy parents, never go smoothly, mainly because of the uneasy relationship she has with her imperious 75-year-old mother, Birdie, Kate expects the next visit will be even more upsetting because she's written a novel based on journals kept by her aunt and grandmother that's a thinly veiled story of a love affair that ended in tragedy on the remote island. Meanwhile, Birdie has visions of a dark intruder prowling Heart Island at all hours. Finally, Emily, a waitress drifting through life, feels powerless to resist as her boyfriend pulls her into schemes that will betray the people closest to her." (Publishers Weekly)

Unsworth, Barry, 1930-2012
  ★ **After** Hannibal. Talese 1997 250p il
  ISBN 0-385-48651-0
                                        LC 96-20856
  First published 1996 in the United Kingdom
  In this novel "five sets of outsiders invade Umbria by renovating houses along a country track. Trouble is made for them by local peasants and by an exploitative speculating Brit, but the real story is the way their various hopes and intrigues retrace ingrained historical patterns. Recognizing these patterns and, in a sense, presiding over them is an Italian lawyer so shrewd and wizardly that he seems supernatural." New Yorker

Unsworth, Barry
  Land of marvels; a novel. Nan A. Talese 2009 287p $26
  ISBN 978-0-385-52007-2
                                        LC 2008-09201
  "It is 1914, and, after three years in the deserts of Mesopotamia, the British archeologist John Somerville believes he is on the brink of a great discovery. Before he can uncover what he thinks was the residence of the last Assyrian king, Somerville must fight off plans for a railway that will encroach on his dig site, and thwart the efforts of Elliot, a charismatic, straight-talking American (in British historical novels there is rarely any other kind) who is bent on finding oil and on destroying what remains of Somerville's marriage. There is something of E. M. Forster in Unsworth's knowing depiction of a decaying empire run by upper-class incompetents, and in his generous and sympathetic portrayal of women caught between cultures." New Yorker

Unsworth, Barry
  Losing Nelson; a novel. Talese 1999 338p $23.95
  ISBN 0-385-48652-9
                                        LC 99-28757
  "Unsworth is in complete control of his material, effortlessly sustaining an almost unbearable level of tension that is suddenly resolved in an unusually effective surprise ending." Libr J

Unsworth, Barry
  Morality play. Talese 1995 192p
                                        LC 95-4106
  This novel, set in 14th century England, is narrated by "Nicholas Barber, a young monk who has forsaken his calling and joined an itinerant troupe of players that gets caught up in the real-life drama of a small-town murder. The crime presents Barber and his fellows with an opportunity to attract a larger-than-usual audience, and they turn sleuths, weaving the bits of information yielded by their investigation into an improvised play that eventually reveals the surprising, sordid truth. Rich in historical detail, Unsworth's well-told tale explores some timeless moral dilemmas and reads like a modern page-turner." Libr J

Unsworth, Barry, 1930-2012
  The **quality** of mercy; a novel. Barry Unsworth. Nan A. Talese/Doubleday 2011 319 p. $26.95
  ISBN 0091937124 Hutchinson; 0385534779 Nan A. Talese; 9780091937126 Hutchinson; 9780307948045; 9780385534772 Nan A. Talese
                                        LC 2011010110
  Sequel to: Sacred hunger.
  In this historical novel, "Erasmus Kemp has tracked down the crew members who absconded to Florida with his late father's slave ship and has hauled them back to Newgate Prison [in England]. But the long-delayed satisfaction he hopes to exact from these sailors is being challenged. . . . A wealthy abolitionist has taken up the crew members' defense, arguing that when they killed their captain, they weren't committing mutiny; they were protecting innocent Africans from drowning." (Washington Post)

"Unsworth's finely crafted plot brings together a vivid cast of seamen, miners, and landowners at a moment in history when crimes of property were considered more serious than crimes against persons and a more enlightened future lay just around the corner." LJ

Unsworth, Barry

The **ruby** in her navel; a novel of love and intrigue in the twelfth century. Nan A. Talese 2006 399p $26

    ISBN 0-385-50963-4

                            LC 2006-40370

"Like the best historical fiction writers, Unsworth tells his story while also fleshing out the backdrop with details that ground us in the moment and make it tangibly real. He makes his characters' individual experiences representative of larger concerns." Washington Post Book World

Unsworth, Barry

Sacred hunger. Doubleday 1992 629p

                            LC 91-33237

"Deftly utilizing a flood of period detail, Unsworth has written a book whose stately pace, like the scope of its meditations, seems accurately to evoke the age. Tackling here a central perversity of our history—the keeping of slaves in a land where 'all men are created equal'—Unsworth illuminates the barbaric cruelty of slavery, as well as the subtler habits of politics and character that it creates." Publ Wkly

Unsworth, Barry

★ The **songs** of the kings; a novel. Doubleday 2003 338p $26

    ISBN 0-385-50114-5

                            LC 2002-66845

"A stubborn wind from the northeast ushers in rough times for the House of Atreus, and the Greek ships, en route to Troy, remain trapped in the straits at Aulis. Unsworths' retelling of the story, familiar from Euripides, of the sacrifice of Iphigeneia to appease the gods so that the boats can sail is a bold, modern tale with cynical riffs on the themes of duty and power, truth and fiction. His Greek warriors are schemers and media-savvy self-promoters who are desperate to look good in the sung reports that are their equivalent of the news media—songs that are, we realize, the seeds of the Homeric tradition." New Yorker

Unsworth, Barry

★ **Stone** virgin. Houghton Mifflin 1986 309p

    ISBN 0-395-35412-9

                            LC 85-24897

"The strength of Unsworth's novel doesn't lie simply in its critique of masculine love, courtly and carnal, sacred and profane. For Stone Virgin is also a murder mystery, a reflection on mediaevalism versus Renaissance humanism, creator versus critic and—last but not least—an elegy to Venice, its water and stone." New Statesman

Upadhyay, Samrat

The **guru** of love. Houghton Mifflin 2003 290p $23

    ISBN 0-618-24727-0

                            LC 2002-32234

The author "excels at depicting the thousand small cuts that afflict a middle-class married man having an affair. . . . The writing is emotionally restrained and doesn't call attention to itself. There are no lyrical bursts of exuberance over the country's beauty or the torments of love. At points the novel is excessively terse; when three words would have sufficed, Upadhyay uses two. In spite of that it is gripping, because you like the characters so much, and wish them well." N Y Times Book Rev

Updike, John

The **afterlife** and other stories. Knopf 1994 316p $24

    ISBN 0-679-43583-2

                            LC 94-9818

"In these mellow, reflective stories, where parents die and grandchildren are born, Updike's heroes are acutely aware of lost glory yet discover the strength to persevere." Libr J

Updike, John

Bech at bay; a quasi-novel. Knopf 1998 240p $23

    ISBN 0-375-40368-X

                            LC 98-27868

This book "brings readers amusingly up to date on the life and times of Bech, a neurotic Jewish novelist. Skipping merrily along, the real author describes the imaginary author's trip to Czechoslovakia, his stint as head of a pretentious and marginal writers' group, a period of true weirdness in which he literally murders his critics, his late arrival at fatherhood and his receipt of a Nobel prize." Economist

Updike, John

Bech is back. Knopf 1982 195p

                            LC 82-161

Further episodes in the life of Henry Bech. "The novella-length 'Bech Wed' finds him married to suburban Bea who provides three teenagers, a dog, and a house in Ossining where Bech finally finishes his fourth novel, 'Think Big,' which is hyped and heralded after his 15-year silence: 'The squalid book we all deserve,' said Alfred Kazin in the 'New York Times Book Review.' In the other stories . . . Bech tours Third-World countries; writes his name 28,500 times for a new signed edition of an old novel; is interviewed in Canada and Australia; and visits Israel with his Episcopalian bride. An atmospheric travelogue and funny satire of the literary scene." Libr J

Updike, John

★ **Bech**: a book. Knopf 1970 206p

"In seven episodes presented in the guise of lectures with a spurious bibliography, the work reveals the literary and personal life of Henry Bech, a distinguished Jewish author of New York. Revelatory incidents include Bech's travels in the 1960s as a kind of cultural ambassador in Russia and Eastern Europe, his visit as a lecturer to adulatory pupils at a girls' school, his diverse romantic affairs, his difficulties in writing as he ages, and his ultimate enshrinement as a major American author." Oxford Companion to Am Lit. 6th edition

Updike, John

Brazil. Knopf 1994 260p $23

ISBN 0-679-43071-7

LC 93-28632

This novel, "for all its political incorrectness, seems good-natured and bent on self-parody. . . . If the book's surface is sometimes a little sticky, its allegorical underpinnings are graceful and firm." N Y Times Book Rev

Updike, John

★ The **centaur**. Knopf 1963 302p $24.95

ISBN 0-394-41881-6

"Utilizing a contemporay setting in Olinger, Pennsylvania, Updike attempts to retell the myth of Chiron, wisest of the centaurs, a creature who gave up his immortality on behalf of Prometheus. In this modern version, Chiron is a high-school science teacher, George Caldwell, and Prometheus is his 15-year-old son, Peter. The story revolves around three critical days in their lives." Shapiro. Fic for Youth. 3d edition

Updike, John

Gertrude and Claudius. Knopf 2000 212p $23

ISBN 0-375-40908-4

LC 99-57601

"Updike turns to Shakespeare's 'Hamlet,' exploring the origin of Gertrude and Claudius' 'reechy kisses.' When the sixteen-year-old Gertrude is unwillingly betrothed to the elder Hamlet, Horwendil, by her father . . . she quickly falls for his brother, Claudius. The two honorably resist their feelings until they are beset by the anxieties of aging; as it turns out, the murder of Horwendil is an act of emotional (and political) desperation rather than cold calculation. Likewise, Updike's portrayal of Gertrude and Claudius' thwarted affections is not just a deft literary exercise but an affecting—and funny—invocation of the abundant desires of what Hamlet called 'this too too solid flesh." New Yorker

Updike, John

In the beauty of the lilies. Knopf 1996 491p $25.95

ISBN 0-679-44640-0

LC 95-23467

The novel "opens in Paterson, New Jersey, in 1910. 'At the moment Mary Pickford fainted' while making a movie close by, Presbyterian minister Clarence Wilmot loses his faith. That loss precipitates another loss: his job. Since 'now he was free—free to sink,' he turns to selling encyclopedias door to door and to an addictive habit of watching the fabulous new medium, moving pictures. Updike then tells of the following three generations of Clarence's family. . . . Updike's soaring novel becomes an extended yet taut metaphor for the secularization of religion and the concomitant infatuation with movies as a substitute for religion." Booklist

Updike, John

Licks of love; short stories and a sequel. Knopf 2000 359p $25

ISBN 0-375-41113-5

LC 00-34906

"This book of stories, mostly about old wives and girl-friends recollected in middle-aged tranquillity, also includes a novella—a return to the world of Harry Angstrom, Up-

dike's unlikely alter ego. In 'Rabbit Remembered,' it turns out that Rabbit's untimely demise has not diminished his ability to shake up the lives of those around him. His family may not miss him, exactly, but, like the rest of us, they still can't get over him." New Yorker

Updike, John

Memories of the Ford Administration; a novel. Knopf 1992 371p

ISBN 0-679-41681-1

LC 92-52955

Professor Alfred Clayton "has received a request from the Northern New England Association of American Historians for his memories and impressions of the Gerald Ford Administration (1974-77). 'Alf' obliges with his memories of a turbulent period in his personal history, as well as pages of an unpublished book he was writing at the time, on the life of James Buchanan, the fifteenth President of the United States (1857-61)." Publisher's note

"Updike's elegant, yet slangy portrait of the Ford era demonstrates considerable finesse. Even more impressive is his authentic, yet unstilted, evocation of Buchanan's era." Christ Sci Monit

Updike, John

My father's tears and other stories. Alfred A. Knopf 2009 292p $25.95

ISBN 978-0-307-27156-3; 0-307-27156-0

LC 2008-54376

"A perfect bookend to Pigeon Feathers, the precocious collection of stories that nearly five decades ago announced their 30-year-old writer's discovery of his own inimitable voice. . . . Mr. Updike writes in these stories . . . with the quiet assurance of someone in complete control of his craft." N Y Times (Late N Y Ed)

Updike, John

Pigeon feathers, and other stories. Knopf 1962 278p hardcover o.p. pa $14

ISBN 0-394-44056-0; 0-449-91225-6 pa

These stories "are filled with gentle humor and irony. Youth, marriage, and family life provide most of the themes." Cincinnati Public Libr

Updike, John

The **poorhouse** fair. Knopf 1959 185p

A reissue with a new introduction of the title first published 1959

This novel concerns the lives of a handful of marvelously eccentric and understandable people in a poorhouse on the undulating plains of central New Jersey. It begins on the morning of the annual Fair, an innovation of Conner, the new and very ambitious prefect. Conner's struggle to institutionalize old age inevitably meets the stiff opposition of those who want to individualize it

"This is a wise book with much to say on individualism and conformity, mechanization and craftsmanship, the 'welfare state' and the 'old days'—and, foremost, on 'death' as it is looked upon by the aged and the young. Updike's old people are memorable." Libr J

Updike, John
Rabbit Angstrom; a tetralogy. with an introduction by author. Knopf 1995 xxxi, 1519p $30
ISBN 0-679-44459-9

Four novels trace the life of Harry "Rabbit" Angstrom against the changing American society from the sixties to the eighties. -WorldCat

Updike, John
Rabbit at rest. Knopf 1990 512p
ISBN 0-394-58815-0

LC 90-52953

Sequel to Rabbit is rich

"The being that most illuminates the Rabbit quartet is not finally Harry Angstrom himself but the world through which he moves in his slow downward slide, meticulously recorded by one of our most gifted American realists." N Y Times Book Rev

Updike, John
Rabbit is rich. Knopf 1981 467p $30
ISBN 0-394-52087-4

LC 81-1287

Sequel to Rabbit redux

"A superlative comic novel that is also an American romance." Time

Followed by Rabbit at rest

Updike, John
Rabbit redux. Knopf 1971 406p
ISBN 0-394-47273-X

Sequel to Rabbit, run

"Updike profiles Harry (Rabbit) Angstrom, 10 years after his first appearance, as a conservative suburbanite no longer running away from responsibilities but unable to resolve the anxieties that are brought to him from outside. His wife takes a lover and, after decrying Rabbit's lack of will to keep her, leaves their home. Rabbit and his thirteen-year-old son Nelson become involved with Jill Pendleton, a young hippie girl whom Rabbit takes into his house; to him she is a sometimes baffling sexual partner, to Nelson an older sister. Jill's friend Skeeter then arrives, a black man of devastating wit and antic humor who initiates Rabbit to marijuana and encourages him to read black history." Booklist

"There are some structural faults, and moments when characters don't ring true. But I can think of no stronger vindication of the claims of essentially realistic fiction than this extraordinary synthesis of the disparate elements of contemporary experience." N Y Times Book Rev

Followed by Rabbit is rich

Updike, John
★ **Rabbit,** run. Knopf 1960 307p

"Contemporary in setting and tone, and brilliant in its evocation of everyday life in America, the novel is about Harry Angstrom ('Rabbit'), a salesman who, on an impulse, leaves home, his alcoholic wife, Janice, and his child, Nelson, to find freedom. After several escapades and a liaison with an ex-prostitute, he returns to his wife and child and attempts to settle down again. In this novel, Updike conveys the longings and frustrations of family life. Rabbit's malaise is not so much a yearning for freedom as, perhaps, a yearn-

ing for guiding spiritual values and meaning. At the end, still dissatisfied and guilt-ridden because of the responsibility he feels for the death of his second child, he begins running again." Reader's Ency. 3d edition

Followed by Rabbit redux

Updike, John
★ **Roger's** version. Knopf 1986 328p
ISBN 0-394-55435-3

LC 86-45298

"Divinity professor Roger Lambert is visited by Dale Kohler, an earnest young student who wants a grant to prove the existence of God by computer. The visit disrupts Roger's ordinary existence, bringing him into contact with . . . Verna (his half-sister's daughter), and leading to his wife's affair with Dale." Libr J

This novel "succeeds in spite of its symbolic structure. Its power and charm lie in the terrific appeal it makes to our capacity for intellectual wonderment. It's rather thrilling to watch Updike assimilate the new vocabularies of particle physics and computer technology—and then fuse them with the ancient vocabulary of religious belief." Newsweek

Updike, John
S. Knopf 1988 279p

LC 87-40496

This novel "concerns Sarah Worth, a latter-day Hester Prynne who has become enamored of a Hindu religious leader called the Arhat. A New Englander, she goes west to join his commune in Arizona, and there mingles with the other sannyasins (pilgrims) in the . . . attempt to subdue ego and achieve moksha (salvation, release from illusion)." Publisher's note

This "is an acid comedy of illusions and delusions told entirely in the words of a woman who is both deceived and deceiver." Atlantic

Updike, John
Seek my face. Knopf 2002 276p $23
ISBN 0-375-41490-8

LC 2002-18442

"The action of the novel, such as it is, takes place over a single early-April day at the house in the Vermont countryside of the septuagenarian Hope Chafetz, an artist in her own right and, more famously, widow of the action painter Zack McCoy and ex-wife of the Pop artist Guy Holloway. Kathryn, an ambitious young journalist, has come up from New York to interview this living repository of the history of postwar American art. Through the course of the long day the two women talk, attended by a tape recorder, that ubiquitous tool of contemporary journalism." N Y Times Book Rev

"Despite its uncomplicated premise, the novel achieves a remarkable depth of characterization and a glowing beauty in its articulation of the artistic sensibility." Booklist

Updike, John
Terrorist. Alfred A. Knopf 2006 320p $24.95
ISBN 0-307-26465-3

LC 2005-57985

This novel tells the story "of eighteen-year-old Ahmad Ashmawy Mulloy and his devotion to Allah and the words of the Holy Qur'an, as expounded to him by a local mosque's imam. The son of an Irish-American mother and an Egyptian father who disappeared when he was three, Ahmad turned to Islam at the age of eleven. He feels his faith threatened by the materialistic, hedonistic society he sees around him in the slumping factory town of New Prospect, in northern New Jersey. . . . When he finds employment in a furniture store owned by a family of recently immigrated Lebanese, the threads of a plot gather around him, with reverberations that rouse the Department of Homeland Security." Publisher's note

"The last part of the novel is suspenseful. It brings together a serviceable plot, which leans a little heavily on coincidental connections, a questionable provocation and some broadly motivated acts of heroism. It seems meant as a fable, and any good fable requires some derring-do. The most satisfactory elements in 'Terrorist' are those that remind us that no amount of special pleading can set us free of history, no matter how oblivious and unresponsive to it we may be." N Y Times Book Rev

Updike, John

Toward the end of time. Knopf 1997 334p $25
ISBN 0-375-40006-0

LC 97-5167

"Like Updike, Ben can write elegant sentences. Although his temporal excursions (and Updike's researched inventions) at first seem random, they fit together into a paranoid structure by novel's end. Ben's report from the body front and reflections on his failures . . . are simultaneously sad and comic, often worthy of that old endgamer Beckett." Nation

Updike, John

Trust me; short stories. Knopf 1987 302p
LC 86-46018

A collection of 22 short stories which share the theme of trust, mostly betrayed, but sometimes fulfilled. -WorldCat

Updike, John

Villages. Knopf 2004 321p $25
ISBN 1-400-04290-9

LC 2004-43845

This novel "novel follows its hero, Owen Mackenzie, from his birth in the semirural Pennsylvania town of Willow to his retirement in the rather geriatric community of Haskells Crossing, Massachusetts. In between these two settlements comes Middle Falls, Connecticut, where Owen, an early computer programmer, founds with a partner, Ed Mervine, the successful firm of E-O Data, which is housed in an old gun factory on the Chunkaunkabaug River. Owen's education is not merely technical but liberal, as the humanity of his three villages, especially that of their female citizens, works to disengage him from his youthful innocence." Publisher's note

Updike, John

The **widows** of Eastwick. Knopf 2008 308p $24.95
ISBN 978-0-307-26960-7; 0-307-26960-4

LC 2008-18513

"One wonders whether anybody has ever described the small physical indignities of the aging process with as much tenderness and good humor as Updike. . . . Now the witches' sex lives are over, but their lives aren't, and you sense Updike's twinkly eyes peering cautiously into the darkness, be-

yond the glow of the merely fleshly, trying to make out what the world beyond might look like." Time

Updike, John

★ The **witches** of Eastwick. Knopf 1984 307p
LC 83-49048

"A novel about three Rhode Island women whose marriages have collapsed and who turn to devil worship and witchcraft." Reader's Ency. 4th edition

"While not a typical Updike narrative, the author's glittering wit, pungent observations, and fabled legerdemain at tabulating mundane particulars reach their peaks in the first half of the novel. Only in the last sections does the reader's attention flag." Booklist

Upson, Nicola

Two for sorrow. HarperCollins 2011 488 p.
ISBN 9780571246335; 9780061451584

LC 2010497725

This book is a mystery novel based on "the murders of newborn innocents for which two British women were hanged at Holloway Prison in 1903. Decades later, mystery writer Josephine Tey has decided to write a novel based on Amelia Sach and Annie Walters, the notorious 'Finchley baby farmers,' unaware that her research will entangle her in the desperate hunt for a modern-day killer. A young seamstress . . . has been found brutally slain in the studio of Tey's friends, the Motley sisters, amid preparations for a star-studded charity gala. Despite initial appearances, Inspector Archie Penrose is not convinced this murder is the result of a long-standing domestic feud--and a horrific accident involving a second young woman soon after supports his convictions. Now he and his friend Josephine must unmask a sadistic killer before more blood flows." (Publisher's note)

Ure, Louise

The **fault** tree. St. Martin's Minotaur 2008 336p $24.95
ISBN 978-0-312-37585-0; 0-312-37585-9

LC 2007-38730

Ure "makes a convincing case for a woman who overcomes her overwhelming sense of inadequacy to become a heroine. Heart-stopping suspense that builds to a crescendo and well-defined characters make this a topnotch mystery." Libr J

Uris, Leon

Armageddon; a novel of Berlin. Doubleday 1964 632p

Berlin from the close of World War II to the end of the airlift is the setting of this novel. Sean O'Sullivan, an American captain responsible for the military government of the city of Rombaden, nurses a fierce hatred of the Germans, and is faced with a dilemma when he falls in love with a German girl

The author "provides a broad and moving panorama of the rebuilding of post-war Germany at the time when the Allies and the Russians first came to clash over Berlin and its routes of access." Atlantic

Uris, Leon

Battle cry. Putnam 1953 505p

"Taking an average group of American boys from their home environment through the ordeal of boot camp, to the battlefields of Guadalcanal, Tarawa, and Saipan, the author fills in a detailed picture of Marine training and traditions." Booklist

Uris, Leon

★ **Exodus**. Doubleday 1958 626p il hardcover o.p. pa $7.99

ISBN 0-385-05082-8; 0-553-25847-8 pa

"Following World War II the British forbade immigration of the Jews to Israel. European Jewish underground groups, aided by Palestinian agent Ari Ben Canaan, made every effort to aid these unfortunate victims of Nazi persecution. The novel provides insight into the heritage of the Jews and understanding of the danger involved in helping them reach a safe haven. It also includes the warm love story of Ari and a gentile nurse, Kitty Fremont, who cared very much for the welfare of the Jewish children caught in this nightmare." Shapiro. Fic for Youth. 3d edition

Uris, Leon

Mila 18. Doubleday 1961 539p $19.95

ISBN 0-385-02076-7

"Uris' major talent is that he is a master storyteller. And in 'Mila 18' he uses this talent fully and unhampered, in a straight narrative that generates an almost unbelievable dramatic intensity." San Francisco Chron

Uris, Leon

QB VII. Doubleday 1970 504p

"Two thirds of this jumbo novel are concerned with the trial, Kelna versus Cady. The judge allows this and overrules that. Dramatic, impassioned confrontations before the Queen's Bench alternate with contributory scenes: the two principals surrounded by worried families, mistresses and friends, the police pressing their search for missing witnesses, the speculation about who's guilty and who's innocent." N Y Times Book Rev

Uris, Leon

Redemption; a novel. HarperCollins Pubs. 1995 827p

ISBN 0-06-018333-0

LC 95-10834

The focus of this sequel is "the conflict between two of the three dominant families of Trinity, the tempestuous Larkins and their staid British counterparts, the Hubbles. . . . Uris begins by tracing the Larkin legacy from patriarch Liam's exile to New Zealand, where he becomes squire of a sheep farm; his brother, Conor, becomes a legendary Irish revolutionary. Another Larkin progeny, Liam's son Rory, is acclaimed as a war hero after fighting with the British at Gallipoli, while Rory's brother Dary takes Catholic clerical vows, only to have a powerful love drive him to question both celibacy and his calling. Uris balances the struggles of the Larkins with the more repressed travails of Caroline Hubble, who battles the efforts of her husband to oppress the Irish after losing a pair of sons in the disastrous British battle against the Turks." Publ Wkly

Uris, Leon

★ **Trinity**. Doubleday 1976 751p il $21.95

ISBN 0-385-03458-X

"The story has a kind of relentless power, based on the real tragedy of Ireland, and Uris's achievement is that he has neither cheapened nor trivialized that tragedy." N Y Times Book Rev

Urquhart, Jane

Away; a novel. Viking 1994 356p

LC 94-178660

"Urquhart's blending of the spiritual and political sides of the Irish makes an amazing story told in a language that is melodious and laden with complex imagery." Booklist

Urquhart, Jane

A **map** of glass. MacAdam/Cage Pub. 2006 371p $25

ISBN 1-596921-70-6

LC 2006-360

First published 2005 in Canada

"Set in present-day Toronto and in the 19th-century world of rural Ontario timber barons, [this novel] opens with the wintry death of Alzheimer's sufferer Andrew, whose body, borne by an ice floe, runs aground on the small Lake Ontario island where artist Jerome McNaughton is seeking inspiration. The story steps back a century, to when Andrew's ancestors, owners of the same island, razed forests to build ships, then it jumps forward a year from the opening scene of Andrew's death, to when Sylvia, Andrew's married lover of 20 years, sets out to meet with Jerome, who discovered Andrew's body, and, through Jerome, to reconnect one last time with Andrew. Meanwhile, Jerome, the relationship-shy adult child of an abusive, alcoholic father, is slowly coming to trust that girlfriend Mira's love for him is real. Urquhart reveals all of their haunted personal histories in the lyrical first and third parts of the novel. But it's in the compact family-saga middle, where a slew of Andrew's memorable forebears take the stage, that this novel's luminous heart truly lies." Publ Wkly

Urquhart, Jane

★ The **underpainter**. Viking 1997 340p

LC 97-225317

"Urquhart writes forcefully; her imagery is vivid, and her evocation of time and place is accomplished and assured. There is an impressive density of character and narrative, and her use of illustrative detail is, at times, striking." Times Lit Suppl

Urrea, Luis Alberto

The **hummingbird's** daughter; a novel. Luis Alberto Urrea. Little, Brown, and Co. 2005 499p $24.95; $14.99

ISBN 0316745464; 9780316154529

LC 2004027849

Kiriyama Prize: Fiction category (2005)

This work of historical fiction "is based on the first 19 years in the life of the author's Mexican great aunt, Teresa Urrea, or Saint Teresa of Cabora (1873-1906). The illegitimate daughter of a poor Indian woman and a wealthy landowner, Teresa is raised on a farm and taught the healing arts by a curandera (female healer) until a near-death experience endows her with the divine gift of healing. Teresa's popularity soars, and she serves as the battle cry for an antigovernment insurrection, after which she and her father are exiled to the United States, where she is not officially recognized as a saint owing to the somewhat unorthodox nature of her work." (Library Journal)

Urrea, Luis Alberto

Into the beautiful North; a novel. Little, Brown and Company 2009 342p $24.99

ISBN 978-0-316-02527-0; 0-316-02527-5

LC 2008-39962

This novel is "about Nayeli, who is 19 years old and working in a taco shop in what would conventionally be referred to as a 'sleepy Mexican village.' The town is not as sleepy as the residents would like. Bandidos — drug dealers — have appeared and are threatening their way of life. There aren't enough men left in town to defend the women, children and old people from their incursions. Nayeli comes up with a solution after seeing 'The Magnificent Seven' at the local cinema. . . . She decides to go to the United States and find seven men to bring back home. They will marry, start families and be the salvation of the village. Their mere presence will deter bandidos. Her Tia Irma won't let her go alone, so she takes Irma's American Express card; Tacho, the gay owner of the taco shop; and her two best friends, Yolo, the reader, and Veronica, the goth girl. So begins their picaresque adventure. The escapades of these four and the people they meet, who help or hinder them, are alternately hilarious, poignant, scary and sad." Seattle Times

Urrea, Luis Alberto

Queen of America; Luis Alberto Urrea. Little, Brown 2011 491p.

ISBN 9780316154864; 0316154865

LC 2011023065

Sequel to: The Hummingbird's Daughter.

This novel takes place "[a]fter the bloody Tomochic rebellion, [when] Teresita Urrea, beloved healer and 'Saint of Cabora,' flees with her father to Arizona. But their plans are derailed when she once again is claimed as the spiritual leader of the Mexican Revolution. Besieged by pilgrims and pursued by assassins, Teresita embarks on a journey through turn-of-the-century industrial America-New York, San Francisco, St. Louis. She meets immigrants and tycoons, European royalty and Cuban poets, all waking to the new American century." (Publisher's note)

V

Vachss, Andrew H.

Another life; a Burke novel. Pantheon Books 2008 271p $24.95

ISBN 978-0-307-37741-8; 0-307-37741-5

LC 2008-00213

"When a sniper shoots Burke's father, the Prof, the Prof's uneasy relationship with the law means that his life-threatening wounds can't be treated at a hospital. While his father's fate remains uncertain, a shadowy figure connected with U.S. intelligence draws Burke, an ex-con turned avenging angel for hire, into a kidnapping case. Early one morning, somebody removed the infant son of a Saudi prince from his father's custom Rolls, parked near an abandoned pier near the Hudson River, after the prince was serviced by a prostitute, who didn't realize the child was in the back seat. Burke visits his usual seamy corners of New York City in the ensuing investigation." Publ Wkly

Vachss, Andrew H.

Choice of evil; {by} Andrew Vachss. Knopf 1999 305p $23

ISBN 0-375-40647-6

LC 99-61596

"At a gay rally in New York City, Burke's friend Crystal Beth is killed in a drive-by shooting. Burke and his tribe of shadowy, semicriminal associates set out to track down the killer, but their investigation is soon impeded by a retaliatory series of murders perpetrated against known gay bashers. . . . Vachss creates a gun-metal gray, paranoid milieu where few can be trusted, where to be mainstream is to be compromised, and where children and women are always—yes, always—at risk." Booklist

Vachss, Andrew H.

Dead and gone; [by] Andrew Vachss. Knopf 2000 333p

ISBN 0-375-41121-6

LC 00-40565

"The left-for-dead-but-back-for-revenge plot is an old one, but Vachss manages to give it new life. Burke isn't quite as dark as he's been in the past, finding time to wax poetic on Chicago bluesman Son Seals and to discuss hot cars with other gear heads. But the message is the same: no mercy for the exploiters of children." Booklist

Vachss, Andrew H.

Down here; [by] Andrew Vachss. Knopf 2004 289p $19.95

ISBN 1-400-04173-2

LC 2003-58860

"This is yet another carefully crafted descent into a hellish environment in which sexual predators roam virtually unchecked, at least until targeted by Burke. One would think the same revenge plot would get old when recast again and again, but, amazingly, Vachss adds enough subtle differences to keep each novel unique and engaging." Booklist

Vachss, Andrew H.

Down in the zero; a novel. by Andrew Vachss. Knopf 1994 259p

LC 94-12312

In this mystery Burke is "confronted with young adult suicides and sexual blackmail in an affluent Connecticut suburb. Hired to watch the young son of a former lover, Burke is drawn into a bizarre situation populated by characters almost as strange as his friends. The suicides and the sadomasochistic sex, which are weirdly connected, force Burke to enlist his usual cohorts. Fans will want this crisply written work." Libr J

Vachss, Andrew H.

Footsteps of the hawk; {by} Andrew Vachss. Knopf 1995 237p

LC 95-17596

"The action begins when Burke is approached by a female police officer, Belinda, who wants him to exonerate her lover, now serving time as a serial killer. Belinda contends that the real killer is still on the loose; her lover is a connected guy who probably deserves to be in prison, but he's no killer. So she says. She also pins the cover-up on Morales, a psycho cop with a desire to send Burke to prison for his role in the violent breakup of a child pornography ring. Burke employs his familiar Fagin's army of street types to discover the real killer and the real motives behind the crime. As always in Vachss' work, New York's underbelly is vividly evoked." Booklist

Vachss, Andrew H.

Hard candy; a novel. by Andrew Vachss. Knopf 1989 241p

LC 89-45272

In this "novel featuring unlicensed New York private eye Burke, word is out that the ex-con PI has become a gun-for-hire. Besides coping with this crazy rumor, Burke contends with two figures from his youth who suddenly turn up. One of them, Candy, now a miniskirted call girl fond of whips and leashes, wants Burke to rescue her teenaged daughter from a cult in Brooklyn; the other, Wesley, an Uzi-toting hit man, already has the cult's leader, Train, in his sights. When Burke learns that the cult safehouse is a baby-breeding operation, vigilante-style justice ensues." Publ Wkly

Vachss, Andrew H.

Pain management; [by] Andrew Vachss. Knopf 2001 307p

ISBN 0-375-41322-7

LC 2001-29868

Burke "resurfaces in Portland, Oregon, after an assassin left him for dead in New York. He's living from hand to mouth when he stumbles into a missing-child case. Burke suspects parental involvement in the disappearance of young teen Rosa, but nothing supports the theory. The trail leads first to Portland's red light district, where he hears about a serial killer whom the cops seem unwilling or unable to catch." Booklist

"Vachss finally lets his secondary characters speak for themselves, as opposed to being wholly defined by Burke's inner growl." Publ Wkly

Vachss, Andrew H.

★ **Sacrifice**; a novel. by Andrew Vachss. Knopf 1991 271p

LC 90-53582

"Vachss' clipped, blunt, ocassionally overly melodramatic sentences may, in some way, be ripe for parody (à la Mickey Spillane), but they also convey the frightening impact of the somber, shocking, emotionally deadening hellholes that Burke, breaking every civilized rule, battles gamely through." Booklist

Vachss, Andrew H.

Safe house; {by} Andrew Vachss. Knopf 1998 291p

LC 97-50557

"At the request of Crystal Beth, operator of a Manhattan safe house, Burke agrees to take the case of a mother being stalked by her estranged husband, the leader of a neo-Nazi cell. As Burke untangles the web that connects the white supremacists to protectors in the federal government, he helps foil a terrorist plot that echoes the real Oklahoma City bombing. As always, Burke's exploits are an occasion to provide updates on Max the Silent, Michelle the transsexual and other veterans of his guerrilla underground—and to offer a quick study of the ways in which the justice system fails victims of crime." Publ Wkly

Vachss, Andrew H.

That's how I roll; Andrew Vachss. Pantheon Books 2011 213 p.

ISBN 9780307379948

LC 2011013503

In this book, "Esau, who's crippled by spina bifida, recounts a horrific childhood of parental abuse. He finds purpose in protecting his strapping little brother, Tory-boy, whose only defect is being a little 'slow'. Esau later becomes a bomb maker and assassin, carving out a precariously balanced life plying his deadly trade for both of the two crime bosses who share his unnamed community. When the authorities finally catch up with him, Esau continues to plan to protect Tory-boy whether Esau is dead or alive by cleverly playing both sides of the law." (Publishers Weekly)

Vachss, Andrew H.

★ **Two** trains running; [by] Andrew Vachss. Pantheon Books 2005 447p $25

ISBN 0-4000-4381-6

LC 2004-60127

"Locke City, a Southern mill town turned tourist mecca, is controlled by the firm but benevolent hand of local crime tsar Royal Beaumont. When the New York mafia arrives, he hires former undercover FBI agent Walker Dett to protect his interests. In short snippets of action and dialog, Vachss . . . creates a broad picture of crime in Locke City, from teenage street gangs to crooked national politicians, with the Ku Klux Klan, militant African Americans, and other factions woven into a shocking climax. A riveting page-turner that marks a definite change of direction from the author's dark Burke thrillers." Libr J

Valdes-Rodriguez, Alisa

Dirty girls on top. St. Martin's Press 2008 324p $24.95

ISBN 978-0-312-34967-7; 0-312-34967-X

LC 2008-12930

Sequel to: The Dirty Girls Social Club (2003)

"The six sucias (dirty girls) return with hilarious and raunchy tales of Latina-tinged love, marriage, and sex told from each character's point of view. Pop star Cuicatl likens the touch of one of her groupie lovers to 'uncooked tofu from the refrigerator,' while man-izer Usnavys describes her husband's wardrobe style as 'like a college student on welfare cheese.' Despite a plot full of guilty-pleasure material,

Dirty Girls admirably dives into darker areas like infidelity, mortality, addiction, and abuse. Hey, life can't be a fiesta 24/7." Entertainment Wkly

Valentine, Genevieve

Mechanique; a tale of Circus Tresaulti. Prime Books 2011 284p il pa $14.95

ISBN 978-1-60701-253-5

The author "raises the novel above the ordinary through her ability to convey the richness of the circus performers' emotional lives, coupled with impressive writing—as in a description of Alec's surgically attached wings, every bone-and-brass feather 'jigsawed and hammered and smoothed so thin that when it strikes another feather it rings out a clear note.'" N Y Times Book Rev

Vallgren, Carl-Johan

The **horrific** sufferings of the mind-reading monster Hercules Barefoot; his wonderful love and his terrible hatred. HarperCollins 2006 288p $23.95

ISBN 0-06-084199-0

LC 2005-52695

Original Swedish edition, 2002

"Overflowing with engrossing drama and superlative characterizations, Vallgren's novel is a masterful meditation on the triumph of love over human degradation." Booklist

Vamos, Miklos

The **book** of fathers; a novel. translated from the Hungarian by Peter Sherwood. Other Press 2009 474p pa $15.95

ISBN 978-1-59051-339-2; 1-59051-339-8

LC 2009-02614

Original Hungarian edition, 2000; this translation first published 2006 in the United Kingdom

"Vámos's novel chronicles a Hungarian family from 1705 until the present, as its members pass down their recollections of joy and hardship in the carefully preserved manuscript of the title. The novel proceeds via discrete episodes, each focussing on the life and death of a male progenitor with the ability to see into the past and, often, into the future. Steadily, a portrait emerges of an artistic, emotional group of men with a tendency toward violent death. . . . Vámos's fatalistic narrative follows in the tradition of 'One Hundred Years of Solitude,' but it stands as a unique and affecting illustration of the vicissitudes of Hungarian history." New Yorker

Van Booy, Simon

Everything beautiful began after; a novel. Harper Perennial 2011 404p pa $14.99

ISBN 978-0-06-166148-8; 0-06-166148-1

In this novel, "flight attendant Rebecca Baptiste moves to Athens, Greece, where she meets George Cavendish, an American with a passion for languages and drinking. Their romance blooms quickly, but when Rebecca falls for a Welsh archeologist named Henry, George drinks so much that he stumbles in front of a car—Henry's car. Without knowing what they share, Henry tends to George's injuries, cementing an immediate and long-lasting alliance. But some time later, George sees Rebecca with Henry, and the shock of recognition leaves these three sensitive souls shaken, snapping

George into sobriety and sending Henry adrift. When Henry finally returns two years later, after a devastating earthquake, both he and Athens have changed dramatically. Finally, his discovery of a journal that may have belonged to Rebecca makes him wonder how well he knew her. The rhythms of Henry's tender, damaged heart propel the narrative, and Van Booy wisely resists romanticizing torment, instead suggesting that grief—tied as it is to fate and faith—can give way to promise." Publ Wkly

Van de Wetering, Janwillem

The **Amsterdam** cops; collected stories. Soho Crime 1999 254p $22

ISBN 1-56947-171-1

LC 99-23243

"Written during the past 16 years, the stories feature the Amsterdam Murder Brigade's cynical, jowly Detective-Adjutant Henk Grijpstra and his handsome assistant Detective-Sergeant Rinus de Gier." Publ Wkly

Van de Wetering, Janwillem

The **blond** baboon; a novel. Houghton Mifflin 1978 194p

LC 77-17338

"Elaine Carnet, one-time chanteuse, is found by her daughter at the bottom of the stairs leading to the garden. Elaine, retired from the cabaret world, has run a profitable furniture business for some years now. It is not clear who might wish her dead, if anyone did. But . . . {detectives Grijpstra and de Gier} feel Carnet's daughter and her explanation of the events don't ring true." Publ Wkly

Van de Wetering, Janwillem

★ The **hollow**-eyed angel. Soho Press 1996 282p $22

ISBN 1-56947-056-1

LC 95-26296

"A young gay reserve policeman asks the commissaris, who happens to be going to a conference in New York, to investigate the mysterious death of his uncle in Central Park. Rinus de Gier follows the commissaris, who is now very old and nods off during lectures. Meanwhile, Henk Grijpstra investigates the death of a baron on a golf course as a possible homicide." Murphy. Ency of Murder and Mystery

Van de Wetering, Janwillem

Just a corpse at twilight. Soho Press 1994 265p $20

ISBN 1-56947-016-2

LC 94-9499

"Responding to de Gier's trans-Atlantic call for help, Grijpstra leaves the cozy embrace of his mistress, Nellie, for a daunting journey to a small coastal island in Maine where his former partner has gone to seek solitude and wisdom . . . and is being blackmailed for having pushed a local woman, his sometime lover, over a cliff to her death. . . . More than one drug-running operation, a money-making scam of lesser proportion, gratuitous cruelty, venality, a Papuan rite of revenge and intelligent, unpredictable humor wrap up this narrative delight." Publ Wkly

Van de Wetering, Janwillem

★ The **perfidious** parrot. Soho Press 1997 280p $22

ISBN 1-56947-102-9

LC 97-2548

In this novel "Grijpstra and de Gier have retired and started a private detective agency. A sleazy character named Carl Ambagt twists their arms into investigating piracy on the high seas—the theft of a chartered oil tanker in the Caribbean. The case takes them to Key West and The Perfidious Parrot, a lap dancing bar, then on to St. Eustatius. Van de Wetering's ribald streak is getting stronger and stronger, his writing looser and looser; in The Perfidious Parrot, he writes like a Dutch Carl Hiaasen." Murphy. Ency of Murder and Mystery

Van Essen, Thomas

The **Center** of the World; by Thomas Van Essen. Random House Inc. 2013 384 p. (paperback) $15.95

ISBN 9781590515495

LC 2013003848

This novel, by Thomas Van Essen, "is the story of renowned British painter J. M. W. Turner and his circle of patrons and lovers. It is also the story of Henry Leiden, a middle-aged family man with a troubled marriage and a dead-end job, who finds his life transformed by his discovery of Turner's 'The Center of the World', a mesmerizing and unsettling painting of Helen of Troy that was thought to have been lost forever." (Publisher's note)

Van Niekerk, Marlene

Agaat; translated by Michiel Heyns. Tin House Books 2010 581p pa $19.95

ISBN 978-0-98250-309-6; 0-98250-309-1

LC 2009-39476

First published 2006 in South Africa with title: The way of the women

"In 1947, Milla Redelinghuys is determined to turn her wealthy new husband, Jak, into the latest salt-of-the-earth farmer in her family's line. But her demands and manipulative personality cause an early marital rift that only worsens with time. As Van Niekerk follows young Milla through the decades, the author parallels it with the last days of an elderly Milla in 1996—miserable, afflicted with ALS, and reliant on her black maid, Agaat, for survival. Slowly, Milla's story—her abandonment and her masochistic relationship with Agaat—is revealed in all its ugliness. Clearly an allegory for race relations in South Africa, the novel succeeds on numerous other grounds: a rich evocation of family dynamics; a chilling portrait of bodily and mental decay; and a successful experiment in combining diaries, the second-person, and stream of consciousness." Publ Wkly

Van Rooy, Michael

An **ordinary** decent criminal. Minotaur Books 2010 278p

ISBN 978-0-312-60628-2

LC 2010-12889

First published 2005 in Canada

This "novel tracks the travails of an ex-con whose plan to settle down, go straight, and put his past behind him is rather rudely interrupted by a trio of home invaders, a vindictive mid-level crime lord, and a cop who has such a big chip on his shoulder, you're surprised he can even stand up. Monty Haaviko, the well-meaning ex-con who defends his home and winds up fighting for his life, is a very engaging protagonist and narrator with a story arc that takes him in one direction and then another, back and forth, until the tale reaches its rewarding and appropriate conclusion. . . . Van Rooy is not merely a capable writer but a quite gifted one; he draws us into the story pretty much immediately and never really gives us an opportunity to turn away." Booklist

Van Rooy, Michael

Your friendly neighborhood criminal. Minotaur Books 2011 325p $24.99

ISBN 978-0-312-60630-5; 0-312-60630-3

LC 2011-08786

"In this superb follow-up to An Ordinary Decent Criminal from the late Canadian author Van Rooy, ex-con Monty Haaviko, who's been a thief, a burglar, an armed robber, a smuggler, and a drug dealer, continues to try to put his past behind him and live quietly with his wife and son in Winnipeg. But Haaviko falls back into his old ways after Marie Blue Duck, a do-gooder seeking to smuggle refugees into the U.S. and Canada who can't enter legally despite their desperate situations, seeks to enlist his professional experience on the side of the angels. Of course, things don't go smoothly, and Haaviko must resort to violence to protect both Blue Duck's operation and his family." Publ Wkly

Van Slyke, Helen

Public smiles, private tears; [by] Helen Van Slyke with James Elward. Harper & Row 1982 250p

ISBN 0-06-014961-2

LC 81-47794

"On her death in 1979 Van Slyke . . . left the uncompleted first half of a novel that has now been completed by Elward, a playwright and author of three pseudonymous novels. The result is an expert combination; one cannot tell where the splice occurs, and the spirit and tone are consistent." Publ Wkly

Van Vogt, A. E.

★ **Slan**; An Orb ed.; Orb 1998 255p pa $13.95

ISBN 0-312-85236-3

LC 97-38438

First published 1940

"One of the landmark novels of the genre, Van Vogt's 1940 tale follows the 'Slan,' a new breed of telepathic humans and their search for a society free from persecution. Essential for all libraries." Libr J

Followed by Slan hunter

Van Vogt, A. E.

Slan hunter; [by] A.E. van Vogt and Kevin J. Anderson. TOR 2007 270p $24.95

ISBN 978-0-7653-1675-2; 0-7653-1675-7

LC 2007-8357

"This sequel to the late Van Vogt's cult sf classic Slan [1940] combines notes from the author and his son Greg with the storytelling skill of sf veteran Anderson, working with the Van Vogt family's permission. [The result is] a blend of astute social commentary and pulp sf action/adventure." Libr J

Vanderbes, Jennifer

Easter Island; a novel. Dial Press (NY) 2003 304p $24.95

ISBN 0-385-33673-X

LC 2002-31588

This novel "parallels two stories: that of Elsa Pendleton, who travels to Easter Island in 1913 with her much older husband and her mentally impaired sister to study the toppled moai statues, and of Dr. Greer Farraday, who in the 1970s escapes grief after the death of her famed scientist husband, accused of fraud, by studying ancient pollen on the island. Both women have been suppressed by circumstance—Elsa, always her sister's caretaker, has made a bid for security by marrying a colleague of her father after his death, and Greer battles prejudice against women scientists." Libr J

Vanderbes, Jennifer

Strangers at the feast; a novel. Scribner 2010 334p $26

ISBN 978-1-4391-6695-6; 1-4391-6695-1

LC 2009-49756

"A Thanksgiving Day showdown between a well-to-do family and the impoverished residents of a housing project. Anthropology professor and new mother Ginny Olson is hosting the Thanksgiving Day festivities for the first time. She has just returned from India, where she adopted a mute seven-year-old girl. . . . The guests include her taciturn dad, her well-meaning but clueless mom, and her wealthy brother, whose overinvestment in an office project just as the real-estate downturn hit has made his wife one angry lady (her cold-eyed pragmatism provides much of the book's entertainment value). A stove malfunction forces the family to move houses and sets them on an inevitable collision course with two young black men. Vanderbes lays on the cultural ironies a little too thickly in what is otherwise an inventively plotted, highly readable novel about white Americans' overweening sense of entitlement." Booklist

Vanderhaeghe, Guy

The **last** crossing. Alantic Monthly Press 2004 393p $24

ISBN 0-87113-912-X

LC 2003-60152

"Centered on three English brothers who venture to the American West—one as a missionary, the two others in pursuit when he disappears—this saga encompasses a wide range of characters through alternating narrative voices. In a panorama of late-nineteenth-century Montana and western Canada, Vanderhaeghe details the lawlessness of the early frontier towns and the desperate ferocity of the dying indigenous tribes. He dwells with particular pathos on the children of white traders and Native American women, who are caught between two cultures. The prose can be overripe, particularly in the opening chapters, and moments of historical exposition are clumsily inserted. However, the sweep of the narrative gradually overcomes these missteps, and as the various searches for revenge or redemption get under way the writing achieves unforced grace and power." New Yorker

VanderMeer, Jeff

Finch. Underland Press 2009 339p pa $14.95

ISBN 978-0-98022-601-0; 0-98022601-5

"Surreal and at times intoxicating, Finch is ambitious in a way that few genre novels ever are. VanderMeer has tried and, often, succeeded in blending fantasy, science fiction, and crime fiction into something delightfully evil and strange. He's converted the traditional hard edges of noir fiction into the foggy, fungal shapes of magical science realism." io9

VanderMeer, Jeff

The **third** bear. Tachyon 2010 273p pa $14.95

ISBN 978-1-892391-98-8

"These 15 elegantly crafted stories ably demonstrate VanderMeer's skill at telling tales of wonder in language that enhances the reading experience. Fans of imaginative literature and true speculative fiction should appreciate this groundbreaking collection by a World Fantasy Award winner that calls to mind the works of Borges, Kafka, and Stanislaw Lem." Libr J

Vann, David

Caribou Island; a novel. Harper 2011 293p $25.99

ISBN 978-0-06-187572-4; 0-06-187572-4

LC 2010-15703

"Vann locates his characters in an utterly convincing Alaska, but the natural world provides no ease for human anguish — nor is nature anything except a mirror in which these characters see what they wish to see. . . . [His] writing is confident — concrete and efficient. His characters' emotions and experiences bleed directly into the reader." Los Angeles Times Book Rev

Vann, David

Legend of a suicide. University of Massachusetts Press 2008 172p $24.95

ISBN 978-1-55849-672-9; 1-55849-672-6

LC 2008-35381

This "collection, five stories and a novella, . . . revolves obsessively around the suicide of an Alaskan father. Hopscotching through time, each tale examines the father's death from the perspective of his young son, Roy. . . . Vann uses startling powers of observation to create strong characters, tense scenes and genuine surprises, leading to a ghastly conclusion that's sure to linger." Publ Wkly

Vantrease, Brenda Rickman

The **illuminator**; Brenda Rickman Vantrease. St. Martin's Press 2005 406p $24.95; (pbk.) $13.95

ISBN 0312331916; 9780312331924

LC 2004030095

In this book, "a medieval illuminator with radical views finds himself sharing quarters with a widow struggling to preserve her independence. . . . Lady Kathryn . . . must be practical to ensure the future of her 15-year-old twin sons. Little as she cares for . . . the local abbey, she is happy to do them a favor by taking in a master illuminator as lodger. . . . Their subsequent passionate affair blinds them to the romance developing between Finn's innocent daughter, Rose, and Kathryn's pious son, Colin. Meanwhile, the unsolved murder of an unscrupulous priest on the manor grounds puts everyone in jeopardy, and Finn's secret sympathy with John Wycliffe and his Lollard followers, who champion an English translation of the Scriptures, endangers his livelihood, not to mention his life." (Publishers Weekly)

Vapnyar, Lara

Broccoli and other tales of food and love. Pantheon Books 2008 148p $20

ISBN 978-0-375-42487-8; 0-375-42487-3

LC 2007-41537

"This slim collection of six short stories (plus recipes) focuses on Russian and Eastern European immigrants to the US. They are lonely, they are disoriented, and they hope dinner will assuage their longings. Food is the slender thread that connects their pasts to their presents. Vapnyar's characters are funny, vulnerable, somewhat deluded, but also courageous. . . . [They] drift wistfully through landscapes they have not yet learned how to embrace. Yet Vapnyar's sly humor keeps her narratives light along with their poignance." Christ Sci Monit

Vargas Llosa, Mario, 1936-

★ **Aunt** Julia and the scriptwriter; translated by Helen R. Lane. Farrar, Straus & Giroux 1982 374p

LC 82-5159

Original Spanish edition, 1977

In this novel Vargas Llosa "draws on memories of his youth during the mid-1950s, namely his marriage to an aunt despite strong family opposition, and the action-packed soap operas penned by a mad colleague at a Lima radio station where Vargas Llosa was employed. The work's overriding irony stems from the juxtaposition of the two plot lines, the first based on fact and the second on imaginary events. The end result is a kind of metanovel in which the author sees the objective account of his courtship and marriage gradually assume the characteristics of melodrama." Ency of World Lit in the 20th Century

Vargas Llosa, Mario

The **bad** girl; translated from the Spanish by Edith Grossman. Farrar, Straus & Giroux 2007 276p $25

ISBN 978-0-374-18243-4

LC 2007-04941

Original Spanish edition, 2006

"Each chapter in Ricardo's life, in Edith Grossman's tart, fluent translation, is a small novel unto itself with its own amiable or striking protagonists, offering a whole fabric of reality waiting to be shredded to pieces by the reappearance of the bad girl. In this way, Vargas Llosa lures us into the world of Latin American revolutionaries; the tony equestrian crowd of Norfolk, England; the denizens of sex clubs in Tokyo; and much more. . . . Vargas Llosa, pulling back one illusory screen after another, eventually reveals the bad girl's true story in a manner that couldn't be more satisfying." Seattle Times

Vargas Llosa, Mario

Captain Pantoja and the Special Service; translated from the Spanish by Gregory Kolovakos and Ronald Christ. Harper & Row 1978 244p

ISBN 0-06-014494-7

LC 76-26280

Original Spanish edition, 1973

"Pantoja is a diligent young army officer who is sent to the Peruvian tropics to organize a squadron of prostitutes and thus make life more bearable for lonely soldiers stationed in remote out-posts. Because of his puritanical nature and zealously analytical approach to his assignment, Pantoja elicits the reader's guffaws from the beginning, but ultimately he comes to typify the absurd hero who continues to struggle against overwhelming odds. The theme of absurdity is underscored, moreover, by the hilarious parodies of military procedures, the clashing montage of incompatible episodes, and generous doses of irony and the grotesque." Ency of World Lit in the 20th Century

Vargas Llosa, Mario

Conversation in the cathedral; a novel. translated by Gregory Rabassa. Rayo 2005 601p pa $15.99

ISBN 978-0-06-073280-6

LC 2004-63263

Original Spanish edition, 1969; this translation first published 1975 by Harper & Row

This novel "takes place in 1950s Peru during the dictatorship of Manuel A. Odría. Over beers and a sea of freely spoken words, the conversation flows between two individuals, Santiago and Ambrosia, who talk of their tormented lives and of the overall degradation and frustration that has slowly taken over their town." Publisher's note

Vargas Llosa, Mario

Death in the Andes; translated by Edith Grossman. Farrar, Straus & Giroux 1996 275p

LC 95-40883

Original Spanish edition, 1993

This novel "begins with a mystery. . . . It concludes with an enigma: How slender is the boundary between civilization and tenebrous horror? The novel's indecipherable mystery is exquisitely attractive to the clear, transparent country that is a genial reader's mind." Atl Mon

Vargas Llosa, Mario, 1936-

The **dream** of the Celt; Mario Vargas Llosa; translated from the Spanish by Edith Grossman. Farrar, Straus and Giroux 2012 358 p.

ISBN 0374143463; 9780374143466

LC 2011052181

In this book, "Nobel Prize for Literature winner (in 2010) and one-time Peruvian presidential candidate, [Mario] Vargas Llosa chronicles the life of Roger Casement, an Irish patriot and human rights activist, or 'specialist in atrocities,' who was executed by the British in 1916 after the Easter Rising, which heralded the beginning of Irish independence." (Publishers Weekly)

Vargas Llosa, Mario

The **Feast** of the Goat; translated from the Spanish by Edith Grossman. Farrar, Straus & Giroux 2001 404p $25; pa $14

ISBN 0-374-15476-7; 0-312-42027-7 pa

LC 2001-33480

Original Spanish edition, 2000

"This fictional portrait of ruthless Dominican Republic dictator Rafael Trujillo focuses on the end of the old 'goat's' life. . . . Vargas Llosa relates Trujillo's story from the perspective of Urania Cabral, a successful New York lawyer who has spent a lifetime in exile but returns to her homeland when the tyrant is finally murdered. Urania hopes to rid herself of the demons that have possessed her since 1961, when as a teenager she was battered and humiliated by the impotent and vindictive old dictator." Libr J

Vargas Llosa, Mario

The **Green** House; a novel. translated by Gregory Rabassa. Rayo 2005 405p pa $14.99

ISBN 978-0-06-073279-0; 0-06-073279-2

LC 2004-63259

Original Spanish edition, 1965; this translation first published 1968 by Harper & Row

This "novel takes place in a Peruvian town, situated between desert and jungle, which is torn by boredom and lust. Don Anselmo, a stranger in a black coat, builds a brothel on the outskirts of the town while he charms its innocent people, setting in motion a chain reaction with extraordinary consequences. This brothel, called the Green House, brings together the innocent and the corrupt: Bonifacia, a young Indian girl saved by the nuns only to become a prostitute; Father Garcia, struggling for the church; and four best friends drawn to both excitement and escape." Publisher's note

Vargas Llosa, Mario

★ The **notebooks** of Don Rigoberto; translated by Edith Grossman. Farrar, Straus & Giroux 1998 259p il $23

ISBN 0-374-22327-0

LC 98-70961

Original Spanish edition, 1997

"Vargas Llosa's complex, gorgeous prose, heroically translated by Edith Grossman, sweeps the reader into a rich confusion of art and fact, fiction and reality, fantasy and deed, where there are no vices and the only virtue is imagination." N Y Times Book Rev

Vargas Llosa, Mario

The **time** of the hero; translated by Lysander Kemp. Farrar, Strauss & Giroux 1986 409p pa $18

ISBN 978-0-374-52021-2; 0-374-52021-6

Original Spanish edition, 1962; this translation first published 1966 by Grove Press

This "novel is a remarkably mature (and, one imagines, highly autobiographical) account. . . . In a sense Llosa is too clever a writer, for his novel gets swamped in places with unnecessary attempts at literary sophistication, repeated flashbacks, multiple viewpoints, and so on. The first hundred pages or so are inordinately prolix, but it is worth making an effort. . . . If [the] novel had been severely edited at an early stage its dramatic core would, I think, have emerged more

effectively: despite its prolixity, it is still a harsh and honest piece of fiction." N Y Rev of Books

Vargas Llosa, Mario

The **war** of the end of the world; translated by Helen R. Lane. Picador; Farrar, Strauss and Giroux 2008 568p pa $17

ISBN 978-0-312-43798-6; 0-312-42798-0

Original Spanish edition, 1981; this translation first published 1984 by Farrar, Straus and Giroux

"Vargas Llosa depicts a clash not only between two opposing factions but also between two societies inhabiting the same nation, who share only one thing in common: their ignorance of one another. This work represents his most ambitious novel to date in terms of the vastness of the world it portrays and the intensity of its epic action. Helen R. Lane's superb translation now makes this novel available to the English-speaking reader who will find the book to be a memorable literary experience." Choice

Vargas Llosa, Mario

★ The **way** to paradise; translated by Natasha Wimmer. Farrar, Straus & Giroux 2003 373p $25

ISBN 0-374-22803-5

LC 2003-56379

"A whiff of the lecture hall is detectable all through this book. (Some passages have more dates than an almanac.) But the juxtaposition of Tristan's and Gauguin's stories is fascinating all the same. In their different ways, both were moralists and proselytizers." N Y Time Book Rev

Vargas, Fred, 1957-

The **Ghost** Riders of Ordebec; a commissaire adamsberg mystery. Fred Vargas; translated from the French by Siân Reynolds. Penguin Books 2013 368 p. $15

ISBN 0143123122; 9780143123125

LC 2012042668

In this novel by Fred Vargas "Commissaire Adamsberg has no jurisdiction in Ordebec. Yet, he cannot ignore a widow's plea. Her daughter Lina has seen a vision of the Ghost Riders with four nefarious men. According to the thousand-year-old legend, the vision means that the men will soon die a grisly death. When one of them disappears, Adamsberg races to Ordebec, where he becomes entranced by the gorgeous Lina—and embroiled in the small Normandy town's ancient feud." (Publisher's note)

Varley, John

Demon. Putnam 1984 464p

LC 84-4814

The author "concludes his trilogy about Gaea, the sentient asteroid circling Titan. Cirocco Jones and her allies, including various Titanides and a Terran bodybuilder, struggle to provide the last refuge for fugitives from an Earth devastated by nuclear war." Booklist

Varley, John

The **golden** globe. Ace Bks. 1998 425p $22.95

ISBN 0-441-00558-6

LC 98-14612

"Galactic actor and con man Sparky Valentine runs afoul of the Charonese Mafia on Pluto and takes on the most important role of his long and illustrious career—that of a desperate survivor. Varley . . . artfully combines a rousing sf adventure with generous doses of Shakespearean lore and theater history, all of which serve as an elaborate backdrop for a moving portrait of a child actor who never quite grew up." Libr J

Varley, John

Red lightning. Ace Books 2006 330p $24.95

ISBN 0-441-01364-3

LC 2005-34226

"Drawing unabashedly on current events from 9/11 to Hurricane Katrina, the author mixes space opera-esque adventure and merriment with uncensored images of disaster areas and teenage sex. At his Heinlein-channeling best, Varley preaches the gospel of individual responsibility with all the fervor of a space-age libertarian revival preacher." Publ Wkly

Varley, John

Red thunder. Ace Bks. 2003 411p $23.95

ISBN 0-441-01015-6

LC 2002-38231

"When a Chinese spacecraft, Heavenly Harmony, threatens to land on Mars a few days before the U.S. shuttle vehicle Ares Seven, washed-up ex-astronaut Travis Broussard, his brilliant but unconventional cousin, Jubal, and four kids from Florida decide to build their own private spaceship, Red Thunder, and get there first in this riveting SF thriller... . With hilarious, well-drawn characters, extraordinary situations presented plausibly, plus exciting action and adventure, this book should do thunderously well." Publ Wkly

Varley, John

Rolling thunder. Ace Books 2008 344p $24.95

ISBN 978-0-441-01563-4; 0-441-01563-8

LC 2007-46581

"In the distant future, Mars is a colony of Earth, and Lt. Patricia Podkayne is a third-generation Martian with something to prove. As a member of the Music, Arts, and Drama Division of the Martian Navy, she accepts an assignment as an entertainer on the planet Europa, not realizing that trouble is brewing on that world. . . . Varley's style of future sf is immediate and gritty, filled with realistic details and believable characters. His conclusion to a trilogy begun with Red Lightning and Red Thunder demonstrates his skill as both raconteur and master of science-based fiction." Libr J

Varley, John

★ Titan; illustrated by Freff. Berkley Pub. Corp. 1979 302p il

LC 78-23865

The first volume of a trilogy that includes Wizard and Demon

"The heroine finds an artificial world among the satellites of Saturn and becomes an agent of its resident intelligence, the godlike Gaea, before being forced to turn against 'her.' Conscientiously nonsexist action-adventure SF." Anatomy of Wonder. 3d edition

Followed by Wizard

Varley, John

Wizard; illustrated by Freff. Berkley Pub. Corp. 1980 354p il

LC 79-24871

"In this sequel to . . . 'Titan,' Varley continues his exploration of the sentient, wheel-shaped world called Gaea. Twenty years have passed, and now that Earth is aware of her, Gaea has tried to protect herself by becoming valuable to humanity—offering us 'miracles' based on her immense scientific knowledge. Two supplicants for such boons are the central characters: Chris, a man from Earth, and Robin, a woman from the Coven, an all-female orbital colony. To earn their miracles, Gaea requires them to become heroes. To achieve this, they accompany Rocky and Gaby (heroines of the first book, back in supporting roles) on a dangerous odyssey through Gaea's rebellious regions and learn that Gaea herself is the real enemy." Publ Wkly

Followed by Demon

Vassanji, M. G., 1950-

The assassin's song. Alfred A. Knopf 2007 313p $25

ISBN 978-1-4000-4217-3; 1-400-04217-8

LC 2007-8562

"Karsan Dargawalla is destined from boyhood to succeed his father and his father's father as avatar of Pirbaag, a 13th-century Sufi shrine. As the novel unfolds in fits and starts, Karsan rejects his spiritual inheritance and decamps for Harvard in 1970, against his chagrined father's wishes. The three decades of stubborn self-exile that follow represent a sorrowful generational rift between father and son that ends when Karsan returns home after his ascetic father's death." Publ Wkly

Vassanji, M. G.

The in-between world of Vikram Lall. Knopf 2004 369p $25

ISBN 1-400-04216-X

LC 2004-48967

"In this novel set among Kenya's Indian diaspora, two ill-fated loves—Vikram Lall's for a young English girl, his sister's for a young African man—symbolize their family's tenuous social position as neither privileged oppressor nor righteous oppressed. Vikram, now in exile in Canada, recounts Kenya's painful process of decolonization and his own role laundering money for government officials, an activity that he justifies as the survival tactic of one considered 'inherently disloyal' because of his race. . . . The book admirably captures the tenor of the postcolonial period: the predicament of the Asian minority, the corruption that marred Kenya's fledgling independence, and the individual tragedies that were the cost of revolution." New Yorker

Vassanji, M. G., 1950-

★ The Magic of Saida; A novel. M.G. Vassanji. 1st U.S. ed. Knopf 2013 303 p. (hardcover) $25.95

ISBN 0307961508; 9780307961501

LC 2012041081

This novel, by M. G. Vassanji, is a story of "an African/ Indian man who returns to the town of his birth in search of the girl he once loved--and the sense of self that has always eluded him. . . . Kamal [Punja] had reached a stage of both undreamed-of material success and disintegrating personal ties. Then, suddenly, he . . . 'allowed an old regret to awaken,' and set off to find the girl he had known as a child, to finally keep his promise to her that he would return." (Publisher's note)

Verdon, John

Shut your eyes tight. Crown Publishers 2011 509p $24

ISBN 978-0-307-71789-4

LC 2010-53589

Sequel to: Think of a number (2010)

Superstar detective Dave Gurney's renewed efforts to retire are halted by the brutal murder of a young bride at her wedding reception, a crime subsequently linked to a brilliant criminal who targets Gurney's family to further his agendas.

"Red herrings come thick and fast in the labyrinthine plot, and the suspense builds until the violent denouement. But it is the nature of the criminal conspiracy—utterly vile, fantastic, and yet curiously plausible—that will have crime readers willingly losing sleep." Booklist

Verdon, John

Think of a number; a novel. Crown Publishers 2010 418p $22

ISBN 978-0-307-58892-0; 0-307-58892-0

LC 2009-28512

"Verdon is a master at controlling pace, illustrating the story of a rich but complicated marriage, pondering what it means to be sucked back into your life's work even if it might kill you, and demanding that the reader use his or her brain to figure out what comes next. When you're finished, you may not trust silly parlor games ever again." Salon

Verghese, Abraham

Cutting for stone; a novel. Alfred A. Knopf 2009 541p $26.95

ISBN 978-0-375-41449-7; 0-375-41449-5

LC 2008-28252

A "novel about identical twin boys born in Addis Ababa in 1954 and instantly orphaned—their mother dies, their father flees. Raised by doctors at the hospital, Shiva and Marion soon begin practicing medicine themselves, but their lives unhappily diverge. . . . Verghese, a doctor, has an affinity for unstinting detail and unscientific intuition. The exhaustive gore of the medical procedures is matched by a poetic perception of the outside world—arriving in New York, Marion misses the cacophony of Addis Ababa's roads, observing that in America 'the cars were near silent, like a school of fish.' Verghese bends history and coincidence to his narrative needs—characters cross paths when they should and find the information they seek—creating a story much like the human bodies Marion painstakingly describes: beautiful, amazing, and a bit of a mess." New Yorker

Verissimo, Luis Fernando

Borges and the eternal orangutans; translated from the Portuguese by Margaret Jull Costa. New Directions 2005 135p pa $13.95

ISBN 0-8112-1592-x

LC 2004-28203

Original Portuguese edition, 2000

"Most writers feel passionate about Borges, but few would have the temerity to put the enigmatic sage into their fiction. That's because evoking Borges's presence would likely overwhelm any meager thoughts of their own. Yet Brazilian novelist Luis Fernando Verissimo has such temerity, as well as the talent to pull it off." Washington Post Book World

Verne, Jules

★ **Around** the world in eighty days; translated with an introduction and notes by William Butcher. Oxford University Press 2008 xlv, 247p (Oxford world's classics) pa $9.95

ISBN 978-0-19-955251-1

LC 2008-482138

Original French edition, 1873

"The hero, Phileas Fogg, undertakes his hasty world tour as the result of a bet made at his London club. He and his French valet Passepartout, meet with some fantastic adventures, but these are overcome by the loyal servant and the endlessy inventive Fogg. The feat they perform is incredible for its day; Fogg wins his bet, having circled the world in only eighty days." Reader's Ency. 4th edition

Includes bibliographical references

Verne, Jules

★ The **extraordinary** journeys: Twenty thousand leagues under the sea; translated with an introduction and notes by William Butcher. Oxford University Press 2009 xlviii, 445p pa $11.95

ISBN 978-0-19-953927-7

LC 2009-464589

Original French edition, 1870; This translation first published 1998

"The voyage of the Nautilus permitted Verne to describe the wonders of an undersea world almost totally unknown to the general public of the period. Indebted to literary tradition for his Atlantis, he made his major innovation in having the submarine completely powered by electricity, although the interest in electrical forces goes back to Poe and Shelley. So far as the enigmatic ending is concerned, his readers had to wait for the three-part The Mysterious Island (1874-1875) to learn that Nemo had been the Indian warrior-prince Dakkar, who had been involved in the Sepoy Mutiny of 1857." Anatomy of Wonder 4

Includes bibliographical references

Verne, Jules

From the earth to the moon, and Round the moon; With pictures of the author and his environment and illus. of the setting of the book, together with an introd. by Arthur C. Clarke. Dodd, Mead 1962 308p il (Great illustrated classics)

LC 63-07412

The two books comprising this volume were first published 1865 and 1872 respectively

These titles provide a "striking example of early hard SF, detailing with great precision the preparations and scientific premises (still mostly correct, apart from the deadly effect of acceleration on the passengers) for a voyage to the moon." New Ency of Sci Fic

Verne, Jules

★ A **journey** to the centre of the earth; introduction by David Brin. Modern Library 2003 195p
pa $8.95

ISBN 0-8129-7009-8

LC 2003-59947

Original French edition, 1864. Variant title: A trip to the
center of the earth

"More than half the book is given to the preliminaries
before the actual descent begins, the first two chapters relying on a standard point of departure, the discovery of a
manuscript giving the location of the caverns in Iceland. The
narrative shows Verne's intense care in presenting the latest
scientific thought of his age, while the sighting of the ple-
siosaurus and the giant humanoid shepherding mammoths
indicates how well he incorporated lengthy imaginary episodes to flesh out the factual report." Anatomy of Wonder 4

Verne, Jules

The **mysterious** island; pictures by N. C. Wyeth.
Scribner 1988 493p il $25.95

ISBN 0-684-18957-7

LC 88-3167

Sequel to Twenty thousand leagues under the sea

Original French edition, 1874; first United States edition published 1883 by J. W. Lovell; this is a reissue of the
1918 edition

A story of adventure in three parts: Dropped from the
clouds; Abandoned; and The secret of the island

"Five men and a dog are carried out to sea in a balloon
and drop from the clouds on the mysterious island. Their
Crusoe-like resourcefulness and adventures are the theme of
the book." Toronto Public Libr

Verne, Jules

Paris in the twentieth century; translated by
Richard Howard; introduction by Eugen Weber. Random House 1996 222p il $21

ISBN 0-679-44434-3

LC 95-31750

Written in 1863; original French edition published 1994

Set in the 1960s, "the novel depicts Michel Dufrenoy as
a poet and humanities scholar at sea in a crass commercial
world that has strong overtones of Soviet realism. He befriends a young musician with whom he works; reconnects
with his long-lost uncle, a literature professor; and even falls
in love with the professor's granddaughter. But despite the
kindnesses of his friends, Michel fails to succeed with the
technological culture around him. Notable are the predictions about the subway, electric lights, and electronic music." Libr J

Vernon, Olympia

Eden. Grove Press 2003 272p $23

ISBN 0-8021-1728-7

LC 2002-33863

"Fourteen-year-old Maddy Dangerfield is called upon
to help her cancer-afflicted aunt Pip live out her last days.
Maddy's mother, Faye, can't forgive her sister's betrayal of
her with her own husband. Maddy is caught in the vortex of
unresolved conflicts among the adults: a stoic, overworked
mother who can't make peace with a dying sister; an alco-

holic husband addicted to gambling; and a fiery aunt who
has lived her life on her own terms. The small black community of Pyke County, Mississippi, is also saturated with unresolved conflicts, seething resentments, and violence. . . .Ver-
non's writing is lyrical and emotionally powerful." Booklist

Vernon, Olympia

A **killing** in this town. Grove Press 2006 246p
$22

ISBN 0-8021-1813-5

LC 2005-52547

"The novel shows the debilitating cancer of hatred and
prejudice and the beauty of the effort to stop the violence.
In language reminiscent of Toni Morrison and William
Faulkner, Vernon weaves a powerful yet dreamlike story of
our not-too-distant past." Booklist

Veselka, Vanessa

Zazen. Red Lemonade 2011 264p pa $15.95

ISBN 978-1-935869-05-4

"The deeply disaffected young woman narrator of Veselka's . . . [novel] must decide whether to flee a dystopian
America or try to endure it, and, in the process maybe help
save it a little. Della is a waitress with an obsessive interest in self-immolation, a sharp wit, and a dwindling hope
in humanity. When a bomb goes off in an office building in
her faceless industrial city's downtown, Della finds that the
distant wars the country's been fighting are coming closer
to home. At first she considers leaving like many others,
but then the chaos becomes attractive to Della and she calls
in a series of phony bomb threats around town, taking big
delight in watching people scramble from, for instance, a
mall-church complex. But when someone starts setting off
bombs at places from her list of 'targets,' Della realizes that
she might be part of something bigger than her own absurd
protest. Veselka's prose is chiseled and laced with arsenic
observations, and though she unleashes some savage social
satire, her focus is more on the hypocrisy, heartache, and
confusion that drive Della and those around her." Publ Wkly

The **vicious** circle; mystery and crime stories by
members of the Algonquin Round Table. edited
by Otto Penzler. Pegasus Books 2007 205p $25;
pa $13.95

ISBN 978-1-933648-67-5; 1-933648-67-8; 978-1-
605980-24-9 pa; 1-605980-24-2 pa

"As mystery expert Penzler admits in his introduction,
this volume contains 'little classic detection . . . and less nail-
biting suspense' than the usual crime fiction anthology, but
those curious about the legendary figures of the Algonquin
Round Table—a group of New York City writers and critics
from the 1920s, many affiliated with the New Yorker—will
get at least a taste of the wit and sophistication for which
they were known." Publ Wkly

Vida, Vendela

And now you can go; a novel. Knopf 2003 189p
$19.95

ISBN 1-400-04027-2

LC 2002-35688

"An armed man waylays a twenty-one-year-old woman,
Ellis, in Riverside Park, seeking a partner in suicide, but she

survives. . . . Ellis alternately fends off and submits to the consolations of various men; thinks about the child an infertile couple conceived with her eggs; broods over her father's four-year disapearance and unexplained return; jets off to the Philippines on a volunteer mission; then, back in Manhattan, cuts her hair into a mullet. There's plenty of mordant humor along the way." New Yorker

Vida, Vendela

Let the Northern Lights erase your name; a novel. Ecco 2007 226p $23.95

ISBN 978-0-06-082837-0; 0-06-082837-4

LC 2006-45030

In this novel, "a twenty-eight-year-old editor of film subtitles discovers on her father's death that he is not her biological parent: her mother, who abandoned her as a teenager, had been married to another man. Feeling betrayed by her fiancé, who has known about the deception for years, she abruptly leaves him to search for her real father in the northern reaches of Finland. Vida gives the icy landscape an eerie, forbidding beauty, and her writing has moments of great emotional acuity. Her heroine is inexplicable and often unlikable, but Vida skillfully draws a parallel between her harsh and thoughtless behavior and that of her mother." New Yorker

Vida, Vendela

The lovers; a novel. Ecco 2010 228p $23.99

ISBN 978-0-06-082839-4; 0-06-082839-0

"An American schoolteacher named Yvonne decides to rent a house by herself in Turkey shortly after her husband dies. It's a familiar impulse: When tragedy strikes, move as far away as possible. But Yvonne isn't just running away from grief; she's also running into it. Datça, the site of her vacation, is the spot where she and her late husband honeymooned decades before. The possibility of leaving her loss behind is The Lovers' main concern. The threadbare plot offers few specifics about the present: Yvonne arrives at Datça only to depart, frequently, into flights of reverie about her husband and their alcoholic daughter. She befriends new people, but they remind her of her former life. There's the estranged wife of her landlord, whose strained marriage oddly reflects her own, and a 12-year-old boy, whose mute responsiveness to Yvonne reminds her of her daughter. No matter how much she tries to take leave of the mourning process, it returns." Time Out N Y

Vidal, Gore, 1925-2012

1876; a novel. Modern Lib. 1998 524p $22.95

ISBN 0-679-60294-1

LC 98-21216

A volume in the author's American chronicle series

A reissue of the title first published 1976 by Random House

"As in 'Burr,' Charles Schuyler, hinted-at as the illegitimate son of Aaron Burr, again narrates. Now a respected and popular journalist-historian, Schuyler at 63 has returned, after years abroad, to the U.S. in the company of his widowed daughter, the Princess d'Agrigente, who is in need of a well-connected husband—thereby giving Vidal another occasion to crash society's party as he follows Schuyler on his journalistic assignments through New York, the city of Washington, later to Philadelphia for the Centennial, then Cincinnati for the Republican Convention." Publ Wkly

Vidal, Gore

Burr. Modern Lib. 1998 697p $20

ISBN 0-679-60285-2

LC 97-39825

A volume in the author's American chronicle series

"Burr is a novel in the form of a memoir told in part by Burr and in part by the young journalist Charles Schuyler, a fictional creation and Vidal's strongest character." Choice

Vidal, Gore, 1925-2012

The city and the pillar. Vintage 2003 207p pa $15

ISBN 1-4000-3037-4; 978-1-4000-3037-8

First published 1948 by Dutton

"Jim, a handsome, all-American athlete, has always been shy around girls. But when he and his best friend, Bob, partake in 'awful kid stuff,' the experience forms Jim's ideal of spiritual completion. Defying his parents' expectations, Jim strikes out on his own, hoping to find Bob and rekindle their amorous friendship. Along the way he struggles with what he feels is his unique bond with Bob and with his persistent attraction to other men." Publisher's note

Vidal, Gore

Clouds and eclipses; the collected short stories. Carroll & Graf 2006 166p pa $13.95

ISBN 0-78671-810-2

"This volume collects the short fiction of Vidal . . . , including the recently rediscovered story from which the book takes its title. All eight pieces date to the author's early career and, with the exception of the title story, were previously published in 1956. Diverse, engaging, and full of surprising twists and turns, the stories take the general theme of homosexual encounter from various points of view. The writing is crisp; the images, crystal clear and often breathtaking." Libr J

Vidal, Gore

Creation; a novel. Random House 1981 510p il

LC 79-5528

"The narrator, old and blind and finishing out his days as Persian ambassador to Pericles' Athens, is recounting his life's experiences, mostly as acquired in the service of Darius the Great and his son Xerxes. . . . In particular, he describes his special missions to India, where, as well as meeting a variety of world princes, he converses with the Buddha, and to what is now China, where he becomes a friend and admirer of Confucius." Publ Wkly

Vidal, Gore

★ Empire; a novel. Modern Lib. 1998 651p $23.95

ISBN 0-679-60293-3

LC 98-21224

A volume in the author's American chronicle series

A reissue of the title first published 1987 by Random House

"Interesting and well-developed real-life characters abound, including, most memorably, Secretary of State and

Lincoln's old friend John Hay. Intermixed with the well-researched backdrop of historical characters and events is Caroline's personal story." Libr J

Vidal, Gore

The **golden** age; a novel. Doubleday 2000 467p $27.50

ISBN 0-385-50075-0

LC 00-43071

Seventh and final volume in the author's American chronicle series. Set chronologically after Washington, D.C.

"Vidal is best on the surface. His account of the 1940 conventions is a real romp. He depicts F.D.R. with irreverent skill. . . . It's good to know how badly Wendell Willkie could give a public speech; and there are some wonderful scenes in which Eleanor Roosevelt skillfully manipulates her husband and the bosses of the old Democratic Party." N Y Times Book Rev

Vidal, Gore

Hollywood; a novel of America in the 1920s. Modern Lib. 1999 558p $24.95

ISBN 0-679-60292-5

LC 98-46174

A volume in the author's American chronicle series

A reissue of the title first published 1990 by Random House

Vidal's "highly polished prose style, in part the fruit of his classical training, is a constant delight." N Y Times Book Rev

Vidal, Gore

★ **Lincoln**. Modern Lib. 1993 712p hardcover o.p.

LC 92-27273

A reissue of the title first published 1984 by Random House

This novel "is not so much an imaginative reconstruction of an era as an intelligent, lucid and highly informative transcript of it, never less than workmanlike in its blocking out of scenes and often extremely compelling." N Y Times Book Rev

Vidal, Gore

★ **Myra** Breckinridge [and] Myron. Random House 1986 417p $19.95

ISBN 0-394-55376-4

LC 86-11423

Combined edition of two titles first published 1968 and 1974 respectively

In the first novel, Myra who was once Myron seduces both Rusty Godowsky and his girlfriend Mary-Ann Pringle. The sequel is set in 1973. Myron Breckinridge, the alter ego of the transsexual heroine, is pushed through his television screen and onto the set of a 1948 film "Siren of Babylon" starring Maria Montez. He has difficulty in getting out. Myra periodically takes command of Myron's body. She attempts to save the world from overpopulation by altering the male sex

Vidal, Gore

The **Smithsonian** Institution; a novel. Random House 1998 260p $23

ISBN 0-375-50121-5

LC 97-38615

"Fans of Vidal's comic novels can expect the usual mixture of earthiness and erudition, though on a more restrained level; the novel provides the author with the chance to put words in the mouths of a dozen presidents, noted scientists, and pop culture heroes." Libr J

Vidal, Gore

Washington, D.C. a novel. Modern Lib. 1999 422p $24.95

ISBN 0-679-60291-7

LC 98-46173

A volume in the author's American chronicle series

Set from the New Deal to the McCarthy years this "political novel features the ambitions of both a senator and his young secretary for the Presidency. The senator loses his chance for the Democratic nomination when Roosevelt decides to run for a third term. The secretary, mapping his course to the top, with the help of a journalist invents a non-happening which makes him a national hero. He then blackmails the senator into withdrawing from the race and wins the senatorial seat for himself." Booklist

Vila-Matas, Enrique

★ **Montano's** malady; translated from the Spanish by Jonathan Dunne. New Directions 2007 $14.95 pa $14.95

ISBN 978-0-8112-1628-9; 0-8112-1628-4

LC 2006-102330

Original Spanish edition, 2002

"Written in the form of a journal, which becomes a novel, then a dictionary of writers' journals, then a lecture on the writing of such journals, Montano tells of its narrator's obsession with literature. Middle-aged and married to Rosa, he has become 'a walking dictionary of quotations', unable to do anything without it triggering a memory of something he's read or, worse, something remembered by a writer that he's read, which in turn recalls a thought from the head of yet another writer. Following him and his overactive brain from his native Barcelona to Nantes, Chile, the Azores, Lisbon and Budapest—via Walter Benjamin, Kafka, W. G. Sebald, Pessoa and Robert Walser among others—is like playing a mental version of Twister. . . . Shunning narrative, the book continues to seduce with writerly observations—both the narrator's, and quotations from other writers." Telegraph (London)

Vila-Matas, Enrique

Never any end to Paris; translated from the Spanish by Anne McLean. New Directions Books 2011 197p $15.95

ISBN 978-0-8112-1813-9

LC 2011-02601

Original Spanish edition, 2003

This novel is "is told in the form of a lecture delivered by a novelist clearly a version of the author himself. The 'lecturer' tells of his two-year stint living in Marguerite Duras's garret during the seventies, spending time with writers, intellectuals, and eccentrics, and trying to make it as a creator of literature. . . . Encountering such luminaries as Duras, Roland Barthes, Georges Perec, Sergio Pitol, Samuel Beckett, and Juan Marsé, our narrator embarks on a novel whose text will 'kill' its readers and put him on a footing with his beloved Hemingway." Publisher's note

Villars, Elizabeth

The **Normandie** affair. Doubleday 1982 319p

LC 81-43727

This novel is "set aboard an opulent cruise liner, the 'Normandie,' in the days when luxury and sumptuousness were taken for granted. Villars' story covers six days of irrevocable change in the lives of several passengers crossing from New York to France in 1936. At the center of this drama is mysterious Anson Sherwood, a wealthy Bostonian with a passion for and inordinate knowledge of the 'Normandie.' Sherwood turns out to be a dedicated meddler who interferes in the lives of his fellow passengers, involving himself in both romantic entanglements and political intrigues, usually with fortuitous results. Neatly bundling drama and romance, Villars has captured the dichotomous nature of shipboard life." Booklist

Vine, Barbara

Anna's book; [by] Ruth Rendell writing as Barbara Vine. Harmony Bks. 1993 394p

LC 92-34309

This "tale of psychological suspense revolves around a woman's discovery that the published memoirs of her deceased grandmother hid evidence of an elderly woman's murder and the disappearance of a little girl." Libr J

"Vine's story is utterly riveting, rich and multifaceted in its complexity. Her characters are wonderfully real and fascinatingly unconventional." Booklist

Vine, Barbara

The **blood** doctor; a novel. Crown 2002 369p il $25

ISBN 1-400-04504-5

LC 2002-18491

"The story lacks the usual page-turner suspense of the Rendell/Vine novels but makes up for that with unusually detailed glimpses into Victorian life and the inner workings of the House of Parliament, which American readers will find particularly intriguing." Libr J

Vine, Barbara

The **brimstone** wedding. Harmony Bks. 1996 330p $24

ISBN 0-517-70339-4

LC 95-30280

"Both Jenny and Stella embrace their pain with the sense of fatalism that has always been Ms. Vine's literary hallmark. The wonder is that they can speak their hearts in such clear and distinctive voices and yet retain their interior mystery." N Y Times Book Rev

Vine, Barbara

★ The **chimney** sweeper's boy; a novel. Harmony Bks. 1998 344p $24

ISBN 0-609-60287-X

LC 98-10567

This novel revolves around the "sudden death of Gerald Candless, a celebrated English novelist who lived on the Devon coast with his wife, Ursula, and two daughters to whom he was conspicuously devoted. When one daughter, Sarah, starts researching her father's early history for the biography she has been asked to write, she discovers that he was living under a false identity for most of his life. As more facts emerge from Sarah's research, they both illuminate and contradict the dark views of Gerald's personality supplied by his bitter wife and the deep, if ambiguous, insights contained in his own novels." N Y Times Book Rev

Vine, Barbara

★ **Gallowglass**. Harmony Bks. 1990 272p $19.95

ISBN 0-517-57744-5

LC 89-29026

"Miss Vine's most penetrating foray yet into the dark mysteries of the heart's obsessions, this haunting novel examines love in many guises—romantic, parental, idolatrous, possessive, selfless, erotic, platonic and sick. The scope of observation is dazzling; the tone, remarkably nonjudgmental." N Y Times Book Rev

Vine, Barbara

Grasshopper; a novel. Harmony Bks. 2000 392p $25

ISBN 0-609-60789-8

LC 00-38281

"Only a handful of writers, in any genre, can match Barbara Vine for imaginative originality and ingenuity. . . . Grasshopper is about good intentions gone wrong, violence, innocence and an encounter with true evil. . . . To say that a book can open your eyes to a different world is a cliché, but rarely has it been more apt than in describing this novel." New Statesman (Engl)

Vine, Barbara

The **house** of stairs; [by] Ruth Rendell writing as Barbara Vine. Harmony Bks. 1989 277p

LC 88-38303

First published 1988 in the United Kingdom

"Elizabeth Vetch, a writer, recalls her adolescence and young womanhood living with her cousin Cosette in a big, eccentric house in the Notting Hill section of London. Lots of people besides Elizabeth and Cosette lived in the House of Stairs, though; it was nest to many of their friends as well. Cosette is intent on recovering her lost youth, and because of her vulnerability in that direction, two residents conspire against her to gain her money. The consequence is violent death, with Elizabeth losing the one person she truly loved. A complex, eloquent novel—sure to retain Vine's large readership and undoubtedly gain her even more followers." Booklist

Vine, Barbara

King Solomon's carpet. Harmony Bks. 1992
355p

LC 91-43668

First published 1991 in the United Kingdom

The author "displays her remarkable ability to spot and
dissect the terrifying beneath the ordinary, to imbue a setting with its own, almost palpable terror, and to construct
in the process a narrative maze filled with constant, fearful
surprise." Booklist

Vine, Barbara

The minotaur; a novel. Shaye Areheart Books
2005 341p $25
ISBN 0-307-23760-5

LC 2005-10837

"In this novel, set in the late 1960s, an autistic man, a
dysfunctional family, and an innocent young woman become entangled in a web of deceit. Swedish nursing student
Kerstin Kvist comes to Essex, England, to care for 39-year-
old John Cosway, who is being heavily sedated for a mental
illness he doesn't actually have. John's mother and sisters
live with him on a drafty estate at the mercy of a trust. Naturally inquisitive, Kerstin wants to explore the bizarre, labyrinthine library built on the estate but ends up coming across
secrets best left hidden." Libr J

"This is very satisfying reading, a sort of blend of Edgar
Allan Poe and Anthony Trollope." Booklist

Vine, Barbara

★ No night is too long. Harmony Bks. 1995
315p $23
ISBN 0-517-79964-2

LC 94-13064

First published 1994 in the United Kingdom

"This is a novel about the effects of passion in which the
mood is as bleak as the cold North Sea; a murder mystery
in which the crucial killing is imaginary, and the actual killing arbitrary. . . . Nevertheless—the novel does grip and its
scheme is impressive; it is hard to withhold applause from
an author so lavishly endowed with the capacity to invent
interlocking segments of plot." Times Lit Suppl

Vinge, Joan D.

★ The Snow Queen. Dial Press (NY) 1980
536p

LC 79-20555

"An amalgam of SF and heroic fantasy borrowing the
structure of Hans Christian Andersen's famous story, set
on a barbarian world exploited by technologically superior
outworlders, against the background of a fallen galactic empire." Anatomy of Wonder 4

Followed by World's end

Vinge, Joan D.

The Summer Queen. Warner Bks. 1991 670p

LC 90-50521

Sequel to World's end

"Plots and subplots proliferate, and although the prose is
sometimes florid and the romance and sex scenes overly sentimental, the book is so full of drama, conflict and tragedy
that it justifies its length." Publ Wkly

Vinge, Joan D.

World's end. Bluejay Bks. 1984 230p

LC 83-21374

In this novel "BZ Gundhalinu, a police inspector who
played a minor role in . . . {The Snow Queen} is the central
character. Having left Carbuncle at the time of the Change
he has traveled to World's End in search of his two irresponsible older brothers. World's End, a barely habitable frontier
planet, is center of a 'Company' mining operation but also
contains Fire Lake, an unexplained anomaly that appears to
drive those who approach it insane." Voice Youth Advocates

Followed by: The Summer Queen

Vinge, Vernor

The children of the sky. Tor Books 2011 444p
il (Zones of thought) $25.99
ISBN 978-0-312-87562-6

LC 2011024210

Sequel to A fire upon the deep (1992)

"It has been ten years since Ravna Bergnsdot brought
150 children to the primitive planet Tines World and, with
the assistance of the native species, caninelike creatures
with a pack mind, formed the last stronghold of humanity in
the galaxy. Residing in the universe's 'slow zone,' in which
faster-than-light travel is impossible and technological developments are limited, Ravna hopes to keep her colony safe
from the alien Blight, which has already destroyed high-
tech worlds. Not all the children brought to safety, however, believe in Ravna's tale of technology gone wrong or
in the existence of the Blight, and their actions might bring
about the cataclysmic disaster Ravna and her Tinish partner, Woodcarver, hoped to avoid. . . . Vinge has crafted a
tale that should captivate his fans and win for him a larger
and well-deserved audience. Libraries should anticipate demand." Libr J

Vinge, Vernor

A deepness in the sky. TOR Bks. 1999 606p
ISBN 0-312-85683-0

LC 98-43457

Prequel to A fire upon the deep

Vinge "is among the very best of the current crop of hard
SF writers, producing work that is not only fast-paced and
intellectually challenging, but also stylishly written and centered on carefully drawn characters." Publ Wkly

Vinge, Vernor

★ A fire upon the deep. TOR Bks. 1992 391p

LC 91-39020

"Thoughtful space opera at its best, this book delivers
everything it promises in terms of galactic scope, audacious
concepts and believable characters both human and nonhuman." N Y Times Book Rev

Vinge, Vernor

Rainbows end. Tor 2006 364p $25.95
ISBN 0-312-85684-9

LC 2006-278136

"Vinge's world is saturated with the logical extensions
of current R&D. He has thought long and hard about how
pervasive and ubiquitous information technology will transform our lives." Sci Fic Wkly

Viswanathan, Padma

The **toss** of a lemon. Harcourt 2008 619p il $26

ISBN 978-0-15-101533-7; 0-15-101533-3

LC 2008-13369

This "novel spans 66 years-from 1896 to 1962—in the life of one Tamil family. The matriarch of the clan, Sivakami, a Brahmin, was married at ten and widowed at 18. Already a mother of two, Sivakami was determined to set a pious example. This meant that she shaved her head, wore only white, and touched no one, not even her children or grand-children, between dusk and dawn. What's more, she obeyed the custom of staying inside her home, venturing outdoors only three times in the many decades before her death. Siv-akami's proscribed world is portrayed in amazing detail, and the life of the Brahmin elite is vividly captured. . . . Gender rules, class relations, and the political castes of late 19th- and early to mid-20th-century India are well presented, making this an important work of historical fiction." Libr J

Vlautin, Willy

Lean on Pete; a novel. Harper Perennial 2010 277, 16p pa $13.99

ISBN 978-0-06-145653-4; 0-06-145653-5

LC 2009-20460

"Charley Thompson is a 15-year-old boy who dreams of a normal home and the chance to play high-school football. Newly arrived in Portland with a mostly absent father, Char-ley hopes for the best and gets the worst. Suddenly home-less, he hangs out on the backstretch at Portland Meadows racetrack and finds a friend—an aging Thoroughbred named Lean on Pete. That's exactly what Charley does, at least for a while, until Pete, bound for the slaughterhouse, needs to lean on Charley. The perilous journey on which Charley and Pete embark must end badly—think of Kirk Douglas and another loyal horse on the run from civilization in Lonely Are the Brave—but on the road Charley tells Pete the story of his life, and in this young boy's flatly descriptive but heartbreaking words, reprising a lifetime of barely getting by . . . , Vlautin transforms what might have been a weepy, unbelievable TV-movie of a novel into a tough-and-tender account of a boy, a big-hearted horse, and a mostly unforgiv-ing world." Booklist

Vlautin, Willy

Northline; a novel. Harper Perennial 2008 192, 18p pa $14.95

ISBN 978-0-06-145652-7; 0-06-145652-7

LC 2008-297989

"Vlautin's writing style is perfectly suited to his mate-rial: Things happen the way they happen, slowly but inexo-rably, with the significance of any moment rarely evident until after the fact, or maybe never evident at all. There are no epiphanies here; new lives are built one unassuming sen-tence at a time." Portland Mercury

Vollmann, William T.

Argall. Viking 2001 746p il $40

ISBN 0-670-91030-9

LC 2001-17744

"The eponymous Captain Argall edges into the fore-ground in the second part, succeeding Smith as Jamestown's

leading spirit; he has the sinister bearing of some Jacobean theater devil—like Iago, there's menace in his meanings. He kidnaps Pokahuntas and manipulates her assimilation into settler culture. Vollman's ability to write in Smith's English and endow it with a contemporary snap is an extraordinary feat." Publ Wkly

Includes bibliographical references

Vollmann, William T.

★ **Butterfly** stories; a novel. Grove Press 1993 279p il

ISBN 0-8021-1502-0

LC 93-2489

The protagonist of this novel, "known as 'the butterfly boy' in grade school but now simply called 'the journalist,' travels to Southeast Asia to investigate the prostitution prob-lem, accompanied by a photographer. The latter proves to be an impeccable sex tourist, but the journalist is inept. He for-gets to use a condom the very first night and suffers from an ever-worsening barrage of fevers and infections thereafter. Then he falls in love with one of the prostitutes and decides to marry." Libr J

Vollmann, William T.

★ **Europe** central. Viking 2005 832p il $39.95

ISBN 0-670-03392-8

LC 2004-61170

"What sets 'Europe Central' apart from Vollmann's other large-scale historical productions is its strong narrative lines. The pieces are dated and arranged chronologically to give the book a plot that arcs from prewar political machinations to Germany's surge east to Russia's counteroffensive, and that ends with cold war politics in divided Berlin." N Y Times Book Rev

Vollmann, William T.

★ **Fathers** and crows. Viking 1992 990p

ISBN 0-670-84333-4

LC 92-18315

The language "moves interestingly between contempo-rary colloquial, Hollywood historical, Middle High Tolk-ientalk, and a quirky and enjoyable poetry: never less than vigorous and inventive. . . . Despite nudges, the narrative grips." Times Lit Suppl

Includes bibliographical references

Vollmann, William T.

The **ice**-shirt. Viking 1990 415p il maps

ISBN 0-670-83239-1

LC 90-50051

"Without apparent strain, the story interweaves numer-ous characters, sea voyages, murders and supernatural hor-rors, digressing with relish. . . . 'The Ice-Shirt' impresses mightily in its scope, its scene-painting and its enciphered social messages." N Y Times Book Rev

Vollmann, William T.

The **rifles**. Viking 1994 411p il maps

ISBN 0-670-84856-5

LC 93-31577

"What The Rifles demonstrates, and what magnetizes the narrative's scattered contexts is the real and binding continuity between nineteenth and twentieth-century patterns of mind-above all, this terrible insistence on our will to power over the world." Yale Rev

Vollmann, William T.

The **royal** family. Viking 2000 780p $40

ISBN 0-670-89167-3

LC 99-56587

"Vollmann is after large-scale social chronicle; he includes characters from nearly every walk of life, and trains his attentions on processes not often seen by the faint of heart. . . . But this hypperrealistic novelist also aims to present a metaphysics: the two brothers stand for two kinds of human being, the chosen and the outcast. As in all Vollmann's novels, the author's encyclopedic ambition sometimes overwhelms the human scale; some supporting characters, though, do stay vivid. Vollmann avoids simply glamorizing the outcasts but remains, deep down, a Blakean romantic: prostitution is for him not only the universal indictment of the human race but also, paradoxically, the only paradise we can actually visit." Publ Wkly

Volpi, Jorge

In search of Klingsor; translated by Kristina Cordero. Scribner 2002 414p $26

ISBN 0-7432-0118-3

LC 2002-17582

Original Spanish edition published 1999 in Mexico

The author "delivers a novel that manages to function as a crackling spy thriller while delivering a thoughtful treatist on the nature of love and deception." Booklist

Voltaire

★ **Candide**; translated by Peter Constantine. Modern Library 2005 119p hardcover o.p. pa $8.95

ISBN 0-679-64313-3; 0-8129-7201-5 pa

LC 2004-55244

Original French edition, 1759

"In this philosophical fantasy, naive Candide sees and suffers such misfortune that he ultimately rejects the philosophy of his tutor Doctor Pangloss, who claims that 'all is for the best in this best of all possible worlds.' Candide and his companions—Pangloss, his beloved Cunegonde, and his servant Cacambo—display an instinct for survival that provides them hope in an otherwise somber setting. When they all retire together to a simple life on a small farm, they discover that the secret of happiness is 'to cultivate one's garden,' a practical philosophy that excludes excessive idealism and nebulous metaphysics." Merriam-Webster's Ency of Lit

Voltaire

Candide and other stories; translated from the French, with an introduction and notes, by Roger Pearson. Knopf 1992 307p $17

ISBN 0-679-41746-X

Voltaire

Voltaire's Candide, Zadig, and selected stories; translated with an introduction by Donald M. Frame. Candide illustrations by Paul Klee. Indiana Univ. Press 1961 351p il

Contains 14 satiric tales in addition to Candide (1759) and Zadig (1748)

Vonnegut, Kurt

Armageddon in retrospect; and other new and unpublished writings on war and peace. [illustrations by the author; introduction by Mark Vonnegut] G. P. Putnam's Sons 2008 232p il $24.95

ISBN 978-0-399-15508-6; 0-399-15508-2

Twelve previously unpublished writings on war and peace include such pieces as an essay on the destruction of Dresden, a story about the first-meal fantasies of three soldiers, and a meditation on the impossibility of shielding children from the temptations of violence.

"Only a few of the . . . stories rely on the twists of reality and narrative present in Vonnegut's novels; the majority are carried by the characters' struggle with the absurdities of war and peace. Vonnegut's World War II experience as a prisoner of war in Dresden haunts the work, with multiple stories featuring American POWs in Germany. . . . Readers of Vonnegut's books won't find any surprises here, but because he is at his sardonic best when working in short form, they won't be let down by his humor and poignancy, either." Libr J

Vonnegut, Kurt

Bagombo snuff box: uncollected short fiction. Putnam 1999 295p hardcover o.p. pa $13.95

ISBN 0-399-14505-2; 0-425-17446-8 pa

LC 99-13665

"The 23 stories in this collection were published in magazines . . . during the Fifties and are collected here for the first time. The topics covered include space travel ('Thanasphere'), which describes the first manned orbit of Earth; finding the American dream ('The package'), about a new home full of the latest accessories; and an attempt to impress an old girlfriend (the title story). . . . Although many of the stories are topically dated, the ironic insights and illumination of character are timeless, and no one does it better than Vonnegut." Libr J

Vonnegut, Kurt

★ **Breakfast** of champions; or, Goodbye blue Monday! by Kurt Vonnegut, Jr; with drawings by the author. Delacorte Press 1973 295p il

"In this novel Vonnegut is . . . clearing his head by throwing out acquired ideas, and also liberating some of the characters from his previous books. . . . This explosive meditation ranks with Vonnegut's best." N Y Times Book Rev

Vonnegut, Kurt

★ **Cat's** cradle; by Kurt Vonnegut, Jr. Holt, Rinehart & Winston 1963 233p

"In this mordant satire on religion, research, government, and human nature, a free-lance writer becomes the catalyst in a chain of events that unearths the secret of ice-nine. This is an element potentially more lethal than that produced by nuclear fission. The search leads to a mythical island, San Lorenzo, where the writer also discovers the leader of a new religion, Bokonon." Shapiro. Fic for Youth. 3d edition

Vonnegut, Kurt

Deadeye Dick. Delacorte Press/Seymour Lawrence 1982 240p

ISBN 0-440-01780-7

LC 82-13024

"In Midland City, Ohio, the {Waltz} family is isolated and scorned by the community for patriarch Otto's ersatz career as an artist and his strident support for Nazi policies. Their wealth and what's left of their social position is decimated when younger son Rudy (Deadeye Dick) accidently shoots a pregnant woman. Father pleads guilty to the crime, Rudy becomes a night-shift pharmacist, author of the prize-winning but unsuccessful play 'Katmandu' and cook and maid for his useless mother. Brother Felix becomes the president of NBC, and mother dies of radiation emitted from the fireplace of their 'shitbox' home. The entire populace is eventually exterminated . . . by the inadvertent dropping of a neutron bomb." SLJ

Vonnegut, Kurt

★ **Galapagos**; a novel. Delacorte Press/Seymour Lawrence 1985 295p

LC 85-4581

"A group of tourists on a cruise survive the end of the world, settling on a small Galapagos Island and beginning a new evolutionary sequence. The ghostly narrator looks back on things from a perspective one million years later." Anatomy of Wonder 4

Vonnegut, Kurt

God bless you, Mr. Rosewater; or, Pearls before swine. by Kurt Vonnegut, Jr. Holt, Rinehart & Winston 1965 217p

"With a satirist's eye for the meanness of man, especially his greed, Vonnegut tells the story of Eliot Rosewater, president of the Rosewater Foundation, who uses his position to help all petitioners. Discovering a plot to remove him from authority Rosewater gives all his money to over 50 children he is falsely accused of fathering." Booklist

Vonnegut, Kurt

Hocus pocus. Putnam 1990 302p

LC 90-34535

"Vonnegut remains an effectual stylist, combining deadpan irony and faux naiveté. As usual, his central narrative winds through a mosaic of aphorisms, verbal tics, digressions, homilies, obscure facts. . . . This compendium of devices and concerns may have hardened into a formula, but it has not yet ceased to be a diverting one." Times Lit Suppl

Vonnegut, Kurt

Jailbird; a novel. by Kurt Vonnegut, Jr. Delacorte Press/Seymour Lawrence 1979 246p

ISBN 0-440-05449-4

LC 79-12881

This novel "opens with Walter F. Starbuck, a 64-year-old victim of Watergate, about to be released from a Georgia prison for white-collar workers. Bereft of fortune and family (his wife is dead, his son is ungrateful) Starbuck retreats to the past via flashbacks of World War II, old love affairs, and past occupations. Eventually he regains respectability in the ubiquitous RAMJAC Corporation . . . which owns 19% of America and continues to swallow every major enterprise in its path." Libr J

Vonnegut, Kurt

Look at the birdie; unpublished short fiction. Delacorte Press 2009 251p il $27

ISBN 978-0-385-34371-8; 0-385-34371-X

LC 2009-34612

"Vonnegut is hardly an American Kafka, but more in the vein of Twain and Swift. He delivers kicks to the sacred cows of the era (psychoanalysis, big corporations, money, success, the dawn of sexual liberation) with such hilarity that readers forget we have just witnessed a body blow. Vonnegut's power to work that magic is already on display in these early stories." Boston Globe

Vonnegut, Kurt

★ **Novels** & stories, 1963-1979; Sidney Offit, editor. Library of America 2011 851p $35

ISBN 978-1-59853-098-8; 1-59853-098-4

This volume opens with Cat's Cradle (1963), "in which a would-be historian of the bombing of Hiroshima finds himself a privileged witness to the icy end of the world. God Bless You, Mr. Rosewater (1965) chronicles the alcoholic unraveling and spiritual rebirth of a goodhearted dreamer tormented by the question 'What are people for?' Slaughterhouse-Five (1969) . . . is the jump-cutting saga of Billy Pilgrim, who, having come unstuck in time, is doomed to relive continually both the destruction of Dresden and his abduction by space aliens. And in a text enhanced by the author's spirited line drawings, Breakfast of Champions (1973) describes the fateful meeting of a luckless science-fiction writer and an unhinged Pontiac dealer who disastrously believes that everyone but himself is a robot." Publisher's note

Vonnegut, Kurt

★ **Player** piano; by Kurt Vonnegut, Jr. Scribner 1952 295p

"Paul Proteus, engineer, leads revolt against machine-computer conformist civilization, only to find that when it succeeds, people wish for the machines again. In order or in chaos, mob psychology is stupid. Modern civilization has hate-love affinity for machines. Incisive satire; a classic modern dystopia." Anatomy of Wonder. 3d edition

Vonnegut, Kurt

★ The **sirens** of Titan; by Kurt Vonnegut, Jr. Houghton Mifflin 1961 319p

First published 1959 in paperback by Dell

This novel "attacks the concept of causality and the confusion of luck with God's will {and} reveals human history as a trivial incident manipulated by the alien Tralfamadorians to further an equally trivial scheme." New Ency of Sci Fic

Vonnegut, Kurt

Slapstick; or, Lonesome no more! a novel. Delacorte Press/Seymour Lawrence 1976 243p

In this satirical fantasy, President of the United States Dr. Wilbur Daffodil-11 Swain sits in the ruins of Manhattan's Skyscraper National Park writing his memoirs. As deformed children, he and his twin sister were separately regarded as idiots but discovered that together they were super-intelligent and went on to write a best-selling child-rearing manual. As president, Wilbur instituted a program to combat loneliness by forming artificial extended families

"Slapstick is a deceptively short and simple book. Its readability should not distract one from the fact that Vonnegut has found a fictional situation which considers serious human problems." New Repub

Vonnegut, Kurt

★ **Slaughterhouse**-five; or, The children's crusade: a duty-dance with death. 25th anniversary ed; Delacorte Press 1994 205p il $22.50; pa $6.99
ISBN 0-385-31208-3; 0-440-18029-5 pa
LC 94-171120

A reissue of the title first published 1969

This novel "mixes a fictionalized account of the author's experience of the fire bombing of Dresden with a compensatory fantasy of the planet Tralfamadore, the science-fiction element is progressively dominated by the overall concerns of satire, black humor, and absurdism." Reader's Ency. 3d edition

"A masterpiece, in which Vonnegut penetrated to the heart of the issues developed in his earlier absurdist fabulations. A key work of modern SF." Anatomy of Wonder 4

Vonnegut, Kurt

Timequake. Putnam 1997 219p il $23.95
ISBN 0-399-13737-8
LC 97-14508

"The cataclysm of the title—in 2001, time undergoes a tremor, and everyone must relive the nineties—provides an excuse for Vonnegut and his longtime alter ego, Kilgore Trout, to trade rants: on desert camouflage, thirties socialism, the joys of waiting in line at the post office, the traitorousness of Dillinger's Hungarian girlfriend, semicolons. The resulting quilt of snippets is equal parts memoir, literary charm, self-congratulation, humanist sermon, randy geriatric fantasy, and toastmasterly jokefest." New Yorker

Vonnegut, Kurt

Welcome to the monkey house; a collection of short works. by Kurt Vonnegut, Jr. Delacorte Press 1968 298p

Vonnegut, Kurt

While mortals sleep; unpublished short fiction. Delacorte Press 2011 253p il $27
ISBN 978-0-385-34373-2
LC 2010-33817

"In well over a dozen novels and hundreds of short stories, Vonnegut wrote about the madness of war and about alienation in the modern machine age. When he died in 2007, he was acclaimed as a great American writer with a signature style. [This] is the second collection of his previously unpublished short stories. Written early in his career, they are concerned less with war and corporate malfeasance than with the pursuit of success, happiness and love. Vintage Vonnegut, for better and worse, they put characters, settings and stories in the service of moral messages. At their best, these messages achieve a simple and powerful eloquence." Pittsburgh Post-Gazette

Vreeland, Susan

Clara and Mr. Tiffany; a novel. Random House 2011 405p $26
ISBN 978-1-4000-6816-6
LC 2010-07758

"Vreeland traces the secret history of an objet d'art— . . . the iconic Tiffany lamp. Her heroine is Clara Driscoll, head of the all-female glass-cutting department at Tiffany Studios, who designed many of the fanciful, nature-inspired leaded-glass lamps for which Louis Comfort Tiffany earned fame.... Through Driscoll's life, Vreeland offers a fascinating look at turn-of-the-century New York City." People

Includes bibliographical references

Vreeland, Susan

Girl in hyacinth blue. MacMurray & Beck 1999 242p $17.50
ISBN 1-87844-890-0
LC 99-27405

"Vreeland strikes a pleasing balance between the timeless world of the painting as a work of art and the finite worlds of its possessors and admirers—not to mention the world of its subject and its creator. Intelligent, searching and unusual, the novel is filled with luminous moments; like the painting it describes so well, it has a way of lingering in the reader's mind." N Y Times Book Rev

Vreeland, Susan

Luncheon of The Boating Party. Viking 2007 434p il map
ISBN 978-0-670-03854-1; 0-670-03854-7
LC 2006-35324

In this novel Vreeland turns "to French impressionist master Auguste Renoir's famous painting Luncheon of the Boating Party , which depicts a group of people (in 1880) enjoying leisure time on the terrace of a riverside restaurant. The current conditions in the life of the painter himself launch the author on an amazingly engrossing reinvigoration of the lives of the individuals who modeled for Renoir for that work, all of whom were actual people, and all are given a third dimension in Vreeland's lovely prose." Booklist

Vreeland, Susan

The **passion** of Artemesia. Viking 2002 288p
ISBN 0-670-89449-4
LC 2001-26119

"Vreeland palpably captures Artemisia's joy as she blends colors and watches her artistic imaginings take shape. . . . Although her final confrontation with her father, artist Orazio Gentileschi, feels forced, the novel brilliantly captures the life of an extraordinary artist." Libr J

Vásquez, Juan Gabriel, 1973-

The **secret** history of Costaguana; Juan Gabriel Vasquez; translated from the Spanish by Anne McLean. Riverhead Books 2011 283p.
ISBN 978-1-4088-0018-8 Bloomsbury; 1-4088-0018-7 Bloomsbury; 978-1-59448-803-0 Riverhead Books; 1-59448-803-7 Riverhead Books
LC 2011005706

"The narrator of this novel emends Joseph Conrad's 'Nostromo.'" (N Y Times Book Rev)

W

Wagner, Bruce

The **chrysanthemum** palace. Simon & Schuster 2005 210p $23

ISBN 0-7432-4339-0

LC 2004-43059

"On the set of a schlocky TV space opera called 'Starwatch,' three children of wealthy and talented parents struggle to attain success of their own. The narrator, Bertie, is the son of the show's creator, and his current acting job is the nadir in a career of ever-shrinking ambition. His companions are Clea, the pill-popping daughter of a sexy actress who died young, and Thad, who is plagued by a personality disorder and the outsized legend of his father, an award-winning author. Suffering in the shadow of parental fame is a familiar trope of tabloid pathos, and the parents here are predictably malevolent. . . . [Wagner's] ability to eviscerate the absurdities of Hollywood, while occasionally hinting at its basic humanity, remains undiminished." New Yorker

Waite, Urban

The **terror** of living; a novel. Little, Brown and Co. 2011 306p $24.99

ISBN 978-0-316-09789-5; 0-316-09789-6

LC 2010021840

"Waite brings a nimble touch to the material. Throwaway lines are rendered with surprising delicacy, and Living's knife-fetishist villain makes for an oddly endearing sociopath." Entertainment Wkly

Wakefield, Dan

★ **Starting** over. Delacorte Press/Seymour Lawrence 1973 290p

"A powerful, naturalistic depiction of the agony suffered by a man whose affluence merely conceals an utter absence of value and direction." Libr J

Walbert, Kate

The **gardens** of Kyoto; a novel. Scribner 2001 288p

ISBN 0-684-86948-9

LC 2001-18876

"Ellen, the self-effacing narrator, mourns the disappearance of her cousin on Iwo Jima during the Second World War, and tries to decipher a book he has left her about the Kyoto gardens. The beauty of these landscapes lies in their impenetrability: one, made up entirely of shadows, must be viewed at night; another may be seen only through a window whose blind is forever drawn. Similarly, Ellen stands on the fringes of other, more dramatic lives, first befriending a fellow-coed whose affair with a married professor ends in an illegal abortion, then falling in love with a traumatized veteran of the Korean War. In precise, delicate prose, the author renders with equal power the quiet desperation of a girl growing up in nineteen-fifies America . . . and the ethereal." New Yorker

Walbert, Kate

Our kind. Scribner 2004 195p $23

ISBN 0-7432-4559-8

LC 2003-66294

"Walbert's characters are caught like insects in amber as they make late-in-life discoveries no school could ever teach. Brittle, funny and poignant, this is a prickly treat." Publ Wkly

Walbert, Kate

A **short** history of women; a novel. Scribner 2009 239p $24

ISBN 978-1-4165-9498-7; 1-4165-9498-1

LC 2008-38312

"This novel follows five generations of women as each "tries (or declines) to find balance between career, marriage and motherhood. Dorothy Trevor is a suffragette in early World War I England who starves herself to death for her cause, leaving her young children behind. Her daughter, Evelyn Townsend, makes her way to America and academia, focusing her life on her work. Evelyn's niece Dorothy Townsend endures 1970s consciousness-raising, a lost child and a marriage that grows stale. Dorothy's daughter Liz, a privileged Manhattan mom, seeks reassurance from her 6-year-old. And Liz's niece Dora, set to graduate as part of Yale's class of 2011, is introduced to us via her Facebook profile and a few impatient words on the phone." Seattle Times

Characters are recognizable but not clichéd and will stay with readers as wise, if also flawed and struggling, exemplars of political and intellectual engagement." Libr J

Waldman, Amy

The **submission**. Farrar, Straus and Giroux 2011 299p

ISBN 0-374-27156-9; 9780374271565

LC 2011007509

"A jury gathers in Manhattan to select a memorial for the victims of a devastating terrorist attack. Their fraught deliberations complete, the jurors open the envelope containing the anonymous winner's name—and discover he is an American Muslim." (Publisher's note)

"It's two years after the events of 9/11, and a (fictional) high-profile committee has convened in Manhattan to select a monument that will transform the still-raw wound at Ground Zero into a safe haven of healing and remembrance. The winner, chosen from a pool of anonymously submitted blueprints, is a beauty: a walled garden whose spare geometry poetically echoes the fallen towers. And its designer? A brilliant young architect, Virginia-born and Yale-educated, named Mohammad Khan. Or as one dismayed committee member exclaims behind the doors of Gracie Mansion, "It's a goddamn Muslim!" Within hours, a tabloid reporter has sniffed out the story, and so begins the ugly political dosi-do of a national scandal, one pushed along as much by personal agendas as by genuine outrage. Among the players: the hapless, overmatched committee head; two grieving widows, one wealthy and white, the other poor and Bangladeshi; and the black-sheep brother of a fallen firefighter. And at its center, of course, 'Mo' Khan himself: Wary and increasingly weary, he refuses all easy outs, even as he is tried and convicted in the kangaroo court of public opinion." Entertainment Wkly

Waldman, Ayelet

Red Hook Road. Doubleday 2010 343p $25.95

ISBN 978-0-385-51786-7; 0-385-51786-6

LC 2009-20023

The book "begins with a prelude, appropriately, since so much of this novel involves music. The wedding of a young couple, Becca Copaken and John Tetherly, has just taken place in a small town on the Maine coast. The setting is described gloriously. Then, in a moment of breathtaking horror, a speeding driver crashes into the bridal couple's limousine and kills them. . . . [The novel] follows the relatives of the bride and groom over the four summers following the tragedy, revealing how they cope with grief and loss, and how they don't. Waldman writes with practiced skill. She's familiar with her subject matter: Maine, classical music, yacht building, violins, lobster molting." Boston Globe

Walker, Alice

By the light of my father's smile; a novel. Random House 1998 222p $22.95

ISBN 0-375-50152-5

LC 98-5464

"Susannah and Magdalena are sisters estranged from each other and their parents since adolescence, after Magdalena is beaten by their father for having sex. As each woman expresses her loneliness and anger—Susannah through sexual exploration, Magdalena through food—they are observed by their father's ghost, who seeks a reconciliation with them that comes only after their deaths." Libr J

"Walker has created a romantic but propagandistic fairy tale that veers disconcertingly from the facile to the heartfelt." Booklist

Walker, Alice

★ The **color** purple; 10th anniversary ed; Harcourt Brace Jovanovich 1992 290p il $24; pa $14

ISBN 0-15-119154-9; 0-15-602835-2 pa

LC 91-47202

A reissue of the title first published 1982

"A feminist novel about an abused and uneducated black woman's struggle for empowerment, the novel was praised for the depth of its female characters and for its eloquent use of black English vernacular." Merriam-Webster's Ency of Lit

Walker, Alice

Now is the time to open your heart; a novel. Random House 2004 240p $24.95

ISBN 1-400-06173-3

LC 2003-54766

"A well-published author, married many times, [Kate] has lived a life rich with explorations of the natural world and the human soul. Now, at fifty-seven, she leaves her lover, Yolo, to embark on a new excursion, one that begins on the Colorado River, proceeds through the past, and flows, inexorably, into the future. As Yolo begins his own parallel voyage, Kate encounters celibates and lovers, shamans and snakes, memories of family disaster and marital discord, and emerges at a place where nothing remains but love." Publisher's note

"Walker's dreamlike novel incorporates the political and spiritual consciousness and emotional style for which she is known and appreciated." Booklist

Walker, Alice

Possessing the secret of joy. Harcourt Brace Jovanovich 1992 286p $25

ISBN 0-15-173152-7

LC 92-6883

"The people in Ms. Walker's book are archetypes rather than characters as we have come to expect them in the 20th-century novel, and this is by defiant intention. . . . When the novel is operating genuinely on this archetypal level, it has a mythic strength. Its many voices are not rendered as stream-of-consciousness monologues, nor are they made to belong to distinct individuals. Instead, they are highly stylized, operatic, prophetic—and powerfully poetic." N Y Times Book Rev

Walker, Alice

The **temple** of my familiar. Harcourt Brace Jovanovich 1989 416p $19.95

ISBN 0-15-188533-8

LC 88-7995

This is a "novel only in a loose sense. Rather, it is a mixture of mythic fantasy, revisionary history, exemplary biography and sermon. It is short on narrative tension, long on inspirational message." N Y Times Book Rev

Walker, Alice

The **way** forward is with a broken heart. Random House 2000 200p $23.95

ISBN 0-679-45587-6

LC 00-27172

"In seven beautifully written and astoundingly perceptive short stories—admittedly based in fact, then fictionalized—{Walker} homes in on the problems endemic to interracial romance and offers a near stream-of-consciousness reflection on her own ten-year marriage to a white civil rights attorney." Libr J

Walker, Alice

You can't keep a good woman down; stories. Harcourt Brace Jovanovich 1981 167p

LC 80-8761

Walker, Karen Thompson, 1980-

★ The **age** of miracles; a novel. Karen Thompson Walker. Random House 2012 272 p.

ISBN 0812992970; 9780812992977; 9780679644385

LC 2011040664

This novel, by Karen Thompson Walker, is a story of "coming of age set against the backdrop of an utterly altered world. On a seemingly ordinary Saturday in a California suburb, Julia and her family awake to discover, along with the rest of the world, that the rotation of the earth has suddenly begun to slow. . . . Yet as she struggles to navigate an ever-shifting landscape, Julia is also coping with the normal disasters of everyday life." (Publisher's note)

Walker, Margaret

★ **Jubilee**. Houghton Mifflin 1966 497p

"Vyry was a slave and the daughter of a slave. She suffered slavery's tribulations and looked forward to the time of freedom to bring her a home of her own and provide an education for her children. The Civil War and the Reconstruction period brought the possibility of that day of jubilation, but the attainment of her two desires still seemed remote. The author gives a clear picture of the everyday life of slaves, their modes of behavior, and the patterns and rhythms of their speech." Shapiro. Fic for Youth. 3d edition

Walker, Martin

The **crowded** grave; Martin Walker. 1st U.S. ed. Alfred A. Knopf 2011 313 [1] p. map (hardcover) $24.95

ISBN 0307700194; 9780307700193

LC 2011050746

This mystery novel, by Martin Walker, begins in "spring in . . . St. Denis, [France] and for Chief of Police Bruno Courreges that means . . . a new string of regional crimes and international capers. When a local archaeological team . . . turns up a corpse with a watch on its wrist and a bullet in its head, it's up to Bruno to solve the case. . . . Complicating events, . . . the professor in charge of the dig is soon reported missing." (Publisher's note)

Walker, Martin

The **dark** vineyard. Alfred A. Knopf 2010 303p $23.95

ISBN 978-0-307-27018-4; 0-307-27018-1

LC 2009-45814

First published 2009 in the United Kingdom

"Bruno handles both cases with great discretion, circulating so quietly and tactfully among his neighbors that his interviews are more like friendly visits. Its a wonderful detection method and an even cannier literary strategy, allowing Walker to pursue the plot of his mystery while beguiling the reader with extended scenes of village market days, old-fashioned wine harvests and some exceptionally congenial dinner parties." N Y Times Book Rev

Walker, Mary Willis

All the dead lie down. Doubleday 1998 308p $22.95

ISBN 0-385-47858-5

LC 97-24131

"Several topics concern magazine writer Molly Cates: the upcoming concealed handgun bill in the Texas legislature, the plight of homeless women in Austin, and her refusal to believe her father's suicide some 28 years earlier. So Molly learns how to shoot, interviews bag ladies, and pursues a new source of material about her father. Literate prose, in-depth characterization, and a cleverly manipulated plot." Libr J

Walker, Mary Willis

Under the beetle's cellar. Doubleday 1995 311p

ISBN 0-385-46859-8

LC 95-10708

"If there can be such a thing as a heartwarming suspense thriller, then Mary Willis Walker has written a nifty one. . . . The real drama is played underground, where the heroic bus driver draws on his war experiences in Vietnam and every

bit of his strength to comfort the children and prepare them for what may well be the end of their world." N Y Times Book Rev

Walker, Walter

Crime of Privilege; a novel. Walter Walker. Random House Inc. 2013 432 p. (hardcover) $26

ISBN 0345541537; 9780345541536

LC 2013004332

This novel, by Walter Walker, begins with "a murder on Cape Cod . . . [and] a rape in Palm Beach. All they have in common is the presence of one of America's most . . . influential families. But nobody is asking questions. . . . Certainly not George Becket . . . of the Cape & Islands district attorney's office. . . . Now, an investigation brings him deep inside the world of the truly wealthy--and shows him what a perilous place it is." (Publisher's note)

Wall, Kathryn R.

The **Mercy** Oak. St. Martin's Minotaur 2008 310p $24.95

ISBN 978-0-312-37534-8; 0-312-37534-4

LC 2008-3304

In this episode, South Carolina Lowcountry PI Bay Tanner "must tackle two cases that hit close to home. Her housekeeper's son disappears after the suspicious hit-and-run death of a young Hispanic woman who had been advocating for the rights of illegal immigrants. Then, during a bank robbery, Lavinia, the woman who raised Bay and still lives with her father, tries to help an old man who has recognized one of the robbers. At the risk of her own life, Bay is desperate to keep those she cares about safe. Sue Grafton, Sara Paretsky, and Marcia Muller come to mind as the quintessential writers of the modern female private eye novel. Wall, in a quiet and unassuming way, has produced a body of work of equal quality as she tackles complex modern issues that trouble her very human characters." Libr J

Wall, P. S.

The **Wilde** women; a novel. [by] Paula Wall. Atria Books 2007 310p

ISBN 978-0-7434-9621-6; 0-7434-9621-3

LC 2006-48023

Having left her southern hometown of Five Points five years earlier after discovering that her sister and fiancé had been having an affair, unpredictable Pearl Wilde returns home to exact revenge.

"Each and every character in Wall's tall tale has a uniquely flawed personality, and Wall has a wonderful sense of place and an adept way with words, adding up to an enthralling novel." Booklist

Wallace, Carey

The **blind** contessa's new machine. Pamela Dorman Books/Viking 2010 207p $23.95

ISBN 978-0-670-02189-5; 0-670-02189-X

LC 2010-03332

"The time is the late 19th century, the place the northern Italian countryside, where minor aristocrats flourish as abundantly as grapevines. A blooming rose, Contessa Carolina Fantoni is about to marry Pietro, a neighboring landowner. Neither Pietro nor her parents take her seriously, however, when Carolina tells them she is going blind. With a love deeper than Pietro's fickle infatuation, Carolina's devoted admirer, Turri, a local eccentric and amateur inventor, gives her a precious gift, the ability to communicate with an outside world locked out by her blindness and her over-protective husband. He invents a machine, the typewriter, which Carolina uses to arrange their increasingly indiscreet — and ill-fated — assignations. A small gem of sensuality." Boston Globe

Wallace, Daniel
★ **Big** fish; a novel of mythic proportions. Algonquin Bks. 1998 180p

ISBN 1-56512-217-8

LC 98-26216

"William Bloom's father, Edward, is dying. He dies in fact in four different takes, all of which have William and his mother waiting outside a bedroom door as the family doctor tells them it's time to say their goodbyes. He intersperses the four takes with stories (all filtered through William's mind and voice) about the elusive Edward. . . . In a plainspoken style dotted with transcendent passages, Wallace mixes the mundane and the mythical. His chapters have the transformative quality of fable and fairy tale, and the novel's roomy structure allows the mystery and lyricism of the story to coalesce." Publ Wkly

Wallace, Daniel
Mr. Sebastian and the Negro magician; a novel. Doubleday 2007 257p

ISBN 978-0-385-52109-3; 0-385-52109-X

LC 2006-28103

"An inept African-American illusionist is dogged by the deal he struck with the devil in Wallace's . . . novel, a circus picaresque that barnstorms its way through the 1950s American South. Henry Walker, once the 'greatest magician in the world,' has been reduced to a minstrel show–like novelty act in a traveling circus. Henry's story, told by a succession of narrators—including members of the circus and a private detective—begins during the Depression, when Henry's family fell on hard times. While down and out, Henry meets and apprentices with the devilish magician Mr. Sebastian. Henry learns the secrets of magic, but his ambition and ability are crimped when his beloved sister, Hannah, disappears." Publ Wkly

"The unraveling of a man's myth to illuminate the essence of his life is the charm of this accomplished and inventive novel." Paste

Wallace, Daniel
The **Watermelon** King. Houghton Mifflin 2003 226p $23

ISBN 0-618-22138-7

LC 2002-75941

"An inept African-American illusionist is dogged by the deal he struck with the devil in Wallace's . . . novel, a circus picaresque that barnstorms its way through the 1950s American South. Henry Walker, once the 'greatest magician in the world,' has been reduced to a minstrel show–like novelty act in a traveling circus. Henry's story, told by a succession of narrators—including members of the circus and a private detective—begins during the Depression, when Henry's family fell on hard times. While down and out, Henry meets and apprentices with the devilish magician Mr. Sebastian. Henry learns the secrets of magic, but his ambition and ability are crimped when his beloved sister, Hannah, disappears." Publ Wkly

"This is a unique and spellbinding novel, an unforgettable southern tall tale with extraordinary characters." Booklist

Wallace, David Foster
★ **Infinite** jest; a novel. Little, Brown 1996 1079p $29.95

ISBN 0-316-92004-5

LC 95-30619

This novel is "set sometime in the next century, on the grounds of a New England tennis academy and in a rehab clinic. Among other things, the book contains perhaps the most moving and hypnotic writing on the psychology of addiction and recovery to be found in modern fiction. There are obsessive riffs on sports, on drugs, and on the hidden horrors of entertainment: the title of the novel refers to the title of a movie that is said to be so 'terminally compelling' that viewers will watch it passively and repeatedly to the point of death. Comparisons with Pynchon are inevitable, and in this case they are fully justified." New Yorker

Wallace, David Foster
Oblivion; stories. Little, Brown 2004 329p $25.95

ISBN 0-316-91981-0

"Unpacking our inner lives with empathy and care, Oblivion showcases the incredibly rich textures and crystalline clarity of Wallace's prose, confirming the singular genius of his expansive imagination and resonating with the complexities of minds in motion." American Book Review

Wallace, David Foster
★ The **pale** king; an unfinished novel. Little, Brown and Co. 2011 548p $27.99

ISBN 978-0-316-07423-0; 0-316-07423-3

LC 2010-45489

The novel "treats its central subject—boredom itself—not as a texture (as in Fernando Pessoa), or a symptom (as in Thomas Mann), or an attitude (as in Bret Easton Ellis), but as the leading edge of truths we're desperate to avoid. It is the mirror beneath entertainment's smiley mask, and The Pale King aims to do for it what Moby-Dick did for the whale. . . . In the end, Wallace's body of work amounts to an extended philosophical experiment. Can 'morally passionate, passionately moral' fiction help free us from the prisons we make? To judge solely by his suicide, the experiment would seem to have failed. Then again, watching him loosed one last time upon the fields of language, we're apt to feel the way he felt at the end of his celebrated essay on Federer at Wimbledon: called to attention, called out of ourselves. Jesus, just look at him out there." New York

Wallace, Irving
The **man**; a novel. Simon & Schuster 1964 766p

This is the story of a black Senator who becomes the first black President of the United States after the deaths, in rapid succession, of first the Vice President and then both the President and the Speaker of the House

The portrayal of the "President as a man, an able, intelligent, politically moderate man who has never been to the fore but must take responsibility overnight, is excellent. With a huge cast of characters and one crisis after another in the plot, this makes an absorbing story." Publ Wkly

Wallace, Irving

The **prize**. Simon & Schuster 1962 768p

This novel is an "inquiry into the private lives of a batch of Nobel Prize winners. . . . The prize winners are . . . a French husband-and-wife team of chemists whose marriage is collapsing, a neurotic American heart surgeon broodingly resentful that he must share the award in medicine with an Italian doctor, a gentle German-born physicist from Atlanta who is being wooed by the Communists of East Germany, and an American novelist who is just coming out of a long alcoholic trance. Wallace . . . assembles them all in Stockholm and embarks them on the frenzied series of public and private events that surround Nobel award weeks in the Swedish capital." NY Her Trib Books

Wallace, Lew

★ **Ben**-Hur; a tale of the Christ. Harper 1880 552p

This novel "depicts the oppressive Roman occupation of ancient Palestine and the origins of Christianity. The Jew Judah Ben-Hur is wrongly accused by his former friend, the Roman Messala, of attempting to kill a Roman official. He is sent to be a slave and his mother and sister are imprisoned. Years later he returns, wins a chariot race against Messala, and is reunited with his now leprous mother and sister. Mother and daughter are cured on the day of the Crucifixion, and the family is converted to Christianity." Merriam-Webster's Ency of Lit

Wallace, Stone

Montana dawn. Avalon Books 2010 231p $23.95

ISBN 978-0-8034-7770-4; 0-8034-7770-8

LC 2009-53848

When the remnants of a ruthless outlaw gang invade the peaceful desert setting Montana Dawn shares with her gentleman husband, little does the girl suspect that her long-dormant spirit for a life far removed from her domestic existence will be passionately re-ignited and that circumstances will soon brand her as the most wanted female criminal in the Southwest. With a bounty on their head and a determined posse hot in pursuit, Montana Dawn and her outlaw companion Walt Egan share romance and danger across the unrelenting Nevada terrain as they attempt to stay ahead of the law and escape into Mexico to start a new life.

"This unusual western mines some fairly fresh ground: female outlaws are in relatively short supply, as are love stories about pairs of outlaws. but the author sells it completely. The characters are quite well drawn—villains who capture our interest and compassion—and the plot is engaging in a Butch Cassidy and the Sundance Kid kind of way: exciting but with a colorful, light feel to it—until the end." Booklist

Wallace, Wendy

The **painted** bridge; Wendy Wallace. Simon & Schuster 2012 386 p. (hardcover) $25.00

ISBN 1451660820; 9780857209276; 9780857209306; 9781451660821

LC 2012453375

This historical novel, by Wendy Wallace, "is a story of family betrayals, illicit power, and a woman sent to an asylum against her will in Victorian England. Just outside London . . . lies Lake House, a private asylum for genteel women of a delicate nature. In the winter of 1859, Anna Palmer becomes its newest patient. . . . Confused and angry, Anna sets out to prove her sanity, but with her husband and doctors unwilling to listen, her freedom will not be won easily." (Publisher's note)

Wallach, Janet

Seraglio. Talese 2003 316p $24.95

ISBN 0-385-49046-1

LC 2002-28698

"It is to Wallach's credit that at no point does her story seem preposterous. The intrigue and drama of the palace are balanced by capable, authoritative prose and admirable restraint, resulting in a novel at once serious and enchanting." Publ Wkly

Wallant, Edward Lewis

The **pawnbroker**; {by} Edward L. Wallant. Harcourt, Brace & World 1961 279p

"Sol Nazerman is a survivor of the Holocaust. In the past he had been a university teacher in Poland; now he runs a pawnshop in Harlem in which Murillio, a ruthless racketeer, has a financial interest. Into Nazerman's shop come people who are sad, sick, or criminal. He also meets Marilyn Birchfield, a friendly social worker who tries to get past the frozen outward indifference of the pawnbroker. In flashbacks that describe the horror and torture suffered by Nazerman and his family, the reader begins to understand his withdrawal from humanity. The relationship between him and his young, ambitious, and confused assistant, Jesus Ortiz, provides the novel's shattering climax." Shapiro. Fic for Youth. 3d edition

Waller, Robert James

★ The **bridges** of Madison County. Warner Bks. 1992 171p il

LC 91-50416

"This is the story of four days that change forever the lives of two lonely people. Robert Kincaid is a roving photographer for National Geographic and Francesca Johnson is a housewife whose marriage suffers from a lack of romance. Francesca's family is out of town when Kincaid arrives on the scene, and the pair are instantly attracted. They soon become lovers, and Kincaid asks Francesca to run away with him, but she refuses. Francesca stays loyal to her family, and memories of Kincaid are all that remain." Libr J

"An erotic, bittersweet tale of lingering memories and forsaken possibilities." Publ Wkly

Walls, Jeannette

The **Silver** Star; a novel. Jeannette Walls. 1st Scribner hardcover ed. Simon & Schuster 2013 288 p. (hardcover) $26

ISBN 1451661509; 9781451661507

LC 2012050790

This novel, by Jeannette Walls, begins in "1970. . . . 'Bean' Holladay is twelve and her sister, Liz, is fifteen when their artistic mother, Charlotte . . . takes off to find herself, leaving her girls enough money to last a month or two. . . . She and Liz decide to take the bus to Virginia, where their Uncle Tinsley lives in the decaying mansion that's been in Charlotte's family for generations." (Publisher's note)

"[A] captivating, read-in-one-sitting, coming-of-age adventure." Booklist

Walser, Robert

The **assistant**; translated from the German by Susan Bernofsky. New Directions 2007 302p pa $16.95

ISBN 978-0-8112-1590-9; 0-8112-1590-3

LC 2007-6865

Original German edition, 1908

"Walser's clerks and layabouts are perhaps the nicest, most considerate people you can meet in modernist fiction, but they can also be cuttingly ironic in the way of only the very polite. . . . Susan Bernofsky reproduces this effect and others with impressive fluency and naturalness." New Yorker

Walsh, Helen

Brass. Canongate 2004 296p pa $14

ISBN 1-8419-5484-5 pa

LC 2005-415744

In this novel set in Liverpool, "nineteen-year-old university student Millie O'Reilley has not taken the news of the impending nuptials of her best mate, 28-year-old Jamie Keeley, very well. Drinking and drugging her way through the evenings, she usually ends up trolling the seedy section of town in search of female prostitutes (the 'brass' of the title). Jamie is growing increasingly impatient with and worried by Millie's behavior and is at a loss to explain their relationship to his dim-witted, social-climbing fiancee. What sets this first novel apart within a burgeoning subgenre is Walsh's lyrical prose. Her evocative phrasing both contains and stands in direct contrast to incredibly graphic scenes of depravity, and the result is both disturbing and compelling." Booklist

Waltari, Mika

The **Roman**; The memoirs of Minutus Launsus Manilianus, who has won the Insignia of a Triumph, who has the rank of consul, who is chairman of the Priests' Collegium of the god Vespasian and a member of the Roman S. English version by Joan Tate. Putnam 1966 637p

This is the final volume of the trilogy, the first being The Egyptian, and the second, The Etruscan

Original Finnish edition, 1964

The story is set in the first century A.D. during the reigns of Claudius and Nero. Minutus is born in Antioch, comes to Rome at the age of fifteen, visits Jerusalem and Britain with the army, and wins honors and power and has several love affairs. He becomes intimate with Nero and helps him persecute the Christians

"Though Minutus is somewhat wooden, his adventures are astonishing. Waltari shuttles his hero around the empire, from Britain to Ephesus, in order to describe the growing decadence of Rome, the rise of Christianity, and the existence of other religions. Waltari's sense of humor and irony points up his pageant of Roman life." Publ Wkly

Walter, Jess

★ **Beautiful** Ruins; A Novel. Jess Walter. Harper 2012 352 p.

ISBN 0061928127; 9780061928123

This book presents a "romance [story that] begins in April 1962, when a young innkeeper, Pasquale Tursi, puts up . . . American actress Dee Moray, who has arrived supposedly sick with stomach cancer at the remote Italian port of Vergogna. . . . Pasquale soon discovers that 20th Century-Fox's chief troubleshooter, the young Michael Deane, has in fact whisked Dee, pregnant with the married Burton's child, away from the public eye to avoid scandal. . . . Pasquale falls in love with the beleaguered, vulnerable Dee." (Publishers Weekly)

Walter, Jess

Citizen Vince; a novel. Jess Walter. Perennial 2008 293p (pbk.) $14.99; (acid-free paper) o.p.; o.p.

ISBN 9780061577659; 0060394412; 9780060394417

LC 2004046828

Edgar Allan Poe Award: Best Novel (2006)

This book, winner of the 2005 Edgar Allan Poe Award, begins "[a]t 1:59 a.m. in Spokane, Washington—eight days before the 1980 presidential election—[when] Vince Camden pockets his stash of stolen credit cards and drops by an all-night poker game before heading to his witness-protection job dusting crullers at Donut Make You Hungry. Along with a neurotic hooker girlfriend, this is the total sum of Vince's new life. But when a familiar face shows up in town, Vince realizes his sordid past is still too close behind him. During the next unforgettable week, he'll negotiate a coast-to-coast maze of obsessive cops, eager politicians, and assorted mobsters—only to find that redemption might exist, of all places, in the voting booth." (Publisher's note)

Walter, Jess

The **financial** lives of the poets; a novel. Harper 2009 290p $25.99

ISBN 978-0-06-191604-5; 0-06-191604-8

The protagonist of this novel is a "former financial journalist turned proprietor of poetfolio.com, an ill-conceived Web site featuring investment advice written in verse. Having gambled everything on this quixotic idea, he finds himself hobbled by debt and six days from losing his family home to a mortgage company. The only way out of his predicament, he decides, is to start dealing pot. The novel riffs (often in blank verse) on everything from balloon mortgages to thong-wearing suburban moms. Despite its unlikely conceit, the novel has warmth, and its protagonist emerges as a bourgeois Everyman of the downturn." New Yorker

Walter, Jess

★ **We** Live in Water; Stories. Jess Walter. HarperCollins 2013 192 p. (paperback) $14.99

ISBN 0061926620; 9780061926624

The short stories of this collection, by Jess Walter, "range from comic tales of love to social satire and suspenseful crime fiction. Traveling from hip Portland to once-hip Seattle to never-hip Spokane, to a condemned casino in Las Vegas and a bottomless lake in the dark woods of Idaho, this is a world of lost fathers and redemptive con men, of personal struggles and diminished dreams." (Publisher's note)

"Drug addicts and hard-luck cases abound here, but these stories aren't melodramatic or even dour. Walter's prose is straightforward and funny, and like Richard Russo, he knows his protagonists are concerned with their immediate predicaments, not the socioeconomic mechanisms that put them there. ... A witty and sobering snapshot of recession-era America." Kirkus

Walters, Minette

The **breaker**. Putnam 1999 351p $23.95

ISBN 0-399-14492-7

LC 98-51836

"Walters limits the suspects to two men with sufficient reason (and appropriate perversions) to have wanted the victim dead—the husband she betrayed and the lover she betrayed him with. Instead of making it easier to identify the killer, the narrow field only intensifies the challenge by demanding closer analysis." N Y Times Book Rev

Walters, Minette

★ The **dark** room. Putnam 1995 381p

LC 95-10616

"Motivation is at the heart of The Dark Room. Like all the best detective fiction it challenges readers to work out how a particular character would act faced with specific circumstances. . . . The quest for truth is punctuated by touches of humanity that lift this novel way above others of its genre." New Statesman Soc

Walters, Minette

The **devil's** feather. Alfred A. Knopf 2006 349p $24

ISBN 0-307-26462-9

LC 2006-41033

First published 2005 in the United Kingdom

In this "thriller, Connie Burns, a white Zimbabwean war correspondent for Reuters, investigates five gruesome murders in Sierra Leone and follows a hunch, convinced that a British mercenary is using the mayhem of war zones to disguise his taste for raping and killing women. After a mysterious assailant kidnaps her and holds her prisoner for three days in Iraq, she becomes convinced that her quarry is now hunting her. She flees to Dorset, rents an isolated house that turns out to have a troubled history, and is befriended by a reclusive neighbor who, some years before, lost her entire family in a car crash. Given the ultra-contemporary world of the early part of the novel, the scenes in Dorset . . . seem parochial, but this does not lessen Walters's ability to use horror-movie logic to terrifying effect." New Yorker

Walters, Minette

The **echo**. Putnam 1997 338p

LC 96-37485

"The discovery of a homeless man's body in the garage of a banker's wife leads her—and a journalist interested in the homeless—to find out more about the man. They also reinvestigate the disappearance, years ago, of the banker and a sizable sum of cash. . . . Well-crafted psychological suspense from a master." Libr J

Walters, Minette

The **sculptress**. St. Martin's Press 1993 308p

LC 93-21527

"Roz Leigh, an author embittered by the tragic death of a child and a split from her husband, agrees to write the story of Olive Martin, a grossly fat, untidy woman serving a long prison sentence for the particularly grisly murder of her mother and sister. Visiting Olive in jail, Roz finds herself drawn to the woman, and despite the fact that 'the sculptress' readily confessed to the crime, she begins to find odd discrepancies in the evidence against her." Publ Wkly

"Walters mesmerizes her readers with a sleek, exciting tale whose slick veneer disguises a sinister, menacing evil." Booklist

Walters, Minette

The **shape** of snakes. Putnam 2001 384p $24.95

ISBN 0-399-14733-0

LC 00-65319

The novel's protagonist "was traumatized in 1978 by the violent death of a London neighbor who suffered from Tourette's syndrome. 'I could never decide whether 'Mad Annie' was murdered because she was mad or because she was black,' she says. But the cruel nature of the woman's death and the torments she endured from prejudiced neighbors have haunted Mrs. Ranelagh for 20 years. And now it is time for the reckoning. Although the narrator obviously has a hidden agenda, the master manipulator here is Walters, whose commanding control over her inflammatory material—and her readers—distracts the eye from potential murder suspects and directs the mind to the everyday acts of casual inhumanity that are the real issue." N Y Times Book Rev

Walton, Jo

★ **Among** others. Tor 2011 302p $24.99

ISBN 978-0-7653-2153-4; 0-7653-2153-X

LC 2010-36108

2012 Hugo Award Winner, Best Novel

"Her mother half insane and her twin sister killed in a car accident, Morwenna Phelps finds herself in the custody of her estranged, feckless father, who almost immediately ships her off to boarding school. Used to conversing with the spirits of the woods in her Welsh hometown, Mori has a difficult time adjusting to a regimented place that seems almost devoid of magic. Even more daunting for her is the necessity to conform to school rules and make friends with girls who regard her with mistrust and envy. Desperate for companionship, Mori casts a spell that seems to bring her the support of a reading group of like-minded science fiction fans, but she fears that her supernatural meddling has attracted the attention of her mother. Despite her growing interest in one of the boys in the group, she must return to Wales to set everything right once and for all." San Francisco Chron

Walton, Jo

Farthing. Tor 2006 319p $25.95

ISBN 0-765-31421-5

LC 2005-34487

"In an alternate reality in which a group of English nobles overthrew Winston Churchill and made peace with Adolf Hitler in 1941, a murder is committed at the home of Lord and Lady Eversley, and suspicion falls on David Kahn, the Jewish husband of Lucy Eversley. Only Inspector Carmichael of Scotland Yard believes that something else might be at work and that the Kahns could, in fact, be victims themselves. . . . An excellent example of alternate history." Libr J

Walton, Jo

Ha'penny. Tor 2007 319p $25.95

ISBN 978-0-7653-1853-4; 0-7653-1853-9

LC 2007-21113

Sequel to: Farthing

This second volume of the author's Small Change trilogy "delves deeper into the intrigue and paranoia of 1940s fascist Great Britain. Denied help from the United States, England negotiated the Farthing Peace with the Nazis to end WWII, surrendering freedom for a narrow kind of safety. Eight years later, Scotland Yard investigators like Inspector Carmichael spend as much time monitoring the activities of gays, Jews and foreigners as they do hunting criminals. Carmichael, outed to his superiors as a homosexual and blackmailed into keeping deadly political secrets, plans to retire after his current case, a bombing at the country house of respected actress Lauria Gilmore. Meanwhile, Viola Lark is preparing for the role of her life as a female Hamlet when she's coerced into a plot to kill the prime minister and Hitler on opening night. World Fantasy Award-winner Walton masterfully illustrates how fear can overwhelm common sense." Publ Wkly

Walton, Jo

Half a crown. Tor 2008 316p $25.95

ISBN 978-0-7653-1621-9; 0-7653-1621-8

LC 2008-31019

Conclusion of the author's Small Change alternative-history trilogy; earlier titiles: Farthing and Ha'penny

"A difficult — and important — book to read about a world gone mad. The characterization is first-rate, the plot is compelling and most important of all, even in this world, there is hope." Romantic Times

Wambaugh, Joseph

★ The **blue** knight. Little, Brown 1972 338p

"The caricature is deliberate; the author means to endow a stereotype with complexity and sentiment. Bumper has his own street ethics. . . . The book tends to be a bit ostentatious in such honesties, as if they established Bumper's credibility. In the end, Wambaugh sentimentalizes Bumper as a sort of repellently lovable super-cop who, whenever he is not strongarming 'pukepots,' is bantering in Yiddish, Spanish or Arabic with the ethnics on the beat." Time

Wambaugh, Joseph

Finnegan's week. Morrow 1993 348p

LC 93-24890

"There is a boyish excessiveness to Mr. Wambaugh's writing that produces an odd synergy with his carefully constructed plots and his colorful characters." N Y Times Book Rev

Wambaugh, Joseph

Floaters. Bantam Bks. 1996 293p

LC 95-26625

In this novel, "two clumsy conspirators try to fix the America's Cup race. A hot number named Blaze Duvall does the grunt work of seducing a dumb sailor into sabotaging the Black Magic, the formidable New Zealand contender. Blaze stands to make a buck from this scheme, but it is really a crime of passion devised by Ambrose Lutterworth, the keeper of the cup, who can't bear to give up his beloved charge. As a spy, the flame-haired Blaze is a bit conspicuous, catching the eye of Fortney and Leeds, a couple of calloused veterans with the harbor police unit that cruises Mission Bay in San Diego." N Y Times Book Rev

Wambaugh, Joseph

Harbor nocturne; Joseph Wambaugh. Grove/Atlantic 2012 320 p.

ISBN 9780802126108

In this book, "Sgt. Thaddeus Hawthorne of Hollywood Vice thinks he sees a way to put pressure on Hector Cozzo, an errand boy for a gang that's smuggling and prostituting illegals: Persuade [a] surfer officer . . . to use his amputated foot to ingratiate himself with a shadowy Russian associate with a fixation on amputations. . . . A fight among superhero panhandlers leads to the hot pursuit of a purse snatcher. A domestic violence call discloses a kinky sex contract gone wrong. A homeless man beds down in a dumpster that's already hosting a corpse. In the middle of this junkyard, a flower struggles to bloom: the unlikely romance between Lita Medina Flores, an incoming Mexican illegal hired to dance even though she's a terrible dancer, and Dinko Babich, the old school friend Hector pays to deliver her to Club Samara." (Kirkus)

Wambaugh, Joseph

Hollywood crows; a novel. Little, Brown 2008 343p $26.99

ISBN 978-0-316-02528-7; 0-316-02528-3

LC 2007-33059

"Wambaugh is an important writer not simply because he's ambitious and technically accomplished, but also because he 'owns' a critical slice of L.A.'s literary real estate: the Los Angeles Police Department not just its inner workings, but also its relationship to the city's political establishment and to its intricately enmeshed social classes." Los Angeles Times Book Rev

Wambaugh, Joseph

Hollywood Hills; a novel. Little, Brown and Co. 2010 356p il $26.99

ISBN 978-0-316-12950-3; 0-316-12950-X

LC 2010-26155

"The main event in this seriocomic production involves the collision of two separate but equally inept pairs of thieves: a sleazy art dealer who plans to defraud a movie producer's widow by making an accomplice of her butler, and an OxyContin addict who talks his druggie girlfriend into robbing mansions in the Hollywood Hills. While keeping these clowns busy tripping over their own shoelaces, Wambaugh salts the narrative with variously funny, sad and thoughtful anecdotes featuring a cast of characters we've come to treasure: handsome Hollywood Nate, the surfer cops Flotsam and Jetsam, and veterans like Viv Daley and Della Ravelle, burned by experience, but conscientiously training the next generation to face the fire." N Y Times Book Rev

Wambaugh, Joseph
★ **Hollywood** Station; a novel. Little, Brown and Co. 2006 340p $24.99

ISBN 9780316066143; 0-316-06614-1

LC 2006-15759

"Wambaugh has his finger on the pulse of today's police force in a way that most other authors simply can't match, and that makes his work a delight to read." Chicago Sun-Times

Wambaugh, Joseph
★ The **new** centurions. Little, Brown 1971 376p

"As a novel the book has lapses, it wears its exposition on its sleeve—necessarily, perhaps, in view of what it's trying to do—and the three protagonists, though very different in type, are perhaps not sufficiently different in sensibility. . . . But never mind that. What he knows Wambaugh tells truly, perceptively, and well." Book World

Wander, Fred
The **seventh** well; translated by Michael Hofmann. W.W. Norton & Co. 2008 160p $23.95; pa $13.95

ISBN 978-0-393-06538-1; 0-393-06538-3; 978-0-393-33362-6 pa; 0-393-33362-0 pa

LC 2007-28897

Original German edition, 1971

This is a "novel narrated by a young man who attempts to maintain his own sanity in the death camps by immersing himself in the lives of his fellow prisoners. Originally published in 1971, it is now available in a superb new translation by Michael Hofmann. Wander does not guide the reader on his own journey from boxcar to barbed wire, as Elie Wiesel and Primo Levi have done. Rather, his anonymous narrator undergoes a sort of spiritual education as he studies the doomed men and boys around him. The result is an indirect portrait of a man trying to grasp an unthinkable trauma." N Y Times Book Rev

Wang Anyi
The **song** of everlasting sorrow; a novel of Shanghai. translated by Michael Berry and Susan Chan Egan. Columbia University Press 2008 440p (Weatherhead books on Asia) $29.95

ISBN 0-231-14342-7; 978-0-231-14342-4

LC 2007-10812

Original Chinese edition, 1996

This novel "follows the adventures of Wang Qiyao, a girl born of the longtang, the crowded . . . alleys of Shanghai's working-class neighborhoods." (Publisher's note)

"Michael Berry and Susan Chang Egan's graceful translation, only rarely marred by jarring Americanisms ('grunt work,' 'deal breaker'), helps us understand why Wang Anyi is one of the most critically acclaimed writers in the Chinese-speaking world. . . . [As the novel] moves toward its violent, melodramatic and distressingly appropriate ending, readers may feel a Proustian nostalgia for the novel's lost time, a sadness that mirrors the melancholy that haunts Wang Qiyao and pervades the fascinating, mostly vanished longtang of Shanghai." N Y Times Book Rev

Includes bibliographical references

Ward, Amanda Eyre
Close your eyes; a novel. Random House 2010 249p $25

ISBN 978-0-345-49448-1

LC 2010-21115

"After spending a summer night sleeping in their tree house, six-year-old Lauren Mahdian and her brother, Alex, discover their mother's body. The police arrest their Egyptian father for the murder, and he is sentenced to life in prison. Alex believes their father is innocent; Lauren accepts the verdict and suppresses her memories. Twenty-four years later, Lauren is a real estate agent and her brother a medical student. When Alex joins Doctors Without Borders, Lauren begins to experience panic attacks and must find the courage to face her past and explore her feelings about her father." Libr J

"A captivating story of loss, forgiveness and ultimate redemption." Kirkus

Ward, Amanda Eyre
Forgive me; a novel. Random House 236p $23.95

ISBN 978-0-345-49446-7; 0-345-49446-6

LC 2006-50436

The protagonist of this novel is "Nadine, a fly-by-night journalist in her mid-30s who can't quite focus on anything beyond the next hot story. Continually jetting off for international trouble spots, Nadine is thoroughly unwilling to recognize just how utterly, and ultimately rather despicably, addicted she is to other peoples' misery. It doesn't help that she's also the kind of person who will harp on about troubles in faraway lands while remaining utterly blind to those existing right before her nose. After a troubled recovery in her home town of Nantucket (she got in over her head in Mexico, not surprisingly), Nadine heads off to South Africa, where she had once spent some time, to cover the Truth and Reconciliation Commission hearings on apartheid atrocities, and confronts some ugly truths about herself. Ward's plotting may not always be the best, this is a start-and-stop kind of book, but her sharp evocation of Nadine—newsgatherer as self-absorbed vampire—is one that's hard to forget." PopMatters

Ward, Jesmyn
Salvage the bones; Jesmyn Ward. Bloomsbury USA 2011 261p. $24

ISBN 978-1-608-19522-0; 1-608-19522-8; 9781608196265

LC 201053025

Alex Award (2012)

National Book Award: Fiction (2011)

This book, a winner of the 2011 National Book Award, chronicles a family's experiences when a "hurricane is building over the Gulf of Mexico, threatening the coastal town of Bois Sauvage, Mississippi, and Esch's father is growing concerned. A hard drinker, largely absent, he doesn't show concern for much else. Esch and her three brothers are stocking food, but there isn't much to save. Lately, Esch can't keep down what food she gets; she's fourteen and pregnant. Her brother Skeetah is sneaking scraps for his prized pitbull's new litter, dying one by one in the dirt. Meanwhile, brothers Randall and Junior try to stake their claim in a family long on child's play and short on parenting.

"The Gulf of Mexico is about to birth a storm, and it's headed straight for Bois Sauvage, Mississippi. But Hurricane Katrina's approach isn't the first thing on teenage Esch Batiste's mind; she's more concerned about her newly discovered pregnancy and the baby's father, Manny, who is dating another girl. Her brother Skeetah, on the other hand, is fixated on his pit bull China's newborn puppies. If they live, the dogs may provide money for the Batiste children, who are living in poverty and fending for themselves as their father drinks to dull the pain of their mother's death. There's an unmistakable contrast between Skeetah's love for China and the indifference of Manny toward Esch. Manny dotes on his girlfriend but approaches Esch for sex; he pushes her away when she seeks emotional connection. Esch repeatedly draws parallels between her situation and her assigned school reading about the mythological Medea, whose husband Jason betrays her. Manny refuses her, but Esch finds support from her brothers, her father and their friends." BookPage

Ward, Liza

Outside valentine. Holt & Co. 2004 301p $23

ISBN 0-8050-7598-4

"A gifted writer, Ward uses simple imagery to chilling effect. A dog with a broken neck hiding under the bed after its owner has been murdered and a dead schoolgirl with her skirt pulled up—Starkweather says he just wanted to look—are as vivid as anything filmmakers have fashioned from the same raw material." Washington Post Book World

Ward, Mary Jane

The **snake** pit. Random House 1946 278p

Related in the first person, this tells of the experiences undergone by the patient, Virginia Cunningham, in a state mental hospital. It follows the course of her insanity from her commitment to her final release. It also takes the reader through mental hospital routine in all its reality

"Chronicled so quietly and unemphatically, the horrors of asylum life become infinitely more poignant than they appear in the hands of grimmer writers who are out to shock. Obviously an incomplete picture, but an extraordinarily moving one." New Yorker

Ware, Chris

★ **Building** stories; Chris Ware. Pantheon Books 2012 p. cm. $50.00

ISBN 9780375424335

LC 2012007946

"Building Stories imagines the inhabitants of a three-story Chicago apartment building: a 30-something woman who has yet to find someone with whom to spend the rest of her life; a couple, possibly married, who wonder if they can bear each other's company another minute; and the building's landlady, an elderly woman who has lived alone for decades. Taking advantage of the absolute latest advances in wood pulp technology, Building Stories is a book with no deliberate beginning nor end, the scope, ambition, artistry and emotional prevarication beyond anything yet seen from this artist or in this medium, probably for good reason." (Publisher's note)

Ware, Danie

Ecko Rising; Danie Ware. Random House Inc. 2013 480 p. (paperback) $14.95

ISBN 085768762X; 9780857687623

In this book, in "a tech-filled future London, Ecko is considered different. He's maxed out on body modifications and gleefully willing to do anything to take on Pilgrim, the organization bent on rendering society docile and compliant. While on a mission to infiltrate Pilgrim, he falls and comes to in a place without electricity, technology, or anything else that would make it resemble modern society. . . . Ecko is convinced it's a test, a program built to push him to his limits." (Library Journal)

Warner, Kaki

Bride of the high country; Kaki Warner. Berkley Sensation 2012 390 p. $15

ISBN 0425247503; 9780425247501

LC 2012005041

In this novel by Kaki Warner, book 3 of the Runaway Brides series, "Margaret Hamilton escaped the Irish slums of Five Points as the ward of a wealthy Manhattan widow, but only marriage can make her future secure. Railroad mogul Doyle Kerrigan needs a well-connected wife. It seems a perfect match...until a shocking revelation sends her fleeing from the wedding reception. . . . Margaret takes on a new identity and heads West, finally stopping in Heartbreak Creek, Colorado. . . . But two men from Margaret's past are on her trail." (Publisher's note)

Warren, Diane

Juliet in August; Dianne Warren. 1st American ed. Penguin Group USA 2012 324 p. (paperback) $16.00; (hardcover) $25.95

ISBN 9780425261002; 0399157999; 9780399157998

LC 2012006196

Governor General's Award, 2010.

Author Dianne Warren tells the story of "the inhabitants of several households in Juliet (population 1,011). Lee Torgeson, 26, isn't sure he's capable of managing the farm left to him by his adoptive parents. Willard Shoenfeld and his brother's widow, Marian, [and] he can't admit to himself how much he loves her, [and] . . . Blaine Dolson has lost most of his family's farmland and faces bankruptcy. . . . Norval Birch . . . is also troubled by wife Lila's plans for an elaborate wedding for their pregnant daughter Rachelle." (Kirkus Reviews)

Warren, Robert Penn

★ **All** the king's men. Harcourt Brace Jovanovich 1990 531p $19

ISBN 0-15-104772-3

LC 90-36181

First published 1946

"In the South during the 1920s a young journalist, Jack Burden, becomes involved in the drive for political power by soon-to-be governor Willie Stark. The journey is a rocky, disillusioning one, and involves exploitation, deceit, and violence. When asked by Stark to uncover a scandal in the past of Judge Irwin, Jack must weigh the many consequences of such action." Shapiro. Fic for Youth. 3d edition

Warren, Robert Penn

★ **Band** of angels. Random House 1955 375p

"A lush, full-bodied Civil War story about a Kentucky plantation owner's daughter sold into slavery whose fight becomes an inquiry into the nature of freedom and the quest for individual identity." Oxford Companion to Am Lit. 6th edition

Warren, Robert Penn

★ **World** enough and time; a romantic novel. Random House 1950 512p

"The murder in Kentucky of Col. Solomon P. Sharp by Jeroboam O. Beauchamp, whose trial was the sensation of 1826, has been a popular theme for novelists ever since. Warren's version in this novel is based on The Confession, which Beauchamp published in 1826. Warren introduced many variations, however, and his quotations from documents are his own inventions." Benet's Reader's Ency of Am Lit

Warren, Susan May

Take a chance on me; Susan May Warren. Tyndale House Publishers, Inc. 2013 416 p. (Christiansen family) (paperback) $13.99

ISBN 1414378416; 9781414378411

LC 2012050809

This novel, by Susan May Warren, is part of the "Christiansen Family" series. "Darek Christiansen is almost a dream bachelor . . . but he's also wounded and angry since the tragic death of his wife, Felicity. . . . New assistant county attorney Ivy Madison . . . doesn't know . . . that . . . she . . . [released] the man responsible for Felicity's death. All Ivy knows is that the Christiansens feel like the family she's always longed for." (Publisher's note)

Warrington, Freda

Elfland. Tor 2009 464 p. (Aetherial tales)

ISBN 9780765318695; 0765318695

LC 2009012918

Romantic Times Reviewers' Choice Award: Best Science Fiction & Fantasy (2009)

When the passage to the Other World fails to open on the designated Night of the Summer Stars due to great danger in the realm, Aetherials Auberon and Rose form a forbidden alliance to breach the gates.

"Solid wordplay, great pacing and a thrilling conclusion." Pub Wkly

Warrington, Freda

Grail of the summer stars; Freda Warrington. 1st ed. Tor 2013 384 p. (Aetherial tales) (hardcover) $27.99

ISBN 0765318717; 9780765318718

LC 2012042626

This is the third installment in Freda Warrington's Aetherial Tales series. "When Stephanie Silverwood, curator of the Museum of Metalwork in Birmingham, England, receives a triptych . . . , she recognizes the work as belonging to her former friend and one-time lover, Daniel Manifold. At the same time, a man calling himself Mist, one of the ancient Aetherials, emerges from the sea to resume the search for his brother. The strange painting" leads both to an ancient, hidden faerie race. (Library Journal)

Warrington, Freda

Midsummer night; Freda Warrington. 1st ed. Tor 2010 412 p. (Aetherial tales.) (hardcover) $27.99

ISBN 0765318709; 9780765318701

LC 2010036680

This is the first in Freda Warrington's Aetherial Tales series. Decades ago, a deadly prank occurred at a place where the human and fairy worlds meet. Years later, the spot is home to an art museum. "One day, during a violent storm, a young woman studying art at the estate stumbles upon a portal to the Otherworld. A handsome young man comes through the portal and seeks shelter with her." He's charming, but others are suspicious. (Publisher's note)

Wascom, Kent, 1986-

★ The **Blood** of Heaven. Pgw 2013 432 p. $25

ISBN 0802121187; 9780802121189

This historical novel is Kent Wascom's debut. Set "mainly in West Florida (comprised of parts of current-day Florida, Alabama, Mississippi, and Louisiana) around 1800, the book follows Angel Woolsack through his transformation from preacher to robber to freedom fighter to hero for independence from Spanish rule as Angel joins his adopted brothers in the effort to free West Florida." (Library Journal)

Waters, Sarah

Fingersmith. Riverhead Bks. 2002 511p

ISBN 1-573-22203-8

LC 2001-51053

"Sue Trinder, who also goes by a number of other names, appears to be a foundling, left for safekeeping at Mrs. Sucksby's baby farm by her thieving mother. . . . Raised by Mrs. Sucksby as her own, Sue picks up a few tricks from a crooked locksmith. . . . One day a young man, Richard Rivers, known as Gentleman, comes knocking at the door with a scheme to marry himself off to a lonely heiress, Maud Lilly, then have her shut up in a madhouse once her money is his. He enlists Sue to be the young woman's maid, promising her a cut of the proceeds. But having attached herself to Maud for the sake of the money, Sue finds herself drawn into an unexpected and fearful intimacy." N Y Times Book Rev

Waters, Sarah

The **little** stranger. Riverhead Books 2009 466p $26.95

ISBN 978-1-59448-880-1; 1-59448-880-0

LC 2009-09338

"In post-World War II Britain, the financially struggling Dr. Faraday is called to Hundreds Hall, home of the upper-class Ayreses, now fallen on hard times. Ostensibly there to treat Roderick Ayres for a war injury, Faraday soon sees signs of mental decline—first in Roderick and later in his mother, Mrs. Ayres. Waters builds the suspense slowly, with the skeptical Faraday refusing to accept the explanations of Roderick or of the maid Betty, who believe that there is a supernatural presence in the house. Meanwhile, Faraday becomes enamored of Roderick's sister Caroline and begins to dream of building a family within the confines of the ruined Hundreds Hall. This spooky, satisfying read has the added pleasure of effectively detailing postwar village life, with its rationing, social strictures, and gossip." Libr J

Waters, Sarah

The **night** watch. Riverhead Books 2006 450p $25.95

ISBN 1-59448-905-X

LC 2005-44927

"In the fall of 1947, an androgynous woman walks aimlessly through the scarred streets of London, adjusting her cufflinks. An ambulance driver during the Blitz, she now does nothing more dramatic than go to the cinema, arriving midway through a film and watching the second half first–'People's pasts, you know, being so much more interesting than their futures.' Likewise, this historical novel begins at the end and moves backward, tracing the lives of its characters from peacetime Britain to the early years of the war. The centerpiece of the book is set in 1944, when the characters come fully alive, creeping through blackout London–an apocalyptic landscape of rubble and ash, searchlights and fires. Waters, acclaimed for her Victorian-era romps, has done meticulous research, and renders wartime scenes with unnerving authenticity." New Yorker

Watkins, Claire Vaye

Battleborn; Claire Vaye Watkins. Riverhead Books 2012 304 p. $25.95

ISBN 9781594488252

LC 2012009175

This collection of short stories, by Claire Vaye Watkins, set in "the author's home state, Nevada . . . cover[s] . . . a lot of ground, from the failed mining efforts of the forty-niners to Charles Manson's debauchery in his desert enclave . . . to the near-present with a legal brothel known as the Cherry Patch Ranch. The characters include small-town teenage girls looking for fun on a Vegas road trip . . . and a young Reno woman with a destructive streak." (Library Journal)

Watkins, Paul

★ The **forger**. Picador 2000 322p $25

ISBN 0-312-26593-X

LC 00-33631

"Watkins is an extremely facile writer. His novels are thrilling, fast-paced, intricately plotted and extraordinarily atmospheric. Cerebral in the manner of Graham Greene, . . Watkins, like Greene, can create a wartime sensibility in which every footfall on the stairs has you holding your breath in anticipation. In 'The Forger', he has created a shifting—and shifty—cast of characters whose loyalties and alliances keep changing as the events of the war advance." N Y Times Book Rev

Watkins, Paul

The **ice** soldier. H. Holt 2006 341p $25

ISBN 0-8050-7867-3

LC 2005-46237

"Narrator William Bromley leads a quiet, isolated life in England circa 1950, socializing only with his similarly inclined friend and mountaineering partner Stanley Carton. Much to the dismay of Stanley's uncle Henry (who not only inspired them to become climbers but was also the first to climb a peak in the Italian Alps, which was named Carton Peak after him), both have given up mountaineering. When a former friend and mountaineer, Sturges, shows up, William begins having flashbacks to his mission as an ice soldier during World War II. The death of Uncle Henry forces both William and Stanley to confront their pasts in a dramatic fashion. With a narrative so strong in imagery and detail that the reader can almost feel the gusts of an Alpine blizzard, this adventurous tale builds to a final climax on Carton Peak, where William's horrific wartime experience occurred." Libr J

Watrous, Malena

If you follow me; a novel. Harper Perennial 2010 356p pa $14.99

ISBN 978-0-06-173285-0 pa; 0-06-173285-0 pa

LC 2009-18301

"The narrator, Marina, has agreed to teach English in rural Japan along with Carolyn, a woman from her college grief counseling group with whom she has fallen in love. Marina's father has recently committed suicide, and Marina, unmoored, thinks Carolyn's plan to head for Japan after graduation is as good as any. But changing places rarely solves problems, and each misstep through this formal and tradition-bound culture sinks Marina deeper into despair. She can't even throw her garbage out correctly, much less be honest about the relationship she arrived with." N Y Times Book rev

A "deft, funny, and emotionally acute first novel. . . . Watrous's book crackles with atmospheric detail and sharp dialogue, and tells a vivid story of an American confronting grief and self-knowledge in an unfamiliar place." Boston Globe

Watson, Brad

Aliens in the prime of their lives; stories. W. W. Norton 2010 268p $23.95

ISBN 978-0-393-05711-9; 0-393-05711-9

LC 2009-23469

"Domestic dramas, failed marriages, gunshots in the night and a dash of alien intrigue punctuate a collection of gothic tales. Returning to the pungent stories that represent his best work, . . . [the author], reaches new creative heights with some pieces and falls prey to literary navel-gazing in others. Fortunately, great works outnumber baffling ones in this mostly splendid collection." Kirkus

Watson, Brad

The **heaven** of Mercury. Norton 2002 333p $23.95

ISBN 0-393-04757-1

In this "southern gothic tale, Finus Bates, an 89-year-old radio announcer, reflects on his thwarted love affair with Birdie Wells. As a child, Finus falls in love with the winsome Birdie when he spies her executing a naked cartwheel. Despite their mutual attraction, Birdie and Finus end up betrothed to others: Birdie to the lecherous son of one of the town's wealthiest families, and Finus to Birdie's best friend, a severe woman with unexpected reservoirs of strength. As Watson traces the lovers' sad histories, he flips to the present day, when Finus investigates the decades-old poisoning of Birdie's husband." Booklist

Watson, Christie

Tiny sunbirds, far away; a novel. Christie Watson. Other Press 2011 438 p.

ISBN 1590514661; 159051467X; 9781590514665; 9781590514672

LC 2010054187

In this book, the winner of the 2011 Costa First Novel Award, "[w]hen their mother catches their father with another woman, twelve year-old Blessing and her fourteen-year-old brother, Ezikiel, are forced to leave their comfortable home in Lagos for a village in the Niger Delta, to live with their mother's family. . . . Blessing's grandmother . . . soon becomes a beloved mentor, teaching Blessing the ways of the midwife in rural Nigeria. Blessing is exposed to the horrors of genital mutilation and the devastation wrought on the environment by British and American oil companies. As Warri comes to feel like home, Blessing becomes . . . aware of the threats to its safety, both from its unshakable but dangerous traditions and the relentless carelessness of the modern world." (Publisher's note)

Watson, Jan Elizabeth

Asta in the wings. Tin House Books 2009 314p (Tin House new voice) pa $14

ISBN 978-0-9802436-1-1; 0-9802436-1-0

LC 2008-40525

This is the "story of what happens when the outside world discovers that a widowed mother in Maine has removed her two children, seven-year-old Asta and her nine-year-old brother, Orion, from any contact with the outside world. Unaware that their mother is delusional, the two children do not feel deprived under her care, appreciating her for what she is able to provide. When their isolated living situation is discovered, the children find themselves at the mercy of kind yet sometimes misguided adults. Asta emerges as the stronger, more communicative child. Bright and sometimes wily, she remains steadfastly devoted to her gifted yet now mute brother." Libr J

Watson, Larry

American boy. Milkweed Editions 2011 251p $24

ISBN 978-1-57131-078-1

LC 2011-21334

"The environment around Willow Falls — its heavy emptiness, its shadowy ground — looms over the story, sometimes ominous, sometimes hopeful. Watson paints it with a restrained vividness. . . . A soft but urgent rendering of a young man coming of age in a rural America that is recognizable even to those of us who were never there." Denver Post

Watson, S. J.

Before I go to sleep. Harper 2011 360p $25.99

ISBN 978-0-06-206055-6; 0-06-206055-4

LC 2010-43159

British Book Awards (the Nibbies): Crime Thriller of the Year (2011)

Dagger Awards: CWA John Creasey (New Blood) Dagger (2011)

"Christine Lucas awakens each morning in London with no idea who she is or why she's in bed with a strange man, until he tells her that his name is Ben and they've been married for 22 years. Slowly, Christine learns that she has amnesia and is unable to remember her past or retain new memories: every night when she falls asleep, the slate is wiped clean. Dr. Nash, her therapist, has encouraged her to write in a journal that she keeps secret from Ben. Christine realizes how truly tangled-and dangerous-her life is after she sees the words 'don't trust Ben' written in her journal, whose contents reveal that the only person she can trust is herself." Publ Wkly

Watts, Peter

Blindsight. Tor 2006 384p $25.95

ISBN 978-0-7653-1218-1; 0-7653-1218-2

LC 2006-5917

"A swarm of Fireflies—lighted alien objects in the sky—now orbits Earth, speaking among themselves and ignoring human attempts at communication. In desperation, a group consisting of a linguist with multiple personality disorder, a biologist more machine than man, a paleogenetic vampire, and a pacifist is sent to confront this unfathomable alien presence." Libr J

Watts "remains one of the most exacting hard SF writers in the field, with a meticulous approach to the science in his works." Sci Fi Wkly

Watts, Peter

Starfish. Tor 1999 317p hardcover o.p. pa $14.95

ISBN 978-0-7653-1596-0; 0-7653-1596-3

LC 99-22967

First title in the author's Rifter's trilogy

"In the near future, energy comes from the geothermal waters of the deep ocean, but the cost of providing power for the surface has a price-the sanity of the physically modified humans ('rifters') who live in an alien and dangerous environment. Watts's first novel elegantly captures the isolation and claustrophobia of the lightless ocean depths, smoothly blending psychological suspense with high-tech sf adventure." Libr J

Followed by: Maelstrom (2001) and Behemoth (2004)

Waugh, Evelyn

★ **Brideshead** revisited; with an introduction by Frank Kermode. Knopf 1993 xxxvii, 315p $17

ISBN 0-679-42300-1

LC 93-1854

A reissue of the title first published 1945 by Little, Brown

"The novel, which takes the form of an extended flashback, is narrated by Charles Ryder, an army officer billeted at the eponymous country house, owned by an aristocratic Roman Catholic family headed by Lord and Lady Marchmain. Charles had visited Brideshead with Sebastian Flyte, the Marchmains' younger son, when both were Oxford undergraduates. In the course of the narrative Ryder conveys his fascination with the family, all of whom are eccentric or unhappy in some way." Oxford Companion to 20th Cent Lit in Engl

Waugh, Evelyn

★ The **complete** stories of Evelyn Waugh. Little, Brown 1999 535p $29.95

ISBN 0-316-92546-2

LC 99-20837

"These 39 stories span Waugh's writing career, and to a one they demonstrate his trademark wit and sophistication." Booklist

Waugh, Evelyn

Decline and fall. Doubleday, Doran 1929 293p

First published 1928 in the United Kingdom

This novel "recounts the chequered career of Paul Pennyfeather, sent down from Scone College, Oxford, for 'indecent behaviour', as the innocent victim of a drunken orgy. Thus forced to abandon a career in the church, he becomes a schoolmaster at Llanabba Castle, where he encounters headmaster Fagan and his daughters, the dubious, bigamous, and reappearing Captain Grimes, and young Beste-Chetwynde, whose glamorous mother Margot carries him off to the dangerous delight of high society. They are about to be married when Paul is arrested at the Ritz and subsequently imprisoned for Margot's activities in the white slave trade." Oxford Companion to Engl Lit. 6th edition

Waugh, Evelyn

The **end** of the battle. Little, Brown 1962 319p

Sequel to Officers and gentlemen

First published 1961 in the United Kingdom with title: Unconditional surrender

In this final volume of the trilogy "Guy volunteers for service in Italy with the military government, and he eventually goes to Yugoslavia as a liaison officer with the Partisans. Virginia gives birth to a son (not Guy's) and is killed in an air raid. At the end of the book Guy has again asserted himself, in the rescue of a group of Jewish refugees, and realizes what kind of man he used to be: one who believed that his private honour would be satisfied by war. In an Epilogue we learn that he has remarried and surrounded himself with a family." Camb Guide to Lit in Engl

Waugh, Evelyn

The **loved** one; an Anglo-American tragedy. Little, Brown 1948 164p hardcover o.p. pa $13.95

ISBN 0-316-92608-6

"Depicting romance in a mortuary could be gruesome but the author succeeds both in poking satirical fun at the maudlin pretentiousness of the funeral industry and in delighting the reader with a hilarious love story." Shapiro. Fic for Youth. 3d edition

Waugh, Evelyn

Men at arms. Little, Brown 1952

This is the first volume of the trilogy that includes Officers and gentlemen and The end of the battle

This novel "introduces 35-year-old divorced Catholic Guy Crouchback, who after much effort succeeds in enlisting in the Royal Corps of Halberdiers just after the outbreak of the Second World War. Much of the plot revolves around his eccentric fellow officer Apthorpe, an old Africa hand who suffers repeatedly from 'Bechuana tummy', is deeply devoted to his 'thunder box' (or chemical closet), and dies in West Africa at the end of the novel of some unspecified tropical disease, aggravated by Guy's thoughtful gift of a bottle of whisky. Other characters include Guy's ex-wife, the beautiful socialite Virginia Troy, her second (but not her final) husband, Tommy Blackhouse, and the ferocious one-eyed Brigadier Ritchie-Hook, who involves Guy in a near-disastrous escapade." Oxford Companion to Engl Lit. 6th edition

Followed by Officers and gentlemen

Waugh, Evelyn

Officers and gentlemen. Little, Brown 1955 339p

Sequel to Men at arms

This novel "continues Waugh's semi-satiric, semi-emotional portrayal of civilian and military life with an account of Guy's training on the Hebridean island of Mugg with a commando unit, and of the exploits of ex-hairdresser Trimmer, now Captain McTavish, which include an affair with Virginia and the blowing up of a French railway; the action moves to Alexandria, then to the withdrawal from Crete, with all but four of 'Hookforce' taken prisoner." Oxford Companion to Engl Lit. 6th edition

Followed by The end of the battle

Waugh, Evelyn

★ **Vile** bodies. Little, Brown 1930 321p

"Set in England between the wars, the novel examines the frenetic but empty lives of the Bright Young Things, young people who indulge in constant party-going, heavy drinking, and promiscuous sex. At the novel's end, the realities of the world intrude, with Adam Fenwick-Symes, the protagonist, serving on a battlefield at the onset of another world war." Merriam-Webster's Ency of Lit

Wax, Wendy

Single in Suburbia; Wendy Wax. Bantam Dell 2006 367p $6.99

ISBN 0553588974; 9780553588972

LC 2007583798

In this book, "Amanda's husband has just traded her in for an affair with a teenybopper. Brooke is a trophy wife collecting dust. And Candace . . . has had too many husbands and too little love. . . . [Their company] Maid for You starts as a way for Amanda to make enough money to keep the roof over her kids' heads after her husband splits for his midlife crisis. But when Candace and Brooke join her, . . . [d]onning disguises, they enter the homes of those who once spurned them and discover more than just clutter in the closets of their neighbors' otherwise tidy lives. But when Amanda takes on the job of cleaning the home of the town's most eligible hunk, someone decides to do her dirty." (Publisher's note)

Wayne, Teddy

★ The **Love** Song of Jonny Valentine; a novel. by Teddy Wayne. Free Press 2013 304 p. $24.99

ISBN 1476705852; 9781476705859

LC 2012038331

This book by Whiting Writers' Award-winning author Teddy Wayne follows "'tween sensation Jonny Valentine" whose bubblegum hits made him a superstar and whose mother Jane is micromanaging every piece of his life. Offered here are "the wholehearted yearnings of a conflicted 11-year-old: his obsession with getting a successful erection, a desire to be like his musical idols, and most of all a quest to reconnect with his father." (Publishers Weekly)

Weaver, Michael

Deceptions. Warner Bks. 1995 454p

LC 94-17382

"Enhanced by strong, sinewy writing, numerous plot twists and a potent melding of sex and violence, this expertly wrought novel proves that Weaver knows what most thriller fans want—and can deliver it in spades." Publ Wkly

Webb, Jim

A **sense** of honor. Prentice-Hall 1981 308p

LC 80-25852

"In this powerful novel, Webb . . . a graduate of the Academy, pulls the reader right into the caldron of Annapolis for a vivid picture of heroes and martinets living according to their various interpretations of 'honor'; and he illuminates the mystique that makes men voluntarily stay in such a meat grinder." Publ Wkly

Weber, David, 1952-

By schism rent asunder; David Weber. Tor 2008 510p maps o.p.; o.p.; $8.99

ISBN 9780765315014; 0765315017; 9780765353986

LC 2008016957

In this science fiction novel, "[t]he mercantile kingdom of Charis has prevailed over the alliance designed to exterminate it. Armed with better sailing vessels, better guns and better devices of all sorts, Charis faced the combined navies of the rest of the world . . . and broke them. Despite the implacable hostility of the Church of God Awaiting, Charis . . . [is] still an island of innovation in a world in which the Church has worked for centuries to keep humanity locked at a medieval level of existence. But the powerful men who run the Church aren't going to take their defeat lying down. Charis may control the world's seas, but it barely has an army worthy of the name. And as King Cayleb knows, far too much of the kingdom's recent good fortune is due to the secret manipulations of the being that calls himself Merlin— a being that, the world must not find out too soon, is more than human." (Publisher's note)

Weber, David

Off Armageddon Reef; David Weber. Tor 2007 605p map (pbk.) $7.99

ISBN 9780765353979; 9780765315007; 0765315009

LC 2006025838

In this science fiction, "[h]umanity pushed its way to the stars – and encountered the Gbaba, a ruthless alien race that nearly wiped us out. . . . [The] few survivors have fled to distant, Earth-like Safehold, to try to rebuild. But the Gbaba can detect the emissions of an industrial civilization, so the human rulers of Safehold have taken extraordinary measures: with mind control and hidden high technology, they've built a . . . religion designed to keep Safehold society medieval forever. 800 years pass. In a hidden chamber on Safehold, an android from the far human past awakens. . . . Via automated recordings, 'Nimue' . . . is told her fate: she will emerge into Safeholdian society . . . and begin the process of provoking the technological progress which the Church of God Awaiting has worked for centuries to prevent." (Publisher's note)

The author launches an epic series with this far-future saga, "which springboards off the near-destruction of humanity in a massive war with the alien Gbaba. The survivors of the human race retreat to the planet Safehold, where they sacrifice basic human rights—and an accurate memory of the Gbaba—for the preservation of the species. The colony's founders psychologically program the colonists to prevent the re-emergence of scientific inquiry, higher mathematics or advanced technology, which the Gbaba would detect and destroy. Centuries later, cultural stagnation on this feudal but thriving planet is enforced by the all-powerful Church of God Awaiting. But one kingdom—with the aid of the war's last survivor, a cybernetic avatar that awakens to reinvent itself as a man named Merlin Athrawes—risks committing the ultimate heresy. Shifting effortlessly between battles among warp-speed starships and among oar-powered galleys, Weber brings the political maneuvering, past and future technologies, and vigorous protagonists together for a cohesive, engrossing whole." Publ Wkly

Weber, David, 1952-

Shadow of freedom; David Weber. Baen Books 2013 448 p. (hardcover) $25

ISBN 1451638698; 9781451638691

LC 2012047561

This entry in David Weber's Honor Harrington series retells some of the events from the previous book "Mission of Honor" from "the point of view of Michelle Henke, Harrington's best friend and the commanding officer of the troops stationed in the Talbott Quadrant. . . . Nearly all the action will be new to fans, including a great deal of unrest in the nearby sectors of the League, unrest that Mesan agents may be stirring up but that draws in Michelle's 10th Fleet." (Booklist)

Weber, Katharine

The **little** women. Farrar, Straus & Giroux 2003 240p $22

ISBN 0-374-18959-5

LC 2003-44062

"In places, the readers' and author's notes do cause the pace to drag. But fortunately, the story of three teenage girls making a go of living in a New Haven apartment with a cute male roommate is lively, interesting and funny enough to carry one over the sluggish bits. . . . Novels with spurious critical apparatus don't often wear it lightly, but Weber's use of the form is both easy and playful." N Y Times Book Rev

Weber, Katharine

The **Music** Lesson. Crown 1999 178p

ISBN 0-609-60317-5

LC 98-9346

This "mystery is as intricate as an acrostic. A trio of clues—the motives of the narrator, who is a woman recovering from the accidental death of her child; the paintings of Vermeer, and the ideals of Irish nationalism—yield, by the book's close, an almost perfect, if chilling, answer." New Yorker

Weber, Katharine

True confections; a novel. Shaye Areheart Books 2010 274p il $22

ISBN 978-0-307-39586-3; 0-307-39586-3

LC 2010-277542

"Katharine Weber is one of the wittiest, most stimulating novelists at work today. . . . Reading True Confections is an intellectual rather than an emotional experience, but on those terms, it's wonderful fun and endlessly provocative." Chicago Trib

Wecker, Helene

The **Golem** and the Jinni; Helene Wecker. HarperCollins 2013 496 p. (hardcover) $26.99

ISBN 0062110837; 9780062110831

This novel, by Helene Wecker, is set "in turn-of-the-century New York. Chava is a golem, a creature made of clay, brought to life to by a disgraced rabbi who dabbles in dark Kabbalistic magic and dies at sea on the voyage from Poland. . . . Ahmad is a jinni, a being of fire born in the ancient Syrian desert, trapped in an old copper flask, and released in New York City. . . . Ahmad and Chava become unlikely friends and soul mates with a mystical connection." (Publisher's note)

Wein, Elizabeth

★ **Code** name Verity; Elizabeth Wein. Hyperion Books 2012 343 p.

ISBN 1423152190; 9781423152194

LC 2011024857

Michael L. Printz Honor Book (2013)

This young adult historical fiction novel presents a "tale of friendship during World War II. In a cell in Nazi-occupied France, a young woman writes. Like Scheherezade, to whom she is compared by the SS officer in charge of her case, she dribbles out information . . . in exchange for time and a reprieve from torture. . . . [S]he describes her friendship with Maddie, the pilot who flew them to France. . . . She also describes . . . her unbearable current situation." (Kirkus Reviews)

Weiner, Jennifer

Certain girls; a novel. Atria Books 2008 386p $26.95

ISBN 978-0-7432-9425-6; 0-7432-9425-4

LC 2007-38373

This is the "kind of book that gets under your skin, reminding you what it felt like to listen to your friend snap her retainer in the dark during a sleepover when you were 13 and capturing exactly what it feels like now, watching your child grow away from you and praying that someday she comes back." Washington Post Book World

Weiner, Jennifer

Good in bed; a novel. Pocket Books 2001 376p

ISBN 0-7434-1816-6

LC 00-68212

"Cannie Shapiro is in her late twenties, funny, independent, and a talented reporter for the Philadelphia Inquirer. After a 'temporary' breakup with her boyfriend of three years, she reads his debut column, 'Good in Bed,' in the women's magazine Moxie. Titled 'Loving a Larger Woman,' this very personal piece triggers events that completely transform her and those around her. Cannie's adventures will strike a chord with all young women struggling to find their place in the world, especially those larger than a size eight." Libr J

Weiner, Jennifer

In her shoes; a novel. Atria Books 2002 424p $25

ISBN 0-7434-1819-0

LC 2003-537614

"Meet plump, dependable Rose Feller and her gorgeous, out-of-control sister, Maggie. As children, they lost their mother and contact with grandmother Ella. Now, 20 years later, we follow their struggles to forgive the past, reclaim each other's love, and become their best selves. . . . Reworking the age-old theme that self-knowledge and acceptance are needed before love and happiness can be achieved, Weiner embroiders serious matters with threads of humor to produce a novel full of memorable characters and situations." Libr J

Weiner, Jennifer

Little earthquakes. Atria Bks. 2004 417p $26

ISBN 0-7434-7009-5

This is the "story of four women in Philadelphia who bond over pregnancy and motherhood. Becky, Kelly, and Ayinde meet in yoga class, and the three become friends when Ayinde's water breaks one day after class and they take her to the hospital. Becky is a chef with an adoring husband and an annoying mother-in-law; Kelly is frustrated when her husband loses his job and drags his feet looking for another; Ayinde's husband is a famous basketball player whom she suspects of infidelity. What brings the women together is their love for their newborns. The fourth woman, Lia, watches the group from afar; she's an actress who walked out on her husband after a devastating tragedy. Weiner seamlessly and gracefully weaves the four women's stories together." Booklist

Weiner, Jennifer

The **next** best thing; a novel. Jennifer Weiner. Atria Books 2012 389 p.

ISBN 1451617755; 9781451617757; 9781451617771

LC 2012015557

In this novel, by Jennifer Weiner, "Ruth Saunders . . . headed west with her seventy-year-old grandma in tow, hoping to make it as a screenwriter. Six years later, she . . . gets The Call: the sitcom she wrote, 'The Next Best Thing,' has gotten the green light. . . . But her dreams of Hollywood happiness are threatened by demanding actors, number-crunching executives, an unrequited crush on her boss, and her grandmother's impending nuptials." (Publisher's note)

Weiner, Jennifer

Then came you; a novel. Atria Books 2011 338p $26.99

ISBN 978-1-4516-1772-6

LC 2011-14411

This book "revolves around an unborn child with one hell of a potential extended family: a Princeton coed who's donated her eggs to a surgically enhanced gold digger and her millionaire husband, said husband's daughter, and a woman considering surrogacy to pay the bills. . . . Weiner's subject is topical, her characters richly drawn." People

Weinstein, Debra

Apprentice to the flower poet Z. Random House 2004 242p $23.95

ISBN 1-400-06155-5

"What's sharpest about Weinstein's well-metered wit is the way she sinks down into this elite subculture. The whole shameful business has been presatirzed for decades, but Weinstein, a published poet herself, knows where all the bodies are buried." Christ Sci Monit

Weir, Alison

Captive queen; a novel of Eleanor of Aquitaine. Ballantine Books 2010 478p $26

ISBN 978-0-345-51187-4; 0-345-51187-5

LC 2010-14855

A "portrayal of 12th century virago Eleanor of Aquitaine as a lusty temptress, all too happy to abandon her doddering husband, France's King Louis VII, for up-and-comer Henry of Anjou, more than a decade her junior. As in her previous novels, Weir frequently straddles a fine line between bodice ripper and historical fiction. Here, too, Eleanor's imagined erotic escapades prove a pleasant backdrop to her political plotting. . . . Even if the author's prose occasionally borders on . . . sexual silliness, Weir knows how to wrest the most pleasure from the lives of long-dead royalty." Denver Post

Weir, Alison

A **dangerous** inheritance; a novel of Tudor rivals and the secret of the Tower. Alison Weir. Ballantine 2012 544 p. (hardcover: acid-free paper) $27

ISBN 0345511891; 9780345511898; 9780345535948

LC 2012027867

In this book, "[w]hen her older sister, Lady Jane Grey, the Nine Days' Queen, is executed in 1554 for unlawfully accepting the English crown, Lady Katherine Grey's world falls apart. Barely recovered from this tragic loss she risks all for love, only to incur the wrath of her formidable cousin Queen Elizabeth I, who sees Katherine as a rival for her insecure throne. Interlaced with Katherine's story is that of her distant kinswoman Kate Plantagenet, the bastard daughter of Richard III." (Publisher's note)

Weir, Alison

Innocent traitor; a novel of Lady Jane Grey. Ballantine Books 2007 402p $24.95

ISBN 0-345-49485-7

LC 2006-49860

"Lady Jane, known to history as the Nine Days Queen, is a tragic and appealing figure. Abused by her parents, this talented and intelligent girl was bullied into a hateful marriage and pushed into accepting the Crown after the death of King Edward VI. Edward's older sister, Princess Mary (later known as Bloody Mary, and for good reason), rightfully claimed the Crown as her own, and Jane was sent to the Tower of London and eventually executed. Weir tells the story of Jane's short life from multiple viewpoints, which might initially confuse readers unfamiliar with the history, but this is a small fault in an otherwise entertaining and moving novel." Libr J

Weir, Alison

The **Lady** Elizabeth; a novel. Ballantine Books 2008 480p $25

ISBN 978-0-345-49535-8; 0-345-49535-7

LC 2008-284

A novel about the life of the young Elizabeth Tudor before she ascended to the throne. "From the time of her mother's death when she was three to her inheritance of the throne in her twenties, danger always came at Elizabeth from some corner. Early in her life, she was stripped of her title of princess; later, she had to defend her virtue from the roving eyes and hands of her stepfather; and, finally, she had to navigate the deadly waters between her Protestant faith and her sister's fanatical Catholicism. Several times Elizabeth barely escaped alive; hers was not a life that could be borne by the average person. Weir successfully depicts this extraordinary young woman who beat the odds to become one of the world's greatest rulers." Libr J

Weisgall, Deborah

The **world** before her. Houghton Mifflin 2008 278p $25

ISBN 978-0-618-74657-6; 0-618-74657-9

LC 2008-4734

"Mary Ann Evans, known to the world as George Eliot, the author of such great works as Middlemarch, is in Venice in 1880, to spend her honeymoon with Johnnie Cross, an uxorious American banker. Mary Ann had a long, passionate affair with philosopher and critic George Lewes, who was married to another woman. The two lived together until Lewes' death in 1878. . . . The other story is of Caroline Edgar Spingold, who arrives in Venice exactly a century after Evans, in 1980, on a business trip with her husband, Malcolm. He is 'commerce,' taking care of the finances, while she is 'art,' capricious and impulsive. Her views on marriage are tainted by her father's long-ago desertion of her mother. Describing the stories of Mary Ann and Caroline in alternate chapters, Weisgall draws parallel portraits of marital dissatisfaction and the attraction of the fleeting past to nullify the dreariness of the present. Her writing is tender, drowning you in its drunken energy, with the city of Venice providing a tasteful backdrop." St. Petersburg Times

Weisgarber, Ann

The **personal** history of Rachel Dupree; a novel.
Viking 2010 321p $25.95

ISBN 978-0-670-02201-4; 0-670-02201-2

LC 2010-04713

"The story begins as Rachel DuPree, wife of one of the only African-American ranchers in the Badlands in 1917, watches her husband, Isaac, lower their six-year-old daughter, Liz, down a well to fetch water in the midst of a terrible drought. Though she concedes it must be done, Rachel-heavily pregnant with her eighth child-is distraught, and her worries set off a chain reaction of second-guessing her loyalty to Isaac, whose schemes include buying out the neighboring ranch and leaving the family to find work during the winter. As a series of calamities befall the family, Rachel must decide whether to follow the only man she has ever loved or strike a new path of her own." Publ Wkly

"An eye-opening look at the little explored area of a black frontier woman in the American West." Chicago Sun-Times

Welch, James

★ The **heartsong** of Charging Elk; a novel.
Doubleday 2000 440p $24.95

ISBN 0-385-49674-5

LC 99-58875

"As a young Oglala Sioux, Charging Elk saw the massacre of General Custer's forces at Little Big Horn. . . . Now in his early 20s and on a tour of Europe as part of Buffalo Bill Cody's 'Wild West show' in the 1890s, Charging Elk has become stranded in Marseille, France." Christ Sci Monit

The author "estranges our vision. We have no choice but to feel, as we look through Charging Elk's eyes, what it is like to live in a no man's land forever." N Y Times Book Rev

Welch, James

★ The **Indian** lawyer. Norton 1990 349p

ISBN 0-393-02896-8

LC 90-6894

"Sylvester Yellow Calf, the hero of this novel, has fought his way, despite the odds, to a top post in a prestigious Montana law firm and now is being wooed as a candidate for Congress by political power brokers. Sylvester, ex-basketball star and Stanford Law School graduate, recognizes that such a move could put him in a position to help his fellow Native Americans and at the same time to work for the preservation of the environment. While his responsibilities are all too clear to him, Yellow Calf hesitates, and, as he ponders his decision, he is drawn by a convict into a web that nearly strangles him." Choice

"The novel contains good, fast-paced action with succinct insight into our ordinary dilemmas." Nation

Weldon, Fay

Big girls don't cry. Atlantic Monthly Press 1998 345p $24

ISBN 0-87113-720-8

LC 98-35702

First published 1997 in the United Kingdom with title: Big women

"Just when Weldon's wit starts to sound like fingernails on a blackboard, she relents and reminds us that even in comedy, she's dead serious. . . . It's tempting to find the zany conclusion unsatisfying because it leaves no answers, but that's the privilege of smart satire." Christ Sci Monit

Weldon, Fay

Chalcot Crescent. Europa Editions 2010 269p pa $15

ISBN 978-1-933372-79-2; 1-933372-79-6

First published 2009 in the United Kingdom

"It's 2013. Fay Weldon's alter ego Frances, an 80-year-old novelist, sits waiting for the bailiffs (or the secret police of near-future dystopia) to break in, and muses on the greed-is-good decades of celebrity, cheery traffic jams and maxed-out credit cards that brought her to this pass. The house on Chalcot Crescent is very like the real house in London's Primrose Hill that Weldon occupied in the glory days of her generation. Frances's past, delivered in bite-sized chapters, is close to Weldon's. There is an ironic subplot about industrial-scale cannibalism, and a sketchy conspiracy to overthrow the brutal government but this is Orwellian nightmare recast for the Twittering classes. There is more skewed memoir than grim future or alternate universe, but you'll be entertained if you enjoy Weldon's trademark barbed frivolity." New Scientist

Weldon, Fay

A **hard** time to be a father. St. Martin's Press 1999 242p $23.95

ISBN 1-58234-011-0

Weldon "is at her wry, risk-taking best in this broad collection of 19 stories. . . . In her signature style, Weldon peoples many of these pieces with women who wreak catastrophe in ways that thrill the misanthropic reader." Publ Wkly

Weldon, Fay

★ The **life** and loves of a she-devil. Pantheon Bks. 1984 241p

LC 84-7070

First published 1983 in the United Kingdom

"A fable about female power and powerlessness, telling the story of Ruth, an ugly woman married to a philandering man, who transforms herself by sheer strength of will into the image of her hated rival." Oxford Companion to 20th-Century Lit in Engl

Weldon, Fay

Rhode Island blues. Atlantic Monthly Press 2000 325p $24

ISBN 0-87113-775-5

LC 00-38576

"Weldon employs a merciless form of satire here; she also takes on favorite themes: love and the war between the sexes. But 'Rhode Island Blues'—is about more than that. Just how much more, in fact, is staggering. Here's a short list of topics covered: rape, adoption, prostitution, murder, romance between the elderly, compulsive gambling, family bonds, madness Hollywood, immigration and sadomasochism." N Y Time Book Rev

Weldon, Fay

She may not leave. Atlantic Monthly Press 2006 284p $24

ISBN 0-8711-3942-1

LC 2005-7227

"In their mid-thirties—handsome, healthy, and well educated—literary agent Hattie and crusading journalist Martyn have been thrown off their game by the arrival of their infant daughter. While on maternity leave, Hattie feels particularly oppressed by the domestic routine. . . . She suggests they hire an au pair, but Martyn has serious qualms about the ethics of having a servant. However, once Martyn experiences the calming effect the Polish nanny has on his household— which allows him to sleep late and eat gourmet meals, not to mention witness demonstrations of her belly-dancing lessons—his political principles crumble, but so does his relationship with Hattie. Narrating the whole turn of events is Hattie's 72-year-old grandmother, Frances, a character who allows Weldon to describe the changing attitudes toward children and marriage over four generations. . . . Throwing in one final unexpected but delicious twist at the end, Weldon delivers another of her trademark takes on the domestic wars." Booklist

Weldon, Fay

Worst fears; a novel. Atlantic Monthly Press 1996 200p

LC 95-52367

Fay Weldon is the "quintessential anti-romance novelist and always will be. But she's filed down a few sharp edges in 'Worst Fears,' and that makes it one of her best novels yet." N Y Times Book Rev

Wellington, David

Monster Island; a zombie novel. Thunder's Mouth 2006 282p pa $13.95

ISBN 1-56025-850-0

In this first volume of a projected horror trilogy, "most of the world has fallen to the undead, with pockets of survivors clinging to a precarious existence. At the behest of the leader of the Free Women's Republic of Somaliland, a shipload of those makes the ludicrous trip from Africa to New York in a desperate quest for medicine. New York is a wasteland, and everything depends on a small, incredibly dedicated band of teenage girls, armed to the teeth, and native guide Dekalb, formerly a UN arms inspector. Also, in NYC there is Gary, a zombie who, completely unexpectedly, retains live human mental faculties. . . . There are many layers to this zombie apocalypse, and this book just gets things rolling." Booklist

Wells, Dan

The hollow city; Dan Wells. 1st ed. St. Martin's Press 2012 333 p. (hardcover) $25.99

ISBN 0765331705; 9780765331700; 9781429950619

LC 2012011663

In this book by Dan Wells, "an amnesiac paranoid schizophrenic holds the key to a serial killer's motivation. . . . Michael Shipman is . . . tortured by his senses and afflicted with delusions about being pursued by Faceless Men. Now the authorities want to know whether Michael's Faceless Men are involved with the Red Line Killer, whose de-faced victims were associated with the Children of the Earth, a

cult based in the former home of notorious murderer Milos Cerny." (Publishers Weekly)

Wells, H. G.

The complete short stories of H. G. Wells. St. Martin's Press 1987 1038p $19.95

ISBN 0-312-15855-6

LC 87-27478

First published 1927 in the United Kingdom with title: The short stories of H. G. Wells

A collection of 62 short stories and the complete work: The time machine, first published 1895

"A fat, heavy volume packed with humour, strangeness, horror and imaginative stimulus." Daily Telegraph

Wells, H. G.

★ The invisible man. Penguin 2005 xxiv, 161p pa $6

ISBN 0-14-143998-X

First published 1897

"The story concerns the life and death of a scientist named Griffin who has gone mad. Having learned how to make himself invisible, Griffin begins to use his invisibility for nefarious purposes, including murder. When he is finally killed, his body becomes visible again." Merriam-Webster's Ency of Lit

Wells, H. G.

★ The island of Doctor Moreau; edited by Patrick Parrinder; with an introduction by Margaret Atwood and notes by Steven McLean. Penguin Books 2005 xxxiv, 139p (Penguin classics)

ISBN 0-14-144102-X

First published 1896

This is "an evolutionary fantasy about a shipwrecked naturalist who becomes involved in an experiment to 'humanize' animals by surgery." Oxford Companion to Engl Lit. 6th edition

Wells, H. G.

Seven famous novels; with a preface by the author. Knopf 1934 860p

Contents: The time machine (1895); The island of Dr. Moreau (1896); The invisible man (1897); The war of the worlds (1898); The first men in the moon (1901); The food of the gods (1904); In the days of the comet (1906)

Wells, H. G.

★ The time machine. Penguin 2005 xxviii, 104p pa $9

ISBN 0-14-143997-1

First published 1895

"Wells advanced his social and political ideas in this narrative of a nameless Time Traveller who is hurtled into the year 802,701 by his elaborate ivory, crystal, and brass contraption. The world he finds is peopled by two races: the decadent Eloi, fluttery and useless, are dependent for food, clothing, and shelter on the simian subterranean Morlocks, who prey on them. The two races—whose names are borrowed from the Biblical Eli and Moloch—symbolize Wells's vision of the eventual result of unchecked capitalism: a neurasthenic upper class that would eventually be devoured by a proletariat driven to the depths." Merriam-Webster's Ency of Lit

Wells, H. G.

Tono-Bungay; edited by Patrick Parrinder; with an introduction and notes by Edward Mendelson. Penguin 2005 xxxiii, 414p pa $14

ISBN 0-14-144111-9

First published 1908

"The narrator is George Ponderevo, son of the housekeeper on a large estate, who is apprenticed to his uncle, Edward Ponderevo, a small-town druggist. His fantastic uncle soon moves to London and makes a fortune from his quack medicine Tono-Bungay. George helps his uncle, ironically observes his rise in the world, and uses some of his money to set himself up as an airplane designer. George resembles H. G. Wells himself—the son of a housekeeper, apprenticed to a druggist, a socialist, and a man with a vision of progress through properly used science." Reader's Ency. 4th edition

Wells, H. G.

★ The war of the worlds; illustrated by Edward Gorey. New York Review Books 2005 251p il $16.95

ISBN 1-59017-158-6

LC 2005-3693

First published 1898

In this novel the author "introduced the 'Alien' being into the role which became a cliché—a monstrous invader of Earth, a competitor in a cosmic struggle for existence. Though the Martians were a ruthless and terrible enemy, HGW was careful to point out that Man had driven many animal species to extinction, and that human invaders of Tasmania had behaved no less callously in exterminating their cousins." Sci Fic Ency

Wells, Ken

Crawfish mountain; a novel. Random House 2007 364p $25.95

ISBN 978-0-375-50876-9; 0-375-50876-7

LC 2007-5612

A "cautionary tale about the environment, set five years before Hurricane Katrina. It's both a political satire and a page-turning mystery. Like the best jambalaya, it's liberally spiced. Readers can almost taste the boiled crawfish and oyster po' boys with extra pickles and mayonnaise (pronounced MY-Nez, by one character). Wells . . . makes the most of Louisiana's legendary political corruption and its roguish politicians." USA Today

Wells, Martha

Wheel of the infinite; Martha Wells. Eos 2000 355 p. $24.00

ISBN 0380973359 (alk. paper)

LC 00021726

This book is set in "the great Temple city of Duvalpore, [where every year] the image of the Wheel of the Infinite must be painstakingly remade to ensure another year of peace and harmony for the Celestial Empire. . . . But a black storm is spreading across the Wheel. Every night . . . the Wheel's constructors and caretakers brush the darkness away and repair the damage with brightly colored sands and

potent magic. Each morning the storm reappears, bigger and darker than before. . . . A murderer and traitor, . . . Maskelle has been summoned back to help put the world right. . . . Now, in the company of Rian-a skilled and dangerously alluring swordsman-she must confront dread enemies old and new and a cold, stalking malevolence unlike any she has ever encountered." (Publisher's note)

Welsh, Irvine, 1958-

Porno. Norton 2002 483p $24.95

ISBN 0-393-05723-2

LC 2002-26362

Sequel to: Trainspotting (1994)

This novel "signals, if not a return to form, then at least a return to enthusiastic formlessness—to something like the raw, jagged energy of old." N Y Times Book Rev

Welsh, Irvine, 1958-

Skagboys; Irvine Welsh. W. W. Norton 2012 532 p. (hardcover) $26.95

ISBN 9780224087902; 9780393088731; 0393088731

LC 2012018043

This book a prequel to Irvine Welsch's "Transpotting," follows "Mark Renton, a philosophical young man who seems poised to rise above his lower-middle-class station until heroin (i.e., skag) implodes him. Not long after he starts using, he's dropped out of university and wants to quit drugs but not very badly. . . . Shifting among various characters' perspectives, Welsh shows how rapidly addiction sank Mark and his friends." (Kirkus Reviews)

Welsh, Irvine

Trainspotting. W.W. Norton 2002 343p $23.95

ISBN 0-393-05724-0

First published 1993 in the United Kingdom

This novel is set in a working class neighborhood in Edinburgh. Narrator Mark Renton tells the story "of young junkies in their 20s living on the dole, fending off adulthood and trying to escape from a world of AIDS, death and national despair." New Repub

Welsh, Louise

The cutting room. Canongate 2002 294p $24

ISBN 1-8419-5280-X

LC 2002-437974

"A remarkable first novel. Like all the best exponents of the genre, Louise Welsh sets up her template and then manipulates it, using the glamour of crime to examine more humdrum kinds of suffering and loss. She piles on atmosphere to produce a Glasgow that is predictably dark and yet still plausible." N Y Times Book Rev

Welty, Eudora

★ The collected stories of Eudora Welty. Harcourt Brace Jovanovich 1980 622p hardcover o.p. pa $16

ISBN 0-15-118994-3; 0-15-618921-6 pa

LC 80-7947

This volume contains four previously published collections: A curtain of green, and other stories; The wide net, and other stories; The golden apples and The bride of the Innisfallen, and other stories. Also included in this volume are two uncollected pieces: Where is the voice coming from? and The demonstrators.

Welty, Eudora

★ **Complete** novels. Library of Am. 1998 1009p $35

ISBN 1-883011-54-X

LC 97-46702

Includes bibliographical references

Welty, Eudora

★ **Delta** wedding; a novel. Harcourt Brace & Co. 1946 247p

A "portrait of a Southern plantation family in 1923. Set in the context of the wedding of one of the daughters, the novel explores the relationships among members of the Fairchild family, most of whom have been sheltered from any contact with the world outside the Mississippi Delta. Although they quarrel among themselves, they also unite against any threats to the family's status, honoring the belief in the family as a sacred and unchanging entity." Merriam-Webster's Ency of Lit

Welty, Eudora

Losing battles. Random House 1970 436p il

"At a large family gathering in Banner, Mississippi, the Renfro and Beecham families have assembled to celebrate Granny's ninetieth birthday. They are also celebrating Jack Renfro's return from the prison farm. As one might expect, the day is made up of reminiscences and recountings of earlier events, so that the novel actually spans many years. One of the key figures is Gloria, an orphan. She is frequently teased about being the daughter of another orphan, Rachel Sojourner, and of one of the Beecham boys who died in World War I. Gloria, who had married Jack just prior to his imprisonment, feels that they must get away from the clan, all of whom seem proud of their ignorance in spite of Miss Julia Mortimer's lifelong struggle to teach them something. It was a losing battle, probably even for Gloria." Shapiro. Fic for Youth. 3d edition

Welty, Eudora

The **optimist's** daughter. Random House 1972 180p

"This novel is considered the high point of Welty's lengthy career. The strong character study examines 45-year-old Laurel McKelva Hand, who returns from Chicago to Mississippi, where her father is dying. She is forced to consider her complex and ambiguous emotions about her powerful and dynamic father, the impact of this relationship on her life, and her puzzlement at his late marriage to a coarse and shallow woman who is Laurel's own age." Shapiro. Fic for Youth. 3d edition

Welty, Eudora

★ The **Ponder** heart; drawings by Joe Krush. Harcourt Brace & Co. 1954 156p il

"Cast as a monologue, {this comic novella} is rich with colloquial speech and descriptive imagery. The narrator of the story is Miss Edna Earle Ponder, one of the last living members of a once-prominent family, who manages the Beulah Hotel in Clay, Miss. She tells a traveling salesman the history of her family and fellow townsfolk." Merriam-Webster's Ency of Lit

Welty, Eudora

★ The **robber** bridegroom; designed and illustrated by Barry Moser. Harcourt Brace Jovanovich 1987 134p il $19.95

ISBN 0-15-178318-7

LC 87-21195

A reissue of the title first published 1942 by Doubleday

"Miss Welty uses the magic of metaphor and simile like a lyric poet, and writes with a limpid purity, and exquisite sense of descriptive coloring that gives a warm glow of beauty to a fantastic, and unfortunately sometimes tiresome story." Springfield Repub

Welty, Eudora

Stories, essays & memoir; [selected and annotated by Richard Ford and Michael Kreyling] Library of Am. 1998 976p il $35

ISBN 1-88301-155-8

LC 97-46691

The story collections included in this volume are in The collected stories of Eudora Welty. Included are two additional stories: Where is the voice coming from? and The demonstrators

Includes bibliographical references

Wenner, Kate

Dancing with Einstein; a novel. Kate Wenner. Scribner 2004 223p $24

ISBN 0-7432-5164-4

LC 2003-65681

"Marea Hoffman, now approaching 30, arrives in New York after years of backpacking around the world. She quickly locates an apartment in Greenwich Village, gets a night job in an organic bakery, and sets to work on unpacking the emotional baggage of her childhood. The daughter of a Princeton physicist, Marea harbors affectionate memories of her surrogate 'grandpa,' Albert Einstein. But her father's work on the hydrogen bomb alienated him from both the pacifist Einstein and Marea's mother, who was raised Quaker. Marea's parents were on the verge of divorce when her father died in a car accident. Determined to deal with her father's death, Marea signs on with four therapists: a Freudian analyst, a New Age Jungian, a feminist, and one, found by chance, without any evident personal agenda." Libr J

Werfel, Franz

★ The **forty** days of Musa Dagh. Viking 1934 824p

Original German edition, 1933; published in the United Kingdom with title: The forty days

"Gabriel Bagradian returns to his ancestral village in Syria, where he learns that the Turks are disarming the Armenians and sending them into exile. Gabriel plans the resistance to the Turks and directs the fortification of the mountain Musa Dagh. The Turks are successfully repulsed a number of times but at great cost in lives to the Armenians on the mountain. On the fortieth day the remnant of the Armenian force is rescued by the French." Shapiro. Fic for Youth. 3d edition

Werfel, Franz

The **song** of Bernadette; translated by Ludwig Lewisohn. Viking 1942 575p

Original German edition, 1941

A slightly fictionalized version of "the life of Saint Bernadette of Lourdes. While it is not exactly a religious work, it is truly reverent in its approach to the inscrutable, the unfathomable, the divine. There is an engrossing picture of emperor, bishops, priests, nuns, merchants and artisans. A living pageant of the second Empire in France." Ont Libr Rev

Wesley, Mary

Part of the furniture. Viking 1997 256p

LC 96-46226

"Wesley's skill with character development and her subtle, amusing dissection of that paramount British preoccupation, family background and breeding, endow this novel with the charm of a comedy of manners and the enduring appeal of a satisfying love story." Publ Wkly

The **Wesleyan** anthology of science fiction; edited by Arthur B. Evans . . . [et al.] Wesleyan University Press 2010 767p $85; pa $39.95

ISBN 978-0-8195-6954-7; 978-0-8195-6955-4 pa

LC 2009-53144

"This anthology offers an overview from the works of Nathaniel Hawthorne and Jules Verne to those of William Gibson—so thorough with its brief, informative analyses at the start of each story, reading this collection is like taking a course without the bother of tests." Washington City Paper

Wesselmann, Debbie Lee

Captivity. John F. Blair, Publisher 2008 295p $22.95

ISBN 978-089587-353-8; 0-89587-353-2

LC 2007-37816

"Primatologist Dana Armstrong is passionate about making a difference in the lives of the animals living at a South Carolina chimpanzee sanctuary. But a break-in resulting in the escape of numerous chimpanzees forces Dana to not only determine who was responsible for the vandalism but also deal with her traumatic memories of the past—for Dana is a survivor of a psychological experiment, raised as a child with a chimp named Annie. She now faces opposition from the local community, political pressure from her university, and a ghost from her past who is bent upon her destruction. . . . [The author combines] a riveting plot with exciting characters to hold you spellbound until the last page." Libr J

West, Dorothy

★ The **wedding**. Doubleday 1995 240p hardcover o.p. pa $12.95

ISBN 0-385-47143-2; 0-385-47144-0 pa

LC 94-27285

"Through the ancestral histories of the Coles family, West . . . subtly reveals the ways in which color can burden and codify behavior. The author makes her points with a delicate hand, maneuvering with confidence and ease through a sometimes incendiary subject." Publ Wkly

West, Jessamyn

Collected stories of Jessamyn West. Harcourt Brace Jovanovich 1986 480p

LC 86-12031

West, Jessamyn

★ The **friendly** persuasion. Harcourt 1945 214p hardcover o.p. pa $13

ISBN 0-15-133605-9; 0-15-602909-X pa

"The Birdwell family of Indiana led a quiet life until the Civil War came into their lives. They were Quakers and tried to live according to the teachings of William Penn. Jess Birdwell, a nurseryman, loved a fast horse as well as his trees and the people he knew. Eliza, his wife, was a Quaker minister and a gentle, albeit strict, soul. When the war reached Indiana, Josh, the oldest son, was torn between his Quaker upbringing and his belief in the rightness of the Union cause; Mattie was at that difficult age between childhood and womanhood; and Little Jess, the youngest, ran into trouble with Eliza's geese. This is a wonderful family chronicle, with the laughter, tears, and tenderness that can be found in many families." Shapiro. Fic for Youth. 3d edition

West, Morris L.

★ The **clowns** of God; [by] Morris West. St. Martin's Press 1990 370p $19.95

ISBN 0-312-04459-3

LC 89-70344

A reissue of the title first published 1981 by Morrow

"The fugitive ex-pope posits all the fearful questions about life that have perplexed us since Hiroshima. West's ultimate answers will disturb some and be dismissed by others, but no one will be left unmoved. The sheer power of his prose and his keen understanding of human nature make this novel a stunning accomplishment." Libr J

Followed by Lazarus

West, Morris L.

The **devil's** advocate. Morrow 1959 319p

"The characters all are firmly, brightly established. The writing, without fanciness or flourish, goes along with a fine, steady drive. There are no profound insights, no remarkable illuminations. But there is an engrossing story, expertly told, about a set of fascinating people whose lives are viewed as meaningful." Chicago Sunday Trib

West, Morris L.

Lazarus; {by} Morris West. St. Martin's Press 1990 293p

LC 89-77919

"A tense and exciting thriller, Lazarus also explores world crises and theological politics quite as fascinating to non-Catholics as to Catholics. . . . While the book can be read as a complement to the other two novels, it stands alone as a superb, absorbing novel." Libr J

West, Morris L.

Masterclass; {by} Morris West. St. Martin's Press 1991 330p

LC 90-28090

Max Mather "served as the paleographer (manuscript archivist) for a well-known Italian family. But when he comes into possession of two Raphael originals, Max becomes incredibly wily, both about the effect his discovery will have on the international art world and about his prospects for cashing in. Big-time collectors, dealers, and auctioneers are drawn into Mather's game, with the players flitting easily from New York to Zurich to Florence to Amsterdam and back again. Amid all the artsy oneupmanship, West gives us a subplot involving the murder of a Manhattan painter whose brilliance extended from her way with palette and brush to kinky, omnivorous sex. Solid plotting and interesting characters make this flashy novel of intrigue fully enjoyable." Booklist

West, Morris L.

The **shoes** of the fisherman; a novel. Morrow 1963 374p

In this first title in the author's Vatican trilogy, "a humble Ukrainian pope finds himself the central negotiator in an attempt to prevent the United States and the Soviet Union from starting World War III. During the negotiations, the pope must confront the Russian who once tortured him. The work, a popular and critical success, demonstrates West's concern with modern man's inability to communicate with his brother." McCormick and Fletcher. Spy Fic

Followed by The clowns of God

West, Nathanael

★ **Miss** Lonelyhearts. Liveright 1933 213p

"The story of a man who writes an 'advice to the lovelorn' column, the theme of the book is the loneliness of the individual in modern society. The hero tries to live the role of omniscient counselor he has assumed for the paper, but his attempts to reach out to suffering humanity are twisted by circumstances, and he is finally murdered by a man he has tried to help." Reader's Ency. 4th edition

West, Nathanael

Miss Lonelyhearts & The day of the locust. Modern Lib. 1998 289p $15.50

ISBN 0-679-60278-X

LC 97-39828

Combined edition of two titles first published 1933 and 1939 respectively. The day of the locust is about Hollywood and the misfits who flock to it in search of the American dream

West, Nathanael

Novels and other writings. Library of Am. 1997 829p $35

ISBN 1-88301-128-0

LC 96-49007

"Each of West's novels is distinct in style and theme. In the Dada-inspired The Dream Life of Balso Snell (1931), he freely mixes high-flown literary and religious allusions with erotic and scatological humor. Miss Lonelyhearts (1933) presents, in a series of grotesque, starkly etched episodes, the spiritual breakdown of a newspaper columnist overwhelmed by his readers' suffering. By contrast, A Cool Million (1934) reduces the eternal optimism of Horatio Alger's novels to a brutal, cartoonish farce. In his last work, The Day of the Locust (1939), West renders with hallucinatory precision the reverse side of the Hollywood dream, as he choreographs a

cast of failures, has-beens, and deluded glamour-seekers in what becomes an apocalyptic dance of death. Also included is a generous sampling of West's other surviving work, ranging from freewheeling improvisations and grotesque comic tales to more mainstream work written with Hollywood or Broadway in mind." Publisher's note

West, Paul

★ **Lord** Byron's doctor; a novel. Doubleday 1989 277p

ISBN 0-385-26129-2

LC 89-7735

"Through Polidori, West compiles a lurid case history on the cruelty of genius. Shelley may have been 'polite to God and pious towards women,' but Byron was arrogant about both. His disdain toward lesser literary figures was godlike, and his venery demonic. . . . Romanticism and egoism normally go hand in hand. Here they are passionately entwined. Rocking and rolling in Byron's carriage, sailing through storms, discussing the uses of opium or exchanging ghost stories at the Villa Diodati, the group is principally concerned with who will be favored by the muse." Time

West, Paul

★ **Love's** mansion. Random House 1992 339p

ISBN 0-394-58734-0

LC 92-6804

"As Mr. West has made vividly clear, we have much to learn from the Moxons and their changing world. It is perhaps unfashionable to write about the pain and transformations that characterize the love of a long-married couple, but Mr. West is concerned with something much more personal than literary fashion. At times the astounding 'diligence of human memory' takes off in his book and produces passages that are close to poetry, almost always when his style is at its least extended and inclusive." N Y Times Book Rev

West, Paul

O.K. the corral, the Earps, and Doc Holliday: a novel. Scribner 2000 302p $24

ISBN 0-684-84865-1

LC 99-89924

West "cares more about character and color than action, and his prose can at times be ponderous. But although some details, like those of Doc's ravaging consumption, require a strong stomach, they serve to depict Holliday as a moving and complex character." N Y Times Book Rev

West, Paul

Sporting with Amaryllis. Overlook Press 1996 158p $19.95

ISBN 0-87951-666-6

LC 96-22766

"Readers who accept unreservedly Milton's solemn, extravagant sense of his destiny are not likely to be amused by West's conception of how muse Amaryllis worked over youth Milton. West makes the muse anything but 'thankless.' But one doesn't have to swallow a word of West's flamboyant writing to find it piquant. It's pleasanter and more comfortable, certainly, to imagine Milton exuberantly enjoying, and benefiting from, fleshly indulgence than to endure seeing him cruelly cartooned as a bigoted thug and assassin." American Scholar

West, Rebecca

The **birds** fall down. Viking 1966 435p

LC 67-10214

"This is a great work of literature. . . . Rebecca West was fascinated by espionage and from her knowledge of Russian emigres she created a comprehensive picture of their preoccupations and torments at the turn of the century." McCormick and Fletcher. Spy Fic

Westerfeld, Scott

The **killing** of worlds. TOR Bks. 2003 336p (Succession) hardcover o.p. pa $14.95

ISBN 0-7653-0850-9; 0-7653-2052-5 pa

LC 2003-56304

Sequel to The risen empire

"Captain Laurent Zai demonstrates his strategic cleverness as well as an unusual amount of luck, when he unexpectedly defeats the Rix ship he was sent to destroy—an assignment intended to be a suicide mission. Meanwhile, in the imperial senate, Nara Oxham walks a fine line between treason and her party's agenda as she fights the emperor himself. . . . [This is] a rip-roaring space opera, with its strength residing in the characters, all of them involved in believable dilemmas." Booklist

Westerfeld, Scott

The **risen** empire. TOR Bks. 2003 304p (Succession) hardcover o.p. pa $14.95

ISBN 0-7653-0555-0; 0-7653-1998-5 pa

LC 2002-42952

"Westerfeld's speculations about the rise and fall of civilizations are appealingly quirky . . . and his action scenes have a breathless realism that does not gloss over the bloody nature of combat. Perhaps most important, his moral calculus never lapses into Q.E.D. As the narrative jumps from intimate glimpses of the Empire to the Rix Cult and back again, we grow less and less clear about whom we are rooting for." N Y Times Book Rev

Followed by The killing of worlds (2003)

Western Writers of America

American West: twenty new stories from the Western Writers of America; edited with an introduction by Loren D. Estleman. Forge 2001 367p $25.95

ISBN 0-312-87317-4

LC 00-48446

This collection of stories about the West includes works by Don Coldsmith, Jory Sherman, Elmer Kelton, Richard S. Wheeler, Johnny D. Boggs, and Max Evans

"Uniformly fine writing makes this a welcome addition to any western collection." Booklist

Western Writers of America

Westward; a fictional history of the American West: 28 original stories celebrating the 50th anniversary of the Western Writers of America. edited by Dale L. Walker. Forge 2003 432p $25.95

ISBN 0-7653-0451-1

LC 2002-45481

"The collection reveals both the vitality and the diversity of the western genre as well as the enduring appeal of the short story." Booklist

Westheimer, David

★ **Von** Ryan's Express. Doubleday 1964 327p

"Colonel Joseph Ryan is shot down over Italy and is sent to a prisoner-of-war camp, where he imposes military discipline upon the other prisoners. After Italy's surrender, when the prisoners are put on a train for Germany, Ryan plans a daring takeover of the train and gets the men to Switzerland." Shapiro. Fic for Youth. 2d edition

Followed by Von Ryan's return (1980)

Westlake, Donald E.

★ The **ax**. Mysterious Press 1997 273p

LC 96-52068

"As novels go, 'The Ax' is pretty much flawless, with a surprise ending that will unplug your expectations. Burke Devore is American Man at the millennium—as emblematic of his time as George F. Babbitt and Holden Caulfield and Capt. John Yossarian were of theirs. Westlake has written a remarkable book. If you can't relate to it, be thankful." N Y Times Book Rev

Westlake, Donald E.

Baby, would I lie? a romance of the Ozarks. Mysterious Press 1994 291p

LC 93-40485

This comic mystery, featuring characters from the author's Trust me on this, "is set in 'the new Nashville': Branson, Missouri. Singer Ray Jones is accused of one murder and then of a second. Out on bail, he continues to entertain in this theater. Meanwhile, an army of troops from the sleazy tabloid Weekly Galaxy descends to bug offices, lie, infiltrate, and do anything else necessary to get some sort of story on the upcoming trial. Also arriving are reporters Sara and Jack, lovers and representatives of a trendy New York magazine called Trend: The Magazine for the Way We Live This Instant. The action is jet-fast, and the satiric commentary on country western stars and fans is wonderfully wicked." Libr J

Westlake, Donald E.

Bad news; by Donald Westlake. Mysterious Press 2001 342p $30

ISBN 0-89296-717-X

LC 00-45592

"Westlake has a genius for comic strategy, and the complications he devises when the casino operators initiate a counterplot to discredit Little Feather have a lunatic brilliance worthy of Abbott and Costello. But Westlake is also a card with characters, and he flashes that talent to terrific effect here." N Y Times Book Rev

Westlake, Donald E.

★ **Bank** shot. Simon & Schuster 1972 224p

It is Westlake's "triumph that whereas on one hand the reader knows he simply can't take the characters and situations seriously, those characters are so deftly drawn that they are eminently believable." N Y Times Book Rev

Westlake, Donald E.

Don't ask. Mysterious Press 1993 327p $18.95

ISBN 0-89296-469-3

LC 92-53721

In this novel John Dormunder "and his cohorts agree to steal a religious relic, the femur of a thirteenth-century saint, that is a bone of contention between two fledgling Eastern European countries. Possession of the bone will lead to a seat in the United Nations." Booklist

"If the plot is of no great concern, it is the effortlessness, wit, and sheer good-heartedness of the telling that make 'Don't Ask' such a consistent delight." N Y Times Book Rev

Westlake, Donald E.

Drowned hopes. Mysterious Press 1990 422p

ISBN 0-89296-178-3

LC 89-35859

In this "comedy-mystery, ex-con John Dortmunder and his benevolent criminal cohorts are continuously frustrated in their attempts to recover $700,000 in stolen money from a 50-foot-deep reservoir in upper New York State." Booklist

Westlake, Donald E.

Get real. Grand Central Publishing 2009 278p $23.99

ISBN 978-0-446-17860-0; 0-446-17860-8

LC 2008-933234

"When Dortmunder and his associates—okay, his criminal gang—are offered a role on a reality show dramatizing their exploits, they initially think it's a terrible idea. However, they soon see it as an opportunity to aid in their usual criminal pursuits. While the producers of their show believe that the group is staging a smalltime robbery, they're actually working on a way to find what they believe is a large amount of money being housed by the production company." Libr J

"A rollicking crime caper that pulls the pants right off the reality TV industry." N Y Times Book Rev

Westlake, Donald E.

Good behavior. Mysterious Press 1985 244p

ISBN 0-89296-240-2

LC 85-43178

The author "manages to create characters who are a curious mixture of stereotypes and archetypes. If he is a master of the comic crime caper, and he is, he also does what the best comic writers throughout history have done—make a comment on society." N Y Times Book Rev

Westlake, Donald E.

The **hook**. Mysterious Press 2000 280p $30

ISBN 0-89296-588-6

LC 99-36273

"Westlake salts the stew with lots of fascinating publishing shoptalk, and his portrayal of the psychological unraveling of a writer is made all the more chilling by the quiet realism of its presentation. A fine thriller." Booklist

Westlake, Donald E.

★ The **hot** rock. Simon & Schuster 1970 249p

"The hot rock is the Balambo Emerald, part of an African exhibit at the New York Coliseum, owned by Akinzi,

and coveted by the breakaway state of Talabwo. Major Iko of Talabwo selects John Dortmunder as the mastermind for the heist. But lifting the stone from the Coliseum is only the first caper for Dortmunder's carefully chosen crew." Libr J

This novel "comes awesomely close to the ultimate in comic, big-caper novels; it's . . . filled with mocking style and action and imagination." N Y Times Book Rev

Westlake, Donald E.

★ **Memory**. Hard Case Crime 2010 366p pa $7.99

ISBN 0-8439-6375-1; 978-0-8439-6375-5

In this "novel that Westlake wrote in the early 1960s and never published, Paul Cole suffers from partial amnesia — his past is just beyond the reach of his mind. He keeps moving, like a fugitive, through a succession of working-class jobs; he falls in love; he gets in trouble with the law. Westlake never again dabbled in social realism, which is a shame: Memory is terse and bleak and low-key emotional, and as indelible as Westlake's other books." Entertainment Wkly

Westlake, Donald E.

Money for nothing. Mysterious Press 2003 294p $24.95

ISBN 0-89296-787-0

LC 2002-35888

"Although Westlake has written funnier books and his characters could use more dimension, 'Money for Nothing' has all of his trademarks: an ample supply of silliness and suspense wrapped up in a wacky plot." N Y Times Book Rev

Westlake, Donald E.

Put a lid on it. Mysterious Press 2002 247p $23.95

ISBN 0-89296-718-8

LC 2001-51435

This is a "crime caper that also gets some nice digs in as political satire. . . . Although Meehan isn't quite as ingenious a thief as some of Westlake's other criminal protagonists, he's a born philosopher." N Y Times Book Rev

Westlake, Donald E.

The **road** to ruin. Mysterious Press 2004 342p $25

ISBN 0-89296-801-X

LC 2003-65007

In this Dortmunder caper the "conspicuous target of larcenous intent is one Monroe Hall, the broadly drawn, babyish CEO and chief perpetrator of an Enron-like financial debacle, which has made him a pariah to friends and potential employees but still rich in funds and enemies. When a disgruntled former chauffeur hires Dortmunder and his crew to steal Hall's classic-car collection for the insurance, together with all the swag they can haul, our clumsy confederation of bandits decides to sidestep the estate's elaborate security system by hiring themselves on as staff, with rumpled second-story man Dortmunder in the unlikely role of butler." Booklist

"Ingenuity fuels the plot, but what puts the match to the comedy is the moral outrage of the furiously funny characters." N Y Times Book Rev

Westlake, Donald E.

    Smoke. Mysterious Press 1995 454p

    ISBN 0-89296-534-7

                              LC 94-48254

"Though Mr. Westlake is a virtuoso plotter, the point of his books, here as ever, is to be found in the interstices. Wicked one-liners and testy miniature monologues about whatever happens to be on the author's mind are scattered generously throughout. The implications of invisibility are played for laughs with near-arrogant skill." N Y Times Book Rev

Westlake, Donald E.

    Thieves' dozen. Mysterious Press 2004 183p pa $12.95

    ISBN 0-446-69302-2 pa

                              LC 2003-70612

A collection of Dortmunder stories. "The swift succession of heists, getaways, scrapes, and screwups gathered in Thieves' Dozen epitomizes the venal joys of the comic caper. . . . The short-story form is well suited to Westlake's sly shenanigans, and he even finds room for snippets of the Runyonesque repartee that gives this inspired nonsense just the right touch of absurd panache." Booklist

Westlake, Donald E.

    Trust me on this. Mysterious Press 1988 293p

                              LC 87-22098

"In between stories about space battles, 100-year-old twins, dead country music stars and bizarre medical happenings, Mr. Westlake has sandwiched a nice romance and a fairish murder mystery." N Y Times Book Rev

Westlake, Donald E.

    Watch your back. Mysterious Press 2005 310p $24.95

    ISBN 0-89296-802-8

                              LC 2004-61064

"Arnie Albright, a fence so obnoxious his family intervened and sent him to Club Med in hopes he'd become more likable, has returned from the resort minimally improved, but having met the man of his dreams Preston Fareweather, a millionaire who's as comically distasteful as Arnie and who, more importantly, plans to be away from his art-filled New York penthouse indefinitely, on the run from hordes of furious ex-wives. Albright calls in Dortmunder and his pals to take advantage of Fareweather's absence. . . . Events unfold in a delicious sequence, and every step is complemented by great writing." Publ Wkly

Westlake, Donald E.

    What's so funny? Warner 2007 359p $24.99

    ISBN 9780446582407; 0-446-58240-9

This caper has "an ending so laden with irony it almost has you thinking that crime doesn't pay. But of course it does pay, in those laughs that land on every page." N Y Times Book Rev

Westlake, Donald E.

    What's the worst that could happen? Mysterious Press 1996 373p

                              LC 96-12770

"Although the gang's dirty tricks are wonderfully ingenious, the characters deliver the real razzle-dazzle. A grandiose guy like Max is cut to order for Mr. Westlake's droll comic style, which reflects a kind of gleeful horror at the schlocky esthetics of the rich and the morally damned." N Y Times Book Rev

Wharton, Edith

    ★ The **age** of innocence. D. Appleton & Co. 1920 364p

New York City in the 1870s "was a place of tight social stratification with rituals for everything from romance to etiquette at the opera. The young attorney Newland Archer was engaged to lovely, socially acceptable May Welland. He faced the power of family and social mores when he became attracted to May's bohemian cousin, Ellen." Shapiro. Fic for Youth. 3d edition

Wharton, Edith

    The **children**. Scribner 282p $25

    ISBN 0-684-18453-2

    First published 1928 by D. Appleton & Co.

Standing at the rail of the liner, Martin Boyne surveyed his fellow-passengers in the act of coming aboard. 'Not a soul I shall want to speak to—as usual!' was his comment. Then he saw Judy Wheater carrying a fat, rosy baby up the gang plank and he changed his mind. Judy was only sixteen, but there was nothing inexperienced in the way she herded her troupe of brothers and sisters and 'steps' over to Europe while her father and mother played at divorce and remarriage. For a whole summer, Martin, old bachelor that he was, joined forces with Judy in her gallant attempt to keep her flock together

Wharton, Edith

    Collected stories, 1891-1910; [Maureen Howard selected the contents and wrote the notes for this volume] Library of Am. 2001 928p $35

    ISBN 1-88301-193-0

                              LC 00-57596

    Includes bibliographical references

Wharton, Edith

    Collected stories, 1911-1937; edited by Maureen Howard. Library of Am. 2001 848p $35

    ISBN 1-88301-194-9

                              LC 00-57595

    Includes bibliographical references

Wharton, Edith

    The **custom** of the country. Scribner 594p $55

    ISBN 0-684-14655-X

    First published 1913

"The story of Undine Spragg, a young woman with social aspirations who convinces her nouveau riche parents to leave the Midwest and settle in New York. There she captures and marries a young man from New York's high society. This and each subsequent relationship she engineers prove unsatisfactory, chiefly because of her greed and great ambition." Merriam-Webster's Ency of Lit

Wharton, Edith
★ **Ethan** Frome. Scribner 1997 195p hardcover o.p. pa $13
ISBN 0-684-82591-0 pa
First published 1911
This is "an ironic tragedy of love, frustration, jealousy,
and sacrifice. The scene is a New England village, where
Ethan barely makes a living out of a stony farm and is at
odds with his wife Zeena (short for Zenobia), a whining
hypochondriac. Mattie, a cousin of Zeena's comes to live
with them, and love develops between her and Ethan. They
try to end their impossible lives by steering a bobsled into a
tree; instead ending up crippled and tied for the rest of their
unhappy time on earth to Zeena and the barren farm. Zeena,
however, is transformed into a devoted nurse and Mattie
becomes the nagging invalid." Benet's Reader's Ency of
Am Lit

Wharton, Edith
★ The **house** of mirth. Scribner 329p $50
ISBN 0-684-14658-4
First published 1905
"The story concerns the tragic fate of the beautiful and
well-connected but penniless Lily Bart, who at age 29 lacks
a husband to secure her position in society. Maneuvering to
correct this situation, she encounters both Simon Rosedale, a
rich man outside her class, and Lawrence Selden, who is personally appealing and socially acceptable but not wealthy.
She becomes indebted to an unscrupulous man, has her
reputation sullied by a promiscuous acquaintance, and slides
into genteel poverty. Unable or unwilling to ally herself with
either Rosedale or Selden, she finally despairs and takes an
overdose of pills." Merriam-Webster's Ency of Lit

Wharton, Edith
New York novels; foreword by Louis Auchin-
closs. Modern Lib. 1998 xxi, 958p $27.95
ISBN 0-679-60302-6
LC 98-5465
Contents: The house of mirth (1905); The custom of the
country (1913); The age of innocence (1920)

Wharton, Edith
Novels. Library of America 1985 1328p $40
ISBN 0-940450-31-3
LC 85-191816
The house of mirth, The custom of the country, and the
age of innocence are entered separately. In the reef (1912),
the "action is confined almost exclusively to a chateau in
France and the issue narrowed to a psychological struggle in
the mind of the heroine, Anna Leath, who discovers that the
man she has agreed to marry has had an affair with the young
woman who is about to marry her stepson." Ref Guide to
Am Lit. 2d edition

Wharton, Edith
Novellas and other writings. Library of Am.
1990 1137p il $45
ISBN 0-940450-53-4
LC 89-62930
In Madame de Treymes (1907), an American woman liv-
ing in Paris tries to break her engagement with a local aris-

tocrat. Ethan Frome is entered separately. Summer (1917)
tells the story of Charity Royall, an adopted New England
girl in a poor village who falls in love with a young architect
from the city. Old New York (1924) is a collection of four
novellas, each set in four different decades: False dawn, The
old maid, The spark, and New Year's Day. In The mother's
recompense (1925), a promiscuous mother moves in with
her daughter only to discover her daughter's fiancee was
once one of her own lovers. A backward glance (1934) is
the author's autobiography.
Includes bibliographical references

Wharton, Edith
The **selected** short stories of Edith Wharton; introduced and edited by R.W.B. Lewis. Scribner 1991
xxi, 390p $24.95
ISBN 0-684-19304-3
LC 91-11433
A "collection of 21 of the author's best stories. Lewis'
excellent introduction explains Wharton's appeal and
provides a brief overview of her life and prolific literary
output." Booklist

Wharton, William
★ **Birdy**. Knopf 1979 309p
ISBN 0-394-42569-3
LC 77-28023
"At the close of World War II, in the mental ward of a
veteran's hospital, there is a patient whose behavior quite
baffles the psychiatrists. The patient's only childhood friend,
another soldier who has a severe facial wound, is transferred
to the hospital in the hope he may be of help. The friend instantly recognizes that the patient is behaving exactly like a
bird. (The keeping of birds had always been an obsession of
the patient throughout his adolescence.)" Choice
"Only the most rigorous imagination can make a story
of this sort work for a reader who is generally indifferent
to birds. Wharton has just such an imagination." Newsweek

Wharton, William
Dad; a novel. Knopf 1981 449p
LC 80-2725
"It's an old story, this man-in-the-middle business, but
fresh in Wharton's telling because he lets experience—
lunch, a crisis, baseball on TV—accumulate as naturally and
surely as aging itself." Saturday Rev

Wheeler, Richard S.
The **canyon** of bones. Forge 2007 330p $24.95
ISBN 978-0-7653-1324-9; 0-7653-1324-3
LC 2006-102846
"Overall, this is genial, character-driven western writing
with plenty of action and appreciation for Native American
customs. Skye's foulmouthed Crow wife, Victoria, is absolutely delightful, and even his cantankerous horse, Jawbone,
has more personality than most western leads. Not just for
fans of the series, this will appeal to anyone in search of
solidly adventuresome tales." Booklist

Wheeler, Richard S.

Eclipse. Forge 2002 380p $27.95

ISBN 0-312-87846-X

LC 2001-58978

After returning home to a hero's welcome in 1806 "Meriwether Lewis floundered as the governor of the Louisiana Territory, Beset by financial and political difficulties, a depressed and despondent Lewis apparently either committed suicide or was murdered in the Tennessee backwoods in 1809. Wheeler ponders that puzzle, constructing a chilling scenario in which a delusional, syphilis-wracked Lewis feels duty bound to end his fife rather than bring shame upon his name, his family, and his beloved Corps of Discovery. A riveting re-creation of the tragic final years of an American legend." Booklist

Wheeler, Richard S.

North Star; a Barnaby Skye novel. Forge 2009 320p $25.95

ISBN 978-0-7653-1663-9; 0-7653-1663-3

LC 2009-278179

This novel in the author's series "featuring venerable mountain man Barnaby Skye, finds Skye—after more than 50 years of trapping beaver, hunting bear, fighting Indians and living outdoors—in constant rheumatic pain, losing his eyesight and wishing to live out his days in a house with a roof, a floor and a real bed. It is 1870, the fur business is dead and white men are taking all the Indian lands. His two Indian wives, Victoria and Mary, have different feelings about these changes. Victoria dreads leaving her Indian family for a white man's life, and Mary longs to see her son, Dirk, whom Skye had sent away to school several years earlier. There is little gun smoke, but plenty of suspense as Skye and Victoria confront brutal Texas cattlemen and cheating Indian agents, and Mary travels to St. Louis to find her son." Publ Wkly

White, Bailey

Quite a year for plums; a novel. Knopf 1998 220p $22

ISBN 0-679-44531-5

LC 97-41124

"The women in town are worried about Roger, the peanut virologist. Hilma and Meade discuss him at their weekly readings. Eula frets over his welfare—not to mention his appetite. And everyone else just seems to be content with giving opinions on his budding romance with the strange bird artist, Della. . . . {The author} will make the reader care about this nurturing gaggle of women and other community members in a small, sleepy town in southern Georgia." Libr J

White, Edmund, 1940-

The **beautiful** room is empty. Knopf 1988 227p

LC 87-40495

In this sequel to A boy's own story, the author "follows our nameless hero from his final year at prep school in the mid-1950s through his cruisy but self-deprecating college years to the 'turning point' in his life—the famous Stonewall uprising of 1969 in which the clients of a New York gay bar stood up to the policemen trying to close it down. What emerges is the picture of a young man desperately struggling to come to terms with himself, a struggle that is a universal even if the context for every individual is different. Artfully

constructed, this work clearly transcends its 'gay' theme." Libr J

Followed by The farewell symphony

White, Edmund

★ A **boy's** own story. Dutton 1982 217p hardcover o.p. pa $14

ISBN 978-0-14-311484-0

LC 82-9536

This first-person novel is "written with the flourish of a master stylist. . . . It is an endearing portrait of a child's longing to be charming, popular, powerful, and loved, and of his struggles with adults . . . {told with} sensitivity and elegance." Harpers

Followed by The beautiful room is empty (1988) and The farewell symphony (1997)

White, Edmund

Hotel de Dream; a New York novel. Ecco 2007 225p $23.95

ISBN 978-0-06-085225-2; 0-06-085225-9

LC 2007-29872

"The American novelist Stephen Crane, according to an unreliable contemporary, began a book about a male prostitute. As no such manuscript survives, White steps in with an artfully pulpy tale about Elliott, a teenage newsboy in New York, who is kept by a married banker. As frame and counterpoint, he shows us Crane, terminally tubercular, summoning his remaining strength to dictate "The Painted Boy" to his common-law wife, who transports him from England to the Black Forest in a vain search for a cure. White illuminates Crane's literary milieu, the urban gay subculture of his time, and the relationship of a writer's experience to his fiction." New Yorker

White, Edmund, 1940-

Jack Holmes and his friend; Edmund White. Bloomsbury 2012

ISBN 1608197034; 9781608197033

LC 2011014728

'This "book maps . . . the friendship of a gay man and a heterosexual in the buttoned-up 1950s, the experimental '60s and, finally, to the first intimations of AIDS. . . . The young men meet in New York when they're both fresh from college. Jack, a Midwesterner with a 'Gothic horror novel' of a childhood, attended the University of Michigan; Will, a foxhunting Southerner of large lineage and small funds, attended Princeton. . . . Relatively early on, Jack introduces Will to Alex, the girl he will eventually marry, and the novel tracks the three of them through years of romantic strife." (Washington Post)

White, Edmund

The **married** man; a love story. Knopf 2000 321p $25

ISBN 0-375-40005-2

LC 99-53980

This is the "tale of Austin Smith, an expatriated scion of decayed Southern gentry, who lives on Ile Saint Louis, in Paris. Austin, an expert on 18th-century French furniture, is HIV positive but healthy when he becomes the lover of

Julien, a married architect more than 20 years Austin's junior who is in the process of divorcing his wife." Publ Wkly

"A shrewd social observer with a great gift for dialogue, White composes quicksilver scenes bright with wit, then sets aside comedy-of-manners for the luster of tragedy." Booklist

White, Kate

A **body** to die for. Warner Bks. 2003 294p $23.95

ISBN 0-446-53148-0

LC 2003-41081

"Once again, White's background as editor-in-chief of 'Cosmopolitan' shines through in her snappy dialog, tight plotting, and insider humor. . . . A breezy beach read for mystery fans." Libr J

White, Kate

Lethally blond. Warner Books 2007 323p $24.99

ISBN 978-0-446-57795-3; 0-446-57795-2

LC 2007-447

"When former fling and sweet stud Chris Wickersham asks Bailey [Weggins] to look into the disappearance of a fellow actor on his TV show, Morgue, she agrees. Someone else might make a couple of phone calls, but rather inexplicably Bailey drives upstate to the missing man's country home. He's there, dead in the bathtub, where he's been for a couple of weeks. Not pretty. That puts Bailey right in the middle of a mystery teeming with TV types, actors, producers, and PR people, one of whom seriously wants Bailey dead." Booklist

"White's flair for pop culture and affection for single career women make this trendy romantic suspense cocktail an addictive read." Publ Wkly

White, Patrick

★ The **eye** of the storm. Viking 1974 608p

First published 1973 in the United Kingdom

"Elizabeth Hunter, once a brilliant socialite and a rich, sensual, materialistic woman, now into her eighties, is dying in her Sydney mansion, perceived as a house-shrine by the nurses and servants who devotedly revolve around her. Mrs. Hunter's crucial experience, during the eye of a cyclone, of harmony between her inner, essential self and the outer void has determined the rest of her life, especially the act of dying. Flawed as she is, her strength and intense authenticity of being is communicated in varying degrees to her servants, her lawyer and to her two inauthentic children, the Princess de Lascabanes and Sir Basil Hunter. The comic brilliance of White's conception of Sir Basil, the weary actor for whom life and acting are perpetually fused, is one of the novel's highlights." Oxford Companion to Australian Lit

White, Randy Wayne

Black widow. G.P. Putnam's Sons 2008 337p $24.95

ISBN 978-0-399-15456-0; 0-399-15456-6

LC 2008-859

"Like Robert B. Parker and John D. MacDonald at their best, White draws readers into his world with characters you'd pay just to hang out with and then hooks us with

straight-ahead action. It's an old-school combination, but it still works just fine." Booklist

White, Randy Wayne

Deep shadow. G.P. Putnam's Sons 2010 353p $25.95

ISBN 978-0-399-15626-7

LC 2009-51083

At the outset of this Doc Ford thriller, "two low-life excons, King and Perry, are on the lam after killing a family of five in a burglary. They end up in Doc's neck of the woods, or rather his neck of the swamp, in central Florida. Doc; his boat-bum hipster pal, Tomlinson; troubled Indian teen Will Chaser, who played a key role in Dead Silence; and Arlis Futch, a crusty old fisherman, have arrived at a small lake, which they intend to search for Batista's treasure plane, which disappeared in 1958 while flying the ex-dictator's looted booty out of Cuba during the Castro takeover. King and Perry, who are as bad as they come, quickly take control of the others, forcing Doc and friends to continue diving in the lake, after which the pair plan to kill them all. Throw in a giant, mysterious swamp creature with an appetite for cattle, horses, and divers, and you've got a nail-biter that's virtually impossible to put down." Publ Wkly

White, Stephen Walsh

Dry ice; a novel. Dutton 2007 401p $25.95

ISBN 978-0-525-94997-8

LC 2006-26771

Sequel to Kill me

"Psychologist Alan Gregory has a secret, and one of his former patients, a deranged killer, is taunting him with it. Michael McClelland . . . has escaped a mental institution and is coming after Gregory's friends and family, including his wife, a deputy district attorney suffering from multiple sclerosis. Gregory becomes a suspect in a series of crimes ranging from the murder of a new patient on a neighbor's property to the disappearance of a star witness in his wife's current grand jury case." Libr J

"Contemporary cerebral thrillers don't get much better than . . . [this novel], which deftly combines complex characterization and intricate plotting." Publ Wkly

White, Stephen Walsh

Kill me; a novel. [by] Stephen White. Dutton 2006 402p $25.95

ISBN 0-525-94930-5

LC 2005-24296

"In this installment of the . . . series starring clinical psychologist Dr. Alan Gregory, the setting remains the picturesque Colorado countryside, but White sends Dr. Gregory to the background and instead features one of his patients, an unnamed, happily married businessman with an adventurous streak. After a near-fatal crash during a Canadian skiing expedition, coupled with a friend's accident, our hero begins to question his own mortality and vows never to be a burden to his family. When he gets word of an organization that, for a hefty fee, will end your life should you become 'a burden,' he rather hastily signs up. But what if you discover you have a slowly ticking time bomb in your head, and while death could come at any moment, it might not be right away? How do you say 'not quite yet' to your personal hit men?. . . . Bizarre, thrilling, and oh so much fun." Booklist

White, Stephen Walsh

Missing persons; [by] Stephen White. Dutton 2005 391p $25.95

ISBN 0-525-94859-7

LC 2004-27172

"Eight years to the day after JonBenet Ramsey was murdered, her childhood friend and neighbor, Mallory, winds up missing. At first, her disappearance seems unconnected to the disappearance of Diane, one of Boulder (Colorado) psychologist Alan Gregory's colleagues, or the apparent murder of Diane's friend Hannah. But nothing is coincidental in a White murder mystery, and once again, he expertly places the good doctor in the middle of one doozy of a whodunit." Booklist

White, T. H.

The **book** of Merlyn; the unpublished conclusion to The once and future king. prologue by Sylvia Townsend Warner; illustrated by Trevor Stubley. University of Tex. Press 1977 xx, 137p il

LC 77-3454

Sequel to The once and future king

"Writing during World War II, White vented his feelings about the futility of war with a fierceness that sometimes overwhelms the intriguing mixture of fantasy, humor, and rationality which pervaded the tetralogy." Booklist

White, T. H.

★ The **once** and future king. Putnam 1958 677p $25.95

ISBN 0-399-10597-2

LC 58-10760

An omnibus edition of four novels; The sword in the stone (1939), The witch in the wood (1939, now called The Queen of Air and Darkness) and The ill-made knight (1940). A number of alterations have been made in the earlier books. Previously unpublished, The candle in the wind "deals with the plotting of Mordred and his kinsmen of the house of Orkney, and their undying enmity to King Arthur." Times Lit Suppl

"White's contemporary retelling of Malory's Le Morte d'Arthur is both romantic and exciting." Shapiro. Fic for Youth. 3d edition

White, T. H.

The **sword** in the stone; with decorations by the author and end papers by Robert Lawson. Putnam 1939

First published 1938 in the United Kingdom

An "account of everyday life in a great medieval manor, with two boys, Kay and Wart (who turns out to be King Arthur) learning the code of being a gentleman, busy with hawking, jousting, sword play, and hunting. The whole trend of the story is how the boy Wart was made worthy to become a king." Ont Libr Rev

"Delightful, fantastic, satirical nonsense, for the reader with a background of Arthurian legend." Wis Libr Bull

Followed by The witch in the wood

Whitehead, Colson

Apex hides the hurt. Doubleday 2006 212p $22.95

ISBN 0-385-50795-X

LC 2005-49391

"A secretive narrator often means the story is weak and has to be puffed up with mystery, but Whitehead's gorgeous, expertly crafted sentences help the reader past the novel's slow start. . . . We are slowly filled in on the limp, the misfortune, the meaning of the title–and we're treated to an eloquent novel about racial identity in America. . . . What could have been an academic exercise becomes a smart tale about who we are under our labels." Newsweek

Whitehead, Colson

The **intuitionist**; a novel. Anchor Bks. (NY) 1999 255p $19.95

ISBN 0-385-49299-5

LC 98-6756

This "novel follows the travails of the redoubtable Lila Mae Watson, the first black woman Elevator Inspector in a nameless city very much like New York. Caught between the political machinations of the two factions of the Elevator Guild (the Intuitionists, like Lila, inspect the elevators by a sort of sympathetic insight, whereas the Empiricists actually examine the cables and helical springs), Lila Mae finds herself in the midst of a murky underground war for control over the kingdom of Vertical Transport. Whitehead's prose is graceful and often lyrical and his elevator underworld is a complex, lovingly realized creation." New Yorker

Whitehead, Colson

John Henry Days; a novel. Doubleday 2001 389p $24.95

ISBN 0385498195

LC 00-43143

The protagonist of this novel is "a young freelance journalist named J. Sutter. . . . J. is black. . . . He is a 'junketeer,' an 'inveigler of invites,' an 'open bar opportunist.' . . . His love life consists of sterile biweekly couplings with a publicist named Monica. He has no discernible connection with his family. He lives in a bubble of educational privilege and ironic knowingness. . . . The novel's main action unfolds on a weekend in July 1996, when a Web site sends J. to Talcott, W.Va., to cover the unveiling of a John Henry postage stamp and the inauguration of a local festival called John Henry Days." (N Y Times Book Rev)

"Whitehead relishes slashing through the mindlessness of the age in a voice so intelligent and an idiom so imaginative that it can lift a reader right out of his chair. But he is not remorseless. He likes these people and respects their longings. They have no moral compass, but he has, so we can laugh at them but still grieve for the loss of so much possiblility." N Y Times Book Rev

Whitehead, Colson

Sag Harbor; a novel. Doubleday 2009 288p $24.95

ISBN 978-0-385-52765-1; 0-385-52765-9

LC 2008-13510

Benji, one of the only black kids at an elite prep school in Manhattan, tries desperately to fit in, but every summer, he and his brother, Reggie, escape to the East End of Sag Harbor, where a small community of African American professionals has built a world of its own.

The author "serves up whole sundaes worth of riffs on the quotidian, all hung on the skinny frame of a 15-year-old everyman virgin and his marginally less distinct friends, give or take a repressive father and a particularly evocative shoreline landscape." Village Voice

Whitehead, Colson
Zone one. Doubleday 2011 259p $25.95
ISBN 0385528078; 9780385528078
LC 2011-08339
"It's a book you want to read rather than one you should read. Sure, there are familiar paradigms: the pandemic subsides behind a foreground of chase scenes, us-or-them admonitions, even the occasional bite sequence. But Zone One is mercilessly free of cookie-cutter social commentaries—office culture is for mindless drones; technology destroys our ability to connect—while still providing the chilling, fleshy pleasures of zombies who lurch, pursue, hunger." Esquire

Whitney, Phyllis A.
Amethyst dreams. Crown 1997 276p $25
ISBN 0-517-70759-4
LC 97-5000
"What matters here are the characters' wonderfully wrought temperaments—no sinners, no saints, but ultimately lots of forgiveness—and the subtle, little glimpses of fear that keep readers looking for answers right up to the satisfying conclusion." Libr J

Whitney, Phyllis A.
Domino. Doubleday 1979 351p
LC 79-7331
"Domino is a ghost town, an abandoned silver mine camp in the Colorado Rockies that holds the secret to young Laurie Morgan's psychic wound. During the 20 years since she left her grandmother's mansion, she has endured nightmarish recollections of a peripheral role in her father's shooting. Now Laurie is summoned to the bedside of that imperious old woman, who needs the assistance of a blood relative if the Morgan territory is to resist the overtures of opportunist land developers." Publ Wkly

Whitney, Phyllis A.
Poinciana. Doubleday 1980 345p
LC 80-949
"Poinciana is the exquisite Palm Beach estate to which young and naive Sharon comes as chatelaine. Married at a vulnerable period in her life to Ross Logan, 60-year-old robber baron, she becomes another of his possessions, a beautiful object like the netsuke collection in his museum-home. There are counterforces in ex-wives, a senile mother, a scheming daughter and Logan's death before Sharon develops her own resources." Publ Wkly

Whitney, Phyllis A.
The **singing** stones. Doubleday 1990 507p
LC 89-37137
Lynn McLeod "is an ombudsman for terminally ill children who is suddenly summoned to assist the daughter of her first husband. But the child is not physically ill. She is haunted by the near-fatal accident that crippled her father and the threatening presence of her wicked stepmother (whom everyone believes to be the epitome of quiet kindness). Lynn enters the complicated family situation with great reluctance, bewitched by the spiritualist philosophies of one character yet driven by her own sympathy for a child in distress. A terrific work of romantic suspense in a contemporary setting." Booklist

Whitney, Phyllis A.
Spindrift. Doubleday 1975 301p
This novel is set in Newport, Rhode Island. "Christy Moreland, having recovered from a breakdown after the apparent suicide of her father, newspaperman Adam Keene, arrives at 'Spindrift,' her domineering mother-in-law's estate. Theo {her mother-in-law} is set on keeping young Peter, son of Christy and her passive husband, Joel. Christy is equally determined to get the boy back and to prove her father was murdered. She suspects Theo and others in the lush company, except strong, personable Bruce Perry. With her marriage failing, Christy turns to Bruce who she hopes will help her and with whom she feels she's falling in love." Publ Wkly

Whittall, Zoe
Holding still for as long as possible; Zoe Whittall. Anansi 2009 301 p. (pbk.) $15.95
ISBN 9780887849640; 9780887842344
LC 2009510336
Lambda Literary Awards: Transgender/Bisexual/Gay (2010)
In this book, author "Zoe Whittall follows a group of twentysomethings struggling to cope with their complicated lives. Trapped somewhere between growing up and being grown-ups, these would-be adults hide behind excessive drinking and partying, and use text messages to relay their emotions. The story focuses on three troubled young people: Billy, a former teen pop starlet who suffers from severe panic attacks; Josh, a paramedic whose ability to patch up injured patients parallels his inability to repair his own emotional damages; and Amy, a rich kid trying to live the Bohemian indie girl life while dealing with her first broken heart." (Quill & Quire)

Whittle, Tina
Blood, Ash, and Bone; A Tai Randolph Series. Poisoned Pen Press 2013 250 p. (Tai Randolph mysteries) $14.95
ISBN 1464200955; 9781464200953
In this, Tina Whittle's third Tai Randolph mystery, Tai decides "to help an ex-boyfriend retrieve a missing Civil War relic. . . . Some collectors are simply obsessed with owning valuable things, but others—such as members of the spruced-up, squeaky-clean-looking Ku Klux Klan—feed on the racist rage that saturates certain historical memorabilia." Tai pursues her investigation at a Civil War expo in Georgia. (Publishers Weekly)

Whittle, Tina
★ The **Dangerous** Edge of Things; a Tai Randolph mystery. Poisoned Pen Press 2011 281 p. (Tai Randolph mysteries) $24.95
ISBN 1590588177; 9781590588178; 9781590588192

In this Tai Randolph mystery from Tina Whittle, "Tai Randolph thinks inheriting a Confederate-themed gun shop is her biggest headache—until she finds a murdered corpse in her brother's driveway. Even worse, her supposedly respectable brother begins behaving in decidedly non-innocent ways, like fleeing to the Bahamas and leaving her with both a homicide in her lap and the pointed suspicions of the Atlanta PD directed her way." (Publisher's note)

Whittle, Tina

Darker than any shadow; a Tai Randolph mystery. 1st ed. Poisoned Pen Press 2012 (hardcover) $24.95; (paperback) $14.95; (paperback) $22.95
ISBN 1590585488; 9781590585467; 9781590585481; 9781590585474 large print
LC 2011933442

This is the second of Tina Whittle's Tai Randolph mysteries. Here, "Atlanta's performance poetry scene is sizzling, and Tai Randolph's friends are preparing to debut their team in a major competition. But this hipster world goes decidedly cold when one of the team members is knifed to death. Then there is another killing; suddenly a 'Dead Poet Killer' panic sets in. Tai's friend Rico (one of the poets) is suspected of the murder and needs her help." (Library Journal)

Whyte, Jack

The **singing** sword. Forge 1996 383p
LC 96-19966

"As the novel progresses, and the Roman Empire continues to decay, the colony of Camulod flourishes. But the lives of the colony's main characters, Gaius Publius Varrus—ironsmith, innovator and soldier—and his brother-in-law, former Roman Senator Caius Britannicus, are not trouble-free, especially when their most bitter enemy, Claudius Seneca, reappears. . . . Whyte provides rich detail about the forging of superior weaponry, the breeding of horses, the training of cavalrymen, the growth of a lawmaking body within the community and the origins of the Round Table." Publ Wkly

Followed by The eagles' brood

Wibberley, Leonard

★ The **mouse** that roared. Little, Brown 1955 279p
LC 54-8294

"The 'Tiny Twenty' overtake the major powers of the world after plotting a bold maneuver to steal the atomic secrets of the United States. Centuries of industrialization and sophistication separate the tiny European nation from the enraged larger countries, who must acquiesce to the will of the former. Underneath this lighthearted tale is a serious warning about the dangers of nuclear power." Shapiro. Fic for Youth. 3d edition

Wickersham, Joan

The **news** from Spain; seven variations on a love story. Joan Wickersham. Alfred A. Knopf 2012 208 p. $24.95
ISBN 0307958884; 9780307958884
LC 2012005073

"Each of the seven stories in this . . . collection [by Joan Wickersham] is titled 'The News from Spain' and makes . . . use of that phrase somewhere in the narrative. A mother consigned to a nursing home and her adult daughter engage in an intricate dance of filial obligation after the mother's condition improves. At an all-boys school, a lone female student, 13, develops a friendship with her married Spanish teacher." (Publishers Weekly)

Wideman, John Edgar

★ The **cattle** killing. Houghton Mifflin 1996 212p
LC 96-19305

"Wideman hauntingly evokes the tragic consequences of racial prejudice. Brimming with mysteries and shadowy secrets, the narrative winds elliptically among the stories of blacks whose attempts to rise above bigotry and lead free lives come to heartbreaking conclusions." Publ Wkly

Wideman, John Edgar

Fanon. Houghton Mifflin 2008 240p $24
ISBN 0618942637; 9780618942633
LC 2007-9420

This is a novel by the author of Brothers and Keepers (1984). The novel "weaves together fiction, biography, and memoir to evoke the life and message of Frantz Fanon, the . . . author of The Wretched of the Earth." (Publisher's note)

"This is Wideman's mulligan stew—on the one hand, the Homewood boy who went on scholarship to Penn, and from Penn to Oxford, and from Oxford to the Iowa Writers' Workshop, nods his head to Marx, Freud, Yeats, Sartre, Joyce, Nabokov, and Baudelaire; on the other, the novelist and college professor who still feels guilty about going to Europe instead of jail signifies his solidarity with W.E.B. DuBois, James Baldwin, and Frantz Fanon by riff, scat, and Igbo. How this mixture works is mysterious, but it always has." Harper's

Wideman, John Edgar

God's gym; John Edgar Wideman. Houghton Mifflin 2005 175p $23
ISBN 0-618-51525-9
LC 2004-54071

The author "offers ten stories that range widely from family and basketball to illness and death. In addition, race is an important element. . . . Wideman's stories are feasts of language offering up new metaphors and original imagery. He often uses a dreamlike, stream-of-consciousness style, wandering seemingly far from the original story but eventually resolving back to the starting elements. Each story is a gem that grows more brilliant with rereading." Libr J

Wideman, John Edgar

★ **Philadelphia** fire; a novel. Holt & Co. 1990 199p
LC 90-30590

"Wideman is best when he is most personal. . . . By turns brilliant and murky, seamless and ragged, Philadelphia Fire is on to something big. Wideman's vision of racism in the U.S. suggests nothing less than a genetic disorder present at the birth of the nation." Time

Wideman, John Edgar

The **stories** of John Edgar Wideman. Pantheon Bks. 1992 432p

LC 91-50839

"The 25 stories pulled together here demonstrate {the author's} eloquence in picturing various elements in the constant friction between black and white societies in the U.S. Family and place are, thus, two prominent themes. He writes lushly, beautifully, yet loudly as well; his voice is deep, rich, booming." Booklist

Wideman, John Edgar

Two cities. Houghton Mifflin 1998 242p $24

ISBN 0-395-85730-9

LC 98-22915

"Kassima, her husband and sons dead, meets Robert Jones in her native Pittsburgh, sleeps with him, and spends much of the rest of the book doing her best to avoid him: this is a cautious love story. The narrative's anchor is Kassima's elderly tenant, who wanders about Pittsburgh and Philadelphia with a camera, making the invisible visible. Wideman, similarly, is a writer who shows you things you would never have seen without him; his prose at once bears the weight of a brutal, complex legacy and exults in a sort of weightlessness." New Yorker

Wiesel, Elie

A **beggar** in Jerusalem; a novel. translated from the French by Lily Edelman and the author. Random House 1970 211p

Original French edition, 1969

"Reading Elie Wiesel is not an easy experience. It is certainly by no means an act of escape, the traditional function of literary entertainment. His works touch all of one's fibers. . . . After we have listened to what Wiesel has to say, other literature seems meaningless." Saturday Rev

Wiesel, Elie

★ **Dawn**; translated from the French by Frances Frenaye. Hill & Wang 1961 89p

Original French edition, 1960

"Elisha, a young Jewish terrorist fighting for the creation of Israel in the 1940s, is faced with an agonizing moral dilemma. He is to be the executioner of a British officer in reprisal for the hanging of a captured terrorist. A survivor of the concentration camps and a victim all of his life, Elisha considers whether he is any different from his oppressors if he can execute a helpless prisoner in cold blood." Shapiro. Fic for Youth. 3d edition

Wiesel, Elie

The **forgotten**; translated by Stephen Becker. Summit Bks. 1992 237p

LC 91-46826

Original French edition, 1989

"Mr. Wiesel is a writer of contention and his characters, even when affectionate, speak with a bitter music. The most loving—and the saddest—of these sounds occur in the dark duets between father and son, especially as Elhanan admits to Malkiel that he 'cannot recall the essential thing that I want so much to pass on to you.' Elhanan's faith, his temptation to faith . . . is as stunning as the loss he confronts." N Y Times Book Rev

Wiesel, Elie

The **Golem**; the story of a legend. as told by Elie Wiesel and illustrated by Mark Podwal; translated by Anne Borchardt. Summit Bks. 1983 105p il

LC 83-9304

"The Golem exists only to save his people, the Jews of sixteenth century Prague in this case, from the heinous, antisemitic acts of the gentile population. Mute, made of clay, and given life through the faith of Rabbi Yehuda Loew, the Golem goes about Prague in secret, uncovering the trumped up charges of the gentiles against individual members of the local community. Eventually, at the behest of the Rabbi, the Golem leaves. The narrator asks for his return, knowing the Golem's work is not done." Best Sellers

"This fable is eloquently presented through the combination of Wiesel's facile storytelling skills and Mark Podwal's evocative line drawings." Booklist

Wiesel, Elie, 1928-

Hostage; Elie Wiesel; translated from the French by Catherine Temerson. 1st ed. Random House Inc. 2012 224 p. (hardcover) $25.95

ISBN 0307599582; 9780307599582

LC 2011050747

Author Elie Wiesel tells the story of "Shaltiel Feigenberg, who in 1975, is captured and imprisoned for 80 hours [by an Italian political revolutionary and a Palestinian advocate]. . . . This forced period of darkness ironically provides him with an extended period of enlightenment, as he has time to reflect on his life--the death of his grandmother at Auschwitz, his frequently absent but observant father, his initial meeting with Blanca (the woman who eventually becomes his wife), and the growing Communist sympathies of his older brother." (Kirkus Reviews)

Wiesel, Elie

The **judges**; a novel. translated from the French by Geoffrey Strachan. Knopf 2002 209p $24

ISBN 0-375-40909-2

LC 2002-25462

Original French edition, 1999

As the characters "talk about themselves and remember crucial turning points in their lives. Wiesel weaves in Jewish history and mysticism with the characters' personal memories, and he raises the big existential questions about life and death and memory and guilt and forgiveness, with lots of metaphors about scapegoat, fellow traveler, messenger, etc." Booklist

Wiesel, Elie

Night, Dawn, The accident: three tales. Hill & Wang 1972 318p hardcover o.p. pa $14

ISBN 0-374-52140-9

In Dawn, Elisha, a young Jewish terrorist fighting for the creation of Israel in the 1940s is faced with an agonizing moral dilemma. He is to be the executioner of a British officer in reprisal for the hanging of a captured terrorist. A survivor of the concentration camps and a victim all of his life, Elisha considers whether he is any different from his oppressors if he can execute a helpless prisoner in cold blood. Night is a memoir. The accident concerns a survivor of Auschwitz who, recovering from a near-fatal accident, questions the meaning of man's existence and purpose, and death

Wiesel, Elie

★ The **oath**; translated from the French by Marion Wiesel. Random House 1973 283p

ISBN 0-394-48779-6

"Azriel meets a young man attempting to commit suicide. Azriel tries to take the man's mind off his plight by interesting him in a story. It is the story of Kolvillag, where all Jews (but one) were killed on the merest pretext by those whose excuse was the charge of Christ-killers. All of the Jews, however, had taken an oath (of the title) never to tell how they suffered—a kind of weapon of silence against their persecutors. Azriel is now faced with breaking that vow to help save the would-be suicide's life. He tells the tale." America

A "powerful novel, interwoven with threads of Hasidic tales, cabalistic mysticism, Talmudic sayings, and pietistic folklore." Libr J

Wiesel, Elie

The **testament**; a novel. translated from the French by Marion Wiesel. Summit Bks. 1981 346p

ISBN 0-671-44833-1

LC 80-27251

Original French edition, 1980

"In none of Wiesel's earlier novels are the characters so earthy, so real, so finely chiseled, as in this one. Women advance more fully to center stage and play more dominant roles. . . . The almost photographic realism of the narrative gives it a cumulative power that is overwhelming." Christ Century

Wiesel, Elie

Twilight; translated from the French by Marion Wiesel. Summit Bks. 1988 217p

LC 88-2634

Original French edition, 1987

"Despite the Holocaust and its atrocities, so specially devised to destroy human life and dignity, we experience in Mr. Wiesel's novel how good the family is, how good people are. Utterly without sentimentality, he gives us a small but real measure of what the world's loss has been." N Y Times Book Rev

Wiggins, Marianne

Evidence of things unseen; a novel. Simon & Schuster 2003 383p $25

ISBN 0-684-86969-1

LC 2003-45611

"Born in Kitty Hawk, where the Wright brothers first rose towards the sun, Ray Foster, or 'Fos', . . . is fascinated by radiance. A portrait photographer who deals with the dynamics of light, Fos . . . keeps a lump of phosphorous glowing in a fish tank by his bedside. . . . After signing on as an official photographer for the Tennessee Valley Authority–hence becoming complicit in kicking countless farmers off their ancestral lands to make way for hydroelectric dams–Fos assumes a similar recordkeeping role at the Oak

Ridge Laboratory in Tennessee, one of three research sites for the Manhattan project." Economist

Wiggins, Marianne

★ **John** Dollar. Harper & Row 1989 214p

LC 88-45538

"Writing with an impressive degree of control and sophistication, Marianne Wiggins investigates the ghastly processes which crush the marooned children. . . . The phenomenon that particularly fascinates Wiggins in the spiritual disintegration she depicts as the consequence of this spectacle is the growth of a parodic religion." London Rev Books

Wiggins, Marianne

The **shadow** catcher. Simon & Schuster 2007 323p il $25

ISBN 978-0-7432-6520--1; 0-7432-6520-3

LC 2007-11842

A fictionalization of the life of photographer Edward Sheriff Curtis. "Digging into the photographer's past in a parallel story line is the modern-day, fictional Marianne Wiggins, an Angeleno who has written a novel about Curtis and is resisting Hollywood's attempts to glamorize him. . . . This faux Wiggins—the real one thanks her sister in the acknowledgments for 'license to decorate our shared history'—stumbles into a mystery involving her family, but the personal developments are considerably less interesting than the detailed reconstruction of Curtis' wife Clara. . . . The beautifully rendered Clara gives resonant shape to Wiggins' musings on the enigmatic Curtis—wayward husband, absent father, acquaintance of Teddy Roosevelt, emblem of a great national restlessness—and leads the author to intriguing insights into sexual politics, the mythology of the West and the relationship between physical and emotional distance." PopMatters

Wiggs, Susan

The **Apple** Orchard; Susan Wiggs. Harlequin Books 2013 432 p. (hardcover) $24.95

ISBN 0778314936; 9780778314936

In this romance novel, by Susan Wiggs, "Tess's . . . history is filled with gaps: a father she never met, a mother who spent more time traveling than with her daughter. So Tess is shocked when she discovers the grandfather she never knew is in a coma. And that she has been named in his will to inherit half of Bella Vista, a hundred-acre apple orchard in the magical Sonoma town called Archangel. . . . Tess begins to discover a world filled with the simple pleasures of food and family." (Publisher's note)

Wiggs, Susan

The **ocean** between us. Mira 2004 382p $19.95

ISBN 0-7783-2035-9

LC 2004-557716

"Steve Bennett is a perfect navy officer with a perfect navy family, and he's confident that his world is just the way it should be. But his son wants to be an artist instead of attending the U.S. Naval Academy, and his stalwart and capable wife of 20 years, Grace, is tired of being the perfect navy wife. She wants her own home, and she wants her own career. She's feeling altogether unsettled, but nothing is more unsettling than the secret her husband has hidden from her their entire marriage. Nothing, that is, until the accident on the carrier. Wiggs has done an excellent job of depicting what lies beneath the surfaces of relationships—assumptions, misunderstandings, and expectations." Booklist

Wignall, Kevin

For the dogs. Simon & Schuster 2004 209p $22
ISBN 0-7432-4756-6

LC 2004-45386

"Stephen Lucas, a recently retired, emotionally stunted hit man, emerges from his Swiss hideaway as a favor to old friend Londoner Mark Hatto, who hires Lucas to surreptitiously guard his daughter, bright, extroverted Ella, while she's vacationing in Italy with her boyfriend. After Ella's entire family is murdered, Lucas foils several serious attempts on Ella's life, and the two of them form an odd, almost familial relationship. The boyfriend soon drops out of the picture as the hit man reluctantly helps Ella exact revenge on those who killed her family. There's plenty of action, but it's the twisting, turning, complicated relationship between Ella and Lucas that forms the core of this compelling novel." Publ Wkly

Wilcken, Hugo

The **execution**; a novel. HarperCollins Pubs. 2002 213p $23.95
ISBN 0-06-018823-5

LC 2001-42410

"Wilcken can be forgiven for resolving knotty plot problems with a well-timed coincidence here and there; his book is an exciting, nervy thriller that fulfills the demands of the genre while resonating on deeper frequencies." N Y Times Book Rev

Wilcox, Collin

Dead center. Holt & Co. 1992 262p

LC 91-31076

In this Frank Hastings mystery "a series of powerful and wealthy men are shot to death on the street, the weapon the .22 favored by professional hitmen. The cops finally connect the victims as rather nasty members of the ultra-exclusive Rabelais Club. . . . Old scandals (a hooker's death covered up, a notorious high-stakes poker circle), heavy political and media pressure and glimpses (for us) of the killer's mindset lead up to Hastings's harrowing, climactic confrontation with the murderer." Publ Wkly

Wilcox, Collin

Except for the bones. Doherty Assocs. 1991 282p

LC 91-21579

"Detective Alan Bernhardt looks into the suspicious death of a New York real estate tycoon's latest girlfriend—a death secretly witnessed by the man's estranged stepdaughter in Cape Cod." Libr J

"Wilcox delivers a taut, suspenseful mystery with credible dialogue and good local color." Publ Wkly

Wilcox, Collin

Find her a grave. Forge 1993 288p

LC 93-26557

"Alan Bernhardt is a San Francisco stage director who moonlights as a private eye. He's hired to help the illegitimate daughter of a late Mafia chieftain collect her inheritance, which is buried by the headstone of her mother's grave." Booklist

The author "gradually establishes an authentic mobster milieu, offering the required mix of brutality and honor." Publ Wkly

Wilcox, Collin

Full circle. Forge 1994 352p

LC 94-32703

In Bernhardt's Edge (1988) San Francisco sleuth Alan Bernhardt "saved the life of art expert Betty Giles, who, along with her boyfriend, was blackmailing aged millionaire Raymond DuBois, owner of several pieces of stolen art. Now the FBI is putting heat on Bernhardt to reveal Betty's whereabouts, while DuBois, who would like to preserve his reputation by returning the purloined pieces to their rightful owners, hires Bernhardt to do so." Publ Wkly

Wilcox, Collin

Switchback. Holt & Co. 1993 256p

LC 93-18197

San Francisco's Lt. Frank Hastings "pursues the murderer of a beautiful but selfish young woman who revelled in controlling others. Hastings questions both Haight-Ashbury acquaintances and Nob Hill lovers; meanwhile, constant erotic tension flows from the mutual attraction between Hastings (who lives with divorcée Ann) and bunco squad cop Janet. Wilcox's practiced hand lends a deft descriptive touch, whether to setting, plot or character: add this to the better police procedurals list." Libr J

Wilcox, James

Heavenly days; a novel. Viking 2003 199p $23.95
ISBN 0-670-03247-6

LC 2003-50164

A novel set in the small Louisiana town of Tula Springs. "Lou Jones, moving through her fifties at too rapid a pace, is unhappy: her husband lost his job and moved out of their $300,000 'Cajun cabin' and is now living in his parents' house. Plus, Lou, who minds everyone's business except her own, has a doctorate in music but makes more money working as the receptionist for a fundamentalist health club than she could ever earn at the state college. Wilcox adds in some dizzying subplots involving Lou's oldest friend, a scandal at the college, a group of militant lesbians, and marital infidelity." Booklist

Wilcox, James

Hunk City; a novel. Viking 2007 199p $25.95
ISBN 978-0-670-03152-8; 0-670-03152-6

LC 2006-48687

"Wilcox has always been about more than broad comedy. His men and women, though often clownish, are rarely cartoonish. He has a Dickensian knack for animating minor characters and an eye for the telling detail." N Y Times Book Rev

Wilde, Oscar

★ The **picture** of Dorian Gray. Modern Library 1992 254p $16.95

ISBN 0-679-60001-9

LC 92-11593

First published 1891 in the United Kingdom; first United States edition published 1895 by G. Munro's Sons

"An archetypal tale of a young man who purchases eternal youth at the expense of his soul, the novel was a romantic exposition of Wilde's Aestheticism. Dorian Gray is a wealthy Englishman who gradually sinks into a life of dissipation and crime. Despite his unhealthy behavior, his physical appearance remains youthful and unmarked by dissolution. Instead, a portrait of himself catalogues every evil deed by turning his once handsome features into a hideous mask." Merriam-Webster's Ency of Lit

Wilder, Thornton

★ The **bridge** of San Luis Rey; illustrated by Amy Drevenstedt. Boni, A. C. 1967 235p il

First published 1927

"On Friday, July 20, 1714, high in the Andes of Peru, the famous bridge of San Luis Rey collapsed, killing the five people who were crossing it. A priest who was witness to the event decided that the tragedy provided the chance to prove the wisdom of God in that instance, and thereafter spent years investigating the lives of the people who had been killed." Shapiro. Fic for Youth. 3d edition

Wilder, Thornton

The **bridge** of San Luis Rey and other novels 1926-1948; [edited by J. D. McClatchy] Library of America 2009 731p $35

ISBN 978-1-59853-045-2

The cabala (1926) is a tale of youthful enchantment with Rome in the form of a fictitious memoir of an American student. Set in 18th-century Peru, The bridge of San Luis Rey (1927), "is a kind of theological detective story concerning a friar's investigations into the lives of five individuals before they were killed in a bridge collapse. . . . The Woman of Andros [1930], based on the Andria of Roman writer Terence, is a consideration of the ancient world filtered through the sensibility of a meditative courtesan; Heaven's My Destination [1935], a departure from Wilder's historical themes, is a picaresque romp through Depression-era America; and The Ides of March [1948] takes up the story of Julius Caesar's assassination by imagining the exchange of letters among such prominent ancient figures as Catullus, Cleopatra, Cicero, and Caesar himself." Publisher's note

Wilder, Thornton

The **eighth** day. Harper & Row 1967 435p

"A chronicle of two early 20th-century Midwestern families and their involvement in a murder case raising serious questions about human nature." Oxford Companion to Am Lit. 6th edition

Wilder, Thornton

The **ides** of March. Harper 1948 246p

This novel offers "divergent views of Caesar's last months seen through letters and documents." Oxford Companion to Am Lit. 6th edition

Wilder, Thornton

★ **Theophilus** North. Harper & Row 1973 374p

"In the summer of 1926, a 30-year-old teacher named Theophilus North comes to Newport, R.I., to tutor the children of the fashionably rich and to read out loud. . . . In Newport he discovers nine separate cities differing in age and social class. In these stories of which this novel is composed, North marches through them all—careers and cities—healing the sick, repairing marriages, rescuing a damsel from injustice, restoring life and health to the old and frail, and freedom to the confined." Newsweek

Wiles, Will

Care of wooden floors; a novel. Will Wiles. Houghton Mifflin Harcourt 2012 295 p. (hardcover) $24

ISBN 0547953569; 9780547953564

LC 2012014251

In author Will Wiles' book, a "nameless narrator is on a night to a foreign city, where he has been asked to look after an old friend's [or Oskar's] apartment. . . . The intrusion of an outside element upsets Oskar's ordered system . . . The crisis begins with what a landlord would call 'wear and tear' when what starts out as a small wine stain on the floor quickly complicates itself into a calamity of dead cats, broken glass, accidental stabbings and drunkenly demolished furniture." (Times Literary Supplement)

Wilhelm, Kate

The **best** defense. St. Martin's Press 1994 342p

LC 94-2039

In this legal thriller Barbara Holloway "defends Paula Kennerman, a battered wife accused of killing her daughter and burning down the safe house in which they had been sheltered. . . . The Holloways' crack team of private investigators assures that important clues are developed in time to use as evidence as Barbara skillfully conducts the defense in a suspenseful trial. The ambitious plot-subplot net threads together abortion rights, antifeminist backlash, and the inequities of legal aid for rich and poor." Libr J

Wilhelm, Kate

Death qualified; a mystery of chaos. St. Martin's Press 1991 438p

LC 90-27504

"It is difficult to describe the novel's many dimensions, ranging from tense courtroom scenes to the almost fantastic descriptions of the scientific study. Most astonishing is the author's ability to peel off one layer after another, revealing new ways of looking at the same facts." Libr J

Wilhelm, Kate

★ The **deepest** water. St. Martin's Minotaur 2000 279p $23.95

ISBN 0-312-26143-8

LC 00-31724

"Abby Connors is mourning the death of her father, bestselling novelist Jud Vickers, at the age of 48. Jud was a womanizing former ne'er-do-well who had recently found success, only to be murdered at his remote lakefront cabin. The local police baffled, Abby soon finds herself doing her own sleuthing, much to the dismay of her husband, Brice, a financial planner who was always jealous of Jud's primary place in Abby's heart. As Abby investigates further, she discovers secrets in Jud's past as well as an unfinished novel." Publ Wkly

Wilhelm's "characters are well drawn, the setting is real, and the pace keeps the reader raptly involved to the last page." Libr J

Wilhelm, Kate

Defense for the devil. St. Martin's Press 1999 389p $24.95

ISBN 0-312-19854-X

LC 98-44576

"Mitch Arno is a spouse abuser, small-time thug, and general ne'er-do-well. When he trashes wife Maggie's cozy Oregon B&B after his latest 'job,' she kicks him out, and he heads for his brother's house. Meanwhile, Maggie turns to attorneys Barbara Holloway and her father, Frank, to get a restraining order against Mitch and file for damages. Then Mitch turns up dead, and brother Ray is arrested for murder. Maggie persuades Barbara to defend Ray, placing her and her father in the middle of a deadly web of deception and greed." Libr J

"The nuances of courtroom procedure are compellingly presented, . . . including a sophisticated look at the complex psychology of a jury." Publ Wkly

Wilhelm, Kate

Desperate measures. St. Martin's Minotaur 2001 387p

ISBN 0-312-27663-X

Barbara Holloway's "latest client is a brilliant young man named Alex Feldman, who has been left hideously deformed by a birth defect. He is accused of killing his next-door neighbor, Gus Marchand, a tyrannical religious Zealot who saw Alex's deformity as the mark of the devil. There is little evidence against him, but Marchand has created such hostility and fear toward Alex in their small, rural community that it seems likely he will be convicted on the basis of his appearance alone. . . . Readers are given all the necessary facts and Alex is an excellent character. Wilhelm does a good job of conveying his anguish and isolation." Publ Wkly

Wilhelm, Kate

The **good** children. St. Martin's Press 1998 246p $22.95

ISBN 0-312-17914-6

LC 97-37101

"Brilliantly plotted, lyrically written, alluring and magical, mesmerizing, terrifying, and heartbreakingly funny, Wilhelm's story is a wrenching masterpiece about love, loyalty, and lies that will lodge itself in readers' psyches long after they've finished the last, stunning chapter." Booklist

Wilhelm, Kate

The **Hamlet** trap. St. Martin's Press 1987 234p

LC 87-16368

This "is a psychological mystery, and a classic murder puzzle as well. Constance and Charlie are a loving couple and skillful detectives; good company for one another and for the reader." Wilson Libr Bull

Wilhelm, Kate

Justice for some. St. Martin's Press 1993 260p

LC 93-15046

"Heading for a family gathering at her father's home/water garden business in rural California, widowed Sarah Drexler anticipates a respite from her work as an Oregon state judge. Instead she finds her deductive skills challenged and the lives of those dearest to her threatened. Joining the tense family dinner is Fran Donatio, a woman whose presence Sarah's father Ralph does not explain. The next morning, after Ralph's body is pulled from a lily pond, police Lt. Arthur Fernandez arrives with questions on another matter. . . . This tale . . . offers a bonus in Fernandez who, running his own, equally intelligent investigation in the background, provides a welcome change from the expected solitary-sleuth plot structure." Publ Wkly

Wilhelm, Kate

Malice prepense. St. Martin's Press 1996 412p

LC 96-1190

"As Wilhelm spins her riveting tale, she not only makes the legal system comprehensible and compelling but also makes her readers care about her characters, particularly the efficient yet vulnerable Barbara." Publ Wkly

Wilhelm, Kate

No defense. St. Martin's Press 2000 376p $24.95

ISBN 0-312-20953-3

LC 99-56355

In this legal thriller Oregon attorney Barbara Holloway defends "Lara Jessup, a young widow accused of murdering her much older husband, Vinny, a man with a large insurance policy, a terminal case of cancer, and some very powerful enemies. Jessup's alibi begins to evaporate when her adolescent son contradicts her story, and Holloway is left with no way to defend her except to expose those powerful enemies. . . . Although there is nothing particularly original or surprising here, this well-written novel skillfully captures small-town life in a rural western community with all its benefits and drawbacks." Booklist

Wilhelm, Kate

Sweet, sweet poison. St. Martin's Press 1990 262p

LC 89-77847

Wilhelm "offers studied prose, an almost too heavy dose of local color, and tightly knit plotting in a novel that isn't like most mysteries. Here, hidden fantasies emerge from the subtext, and narrative detours that would lose most crime writers are handled adroitly." Booklist

Wilhelm, Kate

★ **Where** late the sweet birds sang. Harper & Row 1976 251p

"Pollution and pestilence are the consequences of a war that destroys most of the earth and its inhabitants. The elder Sumners have created a scientific research center whose goal is to perfect a technique for cloning since, among the other results of the world disaster, men and women have become sterile. The younger Sumners are victimized by these clones, who perpetuate the form of humans but have no humaneness or humanity." Shapiro. Fic for Youth. 3d edition

Wilhide, Elizabeth

Ashenden; a novel. Elizabeth Wilhide. 1st Simon & Schuster ed. Simon & Schuster 2013 339 p. (hardcover) $24.99; (paperback) $16

ISBN 145168486X; 9781451684865; 9781451697896
LC 2012014720

This book tells the story of an 18th-century English estate house. "When Charlie Minton and his sister, Ros, inherit Ashenden Park (based on an actual estate in Berkshire, England) from their recently deceased aunt, they are forced to decide its fate. The house's history is revealed through chronologically ordered flashbacks, one per chapter." (Publishers Weekly)

Wilkins, Kim

Veil of gold. Tor 2008 495p $25.95

ISBN 978-0-7653-2006-3; 0-7653-2006-1

First published 2005 in Australia with title: Rosa and the veil of gold

"The discovery of an ancient gold bear hidden in the walls of a St. Petersburg bathhouse brings researchers Daniel St. Clair and Em Hayward to verify its age. On their way to the university in Arkhangelsk, however, they lose their way; maps become useless, and they have no choice but to venture on—and into an unfamiliar, strange Russia. Seeking Daniel, his lost love Rosa ventures forth into her own mystical journey, confronting her past in an attempt to save Daniel's—and possibly the world's—future." Libr J

"Wilkins's human characters are endearing and her mythic monsters spring into vibrant life. Adult fairy tales don't come any better than this." Publ Wkly

Willard, Tom

★ **Buffalo** soldiers. Forge 1996 331p $22.95

ISBN 0-312-86041-2
LC 95-53295

"Held captive by the Kiowa and then bartered to a white buffalo hunter, Augustus Sharps is freed in 1869 by troopers of the all-black Tenth U.S. Cavalry, in which he enlists. First in a series chronicling African American contributions to U.S. military history, Willard's . . . well-researched novel traces Augustus's soldiering from Fort Wallace, Kansas, until his retirement to an Arizona ranch." Libr J

Williams, Amanda Kyle

The **stranger** you seek; a novel. Bantam Books 2011 292p $25

ISBN 978-0-553-80807-0; 0-553-80807-9
LC 2010-53044

"Lt. Aaron Rauser needs help catching what seems to be a new serial killer in his Atlanta stomping ground. He knows that the woman for the job is his old friend and crime-solving compatriot Keye Street. Keye's not the kind of woman you mess around with, and while the folks on the force don't like that she's freelancing in their department, there's not much they can do about it. Keye was on track to be a well-respected FBI profiler before an inconvenient addiction to booze got in the way. Now that she's back on her feet, this tough and whip-smart investigator has opened her own small-time business. Although chasing bail jumpers keeps Keye and her hacker sidekick Neil in modest money, hunting down the deranged psychopath the Atlanta papers have dubbed the Wishbone Killer is just Keye's piece of pie. . . . [Williams] creates a frightening and occasionally witty novel, perfect for those who can sleep with one eye open. Think Mary Higgins Clark with an edge." Kirkus Rev

Williams, Ann Joslin

Down from Cascom Mountain; a novel. Bloomsbury USA 2011 325p $25

ISBN 978-1-60819-306-6; 1-60819-306-3
LC 2010-34477

"Ann Williams' novel contains a smaller world than her father's novels; more accessible, the problems more familiar. She follows her characters' moods more closely, with less of an emphasis on the cultural and historical context of her story. The reader is deeply invested, caught up in Mary's grieving, or in Tobin's failure to forgive his mother. Their stories are made memorable." Los Angeles Times

Williams, Charlie

★ **Stairway** to hell. Serpent's Tail 2010 281p pa $14.95

ISBN 978-1-84668-689-4; 184668689X

First published 2009 in the United Kingdom

"This is one of those rare books when, really, anything might happen in the next few pages. Rather than feeling contrived, Williams manages to create a milieu in which even the wackiest developments are both seamlessly logical and thoroughly unexpected, not to mention funny. Pop music, time travel, soul displacement? You bet!" PopMatters

Williams, Joy

Honored guest; stories. Knopf 2004 213p

ISBN 0-679-44647-8
LC 2004-44199

"The troubled characters in Williams' latest short stories, set in locales as diverse as Maine and Mexico, don't have the wherewithal to do anything but brood, with the exception of a forensic anthropologist who solves the mysteries of scattered bones, hair, and teeth, a feat not unlike the one Williams pulls off in these canny and dissecting tales of fractured lives." Booklist

Williams, Karen

Dirty to the grave. Urban Books 2010 216 p.

ISBN 1601622694; 9781601622693

This novel tells the story of "Cha, Goldie, and Red, who come together for fun, laughs, and sometimes treachery in Long Beach, California. For these three ladies, survival was always about . . . using lies, deceit, and sex. But when a plan goes dangerously wrong, Cha and Goldie take a step back out of the life. Cha desperately wants to rid herself of the demons of her past so she can at least feel normal enough to raise her son, Omari. Goldie . . . [is] tired of going from man to man, and knows her parents are rolling over in their graves at the life she chose for herself. Red craves the streets, and will cross anyone, friends included, to get what she wants. She . . . will betray both Cha and Goldie, leading to horrifying consequences." (Publisher's note)

Williams, Niall

John; a novel. Bloomsbury 2008 276p $24.95

ISBN 978-1-59691-467-4; 1-59691-467-X

LC 2007-25810

"A fictional portrayal of the last years of John, Williams' story explores the exiled Christian community on the island of Patmos. In his hope to preserve the message of love before his own death and the extermination of Christianity, the aging apostle records his encounters with Jesus amid the turmoil of the Roman Empire in the first century." BookPage

"This novel will appeal to readers who like imaginative and gritty sagas of the lives of key Christians in the early church as well as those who value lyricism." Publ Wkly

Williams, Tennessee

★ **Collected** stories; with an introduction by Gore Vidal. New Directions 1985 xxv, 574p

LC 85-10642

Williams, Tennessee

★ The **Roman** spring of Mrs. Stone. New Directions 1950 148p

A wealthy widowed American ex-actress is the heroine of this short novel. At fifty Mrs. Stone is losing her beauty, her stage career is ended, and she finds herself just 'drifting' through an aimless existence in Rome. When an unscrupulous countess introduces a handsome young gigolo to Mrs. Stone it is the beginning of the end

"There are many superb moments, scenes which move with a dramatist's ease. There is a hard candor about Mrs. Stone, about all people who fail at real living and attempt a life of fantasy and fail at that, leaving them vulnerable to annihilation. . . . This different version of Mr. Williams' repeated theme has resulted in a sharp, witty and moving novel." Chicago Sunday Trib

Williams, Walter Jon, 1953-

The **fourth** wall; Walter Jon Williams. Orbit 2012 402 p.

ISBN 9780316133395

LC 2011022494

In this novel, "[f]ormer child actor Sean Makin finds himself reduced to taking gigs on the lowest type of reality television shows to make ends meet--and support his agent. A chance meeting with producer Dagmar Shaw, who is suspected of having connections with unsavory international cults and activist groups, lands him a starring role in a revolutionary film that is part reality TV and part scripted story. However, Sean discovers to his dismay that death seems to follow Dagmar, striking those close to her--thus making Sean a prime target." (Libr J)

Williamson, Penelope

Heart of the west; a novel. Simon & Schuster 1995 591p

LC 94-33487

"Williamson gives these characters convincing voices . . . and demonstrates how women could bond and find new identities on the frontier. Williamson tells her story with brio, if a little too much florid prose." Publ Wkly

Williamson, Penelope

The **outsider**. Simon & Schuster 1996 464p

LC 96-7291

"Rachel Yoder is a young widow with a son trying to survive on a Montana sheep farm in the 1880s. She still grieves for her husband, murdered by the local cattleman's association, but her faith carries her through. As a member of a religious community called the Plain people, she believes that one must not question God's workings. Her beliefs are about to be challenged when a wounded gunfighter named Johnny Cain stumbles onto the Yoder cabin in the midst of a severe snowstorm." Booklist

"This is rich, wonderful reading sure to please any fan of good old-fashioned storytelling." Libr J

Willig, Lauren

The **Ashford** affair; Lauren Willig. St. Martin's Press 2013 368 p. (hardcover) $24.99

ISBN 1250014492; 9781250014498; 9781250027191; 9781250027863

LC 2012037787

In this historical romance, "Addie is 99 and beloved by her granddaughter, Clemmie, a lawyer looking to make partner. Clemmie sees the marriage between her grandmother and grandfather, Frederick, as her model for love and has recently ended an engagement because her fiancé did not measure up. After Addie dies, Clemmie, aided by her stepcousin, historian Jon, learns that their family's history is more complicated than she imagined." (Publishers Weekly)

Willig, Lauren

The **seduction** of the crimson rose. Dutton 2008 385p $24.95; pa $15

ISBN 978-0-525-95033-2; 0-525-95033-8; 978-0-451-22441-5 pa; 0-451-22441-8 pa

LC 2007-43044

"The flower-named spies of Regency England return as Willig's smart, sassy style cleverly incorporates a modern-day historian's hunt for information with Regency characters and events. Willig switches from a historical voice to a modern tone with ease, drawing readers back and forth in time as they hold their breath to see what happens next." Romantic Times

Willis, Connie

Blackout. Spectra/Ballantine Books 2010 $26

ISBN 978-0-553-80319-8; 0-553-80319-0

LC 2009-44673

In this novel "Willis expands the conceit of her Hugo and Nebula winning 1982 story 'Fire Watch'. . . . Three young historians travel from 2060 to early 1940s Britain for firsthand research. As Eileen handles a measles outbreak during the children's evacuation and Polly struggles to work as a London shopgirl, hints of trouble with the time-travel equipment barely register on their radar. Historians aren't supposed to be able to change the course of history, but Mike's actions at Dunkirk may disrupt both the past and the future." Publ Wkly

"Despite the conceit of time travel, the book shows the attention to period detail that defines historical novels." Cleveland Plain Dealer

Willis, Connie

★ **Doomsday** book. Bantam Bks. 1992 445p

ISBN 0-553-08131-4

LC 91-42819

"Kivrin, a student of medieval history, is sent back in time to 14th-century Oxfordshire to do some hands-on study. Meanwhile, in the near-future present day of the book, an old disease comes back to smite Oxford. In the resultant chaos, no one realises that because of a slip-up, Kivrin has arrived bang in the middle of the Black Death." New Statesman Soc

"As much as I enjoyed [Willis's] story, . . . the time travel device is given no justification, and none of the paradoxical implications of time travel are explored. Doomsday Book is a historical novel with tenuous SF connections. . . . Warts and all, though, this is a cracking good story, and that is the bottom line criterion for any novel, SF or other." New Scientist

Willis, Connie

Passage. Bantam Bks. 2001 594p

ISBN 0-553-11124-8

LC 00-68052

This novel "concerns the scientific study of near death experiences (NDEs). . . . Psychologist Joanna Lander, an NDE specialist, joins neurologist Richard Wright in a research project employing a psychoactive drug to simulate NDEs. When most of the volunteer subjects drop out, Joanna agrees to go under and finds herself aboard the Titanic. She returns time after time to the ill-fated ship and becomes increasingly obsessed with the experience and why it seems so real and familiar. . . . With memorable characters, believable science, and convincing hospital ambiance, an initially slow-moving yarn turns into a page-turner whose explosive climax will rock readers back on their heels." Booklist

Willis, Connie

To say nothing of the dog; or, How we found the bishop's bird stump at last. Bantam Bks. 1998 434p hardcover o.p. pa $7.99

ISBN 0-553-09995-7; 0-553-57538-4 pa

LC 97-16002

"Rich dowager Lady Schrapnell has invaded Oxford University's time travel research project in 2057, promising to endow it if they help her rebuild Coventry Cathedral, destroyed by a Nazi air raid in 1940. . . . Time traveler Ned Henry is suffering from advanced time lag and has been sent, he thinks, for rest and relaxation to 1888, where he connects with time traveler Verity Kindle and discovers that he is actually there to correct an incongruity created when Verity inadvertently brought something forward from the past." Booklist

"No one mixes scientific mumbo jumbo and comedy of manners with more panache than Willis." N Y Times Book Rev

Willocks, Tim

The **religion**. Sarah Crichton Books 2007 618p $26

ISBN 978-0-374-24865-9; 0-374-24865-6

LC 2006-30419

First published 2006 in the United Kingdom

The author is "especially convincing on the battle lust which overtakes both sides, and vividly places us among the besieged. If you don't mind a bit of romance tacked around the fighting, it is a gripping story with reliable factual underpinnings: history as heroics." Times Lit Suppl

Wilson, A. N.

Winnie and Wolf. Farrar, Straus & Giroux 2008 363p $25

ISBN 978-0-374-29096-2

LC 2008-932297

First published 2007 in the United Kingdom

This is a "remarkable effort, simultaneously dazzling and sluggish. Wilson pulls off a daring risk in seeking to humanize an unspeakable monster by giving him a domestic life and a mundane past, because he realizes that to explain is not to exonerate." Denver Post

Wilson, Adam

Flatscreen. Harper Perennial 2012 352 p.

ISBN 9780062090331

This book tells the story of "Eli Schwartz, the narrator, . . . [who] is the classic couch-bound failure-to-launch whiling away his 20s 'denying real time, like an anthropologist attempting to study a distant, extinct species, wondering what went wrong.' Eli's simple passions—pop culture, cooking, and watching the Food Network—render his life a pleasant stupor suddenly interrupted when his mother sells the house to one 'Seymour J. Kahn: actor, cripple.' The once accomplished and beloved but now elderly and wheelchair-bound Seymour acts as a time-lapsed version of Eli. . . . And under the old man's terrible tutelage, Eli awakens to a wholly incongruous lifestyle of hillbilly heroin and gunplay." (Publishers Weekly)

Wilson, Chris

Cotton; Chris Wilson. Harcourt 2005 314p (pbk.) $26.00; o.p.; (hbk.) o.p.

ISBN 9780156030458; 0151011230; 9780151011230

LC 2004023117

This novel tells the story of Cotton, "a blonde, white, blue-eyed boy born of a black mother. Lee Cotton's problems are compounded by an . . . oddity, his ability to hear the thoughts of both the living and the dead. If that were not enough, Lee discovers that his life holds surprising, even shocking, turns that ensure he will never fit in anywhere. First he survives a brutal, racially motivated assault that leaves him a John Doe, assumed to be white, in a neurological ward, and then, through a series of events, he undergoes major transformations that always leave him different on the outside than on the inside. No matter what guise he assumes, he remains an honest, homespun, good-humored, observant individual." (Dactyl Review)

Wilson, Daniel H.

Robopocalypse; Daniel H. Wilson. Doubleday 2011 347p. $25

ISBN 978-0-385-53385-0; 0-385-53385-3

LC 201043134

Alex Award (2012)

Two decades into the future humans are battling for their very survival when a powerful AI computer goes rogue, and all the machines on earth rebel against their human controllers

"In this story of a global robotic revolution, Wilson's malevolent machines have surprisingly nuanced motives, and a few of the vignettes, particularly one about the chilling fate of an Alaskan drill team, could even stand alone as great horror short fiction." Entertainment Wkly

Wilson, Edward O.

Anthill; a novel. [by] E. O. Wilson. W.W. Norton & Co. 2010 378p $24.95

ISBN 978-0-393-07119-1; 0-393-07119-7

LC 2009-52140

"Wilson indeed captures in Anthill the rapture of a boyhood amid the snakes and ants, pine and palmetto, of Alabama. He explores the simmering persistence of its painful history, the tensions between whites and blacks, rich and poor, men and women, as the Old South gave way to the New South a generation ago, sometimes languidly, sometimes not. The result is a charming and intriguing novel, elegant especially in a passage on warring ants, but a novel more impressive as advocacy than as artistry, more resonant in its views of nature and humanity than as fiction." Boston Globe

Wilson, F. Paul

Conspiracies; a Repairman Jack novel. Forge 2000 317p

ISBN 0-312-86797-2

LC 99-52372

"Jack, a fix-it man who specializes in problems that frequently require him to face powerful foes and slip into the world of the supernatural, is hired to locate the missing wife of a businessman. This time he must find a missing woman who happens to be one of the world's leading conspiracy theorists (she was preparing to reveal her Grand Unification Theory, which would explain the truth behind all manner of strange goings-on). To find her, Jack must attend a convention of conspiracy buffs, most of whom seem more than a little strange. . . . Those who look at conspiracy theories with a skeptical eye will have a great time, as will anyone who likes a well-plotted, spooky thriller. Wilson tells a great story." Booklist

Wilson, F. Paul

Deep as the marrow. Forge 1997 352p $24.95

ISBN 0-312-86264-4

LC 96-30502

"When President Thomas Winston announces a plan to attack the drug problem by making drugs legal, he's met first with public outrage, then with an assassination plot involving his boyhood friend and personal physician, Dr. John VanDuyne. In a plan masterminded by a Colombian drug lord, six-year-old Katie VanDuyne is kidnapped to persuade her father to give the president an antibiotic that will destroy his bone marrow. The kidnapping goes awry early on, because of the doctor's ethics and a kidnapper's attachment to Katie, but Wilson spins out the action to the last pages, making some persuasive arguments for drug legalization along the way." Libr J

Wilson, F. Paul

The haunted air; a Repairman Jack novel. Forge 2002 415p $24.95

ISBN 0-312-87868-0

LC 2002-72059

This Repairman Jack novel "teams the righteous urban mercenary with his strangest bedfellows yet: a pair of sham spirit mediums who openly operate their occult con game out of a brownstone in Queens. . . . Jack takes the case of brothers Lyle and Charlie Kenton, who've been threatened by other Big Apple pseudo-psychics for horning in on the lucrative seance scene. No sooner has Jack begun . . . than real ghosts begin popping up along with a secret cult of ritual child murderers. . . . Above all, the novel enhances the enigma of Jack, a hero who commands respect despite his curmudgeonly disdain for contemporary culture, his morally ambiguous work-for-hire ethic and his unsettling appeal to the vigilante in every reader." Publ Wkly

Wilson, F. Paul

Legacies. Forge 1998 381p $24.95

ISBN 0-312-86414-0

LC 98-14322

"Jack, a fix-it man who specializes in solving people's problems (and who, as far as the authorities are concerned, doesn't even exist), does a favor for a friend—he recovers some toys stolen from a hospital—and winds up helping a woman solve a deadly mystery from her past. Repairman Jack is a strong man whose moments of compassion don't seem forced, an enigma without being annoyingly mysterious." Booklist

Wilson, G. Willow

★ Alif the unseen; G. Willow Wilson. Grove Press 2012 433 p. (hbk.) $25.00

ISBN 0802120202; 9780802120205

In this novel, by G. Willow Wilson, "a young Arab-Indian hacker shields his clients . . . from surveillance and tries to stay out of trouble. He goes by Alif. . . . When Alif discovers . . . the secret book of the jinn, which . . . he . . . suspect[s] may unleash a new level of information technology, the stakes are raised and Alif must struggle for life or death, aided by forces seen and unseen." (Publisher's note)

"Wilson skillfully weaves a story linking modern-day technologies and computer languages to the folklore and religion of the Middle East." LJ

Wilson, Kevin

The family Fang. Ecco 2011 309p $23.99

ISBN 978-0-06-157903-5; 0-06-157903-3

"Caleb and Camille Fang are gallery darlings of a particularly discomfiting sort, staging public confrontations to provoke an extreme reaction from unwitting bystanders — and recording the results for posterity. In a move that Dr. Spock would never endorse, they've raised their two young children to be accomplices in their work. They take their Santa-fearing daughter, Annie, to every mall they can find so she'll wail the moment she touches the jolly man's lap. They enter their son, Buster, in the Little Miss Crimson Clover pageant disguised as a girl. And so on. As you might imagine, the kids flee the first moment they can. Annie heads to Hollywood and takes up acting; Buster becomes a freelance writer and sometime novelist. But the Fang umbilical cord proves oddly bungee-like, and the offspring soon return for adult-size doses of psychological torment. Wilson writes with the studied quirkiness of George Saunders or filmmaker Wes Anderson, and there's some genuine warmth beneath all the surface eccentricity." Entertainment Wkly

Wilson, Robert

The **blind** man of Seville. Harcourt 2003 434p $26

ISBN 0-15-100835-3

LC 2002-68495

"Wilson . . . is able to hold reader interest at an almost unbearable pitch of excitement throughout this shocker with exquisite plot pacing and intriguing character revelations." Booklist

Wilson, Robert

Capital Punishment. Houghton Mifflin Harcourt 2013 416 p. (Charlie Boxer books) $28

ISBN 0547935196; 9780547935195

This is the first in Gold Dagger Award-winner Robert Wilson's Charles Boxer series. "When 25-year-old Alyshia D'Cruz, the daughter of a self-made Indian billionaire, is kidnapped after an evening out with her co-workers, Boxer is charged with getting Alyshia back alive. The kidnapper, who insists that the crime 'is not about money,' urges the family not to involve the press or the police." (Publishers Weekly)

Wilson, Robert

The **hidden** assassins. Harcourt 2006 453p $25

ISBN 978-0-15-101239-8; 0-15-101239-3

LC 2006-17507

"Falcón is smart and relentless and thoroughly decent, which makes him a capable, if less than captivating, guide through the complicated tangle of motives and suspects. . . . [The novel] is smart and challenging, a mystery that demonstrates the flexibility of a genre that is too often constrained by convention and stereotypes." Cleveland Plain Dealer

Wilson, Robert Charles

Blind Lake. TOR Bks. 2003 399p $24.95

ISBN 0-7653-0262-4

LC 2003-47345

"No one knows better than Wilson how to manipulate the language of science to suggest the essential unknowability of the universe. . . . The drama at Blind Like gradually expands to encompass humans and aliens in entirely unforeseen ways." N Y Times Book Rev

Wilson, Robert Charles

Julian Comstock; a story of 22nd-century America. Tor Bks. 2009 413p $25.95

ISBN 0765319713; 9780765319715

LC 2008-53400

This novel is set in a post-apocalyptic semifeudal America. "In Colorado Springs, the Dominion sees to the nation's spiritual needs. In Labrador, the Army wages war on the Dutch. America, unified, is rising once again. Then out of Labrador come tales of a . . . Captain Commongold, the Youthful Hero of the Saguenay. The ordinary people follow his adventures in the popular press. The Army adores

him. The President is troubled. Especially when the dashing Captain turns out to be his nephew Julian, son of the falsely accused and executed Bryce. Treachery and intrigue dog Julian's footsteps." (Publisher's note)

The narrative is "beautifully written, populated with engaging and sympathetic, if conflicted, characters, and unlike anything else [Wilson's] done to date . . . . It's also a fascinating example of SF's ongoing negotiations with ideas of history and identity, and a good deal more complex than its faux-naif narrative voice and boys'- book adventure plotting would seem to suggest." Locus

Wilson, Robert Charles

Spin. Tor 2005 364p

ISBN 0-7653-0938-6

LC 2004-58862

"The narrative time oscillates effortlessly between Tyler Dupree's early adolescence and his near-future young manhood haunted by the impending death of the sun and the earth. Tyler's best friends, twins Diane and Jason Lawton, take two divergent paths: Diane into a troubling religious cult of the end, Jason into impassioned scientific research to discover the nature of the galactic Hypotheticals whose 'Spin' suddenly sealed Earth in a 'cosmic baggie,' making one of its days equal to a hundred million years in the universe beyond. As convincing as Wilson's scientific hypothesizing is—biological, astrophysical, medical—he excels even more dramatically with the infinitely intricate, minutely nuanced relationships among Jason, Diane and Tyler, whose older self tries to save them both with medicines from Mars, terraformed through Jason's genius into an incubator for new humanity." Publ Wkly

Wilson, Sloan

★ The **man** in the gray flannel suit. Simon & Schuster 1955 304p

The man of the title is the ordinary, upper middle class New York business employee, who at five o'clock heads for his home, wife, and children in Connecticut. Thomas Rath is his name in this book. Tom joins a large corporation, does an honest job, and is evidently headed for bigger money. As an undercurrent to his daily life Tom remembers his war service, the girl he met in Rome, and his illegitimate son

"Thoughtful, searching novel. . . . Sloan Wilson manages to hold the reader's interest and at the same time to solve Rath's problems without distorting his character." N Y Her Trib Books

Wilson, Susan

The **fortune** teller's daughter; Susan Wilson. Atria Books 2002 342 p. o.p.

ISBN 074344230X

LC 20020104271

This book follows Sabine Heartwood, who is "happy in her newly settled life until her flighty mother, Madame Ruby, starts proclaiming visions of a coming upheaval. Meanwhile, Danford Smith has returned from New York City to nurse his ailing grandmother through her final days and set his family's affairs in order before returning to a promising career as a filmmaker. Of course life has other plans, and Dan finds himself mired in . . . family loyalties and new obligations. As his long-distance relationship with rising starlet Karen Whitcomb unravels, Dan is increasingly drawn to the lovely and forthright Sabine, who seems to understand something about him that he himself does not. As for Sabine, the psychic gift she has long rejected awakens, intimating dark secrets in Dan's past and that of Moose River." (Publishers Weekly)

Wiltse, David
Blown away. Putnam 1996 343p

LC 96-2387

"Wiltse illuminates a broad spectrum of heroism and villainy with a colorful, often humorous cast of characters that makes agent Becker seem drab by comparison. These engaging folk will hold readers in thrall through a fastpaced, cleverly plotted tale that features plenty of action, on the street and off, and that will leave readers just as the title says." Publ Wkly

Wiltse, David
Bone deep. Putnam 1995 340p

LC 95-11089

This suspense novel features FBI agent John Becker. Connecticut's "rain-swollen Saugatuck River floats a bone into a local backyard, prompting the attention of the vacationing Becker and his old friend 'Tee' Terhune, the town's police chief. . . . After marks on the bone reveal that the body it belongs to was cut in pieces before burial, an upriver search turns up a charnel house of companion bones in the loose soil of a Christmas tree farm. A prime suspect arises when Tee gets anonymous tips that one of his officers, the loathsome McNeil, who likes to sleep with high-school girls, is involved in the killings." Publ Wkly

Wimberley, Darryl
The **king** of Colored Town. Toby 2007 353p $24.95

ISBN 978-1-59264-181-9; 1-59264-181-4

This "novel explores school integration in Florida in the 1960s through the eyes of tall, musically gifted Cilla Handsom, the black teenage daughter of an autistic mother who requires a lot of care. The section of Laureate, where she lives, is dubbed 'Colored Town' and lacks running water and music, but for one well and radio. Cilla's old life of toting water and helping her mother perform at church is interrupted by the arrival of charismatic Joe Billy King by train one day and by her teacher's request that she join the marching band at the county's formerly all-white school in exchange for music lessons." Libr J

"An impassioned and eloquent piece of storytelling set in the last days of the Jim Crow South." Texas Monthly

Wind, Ruth
In the midnight rain; Ruth Wind. Harper Torch 2000 406p (pbk.) o.p.

ISBN 0061030120

LC 2001555211

In this book, "[o]n a quest both professional and personal, biographer Ellie Connor accepts the invitation of experimental botanist and music lover Laurence 'Blue' Reynard and heads for Pine Bend, TX, to gather information on an obscure Thirties blues singer and, if she can, learn something about her unknown father. However, her search nets her far more than she expects, and Ellie is suddenly faced with a

surprising family, the answer to a mysterious disappearance, and a love she never hoped to find." (Library Journal)

Windle, Jeanette
Congo dawn; Jeanette Windle. Tyndale House Publishers 2013 496 p. (sc) $12.99

ISBN 1414371586; 9781414371580

LC 2012036151

In this Christian novel, "Robin Duncan, member of a global security force for a precious metals mine, learns she is meant for more than providing security for a multinational corporation. She must also overcome her personal grief and betrayal by Michael Stewart if, together, the two are to help liberate people oppressed in once-beautiful, smoldering rain forests that the government and corporate greed have laid to waste." (Publishers Weekly)

Winegardner, Mark
The **Godfather** returns. Random House 2004 430p $26.95

ISBN 1-400-06101-6

LC 2004-51380

"This is a phenomenally entertaining, psychologically rich saga that spans the entire Godfather years imagined in novel and film by Mario Puzo (the latter via his screenplays), filling in the blanks, fleshing out the characters, focusing primarily on the time (mid 1950s-early '60s) between when Puzo's landmark novel ended and the film Godfather II begins." Publ Wkly

Winer, Andrew
The **marriage** artist; a novel. Henry Holt and Company 2010 367p $26

ISBN 978-0-8050-9178-6; 0-8050-9178-5

LC 2009-52432

"As the two story lines converge, readers discern the central secret long before it's revealed, and Winer's prose flickers between ravishing and contrived. Yet structural flaws do not diminish the audacity and beauty of this elaborate psycho-political-sexual puzzle, with its hard truths, startling visions, and eerie insights into the mystical and memorializing powers of art, and that endless hunger we call love." Booklist

Wingate, Steven
Wifeshopping; stories. Houghton Mifflin 2008 190p pa $13.95

ISBN 978-0-547-05365-3

LC 2008-4733

"One of the cruelest ironies of modern letters is that so many books are written about male insecurity — consider the oeuvres of Bellow and Updike, and work down from there — and yet so few readers of serious fiction seem to be men. This irony is especially piquant in the case of Steven Wingate's new story collection, 'Wifeshopping.' Trust me, fellas, even if you think you'e been a bad boyfriend, the protagonists assembled here could teach you a thing or two about despicable conduct. Nearly all are in the thrall of misguided wooing. They want sex (naturally) and companionship (to some vague extent), but mostly they want to bask in the glamorous notion that they are the marrying kind.

It's almost sweet, really — until it turns toxic." Los Angeles Times Book Rev

Winkler, Anthony C.

Dog war. Akashic Books 2007 195p pa $14.95

ISBN 978-1-93335-428-6; 1-93335-428-3

LC 2006-936538

"Newly widowed, Precious, an upstanding Jamaican with practical ideas and a conversational relationship with Jesus, becomes a maid in a Miami mansion for a pampered dog, who soon develops overfond feelings for her person. The dog belongs to the spiritually questing Mistress Lucy, a multimillionaire among whose most pressing concerns is whether to have her Rolls 'decowed'—the leather removed on moral grounds. Winkler has a fine ear for patois and dialogue, and a love of language that makes bawdy jokes crackle." New Yorker

Winman, Sarah

When God was a rabbit; a novel. Bloomsbury 2011 296p $25

ISBN 978-1-60819-934-3; 1-60819-534-1

"Don't be fooled by When God Was a Rabbit, the existential-sounding title of Winman's debut novel. Her protagonist, Elly (whom we're introduced to as a child growing up in late-1960s England), simply has a pet rabbit named God. God the rabbit is a bit magical — he's able to speak with Elly — but that's par for the course in this eccentric coming-of-age story. Winman's prose is elegantly restrained as she sketches Elly's family life, touching lightly upon both good and bad moments. It's these little moments — some small, one monumental — that are the most affecting and poignant." Entertainment Wkly

Winslow, Don

The **Dawn** Patrol. Alfred A. Knopf 2008 303p $23.95

ISBN 978-0-307-26620-0; 0-307-26620-6

LC 2008-6531

"Winslow horses around early with a lightweight plot about San Diego cop turned PI Boone Daniels searching for an AWOL stripper scheduled to testify against a nightclub owner running an insurance scam. Riotous beach-rat banter abounds, and the 'endless summer' vibe is blissful. But a dreadful undercurrent emerges in which Winslow's amiable 'Dawn Patrol' (the day's earliest surfers) see their carefree lifestyle threatened by the modern virus of gangs, drugs and violence. Winslow transforms his blithe trifle into an elegiac riff on the Pacific Coast's paradise lost, and produces a classic. If you haven't read Winslow yet, get to it." San Francisco Chron

Winslow, Don

The **gentlemen's** hour. Simon & Schuster 2011 338p $25

ISBN 978-1-4391-8339-7; 1-4391-8339-2

LC 2011-10781

"Boone Daniels, underemployed private eye and obsessive surfer, ... [continues] his search for a simple life that he nonetheless complicates at every turn. Narrated in an omniscient third-person voice that is both smart-alecky and world-weary, the book finds Daniels in a conundrum when

he is hired by a law firm to attempt to obtain mitigating evidence for the defense in a murder case. The problem is that the late victim, Kelly Kuhio, is a local surfing icon revered by the community, including Daniels and his surfer buddies. . . . Winslow's matter-of-fact but dark narration is the key to this plot-driven work about the fragility and strength of friendships and principles." Bookreporter

Winslow, Don

The **kings** of cool; Don Winslow. Simon & Schuster 2012 322 p. (paperback) $15.00; (downloadable audio) $17.95; (hardcover) $25.00

ISBN 9781451665338; 9781442349803; 1451665326; 9781451665321

LC 2012010619

In this book by Don Winslow, the "prequel to 2010's 'Savages' . . . readers learn the blistering backstories of twentysomething buds Ben and Chon as well as O, the rebellious babe they both love. Beginning his tale in the 1960s, Winslow paints an unsettling portrait of the underbelly of Southern California, from pot- and coke-dealing hippie parents to Mexican gang leaders who compose messages with human entrails." (Booklist)

Winslow, Don

Satori. Grand Central Pub. 2010 504p $25.99

ISBN 978-0-446-56192-1; 0-446-56192-4

LC 2010-12415

"In this homage to Trevanian's cult classic Shibumi (1979), Winslow . . . fills in some of Trevanian's main character's back story. In Shibumi, Nicholai Hel was already an accomplished assassin, called out of retirement to perform one more job. Winslow takes the reader back a few decades to the early 1950s to explain how Hel got into the assassination business in the first place. He picks up the thread after Hel's three-year stint in an American jail for the murder of his mentor in the chaos of post–World War II Japan. The Americans recognize his unique abilities—including his mastery of several languages and thehoda korosumartial art—and offer him a deal: He can have his freedom and a chance to even the score with those who have mistreated him in prison if he will travel to Beijing under the guise of a French arms dealer and assassinate a Soviet official. . . . Perfect for Shibumi fans and anyone else who likes their espionage over the top." Kirkus

Winslow, Don

★ **Savages**. Simon & Schuster 2010 302p $25

ISBN 978-1-4391-8336-6; 1-4391-8336-8

LC 2010-16924

"Ben and Chon are two Americans running a lucrative marijuana operation out of ritzy Laguna Beach, California. Their business is buzzing along nicely until members of the Mexican Baja Cartel decide they want a piece of the action. Ben, a charitable, environmentally conscious Berkeley grad, doesn't want any trouble. Former Navy Seal Chon prefers peace as well but not if it means giving up primo weed. When Ben and Chon resist the Mexicans' demands, the cartel kidnaps 'O' (short for Ophelia), the boys' close confidante and frequent bedroom playmate. Ben and Chon conjure clever schemes to outwit their adversaries and win back O, using everything from improvised explosive devices to Letterman and Leno masks. . . . [Winslow] dispenses short chapters that drive his plot breathlessly forward. He also serves up plenty of savage wit." Booklist

Winslow, Don

The **winter** of Frankie Machine. Alfred A. Knopf 2006 299p $23.95

ISBN 1-4000-4498-7

LC 2006-45263

"Frank Machianno, a retired mob hit man known as Frankie Machine as a tribute to his efficiency, has put his past behind him and is living a tranquil life in San Diego running a bait shop and supplying restaurants with linens and seafood. When the son of a local mob boss asks for his backup in resolving a dispute with the Detroit mob, Frank agrees, only to find that he's been set up as the intended victim of a hit. Using his survival skills and street smarts, the executioner follows a trail of bodies to identify which of his past crimes has caught up with him. While the plot is familiar, Winslow has created plausible characters and taut scenes of suspense that will keep readers turning pages." Publ Wkly

Winspear, Jacqueline

Among the mad; a Maisie Dobbs novel. Henry Holt and Company 2009 303p $25

ISBN 978-0-8050-8216-6; 0-8050-8216-6

LC 2008-32576

Sequel to: An incomplete revenge (2008)

"The lamentation over economic crisis, terrorism and traumatized veterans feels both true to its setting and disquietingly contemporary. Well-crafted and well worth reading." Kirkus

Followed by The mapping of love and death (2010)

Winspear, Jacqueline

Birds of a feather; a novel. Soho Press 2004 311p $25

ISBN 1-569-47368-4

LC 2003-25732

Sequel to Maisie Dobbs (2003)

P.I. Maisie Dobbs "has been hired to find the missing daughter of a wealthy London magnate. As Maisie and her Cockney assistant, Billy Beale, try to track Charlotte Waite down, they discover that three of her old friends have been murdered-poisoned and then bayoneted." Libr J

Followed by Pardonable lies (2005)

Winspear, Jacqueline

Elegy for Eddie; Jacqueline Winspear. Harper/HarperCollins 2012 352 pp. $25.99

ISBN 9780062049575

LC 2011278583

In this book, "[Maisie Dobbs, a] determined psychologist and private investigator looks into the death of Eddie, a gentle man who seemed to have no enemies, certainly not among the horses he charmed. . . . But she can never forget the poor neighborhood in which she was raised. So she doesn't hesitate when the costermongers of Covent Garden ask her to investigate Eddie's death after he's crushed by a roll of paper at the factory of wealthy Canadian newspaper baron John Otterburn. The more Maisie finds out, the more she's convinced that Otterburn is using his considerable influence to steer Britain toward a confrontation with a resur-

gent Germany led by Hitler. . . . Despite mounting danger, she continues to investigate while trying to put her own life in order." (Kirkus)

Winspear, Jacqueline

An **incomplete** revenge; a Maisie Dobbs novel. H. Holt 2008 306p $24; pa $14

ISBN 978-0-8050-8215-9; 0-8050-8215-8; 978-0-312-42818-1 pa; 0-312-42818-9 pa

LC 2007-40639

Sequel to Messenger of truth (2006)

Maisie Dobbs, the extraordinary psychologist and investigator, delves into a strange series of crimes in a small rural community involving mysterious fires, petty crimes, and the legacy of a wartime Zeppelin raid.

"Maisie is absolutely compelling not only as an investigator but also as a psychologist while she probes the hearts and minds of those she meets." Libr J

Followed by Among the mad (2009)

Winspear, Jacqueline

Leaving Everything Most Loved; a Maisie Dobbs Novel. Maisie Dobbs. HarperCollins 2013 352 p. (hardcover) $26.99

ISBN 0062049607; 9780062049605

This is the 10th Maisie Dobbs novel from Jacqueline Winspear. Here, in "the summer of 1933, a young Indian immigrant, Usha Pramal, is found dead in a London canal with a gunshot wound in her forehead. More than two months later, the victim's devastated brother, freshly arrived by boat from India, hires Daisy to solve his sister's murder. With the trail gone cold and the evidence thin, Maisie has her work cut out for her." (Publishers Weekly)

Winspear, Jacqueline

★ **Maisie** Dobbs; a novel. Soho Press 2003 294p $24

ISBN 1-56947-330-7

LC 2002-44656

"For a clever and resourceful young woman who has just set herself up in business as a private investigator, Maisie seems a bit too sober and much too sad. Romantic readers sensing a story-within-a-story won't be disappointed. But first, they must prepare to be astonished at the sensitivity and wisdom with which Maisie resolves her first professional assignment." N Y Times Book Rev

Winspear, Jacqueline

The **mapping** of love and death; a Maisie Dobbs novel. Harper 2010 338p $25.99; pa $14.99

ISBN 978-0-06-172766-5; 0-06-172766-0; 978-0-06-172768-9 pa; 0-06-172768-7 pa

LC 2009-49970

Sequel to Among the mad (2009)

London investigator Maisie Dobbs must unravel a case of wartime love and death—an investigation that leads her to a doomed affair between a young cartographer, listed as missing in action when World War I ends, and a mysterious nurse.

In this installment Maisie Dodds, a "private investigator and former World War I field nurse, tries to help the parents of an American soldier, missing since 1916, whose remains aren't recovered until 1932 on a farm in the Somme Valley. A mapmaker ('an adventurer with his feet on the ground'), Michael Clifton became a military cartographer and presumably perished in the same shelling that wiped out the rest of his unit. But when a necropsy shows he was murdered, Maisie must rely on his diary and the letters of an unknown English nurse to figure out how he died. Always the thorough researcher, Winspear surpasses herself in this absorbing novel by giving Maisie an exacting assignment: learning the skills cartographers bring into battle and then discovering why someone would want to kill one of them." N Y Times Book Rev

Followed by A lesson in secrets (2011)

Winspear, Jacqueline
Messenger of truth; a Maisie Dobbs novel. H. Holt 2006 322p $24; pa $14

ISBN 978-0-8050-7898-5; 0-8050-7898-3; 978-0-312-42685-9 pa; 0-312-42685-2 pa

LC 2006-43626

Sequel to Pardonable lies (2005)

This installment in the historical mystery series "finds our fearless psychologist/inquiry agent investigating the death of artist Nick Bassington-Hope. According to Detective Inspector Stratton, Nick's fall from a set of scaffolding was merely a tragic accident. Nick's twin sister, Georgina, however, insists he was murdered and hires Maisie to discover the truth. . . . The mystery itself is rather transparent, but what makes this book delightful is how Winspear shows Maisie's emotional development amid the bitter legacy of the Great War." Libr J

Followed by An incomplete revenge (2008)

Winspear, Jacqueline
Pardonable lies; a Maisie Dobbs novel. Henry Holt 2005 342p hardcover o.p. pa $15

ISBN 0-8050-7897-5; 0-312-42621-6 pa

LC 2005-46388

Sequel to Birds of a feather (2004)

In this installment, "British psychologist and investigator Maisie Dobbs, who attended university after serving as a nurse in France during World War I, tackles a trio of cases that ranges from the unsettling to the surreal. There's 13-year-old Avril Jarvis, accused of first-degree murder. And Sir Cecil Lawton, QC, who is attempting to honor his late wife's request to determine if their fighter-pilot son is living or dead. And Maisie's rich, trendy friend, Priscilla, desperate for details about her brother, who was killed in the Great War. Maisie pursues clues with the help of her Cockney assistant, Billy, and wisdom imparted by her elegant, if enigmatic, mentor, Maurice. . . . A trip to France reveals a startling connection between the cases but proves traumatic for the former nurse still haunted by her experiences tending to wounded soldiers during the war." Booklist

Followed by Messenger of truth (2006)

Winston, Lolly
Good grief. Warner Books 2004 344p $18

ISBN 0-446-53304-1

LC 2003-15207

After thirty-six-year-old Sophie Stanton's husband Ethan dies of cancer, she leaves her job with a technology company in Silicon Valley and winds up in Oregon where she reinvents herself as a baker and finds a new love interest

"Throughout this heartbreaking, gorgeous look at loss, Winston imbues her heroine and her narrative with the kind of grace, bitter humor and rapier-sharp realness that will dig deep into a reader's heart and refuse to let go. Sophie is wounded terribly, but she's also funny, fresh and utterly believable." Publ Wkly

Winter, Kathleen
Annabel; Kathleen Winter. Black Cat 2010 465p $14.95

ISBN 9780802170828

LC 2010481429

Writers' Federation of Nova Scotia Book Prizes: Thomas Head Raddall Atlantic Fiction Prize (2011)

In this book, which is set "[i]n 1968, into the beautiful, spare environment of remote coastal Labrador, a mysterious child is born: a baby who appears to be neither fully boy nor girl, but both at once. Only three people are privy to the secret—the baby's parents, Jacinta and Treadway, and a trusted neighbour, Thomasina. Together the adults make a difficult decision: to raise the child as a boy named Wayne. But as Wayne grows to adulthood within the hyper-masculine hunting culture of his father, his shadow-self—a girl he thinks of as 'Annabel'—is never entirely extinguished, and indeed is secretly nurtured by the women in his life." (Publisher's note)

Winters, Ben H.
Bedbugs. Quirk Books 2011 253p pa $14.95

ISBN 978-1-59474-523-2; 1-59474-523-4

LC 2011-922691

"The idea of supernatural bedbugs is a stroke of horror genius. Regular bedbugs are enough to inspire shuddering revulsion in most people, and stories abound about how hard they are to purge and how a bad case of them can cause enough strain to break up a stable relationship. Badbugs are bedbugs on steroids, and the death of the person who brought them into being is the only way they can be destroyed. The book sings when it sinks into the scary muck of this mythology." Los Angeles Times Book Rev

Winters, Ben H.
The **last** policeman. Quirk Books 2012 316 p. (paperback) $14.95; (ebook) $14.95

ISBN 1594745765; 9781594745768; 9781594745775

LC 2012454509

In this detective novel by Ben H. Winters, "Hank Palace is investigating a suspicious death that may be a murder or might be part of an epidemic of suicides. Both the promotion and the suicides are rooted in the fact that an asteroid is on a collision course with Earth and will destroy all life in a few months. Palace faces indifference from many of his colleagues who don't see the point of solving one death when everyone is under the same sentence." (Library Journal)

Winterson, Jeanette
Oranges are not the only fruit. Grove Press 1997 176p pa $14

ISBN 0-8021-3516-1

First published 1985 in the United Kingdom

"Raised by an oppressively evangelical mother, Jeanette grows up a good little Christian soldier, even going so far as to stitch samplers whose apocalyptic themes terrify her classmates. . . . Jeanette would have remained in the fold but for her unconventional desires; though she can reconcile her love of women with her love of God, the church cannot. It could have been a grim tale, but this [novel] . . . is in fact a wry and tender telling of a young girl's triumphantly coming into her own." Libr J

Winterson, Jeanette

★ **Sexing** the cherry. Atlantic Monthly Press 1990 167p

ISBN 0-87113-350-4

LC 90-30682

This is a novel "about a prodigious giantess and her explorer son in 17th-century London. Jordan fetches the first pineapple to the court of Charles II, while his mother, The Dog Woman, wreaks vengeance upon Puritans in a brothel. The plague; the flying princesses who defy laws of the courts and gravity; Jordan's travels to the floating city and the botanical wonders of the New World–the tale . . . [involves both] history and fantasy. The two characters eventually merge into the grievously polluted life of modern London." Libr J

"Winterson, whose work is full of profound truths disguised as simple statements, is at her epigrammatic best on the subject of romantic love." Quill Quire

Winterson, Jeanette

The **stone** gods. Harcourt 2008 206p $24

ISBN 978-0-15-101491-0; 0-15-101491-4

LC 2007-47079

First published 2007 in the United Kingdom

"A playful but impassioned novel. Winterson cloaks her disillusionment without political excesses in a sustained imaginative jeu d'esprit. Her writing is funny and beautiful." London Times

Winthrop, Elizabeth

Island justice. Morrow 1998 356p $25

ISBN 0-688-15920-6

LC 97-36566

"Along with the satisfying plot . . . readers are also provided with a good deal of information about the flora and fauna of coastal New England and the delicate balance of its human society. 'Island Justice' is the kind of book that used to be called a 'good read'—and sometimes there's nothing better." N Y Times Book Rev

Winthrop, Elizabeth Hartley

December. Alfred A. Knopf 2008 239p $23.95

ISBN 978-0-307-26830-3; 0-307-26830-6

LC 2007-37095

"To appreciate December, which offers the pleasures of beautifully composed scenes and, when it shifts to Isabelle's point of view, an exact rendering of a child's acute perceptions, the reader must accept that Isabelle has fallen under a sort of existential spell. The fact that her father, Wilson, calls her Belle bolsters the impression that this is a modern fairy tale, and so does the novel's deadline-driven structure. . . . December posits the old-fashioned thesis that family love can conquer many ills. Some may discount this notion as too

hopeful, but others will find, in Winthrop's exact but tender portraits of domestic rituals, enough evidence to support it." N Y Times Book Rev

Winthrop, Elizabeth Hartley

★ The **why** of things; by Elizabeth Hartley Winthrop. Simon & Schuster 2013 320 p. $24.99

ISBN 1451695756; 9781451695755

LC 2012041122

In this novel by Elizabeth Hartley Winthrop "since the tragic loss of her . . . daughter less than a year ago, Joan Jacobs has been working hard to keep her . . . family [together]. The Jacobses flee to their summer home in search of peace. That same evening a pickup truck had driven into the quarry in their backyard. The local police drag up the body of . . . James Favazza. As the Jacobs family learns more about the . . . events that led up to that . . . evening, each of them becomes increasingly tangled in . . . James' life and death." (Publisher's note)

Winton, Tim

Breath; a novel. Farrar, Straus and Giroux 2008 320p $23

ISBN 978-0-374-11634-7; 0-374-11634-2

LC 2007-47879

"The novel's complexity is poetic, psychological and ethical. Winton's descriptions of changing seas and changing seasons are outstanding. His insights into what motivates people like the bitter Eva or the profoundly irresponsible Sando disclose unsettling ethical implications with a sure hand." Sydney Morning Herald

Winton, Tim

Dirt music; a novel. Scribner 2002 411p $26

ISBN 0-7432-2802-2

LC 2002-17583

First published 2001 in Australia

"As well as offering nuanced portraits of three very different characters, [this] is a cracking page-turner which deftly splices together separate narrative threads without ever losing its headlong momentum. . . . Mr Winton comes from Western Australia, a vast state of exceptional natural beauty. . . . He brilliantly conjures its hostile desert spaces and its magnificent coastline. His characters, like the landscape they inhabit, are by turns callous and poetic, vulgar and seductive." Economist

Wiprud, Brian M.

Ringer. Minotaur Books 2011 338p $26.99

ISBN 978-0-312-60189-8; 0-312-60189-1

LC 2011-08724

Sequel to: Feelers (2009)

Morty Martinez pursues a sacred ring currently in the possession of a New York City billionaire, a situation that traps him between the billionaire and his tabloid-prone stepdaughter, all before Morty's sensational murder trial in Mexico.

"Told from Martinez's jail cell the night before he's to be executed, this relentlessly amusing novel is powered by a cast of decidedly quirky characters and its idiosyncratic narrator's frequent digressions (like his defense of breast implants). Fans of the comic crime fiction of Donald E. Westlake and Charles Willeford will find a lot to like." Publ Wkly

Wiseman, Beth

Plain paradise; a Daughters of the promise novel. Beth Wiseman. Thomas Nelson 2010 vi, 313p.p (soft cover) $15.99

ISBN 9781595548238

LC 2009052637

This novel tells the story of "Linda . . . [whose] Amish life seemed like paradise. Until she found out her family had been hiding a secret since the day of her birth. Josie was just a frightened teenager when she left her baby in the care of an Old Order Amish couple in Lancaster County. Since then, seventeen years have passed and while much has changed, one thing hasn't. Josie still longs to reconnect with her daughter Linda. But Linda is unaware of Josie--and living an idyllic life within the Amish community. The bishop's grandson, Stephen, is courting her and she hopes that he will propose soon. When her birth mother comes to Paradise, Linda finds herself unexpectedly drawn to Josie's world." (Publisher's note)

Witchel, Alex

The **spare** wife. Alfred A. Knopf 2008 286p $23.95

ISBN 978-1-4000-4149-7; 1-4000-4149-X

LC 2007-40320

"Former model, widow, and sometime lawyer Ponce Morris (named for Ponce de León and his fountain of youth) has made it perfectly clear that she isn't interested in sex and romance anymore. So her girlfriends don't mind when she acts as a 'spare wife' and attends events and such with their husbands. The wives benefit from Ponce's friendship, too, in the form of girl talk and shopping expositions. But when Babette, a young aspiring writer and editorial assistant, discovers that Ponce is having an affair with one of the husbands, she finds herself with a scoop that could kick her writing career into high gear." Libr J

Wittenborn, Dirk

Pharmakon. Viking 2008 406p $25.95

ISBN 978-0-670-01942-7; 0-670-01942-9

LC 2007-40456

This is a "smart, eccentric coming-of-age story about an entire culture's maturation process, not just one about the workings of a single family. And Mr. Wittenborn is able to channel a lifetime's worth of psychiatric symptoms into one improbably universal story." N Y Times (Late N Y Ed)

Wodehouse, P. G.

The **code** of the Woosters. Doubleday, Doran 1938 298p

"It was only the fact that Jeeves belonged to an exclusive club of gentlemen's personal gentlemen, where all the secrets in the lives of employers were filed for reference, that saved Bertie Wooster when the disappearance of an eighteenth-century silver cows-creamer threatened to land him in jail. Two rival collectors who coveted the piece of silver, and two pairs of bickering lovers, made Bertie's life a burden until Jeeves unearthed evidence that was a weapon." Booklist

Wodehouse, P. G.

The **inimitable** Jeeves; Autograph ed; British Bk. Centre 1956 192p

First published 1923 in the United Kingdom

The resourceful valet again takes command of a typical Wodehouse situation

Wodehouse, P. G.

Tales from the Drones Club. International Polygonics 1991 352p

LC 91-8386

First published 1982 in the United Kingdom

Contents: Fate; Tried in the furnace; Trouble down at Tudsleigh; The amazing hat mystery; Goodbye to all cats; The luck of the Stiffhams; Noblesse oblige; Uncle Fred flits by; The masked troubadour; All's well with Bingo; Bingo and the Peke crisis; The editor regrets; Sonny boy; The shadow passes; Bramley is so bracing; The fat of the land; The word in season; Leave it to Algy; Oofy, Freddie and the beef trust; Bingo bans the bomb; Stylish stouts

Wodehouse, P. G.

A **Wodehouse** bestiary; edited and with a preface by D.R. Bensen; foreword by Howard Phipps, Jr. Ticknor & Fields 1985 329p

LC 85-7999

"An anthology of tales featuring animals of all sorts wreaking havoc in the lives of Bertie Wooster, the indomitable Jeeves, Mr. Muliner's various relations, and other familiar characters from the madcap Wodehousian world. The numerous mishaps, involving snakes, pigs, gorillas, swans, dogs, and cats, prove as amusing as ever." Booklist

Wodehouse, P. G.

★ The **world** of Jeeves. Harper & Row 1988 654p

LC 88-45072

Contents: Jeeves takes charge; Jeeves in the springtime; Scoring off Jeeves; Sir Roderick comes to lunch; Aunt Agatha takes the count; The artistic career of Corky; Jeeves and Chump Cyril; Jeeves and the unbidden guest; Jeeves and the hard-boiled egg; The aunt and the sluggard; Comrade Bingo; The great sermon handicap; The purity of the turf; The metropolitan touch; The delayed exit of Claude and Eustace; Bingo and the little woman; The rummy affair of Old Biffy; Without the option; Fixing it for Freddie; Clustering round young Bingo; Jeeves and the impending doom; The inferiority complex of Old Sippy; Jeeves and the Yule-tide spirit; Jeeves and the song of songs; Episode of the dog Mcintosh; The spot of art; Jeeves and the kid Clementina; The love that purifies; Jeeves and the old school chum; Indian summer of an uncle; The ordeal of young Tuppy; Bertie changes his mind; Jeeves makes an omelette; Jeeves and the greasy bird

First published 1967 in the United Kingdom

Wolcott, James

The **catsitters**; a novel. HarperCollins Pubs. 2001 314p $25

ISBN 0-06-019414-6

LC 00-50635

"This novel has so many hilarious twists and turns that it keeps even the most jaded romance reader turning the pages. Wolcott expertly blends his careening plot with wit, sarcasm, and insight." Libr J

Wolf, Christa, 1929-2011

City of angels or; The overcoat of Dr. Freud. Christa Wolf; translated from the German by Damion Searls. Farrar, Straus and Giroux 2013 336 p. (alk. paper) $27

ISBN 0374269351; 9780374269357

LC 2012018515

This novel is the last from the late author Christa Wolf, winner of the first Deutscher Bücherpress for lifetime achievement. The book "draws on an unsettling discovery she made while perusing her Stasi files: she herself had informed in the early 1960s--something she recalled not at all." (Library Journal)

Wolf, Joan

This scarlet cord; Joan Wolf. Thomas Nelson 2012 307 p. (trade paper) $15.99

ISBN 1595548777; 9781595548771

LC 2012010908

This novel, by Joan Wolf, revisits the Old Testament story of Rahab. "Rahab is the youngest daughter of a Canaanite farmer, taken to Jericho . . . so her father can find her a wealthy spouse. Sala, the Israelite boy who had once saved her from being kidnapped, is also in Jericho. When the two young people meet again they admit their love for one another, but . . . [i]t is only when the One True God of Israel comes into Rahab's life . . . that she and Sala can come together." (Publisher's note)

Wolfe, Gene

★ The best of Gene Wolfe; a definitive retrospective of his finest short fiction. Tor 2009 478p $27.95

ISBN 9780765321350; 0-7653-2135-1

LC 2009-12889

This "is a highly flattering career retrospective of a post-modern fabulist disguised as a mild-mannered SF writer." Publ Wkly

Wolfe, Gene

★ Castleview. Doherty Assocs. 1990 278p

LC 89-25712

"The inhabitants of the small town of Castleview, in a 'forgotten and countrified corner of upstate Illinois,' have grown accustomed to glimpsing a 'mirage' that resembles a medieval castle suspended in air. With the arrival in town of Will E. Shields, who has just bought a local automobile dealership, mysteries multiply like goose bumps. The town's hospital and funeral home fill with the victims of peculiar accidents, unsavory strangers knock on doors or peer through windows or suddenly appear on rainy highways riding horses with too many legs—and you just know Castleview is in for a major crisis." N Y Times Book Rev

Wolfe's "deceptively simple prose masks a wealth of complexity." Libr J

Wolfe, Gene

The **Citadel** of the Autarch. Timescape Bks. 1983 317p (Book of the new Sun)

LC 82-5964

"Wolfe plays with the language like a master wordsmith, yet never loses control of the multi-layered story he's weaving. His style is paradoxically both baroque and simple—the lush beauty of the words never renders the tale impenetrable." Best Sellers

Wolfe, Gene

The **claw** of the conciliator. Timescape Bks. 1981 303p (Book of the new Sun)

LC 80-20569

In this second volume of the series "Severian, a journeyman torturer, struggles to return the magical Claw of the Conciliator to its guardians. His quest is delayed when men under the leadership of the bandit Vodalus capture him to prevent the execution of a comrade. Severian and his companion Jonas win their freedom by agreeing to carry a message to an agent of Vodalus' at the Castle Absolute, seat of power for the ruling Autarch. Severian has no intention of carrying the promise through, in spite of his admiration for Vodalus. His intention to find his lover and continue his personal quest suffers a temporary setback at the hands of Castle guards." West Coast Rev Books

Followed by The sword of the Lictor

Wolfe, Gene

An **evil** guest. Tor 2008 304p $25.95

ISBN 978-0-7653-2133-6; 0-7653-2133-5

LC 2008-28716

The novel is set in the "future, but despite the holographic video broadcasts and intergalactic space transports, the world feels like that of the 1930s, complete with tough-talking cops, wily dames and shady operatives; it's more pulp thriller than Space Age adventure. Though this results in a future with some oddly old-fashioned gender roles, it allows Wolfe to mine his many sources and inspirations—from the detective novels of Raymond Chandler to the fantastic tales of H.P. Lovecraft—to dazzling effect." BookPage

Wolfe, Gene

Home fires. Tor 2011 304p $24.99

ISBN 978-0-7653-2818-2; 0-7653-2818-6

LC 2010-36106

"With complications involving spies, murderers, cyborgs and pirates, Wolfe cross-examines his characters with a subtle, intelligent series of psychological and logical challenges. A somber, almost brooding tone permeates this compelling work from one of the genre's grandmasters." Kirkus

Wolfe, Gene

Pirate freedom. Tor 2007 320p il $24.95

ISBN 978-0-7653-1878-7; 0-7653-1878-4

LC 2007-14348

"The one issue Wolfe tap-dances around is slavery. Chris treats slaves as fellow men and frees them whenever possible without anything more than the occasional light question from others. Wolfe's writing is reminiscent of Carol Emshwiller. . . . There's the same concrete level of detail mixed with an occasionally hazy sense of time and events.

The novel is as simple as Wolfe's straightforward, lean prose and easily pulls the reader through to an enjoyable circular ending." BookPage

Wolfe, Gene

The **shadow** of the torturer. Simon & Schuster 1980 303p (Book of the new Sun)

LC 79-22371

"The book combines elements of fantasy and sf, and the slow pacing is balanced by the excellent characterization and the richly detailed, thoroughly compelling future world." Booklist

Followed by The claw of the conciliator

Wolfe, Gene

The **sorcerer's** house. Tor 2010 302p $24.99

ISBN 978-0-7653-2458-0; 0-7653-2458-X

LC 2009-40726

"Early on in the novel, Wolfe hints at a great darkness, and a world of tremendous power that may destroy Bax if he doesn't master it — but there's very little darkness in this book after the first hundred pages or so. It's almost as if Wolfe couldn't bear to have anything unpleasant happen to his main character, whose good fortune keeps getting better and better. It's a remarkably sunny version of fantasy literature, and though the novel runs out of narrative steam towards the end, by that point you're already drawn in by Wolfe's prodigious invention." io9

Wolfe, Gene

The **sword** of the Lictor. Timescape Bks. 1981 302p (Book of the new Sun)

LC 81-9427

In this third volume of the series "Severian, the torturer demoted to executioner, has reached Thrax, city of his exile, only to find that he can no longer do his work. He lets a prisoner escape rather than kill her (his original crime was to offer a prisoner the escape of death) and flees to the mountains. He meets the Alzabo, a terrifying creature in whom those eaten seem to live on, adopts a son and loses him, fights a revivified tyrant of the past and wins, helps the people of the floating islands, meets aliens and learns something of their true nature. The magical jewel called the Claw of the Conciliator is smashed, but Severian finds its essential heart, which is indeed a claw." Publ Wkly

Followed by The Citadel of the Autarch

Wolfe, Gene

The **Urth** of the new sun. Doherty Assocs. 1987 372p (Book of the new Sun)

LC 87-50478

For all its obvious unity, the book also has a strongly picaresque quality, with many episodes and characters developed as lovingly and skillfully as Wolfe can manage—which is very well indeed." Booklist

Wolfe, Inger Ash

The **calling**. Harcourt 2008 371p $24

ISBN 978-0-15-101347-0

LC 2007-29290

This mystery "opens with the grisly slaying of an elderly cancer sufferer in Port Dundas, a remote Ontario town that has gone years without a homicide. The murder hits at a particularly tough time for 61-year-old Det. Insp. Hazel Micallef, who's struggling to come to terms with a surprise divorce and battles daily with her acerbic 87-year-old mother. A serious staff shortage and an injured back add to the department commander's woes. A second, even more disturbing killing raises the ante for Micallef, who's already doubtful she can solve the first case. As Micallef marshals her forces, Wolfe fans the already high suspense by cutting between them and their elusive quarry. With the body count climbing, the detective puts herself increasingly at risk in a desperate attempt to foil the grand, demented plan that the killer regards as a mission." Publ Wkly

"An excellent literary thriller, both riveting and precise. The ending is a shocker." Libr J

Wolfe, Inger Ash

The **taken**. Houghton Mifflin Harcourt 2010 415p $25

ISBN 978-0-15-101353-1; 0-15-101353-5

LC 2010-05774

A "police procedural featuring Canadian Det. Insp. Hazel Micallef . . . . A bizarre case brings Micallef, who depends on her ex-husband and his new wife as she recovers from a serious back injury suffered in the line of duty, back into action sooner than planned. A body fishermen dredge up from the bottom of a lake in Port Dundas, Ont., turns out just to be a mannequin, but numbers on the dummy lead Micallef to a Web site streaming video that appears to show a man being tortured by his abductor. In a frantic search for clues, Micallef concludes that the kidnapping is somehow linked to a fictional story being run in installments in the local newspaper. It's a testament to Wolfe's storytelling gifts that her reveal of the criminal's identity about midway through heightens rather than diminishes the tension." Publ Wkly

Wolfe, Thomas

The **complete** short stories of Thomas Wolfe; edited by Francis E. Skipp; foreword by James Dickey. Scribner 1987 xxix, 621p hardcover o.p. pa $27.50

ISBN 0-02-040891-9 pa

LC 86-13782

"All 58 of Wolfe's short stories . . . have been edited by Skipp in a way that represents what Wolfe himself may have wanted his audience to read." Booklist

Wolfe, Thomas

★ **Look** homeward, angel; a story of the buried life. with an introduction by Maxwell E. Perkins. Scribner 563p $45; pa $14

ISBN 0-684-15158-8; 0-684-80443-3 pa

First published 1929

This novel, autobiographical in character, "describes the childhood and youth of Eugene Gant in the town of Altamont, state of Catawba (said to be Asheville, North Carolina). As Gant grows up, he becomes aware of the relations among his family, meets the eccentric people of the town, goes to college, discovers literature and ideas, has his first love affairs, and at last sets out alone on a mystic and romantic 'pilgrimage.'" Reader's Ency. 4th edition

Followed by Of time and the river (1935)

Wolfe, Thomas

O lost; a story of the buried life. text established by Arlyn and Matthew J. Bruccoli. Centenary ed; University of S.C. Press 2000 xli, 694p il $34.95

ISBN 1-57003-369-2

LC 00-9503

"The reinsertion of expurgated material puts the marrow back in the novel's bones, making for a richer reading experience." Libr J

Wolfe, Thomas

★ Of time and the river; a legend of man's hunger in his youth. Scribner 912p $35

ISBN 0-684-14739-4

First published 1935

In this sequel to Look homeward, angel, "Eugene Gant, the hero, spends two years as a graduate student at Harvard, returns home for the dramatic death of his father, and teaches literature in New York City at the 'School for Utility Culture' (New York University). Eventually he tours France, returning home financially and emotionally exhausted." Reader's Ency. 4th edition

Wolfe, Thomas

★ The **web** and the rock. Harper 1939 695p

"Wolfe's large scheme has the scope, massive detail and sense of space and time of an epic structure, but also the redundancy of its cyclic conception. The interest lies with the accurate dialogues, realistic descriptions and passages of poetic rhetoric sometimes of considerable power." Penguin Companion to Am Lit

Followed by You can't go home again

Wolfe, Thomas

★ **You** can't go home again. Harper 1940 743p

This sequel to The web and the rock "deals with George's life after his return to the U.S.: his continued unsatisfactory romance; his success in writing novels reminiscent of Wolfe's own; his kindly relation and later dissatisfaction with an internationally famous but disillusioned novelist and with his editor, who fatalistically accepts the sickness of civilization; his unsuccessful attempt to return to the roots of his hometown, whose morality has become shoddy during the prosperous decade of the '20s; and his horrid discovery of the destruction of the Germany he had once loved." Oxford Companion to Am Lit. 6th edition

Wolfe, Tom, 1931-

★ **Back** to blood; a novel. Tom Wolfe. Little, Brown 2012 x, 704 p.p $30

ISBN 0316036315; 9780316036313; 9780316221795; 9780316224246

LC 2012019545

This novel by Tom Wolfe focuses on characters living in Miami, Florida including "the Cuban mayor, the black police chief, a . . . young journalist and his Yale-marinated editor; . . . a billionaire porn addict, crack dealers in the 'hoods, 'de-skilled' conceptual artists at the Miami Art Basel Fair, 'spectators' at the annual Biscayne Bay regatta looking only for that night's orgy, yenta-heavy ex-New Yorkers at an 'Active Adult' condo, and a nest of shady Russians." (Publisher's note)

"Wolfe is back to some old tricks, including an ever-shifting, sometimes untrustworthy point of view, dizzying pans from one actor to another and rat-a-tat prose...a welcome pleasure from an old master and the best from his pen in a long while." Kirkus

Wolfe, Tom, 1931-

★ The **bonfire** of the vanities. Farrar, Straus & Giroux 1987 659p $25

ISBN 0-374-11534-6

LC 87-17691

In this book, "on a clandestine date with his mistress one night, top Wall Street investment banker and snobbish WASP Sherman McCoy misses his turn on the thruway and gets lost in the South Bronx; his Mercedes hits and seriously injures a young black man. The incident is inflated by a manipulative black leader, a district attorney seeking reelection and a sleazy tabloid reporter into a full-blown scandal. . . . The book . . . stand[s] as a[n] . . . evocation of New York's class, racial and political structure in the 1980s." (Publishers Weekly)

"The novel relates the fall of Sherman McCoy, an investment banker making a million a year who seems blind to everything except appearances, sex and money. He lives in the middle of New York City without knowing New York City. He seems barely to know his decorative wife, his decorative daughter or his libidinous mistress, to say nothing of himself. He's all surface is Sherman, and when he blunders off the expressway into the welfare jungle of the South Bronx in his $48,000 Mercedes, into the biggest trouble of his heretofore charmed life, he is without reserves of experience, imagination or moral awareness with which to guide himself." N Y Times Book Rev

Wolfe, Tom

I am Charlotte Simmons. Farrar, Straus and Giroux 2004 676p $28.95

ISBN 0-374-28158-0

LC 2004-47131

Dupont University-the Olympian halls of learning housing the cream of America's youth, the roseate Gothic spires and manicured lawns suffused with tradition . . . Or so it appears to beautiful, brilliant Charlotte Simmons, a sheltered freshman from North Carolina. But Charlotte soon learns, to her mounting dismay, that for the uppercrust coeds of Dupont, sex, Cool, and kegs trump academic achievement every time. As Charlotte encounters Dupont's privileged elite . . . she gains a new, revelatory sense of her own power, that of her difference and of her very innocence, but little does she realize that she will act as a catalyst in all of their lives." Publisher's note

Wolfe, Tom

★ A **man** in full; a novel. Farrar, Straus & Giroux 1998 742p $28.95

ISBN 0-374-27032-5

LC 98-29842

"Among all the animal appetites that are slaked or comically thwarted during the novel there appears one new to Wolfe's fiction. For all their affluence, or their pained lack of same, his chief characters hunger for a code of conduct or a framework of beliefs that will make sense of their lives right now, a blink before the millennium. At its heart, A Man in Full is a cliff-hanging morality tale." Time

Wolff, Isabel

A **vintage** affair; a novel. Bantam Books 2010 346p pa $15; $25

ISBN 055338662X; 0553807838; 9780553386622 pa; 9780553807837

LC 2010-1830

"Vintage clothing lover Phoebe opens her own resale boutique in London's Blackheath neighborhood, meeting much success. She's grateful for the hustle and bustle the shop provides, because it lets her forget her guilt over the death of her best childhood friend, not to mention that she just left her fiancé at the altar. When the elderly Mrs. Bell contracts with Phoebe to sell her entire wardrobe, Phoebe finds herself reeled in by the story of Mrs. Bell's childhood friend, thought lost in the horrors of the Holocaust. Additionally, our heroine's got not one but two new suitors keeping her on her toes." Libr J

"Innocent, tidy and simple escapism, with frocks." Kirkus

Wolff, Maritta M.

Sudden rain; [by] Maritta Wolff. Scribner 2005 434p $26

ISBN 0-7432-5482-1

LC 2004-52149

"Written in the prefeminist early 1970s, this novel features an Alice Adams like cast of well-heeled West Coast characters. The men go off to work, have casual affairs, and come home for cocktail hour expecting their pampered wives to tolerate their indiscretions and look after their homes and children without complaint. The leisurely plot deals with four interconnected couples whose relationships undergo dramatic changes as a Santa Ana wind blows through town. During a four-day weekend of drinking, smoking, and conversation, a long-estranged father and daughter come together, an aerospace engineer resolves to end his fractious marriage and marry his longtime mistress, and a newly divorced young couple attempt a reconciliation. When Wolff . . . died in 2002, her husband found this manuscript in their refrigerator, and it thaws out like a well-preserved artifact." Libr J

Wolff, Rebecca

The **beginners**. Riverhead Books 2011 291p $26.95

ISBN 978-1-59448-799-6; 1-59448-799-5

LC 2011-02768

"Ginger, the heroine of the novel, is a bookish 15-year-old girl whose life thus far has been circumscribed by her family, her job at a local restaurant and hanging out with her sole close friend, Cherry. Her hometown of Wick, Mass., is unassuming as well, though it has hints of a dark history relating to the Salem witch trials. Arriving to break Ginger out of her just-so existence are Theo and Raquel Motherwell, who charm her with their big-city sophistication, wit and candor about sex. That last part is especially important: This is ultimately a book about sexual awakening (the title derives from a virgin-themed porn mag Ginger discovers called The Beginner), but Wolff's prose is deliberately stripped of sensuousness, striking a grim, gothic tone instead. (As it happens, Ginger is a fan of Poe and Franken-

stein.) The writing is engaging, simple and sometimes pleasantly cryptic." Kirkus

Wolff, Tobias

★ **Old** school; a novel. Knopf 2003 195p $22

ISBN 0-375-40146-6

LC 2003-52930

"A fine offering, manly in spirit and style . . . Wolff displays exceptional skill in capturing the small sights and sensations that evoke the whole rarefied world he's taking us back to." Atl Mon (1993)

Wolff, Tobias

Our story begins; new and selected stories. Alfred A. Knopf 2008 379p $26.95

ISBN 978-1-4000-4459-7

LC 2007-44262

"It does not seem coincidental that Wolff's most protean narratives draw heavily upon his autobiographical experiences. Wolff, at his best, is truly a novelist of himself. His feats of self-invention offer a compelling rebuttal both to the fabulists whose stories fall so short of reality that they have to borrow the truth guarantee of memoir—if the lies rang truer, they could be published as fiction—and to those who denounce the faking of memoir as some sort of heinous crime, rather than the failed act of literature it is." Slate

Wolitzer, Hilma

★ **Hearts**. Farrar, Straus & Giroux 1980 342p

LC 80-18556

"This is a comedy about the heart-wrenching process of growth; it is written with great skill and no condescension. Few readers will fail to be moved." New Repub

Wolitzer, Hilma

Summer reading; a novel. Ballantine Books 2007 251p $24.95

ISBN 978-0-345-48586-1; 0-345-48586-6

LC 2006-35771

"Maintaining three perspectives throughout a comparatively short book without labored or slick effect is no mean feat. But once she gets things up and running, Wolitzer accomplishes it with unforced smoothness." N Y Times Book Rev

Wolitzer, Hilma

Tunnel of love. HarperCollins Pubs. 1994 376p

LC 93-51064

"Linda Reismann is a 24-year-old widow, saddled with an unborn child and teenage Robin, the daughter of her former husband. She travels from Newark to Los Angeles looking for a new start. An aging liquor-store owner hires her, proposes marriage, then is shot by a robber. A Latino dance instructor helps her get work at an upscale aerobic salon, but he turns out to be married. Cynthia Sterling, a wealthy soap-opera producer, hires her as a personal trainer; she supplies incredible medical care and moral support in the aftermath of a terrible car accident (caused by Robin), then files suit for custody of Linda's baby, calling her an unfit mother." Booklist

Wolitzer, Meg

The **Interestings**; Meg Wolitzer. Penguin Group USA 2013 480 p. (hardcover) $27.95

ISBN 1594488398; 9781594488399

LC 2012050294

In this novel, by Meg Wolitzer, "the summer that Nixon resigns, six teenagers at a summer camp for the arts become inseparable. Decades later the bond remains powerful, but so much else has changed. . . . Wolitzer follows these characters from the height of youth through middle age, as their talents, fortunes, and degrees of satisfaction diverge." (Publisher's note)

Wolitzer, Meg

The **position**; a novel. Meg Wolitzer. Scribner 2005 307p $24

ISBN 074326178X; 9780743261784

LC 2004056577

In this book, married couple "Paul and Roz Mellow . . . write a how-to sex book . . . that features illustrations of them in every imaginable position. The book becomes a runaway bestseller. When the children find the book and read it together, they're forever traumatized. . . . Flash forward 30 years: Paul and Roz are long divorced and remarried . . . [and] the grown children fumble through their lives on the eve of the publisher's reissue of the sex classic. The oldest, Holly, has settled into late motherhood after a lifetime of nomadic drug-taking; uptight Michael suffers from chronic depression; Dashiell, a gay Log Cabin Republican speechwriter, is diagnosed with Hodgkin's disease; and insecure late-bloomer Claudia returns to her Long Island hometown to finally figure out how to be a fully functioning adult." (Publishers Weekly)

Wolitzer, Meg

Surrender, Dorothy; a novel. Scribner 1999 224p $22

ISBN 0-684-84844-9

LC 98-47007

"Buried within this affecting novel is the troubling question of whether close friendships and close family ties can keep a person from finding romantic intimacy. Wolitzer's Sara didn't live long enough to explore that possibility; perhaps her survivors will be luckier." N Y Times Book Rev

Wolitzer, Meg

The **ten**-year nap. Riverhead Books 2008 351p $24.95

ISBN 978-1-59448-978-5; 1-59448-978-5

LC 2007-38759

This novel "tells the story of a group of formerly high-achieving women who forsook their careers when they had children. Ten years later, as the book's title implies, these mothers are waking up, and realizing that they are bored, directionless, worried about money, and perhaps overinvested in the lives of their husbands, their children and their friends. At their center is Amy Lamb, a former lawyer whose mother, a successful, and very happy, novelist, incessantly nudges her daughter about getting back to work. Amy considers returning to the law, but is crippled by the insecurity born of being out of the workforce, away from the technological innovations that have transformed her profession. Listless,

with a 10-year-old who is no longer dependent on her, Amy becomes embroiled in the entanglements of another mother — a working mother — whom she meets at her son's prep school. 'The Ten-Year Nap' is an engrossing, juicy read about girlfriends, marriages, jealousies and money. But it's also an occasionally brutal dissection of the habits and hang-ups of a rarefied group of mega-mamas." Salon.com

Wolitzer, Meg

The **uncoupling**. Riverhead Books 2011 271p $25.95

ISBN 978-1-59448-788-0; 1-59448-788-X

LC 2010039495

In this novel, "a high school rehearses 'Lysistrata,' and none of the women want to have sex anymore." (N Y Times Book Rev)

"The spell isn't the best fit for a writer of Wolitzer's comic gifts, and at first it seems like a long way to go to get to the novel's best scene, in which five female teachers ruefully remember the thrill of youthful physical love and its slow devolution into routine or obligation. The wincing recognition prompted by their comments is matched by the author's compassionate portraits of mostly decent, loving men unnerved by a sea change they can't comprehend or cope with. . . . A risky strategy pays off for a smart author whose work both amuses and hits home." Kirkus

Wolitzer, Meg

The **wife**; a novel. Scribner 2003 219p $23

ISBN 0-684-86940-3

LC 2002-36660

"Joan Castleman is en route to Finland to watch her husband, the renowned author Joe Castleman, win the Helsinki Prize when she decides to leave him. What follows is Joan's fascinating recollection of their marriage, his career, and her fading dreams. Telling her story in alternating segments, she starts in the 1950s with the beginning of the couple's professor-student relationship and continues through to the present, their 40 years of marriage stacking up unspoken regrets." Libr J

"Wolitzer's crisp pacing and dry wit carry us headlong into a devastating message about the price of love and fame." Publ Wkly

A **Woman's** eye; edited by Sara Paretsky. Delacorte Press 1991 448p

LC 90-28102

Stories included are: Lucky dip, by L. Cody; Murder without a text, by A. Cross; The puppet, by D. S. Davis; Death and diamonds, by S. Dunlap; Getting to know you, by A. Fraser; Full circle, by S. Grafton; Her good name, by C. G. Hart; That summer at Quichiquois, by D. B. Hughes; Discards, by F. Kellerman; Deborah's judgement, by M. Maron; Benny's space, by M. Muller; Where are you, Monica?, by M. A. Oliver; Settled score, by S. Paretsky; The scar, by N. Pickard; A man's home, by S. Singer; Looking for Thelma, by G. Slovo; A match made in hell, by J. Smith; The cutting edge, by M. Wallace; Ghost station, by C. Wheat; Theft of the poet, by B. Wilson; Kill the man for me, by M. Wings

Woo, Sung J.

Everything Asian. Thomas Dunne Books 2009 328p $23.95

ISBN 978-0-312-53885-9; 0-312-53885-5

LC 2008-37673

"A charming tale of family, community and the struggle for understanding. . . . Woo eschews immigrant clichés to focus on complicated familial relationships and surprising, sympathetic characters. Alternating between humor and melancholy, Woo's text strikes a true chord." Publ Wkly

Wood, Barbara

The **dreaming**; a novel of Australia. Random House 1991 453p

LC 90-52883

"After her parents tragic deaths in 1871, Joanna Drury leaves her native India for Australia, to unlock the secret past that haunted her mother, Lady Emily, and led to her mysterious, sudden death at age 40. In Melbourne, Joanna meets dashing and sensitive frontiersman Hugh Westbrook, and together they build Hugh's sheep station into a thriving enterprise, all the while looking for the source of the 'curse' on Joanna's family that took hold in an ancient time the aborigines call 'the dreaming.' . . . Wood's soft-edged prose, likable characters, and period details are always a big hit with her many fans." Booklist

Wood, Barbara

Perfect Harmony; a novel. Little, Brown 1998 429p $23.95

ISBN 0-316-81653-1

LC 97-37623

"Charlotte Lee is the head of Harmony, a major player in the international herbal-medicine industry. Charlotte has taken the ancient Chinese remedies once concocted in her grandmother's kitchen and turned them into a multimillion-dollar business. But now three people have died after taking Harmony products, and when Charlotte receives a series of threatening e-mail messages, it's clear someone is out to ruin the company. Enter Jonathan Sutherland former FBI agent, computer whiz, and—coincidentally—the man Charlotte has loved since she was a teenager." Booklist

Wood, Barbara

★ **Vital** signs. Doubleday 1985 326p

LC 84-13639

"Wood's expert knowledge of medicine and her deft interplay of plot and character make this a richly textured and quite credible story that is delightfully unpredictable from the first page through the last." Booklist

Wood, Summer

Wrecker; a novel. Bloomsbury 2010 290p $20

ISBN 978-1-608-19280-9; 1-608-19280-6

LC 2010-20824

"It's June of 1965 when Wrecker enters the world. The war is raging in Vietnam, San Francisco is tripping toward flower power, and Lisa Fay, Wrecker's birth mother, is knocked nearly sideways by life as a single parent in a city she can barely manage to navigate on her own. Three years later, she's in prison, and Wrecker is left to bounce around in the system before he's shipped off to live with distant relatives in the wilds of Humboldt County, California. When he arrives he's scared and angry, exploding at the least thing, and quick to flee. Wrecker is the story of this boy and the motley group of isolated eccentrics who come together to raise him and become a family along the way." Publisher's note

Wood "moves her characters gracefully through trying times, both cultural and personal." Kirkus

Wooding, Chris

Retribution falls; Chris Wooding. Ballantine Books 2011 461p. (pbk.: alk. paper) $16

ISBN 0345522516; 0345522583; 9780345522511; 9780345522580

LC 2010047793

In this book, "Dorian Frey's Ketty Jay is a hugely battered old freighter which just about runs. Frey keeps accepting jobs for himself and his crew in the hope of a big pay cheque. His current job turns out to be too good to be true. Suddenly Frey and his crew are running from the Navy Coalition and hired bounty hunters, as he is set up to take the fall after a freighter he is chasing explodes. Dorian Frey must outwit them all to prove his innocence and catch the real culprits." (Fantasy Book Review)

Woodrell, Daniel

★ The **death** of sweet mister; a novel. Putnam 2001 196p $23.95

ISBN 0-399-14751-9

LC 00-45972

Set in the Missouri hill country, this novel "presents one eventful summer in the life of Shug, a friendless, overweight 13-year-old living with his mother in the caretaker's cottage at the local cemetery. Glenda flirts incessantly, even with her son, who is becoming increasingly aware of her charms. Glenda's husband, Red (who may or may not be Shug's father), comes and goes, bringing money occasionally and strife a lot more often. . . . Shug's efforts to protect his mother from Red, from other admirers, and from her own rash decisions come to a head one hot summer night." Libr J

Woodrell, Daniel

★ **Give** us a kiss; a country noir. Holt & Co. 1996 237p

ISBN 0-8050-2298-8

LC 95-23458

A "novel set in the Missouri Ozarks, this is the . . . tale of tough-guy midlist novelist Doyle Redmond's transformation into the writer he only dreamed of being. Escaping from trendy California in his estranged wife's Volvo, Doyle reconnects with his roughneck heritage: gun-crazy grandpa and older brother, . . . marijuana farms, and a 50-year-old blood feud with the infamous Dolly clan." (Libr J)

The author creates a "vanishing South with an accuracy and understanding beyond any genre writer's capability. . . . If one is tempted to hear echoes of William Faulkner, Erskine Caldwell or Andrew Lytle in such themes, no matter. Mr. Woodrell isn't imitating any of them. He's only drawing from the same well they did, but with a different take, a different voice, a sharper sense of irony and satire." N Y Times Book Rev

Woodrell, Daniel

The **outlaw** album; stories. by Daniel Woodrell.
Little, Brown 2011 167p $24.99
ISBN 9780316057561; 0316057568

LC 2011-01107

This collection of short stories, by Dabniel Woodrell, presents "Ozarkian tales of those on the fringes of society. . . . A husband cruelly avenges the killing of his wife's pet; an injured rapist is cared for by a young girl, until she reaches her breaking point; a disturbed veteran of Iraq is murdered for his erratic behavior. . . . There is also the tenderness and loyalty of the vulnerable in these stories--between spouses, parents and children, siblings, and comrades in arms." (Publisher's note)

"'Once Boshell finally killed his neighbor he couldn't seem to quit killing him.' That's the opening line of The Outlaw Album, a collection of country-noir stories by the author of Winter's Bone, and it's also a warning: People don't just die in the book. Instead, they go insane (as a Vietnam vet does in 'Night Stand') or get viciously tortured (as a rapist does in 'Uncle')—and then they die. At times, Woodrell seems too eager to punish his characters. But in his best tales, the human desperation behind the violence is gripping. If anyone understands what motivates a man to keep shooting a corpse with a squirrel rifle, it's Woodrell." Entertainment Wkly

Woodrell, Daniel

Winter's bone; a novel. Little, Brown and Co. 2006 193p $22.95
ISBN 0-316-05755-X

LC 2005-17349

"Like his characters, and especially his teen characters, Woodrell's prose mixes tough and tender so thoroughly yet so delicately that we never taste even a hint of false bravado, on the one hand, or sentimentality, on the other. And Ree is one of those heroines whose courage and vulnerability are both irresistible and completely believable—think of not just Mattie Ross in True Grit but also Scout in To Kill a Mockingbird or even Eliza Naumann in Bee Season. One runs out of superlatives to describe Woodrell's fiction." Booklist

Woodruff, Lee

Those we love most; Lee Woodruff. Voice/Hyperion 2012 305 p. (hardcover) $26.99
ISBN 1401341780; 9781401341787

LC 2011049422

In this novel, by Lee Woodruff, "[l]ife is good for Maura Corrigan. . . . Then one day, in a single turn of fate, that entire world comes crashing down and everything that she thought she knew changes. . . . [The novel] chronicles how these . . . characters confront their choices, examine their mistakes, fight for their most valuable relationships, and ultimately find their way back to each other." (Publisher's note)

Woods, Sara

The **lie** direct. St. Martin's Press 1983 191p

LC 83-2982

London barrister/detective "Maitland agrees to defend John Ryder, on trial for treason, in spite of the overwhelming evidence against him. Dr. Boris Gollnow defects from Russia and identifies Ryder as the man who has been selling secrets to the Soviets. Winifred Paull, who claims Ryder has married her in a bigamous ceremony, confirms the identification and so do others. Only the accused's legal wife, Carol, and Antony believe in him. Maitland . . . turns detective and searches for proof of perjury by the witnesses for the prosecution. When Winifred is murdered and Carol is charged with that crime, the lawyer's problems magnify." Publ Wkly

Woods, Sara

Naked villainy. St. Martin's Press 1987 269p

LC 86-27925

This case featuring barrister-sleuth Antony Maitland, "begins with one of Maitland's friends telling him about cosmetics king Georges Letendre who, while visiting her sister in London, found a photograph of her naked on an altar at the climactic moment of a Black Mass. Letendre is subsequently murdered, and Maitland is asked to defend the chief suspect, the dead man's son. Maitland delves deeply into the occult and financial chicanery before putting together a brilliant Old Bailey performance." Booklist

Woods, Stuart

★ **Chiefs**. Norton 1981 427p
ISBN 0-03-901461-4

LC 80-27350

"Set in the small town of Delano, Ga., the novel tells of three Delano police chiefs—a farmer, a sadistic racist and a black—who must deal with the same case: the disappearances and murders of a number of white, teenaged boys over the course of 40 years. The mystery—readers will discern the killer's identity quite early—is played against the South in transition as local politics acquire national prominence when the son of the first chief becomes a candidate for governor and is eyed by the JFK White House as a potential running mate in the reelection campaign." Publ Wkly

Woods, Stuart

Choke; a novel. HarperCollins Pubs. 1995 280p

LC 95-37300

Chuck Chandler "teaches tennis at an exclusive club in Key West and meets his 'match' in gorgeous Claire Carras and her much older, wealthy husband, Harry. Chuck boats, wines, and dines with the Carrases, beds Claire, then finds himself accused of Harry's apparent murder. . . . Enter Tommy Sculley, formerly with the New York Police Department, now augmenting his pension working for the Key West police. Tommy is street-wise and intelligent, and he won't quit until he finds the truth." Libr J

"Mr. Woods knows how to keep the narrative pace in overdrive, and the twists of the plot, if not always surprising, are satisfactorily developed." N Y Times Book Rev

Woods, Stuart

Cold paradise. Putnam 2001 326p
ISBN 0-399-14736-5

LC 00-45974

When millionaire Thad Shames asks Stone Barrington "to go to Palm Beach to track down a mysterious woman he met at a party, Barrington sees the mission as little more than a wild goose chase. . . . To his surprise, it doesn't take long to find the woman, but it's an even bigger shock to him to discover that she is Allison Manning, now calling herself Liz, whom he helped when she was accused of killing her husband. . . . That husband is still very much alive, and Liz wants to pay him to leave her alone with some of the money from the insurance scam they pulled off together." Booklist

Woods, Stuart

Dead eyes. HarperCollins Pubs. 1994 303p

LC 93-14221

"Young Hollywood actress Chris Callaway is poised at the brink of stardom when her world collapses. Shortly after she begins receiving disquieting letters signed 'Admirer,' she is nearly blinded in a fall at the construction site of her new Malibu home. As Admirer becomes a menacing stalker, sending gifts and a gruesome photo and calling on the phone, Chris is stoutly guarded by her best friend and confidant, hairdresser Danny Devere. Also on duty is Beverly Hills police detective and stalker expert Jon Larsen. . . . Woods's style is lean and staccato, if unsubtle, and he's a pro at turning up the suspense." Publ Wkly

Woods, Stuart

Dead in the water; a novel. HarperCollins Pubs. 1997 325p

LC 97-14255

"City Attorney Stone Barrington is on the small island of St. Marks off the coast of Antigua for vacation. His live-in girlfriend is unable to join him. Since he is at loose ends, he attends the coroner's inquest into the death of Paul Manning, a famous mystery writer who was sailing across the Atlantic when, according to his wife, he died. She is arrested for murder because the island prosecutor has political ambitions of being the next prime minister, and a good murder case is just what he needs. Manning was heavily insured, and within a day or so, $15 million is paid to his estate and then transferred to a Cayman Island account. Barrington takes on Allison Manning's defense with the help of a local barrister." Libr J

"This is a cleverly plotted, witty crime caper with a dash of sex, a likably roughish hero, and a surprising twist at the finish." Booklist

Woods, Stuart

Dirt; a novel. HarperCollins Pubs. 1996 272p

LC 96-199910

"Dripping with name-dropping, haute couture and pricey playthings, and spiced with hormonal aerobics as Stone trolls the siren-infested waters of upscale Manhattan, the narrative rockets toward an abrupt but absolutely stunning denouement." Publ Wkly

Woods, Stuart

Dirty work. Putnam 2003 322p $25.95
ISBN 0-399-14982-1

LC 2002-32975

"Suave cop-turned-lawyer Stone Barrington is asked to hire someone to take photos of Lawrence Fortescue, the husband of a wealthy socialite, with a woman who is presumably his mistress. Stone hires the nephew of an old friend, who proves to be grossly incompetent when he falls through the skylight onto the man he's supposed to be photographing. Fortescu ends up dead, the supposed mistress disappears, and the photographer is charged with manslaughter. As Stone digs deeper, he discovers that Fortescue wasn't killed by the photographer's fall, but by an injection of poi-

son. Enter Carpenter, aka Felicity Devonshire, Stone's contact in British intelligence. Carpenter suspects the woman involved with Fortescue is actually . . . a trained assassin with a grudge." Booklist

Woods, Stuart

Grass roots; a novel. Simon & Schuster 1989 459p
ISBN 0-671-66739-4

LC 89-32198

"After years as chief of staff for a venerable Georgia senator, Will Lee decides to run for the seat himself when a stroke cripples his mentor. Standing in his way are an ambitious governor in the Democratic primary and, possibly, a far-right fundamentalist in the general election. In addition, Will must interrupt his campaign to serve as the defense lawyer in a controversial race-murder trial, while elsewhere, a dedicated ex-cop pursues the head of a Klan-like vigilante group that's been carrying out gangland-style killings." Publ Wkly

"A consummate storyteller, Woods . . . demonstrates his narrative ability by intertwining contemporary southern politics and the murder trial into a most satisfying tale." Libr J

Woods, Stuart

Heat. HarperCollins Pubs. 1994 346p
ISBN 0-06-017776-4

LC 94-4175

"Despite a few momentary lapses into banal predictability, Woods has concocted a high-octane story filled with nail-biting suspense and enough unusual twists to keep even experienced puzzle-solvers guessing." Booklist

Woods, Stuart

Imperfect strangers. HarperCollins Pubs. 1995 269p

LC 94-34506

"Woods' 'imperfect' strangers meet on an airplane. Sandy Kinsolving is an attractive, well-dressed man of means. He's flying from London to New York because his father-in-law, who's bankrolled his lucrative wine-selling business, has just had a stroke. Sandy and his wife are far from close, and he's concerned that his father-in-law's death will have unpleasant financial consequences. His seatmate, Peter Martindale, also a well-dressed man of means, is a gallery owner based in San Francisco. It seems that he and his wife are also on the outs, and he, too, stands to lose his livelihood. . . . Peter proposes that they murder each other's wives. The trick here is to complicate matters, and Woods succeeds admirably." Booklist

Woods, Stuart

Kisser. G. P. Putnam's Sons 2010 291p $25.95
ISBN 978-0-399-15611-3; 0-399-15611-9

LC 2009-36934

At the start of this Stone Barrington novel, "the handsome New York lawyer smoothly picks up Carrie Cox, an aspiring actress who's recently moved from Georgia to New York City, at Elaine's, his favorite Manhattan restaurant. . . . Barrington manages to shield Carrie from her ex-husband, protect young heiress Hildy Parsons from a con artist/drug dealer, and plot to take down Ponzi scammer Sig Larsen.

Too crafty to let Barrington sail unscathed through encounters with women or criminals, Woods devises plenty of snarls to provoke laughs and keep the action interesting in a series that excels at playing out male fantasies." Publ Wkly

Woods, Stuart

L.A. dead. Putnam 2000 338p

ISBN 0-399-14664-4

LC 00-28059

This Stone Barrington thriller "finds the lawyer/sleuth from New York back in Los Angeles on a murder case. . . . His ex-lover, Arrington Calder, stands accused of murdering her husband, movie star and renowned man-about-town Vance Calder, found dead of a gunshot wound in the couple's Bel Air mansion. Upon hearing the news, Barrington, in Italy for his imminent wedding to the lovely but unpredictable Dolce Bianchi, rushes to L.A. to take over Arrington's defense." Publ Wkly

Woods, Stuart

L.A. Times; a novel. HarperCollins Pubs. 1993 329p

LC 92-54724

"Vincente Michaele Callabrese works as a shakedown artist for the mob in New York City's Little Italy, but moviegoing is his passion. Early in the story, he changes his name to Michael Vincent and makes a break for L.A., where with the help of powerful studio head Leo Goldman he fulfills his dream of becoming a big-time producer. Vincent's cosa nostra connections keep in touch, particularly old pal Tommy Provenzano whose rise to power in New York parallels Vincent's in Hollywood. Eventually, Vincent's desire to bring a gentle turn-of-the-century novel to the screen leads him to employ the sorts of techniques and friends that served him in his mafia days." Publ Wkly

Woods, Stuart

Lucid intervals. G. P. Putnam's Sons 2010 291p $25.95

ISBN 978-0-399-15644-1; 0-399-15644-5

LC 2010-00527

This "Stone Barrington mystery features the charismatic lawyer juggling an unwanted new client and a hunt for a former British intelligence operative. Stone is less than thrilled when Herbie Fisher, the feckless nephew of his friend Bob Cantor, walks up to him at Elaine's and drops $1 million in his lap in exchange for representation. But Stone has bills to pay, so he helps Herbie with everything from a real-estate deal to a prenuptial agreement. But soon Stone has more pressing matters on his hands: Felicity Devonshire, a beautiful member of British intelligence, has need of his services, in and out of the bedroom. . . . Fans of Woods' long-running series will not be disappointed by this romp." Booklist

Woods, Stuart

New York dead. HarperCollins Pubs. 1991 303p

LC 90-56374

A mystery "set in Manhattan's Upper East Side, the stomping ground of Stone Barrington, a well-bred but unpretentious detective. . . . Late one evening, as Stone trudges home from Elaine's Restaurant, popular TV newscaster Sasha Nijinsky plummets 12 stories from her terrace and lands

on a heap of dirt 20 yards away from him—remarkably, still alive. Stone fails to apprehend the person who flees Sasha's penthouse and, after the ambulance carrying her collides with a fire truck, Sasha herself disappears. Despite the fact that no corpse is in evidence, the baffled NYPD eagerly pins a murder rap on Sasha's distraught lesbian lover. Stone refuses to accept his colleagues' pat solution." Publ Wkly

Woods, Stuart

Orchid Beach. HarperCollins Pubs. 1998 325p $25

ISBN 0-06-019181-3

LC 98-23628

"Army Sergeant Holly Barker has just lost a sexual-harassment case against Colonel Bruno, her former boss. . . . Fortunately, her father, a soon-to-retire master sergeant, knows Chet Marley, the chief of police in Orchid Beach, Florida. Chet is looking for a new deputy chief. It sounds good to Holly, so she packs her gear and sets off for Florida. But when she arrives, she steps into big trouble. The night before, Chet Marley and his best friend were murdered. Shocked at such brutality in peaceful-looking Orchid Beach, Holly sets out to find the killer, only to run into an elaborate conspiracy plot." Booklist

"The story gets extra bite from Holly's intriguing relationship with an inherited canine named Daisy, the clairvoyant Doberman that belonged to her mentor." Publ Wkly

Woods, Stuart

Palindrome. Harper & Row 1991 344p

ISBN 0-06-017911-2

LC 90-55587

"When Liz Barwick is beaten nearly to death by her steroid-crazed husband, Baker Ramsey, a star NFL running back, she quickly divorces him, takes a large cash settlement and disappears from public view. Liz, whose book of sports photographs has just been released, takes advantage of her publisher's offer to live in his cottage on an isolated private island off the Georgia coast. But when Ramsey goes on a murderous rampage, Liz's lawyer and publisher and his wife are among his victims. Meanwhile other events are unfolding on Cumberland Island, where Liz becomes involved with the Drummond family." Publ Wkly

Woods, Stuart

Reckless abandon. G.P. Putnam's Sons 2004 289p $25.95

ISBN 0-399-15151-6

LC 2003-64799

This thriller features cop-turned-lawyer Stone Barrington and Holly Barker, chief of the Orchid Beach, Florida, police department. "Holly's come to New York hot on the trail of Trini Rodriguez, a bad guy she thought she'd stabbed to death in an earlier adventure. He's currently wanted for (among other things) blowing up a dozen people by hiding bombs in the caskets of two of his earlier victims and detonating them at the funeral. But finding him won't be so simple: he's been placed in the FBI Witness Protection Program and is working with the Feds and the CIA to catch an Arab terrorist group trying to employ the Mafia in a money-laundering scheme. Shortly after Holly takes up residence in Stone's guest room, the two of them are hip deep in the dangerous case and likewise each other. . . . Cross-pollinating all these characters from various books makes for some heavyhanded background exposition at times, but readers with no previous experience will still enjoy this amusing, full-throttle sex and crime romp." Publ Wkly

Woods, Stuart

The **run**. HarperCollins Pubs. 2000 356p

ISBN 0-06-019187-2

Sequel to Grass roots (1989)

"Will and Kate Lee, now a Washington power couple, decide to go for broke in their service to the country. Will, a popular senator from Georgia, jumps into the race for the presidency, while Kate, a deputy director at the CIA, cheers him on. . . . The candidate's liberal leanings are anathema to a right-wing militia group from Idaho, whose leader, Zeke Tennant, tracks Will from one campaign stop to another with a duffel bag full of weapons. In a final showdown, Tennant makes one last assassination attempt." Publ Wkly

"A clever, well-constructed story of political ambition and behind-the-scenes skulduggery." Booklist

Woods, Stuart

Santa Fe rules. HarperCollins Pubs. 1992 303p

LC 91-58476

"You're a rich, successful Hollywood producer who awakens the morning before Thanksgiving in your Santa Fe home with no memory of the previous night. Ignoring your dog's attempts to get you to visit the guest wing of the house, you leave and fly your private plane to Los Angeles. But you never get there: a breakdown forces you to spend the holiday isolated in a small airport town. When you finally see the newspaper the next day, you read that the bodies of your wife, your business partner and a third man—assumed to be you—have been found in the guest room of the Santa Fe residence. . . . Wolf Willett decides to stay 'dead' for a while and finish work on his new film, then hires a top defense attorney and turns himself in." Publ Wkly

Woods, Stuart

The **short** forever. Putnam 2002 321p $24.95

ISBN 0-399-14868-X

LC 2001-48725

Mogul John Bartholomew hires Stone Barrington "to fly to London and persuade his niece, Erica, to leave her cocaine-smuggling boyfriend, Lance Cabot, and to make sure Lance winds up in jail. Dapper Stone charms Erica, who offers to set him up with her sister, Monica, and then introduces him to Lance. With help from two British investigators, Stone learns John Bartholomew is not who he seems." Publ Wkly

"Filling his story with enough twists and turns to dizzy even the most seasoned reader, Woods keeps the tension high until the last page." Booklist

Woods, Stuart

Short straw. G. P. Putnam's Sons 2006 289p $25.95

ISBN 0-399-15368-3

LC 2006-41643

When Santa Fe defense lawyer Ed Eagle "wakes up on the morning of his fiftieth birthday, he discovers his wife has left him and taken him for a cool million. The second shock Eagle receives is news that a local lawyer has blown

his brains out in the courthouse, after murdering his wife and children. The plot races off in two directions: with two edgy characters, an ex-LAPD detective and an Apache Indian tracker, whom Eagle hires to find his wife in Mexico; and with Eagle's efforts to clear a man wrongly charged, he believes, with a triple homicide. Woods keeps the wattage high as the two plots intersect, and Eagle finds himself more and more entangled in a deadly criminal scheme. The homicidal desperation of Eagle's wife and the dodginess of the men he sends after her keep the surprises coming." Booklist

Woods, Stuart

Swimming to Catalina; a novel. HarperCollins Pubs. 1998 311p

LC 97-51173

Former NYPD cop turned lawyer Stone "Barrington's former girlfriend Arrington has married Barrington's friend Vance Calder, Hollywood's hottest actor. Three months into the marriage, Arrington's been kidnapped, and Vance calls Barrington to beg for his help. Barrington comes to L.A. only to find a hornet's nest. . . . Despite the fact that this book is definitely politically incorrect and Barrington has apparently never heard of safe sex, it's a highly entertaining read that's chock-full of slam-bang action, fast cars, beautiful women, fine wine, and tart, tongue-in-cheek humor." Booklist

Woods, Stuart

Two-dollar bill. G.P. Putnam's Sons 2005 298p $25.95

ISBN 0-399-15251-2

LC 2004-60068

Stone Barrington "becomes involved with a loud-talking Texan improbably named Billy Bob Barnstormer. It isn't long before Stone regrets ever being introduced to Billy Bob, especially when he leaves a dead body in Stone's guest room. But that is only the beginning of a tale that finds Stone, along with his best friend, Dino Bacchetti, following a twisted trail as they attempt to capture Billy Bob, who, it turns out, is much more dangerous than Stone could ever have imagined. Narrator Roberts slips comfortably into his performance, bringing a nice, down-to-earth quality to his portrayal of Stone." Publ Wkly

Woods, Stuart

Worst fears realized. HarperCollins Pubs. 1999 332p $25

ISBN 0-06-019182-1

LC 98-52924

In this Stone Barrington adventure, "the Manhattan lawyer turned investigator faces an indictment for the murder of a woman he's just met. When other brutal murders quickly pile up—all women connected to him or his best friend, Dino Bacchetti of the 19th Precinct—Stone knows that one of a cop's worst fears has been realized: a con with a grudge is bent on vengeance. While trying to save the lives of the women he cares about, Stone struggles to track down the killer and head off a DA who's out to get him for murder." Libr J

Woods, Teri

Alibi; Teri Woods. Grand Central Pub. 2009 257 p.

ISBN 0446581690; 9780446581691

LC 2008048145

This book "introduces 22-year-old Daisy Fothergill, a naive African-American stripper. Daisy accepts $2,000 from an organized crime rep to provide an alibi for Bernard 'Nard' Guess after he shoots two thieves to death as well as a buddy by accident in a North Philly drug house. An innocent witness to the bloodbath identifies Nard to the police, but pays a fatal price. When Daisy arrives home to tell her mother, Abigail, of her windfall and finds Abigail dead of natural causes, she discovers the $2,000 barely covers funeral costs. Her life takes an even nastier turn once Daisy starts dating Reggie Carter, . . . who soon deserts her. Later, a pregnant Daisy flees to Murfreesboro, Tenn., to seek refuge with her aunt, but eventually she must return to Philly for a day of reckoning." (Publishers Wkly)

Woodward, Gerard

Letters from an unknown woman; a novel. Arcade Pub. 2011 339p $24.95

ISBN 978-1-61145-312-6; 1-61145-312-7

First published 2010 in the United Kingdom with title: Nourishment

The author "takes a unique approach to the hardships women faced during wartime, the impact of the war on the men who survived, and the ways in which the children who lived through it tried to make sense of their upended lives, turning a story about one family's struggles into a tale of self-discovery, overcoming despair, and finding one's rightful place in the world. Best of all is the ingenious use of Toby's salacious letters and Woodward's not-so-subtle indictment of commercial publishing." Publ Wkly

Woof, Emily

The **whole** wide beauty; a novel. W. W. Norton & Co. 2010 250p $23.95

ISBN 978-0-393-07658-5; 0-393-07658-X

LC 2010-05412

"David Freeman has brought his poetry foundation in the North of England to the brink of financial ruin through the same combination of idealism and extravagance that has made him beloved among artists and patrons. When he cajoles his wary daughter, Katherine, and his protégé, Stephen, into attending the foundation's all-important benefit one rainy night in London, the patterns of all three lives are disrupted. Katherine, a former dancer who has deliberately turned her back on words, hasn't the language for why her marriage no longer makes sense to her. Stephen is purportedly writing a much anticipated cycle of poems about his parents' flight from Poland, but in fact he is hopelessly blocked. Is sex the siren or the muse? As the novel's guilty lovers feverishly grapple with that question, we are gently reminded that beauty can spring from sublimation, too." New Yorker

Woolf, Virginia

Between the acts. Harcourt Brace & Co. 1941 219p

This novel "describes a pageant on English history, written and directed by Miss La Trobe, and its effects on the people who watch it. Most of the audience misunderstand it in various ways; a clergyman reduces its vision to a sermon. But, for a moment, Woolf implies art, has imposed order on the chaos of human life" Reader's Ency. 4th edition

Woolf, Virginia

The **complete** shorter fiction of Virginia Woolf; edited by Susan Dick. Harcourt Brace Jovanovich 1985 313p

"Woolf's 46 short stories demonstrate her fondness for experimenting with narrative forms and voices. Arranged chronologically, the pieces range from tales with traditional plot lines to denser interior monologues, and enable the reader to appreciate Woolf's development as a writer of fiction." Publ Wkly

Woolf, Virginia

Jacob's room. Harcourt Brace & Co. 1923 303p

First published 1922 in the United Kingdom

"The life story, character, and friends of Jacob Flanders are presented in a series of separate scenes and moments. The story of this sensitive, promising young man carries him from his childhood, through college at Cambridge, love affairs in London, and travels in Greece, to his death in the war. At the end, instead of describing his death, Virginia Woolf describes his empty room." Reader's Ency. 4th edition

Woolf, Virginia

★ **Mrs.** Dalloway. Knopf 1993 xxviii, 219p $16

ISBN 0-679-42042-8

LC 92-54300

A reissue of the title first published 1925 by Harcourt Brace & Co.

"In this stream-of-consciousness novel all action takes place on a single day. By probing the thoughts and memories of various characters, the author has encompassed several people's lives. Clarissa has a party planned for the evening and is thinking of her daughter's involvement with a religious fanatic. Also in her thoughts are old friends like Sally Seton, who drops by at the party, and Clarissa's former lover, Peter Walsh, who is drawn to Sally, much to Clarissa's chagrin. When a noted psychiatrist arrives late at the party because one of his patients, Septimus Smith, has committed suicide, Clarissa is affected, not because she knew the victim, but because suicide is tantamount to wastefulness." Shapiro. Fic for Youth. 3d edition

Woolf, Virginia

Orlando; a biography. Harcourt Brace & Co. 1928 333p il

"Orlando begins as a young Elizabethan nobleman and ends, three hundred years later, as a contemporary young woman, based on the author's friend Victoria Sackville-West. The novel contains a great deal of literary history and brilliant, ironic insights into the social history of the ages through which Orlando lives. Orlando starts life as a male poet and ends as an equally intense and able woman poet, in order to emphasize the author's belief that women are intellectually men's equals." Reader's Ency. 4th edition

Woolf, Virginia

★ **To** the lighthouse. Harcourt Brace & Co. 1927 310p $17; pa $9

ISBN 0-15-190737-4; 0-15-690739-9 pa

Arranged in three sections, the first "called 'The window,' describes a day during Mr. and Mrs. Ramsay's house party at their country home by the sea. Mr. Ramsay is a distinguished scholar . . . whose mind works rationally, heroically and rather icily. . . . The Ramsays have arranged to take a boat out to the lighthouse, the next morning, and their little son James is bitterly disappointed when a change in weather makes it impossible. The second section, called 'Time passes' describes the seasons and the house, unused and decaying, in the years after Mrs. Ramsay's death. In the third section, the 'Lighthouse,' Mr. Ramsay and his friends are back at the house. He takes the postponed trip to the lighthouse with his now 16-year-old son, who is at last able to communicate silently with him and forgive him for being different from his mother." Reader's Ency. 4th edition

Woolf, Virginia

The **voyage** out. Modern Lib. 2000 xliv, 473p $17.95

ISBN 0-679-64028-2

LC 99-54259

First published 1915 in the United Kingdom; first United States edition 1920 by Harcourt Brace & Co.

"The story concerns a young woman of 24, Rachel Vinrace, an innocent, 'unlicked' girl who voyages to South America on board her father's ship, the Euphrosyne. Accompanying her are her aunt, Helen Ambrose, and uncle Ridley, together with an assortment of English characters whose social interaction is delicately observed. In South America Rachel meets a young Englishman, Terence Hewet, an aspiring writer working on his first novel. . . . He and Rachel fall in love and become engaged, determined to establish their future marriage on a new basis of equality. However, during an expedition Rachel contracts an unspecified disease and is confined to her bed with a fever. After a fortnight's illness she dies." Camb Guide to Lit in Engl

Woolf, Virginia

★ The **waves**. Harcourt Brace & Co. 1931 297p

"Highly original, unconventional, and poetic, it describes the characters, lives, and relationships of six persons living in England. The book is composed of interior monologues, spoken by the six characters in rotation, and of interludes describing the ascent and descent of the sun, the rise and fall of the waves, and the passing of the seasons. These natural cycles symbolize the progress of time, which carries the individual from birth to death." Reader's Ency. 4th edition

Woolf, Virginia

★ The **years**. Harcourt Brace & Co. 1937 435p

This novel "traces the history of a family, opening in 1880 as the children of Colonel and Mrs. Pargiter, living together in a large Victorian London house (later described by one of them as 'Hell') wait for their mother's death and the freedom it will bring; it takes them through several carefully dated and documented sections to the 'Present Day' of 1936, and a large family reunion, where two generations gather." Oxford Companion to Engl Lit. 6th edition

Worsley, Kate

She rises; by Kate Worsley. 1st U.S. ed. Bloomsbury USA 2013 432 p. (hardcover) $26

ISBN 1620400979; 9781620400975

LC 2012047087

In this novel, by Kate Worsley, "It is 1740 and Louise Fletcher . . . is offered work in the bustling naval port of Harwich. . . . Intertwined with her story is fifteen-year-old Luke's: He is . . . sent to sea on board the warship Essex. . . . Louise navigates her new life among the streets and crooked alleys of Harwich. . . . Luke, aching for the girl he left behind and determined to one day find his way back to her, embarks on a long and perilous journey across the ocean." (Publisher's note)

Wortham, Reavis

The **rock** hole; Reavis Z. Wortham. Poisoned Pen Press 2011 250p.

ISBN 9781590588864; 9781590588840

LC 2011920305

This book is set "[i]n 1964, [when] farmer and part-time Constable Ned Parker combine forces with John Washington, the almost mythical black deputy sheriff from nearby Paris, to track down a disturbed individual who is rapidly becoming a threat to the entire small Texas community of Center Springs. When Ned is summoned to a hot cornfield one morning to examine the remains of a tortured bird dog, he finds a dark presence in their quiet community. A farmer by trade, Ned is usually confident when it comes to handling moonshiners, drunks and domestic disputes. But the animal atrocities turn to murder, and the investigation spins beyond his abilities." (Publisher's note)

Wouk, Herman

★ The **Caine** mutiny; a novel of World War II. Doubleday 1951 494p

"The old American mine sweeper 'Caine' patrols the Pacific during World War II. The action shifts from the bridge of the ship to the wardroom and from scenes of petty tyranny on the part of the skipper to incidents of fierce action and heroism on the part of the men. Ensign Willie Keith is assigned to the ship and leads a mutiny against paranoid Captain Queeg, who is eventually brought to trial in a scene that poses the difficulty of weighing evidence to prove that the takeover by the men was justifiable." Shapiro. Fic for Youth. 3d edition

Wouk, Herman

A **hole** in Texas. Little, Brown 2004 278p $25

ISBN 0-316-52590-1

"Unassuming NASA physicist Guy Carpenter, who abandoned his hunt for a particle called the Higgs Boson, is suddenly in the limelight when the Chinese claim they've made the discovery." Libr J

"The plot is busy but secondary to Carpenter's banter and romantic escapades. Occasionally corny but also playful, thoughtful and passionate." Publ Wkly

Wouk, Herman

The **lawgiver**; a novel. Herman Wouk. Simon & Schuster 2012 234 p. (hardcover: alk. paper) $25.99

ISBN 1451699387; 9781451699388; 9781451699395;

9781451699401

LC 2012038205

2013 Sophie Brody Medal Honor Book

This novel by Herman Wouk focuses on "Margo Solovei, a brilliant young writer-director who has rejected her rabbinical father's strict Jewish upbringing to pursue a career in the arts. When an Australian multibillionaire promises to finance a movie about Moses if the script meets certain standards, Margo does everything she can to land the job. . . . Herman Wouk himself and his wife . . . , Betty Sarah . . . almost against their will, find themselves entangled in the Moses movie." (Publisher's note)

Includes bibliographical references

Wouk, Herman

★ **Marjorie** Morningstar. Doubleday 1955 565p

"The story of a middle-class Jewish girl who temporarily rejects her upbringing in her infatuation with the world of show business." Reader's Ency. 4th edition

Wouk, Herman

★ **War** and remembrance; a novel. Little, Brown 1978 1042p

ISBN 0-316-95501-9

LC 78-17746

Sequel to The winds of war

Wouk's "work is a journey of extraordinary emotional riches. Quantity in time becomes quality, movement becomes scope, and history becomes human yearning." NY Times Book Rev

Wouk, Herman

★ The **winds** of war; a novel. Little, Brown 1971 885p hardcover o.p. pa $16.99

ISBN 0-316-95266-8

"On the broadest of tapestries, Wouk weaves the effect of the preparation and the actual outbreak of World War II upon the family of Commander 'Pug' Henry. The affairs of the Henry family became intertwined with those of others, in such varying scenes as Washington, Berlin, Rome, London, and Moscow. . . . Despite the novel's breadth, the development of Henry's character as the middle-class military leader America needed in the 1940's is surprisingly credible." Choice

Another title featuring the Henry family is:
War and remembrance (1978)

Wray, John

Canaan's tongue. Alfred A. Knopf 2005 341p $25

ISBN 1-400-04086-8

LC 2004-64902

"Loosely based on the story of pre-Civil War slave stealer John Murrell, a.k.a. 'The Redeemer,' and his 'Mystic Clan' gang, this novel centers on the relationship between gang member Virgil Ball and charismatic leader Thaddeus Morelle. Ball, the son of a Kansas preacher, is simultaneously captivated and repelled by the criminal Morelle. Though he quickly becomes part of the gang's inner circle, he finds himself deeply conflicted about his involvement, a tension that will eventually lead to a violent act of expiation. Yet, in the end, even murder will not free him from the sway of a power older and deeper than Morelle. Wray has crafted an ambitious and strongly allegorical tale about the ability of belief to structure reality." Libr J

Wray, John

Lowboy. Farrar, Straus and Giroux 2009 258p $25

ISBN 978-0-374-19416-1; 0-374-19416-5

LC 2008-17921

"Will Heller, aka Lowboy, is a brilliant but troubled 16-year-old paranoid schizophrenic in New York City. Recently escaped from a mental hospital and obsessed with the notion that the world is about to be destroyed by global warming, he boards the subway one morning seeking to save the world in the only way he believes it can be-by having sex with a woman. He attempts to locate former girlfriend Emily Wallace, whom he has not seen since he pushed her onto the subway tracks a year earlier, the act that led to his stay in a mental hospital. Throughout his daylong adventures in the tunnels and streets, he is pursued by police detective Ali Lateef and his mother, Violet, a woman with her own secrets, who seek to bring him home before he harms himself or others." Libr J

Wright, Alexis

★ **Carpentaria**; a novel. Atria Books 2009 517p $26

ISBN 978-1-4165-9310-2; 1-4165-9310-1

First published 2006 in Australia

"This book is a sprawling, surreal anti-Odyssey in which time and space contract and expand and experience takes place in the Dreamtime, on the sea, and on and under the continent of Australia. . . . [This novel] will surely stand as a masterpiece of modern English-language literature." Libr J

Wright, Eric

The **last** hand. Thomas Dunne Bks. 2002 231p

ISBN 0-312-28330-X

LC 2001-51295

"As usual, Salter has an insight that proves the unraveling of the unconventional case. The real action, however, is internal, as Salter faces down his own fears. A sensitive end to a marvelous series." Booklist

Wright, John C.

The **golden** age; a romance of the far future. TOR Bks. 2002 336p

ISBN 0-312-84870-6

LC 2001-58468

In this future novel, the first of a projected two-volume saga, Phaethon Radamanthus, the 3,000 year-old scion of one of Earth's most powerful families begins a search for his lost memories

The author "chooses simple pulp-fiction plots to drive us through the technological complexities of Phaethon's world. The hero's quest to regain his lost memories, learn his true identity and reach the stars is undeniably compelling. As a result, having to wait for the next volume is frustrating. Wright's ornate and conceptually dense prose will not be to everyone's taste but, for those willing to be challenged, this is a rare and mind-blowing treat." Publ Wkly

Wright, Richard

Eight men. World Pub. 1961 250p

Contents: The man who was almost a man; The man who lived underground; Big black good man; The man who saw the flood; Man, God ain't like that . . .; The man who killed a shadow; The man who went to Chicago

Wright, Richard

★ Native son. Harper & Brothers 1940 359p

"Bigger Thomas is black. He is driven by anger, hate, and frustration, which are born out of the poverty that has dominated his life. When he gets a job with the Daltons, a white family, he is confused by their behavior and misinterprets their patronizing friendship. Tragedy follows when he accidentally kills Mary Dalton and escalates when Bigger murders his black girlfriend, Bessie." Shapiro. Fic for Youth. 3d edition

Wright, Richard

The outsider. Harper & Row 1953 440p

"Cross Damon, a black man who works in the Chicago post office, is caught in a subway accident but escapes without serious injury, though because of a mistaken identity his death is announced. He decides to take advantage of this error to start life anew and thus free himself of his entanglements with women and debts. He goes to New York to live under an assumed name and before long becomes enmeshed in the Communist party. By it he is used as a murderer, until he is himself killed by a Party member." Oxford Companion to Am Lit. 6th edition

Wright, Richard

Uncle Tom's children; five long stories. Harper & Row 1938 xxx, 384p hardcover o.p. pa $13.95

ISBN 0-06-058714-8 pa

The stories in this collection deal with conflicts between whites and blacks in the South.

Wright, Richard

Works. Library of Am. 1991 2v ea $35

ISBN 0-940450-66-6 v1; 0-940450-67-4 v2

LC 91-60540

This set contains the complete novels Native son; The outsider (1953); and Lawd today! (1963); the story collection Uncle Tom's children; and the memoir Black boy

Wright, Stephen

The Amalgamation Polka. Knopf 2006 323p $24.95

ISBN 0-679-45117-X

LC 2005-938382

"Wright is nothing if not ambitious, and the energy with which he throws himself into this world which bears only a passing resemblance to 19th-century America is a wonder to behold. The novel overflows with charlatans, whores, preachers, soldiers-of-fortune, madmen and even a handful of pirates, all of them declaiming, at the tops of their lungs, in language that often borders on free verse. The prose is unapologetically purple." Washington Post Book World

Wright, Stephen

★ Going native; a novel. Farrar, Straus & Giroux 1994 305p

ISBN 0-374-16490-8

LC 93-10944

This novel explores the "psyches of various distressed characters. The first belongs to an unhappy Chicago-area suburbanite whose husband, Wylie, an average-looking guy with an enigmatic and elusive temperament, disappears one evening while they're entertaining their friends Gerri and Tom H'anna. End of first chapter. Next, Wright thrusts us into the manic realm of Wylie's slovenly crack-head neighbors, who alternate bouts of rough sex with chaotic outings in a beat-up Ford Galaxy. This car reappears in the following chapter when its driver picks up a hitchhiker, who, incidentally, has just stabbed a trucker to death. When the driver introduces himself as Tom Hanna, we realize we've picked up Wylie's trail. He's heading West, and his trip is a grim one." Booklist

Wright, Stephen

★ Meditations in green. Scribner 1983 342p

ISBN 0-684-18010-3

LC 83-11666

"The narrative works several time frames and points of view into a mesmerizing mosaic of men in combat. . . . The absence of feasible political and military goals turns these soldiers in on themselves, and they take out their frustrations on each other rather than an intangible enemy. Exactly how and why this happens is made graphically clear in this superb [novel]." Quill Quire

Wrinkle, Margaret

Wash. Atlantic Monthly Press 2013 384 p. (hardcover) $25

ISBN 0802120660; 9780802120663

This historical novel focuses on "Revolutionary War veteran Gen. James Richardson and his slave, Wash. . . . Richardson had depended on slaves to 'carve out of nothing' a plantation on the Tennessee frontier. Though Richardson had wanted to leave slavery behind, he's driven by greed and still involved with it. . . . Imagining that the waves of settlers heading further west will need even more slaves, Richardson studs out Wash to neighboring plantations and fills the region with his visage." (Publishers Weekly)

Wroblewski, David

The story of Edgar Sawtelle; a novel. Ecco 2008 566p hardcover o.p. pa $16.99

ISBN 978-0-06-137422-7; 0-06-137422-9; 978-0-06-137423-4 pa; 0-06-137423-7 pa

"Set in rural nineteen-seventies Wisconsin, this loose retelling of Hamlet focusses on Edgar, a boy born mute and with a preternatural ability to commune with the dogs whose breeding and training is his family's business. Idyllic routine is threatened when Edgar's ne'er-do-well uncle comes to live with the family, and the menace persists even after his sudden departure. Soon afterward, Edgar's father dies of an apparent aneurysm; Edgar becomes convinced, but can't prove, that his uncle—who soon inserts himself back into the family—is to blame. . . . [The author] illustrates the relationship between man and canine (at times, from the dog's point of view) in a way that is both lyrical and unsentimental, and demonstrates an ability to create a coherent, captivating fictional world in which even supernatural elements feel entirely persuasive." New Yorker

Wu, Julie

The **third** son; a novel. by Julie Wu. 1st ed. Algonquin Books of Chapel Hill 2013 320 p. (hardcover) $24.95

ISBN 1616200790; 9781616200794

LC 2012051161

In this book by Julie Wu, "growing up in Japanese-occupied Taiwan, Saburo feels rejected by his family. He finds love with Yoshiko, and, after their marriage, he leaves her and their baby son to find them a home in the U.S., but it takes years to get a college education and find work in Michigan, which will allow him to bring his loved ones to join him. The 1950s political history is always in the background." (Booklist)

Wurlitzer, Rudolph

★ **Drop** edge of yonder; a novel. Two Dollar Radio 2008 304p pa $15

ISBN 978-0-9763895-5-2; 0-9763895-5-X

LC 2007-924062

"The novel tracks the wayward drift of a mountain man named Zebulon Shook, who is cursed by his dying Shoshone lover—named Not Here Not There—to 'drift like a blind man between the worlds, not knowing if you're dead or alive, or if the unseen world exists, or if you're dreaming.' With the collapse of the fur trade, Zebulon quits the mountains, crawls out of an arroyo after being shot in the heart and left for dead, and becomes an outlaw. In seedy Vera Cruz, he runs into a Russian count and his mysterious half-Abyssinian consort, Delilah, who pay him to sail with them to the gold fields of northern California. The story ends in the Pacific Northwest, at the Trail's End Saloon, but before we get there, we are treated to a Wunderkammer of western tropes and historical residues: wardens and wanted posters, rancheros and opium dens, freedom and fate, the Great Spirit and the Colt .45. Wurlitzer trots through this magic theater like a restless auteur. Chapters are short, the dialogue tangy and declarative, and scenes established and characters described with the visual fetishism of a Leone film." Bookforum

Wyld, Evie

After the fire, a still small voice. Pantheon Books 2009 296p $24

ISBN 978-0-307-37846-0; 0-307-37846-2

LC 2009-14832

"Frank last visited his family's shack, on a Queensland beach, as a gas-huffing teenager, battered by his mother's death and his father's abusive neglect. He returns an alcoholic man, . . . having lashed out at his girlfriend until she left. The shack has served as a retreat before: for Frank's grandfather, reeling from the Korean War, and for his father, who holed up there after serving in Vietnam. The stories of these wounded forebears are layered into Frank's tormented recovery, trauma seeping from one man into the next. Wyld has a feel both for beauty and for the ugliness of inherited pain. The mood is creepy—strange creatures in the sugar

cane, grieving neighbors, a missing local girl—and the sentiment is plain." New Yorker

Wyman, Willard

Blue heaven. University of Nebraska Press 195p il $21.95

ISBN 978-0-8061-4218-0; 0-8061-4218-9

"Wyman's keen eye for landscape and his knowledge of pack and ranch animals enhance his prose style. He's a good, solid writer, too, a man of welcome sparseness and few fillers. . . . [The novel] has a philosophical edge in its story of friendship and constancy. It speaks to the resilience of humans, their ability to adapt, bend and accept change, or buckle and be sacrificed. Women and whiskey, music and camp meals pepper the pages, often with a bittersweet tone." Billings Gazette

Y

Yalom, Irvin D.

The **Schopenhauer** cure; a novel. Irvin D. Yalom. HarperCollins 2005 viii, 358p (alk. paper) $24.95; (pbk.) $13.99

ISBN 0066214416; 9780060938109

LC 2004047580

This book follows "Julius Hertzfeld, a successful therapist in San Francisco, [who] is shocked by the news that he suffers from terminal cancer. Moved to reassess his life's work, he contacts Philip Slate, whose three years of therapy for sexual addiction Julius describes as an 'old-time major-league failure.' Philip is now training to be a therapist himself, guided by the writings of Arthur Schopenhauer, and he offers to teach Julius about Schopenhauer as a way of helping him deal with his looming death. Julius and Philip strike a deal: Julius will serve as Philip's clinical supervisor, but only if Philip joins the ongoing therapy group Julius leads. To complicate matters further, Pam, a group member, is one of the hundreds of women Philip seduced and then rejected." (Publishers Weekly)

Includes bibliographical references

Yanagihara, Hanya

The **people** in the trees; Hanya Yanagihara. Doubleday 2013 384 p. (hardcover: alk. paper) $26.95

ISBN 0385536771; 9780385536776; 9780385536783

LC 2012034034

Hanya Yanagihara's novel "details the life of fictional doctor and Nobel Prize-winning scientist Dr. Abraham Norton Perina, who narrates his travels to the Micronesian islands of Ivu'ivu and U'ivu, where the secret to longevity is revealed to him. Perina learns that members of a primitive tribe who live to be 60 years old (o'anas) are given the privilege during a special ceremony of consuming the meat of the opa'ivu'eke, a rare turtle." He discovers there is a dark side to longevity, however. (Library Journal)

Yancey, Richard

The **highly** effective detective; a Teddy Ruzak novel. Thomas Dunne Books/St Martin's Minotaur 2006 294p $23.95

ISBN 0-312-34752-9

LC 2006-42512

"When his mother dies and leaves him quite a bit of money, night security officer Theodore Ruzak opens a detective agency with no license and no clients. Teddy may be overweight and uneducated, but he has heart and good moral character. He also has flashes of insight and keen powers of observation, making him just the person to consult when you witness the SUV hit-and-run slaughter of a family of geese or your stepmom goes missing the same day as the avian murders. The city of Knoxville will never be the same. Yancey . . . introduces a colorful, memorable detective and tells a suspenseful story full of great humor and careful plotting." Libr J

Yarbro, Chelsea Quinn

Blood roses; a novel of Saint-Germain. TOR Bks. 1998 382p $24.95

ISBN 0-312-86529-5

LC 98-23671

Yarbro "balances description, action, and romance excellently, producing a briskly paced, highly readable historical fantasy and the only recent series installment that is a good starting point for entering the St. Germain saga." Booklist

Yarbro, Chelsea Quinn

Come twilight; a novel of Saint-Germain. TOR Bks. 2000 479p il

ISBN 0-312-87330-1

LC 00-31710

"While traveling through Spain in the seventh century, Saint-Germain, against his better judgment, saves the life of the mortally wounded Csimenae through a mingling of their blood. Despite his efforts to instruct her in the necessity of unobtrusive coexistence with humans, the haughty, impetuous Csimenae intimidates her countrymen into worshiping her and her son, Aulutis, eventually driving her vampire mentor away. Over the next 500 years, Saint-Germain's travels bring him into contact several times with Csimenae, who engenders a personal vampire army that preys on both unwary pilgrims and invading Moors. . . . Though the incessant details of daily life in the Dark Ages can grow wearisome, they are offset by Saint-Germain's poignant moments of soul-searching over his rare, regrettable moment of fallibility." Publ Wkly

Yarbro, Chelsea Quinn

Communion blood; a novel of Saint-Germain. TOR Bks. 1999 477p $26.95

ISBN 0-312-86793-X

LC 99-38760

The vampire Count "Saint-Germain is in late-seventeenth-century Italy after the true death of his beloved Olivia Clemens. Trying to settle her affairs as she would have wished, he has to fight fraudulent efforts to settle her estate on an imposter instead of on her faithful servant. Meanwhile, he inevitably runs afoul of the church, this time in the person of a cardinal who is scheming to increase the power of the Papal States and, on the side, abusing his sister. All this makes for quite lively reading in its own right, but the romance's real strength . . . lies in the meticulously researched and vividly written depiction of a long-ago and largely long-forgotten time and place." Booklist

Yarbro, Chelsea Quinn

Night blooming. Aspect 2002 429p map $24.95

ISBN 0-446-52981-8

LC 2002-16876

"Yarbro's vampire hero Saint-Germain continues his wanderings through history, this time in the late eighth century. The great French king Karl-lo-Magne summons Saint-Germain, here known as Hiernom Rakoczy, to his court. On the way, Rakoczy and his entourage meet Gynethe Mehaut, a young albino afflicted with a stigmata and awaiting news of her fate at a convent. . . . Volunteering to accompany {Gynethe} to the papal court in Rome, Rakoczy soon finds himself haunting his old haunts and falling in love with his charge. But Gynethe . . . is in great danger from those who feel threatened by her, and all Rakoczy's efforts may not be enough to save her." Booklist

"Richly rewarding for longtime readers, the novel also provides a good entry point for new recruits with its subtly supplied back story." Publ Wkly

Yarbrough, Steve

The **end** of California. Knopf 2006 303p $23.95

ISBN 1-4000-4438-3

LC 2005-57750

In this "novel, a 42-year-old doctor named Pete Barrington returns from California to his little home town in Mississippi. He started there as a poor farm boy, but brains, looks and football talent helped him advance to college, medical school and a good life out West. An adulterous affair with a patient ended that, and now he, his wife and their 15-year-old daughter are starting over back home. Yarbrough's story blends elements we have seen in other novels—the small-town South, the football hero grown up, passions that reach back to high school, a little incest and a lot of extramarital sex, racial tensions, hypocrisy among the pious—but it all works because Yarbrough knows his characters so well, cares for them so deeply and writes of them in prose that is graceful, precise and packed with surprises." Washington Post Book World

Yarbrough, Steve

★ **Prisoners** of war; a novel. Knopf 2004 287p $23

ISBN 0-375-41478-9

LC 2003-40071

"Yarbrough writes with quiet compassion about Loring's black population, its reluctance to fight for a country that has so consistently betrayed its democratic promise. To this combustible setting will come a peculiar prisoner, one with an 'angry purple stain, either a birthmark or a rash,' who speaks broken English and haunts one of the Loring natives assigned to guard him. It is the fate of this mysterious captive that once again forces the people of Loring to confront what it means to be American, and all the unexpected and often unwarranted sacrifices that identity might comprise." N Y Times Book Rev

Yarbrough, Steve

The **realm** of last chances; Steve Yarbrough. Alfred A. Knopf 2013 288 p. (hardback) $25.95

ISBN 0385349505; 9780345804884; 9780385349505

LC 2012050904

In this book, "Kristin has lost her job at a California university and has had to relocate to a less prestigious college in the northeast. She brings along her husband Cal, an unemployed woodworker and musician, and her troubled marriage. Kristin and Cal are both in their 50s, and Yarbrough focuses here primarily on how busy lives, past histories, and largely unexamined ideas about love and romance can threaten a marriage." (Library Journal)

Yarbrough, Steve

★ **Safe** from the neighbors. Alfred A. Knopf 2010 259p $25.95

ISBN 978-0-307-27170-9; 0-307-27170-6

LC 2009-22311

"The story is told from the point of view of Luke May, a high school teacher and history buff living in a small Mississippi River delta town where he and his wife carry on a passionless marriage. During Luke's childhood, a family friend killed his wife, and Luke never fully understood the circumstances. After Maggie, one of the slain mother's children, returns to town as the new high school French teacher, Luke begins to unravel the murder, which coincided with one of the key moments in the civil rights movement. He also begins an affair with Maggie." Publ Wkly

Yates, Alex

Moondogs; a novel. Doubleday 2011 339p $25.95

ISBN 978-0-385-53378-2; 0-385-53378-0

LC 2010-07947

"A cloud of exasperated doom hangs over the characters in this weird and weirdly affecting Philippines-set novel. The multiple story lines — involving an American businessman, his bumbling kidnappers, his estranged son, an embassy worker having an affair with a Filipino national hero, and an A-Team of supernaturally enhanced soldiers — languorously intertwine, thankfully without the soulless Swiss-watch efficiency that often governs books with such large casts." Entertainment Wkly

Yates, Richard

★ The **collected** stories of Richard Yates; introduction by Richard Russo. Holt & Co. 2001 xx, 472p

ISBN 0-8050-6693-4

LC 00-61400

"Bitterness, loneliness and lack of fulfillment are the central themes of this grim posthumous collection." Publ Wkly

The **Year's** best fantasy and horror; 1st-21st annual collections. edited by Ellen Datlow and Kelly Link & Gavin J. Grant. St. Martin's Press 1988 21v

First two annual compilations published with title: The Year's best fantasy

Each annual collection includes short stories, poems, and essays. The nonfiction sections cover such topics as trends in fantasy and horror publishing; fantasy and horror films, television and comics; nonprint media; and obituaries. Over the years contributors of stories have included Charles De Lint, Steve Rasnic Tem, Garry Kilworth, Angela Carter, Karel Capek, Isabel Allende, Stephen King, Jane Yolen, Thomas Ligotti and Clive Barker

The **year's** best science fiction; thirtieth annual collection. edited by Gardner Dozois. St. Martin's Griffin 2013 704 p. (hardcover) $40

ISBN 1250028051; 9781250028051; 9781250029133

LC 2013009319

In this collection of short stories, edited by Gardner Dozois, science fiction "authors explore ideas of a new world through their short stories. This venerable collection brings together award winning authors and masters of the field such as Robert Reed, Alastair Reynolds, Damien Broderick, Elizabeth Bear, Paul McAuley and John Barnes." (Publisher's note)

Year's best science fiction; 1st-26th annual collections. edited by Gardner Dozois. St. Martin's Press 1984

First three annual collections published by Bluejay Books

Each annual collection contains stories, a summation of developments in the field, and a list of honorable mentions. Over the years contributors have included Michael Swanwick, Maureen F. McHugh, Charles Sheffield, Cory Doctorow, Kage Baker, Brian Stableford, Gene Wolfe, Nancy Kress, Gregory Benford, Stephen Baxter, Elizabeth Bear, Paolo Bacigalupi, Jay Lake, and Mary Rosenblum

Yiyun Li

The **vagrants**; a novel. Random House 2009 337p $25

ISBN 1-4000-6313-2; 978-1-4000-6313-0

LC 2008-23467

This novel "is set in China in the late 1970s. . . . A young woman, Gu Shan, . . . a follower of Chairman Mao, has renounced her faith in Communism. Now a political prisoner, she is set to be executed for her dissent." (Publisher's note)

This novel "begins and ends with an execution, in 1979, in a small city in China, where democratic reform movements are beginning to ripple through the nation. Gu Shan is a former Red Guard leader turned counter-revolutionary, whose execution, at the age of twenty-eight, devastates her parents and entwines their lives with those of a crippled twelve-year-old girl, the feckless nineteen-year-old son of a Communist hero, an elderly street-cleaning couple, and a radio announcer who comes to question her role in the spread of government propaganda. Li offers both a bleak view of a historical moment when 'people were the most dangerous animals in the world' and a meditation on the act of martyrdom, which is presented both as a duty and as a 'luxury that few could afford.'" New Yorker

Yolen, Jane

Briar Rose. Doherty Assocs. 1992 190p (Fairy tale series) hardcover o.p. pa $6.99

ISBN 0-312-85135-9; 0-7653-4230-8 pa

LC 92-25456

"Yolen takes the story of Briar Rose (commonly known as Sleeping Beauty) and links it to the Holocaust. . . . Rebecca Berlin, a young woman who has grown up hearing her grandmother Gemma tell an unusual and frightening version of the Sleeping Beauty legend, realizes when Gemma dies that the fairy tale offers one of the very few clues she has to her grandmother's past. . . . By interpolating Gemma's vivid and imaginative story into the larger narrative, Yolen has created an engrossing novel." Publ Wkly

Yoon, Paul

Once the shore; stories. Sarabande Books 2009 270p pa $15.95

ISBN 978-1-932511-70-3; 1-932511-70-9

LC 2008-19331

"Yoon's collection of eight richly textured stories explore the themes of family, lost love, silence, alienation and the effects of the Japanese occupation and the Korean War on the poor communities of a small South Korean island." Publ Wkly

Yorke, Margaret

Act of violence. St. Martin's Press 1998 282p $22.95

ISBN 0-312-18522-7

LC 98-16546

First published 1997 in the United Kingdom

"The tension leading to the young toughs' arrest is taut, and the identity of the murderess-turned-counselor kept cleverly obscured until the very end." Publ Wkly

Yorke, Margaret

Almost the truth. Mysterious Press 1995 278p

LC 94-36601

First published 1994 in the United Kingdom

"Without sacrificing entertainment to message, this absorbing, utterly unsentimental narrative reminds us that behind crime-related headlines live real people whose futures are marked by the crimes' effects." Publ Wkly

Yorke, Margaret

Criminal damage. Mysterious Press 1992 248p

LC 91-51182

"Mrs. Newton, a widow, enjoys a quiet and determinedly tidy life in the picturesque English village of Middle Bardolph, but storms are brewing that seem likely to unsettle it. Geoffrey, her boring and not very pleasant son, thinks his mother should underwrite the larger home his ambitious wife demands. Temperamental daughter Jennifer is increasingly obsessed with her former lover and his new fiancée and seems bent on disrupting their lives. . . . Yorke . . . mixes this deftly drawn, untrustworthy cast with robbery, violence and a hidden past, keeping readers guessing about what will be done and who will do it." Publ Wkly

Yorke, Margaret

False pretences. St. Martin's Press 1999 310p $23.95

ISBN 0-312-19975-9

LC 98-51198

First published 1998 in the United Kingdom

This psychological thriller, set in a small English village, traces "the local secrets exposed by a stranger and the aftermath when her true identity is discovered. Captivating and full-bodied." Libr J

Yorke, Margaret

The price of guilt. St. Martin's Press 2000 297p $24.95

ISBN 0-312-25332-X

LC 99-88102

First published 1999 in the United Kingdom

"Yorke is a master at making the reader care about meek and lonely middle-aged women. While the latter part of the novel largely fills in the motivations of minor characters in flashback, Colin's fate remains up in the air until the very end—and is as ironic as Louise's, if more just." Publ Wkly

Yorke, Margaret

★ A question of belief. Mysterious Press 1997 282p

LC 97-20833

First published 1996 in the United Kingdom

In this novel of psychological suspense, an English "department store executive is falsely accused of sexual harassment by a vindictive customer. After losing both his job and the trust of his family, the poor chump fakes his suicide and tramps off to a little village where nobody knows of his shame. Here his fate intersects with that of another outcast, an illiterate teenager who has been shabbily manipulated by a militant animal rights activist with a hidden agenda. Several other folks come out of the woods to play, and although their convergences are strictly contrived, their characters are sharply defined in this fatalistic tale of modern morality in tatters." N Y Times Book Rev

Yoshida, Shuichi

Villain; translated from the Japanese by Philip Gabriel. Pantheon Books 2010 295p $25.95

ISBN 9780307378873; 0-307-37887-X

LC 2010-00159

"Villain can be confusing. Its many characters, multiple points of view and shifts in time require close attention. But that attention is rewarded. Each of Yoshida's characters, whether major or minor, is carefully defined. The title of the novel is finally ironic: No one villain can be separated out of the fabric of actions that led to Yoshino's death, and the line between villain and victim is almost translucent." Columbus Dispatch

Yoshimoto, Banana, 1964-

Asleep; translated from the Japanese by Michael Emmerich. Grove Press 2000 177p

ISBN 0-8021-1669-8

LC 99-88699

This volume consists "of three novellas, each telling a somewhat mystical tale of haunted slumber. In the first story, a woman mourning a dead lover finds herself sleepwalking; in the next, a woman involved in a relationship with a man, whose wife is in a coma, realizes that she is unable to remain awake; and in the third, a woman finds her dreams inhabited by a dead woman, her former rival in a love triangle. The stories flow easily and quietly from one to the next, and while they have a lyrical, almost poetic, quality, they remain gripping, dramatic, intense, and real." Booklist

Yoshimoto, Banana

Goodbye Tsugumi; a novel. translated from the Japanese by Michael Emmerich. Grove Press 2002 186p $23

ISBN 0-8021-1638-8

LC 2001-58460

Original Japanese edition, 1999

"Maria Shirakawa is a thoughtful young woman thrown by family circumstance (her parents never married; with her mother, she is waiting for her father's divorce from his current wife) into growing up with her cousin, Tsugumi Yamamoto, in her aunt and uncle's small inn. Tsugumi, who is chronically ill, possesses a mischievous charm that both maddens and amuses her family. . . . Tsugumi's tenuous health seems to free her from the behavioral norms that govern Maria and Tsugumi's long-suffering older sister, Yoko, allowing her to curse, flirt with boys, concoct elaborate pranks and shock adults in a way Maria resents, envies and admires." Publ Wkly

Yoshimoto, Banana

★ **Kitchen**; translated from the Japanese by Megan Backus. Grove Press 1993 152p

LC 92-12871

Original Japanese edition, 1987

"In supple, precise prose Yoshimoto conveys her protagonists' emotional states by according them unusual sensitivity to the natural world; they share an enhanced vision that makes things shine with luminous clarity or emanate the gloom of mortality." Publ Wkly

Yoshimoto, Banana, 1964-

The lake; translated by Michael Emmerich. Melville House 2011 188p $15.95

ISBN 1-933633-77-8; 978-1-933633-77-0

LC 2011-06711

Original Japanese edition, 2005

This novel "tells the tale of a young woman who moves to Tokyo after the death of her mother, hoping to get over her grief and start a career as a graphic artist. She finds herself spending too much time staring out her window, though . . . until she realizes she's gotten used to seeing a young man across the street staring out his window, too." (Publisher's note)

"Chihiro, an artist, and Nakajima, a graduate student in genetics, finally meet after watching and waving to each other from their respective apartment windows across a Tokyo street. They're both unconventional and seemingly untethered souls; they've both lost their beloved mothers. They meander into a sweet, simple life together, although past secrets involving a mysterious brother and sister who live by an ethereal lake threaten to create an emotional divide. . . .Yoshimoto aficionados . . . will recognize her signature crisp, clipped style (thanks to exacting translator Emmerich's constancy) and revel in her latest cast of quirky characters." Libr J

Youmans, Marly

★ **The wolf pit.** Farrar, Straus & Giroux 2001 342p $24

ISBN 0-374-29195-0

LC 2001-42278

This Civil War novel focuses on "Robin, a young Confederate soldier, and Agate, a mulatto slave girl. In his . . . double tale, each of the characters suffers untold miseries. Robin's are endured in the heat of battle and the horrors of prison camp. while Agate must bear the indignities of slavery. . . . The novel's many dramatic and traumatic events will keep the reader breathless, while the haunting, lyrical language and the fierce intelligence behind it reminds us we are reading a writer and storyteller of the first order." Publ Wkly

Young, Thomas W.

The renegades; Tom Young. G.P. Putnam's Sons 2012 336 p.

ISBN 0399158464; 9780399158469

LC 2012010954

This is the third novel with "Air Force Lt. Col. Michael Parson . . . . Now an adviser to a helicopter unit in Afghanistan, Parson requests that his interpreter friend, Sgt. Maj. Sophia Gold, be deployed back to Afghanistan." Parson and Gold have to deal with the actions of "a group called the Black Crescent"; they "get on the trail of the Crescent leader, Chaaku . . . , and in a last deadly battle bring a measure of justice to their corner of the war." (Publishers Weekly)

Yourcenar, Marguerite

★ **Memoirs of Hadrian**; translated from the French by Grace Frick in collaboration with the author. Farrar, Straus and Young 1954 313p

Original French edition, 1951

"The memoirs portray the emperor on the eve of his death and describe his reflections as he gazes out upon the city that seemed to him indestructible and that he now fears will fall. As with most of her work, the book is a minutely researched reconstruction of actual events in the distant past through which she develops penetrating and fully credible portraits of the people she describes." Reader's Ency. 4th edition

Yrsa Sigurdardottir

Last rituals; an Icelandic novel of secret symbols, medieval witchcraft, and modern murder. translated from the Icelandic by Bernard Scudder. HarperCollins Publishers 2007 314p $23.95

ISBN 978-0-06-114336-6; 0-06-114336-7

Original Icelandic edition, 2005

"Thóra is a thirtysomething divorcée, mother of two, and a partner in a small law firm. She is reluctantly drawn into a murder investigation when approached by the Guntlieb family, whose son, Harald, was killed at the university. With the pay at twice her usual rate and the assistance of Matthew Reich, the Guntlieb family representative, Thóra can't refuse, even though the gruesome murder appalls her. To find the murderer, Thóra and Matthew must delve into Harald's interests in witchcraft and witch burnings and investigate his university friends. Scudder provides such a smooth translation, right down to the slang used by Harald's college friends, that an engaged reader can easily forget this was originally written in Icelandic." Libr J

Yu Hua

Brothers; translated from the Chinese by Eileen Chow and Carlos Rojas. Pantheon Books 2009 641p $29.95

ISBN 978-0-375-42499-1; 0-375-42499-7

LC 2008-21617

Original Chinese edition, 2005

This novel, "a family history documenting four decades of profound social and cultural transformation in China, begins on a toilet. In a sleepy rural outpost known as Liu Town, fourteen-year-old Baldy Li is caught peeping at women's bottoms in a latrine. He becomes known as a compulsive public masturbator, and his obsession continues into adulthood: he ends up hosting a beauty pageant for virgins (all of whom rely on doctored hymens to gain entrance). The book has sold more than a million copies in China, despite its irreverent take on everything from the Cultural Revolution to the capitalist boom." New Yorker

Yu, Charles, 1976-

★ **How** to live safely in a science fictional universe. Pantheon Books 2010 239p $24

ISBN 0-307-37920-5; 978-0-307-37920-7

LC 2010-01837

"Yu's protagonist, a time machine repairman also named Charles Yu, has lived the past decade of his life boxed up in a tiny TM-31 Recreational Time Travel Device. His two companions are TAMMY . . . and Ed, a nonexistent yet 'ontologically valid' dog." (N Y Times Book Rev)

"Our protagonist begins by explaining that he's gotten trapped in a time loop of his own making, caused when he thoughtlessly shot his own future self as he emerged from a time machine. As we ponder what it means, psychologically, to have murdered your future self, Yu takes us on a journey that gets progressively more emotionally intense. We learn about his protagonist's job as a time machine mechanic where his colleagues are mostly artificial intelligences who act more human than he does or who actually believe they are human. Yu effortlessly switches between comic vignettes about the fate of Luke Skywalker's less-famous son (who has messed up his time machine in a fictional universe), and his protagonist's painful memories of growing up at the center of a Venn diagram whose circles include the alien universes of Taiwan, America, and Tatooine. Yu is fond of meta-narrative, and packs the novel with adventures that take place entirely in theoretical universes, nostalgia-altered pasts, fictional worlds, and inside the protagonist's own time-looped mind." io9

Yunis, Alia

The night counter; a novel. Shaye Areheart Books 2009 365p $24

ISBN 978-0-307-45362-4; 0-307-45362-6

LC 2009-281269

"Fatima is an elderly Lebanese woman living in Los Angeles with her favorite grandson, Amir. She moved to Detroit from Lebanon seven decades ago and has since had two husbands, 10 children, and 14 grandchildren. At this point, she's ready to say goodbye to all of it. Or almost ready, that is. First, she must find a wife for wannabe actor Amir (blithely overlooking his constant insistence that he's gay) and then arrange for him to inherit her beloved mother's house in Lebanon. In the meantime, as the successful conclusion of that task drags on, Fatima is content to stay alive for another 1,001 days, spending each night telling her stories to Scheherazade." Christ Sci Monit

This "novel, mixes equal parts of magical realism, social commentary, family drama and light-hearted humor to create a delicious and intriguing indulgence worth savoring." Minneapolis Star Trib

Z

Zahn, Timothy

The last command. Bantam Bks. 1993 407p (Star wars)

LC 92-43876

Earlier titles in the author's Thrawn trilogy: Heir to empire (1991); Dark force rising (1992)

In this concluding volume of the Star wars trilogy "Thrawn mounts a final siege against the Republic. While Han and Chewbacca struggle to form a wary alliance of smugglers in a last-ditch attack against the Empire, Leia keeps the Alliance together and prepares for the birth of her Jedi twins. But the Empire has too many ships and too many clones to combat. The Republic's only hope lies in sending a small force, led by Luke, into the very stronghold that houses Thrawn's terrible cloning machines." Publisher's note

Zamiatin, Evgenii Ivanovich

★ **We**; [by] Yevgeny Zamyatin; translated by Mirra Ginsburg. Viking 1972 204p

First translation published 1924

"The ultimate dystopian novel, presenting a vision of the United States: a society whose suppression of individuality in the cause of order proceeds to the logical limit of eliminating the imagination. Its origin, and the fact that it circulated surreptitiously in Russia as a samizdat publication, encourages a reading that construes it as an attack on Soviet communism, but it actually refers to a much more fundamental tendency in human nature towards conformity and autmatism. Not published in Russia until 1988." Anatomy of Wonder. 5th edition

Zamora Linmark, R.

Leche; a novel. Coffee House Press 2011 355p il pa $15.95

ISBN 978-1-56689-254-4; 1-56689-254-6

LC 2010-39304

Sequel to: Rolling the R's

As "cheeky a novel as you'll encounter. . . . The book's nonstop energy and nonstop attitude are addictive. And in Vince you won't find a less predictable tour guide. A lively satiric return to early '90s Manila, seen from both sides of the Filipino American divide." Kirkus

Zan, Koethi

The **Never** List; Koethi Zan. Penguin Group USA 2013 320 p. $27.95

ISBN 0670026514; 9780670026517

LC 2013007348

In this novel by Koethi Zan "Sarah and Jennifer . . . accept a cab ride with grave . . . consequences. For . . . three years, they are held captive . . . by a connoisseur of sadism. Ten years later . . . Sarah [struggles] to resume a normal life . . . unable to come to grips with Jennifer['s death]. Sarah decides to confront her phobias and . . . goes on a cross-country chase that takes her into the perverse world of BDSM, secret cults, and the arcane study of torture, . . .unraveling a mystery.' (Publisher's note)

Zelazny, Roger

Blood of Amber. Arbor House 1986 215p

ISBN 0-87795-829-7

LC 86-3530

Sequel to Trumps of doom

In this seventh installment in the author's Amber fantasy series "the sorcerer Merlin of Amber—aka Merle Corey of San Francisco—learns the identities of two would-be assassins but makes a truce with one to pursue the greater, more dangerous power beyond them. Once again, the limited plot is enlivened by Zelazny's irony, his bravura sequences . . . and his laconic sense of the incongruous." Publ Wkly

Followed by Sign of chaos

Zelazny, Roger

The **courts** of chaos. Doubleday 1978 183p

ISBN 0-385-13685-4

LC 78-3263

Sequel to The hand of Oberon

This fifth title in the author's "Amber fantasy series answers many of the questions central to previous installments; the nature of the magical kingdom of Amber and the tangents it sometimes forms with the real world; the mystery behind the disappearance of Oberon the King—which forms the plot of the stories—and the machinations of Corwin, Prince of Amber, and his siblings, who thrive on intrigue." Booklist

Followed by Trumps of doom

Zelazny, Roger

The **dead** man's brother. Hard Case Crime 2009 256p pa $6.99

ISBN 978-0-8439-6115-7; 0-8439-6115-5

"The story follows Ovid Wiley, a former art smuggler turned respectable gallery owner who finds his former smuggling partner dead in his place of work. He is quickly picked up by the police, and then the CIA, which offers to make his trouble go away for a price. Wiley must track down a priest who has absconded with $3 million of the Vatican's dollars. This unwelcome assignment takes Wiley to Rome, where he meets up with his smuggling partner's ex-girlfriend, and then to Brazil, where he and Maria end up involved in local politics. The story is solid, but not spectacular. Zelazny keeps everything moving along nicely, but it's all territory that's been trod before. It's entertaining, and it shows Zelazny could have easily branched out into other genres, but The Dead Man's Brother is remarkable mainly for its status as a forgotten novel." Independent Crime

Zelazny, Roger

Donnerjack; {by} Roger Zelazny, Jane Lindskold. Avon Bks. 1997 503p $24

ISBN 0-380-97326-X

LC 96-48705

"The late Zelazny's last novel, completed by Lindskold, is one of his largest and most ambitious. . . . All the mythic resonances we have come to expect from Zelazny are here in abundance." Booklist

Zelazny, Roger

The **guns** of Avalon. Doubleday 1972 180p (Amber)

Sequel to Nine princes in Amber

In this second volume of the author's Amber series Corwin "again walks the shadow worlds in search of his stolen birthright and encounters dreaded forces of evil conjured up by his own terrible curse." Booklist

Followed by Sign of the unicorn

Zelazny, Roger

The **hand** of Oberon. Doubleday 1976 181p

ISBN 0-385-08541-9

"Oberon, the royal leader of the land of Amber, is unexpectedly missing, and his large family of sons and daughters is engaged in searching for him, or else trying to keep him missing." Publ Wkly

Followed by The courts of chaos

Zelazny, Roger

Knight of shadows. Morrow 1989 251p (Amber)

LC 89-34658

Sequel to Sign of chaos

"The ninth book in Zelazny's Amber sagas. . . . Merlin, son of Corwin, escapes at the last minute from the Citadel of the FourWorlds. He is immediately plunged into intrigue and adventure. By book's end, it is apparent that his travels are not yet complete. Zelazny's pacing and the ingenious games he plays with magic continue to be rewarding." Booklist

Followed by Prince of chaos

Zelazny, Roger

★ **Lord** of light. Doubleday 1967 257p

This novel "describes a planet colonized by refugees from India who are tyrannized by a few of their fellow citizens who have assumed the guise and powers of the Hindu gods. Instead of easing his readers into the strange setting and unfamiliar mythology, Zelazny began the story in the middle, centuries after the initial landing; that the reader can absorb—and care to absorb—the complexities of the plot and setting is a tribute to the author's storytelling ability." New Ency of Sci Fic

Zelazny, Roger

★ **Nine** princes in Amber. Doubleday 1970 188p (Amber)

This tale, the first in the author's Amber series, is a fantasy and adventure story about Corwin, who, following an attack of amnesia, realizes that he is one of nine princes in the kingdom of Amber. Each one of the nine princes and four princesses wants the throne, and war breaks out between the brothers

Followed by The guns of Avalon

Zelazny, Roger

Prince of chaos. Morrow 1991 225p (Amber)

LC 91-17296

Sequel to Knight of shadows

The tenth book in the Amber sagas "takes Merlin Corey to the actual Courts of Chaos, which have figured as offstage presences in the series beginning with Trumps of Doom. We now see the Courts from the inside, and a certain amount of the mystery about Corey's world and future is dispelled, although not without the usual quota of intrigues and dangers. The finer nuances of the series are becoming a little hard to appreciate without having followed it from the beginning. The vivid imagination and high command of language, however, can still be enjoyed on a volume-by-volume basis." Booklist

Zelazny, Roger

Sign of chaos. Arbor House 1987 214p (Amber)

LC 87-14509

Sequel to Blood of Amber

In the eighth volume of the author's Amber fantasy series "Merlin Corey follows a confused trail to the Keep of Four Worlds, where he learns the secret of the involvement of the Courts of Chaos in all the intrigues and wars to which he is heir." Booklist

Followed by Knight of shadows

Zelazny, Roger

Sign of the unicorn. Doubleday 1975 186p (Amber)

Sequel to The guns of Avalon

"Third in a series of science fiction-fantasy adventures featuring Corwin, Prince of Amber. . . . Court intrigue is rampant among the surviving princes and princesses of Amber, all of whom weave in and out of Shadow, a multi-dimensional world they can manipulate, and unite to rescue a brother imprisoned by evil beings threatening the kingdom. This, though action packed, does not advance the fortunes of Corwin to any extent but does fill in background." Booklist

Followed by The hand of Oberon

Zelazny, Roger

Trumps of doom. Arbor House 1985 183p

ISBN 0-87795-718-5

LC 84-299

Sequel to The courts of chaos

"A new sequence {in the Amber fantasy series} begins in this sixth volume centering on Corwin's son Merlin, a sorcerer who has followed the father he barely knew from their powerful realm of Amber to an Earth that is one of Amber's many shadowy alternate worlds. Attempts on Merlin's life force him to return to Amber, where he becomes embroiled once more in family quarrels and finally confronts the man who has been stalking him. This fast-paced, colorful tale is enriched by Zelazny's literary analogs of his alternate worlds as he flips from one frame of reference to another (tarot, computers, lawyerly logic) and from one voice to another (hard-boiled detective, classical allusions, high fantasy)." Publ Wkly

Followed by Blood of Amber

Zeltserman, Dave

★ The **caretaker** of Lorne Field. Overlook Press 2010 237p $23.95

ISBN 978-1-59020-303-3; 1-59020-303-8

This novel "focuses on Jack Durkin, the ninth generation of firstborn sons in his family who have daily weeded Lorne Field to purge it of Aukowies, bloodthirsty plants that could overrun the world in weeks if not attended to. Though Jack takes his job seriously, no one else does: his oldest son doesn't want to follow in his footsteps; his wife is tired of living poorly on his caretaker's salary; and the townspeople who subsidize him are increasingly skeptical of purported menaces that no one has ever seen because Jack diligently nips them in the bud. With his support dwindling, Jack finds himself driven to desperate measures to prove that he's truly saving the world. Zeltserman . . . orchestrates events perfectly, making it impossible to tell if Jack is genuinely humankind's unsung hero or merely the latest descendant of a family of superstitious loonies." Publ Wkly

Zeltserman, Dave

Small crimes. Serpent's Tail 2008 263p pa $14.95

ISBN 978-1-85242-971-3; 1-85242-971-2

"This tale is told by one of fortune's fools: Joe Denton is a crooked ex-cop in Vermont who's just been released from jail after serving seven years for stabbing the local district attorney in the face. Since what's past is never truly past in crime noir, no sooner does Joe step out of the slammer than cosmic IOU's begin to rain down on his head. First, the disfigured DA cheerfully greets Joe outside the prison and announces that a local crime kingpin (and Joe's secret boss) is dying of cancer and has found religion. The kingpin's expected confession should send Joe straight back behind bars. Then, the local sheriff (also crooked) orders Joe to murder the DA before the crime kingpin can confess. The plot of Small Crimes ricochets out from this claustrophobic opening, and it's a thing of sordid beauty." NPR

Zevin, Gabrielle

The **hole** we're in; a novel. Black Cat 2010 283p pa $14

ISBN 978-0-8021-1923-0; 0-8021-1923-9

"Roger Pomeroy is an evangelical patriarch who, at 42, decides that what he needs is to quit his job and return to school full-time. Roger's wife, Georgia, takes a second job, but without Roger's salary, and with the wedding of their eldest daughter, Helen, coming up, the family is financially strapped. Unable to pay the bills, Georgia hides them in drawers, pretending everything is fine. When her credit cards are maxed out, she applies for new ones in her children's names, with dire results. Meanwhile, Roger outdoes himself by carrying on an affair with his academic advisor." BookPage

"All five Pomeroys — flawed, devoted, cranky, impetuous, utterly relatable — come blazingly alive on the page." Entertainment Wkly

Zimler, Richard
★ The **last** kabbalist of Lisbon. Overlook Press 1998 318p $24.95
    ISBN 0-87951-834-0
                    LC 97-46184

This novel "first published in Portuguese, vividly re-creates the world of ancient Lisbon, presenting Berekiah's mysticism in graceful, albeit occasionally florid, prose. Zimler's portrait of the city (and the New Christians' uneasy place within it) enriches his many-layered narrative, in which a suitably complex cast of characters plays a dangerous game with fate." N Y Times Book Rev

Zimler, Richard
The **seventh** gate; a novel. Richard Zimler. Overlook Press 2012 577 p. ill., map (hardcover) $26.95
    ISBN 1590207130; 9781590207130
                   LC 2007405815

This book by Richard Zimler presents a "coming-of-age epic set in Berlin at the start of the Nazi era. . . . Precocious 14-year-old Sophie Riedesel is adjusting to her changing body and desires, but she soon has other concerns as Hitler consolidates his power. . . . Although Sophie herself isn't Jewish, she's alarmed by the uptick in anti-Semitism and the threats posed to her Jewish friends." (Publishers Weekly)

Zimmer, Michael
The **long** hitch; a western story. Five Star 2011 364p $25.95
    ISBN 978-1-43282-524-9; 1-43282-524-0
                 LC 2011-13162

"In 1874 Utah territory, young teamster Buck McCready becomes wagon boss for the Kavanaugh freight outfit after his mentor, old Mason Campbell, is murdered. With the Kavanaugh outfit engaged in a wagon train race that will decide whether Kavanaugh or a competitor lands a lucrative freight-hauling contract, Buck vows to find Campbell's killer. But first he must win the race, a difficult task considering there's a saboteur among his crew and a hired gun out to take him down, plus the possibility that Campbell's killer is after Buck, too. . . . Zimmer has put together a believable, gritty, and action-packed tale of the real Old West." Publ Wkly

Zimmer, Michael
Wild side of the river; a western story. Five Star 2011 216p $25.95
    ISBN 978-1-59414-946-7; 1-59414-946-1
                 LC 2010-43349

"Ethan, eldest son of the Wilder clan, returns home after having been away only a couple of months. He finds his family near the point of self-destruction. One of his brothers is on the run, accused of beating a young girl. His father is warring with another brother, who is presently keeping his father locked up in the privy. As if that isn't enough, Ethan learns that local ranchers are being murdered by an unknown culprit, and when his own father becomes a victim, he puts everything he has on the line to make the killer pay. A man's single-minded quest for vengeance is a traditional western theme, but this one doesn't feel like a traditional western. It's darker, harder around the edges, a noir crime drama wearing western clothing." Booklist

Zimmerman, David
Sandbox; a novel. Soho Press 2010 350p $25
    ISBN 978-1-56947-628-4
                 LC 2009-43994

"Set at a remote military base in the Iraqi desert, this debut novel unsparingly portrays the experience of fighting in the Iraq War. Private Toby Durrant is on a routine mission when his convoy gets ambushed. After the shooting has stopped, Durrant briefly leaves his vehicle to get sick. This seemingly minor infraction draws him into a complex conspiracy that involves the base's senior officers, an Iraqi translator, and many of his fellow soldiers." Libr J

Zimmerman, Jean
★ The **orphanmaster**; Jean Zimmerman. Viking 2012 418 p. maps $27.95
    ISBN 0670023647; 9780670023646
                 LC 2011038593

In this historical thriller, a "feisty young Dutch woman, an English spy, and a local demon all cross paths in 1663 New Amsterdam. . . . Orphaned as a child, Blandine van Couvering now . . . looks out for the orphans around the small town . . . . But first one orphan disappears, and then another is found molested and murdered. Evidence of a witika, a fiend of Native American folklore, is found near the remains. . . . As the little bodies pile up, fears run wild." (Library Journal)

Zito, V. M.
The **return** man. Orbit 2012 400p (paperback) $9.99
    ISBN 0316218286; 9780316218283

In this book, in the "desolate heat and haunting emptiness of the zombie-infested American Southwest, exneurologist Henry Marco is hired by the living to 'return' their undead loved ones, a euphemism for blowing their brains out. Marco also yearns to find and 'return' his own wife. Hired by the Department of Homeland Security to track down a scientist who may have developed a cure, Marco embarks on a journey across the desert." (Publishers Weekly)

Zola, Emile
★ **Germinal**; translated with an introduction and notes by Roger Pearson. Penguin Books 2004 xlv, 546p (Penguin classics) pa $10
    ISBN 978-0-14-044742-2; 0-14-044742-3

Original French edition, 1885, one of the Rougon-Macquart series

"A study of life in the mines. . . . Étienne Lanier, a socialist, is forced to work in the mines. Low wages and fines cause a strike, of which Lanier is one of the leaders. He counsels moderation; but hunger drives the miners to desperation, and force is met by force. Several are killed, Lanier is deported, and the miners fall back into their old slavery." Keller. Reader's Dig of Books

Zola, Emile
★ **Nana**; translated with an introduction by Douglas Parmée. Oxford University Press 1998 xxix, 430p (Oxford world's classics)
    ISBN 0-19-283670-6

Original French edition, 1880, one of the Rougon-Macquart series

"The title character grows up in the slums of Paris. She has a brief career as an untalented actress before finding success as a courtesan. Although vulgar and ignorant, she has a destructive sexuality that attracts many rich and powerful men. Cruelly contemptuous of her lovers' emotions, Nana wastes their fortunes, driving many of them to ruin and even suicide." Merriam-Webster's Ency of Lit

Zola, Emile

Three faces of love; especially translated for this volume by Roland Gant. Vanguard Press 1969 151p

These three early Zola stories explore different kinds of love. In For One Night of Love "Zola tells of a dullard whose passion leads to suicide through his having been accessory in the murder of his rival, killed by the girl, a marquise. 'Round Trip' is a lyric of youthful sensuality triumphing over middle-aged insensitivity. In 'Winkles for M. Chabre' Zola deals with a triangle (aging husband, young wife, young man); the husband has been told to expect a child if he follows a diet of shellfish; he gets the child, unaware that it is not because of winkles. Slight things, these stories, but welcome additions to the austere works usually associated with Zola." Libr J

Zuber, Isabel

Salt. Picador 2002 352p

ISBN 0-312-28133-1

LC 2001-54892

The author depicts "one woman's life in the American South at the turn of the 20th century. . . . Central to her portrait are the relationships between Anna Maud Stockton Bayley, her adulterous, twice-married husband, John, and their offspring. Forced into marriage after John seduces her, Anna makes the best of it, sewing, gardening and keeping house in the small town of Faith, N.C. Still, she dreams of music, singing, travel and love. But single-minded John, who is avid to increase his land, children and stock, is less interested in his young wife's desires than his own personal gain." Publ Wkly

"Zuber gets the historical details right, and her characters' emotions (especially Anna's—romantic, tender and full of quiet desperation) are handled just as deftly." N Y Times Book Rev

Includes bibliographical references

Zumas, Leni

Farewell navigator; stories. Open City Books 2008 168p pa $14

ISBN 978-1-890447-49-6; 1-890447-49-8

LC 2008-5955

"Zumas's penchant for rhythmic language and experimentation is paralleled (and possibly influenced) by her work as a drummer. . . . [She focuses] on the culture of rebellious musicians, rock clubs and 'trapped people.' Zumas's stories deal with suicide and bleeding rectums, and take place in rehab centers and towns that don't exist on maps—microcosms of the great community of solitude. Like powerful music, the phenomenon of Zumas's fiction happens when the rhythms are perfectly in time with the pitch of loneliness. She pounds away at her words until they make a melancholy sound." Paste

NAME INDEX

This index of author names and pseudonyms provides a quick reference for finding authors who have written under multiple names. Included, also, are name listings that may require clarification with regard to accurate alphabetization (e.g. Honore de Balzac is filed under *Balzac, Honore de*.) The names are arranged alphabetically, and are listed according to Library of Congress name authority files. Furthermore, this list provides a two-way reference point for pseudonyms. For example, Mark Twain can be found under both *Twain, Mark, 1835-1910*, and *Clemens, Samuel Langhorne*. Works by authors included in this index may be found in Part 1 of this collection, listed under the name used in the responsibility statement of the work. As only authors listed in the *Fiction Core Collection* are included in this index, it should not be considered an exhaustive listing of current and past pseudonyms.

Cauwelaert, Didier van, 1960-
 See Van Cauwelaert, Didier
Cavallo, Evelyn
 See also Spark, Muriel
Celine, Louis-Ferdinand, 1894-1961
 See also Destouches, Henri-Louis
Challans, Mary
 See also Renault, Mary, 1905-1983
Chekhonte, Antosha
 See also Chekhov, Anton Pavlovich, 1860-
 1904
Chekhov, Anton Pavlovich, 1860-1904
 See Chekhonte, Antosha
Chesney, Marion
 See also Tremaine, Jennie; Beaton, M.C.;
 Chesterton, G. K.
Chesterton, G.K.
 See also Chesney, Marion; Tremaine, Jennie;
 Beaton, M.C.
Chisholm, P. F., 1958-
 See Patricia Finney
Chkhartishvili, Grigory
 See also Akunin, Boris, 1956-
Chu, T'ien-Hsin, 1958-
 See also Zhu Tianxin
Claudine, Sidonie Gabrielle
 See also Colette, 1873-1954
Clemens, Samuel Langhorne
 See Twain, Mark, 1835-1910
Clement, Hal, 1922-2003
 See Stubbs, Harry Clement
Clezio, J.-M. G. le
 See Le Clezio, J.-M. G., 1940-
Cohen, Janet
 See also Neel, Janet, 1940-
Coleman, William Laurence
 See Coleman, Lonnie, 1920-1982
Colette, 1873-1954
 See also Claudine, Sidonie Gabrielle
Collins, Hunt, 1926-2005
 See also Cannon, Curt, 1926-2005; Hunter,
 Evan, 1926-2005; Hannon, Ezra, 1926-2005;
 Hudson, Dean, 1926-2005; Marsten, Richard,
 1926-2005; McBain, Ed, 1926-2005
Conde, Maryse, 1937-
 See also Boucolon, Maryse
Conroy, Joseph Robert
 See also Conroy, Robert, 1938-
Conroy, Robert, 1938-
 See also Conroy, Joseph Robert
Cookson, Catherine
 See also Marchant, Catherine
Cornwell, Bernard
 See also Kells, Susannah
Cornwell, David John Moore
 See also Le Carre, John, 1931-

Craig, Alisa
 See also MacLeod, Charlotte
Crayencour, Marguerite De
 See also Yourcenar, Marguerite
Crayon, Geoffrey
 See also Irving, Washington, 1783-1859;
 Knickerbocker, Diedrich
Crichton, Michael, 1942-2008
 See also Douglas, Michael; Hudson, Jeffery;
 Lange, John
Cross, Amanda, 1926-2003
 See also Heilbrun, Carolyn G., 1926-2003
Cross, Mary Ann Evans
 See Eliot, George, 1819-1880
Cunningham, E.V.
 See also Fast, Howard, 1914-2003
Czaczkes, Shmuel Josef
 See also Agnon, Shmuel Yosef, 1888-1970
Daniel, Margaret Truman
 See also Truman, Margaret, 1924-2008
Dargatz, Gail Anderson-
 See Anderson-Dargatz, Gail, 1963-
Davenport, Diana
 See also Davenport, Kiana
Davenport, Kiana
 See also Davenport, Diana
Davies, Douglas Brooks
 See Brooks-Davies, Douglas
Davies, Robertson, 1913-1995
 See Davies, William Robertson
Davies, William Robertson
 See Davies, Robertson, 1913-1995
Dawlatabadi, Mahmud, 1940-
 See Dowlatabadi, Mahmud
De Alba, Alicia Gaspar
 See Gaspar de Alba, Alicia, 1958-
De Balzac, Honore
 See Balzac, Honore de, 1799-1850
De Beauvoir, Simone
 See Beauvoir, Simone de, 1908-1986
De Crayencour, Marguerite
 See Yourcenar, Marguerite
De Hartog, Jan, 1914-2002
 See Hartog, Jan de
De Heriz, Enrique
 See Heriz, Enrique de, 1964-
De Jonge, Peter
 See Jonge, Peter de
De Loo, Tessa
 See Loo, Tessa de
De Moor, Margriet
 See Moor, Margriet de
De Saint-Aubin, Horace
 See also Balzac, Honore de, 1799-1850
De Saint-Exupery, Antoine
 See Saint-Exupery, Antoine de, 1900-1944

Deane, Conor Fitzgerald
 See also Fitzgerald, Conor

Deaver, Jeffery
 See also Jefferies, William, 1950-

Defoe, Daniel, 1661?-1731
 See also Foe, Daniel; Moreton, Andrew

DeLillo, Don
 See also Birdwell, Cleo

Delinsky, Barbara
 See also Douglass, Billie; Drake, Bonnie

Deng Xiaohua
 See also Tsan-hsueh, 1953-; Can Xue

Denning, Troy
 See also Awlinson, Richard

Dennis, Patrick, 1921-1976
 See also Tanner, Edward Everett

Destouches, Henri-Louis
 See Celine, Louis-Ferdinand, 1894-1961

Di Lampedusa, Giuseppe Tomasi
 See Tomasi di Lampedusa, Giuseppe, 1896-1957

Diago, Evelio Rosero
 See Rosero Diago, Evelio, 1958-

Dick, R. A.
 See also Leslie, Josephine Aimee Campbell, 1898-1979

Dickens, Charles, 1812-1870
 See also Boz; Sparks, Timothy

Dikty, Julian May
 See May, Julian, 1931-

Ditzen, Rudolf
 See also Fallada, Hans, 1893-1947

Dominic, R. B.
 See also Lathen, Emma

Dos Passos, John
 See Passos, John Dos

Dostoevskii, Fedor Mikhailovich
 See Dostoyevsky, Fyodor, 1821-1881

Douglas, Michael
 See also Crichton, Michael, 1942-2008; Hudson, Jeffery; Lange, John

Douglass, Billie
 See Delinsky, Barbara; Drake, Bonnie

Doyle, Conan
 See Doyle, Sir Arthur Conan, 1859-1930

Drabble, Margaret, 1939-
 See also Swift, Margaret

Drake, Bonnie
 See Delinsky, Barbara; Douglass, Billie

Drawcansir, Alexander
 See also Fielding, Henry, 1707-1754

Ducornet, Rikki
 See also Rikki

Dudevant, Amantine Lucile Aurore Dupin
 See also Dudevant, Mme; Dupin, Amantine Aurore Lucile; Sand, George, 1804-1876;

Sand, Jules

Dudevant, Mme
 See also Dudevant, Amantine Lucile Aurore Dupin; Dupin, Amantine Aurore Lucile; Sand, George, 1804-1876; Sand, Jule

Dukes, Carol Muske, 1945-
 See Muske-Dukes, Carol

Dunn, Kathleen
 See also Fleming, Irene, 1939-

Dupin, Amantine Aurore Lucile, 1804-1876
 See also Dudevant, Amantine Lucile Aurore Dupin; Dudevant, Mme; Sand, George; Sand, Jules

Eagles, Cynthia Harrod
 See Harrod-Eagles, Cynthia

Echevarria, Roberto Gonzalez
 See Gonzalez Echevarria, Roberto

Edric, Robert, 1956-
 See also Armitage, G. E.

Eliot, Alice C.
 See also Jewett, Sarah Orne, 1849-1909

Eliot, George, 1819-1880
 See also Cross, Mary Ann Evans

Elliot, Jessie
 See also Grodstein, Lauren

English, Isobel
 See also Braybrooke, June, 1920-1994; Jolliffe, June

Ephron, Hallie
 See also Touger, Hallie Ephron

Epstein, Joseph, 1937-
 See also Aristides

Escobar, Marisol
 See also Marisol, 1930-

Evanovich, Janet
 See also Hall, Steffie

Evans, Evan
 See also Brand, Max, 1892-1944; Faust, Frederick

Evelyn, John Michael
 See also Underwood, Michael, 1916-

Exupery, Antoine de Saint
 See Saint-Exupery, Antoine de, 1900-1944

Fair, A. A.
 See also Gardner, Erle Stanley, 1889-1970; Kendrake, Carleton; Kenny, Charles J.

Fairbairn, Ann, 1901 or 2-1972
 See also Tait, Dorothy

Fallada, Hans, 1893-1947
 See also Ditzen, Rudolf

Fallon, Martin
 See also Graham, James; Higgins, Jack, 1929-; Marlowe, Hugh; Patterson, Harry

Fast, Howard, 1914-2003
 See also Cunningham, E. V.

Faust, Frederick

Hamilton, Clive
    See also Lewis, C. S., 1898-1963
Hammett, Samuel Dashiell
    See Hammett, Dashiell, 1894-1961
Hannon, Ezra, 1926-2005
    See also Cannon, Curt, 1926-2005; Collins, Hunt, 1926-2005; Hannon, Ezra, 1926-2005; Hudson, Dean, 1926-2005; Hunter, Evan, 1926-2005; Marsten, Richard, 1926-2005; McBain, Ed, 1926-2005
Harding, John Wesley, 1965-
    See also Stace, Wesley Harding
Harris, Mark, 1922-2007
    See also Wiggen, Henry W.
Hart, Harry
    See also Frank, Pat, 1907-1964
Hartog, Jan de
    See De Hartog, Jan, 1914-2002
Harvey, Caroline
    See also Trollope, Joanna
Harvey, Jack
    See also Rankin, Ian, 1960-
Hauck, Stephanie
    See also Bancroft, Stephanie; Bond, Stephanie
Hawk, Alex
    See also Kelton, Elmer, 1926-2009; McElroy, Lee
Hawkins, Anthony Hope
    See Hope, Anthony, 1863-1933
Haynes, Conrad
    See also Haynes, Dana
Haynes, Dana
    See also Haynes, Conrad
Haywood, Gar Anthony
    See also Shannon, Ray
Head, Ann
    See also Morse, Anne Christensen
Hedge, John
    See also Buck, Pearl S., 1892-1973; Walsh, Pearl S.
Hegarty, Frances
    See also Fyfield, Frances, 1948-
Heilbrun, Carolyn G., 1926-2003
    See also Cross, Amanda, 1926-2003
Helgason, Hallgrimur
    See Hallgrimur Helgason, 1959-
Henry, O., 1862-1910
    See also Porter, William Sydney
Hervey, Evelyn
    See also Keating, H. R. F., 1926-2011; Keating, Henry Reymond Fitzwalter
Higgins, Jack, 1929-
    See also Fallon, Martin; Graham, James; Marlowe, Hugh; Patterson, Harry
Highet, Helen MacInnes
    See also MacInnes, Helen, 1907-1985

Highsmith, Patricia, 1921-1995
    See also Morgan, Claire
Hill, Joe
    See also King, Joseph Hillstrom
Hill, John, 1945-
    See also Koontz, Dean R.
Hill, Reginald, 1936-
    See also Morland, Dick; Ruell, Patrick; Underhill, Charles
Hiraoka, Kimitake
    See also Mishima, Yukio, 1925-1970
Hobb, Robin
    See also Lindholm, Megan; Ogden, Margaret Astrid Lindholm
Holton, Leonard
    See also O'Connor, Patrick; Wibberley, Leonard, 1915-1983
Hope, Anthony, 1863-1933
    See also Hawkins, Anthony Hope
Horowitz, James
    See also Salter, James
Hudson, Dean, 1926-2005
    See also Cannon, Curt, 1926-2005; Collins, Hunt, 1926-2005; Hannon, Ezra, 1926-2005; Hunter, Evan, 1926-2005; Marsten, Richard, 1926-2005; McBain, Ed, 1926-2005
Hudson, Jeffery
    See also Crichton, Michael, 1942-2008; Douglas, Michael; Lange, John
Hueffer, Ford Madox
    See Ford, Ford Madox, 1873-1939
Hulme, Juliet
    See also Perry, Anne, 1938-
Humphreys, C. C.
    See also Humphreys, Chris
Humphreys, Chris
    See also Humphreys, C. C.
Hunter, Evan, 1926-2005
    See also Cannon, Curt, 1926-2005; Collins, Hunt, 1926-2005; Hannon, Ezra, 1926-2005; Hudson, Dean, 1926-2005; Marsten, Richard, 1926-2005; McBain, Ed, 1926-2005
Ibanez, Vicente Blasco
    See Blasco Ibanez, Vicente, 1867-1928
Irving, Clifford
    See also Luckless, John
Irving, Washington, 1783-1859
    See also Crayon, Geoffrey; Knickerbocker, Diedrich
Isherwood, Christopher, 1904-1986
    See also Bradshaw-Isherwood, Christopher William
Jaber, Diana Abu-
    See Abu-Jaber, Diana
James, P. D.
    See also White, Phyllis Dorothy James

Lathen, Emma
   See also Dominic, R. B.
Lawhead, Stephen R.
   See Lawhead, Steve, 1950-
Lawless, Anthony
   See also Fleming, Oliver; Macdonald, Filip; MacDonald, Philip, 1899-1981; Porlock, Martin
Lax, Andromeda Romano-
   See Romano-Lax, Andromeda, 1971-
Le Carre, John, 1931-
   See also Cornwell, David John Moore
Lear, Peter
   See also Lovesey, Peter
Lee, Lilian
   See also Li, Pi-hua
Lennon, J. Robert, 1970-
   See also Lennon, John Robert
Lennon, John Robert
   See also Lennon, J. Robert, 1970-
Leslie, Josephine Aimee Campbell, 1898-1979
   See also Dick, R. A.
Lessing, Doris May, 1919-
   See also Somers, Jane
Leventhal, Alice Walker
   See also Walker, Alice, 1944-
Lewis, C. S. (Clive Staples), 1898-1963
   See also Hamilton, Clive
Lewis, M. G. (Matthew Gregory), 1775-1818
   See also Lewis, Monk
Lewis, Monk
   See Lewis, M. G., 1775-1818
Lewis, Sinclair, 1885-1951
   See also Graham, Tom
Li, Pi-hua
   See also Lee, Lilian
Lindsay, Jeffry P., 1952-
   See also Freundlich, Jeffry P.; Lindsay, Jeff
Lindsay, Jeff
   See also Lindsay, Jeffry P., 1952-; Freundlich, Jeffry P.
Lindholm, Megan
   See also Hobb, Robin; Ogden, Margaret Astrid Lindholm
Linmark, R. Zamora
   See also Zamora Linmark, R.
Litwos
   See also Sienkiewicz, Henryk, 1846-1916
Llosa, Mario Vargas
   See Vargas Llosa, Mario, 1936-
Loo, Tessa de
   See also De Loo, Tessa
Lovesey, Peter
   See also Lear, Peter
Lu Jiamin
   See also Jiang Rong, 1946-

Lucas, Victoria
   See also Plath, Sylvia
Luckless, John
   See also Irving, Clifford
Ludlum, Robert, 1927-2001
   See also Ryder, Jonathan; Shepherd, Michael
Lynch, James Mitchell
   See Lynch, Jim, 1961-
Lynch, Jim, 1961-
   See also Lynch, James Mitchell
Lytton, Edward Bulwer Lytton, 1803-1873
   See Bulwer-Lytton, Edward
MacAlister, Katie
   See also Arends, Marthe; Maxwell, Katie
Macdonald, Filip
   See MacDonald, Philip, 1899-1981
   Lawless, Anthony; Porlock, Martin; Fleming, Oliver
Macdonald, John
   See Macdonald, John Ross; Macdonald, Ross, 1915-1983; Millar, Kenneth
Macdonald, John Ross
   See Macdonald, John; Macdonald, Ross, 1915-1983; Millar, Kenneth
Macdonald, Malcolm, 1932-
   See also Ross-Macdonald, Malcolm
MacDonald, Philip, 1899-1981
   See also Fleming, Oliver; Lawless, Anthony; Macdonald, Filip; Porlock, Martin
Macdonald, Ross, 1915-1983
   See also Macdonald, John; Macdonald, John Ross; Millar, Kenneth
MacInnes, Helen, 1907-1985
   See also Highet, Helen MacInnes
Mackintosh, Elizabeth
   See also Tey, Josephine, 1896-1952
MacLean, Alistair, 1922-1987
   See also Stuart, Ian
MacLeod, Charlotte
   See also Craig, Alisa
MacNeil, Duncan
   See also McCutchan, Philip, 1920-
Mahfouz, Naguib
   See Mahfuz, Najib, 1911-2006
Malraux, Georges Andre
   See Malraux, Andre, 1901-1976
Mandel, Emily St. John
   See St. John Mandel, Emily, 1979-
Mankind (Wrestler)
   See Foley, Mick, 1965-
Mann, Erica
   See also Jong, Erica
Manor, Jason
   See also Hall, Oakley M.
Mansfield, Kathleen Beauchamp
   See Mansfield, Katherine, 1888-1923

Marchant, Catherine
   See also Cookson, Catherine
Marisol, 1930-
   See also Escobar, Marisol
Markandaya, Kamala, 1924-2004
   See also Taylor, Kamala Purnaiya
Marlowe, Hugh
   See also Fallon, Martin; Graham, James; Higgins, Jack, 1929-; Patterson, Harry
Marlowe, Ralph
   See Manheim, Ralph, 1907-1992
Marquez, Gabriel Garcia
   See Garcia Marquez, Gabriel, 1928-
Marshall, Sarah Catherine Wood
   See Marshall, Catherine, 1914-1983
Marsten, Richard, 1926-2005
   See also Cannon, Curt, 1926-2005; Collins, Hunt, 1926-2005; Hannon, Ezra, 1926-2005; Hudson, Dean, 1926-2005; Hunter, Evan, 1926-2005; Marsten, Richard, 1926-2005; McBain, Ed, 1926-2005
Marston, Edward
   See also Allen, Conrad, 1940-
Martin, Peter
   See Melville, James, 1931-; Martin, Roy Peter
Martin, Roy Peter
   See Melville, James, 1931-; Martin, Peter
Marut, Ret
   See also Feige, Hermann Albert Otto Max; Torsvan, Berick Traven; Torsvan, Traven; Traven, B.
Matas, Enrique Vila-
   See Vila-Matas, Enrique, 1948-
Maugham, Somerset
   See Maugham, W. Somerset (William Somerset), 1874-1965
Maxwell, Katie
   See also MacAlister, Katie
May, Julian, 1931-
   See also Dikty, Julian May
McBain, Ed, 1926-2005
   See also Cannon, Curt, 1926-2005; Collins, Hunt, 1926-2005; Hannon, Ezra, 1926-2005; Hudson, Dean, 1926-2005; Hunter, Evan, 1926-2005; Marsten, Richard, 1926-2005; McBain, Ed, 1926-2005
McCall Smith, Alexander, 1948-
   See also McCall Smith, R. A. (R. Alexander)
McCall Smith, R. A. (R. Alexander),
   See also McCall Smith, Alexander, 1948-
McCutchan, Philip, 1920-
   See also MacNeil, Duncan
McElroy, Lee
   See also Kelton, Elmer, 1926-2009; Hawk, Alex
McGarrity, Mark

See also Gill, Bartholomew, 1943-2002
McGuire, Seanan
   See also Grant, Mira
McMahon, Neil
   See also Rhodes, Daniel
McPherson, Jessamyn West
   See West, Jessamyn, 1902-1984; West, Mary Jessamyn
Melville, James, 1931-
   See also Martin, Peter; Martin, Roy Peter
Mercado, Sergio Ramirez
   See Ramirez Mercado, Sergio, 1942-
Mertz, Barbara Gross
   See also Michaels, Barbara; Peters, Elizabeth, 1927-
Michaels, Barbara
   See also Mertz, Barbara Gross; Peters, Elizabeth, 1927-
Millar, Kenneth
   See also Macdonald, Ross, 1915-1983
Miller, A. D.
   See Miller, Andrew, 1974-
Mishima, Yukio, 1925-1970
   See also Hiraoka, Kimitake
Miss Read
   See also Read, 1913-
   Saint, Dora Jessie
Mo, Yen
   See Mo Yan, 1956-
Moberg, Carl Artur Vilhelm
   See Moberg, Vilhelm, 1898-1973
Molina, Antonio Munoz
   See Munoz Molina, Antonio, 1956-
Morales, Adelaida Garcia
   See Garcia Morales, Adelaida
Moravia, Alberto, 1907-1990
   See also Pincherle, Alberto
Moreton, Andrew
   See also Defoe, Daniel, 1661?-1731; Foe, Daniel
Morgan, Claire
   See also Highsmith, Patricia, 1921-1995
Morland, Dick
   See also Hill, Reginald, 1936-; Ruell, Patrick; Underhill, Charles
Morris, Roger N.
   See Morris, R. N., 1960-
Morrison, Patricia Kennealy-
   See Kennealy-Morrison, Patricia
Morse, Anne Christensen
   See also Head, Ann
Moulessehoul, Mohammed, 1955-
   See also Khadra, Yasmina
Moya, Horacio Castellanos
   See Castellanos Moya, Horacio, 1957-
Munro, H. H.

See Murasaki Shikibu, b. 978?; Fujiwara, Murasaki

Shraer, Maksim
    See Shrayer, Maxim, 1967-

Shugaar, Tony
    See Shugaar, Antony

Shute, Nevil, 1899-1960
    See also Norway, Nevil Shute

Sienkiewicz, Henryk, 1846-1916
    See also Litwos

Sigurdardottir, Yrsa
    See also Yrsa Sigurdardóttir

Siler, Jenny
    See also Carr, Alex

Sjowall, Maj, 1935-
    See also Wahloo, Maj Sjowall

Skinner, Marie Bostwick
    See also Bostwick, Marie

Smith, Alexander McCall
    See McCall Smith, Alexander, 1948-

Smith, B. J.
    See also Smith, Brad, 1957-

Smith, Brad, 1957-
    See also Smith, B. J.

Smith, Florence Margaret
    See also Smith, Stevie, 1902-1971

Smith, Mary-Ann Tirone
    See Tirone Smith, Mary-Ann, 1944-

Smith, R. A. McCall
    See McCall Smith, Alexander, 1948-

Smith, Richard Liebmann-
    See Liebmann-Smith, Richard, 1942-

Smith, Stevie, 1902-1971
    See also Smith, Florence Margaret

Snow, Lucy
    See also Aubert, Rosemary, 1946-

Soldan, Edmundo Paz
    See Paz Soldan, Edmundo, 1967-

Somers, Jane
    See also Lessing, Doris May, 1919-

Spark, Muriel
    See also Cavallo, Evelyn

Sparks, Timothy
    See also Dickens, Charles, 1812-1870; Boz

Spillane, Frank Morrison
    See also Spillane, Mickey, 1918-2006

Spillane, Mickey, 1918-2006
    See also Spillane, Frank Morrison

Stace, Wesley Harding
    See also Harding, John Wesley, 1965-

Stack, Andy
    See also Rule, Ann

Stafford, Jean, 1915-1979
    See also Jensen, Mrs. Oliver

Stanley, Michael
    See also Sears, Michael; Trollip, Stanley

Stendhal, 1783-1842
    See also Beyle, Marie Henri; Brulard, Henry

Stephens, Eve
    See Anthony, Evelyn, 1928-

Steptoe, Lydia
    See Barnes, Djuna, 1892-1982

Stevens, Chevy
    See also Unischewski, Rene

Stowe, Harriet Elizabeth
    See Stowe, Harriet Beecher, 1811-1896

Stuart, Ian
    See also MacLean, Alistair, 1922-1987

Stubbs, Harry Clement
    See also Clement, Hal, 1922-2003

Sullivan, Vernon
    See also Vian, Boris, 1920-1959

Sutherland, J. A.
    See Sutherland, John, 1938-

Svevo, Italo, 1861-1928
    See also Schmitz, Ettore

Swift, Margaret
    See also Drabble, Margaret, 1939-

Tait, Dorothy
    See Fairbairn, Ann, 1901 or 2-1972

Tan Twan Eng
    See Eng, Tan Twan

Tanner, Edward Everett
    See Dennis, Patrick, 1921-1976

Taylor, Kamala Purnaiya
    See Markandaya, Kamala, 1924-2004

Templeton, Edith, 1916-
    See also Walbrook, Louise

Tey, Josephine, 1896-1952
    See also Mackintosh, Elizabeth

Thackeray, William Makepeace, 1811-1863
    See also Titmarsh, Michael Angelo

Thomas, Ross, 1926-1995
    See also Bleeck, Oliver

Thompson, Margaret Cezair
    See Cezair-Thompson, Margaret

Titmarsh, Michael Angelo
    See also Thackeray, William Makepeace, 1811-1863

Toer, Pramoedya Ananta, 1925-2006
    See Pramoedya Ananta Toer

Toole, F. X., 1930-2002
    See also Boyd, Jerry

Torsvan, Berick Traven
    See also Feige, Hermann Albert Otto Max; Marut, Ret; Traven, B.; Torsvan, Traven

Torsvan, Traven
    See also Feige, Hermann Albert Otto Max; Marut, Ret; Traven, B.; Torsvan, Berick Traven;

Touger, Hallie Ephron
    See Ephron, Hallie

See Burgess, Anthony, 1917-1993
Wolfe, J. Thomas
　See Wolfe, Tom
Woodhouse, Susan T.
　See Carlyle, Liz, 1958-
Woods, Sara
　See also Bowen-Judd, Sara Hutton
Yan Ni
　See also Shan Sa, 1972-

Yen, Ko-ling
　See Yan, Geling, 1958-
Yorke, Margaret
　See also Larminie, Margaret Beda; Nicholson, Margaret Beda
Yrsa Sigurdardottir
　See also Sigurdardottir, Yrsa
Zafon, Carlos Ruiz
　See Ruiz Zafon, Carlos, 1964-

TITLE AND SUBJECT INDEX

This index to the books listed in part 1 includes title and subject entries, arranged in one alphabet. Full information for each book is given in part 1 under the main entry, which is usually the author.

Title entries. Novels are listed by title. The author's name, if applicable, is listed immediately after.

Subject entries. Subject headings are printed in capital letters. The listing of a work under a subject indicates that a major portion of the work is about that subject. Under genre headings, such as SCIENCE FICTION or ADVENTURE FICTION, works of that genre are listed. The subject headings listed reflect the merging of H. W. Wilson indexing and EBSCO Information Services indexing. While the formatting has been adjusted, every effort has been made to provide multiple access points to the works included in this collection.

10 lb. penalty. Francis, D.

100 YEARS' WAR *See* Hundred Years' War, 1339-1453

The **100-year-old** man who climbed out the window and disappeared. Jonasson, Jonas

101 Reykjavik. Hallgrimur Helgason

11/22/63. King, S.

The **13.** Allen, S.

1356. Cornwell, B.

1861-1865

Gohlke, C. I have seen him in the watchfires

1876. Vidal, G.

1916. Llywelyn, M.

1919. Dos Passos, J.

1921. Llywelyn, M.

1929. Turner, F. W.

1940. Neugeboren, J.

1949. Llywelyn, M.

1972. Llywelyn, M.

The **19th** wife. Ebershoff, D.

1Q84. Murakami, H.

1st to die. Patterson, J.

200 years of great American short stories.

2001: a space odyssey. Clarke, A. C.

2010: odyssey two. Clarke, A. C.

2012: the war for souls. Strieber, W.

2017. Slavnikova, Olga

2030. Brooks, A.

2061: odyssey three. Clarke, A. C.

20th century ghosts. Hill, J.

22 Britannia Road. Hodgkinson, A.

2312. Robinson, K. S.

2666. Bolano, R.

The **27** ingredient chili con carne murders. Pickard, N.

3 by Irving. Irving, J.

3001: the final odyssey. Clarke, A. C.

36 arguments for the existence of God. Goldstein, R.

3: This gun for hire, The confidential agent, The ministry of fear. Greene, G.

The **42nd** parallel. Dos Passos, J.

The **47th** samurai. Hunter, S.

4TH OF JULY *See* Fourth of July

61 hours. Child, L.

82 Desire. Smith, J.

871-899

Cornwell, B. Lords of the North

A

a + e 4ever. Merey, I.

A is for alibi. Grafton, S.

The **A.B.C.** murders. Christie, A.

Abaddon's Gate. Corey, J. S. A.

Abandon. Iyer, P.

ABANDONED CHILDREN

See also Child welfare; Children

Beverley, J. Winter Fire

Celona, M. Y

Oates, J. C. Mudwoman

Quindlen, A. Blessings

Sallis, J. The killer is dying

Shreve, A. Light on snow

ABANDONED TOWNS *See* Extinct cities; Ghost towns

The **Abbess** of Crewe. Spark, M.

ABBEYS

Austen, J. Northanger Abbey

ABBEYS -- ENGLAND

Dean, A. A woman of consequence

Huggins, J. B. Nightbringer

Abbott awaits. Bachelder, C.

Abdication. Nicolson, J.

The **abduction.** Grippando, J.

ABDUCTION

See also Kidnapping

Hayder, M. The treatment

Robards, K. Shiver

Stevens, C. Still missing

Abel (Biblical figure)

About

Maine, D. Fallen

ABERDEEN (SCOTLAND)

MacBride, S. Blind eye

MacBride, S. Cold granite

MacBride, S. Dying Light

Abide with me. Strout, E.

Ablutions. DeWitt, P.

ABNORMAL PSYCHOLOGY *See* Mind and body; Nervous system

ABOLITION OF SLAVERY *See* Abolitionists; Slavery; Slaves -- Emancipation

ABOLITIONISTS

Banks, R. Cloudsplitter

Heidish, M. A woman called Moses

Stowe, H. B. Uncle Tom's cabin

Tryon, T. In the fire of spring

Wright, S. The Amalgamation Polka

ABOLITIONISTS -- FICTION

Leveen, L. The secrets of Mary Bowser

ABORIGINAL AUSTRALIAN ART *See* Art

ABORIGINAL AUSTRALIANS

See also Australians; Indigenous peoples

Scott, K. That deadman dance

ABORIGINES *See* Indigenous peoples

ABORTION

Earle, S. I'll never get out of this world alive

Irving, J. The cider house rules

Jordan, H. When she woke

McKinney-Whetstone, D. Leaving Cecil Street

Patterson, R. N. No safe place

Patterson, R. N. Protect and defend

Piercy, M. Braided lives

Pottinger, S. The fourth procedure

Searles, J. Boy still missing

ABORTION -- ETHICAL ASPECTS *See* Ethics

About a boy. Hornby, N.

About face. Leon, D.

About Schmidt. Begley, L.

Above suspicion. MacInnes, H.

Abraham Lincoln: vampire hunter. Grahame-Smith, S.

Absalom, Absalom! Faulkner, W.

ABSAROKA RANGE (MONT. AND WYO.)

Hagy, A. Boleto

The **absent** one. Adler-Olsen, J.

ABSENTEE FATHERS

Priest, C. Dreadnought

Absolute friends. Le Carre, J.

An **absolute** gentleman. Kinder, R. M.

Absolute power. Baldacci, D.

Absolute truths. Howatch, S.

Absolution. Flanery, P.

The **absolutist.** Boyne, J.

The **abstinence** teacher. Perrotta, T.

ABSTRACT ART *See* Art

Absurdistan. Shteyngart, G.

Abundance. Naslund, S. J.

ABUSE OF ANIMALS *See* Animal welfare

ABUSE OF CHILDREN *See* Child abuse

Abuse of power. Rosenberg, N. T.

ABUSE OF WIVES *See* Wife abuse

ABUSED CHILDREN *See* Child abuse

ABUSED WIVES *See* Abused women; Wife abuse

ABUSED WIVES -- WEST VIRGINIA

McCall, D. Dreamcatcher

ABUSED WOMEN

See also Victims of crimes; Women

Anderson, C. Star bright

Eagle, K. Ride a painted pony

Edwards, Y. A Cupboard full of coats

McCall, D. Dreamcatcher

Rice, L. Little night

Roberts, N. Dance upon the air

Abyss. Hagberg, D.

The **abyss** of human illusion. Sorrentino, G.

Acacia. Durham, D. A.

ACADEMIC ACHIEVEMENT *See* Success

ACADEMIC LIBRARIES *See* Libraries

ACADEMY AWARDS (MOTION PICTURES) *See* Motion pictures

ACADIANS

Morsi, P. The love charm

ACADIANS -- LOUISIANA *See* Cajuns

Accelerando. Stross, C.

Acceptance. Coll, S.

The **accident.** Kadare, I.

ACCIDENT VICTIMS

Cramer, W. D. Bad ground

Davidson, A. The gargoyle

Gould, J. A moment in time

Jones, S. The uninvited guests

Kadare, I. The accident

King, S. Duma Key

Packer, A. The dive from Clausen's pier

Parkhurst, C. The dogs of Babel

Picoult, J. Lone wolf

Simmons, D. Drood

The **accidental.** Smith, A.

An **accidental** man. Murdoch, I.

The **accidental** time machine. Haldeman, J. W.

The **accidental** tourist. Tyler, A.

ACCIDENTS

Aira, C. An afternoon in the life of a landscape painter

Brown, R. Tender mercies

Carroll, J. The ghost in love

De los Santos, M. Belong to me

Delinsky, B. The summer I dared

Evans, N. The horse whisperer

Hamilton, J. When Madeline was young

Heriz, E. d. Lies

King, S. Duma Key

Lawrence, S. The lightning keeper

Mawer, S. The fall

Oates, J. C. American appetites

Grondahl, J. C. Lucca
Harris, E. L. Not a day goes by
Iyer, P. Abandon
Korda, M. Curtain
Leonard, E. LaBrava
Lipman, E. The family man
Lord, B. B. The middle heart
McElroy, J. Actress in the house
McPhee, J. A man of no moon
Michael, J. Acts of love
Oates, J. C. Blonde
O'Connor, J. Ghost light
Pilcher, R. Winter solstice
Sontag, S. In America
Steel, D. Sunset in St. Tropez
Taylor, D. J. Ask Alice
Thomas, R. Voodoo, Ltd
Trollope, J. Second honeymoon
Walton, J. Ha'penny
Weldon, F. Worst fears
Williams, T. The Roman spring of Mrs. Stone
Wilson, K. The family Fang
Wolfe, G. An evil guest
Acts of faith. Caputo, P.
Acts of love. Michael, J.
Ada. Nabokov, V. V.
Adam (Biblical figure)
About
Maine, D. Fallen
Adam and Eve and Pinch me. Rendell, R.
Adam Bede. Eliot, G.
Adams, Abigail, 1744-1818
About
Hambly, B. Patriot hearts
Adams, John Quincy, 1767-1848
About
Pesci, D. Amistad
Adams, John, 1735-1826
About
Shaara, J. Rise to rebellion
ADAPTATION (BIOLOGY) *See* Biology; Ecology; Genetics; Variation (Biology)
ADDICTION -- FICTION
Palahniuk, C. Choke
ADDICTION TO ALCOHOL *See* Alcoholism
ADDICTION TO DRUGS *See* Drug abuse
ADDICTIVE BEHAVIOR *See* Compulsive behavior
ADDICTS *See* Drug addicts
Addie Pray. Brown, J. D.
ADIRONDACK MOUNTAINS (N.Y.)
Doctorow, E. L. Loon Lake
Robinson, R. Sweetwater
Unger, L. Heartbroken
ADMINISTRATION *See* Civil service; Management; Public administration

ADMINISTRATION OF CRIMINAL JUSTICE
See Administration of justice; Criminal law
Admiral Hornblower in the West Indies. Forester, C. S.
ADMIRALS
Donoghue, E. The sealed letter
Nordhoff, C. Men against the sea
Nordhoff, C. Mutiny on the Bounty
O'Brian, P. The golden ocean
Sontag, S. The volcano lover
Unsworth, B. Losing Nelson
ADOLESCENCE
Abbott, M. E. The end of everything
Abraham, P. The romance reader
Aciman, A. A. Call me by your name
Alexie, S. Flight
Barbery, M. The elegance of the hedgehog
Beachy, S. Boneyard
Beale, E. Another life altogether
Beard, J. A. In Zanesville
Berg, E. We are all welcome here
Betts, D. Souls raised from the dead
Bilenchi, R. The chill
Bock, C. Beautiful children
Bognanni, P. The house of tomorrow
Brown, L. Joe
Burns, O. A. Cold Sassy tree
Campbell, B. J. Once upon a river
Chevalier, T. Burning bright
Coe, J. The Rotters' Club
Cohen, L. H. Heart, you bully, you punk
Cooke, C. Daughters of the revolution
Dallas, S. Tallgrass
De Gramont, N. Gossip of the starlings
Dean, M. L. The time it takes to fall
Delaney, E. J. Broken Irish
DeLillo, D. Ratner's star
DeNiro, A. Total oblivion, more or less
Desai, K. The inheritance of loss
DeWoskin, R. Big girl small
Diaz, J. The brief wondrous life of Oscar Wao
Doctorow, E. L. Billy Bathgate
Doig, I. The bartender's tale
Doig, I. English Creek
Doyle, L. Go, mutants!
Dragoman, G. The white king
Durham, D. A. Gabriel's story
Durrow, H. W. The girl who fell from the sky
Earley, T. The blue star
Earley, T. Jim the boy
Eugenides, J. Middlesex
Eugenides, J. The virgin suicides
Evenson, B. The open curtain
Evison, J. All about Lulu
Fielding, J. Heartstopper
Fitch, J. White oleander

Portes, A. Hick

Powell, P. Edisto

Powers, J. R. Do black patent-leather shoes really reflect up?

Price, R. The tongues of angels

Prose, F. Goldengrove

Quindlen, A. Object lessons

Raucher, H. Summer of '42

Riordan, R. Cold Springs

Rock, P. My abandonment

Rolvaag, O. E. Peder Victorious

Rosenberg, N. T. Interest of justice

Rossner, J. Perfidia

Roth, H. A diving rock on the Hudson

Roth, H. A star shines over Mt. Morris Park

Roth, P. Nemesis

Salinger, J. D. The catcher in the rye

Schulman, H. This beautiful life

Shakespeare, N. Secrets of the sea

Shange, N. Betsey Brown

Sharpe, M. The sleeping father

Shields, D. Dead languages

Shreve, A. Testimony

Shriver, L. We need to talk about Kevin

Siddons, A. R. Nora, Nora

Siddons, A. R. Sweetwater Creek

Sinclair, A. Coffee will make you black

Sittenfeld, C. Prep

Smith, A. The accidental

Smith, B. A tree grows in Brooklyn

Smith, D. I capture the castle

Sparks, N. A walk to remember

Stern, S. The frozen rabbi

Strauss, J. The dubious salvation of Jack V.

Strout, E. Amy and Isabelle

Swann, M. Flower children

Swarthout, G. F. Bless the beasts and children

Tea, M. Rose of no man's land

Thayer, N. An act of love

Toews, M. A complicated kindness

Townsend, S. The Adrian Mole diaries

Tremain, R. The way I found her

Tussing, J. The best people in the world

Ulinich, A. Petropolis

Updike, J. Terrorist

Vernon, O. Eden

Vernon, O. A killing in this town

Vlautin, W. Lean on Pete

Walton, J. Among others

Ward, J. Salvage the bones

Watson, L. American boy

Weber, K. The little women

Weiner, J. Certain girls

White, E. A boy's own story

Whitehead, C. Sag Harbor

Williams, A. J. Down from Cascom Mountain

Wimberley, D. The king of Colored Town

Winton, T. Breath

Wolff, R. The beginners

Wolff, T. Old school

Wolitzer, H. Hearts

Woo, S. J. Everything Asian

Woodrell, D. Winter's bone

Wray, J. Lowboy

Yoshimoto, B. Goodbye Tsugumi

ADOPTED CHILDREN

See also Adoptees; Children

Mazzarella, N. This heavy silence

McCall Smith, A. The forgotten affairs of youth

Palwick, S. Mending the moon

Stedman, M. L. The light between oceans

Ullman, E. By blood

ADOPTEES

Parker, T. J. Silent Joe

Trollope, J. Brother and sister

Ullman, E. By blood

ADOPTION

Clark, M. H. Nighttime is my time

D'Amato, B. White male infant

Goudge, E. Trail of secrets

Hagen, G. The Laments

Hallinan, T. A nail through the heart

Hood, A. The red thread

James, P. D. Innocent blood

Kingsolver, B. Pigs in heaven

Lee A gesture life

Mishima, Y. The decay of the angel

Moore, L. A gate at the stairs

Morrison, T. A mercy

Mortman, D. True colors

Parker, T. J. Silent Joe

Patchett, A. Run

Reed, K. The baby merchant

Tevis, W. S. The queen's gambit

Trollope, J. Brother and sister

Tyler, A. Digging to America

Umrigar, T. N. The weight of heaven

Weiner, J. Then came you

ADOPTION -- CORRUPT PRACTICES

See also Criminal law

ADOPTION -- FICTION

Gaspar de Alba, A. Desert blood

Gilmore, J. The Mothers

Lee, M. Somebody's daughter

Siegel, J. Detour

Adored. Bagshawe, T.

Adrian Mole. Townsend, S.

The **Adrian** Mole diaries. Townsend, S.

Adrian Mole: the lost years. Townsend, S.

ADULT CHILD ABUSE VICTIMS *See* Victims of crimes

ADULT CHILDREN

Gilman, D. A palm for Mrs. Pollifax
Gilman, D. The unexpected Mrs. Pollifax
Greene, G. Our man in Havana
Greene, G. Travels with my aunt
Grimes, M. Biting the moon
Grisham, J. The testament
Haggard, H. R. King Solomon's mines
Haggard, H. R. She
Harrison, H. The Stainless Steel Rat joins the circus
Harrison, H. The Stainless Steel Rat sings the blues
Hesse, H. Narcissus and Goldmund
Higgins, J. Flight of eagles
Higgins, J. Storm warning
Hilton, J. Lost horizon
Hoffman, A. The probable future
Holland, C. The angel and the sword
Holland, C. The firedrake
Holland, C. Jerusalem
Hope, A. The prisoner of Zenda
Hughes, R. A. W. A high wind in Jamaica
Iagnemma, K. The expeditions
Innes, H. The wreck of the Mary Deare
Jakes, J. American dreams
Jakes, J. California gold
Jennings, G. Raptor
Johnston, T. C. Dance on the wind
Johnston, T. C. Wind walker
Kay, G. G. The last light of the sun
Kelton, E. The way of the coyote
Keneally, T. To Asmara
Lackey, M. Firebird
Lambdin, D. King's captain
L'Amour, L. Last of the breed
L'Amour, L. May there be a road
L'Amour, L. The walking drum
Lebbon, T. Fallen
Llywelyn, M. Druids
Llywelyn, M. The last prince of Ireland
Llywelyn, M. Pride of lions
Llywelyn, M. Red Branch
London, J. The Sea-Wolf
Lowell, E. Pearl Cove
Ludlum, R. The Bourne identity
Ludlum, R. The Bourne supremacy
Ludlum, R. The Bourne ultimatum
Lustbader, E. V. Floating city
Lustbader, E. V. Second skin
MacInnes, H. Above suspicion
MacInnes, H. The Venetian affair
MacLean, A. Force 10 from Navarone
MacLean, A. The guns of Navarone
MacLean, A. Ice Station Zebra
MacLean, A. Night without end
MacLean, A. When eight bells toll
Marias, J. Voyage along the horizon
Martel, Y. Life of Pi

Martin, G. R. R. Hunter's run
Martin, W. Cape Cod
McCammon, R. R. Gone south
McCutchan, P. Apprentice to the sea
McCutchan, P. Cameron's crossing
McCutchan, P. The last farewell
McCutchan, P. The new lieutenant
McCutchan, P. The second mate
McDonald, R. Mr. Darwin's shooter
McMurtry, L. Comanche moon
McMurtry, L. Dead man's walk
McMurtry, L. Lonesome dove
McMurtry, L. Streets of Laredo
Michener, J. A. Alaska
Michener, J. A. Caravans
Michener, J. A. Caribbean
Michener, J. A. The drifters
Michener, J. A. Hawaii
Mitchard, J. Still summer
Naslund, S. J. Ahab's wife; or, The star-gazer
Nichols, P. Voyage to the North Star
Nordhoff, C. Botany Bay
Nordhoff, C. Pitcairn's Island
O'Brian, P. Blue at the mizzen
O'Brian, P. The commodore
O'Brian, P. The golden ocean
O'Brian, P. The hundred days
O'Brian, P. The unknown shore
O'Brian, P. The wine-dark sea
O'Brian, P. The yellow admiral
Orczy, E. Adventures of the Scarlet Pimpernel
Orczy, E. The elusive Pimpernel
Orczy, E. The Scarlet Pimpernel
Parkhurst, C. Lost and found
Parks, T. Rapids
Penney, S. The tenderness of wolves
Perez-Reverte, A. Captain Alatriste
Perez-Reverte, A. The nautical chart
Perez-Reverte, A. Purity of blood
Poyer, D. Black storm
Poyer, D. China Sea
Poyer, D. The circle
Poyer, D. The command
Poyer, D. Fire on the waters
Poyer, D. The gulf
Preston, D. The codex
Preston, D. Riptide
Pynchon, T. Against the day
Redfield, J. The celestine prophecy
Riley, J. M. In pursuit of the green lion
Roberts, K. L. Lydia Bailey
Roberts, K. L. Rabble in arms
Sabatini, R. Captain Blood
Sabatini, R. Scaramouche
Scott, W. Rob Roy
Seton, A. Avalon

Stevens, C. Always watching

Stevens, T. The informationist

Strugatsky, A. N. Roadside picnic

Tuomainen, A. The healer

Unger, L. Heartbroken

Verne, J. Around the world in eighty days

Verne, J. The extraordinary journeys: Twenty thousand leagues under the sea

Wilson, G. W. Alif the unseen

Wooding, C. Retribution falls

ADVENTURE FILMS See Motion pictures

ADVENTURE GRAPHIC NOVELS

See also Graphic novels

Henson, J. Jim Henson's tale of sand

ADVENTURE RADIO PROGRAMS See Radio programs

ADVENTURE STORIES

See also Adventure

Crichton, M. Pirate latitudes

Dumas, A. The last cavalier

Motion, A. Silver

ADVENTURE TELEVISION PROGRAMS See Television programs

ADVENTURE TRAVEL See Travel; Voyages and travels

ADVENTURERS

Halter, M. Messiah

Vollmann, W. T. Argall

The **adventures** and the memoirs of Sherlock Holmes. Doyle, A. C. S.

The **adventures** of Augie March. Bellow, S.

The **adventures** of Huckleberry Finn. Twain, M.

The **adventures** of Johnny Vermillion. Estleman, L. D.

The **adventures** of Menahem-Mendl. Sholem Aleichem

The **adventures** of Mottel, the cantor's son. Sholem Aleichem

Adventures of the Scarlet Pimpernel. Orczy, E.

The **adventures** of Tom Sawyer. Twain, M.

The **adventures** of Tom Sawyer, Tom Sawyer abroad, Tom Sawyer, detective. Twain, M.

The **adventuress.** Coleridge, N. D.

Adverbs. Handler, D.

The **adversary.** May, J.

ADVERTISING

See also Business; Retail trade

Kenney, J. Truth in advertising

Pohl, F. The space merchants

Roth, P. Everyman

Wells, H. G. Tono-Bungay

Whitehead, C. Apex hides the hurt

ADVERTISING AND CHILDREN See Advertising; Children

ADVERTISING COPY See Advertising; Authorship

ADVERTISING EXECUTIVES

Ballard, J. G. Kingdom come

Kenney, J. Truth in advertising

ADVERTISING LAYOUT AND TYPOGRAPHY

See Advertising; Printing; Typography

Advise and consent. Drury, A.

AENEAS (LEGENDARY CHARACTER)

Graham, J. Black ships

AERIAL BOMBS See Bombs

AERIAL PROPELLERS See Airplanes

AERIAL RECONNAISSANCE See Military aeronautics; Remote sensing

AERIALISTS

McCann, C. Let the great world spin

AERODROMES See Airports

AERONAUTICAL SPORTS See Aeronautics; Sports

AERONAUTICS

Faulkner, W. Pylon

Michener, J. A. Space

AERONAUTICS -- FLIGHTS See Voyages and travels

AERONAUTICS AND CIVILIZATION See Aeronautics; Civilization

AERONAUTICS IN AGRICULTURE See Aeronautics; Agriculture; Spraying and dusting

AERONAUTICS, COMMERCIAL See Commercial aeronautics

AERONAUTICS, MILITARY See Military aeronautics

AEROPLANES See Airplanes

AEROSPACE ENGINEERING See Aeronautics; Astronautics; Engineering

Aetherial tales [series]

Warrington, F. Elfland

Warrington, F. Grail of the summer stars

Warrington, F. Midsummer night

The **affair.** Child, L.

Affairs at Thrush Green. Read

AFFECTION See Friendship; Love

Affliction. Banks, R.

AFFLICTION See Joy and sorrow; Suffering

AFGHAN WAR, 2001-

Hunter, S. Dead zero

Roy-Bhattacharya, J. The watch

Young, T. W. The renegades

AFGHANISTAN

Ahmad, J. The wandering falcon

Aslam, N. The Blind Man's Garden

Aslam, N. The wasted vigil

Fesperman, D. The warlord's son

Hosseini, K. The kite runner

Hosseini, K. A thousand splendid suns

Michener, J. A. Caravans

Moulessehoul, M. The swallows of Kabul

AFGHANISTAN -- 19TH CENTURY

Estleman, L. D. Jitterbug

AFRICAN AMERICANS -- EDUCATION *See*
Blacks -- Education; Education

AFRICAN AMERICANS -- FAMILY LIFE
Mathis, A. The twelve tribes of Hattie
Straight, S. Take one candle light a room

AFRICAN AMERICANS -- FICTION
Diamond, D. A gangster and a gentleman
Rawles, N. My Jim
Rutland, E. No crystal stair
Styles, T. Miss Wayne & the queen of DC
Wilson, C. Cotton

AFRICAN AMERICANS -- FLORIDA
Hiaasen, C. Lucky you
Wimberley, D. The king of Colored Town

AFRICAN AMERICANS -- GEORGIA
Ansa, T. M. The hand I fan with
Bambara, T. C. The salt eaters
Jones, T. Silver sparrow
Kay, T. The runaway
Randall, A. The wind done gone
Woods, S. Chiefs

AFRICAN AMERICANS -- GERMANY
Beatty, P. Slumberland

AFRICAN AMERICANS -- LOUISIANA
Gaines, E. J. A gathering of old men
Gaines, E. J. A lesson before dying
Piazza, T. City of refuge
Rhodes, J. P. Voodoo dreams
Rhodes, J. P. Yellow moon
Tademy, L. Cane River

AFRICAN AMERICANS -- MARYLAND
Bell, M. S. Ten Indians
McBride, J. Song yet sung

AFRICAN AMERICANS -- MASSACHUSETTS
Grant, S. Map of Ireland
West, D. The wedding

AFRICAN AMERICANS -- MICHIGAN
Cleage, P. I wish I had a red dress
Cleage, P. What looks like crazy on an ordinary day--
McMillan, R. Blue collar blues

AFRICAN AMERICANS -- MIGRATIONS -- HISTORY -- 20TH CENTURY
Mathis, A. The twelve tribes of Hattie

AFRICAN AMERICANS -- MISSISSIPPI
Faulkner, W. Light in August
Faulkner, W. Absalom, Absalom!
Faulkner, W. Intruder in the dust
Faulkner, W. Requiem for a nun
Faulkner, W. The sound and the fury
Franklin, T. Crooked letter, crooked letter
French, A. Billy
Grisham, J. A time to kill
Jordan, H. Mudbound
Nordan, L. Wolf whistle

Vernon, O. A killing in this town
Ward, J. Salvage the bones
Yarbrough, S. Prisoners of war

AFRICAN AMERICANS -- MISSOURI
Shange, N. Betsey Brown
Terrell, W. The huntsman

AFRICAN AMERICANS -- NEW JERSEY
Price, R. Freedomland

AFRICAN AMERICANS -- NEW YORK (N.Y.)
Baker, D. Young man with a horn
Baker, K. Strivers Row
Baldwin, J. Another country
Baldwin, J. Go tell it on the mountain
Baldwin, J. If Beale Street could talk
Baldwin, J. Tell me how long the train's been gone
Ellison, R. Invisible man
Marshall, P. The fisher king
McMillan, T. Disappearing acts

AFRICAN AMERICANS -- NEW YORK (STATE)
Oates, J. C. I lock my door upon myself

AFRICAN AMERICANS -- NORTH CAROLINA
Edgerton, C. The night train
Huyler, F. The laws of invisible things

AFRICAN AMERICANS -- OHIO
Morrison, T. The bluest eye
Morrison, T. Sula

AFRICAN AMERICANS -- OKLAHOMA
Morrison, T. Paradise

AFRICAN AMERICANS -- PENNSYLVANIA
McKinney-Whetstone, D. Leaving Cecil Street
Wideman, J. E. Two cities

AFRICAN AMERICANS -- PHILADELPHIA (PA.)
McKinney-Whetstone, D. Blues dancing
McKinney-Whetstone, D. Tempest rising
Wideman, J. E. The cattle killing

AFRICAN AMERICANS -- RACE IDENTITY
Straight, S. Take one candle light a room

AFRICAN AMERICANS -- RELATIONS WITH JEWS
Malamud, B. The tenants

AFRICAN AMERICANS -- RELIGION *See*
Blacks -- Religion; Religion

AFRICAN AMERICANS -- SOUTHERN STATES
Heidish, M. A woman called Moses
Lester, J. Do Lord remember me
Walker, A. The color purple

AFRICAN AMERICANS -- TEXAS
Grisham, J. The confession

AFRICAN AMERICANS -- VIRGINIA
Fuller, D. Sweetsmoke
McCaig, D. Jacob's ladder
Shreve, S. R. A country of strangers

AFRICAN AMERICANS -- WASHINGTON (D.C.)
Pelecanos, G. P. Right as rain

Miles, J. Dear American Airlines

Minot, S. Monkeys

O'Hara, J. Appointment in Samarra

Paretsky, S. Ghost country

Pilch, J. A thousand peaceful cities

Richler, M. Solomon Gursky was here

Rinehart, S. Built in a day

Rossner, J. Perfidia

Saul, J. The right hand of evil

Shreve, A. Rescue

Southgate, M. The taste of salt

Spanidou, I. Before

Stirling, J. The island wife

Styron, W. Set this house on fire

Suri, M. The death of Vishnu

Tremain, R. Trespass

Turner, F. W. 1929

Van Booy, S. Everything beautiful began after

Woodrell, D. The death of sweet mister

Wyld, E. After the fire, a still small voice

ALEUTS

Harrison, S. Call down the stars

Harrison, S. Cry of the wind

Harrison, S. Song of the river

Alexander Pushkin: complete prose fiction. Pushkin, A. S.

Alexander VI, Pope, 1431-1503
About
Poole, S. The Borgia mistress

Alexander, the Great, 356-323 B.C.
About
Doherty, P. C. The gates of hell

Doherty, P. C. The godless man

Doherty, P. C. The house of death

Renault, M. Funeral games

Renault, M. The Persian boy

The **Alexandria** quartet: Justine; Balthazar; Mountolive {and} Clea. Durrell, L.

Alfred, the Great, King of England, 849-899
About
Cornwell, B. Burning land

Cornwell, B. The last kingdom

Cornwell, B. Lords of the North

Cornwell, B. The pale horseman

Cornwell, B. Sword song

ALGEBRA *See* Mathematical analysis; Mathematics

ALGERIA -- ORAN

Camus, A. The plague

ALGONQUIAN INDIANS

Gear, K. O. People of the mist

Alias Grace. Atwood, M.

The **alibi.** Brown, S.

Alibi. Woods, T.

Alice Adams. Tarkington, B.

Alice Bliss. Harrington, L.

Alice I have been. Benjamin, M.

Alice in exile. Read, P. P.

Alice in jeopardy. McBain, E.

An **alien** heat. Moorcock, M.

ALIENATION (SOCIAL PSYCHOLOGY)

Adams, P. The sister

Bell, M. S. The color of night

Burroughs, W. S. Naked lunch

Ford, R. Independence Day

Ford, R. The lay of the land

Heinemann, L. Paco's story

Hoeg, P. Borderliners

Hoffman, A. Skylight confessions

Kantner, S. Ordinary wolves

Kashua, S. Dancing Arabs

Klima, I. No saints or angels

Lessing, D. M. Ben, in the world

Lessing, D. M. The fifth child

Malae, P. N. What we are

McGinniss, J. The delivery man

Mengestu, D. How to read the air

Picoult, J. Nineteen minutes

Spiegelman, I. Everyone's burning

Stamm, P. Seven years

Trevor, W. Felicia's journey

Vine, B. Grasshopper

Wideman, J. E. Philadelphia fire

Winton, T. Dirt music

ALIENATION (SOCIAL PSYCHOLOGY) -- FICTION

Doyon, S. The greatest man in Cedar Hole

Grant, H. The vanishing of Katharina Linden

The **alienist.** Carr, C.

ALIENS

Aslam, N. Maps for lost lovers

Pavone, C. The expats

ALIENS FROM OUTER SPACE *See* Extraterrestrial beings

Aliens in the prime of their lives. Watson, B.

Alif the unseen. Wilson, G. W.

ALIMONY *See* Divorce

Alive in Necropolis. Dorst, D.

All aboard. Porter, J. A.

All about Lulu. Evison, J.

All Aunt Hagar's children. Jones, E.

All for love. Jacobson, D.

All hat. Smith, B.

All he ever wanted. Shreve, A.

All I did was shoot my man. Mosley, W.

All in the family. O'Connor, E.

All is forgotten, nothing is lost. Chang, L. S.

All is vanity. Schwarz, C.

All mortal flesh. Spencer-Fleming, J.

All my sins remembered. Thomas, R.

All or nothing. Adler, E.

All other nights. Horn, D.

Whitehead, C. The intuitionist

Wiggins, M. John Dollar

Wilde, O. The picture of Dorian Gray

Allende Gossens, Salvador, 1908-1973
About
Ampuero, R. The Neruda case

Alley Kat blues. Kijewski, K.

Allgood, Molly, 1887-1952
About
O'Connor, J. Ghost light

ALLIANCES
Bear, E. Range of ghosts

ALLIGATORS
Russell, K. Swamplandia!

ALLOSAURUS *See* Dinosaurs

Almost criminal. Brown, E. R.

The **almost** moon. Sebold, A.

Almost never. Sada, D.

Almost paradise. Isaacs, S.

An **almost** perfect moment. Kirshenbaum, B.

Almost the truth. Yorke, M.

ALMSHOUSES
Trollope, A. The warden

Aloft. Lee

Aloha, lady blue. Memminger, C.

Alone. Gardner, L.

Alone. Estleman, L. D.

Alone in the crowd. Garcia-Roza, L. A.

Along Came a Duke. Boyle, E.

Along came a spider. Patterson, J.

Alphabet of thorn. McKillip, P. A.

ALPS
Johnson, D. L'affaire

Mann, T. The magic mountain

Mawer, S. The fall

Parks, T. Cleaver

Parks, T. Rapids

Thirlwell, A. The escape

Watkins, P. The ice soldier

ALPS, ITALIAN (ITALY)
Huggins, J. B. Nightbringer

Already dead. Huston, C.

Altered carbon. Morgan, R. K.

Altered states. Chayefsky, P.

ALTERNATIVE EDUCATION *See* Education

The **alternative** hero. Thornton, T.

ALTERNATIVE HISTORIES
See also Fantasy fiction
Beard, R. Lazarus is dead

Brennan, T. Doktor Glass

Burgess, A. A clockwork orange

Carriger, G. Blameless

Carriger, G. Timeless

Ciotta, B. Her Sky Cowboy

Ciotta, B. His Clockwork Canary

Connolly, T. Ironskin

Frei, M. The stranger's magic

Hodder, M. Expedition to the Mountains of the Moon

Kay, G. G. River of Stars

Kowalski, D. The company of the dead

Masello, R. The Romanov cross

McFadden, B. L. Gathering of waters

Pearl, M. The technologists

Shepherd, L. A fatal likeness

ALTERNATIVE HISTORIES (FICTION)
Priest, C. Dreadnought

Priest, C. Ganymede

ALTERNATIVE MEDICINE *See* Medicine

Alternatives [series]
Doyle, A. C. The best science fiction of Arthur Conan Doyle

Alternatives to sex. McCauley, S.

ALTRUISTS *See* Philanthropists

Alva & Irva. Carey, E.

Alvin Journeyman. Card, O. S.

Always outnumbered, always outgunned. Mosley, W.

Always watching. Stevens, C.

Alys, always. Lane, H.

ALZHEIMER'S DISEASE
Baldwin, R. You lost me there

Cumyn, A. Losing it

Dean, L. Becoming strangers

Gutcheon, B. R. Five fortunes

Hays, T. The pleasure was mine

Laplante, A. Turn of mind

O'Farrell, M. The vanishing act of Esme Lennox

Robinson, R. Cost

Sparks, N. The notebook

Stuckey-French, E. Revenge of the radioactive lady

ALZHEIMER'S DISEASE -- FICTION
Laplante, A. Turn of mind

Sparks, N. The notebook

Amagansett. Mills, M.

The **Amalgamation** Polka. Wright, S.

AMATEUR FILMS *See* Motion pictures

The **amateur** marriage. Tyler, A.

The **amateur** spy. Fesperman, D.

AMATEUR THEATRICALS
House, T. The beginning of calamities

The **amazing** adventures of Kavalier and Clay. Chabon, M.

Amazing grace. Steel, D.

The **amazing** Mrs. Pollifax. Gilman, D.

AMAZON RIVER REGION
King, R. The sound of butterflies

Patchett, A. State of wonder

AMAZON RIVER VALLEY
Cussler, C. Inca gold

Hamilton-Paterson, J. Gerontius

King, R. The sound of butterflies

AMERICAN MUSIC *See* Music

AMERICAN NOVELISTS *See* American authors; Novelists

American odysseys. Alarcón, D.

American pastoral. Roth, P.

AMERICAN POETRY *See* American literature; Poetry

AMERICAN POETS *See* American authors; Poets

AMERICAN PROPAGANDA *See* Propaganda

AMERICAN PROSE LITERATURE *See* American literature

American purgatorio. Haskell, J.

AMERICAN REVOLUTION BICENTENNIAL, 1776-1976 -- COLLECTIBLES *See* Collectors and collecting

American rust. Meyer, P.

American salvage. Campbell, B. J.

AMERICAN SATIRE *See* American literature; Satire

AMERICAN SERMONS *See* American literature; Sermons

AMERICAN SONGS *See* Songs

AMERICAN SPEECHES *See* American literature; Speeches

An **American** spy. Steinhauer, O.

American subversive. Goodwillie, D.

American tabloid. Ellroy, J.

An **American** tragedy. Dreiser, T.

AMERICAN TRAVELERS *See* Travelers

The **American** trilogy, 1997-2000. Roth, P.

American West: twenty new stories from the Western Writers of America.

AMERICAN WIT AND HUMOR
> *See also* American literature; Wit and humor

Hudgins, A. The joker

AMERICANA *See* Collectors and collecting; Popular culture -- United States; United States -- Civilization; United States -- History

Americanah. Adichie, C. N.

AMERICANIZATION

Alvarez, J. How the Garcia girls lost their accents

Cather, W. My Antonia

Cather, W. O pioneers!

Jen, G. Mona in the promised land

Jen, G. Typical American

Rolvaag, O. E. Peder Victorious

AMERICANS -- AFGHANISTAN

Fesperman, D. The warlord's son

Michener, J. A. Caravans

AMERICANS -- AFRICA

Bellow, S. Henderson the rain king

Hamilton, M. The camel bookmobile

Rush, N. Mating

Stevens, T. The informationist

AMERICANS -- ARGENTINA

Shiner, L. Dark tangos

Swann, M. The foreigners

AMERICANS -- AUSTRALIA

Nordhoff, C. Botany Bay

AMERICANS -- BELGIUM

Shreve, A. Resistance

AMERICANS -- BELIZE

Millet, L. Ghost lights

AMERICANS -- BOTSWANA

McCall Smith, A. The Limpopo Academy of Private Detection

Rush, N. Mortals

AMERICANS -- BURMA

Sendker, J. The art of hearing heartbeats

Tan, A. Saving fish from drowning

AMERICANS -- CAMBODIA

Long, J. The reckoning

AMERICANS -- CANADA

Ford, R. Canada

Freedman, B. Mrs. Mike

Urquhart, J. The underpainter

AMERICANS -- CARIBBEAN REGION

Marshall, P. Praisesong for the widow

Styron, A. All the finest girls

AMERICANS -- CENTRAL AMERICA

Didion, J. A book of common prayer

Stone, R. A flag for sunrise

AMERICANS -- CENTRAL EUROPE

Egan, J. The keep

AMERICANS -- CHINA

Hersey, J. A single pebble

Jin, H. Nanjing requiem

Michael, J. A certain smile

AMERICANS -- COLOMBIA

Grippando, J. A king's ransom

Siegel, J. Detour

AMERICANS -- CONGO (DEMOCRATIC REPUBLIC)

Kingsolver, B. The poisonwood Bible

Windle, J. Congo dawn

AMERICANS -- CUBA

Kennedy, W. Chango's beads and two-tone shoes

Kushner, R. Telex from Cuba

AMERICANS -- EASTERN EUROPE

Mewshaw, M. Shelter from the storm

AMERICANS -- ECUADOR

Kunkel, B. Indecision

AMERICANS -- EGYPT

Ducornet, R. Gazelle

AMERICANS -- ENGLAND

Boyd, W. Ordinary thunderstorms

Fyfield, F. Undercurrents

Goodwin, D. The American heiress

Grant, L. We had it so good

Griesemer, J. Signal & noise

Hale, S. Austenland

Higgins, J. The eagle has landed

Stone, R. Damascus Gate
Uris, L. Exodus

AMERICANS -- ITALY
Aciman, A. A. Call me by your name
Bausch, R. Peace
Epstein, L. The eighth wonder of the world
Fortier, A. Juliet
Goodman, C. The night villa
Gordon, M. The love of my youth
Greeley, A. M. Irish stew!
Grisham, J. The broker
Grisham, J. Playing for pizza
Gruber, M. The forgery of Venus
Hawthorne, N. The marble faun
Hayter, S. Bandit queen boogie
Hellenga, R. The Italian lover
Hemingway, E. Across the river and into the trees
Hemingway, E. A farewell to arms
James, H. Daisy Miller
James, H. Roderick Hudson
Leonard, E. Pronto
Martin, M. Vatican
Martin, V. Italian fever
McBride, J. Miracle at St. Anna
McPhee, J. A man of no moon
Rabb, J. The book of Q
Rachman, T. The imperfectionists
Rice, L. The deep blue sea for beginners
Russo, R. Bridge of sighs
Scott, J. Tourmaline
Styron, W. Set this house on fire
Williams, T. The Roman spring of Mrs. Stone

AMERICANS -- IVORY COAST
D'Souza, T. Whiteman

AMERICANS -- JAPAN
Bird, S. The Yokota Officers Club
Dickey, J. To the white sea
Knight, M. The typist
Lee, D. Country of origin
Murakami, R. In the miso soup
Smith, M. C. December 6
Watrous, M. If you follow me

AMERICANS -- JAPAN -- FICTION
Knight, M. The typist
Lee, D. Country of origin
Smith, M. C. December 6

AMERICANS -- KENYA
Hoagland, E. Children are diamonds

AMERICANS -- KOREA
Limón, M. Mr. Kill

AMERICANS -- LUXEMBOURG
Pavone, C. The expats

AMERICANS -- MARQUESAS ISLANDS
Stahlberg, L. Typee: a peep at Polynesian life

AMERICANS -- MEXICO
Christensen, K. Trouble

D'Erasmo, S. The sky below
Doerr, H. Consider this, senora
Doerr, H. Stones for Ibarra
Fuentes, C. The old gringo
Hambly, B. Days of the dead
Hansen, R. Atticus
Johansen, I. And then you die--
Kellerman, J. Sunstroke
Kingsolver, B. The lacuna
Michener, J. A. Mexico
Olmstead, R. Far bright star
Portis, C. Gringos
Traven, B. The treasure of the Sierra Madre

AMERICANS -- MEXICO -- FICTION
Doerr, H. Consider this, senora
Gaspar de Alba, A. Desert blood
Hambly, B. Days of the dead
Kingsolver, B. The lacuna
Portis, C. Gringos

AMERICANS -- MIDDLE EAST
Menendez, A. The last war

AMERICANS -- MOROCCO
Johnson, D. Lulu in Marrakech

AMERICANS -- NORTH AFRICA
Bowles, P. The sheltering sky

AMERICANS -- PERU
Lynn, A. Now you see it

AMERICANS -- PHILIPPINES
Yates, A. Moondogs
Zamora Linmark, R. Leche

AMERICANS -- PORTUGAL
L'Engle, M. The love letters

AMERICANS -- ROMANIA
Marks, J. Fangland
Wiesel, E. The forgotten

AMERICANS -- RUSSIA
D'Amato, B. White male infant
DeMille, N. The charm school
Harris, R. Archangel
L'Amour, L. Last of the breed
Shonk, K. The red passport

AMERICANS -- RUSSIA (FEDERATION)
Shonk, K. The red passport

AMERICANS -- RWANDA
Leonard, E. Pagan babies

AMERICANS -- SCOTLAND
Stemple, A. Singer of souls

AMERICANS -- SICILY
Hersey, J. A bell for Adano

AMERICANS -- SINGAPORE
Clavell, J. King Rat

AMERICANS -- SOUTH AFRICA
Ward, A. E. Forgive me

AMERICANS -- SOUTH SUDAN
Hoagland, E. Children are diamonds

AMERICANS -- SOUTHEAST ASIA

Howatch, S. Ultimate prizes
Howatch, S. The wonder-worker
Karon, J. A common life
Karon, J. In this mountain
Karon, J. A new song
Karon, J. Out to Canaan
L'Engle, M. A live coal in the sea
L'Engle, M. A severed wasp
MacNeil, R. Burden of desire
Nicholson, W. The secret intensity of everyday life
Paton, A. Cry, the beloved country
Pym, B. An unsuitable attachment
Trollope, A. Barchester Towers
Trollope, A. Framley parsonage
Trollope, A. The last chronicle of Barset
Trollope, J. The choir
Trollope, J. The rector's wife
ANGLICAN CHURCH *See* Church of England
ANGLING *See* Fishing
ANGLO-SAXONS
Rathbone, J. The last English king
Sutcliff, R. Sword at sunset
ANGLO-SAXONS -- FICTION
Cornwell, B. The last kingdom
Cornwell, B. Lords of the North
Cornwell, B. The pale horseman
Cornwell, B. Sword song
Griffiths, E. A Dying Fall
An **angry-ass** black woman. Miller, K. E. Q.
Anil's ghost. Ondaatje, M.
Animal. K'wan
ANIMAL ABUSE *See* Animal welfare
ANIMAL BABIES *See* Animals
ANIMAL BEHAVIOR *See* Animals; Zoology
Animal crackers. Tinti, H.
Animal dreams. Kingsolver, B.
ANIMAL EXPERIMENTATION *See* Research
ANIMAL EXPLOITATION *See* Animal welfare
Animal farm. Orwell, G.
ANIMAL HOUSING *See* Animals
ANIMAL INTELLIGENCE
    See also Animals
Hale, B. The evolution of Bruno Littlemore
ANIMAL LOCOMOTION *See* Animals; Locomotion
ANIMAL MAGNETISM *See* Hypnotism
ANIMAL PARASITES *See* Parasites
ANIMAL PSYCHOLOGY *See* Animal intelligence; Comparative psychology
ANIMAL REPRODUCTION *See* Animals; Reproduction
ANIMAL RESCUE *See* Animal welfare
ANIMAL RIGHTS ACTIVISTS
Gruen, S. Ape house
Smith, A. Judas horse
ANIMAL RIGHTS MOVEMENT

Gruen, S. Ape house
ANIMAL SHELTERS *See* Animal welfare
ANIMAL STORIES *See* Animals -- Fiction
ANIMAL WELFARE
Boyle, T. C. When the killing's done
Coetzee, J. M. Disgrace
Grimes, M. Dakota
Gruen, S. Ape house
Pelecanos, G. P. Drama city
Stott, R. Ghostwalk
Wesselmann, D. L. Captivity
Yorke, M. A question of belief
Animal's people. Sinha, I.
ANIMALS
Birch, C. Jamrach's menagerie
Burnford, S. Bel Ria
Burnford, S. The incredible journey
Grimes, M. Biting the moon
Martel, Y. Beatrice and Virgil
Michener, J. A. Creatures of the kingdom
Millet, L. How the dead dream
Orwell, G. Animal farm
Stuart, J. The tower, the zoo, and the tortoise
Wells, H. G. The island of Doctor Moreau
White, T. H. The book of Merlyn
Wodehouse, P. G. A Wodehouse bestiary
ANIMALS -- COLOR *See* Color
ANIMALS -- DISEASES *See* Diseases
ANIMALS -- FICTION
Bergman, M. M. Birds of a lesser paradise
Beukes, L. Zoo city
ANIMALS -- FOOD *See* Animal behavior; Food
ANIMALS -- MISTREATMENT *See* Animal welfare
ANIMALS -- PROTECTION *See* Animal welfare
ANIMALS -- TREATMENT *See* Animal welfare
ANIMALS IN MOTION PICTURES *See* Motion pictures
ANIMALS IN POLICE WORK *See* Police; Working animals
ANIMATED FILMS *See* Cartoons and caricatures; Motion pictures
ANIMATED TELEVISION PROGRAMS *See* Television programs
ANIMISM *See* Religion
Anna in-between. Nunez, E.
Anna Karenina. Tolstoy, L.
Anna's book. Vine, B.
Annabel. Winter, K.
The **annals** of the Heechee. Pohl, F.
Annapolis. Martin, W.
Anne Boleyn, Queen, consort of Henry VIII, King of England, 1507-1536
                    About
Andersen, L. The Boleyn King
Gregory, P. The other Boleyn girl

Maxwell, R. The secret diary of Anne Boleyn
Plaidy, J. Murder most royal
Anne of Cleves, Queen, consort of Henry VIII, King of England, 1515-1557
About
Gregory, P. The Boleyn Inheritance
Anne, Queen, consort of Louis XIII, King of France, 1601-1666
About
Dumas, A. Twenty years after
Anne, Queen, consort of Richard III, King of England, 1456-1485
About
Gregory, P. The kingmaker's daughter
Annie John. Kincaid, J.
Annie's people [series]
Lewis, B. The preacher's daughter
Anning, Mary, 1799-1847
About
Chevalier, T. Remarkable creatures
The **Anniversary** Man. Ellory, R. J.
ANNUALS *See* Almanacs; Calendars; Periodicals; School yearbooks; Yearbooks
ANNUALS (PLANTS) *See* Cultivated plants; Flower gardening; Flowers
ANNUITIES *See* Investments; Retirement income
The **Anodyne** Necklace. Grimes, M.
ANOREXIA NERVOSA
Levenkron, S. The best little girl in the world
Another country. Baldwin, J.
Another life. Vachss, A. H.
Another life altogether. Beale, E.
Another man's moccasins. Johnson, C.
Another piece of my heart. Green, J.
Another time, another life. Persson, L. G. W.
Anson, George Anson, Baron, 1697-1762
About
O'Brian, P. The golden ocean
The **answer** is always yes. Ferrell, M.
The **antagonist.** Coady, L.
ANTARCTIC REGIONS
Bainbridge, B. The birthday boys
Cussler, C. Shock wave
Johnson, M. Pym
Robinson, K. S. Antarctica
Antarctica. Robinson, K. S.
ANTARCTICA
Bainbridge, B. The birthday boys
Robinson, K. S. Antarctica
Semple, M. Where'd you go, Bernadette
Anthem. Rand, A.
Anthill. Wilson, E. O.
ANTHOLOGIES
See also Books
Alarcón, D. American odysseys
The **anthologist.** Baker, N.

ANTHROPOLOGISTS
Barker, P. The eye in the door
Barker, P. The ghost road
Berlinski, M. Fieldwork
Hellenga, R. Snakewoman of Little Egypt
Jackson, S. The haunting of Hill House
Johnson, A. Parasites like us
Lively, P. Spiderweb
Oliver, C. From other shores
Ondaatje, M. Anil's ghost
Pym, B. An unsuitable attachment
Vanderbes, J. Easter Island
ANTHROPOMETRY *See* Anthropology; Ethnology; Human beings
ANTI-WAR STORIES *See* War stories
Antiagon fire. Modesitt, L. E.
ANTICOMMUNIST MOVEMENTS *See* Communism
Antietam. Reasoner, J.
ANTIETAM (MD.), BATTLE OF, 1862
See also Battles; United States -- History -- 1861-1865, Civil War -- Campaigns
Reasoner, J. Antietam
ANTIGUA AND BARBUDA
Kincaid, J. Annie John
Kincaid, J. Mr. Potter
Le Carre, J. Our kind of traitor
ANTIHEROES
Diaz, J. The brief wondrous life of Oscar Wao
Doyon, S. The greatest man in Cedar Hole
Elkin, S. The MacGuffin
Gibson, W. Spook country
Hill, J. Horns
Hodgen, C. Elegies for the brokenhearted
Hynes, J. Kings of infinite space
Kelman, J. How late it was, how late
Kunkel, B. Indecision
Leonard, E. Tishomingo blues
McGinniss, J. The delivery man
McGuane, T. Keep the change
McGuane, T. Nothing but blue skies
Porter, J. A. The near future
Reuss, F. Horace afoot
Tillman, L. American genius
ANTINUCLEAR MOVEMENT *See* Arms control; Nuclear weapons; Social movements
Antiphon. Scholes, K.
ANTIQUARIAN BOOKS *See* Rare books
ANTIQUARIANS
Sontag, S. The volcano lover
ANTIQUE AND CLASSIC CARS *See* Automobiles
ANTIQUE DEALERS
Calvo, J. Wonderful world
Krauss, N. Great house
McMurtry, L. Cadillac Jack

Abu-Jaber, D. Origin

Gruen, S. Ape house

Apex hides the hurt. Whitehead, C.

The **apocalypse** codex. Stross, C.

The **apocalypse** watch. Ludlum, R.

APOCALYPTIC

Dekker, T. Forbidden

Evenson, B. Immobility

Heller, P. The dog stars

Kazinski, A. J. The last good man

McHugh, M. F. After the apocalypse

Winters, B. H. The last policeman

APOCALYPTIC FILMS *See* Motion pictures

APOLLO PROJECT *See* Life support systems
(Space environment); Orbital rendezvous (Space
flight); Space flight to the moon

The **Apostle.** Asch, S.

APOSTLES

Asch, S. The Apostle

Asch, S. The Nazarene

Kazantzakis, N. The last temptation of Christ

Tóibín, C. The testament of Mary

Williams, N. John

APPALACHIAN MOUNTAINS

McCrumb, S. The ballad of Frankie Silver

McCrumb, S. The hangman's beautiful daughter

McCrumb, S. The rosewood casket

McCrumb, S. She walks these hills

APPALACHIAN REGION

Adams, S. K. My old true love

Greene, A. Bloodroot

Holman, S. Witches on the road tonight

Kingsolver, B. Prodigal summer

Laskas, G. M. The midwife's tale

Marshall, C. Christy

McCrumb, S. Foggy Mountain breakdown and
other stories

Smith, L. Fair and tender ladies

Smith, L. Oral history

APPALACHIAN REGION -- FICTION

Harman, P. The midwife of Hope River

Rash, R. The cove

Appaloosa. Parker, R. B.

Apparition alley. Forrest, K. V.

Appassionata. Hoffman, E.

The **appeal.** Grisham, J.

The **appearance** of a hero. Levine, P.

The **Apple** Orchard. Wiggs, S.

Apple tree lean down. Pearce, M. E.

Appleseed. Clute, J.

APPLIED MECHANICS *See* Mechanics

APPLIQUÉ *See* Needlework

Appointment in Samarra. O'Hara, J.

APPRAISAL OF BOOKS *See* Book reviewing;
Books and reading; Criticism; Literature -- History and criticism

The **apprentice.** Gerritsen, T.

Apprentice Adept [series]

Anthony, P. Split infinity

The **apprentice** lover. Parini, J.

Apprentice to the flower poet Z. Weinstein, D.

Apprentice to the sea. McCutchan, P.

APPRENTICES

Andersen Nexo, M. Pelle the conqueror: v2 Apprenticeship

Modesitt, L. E. Imager's challenge

APPRENTICESHIP NOVELS *See* Bildungsromans

Apricot jam, and other stories. Lantz, K. A.

April Fool's Day. Novakovich, J.

AQUATIC ANIMALS *See* Animals

The **Aquitaine** progression. Ludlum, R.

ARAB AMERICAN WOMEN

Abu-Jaber, D. Crescent

ARAB AMERICANS

Abu-Jaber, D. Crescent

Fesperman, D. The amateur spy

Yunis, A. The night counter

ARAB REFUGEES *See* Refugees

ARAB-ISRAEL CONFLICTS *See* Israel-Arab
conflicts

ARAB-ISRAEL WAR, 1948-1949 *See* Israel-Arab
War, 1948-1949

ARAB-ISRAEL WAR, 1967 *See* Israel-Arab War,
1967

ARAB-ISRAELI CONFLICTS *See* Israel-Arab
conflicts

ARAB-JEWISH RELATIONS *See* Jewish-Arab
relations

ARABIC LANGUAGE *See* Language and languages

ARABS

Higgins, J. Edge of danger

Spark, M. The Mandelbaum Gate

ARABS -- PALESTINE *See* Palestinian Arabs

ARABS -- UNITED STATES

Adams, L. Harbor

ARACHNIDS *See* Animals

ARBORICULTURE *See* Forests and forestry;
Fruit culture; Trees

Arbuckle, Fatty, 1887-1933
                        About

Atkins, A. Devil's garden

Arcadia. Groff, L.

Arcadia Falls. Goodman, C.

Arch of triumph. Remarque, E. M.

ARCHAEOLOGISTS

See also Archeologists

Griffiths, E. The crossing places

Griffiths, E. A Dying Fall

Hart, E. The book of Killowen

Hart, E. Haunted ground

ARGENTINA -- FICTION

Puenzo, L. The fish child

ARGENTINA -- HISTORY -- DIRTY WAR, 1976-1983

De Robertis, C. Perla

ARGENTINA -- HISTORY

De Robertis, C. Perla

ARGENTINA -- RURAL LIFE

Greene, G. The honorary consul

ARGENTINES -- FRANCE

Cortazar, J. Hopscotch

ARGONAUTS (GREEK MYTHOLOGY)

Greenwood, K. Medea

ARISTOCRACY (SOCIAL CLASS)

Ali, M. Untold story

Auchincloss, L. Her infinite variety

Carey, P. Parrot and Olivier in America

Fellowes, J. Snobs

Goodwin, D. The American heiress

Nicolson, J. Abdication

ARISTOCRACY (SOCIAL CLASS) -- GERMA-NY

Moore, S. The life of objects

ARISTOCRACY -- ENGLAND

Balogh, M. The secret mistress

Balogh, M. Simply perfect

Chase, L. L. Silk is for seduction

Colegate, I. The shooting party

Gee, S. The scandal of the season

Goodwin, D. The American heiress

Hardwick, M. The Duchess of Duke Street

Riley, J. M. The serpent garden

Sackville-West, V. The Edwardians

Wodehouse, P. G. The code of the Woosters

Wodehouse, P. G. Tales from the Drones Club

ARISTOCRACY -- FRANCE

Carey, P. Parrot and Olivier in America

Dickens, C. A tale of two cities

Haasse, H. S. In a dark wood wandering

James, H. The American

Laker, R. To dance with kings

Orczy, E. Adventures of the Scarlet Pimpernel

Orczy, E. The elusive Pimpernel

Orczy, E. The Scarlet Pimpernel

Proust, M. The Guermantes way

Proust, M. Sodom and Gomorrah

Riley, J. M. The serpent garden

Stendhal The red and the black

ARISTOCRACY -- GREAT BRITAIN

Dean, A. A gentleman of fortune, or, The suspicions of Miss Dido Kent

Fellowes, J. Snobs

Nicolson, J. Abdication

ARISTOCRACY -- ITALY

Stendhal The charterhouse of Parma

ARISTOCRACY -- JAPAN

Mishima, Y. Spring snow

Schwartz, J. B. The commoner

ARISTOCRACY -- RUSSIA

West, R. The birds fall down

ARISTOCRACY -- SCOTLAND

Coleridge, N. Godchildren

ARISTOCRACY -- SICILY

Unsworth, B. The ruby in her navel

ARISTOCRACY -- WALES

James, E. When beauty tamed the beast

Aristotle

About

Lyon, A. The sweet girl

ARITHMETIC *See* Mathematics; Set theory

ARIZONA

Bull, E. Territory

Caputo, P. Crossers

Faust, C. Choke hold

Jance, J. A. Kiss of the bees

Jance, J. A. Queen of the night

Kingsolver, B. Animal dreams

Kingsolver, B. The bean trees

Kingsolver, B. Pigs in heaven

Mapson, J. Loving Chloe

Preston, D. Blasphemy

Rosenberg, R. This is not civilization

Walls, J. Half broke horses

ARIZONA -- 19TH CENTURY

Silko, L. Gardens in the dunes

Turner, N. E. These is my words

ARIZONA -- 20TH CENTURY

Jance, J. A. Kiss of the bees

Kingsolver, B. Animal dreams

Kingsolver, B. The bean trees

Kingsolver, B. Pigs in heaven

Mapson, J. Loving Chloe

ARIZONA -- FICTION

Krentz, J. A. White lies

Preston, D. Blasphemy

ARIZONA -- PHOENIX

Abbott, M. E. Bury me deep

McMillan, T. Waiting to exhale

Sallis, J. The killer is dying

ARIZONA -- TUCSON

Cullin, M. Undersurface

Kingsolver, B. Pigs in heaven

Ure, L. The fault tree

Arkansas. Brandon, J.

ARKANSAS

Brandon, J. Arkansas

Grisham, J. A painted house

Harington, D. Enduring

Harington, D. With

Hunter, S. Black light

McFadden, B. L. Sugar

Paddock, J. A secret word

Tanenbaum, R. Act of revenge
ASIAN ART *See* Art
ASIAN REFUGEES
Dau, S. The book of Jonas
Asimov, Isaac, 1920-1992
About
Benford, G. Foundation's fear
The **ask.** Lipsyte, S.
Ask Alice. Taylor, D. J.
Ask the parrot. Stark, R.
Asleep. Yoshimoto, B.
ASPERGER'S SYNDROME
See also Autism
Picoult, J. House rules
Simsion, G. The Rosie project
Assassin's apprentice. Hobb, R.
The **assassin's** song. Vassanji, M. G.
ASSASSINATION
Anthony, E. The Janus imperative
Baldacci, D. Divine justice
Block, L. Killing Castro
Buckley, W. F. Mongoose, R.I.P
Costello, M. Big if
Deaver, J. Garden of beasts
Ellroy, J. Blood's a rover
Ellroy, J. The cold six thousand
Folsom, A. R. The day after tomorrow
Folsom, A. R. Day of confession
Forsyth, F. The day of the jackal
Forsyth, F. The dogs of war
Griffin, W. E. B. Blood and honor
Griffin, W. E. B. Secret honor
Grisham, J. The pelican brief
Hanif, M. A case of exploding mangoes
Higgins, J. The eagle has flown
Higgins, J. Edge of danger
Higgins, J. Eye of the storm
Higgins, J. Touch the devil
Higgins, J. The White House connection
Higgins, J. The wolf at the door
Hunter, S. Havana
Hunter, S. I, sniper
Hunter, S. Time to hunt
Kertesz, I. Detective story
Ludlum, R. The apocalypse watch
Ludlum, R. The scorpio illusion
Lustbader, E. V. Dark homecoming
McEuen, P. Spiral
Milligan, J. Jack Fish
Mishima, Y. Runaway horses
Morrell, D. The brotherhood of the rose
Murakami, H. 1Q84
Neville, S. The ghosts of Belfast
Pilch, J. A thousand peaceful cities
Shelby, P. Days of drums
Shelby, P. Gatekeeper

Trevanian The Eiger sanction
Trevanian Shibumi
Walton, J. Ha'penny
Westlake, D. E. Money for nothing
Winslow, D. Satori
Woods, S. Dirty work
Woods, S. The run
ASSASSINATION -- FICTION
Block, L. Hit me
Havley, N. The good father
Stross, C. Neptune's brood
ASSASSINATION -- INVESTIGATION -- SWE-DEN
Persson, L. G. W. Between summer's longing and winter's end
The **assassination** of Jesse James by the coward Robert Ford. Hansen, R.
ASSASSINS
Block, L. Hit me
Knopf, C. Dead anyway
Scholes, K. Canticle
Vachss, A. That's how I roll
ASSAULT AND BATTERY
Amidon, S. Security
Assault with intent. Kienzle, W. X.
ASSAULT, SEXUAL *See* Rape
The **assistant.** Malamud, B.
The **assistant.** Walser, R.
Asta in the wings. Watson, J. E.
ASTEROIDS
Harrington, M. J. The goliath stone
Pohl, F. Beyond the blue event horizon
Pohl, F. Gateway
Pohl, F. Heechee rendezvous
Astor Place Vintage. Lehmann, S.
The **Astral.** Christensen, K.
ASTRAL PROJECTION
Lupton, R. Afterwards
Astrid & Veronika. Olsson, L.
ASTROBIOLOGY *See* Life on other planets; Space biology
ASTROLOGY
See also Astronomy; Divination; Occultism
Leon, D. A question of belief
ASTRONAUTICS *See* Aeronautics
ASTRONAUTICS -- COMMUNICATION SYSTEMS *See* Interstellar communication; Telecommunication
ASTRONAUTS
See also Air pilots; Space flight
Friedman, M. Martian Dawn
Kiefer, C. The infinite tides
Michener, J. A. Space
Sher, I. Gentlemen of space
ASTRONOMERS
See also Scientists

Psychology

The **attorney.** Martini, S. P.

ATTORNEY AND CLIENT

Connelly, M. The fifth witness

ATTORNEYS *See* Lawyers

ATTORNEYS

Greaves, C. Hush money

AU PAIRS

Berne, S. A perfect arrangement

Kincaid, J. Lucy

Lively, P. Family album

Moore, L. A gate at the stairs

Prose, F. Primitive people

Weldon, F. She may not leave

AUCTIONS

Shapton, L. Important artifacts and personal property from the collection of Lenore Doolan and Harold Morris, including books, street fashion, and jewelry

Welsh, L. The cutting room

AUDIENCES *See* Communication; Social psychology

AUDIO CASSETTES *See* Sound recordings

AUDIOBOOKS *See* Sound recordings

AUDIOTAPES *See* Sound recordings

AUDIOVISUAL EDUCATION *See* Education

AUDITORIUMS *See* Buildings; Centers for the performing arts

August. Rossner, J.

Augusta Locke. Henderson, W. H.

Augustus, Emperor of Rome, 63 B.C.-14 A.D.
About

Graves, R. I, Claudius

Aunt Dimity digs in. Atherton, N.

Aunt Julia and the scriptwriter. Vargas Llosa, M.

Auntie Mame. Dennis, P.

AUNTS
See also Family

Braybrooke, J. Every eye

Childress, M. Crazy in Alabama

Dennis, P. Auntie Mame

Dickens, C. David Copperfield

Frazier, C. Nightwoods

Gaffney, P. Flight lessons

Gibbons, K. Divining women

Goudge, E. Such devoted sisters

Greene, G. Travels with my aunt

Heyer, G. Black sheep

Jamison, L. The gin closet

Lodge, D. Paradise news

McDermott, A. At weddings and wakes

O'Farrell, M. The vanishing act of Esme Lennox

Perez Galdos, B. Dona Perfecta

Proulx, A. The shipping news

Purdy, J. The nephew

Rice, L. Little night

Smith, S. Novel on yellow paper

Thorne, M. Hand me down

Vargas Llosa, M. Aunt Julia and the scriptwriter

Vernon, O. Eden

AUNTS -- CRIMES AGAINST

Mogford, T. Sign of the cross

AUNTS -- FICTION

Frazier, C. Nightwoods

Rice, L. Little night

Thorne, M. Hand me down

AURICULAR CONFESSION *See* Confession

Auriel rising. Redfern, E.

AUSCHWITZ (POLAND: CONCENTRATION CAMP)
See also Concentration camps

Wander, F. The seventh well

Austen, Jane, 1775-1817
About

Fowler, K. J. The Jane Austen book club

Hale, S. Austenland

Tennant, E. Pemberley

Tennant, E. An unequal marriage

Austenland. Hale, S.

Austerlitz. Sebald, W. G.

AUSTRALIA

Coetzee, J. M. Elizabeth Costello

De Kretser, M. The lost dog

Flanagan, R. The unknown terrorist

Hospital, J. T. Oyster

Irwin, S. M. The dead path

Keneally, T. A family madness

Keneally, T. Office of innocence

Keneally, T. River town

Keneally, T. Woman of the inner sea

London, J. The good parents

Malouf, D. The complete stories

McCullough, C. The thorn birds

McGahan, A. The white earth

McInerney, M. Upside down, inside out

Moriarty, L. What Alice forgot

Nooteboom, C. Lost paradise

Perlman, E. Seven types of ambiguity

Tsiolkas, C. The slap

White, P. The eye of the storm

Winton, T. Breath

Winton, T. Dirt music

Wyld, E. After the fire, a still small voice

AUSTRALIA -- 18TH CENTURY

Grenville, K. The lieutenant

McCullough, C. Morgan's run

AUSTRALIA -- 19TH CENTURY

Flanagan, R. Gould's book of fish

Franklin, M. The end of my career

Franklin, M. My brilliant career

Grenville, K. The secret river

Holt, V. The black opal

Clarke, B. Exley

Clinch, J. Finn

Coe, J. The closed circle

Coetzee, J. M. Foe

Coetzee, J. M. Summertime

Collins, J. Beginner's Greek

Conroy, P. Beach music

Cook, T. H. Instruments of night

Cooley, M. The archivist

Coover, R. Pinocchio in Venice

Craig, A. Love in idleness

Crowley, J. Lord Byron's novel

Cullin, M. A slight trick of the mind

Cunningham, M. The hours

Cunningham, M. Specimen days

D'Amato, B. Hard road

Davies, R. The lyre of Orpheus

Davies, R. What's bred in the bone

De Kretser, M. The lost dog

Deaver, J. Carte blanche: 007

Delaney, E. J. Broken Irish

Dixon, S. Frog

Dixon, S. I

Dixon, S. Old friends

Docx, E. The calligrapher

Downing, D. C. Looking for the king

Dufresne, J. Requiem, Mass.

Dunne, D. Too much money

Dunning, J. Two o'clock, eastern wartime

Durrell, L. Balthazar

Durrell, L. Clea

Egan, J. The keep

Ehrenreich, B. The suitors

Ellis, B. E. Imperial bedrooms

Ellis, B. E. Lunar Park

Estrin, M. Insect dreams

Everett, P. L. The water cure

Fairstein, L. Entombed

Faulks, S. Devil may care

Fielding, J. Charley's web

Fitzgerald, P. The blue flower

Flanagan, R. Wanting

Foer, J. S. Everything is illuminated

Foulds, A. The quickening maze

Fowler, K. J. The Jane Austen book club

Freeling, N. One more river

Fresan, R. Kensington Gardens

Fuchs, J. Conrad in Beverly Hills

Fuentes, C. The old gringo

Furst, A. Blood of victory

Gaddis, W. A frolic of his own

Gee, S. The scandal of the season

Gessen, K. All the sad young literary men

Gide, A. The counterfeiters (Les faux-monnayeurs)

Godwin, G. The good husband

Goldman, F. Say her name

Goldsborough, R. The missing chapter

Goodman, C. The seduction of water

Gottlieb, E. Now you see him

Grass, G. The box

Gray, A. Old men in love

Greene, G. The end of the affair

Greene, G. The honorary consul

Greene, G. Monsignor Quixote

Grimes, M. Foul matter

Gruber, M. The book of air and shadows

Haasse, H. S. In a dark wood wandering

Haig, M. The dead fathers club

Hale, S. Austenland

Hallinan, T. A nail through the heart

Hansen, R. Exiles

Harris, R. The ghost

Hassler, J. Rookery blues

Heller, J. Good as Gold

Heller, J. Portrait of an artist, as an old man

Hemingway, E. True at first light

Hemon, A. The Lazarus project

Henkin, J. Matrimony

Hill, S. Mrs. de Winter

Hockensmith, S. Holmes on the range

Hockensmith, S. On the wrong track

Hofmann, G. Lichtenberg and the little flower girl

Hofmann, G. Luck

Holland, T. The archivist's story

Hollinghurst, A. The stranger's child

Holman, S. Witches on the road tonight

Horowitz, A. The House of Silk

Hosseini, K. The kite runner

Hurwitz, G. The crime writer

Iles, G. The devil's punchbowl

Irving, J. The world according to Garp

Jance, J. A. Kiss of the bees

Jance, J. A. Queen of the night

Johnson, B. S. The unfortunates

Johnson, M. Pym

Jong, E. Sappho's leap

Jordan, H. When she woke

Kalfus, K. The commissariat of enlightenment

Kehlmann, D. Fame

Keillor, G. Love me

Kellerman, F. The quality of mercy

Keneally, T. The tyrant's novel

Kennedy, D. The moment

Kinder, C. Honeymooners

King, L. R. The beekeeper's apprentice, or, On the segregation of the queen

King, L. R. The game

King, L. R. The god of the hive

King, L. R. Justice Hall

King, L. R. A letter of Mary

King, L. R. Locked rooms

King, L. R. The moor

Roth, H. Requiem for Harlem
Roth, P. The anatomy lesson
Roth, P. Exit ghost
Roth, P. The ghost writer
Roth, P. My life as a man
Roth, P. Zuckerman bound
Roth, P. Zuckerman unbound
Ruiz Zafon, C. The angel's game
Russell, M. D. Dreamers of the day
Schwarz, C. All is vanity
Self, W. Dorian
Shaara, J. The glorious cause
Shaara, J. Rise to rebellion
Sherwood, F. The book of splendor
Simmons, D. Drood
Simmons, D. Ilium
Simmons, D. Muse of fire
Simmons, D. Olympos
Sledge, M. The more I owe you
Smith, A. The accidental
Spark, M. Loitering with intent
Spencer, S. Willing
Steinke, R. Holy skirts
Stevenson, J. The shadow king
Stone, K. Happy endings
Straub, P. The Hellfire Club
Straub, P. In the night room
Straub, P. Lost boy lost girl
Strieber, W. 2012: the war for souls
Strieber, W. Warday
Styron, W. Sophie's choice
Syjuco, M. Ilustrado
Tearne, R. Mosquito
Tennant, E. Pemberley
Tennant, E. An unequal marriage
Theroux, P. A dead hand
Theroux, P. Hotel Honolulu
Theroux, P. My secret history
Toibin, C. The master
Tournier, M. Friday
Truong, M. T. D. The book of salt
TSypkin, L. Summer in Baden-Baden
Tyler, A. The accidental tourist
Updike, J. Bech at bay
Updike, J. Bech is back
Updike, J. Bech: a book
Updike, J. Gertrude and Claudius
Uris, L. QB VII
Vargas Llosa, M. Aunt Julia and the scriptwriter
Verissimo, L. F. Borges and the eternal orangutans
Vidal, G. Burr
Vine, B. The blood doctor
Vine, B. The chimney sweeper's boy
Vonnegut, K. Breakfast of champions
Vonnegut, K. Timequake
Walker, A. The way forward is with a broken heart

Wallace, I. The prize
Weisgall, D. The world before her
West, P. Lord Byron's doctor
West, P. Sporting with Amaryllis
Westlake, D. E. The hook
White, E. Hotel de Dream
Wideman, J. E. The cattle killing
Wideman, J. E. Fanon
Wilhelm, K. The deepest water
Wilson, K. The family Fang
Winegardner, M. The Godfather returns
Winslow, D. Satori
Wolfe, T. Of time and the river
Wolfe, T. The web and the rock
Wolfe, T. You can't go home again
Wolff, T. Old school
Wolitzer, M. The wife
Woodrell, D. Give us a kiss

AUTHORS -- FICTION
Barnes, L. The Perfect Ghost
Buzzelli, E. K. Dead dogs and Englishmen
Fields, J. The age of desire
Jansma, K. The unchangeable spots of leopards
Jio, S. The violets of March
Lafferty, M. The shambling guide to New York City
Landis, J. M. Heartbreak Hotel
Makine, A. The life of an unknown man
Mansbach, A. The end of the Jews
Pilch, J. My first suicide
Pearl, M. The Poe shadow
Upson, N. Two for sorrow
Wind, R. In the midnight rain

AUTHORS AND PUBLISHERS *See* Authorship; Contracts; Publishers and publishing

AUTHORS' SPOUSES
Fowler, T. A. Z
Wolitzer, M. The wife

AUTHORS, AMERICAN -- 19TH CENTURY -- DEATH
Pearl, M. The Poe shadow

AUTHORSHIP
Auster, P. Oracle night
Beachy, S. Boneyard
Bushnell, C. The Carrie diaries
Carey, P. My life as a fake
Christensen, I. Azorno
Clarke, B. An arsonist's guide to writers' homes in New England
Coetzee, J. M. Diary of a bad year
Coetzee, J. M. Elizabeth Costello
Currie, R. Flimsy little plastic miracles
DeWitt, P. Ablutions
Fossum, K. Broken
Hellenga, R. The Italian lover
Howard, M. The rags of time

Portes, A. Hick

Powell, A. A dance to the music of time

Powers, J. R. Do black patent-leather shoes really reflect up?

Powers, J. R. The last Catholic in America

Powers, R. Galatea 2.2

Proust, M. The captive [and] The fugitive

Proust, M. The Guermantes way

Proust, M. Remembrance of things past

Proust, M. Sodom and Gomorrah

Proust, M. Swann's way

Proust, M. Time regained

Proust, M. Within a budding grove

Ridley, J. A conversation with the Mann

Roth, H. A diving rock on the Hudson

Roth, H. From bondage

Roth, H. Requiem for Harlem

Roth, H. A star shines over Mt. Morris Park

Roth, P. The anatomy lesson

Roth, P. The ghost writer

Roth, P. My life as a man

Roth, P. Zuckerman bound

Roth, P. Zuckerman unbound

Sand, G. Lelia

Smith, S. Novel on yellow paper

The sorrow of war

Stahlberg, L. Omoo: a narrative of adventures in the South Seas

Stahlberg, L. Typee: a peep at Polynesian life

Stanisic, S. How the soldier repairs the gramophone

Styron, W. Sophie's choice

Svevo, I. Zeno's conscience

Theroux, P. My secret history

Tolstoy, L. Childhood, Boyhood and Youth

TSypkin, L. Summer in Baden-Baden

Vann, D. Legend of a suicide

Vonnegut, K. Slaughterhouse-five

Vonnegut, K. Timequake

Ward, M. J. The snake pit

Whitehead, C. Sag Harbor

Wolfe, T. Look homeward, angel

Wolfe, T. O lost

Wolfe, T. Of time and the river

Wolfe, T. The web and the rock

The **autobiography** of Fidel Castro. Fuentes, N.

The **autobiography** of Miss Jane Pittman. Gaines, E. J.

The **autobiography** of Mrs. Tom Thumb. Benjamin, M.

Autobiography of my mother. Kincaid, J.

The **autograph** man. Smith, Z.

AUTOIMMUNE DISEASES *See* Diseases

AUTOMATA *See* Robots

The **automatic** detective. Martinez, A. L.

AUTOMATIC MACHINERY *See* Automation

AUTOMATION

Vonnegut, K. Player piano

AUTOMATONS *See* Robots

AUTOMOBILE ACCIDENTS *See* Traffic accidents

AUTOMOBILE DRIVER EDUCATION *See* Education

AUTOMOBILE DRIVERS

Sallis, J. Drive

Sallis, J. Driven

AUTOMOBILE INDUSTRY

Jakes, J. American dreams

McMillan, R. Blue collar blues

AUTOMOBILE INSURANCE *See* Insurance

AUTOMOBILE PARTS *See* Automobiles

AUTOMOBILE RACES

Hunter, S. Night of thunder

Jakes, J. American dreams

Stein, G. The art of racing in the rain

AUTOMOBILE RACING *See* Racing

AUTOMOBILE RACING DRIVERS

McCrumb, S. St. Dale

AUTOMOBILE TRAVEL

See also Transportation; Travel; Voyages and travels

Portes, A. Hick

AUTOMOBILES

Boucher, C. How to keep your Volkswagen alive

Hawke, E. Ash Wednesday

King, S. Christine

King, S. From a Buick 8

AUTOMOBILES -- ACCIDENTS *See* Traffic accidents

AUTOMOBILES -- TOURING

Coe, J. The terrible privacy of Maxwell Sim

McMurtry, L. Cadillac Jack

McMurtry, L. Loop group

Merullo, R. Breakfast with Buddha

AUTOMOTIVE INDUSTRY *See* Automobile industry

AUTOSUGGESTION *See* Hypnotism; Mental suggestion

The **Autumn** Bride. Gracie, A.

The **autumn** of the patriarch. Garcia Marquez, G.

An **autumn** war. Abraham, D.

Available dark. Hand, E.

AVALANCHES

Joyce, G. The silent land

Avalon. Seton, A.

Avalon. Lawhead, S.

AVARICE

Atwood, M. The blind assassin

Barbash, T. The last good chance

Boyd, W. Ordinary thunderstorms

Caputo, P. Acts of faith

Cleage, P. Babylon sisters

Coleridge, N. Godchildren

Bad Boy Brawly Brown. Mosley, W.

Bad company. Higgins, J.

The **bad** detective. Keating, H. R. F.

Bad dirt. Proulx, A.

The **bad** girl. Vargas Llosa, M.

Bad Girl Creek. Mapson

Bad ground. Cramer, W. D.

Bad intentions. Fossum, K.

Bad Little Falls. Doiron, P.

Bad love. Kellerman, J.

Bad luck and trouble. Child, L.

Bad men. Connolly, J.

Bad monkey. Hiaasen, C.

Bad monkeys. Ruff, M.

Bad moon rising. Gorman, E.

Bad news. Westlake, D. E.

The **bad** place. Koontz, D. R.

The **bad** seed. March, W.

Bad things happen. Dolan, H.

Badenheim 1939. Appelfeld, A.

Badger boy. Kelton, E.

Badlands. Bowen, P.

BADLANDS (S.D.)
    Weisgarber, A. The personal history of Rachel Dupree

Bag of bones. King, S.

Bagombo snuff box: uncollected short fiction. Vonnegut, K.

Bahlmann, Anna Catherine, 1849-1916
                About
    Fields, J. The age of desire

BAIL
    Leonard, E. Rum punch

Bailey's Cafe. Naylor, G.

Baja Florida. Morris, B.

Baked. Smith, M. H.

The **baked** bean supper murders. Rich, V.

Baker towers. Haigh, J.

Baker, Chet
                About
    Moody, B. Looking for Chet Baker

BAKERS
    Picoult, J. The Storyteller

BAKERS AND BAKERIES
    Burrowes, G. The soldier

BALANCE OF NATURE *See* Ecology

Balance of power. Patterson, R. N.

A **Bali** conspiracy most foul. Flint, S.

BALKAN PENINSULA
    Kadare, I. The accident
    McNally, T. M. The goat bridge
    Obreht, T. The tiger's wife

BALL GAMES *See* Games

The **ballad** of Frankie Silver. McCrumb, S.

The **ballad** of Peckham Rye. Spark, M.

The **ballad** of Tom Dooley. McCrumb, S.

The **ballad** of Trenchmouth Taggart. Taylor, M. G.

BALLADS *See* Literature; Poetry; Songs

BALLERINAS
    Roorbach, B. Life among giants

BALLET
    Godden, R. Pippa passes
    McCann, C. Dancer
    Sharp, A. The true memoirs of Little K

BALLET DANCERS
    See also Dancers
    Buchanan, C. M. The painted girls
    McCann, C. Dancer

BALLETS *See* Ballet

BALLISTIC MISSILES *See* Guided missiles; Nuclear weapons; Rockets (Aeronautics)

BALLOONS *See* Aeronautics

BALLOT *See* Elections

Balthasar's odyssey. Maalouf, A.

Balthazar. Durrell, L.

BALTIMORE (MD.)
    Coleman, J. The dopeman's wife
    Criswell, M. What to do about Annie?

Bamboo and blood. Church, J.

Band of angels. Warren, R. P.

Bandbox. Mallon, T.

Bandit queen boogie. Hayter, S.

Bandits. Leonard, E.

BANDITS *See* Thieves

BANDMASTERS *See* Conductors (Music)

BANDS (MUSIC)
    Wimberley, D. The king of Colored Town

Banewreaker. Carey, J.

Bang the drum slowly. Harris, M.

BANGALORE (INDIA)
    Mukherjee, B. Miss New India
    Sankaran, L. The hope factory

BANGKOK (THAILAND)
    Burdett, J. Bangkok 8
    Burdett, J. Bangkok haunts
    Burdett, J. Bangkok Tattoo
    Hallinan, T. The fear artist

Bangkok 8. Burdett, J.

Bangkok haunts. Burdett, J.

Bangkok Tattoo. Burdett, J.

BANGLADESH
    Hensher, P. Scenes from early life

BANGLADESH -- HISTORY -- REVOLUTION, 1971
    Hensher, P. Scenes from early life

BANGLADESHIS -- ENGLAND
    Ali, M. Brick lane

Banishing Verona. Livesey, M.

BANK ROBBERIES
    See also Theft
    Hurwitz, G. The survivor
    Laukkanen, O. Criminal enterprise

Leonard, E. Raylan
BANK ROBBERIES -- UNITED STATES
Ford, R. Canada
BANK ROBBERS
Black, L. Takeover
Connelly, J. Crumbtown
Cussler, C. The chase
DeWeese, D. You don't love this man
Estleman, L. D. The adventures of Johnny Vermillion
Higgins, G. V. The friends of Eddie Coyle
Mullen, T. The many deaths of the Firefly Brothers
Robotham, M. The wreckage
Stross, C. Halting state
Tyler, A. Earthly possessions
Westlake, D. E. Bank shot
Bank shot. Westlake, D. E.
BANKERS
Connelly, M. The fifth witness
Dickens, C. Hard times
Haslett, A. Union Atlantic
Higgins, G. V. The Mandeville talent
Le Carre, J. Single & Single
Plain, B. Tapestry
Robotham, M. The wreckage
Sarton, M. Anger
Wolfe, T. The bonfire of the vanities
BANKERS -- FICTION
Cartwright, J. Other people's money
Robotham, M. The wreckage
BANKRUPTCY See Business failures; Commercial law; Debtor and creditor; Finance
BANKS
Browne, M. Eye of the abyss
Campbell, B. M. Brothers and sisters
Dickens, C. Hard times
Le Carre, J. A most wanted man
Le Carre, J. Our kind of traitor
BANKS AND BANKING See Business; Capital; Commerce; Finance
Banners of silk. Laker, R.
BANQUETS See Dining; Dinners
BAR See Lawyers
Barabbas. Lagerkvist, P.
Barabbas (Biblical figure)
                    About
Lagerkvist, P. Barabbas
The **barbarian** nurseries. Tobar, H.
The **Barbed** Crown. Dietrich, W.
The **barbed-wire** kiss. Stroby, W.
Barber, Frank, d. 1801
                    About
Phillips, C. Foreigners
BARBERS
Berry, W. Jayber Crow
Dovey, C. Blood kin

BARCELONA (SPAIN)
Hill, A. The summer of dead toys
Ruiz Zafon, C. The prisoner of heaven
Barchester Towers. Trollope, A.
Bare bones. Reichs, K. J.
Barely a lady. Dreyer, E.
Barnaby Rudge. Dickens, C.
Barnacle love. De Sa, A.
Barney's version. Richler, M.
BARNUM'S AMERICAN MUSEUM (NEW YORK, N.Y.)
Bryson, E. The transformation of Bartholomew Fortuno
Barnum, P. T. (Phineas Taylor), 1810-1891
                    About
Bryson, E. The transformation of Bartholomew Fortuno
Baron in the trees. Calvino, I.
The **Baron** war. Sherman, J.
BAROQUE ART See Art
Barrie, J. M. (James Matthew), 1860-1937
                    About
Fresan, R. Kensington Gardens
BARRISTERS See Lawyers
BARS (DRINKING ESTABLISHMENTS)
DeWitt, P. Ablutions
Doig, I. The bartender's tale
BARS
Colfer, E. Screwed
Doig, I. The bartender's tale
The **bartender's** tale. Doig, I.
BARTENDERS
Drury, T. The driftless area
Huston, C. Caught stealing
Koontz, D. R. Velocity
BARTER See Commerce; Economics; Money; Subsistence economy; Underground economy
BASCOM, ERNIE (FICTITIOUS CHARACTER)
Limón, M. Mr. Kill
BASEBALL
Deford, F. The entitled
Hamill, P. Snow in August
Harbach, C. The art of fielding
Harris, M. Bang the drum slowly
Hudgens, D. Season of Gene
King, S. Blockade Billy
Lombardo, B. The man with two arms
Lupica, M. Wild pitch
Malamud, B. The natural
Parker, R. B. Double play
Ring around the bases
Roth, P. The great American novel
Starr, J. Lights out
BASEBALL -- FICTION
Harbach, C. The art of fielding

Malamud, B. The natural

Ring around the bases

BASEBALL EXECUTIVES

Everett, P. L. I am Not Sidney Poitier

BASEBALL PLAYERS

See also Athletes

Harbach, C. The art of fielding

Lupica, M. Wild pitch

Parker, R. B. Double play

Sayers, V. The powers

BASEBALL STORIES -- UNITED STATES

Sayers, V. The powers

BASEBALL TEAMS *See* Baseball; Sports teams

BASIC EDUCATION *See* Education

Basket case. Hiaasen, C.

BASQUE AMERICANS

Etchart, M. The last shepherd

Johnson, C. Death without company

BASQUES -- FRANCE

Etchart, M. The last shepherd

Bass cathedral. Mackey, N.

The **bastard** of Istanbul. Shafak, E.

Bastard out of Carolina. Allison, D.

BASTILLE

Black, C. Murder in the Bastille

The **bathing** women. Tie Ning

Batman. Glapion, J.

BATMAN (FICTIONAL CHARACTER)

Glapion, J. Batman

BATTERING OF WIVES *See* Wife abuse

Battle cry. Uris, L.

The **battle** of the Villa Fiorita. Godden, R.

BATTLE SHIPS *See* Warships

The **battle** sylph. McDonald, L. J.

Battleborn. Watkins, C. V.

BATTLEFIELDS *See* Battles

BATTLES

See also Military art and science; Military history; War

Abercrombie, J. The heroes

Jordan, R. A memory of light

Weber, D. By schism rent asunder

BATTLESHIPS *See* Warships

Batwoman. Rucka, G.

BATWOMAN (FICTITIOUS CHARACTER) -- COMIC BOOKS, STRIPS, ETC.

Rucka, G. Batwoman

Baudolino. Eco, U.

The **Baum** plan for financial independence and other stories. Kessel, J.

Baum, L. Frank, 1856-1919

About

D'Amato, B. Hard road

Maguire, G. Son of a witch

The **Bawdy** basket. Marston, E.

The **bay** of love and sorrows. Richards, D. A.

Bay of souls. Stone, R.

BAZAARS *See* Fairs

Be cool. Leonard, E.

Be my knife. Grossman, D.

Be near me. O'Hagan, A.

The **beach** house. Green, J.

Beach music. Conroy, P.

BEACHES *See* Seashore

The **bean** trees. Kingsolver, B.

The **Beans** of Egypt, Maine. Chute, C.

The **bear** went over the mountain. Kotzwinkle, W.

Bearing the body. Havazelet, E.

BEARS

King, S. The girl who loved Tom Gordon

Kotzwinkle, W. The bear went over the mountain

Pollen, B. The summer of the bear

Beast Master's ark. Norton, A.

Beastly Things. Leon, D.

BEASTS *See* Animals

BEAT GENERATION *See* American literature; Bohemianism

Beat to quarters. Forester, C. S.

Beatrice

About

Jones, S. Four sisters, all queens

Beatrice and Virgil. Martel, Y.

Beaufort. Leshem, R.

The **beautiful** and damned. Fitzgerald, F. S.

A **beautiful** blue death. Finch, C.

Beautiful children. Bock, C.

A **beautiful** death. Haymon, S. T.

The **Beautiful** indifference. Hall, S.

Beautiful Inez. Schneider, B.

Beautiful lies. Clark, C.

Beautiful Maria of my soul. Hijuelos, O.

The **beautiful** miscellaneous. Smith, D.

The **beautiful** mystery. Penny, L.

The **beautiful** room is empty. White, E.

Beautiful Ruins. Walter, J.

The **beautiful** things that heaven bears. Mengestu, D.

BEAUTY CONTESTS *See* Contests

BEAUTY SHOPS

Boykin, K. The wisdom of hair

Because it is bitter, and because it is my heart. Oates, J. C.

Bech at bay. Updike, J.

Bech is back. Updike, J.

Bech: a book. Updike, J.

Becoming Madame Mao. Min, A.

Becoming strangers. Dean, L.

BED AND BREAKFAST ACCOMMODATIONS

Binchy, M. A week in winter

Shames, L. Mangrove squeeze

Bedbugs. Winters, B. H.

Bedding Lord Ned. MacKenzie, S.

BEREAVEMENT

See also Emotions

Adrian, C. The great night
Banks, R. The sweet hereafter
Block, B. E. The language of sand
Boswell, R. Century's son
Clay, H. Losing Charlotte
Cohen, L. H. The grief of others
Fitch, J. Paint it black
Goldman, F. Say her name
Gottlieb, E. Now you see him
Hadley, T. The London train
Haig, M. The possession of Mr Cave
Hall, S. The raw shark texts
Hart, J. The truth about love
Hawkes, J. Second skin
Hearon, S. Footprints
Hegi, U. The worst thing I've done
Hood, A. The knitting circle
Joss, M. The night following
Kallos, S. Sing them home
Keegan, N. Swimming
King, S. Lisey's story
The lake
Land, B. Pilgrims upon the earth
Lodato, V. Mathilda Savitch
McCann, C. Let the great world spin
McFarland, D. Singing boy
Miller, S. Lost in the forest
Moloney, S. The dwelling
Monette, P. Afterlife
Moore, L. February
Morley, I. Come Sunday
Naylor, P. R. After
Noyes, D. Captivity
Oe, K. An echo of heaven
Petterson, P. In the wake
Pollen, B. The summer of the bear
Prose, F. Goldengrove
Pywell, S. L. What happened to Henry
Rice, L. Last kiss
Rice, L. The letters
Romano, T. When the world was young
Schwartz, J. B. Reservation Road
Sebold, A. The lovely bones
Shreve, A. Light on snow
Shreve, S. R. A student of living things
Steel, D. The house on Hope Street
Strayed, C. Torch
Strout, E. Abide with me
Stuart, J. The tower, the zoo, and the tortoise
Trollope, J. The other family
Tropper, J. How to talk to a widower
Tuck, L. I married you for happiness
Umrigar, T. N. The weight of heaven
Vida, V. The lovers

Walbert, K. The gardens of Kyoto
Waldman, A. Red Hook Road
Watrous, M. If you follow me
Williams, A. J. Down from Cascom Mountain
Winston, L. Good grief
Wolitzer, M. Surrender, Dorothy
Yoshimoto, B. Kitchen

BEREAVEMENT -- FICTION

Bacon, C. Split estate
Doughty, L. Whatever you love
Frankel, L. Goodbye for now
Henkin, J. The world without you
Lasser, S. Say nice things about Detroit
McIntosh, W. Hitchers
Odell, J. The healing
Roy-Bhattacharya, J. The watch
St. Aubyn, E. At last
Swift, G. Wish you were here
Tyler, A. The beginner's goodbye

BEREAVEMENT IN YOUTH

Collins, C. The gamal

BERGEN-BELSEN (GERMANY: CONCEN-TRATION CAMP) *See* Concentration camps

BERKELEY (CALIF.)

Block, F. L. The elementals
Chabon, M. Telegraph Avenue

Berkley Sensation contemporary romance [series]

James, J. A lot like love
James, J. Something about you

Berkley Sensation historical romance [series]

Bourne, J. The forbidden rose

BERLIN (GERMANY)

Kerr, P. If the dead rise not
Zimler, R. The seventh gate

BERLIN (GERMANY) -- HISTORY -- 1918-1945

Edugyan, E. Half-blood blues
Gillham, D. R. City of women
Grossman, P. Children of wrath

BERLIN (GERMANY) -- HISTORY

Grossman, P. Children of wrath

Berlin game. Deighton, L.

The **Berlin** stories. Isherwood, C.

Bernadette, Saint, 1844-1879

About

Werfel, F. The song of Bernadette

Bernie Gunther novel [series]

Kerr, P. Prague fatale

Berrybender narratives [series]

McMurtry, L. By sorrow's river
McMurtry, L. Folly and glory
McMurtry, L. Sin killer
McMurtry, L. The wandering hill

Berserker fury. Saberhagen, F.

Berserker's star. Saberhagen, F.

Bertie and the seven bodies. Lovesey, P.

Best American mystery stories [date]

Sarah/English Sarah

Tarr, J. Pillar of fire

BIBLICAL STORIES

Asch, S. The Apostle

Asch, S. The Nazarene

Cain

Caldwell, T. Dear and glorious physician

Crace, J. Quarantine

Diamant, A. The red tent

Edghill, I. Queenmaker

Kazantzakis, N. The last temptation of Christ

Lagerkvist, P. Barabbas

Mailer, N. The Gospel according to the Son

Maine, D. The book of Samson

Maine, D. Fallen

Maine, D. The preservationist

Mann, T. Joseph and his brothers

Rice, A. Christ the Lord: out of Egypt

Rice, A. Christ the Lord: the road to Cana

Sarah/English Sarah

Tarr, J. Pillar of fire

Wallace, L. Ben-Hur

Williams, N. John

BIBLIOGRAPHY -- RARE BOOKS *See* Rare books

BICYCLE RACING *See* Cycling; Racing

BICYCLE TOURING *See* Camping; Cycling; Travel

Bierce, Ambrose, 1842-1914?

About

Fuentes, C. The old gringo

Big as life. Howard, M.

The **big** bad city. McBain, E.

The **big** blowdown. Pelecanos, G. P.

The **Big** book of adventure stories.

Big Brother. Shriver, L.

Big Cherry Holler. Trigiani, A.

The **big** exit. Carnoy, D.

Big fish. Wallace, D.

BIG FOOT *See* Sasquatch

The **big** gamble. McGarrity, M.

BIG GAME HUNTING *See* Hunting

Big girl small. DeWoskin, R.

The **big** girls. Moore, S.

Big girls don't cry. Weldon, F.

BIG HOLE, BATTLE OF THE, 1877

Johnston, T. C. Lay the mountains low

Big if. Costello, M.

The **big** love. Dunn, S.

Big machine. LaValle, V. D.

The **big** picture. Kennedy, D.

The **Big** Rock Candy Mountain. Stegner, W. E.

The **big** silence. Kaminsky, S. M.

The **big** sky. Guthrie, A. B.

The **big** sleep. Chandler, R.

Big Stone Gap. Trigiani, A.

A **big** storm knocked it over. Colwin, L.

The **big** switch. Turtledove, H.

BIGAMY

Haigh, J. Mrs. Kimble

BIGFOOT *See* Sasquatch

A **bigger** life. Smith, A.

BIGHORN MOUNTAINS (WYO. AND MONT.)

Johnson, C. Death without company

BIGOTRY *See* Prejudices; Toleration

BILDUNGSROMAN

Earley, T. The blue star

Eberstadt, F. Rat

Everett, P. L. I am Not Sidney Poitier

Leithauser, B. The art student's war

Ondaatje, M. The cat's table

Prose, F. Goldengrove

Romano-Lax, A. The Spanish bow

Schwartzman, A. Eddie Signwriter

Walton, J. Among others

BILDUNGSROMANS

Akhtar, A. American dervish

Allende, I. Maya's Notebook

Bank, M. The wonder spot

Bartlett, D. It's fine by me

Bender, A. The particular sadness of lemon cake

Block, F. L. The elementals

Boyagoda, R. Beggar's feast

Dermont, A. The starboard sea

Groff, L. Arcadia

Hannah, K. Firefly Lane

Harrington, R. Penelope

Henry, P. C. And then I found you

Jacobson, H. The mighty Walzer

Johnson, D. Elsewhere, California

Krueger, W. K. Ordinary grace

Levine, P. The appearance of a hero

Lewis, B. The preacher's daughter

McDermott, A. Someone

Merullo, R. The talk-funny girl

Moore, S. The life of objects

O'Donnell, L. The death of bees

Walker, K. T. The age of miracles

Wayne, T. The Love Song of Jonny Valentine

Winter, K. Annabel

Wolitzer, M. The Interestings

BILINGUAL BOOKS *See* Books; Editions

BILINGUALISM *See* Language and languages

BILLIARDS

Kimmel, H. Something rising (light and swift)

Billie's kiss. Knox, E.

Billy. French, A.

Billy Bathgate. Doctorow, E. L.

Billy Boyle. Benn, J. R.

Billy Budd, sailor. Stahlberg, L.

Billy Lynn's long halftime walk. Fountain, B.

Billy Straight. Kellerman, J.

Drayson, N. Guide to the birds of East Africa
Harries, A. Manly pursuits
Wharton, W. Birdy

BIRDS -- COLOR

See also Color

BIRDS -- INDIA

Festing, I. A. The birdkeeper
The **birds** fall down. West, R.
Birds of a feather. Winspear, J.
Birds of a lesser paradise. Bergman, M. M.
Birds of America. McCarthy, M.
Birds of America. Moore, L.
Birds of paradise. Abu-Jaber, D.
Birds of prey. Smith, W. A.

BIRDS OF PREY *See* Birds; Predatory animals

Birds of prey. Jance, J. A.
Birds without wings. De Bernieres, L.
Birdsong. Faulks, S.
Birdy. Wharton, W.

BIRTH *See* Childbirth

BIRTH ATTENDANTS *See* Midwives

BIRTH CONTROL -- ETHICAL ASPECTS *See* Ethics

BIRTH CUSTOMS *See* Childbirth

BIRTH DEFECTS

Novak, C. Breed
The **birth** of love. Kavenna, J.
The **birth** of Venus. Dunant, S.

BIRTH ORDER *See* Children; Family

BIRTHDAY BOOKS *See* Birthdays; Calendars

The **birthday** boys. Bainbridge, B.
The **birthday** of the world and other stories. Le Guin, U. K.

BIRTHDAYS

Welty, E. Losing battles

BIRTHFATHERS

Thompson, V. Murder on Lenox Hill

BISEXUAL MEN

Irving, J. In one person

BISEXUALITY

See also Sex

Baldwin, J. Giovanni's room
Barker, P. The eye in the door
Harris, E. L. Not a day goes by
Piercy, M. Summer people
White, E. The married man

BISEXUALITY -- FICTION

Irving, J. In one person
Bishop as pawn. McInerny, R. M.
The **bishop** in the West Wing. Greeley, A. M.
Bishop, Elizabeth, 1911-1979

About

Sledge, M. The more I owe you

BISHOPS

See also Clergy

Robb, C. M. The cross-legged knight

BISMARCK (BATTLESHIP)

Forester, C. S. The last nine days of the Bismarck

BISON

Kelton, E. Slaughter
A **bit** on the side. Trevor, W.
Bitch Creek. Tapply, W. G.
Biting the moon. Grimes, M.
Bitten. Armstrong, K.
Bitter in the mouth. Truong, M.
Bitter medicine. Paretsky, S.
Bitter sweet. Spencer, L.
Black & white. Shapiro, D.

BLACK ACTORS *See* Actors

BLACK AMERICANS *See* African Americans

Black and blue. Rankin, I.
Black and blue. Quindlen, A.
Black and white and dead all over. Darnton, J.

BLACK ART *See* Art

BLACK ART (MAGIC) *See* Magic; Witchcraft

BLACK ARTISTS *See* Artists

BLACK ATHLETES *See* Athletes

BLACK AUTHORS *See* Authors

Black Betty. Mosley, W.
Black Blade. Lustbader, E. V.
The **black** book. Rankin, I.
The **Black** cat. Grimes, M.
Black cherry blues. Burke, J. L.

BLACK CHILDREN *See* Children

The **black** country. Grecian, A.
Black cross. Iles, G.
The **black** dahlia. Ellroy, J.
Black dahlia & white rose. Oates, J. C.

BLACK DEATH *See* Plague

Black dogs. McEwan, I.
Black flies. Burke, S.
Black Fridays. Sears, M.
Black girl/White girl. Oates, J. C.
Black hats. Collins, M. A.
The **black** hawk. Bourne, J.
Black Hills. Simmons, D.
Black hole. Burns, C.

BLACK HOLES (ASTRONOMY)

Egan, G. Incandescence
Black house. King, S.

BLACK HUMOR (LITERATURE) *See* Fiction; Literature; Wit and humor

The **black** ice. Connelly, M.
Black Irish. Talty, S.

BLACK LIBRARIANS *See* Librarians

Black light. Hunter, S.
The **Black** Lizard big book of Black Mask stories. Black mask; a magazine.

BLACK MAGIC (WITCHCRAFT) *See* Magic; Witchcraft

Black maps. Spiegelman, P.

BLACK MARKET

Leonard, E. Raylan

BLACK MARKETS

Clavell, J. King Rat

Black money. Thomas, M. M.

Black Mountain. Standiford, L.

BLACK MUSIC *See* Music

BLACK MUSICIANS *See* Musicians

BLACK MUSLIM LEADERS

Baker, K. Strivers Row

Black Narcissus. Godden, R.

BLACK NATIONALISM *See* African Americans -- Political activity; African Americans -- Race identity; Blacks -- Political activity; Blacks -- Race identity

The **black** opal. Holt, V.

The **black** opera. Gentle, M.

Black orchids; &, the silent speaker. Stout, R.

Black powder, white smoke. Estleman, L. D.

Black robe. Moore, B.

Black sheep. Heyer, G.

Black ships. Graham, J.

Black storm. Poyer, D.

Black Sunday. Harris, T.

The **black** swan. Mann, T.

Black swan. Knopf, C.

Black swan green. Mitchell, D.

The **black** tower. James, P. D.

The **black** tower. Bayard, L.

Black water. Oates, J. C.

Black water. Parker, T. J.

Black widow. White, R. W.

Black wind. Cussler, C.

BLACK WOMEN

See also Women

Miller, K. E. Q. An angry-ass black woman

Black women writers series

Butler, O. E. Kindred

Blackbird house. Hoffman, A.

The **blackboard** jungle. Hunter, E.

Blackest bird. Rose, J.

The **Blackhouse.** May, P.

Blacklands. Bauer, B.

Blacklist. Paretsky, S.

BLACKMAIL

See also Extortion

Abbott, M. E. The song is you

Baldacci, D. Absolute power

Clark, M. The legal limit

Cornwell, B. Sharpe's fury

Ellis, D. Life sentence

Fesperman, D. The amateur spy

Goddard, R. Into the blue

Greene, G. The heart of the matter

Grippando, J. Found money

Grisham, J. The brethren

Higgins, J. The president's daughter

Hill, S. Mrs. de Winter

Marlette, D. Magic time

Meltzer, B. The first counsel

Meltzer, B. The tenth justice

Richards, D. A. The bay of love and sorrows

Riordan, R. Cold Springs

Roberts, N. Honest illusions

Shelby, P. Days of drums

Spark, M. The bachelors

Woods, S. Dirt

Blackout. Willis, C.

BLACKS

Bell, M. S. All souls' rising

Conde, M. I, Tituba, black witch of Salem

Conrad, J. The Nigger of the Narcissus

Hill, L. Someone knows my name

Kincaid, J. Autobiography of my mother

Nunez, E. Grace

Phillips, C. A distant shore

Strauss, J. The dubious salvation of Jack V.

BLACKS -- EDUCATION *See* Education

BLACKS -- ENGLAND

Phillips, C. Foreigners

BLACKS

Sanders, D. Clover

Straight, S. Take one candle light a room

Walker, A. Possessing the secret of joy

BLACKS -- RELIGION *See* Religion

BLACKS -- UNITED STATES *See* African Americans

BLACKS IN MOTION PICTURES *See* Minorities in motion pictures; Motion pictures

BLACKS IN THE MOTION PICTURE INDUSTRY *See* Minorities in the motion picture industry; Motion picture industry

BLACKSMITHS

Pearce, M. E. Cast a long shadow

The **blackwater** lightship. Toibin, C.

Blackwater sound. Hall, J. W.

Blackwater spirits. Monfredo, M. G.

Blackwood Farm. Rice, A.

The **blade** itself. Sakey, M.

The **blade** itself. Abercrombie, J.

Blake, William, 1757-1827

About

Chevalier, T. Burning bright

Blame. Huneven, M.

Blameless. Carriger, G.

BLANCHARD, URSULA (FICTITIOUS CHARACTER)

Buckley, F. The doublet affair

Buckley, F. The fugitive queen

Buckley, F. Queen of ambition

Buckley, F. Queen's ransom

Buckley, F. The siren queen

Blanche cleans up. Neely, B.

Blood Trillium. May, J.

Blood type. Greenleaf, S.

Blood work. Connelly, M.

Blood's a rover. Ellroy, J.

Blood, Ash, and Bone. Whittle, T.

Bloodhounds. Lovesey, P.

Bloodland. Glynn, A.

Bloodmoney. Ignatius, D.

Bloodroot. Greene, A.

A **Bloodsmoor** romance. Oates, J. C.

BLOODY SUNDAY, DERRY, NORTHERN IRE-LAND, 1972

Spencer, S. The ring of death

Blooms of darkness. Appelfeld, A.

The **blow-off.** Knipfel, J.

Blown away. Wiltse, D.

Blue angel. Prose, F.

Blue at the mizzen. O'Brian, P.

Blue Calhoun. Price, R.

Blue collar blues. McMillan, R.

Blue corn murders. Pickard, N.

Blue death. O'Donnell, L.

Blue Deer thaw. Harrison, J.

Blue diary. Hoffman, A.

Blue dog, green river. Brower, B.

The **blue** door. Fulmer, D.

The **blue** flower. Fitzgerald, P.

The **blue** fox.

Blue heaven. Wyman, W.

The **blue** hour. Parker, T. J.

The **blue** knight. Wambaugh, J.

Blue light in the sky & other stories. Tsan-hsueh

Blue lonesome. Pronzini, B.

The **blue** manuscript. Khemir, S.

Blue Mars. Robinson, K. S.

Blue Monday. French, N.

Blue moon. Rice, L.

Blue Ridge. Pearson, T. R.

BLUE RIDGE MOUNTAINS

Hamner, E. The homecoming

Hamner, E. Spencer's Mountain

Blue shoe. Lamott, A.

Blue shoes and happiness. McCall Smith, A.

The **blue** star. Earley, T.

Blue-eyed devil. Parker, R. B.

Bluebirds used to croon in the choir. Meno, J.

Bluegate Fields. Perry, A.

BLUEGRASS MUSIC *See* Music

Blueprints for building better girls. Schappell, E.

Blues dancing. McKinney-Whetstone, D.

BLUES MUSICIANS

Wind, R. In the midnight rain

The **bluest** blood. Roberts, G.

The **bluest** eye. Morrison, T.

The **bluest** eye. Morrison, T.

Blunt Impact. Black, L.

BOARD GAMES

See also Games

Bolaño, R. The Third Reich

BOARDING HOUSES

Balzac, H. d. Pere Goriot (Old Goriot)

Doig, I. Work song

Egolf, T. Skirt and the fiddle

Koryta, M. The Cypress House

Levy, A. Small island

Naylor, G. Bailey's Cafe

Racculia, K. This must be the place

Ross-Macdonald, M. Tamsin Harte

Spark, M. A far cry from Kensington

Tyler, A. Celestial navigation

BOAT RACERS

Everett, P. L. I am Not Sidney Poitier

BOAT RACING *See* Boats and boating; Racing

The **bodies** left behind. Deaver, J.

BODY AND MIND *See* Mind and body

Body and soil. McInerny, R. M.

The **body** artist. DeLillo, D.

Body count. Kienzle, W. X.

Body double. Gerritsen, T.

BODY IMAGE *See* Human body; Mind and body; Personality; Self-perception

The **body** in the Big Apple. Page, K. H.

The **body** in the bog. Page, K. H.

The **body** in the bookcase. Page, K. H.

The **body** in the library. Christie, A.

The **body** in the vestibule. Page, K. H.

The **body** of David Hayes. Pearson, R.

Body of lies. Ignatius, D.

Body surfing. Shreve, A.

A **body** to die for. White, K.

BODYGUARDS

Kadrey, R. Kill the dead

Parker, R. B. Double play

Parker, T. J. Storm runners

BODYGUARDS -- FICTION

Huston, C. Skinner

Sharp, Z. Die easy

Sharp, Z. Fourth Day

BOERS *See* Afrikaners

BOG BODIES

Hart, E. Lake of sorrows

BOHEMIANISM

See also Counter culture; Manners and customs

Kerouac, J. On the road

Kerouac, J. And the hippos were boiled in their tanks

Kerouac, J. The Dharma bums

Kerouac, J. On the road: the original scroll

Kerouac, J. Road novels 1957-1960

Maugham, W. S. Of human bondage

McCarthy, M. A charmed life

Boleto. Hagy, A.

The **Boleyn** Inheritance. Gregory, P.

The **Boleyn** King. Andersen, L.

Boleyn, Jane, Viscountess Rochford, d. 1542
            About
Gregory, P. The Boleyn Inheritance

Boleyn, Mary, 1508-1543
            About
Gregory, P. The other Boleyn girl

Boleyn, Mary, ca. 1500-1543
            About
Gregory, P. The other Boleyn girl

Bolívar, Simón, 1783-1830
            About
Garcia Marquez, G. The general and his labyrinth

BOLIVIA
Alfieri, A. City of silver

BOLSHEVISM *See* Communism

Bolt. Francis, D.

Bomb grade. Freemantle, B.

Bomber's law. Higgins, G. V.

BOMBERS *See* Airplanes; Military airplanes

BOMBINGS
        See also Offenses against public safety; Po-
        litical crimes and offenses; Terrorism
Black, C. Murder in Belleville

BOMBS
Choi, S. A person of interest
Crais, R. Demolition angel
Grisham, J. The chamber
Holt, T. Blonde bombshell
Knox, E. Billie's kiss
Lutz, J. Final seconds
Nance, J. J. Medusa's child
Snyder, D. J. Night crossing
Veselka, V. Zazen
Wiltse, D. Blown away

Bonanno, Joseph, 1905-2002
            About
Latour, J. The Havana World Series

BOND, JAMES (FICTITIOUS CHARACTER)
Deaver, J. Carte blanche: 007
Faulks, S. Devil may care

BONDAGE (SEXUAL BEHAVIOR)
Zan, K. The Never List

BONDS *See* Finance; Investments; Negotiable in-
    struments; Securities; Stock exchanges

The **bondswomans** narrative. Crafts, H.

Bone. Ng, F. M.

Bone by bone. Matthiessen, P.

Bone deep. Wiltse, D.

Bone fire. Spragg, M.

The **bone** house. Freeman, B.

Bone Key. Standiford, L.

The **bone** people. Hulme, K.

The **bone** season. Shannon, S.

The **bone** vault. Fairstein, L.

Bones. Pronzini, B.

Bones. Kellerman, J.

BONES -- DISEASES *See* Diseases

Bones and silence. Hill, R.

Bones of the earth. Swanwick, M.

The **bonesetter's** daughter. Tan, A.

Boneshaker. Priest, C.

Boneyard. Beachy, S.

The **bonfire** of the vanities. Wolfe, T.

Bonjour tristesse. Sagan, F.

BONOBO
Gruen, S. Ape house

The **book** about Blanche and Marie. Enquist, P. O.

The **book** and the brotherhood. Murdoch, I.

The **book** class. Auchincloss, L.

BOOK CLUBS (DISCUSSION GROUPS)
        See also Clubs
Majors, I. Love's winning plays

BOOK COLLECTING *See* Book selection; Col-
    lectors and collecting

BOOK EDITORS
Gruber, M. The return
Salter, J. All that is

The **book** of Abraham. Halter, M.

The **book** of air and shadows. Gruber, M.

A **book** of common prayer. Didion, J.

The **book** of Dahlia. Albert, E.

The **book** of Daniel. Doctorow, E. L.

The **Book** of Dave. Self, W.

The **book** of evidence. Banville, J.

The **book** of fathers. Vamos, M.

The **book** of getting even. Taylor, B.

The **book** of Jonas. Dau, S.

BOOK OF KELLS
Gill, B. Death in Dublin

The **book** of Killowen. Hart, E.

The **book** of kills. McInerny, R. M.

The **book** of knowledge. Grumbach, D.

The **book** of laughter and forgetting. Kundera, M.

The **book** of lies. Meltzer, B.

The **book** of lies. Horlock, M.

The **book** of lost tales. Tolkien, J. R. R.

The **book** of lost things. Connolly, J.

The **book** of Merlyn. White, T. H.

The **book** of Murdock. Estleman, L. D.

The **book** of night women. James, M.

The **book** of Q. Rabb, J.

The **book** of salt. Truong, M. T. D.

The **book** of Samson. Maine, D.

The **book** of splendor. Sherwood, F.

The **book** of summers. Hall, E.

Book of the new Sun [series]
Wolfe, G. The Citadel of the Autarch
Wolfe, G. The claw of the conciliator
Wolfe, G. The shadow of the torturer

About

Verissimo, L. F. Borges and the eternal orangutans

Borgia family

About

Dunant, S. Blood and beauty

Poole, S. The Borgia mistress

Puzo, M. The family

The **Borgia** mistress. Poole, S.

Borgia, Cesare, 1476?-1507

About

Poole, S. The Borgia mistress

Bormann, Martin, 1900-1945

About

Polsan/English Hash

Born to darkness.

Born to run. Grippando, J.

Borrowed hearts. DeMarinis, R.

The **borrower.** Makkai, R.

BOSCH, HARRY (FICTITIOUS CHARACTER)

Connelly, M. City of bones

BOSNIA AND HERCEGOVINA

Stanisic, S. How the soldier repairs the gramophone

BOSNIA AND HERCEGOVINA -- SARAJEVO

Hemon, A. Nowhere man

BOSNIAN AMERICANS

Prcic, I. Shards

BOSNIANS -- UNITED STATES

Hemon, A. Nowhere man

BOSSINESS

See also Personality

BOSTON (MASS.)

Higgins, G. V. The Digger's game

Lehane, D. Live by night

Pearl, M. The technologists

Shrier, H. Boston cream

Boston cream. Shrier, H.

The **Bostonians.** James, H.

BOTANICAL GARDENS *See* Gardens; Parks

BOTANICAL ILLUSTRATION *See* Art; Illustration of books

BOTANISTS

See also Naturalists

Gregory, P. Virgin earth

Hay, E. A student of weather

Humphreys, H. The lost garden

Jio, S. The last camellia

Vanderbes, J. Easter Island

Botany Bay. Nordhoff, C.

Both ends of the night. Muller, M.

BOTSWANA

Stanley, M. Death of the mantis

BOTSWANA -- FICTION

McCall Smith, A. The full cupboard of life

McCall Smith, A. The Kalahari typing school for men

McCall Smith, A. The Limpopo Academy of Private Detection

McCall Smith, A. The No. 1 Ladies' Detective Agency

McCall Smith, A. The Saturday big tent wedding party

McCall Smith, A. Tea time for the traditionally built

BOTSWANA -- SOCIAL LIFE AND CUSTOMS

McCall Smith, A. The Saturday big tent wedding party

McCall Smith, A. Tea time for the traditionally built

The **bottoms.** Lansdale, J. R.

BOULDER (COLO.)

White, S. W. Dry ice

Bound. Nelson, A.

BOUNDARY WATERS CANOE AREA (MINN.)

Johnson, W. The devil you know

BOUNTY (SHIP) -- FICTION

Nordhoff, C. The Bounty trilogy

Nordhoff, C. Men against the sea

Nordhoff, C. Mutiny on the Bounty

The **Bounty** trilogy. Nordhoff, C.

The **Bourne** identity. Ludlum, R.

The **Bourne** supremacy. Ludlum, R.

The **Bourne** ultimatum. Ludlum, R.

BOWHUNTING *See* Hunting

Bowl of cherries. Kaufman, M.

Bowser, Mary Elizabeth, ca. 1840-

About

Leveen, L. The secrets of Mary Bowser

The **box.** Grass, G.

Box office poison. Bornikova, P.

BOXERS (PERSONS)

Phillips, C. Foreigners

BOXES -- COLLECTORS AND COLLECTING

See Collectors and collecting

BOXING

DeVido, B. Every time I talk to Liston

Lee, G. China boy

Lovesey, P. The detective wore silk drawers

Toole, F. X. Pound for pound

The **boy** detective fails. Meno, J.

The **boy** on the bus. Schupack, D.

BOY SCOUTS *See* Boys' clubs; Scouts and scouting

Boy still missing. Searles, J.

The **boy** who couldn't sleep and never had to. Pierson, D. C.

The **boy** who followed Ripley. Highsmith, P.

The **boy** who would live forever. Pohl, F.

Boy's life. McCammon, R. R.

A **boy's** own story. White, E.

The **boyfriend.** Perry, T.

Boyos. Marinick, R.

BOYS

Ruiz Zafon, C. The shadow of the wind
Sallis, J. The killer is dying
Saroyan, W. The human comedy
Saul, J. Shadows
Schwartzman, A. Eddie Signwriter
Scott, J. Tourmaline
Searles, J. Boy still missing
Shakespeare, N. Secrets of the sea
Sharfeddin, H. Mineral spirits
Silver, M. The god of war
Southgate, M. The fall of Rome
Stanisic, S. How the soldier repairs the gramophone
Stern, S. The frozen rabbi
Strauss, J. The dubious salvation of Jack V.
Swarthout, G. F. Bless the beasts and children
Tinti, H. The good thief
Tobar, H. The barbarian nurseries
Torres, J. We the animals
Townsend, S. The Adrian Mole diaries
Tremain, R. The way I found her
Trollope, J. The choir
Tucker, T. Over and under
Twain, M. The adventures of Huckleberry Finn
Twain, M. The adventures of Tom Sawyer
Vargas Llosa, M. The notebooks of Don Rigoberto
Vlautin, W. Lean on Pete
White, E. A boy's own story
Whitehead, C. Sag Harbor
Wilson, E. O. Anthill
Winton, T. Breath
Wolff, T. Old school
Woo, S. J. Everything Asian
Woodrell, D. The death of sweet mister
Woolf, V. Jacob's room
Wray, J. Lowboy

BOYS -- EDUCATION
 See also Education
BOYS -- ENGLAND
Stace, W. By George
BOYS -- FICTION
Connolly, J. The infernals
Gaiman, N. The Ocean at the End of the Lane
Stace, W. By George
The **boys** from Brazil. Levin, I.
BOYS' CLUBS *See* Clubs; Societies
BRACHIOSAURUS *See* Dinosaurs
Bradbury stories. Bradbury, R.
The **Bradshaw** variations. Cusk, R.
Brahe, Tycho, 1546-1601
   About
Sherwood, F. The book of splendor
Braided lives. Piercy, M.
BRAILLE BOOKS *See* Books
BRAIN
Darnton, J. Mind catcher
Krauss, N. Man walks into a room

Powers, R. The echo maker
BRAIN -- DISEASES *See* Diseases
BRAIN -- WOUNDS AND INJURIES
Picoult, J. Lone wolf
BRAIN DAMAGE
Genova, L. Left neglected
BRAIN DEATH *See* Death
BRAINWASHING
Higgins, J. Day of judgment
Koontz, D. R. Strangers
The **Bram** Stoker bedside companion. Stoker, B.
The **Brambles.** Minot, E.
Brandling, Henry C. (Henry Charles), b. 1818
   About
Carey, P. The chemistry of tears
BRANDT, SARAH (FICTITIOUS CHARACTER)
Thompson, V. Murder in Chinatown
Thompson, V. Murder on Fifth Avenue
Thompson, V. Murder on Lenox Hill
Thompson, V. Murder on Lexington Avenue
Thompson, V. Murder on Waverly Place
Brass. Walsh, H.
The **brass** verdict. Connelly, M.
Brasyl. McDonald, I.
Brat Farrar. Tey, J.
The **brave.** Evans, N.
Brave new world. Huxley, A.
Brave new worlds.
BRAVERY *See* Courage
Brazil. Updike, J.
BRAZIL
Amado, J. Dona Flor and her two husbands
Amado, J. Gabriela, clove and cinnamon
Grisham, J. The testament
Hatoum, M. The brothers
Levin, I. The boys from Brazil
McDonald, I. Brasyl
Peebles, F. d. P. The seamstress
Sledge, M. The more I owe you
Updike, J. Brazil
BRAZIL -- 19TH CENTURY
Vargas Llosa, M. The war of the end of the world
BRAZIL -- BAHIA
Amado, J. Dona Flor and her two husbands
Amado, J. Gabriela, clove and cinnamon
BRAZIL -- FICTION
Grisham, J. The testament
Levin, I. The boys from Brazil
Peebles, F. d. P. The seamstress
Updike, J. Brazil
BRAZILIANS -- UNITED STATES
Stumpf, D. Confessions of a Wall Street shoeshine boy
Breach of duty. Jance, J. A.
Breach of promise. O'Shaughnessy, P.

A **breach** of promise. Perry, A.
BREAD
    See Baking; Cooking; Food
Bread and wine. Silone, I.
Bread upon the waters. Shaw, I.
Break no bones. Reichs, K. J.
Break the skin. Martin, L.
Breakdown. Paretsky, S.
The **breakdown** lane. Mitchard, J.
The **breaker.** Walters, M.
Breakfast at Tiffany's: a short novel and three stories. Capote, T.
Breakfast of champions. Vonnegut, K.
Breakfast with Buddha. Merullo, R.
Breakheart Hill. Cook, T. H.
Breaking news. MacNeil, R.
The **breaking** of eggs. Powell, J.
Breaking silence. Castillo, L.
Breaking the tongue. Loh, V.
Breaking up is hard to do. Gorman, E.
Breakout. Stark, R.
BREAST CANCER *See* Cancer; Women -- Diseases
Breath. Winton, T.
A **breath** of snow and ashes. Gabaldon, D.
Breathing lessons. Tyler, A.
Brébeuf, Jean de, Saint, 1593-1649
       About
Vollmann, W. T. Fathers and crows
Breed. Novak, C.
The **brethren.** Grisham, J.
The **brethren.** Lewis, B.
BREWERIES *See* Factories
Brewing up a storm. Lathen, E.
Briar Rose. Yolen, J.
Briar Rose. Coover, R.
BRIBERY
    Keating, H. R. F. The bad detective
Bribery, corruption also. Keating, H. R. F.
Brick lane. Ali, M.
BRICKLAYING *See* Building
The **bride.** Garwood, J.
The **bride** from Odessa. Cozarinsky, E.
The **bride** of Lammermoor. Scott, W.
Bride of New France. Desrochers, S.
Bride of Pendorric. Holt, V.
Bride of the high country. Warner, K.
The **bride** sale. Hern, C.
The **Bride** Wore Pearls. Carlyle, L.
The **bride** wore scarlet. Carlyle, L.
The **bridegroom.** Ha Jin
The **brides** of Rollrock Island. Lanagan, M.
Brideshead revisited. Waugh, E.
The **bridesmaid.** Rendell, R.
BRIDGE (GAME) *See* Card games
The **bridge** of San Luis Rey. Wilder, T.

The **bridge** of San Luis Rey and other novels 1926-1948. Wilder, T.
Bridge of sand. Burroway, J.
The **Bridge** of Sighs. Steinhauer, O.
Bridge of sighs. Russo, R.
The **bridge** over the River Kwai. Boulle, P.
BRIDGES
    Barton, E. Brookland
    Boulle, P. The bridge over the River Kwai
    Kadare, I. The three-arched bridge
The **bridges** at Toko-ri. Michener, J. A.
The **bridges** of Madison County. Waller, R. J.
Bridget Jones's diary. Fielding, H.
Bridget Jones: the edge of reason. Fielding, H.
The **brief** history of the dead. Brockmeier, K.
Brief lives. Brookner, A.
The **brief** wondrous life of Oscar Wao. Diaz, J.
BRIGANDS *See* Thieves
BRIGANDS AND ROBBERS
    Blackmore, R. D. Lorna Doone
    Puzo, M. The Sicilian
    Urrea, L. A. Into the beautiful North
BRIGANDS AND ROBBERS -- FICTION
    Moehringer, J. R. Sutton
BRIGATE ROSSE
    Kushner, R. The flamethrowers
Bright and distant shores. Smith, D.
BRIGHT CHILDREN *See* Gifted children
The **bright** forever. Martin, L.
Bright lights, big city. McInerney, J.
Bright shiny morning. Frey, J.
Brightness reef. Brin, D.
BRIGHTON (ENGLAND)
    Guttridge, P. The thing itself
Brighton rock. Greene, G.
Brilliance. Sakey, M.
Brimstone. Preston, D.
Brimstone. Parker, R. B.
The **brimstone** wedding. Vine, B.
Bring up the bodies. Mantel, H.
BRITAIN, BATTLE OF, 1940 *See* Battles; World War, 1939-1945 -- Campaigns
BRITISH -- AFGHANISTAN
    Hensher, P. The Mulberry empire
    Trollope, J. Legacy of love
BRITISH -- AFRICA
    Conrad, J. Heart of darkness
    Gordimer. N. A guest of honor
    Lessing, D. M. The sweetest dream
    Maxwell, R. Jane
    Ruark, R. Uhuru
BRITISH -- ARGENTINA
    Greene, G. The honorary consul
BRITISH -- ASIA
    Gardam, J. Old Filth
BRITISH -- AUSTRIA

Stewart, M. Airs above the ground

BRITISH -- BRAZIL

Hamilton-Paterson, J. Gerontius

King, R. The sound of butterflies

Lessing, D. M. Ben, in the world

BRITISH -- BURMA

Ghosh, A. The glass palace

Mason, D. The piano tuner

BRITISH -- CARIBBEAN REGION

Dean, L. Becoming strangers

BRITISH -- CHINA

Ballard, J. G. Empire of the Sun

Ishiguro, K. When we were orphans

BRITISH -- CRETE

Stewart, M. The moon-spinners

BRITISH -- CROATIA

Seymour, G. The heart of danger

BRITISH -- CYPRUS

Jones, S. Small wars

BRITISH -- DENMARK

Tremain, R. Music & silence

BRITISH -- EGYPT

Deighton, L. City of gold

Durrell, L. Mountolive

BRITISH -- ETHIOPIA

Gibb, C. Sweetness in the belly

BRITISH -- FRANCE

Bates, H. E. Fair stood the wind for France

Cornwell, B. Vagabond

Faulks, S. Birdsong

Freeling, N. One more river

Godden, R. The greengage summer

Graham, W. Bella Poldark

Hemingway, E. The sun also rises

Joyce, G. The silent land

Laker, R. Banners of silk

Lessing, D. M. Ben, in the world

Mayle, P. Anything considered

Mayle, P. A good year

Mayle, P. Hotel Pastis

Orczy, E. Adventures of the Scarlet Pimpernel

Orczy, E. The elusive Pimpernel

Orczy, E. The Scarlet Pimpernel

Rhys, J. Quartet

Stewart, M. Nine coaches waiting

Stewart, M. Thunder on the right

Tremain, R. Trespass

Tremain, R. The way I found her

BRITISH -- GERMANY

Hall, A. The Quiller memorandum

Le Carre, J. The spy who came in from the cold

MacLean, A. Where eagles dare

Shakespeare, N. Snowleg

BRITISH -- GREECE

Fowles, J. The magus

Goddard, R. Into the blue

Hill, T. The hidden

Stewart, M. My brother Michael

BRITISH -- HONG KONG

Clavell, J. Tai-Pan

Lanchester, J. Fragrant Harbor

Lee, J. Y. K. The piano teacher

Theroux, P. Kowloon Tong

BRITISH -- INDIA

Dyer, G. Jeff in Venice, death in Varanasi

Forster, E. M. A passage to India

Ghosh, A. The glass palace

Godden, R. Black Narcissus

Jhabvala, R. P. Heat and dust

Kaye, M. M. The far pavilions

Kaye, M. M. Shadow of the moon

Scott, P. The day of the scorpion

Scott, P. A division of the spoils

Scott, P. The jewel in the crown

Scott, P. The Raj quartet

Scott, P. Staying on

Scott, P. The towers of silence

BRITISH -- INDIA -- FICTION

Festing, I. A. The birdkeeper

BRITISH -- IRAQ

Unsworth, B. Land of marvels

BRITISH -- IRELAND

Davis-Goff, A. This cold country

Llywelyn, M. 1921

Uris, L. Redemption

Uris, L. Trinity

BRITISH -- ISRAEL

Spark, M. The Mandelbaum Gate

BRITISH -- ITALY

Amis, M. The pregnant widow

Craig, A. Love in idleness

Dyer, G. Jeff in Venice, death in Varanasi

Forster, E. M. A room with a view

Freud, E. Love falls

Godden, R. The battle of the Villa Fiorita

Godden, R. Pippa passes

Kneale, M. When we were Romans

Mortimer, J. Summer's lease

Parks, T. Destiny

Parks, T. Rapids

Roberts, M. Reader, I married him

Scott, J. Tourmaline

Seymour, G. Killing ground

Watkins, P. The ice soldier

West, M. L. The devil's advocate

Wignall, K. For the dogs

BRITISH -- JAPAN

Clavell, J. Gai-Jin

Clavell, J. Shogun

Hazzard, S. The great fire

BRITISH -- LEBANON

Stewart, M. The Gabriel hounds

BROOKLYN (NEW YORK, N.Y.) -- FICTION
Huston, C. Half the blood of Brooklyn
K'wan Section 8
McDermott, A. Someone
The **Brooklyn** follies. Auster, P.
Brother and sister. Trollope, J.
Brother Cadfael's penance. Peters, E.
Brother Odd. Koontz, D. R.
Brother Wind. Harrison, S.
The **brotherhood** of the rose. Morrell, D.
Brotherhood of war [series]
Griffin, W. E. B. The aviators
Griffin, W. E. B. Special ops
The **brothers.** Hatoum, M.
Brothers. Chen, D.
Brothers. Yu Hua
BROTHERS
See also Men; Siblings
Amis, M. House of meetings
Bakker, G. The twin
Baldwin, J. Tell me how long the train's been gone
Banks, R. Affliction
Barbash, T. The last good chance
Barthelme, F. Waveland
Burgess, M. Dogfight, a love story
Caldwell, T. Testimony of two men
Chaon, D. Await your reply
Clark, M. The legal limit
Clinch, J. Kings of the earth
Coben, H. Gone for good
Coe, J. The closed circle
Cook, T. H. Places in the dark
Cornwell, B. Stonehenge, 2000 B.C.
De la Roche, M. Jalna
DeWitt, P. The Sisters brothers
Dexter, P. The paperboy
Doctorow, E. L. Homer & Langley
Doig, I. Bucking the sun
Dostoyevsky, F. The brothers Karamazov
Dunne, J. G. True confessions
Folsom, A. R. Day of confession
Glass, J. Three Junes
Grisham, J. The client
Gross, A. Eyes wide open
Habila, H. Measuring time
Handke, P. Repetition
Hart, J. Iron house
Hatoum, M. The brothers
Havazelet, E. Bearing the body
Higgins, J. Flight of eagles
Hijuelos, O. Beautiful Maria of my soul
Hijuelos, O. The Mambo Kings play songs of love
Huston, C. The shotgun rule
Johnson, D. Tree of smoke
Kadare, I. The ghost rider
Kelman, J. Kieron Smith, boy

Kelton, E. Texas sunrise
Koontz, D. R. By the light of the moon
Lamb, W. I know this much is true
Lansdale, J. R. Leather maiden
Leithauser, B. A few corrections
Llywelyn, M. Pride of lions
Lourie, R. A hatred for tulips
Martin, C. W. How to sell
Martin, M. Windswept House
McCann, C. Let the great world spin
McCarthy, C. The crossing
McFarland, D. The music room
McNamer, D. Red rover
Miller, A. Oxygen
Mosley, W. Fortunate son
Mullen, T. The many deaths of the Firefly Brothers
Murdoch, I. The green knight
O'Dell, T. Fragile beasts
Orringer, J. The invisible bridge
Parini, J. The apprentice lover
Parker, T. J. California girl
Price, R. Clockers
Robertson, M. The brothers of Baker Street
Robinson, L. Water dogs
Robison, M. One D.O.A., one on the way
Rush, N. Mortals
Russo, R. Empire Falls
Shakar, A. Luminarium
Sidor, S. The mirror's edge
Silver, M. The god of war
Singer, I. J. The brothers Ashkenazi
Smith, W. A. Monsoon
Torres, J. We the animals
Tsukiyama, G. The street of a thousand blossoms
Vanderhaeghe, G. The last crossing
Verghese, A. Cutting for stone
Vollmann, W. T. The royal family
Whitehead, C. Sag Harbor
BROTHERS -- FICTION
Barclay, L. Trust your eyes
Braffet, K. Save yourself
Cash, W. A land more kind than home
Harrison, K. Envy
Kerstan, L. Heart of the tiger
Kowalski, W. Something noble
Longworth, M. L. Death at the Chateau Bremont
Lundrigan, N. Glass boys
Strout, E. The burgess boys
Swift, G. Wish you were here
Vachss, A. That's how I roll
Brothers and sisters. Campbell, B. M.
BROTHERS AND SISTERS
Abu-Jaber, D. Birds of paradise
Auster, P. Invisible
Baker, K. The bird of the river
Barth, J. The sot-weed factor

The **brothers** of Baker Street. Robertson, M.
BROTHERS-IN-LAW
  Clay, H. Losing Charlotte
  Cook, R. Crisis
  McGrath, P. Trauma
  Oe, K. The changeling
Brown eyes blue. Meyer, C.
Brown girl, brownstones. Marshall, P.
BROWN UNIVERSITY
  Eugenides, J. The marriage plot
Brown, John, 1800-1859
                  About
  Banks, R. Cloudsplitter
BROWNS (MUSICAL GROUP)
  Bass, R. Nashville chrome
Brueghel, Pieter, the Elder, 1522?-1569
                  About
  Frayn, M. Headlong
**BRUNETTI, GUIDO (FICTITIOUS CHARAC-
  TER)**
  Leon, D. Blood from a stone
  Leon, D. Doctored evidence
  Leon, D. A question of belief
Bruno, Giordano, 1548-1600
                  About
  Parris, S. J. Sacrilege
Brushback. Constantine, K. C.
BRUTALITY See Cruelty
Brutus, Lucius Junius
                  About
  Massie, A. Caesar
BUBONIC PLAGUE See Plague
BUCCANEERS See Pirates
Buchanan, James, 1791-1868
                  About
  Updike, J. Memories of the Ford Administration
**BUCHANAN, PAMELA (FICTITIOUS CHAR-
  ACTER)**
  Carson, T. Daisy Buchanan's daughter
**BUCHENWALD (GERMANY: CONCENTRA-
  TION CAMP)** See Concentration camps
Bucking the sun. Doig, I.
Buckingham Palace gardens. Perry, A.
Buddenbrooks. Mann, T.
Buddha Da. Donovan, A.
The **Buddha** in the attic. Otsuka, J.
The **Buddha** of suburbia. Kureishi, H.
BUDDHISM
  Burdett, J. Bangkok 8
  Burdett, J. Bangkok haunts
  Burdett, J. Bangkok Tattoo
  Donovan, A. Buddha Da
  Endo, S. Deep river
  Hesse, H. Siddhartha
  Merullo, R. Breakfast with Buddha
  Mishima, Y. The Temple of Dawn

  Mishima, Y. The temple of the golden pavilion
  Pattison, E. The skull mantra
  Zelazny, R. Lord of light
BUDDHIST ART See Art
BUDDHIST LEADERS
  Mishima, Y. The Temple of Dawn
  Mishima, Y. The temple of the golden pavilion
BUDDHIST NUNS
  Ozeki, R. L. A tale for the time being
BUFFALO BILL'S WILD WEST COMPANY
  Welch, J. The heartsong of Charging Elk
Buffalo Bill, 1846-1917
                  About
  McMurtry, L. Buffalo girls
  McMurtry, L. Telegraph days
Buffalo girls. McMurtry, L.
Buffalo soldiers. O'Connor, R.
Buffalo soldiers. Willard, T.
BUFFALO, AMERICAN See Bison
BUGGING, ELECTRONIC See Eavesdropping
BUILDING
  Hodgins, E. Mr. Blandings builds his dream house
BUILDING INDUSTRY See Construction industry
Building stories. Ware, C.
BUILDINGS
  Ware, C. Building stories
BUILDINGS -- EARTHQUAKE EFFECTS See
  Earthquakes
Built in a day. Rinehart, S.
BULGARIA
  Penkov, M. East of the West
BULGARIA -- SOFIA
  Gilman, D. The elusive Mrs. Pollifax
BULIMIA
  Minot, E. The Brambles
The **bull** from the sea. Renault, M.
BULL RUN, 1ST BATTLE, 1861
  Cornwell, B. Rebel
Bullet Park. Cheever, J.
BULLFIGHTERS AND BULLFIGHTING
  Garcia, C. The lady matador's hotel
  Hemingway, E. The sun also rises
  Michener, J. A. Mexico
  O'Dell, T. Fragile beasts
Bullfighting and other stories. Doyle, R.
BULLIES
  Lancaster, J. Here I go again
  Rowell, R. Eleanor & Park
BULLYING
  Picoult, J. Nineteen minutes
Bum steer. Pickard, N.
BUNGO CHANNEL (JAPAN)
  Deutermann, P. T. The ghosts of Bungo Suido
**BUNKER HILL (BOSTON, MASS.), BATTLE
  OF, 1775** See Battles; United States -- History
  -- 1775-1783, Revolution -- Campaigns

Finder, J. Killer instinct
Galgut, D. The impostor
Goddard, R. Into the blue
Grisham, J. The appeal
Huston, C. Sleepless
Ignatius, D. A firing offense
Larsson, S. The girl with the dragon tattoo
Le Carre, J. The constant gardener
Martin, C. W. How to sell
Norris, F. The octopus
Wells, H. G. Tono-Bungay

BUSINESS BUDGETS *See* Business
BUSINESS DEPRESSION, 1929
Adams, A. A southern exposure
Algren, N. A walk on the wild side
Brown, J. D. Addie Pray
Doctorow, E. L. Loon Lake
Doig, I. Bucking the sun
Hamner, E. The homecoming
Kennedy, W. Ironweed
Koryta, M. The Cypress House

BUSINESS EDUCATION *See* Education
BUSINESS ENTERPRISES *See* Business
BUSINESS ENTERTAINING *See* Entertaining;
Public relations
BUSINESS ETHICS *See* Ethics; Professional ethics
BUSINESS FAILURES *See* Business
BUSINESS FORECASTING *See* Economic fore-
casting; Forecasting
BUSINESS INTELLIGENCE
Gibson, W. Pattern recognition
Jones, C. M. The silent oligarch
Stevens, T. The informationist

BUSINESS MATHEMATICS *See* Mathematics
BUSINESSMEN
Adiga, A. The white tiger
Atwood, M. The blind assassin
Boyle, T. C. When the killing's done
Collins, J. Beginner's Greek
Dahl, A. Misterioso
DeLillo, D. Cosmopolis
Finder, J. Company man
Finder, J. Power play
Guterson, D. Ed King
Harrison, C. Afterburn
Ignatius, D. The Sun King
Korda, M. Worldly goods
Lanchester, J. Fragrant Harbor
Leithauser, B. A few corrections
Lewis, S. Babbitt
Lightman, A. P. The diagnosis
McGuane, T. Nothing but blue skies
Millhauser, S. Martin Dressler
Percy, W. The moviegoer
Roth, P. American pastoral
Updike, J. Villages

Westlake, D. E. The ax
Yates, A. Moondogs

BUSINESSMEN -- FICTION
Eggers, D. A hologram for the king
BUSINESSPEOPLE *See* Business
BUSINESSWOMEN
Auchincloss, L. Her infinite variety
Bradford, B. T. A woman of substance
Bushnell, C. Lipstick jungle
Campbell, B. M. Brothers and sisters
Cleage, P. Babylon sisters
Dee, J. A thousand pardons
Goodman, A. The cookbook collector
Hill, R. When all is said and done
Lippman, L. And when she was good
McMillan, T. How Stella got her groove back
McNaught, J. Paradise
Michael, J. A certain smile
Michaels, F. Celebration
Sheldon, S. Master of the game
Thayer, N. Everlasting
Van Slyke, H. Public smiles, private tears
Vidal, G. Empire
Wood, B. Perfect Harmony

Busman's honeymoon. Sayers, D. L.
Busy bodies. Hess, J.
Busy monsters. Giraldi, W.
But come ye back. Lordan, B.
But I wouldn't want to die there. Pickard, N.
The **butcher** boy. McCabe, P.
BUTLERS
Ishiguro, K. The remains of the day
McGrath, P. The grotesque
Wodehouse, P. G. The world of Jeeves
BUTTE (MONT.)
Doig, I. Work song
Butterfield 8. O'Hara, J.
BUTTERFLIES
See also Insects
King, R. The sound of butterflies
**BUTTERFLIES -- COLLECTION AND PRES-
ERVATION**
McGill, B. The butterfly cabinet
The **butterfly** cabinet. McGill, B.
Butterfly stories. Vollmann, W. T.
Buying a fishing rod for my grandfather. Gao
Xingjian
Buzz Aldrin, what happened to you in all the confu-
sion? Harstad, J.
Buzz cut. Hall, J. W.
The **buzzard** table. Maron, M.
BUZZARDS BAY (MASS.)
Graver, E. The end of the point
By blood. Ullman, E.
By George. Stace, W.
By love possessed. Cozzens, J. G.

Mapson Bad Girl Creek
Mapson Solomon's oak
Martini, S. P. The judge
McMillan, T. The interruption of everything
Miller, S. Lost in the forest
Muller, M. Cyanide Wells
Otsuka, J. When the emperor was divine
Otto, W. How to make an American quilt
Packer, A. Songs without words
Parker, T. J. California girl
Parker, T. J. Little Saigon
Parker, T. J. Silent Joe
Parker, T. J. Storm runners
Pronzini, B. The hidden
Pronzini, B. In an evil time
Pronzini, B. A wasteland of strangers
Puchner, E. Model home
Pynchon, T. The crying of lot 49
Pynchon, T. Vineland
Pyne, D. Twentynine Palms
Rosenberg, N. T. Abuse of power
Rosenberg, N. T. Interest of justice
Rosenberg, N. T. Mitigating circumstances
Saroyan, W. The human comedy
Saul, J. The homing
Schwartz, J. B. Northwest corner
Schwartz, L. Angels Crest
Siegel, J. Deceit
Silver, M. The god of war
Steel, D. The house on Hope Street
Stegner, W. E. All the little live things
Steinbeck, J. East of Eden
Steinbeck, J. The grapes of wrath
Steinbeck, J. In dubious battle
Steinbeck, J. The long valley
Steinbeck, J. Of mice and men
Steinbeck, J. The wayward bus
Steinbeck, T. In the shadow of the cypress
Straight, S. The gettin place
Straight, S. Highwire moon
Thomas, R. The fourth Durango
Tobar, H. The barbarian nurseries
Tsukiyama, G. Dreaming water
Winslow, D. Savages
Wood, S. Wrecker
Woods, S. Dead eyes

CALIFORNIA -- 1846-1900
Allende, I. Daughter of fortune
Baker, K. Mendoza in Hollywood
DeWitt, P. The Sisters brothers
Holland, C. Pacific Street
Houston, J. D. Bird of another heaven
Norris, F. The octopus
Steinbeck, J. East of Eden

CALIFORNIA -- 19TH CENTURY
Bristow, G. Jubilee Trail

Fowler, K. J. Sister Noon
Holland, C. An ordinary woman
L'Amour, L. The Californios
L'Amour, L. The lonesome gods

CALIFORNIA -- 20TH CENTURY
Cunningham, M. The hours
Goudge, E. Stranger in paradise
Koontz, D. R. False memory
Koontz, D. R. Fear nothing
Koontz, D. R. Intensity
Koontz, D. R. Seize the night
Lemann, N. Malaise
Mapson Bad Girl Creek
Martini, S. P. The judge
Muller, M. Cyanide Wells
Otsuka, J. When the emperor was divine
Parker, T. J. Little Saigon
Parker, T. J. Silent Joe
Pronzini, B. In an evil time
Pronzini, B. A wasteland of strangers
Pynchon, T. The crying of lot 49
Pynchon, T. Vineland
Rosenberg, N. T. Abuse of power
Saul, J. The homing
Steel, D. The house on Hope Street
Steinbeck, J. East of Eden
Steinbeck, J. The grapes of wrath
Steinbeck, J. In dubious battle
Steinbeck, J. The long valley
Steinbeck, J. Of mice and men
Steinbeck, J. The wayward bus
Woods, S. Dead eyes

CALIFORNIA -- BERKELEY
Goodman, A. The cookbook collector
Meidav, E. Lola, California

CALIFORNIA -- BEVERLY HILLS
Dexter, P. Train
Fuchs, J. Conrad in Beverly Hills
Martin, S. Shopgirl

CALIFORNIA -- FICTION
Johnson, D. Elsewhere, California
Williams, K. Dirty to the grave

CALIFORNIA -- GOLD DISCOVERIES
Allende, I. Daughter of fortune

CALIFORNIA -- HISTORY -- 1950-
Ullman, E. By blood

CALIFORNIA -- HOLLYWOOD
Abbott, M. E. The song is you
Adler, E. All or nothing
Barker, C. Coldheart Canyon
DeWitt, P. Ablutions
Didion, J. Play it as it lays
Dunne, D. An inconvenient woman
Epstein, L. San Remo Drive
Erickson, S. Zeroville
Evans, N. The brave

Houston, J. D. Bird of another heaven
Jamison, L. The gin closet
Lee, C. Y. The flower drum song
Lee, G. China boy
Lescroart, J. T. The first law
Lescroart, J. T. Guilt
Lescroart, J. T. The hearing
Lescroart, J. T. The mercy rule
Lescroart, J. T. Nothing but the truth
Lescroart, J. T. The oath
Lescroart, J. T. The second chair
Maupin, A. Mary Ann in autumn
Maupin, A. Michael Tolliver lives
Mohr, J. Damascus
Moore, C. A dirty job
Ng, F. M. Bone
Norris, F. McTeague
Otsuka, J. The Buddha in the attic
Palwick, S. Shelter
Patterson, J. 1st to die
Patterson, R. N. Degree of guilt
Patterson, R. N. Eyes of a child
Paul, J. Elsewhere in the land of parrots
Richmond, M. No one you know
Shafak, E. The bastard of Istanbul
Siegel, S. Final verdict
Smiley, J. Private life
Steel, D. Amazing grace
Tan, A. The bonesetter's daughter
Tan, A. The Joy Luck Club
Vollmann, W. T. The royal family
CALIFORNIA -- SAN JOSE
  Malae, P. N. What we are
CALIFORNIA -- SANTA BARBARA
  Iyer, P. Abandon
  Rosenberg, N. T. Buried evidence
CALIFORNIA -- SANTA MONICA
  Smith, A. Good morning, killer
California girl. Parker, T. J.
California gold. Jakes, J.
CALIFORNIA, SOUTHERN
  Gavin, J. Middle men
  Hagy, A. Boleto
The **Californios.** L'Amour, L.
The **call.** Murphy, Y.
Call down the stars. Harrison, S.
Call it sleep. Roth, H.
Call me by your name. Aciman, A. A.
Call me irresistible. Phillips, S. E.
The **call** of the toad. Grass, G.
The **call** of the wild. London, J.
Callahan's con. Robinson, S.
Callender, James Thomson, 1758-1803
              About
  Safire, W. Scandalmonger
The **caller.** Fossum, K.

The **calligrapher.** Docx, E.
CALLIGRAPHERS
  Docx, E. The calligrapher
The **calling.** Wolfe, I. A.
Calling Me Home. Kibler, J.
Calling Mr. King. De Feo, R.
Calling the wind.
Calpurnia. Scott, A.
Calumet City. Newton, C.
CALVINISM *See* Reformation
CAMBODIA
  Hall, A. Quiller Salamander
CAMBODIA -- HISTORY -- 1975-
  Ratner, V. In the shadow of the banyan
CAMBODIA -- HISTORY -- 1975-1979
  Ratner, V. In the shadow of the banyan
CAMBODIAN REFUGEES
  Ratner, V. In the shadow of the banyan
CAMBODIANS -- CANADA
  Echlin, K. The disappeared
CAMBODIANS -- UNITED STATES
  Jen, G. World and town
CAMBRIDGE (ENGLAND)
  Atkinson, K. Case histories
  Cumming, C. The Trinity Six
  Harris, R. Enigma
  Stott, R. Ghostwalk
CAMBRIDGE (MASS.)
  Aciman, A. Harvard Square
  Cohen, R. Inspired sleep
  Cook, R. Seizure
  Goodman, A. The cookbook collector
  Langton, J. The Escher twist
  Langton, J. The face on the wall
  Langton, J. The thief of Venice
  Martin, W. Harvard Yard
CAMBRIDGESHIRE (ENGLAND)
  Kelly, J. The fire baby
The **camel** bookmobile. Hamilton, M.
Cameron's crossing. McCutchan, P.
Camille. Dumas, A.
The **campaign.** Fuentes, C.
CAMPAIGN FUNDS *See* Elections; Politics
CAMPUS POLICE
  Rodriguez, L. Every last secret
Can you forgive her? Trollope, A.
Canaan's tongue. Wray, J.
Canada. Ford, R.
CANADA
  Adamson, G. The outlander
  Atwood, M. The blind assassin
  Davies, R. The cunning man
  Davies, R. Fifth business
  Davies, R. The manticore
  Davies, R. Murther & walking spirits
  Davies, R. What's bred in the bone

Patterson, R. N. Conviction
Picoult, J. Change of heart
Tirone Smith Love her madly
Turow, S. Reversible errors
CAPITALISTS AND FINANCIERS
Clavell, J. Noble house
Coleridge, N. Godchildren
Dickens, C. Dombey and Son
Doctorow, E. L. Loon Lake
Durrell, L. Justine
Fuentes, C. The death of Artemio Cruz
Gordimer, N. The conservationist
Grippando, J. Money to burn
Gross, A. Reckless
Le Carre, J. Single & Single
Norris, F. The pit
Ondaatje, M. In the skin of a lion
O'Neill, J. Netherland
Pears, I. Stone's fall
Rand, A. Atlas shrugged
Singer, I. J. The brothers Ashkenazi
Thomas, M. M. Hanover Place
Trenhaile, J. The gates of exquisite view
CAPITALS (CITIES) *See* Cities and towns
Capone, Al, 1899-1947
                    About
Collins, M. A. Black hats
Capote in Kansas. Powers, K.
Capote, Truman, 1924-1984
                    About
Powers, K. Capote in Kansas
CAPRI
Goodman, C. The night villa
Parini, J. The apprentice lover
Rice, L. The deep blue sea for beginners
Caprice and Rondo. Dunnett, D.
Captain Alatriste. Perez-Reverte, A.
The **captain** and the enemy. Greene, G.
Captain Blood. Sabatini, R.
Captain Newman, M.D. Rosten, L.
Captain Pantoja and the Special Service. Vargas Llosa, M.
Captain Saturday. Inman, R.
Captains and kings. Caldwell, T.
The **captive** [and] The fugitive. Proust, M.
Captive queen. Weir, A.
The **captive** Queen of Scots. Plaidy, J.
Captivity. Noyes, D.
Captivity. Wesselmann, D. L.
CAR ACCIDENTS *See* Traffic accidents
CAR INDUSTRY *See* Automobile industry
CAR WRECKS *See* Traffic accidents
Caramba! Martinez, N. M.
The **Caravaggio** obsession. Banks, O. T.
Caravan of thieves. Rich, D.
Caravans. Michener, J. A.

CARBOLIC ACID *See* Acids; Chemicals
CARBON DIOXIDE GREENHOUSE EFFECT
    See Global warming
CARCINOMA *See* Cancer
CARD GAMES
        See also Games
    Stroby, W. Cold shot to the heart
CARD TRICKS *See* Card games; Magic tricks; Tricks
CARDIFF (WALES)
    Bingham, H. Talking to the dead
A **cardinal** offense. McInerny, R. M.
The **cardinal** virtues. Greeley, A. M.
CARDINALS
    Vallgren The horrific sufferings of the mind-reading monster Hercules Barefoot
CARDINALS -- FICTION
    Berry, S. The third secret
Cardington Crescent. Perry, A.
CARE GIVERS *See* Caregivers
Care of wooden floors. Wiles, W.
CAREGIVERS
    Berg, E. We are all welcome here
    Evison, J. The revised fundamentals of caregiving
Careless in red. George, E.
The **Caretaker.** Ahmad, A. X.
The **caretaker** of Lorne Field. Zeltserman, D.
Caribbean. Michener, J. A.
CARIBBEAN REGION
    Buffett, J. A salty piece of land
    Crichton, M. Pirate latitudes
    Dean, L. Becoming strangers
    Green cane and juicy flotsam
    Hemingway, E. Islands in the stream
    Kincaid, J. Autobiography of my mother
    Matthiessen, P. Far Tortuga
    Michener, J. A. Caribbean
    Mitchard, J. Still summer
    Nunez, E. Anna in-between
    Stone, R. Bay of souls
    Styron, A. All the finest girls
    Vonnegut, K. Cat's cradle
    Wolfe, G. Pirate freedom
    Woods, S. Dead in the water
CARIBBEAN REGION -- FICTION
    Allende, I. Island beneath the sea
    Buffett, J. A salty piece of land
    Crichton, M. Pirate latitudes
Caribou Island. Vann, D.
Carmen. Merimee, P.
Carnarvon, Henry Howard Molyneux Herbert, 4th Earl of, 1831-1890
                    About
    Holland, C. Valley of the Kings
CARNIVAL
        See also Festivals

CARNIVALS

See also Amusements; Festivals

Dunn, K. Geek love

CARNIVOROUS ANIMALS *See* Animals

Carolina moon. McCorkle, J.

CAROLS *See* Church music; Folk songs; Hymns; Songs; Vocal music

CARPATHIAN MOUNTAINS

Wiesel, E. The oath

Carpentaria. Wright, A.

CARPENTERS

Eliot, G. Adam Bede

CARPENTRY *See* Building

The carpet makers. Eschbach, A.

Carrie. King, S.

The Carrie diaries. Bushnell, C.

Carried away. Munro, A.

A carrion death. Stanley, M.

Carroll, Lewis, 1832-1898

About

Benjamin, M. Alice I have been

Carry me down. Hyland, M. J.

Carry the one. Anshaw, C.

CARS (AUTOMOBILES) *See* Automobiles

CARSINGTON FAMILY (FICTITIOUS CHARACTERS)

Chase, L. Not quite a lady

Carte blanche: 007. Deaver, J.

Carter, Howard

About

Holland, C. Valley of the Kings

CARTHAGE (EXTINCT CITY) *See* Extinct cities

CARTOGRAPHERS

Humphreys, H. Afterimage

CARTOGRAPHY *See* Map drawing; Maps

CARTOONING *See* Cartoons and caricatures; Wit and humor

CARTOONISTS

Ha Jin In the pond

Jacobson, H. Kalooki nights

CARTOONS AND COMICS

Pierson, D. C. The boy who couldn't sleep and never had to

CARVING, WOOD *See* Wood carving

The caryatids. Sterling, B.

The case has altered. Grimes, M.

Case histories. Atkinson, K.

A case of exploding mangoes. Hanif, M.

The case of the deadly butter chicken. Hall, T.

The case of the deadly desperados. Lawrence, C.

The case of the missing books. Sansom, I.

Casement, Roger, Sir, 1864-1916

About

The dream of the Celt

Cashelmara. Howatch, S.

Casino Royale. Fleming, I.

CASINOS

Hilton, E. Dirty money Honey

The **Cassandra** project. McDevitt, J.

CASSETTE TAPES, AUDIO *See* Sound recordings

Cassidy, David

About

Pearson, A. I think I love you

Cast a long shadow. Pearce, M. E.

CASTAWAYS *See* Survival after airplane accidents, shipwrecks, etc.

CASTE -- INDIA

Mistry, R. A fine balance

Roy, A. The god of small things

Viswanathan, P. The toss of a lemon

The castle. Kafka, F.

Castle. Lennon, J. R.

The castle in the forest. Mailer, N.

Castle Rackrent. Edgeworth, M.

CASTLES

See also Buildings

Egan, J. The keep

Holt, V. Bride of Pendorric

Stewart, M. Nine coaches waiting

Castleview. Wolfe, G.

Castro, Fidel, 1926-

About

Block, L. Killing Castro

Fuentes, N. The autobiography of Fidel Castro

Hunter, S. Havana

The casual vacancy. Rowling, J. K.

CASUALTY INSURANCE

See also Insurance

Cat & mouse. Patterson, J.

Cat and mouse. Grass, G.

Cat chaser. Leonard, E.

The cat dancers. Deutermann, P. T.

Cat in a midnight choir. Douglas, C. N.

Cat in a neon nightmare. Douglas, C. N.

The cat who ate Danish modern. Braun, L. J.

The cat who brought down the house. Braun, L. J.

The cat who sang for the birds. Braun, L. J.

The cat who smelled a rat. Braun, L. J.

The cat who went underground. Braun, L. J.

Cat's cradle. Vonnegut, K.

Cat's eye. Atwood, M.

The cat's table. Ondaatje, M.

CATACOMBS *See* Burial; Cemeteries; Christian antiquities; Tombs

Catalyst. Hoffman, N. K.

CATASTROPHES *See* Disasters

The catch. Mayor, A.

Catch me. Gardner, L.

Catch-22. Heller, J.

The catcher in the rye. Salinger, J. D.

Catching Katie. Hatcher, R. L.

Prose, F. Household saints
Quindlen, A. Object lessons
Rabb, J. The book of Q
Rosero, E. Good offices
Stendhal The red and the black
Sullivan, J. C. Maine
Waugh, E. Brideshead revisited
Waugh, E. The end of the battle
Werfel, F. The song of Bernadette
West, M. L. The clowns of God
West, M. L. Lazarus
West, M. L. The shoes of the fisherman

CATHOLIC PRIESTS

Binchy, M. Whitethorn Woods
Blatty, W. P. The exorcist
Bolano, R. By night in Chile
Camus, A. The plague
Cather, W. Death comes for the archbishop
Cornwell, B. Sharpe's fury
Cronin, A. J. The keys of the kingdom
Delaney, E. J. Broken Irish
Dunne, J. G. True confessions
Eliot, G. Romola
Endo, S. Silence
Erdrich, L. The last report on the miracles at Little No Horse
Flynn, M. Eifelheim
Folsom, A. R. Day of confession
Gordon, M. The company of women
Greeley, A. M. The cardinal virtues
Greeley, A. M. White smoke
Greene, G. A burnt-out case
Greene, G. The honorary consul
Greene, G. Monsignor Quixote
Greene, G. The power and the glory
Haigh, J. Faith
Henley, P. Hummingbird house
Higgins, J. Confessional
Keneally, T. Office of innocence
Kienzle, W. X. Assault with intent
Kienzle, W. X. Body count
Kienzle, W. X. The gathering
Kienzle, W. X. The greatest evil
Kienzle, W. X. The man who loved God
Kienzle, W. X. The rosary murders
Martin, M. Windswept House
McCullough, C. The thorn birds
McGowan, K. The expected one
McNicholl, D. A son called Gabriel
Moore, B. Black robe
Moore, B. The statement
O'Hagan, A. Be near me
Picoult, J. Change of heart
Powers, J. F. Morte d'Urban
Powers, J. F. Wheat that springeth green
Rabb, J. The book of Q

Reimringer, J. Vestments
Roberts, M. Reader, I married him
Rosero, E. Good offices
Schulberg, B. Waterfront
Vargas Llosa, M. The Green House
West, M. L. The devil's advocate
Wilder, T. The bridge of San Luis Rey
Wolfe, G. Pirate freedom
Zelazny, R. The dead man's brother

CATHOLICS

Berry, S. The third secret
Endo, S. Deep river
Endo, S. The final martyrs
McInerny, R. M. Grave undertakings
McKinty, A. The cold cold ground
O'Connor, F. Collected works

CATS

Burnford, S. The incredible journey
Douglas, C. N. Cat in a neon nightmare
Roger Caras' Treasury of great cat stories

CATS -- FICTION

Braun, L. J. The cat who brought down the house
Braun, L. J. The cat who smelled a rat
Roger Caras' Treasury of great cat stories
The **catsitters.** Wolcott, J.
A **Catskill** eagle. Parker, R. B.

CATSKILL MOUNTAINS (N.Y.)

Goodman, C. The seduction of water
Kay, T. Shadow song
Lurie, A. Only children

CATTLE

Hawkes, J. Second skin

CATTLE DRIVERS

McMurtry, L. Lonesome dove
The **cattle** killing. Wideman, J. E.

CAUCASUS, NORTHERN (RUSSIA)

Lapierre, A. Between love and honor
Caught. Coben, H.
Caught stealing. Huston, C.
Caught up in the rapture. Jackson, S.

CAUTIONARY TALES AND VERSES See Didactic fiction; Didactic poetry; Fables; Parables

The **cave.** Saramago, J.

CAVE ECOLOGY See Ecology

Caveat emptor. Downie, R.
Celebration. Michaels, F.

CELEBRITIES

Altschul, A. F. Lady Lazarus
Hiaasen, C. Star Island
Rebeck, T. Three girls and their brother
Rushdie, S. The ground beneath her feet
Sherrill, M. My last movie star
Williams, C. Stairway to hell

CELEBRITIES -- FICTION

Wayne, T. The Love Song of Jonny Valentine

CELEBRITY See Fame

About

Gold, G. D. Sunnyside

Chapterhouse: Dune. Herbert, F.

CHARACTER *See* Ethics; Personality

Charbonneau, Jean-Baptiste, 1805-1866

About

Sargent, C. Museum of human beings

CHARITY *See* Ethics; Virtue

Charity girl. Lowenthal, M.

The **Charlemagne** pursuit. Berry, S.

A **Charles** Dickens Christmas. Dickens, C.

Charles II, King of Great Britain, 1630-1685

About

Koen, K. Dark angels

Plaidy, J. The pleasures of love

Charles, d'Orléans, 1394-1465

About

Haasse, H. S. In a dark wood wandering

Charleston. Jakes, J.

**CHARLESTON (S.C.) -- HISTORY -- COLO-
NIAL PERIOD, CA. 1600-1775**

Gabaldon, D. Drums of autumn

Charley Bland. Settle, M. L.

Charley's web. Fielding, J.

Charlie Boxer books [series]

Wilson, R. Capital Punishment

Charlotte Gray. Faulks, S.

The **Charlotte** Perkins Gilman reader. Gilman, C. P.

Charlotte Perkins Gilman's Utopian novels.

The **charm** school. DeMille, N.

A **charmed** life. McCarthy, M.

Charming Billy. McDermott, A.

CHARMS *See* Folklore; Superstition

Charms for the easy life. Gibbons, K.

The **charterhouse** of Parma. Stendhal

The **chase.** Cussler, C.

Chaser. Miasha

CHASIDISM *See* Hasidism

Chasing Cezanne. Mayle, P.

Chasing darkness. Crais, R.

Chat. Mayor, A.

CHATEAUX *See* Castles

The **Chatham** School affair. Cook, T. H.

CHAUFFEURS

Adiga, A. The white tiger

Cheating at canasta. Trevor, W.

Cheating at solitaire. Haddam, J.

Cheating death. Keating, H. R. F.

**CHECHNYA (RUSSIA) -- HISTORY -- CIVIL
WAR, 1994-**

Marra, A. A constellation of vital phenomena

CHECHNYA (RUSSIA)

Marra, A. A constellation of vital phenomena

CHECKERS *See* Board games

Checkmate. Dunnett, D.

CHEERFUL STORIES

Austen, J. Emma

Benson, E. F. Make way for Lucia

Colwin, L. Happy all the time

Davies, V. Miracle on 34th Street

Heyer, G. The grand Sophy

Karon, J. A common life

Karon, J. In this mountain

Karon, J. A new song

Karon, J. Out to Canaan

Keillor, G. Lake Wobegon days

Keillor, G. Lake Wobegon summer 1956

Powers, J. R. Do black patent-leather shoes really reflect up?

Powers, J. R. The last Catholic in America

Read Affairs at Thrush Green

Read At home in Thrush Green

Read Chronicles of Fairacre

Read Farewell to Fairacre

Read Friends at Thrush Green

Read Mrs. Pringle

Read Return to Thrush Green

Read Thrush Green

West, J. The friendly persuasion

White, B. Quite a year for plums

Wodehouse, P. G. The code of the Woosters

Wodehouse, P. G. The inimitable Jeeves

Wodehouse, P. G. Tales from the Drones Club

Wodehouse, P. G. A Wodehouse bestiary

Wodehouse, P. G. The world of Jeeves

CHEERLEADING -- COACHING

Abbott, M. E. Dare me

CHEERLEADING

Abbott, M. E. Dare me

CHEESEMAKERS

Milton, G. Edward Trencom's nose

Cheeshahteaumuck, Caleb, ca. 1646-1666

About

Brooks, G. Caleb's crossing

CHEMICAL INDUSTRY -- ACCIDENTS *See* Industrial accidents

CHEMICAL POLLUTION *See* Pollution

CHEMICAL WARFARE *See* Military art and science; War

CHEMICALS

Grisham, J. The appeal

CHEMISTRY -- DICTIONARIES *See* Encyclopedias and dictionaries

The **chemistry** of tears. Carey, P.

CHEMISTS

See also Scientists

Deighton, L. Funeral in Berlin

Enquist, P. O. The book about Blanche and Marie

Levi, P. The monkey's wrench

O'Connell, J. The resurrectionist

Rubenfeld, J. The death instinct

Wallace, I. The prize

Mapson, J. Loving Chloe

Childhood's end. Clarke, A. C.

Childhood, Boyhood and Youth. Tolstoy, L.

CHILDLESS MARRIAGE

Lynn, A. Now you see it

Moore, L. A gate at the stairs

Rosenfeld, L. I'm so happy for you

Ross, A. Mr. Peanut

Shakespeare, N. Secrets of the sea

Swift, G. Waterland

Tennant, E. Pemberley

CHILDLESSNESS

See also Children; Family size

Green, J. Another piece of my heart

Oates, J. C. I lock my door upon myself

The **children.** Wharton, E.

CHILDREN

See also Age; Family

Adrian, C. The children's hospital

Benjamin, M. Alice I have been

Elkin, S. Stanley Elkin's The magic kingdom

Godden, R. The battle of the Villa Fiorita

Godden, R. The greengage summer

Hughes, R. A. W. A high wind in Jamaica

Ishiguro, K. Never let me go

Lee, H. To kill a mockingbird

Lively, P. Family album

Lourie, R. A hatred for tulips

McCullers, C. The member of the wedding

McDermott, A. At weddings and wakes

McGill, B. The butterfly cabinet

Patton, F. G. Good morning, Miss Dove

Pollen, B. The summer of the bear

Powers, R. Operation wandering soul

Roth, H. Call it sleep

Swann, M. Flower children

Walker, M. W. Under the beetle's cellar

CHILDREN -- ABUSE *See* Child abuse

CHILDREN -- ADOPTION *See* Adoption

CHILDREN -- BOOKS AND READING *See* Books and reading

CHILDREN -- CRIMES AGAINST

Ballantyne, L. The guilty one

CHILDREN -- CUSTODY *See* Child custody

CHILDREN -- DEATH

See also Death

Winthrop, E. H. The why of things

CHILDREN -- DEATH -- FICTION

Fyfield, F. Undercurrents

Woodruff, L. Those we love most

CHILDREN -- DISEASES *See* Diseases

CHILDREN -- EMPLOYMENT *See* Child labor

CHILDREN -- LANGUAGE *See* Language and languages

CHILDREN -- MOLESTING *See* Child sexual abuse

CHILDREN -- MONTANA

Rock, P. The Shelter Cycle

CHILDREN -- PLACING OUT *See* Adoption; Foster home care

CHILDREN -- SURGERY *See* Surgery

CHILDREN AND DEATH *See* Death

Children and fire. Hegi, U.

CHILDREN AND WAR *See* Children; War

Children are diamonds. Hoagland, E.

CHILDREN IN LITERATURE

Ivey, E. The snow child

Children in Reindeer Woods. Omarsdottir, K.

CHILDREN OF ALCOHOLICS

See also Children

Boykin, K. The wisdom of hair

Braffet, K. Save yourself

CHILDREN OF ALCOHOLICS -- FICTION

Boykin, K. The wisdom of hair

Braffet, K. Save yourself

CHILDREN OF CLERGY

Billingsley, R. T. Let the church say amen

Lewis, B. The brethren

Lewis, B. The preacher's daughter

Sparks, N. A walk to remember

CHILDREN OF DIVORCED PARENTS

See also Children; Divorce; Parent-child relationship

CHILDREN OF DIVORCED PARENTS -- FICTION

Evans, N. The divide

Wolitzer, M. The position

CHILDREN OF DRUG ADDICTS *See* Children; Drug addicts

Children of Dune. Herbert, F.

CHILDREN OF GANGSTERS -- ENGLAND -- LONDON

Harkaway, N. Angelmaker

CHILDREN OF GAY PARENTS *See* Children

Children of God. Russell, M. D.

CHILDREN OF IMMIGRANTS

See also Children; Immigration and emigration

Castellani, C. All this talk of love

Slouka, M. The visible world

Stefaniak, M. H. The Turk and my mother

CHILDREN OF PROMINENT PERSONS

Crowley, J. Lord Byron's novel

CHILDREN OF SINGLE PARENTS

See also Children; Single parents

Thorne, M. Hand me down

Children of the alley. Mahfouz, N.

Children of the mind. Card, O. S.

CHILDREN OF THE RICH

Forster, E. M. Maurice

Gordimer, N. The pickup

McOmber, A. The white forest

Yiyun Li   The vagrants

CHINA -- 19TH CENTURY

Garcia, C. Monkey hunting

Min, A. Empress Orchid

Min, A. The last empress

CHINA -- 20TH CENTURY

Gao Xingjian   Soul mountain

Garcia, C. Monkey hunting

Lianke, Y. Dream of Ding Village

Tan, A. The Joy Luck Club

CHINA -- BEIJING

Guo Xiaolu   Twenty fragments of a ravenous youth

Michael, J. A certain smile

CHINA -- FICTION

Joinson, S. A lady cyclist's guide to Kashgar

Lin, J. The Dragon and the Pearl

Steinhauer, O. An American spy

CHINA -- GUANGZHOU

Clavell, J. Tai-Pan

Ghosh, A. River of smoke

CHINA -- HISTORY

Chen, P. A. The red chamber

Lin, J. My fair concubine

Tie Ning   The bathing women

CHINA -- HISTORY -- TIANAMEN SQUARE INCIDENT, 1989

Ma Jian   Beijing coma

CHINA -- PEOPLE'S LIBERATION ARMY

Bosse, M. J. The warlord

CHINA -- RURAL LIFE

Talarigo, J. The ginseng hunter

CHINA -- SHANGHAI

Ballard, J. G. Empire of the Sun

Harrison, K. The binding chair

Ishiguro, K. When we were orphans

Malraux, A. Man's fate (La condition humaine)

Qiu Xiaolong   Years of Red Dust

Reuss, F. Mohr

Stephenson, N. Reamde

Wang Anyi   The song of everlasting sorrow

CHINA -- SOCIAL LIFE AND CUSTOMS -- 21ST CENTURY

Tie Ning   The bathing women

CHINA -- TIBET

Hilton, J. Lost horizon

Ma Jian   Stick out your tongue

Pattison, E. The skull mantra

CHINA -- TO 1643

Kay, G. G. Under heaven

Larsen, J. Silk road

CHINA -- WAR OF 1840-1842

Clavell, J. Tai-Pan

China boy. Lee, G.

The **China** lover. Buruma, I.

China Sea. Poyer, D.

CHINATOWN (NEW YORK, N.Y.)

Thompson, V. Murder in Chinatown

CHINESE -- CALIFORNIA

Steinbeck, T. In the shadow of the cypress

CHINESE -- CUBA

Garcia, C. Monkey hunting

CHINESE -- ENGLAND

Guo Xiaolu   A concise Chinese-English dictionary for lovers

CHINESE

Bates, J. F. Midnight at the Dragon Café

CHINESE -- HAWAII

Michener, J. A. Hawaii

CHINESE -- MASSACHUSETTS

Shepard, K. The Celestials

CHINESE -- NEW YORK (STATE) -- NEW YORK

Kwok, J. Girl in translation

CHINESE -- NEW ZEALAND

Tremain, R. The color

CHINESE -- ONTARIO

Bates, J. F. Midnight at the Dragon Café

CHINESE -- SINGAPORE

Loh, V. Breaking the tongue

CHINESE -- UNITED STATES

Allende, I. Daughter of fortune

Fowler, K. J. Sarah Canary

Freudenberger, N. The dissident

Ha Jin   A free life

Hand, D. Deep Creek

Harrison, C. The finder

Jin, H. A good fall

Kwok, J. Girl in translation

Lee, C. Y. The flower drum song

Raban, J. Waxwings

See, L. Shanghai girls

Steinbeck, J. Cannery Row

Williamson, P. Heart of the west

CHINESE -- UNITED STATES

Fowler, K. J. Sarah Canary

Jin, H. A good fall

CHINESE AMERICAN TEENAGERS

Kwok, J. Girl in translation

CHINESE AMERICANS

Jen, G. The love wife

Jen, G. Mona in the promised land

Jen, G. Typical American

Jen, G. Who's Irish?

Jen, G. World and town

Lee, G. China boy

Li Yiyun   A thousand years of good prayers

Ng, F. M. Bone

Tan, A. The bonesetter's daughter

Tan, A. The hundred secret senses

Tan, A. The Joy Luck Club

Tan, A. The kitchen god's wife

Wood, B. Perfect Harmony

L'Engle, M. Certain women

McEwan, I. Enduring love

Sienkiewicz, H. Quo Vadis

Williams, N. John

CHRISTIANITY -- RELATIONS -- JUDAISM
  See Christianity and other religions; Judaism

CHRISTIANITY AND ECONOMICS *See* Christianity; Economics

CHRISTIANS -- PERSECUTIONS *See* Church history; Persecution

Christiansen family [series]

Warren, S. M. Take a chance on me

Christine. King, S.

Christine Falls. Banville, J.

CHRISTMAS

Beverley, J. Winter Fire

A **Christmas** carol. Dickens, C.

CHRISTMAS STORIES

Davies, V. Miracle on 34th Street

Dickens, C. A Charles Dickens Christmas

Dickens, C. A Christmas carol

Dickens, C. The cricket on the hearth

Faulks, S. A week in December

Hamner, E. The homecoming

O'Nan, S. Last night at the Lobster

Pilcher, R. Winter solstice

Stubbs, J. Family games

CHRISTMAS TREES *See* Christmas decorations; Trees

Christy. Marshall, C.

CHROMOSOMES *See* Genetics; Heredity

Chronic city. Lethem, J.

CHRONIC DISEASES *See* Diseases

CHRONIC FATIGUE SYNDROME *See* Diseases

Chronicle of a death foretold. Garcia Marquez, G.

Chronicles of Barsetshire [series]

Trollope, A. Barchester Towers

Trollope, A. Doctor Thorne

Trollope, A. Framley parsonage

Trollope, A. The last chronicle of Barset

Trollope, A. The small house at Allington

Trollope, A. The warden

Chronicles of Fairacre. Read

The **chronicles** of Pern. McCaffrey, A.

Chronicles of Thomas Covenant, the Unbeliever [series]

Donaldson, S. R. The Illearth war

Donaldson, S. R. Lord Foul's bane

Donaldson, S. R. The One Tree

Donaldson, S. R. The power that preserves

Donaldson, S. R. White gold wielder

Donaldson, S. R. The wounded Land

CHRONOLOGY *See* Astronomy; History; Time

The **chrysanthemum** chain. Melville, J.

The **chrysanthemum** palace. Wagner, B.

CHURCH AND EDUCATION *See* Church; Education

CHURCH AND SOCIAL PROBLEMS *See* Church; Social problems

CHURCH AND STATE

Dunant, S. Blood and beauty

Poole, S. The Borgia mistress

CHURCH ARCHITECTURE

Follett, K. Pillars of the earth

CHURCH BUILDINGS *See* Buildings

CHURCH DENOMINATIONS *See* Christian sects; Sects

CHURCH FINANCE

  See also Finance

CHURCH HISTORY -- 600-1500, MIDDLE AGES *See* Middle Ages

CHURCH HISTORY -- PRIMITIVE AND EARLY CHURCH

Caldwell, T. Dear and glorious physician

Sienkiewicz, H. Quo Vadis

Waltari, M. The Roman

CHURCH LIBRARIES *See* Libraries

CHURCH MEMBERSHIP

Billingsley, R. T. Let the church say amen

CHURCH MUSIC *See* Music

CHURCH OF ENGLAND

Howatch, S. Absolute truths

Howatch, S. Glamorous powers

Howatch, S. Glittering images

Howatch, S. The heartbreaker

Howatch, S. Mystical paths

Howatch, S. Scandalous risks

Howatch, S. Ultimate prizes

CHURCH SCHOOLS

Godwin, G. Unfinished desires

House, T. The beginning of calamities

Powers, J. R. Do black patent-leather shoes really reflect up?

Powers, J. R. The last Catholic in America

CHURCH UNIVERSAL AND TRIUMPHANT

Rock, P. The Shelter Cycle

CHURCH WORK WITH YOUTH *See* Church work; Youth

CHURCHES

Barrett, W. E. The lilies of the field

Churchill, Winston Sir, 1874-1965

About

Hunt, R. Mr. Chartwell

Russell, M. D. Dreamers of the day

CHURCHYARDS *See* Cemeteries

Cicero, Marcus Tullius, 106-43 B.C.

About

Harris, R. Conspirata

Harris, R. Imperium

The **cider** house rules. Irving, J.

CIGARETTES *See* Smoking; Tobacco

CIGARS *See* Smoking; Tobacco

Wilson, C. Cotton

CIVIL SERVANTS *See* Civil service

CIVIL SERVICE

Dickens, C. Little Dorrit

Greene, G. The heart of the matter

Snow, C. P. Homecoming

Civil to strangers and other writings. Pym, B.

CIVIL UNIONS *See* Rites and ceremonies

CIVIL WAR

Bear, E. Range of ghosts

CIVILIZATION AND TECHNOLOGY *See* Technology and civilization

Claire DeWitt and the city of the dead. Gran, S.

CLAIRVOYANCE

> *See also* Extrasensory perception; Occultism

Ansa, T. M. The hand I fan with

Garcia, C. Dreaming in Cuban

Gregory, P. The queen's fool

Hoffman, A. The probable future

McCrumb, S. The hangman's beautiful daughter

CLAIRVOYANCE -- FICTION

Cotterill, C. The woman who wouldn't die

Sayers, V. The powers

Shannon, S. The bone season

CLAIRVOYANTS

> *See also* Psychics

Cotterill, C. The woman who wouldn't die

Shannon, S. The bone season

The **Clan** of the Cave Bear. Auel, J. M.

CLANS

> *See* Family

Clara. Galloway, J.

Clara and Mr. Tiffany. Vreeland, S.

Clare, John, 1793-1864

About

Foulds, A. The quickening maze

The **clarinet** polka. Maillard, K.

Clarissa. Richardson, S.

Clark, William, 1770-1838

About

Hall, B. I should be extremely happy in your company

Sargent, C. Museum of human beings

A **clash** of kings. Martin, G. R. R.

CLASS CONSCIOUSNESS

> *See also* Social classes; Social psychology

Hadley, T. Married love and other stories

Soli, T. The forgetting tree

CLASS DISTINCTION

Brown, R. M. Southern discomfort

Chevalier, T. Girl with a pearl earring

Cusk, R. Arlington Park

Dean, L. The old romantic

Dreiser, T. An American tragedy

Dunne, D. People like us

Forster, E. M. A room with a view

Greene, G. The tenth man

Grisham, J. A painted house

Harris, J. Gentlemen and players

Hijuelos, O. Empress of the splendid season

Ishiguro, K. The remains of the day

James, H. The American

Leavitt, D. While England sleeps

McNaught, J. Paradise

Paddock, J. A secret word

Quindlen, A. Blessings

Rice, A. The Feast of All Saints

Richler, M. Solomon Gursky was here

Stirling, J. The marrying kind

Tarkington, B. Alice Adams

Towles, A. Rules of civility

Umrigar, T. N. The space between us

Wolff, T. Old school

CLASS DISTINCTION *See* Social classes

Class reunion. Jaffe, R.

CLASS REUNIONS

Harrison, K. Envy

The **classic** Philip Jose Farmer, 1952-1964--1964-1973. Farmer, P. J.

CLASSICAL ANTIQUITIES *See* Antiquities

CLASSICAL DICTIONARIES *See* Ancient history; Encyclopedias and dictionaries

CLASSICAL EDUCATION *See* Education

CLASSICAL MUSIC *See* Music

CLASSICAL MYTHOLOGY

> *See also* Mythology

Renault, M. The king must die

Claudia Silver to the rescue. Ebel, K.

Claudius, Emperor of Rome, 10 B.C.-54

About

Graves, R. Claudius, the god and his wife Messalina

Graves, R. I, Claudius

Claudius, the god and his wife Messalina. Graves, R.

The **claw** of the conciliator. Wolfe, G.

Clea. Durrell, L.

CLEANING WOMEN

Doyle, R. Paula Spencer

Hijuelos, O. Empress of the splendid season

Hunt, S. The invention of everything else

Clear and present danger. Clancy, T.

Clear light of day. Desai, A.

Cleaver. Parks, T.

Clementine. Priest, C.

Cleopatra's sister. Lively, P.

Cleopatra, Queen of Egypt, d. 30 B.C.

About

Essex, K. Kleopatra

Essex, K. Pharaoh

George, M. The memoirs of Cleopatra

McCullough, C. The October horse

Clouds of witnesses. Sayers, D. L.

Cloudsplitter. Banks, R.

Clover. Sanders, D.

The **clown.** Boll, H.

CLOWNS

    See also Circus; Entertainers

  Boll, H. The clown

The **clowns** of God. West, M. L.

The **Club** Dumas. Perez-Reverte, A.

CLUBS

  Auchincloss, L. The book class

  Dickens, C. The posthumous papers of the Pickwick Club

  Santmyer, H. H. --and ladies of the club

  Spark, M. The girls of slender means

  Tan, A. The Joy Luck Club

  Wodehouse, P. G. Tales from the Drones Club

CLUBS -- FICTION

  Palahniuk, C. Fight Club

CO-OPS *See* Cooperative societies

COACHING *See* Coaching (Athletics); Horsemanship

COACHING (ATHLETICS)

  Perrotta, T. The abstinence teacher

Coal black horse. Olmstead, R.

COAL MINES AND MINING

  O'Dell, T. Coal Run

  O'Dell, T. Sister mine

  Pancake, A. Strange as this weather has been

COAL MINES AND MINING -- ENGLAND

  Smith, M. C. Rose

COAL MINES AND MINING -- FICTION

  Haigh, J. Baker towers

  O'Dell, T. Coal Run

  Smith, M. C. Rose

  Unsworth, B. The quality of mercy

COAL MINES AND MINING -- FRANCE

  Zola, E. Germinal

COAL MINES AND MINING -- WALES

  Llewellyn, R. How green was my valley

Coal Run. O'Dell, T.

COASTAL ECOLOGY *See* Ecology

Coastliners. Harris, J.

Cobbett, William, 1763-1835

    About

  Safire, W. Scandalmonger

The **Cobra** event. Preston, R.

COCAINE

  McCann, C. Let the great world spin

  Pelecanos, G. P. The sweet forever

  Price, R. Clockers

COCKROACHES

    See also Insects

  Lashner, W. Kockroach

The **cocktail** waitress. Cain, J. M.

COCOONS *See* Butterflies; Caterpillars; Moths;

Silkworms

CODE DECIPHERING *See* Cryptography

CODE ENCIPHERING *See* Cryptography

Code name Verity. Wein, E.

Code of the West. Latham, A.

The **code** of the Woosters. Wodehouse, P. G.

Code sixty-one. Harstad, D.

Codes of betrayal. Uhnak, D.

CODES, PENAL *See* Criminal law

The **codex.** Preston, D.

Codrington, Henry John Sir, 1808-1877

    About

  Donoghue, E. The sealed letter

COEDUCATION *See* Education

Coffee will make you black. Sinclair, A.

The **Coffin** Dancer. Deaver, J.

The **coffins** of Little Hope. Schaffert, T.

COHABITATION *See* Unmarried couples

COINAGE *See* Money

COINS *See* Money

COLD (DISEASE) *See* Communicable diseases; Diseases

Cold blood. La Plante, L.

Cold case. Barnes, L.

COLD CASES (CRIMINAL INVESTIGATION)

  Adler-Olsen, J. The absent one

  Adler-Olsen, J. The keeper of lost causes

  Black, L. Trail of blood

The **cold** cold ground. McKinty, A.

Cold company. Henry, S.

Cold cruel winter. Nickson, C.

Cold Flat Junction. Grimes, M.

Cold granite. MacBride, S.

Cold Harbour. Higgins, J.

Cold heaven. Moore, B.

Cold in hand. Harvey, J.

Cold is the grave. Robinson, P.

Cold light. Harvey, J.

Cold Mountain. Frazier, C.

Cold paradise. Woods, S.

Cold pursuit. Parker, T. J.

A **cold** red sunrise. Kaminsky, S. M.

Cold Sassy tree. Burns, O. A.

Cold service. Parker, R. B.

Cold shot to the heart. Stroby, W.

The **cold** six thousand. Ellroy, J.

Cold Springs. Riordan, R.

COLD WAR

  Kanon, J. Istanbul passage

  Littell, R. Young Philby

  Powers, T. Declare

  Tregillis, I. The coldest war

COLD WAR -- FICTION

  Fesperman, D. The double game

  Kanon, J. Istanbul passage

  Tregillis, I. The coldest war

The **coldest** blood. Kelly, J.
The **coldest** night.
The **coldest** war. Tregillis, I.
Coldheart Canyon. Barker, C.
COLLAGE *See* Art; Handicraft
Collected fictions. Borges, J. L.
Collected novellas. Garcia Marquez, G.
Collected novels. Hawthorne, N.
COLLECTED PAPERS (ANTHOLOGIES) *See* Anthologies
The **collected** short fiction of C.J. Cherryh. Cherryh, C. J.
Collected short stories. Huxley, A.
The **collected** short stories. Rhys, J.
Collected stories. Greene, G.
Collected stories. Garcia Marquez, G.
Collected stories. Rendell, R.
Collected stories. Lawrence, D. H.
Collected stories. Kafka, F.
Collected stories. Dahl, R.
Collected stories. Carver, R.
The **collected** stories. Theroux, P.
The **collected** stories. Paley, G.
The **collected** stories. Trevor, W.
The **collected** stories. Price, R.
Collected stories. Kipling, R.
Collected stories. McCullers, C.
Collected stories. Williams, T.
The **collected** stories. Michaels, L.
The **collected** stories. Thomas, D.
Collected stories. O'Connor, F.
Collected stories & later writings. Bowles, P.
Collected stories and other writings. Porter, K. A.
Collected stories and other writings. Cheever, J.
The **collected** stories of Amanda Cross. Cross, A.
The **collected** stories of Amy Hempel. Hempel, A.
The **collected** stories of Andre Maurois. Maurois, A.
The **collected** stories of Arthur C. Clarke. Clarke, A. C.
The **collected** stories of Chester Himes. Himes, C.
The **collected** stories of Colette. Colette
The **collected** stories of Deborah Eisenberg. Eisenberg, D.
The **collected** stories of Eudora Welty. Welty, E.
The **collected** stories of Greg Bear. Bear, G.
The **collected** stories of Hortense Calisher. Calisher, H.
The **collected** stories of Jack Schaefer. Schaefer, J. W.
The **collected** stories of Jean Stafford. Stafford, J.
Collected stories of Jessamyn West. West, J.
Collected stories of John O'Hara. O'Hara, J.
The **collected** stories of Joseph Roth. Roth, J.
The **collected** stories of Katherine Anne Porter. Porter, K. A.
The **collected** stories of Lydia Davis. Davis, L.

The **collected** stories of Max Brand. Brand, M.
The **collected** stories of Noel Coward. Coward, N.
The **collected** stories of Philip K. Dick. Dick, P. K.
The **collected** stories of Richard Yates. Yates, R.
The **collected** stories of Robert Silverberg. Silverberg, R.
The **collected** stories of Sean O'Faolain. O'Faolain, S.
Collected stories of Wallace Stegner. Stegner, W. E.
Collected stories of William Faulkner. Faulkner, W.
Collected stories, 1891-1910. Wharton, E.
Collected stories, 1911-1937. Wharton, E.
Collected stories, 1948-1986. Morris, W.
Collected stories: A friend of Kafka to Passions. Singer, I. B.
Collected stories: Gimpel the fool to The letter writer. Singer, I. B.
Collected stories: One night in Brazil to The death of Methuselah. Singer, I. B.
Collected tales. De la Mare, W.
The **collected** tales and poems of Edgar Allan Poe. Poe, E. A.
The **collected** tales of E. M. Forster. Forster, E. M.
The **collected** tales of Nikolai Gogol. Gogol', N. V.
Collected works. O'Connor, F.
COLLECTED WORKS *See* Anthologies; Literature -- Collections; Storytelling -- Collections
COLLECTIBLE CARD GAMES *See* Card games
COLLECTIBLES *See* Collectors and collecting
COLLECTING *See* Collectors and collecting
COLLECTIONS (ANTHOLOGIES) *See* Anthologies
COLLECTIONS OF LITERATURE *See* Anthologies; Literature -- Collections; Storytelling -- Collections
COLLECTIONS OF OBJECTS *See* Collectors and collecting
COLLECTIVE BARGAINING *See* Industrial relations; Labor; Labor disputes; Negotiation
COLLECTIVE FARMS *See* Collective settlements; Cooperative agriculture
COLLECTIVE SETTLEMENTS
　See also Communism; Cooperation; Socialism
　Carey, P. His illegal self
　Gardam, J. Faith Fox
　Kasischke, L. Eden Springs
　McPhee, M. Gorgeous lies
　Raymond, J. The half-life
　Sontag, S. In America
　Updike, J. S
The **collector** of hearts. Oates, J. C.
COLLECTORS
　Doctorow, E. L. Homer & Langley
　Lazar, Z. Sway
COLLECTORS AND COLLECTING

COMMUNITY CHESTS *See* Fund raising

COMMUNITY GARDENS *See* Gardens

COMMUNITY LIFE

Carr, R. The Wanderer

Neuhaus, N. Snow White must die

Rhodes, D. Jewelweed

COMPACT CARS *See* Automobiles

COMPACT DISCS *See* Optical storage devices; Sound recordings

COMPANIONS

Marias, J. The man of feeling

Quick, A. I thee wed

Quick, A. The paid companion

The **company**. Littell, R.

Company. Barry, M.

The **company**. Parker, K. J.

Company man. Finder, J.

The **company** man. Bennett, R. J.

The **company** of the dead. Kowalski, D.

The **company** of women. Gordon, M.

The **company** you keep. Gordon, N.

Compass rose. Casey, J.

COMPASSION *See* Emotions

Compelling evidence. Martini, S. P.

COMPETITION

See also Business; Business ethics; Commerce

Coll, S. Acceptance

COMPETITION (PSYCHOLOGY)

See also Interpersonal relations; Motivation (Psychology); Psychology

Cleave, C. Gold

COMPETITIONS *See* Awards; Contests

The **complaints**. Rankin, I.

The **complete** Claudine. Colette

Complete collected stories. Pritchett, V. S.

The **complete** Drive-in. Lansdale, J. R.

The **complete** ghost stories of Charles Dickens. Dickens, C.

Complete novels. Welty, E.

Complete novels. Hammett, D.

The **complete** novels. O'Brien, F.

Complete novels. Cheever, J.

Complete novels. McCullers, C.

Complete novels and stories. Chopin, K.

The **complete** novels of Mark Twain. Twain, M.

The **complete** novels of Stephen Crane. Crane, S.

The **complete** Sherlock Holmes. Doyle, A. C.

The **complete** short fiction of Joseph Conrad.

Complete short stories. Maugham, W. S.

Complete short stories.

The **complete** short stories. Stevenson, R. L.

The **complete** short stories & sketches of Stephen Crane. Crane, S.

The **complete** short stories of Ambrose Bierce. Bierce, A.

The **complete** short stories of H. G. Wells. Wells, H. G.

The **complete** short stories of Jack London.

The **complete** short stories of Marcel Proust. Proust, M.

The **complete** short stories of Mark Twain. Twain, M.

Complete short stories of Nathaniel Hawthorne. Hawthorne, N.

The **complete** short stories of Robert Louis Stevenson. Stevenson, R. L.

The **complete** short stories of Thomas Wolfe.

The **complete** shorter fiction. Trollope, A.

The **complete** shorter fiction. Stahlberg, L.

The **complete** shorter fiction of Virginia Woolf. Woolf, V.

The **complete** stories. Kafka, F.

The **complete** stories. Hurston, Z. N.

The **complete** stories. Malouf, D.

The **complete** stories. Malamud, B.

The **complete** stories. O'Connor, F.

The **complete** stories. Asimov, I.

Complete stories and poems of Edgar Allan Poe. Poe, E. A.

The **complete** stories of Evelyn Waugh. Waugh, E.

The **complete** stories of J.G. Ballard. Ballard, J. G.

The **complete** stories of Truman Capote. Capote, T.

Complete stories, 1864-1874. James, H.

Complete stories, 1874-1884. James, H.

Complete stories, 1884-1891. James, H.

Complete stories, 1892-1898. James, H.

Complete stories, 1898-1910. James, H.

The **complete** tales of Henry James. James, H.

The **complete** tales of Washington Irving. Irving, W.

The **complete** Wendel. Cruse, H.

The **complete** Western stories of Elmore Leonard. Leonard, E.

The **complete** works of Isaac Babel. Babel, I.

The **complete** works of O. Henry. Henry, O.

A **complicated** kindness. Toews, M.

COMPOSERS

See also Musicians

Bernhard, T. The loser

Davies, R. The lyre of Orpheus

Duncker, P. The strange case of the composer and his judge

Frame, R. The lantern bearers

Galloway, J. Clara

Grushin, O. The line

Hamilton-Paterson, J. Gerontius

Hesse, H. Gertrude

Hijuelos, O. A simple Habana melody: from when the world was good

Hodgen, C. Elegies for the brokenhearted

Mann, T. Doctor Faustus

McEwan, I. Amsterdam

Cornwell, B. Rebel

Shaara, J. Gods and generals

Shaara, J. The last full measure

Youmans, M. The wolf pit

**CONFEDERATE STATES OF AMERICA -- FIC-
TION**

Leveen, L. The secrets of Mary Bowser

**CONFEDERATE STATES OF AMERICA.
ARMY -- OFFICERS**

Kowalski, D. The company of the dead

Confession. Pickard, N.

CONFESSION

Banville, J. The book of evidence

Rosero, E. Good offices

The **confession.** Grisham, J.

CONFESSION -- FICTION

Kelly, J. The fire baby

Confessional. Higgins, J.

Confessions of a Wall Street shoeshine boy. Stumpf,
D.

Confessions of an ugly stepsister. Maguire, G.

The **confessions** of Edward Day. Martin, V.

Confessions of Felix Krull, confidence man. Mann,
T.

The **confessions** of Nat Turner. Styron, W.

The **confidant.** Gremillon, H.

CONFIDENCE GAME *See* Swindlers and swindling

The **confidence-man:** his masquerade. Stahlberg, L.

CONFLICT OF CULTURES *See* Culture conflict

CONFLICT OF GENERATIONS

See also Child-adult relationship; Interpersonal relations; Parent-child relationship; Social conflict

Cummins, A. Yellowcake

Cunningham, M. Flesh and blood

Jen, G. Mona in the promised land

Lee, C. Y. The flower drum song

Lurie, A. The war between the Tates

Meloy, M. Liars and saints

Read, P. P. The professor's daughter

Stegner, W. E. All the little live things

Thayer, N. Family secrets

Toynton, E. The Oriental wife

Trollope, J. The men and the girls

Turgenev, I. S. Fathers and sons

Tyler, A. A slipping-down life

Vassanji, M. G. The assassin's song

West, D. The wedding

Wharton, W. Dad

CONFLICT OF GENERATIONS -- FICTION

McAfee, A. The spoiler

CONFLICT OF INTERESTS *See* Political ethics

CONFORMITY

Berger, T. Neighbors

Hoeg, P. Borderliners

Lewis, S. Babbitt

McCann, C. Zoli

McNicholl, D. A son called Gabriel

Trollope, J. The rector's wife

Wilson, S. The man in the gray flannel suit

CONGO (REPUBLIC)

Kingsolver, B. The poisonwood Bible

Congo dawn. Windle, J.

CONGRESSIONAL INVESTIGATIONS *See*
Governmental investigations

CONJOINED TWINS

Slouka, M. God's fool

CONNECTICUT

Clark, M. H. Two little girls in blue

Hobson, L. K. Z. Gentleman's agreement

Hodgins, E. Mr. Blandings builds his dream house

Hoffman, A. Skylight confessions

Lawrence, S. The lightning keeper

O'Nan, S. Last night at the Lobster

O'Nan, S. The night country

Rice, L. Last kiss

Rice, L. Safe harbor

Schine, C. The love letter

Schine, C. The three Weissmanns of Westport

Schwartz, J. B. Reservation Road

Shulman, M. Rally round the flag, boys!

Straub, P. The Hellfire Club

Tryon, T. The other

Updike, J. Villages

Weber, K. True confections

Westlake, D. E. The ax

Wittenborn, D. Pharmakon

CONNECTICUT -- 19TH CENTURY

Tryon, T. In the fire of spring

Tryon, T. The wings of the morning

CONNECTICUT -- BRIDGEPORT

Howard, M. Natural history

CONNECTICUT -- HARTFORD

Pearson, R. Chain of evidence

CONNECTICUT -- NEW HAVEN

Mattison, A. The wedding of the two-headed woman

Perrotta, T. Joe College

Weber, K. The little women

A **Connecticut** Yankee in King Arthur's court.
Twain, M.

The **conquest** of Lady Cassandra. Hunter, M.

Conquistadora. Santiago, E.

Conrad in Beverly Hills. Fuchs, J.

Cons, scams & grifts. Gores, J.

CONSCIENCE

See also Christian ethics; Duty; Ethics

Conrad, J. Lord Jim

Dostoyevsky, F. Crime and punishment

Hawthorne, N. The marble faun

Hawthorne, N. The scarlet letter

Palmer, M. The fifth vial
Patterson, J. Four blind mice
Patterson, R. N. Eclipse
Porter, H. The bell ringers
Pottinger, S. The fourth procedure
Poyer, D. Down to a sunless sea
Rabb, J. The book of Q
Redfern, E. Auriel rising
Reed, B. The indictment
Reich, C. Rules of deception
Ricks, T. E. A soldier's duty
Rollins, J. The devil colony
Ruiz, L. M. Only one thing missing
Shelby, P. Days of drums
Sheldon, S. The doomsday conspiracy
Sheldon, S. Windmills of the gods
Siegel, J. Deceit
Silva, D. The mark of the assassin
Snyder, D. J. Night crossing
Stephenson, N. Cryptonomicon
Strieber, W. The Grays
Sullivan, M. J. Theft of swords
Tanenbaum, R. Corruption of blood
Thomas, M. M. Black money
Tolkien, S. Orders from Berlin
Toyne, S. The key
Toyne, S. Sanctus
Vinge, V. Rainbows end
Walton, J. Farthing
Walton, J. Ha'penny
Weldon, F. Chalcot Crescent
West, M. L. Masterclass
Wiprud, B. M. Ringer
Wood, B. Perfect Harmony
Woods, S. Orchid Beach

CONSPIRACIES -- FICTION
Box, C. J. Force of nature
Buckley, F. The siren queen
Church, J. A corpse in the Koryo
Geagley, B. Year of the hyenas
Grant, M. Deadline
McDevitt, J. The Cassandra project
Moore, J. The extinction club
Newton, M. C. Nights of Villjamur
O'Brien, T. L. The Lincoln conspiracy
Rollins, J. The devil colony
Sullivan, M. J. Theft of swords
Tolkien, S. Orders from Berlin
Toyne, S. The key
Walton, J. Ha'penny
A **Conspiracy** of Faith. Adler-Olsen, J.
A **conspiracy** of friends. McCall Smith, A.
Conspirata. Harris, R.
Constance. McGrath, P.
The **constant** gardener. Le Carre, J.
The **constant** princess. Gregory, P.

A **constellation** of vital phenomena. Marra, A.
CONSTRUCTION See Architecture; Building; Engineering
CONSTRUCTION INDUSTRY
See also Building; Industries
Clark, M. H. Before I say goodbye
Kelly, T. Empire rising
Ondaatje, M. In the skin of a lion
Trigiani, A. Big Cherry Holler
CONSTRUCTION INDUSTRY -- FICTION
Putney, M. J. The burning point
CONSTRUCTION WORKERS
Cramer, W. D. Bad ground
CONSULS See Diplomats
CONSUMER EDUCATION See Education; Home economics
CONSUMER ORGANIZATIONS See Cooperative societies
CONSUMERS' COOPERATIVE SOCIETIES See Cooperative societies
The **Consummata.** Spillane, M.
Consumption. Patterson, K.
CONSUMPTION (ECONOMICS) -- SOCIAL ASPECTS -- ENGLAND
Ballard, J. G. Kingdom come
Contact. Sagan, C.
Contagious. Sigler, S.
CONTAMINATION OF ENVIRONMENT See Pollution
Contemporary art of the novella [series]
Ballestrini, N. Sandokan
Contemporary classics [series]
Buck, P. S. The good earth
CONTESTS
Drayson, N. Guide to the birds of East Africa
Parkhurst, C. Lost and found
CONTESTS -- FICTION
Harms, K. The Good Luck Girls of Shipwreck Lane
CONTINUING EDUCATION See Education
CONTRABAND TRADE See Smuggling
Contract null & void. Gores, J.
The **contract** surgeon. O'Brien, D.
CONTRACTORS
Hurwitz, G. You're next
CONVENIENCE FOODS See Food
CONVENT LIFE
Godden, R. Black Narcissus
Gregory, P. The wise woman
Hansen, R. Mariette in ecstasy
Hulme, K. The nun's story
L'Engle, M. The love letters
Roberts, M. Reader, I married him
Spark, M. The Abbess of Crewe
Stewart, M. Thunder on the right
Westlake, D. E. Good behavior
A **conventional** corpse. Hess, J.

Le Carre, J. The constant gardener
Westlake, D. E. The road to ruin
CORPORATIONS -- FINANCE *See* Finance
Corps [series]
  Griffin, W. E. B. Close combat
  Griffin, W. E. B. In danger's path
  Griffin, W. E. B. Line of fire
A **corpse** in the Koryo. Church, J.
CORPSE REMOVALS
  Guinn, M. The resurrectionist
CORPSES *See* Dead
CORPULENCE *See* Obesity
The **corrections.** Franzen, J.
Corridors of power. Snow, C. P.
CORRUPT PRACTICES
  Atxaga, B. Seven houses in France
CORRUPTION (IN POLITICS)
  Adams, H. Democracy
  Atkins, A. Wicked city
  Bolaño, R. The skating rink
  Diehl, W. Reign in hell
  Dovey, C. Blood kin
  Ellis, D. Life sentence
  Ellroy, J. American tabloid
  Ellroy, J. The cold six thousand
  Estleman, L. D. Gas City
  Estleman, L. D. Port hazard
  Goddard, R. Into the blue
  Greeley, A. M. Irish lace
  Grisham, J. The brethren
  Grisham, J. The pelican brief
  Hiaasen, C. Sick puppy
  Hiaasen, C. Strip tease
  Higgins, G. V. A change of gravity
  Isegawa, M. Snakepit
  Kadare, I. Spring flowers, spring frost
  Kelly, T. Empire rising
  Kennedy, W. Roscoe
  Koontz, D. R. Dark rivers of the heart
  Meltzer, B. The zero game
  Moore, B. The statement
  Oates, J. C. The falls
  Parker, B. Blood relations
  Parker, T. J. The fallen
  Patterson, R. N. Dark lady
  Patterson, R. N. Eyes of a child
  Puzo, M. The godfather
  Reed, B. The indictment
  Rogers, R. Devil's Cape
  Roncagliolo, S. Red April
  Rosenberg, N. T. Abuse of power
  Silva, D. The mark of the assassin
  Tanenbaum, R. Corruption of blood
  Tanenbaum, R. Falsely accused
  Tanenbaum, R. Reversible error
  Thomas, R. Ah, treachery!

  Thomas, R. The fourth Durango
  Turow, S. Presumed innocent
  Vachss, A. H. Two trains running
  Vassanji, M. G. The in-between world of Vikram
    Lall
  Vidal, G. Hollywood
  Vonnegut, K. Jailbird
  Warren, R. P. All the king's men
  Wells, K. Crawfish mountain
  Wolfe, T. A man in full
CORRUPTION -- FICTION
  Hunt, A. City of saints
  Newton, C. Start shooting
  Rash, R. Serena
Corruption of blood. Tanenbaum, R.
CORSAIRS *See* Pirates
Cortés, Hernán, 1485-1547
                    About
  Falconer, C. Feathered serpent
  Sherwood, F. Night of sorrows
COSMOGONY *See* Cosmology; Universe
COSMOGRAPHY *See* Cosmology; Universe
COSMOLOGY *See* Universe
COSMONAUTS *See* Astronauts
Cosmopolis. DeLillo, D.
COSSACKS
  Sholokhov, M. A. And quiet flows the Don
  Sholokhov, M. A. The Don flows home to the sea
  Sienkiewicz, H. With fire and sword
Cost. Robinson, R.
COST AND STANDARD OF LIVING *See* Eco-
    nomics; Home economics; Quality of life; Social
    conditions; Wealth
COSTUME DESIGN
  Gibson, W. Zero history
Coswell's guide to Tambralinga. Landers, S.
COT DEATH *See* Sudden infant death syndrome
COTSWOLDS (ENGLAND)
  Lively, P. Passing on
  Pilcher, R. The shell seekers
Cotton. Wilson, C.
Cotton comes to Harlem. Himes, C.
COTTON INDUSTRY
  Meacham, L. Roses
COTTON MANUFACTURE *See* Textile industry
COUNCILS AND SYNODS *See* Christianity;
    Church history
The **Count** of Monte Cristo. Dumas, A.
COUNTER CULTURE
  Abrahams, P. Hard rain
  Gordon, N. The company you keep
  Keating, C. Layla
  Lazar, Z. Sway
  Lessing, D. M. The good terrorist
  Nunez, S. The last of her kind
  Pynchon, T. Vineland

Robbins, T. Still life with Woodpecker

Swann, M. Flower children

COUNTER-REFORMATION *See* Christianity; Church history -- 1500- , Modern period

COUNTERCULTURE *See* Counter culture

COUNTERFEITERS

Kerr, P. Dark matter

The **counterfeiters** (Les faux-monnayeurs) Gide, A.

COUNTERFEITS AND COUNTERFEITING

See also Coinage; Crime; Forgery; Impostors and imposture; Money; Swindlers and swindling

Gaddis, W. The recognitions

Counting heads. Marusek, D.

COUNTRY AND WESTERN MUSIC *See* Country music

The **country** doctor. Balzac, H. d.

The **country** girls trilogy and epilogue. O'Brien, E.

COUNTRY HOMES -- ENGLAND

Dean, A. Bellfield Hall, or, The observations of Miss Dido Kent

Dean, A. A gentleman of fortune, or, The suspicions of Miss Dido Kent

Wilhide, E. Ashenden

COUNTRY HOMES

Fellowes, J. Snobs

Joss, M. Half broken things

Kelly, E. The burning air

King, L. R. Justice Hall

Quick, A. Late for the wedding

COUNTRY LIFE

Allison, D. Bastard out of Carolina

Chute, C. The school on Heart's Content Road

Gloss, M. The hearts of horses

Holman, S. Witches on the road tonight

Murphy, Y. The call

Nicholson, W. The secret intensity of everyday life

Pilcher, R. Winter solstice

Rhodes, D. Driftless

Roy, L. Bent Road

Taylor, M. G. The ballad of Trenchmouth Taggart

Wiggins, M. Evidence of things unseen

COUNTRY LIFE -- ENGLAND

Simonson, H. Major Pettigrew's last stand

COUNTRY LIFE -- FICTION

Harris, J. Peaches for Father Francis

Hoff, B. J. River of mercy

Manfredi, V. M. A Winter's Night

Myśliwski, W. Stone upon stone

COUNTRY LIFE -- FRANCE

Harris, J. Peaches for Father Francis

COUNTRY LIFE -- NIGERIA

Watson, C. Tiny sunbirds, far away

COUNTRY MUSIC

Bass, R. Nashville chrome

Hall, A. L. The rhythm of the road

Portis, C. Norwood

Smith, L. The devil's dream

Spencer, L. Small town girl

Westlake, D. E. Baby, would I lie?

COUNTRY MUSICIANS

Earle, S. I'll never get out of this world alive

A **country** of old men. Hansen, J.

Country of origin. Lee, D.

A **country** of our own. Poyer, D.

A **country** of strangers. Shreve, S. R.

The **country** of the pointed firs. Jewett, S. O.

The **country** of the pointed firs and other stories. Jewett, S. O.

COUPONS (RETAIL TRADE) *See* Advertising

COUPS D'ÉTAT

See also Revolutions

Dovey, C. Blood kin

Forsyth, F. The dogs of war

Knebel, F. Seven days in May

COURAGE

Forester, C. S. The last nine days of the Bismarck

Hemingway, E. The old man and the sea

Hersey, J. The wall

Nordhoff, C. Men against the sea

Saint-Exupery, A. d. Night flight

Uris, L. Mila 18

The **courage** consort. Faber, M.

COURT LIFE *See* Courts and courtiers

The **court-martial** of George Armstrong Custer. Jones, D. C.

COURTESANS

Dumas, A. Camille

Dunant, S. In the company of the courtesan

COURTIERS

See also Courts and courtiers

Bennett, V. The queen's lover

George, M. Elizabeth I

Gregory, P. The Boleyn Inheritance

Gregory, P. The queen's fool

Maxwell, R. The Queen's bastard

Naipaul, V. S. A way in the world

COURTING *See* Courtship

Courting Greta. Hootman, R.

COURTS AND COURTIERS

Hope, A. The prisoner of Zenda

Tarr, J. Queen of swords

Weir, A. Captive queen

COURTS AND COURTIERS -- DENMARK

Tremain, R. Music & silence

Updike, J. Gertrude and Claudius

COURTS AND COURTIERS -- EGYPT

Smith, W. A. River god

COURTS AND COURTIERS -- ENGLAND

Bennett, V. The queen's lover

George, M. Elizabeth I

Gregory, P. Earthly joys

Holt, V. My enemy the Queen
Koen, K. Dark angels
Mantel, H. Wolf Hall
Maxwell, R. The Queen's bastard
Maxwell, R. The secret diary of Anne Boleyn
Penman, S. K. Devil's brood
Penman, S. K. Falls the shadow
Penman, S. K. Here be dragons
Penman, S. K. The reckoning
Penman, S. K. The sunne in splendour
Penman, S. K. Time and chance
Penman, S. K. When Christ and his saints slept
Plaidy, J. The captive Queen of Scots
Plaidy, J. Murder most royal
Plaidy, J. The pleasures of love
Plaidy, J. William's wife
Riley, J. M. The serpent garden
Seton, A. Katherine
Weir, A. Innocent traitor
Weir, A. The Lady Elizabeth

COURTS AND COURTIERS -- FICTION
Buckley, F. The doublet affair
Buckley, F. The fugitive queen
Buckley, F. Queen of ambition
Buckley, F. Queen's ransom
Buckley, F. The siren queen
Byrd, S. The secret keeper
Newton, M. C. Nights of Villjamur

COURTS AND COURTIERS -- FRANCE
Davis, K. Versailles
Dumas, A. The man in the iron mask
Dumas, A. The three musketeers
Haasse, H. S. In a dark wood wandering
Laker, R. To dance with kings
Naslund, S. J. Abundance
Riley, J. M. The serpent garden

COURTS AND COURTIERS -- ITALY
Sontag, S. The volcano lover
Stendhal The charterhouse of Parma

COURTS AND COURTIERS -- JAPAN
Mishima, Y. Spring snow
Murasaki Shikibu The tale of Genji

COURTS AND COURTIERS -- SCOTLAND
Dunnett, D. Gemini

COURTS AND COURTIERS -- TURKEY
Wallach, J. Seraglio

**COURTS MARTIAL AND COURTS OF INQUI-
RY** *See* Courts; Trials
The **courts** of chaos. Zelazny, R.

COURTS-MARTIAL
DeMille, N. Word of honor
Jones, D. C. The court-martial of George Arm-
strong Custer
Nordhoff, C. Mutiny on the Bounty
Poyer, D. The circle

COURTSHIP

See also Love
Colwin, L. Happy all the time
Gee, S. The scandal of the season
James, H. Daisy Miller
James, H. Washington Square
Purdy, J. In a shallow grave
Cousin Bette. Balzac, H. d.
COUSINS
See also Family
Balzac, H. d. Cousin Bette
Bradford, B. T. The Ravenscar dynasty
Chabon, M. The amazing adventures of Kavalier
and Clay
Coe, J. The rain before it falls
Colwin, L. Happy all the time
Dew, R. F. The evidence against her
Egan, J. The keep
Faulkner, W. The mansion
Hamilton, J. When Madeline was young
Jakes, J. American dreams
James, H. The Europeans
Krivak, A. The sojourn
McCorkle, J. Ferris Beach
McDermott, A. Child of my heart
Morris, M. M. Fiona Range
Pearson, T. R. Blue Ridge
Robards, K. Ghost moon
Seton, A. Dragonwyck
Siddons, A. R. Nora, Nora
St. John Mandel, E. The singer's gun
Stewart, M. The Gabriel hounds
Thomas, R. All my sins remembered
Thompson, J. The year we left home
Walbert, K. The gardens of Kyoto
Weber, K. The Music Lesson
Yoshimoto, B. Goodbye Tsugumi
COUSINS -- FICTION
Godwin, G. Flora
Cousins' war [series]
Gregory, P. The red queen
The **cove.** Rash, R.
The **covenant.** Michener, J. A.
COVENS *See* Witches
Coventry. Humphreys, H.
COVERLETS *See* Bedspreads; Quilts
Covet. Graves, T. G.
COVETOUSNESS *See* Avarice
Covington, Syms, 1813-1861
About
McDonald, R. Mr. Darwin's shooter
COWARDICE
Conrad, J. Lord Jim
COWBOYS
Clark, W. V. T. The Ox-bow incident
Durham, D. A. Gabriel's story
Evans, N. The horse whisperer

Houston, P. Cowboys are my weakness
Kittredge, W. The Willow Field
McCarthy, C. All the pretty horses
Schaefer, J. W. Monte Walsh
COWBOYS -- FICTION
Paul, B. Under Tower Peak
Cowboys are my weakness. Houston, P.
COWHANDS
     See also Frontier and pioneer life; Ranch life
Evans, N. The horse whisperer
McCarthy, C. All the pretty horses
McCarthy, C. The crossing
McMurtry, L. Lonesome dove
COWHANDS -- SONGS *See* Music; Songs
COWS *See* Cattle
Coyote. Steele, A. M.
Coyote summer. Gear, W. M.
Coyote waits. Hillerman, T.
COYOTES
Kingsolver, B. Prodigal summer
Crabwalk. Grass, G.
CRACK (DRUG)
     See also Cocaine
Burke, S. Black flies
Carcaterra, L. Apaches
CRACK COCAINE *See* Crack (Drug)
The **cradle.** Somerville, P.
The **cradle** in the grave. Hannah, S.
The **cradle** will fall. Clark, M. H.
CRAFT SHOWS *See* Exhibitions; Festivals; Handicraft
Crane, Cora Howarth Stewart Taylor, 1868-1910
        About
White, E. Hotel de Dream
Crane, Stephen, 1871-1900
        About
White, E. Hotel de Dream
Cranford. Gaskell, E. C.
CRANKS *See* Eccentrics and eccentricities
Crashers. Haynes, D.
CRASHES (FINANCE) *See* Financial crises
Crawfish mountain. Wells, K.
CRAWFORD, BESS (FICTITIOUS CHARACTER)
Todd, C. A duty to the dead
Todd, C. An unmarked grave
The **crazed.** Ha Jin
Crazy Horse, Sioux Chief, ca. 1842-1877
        About
O'Brien, D. The contract surgeon
Crazy in Alabama. Childress, M.
Crazybone. Pronzini, B.
Creation. Vidal, G.
CREATION (LITERARY, ARTISTIC, ETC.)
Ishiguro, K. The unconsoled
CREATION

Bennett, R. J. The troupe
CREATIVE WRITING *See* Authorship; Creation (Literary, artistic, etc.); Language arts
Creatures of the kingdom. Michener, J. A.
CREDIBILITY *See* Truthfulness and falsehood
CREDIT *See* Finance; Money
CREDIT CARD FRAUD *See* Fraud; Swindlers and swindling
CREE INDIANS
Boyden, J. Three-day road
A **creek** called Wounded Knee. Jones, D. C.
Creek Mary's blood. Brown, D. A.
The **creeper.** Carver, T.
CREOLES
Hambly, B. Days of the dead
Hambly, B. Dead water
Hambly, B. Die upon a kiss
Hambly, B. A free man of color
Hambly, B. Graveyard dust
Hambly, B. Sold down the river
Hambly, B. Wet grave
Tademy, L. Cane River
CREOLES -- FICTION
Fulmer, D. Jass
Hambly, B. A free man of color
Crescent. Abu-Jaber, D.
Crescent City. Plain, B.
Crescent city kill. Smith, J.
CRETE
Kazantzakis, N. Zorba the Greek
Renault, M. The king must die
Stewart, M. The moon-spinners
CRIB DEATH *See* Sudden infant death syndrome
CRICKET
Gunesekera, R. The match
O'Neill, J. Netherland
CRICKET (SPORT)
Karunatilaka, S. The legend of Pradeep Mathew
The **cricket** on the hearth. Dickens, C.
CRICKETS
     See also Insects
Dickens, C. The cricket on the hearth
CRIME
     See also Administration of criminal justice; Social problems
Blackmoore, S. City of the lost
Box, C. J. Force of nature
Box, C. J. Free fire
Brookmyre, C. Where the bodies are buried
Coleman, A. Murderville
Crais, R. Taken
DeSilva, B. Rogue island
Doetsch, R. Half-past dawn
Ellory, R. J. A simple act of violence
Faletti, G. A pimp's notes
Fossum, K. The caller

Gardner, L. Catch me
Gruber, M. The return
Harvey, J. A darker shade of blue
Higashino, K. The devotion of suspect X
Jio, S. The last camellia
Kardos, M. The Three-Day Affair
Kelly, J. The fire baby
Lansdale, J. R. Edge of dark water
Leonard, E. Raylan
Manfredo, L. Rizzo's fire
Meyer, D. Trackers
Miasha Chaser
Mina, D. Field of blood
Mofina, R. They disappeared
Newton, C. Start shooting
Pettersson, V. The taken
Piccirilli, T. The Last Whisper in the Dark
Shepherd, L. The solitary house
Speller, E. The strange fate of Kitty Easton
Transgressions
Turner, N. Natural born hustler
Tursten, H. Night rounds
Walter, J. Citizen Vince
Walter, J. We Live in Water

CRIME -- NEW JERSEY
Colfer, E. Screwed

CRIME AND CRIMINALS
Abani, C. GraceLand
Adams, L. Harbor
Atkins, A. White shadow
Atkins, A. Wicked city
Baldacci, D. Absolute power
Ballestrini, N. Sandokan
Brandon, J. Arkansas
Breslin, J. The gang that couldn't shoot straight
Calvo, J. Wonderful world
Camus, A. The plague
Carcaterra, L. Apaches
Cheever, J. Falconer
Clark, M. H. The cradle will fall
Colfer, E. Plugged
Connelly, M. The brass verdict
Connelly, M. The Lincoln lawyer
Daley, R. Nowhere to run
Dee, E. The con man's daughter
Defoe, D. Moll Flanders
Dickens, C. Great expectations
Dickens, C. Oliver Twist
Dixon, K. The art of losing
Dostoyevsky, F. Crime and punishment
Dreiser, T. An American tragedy
Drury, T. The driftless area
Durham, M. The man who loved Cat Dancing
Ellroy, J. L.A. confidential
Ellroy, J. L.A. noir
Ellroy, J. White jazz

Estleman, L. D. Jitterbug
Faulkner, W. Intruder in the dust
Forsyth, F. The day of the jackal
Freeman, C. All that I have
George, E. What came before he shot her
Godey, J. The taking of Pelham one two three
Goodis, D. Nightfall
Gores, J. Cons, scams & grifts
Gores, J. Contract null & void
Green, N. Shooting Dr. Jack
Greene, G. Brighton rock
Grisham, J. The brethren
Hage, R. De Niro's game
Hallinan, T. A nail through the heart
Hamill, P. Snow in August
Harrison, C. Afterburn
Harrison, C. The finder
Hart, J. Iron house
Hayter, S. Bandit queen boogie
Hemingway, E. To have and have not
Hiaasen, C. Lucky you
Hiaasen, C. Native tongue
Hiaasen, C. Skin tight
Hiaasen, C. Skinny dip
Hiaasen, C. Stormy weather
Hiaasen, C. Strip tease
Higgins, G. V. At end of day
Higgins, G. V. Bomber's law
Higgins, G. V. The friends of Eddie Coyle
Highsmith, P. The boy who followed Ripley
Highsmith, P. Ripley's game
Highsmith, P. The talented Mr. Ripley; Ripley under ground; Ripley's game
Hogan, C. Devils in exile
Holden, C. The jazz bird
Hugo, V. Les miserables
Hunter, S. Black light
Hunter, S. Dirty white boys
Huston, C. Caught stealing
Huston, C. The mystic arts of erasing all signs of death
Isaacs, S. Lily White
James, P. D. Innocent blood
Johnson, D. Nobody move
Katkov, N. Blood & orchids
Katzenbach, J. Just cause
Keating, H. R. F. The bad detective
King, S. Blaze
Klein, M. Con ed
Krist, G. Chaos theory
Latour, J. The Havana World Series
Leonard, E. Be cool
Leonard, E. Freaky Deaky
Leonard, E. Get Shorty
Leonard, E. The hot kid
Leonard, E. Killshot

TITLE AND SUBJECT INDEX

pen?

Wiltse, D. Blown away

Winegardner, M. The Godfather returns

Winslow, D. Savages

Woods, S. Grass roots

Woods, S. Reckless abandon

Woods, S. Two-dollar bill

Zelazny, R. The dead man's brother

Zeltserman, D. Small crimes

Crime and Mr. Campion. Allingham, M.

Crime and punishment. Dostoyevsky, F.

Crime novels: American noir of the 1930s and 40s.

Crime novels: American noir of the 1950s.

Crime of Privilege. Walker, W.

Crime school. O'Connell, C.

CRIME STORIES *See* Mystery fiction

Crime stories and other writings. Hammett, D.

CRIME VICTIMS *See* Victims of crimes

The **crime** writer. Hurwitz, G.

Crimes in southern Indiana. Bill, F.

The **crimes** of Jordan Wise. Pronzini, B.

CRIMES OF PASSION

Cook, T. H. The last talk with Lola Faye

CRIMES WITHOUT VICTIMS *See* Crime; Criminal law

Criminal damage. Yorke, M.

Criminal enterprise. Laukkanen, O.

CRIMINAL INVESTIGATION

Arsenault, E. In search of the Rose notes

Finder, J. Buried secrets

Sidor, S. The mirror's edge

CRIMINAL INVESTIGATION -- ENGLAND -- LONDON

Hodder, M. The strange affair of Spring Heeled Jack

CRIMINAL INVESTIGATION -- FICTION

Black, B. Vengeance

Blake, R. A dark anatomy

Castillo, L. Her last breath

Elias, G. Danse macabre

Griffiths, E. A Dying Fall

Harrod-Eagles, C. Blood Never Dies

Irwin, S. M. The broken ones

Lackberg, C. The Stranger

Mark, D. The dark winter

Mark, D. Original skin

May, P. The Blackhouse

Mosley, W. Little Scarlet

Nesbø, J. The leopard

Penny, L. The beautiful mystery

The redeemer

Robertson, I. Circle of shadows

Smith, M. C. Tatiana

Tallis, F. Fatal lies

Tolkien, S. Orders from Berlin

Wells, D. The hollow city

Winthrop, E. H. The why of things

Criminal justice. Parker, B.

CRIMINAL LAW

De la Pava, S. A naked singularity

Criminals. Livesey, M.

CRIMINALS -- FAMILY RELATIONSHIPS

Turner, N. Heartbreak of a hustler's wife

CRIMINALS

Amis, M. Lionel Asbo

Bayard, L. The black tower

Beukes, L. Zoo city

Gavin, R. Beluga

Hellstrom, B. Cell 8

Sears, M. Black Fridays

Turner, N. Heartbreak of a hustler's wife

CRIMINALS -- IDENTIFICATION *See* Criminal investigation; Identification

Crimson eve. Collins, B.

Crimson joy. Parker, R. B.

The **crimson** petal and the white. Faber, M.

Crippen. Boyne, J.

Crippen, Hawley Harvey, 1862-1910
About

Boyne, J. Crippen

Cripple Creek. Sallis, J.

CRIPPLED CHILDREN *See* Physically handicapped children

CRIPPLED PEOPLE *See* Physically handicapped

Crisis. Cook, R.

Critical injuries. Barfoot, J.

Critical mass. Martini, S. P.

CROATIA

Novakovich, J. April Fool's Day

Seymour, G. The heart of danger

CROATIAN AMERICANS

Martin, V. Trespass

Stefaniak, M. H. The Turk and my mother

CROATS -- AUSTRALIA

Coetzee, J. M. Slow man

CROCHETING *See* Needlework

The **Crocodile.** De Giovanni, M.

The **crocodile** bird. Rendell, R.

Cromwell, Thomas, Earl of Essex, 1485?-1540
About

Mantel, H. Bring up the bodies

Mantel, H. Wolf Hall

Crooked letter, crooked letter. Franklin, T.

Crooked little vein. Ellis, W.

Cross. Bruen, K.

Cross. Patterson, J.

CROSS CULTURAL CONFLICT *See* Culture conflict

CROSS-EXAMINATION *See* Witnesses

The **cross-legged** knight. Robb, C. M.

Crossbones. Farah, N.

Crossers. Caputo, P.

Oyeyemi, H. The opposite house

CUBANS -- FRANCE

Hijuelos, O. A simple Habana melody: from when the world was good

CUBANS -- UNITED STATES

Atkins, A. White shadow

Bell, C. The Perez family

Garcia, C. The Aguero sisters

Garcia, C. Dreaming in Cuban

Hijuelos, O. The Mambo Kings play songs of love

Rosales, G. The halfway house

Spillane, M. The Consummata

CUBISM See Art

CUCHULAIN (LEGENDARY CHARACTER)

Llywelyn, M. Red Branch

The **cuckoo's** calling. Rowling, J. K.

Cujo. King, S.

CULLODEN, BATTLE OF, SCOTLAND, 1746

Gabaldon, D. Outlander

CULTS

Atwood, M. The year of the flood

Bell, M. S. The color of night

Cussler, C. Plague ship

DeLillo, D. The names

Goodman, C. The night villa

Harrison, J. The great leader

Hooper, K. Blood sins

Hospital, J. T. Oyster

Houellebecq, M. The possibility of an island

Jhabvala, R. P. Shards of memory

Johansen, I. Eight days to live

King, L. R. A darker place

Koontz, D. R. One door away from heaven

LaValle, V. D. Big machine

Magary, D. The postmortal

McGowan, K. The expected one

Mieville, C. Kraken

Murakami, H. 1Q84

Oe, K. An echo of heaven

Oe, K. Somersault

Perrotta, T. The leftovers

Prose, F. Hunters and gatherers

Rabb, J. The book of Q

Sidor, S. The mirror's edge

Sidor, S. Pitch dark

Tirone Smith Love her madly

Vargas Llosa, M. The war of the end of the world

Walker, M. W. Under the beetle's cellar

Wilson, R. C. Spin

Woods, S. Heat

CULTS -- FICTION

Bear, E. Range of ghosts

McOmber, A. The white forest

Merullo, R. The talk-funny girl

Parris, S. J. Sacrilege

Rock, P. The Shelter Cycle

Stevens, C. Always watching

Zan, K. The Never List

CULTURAL PROPERTY See Property

CULTURAL TOURISM See Tourist trade

CULTURE CONFLICT

See also Ethnic relations; Ethnopsychology; Race relations

Achebe, C. Things fall apart

Alvarez, J. How the Garcia girls lost their accents

Conde, M. I, Tituba, black witch of Salem

De Bernieres, L. Birds without wings

Doerr, H. Consider this, senora

Doerr, H. Stones for Ibarra

D'Souza, T. The Konkans

Erdrich, L. Love medicine

Erdrich, L. Tracks

Garcia, C. Dreaming in Cuban

Gordimer, N. The pickup

Grenville, K. The secret river

Guo Xiaolu A concise Chinese-English dictionary for lovers

Han, S. Till morning comes

Ishiguro, K. An artist of the floating world

Jen, G. Mona in the promised land

Jennings, G. Aztec

Johnson, D. Le divorce

Kingsolver, B. Pigs in heaven

Kwok, J. Girl in translation

Lahiri, J. The namesake

Lee, C. Y. The flower drum song

Lee, D. Country of origin

Lee, G. China boy

Malouf, D. Remembering Babylon

Michael, J. A certain smile

Michener, J. A. Caribbean

Momaday, N. S. House made of dawn

Moore, B. Black robe

Naipaul, V. S. A way in the world

Ng, F. M. Bone

Nunez, E. Anna in-between

Patterson, K. Consumption

Phillips, A. Prague

Power, S. The grass dancer

Richter, C. The light in the forest

Rosenberg, R. This is not civilization

Shafak, E. The bastard of Istanbul

Silko, L. Gardens in the dunes

Sundaresan, I. The splendor of silence

Tan, A. The Joy Luck Club

Thom, J. A. The red heart

Tyler, A. Digging to America

Updike, J. Terrorist

Watrous, M. If you follow me

CULTURE CONFLICT -- FICTION

Alvarez, J. How the Garcia girls lost their accents

Kingsolver, B. Pigs in heaven

CZECHS -- UNITED STATES
  Cather, W. My Antonia
  Cather, W. O pioneers!
  Kafka, F. Amerika
  Slouka, M. The visible world

D

D is for deadbeat. Grafton, S.
The **Da** Vinci code. Brown, D.
Dad. Wharton, W.
Daddy Love. Oates, J. C.
Daddy's little girl. Clark, M. H.
DAIRY CATTLE See Cattle; Dairying
Daisy Buchanan's daughter. Carson, T.
The **Daisy** Ducks. Boyer, R.
Daisy Miller. James, H.
Dakota. Grimes, M.
DAKOTA INDIANS
  Harrison, J. The road home
  Hill, R. B. Hanta yo
  Jones, D. C. Arrest Sitting Bull
  Power, S. The grass dancer
  Simmons, D. Black Hills
DAKOTA INDIANS -- FICTION
  Power, S. The grass dancer
**DALHOUSIE, ISABEL (FICTITIOUS CHAR-
    ACTER)**
  McCall Smith, A. The forgotten affairs of youth
DALLAS (TEX.)
  Ellroy, J. The cold six thousand
  Grafton, S. L is for lawless
  Noire (Author) Natural born liar
**DALZIEL, ANDREW (FICTITIOUS CHARAC-
    TER)**
  Hill, R. Death comes for the Fat Man
Damage. Hart, J.
Damaged goods. Solomita, S.
Damascus. Mohr, J.
Damascus Countdown. Rosenberg, J. C.
Damascus Gate. Stone, R.
DAMS
  Doig, I. Bucking the sun
  Evison, J. West of here
  Wiggins, M. Evidence of things unseen
Dance for the dead. Perry, T.
Dance hall of the dead. Hillerman, T.
DANCE MUSIC See Music
Dance on the wind. Johnston, T. C.
DANCE TEACHERS
  Sharp, A. The true memoirs of Little K
A **dance** to the music of time. Powell, A.
Dance upon the air. Roberts, N.
A **dance** with dragons. Martin, G. R. R.
Dancer. McCann, C.
The **dancer** and the thief. Skarmeta, A.
DANCERS

  See also Entertainers
  Brown, C. The hatbox baby
  Durrell, L. Justine
  Hamilton, J. The short history of a prince
  Hiaasen, C. Strip tease
  Lutz, J. Dancing with the dead
  McMurtry, L. The desert rose
  Sharp, A. The true memoirs of Little K
  Skarmeta, A. The dancer and the thief
DANCERS -- FICTION
  Chao, P. Mambo peligroso
Dancers at the end of time [series]
  Moorcock, M. An alien heat
  Moorcock, M. The end of all songs
  Moorcock, M. The hollow lands
Dancing Arabs. Kashua, S.
Dancing at the Rascal Fair. Doig, I.
The **dancing** floor. Michaels, B.
Dancing in the dark. Kaminsky, S. M.
Dancing in the dark. Phillips, C.
Dancing with bears. Swanwick, M.
Dancing with Einstein. Wenner, K.
Dancing with the dead. Lutz, J.
Dandelion wine. Bradbury, R.
DANES -- ENGLAND
  Hoeg, P. The woman and the ape
DANGEROUS ANIMALS See Animals
The **Dangerous** Edge of Things. Whittle, T.
The **dangerous** hour. Muller, M.
A **dangerous** inheritance. Weir, A.
Dangerous laughter. Millhauser, S.
A **dangerous** mourning. Perry, A.
A **dangerous** woman. Morris, M. M.
Dangling man. Bellow, S.
Daniel isn't talking. Leimbach, M.
DANISH LANGUAGE See Language and lan-
    guages; Norwegian language; Scandinavian lan-
    guages
Danse macabre. Elias, G.
Dante Alighieri, 1265-1321
                                About
  Pearl, M. The Dante Club
The **Dante** Club. Pearl, M.
Dante's equation. Jensen, J.
Dante's wood. Raimondo, L.
The **Danzig** trilogy. Grass, G.
Daphne du Maurier's classics of the macabre. Du
    Maurier, D.
Darconville's cat. Theroux, A.
Dare me. Abbott, M. E.
The **dark.**
DARK AGES See Middle Ages
A **dark** anatomy. Blake, R.
Dark angels. Koen, K.
Dark back of time. Marias, J.
Dark currents. Carey, J.

The **day** of creation. Ballard, J. G.

Day of judgment. Higgins, J.

Day of reckoning. Higgins, J.

The **day** of the jackal. Forsyth, F.

Day of the oprichnik.

The **day** of the scorpion. Scott, P.

Day out of days. Shepard, S.

The **day** the rabbi resigned. Kemelman, H.

Daylight. Knox, E.

Days of drums. Shelby, P.

Days of the dead. Hambly, B.

Daytripper. Bá, G.

De Niro's game. Hage, R.

De Quincey, Thomas, 1785-1859

About

Morrell, D. Murder as a fine art

DEAD

> *See also* Burial; Cremation; Death; Funeral rites and ceremonies; Obituaries

Blake, R. A dark anatomy

Dorst, D. Alive in Necropolis

Keilson, H. Comedy in a minor key

King, S. The dark half

King, S. Pet sematary

Marr, M. Graveminder

Moloney, S. The dwelling

Reynolds, S. A gracious plenty

Stross, C. The Jennifer morgue

Dead and gone. Vachss, A. H.

Dead and gone. Simpson, D.

Dead anyway. Knopf, C.

Dead as a dodo. Langton, J.

Dead by morning. Simpson, D.

Dead center. Wilcox, C.

Dead crazy. Pickard, N.

The **dead** detective. Heffernan, W.

Dead dogs and Englishmen. Buzzelli, E. K.

Dead even. Meltzer, B.

Dead eyes. Woods, S.

The **dead** fathers club. Haig, M.

The **dead** fish museum. D'Ambrosio, C.

A **dead** hand. Theroux, P.

The **dead** hour. Mina, D.

Dead in the water. Woods, S.

Dead languages. Shields, D.

The **dead** man's brother. Zelazny, R.

Dead man's ransom. Peters, E.

Dead man's walk. McMurtry, L.

Dead meat. Tapply, W. G.

Dead men living. Freemantle, B.

Dead midnight. Muller, M.

Dead north. Henry, S.

The **dead** of winter. Gosling, P.

The **dead** path. Irwin, S. M.

Dead reckoning. Harris, C.

The **dead** republic. Doyle, R.

Dead ringer. Scottoline, L.

The **dead** sit round in a ring. Lawrence, D.

Dead souls. Gogol', N. V.

Dead souls. Rankin, I.

Dead to rights. Jance, J. A.

Dead water. Marsh, N.

Dead water. Hambly, B.

Dead winter. Tapply, W. G.

Dead zero. Hunter, S.

The **dead** zone. King, S.

Deadeye Dick. Vonnegut, K.

Deadline. Grant, M.

Deadly decisions. Reichs, K. J.

Deadly Harvest. Stanley, M.

Deadly lies. Eden, C.

Deadly rich. Stewart, E.

A **deadly** shade of gold. MacDonald, J. D.

Deadwood. Dexter, P.

DEAF

> *See also* Hearing impaired; Physically handicapped

Greenberg, J. In this sign

Itani, F. Deafening

Lodge, D. Deaf sentence

McCullers, C. The heart is a lonely hunter

Seth, V. An equal music

Thompson, V. Murder on Lexington Avenue

DEAF -- EDUCATION

> *See also* Education

Thompson, V. Murder on Lexington Avenue

DEAF -- MEANS OF COMMUNICATION *See* Communication

Deaf sentence. Lodge, D.

Deafening. Itani, F.

Deal on ice. Standiford, L.

Deal with the dead. Standiford, L.

The **dean's** list. Hassler, J.

Dear American Airlines. Miles, J.

Dear and glorious physician. Caldwell, T.

Dear husband, Oates, J. C.

Dear John. Sparks, N.

Dear life. Munro, A.

Dear money. McPhee, M.

The **dearly** departed. Lipman, E.

Dearly devoted Dexter. Lindsay, J. P.

DEATH

Agee, J. A death in the family

Banks, R. The sweet hereafter

Bausch, R. Peace

Betts, D. Souls raised from the dead

Brockmeier, K. The brief history of the dead

Clay, H. Losing Charlotte

Clinch, J. Kings of the earth

Coetzee, J. M. Age of iron

Cohen, L. H. The grief of others

Crace, J. Being dead

Death in Venice. Mann, T.

Death in Venice and other tales. Mann, T.

A **death** in Vienna. Tallis, F.

The **death** instinct. Rubenfeld, J.

Death is now my neighbor. Dexter, C.

Death lives next door. Butler, G.

Death of a cattle king. Overholser, W. D.

Death of a hero. Haymon, S. T.

Death of a hussy. Beaton, M. C.

Death of a literary widow. Barnard, R.

Death of a macho man. Beaton, M. C.

Death of a nationalist. Pawel, R.

Death of a Russian priest. Kaminsky, S. M.

Death of a stranger. Perry, A.

Death of a Valentine. Beaton, M. C.

Death of a writer. Collins, M.

Death of an expert witness. James, P. D.

The **death** of an Irish lover. Gill, B.

The **death** of an Irish sea wolf. Gill, B.

Death of an ordinary man. Duncan, G.

The **death** of Artemio Cruz. Fuentes, C.

The **death** of bees. O'Donnell, L.

The **death** of Bunny Munro. Cave, N.

The **death** of Ivan Ilyitch, and other stories. Tolstoy, L.

Death of kings. Cornwell, B.

The **death** of sweet mister. Woodrell, D.

Death of the mantis. Stanley, M.

The **death** of Vishnu. Suri, M.

Death on a cold, wild river. Gill, B.

DEATH PENALTY See Capital punishment

Death qualified. Wilhelm, K.

DEATH ROW INMATES

Grisham, J. The confession

McCrumb, S. The ballad of Frankie Silver

Picoult, J. Change of heart

Tirone Smith Love her madly

Vachss, A. That's how I roll

Death song. McGarrity, M.

Death takes passage. Henry, S.

Death to go. Harrod-Eagles, C.

Death to the landlords! Peters, E.

Death trap. Henry, S.

DEATH VALLEY (CALIF. AND NEV.)

Pronzini, B. The other side of silence

Death walked in. Hart, C. G.

Death watch. Harrod-Eagles, C.

Death with interruptions. Saramago, J.

Death without company. Johnson, C.

DEATHBED SCENES

Fuentes, C. The death of Artemio Cruz

White, P. The eye of the storm

Debris. Anderton, J.

DEBT See Finance

The **debt** to pleasure. Lanchester, J.

DEBTS

Zevin, G. The hole we're in

The **decay** of the angel. Mishima, Y.

DECEASED See Dead

Deceit. Siegel, J.

DECEIT See Deception; Fraud

December. Winthrop, E. H.

December 6. Smith, M. C.

December heat. Garcia-Roza, L. A.

Deception. Mina, D.

DECEPTION

See also Truthfulness and falsehood

Brockway, C. The golden season

Cartwright, J. Other people's money

Deceptions. Michael, J.

Deceptions. Weaver, M.

DECEPTIVE ADVERTISING See Advertising; Business ethics

Decked. Clark, C. H.

DECLAMATIONS See Monologues; Recitations

Declare. Powers, T.

Decline and fall. Waugh, E.

DECORATION AND ORNAMENT See Art; Decorative arts

DECOYS (HUNTING) See Hunting; Shooting

The **deeds** of the disturber. Peters, E.

DEEJAYS See Disc jockeys

Deep as the marrow. Wilson, F. P.

The **deep** blue good-by. MacDonald, J. D.

The **deep** blue sea for beginners. Rice, L.

Deep Creek. Hand, D.

Deep down true. Fay, J.

The **deep** end of the ocean. Mitchard, J.

Deep in the shade of paradise. Dufresne, J.

Deep river. Endo, S.

Deep shadow. White, R. W.

A **deeper** sleep. Stabenow, D.

The **deepest** water. Wilhelm, K.

A **deepness** in the sky. Vinge, V.

Deepsix. McDevitt, J.

The **Deer** Leap. Grimes, M.

The **Deerslayer.** Cooper, J. F.

DEFECTORS

Clancy, T. The hunt for Red October

Deighton, L. Mexico set

Ford, R. The student conductor

Judd, A. Legacy

Le Carre, J. Our kind of traitor

DEFECTORS -- FICTION

Kanon, J. Istanbul passage

Defend and betray. Perry, A.

Defending Jacob. Landay, W.

DEFENSE CONTRACTS

Gibson, W. Zero history

Defense for the devil. Wilhelm, K.

DEFENSE INFORMATION, CLASSIFIED -- CHINA

Alpert, M. Extinction

DEFENSE INFORMATION, CLASSIFIED -- SOVIET UNION

Eastland, S. Shadow pass

DEFLATION (FINANCE) *See* Finance

Defoe, Daniel, 1661?-1731

About

Coetzee, J. M. Foe

Tournier, M. Friday

DEFORMITIES

Dalton, J. The inverted forest

Golding, W. Darkness visible

Grass, G. Cat and mouse

Lessing, D. M. Ben, in the world

McCammon, R. R. Gone south

McGrath, P. Martha Peake

Vallgren The horrific sufferings of the mind-reading monster Hercules Barefoot

Wilhelm, K. Desperate measures

DEGENERATION

Algren, N. A walk on the wild side

Caldwell, E. Tobacco road

Chute, C. The Beans of Egypt, Maine

Dickey, J. Deliverance

Faulkner, W. Absalom, Absalom!

Faulkner, W. As I lay dying

Faulkner, W. The hamlet

Faulkner, W. Sanctuary

Faulkner, W. The sound and the fury

Gide, A. The immoralist

Herlihy, J. L. Midnight cowboy

James, H. Roderick Hudson

Kennedy, W. Ironweed

Kosinski, J. N. The devil tree

Norris, F. McTeague

Proulx, A. Postcards

Rossner, J. Looking for Mr. Goodbar

Styron, W. Lie down in darkness

Wilde, O. The picture of Dorian Gray

Zola, E. Nana

Degree of guilt. Patterson, R. N.

DEISM *See* Religion; Theology

Deja dead. Reichs, K. J.

DELAWARE INDIANS

Richter, C. The light in the forest

Delicate edible birds and other stories. Groff, L.

A Delicate Truth. Le Carré, J.

Delicious. Thomas, S.

Delilah (Biblical figure)

About

Maine, D. The book of Samson

DELINQUENCY, JUVENILE *See* Juvenile delinquency

DELINQUENTS *See* Criminals

Deliver us from evil. Baldacci, D.

Deliverance. Dickey, J.

The delivery man. McGinniss, J.

The delivery room. Brownrigg, S.

DELTA (MISS. : REGION)

Gavin, R. Beluga

Morris, W. Taps

Yarbrough, S. Prisoners of war

Delta wedding. Welty, E.

The deluge. Sienkiewicz, H.

DELUSIONS *See* Hallucinations and illusions

DEMENTIA

Lichtenstein, A. Lost

Demian. Hesse, H.

Democracy. Adams, H.

Demolition angel. Crais, R.

Demon. Varley, J.

Demon of the air. Levack, S.

DEMONIAC POSSESSION

See also Demonology

Gregory, D. Pandemonium

Saul, J. The right hand of evil

Seton, A. Green darkness

DEMONOLOGY

See also Occultism

Shirley, J. Demons

Stross, C. The apocalypse codex

Stross, C. The Fuller memorandum

Demons. Shirley, J.

Deng, Valentino Achak

About

Eggers, D. What is the what

A **Deniable** Death. Seymour, G.

DENMARK

Hoeg, P. Borderliners

Hoeg, P. The history of Danish dreams

Ramsland, M. Doghead

DENMARK -- 17TH CENTURY

Tremain, R. Music & silence

DENMARK -- 19TH CENTURY

Andersen Nexo, M. Pelle the conqueror: v1 Childhood

Andersen Nexo, M. Pelle the conqueror: v2 Apprenticeship

Dinesen, I. Winter's tales

DENMARK -- COPENHAGEN

Cornwell, B. Sharpe's prey: Richard Sharpe and the Expedition to Copenhagen, 1807

Hoeg, P. Smilla's sense of snow

Kennedy, T. E. In the company of angels

DENMARK -- FICTION

Adler-Olsen, J. The absent one

Adler-Olsen, J. The keeper of lost causes

Kazinski, A. J. The last good man

DENMARK -- TO 1241

Anderson, P. War of the Gods

DENOMINATIONAL SCHOOLS *See* Church schools

DENOMINATIONS, RELIGIOUS *See* Sects

Denting the Bosch. Link, T.

DENTISTRY *See* Medicine

DENTISTS
Bull, E. Territory
Norris, F. McTeague
Russell, M. D. Doc
West, P. O.K.

DEPARTMENT STORES
See also Business; Retail trade; Stores
Archer, J. As the crow flies
Bradford, B. T. A woman of substance
Davies, V. Miracle on 34th Street
Martin, S. Shopgirl
McNaught, J. Paradise

DEPENDENCIES *See* Colonies

The **deportees** and other stories. Doyle, R.

DEPRESSION (PSYCHOLOGY) *See* Abnormal
psychology; Affective disorders; Neuroses

DEPRESSIONS -- 1929
Brennert, A. Palisades Park
Silver, M. Mary Coin

DEPROGRAMMING *See* Brainwashing

Derailed. Siegel, J.

DERELICTS
Innes, H. The wreck of the Mary Deare

The **Dervish** House. McDonald, I.

The **descendants.** Hemmings, K. H.

DESCENT *See* Genealogy; Heredity

DESERT ANIMALS *See* Animals; Deserts

Desert blood. Gaspar de Alba, A.

DESERT ECOLOGY *See* Ecology

DESERT PLANTS *See* Deserts; Plant ecology;
Plants

The **desert** rose. McMurtry, L.

DESERTED HOUSES
Rayne, S. Property of a lady

The **deserter.** Langton, J.

DESERTIFICATION *See* Climate; Deserts

DESERTION *See* Desertion and nonsupport; Military desertion

DESERTION AND NONSUPPORT *See* Divorce;
Domestic relations

DESERTION, MILITARY *See* Military desertion

DESERTS
Aira, C. The seamstress and the wind
Bolano, R. 2666
Caputo, P. Horn of Africa
Herbert, F. Children of Dune
Pyne, D. Twentynine Palms
Silko, L. Gardens in the dunes

DESERTS -- GRAPHIC NOVELS
Henson, J. Jim Henson's tale of sand

DESIGNED GENETIC CHANGE *See* Genetic
engineering

DESIGNER DRUGS *See* Drugs

DESIGNERS
Lively, P. How it all began

DESIGNERS *See* Artists

DESIRE
Wolitzer, M. The uncoupling

DESKS
Krauss, N. Great house

Desperate measures. Wilhelm, K.

Desperation. King, S.

Destiny. Parks, T.

DESTINY *See* Fate and fatalism

Destiny and desire. Fuentes, C.

Destiny: child of the sky. Haydon, E.

DESTITUTION *See* Poverty

The **destruction** of the books. Odom, M.

Detective. Hailey, A.

DETECTIVE AND MYSTERY STORIES
See also Mystery fiction
Abrahams, P. Dog on it
Akunin, B. Murder on the Leviathan
Atkinson, K. Case histories
Atkinson, K. When will there be good news?
Banville, J. A death in summer
Banville, J. Elegy for April
Bauer, B. Darkside
Berlinski, M. Fieldwork
Block, L. A drop of the hard stuff
Bradley, A. A red herring without mustard
Bradley, A. The sweetness at the bottom of the pie
Bradley, A. The weed that strings the hangman's
bag
Burdett, J. Bangkok haunts
Burdett, J. Bangkok Tattoo
Burke, J. L. The glass rainbow
Cain, C. Heartsick
Carter, S. L. New England white
Chabon, M. The Yiddish policemen's union
Chandler, R. Raymond Chandler
Child, L. 61 hours
Child, L. The enemy
Child, L. The hard way
Child, L. One shot
Connelly, M. The brass verdict
Connelly, M. The closers
Connelly, M. Echo Park
Connelly, M. The narrows
Cotterill, C. Anarchy and old dogs
Cotterill, C. Killed at the whim of a hat
Cotterill, C. Love songs from a shallow grave
Crais, R. First rule
Cullin, M. A slight trick of the mind
Dicks, M. Unexpectedly, Milo
Doiron, P. The poacher's son
Elkins, A. J. Unnatural selection
French, T. Faithful Place
French, T. In the woods

Barnard, R. A fall from grace

Barnes, L. Cold case

Barnes, L. The snake tattoo

Barr, N. Burn

Barr, N. High country

Barr, N. Winter study

Bayard, L. The black tower

Beaton, M. C. Death of a hussy

Beaton, M. C. Death of a macho man

Beaton, M. C. Death of a Valentine

Beaton, M. C. Love, lies, and liquor

Bell, A. A. The blood of Caesar

Belzer, R. I am not a cop!

Benn, J. R. Billy Boyle

Benn, J. R. The first wave

Benn, J. R. A mortal terror

Black, C. Murder in Passy

Black, C. Murder in the Sentier

Bland, E. T. See no evil

Block, L. All the flowers are dying

Block, L. The burglar in the library

Block, L. A drop of the hard stuff

Block, L. Eight million ways to die

Block, L. The sins of the fathers

Block, L. A ticket to the boneyard

Block, L. When the sacred ginmill closes

Bond, M. Monsieur Pamplemousse

Bowen, P. Badlands

Box, C. J. Back of beyond

Box, C. J. Blood trail

Box, C. J. Nowhere to run

Box, C. J. Savage run

Boyer, R. The Daisy Ducks

Bradley, A. A red herring without mustard

Braun, L. J. The cat who ate Danish modern

Braun, L. J. The cat who brought down the house

Braun, L. J. The cat who sang for the birds

Braun, L. J. The cat who smelled a rat

Braun, L. J. The cat who went underground

Brett, S. Mrs. Pargeter's package

Brett, S. Murder unprompted

Brett, S. The torso in the town

Brown, R. M. Murder at Monticello; or, Old sins

Brown, R. M. Wish you were here

Bruen, K. Cross

Bruen, K. The guards

Buchanan, E. Love kills

Buchanan, E. Suitable for framing

Buchanan, E. You only die twice

Burke, A. Angel's tip

Burke, J. L. Black cherry blues

Burke, J. L. The glass rainbow

Burke, J. L. Heaven's prisoners

Burke, J. L. Last car to Elysian Fields

Burke, J. L. A stained white radiance

Burke, J. L. The tin roof blowdown

Burke, J. Disturbance

Burke, J. Remember me, Irene

Butler, G. Death lives next door

Cannell, D. How to murder your mother-in-law

Chandler, R. The big sleep

Chandler, R. The high window

Chandler, R. The lady in the lake

Chandler, R. Later novels and other writings

Chandler, R. The long goodbye

Chandler, R. Stories and early novels

Chesterton, G. K. Father Brown mystery stories

Chesterton, G. K. The Father Brown omnibus

Chesterton, G. K. The innocence of Father Brown

Child, L. 61 hours

Child, L. The affair

Child, L. Bad luck and trouble

Child, L. Echo burning

Child, L. The enemy

Child, L. The hard way

Child, L. Nothing to lose

Child, L. One shot

Child, L. Persuader

Child, L. Without fail

Child, L. Worth dying for

Christie, A. The A.B.C. murders

Christie, A. The body in the library

Christie, A. Curtain

Christie, A. The Hollow

Christie, A. Mrs. McGinty's dead

Christie, A. The murder at the vicarage

Christie, A. Murder in the Calais coach

Christie, A. A murder is announced

Christie, A. The murder of Roger Ackroyd

Christie, A. Towards zero

Clark, C. H. Decked

Cleverly, B. Strange images of death

Coben, H. Darkest fear

Coben, H. One false move

Cockey, T. Hearse case scenario

Cockey, T. Murder in the hearse degree

Coel, M. The dream stalker

Coel, M. The ghost walker

Collins, M. A. Bye bye, baby

Connelly, M. City of bones

Connelly, M. The black ice

Connelly, M. The closers

Connelly, M. A darkness more than night

Connelly, M. Echo Park

Connelly, M. Lost light

Connelly, M. The narrows

Connelly, M. Nine dragons

Connelly, M. The overlook

Connolly, J. The burning soul

Connolly, J. The unquiet

Constantine, K. C. Blood mud

Constantine, K. C. Brushback

Gardner, L. Love you more

Gash, J. Prey dancing

Gash, J. A rag, a bone, and a hank of hair

Gash, J. The rich and the profane

George, E. Careless in red

George, E. This body of death

George, E. A traitor to memory

Gill, B. Death in Dublin

Gill, B. The death of an Irish lover

Gill, B. The death of an Irish sea wolf

Gill, B. Death on a cold, wild river

Gilman, D. The amazing Mrs. Pollifax

Gilman, D. The elusive Mrs. Pollifax

Gilman, D. Kaleidoscope

Gilman, D. Mrs. Pollifax and the whirling dervish

Gilman, D. Mrs. Pollifax pursued

Gilman, D. Mrs. Pollifax, innocent tourist

Gilman, D. A palm for Mrs. Pollifax

Gilman, D. The unexpected Mrs. Pollifax

Gilman, K. Father's Day

Giroux, E. X. A death for a dancer

Goldsborough, R. The missing chapter

Gorman, E. Bad moon rising

Gorman, E. Breaking up is hard to do

Gorman, E. Fools rush in

Gorman, E. Save the last dance for me

Gorman, E. Sleeping dogs

Gorman, E. Ticket to ride

Gosling, P. The dead of winter

Gosling, P. A few dying words

Grafton, S. B is for burglar

Grafton, S. C is for corpse

Grafton, S. D is for deadbeat

Grafton, S. E is for evidence

Grafton, S. F is for fugitive

Grafton, S. G is for gumshoe

Grafton, S. H is for homicide

Grafton, S. I is for innocent

Grafton, S. A is for alibi

Grafton, S. J is for judgment

Grafton, S. K is for killer

Grafton, S. L is for lawless

Grafton, S. M is for malice

Grafton, S. N is for noose

Grafton, S. O is for outlaw

Grafton, S. P is for peril

Grafton, S. Q is for quarry

Grafton, S. R is for ricochet

Grafton, S. S is for Silence

Grafton, S. T is for trespass

Gran, S. Claire DeWitt and the city of the dead

Granger, B. The el murders

Greeley, A. M. The bishop in the West Wing

Greenleaf, S. Blood type

Greenleaf, S. False conception

Greenleaf, S. Flesh wounds

Greenleaf, S. Past tense

Greenleaf, S. Strawberry Sunday

Greer, R. O. First of state

Grimes, M. The Anodyne Necklace

Grimes, M. The Black cat

Grimes, M. The case has altered

Grimes, M. The Deer Leap

Grimes, M. The Dirty Duck

Grimes, M. The five bells and bladebone

Grimes, M. Help the poor struggler

Grimes, M. The Horse You Came In On

Grimes, M. I am the only running footman

Grimes, M. Jerusalem Inn

Grimes, M. The Lamorna wink

Grimes, M. The man with a load of mischief

Grimes, M. The Old Contemptibles

Grimes, M. The old fox deceiv'd

Grimes, M. The Old Silent

Grimes, M. The Old Wine Shades

Grimes, M. Rainbow's end

Grimes, M. The Stargazey

Grimes, M. The winds of change

Gulik, R. H. v. The Chinese bell murders

Gulik, R. H. v. The haunted monastery

Gulik, R. H. v. The lacquer screen

Gulik, R. H. v. The Red Pavilion

Gulik, R. H. v. The willow pattern

Haddam, J. Bleeding hearts

Haddam, J. Cheating at solitaire

Haddam, J. Flowering Judas

Haddam, J. Hardscrabble road

Haddam, J. Somebody else's music

Haddam, J. True believers

Hager, J. The spirit caller

Hall, J. W. Blackwater sound

Hall, J. W. Buzz cut

Hall, J. W. Off the chart

Hall, J. W. Red sky at night

Hammett, D. The glass key

Hammett, D. The Maltese falcon

Hammett, D. The thin man

Hansen, J. A country of old men

Hansen, J. Early graves

Hansen, J. Gravedigger

Hansen, J. The little dog laughed

Hardwick, M. Malice domestic

Hardwick, M. Parson's pleasure

Harper, K. The Poyson garden

Harper, K. The queene's Christmas

Harper, K. The tidal poole

Harrison, J. Blue Deer thaw

Harrison, J. An unfortunate prairie occurrence

Harrod-Eagles, C. Blood lines

Harrod-Eagles, C. Death to go

Harrod-Eagles, C. Death watch

Harrod-Eagles, C. Game over

Jungstedt, M. The inner circle
Kaminsky, S. M. The big silence
Kaminsky, S. M. Blood and rubles
Kaminsky, S. M. A cold red sunrise
Kaminsky, S. M. Dancing in the dark
Kaminsky, S. M. Death of a Russian priest
Kaminsky, S. M. The dog who bit a policeman
Kaminsky, S. M. A fatal glass of beer
Kaminsky, S. M. Hard currency
Kaminsky, S. M. Lieberman's choice
Kaminsky, S. M. Lieberman's day
Kaminsky, S. M. Lieberman's folly
Kaminsky, S. M. Lieberman's thief
Kaminsky, S. M. The man who walked like a bear
Kaminsky, S. M. Murder on the Trans-Siberian Express
Kaminsky, S. M. Not quite kosher
Kaminsky, S. M. Retribution
Kaminsky, S. M. Rostnikov's vacation
Kaminsky, S. M. To catch a spy
Kaminsky, S. M. Tomorrow is another day
Kava, A. Hotwire
Keating, H. R. F. Bribery, corruption also
Keating, H. R. F. Cheating death
Keating, H. R. F. Doing wrong
Keating, H. R. F. Inspector Ghote trusts the heart
Kellerman, F. Day of atonement
Kellerman, F. The forgotten
Kellerman, F. Grievous sin
Kellerman, F. Jupiter's bones
Kellerman, F. Justice
Kellerman, F. Milk and honey
Kellerman, F. Prayers for the dead
Kellerman, F. Sanctuary
Kellerman, F. Serpent's tooth
Kellerman, F. Stone kiss
Kellerman, F. Street dreams
Kellerman, J. Bad love
Kellerman, J. Bones
Kellerman, J. The clinic
Kellerman, J. Devil's waltz
Kellerman, J. Dr. Death
Kellerman, J. Gone
Kellerman, J. Monster
Kellerman, J. The murder book
Kellerman, J. Private eyes
Kellerman, J. Self-defense
Kellerman, J. Survival of the fittest
Kellerman, J. Therapy
Kellerman, J. Time bomb
Kellerman, J. The web
Kellerman, J. When the bough breaks
Kelly, J. The coldest blood
Kemelman, H. The day the rabbi resigned
Kemelman, H. Friday the rabbi slept late
Kemelman, H. Monday the rabbi took off

Kemelman, H. One fine day the rabbi bought a cross
Kemelman, H. Saturday the rabbi went hungry
Kemelman, H. Sunday the rabbi stayed home
Kemelman, H. Thursday the rabbi walked out
Kemelman, H. Wednesday the rabbi got wet
Kerr, P. Field gray
Kerr, P. A quiet flame
Kienzle, W. X. Assault with intent
Kienzle, W. X. Body count
Kienzle, W. X. The gathering
Kienzle, W. X. The greatest evil
Kienzle, W. X. The man who loved God
Kienzle, W. X. The rosary murders
Kijewski, K. Alley Kat blues
Kijewski, K. Copy Kat
Kijewski, K. Honky tonk Kat
Kijewski, K. Kat scratch fever
Kijewski, K. Kat's cradle
Kijewski, K. Stray Kat waltz
King, L. R. The beekeeper's apprentice, or, On the segregation of the queen
King, L. R. The game
King, L. R. The god of the hive
King, L. R. Justice Hall
King, L. R. A letter of Mary
King, L. R. Locked rooms
King, L. R. The moor
King, L. R. O Jerusalem
King, L. R. Pirate king
Knopf, C. Black swan
Knopf, C. Hard stop
Knopf, C. Head wounds
Knopf, C. The last refuge
Knopf, C. Two time
Koryta, M. The silent hour
Krueger, W. K. Northwest angle
Krueger, W. K. Vermilion drift
La Plante, L. Blind fury
La Plante, L. Cold blood
Lackberg, C. The preacher
Langton, J. Dead as a dodo
Langton, J. The deserter
Langton, J. Emily Dickinson is dead
Langton, J. The Escher twist
Langton, J. The face on the wall
Langton, J. Murder at Monticello
Langton, J. The thief of Venice
Lansdale, J. R. Devil red
Lansdale, J. R. Vanilla Ride
Larsson, A. Until thy wrath be past
Lathen, E. Brewing up a storm
Lathen, E. Double, double, oil and trouble
Lathen, E. East is east
Lathen, E. Going for the gold
Lathen, E. Right on the money

McBain, E. There was a little girl
McBain, E. Three blind mice
McBain, E. Vespers
McBain, E. Widows
McCaffrey, V. A slepyng hound to wake
McCall Smith, A. Blue shoes and happiness
McCall Smith, A. The comforts of a muddy Saturday
McCall Smith, A. The Double Comfort Safari Club
McCall Smith, A. The good husband of Zebra Drive
McCall Smith, A. In the company of cheerful ladies
McCall Smith, A. The lost art of gratitude
McCammon, R. R. The Queen of Bedlam
McClure, J. The steam pig
McCrumb, S. If I'd killed him when I met him
McCrumb, S. MacPherson's lament
McCrumb, S. Missing Susan
McCrumb, S. The Windsor knot
Mcdonald, G. Fletch
Mcdonald, G. The Fletch chronicles
Mcdonald, G. Son of Fletch
McGarrity, M. The big gamble
McGarrity, M. Death song
McGarrity, M. Everyone dies
McGarrity, M. The Judas judge
McGarrity, M. Nothing but trouble
McGarrity, M. Under the color of law
McGilloway, B. Bleed a river deep
McGown, J. Murder at the old vicarage
McGown, J. Picture of innocence
McGown, J. Plots and errors
McGown, J. Verdict unsafe
McInerny, R. M. Bishop as pawn
McInerny, R. M. Body and soil
McInerny, R. M. The book of kills
McInerny, R. M. A cardinal offense
McInerny, R. M. Celt and pepper
McInerny, R. M. Grave undertakings
McInerny, R. M. Irish coffee
McInerny, R. M. Irish tenure
McInerny, R. M. Judas Priest
McInerny, R. M. Last things
McInerny, R. M. Requiem for a realtor
McInerny, R. M. Second vespers
McInerny, R. M. Still life
McInerny, R. M. Thicker than water
McKinzie, C. Crossing the line
Melville, J. The chrysanthemum chain
Meyer, D. Devil's peak
Meyer, N. The seven-per-cent solution
Meyer, N. The West End horror
Mina, D. The dead hour
Mina, D. Slip of the knife
Mitchell, J. C. Lovers crossing
Monfredo, M. G. Blackwater spirits

Monfredo, M. G. The stalking horse
Moody, B. Looking for Chet Baker
Morris, B. Baja Florida
Morris, R. N. The gentle axe
Mosley, W. Bad Boy Brawly Brown
Mosley, W. Black Betty
Mosley, W. Cinnamon kiss
Mosley, W. Devil in a blue dress
Mosley, W. Fear itself
Mosley, W. Fear of the dark
Mosley, W. Gone fishin'
Mosley, W. Known to evil
Mosley, W. A little yellow dog
Mosley, W. The long fall
Mosley, W. A red death
Mosley, W. Six easy pieces
Mosley, W. When the thrill is gone
Mosley, W. White butterfly
Muller, M. Both ends of the night
Muller, M. The broken promise land
Muller, M. Burn out
Muller, M. City of whispers
Muller, M. The dangerous hour
Muller, M. Dead midnight
Muller, M. Listen to the silence
Muller, M. Pennies on a dead woman's eyes
Muller, M. The shape of dread
Muller, M. There's something in a Sunday
Muller, M. Till the butchers cut him down
Muller, M. Trophies and dead things
Muller, M. A walk through the fire
Muller, M. Where echoes live
Muller, M. While other people sleep
Muller, M. A wild and lonely place
Muller, M. Wolf in the shadows
Nabb, M. Some bitter taste
Neel, J. To die for
Neely, B. Blanche cleans up
Nelscott, K. Stone cribs
Nesbo, J. The devil's star
Nesbo, J. The redbreast
Newman, S. Strong as death
O'Connell, C. Crime school
O'Connell, C. Killing critics
O'Connell, C. The man who cast two shadows
O'Connell, C. Stone angel
O'Donnell, L. Blue death
O'Donnell, L. Pushover
O'Donnell, L. The raggedy man
O'Donovan, G. The priest
Page, K. H. The body in the Big Apple
Page, K. H. The body in the bog
Page, K. H. The body in the bookcase
Page, K. H. The body in the vestibule
Pajer, B. A spark of death
Paretsky, S. Bitter medicine

Pickard, N. But I wouldn't want to die there
Pickard, N. Confession
Pickard, N. Dead crazy
Pickard, N. Generous death
Pickard, N. Marriage is murder
Pickard, N. No body
Pickard, N. The truth hurts
Pickard, N. The whole truth
Pintoff, S. In the shadow of Gotham
Qiu Xiaolong   Red mandarin dress
Qiu Xiaolong   When red is black
Quartey, K. J. Children of the street
Queen, E. A fine and private place
Queen, E. The Roman hat mystery
Queen, E. The XYZ murders
Rankin, I. Black and blue
Rankin, I. The black book
Rankin, I. Dead souls
Rankin, I. Exit music
Rankin, I. The falls
Rankin, I. The naming of the dead
Rankin, I. A question of blood
Rankin, I. Resurrection men
Rankin, I. Set in darkness
Read, C. Invisible boy
Reichs, K. J. Bare bones
Reichs, K. J. Break no bones
Reichs, K. J. Deadly decisions
Reichs, K. J. Death du jour
Reichs, K. J. Grave secrets
Reichs, K. J. Monday mourning
Rendell, R. Harm done
Rendell, R. Kissing the gunner's daughter
Rendell, R. Not in the flesh
Rendell, R. Road rage
Rendell, R. Simisola
Rendell, R. A sleeping life
Rich, V. The baked bean supper murders
Rich, V. The cooking school murders
Rich, V. The Nantucket diet murders
Rinehart, M. R. The circular staircase
Rinehart, M. R. Miss Pinkerton: adventures of a
  nurse detective
Robb, C. M. The cross-legged knight
Robb, C. M. A gift of sanctuary
Robb, C. M. The riddle of St. Leonard's
Robb, J. D. Naked in death
Roberts, G. The bluest blood
Roberts, G. Helen hath no fury
Roberts, G. The mummers' curse
Robinson, L. S. Murder at the feast of rejoicing
Robinson, L. S. Murder at the God's gate
Robinson, P. Cold is the grave
Robinson, P. Innocent grave
Robinson, P. Piece of my heart
Roosevelt, E. The Hyde Park murder

Roosevelt, E. Murder and the First Lady
Roosevelt, E. Murder at midnight
Roosevelt, E. Murder at the palace
Roosevelt, E. Murder in the Blue Room
Roosevelt, E. Murder in the map room
Roosevelt, E. Murder in the Oval Office
Roosevelt, E. Murder in the Rose Garden
Roosevelt, E. The White House pantry murder
Rozan, S. J. Winter and night
Russell, S. This insane train
Sallis, J. Cripple Creek
Sallis, J. Cypress Grove
Sallis, J. Salt River
Sanders, L. The fourth deadly sin
Sanders, L. McNally's dilemma
Sanders, L. McNally's gamble
Sanders, L. McNally's luck
Sanders, L. McNally's puzzle
Sanders, L. McNally's secret
Sanders, L. McNally's trial
Sanders, L. The Timothy files
Sanders, L. Timothy's game
Sandford, J. Broken prey
Sandford, J. Buried prey
Sandford, J. Certain prey
Sandford, J. Chosen prey
Sandford, J. Easy prey
Sandford, J. Hidden prey
Sandford, J. Mind prey
Sandford, J. Mortal prey
Sandford, J. Naked prey
Sandford, J. Night prey
Sandford, J. Rules of prey
Sandford, J. Shock wave
Sandford, J. Silent prey
Sandford, J. Sudden prey
Sandford, J. Winter prey
Sansom, I. The case of the missing books
Sayers, D. L. Busman's honeymoon
Sayers, D. L. Clouds of witnesses
Sayers, D. L. The Dawson pedigree
Sayers, D. L. The documents in the case
Sayers, D. L. The five red herrings
Sayers, D. L. Gaudy Night
Sayers, D. L. Have his carcase
Sayers, D. L. Lord Peter
Sayers, D. L. Murder must advertise
Sayers, D. L. The nine tailors
Sayers, D. L. Strong poison
Sayers, D. L. Thrones, dominations
Sayers, D. L. The unpleasantness at the Bellona
  Club
Sayers, D. L. Whose body?
Saylor, S. The house of the Vestals
Saylor, S. The judgment of Caesar
Saylor, S. A mist of prophecies

Vachss, A. H. Sacrifice
Vachss, A. H. Safe house
Van de Wetering, J. The Amsterdam cops
Van de Wetering, J. The blond baboon
Van de Wetering, J. The hollow-eyed angel
Van de Wetering, J. Just a corpse at twilight
Van de Wetering, J. The perfidious parrot
Verdon, J. Shut your eyes tight
Walker, M. The dark vineyard
Walker, M. W. All the dead lie down
Wall, K. R. The Mercy Oak
White, K. A body to die for
White, K. Lethally blond
White, R. W. Black widow
White, R. W. Deep shadow
Wilcox, C. Dead center
Wilcox, C. Except for the bones
Wilcox, C. Find her a grave
Wilcox, C. Full circle
Wilcox, C. Switchback
Wilhelm, K. The Hamlet trap
Wilhelm, K. Sweet, sweet poison
Williams, A. K. The stranger you seek
Wilson, F. P. Conspiracies
Wilson, F. P. The haunted air
Wilson, F. P. Legacies
Winslow, D. The Dawn Patrol
Winslow, D. The gentlemen's hour
Winspear, J. Among the mad
Winspear, J. Birds of a feather
Winspear, J. An incomplete revenge
Winspear, J. Maisie Dobbs
Winspear, J. The mapping of love and death
Winspear, J. Messenger of truth
Winspear, J. Pardonable lies
Wolfe, I. A. The taken
Woods, S. The lie direct
Woods, S. Naked villainy
Wright, E. The last hand
Yancey, R. The highly effective detective

DETECTIVES -- DENMARK

Kazinski, A. J. The last good man

DETECTIVES -- ENGLAND

Bradley, A. Speaking from among the bones
Grecian, A. The black country

DETECTIVES -- FICTION

Atkinson, K. Started early, took my dog
Bradley, A. The weed that strings the hangman's
bag
Burke, J. L. Light of the world
Butcher, J. Proven guilty
Cain, C. Let me go
Coben, H. Stay close
Conlon, E. Red on red
Cross, N. Luther
Dahl, A. Bad Blood

Eastland, S. Shadow pass
Gallagher, S. The bedlam detective
Gardner, L. Live to tell
George, E. Believing the lie
Grossman, P. Children of wrath
Harvey, J. A darker shade of blue
Hayder, M. Poppet
Higashino, K. The devotion of suspect X
Kerley, J. The death collectors
Kerr, P. If the dead rise not
Kerr, P. Prague fatale
Koryta, M. The prophet
Lackberg, C. The stonecutter
MacBride, S. Cold granite
Mosley, W. All I did was shoot my man
Nadel, B. The Ottoman cage
Oldham, N. Fighting for the dead
Pearl, M. The Poe shadow
Penney, S. The invisible ones
Shrier, H. Boston cream
Smith, M. C. Tatiana
Steele, J. Angel City
Tolkien, S. The king of diamonds
Wambaugh, J. Harbor nocturne

DETECTIVES -- FRANCE

Syndrome E

DETECTIVES -- IRELAND -- DUBLIN

O'Donovan, G. Dublin dead

DETECTIVES -- SWEDEN

Lackberg, C. The stonecutter

DETECTIVES, PRIVATE

Adler, E. All or nothing
Barnes, J. The somnambulist
Berry, J. The manual of detection
Collins, M. A. Black hats
Coover, R. Noir
Cunningham, E. Shadows in the starlight
Cussler, C. The chase
Cussler, C. The race
Ellis, W. Crooked little vein
Fulmer, D. The blue door
Gores, J. Cons, scams & grifts
Gores, J. Contract null & void
Hallinan, T. A nail through the heart
Hughes, M. Hespira
Ishiguro, K. When we were orphans
Jones, D. Second grave on the left
Kaminsky, S. M. Vengeance
Koontz, D. R. The bad place
Lethem, J. Motherless Brooklyn
Levien, D. City of the sun
Lutz, L. Curse of the Spellmans
Lutz, L. Revenge of the Spellmans
Lutz, L. The Spellman files
Masters, H. Post
McPhee, J. No ordinary matter

Trollope, A. The Eustace diamonds

Diana, Princess of Wales, 1961-1997
About
Ali, M. Untold story

DIARIES (STORIES ABOUT)
Brockmeier, K. The Illumination
Cooley, M. The archivist
Couto, M. Sleepwalking land
Erdrich, L. Shadow tag
Higgins, J. Bad company
Hustvedt, S. The sorrows of an American
MacNeil, R. Burden of desire
Maxwell, R. The secret diary of Anne Boleyn
Miller, S. The world below
Moore, G. The Sherlockian
Van Booy, S. Everything beautiful began after

DIARIES (STORIES IN DIARY FORM)
Bellow, S. Dangling man
Bronte, A. The tenant of Wildfell Hall
Cheever, J. The Wapshot chronicle
Collins, W. The woman in white
Dallas, S. The diary of Mattie Spenser
Fielding, H. Bridget Jones: the edge of reason
Fielding, H. Bridget Jones's diary
Golding, W. Close quarters
Golding, W. Fire down below
Golding, W. Rites of passage
Guo Xiaolu A concise Chinese-English dictionary
  for lovers
Heriz, E. d. Lies
Hersey, J. The wall
Horlock, M. The book of lies
Kaufman, S. Diary of a mad housewife
Keyes, D. Flowers for Algernon
Kingsolver, B. The lacuna
Klein, R. The moth diaries
Leshem, R. Beaufort
Lessing, D. M. The golden notebook
Lodge, D. Deaf sentence
McGill, B. The butterfly cabinet
Oe, K. A quiet life
Olafur Johann Olafsson The journey home
Palahniuk, C. Diary
Patterson, J. Suzanne's diary for Nicholas
Sams, F. Down town
Sarton, M. As we are now
Shields, C. The stone diaries
Smith, L. On Agate Hill
Townsend, S. Adrian Mole
Townsend, S. The Adrian Mole diaries
Townsend, S. Adrian Mole: the lost years
Turner, N. E. These is my words
Updike, J. Toward the end of time
Vine, B. Anna's book
Walton, J. Among others
Watson, S. J. Before I go to sleep

West, P. Lord Byron's doctor

DIARIES
Jio, S. The violets of March
Moore, M. M. So far away
Ozeki, R. L. A tale for the time being
Stabenow, D. Though not dead

DIARISTS
Lourie, R. A hatred for tulips
Diary. Palahniuk, C.
Diary of a bad year. Coetzee, J. M.
Diary of a mad housewife. Kaufman, S.
The **diary** of Mattie Spenser. Dallas, S.
The **Dick** Francis treasury of great racing stories.

Dickens, Charles, 1812-1870
About
Flanagan, R. Wanting
Pearl, M. The last Dickens
Simmons, D. Drood

Dickinson, Emily, 1830-1886
About
Charyn, J. The secret life of Emily Dickinson
Dictation. Ozick, C.

DICTATORS
See also Heads of state; Totalitarianism
Garcia Marquez, G. The autumn of the patriarch
Greene, G. The comedians
Keneally, T. The tyrant's novel
Lewis, S. It can't happen here
Orwell, G. Animal farm
Steinbeck, J. The moon is down
Vargas Llosa, M. The Feast of the Goat

DICTATORS -- FICTION
Orwell, G. Animal farm
Vargas Llosa, M. The Feast of the Goat

DICTIONARIES See Encyclopedias and dictionaries
DIDACTIC POETRY See Poetry
Diderot, Denis, 1713-1784
About
Bradbury, M. To the Hermitage
Dido Kent mystery [series]
Dean, A. A woman of consequence
Die easy. Sharp, Z.
Die in plain sight. Lowell, E.
Die upon a kiss. Hambly, B.
Dies the fire. Stirling, S. M.
DIESEL AUTOMOBILES See Automobiles
DIETETIC FOODS See Diet; Food
DIFFERENCE (PSYCHOLOGY)
Dermansky, M. Twins
Ruby, I. The salt god's daughter
Different seasons. King, S.
The **Digger's** game. Higgins, G. V.
Digging to America. Tyler, A.
DIGITAL LIBRARIES See Information systems;
  Libraries
DiMaggio, Joe, 1914-1999

King, S. Cujo
Koontz, D. R. The darkest evening of the year
Koontz, D. R. Watchers
Kress, N. Dogs
London, J. The call of the wild
London, J. White Fang
London, J. White Fang, and other stories
Nelson, P. I thought you were dead: a love story
Parkhurst, C. The dogs of Babel
Pletzinger, T. Funeral for a dog
Roger Caras' Treasury of great dog stories
Rosenblatt, R. Lapham rising
Schine, C. The New Yorkers
Siddons, A. R. Sweetwater Creek
Sparks, N. The guardian
Spencer, S. Man in the woods
Stein, G. The art of racing in the rain
Ward, J. Salvage the bones
Winkler, A. C. Dog war
Wroblewski, D. The story of Edgar Sawtelle

DOGS -- FICTION
McCall Smith, A. A conspiracy of friends

DOGS -- PSYCHOLOGY *See* Animal intelligence;
  Comparative psychology; Psychology

The **dogs** of Babel. Parkhurst, C.

Dogs of Riga. Mankell, H.

The **dogs** of war. Forsyth, F.

Doing wrong. Keating, H. R. F.

Doktor Glass. Brennan, T.

Dolley. Brown, R. M.

The **dollmaker.** Arnow, H. L. S.

Dolores Claiborne. King, S.

DOLPHINS
Ghosh, A. The hungry tide

Dombey and Son. Dickens, C.

DOMESTIC ANIMALS *See* Animals

DOMESTIC FICTION
Barry, S. On Canaan's side
Casey, J. Compass rose
Dexter, P. Spooner
Dillard, A. The Maytrees
Ferris, J. The unnamed
Greene, A. Bloodroot
Habila, H. Measuring time
Henkin, J. The world without you
Hershon, J. The German bride
Hoover, M. The quickening
Howrey, M. Blind sight
Jaime-Becerra, M. This time tomorrow
Leithauser, B. The art student's war
Lipman, E. The family man
Lively, P. Consequences
Melnyczuk, A. The house of widows
Meloy, M. A family daughter
Miller, S. The senator's wife
Minot, E. The Brambles

Phillips, J. A. Lark and Termite
Winthrop, E. H. December

DOMESTIC FICTION, AMERICAN
Mattison, A. In case we're separated

DOMESTIC RELATIONS
See also Interpersonal relations
Chung, C. Forgotten country
Cook, C. Best staged plans
Jackson, J. A grown up kind of pretty
Jensen, N. The sisters
McNeal, T. To be sung underwater
Merullo, R. The talk-funny girl

DOMESTIC TERRORISM *See* Terrorism

DOMESTIC VIOLENCE
See also Violence
Haynes, E. Into the darkest corner
Hunt, L. Kind one
Rivas, M. In the wilderness
Straight, S. Take one candle light a room

DOMESTIC WORKERS *See* Household employees

DOMESTICS
Phillips, C. Foreigners

Dominance. Lavender, W.

DOMINICA
Kincaid, J. Autobiography of my mother

DOMINICAN AMERICANS
Alvarez, J. How the Garcia girls lost their accents
Alvarez, J. Yo!
Diaz, J. The brief wondrous life of Oscar Wao
Diaz, J. Drown
Michaud, J. When Tito loved Clara

DOMINICAN AMERICANS -- FICTION
Alvarez, J. How the Garcia girls lost their accents
Alvarez, J. Yo!
Diaz, J. The brief wondrous life of Oscar Wao
Michaud, J. When Tito loved Clara

DOMINICAN REPUBLIC
Danticat, E. The farming of bones
Vargas Llosa, M. The Feast of the Goat

DOMINICAN REPUBLIC -- FICTION
Danticat, E. The farming of bones
Vargas Llosa, M. The Feast of the Goat

DOMINICAN-HAITIAN CONFLICT, 1937
Danticat, E. The farming of bones

Domino. Whitney, P. A.

Domino. King, R.

The **Don** flows home to the sea. Sholokhov, M. A.

Don Juan. Handke, P.

DON JUAN (LEGENDARY CHARACTER)
Handke, P. Don Juan

Don Quixote de la Mancha. Cervantes Saavedra, M.
d.

Don't ask. Westlake, D. E.

Don't breathe a word. McMahon, J.

Don't call it night. Oz, A.

McCaffrey, A. Dragonquest

McCaffrey, A. Dragon's Kin

McCaffrey, A. Dragon's time

McCaffrey, A. Dragonsdawn

McCaffrey, A. Dragonseye

McCaffrey, A. The Masterharper of Pern

McCaffrey, A. The renegades of Pern

McCaffrey, A. The skies of Pern

McCaffrey, A. The white dragon

Norton, A. The elvenbane

Norton, A. Elvenblood

Novik, N. His majesty's dragon

DRAGONS -- FICTION

Brennan, M. A natural history of dragons

Cross, J. Touched by venom

Harrison, T. Dragon bound

McCaffrey, T. Dragonsblood

Dragonsblood. McCaffrey, T.

Dragonsdawn. McCaffrey, A.

Dragonseye. McCaffrey, A.

Dragonwyck. Seton, A.

The **draining** lake. Arnaldur Indridason

DRAMA -- TECHNIQUE *See* Authorship

Drama city. Pelecanos, G. P.

DRAMATIC MUSIC *See* Musicals; Opera; Operetta

DRAMATISTS

    See also Authors; Drama

Adrian, C. The great night

Aira, C. The literary conference

Bear, E. Ink and steel

Cooley, M. The archivist

Craig, A. Love in idleness

D'Amato, B. Hard road

Fresan, R. Kensington Gardens

Greene, G. Monsignor Quixote

Gruber, M. The book of air and shadows

Haig, M. The dead fathers club

Hazzard, S. The transit of Venus

Holland, T. The archivist's story

Kalfus, K. The commissariat of enlightenment

Kellerman, F. The quality of mercy

Lessing, D. M. Love, again

Maguire, G. Son of a witch

Marsh, N. Light thickens

Martin, W. Harvard Yard

Murdoch, I. The sea, the sea

Nye, R. The late Mr. Shakespeare

O'Connor, J. Ghost light

Phillips, A. The tragedy of Arthur

Reyn, I. What happened to Anna K.

Self, W. Dorian

Simmons, D. Muse of fire

Stevenson, J. The shadow king

Updike, J. Gertrude and Claudius

DRAMATISTS -- FICTION

Barber, R. The Marlowe papers

DRAWING *See* Art; Graphic arts

Drawing conclusions. Leon, D.

DRAWN WORK *See* Embroidery; Needlework

The **dreadful** lemon sky. MacDonald, J. D.

Dreadnought. Priest, C.

Dream eyes. Krentz, J. A.

Dream house. Laken, V.

DREAM INTERPRETATION *See* Dreams

The **dream** life of Sukhanov. Grushin, O.

Dream new dreams. Pausch, J.

Dream of darkness. Hill, R.

Dream of Ding Village. Lianke, Y.

The **dream** of perpetual motion. Palmer, D. C.

The **dream** of Scipio. Pears, I.

The **dream** of the Celt.

The **dream** stalker. Coel, M.

Dreamcatcher. King, S.

Dreamcatcher. McCall, D.

Dreamer. Johnson, C. R.

Dreamers of the day. Russell, M. D.

The **dreaming.** Wood, B.

DREAMING *See* Dreams

Dreaming in Cuban. Garcia, C.

The **dreaming** void. Hamilton, P. F.

Dreaming water. Tsukiyama, G.

DREAMS

    See also Visions

Downing, D. C. Looking for the king

Hill, R. Dream of darkness

Le Guin, U. K. The lathe of heaven

O'Brien, T. Going after Cacciato

Ruiz, L. M. Only one thing missing

Sallis, J. The killer is dying

DREAMS -- FICTION

McCall, D. Dreamcatcher

Dreams and Shadows. Cargill, C. R.

Dreams of glory. Fleming, T. J.

Dreams of joy. See, L.

Dreams of my Russian summers. Makine, A.

Dreamsnake. McIntyre, V. N.

The **dreamthief's** daughter. Moorcock, M.

DRESDEN, HARRY (FICTITIOUS CHARACTER)

Butcher, J. Proven guilty

Dress her in indigo. MacDonald, J. D.

DRESSMAKERS

Aira, C. The seamstress and the wind

Chase, L. L. Silk is for seduction

Peebles, F. d. P. The seamstress

Wolff, I. A vintage affair

DRESSMAKING

    See also Clothing and dress; Clothing industry

Chase, L. Scandal wears satin

DRIED FOODS *See* Food

Dugoni, R. Murder one
Ellroy, J. Blood's a rover
Ellroy, J. The cold six thousand
Faulks, S. Devil may care
George, E. What came before he shot her
Grant, M. Officer down
Henry, A. Learning to fly
Huston, C. The shotgun rule
Johansen, I. The ugly duckling
Krist, G. Chaos theory
Le Carre, J. The night manager
Leonard, E. Rum punch
Leonard, E. Stick
Lessing, D. M. Ben, in the world
Ludlum, R. The Matlock paper
Marinick, R. Boyos
Martini, S. P. The attorney
Parker, B. Criminal justice
Pelecanos, G. P. The sweet forever
Pelecanos, G. The cut
Poyer, D. Down to a sunless sea
Price, R. Clockers
Robbins, T. Villa incognito
Seymour, G. Killing ground
Seymour, G. Rat run
Stewart, M. Airs above the ground
Stone, R. Dog soldiers
Thomas, M. M. Black money
Waite, U. The terror of living
Wilson, F. P. Deep as the marrow
Winslow, D. Savages
Woodrell, D. Winter's bone

DRUG TRAFFIC -- FICTION
Born to darkness
Coleman, A. Murder mamas
Coleman, J. The dopeman's wife
Diamond, D. Hustlin' divas
Land, J. Strong at the break
Lange, R. Angel baby
O'Donovan, G. Dublin dead
Palmer, D. Helpless
Robards, K. Shiver
Siegel, J. Detour
Winslow, D. The kings of cool

DRUG USE See Drug abuse; Drugs

DRUGS
Boyd, W. Ordinary thunderstorms
Byrne, T. Ghosts and lightning
Cohen, R. Inspired sleep
DeMarinis, R. Sky full of sand
Dierbeck, L. One pill makes you smaller
Ellis, B. E. Lunar Park
Gaitskill, M. Veronica
Hagedorn, J. T. Toxicology
Henderson, E. Ten thousand saints
Hiaasen, C. Star Island

Hogan, C. Devils in exile
Kunkel, B. Indecision
Land, B. Pilgrims upon the earth
Lazar, Z. Sway
Martin, C. W. How to sell
McGuane, T. Panama
Richards, D. A. The bay of love and sorrows
Robbins, T. Fierce invalids home from hot climates
Schwegel, T. Person of interest
Smith, C. Three delays
Spanidou, I. Before
Spiegelman, I. Everyone's burning
Tea, M. Rose of no man's land
Vollmann, W. T. The royal family
Walker, A. Now is the time to open your heart
Walsh, H. Brass
Wittenborn, D. Pharmakon

DRUGS -- ABUSE See Drug abuse

DRUGS -- FICTION
Burgess, A. A clockwork orange
Cohen, J. Four new messages

DRUGS -- MISUSE See Drug abuse

DRUGS AND CRIME See Crime; Drugs

DRUGSTORES See Retail trade; Stores

The **druid** of Shannara. Brooks, T.

Druids. Llywelyn, M.

DRUIDS AND DRUIDISM
    See also Celts; Religions
Llywelyn, M. Druids
Rose, M. J. Seduction

DRUM MAJORING See Bands (Music)

DRUMMERS
Sanchez, T. King Bongo

Drums along the Mohawk. Edmonds, W. D.

Drums of autumn. Gabaldon, D.

DRUNKENNESS
    See also Alcoholism; Temperance
Rosero, E. Good offices

Dry ice. White, S. W.

DRYDEN, PHILIP (FICTITIOUS CHARACTER)
Kelly, J. The fire baby
Kelly, J. The moon tunnel

DS Aector McAvoy [series]
Mark, D. Original skin

Du Maurier, Daphne Dame, 1907-1989
            About
Hill, S. Mrs. de Winter

DUAL PERSONALITY
Hesse, H. Steppenwolf
Martin, V. Mary Reilly
Stevenson, R. L. The strange case of Dr. Jekyll and Mr. Hyde

DUAL-CAREER FAMILIES See Family

Duane's depressed. McMurtry, L.

The **dubious** salvation of Jack V. Strauss, J.

E

E is for evidence. Grafton, S.

E.T. Kotzwinkle, W.

The **eagle** has flown. Higgins, J.

The **eagle** has landed. Higgins, J.

The **eagle's** throne. Fuentes, C.

EAGLES *See* Birds; Birds of prey

EARLY CHILDHOOD EDUCATION *See* Education

EARLY CHRISTIANS

Asch, S. The Apostle

Asch, S. The Nazarene

Lagerkvist, P. Barabbas

Sienkiewicz, H. Quo Vadis

Waltari, M. The Roman

Williams, N. John

Early graves. Hansen, J.

EARLY MEMORIES

Kiesbye, S. Your house is on fire, your children all gone

Early novels and stories. Cather, W.

Early novels and stories. Maxwell, W.

Early novels and stories. Baldwin, J.

EARLY PRINTED BOOKS *See* Books

Early short stories, 1883-1888.

Earnhardt, Dale, 1951-2001

About

McCrumb, S. St. Dale

Earp, Morgan, 1851-1882

About

West, P. O.K.

Earp, Wyatt, 1848-1929

About

Bull, E. Territory

Collins, M. A. Black hats

Parker, R. B. Gunman's rhapsody

Parry, R. The winter wolf

Russell, M. D. Doc

West, P. O.K.

Earth. Brin, D.

Earth abides. Stewart, G. R.

Earth Afire. Card, O. S.

EARTH SHELTERED HOUSES *See* House construction; Houses; Underground architecture

Earth unaware. Card, O. S.

Earth's children [series]

Auel, J. M. The Clan of the Cave Bear

Auel, J. M. The land of painted caves

EARTH, DESTRUCTION OF

Bear, G. Anvil of stars

Bear, G. The forge of God

Hoban, R. Riddley Walker

Niven, L. Lucifer's hammer

Earthfall. Card, O. S.

Earthly joys. Gregory, P.

Earthly possessions. Tyler, A.

Earthquake weather. Lankford, T.

EARTHQUAKES

Brooks, A. 2030

Gardiner, M. The Dirty Secrets Club

Rosenberg, R. This is not civilization

Steel, D. Amazing grace

EARTHQUAKES -- FICTION

Brooks, A. 2030

Walker, K. T. The age of miracles

Young, T. W. The renegades

EARTHWORKS (ART) *See* Art

EAST AFRICA

Hemingway, E. True at first light

EAST AND WEST

Clavell, J. Gai-Jin

Clavell, J. Noble house

Clavell, J. Shogun

Endo, S. Silence

Forster, E. M. A passage to India

Han, S. Till morning comes

Hersey, J. A single pebble

Mitchell, D. The thousand autumns of Jacob de Zoet

Rushdie, S. The ground beneath her feet

Scott, P. The day of the scorpion

Scott, P. The jewel in the crown

Tan, A. The Joy Luck Club

EAST AND WEST -- FICTION

Osborne, L. The forgiven

EAST EUROPEANS -- ENGLAND

Tremain, R. The road home

EAST INDIAN AMERICANS

Mehta, R. Quarantine

EAST INDIANS -- AFRICA

Naipaul, V. S. A bend in the river

Naipaul, V. S. Half a life

EAST INDIANS -- CANADA

Alam, S. The groom to have been

Vassanji, M. G. The assassin's song

EAST INDIANS -- ENGLAND

Kunzru, H. The impressionist

Kureishi, H. The Buddha of suburbia

Leavitt, D. The Indian clerk

Naipaul, V. S. Half a life

Naipaul, V. S. Magic seeds

Seton, A. Green darkness

EAST INDIANS -- FRANCE

Morais, R. C. The hundred-foot journey

EAST INDIANS -- GUYANA

Bhattacharya, R. The sly company of people who care

EAST INDIANS -- ITALY

Ondaatje, M. The English patient

EAST INDIANS -- MALAYSIA

Samarasan, P. Evening is the whole day

EAST INDIANS -- TRINIDAD AND TOBAGO

Rosenblatt, R. Lapham rising
Schaffert, T. The coffins of Little Hope
Smith, D. Pictures from an expedition
Smith, D. I capture the castle
Spark, M. A far cry from Kensington
Spark, M. Loitering with intent
Spiotta, D. Stone Arabia
Steinke, R. Holy skirts
Stuart, J. The tower, the zoo, and the tortoise
Theroux, P. Hotel Honolulu
Todos las almas/English All souls
Toole, J. K. A confederacy of dunces
Townsend, S. Number 10
Tyler, A. Back when we were grownups
Tyler, A. Morgan's passing
Unsworth, B. Losing Nelson
Vine, B. King Solomon's carpet
Wilcox, J. Heavenly days
Wilcox, J. Hunk City
Wilson, K. The family Fang
Wood, S. Wrecker

ECCENTRICS AND ECCENTRICITIES -- FIC-TION

Brewer, S. The poet of Tolstoy Park
Gallagher, S. The bedlam detective
Roberts, V. After the fall

ECCLESIASTICAL RITES AND CEREMONIES
See Rites and ceremonies

The **echo.** Walters, M.
Echo burning. Child, L.
An **echo** in the bone. Gabaldon, D.
The **echo** maker. Powers, R.
An **echo** of heaven. Oe, K.
Echo Park. Connelly, M.
Echoes from the dead. Theorin, J.
Echoes of the dead. Spencer, S.
Ecko Rising. Ware, D.
Eclipse. Wheeler, R. S.
Eclipse. Patterson, R. N.

ECOLOGICAL DISTURBANCES
Boyle, T. C. When the killing's done
Ghosh, A. The hungry tide

ECOLOGISTS
Gordimer, N. Get a life

ECOLOGY
Boyle, T. C. When the killing's done
Llywelyn, M. The elementals
Michener, J. A. Chesapeake
Robinson, K. S. Antarctica
Winterson, J. The stone gods

ECONOMIC CONDITIONS *See* Business; Eco-nomics; Social conditions; Wealth

ECONOMIC FORECASTING *See* Business cy-cles; Economics; Forecasting

ECOSYSTEMS *See* Ecology
ECOTERRORISM

See also Environmental movement; Terrorism
Evans, N. The divide
ECOTOURISM *See* Tourist trade
The **ecstatic.** LaValle, V. D.
ECUADOR
Paul, J. Elsewhere in the land of parrots
Ed King. Guterson, D.
The edda of burdens [series]
Bear, E. All the windwracked stars
EDDAS *See* Old Norse literature; Poetry; Scandi-navian literature
Eddie Signwriter. Schwartzman, A.
Eden. Lem, S.
Eden. Hedaya, Y.
Eden. Vernon, O.
Eden Close. Shreve, A.
Eden Springs. Kasischke, L.
EDGAR ALLAN POE AWARDS *See* Literary prizes; Mystery fiction
Edge of danger. Higgins, J.
Edge of dark water. Lansdale, J. R.
The **edge** of ruin. Fleming, I.
The **Edge** of the Earth. Schwarz, C.
EDIBLE PLANTS *See* Economic botany; Food; Plants
EDIFICES *See* Buildings
EDINBURGH (SCOTLAND)
McCall Smith, A. The forgotten affairs of youth
O'Neill, A. The lamplighter
Rankin, I. Black and blue
Rankin, I. The falls
Rankin, I. A question of blood
Rankin, I. Set in darkness
Stemple, A. Singer of souls
Welsh, I. Skagboys
Edison, Thomas A. (Thomas Alva), 1847-1931
About
Echenoz, J. Lightning
Edisto. Powell, P.
Edisto revisited. Powell, P.
EDITING *See* Authorship; Publishers and publish-ing
EDITORS
Akst, D. The Webster chronicle
Bushnell, C. Lipstick jungle
Castellanos Moya, H. Senselessness
Cleave, C. Little Bee
Cooley, M. The archivist
Dolan, H. Bad things happen
Dolan, H. Very bad men
Harris, R. Conspirata
Nunez, E. Anna in-between
Rosenfeld, L. I'm so happy for you
Walker, A. The way forward is with a broken heart
EDMONTOSAURUS *See* Dinosaurs
EDUCATION

Gaspar de Alba, A. Desert blood

EL SALVADOR

Castellanos Moya, H. Tyrant memory

Garcia, C. A handbook to luck

EL SALVADOR -- HISTORY

Castellanos Moya, H. Tyrant memory

Elantris. Sanderson, B.

ELDERLY -- DISEASES *See* Diseases

ELDERLY -- EDUCATION *See* Education

ELDERLY

Brewer, S. The poet of Tolstoy Park

ELDERLY MEN

Friedman, D. Don't ever get old

Jonasson, J. The 100-year-old man who climbed out the window and disappeared

Mosley, W. The last days of Ptolemy Grey

Savage, S. The way of the dog

Eleanor & Park. Rowell, R.

Eleanor Rigby. Coupland, D.

Eleanor, of Aquitaine, Queen, consort of Henry II, King of England, 1122?-1204

About

Franklin, A. The serpent's tale

Penman, S. K. Cruel as the grave

Penman, S. K. Devil's brood

Penman, S. K. Dragon's lair

Penman, S. K. The queen's man

Penman, S. K. Time and chance

Weir, A. Captive queen

Eleanor, of Provence, Queen, consort of Henry III, King of England

About

Jones, S. Four sisters, all queens

ELECTION *See* Elections

ELECTION (THEOLOGY) *See* Predestination

ELECTIONS

O'Connor, E. The last hurrah

Vidal, G. 1876

ELECTIONS -- FICTION

Lynch, J. Truth like the sun

Rowling, J. K. The casual vacancy

ELECTRIC AUTOMOBILES *See* Automobiles

ELECTRIC CIRCUITS *See* Electric lines; Electricity

ELECTRIC CURRENTS *See* Electricity

ELECTRIC POWER *See* Electricity; Energy resources; Power (Mechanics)

ELECTRIC POWER FAILURES

Stirling, S. M. Dies the fire

ELECTRIC RAILROADS *See* Railroads

ELECTRIC SIGNS *See* Advertising; Signs and signboards

ELECTRIC WAVES *See* Electricity; Waves

ELECTRICAL ENGINEERS

Echenoz, J. Lightning

Hunt, S. The invention of everything else

ELECTRICITY

See also Physics

Lawrence, S. The lightning keeper

ELECTRICITY IN AGRICULTURE *See* Agricultural engineering; Agricultural machinery; Electricity

ELECTRICITY IN MINING *See* Electrical engineering; Electricity

ELECTRONIC BOOKS *See* Books; Digital media

ELECTRONIC BUGGING *See* Eavesdropping

ELECTRONIC EAVESDROPPING *See* Eavesdropping

ELECTRONIC GAMES *See* Video games

ELECTRONIC LISTENING DEVICES *See* Eavesdropping

ELECTRONIC MAIL MESSAGES

Hamilton, J. Disobedience

ELECTRONIC MUSIC *See* Music

ELECTRONIC PUBLISHING *See* Information services; Publishers and publishing

ELECTRONIC SURVEILLANCE

Hurwitz, G. They're watching

Raban, J. Surveillance

ELECTRONIC SURVEILLANCE -- FICTION

Hallinan, T. The fear artist

ELECTRONICS *See* Engineering; Physics; Technology

The **elegance** of the hedgehog. Barbery, M.

ELEGIAC POETRY *See* Poetry

Elegies for the brokenhearted. Hodgen, C.

Elegy for April. Banville, J.

Elegy for Eddie. Winspear, J.

The **elementals.** Llywelyn, M.

The **elementals.** Block, F. L.

ELEMENTARY EDUCATION *See* Education

ELEMENTARY SCHOOL TEACHERS

Messud, C. The woman upstairs

The **elephant** keeper. Nicholson, C.

The **elephant** keepers' children. Høeg, P.

The **elephant's** journey.

The **Elephanta** suite. Theroux, P.

ELEPHANTS

The elephant's journey

Gruen, S. Water for elephants

Nicholson, C. The elephant keeper

ELEVATORS

Whitehead, C. The intuitionist

Eleven on top. Evanovich, J.

The **eleventh** man. Doig, I.

Elfland. Warrington, F.

Elgar, Edward, 1857-1934

About

Hamilton-Paterson, J. Gerontius

Eliot, George, 1819-1880

About

Weisgall, D. The world before her

Katzenbach, J. The madman's tale

The **emperor** of Ocean Park. Carter, S. L.

The **emperor's** children. Messud, C.

EMPERORS

> *See also* Kings and rulers

Levack, S. Demon of the air

Empire. Vidal, G.

Empire Falls. Russo, R.

The **empire** of ice cream. Ford, J.

Empire of lies. Klavan, A.

Empire of the Sun. Ballard, J. G.

Empire rising. Kelly, T.

Empire rising. Barone, S.

EMPIRE STATE BUILDING (NEW YORK, N.Y.)

Kelly, T. Empire rising

EMPLOYEES -- ACCIDENTS *See* Industrial accidents

EMPLOYEES AND OFFICIALS *See* Civil service

EMPLOYMENT OF CHILDREN *See* Child labor

Empress of the splendid season. Hijuelos, O.

The **Empress** of Weehawken. Dische, I.

Empress Orchid. Min, A.

EMPRESSES

Eastland, S. Eye of the Red Tsar

Graves, R. I, Claudius

Min, A. Empress Orchid

Min, A. The last empress

Penman, S. K. When Christ and his saints slept

Scholes, K. Requiem

The **empty** family. Toibin, C.

EMPTY NESTERS

Link, T. Denting the Bosch

EMTS (MEDICINE) *See* Emergency medical technicians

The **enchanted** wanderer and other stories. Leskov, N. S.

Enchantments. Harrison, K.

The **enchantress.** Han, S.

The **enchantress** of Florence. Rushdie, S.

Enclave. Reed, K.

ENCOURAGEMENT *See* Courage; Helping behavior

ENCYCLOPEDIAS *See* Encyclopedias and dictionaries

ENCYCLOPEDIAS AND DICTIONARIES

Levithan, D. The lover's dictionary

ENCYCLOPEDISTS

Bradbury, M. To the Hermitage

The **end** of all songs. Moorcock, M.

The **end** of California. Yarbrough, S.

End of days. Gleason, R.

The **end** of everything. Abbott, M. E.

The **end** of my career. Franklin, M.

The **end** of sleep. Somerville, R.

The **end** of the affair. Greene, G.

The **end** of the alphabet. Richardson, C. S.

The **end** of the battle. Waugh, E.

End of the chapter. Galsworthy, J.

End of the drive. L'Amour, L.

END OF THE EARTH *See* End of the world

The **end** of the Jews. Mansbach, A.

The **end** of the point. Graver, E.

The **end** of the wasp season. Mina, D.

END OF THE WORLD

Adrian, C. The children's hospital

Butler, O. E. Adulthood rites

Butler, O. E. Dawn

Butler, O. E. Imago

Currie, R. Everything matters!

Gaiman, N. Good omens

Glavinic, T. Night work

Gleason, R. End of days

Percy, W. Love in the ruins

Shute, N. On the beach

Updike, J. Toward the end of time

West, M. L. The clowns of God

Wilson, R. C. Spin

END OF THE WORLD (ASTRONOMY) *See* End of the world

END OF THE WORLD -- FICTION

Adrian, C. The children's hospital

Currie, R. Everything matters!

Harkaway, N. Angelmaker

Heller, P. The dog stars

McCarthy, C. The road

Updike, J. Toward the end of time

Whitehead, C. Zone one

END-OF-THE-WORLD FICTION *See* Apocalyptic fiction

ENDANGERED SPECIES

> *See also* Environmental protection; Nature conservation

Anderson, A. Darwin's wink

Millet, L. How the dead dream

ENDANGERED SPECIES -- CANADA

Moore, J. The extinction club

Ender Wiggin [series]

Card, O. S. Ender's shadow

Ender's game. Card, O. S.

Ender's Game [series]

Card, O. S. Children of the mind

Card, O. S. Xenocide

Ender's Saga [series]

Card, O. S. Speaker for the Dead

Ender's shadow. Card, O. S.

Endless love. Spencer, S.

Endless night. Christie, A.

ENDOCRINOLOGY *See* Medicine

ENDOWED CHARITIES *See* Charities; Endowments

ENDOWMENTS

Townsend, S. Adrian Mole: the lost years
Townsend, S. Number 10
Tremain, R. Sacred country
Trevor, W. Felicia's journey
Trollope, J. The best of friends
Trollope, J. The choir
Trollope, J. Other people's children
Trollope, J. A Spanish lover
Uris, L. QB VII
Vine, B. The brimstone wedding
Walters, M. The sculptress
Walton, J. Ha'penny
Waugh, E. Brideshead revisited
Waugh, E. Decline and fall
Weldon, F. Chalcot Crescent
Weldon, F. Worst fears
Wells, H. G. Tono-Bungay
Wesley, M. Part of the furniture
Williams, C. Stairway to hell
Winterson, J. Oranges are not the only fruit
Wodehouse, P. G. The code of the Woosters
Wodehouse, P. G. The inimitable Jeeves
Wodehouse, P. G. Tales from the Drones Club
Woolf, V. Jacob's room
Woolf, V. Orlando
Woolf, V. The years
Yorke, M. Almost the truth
Yorke, M. A question of belief

ENGLAND -- 11TH CENTURY
Rathbone, J. The last English king

ENGLAND -- 12TH CENTURY
Follett, K. Pillars of the earth
Franklin, A. Mistress of the art of death
Franklin, A. The serpent's tale
Penman, S. K. Devil's brood
Penman, S. K. Lionheart
Penman, S. K. Time and chance
Penman, S. K. When Christ and his saints slept
Rice, A. Angel time
Scott, W. Ivanhoe
Weir, A. Captive queen

ENGLAND -- 13TH CENTURY
Penman, S. K. Falls the shadow
Penman, S. K. Here be dragons
Penman, S. K. The reckoning
White, T. H. The once and future king
White, T. H. The sword in the stone

ENGLAND -- 14TH CENTURY
Cornwell, B. Vagabond
Follett, K. World without end
Riley, J. M. In pursuit of the green lion
Riley, J. M. A vision of light
Seton, A. Katherine
Unsworth, B. Morality play

ENGLAND -- 15TH CENTURY
Bennett, V. The queen's lover

Penman, S. K. The sunne in splendour

ENGLAND -- 16TH CENTURY
Baker, K. In the garden of Iden
Bayard, L. The school of night
Bear, E. Ink and steel
Finney, P. Gloriana's torch
Fraser, G. M. The reavers
George, M. Elizabeth I
Gregory, P. The other Boleyn girl
Gregory, P. The Boleyn Inheritance
Gregory, P. The queen's fool
Gregory, P. The wise woman
Holt, V. My enemy the Queen
L'Amour, L. To the far blue mountains
Mantel, H. Wolf Hall
Maxwell, R. The Queen's bastard
Maxwell, R. The secret diary of Anne Boleyn
Maxwell, R. The wild Irish
Nye, R. The late Mr. Shakespeare
Plaidy, J. The captive Queen of Scots
Plaidy, J. Murder most royal
Riley, J. M. The serpent garden
Seton, A. Green darkness
Weir, A. Innocent traitor
Weir, A. The Lady Elizabeth

ENGLAND -- 17TH CENTURY
Barth, J. The sot-weed factor
Blackmore, R. D. Lorna Doone
Brooks, G. Year of wonders
Chevalier, T. Burning bright
Defoe, D. Moll Flanders
Du Maurier, D. Frenchman's Creek
Dumas, A. Twenty years after
Gregory, P. Earthly joys
Gregory, P. Virgin earth
Koen, K. Dark angels
Morrow, J. The last witchfinder
Nye, R. The late Mr. Shakespeare
Pears, I. An instance of the fingerpost
Plaidy, J. The pleasures of love
Plaidy, J. William's wife

ENGLAND -- 18TH CENTURY
Bronte, C. Emma
Chase, L. L. Lord of scoundrels
Fielding, H. The history of Tom Jones, a foundling
Fielding, H. Joseph Andrews and Shamela
Koen, K. Through a glass darkly
Nicholson, C. The elephant keeper
Richardson, S. Pamela
Robertson, I. Instruments of darkness
Smollett, T. G. The expedition of Humphry Clinker
Thackeray, W. M. The Virginians

ENGLAND -- 19TH CENTURY
Austen, J. Emma
Austen, J. Mansfield Park
Austen, J. Northanger Abbey

ENGLAND -- 20TH CENTURY

Lively, P. Passing on
Lodge, D. Nice work
Lodge, D. Therapy
Lodge, D. Thinks--
McEwan, I. Enduring love
McGowan, H. Schooling
McGrath, P. Asylum
McGrath, P. The grotesque
Miller, A. Oxygen
Mortimer, J. Paradise postponed
Mortimer, J. The sound of trumpets
Mortimer, J. Titmuss regained
Murdoch, I. The book and the brotherhood
Murdoch, I. Jackson's dilemma
Nicholls, D. A question of attraction
Perry, A. No graves as yet
Powell, A. A dance to the music of time
Rendell, R. The crocodile bird
Self, W. Dorian
Sillitoe, A. The loneliness of the long-distance run-
ner
Sillitoe, A. Saturday night and Sunday morning
Smith, S. Novel on yellow paper
Snow, C. P. Corridors of power
Snow, C. P. Last things
Snow, C. P. The new men
Snow, C. P. Time of hope
Spark, M. Memento mori
Swift, G. Waterland
Swift, G. Last orders
Townsend, S. Adrian Mole
Townsend, S. The Adrian Mole diaries
Townsend, S. Adrian Mole: the lost years
Trevor, W. Felicia's journey
Trollope, J. The best of friends
Trollope, J. The choir
Trollope, J. Other people's children
Trollope, J. A Spanish lover
Uris, L. QB VII
Waugh, E. Brideshead revisited
Weldon, F. Worst fears
Wells, H. G. Tono-Bungay
Wesley, M. Part of the furniture
Woolf, V. The years
Yorke, M. A question of belief

ENGLAND -- 20TH CENTURY -- FICTION
Speller, E. The strange fate of Kitty Easton

**ENGLAND -- ANGLO-SAXON PERIOD, 449-
1066**
Berger, T. Arthur Rex
Bradley, M. Z. The mists of Avalon
Cornwell, B. Burning land
Cornwell, B. Enemy of God
Cornwell, B. Excalibur
Cornwell, B. The winter king
Rathbone, J. The last English king

Seton, A. Avalon
Stewart, M. The crystal cave
Stewart, M. The hollow hills
Stewart, M. The last enchantment
Stewart, M. Mary Stewart's Merlin trilogy
Stewart, M. The wicked day
Sutcliff, R. Sword at sunset
Twain, M. A Connecticut Yankee in King Arthur's
court

ENGLAND -- BATH
Balogh, M. Simply love
Balogh, M. Simply magic

ENGLAND -- BIRMINGHAM
Coe, J. The closed circle
Coe, J. The Rotters' Club
O'Flynn, C. The news where you are

ENGLAND -- BRIGHTON
Greene, G. Brighton rock

ENGLAND -- BRISTOL
Archer, J. Only time will tell

ENGLAND -- CAMBRIDGE
Franklin, A. Mistress of the art of death
Harris, R. Enigma
Harvey, J. Far cry
Harvey, J. Gone to ground
Stott, R. Ghostwalk

ENGLAND -- CHESHIRE
Gaskell, E. C. Cranford
Murphy, M. Darkness falls

ENGLAND -- CORNWALL
Cartwright, J. The promise of happiness
Du Maurier, D. Frenchman's Creek
Du Maurier, D. Jamaica Inn
Du Maurier, D. Rebecca
Goddard, R. Beyond recall
Graham, W. Bella Poldark
Heyer, G. Penhallow
Hill, S. Mrs. de Winter
Holt, V. Bride of Pendorric
Holt, V. Mistress of Mellyn
Howatch, S. Penmarric
Pilcher, R. Coming home
Pilcher, R. Voices in summer
Ross-Macdonald, M. Tamsin Harte
Ross-Macdonald, M. The Trevarton inheritance
Shannon, D. The Manson curse
Stubbs, J. Family games
Trollope, J. Legacy of love

ENGLAND -- COVENTRY
Humphreys, H. Coventry

ENGLAND -- CUMBRIA
Hill, R. The woodcutter

ENGLAND -- DERBYSHIRE
Brooks, G. Year of wonders
Lawrence, D. H. Lady Chatterley's lover

ENGLAND -- DEVON

Yorke, M. The price of guilt

ENGLAND -- HAMPSHIRE

Drabble, M. The witch of Exmoor

ENGLAND -- HISTORY See Great Britain -- History

ENGLAND -- KENT

Barker, N. Darkmans

Dickens, C. The mystery of Edwin Drood

ENGLAND -- KINGS AND RULERS

Gregory, P. The other Boleyn girl

Gregory, P. The Boleyn Inheritance

Gregory, P. The queen's fool

ENGLAND -- LANCASHIRE

De Hartog, J. The peaceable kingdom

Sharratt, M. Daughters of the Witching Hill

Smith, M. C. Rose

ENGLAND -- LIVERPOOL

Walsh, H. Brass

ENGLAND -- LONDON

Ali, M. Brick lane

Ali, M. In the kitchen

Amis, K. The Russian girl

Amis, M. London fields

Ballard, J. G. Millennium people

Balogh, M. Seducing an angel

Barnard, R. A murder in Mayfair

Barnard, R. Out of the blackout

Barnes, J. The somnambulist

Beckett, S. Murphy

Birch, C. Jamrach's menagerie

Blake, S. The postmistress

Bolton, S. J. Now you see me

Bowen, E. The heat of the day

Boyd, W. Ordinary thunderstorms

Bradford, B. T. The Ravenscar dynasty

Brennan, M. With fate conspire

Brookner, A. Family and friends

Brookner, A. Undue influence

Byatt, A. S. Possession

Cary, J. The horse's mouth

Chase, L. L. Silk is for seduction

Chevalier, T. Burning bright

Coe, J. The closed circle

Coe, J. The rain before it falls

Cox, M. The meaning of night

Cronin, A. J. The citadel

Dark, A. E. Think of England

De Bernieres, L. A partisan's daughter

Docx, E. The calligrapher

Donoghue, E. The sealed letter

Eberstadt, F. Rat

Faulks, S. Engleby

Faulks, S. A week in December

Fielding, H. Bridget Jones: the edge of reason

Fielding, H. Bridget Jones's diary

Fonseca, I. Attachment

Foulds, A. The quickening maze

Frayn, M. Spies

French, N. Beneath the skin

French, N. Land of the living

Fresan, R. Kensington Gardens

Fyfield, F. Blind date

Galsworthy, J. End of the chapter

Galsworthy, J. A modern comedy

Gardam, J. The queen of the tambourine

George, E. What came before he shot her

Gibb, C. Sweetness in the belly

Gibson, W. Pattern recognition

Gibson, W. Zero history

Grant, L. We had it so good

Greene, G. The end of the affair

Greene, G. The human factor

Greene, G. The ministry of fear

Guo Xiaolu A concise Chinese-English dictionary for lovers

Hadley, T. The London train

Hambly, B. Those who hunt the night

Hand, E. Mortal love

Hardwick, M. The Duchess of Duke Street

Hart, J. The reconstructionist

Hilton, J. Random harvest

Hoban, R. Her name was Lola

Hoeg, P. The woman and the ape

Hoffman, A. The third angel

Hornby, N. About a boy

Hornby, N. High fidelity

Hornby, N. How to be good

Hornby, N. A long way down

Howatch, S. The heartbreaker

Howatch, S. The high flyer

Hunt, R. Mr. Chartwell

Huxley, A. Point counter point

Kavenna, J. Inglorious

Kelly, E. The poison tree

Keyes, M. Last Chance Saloon

Korda, M. Curtain

Kureishi, H. The Buddha of suburbia

Kureishi, H. Something to tell you

Laird, N. Utterly monkey

Le Carre, J. The looking glass war

Leavitt, D. While England sleeps

Lebrecht, N. The song of names

Leebron, F. G. In the middle of all this

Lessing, D. M. Ben, in the world

Lessing, D. M. The good terrorist

Lessing, D. M. Love, again

Lessing, D. M. The sweetest dream

Levy, A. Fruit of the lemon

Levy, A. Small island

Lively, P. Consequences

Livesey, M. Banishing Verona

Livesey, M. The house on Fortune Street

Hill, T. The love of stones
Jakeman, J. In the Kingdom of mists
James, H. The golden bowl
Martin, V. Mary Reilly
Moorcock, M. An alien heat
Moorcock, M. The hollow lands
Palliser, C. The quincunx
Quick, A. Slightly shady
Quick, A. Wicked widow
Simmons, D. Drood
Smith, Z. White teeth
Stevenson, R. L. The strange case of Dr. Jekyll and
  Mr. Hyde
Wilde, O. The picture of Dorian Gray

ENGLAND -- LONDON -- 20TH CENTURY
Ali, M. Brick lane
Amis, K. The Russian girl
Amis, M. London fields
Barnard, R. A murder in Mayfair
Barnard, R. Out of the blackout
Beckett, S. Murphy
Bowen, E. The heat of the day
Brookner, A. Family and friends
Brookner, A. Undue influence
Byatt, A. S. Possession
Cary, J. The horse's mouth
Cronin, A. J. The citadel
Fielding, H. Bridget Jones: the edge of reason
Fielding, H. Bridget Jones's diary
Frayn, M. Spies
Fyfield, F. Blind date
Galsworthy, J. End of the chapter
Galsworthy, J. A modern comedy
Greene, G. The end of the affair
Greene, G. The human factor
Hambly, B. Those who hunt the night
Hardwick, M. The Duchess of Duke Street
Hoeg, P. The woman and the ape
Hornby, N. About a boy
Hornby, N. How to be good
Howatch, S. The high flyer
Huxley, A. Point counter point
Korda, M. Curtain
Leebron, F. G. In the middle of all this
Lessing, D. M. Ben, in the world
Lessing, D. M. The good terrorist
Lessing, D. M. Love, again
Lessing, D. M. The sweetest dream
Livesey, M. The missing world
Lovesey, P. On the edge
Maugham, W. S. Of human bondage
McEwan, I. Amsterdam
McGrath, P. Spider
Moorcock, M. The end of all songs
Murdoch, I. An accidental man
Murdoch, I. A fairly honourable defeat

Murdoch, I. The green knight
Murdoch, I. The nice and the good
Murdoch, I. Nuns and soldiers
Naipaul, V. S. Half a life
O'Brien, E. Time and tide
Pym, B. An unsuitable attachment
Pynchon, T. Gravity's rainbow
Read, P. P. A season in the West
Rendell, R. Adam and Eve and Pinch me
Rendell, R. The bridesmaid
Rendell, R. Going wrong
Rendell, R. The keys to the street
Rendell, R. The tree of hands
Snow, C. P. The conscience of the rich
Snow, C. P. Homecoming
Spark, M. Aiding and abetting
Spark, M. The ballad of Peckham Rye
Spark, M. A far cry from Kensington
Spark, M. The girls of slender means
Taylor, E. Mrs. Palfrey at the Claremont
Vine, B. Anna's book
Vine, B. The house of stairs
Waugh, E. Vile bodies
Weldon, F. Big girls don't cry
Weldon, F. Rhode Island blues
Woolf, V. Mrs. Dalloway

ENGLAND -- LONDON -- 21ST CENTURY
Docx, E. The calligrapher
Gibson, W. Pattern recognition
Steel, D. The kiss

ENGLAND -- LONDON -- PLAGUE, 1665
Defoe, D. A journal of the plague year

ENGLAND -- MANCHESTER
Noon, J. Vurt

ENGLAND -- MIDLANDS
Pietroni, A. L. Ruby's spoon

ENGLAND -- NORFOLK
Smith, A. The accidental

ENGLAND -- NORTHUMBERLAND
Stewart, M. The ivy tree

ENGLAND -- NOTTINGHAM
Johnson, B. S. The unfortunates
Monaghan, N. The killing jar
Sillitoe, A. Saturday night and Sunday morning

ENGLAND -- NOTTINGHAMSHIRE
Haig, M. The dead fathers club
Lawrence, D. H. The rainbow
Lawrence, D. H. Women in love

ENGLAND -- OXFORD
Benjamin, M. Alice I have been
Herron, M. Reconstruction
Marias, J. Dark back of time
Todos las almas/English All souls
Trollope, J. The men and the girls
Willis, C. Doomsday book

ENGLAND -- OXFORDSHIRE

ENGLAND -- SURREY
Forster, E. M. A room with a view
ENGLAND -- SUSSEX
Nicholson, W. The secret intensity of everyday life
Robertson, I. Instruments of darkness
Symons, J. Something like a love affair
White, E. Hotel de Dream
ENGLAND -- TO 55 B.C.
Cornwell, B. Stonehenge, 2000 B.C.
Holland, C. Pillar of the Sky
ENGLAND -- WARWICKSHIRE
Eliot, G. Middlemarch
Eliot, G. Silas Marner
Waters, S. The little stranger
ENGLAND -- WILTSHIRE
Dickens, C. Martin Chuzzlewit
ENGLAND -- WORCESTERSHIRE
Mitchell, D. Black swan green
Pearce, M. E. Cast a long shadow
ENGLAND -- YORKSHIRE
Bronte, A. The tenant of Wildfell Hall
Bronte, C. Jane Eyre
Bronte, E. Wuthering Heights
ENGLAND, CHURCH OF See Church of England
ENGLAND, SOUTHERN
Lelic, S. The child who
Engleby. Faulks, S.
ENGLISH -- FRANCE
Todd, C. An unmarked grave
ENGLISH -- INDIA -- NĀGPUR
Festing, I. A. The birdkeeper
ENGLISH -- MOROCCO
Osborne, L. The forgiven
ENGLISH -- SIERRA LEONE
Forna, A. The memory of love
ENGLISH AUTHORS See Authors
English Creek. Doig, I.
ENGLISH FICTION
Trial and error
ENGLISH HISTORY See Great Britain -- History
ENGLISH LANGUAGE See Language and languages
ENGLISH LANGUAGE -- DICTIONARIES See Encyclopedias and dictionaries
ENGLISH LANGUAGE -- DICTIONARIES -- FRENCH See Encyclopedias and dictionaries
The **English** major. Harrison, J.
ENGLISH NOVELISTS
See also Novelists
McEwan, I. Sweet tooth
English passengers. Kneale, M.
The **English** patient. Ondaatje, M.
ENGLISH PERIODICALS See Periodicals
ENGLISH POETRY See English literature; Poetry
ENGLISH POETS See Poets
ENGLISH SATIRE See English literature; Satire

ENGLISH WIT AND HUMOR See English literature; Wit and humor
English, August. Chatterjee, U.
ENGRAVERS
See also Artists
Chevalier, T. Burning bright
ENGRAVING See Art; Graphic arts; Illustration of books; Pictures
Enigma. Harris, R.
Enlightenment. Freely, M.
ENSEMBLES (MUSIC) See Music; Musical form; Musicians
ENTERTAINERS
Ackroyd, P. The trial of Elizabeth Cree
Benjamin, M. The autobiography of Mrs. Tom Thumb
Delaney, F. Venetia Kelly's traveling show
Gruen, S. Water for elephants
McMurtry, L. Buffalo girls
Nicholls, D. One day
Pelevin, V. The hall of singing caryatids
Phillips, C. Dancing in the dark
Roth, P. I married a communist
Singer, I. B. The magician of Lublin
Turner, F. W. 1929
Tyler, A. A slipping-down life
ENTERTAINERS -- FICTION
Stace, W. By George
The **entitled.** Deford, F.
Entombed. Fairstein, L.
ENTOMOLOGISTS
Abe, K. The woman in the dunes
Kingsolver, B. Prodigal summer
Saul, J. The homing
ENTOZOA See Parasites
ENTREPRENEURSHIP See Business; Capitalism; Small business
ENVIRONMENTAL ETHICS
See also Ethics
ENVIRONMENTAL POLLUTION See Pollution
ENVIRONMENTAL PROTECTION
See also Ecology; Environment
Carr, R. The Wanderer
Windle, J. Congo dawn
ENVIRONMENTALISTS
Bernhardt, W. Dark justice
Cussler, C. White death
Friedman, M. Martian Dawn
Glass, J. The widower's tale
Gruber, M. Night of the jaguar
Hiaasen, C. Native tongue
Hiaasen, C. Sick puppy
Pancake, A. Strange as this weather has been
Parks, T. Rapids
Rash, R. Saints at the river
Rash, R. Serena

Oates, J. C. Wild nights!

Pearl, M. The Dante Club

Pearl, M. The Poe shadow

Pipkin, J. Woodsburner

Powers, K. Capote in Kansas

Rose, J. Blackest bird

Tournier, M. Friday

Truong, M. T. D. The book of salt

Vargas Llosa, M. The way to paradise

Verissimo, L. F. Borges and the eternal orangutans

Walker, A. The way forward is with a broken heart

Weisgall, D. The world before her

West, P. Sporting with Amaryllis

Winegardner, M. The Godfather returns

ESSENES See Jews

The **estate.** Singer, I. B.

ESTRANGEMENT (SOCIAL PSYCHOLOGY)
See Alienation (Social psychology)

ETCHERS See Artists; Engravers

ETCHING See Art; Pictures

ETERNAL LIFE See Eternity; Future life; Immortality

ETERNAL PUNISHMENT See Hell

Eternal sky [series]
Bear, E. Shattered pillars

Ethan Frome. Wharton, E.

Ethelred II, King of England, 968?-1016
About
Bracewell, P. Shadow on the crown

Ether. Ehrenreich, B.

The **ethical** assassin. Liss, D.

ETHICS
Barbash, T. The last good chance

Canin, E. America America

Caputo, P. Horn of Africa

Clark, M. The legal limit

Dexter, P. The paperboy

Ducker, B. Dizzying heights

Haig, M. The Labrador Pact

Horn, D. All other nights

Reed, B. The choice

Reuland, R. Semiautomatic

Shreve, A. Strange fits of passion

Snow, C. P. The new men

Steinbeck, J. The winter of our discontent

ETHICS -- FICTION
Clark, M. The legal limit

Franzen, J. Freedom

Mosley, W. Always outnumbered, always outgunned

ETHIOPIA
Gibb, C. Sweetness in the belly

Keneally, T. To Asmara

Verghese, A. Cutting for stone

ETHIOPIANS -- UNITED STATES
Mengestu, D. The beautiful things that heaven bears

Mengestu, D. How to read the air

ETHNIC ART See Art; Ethnic groups

ETHNIC RELATIONS
See also Acculturation; Ethnology; Sociology
Desai, K. The inheritance of loss

Gordimer, N. The pickup

Smith, Z. White teeth

ETHNICITY See Identity (Psychology)

ETHNOCENTRISM See Ethnopsychology; Nationalism; Prejudices; Race

ETHNOLOGY See Human beings

ETIQUETTE -- ENGLAND -- LONDON -- HISTORY -- 19TH CENTURY
Carriger, G. Soulless

ETIQUETTE
Jones, S. The uninvited guests

ETRUSCAN ART See Art

Eucalyptus. Bail, M.

EUGENICS See Genetics; Population

EUNUCHS
Amirrezvani, A. Equal of the sun

King, R. Domino

Smith, W. A. River god

EURO See Capital market; Money

EUROPE
Archer, J. A matter of honor

Greene, G. Orient Express

Ishiguro, K. The unconsoled

Pynchon, T. Gravity's rainbow

Sartre, J. P. The reprieve

Tournier, M. The ogre

West, R. The birds fall down

EUROPE -- 11TH CENTURY
Holland, C. The firedrake

EUROPE -- 12TH CENTURY
Eco, U. Baudolino

L'Amour, L. The walking drum

EUROPE -- 15TH CENTURY
Dunnett, D. Caprice and Rondo

Dunnett, D. Niccolo rising

Dunnett, D. Race of scorpions

Dunnett, D. Scales of gold

Dunnett, D. The spring of the ram

Dunnett, D. To lie with lions

Dunnett, D. The unicorn hunt

EUROPE -- 16TH CENTURY
Dunnett, D. Checkmate

Halter, M. Messiah

EUROPE -- 17TH CENTURY
Maalouf, A. Balthasar's odyssey

EUROPE -- 19TH CENTURY
Cornwell, B. Sharpe's battle

Eco, U. The Prague cemetery

James, H. The portrait of a lady

EVOLUTION

Baxter, S. Evolution

McDonald, R. Mr. Darwin's shooter

Stott, R. The coral thief

Vonnegut, K. Galapagos

The **evolution** of Bruno Littlemore. Hale, B.

EX-CONCENTRATION CAMP INMATES

Edugyan, E. Half-blood blues

EX-CONVICTS

Banks, R. Lost memory of skin

Burgess, M. Dogfight, a love story

Carlson, R. The signal

Cartwright, J. The promise of happiness

Clark, M. H. Daddy's little girl

Clarke, B. An arsonist's guide to writers' homes in New England

Coben, H. The innocent

Connelly, J. Crumbtown

Connelly, M. Void moon

Crais, R. The two minute rule

Durham, M. The man who loved Cat Dancing

Harrison, C. Afterburn

Hart, B. Then came the evening

Heinlein, R. A. The moon is a harsh mistress

Hellenga, R. Snakewoman of Little Egypt

Hill, R. The woodcutter

Huneven, M. Blame

James, P. D. Innocent blood

Jones, S. Outcast

Joss, M. Among the missing

Klein, M. Con ed

Le Carre, J. The tailor of Panama

Lehane, D. Mystic river

Leonard, E. Glitz

Leonard, E. Pagan babies

Leonard, E. Road dogs

Leonard, E. Rum punch

Leonard, E. Stick

Margolin, P. Fugitive

McEwan, I. Atonement

Mortimer, J. Quite honestly

Oates, J. C. Missing mom

Pekearo, N. T. The wolfman

Pelecanos, G. P. Drama city

Pickard, N. The scent of rain and lightning

Richards, D. A. The bay of love and sorrows

Sakey, M. The blade itself

Schlink, B. The weekend

Schwartz, J. B. Northwest corner

Skarmeta, A. The dancer and the thief

Smith, B. All hat

Spencer, L. Morning glory

Stroby, W. Cold shot to the heart

Stross, C. Rule 34

Terrell, W. The huntsman

Van Rooy, M. An ordinary decent criminal

Van Rooy, M. Your friendly neighborhood criminal

Waite, U. The terror of living

Wolfe, G. The sorcerer's house

Zeltserman, D. Small crimes

EX-CONVICTS -- FICTION

Carnoy, D. The big exit

Higgins, G. V. The Digger's game

Somerville, P. This bright river

EX-NAZIS

Picoult, J. The Storyteller

EX-NUNS

See also Nuns

Leonard, E. Bandits

Murdoch, I. Nuns and soldiers

EX-POLICE OFFICERS

Bennett, R. J. American elsewhere

Child, L. A wanted man

Dee, E. The con man's daughter

Friedman, D. Don't ever get old

Hoag, T. Dark horse

King, S. Black house

Lamanda, A. Sunset

Lansdale, J. R. A fine dark line

Pattison, E. The lord of death

EX-PRIESTS

See also Catholic Church -- Clergy; Priests

Hailey, A. Detective

Lodge, D. Paradise news

EX-PRIESTS -- FICTION

Criswell, M. What to do about Annie?

Wells, M. Wheel of the infinite

Excalibur. Cornwell, B.

EXCAVATIONS (ARCHAEOLOGY)

See also Archeology

Kelly, J. The moon tunnel

Khemir, S. The blue manuscript

Unsworth, B. Land of marvels

Excellent women. Pym, B.

Except for the bones. Wilcox, C.

EXCEPTIONAL CHILDREN *See* Children; Elementary education

EXCHANGE OF PRISONERS OF WAR *See* Prisoners of war

The **execution.** Wilcken, H.

The **executioner's** song. Mailer, N.

EXECUTIONS AND EXECUTIONERS

See also Criminal law; Criminal procedure

Doctorow, E. L. The book of Daniel

Estleman, L. D. The master executioner

French, A. Billy

Mailer, N. The executioner's song

Wiesel, E. Dawn

EXECUTIONS AND EXECUTIONERS -- FICTION

Deutermann, P. T. The cat dancers

Estleman, L. D. The master executioner

Gaddis, W. A frolic of his own
Gaddis, W. The recognitions
Garcia Marquez, G. The autumn of the patriarch
Grass, G. My century
Gray, A. Old men in love
Gray, A. Poor things
Handke, P. The left-handed woman
Hoban, R. Her name was Lola
Howard, M. Natural history
Howard, M. The rags of time
Hunt, L. The exquisite
Johnson, B. S. The unfortunates
Joyce, J. Finnegans wake
Joyce, J. Ulysses
Kesey, K. Sailor song
Kingsolver, B. The lacuna
Lashner, W. Kockroach
Levithan, D. The lover's dictionary
Marias, J. Voyage along the horizon
Markson, D. The last novel
Markson, D. Vanishing point
Markson, D. Wittgenstein's mistress
McGregor, J. Even the dogs
Mitchell, D. Cloud atlas
Naipaul, V. S. A way in the world
Oe, K. The pinch runner memorandum
Oz, A. The same sea
Perec, G. Life
Perec, G. A void
Perez-Reverte, A. The Club Dumas
Pessl, M. Special topics in calamity physics
Pletzinger, T. Funeral for a dog
Powell, P. The interrogative mood
Powers, R. The gold bug variations
Pynchon, T. Against the day
Pynchon, T. Gravity's rainbow
Ramirez Mercado, S. A thousand deaths plus one
Saramago, J. The history of the siege of Lisbon
Shapton, L. Important artifacts and personal property from the collection of Lenore Doolan and Harold Morris, including books, street fashion, and jewelry
Silko, L. Gardens in the dunes
Sorrentino, G. The abyss of human illusion
Sorrentino, G. A strange commonplace
Syjuco, M. Ilustrado
Tillman, L. American genius
TSypkin, L. Summer in Baden-Baden
Unferth, D. O. Vacation
Vila-Matas, E. Montano's malady
Vollmann, W. T. The ice-shirt
Walker, A. The temple of my familiar
Wallace, D. F. Infinite jest
Wideman, J. E. The cattle killing
Wideman, J. E. Philadelphia fire
EXPERT SYSTEMS (COMPUTER SCIENCE)
See Artificial intelligence; Data processing; Information systems
Expiration date. Swierczynski, D.
EXPLORERS
Bainbridge, B. The birthday boys
Dorris, M. The crown of Columbus
Falconer, C. Feathered serpent
Flanagan, R. Wanting
Forester, C. S. To the Indies
Gilman, C. P. Herland
Gilman, C. P. With her in Ourland
Hall, B. I should be extremely happy in your company
Hensher, P. The Mulberry empire
Johnston, W. The navigator of New York
Maalouf, A. Leo Africanus
McDonald, R. Mr. Darwin's shooter
Naipaul, V. S. A way in the world
Nordhoff, C. Men against the sea
Nordhoff, C. Mutiny on the Bounty
Russell, M. D. Dreamers of the day
Sargent, C. Museum of human beings
Sherwood, F. Night of sorrows
Simmons, D. The terror
Vollmann, W. T. Argall
Vollmann, W. T. The rifles
Wheeler, R. S. Eclipse
EXPLOSIONS *See* Accidents
EXPO 92 (SEVILLE, SPAIN) *See* Exhibitions; Fairs
EXPOSED CHILDREN *See* Abandoned children
EXPRESS SERVICE *See* Railroads; Transportation
EXPRESSIONISM (ART) *See* Art
The **exquisite.** Hunt, L.
EXTINCT ANIMALS *See* Animals
EXTINCT CITIES
See also Archeology; Cities and towns
Whitney, P. A. Domino
Extinction. Alpert, M.
The **extinction** club. Moore, J.
EXTORTION
Dickens, C. Our mutual friend
Godey, J. The taking of Pelham one two three
Gruber, M. The forgery of Venus
Leonard, E. Freaky Deaky
Leonard, E. LaBrava
Lindsey, D. L. The rules of silence
Siegel, J. Derailed
Trevanian The Loo sanction
Weber, K. The Music Lesson
EXTORTION -- FICTION
Clark, W. Thug lovin'
Greaves, C. Hush money
The **extraordinary** journeys: Twenty thousand leagues under the sea. Verne, J.

Allen, S. A. The sugar queen
Bernheimer, K. Horse, flower, bird
Goodman, C. Arcadia Falls
Hesse, H. The fairy tales of Hermann Hesse
Joyce, G. Some kind of fairy tale
Maguire, G. Confessions of an ugly stepsister
Maguire, G. Mirror mirror
The Oxford book of modern fairy tales
Pullman, P. Fairy tales from the Brothers Grimm
Saint-Exupery, A. d. The little prince

FAIRY TALES -- ADAPTATIONS
Coover, R. Briar Rose
Ivey, E. The snow child
Lee, T. White as snow
Maguire, G. Confessions of an ugly stepsister
Maguire, G. Mirror mirror

FAIRY TALES -- GERMANY
Pullman, P. Fairy tales from the Brothers Grimm
Fairy tales from the Brothers Grimm. Pullman, P.
The **fairy** tales of Hermann Hesse. Hesse, H.
Faith. Haigh, J.

FAITH
> *See also* Religion; Salvation; Spiritual life;
> Theology; Virtue
Ansay, A. M. River angel
Cooley, M. The archivist
Cutter, K. The maid
Davies, R. The cunning man
Ehrenreich, B. Ether
Endo, S. Deep river
Godwin, G. Evensong
Grisham, J. The testament
Guterson, D. Our Lady of the Forest
Hansen, R. Mariette in ecstasy
Hoffman, A. The third angel
Howatch, S. Absolute truths
Howatch, S. Glamorous powers
Howatch, S. Mystical paths
Howatch, S. Scandalous risks
Howatch, S. Ultimate prizes
Howatch, S. The wonder-worker
L'Engle, M. Certain women
Maine, D. The preservationist
Marcantel, P. An army of angels
McDonald, R. Mr. Darwin's shooter
McEwan, I. Enduring love
Picoult, J. Keeping Faith
Robinson, M. Home
Rogers, J. Mr. Wroe's virgins
Russell, M. D. Children of God
Russell, M. D. The sparrow

FAITH -- FICTION
Markovits, A. I am forbidden
Sullivan, M. J. Necessary heartbreak

FAITH CURE
Bambara, T. C. The salt eaters

Leonard, E. Touch
Faith Fox. Gardam, J.
Faithful Place. French, T.
Faithfull, Emily, 1835-1895
> **About**
Donoghue, E. The sealed letter
Faithless. Oates, J. C.
Faking it. Crusie, J.
Falconer. Cheever, J.
FALCONRY *See* Game and game birds; Hunting
The **fall.** Camus, A.
The **fall.** Mawer, S.
A **fall** from grace. Barnard, R.
Fall from pride. Harper, K.
Fall of giants. Follett, K.
The **fall** of Hyperion. Simmons, D.
The **fall** of Rome. Southgate, M.
The **fall** of Troy. Ackroyd, P.
Fall on your knees. MacDonald
The **fallen.** Parker, T. J.
Fallen. Slaughter, K.
Fallen. Maine, D.
Fallen. Lebbon, T.
Fallen angels. Dial, C.
Fallen into the pit. Peters, E.
The **fallen** man. Hillerman, T.
Falling man. DeLillo, D.
The **falls.** Oates, J. C.
The **falls.** Rankin, I.
Falls the shadow. Penman, S. K.

FALSE ACCUSATION
Baldwin, J. If Beale Street could talk
Coben, H. Caught
Eliot, G. Silas Marner
Freeman, B. The bone house
Gaines, E. J. A lesson before dying
Grippando, J. Money to burn
Grisham, J. The confession
Hamilton, J. A map of the world
Haywood, G. A. Cemetery Road
Holt, V. The black opal
Katkov, N. Blood & orchids
Katzenbach, J. Hart's war
Lee, H. To kill a mockingbird
Lewin, M. Z. Oh Joe
Malamud, B. The fixer
McEwan, I. Atonement
Mina, D. Deception
Parker, B. Suspicion of vengeance
Patterson, R. N. Eclipse
Picoult, J. House rules
Rankin, I. The complaints
Richmond, M. No one you know
Rosenfelt, D. Don't tell a soul
Tey, J. The Franchise affair
Wilder, T. The eighth day

Carter, S. L. The emperor of Ocean Park
Cheever, J. The Wapshot chronicle
Cheever, J. The Wapshot scandal
Conroy, P. The prince of tides
Cooper, J. C. The wake of the wind
Cunningham, M. Flesh and blood
Davidar, D. The house of blue mangoes
Davies, R. The manticore
Davies, R. Murther & walking spirits
De la Roche, M. Jalna
Delbanco, N. Sherbrookes
Delbanco, N. What remains
Doig, I. Bucking the sun
Doig, I. Ride with me, Mariah Montana
Dorris, M. Cloud chamber
Dorris, M. A yellow raft in blue water
Dunne, D. A season in purgatory
Dunnett, D. Niccolo rising
Dunnett, D. Race of scorpions
Dunnett, D. The spring of the ram
Edgeworth, M. Castle Rackrent
Eve, N. The family orchard
Faulkner, W. Flags in the dust
Faulkner, W. Sartoris
Galsworthy, J. End of the chapter
Galsworthy, J. The Forsyte saga
Galsworthy, J. A modern comedy
Garcia Marquez, G. One hundred years of solitude
Garcia, C. The Aguero sisters
Garcia, C. Dreaming in Cuban
Garcia, C. Monkey hunting
Gibbons, K. Charms for the easy life
Gilmore, J. Golden country
Graham, W. Bella Poldark
Grau, S. A. The keepers of the house
Greene, A. Bloodroot
Haley, A. Mama Flora's family
Halter, M. The book of Abraham
Harmonia caelestis/English   Celestial harmonies
Harrison, J. The road home
Hatoum, M. The brothers
Hawthorne, N. The House of the Seven Gables
Hegi, U. The vision of Emma Blau
Hijuelos, O. The fourteen sisters of Emilio Montez
  O'Brien
Hill, R. B. Hanta yo
Hoeg, P. The history of Danish dreams
Houston, J. D. Bird of another heaven
Howard, M. Natural history
Howatch, S. Cashelmara
Howatch, S. Penmarric
Howatch, S. The wheel of fortune
Hunter, E. The Chisholms
Isaacs, S. Almost paradise
Isaacs, S. Red, white and blue
Jakes, J. American dreams

Jakes, J. Charleston
Jakes, J. Heaven and hell
Jakes, J. Love and war
Jakes, J. North and South
Jennings, G. Aztec
Jhabvala, R. P. Shards of memory
Kennedy, W. Very old bones
Kesey, K. Sometimes a great notion
Kittredge, W. The Willow Field
Krantz, J. Mistral's daughter
Laker, R. To dance with kings
L'Amour, L. The Sacketts: beginnings of a dynasty
Laskas, G. M. The midwife's tale
Lawrence, D. H. The rainbow
L'Engle, M. Certain women
L'Engle, M. A live coal in the sea
Lessing, D. M. The sweetest dream
Lott, B. Ancient highway
MacDonald Fall on your knees
Mahfouz, N. Palace of desire
Mahfouz, N. Palace walk
Mahfouz, N. Sugar Street
Manicka, R. The rice mother
Mann, T. Buddenbrooks
Mansbach, A. The end of the Jews
Martin, W. Annapolis
Martin, W. Cape Cod
McCrumb, S. The songcatcher
McCullough, C. The thorn birds
McDermott, A. At weddings and wakes
Meacham, L. Roses
Michener, J. A. Chesapeake
Michener, J. A. Mexico
Michener, J. A. Poland
Miller, S. Family pictures
Morrison, T. Jazz
Morrison, T. Song of Solomon
Nabokov, V. V. Ada
Naylor, G. Linden Hills
Ng, F. M. Bone
Oates, J. C. Bellefleur
Pearce, M. E. Apple tree lean down
Piercy, M. Three women
Pilcher, R. September
Pilcher, R. The shell seekers
Plain, B. Evergreen
Plain, B. The golden cup
Plain, B. Harvest
Plain, B. Random winds
Plain, B. Tapestry
Powers, R. The time of our singing
Price, E. Savannah
Puzo, M. The family
Rice, A. Lasher
Rice, A. The witching hour
Richler, M. Solomon Gursky was here

Cook, C. Best staged plans

Cook, T. H. The cloud of unknowing

Cummins, A. Yellowcake

Cunningham, M. Flesh and blood

Cusk, R. The Bradshaw variations

Cusk, R. In the fold

Dark, A. E. Think of England

De la Roche, M. Jalna

Dean, M. L. The time it takes to fall

Deane, S. Reading in the dark

Dee, J. The privileges

Delbanco, N. What remains

DeLillo, D. White noise

Demetz, H. The house on Prague Street

DeNiro, A. Total oblivion, more or less

Desai, A. Clear light of day

Dew, R. F. The truth of the matter

Diaz, J. The brief wondrous life of Oscar Wao

Doig, I. Dancing at the Rascal Fair

Doig, I. English Creek

Donovan, A. Buddha Da

Doyle, R. Paddy Clarke, ha ha ha

Doyle, R. The woman who walked into doors

Drabble, M. The witch of Exmoor

D'Souza, T. The Konkans

Dufresne, J. Deep in the shade of paradise

Dufresne, J. Requiem, Mass.

Dunmore, H. The betrayal

Dunn, K. Geek love

Eliot, G. The mill on the Floss

Ellis, B. E. Lunar Park

Elwork, P. The girl who would speak for the dead

Enright, A. The gathering

Epstein, L. San Remo Drive

Evans, N. The brave

Faulkner, W. As I lay dying

Faulkner, W. Flags in the dust

Faulkner, W. The mansion

Faulkner, W. Sartoris

Faulkner, W. The sound and the fury

Faulkner, W. The town

Ferber, E. So Big

Ferris, J. The unnamed

Flynn, G. Sharp objects

Forster, E. M. Howards End

Franck, J. The blindness of the heart

Franzen, J. Freedom

Franzen, J. The corrections

Freda, J. The patience of rivers

French, T. Faithful Place

Freudenberger, N. The dissident

Fuentes, C. Happy families

Galsworthy, J. The Forsyte saga

Gibbons, K. Sights unseen

Gilmore, J. Something red

Goddard, R. Beyond recall

Godwin, G. A mother and two daughters

Goldberg, M. Bee season

Goudge, E. One last dance

Grant, H. The glass demon

Grant, L. We had it so good

Greeley, A. M. Second spring

Greeley, A. M. September song

Greenberg, J. In this sign

Grenville, K. The secret river

Grey, Z. Woman of the frontier

Grushin, O. The line

Guest, J. Ordinary people

Haddon, M. A spot of bother

Hagen, G. The Laments

Haig, M. The Labrador Pact

Haig, M. The Radleys

Haigh, J. Baker towers

Haigh, J. The condition

Hailey, E. F. A woman of independent means

Hamilton, J. Disobedience

Hamilton, J. A map of the world

Hamilton, J. The short history of a prince

Hamilton, J. When Madeline was young

Hamner, E. The homecoming

Hamner, E. Spencer's Mountain

Harrison, J. Returning to earth

Hart, B. Then came the evening

Hart, J. Down river

Hart, J. The truth about love

Haruf, K. Plainsong

Hatoum, M. The brothers

Hay, E. Garbo laughs

Hedaya, Y. Eden

Heller, J. Good as Gold

Heller, J. Something happened

Heller, Z. The believers

Hemmings, K. H. The descendants

Heriz, E. d. Lies

Hijuelos, O. Empress of the splendid season

Hill, R. When all is said and done

Hilton, J. Random harvest

Hoffman, A. At risk

Hoffman, A. Blue diary

Hoffman, A. Second nature

Hofmann, G. Luck

Hood, A. Places to stay the night

Hooper, K. Finding Laura

Hosseini, K. A thousand splendid suns

Hughes, L. Not without laughter

Hustvedt, S. What I loved

Hyland, M. J. Carry me down

Irving, J. The Hotel New Hampshire

Irving, J. The world according to Garp

Jacobson, H. Kalooki nights

Jen, G. The love wife

Jewett, S. O. The country of the pointed firs

Rice, L. Home fires
Richter, C. The awakening land
Robinson, R. Cost
Rolvaag, O. E. Giants in the earth
Rolvaag, O. E. Peder Victorious
Romano, T. When the world was young
Rossner, J. Emmeline
Roth, H. Call it sleep
Roth, H. A star shines over Mt. Morris Park
Roy, A. An atlas of impossible longing
Roy, A. The god of small things
Runcie, J. Canvey Island
Russo, R. Nobody's fool
Salinger, J. D. Franny & Zooey
Salinger, J. D. Raise high the roof beam, carpenters, and Seymour: an introduction
Samarasan, P. Evening is the whole day
Sanders, L. Guilty pleasures
Saroyan, W. The human comedy
Schwartz, J. B. Reservation Road
Schwartz, L. S. Disturbances in the field
Schwartz, L. S. In the family way
Scott, J. Tourmaline
Searles, J. Boy still missing
Sebold, A. The lovely bones
Settle, M. L. Charley Bland
Shafak, E. The bastard of Istanbul
Sharpe, M. The sleeping father
Shaw, I. Bread upon the waters
Shepard, L. Softspoken
Shields, D. Dead languages
Shreve, A. Body surfing
Shreve, A. The weight of water
Shreve, S. R. A student of living things
Siddons, A. R. Sweetwater Creek
Sinclair, A. Coffee will make you black
Singer, I. B. The estate
Singer, I. B. The family Moskat
Smiley, J. A thousand acres
Smith, A. The accidental
Smith, B. A tree grows in Brooklyn
Smith, D. I capture the castle
Smith, R. K. Jane's house
Smith, Z. On beauty
Snow, C. P. The conscience of the rich
Snow, C. P. Last things
Snow, C. P. Time of hope
Sofer, D. The Septembers of Shiraz
Spencer, S. Endless love
Spragg, M. Bone fire
St. John Mandel, E. The singer's gun
Starr, J. Panic attack
Stead, C. The man who loved children
Stefaniak, M. H. The Turk and my mother
Stegner, W. E. The Big Rock Candy Mountain
Stein, G. The art of racing in the rain

Steinbeck, J. The grapes of wrath
Stirling, J. The penny wedding
Straight, S. The gettin place
Strayed, C. Torch
Stubbs, J. Family games
Stubbs, J. Like we used to be
Styron, A. All the finest girls
Styron, W. Lie down in darkness
Tanizaki, J. The Makioka sisters
Tarkington, B. Alice Adams
Tartt, D. The little friend
Taylor, B. The book of getting even
Taylor, P. H. A summons to Memphis
Tennant, E. An unequal marriage
Thayer, N. An act of love
Thompson, J. The year we left home
Thompson, J. Wide blue yonder
Tóibín, C. The heather blazing
Toibin, C. The blackwater lightship
Torres, J. We the animals
Townsend, S. The Adrian Mole diaries
Toynton, E. The Oriental wife
Trevor, W. The silence in the garden
Trollope, J. Brother and sister
Trollope, J. Marrying the mistress
Trollope, J. The men and the girls
Trollope, J. Next of kin
Trollope, J. The other family
Trollope, J. Other people's children
Trollope, J. The rector's wife
Trollope, J. Second honeymoon
Tryon, T. The other
Tsiolkas, C. The slap
Turow, S. The burden of proof
Twain, M. The adventures of Tom Sawyer
Tyler, A. The amateur marriage
Tyler, A. Back when we were grownups
Tyler, A. Breathing lessons
Tyler, A. The clock winder
Tyler, A. Digging to America
Tyler, A. Dinner at the Homesick Restaurant
Tyler, A. Earthly possessions
Tyler, A. Ladder of years
Tyler, A. Morgan's passing
Tyler, A. Saint maybe
Tyler, A. The tin can tree
Udall, B. The lonely polygamist
Updike, J. Rabbit at rest
Updike, J. Rabbit is rich
Vernon, O. Eden
Viswanathan, P. The toss of a lemon
Waldman, A. Red Hook Road
Ward, A. E. Close your eyes
Ward, J. Salvage the bones
Weiner, J. In her shoes
Weiner, J. Then came you

King, S. Insomnia
Meek, J. The people's act of love
Moulessehoul, M. The swallows of Kabul
Yorke, M. A question of belief
Fangland. Marks, J.
Fanon. Wideman, J. E.
Fanon, Frantz, 1925-1961
                    About
Wideman, J. E. Fanon
FANS (PERSONS)
Pearson, A. I think I love you
FANTASIES
Abercrombie, J. Before they are hanged
Abercrombie, J. The blade itself
Abercrombie, J. Last argument of kings
Abraham, D. An autumn war
Abraham, D. A shadow in summer
Adams, R. Watership Down
Adrian, C. The children's hospital
Adrian, C. The great night
Aiken, J. The monkey's wedding, and other stories
Aira, C. Ghosts
American fantastic tales: terror and the uncanny
    from Poe to the pulps
American fantastic tales: terror and the uncanny
    from the 1940s to now
Anderson, P. War of the Gods
Anthony, P. Split infinity
Anthony, P. Virtual mode
Baker, K. The bird of the river
Baker, K. The house of the stag
Baker, K. Mother Aegypt and other stories
Baker, K. Not less than gods
Baker, N. House of holes
Ballard, J. G. The day of creation
Barker, C. Imajica
Barker, C. Weaveworld
Beagle, P. S. The last unicorn
Bear, E. Blood and iron
Bear, E. Ink and steel
Berger, T. Being invisible
The Best from fantasy & science fiction: the fiftieth
    anniversary anthology
Bledsoe, A. The hum and the shiver
Borchardt, A. The silver wolf
Bradbury, R. Something wicked this way comes
Bradley, M. Z. The mists of Avalon
Brennan, M. With fate conspire
Brockmeier, K. The brief history of the dead
Brockmeier, K. The Illumination
Brook, M. The Iron Duke
Brooks, T. The druid of Shannara
Brooks, T. First king of Shannara
Brooks, T. The measure of the magic
Brooks, T. The sword of Shannara
Bujold, L. M. The paladin of souls

Bull, E. Territory
Bull, E. War for the Oaks
Butcher, J. Changes
Butcher, J. Ghost story
Butcher, J. Side jobs
Butcher, J. Small favor
Calvino, I. Baron in the trees
Calvino, I. Invisible cities
Capote, T. The grass harp
Card, O. S. Alvin Journeyman
Card, O. S. Keeper of dreams
Card, O. S. Seventh son
Carey, E. Alva & Irva
Carey, J. Kushiel's dart
Carriger, G. Heartless
Carroll, J. The ghost in love
Carter, A. Nights at the circus
Charlton, B. Spellbound
Charlton, B. Spellwright
Chayefsky, P. Altered states
Cherryh, C. J. The collected short fiction of C.J.
    Cherryh
Connolly, J. The book of lost things
Coover, R. Briar Rose
Coover, R. Pinocchio in Venice
Craig, A. Love in idleness
Crowley, J. Little, big
Cunningham, E. Shadows in the starlight
Dark matter
Davies, R. Murther & walking spirits
Davies, V. Miracle on 34th Street
De Lint, C. Memory and dream
De Lint, C. Someplace to be flying
De Lint, C. Trader
De Lint, C. Widdershins
Dickens, C. The cricket on the hearth
Dickinson, C. A shortcut in time
Donaldson, S. R. The Illearth war
Donaldson, S. R. Lord Foul's bane
Donaldson, S. R. The One Tree
Donaldson, S. R. The power that preserves
Donaldson, S. R. The runes of the earth
Donaldson, S. R. White gold wielder
Donaldson, S. R. The wounded Land
Donohue, K. The stolen child
Durham, D. A. Acacia
Ennen paivanlaskua ei voi/English Troll
Estrin, M. Insect dreams
Everett, P. L. American desert
Feeling very strange
Fforde, J. The Eyre affair
Fforde, J. Shades of grey
Fforde, J. Thursday Next in Lost in a good book
Fforde, J. Thursday Next in Something rotten
Fforde, J. Thursday Next in The well of lost plots
Ford, J. The empire of ice cream

McCaffrey, A. Dragonquest
McCaffrey, A. Dragon's Kin
McCaffrey, A. Dragon's time
McCaffrey, A. Dragonsdawn
McCaffrey, A. Dragonseye
McCaffrey, A. Killashandra
McCaffrey, A. The Masterharper of Pern
McCaffrey, A. Pegasus in space
McCaffrey, A. The renegades of Pern
McCaffrey, A. The skies of Pern
McCaffrey, A. The white dragon
McDermott, J. M. Last dragon
McKillip, P. A. Alphabet of thorn
McKillip, P. A. The sorceress and the Cygnet
McMullen, S. Glass dragons
Mendelsohn, J. American music
Mieville, C. The city & the city
Mieville, C. Kraken
Mieville, C. Perdido Street Station
Mieville, C. The scar
Miller, W. M. A canticle for Leibowitz
Millhauser, S. Martin Dressler
Milligan, J. Jack Fish
Modesitt, L. E. Viewpoints critical
Moning, K. M. The immortal highlander
Moon, E. Moon flights
Moorcock, M. An alien heat
Moorcock, M. The best of Michael Moorcock
Moorcock, M. The dreamthief's daughter
Moorcock, M. The end of all songs
Moorcock, M. The hollow lands
Moorcock, M. The skrayling tree
Mosse, K. Labyrinth
Nabokov, V. V. Pale fire
Nathan, R. Portrait of Jennie
Niven, L. The burning city
Norton, A. The elvenbane
Norton, A. Elvenblood
Norton, A. Golden Trillium
Novik, N. His majesty's dragon
O'Connell, J. The resurrectionist
Odom, M. The destruction of the books
Orwell, G. Animal farm
The Oxford book of modern fairy tales
Oyeyemi, H. Mr. Fox
Palmer, D. C. The dream of perpetual motion
Parker, K. J. The company
Parker, K. J. Devices and desires
Pelevin, V. The sacred book of the werewolf
Phillips, M. Gods behaving badly
Piercy, M. Woman on the edge of time
Polansky, D. Low Town
Powers, T. Three days to never
Pratchett, T. The color of magic
Pratchett, T. The fifth elephant
Pratchett, T. Going postal

Pratchett, T. Monstrous regiment
Pratchett, T. Thief of time
Pratchett, T. Thud!
Pratchett, T. The truth
Putney, M. J. A kiss of fate
Rand, A. Atlas shrugged
Rawn, M. The diviner
Riley, J. M. The serpent garden
Robbins, T. Jitterbug perfume
Robbins, T. Villa incognito
Robson, J. Keeping it real
Rothfuss, P. The name of the wind
Rothfuss, P. The wise man's fear
Ruiz Zafon, C. The angel's game
Ruiz Zafon, C. The shadow of the wind
Rushdie, S. The satanic verses
Rushdie, S. The Moor's last sigh
Ryman, G. Paradise tales
Saberhagen, F. The fifth book of lost swords: Coin-
    spinner's story
Saberhagen, F. The first book of lost swords:
    Woundhealer's story
Saberhagen, F. The fourth book of lost swords:
    Farslayer's story
Saberhagen, F. The last book of swords: Shield-
    breaker's story
Saberhagen, F. The second book of lost swords:
    Sightblinder's story
Saberhagen, F. The seventh book of lost swords:
    Wayfinder's story
Saberhagen, F. The sixth book of lost swords:
    Mindsword's story
Saberhagen, F. The third book of lost swords:
    Stonecutter's story
Saint, H. F. Memoirs of an invisible man
Saint-Exupery, A. d. The little prince
Salvatore, R. A. Immortalis
Sanderson, B. Elantris
Sanderson, B. Mistborn: the final empire
Savage, S. Firmin
Sedia, E. Alchemy of stone
Shaw, A. The girl with glass feet
Silverberg, R. Lord Valentine's castle
Snow white, blood red
Spark, M. The ballad of Peckham Rye
Steinbeck, J. The short reign of Pippin IV
Swanwick, M. The best of Michael Swanwick
Swift, J. Gulliver's travels
Tarr, J. Lady of horses
Tolkien, J. R. R. The book of lost tales
Tolkien, J. R. R. The fellowship of the ring
Tolkien, J. R. R. The hobbit
Tolkien, J. R. R. The lord of the rings
Tolkien, J. R. R. Narn i chin Hurin
Tolkien, J. R. R. The return of the king
Tolkien, J. R. R. The Silmarillion

O'Brien, E. Wild Decembers

FARM LIFE -- KANSAS
Roy, L. Bent Road

FARM LIFE -- KENTUCKY
Mason, B. A. Feather crowns
Morgan, C. E. All the living

FARM LIFE -- MINNESOTA
Clark, M. H. A cry in the night

FARM LIFE -- MISSISSIPPI
Jordan, H. Mudbound

FARM LIFE -- NEBRASKA
Cather, W. O pioneers!

FARM LIFE -- NEW ENGLAND
Wharton, E. Ethan Frome

FARM LIFE -- NEW HAMPSHIRE
Benet, S. V. The Devil and Daniel Webster

FARM LIFE -- NORTH CAROLINA
Frazier, C. Cold Mountain

FARM LIFE -- NORWAY
Undset, S. Kristin Lavransdatter

FARM LIFE -- SOUTH AFRICA
Lessing, D. M. The grass is singing

FARM LIFE -- SOUTH DAKOTA
Rolvaag, O. E. Giants in the earth
Rolvaag, O. E. Peder Victorious

FARM LIFE -- SOUTHERN STATES
Kingsolver, B. Prodigal summer

FARM LIFE -- SWEDEN
Moberg, V. The emigrants

FARM LIFE -- TENNESSEE
McCrumb, S. The rosewood casket

FARM LIFE -- TEXAS
Proulx, A. That old ace in the hole

FARM LIFE -- VERMONT
Peck, R. N. A day no pigs would die
Proulx, A. Postcards

FARM LIFE -- VIRGINIA
Shreve, S. R. A country of strangers

FARM LIFE -- WESTERN STATES
Stegner, W. E. The Big Rock Candy Mountain

FARM LIFE -- WISCONSIN
Hamilton, J. A map of the world
Schwarz, C. Drowning Ruth

FARM LIFE -- ZAMBIA
Mankell, H. The eye of the leopard

FARM PRODUCE *See* Food; Raw materials
FARM TENANCY *See* Farms; Land tenure
The **farmer's** daughter. Harrison, J.
FARMERS
McCall Smith, A. The Saturday big tent wedding party
The **farming** of bones. Danticat, E.
FARMS
See also Land use; Real estate
Warren, D. Juliet in August
Farriers' Lane. Perry, A.

Farthing. Walton, J.
FASCISM
See also Totalitarianism
Furst, A. The foreign correspondent
Roth, P. The plot against America
Walton, J. Half a crown
Walton, J. Ha'penny
FASCISM -- ITALY
Silone, I. Bread and wine
FASCISM -- UNITED STATES
Lewis, S. It can't happen here
FASHION -- FICTION
Steel, D. First sight
FASHION DESIGN *See* Clothing industry; Commercial art; Design
FASHION DESIGNERS
See also Designers
Steel, D. First sight
Szado, A. Studio saint-ex
FASHION INDUSTRY *See* Clothing industry
FASHION INDUSTRY AND TRADE
Bushnell, C. Lipstick jungle
Gibson, W. Zero history
Laker, R. Banners of silk
FASHION MODELS
See also Advertising
Gaitskill, M. Veronica
Rendell, R. Thirteen steps down
Rowling, J. K. The cuckoo's calling
Fat Ollie's book. McBain, E.
A **fatal** glass of beer. Kaminsky, S. M.
Fatal induction. Pajer, B.
Fatal lies. Tallis, F.
A **fatal** likeness. Shepherd, L.
A **fatal** winter. Malliet, G. M.
Fatale. Manchette
FATE AND FATALISM
Garcia Marquez, G. Chronicle of a death foretold
Garcia, C. A handbook to luck
Guterson, D. Ed King
Mooney, T. The same river twice
Wilder, T. The bridge of San Luis Rey
FATE AND FATALISM -- FICTION
Browne, S. G. Lucky bastard
Lively, P. How it all began
The **fate** of Katherine Carr. Cook, T. H.
The **fates** will find their way. Pittard, H.
Father Brown mystery stories. Chesterton, G. K.
The **Father** Brown omnibus. Chesterton, G. K.
The **father** of the rain. King, L.
Father's Day. Gilman, K.
FATHER-CHILD RELATIONSHIP
See also Children; Fathers; Parent-child relationship
Nichols, J. On top of Spoon Mountain
Thompson, J. The humanity project

Hannah, K. On Mystic lake

Harrington, L. Alice Bliss

Harris, J. Coastliners

Hellenga, R. Philosophy made simple

Hunter, S. Night of thunder

Ishiguro, K. An artist of the floating world

Jaime-Becerra, M. This time tomorrow

James, H. The golden bowl

James, H. Washington Square

Joe, Y. My fine lady

Jones, T. Silver sparrow

Kafka, K. Miranda's vines

Kay, G. G. River of Stars

Kimmel, H. Something rising (light and swift)

Kincaid, J. Mr. Potter

King, L. The father of the rain

Kingsolver, B. Animal dreams

Larison, J. Holding lies

Larsson, S. The girl who kicked the hornets' nest

Le, T. D. T. The gangster we are all looking for

Lee, H. To kill a mockingbird

L'Engle, M. Certain women

Lipman, E. The family man

Lively, P. The road to Lichfield

Livesey, M. The house on Fortune Street

Lyon, A. The sweet girl

Malone, M. The four corners of the sky

Manfredo, L. Rizzo's daughter

McGrath, P. Constance

McGrath, P. Martha Peake

McNaught, J. Paradise

McPhee, M. Gorgeous lies

Miles, J. Dear American Airlines

Moore, C. A dirty job

Morrell, D. Murder as a fine art

Norman, H. What is left the daughter

Oates, J. C. Black girl/White girl

Pears, I. Stone's fall

Pessl, M. Special topics in calamity physics

Picoult, J. Vanishing acts

Pötzsch, O. The beggar king

Pronzini, B. In an evil time

Proulx, A. The shipping news

Read, P. P. The professor's daughter

Rendell, R. Heartstones

Reuss, F. Mohr

Robinson, M. Home

Rock, P. My abandonment

Roth, P. American pastoral

Russo, R. Empire Falls

Sagan, F. Bonjour tristesse

Sakamoto, K. One hundred million hearts

Saramago, J. The cave

Scottoline, L. Don't Go

Scottoline, L. Moment of truth

See, L. Dreams of joy

Segal, E. Love story

Sharp, Z. Third strike

Shreve, A. Light on snow

Shreve, A. Rescue

Sittenfeld, C. The man of my dreams

Smiley, J. A thousand acres

Smith, L. Saving Grace

Spark, M. Reality and dreams

Sparks, N. The last song

Stevens, M. Useful girl

Strout, E. Abide with me

Sullivan, M. J. Necessary heartbreak

Toews, M. A complicated kindness

Trevor, W. Death in summer

Trollope, J. Next of kin

Tyler, A. Noah's compass

Ulinich, A. Petropolis

Vidal, G. 1876

Vine, B. The chimney sweeper's boy

Walker, A. By the light of my father's smile

Walton, J. Among others

Wenner, K. Dancing with Einstein

Wiggins, M. The shadow catcher

Wilhelm, K. The deepest water

Woodrell, D. Winter's bone

Woof, E. The whole wide beauty

Yorke, M. Almost the truth

Fathers and sons. Turgenev, I. S.

FATHERS AND SONS

    See also Father-son relationship Abani, C. GraceLand

Akst, D. The Webster chronicle

Andersen Nexo, M. Pelle the conqueror: v1 Childhood

Archer, J. Only time will tell

Bakker, G. The twin

Banks, R. Cloudsplitter

Banville, J. The infinities

Barker, N. Darkmans

Barthelme, F. Waveland

Berry, S. The Charlemagne pursuit

Boucher, C. How to keep your Volkswagen alive

Braff, J. Peep show

Bragg, M. The soldier's return

Bragg, M. A son of war

Cave, N. The death of Bunny Munro

Chaon, D. Await your reply

Clarke, B. Exley

Coetzee, J. M. Summertime

Cook, T. H. The last talk with Lola Faye

Cook, T. H. Master of the delta

Cusk, R. In the fold

Darnton, J. Mind catcher

De los Santos, M. Belong to me

De Sa, A. Barnacle love

Dean, L. The old romantic

Russo, R. Nobody's fool
Russo, R. The risk pool
Saul, J. The right hand of evil
Schlink, B. Homecoming
Schwartz, J. B. Northwest corner
Schwartz, J. B. Reservation Road
Segal, E. Love story
Sher, I. Gentlemen of space
Smith, D. The beautiful miscellaneous
Smith, W. A. Birds of prey
Smith, W. A. Monsoon
Snow, C. P. The conscience of the rich
Stewart, M. The wicked day
Stone, R. Bay of souls
Straub, P. Mr. X
Taylor, R. L. The travels of Jaimie McPheeters
Townsend, S. Adrian Mole
Tucker, T. Over and under
Turow, S. Ordinary heroes
Updike, J. The centaur
Vamos, M. The book of fathers
Vanderhaeghe, G. The last crossing
Vargas Llosa, M. The notebooks of Don Rigoberto
Vassanji, M. G. The assassin's song
Verghese, A. Cutting for stone
Wallace, D. Big fish
Wharton, W. Dad
Wiesel, E. The forgotten
Wilson, R. The blind man of Seville
Wittenborn, D. Pharmakon
Wyld, E. After the fire, a still small voice
Yates, A. Moondogs

FATHERS AND SONS -- FICTION

Akst, D. The Webster chronicle
Bradbury, R. Something wicked this way comes
Clarke, B. Exley
Coady, L. The antagonist
Deb, S. The point of return
Dexter, P. Spooner
Doig, I. The bartender's tale
Doiron, P. The poacher's son
Dragoman, G. The white king
Estleman, L. D. Retro
Fesperman, D. The double game
Foer, J. S. Extremely loud & incredibly close
Garey, J. Too bright to hear too loud to see
Habila, H. Measuring time
Hadley, T. The master bedroom
Harding, P. Tinkers
Harkaway, N. Angelmaker
Hart, J. Down river
Havazelet, E. Bearing the body
Havley, N. The good father
Irving, J. Last night in Twisted River
Irving, J. Until I find you
Johnson, W. The devil you know

Lamb, W. I know this much is true
Le Carre, J. Single & Single
Lodge, D. Deaf sentence
Lupica, M. Wild pitch
Malouf, D. Ransom
Mansbach, A. Rage is back
Maxwell, R. The Queen's bastard
McCarthy, C. The road
McGarrity, M. The big gamble
McNally, T. M. The goat bridge
Mengiste, M. Beneath the lion's gaze
Mosley, W. Gone fishin'
Oe, K. The pinch runner memorandum
Olmstead, R. Coal black horse
Parks, T. Destiny
Pattison, E. The lord of death
Percy, B. The wilding
Preston, D. The codex
Price, R. The good priest's son
Price, R. The promise of rest
Ramsland, M. Doghead
Rice, L. Summer light
Robinson, M. Home
Schwartz, J. B. Northwest corner
Schwartz, L. Angels Crest
Sher, I. Gentlemen of space
Turow, S. Ordinary heroes
Vamos, M. The book of fathers
Vanderhaeghe, G. The last crossing
Verghese, A. Cutting for stone
Wittenborn, D. Pharmakon
Yu, C. How to live safely in a science fictional universe

FATHERS-IN-LAW

Mewshaw, M. Shelter from the storm
Plain, B. Looking back
The **fatigue** artist. Schwartz, L. S.

FATIMA, OUR LADY OF

Berry, S. The third secret

FATNESS *See* Obesity

The **Faulkner** reader. Faulkner, W.

Fault lines. Carroll, J.

The **fault** tree. Ure, L.

FAUNA *See* Animals; Zoology

FAUST LEGEND

Mann, T. Doctor Faustus

FEAR

Du Maurier, D. Rebecca
French, N. Land of the living
Heller, J. Something happened
King, S. The girl who loved Tom Gordon
Koontz, D. R. False memory
Mullen, T. The last town on earth
See, C. There will never be another you

FEAR

See also Emotions

The **first** cut. Caedmon's song
The **first** deadly sin. Sanders, L.
The **first** desire. Reisman, N.
The **first** eagle. Hillerman, T.
First Edition [series]
    Aslam, N. The Blind Man's Garden
First king of Shannara. Brooks, T.
FIRST LADIES
    Chiaverini, J. Mrs. Lincoln's dressmaker
First lady. Phillips, S. E.
The **first** law. Lescroart, J. T.
First light. Tapply, W. G.
First love and other stories. Turgenev, I. S.
FIRST LOVES
    Fyfield, F. Undercurrents
    Gordon, M. The love of my youth
    Lytal, B. A map of Tulsa
The **first** man in Rome. McCullough, C.
First of state. Greer, R. O.
First offense. Rosenberg, N. T.
First rule. Crais, R.
The **First** Rule of Swimming. Brkic, C. A.
First sight. Steel, D.
First thrills.
The **first** victim. Pearson, R.
The **first** wave. Benn, J. R.
The **First** Wives Club. Goldsmith, O.
FIRST WORLD WAR *See* World War, 1914-1918
FISH *See* Fish as food; Fishes
FISH AS FOOD *See* Cooking; Fishes; Food
The **fish** child. Puenzo, L.
A **fish** trapped inside the wind. Gholson, C.
The **fisher** king. Marshall, P.
FISHERIES
    Torday, P. Salmon fishing in the Yemen
FISHERMEN
    Casey, J. Compass rose
    Casey, J. Spartina
    Grass, G. The flounder
    Guterson, D. Snow falling on cedars
    Mills, M. Amagansett
    Mishima, Y. The sound of waves
    Rice, L. Blue moon
    Winton, T. Dirt music
FISHES
    Grass, G. The flounder
FISHES -- ECOLOGY
    See also Ecology
FISHES -- FICTION
    Gholson, C. A fish trapped inside the wind
FISHING
    Hemingway, E. Islands in the stream
    Larison, J. Holding lies
    McGuane, T. Ninety-two in the shade
FISHING -- FICTION
    Edwardson, A. Sail of stone

FISHING VILLAGES -- SWEDEN
    Lackberg, C. The ice princess
The **Fitzgerald** reader. Fitzgerald, F. S.
Fitzgerald, F. Scott (Francis Scott), 1896-1940
        About
    Carson, T. Daisy Buchanan's daughter
    Fowler, T. A. Z
Fitzgerald, Zelda, 1900-1948
        About
    Fowler, T. A. Z
The **five** bells and bladebone. Grimes, M.
Five fortunes. Gutcheon, B. R.
Five novels of the 1960s & 70s. Dick, P. K.
Five quarters of the orange. Harris, J.
The **five** red herrings. Sayers, D. L.
Five skies. Carlson, R.
Five Star standard print romance series
    Chase, L. L. The last hellion
    Chase, L. L. Lord of scoundrels
FIXED IDEAS *See* Obsessive-compulsive disorder
The **fixed** stars. Conn, B.
The **fixer.** Malamud, B.
A **flag** for sunrise. Stone, R.
Flags in the dust. Faulkner, W.
The **flame** alphabet. Marcus, B.
Flame of resistance. Groot, T.
The **flamethrowers.** Kushner, R.
Flannery O'Connor Award for Short Fiction [series]
    Selgin, P. Drowning lessons
Flannigan, Katherine Mary O'Fallon
        About
    Freedman, B. Mrs. Mike
FLASH MOBS *See* Crowds; Performance art
Flashback. Simmons, D.
Flashover. Chazin, S.
FLATS *See* Apartments
Flatscreen. Wilson, A.
Flaubert, Gustave, 1821-1880
        About
    Shomer, E. The twelve rooms of the Nile
FLAVORING ESSENCES *See* Cooking; Essences and essential oils; Food
Fleming, Ian, 1908-1964
        About
    Deaver, J. Carte blanche: 007
    Faulks, S. Devil may care
Flesh and blood. Cunningham, M.
Flesh and blood. Harvey, J.
Flesh and fire. Gilman, L. A.
Flesh house. MacBride, S.
Flesh wounds. Greenleaf, S.
Fletch. Mcdonald, G.
The **Fletch** chronicles. Mcdonald, G.
A **flickering** light. Kirkpatrick, J.
FLIES *See* Household pests; Insects; Pests

Hall, J. W. Rough draft

Hoffman, J. Retribution

Leonard, E. LaBrava

Leonard, E. Pronto

Lindsay, J. P. Darkly dreaming Dexter

Lindsay, J. P. Dearly devoted Dexter

Lindsay, J. P. Dexter in the dark

Lindsay, J. P. Dexter is delicious

Parker, B. Blood relations

Parker, B. Criminal justice

Parker, B. Suspicion of betrayal

Parker, B. Suspicion of deceit

Parker, B. Suspicion of vengeance

Rosales, G. The halfway house

Spillane, M. The Consummata

Stone, N. The king of swords

FLORIDA -- PALM BEACH

Fielding, J. Missing pieces

Hoag, T. Dark horse

Whitney, P. A. Poinciana

FLORIDA -- TAMPA

Atkins, A. White shadow

Heffernan, W. The dead detective

FLORISTS

Diffenbaugh, V. The language of flowers

The **flounder**. Grass, G.

FLOWER ARRANGEMENT *See* Decoration and
ornament; Flowers; Table setting and decoration

Flower children. Swann, M.

The **flower** drum song. Lee, C. Y.

Flowering Judas. Haddam, J.

Flowering Judas and other stories. Porter, K. A.

The **flowers**. Gilb, D.

FLOWERS

Diffenbaugh, V. The language of flowers

FLOWERS -- ENGLAND

Jio, S. The last camellia

FLOWERS -- FICTION

Jio, S. The last camellia

Flowers for Algernon. Keyes, D.

Flowers in the rain & other stories. Pilcher, R.

FLU *See* Influenza

FLUID MECHANICS *See* Mechanics

Fluke; or, I know why the winged whale sings.
Moore, C.

FLUTISTS

Piercy, M. Summer people

Fly Away. Hannah, K.

FLY CASTING *See* Fishing

Flying colours. Forester, C. S.

Flying hero class. Keneally, T.

FLYING SAUCERS

See also Unidentified flying objects

Heinlein, R. A. The puppet masters

Koontz, D. R. One door away from heaven

Flyover fiction [series]

Blew, M. C. Jackalope dreams

FOALS *See* Horses; Ponies

Fobbit. Abrams, D.

Foe. Coetzee, J. M.

Foggy Mountain breakdown and other stories. Mc-
Crumb, S.

FOLK ART *See* Art; Art and society

FOLK BELIEFS *See* Folklore; Superstition

FOLK MUSIC *See* Music

FOLK SONGS *See* Folklore; Songs; Vocal music

FOLK TALES *See* Folklore; Legends

FOLKLORE -- CAMBODIA

Ratner, V. In the shadow of the banyan

FOLKLORE -- IRELAND

Delaney, F. Ireland

FOLKLORE -- PARAGUAY

Puenzo, L. The fish child

Follies. Beattie, A.

Follow me. Scott, J.

Folly. Minot, S.

Folly and glory. McMurtry, L.

Folly Beach. Frank, D. B.

FOOD

Lanchester, J. The debt to pleasure

Mayle, P. Anything considered

O'Reilly, B. Angelina's bachelors

FOOD CHAINS (ECOLOGY) *See* Animals --
Food; Ecology

FOOD OF ANIMAL ORIGIN *See* Food

FOOD RELIEF *See* Charities; Disaster relief;
Public welfare; Unemployed

FOOLS AND JESTERS *See* Comedians; Courts
and courtiers; Entertainers

Fools of fortune. Trevor, W.

Fools rush in. Gorman, E.

FOOT -- PARALYSIS *See* Paralysis

FOOTBALL

Grisham, J. Playing for pizza

Harris, E. L. And this too shall pass

Phillips, S. E. It had to be you

FOOTBALL -- COACHING

See also Coaching (Athletics)

Majors, I. Love's winning plays

FOOTBALL -- FICTION

Fountain, B. Billy Lynn's long halftime walk

FOOTBALL AND WAR -- UNITED STATES

Fountain, B. Billy Lynn's long halftime walk

FOOTBALL COACHES

Majors, I. Love's winning plays

Footprints. Hearon, S.

The **footprints** of God. Iles, G.

Footsteps of the hawk. Vachss, A. H.

For love. Miller, S.

For the dogs. Wignall, K.

For they shall inherit. Ross-Macdonald, M.

Forbidden. Dekker, T.

FORTUNE *See* Fate and fatalism; Probabilities; Success

FORTUNE
Browne, S. G. Lucky bastard
Livesey, M. The house on Fortune Street

FORTUNE HUNTERS
Brockway, C. The golden season
Fortune is a woman. Adler, E.
The **fortune** teller's daughter. Wilson, S.

FORTUNE TELLING
See also Amusements; Divination
Senate, M. The love goddess' cooking school

FORTUNE TELLING -- FICTION
Bishop, A. Written in red
Engelmann, K. The Stockholm Octavo
Fortune's favorites. McCullough, C.
Fortune's Rocks. Shreve, A.

FORTUNES *See* Income; Wealth
The **forty** days of Musa Dagh. Werfel, F.
Forward the Foundation. Asimov, I.
Forward, Gunner Asch! Kirst, H. H.

FOSSIL HOMINIDS *See* Archeology; Fossils
FOSSIL MAMMALS *See* Fossils; Mammals
FOSSIL PLANTS *See* Fossils; Plants
FOSSIL REPTILES *See* Fossils; Reptiles

FOSSILS
Chevalier, T. Remarkable creatures
Doyle, A. C. The lost world
Smith, D. Pictures from an expedition

FOSTER CHILDREN
Alexie, S. Flight
Austen, J. Mansfield Park
Diffenbaugh, V. The language of flowers
Eliot, G. Silas Marner
Fitch, J. White oleander
Gibbons, K. Ellen Foster
Hurwitz, G. You're next
Mapson Solomon's oak
March, W. The bad seed
McKinney-Whetstone, D. Tempest rising
Rinehart, S. Built in a day

FOSTER CHILDREN -- FICTION
Celona, M. Y

FOSTER GRANDPARENTS *See* Grandparents; Volunteer work

FOSTER HOME CARE
Gibbons, K. Ellen Foster
Gibbons, K. The life all around me by Ellen Foster
Foucault's pendulum. Eco, U.
Foul matter. Grimes, M.
Found money. Grippando, J.
Found wanting. Goddard, R.
Foundation. Asimov, I.
Foundation [series]
Asimov, I. Forward the Foundation
Asimov, I. Foundation

Asimov, I. Foundation and earth
Asimov, I. Foundation and empire
Asimov, I. Foundation's edge
Asimov, I. Prelude to Foundation
Asimov, I. Second Foundation
Foundation and earth. Asimov, I.
Foundation and empire. Asimov, I.
Foundation's edge. Asimov, I.
Foundation's fear. Benford, G.

FOUNDATIONS *See* Architecture -- Details; Buildings; Structural engineering

FOUNDATIONS (ENDOWMENTS) *See* Endowments

FOUNDLINGS
See also Orphans
Grey, Z. Woman of the frontier
Stedman, M. L. The light between oceans
The **fountainhead.** Rand, A.
Four blind mice. Patterson, J.
The **four** corners of the sky. Malone, M.
The **four** fingers of death. Moody, R.
Four freedoms. Crowley, J.
Four new messages. Cohen, J.
Four novels of the 1960s. Dick, P. K.
Four past midnight. King, S.
Four sisters, all queens. Jones, S.
Four souls. Erdrich, L.
Four spirits. Naslund, S. J.
Four ways to forgiveness. Le Guin, U. K.
Four, five and six by Tey. Tey, J.
The **fourteen** sisters of Emilio Montez O'Brien. Hijuelos, O.
The **fourth** book of lost swords: Farslayer's story. Saberhagen, F.
Fourth Day. Sharp, Z.
The **fourth** deadly sin. Sanders, L.

FOURTH DIMENSION *See* Mathematics
The **fourth** Durango. Thomas, R.
The **fourth** hand. Irving, J.

FOURTH OF JULY
Lockridge, R. Raintree County
Lurie, A. Only children
The **fourth** procedure. Pottinger, S.
The **fourth** protocol. Forsyth, F.
The **fourth** wall. Williams, W. J.
The **fourth** world. Danvers, D.

FOX HUNTING
The blue fox

FOX, CHARLIE (FICTITIOUS CHARACTER)
Sharp, Z. Third strike

Fox, George, 1624-1691
About
De Hartog, J. The peaceable kingdom

Fox, Margaret Askew Fell, 1614-1702
About
De Hartog, J. The peaceable kingdom

Kundera, M. Identity
Kundera, M. Slowness
Proust, M. The captive [and] The fugitive
Proust, M. The Guermantes way
Proust, M. Remembrance of things past
Proust, M. Sodom and Gomorrah
Proust, M. Time regained
Sartre, J. P. The reprieve

FRANCE -- AIX-EN-PROVENCE
Kay, G. G. Ysabel

FRANCE -- BRITTANY
Stewart, M. The crystal cave
Stewart, M. Mary Stewart's Merlin trilogy

FRANCE -- CANNES
Shaw, I. Evening in Byzantium

FRANCE -- COURT AND COURTIERS -- HISTORY -- 19TH CENTURY -- FICTION
Moran, M. The second empress

FRANCE -- FICTION
Black, C. Murder below Montparnasse
Black, C. Murder in the rue de Paradis
Bourne, J. The black hawk
The map and the territory
Moran, M. Madame Tussaud
Three strong women
Walker, M. The crowded grave

FRANCE -- GASCONY
Dumas, A. The three musketeers

FRANCE -- HISTORY -- 1328-1589, HOUSE OF VALOIS
Hugo, V. The hunchback of Notre Dame

FRANCE -- HISTORY -- 14TH CENTURY
Buehlman, C. Between two fires
Yarbro, C. Q. Blood roses

FRANCE -- HISTORY -- 1589-1789, BOURBONS
Koen, K. Before Versailles
Rosenthal, P. The bookseller's daughter

FRANCE -- HISTORY -- 1789-1799, REVOLUTION
See also Revolutions
Miller, A. Pure
Moran, M. Madame Tussaud

FRANCE -- HISTORY -- 1799-1815
Putney, M. J. No longer a gentleman
Sacre bleu

FRANCE -- HISTORY -- 1815-1914
Stendhal The red and the black

FRANCE -- HISTORY -- 1940-1945, GERMAN OCCUPATION -- FICTION
de Rosnay, T. Sarah's key
Faulks, S. Charlotte Gray
Follett, K. Jackdaws
Furst, A. Red gold
Kricorian, N. All the Light There Was
Steiner, P. The resistance
Wein, E. Code name Verity

FRANCE -- KINGS AND RULERS
Koen, K. Before Versailles

FRANCE -- PARIS
Baldwin, J. Giovanni's room
Barbery, M. The elegance of the hedgehog
Barnes, D. Nightwood
Beauvoir, S. d. The mandarins
Bolano, R. Monsieur Pain
Cortazar, J. Hopscotch
Cosse, L. A novel bookstore
Dumas, A. Camille
Furst, A. Red gold
Gide, A. The counterfeiters (Les faux-monnayeurs)
Harris, J. The girl with no shadow
Hemingway, E. The sun also rises
Hijuelos, O. A simple Habana melody: from when the world was good
Johnson, D. Le mariage
Kostova, E. The swan thieves
Krantz, J. Mistral's daughter
MacInnes, H. The Venetian affair
Makine, A. Dreams of my Russian summers
Marshall, P. The fisher king
McCarthy, M. Birds of America
McLain, P. The Paris wife
Miller, A. Oxygen
Miller, H. Tropic of Cancer
Mooney, T. The same river twice
Orringer, J. The invisible bridge
Ozick, C. Foreign bodies
Powell, J. The breaking of eggs
Remarque, E. M. Arch of triumph
Rhys, J. Quartet
Richler, M. Barney's version
Sartre, J. P. The age of reason
Stamm, P. On a day like this
Steinbeck, J. The short reign of Pippin IV
Sussman, E. French lessons
Tremain, R. The way I found her
Truong, M. T. D. The book of salt
Vargas Llosa, M. The bad girl
Verne, J. Paris in the twentieth century
Vila-Matas, E. Never any end to Paris
Watkins, P. The forger
White, E. The married man

FRANCE -- PARIS -- 15TH CENTURY
Hugo, V. The hunchback of Notre Dame

FRANCE -- PARIS -- 18TH CENTURY
Dickens, C. A tale of two cities
Sabatini, R. Scaramouche

FRANCE -- PARIS -- 19TH CENTURY
Balzac, H. d. Cousin Bette
Balzac, H. d. Pere Goriot (Old Goriot)
Dumas, A. The Count of Monte Cristo
James, H. The ambassadors
James, H. The American

Texier, C. Victorine

FRENCH -- IRELAND

Flanagan, T. The year of the French

FRENCH -- POLAND

Furst, A. The spies of Warsaw

FRENCH -- RUSSIA

Bradbury, M. To the Hermitage

Makine, A. Dreams of my Russian summers

FRENCH -- UNITED STATES

Carey, P. Parrot and Olivier in America

Cather, W. Death comes for the archbishop

Clark, C. Savage lands

Hansen, R. Isn't it romantic?

FRENCH FICTION -- TRANSLATIONS INTO ENGLISH

Barbery, M. The elegance of the hedgehog

Conde, M. I, Tituba, black witch of Salem

Dumas, A. The last cavalier

Dumas, A. The three musketeers

Flaubert, G. Madame Bovary

Houellebecq, M. The possibility of an island

Littell, J. The kindly ones

Maalouf, A. Balthasar's odyssey

Makine, A. Dreams of my Russian summers

Makine, A. Music of a life

Makine, A. The woman who waited

Makine, A. The life of an unknown man

Manchette Fatale

Moulessehoul, M. The swallows of Kabul

Nemirovsky, I. Fire in the blood

Nemirovsky, I. Suite Francaise

Nothomb, A. Tokyo fiancee

Paasilinna, A. The howling miller

Perec, G. Life

Perec, G. A void

Verne, J. Paris in the twentieth century

Wiesel, E. Twilight

FRENCH LANGUAGE *See* Language and languages; Romance languages

FRENCH LANGUAGE -- DICTIONARIES -- ENGLISH *See* Encyclopedias and dictionaries

French lessons. Sussman, E.

The **French** lieutenant's woman. Fowles, J.

FRENCH POETRY *See* French literature; Poetry

Frenchman's Creek. Du Maurier, D.

The **frenzy** way. Lamberson, G.

FRESHWATER ECOLOGY *See* Ecology

Freud, Sigmund, 1856-1939

About

Meyer, N. The seven-per-cent solution

Rubenfeld, J. The death instinct

Skibell, J. A curable romantic

Thomas, D. M. The white hotel

Freytag-Loringhoven, Elsa von, Baroness, 1874-1927

About

Steinke, R. Holy skirts

Friday. Heinlein, R. A.

Friday. Tournier, M.

Friday nights. Trollope, J.

Friday the rabbi slept late. Kemelman, H.

Fried green tomatoes at the Whistle-Stop Cafe. Flagg, F.

Friend of my youth. Munro, A.

A **friend** of the family. Grodstein, L.

The **friendly** persuasion. West, J.

FRIENDS

See also Friendship

Palwick, S. Mending the moon

Friends at Thrush Green. Read

The **friends** of Eddie Coyle. Higgins, G. V.

FRIENDSHIP

Abbott, M. E. The end of everything

Adler, E. Fortune is a woman

Allen, S. A. The peach keeper

Arsenault, E. In search of the Rose notes

Attenberg, J. The melting season

Barnes, J. The sense of an ending

Bauermeister, E. Joy for beginners

Beard, J. A. In Zanesville

Beattie, A. My life, starring Dara Falcon

Binchy, M. Circle of friends

Birch, C. Jamrach's menagerie

Brookner, A. Brief lives

Buckley, W. F. Elvis in the morning

Carey, P. Parrot and Olivier in America

Carlson, R. Five skies

Chang, L. S. All is forgotten, nothing is lost

Chevalier, T. Remarkable creatures

Christensen, K. Trouble

Cleave, C. Little Bee

Coe, J. The Rotters' Club

Collins, J. Beginner's Greek

Colwin, L. A big storm knocked it over

Connelly, K. The lizard cage

Conroy, P. South of Broad

Dallas, S. The Persian Pickle Club

De Gramont, N. Gossip of the starlings

Dixon, S. Old friends

Doig, I. Dancing at the Rascal Fair

Edgerton, C. The night train

Ellis, B. E. Imperial bedrooms

Erdrich, L. The Beet Queen

Feldman, E. Next to love

Franklin, T. Crooked letter, crooked letter

Frayn, M. Spies

Fuentes, C. Destiny and desire

Gaitskill, M. Veronica

Galgut, D. The impostor

Gander, F. As a friend

Gardam, J. The flight of the maidens

Garner, H. The spare room

FRIENDSHIP -- FICTION

Brunt, C. R. Tell the wolves I'm home

Cargill, C. R. Dreams and Shadows

Chabon, M. Telegraph Avenue

Conlon, E. Red on red

Connelly, K. The lizard cage

Doig, I. The bartender's tale

Evison, J. The revised fundamentals of caregiving

Gordimer, N. No time like the present

Gremillon, H. The confidant

Jansma, K. The unchangeable spots of leopards

Johnson, B. More of this world or maybe another

Joyce, R. The unlikely pilgrimage of Harold Fry

Kardos, M. The Three-Day Affair

Kiefer, C. The infinite tides

Picoult, J. The Storyteller

Pierson, D. C. The boy who couldn't sleep and never had to

Powers, K. The yellow birds

Samuel, B. No place like home

Umrigar, T. The world we found

White, E. Jack Holmes and his friend

Wilson, A. Flatscreen

Winslow, D. The kings of cool

FRIENDSHIP -- GRAPHIC NOVELS
Merey, I. a + e 4ever

FRIENDSHIP IN ADOLESCENCE
Hannah, K. Firefly Lane

FRIENDSHIP IN YOUTH
Collins, C. The gamal

Frog. Dixon, S.

A **frolic** of his own. Gaddis, W.

From a Buick 8. King, S.

From away. Carkeet, D.

From bondage. Roth, H.

From here to eternity. Jones, J.

From other shores. Oliver, C.

From Russia, with love. Fleming, I.

From the corner of his eye. Koontz, D. R.

From the earth to the moon, and Round the moon. Verne, J.

From the terrace. O'Hara, J.

From time to time. Finney, J.

FRONTIER AND PIONEER LIFE
Hall, B. I should be extremely happy in your company

Pynchon, T. Mason & Dixon

Richter, C. The light in the forest

Sargent, C. Museum of human beings

Thom, J. A. The red heart

Wheeler, R. S. Eclipse

FRONTIER AND PIONEER LIFE -- ALASKA
Brand, M. Chinook

Parry, R. The winter wolf

FRONTIER AND PIONEER LIFE -- ALASKA -- FICTION
Ivey, E. The snow child

FRONTIER AND PIONEER LIFE -- ARIZONA
Grey, Z. Woman of the frontier

Turner, N. E. These is my words

FRONTIER AND PIONEER LIFE -- AUSTRALIA
Grenville, K. The secret river

Malouf, D. Remembering Babylon

Nordhoff, C. Botany Bay

FRONTIER AND PIONEER LIFE -- CALIFORNIA
Bristow, G. Jubilee Trail

FRONTIER AND PIONEER LIFE -- CANADA
Adamson, G. The outlander

Freedman, B. Mrs. Mike

Urquhart, J. Away

Vanderhaeghe, G. The last crossing

FRONTIER AND PIONEER LIFE -- COLORADO
Dallas, S. The diary of Mattie Spenser

Michener, J. A. Centennial

FRONTIER AND PIONEER LIFE -- FICTION
Desrochers, S. Bride of New France

Evison, J. West of here

Keesey, A. Little century

Schanbacher, G. Crossing Purgatory

FRONTIER AND PIONEER LIFE -- KANSAS
Durham, D. A. Gabriel's story

FRONTIER AND PIONEER LIFE -- LOUISIANA
Clark, C. Savage lands

FRONTIER AND PIONEER LIFE -- MIDDLE WESTERN STATES
Cooper, J. F. The prairie

FRONTIER AND PIONEER LIFE -- MINNESOTA
Moberg, V. The last letter home

Moberg, V. Unto a good land

FRONTIER AND PIONEER LIFE -- MONTANA
Williamson, P. Heart of the west

Williamson, P. The outsider

FRONTIER AND PIONEER LIFE -- NEBRASKA
Cather, W. My Antonia

Cather, W. O pioneers!

FRONTIER AND PIONEER LIFE -- NEW YORK (STATE)
Cooper, J. F. The Deerslayer

Cooper, J. F. The last of the Mohicans

Cooper, J. F. The Leatherstocking tales

Cooper, J. F. The Pathfinder

Cooper, J. F. The pioneers

Edmonds, W. D. Drums along the Mohawk

FRONTIER AND PIONEER LIFE -- NEW ZEALAND
Goudge, E. Green Dolphin Street

FRONTIER AND PIONEER LIFE -- OHIO

Bates, E. Her Amish man

Fugitives' fire. Brand, M.

Full circle. Wilcox, C.

The **full** cupboard of life. McCall Smith, A.

Full dark, no stars. King, S.

The **Fuller** memorandum. Stross, C.

Fuller, R. Buckminster, 1895-1983
About
Bognanni, P. The house of tomorrow

Fun and games. Swierczynski, D.

Fun with problems. Stone, R.

FUNCTIONS *See* Differential equations; Mathematical analysis; Mathematics; Set theory

FUND RAISING
> *See also* Finance

Lipsyte, S. The ask

FUNDAMENTALISM
Atwood, M. The Handmaid's tale

Hamid, M. The reluctant fundamentalist

Nunez, S. Salvation city

Wilcox, J. Hunk City

FUNDAMENTALISTS
Hellenga, R. Snakewoman of Little Egypt

Nunez, S. Salvation city

Paretsky, S. Bleeding Kansas

Wilcox, J. Hunk City

Winterson, J. Oranges are not the only fruit

FUNDAMENTALISTS -- FICTION
Cash, W. A land more kind than home

FUNDING *See* Finance

FUNDS *See* Finance

FUNERAL CUSTOMS AND RITES *See* Funeral rites and ceremonies

FUNERAL DIRECTORS *See* Undertakers and undertaking

Funeral for a dog. Pletzinger, T.

Funeral games. Renault, M.

Funeral in Berlin. Deighton, L.

Funeral in blue. Perry, A.

FUNERAL RITES AND CEREMONIES
> *See also* Manners and customs; Rites and ceremonies

Agee, J. A death in the family

Duncan, G. Death of an ordinary man

Faulkner, W. As I lay dying

Lipman, E. The dearly departed

Styron, A. All the finest girls

Styron, W. Lie down in darkness

Tyler, A. Breathing lessons

Waugh, E. The loved one

Welty, E. Losing battles

Welty, E. The optimist's daughter

FUNERAL RITES AND CEREMONIES -- FICTION
St. Aubyn, E. At last

FUNNIES *See* Comic books, strips, etc.

FUR TRADE
Guthrie, A. B. The big sky

FUR TRADERS
Sargent, C. Museum of human beings

FURBEARING ANIMALS *See* Animals; Economic zoology

The **further** adventures of Menachem-Mendl. Sholem Aleichem

FUTURE
Amis, M. London fields

Anderson, P. Genesis

Asaro, C. Primary inversion

Asimov, I. Forward the Foundation

Asimov, I. Foundation

Asimov, I. Foundation and earth

Asimov, I. Foundation and empire

Asimov, I. Foundation's edge

Asimov, I. Prelude to Foundation

Asimov, I. Second Foundation

Atwood, M. The Handmaid's tale

Atwood, M. The year of the flood

Auster, P. In the country of last things

Bacigalupi, P. The windup girl

Ball, J. The curfew

Banks, I. Matter

Barnes, J. The armies of memory

Bear, G. Anvil of stars

Bear, G. The forge of God

Benford, G. Foundation's fear

Benford, G. Timescape

Bova, B. Saturn

Brin, D. Earth

Brooks, A. 2030

Brunner, J. Stand on Zanzibar

Bynum, L. Veracity

Cherryh, C. J. Foreigner

Cline, E. Ready player one

Conn, B. The fixed stars

Crace, J. All that follows

Crace, J. The pesthouse

Cunningham, M. Specimen days

Cussler, C. Shock wave

Danvers, D. The fourth world

Day of the oprichnik

Delany, S. R. Stars in my pocket like grains of sand

Doctorow, C. Down and out in the Magic Kindgom

Egan, G. Zendegi

Eskridge, K. Solitaire

Ferrigno, R. Prayers for the assassin

Foster, A. D. The mocking program

Fuentes, C. The eagle's throne

Gibson, W. Neuromancer

Gleason, R. End of days

Goonan, K. A. Light music

Grant, M. Feed

Grippando, J. The abduction

found the bishop's bird stump at last
Wilson, D. H. Robopocalypse
Wilson, R. C. Julian Comstock
Wolfe, G. The Citadel of the Autarch
Wolfe, G. The claw of the conciliator
Wolfe, G. An evil guest
Wolfe, G. Home fires
Wolfe, G. The shadow of the torturer
Wolfe, G. The sword of the Lictor
Wolfe, G. The Urth of the new sun
Zamiatin, E. I. We
Zelazny, R. Lord of light
The **future** has a past. Cooper, J. C.
The **Future** Is Japanese.
FUTURE LIFE
> *See also* Death; Eschatology
Brockmeier, K. The brief history of the dead
Farmer, P. J. The fabulous riverboat
Krusoe, J. Toward you
FUTURE LIFE -- FICTION
Domingue, R. The mercy of thin air
FUTURE SHOCK *See* Culture conflict
FUTURES *See* Investments; Securities
FUTURISM (ART) *See* Art
FUTURISM
Kushner, R. The flamethrowers
The **futurist.** Othmer, J. P.
FUTUROLOGY *See* Forecasting

G

G is for gumshoe. Grafton, S.
G.I. bones. Limon, M.
The **Gabriel** hounds. Stewart, M.
Gabriel's story. Durham, D. A.
Gabriela, clove and cinnamon. Amado, J.
Gad's Hall. Lofts, N.
GAELS *See* Celts
Gage, Thomas, 1721-1787
> **About**
Shaara, J. Rise to rebellion
Gai-Jin. Clavell, J.
GAIA HYPOTHESIS *See* Biology; Earth; Ecology; Life (Biology)
Galapagos. Vonnegut, K.
GALAPAGOS ISLANDS
Vonnegut, K. Galapagos
Galatea 2.2. Powers, R.
Galilei, Galileo, 1564-1642
> **About**
Robinson, K. S. Galileo's dream
Galileo's dream. Robinson, K. S.
Gallatin Canyon. McGuane, T.
GALLOWAY, RUTH (FICTITIOUS CHARACTER)
Griffiths, E. The crossing places
Griffiths, E. A Dying Fall

Griffiths, E. The house at sea's end
Gallowglass. Vine, B.
Gallows thief. Cornwell, B.
Galore. Crummey, M.
The **Galton** case. Macdonald, R.
GALVESTON (TEX.)
Black, E. The drowning house
GAMACHE, ARMAND (FICTITIOUS CHARACTER)
Penny, L. The beautiful mystery
Penny, L. How the light gets in
The **gamal.** Collins, C.
Gambit. Stout, R.
The **gambler.** Dostoyevsky, F.
GAMBLERS
Bull, E. Territory
Russell, M. D. Doc
West, P. O.K.
GAMBLING
> *See also* Games
Amado, J. Dona Flor and her two husbands
Atkins, A. White shadow
Dickens, C. The old curiosity shop
Dixon, K. The art of losing
Dostoyevsky, F. The gambler
Fleming, I. Casino Royale
Francis, D. Even money
Iles, G. The devil's punchbowl
Johnson, D. Nobody move
Latour, J. The Havana World Series
Rigosi, G. Night bus
Robbins, H. Sin city
Schwegel, T. Person of interest
Westlake, D. E. Bad news
GAMBLING -- FICTION
Grant, C. A gentleman undone
Higgins, G. V. The Digger's game
MacLean, S. A rogue by any other name
O'Nan, S. The odds
The **game.** King, L. R.
GAME AND GAME BIRDS
> *See also* Animals; Birds; Wildlife
A **game** of thrones. Martin, G. R. R.
Game over. Harrod-Eagles, C.
GAME PROTECTION
> *See also* Game and game birds; Hunting; Wildlife conservation
Doiron, P. The poacher's son
GAME PROTECTION -- FICTION
Box, C. J. Open season
Box, C. J. Out of range
GAME RESERVES *See* Hunting; Wildlife conservation
GAME THEORY *See* Mathematical models; Mathematics; Probabilities
GAME WARDENS

Gathering of waters. McFadden, B. L.

Gaudy Night. Sayers, D. L.

Gauguin, Paul, 1848-1903
About
Maugham, W. S. The moon and sixpence

Vargas Llosa, M. The way to paradise

GAUL
Llywelyn, M. Druids

Gaulle, Charles de, 1890-1970
About
Forsyth, F. The day of the jackal

Gauss, Carl Friedrich, 1777-1855
About
Kehlmann, D. Measuring the world

Gautama Buddha
About
Mishima, Y. The Temple of Dawn

Mishima, Y. The temple of the golden pavilion

GAY LIBERATION MOVEMENT *See* Homosexuality

GAY LIFESTYLE *See* Homosexuality

GAY MEN -- COMIC BOOKS, STRIPS, ETC
Cruse, H. The complete Wendel

GAY MEN -- CRIMES AGAINST
Harvey, J. Gone to ground

McGarrity, M. Everyone dies

McKinty, A. The cold cold ground

GAY MEN -- FICTION
See also Men

Alenyikov, M. Ivan and Misha

Boyne, J. The absolutist

Brunt, C. R. Tell the wolves I'm home

Festing, I. A. The birdkeeper

Jones, J. S. The silence

Mehta, R. Quarantine

White, E. Jack Holmes and his friend

GAY MEN -- INDIA -- NĀGPUR
Festing, I. A. The birdkeeper

GAY YOUTH
See also Youth

Cruse, H. The complete Wendel

Gazelle. Ducornet, R.

Geek love. Dunn, K.

GEEKS (COMPUTER ENTHUSIASTS)
Stross, C. The apocalypse codex

GEESE *See* Birds; Poultry

GEISHAS
See also Entertainers

Golden, A. Memoirs of a geisha

Gemini. Dunnett, D.

The **Gemini** contenders. Ludlum, R.

GEMINI PROJECT *See* Orbital rendezvous (Space flight); Space flight

GEMS *See* Archeology; Art; Decoration and ornament; Engraving; Minerals

GENDER ROLE

See also Sex; Sex differences (Psychology); Social role

Winter, K. Annabel

GENE MAPPING *See* Genetics

GENE SPLICING *See* Genetic engineering

GENE THERAPY *See* Genetic engineering; Therapeutics

GENE TRANSFER *See* Genetic engineering

GENEALOGY
Groff, L. The monsters of Templeton

Halter, M. The book of Abraham

The **general** and his labyrinth. Garcia Marquez, G.

The **general** of the dead army. Kadare, I.

GENERAL STORES *See* Retail trade; Stores

The **general's** daughter. DeMille, N.

GENERALS
Bell, M. S. All souls' rising

Byrd, M. Grant

Castellanos Moya, H. Tyrant memory

Charyn, J. Johnny One-Eye

De Bernieres, L. Birds without wings

Doctorow, E. L. The march

Fleming, T. J. Dreams of glory

Forsyth, F. The day of the jackal

George, M. The memoirs of Cleopatra

Gingrich, N. Grant comes east

Griffin, W. E. B. Secret honor

Hanif, M. A case of exploding mangoes

Jakes, J. Savannah; or, A gift for Mr. Lincoln

Jones, D. C. The court-martial of George Armstrong Custer

Massie, A. Caesar

McCullough, C. The first man in Rome

McCullough, C. Fortune's favorites

McCullough, C. The grass crown

Mrazek, R. J. Unholy fire

Naipaul, V. S. A way in the world

Penman, S. K. Falls the shadow

Ricks, T. E. A soldier's duty

Roth, P. The plot against America

Shaara, J. The glorious cause

Shaara, J. Gods and generals

Shaara, J. Gone for soldiers

Shaara, J. The last full measure

Shaara, J. Rise to rebellion

Simmons, D. Black Hills

Vargas Llosa, M. The Feast of the Goat

GENERALS -- FICTION
Kerr, P. Prague fatale

GENERATION GAP *See* Conflict of generations

Generation loss. Hand, E.

GENERIC DRUGS *See* Drugs; Generic products

Generosity. Powers, R.

Generous death. Pickard, N.

Genesis. Anderson, P.

GENETIC ENGINEERING

McCullers, C. The member of the wedding
Siddons, A. R. Heartbreak Hotel
Siddons, A. R. Nora, Nora
Smith, L. E. Strange fruit
Woods, S. Grass roots
Woods, S. Palindrome
GEORGIA -- ATLANTA
Cleage, P. Babylon sisters
Ha Jin A free life
Hooper, K. Finding Laura
Jones, T. Silver sparrow
Randall, A. The wind done gone
Wolfe, T. A man in full
GEORGIA -- FICTION
Burns, O. A. Cold Sassy tree
Dexter, P. Paris Trout
Doctorow, E. L. The march
Ellison, R. Three days before the shooting--
Jackson, J. Between, Georgia
Johansen, I. The killing game
McCullers, C. The member of the wedding
Morrison, T. Home
Siddons, A. R. Nora, Nora
White, B. Quite a year for plums
GEORGIA -- SAVANNAH
Battle, L. Southern women
Jakes, J. Savannah; or, A gift for Mr. Lincoln
Price, E. Savannah
Gerald's game. King, S.
Géricault, Théodore, 1791-1824
About
Edge, A. The god of spring
GERM WARFARE *See* Biological warfare
GERMAN AMERICANS
Erdrich, L. The Master Butchers Singing Club
Hegi, U. The vision of Emma Blau
Jakes, J. American dreams
The **German** bride. Hershon, J.
GERMAN FICTION -- 20TH CENTURY
Thelen, A. V. The island of second sight
GERMAN FICTION -- TRANSLATIONS INTO ENGLISH
Adler, H. G. Panorama
Bernhard, T. The loser
Bernhard, T. Woodcutters
Boll, H. The silent angel
The emigrants
Fallada, H. Every man dies alone
Grass, G. The box
Grass, G. The call of the toad
Handke, P. Don Juan
Hein, C. Settlement
Hofmann, G. Lichtenberg and the little flower girl
Hofmann, G. Luck
Kehlmann, D. Fame
Kehlmann, D. Measuring the world

Keilson, H. Comedy in a minor key
Musil, R. The man without qualities
Pletzinger, T. Funeral for a dog
Schlink, B. Homecoming
Schlink, B. The reader
Schlink, B. The weekend
Schulze, I. New lives
Sebald, W. G. Vertigo
Stamm, P. Seven years
Stanisic, S. How the soldier repairs the gramophone
Walser, R. The assistant
GERMAN LANGUAGE *See* Language and languages
GERMAN REFUGEES
Remarque, E. M. Arch of triumph
Remarque, E. M. The night in Lisbon
GERMANS -- ARGENTINA
Aira, C. An afternoon in the life of a landscape painter
GERMANS -- BRAZIL
Levin, I. The boys from Brazil
GERMANS -- CANADA
Norman, H. What is left the daughter
GERMANS -- CHINA
Reuss, F. Mohr
GERMANS -- CZECHOSLOVAKIA
Demetz, H. The house on Prague Street
GERMANS -- DENMARK
Follett, K. Hornet flight
GERMANS -- ENGLAND
Follett, K. Eye of the needle
Higgins, J. The eagle has landed
GERMANS
Thelen, A. V. The island of second sight
GERMANS -- FRANCE
Remarque, E. M. All quiet on the western front
Remarque, E. M. Arch of triumph
GERMANS -- GREAT BRITAIN -- FICTION
Griffiths, E. The house at sea's end
GERMANS -- ISLANDS OF THE PACIFIC
Conrad, J. Victory
GERMANS -- NAMIBIA
Brink, A. P. The other side of silence
GERMANS -- NORWAY
Steinbeck, J. The moon is down
GERMANS -- POLAND
Hersey, J. The wall
Uris, L. Mila 18
GERMANS -- RUSSIA
Anatoli, A. Babi Yar
Kirst, H. H. Forward, Gunner Asch!
Robbins, D. L. War of the rats
GERMANS -- SPAIN
Bolaño, R. The Third Reich
GERMANS -- UNITED STATES
Dische, I. The Empress of Weehawken

Golden, A. Memoirs of a geisha
Gowdy, B. Helpless
Grimes, M. Belle ruin
Grimes, M. Biting the moon
Grimes, M. Cold Flat Junction
Grimes, M. Hotel Paradise
Guene, F. Kiffe kiffe tomorrow
Guterson, D. Our Lady of the Forest
Hall, A. L. The rhythm of the road
Hannah, K. On Mystic lake
Harington, D. With
Harrington, L. Alice Bliss
Harris, J. The girl with no shadow
Hegi, U. The worst thing I've done
Henley, P. Hummingbird house
Hoffman, A. Illumination night
Hubbard, S. The Society of S
Jen, G. Mona in the promised land
Johansen, I. Final target
Johnson, S. The sailmaker's daughter
Jones, L. Mister Pip
Jones, T. Silver sparrow
Julavits, H. The uses of enchantment
Keegan, N. Swimming
Kidd, S. M. The secret life of bees
King, S. The girl who loved Tom Gordon
Kirshenbaum, B. An almost perfect moment
Klein, R. The moth diaries
Koontz, D. R. One door away from heaven
Krauss, N. The history of love
Krilanovich, G. The orange eats creeps
Kring, S. Thank you for all things
Kwok, J. Girl in translation
Kyle, A. The god of animals
Lawson, M. Crow Lake
Le, T. D. T. The gangster we are all looking for
Lipman, E. My latest grievance
Lodato, V. Mathilda Savitch
Lukas, M. D. The Oracle of Stamboul
Lurie, A. Only children
MacDonald The way the crow flies
Mapson Solomon's oak
March, W. The bad seed
Mason, D. A far country
Maynard, J. The usual rules
McCorkle, J. Ferris Beach
McDermott, A. Child of my heart
McEwan, I. Atonement
McGowan, H. Schooling
McMahon, J. Dismantled
Meidav, E. Lola, California
Miller, S. Lost in the forest
Monaghan, N. The killing jar
Moriarty, L. The center of everything
Morrison, T. The bluest eye
Nadzam, B. Lamb

Oates, J. C. Foxfire
Oates, J. C. Rape
O'Connell, C. Judas child
Pearson, A. I think I love you
Pessl, M. Special topics in calamity physics
Picoult, J. Keeping Faith
Picoult, J. My sister's keeper
Pietroni, A. L. Ruby's spoon
Pilcher, R. Coming home
Portes, A. Hick
Powell, S. The Mushroom Man
Prose, F. Goldengrove
Raymond, J. The half-life
Revoyr, N. Wingshooters
Reynolds, M. The Starlite Drive-in
Rice, L. Safe harbor
Riordan, R. Cold Springs
Rock, P. My abandonment
Roy, L. Bent Road
Russell, K. Swamplandia!
Samarasan, P. Evening is the whole day
Sanders, D. Clover
Sebold, A. The lovely bones
Shreve, A. Light on snow
Siddons, A. R. Nora, Nora
Siddons, A. R. Sweetwater Creek
Sinclair, A. Coffee will make you black
Sittenfeld, C. Prep
Smith, D. I capture the castle
Spark, M. The prime of Miss Jean Brodie
Tarkington, B. Alice Adams
Tartt, D. The little friend
Tea, M. Rose of no man's land
Tepper, S. S. The Margarets
Toews, M. A complicated kindness
Ulinich, A. Petropolis
Vernon, O. Eden
Walton, J. Among others
Watson, J. E. Asta in the wings
Weiner, J. Certain girls
Whitney, P. A. The singing stones
Wilson, R. C. Blind Lake
Winthrop, E. H. December
Wolff, R. The beginners
Woodrell, D. Winter's bone
Yoshimoto, B. Goodbye Tsugumi
GIRLS -- CRIMES AGAINST
  Martin, L. The bright forever
GIRLS -- EDUCATION *See* Education
GIRLS -- FICTION
  Abbott, M. E. Dare me
  Grant, H. The vanishing of Katharina Linden
  Hassman, T. Girlchild
  Merullo, R. The talk-funny girl
  Moore, M. M. So far away
  Ozeki, R. L. A tale for the time being

Paretsky, S. Breakdown
Urrea, L. A. Queen of America
GIRLS -- ITALY
Avallone, S. Swimming to Elba
GIRLS -- JUVENILE FICTION
London, K. Cali boys
GIRLS -- PSYCHOLOGY
Kushner, D. M. The conditions of love
GIRLS -- SEXUAL BEHAVIOR
Avallone, S. Swimming to Elba
Girls in trucks. Crouch, K.
Girls in white dresses. Close, J.
The **girls** of slender means. Spark, M.
GIRLS' CLUBS *See* Clubs; Societies
The **girls'** guide to hunting and fishing. Bank, M.
Give us a kiss. Woodrell, D.
The **given** day. Lehane, D.
GLADIATORS
Lytton, E. B. L. The last days of Pompeii
Sienkiewicz, H. Quo Vadis
GLADIATORS -- FICTION
Kane, B. Spartacus
GLADNESS *See* Happiness
The **Gladstone** bag. MacLeod, C.
Glamorous powers. Howatch, S.
GLASGOW (SCOTLAND)
Brookmyre, C. Where the bodies are buried
Glass. Savage, S.
GLASS ARTISTS
Vreeland, S. Clara and Mr. Tiffany
The **glass** bead game (Magister Ludi) Hesse, H.
GLASS BLOWING AND WORKING
Vreeland, S. Clara and Mr. Tiffany
Glass boys. Lundrigan, N.
The **glass** demon. Grant, H.
Glass dragons. McMullen, S.
Glass God. Griffin, K.
The **glass** key. Hammett, D.
The **glass** lake. Binchy, M.
The **Glass** Ocean. Baker, L.
The **glass** of time. Cox, M.
The **glass** palace. Ghosh, A.
The **glass** rainbow. Burke, J. L.
The **glass** room. Mawer, S.
Glasshouse. Stross, C.
GLEN CANYON NATIONAL RECREATION AREA (UTAH AND ARIZ.)
Barr, N. The rope
GLIDERS (AERONAUTICS) *See* Aeronautics; Airplanes
GLIDING AND SOARING *See* Aeronautics
Glister. Burnside, J.
Glittering images. Howatch, S.
Glitz. Leonard, E.
GLOBAL WARMING
McEwan, I. Solar

Wray, J. Lowboy
Gloriana's torch. Finney, P.
The **glorious** cause. Shaara, J.
GLOSSARIES *See* Encyclopedias and dictionaries
Go down, Moses. Faulkner, W.
Go tell it on the mountain. Baldwin, J.
Go with me. Freeman, C.
Go, mutants! Doyle, L.
The **go-between.** Turner, F. W.
The **goat** bridge. McNally, T. M.
GOD
Ehrenreich, B. Ether
God bless you, Mr. Rosewater. Vonnegut, K.
God Emperor of Dune. Herbert, F.
The **god** of animals. Kyle, A.
The **god** of small things. Roy, A.
The **god** of small things. Roy, A.
The **god** of spring. Edge, A.
The **god** of the hive. King, L. R.
The **god** of war. Silver, M.
God on the rocks. Gardam, J.
God's fool. Slouka, M.
God's gym. Wideman, J. E.
God's little acre. Caldwell, E.
God's mercy. Ekman, K.
Godchildren. Coleridge, N.
GODDESS RELIGION *See* Paganism
The **godfather.** Puzo, M.
The **godfather** of Kathmandu. Burdett, J.
The **Godfather** returns. Winegardner, M.
The **godless** man. Doherty, P. C.
Godplayer. Cook, R.
GODS
Baker, K. Sky coyote
Gaiman, N. American gods
Jemisin, N. K. The hundred thousand kingdoms
Lake, J. Endurance
Phillips, M. Gods behaving badly
Gods and beasts. Mina, D.
Gods and generals. Shaara, J.
GODS AND GODDESSES
Card, O. S. The Gate Thief
Carey, J. Banewreaker
Greenwood, K. Out of the black land
Gods behaving badly. Phillips, M.
The **gods** of Gotham. Faye, L.
Gods of Riverworld. Farmer, P. J.
The **gods** themselves. Asimov, I.
Gods without men. Kunzru, H.
Gogh, Vincent van, 1853-1890
About
Stone, I. Lust for life
Going after Cacciato. O'Brien, T.
Going for the gold. Lathen, E.
Going native. Wright, S.
Going postal. Pratchett, T.

Going to bend. Hammond, D. C.

Going to meet the man. Baldwin, J.

Going to see the elephant. Fishburne, R.

Going wrong. Rendell, R.

Gold. Cleave, C.

GOLD

Brand, M. Chinook

Dunnett, D. Scales of gold

Fleming, I. Goldfinger

Higgins, J. Drink with the Devil

L'Amour, L. The Californios

Stephenson, N. Cryptonomicon

GOLD -- FICTION

Friedman, D. Don't ever get old

The **gold** bug variations. Powers, R.

The **Gold** Coast. DeMille, N.

GOLD MINES AND MINING

Hand, D. Deep Creek

Overholser, W. D. Law at Angel's Landing

Parry, R. The winter wolf

Traven, B. The treasure of the Sierra Madre

Tremain, R. The color

GOLD MINES AND MINING -- FICTION

Priest, C. The inexplicables

GOLD RUSH *See* Gold mines and mining

GOLD RUSHES *See* Gold mines and mining

GOLD, SOPHIA (FICTITIOUS CHARACTER)

Young, T. W. The renegades

The **golden** age. Vidal, G.

The **golden** age. Wright, J. C.

The **golden** bowl. James, H.

Golden country. Gilmore, J.

The **golden** cup. Plain, B.

The **Golden** Egg. Leon, D.

Golden fox. Smith, W. A.

GOLDEN GATE BRIDGE (SAN FRANCISCO, CALIF.) *See* Bridges

The **golden** globe. Varley, J.

The **golden** leopard. Kerstan, L.

Golden lies. Freethy, B.

The **golden** notebook. Lessing, D. M.

The **golden** ocean. O'Brian, P.

The **golden** one. Peters, E.

GOLDEN RULE *See* Ethics

The **golden** season. Brockway, C.

The **golden** torc. May, J.

Golden Trillium. Norton, A.

The **golden** tulip. Laker, R.

Goldengrove. Prose, F.

Goldfinger. Fleming, I.

GOLDFISH

See also Fishes

GOLDWORK

See also Art metalwork; Gold; Metalwork

The **Golem.** Wiesel, E.

GOLEM

See also Jewish legends; Mysticism/Judaism

Wiesel, E. The Golem

GOLEM -- FICTION

Wecker, H. The Golem and the Jinni

The **Golem** and the Jinni. Wecker, H.

GOLF

Dexter, P. Train

The **Goliath** bone. Spillane, M.

The **goliath** stone. Harrington, M. J.

Gone. Kellerman, J.

Gone. Hayder, M.

Gone. Hanauer, C.

Gone fishin' Mosley, W.

Gone for good. Coben, H.

Gone for soldiers. Shaara, J.

Gone girl. Flynn, G.

Gone missing. Castillo, L.

Gone south. McCammon, R. R.

Gone to ground. Harvey, J.

Gone to soldiers. Piercy, M.

Gone to the dogs. Guterson, M.

Gone with the wind. Mitchell, M.

The **gone-away** world. Harkaway, N.

Gonna take a homicidal journey. Scoppettone, S.

GOOD AND EVIL

See also Ethics; Philosophy; Theology

Barker, C. Imajica

Barker, C. Weaveworld

Brooks, T. The druid of Shannara

Brooks, T. First king of Shannara

Brooks, T. The measure of the magic

Brooks, T. The sword of Shannara

Browne, R. The paradise prophecy

Bulgakov, M. A. The master and Margarita

De la Cruz, M. Witches of East End

Dickey, J. Deliverance

Doctorow, E. L. Welcome to Hard Times

Garcia Marquez, G. In evil hour

Gay, W. Twilight

Greene, G. The captain and the enemy

James, H. The turn of the screw

King, S. The dark half

King, S. Insomnia

King, S. The stand

Koontz, D. R. From the corner of his eye

Lewis, C. S. Out of the silent planet

Lewis, C. S. Perelandra

Lewis, C. S. That hideous strength

Lewis, C. S. Till we have faces

Mailer, N. The castle in the forest

Martin, M. Windswept House

McCammon, R. R. Boy's life

McEwan, I. Black dogs

Murdoch, I. The green knight

Murdoch, I. The nice and the good

Rice, A. Lasher

Shelley, M. W. Frankenstein; or, The modern Prometheus

Stewart, M. The Gabriel hounds

Stewart, M. The ivy tree

Stewart, M. Nine coaches waiting

Stewart, M. Thunder on the right

Stewart, M. Touch not the cat

Stewart, M. Wildfire at midnight

Stoker, B. Dracula

Trevanian The summer of Katya

Whitney, P. A. Poinciana

Whitney, P. A. The singing stones

Whitney, P. A. Spindrift

Wood, B. The dreaming

Gould's book of fish. Flanagan, R.

Gould, Glenn, 1932-1982

About

Bernhard, T. The loser

Gould, William Buelow, 1803-1853

About

Flanagan, R. Gould's book of fish

GOVERNESSES

Bronte, C. Jane Eyre

Faber, M. The crimson petal and the white

Holt, V. Mistress of Mellyn

James, H. The turn of the screw

McLaughlin, E. The nanny diaries

McLaughlin, E. Nanny returns

Read, P. P. Alice in exile

Seton, A. Dragonwyck

Stewart, M. Nine coaches waiting

GOVERNESSES -- FICTION

Connolly, T. Ironskin

GOVERNMENT EMPLOYEES *See* Civil service

GOVERNMENT INVESTIGATIONS *See* Governmental investigations

GOVERNMENT INVESTIGATORS

Harris, T. Red Dragon

Higgins, J. Day of reckoning

Isaacs, S. Red, white and blue

King, L. R. A darker place

Laukkanen, O. Criminal enterprise

Ludlum, R. The Sigma protocol

McKinzie, C. Crossing the line

Perry, T. The informant

Rush, N. Mortals

Tirone Smith Love her madly

Tirone Smith She smiled sweetly

GOVERNMENT OFFICIALS

Caldwell, T. Dear and glorious physician

Donoghue, E. Slammerkin

Harries, A. Manly pursuits

Millet, L. Oh pure and radiant heart

Nordhoff, C. Men against the sea

Nordhoff, C. Mutiny on the Bounty

Shaara, J. The glorious cause

Shaara, J. Rise to rebellion

Smith, M. C. Stallion Gate

GOVERNMENT OWNERSHIP *See* Economic policy; Industrial policy; Socialism

GOVERNMENT SERVICE *See* Civil service

GOVERNMENT, RESISTANCE TO *See* Resistance to government

GOVERNMENTAL INVESTIGATIONS

Porter, H. The bell ringers

GOVERNORS

Mallon, T. Dewey defeats Truman

Standiford, L. Black Mountain

Grace. Nunez, E.

Grace in thine eyes. Higgs, L. C.

GraceLand. Abani, C.

A **gracious** plenty. Reynolds, S.

GRADUATE STUDENTS

Aciman, A. Harvard Square

Baxter, C. The soul thief

Cameron, P. The city of your final destination

Morrow, J. The philosopher's apprentice

GRAFFITI

Mansbach, A. Rage is back

GRAIL

Cornwell, B. The archer's tale

Cornwell, B. Vagabond

Eco, U. Baudolino

Hemingway, A. The Greenstone grail

Grail of the summer stars. Warrington, F.

GRAMMAR *See* Language and languages; Linguistics

GRAMMY AWARDS *See* Sound recordings

The **grand** complication. Kurzweil, A.

The **grand** Sophy. Heyer, G.

GRANDCHILDREN

McMurtry, L. The evening star

Tyler, A. The amateur marriage

GRANDDAUGHTERS

Desai, K. The inheritance of loss

Hawkes, J. Second skin

Weldon, F. Rhode Island blues

GRANDFATHERS

See also Grandparents

Allen, S. A. The girl who chased the moon

Bilenchi, R. The chill

Burns, O. A. Cold Sassy tree

Dezenhall, E. Money wanders

Dickens, C. Martin Chuzzlewit

Dickens, C. The old curiosity shop

Foer, J. S. Everything is illuminated

Foer, J. S. Extremely loud & incredibly close

Grisham, J. The chamber

Kring, S. Thank you for all things

Lowell, E. Die in plain sight

McGuane, T. Nobody's angel

Obreht, T. The tiger's wife

Cornwell, B. Sharpe's fury

Cornwell, B. Sharpe's prey: Richard Sharpe and the Expedition to Copenhagen, 1807

Cornwell, B. Sharpe's Trafalgar

Kaye, M. M. The far pavilions

Kaye, M. M. Shadow of the moon

Waugh, E. Men at arms

Waugh, E. Officers and gentlemen

GREAT BRITAIN -- ARMY -- OFFICERS

Boulle, P. The bridge over the River Kwai

Forester, C. S. Hornblower and the Atropos

Forester, C. S. Ship of the line

Mallinson, A. A close run thing

Waugh, E. The end of the battle

GREAT BRITAIN -- COLONIES

See also Colonies

Clavell, J. Tai-Pan

GREAT BRITAIN -- COURT AND COURTIERS

Weir, A. A dangerous inheritance

GREAT BRITAIN -- FICTION

Bourne, J. The black hawk

Bradley, A. The sweetness at the bottom of the pie

Bradley, A. The weed that strings the hangman's bag

Carriger, G. Blameless

Dare, T. A night to surrender

Dean, A. A woman of consequence

Fellowes, J. Snobs

Gallagher, S. The bedlam detective

Hodder, M. Expedition to the Mountains of the Moon

Kelly, J. The fire baby

Kelly, J. The moon tunnel

Swift, G. Wish you were here

Winspear, J. Elegy for Eddie

GREAT BRITAIN -- HISTORY

Kearsley, S. Mariana

MacColl, G. To marry an English Lord

GREAT BRITAIN -- HISTORY -- 0-1066

Bracewell, P. Shadow on the crown

Cornwell, B. Death of kings

Cornwell, B. The last kingdom

Cornwell, B. Lords of the North

Cornwell, B. The pale horseman

Cornwell, B. Sword song

Llywelyn, M. After Rome

GREAT BRITAIN -- HISTORY -- 1154-1399, PLANTAGENETS

Doherty, P. C. The Mysterium

Follett, K. Pillars of the earth

Vantrease, B. R. The illuminator

GREAT BRITAIN -- HISTORY -- 1455-1485, WARS OF THE ROSES

Gregory, P. The lady of the rivers

Gregory, P. The red queen

Smith, A. E. Royal mistress

GREAT BRITAIN -- HISTORY -- 1485-1603, TUDORS

Andersen, L. The Boleyn King

Bilyeau, N. The chalice

Buckley, F. The doublet affair

Buckley, F. The fugitive queen

Buckley, F. Queen of ambition

Buckley, F. Queen without a crown

Buckley, F. Queen's ransom

Buckley, F. The siren queen

Clements, R. Revenger

Gregory, P. The constant princess

Gregory, P. The white princess

Higginbotham, S. Her highness, the traitor

Mantel, H. Bring up the bodies

GREAT BRITAIN -- HISTORY -- 14TH CENTURY

Vantrease, B. R. The illuminator

GREAT BRITAIN -- HISTORY -- 1642-1660, CIVIL WAR AND COMMONWEALTH

Brown, S. M. Accidents of providence

GREAT BRITAIN -- HISTORY -- 1714-1837

Blake, R. A dark anatomy

Brockway, C. The golden season

Chase, L. Miss Wonderful

Chase, L. Not quite a lady

Hern, C. The bride sale

Hern, C. Once a gentleman

Kinsale, L. Lessons in French

Putney, M. J. The marriage spell

GREAT BRITAIN -- HISTORY -- 1800-1837

Motion, A. Silver

GREAT BRITAIN -- HISTORY -- 18TH CENTURY

Robertson, I. Island of bones

GREAT BRITAIN -- HISTORY -- 1936-1945

Wein, E. Code name Verity

GREAT BRITAIN -- HISTORY -- 1945-1952

Cameron, P. Coral Glynn

GREAT BRITAIN -- HISTORY -- 19TH CENTURY

Dean, A. A gentleman of fortune, or, The suspicions of Miss Dido Kent

Hodder, M. The strange affair of Spring Heeled Jack

Shepherd, L. The solitary house

GREAT BRITAIN -- HISTORY -- 20TH CENTURY

Baker, J. The undertow

Nicolson, J. Abdication

GREAT BRITAIN -- HISTORY -- ALFRED, 871-899

Cornwell, B. The last kingdom

Cornwell, B. Lords of the North

Cornwell, B. The pale horseman

Cornwell, B. Sword song

Hodder, M. The strange affair of Spring Heeled Jack

GREAT BRITAIN -- SOCIAL LIFE AND CUS-TOMS

Amis, M. Lionel Asbo

Dean, A. A woman of consequence

GREAT BRITAIN -- SOCIAL LIFE AND CUS-TOMS -- 20TH CENTURY

Baker, J. The undertow

GREAT BRITAIN. ARMY -- OFFICERS -- CRIMES AGAINST

Todd, C. An unmarked grave

GREAT DEPRESSION, 1929-1939 -- FICTION

Lansdale, J. R. Edge of dark water

Silver, M. Mary Coin

Great dream of heaven. Shepard, S.

The **great** escape. Phillips, S. E.

Great expectations. Dickens, C.

The **great** fire. Hazzard, S.

The **great** Gatsby. Fitzgerald, F. S.

Great house. Krauss, N.

Great illustrated classics [series]

Verne, J. From the earth to the moon, and Round the moon

The **great** leader. Harrison, J.

The **great** man. Christensen, K.

The **great** night. Adrian, C.

Great north road. Hamilton, P. F.

The **great** perhaps. Meno, J.

Great short works of Joseph Conrad. Conrad, J.

GREAT SMOKY MOUNTAINS (N.C. AND TENN.)

Bledsoe, A. Wisp of a thing

Godwin, G. Evensong

Great stories of the American West.

The **greatest** evil. Kienzle, W. X.

Greatest hits.

The **greatest** man in Cedar Hole. Doyon, S.

GRECO-TURKISH WAR, 1921-1922

Karnezis, P. The maze

GREECE

Cook, E. Achilles

Doherty, P. C. The godless man

Doherty, P. C. The house of death

Fowles, J. The magus

Glass, J. Three Junes

Goddard, R. Into the blue

Jong, E. Sappho's leap

Malouf, D. Ransom

Michaels, A. Fugitive pieces

Murray, S. Forgery

Renault, M. The bull from the sea

Renault, M. Funeral games

Renault, M. The king must die

Renault, M. The last of the wine

Stewart, M. My brother Michael

Unsworth, B. The songs of the kings

GREECE -- ATHENS

Renault, M. The last of the wine

Van Booy, S. Everything beautiful began after

Vidal, G. Creation

GREECE -- DELPHI

Stewart, M. My brother Michael

GREECE -- HISTORY -- 1967-1974

Bakopoulos, N. The green shore

GREECE -- HISTORY -- TO 146 B.C.

Lyon, A. The sweet girl

Miller, M. The song of Achilles

GREECE -- SALONIKA

Furst, A. Spies of the Balkans

GREED

Swinson, K. Playing dirty

GREEK AMERICANS

Cunningham, M. Flesh and blood

Eugenides, J. Middlesex

Pelecanos, G. P. The big blowdown

GREEK ART See Ancient art; Art; Classical antiquities

GREEK LANGUAGE See Language and languages

GREEK MYTHOLOGY

Banville, J. The infinities

Phillips, M. Gods behaving badly

GREEKS -- EGYPT

Jong, E. Sappho's leap

GREEKS -- TURKEY

Miller, M. The song of Achilles

Green cane and juicy flotsam.

Green darkness. Seton, A.

Green Dolphin Street. Goudge, E.

The **Green** House. Vargas Llosa, M.

The **green** knight. Murdoch, I.

Green mansions. Hudson, W. H.

The **green** ripper. MacDonald, J. D.

The **green** shore. Bakopoulos, N.

Greene, Nathanael, 1742-1786

About

Shaara, J. The glorious cause

The **greengage** summer. Godden, R.

GREENHOUSE EFFECT See Global warming

GREENLAND

MacLean, A. Night without end

Smiley, J. The Greenlanders

Vollmann, W. T. The ice-shirt

The **Greenlanders.** Smiley, J.

The **Greenstone** grail. Hemingway, A.

Grey, Jane, Lady, 1537-1554

About

Higginbotham, S. Her highness, the traitor

Weir, A. Innocent traitor

Greywalker. Richardson, K.

GRIEF

Huneven, M. Blame
Irwin, S. M. The dead path
Joss, M. The night following
Kallos, S. Broken for you
Kasischke, L. The life before her eyes
Kennedy, W. Ironweed
Lamb, W. I know this much is true
LaValle, V. D. Big machine
Leavitt, C. Pictures of you
Lehrer, J. The special prisoner
Lourie, R. A hatred for tulips
Martin, V. The confessions of Edward Day
McEwan, I. Atonement
McEwan, I. The innocent
McGrath, P. Trauma
Miller, S. Family pictures
Morrison, T. Jazz
Neville, S. The ghosts of Belfast
Nordan, L. Wolf whistle
Oates, J. C. The gravedigger's daughter
O'Dell, T. Coal Run
Oe, K. An echo of heaven
Petterson, P. In the wake
Robinson, L. Water dogs
Rossner, J. Looking for Mr. Goodbar
Schlink, B. The reader
Schwartz, J. B. Reservation Road
Schwarz, C. Drowning Ruth
Shakespeare, N. Snowleg
Shreve, A. The weight of water
Smith, S. A simple plan
Spencer, S. Man in the woods
Styron, W. Sophie's choice
Trevor, W. The silence in the garden
Tyler, A. Saint maybe
Ward, A. E. Forgive me
Wiesel, E. Twilight

GUILT -- FICTION
Ballantyne, L. The guilty one
Edwards, Y. A Cupboard full of coats
Koryta, M. The prophet
Guilt by association. Clark, M.
Guilt by degrees. Clark, M.
Guilty as sin. Hoag, T.
The **guilty** one. Ballantyne, L.
Guilty pleasures. Sanders, L.
The **gulf.** Poyer, D.
GULF OF ADEN
Leonard, E. Djibouti
GULF STREAM
Hemingway, E. The old man and the sea
Gulliver's travels. Swift, J.
GUNDAM (FICTIONAL CHARACTER) *See* Fictional characters; Fictional robots; Manga; Mecha
Gunman's rhapsody. Parker, R. B.

GUNPOWDER *See* Explosives; Firearms
GUNS *See* Firearms; Ordnance; Rifles; Shotguns
The **guns** of Avalon. Zelazny, R.
The **guns** of Navarone. MacLean, A.
GUNTHER, BERNHARD (FICTITIOUS CHARACTER)
Kerr, P. If the dead rise not
Kerr, P. A Man Without Breath
Kerr, P. The one from the other
Kerr, P. Prague fatale
The **guru** of love. Upadhyay, S.
GUYANA
Bhattacharya, R. The sly company of people who care
Guys and dolls. Runyon, D.
GYPSIES
Gores, J. Cons, scams & grifts
Hugo, V. The hunchback of Notre Dame
King, S. Thinner
McCann, C. Zoli
Merimee, P. Carmen
Penney, S. The invisible ones

H

H is for homicide. Grafton, S.
H. P. Lovecraft. Lovecraft, H. P.
Ha'penny. Walton, J.
The **ha-ha.** King, D.
HABITAT (ECOLOGY) *See* Ecology
HADES *See* Hell
Hadrian, Emperor of Rome, 76-138
About
Yourcenar, M. Memoirs of Hadrian
HAIKU
See also Poetry
HAIR
Boykin, K. The wisdom of hair
HAITI
Danticat, E. The dew breaker
Danticat, E. Krik? Krak!
Greene, G. The comedians
HAITI -- 20TH CENTURY
Danticat, E. Krik? Krak!
HAITI -- FICTION
Allende, I. Island beneath the sea
Danticat, E. Krik? Krak!
HAITI -- PORT-AU-PRINCE
Greene, G. The comedians
HAITI -- REVOLUTION, 1791-1804
Allende, I. Island beneath the sea
Bell, M. S. All souls' rising
Roberts, K. L. Lydia Bailey
HAITIAN AMERICANS
Danticat, E. Krik? Krak!
HAITIANS -- DOMINICAN REPUBLIC
Danticat, E. The farming of bones

Hard evidence. D'Amato, B.

Hard magic. Gilman, L. A.

Hard rain. Abrahams, P.

Hard revolution. Pelecanos, G. P.

Hard road. D'Amato, B.

Hard stop. Knopf, C.

Hard time. Paretsky, S.

A hard time to be a father. Weldon, F.

Hard times. Dickens, C.

Hard twisted. Greaves, C. J.

The hard way. Child, L.

HARDANGER NEEDLEWORK See Drawn
work; Embroidery; Needlework

Hardball. Paretsky, S.

Hardcase. Pronzini, B.

Hardly knew her. Lippman, L.

Hardscrabble road. Haddam, J.

Hardy, Godfrey Harold, 1877-1947
About
Leavitt, D. The Indian clerk

HAREM LIFE
Wallach, J. Seraglio

HARES See Rabbits

Hargreaves, Alice Pleasance Liddell, 1852-1934
About
Benjamin, M. Alice I have been

Hark! McBain, E.

Hark! A vagrant. Beaton, K.

HARLAN COUNTY (KY.)
Leonard, E. Raylan

HARLEM (NEW YORK, N.Y.) -- BIOGRAPHY
Miller, K. E. Q. An angry-ass black woman

HARLEM (NEW YORK, N.Y.)
Miller, K. E. Q. An angry-ass black woman

Harlem Renaissance: five novels of the 1920s.

Harlem Renaissance: four novels of the 1930s.

Harlot's ghost. Mailer, N.

Harm done. Rendell, R.

HARMONY See Composition (Music); Music;
Music -- Theory

Harold II, King of England, 1022?-1066
About
Rathbone, J. The last English king

Haroun and the sea of stories. Rushdie, S.

Harper Perennial modern classics [series]
Crowley, J. Little, big

HARPERS FERRY (W.VA.) -- JOHN BROWN'S
RAID, 1859
Banks, R. Cloudsplitter

HARRINGTON, HONOR (FICTITIOUS CHAR-
ACTER)
Weber, D. Shadow of freedom

The harrowing of Gwynedd. Kurtz, K.

Hart's war. Katzenbach, J.

Harvard Square. Aciman, A.

HARVARD UNIVERSITY

Brooks, G. Caleb's crossing

Martin, W. Harvard Yard

McDonell, N. An expensive education

Wolfe, T. Of time and the river

HARVARD UNIVERSITY -- FICTION
Harrington, R. Penelope

Harvard Yard. Martin, W.

Harvest. Plain, B.

Harvest. Crace, J.

HARWICH (ENGLAND)
Worsley, K. She rises

Hash. Polsan/English

HASHISH See Marijuana

HASIDISM
See also Judaism
Abraham, P. The romance reader
Lebrecht, N. The song of names
Mirvis, T. The outside world
Potok, C. The chosen
Potok, C. The gift of Asher Lev
Potok, C. My name is Asher Lev
Potok, C. The promise

HASSIDISM See Hasidism

HASTINGS (EAST SUSSEX, ENGLAND), BAT-
TLE OF, 1066 See Battles; Great Britain -- History -- 1066-1154, Norman period

The hatbox baby. Brown, C.

HATE See Emotions

HATE CRIMES See Crime; Discrimination; Violence

Hater. Moody, D.

Hateship, friendship, courtship, loveship, marriage.
Munro, A.

A hatred for tulips. Lourie, R.

Haunted. Oates, J. C.

The haunted air. Wilson, F. P.

Haunted ground. Hart, E.

HAUNTED HOUSES
See also Houses
Herbert, J. Ash

The haunted mesa. L'Amour, L.

The haunted monastery. Gulik, R. H. v.

HAUNTED PLACES
Dean, A. A woman of consequence

The haunting of Hill House. Jackson, S.

The haunting of L. Norman, H.

The haunting of Maddy Clare. Saint James, S.

Haunting Rachel. Hooper, K.

Havana. Hunter, S.

Havana Bay. Smith, M. C.

The Havana room. Harrison, C.

Havana run. Standiford, L.

The Havana World Series. Latour, J.

Have his carcase. Sayers, D. L.

HAVERS, BARBARA (FICTITIOUS CHARAC-
TER)

The **heather** blazing. Tóibín, C.

HEAVEN

    See also Eschatology; Future life

  Heinlein, R. A. Job: a comedy of justice

  Sebold, A. The lovely bones

Heaven and hell. Jakes, J.

The **heaven** of Mercury. Watson, B.

Heaven's prisoners. Burke, J. L.

Heaven's reach. Brin, D.

Heavenly days. Wilcox, J.

Heavy planet. Clement, H.

HEBREW FICTION -- TRANSLATIONS INTO ENGLISH

  Appelfeld, A. Blooms of darkness

  Grossman, D. Someone to run with

  Leshem, R. Beaufort

  Oz, A. Panther in the basement

  Oz, A. The same sea

  Oz, A. Scenes from village life

  Shalev, M. A pigeon and a boy

  To the end of the land

HEBREW LANGUAGE *See* Language and languages

HEBREWS *See* Jews

HEBRIDES (SCOTLAND)

  Pollen, B. The summer of the bear

  Stewart, M. The stormy petrel

  Woolf, V. To the lighthouse

HEDGE FUNDS

  Harris, R. The fear index

HEDONISM

  Cave, N. The death of Bunny Munro

  Kazantzakis, N. Zorba the Greek

  Kundera, M. Slowness

  Miller, A. D. Snowdrops

  Pierre, D. B. C. Lights out in Wonderland

  See, C. The handyman

Heechee rendezvous. Pohl, F.

The **Heights.** Hedges, P.

The **heir.** Burrowes, G.

Heir to the glimmering world. Ozick, C.

HEIRESSES

  Hughes, A. Market Street

HEIRS *See* Inheritance and succession

Heirs of Saint Camber [series]

  Kurtz, K. The harrowing of Gwynedd

Helen hath no fury. Roberts, G.

Helen of Troy. George, M.

HELEN OF TROY (LEGENDARY CHARACTER)

  George, M. Helen of Troy

HELICOPTERS *See* Aeronautics; Airplanes

HELIPORTS *See* Airports

Hell. Butler, R. O.

HELL

    See also Eschatology; Future life

  Butler, R. O. Hell

HELL -- FICTION

  Connolly, J. The infernals

Hell at the breech. Franklin, T.

Hell is empty. Johnson, C.

Hell or high water. Castro, J.

Hell to pay. Pelecanos, G. P.

Hellbox. Pronzini, B.

HELLER, NATHAN (FICTITIOUS CHARACTER)

  Collins, M. A. Target Lancer

The **Hellfire** Club. Straub, P.

Helliconia spring. Aldiss, B. W.

Helliconia summer. Aldiss, B. W.

Helliconia winter. Aldiss, B. W.

Hello goodbye. Chenoweth, E.

HELLS CANYON (IDAHO AND OR.)

  Hand, D. Deep Creek

The **help.** Stockett, K.

Help the poor struggler. Grimes, M.

HELPING BEHAVIOR *See* Human behavior; Interpersonal relations

Helpless. Gowdy, B.

Helpless. Palmer, D.

HELPLESSNESS (PSYCHOLOGY) *See* Emotions

HELSINKI (FINLAND)

  Hand, E. Available dark

Hemings, Sally, 1773-1835

        About

  Chase-Riboud, B. Sally Hemings

  Hambly, B. Patriot hearts

The **Hemingway** reader. Hemingway, E.

Hemingway, Ernest, 1899-1961

        About

  McLain, P. The Paris wife

Hemingway, Hadley

        About

  McLain, P. The Paris wife

Henderson the rain king. Bellow, S.

Henry II, King of England, 1133-1189

        About

  Franklin, A. Mistress of the art of death

  Franklin, A. The serpent's tale

  Penman, S. K. Devil's brood

  Penman, S. K. Time and chance

  Penman, S. K. When Christ and his saints slept

Henry III, King of England, 1207-1272

        About

  Penman, S. K. Falls the shadow

The **Henry** James reader. James, H.

Henry of Atlantic City. Reuss, F.

Henry VIII, King of England, 1491-1547

        About

  Andersen, L. The Boleyn King

  Gregory, P. The constant princess

The **highway.** Box, C. J.

HIGHWAY ACCIDENTS *See* Traffic accidents

HIGHWAYMEN *See* Thieves

Highwire moon. Straight, S.

HIJACKING OF AIRCRAFT *See* Hijacking of airplanes

HIJACKING OF AIRPLANES
Griffin, W. E. B. By order of the President
Hospital, J. T. Due preparations for the plague
Keneally, T. Flying hero class
Nance, J. J. The last hostage

HIJACKING OF SHIPS
Coonts, S. America
Follett, K. Triple
MacLean, A. When eight bells toll
Smith, W. A. Those in peril

HIJACKING OF SUBWAYS
Godey, J. The taking of Pelham one two three

HIKING
Nevill, A. The ritual

Hildegard, Saint, 1098-1179
                    About
Sharratt, M. Illuminations

The **hill** bachelors. Trevor, W.

HILLBILLY MUSIC *See* Country music

The **Hills** at home. Clark, N.

HIMALAYA MOUNTAINS
Godden, R. Black Narcissus

HINDI LANGUAGE *See* Indian languages; Language and languages

HINDUS
Kaye, M. M. The far pavilions
Seth, V. A suitable boy

HIP-HOP FICTION *See* Urban fiction

HIPPIES
       See also Bohemianism
Carey, P. His illegal self
Dierbeck, L. One pill makes you smaller
McPhee, M. L'America
Swann, M. Flower children

HIPPIES -- FAMILY RELATIONSHIPS
Swann, M. Flower children

HIPPIES -- FICTION
Groff, L. Arcadia
Swann, M. Flower children

The **hippopotamus** pool. Peters, E.

Hirasawa, Sadamichi, 1892-1987
                    About
Peace, D. Occupied city

HIRED KILLERS
Brown, S. The crush
Collins, M. A. Quarry's ex
De Féo, R. Calling Mr. King
DeWitt, P. The Sisters brothers
Estleman, L. D. Something borrowed, something black

Gay, W. Twilight
Greatest hits
Hunter, S. Havana
Leonard, E. Mr. Paradise
Liss, D. The ethical assassin
Littell, R. Walking back the cat
Manchette Fatale
McCarthy, C. No country for old men
Neville, S. The ghosts of Belfast
Perry, T. Fidelity
Perry, T. The informant
Perry, T. Pursuit
Perry, T. Runner
Perry, T. Shadow woman
Rice, A. Angel time
Rice, A. Of love and evil
Sallis, J. The killer is dying
Silva, D. The mark of the assassin
Standiford, L. Black Mountain
Stroby, W. Cold shot to the heart
Vachss, A. H. Two trains running
Waite, U. The terror of living
Weaver, M. Deceptions
Westlake, D. E. The hook
Wignall, K. For the dogs
Winslow, D. The winter of Frankie Machine

HIRED MEN
Malamud, B. The fixer
Quindlen, A. Blessings
See, C. The handyman
Tyler, A. A patchwork planet

HIRED WOMEN
Tyler, A. The clock winder

His Clockwork Canary. Ciotta, B.

His illegal self. Carey, P.

His majesty's dragon. Novik, N.

His Master's Voice. Lem, S.

His mother's son. Emmons, C.

HISPANIC AMERICANS
       See also Latinos (U.S.)
Burgess, M. Dogfight, a love story
Valdes-Rodriguez, A. Dirty girls on top

The **historian.** Kostova, E.

HISTORIANS
       See also Authors
Bayard, L. The school of night
Bell, A. A. The blood of Caesar
Coetzee, J. M. Foe
Cook, T. H. The last talk with Lola Faye
Flynn, M. Eifelheim
George, M. The memoirs of Cleopatra
Harris, R. Archangel
Hunt, R. Mr. Chartwell
Lively, P. How it all began
Lively, P. Family album
Lurie, A. The nowhere city

Duncan, D. When the saints
Finch, C. A beautiful blue death
Follett, K. Winter of the world
Frazier, C. Nightwoods
Furst, A. Mission to Paris
Gabaldon, D. The fiery cross
Gardam, J. Last Friends
Gentle, M. The black opera
Gillham, D. R. City of women
Godwin, G. Flora
Gohlke, C. I have seen him in the watchfires
Gohlke, C. Promise me this
Goodman, J. Season to be sinful
Gracie, A. The Autumn Bride
Grant, C. A gentleman undone
Grant, C. A lady awakened
Graver, E. The end of the point
Gray, J. A Duke Never Yields
Grecian, A. The black country
Greenwood, K. Out of the black land
Gregory, P. The constant princess
Gregory, P. The kingmaker's daughter
Gregory, P. The lady of the rivers
Gregory, P. The red queen
Grenville, K. Sarah Thornhill
Grindle, L. Villa triste
Groot, T. Flame of resistance
Hambly, B. Good man Friday
Harkness, D. Shadow of night
Harman, P. The midwife of Hope River
Harrison, K. Enchantments
Hatcher, R. L. Catching Katie
Hensher, P. Scenes from early life
Hern, C. The bride sale
Higginbotham, S. Her highness, the traitor
Higgs, L. C. Grace in thine eyes
Higley, T. L. Pompeii
Hodder, M. Expedition to the Mountains of the Moon
Holbert, B. Lonesome animals
Hood, A. The Obituary Writer
Hoyt, E. Scandalous desires
Hoyt, E. Thief of Shadows
Hunt, L. Kind one
Hunter, M. The conquest of Lady Cassandra
Ivey, E. The snow child
James, E. When beauty tamed the beast
James, P. D. Death comes to Pemberley
Jensen, N. The sisters
Jones, E. P. The known world
Jones, J. S. The silence
Jones, S. The uninvited guests
Jones, S. Four sisters, all queens
Kane, B. Spartacus
Karp, L. A perilous conception
Kerr, P. A Man Without Breath

Kerstan, L. The golden leopard
Khair, T. The thing about thugs
Kibler, J. Calling Me Home
King, L. R. Garment of shadows
Kinsale, L. Lessons in French
Kirkpatrick, J. A flickering light
Kneale, M. English passengers
Koen, K. Before Versailles
Kowal, M. R. Without a summer
Lambdin, D. Hostile Shores
Lehmann, S. Astor Place Vintage
Lethem, J. Dissident Gardens
Lin, J. The Dragon and the Pearl
Livesey, M. The flight of Gemma Hardy
Locke, A. The cutting season
Lyndon, R. Hawk quest
MacLean, S. One Good Earl Deserves a Lover
Majmudar, A. Partitions
Mallon, T. Watergate
Manfredi, V. M. A Winter's Night
Mantel, H. Bring up the bodies
Marcantel, P. An army of angels
Medeiros, T. The Temptation of Your Touch
Meno, J. Office girl
Meyer, P. The Son
Moore, K. To seduce an angel
Moore, S. The life of objects
Moran, M. The second empress
Morgenstern, E. The night circus
Morris, M. Man in the blue moon
Morrow, J. The last witchfinder
Morsi, P. The love charm
Morton, C. Stealing Mona Lisa
Nicholas, D. Something red
Nickson, C. Cold cruel winter
Nicolson, J. Abdication
Norfolk, L. John Saturnall's feast
Oates, J. C. The Accursed
O'Brien, T. L. The Lincoln conspiracy
Odell, J. The healing
Pajer, B. Capacity for murder
Pajer, B. Fatal induction
Parris, S. J. Sacrilege
Pearl, M. The last Dickens
Perry, A. A sunless sea
Pitts, L. Freeman
The Poisoned Pilgrim
Pötzsch, O. The beggar king
Powers, T. Hide me among the graves
Powning, B. The sea captain's wife
Preston, C. The scrapbook of Frankie Pratt
Putney, M. J. Nowhere near respectable
Rash, R. The cove
Rindell, S. The Other Typist
Robertson, I. Island of bones
Roy, L. Until she comes home

Holding lies. Larison, J.
Holding still for as long as possible. Whittall, Z.
A hole in Texas. Wouk, H.
The hole we're in. Zevin, G.
HOLE, HARRY (FICTITIOUS CHARACTER)
  Nesbø, J. The leopard
  Nesbø, J. Phantom
HOLISTIC MEDICINE *See* Alternative medicine;
  Medicine
Holliday, John Henry, 1851-1887
          About
  Bull, E. Territory
  Russell, M. D. Doc
  West, P. O.K.
The **Hollow.** Christie, A.
The **hollow** city. Wells, D.
The **hollow** hills. Stewart, M.
The **hollow** lands. Moorcock, M.
The **hollow-eyed** angel. Van de Wetering, J.
A **holly,** jolly murder. Hess, J.
Hollywood. Vidal, G.
HOLLYWOOD (CALIF.)
  Bagshawe, T. Adored
  Bornikova, P. Box office poison
  Sallis, J. Drive
  Wambaugh, J. Harbor nocturne
  Weiner, J. The next best thing
HOLLYWOOD (LOS ANGELES, CALIF.)
  Bagshawe, T. Adored
  DeWitt, P. Ablutions
  Erickson, S. Zeroville
  Gold, G. D. Sunnyside
  Kaminsky, S. M. To catch a spy
  Oates, J. C. Blonde
  Sherrill, M. My last movie star
  Vidal, G. Hollywood
  Wagner, B. The chrysanthemum palace
  Wambaugh, J. Hollywood Hills
  Wambaugh, J. Hollywood Station
  Weiner, J. The next best thing
  Wouk, H. The lawgiver
Hollywood crows. Wambaugh, J.
Hollywood Hills. Wambaugh, J.
Hollywood Station. Wambaugh, J.
Holmes on the range. Hockensmith, S.
Holmes, Oliver Wendell, 1809-1894
          About
  Pearl, M. The Dante Club
**HOLMES, SHERLOCK (FICTITIOUS CHAR-
  ACTER)**
  Cullin, M. A slight trick of the mind
  Doyle, A. C. S. The adventures and the memoirs of
    Sherlock Holmes
  King, L. R. The game
  King, L. R. Garment of shadows
  King, L. R. Justice Hall

  King, L. R. O Jerusalem
  Moore, G. The Sherlockian
HOLOCAUST SURVIVORS
  Adler, H. G. Panorama
  Auslander, S. Hope
  Bellow, S. Mr. Sammler's planet
  Chatwin, B. Utz
  Conroy, P. Beach music
  Demetz, H. The house on Prague Street
  Federman, R. Shhh
  Havazelet, E. Bearing the body
  Krauss, N. The history of love
  Michaels, A. Fugitive pieces
  Ozick, C. The shawl
  Perlman, E. The street sweeper
  Phillips, C. The nature of blood
  Prose, F. A changed man
  Pye, M. The pieces from Berlin
  Rosen, J. Joy comes in the morning
  Singer, I. B. Shadows on the Hudson
  Wallant, E. L. The pawnbroker
  Wiesel, E. The forgotten
  Wiesel, E. Twilight
  Winer, A. The marriage artist
HOLOCAUST VICTIMS
  Lourie, R. A hatred for tulips
  Ozick, C. The Messiah of Stockholm
HOLOCAUST, 1933-1945
  Bellow, S. The Bellarosa connection
  The emigrants
  Keneally, T. Schindler's list
  Wiesel, E. Twilight
  Yolen, J. Briar Rose
HOLOCAUST, 1939-1945
    See also Antisemitism; Germany -- History
    -- 1933-1945; Jews -- Persecutions
  de Rosnay, T. Sarah's key
  Jensen, J. Dante's equation
HOLOCAUST, JEWISH (1933-1945)
  Amis, M. Time's arrow
  Appelfeld, A. Badenheim 1939
  Appelfeld, A. Blooms of darkness
  Bellow, S. The Bellarosa connection
  Cooley, M. The archivist
  Delbanco, N. What remains
  Demetz, H. The house on Prague Street
  The emigrants
  Fallada, H. Every man dies alone
  Harris, R. Fatherland
  Hersey, J. The wall
  Iles, G. Black cross
  Keneally, T. Schindler's list
  Korda, M. Worldly goods
  Krauss, N. Great house
  Lebrecht, N. The song of names
  Littell, J. The kindly ones

Aslam, N. Maps for lost lovers

Barclay, L. Trust your eyes

Bell, A. The reapers are the angels

Black, C. Murder in Clichy

Black, C. Murder in the Bastille

Black, C. Murder in the Marais

Box, C. J. Force of nature

Box, C. J. Free fire

Box, C. J. Out of range

Bradley, A. I am half-sick of shadows

Burns, C. Black hole

Buzzelli, E. K. Dead dogs and Englishmen

Cain, C. Kill you twice

Callihan, K. Firelight

Carey, J. Dark currents

Carkeet, D. Double negative

Castillo, L. Gone missing

Child, L. A wanted man

Church, J. A corpse in the Koryo

Clark, M. Guilt by association

Clark, W. Thug lovin'

Cleave, P. Cemetery Lake

Cleverly, B. The last kashmiri rose

Coben, H. The innocent

Coben, H. Stay close

Coleman, A. Murder mamas

Cotterill, C. Slash and burn

DeSilva, B. Cliff Walk

Deutermann, P. T. The cat dancers

Eastland, S. Archive 17

Edwards, Y. A Cupboard full of coats

Elias, G. Danse macabre

Elkins, A. J. Dying on the vine

Ellis, D. In the company of liars

Ellory, R. J. A quiet vendetta

Faletti, G. A pimp's notes

Flynn, G. Gone girl

French, N. Tuesday's gone

French, T. Broken Harbor

Fulmer, D. Jass

Gardner, L. Catch me

Gardner, L. Live to tell

Gaspar de Alba, A. Desert blood

Geagley, B. Year of the hyenas

Greaves, C. J. Hard twisted

Grecian, A. The black country

Griffiths, E. The Janus stone

Hambly, B. Ran away

Hamilton, P. F. Great north road

Hart, E. Haunted ground

Haynes, E. Dark tide

Higashino, K. The devotion of suspect X

Holbert, B. Lonesome animals

Hunt, A. City of saints

James, P. D. Death comes to Pemberley

James, S. The queen

Jensen, L. The uninvited

Johnson, C. Hell is empty

Johnson, C. Death without company

Karp, L. A perilous conception

Kerley, J. The death collectors

Klaussmann, L. Tigers in red weather

Knopf, C. Dead anyway

Lackberg, C. The Stranger

Lackberg, C. The stonecutter

Leon, D. Blood from a stone

Levack, S. Demon of the air

Longworth, M. L. Death at the Chateau Bremont

Malliet, G. M. A fatal winter

Maron, M. The buzzard table

Martin, L. The bright forever

May, P. The Blackhouse

Miller, M. G. Stalking season

Mogford, T. Shadow of the rock

Mosley, W. The last days of Ptolemy Grey

Neuhaus, N. Snow White must die

Newton, M. C. Nights of Villjamur

Nickson, C. Cold cruel winter

O'Connell, C. The chalk girl

Ohlsson, K. Silenced

Palmer, D. Helpless

Paretsky, S. Breakdown

Parks, B. The girl next door

Parshall, S. Bleeding through

Penny, L. How the light gets in

Priest, C. The islanders

Raimondo, L. Dante's wood

The redeemer

Robertson, I. Circle of shadows

Robotham, M. Suspect

Rodriguez, L. Every broken trust

The Russian Donation

Scott, A. D. Beneath the abbey wall

Sears, M. Black Fridays

Shafak, E. Honor

Sullivan, M. J. Theft of swords

Tallis, F. Death and the maiden

Talty, S. Black Irish

Thompson, J. Lucifer's tears

Thompson, V. Murder in Chinatown

Thompson, V. Murder on Lenox Hill

Thompson, V. Murder on Lexington Avenue

Thompson, V. Murder on Waverly Place

Tolkien, S. The king of diamonds

Upson, N. Two for sorrow

Walker, W. Crime of Privilege

Wortham, R. The rock hole

HOMICIDE TRIALS *See* Trials (Homicide)

The **homing.** Saul, J.

HOMING PIGEONS

Shalev, M. A pigeon and a boy

HOMO SAPIENS *See* Human beings

TITLE AND SUBJECT INDEX

Stoker, B. Dracula

Stoker, B. Midnight tales

Straub, P. A dark matter

Straub, P. Ghost story

Straub, P. The Hellfire Club

Straub, P. In the night room

Straub, P. Lost boy lost girl

Straub, P. Magic terror

Straub, P. Mr. X

Straub, P. A special place

Strieber, W. The forbidden zone

Strieber, W. The hunger

Strieber, W. The last vampire

Strieber, W. The Wolfen

Stross, C. The Jennifer morgue

Tryon, T. The other

Wellington, D. Monster Island

The white people and other weird stories

Whitehead, C. Zone one

Winters, B. H. Bedbugs

The Year's best fantasy and horror

Zeltserman, D. The caretaker of Lorne Field

HORROR STORIES *See* Horror fiction

HORROR TALES

See also Horror fiction

Grant, H. The glass demon

Harris, T. Hannibal rising

King, S. Duma Key

Morrow, B. The diviner's tale

Smith, M. M. The intruders

Straub, P. A dark matter

Strieber, W. The last vampire

Whitehead, C. Zone one

HORROR TALES, AMERICAN

Jackson, S. The lottery and other stories

King, S. Cell

King, S. Everything's eventual: 14 dark tales

King, S. Just after sunset

Koontz, D. R. The darkest evening of the year

Novels Three Gothic novels

Oates, J. C. The collector of hearts

Straub, P. Magic terror

HORROR TELEVISION PROGRAMS *See* Television programs

HORSE BREEDING

Machart, B. The wake of forgiveness

HORSE FARMS

Hoag, T. Dark horse

The **horse** goddess. Llywelyn, M.

Horse heaven. Smiley, J.

HORSE RACING

See also Racing

The Dick Francis treasury of great racing stories

Dixon, K. The art of losing

Francis, D. 10 lb. penalty

Francis, D. Bolt

Francis, D. Even money

Francis, D. Field of thirteen

Francis, D. Longshot

Francis, D. Nerve

Francis, D. Smokescreen

Francis, D. Whip hand

Gordon, J. Lord of Misrule

The New treasury of great racing stories

Shoemaker, B. Stalking horse

Smiley, J. Horse heaven

Smith, B. All hat

HORSE RACING -- FICTION

Francis, D. 10 lb. penalty

Francis, D. Shattered

Gordon, J. Lord of Misrule

Smiley, J. Horse heaven

HORSE TRAINERS

Hagy, A. Boleto

The **horse** whisperer. Evans, N.

The **Horse** You Came In On. Grimes, M.

The **horse's** mouth. Cary, J.

Horse, flower, bird. Bernheimer, K.

HORSEMANSHIP

Hagy, A. Boleto

HORSES

Evans, N. The horse whisperer

Gloss, M. The hearts of horses

Gordon, J. Lord of Misrule

McCarthy, C. All the pretty horses

Meyers, K. The work of wolves

Olmstead, R. Coal black horse

Tarr, J. Lady of horses

Vlautin, W. Lean on Pete

HORSES -- FICTION

Greaves, C. Hush money

Hagy, A. Boleto

HORSES -- TRAINING

Hagy, A. Boleto

HOSIERY *See* Clothing and dress; Textile industry

HOSPITAL ADMINISTRATORS

Boyle, T. C. Road to Wellville

HOSPITAL LIBRARIES *See* Libraries

HOSPITAL SHIPS *See* Hospitals; Ships

HOSPITALS -- RUSSIA

Marra, A. A constellation of vital phenomena

HOSPITALS AND SANATORIUMS

Adrian, C. The children's hospital

Barker, P. The eye in the door

Barker, P. The ghost road

Barker, P. Regeneration

Blatty, W. P. Dimiter

Clark, M. H. The cradle will fall

Cook, R. Coma

Cook, R. Godplayer

Greene, G. A burnt-out case

Hemingway, E. A farewell to arms

A **house** for Mr. Biswas. Naipaul, V. S.

The **house** girl. Conklin, T.

House lights. Cohen, L. H.

House made of dawn. Momaday, N. S.

The **house** of blue mangoes. Davidar, D.

House of blues. Smith, J.

HOUSE OF DAVID

Kasischke, L. Eden Springs

The **house** of death. Doherty, P. C.

House of holes. Baker, N.

The **House** of Impossible Loves. López Barrio, C.

House of many gods. Davenport, K.

House of meetings. Amis, M.

The **house** of mirth. Wharton, E.

House of Niccolò [series]

Dunnett, D. Caprice and Rondo

Dunnett, D. Gemini

Dunnett, D. Niccolo rising

Dunnett, D. Race of scorpions

Dunnett, D. Scales of gold

Dunnett, D. The spring of the ram

Dunnett, D. To lie with lions

Dunnett, D. The unicorn hunt

The **house** of paper. Dominguez, C. M.

House of reeds. Harlan, T.

House of Romanov

About

Eastland, S. Eye of the Red Tsar

The **house** of rumour. Arnott, J.

The **House** of Silk. Horowitz, A.

The **house** of special purpose. Boyne, J.

House of splendid isolation. O'Brien, E.

The **house** of stairs. Vine, B.

The **House** of the Seven Gables. Hawthorne, N.

The **house** of the spirits. Allende, I.

The **house** of the stag. Baker, K.

The **house** of the Vestals. Saylor, S.

The **house** of tomorrow. Bognanni, P.

The **house** of widows. Melnyczuk, A.

The **house** on Fortune Street. Livesey, M.

The **house** on Hope Street. Steel, D.

The **house** on Mango Street. Cisneros, S.

The **house** on Prague Street. Demetz, H.

House rules. Picoult, J.

The **house** sitter. Lovesey, P.

HOUSEBOATS

Haynes, E. Dark tide

HOUSEHOLD EMPLOYEES

Burrowes, G. The heir

Lin, J. My fair concubine

Ozick, C. Heir to the glimmering world

Umrigar, T. N. The space between us

Van Niekerk, M. Agaat

Wax, W. Single in Suburbia

Household saints. Prose, F.

The **housekeeper** and the professor. Ogawa, Y.

HOUSEKEEPERS

Adams, A. After the war

Doig, I. The whi stling season

Labiner, N. Miniatures

McBain, E. Alice in jeopardy

McFarland, D. School for the blind

Ogawa, Y. The housekeeper and the professor

Piercy, M. The longings of women

Stein, G. Three lives

Tobar, H. The barbarian nurseries

Winkler, A. C. Dog war

HOUSEMAIDS *See* Household employees

HOUSES

See also Buildings

Clark, M. H. No place like home

De la Roche, M. Jalna

Delinsky, B. Flirting with Pete

Erpenbeck, J. Visitation

Forster, E. M. Howards End

Hawthorne, N. The House of the Seven Gables

Hodgins, E. Mr. Blandings builds his dream house

Howatch, S. Cashelmara

Howatch, S. Penmarric

Howatch, S. The wheel of fortune

James, H. The spoils of Poynton

Laken, V. Dream house

Lofts, N. Gad's Hall

Mawer, S. The glass room

Moloney, S. The dwelling

Morris, M. Man in the blue moon

Naipaul, V. S. A house for Mr. Biswas

Rendell, R. Thirteen steps down

Rosenblatt, R. Lapham rising

Scott, A. Calpurnia

Speller, E. The strange fate of Kitty Easton

Stewart, M. Touch not the cat

Swerling, B. Shadowbrook

Tilghman, C. The right-hand shore

Unsworth, B. After Hannibal

Wilhide, E. Ashenden

Wolfe, G. The sorcerer's house

HOUSES -- BUYING AND SELLING *See* Real estate business

HOUSES -- MAINTENANCE AND REPAIR

Higgins, K. Somebody to love

Houses of stone. Michaels, B.

HOUSESITTING

Joss, M. Half broken things

HOUSEWIVES

Hood, A. The Obituary Writer

HOUSING *See* Houses; Landlord and tenant

HOUSTON (TEX.)

Billingsley, R. T. Let the church say amen

Brown, R. Half a heart

How far is the ocean from here. Shearn, A.

How green was my valley. Llewellyn, R.

See also Philanthropists

Keneally, T. Schindler's list

Roosevelt, E. Murder at midnight

The **humanity** project. Thompson, J.

The **humans**. Haig, M.

HUMANS IN SPACE *See* Space flight

The **humbling**. Roth, P.

Humboldt's gift. Bellow, S.

Humboldt, Alexander, Freiherr von, 1769-1859
About

Kehlmann, D. Measuring the world

HUMIDITY *See* Meteorology; Weather

Hummingbird house. Henley, P.

The **hummingbird's** daughter. Urrea, L. A.

HUMOR

See also Wit and humor

Adams, D. The hitchhiker's guide to the galaxy

Adams, D. Life, the universe, and everything

Adams, D. The restaurant at the end of the universe

Adams, D. So long, and thanks for all the fish

Aira, C. The literary conference

Alvarez, J. How the Garcia girls lost their accents

Alvarez, J. Yo!

Amis, K. Lucky Jim

Baldwin, J. The Wilshire sun

Beatty, P. Slumberland

Bell, C. The Perez family

Belle, J. The seven year bitch

Bellow, S. Henderson the rain king

Bellow, S. Mr. Sammler's planet

Berger, T. Little Big Man

Bird, S. The gap year

Boucher, C. How to keep your Volkswagen alive

Bragi Olafsson The pets

Breslin, J. The gang that couldn't shoot straight

Capote, T. The grass harp

Carkeet, D. From away

Cary, J. The horse's mouth

Cheever, J. The Wapshot chronicle

Cheever, J. The Wapshot scandal

Cline, R. What to keep

Colfer, E. Plugged

Davies, V. Miracle on 34th Street

Dennis, P. Auntie Mame

Dezenhall, E. Money wanders

Dickens, C. The posthumous papers of the Pickwick Club

Dische, I. The Empress of Weehawken

Donovan, A. Buddha Da

Ducker, B. Dizzying heights

Edgerton, C. The Bible salesman

Faulkner, W. The reivers

Fielding, H. Bridget Jones: the edge of reason

Fielding, H. Bridget Jones's diary

Flagg, F. Fried green tomatoes at the Whistle-Stop Cafe

Flagg, F. Standing in the rainbow

Fraser, G. M. The reavers

Frayn, M. Headlong

Goldstein, R. 36 arguments for the existence of God

Goodman, A. Paradise park

Greene, G. Monsignor Quixote

Greene, G. Travels with my aunt

Guo Xiaolu A concise Chinese-English dictionary for lovers

Guterson, M. Gone to the dogs

Harrison, J. The English major

Hasek, J. The good soldier Svejk

Heffernan, W. The Dinosaur Club

Heller, J. Catch-22

Hemingway, E. The torrents of spring

Hiaasen, C. Lucky you

Hiaasen, C. Skinny dip

Hodgins, E. Mr. Blandings builds his dream house

Hooker, R. MASH

Hornby, N. How to be good

Hughes, L. Simple speaks his mind

Hughes, L. Simple stakes a claim

Hughes, L. Simple takes a wife

Hughes, L. Simple's Uncle Sam

Irving, J. The Hotel New Hampshire

Kafka, F. Amerika

Karbo, K. Motherhood made a man out of me

Keillor, G. Lake Wobegon days

Keillor, G. Lake Wobegon summer 1956

Keillor, G. WLT

Kingsolver, B. The bean trees

Kotzwinkle, W. The bear went over the mountain

Krusoe, J. Toward you

Kundera, M. The book of laughter and forgetting

Levi, P. The monkey's wrench

Liebmann-Smith, R. The James boys

Lipman, E. The Inn at Lake Devine

Lipman, E. The ladies' man

Lipsyte, S. Home land

Liss, D. The ethical assassin

Lodato, V. Mathilda Savitch

Lupica, M. Wild pitch

Lurie, A. Only children

Lutz, L. Curse of the Spellmans

Lutz, L. Revenge of the Spellmans

Lutz, L. The Spellman files

Makkai, R. The borrower

Martin, S. The pleasure of my company

McCall Smith, A. Corduroy mansions

McCall Smith, A. Love over Scotland

McCall Smith, A. The world according to Bertie

McInerney, J. Bright lights, big city

McLarty, R. Art in America

McLaughlin, E. The nanny diaries

McLaughlin, E. Nanny returns

HUMOR -- FORM -- ESSAYS
HUMORISTS
HUMOROUS FICTION

Browne, S. G. Lucky bastard

Claudel, P. The investigation

Jones, S. The uninvited guests

Keillor, G. Leaving home

Kotzwinkle, W. The bear went over the mountain

Levine, S. Treasure Island!!!

Mayle, P. Anything considered

McInerney, J. Bright lights, big city

Parameswaran, R. I am an executioner

Perec, G. Life

Portis, C. Gringos

Roth, P. Sabbath's theater

Schine, C. The love letter

Westlake, D. E. Don't ask

Westlake, D. E. What's the worst that could happen?

HUMOROUS GRAPHIC NOVELS
See also Graphic novels

HUMOROUS PICTURES *See* Comic books, strips, etc.

HUMOROUS POETRY
See also Poetry; Wit and humor

HUMOROUS STORIES
Cadwalladr, C. The family tree

Harrison, J. The English major

Hiaasen, C. Nature girl

Hiaasen, C. Star Island

Hodgen, C. Elegies for the brokenhearted

Kunkel, B. Indecision

Milligan, J. Jack Fish

Moody, R. The four fingers of death

Mortimer, J. Quite honestly

Rebeck, T. Three girls and their brother

Stuckey-French, E. Revenge of the radioactive lady

Tillman, L. American genius

Walter, J. The financial lives of the poets

HUMOROUS STORIES *See* Humorous fiction
The **hunchback** of Notre Dame. Hugo, V.

HUNCHBACKS
Hugo, V. The hunchback of Notre Dame

Rosero, E. Good offices

The **hundred** days. O'Brian, P.

The **hundred** secret senses. Tan, A.

The **hundred** thousand kingdoms. Jemisin, N. K.

HUNDRED YEARS' WAR, 1339-1453
Cornwell, B. The archer's tale

Cornwell, B. Vagabond

Doyle, A. C. The White Company

Druon, M. The Iron King

Haasse, H. S. In a dark wood wandering

The **hundred-foot** journey. Morais, R. C.

The **hundredth** man. Kerley, J.

HUNGARIANS -- FRANCE
Furst, A. Kingdom of shadows

Miller, A. Oxygen

HUNGARY

Furst, A. Kingdom of shadows

Harmonia caelestis/English Celestial harmonies

Vamos, M. The book of fathers

HUNGARY -- BUDAPEST
Hall, E. The book of summers

Orringer, J. The invisible bridge

Parallel stories

Phillips, A. Prague

HUNGARY -- HISTORY -- 1956, REVOLUTION
See Revolutions

The **hunger.** Strieber, W.

HUNGER
The hunger angel

The **hunger** angel.

HUNGER STRIKES *See* Demonstrations; Fasting; Nonviolence; Passive resistance; Resistance to government

The **hungry** tide. Ghosh, A.

Hunk City. Wilcox, J.

The **hunt** for Red October. Clancy, T.

Hunted past reason. Matheson, R.

The **hunter.** Stark, R.

Hunter's moon. Stabenow, D.

Hunter's run. Martin, G. R. R.

The **hunters.** Messud, C.

HUNTERS
McMurtry, L. Buffalo girls

McMurtry, L. Telegraph days

HUNTERS -- ICELAND -- 19TH CENTURY
The blue fox

Hunters and gatherers. Prose, F.

HUNTING
Colegate, I. The shooting party

Cooper, J. F. The pioneers

Guterson, D. East of the mountains

Guthrie, A. B. The big sky

King, S. Dreamcatcher

Nichols, P. Voyage to the North Star

Percy, B. The wilding

Thomas, E. M. Reindeer Moon

HUNTING -- AFRICA
Hemingway, E. True at first light

Smith, W. A. A time to die

HUNTING ACCIDENTS
Murphy, Y. The call

Hunting badger. Hillerman, T.

HUNTINGTON'S CHOREA
Fay, J. The shortest way home

The **huntsman.** Terrell, W.

HURRICANE KATRINA, 2005
See also Hurricanes

Burke, J. L. The tin roof blowdown

Piazza, T. City of refuge

Ward, J. Salvage the bones

HURRICANES
See also Cyclones; Storms; Winds

Hiaasen, C. Stormy weather
The **husband.** Koontz, D. R.
Husband and wife. Shalev, T.
HUSBAND AND WIFE
Abrahams, P. Nerve damage
Ackroyd, P. The fall of Troy
Chenoweth, E. Hello goodbye
Crace, J. Being dead
Gardam, J. The man in the wooden hat
Graves, T. G. Covet
Hays, T. The pleasure was mine
Hodgkinson, A. 22 Britannia Road
Hollingshead, G. Bedlam
Joyce, G. The silent land
King, R. The sound of butterflies
Krauss, N. Great house
Lewis, S. Dodsworth
Lichtenstein, A. Lost
Martin, C. Where the river ends
McEwan, I. On Chesil Beach
McFarland, D. A face at the window
Oates, J. C. American appetites
Oyeyemi, H. Mr. Fox
Pronzini, B. The hidden
Rash, R. Serena
Reuss, F. Mohr
Richardson, C. S. The end of the alphabet
Shalev, T. Husband and wife
Sparks, N. The notebook
Stamm, P. Seven years
Strauss, D. More than it hurts you
Tremain, R. The color
Tuck, L. I married you for happiness
Unferth, D. O. Vacation
Watson, S. J. Before I go to sleep
Wiggins, M. Evidence of things unseen
Wiggins, M. The shadow catcher
Wolitzer, M. The wife
HUSBANDS
   See also Family; Marriage; Married people;
   Men
Flynn, G. Gone girl
HUSBANDS AND WIVES
Putney, M. J. Loving a lost lord
Hush money. Parker, R. B.
Hush money. Greaves, C.
Hustlin' divas. Diamond, D.
HYBRID AUTOMOBILES *See* Automobiles
The **Hyde** Park headsman. Perry, A.
The **Hyde** Park murder. Roosevelt, E.
HYDRAULICS *See* Fluid mechanics; Liquids;
   Mechanics; Physics
HYDRODYNAMICS *See* Dynamics; Fluid me-
   chanics; Hydraulic engineering; Hydraulics;
   Liquids; Mechanics
HYDROGEN BOMB *See* Bombs; Nuclear weap-

ons
The **hydrogen** sonata. Banks, I.
HYDROPHOBIA *See* Rabies
HYDROSTATICS *See* Fluid mechanics; Hydraulic
   engineering; Hydraulics; Hydrodynamics; Liq-
   uids; Mechanics; Physics; Statics
HYGIENE *See* Medicine; Preventive medicine
Hylozoic. Rucker, R. v. B.
HYMNS *See* Church music; Liturgies; Songs; Vo-
   cal music
HYPERACTIVITY *See* Diseases
Hyperion. Simmons, D.
HYPNEROTOMACHIA POLIPHILI
   Caldwell, I. The rule of four
HYPNOSIS *See* Hypnotism
HYPNOTISM
   Kepler, L. The hypnotist
   Koontz, D. R. False memory
   Stoker, B. Dracula
   Thomas, R. Voodoo, Ltd
The **hypnotist.** Kepler, L.
HYPOCRISY
   Collins, M. Lost souls
   Dickens, C. Martin Chuzzlewit
   Ellis, W. Crooked little vein
   Rosero, E. Good offices

I

I. Dixon, S.
I am an executioner. Parameswaran, R.
I am Charlotte Simmons. Wolfe, T.
I am forbidden. Markovits, A.
I am half-sick of shadows. Bradley, A.
I am legend. Matheson, R.
I am no one you know. Oates, J. C.
I am not a cop! Belzer, R.
I am Not Sidney Poitier. Everett, P. L.
I am the only running footman. Grimes, M.
I been in sorrow's kitchen and licked out all the pots.
   Straight, S.
I capture the castle. Smith, D.
I curse the river of time. Petterson, P.
I hate to see that evening sun go down. Gay, W.
I have seen him in the watchfires. Gohlke, C.
I is for innocent. Grafton, S.
I know this much is true. Lamb, W.
I lock my door upon myself. Oates, J. C.
I married a communist. Roth, P.
I married you for happiness. Tuck, L.
I never promised you a rose garden. Greenberg, J.
I sailed with Magellan. Dybek, S.
I see you everywhere. Glass, J.
I served the King of England. Hrabal, B.
I should be extremely happy in your company. Hall,
   B.
I thee wed. Quick, A.

I think I love you. Pearson, A.

I thought you were dead: a love story. Nelson, P.

I wish I had a red dress. Cleage, P.

I'd know you anywhere. Lippman, L.

I'll never get out of this world alive. Earle, S.

I'm so happy for you. Rosenfeld, L.

I've got your number. Kinsella, S.

I, Alex Cross. Patterson, J.

I, Claudius. Graves, R.

I, Hogarth. Dean, M.

I, robot. Asimov, I.

I, sniper. Hunter, S.

I, Tituba, black witch of Salem. Conde, M.

12. Bannon, J.

IBIZA (SPAIN)

Braybrooke, J. Every eye

IBO (AFRICAN PEOPLE)

Achebe, C. Things fall apart

Ice. McBain, E.

Ice. Sorokin, V.

The ice child. McGregor, E.

ICE FISHING See Fishing; Winter sports

ICE HOCKEY See Hockey

The ice princess. Lackberg, C.

The ice queen. Hoffman, A.

ICE SKATING

Bolaño, R. The skating rink

The ice soldier. Watkins, P.

Ice Station Zebra. MacLean, A.

The ice-shirt. Vollmann, W. T.

ICEBERGS See Ice; Ocean; Physical geography

ICELAND

Hand, E. Available dark

Olafur Johann Olafsson The journey home

ICELAND -- 10TH CENTURY

Seton, A. Avalon

ICELAND -- REYKJAVIK

Bragi Olafsson The pets

Hallgrimur Helgason 101 Reykjavik

Yrsa Sigurdardottir Last rituals

ICELANDERS -- ENGLAND

Olafur Johann Olafsson The journey home

ICELANDERS -- LITHUANIA

Bragi Olafsson The ambassador

ICELANDIC AMERICANS

Wilson, C. Cotton

ICELANDIC LANGUAGE See Language and languages; Scandinavian languages

ICHTHYOLOGY See Fishes

ICHTHYOSAURUS See Dinosaurs

IDAHO

Carlson, R. Five skies

Collins, B. Crimson eve

Hart, B. Then came the evening

Hatcher, R. L. Catching Katie

Parkinson, H. Across open ground

Woods, S. Heat

The idea of perfection. Grenville, K.

The ideal man. Garwood, J.

IDEAL STATES See Utopian fiction; Utopias

Ideas of heaven. Silber, J.

Identity. Kundera, M.

IDENTITY (PSYCHOLOGY)

See also Personality; Psychology; Self

Alarcón, D. American odysseys

Celona, M. Y

Coady, L. The antagonist

Cole, T. Open city

Company, F. The Island of Last Truth

Divakaruni, C. B. Oleander girl

Ferris, J. The unnamed

Gaige, A. Schroder

Gass, W. H. Middle C

Harding, P. Tinkers

Joss, M. Among the missing

Kunzru, H. My revolutions

Larsen, N. Passing

Mehta, R. Quarantine

Pletzinger, T. Funeral for a dog

Saunders, G. Tenth of December

Smith, A. There but for the

Vida, V. Let the Northern Lights erase your name

Watson, S. J. Before I go to sleep

IDENTITY

See also Identity (Psychology); Individuality; Personality

Huston, N. Infrared

IDENTITY THEFT

See also Offenses against the person; Theft

Chaon, D. Await your reply

Compton, J. Thieves get rich, saints get shot

The ides of March. Wilder, T.

The idiot. Dostoyevsky, F.

If Beale Street could talk. Baldwin, J.

If ever I return, pretty Peggy-O. McCrumb, S.

If I'd killed him when I met him. McCrumb, S.

If not now, when? Levi, P.

If on a winter's night a traveler. Calvino, I.

If the dead rise not. Kerr, P.

If this world were mine. Harris, E. L.

If you follow me. Watrous, M.

IGLOOS See Houses; Inuit

Ignorance. Kundera, M.

Ignorance. Roberts, M.

IGUANODON See Dinosaurs

Ilium. Simmons, D.

The Illearth war. Donaldson, S. R.

ILLEGAL ALIENS

Adams, L. Harbor

Wambaugh, J. Harbor nocturne

ILLEGAL ARMS TRANSFERS

Le Carré, J. A Delicate Truth

Marley, L. The child goddess
Marusek, D. Counting heads
Robbins, T. Jitterbug perfume
Saramago, J. Death with interruptions
Sterling, B. Holy fire
Westerfeld, S. The killing of worlds
Westerfeld, S. The risen empire
Yanagihara, H. The people in the trees
The **immortals.** Korda, M.
The **immortals.** Chaudhuri, A.
IMMUNOLOGY *See* Medicine
Impact. Preston, D.
Imperfect birds. Lamott, A.
An **imperfect** lens. Roiphe, A. R.
An **imperfect** spy. Cross, A.
Imperfect strangers. Woods, S.
The **imperfectionists.** Rachman, T.
Imperial bedrooms. Ellis, B. E.
IMPERIALISM
De Kretser, M. The Hamilton case
Fuentes, C. The campaign
Ghosh, A. The glass palace
Hensher, P. The Mulberry empire
King, R. The sound of butterflies
Kingsolver, B. The poisonwood Bible
Lapierre, A. Between love and honor
Naipaul, V. S. A way in the world
Scott, P. The day of the scorpion
Scott, P. The jewel in the crown
Silverberg, R. Roma eterna
Timm, U. Morenga
Vassanji, M. G. The in-between world of Vikram Lall
Westerfeld, S. The killing of worlds
Westerfeld, S. The risen empire
Imperium. Harris, R.
IMPERSONATION
Lin, J. My fair concubine
IMPERSONATIONS
Allende, I. Daughter of fortune
DeMille, N. The charm school
Dickens, C. Our mutual friend
Dickens, C. A tale of two cities
Erdrich, L. The last report on the miracles at Little No Horse
Greene, G. The tenth man
Higgins, J. Night of the fox
Holland, C. The angel and the sword
Hope, A. The prisoner of Zenda
Leonard, E. Pagan babies
Michael, J. Deceptions
Rice, A. Angel time
Stewart, M. The ivy tree
Tey, J. Brat Farrar
Townsend, S. Number 10
Twain, M. Pudd'nhead Wilson;

Yorke, M. False pretences
The **importance** of a piece of paper. Baca, J. S.
Important artifacts and personal property from the collection of Lenore Doolan and Harold Morris, including books, street fashion, and jewelry. Shapton, L.
The **impossible** dead. Rankin, I.
The **impostor.** Cocteau, J.
The **impostor.** Galgut, D.
IMPOSTORS
Kunzru, H. The impressionist
Makine, A. Music of a life
Mathews, H. My life in CIA
Starr, J. Panic attack
Strauss, D. The real McCoy
IMPOSTORS AND IMPOSTURE *See* Crime; Criminals
IMPOTENCE *See* Diseases
IMPRESSIONISM (ART) *See* Art
The **impressionist.** Kunzru, H.
IMPRISONMENT
Barr, N. The rope
In a dark wood wandering. Haasse, H. S.
In a fix. Grimes, L.
In a perfect world. Kasischke, L.
In a shallow grave. Purdy, J.
In America. Sontag, S.
In an evil time. Pronzini, B.
In case we're separated. Mattison, A.
In country. Mason, B. A.
In danger's path. Griffin, W. E. B.
In dubious battle. Steinbeck, J.
In evil hour. Garcia Marquez, G.
In her absence. Munoz Molina, A.
In her shoes. Weiner, J.
In one person. Irving, J.
In other rooms, other wonders. Mueenuddin, D.
In our time. Hemingway, E.
In persuasion nation. Saunders, G.
In pursuit of the green lion. Riley, J. M.
In search of Klingsor. Volpi, J.
In search of lost time [series]
Proust, M. The captive [and] The fugitive
Proust, M. The Guermantes way
Proust, M. Sodom and Gomorrah
Proust, M. Swann's way
Proust, M. Time regained
Proust, M. Within a budding grove
In search of the Rose notes. Arsenault, E.
In sunlight and in shadow. Helprin, M.
In the beauty of the lilies. Updike, J.
In the bleak midwinter. Spencer-Fleming, J.
In the company of angels. Kennedy, T. E.
In the company of cheerful ladies. McCall Smith, A.
In the company of liars. Ellis, D.
In the company of the courtesan. Dunant, S.

Narayan, R. K.   Under the banyan tree and other
  stories
Roy, A.   The god of small things
Rushdie, S.   Midnight's children
Rushdie, S.   Shalimar the clown
Scott, P.   Staying on
Seth, V.   A suitable boy
Sundaresan, I.   In the Convent of Little Flowers
Suri, M.   The age of Shiva
Theroux, P.   The Elephanta suite
Vassanji, M. G.   The assassin's song

INDIA -- BENARES
Mishima, Y.   The Temple of Dawn

INDIA -- BOMBAY
Chaudhuri, A.   The immortals
Irving, J.   A son of the circus
Joseph, M.   Serious men
Mistry, R.   Family matters
Mistry, R.   A fine balance
Rushdie, S.   The ground beneath her feet
Rushdie, S.   Midnight's children
Rushdie, S.   The Moor's last sigh
Suri, M.   The death of Vishnu
Umrigar, T. N.   The space between us

INDIA -- BRITISH OCCUPATION, 1765-1947
Cornwell, B.   Sharpe's fortress
Forster, E. M.   A passage to India
Ghosh, A.   The glass palace
Godden, R.   Black Narcissus
Jhabvala, R. P.   Heat and dust
Kaye, M. M.   The far pavilions
Kaye, M. M.   Shadow of the moon
Kunzru, H.   The impressionist
Mehta, G.   Raj
Narayan, R. K.   Swami and friends, The bachelor of
  arts, The dark room, The English teacher
Scott, P.   The day of the scorpion
Scott, P.   A division of the spoils
Scott, P.   The jewel in the crown
Scott, P.   The Raj quartet
Scott, P.   The towers of silence
Sundaresan, I.   The splendor of silence

INDIA -- CALCUTTA
Ghosh, A.   Sea of poppies
Theroux, P.   A dead hand

INDIA -- DELHI
Desai, A.   Clear light of day

**INDIA -- HISTORY -- 1765-1947, BRITISH OC-
CUPATION**
Cleverly, B.   The last kashmiri rose
Kerstan, L.   The golden leopard

INDIA -- HISTORY -- 19TH CENTURY
Khair, T.   The thing about thugs

**INDIA -- POLITICS AND GOVERNMENT --
1947-**
Festing, I. A.   The birdkeeper

INDIA -- RACE RELATIONS
Forster, E. M.   A passage to India

INDIA -- RURAL LIFE
Jhabvala, R. P.   Heat and dust
Narayan, R. K.   The grandmother's tale and select-
  ed stories
Narayan, R. K.   Malgudi days

**INDIA -- SOCIAL CONDITIONS -- 20TH CEN-
TURY**
Festing, I. A.   The birdkeeper

INDIA -- SOCIAL CONDITIONS -- FICTION
Festing, I. A.   The birdkeeper

INDIA-PAKISTAN CONFLICT, 1971
Hensher, P.   Scenes from early life

INDIAN ART *See* Art

INDIAN CAPTIVES
Larsen, D.   The white

INDIAN CHIEFS
Jones, D. C.   Arrest Sitting Bull
O'Brien, D.   The contract surgeon
Thom, J. A.   Panther in the sky
The **Indian** clerk. Leavitt, D.

INDIAN FAMILIES
Erdrich, L.   The round house
Indian killer. Alexie, S.

INDIAN LANGUAGES *See* Language and languages
The **Indian** lawyer. Welch, J.

INDIAN LEADERS
McMurtry, L.   Zeke and Ned
Vollmann, W. T.   Argall

INDIAN OCEAN *See* Ocean

INDIAN POETRY *See* Indian literature; Poetry

INDIAN RESERVATIONS
Erdrich, L.   The round house
Erdrich, L.   The last report on the miracles at Little
  No Horse

**INDIAN WOMEN -- CRIMES AGAINST -- FIC-
TION**
Erdrich, L.   The round house

INDIANA
Bill, F.   Crimes in southern Indiana
Collins, M.   Lost souls
Day, C.   The circus in winter
Henley, P.   In the river sweet
Kimmel, H.   Something rising (light and swift)
Kimmel, H.   The used world
Martin, L.   The bright forever
Nunez, S.   Salvation city
Reynolds, M.   The Starlite Drive-in
Tarkington, B.   Alice Adams
Tucker, T.   Over and under
Vonnegut, K.   God bless you, Mr. Rosewater
West, J.   The friendly persuasion

INDIANA -- 19TH CENTURY
Fleming, T. J.   When this cruel war is over

Edmonds, W. D. Drums along the Mohawk

O'Brien, D. The contract surgeon

**INDIANS OF NORTH AMERICA -- WASHING-
TON (STATE)**

Alexie, S. Indian killer

Alexie, S. Reservation blues

INDIANS OF SOUTH AMERICA

Aira, C. An afternoon in the life of a landscape
painter

Hudson, W. H. Green mansions

INDIC FICTION (ENGLISH)

Khair, T. The thing about thugs

The **indictment.** Reed, B.

INDIGENOUS PEOPLES

Stanley, M. Death of the mantis

Indignation. Roth, P.

Indigo slam. Crais, R.

Indigo Springs. Dellamonica, A. M.

INDIVIDUALISM

Orwell, G. Nineteen eighty-four

Pasternak, B. L. Doctor Zhivago

Rand, A. Anthem

Rand, A. Atlas shrugged

Rand, A. The fountainhead

INDOCTRINATION, FORCED See Brainwashing

INDONESIA

Toer, P. A. The girl from the coast

INDOOR GAMES See Games

INDUCED ABORTION See Abortion

INDUSTRIAL ACCIDENTS

Cussler, C. Sahara

DeLillo, D. White noise

Sinha, I. Animal's people

INDUSTRIAL ACCIDENTS See Accidents

INDUSTRIAL ARBITRATION See Industrial relations; Labor; Labor disputes; Labor unions;
Negotiation

INDUSTRIAL ARCHEOLOGY See Archeology;
Industries -- History

INDUSTRIAL BUILDINGS See Buildings

**INDUSTRIAL BUILDINGS -- DESIGN AND
CONSTRUCTION** See Architecture; Building

INDUSTRIAL CONDITIONS

Dickens, C. Hard times

Singer, I. J. The brothers Ashkenazi

INDUSTRIAL DISASTERS See Industrial accidents

INDUSTRIAL DISPUTES See Labor disputes

INDUSTRIAL INJURIES See Industrial accidents

INDUSTRIAL PLANTS See Factories

INDUSTRIAL RESEARCH See Research

INDUSTRIAL ROBOTS See Automation; Industrial equipment; Robots

INDUSTRIALISTS

Sankaran, L. The hope factory

The **inexplicables.** Priest, C.

INFANT SUDDEN DEATH See Sudden infant
death syndrome

INFANTICIDE

Abu-Jaber, D. Origin

Tanenbaum, R. True justice

INFANTILE PARALYSIS See Poliomyelitis

INFANTS

See also Children

Brown, C. The hatbox baby

Clay, H. Losing Charlotte

Strauss, D. More than it hurts you

INFANTS -- DEATH See Death

INFANTS -- DISEASES See Diseases

Infected. Sigler, S.

Infernal angels. Estleman, L. D.

The **infernals.** Connolly, J.

INFERTILITY

Gilmore, J. The Mothers

Weiner, J. Then came you

Infinite jest. Wallace, D. F.

The **infinite** tides. Kiefer, C.

The **infinities.** Banville, J.

Infinity beach. McDevitt, J.

Infinity's shore. Brin, D.

INFLATION (FINANCE) See Finance

**INFLUENCE (LITERARY, ARTISTIC, ETC.) --
FICTION**

Hacker, C. The Morels

INFLUENZA

See also Communicable diseases; Diseases

Goldberg, M. Wickett's remedy

Masello, R. The Romanov cross

Mullen, T. The last town on earth

INFLUENZA EPIDEMIC, 1918-1919 -- FICTION

Todd, C. An unmarked grave

The **informant.** Grippando, J.

The **informant.** Perry, T.

The **information** officer. Mills, M.

INFORMATION SCIENCE See Communication

INFORMATION SUPERHIGHWAY See Computer networks; Information networks; Internet

INFORMATION SYSTEMS See Bibliographic
control; Computers; Information science

The **informationist.** Stevens, T.

The **informer.** Nova, C.

INFORMERS

Bayard, L. The black tower

Perry, T. The informant

Infrared. Huston, N.

Inglorious. Kavenna, J.

The **inhabited** world. Long, D.

Inherent vice. Pynchon, T.

INHERITANCE AND SUCCESSION

See also Wealth

Bear, E. Range of ghosts

Straub, P. The Hellfire Club
Straub, P. A special place
INSANITY
Bohjalian, C. The night strangers
Bronte, C. Jane Eyre
Cheever, J. Bullet Park
Evenson, B. The open curtain
Faulkner, W. The sound and the fury
Jackson, S. We have always lived in the castle
Keneally, T. A family madness
Krilanovich, G. The orange eats creeps
McCabe, P. Winterwood
McGrath, P. Asylum
Rendell, R. Adam and Eve and Pinch me
Ward, M. J. The snake pit
West, M. L. The clowns of God
Wiesel, E. Twilight
INSANITY DEFENSE See Criminal law
INSCRIPTIONS See Ancient history; Archeology
Insect dreams. Estrin, M.
INSECT PESTS See Economic zoology; Insects; Pests
INSECTS
See also Animals
Estrin, M. Insect dreams
Kafka, F. Metamorphosis
Saul, J. The homing
Insomnia. King, S.
INSOMNIA
See Sleep
Cohen, R. Inspired sleep
Huston, C. Sleepless
Inspector Ghote trusts the heart. Keating, H. R. F.
Inspector Maigret and the killers. Simenon, G.
INSPIRATION See Creation (Literary, artistic, etc.)
Inspired sleep. Cohen, R.
INSTALLMENT PLAN See Business; Consumer credit; Credit; Purchasing
An **instance** of the fingerpost. Pears, I.
INSTRUCTION See Education; Teaching
INSTRUCTIONAL MATERIALS CENTERS See Libraries
INSTRUMENTAL MUSIC See Music
INSTRUMENTALISTS See Musicians
INSTRUMENTATION AND ORCHESTRATION
See Bands (Music); Composition (Music); Music; Orchestra
Instruments of darkness. Robertson, I.
Instruments of night. Cook, T. H.
INSURANCE
See also Estate planning; Finance; Personal finance
Greaves, C. Hush money
Shriver, L. So much for that
INSURANCE BROKERS
Shreve, A. Where or when

INSURANCE CRIMES
Greaves, C. Hush money
INSURGENCY
See also Revolutions
Wein, E. Code name Verity
INTEGRATION, RACIAL See Race relations
INTELLECTUAL PROPERTY See Property
INTELLECTUALS
See also Persons; Social classes
Davies, R. The cunning man
Kundera, M. Slowness
Mendelson, C. Morningside Heights
Oz, A. Fima
INTELLIGENCE AGENTS
See also Spies
Kanon, J. Istanbul passage
INTELLIGENCE OF ANIMALS See Animal intelligence
INTELLIGENCE OFFICERS
Fesperman, D. The double game
Higgins, J. Midnight runner
Huston, C. Skinner
King, L. R. The game
Le Carre, J. The mission song
Le Carre, J. A most wanted man
Littell, R. The company
Littell, R. Young Philby
Ludlum, R. The Prometheus deception
Mathews, H. My life in CIA
McCarry, C. Old boys
McDonell, N. An expensive education
Silva, D. The mark of the assassin
Snyder, D. J. Night crossing
INTELLIGENCE OFFICERS -- GREAT BRITAIN
Jones, C. M. The silent oligarch
INTELLIGENCE OFFICERS -- UNITED STATES
MacDonald, G. The prisoner's wife
Rosenberg, J. C. Damascus Countdown
Rosenberg, J. C. The Tehran initiative
Rosenberg, J. C. The twelfth Imam
INTELLIGENCE SERVICE
See also Public administration; Research
Clarke, R. A. The scorpion's gate
INTELLIGENCE SERVICE -- GERMANY (EAST)
City of angels or
INTELLIGENCE SERVICE -- GREAT BRITAIN
Stross, C. The apocalypse codex
INTELLIGENCE SERVICE -- UNITED STATES
Allen, S. The 13
Kanon, J. Istanbul passage
INTELLIGENCE SERVICE AGENTS
Deaver, J. Carte blanche: 007
Faulks, S. Devil may care

Ludlum, R. The scorpio illusion

Lustbader, E. V. Floating city

MacInnes, H. Prelude to terror

MacInnes, H. Ride a pale horse

MacInnes, H. The Venetian affair

MacLean, A. Ice Station Zebra

MacLean, A. Where eagles dare

Mailer, N. Harlot's ghost

Martini, S. P. Critical mass

McEuen, P. Spiral

Morrell, D. The brotherhood of the rose

Neville, K. The eight

Neville, K. The fire

The Oxford book of spy stories

Reich, C. Rules of deception

Robinson, P. Kilo class

Robinson, P. Nimitz class

Sheldon, S. Windmills of the gods

Steinhauer, O. The nearest exit

Steinhauer, O. The tourist

Thomas, C. Firefox

Trenhaile, J. The gates of exquisite view

Westlake, D. E. Money for nothing

INTERNATIONAL MARRIAGES

Gordimer, N. The pickup

James, H. The golden bowl

Just, W. S. Exiles in the garden

INTERNATIONAL POLITICS *See* World politics

INTERNATIONAL RELATIONS

Cussler, C. Fire ice

Kerr, P. The one from the other

Littell, R. The company

Rosenberg, J. C. Damascus Countdown

Rosenberg, J. C. The Tehran initiative

INTERNATIONAL SPACE STATION *See* Space stations

INTERNET

Coben, H. Hold tight

Deaver, J. Roadside crosses

INTERNET (COMPUTER NETWORK) *See* Internet

INTERNET ADDRESSES *See* Internet

INTERNET AND CHILDREN *See* Children

INTERNET AUCTIONS *See* Auctions; Electronic commerce

INTERNET GAMBLING *See* Gambling

INTERNET IN EDUCATION *See* Education

INTERNET RESOURCES *See* Information resources; Internet

INTERNMENT CAMPS *See* Concentration camps

INTERPERSONAL RELATIONS

Anshaw, C. Carry the one

Bronsky, A. The Hottest Dishes of the Tartar Cuisine

Dekker, T. Immanuel's veins

Eggers, D. How we are hungry

Forna, A. The memory of love

George, E. Believing the lie

Green, J. Another piece of my heart

Harstad, J. Buzz Aldrin, what happened to you in all the confusion?

Higley, T. L. Pompeii

Hootman, R. Courting Greta

Jio, S. The violets of March

Joss, M. Half broken things

Keesey, A. Little century

Lasser, S. Say nice things about Detroit

Lively, P. How it all began

MacLeod, A. Light lifting

Manual of painting & calligraphy

McAfee, A. The spoiler

McCall Smith, A. The forgotten affairs of youth

McCorkle, J. Life after life

Morris, M. Man in the blue moon

Neugeboren, J. Other side of the world

O'Nan, S. The odds

Oz, A. Scenes from village life

Perlman, E. The street sweeper

Phillips, S. E. Call me irresistible

Steel, D. First sight

Steele, J. The watchers

Summer lies

INTERPLANETARY COMMUNICATION *See* Interstellar communication

INTERPLANETARY VISITORS

See also Extraterrestrial beings

Anthony, P. Virtual mode

Bear, G. Anvil of stars

Bear, G. The forge of God

Clarke, A. C. Rama II

Clarke, A. C. Rendezvous with Rama

Doyle, L. Go, mutants!

Emshwiller, C. The secret city

Flynn, M. Eifelheim

Haldeman, J. W. The coming

King, S. Dreamcatcher

Koontz, D. R. The taking

Kotzwinkle, W. E.T.

Meyer, S. The host

Oliver, C. From other shores

Rucker, R. v. B. Hylozoic

Saint-Exupery, A. d. The little prince

Sheldon, S. The doomsday conspiracy

Strieber, W. 2012: the war for souls

Strieber, W. The Grays

Watts, P. Blindsight

Wells, H. G. The war of the worlds

INTERPLANETARY VOYAGES

Adams, D. The hitchhiker's guide to the galaxy

Adams, D. Life, the universe, and everything

Adams, D. The restaurant at the end of the universe

Adams, D. So long, and thanks for all the fish

INVALIDS
Cather, W. Sapphira and the slave girl
Dickens, C. Dombey and Son
Elkin, S. Stanley Elkin's The magic kingdom
Wharton, E. Ethan Frome
Invasion of privacy. Healy, J. F.
Invasion of privacy. O'Shaughnessy, P.
INVECTIVE See Satire
Inventing the Abbotts and other stories. Miller, S.
The **invention** of everything else. Hunt, S.
INVENTIONS
Echenoz, J. Lightning
INVENTORS
Bognanni, P. The house of tomorrow
Echenoz, J. Lightning
Fishburne, R. Going to see the elephant
Harris, R. Conspirata
Hunt, S. The invention of everything else
Morrow, J. The last witchfinder
Shaara, J. The glorious cause
Shaara, J. Rise to rebellion
Theroux, P. The Mosquito Coast
Wallace, C. The blind contessa's new machine
INVERTEBRATES See Animals
The **inverted** forest. Dalton, J.
The **investigation.** Uhnak, D.
The **investigation.** Claudel, P.
INVESTMENTS
See also Banks and banking; Capital; Finance
Cartwright, J. Other people's money
Ducker, B. Dizzying heights
Finder, J. Buried secrets
INVISIBILITY
Berger, T. Being invisible
Klosterman, C. The visible man
Saint, H. F. Memoirs of an invisible man
Westlake, D. E. Smoke
Invisible. Auster, P.
Invisible boy. Read, C.
The **invisible** bridge. Orringer, J.
Invisible cities. Calvino, I.
Invisible man. Ellison, R.
The **invisible** man. Wells, H. G.
The **invisible** ones. Penney, S.
The **invisibles.** Sheehy, H.
Iodine. Kimmel, H.
IOWA
Bognanni, P. The house of tomorrow
Bruni, S. The Night Gwen Stacy Died
Drury, T. The driftless area
Harstad, D. Code sixty-one
Robinson, M. Gilead
Smiley, J. A thousand acres
Thompson, J. The year we left home
Waller, R. J. The bridges of Madison County
The **Ipcress** file. Deighton, L.

IPHIGENIA (LEGENDARY CHARACTER)
Unsworth, B. The songs of the kings
Ira Foxglove. McMahon, T. A.
IRAN
Bond, L. Exit plan
Clavell, J. Whirlwind
Dowlatabadi, M. The colonel
Egan, G. Zendegi
Rosenberg, J. C. The twelfth Imam
IRAN -- 20TH CENTURY
Clavell, J. Whirlwind
IRAN -- TEHRAN
Garcia, C. A handbook to luck
Ignatius, D. The increment
Sofer, D. The Septembers of Shiraz
IRAN -- TO 640 A.D.
Vidal, G. Creation
IRANIAN AMERICANS
Tyler, A. Digging to America
IRAQ
Bunn, T. D. Lion of Babylon
Unsworth, B. Land of marvels
IRAQ -- BAGHDAD
Menendez, A. The last war
Robotham, M. The wreckage
**IRAQ -- HISTORY -- 2003- , ANGLO-AMERI-
CAN INVASION** See Iraq War, 2003-2011
IRAQ WAR, 2003-
DeLillo, D. Point Omega
Fallon, S. You know when the men are gone
Harrington, L. Alice Bliss
Haslett, A. Union Atlantic
Paretsky, S. Bleeding Kansas
Zimmerman, D. Sandbox
IRAQ WAR, 2003-2011
Abrams, D. Fobbit
DeLillo, D. Point Omega
Fountain, B. Billy Lynn's long halftime walk
Harrington, L. Alice Bliss
Haslett, A. Union Atlantic
Paretsky, S. Bleeding Kansas
Powers, K. The yellow birds
Zimmerman, D. Sandbox
IRAQ WAR, 2003-2011 -- VETERANS
Robinson, R. Sparta
Ireland. Delaney, F.
IRELAND
Banville, J. The infinities
Banville, J. The book of evidence
Banville, J. The sea
Barry, K. City of Bohane
Binchy, M. A week in winter
Binchy, M. Circle of friends
Binchy, M. The glass lake
Delaney, F. Ireland
Delaney, F. The matchmaker of Kenmare

ITALIAN AMERICAN FAMILIES
Castellani, C. All this talk of love
Samuel, B. No place like home

ITALIAN AMERICANS
Castellani, C. All this talk of love
Criswell, M. What to do about Annie?
Lee Aloft
Pelecanos, G. P. The big blowdown
Puzo, M. The last Don
Quindlen, A. Object lessons
Samuel, B. No place like home
Scottoline, L. Killer smile
Scottoline, L. The vendetta defense
Shulman, M. Rally round the flag, boys!
Trigiani, A. Very Valentine
Winegardner, M. The Godfather returns
Italian fever. Martin, V.
The **Italian** lover. Hellenga, R.

ITALIANS -- GREECE
De Bernieres, L. Corelli's mandolin

ITALIANS -- NEW YORK (N.Y.)
Prose, F. Household saints

ITALIANS -- RUSSIA
Levi, P. The monkey's wrench

ITALIANS -- SOUTH AMERICA
Conrad, J. Nostromo

ITALIANS -- UNITED STATES
Breslin, J. The gang that couldn't shoot straight
Malamud, B. The assistant
Puzo, M. The godfather
Romano, T. When the world was young
Waller, R. J. The bridges of Madison County

ITALY
Aciman, A. A. Call me by your name
Ballestrini, N. Sandokan
Dibdin, M. Ratking
Eco, U. The mysterious flame of Queen Loana
Ferrante, E. The lost daughter
Furst, A. The foreign correspondent
Godden, R. The battle of the Villa Fiorita
Godden, R. Pippa passes
Heller, J. Catch-22
Helprin, M. A soldier of the great war
Kushner, R. The flamethrowers
Leonard, E. Pronto
Maguire, G. Mirror mirror
Martin, V. Italian fever
McPhee, M. L'America
Moravia, A. Two friends
Rich, N. The mayor's tongue
Roberts, M. Reader, I married him
Seymour, G. Killing ground
Silone, I. Bread and wine
Unsworth, B. After Hannibal
Walter, J. Beautiful Ruins

ITALY -- 14TH CENTURY

Eco, U. The name of the rose

ITALY -- 15TH CENTURY
Dunant, S. The birth of Venus
Eliot, G. Romola
Essex, K. Leonardo's swans
Puzo, M. The family
Rice, A. Of love and evil
Rice, A. Vittorio the vampire
Stone, I. The agony and the ecstasy

ITALY -- 16TH CENTURY
Dunant, S. In the company of the courtesan
Rushdie, S. The enchantress of Florence
Stone, I. The agony and the ecstasy

ITALY -- 17TH CENTURY
Vreeland, S. The passion of Artemesia
Yarbro, C. Q. Communion blood

ITALY -- 18TH CENTURY
Stendhal The charterhouse of Parma

ITALY -- 19TH CENTURY
Calvino, I. Baron in the trees
Hawthorne, N. The marble faun
James, H. Daisy Miller
Wallace, C. The blind contessa's new machine

ITALY -- ANTIQUITIES *See* Antiquities

ITALY -- BOLOGNA
Rigosi, G. Night bus

ITALY -- CALABRIA
West, M. L. The devil's advocate

ITALY -- ELBA
Scott, J. Tourmaline

ITALY -- FLORENCE
Dunant, S. The birth of Venus
Eliot, G. Romola
Forster, E. M. A room with a view
Hellenga, R. The Italian lover
Rushdie, S. The enchantress of Florence
Stone, I. The agony and the ecstasy

ITALY -- HISTORY -- 0-1559
Dunant, S. Blood and beauty

ITALY -- HISTORY -- 1492-1559
Dunant, S. Blood and beauty
Puzo, M. The family

ITALY -- MILAN
Eco, U. Foucault's pendulum
Essex, K. Leonardo's swans
Greeley, A. M. Irish stew!
King, R. Domino

ITALY -- NAPLES
Ferrante, E. Troubling love
Sontag, S. The volcano lover

ITALY -- PARMA
Grisham, J. Playing for pizza
Stendhal The charterhouse of Parma

ITALY -- ROME
Bezmozgis, D. The free world
Gordon, M. The love of my youth

Hansen, E. F. Tales of protection
Hawthorne, N. The marble faun
James, H. Roderick Hudson
Kneale, M. When we were Romans
Martin, M. Vatican
McGowan, H. Duchess of nothing
McPhee, J. A man of no moon
Rabb, J. The book of Q
Rachman, T. The imperfectionists
Rice, A. Of love and evil
Stone, I. The agony and the ecstasy
West, M. L. The shoes of the fisherman
Williams, T. The Roman spring of Mrs. Stone

ITALY -- RURAL LIFE
Styron, W. Set this house on fire

ITALY -- SIENA
Fortier, A. Juliet

ITALY -- TUSCANY
Bilenchi, R. The chill
Craig, A. Love in idleness
Freud, E. Love falls
Ondaatje, M. The English patient

ITALY -- VENICE
Chase, L. Your scandalous ways
Dunant, S. In the company of the courtesan
Dyer, G. Jeff in Venice, death in Varanasi
Godden, R. Pippa passes
Hemingway, E. Across the river and into the trees
Hewson, D. Lucifer's shadow
Lovric, M. The floating book
MacInnes, H. The Venetian affair
Mann, T. Death in Venice
Phillips, C. The nature of blood
Unsworth, B. Stone virgin
Weisgall, D. The world before her
Wharton, E. The children

ITALY -- VESUVIUS
Pohl, F. All the lives he led

ITINERANT CLERGY
Eliot, G. Adam Bede
Ivan and Misha. Alenyikov, M.
Ivanhoe. Scott, W.
IVORY COAST
D'Souza, T. Whiteman
The **ivy** tree. Stewart, M.

J

J is for judgment. Grafton, S.
Jack and Jill. Patterson, J.
Jack Fish. Milligan, J.
Jack Holmes and his friend. White, E.
Jack the bodiless. May, J.
JACK THE RIPPER MURDERS, LONDON, ENGLAND, 1888 *See* Serial killers
The **jackal's** share. Morgan-Jones, C.
Jackalope dreams. Blew, M. C.

Jackdaws. Follett, K.
Jackson's dilemma. Murdoch, I.
Jackson, Stonewall, 1824-1863
About
Shaara, J. Gods and generals
Jacob's folly. Miller, R.
Jacob's ladder. McCaig, D.
Jacob's room. Woolf, V.
JACOBITE REBELLION, 1745-1746
Gabaldon, D. Outlander
Jacquetta, Duchess of Bedford, 1416?-1472
About
Gregory, P. The lady of the rivers
JADE ART OBJECTS
Black, C. Murder in Clichy
Jailbird. Vonnegut, K.
Jalna. De la Roche, M.
JAMAICA
Crichton, M. Pirate latitudes
Fleming, I. The man with the golden gun
Hughes, R. A. W. A high wind in Jamaica
James, M. The book of night women
Levy, A. The long song
McMillan, T. How Stella got her groove back
Jamaica Inn. Du Maurier, D.
JAMAICANS -- ENGLAND
Levy, A. Fruit of the lemon
Levy, A. Small island
JAMAICANS -- UNITED STATES
Winkler, A. C. Dog war
James A. Michener fiction series
Hearon, S. Year of the dog
The **James** boys. Liebmann-Smith, R.
James, Frank, 1844-1915
About
Liebmann-Smith, R. The James boys
James, Garth Wilkinson, 1845-1883
About
Liebmann-Smith, R. The James boys
James, Henry, 1843-1916
About
Liebmann-Smith, R. The James boys
Toibin, C. The master
James, Jesse, 1847-1882
About
Hansen, R. The assassination of Jesse James by the coward Robert Ford
Liebmann-Smith, R. The James boys
James, Robertson, 1846-1910
About
Liebmann-Smith, R. The James boys
James, William, 1842-1910
About
Liebmann-Smith, R. The James boys
Jamrach's menagerie. Birch, C.
Jane. Maxwell, R.

Jane and Prudence. Pym, B.

The **Jane** Austen book club. Fowler, K. J.

Jane Eyre. Bronte, C.

Jane's house. Smith, R. K.

The **Janson** directive. Ludlum, R.

The **January** dancer. Flynn, M.

The **Janus** imperative. Anthony, E.

The **Janus** stone. Griffiths, E.

JAPAN

Buruma, I. The China lover

Dickey, J. To the white sea

The Future Is Japanese

Golden, A. Memoirs of a geisha

Higashino, K. The devotion of suspect X

Ishiguro, K. An artist of the floating world

Mishima, Y. The sound of waves

Mishima, Y. The Temple of Dawn

Murakami, H. The wind-up bird chronicle

Oe, K. The changeling

Oe, K. Nip the buds, shoot the kids

Ogawa, Y. The housekeeper and the professor

Watrous, M. If you follow me

JAPAN -- 11TH CENTURY

Murasaki Shikibu The tale of Genji

JAPAN -- 1787-1868

Mitchell, D. The thousand autumns of Jacob de Zoet

JAPAN -- 17TH CENTURY

Clavell, J. Shogun

Endo, S. Silence

JAPAN -- 1867-1945

Kawabata, Y. Snow country, and Thousand cranes

Kawabata, Y. Thousand cranes

Mishima, Y. Runaway horses

Mishima, Y. Spring snow

Tanizaki, J. The Makioka sisters

JAPAN -- 1945-

Hazzard, S. The great fire

Kawabata, Y. The sound of the mountain

Knight, M. The typist

Michener, J. A. Sayonara

Mishima, Y. The decay of the angel

Miyamoto, T. Kinshu: Autumn brocade

Murakami, H. Kafka on the shore

Murakami, H. South of the border, west of the sun

Oe, K. The pinch runner memorandum

Oe, K. A quiet life

Oe, K. Somersault

Okuizumi, H. The stones cry out

Peace, D. Occupied city

Schwartz, J. B. The commoner

Yoshida, S. Villain

Yoshimoto, B. Goodbye Tsugumi

Yoshimoto, B. Kitchen

JAPAN -- 19TH CENTURY

Clavell, J. Gai-Jin

JAPAN -- 20TH CENTURY

Dickey, J. To the white sea

Golden, A. Memoirs of a geisha

Ishiguro, K. An artist of the floating world

Mishima, Y. The sound of waves

Mishima, Y. The Temple of Dawn

Murakami, H. The wind-up bird chronicle

Oe, K. Nip the buds, shoot the kids

JAPAN -- HIROSHIMA

Bock, D. The ash garden

Pywell, S. L. What happened to Henry

JAPAN -- HISTORY

Knight, M. The typist

JAPAN -- KAMAKURA

Kawabata, Y. The sound of the mountain

JAPAN -- KYOTO

Walbert, K. The gardens of Kyoto

JAPAN -- NAGASAKI

Mitchell, D. The thousand autumns of Jacob de Zoet

JAPAN -- OKINAWA

Bird, S. The Yokota Officers Club

JAPAN -- RURAL LIFE

Abe, K. The woman in the dunes

JAPAN -- TOKYO

Hill, T. The love of stones

Hunter, S. The 47th samurai

Kawabata, Y. The sound of the mountain

The lake

Lee, D. Country of origin

Mishima, Y. Spring snow

Mitchell, D. Number9dream

Murakami, H. After dark

Murakami, R. In the miso soup

Nothomb, A. Tokyo fiancee

Peace, D. Occupied city

Peace, D. Tokyo year zero

Perdue, L. Slatewiper

Smith, M. C. December 6

Tsukiyama, G. The street of a thousand blossoms

Vargas Llosa, M. The bad girl

JAPANESE -- CALIFORNIA

Otsuka, J. The Buddha in the attic

JAPANESE -- CANADA

Itani, F. Requiem

Sakamoto, K. One hundred million hearts

JAPANESE -- CANADA -- EVACUATION AND RELOCATION, 1942-1945 -- FICTION

Itani, F. Requiem

JAPANESE -- CHINA

Ballard, J. G. Empire of the Sun

Shan Sa The girl who played go

JAPANESE -- GERMANY

Oe, K. The changeling

JAPANESE -- HAWAII

Michener, J. A. Hawaii

Oz, A. Fima

Oz, A. Panther in the basement

Spark, M. The Mandelbaum Gate

Stone, R. Damascus Gate

Sullivan, M. J. Necessary heartbreak

Tarr, J. Queen of swords

Wiesel, E. A beggar in Jerusalem

Jerusalem Inn. Grimes, M.

JESUITS

Blatty, W. P. The exorcist

Eco, U. The island of the day before

Hansen, R. Exiles

Higgins, J. Day of judgment

McDonald, I. Brasyl

Russell, M. D. Children of God

Russell, M. D. The sparrow

Vollmann, W. T. Fathers and crows

JESUITS -- MISSIONS -- CANADA -- HISTORY

Vollmann, W. T. Fathers and crows

Jesus Christ

About

Asch, S. The Nazarene

Beard, R. Lazarus is dead

Bulgakov, M. A. The master and Margarita

Cantrell, R. The blood Gospel

Crace, J. Quarantine

Kazantzakis, N. The last temptation of Christ

Mailer, N. The Gospel according to the Son

Rice, A. Christ the Lord: out of Egypt

Rice, A. Christ the Lord: the road to Cana

Tóibín, C. The testament of Mary

Wallace, L. Ben-Hur

JESUS CHRIST -- PARABLES See Parables

Jesus' son. Johnson, D.

JET PLANES See Airplanes

The **Jew** of Home Depot and other stories. Apple, M.

The **jewel** in the crown. Scott, P.

The **jewel** that was ours. Dexter, C.

JEWELERS

Martin, C. W. How to sell

JEWELRY

Hill, T. The love of stones

Parks Getting mother's body

Tolkien, J. R. R. The Silmarillion

Trollope, A. The Eustace diamonds

JEWELS See Gems; Jewelry; Precious stones

Jewelweed. Rhodes, D.

JEWISH CARTOONISTS

Jacobson, H. Kalooki nights

JEWISH CHILDREN

Toynton, E. The Oriental wife

JEWISH DIASPORA See Human geography; Jews

JEWISH ETHICS See Ethics

JEWISH FAMILIES

Bank, M. The wonder spot

Bezmozgis, D. The free world

Delbanco, N. What remains

Eve, N. The family orchard

Foer, J. S. Everything is illuminated

Gilmore, J. Golden country

Gilmore, J. Something red

Gregory, P. The queen's fool

Havazelet, E. Bearing the body

Jacobson, H. Kalooki nights

Kellerman, F. Stone kiss

Kirshenbaum, B. An almost perfect moment

Mattison, A. In case we're separated

Miller, R. Welcome to Heavenly Heights

Mirvis, T. The outside world

Ozick, C. Heir to the glimmering world

Reisman, N. The first desire

Roth, P. The plot against America

Sofer, D. The Septembers of Shiraz

JEWISH HOLIDAYS See Judaism; Religious holidays

JEWISH LEGENDS

See also Legends

Kazinski, A. J. The last good man

JEWISH MEN

See also Men

JEWISH REFUGEES

Bellow, S. Mr. Sammler's planet

Delbanco, N. What remains

The emigrants

Gregory, P. The queen's fool

Uris, L. Exodus

JEWISH RELIGION See Judaism

JEWISH WIT AND HUMOR

See also Wit and humor

JEWISH WOMEN

See also Women

Anton, M. Rav Hisda's daughter, book I, apprentice

Bank, M. The wonder spot

Braff, J. Peep show

Ozick, C. The Puttermesser papers

Sherwood, F. The book of splendor

Solomon, A. The little bride

JEWISH-ARAB RELATIONS

See also Arabs; Jews

Harris, T. Black Sunday

Littell, R. Vicious circle

JEWS

Albert, E. The book of Dahlia

Auslander, S. Hope

Ausubel, R. No one is here except all of us

Bellow, S. The Bellarosa connection

Bezmozgis, D. The free world

Cohen, J. Witz

Diamant, A. The red tent

The emigrants

Epstein, L. The eighth wonder of the world

JEWS -- NEW YORK (N.Y.)
Bellow, S. Mr. Sammler's planet
Braff, J. Peep show
Chabon, M. The amazing adventures of Kavalier and Clay
Colwin, L. Family happiness
Hamill, P. Snow in August
Kirshenbaum, B. An almost perfect moment
Malamud, B. The assistant
Mirvis, T. The outside world
Ozick, C. Heir to the glimmering world
Ozick, C. The Puttermesser papers
Plain, B. The golden cup
Potok, C. The chosen
Potok, C. The gift of Asher Lev
Potok, C. My name is Asher Lev
Potok, C. The promise
Reyn, I. What happened to Anna K.
Reznikoff, C. By the waters of Manhattan
Rosen, J. Joy comes in the morning
Roth, H. Call it sleep
Roth, H. A diving rock on the Hudson
Roth, H. From bondage
Roth, H. Requiem for Harlem
Roth, H. A star shines over Mt. Morris Park
Sholem Aleichem   The adventures of Mottel, the cantor's son
Singer, I. B. Shadows on the Hudson
Stern, S. The angel of forgetfulness
Styron, W. Sophie's choice
Tax, M. Rivington Street
Wallant, E. L. The pawnbroker
Wouk, H. Marjorie Morningstar

JEWS -- NEW YORK (STATE)
Abraham, P. The romance reader
Kay, T. Shadow song
Reisman, N. The first desire
Toynton, E. The Oriental wife
Wiesel, E. Twilight

JEWS -- PALESTINE
Asch, S. The Apostle
Wallace, L. Ben-Hur
Wiesel, E. Dawn

JEWS -- PERSECUTIONS
See also Antisemitism; Persecution
Anatoli, A. Babi Yar
Appelfeld, A. Badenheim 1939
Keneally, T. Schindler's list
Levi, P. If not now, when?
Lourie, R. A hatred for tulips
Malamud, B. The fixer
Phillips, C. The nature of blood
Schwarz-Bart, A. The last of the just
Uris, L. Exodus
Uris, L. QB VII
Wiesel, E. The oath

Wiesel, E. The testament
Zimler, R. The last kabbalist of Lisbon

JEWS -- POLAND
Hersey, J. The wall
Ozick, C. The Messiah of Stockholm
Singer, I. B. The estate
Singer, I. B. The family Moskat
Singer, I. B. The magician of Lublin
Singer, I. J. The brothers Ashkenazi
Uris, L. Mila 18
Yolen, J. Briar Rose

JEWS -- PORTUGAL
Zimler, R. The last kabbalist of Lisbon

JEWS -- RELIGION *See* Judaism

JEWS -- ROME
Asch, S. The Apostle

JEWS -- RUSSIA
Amis, M. House of meetings
Anatoli, A. Babi Yar
Malamud, B. The fixer
Richler, N. Your mouth is lovely
Sholem Aleichem   The adventures of Menahem-Mendl
Sholem Aleichem   The further adventures of Menachem-Mendl
Sholem Aleichem   The nightingale
Sholem Aleichem   Tevye's daughters
Wiesel, E. The testament

JEWS -- SEGREGATION
Hersey, J. The wall
Uris, L. Mila 18

JEWS -- SOUTH AFRICA
Gordimer, N. No time like the present

JEWS -- SOUTHERN STATES
Cheuse, A. Song of slaves in the desert

JEWS -- SOVIET UNION
Amis, M. House of meetings
Bezmozgis, D. The free world

JEWS -- TENNESSEE
Stern, S. The frozen rabbi

JEWS -- UKRAINE
Sherman, S. The little Russian

JEWS -- UNITED STATES
Bellow, S. Herzog
Bellow, S. The adventures of Augie March
Bellow, S. Mr. Sammler's planet
Chabon, M. The Yiddish policemen's union
Delbanco, N. What remains
Doctorow, E. L. The book of Daniel
Doctorow, E. L. Ragtime
Epstein, J. Fabulous small Jews
Epstein, J. The love song of A. Jerome Minkoff and other stories
Gilmore, J. Golden country
Gilmore, J. Something red
Goldberg, M. Bee season

JOURNALISTS

See also Authors

Adams, L. The room and the chair
Anthony, E. The Janus imperative
Barbash, T. The last good chance
Barker, P. Double vision
Belfer, L. A fierce radiance
Bhattacharya, R. The sly company of people who care
Bolano, R. 2666
Busch, F. The night inspector
Byrd, M. Grant
Camus, A. The plague
Carr, C. The alienist
Clark, C. Beautiful lies
Cleage, P. Babylon sisters
Connelly, M. The scarecrow
Cook, T. H. The fate of Katherine Carr
D'Amato, B. Hard road
Danvers, D. The fourth world
Darnton, J. Black and white and dead all over
Darnton, J. The experiment
Deaver, J. Carte blanche: 007
Delinsky, B. Lake news
DeSilva, B. Cliff Walk
DeSilva, B. Rogue island
Dexter, P. The paperboy
Doctorow, E. L. The waterworks
Doig, I. The eleventh man
Doig, I. Mountain time
Dolan, H. Very bad men
Downing, D. Potsdam station
Dunn, S. The big love
Dunne, J. G. Nothing lost
Dyer, G. Jeff in Venice, death in Varanasi
Egan, G. Zendegi
Estleman, L. D. Gas City
Farah, N. Crossbones
Faulks, S. Devil may care
Faulks, S. On Green Dolphin Street
Ferber, E. Cimarron
Fesperman, D. The double game
Fesperman, D. The warlord's son
Fielding, J. Charley's web
Fishburne, R. Going to see the elephant
Flanagan, R. The unknown terrorist
Fleishman, J. Promised virgins
Freely, M. Enlightenment
Fuentes, C. The old gringo
Furst, A. The foreign correspondent
Gibson, W. Spook country
Glass, J. Three Junes
Gleason, R. End of days
Glynn, A. Bloodland
Goodwillie, D. American subversive
Grant, M. Feed

Grass, G. Crabwalk
Greeley, A. M. White smoke
Greene, G. The quiet American
Grippando, J. The informant
Grisham, J. The last juror
Grisham, J. The pelican brief
Guterson, D. Snow falling on cedars
Hamill, P. Tabloid city
Harris, R. Archangel
Hiaasen, C. Basket case
Hiaasen, C. Lucky you
Hobson, L. K. Z. Gentleman's agreement
Ignatius, D. A firing offense
Ignatius, D. The Sun King
Irving, J. The fourth hand
Johnson, A. D. Moonshine
Johnson, D. Le mariage
Jones, D. C. A creek called Wounded Knee
Kanon, J. The good German
Karunatilaka, S. The legend of Pradeep Mathew
Katzenbach, J. Just cause
Kelly, J. The fire baby
Kelly, J. The moon tunnel
Keneally, T. To Asmara
Kennedy, W. Chango's beads and two-tone shoes
Knipfel, J. The blow-off
Lanchester, J. Fragrant Harbor
Lansdale, J. R. Leather maiden
Larsson, S. The girl with the dragon tattoo
Larsson, S. The girl who kicked the hornets' nest
Larsson, S. The girl who played with fire
Lee, M. The canal house
Leonard, E. The hot kid
Leonard, E. Split images
Littell, R. Vicious circle
Llywelyn, M. 1921
Lynn, A. Now you see it
MacInnes, H. The Venetian affair
MacNeil, R. Breaking news
Maguire, G. Son of a witch
Mallon, T. Bandbox
Marlette, D. Magic time
McCabe, P. Winterwood
McDonald, I. Brasyl
McEwan, I. Amsterdam
McEwan, I. Enduring love
McGregor, E. The ice child
Meek, J. We are now beginning our descent
Meltzer, B. The tenth justice
Menendez, A. The last war
Messud, C. The emperor's children
Michener, J. A. Mexico
Mortman, D. True colors
Murray, S. Forgery
Naipaul, V. S. A house for Mr. Biswas
Ozick, C. The Messiah of Stockholm

Palahniuk, C. Lullaby
Parks, B. The girl next door
Parks, T. Cleaver
Parks, T. Destiny
Peacock, J. Blind man's alley
Pears, I. Stone's fall
Piazza, T. City of refuge
Plath, S. The bell jar
Pletzinger, T. Funeral for a dog
Polsan/English Hash
Pratchett, T. The truth
Preston, D. The cabinet of curiosities
Proulx, A. The shipping news
Rachman, T. The imperfectionists
Rash, R. Saints at the river
Robotham, M. The wreckage
Safire, W. Scandalmonger
Salak, K. The white Mary
Schaffert, T. The coffins of Little Hope
Schneider, B. Beautiful Inez
Sherrill, M. My last movie star
Sidor, S. The mirror's edge
Siegel, J. Deceit
Somerville, R. The end of sleep
Stone, R. Damascus Gate
Strieber, W. Majestic
Stumpf, D. Confessions of a Wall Street shoeshine boy
Thayer, S. The weatherman
Theroux, A. Laura Warholic; or, The sexual intellectual
Thornton, T. The alternative hero
Toyne, S. Sanctus
Turner, F. W. The go-between
Vidal, G. 1876
Vollmann, W. T. Butterfly stories
Waldman, A. The submission
Walters, M. The echo
West, N. Miss Lonelyhearts
Westlake, D. E. Baby, would I lie?
White, E. Hotel de Dream
Whitehead, C. John Henry Days
Wilson, R. C. Blind Lake

JOURNALISTS -- WASHINGTON (D.C.)
Fesperman, D. The double game
JOURNALS *See* Periodicals
Journey. Steel, D.
The **journey** home. Olafur Johann Olafsson
A **journey** to the centre of the earth. Verne, J.
Journey to the end of the night. Celine
JOURNEYS *See* Travel; Voyages and travels
Joust. Lackey, M.
JOY AND SORROW *See* Emotions
Joy comes in the morning. Rosen, J.
Joy for beginners. Bauermeister, E.
Joy in the morning. Smith, B.

The **Joy** Luck Club. Tan, A.
Jubal Sackett. L'Amour, L.
Jubilee. Walker, M.
Jubilee. Dann, J.
Jubilee Trail. Bristow, G.
Judah Loew ben Bezalel, ca. 1525-1609
About
Sherwood, F. The book of splendor
Wiesel, E. The Golem
JUDAISM
Agnon, S. Y. Only yesterday
Brooks, G. People of the book
Jen, G. Mona in the promised land
Mirvis, T. The outside world
Potok, C. The chosen
Potok, C. The gift of Asher Lev
Potok, C. My name is Asher Lev
Potok, C. The promise
Roiphe, A. R. Lovingkindness
Singer, I. B. The estate
Singer, I. B. The magician of Lublin
Wiesel, E. The Golem
Zimler, R. The last kabbalist of Lisbon
JUDAISM -- CUSTOMS AND PRACTICES *See*
Rites and ceremonies
JUDAISM -- RELATIONS -- CHRISTIANITY
See Christianity and other religions; Judaism
JUDAISM -- RELATIONS -- ISLAM *See* Islam;
Judaism
Judas child. O'Connell, C.
The **Judas** Field. Bahr, H.
Judas horse. Smith, A.
Judas Iscariot
About
Asch, S. The Nazarene
Kazantzakis, N. The last temptation of Christ
The **Judas** judge. McGarrity, M.
The **Judas** kiss. Holt, V.
Judas Priest. McInerny, R. M.
Jude the obscure. Hardy, T.
The **judge.** Martini, S. P.
The **judges.** Wiesel, E.
JUDGES
See also Lawyers
Carter, S. L. The emperor of Ocean Park
Coulter, C. The target
Desai, K. The inheritance of loss
Grisham, J. The appeal
Grisham, J. The brethren
Hand, D. Deep Creek
Leonard, E. Maximum Bob
Longworth, M. L. Death at the Chateau Bremont
Mankell, H. The man from Beijing
Margolin, P. After dark
Marlette, D. Magic time
Martini, S. P. The judge

Patterson, R. N. Protect and defend

Picoult, J. Nineteen minutes

Pottinger, S. The fourth procedure

Rosenberg, N. T. Interest of justice

Schwartz, L. Angels Crest

Tóibín, C. The heather blazing

Trollope, J. Marrying the mistress

Turow, S. Innocent

Turow, S. Limitations

JUDGES -- FRANCE

Longworth, M. L. Death in the Vines

JUDGMENT DAY *See* End of the world; Second Advent

A **judgment** in stone. Rendell, R.

The **judgment** of Caesar. Saylor, S.

JUDICIAL ERROR

Coben, H. The innocent

Grisham, J. The confession

JUDICIAL INVESTIGATIONS *See* Governmental investigations

JUDO *See* Martial arts; Self-defense

The **jugger.** Stark, R.

Julian Comstock. Wilson, R. C.

Juliet. Fortier, A.

Juliet in August. Warren, D.

Juliet, naked. Hornby, N.

JULY FOURTH *See* Fourth of July

July's people. Gordimer, N.

Jump and other stories. Gordimer, N.

The **jungle.** Sinclair, U.

JUNGLE ANIMALS *See* Animals; Forest animals

JUNGLE ECOLOGY *See* Ecology; Forest ecology

JUNGLES

Conrad, J. Heart of darkness

Forester, C. S. The African Queen

Hamilton-Paterson, J. Gerontius

King, R. The sound of butterflies

Millet, L. Ghost lights

Patchett, A. State of wonder

Salak, K. The white Mary

Jupiter. Bova, B.

JUPITER (PLANET)

Bova, B. Jupiter

Bova, B. Leviathans of Jupiter

Jupiter's bones. Kellerman, F.

Jurassic Park. Crichton, M.

JURISTS *See* Lawyers

The **juror.** Green, G. D.

The **jury.** Martini, S. P.

JURY

See also Courts; Criminal law

Doctorow, C. Rapture of the nerds

Just a corpse at twilight. Van de Wetering, J.

Just after sunset. King, S.

Just an ordinary day. Jackson, S.

Just cause. Katzenbach, J.

Just one look. Coben, H.

Justice. Kellerman, F.

JUSTICE

See also Ethics; Law; Virtue

Gruber, M. The return

Spark, M. Aiding and abetting

Justice for some. Wilhelm, K.

Justice Hall. King, L. R.

Justine. Durrell, L.

JUVENILE DELINQUENCY

See also Crime; Social problems

Edgerton, C. Walking across Egypt

Garigliano, J. Dogface

Hunter, E. The blackboard jungle

Levin, M. Compulsion

Oe, K. Nip the buds, shoot the kids

JUVENILE DELINQUENCY -- FICTION

Lelic, S. The child who

JUVENILE DELINQUENTS *See* Juvenile delinquency

JUVENILE DELINQUENTS -- FICTION

Lelic, S. The child who

JUVENILE FICTION -- FANTASY & MAGIC

Lanagan, M. The brides of Rollrock Island

JUVENILE FICTION -- LEGENDS, MYTHS, FABLES -- OTHER

Lanagan, M. The brides of Rollrock Island

JUVENILE FICTION -- LOVE & ROMANCE

Rowell, R. Eleanor & Park

JUVENILE FICTION -- SOCIAL ISSUES -- EMOTIONS & FEELINGS

Lanagan, M. The brides of Rollrock Island

JUVENILE PROSTITUTION

See also Juvenile delinquency; Prostitution

Coplin, A. The orchardist

K

K is for killer. Grafton, S.

KANCHENJUNGA (NEPAL AND INDIA)

Desai, K. The inheritance of loss

KABUL (AFGHANISTAN)

Hosseini, K. The kite runner

Moulessehoul, M. The swallows of Kabul

Kafka on the shore. Murakami, H.

Kafka, Franz, 1883-1924

About

Estrin, M. Insect dreams

Lashner, W. Kockroach

Kahlo, Frida, 1907-1954

About

Kingsolver, B. The lacuna

The **Kalahari** typing school for men. McCall Smith, A.

Kalakaua, David, King of Hawaii, 1836-1891

About

KENTUCKY -- FICTION
Berry, W. Jayber Crow
Koryta, M. The ridge
Mason, B. A. In country
Morgan, C. E. All the living

KENYA
Ruark, R. Uhuru
Vassanji, M. G. The in-between world of Vikram Lall

KENYA -- FICTION
Crompton, R. Hour of the Red God

KENYA -- NAIROBI
Drayson, N. Guide to the birds of East Africa
Le Carre, J. The constant gardener

KENYANS -- CANADA
Vassanji, M. G. The in-between world of Vikram Lall

The **key.** Toyne, S.
Key West tales. Hersey, J.
KEYS *See* Locks and keys
The **keys** of the kingdom. Cronin, A. J.
The **keys** to the street. Rendell, R.

Khrushchev, Nikita Sergeevich, 1894-1971
About
Lawton, J. Old flames

KIDNAPPING
See also Criminal law; Offenses against the person
Aira, C. The seamstress and the wind
Carcaterra, L. Apaches
Carey, P. His illegal self
Clark, M. H. A stranger is watching
Clark, M. H. Two little girls in blue
Clark, M. H. Where are the children?
Coben, H. Just one look
Coben, H. No second chance
Coulter, C. The target
D'Amato, B. White male infant
Dee, E. The con man's daughter
Durham, M. The man who loved Cat Dancing
Eden, C. Deadly lies
Everett, P. L. American desert
Farah, N. Links
Fergus, J. The wild girl: the notebooks of Ned Giles, 1932
Fielding, J. Heartstopper
Finder, J. Buried secrets
French, N. Land of the living
Fresan, R. Kensington Gardens
Gautreaux, T. The missing
Goudge, E. Trail of secrets
Gowdy, B. Helpless
Greene, G. The honorary consul
Grippando, J. The abduction
Grippando, J. A king's ransom
Gruber, M. The good son

Harington, D. With
Hiaasen, C. Sick puppy
Hiaasen, C. Star Island
Higgins, J. The president's daughter
Highsmith, P. The boy who followed Ripley
Hoag, T. Dark horse
Hoag, T. Guilty as sin
Hoag, T. Night sins
Howard, L. Cry no more
Jance, J. A. Kiss of the bees
Julavits, H. The uses of enchantment
Keating, H. R. F. Inspector Ghote trusts the heart
Kelton, E. The way of the coyote
King, L. R. Keeping watch
King, S. Blaze
Koontz, D. R. The face
Koontz, D. R. The husband
Lehane, D. Mystic river
Leonard, E. Riding the rap
Levin, M. Compulsion
Lindsey, D. L. The rules of silence
Lippman, L. I'd know you anywhere
Lippman, L. What the dead know
Littell, R. Vicious circle
Ludlum, R. The Janson directive
Martinez, A. L. The automatic detective
Matar, H. Anatomy of a disappearance
McBain, E. Alice in jeopardy
McCrumb, S. The songcatcher
McEwan, I. The child in time
Mewshaw, M. Shelter from the storm
Michaels, F. Finders keepers
Mitchard, J. The deep end of the ocean
Morrell, D. Scavenger
Murphy, M. Darkness falls
O'Connell, C. Judas child
Parker, T. J. Little Saigon
Patterson, J. Along came a spider
Peebles, F. d. P. The seamstress
Perlman, E. Seven types of ambiguity
Rendell, R. The tree of hands
Sakey, M. The blade itself
Searles, J. Boy still missing
Silva, D. The secret servant
Slaughter, K. Fallen
Smith, A. Good morning, killer
Smith, W. A. Golden fox
Smith, W. A. Those in peril
Smith, W. A. A time to die
Stephenson, N. Reamde
Stevens, C. Still missing
Straub, P. The Hellfire Club
Trevor, W. Death in summer
Vine, B. Gallowglass
Walker, M. W. Under the beetle's cellar
Wallach, J. Seraglio

Cornwell, B. The winter king
Doherty, P. C. The gates of hell
Doherty, P. C. The godless man
Doherty, P. C. The house of death
Downing, D. C. Looking for the king
Drake, N. Tutankhamun
Dumas, A. The man in the iron mask
Eco, U. Baudolino
Edghill, I. Queenmaker
Franklin, A. Mistress of the art of death
Franklin, A. The serpent's tale
Gregory, P. The other Boleyn girl
Gregory, P. The Boleyn Inheritance
Hardwick, M. The Duchess of Duke Street
Holland, C. Valley of the Kings
Houston, J. D. Bird of another heaven
Koen, K. Dark angels
Laker, R. To dance with kings
Lawhead, S. Avalon
L'Engle, M. Certain women
Mantel, H. Wolf Hall
Maxwell, R. The secret diary of Anne Boleyn
Penman, S. K. Devil's brood
Penman, S. K. Falls the shadow
Penman, S. K. Here be dragons
Penman, S. K. Lionheart
Penman, S. K. The reckoning
Penman, S. K. The sunne in splendour
Penman, S. K. Time and chance
Penman, S. K. When Christ and his saints slept
Plaidy, J. Murder most royal
Plaidy, J. The pleasures of love
Plaidy, J. William's wife
Puzo, M. The family
Rathbone, J. The last English king
Renault, M. Funeral games
Renault, M. The Persian boy
Scott, W. Ivanhoe
Sprott, D. The Ptolemies
Stewart, M. Mary Stewart's Merlin trilogy
Stewart, M. The wicked day
Sutcliff, R. Sword at sunset
Tarr, J. Pillar of fire
Tey, J. The daughter of time
Twain, M. A Connecticut Yankee in King Arthur's court
White, T. H. The book of Merlyn
White, T. H. The once and future king
White, T. H. The sword in the stone

KINGS AND RULERS
    See also Heads of state
Anderson, P. War of the Gods
Tremain, R. Music & silence
Wallach, J. Seraglio

KINGS AND RULERS -- FICTION
Carey, J. Kushiel's Scion

Greenwood, K. Out of the black land
Koen, K. Before Versailles
McClellan, B. Promise of blood
McKillip, P. A. Ombria in shadow

KINGS AND RULERS -- SUCCESSION
Carey, J. Kushiel's Scion
Gregory, P. The queen's fool
The **kings** of cool. Winslow, D.
Kings of infinite space. Hynes, J.
Kings of midnight. Stroby, W.
Kings of the earth. Clinch, J.
KINGS, QUEENS, RULERS, ETC. *See* Kings and rulers
KINSHIP *See* Ethnology; Family
Kinshu: Autumn brocade. Miyamoto, T.
KIOWA INDIANS
    Momaday, N. S. The ancient child
Kiss. McBain, E.
The **kiss.** Steel, D.
A **kiss** before dying. Levin, I.
Kiss me, Annabel. James, E.
A **kiss** of fate. Putney, M. J.
Kiss of the bees. Jance, J. A.
Kiss of the spider woman. Puig, M.
Kiss the girls. Patterson, J.
Kissed a sad goodbye. Crombie, D.
Kisser. Woods, S.
Kissing the gunner's daughter. Rendell, R.
Kitchen. Yoshimoto, B.
The **kitchen** god's wife. Tan, A.
KITCHENS *See* Houses; Rooms
The **kite** runner. Hosseini, K.
KITES *See* Aeronautics
KITTENS *See* Cats
Kleopatra. Essex, K.
KLOSTER ANDECHS (ANDECHS, GERMANY)
    The Poisoned Pilgrim
The **knife** thrower and other stories. Millhauser, S.
Knight of shadows. Zelazny, R.
KNIGHTHOOD *See* Knights and knighthood
KNIGHTS AND KNIGHTHOOD
    See also Middle Ages; Nobility
Berger, T. Arthur Rex
Cervantes Saavedra, M. d. Don Quixote de la Mancha
Connell, E. S. Deus lo volt!
Cornwell, B. Enemy of God
Cornwell, B. Excalibur
Cornwell, B. The winter king
Doyle, A. C. The White Company
Follett, K. World without end
Harris, D. T. The temple and the stone
Holland, C. The angel and the sword
Holland, C. The firedrake
Holland, C. Jerusalem
Scott, W. Ivanhoe

L.A. dead. Woods, S.

L.A. noir. Ellroy, J.

L.A. outlaws. Parker, T. J.

L.A. requiem. Crais, R.

L.A. Times. Woods, S.

La Tour dreams of the wolf girl. Huddle, D.

La Tour, Georges de, 1593-1652

About

Huddle, D. La Tour dreams of the wolf girl

LABOR (CHILDBIRTH) *See* Childbirth

LABOR -- ACCIDENTS *See* Industrial accidents

LABOR -- EDUCATION *See* Education

LABOR AND LABORING CLASSES -- DENMARK

Andersen Nexo, M. Pelle the conqueror: v2 Apprenticeship

LABOR AND LABORING CLASSES -- ENGLAND

Pearce, M. E. Apple tree lean down

Sillitoe, A. Saturday night and Sunday morning

Swift, G. Last orders

LABOR AND LABORING CLASSES -- FRANCE

Zola, E. Germinal

LABOR AND LABORING CLASSES -- PENNSYLVANIA

Poyer, D. Thunder on the mountain

LABOR AND LABORING CLASSES -- POLAND

Singer, I. J. The brothers Ashkenazi

LABOR AND LABORING CLASSES -- UNITED STATES

Doig, I. Bucking the sun

Hemingway, E. The torrents of spring

Lehane, D. The given day

Steinbeck, J. In dubious battle

Tax, M. Rivington Street

LABOR AND LABORING CLASSES -- WALES

Llewellyn, R. How green was my valley

LABOR CAMPS

The hunger angel

Labor Day. Maynard, J.

LABOR DISPUTES

Tucker, T. Over and under

LABOR ORGANIZATIONS *See* Labor unions

LABOR UNIONS

Bennett, R. J. The company man

Doig, I. Work song

Lehane, D. The given day

Poyer, D. Thunder on the mountain

Schulberg, B. Waterfront

LABOR UNIONS -- MASSACHUSETTS

Shepard, K. The Celestials

LABORATORY ANIMAL WELFARE *See* Animal welfare

LABORATORY FERTILIZATION *See* Fertilization in vitro

LABORATORY TECHNICIANS

Enquist, P. O. The book about Blanche and Marie

LABORERS

Eschbach, A. The carpet makers

The **Labrador** Pact. Haig, M.

LaBrava. Leonard, E.

Labyrinth. Mosse, K.

LACE AND LACE MAKING *See* Crocheting; Needlework; Weaving

The **lace** reader. Barry, B.

The **lacquer** screen. Gulik, R. H. v.

The **lacuna.** Kingsolver, B.

Ladder of years. Tyler, A.

Ladies and gentlemen. Ross, A.

The **ladies** of Covington send their love. Medlicott, J. A.

The **ladies'** man. Lipman, E.

Ladies' night. Andrews, M. K.

A **lady** awakened. Grant, C.

A **lady** by midnight. Dare, T.

Lady Chatterley's lover. Lawrence, D. H.

A **lady** cyclist's guide to Kashgar. Joinson, S.

The **Lady** Elizabeth. Weir, A.

The **lady** in the lake. Chandler, R.

Lady Lazarus. Altschul, A. F.

Lady Louisa's Christmas knight. Burrowes, G.

Lady Maggie's secret scandal. Burrowes, G.

The **lady** matador's hotel. Garcia, C.

The **Lady** Most Willing. Brockway, C.

A **lady** never lies. Gray, J.

Lady of horses. Tarr, J.

The **lady** of the rivers. Gregory, P.

A **lady's** lessons in scandal. Duran, M.

LADY'S MAIDS

Worsley, K. She rises

LAGUNA BEACH (CALIF.)

Winslow, D. The kings of cool

Winslow, D. Savages

Laguna heat. Parker, T. J.

The **lake.**

Lake country. Doolittle, S.

LAKE DISTRICT (ENGLAND)

McDermid, V. Grave tattoo

Robertson, I. Island of bones

LAKE ECOLOGY *See* Ecology

Lake news. Delinsky, B.

Lake of sorrows. Hart, E.

LAKE ONTARIO (N.Y. AND ONT.)

Cooper, J. F. The Pathfinder

The **Lake** Shore Limited. Miller, S.

LAKE SUPERIOR

Sosin, D. The long-shining waters

LAKE TAHOE (CALIF. AND NEV.)

O'Shaughnessy, P. Breach of promise

O'Shaughnessy, P. Invasion of privacy

O'Shaughnessy, P. Motion to suppress

The **last** book of swords: Shieldbreaker's story. Saberhagen, F.

The **last** camel died at noon. Peters, E.

The **last** camellia. Jio, S.

Last car to Elysian Fields. Burke, J. L.

The **last** Catholic in America. Powers, J. R.

The **last** cavalier. Dumas, A.

Last chance for glory. Solomita, S.

Last Chance Saloon. Keyes, M.

The **last** child. Hart, J.

The **last** chronicle of Barset. Trollope, A.

Last chronicles of Thomas Covenant [series]
  Donaldson, S. R. The runes of the earth

The **last** citadel. Robbins, D. L.

The **last** command. Zahn, T.

The **last** crossing. Vanderhaeghe, G.

The **last** dance. McBain, E.

Last days of Dogtown. Diamant, A.

The **last** days of Pompeii. Lytton, E. B. L.

The **last** days of Ptolemy Grey. Mosley, W.

The **last** detective. Lovesey, P.

The **last** detective. Crais, R.

The **last** Dickens. Pearl, M.

Last ditch. Marsh, N.

The **last** Don. Puzo, M.

Last dragon. McDermott, J. M.

The **last** empress. Min, A.

The **last** enchantment. Stewart, M.

The **last** English king. Rathbone, J.

Last evenings on Earth. Bolano, R.

The **last** farewell. McCutchan, P.

Last Friends. Gardam, J.

The **last** full measure. Shaara, J.

The **last** gentleman. Percy, W.

The **last** girls. Smith, L.

The **last** good chance. Barbash, T.

The **last** good kiss. Crumley, J.

The **last** good man. Kazinski, A. J.

The **last** hand. Wright, E.

The **last** hellion. Chase, L. L.

The **last** heroes. Griffin, W. E. B.

The **last** hostage. Nance, J. J.

The **last** hurrah. O'Connor, E.

The **last** judgment. Pears, I.

The **last** juror. Grisham, J.

The **last** kabbalist of Lisbon. Zimler, R.

The **last** kashmiri rose. Cleverly, B.

The **last** kingdom. Cornwell, B.

Last kiss. Rice, L.

Last last chance. Maazel, F.

The **last** letter from your lover. Moyes, J.

The **last** letter home. Moberg, V.

The **last** light of the sun. Kay, G. G.

Last man in tower. Adiga, A.

The **last** Nazi. Pottinger, S.

Last night. Salter, J.

Last night at the Lobster. O'Nan, S.

Last night in Twisted River. Irving, J.

The **last** nine days of the Bismarck. Forester, C. S.

Last nocturne. Eccles, M.

The **last** novel. Markson, D.

The **last** nude. Avery, E.

The **last** of her kind. Nunez, S.

Last of the breed. L'Amour, L.

The **last** of the just. Schwarz-Bart, A.

The **last** of the Mohicans. Cooper, J. F.

The **last** of the wine. Renault, M.

Last orders. Swift, G.

The **last** policeman. Winters, B. H.

The **last** prince of Ireland. Llywelyn, M.

The **last** refuge. Knopf, C.

The **last** report on the miracles at Little No Horse. Erdrich, L.

The **last** resort. Lurie, A.

Last resort. Alexander, H.

Last rites. Harvey, J.

Last rituals. Yrsa Sigurdardottir

The **last** runaway. Chevalier, T.

Last seen alive. Simpson, D.

The **last** shepherd. Etchart, M.

The **last** song. Sparks, N.

The **last** suppers. Davidson, D. M.

The **last** surgeon. Palmer, M.

The **last** talk with Lola Faye. Cook, T. H.

The **last** temptation of Christ. Kazantzakis, N.

The **last** thing he wanted. Didion, J.

Last things. Snow, C. P.

Last things. McInerny, R. M.

The **last** time I saw you. Berg, E.

The **last** time they met. Shreve, A.

The **last** town on earth. Mullen, T.

The **last** tycoon. Fitzgerald, F. S.

The **last** unicorn. Beagle, P. S.

The **last** vampire. Strieber, W.

The **last** war. Menendez, A.

The **last** werewolf. Duncan, G.

The **Last** Whisper in the Dark. Piccirilli, T.

The **last** witchfinder. Morrow, J.

The **last** word. Lutz, L.

The **last** word and other stories. Greene, G.

Late for the wedding. Quick, A.

The **late** Mr. Shakespeare. Nye, R.

Late nights on air. Hay, E.

Later novels. Cather, W.

Later novels and other writings. Chandler, R.

Later novels and stories. Maxwell, W.

Later short stories, 1888-1903.

The **lathe** of heaven. Le Guin, U. K.

LATIN AMERICA
  Allende, I. Eva Luna
  Garcia Marquez, G. Love in the time of cholera
  Garcia, C. The lady matador's hotel

Margolin, P. The burning man

Margolin, P. Fugitive

Martin, M. Windswept House

Martini, S. P. The attorney

Martini, S. P. Compelling evidence

Martini, S. P. The judge

Martini, S. P. The jury

Martini, S. P. Prime witness

Martini, S. P. Undue influence

McElroy, J. Actress in the house

Meltzer, B. Dead even

Meltzer, B. The first counsel

Meltzer, B. The tenth justice

Miller, S. The good mother

Mishima, Y. The decay of the angel

Mishima, Y. Runaway horses

Mishima, Y. The Temple of Dawn

Mortimer, J. Rumpole a la carte

Mortimer, J. Rumpole and the angel of death

Mortimer, J. Rumpole misbehaves

Mortimer, J. Rumpole on trial

Mortimer, J. Rumpole rests his case

Mortimer, J. Rumpole's return

Mortimer, J. The second Rumpole omnibus

Parker, B. Blood relations

Parker, B. Criminal justice

Parker, B. Suspicion of betrayal

Parker, B. Suspicion of deceit

Parker, B. Suspicion of vengeance

Patchett, A. Run

Patterson, R. N. Balance of power

Patterson, R. N. Conviction

Patterson, R. N. Dark lady

Patterson, R. N. Degree of guilt

Patterson, R. N. Eclipse

Patterson, R. N. Eyes of a child

Patterson, R. N. Silent witness

Peacock, J. Blind man's alley

Picoult, J. Change of heart

Picoult, J. My sister's keeper

Plain, B. Blessings

Reed, B. The choice

Reed, B. The indictment

Reuland, R. Semiautomatic

Roberts, K. L. Lydia Bailey

Robertson, M. The brothers of Baker Street

Roosevelt, K. In the shadow of the law

Sams, F. Down town

Schlink, B. The reader

Scottoline, L. Dead ringer

Scottoline, L. Killer smile

Scottoline, L. Moment of truth

Sheehan, A. The anxiety of everyday objects

Siegel, S. Final verdict

Simenon, G. Strangers in the house

Snow, C. P. Strangers and brothers

Snow, C. P. Time of hope

Tanenbaum, R. Act of revenge

Tanenbaum, R. Falsely accused

Tanenbaum, R. Hoax

Tanenbaum, R. Immoral certainty

Tanenbaum, R. Irresistible impulse

Tanenbaum, R. Reckless endangerment

Tanenbaum, R. Reversible error

Tanenbaum, R. True justice

Tey, J. The Franchise affair

Traver, R. Anatomy of a murder

Trial and error

Turow, S. The burden of proof

Turow, S. Innocent

Turow, S. The laws of our fathers

Turow, S. Limitations

Turow, S. Personal injuries

Turow, S. Presumed innocent

Turow, S. Reversible errors

Unsworth, B. After Hannibal

Warren, R. P. All the king's men

Warren, R. P. World enough and time

Welch, J. The Indian lawyer

Wilhelm, K. The best defense

Wilhelm, K. Defense for the devil

Woods, S. Cold paradise

Woods, S. Dead in the water

Woods, S. Dirty work

Woods, S. Grass roots

Woods, S. Kisser

Woods, S. L.A. dead

Woods, S. Lucid intervals

Woods, S. Orchid Beach

Woods, S. Reckless abandon

Woods, S. The short forever

Woods, S. Short straw

Woods, S. Swimming to Catalina

Woods, S. Two-dollar bill

Woods, S. Worst fears realized

Law at Angel's Landing. Overholser, W. D.

LAW ENFORCEMENT

Leonard, E. Raylan

The **lawgiver.** Wouk, H.

LAWN TENNIS *See* Tennis

Lawrence, T. E. (Thomas Edward), 1888-1935

About

Russell, M. D. Dreamers of the day

The **laws** of invisible things. Huyler, F.

The **laws** of our fathers. Turow, S.

LAWYERS

See also Legal stories

Benet, S. V. The Devil and Daniel Webster

Grahame-Smith, S. Abraham Lincoln: vampire hunter

Safire, W. Freedom

Stone, I. Love is eternal

Lelic, S. The child who
Lutz, L. The last word
Margolin, P. After dark
Martini, S. P. Undue influence
Meltzer, B. The tenth justice
O'Shaughnessy, P. Motion to suppress
Patterson, R. N. Degree of guilt
Perry, A. A sunless sea
Rogan, C. The lifeboat
Roosevelt, K. In the shadow of the law
Rosenberg, N. T. Mitigating circumstances
Turow, S. The burden of proof
Turow, S. Innocent
Turow, S. Presumed innocent
Unsworth, B. The quality of mercy
Unsworth, B. After Hannibal
Walker, W. Crime of Privilege
Welch, J. The Indian lawyer
Wilhelm, K. The best defense
LEGAL STORIES -- FICTION
Mogford, T. Sign of the cross
Legal tender. Scottoline, L.
LEGAL TENDER *See* Money
Legend of a suicide. Vann, D.
The **legend** of Pradeep Mathew. Karunatilaka, S.
LEGENDARY CHARACTERS *See* Legends;
Mythology
LEGENDS
The Ghost Riders of Ordebec
LEGENDS -- IRELAND
Delaney, F. Ireland
LEGENDS AND FOLK TALES
Benet, S. V. The Devil and Daniel Webster
Berger, T. Arthur Rex
Bradley, M. Z. The mists of Avalon
Lewis, C. S. Till we have faces
Llywelyn, M. The horse goddess
Mailer, N. Ancient evenings
Mehta, G. A river Sutra
Renault, M. The bull from the sea
Renault, M. The king must die
Schwarz-Bart, A. The last of the just
Steinbeck, J. The pearl
Stewart, M. The hollow hills
Stewart, M. The last enchantment
Stewart, M. The wicked day
Sutcliff, R. Sword at sunset
Updike, J. The centaur
Welty, E. The robber bridegroom
White, T. H. The once and future king
White, T. H. The sword in the stone
Wiesel, E. The Golem
LEGENDS AND FOLK TALES -- AFRICA
Lord, K. Redemption in indigo
LEGENDS, JEWISH *See* Jewish legends
LEGISLATIVE INVESTIGATIONS *See* Govern-

mental investigations
LEGISLATORS *See* Statesmen
LEGITIMACY (LAW) *See* Illegitimacy
Leicester, Robert Dudley, Earl of, 1532?-1588
About
George, M. Elizabeth I
Gregory, P. The queen's fool
Maxwell, R. The Queen's bastard
Lelia. Sand, G.
Lempicka, Tamara de, 1898-1980
About
Avery, E. The last nude
Lenin, Vladimir Il¿ich, 1870-1924
About
Kalfus, K. The commissariat of enlightenment
Leno, Dan, 1860-1904
About
Ackroyd, P. The trial of Elizabeth Cree
**LENOX, CHARLES (FICTITIOUS CHARAC-
TER)**
Finch, C. A beautiful blue death
Leo Africanus. Maalouf, A.
Leo Africanus, ca. 1492-ca. 1550
About
Maalouf, A. Leo Africanus
Leonardo's swans. Essex, K.
Leonardo, da Vinci, 1452-1519
About
Brown, D. The Da Vinci code
Essex, K. Leonardo's swans
The **leopard.** Nesbø, J.
Leopold, Nathan Freundenthal, 1904 or 5-1971
About
Levin, M. Compulsion
The **leper.** Thayer, S.
LEPIDOPTERA *See* Butterflies; Moths
LEPROSY
See also Diseases
Greene, G. A burnt-out case
Thayer, S. The leper
Les miserables. Hugo, V.
LESBIANISM
See also Homosexuality
Barnes, D. Nightwood
Byrne, T. Ghosts and lightning
Grant, S. Map of Ireland
Grumbach, D. The book of knowledge
Hagedorn, J. T. Toxicology
Hall, R. The well of loneliness
Hallgrimur Helgason 101 Reykjavik
Henley, P. In the river sweet
Humphreys, H. Afterimage
Hunter, E. Lizzie
Lurie, A. The last resort
Meyer, C. Brown eyes blue
Muller, M. Cyanide Wells

LEWIS AND CLARK EXPEDITION (1804-1806)
Hall, B. I should be extremely happy in your company
Sargent, C. Museum of human beings
Wheeler, R. S. Eclipse
LEWIS WITH HARRIS ISLAND (SCOTLAND)
May, P. The Blackhouse
Lewis, C. S. (Clive Staples), 1898-1963
About
Downing, D. C. Looking for the king
Lewis, Meriwether, 1774-1809
About
Hall, B. I should be extremely happy in your company
Wheeler, R. S. Eclipse
LEXICOGRAPHERS
Arsenault, E. The broken teaglass
Lexicon. Barry, M.
LEXINGTON (MASS.), BATTLE OF, 1775 *See*
Battles; United States -- History -- 1775-1783,
Revolution -- Campaigns
LIABILITY, PROFESSIONAL *See* Malpractice
Liars and saints. Meloy, M.
LIBEL AND SLANDER *See* Journalism
Liberation. Slattery, B. F.
LIBERIA
Maksik, A. A marker to measure drift
LIBERTY
Coetzee, J. M. Life & times of Michael K.
Sartre, J. P. The age of reason
Liberty Square. Forrest, K. V.
Libra. DeLillo, D.
LIBRARIANS
Cooley, M. The archivist
Doig, I. Work song
Glass, J. The widower's tale
Hamilton, M. The camel bookmobile
Hegi, U. Stones from the river
Hoffman, A. The ice queen
Krentz, J. A. Smoke in mirrors
Kurzweil, A. The grand complication
Makkai, R. The borrower
McCracken, E. The giant's house
Michaud, J. When Tito loved Clara
Pym, B. An unsuitable attachment
Schwartz, L. S. The writing on the wall
LIBRARIANS -- FICTION
Millet, L. Oh pure and radiant heart
LIBRARIANS' UNIONS *See* Labor unions
LIBRARIES
Larson, N. The Dewey Decimal system
Treuer, D. The translation of Dr Apelles
LIBRARIES -- AUTOMATION *See* Automation
LIBRARIES -- FICTION
Fforde, J. Thursday Next in The well of lost plots
Scholes, K. Antiphon

LIBRARIES AND AFRICAN AMERICANS *See*
African Americans; Library services
LIBRARIES AND COMMUNITY *See* Libraries
LIBRARIES AND SCHOOLS *See* Libraries;
Schools
LIBRARY ARCHITECTURE *See* Architecture;
Libraries
LIBRARY CATALOGS *See* Libraries
LIBRARY COOPERATION *See* Libraries
LIBRARY EDUCATION *See* Education; Professional education
LIBRARY FINANCE *See* Finance; Libraries --
Administration
Library of America [series]
Nabokov, V. V. Novels and memoirs, 1941-1951
Twain, M. Historical romances
The library of America [series]
Alcott, L. M. Little women; Little men; Jo's boys
Dos Passos, J. Novels, 1920-1925
Farrell, J. T. Studs Lonigan
LIBRARY OF CONGRESS
See also Libraries
Truman, M. Murder at the Library of Congress
LIBRARY RESOURCES *See* Libraries
LIBRARY SERVICES *See* Libraries
LIBRARY TECHNICAL PROCESSES *See* Libraries; Library science
LIBRARY TECHNICIANS *See* Librarians; Paraprofessionals
LIBRETTOS *See* Books
LIBYA
Matar, H. In the country of men
LIBYANS -- UNITED STATES
DeMille, N. The lion's game
Lichtenberg and the little flower girl. Hofmann, G.
Lichtenberg, Georg Christoph, 1742-1799
About
Hofmann, G. Lichtenberg and the little flower girl
Licks of love. Updike, J.
LIE DETECTORS AND DETECTION *See* Criminal investigation; Medical jurisprudence; Truthfulness and falsehood
The lie direct. Woods, S.
Lie down in darkness. Styron, W.
Lie down with lions. Follett, K.
Lieberman's choice. Kaminsky, S. M.
Lieberman's day. Kaminsky, S. M.
Lieberman's folly. Kaminsky, S. M.
Lieberman's thief. Kaminsky, S. M.
LIEBERMANN, MAX (FICTITIOUS CHARACTER)
Tallis, F. Death and the maiden
Tallis, F. Fatal lies
Tallis, F. Vienna Twilight
Lies. Heriz, E. d.
The lies of Locke Lamora. Lynch, S.

Vinge, V. The children of the sky

Vinge, V. A deepness in the sky

Vinge, V. A fire upon the deep

Westerfeld, S. The killing of worlds

Westerfeld, S. The risen empire

Wilson, R. C. Blind Lake

LIFE ON OTHER PLANETS -- FICTION

McCaffrey, T. Dragonsblood

Weber, D. Off Armageddon Reef

Life sentence. Ellis, D.

LIFE SKILLS *See* Interpersonal relations; Success

LIFE SPAN PROLONGATION *See* Longevity

Life times. Gordimer, N.

LIFE, FUTURE *See* Future life

Life, the universe, and everything. Adams, D.

The **lifeboat.** Rogan, C.

LIFTS *See* Elevators; Hoisting machinery

LIGHT *See* Electromagnetic waves; Physics

The **light** and the dark. Snow, C. P.

The **light** between oceans. Stedman, M. L.

Light in August. Faulkner, W.

The **light** in the forest. Richter, C.

Light lifting. MacLeod, A.

Light music. Goonan, K. A.

Light of the world. Burke, J. L.

Light on snow. Shreve, A.

Light thickens. Marsh, N.

The **lighthouse.** James, P. D.

The **Lighthouse.** Moore, A.

LIGHTHOUSE KEEPERS

Schwarz, C. The Edge of the Earth

LIGHTHOUSES

Hansen, E. F. Tales of protection

Koryta, M. The ridge

LIGHTHOUSES -- FICTION

Schwarz, C. The Edge of the Earth

Lightning. McBain, E.

Lightning. Koontz, D. R.

Lightning. Echenoz, J.

LIGHTNING

See also Electricity; Meteorology; Thunderstorms

Hoffman, A. The ice queen

Lightning. Lutz, J.

The **lightning** keeper. Lawrence, S.

Lightning rods. Dewitt, H.

Lights out. Starr, J.

Lights out in Wonderland. Pierre, D. B. C.

LIGHTSHIPS *See* Lighthouses; Ships

Like trees, walking. Howard, R.

Like water for chocolate. Esquivel, L.

Like we used to be. Stubbs, J.

Like you'd understand, anyway. Shepard, J.

The **likeness.** French, T.

The **lilies** of the field. Barrett, W. E.

Lily White. Isaacs, S.

Limitations. Turow, S.

The **limits** of enchantment. Joyce, G.

The **Limpopo** Academy of Private Detection. McCall Smith, A.

Lincoln. Vidal, G.

The **Lincoln** conspiracy. O'Brien, T. L.

The **Lincoln** lawyer. Connelly, M.

Lincoln, Abraham, 1809-1865

About

Grahame-Smith, S. Abraham Lincoln: vampire hunter

O'Brien, T. L. The Lincoln conspiracy

Safire, W. Freedom

Stone, I. Love is eternal

Vidal, G. Lincoln

Lincoln, Mary Todd, 1818-1882

About

Chiaverini, J. Mrs. Lincoln's dressmaker

Newman, J. C. Mary

O'Brien, T. L. The Lincoln conspiracy

Stone, I. Love is eternal

Lindbergh, Anne Morrow, 1906-2001

About

Benjamin, M. The aviator's wife

Lindbergh, Charles A. (Charles Augustus), 1902-1974

About

Benjamin, M. The aviator's wife

Lindbergh, Charles, 1902-1974

About

Roth, P. The plot against America

Linden Hills. Naylor, G.

The **line.** Grushin, O.

Line of fire. Griffin, W. E. B.

Linger awhile. Hoban, R.

LINGUISTICS

See also Language and languages

LINGUISTICS -- FICTION

Carkeet, D. Double negative

LINGUISTS

Downing, D. C. Looking for the king

Harris, R. Conspirata

Karinthy, F. Metropole

Links. Farah, N.

A **lion** among men. Maguire, G.

Lion in the valley. Peters, E.

Lion of Babylon. Bunn, T. D.

The **lion's** game. DeMille, N.

Lionel Asbo. Amis, M.

Lionheart. Penman, S. K.

LIONS

Maguire, G. A lion among men

LIPPIZANER HORSES

Stewart, M. Airs above the ground

Lipstick jungle. Bushnell, C.

LIQUIDS *See* Fluid mechanics; Physics

About

Penman, S. K. The reckoning

LOANS

See also Finance

Higgins, G. V. The Digger's game

LOBBYING See Politics; Propaganda

LOCAL ELECTIONS

Rowling, J. K. The casual vacancy

Local girls. Hoffman, A.

LOCH NESS MONSTER See Monsters

The **lock** artist. Hamilton, S.

LOCK PICKING

Hamilton, S. The lock artist

The **locked** room. Sjowall, M.

Locked rooms. King, L. R.

LOCKS AND KEYS

Hamilton, S. The lock artist

LOCOMOTIVES See Railroads

LOCUSTS See Insect pests; Insects

Loeb, Richard A., 1905-1936

About

Levin, M. Compulsion

LOG CABINS AND HOUSES See House construction; Houses

LOGGERS

Guterson, D. Our Lady of the Forest

Irving, J. Last night in Twisted River

Rash, R. Serena

Urquhart, J. A map of glass

Loitering with intent. Spark, M.

Lola, California. Meidav, E.

Lolita. Nabokov, V. V.

London. Rutherfurd, E.

LONDON (ENGLAND)

Burrowes, G. The heir

Cornwell, B. Sword song

French, N. Blue Monday

Griffin, K. Stray souls

Hayder, M. Birdman

Joinson, S. A lady cyclist's guide to Kashgar

Khair, T. The thing about thugs

MacLean, S. A rogue by any other name

McCall Smith, A. A conspiracy of friends

Robertson, I. Anatomy of murder

Smith, Z. NW

LONDON (ENGLAND) -- HISTORY -- 16TH CENTURY

Parris, S. J. Sacrilege

LONDON (ENGLAND) -- HISTORY -- 1800-1950

Perry, A. A sunless sea

LONDON (ENGLAND) -- HISTORY -- 18TH CENTURY

Donoghue, E. Slammerkin

King, R. Domino

Liss, D. A spectacle of corruption

Robertson, I. Anatomy of murder

Unsworth, B. The quality of mercy

LONDON (ENGLAND) -- HISTORY -- 19TH CENTURY

Atlee, A. The typewriter girl

Clark, C. Beautiful lies

Simmons, D. Drood

LONDON (ENGLAND) -- HISTORY -- 20TH CENTURY

McAfee, A. The spoiler

LONDON (ENGLAND) -- HISTORY -- TO 1500

Cornwell, B. Sword song

LONDON (ENGLAND) -- SOCIAL CONDITIONS -- 19TH CENTURY

Shepherd, L. The solitary house

LONDON (ENGLAND) -- SOCIAL LIFE AND CUSTOMS -- 19TH CENTURY

Carriger, G. Soulless

Morrell, D. Murder as a fine art

LONDON (ENGLAND) -- SOCIAL LIFE AND CUSTOMS -- 20TH CENTURY

Joinson, S. A lady cyclist's guide to Kashgar

Nicolson, J. Abdication

London bridges. Patterson, J.

London fields. Amis, M.

London match. Deighton, L.

The **London** train. Hadley, T.

Lone wolf. Picoult, J.

LONELINESS

See also Emotions

Bakker, G. The twin

Brookner, A. Undue influence

Coupland, D. Eleanor Rigby

Davenport, K. House of many gods

Glavinic, T. Night work

Harrison, K. The seal wife

Heller, Z. What was she thinking?

Hornby, N. Juliet, naked

Keegan, N. Swimming

Kimmel, H. The used world

Martin, L. Break the skin

Martin, S. Shopgirl

Moore, B. The lonely passion of Judith Hearne

Phillips, A. The song is you

Pym, B. Excellent women

Pym, B. Quartet in autumn

Pym, B. The sweet dove died

Rossner, J. Looking for Mr. Goodbar

Schine, C. The New Yorkers

Taylor, E. Mrs. Palfrey at the Claremont

Tyler, A. The accidental tourist

Vann, D. Caribou Island

West, N. Miss Lonelyhearts

LONELINESS IN CHILDREN

O'Malley, T. This magnificent desolation

The **loneliness** of the long-distance runner. Sillitoe, A.

Howatch, S. Scandalous risks

Howatch, S. Ultimate prizes

Huddle, D. La Tour dreams of the wolf girl

Hunter, E. Privileged conversation

Irving, J. A widow for one year

Isaacs, S. Close relations

Jacobson, D. All for love

Jaime-Becerra, M. This time tomorrow

James, H. The ambassadors

Jen, G. Typical American

Jhabvala, R. P. Heat and dust

Johnson, D. L'affaire

Johnson, D. Lulu in Marrakech

Jones, J. From here to eternity

Jordan, H. When she woke

Kadare, I. The accident

Kawabata, Y. Thousand cranes

Keneally, T. A family madness

Keyes, M. Last Chance Saloon

Keyes, M. The other side of the story

Kim, S. The interpreter

King, T. Survivor

Korda, M. Curtain

Korda, M. The immortals

Kostova, E. The swan thieves

Krantz, J. Mistral's daughter

Kundera, M. Immortality

Kundera, M. The unbearable lightness of being

Leavitt, D. While England sleeps

LeCraw, H. The swimming pool

Lee, J. Y. K. The piano teacher

Lee, M. The canal house

L'Engle, M. A live coal in the sea

Leonard, E. Cat chaser

Lescroart, J. T. Guilt

Lethem, J. You don't love me yet

Lipman, E. The dearly departed

Lipman, E. My latest grievance

Lively, P. The photograph

Lively, P. The road to Lichfield

Lively, P. Spiderweb

Llywelyn, M. 1949

Lodge, D. Thinks--

Long, D. The inhabited world

Lurie, A. Foreign affairs

Lurie, A. The last resort

Mallon, T. Fellow travelers

Marias, J. The man of feeling

Martin, L. Break the skin

Martin, V. The confessions of Edward Day

Martin, V. Italian fever

Martini, S. P. Compelling evidence

Mattison, A. The wedding of the two-headed woman

McEwan, I. Solar

McEwan, I. Amsterdam

McEwan, I. The innocent

McGrath, P. Asylum

McGrath, P. Trauma

McGuane, T. Keep the change

McGuane, T. Nobody's angel

McGuane, T. Nothing but blue skies

McInerney, J. The good life

McMillan, T. Disappearing acts

McMillan, T. Waiting to exhale

McMurtry, L. Cadillac Jack

McMurtry, L. The evening star

McMurtry, L. Rhino Ranch

McMurtry, L. Terms of endearment

McMurtry, L. Texasville

McPhee, J. A man of no moon

McPhee, M. L'America

Miller, A. D. Snowdrops

Miller, S. The good mother

Miller, S. Lost in the forest

Miller, S. The senator's wife

Mills, M. The information officer

Moore, L. A gate at the stairs

Moravia, A. Two friends

Morris, M. M. Fiona Range

Morton, K. The house at Riverton

Murdoch, I. An accidental man

Murdoch, I. The nice and the good

Naipaul, V. S. Magic seeds

Nayman, S. The listener

Nelson, A. Bound

Nichols, J. T. The sterile cuckoo

Nicholson, W. The secret intensity of everyday life

Nin, A. Cities of the interior

Norman, H. The museum guard

Oates, J. C. I lock my door upon myself

Oates, J. C. Missing mom

O'Brien, E. Time and tide

O'Connor, J. Ghost light

O'Dell, T. Back roads

O'Hara, J. From the terrace

Ondaatje, M. In the skin of a lion

Ostermiller, D. Outside the ordinary world

Oz, A. Fima

Packer, A. The dive from Clausen's pier

Parks, T. Rapids

Patterson, R. N. Degree of guilt

Perrotta, T. Little children

Piercy, M. Vida

Plain, B. Looking back

Pletzinger, T. Funeral for a dog

Price, R. Blue Calhoun

Pyne, D. Twentynine Palms

Rendell, R. The bridesmaid

Reyn, I. What happened to Anna K.

Reynolds, M. The Starlite Drive-in

Rosenberg, N. T. First offense

Ross-Macdonald, M. For they shall inherit

Andrews, M. K. Summer rental
Angell, R. Nothing but you
Atlee, A. The typewriter girl
Austen, J. Emma
Austen, J. Mansfield Park
Austen, J. Persuasion
Austen, J. Sense and sensibility
Avery, E. The last nude
Bagshawe, T. Adored
Bail, M. Eucalyptus
Baker, K. In the garden of Iden
Baker, L. The Glass Ocean
Baldwin, J. If Beale Street could talk
Balogh, M. More than a mistress
Balogh, M. The secret mistress
Balogh, M. Seducing an angel
Balogh, M. Simply love
Balogh, M. Simply magic
Balogh, M. Simply perfect
Balogh, M. Slightly dangerous
Banks, I. Stonemouth
Bannon, J. I2
Bates, E. Her Amish man
Baxter, C. The feast of love
Belfer, L. A fierce radiance
Benjamin, M. Alice I have been
Bennett, V. The queen's lover
Berry, W. Jayber Crow
Beverley, J. Winter Fire
Binchy, M. The glass lake
Binchy, M. Whitethorn Woods
Blackstock, T. Shadow in serenity
Blake, S. The postmistress
Bohjalian, C. The sandcastle girls
Bolano, R. Monsieur Pain
Bolaño, R. The skating rink
Boll, H. The silent angel
Bourne, J. The black hawk
Bourne, J. The forbidden rose
Bourne, J. My lord and spymaster
Bourne, J. The spymaster's lady
Boyle, E. Along Came a Duke
Boyle, E. Mad about the duke
Brill, A. The movement of stars
Brockway, C. The Lady Most Willing
Bronte, A. The tenant of Wildfell Hall
Bronte, C. Jane Eyre
Bronte, E. Wuthering Heights
Brook, M. The Iron Duke
Brookner, A. Brief lives
Brown, C. The hatbox baby
Brown, C. Lamb in love
Bruni, S. The Night Gwen Stacy Died
Bryson, E. The transformation of Bartholomew
 Fortuno
Burgess, M. Dogfight, a love story

Burroway, J. Bridge of sand
Burrowes, G. The heir
Burrowes, G. Lady Louisa's Christmas knight
Burrowes, G. Lady Maggie's secret scandal
Burrowes, G. The soldier
Byatt, A. S. Possession
Byrd, S. The secret keeper
Byrd, S. To die for
Callihan, K. Firelight
Cameron, P. The city of your final destination
Cameron, P. Coral Glynn
Carlyle, L. The Bride Wore Pearls
Carlyle, L. The bride wore scarlet
Carroll, J. The ghost in love
Carroll, S. Midnight bride
Chase, L. L. The last hellion
Chase, L. L. Lord of scoundrels
Chase, L. L. Silk is for seduction
Chase, L. Miss Wonderful
Chase, L. Not quite a lady
Chase, L. Scandal wears satin
Chase, L. Your scandalous ways
Chen, D. Brothers
Ciotta, B. Her Sky Cowboy
Cleage, P. I wish I had a red dress
Climates
Coetzee, J. M. Diary of a bad year
Cohen, L. H. Heart, you bully, you punk
Coleman, A. Murderville
Collins, J. Beginner's Greek
Colwin, L. Happy all the time
Conley, R. J. Mountain windsong
Cook, T. H. Breakheart Hill
Cooper, I. No proper lady
Cosse, L. A novel bookstore
Crace, J. The pesthouse
Criswell, M. What to do about Annie?
Crowley, J. Little, big
Crowley, J. The translator
Crusie, J. Anyone but you
Crusie, J. Bet me
Crusie, J. Faking it
Currie, R. Flimsy little plastic miracles
Dai Sijie Once on a moonless night
Danielewski, M. Z. Only revolutions
Dare, T. Any Duchess Will Do
Dare, T. A lady by midnight
Dare, T. A night to surrender
Dare, T. A week to be wicked
Davidson, A. The gargoyle
Davies, P. H. The Welsh girl
Davis, L. Master and God
De Bernieres, L. Corelli's mandolin
De los Santos, M. Belong to me
De los Santos, M. Love walked in
Delaney, F. The matchmaker of Kenmare

Harris, E. L. And this too shall pass
Harrison, J. The English major
Harrison, K. The seal wife
Hassler, J. The dean's list
Hassler, J. Rookery blues
Hatcher, R. L. Catching Katie
Hawke, E. Ash Wednesday
Hay, E. A student of weather
Hazzard, S. The great fire
Hearon, S. Year of the dog
Heinlein, R. A. (. A. Variable star
Hellenga, R. Snakewoman of Little Egypt
Helprin, M. In sunlight and in shadow
Hemingway, E. A farewell to arms
Henley, P. Hummingbird house
Henry, P. C. And then I found you
Henry, P. C. Coming up for air
Hern, C. The bride sale
Hern, C. Once a gentleman
Heti, S. How should a person be?
Hewson, D. Lucifer's shadow
Heyer, G. Black sheep
Heyer, G. The grand Sophy
Higgins, K. The Best Man
Higgins, K. Somebody to love
Hilderbrand, E. Silver girl
Hilton, J. Random harvest
Hoban, R. Her name was Lola
Hoban, R. Linger awhile
Hoeg, P. The woman and the ape
Hoff, B. J. River of mercy
Hoffman, A. The dovekeepers
Hoffman, A. Here on Earth
Hoffman, A. The ice queen
Hoffman, A. The third angel
Hoffman, A. Turtle Moon
Hofmann, G. Lichtenberg and the little flower girl
Hollinghurst, A. The stranger's child
Holt, V. The black opal
Holt, V. Secret for a nightingale
Hood, A. The Obituary Writer
Hornby, N. High fidelity
Hospital, J. T. Orpheus lost
House, S. A parchment of leaves
Howatch, S. Glittering images
Howatch, S. Penmarric
Hoyt, E. Scandalous desires
Hoyt, E. Thief of Shadows
Hughes, A. Market Street
Humphreys, J. The fireman's fair
Humphreys, J. Nowhere else on earth
Ignatius, D. The Sun King
Irving, J. The fourth hand
Isaacs, S. Red, white and blue
Isaacs, S. Shining through
Itani, F. Deafening

Iyer, P. Abandon
Jackson, S. Caught up in the rapture
Jakes, J. California gold
James, E. Kiss me, Annabel
James, E. The ugly duchess
James, E. When beauty tamed the beast
James, J. A lot like love
James, J. Something about you
Jeffries, S. 'Twas the night after Christmas
Jiles, P. Enemy women
Jio, S. The violets of March
Johansen, I. The ugly duckling
Jones, D. Second grave on the left
Jones, L. The Dixie Belle's Guide to Love
Jones, S. Outcast
Kamensky, J. Blindspot
Kay, T. Shadow song
Kaye, M. M. The far pavilions
Kaye, M. M. Shadow of the moon
Kearsley, S. Mariana
Kellerman, F. The quality of mercy
Kelly, T. Empire rising
Kenin, E. Driven
Kennedy, D. The moment
Kennedy, K. The lord of illusion
Kennedy, T. E. In the company of angels
Kerstan, L. The golden leopard
Kerstan, L. Heart of the tiger
Kincaid, N. Verbena
Kingsolver, B. Animal dreams
Kinsale, L. Lessons in French
Kinsella, S. I've got your number
Kitt, S. Celluloid memories
Kittredge, W. The Willow Field
Kleypas, L. Crystal Cove
Kleypas, L. Rainshadow road
Knox, E. Billie's kiss
Koen, K. Dark angels
Koen, K. Through a glass darkly
Krauss, N. The history of love
Krentz, J. A. Dream eyes
Krentz, J. A. Lost and found
Krentz, J. A. Running hot
Krentz, J. A. Smoke in mirrors
Kundera, M. Ignorance
Kushner, D. M. The conditions of love
La Farge, O. Laughing Boy
Laker, R. Banners of silk
Laker, R. The golden tulip
Land, B. Pilgrims upon the earth
Law, S. K. The paper marriage
Lawrence, S. The lightning keeper
Layton, E. To wed a stranger
Ledgard, J. M. Submergence
Leithauser, B. The art student's war
Lemann, N. Malaise

Norman, H. The bird artist
Norman, H. What is left the daughter
Nothomb, A. Tokyo fiancee
Oates, J. C. A Bloodsmoor romance
O'Farrell, M. The hand that first held mine
O'Nan, S. Snow angels
Orringer, J. The invisible bridge
Owens, R. D. Heart thief
The Oxford book of English love stories
Oz, A. Don't call it night
Pamuk, O. The museum of innocence
Parameswaran, R. I am an executioner
Park, S. This burns my heart
Parkinson, H. Across open ground
Patterson, J. Suzanne's diary for Nicholas
Paul, J. Elsewhere in the land of parrots
Pears, I. The dream of Scipio
Penman, S. K. Here be dragons
Percy, W. The last gentleman
Percy, W. The second coming
Perlman, E. Seven types of ambiguity
Pettersson, V. The taken
Phillips, A. The song is you
Phillips, M. Gods behaving badly
Phillips, S. E. Ain't she sweet
Phillips, S. E. Call me irresistible
Phillips, S. E. First lady
Phillips, S. E. The great escape
Phillips, S. E. It had to be you
Phillips, S. E. Natural born charmer
Pilcher, R. Coming home
Pilcher, R. September
Plain, B. Blessings
Plain, B. Random winds
Porter, J. A. The near future
Powers, R. Galatea 2.2
Powers, R. The gold bug variations
Powning, B. The sea captain's wife
Preston, C. The scrapbook of Frankie Pratt
Price, E. Savannah
Price, R. Blue Calhoun
Price, R. The tongues of angels
Putney, M. J. The burning point
Putney, M. J. Loving a lost lord
Putney, M. J. The marriage spell
Putney, M. J. No longer a gentleman
Putney, M. J. Nowhere near respectable
Pym, B. An unsuitable attachment
Quick, A. I thee wed
Quick, A. The paid companion
Quick, A. Slightly shady
Quick, A. Wicked widow
Rand, A. The fountainhead
Rand, A. We the living
Rash, R. The cove
Rayner, R. The cloud sketcher

Read, P. P. Alice in exile
Reimringer, J. Vestments
Remarque, E. M. The night in Lisbon
Remarque, E. M. A time to love and a time to die
Reuss, F. Mohr
Reynolds, M. The Starlite Drive-in
Rice, L. Home fires
Rice, L. Last kiss
Rice, L. Safe harbor
Richter, C. The sea of grass
Robards, K. Ghost moon
Robards, K. Shiver
Robards, K. To trust a stranger
Roberts, N. Dance upon the air
Roberts, N. Whiskey Beach
Roberts, N. The witness
Roberts, N. Angel's fall
Roberts, N. Honest illusions
Roberts, N. Midnight Bayou
Roberts, N. River's end
Robinson, E. The true and outstanding adventures
    of the Hunt sisters
Roiphe, A. R. An imperfect lens
Rosenthal, P. The bookseller's daughter
Ross-Macdonald, M. Tamsin Harte
Ross-Macdonald, M. The Trevarton inheritance
Rowell, R. Eleanor & Park
Roy, A. An atlas of impossible longing
Rush, N. Mating
Rushdie, S. The ground beneath her feet
Russell, M. D. Dreamers of the day
Rutland, E. No crystal stair
Sada, D. Almost never
Saint, H. F. Memoirs of an invisible man
Salter, J. All that is
Sand, G. Marianne
Saramago, J. The history of the siege of Lisbon
Sayers, D. L. Busman's honeymoon
Schickler, D. Sweet and vicious
Schine, C. The love letter
Schine, C. The New Yorkers
Schine, C. The three Weissmanns of Westport
Schlink, B. The reader
Schwartz, J. B. The commoner
Schwartzman, A. Eddie Signwriter
Scott, W. Rob Roy
See, L. Peony in love
Segal, E. Love story
Senate, M. The love goddess' cooking school
Seth, V. An equal music
Settle, M. L. Charley Bland
Shakespeare, N. Secrets of the sea
Shakespeare, N. Snowleg
Shalev, M. A pigeon and a boy
Shan Sa The girl who played go
Shapton, L. Important artifacts and personal prop-

Willig, L. The Ashford affair

Willig, L. The seduction of the crimson rose

Wilson, S. The fortune teller's daughter

Wind, R. In the midnight rain

Winspear, J. Elegy for Eddie

Winthrop, E. Island justice

Wiseman, B. Plain paradise

Wolf, J. This scarlet cord

Wood, B. Perfect Harmony

Wood, B. Vital signs

Worsley, K. She rises

Wouk, H. A hole in Texas

Yarbrough, S. The realm of last chances

Yoshimoto, B. Asleep

LOVE STORIES -- TECHNIQUE *See* Authorship

LOVE STORIES, AMERICAN

Soli, T. The lotus eaters

LOVE STORIES, ENGLISH

Hollinghurst, A. The stranger's child

Love story. Segal, E.

Love walked in. De los Santos, M.

The **love** wife. Jen, G.

Love you more. Gardner, L.

Love's mansion. West, P.

Love's winning plays. Majors, I.

Love, again. Lessing, D. M.

Love, lies, and liquor. Beaton, M. C.

LOVE-LETTERS

Brockmeier, K. The Illumination

Rose, M. J. Seduction

The **loved** one. Waugh, E.

Lovelace, Ada King, Countess of, 1815-1852
About

Crowley, J. Lord Byron's novel

The **lovely** bones. Sebold, A.

The **lover's** dictionary. Levithan, D.

The **lovers.** Vida, V.

LOVERS

Beattie, A. Walks with men

Ehrenreich, B. The suitors

Kundera, M. Identity

McGowan, H. Duchess of nothing

Piercy, M. Summer people

Trueblood, V. Seven loves

Lovers crossing. Mitchell, J. C.

Loves music, loves to dance. Clark, M. H.

Loving a lost lord. Putney, M. J.

Loving Chloe. Mapson, J.

The **loving** dead. Beamer, A.

Loving Frank. Horan, N.

Lovingkindness. Roiphe, A. R.

Low down & dirty. Stringer, V. M.

LOW TEMPERATURE ENGINEERING

Evenson, B. Immobility

Low Town. Polansky, D.

Lowboy. Wray, J.

LOWER EAST SIDE (NEW YORK, N.Y.)

Mosley, W. RL's dream

Price, R. Lush life

Stern, S. The angel of forgetfulness

The **lower** river. Theroux, P.

LOYALTY *See* Ethics; Virtue

Lucan, Richard John Bingham, Earl of, 1934-
About

Spark, M. Aiding and abetting

Lucca. Grondahl, J. C.

Luciano's luck. Higgins, J.

Luciano, Lucky, 1897-1962
About

Higgins, J. Luciano's luck

Lucid intervals. Woods, S.

Lucifer's hammer. Niven, L.

Lucifer's shadow. Hewson, D.

Lucifer's tears. Thompson, J.

Luck. Hofmann, G.

The **Luck** of Roaring Camp, and other tales. Harte, B.

Lucky bastard. Browne, S. G.

Lucky break. Freud, E.

Lucky girls. Freudenberger, N.

Lucky Jim. Amis, K.

The **lucky** ones. Mortman, D.

Lucky you. Hiaasen, C.

LUCUMI (RELIGION) *See* Santeria

Lucy. Kincaid, J.

Lucy. Gonzales, L.

Luke, Saint
About

Caldwell, T. Dear and glorious physician

LULLABIES *See* Bedtime; Children's poetry; Children's songs; Songs

Lullaby. McBain, E.

Lullaby. Palahniuk, C.

Lulu in Marrakech. Johnson, D.

LUMBER AND LUMBERING *See* Forest products; Forests and forestry; Trees; Wood

LUMBER INDUSTRY

Bernhardt, W. Dark justice

Kesey, K. Sometimes a great notion

Rash, R. Serena

Luminarium. Shakar, A.

Luminous airplanes. LaFarge, P.

LUNAR EXPEDITIONS *See* Space flight to the moon

Lunar Park. Ellis, B. E.

LUNAR PROBES *See* Space probes

Luncheon of The Boating Party. Vreeland, S.

LUNG CANCER *See* Cancer; Lungs -- Diseases

LUNGS -- DISEASES

See also Diseases

Lush life. Price, R.

Lust & other stories. Minot, S.

Lust for life. Stone, I.

Luther. Cross, N.
Lydia Bailey. Roberts, K. L.
LYING *See* Truthfulness and falsehood
Lying awake. Salzman, M.
Lying in wait. Jance, J. A.
Lying with strangers. Grippando, J.
LYME DISEASE *See* Diseases
LYNCHING
  Clark, W. V. T. The Ox-bow incident
  Howard, R. Like trees, walking
  Lansdale, J. R. The bottoms
  Nordan, L. Wolf whistle
  Smith, L. E. Strange fruit
  Vernon, O. A killing in this town
LYNLEY, THOMAS (FICTITIOUS CHARAC-TER)
  George, E. Believing the lie
  George, E. A traitor to memory
The **lyre** of Orpheus. Davies, R.
LYRICISTS *See* Poets

M

M is for malice. Grafton, S.
MAASAI (AFRICAN PEOPLE)
  Crompton, R. Hour of the Red God
MacArthur, Douglas, 1880-1964
          About
  Knight, M. The typist
The **MacGuffin.** Elkin, S.
MACHINE INTELLIGENCE *See* Artificial intelligence
MACHINE READABLE DICTIONARIES *See* Encyclopedias and dictionaries
MACINTOSH (COMPUTER) *See* Computers
MACLEAN, THERESA (FICTITIOUS CHAR-ACTER)
  Black, L. Evidence of murder
  Black, L. Trail of blood
MacPherson's lament. McCrumb, S.
Mad about the duke. Boyle, E.
The **mad** ship. Hobb, R.
Madame Bovary. Flaubert, G.
Madame Bovary. Flaubert, G.
Madame Tussaud. Moran, M.
Made in Michigan writers series
  Kasischke, L. Eden Springs
MADE-FOR-TV MOVIES
  Moody, R. The diviners
Madison, Dolley, 1768-1849
          About
  Brown, R. M. Dolley
  Hambly, B. Patriot hearts
Madison, James, 1751-1836
          About
  Brown, R. M. Dolley
The **madman's** tale. Katzenbach, J.

Madness in Maggody. Hess, J.
The **Madonna** of Excelsior. Mda, Z.
The **Madonnas** of Echo Park. Skyhorse, B.
The **madonnas** of Leningrad. Dean, D.
MAFIA
  Breslin, J. The gang that couldn't shoot straight
  Connelly, M. Void moon
  Cristofano, D. The girl she used to be
  DeMille, N. The gate house
  DeMille, N. The Gold Coast
  Ellroy, J. American tabloid
  Ellroy, J. The cold six thousand
  Estleman, L. D. Gas City
  Green, G. D. The juror
  Green, N. The angel of Montague Street
  Grisham, J. The client
  Grisham, J. The firm
  Higgins, G. V. At end of day
  Higgins, G. V. Bomber's law
  Higgins, J. Day of reckoning
  Higgins, J. Luciano's luck
  Latour, J. The Havana World Series
  Leonard, E. Pronto
  Littell, R. Walking back the cat
  Patterson, R. N. Dark lady
  Perry, T. Blood money
  Perry, T. The informant
  Puzo, M. The godfather
  Puzo, M. The last Don
  Puzo, M. The Sicilian
  Robbins, H. Sin city
  Robinson, S. Callahan's con
  Scottoline, L. The vendetta defense
  Seymour, G. Killing ground
  Shames, L. Virgin heat
  Shames, L. Welcome to paradise
  Sheldon, S. Rage of angels
  Tanenbaum, R. Act of revenge
  Tanenbaum, R. Immoral certainty
  Turner, F. W. The go-between
  Uhnak, D. Codes of betrayal
  Vachss, A. H. Two trains running
  Weaver, M. Deceptions
  Winegardner, M. The Godfather returns
  Winslow, D. The winter of Frankie Machine
  Woods, S. L.A. Times
  Woods, S. Reckless abandon
MAFIA -- FICTION
  Doss, J. D. The old gray wolf
  Ellory, R. J. A quiet vendetta
  Harkaway, N. Angelmaker
  Swinson, K. Playing dirty
MAFIA -- NEW YORK (STATE) -- NEW YORK
  Collins, M. A. Black hats
MAGAZINES *See* Periodicals
Magdalene line [series]

McGowan, K. The expected one

Mage winds [series]
  Lackey, M. Winds of fate
  Lackey, M. Winds of fury

The **Magellan** House. Gardiner, J. R.

Maggie: a girl of the streets (a story of New York)
  Crane, S.

Maggody and the moonbeams. Hess, J.

MAGI
  Card, O. S. The Gate Thief

MAGIC
    See also Occultism
  Adrian, C. The great night
  Baker, K. The house of the stag
  Bear, E. All the windwracked stars
  Card, O. S. Alvin Journeyman
  Card, O. S. Seventh son
  Charlton, B. Spellbound
  Charlton, B. Spellwright
  Clarke, S. Jonathan Strange & Mr. Norrell
  Crowley, J. Little, big
  Esquivel, L. Like water for chocolate
  Gilman, L. A. Hard magic
  Gregory, P. The wise woman
  Grossman, L. The magician king
  Grossman, L. The magicians
  Harkness, D. E. A discovery of witches
  Harris, J. The girl with no shadow
  The hobbit
  Kowal, M. R. Shades of milk and honey
  Lake, J. Endurance
  Lanagan, M. The brides of Rollrock Island
  Mailer, N. Ancient evenings
  Mieville, C. Kraken
  Nordan, L. Wolf whistle
  Rawn, M. The diviner
  Tolkien, J. R. R. The fellowship of the ring
  Tolkien, J. R. R. The lord of the rings
  Tolkien, J. R. R. The return of the king
  Tolkien, J. R. R. The two towers
  Updike, J. The widows of Eastwick
  Updike, J. The witches of Eastwick
  Walton, J. Among others
  Wilkins, K. Veil of gold
  Wolfe, G. The sorcerer's house

MAGIC -- FICTION
  Anderton, J. Debris
  Anton, M. Rav Hisda's daughter, book I, apprentice
  Bledsoe, A. Wisp of a thing
  Butcher, J. Proven guilty
  Card, O. S. The Gate Thief
  De Robertis, C. Perla
  Dellamonica, A. M. Indigo Springs
  Duncan, D. When the saints
  Evans, C. A darkness forged in fire
  Frei, M. The stranger's magic

Gilman, L. A. Flesh and fire
Griffin, K. Glass God
Griffin, K. Stray souls
Jemisin, N. K. The killing moon
Kennedy, K. The lord of illusion
McDonald, L. J. The battle sylph
McGarry, T. Illumination
McKillip, P. A. Ombria in shadow
Okorafor, N. Who fears death
Putney, M. J. The marriage spell
Putney, M. J. Stolen magic
Rawn, M. Touchstone
Roberts, N. Dance upon the air
Scholes, K. Antiphon
Tregillis, I. The coldest war

Magic for beginners. Link, K.

Magic hour. Isaacs, S.

The **magic** labyrinth. Farmer, P. J.

The **magic** mountain. Mann, T.

The **Magic** of Saida. Vassanji, M. G.

Magic seeds. Naipaul, V. S.

Magic terror. Straub, P.

Magic time. Marlette, D.

Magic words. Koplan, G.

The **magician** king. Grossman, L.

The **magician** of Lublin. Singer, I. B.

The **magicians.** Grossman, L.

MAGICIANS
  Barnes, J. The somnambulist
  Butcher, J. Changes
  Butcher, J. Ghost story
  Butcher, J. Side jobs
  Butcher, J. Small favor
  Davies, R. World of wonders
  Foster, A. D. Kingdoms of light
  Garcia, C. A handbook to luck
  Kadrey, R. Kill the dead
  Kay, G. G. The summer tree
  Roberts, N. Honest illusions
  Stewart, M. The crystal cave
  Stewart, M. The hollow hills
  Stewart, M. The last enchantment
  Stewart, M. Mary Stewart's Merlin trilogy
  Tanner, H. Vaclav and Lena
  Wallace, D. Mr. Sebastian and the Negro magician
  White, T. H. The book of Merlyn

MAGICIANS -- FICTION
  Koplan, G. Magic words
  Morgenstern, E. The night circus

MAGNA CARTA *See* Charters; Great Britain -- History -- 1154-1399, Plantagenets

MAGNETISM *See* Physics

Magnificat. May, J.

Magnificence. Millet, L.

The **magnificent** Ambersons. Tarkington, B.

The **magus.** Fowles, J.

Doiron, P. The poacher's son

Gutcheon, B. R. More than you know

King, S. Bag of bones

King, S. Carrie

King, S. Cujo

King, S. Dolores Claiborne

King, S. Dreamcatcher

King, S. It

King, S. Needful things

King, S. Pet sematary

King, S. Salem's Lot

King, S. Under the dome

Preston, D. Riptide

Rickards, J. Winter's end

Robinson, L. Water dogs

Russo, R. Empire Falls

Strout, E. Olive Kitteridge

Sullivan, J. C. Maine

Mainspring. Lake, J.

MAINSTREAMING IN EDUCATION *See* Education; Exceptional children; Handicapped children

Maisie Dobbs. Winspear, J.

Majestic. Strieber, W.

Major Pettigrew's last stand. Simonson, H.

Make way for Lucia. Benson, E. F.

The **making** of us. Jewell, L.

The **Makioka** sisters. Tanizaki, J.

MALADJUSTED CHILDREN *See* Emotionally disturbed children

Malaise. Lemann, N.

A **Malamud** reader. Malamud, B.

MALARIA

     See also Diseases

  Mallon, T. Two moons

MALAWI

  Theroux, P. The lower river

MALAYA

  Eng, T. T. The gift of rain

MALAYA -- FICTION

  Tan, T. E. The Garden of Evening Mists

MALAYSIA

  Conrad, J. Lord Jim

  Manicka, R. The rice mother

  Samarasan, P. Evening is the whole day

Malcolm X, 1925-1965

About

  Baker, K. Strivers Row

MALE ACTORS *See* Actors

MALE CLIMACTERIC *See* Aging

MALE FRIENDSHIP

  Bradbury, R. Something wicked this way comes

  Coe, J. The Rotters' Club

  Dermont, A. The starboard sea

  Kiefer, C. The infinite tides

  Kinder, C. Honeymooners

Lehane, D. Mystic river

McCracken, E. Niagara Falls all over again

O'Neill, J. At swim, two boys

Pywell, S. L. What happened to Henry

Smith, Z. White teeth

White, E. Jack Holmes and his friend

MALE HOMOSEXUALITY

  White, E. Jack Holmes and his friend

Malgudi days. Narayan, R. K.

Malice domestic. Hardwick, M.

Malice prepense. Wilhelm, K.

MALIGNANT TUMORS *See* Cancer

Mallory's oracle. O'Connell, C.

MALLORY, KATHLEEN (FICTITIOUS CHARACTER)

  O'Connell, C. The chalk girl

  O'Connell, C. Crime school

MALLOY, FRANK (FICTITIOUS CHARACTER)

  Thompson, V. Murder in Chinatown

  Thompson, V. Murder on Fifth Avenue

  Thompson, V. Murder on Lexington Avenue

  Thompson, V. Murder on Waverly Place

MALPRACTICE

  Cook, R. Crisis

MALPRACTICE INSURANCE *See* Insurance

MALTA

  Mills, M. The information officer

  Willocks, T. The religion

MALTA -- FICTION

  Mogford, T. Sign of the cross

MALTA -- HISTORY -- SIEGE, 1565

  Willocks, T. The religion

The **Maltese** falcon. Hammett, D.

Mama Day. Naylor, G.

Mama Flora's family. Haley, A.

MAMBO (DANCE)

  Chao, P. Mambo peligroso

The **Mambo** Kings play songs of love. Hijuelos, O.

Mambo peligroso. Chao, P.

MAMMALS *See* Animals

The **mammoth** book of steampunk.

The **man.** Wallace, I.

MAN *See* Human beings

The **man** from Beijing. Mankell, H.

The **man** from Saigon. Leimbach, M.

A **man** in full. Wolfe, T.

The **man** in my basement. Mosley, W.

MAN IN SPACE *See* Space flight

Man in the blue moon. Morris, M.

The **man** in the gray flannel suit. Wilson, S.

The **man** in the high castle. Dick, P. K.

The **man** in the iron mask. Dumas, A.

Man in the Iron Mask

About

  Dumas, A. The man in the iron mask

Haimoff, M. These days are ours

Heller, J. Best enemies

Lehmann, S. Astor Place Vintage

McLaughlin, E. The nanny diaries

Paddock, J. A secret word

Sharp, Z. Third strike

MANHATTAN (NEW YORK, N.Y.) -- SOCIAL LIFE AND CUSTOMS

Haimoff, M. These days are ours

Manhattan transfer. Dos Passos, J.

MANHUNTS

Forsyth, F. The Odessa file

MANIC-DEPRESSIVE ILLNESS

See also Affective disorders; Mental illness

Alenyikov, M. Ivan and Misha

Garey, J. Too bright to hear too loud to see

Manifold. Baxter, S.

Manifold. Baxter, S.

MANIKINS (FASHION MODELS) *See* Fashion models

Manly pursuits. Harries, A.

MANNED SPACE FLIGHT *See* Space flight

MANNEQUINS (FASHION MODELS) *See* Fashion models

MANNEQUINS (FIGURES)

Stace, W. By George

MANORS -- ENGLAND -- 20TH CENTURY

Jones, S. The uninvited guests

Mansfield Park. Austen, J.

The **mansion.** Faulkner, W.

MANSIONS

Koontz, D. R. Odd apocalypse

Millet, L. Magnificence

The **Manson** curse. Shannon, D.

Manson, Charles, 1934-

About

Lazar, Z. Sway

The **manticore.** Davies, R.

The **manual** of detection. Berry, J.

Manual of painting & calligraphy.

MANUFACTURING EXECUTIVES

Keneally, T. Schindler's list

A **manuscript** of ashes. Munoz Molina, A.

MANUSCRIPTS

See also Archives; Bibliography; Books

Archer, J. A matter of honor

Caldwell, I. The rule of four

Crowley, J. Lord Byron's novel

Dai Sijie Once on a moonless night

Durrell, L. Balthazar

Gruber, M. The book of air and shadows

Holland, T. The archivist's story

Khemir, S. The blue manuscript

Kiernan, C. R. The red tree

Langer, A. The thieves of Manhattan

Ludlum, R. The Gemini contenders

Martin, W. Harvard Yard

McCarry, C. Old boys

McDermid, V. Grave tattoo

Michaels, B. Houses of stone

Ozick, C. The Messiah of Stockholm

Redfield, J. The celestine prophecy

Stern, S. The angel of forgetfulness

Weber, K. The little women

MANUSCRIPTS -- COLLECTORS AND COLLECTING

Byatt, A. S. Possession

Martin, W. Harvard Yard

MANUSCRIPTS -- FICTION

Harkness, D. Shadow of night

The **many** deaths of the Firefly Brothers. Mullen, T.

The **many** loves of Dobie Gillis. Shulman, M.

The **many-colored** land. May, J.

MAORIS

See also Indigenous peoples

Hulme, K. The bone people

Tremain, R. The color

The **map** and the territory.

MAP DRAWING

Larsen, R. The selected works of T. S. Spivet

A **map** of glass. Urquhart, J.

Map of Ireland. Grant, S.

The **map** of lost memories. Fay, K.

The **map** of the sky. Palma, F. J.

A **map** of the world. Hamilton, J.

The **map** of true places. Barry, B.

A **map** of Tulsa. Lytal, B.

The **mapping** of love and death. Winspear, J.

Maps for lost lovers. Aslam, N.

Maps in a mirror. Card, O. S.

Mara and Dann. Lessing, D. M.

MARAIS (PARIS, FRANCE)

Black, C. Murder in the Marais

Marathon man. Goldman, W.

MARATHON SWIMMING *See* Swimming

The **marble** faun. Hawthorne, N.

The **march.** Doctorow, E. L.

MARDI GRAS

Faulkner, W. Pylon

The **Margarets.** Tepper, S. S.

Marguerite, Queen, consort of Louis IX, King of France

About

Jones, S. Four sisters, all queens

Mariana. Kearsley, S.

Marianne. Sand, G.

Marie Antoinette, Queen, consort of Louis XVI, King of France, 1755-1793

About

Davis, K. Versailles

Naslund, S. J. Abundance

Mariette in ecstasy. Hansen, R.

Ford, F. M. The good soldier
Franzen, J. Freedom
Franzen, J. The corrections
Galchen, R. Atmospheric disturbances
Galloway, J. Clara
Gardam, J. The man in the wooden hat
Gardam, J. The queen of the tambourine
Genova, L. Left neglected
Gibbons, K. On the occasion of my last afternoon
Goodwin, D. The American heiress
Goolrick, R. A reliable wife
Gordon, E. F. It will come to me
Grant, L. We had it so good
Hamilton, J. When Madeline was young
Haskell, J. American purgatorio
Hay, E. Garbo laughs
Hays, T. The pleasure was mine
Hedges, P. The Heights
Henkin, J. Matrimony
Hill, R. When all is said and done
Hoffman, A. Blue diary
Hoffman, A. Skylight confessions
Hornby, N. How to be good
Isaacs, S. As husbands go
Jaffe, R. Class reunion
James, H. The Europeans
James, H. The spoils of Poynton
James, H. The wings of the dove
Jones, S. Small wars
Joss, M. The night following
Karon, J. Out to Canaan
Kasischke, L. In a perfect world
Kinder, C. Honeymooners
King, S. Lisey's story
Kittredge, W. The Willow Field
Koen, K. Through a glass darkly
Leebron, F. G. In the middle of all this
Lodge, D. Deaf sentence
Lordan, B. But come ye back
MacColl, G. To marry an English Lord
Marias, J. A heart so white
Mawer, S. The glass room
McEwan, I. Black dogs
McEwan, I. On Chesil Beach
McFarland, D. Letter from Point Clear
McLain, P. The Paris wife
McPhee, M. Dear money
Meloy, M. Liars and saints
Meltzer, B. Dead even
Miller, S. The senator's wife
Minot, E. The Brambles
Minot, S. Folly
Mooney, T. The same river twice
Morley, I. Come Sunday
Nelson, A. Bound
Nicholson, W. The secret intensity of everyday life

Nunez, E. Anna in-between
Oates, J. C. The falls
O'Nan, S. The good wife
Otsuka, J. The Buddha in the attic
Pletzinger, T. Funeral for a dog
Pouncey, P. R. Rules for old men waiting
Price, R. Roxanna Slade
Rice, L. Blue moon
Ross, A. Mr. Peanut
Russo, R. Bridge of sighs
Russo, R. That old Cape magic
Sarton, M. Anger
Savage, S. Glass
Seth, V. A suitable boy
Shakespeare, N. Secrets of the sea
Shreve, A. All he ever wanted
Shreve, A. Sea glass
Shriver, L. So much for that
Smiley, J. Private life
Solomon, A. The little bride
Stamm, P. Seven years
Stegner, W. E. Crossing to safety
Stirling, J. The piper's tune
Stone, R. Outerbridge Reach
Stuart, J. The tower, the zoo, and the tortoise
Suri, M. The age of Shiva
Swift, G. Tomorrow
Tennant, E. An unequal marriage
Thayer, N. Between husbands and friends
Thayer, N. Family secrets
Theroux, P. My secret history
Toer, P. A. The girl from the coast
Trollope, J. The men and the girls
Trollope, J. Next of kin
Tuck, L. I married you for happiness
Tyler, A. The amateur marriage
Tyler, A. Breathing lessons
Vidal, G. 1876
Weber, K. True confections
Weiner, J. Little earthquakes
West, P. Love's mansion
Winer, A. The marriage artist
Wolff, M. M. Sudden rain
Wolitzer, M. The ten-year nap
Wood, B. The dreaming

MARRIAGE -- FICTION
Burrowes, G. The heir
Gilmore, J. The Mothers
Grant, S. The star princess
Graves, T. G. Covet
Hannah, K. Home front
Higgins, K. My one and only
James, E. When beauty tamed the beast
Kincaid, J. See now then
MacLean, S. A rogue by any other name
Moore, A. The Lighthouse

MARTIANS
  Haldeman, J. W. Starbound
  Heinlein, R. A. Stranger in a strange land
Martin Bauman. Leavitt, D.
Martin Chuzzlewit. Dickens, C.
Martin Dressler. Millhauser, S.
Martin Eden. London, J.
MARTYRS
  Eliot, G. Romola
  Penman, S. K. Time and chance
Mary. Newman, J. C.
MARY (BLESSED VIRGIN, SAINT)
    See also Saints
  Berry, S. The third secret
  Tóibín, C. The testament of Mary
MARY (BLESSED VIRGIN, SAINT) -- ART *See*
  Art; Christian art
Mary Ann in autumn. Maupin, A.
Mary Coin. Silver, M.
Mary I, Queen of England, 1516-1558
    About
  Gregory, P. The queen's fool
  Harper, K. The Poyson garden
Mary II, Queen of Great Britain, 1662-1694
    About
  Plaidy, J. William's wife
Mary Magdalene, Saint
    About
  McGowan, K. The expected one
Mary Reilly. Martin, V.
Mary Stewart's Merlin trilogy. Stewart, M.
Mary, Blessed Virgin, Saint
    About
  Berry, S. The third secret
  Guterson, D. Our Lady of the Forest
  Kirshenbaum, B. An almost perfect moment
  Tóibín, C. The testament of Mary
Mary, Mary. Parsons, J.
Mary, Queen of Scots, 1542-1587
    About
  Buckley, F. The fugitive queen
  Plaidy, J. The captive Queen of Scots
Marya. Oates, J. C.
MARYLAND
  Gaffney, P. Flight lessons
  Lippman, L. I'd know you anywhere
  Lippman, L. The most dangerous thing
  McBride, J. Song yet sung
  Michener, J. A. Chesapeake
  Tyler, A. Searching for Caleb
MARYLAND -- 17TH CENTURY
  Barth, J. The sot-weed factor
MARYLAND -- ANNAPOLIS
  Deutermann, P. T. Darkside
  Martin, W. Annapolis
MARYLAND -- BALTIMORE

  Bell, M. S. Ten Indians
  Lippman, L. What the dead know
  Palmer, M. The last surgeon
  Tyler, A. The amateur marriage
  Tyler, A. Back when we were grownups
  Tyler, A. Celestial navigation
  Tyler, A. The clock winder
  Tyler, A. Digging to America
  Tyler, A. Dinner at the Homesick Restaurant
  Tyler, A. Ladder of years
  Tyler, A. Morgan's passing
  Tyler, A. Noah's compass
  Tyler, A. A patchwork planet
  Tyler, A. Saint maybe
MARYLAND -- FICTION
  Tilghman, C. The right-hand shore
MASADA SITE (ISRAEL)
  Hoffman, A. The dovekeepers
MASAI (AFRICAN PEOPLE) *See* Africans; Indigenous peoples
Masaryk Station. Down, D.
MASH. Hooker, R.
MASKS (PLAYS) *See* Drama; Pageants; Theater
MASOCHISM
  Templeton, E. Gordon
Mason & Dixon. Pynchon, T.
MASON (OHIO)
  Tatlock, A. Things we once held dear
Mason, Charles, 1730-1787
    About
  Pynchon, T. Mason & Dixon
MASONRY *See* Building; Stone
MASS COMMUNICATION *See* Communication;
  Mass media; Telecommunication
MASS MEDIA *See* Communication
MASS MURDER
  Deutermann, P. T. The cat dancers
  Mankell, H. The man from Beijing
MASSACHUSETTS
  Adams, L. Harbor
  Arsenault, E. The broken teaglass
  Blake, S. The postmistress
  Clark, N. The Hills at home
  Cook, T. H. The Chatham School affair
  Dufresne, J. Requiem, Mass.
  Giffin, E. Heart of the matter
  Glass, J. The widower's tale
  Haigh, J. The condition
  Haslett, A. Union Atlantic
  Higgins, G. V. A change of gravity
  Higgins, G. V. The Mandeville talent
  Hoffman, A. Blue diary
  Hoffman, A. Here on Earth
  Hoffman, A. Practical magic
  Hoffman, A. The red garden
  Hoffman, A. The river king

Hoffman, A. Blue diary

Hoffman, A. Practical magic

Lahiri, J. The namesake

Landay, W. Defending Jacob

Lehane, D. Shutter Island

Miller, J. The year of the gadfly

Morris, M. M. Fiona Range

Page, K. H. The body in the bookcase

Parker, R. B. Death in paradise

Pipkin, J. Woodsburner

Searles, J. Boy still missing

Sittenfeld, C. Prep

Updike, J. Toward the end of time

MASSACHUSETTS -- HISTORY -- 19TH CENTURY

Shepard, K. The Celestials

MASSACHUSETTS -- LOWELL

Rossner, J. Emmeline

MASSACHUSETTS -- MARBLEHEAD

Howe, K. The physick book of Deliverance Dane

MASSACHUSETTS -- PROVINCETOWN

Dillard, A. The Maytrees

Mailer, N. Tough guys don't dance

MASSACHUSETTS -- SALEM

Barry, B. The lace reader

Barry, B. The map of true places

Conde, M. I, Tituba, black witch of Salem

Hawthorne, N. The House of the Seven Gables

Howe, K. The physick book of Deliverance Dane

Julavits, H. The uses of enchantment

Kent, K. The heretic's daughter

Morrow, J. The last witchfinder

MASSACHUSETTS -- SOCIAL LIFE AND CUSTOMS

Graver, E. The end of the point

MASSACHUSETTS INSTITUTE OF TECHNOLOGY

Pearl, M. The technologists

MASSACHUSETTS INSTITUTE OF TECHNOLOGY -- HISTORY -- 19TH CENTURY

Pearl, M. The technologists

MASSACRES

See also Atrocities; History; Persecution

Danticat, E. The farming of bones

DeMille, N. Word of honor

O'Brien, T. In the Lake of the Woods

Stanisic, S. How the soldier repairs the gramophone

Zimler, R. The last kabbalist of Lisbon

MASSACRES -- FICTION

Mankell, H. The man from Beijing

The **master.** Toibin, C.

Master and God. Davis, L.

The **master** and Margarita. Bulgakov, M. A.

MASTER AND SERVANT

Carey, P. Parrot and Olivier in America

Osborne, L. The forgiven

Umrigar, T. N. The space between us

The **master** bedroom. Hadley, T.

The **Master** Butchers Singing Club. Erdrich, L.

The **master** executioner. Estleman, L. D.

Master of the delta. Cook, T. H.

Master of the game. Sheldon, S.

Master's choice [v1]-2: mystery stories by today's top writers and the masters who inspired them.

Masterclass. West, M. L.

The **Masterharper** of Pern. McCaffrey, A.

The **masters.** Snow, C. P.

Masters of Atlantis. Portis, C.

Mata Hari, 1876-1917

About

Murphy, Y. Signed, Mata Hari

The **Matarese** Circle. Ludlum, R.

The **match.** Gunesekera, R.

Match me if you can. Phillips, S. E.

The **matchmaker** of Kenmare. Delaney, F.

MATERIA MEDICA See Medicine; Therapeutics

MATERNITY See Mothers

MATHEMATICAL ANALYSIS See Mathematics

MATHEMATICAL MODELS

See also Mathematics

MATHEMATICAL RECREATIONS See Amusements; Puzzles; Scientific recreations

MATHEMATICIANS

See also Scientists

Banville, J. The infinities

Benjamin, M. Alice I have been

Choi, S. A person of interest

Crowley, J. Lord Byron's novel

DeLillo, D. Ratner's star

Goodman, C. The night villa

Hospital, J. T. Orpheus lost

Kehlmann, D. Measuring the world

Kerr, P. Dark matter

Leavitt, D. The Indian clerk

Morrow, J. The last witchfinder

Ogawa, Y. The housekeeper and the professor

Rucker, R. v. B. Mathematicians in love

Stott, R. Ghostwalk

Zamiatin, E. I. We

Mathematicians in love. Rucker, R. v. B.

MATHEMATICS

Kehlmann, D. Measuring the world

Richmond, M. No one you know

Taylor, B. The book of getting even

Mathew, Pradeep Sivanathan, 1965-

About

Karunatilaka, S. The legend of Pradeep Mathew

Mathilda Savitch. Lodato, V.

Matilda, Empress, consort of Henry V, Holy Roman Emperor, 1102-1167

About

Penman, S. K. When Christ and his saints slept

Iles, G. The footprints of God
Lescroart, J. T. The oath
Michener, J. A. Recessional
Moon, E. The speed of dark
Picoult, J. My sister's keeper
MEDICAL EXAMINERS
Cook, R. Crisis
Cook, R. Marker
Patterson, J. 1st to die
MEDICAL FICTION *See* Medical novels
MEDICAL GENETICS *See* Genetics; Pathology
MEDICAL MISSIONS *See* Medicine
MEDICAL NOVELS
Kellerman, J. Devil's waltz
Powers, R. Operation wandering soul
Yanagihara, H. The people in the trees
MEDICAL PERSONNEL -- MALPRACTICE
See Malpractice; Medicine -- Law and legislation
MEDICAL PRACTICE *See* Medicine
MEDICAL PROFESSION *See* Medical personnel;
Medical practice; Medicine
MEDICAL SCHOOLS *See* Medical colleges
MEDICAL SCIENCES *See* Medicine
MEDICAL STUDENTS
Guinn, M. The resurrectionist
MEDICAL TECHNOLOGY *See* Medicine
MEDICAL TRANSPLANTATION *See* Trans-
plantation of organs, tissues, etc.
MEDICATION ABUSE *See* Drug abuse; Sub-
stance abuse
MEDICINE
Caldwell, T. Testimony of two men
MEDICINE -- ETHICAL ASPECTS *See* Medical
ethics
MEDICINE -- RESEARCH
See also Research
Martini, S. P. The jury
Mosley, W. The last days of Ptolemy Grey
Palmer, M. The fifth vial
Patchett, A. State of wonder
Sanders, L. The sixth commandment
Saul, J. Shadows
Uris, L. QB VII
MEDICINE -- RESEARCH -- FICTION
Martini, S. P. The jury
Patchett, A. State of wonder
MEDICINE MEN *See* Shamans
MEDICINES, PATENT, PROPRIETARY, ETC.
Capote, T. The grass harp
Wells, H. G. Tono-Bungay
Medicus. Downie, R.
MEDIEVAL ART *See* Art; Medieval civilization
MEDIEVAL TOURNAMENTS *See* Chivalry;
Medieval civilization; Pageants
Meditations in green. Wright, S.
MEDITERRANEAN REGION

Dunnett, D. Pawn in frankincense
MEDIUMS
Noyes, D. Captivity
MEDIUMS -- FICTION
Koontz, D. R. Odd apocalypse
Mantel, H. Beyond black
Medusa. Dibdin, M.
MEDUSA (FRIGATE)
Edge, A. The god of spring
Medusa's child. Nance, J. J.
**MEEHAN, PADDY (FICTITIOUS CHARAC-
TER)**
Mina, D. Field of blood
MEGALITHIC MONUMENTS
See also Antiquities; Archeology; Monu-
ments
Cornwell, B. Stonehenge, 2000 B.C.
MELANCHOLY
See also Emotions; Mood (Psychology)
Snow, C. P. The light and the dark
Melancholy baby. Parker, R. B.
**Melisinda, Queen, consort of Fulk V, King of Jeru-
salem, d. 1160**
About
Tarr, J. Queen of swords
Melmoth the wanderer. Maturin, C. R.
The **melting** season. Attenberg, J.
Melville, Herman, 1819-1891
About
Busch, F. The night inspector
Naslund, S. J. Ahab's wife; or, The star-gazer
Parini, J. The passages of H.M.
The **member** of the wedding. McCullers, C.
MEMBERS OF CONGRESS
Brown, R. M. Dolley
Buckley, W. F. Mongoose, R.I.P
DeLillo, D. Libra
Ellroy, J. American tabloid
Grahame-Smith, S. Abraham Lincoln: vampire
hunter
Korda, M. The immortals
Morrow, J. The last witchfinder
Pesci, D. Amistad
Safire, W. Freedom
Shaara, J. The glorious cause
Shaara, J. Rise to rebellion
Stone, I. Love is eternal
Tanenbaum, R. Corruption of blood
Turner, F. W. The go-between
Updike, J. Memories of the Ford Administration
Vidal, G. Lincoln
MEMBERS OF PARLIAMENT
Docx, E. The calligrapher
Holland, C. Valley of the Kings
Hunt, R. Mr. Chartwell
Kadare, I. The Successor

MEN -- SOCIETIES *See* Clubs; Societies
Men against the sea. Nordhoff, C.
Men and dogs. Crouch, K.
The men and the girls. Trollope, J.
Men at arms. Waugh, E.
MEN IN BUSINESS *See* Businessmen
The men of Brewster Place. Naylor, G.
Men without women. Hemingway, E.
Mending. Bingham, S.
Mending the moon. Palwick, S.
Mendoza in Hollywood. Baker, K.
MENNONITES
  Toews, M. A complicated kindness
MENOPAUSE *See* Aging
MENTAL DEPRESSION
  Hall, B. The music teacher
MENTAL DISEASES *See* Abnormal psychology;
  Mental illness
MENTAL HEALTH
      See also Happiness; Health
  Lennon, J. R. Familiar
MENTAL HYGIENE *See* Mental health
MENTAL ILLNESS
      See also Abnormal psychology; Diseases
  Alexie, S. Indian killer
  Banville, J. The book of evidence
  Barry, B. The lace reader
  Beale, E. Another life altogether
  Beattie, A. Chilly scenes of winter
  Bulgakov, M. A. The master and Margarita
  Cooley, M. The archivist
  Cotter, B. Fever chart
  Didion, J. Play it as it lays
  Doctorow, E. L. The book of Daniel
  Dostoyevsky, F. The idiot
  Duisberg, K. W. The good patient
  Findley, T. The piano man's daughter
  Gibbons, K. Sights unseen
  Gross, A. Eyes wide open
  Guest, J. Ordinary people
  Hirshberg, G. The Snowman's children
  Hunt, L. The exquisite
  Matheson, R. Hunted past reason
  McCabe, P. The butcher boy
  McEwan, I. Enduring love
  McGrath, P. Spider
  Meno, J. The boy detective fails
  Morris, M. M. A dangerous woman
  Murr, N. The perfect man
  Nayman, S. The listener
  Neugeboren, J. 1940
  Noel, K. Halfway house
  O'Farrell, M. The vanishing act of Esme Lennox
  Percy, W. The moviegoer
  Percy, W. The second coming
  Plath, S. The bell jar

  Price, N. Night woman
  Pyper, A. The killing circle
  Rendell, R. Going wrong
  Rhys, J. Wide Sargasso Sea
  Roth, P. When she was good
  Schupack, D. The boy on the bus
  Spark, M. The driver's seat
  Vonnegut, K. Breakfast of champions
  Vonnegut, K. Slaughterhouse-five
  Walker, A. Possessing the secret of joy
MENTAL ILLNESS -- FICTION
  Bauer, C. Frances and Bernard
  Frame, J. Between my father and the king
  Rock, P. The Shelter Cycle
MENTAL PATIENTS *See* Mentally ill
MENTAL SUGGESTION *See* Mind and body;
  Parapsychology; Subconsciousness
MENTAL TELEPATHY *See* Telepathy
MENTALLY DERANGED *See* Mentally ill
MENTALLY HANDICAPPED
  Brown, C. Lamb in love
  Dalton, J. The inverted forest
  Dickens, C. Barnaby Rudge
  Faulkner, W. The sound and the fury
  Gaines, E. J. A lesson before dying
  Hamilton, J. When Madeline was young
  Hunter, S. Dirty white boys
  Keyes, D. Flowers for Algernon
  King, S. Blaze
  Moon, E. The speed of dark
  Murakami, H. Kafka on the shore
  Oe, K. The pinch runner memorandum
  Oe, K. A quiet life
  Raimondo, L. Dante's wood
  Steinbeck, J. Of mice and men
  Welty, E. The Ponder heart
MENTALLY HANDICAPPED CHILDREN
      See also Child psychiatry; Handicapped chil-
      dren; Mentally handicapped
  Heller, J. Something happened
  Steel, D. The house on Hope Street
MENTALLY HANDICAPPED CHILDREN --
  EDUCATION *See* Education; Special education
MENTALLY HANDICAPPED CHILDREN --
  FICTION
  Edwards, K. The memory keeper's daughter
MENTALLY ILL
  Goodman, C. The drowning tree
  Matheson, R. Hunted past reason
  Meno, J. The boy detective fails
MENTALLY ILL -- CARE AND TREATMENT
  Enquist, P. O. The book about Blanche and Marie
  Foulds, A. The quickening maze
  Greenberg, J. I never promised you a rose garden
  Hollingshead, G. Bedlam
  Katzenbach, J. The madman's tale

Boyle, T. C. The tortilla curtain
Cisneros, S. The house on Mango Street
Forbes, C. The good works of Ayela Linde
Frey, J. Bright shiny morning
Gilb, D. The flowers
Jaime-Becerra, M. This time tomorrow
Martinez, N. M. Caramba!
Nichols, J. T. The Milagro beanfield war
Piercy, M. Woman on the edge of time
Skyhorse, B. The Madonnas of Echo Park
Tobar, H. The barbarian nurseries
Toole, F. X. Pound for pound
Wiprud, B. M. Ringer

MEXICAN AMERICANS -- FICTION
Cisneros, S. The house on Mango Street
Gilb, D. The flowers
Jaime-Becerra, M. This time tomorrow
Skyhorse, B. The Madonnas of Echo Park

MEXICAN-AMERICAN BORDER REGION
Olmstead, R. Far bright star

MEXICAN-AMERICAN BORDER REGION -- FICTION
Caputo, P. Crossers
Fields, T. Scratchgravel Road
Forbes, C. The good works of Ayela Linde

MEXICANS -- NEW YORK (N.Y.)
Wiprud, B. M. Ringer

MEXICANS -- UNITED STATES
Urrea, L. A. Into the beautiful North

Mexico. Michener, J. A.

MEXICO
Bolano, R. 2666
Clancy, T. Against all enemies
Cussler, C. Inca gold
Danvers, D. The fourth world
Doerr, H. Consider this, senora
Doerr, H. Stones for Ibarra
Esquivel, L. Like water for chocolate
Fuentes, C. Destiny and desire
Fuentes, C. The eagle's throne
Fuentes, C. The old gringo
Fuentes, C. The years with Laura Diaz
Greene, G. The power and the glory
Hansen, R. Atticus
Howard, L. Cry no more
Johansen, I. And then you die--
Lowry, M. Under the volcano
McCarthy, C. All the pretty horses
Michener, J. A. Mexico
Portis, C. Gringos
Urrea, L. A. Into the beautiful North

MEXICO -- 16TH CENTURY
Falconer, C. Feathered serpent
Jennings, G. Aztec
Jennings, G. Aztec blood
Sherwood, F. Night of sorrows

MEXICO -- 19TH CENTURY
Fuentes, C. The death of Artemio Cruz
Hambly, B. Days of the dead

MEXICO -- BAJA CALIFORNIA
Steinbeck, J. The pearl

MEXICO -- FICTION
Gaspar de Alba, A. Desert blood
Urrea, L. A. The hummingbird's daughter

MEXICO -- HISTORY -- 1910-1920, REVOLUTION
Urrea, L. A. Queen of America

MEXICO -- JUAREZ
McCarthy, C. Cities of the plain

MEXICO -- MEXICO CITY
Bolano, R. Amulet
Christensen, K. Trouble
Gilman, D. The unexpected Mrs. Pollifax
Kingsolver, B. The lacuna

Mexico set. Deighton, L.

MIAMI (FLA.)
Swinson, K. Playing dirty
Wolfe, T. Back to blood

MIAMI INDIANS
Thom, J. A. The red heart

Michael Tolliver lives. Maupin, A.

Michal
About
Edghill, I. Queenmaker

Michelangelo Buonarroti, 1475-1564
About
Stone, I. The agony and the ecstasy

MICHIGAN
Baxter, C. Saul and Patsy
Campbell, B. J. Once upon a river
Cleage, P. I wish I had a red dress
Cleage, P. What looks like crazy on an ordinary day--
Eugenides, J. The virgin suicides
Finder, J. Company man
Harrison, J. The great leader
Harrison, J. Returning to earth
Iagnemma, K. The expeditions
Kasischke, L. The raising
Kasischke, L. Eden Springs
Mallon, T. Dewey defeats Truman
Traver, R. Anatomy of a murder

MICHIGAN -- ANN ARBOR
Baxter, C. The feast of love
Dolan, H. Bad things happen
Dolan, H. Very bad men
Laken, V. Dream house

MICHIGAN -- BATTLE CREEK
Boyle, T. C. Road to Wellville

MICHIGAN -- DETROIT
Arnow, H. L. S. The dollmaker
Bolano, R. 2666

Updike, J. Rabbit is rich
Updike, J. Rabbit redux
Wilson, S. The man in the gray flannel suit
Wouk, H. Marjorie Morningstar

MIDDLE EAST
Clancy, T. Against all enemies
Ignatius, D. Body of lies
Keneally, T. The tyrant's novel
Poyer, D. The gulf
Silva, D. The messenger
Silva, D. Prince of Fire

MIDDLE EAST -- FICTION
Clarke, R. A. The scorpion's gate
MacDonald, G. The prisoner's wife
Wilson, G. W. Alif the unseen
The **middle** heart. Lord, B. B.
Middle men. Gavin, J.
Middle of nowhere. Pearson, R.
Middle passage. Johnson, C. R.

MIDDLE WEST
Attenberg, J. The Middlesteins
Boswell, R. Century's son
Hynes, J. The lecturer's tale
Leithauser, B. A few corrections
Lewis, S. Main Street & Babbitt
Reuss, F. Horace afoot
Smiley, J. Moo

MIDDLE WESTERN STATES
Boswell, R. Century's son
Choi, S. A person of interest
DeLillo, D. White noise
Hoover, M. The quickening
Hynes, J. The lecturer's tale
Leithauser, B. A few corrections
Maxwell, W. Early novels and stories
Moore, L. A gate at the stairs
Mullen, T. The many deaths of the Firefly Brothers
Patterson, R. N. Dark lady
Powers, J. F. Wheat that springeth green
Reuss, F. Horace afoot
Roth, P. When she was good
Simpson, M. Anywhere but here
Smiley, J. Moo
Somerville, P. The cradle

MIDDLE-AGED MEN
Begley, L. About Schmidt
Harrison, K. Envy
Tyler, A. The beginner's goodbye

MIDDLE-AGED PERSONS
Link, T. Denting the Bosch

MIDDLE-AGED WOMEN -- CRIMES AGAINST
Scott, A. D. Beneath the abbey wall

MIDDLE-AGED WOMEN
Seitz, N. Trouble the water

Middlemarch. Eliot, G.

Middlesex. Eugenides, J.

The **Middlesteins.** Attenberg, J.
MIDLIFE CRISIS
See also Middle age
Harrison, K. Envy
Midnight at the Dragon Café. Bates, J. F.
Midnight Bayou. Roberts, N.
Midnight bride. Carroll, S.
Midnight cowboy. Herlihy, J. L.
Midnight magic. Mason, B. A.
Midnight movie. Hooper, T.
Midnight rambler. Swain, J.
Midnight runner. Higgins, J.
Midnight tales. Stoker, B.
Midnight voices. Saul, J.
Midnight's children. Rushdie, S.
MIDSHIPMEN
Webb, J. A sense of honor
Midsummer night. Warrington, F.
The **midwife** of Hope River. Harman, P.
The **midwife's** tale. Laskas, G. M.
MIDWIFERY *See* Midwives
MIDWIVES
See also Childbirth; Natural childbirth; Nurses
Ekman, K. God's mercy
Henley, P. Hummingbird house
Joyce, G. The limits of enchantment
Laskas, G. M. The midwife's tale
Riley, J. M. A vision of light

MIDWIVES -- FICTION
Harman, P. The midwife of Hope River
Watson, C. Tiny sunbirds, far away

MIDWIVES -- NEW YORK (STATE) -- NEW YORK
Thompson, V. Murder on Fifth Avenue
The **mighty** Walzer. Jacobson, H.
MIGRANT LABOR
Guterson, D. Our Lady of the Forest
Oates, J. C. A garden of earthly delights
Steinbeck, J. The grapes of wrath
Steinbeck, J. In dubious battle
Steinbeck, J. Of mice and men
Straight, S. Highwire moon

MIGRATORY WORKERS *See* Migrant labor
The **Mike** Hammer collection [v1] Spillane, M.
The **Mike** Hammer collection [v2] Spillane, M.
Mila 18. Uris, L.
The **Milagro** beanfield war. Nichols, J. T.
MILITARY AERONAUTICS
See also Aeronautics; Military art and science; War
Brown, D. Hammerheads
Brown, D. Storming heaven
Coonts, S. Final flight
Coonts, S. Flight of the Intruder
Heller, J. Catch-22
Malraux, A. Man's hope

Doig, I. Work song

Mineral spirits. Sharfeddin, H.

MINERALS IN HUMAN NUTRITION *See* Food; Minerals; Nutrition

MINERS

Cramer, W. D. Bad ground

Cummins, A. Yellowcake

Doig, I. Work song

MINES AND MINING

Stegner, W. E. Angle of repose

MINIATURE GARDENS *See* Gardens; Miniature objects

MINIATURE OBJECTS *See* Art objects

Miniatures. Labiner, N.

MINING ENGINEERING *See* Civil engineering; Coal mines and mining; Engineering; Mines and mineral resources

MINISTERS (DIPLOMATIC AGENTS) *See* Diplomats

MINISTERS OF THE GOSPEL *See* Clergy

The **ministry** of fear. Greene, G.

The **Ministry** of Special Cases. Englander, N.

MINNEAPOLIS (MINN.)

Hoag, T. Dust to dust

Sandford, J. Silken prey

Sandford, J. Chosen prey

Sandford, J. Easy prey

Sandford, J. Hidden prey

Sandford, J. Mortal prey

Sandford, J. Naked prey

Tracy, P. J. Monkeewrench

MINNESOTA

Enger, L. Undiscovered country

Hart, E. False mermaid

Hassler, J. The dean's list

Hassler, J. Rookery blues

Hassler, J. The Staggerford flood

Hoag, T. Guilty as sin

Hoag, T. Night sins

Hustvedt, S. The sorrows of an American

Johnson, W. The devil you know

Keillor, G. Lake Wobegon days

Keillor, G. Lake Wobegon summer 1956

Keillor, G. WLT

Lewis, S. Main Street

O'Brien, T. In the Lake of the Woods

Powers, J. F. Morte d'Urban

Sidor, S. Pitch dark

Strayed, C. Torch

Watson, L. American boy

MINNESOTA -- 19TH CENTURY

Moberg, V. The last letter home

Moberg, V. Unto a good land

MINNESOTA -- FICTION

Hassler, J. The dean's list

Hassler, J. Rookery blues

Hassler, J. The Staggerford flood

Hoag, T. Guilty as sin

Hunter, S. Soft target

Keillor, G. Leaving home

Keillor, G. Love me

Lewis, S. Main Street & Babbitt

O'Malley, T. This magnificent desolation

MINNESOTA -- MINNEAPOLIS

Hoag, T. Dust to dust

Thayer, S. The weatherman

Tracy, P. J. Monkeewrench

MINNESOTA -- ST. PAUL

Franzen, J. Freedom

Keillor, G. Love me

Reimringer, J. Vestments

MINOR PLANETS *See* Asteroids

MINORITIES IN MOTION PICTURES *See* Motion pictures

MINORITIES IN THE MOTION PICTURE IN-DUSTRY *See* Motion picture industry

MINORITIES ON TELEVISION *See* Minorities; Television

The **minority** report. Dick, P. K.

MINORITY WOMEN *See* Minorities; Women

MINORITY YOUTH *See* Minorities; Youth

The **minotaur.** Vine, B.

MINSTRELS *See* Poets

Mint julep murder. Hart, C. G.

MINTS *See* Money

Miracle at St. Anna. McBride, J.

Miracle cure. Palmer, M.

Miracle on 34th Street. Davies, V.

MIRACLES

Paretsky, S. Ghost country

Werfel, F. The song of Bernadette

MIRACLES -- FICTION

Magnin, J. The prayers of Agnes Sparrow

Miranda's vines. Kafka, K.

Miranda, Francisco de, 1750-1816

About

Naipaul, V. S. A way in the world

Mirror mirror. Maguire, G.

The **mirror's** edge. Sidor, S.

Misadventure. Kaufman, M.

MISCARRIAGE *See* Pregnancy

MISCEGENATION

Brown, R. M. Southern discomfort

Chase-Riboud, B. Sally Hemings

Paton, A. Too late the phalarope

Randall, A. The wind done gone

Tademy, L. Cane River

Mischief. McBain, E.

Mischief in Maggody. Hess, J.

MISCONDUCT IN OFFICE *See* Conflict of interests; Criminal law

MISDEMEANORS (LAW) *See* Criminal law

Lynn, A. Now you see it
Mason, D. A far country
Matar, H. Anatomy of a disappearance
McGregor, E. The ice child
McMahon, J. Don't breathe a word
Michener, J. A. Caravans
Moore, B. Cold heaven
Muller, M. Cyanide Wells
O'Brien, T. In the Lake of the Woods
O'Nan, S. Songs for the missing
Ondaatje, M. In the skin of a lion
Picoult, J. Vanishing acts
Pittard, H. The fates will find their way
Pronzini, B. The other side of silence
Reisman, N. The first desire
Robinson, L. Water dogs
Salak, K. The white Mary
Sanchez, T. King Bongo
Sanders, L. The tenth commandment
Scott, J. Tourmaline
Shiner, L. Dark tangos
Smith, M. C. Rose
Solomon, N. Single wife
Spark, M. Aiding and abetting
Stevens, M. The curve of the world
Straub, P. Lost boy lost girl
Sundaresan, I. The splendor of silence
Tan, A. Saving fish from drowning
Tremain, R. The way I found her
Tyler, A. Searching for Caleb
Vanderhaeghe, G. The last crossing
Walters, M. The echo
White, S. W. Missing persons
Whitney, P. A. Amethyst dreams

MISSING PERSONS -- DRAMA

Edwardson, A. Sail of stone

MISSING PERSONS -- FICTION

Alexander, H. Last resort
Atkinson, K. Started early, took my dog
Black, C. Murder in the Sentier
Block, F. L. The elementals
Box, C. J. The highway
Brkic, C. A. The First Rule of Swimming
Caletti, D. He's gone
Church, J. A drop of Chinese blood
Coben, H. Stay close
Delaney, F. The matchmaker of Kenmare
Doiron, P. Bad Little Falls
Doolittle, S. Lake country
Edugyan, E. Half-blood blues
Ferraris, Z. Kingdom of strangers
Flynn, G. Gone girl
Flynn, M. In the Lion's Mouth
Flynn, M. Up Jim River
Galloway, G. As simple as snow
Gardner, L. The neighbor

Gaspar de Alba, A. Desert blood
Gracie, A. To catch a bride
Griffin, K. Glass God
Gross, G. When she was gone
Hambly, B. Good man Friday
Hill, S. Shadows in the street
Indridason, A. Outrage
Joyce, G. Some kind of fairy tale
Kelly, E. The burning air
MacBride, S. Close to the Bone
McCall Smith, A. The No. 1 Ladies' Detective Agency
McMahon, J. The One I Left Behind
Mofina, R. They disappeared
Mosley, W. Little Scarlet
Oldham, N. Fighting for the dead
Penney, S. The invisible ones
Robotham, M. Say you're sorry
Romano, S. Resurrection Express
Roy, L. Until she comes home
Semple, M. Where'd you go, Bernadette
Shields, K. A Study in Revenge
Shrier, H. Boston cream
Speller, E. The strange fate of Kitty Easton
Stevens, T. The informationist

MISSING PERSONS -- INVESTIGATION -- FICTION

Adler-Olsen, J. The keeper of lost causes
Castillo, L. Gone missing
Dean, A. Bellfield Hall, or, The observations of Miss Dido Kent
Grant, H. The vanishing of Katharina Linden
Missing pieces. Fielding, J.
Missing Susan. McCrumb, S.
The **missing** world. Livesey, M.
The **mission** song. Le Carre, J.
Mission to Paris. Furst, A.

MISSIONARIES

Achebe, C. Things fall apart
Berlinski, M. Fieldwork
Bosse, M. J. The warlord
Cather, W. Death comes for the archbishop
Cronin, A. J. The keys of the kingdom
Endo, S. Silence
Forester, C. S. The African Queen
Grisham, J. The testament
Jin, H. Nanjing requiem
Kingsolver, B. The poisonwood Bible
Lee The surrendered
Marks, J. Fangland
Marshall, C. Christy
Michener, J. A. Hawaii
Phillips, C. Crossing the river
Stahlberg, L. Omoo: a narrative of adventures in the South Seas
Vollmann, W. T. Fathers and crows

TITLE AND SUBJECT INDEX

MISSISSIPPI

Atkins, A. The ranger
Barthelme, F. Waveland
Berg, E. We are all welcome here
Brown, L. Joe
Campbell, B. M. Your blues ain't like mine
Cook, T. H. Master of the delta
Faulkner, W.   Light in August
Faulkner, W. Flags in the dust
Faulkner, W. Go down, Moses
Faulkner, W. The hamlet
Faulkner, W. Intruder in the dust
Faulkner, W. The mansion
Faulkner, W. Requiem for a nun
Faulkner, W. Sanctuary
Faulkner, W. Sartoris
Faulkner, W. The sound and the fury
Faulkner, W. The town
Franklin, T. Crooked letter, crooked letter
French, A. Billy
Grisham, J. The appeal
Grisham, J. The chamber
Grisham, J. Ford County
Grisham, J. The last juror
Grisham, J. The runaway jury
Grisham, J. A time to kill
Hunter, S. Pale horse coming
Iles, G. The devil's punchbowl
Iles, G. Third degree
Logan, C. South of Shiloh
Marlette, D. Magic time
Morris, W. Taps
Nordan, L. Wolf whistle
Phillips, S. E. Ain't she sweet
Spencer, E. The stories of Elizabeth Spencer
Tartt, D. The little friend
Vernon, O. Eden
Vernon, O. A killing in this town
Ward, J. Salvage the bones
Watson, B. The heaven of Mercury
Welty, E. Delta wedding
Welty, E. Losing battles
Welty, E. The optimist's daughter
Welty, E. The Ponder heart
Yarbrough, S. The end of California
Yarbrough, S. Prisoners of war
Yarbrough, S. Safe from the neighbors

MISSISSIPPI -- 19TH CENTURY

Faulkner, W. Absalom, Absalom!
Faulkner, W. The unvanquished

MISSISSIPPI -- FICTION

Atkins, A. The broken places
Cheng, B. Southern Cross the Dog
Wilson, C. Cotton

MISSISSIPPI -- JACKSON

Stockett, K. The help

MISSISSIPPI -- NATCHEZ

Iles, G. Turning angel

MISSISSIPPI -- RACE RELATIONS

Jordan, H. Mudbound
McFadden, B. L. Gathering of waters
Stockett, K. The help

MISSISSIPPI RIVER

Clinch, J. Finn
DeNiro, A. Total oblivion, more or less
Gautreaux, T. The missing
Smith, L. The last girls
Twain, M. The adventures of Huckleberry Finn
Twain, M. The adventures of Tom Sawyer
Twain, M. Mississippi writings
Welty, E. The robber bridegroom

Mississippi writings. Twain, M.

MISSOURI

Clinch, J. Finn
Dalton, J. The inverted forest
Flagg, F. Standing in the rainbow
Flynn, G. Sharp objects
Kinder, R. M. An absolute gentleman
Murr, N. The perfect man
Spencer, L. Small town girl
Twain, M. The adventures of Tom Sawyer
Twain, M. Pudd'nhead Wilson;
Woodrell, D. The death of sweet mister
Woodrell, D. Give us a kiss

MISSOURI -- 19TH CENTURY

Jiles, P. Enemy women

MISSOURI -- FICTION

Jiles, P. Enemy women
Twain, M. The adventures of Huckleberry Finn
Twain, M. The adventures of Tom Sawyer

MISSOURI -- KANSAS CITY

Connell, E. S. Mr. Bridge
Connell, E. S. Mrs. Bridge
Terrell, W. The huntsman

MISSOURI -- SAINT LOUIS

Shange, N. Betsey Brown

MISSOURI RIVER

McMurtry, L. Sin killer

Missy. Hannan, C.
A mist of prophecies. Saylor, S.
Mistaken identity. Scottoline, L.

MISTAKEN IDENTITY

Carkeet, D. From away
Collins, W. The woman in white
Henry, A. Learning to fly
Stewart, M. The ivy tree
Wiprud, B. M. Ringer

MISTAKEN IDENTITY -- FICTION

Putney, M. J. Loving a lost lord
Mistborn: the final empire. Sanderson, B.
Mister Pip. Jones, L.
Mister Roberts. Heggen, T.

Misterioso. Dahl, A.

Mistral's daughter. Krantz, J.

Mistress of Mellyn. Holt, V.

Mistress of the art of death. Franklin, A.

Mistress of the pearl. Lustbader, E. V.

MISTRESSES

Cameron, P. The city of your final destination

Chase-Riboud, B. Sally Hemings

Christensen, K. The great man

Faber, M. The crimson petal and the white

Gould, J. The best is yet to come

Gregory, P. The other Boleyn girl

Hambly, B. Patriot hearts

King, R. Domino

Martin, V. Property

Sharp, A. The true memoirs of Little K

Trollope, J. Marrying the mistress

Turner, F. W. The go-between

MISTRESSES -- GREAT BRITAIN

Smith, A. E. Royal mistress

The **mists** of Avalon. Bradley, M. Z.

Mitchell, Margaret, 1900-1949

About

Randall, A. The wind done gone

Mitigating circumstances. Rosenberg, N. T.

MIXED BLOODS

Alexie, S. Flight

Eng, T. T. The gift of rain

Erdrich, L. The Beet Queen

Houston, J. D. Bird of another heaven

Humphreys, J. Nowhere else on earth

Jennings, G. Aztec blood

Murr, N. The perfect man

Powers, R. The time of our singing

MIXED MARRIAGE *See* Interfaith marriage; Intermarriage

Mo said she was quirky. Kelman, J.

MOBILE (ALA.)

Kerley, J. The death collectors

MOBSTERS

Collins, M. A. Black hats

Higgins, J. Luciano's luck

Latour, J. The Havana World Series

Turner, F. W. The go-between

Moby-Dick; or, The whale. Stahlberg, L.

MOCK-HEROIC LITERATURE *See* Literature; Wit and humor

The **mocking** program. Foster, A. D.

Mode [series]

Anthony, P. Virtual mode

Model home. Puchner, E.

MODELS *See* Artists' models; Fashion models; Mathematical models; Models and modelmaking

MODELS (PERSONS)

See also Artists' models; Fashion models

Bagshawe, T. Adored

Gaitskill, M. Veronica

MODELS, ARTISTS' *See* Artists' models

A **modern** comedy. Galsworthy, J.

MODERN GREEK LANGUAGE *See* Language and languages

MODERN HISTORY -- 1900-1999 (20TH CENTURY) *See* World history -- 20th century

MODERN LANGUAGES *See* Language and languages

Modern Library classics [series]

Cooper, J. F. The last of the Mohicans

Dostoyevsky, F. The gambler

Larsen, N. Passing

Twain, M. Pudd'nhead Wilson;

MODERNISM IN ART *See* Art; Modernism (Aesthetics)

MOGUL EMPIRE

Rushdie, S. The enchantress of Florence

MOHAWK VALLEY (N.Y.)

Edmonds, W. D. Drums along the Mohawk

MOHEGAN INDIANS

Cooper, J. F. The last of the Mohicans

Mohr. Reuss, F.

Mohr, Max, 1891-1937

About

Reuss, F. Mohr

MOJAVE DESERT (CALIF.)

Kunzru, H. Gods without men

MOLDAVIA

Dekker, T. Immanuel's veins

MOLECULAR CLONING *See* Cloning; Genetic engineering

MOLECULAR TECHNOLOGY *See* Nanotechnology

MOLES (SPIES)

Fesperman, D. The double game

MOLESTING OF CHILDREN *See* Child sexual abuse

Moll Flanders. Defoe, D.

Molloy, Malone dies, The unnamable. Beckett, S.

The **moment.** Kennedy, D.

Moment in Peking. Lin Yutang

A **moment** in the sun. Sayles, J.

A **moment** in time. Gould, J.

Moment of truth. Scottoline, L.

A **moment** on the edge.

The **moment** she was gone. Hunter, E.

Mona in the promised land. Jen, G.

MONACO

Mayle, P. Anything considered

MONACO -- MONTE CARLO

Kelby, N. M. White truffles in winter

MONARCHS *See* Kings and rulers

MONASTERIES

Penny, L. The beautiful mystery

MONASTIC ORDERS *See* Monasticism and religious orders

MONASTICISM *See* Monasticism and religious orders

MONASTICISM AND RELIGIOUS ORDERS
Gulik, R. H. v. The haunted monastery
Miller, W. M. A canticle for Leibowitz

MONASTICISM AND RELIGIOUS ORDERS FOR MEN *See* Monasticism and religious orders

MONASTICISM AND RELIGIOUS ORDERS FOR WOMEN *See* Convents; Monasticism and religious orders

Monday mourning. Reichs, K. J.

Monday the rabbi took off. Kemelman, H.

Mondo and other stories. Le Clezio, G.

Monet, Claude, 1840-1926
                              About
Jakeman, J. In the Kingdom of mists

MONETARY UNIONS *See* Money

MONEY
          See also Economics; Exchange; Finance
Grippando, J. Found money
Grisham, J. The summons
Thomas, M. M. Black money

Money for nothing. Westlake, D. E.

MONEY LAUNDERING
Gavin, R. Beluga

MONEY RAISING *See* Fund raising

Money shot. Faust, C.

MONEY SUPPLY *See* Money

Money to burn. Grippando, J.

Money wanders. Dezenhall, E.

MONEYLENDERS
Dickens, C. Nicholas Nickleby
Perez Galdos, B. Torquemada

MONGOLIA
Jiang Rong Wolf totem

Mongoose, R.I.P. Buckley, W. F.

Monika Paniatowski mysteries [series]
Spencer, S. Backlash
Spencer, S. Echoes of the dead

The **monk.** Lewis, M. G.

Monk's-hood. Peters, E.

MONK, WILLIAM (FICTITIOUS CHARACTER)
Perry, A. A sunless sea
Perry, A. Funeral in blue
Perry, A. Slaves of obsession

Monkeewrench. Tracy, P. J.

Monkey hunting. Garcia, C.

The **monkey's** wedding, and other stories. Aiken, J.

The **monkey's** wrench. Levi, P.

Monkeys. Minot, S.

MONKS
Eco, U. The name of the rose
Eliot, G. Romola

Hesse, H. Narcissus and Goldmund
Kadare, I. The three-arched bridge
Kidd, S. M. The mermaid chair
Lewis, M. G. The monk
McCann, C. Let the great world spin
Pattison, E. The skull mantra
Preston, D. The wheel of darkness
Rathbone, J. The last English king
Toyne, S. Sanctus
Unsworth, B. Morality play

MONKS -- FICTION
Eco, U. The name of the rose
Kadare, I. The three-arched bridge
Penny, L. The beautiful mystery
The Poisoned Pilgrim

MONMOUTH'S REBELLION, 1685
Blackmore, R. D. Lorna Doone

MONMOUTHSHIRE (WALES)
Putney, M. J. Stolen magic

MONOLOGUES
Bernhard, T. Frost
Hamid, M. The reluctant fundamentalist

MONORAIL RAILROADS *See* Railroads

MONOTHEISM *See* Religion; Theism

Monroe, Marilyn, 1926-1962
                              About
Collins, M. A. Bye bye, baby
Korda, M. The immortals
Oates, J. C. Blonde

Monsieur Pain. Bolano, R.

Monsieur Pamplemousse. Bond, M.

Monsignor Quixote. Greene, G.

Monsoon. Smith, W. A.

Monster. Kellerman, J.

Monster Island. Wellington, D.

A **monster's** notes. Sheck, L.

MONSTERS
          See also Animals -- Folklore; Curiosities and wonders; Folklore; Mythology
Groff, L. The monsters of Templeton
Knipfel, J. The blow-off

MONSTERS -- FICTION
Frei, M. The stranger's magic
Kosmatka, T. The games
Lafferty, M. The shambling guide to New York City
Nicholas, D. Something red
Priest, C. The inexplicables

The **monsters** of St. Helena. Hansen, B.

The **monsters** of Templeton. Groff, L.

Monstrous regiment. Pratchett, T.

MONTANA
Blew, M. C. Jackalope dreams
Canty, K. Everything
Davis, C. Winter range
Doig, I. Bucking the sun

Doig, I. Dancing at the Rascal Fair
Doig, I. The eleventh man
Doig, I. English Creek
Doig, I. Mountain time
Doig, I. Prairie nocturne
Doig, I. Ride with me, Mariah Montana
Doig, I. The whistling season
Doig, I. Work song
Evans, N. The brave
Evans, N. The horse whisperer
Fromm, P. As cool as I am
Kennedy, D. The big picture
Kittredge, W. The Willow Field
Laskowski, T. Every good boy does fine
McGuane, T. The cadence of grass
McGuane, T. Driving on the rim
McGuane, T. Keep the change
McGuane, T. Nobody's angel
McGuane, T. Nothing but blue skies
McNamer, D. Red rover
Ray, S. American masculine
Sharfeddin, H. Mineral spirits
Smith, D. Pictures from an expedition
Stevens, M. Useful girl
Welch, J. The Indian lawyer

MONTANA -- 19TH CENTURY
Williamson, P. Heart of the west
Williamson, P. The outsider

MONTANA -- FICTION
Canty, K. Everything
Crumley, J. The final country
Davis, C. Winter range
Doig, I. The bartender's tale
Doig, I. The eleventh man
Doig, I. Ride with me, Mariah Montana
Doig, I. The whistling season
Evans, N. The horse whisperer
Harrison, J. An unfortunate prairie occurrence
Johnston, T. C. Lay the mountains low
McGuane, T. The cadence of grass
McGuane, T. Keep the change
McGuane, T. Nothing but blue skies
McNamer, D. Red rover
Smith, D. Pictures from an expedition
Welch, J. The Indian lawyer
Williamson, P. Heart of the west
Montana dawn. Wallace, S.
Montano's malady. Vila-Matas, E.
Monte Walsh. Schaefer, J. W.
Montezuma II, Emperor of Mexico, ca. 1480-1520
About
Levack, S. Demon of the air
Montfort, Simon de, Earl of Leicester, 1208?-1265
About
Penman, S. K. Falls the shadow
Moo. Smiley, J.

MOON
Heinlein, R. A. The moon is a harsh mistress
Verne, J. From the earth to the moon, and Round the moon
MOON -- EXPLORATION *See* Space flight to the moon
The **moon** and sixpence. Maugham, W. S.
Moon flights. Moon, E.
The **moon** in its flight. Sorrentino, G.
The **moon** is a harsh mistress. Heinlein, R. A.
The **moon** is down. Steinbeck, J.
Moon music. Kellerman, F.
Moon tiger. Lively, P.
The **moon** tunnel. Kelly, J.
MOON WORSHIP *See* Religion
MOON, CHARLIE (FICTITIOUS CHARACTER : DOSS)
Doss, J. D. The old gray wolf
MOON, VOYAGES TO *See* Space flight to the moon
The **moon-spinners.** Stewart, M.
Moondogs. Yates, A.
Moonlight mile. Lehane, D.
The **moons** of Jupiter. Munro, A.
Moonshine. Johnson, A. D.
MOONSHINERS
Faulkner, W. Sanctuary
The **moonstone.** Collins, W.
Moonstruck. Grant, S.
The **moor.** King, L. R.
The **Moor's** last sigh. Rushdie, S.
MOORS *See* Muslims
MORAL AND PHILOSOPHIC STORIES *See* Didactic fiction; Fables; Parables
MORAL EDUCATION *See* Education; Ethics
MORAL PHILOSOPHY *See* Ethics
MORALE
See also Courage
MORALITY
See also Ethics
Morrow, J. The philosopher's apprentice
Morality play. Unsworth, B.
Morality tale. Brownrigg, S.
MORALITY TALES *See* Parables
MORALS *See* Conduct of life; Ethics; Human behavior; Moral conditions
MORDRED (LEGENDARY CHARACTER)
Stewart, M. The wicked day
The **more** I owe you. Sledge, M.
More of this world or maybe another. Johnson, B.
More than a mistress. Balogh, M.
More than it hurts you. Strauss, D.
More than you know. Gutcheon, B. R.
The **Morels.** Hacker, C.
Morenga. Timm, U.
Morenga, Jakob, d. 1907

The **Mothers.** Gilmore, J.

MOTHERS

See also Family; Women

Arnow, H. L. S. The dollmaker
Belle, J. The seven year bitch
Colwin, L. A big storm knocked it over
Colwin, L. Goodbye without leaving
Cusk, R. Arlington Park
Doyle, R. Paula Spencer
Edgarian, C. Three stages of amazement
Genova, L. Left neglected
Giffin, E. Heart of the matter
Goudge, E. Thorns of truth
Grunwald, L. The irresistible Henry House
Hannah, S. The cradle in the grave
Hannah, S. The wrong mother
Hood, A. The red thread
Kavenna, J. The birth of love
Kennedy, D. Leaving the world
Kincaid, N. Verbena
Lively, P. Family album
McGill, B. The butterfly cabinet
Miller, R. The private lives of Pippa Lee
Moses, K. Wintering
Oates, J. C. Them
O'Farrell, M. The hand that first held mine
Pausch, J. Dream new dreams
Pilcher, R. The shell seekers
Quindlen, A. Every last one
Sheldon, S. Master of the game
Smith, L. Family linen
Steel, D. The house on Hope Street
Trollope, J. Second honeymoon
Trueblood, V. Seven loves
Weiner, J. Little earthquakes
Weiner, J. Then came you
Wolitzer, M. The ten-year nap

MOTHERS -- FICTION

Doughty, L. Whatever you love
Lee, M. Somebody's daughter

MOTHERS AND DAUGHTERS

Allen, S. A. The sugar queen
Battle, L. Southern women
Berg, E. Home safe
Berg, E. We are all welcome here
Berg, E. What we keep
Binchy, M. The glass lake
Bird, S. The gap year
Blatty, W. P. The exorcist
Brown, R. Half a heart
Bynum, L. Veracity
Casey, J. Compass rose
Chenoweth, E. Hello goodbye
Cleage, P. Babylon sisters
Cline, R. What to keep
Coetzee, J. M. Age of iron

Davenport, K. House of many gods
Didion, J. A book of common prayer
Dische, I. The Empress of Weehawken
Doerr, H. Consider this, senora
Dorris, M. A yellow raft in blue water
Dubus, A. The garden of last days
Erdrich, L. The painted drum
Evans, N. The horse whisperer
Ferrante, E. The lost daughter
Ferrante, E. Troubling love
Fitch, J. White oleander
French, M. Her mother's daughter
Gaffney, P. Circle of three
Garcia, C. Dreaming in Cuban
Gardam, J. God on the rocks
Gibbons, K. Charms for the easy life
Gibbons, K. Sights unseen
Godwin, G. A mother and two daughters
Goodman, C. Arcadia Falls
Goodman, C. The seduction of water
Goudge, E. Garden of lies
Goudge, E. Stranger in paradise
Goudge, E. Such devoted sisters
Goudge, E. Trail of secrets
Gowdy, B. Helpless
Greene, A. Bloodroot
Gregory, D. Raising Stony Mayhall
Griesemer, J. Signal & noise
Gutcheon, B. R. Five fortunes
Gutcheon, B. R. Saying grace
Hadley, T. The master bedroom
Hagedorn, J. T. Toxicology
Hannah, K. Winter garden
Hannah, S. Little face
Harrington, L. Alice Bliss
Harris, J. Chocolat
Harris, J. Five quarters of the orange
Harris, J. The girl with no shadow
Henderson, W. H. Augusta Locke
Henley, P. In the river sweet
Hilderbrand, E. The island
Hodgen, C. Elegies for the brokenhearted
Hoffman, A. Here on Earth
Hoffman, A. The probable future
Hoffman, A. The story sisters
Hoffman, E. The secret
Hood, A. The knitting circle
Jackson, J. Between, Georgia
Jakes, J. Savannah; or, A gift for Mr. Lincoln
James, P. D. Innocent blood
Johnson, S. The sailmaker's daughter
Jones, L. Mister Pip
Jones, T. Silver sparrow
Joyce, G. The limits of enchantment
Kadare, I. The ghost rider
Karbo, K. Motherhood made a man out of me

MOTHERS AND DAUGHTERS -- FICTION

Harris, J. Five quarters of the orange
Harris, J. The girl with no shadow
Harris, J. Peaches for Father Francis
Hassman, T. Girlchild
Hoffman, A. The story sisters
Hosseini, K. A thousand splendid suns
Jackson, J. Between, Georgia
Jackson, J. A grown up kind of pretty
Kidd, S. M. The mermaid chair
Kingsolver, B. Pigs in heaven
Kwok, J. Girl in translation
Lamott, A. Blue shoe
Lange, R. Angel baby
Larsen, J. Silk road
Laskas, G. M. The midwife's tale
Lessing, D. M. The sweetest dream
Lupton, R. Afterwards
Manicka, R. The rice mother
Mattison, A. In case we're separated
Mazzarella, N. This heavy silence
Moore, M. M. So far away
Morrison, T. A mercy
Morton, K. The distant hours
Oates, J. C. Missing mom
Oates, J. C. Rape
Parsons, J. Mary, Mary
Powell, S. The Mushroom Man
Rice, L. Home fires
Rice, L. Summer light
Ruby, I. The salt god's daughter
Schine, C. The three Weissmanns of Westport
Schwarz, C. Drowning Ruth
Sebold, A. The almost moon
Semple, M. Where'd you go, Bernadette
Serber, N. Shout her lovely name
Shapiro, D. Black & white
Shields, C. Unless
Shreve, S. R. Daughters of the new world
Simpson, M. Off Keck Road
Somerville, P. The cradle
Straight, S. Highwire moon
Tademy, L. Cane River
Tan, A. The bonesetter's daughter
Tan, A. The Joy Luck Club
Tan, A. The kitchen god's wife
Toibin, C. The blackwater lightship
Truong, M. Bitter in the mouth
Vine, B. Anna's book
Walton, J. Among others
Wolitzer, M. Surrender, Dorothy
Mothers and sons. Toibin, C.
MOTHERS AND SONS *See* Mother-son relationship
MOTHERS AND SONS
  Bauer, B. Blacklands
  Beattie, A. Chilly scenes of winter

Calvo, J. Wonderful world
Carey, P. His illegal self
Clarke, B. Exley
Coetzee, J. M. Life & times of Michael K.
Coupland, D. Eleanor Rigby
De Kretser, M. The lost dog
Delaney, E. J. Broken Irish
Donoghue, E. Room
Emmons, C. His mother's son
Erdrich, L. Four souls
Ferber, E. So Big
Fielding, J. Charley's web
Findley, T. The piano man's daughter
Fitch, J. Paint it black
Flagg, F. Standing in the rainbow
Gatewood, R. The sound of the trees
Glass, J. The whole world over
Graver, E. Awake
Green, G. D. The juror
Greer, A. S. The story of a marriage
Gruber, M. The good son
Hallgrimur Helgason 101 Reykjavik
Halperin, D. J. Journal of a UFO investigator
Hamilton, J. Disobedience
Harrison, J. The road home
Harwood, J. The ghost writer
Hassler, J. The dean's list
Hoffman, A. Seventh heaven
Hoffman, A. Turtle Moon
Howrey, M. Blind sight
Humphreys, H. Coventry
Irving, J. The world according to Garp
Isaacs, S. As husbands go
James, H. The spoils of Poynton
Jonsson, R. My life as a dog
Kafka, K. Miranda's vines
Kneale, M. When we were Romans
Lawrence, D. H. Sons and lovers
Leimbach, M. Daniel isn't talking
Letts, B. Shoot the moon
Levy, A. The long song
Lively, P. Passing on
Maguire, G. Son of a witch
Martin, S. The pleasure of my company
Martin, V. Trespass
Maupin, A. Michael Tolliver lives
Maynard, J. Labor Day
McFarland, D. Singing boy
McGrath, P. Spider
McGregor, E. The ice child
Mestre-Reed, E. The second death of Unica Aveyano
Miller, A. Oxygen
Miller, S. The distinguished guest
Millet, L. How the dead dream
Mitcham, J. Sabbath Creek

Mitchard, J. Twelve times blessed
Miyamoto, T. Kinshu: Autumn brocade
Neugeboren, J. 1940
Oates, J. C. Broke heart blues
Oates, J. C. A garden of earthly delights
O'Brien, E. Time and tide
Oe, K. An echo of heaven
Ogawa, Y. The housekeeper and the professor
Parkhurst, C. The nobodies album
Patterson, J. Suzanne's diary for Nicholas
Penney, S. The tenderness of wolves
Petterson, P. I curse the river of time
Picoult, J. House rules
Price, R. Kate Vaiden
Price, R. Freedomland
Priest, C. Boneshaker
Quindlen, A. Black and blue
Restrepo, L. No place for heroes
Rice, L. Last kiss
Rolvaag, O. E. Peder Victorious
Rosenberg, N. T. First offense
Roth, H. Call it sleep
Roth, P. Portnoy's complaint
Saul, J. The presence
Schupack, D. The boy on the bus
Shriver, L. We need to talk about Kevin
Spiotta, D. Eat the document
Steel, D. Johnny Angel
Straight, S. I been in sorrow's kitchen and licked
  out all the pots
Suri, M. The age of Shiva
To the end of the land
Toibin, C. Mothers and sons
Toole, J. K. A confederacy of dunces
Tremain, R. The way I found her
Williamson, P. The outsider
Winterson, J. Sexing the cherry

MOTHERS AND SONS -- FICTION
Carey, P. His illegal self
Essex, K. Pharaoh
Gatewood, R. The sound of the trees
Grunwald, L. The irresistible Henry House
Hamilton, J. Disobedience
Harwood, J. The ghost writer
Jeffries, S. 'Twas the night after Christmas
Leimbach, M. Daniel isn't talking
Martin, V. Trespass
Miller, S. The distinguished guest
Millet, L. How the dead dream
O'Malley, T. This magnificent desolation
Palwick, S. Mending the moon
Parkhurst, C. The nobodies album
Patterson, J. Suzanne's diary for Nicholas
Petterson, P. I curse the river of time
Quindlen, A. Every last one
Samuel, B. No place like home

Schupack, D. The boy on the bus
Spiotta, D. Eat the document
Steel, D. The house on Hope Street
Steel, D. Johnny Angel
Suri, M. The age of Shiva
To the end of the land
MOTHERS-IN-LAW
Dunne, D. The two Mrs. Grenvilles
Jen, G. The love wife
Naipaul, V. S. A house for Mr. Biswas
Trevor, W. Death in summer
MOTHS
  See also Insects
Adams, P. The sister
MOTION PICTURE ACTORS AND ACTRESS-ES
Abbott, M. E. The song is you
Atkins, A. Devil's garden
Barker, C. Coldheart Canyon
Evans, N. The brave
Francis, D. Smokescreen
Friedman, M. Martian Dawn
Harvey, J. Gone to ground
Hoban, R. Linger awhile
Jakes, J. American dreams
Koontz, D. R. The face
Lewis, J. The king is dead
Sherrill, M. My last movie star
Swierczynski, D. Fun and games
Woods, S. Dead eyes
MOTION PICTURE ACTORS AND ACTRESS-ES -- FICTION
Bornikova, P. Box office poison
Buruma, I. The China lover
Gold, G. D. Sunnyside
Oates, J. C. Blonde
Sherrill, M. My last movie star
Smiley, J. Ten days in the hills
MOTION PICTURE CRITICS
Knode, H. The ticket out
MOTION PICTURE DIRECTORS
  See also Motion picture producers and direc-tors
Atkins, A. Devil's garden
Everett, P. L. I am Not Sidney Poitier
Gold, G. D. Sunnyside
Kaplow, R. Me and Orson Welles
Lazar, Z. Sway
MOTION PICTURE EDITORS
Weldon, F. Rhode Island blues
MOTION PICTURE INDUSTRY
Fuchs, J. Conrad in Beverly Hills
Lott, B. Ancient highway
MOTION PICTURE INDUSTRY -- FICTION
Bagshawe, T. Adored
Kitt, S. Celluloid memories

Moody, R. The diviners
Williams, W. J. The fourth wall

MOTION PICTURE PRODUCERS

See also Motion picture producers and directors

Gold, G. D. Sunnyside
Kaplow, R. Me and Orson Welles

MOTION PICTURE PRODUCERS AND DIRECTORS

See also Motion picture industry

Burdett, J. The godfather of Kathmandu
Burke, A. Long gone
Bushnell, C. Lipstick jungle
Collins, M. A. Quarry's ex
DeLillo, D. Point Omega
Delson, R. Maynard and Jennica
Dixon, K. The art of losing
Fleming, I. The edge of ruin
Hagedorn, J. T. Toxicology
Hooper, T. Midnight movie
Just, W. S. The weather in Berlin
Leonard, E. Be cool
Leonard, E. Djibouti
Mooney, T. The same river twice
Oe, K. The changeling
Robinson, E. The true and outstanding adventures of the Hunt sisters
Shaw, I. Evening in Byzantium
Smiley, J. Ten days in the hills
Spark, M. Reality and dreams
Stone, K. Happy endings
Welsh, I. Porno
Woods, S. L.A. Times
Woods, S. Santa Fe rules

MOTION PICTURE PRODUCERS AND DIRECTORS -- FICTION

Moody, R. The diviners
Wilson, S. The fortune teller's daughter

MOTION PICTURE SERIALS *See* Motion pictures

MOTION PICTURE THEATERS

Reynolds, M. The Starlite Drive-in

MOTION PICTURES

Buruma, I. The China lover
Davies, R. Murther & walking spirits
De los Santos, M. Love walked in
Epstein, L. San Remo Drive
Erickson, S. Zeroville
Fitzgerald, F. S. The last tycoon
Gibson, W. Pattern recognition
Gold, G. D. Sunnyside
Harington, D. The pitcher shower
Hay, E. Garbo laughs
Hellenga, R. The Italian lover
Kalfus, K. The commissariat of enlightenment
Kesey, K. Sailor song

King, L. R. Pirate king
Knode, H. The ticket out
Lankford, T. Earthquake weather
Leonard, E. Get Shorty
McPhee, J. A man of no moon
Oates, J. C. Blonde
Percy, W. The moviegoer
Raymond, J. The half-life
Schulberg, B. What makes Sammy run?
Shaw, I. Evening in Byzantium
Sheehan, A. The anxiety of everyday objects
Updike, J. In the beauty of the lilies
Vidal, G. Hollywood
Vidal, G. Myra Breckinridge [and] Myron

MOTION PICTURES -- ETHICAL ASPECTS

See also Ethics

MOTION PICTURES -- FICTION

Bornikova, P. Box office poison
Erickson, S. Zeroville
Raymond, J. The half-life
Spark, M. Reality and dreams
Updike, J. In the beauty of the lilies

MOTION PICTURES -- PRODUCTION AND DIRECTION

See also Motion picture industry

Wouk, H. The lawgiver

MOTION PICTURES AND CHILDREN *See* Children; Motion pictures

MOTION PICTURES IN EDUCATION *See* Audiovisual education; Motion pictures; Teaching -- Aids and devices

Motion to suppress. O'Shaughnessy, P.

MOTOR BUSES *See* Buses

MOTOR CARS *See* Automobiles

MOTOR VEHICLE INDUSTRY *See* Automobile industry

MOTORCYCLES

Kushner, R. The flamethrowers

MOUNDS AND MOUND BUILDERS *See* Archeology; Burial; Tombs

MOUNT EVEREST (CHINA AND NEPAL) *See* Mountains

MOUNT RAINIER (WASH.) *See* Mountains

MOUNTAIN ANIMALS *See* Animals

MOUNTAIN CLIMBING *See* Mountaineering

MOUNTAIN ECOLOGY *See* Ecology

MOUNTAIN LIFE

See also Country life

Harington, D. With
House, S. A parchment of leaves
Pancake, A. Strange as this weather has been
Woodrell, D. Give us a kiss
Woodrell, D. Winter's bone

MOUNTAIN LIFE -- SOUTHERN STATES

Arnow, H. L. S. The dollmaker
Caldwell, E. God's little acre

MUNICIPALITIES *See* Cities and towns; Municipal government

MURDER

Adiga, A. The white tiger

Clark, M. The legal limit

Coleman, A. Murder mamas

Connelly, M. The closers

Cook, T. H. Instruments of night

Crace, J. Being dead

Darnton, J. Black and white and dead all over

Dunne, D. Too much money

Hamill, P. Tabloid city

Hayder, M. The treatment

Hill, J. Horns

Isaacs, S. As husbands go

Kellerman, J. Gone

Kerouac, J. And the hippos were boiled in their tanks

Kertesz, I. Detective story

LeCraw, H. The swimming pool

McOmber, A. The white forest

Meyer, P. American rust

Qiu Xiaolong Red mandarin dress

Russell, S. This insane train

Sallis, J. The killer is dying

Smith, T. R. Agent 6

MURDER -- INVESTIGATION -- ENGLAND

Grecian, A. The black country

MURDER -- INVESTIGATION

Adler-Olsen, J. The absent one

Albert, S. W. The Darling Dahlias and the cucumber tree

Atkins, A. The broken places

Bates, E. Her Amish man

Bauer, B. Blacklands

Black, C. Murder below Montparnasse

Black, L. Evidence of murder

Black, L. Trail of blood

Blake, R. A dark anatomy

Bradley, A. Speaking from among the bones

Brooks, B. Frontier justice

Cain, C. Let me go

Carey, J. Dark currents

Carter, S. L. Palace council

Castillo, L. Her last breath

Child, L. A wanted man

Cleverly, B. Strange images of death

Colfer, E. Screwed

Connelly, M. The brass verdict

Cotterill, C. Killed at the whim of a hat

Crompton, R. Hour of the Red God

Dean, A. A gentleman of fortune, or, The suspicions of Miss Dido Kent

Dean, A. A woman of consequence

Doiron, P. Bad Little Falls

Eastland, S. Shadow pass

Elias, G. Danse macabre

Fitzgerald, C. The namesake

French, N. Tuesday's gone

French, T. Broken Harbor

French, T. In the woods

Gallagher, S. The bedlam detective

George, K. Simple

Greaves, C. J. Hard twisted

Greaves, C. Hush money

Grossman, P. Children of wrath

Hall, T. The case of the deadly butter chicken

Haynes, E. Dark tide

Hiaasen, C. Bad monkey

Hill, A. The summer of dead toys

Hunt, A. City of saints

Jenkins, V. An unattended death

Kazinski, A. J. The last good man

Lackberg, C. The ice princess

Landay, W. Defending Jacob

Laplante, A. Turn of mind

Lasser, S. Say nice things about Detroit

Longworth, M. L. Murder in the Rue Dumas

Lovesey, P. The tooth tattoo

Lupton, R. Sister

Malliet, G. M. A fatal winter

Mark, D. Original skin

May, P. The Blackhouse

Miller, J. The year of the gadfly

Miller, M. G. Stalking season

Morgan-Jones, C. The jackal's share

Mosley, W. When the thrill is gone

Munson, S. The November criminals

Newton, M. C. Nights of Villjamur

Oates, J. C. Little bird of heaven

O'Connell, C. The chalk girl

Ohlsson, K. Unwanted

Pajer, B. Fatal induction

Parks, B. The girl next door

Penny, L. The beautiful mystery

Penny, L. Bury your dead

Perry, A. A sunless sea

Pötzsch, O. The beggar king

Raimondo, L. Dante's wood

Roberts, N. The witness

Robertson, I. Circle of shadows

Robotham, M. Say you're sorry

Rodriguez, L. Every broken trust

Rodriguez, L. Every last secret

Roorbach, B. Life among giants

Salvation for a saint

Scott, A. D. Beneath the abbey wall

Simmons, D. Flashback

Stabenow, D. Restless in the grave

Stabenow, D. Though not dead

Steele, J. Angel City

Steele, J. The watchers

Carkeet, D. From away

Carr, C. The alienist

Carter, S. L. New England white

Carver, T. The surrogate

Childress, M. Crazy in Alabama

Clark, M. The legal limit

Clark, M. H. The cradle will fall

Clark, M. H. Daddy's little girl

Clark, M. H. Loves music, loves to dance

Clark, M. H. Nighttime is my time

Clark, M. H. On the street where you live

Clark, M. H. The shadow of your smile

Coben, H. The innocent

Coben, H. Gone for good

Coben, H. Hold tight

Colfer, E. Plugged

Collins, M. Death of a writer

Collins, M. Lost souls

Connelly, M. The fifth witness

Connelly, M. The brass verdict

Connelly, M. The scarecrow

Cook, R. Godplayer

Cook, T. H. Breakheart Hill

Cook, T. H. The Chatham School affair

Cook, T. H. Instruments of night

Cook, T. H. The interrogation

Cook, T. H. The last talk with Lola Faye

Cook, T. H. Places in the dark

Cosse, L. A novel bookstore

Coulter, C. The maze

Coulter, C. Split second

Cox, M. The glass of time

Crace, J. Being dead

Crais, R. The two minute rule

Cullin, M. Undersurface

Dahl, A. Misterioso

Daley, R. Wall of brass

Dallas, S. The Persian Pickle Club

Dallas, S. Tallgrass

D'Amato, B. White male infant

Darnton, J. Black and white and dead all over

Davies, R. Murther & walking spirits

De Kretser, M. The Hamilton case

Deaver, J. Roadside crosses

DeMille, N. The general's daughter

DeMille, N. The lion's game

DeMille, N. Plum Island

Dickey, J. Deliverance

Dickinson, P. Some deaths before dying

Diehl, W. Primal fear

Diehl, W. Show of evil

Dolan, H. Bad things happen

Dolan, H. Very bad men

Donoghue, E. Slammerkin

Donohue, J. J. Sensei

Donohue, K. Centuries of June

Dostoyevsky, F. The brothers Karamazov

Dostoyevsky, F. Crime and punishment

Dreiser, T. An American tragedy

Du Maurier, D. Rebecca

Dufosse, C. School's out

Dugoni, R. Murder one

Duncker, P. The strange case of the composer and his judge

Dunne, D. A season in purgatory

Dunne, D. The two Mrs. Grenvilles

Dunne, J. G. Nothing lost

Dunne, J. G. True confessions

Eastland, S. Eye of the Red Tsar

Ebershoff, D. The 19th wife

Ellis, D. Life sentence

Ellory, R. J. The Anniversary Man

Ellroy, J. The black dahlia

Enger, L. Undiscovered country

Erdrich, L. The plague of doves

Estleman, L. D. Jitterbug

Evenson, B. The open curtain

Everett, P. L. The water cure

Fairstein, L. Bad blood

Fairstein, L. The bone vault

Fairstein, L. Entombed

Faulkner, W. Requiem for a nun

Faulkner, W. Sanctuary

Faulks, S. Engleby

Fielding, J. Don't cry now

Finder, J. Company man

Fleming, I. The edge of ruin

Flynn, G. Dark places

Flynn, G. Sharp objects

Folsom, A. R. The day after tomorrow

Foster, A. D. The mocking program

Franklin, A. Mistress of the art of death

Franklin, A. The serpent's tale

Freeman, B. The bone house

French, A. Billy

French, N. Beneath the skin

French, T. In the woods

French, T. The likeness

Fuller, D. Sweetsmoke

Fyfield, F. Undercurrents

Gaines, E. J. A gathering of old men

Gallagher, S. The kingdom of bones

Garcia Marquez, G. Chronicle of a death foretold

Gardiner, M. The Dirty Secrets Club

Gerritsen, T. The apprentice

Gerritsen, T. Body double

Gerritsen, T. The sinner

Gilman, L. A. Hard magic

Ginsberg, D. The grift

Goddard, R. Beyond recall

Goddard, R. Into the blue

Goddard, R. Never go back

Laplante, A. Turn of mind
Larison, J. Holding lies
Larsson, S. The girl who kicked the hornets' nest
Larsson, S. The girl who played with fire
Lashner, W. A killer's kiss
Lawrence, M. K. The burning bride
Lawrence, M. K. Hearts and bones
Le Carre, J. The constant gardener
LeCraw, H. The swimming pool
Lehane, D. Mystic river
Leonard, E. Split images
Lescroart, J. T. The first law
Lescroart, J. T. Guilt
Lescroart, J. T. The hearing
Lescroart, J. T. The mercy rule
Lescroart, J. T. Nothing but the truth
Lescroart, J. T. The oath
Lescroart, J. T. The second chair
Letts, B. Shoot the moon
Levin, I. A kiss before dying
Lewin, M. Z. Oh Joe
Lewis, J. The king is dead
Lewis, M. G. The monk
Lindsey, D. L. The color of night
Logan, C. South of Shiloh
Lovesey, P. On the edge
Lowell, E. Die in plain sight
Ludlum, R. The Sigma protocol
Lupton, R. Sister
Lustbader, E. V. Black Blade
Lustbader, E. V. Floating city
Lutz, J. Dancing with the dead
Lutz, J. Final seconds
MacLean, A. Night without end
Mailer, N. The executioner's song
Mailer, N. Tough guys don't dance
Mankell, H.   The man from Beijing
March, W. The bad seed
Margolin, P. After dark
Margolin, P. The burning man
Margolin, P. Fugitive
Margolin, P. Wild justice
Martini, S. P. The attorney
Martini, S. P. The judge
Martini, S. P. Prime witness
Martini, S. P. Undue influence
Matthiessen, P. Bone by bone
Matthiessen, P. Killing Mister Watson
Matthiessen, P. Lost Man's River
Matthiessen, P. Shadow country
McCabe, P. The butcher boy
McCammon, R. R. Boy's life
McCorkle, J. Carolina moon
McCrumb, S. The ballad of Tom Dooley
McCrumb, S. The hangman's beautiful daughter
McCrumb, S. If ever I return, pretty Peggy-O

McDermid, V. The distant echo
McEwan, I. The innocent
McFarland, D. School for the blind
McFarland, D. Singing boy
McGrath, P. The grotesque
Meltzer, B. The book of lies
Meltzer, B. The first counsel
Meyer, P. American rust
Michener, J. A. The novel
Mieville, C. The city & the city
Miller, S. While I was gone
Mills, M. Amagansett
Mills, M. The information officer
Mina, D. Deception
Moore, G. The Sherlockian
Morrison, T. Jazz
Mortimer, J. Felix in the underworld
Mortman, D. True colors
Mosley, W. The last days of Ptolemy Grey
Muller, M. Cyanide Wells
Munoz Molina, A. A manuscript of ashes
Munson, S. The November criminals
Murdoch, I. The green knight
Murray, S. Forgery
My name is Red
Nabokov, V. V. King, queen, knave
Nasaw, J. L. Twenty-seven bones
Norman, H. The bird artist
Norman, H. What is left the daughter
Norris, F. McTeague
Oates, J. C. Because it is bitter, and because it is my heart
Oates, J. C. Broke heart blues
Oates, J. C. Little bird of heaven
Oates, J. C. Missing mom
Ogilvie, E. When the music stopped
O'Hara, J. Butterfield 8
O'Nan, S. Snow angels
O'Neill, A. The lamplighter
O'Shaughnessy, P. Invasion of privacy
O'Shaughnessy, P. Motion to suppress
O'Shaughnessy, P. Unlucky in law
Palliser, C. The unburied
Palmer, M. The society
Parker, B. Blood relations
Parker, B. Suspicion of vengeance
Parker, T. J. Black water
Parker, T. J. California girl
Parker, T. J. Cold pursuit
Parker, T. J. The fallen
Parker, T. J. Silent Joe
Parkhurst, C. The nobodies album
Parsons, J. Mary, Mary
Patterson, J. 1st to die
Patterson, J. Cat & mouse
Patterson, J. Cross

Stade, G. Love is war

Starr, J. Panic attack

Steinhauer, O. The Bridge of Sighs

Stewart, M. Nine coaches waiting

Stewart, M. Wildfire at midnight

Straight, S. The gettin place

Straub, P. The Hellfire Club

Straub, P. In the night room

Straub, P. Lost boy lost girl

Straub, P. A special place

Stross, C. Rule 34

Styron, W. Set this house on fire

Suskind, P. Perfume: the story of a murderer

Swain, J. Midnight rambler

Swierczynski, D. Expiration date

Syjuco, M. Ilustrado

Symons, J. Something like a love affair

Tanenbaum, R. Hoax

Tartt, D. The little friend

Tartt, D. The secret history

Terrell, W. The huntsman

Thayer, S. The weatherman

Thomas, M. M. Black money

Thomas, R. Voodoo, Ltd

Tirone Smith She smiled sweetly

Tirone Smith She's not there

Tracy, P. J. Monkeewrench

Traver, R. Anatomy of a murder

Truscott, L. K. Heart of war

Turow, S. The laws of our fathers

Turow, S. Reversible errors

Uhnak, D. Victims

Unsworth, B. Morality play

Unsworth, B. Stone virgin

Ure, L. The fault tree

Verdon, J. Think of a number

Verissimo, L. F. Borges and the eternal orangutans

Vine, B. Anna's book

Vine, B. No night is too long

Walters, M. The breaker

Walters, M. The dark room

Walters, M. The sculptress

Walters, M. The shape of snakes

Walton, J. Farthing

Wambaugh, J. Floaters

Ward, L. Outside valentine

Warren, R. P. World enough and time

Welsh, L. The cutting room

Welty, E. The Ponder heart

West, M. L. Masterclass

Westlake, D. E. The hook

Whitney, P. A. Domino

Whitney, P. A. The singing stones

Wilhelm, K. Death qualified

Wilhelm, K. The deepest water

Wilhelm, K. Defense for the devil

Wilhelm, K. Desperate measures

Wilhelm, K. Malice prepense

Wilhelm, K. No defense

Wilson, R. The blind man of Seville

Wiltse, D. Bone deep

Wittenborn, D. Pharmakon

Woods, S. Chiefs

Woods, S. Choke

Woods, S. Dead in the water

Woods, S. Dirt

Woods, S. Grass roots

Woods, S. Imperfect strangers

Woods, S. L.A. dead

Woods, S. Orchid Beach

Woods, S. Palindrome

Woods, S. Santa Fe rules

Woods, S. Short straw

Woods, S. Worst fears realized

Yoshida, S. Villain

Yrsa Sigurdardottir Last rituals

Zimler, R. The last kabbalist of Lisbon

MURDER TRIALS *See* Trials (Homicide)

Murder unprompted. Brett, S.

MURDER VICTIMS

Hansen, R. The assassination of Jesse James by the coward Robert Ford

Howard, R. Like trees, walking

Rose, J. Blackest bird

MURDER VICTIMS -- FICTION

Dean, A. Bellfield Hall, or, The observations of Miss Dido Kent

DeLillo, D. Cosmopolis

O'Brien, E. In the forest

Palwick, S. Mending the moon

MURDER VICTIMS -- IRAN

Morgan-Jones, C. The jackal's share

MURDER VICTIMS' FAMILIES -- CONNECTI-CUT

Roorbach, B. Life among giants

MURDER VICTIMS' FAMILIES

Aslam, N. Maps for lost lovers

Clark, M. H. Daddy's little girl

Coben, H. No second chance

Deutermann, P. T. The cat dancers

Fyfield, F. Blind date

Kelman, J. Summer of storms

LeCraw, H. The swimming pool

Pickard, N. The scent of rain and lightning

Sebold, A. The lovely bones

Murder walks the plank. Hart, C. G.

Murder@maggody.com. Hess, J.

MURDERERS

Adamson, G. The outlander

Bauer, B. Blacklands

Boyne, J. Crippen

Clark, M. H. Nighttime is my time

The **music** teacher. Hall, B.

MUSIC TEACHERS

Chaudhuri, A. The immortals

Doig, I. Prairie nocturne

Hall, B. The music teacher

Lee, J. Y. K. The piano teacher

MUSIC TEACHERS -- FICTION

Gass, W. H. Middle C

MUSIC TRADE

Turner, N. Ghetto superstar

MUSICAL FILMS *See* Motion pictures

MUSICAL NOTATION *See* Music

MUSICIANS

See also Music

Baldwin, J. Another country

Bass, R. Nashville chrome

Beatty, P. Slumberland

Davies, R. The lyre of Orpheus

Edgerton, C. The night train

Flagg, F. Standing in the rainbow

Franzen, J. Freedom

Hassler, J. Rookery blues

Hesse, H. Gertrude

Hewson, D. Lucifer's shadow

Hijuelos, O.   Beautiful Maria of my soul

Hijuelos, O. The Mambo Kings play songs of love

Hornby, N. High fidelity

Hospital, J. T. Orpheus lost

L'Engle, M. A severed wasp

Lethem, J. You don't love me yet

MacDonald Fall on your knees

Mackey, N. Bass cathedral

McEwan, I. On Chesil Beach

McGuane, T. Panama

Mendelson, C. Morningside Heights

Mosley, W. RL's dream

Murakami, H. After dark

Reiken, F. Day for night

Romano-Lax, A. The Spanish bow

Sarton, M. Anger

Seth, V. An equal music

Smith, L. The devil's dream

Spiotta, D. Stone Arabia

Taylor, M. G. The ballad of Trenchmouth Taggart

Tremain, R. Music & silence

Turner, F. W. 1929

Tyler, A. Searching for Caleb

Tyler, A. A slipping-down life

Wimberley, D. The king of Colored Town

MUSICIANS -- FICTION

Bledsoe, A. Wisp of a thing

Elias, G. Death and transfiguration

Kalotay, D. Sight Reading

Stemple, A. Singer of souls

MUSLIM FAMILIES

Akhtar, A. American dervish

Smith, Z. White teeth

MUSLIM WOMEN

See also Muslims; Women

Amirrezvani, A. Equal of the sun

MUSLIM WOMEN -- FICTION

Aslam, N. Maps for lost lovers

MUSLIMS

Caputo, P. Acts of faith

De Bernieres, L. Birds without wings

D'Souza, T. Whiteman

Gibb, C. Sweetness in the belly

Guene, F. Kiffe kiffe tomorrow

Kureishi, H. Something to tell you

Lapierre, A. Between love and honor

My name is Red

Seth, V. A suitable boy

Unsworth, B. The ruby in her navel

Updike, J. Terrorist

Waldman, A. The submission

MUSLIMS -- FICTION

Akhtar, A. American dervish

MUSLIMS -- FRANCE

Harris, J. Peaches for Father Francis

Mussolini, Benito, 1883-1945

About

Epstein, L. The eighth wonder of the world

MUTATION (BIOLOGY)

See also Evolution; Variation (Biology)

Gregory, D. The devil's alphabet

MUTE PERSONS

Barnes, J. The somnambulist

Coulter, C. The target

Harrison, K. The seal wife

King, D. The ha-ha

Reuss, F. The wasties

Winthrop, E. H. December

Wroblewski, D. The story of Edgar Sawtelle

MUTE PERSONS -- FICTION

Hamilton, S. The lock artist

Harding, G. Painter of silence

MUTINEERS

McDermid, V. Grave tattoo

MUTINY

Faulkner, W. A fable

Nordhoff, C. Mutiny on the Bounty

Pesci, D. Amistad

Unsworth, B. Sacred hunger

Wouk, H. The Caine mutiny

Mutiny on the Bounty. Nordhoff, C.

MUTUAL FUNDS *See* Investments

My abandonment. Rock, P.

My Antonia. Cather, W.

My big apartment. Oster, C.

My brilliant career. Franklin, M.

My brother Michael. Stewart, M.

My century. Grass, G.

HAMAS

Hart, C. G. Resort to murder

Morris, B. Baja Florida

MYSTERY AND DETECTIVE STORIES -- BO-TSWANA

McCall Smith, A. Blue shoes and happiness

McCall Smith, A. The Double Comfort Safari Club

McCall Smith, A. The good husband of Zebra Drive

McCall Smith, A. In the company of cheerful ladies

Stanley, M. A carrion death

MYSTERY AND DETECTIVE STORIES -- BRAZIL

Garcia-Roza, L. A. Alone in the crowd

Garcia-Roza, L. A. December heat

Garcia-Roza, L. A. The silence of the rain

MYSTERY AND DETECTIVE STORIES -- CANADA

Engel, H. The Cooperman variations

Penny, L. Bury your dead

Penny, L. The cruelest month

Penny, L. Still life

Penny, L. A trick of the light

Reichs, K. J. Deja dead

Reichs, K. J. Monday mourning

Wolfe, I. A. The taken

Wright, E. The last hand

MYSTERY AND DETECTIVE STORIES -- CARIBBEAN REGION

White, R. W. Black widow

MYSTERY AND DETECTIVE STORIES -- CHINA

Gulik, R. H. v. The Chinese bell murders

Gulik, R. H. v. The haunted monastery

Gulik, R. H. v. The lacquer screen

Gulik, R. H. v. The Red Pavilion

Gulik, R. H. v. The willow pattern

Qiu Xiaolong Red mandarin dress

Qiu Xiaolong When red is black

See, L. Dragon bones

MYSTERY AND DETECTIVE STORIES -- CORFU

Brett, S. Mrs. Pargeter's package

MYSTERY AND DETECTIVE STORIES -- CUBA

Kaminsky, S. M. Hard currency

Smith, M. C. Havana Bay

Standiford, L. Havana run

MYSTERY AND DETECTIVE STORIES -- EGYPT

Doherty, P. C. The Anubis slayings

Drake, N. Tutankhamun

Hess, J. Mummy dearest

Peters, E. Children of the storm

Peters, E. The golden one

Peters, E. Guardian of the horizon

Peters, E. He shall thunder in the sky

Peters, E. The hippopotamus pool

Peters, E. Lion in the valley

Peters, E. The mummy case

Peters, E. Night train to Memphis

Peters, E. Seeing a large cat

Peters, E. The snake, the crocodile, and the dog

Robinson, L. S. Murder at the feast of rejoicing

Robinson, L. S. Murder at the God's gate

MYSTERY AND DETECTIVE STORIES -- ENGLAND

Allingham, M. Crime and Mr. Campion

Allingham, M. Three cases for Mr. Campion

Atherton, N. Aunt Dimity digs in

Atkinson, K. Case histories

Atkinson, K. Started early, took my dog

Aubert, R. The ferryman will be there

Babson, M. Canapes for the kitties

Banks, R. No more heroes

Bannister, J. No birds sing

Barnard, R. Death of a literary widow

Barnard, R. A fall from grace

Barnard, R. Out of the blackout

Beaton, M. C. Love, lies, and liquor

Bradley, A. A red herring without mustard

Brett, S. Murder unprompted

Brett, S. The torso in the town

Brook, M. The Iron Duke

Butler, G. Death lives next door

Cannell, D. How to murder your mother-in-law

Carver, T. The surrogate

Chesterton, G. K. Father Brown mystery stories

Chesterton, G. K. The Father Brown omnibus

Chesterton, G. K. The innocence of Father Brown

Christie, A. The A.B.C. murders

Christie, A. And then there were none

Christie, A. The body in the library

Christie, A. Curtain

Christie, A. Endless night

Christie, A. The Hollow

Christie, A. Mrs. McGinty's dead

Christie, A. The murder at the vicarage

Christie, A. A murder is announced

Christie, A. The murder of Roger Ackroyd

Christie, A. The pale horse

Christie, A. Three blind mice and other stories

Christie, A. Towards zero

Collins, W. The moonstone

Collins, W. The woman in white

Cornwell, B. Gallows thief

Crombie, D. And justice there is none

Crombie, D. Kissed a sad goodbye

Crombie, D. Water like a stone

Cullin, M. A slight trick of the mind

Dean, S. F. X. It can't be my grave

Dexter, C. The daughters of Cain

Lovesey, P. The last detective

Lovesey, P. Rough cider

Lovesey, P. Upon a dark night

Lovesey, P. The vault

Lovesey, P. Waxwork

MacDonald, P. The list of Adrian Messenger

Macdonald, R. The drowning pool

Malliet, G. M. Wicked autumn

Marsh, N. Dead water

Marsh, N. False scent

Marsh, N. Grave mistake

Marsh, N. Last ditch

Marsh, N. Light thickens

Marston, E. The Bawdy basket

Marston, E. The Devil's apprentice

Marston, E. The roaring boy

Marston, E. The stallions of Woodstock

Marston, E. The vagabond clown

Marston, E. The wanton angel

Marston, E. The wildcats of Exeter

McCrumb, S. Missing Susan

McGown, J. Murder at the old vicarage

McGown, J. Picture of innocence

McGown, J. Plots and errors

McGown, J. The stalking horse

McGown, J. Verdict unsafe

Meyer, N. The West End horror

Mina, D. The end of the wasp season

Neel, J. To die for

Penman, S. K. Cruel as the grave

Penman, S. K. The queen's man

Perry, A. Bedford Square

Perry, A. Belgrave Square

Perry, A. Bluegate Fields

Perry, A. A breach of promise

Perry, A. Buckingham Palace gardens

Perry, A. Cain his brother

Perry, A. Cardington Crescent

Perry, A. A dangerous mourning

Perry, A. Death of a stranger

Perry, A. Defend and betray

Perry, A. The face of a stranger

Perry, A. Farriers' Lane

Perry, A. Funeral in blue

Perry, A. Half Moon Street

Perry, A. Highgate rise

Perry, A. The Hyde Park headsman

Perry, A. Paragon Walk

Perry, A. Pentecost Alley

Perry, A. Resurrection row

Perry, A. Seven dials

Perry, A. The silent cry

Perry, A. The sins of the wolf

Perry, A. Slaves of obsession

Perry, A. Southampton Row

Perry, A. Traitor's gate

Perry, A. The twisted root

Perry, A. Weighed in the balance

Perry, A. The Whitechapel conspiracy

Peters, E. The deeds of the disturber

Peters, E. The last camel died at noon

Peters, E. The benediction of Brother Cadfael

Peters, E. Brother Cadfael's penance

Peters, E. Dead man's ransom

Peters, E. Fallen into the pit

Peters, E. The hermit of Eyton Forest

Peters, E. The holy thief

Peters, E. Monk's-hood

Peters, E. The pilgrim of hate

Peters, E. The potter's field

Peters, E. A rare Benedictine

Peters, E. The rose rent

Peters, E. Saint Peter's Fair

Peters, E. The sanctuary sparrow

Peters, E. The summer of the Danes

Peters, E. The virgin in the ice

Pickard, N. Bum steer

Pirie, D. The patient's eyes

Rendell, R. Collected stories

Rendell, R. Harm done

Rendell, R. Kissing the gunner's daughter

Rendell, R. Not in the flesh

Rendell, R. Road rage

Rendell, R. Simisola

Rendell, R. A sleeping life

Robb, C. M. The riddle of St. Leonard's

Robinson, P. Cold is the grave

Robinson, P. Innocent grave

Robinson, P. Piece of my heart

Sayers, D. L. Busman's honeymoon

Sayers, D. L. Clouds of witnesses

Sayers, D. L. The Dawson pedigree

Sayers, D. L. The documents in the case

Sayers, D. L. Gaudy Night

Sayers, D. L. Have his carcase

Sayers, D. L. Lord Peter

Sayers, D. L. Murder must advertise

Sayers, D. L. The nine tailors

Sayers, D. L. Strong poison

Sayers, D. L. Thrones, dominations

Sayers, D. L. The unpleasantness at the Bellona
  Club

Sayers, D. L. Whose body?

Simpson, D. Dead and gone

Simpson, D. Dead by morning

Simpson, D. Doomed to die

Simpson, D. Last seen alive

Simpson, D. No laughing matter

Simpson, D. Once too often

Speller, E. The return of Captain John Emmett

Symons, J. The Kentish manor murders

Tallis, F. A death in Vienna

Elkins, A. J. Good blood

Hewson, D. The garden of evil

Hewson, D. A season for the dead

Langton, J. The thief of Venice

Leon, D. About face

Leon, D. Doctored evidence

Leon, D. Drawing conclusions

Leon, D. The girl of his dreams

Leon, D. Uniform justice

Marsh, N. When in Rome

Nabb, M. Some bitter taste

Pears, I. Death and restoration

Pears, I. The immaculate deception

MYSTERY AND DETECTIVE STORIES -- JAPAN

Lathen, E. East is east

Melville, J. The chrysanthemum chain

MYSTERY AND DETECTIVE STORIES -- JORDAN

Gilman, D. Mrs. Pollifax, innocent tourist

MYSTERY AND DETECTIVE STORIES -- LAOS

Cotterill, C. Love songs from a shallow grave

MYSTERY AND DETECTIVE STORIES -- MEXICO

MacDonald, J. D. A deadly shade of gold

MacDonald, J. D. Dress her in indigo

MYSTERY AND DETECTIVE STORIES -- MOROCCO

Gilman, D. Mrs. Pollifax and the whirling dervish

MYSTERY AND DETECTIVE STORIES -- NETHERLANDS

Freeling, N. Sand castles

Moody, B. Looking for Chet Baker

Simenon, G. Maigret in Holland

Van de Wetering, J. The Amsterdam cops

Van de Wetering, J. The blond baboon

MYSTERY AND DETECTIVE STORIES -- NORWAY

Benn, J. R. Billy Boyle

Fossum, K. Bad intentions

Nesbo, J. The redbreast

The snowman

MYSTERY AND DETECTIVE STORIES -- PALESTINE

King, L. R. O Jerusalem

MYSTERY AND DETECTIVE STORIES -- POLAND

Lathen, E. A shark out of water

MYSTERY AND DETECTIVE STORIES -- ROME

Bell, A. A. The blood of Caesar

Davis, L. The accusers

Davis, L. Last act in Palmyra

Davis, L. Poseidon's gold

Davis, L. Three hands in the fountain

Downie, R. Caveat emptor

Downie, R. Medicus

Downie, R. Terra incognita

Saylor, S. The house of the Vestals

Saylor, S. The judgment of Caesar

Saylor, S. A mist of prophecies

Saylor, S. Rubicon

Saylor, S. The triumph of Caesar

MYSTERY AND DETECTIVE STORIES -- RUSSIA

Kaminsky, S. M. Blood and rubles

Kaminsky, S. M. A cold red sunrise

Kaminsky, S. M. Death of a Russian priest

Kaminsky, S. M. The dog who bit a policeman

Kaminsky, S. M. The man who walked like a bear

Kaminsky, S. M. Murder on the Trans-Siberian Express

Kaminsky, S. M. Rostnikov's vacation

Morris, R. N. The gentle axe

Smith, M. C. Gorky Park

Smith, M. C. Polar Star

Smith, M. C. Red Square

Smith, M. C. Stalin's ghost

Smith, M. C. Three stations

Smith, M. C. Wolves eat dogs

MYSTERY AND DETECTIVE STORIES -- SAUDI ARABIA

Ferraris, Z. Finding Nouf

MYSTERY AND DETECTIVE STORIES -- SCOTLAND

Atkinson, K. When will there be good news?

Beaton, M. C. Death of a hussy

Beaton, M. C. Death of a macho man

Beaton, M. C. Death of a Valentine

MacBride, S. Flesh house

McCall Smith, A. The comforts of a muddy Saturday

McCall Smith, A. The lost art of gratitude

Mina, D. The dead hour

Mina, D. Slip of the knife

Mina, D. Still midnight

Rankin, I. Black and blue

Rankin, I. The black book

Rankin, I. Dead souls

Rankin, I. Exit music

Rankin, I. The falls

Rankin, I. The naming of the dead

Rankin, I. A question of blood

Rankin, I. Resurrection men

Rankin, I. Set in darkness

Sayers, D. L. The five red herrings

MYSTERY AND DETECTIVE STORIES -- SOUTH AFRICA

Francis, D. Smokescreen

Mackenzie, J. Random violence

McClure, J. The steam pig

Connelly, M. The narrows
Connelly, M. Nine dragons
Connelly, M. The overlook
Connolly, J. The burning soul
Connolly, J. The unquiet
Constantine, K. C. Blood mud
Constantine, K. C. Brushback
Constantine, K. C. Family values
Constantine, K. C. Grievance
Constantine, K. C. Saving room for dessert
Craig, P. R. A shoot on Martha's Vineyard
Craig, P. R. Third strike
Craig, P. R. Vineyard enigma
Craig, P. R. A vineyard killing
Crais, R. Chasing darkness
Crais, R. First rule
Crais, R. The forgotten man
Crais, R. Indigo slam
Crais, R. L.A. requiem
Crais, R. The last detective
Crais, R. The watchman
Crosby, E. The Viognier vendetta
Cross, A. The collected stories of Amanda Cross
Cross, A. Honest doubt
Cross, A. An imperfect spy
Cross, A. The puzzled heart
Crumley, J. Bordersnakes
Crumley, J. The final country
Crumley, J. The last good kiss
Crumley, J. The wrong case
D'Amato, B. Hard evidence
D'Amato, B. Hard road
Dams, J. M. Death in lacquer red
Davidson, D. M. Killer pancake
Davidson, D. M. The last suppers
Davidson, D. M. Prime cut
Deaver, J. The broken window
Deaver, J. The Coffin Dancer
Deaver, J. The vanished man
DePoy, P. The drifter's wheel
Dicks, M. Unexpectedly, Milo
Dobyns, S. Saratoga strongbox
Doss, J. D. The night visitor
Doss, J. D. The shaman's bones
Douglas, C. N. Cat in a midnight choir
Douglas, C. N. Cat in a neon nightmare
Dunning, J. Booked to die
Dunning, J. The bookman's wake
Dunning, J. The sign of the book
Estleman, L. D. Alone
Estleman, L. D. American detective
Estleman, L. D. Amos Walker
Estleman, L. D. Frames
Estleman, L. D. The hours of the virgin
Estleman, L. D. Infernal angels
Estleman, L. D. Poison blonde

Estleman, L. D. Retro
Estleman, L. D. A smile on the face of the tiger
Evanovich, J. Eleven on top
Evanovich, J. Hard eight
Evanovich, J. Hot six
Evanovich, J. One for the money
Evanovich, J. Three to get deadly
Evanovich, J. To the nines
Evanovich, J. Two for the dough
Finch, C. The September Society
Flanagan, J. Storm peak
Fleming, I. The edge of ruin
Forrest, K. V. Apparition alley
Forrest, K. V. Liberty Square
Forrest, K. V. Sleeping bones
Freeman, B. Stripped
Fulmer, D. The blue door
Gardner, L. Love you more
Gilman, D. Kaleidoscope
Gilman, D. Mrs. Pollifax pursued
Gilman, D. Thale's Folly
Gilman, K. Father's Day
Goldsborough, R. The missing chapter
Gorman, E. Bad moon rising
Gorman, E. Breaking up is hard to do
Gorman, E. Fools rush in
Gorman, E. Save the last dance for me
Gorman, E. Sleeping dogs
Gorman, E. Ticket to ride
Gosling, P. The dead of winter
Gosling, P. A few dying words
Grafton, S. B is for burglar
Grafton, S. C is for corpse
Grafton, S. D is for deadbeat
Grafton, S. E is for evidence
Grafton, S. F is for fugitive
Grafton, S. G is for gumshoe
Grafton, S. H is for homicide
Grafton, S. I is for innocent
Grafton, S. A is for alibi
Grafton, S. J is for judgment
Grafton, S. K is for killer
Grafton, S. L is for lawless
Grafton, S. M is for malice
Grafton, S. N is for noose
Grafton, S. O is for outlaw
Grafton, S. P is for peril
Grafton, S. Q is for quarry
Grafton, S. R is for ricochet
Grafton, S. S is for Silence
Grafton, S. T is for trespass
Gran, S. Claire DeWitt and the city of the dead
Granger, B. The el murders
Greeley, A. M. The bishop in the West Wing
Greenleaf, S. Blood type
Greenleaf, S. False conception

Kaminsky, S. M. Lieberman's folly

Kaminsky, S. M. Lieberman's thief

Kaminsky, S. M. Not quite kosher

Kaminsky, S. M. Retribution

Kaminsky, S. M. To catch a spy

Kaminsky, S. M. Tomorrow is another day

Kaminsky, S. M. Vengeance

Kava, A. Hotwire

Kellerman, F. Day of atonement

Kellerman, F. The forgotten

Kellerman, F. Grievous sin

Kellerman, F. Jupiter's bones

Kellerman, F. Justice

Kellerman, F. Milk and honey

Kellerman, F. Moon music

Kellerman, F. Prayers for the dead

Kellerman, F. Sanctuary

Kellerman, F. Serpent's tooth

Kellerman, F. Stone kiss

Kellerman, F. Street dreams

Kellerman, J. Bad love

Kellerman, J. Billy Straight

Kellerman, J. Bones

Kellerman, J. The clinic

Kellerman, J. Devil's waltz

Kellerman, J. Dr. Death

Kellerman, J. Gone

Kellerman, J. Monster

Kellerman, J. The murder book

Kellerman, J. Private eyes

Kellerman, J. Self-defense

Kellerman, J. Survival of the fittest

Kellerman, J. Therapy

Kellerman, J. Time bomb

Kellerman, J. The web

Kellerman, J. When the bough breaks

Kemelman, H. The day the rabbi resigned

Kemelman, H. Friday the rabbi slept late

Kemelman, H. Saturday the rabbi went hungry

Kemelman, H. Sunday the rabbi stayed home

Kemelman, H. Thursday the rabbi walked out

Kemelman, H. Wednesday the rabbi got wet

Kienzle, W. X. Assault with intent

Kienzle, W. X. Body count

Kienzle, W. X. The gathering

Kienzle, W. X. The greatest evil

Kienzle, W. X. The man who loved God

Kienzle, W. X. The rosary murders

Kijewski, K. Alley Kat blues

Kijewski, K. Copy Kat

Kijewski, K. Honky tonk Kat

Kijewski, K. Kat scratch fever

Kijewski, K. Kat's cradle

Kijewski, K. Stray Kat waltz

King, L. R. Locked rooms

Knopf, C. Black swan

Knopf, C. Hard stop

Knopf, C. Head wounds

Knopf, C. The last refuge

Knopf, C. Two time

Koryta, M. The silent hour

Koryta, M. Tonight I said goodbye

Krueger, W. K. Northwest angle

Krueger, W. K. Vermilion drift

La Plante, L. Cold blood

Langton, J. The deserter

Langton, J. Emily Dickinson is dead

Langton, J. The Escher twist

Langton, J. The face on the wall

Langton, J. Murder at Monticello

Lansdale, J. R. Devil red

Lansdale, J. R. Vanilla Ride

Lathen, E. Brewing up a storm

Lathen, E. Going for the gold

Lathen, E. Right on the money

Lathen, E. Something in the air

Lavender, W. Dominance

Lehane, D. Moonlight mile

Lehane, D. Prayers for rain

Lehane, D. Sacred

Leonard, E. When the women come out to dance, and other stories

Lethem, J. Motherless Brooklyn

Lippman, L. Hardly knew her

Lippman, L. No good deeds

Lovesey, P. Skeleton Hill

Lutz, J. Burn

Lutz, J. Death by jury

Lutz, J. Lightning

Lutz, J. Oops!

Lutz, L. Curse of the Spellmans

Lutz, L. Revenge of the Spellmans

Lutz, L. The Spellman files

MacDonald, J. D. Cinnamon skin

MacDonald, J. D. A deadly shade of gold

MacDonald, J. D. The deep blue good-by

MacDonald, J. D. The dreadful lemon sky

MacDonald, J. D. Free fall in crimson

MacDonald, J. D. The green ripper

MacDonald, J. D. The lonely silver rain

MacDonald, J. D. The long lavender look

MacDonald, J. D. One fearful yellow eye

MacDonald, J. D. A purple place for dying

MacDonald, J. D. The scarlet ruse

MacDonald, J. D. The turquoise lament

Macdonald, R. Archer in Hollywood

Macdonald, R. Archer in jeopardy

Macdonald, R. The far side of the dollar

Macdonald, R. The Galton case

Macdonald, R. The goodbye look

Macdonald, R. Sleeping beauty

Macdonald, R. The underground man

O'Connell, C. Crime school
O'Connell, C. Killing critics
O'Connell, C. Mallory's oracle
O'Connell, C. The man who cast two shadows
O'Connell, C. Stone angel
O'Donnell, L. Blue death
O'Donnell, L. Pushover
O'Donnell, L. The raggedy man
The Oxford book of American detective stories
Page, K. H. The body in the Big Apple
Page, K. H. The body in the bog
Page, K. H. The body in the bookcase
Pajer, B. A spark of death
Paretsky, S. Bitter medicine
Paretsky, S. Blacklist
Paretsky, S. Blood shot
Paretsky, S. Burn marks
Paretsky, S. Fire sale
Paretsky, S. Guardian angel
Paretsky, S. Hard time
Paretsky, S. Hardball
Paretsky, S. Indemnity only
Paretsky, S. Total recall
Paretsky, S. Tunnel vision
Paretsky, S. Windy City blues
Parker, R. B. Back story
Parker, R. B. A Catskill eagle
Parker, R. B. Chance
Parker, R. B. Cold service
Parker, R. B. Crimson joy
Parker, R. B. Death in paradise
Parker, R. B. Double Deuce
Parker, R. B. Family honor
Parker, R. B. Hugger mugger
Parker, R. B. Hush money
Parker, R. B. Melancholy baby
Parker, R. B. Night passage
Parker, R. B. Now and then
Parker, R. B. Painted ladies
Parker, R. B. Paper doll
Parker, R. B. Perchance to dream
Parker, R. B. Potshot
Parker, R. B. Rough weather
Parker, R. B. School days
Parker, R. B. Sea change
Parker, R. B. Shrink rap
Parker, R. B. Sixkill
Parker, R. B. Small vices
Parker, R. B. Taming a sea-horse
Parker, R. B. Thin air
Parker, R. B. Trouble in Paradise
Parker, R. B. Walking shadow
Parker, R. B. Widow's walk
Parker, T. J. Laguna heat
Parker, T. J. Pacific beat
Pearson, R. Killer summer

Pelecanos, G. P. Hard revolution
Pelecanos, G. P. Hell to pay
Pelecanos, G. P. Soul circus
Perry, T. Death benefits
Pickard, N. The 27 ingredient chili con carne murders
Pickard, N. Blue corn murders
Pickard, N. But I wouldn't want to die there
Pickard, N. Confession
Pickard, N. Dead crazy
Pickard, N. Generous death
Pickard, N. Marriage is murder
Pickard, N. No body
Pickard, N. The truth hurts
Pickard, N. The whole truth
Pickens, C. Southern fried
Pintoff, S. In the shadow of Gotham
Pronzini, B. Blue lonesome
Pronzini, B. Bones
Pronzini, B. Crazybone
Pronzini, B. Fever
Pronzini, B. Hardcase
Pronzini, B. Illusions
Pronzini, B. Mourners
Pronzini, B. Nightcrawlers
Pronzini, B. Quarry
Pronzini, B. Savages
Pronzini, B. Spook
Queen, E. A fine and private place
Queen, E. The Roman hat mystery
Read, C. Invisible boy
Reichs, K. J. Bare bones
Reichs, K. J. Break no bones
Rich, V. The baked bean supper murders
Rich, V. The cooking school murders
Rich, V. The Nantucket diet murders
Rinehart, M. R. The circular staircase
Rinehart, M. R. Miss Pinkerton: adventures of a nurse detective
Robb, C. M. The cross-legged knight
Roberts, G. The bluest blood
Roberts, G. Helen hath no fury
Roberts, G. The mummers' curse
Roosevelt, E. The Hyde Park murder
Roosevelt, E. Murder and the First Lady
Roosevelt, E. Murder at midnight
Roosevelt, E. Murder at the palace
Roosevelt, E. Murder in the Blue Room
Roosevelt, E. Murder in the map room
Roosevelt, E. Murder in the Oval Office
Roosevelt, E. Murder in the Rose Garden
Roosevelt, E. The White House pantry murder
Rozan, S. J. Winter and night
Russell, S. This insane train
Sallis, J. Cripple Creek
Sallis, J. Cypress Grove

Wilcox, C. Find her a grave
Wilcox, C. Full circle
Wilcox, C. Switchback
Wilhelm, K. The Hamlet trap
Wilhelm, K. Justice for some
Wilhelm, K. Sweet, sweet poison
Williams, A. K. The stranger you seek
Wilson, F. P. Conspiracies
Wilson, F. P. The haunted air
Wilson, F. P. Legacies
Winslow, D. The Dawn Patrol
Winslow, D. The gentlemen's hour
Woods, S. Chiefs
Woods, S. New York dead
Yancey, R. The highly effective detective

MYSTERY AND DETECTIVE STORIES -- WALES
Penman, S. K. Dragon's lair
Robb, C. M. A gift of sanctuary

MYSTERY AND DETECTIVE STORIES/ FRANCE
Black, C. Murder in the Sentier

MYSTERY COMIC BOOKS, STRIPS, ETC. *See*
Comic books, strips, etc.

MYSTERY FICTION
Adler-Olsen, J. The absent one
Adler-Olsen, J. A Conspiracy of Faith
Adler-Olsen, J. The keeper of lost causes
Ahmad, A. X. The Caretaker
Albert, S. W. The Darling Dahlias and the cucumber tree
Alfieri, A. City of silver
Alpert, M. Extinction
Ampuero, R. The Neruda case
Atkins, A. The broken places
Atkinson, K. Started early, took my dog
Barclay, L. Trust your eyes
Barr, N. The rope
Berry, S. The third secret
The Best American mystery stories of the century
Beukes, L. Zoo city
Bingham, H. Talking to the dead
Black, B. Vengeance
Black, C. Murder below Montparnasse
Black, C. Murder in Belleville
Black, C. Murder in the rue de Paradis
Black, L. Blunt Impact
Black, L. Evidence of murder
Blake, R. A dark anatomy
Bohman, T. Drowned
Box, C. J. Out of range
Bradley, A. I am half-sick of shadows
Bradley, A. Speaking from among the bones
Bradley, A. The sweetness at the bottom of the pie
Bradley, A. The weed that strings the hangman's bag

Brennan, T. Doktor Glass
Brookmyre, C. When the Devil Drives
Brookmyre, C. Where the bodies are buried
Brooks, B. Winter kill
Brown, E. R. Almost criminal
Brown, R. Before and after
Browne, S. G. Lucky bastard
Buckley, F. Queen of ambition
Buckley, F. Queen without a crown
Buckley, F. Queen's bounty
Buckley, F. A Rescue for a Queen
Buckley, F. The siren queen
Bunn, T. D. Lion of Babylon
Burrowes, G. Lady Maggie's secret scandal
Butcher, J. Proven guilty
Buzzelli, E. K. Dead dogs and Englishmen
Cain, C. Kill you twice
Caletti, D. He's gone
Carkeet, D. Double negative
Carlyle, L. One touch of scandal
Carnoy, D. The big exit
Carr, C. The alienist
Carver, T. The creeper
Castillo, L. Breaking silence
Castro, J. Hell or high water
Child, L. A wanted man
Christie, A. The A.B.C. murders
Christie, A. And then there were none
Church, J. Bamboo and blood
Church, J. A drop of Chinese blood
Clark, M. Guilt by association
Clark, M. Guilt by degrees
Clark, M. H. On the street where you live
Clark, M. H. Where are the children?
Clarke, L. Swimming at night
Claudel, P. The investigation
Cleave, P. Cemetery Lake
Clements, R. Revenger
Cleverly, B. The last kashmiri rose
Coben, H. The innocent
Coben, H. Stay close
Collins, B. Crimson eve
Collins, M. A. Target Lancer
Conlon, E. Red on red
Cook, T. H. Sandrine's Case
Corey, J. S. A. Leviathan Wakes
Cotterill, C. Disco for the departed
Cotterill, C. The merry misogynist
Cotterill, C. Slash and burn
Cotterill, C. Thirty-three teeth
Cotterill, C. The woman who wouldn't die
Crais, R. Taken
Crompton, R. Hour of the Red God
Cross, A. An imperfect spy
Cross, N. Luther
Crumley, J. Bordersnakes

Hill, S. The vows of silence

Hillerman, T. The fallen man

Hillerman, T. Hunting badger

Hillerman, T. Sacred clowns

Hillerman, T. The sinister pig

Hillerman, T. Skinwalkers

Hillerman, T. A thief of time

Hines, T. L. Waking Lazarus

Høeg, P. The elephant keepers' children

Holbert, B. Lonesome animals

Indridason, A. Outrage

Irwin, S. M. The broken ones

Jackson, J. A grown up kind of pretty

James, B. Undercover

James, P. D. Death comes to Pemberley

James, P. D. Devices and desires

James, S. The queen

Jenkins, V. An unattended death

Jio, S. The violets of March

Johansen, I. Taking eve

Johnson, C. Another man's moccasins

Johnson, C. Hell is empty

Johnson, C. Death without company

Jones, J. S. The silence

Karp, L. A perilous conception

Katzenbach, J. State of mind

Kazinski, A. J. The last good man

Keating, H. R. F. Doing wrong

Kellerman, F. Prayers for the dead

Kellerman, J. The clinic

Kellerman, J. Devil's waltz

Kelly, E. The burning air

Kelly, J. The fire baby

Kelly, J. The moon tunnel

Kemelman, H. Friday the rabbi slept late

Kerley, J. The death collectors

Kerr, P. If the dead rise not

Kerr, P. A Man Without Breath

Kerr, P. Prague fatale

Khair, T. The thing about thugs

Kijewski, K. Alley Kat blues

King, L. R. The beekeeper's apprentice, or, On the segregation of the queen

King, L. R. Garment of shadows

Koontz, D. R. The bad place

Koontz, D. R. Odd apocalypse

Koryta, M. The prophet

Krentz, J. A. Dream eyes

Lackberg, C. The ice princess

Lackberg, C. The stonecutter

Lamanda, A. Sunset

Lathen, E. A shark out of water

Lawrence, C. The case of the deadly desperados

Le Fanu, J. S. Uncle Silas

Lehane, D. Sacred

Lelic, S. The child who

Leon, D. Beastly Things

Leon, D. Blood from a stone

Leon, D. The Golden Egg

Leon, D. A question of belief

Levack, S. Demon of the air

Limón, M. Mr. Kill

Locke, A. The cutting season

Longworth, M. L. Death in the Vines

Longworth, M. L. Murder in the Rue Dumas

Lovesey, P. The tooth tattoo

Lupton, R. Afterwards

Lutz, L. The last word

MacBride, S. Blind eye

MacBride, S. Close to the Bone

MacBride, S. Cold granite

MacBride, S. Dying Light

MacBride, S. Shatter the bones

Malliet, G. M. A fatal winter

Manfredo, L. Rizzo's daughter

Manfredo, L. Rizzo's fire

The map and the territory

Mark, D. The dark winter

Maron, M. The buzzard table

Maron, M. Killer market

Maron, M. Shooting at loons

Master's choice [v1]-2: mystery stories by today's top writers and the masters who inspired them

McCall Smith, A. The forgotten affairs of youth

McCall Smith, A. The full cupboard of life

McCall Smith, A. The Kalahari typing school for men

McCall Smith, A. The Limpopo Academy of Private Detection

McCall Smith, A. The No. 1 Ladies' Detective Agency

McCall Smith, A. The Saturday big tent wedding party

McCall Smith, A. Tea time for the traditionally built

McCorkle, J. Carolina moon

McMahon, J. The One I Left Behind

McOmber, A. The white forest

Memminger, C. Aloha, lady blue

Miller, J. The year of the gadfly

Miller, M. G. Stalking season

Mina, D. Gods and beasts

Mogford, T. Shadow of the rock

Mogford, T. Sign of the cross

Morgan-Jones, C. The jackal's share

Morton, C. Stealing Mona Lisa

Mosley, W. All I did was shoot my man

Mosley, W. Black Betty

Mosley, W. Devil in a blue dress

Mosley, W. Gone fishin'

Mosley, W. Little green

Mosley, W. A little yellow dog

Straight, S. Between heaven and here

Straight, S. The gettin place

Symons, J. The Kentish manor murders

Syndrome E

Tallis, F. Fatal lies

Tallis, F. Vienna blood

Talty, S. Black Irish

Tey, J. The daughter of time

Thomas, R. The Kashmir Shawl

Thompson, J. Lucifer's tears

Thompson, V. Murder on Fifth Avenue

Todd, C. A duty to the dead

Tolkien, S. The king of diamonds

Transgressions

Turow, S. The burden of proof

Turow, S. Presumed innocent

Tursten, H. Night rounds

Ulfelder, S. Purgatory chasm

Upson, N. Two for sorrow

Vine, B. No night is too long

Walker, M. The crowded grave

Walter, J. Citizen Vince

Walters, M. The echo

Westlake, D. E. The hook

Westlake, D. E. What's the worst that could happen?

Whittle, T. Blood, Ash, and Bone

Whittle, T. The Dangerous Edge of Things

Whittle, T. Darker than any shadow

Williams, W. J. The fourth wall

Wilson, R. Capital Punishment

Winspear, J. Among the mad

Winspear, J. Birds of a feather

Winspear, J. Elegy for Eddie

Winspear, J. An incomplete revenge

Winspear, J. Leaving Everything Most Loved

Winspear, J. Maisie Dobbs

Winspear, J. The mapping of love and death

Winspear, J. Messenger of truth

Winspear, J. Pardonable lies

Winters, B. H. The last policeman

Wortham, R. The rock hole

Zimmerman, J. The orphanmaster

MYSTERY FICTION -- JUVENILE FICTION

Tallis, F. Death and the maiden

MYSTERY FILMS *See* Motion pictures

MYSTERY GRAPHIC NOVELS *See* Graphic novels

The **mystery** of Edwin Drood. Dickens, C.

MYSTERY RADIO PROGRAMS *See* Radio programs

MYSTERY STORIES *See* Mystery fiction

MYSTERY TELEVISION PROGRAMS *See* Television programs

MYSTERY WRITERS

Atkins, A. Devil's garden

Chandler, R. Raymond Chandler

Cullin, M. A slight trick of the mind

Deaver, J. Carte blanche: 007

Faulks, S. Devil may care

Goldsborough, R. The missing chapter

Hockensmith, S. Holmes on the range

Hockensmith, S. On the wrong track

Horowitz, A. The House of Silk

King, L. R. The beekeeper's apprentice, or, On the segregation of the queen

King, L. R. The game

King, L. R. The god of the hive

King, L. R. Justice Hall

King, L. R. A letter of Mary

King, L. R. Locked rooms

King, L. R. The moor

King, L. R. O Jerusalem

King, L. R. Pirate king

Meyer, N. The seven-per-cent solution

Meyer, N. The West End horror

Moore, G. The Sherlockian

Parker, R. B. Perchance to dream

Pirie, D. The patient's eyes

Robertson, M. The brothers of Baker Street

Simmons, D. Drood

The **mystic** arts of erasing all signs of death. Huston, C.

Mystic river. Lehane, D.

Mystical paths. Howatch, S.

MYSTICAL THEOLOGY *See* Mysticism

MYSTICISM

Erdrich, L. Four souls

Hesse, H. Siddhartha

Llywelyn, M. Druids

McEwan, I. Black dogs

Wiesel, E. Twilight

Zimler, R. The last kabbalist of Lisbon

MYSTICISM -- FICTION

Bennett, R. J. The troupe

MYSTICISM -- ISLAM *See* Islam

MYSTICISM -- JUDAISM *See* Judaism

MYTHICAL ANIMALS *See* Mythology

MYTHOLOGY

Gaiman, N. American gods

Lewis, C. S. Till we have faces

Momaday, N. S. The ancient child

Murdoch, I. The green knight

Simmons, D. Ilium

Simmons, D. Olympos

MYTHOLOGY, GREEK *See* Greek mythology

MYTHOLOGY, NORSE

Byatt, A. S. Ragnarok

MYTHS *See* Mythology

N

N is for noose. Grafton, S.

NATIONAL SECURITY -- KOREA (NORTH)
Church, J. A drop of Chinese blood
NATIONAL SELF-DETERMINATION *See* Nationalism
NATIONAL SOCIALISM
> *See also* Fascism; World War, 1939-1945 -- Causes

Amis, M. Time's arrow
Bolano, R. Nazi literature in the Americas
Browne, M. Eye of the abyss
Cussler, C. Atlantis found
Deaver, J. Garden of beasts
Dick, P. K. The man in the high castle
Faulks, S. Charlotte Gray
Forsyth, F. The Odessa file
Furst, A. Kingdom of shadows
Furst, A. Red gold
Grass, G. Dog years
Griffin, W. E. B. Blood and honor
Griffin, W. E. B. Honor bound
Griffin, W. E. B. Secret honor
Hall, A. The Quiller memorandum
Hansen, R. Hitler's niece
Harris, R. Fatherland
Hegi, U. Children and fire
Hegi, U. Stones from the river
Higgins, J. Cold Harbour
Hijuelos, O. A simple Habana melody: from when the world was good
Iles, G. Black cross
Keneally, T. Schindler's list
Korda, M. Worldly goods
Littell, J. The kindly ones
Lourie, R. A hatred for tulips
Ludlum, R. The apocalypse watch
Ludlum, R. The Holcroft covenant
Ludlum, R. The Scarlatti inheritance
MacInnes, H. Above suspicion
Moore, B. The statement
Pottinger, S. The last Nazi
Ramirez Mercado, S. A thousand deaths plus one
Schlink, B. The reader
Shaw, I. The young lions
Tournier, M. The ogre
Ullman, E. By blood
Uris, L. Mila 18
Vollmann, W. T. Europe central
Volpi, J. In search of Klingsor
NATIONAL SONGS *See* Songs
NATIONALISM
Grass, G. The call of the toad
Werfel, F. The forty days of Musa Dagh
NATIONALISM -- TURKEY -- FICTION
Silent house
NATIVE AMERICAN ART *See* Art
NATIVE AMERICAN AUTHORS *See* Authors

NATIVE AMERICAN CHILDREN *See* Children
NATIVE AMERICAN GAMES *See* Games; Native Americans -- Social life and customs
NATIVE AMERICAN LANGUAGES *See* Language and languages
NATIVE AMERICAN MEDICINE *See* Medicine
NATIVE AMERICAN MUSIC *See* Music
NATIVE AMERICAN WOMEN
> *See* Women

Perry, T. Poison flower
NATIVE AMERICANS
> *See also* Indigenous peoples

Alexie, S. Blasphemy
Boyden, J. Three-day road
Brooks, G. Caleb's crossing
Koplan, G. Magic words
NATIVE AMERICANS -- ANTIQUITIES *See* Antiquities
NATIVE AMERICANS -- CAPTIVITIES *See* Frontier and pioneer life
NATIVE AMERICANS -- EDUCATION *See* Education
NATIVE AMERICANS -- HUNTING *See* Hunting
NATIVE AMERICANS -- RELIGION *See* Religion
NATIVE AMERICANS -- RITES AND CEREMONIES *See* Rites and ceremonies
NATIVE AMERICANS -- WYOMING
Johnson, C. Another man's moccasins
NATIVE PEOPLES *See* Indigenous peoples
Native son. Wright, R.
Native tongue. Hiaasen, C.
NATIVES *See* Indigenous peoples
The **natural.** Malamud, B.
Natural born charmer. Phillips, S. E.
Natural born hustler. Turner, N.
Natural born liar. Noire (Author)
NATURAL CHILDBIRTH *See* Childbirth
NATURAL DISASTERS
> *See also* Disasters

Walker, K. T. The age of miracles
NATURAL FOODS *See* Food
Natural history. Howard, M.
NATURAL HISTORY -- ICELAND -- 19TH CENTURY
The blue fox
A **natural** history of dragons. Brennan, M.
NATURAL LAW *See* Ethics; Law
NATURAL MONUMENTS *See* Landscape protection; Monuments; Nature conservation
NATURAL SELECTION *See* Genetics; Variation (Biology)
NATURALISTS
> *See also* Scientists

Anderson, A. Darwin's wink

Kallos, S. Sing them home

Powers, R. The echo maker

Schaffert, T. The coffins of Little Hope

Ward, L. Outside valentine

NEBRASKA -- 19TH CENTURY

Cather, W. My Antonia

Cather, W. O pioneers!

NEBRASKA -- FICTION

Cather, W. My Antonia

Cather, W. O pioneers!

Harrison, J. The road home

Schaffert, T. The coffins of Little Hope

NEBULA AWARD *See* Literary prizes; Science fiction

Nebula Awards Showcase 2013.

The **necessary** beggar. Palwick, S.

Necessary evil. Tregillis, I.

Necessary heartbreak. Sullivan, M. J.

NECROMANCY *See* Divination; Magic

Nectar in a sieve. Markandaya, K.

Needful things. King, S.

NEEDLEPOINT *See* Embroidery; Needlework

NEEDLEWORK

Hendrie, L. Remember me

NEGRO LEAGUES *See* Baseball

NEGROES *See* African Americans; Blacks

The **neighbor.** Gardner, L.

NEIGHBORHOOD

Greenfeld, K. T. Triburbia

McCall Smith, A. A conspiracy of friends

NEIGHBORHOODS -- ENGLAND -- LONDON

McCall Smith, A. A conspiracy of friends

Neighbors. Berger, T.

NEIGHBORS

Baxter, C. The feast of love

Berger, T. Neighbors

Cheever, J. Bullet Park

Gowdy, B. The romantic

Hagedorn, J. T. Toxicology

Hamilton, J. A map of the world

Haslett, A. Union Atlantic

Hedges, P. The Heights

Hensher, P. The northern clemency

Hoffman, A. Illumination night

Hoover, M. The quickening

Lively, P. Spiderweb

McCall Smith, A. Corduroy mansions

McFadden, B. L. Sugar

McKinney-Whetstone, D. Leaving Cecil Street

Mendelson, C. Morningside Heights

Mengestu, D. The beautiful things that heaven bears

Miller, S. For love

Ochsner, G. Russian dreambook of color and flight

Parker, T. J. California girl

Rendell, R. Tigerlily's orchids

Schine, C. The New Yorkers

Shreve, A. Eden Close

Simonson, H. Major Pettigrew's last stand

Stuckey-French, E. Revenge of the radioactive lady

Thornton, T. The alternative hero

Unsworth, B. After Hannibal

NEIGHBORS -- FICTION

O'Donnell, L. The death of bees

Nekropolis. McHugh, M. F.

Nelson, Horatio Nelson, Viscount, 1758-1805

About

Sontag, S. The volcano lover

Unsworth, B. Losing Nelson

Nemesis. Roth, P.

NEO-FASCISM *See* Fascism; Neo-Nazis

NEO-NAZIS *See* Fascism

NEOLITHIC PERIOD *See* Stone Age

NEON GENESIS EVANGELION (FICTIONAL ROBOT) *See* Fictional robots; Manga; Mecha

NEPAL -- FICTION

Desai, K. The inheritance of loss

Upadhyay, S. The guru of love

NEPAL -- KATHMANDU

Upadhyay, S. The guru of love

The **nephew.** Purdy, J.

NEPHEWS

Dennis, P. Auntie Mame

Gross, A. Eyes wide open

Nabokov, V. V. King, queen, knave

Ozick, C. Foreign bodies

Rosenberg, N. T. Interest of justice

Wood, S. Wrecker

Neptune's brood. Stross, C.

Nero, Emperor of Rome, 37-68

About

Sienkiewicz, H. Quo Vadis

The **Neruda** case. Ampuero, R.

Neruda, Pablo, 1904-1973

About

Ampuero, R. The Neruda case

Nerve. Francis, D.

Nerve damage. Abrahams, P.

NERVOUS BREAKDOWN

Kavenna, J. Inglorious

Marlette, D. Magic time

Wilson, R. The blind man of Seville

NERVOUS SYSTEM -- DISEASES

See also Diseases

Kellogg, M. Tell me that you love me, Junie Moon

Netherland. O'Neill, J.

NETHERLANDS

Bakker, G. The twin

Keilson, H. Comedy in a minor key

MacLean, A. Floodgate

Maguire, G. Confessions of an ugly stepsister

Moor, M. d. The storm

Knowles, J. A separate peace
Levin, I. The Stepford wives
Minot, S. Monkeys
Rice, L. Home fires
Strout, E. Amy and Isabelle
Theroux, P. Picture palace

NEW ENGLAND -- FICTION
Irving, J. In one person
New England white. Carter, S. L.

NEW FOREST (ENGLAND)
Rutherfurd, E. The forest

NEW GUINEA
Jones, L. Mister Pip

NEW HAMPSHIRE
Banks, R. Affliction
Beattie, A. My life, starring Dara Falcon
Bohjalian, C. The night strangers
Brown, R. Before and after
Delinsky, B. Lake news
Hegi, U. The vision of Emma Blau
Irving, J. Last night in Twisted River
Irving, J. A prayer for Owen Meany
Lipman, E. The dearly departed
Maynard, J. Labor Day
Patterson, R. N. The final judgment
Picoult, J. Keeping Faith
Picoult, J. Nineteen minutes
Sarton, M. Kinds of love
Shreve, A. Body surfing
Shreve, A. Light on snow
Shreve, A. Sea glass
Updike, J. Memories of the Ford Administration
Williams, A. J. Down from Cascom Mountain

NEW HAMPSHIRE -- 19TH CENTURY
Benet, S. V. The Devil and Daniel Webster
Lent, J. Lost nation
Shreve, A. Fortune's Rocks

NEW HAMPSHIRE -- 20TH CENTURY
Banks, R. Affliction
Beattie, A. My life, starring Dara Falcon
Brown, R. Before and after
Delinsky, B. Lake news
Picoult, J. Keeping Faith
Shreve, A. Sea glass
Updike, J. Memories of the Ford Administration

NEW HAMPSHIRE -- FICTION
Banks, R. Affliction
Brown, R. Before and after
Costello, M. Big if
Hegi, U. The vision of Emma Blau
Irving, J. A prayer for Owen Meany
Lent, J. Lost nation
Lipman, E. The dearly departed
Perry, T. Death benefits
Picoult, J. Nineteen minutes
Shreve, A. Sea glass

NEW JERSEY
Clark, M. H. The cradle will fall
Clark, M. H. On the street where you live
Coben, H. The innocent
Coben, H. Caught
Coben, H. Gone for good
Coben, H. The woods
Colfer, E. Plugged
Diaz, J. The brief wondrous life of Oscar Wao
Dische, I. The Empress of Weehawken
Dunning, J. Two o'clock, eastern wartime
Ford, R. Independence Day
Ford, R. The lay of the land
Grodstein, L. A friend of the family
Meno, J. The boy detective fails
Michaud, J. When Tito loved Clara
Price, R. Clockers
Price, R. Freedomland
Price, R. Samaritan
Prose, F. My new American life
Rosenfelt, D. Don't tell a soul
Roth, P. American pastoral
Updike, J. The poorhouse fair
Updike, J. Terrorist
Wolitzer, M. The uncoupling
Woo, S. J. Everything Asian

NEW JERSEY -- 18TH CENTURY
Fleming, T. J. Dreams of glory

NEW JERSEY -- 20TH CENTURY
Clark, M. H. The cradle will fall
Clark, M. H. On the street where you live
Ford, R. Independence Day
Price, R. Clockers
Roth, P. American pastoral
Updike, J. The poorhouse fair

NEW JERSEY -- ATLANTIC CITY
Dezenhall, E. Money wanders
Leonard, E. Glitz
Reuss, F. Henry of Atlantic City

NEW JERSEY -- FICTION
Brennert, A. Palisades Park
Caldwell, I. The rule of four
Clark, M. H. On the street where you live
Coben, H. The innocent
Coben, H. Caught
Coben, H. Gone for good
Dermansky, M. Twins
Evanovich, J. One for the money
Evanovich, J. Three to get deadly
Ford, R. The lay of the land
Levitt, P. M. Come with me to Babylon
Perrotta, T. Joe College
Price, R. Freedomland
Roth, P. American pastoral
Roth, P. The plot against America
Updike, J. Terrorist

Robb, J. D. Naked in death
Ross, A. Mr. Peanut
Rossner, J. August
Roth, H. A diving rock on the Hudson
Roth, H. From bondage
Roth, H. Requiem for Harlem
Roth, P. The dying animal
Runyon, D. Guys and dolls
Saint, H. F. Memoirs of an invisible man
Salinger, J. D. The catcher in the rye
Salinger, J. D. Franny & Zooey
Salinger, J. D. Raise high the roof beam, carpenters, and Seymour: an introduction
Sanders, L. The sixth commandment
Schwartz, L. S. The fatigue artist
Shakar, A. Luminarium
Shaw, I. Bread upon the waters
Shelby, P. Gatekeeper
Sheldon, S. Rage of angels
Singer, I. B. Shadows on the Hudson
Slattery, B. F. Spaceman blues
Tanenbaum, R. Act of revenge
Tanenbaum, R. Hoax
Towles, A. Rules of civility
Trigiani, A. Very Valentine
Uhnak, D. Codes of betrayal
Van Slyke, H. Public smiles, private tears
Wellington, D. Monster Island
Westlake, D. E. Don't ask
Westlake, D. E. The hook
Westlake, D. E. Money for nothing
Westlake, D. E. Smoke
Wharton, E. The house of mirth
Wolcott, J. The catsitters
Wolfe, T. The web and the rock
Wolfe, T. You can't go home again
Wolfe, T. The bonfire of the vanities
Wray, J. Lowboy
Wright, R. The outsider

NEW YORK (N.Y.) -- 18TH CENTURY
Charyn, J. Johnny One-Eye
Liss, D. The whiskey rebels

NEW YORK (N.Y.) -- 19TH CENTURY
Bryson, E. The transformation of Bartholomew Fortuno
Busch, F. The night inspector
Carr, C. The alienist
Crane, S. Maggie: a girl of the streets (a story of New York)
Doctorow, E. L. The waterworks
Finney, J. Time and again
Millhauser, S. Martin Dressler
Piercy, M. Sex wars
Rose, J. Blackest bird
Swerling, B. City of promise
Vidal, G. 1876

Wharton, E. The age of innocence

NEW YORK (N.Y.) -- 20TH CENTURY
Auchincloss, L. The book class
Auchincloss, L. Her infinite variety
Baker, D. Young man with a horn
Baldwin, J. Another country
Bellow, S. Mr. Sammler's planet
Carcaterra, L. Apaches
Chabon, M. The amazing adventures of Kavalier and Clay
Clark, M. H. Before I say goodbye
Clark, M. H. A stranger is watching
Colwin, L. A big storm knocked it over
Colwin, L. Family happiness
Conroy, P. The prince of tides
Daley, R. Wall of brass
Davies, V. Miracle on 34th Street
Doctorow, E. L. City of God
Dos Passos, J. Manhattan transfer
Dreiser, T. Sister Carrie
Faulks, S. On Green Dolphin Street
Fitzgerald, F. S. The great Gatsby
Godey, J. The taking of Pelham one two three
Goudge, E. Garden of lies
Heller, J. Closing time
Helprin, M. Winter's tale
Hijuelos, O. Empress of the splendid season
Hunter, E. The blackboard jungle
Hunter, E. Candyland
Isaacs, S. Shining through
Jackson, C. The lost weekend
Kelly, T. Empire rising
Leavitt, D. The lost language of cranes
Malamud, B. The tenants
Miller, H. Tropic of Capricorn
Nathan, R. Portrait of Jennie
O'Hara, J. Butterfield 8
Ozick, C. The Puttermesser papers
Plath, S. The bell jar
Preston, D. Reliquary
Rand, A. The fountainhead
Rayner, R. The cloud sketcher
Rossner, J. August
Roth, H. A diving rock on the Hudson
Roth, H. From bondage
Roth, H. Requiem for Harlem
Roth, P. The dying animal
Saint, H. F. Memoirs of an invisible man
Salinger, J. D. The catcher in the rye
Salinger, J. D. Franny & Zooey
Salinger, J. D. Raise high the roof beam, carpenters, and Seymour: an introduction
Schwartz, L. S. The fatigue artist
Sheldon, S. Rage of angels
Singer, I. B. Enemies, a love story
Singer, I. B. Shadows on the Hudson

Stern, S. The angel of forgetfulness

Tax, M. Rivington Street

NEW YORK (N.Y.) -- MANHATTAN

Aciman, A. A. Eight white nights

Auchincloss, L. The book class

Auchincloss, L. Her infinite variety

Bank, M. The girls' guide to hunting and fishing

Beattie, A. Walks with men

Belle, J. The seven year bitch

Blackwell, E. Grub

Burke, A. Long gone

Bushnell, C. Lipstick jungle

Chazin, S. Flashover

Christensen, K. The great man

Clark, M. H. The shadow of your smile

Clay, H. Losing Charlotte

Close, J. Girls in white dresses

Collins, M. A. Black hats

Colwin, L. Happy all the time

Cunningham, M. By nightfall

Darnton, J. Black and white and dead all over

Darnton, J. Mind catcher

Davies, V. Miracle on 34th Street

Dee, J. The privileges

DeLillo, D. Cosmopolis

DeLillo, D. Falling man

Delson, R. Maynard and Jennica

Dennis, P. Auntie Mame

D'Erasmo, S. The sky below

Dierbeck, L. One pill makes you smaller

Doctorow, E. L. Homer & Langley

Donohue, J. J. Sensei

Dunne, D. People like us

Dunne, D. Too much money

Fairstein, L. Bad blood

Fairstein, L. The bone vault

Fairstein, L. Entombed

Fairstein, L. Killer heat

Faulks, S. On Green Dolphin Street

Ferrell, M. The answer is always yes

Fitzgerald, F. S. The beautiful and damned

Fitzgerald, F. S. The great Gatsby

Fonseca, I. Attachment

Gaitskill, M. Veronica

Glass, J. Three Junes

Goldman, W. Marathon man

Goldsmith, O. The First Wives Club

Goldsmith, O. Pen pals

Goodis, D. Nightfall

Goudge, E. Such devoted sisters

Gould, J. The best is yet to come

Grimes, M. Foul matter

Hagedorn, J. T. Toxicology

Harrison, C. The finder

Harrison, C. The Havana room

Heller, J. Best enemies

Heller, J. Good as Gold

Heller, Z. The believers

Herlihy, J. L. Midnight cowboy

Hijuelos, O. The Mambo Kings play songs of love

Howard, M. The rags of time

Hunt, S. The invention of everything else

Hunter, E. The moment she was gone

Hunter, E. Privileged conversation

Jaffe, R. The room-mating season

Kalfus, K. A disorder peculiar to the country

Kaufman, B. Up the down staircase

Kaufman, S. Diary of a mad housewife

Keillor, G. Love me

Kellerman, J. The genius

Kim, S. The interpreter

Korda, M. The fortune

Krauss, N. The history of love

Langer, A. The thieves of Manhattan

Leavitt, D. Martin Bauman

L'Engle, M. A severed wasp

Lethem, J. Chronic city

Levenkron, S. The best little girl in the world

Levin, I. Rosemary's baby

Lipman, E. The family man

Lynn, A. Now you see it

Malamud, B. The tenants

Mallon, T. Bandbox

Martin, V. The confessions of Edward Day

McCann, C. Let the great world spin

McElroy, J. Actress in the house

McGrath, P. Trauma

McInerney, J. The good life

McLaughlin, E. The nanny diaries

McLaughlin, E. Nanny returns

McPhee, J. No ordinary matter

McPhee, M. Dear money

Meltzer, B. Dead even

Mendelson, C. Morningside Heights

Messud, C. The emperor's children

O'Hara, J. Butterfield 8

O'Neill, J. Netherland

Packer, A. The dive from Clausen's pier

Park, E. Personal days

Peacock, J. Blind man's alley

Pearson, T. R. Blue Ridge

Percy, W. The last gentleman

Preston, D. The cabinet of curiosities

Price, R. The good priest's son

Prose, F. Household saints

Rinaldi, N. Between two rivers

Robinson, R. Sweetwater

Rosen, J. Joy comes in the morning

Roth, P. Exit ghost

Sanders, L. The tenth commandment

Saul, J. Midnight voices

Schine, C. The New Yorkers

Cheever, J. Bullet Park

Cook, T. H. Instruments of night

Dreiser, T. An American tragedy

Godwin, G. The finishing school

Hansen, R. Mariette in ecstasy

Lee A gesture life

Oates, J. C. Because it is bitter, and because it is my heart

Oates, J. C. Broke heart blues

Oates, J. C. Foxfire

Oates, J. C. I lock my door upon myself

Oates, J. C. Middle age

Oates, J. C. We were the Mulvaneys

Perry, T. Shadow woman

Prose, F. Primitive people

Puzo, M. The godfather

Quindlen, A. Object lessons

Russo, R. Nobody's fool

Russo, R. The risk pool

Shreve, A. Eden Close

Straub, P. Ghost story

Strieber, W. The forbidden zone

Westlake, D. E. Drowned hopes

Winegardner, M. The Godfather returns

NEW YORK (STATE) -- 21ST CENTURY

Shriver, L. We need to talk about Kevin

NEW YORK (STATE) -- ALBANY

Kennedy, W. Chango's beads and two-tone shoes

Kennedy, W. Ironweed

Kennedy, W. Roscoe

Kennedy, W. Very old bones

NEW YORK (STATE) -- BUFFALO

Baxter, C. The soul thief

Reisman, N. The first desire

NEW YORK (STATE) -- COOPERSTOWN

Cooper, J. F. The pioneers

NEW YORK (STATE) -- CORINTH

Lurie, A. The war between the Tates

NEW YORK (STATE) -- FICTION

Groff, L. Arcadia

NEW YORK (STATE) -- ITHACA

O'Nan, S. The names of the dead

NEW YORK (STATE) -- NIAGARA FALLS

Oates, J. C. The falls

Oates, J. C. Rape

NEW YORK (STATE) -- SYRACUSE

Abu-Jaber, D. Origin

NEW YORK (STATE) -- WESTCHESTER COUNTY

Boyle, T. C. World's end

Green, G. D. The juror

Jen, G. Mona in the promised land

Nayman, S. The listener

NEW YORK

Shumway, C. Ten girls to watch

Zimmerman, J. The orphanmaster

New York dead. Woods, S.

New York novels. Wharton, E.

NEW YORK REGION

Mansbach, A. The end of the Jews

New York Review Books classics [series]

Chatterjee, U. English, August

Simenon, G. The man who watched trains go by

Simenon, G. Strangers in the house

Tolstaia, T. White walls

NEW YORKER (PERIODICAL)

Keillor, G. Love me

The **New** Yorker stories. Beattie, A.

The **New** Yorkers. Schine, C.

NEW ZEALAND

Hulme, K. The bone people

Tremain, R. The color

Uris, L. Redemption

NEW ZEALAND -- 19TH CENTURY

Goudge, E. Green Dolphin Street

NEW ZEALAND -- FICTION

Grenville, K. Sarah Thornhill

NEW ZEALANDERS -- ENGLAND

Frame, J. Towards another summer

NEW ZEALANDERS -- FRANCE

Knox, E. Daylight

NEWARK (N.J.)

Parks, B. The girl next door

Roth, P. Nemesis

Roth, P. The human stain

NEWFOUNDLAND

Lundrigan, N. Glass boys

The **newlyweds.** Freudenberger, N.

NEWLYWEDS

Freudenberger, N. The newlyweds

The **news** from Spain. Wickersham, J.

NEWS PHOTOGRAPHERS

Belfer, L. A fierce radiance

Just, W. S. Exiles in the garden

Leimbach, M. The man from Saigon

Menendez, A. The last war

Soli, T. The lotus eaters

The **news** where you are. O'Flynn, C.

NEWSLETTERS See Journalism; Newspapers

NEWSPAPER ADVERTISING See Advertising; Newspapers

NEWSPAPER EDITORS

Rachman, T. The imperfectionists

NEWSPAPER EMPLOYEES

Scott, A. D. Beneath the abbey wall

NEWSPAPER EXECUTIVES

Safire, W. Scandalmonger

NEWSPAPERS

Akst, D. The Webster chronicle

Darnton, J. Black and white and dead all over

Hamill, P. Tabloid city

Rachman, T. The imperfectionists

Night, Dawn, The accident: three tales. Wiesel, E.

Nightbringer. Huggins, J. B.

Nightcrawlers. Pronzini, B.

Nightfall. Goodis, D.

The nightingale. Sholem Aleichem

Nightingale, Florence, 1820-1910
About
Shomer, E. The twelve rooms of the Nile

The nightingales of Troy. Fulton, A.

Nightlife. Perry, T.

Nightmare town. Hammett, D.

Nightmares & dreamscapes. King, S.

Nights at the circus. Carter, A.

Nights in Rodanthe. Sparks, N.

Nights of Villjamur. Newton, M. C.

Nighttime is my time. Clark, M. H.

Nightwood. Barnes, D.

Nightwoods. Frazier, C.

Nightwoods. Frazier, C.

NILE RIVER
Shomer, E. The twelve rooms of the Nile

Nimitz class. Robinson, P.

Nine coaches waiting. Stewart, M.

Nine dragons. Connelly, M.

Nine princes in Amber. Zelazny, R.

Nine stories. Salinger, J. D.

The nine tailors. Sayers, D. L.

NINETEEN EIGHTIES See World history -- 20th century

Nineteen eighty-four. Orwell, G.

NINETEEN FIFTIES
See also World history -- 20th century
Godwin, G. Unfinished desires
Kennedy, W. Chango's beads and two-tone shoes
Mallon, T. Fellow travelers
Phillips, J. A. Lark and Termite

NINETEEN FORTIES See World history -- 20th century

Nineteen minutes. Picoult, J.

NINETEEN NINETIES See World history -- 20th century

NINETEEN SEVENTIES
See also World history -- 20th century
Amis, M. The pregnant widow
Beard, J. A. In Zanesville
Hannah, K. Firefly Lane
McCann, C. Let the great world spin

NINETEEN SIXTIES
See also World history -- 20th century
Groff, L. Arcadia

NINETEEN THIRTIES See World history -- 20th century

NINETEEN TWENTIES
See also World history -- 20th century
Lehane, D. Live by night

Ninety-two in the shade. McGuane, T.

The ninth step. Jerkins, G.

Nip the buds, shoot the kids. Oe, K.

NISEI See Japanese Americans

NITRATES See Chemicals; Fertilizers

No birds sing. Bannister, J.

No body. Pickard, N.

No country for old men. McCarthy, C.

No crystal stair. Rutland, E.

No defense. Wilhelm, K.

No good deeds. Lippman, L.

No graves as yet. Perry, A.

No greater love. Steel, D.

No laughing matter. Simpson, D.

No longer a gentleman. Putney, M. J.

No man's dog. Jackson, J. A.

No more heroes. Banks, R.

No night is too long. Vine, B.

No one belongs here more than you. July, M.

No one is here except all of us. Ausubel, R.

No one you know. Richmond, M.

No ordinary matter. McPhee, J.

No place for heroes. Restrepo, L.

No place like home. Clark, M. H.

No place like home. Samuel, B.

No proper lady. Cooper, I.

No safe place. Patterson, R. N.

No saints or angels. Klima, I.

No second chance. Coben, H.

No time like the present. Gordimer, N.

No time to wave goodbye. Mitchard, J.

No witnesses. Pearson, R.

No. 1 Ladies Detective Agency [series]
McCall Smith, A. The Limpopo Academy of Private Detection
McCall Smith, A. The good husband of Zebra Drive

The No. 1 Ladies' Detective Agency. McCall Smith, A.

NO. 1 LADIES' DETECTIVE AGENCY (IMAGINARY ORGANIZATION)
McCall Smith, A. The Limpopo Academy of Private Detection
McCall Smith, A. The No. 1 Ladies' Detective Agency
McCall Smith, A. The Saturday big tent wedding party
McCall Smith, A. Tea time for the traditionally built

Noah (Biblical figure)
About
Maine, D. The preservationist

Noah's compass. Tyler, A.

NOBEL LAUREATES FOR LITERATURE
Coetzee, J. M. Summertime
Cooley, M. The archivist
Hunt, R. Mr. Chartwell

Huyler, F. The laws of invisible things
Inman, R. Captain Saturday
Kingsolver, B. The lacuna
Kostova, E. The swan thieves
Malone, M. The four corners of the sky
McCorkle, J. Carolina moon
McCrumb, S. The ballad of Tom Dooley
McCrumb, S. The songcatcher
Medlicott, J. A. Gardens of Covington
Medlicott, J. A. The ladies of Covington send their love
Patterson, J. Four blind mice
Pearson, T. R. A short history of a small place
Percy, W. The second coming
Pessl, M. Special topics in calamity physics
Price, R. Blue Calhoun
Price, R. The good priest's son
Price, R. Kate Vaiden
Price, R. The promise of rest
Price, R. Roxanna Slade
Price, R. The tongues of angels
Rash, R. Serena
Ross, A. B. Miss Julia throws a wedding
Smith, L. On Agate Hill
Sparks, N. The notebook
Sparks, N. A bend in the road
Sparks, N. The guardian
Sparks, N. The last song
Sparks, N. Nights in Rodanthe
Sparks, N. A walk to remember
Truong, M. Bitter in the mouth
Tyler, A. A slipping-down life
Tyler, A. The tin can tree
Wolfe, T. The web and the rock
Zuber, I. Salt

NORTH CAROLINA -- 18TH CENTURY
Gabaldon, D. A breath of snow and ashes
Gabaldon, D. An echo in the bone

NORTH CAROLINA -- 19TH CENTURY
Crafts, H. The bondswomans narrative
Humphreys, J. Nowhere else on earth
Slouka, M. God's fool
Trotter, W. R. The sands of pride

NORTH CAROLINA -- 20TH CENTURY
Adams, A. A southern exposure
Betts, D. Souls raised from the dead
Edgerton, C. Walking across Egypt
Gibbons, K. Charms for the easy life
Godwin, G. Evensong
Godwin, G. A mother and two daughters
Medlicott, J. A. The ladies of Covington send their love
Percy, W. The second coming
Price, R. Kate Vaiden
Price, R. Roxanna Slade
Ross, A. B. Miss Julia throws a wedding

Sparks, N. The notebook
Sparks, N. A bend in the road
Sparks, N. Nights in Rodanthe
Sparks, N. A walk to remember
Tyler, A. A slipping-down life
Tyler, A. The tin can tree
Wolfe, T. The web and the rock
Zuber, I. Salt

NORTH CAROLINA -- FICTION
Gabaldon, D. The fiery cross
Smith, D. The Crossroads Cafe

NORTH CAROLINA -- HISTORY -- 20TH CENTURY
Frazier, C. Nightwoods

NORTH CAROLINA -- HISTORY -- COLONIAL PERIOD, CA. 1600-1775
Gabaldon, D. The fiery cross

NORTH CAROLINA -- RURAL CONDITIONS
Frazier, C. Nightwoods

NORTH DAKOTA
Erdrich, L. The Beet Queen
Erdrich, L. The last report on the miracles at Little No Horse
Erdrich, L. The Master Butchers Singing Club
Erdrich, L. The plague of doves
Erdrich, L. Tracks
Grimes, M. Dakota
Klosterman, C. Downtown Owl
Power, S. The grass dancer

NORTH DAKOTA -- 19TH CENTURY
Jones, D. C. Arrest Sitting Bull

NORTH DAKOTA -- 20TH CENTURY
Erdrich, L. The Beet Queen
Erdrich, L. The last report on the miracles at Little No Horse
Erdrich, L. Tracks
Power, S. The grass dancer

North of Montana. Smith, A.
North of nowhere, south of loss. Hospital, J. T.
North Star. Wheeler, R. S.

NORTHAMPTON, HELENA VON SNAKENBORG, MARCHIONESS OF, 1549-1635
About
Byrd, S. Roses have thorns
Northanger Abbey. Austen, J.
NORTHEAST PASSAGE See Arctic regions; Exploration; Voyages and travels
The **northern** clemency. Hensher, P.
NORTHERN IRELAND
The dream of the Celt
NORTHERN IRELAND -- BELFAST
Dean, L. This human season
Moore, B. The lonely passion of Judith Hearne
Rankin, I. Watchman
NORTHERN IRELAND -- HISTORY -- 1969-1994

Ferrante, E. Troubling love

Gaddis, W. Agape agape

Gander, F. As a friend

Garcia Marquez, G. Chronicle of a death foretold

Garcia Marquez, G. Collected novellas

Gibbons, K. Ellen Foster

Grimes, M. The train now departing: two novellas

Gurganus, A. The practical heart

Hale, E. E. The man without a country

Hamner, E. The homecoming

Handke, P. Don Juan

Handke, P. The left-handed woman

Harrison, J. The farmer's daughter

Hemingway, E. The Hemingway reader

Hemingway, E. The torrents of spring

Hill, O. The incredible Double

Hilton, J. Good-bye Mr. Chips

Hoban, R. Linger awhile

Howard, M. Big as life

Hrabal, B. Too loud a solitude

The Hugo winners

James, H. Complete stories, 1864-1874

James, H. Complete stories, 1874-1884

James, H. Complete stories, 1884-1891

James, H. Complete stories, 1892-1898

James, H. Complete stories, 1898-1910

James, H. The complete tales of Henry James

James, H. The Henry James reader

James, H. Short novels of Henry James

James, H. What Maisie knew, In the cage, The pupil

Johnson, D. Train dreams

Kafka, F. Metamorphosis

Kasischke, L. Eden Springs

Kawabata, Y. Snow country, and Thousand cranes

Kawabata, Y. Thousand cranes

Keilson, H. Comedy in a minor key

Kertesz, I. Detective story

King, S. Blockade Billy

King, S. Different seasons

King, S. Four past midnight

King, S. Full dark, no stars

Kundera, M. Slowness

Le Guin, U. K. Four ways to forgiveness

Lessing, D. M. The fifth child

Levin, I. The Stepford wives

London, J. The call of the wild

Makine, A. Music of a life

Manchette Fatale

Mann, T. The black swan

Mann, T. Death in Venice

Martin, S. The pleasure of my company

Martin, S. Shopgirl

McEwan, I. Black dogs

Merimee, P. Carmen

Messud, C. The hunters

Millhauser, S. The king in the tree: three novellas

Minot, S. Monkeys

Minot, S. Rapture

Moody, R. Right livelihoods

Munoz Molina, A. In her absence

Nemirovsky, I. Fire in the blood

Nin, A. Cities of the interior

Oates, J. C. Black water

Oates, J. C. I lock my door upon myself

Oates, J. C. Rape

Oster, C. My big apartment

Otsuka, J. The Buddha in the attic

Otsuka, J. When the emperor was divine

Oz, A. Panther in the basement

Ozick, C. The Messiah of Stockholm

Pelevin, V. The hall of singing caryatids

Poe, E. A. The imaginary voyages: The narrative of Arthur Gordon Pym; The unparalleled adventure of one Hans Pfaall; The journal of Julius Rodman

Porter, K. A. Pale horse, pale rider: three short novels

Potok, C. Old men at midnight

Rand, A. Anthem

Rendell, R. Heartstones

Richardson, C. S. The end of the alphabet

Rosales, G. The halfway house

Rosero, E. Good offices

Roth, P. The dying animal

Roth, P. The humbling

Sagan, F. Bonjour tristesse

Salinger, J. D. Franny & Zooey

Salinger, J. D. Raise high the roof beam, carpenters, and Seymour: an introduction

Sand, G. Marianne

Savage, S. Firmin

Segal, E. Love story

Shapton, L. Important artifacts and personal property from the collection of Lenore Doolan and Harold Morris, including books, street fashion, and jewelry

Simenon, G. Maigret and the fortune-teller

Simenon, G. Maigret and the Saturday caller

Simenon, G. Maigret goes home

Simmons, D. Muse of fire

Simon, C. The trolley

Sorrentino, G. The abyss of human illusion

Spark, M. The Abbess of Crewe

Spark, M. The driver's seat

Stahlberg, L. Billy Budd, sailor

Steinbeck, J. Of mice and men

Steinbeck, J. The pearl

Stevenson, R. L. The strange case of Dr. Jekyll and Mr. Hyde

Straub, P. A special place

Theroux, P. The Elephanta suite

Theroux, P. Half Moon Street

Novels and other writings. West, N.

Novels and stories. Hurston, Z. N.

Novels and stories. Jackson, S.

Novels and stories, 1920-1922. Fitzgerald, F. S.

Novels and stories, 1932-1937. Steinbeck, J.

NOVELS IN LETTERS *See* Epistolary fiction

Novels, 1875-1886. Howells, W. D.

Novels, 1886-1888. Howells, W. D.

Novels, 1920-1925. Dos Passos, J.

Novels, 1926-1929. Faulkner, W.

Novels, 1930-1935. Faulkner, W.

Novels, 1930-1942. Powell, D.

Novels, 1936-1940. Faulkner, W.

Novels, 1942-1952. Steinbeck, J.

Novels, 1942-1954. Faulkner, W.

Novels, 1944-1953. Bellow, S.

Novels, 1944-1962. Powell, D.

Novels, 1955-1962. Nabokov, V. V.

Novels, 1956-1964. Bellow, S.

Novels, 1957-1962. Faulkner, W.

Novels, 1967-1972. Roth, P.

Novels, 1969-1974. Nabokov, V. V.

Novels, 1970-1982. Bellow, S.

Novels, 1973-1977. Roth, P.

Novels, 1993-1995. Roth, P.

The **November** criminals. Munson, S.

Now and then. Parker, R. B.

Now is the time to open your heart. Walker, A.

Now or never. Adler, E.

Now you see him. Gottlieb, E.

Now you see it. Lynn, A.

Now you see me. Bolton, S. J.

Nowhere but home. Palmer, L.

The **nowhere** city. Lurie, A.

Nowhere else on earth. Humphreys, J.

Nowhere man. Hemon, A.

Nowhere near respectable. Putney, M. J.

Nowhere to run. Daley, R.

Nowhere to run. Box, C. J.

NUCLEAR MEDICINE *See* Medicine

NUCLEAR PHYSICISTS

Millet, L. Oh pure and radiant heart

NUCLEAR PHYSICS *See* Physics

NUCLEAR POWER PLANTS

Pohl, F. Chernobyl

NUCLEAR POWER PLANTS -- FIRES AND FIRE PREVENTION *See* Fire prevention; Fires

NUCLEAR SUBMARINES

See also Nuclear propulsion; Submarines

Clancy, T. The hunt for Red October

Coonts, S. America

MacLean, A. Ice Station Zebra

NUCLEAR WARFARE

See also War

Burdick, E. Fail-safe

Frank, P. Alas, Babylon

Shute, N. On the beach

West, M. L. The clowns of God

NUCLEAR WARFARE -- FICTION

Rosenberg, J. C. The twelfth Imam

NUCLEAR WARFARE -- PREVENTION

Rosenberg, J. C. Damascus Countdown

Rosenberg, J. C. The Tehran initiative

Rosenberg, J. C. The twelfth Imam

NUCLEAR WEAPONS

DeMille, N. Wild fire

Forsyth, F. The fourth protocol

Ignatius, D. The increment

Martini, S. P. Critical mass

Robinson, P. Nimitz class

Scholz, C. Radiance

NUCLEAR WEAPONS -- FICTION

Bond, L. Exit plan

Number 10. Townsend, S.

NUMBER THEORY *See* Algebra; Mathematics; Set theory

Number9dream. Mitchell, D.

Numbers don't lie. Bisson, T.

NUMEROLOGY *See* Occultism; Symbolism of numbers

NUMISMATICS *See* Ancient history; Archeology; History

The **nun's** story. Hulme, K.

NUNS

See also Women

Barrett, W. E. The lilies of the field

Clark, M. H. The shadow of your smile

Godden, R. Black Narcissus

Godwin, G. Unfinished desires

Hulme, K. The nun's story

Lanchester, J. Fragrant Harbor

L'Engle, M. The love letters

Robbins, T. Fierce invalids home from hot climates

Roberts, M. Reader, I married him

Salzman, M. Lying awake

Spark, M. The Abbess of Crewe

Steel, D. Amazing grace

Tremayne, P. Chalice of blood

Trussoni, D. Angelology

NUNS -- FICTION

Alfieri, A. City of silver

Bilyeau, N. The chalice

Coben, H. The innocent

Cross, J. Touched by venom

Sharratt, M. Illuminations

Nuns and soldiers. Murdoch, I.

Nureyev, Rudolf, 1938-1993

About

McCann, C. Dancer

NURSE MIDWIVES *See* Midwives

NURSEMAIDS

Styron, A. All the finest girls

NURSERY SCHOOLS

Glass, J. The widower's tale

NURSES -- CRIMES AGAINST

Robotham, M. Suspect

Tursten, H. Night rounds

NURSES -- ENGLAND

Todd, C. A duty to the dead

NURSES

Cameron, P. Coral Glynn

Keneally, T. The Daughters of Mars

Todd, C. A duty to the dead

NURSES AND NURSING

Coetzee, J. M. Slow man

Faulkner, W. Soldiers' pay

Hamilton, J. A map of the world

Hemingway, E. A farewell to arms

Holt, V. Secret for a nightingale

Hulme, K. The nun's story

Kesey, K. One flew over the cuckoo's nest

McCullough, C. An indecent obsession

McEwan, I. Atonement

Ondaatje, M. The English patient

Rinehart, M. R. Miss Pinkerton: adventures of a nurse detective

Straub, P. The Hellfire Club

Vine, B. The minotaur

NURSING *See* Medicine; Therapeutics

NURSING HOMES

Mestre-Reed, E. The second death of Unica Aveyano

Polsan/English Hash

Weldon, F. Rhode Island blues

NURSING HOMES -- FICTION

McCorkle, J. Life after life

NUTS *See* Food; Seeds

NW. Smith, Z.

NYUNGA (AUSTRALIAN PEOPLE)

Scott, K. That deadman dance

O

O Beulah Land. Settle, M. L.

O is for outlaw. Grafton, S.

O Jerusalem. King, L. R.

O lost. Wolfe, T.

O pioneers! Cather, W.

O'Malley, Grace, 1530?-1603?

About

Maxwell, R. The wild Irish

O'Sullivan Beare, Donal Cam, 1560-1618

About

Llywelyn, M. The last prince of Ireland

The **O.** Henry prize stories 2007.

O.K. West, P.

OAK *See* Trees; Wood

OAKLAND (CALIF.)

Chabon, M. Telegraph Avenue

The **oath.** Wiesel, E.

The **oath.** Lescroart, J. T.

OBELISKS *See* Archeology; Architecture; Monuments

OBESITY

LaValle, V. D. The ecstatic

Walters, M. The sculptress

Weiner, J. Good in bed

OBESITY -- FICTION

Attenberg, J. The Middlesteins

Magnin, J. The prayers of Agnes Sparrow

OBITUARIES -- GRAPHIC NOVELS

Bá, G. Daytripper

The **Obituary** Writer. Hood, A.

Object lessons. Quindlen, A.

Object lessons.

An **object** of beauty. Martin, S.

OBJETS D'ART *See* Art objects

Oblivion. Wallace, D. F.

OBSCENE MATERIALS *See* Obscenity (Law); Pornography

OBSCENITY (LAW) *See* Criminal law

OBSESSION (PSYCHOLOGY) *See* Obsessive-compulsive disorder

OBSESSIONS

Ackroyd, P. The fall of Troy

Bolaño, R. The skating rink

Erickson, S. Zeroville

King, R. The sound of butterflies

Klosterman, C. The visible man

Kostova, E. The swan thieves

McCauley, S. Alternatives to sex

Nayman, S. The listener

Pamuk, O. The museum of innocence

Phillips, A. The song is you

Smiley, J. Private life

Stamm, P. Seven years

Vargas Llosa, M. The bad girl

OBSESSIVE-COMPULSIVE DISORDER

See also Neuroses

Dicks, M. Unexpectedly, Milo

Martin, S. The pleasure of my company

OBSESSIVE-COMPULSIVE DISORDER -- FICTION

Alexander, H. Last resort

McEwan, I. Enduring love

Tillman, L. American genius

OBSESSIVE-COMPULSIVE NEUROSES *See* Obsessive-compulsive disorder

OBSTETRICS *See* Childbirth

Obstruction of justice. O'Shaughnessy, P.

Occam's razor. Mayor, A.

OCCULT FICTION

Aira, C. Ghosts

Barry, M. Lexicon

Bear, E. Shattered pillars

Belcher, R. S. The six-gun tarot

Bishop, A. Written in red

Bolano, R. Monsieur Pain

Bornikova, P. This case is gonna kill me

Carey, J. Dark currents

Cargill, C. R. Dreams and Shadows

Czerneda, J. E. A Turn of Light

Dellamonica, A. M. Indigo Springs

Held, R. Silver

Jemisin, N. K. The killing moon

Kiernan, C. R. Blood oranges

King, S. Christine

King, S. Needful things

King, S. Pet sematary

King, S. Rose Madder

Kleypas, L. Crystal Cove

Kowal, M. R. Without a summer

Krentz, J. A. Dream eyes

McOmber, A. The white forest

Michaels, B. Stitches in time

Modesitt, L. E. Imager

Modesitt, L. E. Imager's challenge

Modesitt, L. E. Imager's intrigue

Naylor, G. Mama Day

Percy, B. Red moon

Rice, A. The queen of the damned

Rice, A. The tale of the body thief

Rice, A. The witching hour

Shields, K. A Study in Revenge

Stanley, M. Deadly Harvest

Trussoni, D. Angelopolis

Zimmerman, J. The orphanmaster

OCCULT SCIENCES *See* Occultism

OCCULTISM

Bolano, R. Monsieur Pain

Eco, U. Foucault's pendulum

Gallagher, S. The kingdom of bones

Howe, K. The physick book of Deliverance Dane

King, S. Firestarter

Kurtz, K. Two crowns for America

LaValle, V. D. Big machine

Shannon, D. The Manson curse

Stross, C. The Fuller memorandum

Williams, C. Stairway to hell

OCCUPATIONAL ACCIDENTS *See* Industrial accidents

OCCUPATIONAL DISEASES *See* Diseases

OCCUPATIONAL INJURIES *See* Industrial accidents

OCCUPATIONAL RETRAINING *See* Employees -- Training; Labor supply; Occupational training; Technical education; Unemployed; Vocational education

OCCUPATIONAL THERAPY *See* Mental health; Physical therapy; Physically handicapped -- Rehabilitation; Therapeutics

Occupied city. Peace, D.

OCEAN

Verne, J. The extraordinary journeys: Twenty thousand leagues under the sea

OCEAN -- ECONOMIC ASPECTS *See* Marine resources; Shipping

The **Ocean** at the End of the Lane. Gaiman, N.

The **ocean** between us. Wiggs, S.

OCEAN BOTTOM *See* Ocean; Submarine geology

OCEAN CURRENTS *See* Navigation; Ocean

OCEAN LIFE *See* Marine biology

OCEAN LINERS

See also Ships

Rogan, C. The lifeboat

OCEAN TRANSPORTATION *See* Shipping

OCEAN TRAVEL

See also Transportation; Travel; Voyages and travels

Galbraith, D. The rising sun

Golding, W. Close quarters

Golding, W. Fire down below

Golding, W. Rites of passage

McCutchan, P. The last farewell

Moberg, V. The emigrants

Ondaatje, M. The cat's table

Porter, K. A. Ship of fools

Preston, D. The wheel of darkness

Villars, E. The Normandie affair

Woolf, V. The voyage out

OCEAN TRAVEL -- FICTION

Davies, J. D. The mountain of gold

OCEAN WAVES *See* Ocean; Waves

OCEANOGRAPHY -- RESEARCH *See* Research

OCEANS *See* Ocean

The **October** horse. McCullough, C.

The **octopus.** Norris, F.

Odd apocalypse. Koontz, D. R.

The **odds.** O'Nan, S.

Odds against tomorrow. Rich, N.

The **Odessa** file. Forsyth, F.

Odyssey. McDevitt, J.

Of blood and honey. Leicht, S.

Of human bondage. Maugham, W. S.

Of love and evil. Rice, A.

Of mice and men. Steinbeck, J.

Of time and the river. Wolfe, T.

Off Armageddon Reef. Weber, D.

Off Keck Road. Simpson, M.

Off the chart. Hall, J. W.

OFFENSES AGAINST PROPERTY *See* Crime; Criminal law

OFFENSES AGAINST PUBLIC SAFETY *See* Crime; Criminal law

OFFENSES AGAINST THE PERSON *See* Crime;

tells all
Harding, P. Tinkers
Hassler, J. The Staggerford flood
Hemingway, E. The old man and the sea
Hilton, J. Good-bye Mr. Chips
Itani, F. Remembering the bones
Kawabata, Y. The sound of the mountain
King, S. Insomnia
Krauss, N. The history of love
Maloy, K. Every last cuckoo
McFarland, D. School for the blind
McMurtry, L. The evening star
McNamer, D. Red rover
Medlicott, J. A. Gardens of Covington
Medlicott, J. A. The ladies of Covington send their love
Mestre-Reed, E. The second death of Unica Aveyano
Michener, J. A. Recessional
Miller, S. The distinguished guest
Mistry, R. Family matters
Mosley, W. RL's dream
O'Flynn, C. The news where you are
Olsson, L. Astrid & Veronika
O'Nan, S. Emily, alone
Polsan/English Hash
Porter, J. A. The near future
Pouncey, P. R. Rules for old men waiting
Price, R. The good priest's son
Purdy, J. The nephew
Quindlen, A. Blessings
Roth, P. Exit ghost
Roth, P. Sabbath's theater
Sackville-West, V. All passion spent
Sarton, M. As we are now
Sarton, M. Kinds of love
Scott, A. Calpurnia
Scott, P. Staying on
Simon, C. The trolley
Spark, M. Memento mori
Sparks, N. The notebook
Stuckey-French, E. Revenge of the radioactive lady
Taylor, E. Mrs. Palfrey at the Claremont
Taylor, M. G. The ballad of Trenchmouth Taggart
Thirlwell, A. The escape
Trollope, J. The men and the girls
Trueblood, V. Seven loves
Tyler, A. A patchwork planet
Updike, J. The poorhouse fair
Updike, J. Seek my face
Updike, J. The widows of Eastwick
Van Niekerk, M. Agaat
Weldon, F. Rhode Island blues
Wharton, W. Dad
White, P. The eye of the storm
Wiesel, E. The forgotten

OLD AGE -- FICTION
  Miller, D. B. Norwegian by night
OLD AGE HOMES
  Sarton, M. As we are now
  Updike, J. The poorhouse fair
Old boys. McCarry, C.
The **Old** Contemptibles. Grimes, M.
The **old** curiosity shop. Dickens, C.
Old Filth. Gardam, J.
Old Filth trilogy [series]
  Gardam, J. Last Friends
Old flames. Lawton, J.
The **old** fox deceiv'd. Grimes, M.
Old friends. Dixon, S.
The **old** gray wolf. Doss, J. D.
The **old** gringo. Fuentes, C.
The **old** man and the sea. Hemingway, E.
Old man's war. Scalzi, J.
Old men at midnight. Potok, C.
Old men in love. Gray, A.
OLD NORSE LANGUAGE *See* Language and languages; Scandinavian languages
OLD NORTHWEST
  Roberts, K. L. Northwest Passage
The **old** romantic. Dean, L.
Old school. Wolff, T.
The **Old** Silent. Grimes, M.
OLD SOUTHWEST
  Richter, C. The sea of grass
The **Old** Wine Shades. Grimes, M.
OLDER MEN -- CRIMES AGAINST
  Mina, D. Gods and beasts
OLDER MEN
  Banville, J. Ancient light
  Crumey, A. Mr. Mee
  Friedman, D. Don't ever get old
  Hoban, R. Angelica's Grotto
  Lurie, A. The last resort
  Nichols, J. On top of Spoon Mountain
  Potok, C. Old men at midnight
OLDER PEOPLE -- CRIMES AGAINST
  Memminger, C. Aloha, lady blue
OLDER PEOPLE
  Brewer, S. The poet of Tolstoy Park
  Brooker, B. R. The Viagra diaries
  Cotterill, C. The coroner's lunch
  Cotterill, C. Curse of the pogo stick
  Cotterill, C. Disco for the departed
  Cotterill, C. The merry misogynist
  Cotterill, C. Slash and burn
  Cotterill, C. Thirty-three teeth
  Jonasson, J. The 100-year-old man who climbed out the window and disappeared
  Kiesbye, S. Your house is on fire, your children all gone
  McCorkle, J. Life after life

OLDER WOMEN

Atwood, M. The blind assassin

Dickinson, P. Some deaths before dying

Gutcheon, B. R. More than you know

Harkaway, N. Angelmaker

Maloy, K. Every last cuckoo

Rawles, N. My Jim

The **oldest** living Confederate widow tells all. Gurganus, A.

Oleander girl. Divakaruni, C. B.

Olive Kitteridge. Strout, E.

Oliver Twist. Dickens, C.

Oliver Wiswell. Roberts, K. L.

OLIVER, GIDEON (FICTITIOUS CHARACTER)

Elkins, A. J. Dying on the vine

Elkins, A. J. Good blood

Elkins, A. J. Skeleton dance

Oluwale, David, 1930 or 1-1969

About

Phillips, C. Foreigners

OLYMPIC ATHLETES *See* Athletes

OLYMPIC GAMES

See also Athletics; Contests; Games; Sports

Keegan, N. Swimming

Kosmatka, T. The games

OLYMPIC GAMES, 1936 (BERLIN, GER.)

Kerr, P. If the dead rise not

OLYMPIC GAMES, 2012 (LONDON, ENGLAND)

Cleave, C. Gold

OLYMPIC PENINSULA (WASH.)

Evison, J. West of here

OLYMPICS

Coldsmith, D. The long journey home

Keegan, N. Swimming

Olympos. Simmons, D.

Ombria in shadow. McKillip, P. A.

Omoo: a narrative of adventures in the South Seas. Stahlberg, L.

On a day like this. Stamm, P.

On Agate Hill. Smith, L.

On beauty. Smith, Z.

On Canaan's side. Barry, S.

On Chesil Beach. McEwan, I.

On Green Dolphin Street. Faulks, S.

On Her Majesty's Secret Service. Fleming, I.

On Kingdom Mountain. Mosher, H. F.

On Mystic lake. Hannah, K.

On secret service. Jakes, J.

On the beach. Shute, N.

On the edge. Lovesey, P.

On the nature of human romantic interaction. Iagnemma, K.

On the occasion of my last afternoon. Gibbons, K.

On the razor's edge. Flynn, M.

On the river Styx and other stories. Matthiessen, P.

On the road. Kerouac, J.

On the road: the original scroll. Kerouac, J.

On the street where you live. Clark, M. H.

On the wrong track. Hockensmith, S.

On top of Spoon Mountain. Nichols, J.

Once a gentleman. Hern, C.

Once a hero. Moon, E.

The **once** and future king. White, T. H.

Once on a moonless night. Dai Sijie

Once the shore. Yoon, P.

Once too often. Simpson, D.

Once upon a river. Campbell, B. J.

Once upon a time, there was you. Berg, E.

One D.O.A., one on the way. Robison, M.

One day. Nicholls, D.

One day in the life of Ivan Denisovich. Solzhenitsyn, A.

One door away from heaven. Koontz, D. R.

One false move. Coben, H.

One fearful yellow eye. MacDonald, J. D.

One fine day the rabbi bought a cross. Kemelman, H.

One flew over the cuckoo's nest. Kesey, K.

One for the money. Evanovich, J.

The **one** from the other. Kerr, P.

One Good Earl Deserves a Lover. MacLean, S.

One hundred million hearts. Sakamoto, K.

One hundred years of solitude. Garcia Marquez, G.

The **One** I Left Behind. McMahon, J.

One last dance. Goudge, E.

One last thing before I go. Tropper, J.

One more river. Freeling, N.

One more Sunday. MacDonald, J. D.

One pill makes you smaller. Dierbeck, L.

One Police Plaza. Caunitz, W. J.

One shot. Child, L.

One step behind. Mankell, H.

One summer. Baldacci, D.

One Sunday morning. Ephron, A.

One touch of scandal. Carlyle, L.

The **One** Tree. Donaldson, S. R.

One true thing. Quindlen, A.

ONLINE CHAT GROUPS *See* Conversation

ONLINE DATING *See* Dating (Social customs)

ONLINE JOURNALISM *See* Journalism

ONLY CHILD *See* Children; Family size

Only children. Lurie, A.

Only one thing missing. Ruiz, L. M.

Only revolutions. Danielewski, M. Z.

Only time will tell. Archer, J.

Only yesterday. Agnon, S. Y.

ONTARIO

Burnford, S. The incredible journey

Itani, F. Requiem

ONTARIO -- FICTION

Bates, J. F. Midnight at the Dragon Café

Engel, H. The Cooperman variations

Itani, F. Deafening

Lawson, M. Crow Lake

Munro, A. Friend of my youth

Shields, C. Unless

Oops! Lutz, J.

OPEN AND CLOSED SHOP *See* Labor; Labor contract; Labor unions

Open city. Cole, T.

The **open** curtain. Evenson, B.

Open season. Box, C. J.

Open secrets. Munro, A.

Open to the public. Spark, M.

OPERA

Davies, R. The lyre of Orpheus

Hambly, B. Die upon a kiss

Marias, J. The man of feeling

Parker, B. Suspicion of deceit

See, L. Peony in love

OPERA -- FICTION

Gentle, M. The black opera

OPERA -- SOUND RECORDINGS *See* Sound recordings

OPERAS *See* Opera

OPERATION OVERLORD

Foden, G. Turbulence

Operation wandering soul. Powers, R.

OPERATIONS RESEARCH *See* Research; System theory

OPERATIONS, SURGICAL *See* Surgery

OPERETTA *See* Musical form; Opera; Vocal music

OPIUM

Hannan, C. Missy

OPIUM TRADE

Ghosh, A. River of smoke

Ghosh, A. Sea of poppies

Oppenheimer, J. Robert, 1904-1967

About

Smith, M. C. Stallion Gate

The **opposite** house. Oyeyemi, H.

OPTICAL ILLUSIONS *See* Hallucinations and illusions; Psychophysiology; Vision

OPTICS *See* Physics

The **optimist's** daughter. Welty, E.

Oracle night. Auster, P.

The **Oracle** of Stamboul. Lukas, M. D.

ORACLES

See also Occultism

Graham, J. Black ships

Lukas, M. D. The Oracle of Stamboul

Oral history. Smith, L.

The **orange** eats creeps. Krilanovich, G.

Oranges are not the only fruit. Winterson, J.

ORATORS

Bell, A. A. The blood of Caesar

George, M. The memoirs of Cleopatra

Harris, R. Conspirata

Harris, R. Imperium

ORBITAL LABORATORIES *See* Space stations

ORBITAL RENDEZVOUS (SPACE FLIGHT) *See* Space flight; Space stations; Space vehicles

ORBITING VEHICLES *See* Artificial satellites; Space stations

The **orchardist.** Coplin, A.

ORCHARDS -- NORTHWEST, PACIFIC

Coplin, A. The orchardist

ORCHESTRAL MUSIC *See* Instrumental music; Music; Orchestra

Orchestrated death. Harrod-Eagles, C.

Orchid Beach. Woods, S.

The **ordeal** of Richard Feverel. Meredith, G.

Orders from Berlin. Tolkien, S.

ORDERS, MONASTIC *See* Monasticism and religious orders

The **ordinary.** Grimsley, J.

An **ordinary** decent criminal. Van Rooy, M.

Ordinary grace. Krueger, W. K.

Ordinary heroes. Turow, S.

Ordinary people. Guest, J.

Ordinary thunderstorms. Boyd, W.

Ordinary wolves. Kantner, S.

An **ordinary** woman. Holland, C.

ORDINATION *See* Rites and ceremonies; Sacraments

OREGON

Gloss, M. The hearts of horses

Hammond, D. C. Going to bend

Kafka, K. Miranda's vines

Kesey, K. Sometimes a great notion

Krilanovich, G. The orange eats creeps

Margolin, P. After dark

Margolin, P. The burning man

Percy, B. The wilding

Rock, P. My abandonment

Smith, A. Judas horse

Wilhelm, K. The deepest water

Wilhelm, K. The good children

Winston, L. Good grief

OREGON -- FICTION

Carr, R. The Wanderer

OREGON -- PORTLAND

Cain, C. Heartsick

Durrow, H. W. The girl who fell from the sky

Margolin, P. Wild justice

Vlautin, W. Lean on Pete

OREGON TRAIL *See* Overland journeys to the Pacific; United States

ORGAN MUSIC *See* Church music; Instrumental music; Music

ORGAN TRANSPLANTS *See* Transplantation of

James, E. Kiss me, Annabel

Keesey, A. Little century

Lawrence, C. The case of the deadly desperados

Le Fanu, J. S. Uncle Silas

Livesey, M. The flight of Gemma Hardy

Lyon, A. The sweet girl

O'Donnell, L. The death of bees

O'Malley, T. This magnificent desolation

Omarsdottir, K. Children in Reindeer Woods

Orullian, P. V. The unremembered

Stedman, M. L. The light between oceans

Zimmerman, J. The orphanmaster

ORPHEUS (LEGENDARY CHARACTER)

Hospital, J. T. Orpheus lost

Orpheus lost. Hospital, J. T.

Orsinian tales. Le Guin, U. K.

ORTHOPEDICS *See* Medicine; Surgery

Osgood, James R., 1836-1892

About

Pearl, M. The last Dickens

OSLO (NORWAY)

Nesbø, J. The leopard

Nesbø, J. Phantom

OSTEOPATHIC MEDICINE *See* Medicine

Oswald, Lee Harvey, 1939-1963

About

DeLillo, D. Libra

The **other.** Tryon, T.

The **other.** Guterson, D.

The **other** Boleyn girl. Gregory, P.

The **other** family. Trollope, J.

The **other** half of me. McCarthy, M.

Other people's children. Trollope, J.

Other people's marriages. Thomas, R.

Other people's money. Cartwright, J.

The **other** side of silence. Brink, A. P.

The **other** side of silence. Pronzini, B.

The **other** side of the story. Keyes, M.

The **other** side of the sun. L'Engle, M.

Other side of the world. Neugeboren, J.

The **Other** Typist. Rindell, S.

The **other** wind. Le Guin, U. K.

The **other** woman. Ryan, H. P.

OTTAWA (ONT.)

Itani, F. Requiem

The **Ottoman** cage. Nadel, B.

Our game. Le Carre, J.

Our kind. Walbert, K.

Our kind of traitor. Le Carre, J.

Our Lady of the Forest. Guterson, D.

Our man in Havana. Greene, G.

Our mutual friend. Dickens, C.

Our story begins. Wolff, T.

Out of India. Jhabvala, R. P.

Out of It. Dabbagh, S.

Out of range. Box, C. J.

Out of sight. Leonard, E.

Out of the black land. Greenwood, K.

Out of the blackout. Barnard, R.

Out of the silent planet. Lewis, C. S.

Out on a limb. Hess, J.

Out stealing horses. Petterson, P.

Out to Canaan. Karon, J.

OUT-OF-WORK PEOPLE *See* Unemployed

The **outcast.** Pirandello, L.

Outcast. Jones, S.

OUTDOOR EDUCATION *See* Education

OUTDOOR SURVIVAL *See* Wilderness survival

Outer banks. Siddons, A. R.

OUTER SPACE -- COLONIES *See* Space colonies

OUTER SPACE -- COMMUNICATION *See* Interstellar communication

OUTER SPACE -- EXPLORATION

See also Exploration; Interplanetary voyages; Space flight

Corey, J. S. A. Abaddon's Gate

McDevitt, J. The Cassandra project

McDevitt, J. Odyssey

Outerbridge Reach. Stone, R.

The **outlander.** Adamson, G.

Outlander. Gabaldon, D.

The **outlaw** album. Woodrell, D.

OUTLAWS

See also Criminals; Thieves

Bull, E. Territory

Estleman, L. D. Black powder, white smoke

Estleman, L. D. The book of Murdock

Franklin, T. Smonk; or, Widow town

Hansen, R. The assassination of Jesse James by the coward Robert Ford

Humphreys, J. Nowhere else on earth

Liebmann-Smith, R. The James boys

Lynch, S. The lies of Locke Lamora

McMurtry, L. Anything for Billy

McMurtry, L. Streets of Laredo

Momaday, N. S. The ancient child

Olmstead, R. Far bright star

Resnick, M. The return of Santiago

Scott, W. Rob Roy

Wallace, S. Montana dawn

Williamson, P. The outsider

OUTLAWS -- FICTION

Brand, M. The survival of Juan Oro

Brooks, B. Winter kill

Outrage. Indridason, A.

Outside the ordinary world. Ostermiller, D.

Outside valentine. Ward, L.

The **outside** world. Mirvis, T.

The **outsider.** Wright, R.

The **outsider.** Williamson, P.

OUTSIDER ART *See* Art

Over and under. Tucker, T.
Overclocked. Doctorow, C.
The **overcoat,** and other tales of good and evil. Gogol', N. V.
OVERLAND JOURNEYS
  Bristow, G. Jubilee Trail
  Holland, C. An ordinary woman
  Hunter, E. The Chisholms
  Wolitzer, H. Hearts
OVERLAND JOURNEYS TO THE PACIFIC
    See also Frontier and pioneer life; Voyages and travels
  Guthrie, A. B. The way West
  Taylor, R. L. The travels of Jaimie McPheeters
  Vanderhaeghe, G. The last crossing
**OVERLAND JOURNEYS TO THE PACIFIC --
  FICTION**
  Priest, C. Dreadnought
The **overlook.** Connelly, M.
OVERWEIGHT See Obesity
OVERWEIGHT PERSONS
  Magnin, J. The prayers of Agnes Sparrow
OWNERSHIP See Property
The **Ox-bow** incident. Clark, W. V. T.
The **Oxford** book of American detective stories.
The **Oxford** book of American short stories.
The **Oxford** book of English ghost stories.
The **Oxford** book of English love stories.
The **Oxford** book of English short stories.
The **Oxford** book of gothic tales.
The **Oxford** book of Irish short stories.
The **Oxford** book of Jewish stories.
The **Oxford** book of Latin American short stories.
The **Oxford** book of modern fairy tales.
The **Oxford** book of science fiction stories.
The **Oxford** book of short stories.
The **Oxford** book of spy stories.
The **Oxford** book of twentieth-century ghost stories.
Oxford world classics [series]
  Bunyan, J. The pilgrim's progress
  Gaskell, E. C. Cranford
Oxford world's classics [series]
  Blackmore, R. D. Lorna Doone
  Cather, W. O pioneers!
  Defoe, D. Robinson Crusoe
  Edgeworth, M. Castle Rackrent
  Fielding, H. Joseph Andrews and Shamela
  Grey, Z. Riders of the purple sage
  Hawthorne, N. The Blithedale romance
  Lewis, M. G. The monk
  Richardson, S. Pamela
  Thackeray, W. M. Vanity fair
  Trollope, A. The prime minister
  Verne, J. Around the world in eighty days
  Zola, E. Nana
 Oxygen. Miller, A.

Oyster. Hospital, J. T.
OZ (IMAGINARY PLACE)
  Maguire, G. A lion among men
  Maguire, G. Son of a witch
  Maguire, G. Wicked
OZARK MOUNTAINS
  Harington, D. Enduring
  McMurtry, L. Zeke and Ned
  Woodrell, D. Give us a kiss
  Woodrell, D. The outlaw album
OZARK MOUNTAINS REGION
  Harington, D. Enduring
  Harington, D. The pitcher shower
  Woodrell, D. The outlaw album
  Woodrell, D. Winter's bone

P

P is for peril. Grafton, S.
PYŎNGYANG (KOREA) -- FICTION
  Church, J. The man with the Baltic stare
P.K. Pinkerton [series]
  Lawrence, C. The case of the deadly desperados
PACHYCEPHALOSAURUS See Dinosaurs
The **Pacific** and other stories. Helprin, M.
Pacific beat. Parker, T. J.
Pacific glory. Deutermann, P. T.
PACIFIC NORTHWEST
  DeWeese, D. You don't love this man
  Fowler, K. J. Sarah Canary
  Larison, J. Holding lies
  Priest, C. Boneshaker
  Raymond, J. The half-life
PACIFIC NORTHWEST -- FICTION
  Evison, J. West of here
  Perillo, L. Happiness is a chemical in the brain
PACIFIC OCEAN
    See also Ocean
  Smith, D. Bright and distant shores
  Watts, P. Starfish
Pacific Street. Holland, C.
PACIFISTS
  Pipkin, J. Woodsburner
Pack of cards and other stories. Lively, P.
PACKAGING See Advertising; Retail trade
PACKING INDUSTRY See Meat industry
Paco's story. Heinemann, L.
Paddy Clarke, ha ha ha. Doyle, R.
Pagan babies. Leonard, E.
PAGANISM
  Renault, M. The king must die
  Sienkiewicz, H. Quo Vadis
PAGEANTS
  Woolf, V. Between the acts
**PAIBOUN, SIRI, DOCTOR (FICTITIOUS
  CHARACTER)**
  Cotterill, C. Curse of the pogo stick

Akhtar, A. American dervish
Palace council. Carter, S. L.
Palace of desire. Mahfouz, N.
The **palace** thief. Canin, E.
Palace walk. Mahfouz, N.
PALACES *See* Buildings
The **paladin** of souls. Bujold, L. M.
Pale fire. Nabokov, V. V.
The **pale** horse. Christie, A.
Pale horse coming. Hunter, S.
Pale horse, pale rider: three short novels. Porter, K.
A.
The **pale** horseman. Cornwell, B.
The **pale** king. Wallace, D. F.
PALEOLITHIC PERIOD *See* Stone Age
PALEONTOLOGISTS
Chevalier, T. Remarkable creatures
Lively, P. Cleopatra's sister
Preston, D. Tyrannosaur Canyon
Smith, D. Pictures from an expedition
Swanwick, M. Bones of the earth
Vine, B. No night is too long
PALESTINE
Agnon, S. Y. Only yesterday
Eve, N. The family orchard
Khoury, E. Gate of the sun
Oz, A. Panther in the basement
Shabtai, Y. Uncle Peretz takes off
Uris, L. Exodus
Wiesel, E. Dawn
PALESTINE -- FICTION
Dabbagh, S. Out of It
PALESTINE -- TO 70 A.D.
Asch, S. The Apostle
Asch, S. The Nazarene
Caldwell, T. Dear and glorious physician
Edghill, I. Queenmaker
Wallace, L. Ben-Hur
PALESTINIAN ARABS
See also Arabs
Kashua, S. Dancing Arabs
Keneally, T. Flying hero class
Khoury, E. Gate of the sun
Littell, R. Vicious circle
PALESTINIAN ARABS -- FICTION
Dabbagh, S. Out of It
PALESTINIANS *See* Palestinian Arabs
Palindrome. Woods, S.
PALISADES AMUSEMENT PARK (N.J.)
Brennert, A. Palisades Park
Palisades Park. Brennert, A.
The **Pallisers.** Trollope, A.
A **palm** for Mrs. Pollifax. Gilman, D.
Palme, Olof, 1927-1986
About
Persson, L. G. W. Between summer's longing and

winter's end
PALMISTRY *See* Divination; Fortune telling; Occultism
Pamela. Richardson, S.
PAMPHLETEERS
Coetzee, J. M. Foe
Safire, W. Scandalmonger
Tournier, M. Friday
Panama. McGuane, T.
PANAMA
Galbraith, D. The rising sun
Le Carre, J. The tailor of Panama
PANCREAS -- CANCER -- PATIENTS -- FAMILY RELATIONSHIPS -- UNITED STATES
Pausch, J. Dream new dreams
Pandemonium. Gregory, D.
Pandora's clock. Nance, J. J.
Pandora's star. Hamilton, P. F.
Panic attack. Starr, J.
PANIC DISORDERS *See* Abnormal psychology; Neuroses
PANICS (FINANCE) *See* Financial crises
Panorama. Adler, H. G.
PANTHEISM *See* Philosophy; Religion
Panther in the basement. Oz, A.
Panther in the sky. Thom, J. A.
PAPAL VISITS *See* Voyages and travels
Paper doll. Parker, R. B.
The **paper** marriage. Law, S. K.
PAPER MONEY *See* Money
PAPERBACK BOOKS *See* Books; Editions
The **paperboy.** Dexter, P.
PAPUA NEW GUINEA
Salak, K. The white Mary
PARABLES
Baker, T. The little giant of Aberdeen County
Crace, J. The gift of stones
Emshwiller, C. The secret city
Girzone, J. F. Joshua and the city
Girzone, J. F. Joshua, the homecoming
Girzone, J. F. The shepherd
Grass, G. Dog years
Han, S. The enchantress
Hemingway, E. The old man and the sea
Hrabal, B. I served the King of England
Kadare, I. The three-arched bridge
Kosinski, J. N. Being there
Kotzwinkle, W. The bear went over the mountain
Le Guin, U. K. The telling
Llywelyn, M. The elementals
Mason, D. A far country
Oates, J. C. I lock my door upon myself
Paretsky, S. Ghost country
Roth, P. Everyman
Saramago, J. Death with interruptions
Spark, M. The Abbess of Crewe

Steinbeck, J. East of Eden
Steinbeck, J. The pearl
Tremain, R. The way I found her
Vonnegut, K. Deadeye Dick
Vonnegut, K. Galapagos
Weldon, F. The life and loves of a she-devil
PARACHUTE TROOPS *See* Military aeronautics; Parachutes
PARACHUTES *See* Aeronautics
Parade's end. Ford, F. M.
PARADES *See* Festivals; Pageants
Paradise. McNaught, J.
Paradise. Morrison, T.
PARADISE *See* Future life
Paradise news. Lodge, D.
Paradise park. Goodman, A.
Paradise postponed. Mortimer, J.
The **paradise** prophecy. Browne, R.
Paradise tales. Ryman, G.
Paragon Walk. Perry, A.
PARAGUAY
Puenzo, L. The fish child
Parallel stories.
PARALYSIS
Barfoot, J. Critical injuries
Kafka, K. Miranda's vines
PARALYSIS -- FICTION
Evenson, B. Immobility
PARAMEDICAL PERSONNEL *See* Allied health personnel; Emergency medical technicians
PARAMEDICS, EMERGENCY *See* Emergency medical technicians
PARAMILITARY MILITIA MOVEMENTS *See* Militia movements
PARANOIA
Baldwin, J. The Wilshire sun
Chaon, D. Await your reply
Galchen, R. Atmospheric disturbances
Gibson, W. Pattern recognition
Gibson, W. Spook country
Gibson, W. Zero history
Goodis, D. Nightfall
Koontz, D. R. False memory
Lazar, Z. Sway
Lethem, J. Chronic city
McNamer, D. Red rover
Nayman, S. The listener
Nersesian, A. The swing voter of Staten Island
Pynchon, T. Vineland
Ruff, M. Bad monkeys
Simmons, D. Drood
Strieber, W. The Grays
Winters, B. H. Bedbugs
Wright, S. Going native
PARANOID SCHIZOPHRENIA
Wells, D. The hollow city

PARANORMAL FICTION
Hines, T. L. Waking Lazarus
Kearsley, S. The Firebird
Kearsley, S. Mariana
PARAPLEGICS
Kellogg, M. Tell me that you love me, Junie Moon
PARAPSYCHOLOGY
See also Psychology; Research; Supernatural
Krentz, J. A. White lies
PARASAUROLOPHUS *See* Dinosaurs
PARASITES
Sigler, S. Contagious
Sigler, S. Infected
Parasites like us. Johnson, A.
The Parasol Protectorate [series]
Carriger, G. Heartless
PARCEL POST *See* Postal service
A **parchment** of leaves. House, S.
Pardonable lies. Winspear, J.
PARENT AND ADULT CHILD
Brooker, B. R. The Viagra diaries
Gaddis, W. Agape agape
Keyes, M. The other side of the story
London, J. The good parents
Meloy, M. Liars and saints
Picoult, J. Lone wolf
Pronzini, B. In an evil time
Wilson, K. The family Fang
Wolitzer, M. The position
PARENT AND CHILD
Abu-Jaber, D. Birds of paradise
Aira, C. The seamstress and the wind
Bacon, C. Split estate
Banks, R. Affliction
Beattie, A. Picturing Will
Berg, E. Once upon a time, there was you
Berne, S. A perfect arrangement
Bock, C. Beautiful children
Bohjalian, C. The night strangers
Brookner, A. Family and friends
Brown, R. Before and after
Byatt, A. S. The children's book
Carroll, J. Fault lines
Carter, S. L. New England white
Christensen, K. The Astral
Clark, M. H. Remember me
Coben, H. Hold tight
Cohen, L. H. The grief of others
Cumyn, A. Losing it
Cunningham, M. By nightfall
Dallas, S. Tallgrass
Dillard, A. The Maytrees
Doctorow, E. L. The book of Daniel
Docx, E. Pravda
Doyle, R. Paula Spencer
Duncan, G. Death of an ordinary man

West, P. Love's mansion
Wilson, E. O. Anthill
Wilson, K. The family Fang
Winthrop, E. H. December
Wolitzer, H. Hearts

PARENT AND CHILD -- FICTION
Beattie, A. Picturing Will
Braffet, K. Save yourself
Christensen, K. The Astral
Edwards, K. The memory keeper's daughter
Henderson, E. Ten thousand saints
Hodgkinson, A. 22 Britannia Road
Lessing, D. M. The fifth child
Marcus, B. The flame alphabet
Perrotta, T. Little children
Price, R. Blue Calhoun
Robison, M. One D.O.A., one on the way

PARENT-CHILD RELATIONSHIP
    See also Child-adult relationship; Children;
    Family; Parents
Edwards, K. The memory keeper's daughter
Lennon, J. R. Familiar
Marcus, B. The flame alphabet
Moore, A. The Lighthouse
Picoult, J. Lone wolf
Powers, T. Hide me among the graves
St. Aubyn, E. At last

PARENTAL CUSTODY *See* Child custody
PARENTAL KIDNAPPING
    See also Child custody
Eagle, K. Ride a painted pony
Jackson, N. Who do I talk to?

PARENTHOOD
    See also Family
Novak, C. Breed

PARENTS -- DEATH
St. Aubyn, E. At last

PARENTS
    See also Family; Parents
Stedman, M. L. The light between oceans

PARENTS OF AUTISTIC CHILDREN
Netzer, L. Shine shine shine

PARENTS OF MURDER VICTIMS
Johansen, I. Taking eve

PARENTS OF PRESIDENTS
Hambly, B. Patriot hearts

PARENTS, UNMARRIED *See* Unmarried fathers;
    Unmarried mothers
Paris. Rutherfurd, E.

PARIS (FRANCE)
Black, C. Murder in the Bastille
Black, C. Murder in the Marais
Black, C. Murder in the Sentier
Furst, A. Mission to Paris

PARIS (FRANCE) -- HISTORY -- 1870-1940
Buchanan, C. M. The painted girls

PARIS (FRANCE) -- HISTORY -- 1940-1944
Edugyan, E. Half-blood blues

PARIS (FRANCE) -- HISTORY
Miller, A. Pure
Rutherfurd, E. Paris
Paris in the twentieth century. Verne, J.
Paris Trout. Dexter, P.
The **Paris** wife. McLain, P.

PARKINSONISM
Esquivel, L. Swift as desire
Franzen, J. The corrections
Miller, S. The distinguished guest
Mistry, R. Family matters

PARKS *See* Cities and towns; Landscape architecture

PAROCHIAL SCHOOLS *See* Church schools
PARODIES
Berger, T. Arthur Rex
Coover, R. Ghost town
Coover, R. Noir
Fielding, H. Joseph Andrews and Shamela
Hemingway, E. The torrents of spring
Nabokov, V. V. Lolita

PARODY *See* Literature; Satire; Wit and humor
PARRICIDE
Rossner, J. Perfidia
Sebold, A. The almost moon
Parrot and Olivier in America. Carey, P.

PARROTS
Paul, J. Elsewhere in the land of parrots
The **Parsifal** mosaic. Ludlum, R.
Parson's pleasure. Hardwick, M.

PARSON, MICHAEL (FICTITIOUS CHARACTER)
Young, T. W. The renegades
Part of the furniture. Wesley, M.
The **particular** sadness of lemon cake. Bender, A.

PARTIES
Pilcher, R. September
Rendell, R. Tigerlily's orchids

PARTIES -- ENGLAND -- 20TH CENTURY
Jones, S. The uninvited guests

PARTIES -- FICTION
Jones, S. The uninvited guests
A **partisan's** daughter. De Bernieres, L.

PARTISANS *See* Guerrillas
Partitions. Majmudar, A.
The **partner.** Grisham, J.

PASCOE, PETER (FICTITIOUS CHARACTER)
Hill, R. Death comes for the Fat Man
Passage. Willis, C.
The **passage.** Cronin, J.
A **passage** to India. Forster, E. M.
The **passages** of H.M. Parini, J.
Passing. Larsen, N.
Passing on. Lively, P.

Penguin book of gay short fiction.

The **Penguin** book of lesbian short stories.

Penguin classics [series]

  Cooper, J. F. The Deerslayer

  Defoe, D. A journal of the plague year

  Dumas, A. The man in the iron mask

  Greene, G. The heart of the matter

  Meredith, G. The ordeal of Richard Feverel

  Radcliffe, A. W. The mysteries of Udolpho

  Tolstoy, L. Resurrection

  Wells, H. G. The island of Doctor Moreau

  The white people and other weird stories

  Zola, E. Germinal

Penguin twentieth-century classics [series]

  Forster, E. M. A room with a view

PENGUINS *See* Birds

Penhallow. Heyer, G.

PENICILLIN

  Belfer, L. A fierce radiance

PENINSULAR WAR, 1807-1814

  Cornwell, B. Sharpe's battle

  Cornwell, B. Sharpe's Waterloo

  Forester, C. S. Commodore Hornblower

  Forester, C. S. Hornblower and the Hotspur

  Forester, C. S. Lieutenant Hornblower

  Forester, C. S. Ship of the line

  Tillyard, S. K. Tides of war

Penmarric. Howatch, S.

Pennies on a dead woman's eyes. Muller, M.

**PENNINE CHAIN (ENGLAND) -- 13TH CEN-
TURY**

  Nicholas, D. Something red

PENNSYLVANIA

  Caldwell, T. Testimony of two men

  Dark, A. E. Think of England

  Donohue, K. Angels of destruction

  Elwork, P. The girl who would speak for the dead

  Haigh, J. Baker towers

  Hijuelos, O. The fourteen sisters of Emilio Montez
    O'Brien

  Hornby, N. Juliet, naked

  King, S. Christine

  King, S. From a Buick 8

  Leebron, F. G. In the middle of all this

  Meyer, C. Brown eyes blue

  Meyer, P. American rust

  Michener, J. A. The novel

  O'Dell, T. Back roads

  O'Dell, T. Coal Run

  O'Dell, T. Fragile beasts

  O'Dell, T. Sister mine

  O'Hara, J. From the terrace

  O'Hara, J. Ten North Frederick

  O'Nan, S. Snow angels

  Poyer, D. Thunder on the mountain

  Russo, R. The straight man

  Scott, J. Follow me

  Smiley, J. Good faith

  Swann, M. Flower children

  Updike, J. The centaur

  Updike, J. Rabbit Angstrom

  Updike, J. Rabbit at rest

  Updike, J. Rabbit is rich

  Updike, J. Rabbit redux

  Updike, J. Rabbit, run

  Wharton, W. Birdy

PENNSYLVANIA -- 18TH CENTURY

  De Hartog, J. The peaceable kingdom

  Larsen, D. The white

  Liss, D. The whiskey rebels

PENNSYLVANIA -- 19TH CENTURY

  Jakes, J. Heaven and hell

  Jakes, J. Love and war

  Jakes, J. North and South

PENNSYLVANIA -- 20TH CENTURY

  Hijuelos, O. The fourteen sisters of Emilio Montez
    O'Brien

  King, S. Christine

  King, S. From a Buick 8

  Leebron, F. G. In the middle of all this

  Michener, J. A. The novel

  Updike, J. The centaur

  Updike, J. Rabbit Angstrom

  Updike, J. Rabbit at rest

  Updike, J. Rabbit is rich

  Updike, J. Rabbit redux

  Updike, J. Rabbit, run

  Wharton, W. Birdy

PENNSYLVANIA -- FICTION

  Constantine, K. C. Brushback

  Constantine, K. C. Grievance

  Constantine, K. C. Saving room for dessert

  Haigh, J. Baker towers

  Hijuelos, O. The fourteen sisters of Emilio Montez
    O'Brien

  King, S. Christine

  King, S. From a Buick 8

  Liss, D. The whiskey rebels

  Magnin, J. The prayers of Agnes Sparrow

  O'Dell, T. Back roads

  O'Dell, T. Sister mine

  O'Nan, S. Snow angels

  Scott, J. Follow me

PENNSYLVANIA -- PHILADELPHIA

  De los Santos, M. Belong to me

  De los Santos, M. Love walked in

  Dunn, S. The big love

  Durham, D. A. A walk through darkness

  Elwork, P. The girl who would speak for the dead

  Fulmer, D. The blue door

  Gallagher, S. The kingdom of bones

  Halperin, D. J. Journal of a UFO investigator

Lashner, W. A killer's kiss
Liss, D. The whiskey rebels
McKinney-Whetstone, D. Leaving Cecil Street
McKinney-Whetstone, D. Tempest rising
Morrow, J. The last witchfinder
Scott, A. Calpurnia
Scottoline, L. Dead ringer
Scottoline, L. Legal tender
Scottoline, L. Mistaken identity
Scottoline, L. Rough justice
Scottoline, L. The vendetta defense
Swierczynski, D. Expiration date
Weiner, J. Certain girls
Weiner, J. Good in bed
Weiner, J. Little earthquakes
Wideman, J. E. The cattle killing
Wideman, J. E. Philadelphia fire
Wideman, J. E. Two cities

PENNSYLVANIA -- PITTSBURGH
O'Nan, S. Emily, alone
Wideman, J. E. Two cities
The **penny** wedding. Stirling, J.
PENTAGON (VA.) TERRORIST ATTACK, 2001
See September 11 terrorist attacks, 2001
Pentecost Alley. Perry, A.
PENTECOSTALISM *See* Christianity
PEONAGE *See* Forced labor
Peony in love. See, L.
PEOPLE *See* Ethnic groups; Indigenous peoples;
Persons
PEOPLE IN SPACE *See* Space flight
The **people** in the trees. Yanagihara, H.
People like us. Dunne, D.
People of Darkness. Hillerman, T.
The **people** of forever are not afraid. Boianjiu, S.
People of the book. Brooks, G.
People of the masks. Gear, K. O.
People of the mist. Gear, K. O.
People of the owl. Gear, K. O.
People of the thunder. Gear, W. M.
The **people** on Privilege Hill and other stories. Gardam, J.
PEOPLE WITH DISABILITIES
Leon, D. The Golden Egg
The **people's** act of love. Meek, J.
Perchance to dream. Parker, R. B.
Percival Everett by Virgil Russell. Everett, P.
Percival's planet. Byers, M.
Perdido Street Station. Mieville, C.
Pere Goriot (Old Goriot) Balzac, H. d.
Perelandra. Lewis, C. S.
PERENNIALS *See* Cultivated plants; Flower gardening; Flowers
The **Perez** family. Bell, C.
A **perfect** arrangement. Berne, S.
The **Perfect** Ghost. Barnes, L.

Perfect Harmony. Wood, B.
Perfect life. Shattuck, J.
The **perfect** man. Murr, N.
A **perfect** spy. Le Carre, J.
A **perfect** stranger. Robinson, R.
PERFECTIONISM (PERSONALITY TRAIT)
See Personality
Perfidia. Rossner, J.
The **perfidious** parrot. Van de Wetering, J.
PERFORMANCE ART
See also Art; Performing arts
DeLillo, D. Falling man
Nooteboom, C. Lost paradise
Wilson, K. The family Fang
PERFORMANCE ARTISTS
Steinke, R. Holy skirts
PERFORMANCE ARTISTS -- FICTION
Wilson, K. The family Fang
Perfume: the story of a murderer. Suskind, P.
PERFUMES
Faber, M. The crimson petal and the white
A **perilous** conception. Karp, L.
PERIODIC HEALTH EXAMINATIONS *See*
Medicine
PERIODICALS
Bushnell, C. Lipstick jungle
Dolan, H. Bad things happen
Mallon, T. Bandbox
The **Peripatetic** Coffin and other stories. Rutherford, E.
Perla. De Robertis, C.
Perlmann's silence. Mercier, P.
PERN (IMAGINARY PLACE)
McCaffrey, T. Dragonsblood
PERSECUTION
See also Atrocities
Vallgren The horrific sufferings of the mind-reading monster Hercules Barefoot
PERSECUTIONS *See* Persecution
PERSEVERANCE *See* Ethics
The **Persian** boy. Renault, M.
The **Persian** Pickle Club. Dallas, S.
PERSISTENCE *See* Personality
A **person** of interest. Choi, S.
Person of interest. Schwegel, T.
PERSONAL BEAUTY
Maguire, G. Confessions of an ugly stepsister
PERSONAL COMPUTERS *See* Computers
Personal days. Park, E.
PERSONAL DEVELOPMENT *See* Personality;
Self-improvement; Success
PERSONAL FINANCE *See* Finance
The **personal** history of Rachel Dupree. Weisgarber, A.
Personal injuries. Turow, S.
PERSONAL PARAPHERNALIA

Shapton, L. Important artifacts and personal property from the collection of Lenore Doolan and Harold Morris, including books, street fashion, and jewelry

Personal recollections of Joan of Arc. Twain, M.

PERSONAL SPACE *See* Interpersonal relations; Nonverbal communication; Space and time

PERSONALITY

Baxter, C. The soul thief

Kehlmann, D. Fame

Keillor, G. Lake Wobegon summer 1956

Ludlum, R. The Bourne identity

Ludlum, R. The Bourne supremacy

McCarthy, T. Remainder

Moon, E. The speed of dark

Tyler, A. Morgan's passing

PERSONALITY DISORDERS

Conroy, P. The prince of tides

Faulks, S. Engleby

Levenkron, S. The best little girl in the world

Percy, W. Lancelot

Rendell, R. A sight for sore eyes

Thomas, D. M. The white hotel

Unsworth, B. Losing Nelson

PERSONS *See* Human beings

Persuader. Child, L.

Persuasion. Austen, J.

PERSUASION (PSYCHOLOGY)

See also Communication; Conformity

PERSUASION (PSYCHOLOGY) -- FICTION

Barry, M. Lexicon

PERU

Alfieri, A. City of silver

Redfield, J. The celestine prophecy

Roncagliolo, S. Red April

Vargas Llosa, M. Captain Pantoja and the Special Service

Vargas Llosa, M. Conversation in the cathedral

Vargas Llosa, M. Death in the Andes

Vargas Llosa, M. The Green House

PERU (VICEROYALTY) -- HISTORY

Alfieri, A. City of silver

PERU -- 18TH CENTURY

Wilder, T. The bridge of San Luis Rey

PERU -- ARMY -- OFFICERS

Vargas Llosa, M. Captain Pantoja and the Special Service

PERU -- FICTION

Wilder, T. The bridge of San Luis Rey

PERU -- LIMA

Vargas Llosa, M. Aunt Julia and the scriptwriter

Vargas Llosa, M. The notebooks of Don Rigoberto

Vargas Llosa, M. The time of the hero

Wilder, T. The bridge of San Luis Rey

The **pesthouse.** Crace, J.

PESTICIDES -- ENVIRONMENTAL ASPECTS

See Environment; Pollution

PESTILENCES *See* Epidemics

Pet sematary. King, S.

Petit, Philippe, 1949-

About

McCann, C. Let the great world spin

Petre, Robert Petre, Baron, 1689-1713

About

Gee, S. The scandal of the season

PETROCHEMICALS *See* Chemicals

PETROLEUM INDUSTRY

Cussler, C. Valhalla rising

Estleman, L. D. Gas City

Ferber, E. Cimarron

Furst, A. Blood of victory

McMurtry, L. Texasville

Patterson, R. N. Eclipse

Poyer, D. Thunder on the mountain

Smith, W. A. Those in peril

Unsworth, B. Land of marvels

Wells, K. Crawfish mountain

PETROLEUM INDUSTRY AND TRADE *See* Petroleum industry

Petropolis. Ulinich, A.

The **pets.** Bragi Olafsson

PETS *See* Animals

PETTING ZOOS *See* Zoos

Phantom. Nesbø, J.

Pharaoh. Essex, K.

PHARISEES

Asch, S. The Nazarene

PHARMACEUTICAL INDUSTRY

Belfer, L. A fierce radiance

Grisham, J. The litigators

Huston, C. Sleepless

Le Carre, J. The constant gardener

Palmer, M. Miracle cure

Patchett, A. State of wonder

Preston, D. The codex

Reed, B. The choice

Wood, B. Perfect Harmony

PHARMACEUTICALS *See* Drugs

PHARMACISTS

Amado, J. Dona Flor and her two husbands

Cather, W. Shadows on the rock

Hearon, S. Year of the dog

Redhill, M. Consolation

PHARMACOLOGY *See* Medicine

PHARMACY *See* Chemistry; Medicine

Pharmakon. Wittenborn, D.

PHEASANTS *See* Birds; Game and game birds

PHILADELPHIA (PA.)

Woods, T. Alibi

Philadelphia fire. Wideman, J. E.

PHILANTHROPISTS

Everett, P. L. I am Not Sidney Poitier

Hustvedt, S. What I loved
Ishiguro, K. Never let me go
Johnson, C. R. Middle passage
Kadare, I. The Successor
Kehlmann, D. Fame
Kundera, M. Identity
Kundera, M. Ignorance
Kundera, M. Immortality
Kundera, M. Slowness
Kundera, M. The unbearable lightness of being
Kurzweil, A. The grand complication
Le Guin, U. K. The dispossessed
Lehrer, J. The special prisoner
Lem, S. Solaris
Lessing, D. M. Mara and Dann
Lewis, C. S. Out of the silent planet
Lewis, C. S. Perelandra
Lewis, C. S. That hideous strength
Lightman, A. P. The diagnosis
Lightman, A. P. Einstein's dreams
Lightman, A. P. Ghost
Lodge, D. Thinks--
Mahfouz, N.   Children of the alley
Mahfouz, N.   Palace of desire
Mahfouz, N.   Sugar Street
Malouf, D. Remembering Babylon
Mann, T. The magic mountain
Marias, J. Dark back of time
Marias, J. The man of feeling
Maugham, W. S. The razor's edge
McCarthy, C. The road
McCarthy, C. All the pretty horses
McCarthy, C. Cities of the plain
McCarthy, M. Birds of America
McCarthy, T. Remainder
McEwan, I. Atonement
McEwan, I. Black dogs
Meek, J. The people's act of love
Michaels, A. Fugitive pieces
Mishima, Y. The temple of the golden pavilion
Mitchell, D. Cloud atlas
Moore, B. Black robe
Moore, B. The statement
Morrow, J. The last witchfinder
Mosley, W. The man in my basement
Murakami, H. The wind-up bird chronicle
Murdoch, I. The book and the brotherhood
Murdoch, I. The good apprentice
Murdoch, I. The green knight
Murdoch, I. Jackson's dilemma
Murdoch, I. The philosopher's pupil
My name is Red
Naylor, G. Linden Hills
Nooteboom, C. All souls' day
Nooteboom, C. Lost paradise
Norman, H. The museum guard

Oe, K. An echo of heaven
Oe, K. Nip the buds, shoot the kids
Ondaatje, M. The English patient
Ondaatje, M. Anil's ghost
Percy, W. The last gentleman
Percy, W. The moviegoer
Percy, W. The second coming
Perez-Reverte, A. The nautical chart
Petterson, P. In the wake
Powers, R. The echo maker
Powers, R. Generosity
Powers, R. The gold bug variations
Powers, R. Operation wandering soul
Powers, R. Plowing the dark
Powers, R. Prisoner's dilemma
Powers, R. The time of our singing
Pywell, S. L. What happened to Henry
Reuss, F. Henry of Atlantic City
Reuss, F. Horace afoot
Robbins, T. Skinny legs and all
Roth, P. Everyman
Russell, M. D. Children of God
Russell, M. D. The sparrow
Saint-Exupery, A. d. The little prince
Saramago, J. All the names
Saramago, J. The cave
Saramago, J. The history of the siege of Lisbon
Sartre, J. P. Nausea
Savage, S. Firmin
Schlink, B. Homecoming
Scott, J. Tourmaline
Sebald, W. G. Austerlitz
Sebald, W. G. Vertigo
Shields, C. Unless
Simon, C. The trolley
Singer, I. B. Shadows on the Hudson
Spark, M. Aiding and abetting
Stephenson, N. Anathem
Stone, R. Bay of souls
Stone, R. Outerbridge Reach
Suri, M. The death of Vishnu
Tournier, M. Friday
Tournier, M. The ogre
Updike, J. Roger's version
Vidal, G. Creation
Vonnegut, K. Galapagos
Whitehead, C. The intuitionist
Wiesel, E. The forgotten
Wiesel, E. The judges
Wiesel, E. Twilight
Zimler, R. The last kabbalist of Lisbon
PHILOSOPHY -- ENCYCLOPEDIAS *See* Encyclopedias and dictionaries
PHILOSOPHY AND RELIGION *See* Philosophy; Religion
Philosophy made simple. Hellenga, R.

Kehlmann, D. Measuring the world

Kerr, P. Dark matter

Le Guin, U. K. The dispossessed

Lightman, A. P. Einstein's dreams

McEwan, I. Solar

McMahon, T. A. Principles of American nuclear chemistry

Morrow, J. The last witchfinder

Powers, T. Three days to never

Preston, D. Blasphemy

Rubenfeld, J. The death instinct

Scholz, C. Radiance

Smith, M. C. Stallion Gate

Snow, C. P. The new men

Somoza, J. C. Zig Zag

Stott, R. Ghostwalk

Strieber, W. The forbidden zone

Wallace, I. The prize

Wouk, H. A hole in Texas

PHYSICISTS -- FICTION

Jensen, J. Dante's equation

Millet, L. Oh pure and radiant heart

Salvation for a saint

The **physick** book of Deliverance Dane. Howe, K.

PHYSICS

Kehlmann, D. Measuring the world

PHYSICS -- FICTION

Holt, T. Doughnut

Rajaniemi, H. The fractal prince

PHYSICS TEACHERS

Salvation for a saint

PHYSIOLOGICAL PSYCHOLOGY

Keyes, D. Flowers for Algernon

PHYSIOLOGISTS

Barker, P. The eye in the door

Barker, P. The ghost road

PHYSIOLOGY *See* Biology; Medicine; Science

PIANISTS

Bernhard, T. The loser

Docx, E. Pravda

Galloway, J. Clara

Hambly, B. Die upon a kiss

Hambly, B. A free man of color

Hamilton, J. Disobedience

Hoffman, E. Appassionata

Ishiguro, K. The unconsoled

L'Engle, M. A severed wasp

Makine, A. Music of a life

Morgan, C. E. All the living

Romano-Lax, A. The Spanish bow

The **piano** man's daughter. Findley, T.

PIANO MUSIC *See* Instrumental music; Music

The **piano** teacher. Lee, J. Y. K.

The **piano** tuner. Mason, D.

PIANO TUNERS

Mason, D. The piano tuner

PICARESQUE LITERATURE

Coover, R. Pinocchio in Venice

Doig, I. Ride with me, Mariah Montana

Hrabal, B. I served the King of England

Kureishi, H. The Buddha of suburbia

Larsen, J. Silk road

Portis, C. Gringos

PICARESQUE NOVELS

See also Picaresque literature

Adamson, G. The outlander

Barth, J. The sot-weed factor

Bellow, S. The adventures of Augie March

Berger, T. Little Big Man

Bolano, R. The savage detectives

Brown, J. D. Addie Pray

Cervantes Saavedra, M. d. Don Quixote de la Mancha

Charyn, J. Johnny One-Eye

Crace, J. The pesthouse

Defoe, D. Moll Flanders

Dexter, P. Spooner

Dickens, C. The posthumous papers of the Pickwick Club

Doctorow, E. L. Billy Bathgate

Doctorow, E. L. Loon Lake

Doig, I. Ride with me, Mariah Montana

Dunn, K. Geek love

Eco, U. Baudolino

Edgerton, C. The Bible salesman

Fielding, H. The history of Tom Jones, a foundling

Fowler, K. J. Sarah Canary

Gogol', N. V. Dead souls

Grossman, D. Someone to run with

Harington, D. The pitcher shower

Harrison, J. The English major

Hellenga, R. Philosophy made simple

Holland, C. The firedrake

Hrabal, B. I served the King of England

Jennings, G. Aztec

Jennings, G. Aztec blood

Kaufman, M. Bowl of cherries

Keneally, T. Woman of the inner sea

Kerouac, J. On the road

Kerouac, J. On the road: the original scroll

King, R. A girl from Zanzibar

Kunzru, H. The impressionist

Kureishi, H. The Buddha of suburbia

Lynch, S. The lies of Locke Lamora

Maalouf, A. Balthasar's odyssey

Maazel, F. Last last chance

Mann, T. Confessions of Felix Krull, confidence man

Manseau, P. Songs for the butcher's daughter

McCullough, C. Morgan's run

McMahon, T. A. Ira Foxglove

Murakami, H. Kafka on the shore

Hughes, R. A. W. A high wind in Jamaica
King, L. R. Pirate king
Leonard, E. Djibouti
Lindsey, J. Gentle rogue
Maxwell, R. The wild Irish
Sabatini, R. Captain Blood
Smith, W. A. Birds of prey
Smith, W. A. Monsoon
Smith, W. A. Those in peril
Wolfe, G. Pirate freedom

PIRATES -- FICTION
Davies, J. D. The mountain of gold
Hoyt, E. Scandalous desires
Levine, S. Treasure Island!!!
Stross, C. Neptune's brood
Wooding, C. Retribution falls

The **pit**. Norris, F.

PITCAIRN ISLAND
Nordhoff, C. Pitcairn's Island

Pitcairn's Island. Nordhoff, C.

Pitch dark. Sidor, S.

The **pitcher** shower. Harington, D.

PITTSBURGH (PA.)
George, K. Simple
Wideman, J. E. Two cities

A **place** called home. Goodman, J.

A **place** of execution. McDermid, V.

Places in the dark. Cook, T. H.

PLACES OF RETIREMENT See Retirement
communities

Places to stay the night. Hood, A.

PLAGIARISM
See also Authorship; Offenses against prop-
erty
Mercier, P. Perlmann's silence
Sarton, M. A small room

The **plague**. Camus, A.

PLAGUE
See also Communicable diseases; Epidemics
Brooks, G. Year of wonders
Camus, A. The plague
Conn, B. The fixed stars
Crace, J. The pesthouse
DeNiro, A. Total oblivion, more or less
Flynn, M. Eifelheim
Follett, K. World without end
Hillerman, T. The first eagle
Johnson, A. Parasites like us
Kasischke, L. In a perfect world
Mann, T. Death in Venice
Oe, K. Nip the buds, shoot the kids
Pears, I. The dream of Scipio
Perdue, L. Slatewiper
Robinson, K. S. The years of rice and salt
Wideman, J. E. The cattle killing
Willis, C. Doomsday book

Yarbro, C. Q. Blood roses

The **plague** of doves. Erdrich, L.

Plague ship. Cussler, C.

Plain paradise. Wiseman, B.

Plainsong. Haruf, K.

Planet of the apes. Boulle, P.

PLANETOIDS See Asteroids

PLANETS -- EXPLORATION
McDevitt, J. Deepsix

**PLANNED COMMUNITIES -- ENGLAND --
LONDON**
Smith, Z. NW

PLANNING See Creation (Literary, artistic, etc.);
Executive ability; Management

PLANS See Geometrical drawing; Map drawing;
Maps; Mechanical drawing

PLANT CONSERVATION See Conservation of
natural resources; Economic botany; Endangered
species; Nature conservation

PLANT DISEASES See Agricultural pests; Diseases; Fungi

PLANT ECOLOGY See Ecology

PLANT SHUTDOWNS See Factories; Unemployment

PLANTATION LIFE
See also Country life
Allende, I. Island beneath the sea
Bell, M. S. All souls' rising
Buehlman, C. Those across the river
Cheuse, A. Song of slaves in the desert
Crafts, H. The bondswomans narrative
Faulkner, W. Absalom, Absalom!
Fuller, D. Sweetsmoke
Gaines, E. J. The autobiography of Miss Jane Pit-
tman
Johnson, S. The sailmaker's daughter
L'Engle, M. The other side of the sun
Levy, A. The long song
Martin, V. Property
Mitchell, M. Gone with the wind
Santiago, E. Conquistadora
Smith, L. On Agate Hill
Stowe, H. B. Uncle Tom's cabin
Straight, S. A million nightingales
Walker, M. Jubilee

PLANTATION LIFE -- AFRICA
Forna, A. Ancestor stones

PLANTATION LIFE -- FICTION
Jones, E. P. The known world

PLANTATION OWNERS
Matthiessen, P. Bone by bone
Matthiessen, P. Killing Mister Watson
Matthiessen, P. Shadow country
Slouka, M. God's fool

PLANTATION OWNERS' SPOUSES
Crafts, H. The bondswomans narrative

Krauss, N. Great house
Lashner, W. Kockroach
Lerner, B. Leaving the Atocha Station
Littell, R. The Stalin epigram
Malae, P. N. What we are
Malouf, D. Ransom
Manseau, P. Songs for the butcher's daughter
Marsh, N. Light thickens
Martin, V. Mary Reilly
Martin, W. Harvard Yard
McCann, C. Zoli
McDermid, V. Grave tattoo
McLain, P. The Paris wife
McPhee, J. A man of no moon
Michaels, A. Fugitive pieces
Miles, J. Dear American Airlines
Morton, K. The house at Riverton
Moses, K. Wintering
Nabokov, V. V. Novels and memoirs, 1941-1951
Nabokov, V. V. Pale fire
Naipaul, V. S. A way in the world
Nye, R. The late Mr. Shakespeare
Oates, J. C. Wild nights!
Pamuk, O. Snow
Paul, J. Elsewhere in the land of parrots
Pearl, M. The Dante Club
Pears, I. The dream of Scipio
Phillips, A. The tragedy of Arthur
Price, R. The promise of rest
Reznikoff, C. By the waters of Manhattan
Rose, J. Blackest bird
Salinger, J. D. Raise high the roof beam, carpenters, and Seymour: an introduction
Self, W. Dorian
Sherwood, F. The book of splendor
Shreve, A. The last time they met
Simmons, D. Ilium
Simmons, D. Muse of fire
Simmons, D. Olympos
Sledge, M. The more I owe you
Spark, M. The girls of slender means
Steinke, R. Holy skirts
Stevenson, J. The shadow king
Truong, M. T. D. The book of salt
Updike, J. Gertrude and Claudius
Verissimo, L. F. Borges and the eternal orangutans
Walker, A. The way forward is with a broken heart
Waugh, E. The loved one
Weinstein, D. Apprentice to the flower poet Z
West, P. Lord Byron's doctor
West, P. Sporting with Amaryllis
Wiesel, E. The testament
Woof, E. The whole wide beauty
POETS -- FICTION
Pearl, M. The Poe shadow
POETS LAUREATE

Foulds, A. The quickening maze
McDermid, V. Grave tattoo
Moses, K. Wintering
POETS, AMERICAN -- 20TH CENTURY -- BIOGRAPHY
Hudgins, A. The joker
POETS, ENGLISH -- 19TH CENTURY
Shepherd, L. A fatal likeness
POETS, ENGLISH -- EARLY MODERN, 1500-1700
West, P. Sporting with Amaryllis
POETS, FINNISH
Tuomainen, A. The healer
Poinciana. Whitney, P. A.
Point counter point. Huxley, A.
The **point** of return. Deb, S.
Point Omega. DeLillo, D.
Poison. McBain, E.
Poison blonde. Estleman, L. D.
Poison flower. Perry, T.
The **poison** tree. Kelly, E.
The **Poisoned** Pilgrim.
POISONING
Peace, D. Occupied city
Pearson, R. No witnesses
Watson, B. The heaven of Mercury
POISONING -- FICTION
Bradley, A. The sweetness at the bottom of the pie
Hall, T. The case of the deadly butter chicken
Robertson, I. Circle of shadows
POISONOUS ANIMALS *See* Animals; Dangerous animals; Economic zoology; Poisons and poisoning
POISONS
Rendell, R. Heartstones
POISONS AND POISONING
See also Accidents; Hazardous substances; Homicide; Medical jurisprudence
Poole, S. The Borgia mistress
The **poisonwood** Bible. Kingsolver, B.
Poitier, Sidney
About
Everett, P. L. I am Not Sidney Poitier
POKER *See* Card games
POKER (GAME)
Pronzini, B. Step to the graveyard easy
Poland. Michener, J. A.
POLAND
Kosinski, J. N. The painted bird
Michener, J. A. Poland
Pilch, J. A thousand peaceful cities
POLAND -- 17TH CENTURY
Sienkiewicz, H. The deluge
Sienkiewicz, H. Fire in the steppe
Sienkiewicz, H. With fire and sword
POLAND -- 19TH CENTURY

POLICE -- COLORADO
Doss, J. D. The old gray wolf
POLICE -- CONNECTICUT
Pearson, R. Chain of evidence
POLICE -- DENMARK
Adler-Olsen, J. The absent one
Adler-Olsen, J. The keeper of lost causes
POLICE -- DETROIT (MICH.)
Estleman, L. D. Jitterbug
Leonard, E. Freaky Deaky
Leonard, E. Mr. Paradise
Leonard, E. Split images
POLICE -- EASTERN EUROPE
Steinhauer, O. The Bridge of Sighs
POLICE -- EDINBURGH (SCOTLAND)
Rankin, I. The complaints
Rankin, I. The impossible dead
POLICE -- ENGLAND
Bauer, B. Darkside
Bolton, S. J. Now you see me
Boyne, J. Crippen
Carver, T. The surrogate
Hannah, S. Little face
Harvey, J. Far cry
Harvey, J. Gone to ground
Keating, H. R. F. The bad detective
McDermid, V. A place of execution
Robotham, M. The wreckage
Walton, J. Farthing
Walton, J. Half a crown
Walton, J. Ha'penny
POLICE -- ENGLAND -- BATH
Lovesey, P. Diamond dust
Lovesey, P. The tooth tattoo
Lovesey, P. The vault
POLICE -- ENGLAND
Grimes, M. The Stargazey
Hill, S. The vows of silence
Mark, D. Original skin
McDermid, V. A place of execution
McGown, J. Picture of innocence
Rendell, R. Harm done
Townsend, S. Number 10
POLICE -- ENGLAND -- LIVERPOOL
Brennan, T. Doktor Glass
POLICE -- ENGLAND -- LONDON
Crombie, D. And justice there is none
George, E. A traitor to memory
Harrod-Eagles, C. Killing time
Hayder, M. Birdman
Lawrence, D. The dead sit round in a ring
Neel, J. To die for
Perry, A. Southampton Row
Perry, A. The Whitechapel conspiracy
Pinborough, S. A matter of blood
POLICE -- ENGLAND -- YORKSHIRE

Hill, R. Death comes for the Fat Man
POLICE -- FICTION
Box, C. J. The highway
Dibdin, M. Ratking
The Ghost Riders of Ordebec
Hunt, A. City of saints
James, B. Undercover
Johnson, C. Hell is empty
Katzenbach, J. What comes next
Laukkanen, O. Criminal enterprise
Leon, D. Blood from a stone
Rodriguez, L. Every broken trust
POLICE -- FICTION -- ITALY -- VENICE -- PO-LICE
Leon, D. A question of belief
POLICE -- FLORIDA
Atkins, A. White shadow
Heffernan, W. The dead detective
Hoffman, A. Turtle Moon
Leonard, E. Maximum Bob
Leonard, E. Rum punch
Woods, S. Choke
Woods, S. Orchid Beach
Woods, S. Reckless abandon
POLICE -- FRANCE
Duncker, P. The strange case of the composer and his judge
POLICE -- GEORGIA
Woods, S. Chiefs
POLICE -- GREAT BRITAIN
Harvey, J. Gone to ground
Walton, J. Ha'penny
POLICE -- INDIANA
Collins, M. Lost souls
POLICE -- IOWA
Harstad, D. Code sixty-one
POLICE -- IRELAND
French, T. Faithful Place
French, T. In the woods
French, T. The likeness
Parsons, J. Mary, Mary
POLICE -- IRELAND -- DUBLIN
French, T. Broken Harbor
POLICE -- IRELAND
Black, B. Vengeance
Gill, B. The death of an Irish lover
POLICE -- ITALY
Dibdin, M. Ratking
POLICE -- ITALY -- ROME
Fitzgerald, C. The namesake
Pears, I. Death and restoration
Pears, I. The immaculate deception
POLICE -- ITALY -- VENICE
Leon, D. Blood from a stone
Leon, D. Doctored evidence
POLICE -- JAPAN -- TOKYO

Hiaasen, C. Bad monkey

POLICE STATIONS -- NEW YORK (STATE) -- NEW YORK

Rindell, S. The Other Typist

POLICEMEN *See* Police

POLICEWOMEN

> *See also* Police; Women

Bolton, S. J. Now you see me

Boyd, W. Ordinary thunderstorms

Deaver, J. The bodies left behind

Deaver, J. Roadside crosses

Dolan, H. Bad things happen

Dolan, H. Very bad men

Mina, D. The end of the wasp season

Mina, D. Still midnight

Newton, C. Calumet City

Nova, C. The informer

Robb, J. D. Naked in death

Slaughter, K. Fallen

Stross, C. Rule 34

Wolfe, I. A. The calling

POLICEWOMEN -- FICTION

Bingham, H. Talking to the dead

Dial, C. Fallen angels

Miller, M. G. Stalking season

Polidori, John William, 1795-1821

> **About**

West, P. Lord Byron's doctor

POLIO *See* Poliomyelitis

POLIOMYELITIS

> *See also* Diseases

Berg, E. We are all welcome here

Roth, P. Nemesis

POLIOMYELITIS -- FICTION

Roth, P. Nemesis

POLISH AMERICANS

Maillard, K. The clarinet polka

POLISH FICTION -- TRANSLATIONS INTO ENGLISH

Lem, S. Eden

Myśliwski, W. Stone upon stone

Sienkiewicz, H. The deluge

Sienkiewicz, H. Fire in the steppe

POLITICAL ACTIVISTS

The dream of the Celt

POLITICAL AND SOCIAL PHILOSOPHERS

Wideman, J. E. Fanon

Political animal. Mizner, D.

POLITICAL CAMPAIGNS

Devoto, P. C. The summer we got saved

Westlake, D. E. Put a lid on it

POLITICAL CORRUPTION

> *See also* Conflict of interests; Political crimes and offenses; Political ethics; Politics

Glynn, A. Bloodland

Lelic, S. The facility

POLITICAL CORRUPTION -- GREAT BRITAIN

Le Carré, J. A Delicate Truth

POLITICAL CRIMES AND OFFENSES *See* Criminal law; Political ethics; Subversive activities

POLITICAL DEFECTORS *See* Defectors

POLITICAL ETHICS

> *See also* Ethics; Political science; Politics; Social ethics

O'Connor, E. All in the family

POLITICAL LEADERS

Harris, R. Archangel

Johnston, W. The colony of unrequited dreams

Kalfus, K. The commissariat of enlightenment

Kingsolver, B. The lacuna

Lawton, J. Old flames

Min, A. Becoming Madame Mao

POLITICAL PARTY LEADERS

Kadare, I. The Successor

POLITICAL PRISONERS

> *See also* Political crimes and offenses; Prisoners

Connelly, K. The lizard cage

Eastland, S. Eye of the Red Tsar

Haasse, H. S. In a dark wood wandering

Higgins, J. Day of judgment

Holland, T. The archivist's story

Kertesz, I. Detective story

Lord, B. B. The middle heart

Mengiste, M. Beneath the lion's gaze

Solzhenitsyn, A. In the first circle

Solzhenitsyn, A. One day in the life of Ivan Denisovich

Wiesel, E. Hostage

POLITICAL PRISONERS -- BURMA

Connelly, K. The lizard cage

POLITICAL PRISONERS -- FICTION

Lelic, S. The facility

POLITICAL REFUGEES *See* Asylum; International law; International relations; Refugees

POLITICAL SATIRE

> *See also* Satire

Maguire, G. Wicked

Nersesian, A. The swing voter of Staten Island

POLITICAL SCIENTISTS

Carey, P. Parrot and Olivier in America

POLITICAL VIOLENCE *See* Sabotage; Terrorism

POLITICIANS *See* Statesmen

POLITICIANS -- CRIMES AGAINST -- CHINA

Pattison, E. The lord of death

POLITICIANS -- SEXUAL BEHAVIOR

Mark, D. Original skin

POLITICIANS -- UNITED STATES

Lynch, J. Truth like the sun

POLITICIANS' SPOUSES -- WEST VIRGINIA
McCall, D. Dreamcatcher
POLITICS -- AFRICA
Gordimer, N. A guest of honor
Naipaul, V. S. A bend in the river
Ruark, R. Uhuru
Smith, W. A. Golden fox
Smith, W. A. A time to die
POLITICS -- BRAZIL
Amado, J. Gabriela, clove and cinnamon
POLITICS -- CANADA
Johnston, W. The colony of unrequited dreams
POLITICS -- CENTRAL AMERICA
Didion, J. A book of common prayer
Stone, R. A flag for sunrise
POLITICS -- CHILE
Allende, I. The house of the spirits
POLITICS -- CHINA
Bosse, M. J. The warlord
Ha Jin In the pond
Min, A. Becoming Madame Mao
POLITICS -- EGYPT
Durrell, L. Mountolive
POLITICS -- ENGLAND
Barnard, R. A murder in Mayfair
Coe, J. The closed circle
Drabble, M. The radiant way
Goddard, R. Into the blue
Hart, J. Damage
Maxwell, R. The secret diary of Anne Boleyn
McEwan, I. Amsterdam
Mortimer, J. The sound of trumpets
Mortimer, J. Titmuss regained
Penman, S. K. Devil's brood
Penman, S. K. Time and chance
Penman, S. K. When Christ and his saints slept
Snow, C. P. Corridors of power
Trollope, A. The Eustace diamonds
Trollope, A. The prime minister
POLITICS -- ETHIOPIA
Keneally, T. To Asmara
Mengiste, M. Beneath the lion's gaze
POLITICS -- EUROPE
Dunnett, D. Niccolo rising
Dunnett, D. Race of scorpions
Dunnett, D. The spring of the ram
Sartre, J. P. The reprieve
POLITICS
Bunn, T. D. Lion of Babylon
Chiaverini, J. Mrs. Lincoln's dressmaker
Dowlatabadi, M. The colonel
Ignatius, D. Bloodmoney
Modesitt, L. E. Princeps
Robbins, C. The accomplice
POLITICS -- FRANCE
Beauvoir, S. d. The mandarins

Steinbeck, J. The short reign of Pippin IV
POLITICS -- GUATEMALA
Henley, P. Hummingbird house
POLITICS -- HAWAII
Michener, J. A. Hawaii
POLITICS -- INDIA
Mehta, G. Raj
Mistry, R. A fine balance
Rushdie, S. Shalimar the clown
Scott, P. A division of the spoils
POLITICS -- IRELAND
Uris, L. Redemption
Uris, L. Trinity
POLITICS -- ITALY
Silone, I. Bread and wine
POLITICS -- KENTUCKY
Warren, R. P. World enough and time
POLITICS -- LATIN AMERICA
Allende, I. Eva Luna
Garcia Marquez, G. The autumn of the patriarch
POLITICS -- MASSACHUSETTS
Martin, W. Cape Cod
POLITICS -- MEXICO
Fuentes, C. The eagle's throne
POLITICS -- MIDDLE WESTERN STATES
Patterson, R. N. Dark lady
POLITICS -- NEW YORK (STATE)
Isaacs, S. Close relations
Kennedy, W. Roscoe
POLITICS -- NIGERIA
Adichie, C. N. Half of a yellow sun
POLITICS -- OKLAHOMA
Ferber, E. Cimarron
POLITICS -- ROME
Massie, A. Caesar
McCullough, C. Caesar
McCullough, C. Caesar's women
McCullough, C. The first man in Rome
McCullough, C. Fortune's favorites
McCullough, C. The grass crown
Waltari, M. The Roman
POLITICS -- RUSSIA
Koestler, A. Darkness at noon
Pasternak, B. L. Doctor Zhivago
POLITICS -- SOUTH AFRICA
Gordimer, N. My son's story
Gordimer, N. None to accompany me
Paton, A. Ah, but your land is beautiful
Smith, W. A. Rage
POLITICS -- SOUTH AMERICA
Conrad, J. Nostromo
POLITICS -- SOUTHERN STATES
Warren, R. P. All the king's men
Woods, S. Grass roots
POLITICS -- SPAIN
Romano-Lax, A. The Spanish bow

ture; Intellectual life; Recreation

POPULAR MEDICINE *See* Medicine

POPULAR MUSIC *See* Music; Songs

Porno. Welsh, I.

PORNOGRAPHY
Banks, R.   Lost memory of skin
Braff, J.   Peep show
Faust, C.   Money shot
Hayder, M.   Hanging hill
Hoban, R.   Angelica's Grotto
Rosenberg, N. T.   Interest of justice
Welsh, I.   Porno
Welsh, L.   The cutting room

PORNOGRAPHY -- FICTION
Cohen, J.   Four new messages
DeSilva, B.   Cliff Walk

Port hazard. Estleman, L. D.

PORTABLE COMPUTERS *See* Computers

The **portable** Conrad. Conrad, J.

The **portable** Stephen Crane. Crane, S.

PORTLAND (OR.)
Cain, C.   Heartsick
Cain, C.   Kill you twice
Deborde, R.   Portlandtown
Durrow, H. W.   The girl who fell from the sky
Perry, T.   Nightlife
Vachss, A. H.   Pain management

Portlandtown. Deborde, R.

Portnoy's complaint. Roth, P.

The **portrait.** Pears, I.

Portrait in sepia. Allende, I.

The **portrait** of a lady. James, H.

Portrait of a spy. Silva, D.

Portrait of an artist, as an old man. Heller, J.

Portrait of Jennie. Nathan, R.

A **portrait** of the artist as a young man. Joyce, J.

Portrait of the mother as a young woman.

PORTRAIT PAINTERS
Modesitt, L. E.   Imager
Modesitt, L. E.   Imager's challenge
Modesitt, L. E.   Imager's intrigue
Pears, I.   The portrait

PORTRAIT PAINTING
Manual of painting & calligraphy

PORTRAITS
See also Art; Biography; Pictures

PORTRAITS -- FICTION
Wilde, O.   The picture of Dorian Gray

PORTUGAL
Antunes, A. L.   The inquisitors' manual
Cornwell, B.   Sharpe's havoc

PORTUGAL -- FICTION
Manual of painting & calligraphy

PORTUGAL -- LISBON
Saramago, J.   The history of the siege of Lisbon
Zimler, R.   The last kabbalist of Lisbon

PORTUGAL -- RURAL LIFE
L'Engle, M.   The love letters

PORTUGUESE -- CANADA
De Sa, A.   Barnacle love

PORTUGUESE -- JAPAN
Endo, S.   Silence

Poseidon's gold. Davis, L.

The **position.** Wolitzer, M.

The **possessed.** Dostoyevsky, F.

Possessing the secret of joy. Walker, A.

Possession. Byatt, A. S.

The **possession** of Mr Cave. Haig, M.

The **possibility** of an island. Houellebecq, M.

Post. Masters, H.

POST OFFICE *See* Postal service

The **post-birthday** world. Shriver, L.

POST-TRAUMATIC STRESS DISORDER
See also Anxiety; Neuroses; Stress (Psychology)
Robinson, R.   Sparta

POSTAGE STAMPS *See* Postal service

POSTAL SERVICE
See also Communication; Transportation
Blake, S.   The postmistress
Brown, C.   Lamb in love

Postcards. Proulx, A.

Postcards from Berlin. Leroy, M.

POSTERS *See* Advertising; Commercial art

The **posthumous** papers of the Pickwick Club.
Dickens, C.

POSTIMPRESSIONISM (ART) *See* Art

The **postman** always rings twice, double indemnity,
Mildred Pierce and selected stories. Cain, J. M.

The **postmistress.** Blake, S.

The **postmortal.** Magary, D.

Postsingular. Rucker, R. v. B.

POT (DRUG) *See* Marijuana

POTOSÍ (BOLIVIA) -- HISTORY -- 17TH CENTURY
Alfieri, A.   City of silver

POTPOURRI *See* Herbs; Nature craft; Perfumes

Potsdam station. Downing, D.

Potshot. Parker, R. B.

The **potter's** field. Peters, E.

POTTERS *See* Artists

POULTRY *See* Birds; Domestic animals

Pound for pound. Toole, F. X.

POVERTY
See also Economic conditions; Social problems
Adiga, A.   The white tiger
Allison, D.   Bastard out of Carolina
Boyle, T. C.   The tortilla curtain
Bragg, M.   A son of war
Brown, L.   Joe
Byrne, T.   Ghosts and lightning

Wilder, T. The bridge of San Luis Rey
PREDICTIONS *See* Forecasting; Prophecies
PREFABRICATED BUILDINGS *See* Buildings
PREFABRICATED HOUSES *See* Domestic architecture; House construction; Houses; Prefabricated buildings
The **prefect.** Reynolds, A.
PREGNANCY
Bachelder, C. Abbott awaits
Berne, S. A perfect arrangement
Burgess, M. Dogfight, a love story
Hallgrimur Helgason 101 Reykjavik
Hannah, K. On Mystic lake
Haruf, K. Plainsong
Hawke, E. Ash Wednesday
Joss, M. Among the missing
Kimmel, H. The used world
McPhee, J. No ordinary matter
Michaud, J. When Tito loved Clara
Parks Getting mother's body
Pottinger, S. The last Nazi
Read, P. P. Alice in exile
Reed, K. The baby merchant
Schwartz, L. S. In the family way
Snyder, D. J. Night crossing
Ward, J. Salvage the bones
Weiner, J. Little earthquakes
PREGNANCY -- FICTION
Novak, C. Breed
PREGNANT TEENAGERS
Coplin, A. The orchardist
The **pregnant** widow. Amis, M.
PREGNANT WOMEN -- CRIMES AGAINST
Gaspar de Alba, A. Desert blood
PREGNANT WOMEN
Goudge, E. Stranger in paradise
Joss, M. Half broken things
PREHISTORIC ANIMALS *See* Animals; Fossils
PREHISTORIC ART *See* Art
PREHISTORIC MAN
Auel, J. M. The Clan of the Cave Bear
Auel, J. M. The land of painted caves
Cornwell, B. Stonehenge, 2000 B.C.
Darnton, J. Neanderthal
Gear, K. O. People of the owl
Gear, W. M. People of the thunder
Golding, W. The inheritors
Harrison, S. Brother Wind
Harrison, S. Call down the stars
Harrison, S. Cry of the wind
Harrison, S. Mother earth, father sky
Harrison, S. My sister the moon
Harrison, S. Song of the river
Holland, C. Pillar of the Sky
Tarr, J. Lady of horses
Thomas, E. M. Reindeer Moon

PREHISTORIC PEOPLES *See* Antiquities; Archeology; Human beings
PREHISTORIC TIMES
Auel, J. M. The Clan of the Cave Bear
Auel, J. M. The land of painted caves
Barone, S. Dawn of empire
Barone, S. Empire rising
Crace, J. The gift of stones
Holland, C. Pillar of the Sky
Thomas, E. M. Reindeer Moon
PREHISTORY *See* Archeology; Fossil hominids; Prehistoric peoples
PREJUDICE *See* Prejudices
PREJUDICES
See also Attitude (Psychology); Emotions; Interpersonal relations
Brown, S. The witness
Coldsmith, D. The long journey home
Dallas, S. Tallgrass
Dexter, P. Paris Trout
Dische, I. The Empress of Weehawken
Grau, S. A. The keepers of the house
Grisham, J. A painted house
Guterson, D. Snow falling on cedars
Katzenbach, J. Hart's war
Keneally, T. River town
Lee, D. Country of origin
Matthiessen, P. Lost Man's River
Morrison, T. Tar baby
Paretsky, S. Bleeding Kansas
Perez Galdos, B. Dona Perfecta
Powers, R. The time of our singing
See, L. Shanghai girls
Straight, S. Highwire moon
Waldman, A. The submission
West, D. The wedding
PREJUDICES -- FICTION
Hamill, P. Snow in August
Lipman, E. The Inn at Lake Devine
Prelude to Foundation. Asimov, I.
Prelude to terror. MacInnes, H.
PREMIERS *See* Prime ministers
PREMONITIONS
King, S. The dead zone
King, S. The shining
PRENATAL CARE *See* Pregnancy
Prep. Sittenfeld, C.
PREPARATORY SCHOOLS
Cooke, C. Daughters of the revolution
Schulman, H. This beautiful life
PREPARED CEREALS *See* Breakfasts; Food
PRESCHOOL CHILDREN *See* Children
PRESCHOOL EDUCATION *See* Education
PRESCHOOLS
Glass, J. The widower's tale
The **presence.** Saul, J.

Harris, J. Peaches for Father Francis
Malliet, G. M. A fatal winter
Marley, L. The child goddess
PRIESTS -- FRANCE
Harris, J. Peaches for Father Francis
PRIESTS -- ICELAND -- 19TH CENTURY
The blue fox
Primal fear. Diehl, W.
PRIMARIES *See* Elections; Political conventions;
Politics
Primary colors. Klein, J.
Primary inversion. Asaro, C.
PRIMATOLOGISTS
Gonzales, L. Lucy
Wesselmann, D. L. Captivity
Prime cut. Davidson, D. M.
The **prime** minister. Trollope, A.
PRIME MINISTERS
Antunes, A. L. The inquisitors' manual
Forsyth, F. The day of the jackal
Harris, R. The ghost
Hunt, R. Mr. Chartwell
Kadare, I. The Successor
Russell, M. D. Dreamers of the day
Townsend, S. Number 10
PRIME MINISTERS -- ASSASSINATION
Walton, J. Ha'penny
**PRIME MINISTERS -- SWEDEN -- ASSASSINA-
TION**
Persson, L. G. W. Another time, another life
Persson, L. G. W. Between summer's longing and
winter's end
PRIME MINISTERS -- SWEDEN -- DEATH
Persson, L. G. W. Between summer's longing and
winter's end
The **prime** of Miss Jean Brodie. Spark, M.
Prime witness. Martini, S. P.
Primitive people. Prose, F.
Prince of chaos. Zelazny, R.
Prince of Fire. Silva, D.
Prince of thorns. Lawrence, M.
The **prince** of tides. Conroy, P.
Princeps. Modesitt, L. E.
PRINCES
See also Courts and courtiers
Doyle, A. C. The White Company
Lawrence, M. Prince of thorns
Penman, S. K. The reckoning
Saint-Exupery, A. d. The little prince
Seton, A. Katherine
PRINCES AND PRINCESSES *See* Princes; Prin-
cesses
The **princes** of Ireland. Rutherfurd, E.
The **princess** bride. Goldman, W.
The **princess** of Burundi. Eriksson, K.
PRINCESSES

See also Courts and courtiers
Ali, M. Untold story
Amirrezvani, A. Equal of the sun
Holland, C. The angel and the sword
Lee, T. White as snow
Mehta, G. Raj
Mishima, Y. The Temple of Dawn
Penman, S. K. When Christ and his saints slept
Seton, A. Katherine
Sherwood, F. Night of sorrows
Vollmann, W. T. Argall
PRINCESSES -- FICTION
Gray, J. How to Tame Your Duke
Moran, M. The second empress
Putney, M. J. Nowhere near respectable
PRINCETON (N.J.)
Oates, J. C. The Accursed
PRINCETON UNIVERSITY
Caldwell, I. The rule of four
Principles of American nuclear chemistry. McMa-
hon, T. A.
Prine, Sarah Agnes
About
Turner, N. E. These is my words
PRINTERS
Donoghue, E. The sealed letter
PRINTERS AND PRINTING
Lovric, M. The floating book
PRINTING *See* Bibliography; Book industry;
Graphic arts; Industrial arts; Publishers and pub-
lishing
PRINTING -- SPECIMENS *See* Advertising; Ini-
tials
PRISON ESCAPES *See* Escapes
PRISON REFORM *See* Social problems
PRISON WARDENS -- GREAT BRITAIN
Lelic, S. The facility
The **prisoner** of heaven. Ruiz Zafon, C.
The **prisoner** of Zenda. Hope, A.
Prisoner's dilemma. Powers, R.
The **prisoner's** wife. MacDonald, G.
PRISONERS
See also Criminals
Flanagan, R. Gould's book of fish
Lazar, Z. Sway
Ward, L. Outside valentine
PRISONERS -- AUSTRALIA
Grenville, K. The secret river
PRISONERS -- FICTION
Lyndon, R. Hawk quest
PRISONERS AND PRISONS
See also Prisoners; Prisoners of war; Prisons
Baldwin, J. If Beale Street could talk
Blatty, W. P. Dimiter
Cheever, J. Falconer
Egan, J. The keep

Brooks, B. Frontier justice

Browne, S. G. Lucky bastard

Child, L. A wanted man

Collins, M. A. Target Lancer

Coover, R. Noir

Cussler, C. The spy

Cussler, C. The striker

Cussler, C. The thief

Estleman, L. D. Amos Walker

Kerr, P. Prague fatale

Lutz, L. The Spellman files

Memminger, C. Aloha, lady blue

Mosley, W. Six easy pieces

Mosley, W. When the thrill is gone

Parker, R. B. Hugger mugger

Perry, T. Fidelity

Pronzini, B. Hellbox

Robards, K. To trust a stranger

Sandford, J. Easy prey

Scott, J. The wrecker

Shepherd, L. A fatal likeness

Stevens, T. The informationist

PRIVATE INVESTIGATORS -- GERMANY

Kerr, P. If the dead rise not

Kerr, P. A Man Without Breath

PRIVATE INVESTIGATORS -- INDIA

Hall, T. The case of the deadly butter chicken

PRIVATE INVESTIGATORS -- MINNESOTA --
MINNEAPOLIS

Sandford, J. Silken prey

Sandford, J. Chosen prey

Sandford, J. Hidden prey

Sandford, J. Mortal prey

Sandford, J. Naked prey

PRIVATE INVESTIGATORS -- NEW YORK
(STATE) -- NEW YORK

Collins, M. A. Black hats

Lethem, J. Motherless Brooklyn

Mosley, W. All I did was shoot my man

Vachss, A. H. Choice of evil

Vachss, A. H. Down here

Woods, S. Cold paradise

Woods, S. Dirty work

Woods, S. Reckless abandon

Woods, S. The short forever

PRIVATE INVESTIGATORS -- NEW ZEALAND
-- CHRISTCHURCH

Cleave, P. Cemetery Lake

Private life. Smiley, J.

The **private** lives of Pippa Lee. Miller, R.

The **private** patient. James, P. D.

PRIVATE SCHOOLS

Miller, J. The year of the gadfly

PRIVATE SECRETARIES

Truong, M. T. D. The book of salt

PRIVATE SECRETARIES -- FICTION

Fields, J. The age of desire

PRIVATEERING *See* International law; Naval art
and science; Naval history; Pirates

Privileged conversation. Hunter, E.

The **privileges**. Dee, J.

The **prize**. Wallace, I.

PRIZE FIGHTING *See* Boxing

Prizes. Frame, J.

PROBABILITIES *See* Algebra; Logic; Mathematics; Statistics

Probability moon. Kress, N.

Probability sun. Kress, N.

The **probable** future. Hoffman, A.

PROBATE LAW AND PRACTICE *See* Civil procedure; Inheritance and succession

PROBATION *See* Corrections; Criminal law;
Prisons; Punishment; Reformatories; Social case
work

PROBATION OFFICERS

Leonard, E. Maximum Bob

Pelecanos, G. P. Drama city

Rosenberg, N. T. First offense

Rosenberg, N. T. Sullivan's law

PROBIOTICS *See* Dietary supplements; Microorganisms

PROBLEM CHILDREN *See* Emotionally disturbed children

PROBLEM DRINKING *See* Alcoholism

PROBLEM FAMILIES

Franzen, J. Freedom

Haig, M. The Radleys

King, L. The father of the rain

Koontz, D. R. One door away from heaven

Lawson, M. Crow Lake

Lundrigan, N. Glass boys

O'Dell, T. Back roads

Woodrell, D. The death of sweet mister

Proctor, Ezekiel, 1831-1907
About

McMurtry, L. Zeke and Ned

PRODIGAL SON (PARABLE) *See* Parables

Prodigal summer. Kingsolver, B.

PROFESSIONAL EDUCATION *See* Education;
Higher education; Learning and scholarship

PROFESSIONAL ETHICS *See* Ethics

PROFESSIONAL LIABILITY *See* Malpractice

The **professionals.** Laukkanen, O.

PROFESSIONS -- TORT LIABILITY *See* Malpractice

The **professor** of desire. Roth, P.

The **professor's** daughter. Read, P. P.

PROFESSORS *See* Educators; Teachers

PROFIT *See* Business; Capital; Economics;
Wealth

PROGRAMMING (COMPUTERS)

Tracy, P. J. Monkeewrench

Garcia Marquez, G. Memories of my melancholy whores

George, E. What came before he shot her

Gruber, M. Valley of bones

Harrison, K. The binding chair

Martini, S. P. Compelling evidence

McGinniss, J. The delivery man

Spencer, S. Willing

Turner, F. W. Redemption

Vargas Llosa, M. Captain Pantoja and the Special Service

Vargas Llosa, M. The Green House

Vollmann, W. T. The royal family

PROSTITUTION -- FICTION

Faletti, G. A pimp's notes

Lippman, L. And when she was good

Perry, T. The boyfriend

Sada, D. Almost never

Watkins, C. V. Battleborn

Protect and defend. Patterson, R. N.

PROTECTION OF ANIMALS *See* Animal welfare

PROTECTION OF GAME *See* Game protection

PROTECTION OF NATURAL SCENERY *See* Landscape protection; Natural monuments; Nature conservation

PROTESTANT REFORMATION *See* Reformation

PROTESTANTISM *See* Christianity; Church history

PROTOZOA *See* Microorganisms

Proven guilty. Butcher, J.

PROVIDENCE (R.I.)

DeSilva, B. Cliff Walk

DeSilva, B. Rogue island

PROVIDENCE AND GOVERNMENT OF GOD *See* God

PRUNING

See also Forests and forestry; Fruit culture; Gardening; Trees

Psalms of Isaak saga [series]

Scholes, K. Lamentation

PSYCHE (GODDESS)

Lewis, C. S. Till we have faces

PSYCHIATRIC HOSPITAL PATIENTS

Kesey, K. One flew over the cuckoo's nest

LaValle, V. D. The devil in silver

Lehane, D. Shutter Island

PSYCHIATRIC HOSPITALS

Kesey, K. One flew over the cuckoo's nest

LaValle, V. D. The devil in silver

Nayman, S. The listener

PSYCHIATRISTS

See also Psychologists

Ablow, K. R. Compulsion

Barker, P. The eye in the door

Barker, P. The ghost road

Barker, P. Regeneration

Faulks, S. Human traces

Friedman, M. Martian Dawn

Galchen, R. Atmospheric disturbances

Glass, J. The whole world over

Greenberg, J. I never promised you a rose garden

Guest, J. Ordinary people

Hand, E. Mortal love

Hart, J. The reconstructionist

Hoban, R. Angelica's Grotto

Hunter, E. Privileged conversation

Hustvedt, S. The sorrows of an American

Jong, E. Fear of flying

Koontz, D. R. False memory

Kostova, E. The swan thieves

Le Guin, U. K. The lathe of heaven

MacNeil, R. Burden of desire

McGrath, P. Asylum

McGrath, P. Trauma

Mina, D. Deception

Moore, S. The big girls

Nayman, S. The listener

Perlman, E. Seven types of ambiguity

Potok, C. The promise

Rosten, L. Captain Newman, M.D.

Schwartz, L. S. In the family way

Sittenfeld, C. The man of my dreams

Templeton, E. Gordon

Wideman, J. E. Fanon

PSYCHIATRISTS -- FICTION

Raimondo, L. Dante's wood

Robotham, M. Suspect

Tallis, F. Fatal lies

PSYCHIATRY *See* Medicine

PSYCHIC ABILITY

Sittenfeld, C. Sisterland

PSYCHICS

Greeley, A. M. Irish stew!

Kearsley, S. The Firebird

Krentz, J. A. Dream eyes

Odell, J. The healing

Owens, R. D. Heart thief

Sittenfeld, C. Sisterland

Wilson, S. The fortune teller's daughter

PSYCHO (MOTION PICTURE: 1960)

DeLillo, D. Point Omega

PSYCHOANALYSIS

Davies, R. The manticore

Lodge, D. Therapy

Rossner, J. August

Roth, P. My life as a man

Roth, P. Portnoy's complaint

Rubenfeld, J. The death instinct

Thomas, D. M. The white hotel

Wenner, K. Dancing with Einstein

Hoffman, J. Retribution
Landay, W. Defending Jacob
Meltzer, B. Dead even
Patterson, R. N. Dark lady
Reuland, R. Semiautomatic
Rosenberg, N. T. Buried evidence
Tanenbaum, R. True justice
Turow, S. Innocent
Vachss, A. H. Down here

PUBLIC RELATIONS
Dezenhall, E. Money wanders
Public smiles, private tears. Van Slyke, H.
PUBLIC SPEAKING *See* Communication
PUBLICITY
Abbott, M. E. The song is you
PUBLISHERS AND PUBLISHING
Bank, M. The girls' guide to hunting and fishing
Blackwell, E. Grub
Canin, E. America America
Colwin, L. A big storm knocked it over
Eco, U. Foucault's pendulum
Grimes, M. Foul matter
Heller, J. Best enemies
Ignatius, D. The Sun King
Kotzwinkle, W. The bear went over the mountain
Langer, A. The thieves of Manhattan
Lemann, N. Malaise
Martini, S. P. The list
Michener, J. A. The novel
Pearl, M. The last Dickens
Sanders, L. Guilty pleasures
Saramago, J. The history of the siege of Lisbon
Schaffert, T. The coffins of Little Hope
Spark, M. A far cry from Kensington
Vidal, G. Empire
Vidal, G. The golden age
Vidal, G. Washington, D.C.
Weldon, F. Big girls don't cry
PUBLISHERS' CATALOGS *See* Publishers and publishing
PUBLISHERS' STANDARD BOOK NUMBERS *See* Publishers and publishing
PUBLISHING *See* Publishers and publishing
PUBLISHING EXECUTIVES
Pearl, M. The last Dickens
Pudd'nhead Wilson. Twain, M.
PUERTO RICO
Santiago, E. Conquistadora
Puffin classics [series]
Crane, S. The red badge of courage
PUFFINS *See* Birds
PUGILISM *See* Boxing
PULLMAN, PHILIP, 1946-
Pullman, P. Fairy tales from the Brothers Grimm
Pulse. Barnes, J.
PUNCTUALITY *See* Time; Virtue

PUNISHMENT
Crace, J. Harvest
PUNK CULTURE *See* Counter culture
PUNK ROCK MUSIC
Bognanni, P. The house of tomorrow
Egan, J. A visit from the Goon Squad
PUNS *See* Wit and humor
The **puppet** masters. Heinlein, R. A.
PUPPETS AND PUPPET PLAYS
Tyler, A. Morgan's passing
PUPPIES *See* Dogs
Pure. Baggott, J.
Pure. Miller, A.
The **pure** in heart. Hill, S.
Purgatory chasm. Ulfelder, S.
PURITANISM
Seton, A. The Winthrop woman
PURITANS
Conde, M. I, Tituba, black witch of Salem
Hawthorne, N. The House of the Seven Gables
Hawthorne, N. The scarlet letter
Nissenson, H. The pilgrim
Purity of blood. Perez-Reverte, A.
Purnell, Benjamin Franklin, 1861-1927
About
Kasischke, L. Eden Springs
Purple dots. Lehrer, J.
A **purple** place for dying. MacDonald, J. D.
Pursuit. Perry, T.
The **pursuit** of Alice Thrift. Lipman, E.
The **pursuit** of love & Love in a cold climate. Mitford, N.
Pushcart prize XXXVII.
Pushcart prize XXXVII.
Pushover. O'Donnell, L.
Put a lid on it. Westlake, D. E.
The **Puttermesser** papers. Ozick, C.
Puzo, Mario, 1920-1999
About
Winegardner, M. The Godfather returns
The **puzzled** heart. Cross, A.
PUZZLES
Cline, E. Ready player one
Pygmy. Palahniuk, C.
Pylon. Faulkner, W.
Pym. Johnson, M.
PYRAMIDS *See* Ancient architecture; Archeology; Monuments
Pyro. Emerson, E. W.
Pythagoras
About
Goodman, C. The night villa

Q

Q is for quarry. Grafton, S.
QAIDA (ORGANIZATION) *See* Terrorism

QUINTUPLETS
Mason, B. A. Feather crowns

Quite a year for plums. White, B.

Quite honestly. Mortimer, J.

Quo Vadis. Sienkiewicz, H.

QUR'AN *See* Islam; Sacred books

R

R is for ricochet. Grafton, S.

RABBIS
See also Clergy; Judaism

Abraham, P. The romance reader

Doctorow, E. L. City of God

Hamill, P. Snow in August

Kemelman, H. The day the rabbi resigned

Kemelman, H. Friday the rabbi slept late

Kemelman, H. Monday the rabbi took off

Kemelman, H. One fine day the rabbi bought a cross

Kemelman, H. Saturday the rabbi went hungry

Kemelman, H. Sunday the rabbi stayed home

Kemelman, H. Thursday the rabbi walked out

Kemelman, H. Wednesday the rabbi got wet

Littell, R. Vicious circle

Potok, C. The promise

Rosen, J. Joy comes in the morning

Sherwood, F. The book of splendor

Stern, S. The frozen rabbi

Wiesel, E. The Golem

RABBIS -- FICTION
Anton, M. Rav Hisda's daughter, book I, apprentice

Jensen, J. Dante's equation

Rabbit Angstrom. Updike, J.

Rabbit at rest. Updike, J.

Rabbit is rich. Updike, J.

Rabbit redux. Updike, J.

Rabbit, run. Updike, J.

RABBITS
Adams, R. Watership Down

Rabble in arms. Roberts, K. L.

RABIES
King, S. Cujo

The **race.** Cussler, C.

RACE AWARENESS *See* Race relations

RACE DISCRIMINATION *See* Discrimination; Race relations; Racism; Social problems

Race for the dying. Havill, S.

RACE HORSES
Gordon, J. Lord of Misrule

Race of scorpions. Dunnett, D.

RACE PROBLEMS *See* Race relations

RACE RELATIONS
See also Acculturation; Ethnology; Sociology

Beatty, P. Slumberland

D'Souza, T. Whiteman

Evaristo, B. Blonde roots

Vassanji, M. G. The in-between world of Vikram Lall

RACE RELATIONS -- FICTION
Arvin, R. Blood of angels

Lansdale, J. R. Edge of dark water

RACIAL INTEGRATION *See* Race relations

RACIAL INTERMARRIAGE *See* Interracial marriage

RACIALLY MIXED CHILDREN
Thompson, V. Murder in Chinatown

RACIALLY MIXED PEOPLE
Lawrence, C. The case of the deadly desperados

Thompson, V. Murder in Chinatown

Wilson, C. Cotton

RACING
McCrumb, S. St. Dale

RACISM
See also Attitude (Psychology); Prejudices; Race awareness; Race relations

Devoto, P. C. The summer we got saved

Everett, P. L. I am Not Sidney Poitier

Marlette, D. Magic time

Morrison, T. Home

Pelecanos, G. P. Right as rain

Strauss, D. More than it hurts you

Vernon, O. A killing in this town

RADAR *See* Navigation; Radio; Remote sensing

Radiance. Scholz, C.

The **radiant** way. Drabble, M.

RADIATION *See* Optics; Physics; Waves

RADIATION -- PHYSIOLOGICAL EFFECT
Cummins, A. Yellowcake

Hill, R. When all is said and done

Shute, N. On the beach

Wiggins, M. Evidence of things unseen

RADICALISM
See also Political science; Revolutions; Right and left (Political science)

Kushner, R. The flamethrowers

RADICALS AND RADICALISM
Carey, P. His illegal self

Goodwillie, D. American subversive

Gordon, N. The company you keep

Keating, C. Layla

Kunzru, H. My revolutions

Leonard, E. Freaky Deaky

Lessing, D. M. The good terrorist

Lessing, D. M. The sweetest dream

Meek, J. The people's act of love

Nunez, S. The last of her kind

Piercy, M. Vida

Plain, B. Harvest

Read, P. P. The professor's daughter

Spiotta, D. Eat the document

Turow, S. The laws of our fathers

Rally round the flag, boys! Shulman, M.

Rama [series]

Clarke, A. C. The Garden of Rama

Clarke, A. C. Rama II

Clarke, A. C. Rama revealed

Clarke, A. C. Rendezvous with Rama

Rama II. Clarke, A. C.

Rama revealed. Clarke, A. C.

Ramanujan Aiyangar, Srinivasa, 1887-1920

About

Leavitt, D. The Indian clerk

RAMOTSWE, PRECIOUS (FICTITIOUS CHARACTER)

McCall Smith, A. The full cupboard of life

McCall Smith, A. The Kalahari typing school for men

McCall Smith, A. The Limpopo Academy of Private Detection

McCall Smith, A. The No. 1 Ladies' Detective Agency

McCall Smith, A. The Saturday big tent wedding party

McCall Smith, A. Tea time for the traditionally built

Ramses III, King of Egypt

About

Geagley, B. Year of the hyenas

Ran away. Hambly, B.

RANCH LIFE

See also Farm life; Frontier and pioneer life

Bacon, C. Split estate

Blew, M. C. Jackalope dreams

Caputo, P. Crossers

Davis, C. Winter range

Doig, I. English Creek

Grey, Z. Woman of the frontier

Kittredge, W. The Willow Field

Kyle, A. The god of animals

L'Amour, L. The Californios

Latham, A. Code of the West

McCarthy, C. All the pretty horses

McCarthy, C. Cities of the plain

McCullough, C. The thorn birds

McGuane, T. Keep the change

McGuane, T. Nobody's angel

Meyers, K. The work of wolves

Overholser, W. D. Death of a cattle king

Richter, C. The sea of grass

Schaefer, J. W. Monte Walsh

Schaefer, J. W. Shane

Sherman, J. The Baron war

Steinbeck, J. Of mice and men

Turner, N. E. These is my words

Walls, J. Half broke horses

Weisgarber, A. The personal history of Rachel Dupree

Williamson, P. The outsider

Zimmer, M. Wild side of the river

RANCH LIFE -- CALIFORNIA

Soli, T. The forgetting tree

RANCH LIFE -- FICTION

Eagle, K. Ride a painted pony

RANCH LIFE -- SOUTH DAKOTA

Eagle, K. Ride a painted pony

RANCHERS -- COLORADO

Doss, J. D. The old gray wolf

RANCHERS

Alexander, T. Rekindled

Brooks, B. Winter kill

Caputo, P. Crossers

Carlson, R. The signal

Walls, J. Half broke horses

RANCHES -- FICTION

Kyle, A. The god of animals

RAND AL'THOR (FICTITIOUS CHARACTER)

Jordan, R. A memory of light

RANDALL, CLAIRE (FICTITIOUS CHARACTER)

Gabaldon, D. Voyager

Random harvest. Hilton, J.

Random violence. Mackenzie, J.

Random winds. Plain, B.

Range of ghosts. Bear, E.

RANGELANDS -- OREGON

Keesey, A. Little century

The **ranger.** Atkins, A.

RANK *See* Social classes

Ransom. Malouf, D.

Rant. Palahniuk, C.

Rape. Oates, J. C.

RAPE

Brink, A. P. The other side of silence

Coetzee, J. M. Disgrace

Dallas, S. Tallgrass

Davis, A. Wonder when you'll miss me

Deford, F. The entitled

Fielding, J. Tell me no secrets

Gerritsen, T. The surgeon

Grisham, J. A time to kill

Kay, T. The runaway

Lawrence, M. K. Hearts and bones

Lewis, M. G. The monk

Michael, J. Sleeping beauty

Nooteboom, C. Lost paradise

Oates, J. C. Rape

Oates, J. C. We were the Mulvaneys

Parker, B. Blood relations

Patterson, R. N. Degree of guilt

Rendell, R. Live flesh

Rosenberg, N. T. Buried evidence

Rosenberg, N. T. Mitigating circumstances

Scott, P. The day of the scorpion

The **rebels** of Ireland. Rutherfurd, E.

REBIRTH *See* Reincarnation

REBUSES *See* Literary recreations; Puzzles; Riddles

Recalled to life. Hill, R.

Recessional. Michener, J. A.

RECESSIONS
 Eggers, D. A hologram for the king

A **recipe** for bees. Anderson-Dargatz, G.

Reckless. Gross, A.

Reckless abandon. Woods, S.

Reckless endangerment. Tanenbaum, R.

A **reckoning.** Sarton, M.

The **reckoning.** Penman, S. K.

The **reckoning.** Long, J.

RECLUSES
 See also Hermits
 Doctorow, E. L. Homer & Langley
 Mosley, W. The last days of Ptolemy Grey

The **recognitions.** Gaddis, W.

The **recognitions.** Gaddis, W.

RECOMBINANT DNA *See* DNA; Genetic engineering; Genetic recombination

RECONCILIATION
 Jeffries, S. 'Twas the night after Christmas
 Pelecanos, G. P. The turnaround

Reconstruction. Herron, M.

RECONSTRUCTION
 Mitchell, M. Gone with the wind
 Smith, L. On Agate Hill

RECONSTRUCTION (1865-1876)
 Mitchell, M. Gone with the wind

RECONSTRUCTION (1939-1951) -- SICILY
 Hersey, J. A bell for Adano

RECONSTRUCTION (U.S. HISTORY, 1865-1877)
 Pitts, L. Freeman

The **reconstructionist.** Hart, J.

RECORDINGS, SOUND *See* Sound recordings

RECORDS, PHONOGRAPH *See* Sound recordings

RECOVERED MEMORY *See* Memory

RECOVERING ADDICTS *See* Drug addicts

RECOVERING ALCOHOLICS
 Ulfelder, S. Purgatory chasm

RECOVERING ALCOHOLICS -- FICTION
 Jerkins, G. The ninth step

The **rector's** wife. Trollope, J.

RECTORS *See* Clergy

RECYCLING *See* Energy conservation; Pollution control industry; Salvage

RED *See* Color

The **red** and the black. Stendhal

Red angel. Heffernan, W.

Red April. Roncagliolo, S.

RED ARMY FACTION

Schlink, B. The weekend

The **red** badge of courage. Crane, S.

The **red** badge of courage and other stories. Crane, S.

Red Branch. Llywelyn, M.

Red cat. Spiegelman, P.

The **red** chamber. Chen, P. A.

The **red** convertible. Erdrich, L.

Red country. Abercrombie, J.

A **red** death. Mosley, W.

The **red** door. Todd, C.

Red Dragon. Harris, T.

The **red** garden. Hoffman, A.

Red gold. Furst, A.

The **red** heart. Thom, J. A.

Red herring. Mayor, A.

A **red** herring without mustard. Bradley, A.

Red Hook Road. Waldman, A.

The **red** house. Haddon, M.

Red lightning. Varley, J.

Red mandarin dress. Qiu Xiaolong

Red Mars. Robinson, K. S.

Red moon. Percy, B.

Red on red. Conlon, E.

The **red** passport. Shonk, K.

The **Red** Pavilion. Gulik, R. H. v.

The **red** queen. Gregory, P.

Red rover. McNamer, D.

The **red** scarf. Furnivall, K.

Red sky at night. Hall, J. W.

Red sparrow. Matthews, J.

Red Spectres.

Red Square. Smith, M. C.

The **red** tent. Diamant, A.

The **red** thread. Hood, A.

Red thunder. Varley, J.

The **red** tree. Kiernan, C. R.

Red, white and blue. Isaacs, S.

The **redbreast.** Nesbo, J.

Redburn, his first voyage; White-jacket, or, The world in a man-of-war; Moby-Dick, or, The whale. Stahlberg, L.

The **redeemer.**

Redemption. Uris, L.

Redemption. Turner, F. W.

REDEMPTION
 Cleaver, S. Saving Erasmus
 Warrington, F. Midsummer night

Redemption in indigo. Lord, K.

Redline the stars. Norton, A.

Redshirts. Scalzi, J.

REDUCING
 Levenkron, S. The best little girl in the world

REEF ECOLOGY *See* Ecology; Marine ecology

REFERENCE BOOKS *See* Bibliography; Books; Books and reading

Mason, B. A. Feather crowns
McGowan, K. The expected one
Meek, J. The people's act of love
Mishima, Y. The temple of the golden pavilion
Murdoch, I. The bell
Murdoch, I. The green knight
O'Connor, F. Wise blood
Oe, K. An echo of heaven
Perez Galdos, B. Dona Perfecta
Picoult, J. Sing you home
Preston, D. Blasphemy
Robbins, T. Skinny legs and all
Salinger, J. D. Franny & Zooey
Self, W. The Book of Dave
Sorokin, V. Ice
Spark, M. The Mandelbaum Gate
Stone, R. Damascus Gate
Updike, J. In the beauty of the lilies
Updike, J. S
Vidal, G. Creation
West, M. L. The devil's advocate

RELIGION -- FICTION
Hansen, R. Mariette in ecstasy
Irving, J. A prayer for Owen Meany
L'Engle, M. A live coal in the sea
Mahfouz, N. Children of the alley
Moore, B. Black robe
Updike, J. In the beauty of the lilies

RELIGION AND POLITICS *See* Politics; Religion

RELIGION AND SCIENCE *See* Religion; Science

RELIGION AND SOCIOLOGY *See* Religion; Sociology

RELIGION IN LITERATURE *See* Literature; Religion

RELIGIOUS ART *See* Art

RELIGIOUS AWAKENING *See* Religion

RELIGIOUS BELIEF *See* Faith

RELIGIOUS CEREMONIES *See* Rites and ceremonies

RELIGIOUS CULTS *See* Cults

RELIGIOUS DENOMINATIONS *See* Sects

RELIGIOUS EDUCATION *See* Education; Religion

RELIGIOUS FUNDAMENTALISM *See* Religion

RELIGIOUS GRAPHIC NOVELS *See* Graphic novels

RELIGIOUS HOLIDAYS *See* Holidays; Rites and ceremonies

RELIGIOUS INSTITUTIONS *See* Associations; Religion

RELIGIOUS LIFE *See* Religion

RELIGIOUS LIFE (CHRISTIAN) *See* Christian life

RELIGIOUS ORDERS *See* Monasticism and religious orders

RELIGIOUS PERSECUTION *See* Persecution

RELIGIOUS POETRY *See* Poetry; Religious literature

RELIGIOUS REFUGEES *See* Refugees

RELIGIOUS TOLERANCE
Høeg, P. The elephant keepers' children

Reliquary. Preston, D.

The **reluctant** fundamentalist. Hamid, M.

Remainder. McCarthy, T.

The **remains** of the day. Ishiguro, K.

Remarkable creatures. Chevalier, T.

REMARRIAGE
See also Marriage
Barfoot, J. Critical injuries
DeMille, N. The gate house
Mitchard, J. Twelve times blessed
Robinson, R. Sweetwater
Trollope, J. Marrying the mistress
Trollope, J. Other people's children

Remember me. Clark, M. H.

Remember me. Hendrie, L.

Remember me, Irene. Burke, J.

Remembering Babylon. Malouf, D.

Remembering the bones. Itani, F.

Remembrance of things past. Proust, M.

Remembrance Rock. Sandburg, C.

REMEMBRANCE SUNDAY
Hill, S. The vows of silence

REMINISCING IN OLD AGE
Banville, J. Ancient light
Benioff, D. City of thieves
Gutcheon, B. R. More than you know
Harding, P. Tinkers
Rawles, N. My Jim

The **remorseful** day. Dexter, C.

Remus, George, 1876-1952
About
Holden, C. The jazz bird

RENAISSANCE
Poole, S. The Borgia mistress

RENAISSANCE -- ITALY -- ROME
Poole, S. The Borgia mistress

Rendezvous with Rama. Clarke, A. C.

The **renegades.** Young, T. W.

The **renegades** of Pern. McCaffrey, A.

Renoir, Auguste, 1841-1919
About
Vreeland, S. Luncheon of The Boating Party

RENOWN *See* Fame

REPARATIONS FOR HISTORICAL INJUSTICES
Conklin, T. The house girl

The **repeat** year. Lochen, A.

Repetition. Handke, P.

REPORT WRITING *See* Authorship

RETROSPECTIVE STORIES
Gardam, J. Old Filth
The **return.** Gruber, M.
The **return** man. Zito, V. M.
The **return** of Captain John Emmett. Speller, E.
The **return** of Gunner Asch. Kirst, H. H.
The **return** of Santiago. Resnick, M.
The **return** of the dancing master. Mankell, H.
The **return** of the king. Tolkien, J. R. R.
The **return** of the native. Hardy, T.
Return to Mars. Bova, B.
Return to Thrush Green. Read
The **Returned.** Mott, J.
Returning to earth. Harrison, J.
Reunion. Lightman, A. P.
REUNIONS
Berg, E. The last time I saw you
Clark, M. H. Nighttime is my time
Drabble, M. The sea lady
Goddard, R. Never go back
Goodman, C. The drowning tree
Jaffe, R. Class reunion
McCrumb, S. If ever I return, pretty Peggy-O
Siddons, A. R. Outer banks
Smith, L. The last girls
REUNIONS -- FICTION
Edugyan, E. Half-blood blues
Reuveni, David, 1490-ca. 1535
                About
Halter, M. Messiah
REVELATION *See* God; Supernatural; Theology
REVENGE
Alexie, S. Flight
Amis, K. The Russian girl
Archer, J. As the crow flies
Baker, K. The house of the stag
Balzac, H. d. Cousin Bette
Banks, I. Surface detail
Bear, G. Anvil of stars
Blatty, W. P. Dimiter
Block, L. Getting off
Bradford, B. T. The Ravenscar dynasty
Brink, A. P. The other side of silence
Bronte, E. Wuthering Heights
Caedmon's song The first cut
Calvo, J. Wonderful world
Carter, S. L. The emperor of Ocean Park
Chen, D. Brothers
Conrad, J. Victory
Cornwell, B. Vagabond
Cox, M. The meaning of night
Davis, C. Winter range
DeMille, N. The lion's game
Dickens, C. Great expectations
Dickens, C. A tale of two cities
Dolan, H. Very bad men

Dumas, A. The Count of Monte Cristo
Enger, L. Undiscovered country
Estleman, L. D. Gas City
Everett, P. L. The water cure
Fairstein, L. Killer heat
Faust, C. Money shot
Frame, R. The lantern bearers
Franklin, T. Hell at the breech
French, A. Billy
Galgut, D. The impostor
Garcia Marquez, G. Chronicle of a death foretold
George, E. What came before he shot her
Goddard, R. Beyond recall
Goldsmith, O. The First Wives Club
Goldsmith, O. Young wives
Goodman, C. Arcadia Falls
Gould, J. The best is yet to come
Grisham, J. The last juror
Grisham, J. A time to kill
Haig, M. The dead fathers club
Harris, J. Gentlemen and players
Harris, T. Hannibal rising
Harrison, S. Cry of the wind
Harrison, S. Song of the river
Haywood, G. A. Cemetery Road
Heffernan, W. The Dinosaur Club
Hiaasen, C. Skinny dip
Higgins, J. Bad company
Higgins, J. Day of reckoning
Higgins, J. Edge of danger
Higgins, J. Midnight runner
Higgins, J. The wolf at the door
Hill, J. Heart-shaped box
Hill, J. Horns
Hill, R. The woodcutter
Hill, S. Mrs. de Winter
Hunter, S. The 47th samurai
Hunter, S. Black light
Hunter, S. Time to hunt
Huston, C. The shotgun rule
Isegawa, M. Snakepit
James, P. D. Innocent blood
Jance, J. A. Kiss of the bees
Jiles, P. The color of lightning
Johansen, I. The ugly duckling
Just, W. S. Forgetfulness
Katzenbach, J. The analyst
Kellerman, J. Sunstroke
King, S. Bag of bones
King, S. Rose Madder
Korda, M. Worldly goods
Koryta, M. So cold the river
Lawrence, M. Prince of thorns
Le Carre, J. The night manager
Lebrecht, N. The song of names
Lehane, D. Mystic river

REVOLUTIONS

Bell, M. S. All souls' rising
Didion, J. A book of common prayer
Flanagan, T. The tenants of time
Gordimer, N. July's people
Heinlein, R. A. The moon is a harsh mistress
Keneally, T. To Asmara
Kushner, R. Telex from Cuba
Mengiste, M. Beneath the lion's gaze
Sienkiewicz, H. With fire and sword
Stone, R. A flag for sunrise

REVOLUTIONS -- FICTION

Flynn, M. On the razor's edge
Kennedy, K. The lord of illusion
Rajaniemi, H. The fractal prince

REYKJAVÍK (ICELAND)

Indridason, A. Outrage

RHETORIC *See* Language and languages

RHEUMATISM *See* Diseases

The **Rhinemann** exchange. Ludlum, R.

Rhino Ranch. McMurtry, L.

RHODE ISLAND

Casey, J. Compass rose
Casey, J. Spartina
Kiernan, C. R. The red tree
Rice, L. Blue moon
Shreve, A. Where or when
Updike, J. The widows of Eastwick
Updike, J. The witches of Eastwick
Weldon, F. Rhode Island blues

RHODE ISLAND -- NEWPORT

Rice, L. The deep blue sea for beginners
Rice, L. The geometry of sisters
Whitney, P. A. Spindrift
Wilder, T. Theophilus North

RHODE ISLAND -- PROVIDENCE

Hood, A. The knitting circle
Hood, A. The red thread
McLarty, R. Traveler

Rhode Island blues. Weldon, F.

Rhodes, Cecil John, 1853-1902

About

Harries, A. Manly pursuits

RHYMES *See* Limericks; Nonsense verses; Nursery rhymes; Poetry -- Collections

The **rhythm** of the road. Hall, A. L.

The **rice** mother. Manicka, R.

RICH

See also Social classes

Gallagher, S. The bedlam detective
Haimoff, M. These days are ours
Jenkins, V. An unattended death
Klaussmann, L. Tigers in red weather
Laukkanen, O. The professionals

The **rich** and the profane. Gash, J.

The **rich** are with you always. Ross-Macdonald, M.

Rich boy. Pomerantz, S.

Rich man, poor man. Shaw, I.

RICH PEOPLE -- ENGLAND

Coleridge, N. D. The adventuress
Gallagher, S. The bedlam detective

RICH PEOPLE

Dee, J. The privileges
Everett, P. L. I am Not Sidney Poitier
Galgut, D. The impostor
Koryta, M. So cold the river
McLaughlin, E. The nanny diaries
Patterson, V. This vacant paradise
Roberts, G. The bluest blood
Schulman, H. This beautiful life
Thompson, V. Murder on Fifth Avenue
Witchel, A. The spare wife

Rich, Virginia

About

Pickard, N. The 27 ingredient chili con carne murders
Pickard, N. Blue corn murders

Richard I, King of England, 1157-1199

About

Penman, S. K. Lionheart
Scott, W. Ivanhoe

Richard III, King of England, 1452-1485

About

Gregory, P. The red queen
Penman, S. K. The sunne in splendour
Tey, J. The daughter of time

Richard Yates. Lin, T.

Richard, Duke of York, 1472-1483

About

Gregory, P. The red queen

RICHES *See* Wealth

RICHMOND (VA.)

Hooper, K. Haunting Rachel
Turner, N. Heartbreak of a hustler's wife

The **riddle** of St. Leonard's. Robb, C. M.

Riddley Walker. Hoban, R.

Ride a painted pony. Eagle, K.

Ride a pale horse. MacInnes, H.

Ride with me, Mariah Montana. Doig, I.

Rider on the buckskin. Dawson, P.

Riders of the purple sage. Grey, Z.

The **ridge.** Koryta, M.

Riding the rap. Leonard, E.

The **rifles.** Vollmann, W. T.

RIFLES *See* Firearms

Right as rain. Pelecanos, G. P.

The **right** hand of evil. Saul, J.

Right livelihoods. Moody, R.

RIGHT OF PROPERTY

See also Civil rights; Property

Morris, M. Man in the blue moon

Right on the money. Lathen, E.

RIGHT TO DIE *See* Death; Medical ethics; Medicine -- Law and legislation

The **right-hand** shore. Tilghman, C.

Ring around the bases.

The **ring** of death. Spencer, S.

Ringer. Wiprud, B. M.

Ringo, John, 1844-1882

About

Bull, E. Territory

RINGS

Tolkien, J. R. R. The fellowship of the ring

Tolkien, J. R. R. The lord of the rings

Tolkien, J. R. R. The return of the king

Tolkien, J. R. R. The two towers

Ringworld. Niven, L.

The **Ringworld** engineers. Niven, L.

The **Ringworld** throne. Niven, L.

Ringworld's children. Niven, L.

RIOTS

Mosley, W. Little Scarlet

Ripley's game. Highsmith, P.

RIPOFFS *See* Fraud

Riptide. Preston, D.

The **rise** of Endymion. Simmons, D.

The **rise** of Silas Lapham. Howells, W. D.

Rise to rebellion. Shaara, J.

The **risen** empire. Westerfeld, S.

The **rising** sun. Galbraith, D.

The **rising** tide. Shaara, J.

The **risk** of darkness. Hill, S.

The **risk** pool. Russo, R.

A **risk** worth taking. Pilcher, R.

RITES AND CEREMONIES

Conn, B. The fixed stars

Straub, P. A dark matter

Wallace, D. The Watermelon King

RITES AND CEREMONIES -- CARIBBEAN REGION

Marshall, P. Praisesong for the widow

RITES AND CEREMONIES -- JAPAN

Kawabata, Y. Thousand cranes

Rites of passage. Golding, W.

Ritual. Hayder, M.

RITUAL *See* Liturgies; Rites and ceremonies

The **ritual.** Nevill, A.

River angel. Ansay, A. M.

RIVER ECOLOGY *See* Ecology

River god. Smith, W. A.

The **river** king. Hoffman, A.

RIVER LIFE

Larison, J. Holding lies

RIVER LIFE -- CHINA

Hersey, J. A single pebble

River of gods. McDonald, I.

River of mercy. Hoff, B. J.

River of smoke. Ghosh, A.

River of Stars. Kay, G. G.

A **river** Sutra. Mehta, G.

River town. Keneally, T.

River's end. Roberts, N.

Rivera, Diego, 1886-1957

About

Kingsolver, B. The lacuna

RIVERS

Ballard, J. G. The day of creation

Brower, B. Blue dog, green river

Campbell, B. J. Once upon a river

Scott, J. Follow me

Rivers, W. H. R. (William Halse Rivers), 1864-1922

About

Barker, P. The eye in the door

Barker, P. The ghost road

Riverworld [series]

Farmer, P. J. The dark design

Farmer, P. J. Gods of Riverworld

Farmer, P. J. The magic labyrinth

Farmer, P. J. To your scattered bodies go

RIVIERA (FRANCE AND ITALY)

Sagan, F. Bonjour tristesse

RIVIERA (FRANCE) -- FICTION

Levy, D. Swimming home

Rivington Street. Tax, M.

Rizzo's daughter. Manfredo, L.

Rizzo's fire. Manfredo, L.

RL's dream. Mosley, W.

ROACHES (INSECTS) *See* Cockroaches

The **road.** McCarthy, C.

The **road** back. Remarque, E. M.

Road dogs. Leonard, E.

The **road** home. Harrison, J.

The **road** home. Tremain, R.

Road novels 1957-1960. Kerouac, J.

Road rage. Rendell, R.

The **road** to Lichfield. Lively, P.

The **road** to ruin. Westlake, D. E.

Road to Wellville. Boyle, T. C.

ROADS -- MONTANA

Box, C. J. The highway

Roads to freedom [series]

Sartre, J. P. The age of reason

Sartre, J. P. The reprieve

Sartre, J. P. Troubled sleep

Roadside crosses. Deaver, J.

Roadside picnic. Strugatsky, A. N.

The **roaring** boy. Marston, E.

Rob Roy. Scott, W.

Rob Roy, 1671-1734

About

Scott, W. Rob Roy

The **robber** bridegroom. Welty, E.

ROBBERS *See* Thieves

ROBBERY

Barfoot, J. Critical injuries

Durham, M. The man who loved Cat Dancing

Latour, J. The Havana World Series

Malamud, B. The assistant

Pelecanos, G. P. Shame the devil

Roberts, N. Honest illusions

Spiegelman, P. Thick as thieves

Stark, R. Comeback

Westlake, D. E. The hot rock

Westlake, D. E. Put a lid on it

Westlake, D. E. What's the worst that could happen?

ROBBERY -- FICTION

Hilton, E. Dirty money Honey

Woods, T. Alibi

A **Robert** Silverberg omnibus. Silverberg, R.

ROBICHEAUX, DAVE (FICTITIOUS CHARACTER)

Burke, J. L. Light of the world

Burke, J. L. Last car to Elysian Fields

ROBINS *See* Birds

Robinson Crusoe. Defoe, D.

Robinson, Jackie, 1919-1972

About

Parker, R. B. Double play

ROBINSONADES *See* Adventure fiction; Imaginary voyages

Robopocalypse. Wilson, D. H.

Robot series

Asimov, I. I, robot

ROBOTICS *See* Robots

ROBOTS

Asimov, I. I, robot

Asimov, I. The rest of the robots

Carey, P. The chemistry of tears

Martinez, A. L. The automatic detective

Sedia, E. Alchemy of stone

Stross, C. Neptune's brood

Stross, C. Saturn's children

Wilson, D. H. Robopocalypse

Winterson, J. The stone gods

ROCK AND ROLL MUSIC *See* Rock music

ROCK CLIMBING *See* Mountaineering

ROCK DRAWINGS, PAINTINGS, AND ENGRAVINGS *See* Archeology; Prehistoric art

ROCK GARDENS *See* Gardens

The **rock** hole. Wortham, R.

ROCK MUSIC

See also Music; Popular music

Alexie, S. Reservation blues

Bull, E. War for the Oaks

Egan, J. A visit from the Goon Squad

Flanagan, B. Evening's empire

Hiaasen, C. Basket case

Hill, J. Heart-shaped box

Hornby, N. High fidelity

Hornby, N. Juliet, naked

Lazar, Z. Sway

Lethem, J. You don't love me yet

McGuane, T. Panama

Parker, B. Criminal justice

Rushdie, S. The ground beneath her feet

Spiotta, D. Stone Arabia

Thornton, T. The alternative hero

Williams, C. Stairway to hell

ROCK MUSIC -- FICTION

Bognanni, P. The house of tomorrow

ROCK MUSICIANS

Abani, C. GraceLand

Buckley, W. F. Elvis in the morning

Tropper, J. One last thing before I go

ROCK MUSICIANS -- FICTION

Lethem, J. You don't love me yet

Robinson, P. Piece of my heart

ROCKET FLIGHT *See* Space flight

ROCKETRY *See* Aeronautics; Astronautics

ROCKETS (AERONAUTICS) *See* Aeronautics; High speed aeronautics; Projectiles; Rocketry

ROCKY MOUNTAINS

See also Mountains

Rollins, J. The devil colony

RODEOS

Borland, H. When the legends die

Roderick Hudson. James, H.

Rodin's debutante. Just, W. S.

Roger Caras' Treasury of great cat stories.

Roger Caras' Treasury of great dog stories.

Roger's version. Updike, J.

Rogers, Mary, 1820-1841

About

Rose, J. Blackest bird

Rogers, Robert, 1731-1795

About

Roberts, K. L. Northwest Passage

A **rogue** by any other name. MacLean, S.

Rogue island. DeSilva, B.

ROGUES AND VAGABONDS

See also Picaresque literature

Brown, J. D. Addie Pray

Doctorow, E. L. Loon Lake

Fraser, G. M. The reavers

Kerouac, J. On the road

Kerouac, J. The Dharma bums

Kerouac, J. On the road: the original scroll

Mann, T. Confessions of Felix Krull, confidence man

Steinbeck, J. Cannery Row

Steinbeck, J. Sweet Thursday

Steinbeck, J. Tortilla Flat

Tinti, H. The good thief

ROLAND (LEGENDARY CHARACTER)

Rose Madder. King, S.

Rose of no man's land. Tea, M.

The **rose** rent. Peters, E.

Rose, Billy, 1899-1966
About
Bellow, S. The Bellarosa connection

Rosemary remembered. Albert, S. W.

Rosemary's baby. Levin, I.

Roses. Meacham, L.

ROSES *See* Flowers

Roses are red. Patterson, J.

Roses have thorns. Byrd, S.

The **rosewood** casket. McCrumb, S.

The **Rosie** project. Simsion, G.

ROSS, CARTER (FICTITIOUS CHARACTER)
Parks, B. The girl next door

Rostnikov's vacation. Kaminsky, S. M.

The **Rotters'** Club. Coe, J.

Rough cider. Lovesey, P.

Rough draft. Hall, J. W.

Rough justice. Scottoline, L.

Rough justice. Higgins, J.

Rough weather. Parker, R. B.

The **round** house. Erdrich, L.

Roxanna Slade. Price, R.

ROYAL CANADIAN MOUNTED POLICE
Freedman, B. Mrs. Mike

The **royal** family. Vollmann, W. T.

ROYAL FAVORITES
Gregory, P. The other Boleyn girl

Sharp, A. The true memoirs of Little K

ROYAL HOUSES *See* Kings and rulers; Monarchy

Royal mistress. Smith, A. E.

ROYALTY *See* Kings and rulers; Monarchy; Princes; Princesses; Queens

The **rubber** band & The red box. Stout, R.

Rubicon. Saylor, S.

RUBIES
Slavnikova, O. 2017

The **ruby** in her navel. Unsworth, B.

Ruby's spoon. Pietroni, A. L.

Rudolf II, Holy Roman Emperor, 1552-1612
About
Sherwood, F. The book of splendor

RUGBY FOOTBALL *See* Football

Rugendas, Johann Moritz, 1802-1858
About
Aira, C. An afternoon in the life of a landscape painter

RUINS *See* Antiquities; Excavations (Archeology); Extinct cities

Rule 34. Stross, C.

The **rule** of four. Caldwell, I.

RULERS *See* Emperors; Heads of state; Kings and rulers; Queens

Rulers of the darkness. Turtledove, H.

Rules for old men waiting. Pouncey, P. R.

Rules of civility. Towles, A.

Rules of deception. Reich, C.

Rules of prey. Sandford, J.

The **rules** of silence. Lindsey, D. L.

Rum punch. Leonard, E.

Rumpole a la carte. Mortimer, J.

Rumpole and the angel of death. Mortimer, J.

Rumpole misbehaves. Mortimer, J.

Rumpole on trial. Mortimer, J.

Rumpole rests his case. Mortimer, J.

Rumpole's return. Mortimer, J.

The **run.** Woods, S.

Run. Patchett, A.

Run silent, run deep. Beach, E. L.

The **runaway.** Kay, T.

Runaway. Munro, A.

RUNAWAY ADULTS *See* Desertion and nonsupport; Missing persons

RUNAWAY CHILDREN
See also Children; Homeless persons; Missing children

Walls, J. The Silver Star

Runaway horses. Mishima, Y.

The **runaway** jury. Grisham, J.

RUNAWAY SLAVES *See* Fugitive slaves

RUNAWAY TEENAGERS
See also Homeless persons; Missing persons; Teenagers

Katzenbach, J. What comes next

RUNAWAY WIVES
Lange, R. Angel baby

RUNAWAYS (YOUTH)
Abu-Jaber, D. Birds of paradise

Byatt, A. S. The children's book

Chaon, D. Await your reply

Davis, A. Wonder when you'll miss me

Eberstadt, F. Rat

Frey, J. Bright shiny morning

Gatewood, R. The sound of the trees

Goudge, E. Stranger in paradise

Grossman, D. Someone to run with

Guterson, D. Our Lady of the Forest

Portes, A. Hick

Pyne, D. Twentynine Palms

Shakespeare, N. Secrets of the sea

Stevens, M. Useful girl

The **runes** of the earth. Donaldson, S. R.

Runner. Perry, T.

RUNNING
Benaron, N. Running the rift

MacLeod, A. Light lifting

Running hot. Krentz, J. A.

Running the rift. Benaron, N.

RURAL FAMILIES
Clinch, J. Kings of the earth

Bulgakov, M. A. The master and Margarita

Freemantle, B. Dead men living

Miller, A. D. Snowdrops

Silva, D. Moscow rules

Tolstoy, L. Childhood, Boyhood and Youth

RUSSIA -- NAVY

Clancy, T. The hunt for Red October

RUSSIA -- RURAL LIFE

Makine, A. The woman who waited

Rutherfurd, E. Russka

Sholokhov, M. A. And quiet flows the Don

Sholokhov, M. A. The Don flows home to the sea

Solzhenitsyn, A. Cancer ward

RUSSIA -- ST. PETERSBURG

Benioff, D. City of thieves

Dean, D. The madonnas of Leningrad

Docx, E. Pravda

Dostoyevsky, F. Crime and punishment

Dostoyevsky, F. The idiot

Dunmore, H. The betrayal

The **Russia** house. Le Carre, J.

RUSSIAN AMERICANS

Boswell, R. Century's son

Dean, D. The madonnas of Leningrad

Hannah, K. Winter garden

Shteyngart, G. The Russian debutante's handbook

Shteyngart, G. Super sad true love story

Stefaniak, M. H. The Turk and my mother

Tanner, H. Vaclav and Lena

The **Russian** debutante's handbook. Shteyngart, G.

The **Russian** Donation.

Russian dreambook of color and flight. Ochsner, G.

RUSSIAN FICTION -- TRANSLATIONS INTO ENGLISH

Akunin, B. Murder on the Leviathan

Day of the oprichnik

Pelevin, V. The sacred book of the werewolf

Petrushevskaya, L. There once lived a woman who tried to kill her neighbor's baby

Solzhenitsyn, A. In the first circle

Sorokin, V. Ice

The **Russian** girl. Amis, K.

RUSSIAN LANGUAGE *See* Language and languages

RUSSIAN LITERATURE

Red Spectres

RUSSIAN REFUGEES

Bosse, M. J. The warlord

Nabokov, V. V. Look at the harlequins!

Nabokov, V. V. Pnin

RUSSIAN SCIENCE FICTION

Roadside picnic Strugatsky, A. N.

RUSSIANS -- AUSTRALIA

Keneally, T. A family madness

RUSSIANS -- ENGLAND

Amis, K. The Russian girl

Judd, A. Legacy

Lawton, J. Old flames

RUSSIANS -- ENGLAND -- LONDON

Boyne, J. The house of special purpose

RUSSIANS

Boyne, J. The house of special purpose

RUSSIANS -- GERMANY

Turgenev, I. S. The torrents of spring

Uris, L. Armageddon

RUSSIANS -- ITALY

Bezmozgis, D. The free world

RUSSIANS -- NEW YORK (STATE) -- NEW YORK -- FICTION

Alenyikov, M. Ivan and Misha

RUSSIANS -- UNITED STATES

Alenyikov, M. Ivan and Misha

Russka. Rutherfurd, E.

Ruth Galloway mystery [series]

Griffiths, E. The crossing places

Griffiths, E. The house at sea's end

RWANDA

Benaron, N. Running the rift

S

S. Updike, J.

S is for Silence. Grafton, S.

SABBATH *See* Judaism

Sabbath Creek. Mitcham, J.

Sabbath's theater. Roth, P.

SABOTAGE

See also Offenses against public safety; Strikes; Subversive activities; Terrorism

MacLean, A. Force 10 from Navarone

MacLean, A. The guns of Navarone

Vonnegut, K. Player piano

SABOTAGE -- FICTION

Banks, I. The hydrogen sonata

Sacagawea, b. 1786

About

Hall, B. I should be extremely happy in your company

Sargent, C. Museum of human beings

The **Sacketts:** beginnings of a dynasty. L'Amour, L.

SACRAMENTS *See* Church; Grace (Theology); Rites and ceremonies

Sacre bleu.

Sacred. Lehane, D.

The **sacred** book of the werewolf. Pelevin, V.

SACRED BOOKS

Jensen, J. Dante's equation

Sacred clowns. Hillerman, T.

Sacred country. Tremain, R.

Sacred hunger. Unsworth, B.

Sacrifice. Vachss, A. H.

Sacrilege. Parris, S. J.

SADISM

Cleaver, S. Saving Erasmus

SALVATION ARMY
 The redeemer

Salvation city. Nunez, S.

Salvation for a saint.

Samaritan. Price, R.

The **same** river twice. Mooney, T.

The **same** sea. Oz, A.

SAME-SEX MARRIAGE *See* Marriage

SAMOAN AMERICANS
 Malae, P. N. What we are

SAMPLERS *See* Embroidery; Needlework

Samson (Biblical figure)
About
 Maine, D. The book of Samson

SAMURAI
 Clavell, J. Gai-Jin
 Clavell, J. Shogun
 Mishima, Y. Runaway horses

SAN FRANCISCO (CALIF.)
 Freethy, B. Golden lies
 Schneider, B. Beautiful Inez

San Miguel. Boyle, T. C.

SAN MIGUEL ISLAND (CALIF.)
 Boyle, T. C. San Miguel

San Remo Drive. Epstein, L.

Sancha, of Provence, Queen, consort of Richard, King of the Romans
About
 Jones, S. Four sisters, all queens

Sanctuary. Faulkner, W.

Sanctuary. Kellerman, F.

The **sanctuary** sparrow. Peters, E.

Sanctus. Toyne, S.

Sand castles. Freeling, N.

SAND DUNES *See* Seashore

Sandbox. Zimmerman, D.

The **sandcastle** girls. Bohjalian, C.

Sandokan. Ballestrini, N.

Sandrine's Case. Cook, T. H.

The **sands** of pride. Trotter, W. R.

SANSKRIT LANGUAGE *See* Indian languages;
 Language and languages

SANTA CLAUS
 Davies, V. Miracle on 34th Street

SANTA FE (N.M.)
 Grimes, M. Biting the moon
 McGarrity, M. The big gamble
 McGarrity, M. Everyone dies
 McGarrity, M. Under the color of law
 Millet, L. Oh pure and radiant heart

Santa Fe rules. Woods, S.

SANTA FE TRAIL
 Bristow, G. Jubilee Trail

SANTERIA
 See also Religion

Oyeyemi, H. The opposite house

Sapphira and the slave girl. Cather, W.

Sappho
About
 Jong, E. Sappho's leap

Sappho's leap. Jong, E.

Sarah. Sarah/English

Sarah (Biblical figure)
About
 Sarah/English Sarah

Sarah Canary. Fowler, K. J.

Sarah Thornhill. Grenville, K.

Sarah's key. de Rosnay, T.

SARAJEVO (BOSNIA AND HERCEGOVINA)
 McNally, T. M. The goat bridge

Saratoga strongbox. Dobyns, S.

SARCOSUCHUS IMPERATOR *See* Dinosaurs

Sartoris. Faulkner, W.

Sarum. Rutherfurd, E.

SASKATCHEWAN
 Ford, R. Canada
 Hay, E. A student of weather
 Warren, D. Juliet in August

SASQUATCH
 See also Monsters; Mythical animals
 Giraldi, W. Busy monsters

Sassafrass, Cypress & Indigo. Shange, N.

Sassoon, Siegfried, 1886-1967
About
 Barker, P. The eye in the door
 Barker, P. Regeneration

SATAN *See* Devil

The **satanic** verses. Rushdie, S.

SATANISM
 Ruiz, L. M. Only one thing missing
 Sidor, S. Pitch dark

SATIRE
 See also Literature; Rhetoric; Wit and humor
 Abrams, D. Fobbit
 Adams, D. The hitchhiker's guide to the galaxy
 Adams, D. Life, the universe, and everything
 Adams, D. The restaurant at the end of the universe
 Adams, D. So long, and thanks for all the fish
 Adiga, A. The white tiger
 Altschul, A. F. Deus ex machina
 Amis, K. The Russian girl
 Austen, J. Northanger Abbey
 Austen, J. Sense and sensibility
 Ballard, J. G. Millennium people
 Barry, M. Company
 Barth, J. Giles goat-boy
 Barth, J. The sot-weed factor
 Begley, L. About Schmidt
 Belle, J. The seven year bitch
 Bellow, S. Humboldt's gift
 Berger, T. Arthur Rex

Hesse, H. The glass bead game (Magister Ludi)

Hiaasen, C. Native tongue

Hiaasen, C. Nature girl

Hiaasen, C. Sick puppy

Hiaasen, C. Star Island

Hiaasen, C. Stormy weather

Hiaasen, C. Strip tease

The hobbit

Hodgins, E. Mr. Blandings builds his dream house

Hoeg, P. The history of Danish dreams

Hoeg, P. The woman and the ape

Homes, A. M. This book will save your life

Hornby, N. About a boy

Houellebecq, M. The possibility of an island

Hrabal, B. I served the King of England

Hughes, R. A. W. A high wind in Jamaica

Huxley, A. Brave new world

Huxley, A. Point counter point

Hynes, J. Kings of infinite space

Hynes, J. The lecturer's tale

Inman, R. Captain Saturday

Irving, J. A prayer for Owen Meany

Irving, J. The world according to Garp

Isaacs, S. After all these years

Isaacs, S. Close relations

Ishiguro, K. The remains of the day

Jacobson, H. The Finkler question

Jacobson, H. Kalooki nights

James, H. The Bostonians

Jen, G. Mona in the promised land

Johnson, A. Parasites like us

Johnson, D. L'affaire

Johnson, M. Pym

Joseph, M. Serious men

Kadare, I. Spring flowers, spring frost

Kafka, F. Amerika

Kalfus, K. The commissariat of enlightenment

Kalfus, K. A disorder peculiar to the country

Kaufman, B. Up the down staircase

Kaufman, M. Bowl of cherries

Keillor, G. Love me

Keilson, H. Comedy in a minor key

Kirst, H. H. Forward, Gunner Asch!

Kirst, H. H. The return of Gunner Asch

Kirst, H. H. The revolt of Gunner Asch

Klein, J. Primary colors

Knipfel, J. The blow-off

Kosinski, J. N. Being there

Kotzwinkle, W. The bear went over the mountain

Krauss, N. The history of love

Kunkel, B. Indecision

Laird, N. Utterly monkey

Langer, A. The thieves of Manhattan

Lasdun, J. The horned man

Le Carre, J. The tailor of Panama

Leavitt, D. Martin Bauman

Lehrer, J. Purple dots

Lelchuk, A. Ziff

Lem, S. Memoirs of a space traveler

Lethem, J. Chronic city

Lewis, C. S. That hideous strength

Lewis, S. Babbitt

Lewis, S. Dodsworth

Lewis, S. Elmer Gantry

Lewis, S. It can't happen here

Lewis, S. Main Street

Lipman, E. My latest grievance

Lipsyte, S. The ask

Lodge, D. Nice work

Lodge, D. Paradise news

Lodge, D. Therapy

Lurie, A. The war between the Tates

Maguire, G. Son of a witch

Mantel, H. Beyond black

Martin, C. W. How to sell

Martin, V. Italian fever

Martini, S. P. The list

Masters, H. Post

Maugham, W. S. Cakes and ale

Mayle, P. Hotel Pastis

McCarthy, M. Birds of America

McCarthy, M. A charmed life

McCarthy, M. The group

McCarthy, M. The groves of Academe

McEwan, I. Solar

McEwan, I. Amsterdam

McGrath, P. The grotesque

McLaughlin, E. The nanny diaries

McLaughlin, E. Nanny returns

McPhee, M. Dear money

Messud, C. The emperor's children

Mo Yan Life and death are wearing me out

Moody, R. The four fingers of death

Moore, C. A dirty job

Moore, C. You suck

Morrow, J. The philosopher's apprentice

Mortimer, J. Felix in the underworld

Mortimer, J. Paradise postponed

Mortimer, J. Quite honestly

Mortimer, J. The sound of trumpets

Mortimer, J. Titmuss regained

Murakami, H. The wind-up bird chronicle

Murdoch, I. The book and the brotherhood

Murdoch, I. A fairly honourable defeat

Nabokov, V. V. Lolita

Nabokov, V. V. Pale fire

Nabokov, V. V. Pnin

Naipaul, V. S. A house for Mr. Biswas

Ochsner, G. Russian dreambook of color and flight

Oe, K. The pinch runner memorandum

O'Neill, J. Kilbrack; or, Who is Nancy Valentine?

Orwell, G. Animal farm

Updike, J. Bech is back

Updike, J. Bech: a book

Updike, J. S

Vargas Llosa, M. Captain Pantoja and the Special Service

Veselka, V. Zazen

Vidal, G. Hollywood

Vidal, G. Myra Breckinridge [and] Myron

Vidal, G. The Smithsonian Institution

Voltaire Candide

Voltaire Voltaire's Candide, Zadig, and selected stories

Vonnegut, K. Breakfast of champions

Vonnegut, K. Cat's cradle

Vonnegut, K. Deadeye Dick

Vonnegut, K. God bless you, Mr. Rosewater

Vonnegut, K. Hocus pocus

Vonnegut, K. Jailbird

Vonnegut, K. Player piano

Vonnegut, K. Slapstick

Vonnegut, K. Timequake

Wagner, B. The chrysanthemum palace

Waugh, E. Brideshead revisited

Waugh, E. Decline and fall

Waugh, E. The end of the battle

Waugh, E. The loved one

Waugh, E. Men at arms

Waugh, E. Officers and gentlemen

Waugh, E. Vile bodies

Weinstein, D. Apprentice to the flower poet Z

Weldon, F. Big girls don't cry

Weldon, F. Chalcot Crescent

Weldon, F. The life and loves of a she-devil

Weldon, F. Rhode Island blues

Weldon, F. She may not leave

Wells, H. G. Tono-Bungay

Wells, K. Crawfish mountain

West, N. Miss Lonelyhearts

Westlake, D. E. Baby, would I lie?

Westlake, D. E. Trust me on this

White, T. H. The sword in the stone

Whitehead, C. Apex hides the hurt

Wibberley, L. The mouse that roared

Wolcott, J. The catsitters

Wolfe, T. The bonfire of the vanities

Wolfe, T. I am Charlotte Simmons

Wolfe, T. A man in full

Wolitzer, M. The wife

Woodrell, D. Give us a kiss

Wright, S. Going native

Yu Hua Brothers

Zamora Linmark, R. Leche

SATIRISTS

Clinch, J. Finn

Downing, D. C. Looking for the king

Fresan, R. Kensington Gardens

Novels The gilded age and later novels

Oates, J. C. Wild nights!

Satori. Winslow, D.

Saturday. McEwan, I.

The **Saturday** big tent wedding party. McCall Smith, A.

Saturday night and Sunday morning. Sillitoe, A.

Saturday the rabbi went hungry. Kemelman, H.

Saturn. Bova, B.

SATURN (PLANET)

Bova, B. Saturn

Saturn's children. Stross, C.

Saturn's race. Niven, L.

SAUCERS, FLYING See Unidentified flying objects

SAUDI ARABIA

Ferraris, Z. Kingdom of strangers

SAUDI ARABIANS -- UNITED STATES

Dubus, A. The garden of last days

Saul and Patsy. Baxter, C.

Saunders, Mary

About

Donoghue, E. Slammerkin

The **savage** detectives. Bolano, R.

Savage lands. Clark, C.

Savage run. Box, C. J.

Savages. Winslow, D.

Savages. Pronzini, B.

Savannah. Price, E.

Savannah; or, A gift for Mr. Lincoln. Jakes, J.

SAVANTS (SAVANT SYNDROME)

Hamilton, S. The lock artist

SAVANTS (SAVANT SYNDROME) -- FICTION

Berman, S. Me, who dove into the heart of the world

Save the last dance for me. Gorman, E.

Save yourself. Braffet, K.

SAVING AND INVESTMENT See Capital; Economics; Personal finance; Wealth

Saving Erasmus. Cleaver, S.

Saving fish from drowning. Tan, A.

Saving Grace. Smith, L.

Saving room for dessert. Constantine, K. C.

SAVINGS AND LOAN ASSOCIATIONS See Banks and banking; Cooperation; Cooperative societies; Investments; Loans; Personal loans; Saving and investment

Savonarola, Girolamo, 1452-1498

About

Eliot, G. Romola

SAXONS -- ENGLAND

Cornwell, B. Sword song

SAXONS

Cornwell, B. Lords of the North

SAXOPHONISTS

Crace, J. All that follows

SCHOOL LIBRARIES *See* Instructional materials
  centers; Libraries
SCHOOL LIFE
    See also Students
  Reed, K. Enclave
  Spark, M. The finishing school
SCHOOL LIFE -- DENMARK
  Hoeg, P. Borderliners
SCHOOL LIFE -- ENGLAND
  Bronte, C. Emma
  Delderfield, R. F. To serve them all my days
  Dickens, C. David Copperfield
  Dickens, C. Nicholas Nickleby
  Faulks, S. Engleby
  Harris, J. Gentlemen and players
  Hilton, J. Good-bye Mr. Chips
  Ishiguro, K. Never let me go
  McGowan, H. Schooling
  Read Chronicles of Fairacre
  Stace, W. By George
  Swift, G. Waterland
  Walton, J. Among others
SCHOOL LIFE -- FRANCE
  Dufosse, C. School's out
  Flaubert, G. Sentimental education
SCHOOL LIFE -- GERMANY
  Hegi, U. Children and fire
SCHOOL LIFE -- IRELAND
  Murray, P. Skippy dies
SCHOOL LIFE -- SCOTLAND
  Spark, M. The prime of Miss Jean Brodie
SCHOOL LIFE -- UNITED STATES
  Beard, J. A. In Zanesville
  Bushnell, C. The Carrie diaries
  Bynum, S. Ms. Hempel chronicles
  Coll, S. Acceptance
  Conroy, P. The lords of discipline
  Cook, T. H. The Chatham School affair
  Cooke, C. Daughters of the revolution
  De Gramont, N. Gossip of the starlings
  DeWoskin, R. Big girl small
  Doyle, L. Go, mutants!
  Earley, T. The blue star
  Goodman, C. Arcadia Falls
  Gutcheon, B. R. Saying grace
  Hoffman, A. The river king
  Hunter, E. The blackboard jungle
  Just, W. S. Rodin's debutante
  Kaufman, B. Up the down staircase
  Klein, R. The moth diaries
  Knowles, J. Peace breaks out
  Knowles, J. A separate peace
  Land, B. Pilgrims upon the earth
  Munson, S. The November criminals
  Patton, F. G. Good morning, Miss Dove
  Pessl, M. Special topics in calamity physics

Picoult, J. Nineteen minutes
Powers, J. R. Do black patent-leather shoes really
  reflect up?
Powers, J. R. The last Catholic in America
Rice, L. The geometry of sisters
Saul, J. Shadows
Schulman, H. This beautiful life
Shreve, A. Testimony
Sinclair, A. Coffee will make you black
Sittenfeld, C. Prep
Southgate, M. The fall of Rome
Sparks, N. A walk to remember
Wolff, T. Old school
The **school** of night. Bayard, L.
The **school** on Heart's Content Road. Chute, C.
SCHOOL PRINCIPALS *See* School superinten-
  dents and principals
SCHOOL PSYCHOLOGISTS *See* Psychologists
SCHOOL SONGBOOKS *See* Songbooks; Songs
SCHOOL SPORTS
  Majors, I. Love's winning plays
SCHOOL STORIES
  Bruni, S. The Night Gwen Stacy Died
  Dermont, A. The starboard sea
  Ishiguro, K. Never let me go
  Knowles, J. Peace breaks out
  Knowles, J. A separate peace
  Nicholls, D. A question of attraction
  Rowell, R. Eleanor & Park
  Sittenfeld, C. Prep
  Southgate, M. The fall of Rome
SCHOOL SUPERINTENDANTS AND PRINCI-
  PALS -- FICTION
  Lam, V. The headmaster's wager
SCHOOL SUPERINTENDENTS AND PRINCI-
  PALS
  Balogh, M. Simply perfect
  Cooke, C. Daughters of the revolution
  Godwin, G. Evensong
  Gutcheon, B. R. Saying grace
SCHOOL VIOLENCE
    See also Juvenile delinquency; Violence
  Picoult, J. Nineteen minutes
School's out. Dufosse, C.
Schooling. McGowan, H.
SCHOOLS
    See also School stories
  Bynum, S. Ms. Hempel chronicles
  Ishiguro, K. Never let me go
  Pierson, D. C. The boy who couldn't sleep and
    never had to
  Rowell, R. Eleanor & Park
SCHOOLS, MILITARY *See* Military education
The **Schopenhauer** cure. Yalom, I. D.
Schopenhauer, Arthur, 1788-1860
       About

Yalom, I. D. The Schopenhauer cure

Schroder. Gaige, A.

Schulz, Bruno, 1892-1942

About

Ozick, C. The Messiah of Stockholm

Schumann, Clara, 1819-1896

About

Galloway, J. Clara

Schumann, Robert, 1810-1856

About

Galloway, J. Clara

SCIENCE -- EXPERIMENTS

MacLean, S. One Good Earl Deserves a Lover

**SCIENCE -- SOCIAL ASPECTS -- HISTORY --
19TH CENTURY**

Barrett, A. Archangel

**SCIENCE -- SOCIAL ASPECTS -- HISTORY --
20TH CENTURY**

Barrett, A. Archangel

SCIENCE FICTION *See* Adventure fiction; Fiction

**SCIENCE FICTION COMIC BOOKS, STRIPS,
ETC.** *See* Comic books, strips, etc.

SCIENCE FICTION FILMS *See* Motion pictures

SCIENCE FICTION GRAPHIC NOVELS *See*
Graphic novels

SCIENCE FICTION POETRY *See* Poetry

SCIENCE FICTION RADIO PROGRAMS *See*
Radio programs

SCIENCE FICTION TELEVISION PROGRAMS
See Television programs

SCIENCE FICTION WRITERS

Benford, G. Foundation's fear

Calvo, J. Wonderful world

SCIENCE FICTION, AMERICAN

The Best from fantasy & science fiction: the fiftieth
anniversary anthology

Bradbury, R. Bradbury stories

Cronin, J. The passage

Dark matter

Dick, P. K. VALIS and later novels

Drake, D. Grimmer than hell

Robinson, K. S. The Martians

Wolfe, G. The best of Gene Wolfe

The year's best science fiction

SCIENCE FICTION, RUSSIAN

Strugatsky, A. N. Roadside picnic

SCIENTIFIC EXPEDITIONS

See also Voyages and travels

Kiernan, S. P. The Curiosity

Maxwell, R. Jane

SCIENTIFIC EXPERIMENTS

Benford, G. Timescape

Doctorow, E. L. The waterworks

Hoeg, P. Smilla's sense of snow

Koontz, D. R. Fear nothing

Koontz, D. R. Seize the night

Lem, S. His Master's Voice

McAuley, P. J. White devils

Wells, H. G. The island of Doctor Moreau

Wilhelm, K. Death qualified

Wittenborn, D. Pharmakon

SCIENTIFIC JOURNALISM *See* Journalism

SCIENTISTS

Baldwin, R. You lost me there

Brown, D. The Da Vinci code

Chayefsky, P. Altered states

Crichton, M. The Andromeda strain

Crichton, M. Jurassic Park

Crichton, M. Sphere

Darnton, J. Mind catcher

DeLillo, D. Ratner's star

Essex, K. Leonardo's swans

Goodman, A. Intuition

Gruen, S. Ape house

Haigh, J. The condition

Hoeg, P. The woman and the ape

Kanon, J. Los Alamos

Klosterman, C. The visible man

Lem, S. His Master's Voice

Lessing, D. M. Ben, in the world

Lodge, D. Thinks--

McMahon, T. A. Ira Foxglove

Morrow, J. The last witchfinder

Patchett, A. State of wonder

Powers, R. The gold bug variations

Powers, R. The time of our singing

Roiphe, A. R. An imperfect lens

Rucker, R. v. B. Postsingular

Shaara, J. The glorious cause

Shaara, J. Rise to rebellion

Snow, C. P. The new men

Volpi, J. In search of Klingsor

Wenner, K. Dancing with Einstein

Wiggins, M. Evidence of things unseen

SCIENTISTS -- FICTION

Harris, R. The fear index

McDevitt, J. Deepsix

Preston, D. Blasphemy

Rich, N. Odds against tomorrow

SCIPIONYX *See* Dinosaurs

The **scorpio** illusion. Ludlum, R.

The **scorpion's** gate. Clarke, R. A.

SCOTLAND

Cronin, A. J. The keys of the kingdom

Foden, G. Turbulence

Garwood, J. The bride

Glass, J. Three Junes

Joss, M. Among the missing

Knox, E. Billie's kiss

Livesey, M. Criminals

McDermid, V. The distant echo

O'Farrell, M. The vanishing act of Esme Lennox

O'Hagan, A. Be near me

Pilcher, R. A risk worth taking

Pilcher, R. September

Yorke, M. Almost the truth

SCOTLAND -- 16TH CENTURY

Plaidy, J. The captive Queen of Scots

SCOTLAND -- 17TH CENTURY

Galbraith, D. The rising sun

SCOTLAND -- 18TH CENTURY

Scott, W. The bride of Lammermoor

Scott, W. Rob Roy

Smollett, T. G. The expedition of Humphry Clinker

SCOTLAND -- 19TH CENTURY

Stirling, J. The workhouse girl

SCOTLAND -- EDINBURGH

McCall Smith, A. Love over Scotland

McCall Smith, A. The world according to Bertie

O'Neill, A. The lamplighter

Rankin, I. The complaints

Rankin, I. Doors open

Rankin, I. The impossible dead

Spark, M. The prime of Miss Jean Brodie

Stross, C. Halting state

Welsh, I. Porno

Welsh, I. Trainspotting

SCOTLAND -- FICTION

Carriger, G. Changeless

Gabaldon, D. Dragonfly in amber

Gabaldon, D. Outlander

Gabaldon, D. Voyager

Higgs, L. C. Grace in thine eyes

James, E. Kiss me, Annabel

MacBride, S. Blind eye

MacBride, S. Cold granite

May, P. The Blackhouse

Mina, D. Field of blood

SCOTLAND -- GLASGOW

Donovan, A. Buddha Da

Gray, A. Old men in love

Gray, A. Poor things

Kelman, J. How late it was, how late

Kelman, J. Kieron Smith, boy

Mina, D. The end of the wasp season

Mina, D. Deception

Mina, D. Still midnight

Stirling, J. The marrying kind

Stirling, J. The penny wedding

Stirling, J. The piper's tune

Welsh, L. The cutting room

SCOTLAND -- HISTORY -- 18TH CENTURY

Gabaldon, D. Outlander

SCOTLAND -- HISTORY -- 19TH CENTURY

Dare, T. A week to be wicked

SCOTLAND -- RURAL LIFE

Buchan, J. The thirty-nine steps

Livesey, M. Eva moves the furniture

MacLean, A. When eight bells toll

Pilcher, R. Winter solstice

Stirling, J. The island wife

Stirling, J. The wind from the hills

SCOTLAND -- TO 1603

Dunnett, D. Gemini

Harris, D. T. The temple and the stone

SCOTS -- ENGLAND

Spark, M. The ballad of Peckham Rye

SCOTS -- FRANCE

Faulks, S. Charlotte Gray

SCOTS -- PANAMA

Galbraith, D. The rising sun

SCOTS -- UNITED STATES

Doig, I. Dancing at the Rascal Fair

Glass, J. Three Junes

Kamensky, J. Blindspot

Pouncey, P. R. Rules for old men waiting

Scott, Robert Falcon, 1868-1912
About

Bainbridge, B. The birthday boys

Scott, Winfield, 1786-1866
About

Shaara, J. Gone for soldiers

SCOTTISH AMERICANS

Gabaldon, D. Drums of autumn

SCOTTISH AMERICANS -- SOUTH CAROLINA -- CHARLESTON -- HISTORY -- 18TH CENTURY

Gabaldon, D. Drums of autumn

SCOUTS

Dexter, P. Deadwood

McMurtry, L. Buffalo girls

McMurtry, L. Telegraph days

SCOUTS AND SCOUTING

See also Clubs; Community life

Berger, T. Little Big Man

Cooper, J. F. The Deerslayer

Cooper, J. F. The last of the Mohicans

Cooper, J. F. The Leatherstocking tales

The **scrapbook** of Frankie Pratt. Preston, C.

SCRAPBOOKS

Hall, E. The book of summers

Scratchgravel Road. Fields, T.

SCREENWRITERS

Carson, T. Daisy Buchanan's daughter

Chandler, R. Raymond Chandler

Lazar, Z. Sway

Parker, R. B. Perchance to dream

Weiner, J. The next best thing

Winegardner, M. The Godfather returns

Screwed. Colfer, E.

SCRIBES

Vantrease, B. R. The illuminator

SCULPTORS

Stone, R. Outerbridge Reach

Unsworth, B. Sacred hunger

Verne, J. The extraordinary journeys: Twenty thousand leagues under the sea

Verne, J. The mysterious island

Wolfe, G. Pirate freedom

Worsley, K. She rises

Sea tales: The pilot, The red rover. Cooper, J. F.

SEA TRANSPORTATION *See* Shipping

SEA TRAVEL *See* Ocean travel

The **sea,** the sea. Murdoch, I.

SEA-SHORE *See* Seashore

The **Sea-Wolf.** London, J.

SEAFARING LIFE

> *See also* Adventure and adventurers; Manners and customs; Voyages and travels

Kneale, M. English passengers

Powning, B. The sea captain's wife

SEAFOOD *See* Food; Marine resources

The **seal** wife. Harrison, K.

The **sealed** letter. Donoghue, E.

SEAMEN

> *See also* Sailors

Beach, E. L. Run silent, run deep

Birch, C. Jamrach's menagerie

Conrad, J. The Nigger of the Narcissus

Cooper, J. F. The pilot

Forester, C. S. Ship of the line

Ghosh, A. River of smoke

Ghosh, A. Sea of poppies

Heggen, T. Mister Roberts

Hough, R. The stowaway

Innes, H. The wreck of the Mary Deare

Lambdin, D. King's captain

London, J. The Sea-Wolf

Matthiessen, P. Far Tortuga

McCutchan, P. Apprentice to the sea

McCutchan, P. Cameron's crossing

McCutchan, P. The last farewell

McCutchan, P. The new lieutenant

McCutchan, P. The second mate

Monsarrat, N. The cruel sea

Nichols, P. Voyage to the North Star

Nordhoff, C. Men against the sea

O'Brian, P. Blue at the mizzen

O'Brian, P. The commodore

O'Brian, P. The golden ocean

O'Brian, P. The hundred days

O'Brian, P. The unknown shore

O'Brian, P. The wine-dark sea

O'Brian, P. The yellow admiral

Poyer, D. Black storm

Poyer, D. China Sea

Poyer, D. The circle

Poyer, D. The command

Poyer, D. The gulf

Smith, W. A. Birds of prey

Smith, W. A. Monsoon

Stahlberg, L. Billy Budd, sailor

Stahlberg, L. Moby-Dick; or, The whale

Wouk, H. The Caine mutiny

The **seamstress.** Peebles, F. d. P.

The **seamstress** and the wind. Aira, C.

SEANCES

Rose, M. J. Seduction

Thompson, V. Murder on Waverly Place

SEARCH AND RESCUE OPERATIONS

Lichtenstein, A. Lost

MacLean, A. Where eagles dare

SEARCH AND RESCUE OPERATIONS -- FICTION

Bond, L. Exit plan

Searching for Caleb. Tyler, A.

SEASHORE

Ferrante, E. The lost daughter

SEASHORE ECOLOGY *See* Ecology

SEASIDE RESORTS

Gholson, C. A fish trapped inside the wind

A **season** for the dead. Hewson, D.

A **season** in purgatory. Dunne, D.

A **season** in the West. Read, P. P.

Season of Gene. Hudgens, D.

Season to be sinful. Goodman, J.

SEATTLE (WASH.)

Lynch, J. Truth like the sun

Semple, M. Where'd you go, Bernadette

SECLUSION

> *See also* Solitude

Rutherford, E. The Peripatetic Coffin and other stories

The **second** book of lost swords: Sightblinder's story. Saberhagen, F.

The **second** chair. Lescroart, J. T.

Second child. Saul, J.

The **second** coming. Percy, W.

The **second** deadly sin. Sanders, L.

The **second** death of Unica Aveyano. Mestre-Reed, E.

The **second** empress. Moran, M.

Second Foundation. Asimov, I.

Second Foundation trilogy [series]

Benford, G. Foundation's fear

Second grave on the left. Jones, D.

Second honeymoon. Trollope, J.

The **second** mate. McCutchan, P.

Second nature. Hoffman, A.

Second person singular.

The **second** Rumpole omnibus. Mortimer, J.

Second skin. Lustbader, E. V.

Second skin. Hawkes, J.

Second spring. Greeley, A. M.

The **second** time around. Clark, M. H.

Downing, D. Potsdam station
Harris, R. Enigma
Smith, T. R. Agent 6
Smith, T. R. Child 44
Smith, T. R. The secret speech

SECRET SERVICE -- GREAT BRITAIN
Cumming, C. The Trinity Six
Sansom, C. J. Winter in Madrid

SECRET SOCIETIES
See also Rites and ceremonies; Societies
Baldacci, D. Divine justice
Bayard, L. The school of night
Bear, E. Ink and steel
Ludlum, R. The Matarese Circle
Neville, K. The eight
Neville, K. The fire
Portis, C. Masters of Atlantis

SECRET SOCIETIES -- FICTION
Gentle, M. The black opera
Miller, J. The year of the gadfly
O'Malley, D. The rook
Rollins, J. The devil colony
The **secret** speech. Smith, T. R.
The **secret** warriors. Griffin, W. E. B.
A **secret** word. Paddock, J.

SECRET WRITING See Cryptography

SECRETARIES
Sheehan, A. The anxiety of everyday objects

SECRETARIES -- FICTION
Rindell, S. The Other Typist

SECRETARIES OF STATE
Benet, S. V. The Devil and Daniel Webster
Brown, R. M. Dolley
Pesci, D. Amistad
Updike, J. Memories of the Ford Administration

SECRETARIES OF THE TREASURY
Liss, D. The whiskey rebels

SECRETARIES OF WAR
Doctorow, E. L. The march
Jakes, J. Savannah; or, A gift for Mr. Lincoln

SECRETS
Byrd, S. The secret keeper
Cash, W. A land more kind than home
Gross, G. When she was gone
Secrets of a proper lady. Alexander, V.
Secrets of Eden. Bohjalian, C. A.
The **secrets** of Mary Bowser. Leveen, L.
Secrets of the sea. Shakespeare, N.
Section 8. K'wan

SECTS
Duncker, P. The strange case of the composer and his judge
Rogers, J. Mr. Wroe's virgins

SECULARISM See Ethics; Utilitarianism

SECURITIES See Finance; Investments; Stock exchanges

SECURITIES FRAUD See Fraud

Security. Amidon, S.

SECURITY (PSYCHOLOGY) See Emotions; Psychology

SEDITION See Political crimes and offenses; Revolutions

Seducing an angel. Balogh, M.

Seduction. Rose, M. J.

SEDUCTION
Dierbeck, L. One pill makes you smaller
Handke, P. Don Juan
Kundera, M. Slowness
Mawer, S. The fall
Nabokov, V. V. Lolita
Tolstoy, L. Resurrection

SEDUCTION -- FICTION
Schneider, B. Beautiful Inez
The **seduction** of the crimson rose. Willig, L.
The **seduction** of water. Goodman, C.
See Jane run. Fielding, J.
See no evil. Bland, E. T.
See now then. Kincaid, J.
Seeing. Saramago, J.
Seeing a large cat. Peters, E.
Seek my face. Updike, J.

SEGREGATION
See also Race relations
Devoto, P. C. The summer we got saved

SEINEN See Manga

SEISMOGRAPHY See Earthquakes

SEISMOLOGY See Earthquakes

Seize the day. Bellow, S.
Seize the night. Koontz, D. R.
Seizure. Cook, R.
Selected short stories. Gorky, M.
The **selected** short stories of Edith Wharton.
Selected short stories of Franz Kafka. Kafka, F.
Selected stories. Munro, A.
Selected stories. Trevor, W.
The **selected** stories of Patricia Highsmith. Highsmith, P.
The **selected** works of T. S. Spivet. Larsen, R.

SELECTIVE SERVICE See Draft

SELF
See also Consciousness; Individuality; Personality
Keillor, G. Lake Wobegon summer 1956
Self's punishment. Selbs Justiz/English

SELF-ACCEPTANCE
Shumway, C. Ten girls to watch

SELF-ACTUALIZATION (PSYCHOLOGY)
Bynum, S. Ms. Hempel chronicles
Eugenides, J. The marriage plot
Goodman, A. The cookbook collector
Lansens, L. The wife's tale
McCarthy, T. C

Sentimental education. Flaubert, G.

A **separate** peace. Knowles, J.

SEPARATION (LAW) *See* Divorce; Marriage

SEPARATION (PSYCHOLOGY)

    Edwards, K. The memory keeper's daughter

    Harris, E. L. Not a day goes by

    O'Nan, S. The good wife

September. Pilcher, R.

SEPTEMBER 11 TERRORIST ATTACKS, 2001

    DeLillo, D. Falling man

    Foer, J. S. Extremely loud & incredibly close

    Kalfus, K. A disorder peculiar to the country

    Maynard, J. The usual rules

    McCauley, S. Alternatives to sex

    McInerney, J. The good life

    McPhee, M. L'America

    Messud, C. The emperor's children

    Price, R. The good priest's son

    Schwartz, L. S. The writing on the wall

    Waldman, A. The submission

**SEPTEMBER 11 TERRORIST ATTACKS, 2001
-- FICTION**

    Grunberg, A. Tirza

The **September** Society. Finch, C.

September song. Greeley, A. M.

The **Septembers** of Shiraz. Sofer, D.

SEQUENCES (MATHEMATICS) *See* Algebra;
    Mathematics

Seraglio. Wallach, J.

SERBIA

    Novakovich, J. April Fool's Day

SERBIANS -- ENGLAND

    Brownrigg, S. The delivery room

    De Bernieres, L. A partisan's daughter

SERBIANS -- UNITED STATES

    Lawrence, S. The lightning keeper

Serena. Rash, R.

SERIAL KILLERS

    See also Criminals; Homicide

    Abu-Jaber, D. Origin

    Bauer, B. Blacklands

    Bauer, B. Darkside

    Benn, J. R. A mortal terror

    Block, L. Getting off

    Bolton, S. J. Now you see me

    Cain, C. Heartsick

    Castillo, L. Sworn to silence

    Coben, H. The woods

    Connelly, M. The scarecrow

    Coulter, C. Split second

    Dahl, A. Misterioso

    Deaver, J. Roadside crosses

    Ellory, R. J. The Anniversary Man

    Estleman, L. D. Gas City

    Fairstein, L. Killer heat

    Fielding, J. Heartstopper

Lavender, W. Dominance

Lindsay, J. P. Dearly devoted Dexter

Lippman, L. I'd know you anywhere

Moore, G. The Sherlockian

Morgan, R. K. Thirteen

Nelson, A. Bound

Nova, C. The informer

Palahniuk, C. Rant

Palmer, M. The last surgeon

Pekearo, N. T. The wolfman

Pronzini, B. The hidden

Smith, T. R. Child 44

Verdon, J. Think of a number

Wolfe, I. A. The calling

SERIAL KILLERS -- FICTION

    Black, C. Murder in the Bastille

    Black, L. Trail of blood

    Box, C. J. The highway

    Burke, J. L. Light of the world

    Cain, C. Kill you twice

    Cain, C. Let me go

    Carver, T. Cage of Bones

    Carver, T. The creeper

    Clark, M. Guilt by degrees

    Colfer, E. Screwed

    Cotterill, C. The merry misogynist

    Dahl, A. Bad Blood

    Doherty, P. C. The Mysterium

    Ellory, R. J. A simple act of violence

    Faye, L. The gods of Gotham

    Ferraris, Z. Kingdom of strangers

    Hand, E. Available dark

    Harrod-Eagles, C. Blood Never Dies

    Hayder, M. Birdman

    Hines, T. L. Waking Lazarus

    Kerley, J. The death collectors

    MacBride, S. Cold granite

    Mark, D. The dark winter

    McMahon, J. The One I Left Behind

    Morrell, D. Murder as a fine art

    Ohlsson, K. Unwanted

    Perry, T. The boyfriend

    Pinborough, S. A matter of blood

    Ryan, H. P. The other woman

    Tallis, F. Vienna blood

    Tuomainen, A. The healer

    Wells, D. The hollow city

    Wortham, R. The rock hole

**SERIAL MURDER INVESTIGATION -- ENG-
    LAND -- LONDON**

    Doherty, P. C. The Mysterium

    Pinborough, S. A matter of blood

SERIAL MURDER INVESTIGATION

    Box, C. J. The highway

    Cleave, P. Cemetery Lake

    Faye, L. The gods of Gotham

Barker, C. Imajica

Barnes, D. Nightwood

Beachy, S. Boneyard

Beatty, P. Slumberland

Bell, M. S. The color of night

Block, L. Getting off

Bock, C. Beautiful children

Burdett, J. Bangkok 8

Burdett, J. Bangkok haunts

Burdett, J. Bangkok Tattoo

Burdett, J. The godfather of Kathmandu

Cave, N. The death of Bunny Munro

Christensen, K. Trouble

Crusie, J. Faking it

DeMarinis, R. Sky full of sand

Dewitt, H. Lightning rods

Dierbeck, L. One pill makes you smaller

Ducornet, R. Netsuke

Ehrenreich, B. The suitors

Ellis, W. Crooked little vein

Ennen paivanlaskua ei voi/English   Troll

Epstein, L. San Remo Drive

Eugenides, J. The virgin suicides

Faust, C. Money shot

Gaitskill, M. Veronica

Garcia Marquez, G. Memories of my melancholy
  whores

Gray, A. Poor things

Gregory, P. The wise woman

Hall, A. L. The rhythm of the road

Harrison, J. The great leader

Harrison, K. The binding chair

Harrison, K. The seal wife

Hart, J. Damage

Herlihy, J. L. Midnight cowboy

Hoban, R. Angelica's Grotto

Hoffman, N. K. Catalyst

Hooper, C. A child's book of true crime

Houellebecq, M. The possibility of an island

Howatch, S. The wonder-worker

Hunter, E. Candyland

Irving, J. The fourth hand

Irving, J. A widow for one year

Jen, G. Mona in the promised land

Jennings, G. Raptor

Johnson, D. Nobody move

Johnson, D. Le divorce

Jong, E. Fear of flying

Jong, E. Sappho's leap

King, S. Gerald's game

Kureishi, H. Something to tell you

Lethem, J. You don't love me yet

Lewis, M. G. The monk

Lipsyte, S. Home land

Lodge, D. Therapy

Lowell, E. Pearl Cove

MacNeil, R. Burden of desire

Martin, C. W. How to sell

McDermott, A. Child of my heart

McEwan, I. On Chesil Beach

McMillan, T. How Stella got her groove back

McMillan, T. Waiting to exhale

McMurtry, L. Loop group

McMurtry, L. Telegraph days

McPhee, J. A man of no moon

Minot, S. Rapture

Mishima, Y. The Temple of Dawn

Murakami, R. In the miso soup

Norman, H. The haunting of L

Oates, J. C. Blonde

Oates, J. C. Foxfire

O'Dell, T. Back roads

Paddock, J. A secret word

Palahniuk, C. Pygmy

Parini, J. The apprentice lover

Patterson, J. Along came a spider

Patterson, R. N. Degree of guilt

Pelevin, V. The hall of singing caryatids

Pelevin, V. The sacred book of the werewolf

Perrotta, T. The abstinence teacher

Perrotta, T. Little children

Portes, A. Hick

Prose, F. Goldengrove

Reynolds, M. The Starlite Drive-in

Richards, D. A. The bay of love and sorrows

Rinehart, S. Built in a day

Robbins, H. Sin city

Robbins, T. Fierce invalids home from hot climates

Roberts, M. Reader, I married him

Roberts, N. Honest illusions

Rossner, J. Perfidia

Roth, H. Requiem for Harlem

Roth, P. Everyman

Roth, P. The humbling

Roth, P. Indignation

Roth, P. The professor of desire

Roth, P. Sabbath's theater

Schlink, B. The reader

Schulman, H. This beautiful life

Self, W. Dorian

Shreve, A. Testimony

Shreve, A. Where or when

Smiley, J. Ten days in the hills

Spanidou, I. Before

Spencer, S. Willing

Spiegelman, I. Everyone's burning

Strout, E. Amy and Isabelle

Sussman, E. French lessons

Tea, M. Rose of no man's land

Templeton, E. Gordon

Theroux, A. Laura Warholic; or, The sexual intellectual

The **shadow** of your smile. Clark, M. H.

Shadow on the crown. Bracewell, P.

SHADOW PANTOMIMES AND PLAYS *See* Amateur theater; Pantomimes; Puppets and puppet plays; Shadow pictures; Theater

Shadow pass. Eastland, S.

Shadow song. Kay, T.

Shadow tag. Erdrich, L.

Shadow woman. Perry, T.

The **shadow** year. Ford, J.

Shadowbrook. Swerling, B.

Shadows. Saul, J.

Shadows in the starlight. Cunningham, E.

Shadows in the street. Hill, S.

Shadows on the Hudson. Singer, I. B.

Shadows on the rock. Cather, W.

SHAKERS

Peck, R. N. A day no pigs would die

Shakespeare's kitchen. Segal, L. G.

Shakespeare, William, 1564-1616

About

Adrian, C. The great night

Barber, R. The Marlowe papers

Bear, E. Ink and steel

Belanger, A. Kill Shakespeare

Craig, A. Love in idleness

Gruber, M. The book of air and shadows

Haig, M. The dead fathers club

Kellerman, F. The quality of mercy

Lovett, C. The bookman's tale

Marsh, N. Light thickens

Martin, W. Harvard Yard

Nye, R. The late Mr. Shakespeare

Phillips, A. The tragedy of Arthur

Simmons, D. Muse of fire

Updike, J. Gertrude and Claudius

SHAKESPEARE, WILLIAM, 1564-1616 -- AUTHORSHIP *See* Authorship

SHAKESPEARE, WILLIAM, 1564-1616 -- DICTIONARIES *See* Encyclopedias and dictionaries

SHAKESPEARE, WILLIAM, 1564-1616 -- ETHICS *See* Ethics

SHAKESPEARE, WILLIAM, 1564-1616 -- RELIGION *See* Religion

Shalimar the clown. Rushdie, S.

Shallow grave. Harrod-Eagles, C.

Shallow graves. Healy, J. F.

The **shaman's** bones. Doss, J. D.

SHAMANS

Gear, K. O. People of the owl

Griffin, K. Glass God

The **shambling** guide to New York City. Lafferty, M.

SHAME *See* Emotions

Shame the devil. Pelecanos, G. P.

SHAN, TAO YUN (FICTITIOUS CHARACTER)

Pattison, E. The lord of death

Pattison, E. The skull mantra

Shane. Schaefer, J. W.

SHANGHAI (CHINA)

Ballard, J. G. Empire of the Sun

Harrison, K. The binding chair

Ishiguro, K. When we were orphans

Qiu Xiaolong Red mandarin dress

Qiu Xiaolong Years of Red Dust

Reuss, F. Mohr

See, L. Shanghai girls

Wang Anyi The song of everlasting sorrow

Shanghai girls. See, L.

SHANNARA (IMAGINARY PLACE)

Brooks, T. Wards of Faerie

The **shape** of desire. Shinn, S.

The **shape** of dread. Muller, M.

The **shape** of snakes. Walters, M.

The **shape** shifter. Hillerman, T.

SHAPESHIFTING

Shinn, S. The shape of desire

Shards. Prcic, I.

Shards of memory. Jhabvala, R. P.

SHARED CUSTODY *See* Child custody

SHARED HOUSING

Millet, L. Magnificence

A **shark** out of water. Lathen, E.

SHARKS

Benchley, P. Jaws

Sharp objects. Flynn, G.

Sharpe's battle. Cornwell, B.

Sharpe's devil. Cornwell, B.

Sharpe's fortress. Cornwell, B.

Sharpe's fury. Cornwell, B.

Sharpe's havoc. Cornwell, B.

Sharpe's prey: Richard Sharpe and the Expedition to Copenhagen, 1807. Cornwell, B.

Sharpe's Trafalgar. Cornwell, B.

Sharpe's Waterloo. Cornwell, B.

Sharps. Parker, K. J.

Shatter the bones. MacBride, S.

Shattered. Francis, D.

Shattered pillars. Bear, E.

Shattered silk. Michaels, B.

The **shawl.** Ozick, C.

SHAWNEE INDIANS

Thom, J. A. Panther in the sky

She. Haggard, H. R.

She may not leave. Weldon, F.

She rises. Worsley, K.

She smiled sweetly. Tirone Smith

She walks these hills. McCrumb, S.

She's not there. Tirone Smith

SHEEP

Hardy, T. Far from the madding crowd

Doctorow, C. Overclocked

Doctorow, E. L. All the time in the world

Doctorow, E. L. Sweet land stories

Doenges, J. What she left me: stories and a novella

Doerr, A. Memory wall

Doerr, H. The tiger in the grass

Donoghue, E. Touchy subjects

Donovan, G. Young Irelanders

Dorst, D. The surf guru

Dostoyevsky, F. The best short stories of Dostoevsky

Doyle, A. C. The best science fiction of Arthur Conan Doyle

Doyle, A. C. The complete Sherlock Holmes

Doyle, R. Bullfighting and other stories

Doyle, R. The deportees and other stories

Dozois, G. R. When the great days come

Drabble, M. A day in the life of a smiling woman

Drake, D. Grimmer than hell

Drummond, L. L. Anything you say can and will be used against you

Du Maurier, D. Daphne du Maurier's classics of the macabre

Dubus, A. Dirty Love

Dumas, A. Short stories

Dybek, S. I sailed with Magellan

Early short stories, 1883-1888

Effinger, G. A. George Alec Effinger live! from planet Earth

Eggers, D. How we are hungry

Eisenberg, D. The collected stories of Deborah Eisenberg

Eisenberg, D. Twilight of the superheroes

Endo, S. The final martyrs

Engel, M. P. Strangers and sojourners

Englander, N. What we talk about when we talk about Anne Frank

Enright, A. Yesterday's weather

Epstein, J. Fabulous small Jews

Epstein, J. The love song of A. Jerome Minkoff and other stories

Erdrich, L. The red convertible

Estleman, L. D. Amos Walker

Evans, D. Before you suffocate your own fool self

Faber, M. Vanilla bright like Eminem

Fallon, S. You know when the men are gone

Farmer, P. J. The classic Philip Jose Farmer, 1952-1964--1964-1973

Faulkner, W. Collected stories of William Faulkner

Faulkner, W. The Faulkner reader

Faulkner, W. Go down, Moses

Faulkner, W. Uncollected stories of William Faulkner

Faulkner, W. The unvanquished

Feeling very strange

Fifty years of the best from Ellery Queen's Mystery Magazine

Finch, S. The guild of xenolinguists

First thrills

Fitzgerald, F. S. The Fitzgerald reader

Fitzgerald, F. S. The short stories of F. Scott Fitzgerald

Fitzgerald, F. S. Six tales of the jazz age, and other stories

Fitzgerald, F. S. The stories of F. Scott Fitzgerald

Fitzgerald, P. The means of escape

Ford, J. The drowned life

Ford, J. The empire of ice cream

Ford, R. A multitude of sins

Ford, R. Women with men

Forester, C. S. Mr. Midshipman Hornblower

Forster, E. M. The collected tales of E. M. Forster

Forsyth, F. The veteran

Fowler, K. J. What I didn't see and other stories

Frame, J. Between my father and the king

Frame, J. Prizes

Francis, D. Field of thirteen

Freed, L. The curse of the appropriate man

Freudenberger, N. Lucky girls

Fuentes, C. The crystal frontier

Fuentes, C. Happy families

Fulton, A. The nightingales of Troy

The Future Is Japanese

Gaiman, N. Fragile things

Gaitskill, M. Don't cry

Gao Xingjian Buying a fishing rod for my grandfather

Garcia Marquez, G. Collected stories

Garcia Marquez, G. Leaf storm, and other stories

Garcia Marquez, G. Strange pilgrims

Gardam, J. The people on Privilege Hill and other stories

Gardiner, J. R. The Magellan House

Gavin, J. Middle men

Gay, W. I hate to see that evening sun go down

Gifford, B. The stars above Veracruz

Gilchrist, E. The age of miracles

Gilchrist, E. The cabal and other stories

Gilchrist, E. Ellen Gilchrist: collected stories

Gilchrist, E. Flights of angels

Gilman, C. P. The Charlotte Perkins Gilman reader

Gogol', N. V. The collected tales of Nikolai Gogol

Gogol', N. V. The overcoat, and other tales of good and evil

Gordimer, N. Beethoven was one-sixteenth black

Gordimer, N. Jump and other stories

Gordimer, N. Life times

Gordimer, N. Loot, and other stories

Gorky, M. Selected short stories

Great stories of the American West

Greatest hits

Green cane and juicy flotsam

Knight, M. Goodnight, nobody

Kundera, M. Laughable loves

Lahiri, J. Interpreter of maladies

Lahiri, J. Unaccustomed earth

L'Amour, L. Beyond the Great Snow Mountains

L'Amour, L. End of the drive

L'Amour, L. May there be a road

Lantz, K. A. Apricot jam, and other stories

Lardner, R. The best short stories of Ring Lardner

Lasdun, J. It's beginning to hurt

Later short stories, 1888-1903

Lawrence, D. H. Collected stories

Le Clezio, G. Mondo and other stories

Le Guin, U. K. The birthday of the world and other stories

Le Guin, U. K. Four ways to forgiveness

Le Guin, U. K. Orsinian tales

Lee, K. Drifting house

Legal fictions

Lem, S. Memoirs of a space traveler

Leonard, E. The complete Western stories of Elmore Leonard

Leonard, E. When the women come out to dance, and other stories

Leskov, N. S. The enchanted wanderer and other stories

Lessing, D. M. African stories

Lessing, D. M. Stories

Leung, B. World famous love acts

Levi, P. The sixth day, and other tales

Levine, P. The appearance of a hero

Lewis, C. S. The dark tower and other stories

Li Yiyun A thousand years of good prayers

Link, K. Magic for beginners

Lippman, L. Hardly knew her

Lively, P. Pack of cards and other stories

The living dead

Lock, N. Love among the particles & other stories

London, J. Novels & stories

London, J. South Sea tales

London, J. White Fang, and other stories

Lovecraft, H. P. At the mountains of madness, and other novels

Lovecraft, H. P. The Dunwich horror, and others

Lovecraft, H. P. H. P. Lovecraft

Lovecraft, H. P. Tales of H.P. Lovecraft

Lurie, A. Women and ghosts

Lychack, W. The architect of flowers

Ma Jian Stick out your tongue

MacLeod, A. Light lifting

MacLeod, A. Island

Malamud, B. The complete stories

Malamud, B. A Malamud reader

Malouf, D. The complete stories

The mammoth book of steampunk

Mann, T. Death in Venice and other tales

Mann, T. Six early stories

Mann, T. Stories of three decades

Mansfield, K. The garden party and other stories

Mansfield, K. The short stories of Katherine Mansfield

Mason, B. A. Love life

Mason, B. A. Midnight magic

Mason, B. A. Nancy Culpepper

Mason, B. A. Shiloh and other stories

Mason, B. A. Zigzagging down a wild trail

Master's choice [v1]-2: mystery stories by today's top writers and the masters who inspired them

Matheson, R. I am legend

Matthiessen, P. On the river Styx and other stories

Mattison, A. In case we're separated

Maugham, W. S. The best short stories of W. Somerset Maugham

Maugham, W. S. Complete short stories

Maurois, A. The collected stories of Andre Maurois

Maxwell, W. All the days and nights

Maxwell, W. Early novels and stories

Maxwell, W. Later novels and stories

McAllister, B. The girl who loved animals and other stories

McBain, E. Learning to kill

McCaffrey, A. The chronicles of Pern

McCaffrey, A. The girl who heard dragons

McCrumb, S. Foggy Mountain breakdown and other stories

McCullers, C. Collected stories

McGuane, T. Gallatin Canyon

McHugh, M. F. After the apocalypse

McInerney, J. How it ended

Means, D. The secret goldfish

Mehta, R. Quarantine

Meno, J. Bluebirds used to croon in the choir

Michaels, L. The collected stories

Michener, J. A. Creatures of the kingdom

Miller, A. L. Water

Miller, A. Homely girl, a life, and other stories

Miller, S. Inventing the Abbotts and other stories

Millhauser, S. Dangerous laughter

Millhauser, S. The king in the tree: three novellas

Millhauser, S. The knife thrower and other stories

Millhauser, S. We others

Minot, S. Lust & other stories

Modesitt, L. E. Viewpoints critical

A moment on the edge

Moon, E. Moon flights

Moorcock, M. The best of Michael Moorcock

Moore, L. Birds of America

Morris, W. Collected stories, 1948-1986

Mortimer, J. Rumpole a la carte

Mortimer, J. Rumpole and the angel of death

Mortimer, J. Rumpole on trial

Mortimer, J. Rumpole rests his case

Porter, K. A. Flowering Judas and other stories

Porter, K. A. The leaning tower, and other stories

Price, R. The collected stories

Price, R. The foreseeable future

Pritchett, V. S. Complete collected stories

Proulx, A. Bad dirt

Proulx, A. Close range

Proulx, A. Fine just the way it is

Proust, M. The complete short stories of Marcel Proust

Pushcart prize XXXVII

Pushkin, A. S. Alexander Pushkin: complete prose fiction

Pym, B. Civil to strangers and other writings

Qiu Xiaolong Years of Red Dust

Queen, E. The best of Ellery Queen

Rash, R. Burning bright

Rawlings, M. K. Short stories

Ray, S. American masculine

Rendell, R. Blood lines

Rendell, R. Collected stories

Rhys, J. The collected short stories

Ring around the bases

Robinson, K. S. The Martians

Robinson, R. A perfect stranger

Roger Caras' Treasury of great cat stories

Roger Caras' Treasury of great dog stories

Ross, A. Ladies and gentlemen

Roth, J. The collected stories of Joseph Roth

Roth, P. Goodbye, Columbus, and five short stories

Roth, P. Novels & stories, 1959-1962

Runyon, D. Guys and dolls

Rushdie, S. East, west

Russell, K. St. Lucy's home for girls raised by wolves

Russell, K. Vampires in the lemon grove

Russo, R. The whore's child

Rutherford, E. The Peripatetic Coffin and other stories

Ryman, G. Paradise tales

Saki The short stories of Saki

Salinger, J. D. Nine stories

Salter, J. Last night

Sartre, J. P. Intimacy, and other stories

Saunders, G. In persuasion nation

Saunders, G. Tenth of December

Sayers, D. L. Hangman's holiday

Sayers, D. L. In the teeth of the evidence and other stories

Sayers, D. L. Lord Peter

Saylor, S. The house of the Vestals

Schaefer, J. W. The collected stories of Jack Schaefer

Schappell, E. Blueprints for building better girls

Scholz, C. The amount to carry

Scott, J. Everybody loves somebody

Segal, L. G. Shakespeare's kitchen

Seiffert, R. Field study

The selected short stories of Edith Wharton

Selections/English Lands of memory

Self, W. The undivided self

Selgin, P. Drowning lessons

Serber, N. Shout her lovely name

Shabtai, Y. Uncle Peretz takes off

Shade, E. Eyesores

Shaw, I. Short stories: five decades

Sheehy, H. The invisibles

Shepard, J. Like you'd understand, anyway

Shepard, J. You think that's bad

Shepard, L. The best of Lucius Shepard

Shepard, S. Day out of days

Shepard, S. Great dream of heaven

Sholem Aleichem The best of Sholom Aleichem

Sholem Aleichem Tevye the dairyman and The railroad stories

Sholem Aleichem Tevye's daughters

Shonk, K. The red passport

Short stories of Jack London

Shulman, M. The many loves of Dobie Gillis

Silber, J. Ideas of heaven

Sillitoe, A. The loneliness of the long-distance runner

Silverberg, R. The collected stories of Robert Silverberg

Simpson, H. In the driver's seat

Singer, I. B. Collected stories: A friend of Kafka to Passions

Singer, I. B. Collected stories: Gimpel the fool to The letter writer

Singer, I. B. Collected stories: One night in Brazil to The death of Methuselah

Singer, I. B. An Isaac Bashevis Singer reader

Skvorecky, J. When Eve was naked

The Sleeper wakes

Smiley, J. The age of grief

Smith, L. Mrs. Darcy and the blue-eyed stranger

Snow white, blood red

Sorrentino, G. The moon in its flight

Spark, M. Open to the public

Spencer, E. The southern woman

Spencer, E. The stories of Elizabeth Spencer

Stafford, J. The collected stories of Jean Stafford

Stahlberg, L. The complete shorter fiction

Stegner, W. E. Collected stories of Wallace Stegner

Steinbeck, J. The long valley

Steinbeck, J. Novels and stories, 1932-1937

Steinbeck, T. Down to a soundless sea

Stevenson, R. L. The complete short stories

Stevenson, R. L. The complete short stories of Robert Louis Stevenson

Stevenson, R. L. The strange case of Dr. Jekyll and Mr. Hyde, and other famous tales

Stoker, B. The Bram Stoker bedside companion
Stoker, B. Midnight tales
Stone, R. Fun with problems
Stories
Straub, P. Magic terror
Strout, E. Olive Kitteridge
Summer lies
Sundaresan, I. In the Convent of Little Flowers
Swanwick, M. The best of Michael Swanwick
Swanwick, M. The dog said bow-wow
Theroux, P. The collected stories
Thomas, D. The collected stories
Thon, M. R. In this light
Tillman, L. Someday this will be funny
Tinti, H. Animal crackers
Toibin, C. The empty family
Toibin, C. Mothers and sons
Tolkien, J. R. R. The book of lost tales
Tolkien, J. R. R. The Silmarillion
Tolstaia, T. White walls
Tolstoy, L. The death of Ivan Ilyitch, and other stories
Tolstoy, L. Divine and human and other stories
Tolstoy, L. Short stories
Tower, W. Everything ravaged, everything burned
Transgressions
Trevor, W. A bit on the side
Trevor, W. Cheating at canasta
Trevor, W. The collected stories
Trevor, W. The hill bachelors
Trevor, W. Selected stories
Trial and error
Trollope, A. The complete shorter fiction
Tsan-hsueh Blue light in the sky & other stories
Twain, M. The complete short stories of Mark Twain
Twain, M. The man that corrupted Hadleyburg, and other stories and essays
Twain, M. Mysterious stranger, and other stories
Under African skies
The Unforgetting heart: an anthology of short stories by African American women (1859-1993)
Updike, J. The afterlife and other stories
Updike, J. Bech at bay
Updike, J. Bech is back
Updike, J. Bech: a book
Updike, J. Licks of love
Updike, J. My father's tears and other stories
Updike, J. Pigeon feathers, and other stories
Updike, J. Trust me
Van de Wetering, J. The Amsterdam cops
VanderMeer, J. The third bear
Vann, D. Legend of a suicide
Vapnyar, L. Broccoli and other tales of food and love
The vicious circle

Vidal, G. Clouds and eclipses
Voltaire Candide and other stories
Voltaire Voltaire's Candide, Zadig, and selected stories
Vonnegut, K. Armageddon in retrospect
Vonnegut, K. Bagombo snuff box: uncollected short fiction
Vonnegut, K. Look at the birdie
Vonnegut, K. Welcome to the monkey house
Vonnegut, K. While mortals sleep
Walker, A. The way forward is with a broken heart
Walker, A. You can't keep a good woman down
Wallace, D. F. Oblivion
Walter, J. We Live in Water
Watkins, C. V. Battleborn
Watson, B. Aliens in the prime of their lives
Waugh, E. The complete stories of Evelyn Waugh
Weldon, F. A hard time to be a father
Wells, H. G. The complete short stories of H. G. Wells
Welty, E. The collected stories of Eudora Welty
We're flying
The Wesleyan anthology of science fiction
West, J. Collected stories of Jessamyn West
West, J. The friendly persuasion
Westlake, D. E. Thieves' dozen
Westward
Wharton, E. Collected stories, 1891-1910
Wharton, E. Collected stories, 1911-1937
While the women are sleeping
The white people and other weird stories
Wickersham, J. The news from Spain
Wideman, J. E. God's gym
Wideman, J. E. The stories of John Edgar Wideman
Williams, J. Honored guest
Williams, T. Collected stories
Wingate, S. Wifeshopping
Wodehouse, P. G. Tales from the Drones Club
Wodehouse, P. G. A Wodehouse bestiary
Wodehouse, P. G. The world of Jeeves
Wolfe, G. The best of Gene Wolfe
Wolff, T. Our story begins
A Woman's eye
Woodrell, D. The outlaw album
Woolf, V. The complete shorter fiction of Virginia Woolf
Wright, R. Eight men
Wright, R. Uncle Tom's children
Yates, R. The collected stories of Richard Yates
The Year's best fantasy and horror
Year's best science fiction
Yoon, P. Once the shore
Yoshimoto, B. Asleep
Zola, E. Three faces of love
Zumas, L. Farewell navigator
The **short** stories. Hemingway, E.

Short stories. Pirandello, L.

SHORT STORIES -- BY INDIVIDUAL AUTHORS

Abbott, L. K. All things, all at once

Adichie, C. N. The thing around your neck

Agee, J. Let us now praise famous men; A death in the family, and shorter fiction

Amsterdam, S. Things we didn't see coming

Anaya, R. A. The man who could fly and other stories

Apple, M. The Jew of Home Depot and other stories

Ballard, J. G. The complete stories of J.G. Ballard

Bank, M. The wonder spot

Barrett, A. Ship fever and other stories

Bausch, R. Something is out there

Bausch, R. The stories of Richard Bausch

Baxter, C. Gryphon

Beattie, A. Follies

Beattie, A. The New Yorker stories

Bingham, S. Mending

Bolano, R. Last evenings on Earth

Boswell, R. The heyday of the insensitive bastards

Boyle, T. C. Wild child

Busch, F. Rescue missions

Capote, T. The complete stories of Truman Capote

Carter, A. Burning your boats

Carver, R. Collected stories

Cheever, J. Collected stories and other writings

Complete short stories

Cozarinsky, E. The bride from Odessa

Danticat, E. Krik? Krak!

Davis, L. The collected stories of Lydia Davis

Doctorow, E. L. All the time in the world

Doctorow, E. L. Sweet land stories

Doerr, A. Memory wall

Donoghue, E. Touchy subjects

Dorst, D. The surf guru

Drabble, M. A day in the life of a smiling woman

Eisenberg, D. The collected stories of Deborah Eisenberg

Eisenberg, D. Twilight of the superheroes

Endo, S. The final martyrs

Enright, A. Yesterday's weather

Erdrich, L. The red convertible

Estleman, L. D. Amos Walker

Evans, D. Before you suffocate your own fool self

Faber, M. The courage consort

Faber, M. Vanilla bright like Eminem

Fallon, S. You know when the men are gone

Freed, L. The curse of the appropriate man

Fuentes, C. The crystal frontier

Fuentes, C. Happy families

Fulton, A. The nightingales of Troy

Gaiman, N. Fragile things

Gaitskill, M. Don't cry

Garcia Marquez, G. Strange pilgrims

Gardam, J. The people on Privilege Hill and other stories

Gilchrist, E. The age of miracles

Gordimer, N. Beethoven was one-sixteenth black

Gordimer, N. Jump and other stories

Gordimer, N. Life times

Grisham, J. Ford County

Gurganus, A. White people

Hannah, B. Long, last, happy

Harrison, J. The farmer's daughter

Heathcock, A. Volt

Helprin, M. The Pacific and other stories

Hemon, A. Love and obstacles

Hempel, A. The collected stories of Amy Hempel

Hersey, J. Key West tales

Highsmith, P. The selected stories of Patricia Highsmith

Hoeg, P. Tales of the night

Houston, P. Cowboys are my weakness

Houston, P. Waltzing the cat

Hughes Double happiness

Jackson, S. Novels and stories

Jin, H. A good fall

Johnson, C. R. Dr. King's refrigerator and other bedtime stories

Johnson, D. Jesus' son

Jones, E. All Aunt Hagar's children

July, M. No one belongs here more than you

Keillor, G. Leaving home

King, S. Full dark, no stars

King, S. Just after sunset

Lahiri, J. Unaccustomed earth

Li Yiyun A thousand years of good prayers

Link, K. Magic for beginners

Lovecraft, H. P. H. P. Lovecraft

Lurie, A. Women and ghosts

MacLeod, A. Light lifting

Malamud, B. The complete stories

Mann, T. Six early stories

Mason, B. A. Nancy Culpepper

Matthiessen, P. On the river Styx and other stories

Maxwell, W. Early novels and stories

McCrumb, S. Foggy Mountain breakdown and other stories

McGuane, T. Gallatin Canyon

McInerney, J. How it ended

Means, D. The secret goldfish

Messud, C. The hunters

Michaels, L. The collected stories

Miller, A. L. Water

Millhauser, S. Dangerous laughter

Millhauser, S. The knife thrower and other stories

Munro, A. Friend of my youth

Munro, A. Hateship, friendship, courtship, loveship, marriage

SHORT STORIES -- COLLECTIONS

SHORT STORIES, AMERICAN

SHORT STORIES, ENGLISH

SHORT STORY

SHORT STORY -- AUTHORSHIP

SHORT STORY WRITERS

Hill, S. Mrs. de Winter
Holland, T. The archivist's story
Johnson, M. Pym
Jordan, H. When she woke
Kalfus, K. The commissariat of enlightenment
Lashner, W. Kockroach
Marks, J. Fangland
Martin, V. Mary Reilly
McLain, P. The Paris wife
Moore, G. The Sherlockian
Morris, R. N. The gentle axe
Nabokov, V. V. Novels and memoirs, 1941-1951
Novels The gilded age and later novels
Oates, J. C. Wild nights!
Ozick, C. The Messiah of Stockholm
Pearl, M. The Poe shadow
Powers, K. Capote in Kansas
Reyn, I. What happened to Anna K.
Rose, J. Blackest bird
TSypkin, L. Summer in Baden-Baden
Vásquez, J. G. The secret history of Costaguana
Verissimo, L. F. Borges and the eternal orangutans
Walker, A. The way forward is with a broken heart
Winegardner, M. The Godfather returns
Short straw. Woods, S.
A **shortcut** in time. Dickinson, C.
The **shortest** way home. Fay, J.
SHORTWAVE RADIO *See* Radio; Radio frequency modulation
SHOSHONI INDIANS
Hall, B. I should be extremely happy in your company
The **shotgun** rule. Huston, C.
SHOTGUNS *See* Firearms
Shoulder the sky. Perry, A.
Shout her lovely name. Serber, N.
SHOW JUMPING
Greaves, C. Hush money
Show of evil. Diehl, W.
SHOW WINDOWS *See* Advertising; Decoration and ornament; Windows
SHOWERS (PARTIES) *See* Parties
SHRINES
Vassanji, M. G. The assassin's song
Shrink rap. Parker, R. B.
SHRUBS
See also Plants; Trees
SHUGAK, KATE (FICTITIOUS CHARACTER)
Stabenow, D. Hunter's moon
Stabenow, D. Killing grounds
Stabenow, D. Restless in the grave
Stabenow, D. Though not dead
Shut your eyes tight. Verdon, J.
Shutter Island. Lehane, D.
SHYNESS
See also Emotions

Harstad, J. Buzz Aldrin, what happened to you in all the confusion?
SIAMESE TWINS
Lansens, L. The girls
McCammon, R. R. Gone south
Slouka, M. God's fool
SIBERIA (RUSSIA)
Freemantle, B. Dead men living
L'Amour, L. Last of the breed
Meek, J. The people's act of love
Pasternak, B. L. Doctor Zhivago
Richler, N. Your mouth is lovely
Theroux, M. Far north
SIBERIA (RUSSIA) -- FICTION
Eastland, S. Archive 17
SIBLING RIVALRY
Chung, C. Forgotten country
SIBLINGS
See also Family
Anshaw, C. Carry the one
Haddon, M. The red house
Jewell, L. The making of us
McCarthy, M. The other half of me
Meek, J. The heart broke in
Morrison, T. Home
The **Sicilian.** Puzo, M.
SICILY
Hersey, J. A bell for Adano
Higgins, J. Luciano's luck
Pirandello, L. The outcast
Puzo, M. The Sicilian
Unsworth, B. The ruby in her navel
SICK
Ondaatje, M. The English patient
Schwartz, L. S. The fatigue artist
Shriver, L. So much for that
Wharton, E. Ethan Frome
SICK CHILDREN
Leroy, M. Postcards from Berlin
Winthrop, E. H. December
Sick puppy. Hiaasen, C.
SICKNESS *See* Diseases
Siddhartha. Hesse, H.
Side jobs. Butcher, J.
Sideshow. Tepper, S. S.
SIDS (DISEASE) *See* Sudden infant death syndrome
SIEGES
See also Battles
Cornwell, B. Lords of the North
Harrigan, S. The gates of the Alamo
SIERRA LEONE
Forna, A. The memory of love
Hill, L. Someone knows my name
SIERRA LEONE -- HISTORY -- CIVIL WAR, 1991-

the world was good
Jackson, S. Caught up in the rapture
Joe, Y. My fine lady
King, R. Domino
Marias, J. The man of feeling
McCrumb, S. If ever I return, pretty Peggy-O
McCrumb, S. The songcatcher
Patchett, A. Bel canto
Patterson, J. Hide & seek
Pearson, A. I think I love you
Phillips, A. The song is you
Phillips, C. Dancing in the dark
Powers, R. The time of our singing
Pynchon, T. The crying of lot 49
Rushdie, S. The ground beneath her feet
Sarton, M. Anger
Smith, L. The devil's dream
Spencer, L. Small town girl
Steel, D. Amazing grace
Thomas, D. M. The white hotel
Turner, F. W. The go-between
Tyler, A. A slipping-down life
Weiner, J. In her shoes
Williams, C. Stairway to hell

SINGERS -- FICTION
Little star

SINGING *See* Music

Singing boy. McFarland, D.

SINGING GAMES *See* Games

The **singing** of the dead. Stabenow, D.

The **singing** sands. Tey, J.

The **singing** stones. Whitney, P. A.

The **singing** sword. Whyte, J.

Singing the sadness. Hill, R.

Single & Single. Le Carre, J.

SINGLE FATHERS
Coben, H. No second chance
Law, S. K. The paper marriage
Sullivan, M. J. Necessary heartbreak

Single in Suburbia. Wax, W.

SINGLE MEN
See also Men; Single people
Alam, S. The groom to have been
Doig, I. Work song
Hornby, N. About a boy
LaFarge, P. Luminous airplanes
Lee A gesture life
Lipman, E. The ladies' man
Pierre, D. B. C. Lights out in Wonderland
Pym, B. Quartet in autumn
Sams, F. Down town
Spark, M. The bachelors
Stamm, P. On a day like this
Talarigo, J. The ginseng hunter
Wolcott, J. The catsitters

SINGLE MOTHERS

Higgins, K. Somebody to love
Jenkins, V. An unattended death
Robards, K. Shiver

SINGLE PARENT FAMILY
Moriarty, L. The center of everything

SINGLE PARENTS
See also Parents; Unmarried couples
Smith, A. A bigger life

A **single** pebble. Hersey, J.

Single wife. Solomon, N.

SINGLE WOMEN
See also Single people; Women
Abu-Jaber, D. Crescent
Albert, E. The book of Dahlia
Allen, S. A. The sugar queen
Ansa, T. M. The hand I fan with
Balzac, H. d. Cousin Bette
Bank, M. The girls' guide to hunting and fishing
Barbery, M. The elegance of the hedgehog
Blew, M. C. Jackalope dreams
Brookner, A. Hotel du Lac
Brookner, A. Undue influence
Bynum, S. Ms. Hempel chronicles
Capote, T. The grass harp
Chevalier, T. Remarkable creatures
Close, J. Girls in white dresses
Cox, M. The glass of time
Crouch, K. Girls in trucks
Crouch, K. Men and dogs
Davenport, K. House of many gods
Davies, P. H. The Welsh girl
Diffenbaugh, V. The language of flowers
Dreyer, E. Barely a lady
Dunn, S. The big love
Faulkner, W. Intruder in the dust
Fielding, H. Bridget Jones: the edge of reason
Fielding, H. Bridget Jones's diary
Fielding, J. Charley's web
Fitch, J. Paint it black
Forester, C. S. The African Queen
Fowler, K. J. Sister Noon
Freeman, C. Go with me
Gaffney, P. Flight lessons
Gaskell, E. C. Cranford
Gloss, M. The hearts of horses
Goodman, A. Paradise park
Gordon, M. Final payments
Gould, J. A moment in time
Graham, W. Bella Poldark
Grimes, M. The train now departing: two novellas
Groff, L. The monsters of Templeton
Gunning, S. The rebellion of Jane Clarke
Guo Xiaolu A concise Chinese-English dictionary
  for lovers
Guo Xiaolu Twenty fragments of a ravenous youth
Guterson, M. Gone to the dogs

Cather, W. Sapphira and the slave girl

Chase-Riboud, B. Sally Hemings

Cheuse, A. Song of slaves in the desert

Conde, M. I, Tituba, black witch of Salem

Crafts, H. The bondswomans narrative

Durham, D. A. A walk through darkness

Fuller, D. Sweetsmoke

Gaines, E. J. The autobiography of Miss Jane Pittman

Garcia, C. Monkey hunting

Gibbons, K. On the occasion of my last afternoon

Hambly, B. Sold down the river

Hansen, B. The monsters of St. Helena

Heidish, M. A woman called Moses

Heinlein, R. A. Citizen of the galaxy

Hill, L. Someone knows my name

Jakes, J. Charleston

James, M. The book of night women

L'Engle, M. The other side of the sun

Levy, A. The long song

Martin, V. Property

McCaig, D. Jacob's ladder

Morrison, T. A mercy

Pesci, D. Amistad

Phillips, C. Crossing the river

Plain, B. Crescent City

Rhodes, J. P. Voodoo dreams

Santiago, E. Conquistadora

Smith, W. A. River god

Stowe, H. B. Uncle Tom's cabin

Straight, S. A million nightingales

Stross, C. Saturn's children

Styron, W. The confessions of Nat Turner

Tademy, L. Cane River

Twain, M. Pudd'nhead Wilson;

Walker, M. Jubilee

Wallach, J. Seraglio

Warren, R. P. Band of angels

Wright, S. The Amalgamation Polka

Youmans, M. The wolf pit

SLAVERY -- FICTION

Anderton, J. Debris

Odell, J. The healing

Unsworth, B. The quality of mercy

Wrinkle, M. Wash

SLAVERY -- UNITED STATES

Jones, E. P. The known world

Leveen, L. The secrets of Mary Bowser

Pitts, L. Freeman

Rawles, N. My Jim

SLAVES

> *See also* Slavery

Chase-Riboud, B. Sally Hemings

Conde, M. I, Tituba, black witch of Salem

Falconer, C. Feathered serpent

Hambly, B. Patriot hearts

Harris, R. Conspirata

Sherwood, F. Night of sorrows

Styron, W. The confessions of Nat Turner

SLAVES -- EMANCIPATION -- SOUTH AFRICA

Brink, A. P. Philida

SLAVES -- FICTION

Guinn, M. The resurrectionist

Hunt, L. Kind one

Kane, B. Spartacus

Slaves of obsession. Perry, A.

SLED DOG RACING

Henry, S. Murder on the Iditarod Trail

SLEEP

> *See also* Health; Hygiene; Mind and body;
> Psychophysiology; Rest; Subconsciousness

Kress, N. Beggars & choosers

Kress, N. Beggars in Spain

Pierson, D. C. The boy who couldn't sleep and never had to

SLEEP APNEA *See* Sleep

SLEEP DISORDERS

Pierson, D. C. The boy who couldn't sleep and never had to

The **Sleeper** wakes.

Sleeping beauty. Macdonald, R.

Sleeping beauty. Michael, J.

SLEEPING BEAUTY -- ADAPTATIONS

Coover, R. Briar Rose

Sleeping bones. Forrest, K. V.

Sleeping dogs. Gorman, E.

The **sleeping** father. Sharpe, M.

A **sleeping** life. Rendell, R.

Sleeping with the enemy. Price, N.

Sleepless. Huston, C.

SLEEPLESSNESS *See* Insomnia

Sleepwalking land. Couto, M.

A **slepyng** hound to wake. McCaffrey, V.

A **slight** trick of the mind. Cullin, M.

Slightly dangerous. Balogh, M.

Slightly shady. Quick, A.

Slip of the knife. Mina, D.

A **slipping-down** life. Tyler, A.

SLOVAKIA

McCann, C. Zoli

Slow dollar. Maron, M.

Slow man. Coetzee, J. M.

Slowness. Kundera, M.

SLUM LIFE

Abani, C. GraceLand

Algren, N. A walk on the wild side

Bellow, S. The adventures of Augie March

Crane, S. Maggie: a girl of the streets (a story of New York)

Dickens, C. Oliver Twist

Farrell, J. T. Studs Lonigan

Naylor, G. The men of Brewster Place

Karon, J. In this mountain

Karon, J. A new song

Karon, J. Out to Canaan

Kay, T. The runaway

Keillor, G. Lake Wobegon days

Keillor, G. Lake Wobegon summer 1956

Keillor, G. Leaving home

Kimmel, H. Something rising (light and swift)

Kimmel, H. The used world

Kincaid, N. Verbena

King, S. Carrie

Klosterman, C. Downtown Owl

Lansdale, J. R. The bottoms

Lansdale, J. R. A fine dark line

Lee, H. To kill a mockingbird

Letts, B. Shoot the moon

Lewis, S. Main Street

Lipman, E. The dearly departed

Lockridge, R. Raintree County

Mallon, T. Dewey defeats Truman

Marlette, D. Magic time

Martin, L. Break the skin

Mason, B. A. In country

McCammon, R. R. Boy's life

McCorkle, J. Carolina moon

McCorkle, J. Ferris Beach

McCrumb, S. The hangman's beautiful daughter

McCrumb, S. If ever I return, pretty Peggy-O

McCrumb, S. She walks these hills

McCullers, C. The heart is a lonely hunter

McFadden, B. L. Sugar

McLarty, R. Art in America

McMurtry, L. Duane's depressed

McMurtry, L. Rhino Ranch

McMurtry, L. Texasville

Medlicott, J. A. Gardens of Covington

Medlicott, J. A. The ladies of Covington send their
  love

Miller, S. While I was gone

Miller, S. The world below

Morris, K. L. The dart league king

Morris, M. M. A dangerous woman

Morris, M. M. Fiona Range

Morris, M. M. Songs in ordinary time

Morris, W. Taps

Mosher, H. F. On Kingdom Mountain

Murr, N. The perfect man

Naylor, G. Mama Day

Nichols, J. T. The Milagro beanfield war

Nordan, L. Wolf whistle

Oates, J. C. Broke heart blues

Oates, J. C. Little bird of heaven

Oates, J. C. Missing mom

Oates, J. C. Rape

O'Dell, T. Back roads

O'Dell, T. Coal Run

O'Dell, T. Sister mine

O'Hara, J. Ten North Frederick

O'Nan, S. Snow angels

Otto, W. How to make an American quilt

Parks, G. The learning tree

Patton, F. G. Good morning, Miss Dove

Pearson, T. R. Blue Ridge

Pearson, T. R. Cry me a river

Pearson, T. R. A short history of a small place

Phillips, S. E. Ain't she sweet

Picoult, J. Nineteen minutes

Pollock, D. R. Knockemstiff

Poyer, D. Thunder on the mountain

Price, R. Roxanna Slade

Pronzini, B. A wasteland of strangers

Purdy, J. The nephew

Rash, R. Saints at the river

Reuss, F. Horace afoot

Revoyr, N. Wingshooters

Reynolds, S. A gracious plenty

Richards, D. A. The bay of love and sorrows

Rinehart, S. Built in a day

Roth, P. When she was good

Roy, L. Bent Road

Russo, R. Bridge of sighs

Russo, R. Empire Falls

Russo, R. Nobody's fool

Russo, R. The risk pool

Sams, F. Down town

Santmyer, H. H. --and ladies of the club

Saroyan, W. The human comedy

Sarton, M. Kinds of love

Schaffert, T. The coffins of Little Hope

Schupack, D. The boy on the bus

Schwartz, J. B. Reservation Road

Settle, M. L. Charley Bland

Sholem Aleichem   The nightingale

Shreve, A. Strange fits of passion

Shreve, S. R. The visiting physician

Siddons, A. R. Nora, Nora

Sidor, S. Pitch dark

Simpson, M. Off Keck Road

Smith, L. Family linen

Sparks, N. A bend in the road

Spencer, L. Bitter sweet

Spencer, L. Morning glory

Spencer, L. That Camden summer

Steinbeck, J. East of Eden

Strout, E. Amy and Isabelle

Strout, E. Olive Kitteridge

Tarkington, B. Alice Adams

Thomas, R. The fourth Durango

Trigiani, A. Big Cherry Holler

Trigiani, A. Big Stone Gap

Trigiani, A. Milk glass moon

Tryon, T. In the fire of spring

Young, T. W. The renegades
SOLDIERS -- FRANCE
Balzac, H. d. The country doctor
Faulkner, W. A fable
Flanagan, T. The year of the French
SOLDIERS -- GERMANY
Boll, H. The silent angel
Friedman, D. Don't ever get old
Higgins, J. The eagle has landed
Kirst, H. H. Forward, Gunner Asch!
Kirst, H. H. The return of Gunner Asch
Kirst, H. H. The revolt of Gunner Asch
Remarque, E. M. All quiet on the western front
Remarque, E. M. A time to love and a time to die
Robbins, D. L. War of the rats
Shaw, I. The young lions
SOLDIERS -- GERMANY -- FICTION
Friedman, D. Don't ever get old
SOLDIERS -- GREAT BRITAIN
Barker, P. The eye in the door
Barker, P. The ghost road
Barker, P. Regeneration
Boulle, P. The bridge over the River Kwai
Cornwell, B. Sharpe's battle
Cornwell, B. Sharpe's fortress
Cornwell, B. Sharpe's fury
Cornwell, B. Sharpe's havoc
Cornwell, B. Sharpe's prey: Richard Sharpe and
  the Expedition to Copenhagen, 1807
Cornwell, B. Sharpe's Trafalgar
Cornwell, B. Sharpe's Waterloo
MacLean, A. Force 10 from Navarone
MacLean, A. The guns of Navarone
Mallinson, A. A close run thing
Ondaatje, M. The English patient
Scott, P. A division of the spoils
Waugh, E. Men at arms
Waugh, E. Officers and gentlemen
SOLDIERS -- GREAT BRITAIN -- FICTION
Swift, G. Wish you were here
SOLDIERS -- ISRAEL
Leshem, R. Beaufort
Reiken, F. Day for night
To the end of the land
SOLDIERS -- JAPAN
Shan Sa The girl who played go
SOLDIERS -- ROME
Llywelyn, M. Druids
SOLDIERS -- RUSSIA
Dekker, T. Immanuel's veins
SOLDIERS -- UNITED STATES
Bausch, R. Peace
Clavell, J. King Rat
Evans, N. The brave
Fleming, T. J. Dreams of glory
Fountain, B. Billy Lynn's long halftime walk

Gold, G. D. Sunnyside
Goonan, K. A. In war times
Griffin, W. E. B. The aviators
Griffin, W. E. B. Special ops
Harrington, L. Alice Bliss
Hawke, E. Ash Wednesday
Hersey, J. A bell for Adano
Higgins, J. Night of the fox
Hooker, R. MASH
Johnson, D. Tree of smoke
Jones, J. From here to eternity
Jones, J. The thin red line
Jones, J. Whistle
Knight, M. The typist
Lee The surrendered
Leimbach, M. The man from Saigon
Mailer, N. The naked and the dead
Melman, P. C. Landsman
Nathanson, E. M. The dirty dozen
O'Brien, T. Going after Cacciato
Olmstead, R. Far bright star
Purdy, J. The nephew
Ricks, T. E. A soldier's duty
Shaara, J. Gone for soldiers
Shaw, I. The young lions
Shulman, M. Rally round the flag, boys!
Sparks, N. Dear John
Sundaresan, I. The splendor of silence
Willard, T. Buffalo soldiers
Wright, S. Meditations in green
Zimmerman, D. Sandbox
SOLDIERS -- UNITED STATES -- FICTION
Fountain, B. Billy Lynn's long halftime walk
SOLDIERS -- VIETNAM
The sorrow of war
SOLDIERS OF FORTUNE
Caputo, P. Horn of Africa
Cussler, C. Plague ship
Forsyth, F. The dogs of war
Walters, M. The devil's feather
SOLDIERS' LIFE *See* Soldiers
Soldiers' pay. Faulkner, W.
SOLICITORS *See* Lawyers
SOLIDS *See* Physical chemistry; Physics
Solitaire. Eskridge, K.
SOLITAIRE (GAME) *See* Card games
The **solitary** house. Shepherd, L.
SOLITUDE
Giordano, P. The solitude of prime numbers
Parks, T. Cleaver
SOLITUDE -- FICTION
Brewer, S. The poet of Tolstoy Park
The **solitude** of prime numbers. Giordano, P.
Solomon Gursky was here. Richler, M.
SOLOMON ISLANDS
London, J. South Sea tales

Solomon's oak. Mapson
SOLVENT ABUSE *See* Social problems; Substance abuse
SOMALI AMERICANS
  Strout, E. The burgess boys
SOMALIA
  Farah, N. Crossbones
  Farah, N. Knots
  Farah, N. Links
  McDonell, N. An expensive education
Some bitter taste. Nabb, M.
Some buried Caesar & The golden spiders. Stout, R.
Some deaths before dying. Dickinson, P.
Some kind of fairy tale. Joyce, G.
Somebody else's music. Haddam, J.
Somebody to love. Higgins, K.
Somebody's daughter. Lee, M.
Someday this will be funny. Tillman, L.
Someone. McDermott, A.
Someone knows my name. Hill, L.
Someone to run with. Grossman, D.
Someplace to be flying. De Lint, C.
Somersault. Oe, K.
Something about you. James, J.
Something borrowed, something black. Estleman, L. D.
Something happened. Heller, J.
Something in the air. Lathen, E.
Something is out there. Bausch, R.
Something like a love affair. Symons, J.
Something noble. Kowalski, W.
Something red. Gilmore, J.
Something red. Nicholas, D.
Something rising (light and swift) Kimmel, H.
Something special. Murdoch, I.
Something to tell you. Kureishi, H.
Something wicked this way comes. Bradbury, R.
Sometimes a great notion. Kesey, K.
The **somnambulist.** Barnes, J.
The **Son.** Meyer, P.
A **son** called Gabriel. McNicholl, D.
Son of a witch. Maguire, G.
Son of Fletch. Mcdonald, G.
A **son** of the circus. Irving, J.
A **son** of war. Bragg, M.
The **song** is you. Phillips, A.
The **song** is you. Abbott, M. E.
The **song** of Achilles. Miller, M.
The **song** of Bernadette. Werfel, F.
The **song** of everlasting sorrow. Wang Anyi
Song of ice and fire [series]
  Martin, G. R. R. A dance with dragons
  Martin, G. R. R. A clash of kings
  Martin, G. R. R. A feast for crows
  Martin, G. R. R. A game of thrones
The **song** of names. Lebrecht, N.

Song of slaves in the desert. Cheuse, A.
Song of Solomon. Morrison, T.
The **song** of the lark. Cather, W.
Song of the river. Harrison, S.
The **song** of Troy. McCullough, C.
Song yet sung. McBride, J.
SONGBOOKS *See* Singing; Songs
The **songcatcher.** McCrumb, S.
SONGS
  See also Poetry; Vocal music
  McCrumb, S. The songcatcher
SONGS -- FICTION
  Bennett, R. J. The troupe
Songs for the butcher's daughter. Manseau, P.
Songs for the missing. O'Nan, S.
Songs in ordinary time. Morris, M. M.
The **songs** of the kings. Unsworth, B.
The songs of the seraphim [series]
  Rice, A. Angel time
Songs without words. Packer, A.
SONGWRITERS
  See also Composers; Lyricists
  Bellow, S. The Bellarosa connection
  Earle, S. I'll never get out of this world alive
  Pearson, A. I think I love you
SONNETS *See* Poetry
SONS *See* Family; Men
SONS -- DEATH
  Harrison, K. Envy
  Steel, D. Johnny Angel
SONS AND FATHERS *See* Father-son relationship
Sons and lovers. Lawrence, D. H.
SONS AND MOTHERS *See* Mother-son relationship
The **sons** of heaven. Baker, K.
SONS-IN-LAW
  Saramago, J. The cave
Soon I will be invincible. Grossman, A.
SOOTHSAYING *See* Divination
Sophie's choice. Styron, W.
The **sorcerer's** house. Wolfe, G.
The **sorceress** and the Cygnet. McKillip, P. A.
SORCERY *See* Magic; Occultism; Witchcraft
SORROW *See* Bereavement; Grief; Joy and sorrow
The **sorrow** of war.
The **sorrows** of an American. Hustvedt, S.
The **sorrows** of young Werther, and Novella. Goethe, J. W. v.
The **sot-weed** factor. Barth, J.
SOUL
  See also Future life; Human beings (Theology); Philosophy
  Williams, C. Stairway to hell
SOUL -- FICTION
  Bannon, J. I2

Soul circus. Pelecanos, G. P.

Soul mountain. Gao Xingjian

The soul thief. Baxter, C.

Soulless. Carriger, G.

Souls in the great machine. McMullen, S.

Souls raised from the dead. Betts, D.

SOUND *See* Physics; Pneumatics; Radiation

The sound and the fury. Faulkner, W.

The sound of butterflies. King, R.

The sound of the mountain. Kawabata, Y.

The sound of the trees. Gatewood, R.

The sound of trumpets. Mortimer, J.

The sound of waves. Mishima, Y.

SOUND RECORDINGS

Egan, J. A visit from the Goon Squad

Sourland. Oates, J. C.

SOUTH AFRICA

Coetzee, J. M. Summertime

Galgut, D. The impostor

Gordimer, N. The conservationist

Gordimer, N. Get a life

Gordimer, N. July's people

Gordimer, N. Jump and other stories

Gordimer, N. Life times

Gordimer, N. None to accompany me

Gordimer, N. The pickup

Lessing, D. M. Children of violence

Lessing, D. M. The grass is singing

Mda, Z. The whale caller

Michener, J. A. The covenant

Morley, I. Come Sunday

Paton, A. Ah, but your land is beautiful

Paton, A. Cry, the beloved country

Paton, A. Tales from a troubled land

Sheldon, S. Master of the game

Smith, W. A. Golden fox

Smith, W. A. Power of the sword

Smith, W. A. A time to die

Ward, A. E. Forgive me

SOUTH AFRICA -- 19TH CENTURY

Harries, A. Manly pursuits

SOUTH AFRICA -- CAPE TOWN

Meyer, D. Heart of the hunter

Smith, R. Wake up dead

SOUTH AFRICA -- COMMISSION FOR TRUTH AND RECONCILIATION

Ward, A. E. Forgive me

SOUTH AFRICA -- FICTION

Beukes, L. Zoo city

Flanery, P. Absolution

Meyer, D. Trackers

SOUTH AFRICA -- HISTORY -- 19TH CENTURY

Brink, A. P. Philida

SOUTH AFRICA -- HISTORY

Brink, A. P. Philida

SOUTH AFRICA -- JOHANNESBURG

Paton, A. Too late the phalarope

Strauss, J. The dubious salvation of Jack V.

SOUTH AFRICA -- NATIVE PEOPLES

Coetzee, J. M. Life & times of Michael K.

SOUTH AFRICA -- RACE RELATIONS

See also Race relations

Coetzee, J. M. Age of iron

Coetzee, J. M. Disgrace

Fugard, L. Skinner's drift

Gien, P. The syringa tree

Gordimer, N. The conservationist

Gordimer, N. July's people

Gordimer, N. My son's story

Gordimer, N. None to accompany me

Lessing, D. M. The grass is singing

Mda, Z. The Madonna of Excelsior

Michener, J. A. The covenant

Paton, A. Ah, but your land is beautiful

Paton, A. Cry, the beloved country

Paton, A. Too late the phalarope

Smith, W. A. Rage

Strauss, J. The dubious salvation of Jack V.

Van Niekerk, M. Agaat

SOUTH AFRICA -- RACE RELATIONS -- FICTION

Gordimer, N. No time like the present

SOUTH AFRICA -- SOCIAL CONDITIONS -- 1994-

Gordimer, N. No time like the present

SOUTH AFRICAN DUTCH *See* Afrikaners

SOUTH AFRICANS -- MIDDLE EAST

Gordimer, N. The pickup

SOUTH AFRICANS -- WEST INDIES

Naipaul, V. S. Guerrillas

SOUTH AFRICANS, AFRIKAANS-SPEAKING

See Afrikaners

SOUTH AMERICA

Alarcon, D. Lost City Radio

Allende, I. Eva Luna

Castellanos Moya, H. Senselessness

Conrad, J. Nostromo

Doyle, A. C. The lost world

Hudson, W. H. Green mansions

Patchett, A. Bel canto

Woolf, V. The voyage out

SOUTH AMERICA -- FICTION

Aira, C. An afternoon in the life of a landscape painter

Alarcon, D. Lost City Radio

Erpenbeck, J. The book of words

Patchett, A. Bel canto

SOUTH AMERICAN ART *See* Art

SOUTH CAROLINA

Allison, D. Bastard out of Carolina

Baldacci, D. One summer

Siddons, A. R. Heartbreak Hotel

Siddons, A. R. Outer banks

Smith, L. The devil's dream

Smith, L. Mrs. Darcy and the blue-eyed stranger

Smith, L. Oral history

Smith, L. Saving Grace

Spencer, E. The southern woman

Tyler, A. Earthly possessions

Walker, A. The color purple

Wallace, D. Mr. Sebastian and the Negro magician

White, B. Quite a year for plums

Woods, S. Chiefs

SOUTHERN STATES -- 19TH CENTURY

Gibbons, K. On the occasion of my last afternoon

Mitchell, M. Gone with the wind

Price, E. Savannah

Walker, M. Jubilee

SOUTHERN STATES -- 20TH CENTURY

Adams, A. A southern exposure

Allison, D. Bastard out of Carolina

Bambara, T. C. The salt eaters

Brown, J. D. Addie Pray

Brown, L. Joe

Brown, R. M. Southern discomfort

Capote, T. The grass harp

Childress, M. Crazy in Alabama

Conroy, P. The prince of tides

Dexter, P. Paris Trout

Dickey, J. Deliverance

Faulkner, W. Pylon

Flagg, F. Fried green tomatoes at the Whistle-Stop Cafe

Gaines, E. J. A gathering of old men

Gibbons, K. Charms for the easy life

Gibbons, K. Ellen Foster

Gilchrist, E. The cabal and other stories

McCorkle, J. Ferris Beach

McCullers, C. The heart is a lonely hunter

McCullers, C. Reflections in a golden eye

Percy, W. The last gentleman

Percy, W. Love in the ruins

Price, R. Roxanna Slade

Reynolds, S. A gracious plenty

Siddons, A. R. Heartbreak Hotel

Siddons, A. R. Outer banks

Smith, L. Saving Grace

Spencer, E. The southern woman

Tyler, A. Earthly possessions

Woods, S. Chiefs

SOUTHERN STATES -- FICTION

Cramer, W. D. Bad ground

Dickey, J. Deliverance

Faulkner, W. Light in August

Faulkner, W. Novels, 1926-1929

Gibbons, K. Ellen Foster

Gibbons, K. The life all around me by Ellen Foster

Gurganus, A. The oldest living Confederate widow tells all

McCullers, C. The heart is a lonely hunter

O'Connor, F. Collected works

Smith, L. Saving Grace

Walker, A. The color purple

SOUTHERN STATES -- HISTORY -- 1865-1877

Pitts, L. Freeman

SOUTHERN STATES -- SOCIAL LIFE AND CUSTOMS

Gilchrist, E. The cabal and other stories

Knight, M. Goodnight, nobody

Welty, E. Complete novels

Welty, E. Stories, essays & memoir

The **southern** woman. Spencer, E.

Southern women. Battle, L.

SOUTHWESTERN STATES

Anaya, R. A. The man who could fly and other stories

Barrett, W. E. The lilies of the field

SOUTHWESTERN STATES -- GRAPHIC NOVELS

Henson, J.   Jim Henson's tale of sand

SOVEREIGNS *See* Emperors; Kings and rulers; Monarchy; Queens

SOVIET LITERATURE *See* Russian literature

SOVIET UNION

Bronsky, A. The Hottest Dishes of the Tartar Cuisine

Smith, T. R. Agent 6

Tregillis, I. The coldest war

SOVIET UNION -- HISTORY -- 1917-1936

Kalfus, K. The commissariat of enlightenment

Sherman, S. The little Russian

SOVIET UNION -- HISTORY -- 1925-1953

Eastland, S. Archive 17

Space. Michener, J. A.

SPACE AND TIME

See also Fourth dimension; Metaphysics; Space sciences; Time

Benford, G. Timescape

Donohue, K. Centuries of June

Heinlein, R. A. Job: a comedy of justice

Murakami, H. 1Q84

Yu, C.   How to live safely in a science fictional universe

SPACE AND TIME -- FICTION

Baxter, S. Manifold

Baxter, S. Sunstorm

The **space** between us. Umrigar, T. N.

SPACE COLONIES

Clement, H. Noise

Haldeman, J. W. Marsbound

Hamilton, P. F. The dreaming void

Heinlein, R. A. The moon is a harsh mistress

Martin, G. R. R. Hunter's run

GREAT BRITAIN
Le Carré, J. A Delicate Truth
SPECIAL LIBRARIES *See* Libraries
Special ops. Griffin, W. E. B.
A **special** place. Straub, P.
The **special** prisoner. Lehrer, J.
Special topics in calamity physics. Pessl, M.
Specimen days. Cunningham, M.
SPECIMENS, PRESERVATION OF *See* Plants
-- Collection and preservation; Taxidermy; Zoo-
logical specimens -- Collection and preservation
A **spectacle** of corruption. Liss, D.
SPECULATION
See also Finance
Moggach, D. Tulip fever
Norris, F. The pit
SPEECH -- HEALTH ASPECTS
Marcus, B. The flame alphabet
SPEECH DISORDERS
Mitchell, D. Black swan green
Wroblewski, D. The story of Edgar Sawtelle
The **speed** of dark. Moon, E.
Spellbound. Charlton, B.
SPELLING BEES *See* Language and languages
The **Spellman** files. Lutz, L.
**SPELLMAN, ISABEL (FICTITIOUS CHARAC-
TER)**
Lutz, L. The last word
SPELLS *See* Charms; Magic
Spellwright. Charlton, B.
Spencer's Mountain. Hamner, E.
SPERM BANKS
Jewell, L. The making of us
Sphere. Crichton, M.
SPICES *See* Food
Spider. McGrath, P.
Spiderweb. Lively, P.
Spies. Frayn, M.
SPIES
Abrahams, P. Hard rain
Baldacci, D. Deliver us from evil
Blatty, W. P. Dimiter
Bourne, J. The forbidden rose
Bourne, J. My lord and spymaster
Bourne, J. The spymaster's lady
Bowen, E. The heat of the day
Buchan, J. The thirty-nine steps
Buckley, W. F. Mongoose, R.I.P
Charyn, J. Johnny One-Eye
City of angels or
Clancy, T. The hunt for Red October
Clavell, J. Noble house
Cook, T. H. The quest for Anna Klein
Cornwell, B. Sharpe's havoc
Cumming, C. The Trinity Six
Davies, R. What's bred in the bone

Deaver, J. Carte blanche: 007
Deaver, J. Garden of beasts
Deighton, L. Berlin game
Deighton, L. City of gold
Deighton, L. Funeral in Berlin
Deighton, L. The Ipcress file
Deighton, L. London match
Deighton, L. Mexico set
DeMille, N. The charm school
Doctorow, E. L. The book of Daniel
Dunning, J. Two o'clock, eastern wartime
Faulks, S. Devil may care
Fesperman, D. The amateur spy
Finney, P. Gloriana's torch
Fleming, I. Casino Royale
Fleming, I. Doctor No
Fleming, I. From Russia, with love
Fleming, I. Goldfinger
Fleming, I. The man with the golden gun
Fleming, I. On Her Majesty's Secret Service
Fleming, I. You only live twice
Fleming, T. J. Dreams of glory
Follett, K. Eye of the needle
Follett, K. Hornet flight
Follett, K. Lie down with lions
Francis, C. Wolf winter
Freemantle, B. Bomb grade
Freemantle, B. Dead men living
Furst, A. Dark voyage
Furst, A. Spies of the Balkans
Furst, A. The spies of Warsaw
Gilman, D. The amazing Mrs. Pollifax
Gilman, D. The elusive Mrs. Pollifax
Gilman, D. A palm for Mrs. Pollifax
Gilman, D. The unexpected Mrs. Pollifax
Goldman, W. Marathon man
Grady, J. Six days of the condor
Greene, G. 3: This gun for hire, The confidential
agent, The ministry of fear
Greene, G. The human factor
Greene, G. The ministry of fear
Greene, G. Our man in Havana
Hall, A. Quiller Balalaika
Hall, A. The Quiller memorandum
Hall, A. Quiller Salamander
Hall, A. Quiller solitaire
Higgins, J. The eagle has flown
Higgins, J. The eagle has landed
Horn, D. All other nights
Ignatius, D. Body of lies
Ignatius, D. The increment
Isaacs, S. Shining through
Jakes, J. On secret service
Johnson, D. Tree of smoke
Johnson, D. Lulu in Marrakech
Judd, A. Legacy

Kennedy, D. The moment
Koontz, D. R. Watchers
Le Carre, J. Absolute friends
Le Carre, J. The honourable schoolboy
Le Carre, J. The little drummer girl
Le Carre, J. The looking glass war
Le Carre, J. The night manager
Le Carre, J. Our game
Le Carre, J. Our kind of traitor
Le Carre, J. A perfect spy
Le Carre, J. The Russia house
Le Carre, J. The secret pilgrim
Le Carre, J. Smiley's people
Le Carre, J. The spy who came in from the cold
Le Carre, J. The tailor of Panama
Le Carre, J. Tinker, tailor, soldier, spy
Leonard, E. Up in Honey's room
Lindsey, D. L. The color of night
Littell, R. The company
Littell, R. Walking back the cat
Ludlum, R. The Bourne identity
Ludlum, R. The Bourne supremacy
Ludlum, R. The Bourne ultimatum
Ludlum, R. The Parsifal mosaic
MacInnes, H. Prelude to terror
MacInnes, H. Ride a pale horse
MacLean, A. Ice Station Zebra
MacLean, A. Where eagles dare
Mailer, N. Harlot's ghost
Marias, J. Your face tomorrow: volume one: Fever and spear
Marias, J. Your face tomorrow: volume three: Poison, shadow and farewell
Marias, J. Your face tomorrow: volume two: Dance and dream
Mathews, H. My life in CIA
McCarry, C. Old boys
McEwan, I. The innocent
Morrell, D. The brotherhood of the rose
Murphy, Y. Signed, Mata Hari
Ondaatje, M. The English patient
The Oxford book of spy stories
Rankin, I. Watchman
Roberts, K. L. Arundel
Roberts, K. L. Rabble in arms
Sansom, C. J. Winter in Madrid
Silva, D. Portrait of a spy
Smith, M. C. Stallion Gate
Spillane, M. The Consummata
Steiner, P. The terrorist
Steinhauer, O. The nearest exit
Steinhauer, O. The tourist
Sundaresan, I. The splendor of silence
Trenhaile, J. The gates of exquisite view
Trevanian The Eiger sanction
Trevanian The Loo sanction

West, R. The birds fall down
Willig, L. The seduction of the crimson rose
SPIES -- FICTION
Buckley, F. Queen without a crown
Chase, L. Your scandalous ways
Fesperman, D. The double game
Kerr, P. Hitler's peace
Powers, T. Declare
Spies of the Balkans. Furst, A.
The **spies** of Warsaw. Furst, A.
Spin. Wilson, R. C.
Spindrift. Whitney, P. A.
SPINNING *See* Textile industry
The **spinning** man. Harrar, G.
SPINOSAURUS *See* Dinosaurs
Spiral. Healy, J. F.
Spiral. McEuen, P.
SPIRIT *See* Soul
The **spirit** caller. Hager, J.
SPIRITISM *See* Spiritualism
SPIRITUAL HEALING
Burney, C. M. Wounded
SPIRITUALISM
    See also Occultism; Supernatural
Elwork, P. The girl who would speak for the dead
Griesemer, J. Signal & noise
Howatch, S. The high flyer
Jackson, S. The haunting of Hill House
Mantel, H. Beyond black
Noyes, D. Captivity
Paretsky, S. Ghost country
Spark, M. The bachelors
Vargas Llosa, M. Death in the Andes
Wilson, C. Cotton
The **splendor** of silence. Sundaresan, I.
SPLICING OF GENES *See* Genetic engineering
Split estate. Bacon, C.
Split images. Leonard, E.
Split infinity. Anthony, P.
Split second. Coulter, C.
The **spoiler.** McAfee, A.
The **spoils** of Poynton. James, H.
SPOKANE (WASH.)
Walter, J. Citizen Vince
SPOKANE INDIANS
Alexie, S. Reservation blues
Spook. Pronzini, B.
Spook country. Gibson, W.
Spooner. Dexter, P.
Sporting with Amaryllis. West, P.
SPORTS -- CORRUPT PRACTICES *See* Criminal law
SPORTS
Hagy, A. Boleto
SPORTS -- GRAPHIC NOVELS *See* Graphic novels

The **Staggerford** flood. Hassler, J.
STAINED GLASS ARTISTS
  Vreeland, S. Clara and Mr. Tiffany
A **stained** white radiance. Burke, J. L.
The **Stainless** Steel Rat joins the circus. Harrison, H.
The **Stainless** Steel Rat sings the blues. Harrison, H.
Stainless steel visions. Harrison, H.
Stairway to hell. Williams, C.
The **Stalin** epigram. Littell, R.
Stalin's ghost. Smith, M. C.
Stalin, Joseph, 1879-1953
          About
  Eastland, S. Archive 17
  Harris, R. Archangel
STALINGRAD, BATTLE OF, 1942-1943
  Robbins, D. L. War of the rats
STALKERS
  Garwood, J. The ideal man
  Percy, B. The wilding
STALKERS -- CRIMES AGAINST
  Coben, H. The innocent
STALKERS -- FICTION
  Parshall, S. Bleeding through
STALKING
  Freeman, C. Go with me
  Hurwitz, G. They're watching
  Katzenbach, J. The wrong man
STALKING -- LAW AND LEGISLATION *See* Stalking
The **stalking** horse. McGown, J.
Stalking horse. Shoemaker, B.
The **stalking** horse. Monfredo, M. G.
Stalking season. Miller, M. G.
Stallion Gate. Smith, M. C.
The **stallions** of Woodstock. Marston, E.
Stamm, Peter, 1963-
          About
  We're flying
STAMP COLLECTING
    See also Collectors and collecting
  Block, L. Hit me
  Bradley, A. The sweetness at the bottom of the pie
The **stand.** King, S.
Stand on Zanzibar. Brunner, J.
STANDARD OF VALUE *See* Money
STANDARD TIME *See* Time
Standing in the rainbow. Flagg, F.
Stanhope, Hester Lucy Lady, 1776-1839
          About
  Stewart, M. The Gabriel hounds
STANLEY CUP (HOCKEY)
    See also Hockey; Sports tournaments
Stanley Elkin's The magic kingdom. Elkin, S.
Star bright. Anderson, C.
A **star** called Henry. Doyle, R.

Star Island. Hiaasen, C.
The **star** princess. Grant, S.
The **star** rover. London, J.
A **star** shines over Mt. Morris Park. Roth, H.
Star wars [series]
  Zahn, T. The last command
STAR WARS FILMS *See* Motion pictures; Science fiction films
The **starboard** sea. Dermont, A.
Starbound. Haldeman, J. W.
Starbuck chronicles [series]
  Cornwell, B. Rebel
Stardust. Gaiman, N.
Starfish. Watts, P.
The **Stargazey.** Grimes, M.
Starkweather, Charles, 1938-1959
          About
  Ward, L. Outside valentine
The **Starlite** Drive-in. Reynolds, M.
The **stars** above Veracruz. Gifford, B.
Stars in my pocket like grains of sand. Delany, S. R.
Starship troopers. Heinlein, R. A.
Start shooting. Newton, C.
Started early, took my dog. Atkinson, K.
Starting over. Wakefield, D.
STATE BIRDS *See* Birds; State emblems
STATE FLOWERS *See* Flowers; State emblems
STATE LEGISLATORS
  Grahame-Smith, S. Abraham Lincoln: vampire hunter
  Safire, W. Freedom
  Stone, I. Love is eternal
  Vidal, G. Lincoln
STATE MEDICINE *See* Medicine
State of mind. Katzenbach, J.
State of wonder. Patchett, A.
STATE POLICE *See* Police
STATE SONGS *See* Songs
STATE, HEADS OF *See* Heads of state
STATE-SPONSORED TERRORISM
  MacDonald, G. The prisoner's wife
The **statement.** Moore, B.
STATESMEN
  Bell, A. A. The blood of Caesar
  Benet, S. V. The Devil and Daniel Webster
  Carey, P. Parrot and Olivier in America
  Forsyth, F. The day of the jackal
  Garcia Marquez, G. The general and his labyrinth
  George, M. The memoirs of Cleopatra
  Harris, R. Conspirata
  Harris, R. Imperium
  Holland, C. Valley of the Kings
  Hunt, R. Mr. Chartwell
  Liss, D. The whiskey rebels
  Mantel, H. Wolf Hall
  Massie, A. Caesar

McCullough, C. Caesar
McCullough, C. Caesar's women
McCullough, C. The first man in Rome
McCullough, C. Fortune's favorites
McCullough, C. The grass crown
McCullough, C. The October horse
Morrow, J. The last witchfinder
Penman, S. K. Falls the shadow
Russell, M. D. Dreamers of the day
Saylor, S. The triumph of Caesar
Shaara, J. The glorious cause
Shaara, J. Rise to rebellion
Wilder, T. The ides of March
STATICS *See* Mechanics; Physics
STATUS, SOCIAL *See* Social status
Stay close. Coben, H.
Staying on. Scott, P.
Steal across the sky. Kress, N.
STEALING *See* Theft
Stealing Mona Lisa. Morton, C.
Stealing shadows. Hooper, K.
The **steam** pig. McClure, J.
STEAMBOATS
    See also Boats and boating; Naval architecture; Ocean travel; Shipbuilding; Ships
Forester, C. S. The African Queen
Gautreaux, T. The missing
Smith, L. The last girls
STEAMPUNK CULTURE *See* Counter culture
STEAMPUNK FICTION
    See also Science fiction
The mammoth book of steampunk
Priest, C. Clementine
Priest, C. Dreadnought
Priest, C. The inexplicables
STEAMSHIPS *See* Steamboats
STEEL CONSTRUCTION *See* Building; Structural engineering
The **steel** wave. Shaara, J.
STEGOSAURUS *See* Dinosaurs
Stein, Gertrude, 1874-1946
        About
Truong, M. T. D. The book of salt
Step to the graveyard easy. Pronzini, B.
STEPBROTHERS
Chen, D. Brothers
Haigh, J. Faith
Thayer, N. An act of love
Yu Hua Brothers
STEPCHILDREN
    See also Children; Parent-child relationship
McPhee, M. Gorgeous lies
Schwartz, L. S. The fatigue artist
Smith, W. A. Power of the sword
Trollope, J. Other people's children
STEPDAUGHTERS

Amis, M. House of meetings
Lipman, E. The family man
Wolitzer, H. Tunnel of love
STEPDAUGHTERS -- FICTION
Green, J. Another piece of my heart
STEPFAMILIES *See* Family
STEPFATHERS
    See also Fathers; Stepparents
Dexter, P. Spooner
Dickens, C. David Copperfield
Michael, J. Sleeping beauty
Saul, J. Midnight voices
STEPFATHERS -- FICTION
Abercrombie, J. Red country
The **Stepford** wives. Levin, I.
STEPMOTHERS
    See also Mothers; Stepparents
Kasischke, L. In a perfect world
Lee, G. China boy
Matar, H. Anatomy of a disappearance
Phillips, J. A. MotherKind
Sanders, D. Clover
Smith, R. K. Jane's house
Vargas Llosa, M. The notebooks of Don Rigoberto
Whitney, P. A. The singing stones
Wolitzer, H. Hearts
STEPMOTHERS -- FICTION
Green, J. Another piece of my heart
Steppenwolf. Hesse, H.
STEPSISTERS
Evison, J. All about Lulu
Maguire, G. Confessions of an ugly stepsister
STEPSONS
Tropper, J. How to talk to a widower
The **sterile** cuckoo. Nichols, J. T.
STERILITY IN ANIMALS *See* Infertility
STERILITY IN HUMANS *See* Infertility
STEROIDS *See* Biochemistry; Drugs
Stevenson, Robert Louis, 1850-1894
        About
Martin, V. Mary Reilly
STEWARDESSES, AIRLINE *See* Flight attendants
STEWARDS, AIRLINE *See* Flight attendants
Stick. Leonard, E.
Stick out your tongue. Ma Jian
STIGMATIZATION
Burney, C. M. Wounded
Still life. McInerny, R. M.
Still life. Penny, L.
Still life with crows. Preston, D.
Still life with Woodpecker. Robbins, T.
Still midnight. Mina, D.
Still missing. Stevens, C.
Still summer. Mitchard, J.
Still waters. Harvey, J.

Stillwatch. Clark, M. H.

Stiltsville. Daniel, S.

STIMULANTS *See* Drugs; Psychotropic drugs

The **Stingaree.** Brand, M.

Stitches in time. Michaels, B.

STOCK EXCHANGE
  Robbins, T. Half asleep in frog pajamas
  Stumpf, D. Confessions of a Wall Street shoeshine boy

STOCK EXCHANGE CRASHES *See* Financial crises

STOCK EXCHANGES *See* Finance; Markets

STOCK MARKET PANICS *See* Financial crises

STOCKHOLM (SWEDEN)
  Dahl, A. Bad Blood
  Larsson, S. The girl with the dragon tattoo
  Ozick, C. The Messiah of Stockholm

The **Stockholm** Octavo. Engelmann, K.

STOCKYARDS *See* Meat industry

STOICS *See* Ancient philosophy; Ethics

Stoker, Bram, 1847-1912
About

  Marks, J. Fangland
  Moore, G. The Sherlockian

The **stolen** child. Donohue, K.

Stolen gold: a western trio. Brand, M.

Stolen magic. Putney, M. J.

STONE AGE
  Harrison, S. Brother Wind
  Harrison, S. Call down the stars
  Harrison, S. Cry of the wind
  Harrison, S. Mother earth, father sky
  Harrison, S. My sister the moon
  Harrison, S. Song of the river

Stone angel. O'Connell, C.

Stone Arabia. Spiotta, D.

STONE CARVING
  Davidson, A. The gargoyle

Stone cribs. Nelscott, K.

The **stone** diaries. Shields, C.

The **stone** gods. Winterson, J.

Stone kiss. Kellerman, F.

Stone upon stone. Myśliwski, W.

Stone virgin. Unsworth, B.

Stone's fall. Pears, I.

The **stonecutter.** Lackberg, C.

STONEHENGE (ENGLAND)
  Cornwell, B. Stonehenge, 2000 B.C.
  Holland, C. Pillar of the Sky

Stonehenge, 2000 B.C. Cornwell, B.

Stonemouth. Banks, I.

The **stones** cry out. Okuizumi, H.

Stones for Ibarra. Doerr, H.

Stones from the river. Hegi, U.

STORES
  Kimmel, H. The used world

Russo, R. Bridge of sighs

Stories. Lessing, D. M.

STORIES *See* Anecdotes; Bible stories; Fairy tales; Fiction; Legends; Romances; Short stories; Stories in rhyme; Stories without words; Storytelling

Stories.

Stories and early novels. Chandler, R.

STORIES FOR CHILDREN *See* Children's stories

The **stories** of Alice Adams. Adams, A.

The **stories** of Elizabeth Spencer. Spencer, E.

The **stories** of F. Scott Fitzgerald. Fitzgerald, F. S.

Stories of five decades. Hesse, H.

The **stories** of John Edgar Wideman. Wideman, J. E.

The **stories** of Paul Bowles. Bowles, P.

The **stories** of Richard Bausch. Bausch, R.

Stories of three decades. Mann, T.

The **stories** of Vladimir Nabokov. Nabokov, V. V.

STORIES WITHIN A NOVEL
  Atwood, M. The blind assassin
  Barnes, J. A history of the world in 101/2 chapters
  Baxter, C. The feast of love
  Conley, R. J. Mountain windsong
  Fowles, J. The magus
  Gray, A. Old men in love
  Hansen, E. F. Tales of protection
  Harwood, J. The ghost writer
  King, S. Misery
  McGrath, P. Martha Peake
  Pouncey, P. R. Rules for old men waiting
  Rinaldi, N. Between two rivers
  Roth, P. The ghost writer
  Slouka, M. The visible world
  Tan, A. The Joy Luck Club
  Vargas Llosa, M. Aunt Julia and the scriptwriter
  Vidal, G. Burr
  Wallace, D. Big fish
  Waller, R. J. The bridges of Madison County
  Wiesel, E. The testament

Stories, essays & memoir. Welty, E.

Stories, novels, & essay. Chesnutt, C. W.

The **storm.** Moor, M. d.

Storm peak. Flanagan, J.

Storm runners. Parker, T. J.

Storm track. Maron, M.

Storm warning. Higgins, J.

Storming heaven. Brown, D.

STORMS
    See also Meteorology; Natural disasters; Weather
  Hailey, A. Airport
  Pronzini, B. The hidden
  Sparks, N. Nights in Rodanthe

The **stormy** petrel. Stewart, M.

Stormy weather. Hiaasen, C.

Proust, M. Sodom and Gomorrah

Proust, M. Swann's way

Proust, M. Time regained

Proust, M. Within a budding grove

Pynchon, T. Gravity's rainbow

Savage, S. Glass

Styron, W. Lie down in darkness

TSypkin, L. Summer in Baden-Baden

Woolf, V. Jacob's room

Woolf, V. Mrs. Dalloway

Woolf, V. To the lighthouse

Woolf, V. The waves

Woolf, V. The years

The **street.** Petry, A. L.

STREET ART *See* Art

Street dreams. Kellerman, F.

STREET GANGS *See* Gangs

The **street** lawyer. Grisham, J.

STREET LIFE

    See also City and town life

Coleman, A. Murder mamas

Coleman, A. Murderville

Diamond, D. Hustlin' divas

K'wan Section 8

Little, T. Where there's smoke

Miasha Chaser

Styles, T. Miss Wayne & the queen of DC

Turner, N. Heartbreak of a hustler's wife

Turner, N. Natural born hustler

Williams, K. Dirty to the grave

STREET MUSICIANS

Stemple, A. Singer of souls

The **street** of a thousand blossoms. Tsukiyama, G.

STREET PEOPLE *See* Homeless persons

STREET RAILROADS *See* Local transit; Railroads

The **street** sweeper. Perlman, E.

STREET VENDORS -- CRIMES AGAINST

Leon, D. Blood from a stone

STREETS *See* Cities and towns; Civil engineering; Transportation

Streets of Laredo. McMurtry, L.

STRENGTH OF MATERIALS *See* Mechanics; Structural analysis (Engineering)

STRESS (PSYCHOLOGY) *See* Mental health; Psychology

The **striker.** Cussler, C.

STRIKES *See* Industrial relations; Labor disputes

STRIKES AND LOCKOUTS

Poyer, D. Thunder on the mountain

Shreve, A. Sea glass

Steinbeck, J. In dubious battle

Strip tease. Hiaasen, C.

Stripped. Freeman, B.

STRIPTEASERS

Bock, C. Beautiful children

Dubus, A. The garden of last days

Flanagan, R. The unknown terrorist

STRIPTEASERS -- CRIMES AGAINST

Hayder, M. Birdman

Strivers Row. Baker, K.

STROLLING PLAYERS

Sabatini, R. Scaramouche

Strong as death. Newman, S.

Strong at the break. Land, J.

Strong poison. Sayers, D. L.

STRUCTURES *See* Buildings

STUBBORNNESS *See* Personality

STUDENT ACTIVITIES *See* Students

The **student** conductor. Ford, R.

STUDENT LIFE *See* College students; Students

A **student** of living things. Shreve, S. R.

A **student** of weather. Hay, E.

STUDENTS

Baxter, C. The soul thief

Cook, R. Coma

Dufosse, C. School's out

Eggers, D. What is the what

Goldman, W. Marathon man

Haslett, A. Union Atlantic

Knowles, J. Peace breaks out

Palahniuk, C. Pygmy

Rahimi, A. A thousand rooms of dream and fear

Stirling, J. The marrying kind

STUDENTS' MILITARY TRAINING CAMPS *See* Military training camps

STUDENTS' SONGS *See* Songs

Studio saint-ex. Szado, A.

Studs Lonigan. Farrell, J. T.

STUDY AND TEACHING *See* Education

A **Study** in Revenge. Shields, K.

A **study** in scarlet. Doyle, A. C.

STUDY SKILLS *See* Education; Life skills; Teaching

STUNT PERFORMERS

    See also Actors

Sallis, J. Drive

Sallis, J. Driven

STUTTERING

Shields, D. Dead languages

STYLE MANIKINS *See* Fashion models

SUBCULTURE *See* Counter culture

SUBJECT DICTIONARIES *See* Encyclopedias and dictionaries

SUBLIMINAL PERCEPTION

Syndrome E

SUBMARINE BOATS *See* Submarines

SUBMARINE CABLES *See* Telecommunication; Telegraph

SUBMARINE CAPTAINS

Bond, L. Exit plan

SUBMARINE MEDICINE *See* Medicine

Palahniuk, C. Lullaby

Sudden prey. Sandford, J.

Sudden rain. Wolff, M. M.

A **sudden** wild magic. Jones, D. W.

SUDOKU *See* Puzzles

SUENO, GEORGE (FICTITIOUS CHARACTER)

Limón, M. Mr. Kill

SUFFERING

Brockmeier, K. The Illumination

SUFFRAGE *See* Citizenship; Constitutional law; Democracy; Elections; Political science

SUFFRAGETTES *See* Suffragists

SUFFRAGISTS

Piercy, M. Sex wars

SUFFRAGISTS -- FICTION

Hatcher, R. L. Catching Katie

SUFISM

Iyer, P. Abandon

Sugar. McFadden, B. L.

SUGAR *See* Food

SUGAR LAND (TEX.)

Evans, S. J. Safe from harm

The **sugar** queen. Allen, S. A.

Sugar Street. Mahfouz, N.

SUICIDAL BEHAVIOR

Hornby, N. A long way down

Lurie, A. The last resort

Plath, S. The bell jar

Schneider, B. Beautiful Inez

SUICIDE

See also Medical jurisprudence; Social problems

Elias, G. Death and transfiguration

Elkins, A. J. Dying on the vine

Hayder, M. Skin

Jones, J. S. The silence

Lackberg, C. The ice princess

Mogford, T. Sign of the cross

O'Donovan, G. Dublin dead

Palwick, S. The necessary beggar

Sacre bleu

Winters, B. H. The last policeman

SUICIDE ATTEMPTS *See* Suicide

SUICIDE BOMBERS *See* Terrorism

SUICIDE VICTIMS

Boswell, R. Century's son

Long, D. The inhabited world

Melnyczuk, A. The house of widows

Palwick, S. Mending the moon

Parks, T. Destiny

A **suitable** boy. Seth, V.

Suitable for framing. Buchanan, E.

Suite Francaise. Nemirovsky, I.

The **suitors.** Ehrenreich, B.

Sula. Morrison, T.

SULFONAMIDES *See* Drugs

Sulla, Lucius Cornelius

About

McCullough, C. The first man in Rome

McCullough, C. Fortune's favorites

McCullough, C. The grass crown

Sullivan's law. Rosenberg, N. T.

Sullivan's sting. Sanders, L.

SULTANS

Wallach, J. Seraglio

SUMMER

Bradbury, R. Dandelion wine

Hilderbrand, E. Summerland

Kelman, J. Summer of storms

Rice, L. Summer light

SUMMER CAMPS

Dalton, J. The inverted forest

Price, R. The tongues of angels

Swarthout, G. F. Bless the beasts and children

The **summer** I dared. Delinsky, B.

Summer in Baden-Baden. TSypkin, L.

Summer lies.

Summer light. Rice, L.

Summer of '42. Raucher, H.

The **summer** of dead toys. Hill, A.

The **summer** of Katya. Trevanian

Summer of storms. Kelman, J.

The **summer** of the bear. Pollen, B.

The **summer** of the Danes. Peters, E.

Summer people. Piercy, M.

The **Summer** Queen. Vinge, J. D.

Summer reading. Wolitzer, H.

Summer rental. Andrews, M. K.

SUMMER RESORTS

Appelfeld, A. Badenheim 1939

Benchley, P. Jaws

Craig, A. Love in idleness

Kay, T. Shadow song

Morrison, T. Love

Raucher, H. Summer of '42

SUMMER RESORTS -- FICTION

Grimes, M. Cold Flat Junction

Hensher, P. King of the badgers

SUMMER SOLSTICE

Adrian, C. The great night

The **summer** tree. Kay, G. G.

The **summer** we got saved. Devoto, P. C.

Summer's lease. Mortimer, J.

Summerland. Hilderbrand, E.

Summertime. Coetzee, J. M.

The **summons.** Grisham, J.

A **summons** to Memphis. Taylor, P. H.

The **sun** also rises. Hemingway, E.

The **Sun** King. Ignatius, D.

SUN WORSHIP *See* Religion

SUNDARBANS (BANGLADESH AND INDIA)

Lofts, N. Gad's Hall

Lord, K. Redemption in indigo

Lovecraft, H. P. At the mountains of madness, and other novels

Lovecraft, H. P. The Dunwich horror, and others

Marr, M. Graveminder

McMahon, J. Don't breathe a word

Michaels, B. The dancing floor

Michaels, B. Stitches in time

Moloney, S. The dwelling

Morrow, B. The diviner's tale

Naylor, G. Mama Day

Picoult, J. Change of heart

Power, S. The grass dancer

Powers, T. Three days to never

Preston, D. The wheel of darkness

Rayne, S. Property of a lady

Reynolds, S. A gracious plenty

Rice, A. Lasher

Rice, A. Taltos

Rice, A. The witching hour

Richardson, K. Greywalker

Riley, J. M. In pursuit of the green lion

Roberts, N. Midnight Bayou

Rogers, R. Devil's Cape

Shepard, L. Softspoken

Simmons, D. Drood

Stoker, B. Dracula

Stott, R. Ghostwalk

Straub, P. Ghost story

Straub, P. Mr. X

Strieber, W. The forbidden zone

Thomas, E. M. Reindeer Moon

Wallace, D. The Watermelon King

Waters, S. The little stranger

Whitney, P. A. The singing stones

Wilde, O. The picture of Dorian Gray

Wolfe, G. Castleview

Wolfe, G. The sorcerer's house

SUPERSTITION

Kadare, I. The ghost rider

Naylor, G. Mama Day

The **Supremes** at Earl's all-you-can-eat. Moore, E. K.

The **surf** guru. Dorst, D.

Surface detail. Banks, I.

SURFERS

Winslow, D. The Dawn Patrol

Winslow, D. The gentlemen's hour

Winton, T. Breath

SURFING -- SONGS See Songs

The **surgeon.** Gerritsen, T.

SURGEONS

See also Physicians

Fielding, J. See Jane run

Hiaasen, C. Skin tight

Irving, J. The fourth hand

Kundera, M. The unbearable lightness of being

Laplante, A. Turn of mind

Palmer, M. The last surgeon

Uris, L. QB VII

SURGERY

See also Medicine

Cook, R. Coma

Cook, R. Godplayer

Cook, R. Marker

Palmer, M. The patient

SURGICAL TRANSPLANTATION See Transplantation of organs, tissues, etc.

SURPLUS GOVERNMENT PROPERTY See Property

SURREALISM

Aira, C. The literary conference

Baldwin, J. The Wilshire sun

Berry, J. The manual of detection

Birch, C. Jamrach's menagerie

Bolano, R. By night in Chile

Burroughs, W. S. Naked lunch

Calvo, J. Wonderful world

Childress, M. Crazy in Alabama

Cotter, B. Fever chart

DeLillo, D. Ratner's star

Donohue, K. Centuries of June

Ellis, B. E. Lunar Park

Erickson, S. Zeroville

Foer, J. S. Everything is illuminated

Garcia Marquez, G. The autumn of the patriarch

Gholson, C. A fish trapped inside the wind

Giraldi, W. Busy monsters

Grushin, O. The dream life of Sukhanov

Harkaway, N. The gone-away world

Hoffman, A. Seventh heaven

Ishiguro, K. The unconsoled

Ishiguro, K. When we were orphans

Lethem, J. Chronic city

Lethem, J. The fortress of solitude

Munoz Molina, A. In her absence

Murakami, H. 1Q84

Murakami, H. Kafka on the shore

Murakami, H. South of the border, west of the sun

Murakami, H. The wind-up bird chronicle

Pelevin, V. The hall of singing caryatids

Pelevin, V. The sacred book of the werewolf

Saramago, J. Blindness

Shaw, A. The girl with glass feet

Shteyngart, G. The Russian debutante's handbook

Wright, S. Going native

Surrender, Dorothy. Wolitzer, M.

The **surrendered.** Lee

SURREY (ENGLAND)

Dean, A. A gentleman of fortune, or, The suspicions of Miss Dido Kent

Ruff, M. Bad monkeys
Schickler, D. Sweet and vicious
Shreve, A. Resistance
Shreve, A. The weight of water
Smith, M. C. Polar Star
Smith, M. C. Rose
Smith, T. R. Child 44
Smith, T. R. The secret speech
Steiner, P. The terrorist
Steinhauer, O. The nearest exit
Stott, R. The coral thief
Tartt, D. The secret history
Verdon, J. Think of a number
Vine, B. Anna's book
Vine, B. Gallowglass
Vine, B. No night is too long
Waite, U. The terror of living
Wilcken, H. The execution
Wouk, H. A hole in Texas

SUSPENSE FICTION
Brown, D. The lost symbol
Buckley, W. F. Mongoose, R.I.P
Caldwell, I. The rule of four
Carter, S. L. Palace council
Carver, T. The creeper
Child, L. 61 hours
Child, L. Bad luck and trouble
Clancy, T. Clear and present danger
Clancy, T. Patriot games
Coben, H. Stay close
Cox, M. The meaning of night
Cussler, C. Shock wave
Doolittle, S. Lake country
Dovey, C. Blood kin
Down, D. Masaryk Station
Eastland, S. Shadow pass
Ellroy, J. Blood's a rover
Epperson, T. Sailor
Evans, J. The white devil
Faulks, S. Devil may care
Fielding, J. Don't cry now
Finder, J. Killer instinct
Finder, J. Power play
Furst, A. The spies of Warsaw
Gibson, W. Spook country
Glynn, A. Bloodland
Gowdy, B. Helpless
Grisham, J. The broker
Grisham, J. The client
Grisham, J. Ford County
Grisham, J. The pelican brief
Hall, J. W. Buzz cut
Hall, S. The raw shark texts
Harris, R. The fear index
Harrison, C. The finder
Harvey, M. T. The third rail

Hayder, M. Hanging hill
Haynes, E. Into the darkest corner
Hiaasen, C. Lucky you
Hiaasen, C. Skinny dip
Hill, J. Heart-shaped box
Hoeg, P. Smilla's sense of snow
Hospital, J. T. Orpheus lost
Hunter, S. Soft target
Huston, C. Sleepless
Ignatius, D. A firing offense
Isaacs, S. After all these years
Jones, C. M. The silent oligarch
Katzenbach, J. What comes next
King, S. Rose Madder
King, S. Under the dome
Knopf, C. Dead anyway
Koontz, D. R. Dark rivers of the heart
Koryta, M. The Cypress House
Krist, G. Chaos theory
Lane, H. Alys, always
Larsson, S. The girl who kicked the hornets' nest
Le Carre, J. The mission song
Le Carre, J. A most wanted man
Limón, M. Mr. Kill
Littell, R. Vicious circle
McEuen, P. Spiral
Meek, J. We are now beginning our descent
Meltzer, B. The tenth justice
Meyer, D. Trackers
Mofina, R. Every fear
Mosley, W. The man in my basement
Mosse, K. Labyrinth
Nicholas, D. Something red
O'Flynn, C. The news where you are
Parris, S. J. Sacrilege
Patterson, J. Along came a spider
Patterson, J. Cat & mouse
Pearl, M. The technologists
Penney, S. The invisible ones
Perry, T. Shadow woman
Peters, E. Guardian of the horizon
Picoult, J. Vanishing acts
Pottinger, S. The fourth procedure
Preston, R. The Cobra event
Reich, C. Rules of deception
Rendell, R. Collected stories
Rendell, R. The keys to the street
Rice, A. Angel time
Ruff, M. Bad monkeys
Schickler, D. Sweet and vicious
Shreve, A. Resistance
Shreve, A. The weight of water
Smith, M. A. The Inquisitor
Smith, M. C. Polar Star
Smith, M. C. Rose
Smith, T. R. Child 44

Deighton, L. The Ipcress file
Deighton, L. London match
Deighton, L. Mexico set
DeMille, N. The lion's game
DeMille, N. Plum Island
DeMille, N. Wild fire
Deutermann, P. T. Darkside
Dickey, J. Deliverance
Diehl, W. Primal fear
Diehl, W. Reign in hell
Diehl, W. Show of evil
Donohue, J. J. Sensei
D'Souza, T. Whiteman
Dufosse, C. School's out
Ellis, D. Life sentence
Emerson, E. W. Pyro
Emerson, E. W. Vertical burn
Estleman, L. D. Something borrowed, something
  black
Fairstein, L. Bad blood
Fairstein, L. The bone vault
Fairstein, L. Entombed
Fairstein, L. Killer heat
Faulks, S. Devil may care
Ferrigno, R. Prayers for the assassin
Fesperman, D. The amateur spy
Fielding, J. Charley's web
Fielding, J. Don't cry now
Fielding, J. Heartstopper
Fielding, J. See Jane run
Fielding, J. Tell me no secrets
Finder, J. Company man
Finder, J. Killer instinct
Finder, J. Power play
Finder, J. Vanished
Flanagan, R. The unknown terrorist
Fleishman, J. Promised virgins
Fleming, I. Casino Royale
Fleming, I. Doctor No
Fleming, I. From Russia, with love
Fleming, I. Goldfinger
Fleming, I. The man with the golden gun
Fleming, I. On Her Majesty's Secret Service
Fleming, I. You only live twice
Fleming, T. J. Dreams of glory
Flynn, G. Dark places
Flynn, G. Sharp objects
Follett, K. Eye of the needle
Follett, K. Hornet flight
Follett, K. Jackdaws
Follett, K. Lie down with lions
Follett, K. Triple
Folsom, A. R. The day after tomorrow
Folsom, A. R. Day of confession
Forsyth, F. Avenger
Forsyth, F. The day of the jackal

Forsyth, F. The dogs of war
Forsyth, F. The fourth protocol
Forsyth, F. The Odessa file
Francis, C. Wolf winter
Freeman, C. Go with me
Freemantle, B. Bomb grade
Freemantle, B. Dead men living
Freemantle, B. Mind/reader
French, N. Beneath the skin
French, N. Land of the living
French, T. Faithful Place
French, T. In the woods
French, T. The likeness
Furst, A. The foreign correspondent
Furst, A. Kingdom of shadows
Furst, A. Red gold
Fyfield, F. Blind date
Galgut, D. The impostor
Gallagher, S. The kingdom of bones
Gardiner, M. The Dirty Secrets Club
Gardner, L. Alone
Gerritsen, T. The apprentice
Gerritsen, T. Body double
Gerritsen, T. The sinner
Gerritsen, T. The surgeon
Gibson, W. Spook country
Gilman, D. The amazing Mrs. Pollifax
Gilman, D. The elusive Mrs. Pollifax
Goddard, R. Into the blue
Goddard, R. Never go back
Godey, J. The taking of Pelham one two three
Goldman, W. Marathon man
Gowdy, B. Helpless
Grady, J. Six days of the condor
Grant, M. Officer down
Green, G. D. The juror
Green, G. D. Ravens
Gregory, P. The wise woman
Griffin, W. E. B. By order of the President
Griffin, W. E. B. The last heroes
Griffin, W. E. B. The secret warriors
Griffin, W. E. B. The soldier spies
Grippando, J. The abduction
Grippando, J. Born to run
Grippando, J. Found money
Grippando, J. Hear no evil
Grippando, J. The informant
Grippando, J. A king's ransom
Grippando, J. Lying with strangers
Grisham, J. The brethren
Grisham, J. The broker
Grisham, J. The client
Grisham, J. The firm
Grisham, J. The last juror
Grisham, J. The partner
Grisham, J. The pelican brief

Katzenbach, J. The analyst
Katzenbach, J. Just cause
Katzenbach, J. The madman's tale
Katzenbach, J. State of mind
Katzenbach, J. The wrong man
Kellerman, F. The quality of mercy
Kellerman, J. The genius
Kellerman, J. Sunstroke
Kelman, J. Summer of storms
Kerley, J. The hundredth man
Khemir, S. The blue manuscript
Kinder, R. M. An absolute gentleman
King, L. R. A darker place
King, L. R. Keeping watch
King, S. The dead zone
King, S. Dolores Claiborne
King, S. Dreamcatcher
King, S. Gerald's game
King, S. Insomnia
King, S. Misery
King, S. Rose Madder
Klavan, A. Empire of lies
Knebel, F. Seven days in May
Knox, E. Daylight
Koontz, D. R. The bad place
Koontz, D. R. Brother Odd
Koontz, D. R. By the light of the moon
Koontz, D. R. Dark rivers of the heart
Koontz, D. R. The darkest evening of the year
Koontz, D. R. The face
Koontz, D. R. False memory
Koontz, D. R. Fear nothing
Koontz, D. R. From the corner of his eye
Koontz, D. R. The husband
Koontz, D. R. Intensity
Koontz, D. R. Lightning
Koontz, D. R. Relentless
Koontz, D. R. Seize the night
Koontz, D. R. The taking
Koontz, D. R. Velocity
Krentz, J. A. Lost and found
Krentz, J. A. Running hot
Krentz, J. A. Smoke in mirrors
Kress, N. Dogs
Krist, G. Chaos theory
Kunzru, H. My revolutions
Larsson, S. The girl with the dragon tattoo
Larsson, S. The girl who played with fire
Lashner, W. A killer's kiss
Lawton, J. Old flames
Le Carre, J. The constant gardener
Le Carre, J. The honourable schoolboy
Le Carre, J. The little drummer girl
Le Carre, J. The mission song
Le Carre, J. The night manager
Le Carre, J. A perfect spy

Le Carre, J. The Russia house
Le Carre, J. Smiley's people
Le Carre, J. The spy who came in from the cold
Le Carre, J. Tinker, tailor, soldier, spy
Lehane, D. Shutter Island
Leonard, E. Bandits
Leonard, E. Cat chaser
Leonard, E. Freaky Deaky
Leonard, E. Glitz
Leonard, E. Killshot
Leonard, E. LaBrava
Leonard, E. Mr. Paradise
Leonard, E. Split images
Leonard, E. Stick
Leonard, E. Touch
Leroy, M. Postcards from Berlin
Lescroart, J. T. The first law
Lescroart, J. T. Guilt
Lescroart, J. T. The hearing
Lescroart, J. T. The mercy rule
Lescroart, J. T. Nothing but the truth
Lescroart, J. T. The oath
Lescroart, J. T. The second chair
Levien, D. City of the sun
Levin, I. The boys from Brazil
Lindsay, J. P. Dearly devoted Dexter
Lindsay, J. P. Dexter in the dark
Lindsey, D. L. The color of night
Lindsey, D. L. The rules of silence
Liss, D. The ethical assassin
Littell, R. Vicious circle
Littell, R. Walking back the cat
Logan, C. South of Shiloh
Long, J. The reckoning
Lovesey, P. On the edge
Lowell, E. Die in plain sight
Lowell, E. Pearl Cove
Ludlum, R. The apocalypse watch
Ludlum, R. The Aquitaine progression
Ludlum, R. The Bourne identity
Ludlum, R. The Bourne supremacy
Ludlum, R. The Bourne ultimatum
Ludlum, R. The Gemini contenders
Ludlum, R. The Holcroft covenant
Ludlum, R. The Janson directive
Ludlum, R. The Matarese Circle
Ludlum, R. The Matlock paper
Ludlum, R. The Parsifal mosaic
Ludlum, R. The Prometheus deception
Ludlum, R. The Rhinemann exchange
Ludlum, R. The Scarlatti inheritance
Ludlum, R. The scorpio illusion
Ludlum, R. The Sigma protocol
Lustbader, E. V. Black Blade
Lustbader, E. V. Dark homecoming
Lustbader, E. V. Floating city

Pearson, R. The first victim

Pearson, R. Middle of nowhere

Pearson, R. No witnesses

Pelecanos, G. P. Shame the devil

Pelecanos, G. P. The sweet forever

Perdue, L. Slatewiper

Perez-Reverte, A. The nautical chart

Perry, T. Blood money

Perry, T. Dance for the dead

Perry, T. The face-changers

Perry, T. Fidelity

Perry, T. Nightlife

Perry, T. Pursuit

Perry, T. Runner

Perry, T. Shadow woman

Perry, T. Vanishing act

Picoult, J. Vanishing acts

Pottinger, S. The fourth procedure

Pottinger, S. The last Nazi

Poyer, D. Down to a sunless sea

Preston, D. Blasphemy

Preston, D. Brimstone

Preston, D. The cabinet of curiosities

Preston, D. The codex

Preston, D. Reliquary

Preston, D. Still life with crows

Preston, D. Tyrannosaur Canyon

Preston, D. The wheel of darkness

Preston, R. The Cobra event

Price, N. Night woman

Pronzini, B. The crimes of Jordan Wise

Pronzini, B. In an evil time

Pronzini, B. The other side of silence

Pronzini, B. Step to the graveyard easy

Pronzini, B. A wasteland of strangers

Pyper, A. The killing circle

Quick, A. I thee wed

Quick, A. Late for the wedding

Quick, A. Slightly shady

Quick, A. Wicked widow

Rabb, J. The book of Q

Rankin, I. Watchman

Redfern, E. Auriel rising

Reich, C. Rules of deception

Reichs, K. J. Deja dead

Rendell, R. The bridesmaid

Rendell, R. Heartstones

Rendell, R. A judgment in stone

Rendell, R. The keys to the street

Rendell, R. Live flesh

Rendell, R. A sight for sore eyes

Rendell, R. Thirteen steps down

Rendell, R. The water's lovely

Reuland, R. Semiautomatic

Rigosi, G. Night bus

Riordan, R. Cold Springs

Robards, K. Ghost moon

Robards, K. To trust a stranger

Robbins, D. L. War of the rats

Robbins, H. Sin city

Roberts, N. Angel's fall

Roberts, N. Honest illusions

Roberts, N. Midnight Bayou

Roberts, N. River's end

Robinson, P. Kilo class

Robinson, P. Nimitz class

Rosenberg, N. T. Buried evidence

Rosenberg, N. T. First offense

Rosenberg, N. T. Interest of justice

Rosenberg, N. T. Sullivan's law

Rosenfelt, D. Don't tell a soul

Ruiz Zafon, C. The shadow of the wind

Ruiz, L. M. Only one thing missing

Sanchez, T. King Bongo

Sanders, L. The first deadly sin

Sanders, L. Guilty pleasures

Sanders, L. The second deadly sin

Sanders, L. The sixth commandment

Sanders, L. Sullivan's sting

Sanders, L. The tenth commandment

Sanders, L. The third deadly sin

Sansom, C. J. Winter in Madrid

Saul, J. The presence

Saul, J. Shadows

Schickler, D. Sweet and vicious

Schwegel, T. Person of interest

Scottoline, L. Legal tender

Scottoline, L. Mistaken identity

Scottoline, L. Moment of truth

Scottoline, L. Rough justice

Seymour, G. Killing ground

Seymour, G. Rat run

Shannon, D. The Manson curse

Shelby, P. Days of drums

Shelby, P. Gatekeeper

Sheldon, S. The doomsday conspiracy

Shreve, A. Resistance

Shreve, A. Testimony

Shreve, A. The weight of water

Shreve, S. R. A student of living things

Sidor, S. Skin River

Siegel, J. Deceit

Siegel, J. Derailed

Siegel, S. Final verdict

Sigler, S. Contagious

Sigler, S. Infected

Silva, D. The mark of the assassin

Silva, D. The messenger

Silva, D. Moscow rules

Silva, D. Prince of Fire

Silva, D. The secret servant

Simmons, D. Drood

Woods, S. The run

Woods, S. Santa Fe rules

Woods, S. The short forever

Woods, S. Short straw

Woods, S. Swimming to Catalina

Woods, S. Two-dollar bill

Woods, S. Worst fears realized

Wouk, H. A hole in Texas

Yorke, M. Almost the truth

Yorke, M. The price of guilt

Yorke, M. A question of belief

SUSPENSE STORIES

Abbott, M. E. Bury me deep

Baldacci, D. Deliver us from evil

Bayard, L. The school of night

Blatty, W. P. Dimiter

Bolton, S. J. Now you see me

Boyd, W. Ordinary thunderstorms

Boyle, T. C. When the killing's done

Bradley, J. You believers

Browne, R. The paradise prophecy

Burke, A. Long gone

Caputo, P. Crossers

Clark, M. H. The shadow of your smile

Coben, H. Caught

Compton, J. Thieves get rich, saints get shot

Cook, T. H. The quest for Anna Klein

Coulter, C. Split second

Deaver, J. Carte blanche: 007

Doiron, P. The poacher's son

Dolan, H. Very bad men

Donoghue, E. Room

Downing, D. Potsdam station

Duncker, P. The strange case of the composer and his judge

Eastland, S. Eye of the Red Tsar

Eco, U. The Prague cemetery

Eden, C. Deadly lies

Finder, J. Buried secrets

First thrills

Frazier, C. Nightwoods

Freeman, B. The bone house

Garwood, J. The ideal man

Gibson, W. Zero history

Goddard, R. Found wanting

Goddard, R. Long time coming

Grippando, J. Money to burn

Grisham, J. The confession

Gross, A. Eyes wide open

Gross, A. Reckless

Gruber, M. The good son

Hagberg, D. Abyss

Hannah, S. The cradle in the grave

Harper, K. Fall from pride

Haynes, D. Crashers

Higgins, J. The wolf at the door

Hill, R. The woodcutter

Hogan, C. Devils in exile

Hooper, K. Blood ties

Hunter, S. I, sniper

Hurwitz, G. They're watching

Hurwitz, G. You're next

Huston, C. Sleepless

Jance, J. A. Queen of the night

Johansen, I. Eight days to live

Joss, M. Among the missing

Kelly, E. The poison tree

Kepler, L. The hypnotist

King, S. Under the dome

Klein, M. Switchback

Koryta, M. The Cypress House

Koryta, M. So cold the river

Larsson, S. The girl who kicked the hornets' nest

Lawrenson, D. The lantern

Lindsay, J. P. Dexter is delicious

Lupton, R. Sister

Martin, L. Break the skin

McEuen, P. Spiral

Meltzer, B. The inner circle

Mooney, T. The same river twice

Mullen, T. The many deaths of the Firefly Brothers

Nesbo, J. The headhunters

Palmer, M. The last surgeon

Patterson, J. I, Alex Cross

Peacock, J. Blind man's alley

Perry, T. The informant

Polansky, D. Low Town

Pollock, D. R. The devil all the time

Preston, D. Impact

Pronzini, B. The hidden

Rankin, I. Doors open

Rice, A. Angel time

Rice, A. Of love and evil

Robotham, M. The wreckage

Rollins, J. The devil colony

Sakey, M. The two deaths of Daniel Hayes

Sallis, J. The killer is dying

Scott, A. D. A double death on the Black Isle

Shiner, L. Dark tangos

Sidor, S. Pitch dark

Silva, D. Portrait of a spy

Simmons, D. Flashback

Slaughter, K. Fallen

Smith, R. Wake up dead

Smith, W. A. Those in peril

Spiegelman, P. Thick as thieves

Steiner, P. The terrorist

Steinhauer, O. The nearest exit

Stephenson, N. Reamde

Straub, P. A dark matter

Stroby, W. Cold shot to the heart

Swierczynski, D. Expiration date

Swierczynski, D. Fun and games
Toyne, S. Sanctus
Trussoni, D. Angelology
Turow, S. Innocent
Verdon, J. Think of a number
Waite, U. The terror of living
Wilson, D. H. Robopocalypse
Winters, B. H. Bedbugs
Suspicion of betrayal. Parker, B.
Suspicion of deceit. Parker, B.
Suspicion of vengeance. Parker, B.
Sutton. Moehringer, J. R.
Sutton, Willie
About
Moehringer, J. R. Sutton
Suzanne's diary for Nicholas. Patterson, J.
SWAGGER, BOB LEE (FICTITIOUS CHARAC-TER) -- FICTION
Hunter, S. Dead zero
Hunter, S. Hot Springs
Hunter, S. Pale horse coming
The **swallows** of Kabul. Moulessehoul, M.
Swami and friends, The bachelor of arts, The dark room, The English teacher. Narayan, R. K.
SWAMP ANIMALS
See also Animals
SWAMP ECOLOGY
See also Ecology; Wetland ecology
Swamplandia! Russell, K.
The **swan** thieves. Kostova, E.
Swann's way. Proust, M.
SWASHBUCKLERS *See* Adventure fiction; Adventure films
Sway. Lazar, Z.
SWEDEN
Kepler, L. The hypnotist
Larsson, S. The girl with the dragon tattoo
Larsson, S. The girl who kicked the hornets' nest
Larsson, S. The girl who played with fire
Mankell, H. The man from Beijing
Olsson, L. Astrid & Veronika
Polsan/English Hash
Theorin, J. Echoes from the dead
SWEDEN -- 19TH CENTURY
Moberg, V. The emigrants
SWEDEN -- FICTION
Dahl, A. Bad Blood
Edwardson, A. Sail of stone
Lackberg, C. The ice princess
Persson, L. G. W. Another time, another life
Persson, L. G. W. Between summer's longing and winter's end
SWEDEN -- RURAL LIFE
Ekman, K. God's mercy
Jonsson, R. My life as a dog
SWEDEN -- STOCKHOLM

Dahl, A. Misterioso
Ozick, C. The Messiah of Stockholm
SWEDES -- DENMARK
Andersen Nexo, M. Pelle the conqueror: v1 Childhood
Andersen Nexo, M. Pelle the conqueror: v2 Apprenticeship
SWEDES -- ENGLAND
Vine, B. The minotaur
SWEDES -- ISLANDS OF THE PACIFIC
Conrad, J. Victory
SWEDES -- UNITED STATES
Cather, W. O pioneers!
Cather, W. The song of the lark
Moberg, V. The emigrants
Moberg, V. The last letter home
Moberg, V. Unto a good land
SWEDES -- ZAMBIA
Mankell, H. The eye of the leopard
SWEDISH AMERICANS
Cather, W. O pioneers!
SWEDISH FICTION -- TRANSLATIONS INTO ENGLISH
Larsson, S. The girl with the dragon tattoo
Larsson, S. The girl who kicked the hornets' nest
Mankell, H. The man from Beijing
Mankell, H. One step behind
SWEDISH LANGUAGE *See* Language and languages; Scandinavian languages
Sweet and vicious. Schickler, D.
The **sweet** dove died. Pym, B.
The **sweet** forever. Pelecanos, G. P.
The **sweet** girl. Lyon, A.
The **sweet** hereafter. Banks, R.
Sweet land stories. Doctorow, E. L.
Sweet salt air. Delinsky, B.
Sweet Thursday. Steinbeck, J.
Sweet tooth. McEwan, I.
Sweet, sweet poison. Wilhelm, K.
The **sweetest** dream. Lessing, D. M.
The **sweetness** at the bottom of the pie. Bradley, A.
Sweetness in the belly. Gibb, C.
SWEETS *See* Candy; Confectionery
Sweetsmoke. Fuller, D.
Sweetwater. Robinson, R.
Sweetwater Creek. Siddons, A. R.
Swift as desire. Esquivel, L.
Swim back to me. Packer, A.
Swimming. Keegan, N.
SWIMMING
Keegan, N. Swimming
Swimming at night. Clarke, L.
Swimming home. Levy, D.
The **swimming** pool. LeCraw, H.
Swimming to Catalina. Woods, S.
Swimming to Elba. Avallone, S.

O'Brien, T. In the Lake of the Woods
Oe, K. An echo of heaven
Oe, K. The pinch runner memorandum
Okuizumi, H. The stones cry out
Percy, W. Lancelot
Porter, K. A. Ship of fools
Powers, R. Operation wandering soul
Pynchon, T. V.
Roy, A. The god of small things
Rushdie, S. The satanic verses
Rushdie, S. The ground beneath her feet
Stahlberg, L. Billy Budd, sailor
Stahlberg, L. Moby-Dick; or, The whale
Tan, A. The bonesetter's daughter
Theroux, P. The Mosquito Coast
Thomas, D. M. The white hotel
Updike, J. Roger's version
Urquhart, J. The underpainter
Vargas Llosa, M. The Green House
Walbert, K. The gardens of Kyoto
Wiesel, E. A beggar in Jerusalem
Woolf, V. Between the acts
Woolf, V. The waves

SYMBOLISM IN LITERATURE *See* Literature; Symbolism

SYMBOLISM OF NUMBERS *See* Symbolism

SYMPATHY *See* Conduct of life; Emotions

SYNAGOGUES *See* Buildings; Religious institutions; Temples

SYNCHRONIZED SWIMMING *See* Swimming

Syndrome E.

Synge, J. M. (John Millington), 1871-1909

About

O'Connor, J. Ghost light

SYPHILIS *See* Sexually transmitted diseases

SYRIA
Caldwell, T. Dear and glorious physician
Werfel, F. The forty days of Musa Dagh

SYRIANS -- BRAZIL
Amado, J. Gabriela, clove and cinnamon

The **syringa** tree. Gien, P.

SYSTEMS ENGINEERING *See* Automation; Cybernetics; Engineering; Industrial design; System analysis; System theory

Szilard, Leo

About

Millet, L. Oh pure and radiant heart

T

T is for trespass. Grafton, S.

Table money. Breslin, J.

TABLE TALK *See* Conversation

TABLE TENNIS
Jacobson, H. The mighty Walzer

TABLE TENNIS PLAYERS
Jacobson, H. The mighty Walzer

Tabloid city. Hamill, P.

Tacitus, Cornelius

About

Bell, A. A. The blood of Caesar

TAE KWON DO
See also Karate; Martial arts; Self-defense
Bell, M. S. Ten Indians

Tag man. Mayor, A.

TAHITI
Maugham, W. S. The moon and sixpence
Stahlberg, L. Omoo: a narrative of adventures in the South Seas

TAI CHI *See* Exercise; Martial arts

Tai Randolph mysteries [series]
Whittle, T. Blood, Ash, and Bone
Whittle, T. The Dangerous Edge of Things

Tai-Pan. Clavell, J.

The **tailor** of Panama. Le Carre, J.

TAILORING *See* Clothing and dress; Clothing industry

TAIWAN -- HISTORY -- 1895-1945
Wu, J. The third son

TAIWAN -- HISTORY
Wu, J. The third son

TAJIKISTAN
Darnton, J. Neanderthal

Take a chance on me. Warren, S. M.

Take one candle light a room. Straight, S.

The **taken.** Wolfe, I. A.

The **taken.** Pettersson, V.

Taken. Crais, R.

Takeover. Black, L.

The **taking.** Koontz, D. R.

Taking eve. Johansen, I.

The **taking** of Pelham one two three. Godey, J.

A **tale** for the time being. Ozeki, R. L.

The **tale** of Genji. Murasaki Shikibu

The **tale** of the body thief. Rice, A.

A **tale** of two cities. Dickens, C.

TALENT *See* Ability; Genius

The **talented** Mr. Ripley; Ripley under ground; Ripley's game. Highsmith, P.

TALES *See* Fables; Fairy tales; Folklore; Legends

Tales and sketches, including Twice-told tales, Mosses from an old manse, and The snow-image; A wonder book for girls and boys; Tanglewood tales for girls and boys, being a second Wonder book. Hawthorne, N.

Tales from a troubled land. Paton, A.

Tales from the Drones Club. Wodehouse, P. G.

Tales of Alvin Maker [series]
Card, O. S. Alvin Journeyman
Card, O. S. Seventh son

Tales of H.P. Lovecraft. Lovecraft, H. P.

Tales of protection. Hansen, E. F.

Tales of the night. Hoeg, P.

Smiley, J. Moo

Smith, Z. On beauty

Southgate, M. The fall of Rome

Spark, M. The prime of Miss Jean Brodie

Sparks, N. A bend in the road

Stade, G. Love is war

Stamm, P. On a day like this

Stone, R. Bay of souls

Strout, E. Amy and Isabelle

Swift, G. Waterland

Tartt, D. The secret history

Thayer, S. The leper

Theroux, A. Darconville's cat

Trollope, J. The men and the girls

Trueblood, V. Seven loves

Tussing, J. The best people in the world

Tyler, A. Noah's compass

Upadhyay, S. The guru of love

Updike, J. The centaur

Updike, J. Memories of the Ford Administration

Vassanji, M. G. The assassin's song

Walls, J. Half broke horses

Watkins, P. The ice soldier

Watrous, M. If you follow me

Weinstein, D. Apprentice to the flower poet Z

Wiesel, E. Twilight

Wiggins, M. John Dollar

Yarbrough, S. Safe from the neighbors

TEACHERS -- FICTION

Gordimer, N. No time like the present

Hootman, R. Courting Greta

Kerouac, J. The sea is my brother

Little, T. Where there's smoke

TEACHING *See* Education

TEASING *See* Aggressiveness (Psychology); Interpersonal relations

TECHNICAL EDUCATION *See* Education; Higher education; Technology

TECHNICAL WRITING *See* Authorship; Technology -- Language

TECHNOLOGICAL INNOVATIONS *See* Inventions; Technology

The **technologists.** Pearl, M.

TECHNOLOGY -- DICTIONARIES *See* Encyclopedias and dictionaries

TECHNOLOGY

Doctorow, C. Rapture of the nerds

TECHNOLOGY AND CIVILIZATION

Burdick, E. Fail-safe

Crace, J. The gift of stones

Huxley, A. Brave new world

Percy, W. Love in the ruins

Vonnegut, K. Cat's cradle

Vonnegut, K. Player piano

Vonnegut, K. The sirens of Titan

TECHNOLOGY TRANSFER *See* Inventions;

Technology

Tecumseh, Shawnee Chief, 1768-1813
About

Thom, J. A. Panther in the sky

TEEN AGE *See* Adolescence

TEENAGE BOYS

Abani, C. GraceLand

Aciman, A. A. Call me by your name

Barfoot, J. Critical injuries

Burgess, A. A clockwork orange

Coe, J. The Rotters' Club

Cooke, C. Daughters of the revolution

Cramer, W. D. Bad ground

Earley, T. The blue star

Edgerton, C. The Bible salesman

Follett, K. Hornet flight

Ford, R. Canada

Galloway, G. As simple as snow

Gilb, D. The flowers

Gohlke, C. I have seen him in the watchfires

Irving, J. Last night in Twisted River

Johnson, W. The devil you know

Kaplow, R. Me and Orson Welles

Kay, G. G. Ysabel

McMurtry, L. Boone's Lick

Mitchell, D. Black swan green

Munson, S. The November criminals

Murakami, H. Kafka on the shore

O'Dell, T. Back roads

O'Neill, J. At swim, two boys

Searles, J. Boy still missing

Shriver, L. We need to talk about Kevin

Sparks, N. A walk to remember

Stern, S. The frozen rabbi

Wilson, E. O. Anthill

TEENAGE FATHERS *See* Fathers; Teenage parents

TEENAGE GANGS *See* Gangs

TEENAGE GIRLS -- CRIMES AGAINST

Moore, J. The extinction club

Sebold, A. The lovely bones

TEENAGE GIRLS -- DEATH

Evans, S. J. Safe from harm

TEENAGE GIRLS

Bank, M. The wonder spot

Beard, J. A. In Zanesville

Brunt, C. R. Tell the wolves I'm home

Buchanan, C. M. The painted girls

Campbell, B. J. Once upon a river

Coben, H. Caught

Cooke, C. Daughters of the revolution

Eberstadt, F. Rat

Gibbons, K. The life all around me by Ellen Foster

Grimes, M. Biting the moon

Harrar, G. The spinning man

Hoag, T. Dark horse

Humphreys, J. Nowhere else on earth
Julavits, H. The uses of enchantment
Kasischke, L. The life before her eyes
Kidd, S. M. The secret life of bees
Kirshenbaum, B. An almost perfect moment
Klein, R. The moth diaries
Lent, J. Lost nation
Lipman, E. My latest grievance
Mason, D. A far country
McEwan, I. Atonement
McGowan, H. Schooling
McKillip, P. A. Alphabet of thorn
Miller, S. Lost in the forest
O'Nan, S. Songs for the missing
Ozeki, R. L. A tale for the time being
Pearson, A. I think I love you
Pittard, H. The fates will find their way
Rawles, N. My Jim
Raymond, J. The half-life
Riordan, R. Cold Springs
Shields, C. Unless
Shreve, A. Testimony
Sittenfeld, C. Prep
Smith, L. On Agate Hill
Stevens, M. Useful girl
Straight, S. A million nightingales
Sullivan, M. J. Necessary heartbreak
Tea, M. Rose of no man's land
Thorne, M. Hand me down
Ulinich, A. Petropolis
Urrea, L. A. The hummingbird's daughter
Vernon, O. Eden

TEENAGE GIRLS -- FICTION
Dermansky, M. Twins

TEENAGE GIRLS -- NIGERIA
Watson, C. Tiny sunbirds, far away

TEENAGE LITERATURE *See* Young adult literature

TEENAGE MARRIAGE *See* Marriage

TEENAGE MOTHERS *See* Mothers; Teenage parents

TEENAGE PARENTS
Kingsolver, B. Flight behavior

TEENAGE PREGNANCY
See also Pregnancy
Thompson, V. Murder on Lenox Hill

TEENAGERS *See* Age; Youth

TEENAGERS -- BOOKS AND READING *See* Books and reading

TEENAGERS -- CONDUCT OF LIFE
Castillo, L. Gone missing

TEENAGERS -- DEVELOPMENT *See* Adolescence

TEENAGERS -- DRUG USE
Little, T. Where there's smoke

TEENAGERS

Burns, C. Black hole
Dau, S. The book of Jonas
Dermansky, M. Twins
Ford, R. Canada
Galloway, G. As simple as snow
Grant, H. The glass demon
Little star
Pierson, D. C. The boy who couldn't sleep and never had to
Thorne, M. Hand me down

TEENAGERS -- GRAPHIC NOVELS
Merey, I. a + e 4ever

TEENAGERS -- LITERATURE *See* Young adult literature

TEENAGERS -- PENNSYLVANIA
Braffet, K. Save yourself

TEENAGERS -- SUICIDE
See also Suicide
Palwick, S. Mending the moon

TEETH -- DISEASES *See* Diseases

The **Tehran** initiative. Rosenberg, J. C.

TELECOMMUNICATION *See* Communication

TELECOMMUTING *See* Automation; Telecommunication

TELECONFERENCING *See* Telephone

TELEGRAPH
Esquivel, L. Swift as desire

Telegraph Avenue. Chabon, M.

Telegraph days. McMurtry, L.

TELEKINESIS *See* Psychokinesis

TELEPATHY
See also Extrasensory perception
Clark, M. H. Two little girls in blue
Everett, P. L. American desert
King, S. Dreamcatcher
Le Guin, U. K. The left hand of darkness
McCaffrey, A. Pegasus in space
Rucker, R. v. B. Hylozoic
Vallgren The horrific sufferings of the mind-reading monster Hercules Barefoot

TELEPHONE
King, S. Cell

TELEVANGELISTS *See* Clergy; Television personalities

TELEVISION
Gilmore, J. Golden country
Holman, S. Witches on the road tonight
Irving, J. The fourth hand
Kosinski, J. N. Being there
Lodge, D. Therapy
MacNeil, R. Breaking news
O'Flynn, C. The news where you are
Thayer, N. Belonging
Thayer, S. The weatherman
Wagner, B. The chrysanthemum palace

TELEVISION ACTORS *See* Actors

TELEVISION ADAPTATIONS *See* Television plays; Television programs; Television scripts

TELEVISION ADVERTISING *See* Advertising; Television broadcasting

TELEVISION AND CHILDREN *See* Children; Television

TELEVISION AND POLITICS *See* Politics; Television

TELEVISION AND YOUTH *See* Television; Youth

TELEVISION AUTHORSHIP *See* Authorship

TELEVISION BROADCASTING *See* Broadcasting; Mass media; Television

TELEVISION GAMES *See* Video games

TELEVISION IN EDUCATION *See* Audiovisual education; Teaching -- Aids and devices; Television

TELEVISION MOVIES *See* Motion pictures; Television programs

TELEVISION PERSONALITIES
    See also Celebrities
  Holman, S. Witches on the road tonight
  Nicholls, D. One day

TELEVISION PLAYS *See* Drama; Television programs

TELEVISION PRODUCERS AND DIRECTORS
  Altschul, A. F. Deus ex machina
  Clark, M. H. Stillwatch
  Hannah, S. The cradle in the grave
  Marks, J. Fangland
  McCauley, S. True enough

TELEVISION PROGRAMS
  Altschul, A. F. Deus ex machina
  Connelly, J. Crumbtown
  Gruen, S. Ape house
  McPhee, J. No ordinary matter
  Nicholls, D. A question of attraction
  Parkhurst, C. Lost and found
  Westlake, D. E. Get real

TELEVISION PROGRAMS -- FICTION
  Connelly, J. Crumbtown
  Fellowes, J. Snobs
  Gruen, S. Ape house
  Parkhurst, C. Lost and found

TELEVISION SERIALS *See* Television programs

Telex from Cuba. Kushner, R.

Tell me a riddle. Olsen, T.

Tell me how long the train's been gone. Baldwin, J.

Tell me no secrets. Fielding, J.

Tell me that you love me, Junie Moon. Kellogg, M.

Tell the wolves I'm home. Brunt, C. R.

The **telling.** Le Guin, U. K.

Telling stories! [series]
  Roy, A. The god of small things

Temeraire series
  Novik, N. His majesty's dragon

TEMPER TANTRUMS *See* Emotions; Human behavior

TEMPERAMENT *See* Mind and body; Psychology; Psychophysiology

Tempest rising. McKinney-Whetstone, D.

TEMPLARS
  Harris, D. T. The temple and the stone
  Holland, C. Jerusalem

The **temple** and the stone. Harris, D. T.

The **Temple** of Dawn. Mishima, Y.

The **temple** of my familiar. Walker, A.

The **temple** of the golden pavilion. Mishima, Y.

TEMPLES
    See also Buildings; Religious institutions
  Black, C. Murder in Clichy

TEMPORARY EMPLOYEES
  Barr, N. The rope

The **Temptation** of Your Touch. Medeiros, T.

Tempting the bride. Thomas, S.

Ten days in the hills. Smiley, J.

Ten girls to watch. Shumway, C.

Ten Indians. Bell, M. S.

Ten North Frederick. O'Hara, J.

Ten thousand saints. Henderson, E.

The **ten-year** nap. Wolitzer, M.

TENANT AND LANDLORD *See* Landlord and tenant

TENANT FARMING
  Faulkner, W. The mansion

The **tenant** of Wildfell Hall. Bronte, A.

The **tenants.** Malamud, B.

The **tenants** of time. Flanagan, T.

Tender mercies. Brown, R.

The **tenderness** of wolves. Penney, S.

TENEMENT HOUSES *See* Apartment houses

TENNESSEE
  Bahr, H. The Judas Field
  Bledsoe, A. The hum and the shiver
  Greene, A. Bloodroot
  Gregory, D. The devil's alphabet
  Hooper, K. Blood ties
  Hunter, S. Night of thunder
  Lewis, J. The king is dead
  McCrumb, S. The ballad of Frankie Silver
  McCrumb, S. The hangman's beautiful daughter
  McCrumb, S. If ever I return, pretty Peggy-O
  McCrumb, S. The rosewood casket
  McCrumb, S. She walks these hills
  O'Connor, F. The violent bear it away
  O'Connor, F. Wise blood
  Pekearo, N. T. The wolfman
  Wall, P. S. The Wilde women
  Wiggins, M. Evidence of things unseen

TENNESSEE -- FICTION
  Agee, J. A death in the family
  Faulkner, W. The reivers

Greene, G. The comedians
Griffin, W. E. B. By order of the President
Gruber, M. The good son
Hagberg, D. Abyss
Hamid, M. The reluctant fundamentalist
Hamill, P. Tabloid city
Harris, T. Black Sunday
Higgins, J. Confessional
Higgins, J. Drink with the Devil
Higgins, J. Edge of danger
Higgins, J. Eye of the storm
Higgins, J. Midnight runner
Higgins, J. Touch the devil
Higgins, J. The White House connection
Hospital, J. T. Orpheus lost
Hynes, J. Next
Ignatius, D. Body of lies
Johansen, I. And then you die--
Johnson, D. Lulu in Marrakech
Just, W. S. Forgetfulness
Keneally, T. Flying hero class
Klavan, A. Empire of lies
Kress, N. Dogs
Le Carre, J. The little drummer girl
Leonard, E. Djibouti
Lessing, D. M. The good terrorist
Littell, R. Vicious circle
Ludlum, R. The Bourne ultimatum
Ludlum, R. The Janson directive
Ludlum, R. The Matarese Circle
Ludlum, R. The Prometheus deception
MacInnes, H. Prelude to terror
MacLean, A. Floodgate
Magary, D. The postmortal
Martini, S. P. Critical mass
McCarry, C. Old boys
Meyer, D. Heart of the hunter
Miller, S. The Lake Shore Limited
Nance, J. J. Medusa's child
O'Brien, E. House of splendid isolation
Oe, K. Somersault
Palahniuk, C. Pygmy
Palmer, M. The patient
Patchett, A. Bel canto
Patterson, J. London bridges
Perdue, L. Slatewiper
Piercy, M. Vida
Pohl, F. All the lives he led
Porter, H. The bell ringers
Pottinger, S. The last Nazi
Reich, C. Rules of deception
Robinson, K. S. Antarctica
Roncagliolo, S. Red April
Rosenfelt, D. Don't tell a soul
Roth, P. American pastoral
Rubenfeld, J. The death instinct

Rushdie, S. Shalimar the clown
Schlink, B. The weekend
See, C. There will never be another you
Sheldon, S. Windmills of the gods
Shreve, S. R. Plum & Jaggers
Shreve, S. R. A student of living things
Silva, D. The mark of the assassin
Silva, D. The messenger
Silva, D. Moscow rules
Silva, D. Portrait of a spy
Silva, D. Prince of Fire
Silva, D. The secret servant
Smith, A. Judas horse
Smith, W. A. Golden fox
Smith, W. A. Those in peril
Smith, W. A. A time to die
Snyder, D. J. Night crossing
Steiner, P. The terrorist
Stone, R. Damascus Gate
Trevanian Shibumi
Updike, J. Terrorist
Wallace, D. F. Infinite jest
West, M. L. Lazarus
West, R. The birds fall down
Wilson, R. The hidden assassins
Wiltse, D. Blown away
Woods, S. Reckless abandon

TERRORISM -- FICTION
Clarke, R. A. The scorpion's gate
Ellis, D. In the company of liars
Huston, C. Skinner
MacDonald, G. The prisoner's wife
Rosenberg, J. C. The Tehran initiative
TERRORISM -- PREVENTION -- CHINA
Alpert, M. Extinction
TERRORISM -- PREVENTION
Allen, S. The 13
Le Carré, J. A Delicate Truth
TERRORISM -- UNITED STATES
Allen, S. The 13
Terrorist. Updike, J.
The **terrorist.** Steiner, P.
TERRORIST ACTS *See* Terrorism
TERRORIST ATTACKS, SEPTEMBER 11, 2001
 See September 11 terrorist attacks, 2001
TERRORISTS
Sakey, M. Brilliance
Tesla, Nikola, 1856-1943
 About
Echenoz, J. Lightning
Hunt, S. The invention of everything else
Tess of the D'Urbervilles. Hardy, T.
TEST PILOTS *See* Air pilots; Airplanes -- Testing
TEST TUBE BABIES *See* Fertilization in vitro
TEST TUBE FERTILIZATION *See* Fertilization
 in vitro

THEATER

Rawn, M. Touchstone

THEATER LIFE

Davies, R. World of wonders

Dickens, C. Nicholas Nickleby

Dreiser, T. Sister Carrie

Gallagher, S. The kingdom of bones

L'Engle, M. Certain women

Lessing, D. M. Love, again

Michael, J. Acts of love

Nye, R. The late Mr. Shakespeare

O'Connor, J. Ghost light

Singer, I. B. The magician of Lublin

Unsworth, B. Morality play

Zola, E. Nana

THEATERS *See* Buildings; Centers for the performing arts; Theaters

THEATRICAL DIRECTORS

Kaplow, R. Me and Orson Welles

THEATRICAL PRODUCERS

Bellow, S. The Bellarosa connection

Kaplow, R. Me and Orson Welles

THEFT

Eliot, G. Silas Marner

Langer, A. The thieves of Manhattan

Leonard, E. Bandits

Nesbo, J. The headhunters

Perez-Reverte, A. The fencing master

Stott, R. The coral thief

Westlake, D. E. Don't ask

THEFT -- FICTION

Hilton, E. Dirty money Honey

Hunter, M. The conquest of Lady Cassandra

Longworth, M. L. Death in the Vines

Morgan-Jones, C. The jackal's share

Theft of swords. Sullivan, M. J.

Their eyes were watching God. Hurston, Z. N.

THEISM

See also Philosophy; Religion; Theology

Thelen, Albert Vigoleis, 1903-1989

About

Thelen, A. V. The island of second sight

Them. Oates, J. C.

THEME PARKS *See* Amusement parks

Then came the evening. Hart, B.

Then came you. Weiner, J.

Theodora. Duffy, S.

Theodora, Empress, consort of Justinian I, Emperor of the East, d. 548

About

Duffy, S. Theodora

Theodoric, King of the Ostrogoths, 454?-526

About

Jennings, G. Raptor

THEOLOGIANS

Downing, D. C. Looking for the king

Theophilus North. Wilder, T.

A **theory** of relativity. Mitchard, J.

THEOSOPHY *See* Mysticism; Religions

THERAPEUTICS *See* Medicine; Pathology

Therapy. Lodge, D.

Therapy. Kellerman, J.

THERAPY, PSYCHOLOGICAL *See* Psychotherapy

There but for the. Smith, A.

There is no year. Butler, B.

There once lived a woman who tried to kill her neighbor's baby. Petrushevskaya, L.

There was a little girl. McBain, E.

There will never be another you. See, C.

There's something in a Sunday. Muller, M.

THERMODYNAMICS *See* Dynamics; Physical chemistry; Physics

These days are ours. Haimoff, M.

These is my words. Turner, N. E.

THESEUS (GREEK MYTHOLOGY)

Renault, M. The bull from the sea

Renault, M. The king must die

They disappeared. Mofina, R.

They're watching. Hurwitz, G.

Thick as thieves. Spiegelman, P.

Thicker than water. McInerny, R. M.

The **thief.** Cussler, C.

Thief of Shadows. Hoyt, E.

A **thief** of time. Hillerman, T.

Thief of time. Pratchett, T.

The **thief** of Venice. Langton, J.

THIEVES

See also Criminals

Connelly, M. Void moon

Crusie, J. Faking it

Cussler, C. Inca gold

Defoe, D. Moll Flanders

Dickens, C. Oliver Twist

Disher, G. Wyatt

Gilman, D. A palm for Mrs. Pollifax

Hansen, R. The assassination of Jesse James by the coward Robert Ford

Herlihy, J. L. Midnight cowboy

Horn, D. The world to come

Keating, H. R. F. The bad detective

Liebmann-Smith, R. The James boys

Parker, T. J. L.A. outlaws

Rankin, I. Doors open

Roberts, N. Honest illusions

Schickler, D. Sweet and vicious

Skarmeta, A. The dancer and the thief

Smith, S. A simple plan

Thomas, C. Firefox

Waters, S. Fingersmith

Westlake, D. E. Smoke

Woodrell, D. The death of sweet mister

Three stations. Smith, M. C.

THREE STOOGES FILMS *See* Comedy films; Motion pictures

Three strong women.

Three to get deadly. Evanovich, J.

The **three** Weissmanns of Westport. Schine, C.

Three women. Piercy, M.

The **three-arched** bridge. Kadare, I.

The **Three-Day** Affair. Kardos, M.

Three-day road. Boyden, J.

THRIFT SHOPS *See* Secondhand trade; Stores

THRILLERS *See* Adventure fiction; Adventure films

Thrones, dominations. Sayers, D. L.

Through a glass darkly. Koen, K.

Thrush Green. Read

Thud! Pratchett, T.

Thug lovin' Clark, W.

THUGS (INDIC CRIMINAL GROUP)

Khair, T. The thing about thugs

Thunder on the mountain. Poyer, D.

Thunder on the right. Stewart, M.

THUNDERSTORMS *See* Meteorology; Storms

Thursday Next in Lost in a good book. Fforde, J.

Thursday Next in Something rotten. Fforde, J.

Thursday Next in The well of lost plots. Fforde, J.

Thursday the rabbi walked out. Kemelman, H.

TIBET AUTONOMOUS REGION (CHINA)

Pattison, E. The lord of death

The **ticket** out. Knode, H.

Ticket to ride. Gorman, E.

A **ticket** to the boneyard. Block, L.

The **tidal** poole. Harper, K.

TIDE POOL ECOLOGY *See* Ecology

TIDES

See also Ocean

Ghosh, A. The hungry tide

Tides of war. Tillyard, S. K.

TIFFANY & CO.

Vreeland, S. Clara and Mr. Tiffany

Tiffany, Louis Comfort, 1848-1933

About

Vreeland, S. Clara and Mr. Tiffany

Tigana. Kay, G. G.

The **tiger** in the grass. Doerr, H.

The **tiger's** wife. Obreht, T.

Tigerlily's orchids. Rendell, R.

TIGERS

Martel, Y. Life of Pi

Tigers in red weather. Klaussmann, L.

Tight lines. Tapply, W. G.

TIJUANA (MEXICO)

Lange, R. Angel baby

Till morning comes. Han, S.

Till the butchers cut him down. Muller, M.

Till we have faces. Lewis, C. S.

Till, Emmett, 1941-1955

About

McFadden, B. L. Gathering of waters

TIMBER *See* Forests and forestry; Lumber and lumbering; Trees; Wood

TIME

Amis, M. Time's arrow

Hoeg, P. Borderliners

Lightman, A. P. The diagnosis

TIME -- FICTION

Kincaid, J. See now then

Time and again. Finney, J.

Time and chance. Penman, S. K.

TIME AND SPACE *See* Space and time

Time and tide. O'Brien, E.

Time bomb. Kellerman, J.

The **time** in between. Duenas, M.

The **time** it takes to fall. Dean, M. L.

The **time** machine. Wells, H. G.

TIME MANAGEMENT *See* Management; Time

Time odyssey [series]

Baxter, S. Sunstorm

Time of hope. Snow, C. P.

The **time** of our singing. Powers, R.

The **time** of the hero. Vargas Llosa, M.

Time regained. Proust, M.

A **time** to die. Smith, W. A.

Time to hunt. Hunter, S.

A **time** to kill. Grisham, J.

A **time** to love and a time to die. Remarque, E. M.

TIME TRAVEL

See also Fourth dimension; Space and time

Alexie, S. Flight

Baker, K. The graveyard game

Baker, K. In the garden of Iden

Baker, K. The life of the world to come

Baker, K. Mendoza in Hollywood

Baker, K. Sky coyote

Baker, K. The sons of heaven

Butler, O. E. Kindred

Crichton, M. Timeline

Danielewski, M. Z. Only revolutions

Dickinson, C. A shortcut in time

Finney, J. From time to time

Finney, J. Time and again

Gabaldon, D. A breath of snow and ashes

Gabaldon, D. An echo in the bone

Gabaldon, D. Outlander

Gabaldon, D. Voyager

Haldeman, J. W. The accidental time machine

Heinlein, R. A. Job: a comedy of justice

Helprin, M. Winter's tale

Kay, G. G. The summer tree

Kearsley, S. Mariana

Koontz, D. R. Lightning

May, J. The adversary

Carey, P. Parrot and Olivier in America

Toklas, Alice B.
About
Truong, M. T. D. The book of salt

TOKYO (JAPAN)
Hill, T. The love of stones
Lee, D. Country of origin
Murakami, H. After dark
Ozeki, R. L. A tale for the time being
Peace, D. Tokyo year zero
Smith, M. C. December 6

Tokyo fiancee. Nothomb, A.
Tokyo year zero. Peace, D.
TOLERATION *See* Interpersonal relations
Tolkien, J. R. R. (John Ronald Reuel), 1892-1973
About
Downing, D. C. Looking for the king

Tolstoy, Leo, graf, 1828-1910
About
Kalfus, K. The commissariat of enlightenment
Reyn, I. What happened to Anna K.

Tombaugh, Clyde, 1906-1997
About
Byers, M. Percival's planet

TOMBS *See* Archeology; Architecture; Burial;
Monuments; Shrines
Tomorrow. Swift, G.
Tomorrow is another day. Kaminsky, S. M.
The **tongues** of angels. Price, R.
Tonight I said goodbye. Koryta, M.
Tono-Bungay. Wells, H. G.
Too bright to hear too loud to see. Garey, J.
Too far afield. Grass, G.
Too late the phalarope. Paton, A.
Too loud a solitude. Hrabal, B.
Too many cooks; & champagne for one. Stout, R.
Too much happiness. Munro, A.
Too much money. Dunne, D.
The **tooth** tattoo. Lovesey, P.
Torch. Strayed, C.

TORNADOES
See also Meteorology; Storms; Winds
Atkins, A. The broken places
Torquemada. Perez Galdos, B.
The **torrents** of spring. Hemingway, E.
The **torrents** of spring. Turgenev, I. S.
The **torso** in the town. Brett, S.
TORT LIABILITY OF PROFESSIONS *See* Mal-
practice
The **tortilla** curtain. Boyle, T. C.
Tortilla Flat. Steinbeck, J.

TORTURE
See also Criminal procedure; Cruelty; Pun-
ishment
Danticat, E. The dew breaker
Everett, P. L. The water cure

Kennedy, T. E. In the company of angels
Kertesz, I. Detective story
Lehrer, J. The special prisoner
Mengiste, M. Beneath the lion's gaze

TORTURE -- FICTION
Katzenbach, J. What comes next
Smith, M. A. The Inquisitor
Zan, K. The Never List

TORTURERS
Smith, M. A. The Inquisitor
The **toss** of a lemon. Viswanathan, P.
Total control. Baldacci, D.
Total oblivion, more or less. DeNiro, A.
Total recall. Paretsky, S.

TOTALITARIANISM
See also Ethnology; Mythology
Antunes, A. L. The inquisitors' manual
Ball, J. The curfew
Bolano, R. By night in Chile
Bynum, L. Veracity
Chatwin, B. Utz
Connelly, K. The lizard cage
Danticat, E. The dew breaker
Day of the oprichnik
Dragoman, G. The white king
Englander, N. The Ministry of Special Cases
Erpenbeck, J. The book of words
Farah, N. Links
Hall, S. Daughters of the north
Hrabal, B. I served the King of England
Isegawa, M. Snakepit
Kadare, I. The Successor
Keneally, T. The tyrant's novel
Koestler, A. Darkness at noon
Kundera, M. The joke
Matar, H. In the country of men
McCann, C. Zoli
Moulessehoul, M. The swallows of Kabul
Orwell, G. Animal farm
Orwell, G. Nineteen eighty-four
Porter, H. The bell ringers
Saramago, J. The cave
Smith, T. R. Child 44
Sorokin, V. Ice
Steele, A. M. Coyote
Vargas Llosa, M. Conversation in the cathedral
Vollmann, W. T. Europe central
Zamiatin, E. I. We

TOTALITARIANISM -- FICTION
Dunn, M. Ella Minnow Pea
Touch. Leonard, E.
Touch not the cat. Stewart, M.
Touch the devil. Higgins, J.
Touched by venom. Cross, J.
Touchstone. Rawn, M.
Touchy subjects. Donoghue, E.

Bryson, E.

TRANSGENICS *See* Genetic engineering

Transgressions.

The **transit** of Venus. Hazzard, S.

TRANSLATING AND INTERPRETING *See* Language and languages

The **translation** of Dr Apelles. Treuer, D.

The **translator.** Crowley, J.

TRANSLATORS

Coetzee, J. M. Summertime

Crowley, J. The translator

Dai Sijie Once on a moonless night

Fleishman, J. Promised virgins

Horan, N. Loving Frank

Kennedy, D. The moment

Kim, S. The interpreter

Le Carre, J. The mission song

Littell, R. The Stalin epigram

Manseau, P. Songs for the butcher's daughter

Marias, J. A heart so white

McKillip, P. A. Alphabet of thorn

Miller, A. Oxygen

Nabokov, V. V. Novels and memoirs, 1941-1951

Ozick, C. The Messiah of Stockholm

Sherwood, F. Night of sorrows

Tremain, R. The way I found her

Treuer, D. The translation of Dr Apelles

Van Booy, S. Everything beautiful began after

Vargas Llosa, M. The bad girl

Verissimo, L. F. Borges and the eternal orangutans

TRANSMIGRATION

London, J. The star rover

Transmission. Kunzru, H.

TRANSMUTATION OF METALS *See* Alchemy; Transmutation (Chemistry)

TRANSPLANTATION *See* Transplantation of organs, tissues, etc.

TRANSPLANTATION OF ORGANS, TISSUES, ETC.

See also Surgery

Cook, R. Coma

Hearon, S. Footprints

Irving, J. The fourth hand

Lustbader, E. V. Dark homecoming

McGregor, E. The ice child

Palmer, M. The fifth vial

Picoult, J. Change of heart

Picoult, J. My sister's keeper

TRANSPLANTATION OF ORGANS, TISSUES, ETC. -- FICTION

Kowalski, W. Something noble

TRANSSEXUALS

Tremain, R. Sacred country

Vidal, G. Myra Breckinridge [and] Myron

TRANSSEXUALS -- FICTION.

Wilson, C. Cotton

TRAPPERS

Sargent, C. Museum of human beings

TRAPPERS AND TRAPPING

Cooper, J. F. The Leatherstocking tales

Cooper, J. F. The pioneers

Cooper, J. F. The prairie

Guthrie, A. B. The big sky

Penney, S. The tenderness of wolves

Raymond, J. The half-life

Traps. Bezos, M.

Trauma. McGrath, P.

TRAVEL

Kerouac, J. On the road

Kerouac, J. On the road: the original scroll

Maugham, W. S. The razor's edge

Richardson, C. S. The end of the alphabet

Simpson, M. Anywhere but here

Smollett, T. G. The expedition of Humphry Clinker

TRAVEL -- FICTION

Bhattacharya, R. The sly company of people who care

Higgins, K. My one and only

McCall Smith, A. Trains and Lovers

Priest, C. Dreadnought

TRAVEL BOOKS *See* Voyages and travels; Voyages around the world

TRAVEL IN LITERATURE *See* Literature -- Themes; Travel

TRAVEL INDUSTRY *See* Tourist trade

TRAVEL WRITERS

Calvino, I. Invisible cities

Clinch, J. Finn

Flanagan, R. Wanting

Kehlmann, D. Measuring the world

Martin, V. Mary Reilly

McDonald, R. Mr. Darwin's shooter

Naipaul, V. S. A way in the world

Novels The gilded age and later novels

Oates, J. C. Wild nights!

Russell, M. D. Dreamers of the day

Simmons, D. The terror

Vollmann, W. T. Argall

Vollmann, W. T. The rifles

TRAVEL WRITING *See* Authorship

Traveler. McLarty, R.

Traveler of the century.

TRAVELERS

See also Voyages and travels

Calvino, I. Invisible cities

Ghosh, A. Sea of poppies

Gregory, P. Earthly joys

Hansen, R. Isn't it romantic?

Hensher, P. The Mulberry empire

Kehlmann, D. Measuring the world

Maalouf, A. Leo Africanus

Russell, M. D. Dreamers of the day

Oates, J. C. American appetites
O'Shaughnessy, P. Breach of promise
O'Shaughnessy, P. Invasion of privacy
O'Shaughnessy, P. Motion to suppress
O'Shaughnessy, P. Obstruction of justice
O'Shaughnessy, P. Writ of execution
Parker, B. Blood relations
Patterson, J. Hide & seek
Patterson, R. N. Degree of guilt
Patterson, R. N. Eyes of a child
Patterson, R. N. The final judgment
Patterson, R. N. Silent witness
Pesci, D. Amistad
Picoult, J. My sister's keeper
Reed, B. The choice
Reuland, R. Semiautomatic
Scottoline, L. Mistaken identity
Scottoline, L. Rough justice
Scottoline, L. The vendetta defense
Sharratt, M. Daughters of the Witching Hill
Siegel, S. Final verdict
Traver, R. Anatomy of a murder
Turow, S. Innocent
Turow, S. The laws of our fathers
Turow, S. Limitations
Turow, S. Presumed innocent
Uris, L. QB VII
Warren, R. P. World enough and time
Welty, E. The Ponder heart
Wilhelm, K. The best defense
Wilhelm, K. Death qualified
Wilhelm, K. Defense for the devil
Wilhelm, K. Desperate measures
Wilhelm, K. Malice prepense
Wilhelm, K. No defense
Wiprud, B. M. Ringer
Woods, S. Dead in the water
Woods, S. Grass roots

TRIALS (HOMICIDE)
Landay, W. Defending Jacob

TRIALS (HOMICIDE)
    See also Homicide; Trials

TRIALS (HOMICIDE) -- FICTION
Lelic, S. The child who

TRIALS (MURDER) *See* Trials (Homicide)

TRIALS (MURDER) -- ENGLAND -- FICTION
Brown, S. M. Accidents of providence

TRIALS (MURDER) -- FICTION
Bernhardt, W. Dark justice
Brown, S. The crush
Connelly, M. The fifth witness
De Kretser, M. The Hamilton case
Ellis, D. Life sentence
Green, T. The letter of the law
Hoffman, A. Blue diary
Holden, C. The jazz bird

Martini, S. P. The jury
Pickard, N. The whole truth
Reuland, R. Semiautomatic
Scottoline, L. The vendetta defense

TRIALS -- FICTION
Grisham, J. The rainmaker
Guterson, D. Snow falling on cedars
Kafka, F. The trial
Kent, K. The heretic's daughter
Pesci, D. Amistad

TRIALS *See* Legal stories

TRIANGLES (INTERPERSONAL RELATIONS)
Cain, J. M. The cocktail waitress
Collins, C. The gamal
Graves, T. G. Covet
Helprin, M. In sunlight and in shadow
Jenoff, P. The Ambassador's Daughter
Kalotay, D. Sight Reading
Levy, D. Swimming home
McOmber, A. The white forest
Neugeboren, J. Other side of the world
Szado, A. Studio saint-ex

TRIBAL GOVERNMENT *See* Political science;
  Tribes

TRIBAL LEADERS
Jennings, G. Raptor

TRIBECA (NEW YORK, N.Y.)
Greenfeld, K. T. Triburbia

TRIBES
    See also Clans; Family
Berlinski, M. Fieldwork
Darnton, J. Neanderthal

TRIBES AND TRIBAL SYSTEM *See* Tribes
Triburbia. Greenfeld, K. T.
TRICERATOPS *See* Dinosaurs
A **trick** of the light. Penny, L.
Tricks. McBain, E.
TRIGONOMETRY *See* Geometry; Mathematics
Trillium [series]
May, J. Blood Trillium
Norton, A. Golden Trillium

TRINIDAD AND TOBAGO
Naipaul, V. S. A house for Mr. Biswas
Naipaul, V. S. A way in the world

Trinity. Uris, L.
The **Trinity** Six. Cumming, C.
Triple. Follett, K.
TRIPLETS
Powell, S. The Mushroom Man
Tristan, Flora, 1803-1844
        About
Vargas Llosa, M. The way to paradise
The **triumph** of Caesar. Saylor, S.
A **triumph** of souls. Foster, A. D.
Trojan gold. Peters, E.
TROJAN WAR

See also Greek mythology; Troy (Extinct city)

George, M. Helen of Troy

McCullough, C. The song of Troy

Simmons, D. Ilium

Simmons, D. Olympos

Unsworth, B. The songs of the kings

TROJAN WAR -- FICTION

Miller, M. The song of Achilles

Troll. Ennen paivanlaskua ei voi/English

The **trolley.** Simon, C.

TROODON *See* Dinosaurs

Trophies and dead things. Muller, M.

Trophy. Griffith, M.

Tropic of Cancer. Miller, H.

Tropic of Capricorn. Miller, H.

TROPICAL FISH *See* Fishes

TROPICAL JUNGLES *See* Jungles

TROPICAL MEDICINE *See* Medicine

TROPICAL RAIN FORESTS *See* Rain forests

Trotsky, Leon, 1879-1940

About

Kingsolver, B. The lacuna

TROUBADOURS *See* French poetry; Minstrels; Poets

Trouble. Christensen, K.

Trouble in Paradise. Parker, R. B.

Trouble the water. Seitz, N.

The **troubled** man. Mankell, H.

Troubled sleep. Sartre, J. P.

Troubling love. Ferrante, E.

The **troupe.** Bennett, R. J.

TROUT FISHING *See* Fishing

TROY (ANCIENT CITY)

Ackroyd, P. The fall of Troy

George, M. Helen of Troy

TROY (EXTINCT CITY)

Cook, E. Achilles

Miller, M. The song of Achilles

TRUCK DRIVERS

Hall, A. L. The rhythm of the road

TRUCKS

See also Automobiles; Highway transportation; Motor vehicles

Hall, A. L. The rhythm of the road

The **true** and outstanding adventures of the Hunt sisters. Robinson, E.

True at first light. Hemingway, E.

True believers. Haddam, J.

True colors. Mortman, D.

True confections. Weber, K.

True confessions. Dunne, J. G.

True enough. McCauley, S.

True grit. Portis, C.

True justice. Tanenbaum, R.

The **true** memoirs of Little K. Sharp, A.

Trujillo Molina, Rafael Leónidas, 1891-1961

About

Vargas Llosa, M. The Feast of the Goat

TRUMPET PLAYERS

Baker, D. Young man with a horn

Moody, B. Looking for Chet Baker

Trumps of doom. Zelazny, R.

TRUST *See* Attitude (Psychology); Emotions

TRUST COMPANIES *See* Business; Corporations

Trust me. Updike, J.

Trust me on this. Westlake, D. E.

Trust your eyes. Barclay, L.

The **truth.** Pratchett, T.

The **truth** about love. Hart, J.

The **truth** hurts. Pickard, N.

Truth in advertising. Kenney, J.

Truth like the sun. Lynch, J.

The **truth** of the matter. Dew, R. F.

TRUTHFULNESS AND FALSEHOOD

Eco, U. Baudolino

Horlock, M. The book of lies

Hyland, M. J. Carry me down

Smith, A. The accidental

TRUTHFULNESS AND FALSEHOOD -- FICTION

Johnson, A. The orphan master's son

Smith, M. A. The Inquisitor

TUBERCULOSIS

Conrad, J. The Nigger of the Narcissus

Gide, A. The immoralist

Mann, T. The magic mountain

Patterson, K. Consumption

Tubman, Harriet, 1820?-1913

About

Heidish, M. A woman called Moses

Tudor, Owen, ca. 1400-1461

About

Bennett, V. The queen's lover

Tuesday's gone. French, N.

Tulip fever. Moggach, D.

TULIP MANIA, 17TH CENTURY

Moggach, D. Tulip fever

TULSA (OKLA.)

Lytal, B. A map of Tulsa

TUNA FISHERIES

Berman, S. Me, who dove into the heart of the world

TUNDRA ECOLOGY *See* Ecology

Tunnel of love. Wolitzer, H.

Tunnel vision. Paretsky, S.

TUNNELS

Kelly, J. The moon tunnel

Turbulence. Foden, G.

The **Turk** and my mother. Stefaniak, M. H.

TURKEY

De Bernieres, L. Birds without wings

Freely, M. Enlightenment

Karnezis, P. The maze
Pamuk, O. Snow
Vida, V. The lovers
TURKEY -- 19TH CENTURY
Wallach, J. Seraglio
TURKEY -- ANTIQUITIES *See* Antiquities
TURKEY -- FICTION
Karnezis, P. The maze
Pamuk, O. Snow
Silent house
TURKEY -- ISTANBUL
Gilman, D. The amazing Mrs. Pollifax
Hill, T. The love of stones
L'Amour, L. The walking drum
Lukas, M. D. The Oracle of Stamboul
McDonald, I. The Dervish House
Menendez, A. The last war
My name is Red
Pamuk, O. The museum of innocence
Rosenberg, R. This is not civilization
Shafak, E. The bastard of Istanbul
TURKEYS *See* Birds; Poultry
TURKISH FICTION -- TRANSLATIONS INTO ENGLISH
My name is Red
Pamuk, O. The museum of innocence
Pamuk, O. Snow
TURKS
Hambly, B. Ran away
A **Turn** of Light. Czerneda, J. E.
Turn of mind. Laplante, A.
The **turn** of the screw. James, H.
The **turnaround.** Pelecanos, G. P.
TURNCOATS *See* Defectors
TURNER'S SYNDROME
Haigh, J. The condition
Turner, J. M. W. (Joseph Mallord William), 1775-1851
About
Van Essen, T. The Center of the World
Turner, Nat, 1800?-1831
About
Styron, W. The confessions of Nat Turner
Turner, Ted, 1938-
About
Everett, P. L. I am Not Sidney Poitier
Turning angel. Iles, G.
Turpin, Randy, 1928-1966
About
Phillips, C. Foreigners
The **turquoise** lament. MacDonald, J. D.
Turtle Moon. Hoffman, A.
TUSCANY (ITALY)
Elkins, A. J. Dying on the vine
Mortimer, J. Summer's lease
Tutankhamen, King of Egypt

About
Drake, N. Tutankhamun
Holland, C. Valley of the Kings
Tutankhamun. Drake, N.
TUTORS
Barth, J. The sot-weed factor
Desai, K. The inheritance of loss
Mann, T. The black swan
Shreve, A. Body surfing
Sussman, E. French lessons
Upadhyay, S. The guru of love
Voltaire Candide
Wilder, T. Theophilus North
TUTSI (AFRICAN PEOPLE)
See also Africans; Indigenous peoples
Benaron, N. Running the rift
TV *See* Television
Twain, Mark, 1835-1910
About
Clinch, J. Finn
'**Twas** the night after Christmas. Jeffries, S.
The **twelfth** Imam. Rosenberg, J. C.
The **twelve** rooms of the Nile. Shomer, E.
Twelve times blessed. Mitchard, J.
The **twelve** tribes of Hattie. Mathis, A.
TWENTIETH CENTURY
See also World history -- 20th century
Follett, K. Winter of the world
Twenty fragments of a ravenous youth. Guo Xiaolu
Twenty years after. Dumas, A.
Twenty-seven bones. Nasaw, J. L.
Twentynine Palms. Pyne, D.
Twice-told tales. Hawthorne, N.
Twilight. Wiesel, E.
Twilight. Gay, W.
Twilight of the superheroes. Eisenberg, D.
The **twin.** Bakker, G.
TWIN BROTHERS
Alenyikov, M. Ivan and Misha
Twins. Dermansky, M.
TWINS
Ablow, K. R. Compulsion
Adichie, C. N. Half of a yellow sun
Bakker, G. The twin
Barth, J. The sot-weed factor
Bohjalian, C. The night strangers
Carey, E. Alva & Irva
Chaon, D. Await your reply
Clark, M. H. Two little girls in blue
Clay, H. Losing Charlotte
Docx, E. Pravda
Elwork, P. The girl who would speak for the dead
Frazier, C. Nightwoods
Golding, W. Darkness visible
Habila, H. Measuring time
Hart, J. The last child

UNCLES -- FICTION
  Amis, M. Lionel Asbo
  Cramer, W. D. Bad ground
  Le Fanu, J. S. Uncle Silas
  Stabenow, D. Though not dead
Uncollected stories of William Faulkner. Faulkner, W.
Uncommon clay. Maron, M.
The **unconsoled.** Ishiguro, K.
The **uncoupling.** Wolitzer, M.
Under African skies.
Under fire. Griffin, W. E. B.
Under heaven. Kay, G. G.
Under the banyan tree and other stories. Narayan, R. K.
Under the beetle's cellar. Walker, M. W.
Under the color of law. McGarrity, M.
Under the dome. King, S.
Under the greenwood tree. Hardy, T.
Under the volcano. Lowry, M.
Under Tower Peak. Paul, B.
UNDERACHIEVERS *See* Students
Undercover. James, B.
UNDERCOVER OPERATIONS
  James, B. Undercover
  Ledgard, J. M. Submergence
  Smith, A. Judas horse
Undercurrents. Pearson, R.
Undercurrents. Fyfield, F.
UNDERGRADUATES *See* College students
The **underground** man. Macdonald, R.
UNDERGROUND RAILROAD
  Heidish, M. A woman called Moses
  Stowe, H. B. Uncle Tom's cabin
UNDERGROUND RAILROAD -- FICTION
  Chevalier, T. The last runaway
UNDERGROUND RAILROADS *See* Subways
The **underpainter.** Urquhart, J.
Undersurface. Cullin, M.
UNDERTAKERS AND UNDERTAKING
  Gay, W. Twilight
The **undertow.** Baker, J.
Underworld. DeLillo, D.
UNDERWORLD
  Algren, N. The man with the golden arm
  Boyd, W. Ordinary thunderstorms
  Busch, F. The night inspector
  DeMarinis, R. Sky full of sand
  Dickens, C. Oliver Twist
  Dos Passos, J. U.S.A.
  Ellroy, J. American tabloid
  Ellroy, J. Blood's a rover
  Ellroy, J. The cold six thousand
  Ellroy, J. L.A. confidential
  Ellroy, J. White jazz
  Faust, C. Choke hold

  Faust, C. Money shot
  Hiaasen, C. Stormy weather
  Higgins, G. V. At end of day
  Johansen, I. Final target
  Mieville, C. Kraken
  Mortimer, J. Felix in the underworld
  Pelecanos, G. P. The big blowdown
  Polansky, D. Low Town
  Puzo, M. The godfather
  Puzo, M. The last Don
  Sanchez, T. King Bongo
  Steinbeck, J. Cannery Row
  Theroux, P. A dead hand
  Turner, F. W. Redemption
  Wambaugh, J. Hollywood crows
  Wambaugh, J. Hollywood Hills
  Wambaugh, J. Hollywood Station
  Weaver, M. Deceptions
  Winegardner, M. The Godfather returns
Undiscovered country. Enger, L.
The **undivided** self. Self, W.
UNDOCUMENTED ALIENS
  Adams, L. Harbor
  Boyle, T. C. The tortilla curtain
  Cleave, C. Little Bee
  Cussler, C. Flood tide
  Glass, J. The widower's tale
  Prose, F. Primitive people
  Straight, S. Highwire moon
  Tobar, H. The barbarian nurseries
UNDOCUMENTED ALIENS *See* Illegal aliens
Undue influence. Martini, S. P.
Undue influence. Brookner, A.
UNEMPLOYED
  Belle, J. The seven year bitch
  Minot, E. The Brambles
  Pilcher, R. A risk worth taking
  Steinbeck, J. Cannery Row
  Steinbeck, J. The grapes of wrath
  Steinbeck, J. Sweet Thursday
  Walter, J. The financial lives of the poets
  Westlake, D. E. The ax
  Wolitzer, M. The ten-year nap
UNEMPLOYED -- FICTION
  Austin, L. All she ever wanted
  Laukkanen, O. The professionals
UNEMPLOYMENT
    See also Employment; Labor supply; Social problems
  Thompson, J. The humanity project
UNEMPLOYMENT INSURANCE
    See also Insurance
An **unequal** marriage. Tennant, E.
The **unexpected** Mrs. Pollifax. Gilman, D.
Unexpectedly, Milo. Dicks, M.
Unfinished desires. Godwin, G.

Fitzgerald, F. S. The beautiful and damned
Fitzgerald, F. S. The great Gatsby
Franzen, J. The corrections
Gaddis, W. A frolic of his own
Greeley, A. M. September song
Heller, J. Something happened
Jakes, J. American dreams
Johnson, C. R. Dreamer
Kerouac, J. On the road
Kerouac, J. The Dharma bums
King, S. Hearts in Atlantis
Kosinski, J. N. Being there
Lewis, S. Babbitt
Mailer, N. Harlot's ghost
Nabokov, V. V. Lolita
Piercy, M. Vida
Proulx, A. Accordion crimes
Proulx, A. Postcards
Roth, P. The great American novel
Shaw, I. Rich man, poor man
Stewart, F. M. Ellis Island
Turner, F. W. 1929
Updike, J. In the beauty of the lilies
Updike, J. Memories of the Ford Administration
Vonnegut, K. Jailbird
Wiggins, M. Evidence of things unseen
Wouk, H. War and remembrance
Wouk, H. The winds of war
Wright, S. Going native

UNITED STATES -- AIR FORCE
Dickey, J. To the white sea
Heller, J. Catch-22
Rosten, L. Captain Newman, M.D.

UNITED STATES -- AIR FORCE -- OFFICERS
L'Amour, L. Last of the breed
Westheimer, D. Von Ryan's Express

UNITED STATES -- ANTIQUITIES *See* Antiquities

UNITED STATES -- ARMED FORCES
Knebel, F. Seven days in May

UNITED STATES -- ARMY
DeMille, N. The general's daughter
Hemingway, E. Across the river and into the trees
Jones, J. From here to eternity
Jones, J. The thin red line
McCullers, C. Reflections in a golden eye
O'Connor, R. Buffalo soldiers
Shaara, J. Gods and generals
Shaara, J. The last full measure
Truscott, L. K. Heart of war
Willard, T. Buffalo soldiers

UNITED STATES -- ARMY -- CAVALRY
Jones, D. C. A creek called Wounded Knee

UNITED STATES -- ARMY -- OFFICERS
DeMille, N. Word of honor
Hersey, J. A bell for Adano

Nathanson, E. M. The dirty dozen
Pynchon, T. Gravity's rainbow
Shulman, M. Rally round the flag, boys!
Traver, R. Anatomy of a murder
Uris, L. Armageddon

UNITED STATES -- ARMY -- SPECIAL FORCES
Griffin, W. E. B. Special ops

UNITED STATES -- ARMY AIR FORCES
Griffin, W. E. B. The aviators

UNITED STATES -- CENTRAL INTELLIGENCE AGENCY
Buckley, W. F. Mongoose, R.I.P
Clancy, T. Against all enemies
DeMille, N. The lion's game
Ellroy, J. American tabloid
Gilman, D. The amazing Mrs. Pollifax
Gilman, D. The elusive Mrs. Pollifax
Gilman, D. A palm for Mrs. Pollifax
Gilman, D. The unexpected Mrs. Pollifax
Grady, J. Six days of the condor
Griffin, W. E. B. Special ops
Griffin, W. E. B. Under fire
Grisham, J. The brethren
Grisham, J. The broker
Harris, R. The ghost
Hospital, J. T. Due preparations for the plague
Ignatius, D. Body of lies
Johansen, I. And then you die--
Johnson, D. Tree of smoke
Johnson, D. Lulu in Marrakech
Lehrer, J. Purple dots
Littell, R. The company
Littell, R. Walking back the cat
Mailer, N. Harlot's ghost
Morrell, D. The brotherhood of the rose
Palmer, M. The patient
Robbins, T. Fierce invalids home from hot climates
Rush, N. Mortals
Silva, D. The mark of the assassin
Steiner, P. The terrorist
Steinhauer, O. The nearest exit
Steinhauer, O. The tourist
Thomas, R. Ah, treachery!

UNITED STATES -- CIVIL WAR, 1861-1865
Adams, S. K. My old true love
Bahr, H. The Judas Field
Byrd, M. Grant
Cornwell, B. Rebel
Doctorow, E. L. The march
Faulkner, W. The unvanquished
Fleming, T. J. When this cruel war is over
Frazier, C. Cold Mountain
Gibbons, K. On the occasion of my last afternoon
Gingrich, N. Gettysburg
Gingrich, N. Grant comes east

Ridley, J. A conversation with the Mann
Robinson, M. Gilead
Roth, P. The human stain
Shreve, S. R. A country of strangers
Siddons, A. R. Nora, Nora
Smith, L. E. Strange fruit
Southgate, M. The fall of Rome
Straight, S. The gettin place
Straight, S. A million nightingales
Styron, W. The confessions of Nat Turner
Tademy, L. Cane River
Taylor, M. G. The Marrowbone Marble Company
Terrell, W. The huntsman
Three days before the shooting--
Vachss, A. H. Two trains running
Vernon, O. Eden
Vernon, O. A killing in this town
Wallace, I. The man
Warren, R. P. Band of angels
West, D. The wedding
Whitehead, C. Apex hides the hurt
Whitehead, C. The intuitionist
Wideman, J. E. The cattle killing
Wideman, J. E. Philadelphia fire
Wimberley, D. The king of Colored Town
Wolfe, T. A man in full
Woods, S. Chiefs
Wright, R. Native son
Yarbrough, S. Prisoners of war

UNITED STATES -- RACE RELATIONS -- FICTION
Perlman, E. The street sweeper

UNITED STATES -- RELIGION *See* Religion

UNITED STATES -- REVOLUTION, 1775-1783
Charyn, J. Johnny One-Eye
Edmonds, W. D. Drums along the Mohawk
Fleming, T. J. Dreams of glory
Gabaldon, D. An echo in the bone
Hambly, B. Patriot hearts
Hill, L. Someone knows my name
Jakes, J. Charleston
Kurtz, K. Two crowns for America
McGrath, P. Martha Peake
Roberts, K. L. Arundel
Shaara, J. The glorious cause
Shaara, J. Rise to rebellion

UNITED STATES -- REVOLUTION, 1775-1783 -- CAMPAIGNS
Roberts, K. L. Oliver Wiswell
Roberts, K. L. Rabble in arms

UNITED STATES -- REVOLUTION, 1775-1783 -- NAVAL OPERATIONS
Cooper, J. F. The pilot

UNITED STATES -- RURAL CONDITIONS
Rhodes, D. Jewelweed

UNITED STATES -- SECRET SERVICE

Costello, M. Big if
Shelby, P. Days of drums

UNITED STATES -- SOCIAL LIFE AND CUSTOMS -- 20TH CENTURY
DeMarinis, R. Borrowed hearts
Doenges, J. What she left me: stories and a novella
Fitzgerald, F. S. Novels and stories, 1920-1922
Gurganus, A. The practical heart
Jen, G. Who's Irish?
Klaussmann, L. Tigers in red weather
Mason, B. A. Zigzagging down a wild trail
Moore, L. Birds of America
Oates, J. C. Faithless
Updike, J. Licks of love
Vonnegut, K. Bagombo snuff box: uncollected short fiction

UNITED STATES -- SOCIAL LIFE AND CUSTOMS
Epstein, J. Fabulous small Jews
Hood, A. The Obituary Writer
Hood, A. An ornithologist's guide to life
Yates, R. The collected stories of Richard Yates

UNITED STATES -- SUPREME COURT
Baldacci, D. The simple truth
Meltzer, B. The tenth justice
Patterson, R. N. Protect and defend

UNITED STATES -- TO 1776
Defoe, D. Moll Flanders
Gabaldon, D. A breath of snow and ashes
L'Amour, L. To the far blue mountains
Morrison, T. A mercy
Pynchon, T. Mason & Dixon
Richter, C. The light in the forest

UNITED STATES -- TRIPOLITAN WAR, 1801-1805
Roberts, K. L. Lydia Bailey

UNITED STATES -- WAR OF 1812
Brown, R. M. Dolley

UNITED STATES -- WAR WITH MEXICO, 1845-1848
Kelton, E. The rebels
Shaara, J. Gone for soldiers

UNITED STATES MARSHALS
Lehane, D. Shutter Island
Leonard, E. Raylan
Parker, R. B. Gunman's rhapsody
West, P. O.K.

UNITED STATES NATIONAL ARCHIVES
Meltzer, B. The inner circle

UNITED STATES NAVAL ACADEMY
Deutermann, P. T. Darkside
Webb, J. A sense of honor

UNITED STATES NAVAL OBSERVATORY
Mallon, T. Two moons

UNITED STATES -- ARMY CRIMINAL INVESTIGATION COMMAND

Limon, M. G.I. bones

UNITED STATES ARMY -- MILITARY LIFE
See Military personnel; Soldiers

UNITED STATES ARMY -- OFFICERS *See*
Military personnel; Soldiers

UNITED STATES ARMY -- SONGS *See* Songs

**UNITED STATES ARMY -- COMMANDO
TROOPS**
Atkins, A. The broken places

**UNITED STATES. ARMY -- SURGEONS -- FIC-
TION**
Scottoline, L. Don't Go

**UNITED STATES. ARMY CRIMINAL INVESTI-
GATION COMMAND -- FICTION**
Limón, M. Mr. Kill

**UNITED STATES CENTRAL INTELLIGENCE
AGENCY**
Fesperman, D. The double game
Huston, C. Skinner

**UNITED STATES. NATIONAL AERONAUTICS
AND SPACE ADMINISTRATION**
McDevitt, J. The Cassandra project

UNITED STATES NAVY SEALS
Bond, L. Exit plan

UNITED STEELWORKERS OF AMERICA *See*
Labor unions

UNIVERSAL LANGUAGE *See* Language and
languages; Linguistics

UNIVERSAL MILITARY TRAINING *See* Draft

UNIVERSE
Lake, J. Mainspring

UNIVERSITIES AND COLLEGES
Carter, S. L. New England white
Coll, S. Acceptance
Lipsyte, S. The ask

UNIVERSITY OF CAMBRIDGE
Leavitt, D. The Indian clerk
Snow, C. P. The light and the dark
Snow, C. P. The masters

UNIVERSITY OF NOTRE DAME
McInerny, R. M. The book of kills
McInerny, R. M. Celt and pepper
McInerny, R. M. Irish coffee
McInerny, R. M. Irish tenure

UNIVERSITY OF OXFORD
Marias, J. Dark back of time
Sayers, D. L. Gaudy Night
Todos las almas/English All souls

UNIVERSITY STUDENTS *See* College students

The **unknown** shore. O'Brian, P.

The **unknown** terrorist. Flanagan, R.

Unless. Shields, C.

The **unlikely** pilgrimage of Harold Fry. Joyce, R.

Unlucky in law. O'Shaughnessy, P.

An **unmarked** grave. Todd, C.

UNMARRIED COUPLES

Dean, L. The old romantic
Hawke, E. Ash Wednesday
Levithan, D. The lover's dictionary
Mapson, J. Loving Chloe
McMillan, T. Disappearing acts
Morgan, C. E. All the living
Reiken, F. Day for night
Shriver, L. The post-birthday world
Spencer, S. Man in the woods
Walker, A. Now is the time to open your heart
Weldon, F. She may not leave

UNMARRIED FATHERS
See also Fathers; Single parents
Law, S. K. The paper marriage
Little, T. Where there's smoke

UNMARRIED MEN *See* Single men

UNMARRIED MOTHERS
See also Mothers; Single parents
Eberstadt, F. Rat
Gordon, M. The company of women
Llywelyn, M. 1949
Reed, K. The baby merchant
Richler, N. Your mouth is lovely
Sheldon, S. Rage of angels
Shreve, A. Fortune's Rocks
Straight, S. I been in sorrow's kitchen and licked
out all the pots
Thayer, N. Belonging
Upadhyay, S. The guru of love

UNMARRIED MOTHERS -- FICTION
Burney, C. M. Wounded
DuPree, K. Silenced
Hannah, K. Home again
K'wan Section 8
K'wan Welfare wifeys
Lippman, L. And when she was good

UNMARRIED PARENTS *See* Unmarried fathers;
Unmarried mothers

UNMARRIED PEOPLE *See* Single people; Unmarried couples

UNMARRIED WOMEN *See* Single women

The **unnamed.** Ferris, J.

Unnatural selection. Elkins, A. J.

The **unpleasantness** at the Bellona Club. Sayers,
D. L.

The **unquiet.** Connolly, J.

The **unremembered.** Orullian, P. V.

An **unsuitable** attachment. Pym, B.

An **unsuitable** job for a woman. James, P. D.

Until I find you. Irving, J.

Until she comes home. Roy, L.

Until the dawn's light. Appelfeld, A.

Until thy wrath be past. Larsson, A.

Unto a good land. Moberg, V.

Untold story. Ali, M.

UNTRUTH *See* Truthfulness and falsehood

The **unvanquished.** Faulkner, W.

Unwanted. Ohlsson, K.

UNWED MOTHERS *See* Unmarried mothers

Up in Honey's room. Leonard, E.

Up Jim River. Flynn, M.

Up jumps the Devil. Maron, M.

Up the down staircase. Kaufman, B.

Upon a dark night. Lovesey, P.

UPPER CLASS -- ENGLAND
　　Dean, A. A gentleman of fortune, or, The suspi-
　　cions of Miss Dido Kent
　　Dean, A. A woman of consequence
　　Lane, H. Alys, always
　　McOmber, A. The white forest

UPPER CLASS
　　　　See also Social classes
　　Dean, A. A woman of consequence
　　Walker, W. Crime of Privilege

UPPER CLASS FAMILIES -- ENGLAND
　　Dean, A. Bellfield Hall, or, The observations of
　　Miss Dido Kent

UPPER CLASS FAMILIES
　　Benjamin, M. Alice I have been
　　Kelly, E. The burning air
　　Miller, J. The year of the gadfly
　　Samarasan, P. Evening is the whole day

Upside down, inside out. McInerney, M.

URANIUM
　　Cummins, A. Yellowcake

URBAN AREAS *See* Cities and towns; Metropoli-
　　tan areas

URBAN ECOLOGY *See* Cities and towns; Ecol-
　　ogy

URBAN FICTION
　　Clark, W. Thug lovin'
　　Diamond, D. A gangster and a gentleman
　　DuPree, K. Silenced
　　K'wan Animal
　　K'wan Welfare wifeys
　　Williams, K. Dirty to the grave
　　Woods, T. Alibi

URBAN LIFE *See* City and town life

URBAN POLICY *See* City and town life; Eco-
　　nomic policy; Social policy; Urban sociology

URBANIZATION *See* Cities and towns; Rural so-
　　ciology; Social change; Social conditions; Urban
　　sociology

Urrea, Teresa
　　　　　　About
　　Urrea, L. A. The hummingbird's daughter

The **Urth** of the new sun. Wolfe, G.

URUGUAY
　　Cameron, P. The city of your final destination

The **used** world. Kimmel, H.

Useful girl. Stevens, M.

The **uses** of enchantment. Julavits, H.

The **usual** rules. Maynard, J.

UTAH
　　Ebershoff, D. The 19th wife
　　Evenson, B. The open curtain
　　Mailer, N. The executioner's song
　　Udall, B. The lonely polygamist

UTAH -- 19TH CENTURY
　　Grey, Z. Riders of the purple sage

UTAH -- 20TH CENTURY
　　Mailer, N. The executioner's song

UTAH -- FICTION
　　Ebershoff, D. The 19th wife
　　Grey, Z. Riders of the purple sage
　　Mailer, N. The executioner's song

UTAH -- SALT LAKE CITY
　　Reiken, F. Day for night

UTE INDIANS
　　Borland, H. When the legends die
　　Doss, J. D. The night visitor
　　Doss, J. D. The shaman's bones

UTILITARIANISM
　　　　See also Ethics
　　Dickens, C. Hard times

UTILIZATION OF WASTE *See* Salvage

UTOPIAN FICTION
　　　　See also Fantasy fiction; Science fiction

UTOPIAN LITERATURE *See* Utopian fiction;
　　Utopias

UTOPIAS
　　　　See also Political science; Socialism
　　Gilman, C. P. Herland
　　Gilman, C. P. With her in Ourland
　　Hawthorne, N. The Blithedale romance
　　Hesse, H. The glass bead game (Magister Ludi)
　　Huxley, A. Brave new world
　　Le Guin, U. K. The dispossessed
　　Murdoch, I. The bell
　　Piercy, M. Woman on the edge of time
　　Rush, N. Mating
　　Skinner, B. F. Walden two
　　Unsworth, B. Sacred hunger

UTOPIAS -- FICTION
　　Charlotte Perkins Gilman's Utopian novels
　　Cline, E. Ready player one
　　Hilton, J. Lost horizon
　　Niven, L. Saturn's race

Utterly monkey. Laird, N.

Utz. Chatwin, B.

V

V. Pynchon, T.

Vacation. Unferth, D. O.

VACATION HOMES
　　　　See also Houses
　　Stonich, S. Vacationland
　　Thayer, N. Island girls

The **vanishing** act of Esme Lennox. O'Farrell, M.

Vanishing acts. Picoult, J.

The **vanishing** of Katharina Linden. Grant, H.

Vanishing point. Markson, D.

VANISHING SPECIES *See* Endangered species

Vanity fair. Thackeray, W. M.

Variable star. Heinlein, R. A. (. A.

VARIATION (BIOLOGY) *See* Biology; Genetics; Heredity

VARIETY SHOWS (RADIO PROGRAMS) *See* Radio programs

VARIETY SHOWS (TELEVISION PROGRAMS) *See* Television programs

The **various** haunts of men. Hill, S.

VASSALS *See* Feudalism

VASSAR COLLEGE
McCarthy, M. The group

Vatican. Martin, M.

VATICAN
Folsom, A. R. Day of confession
Greeley, A. M. White smoke
Martin, M. Vatican
Martin, M. Windswept House
Puzo, M. The family
Rabb, J. The book of Q
West, M. L. Lazarus

VATICAN CITY
Berry, S. The third secret

VAUDEVILLE
McCracken, E. Niagara Falls all over again

VAUDEVILLE -- FICTION
Bennett, R. J. The troupe

The **vault.** Lovesey, P.

Vautrin, Wilhelmina, d. 1941
About
Jin, H. Nanjing requiem

VD *See* Sexually transmitted diseases

Vector. Cook, R.

VEGETABLES *See* Food; Plants

Veil of gold. Wilkins, K.

Veiled worlds trilogy [series]
Anderton, J. Debris

VELOCIRAPTORS *See* Dinosaurs

Velocity. Koontz, D. R.

The **vendetta** defense. Scottoline, L.

VENEREAL DISEASES *See* Sexually transmitted diseases

Venetia Kelly's traveling show. Delaney, F.

The **Venetian** affair. MacInnes, H.

Vengeance. Kaminsky, S. M.

Vengeance. Black, B.

VENGENCE *See* Revenge

VENICE (ITALY)
Chase, L. Your scandalous ways
Leon, D. Beastly Things
Leon, D. Blood from a stone

Leon, D. A question of belief

VENTRILOQUISTS
Stace, W. By George

VENUS (PLANET)
Lewis, C. S. Perelandra
Pohl, F. The space merchants

Venus in copper. Davis, L.

Veracity. Bynum, L.

VERBAL LEARNING *See* Language and languages; Psychology of learning

Verbena. Kincaid, N.

Verdict unsafe. McGown, J.

Vermeer, Johannes, 1632-1675
About
Chevalier, T. Girl with a pearl earring
Vreeland, S. Girl in hyacinth blue

Vermilion drift. Krueger, W. K.

VERMONT
Bohjalian, C. A. Secrets of Eden
Carkeet, D. From away
Delbanco, N. Sherbrookes
Freeman, C. All that I have
Freeman, C. Go with me
Hearon, S. Year of the dog
Henderson, E. Ten thousand saints
Irving, J. Last night in Twisted River
Lipman, E. The Inn at Lake Devine
Maloy, K. Every last cuckoo
McMahon, J. Dismantled
Miller, S. The world below
Morris, M. M. A dangerous woman
Morris, M. M. The lost mother
Morris, M. M. Songs in ordinary time
Mosher, H. F. On Kingdom Mountain
Peck, R. N. A day no pigs would die
Prose, F. Blue angel
Proulx, A. Postcards
Schupack, D. The boy on the bus
Shreve, A. Testimony
Tartt, D. The secret history
Tussing, J. The best people in the world
Updike, J. Seek my face
Zeltserman, D. Small crimes

Veronica. Gaitskill, M.

Versailles. Davis, K.

VERSIFICATION *See* Authorship; Poetics; Rhythm

VERTEBRATES *See* Animals

Vertical burn. Emerson, E. W.

Vertical coffin. Cannell, S. J.

Vertigo. Sebald, W. G.

Very bad men. Dolan, H.

Very old bones. Kennedy, W.

Very Valentine. Trigiani, A.

Vespers. McBain, E.

VESSELS (SHIPS) *See* Ships

Vestments. Reimringer, J.

The **veteran.** Forsyth, F.

VETERANS

     See also Military art and science; Veterans

  Atkins, A. The ranger

  Liss, D. The whiskey rebels

  Parker, K. J. The company

  Purdy, J. In a shallow grave

  Wyld, E. After the fire, a still small voice

VETERANS (AMERICAN CIVIL WAR, 1861-1865)

  Bahr, H. The Judas Field

  Busch, F. The night inspector

  Byrd, M. Grant

  Smith, D. Pictures from an expedition

  Swerling, B. City of promise

VETERANS (IRAQ WAR, 2003-)

  Bledsoe, A. The hum and the shiver

  Clarke, B. Exley

  Hamill, P. Tabloid city

  Hogan, C. Devils in exile

  Lansdale, J. R. Leather maiden

  Lennon, J. R. Castle

  Mendelsohn, J. American music

  Mohr, J. Damascus

  Pelecanos, G. The cut

  Percy, B. The wilding

VETERANS (KOREAN WAR, 1950-1953)

  Hill, R. When all is said and done

  Percy, W. The moviegoer

  Walbert, K. The gardens of Kyoto

VETERANS (PERSIAN GULF WAR, 1991)

  Littell, R. Walking back the cat

VETERANS (VIETNAMESE WAR, 1961-1975)

  Burke, S. Black flies

  Forsyth, F. Avenger

  Green, N. The angel of Montague Street

  Harris, T. Black Sunday

  Harrison, C. Afterburn

  Heinemann, L. Paco's story

  Hunter, S. I, sniper

  Hunter, S. Night of thunder

  Hunter, S. Time to hunt

  King, D. The ha-ha

  King, L. R. Keeping watch

  King, S. Hearts in Atlantis

  Maillard, K. The clarinet polka

  Martin, L. Break the skin

  Mason, B. A. In country

  McCammon, R. R. Gone south

  McFarland, D. Singing boy

  Morris, M. M. Fiona Range

  O'Brien, T. In the Lake of the Woods

  O'Nan, S. The names of the dead

  Pekearo, N. T. The wolfman

  Stone, R. Dog soldiers

  Thayer, S. The weatherman

  Thomas, R. Ah, treachery!

  Thompson, J. The year we left home

  Vonnegut, K. Hocus pocus

  Walker, M. W. Under the beetle's cellar

  Webb, J. A sense of honor

VETERANS (WORLD WAR, 1914-1918)

  Buehlman, C. Those across the river

  Erdrich, L. The Master Butchers Singing Club

  Faulkner, W. Soldiers' pay

  Gautreaux, T. The missing

  Koryta, M. The Cypress House

  Parkinson, H. Across open ground

  Remarque, E. M. The road back

  Rubenfeld, J. The death instinct

  Speller, E. The return of Captain John Emmett

  Thayer, S. The leper

  Wiggins, M. Evidence of things unseen

VETERANS (WORLD WAR, 1939-1945)

  Algren, N. The man with the golden arm

  Boll, H. The silent angel

  Bragg, M. The soldier's return

  Bragg, M. A son of war

  Dickinson, P. Some deaths before dying

  Greeley, A. M. Younger than springtime

  Greer, A. S. The story of a marriage

  Guterson, D. Snow falling on cedars

  Hawkes, J. Second skin

  Hazzard, S. The great fire

  Heller, J. Closing time

  Hunter, S. Hot Springs

  Jones, J. Whistle

  Jordan, H. Mudbound

  Knowles, J. Peace breaks out

  Lee A gesture life

  Lehrer, J. The special prisoner

  Levy, A. Small island

  McEwan, I. Atonement

  McNamer, D. Red rover

  Nayman, S. The listener

  Okuizumi, H. The stones cry out

  Pouncey, P. R. Rules for old men waiting

  Taylor, M. G. The Marrowbone Marble Company

  Turow, S. Ordinary heroes

  Watkins, P. The ice soldier

  Wharton, W. Birdy

  Wilson, S. The man in the gray flannel suit

VETERANS -- CRIMES AGAINST

  Griffiths, E. The house at sea's end

VETERANS -- EDUCATION *See* Education

VETERANS -- FICTION

  Burrowes, G. The soldier

  Campbell, D. When She Came Home

  Doolittle, S. Lake country

  Morrison, T. Home

  Robinson, R. Sparta

Salter, J. All that is

Saunders, G. Tenth of December

VETERANS -- TEXAS

Fountain, B. Billy Lynn's long halftime walk

VETERINARIANS

Deb, S. The point of return

Gould, J. A moment in time

Gruen, S. Water for elephants

Miller, S. While I was gone

Murphy, Y. The call

Reiken, F. Day for night

Stewart, M. Airs above the ground

VETERINARIANS -- FICTION

Leon, D. Beastly Things

VETERINARY MEDICINE *See* Medicine

VIADUCTS *See* Bridges

The **Viagra** diaries. Brooker, B. R.

VIBRATION *See* Mechanics; Sound

VICARS, PAROCHIAL -- ENGLAND -- FIC-TION

Malliet, G. M. A fatal winter

VICE *See* Conduct of life; Ethics; Human behavior

VICE-PRESIDENTS

See also Presidents

Chase-Riboud, B. Sally Hemings

Shaara, J. Rise to rebellion

Updike, J. Memories of the Ford Administration

Vidal, G. Burr

Vicious circle. Littell, R.

The **vicious** circle.

VICKSBURG (MISS.) -- HISTORY -- SIEGE, 1863

Shaara, J. A Chain of Thunder

VICKSBURG (MISS.) -- SIEGE, 1863

Shaara, J. A Chain of Thunder

Victims. Uhnak, D.

VICTIMS OF CRIME *See* Victims of crimes

VICTIMS OF CRIMES

Ellory, R. J. A simple act of violence

Phillips, C. Foreigners

VICTIMS OF CRIMES

Haynes, E. Into the darkest corner

Wilson, C. Cotton

VICTIMS OF TERRORISM

Johansen, I. Final target

Miller, S. The Lake Shore Limited

Patchett, A. Bel canto

VICTIMS OF VIOLENT CRIMES -- FICTION

Wilson, C. Cotton

Victoria, Queen of Great Britain, 1819-1901
About

Hodder, M. The strange affair of Spring Heeled Jack

VICTORIANA *See* Antiques; Collectibles

Victorine. Texier, C.

Victory. Conrad, J.

Vida. Piercy, M.

VIDEO ART *See* Art; Television; Video recording

VIDEO GAMES

See also Electronic toys; Games

Huston, C. Sleepless

Tracy, P. J. Monkeewrench

VIDEO TELEPHONE *See* Data transmission systems; Telephone; Television

Vidocq, Eugène Francois, 1775-1857
About

Bayard, L. The black tower

VIENNA (AUSTRIA)

Boyd, W. Waiting for sunrise

Jones, J. S. The silence

Vienna blood. Tallis, F.

Vienna Twilight. Tallis, F.

VIETNAM

The sorrow of war

VIETNAM -- FICTION

Duong Thu Huong The zenith

VIETNAM -- HO CHI MINH CITY

Greene, G. The quiet American

Soli, T. The lotus eaters

VIETNAM WAR, 1961-1975

Lam, V. The headmaster's wager

Wilson, C. Cotton

VIETNAM WAR, 1961-1975 -- VETERANS

O'Malley, T. This magnificent desolation

VIETNAMESE -- FRANCE

Truong, M. T. D. The book of salt

VIETNAMESE -- UNITED STATES

Parker, T. J. Little Saigon

VIETNAMESE -- UNITED STATES -- FICTION

Johnson, C. Another man's moccasins

VIETNAMESE AMERICANS

Le, T. D. T. The gangster we are all looking for

VIETNAMESE CONFLICT, 1961-1975

Johnson, D. Tree of smoke

Leimbach, M. The man from Saigon

Marlantes, K. Matterhorn

Soli, T. The lotus eaters

VIETNAMESE REFUGEES *See* Refugees

VIETNAMESE WAR, 1961-1975

Coonts, S. Flight of the Intruder

DeMille, N. Word of honor

Griffin, W. E. B. The aviators

Heinemann, L. Paco's story

Henley, P. In the river sweet

Johnson, D. Tree of smoke

King, S. Hearts in Atlantis

Leimbach, M. The man from Saigon

Long, J. The reckoning

Marlantes, K. Matterhorn

Mason, B. A. In country

McCann, C. Let the great world spin

McDermott, A. After this

Jiles, P. The color of lightning
Johnson, D. Nobody move
Johnson, W. The devil you know
Jones, S. Outcast
Jordan, H. Mudbound
Katzenbach, J. State of mind
King, R. The sound of butterflies
Lansdale, J. R. Sunset and sawdust
Lazar, Z. Sway
Lehrer, J. The special prisoner
Lessing, D. M. The memoirs of a survivor
Lively, P. Spiderweb
Llywelyn, M. 1916
Llywelyn, M. 1972
Lustbader, E. V. Black Blade
Mankell, H. The eye of the leopard
Martin, L. Break the skin
Martin, V. Trespass
Matar, H. In the country of men
Matthiessen, P. Bone by bone
Matthiessen, P. Lost Man's River
Matthiessen, P. Shadow country
McCarthy, C. The road
McCarthy, C. Blood meridian
McCarthy, C. No country for old men
McGuane, T. Ninety-two in the shade
Miller, R. Welcome to Heavenly Heights
Monaghan, N. The killing jar
Naslund, S. J. Four spirits
Nersesian, A. The swing voter of Staten Island
Oates, J. C. Black girl/White girl
Oates, J. C. The gravedigger's daughter
O'Dell, T. Back roads
Palahniuk, C. Rant
Patterson, J. Hide & seek
Pawel, R. Death of a nationalist
Pelecanos, G. P. The big blowdown
Pelecanos, G. P. Drama city
Pelecanos, G. P. Shame the devil
Pelecanos, G. P. The sweet forever
Pelecanos, G. P. The turnaround
Picoult, J. Nineteen minutes
Pollock, D. R. The devil all the time
Poyer, D. Thunder on the mountain
Price, R. Samaritan
Quindlen, A. Every last one
Rash, R. Serena
Richards, D. A. The bay of love and sorrows
Rosero Diago, E. The armies
Rushdie, S. Shalimar the clown
Salak, K. The white Mary
Shamsie, K. Kartography
Shriver, L. We need to talk about Kevin
Spiegelman, I. Everyone's burning
Straight, S. The gettin place
Straub, P. A special place

Turner, F. W. Redemption
Vachss, A. H. Two trains running
Vanderbes, J. Strangers at the feast
Vargas Llosa, M. Death in the Andes
Vargas Llosa, M. The war of the end of the world
Vernon, O. Eden
Vine, B. King Solomon's carpet
Vonnegut, K. Armageddon in retrospect
Walker, A. Possessing the secret of joy
Wimberley, D. The king of Colored Town
Woods, S. L.A. Times
Wright, S. Going native

VIOLENCE -- FICTION
  Hoagland, E. Children are diamonds
  Koch, H. The dinner
VIOLENCE IN MASS MEDIA *See* Mass media;
  Violence
VIOLENCE IN POPULAR CULTURE *See* Popu-
  lar culture; Violence
VIOLENCE IN SPORTS *See* Sports; Violence
VIOLENCE IN THE WORKPLACE *See* Vio-
  lence; Work environment
VIOLENCE ON TELEVISION *See* Television;
  Television programs; Violence
The **violent** bear it away. O'Connor, F.
VIOLENT CRIMES
  Lange, R. Angel baby
  Robards, K. Shiver
A **violet** season. Czepiel, K. L.
The **violets** of March. Jio, S.
VIOLIN MUSIC *See* Music
VIOLIN PLAYERS *See* Violinists
VIOLIN TEACHERS
  Elias, G. Death and transfiguration
VIOLINISTS
  Egolf, T. Skirt and the fiddle
  Hall, B. The music teacher
  Lebrecht, N. The song of names
VIOLINISTS -- FICTION
  Elias, G. Danse macabre
  Schneider, B. Beautiful Inez
VIPERS *See* Snakes
Virgil

About
  Graham, J. Black ships
Virgin earth. Gregory, P.
Virgin heat. Shames, L.
The **virgin** in the ice. Peters, E.
VIRGIN ISLANDS OF THE UNITED STATES
  Nasaw, J. L. Twenty-seven bones
  Pronzini, B. The crimes of Jordan Wise
The **virgin** suicides. Eugenides, J.
VIRGINIA
  Baldacci, D. Divine justice
  Bausch, R. Thanksgiving night
  Clark, M. The legal limit

Lytton, E. B. L. The last days of Pompeii
Verne, J. A journey to the centre of the earth
Volt. Heathcock, A.
Voltaire's Candide, Zadig, and selected stories. Voltaire
VOLUNTEER WORKERS
See, C. There will never be another you
Von Ryan's Express. Westheimer, D.
VOODOO *See* Voodooism
Voodoo dreams. Rhodes, J. P.
Voodoo, Ltd. Thomas, R.
VOODOOISM
Due, T. The good house
Rhodes, J. P. Voodoo dreams
Rhodes, J. P. Yellow moon
Stone, R. Bay of souls
VOTER REGISTRATION
See also Elections; Suffrage
Devoto, P. C. The summer we got saved
VOTING *See* Elections; Suffrage
VOUDOU *See* Voodooism
VOUDOUISM *See* Voodooism
The **vows** of silence. Hill, S.
Voyage along the horizon. Marias, J.
The **voyage** out. Woolf, V.
Voyage to the North Star. Nichols, P.
Voyager. Gabaldon, D.
VOYAGERS *See* Explorers; Travelers
VOYAGES AND TRAVELS
Campbell, B. J. Once upon a river
Carey, P. Parrot and Olivier in America
Dunnett, D. Caprice and Rondo
Dunnett, D. Scales of gold
Dunnett, D. To lie with lions
Dunnett, D. The unicorn hunt
Eberstadt, F. Rat
The elephant's journey
Ghosh, A. River of smoke
Ghosh, A. Sea of poppies
Golding, W. Close quarters
Golding, W. Fire down below
Golding, W. Rites of passage
Halter, M. Messiah
Higgins, J. Storm warning
Johnson, C. R. Middle passage
Johnson, M. Pym
Larsen, R. The selected works of T. S. Spivet
Lodge, D. Paradise news
Marias, J. Voyage along the horizon
McCarthy, C. The road
McCutchan, P. Apprentice to the sea
McCutchan, P. The second mate
Melnyczuk, A. The house of widows
Moberg, V. The emigrants
Nichols, P. Voyage to the North Star
O'Brian, P. The golden ocean

Poe, E. A. The imaginary voyages: The narrative of Arthur Gordon Pym; The unparalleled adventure of one Hans Pfaall; The journal of Julius Rodman
Schwartzman, A. Eddie Signwriter
Seton, A. Avalon
Stone, R. Outerbridge Reach
Verne, J. Around the world in eighty days
Villars, E. The Normandie affair
Vollmann, W. T. The ice-shirt
Wright, S. Going native
VOYAGES AND TRAVELS -- FICTION
Boyagoda, R. Beggar's feast
Cornwell, B. 1356
Dare, T. A week to be wicked
Garey, J. Too bright to hear too loud to see
Grossman, L. The magician king
Hall, T. The case of the deadly butter chicken
Held, R. Silver
Joyce, R. The unlikely pilgrimage of Harold Fry
Kerouac, J. The sea is my brother
Morrison, T. Home
Motion, A. Silver
Orullian, P. V. The unremembered
Preston, C. The scrapbook of Frankie Pratt
Thomas, S. Beguiling the beauty
VOYAGES AROUND THE WORLD
See also Travel; Voyages and travels
Silko, L. Gardens in the dunes
Verne, J. Around the world in eighty days
VOYAGES TO THE MOON *See* Imaginary voyages; Space flight to the moon
VOYEURS
Klosterman, C. The visible man
Vurt. Noon, J.

W

Wagner, Winifred, 1897-1980
About
Wilson, A. N. Winnie and Wolf
WAGON TRAINS
Guthrie, A. B. The way West
The **wailing** wind. Hillerman, T.
WAITERS AND WAITRESSES
Cain, J. M. The cocktail waitress
Waiting. Ha Jin
Waiting for sunrise. Boyd, W.
Waiting to exhale. McMillan, T.
WAITRESSES
De los Santos, M. Belong to me
Hemingway, E. The torrents of spring
O'Nan, S. Last night at the Lobster
Robbins, T. Skinny legs and all
Schwartz, L. Angels Crest
Vlautin, W. Northline
WAITRESSES -- FICTION
Schneider, B. Beautiful Inez

Perez-Reverte, A. The painter of battles
Potok, C. Old men at midnight
Prcic, I. Shards
Scholes, K. Antiphon
Seymour, G. The heart of danger
Sheers, O. Resistance
Sienkiewicz, H. The deluge
Sienkiewicz, H. Fire in the steppe
The sorrow of war
Stanisic, S. How the soldier repairs the gramophone
Tearne, R. Mosquito
Tolkien, J. R. R. The Silmarillion
Turtledove, H. Into the darkness
Turtledove, H. Rulers of the darkness
Vonnegut, K. Armageddon in retrospect
White, T. H. The book of Merlyn

WAR -- RELIGIOUS ASPECTS
See also Religion; War
Weber, D. By schism rent asunder

WAR -- SIMULATION GAMES See War games
WAR AND CIVILIZATION See Civilization; War
WAR AND EMERGENCY POWERS
See also Constitutional law; Executive power;
Legislative bodies; War
War and peace. Tolstoy, L.
War and peace. Tolstoy, L.
War and remembrance. Wouk, H.
The **war** between the Tates. Lurie, A.

WAR CASUALTIES See War
WAR CRIME TRIALS
See also Trials
DeMille, N. Word of honor
Schlink, B. The reader

WAR CRIMES
See also Crimes against humanity; International law; War
Thompson, J. Lucifer's tears

WAR CRIMINALS
Forsyth, F. The Odessa file
Levin, I. The boys from Brazil
Moore, B. The statement
Ondaatje, M. Anil's ghost
Seymour, G. The heart of danger
Uris, L. QB VII

WAR FILMS See Historical drama; Motion pictures
War for the Oaks. Bull, E.

WAR GAMES
Bolaño, R. The Third Reich
The **war** of the end of the world. Vargas Llosa, M.
War of the Gods. Anderson, P.
War of the rats. Robbins, D. L.
The **war** of the worlds. Wells, H. G.

WAR ON TERRORISM, 2001-
Adams, L. The room and the chair
Harris, R. The ghost

Le Carre, J. A most wanted man
WAR ON TERRORISM, 2001-2009
Le Carré, J. A Delicate Truth
WAR POETRY See Poetry
WAR RADIO PROGRAMS See Radio programs
WAR SHIPS See Warships
WAR SONGS See National songs; Songs
WAR STORIES
See also Fiction; Historical fiction
Abercrombie, J. The heroes
Bausch, R. Peace
Boll, H. The silent angel
Boyden, J. Three-day road
Byatt, A. S. Ragnarok
Corey, J. S. A. Caliban's war
Cornwell, B. 1356
Delaney, F. The matchmaker of Kenmare
Deutermann, P. T. Pacific glory
Groot, T. Flame of resistance
Gurganus, A. The oldest living Confederate widow tells all
Harris, R. Enigma
Helprin, M. A soldier of the great war
Hicks, R. The widow of the south
Hunter, S. Dead zero
Keneally, T. To Asmara
Marra, A. A constellation of vital phenomena
McClellan, B. Promise of blood
Modesitt, L. E. Imager's battalion
Oe, K. Nip the buds, shoot the kids
Olmstead, R. Coal black horse
Ondaatje, M. The English patient
Rash, R. The cove
Seymour, G. A Deniable Death
Vonnegut, K. Armageddon in retrospect
Weber, D. Shadow of freedom
West, P. Love's mansion
Young, T. W. The renegades

WAR TELEVISION PROGRAMS See Television programs
The **war that came early** [series]
Turtledove, H. The big switch
War trash. Ha Jin
WAR VETERANS See Veterans
WARD, SUSAN (FICTITIOUS CHARACTER)
Cain, C. Let me go
Warday. Strieber, W.
The **warden.** Trollope, A.
Wards of Faerie. Brooks, T.
WARGAMES See War games
WARLOCKS
Tregillis, I. The coldest war
The **warlord.** Bosse, M. J.
Warlord chronicles [series]
Cornwell, B. Enemy of God
Cornwell, B. Excalibur

Pelecanos, G. P. The sweet forever
Roberts, N. Honest illusions
Stead, C. The man who loved children
Steel, D. Journey
Tanenbaum, R. Corruption of blood
Wilson, F. P. Deep as the marrow

WASHINGTON (D.C.) -- FICTION

DuPree, K. Silenced
Styles, T. Miss Wayne & the queen of DC

WASHINGTON (D.C.) -- GEORGETOWN

Blatty, W. P. The exorcist

WASHINGTON (D.C.) -- HISTORY -- 20TH CENTURY

Cussler, C. The spy

WASHINGTON (STATE)

Alexie, S. Reservation blues
Bernhardt, W. Dark justice
Dugoni, R. Murder one
Guterson, D. East of the mountains
Guterson, D. The other
Guterson, D. Our Lady of the Forest
Guterson, D. Snow falling on cedars
Hannah, K. On Mystic lake
Havill, S. Race for the dying
Long, D. The inhabited world
Lynch, J. Border songs
Mullen, T. The last town on earth
Roberts, N. River's end
Smith, M. M. The intruders
Waite, U. The terror of living

WASHINGTON (STATE) -- 20TH CENTURY

Alexie, S. Reservation blues
Bernhardt, W. Dark justice
Guterson, D. East of the mountains
Guterson, D. Snow falling on cedars
Roberts, N. River's end

WASHINGTON (STATE) -- FICTION

Perillo, L. Happiness is a chemical in the brain

WASHINGTON (STATE) -- SEATTLE

Alexie, S. Indian killer
Bauermeister, E. Joy for beginners
Doig, I. Mountain time
Emerson, E. W. Pyro
Emerson, E. W. Vertical burn
Guterson, D. Ed King
Kallos, S. Broken for you
Martini, S. P. The list
Pearson, R. The angel maker
Pearson, R. The art of deception
Pearson, R. Beyond recognition
Pearson, R. The body of David Hayes
Pearson, R. The first victim
Pearson, R. Middle of nowhere
Pearson, R. No witnesses
Pearson, R. Undercurrents
Powers, R. Plowing the dark

Raban, J. Surveillance
Raban, J. Waxwings
Robbins, T. Half asleep in frog pajamas
Washington Square. James, H.
Washington, D.C. Vidal, G.
Washington, George, 1732-1799
About
Charyn, J. Johnny One-Eye
Fleming, T. J. Dreams of glory
Shaara, J. The glorious cause
Washington, Martha, 1731-1802
About
Hambly, B. Patriot hearts
The **wasp** eater. Lychack, W.
WASPS *See* Insects
WASTE PRODUCTS AS FUEL *See* Salvage
WASTE RECLAMATION *See* Salvage
The **wasted** vigil. Aslam, N.
Wasted years. Harvey, J.
A **wasteland** of strangers. Pronzini, B.
The **wasties.** Reuss, F.
The **watch.** Roy-Bhattacharya, J.
Watch your back. Westlake, D. E.
Watchers. Koontz, D. R.
The **watchers.** Steele, J.
WATCHES *See* Clocks and watches
The **watchman.** Crais, R.
Watchman. Rankin, I.
Water. Miller, A. L.
WATER BIRDS *See* Birds
The **water** cure. Everett, P. L.
Water dogs. Robinson, L.
Water for elephants. Gruen, S.
WATER GARDENS *See* Gardens; Landscape architecture
Water like a stone. Crombie, D.
WATER POLLUTION *See* Environmental health; Pollution; Public health
WATER POWER *See* Energy resources; Hydraulics; Power (Mechanics); Renewable energy resources; Rivers; Water resources development
WATER TRANSPORTATION *See* Shipping
The **water's** lovely. Rendell, R.
Waterfront. Schulberg, B.
Watergate. Mallon, T.
WATERGATE AFFAIR, 1972-1974
Mallon, T. Watergate
WATERING PLACES *See* Health resorts
Waterland. Swift, G.
WATERLOO, BATTLE OF, 1815
Cornwell, B. Sharpe's Waterloo
The **Watermelon** King. Wallace, D.
WATERMELONS
Wallace, D. The Watermelon King
Waters family
About

Witchel, A. The spare wife
Wolfe, T. A man in full
Wolitzer, H. Summer reading
Wood, B. The dreaming
Woods, S. Imperfect strangers

WEALTH -- FICTION
Dunne, D. Too much money
Fitzgerald, F. S. The great Gatsby
Naylor, G. Linden Hills
Smith, S. A simple plan

WEAPONS SYSTEMS -- SOVIET UNION
Eastland, S. Shadow pass

WEAPONS, ATOMIC *See* Nuclear weapons

WEAPONS, NUCLEAR *See* Nuclear weapons

WEATHER
Foden, G. Turbulence
Hay, E. A student of weather
Thompson, J. Wide blue yonder

WEATHER CONTROL *See* Meteorology; Weather

WEATHER FORECASTING *See* Forecasting; Meteorology; Weather

The **weather** in Berlin. Just, W. S.

WEATHER UNDERGROUND (ORGANIZATION)
Gordon, N. The company you keep

Weatherhead books on Asia [series]
Wang Anyi The song of everlasting sorrow

The **weatherman.** Thayer, S.

WEAVERS
Eliot, G. Silas Marner
Singer, I. J. The brothers Ashkenazi

Weaveworld. Barker, C.

WEAVING *See* Handicraft; Textile industry

The **web.** Kellerman, J.

The **web** and the rock. Wolfe, T.

The **Webster** chronicle. Akst, D.

Webster, Daniel, 1782-1852
About
Benet, S. V. The Devil and Daniel Webster

The **wedding.** West, D.

The **wedding** of the two-headed woman. Mattison, A.

WEDDINGS
See also Marriage
DeWeese, D. You don't love this man
Garwood, J. The ideal man
Haddon, M. A spot of bother
Johnson, D. Le mariage
Karon, J. A common life
Mapson Solomon's oak
McCullers, C. The member of the wedding
Ross, A. B. Miss Julia throws a wedding
Waldman, A. Red Hook Road
Welty, E. Delta wedding
West, D. The wedding

WEDDINGS -- BOTSWANA
McCall Smith, A. The Saturday big tent wedding party

WEDDINGS -- FICTION
Anshaw, C. Carry the one
Higgins, K. The Best Man
Kinsella, S. I've got your number
McCall Smith, A. The Saturday big tent wedding party
Warren, D. Juliet in August

Wednesday the rabbi got wet. Kemelman, H.

The **weed** that strings the hangman's bag. Bradley, A.

A **week** in December. Faulks, S.

A **week** in winter. Binchy, M.

A **week** to be wicked. Dare, T.

The **weekend.** Schlink, B.

Weep no more, my lady. Clark, M. H.

Weighed in the balance. Perry, A.

WEIGHT *See* Physics

The **weight** of heaven. Umrigar, T. N.

The **weight** of water. Shreve, A.

WEIGHTS AND MEASURES
See also Physics
The **weird** sisters. Brown, E.

Welcome to Hard Times. Doctorow, E. L.

Welcome to Heavenly Heights. Miller, R.

Welcome to paradise. Shames, L.

Welcome to the monkey house. Vonnegut, K.

Welfare wifeys. K'wan

The **well** of loneliness. Hall, R.

Welles, Orson, 1915-1985
About
Kaplow, R. Me and Orson Welles

Wells, H. G. (Herbert George), 1866-1946
About
Palma, F. J. The map of the sky

WELSH -- SPAIN
Gwyn, R. The color of a dog running away

The **Welsh** girl. Davies, P. H.

The **wench** is dead. Dexter, C.

WEREWOLVES
Armstrong, K. Bitten
Borchardt, A. The silver wolf
Duncan, G. The last werewolf
Harris, C. Dead reckoning
Lamberson, G. The frenzy way
Pekearo, N. T. The wolfman
Pelevin, V. The sacred book of the werewolf
Strieber, W. The Wolfen

WEREWOLVES -- ENGLAND -- LONDON
Carriger, G. Soulless

WEREWOLVES -- FICTION
Carriger, G. Changeless
Duncan, G. Talulla rising
Held, R. Silver

Buntline, N. The hero of a hundred fights

A Century of great Western stories

Champlin, T. Beecher island

Clark, W. V. T. The Ox-bow incident

Coldsmith, D. Tallgrass

Coover, R. Ghost town

Cussler, C. The chase

Dawson, P. Rider on the buckskin

Deborde, R. Portlandtown

DeWitt, P. The Sisters brothers

Doctorow, E. L. Welcome to Hard Times

Doig, I. The whistling season

Dunlap, P. Ambush Creek

Durham, M. The man who loved Cat Dancing

Estleman, L. D. The adventures of Johnny Vermillion

Estleman, L. D. Black powder, white smoke

Estleman, L. D. The book of Murdock

Estleman, L. D. The master executioner

Estleman, L. D. Port hazard

Fergus, J. The wild girl: the notebooks of Ned Giles, 1932

Franklin, T. Smonk; or, Widow town

Gear, W. M. Coyote summer

Gilman, F. The half-made world

Great stories of the American West

Grey, Z. Riders of the purple sage

Grey, Z. West of the Pecos

Grey, Z. Woman of the frontier

Guthrie, A. B. The way West

Hand, D. Deep Creek

Hannan, C. Missy

Hansen, R. The assassination of Jesse James by the coward Robert Ford

Harrigan, S. The gates of the Alamo

Havill, S. Race for the dying

Hershon, J. The German bride

Hockensmith, S. Holmes on the range

Hockensmith, S. On the wrong track

Holbert, B. Lonesome animals

Houston, P. Cowboys are my weakness

Jiles, P. The color of lightning

Johnston, T. C. Dance on the wind

Johnston, T. C. Lay the mountains low

Johnston, T. C. Wind walker

Kelton, E. Badger boy

Kelton, E. Long way to Texas

Kelton, E. The rebels

Kelton, E. Slaughter

Kelton, E. Texas sunrise

Kelton, E. Texas vendetta

Kelton, E. The way of the coyote

Kittredge, W. The Willow Field

Koplan, G. Magic words

L'Amour, L. Bendigo Shafter

L'Amour, L. The Californios

L'Amour, L. The Cherokee Trail

L'Amour, L. End of the drive

L'Amour, L. The haunted mesa

L'Amour, L. Jubal Sackett

L'Amour, L. The lonesome gods

L'Amour, L. The Sacketts: beginnings of a dynasty

L'Amour, L. The trail to Seven Pines

Latham, A. Code of the West

Lawrence, C. The case of the deadly desperados

Leonard, E. The complete Western stories of Elmore Leonard

Liebmann-Smith, R. The James boys

McCarthy, C. Blood meridian

McMurtry, L. Anything for Billy

McMurtry, L. Boone's Lick

McMurtry, L. By sorrow's river

McMurtry, L. Comanche moon

McMurtry, L. Folly and glory

McMurtry, L. Sin killer

McMurtry, L. Telegraph days

McMurtry, L. The wandering hill

O'Brien, D. The contract surgeon

Olmstead, R. Far bright star

Overholser, W. D. Death of a cattle king

Overholser, W. D. Law at Angel's Landing

Parker, R. B. Appaloosa

Parker, R. B. Blue-eyed devil

Parker, R. B. Brimstone

Parker, R. B. Gunman's rhapsody

Parker, R. B. Resolution

Parry, R. The winter wolf

Paul, B. Under Tower Peak

Portis, C. True grit

Russell, M. D. Doc

Sargent, C. Museum of human beings

Schaefer, J. W. The collected stories of Jack Schaefer

Schaefer, J. W. Monte Walsh

Schaefer, J. W. Shane

Sharfeddin, H. Mineral spirits

Smith, D. Pictures from an expedition

Stegner, W. E. Angle of repose

Swarthout, G. F. The shootist

Trevanian Incident at Twenty Mile

Wallace, S. Montana dawn

Walls, J. Half broke horses

West, P. O.K.

Westward

Wheeler, R. S. The canyon of bones

Wheeler, R. S. North Star

Williamson, P. Heart of the west

Williamson, P. The outsider

Wurlitzer, R. Drop edge of yonder

Wyman, W. Blue heaven

Zimmer, M. The long hitch

Zimmer, M. Wild side of the river

Where the river ends. Martin, C.

Where there's smoke. Little, T.

Where'd you go, Bernadette. Semple, M.

While England sleeps. Leavitt, D.

While I was gone. Miller, S.

While mortals sleep. Vonnegut, K.

While other people sleep. Muller, M.

While the women are sleeping.

Whip hand. Francis, D.

Whirlwind. Clavell, J.

Whiskey Beach. Roberts, N.

WHISKEY REBELLION, PA., 1794

  Liss, D. The whiskey rebels

The whiskey rebels. Liss, D.

Whisper to the blood. Stabenow, D.

Whistle. Jones, J.

The whistling season. Doig, I.

The white. Larsen, D.

White as snow. Lee, T.

White butterfly. Mosley, W.

The White Company. Doyle, A. C.

White death. Cussler, C.

The white devil. Evans, J.

White devils. McAuley, P. J.

The white dragon. McCaffrey, A.

The white earth. McGahan, A.

White elephant dead. Hart, C. G.

White Fang. London, J.

White Fang, and other stories. London, J.

The white forest. McOmber, A.

White gold wielder. Donaldson, S. R.

The white hotel. Thomas, D. M.

The White House connection. Higgins, J.

The White House pantry murder. Roosevelt, E.

White jazz. Ellroy, J.

The white king. Dragoman, G.

White lies. Krentz, J. A.

White male infant. D'Amato, B.

The white Mary. Salak, K.

White noise. DeLillo, D.

White oleander. Fitch, J.

White people. Gurganus, A.

The white people and other weird stories.

The white princess. Gregory, P.

White shadow. Atkins, A.

White smoke. Greeley, A. M.

WHITE SUPREMACY MOVEMENTS See Race
  relations; Racism; Social movements

White teeth. Smith, Z.

The white tiger. Adiga, A.

White truffles in winter. Kelby, N. M.

White walls. Tolstaia, T.

The Whitechapel conspiracy. Perry, A.

Whiteman. D'Souza, T.

The Whiteness of the Whale. Poyer, D.

Whitethorn Woods. Binchy, M.

Whitman, Walt, 1819-1892
About

Cunningham, M. Specimen days

WHITTLING See Wood carving

Who do I talk to? Jackson, N.

Who fears death. Okorafor, N.

Who's Irish? Jen, G.

WHODUNITS See Mystery and detective plays;
  Mystery fiction; Mystery films; Mystery radio
  programs; Mystery television programs

The whole truth. Pickard, N.

The whole wide beauty. Woof, E.

The whole world over. Glass, J.

The whore's child. Russo, R.

Whose body? Sayers, D. L.

The why of things. Winthrop, E. H.

WICCA See Paganism

Wicked. Maguire, G.

Wicked autumn. Malliet, G. M.

Wicked city. Atkins, A.

The wicked day. Stewart, M.

Wicked widow. Quick, A.

WICKEDNESS See Good and evil

Wickett's remedy. Goldberg, M.

Widdershins. De Lint, C.

Wide blue yonder. Thompson, J.

Wide Sargasso Sea. Rhys, J.

A widow for one year. Irving, J.

The widow of the south. Hicks, R.

Widow's walk. Parker, R. B.

The widower's tale. Glass, J.

WIDOWERS

  See also Men

  Adiga, A. Last man in tower

  Bacon, C. Split estate

  Baldacci, D. One summer

  Baldwin, R. You lost me there

  Banville, J. The sea

  Caputo, P. Crossers

  Coben, H. No second chance

  Cooley, M. The archivist

  De Bernieres, L. A partisan's daughter

  Doig, I. The whistling season

  Drayson, N. Guide to the birds of East Africa

  Finder, J. Company man

  Gardam, J. Old Filth

  Glass, J. Three Junes

  Glass, J. The widower's tale

  Goldman, F. Say her name

  Guterson, D. East of the mountains

  Haig, M. The possession of Mr Cave

  Harrigan, S. Challenger Park

  Hellenga, R. Philosophy made simple

  Hoban, R. Linger awhile

  Hoffman, A. Skylight confessions

  Irwin, S. M. The dead path

O'Brien, E. House of splendid isolation

O'Nan, S. Emily, alone

O'Reilly, B. Angelina's bachelors

Pausch, J. Dream new dreams

Perry, T. Fidelity

Powell, S. The Mushroom Man

Purdy, J. In a shallow grave

Quick, A. Wicked widow

Quindlen, A. Blessings

Raucher, H. Summer of '42

Redhill, M. Consolation

Riley, J. M. The serpent garden

Roberts, M. Reader, I married him

Robinson, R. Sweetwater

Ruiz, L. M. Only one thing missing

Russo, R. Empire Falls

Sackville-West, V. All passion spent

Sarton, M. A reckoning

Savage, S. Glass

See, C. There will never be another you

Shonk, K. Happy now?

Shreve, A. Body surfing

Shreve, A. The pilot's wife

Simonson, H. Major Pettigrew's last stand

Spark, M. A far cry from Kensington

Sparks, N. The guardian

Spencer, L. Bitter sweet

Spencer, L. Morning glory

Steel, D. The house on Hope Street

Trueblood, V. Seven loves

Tuck, L. I married you for happiness

Tyler, A. Back when we were grownups

Tyler, A. The clock winder

Updike, J. Seek my face

Updike, J. The widows of Eastwick

Vida, V. The lovers

Viswanathan, P. The toss of a lemon

Weldon, F. Worst fears

Welty, E. The optimist's daughter

Wideman, J. E. Two cities

Williams, A. J. Down from Cascom Mountain

Williams, T. The Roman spring of Mrs. Stone

Williamson, P. The outsider

Winkler, A. C. Dog war

Winston, L. Good grief

Wolitzer, H. Hearts

Wolitzer, H. Tunnel of love

WIDOWS -- FICTION

Bennett, A. Smut

Gray, J. A lady never lies

Landis, J. M. Heartbreak Hotel

Millet, L. Magnificence

Moore, M. M. So far away

Phillips, S. E. First lady

Vantrease, B. R. The illuminator

The **widows** of Eastwick. Updike, J.

The **wife.** Wolitzer, M.

Wife 22. Gideon, M.

WIFE ABUSE

Bohjalian, C. A. Secrets of Eden

Clark, M. H. No place like home

Doyle, R. The woman who walked into doors

Ferrante, E. Troubling love

King, S. Dolores Claiborne

King, S. Insomnia

King, S. Rose Madder

Oates, J. C. The gravedigger's daughter

Price, N. Sleeping with the enemy

Quindlen, A. Black and blue

Shreve, A. Strange fits of passion

Steel, D. Journey

Wilhelm, K. The best defense

WIFE ABUSE -- FICTION

Adler-Olsen, J. A Conspiracy of Faith

WIFE BATTERING *See* Wife abuse

WIFE BEATING *See* Wife abuse

The **wife's** tale. Lansens, L.

Wifeshopping. Wingate, S.

A **wild** and lonely place. Muller, M.

WILD ANIMALS *See* Animals; Wildlife

Wild child. Boyle, T. C.

WILD CHILDREN

Clark, C. Savage lands

Wild Decembers. O'Brien, E.

Wild fire. DeMille, N.

WILD FLOWERS *See* Flowers

The **wild** girl: the notebooks of Ned Giles, 1932.
Fergus, J.

The **wild** Irish. Maxwell, R.

Wild justice. Margolin, P.

WILD MEN

Hoffman, A. Second nature

Wild nights! Oates, J. C.

Wild pitch. Lupica, M.

Wild side of the river. Zimmer, M.

Wild stars seeking midnight suns. Cooper, J. C.

A **wild** surge of guilty passion. Hansen, R.

The **wildcats** of Exeter. Marston, E.

The **Wilde** women. Wall, P. S.

Wilde, Oscar, 1854-1900

About

Self, W. Dorian

WILDERNESS AREAS

Doiron, P. The poacher's son

Henderson, W. H. Augusta Locke

Lent, J. Lost nation

McCarthy, C. The crossing

Standiford, L. Black Mountain

WILDERNESS AREAS -- FICTION

Kantner, S. Ordinary wolves

Lent, J. Lost nation

Schwartz, L. Angels Crest

Laker, R. The golden tulip
Laker, R. To dance with kings
Larsen, J. Silk road
L'Engle, M. Certain women
Lively, P. Consequences
Lively, P. Moon tiger
Manicka, R. The rice mother
Markson, D. Wittgenstein's mistress
Maupin, A. Mary Ann in autumn
McCauley, S. True enough
McDermott, A. At weddings and wakes
McMillan, T. How Stella got her groove back
Mehta, G. Raj
Momaday, N. S. The ancient child
Morrison, T. Paradise
Munro, A. Open secrets
Naylor, G. The women of Brewster Place
Nin, A. Cities of the interior
Otto, W. How to make an American quilt
Oyeyemi, H. The opposite house
Paddock, J. A secret word
Paretsky, S. Ghost country
Pilcher, R. September
Pilcher, R. The shell seekers
Pym, B. Excellent women
Read, P. P. Alice in exile
Ross, A. B. Miss Julia throws a wedding
Rushdie, S. The enchantress of Florence
Santiago, E. Conquistadora
Sarah/English Sarah
Scott, J. Follow me
See, L. Peony in love
Sheldon, S. Windmills of the gods
Shields, C. The stone diaries
Shreve, S. R. Daughters of the new world
Siddons, A. R. Islands
Sienkiewicz, H. Fire in the steppe
Sosin, D. The long-shining waters
Steel, D. Amazing grace
Strout, E. Olive Kitteridge
Swann, M. The foreigners
Thayer, N. My dearest friend
Thomas, E. M. Reindeer Moon
Towles, A. Rules of civility
Trollope, J. Legacy of love
Trueblood, V. Seven loves
Turner, N. E. These is my words
Updike, J. S
Vine, B. The brimstone wedding
Walbert, K. The gardens of Kyoto
Walbert, K. Our kind
Walbert, K. A short history of women
Walker, A. Possessing the secret of joy
Wallach, J. Seraglio
Williamson, P. Heart of the west
Winthrop, E. Island justice

Wolff, I. A vintage affair
Wolitzer, M. The uncoupling
WOMEN -- CALIFORNIA -- SAN FRANCISCO
Fowler, K. J. Sister Noon
Hughes, A. Market Street
WOMEN -- CHINA -- HISTORY -- 18TH CENTURY
Chen, P. A. The red chamber
WOMEN -- CONNECTICUT
Brown, K. The longings of wayward girls
WOMEN -- CRIMES AGAINST
Cotterill, C. The merry misogynist
French, N. Beneath the skin
Fyfield, F. Blind date
Nesbø, J. The leopard
Pickard, N. The whole truth
WOMEN -- CRIMES AGAINST -- SAUDI ARABIA
Ferraris, Z. Kingdom of strangers
WOMEN -- DISEASES *See* Diseases
WOMEN -- EDUCATION *See* Education
WOMEN -- EMPLOYMENT
Crowley, J. Four freedoms
Wilcox, J. Heavenly days
WOMEN -- ENGLAND -- HISTORY -- RENAISSANCE, 1450-1600
Higginbotham, S. Her highness, the traitor
WOMEN -- FICTION
Bezos, M. Traps
Coleridge, N. D. The adventuress
Cook, C. Best staged plans
Desrochers, S. Bride of New France
Freudenberger, N. The newlyweds
Gideon, M. Wife 22
Graeme-Evans, P. The island house
Huston, N. Infrared
McDermott, A. Someone
McNeal, T. To be sung underwater
Rindell, S. The Other Typist
Simone, A. Note to self
Three strong women
WOMEN -- FRANCE
Three strong women
WOMEN -- GERMANY -- BERLIN
Gillham, D. R. City of women
WOMEN -- GREECE
Greenwood, K. Medea
WOMEN -- HISTORY *See* Feminism; History
WOMEN -- IDENTITY
  See also Identity (Psychology)
Oates, J. C. Mudwoman
Traveler of the century
WOMEN -- INDIA
Umrigar, T. The world we found
WOMEN -- IRAN
Amirrezvani, A. Equal of the sun

Mapson, J. Loving Chloe
Martin, V. Italian fever
Martin, V. Trespass
Mason, B. A. Feather crowns
Mattison, A. The wedding of the two-headed woman
McGowan, H. Duchess of nothing
Menendez, A. The last war
Michael, J. Sleeping beauty
Michaels, F. Celebration
Miller, R. The private lives of Pippa Lee
Miller, S. For love
Miller, S. While I was gone
Miller, S. The world below
Minot, S. Evening
Morgan, C. E. All the living
Morley, I. Come Sunday
Morris, M. M. A dangerous woman
Nelson, A. Bound
Nooteboom, C. Lost paradise
Oates, J. C. Blonde
Oates, J. C. The falls
Oates, J. C. The gravedigger's daughter
Oates, J. C. I lock my door upon myself
O'Brien, E. House of splendid isolation
O'Brien, E. Time and tide
Oe, K. An echo of heaven
O'Farrell, M. The vanishing act of Esme Lennox
Olafur Johann Olafsson   The journey home
O'Nan, S. The good wife
Ostermiller, D. Outside the ordinary world
Ozick, C. Foreign bodies
Packer, A. The dive from Clausen's pier
Patterson, J. Hide & seek
Patterson, K. Consumption
Pearson, A. I think I love you
Phillips, C. A distant shore
Phillips, J. A. MotherKind
Pickard, N. The scent of rain and lightning
Price, N. Night woman
Price, R. Roxanna Slade
Quindlen, A. Black and blue
Quindlen, A. One true thing
Reynolds, S. A gracious plenty
Rice, L. Home fires
Robinson, R. Sweetwater
Rosen, J. Joy comes in the morning
Rosenberg, N. T. Abuse of power
Rush, N. Mating
Schwartz, L. S. Disturbances in the field
Schwartz, L. S. The writing on the wall
Sebold, A. The almost moon
Shields, C. Unless
Shreve, A. The pilot's wife
Shreve, A. Strange fits of passion
Shriver, L. The post-birthday world

Simpson, M. Off Keck Road
Sittenfeld, C. The man of my dreams
Smiley, J. Private life
Snyder, D. J. Night crossing
Solomon, N. Single wife
Spanidou, I. Before
Stevens, C. Still missing
Styron, A. All the finest girls
Swift, G. Tomorrow
Symons, J. Something like a love affair
Tennant, E. Pemberley
Texier, C. Victorine
Thayer, N. Belonging
Trevor, W. Felicia's journey
Truong, M. Bitter in the mouth
Tyler, A. Back when we were grownups
Tyler, A. Ladder of years
Updike, J. Seek my face
Urquhart, J. A map of glass
Vanderbes, J. Easter Island
Walker, A. Now is the time to open your heart
Waller, R. J. The bridges of Madison County
Weber, K. The Music Lesson
Weldon, F. Worst fears
Wenner, K. Dancing with Einstein
Winton, T. Dirt music
Wolitzer, M. The wife

WOMEN -- RELATION TO OTHER WOMEN

Abbott, M. E. Bury me deep
Allen, S. A. The peach keeper
Allen, S. A. The sugar queen
Bauermeister, E. Joy for beginners
Beattie, A. My life, starring Dara Falcon
Binchy, M. Circle of friends
Cleage, P. I wish I had a red dress
Cleave, C. Little Bee
Coe, J. The rain before it falls
Crouch, K. Girls in trucks
De los Santos, M. Belong to me
Enquist, P. O. The book about Blanche and Marie
Furnivall, K. The red scarf
Gaitskill, M. Veronica
Garner, H. The spare room
Golden, A. Memoirs of a geisha
Goldsmith, O. Pen pals
Goldsmith, O. Young wives
Gutcheon, B. R. Five fortunes
Hagedorn, J. T. Toxicology
Heller, J. Best enemies
Heller, Z. What was she thinking?
Hilderbrand, E. Silver girl
Hood, A. The knitting circle
Hosseini, K. A thousand splendid suns
Jaffe, R. The room-mating season
Kafka, K. Miranda's vines
Keyes, M. Last Chance Saloon

Cleave, C. Gold

WOMEN AUTHORS

See also Authors; Women

Alvarez, J. Yo!

Atwood, M. The blind assassin

Battle, L. Southern women

Berg, E. Home safe

Bohjalian, C. A. Secrets of Eden

Brookner, A. Hotel du Lac

Byatt, A. S. The children's book

Caedmon's song The first cut

Carroll, J. Fault lines

Cline, R. What to keep

Coetzee, J. M. Elizabeth Costello

Coetzee, J. M. Slow man

Doig, I. Bucking the sun

Drabble, M. The witch of Exmoor

Fossum, K. Broken

Frame, J. Towards another summer

Gordon, E. F. It will come to me

Hagedorn, J. T. Toxicology

Hall, J. W. Rough draft

Hay, E. Garbo laughs

Howard, M. The rags of time

Irving, J. A widow for one year

Keyes, M. The other side of the story

Lessing, D. M. The golden notebook

Lively, P. Heat wave

McEwan, I. Atonement

McGowan, K. The expected one

McPhee, M. Dear money

Meloy, M. A family daughter

Miller, S. The distinguished guest

Nicholls, D. One day

Oates, J. C. Marya

Ogilvie, E. When the music stopped

Olsson, L. Astrid & Veronika

Parkhurst, C. The nobodies album

Piercy, M. The longings of women

Schwartz, L. S. The fatigue artist

Settle, M. L. Charley Bland

Settle, M. L. The killing ground

Shaffer, M. A. The Guernsey Literary and Potato
 Peel Pie Society

Shields, C. Unless

Shreve, A. Strange fits of passion

Stegner, W. E. Angle of repose

Thomas, R. All my sins remembered

Tremain, R. The way I found her

Watson, S. J. Before I go to sleep

Weiner, J. Certain girls

Weldon, F. Chalcot Crescent

Wiggins, M. The shadow catcher

WOMEN AUTHORS -- FICTION

de Rosnay, T. Sarah's key

Flanery, P. Absolution

Martinusen-Coloma, C. The salt garden

Moore, K. Sexy Lexy

Ozeki, R. L. A tale for the time being

Preston, C. The scrapbook of Frankie Pratt

**WOMEN AUTHORS, AMERICAN -- 20TH
CENTURY -- BIOGRAPHY**

Welty, E. Stories, essays & memoir

WOMEN BIOLOGISTS

Boyle, T. C. When the killing's done

Kingsolver, B. Flight behavior

WOMEN BOTANISTS -- ENGLAND

Jio, S. The last camellia

**WOMEN CAREGIVERS -- UNITED STATES --
BIOGRAPHY**

Pausch, J. Dream new dreams

WOMEN CIRCUS PERFORMERS

Samson, L. Embrace me

WOMEN CLERGY *See* Clergy; Women

WOMEN COLLEGE GRADUATES

Shumway, C. Ten girls to watch

WOMEN COLLEGE PRESIDENTS

Oates, J. C. Mudwoman

WOMEN COLLEGE STUDENTS

Adams, A. After the war

Bird, S. The Yokota Officers Club

Eugenides, J. The marriage plot

Nunez, S. The last of her kind

Oates, J. C. Black girl/White girl

Plath, S. The bell jar

Roth, P. The dying animal

Wolfe, T. I am Charlotte Simmons

WOMEN CRIMINALS

Coleman, A. Murder mamas

Hilton, E. Dirty money Honey

WOMEN DANCERS

Chao, P. Mambo peligroso

WOMEN DETECTIVES

Castillo, L. Breaking silence

WOMEN DETECTIVES -- ENGLAND

Brett, S. The torso in the town

Buckley, F. The doublet affair

Buckley, F. The fugitive queen

Buckley, F. Queen of ambition

Buckley, F. Queen's ransom

Buckley, F. The siren queen

George, E. Believing the lie

King, L. R. Justice Hall

Linscott, G. Blood on the wood

McGown, J. Picture of innocence

WOMEN DETECTIVES -- FICTION

Black, L. Evidence of murder

Brookmyre, C. When the Devil Drives

Buckley, F. The doublet affair

Buckley, F. The fugitive queen

Buckley, F. Queen's ransom

Clark, M. Guilt by degrees

Eagle, K. Ride a painted pony

WOMEN JOURNALISTS

Adler, E. Now or never
Baldacci, D. Deliver us from evil
Buruma, I. The China lover
Cain, C. Heartsick
Clark, M. H. Daddy's little girl
Clark, M. H. The second time around
Coben, H. Caught
Coel, M. Blood memory
Cotterill, C. Killed at the whim of a hat
D'Amato, B. White male infant
Didion, J. The last thing he wanted
Flynn, G. Sharp objects
Godwin, G. Queen of the underworld
Hart, C. G. Letter from home
Isaacs, S. Red, white and blue
Johnston, W. The colony of unrequited dreams
Kavenna, J. Inglorious
Leimbach, M. The man from Saigon
Lively, P. Cleopatra's sister
MacInnes, H. Ride a pale horse
Mortman, D. The lucky ones
Moyes, J. The last letter from your lover
Patterson, J. 1st to die
Patterson, R. N. Degree of guilt
Pottinger, S. The fourth procedure
Price, R. Freedomland
Raban, J. Surveillance
Salak, K. The white Mary
Scott, A. D. A double death on the Black Isle
Soli, T. The lotus eaters
Sparks, N. Message in a bottle
Steel, D. Journey
Thomas, M. M. Black money
Updike, J. Seek my face
Villars, E. The Normandie affair
Walker, M. W. Under the beetle's cellar
Walters, M. The devil's feather
Walters, M. The sculptress
Ward, A. E. Forgive me
Weiner, J. Good in bed
Woods, S. Dirt

WOMEN JOURNALISTS -- ENGLAND

McAfee, A. The spoiler

WOMEN JOURNALISTS -- FICTION

Brooker, B. R. The Viagra diaries
Castro, J. Hell or high water
McAfee, A. The spoiler
Miller, J. The year of the gadfly
Mina, D. Field of blood
Ryan, H. P. The other woman

WOMEN JUDGES See Judges; Women

WOMEN LAW STUDENTS

George, K. Simple

WOMEN LAW TEACHERS

Longworth, M. L. Death in the Vines

WOMEN LAWYERS

Baldacci, D. Total control
Berne, S. A perfect arrangement
Brown, S. The witness
Clark, M. H. The cradle will fall
Clark, M. H. On the street where you live
Fielding, J. Tell me no secrets
Gordimer, N. None to accompany me
Green, T. The letter of the law
Harris, E. L. And this too shall pass
Howatch, S. The high flyer
Isaacs, S. Lily White
James, J. Something about you
Margolin, P. Wild justice
Martini, S. P. Critical mass
Martini, S. P. The list
Meltzer, B. Dead even
Michael, J. Sleeping beauty
Murphy, M. Darkness falls
O'Shaughnessy, P. Breach of promise
O'Shaughnessy, P. Invasion of privacy
O'Shaughnessy, P. Motion to suppress
O'Shaughnessy, P. Obstruction of justice
O'Shaughnessy, P. Unlucky in law
O'Shaughnessy, P. Writ of execution
Patterson, R. N. The final judgment
Piercy, M. Three women
Pottinger, S. The fourth procedure
Pottinger, S. The last Nazi
Rosenberg, N. T. Buried evidence
Rosenberg, N. T. Interest of justice
Rosenberg, N. T. Mitigating circumstances
Scottoline, L. Legal tender
Scottoline, L. Mistaken identity
Scottoline, L. Rough justice
Scottoline, L. The vendetta defense
Sheldon, S. Rage of angels
Steel, D. The house on Hope Street
Stone, K. Happy endings
Truscott, L. K. Heart of war
Weiner, J. In her shoes
Wilhelm, K. The best defense
Wilhelm, K. Death qualified
Wilhelm, K. Defense for the devil
Wilhelm, K. Desperate measures
Wilhelm, K. Malice prepense
Wilhelm, K. No defense
Yrsa Sigurdardottir Last rituals

WOMEN LAWYERS -- FICTION

Bornikova, P. Box office poison
Clark, M. Guilt by degrees
George, K. Simple
Swinson, K. Playing dirty
Warren, S. M. Take a chance on me

WOMEN LIBRARIANS

LAND -- LONDON

Gibson, W. Pattern recognition

Winspear, J. Birds of a feather

Winspear, J. Maisie Dobbs

WOMEN PRIVATE INVESTIGATORS

Cross, A. Honest doubt

Lutz, L. The last word

WOMEN PRIVATE INVESTIGATORS -- FRANCE -- CLICHY

Black, C. Murder in Clichy

WOMEN PRIVATE INVESTIGATORS -- FRANCE -- PARIS

Black, C. Murder below Montparnasse

Black, C. Murder in Belleville

Black, C. Murder in the Bastille

Black, C. Murder in the Marais

Black, C. Murder in the rue de Paradis

WOMEN PRIVATE INVESTIGATORS -- ILLINOIS -- CHICAGO

D'Amato, B. Hard evidence

Paretsky, S. Breakdown

Paretsky, S. Total recall

WOMEN PRIVATE INVESTIGATORS -- INDIA

King, L. R. Garment of shadows

WOMEN PSYCHOTHERAPISTS

French, N. Tuesday's gone

WOMEN REAL ESTATE AGENTS

Collins, B. Crimson eve

WOMEN SCIENTISTS

Enquist, P. O. The book about Blanche and Marie

Hagberg, D. Abyss

Johansen, I. Long after midnight

Perdue, L. Slatewiper

Southgate, M. The taste of salt

Vanderbes, J. Easter Island

Wilson, R. C. Blind Lake

WOMEN SCIENTISTS -- FICTION

Bond, L. Exit plan

Ghosh, A. The hungry tide

WOMEN SCREENWRITERS

Weiner, J. The next best thing

WOMEN SCULPTORS -- FICTION

Johansen, I. The face of deception

Johansen, I. The killing game

Johansen, I. Taking eve

WOMEN SERIAL MURDERERS

Cain, C. Heartsick

Cain, C. Kill you twice

WOMEN SINGERS

Tallis, F. Death and the maiden

WOMEN SLAVES

Allende, I. Island beneath the sea

Martin, V. Property

Morrison, T. A mercy

Rawles, N. My Jim

WOMEN SLAVES -- SOUTH AFRICA

Brink, A. P. Philida

WOMEN SOLDIERS

Bledsoe, A. The hum and the shiver

Holland, C. The angel and the sword

WOMEN SOLDIERS -- FICTION

Boianjiu, S. The people of forever are not afraid

WOMEN SOLDIERS -- ISRAEL

Boianjiu, S. The people of forever are not afraid

WOMEN SPIES

Buckley, F. Queen of ambition

McEwan, I. Sweet tooth

Putney, M. J. No longer a gentleman

WOMEN TEACHERS

Boswell, R. Century's son

Cross, A. Honest doubt

Goodman, C. The seduction of water

Hooper, C. A child's book of true crime

Roberts, G. The bluest blood

WOMEN VIOLINISTS

Schneider, B. Beautiful Inez

Women with men. Ford, R.

WOMEN'S LAND ARMY (GREAT BRITAIN)

Humphreys, H. The lost garden

WOMEN'S MOVEMENT *See* Women -- Social conditions; Women's rights

The **women's** room. French, M.

WOMEN-OWNED BUSINESS ENTERPRISES

Lehmann, S. Astor Place Vintage

WOMEN -- CHINA

Chen, P. A. The red chamber

Tie Ning The bathing women

The **wonder** spot. Bank, M.

Wonder when you'll miss me. Davis, A.

The **wonder-worker.** Howatch, S.

Wonderful world. Calvo, J.

WOOD *See* Building materials; Forest products; Fuel; Trees

The **wood** beyond. Hill, R.

WOOD CARVING

Arnow, H. L. S. The dollmaker

The **woodcutter.** Hill, R.

Woodcutters. Bernhard, T.

Woodhull, Victoria C., 1838-1927

About

Piercy, M. Sex wars

The **woods.** Coben, H.

Woodsburner. Pipkin, J.

Woolf, Virginia, 1882-1941

About

Cunningham, M. The hours

WORD GAMES *See* Games; Literary recreations

Word of God: or, Holy writ rewritten. Disch, T. M.

Word of honor. DeMille, N.

WORD PROBLEMS (MATHEMATICS) *See* Mathematics

Wordsworth, William, 1770-1850

Portrait of the mother as a young woman

WORLD WAR, 1939-1945 -- JAPAN

Dickey, J. To the white sea

Sakamoto, K. One hundred million hearts

Smith, M. C. December 6

Tsukiyama, G. The street of a thousand blossoms

WORLD WAR, 1939-1945 -- JERSEY (CHAN-NEL ISLANDS)

Higgins, J. Night of the fox

WORLD WAR, 1939-1945 -- JEWS

See also Jews

Keneally, T. Schindler's list

Levi, P. If not now, when?

Remarque, E. M. The night in Lisbon

Wander, F. The seventh well

WORLD WAR, 1939-1945 -- JOURNALISTS

See also Journalists

WORLD WAR, 1939-1945 -- MALTA

Mills, M. The information officer

WORLD WAR, 1939-1945 -- MEDITERRANEAN REGION

MacLean, A. The guns of Navarone

WORLD WAR, 1939-1945 -- MOTION PIC-TURES AND THE WAR *See* Motion pictures; War films

WORLD WAR, 1939-1945 -- MUSEUMS *See* Museums

WORLD WAR, 1939-1945 -- NAVAL OPERA-TIONS

Furst, A. Dark voyage

Heggen, T. Mister Roberts

Hickam, H. H. The keeper's son

McCutchan, P. Cameron's crossing

Reeman, D. A ship must die

WORLD WAR, 1939-1945 -- NAVAL OPERA-TIONS -- SUBMARINE

Beach, E. L. Run silent, run deep

WORLD WAR, 1939-1945 -- NETHERLANDS

Lourie, R. A hatred for tulips

WORLD WAR, 1939-1945 -- NORTH AFRICA

Shaara, J. The rising tide

WORLD WAR, 1939-1945 -- NORWAY

Benn, J. R. Billy Boyle

WORLD WAR, 1939-1945 -- PACIFIC OCEAN

Beach, E. L. Run silent, run deep

Griffin, W. E. B. Close combat

Griffin, W. E. B. In danger's path

Griffin, W. E. B. Line of fire

Heggen, T. Mister Roberts

Mailer, N. The naked and the dead

Uris, L. Battle cry

Wouk, H. The Caine mutiny

WORLD WAR, 1939-1945 -- PEACE

Kerr, P. Hitler's peace

WORLD WAR, 1939-1945 -- PHILIPPINES

Holthe, T. U. When the elephants dance

WORLD WAR, 1939-1945 -- POLAND

Hersey, J. The wall

Hodgkinson, A. 22 Britannia Road

Keneally, T. Schindler's list

Kosinski, J. N. The painted bird

Uris, L. Mila 18

WORLD WAR, 1939-1945 -- PRISONERS AND PRISONS

See also Concentration camps; Prisoners of war; Prisons

Ballard, J. G. Empire of the Sun

Boulle, P. The bridge over the River Kwai

Clavell, J. King Rat

Davies, P. H. The Welsh girl

Katzenbach, J. Hart's war

Keneally, T. Schindler's list

Lehrer, J. The special prisoner

Nathanson, E. M. The dirty dozen

Vonnegut, K. Slaughterhouse-five

Westheimer, D. Von Ryan's Express

Yarbrough, S. Prisoners of war

WORLD WAR, 1939-1945 -- PRISONERS AND PRISONS -- FICTION

Friedman, D. Don't ever get old

The hunger angel

Kelly, J. The moon tunnel

WORLD WAR, 1939-1945 -- PROPAGANDA

See also Propaganda

WORLD WAR, 1939-1945 -- ROMANIA

Furst, A. Blood of victory

WORLD WAR, 1939-1945 -- RUSSIA

Benioff, D. City of thieves

Keneally, T. A family madness

Kirst, H. H. Forward, Gunner Asch!

Makine, A. Music of a life

Robbins, D. L. The last citadel

Robbins, D. L. War of the rats

WORLD WAR, 1939-1945 -- SECRET SERVICE

See also Secret service

Follett, K. Eye of the needle

Follett, K. Jackdaws

Griffin, W. E. B. Secret honor

Higgins, J. Cold Harbour

Iles, G. Black cross

Ludlum, R. The Rhinemann exchange

WORLD WAR, 1939-1945 -- SICILY

Hersey, J. A bell for Adano

Higgins, J. Luciano's luck

Shaara, J. The rising tide

WORLD WAR, 1939-1945 -- SINGAPORE

Loh, V. Breaking the tongue

WORLD WAR, 1939-1945 -- SOLOMON IS-LANDS

Griffin, W. E. B. Line of fire

WORLD WAR, 1939-1945 -- UNDERGROUND MOVEMENTS

Fallada, H. Every man dies alone
Faulks, S. Charlotte Gray
Follett, K. Hornet flight
Follett, K. Jackdaws
Furst, A. Blood of victory
Furst, A. The foreign correspondent
Furst, A. Red gold
Furst, A. Spies of the Balkans
Mason, B. A. The girl in the blue beret
Shreve, A. Resistance
Uris, L. Mila 18
WORLD WAR, 1939-1945 -- UNDERGROUND MOVEMENTS -- CZECHOSLOVAKIA
Binet, L. HHhH
WORLD WAR, 1939-1945 -- UNDERGROUND MOVEMENTS -- FICTION
Binet, L. HHhH
Groot, T. Flame of resistance
Zimler, R. The seventh gate
WORLD WAR, 1939-1945 -- UNDERGROUND MOVEMENTS -- FRANCE
Groot, T. Flame of resistance
WORLD WAR, 1939-1945 -- UNITED STATES
Adams, A. After the war
Belfer, L. A fierce radiance
Blake, S. The postmistress
Crowley, J. Four freedoms
Dew, R. F. The truth of the matter
Dunning, J. Two o'clock, eastern wartime
Earley, T. The blue star
Guterson, D. Snow falling on cedars
Hickam, H. H. The keeper's son
Jones, J. Whistle
Leithauser, B. The art student's war
Leonard, E. Up in Honey's room
Otsuka, J. When the emperor was divine
Wouk, H. War and remembrance
Yarbrough, S. Prisoners of war
WORLD WAR, 1939-1945 -- UNITED STATES -- FICTION
Kerouac, J. The sea is my brother
Rutland, E. No crystal stair
WORLD WAR, 1939-1945 -- VETERANS
See also Veterans
WORLD WAR, 1939-1945 -- WALES
Davies, P. H. The Welsh girl
Sheers, O. Resistance
WORLD WAR, 1939-1945 -- WOMEN
See also Women
WORLD WAR, 1939-1945 -- YUGOSLAVIA
MacLean, A. Force 10 from Navarone
The **world** we found. Umrigar, T.
WORLD WIDE WEB *See* Internet
World without end. Follett, K.
The **world** without you. Henkin, J.
World's end. Vinge, J. D.

World's end. Boyle, T. C.
WORLD'S FAIRS *See* Exhibitions; Fairs
Worldly goods. Korda, M.
WORMS *See* Animals
WORRY *See* Emotions
WORSHIP *See* Religion; Theology
Worst fears. Weldon, F.
Worst fears realized. Woods, S.
The **worst** thing I've done. Hegi, U.
Worth dying for. Child, L.
Wouk, Herman, 1915-
                    About
Wouk, H. The lawgiver
Wounded. Burney, C. M.
WOUNDED KNEE CREEK, BATTLE OF, 1890
Jones, D. C. A creek called Wounded Knee
The **wounded** Land. Donaldson, S. R.
WOUNDS AND INJURIES
        See also Accidents
Laskowski, T. Every good boy does fine
WOUNDS AND INJURIES -- FICTION
Kellogg, M. Tell me that you love me, Junie Moon
The **wreck** of the Godspeed. Kelly, J. P.
The **wreck** of the Mary Deare. Innes, H.
The **wreckage.** Robotham, M.
Wrecker. Wood, S.
The **wrecker.** Scott, J.
WRECKS *See* Accidents
Wright, Frank Lloyd, 1867-1959
                    About
Boyle, T. C. The women
Horan, N. Loving Frank
Writ of execution. O'Shaughnessy, P.
WRITERS
        See also Authors
Currie, R. Flimsy little plastic miracles
Palma, F. J. The map of the sky
WRITERS ON FILM
Lazar, Z. Sway
WRITERS ON MEDICINE
Boyle, T. C. Road to Wellville
Meyer, N. The seven-per-cent solution
Pearl, M. The Dante Club
Rubenfeld, J. The death instinct
Thomas, D. M. The white hotel
Wideman, J. E. Fanon
WRITERS ON NATURE
Pipkin, J. Woodsburner
WRITERS ON POLITICS
Carey, P. Parrot and Olivier in America
Coetzee, J. M. Foe
Safire, W. Scandalmonger
Tournier, M. Friday
WRITERS ON RELIGION
Asch, S. The Apostle
Caldwell, T. Dear and glorious physician

De Hartog, J. The peaceable kingdom
Docx, E. The calligrapher
Eliot, G. Romola
Kalfus, K. The commissariat of enlightenment
Reyn, I. What happened to Anna K.

WRITERS ON SCIENCE
Benford, G. Foundation's fear
Benjamin, M. Alice I have been
Bognanni, P. The house of tomorrow
Brown, D. The Da Vinci code
Essex, K. Leonardo's swans
Hofmann, G. Lichtenberg and the little flower girl
Kehlmann, D. Measuring the world
Kerr, P. Dark matter
Liebmann-Smith, R. The James boys
McDonald, R. Mr. Darwin's shooter
Morrow, J. The last witchfinder
Robinson, K. S. Galileo's dream
Shaara, J. The glorious cause
Shaara, J. Rise to rebellion
Stott, R. Ghostwalk

WRITING
> See also Communication; Language and languages; Language arts

Binet, L. HHhH

WRITING (AUTHORSHIP) See Authorship; Creative writing

The **writing** on the wall. Schwartz, L. S.
Written in red. Bishop, A.
Wroe, John, 1782-1863
About
Rogers, J. Mr. Wroe's virgins
The **wrong** case. Crumley, J.
The **wrong** man. Katzenbach, J.
The **wrong** mother. Hannah, S.

WROXETER (ENGLAND) -- HISTORY
Llywelyn, M. After Rome
Wuthering Heights. Bronte, E.
Wyatt. Disher, G.

WYOMING
Bacon, C. Split estate
Carlson, R. The signal
Isaacs, S. Red, white and blue
Roberts, N. Angel's fall
Spragg, M. Bone fire
Standiford, L. Black Mountain

WYOMING -- 19TH CENTURY
Durham, M. The man who loved Cat Dancing
L'Amour, L. Bendigo Shafter
Schaefer, J. W. Shane
Trevanian Incident at Twenty Mile

WYOMING -- FICTION
Box, C. J. Force of nature
Box, C. J. Free fire
Box, C. J. Open season
Johnson, C. Another man's moccasins

Johnson, C. Hell is empty

X

Xenocide. Card, O. S.
Xenogenesis [series]
Butler, O. E. Adulthood rites
Butler, O. E. Dawn
Butler, O. E. Imago
The **XYZ** murders. Queen, E.

Y

Y. Celona, M.
YA LITERATURE See Young adult literature
YACHTING See Yachts and yachting
YACHTS AND YACHTING
> See also Boatbuilding; Boats and boating; Ocean travel; Ships; Voyages and travels; Water sports

Wambaugh, J. Floaters
Yamaguchi, Yoshiko, 1920-
About
Buruma, I. The China lover
YANGTZE RIVER (CHINA)
Hersey, J. A single pebble
Yankee Doodle dead. Hart, C. G.
Year of the dog. Hearon, S.
The **year** of the flood. Atwood, M.
The **year** of the French. Flanagan, T.
The **year** of the gadfly. Miller, J.
Year of the hyenas. Geagley, B.
Year of wonders. Brooks, G.
The **year** we left home. Thompson, J.
The **Year's** best fantasy and horror.
Year's best science fiction.
The **year's** best science fiction.
The **years.** Woolf, V.
Years of Red Dust. Qiu Xiaolong
The **years** of rice and salt. Robinson, K. S.
The **years** with Laura Diaz. Fuentes, C.
The **yellow** admiral. O'Brian, P.
The **yellow** birds. Powers, K.
Yellow moon. Rhodes, J. P.
A **yellow** raft in blue water. Dorris, M.
The **yellow** room conspiracy. Dickinson, P.
Yellow shoe fiction [series]
Bachelder, C. Abbott awaits
Yellowcake. Cummins, A.
YELLOWSTONE NATIONAL PARK
Box, C. J. Back of beyond
Nance, J. J. Fire flight
YEMEN
Torday, P. Salmon fishing in the Yemen
Yesterday will make you cry. Himes, C.
Yesterday's weather. Enright, A.
YETI See Monsters; Mythical animals

Gessen, K. All the sad young literary men
Godden, R. Pippa passes
Guest, J. Ordinary people
Guo Xiaolu Twenty fragments of a ravenous youth
Hesse, H. Demian
Huston, C. The shotgun rule
Jones, S. Outcast
Kay, G. G. Ysabel
Krist, G. Chaos theory
McCarthy, M. Birds of America
Michener, J. A. The drifters
Mishima, Y. The sound of waves
Nichols, J. T. The sterile cuckoo
O'Hagan, A. Be near me
Salinger, J. D. The catcher in the rye
Schwartzman, A. Eddie Signwriter
Siddons, A. R. Heartbreak Hotel
Sillitoe, A. Saturday night and Sunday morning
Smith, B. Joy in the morning
Sparks, N. A walk to remember
Spencer, S. Endless love
Stirling, J. The marrying kind
Stirling, J. The penny wedding
Tarkington, B. Alice Adams
Townsend, S. Adrian Mole: the lost years
Turgenev, I. S. Fathers and sons
Tyler, A. A slipping-down life
Updike, J. Brazil
Weber, K. The little women
Wolfe, T. Of time and the river
Wolfe, T. The web and the rock
Woolf, V. Jacob's room

YOUTH -- FICTION
Bartlett, D. It's fine by me
Collins, C. The gamal
Meno, J. Office girl
Whittall, Z. Holding still for as long as possible

YOUTH -- PSYCHOLOGY
Collins, C. The gamal

YOUTH WITH MENTAL DISABILITIES
Raimondo, L. Dante's wood

YOUTHS' WRITINGS
Collins, C. The gamal

Ysabel. Kay, G. G.

YUGOSLAV WAR, 1991-1995
Prcic, I. Shards

YUGOSLAVIA
Handke, P. Repetition
MacLean, A. Force 10 from Navarone
Seymour, G. The heart of danger

YUKON RIVER VALLEY (YUKON AND ALAS-KA)
London, J. The call of the wild
London, J. White Fang

Z

Z. Fowler, T. A.
ZAIRE
Griffin, W. E. B. Special ops
Hulme, K. The nun's story
Kingsolver, B. The poisonwood Bible
Le Carre, J. The mission song
Stevens, M. The curve of the world
ZAMBIA -- RACE RELATIONS
Mankell, H. The eye of the leopard
Zamenhof, L. L., 1859-1917
About
Skibell, J. A curable romantic
Zazen. Veselka, V.
Zeke and Ned. McMurtry, L.
ZEN BUDDHISM
See also Buddhism
Kerouac, J. The Dharma bums
ZEN, AURELIO (FICTITIOUS CHARACTER)
Dibdin, M. Medusa
Dibdin, M. Ratking
Zendegi. Egan, G.
The **zenith.** Duong Thu Huong
Zeno's conscience. Svevo, I.
The **zero** game. Meltzer, B.
Zero history. Gibson, W.
Zeroville. Erickson, S.
Zia-ul-Haq, Mohammad
About
Hanif, M. A case of exploding mangoes
Ziff. Lelchuk, A.
Zig Zag. Somoza, J. C.
Zigzagging down a wild trail. Mason, B. A.
ZIONISM
Agnon, S. Y. Only yesterday
Iles, G. Black cross
Phillips, C. The nature of blood
Uris, L. Exodus
ZIONIST MOVEMENT *See* Zionism
ZIP CODE *See* Postal service
Zoli. McCann, C.
ZOMBIES
See also Dead; Folklore
Beamer, A. The loving dead
Brook, M. The Iron Duke
Brooks, M. World War Z
Grant, M. Feed
Gregory, D. Raising Stony Mayhall
Hooper, T. Midnight movie
Hynes, J. Kings of infinite space
Kadrey, R. Kill the dead
King, S. Cell
The living dead
Marion, I. Warm bodies
Priest, C. Boneshaker